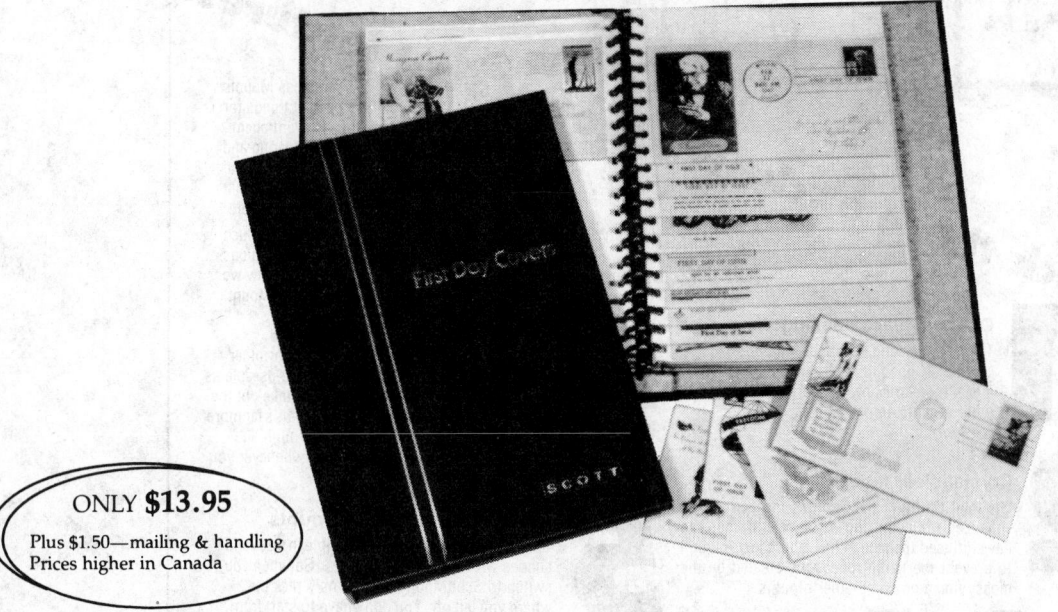

SCOTT®

STANDARD POSTAGE STAMP CATALOGUE

1980

One Hundred and Thirty-sixth Edition in Four Volumes

VOLUME II

EUROPEAN COUNTRIES and COLONIES
INDEPENDENT NATIONS of
AFRICA, ASIA, LATIN AMERICA
A—F

SCOTT PUBLISHING CO.

3 East 57th St., New York, N.Y. 10022

BERT TAUB, *Publisher*
FRANK S. TRUMBOWER, *President*

Chief Catalogue Editor—JAMES B. HATCHER
New Issues Editor—LILLY B. FREED

Staff Editors—WILLIAM W. CUMMINGS, RICHARD GORDON, IRVING KOSLOW, STEVEN Y. MARDIGUIAN, IRWIN SIEGEL, BERT TAUB
Associate Editors—GEORGE A. McNAMARA, WILLIAM N. SALOMON

ACKNOWLEDGMENT

The Editor cordially thanks all those many good friends of Scott who have helped this year or in previous years in the task of revising the Standard Catalogue. They have generously shared their stamp knowledge with others through this medium.

No list of aides can be complete, and several helpers prefer anonymity. The following men are chiefly those who have undertaken to assist on one or more specific countries:

Bruce W. Ball
John K. Bash
Ivan Bedic
Herbert J. Bloch
William G. Bogg
John R. Boker, Jr.
Paul Brenner
George W. Brett
Victor Bukinik

Alex A. Cohen
Herbert E. Conway

Ellery Denison
Pandelis J. Drossos

Daniel S. Franklin
Roger K. Frigstad

Frank P. Geiger
Frederick H. Gloeckner
Brian M. Green
Irving I. Green
David Gronbeck-Jones

Mihran B. Hagopian
Calvet M. Hahn
J. Hannaney
Leo John Harris
Harrison D. S. Haverbeck
Clifford O. Herrick
Juan J. Holler
Robert L. Huggins
J. R. Hughes

Abdullah Izadi

Lewis S. Kaufman

Ernest A. Kehr
Allen D. Kerr

Irving Lapiner
Jim Lemmon
Arthur L. Levine
Andrew Levitt

Robert L. Markovits
Joseph C. Martin

Robert P. Odenweller

Souren Panirian
Frank E. Patterson III
Gilbert N. Plass
Henrik Pollak
Charles Prant

Alex Rendon
Stanley J. Richmond
Col. Milo D. Rowell

Otto G. Schaffling
Alfredo M. Seiferheld
F. Burton Sellers
James N. Sissons
Lt. Col. James W. Smith
Sherwood Springer
Willard F. Stanley
John Stark

M. N. Thacker

John M. Wilson
Paul B. Woodward
William W. Wylie

Among the organizations that have helped are:

AMERICAN AIR MAIL SOCIETY
Gerhard Wolff, c/o Elmer Fox, Westheimer & Co., 540 Investment Bldg., Washington, D.C. 20005

AMERICAN PHILATELIC SOCIETY
P.O. Box 800, State College, Pa. 16801

AMERICAN REVENUE ASSOCIATION
Sherwood Springer, 3761 West 117th St., Hawthorne, Calif. 90250

AMERICAN STAMP DEALERS' ASSOCIATION
840 Willis Ave., Albertson, N.Y. 11507

ARABIAN PHILATELIC ASSOCIATION
Aramco Box 1929, Dhahran, Saudi Arabia

BRAZIL PHILATELIC ASSOCIATION
T.E. Gaughan, Thompson Drive, Washingtonville, N.Y. 10992.

BUREAU ISSUES ASSOCIATION
16 Sammis Lane, White Plains, N.Y. 10605

CANADIAN STAMP DEALERS' ASSOCIATION
L. A. Davenport, Apt. 308, 7 Jackes Ave., Toronto, Ont., Canada M4T 1E3

CANAL ZONE STUDY GROUP
Alfred R. Bew, Sec'y., 29 S. South Carolina Ave., Atlantic City, N.J. 08401

CHINA STAMP SOCIETY
Ellery Denison, Pres., 7207 Thirteenth Pl., Takoma Park, Md. 20012

CONFEDERATE STAMP ALLIANCE
Jack Solomon, 612 East Park Avenue, Long Beach, New York 11561

COSTA RICA COLLECTORS, Society of
Rt. 3, Box 72, Marble Falls, TX 78654

CROATIAN PHILATELIC SOCIETY
260 Vancouver St., London, Ontario, Canada N5W 4R8

CZECHOSLOVAK PHILATELY, Society for
87 Carmita Ave., Rutherford, N.J. 07070

EIRE PHILATELIC ASSOCIATION
John J. Blessington, Sec'y., 4302 St. Clair Ave., Studio City, Calif. 91604

ESTONIAN PHILATELIC SOCIETY
Rudolf Hamar, Pres., 243 E. 34th St., New York, N.Y. 10016

FRANCE & COLONIES PHILATELIC SOCIETY
Walter Parshall, Sec'y., 103 Spruce St., Bloomfield, N.J. 07003

FRIEDL EXPERT COMMITTEE
10 East 40th St., New York, N.Y. 10016

GERMANY PHILATELIC SOCIETY
c/o Fred Behrendt, Sec'y, P.O. Box 563, Westminster, Maryland 21157

GUATEMALA COLLECTORS, International Society of
Richard Canman, Pres., 175 W. Jackson Blvd., Chicago, Ill. 60604

HELLENIC PHILATELIC Society of America
Maurice R. Friend, M.D., Sec'y., 262 Central Park West, New York, N.Y. 10024

JAPANESE PHILATELY, International Society for
Lois M. Evans, Sec'y., P.O. Box 961, State College, Pa. 16801

KOREA STAMP SOCIETY
Forrest W. Calkins, Sec'y., P.O. Box 1057, Grand Junction, Colo. 81501

MEXICO-ELMHURST PHILATELIC SOCIETY INTERNATIONAL
Mrs. Judith Saks, 2310 Veteran, West Los Angeles, CA 90064

NETHERLANDS PHILATELIC SOCIETY
Julius Mansbach, Sec'y., 6323 N. Francisco, Chicago, Ill. 60645

OCEANIA PHILATELIC SOCIETY
William Hagan, Pres., 1523 East Meadowbrook Drive, Loveland, OH 45140

PHILATELIC FOUNDATION
270 Madison Ave., New York, N.Y. 10016

POLONUS PHILATELIC SOCIETY
864 N. Ashland Ave., Chicago, Ill. 60622

PORTUGUESE PHILATELY, International Society for
Robert L. Huggins, 69 Woodland Ave., Glen Ridge, N.J. 07028

ROSSICA, Society of Russian Philately
Norman Epstein, Treas., 33 Crooke Ave., Brooklyn, N.Y. 11226

EL SALVADOR, Associated Collectors of
Joseph D. Hahn, P.O. Box 522, State College, Pa. 16801

SCANDINAVIAN COLLECTORS CLUB
Box 175, Ben Franklin Sta., Washington, D.C. 20044

SOCIETY OF PHILATELIC AMERICANS
Robert B. Brandeberry, P.O. Box 9041, Wilmington, Del. 19809

UNITED POSTAL STATIONERY SOCIETY
Central Office, P.O. Box 1407, Bloomington, Ill. 61701

Soft-Cover Edition: ISBN 0-89487-024-6

Library of Congress Card No. 2-3301

CONTENTS OF VOLUME II

See Index at back of book for page numbers

COPYRIGHT NOTICE

TRADEMARK NOTICE

SPECIAL NOTICES

This Catalogue lists adhesive postage stamps of the various countries, except for the United States where additional listings cover revenue stamps and postal stationery.

To facilitate identification, the following style of listing is used:

Cuba

13 A1 1r p gray green................1.50 40
a. 1r p pale yellow green 3.25 1.00

The number (13) in the first column is the index or identification number; the letter and number combination (A1) indicates the design and refers to the illustration having this (A1) designation; next comes the denomination (1r p) followed by the color (gray green); the prices are in two columns at the right, the first (1.50) being that of an unused stamp and the last (40) of a canceled one. This is known as a major listing or variety.

Variations from so-called "normal" stamps are listed in small type and designated by lowercase letters of the alphabet. These are called minor varieties. When they immediately follow the major listing in the catalogue the original index and design numbers are understood to be the same. In the preceding example, the minor variety, No. 13a, differs from the major variety, No. 13, only in shade; its design, perforation, etc., remain unchanged.

When year, perforation, watermark or printing method is mentioned, the description applies to all succeeding listings until a change is noted. The heading note "Without Gum" applies only to the set it precedes.

When a stamp is printed in black on colored paper, the color of the paper alone is given in italics.

With stamps printed in two or more colors, the color given first is that of the frame or outer parts of the design starting at upper left corner. The colors that follow are those of the vignette or inner parts of the design.

For some sets which include both vertical and horizontal format stamps, a single illustration is used, with the various designs and formats described beneath the illustration.

ABBREVIATIONS

The most frequently used abbreviations are:

Imperf. = Imperforate. Perf. = Perforated. Wmk. = Watermark. Unwmkd. = Unwatermarked. Litho. = Lithographed. Photo. = Photogravure. Engr. = Engraved. Typo. = Typographed.

When no color is given for an overprint or surcharge, it is understood to be in black. Abbreviations are sometimes used, as (B) or (Bk) Black, (Bl) Blue, (R) Red, (G) Green, etc.

NEW ISSUE LISTINGS

Scott's Chronicle of New Issues appears regularly in the Scott's Monthly Stamp Journal and reports new listings.

CONDITION

Condition is the all-important factor of price. Prices quoted are for stamps in fine condition. Extra fine copies often bring higher prices, while unused stamps without gum or with partial gum usually sell for less than copies with full original gum. Prices given in this Catalogue for unused stamps are for specimens which have the major part of the original gum on the back, except, of course, those varieties which were issued without gum. In certain countries, such as Brunswick, a note indicates that prices are for specimens without gum. **Slightly defective stamps which are off-center, heavily canceled, faded or stained are usually sold at large discounts. Damaged stamps which are torn or mutilated or have serious defects seldom bring more than a small fraction of the price of a fine specimen.**

Standards of condition vary greatly in the stamps of different countries. Early United States, Great Britain, Victoria and Japan stamps, for example, were poorly perforated and as a rule heavily canceled. They cannot be obtained in as fine condition as stamps from countries where more care was taken in perforating and lighter cancellations applied.

PRICES

The prices appearing in this Catalogue were estimated after careful study of available wholesale and retail offerings together with recommendations and information submitted by many of the leading philatelic societies. These and other factors were considered in determining the figures which the editors consider represent the proper or present price basis for a fine specimen when offered by an informed dealer to an informed buyer. Sales are frequently made at lower figures occasioned by individual bargaining, changes in popularity, temporary over-supply, local custom, the "vest pocket dealer," or the many other reasons which cause deviations from any accepted standard. Sales at higher prices are usually because of exceptionally fine condition, unusual postal markings, unexpected political changes or newly discovered information. While the minimum price of a stamp is fixed at 3c to cover the dealer's labor and service cost of sorting, cataloguing and filling orders individually, the sum of these list prices does not properly represent the "value" of a packet of unsorted or unmounted stamps sold in bulk which generally consists of only the cheaper stamps.

Prices in italics indicate infrequent sales, lack of pricing information, or that the market value is fluctuating excessively. The condition of early issues of many countries varies greatly. In some instances very fine to superb copies are rarely obtainable. Many of these older issues are priced in italics because the actual value is determined by the condition of each individual stamp.

The absence of price does not necessarily indicate that the stamp is scarce or rare. In the United States listings, a dash in the price column means that the stamp is known in a stated form or variety, but that information is lacking or insufficient for pricing.

Unused prices are for stamps that have been hinged. Where used prices are considerably higher than unused, the price applies to a stamp showing a distinct postmark of origin including a contemporary date.

Beginning around 1900, sometimes earlier, prices for sets are given for most issues of five or more stamps. Unless otherwise noted, the set price excludes minor varieties. The parenthetical number in the set-price line tells the number of stamps in the priced total. Set prices are the sum of the individual prices.

Many countries sell canceled-to-order stamps at a marked reduction of face value. (Exceptions include Australia, Netherlands, France and Switzerland, which sell or have sold CTO stamps at full face value.) It is almost impossible to identify such stamps, if the gum has been removed, as the official government canceling devices are used. Examples on cover and used in the proper period are worth more.

Price Changes affecting this Catalogue are published regularly in Scott's Monthly Stamp Journal. (Subscribe and follow Scott's Chronicle of New Issues as well as the Price Changes.)

HOW TO ORDER FROM YOUR DEALER

It is not necessary to write the full description of a stamp as listed in this Catalogue. All that is needed is the name of the country, the index number and whether unused or used. For example, "Japan No. 422 unused" is sufficient to identify the stamp of Japan listed as: "422 A206 5y brown."

ADDENDA and NUMBER CHANGES

Stamps received too late to be included in the body of the Catalogue are listed in the Addenda at the back of this volume.

A list of stamps whose catalogue numbers have been changed from those of the preceding edition appears at the back of this volume.

Certain currently unlisted stamps are mentioned in "For the Record" at the back of this volume.

EXAMINATION

Scott Publishing Co. cannot undertake to pass upon genuineness or condition of stamps, due to the time and responsibility involved, but refers collectors to the several expert committees which undertake this work. Neither can Scott Publishing Co. undertake to appraise or identify. The Company cannot take responsibility for unsolicited stamps or covers.

INFORMATION FOR COLLECTORS

The anatomy of a stamp can be divided into the following parts: paper, watermark, separation, impression, design and gum.

PAPER

Paper is a material composed of a compacted web of cellulose fibers formed into sheets. The fibers most often used for the paper on which stamps are printed are mulberry bark, wood, straw and certain grasses, with linen or cotton rags added for greater strength. These fibers are ground, bleached and boiled until they are reduced to a slushy pulp known as "stuff." Sizing, or weak glue, and coloring matter may be added to the pulp. Thin coatings of pulp are poured on sieve-like frames which allow the water to run off while retaining the matted pulp. When it is almost dry, the appearance of the pulp is converted by mechanical processes. It may be passed through smooth or engraved rollers (dandy rolls) or placed between cloth in a press that flattens and dries the product under pressure, thus forming a sheet of paper.

Stamp paper falls broadly into two divisions–"wove" and "laid." The differences in appearance are caused by the surface of the frame onto which the pulp is first fed. If the surface is smooth and even, the paper will be of uniform texture throughout, showing no light and dark areas when held up to a light. This is called **Wove Paper.** Early paper making machines poured the pulp on to continuously circulating webs of felt, but modern machines feed the pulp on to a cloth-like screen made of closely interwoven fine wires. This paper, when held up to a light, will show little dots or points, very close together. Technically, it is called "wire wove," but because it is the most common form, it is generally known as "wove paper." Any United States or British stamp printed after 1880 will furnish an example of wire wove paper.

The frames utilized for **Laid Paper** are made of closely spaced parallel wires, with cross wires at wider intervals. Obviously a greater thickness of the pulp will settle between the wires, and the paper, when held up to a light, will show alternate light and dark lines. The spacing and the thickness of the lines may vary, but on any one sheet of paper, they are all alike. (Russia Nos. 31-38.)

If the lines are spaced quite far apart, like the ruling on a writing tablet, the paper is called **Batonné** from the French word meaning a staff. Batonné paper may be either wove or laid. If it is laid, fine laid lines can be seen between the batons. The laid lines, which are actually a form of watermark, may be geometrical figures such as squares, diamonds, rectangles, or wavy lines.

When the lines form little squares, the paper is called **Quadrille.** When they form rectangles instead of squares, the paper is called **Oblong Quadrille.** (Mexico–Guadalajara Nos. 38-41.)

Paper is also classified as thick or thin, hard or soft, and by color if dye was added during production, such as yellowish, greenish, bluish and reddish.

Pelure Paper is an extremely thin, hard and often brittle paper. It is sometimes bluish or grayish. (Serbia No. 170.)

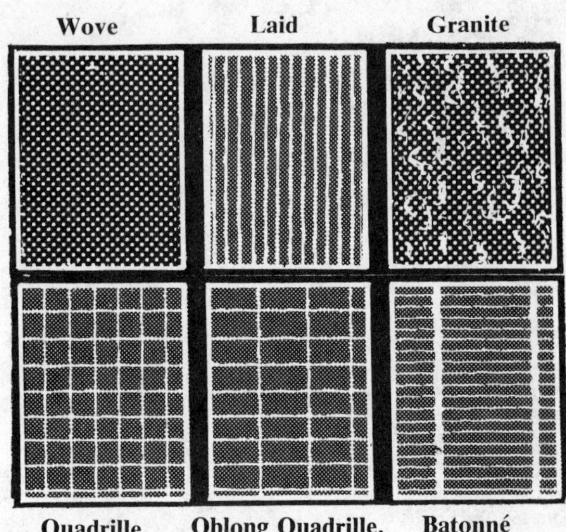

Native Paper is a term applied to the handmade papers on which some of the early stamps of the Indian States were printed. Japanese paper, originally made of mulberry fibers and rice flour, is part of this group. (Japan Nos. 1-18.)

Manila Paper, often used to make stamped envelopes and wrappers, is a coarse textured stock, usually smooth on one side and rough on the other. It is made in a variety of colors.

Silk Paper, introduced by the British in 1847 as a safeguard against counterfeiting, has scattered bits of colored silk thread in it. Silk-thread paper has continuous threads of colored silk arranged so that one or more threads run through the stamp or postal stationery. (Great Britain Nos. 5-8.)

Granite Paper, not to be confused with either of the silk papers, is filled with minute fibers of various colors and lengths in the paper substance. (Austria Nos. 172-175.)

Chalky Paper is coated with a chalk-like substance to discourage the cleaning and reuse of canceled stamps. As the design is imprinted on the water-soluble coating of the stamp, any attempts to remove a cancellation will destroy the stamp. **Collectors are warned not to soak these stamps in any fluid.** If one is to be removed from envelope paper, a good way is to wet the paper from underneath until the gum dissolves enough to slip the stamp off it. (St. Kitts-Nevis Nos. 89-90.)

India Paper, originally introduced from China about 1750, is sometimes referred to as China Paper. It is a thin, opaque paper often used for plate and die proofs by many countries.

Double Paper in philately has two distinct meanings. The first, used experimentally as a means to discourage re-use,is two-ply paper, usually of a thick and thin sheet, joined together during the process of manufacture. Any attempt to remove a cancellation would destroy the design which is printed on the thin paper. The second occurs on the rotary press when the printer glues the end of one paper roll onto the next roll to save time in feeding the paper through the press. Stamp designs are printed over the joined paper and if overlooked by inspectors, may get into post-office stocks.

Goldbeater's Skin, used for the 1886 issue of Prussia, was made of a tough translucent paper. The design was printed in reverse on the back of the stamp, and the gum applied on top of the printing. It is impossible to remove them from the paper to which they are affixed without destroying the design.

Ribbed Paper has an uneven, corrugated surface made by passing it through ridged rollers. (Exists on some copies of U.S. No. 163.)

Various other substances that have been used for stamp manufacture include aluminum, copper, silver and gold foil, plastic, silk and cotton fabrics. Most of these are considered novelties designed for sale to novice collectors.

WATERMARKS

Watermarks are an integral part of the paper as they are formed in the process of manufacture. They consist of small designs such as crowns, stars, anchors, letters, etc. formed of wire or cut from metal that are soldered to the surface of the dandy roll or mold. These pieces of metal (referred to as "bits") impress a design into the paper which may be seen by holding the stamp up to the light. They are more easily seen in a watermark detector, a small black tray. The stamp is placed face down in the tray and dampened with carbon tetrachloride or lighter fluid, which brings up the watermark in dark lines against a lighter background.

WARNING. Some inks used in the photogravure process dissolve in watermark fluids. (See SOLUBLE PRINTING INKS.) There are also electric watermark detectors that come with plastic discs of various colors. When the light is turned on the watermark can be seen through the disc that neutralizes the color of the stamp.

Watermarks may be found reversed, inverted, sideways or diagonal, as seen from the back of the stamp, depending on the position of the printing plates or the manner in which paper was fed through the press. On machine-made paper they normally read from right to left. In a "multiple watermark" the design is repeated closely throughout the sheet. In a "sheet watermark" the design appears only once on the sheet, but extends over many stamps. Individual stamps may carry only a small fraction or none of the watermark.

"Marginal watermarks" occur in the margins of sheets or panes of stamps. Outside the border of some papers a large

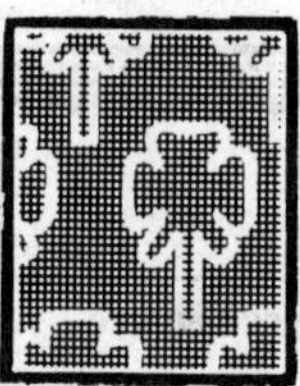

Multiple Watermarks of Crown Agents and Burma

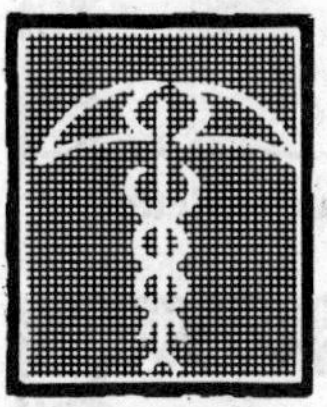

Watermarks of Uruguay, Vatican and Jamaica

row of letters may spell the name of the country or of the manufacturer of the paper. Careless press feeding may cause parts of these letters to show on stamps of the outer rows. **For easier reference watermarks are numbered in the Scott Catalogue. See numerical index of Watermarks at back of this volume.**

SEPARATION

Separation is the general term used to describe methods of separating stamps. The earliest issues, such as the 1840 Penny Blacks, did not have any means provided for separating and were intended to be cut apart with scissors. These are called imperforate stamps. As many stamps that were first issued imperforate were later issued perforated, care must be observed in buying imperforate stamps to be sure they are really imperforate and not perforated copies that have been trimmed. Although sometimes priced as singles, it is recommended that imperforate varieties of normally perforated stamps be collected in pairs or larger pieces as indisputable evidence of their imperforate character.

Separation is effected by two general methods, rouletting and perforating. In rouletting the paper is cut partly or wholly through, but no paper is removed. In perforating a part of the paper is removed. Rouletting derives its name from the French roulette, a spur-like wheel. As the wheel is rolled over the paper, each point makes a small cut. The number of cuts made in two centimeters determines the gauge of the roulette. This is fully explained under "Perforation."

ROULETTING: The shape and arrangement of the teeth on the wheels varies. French names are usually used to describe the various roulettes:

Percé en lignes: rouletted in lines. The paper receives short, straight cuts in lines. (Mexico No. 500.)

Percé en points: pin-perforated. Round, equidistant holes are pricked through the paper, but no paper is removed, which distinguishes it from a small perforation. (Mexico Nos. 242-256.)

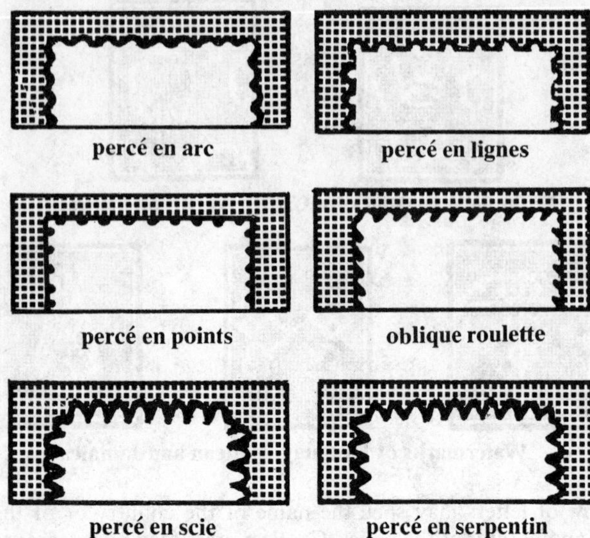
percé en arc
percé en lignes
percé en points
oblique roulette
percé en scie
percé en serpentin

Percé en arc and percé en scie: pierced in an arc or saw-toothed rouletted, forming half circles or small triangles. (Hanover Nos. 25-29.)

Percé en serpentin: serpentine roulette. The cuts form a serpentine or wavy line. (Brunswick Nos. 13-22.)

PERFORATION: The second chief style of separation of stamps, and the one which is in universal use today, is called perforating. By this process the paper between the stamps is cut away in a line of holes, usually round, leaving little bridges of paper between the stamps to hold them together. These little bridges, which project from the stamp when it is torn from the sheet are called the teeth of the perforation. As the size of the perforation is sometimes the only way to differentiate between two otherwise identical stamps, it is necessary to be able to measure and describe them. This is done with a perforation gauge, a ruler-like device that has dots to show how many perforations can be counted in the space of 2 centimeters, the space universally adopted as the length in which perforations are measured. Run your stamp along the gauge until the dots on it fit exactly into the perforations. If the number alongside the dots into which it fits is 11, this means that 11 perforations fit between two centimeters and the stamp is described as "perf. 11." If the gauge of the perforations on the top and bottom of a stamp differs from that on the sides, it is called a "compound perforation." In measuring compound perforations the gauge at the top and bottom is always given first, then the sides. Thus a stamp that measures 10½ at top and bottom and 11 at the sides is described as "10½ x 11." (U.S. No. 1526.)

A perforation with small holes and teeth close together is called a "fine perforation." One with large holes and teeth far apart is a "coarse perforation." If the holes are jagged rather than clean cut, it is called "rough perforation." Blind perforations are the slight impressions left by the perforating pins if they fail to puncture the paper. Multiples showing blind perfs may command a slight premium over normally perforated stamps.

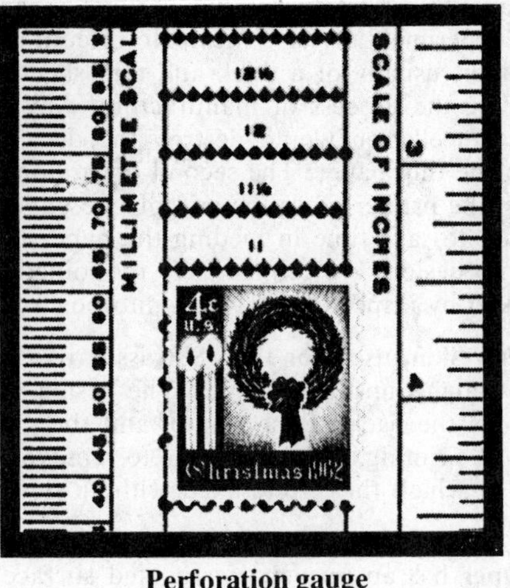

Perforation gauge

PRINTING PROCESSES

ENGRAVING (Intaglio): Master Die—The initial operation in the engraving process is the making of the master die. The die is a small flat block of soft steel on which the stamp design is recess engraved in reverse.

The original art is reduced photographically to the appropriate size, and serves as a tracing guide for the initial outline of the design. After the engraving is completed, the die is hardened to withstand the stress and pressures of subsequent transfer operations.

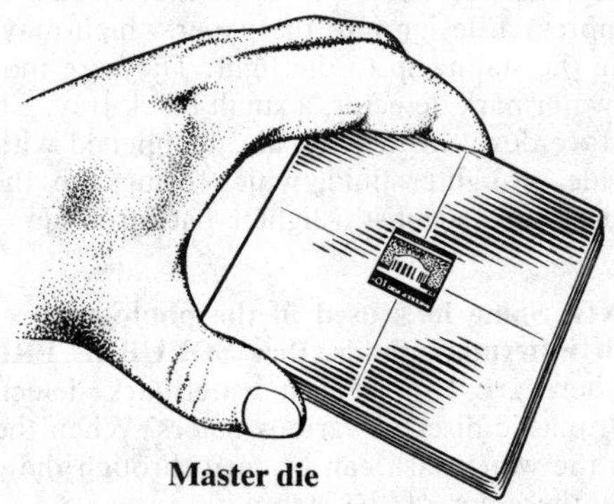
Master die

Transfer Roll—The next operation is the making of the transfer roll which, as the name implies, is the medium used to transfer the subject from the die to the plate. A blank roll of soft steel, mounted on a mandrel, is placed under the bearers of a transfer press, so as to allow it to roll freely on its axis. The hardened die is placed on the bed of the press and the face of the transfer roll is brought to bear on the die under pressure. The bed is then rocked back and forth under increasing pressure until the soft steel of the roll is forced into every engraved line of the die. The resulting impression on the roll is known as a "relief" or a "relief transfer." When the required number of reliefs are "rocked in," the soft steel transfer roll is also hardened.

A "relief" is the normal reproduction of the design on the die in reverse. A "defective relief" may occur during the "rocking in" process due to a minute piece of foreign material lodging on the die, or other causes. Imperfections in the steel of the transfer roll may result in a breaking away of parts of the design. If the damaged relief is continued in use, it will transfer a repeating defect to the plate. Sometimes reliefs are deliberately altered. "Broken relief" and "altered relief" are terms used to designate these changed conditions.

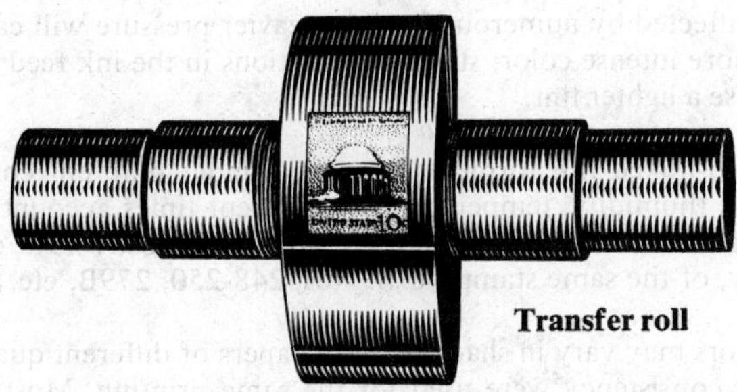

Transfer roll

Plate–The final step in the procedure is the making of the printing plate. A flat piece of soft steel replaces the die on the bed of the transfer press and one of the reliefs on the transfer roll is brought to bear on it. The position on the plate is determined by position dots, which have been lightly marked on the plate in advance. After the position of the relief is determined, pressure is brought to bear and, by following the same method used in making the transfer roll, a transfer is entered, This transfer reproduces in reverse and in detail the design of the relief. As many transfers are entered on the plate as there are to be subjects.

After the required transfers have been entered, the position dots, layout dots and lines, scratches, etc. are generally burnished out. Any required *guide lines, plate numbers* or other *marginal markings* are added. A proof impression is then taken and if "certified" (approved), the plate is machined for fitting to the press, hardened and sent to the plate vault ready for use.

Transferring the design to the plate

On press, the plate is inked and the surface automatically wiped clean, leaving the ink only in the depressed lines. Damp paper under pressure is forced down into the engraved depressed lines, thereby receiving the ink. Consequently, the lines on engraved stamps are slightly raised; and, conversely, slight depressions occur on the back of the stamp.

The expressions *taille douce,* engraved, line engraved and steel plate all designate substantially the same processes for producing engraved stamps.

Rotary Press–Engraved stamps were printed only with flat plates until 1915, when rotary press printing was introduced. *Rotary press plates,* after being certified, require additional machining. They are curved to fit the press cylinder and "gripper slots" are cut into the back of each plate to receive the "grippers," which hold the plate securely on the press, after which the plate is hardened. Stamps printed from rotary press plates are usually longer or wider than the same stamps printed from flat press plates. The stretching of the plate during the curving process causes this enlargement.

Re-entry–In order to execute a re-entry the transfer roll is reapplied to the plate, usually at some time after it has been put to press. Thus worn-out designs can be resharpened by carefully re-entering the transfer roll. If the transfer roll is not precisely in line with the impression on the plate, the registration will not be true and a double transfer will result. After a plate has been curved for the rotary press, it is impossible to make a re-entry.

Double Transfer–A description of the condition of a transfer on a plate that shows evidence of a duplication of all, or a portion of the design. It is usually the result of the changing of the registration between the transfer roll and the plate during the rocking-in of the original entry.

It is sometimes necessary to remove the original transfer from a plate and repeat the process a second time. If the finished re-transfer shows indications of the original impression due to incomplete erasure, the result is also a double transfer.

Re-engraved–Either the die that has been used to make a plate or the plate itself may have its "temper" drawn (softened) and be re-cut. The resulting impressions from such a re-engraved die or plate may differ slightly from the original issue, and are known as "re-engraved."

Short Transfer–It sometimes happens that the transfer roll is not rocked its entire length in entering a transfer on a plate, with the result that the finished transfer fails to show the complete design. This is known as a "short transfer." (U.S. No. 8, type III of 1851-56 1c.)

TYPOGRAPHY (Letterpress, Surface Printing)–As related to the printing of postage stamps, typography is the reverse of engraving. It includes all printing wherein the design is raised above the surface area, whether it is wood, metal, or in some instances hard rubber.

The master die is made in much the same manner as the engraved die. However, in this instance the area not being utilized as a printing surface is cut away, leaving the surface area raised. The original die is then reproduced by stereotyping or electrotyping. The resulting electrotypes are assembled in the required number and format of the desired sheet of stamps. The plate used in printing the stamps is an electroplate of these assembled electrotypes.

Ink is applied to the raised surface and the pressure of the press transfers the ink impression to the paper. Again, as opposed to engraving, the fine lines of typography are impressed on the surface of the stamp. When viewed from the back (as on a typewritten page) the corresponding linework will be raised slightly above the surface.

PHOTOGRAVURE (Rotogravure, Heliogravure)–In this process the basic principles of photography are applied to a sensitized metal plate, as opposed to photographic paper. The design is photographically transferred to the plate through a halftone screen, breaking the reproduction into tiny dots. The plate is treated chemically and the dots form depressions of varying depths, depending on the degrees of shade in the design. The depressions in the plate hold the ink, which is lifted out when the paper is pressed against the plate, in a manner similar to that of engraved printing.

LITHOGRAPHY–This process is based on the principle that oil and water will not mix. The design is drawn by hand or transferred from an engraving to the surface of a lithographic stone or metal plate in a greasy (oily) ink. The stone (or plate) is wet with an acid fluid, causing it to repel the printing ink in all areas not covered by the greasy ink.

Transfers are made from the original stone or plate by means of transfer paper. A series of duplicate transfers are grouped and these in turn are transferred to the final printing plate.

Photolithography–The application of photographic processes to lithography. This process allows greater flexibility of design, relating to use of halftone screens combined with linework.

Offset–A development of the lithographic process. A rubber-covered blanket cylinder takes up the impression from the inked lithographic plate. From the "blanket" the impression is *offset* or transferred to the paper. Because of its greater flexibility and speed, offset printing has largely displaced lithography. Since the processes and results are almost identical, stamps printed by either method are designated as lithographed.

Sometimes two or even three printing methods are combined in producing stamps.

EMBOSSED (RELIEF) PRINTING–A method in which the design is sunk in the metal of the die and the printing is done against a yielding platen, such as leather or linoleum, which is forced up into the depression of the die, thus forming the design on the paper in relief.

Embossing may be done without color (Sardinia Nos. 4-6); with color printed around the embossed area (Great Britain No. 5 and most U.S. envelopes); and with color in exact registration with the embossed subject (Canada Nos. 656-657).

INK COLORS: Pigments or dyes, usually of mineral origin, are used in the manufacture of inks or colored papers on which stamps are printed. The tone of any given color may be affected by numerous factors: heavier pressure will cause a more intense color; slight interruptions in the ink feed will cause a lighter tint.

Hand-mixed ink formulas produced under different conditions (humidity, temperature) at different times account for notable color variations in early printings, mostly 19th century, of the same stamp (U.S. Nos. 248-250, 279B, etc.).

Colors may vary in shade because papers of different quality and consistency were used for the same printing. Most pelure papers, for example, show a richer color when compared to wove or laid papers. (Russia No. 181a.)

The very nature of the printing processes can cause a variety of differences in shades or hues of the same stamp. Some of these shades are scarcer than others, and are of particular interest to the advanced collector.

SOLUBLE PRINTING INKS. WARNING. Most stamp colors are permanent. That is, they are not seriously affected by light or water. Some colors may fade from excessive exposure to light. Other stamps are printed in inks which dissolve easily in water or in benzine, carbon tetrachloride or other fluids used to detect watermarks. These inks were often used intentionally to prevent the removal of cancellations.

Benzine affects most photogravure printings. Water affects all aniline prints, those on safety paper, and some photogravure printings. All the above are called *fugitive colors.*

TAGGED STAMPS

(Luminescence, Fluorescence, Phosphorescence)

Some tagged stamps have bars (Great Britain, Canada), frames (South Africa), or an overall coating of luminescent material applied after the stamps have been printed (United States). Another tagging method is to incorporate the luminescent material into some or all colors of the printing ink (Australia No. 366, Netherlands No. 478). A third is to mix the luminescent material with the pulp during the paper manufacturing process or apply it as a surface coating afterwards. These are called "fluorescent" papers. (Switzerland Nos. 510-514, Germany No. 848.)

The treated stamps show up in specific colors when exposed to ultraviolet light. The wave length of the luminescent material determines the colors and activates the triggering mechanism of the electronic machinery for sorting, facing or canceling letters.

Various fluorescent substances have been used as paper whiteners, but the resulting "hi-brite papers" show up differently under ultraviolet light and do not trigger the machines. They are not noted in the Catalogue.

Introduced in Great Britain in 1959 on an experimental basis, tagging in its various forms is now used by many countries to expedite the handling of mail. Following Great Britain were Germany ('61); Canada and Denmark ('62); United States, Australia, Netherlands and Switzerland ('63); Belgium and Japan ('66); Sweden and Norway ('67); Italy ('68); Russia ('69), and so forth.

Certain stamps were issued both with and without the luminescent factor. In these instances, the "tagged" variety is listed in the United States, Canada, Great Britain and Switzerland, and is noted in some of the other countries.

GUM

The gum on a stamp's back may be smooth, crinkly, dark, white, colored or tinted, and either obvious or virtually invisible as on Canada No. 453 or Rwanda Nos. 287-294. Most stamp gumming has been carried out with adhesives using gum arabic or dextrine as a base, but certain polymers such as polyvinyl alcohol (PVA) have been used extensively since World War II. The PVA gum which Harrison & Sons of Great Britain introduced in 1968 is dull, slightly yellowish and almost invisible.

Stamps having full **original gum** sell for more than those from which the gum has been removed. Reprints may have gum differing from the originals.

REPRINTS AND REISSUES

Reprints are impressions of stamps (usually obsolete) made from the original plates or stones. If valid for postage and from obsolete issues, they are called reissues. If they are from current issues, they are *second, third,* etc. *printings.* If designated for a particular purpose, they are called *special printings.*

When reprints are not valid for postage, but made from original dies and plates by authorized persons they are *official reprints*–to distinguish them from *private reprints* made from original plates and dies by private hands. *Official reproductions* or imitations are made from new dies and plates by government authorization.

For the 1876 Centennial, the U.S. government made official imitations of its first postage stamps, which are listed as Nos. 3-4; official reprints of the demonetized pre-1861 issues; reissued the 1869 stamps and made special printings of the current 1875 denominations. An example of the private reprint is that of the New Haven postmaster's provisional.

Most reprints differ slightly from the original stamp in some characteristic such as gum, paper, perforation, color, watermark (or lack thereof). Sometimes the details have been followed so meticulously that only a student of that stamp can tell the reprint from the original.

REMAINDERS AND CANCELED TO ORDER

Some countries sell their stock of old stamps when a new issue replaces them. The **remainders** are usually canceled with a punch hole, a heavy line or bar, or a more or less regular cancellation to avoid postal use. The most famous merchant of remainders was Nicholas F. Seebeck, who arranged printing contracts between the Hamilton Bank Note Co., of which he was a director, and several Central and Latin American countries in the 1880's and 1890's. The contracts provided that the plates and all remainders of the yearly issues became the property of Hamilton, and Seebeck saw to it that ample stock remained. The "Seebecks," both remainders and reprints, were standard packet fillers for decades.

Some countries also issue stamps **canceled to order** (CTO), either in sheets with original gum or stuck onto pieces of paper or envelopes and canceled. Such CTO items generally are worth less than postally used stamps. Most can be detected by the presence of gum. However, as the CTO practice goes back at least to 1885, the gum inevitably has been washed off some stamps so they could pass for postally used. The normally applied postmarks usually differ slightly and specialists can tell the difference. When applied individually to envelopes by philatelically minded persons, CTO material is known as *favor canceled* and generally sells at large discounts.

CINDERELLAS AND FACSIMILES

Cinderella is a catchall term used by collectors of phantoms, fantasies, bogus items, municipal issues, exhibition seals, local revenues, transportation stamps, labels, poster stamps, etc. Cinderellas are not issued by any national government for postal purposes. Some cinderella collectors include local postage issues, telegraph stamps, essays and proofs, forgeries and counterfeits.

A fantasy is an adhesive created for a nonexisting stamp issuing authority. Fantasy items range from imaginary countries (Kingdom of Sedang or Principality of Trinidad) to nonexisting locals (Winans City Post), or nonexisting transportation lines (McRobish & Co.'s Acapulco-San Francisco Line). On the other hand, if the entity exists and might have issued stamps or did issue other stamps, the items are *bogus* stamps. These would include the Mormon postage stamps of Utah, S. Allan Taylor's Guatemala and Paraguay inventions, the propaganda issues for the South Moluccas and the adhesives of the Page & Keyes local post of Boston.

Both fantasies and bogus issues are sometimes called *phantoms.*

Facsimiles are copies or imitations made to represent original stamps, but which do not pretend to be originals. A catalogue illustration is such a facsimile. Illustrations from the Moëns catalogue of the last century were occasionally colored and passed as stamps. Since the beginning of stamp collecting, facsimiles have been made for collectors as space fillers or for reference. They often carry the words "facsimile," "falsch" (German), "sanko" or "mozo" (Japanese), or "faux" (French) overprinted on the face or stamped on the back. Naturally, they have only curio value.

COUNTERFEITS OR FORGERIES

Postal counterfeits or **postal forgeries** are unauthorized imitations of stamps intended to deprive the post of revenue. They often command higher prices than the genuine stamps they imitate. Sales are illegal and governments can, and do, prosecute.

The first postal forgery was of Spain's 4-cuartos carmine of 1854, No. 25. The forgers lithographed it, though the original was typographed. Apparently they were not satisfied and soon made an engraved forgery which is fairly common, unlike the scarce lithographed counterfeit. Postal forgeries quickly followed in Spain, Austria, Naples, Sardinia and the Roman States.

An infamous counterfeit to defraud the government is the 1-shilling Great Britain "Stock Exchange" forgery of 1872 used on telegrams at the exchange that year. It escaped detection until a stamp dealer noticed it in 1898. Recent postal counterfeits include the U.S. 4c Lincoln and the 8c Eisenhower as well as Canada's 6c orange of 1968 (which was later faked in turn).

Because the governments concerned did not issue them, the *wartime propaganda* stamps of both World Wars may be classed as postal counterfeits. They were put out by other governments or resistance groups.

Philatelic forgeries or *counterfeits* are unauthorized imitations of stamps designed to deceive and defraud collectors. Such spurious items first appeared on the market around 1860 and most old-time collections contain one or more. Many are crude and easily spotted even by the non-specialist, but some can deceive the better-than-average collector.

An important supplier of these early philatelic forgeries was the Hamburg printer, Gebrüder Spiro. Many others indulged in this craft including S. Allan Taylor, George Hussey, James Chute, Georges Foure, Benjamin & Sarpy, Julius Goldner, E. Oneglia and L. H. Mercier. Among the noted 20th century forgers are Francois Fournier, Jean Sperati and the prolific Raoul DeThuin.

Most classic rarities, many medium priced stamps and, in this century, cheap stamps on a wholesale basis destined for beginners' packets, have been fraudulently produced. However, few new philatelic forgeries have appeared in recent decades and virtually no new frauds of valuable classics. Successful imitation of engraved work is virtually impossible. It has proven far easier to produce a fake by altering a genuine stamp than to duplicate a stamp completely.

REPAIRS AND FAKES

Most collectors will not object to restoration of a stamp or cover, although they will not accept repairs on the same basis. *Restoration* in this sense includes cleaning with a soft eraser or soap and water. It may include the ironing out of a crease or removal of a cellophane tape stain. Removal of old hinges is acceptable. Some collectors believe that freshening of a stamp is valid restoration, whether done by the removal of oxides, "toning," or the effect of wax paper left on stamps shipped to the tropics between such sheets. Regumming may have been acceptable restoration half a century ago, but today it is considered faking. Restored stamps or covers do not normally sell at a discount, and may even change hands at a premium.

Repairs include filling in thin spots, mending tears by reweaving, adding a missing corner or perforation "tooth." Repaired stamps sell at substantial discounts.

Fakes are genuine stamps altered in some way to make them more desirable and sold without revealing the alterations. According to one major student, 30,000 varieties of fakes were known in the 1950's. The number has grown. The widespread existence of fakes makes it important for collectors to study their philatelic holdings and relevant literature. For the same reason they should buy from reputable dealers who will guarantee their stamps and make full prompt refund should a purchase be declared not genuine by some mutually agreed-upon authority. Because fakes always have some genuine characteristics, it is not always possible to obtain unanimity among expert students regarding specific items. These students may change their opinions as philatelic knowledge increases. More than 80 per cent of all fakes on the market today are regummed, reperforated or altered in regard to overprints, surcharges or cancellations.

Stamps can be chemically treated to alter or eliminate colors. For example a pale rose can be recolored into a blue of a higher value, or a "missing color" variety created. Designs may be changed by "painting," or a stroke or dot added or bleached out to turn an ordinary variety into a scarce stamp. Part of a stamp can be bleached and reprinted in a different version, achieving an inverted center or frame. Margins can be added or repairs done so deceptively that the stamp moves from the repaired to the fake category.

The fakers have not left the backs of stamps untouched. They may create false watermarks or add fake grills (or press out genuine ones). A thin India paper proof may be glued onto a thicker backing to "create" an issued stamp, or a cardboard proof may be shaved down. Silk threads have been impressed in and stamps have been split so that a rare paper variety, from a cheap stamp, can be applied as a back to falsely identify the stamp. However, the most common back treatment is regumming.

Some operators openly advertise "foolproof" application of "original gum" to stamps that lack it. This is faking, not counterfeiting. As few early stamps have survived without being hinged, the large number of never-hinged examples now offered for sale suggests the extent of regumming that has been and is being done. Regumming may be used to hide repairs and thin spots, but dipping in watermark fluid will often reveal these flaws.

The fakers also tamper with separations. Ingenious ways to add margins are known, and perforated wide-margin stamps may be falsely represented as imperforate when trimmed. Reperforating is commonly done to create scarce coil or perforation varieties and to eliminate the straight-edge stamps found in sheet margin positions of many earlier issues. Custom has made straight edges less desirable and the fakers have obliged by reperforating them so extensively that many are now uncommon if not rare.

Another main field of the faker is that of the overprint, surcharge and cancellation. The forging of rare surcharges or overprints began in the 1880's or 1890's. These forgeries are sometimes difficult to detect, but the better experts have probably identified almost all of them. Only occasionally are the overprints or cancellations removed to create unoverprinted stamps or unused items. The SPECIMEN overprints are sometimes removed–scraping and repainting is one way –to create unoverprinted varieties. Cheap revenues or pen-canceled stamps are used to generate "unused" stamps for further faking by adding other markings. The quartz lamp and a high-powered magnifying glass help in detecting cancellation removals.

The big problem, however, is the addition of overprints, surcharges or cancellations–many quite dangerous. Plating of the stamps or the overprint can be an important detecting method.

Fake postmarks can range from numerous spurious fancy cancellations, to the host of markings applied to transatlantic covers to create rare uses. With the advance of cover collecting and the wide interest in postal history, a fertile new field for fakers arose. Some have tried to create entire covers. Others specialize in adding stamps, tied by fake cancellations, to genuine stampless covers, or replacing cheaper or damaged stamps with more valuable ones. Detailed study of rates and postmarks (including the analysis of "breaks" in each handstamp over a period), ink analysis, etc. will usually unmask the fraud.

TERMINOLOGY

BOOKLETS: Many countries have issued stamps in small booklets for the convenience of users. They are usually sold by the post office at a small premium. Booklets have been issued in all sizes and forms, often with advertising on the covers, on the panes of stamps or on the interleaving. The panes may be printed from special plates or made from regular sheets. All panes from booklets issued by the United States and many from those of other countries are straight edged on the bottom and both sides, but perforated between the stamps. Any unit in the pane, either printed or blank, which is not a postage stamp, is called a *label* in the catalogue listings.

CANCELLATIONS: The marks or obliterations put on a stamp by the postal authorities to show that it has done service and is no longer valid for postage. If it is made with a pen, it is called a pen cancellation. When the location of the post office appears in the cancellation, it is called a town cancellation. When it calls attention to a cause or celebration, it is a slogan cancellation. Many other types and styles of cancellations exist, such as duplex, numerals, targets, etc.

COIL STAMPS–Stamps issued in rolls for use in affixing and vending machines. Those of the United States, Canada, etc., are perforated horizontally or vertically only, with the outer edges imperforate. Coil stamps of some countries (Great Britain) are perforated on all four sides.

COVERS: Envelopes, with or without adhesive postage stamps, which have passed through the mail and bear postal or other markings of philatelic interest. Before the introduction of envelopes (1840), people folded letters and wrote the address on the outside. Many people covered their letters with an extra sheet of paper on the outside for the address. Hence the word "cover." Used air letter sheets, stamped envelopes, and other items of postal stationery are also referred to as "covers."

ERRORS: Stamps having some unintentional deviation from the normal. Errors include, but are not limited to, mistakes in color, paper or watermark; inverted centers (or frames), surcharges or overprints, and double impressions. A factually wrong or misspelled inscription, if it appears on all examples of a stamp, is not classified as a philatelic error. (Panama No. J1).

OVERPRINTED AND SURCHARGED STAMPS: Overprinting is wording placed on stamps to alter the place of use ("Canal Zone" on U.S. issues); to adapt them for a special purpose ("Porto" on Denmark's 1913-20 regular issues for use as postage dues, Nos. J1-J7); or for a special occasion (Guatemala Nos. 374-378).

The term **surcharge** is used when the overprint changes or restates the value (1923 "Inflation Issues" of Germany; Australia No. 580).

Surcharges and overprints may be handstamped, typeset or, occasionally, lithographed or engraved.

PRECANCELS: Stamps canceled by the issuing government before they are sold at the post office. Precanceling is done to expedite the handling of large mailings.

In the United States precancellations generally identify the point of origin. That is, the city and state names (or initials) appear, usually centered by an arrangement of parallel lines.

In France the abbreviation **Affranchts** in a semicircle together with the word **Postes** is the general form. Belgian precancellations are usually a square box in which the name of the city appears. Netherlands' precancellations have the name of the city enclosed between a large and small circle, sometimes called a "life-saver."

Precancellations of other countries usually follow these patterns, but may be any arrangement of bars, boxes and city names.

PROOFS AND ESSAYS: Proofs are impressions taken from an approved die, plate or stone in which the design and color are the same as the stamp issued to the public. Trial color proofs are impressions taken from approved dies, plates or stones in varying colors. An essay is the impression of a design that differs in some way from the stamp as issued.

PROVISIONALS: Stamps issued on short notice and intended for temporary use pending the arrival of regular (definitive) issues. They are usually issued to meet contingencies: changes in government or currency; shortage of necessary postage values, or military occupation.

In the 1840's, postmasters in certain American cities issued stamps that were valid only at specific post offices. Postmasters of the Confederate States also issued stamps with limited validity. These are known as Postmasters' Provisionals.

SE-TENANT: Joined together, referring to an unsevered pair, strip or block of stamps differing in design, denomination or overprint (U.S. Nos. 1530-1537).

TETE BECHE: A pair of stamps in which one is upside down in relation to the other. Some of these are the result of intentional sheet arrangement (Morocco Nos. B10-B11). Others occurred when one or more electrotypes were accidentally placed upside down on the plate (Colombia No. 57a). Separation of course destroys the tête bêche variety.

SPECIMENS: One of the regulations of the Universal Postal Union requires member nations to send samples of all stamps they put into service to the International Bureau in Switzerland. These are then sent to all other member nations as samples of what stamps are valid for postage. Many are overprinted, handstamped or initial-perforated "Specimen," "Canceled" or "Muestra." Some are marked with bars across the denominations (China), punched holes (Czechoslovakia) or back inscriptions (Mongolia).

Stamps distributed to government officials or for publicity purposes, and stamps submitted by private security printers for official approval may also receive such defacements.

These markings prevent postal use, and all such items are generally known as "specimens."

CLASSIFICATION OF STAMPS

The various functions of stamps are classified by their names. Postage stamps; air post stamps; postage due stamps for unpaid postage, collected at time of delivery; late fee stamps, a special fee for forwarding a letter after regular mail delivery; registration stamps, fee for keeping special record of letter and ensuring its delivery; special delivery and express stamps, for delivery of letter in advance of regular delivery. With the exception of regular postage, all numbers in the catalogue include a prefix letter denoting the class to which the stamp belongs. (B=Semi-Postal; C=Air Post; E=Special Delivery; J=Postage Due; O=Official; CO=Air Post Official; etc.).

CATALOGUE TERMS TRANSLATED

English	French	German	Spanish	Italian
Air mail	Poste aérienne	Flugpost	Correo aéreo	Posta aerea
Back	Verso	Rückseitig	Dorso	Dorso
Background	Fond	Hintergrund	Fondo	Sfondo
Bar	Barre	Balken	Barra	Barra
Bisected stamp	Timbre coupé	Halbiert	Partido en dos	Frazionato
Block of four	Bloc de quatre	Viererblock	Bloque de cuatro	Blocco di quattro
Booklet	Carnet	Heftchen	Cuadernillo	Libretto
Bottom	Bas	Unten	Abajo	Basso
Bright	Vif	Lebhaft	Vivo	Vivo
Broken	Interrompu	Unterbrochen	Interrumpido	Interrotto
Cancellation	Oblitération	Entwertung	Matasello	Annullamento
Cancellation to order	Oblitération de complaisance	Gefälligkeitsabstempelung	Matasello de complacencia	Annullamento di compiacenza
Canceled	Annulé	Gestempelt	Cancelado	Annullato
Center	Centre du timbre	Mittelstück	Centro	Centro
Centering	Centrage	Zentrierung	Centrado	Centratura
Chalky paper	Papier couché	Kreidepapier	Papel estucado	Carta gessata
Circle	Cercle	Kreis	Circulo	Circolo
Coat of arms	Armoiries	Wappen	Escudo de armas	Arme
Coil	Rouleau de timbres	Markenrolle	Rollo de sellos	Rollo di francobolli
Color	Couleur	Farbe	Color	Colore
Comb perforation	Dentelure en peigne	Kammzähnung	Dentado de peine	Dentalletura e pettine
Commemorative	Commémoratif	Gedenkausgabe	Conmemorativo	Commemorativo
Corner	Angle	Ecke	Esquina	Angolo
Counterfeit	Faux	Fälschung	Falsificación	Falsificazione
Cover	Lettre	Brief	Carta	Lettera
Crescent	Croissant	Halbmond	Media luna	Luna crescente
Crown	Couronne	Krone	Corona	Corona
Cut square	Coupure	Ausschnitt	Recorte	Ritaglio
Dark	Foncé	Dunkel	Oscuro	Oscuro
Date	Date	Datum	Fecha	Data
Definitive	Définitif	Freimarken	Definitivo	Definitivo
Design	Dessin	Zeichnung	Diseño	Disegno
Die	Matrice	Urstempel	Cuño	Conio
District	District	Bezirk	Distrito	Distretto
Double	Double	Doppelt	Doble	Doppio
Dull	Terne	Trüb	Turbio	Smorto
Embossing	Impression en relief	Prägedruck	Impresión en relieve	Rilievo
Engraved	Gravé	Graviert	Grabado	Inciso
Error	Erreur	Fehler	Error	Errore
Essay	Essai	Probedruck	Ensayo	Saggio
Figure	Chiffre	Ziffer	Cifra	Cifra
Forerunner	Précurseur	Vorläufer	Precursor	Precursore
Forgery	Faux	Fälschung	Falsificación	Falsificazione
Frame	Cadre	Rahmen	Marco	Cornice
Genuine	Authentique	Echt	Auténtico	Autentico
Glossy paper	Papier glacé	Glanzpapier	Papel lustre	Carta patinata
Granite paper	Papier mélangé de fils de soie	Faserpapier	Papel con filamentos	Carta con fili di seta
Gum	Gomme	Gummi	Goma	Gomma
Gutter	Interpanneau	Zwischensteg	Espacio blanco entre dos grupos	Interspazio
Half	Moitié	Hälfte	Mitad	Metà
Handstamp	Cachet à la main	Handstempel	Matasello manual	Annullamento manuale

English	French	German	Spanish	Italian
Imperforate	Non-dentelé	Geschnitten	Sin dentar	Non dentellato
Inscription	Inscription	Inschrift	Inscripción	Dicitura
Inverted	Renversé	Kopfstehend	Invertido	Capovolto
Issue	Emission	Ausgabe	Emisión	Emissione
King	Roi	König	Rey	Re
Kingdom	Royaume	Königreich	Reino	Regno
Laid	Vergé	Gestrichen	Listado	Vergato
Large	Grand	Gross	Grande	Grosso
Late fee stamp	Timbre pour lettres en retard	Verspätungsmarke	Sello para cartas retardadas	Francobollo per le lettere in ritardo
Left	Gauche	Links	Izquierda	Sinistro
Light	Clair	Hell	Claro	Chiaro
Line perforation	Dentelure en lignes	Linienzähnung	Dentado en linea	Dentellatura lineare
Lithography	Lithographie	Steindruck	Litografia	Litografia
Lozenges	Losanges	Rauten	Rombos	Losanghe
Margin	Marge	Rand	Borde	Margine
Multiple	Multiple	Mehrfach	Multiple	Multiplo
Narrow	Étroit	Eng	Estrecho	Stretto
Network	Burelage	Netz	Burelage	Rete
Newspaper stamp	Timbre pour journaux	Zeitungsmarke	Sello para periódicos	Francobollo per giornali
Not issued	Non émis	Nicht verausgabt	No emitido	Non emesso
Numeral	Chiffre	Ziffer	Cifra	Numerale
Occupation	Occupation	Besetzung	Occupación	Occupazione
Official stamp	Timbre de service	Dienstmarke	Sello de servicio	Francobollo servizio
Oval	Ovale	Eiförmig	Óvalo	Ovale
Overprint	Surcharge	Aufdruck	Sobrecarga	Soprastampa
Pair	Paire	Paar	Pareja	Coppia
Pale	Pâle	Blass	Pálido	Pallido
Pane	Panneau	Gruppe	Grupo	Gruppo
Paper	Papier	Papier	Papel	Carta
Parcel post stamp	Timbre pour colis postaux	Paketmarke	Sello para paquete postal	Francobollo per pacchi postali
Pen canceled	Oblitéré à plume	Federzugentwertung	Cancelado a pluma	Annullato a penna
Perforated	Dentelé	Gezähnt	Dentado	Dentellato
Perforation	Dentelure	Zähnung	Dentar	Dentellatura
Photogravure	Héliogravure	Rastertiefdruck	Fotograbado	Rotocalco
Piece	Fragment	Briefstück	Fragmento	Frammento
Pin perforation	Percé en points	In Punkten durchstochen	Horadado con alfileres	Perforato a punti
Plate	Planche	Platte	Plancha	Lastra
Postage due stamp	Timbre-taxe	Portomarke	Sello de tasa	Segnatasse
Postage stamp	Timbre-poste	Briefmarke	Sello de correos	Francobollo postale
Postal forgery	Faux pour servir	Postfälschung	Falso por correo	Falso per posta
Postal tax stamp	Timbre surtaxe obligatoire	Zwangszuschlagsmarke	Sello de sobretasa obligatorio	Francobollo per sopratassa obligatorio
Postmark	Oblitération postale	Poststempel	Matasello	Bollo
Price	Prix	Preis	Precio	Prezzo
Printing	Impression	Druck	Impresión	Stampa
Private	Privé	Privat	Privado	Privato
Proof	Epreuve	Druckprobe	Prueba de impresión	Prova
Quadrille	Quadrillé	Gegittert	Cuadriculado	Quadriglia
Quarter	Un quart	Viertel	Un cuarto	Quarto
Recess printing	Impression en taille douce	Tiefdruck	Grabado	Incisione
Reengraving	Regravure	Neugravierung	Regrabado	Rincisione

English	French	German	Spanish	Italian
Reentry	Double frappe	Nachgravierung	Regrabado	Doppia incisione
Registration stamp	Timbre pour lettre recommandée	Einschreibemarke	Sello de certificado	Francobollo per lettere raccomandate
Reprint	Réimpression	Nachdruck	Reimpresión	Ristampa
Revenue stamp	Timbre fiscal	Stempelmarke	Sello fiscal	Francobollo fiscale
Reversed	Retourné	Umgekehrt	Invertido	Rovesciato
Ribbed	Cannelé	Geriffelt	Acanalado	Scanalatura
Right	Droite	Rechts	A la derecha	Destro
Rotary printing	Impression par cylindre	Walzendruck	Impresión cilindrica	Stampa rotativa
Roulette	Perçage	Durchstich	Picadura	Foratura
Rouletted	Percé	Durchstochen	Picado	Forato
Semipostal stamp	Timbre de bienfaisance	Wohltätigkeitsmarke	Sello de beneficencia	Francobollo di beneficenza
Serpentine roulette	Percé en serpentin	Schlangenartiger Durchstich	Picado a serpentina	Perforazione a serpentina
Set	Série	Satz	Serie	Serie
Set price	Prix de la série	Satzpreis	Precio por serie	Prezzo per serie
Se-tenant	Se-tenant	Zusammendruck	Combinación	Combinazione
Shade	Nuance	Tönung	Tono	Gradazione di colore
Sheet	Feuille	Bogen	Hoja	Foglio
Side	Côté	Seite	Lado	Lato
Small	Petit	Klein	Pequeño	Piccolo
Souvenir sheet	Bloc commémoratif	Block, gedenkblock	Hojita-bloque conmemorativa	Foglietto commemorativo
Special delivery stamp	Timbre pour exprès	Eilmarke	Sello de urgencia	Francobollo per espressi
Specimen	Spécimen	Muster	Muestra	Saggio
Strip	Bande	Streifen	Tira	Striscia
Surcharge	Surcharge	Zuschlag	Sobrecarga	Soprastampa
Surtax	Surtaxe	Zuschlag	Sobretasa	Sopratassa
Tête bêche	Tête-bêche	Kehrdruck	Tête-bêche	Tête-bêche
Thick	Épais	Dick	Grueso	Spesso
Thin	Mince	Dünn	Delgado	Smilzo
Tinted paper	Papier teinté	Getöntes papier	Papel coloreado	Carta colorata
Top	Haut	Oben	Arriba	Alto
Typography	Typographie	Buchdruck	Tipografía	Tipografia
Unused	Neuf	Ungebraucht	Nuevo	Nuovo
Used	Oblitéré	Gebraucht	Usado	Usato
War tax stamp	Timbre d'impôt de guerre	Kriegssteuermarke	Sello de impuesto de guerra	Francobollo per tassa di guerra
Watermark	Filigrane	Wasserzeichen	Filigrana	Filigrana
Wide	Espacé	Weit	Ancho	Largo
With	Avec	Mit	Con	Con
Without	Sans	Ohne	Sin	Senza
Worn	Usé	Abgenutzt	Gastado	Usato
Wove paper	Papier ordinaire	Einfaches Papier	Papel avitelado	Carta unita

CATALOGUE COLORS TRANSLATED

English	French	German	Spanish	Italian
Apple green	Verte-pomme	Apfelgrün	Verde manzana	Verde mela
Bister	Bistre	Bister	Bistre	Bistro
Black	Noir	Schwarz	Negro	Nero
Blue	Bleu	Blau	Azul	Azzurro
Brick red	Rouge-brique	Ziegelrot	Rojo ladrillo	Rosso di mattone
Bronze	Bronze	Bronze	Bronce	Bronzo
Brown	Brun	Braun	Castaño, pardo	Bruno
Buff	Chamois	Sämisch	Anteado	Camoscio
Carmine	Carmin	Karmin	Carmin	Carminio
Cerise	Cerise	Kirschrot	Color de ceresa	Color ciliegia
Chalky blue	Bleu terne	Kreideblau	Azul turbio	Azzurro smorto
Chamois	Chamois	Sämisch	Anteado	Camoscio
Chestnut	Marron	Kastanienbraun	Castaño rojo	Marrone
Chocolate	Chocolat	Schokoladebraun	Chocolate	Cioccolato
Chrome yellow	Jaune-chrome	Chromgelb	Amarillo cromo	Giallo croma
Citron	Citron	Zitronengelb	Cidra	Cedro
Claret	Lie de vin	Weinrot	Rojo vinoso	Vinaccia
Cobalt	Cobalt	Kobaltblau	Cobalto	Cobalto
Copper red	Rouge-cuivre	Kupferrot	Rojo cobre	Rosso di rame
Cream	Crème	Rahmfarbe	Crema	Crema
Crimson	Cramoisi	Karmesin	Carmesi	Cremisi
Emerald	Vert-émeraude	Smaragdgrün	Esmeralda	Smeraldo
Flesh	Chair	Fleischfarben	Carne	Carnicino
Gray	Gris	Grau	Gris	Grigio
Green	Vert	Grün	Verde	Verde
Indigo	Indigo	Indigo	Azul indigo	Indaco
Lake	Lie de vin	Lackfarbe	Laca	Lacca
Lemon	Jaune-citron	Zitronengelb	Limón	Limone
Lilac	Lilas	Lila	Lila	Lilla
Magenta	Magenta	Magentarot	Magenta	Magenta
Mauve	Mauve	Malvenfarbe	Malva	Malva
Milky blue	Bleu laiteux	Milchblau	Azul lechoso	Azzurro di latte
Moss green	Vert mousse	Moosgrün	Verde musgo	Verde muscosa
Multicolored	Polychrome	Mehrfarbig	Multicolores	Policromo
Ocher	Ocre	Ocker	Ocre	Ocra
Olive	Olive	Oliv	Oliva	Oliva
Orange	Orange	Orange	Naranja	Arancio
Pink	Rose	Rosa	Rosa	Rosa
Plum	Prune	Pflaumenfarbe	Color de ciruela	Prugna
Prussian blue	Bleu de Prusse	Preussischblau	Azul de Prusia	Azzurro di Prussia
Purple	Pourpre	Purpur	Púrpura	Porpora
Red	Rouge	Rot	Rojo	Rosso
Rose	Rose	Rosa	Rosa	Rosa
Rosine	Rose vif	Lebhaftrosa	Rosa vivo	Rosa vivo
Royal blue	Bleu-roi	Königsblau	Azul real	Azzurro reale
Rust	Brun-rouille	Rostbraun	Castaño oxidado	Castagna
Sage green	Vert-sauge	Salbeigrün	Verde salvia	Verde salvia
Salmon	Saumon	Lachs	Salmón	Salmone
Scarlet	Écarlate	Scharlach	Escarlata	Scarlatto
Sea green	Vert de mer	Seegrün	Verde mar	Verde mare
Sepia	Sépia	Sepia	Sepia	Seppia
Sienna	Terre de Sienne	Siena	Siena	Siena
Sky blue	Bleu ciel	Himmelblau	Azul celeste	Azzurro cielo
Slate	Ardoise	Schiefer	Pizarra	Ardesia
Steel blue	Bleu acier	Stahlblau	Azul acero	Azzurro acciaio
Straw	Jaune-paille	Strohgelb	Amarillo pajizo	Giallo pallido
Turquoise blue	Bleu-turquoise	Türkisblau	Azul turquesa	Azzurro turchese
Ultramarine	Outremer	Ultramarin	Ultramar	Oltremare
Vermilion	Vermillon	Zinnober	Cinabrio	Vermiglione
Violet	Violet	Violett	Violeta	Violetto
Yellow	Jaune	Gelb	Amarillo	Giallo

List of Colonies, Former Colonies, Offices and Territories Controlled by Parent States

BELGIUM

Belgian Congo
Ruanda-Urundi

DENMARK

Danish West Indies
Faroe Islands
Greenland
Iceland

FRANCE

Colonies, Past and Present, and Controlled Territories

Afars and Issas, Terr. of
Alaouites
Alexandretta
Algeria
Alsace and Lorraine
Ajouan
Annam & Tonkin
Benin
Cambodia (Khmer)
Cameroun
Castellorizo
Chad
Cilicia
Cochin China
Comoro Islands
Dahomey
Diego Suarez
Djibouti (Somali Coast)
Fezzan
French Congo
French Equatorial Africa
French Guiana
French Guinea
French India
French Morocco
French Polynesia (Oceania)
French Southern & Antarctic Territories
French Sudan
French West Africa
Gabon
Germany
Ghadames
Grand Comoro
Guadeloupe
Indo-China
Inini
Ivory Coast
Laos
Latakia
Lebanon
Madagascar
Martinique
Mauritania
Mayotte
Memel
Middle Congo
Mohéli
New Caledonia
New Hebrides
Niger Territory
Nossi-Bé
Obock
Reunion
Rouad, Ile
Ste.-Marie de Madagascar
St. Pierre & Miquelon
Senegal
Senegambia & Niger
Somali Coast
Syria
Tahiti
Togo
Tunisia
Ubangi-Shari
Upper Senegal & Niger
Upper Volta
Viet Nam
Wallis & Futuna Islands

Post Offices in Foreign Countries

China
Crete
Egypt
Turkish Empire
Zanzibar

GERMANY

Early States

Baden
Bavaria
Bergedorf
Bremen
Brunswick
Hamburg
Hanover
Lubeck
Mecklenburg-Schwerin
Mecklenburg-Strelitz
Oldenburg
Prussia
Saxony
Schleswig-Holstein
Wurttemberg

Former Colonies

Cameroun (Kamerun)
Caroline Islands
German East Africa
German New Guinea
German South-West Africa
Kiauchau
Mariana Islands
Marshall Islands
Samoa
Togo

ITALY

Early States

Modena
Parma
Romagna
Roman States
Sardinia
Tuscany
Two Sicilies
- Naples
- Neapolitan Provinces
- Sicily

Former Colonies, Controlled Territories, Occupation Areas

Aegean Islands
- Calimno (Calino)
- Caso
- Cos (Coo)
- Karki (Carchi)
- Leros (Lero)
- Lipso
- Nisiros (Nisiro)
- Patmos (Patmo)
- Piscopi
- Rodi (Rhodes)
- Scarpanto
- Simi
- Stampalia

Castellorizo
Corfu
Cyrenaica
Eritrea
Ethiopia (Abyssinia)
Fiume
Ionian Islands
- Cephalonia
- Ithaca
- Paxos

Italian East Africa
Libya
Oltre Giuba
Saseno
Somalia (Italian Somaliland)
Tripolitania

Post Offices in Foreign Countries

"Estero"*

Austria
China
- Peking
- Tientsin

Crete
Tripoli
Turkish Empire
- Constantinople

Turkish Empire (cont.)
- Durazzo
- Janina

Jerusalem
Salonika
Scutari
Smyrna
Valona

* Stamps overprinted "ESTERO" were used in various parts of the world.

NETHERLANDS

Netherlands Antilles (Curacao)
Netherlands Indies
Netherlands New Guinea
Surinam (Dutch Guiana)

PORTUGAL

Colonies, Past and Present, and Controlled Territories

Angola
Angra
Azores
Cape Verde
Funchal
Horta
Inhambane
Kionga
Lourenço Marques
Macao
Madeira
Mozambique
Mozambique Co.
Nyassa
Ponta Delgada
Portuguese Africa
Portuguese Congo
Portuguese Guinea
Portuguese India
Quelimane
St. Thomas & Prince Isls.
Tete
Timor
Zambezia

RUSSIA

Allied Territories and Republics, Occupation Areas

Armenia
Aunus (Olonets)
Azerbaijan
Batum
Estonia
Far Eastern Republic
Georgia
Karelia
Latvia
Lithuania
North Ingermanland
Ostland
Russian Turkestan
Siberia
South Russia
Tannu Tuva
Transcaucasian Federated Republics
Ukraine
Wenden (Livonia)
Western Ukraine

SPAIN

Colonies, Past and Present, and Controlled Territories

Agüera, La
Cape Juby
Cuba
Elobey, Annobon & Corisco
Fernando Po
Ifni
Mariana Islands
Philippines
Puerto Rico
Rio de Oro
Rio Muni
Spanish Guinea
Spanish Morocco
Spanish Sahara
Spanish West Africa

Post Offices in Foreign Countries

Morocco
Tangier
Tetuan

COMMON DESIGN TYPES

Pictured in this section are issues where one illustration has been used for a number of countries in the Catalogue. Not included in this section are overprinted stamps or those issues which are illustrated in each country.

EUROPA

Europa Issue, 1956

The design symbolizing the cooperation among the six countries comprising the Coal and Steel Community is illustrated in each country.

Belgium 444–445
France 805–806
Germany 748–749
Italy 715–716
Luxembourg 318–320
Netherlands 368–369

Europa Issue, 1958

"E" and Dove
CD1

European Postal Union at the service of European integration.

1958, Sept. 13

Belgium 478–479
France 889–890
Germany 790–791
Italy 750–751
Luxembourg 341–343
Netherlands 375–376
Saar 317–318

Europa Issue, 1959

6-Link Endless Chain
CD2

1959, Sept. 19

Belgium 479–498
France 929–930
Germany 805–806
Italy 791–792
Luxembourg 354–355
Netherlands 379–380

Europa Issue, 1960

19-Spoke Wheel
CD3

First anniversary of the establishment of C.E.P.T. (Conférence Européenne des Administrations des Postes et des Télécommunications.)

The spokes symbolize the 19 founding members of the Conference.

1960, Sept.

Belgium 518–519
Denmark 379
Finland 376–377
France 970–971
Germany 818–820
Great Britain 377–378
Greece 688
Iceland 327–328
Ireland 175–176
Italy 809–810
Luxembourg 374–375
Netherlands 385–386
Norway 387
Portugal 866–867
Spain 941–942
Sweden 562–563
Switzerland 400–401
Turkey 1493–1494

Europa Issue, 1961

19 Doves Flying as One
CD4

The 19 doves represent the 19 members of the Conference of European Postal and Telecommunications Administrations, C.E.P.T.

1961–62

Belgium 536–537
Cyprus 201–203
France 1005–1006
Germany 844–845
Great Britain 383–384
Greece 718–719
Iceland 340–341
Italy 845–846
Luxembourg 382–383
Netherlands 387–388
Spain 1010–1011
Switzerland 410–411
Turkey 1518–1520

Europa Issue 1962

Young Tree with 19 Leaves
CD5

The 19 leaves represent the 19 original members of C.E.P.T.

1962–63

Belgium 546–547
Cyprus 219–221
France 1045–1046
Germany 852–853
Greece 739–740
Iceland 348–349
Ireland 184–185
Italy 860–861
Luxembourg 386–387
Netherlands 394–395
Norway 414–415
Switzerland 416–417
Turkey 1553–1555

Europa Issue, 1963

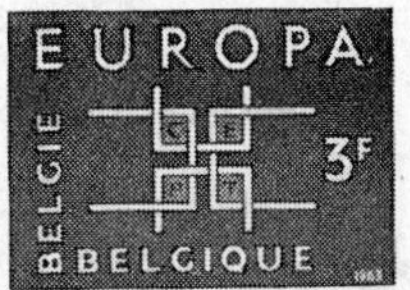

Stylized Links, Symbolizing Unity
CD6

1963, Sept.

Belgium 562–563
Cyprus 229–231
Finland 419
France 1074–1075
Germany 867–868
Greece 768–769
Iceland 357–358
Ireland 188–189
Italy 880–881
Luxembourg 403–404
Netherlands 416–417
Norway 441–442
Switzerland 429
Turkey 1602–1603

Europa Issue, 1964

Symbolic Daisy
CD7

5th anniversary of the establishment of C.E.P.T. The 22 petals of the flower symbolize the 22 members of the Conference.

1964, Sept.

Austria 738
Belgium 578–579
Cyprus 244–246
France 1109–1110
Germany 897–898
Greece 801–802
Iceland 367–368
Ireland 196–197
Italy 894–895
Luxembourg 411–412
Monaco 590–591
Netherlands 428–429
Norway 458
Portugal 931–933
Spain 1262–1263
Switzerland 438–439
Turkey 1628–1629

Europa Issue, 1965

Leaves and "Fruit"
CD8

1965

Belgium 600–601
Cyprus 262–264
Finland 437
France 1131–1132
Germany 934–935
Greece 833–834
Iceland 375–376
Ireland 204–205
Italy 915–916
Luxembourg 432–433
Monaco 616–617
Netherlands 438–439
Norway 475–476
Portugal 958–960
Switzerland 469
Turkey 1665–1666

Europa Issue, 1966

Symbolic Sailboat
CD9

1966, Sept.

Andorra, French 172
Belgium 622–628
Cyprus 275–277
France 1163–1164
Germany 963–964
Greece 862–863
Iceland 384–385
Ireland 216–217
Italy 942–943
Liechtenstein 415
Luxembourg 440–441
Monaco 639–640
Netherlands 441–442
Norway 496–497
Portugal 980–982
Switzerland 477–478
Turkey 1718–1719

Europa Issue, 1967

Cogwheels
CD10

1967

Andorra, French	174–175
Belgium	641–642
Cyprus	297–299
France	1178–1179
Greece	891–892
Germany	969–970
Iceland	389–390
Ireland	232–233
Italy	951–952
Liechtenstein	420
Luxembourg	449–450
Monaco	669–670
Netherlands	444–447
Norway	504–505
Portugal	994–996
Spain	1465–1466
Switzerland	482
Turkey	B120–B121

Europa Issue, 1968

Golden Key with C.E.P.T. Emblem
CD11

1968

Andorra, French	182–183
Belgium	664–665
Cyprus	314–316
France	1209–1210
Germany	983–984
Greece	916–917
Iceland	395–396
Ireland	242–243
Italy	979–980
Liechtenstein	442
Luxembourg	466–467
Monaco	689–691
Netherlands	452–453
Portugal	1019–1021
San Marino	687
Spain	1526
Turkey	1775–1776

Europa Issue, 1969

"EUROPA" and "CEPT"
CD12

Tenth anniversary of C.E.P.T.

1969

Andorra, French	188–189
Austria	837
Belgium	683–684
Cyprus	326–328
Denmark	458
Finland	483
France	1245–1246
Germany	996–997
Great Britain	585
Greece	947–948
Iceland	406–407
Ireland	270–271
Italy	1000–1001
Jugoslavia	1003–1004
Liechtenstein	453
Luxembourg	474–475
Monaco	722–724
Netherlands	475–476
Norway	533–534
Portugal	1038–1040
San Marino	701–702
Spain	1567
Sweden	814–816
Switzerland	500–501
Turkey	1799–1800
Vatican	470–472

Europa Issue, 1970

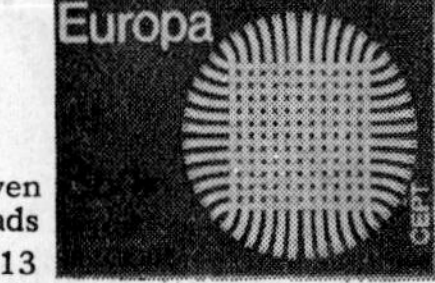

Interwoven Threads
CD13

1970

Andorra, French	196–197
Belgium	708–709
Cyprus	340–342
France	1271–1272
Germany	1018–1019
Greece	985, 987
Iceland	420–421
Ireland	279–281
Italy	1013–1014
Jugoslavia	1024–1025
Liechtenstein	470
Luxembourg	489–490
Monaco	768–770
Netherlands	483–484
Portugal	1060–1062
San Marino	729–730
Spain	1607
Switzerland	515–516
Turkey	1848–1849

Europa Issue, 1971

"Fraternity, Cooperation, Common Effort"—CD14

1971

Andorra, French	205–206
Belgium	742–743
Cyprus	365–367
Finland	504
France	1304
Germany	1064–1065
Greece	1029–1030
Iceland	429–430
Ireland	305–306
Italy	1038–1039
Jugoslavia	1052–1053
Liechtenstein	485
Luxembourg	500–501
Malta	425–427
Monaco	797–799
Netherlands	488–489
Portugal	1094–1096
San Marino	749–750
Spain	1675–1676
Switzerland	531–532
Turkey	1876–1877

Europa Issue, 1972

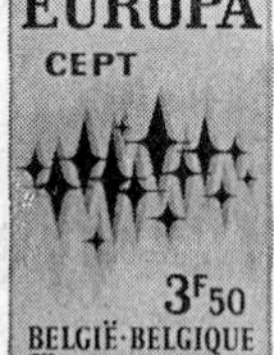

Sparkles, Symbolic of Communications
CD15

1972

Andorra, French	210–211
Andorra, Spanish	62
Belgium	768–769
Cyprus	380–382
Finland	512–513
France	1341
Germany	1089–1090
Greece	1049–1050
Iceland	439–440
Ireland	316–317
Italy	1065–1066
Jugoslavia	1100–1101
Liechtenstein	504
Luxembourg	512–513
Malta	450–453
Monaco	831–832
Netherlands	494–495
Portugal	1141–1143
San Marino	771–772
Spain	1718
Switzerland	544–545
Turkey	1907–1908

Europa Issue, 1973

Post Horn and Arrows
CD16

1973

Andorra, French	319–320
Andorra, Spanish	76
Belgium	782–783
Cyprus	396–398
Finland	526
France	1367
Germany	1114–1115
Greece	1090–1092
Iceland	447–448
Ireland	329–330
Italy	1108–1109
Jugoslavia	1138–1139
Liechtenstein	528–529
Luxembourg	523–524
Malta	469–471
Monaco	866–867
Netherlands	504–505
Norway	604–605
Portugal	1170–1172
San Marino	802–803
Spain	1753
Switzerland	580–581
Turkey	1935–1936

PORTUGAL & COLONIES

Vasco da Gama Issue

Fleet Departing—CD20

Fleet Arriving at Calicut
CD21

Embarking at Rastello—CD22

Muse of History
CD23

Flagship San Gabriel, da Gama and Camoens
CD24

Archangel Gabriel, the Patron Saint
CD25

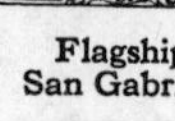

Flagship San Gabriel
CD26

Vasco da Gama
CD27

Fourth centenary of Vasco da Gama's discovery of the route to India.

1898

Azores	93–100
Macao	67–74
Madeira	37–44
Portugal	147–154
Port. Africa	1–8
Port. India	189–196
Timor	45–52

Pombal Issue
POSTAL TAX

Marquis de Pombal
CD28

Planning Reconstruction of Lisbon, 1755
CD29

Pombal Monument, Lisbon
CD30

Sebastiao José de Carvalho e Mello, Marquis de Pombal (1699–1782), statesman, rebuilt Lisbon after earthquake of 1755. Tax was for the erection of Pombal monument. Obligatory on all mail on certain days throughout the year.

1925

Angola	RA1–RA3
Azores	RA9–RA11
Cape Verde	RA1–RA3
Macao	RA1–RA3
Madeira	RA1–RA3
Mozambique	RA1–RA3
Portugal	RA11–RA13
Port. Guinea	RA1–RA3
Port. India	RA1–RA3
St. Thomas & Prince Islands	RA1–RA3
Timor	RA1–RA3

Pombal Issue

POSTAL TAX DUES

Marquis de Pombal
CD31

Planning Reconstruction of Lisbon, 1755
CD32

Pombal Monument, Lisbon
CD33

1925

Angola	RAJ1-RAJ3
Azores	RAJ2-RAJ4
Cape Verde	RAJ1-RAJ3
Macao	RAJ1-RAJ3
Madeira	RAJ1-RAJ3
Mozambique	RAJ1-RAJ3
Portugal	RAJ2-RAJ4
Port. Guinea	RAJ1-RAJ3
Port. India	RAJ1-RAJ3
St. Thomas & Prince Islands	RAJ1-RAJ3
Timor	RAJ1-RAJ3

Vasco da Gama
CD34

Mousinho de Albuquerque
CD35

Dam
CD36

Prince Henry the Navigator
CD37

Affonso de Albuquerque
CD38

1938–39

Angola	274–291
Cape Verde	234–251
Macao	289–305
Mozambique	270–287
Port. Guinea	233–250
Port. India	439–453
St. Thomas & Prince Islands	302–319, 323–340
Timor	223–239

Plane over Globe
CD39

1938–39

Angola	C1–C9
Cape Verde	C1–C9
Macao	C7–C15
Mozambique	C1–C9
Port. Guinea	C1–C9
Port. India	C1–C8
St. Thomas & Prince Islands	C1–C18
Timor	C1–C9

Lady of Fatima Issue

Our Lady of the Rosary, Fatima, Portugal
CD40

1948–49

Angola	315–318
Cape Verde	266
Macao	336
Mozambique	325–328
Port. Guinea	271
Port. India	480
St. Thomas & Prince Islands	351
Timor	254

A souvenir sheet of 9 stamps was issued in 1951 to mark the extension of the 1950 Holy Year. The sheet contains: Angola No. 316, Cape Verde No. 266, Macao No. 336, Mozambique No. 325, Portuguese Guinea No. 271, Portuguese India Nos. 480, 485, St. Thomas & Prince Islands No. 351, Timor No. 254.

The sheet also contains a portrait of Pope Pius XII and is inscribed "Encerramento do Ano Santo, Fatima 1951." It was sold for 11 escudos.

Holy Year Issue

Church Bells and Dove
CD41

Angel Holding Candelabra
CD42

Holy Year, 1950.

1950–51

Angola	331–332
Cape Verde	268–269
Macao	339–340
Mozambique	330–331
Port. Guinea	273–274
Port. India	490–491, 496–503
St. Thomas & Prince Islands	353–354
Timor	258–259

A souvenir sheet of 8 stamps was issued in 1951 to mark the extension of the Holy Year. The sheet contains: Angola No. 331, Cape Verde No. 269, Macao No. 340, Mozambique No. 331, Portuguese Guinea No. 275, Portuguese India No. 490, St. Thomas & Prince Islands No. 354, Timor No. 258, some with colors changed. The sheet contains doves and is inscribed "Encerramento do Ano Santo, Fatima 1951." It was sold for 17 escudos.

Holy Year Conclusion Issue

Our Lady of Fatima
CD43

Conclusion of Holy Year. Sheets contain alternate vertical rows of stamps and labels bearing quotation from Pope Pius XII, different for each colony.

1951

Angola	357
Cape Verde	270
Macao	352
Mozambique	356
Port. Guinea	275
Port. India	506
St. Thomas & Prince Islands	355
Timor	270

Medical Congress Issue

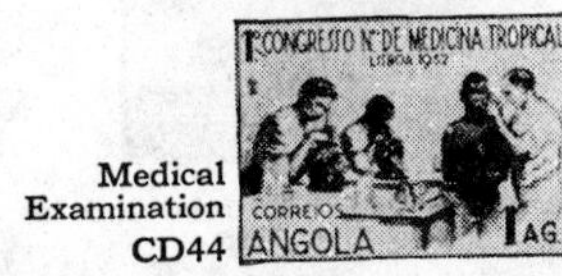

Medical Examination
CD44

First National Congress of Tropical Medicine, Lisbon, 1952.
Each stamp has a different design.

1952

Angola	358
Cape Verde	287
Macao	364
Mozambique	359
Port. Guinea	276
Port. India	516
St. Thomas & Prince Islands	356
Timor	271

POSTAGE DUE STAMPS

CD45

1952

Angola	J37–J42
Cape Verde	J31–J36
Macao	J53–J58
Mozambique	J51–J56
Port. Guinea	J40–J45
Port. India	J47–J52
St. Thomas & Prince Islands	J52–J57
Timor	J31–J36

Sao Paulo Issue

Father Manuel da Nobrega and View of Sao Paulo
CD46

400th anniversary of the founding of Sao Paulo, Brazil.

1954

Angola	385
Cape Verde	297
Macao	382
Mozambique	395
Port. Guinea	291
Port. India	530
St. Thomas & Prince Islands	369
Timor	279

Tropical Medicine Congress Issue

Securidaca Longipedunculata
CD47

Sixth International Congress for Tropical Medicine and Malaria, Lisbon, Sept. 1958.
Each stamp shows a different plant.

1958

Angola	409
Cape Verde	303
Macao	392
Mozambique	404
Port. Guinea	295
Port. India	569
St. Thomas & Prince Islands	371
Timor	289

Sports Issue

Flying
CD48

Each stamp shows a different sport.

1962

Angola	433–438
Cape Verde	320–325
Macao	394–399
Mozambique	424–429
Port. Guinea	299–304
St. Thomas & Prince Islands	374–379
Timor	313–318

Anti-Malaria Issue

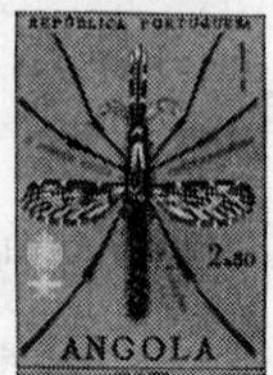

Anopheles Funestus and Malaria Eradication Symbol
CD49

World Health Organization drive to eradicate malaria.

1962

Angola	439
Cape Verde	326
Macao	400
Mozambique	430
Port. Guinea	305
St. Thomas & Prince Islands	380
Timor	319

Airline Anniversary Issue

Map of Africa, Super Constellation and Jet Liner
CD50

Tenth anniversary of Transportes Aéreos Portugueses (TAP).

1963

Angola	490
Cape Verde	327
Mozambique	434
Port. Guinea	318
St. Thomas & Prince Islands	381

National Overseas Bank Issue

Antonio Teixeira de Sousa
CD51

Centenary of the National Overseas Bank of Portugal.

1964, May 16

Angola	509
Cape Verde	328
Port. Guinea	319
St. Thomas & Prince Islands	382
Timor	320

ITU Issue

ITU Emblem and St. Gabriel
CD52

Centenary of the International Communications Union.

1965, May 17

Angola	511
Cape Verde	329
Macao	402
Mozambique	464
Port. Guinea	320
St. Thomas & Prince Islands	383
Timor	321

National Revolution Issue

St. Pauls's Hospital, and Commercial and Industrial School
CD53

40th anniversary of the National Revolution.
Different buildings on each stamp.

1966, May 28

Angola	525
Cape Verde	338
Macao	403
Mozambique	465
Port. Guinea	329
St. Thomas & Prince Islands	392
Timor	322

Navy Club Issue

Mendes Barata and Cruiser Dom Carlos I
CD54

Centenary of Portugal's Navy Club.
Each stamp has a different design.

1967, Jan. 31

Angola	527–528
Cape Verde	339–340
Macao	412–413
Mozambique	478–479
Port. Guinea	330–331
St. Thomas & Prince Islands	393–394
Timor	323–324

Admiral Coutinho Issue

Admiral Gago Coutinho and his First Ship
CD55

Centenary of the birth of Admiral Carlos Viegas Gago Coutinho (1869–1959), explorer and aviation pioneer.
Each stamp has a different design.

1969, Feb. 17

Angola	547
Cape Verde	355
Macao	417
Mozambique	484
Port. Guinea	335
St. Thomas & Prince Islands	397
Timor	335

Administration Reform Issue

Luiz Augusto Rebello da Silva
CD56

Centenary of the administration reforms of the overseas territories.

1969, Sept. 25

Angola	549
Cape Verde	357
Macao	419
Mozambique	491
Port. Guinea	337
St. Thomas & Prince Islands	399
Timor	338

Marshal Carmona Issue

Marshal A. O. Carmona
CD57

Birth centenary of Marshal Antonio Oscar Carmona de Fragoso (1869–1951), President of Portugal.
Each stamp has a different design.

1970, Nov. 15

Angola	563
Cape Verde	359
Macao	422
Mozambique	493
Port. Guinea	340
St. Thomas & Prince Islands	403
Timor	341

Olympic Games Issue

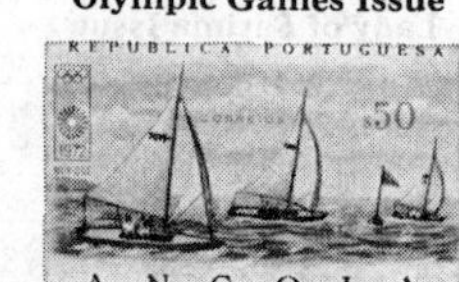

Racing Yachts and Olympic Emblem
CD59

20th Olympic Games, Munich, Aug. 26–Sept. 11.
Each stamp shows a different sport.

1972, June 20

Angola	569
Cape Verde	361
Macao	426
Mozambique	504
Port. Guinea	342
St. Thomas & Prince Islands	408
Timor	343

Lisbon-Rio de Janeiro Flight Issue

"Santa Cruz" over Fernando de Noronha
CD60

50th anniversary of the Lisbon to Rio de Janeiro flight by Arturo de Sacadura and Coutinho, March 30–June 5, 1922.
Each stamp shows a different stage of the flight.

1972, Sept. 20

Angola	570
Cape Verde	362
Macao	427
Mozambique	505
Port. Guinea	343
St. Thomas & Prince Islands	409
Timor	344

WMO Centenary Issue

WMO Emblem
CD61

Centenary of international meteorological cooperation.

1973, Dec. 15

Angola	571
Cape Verde	363
Macao	429
Mozambique	509
Port. Guinea	344
St. Thomas & Prince Islands	410
Timor	345

FRENCH COMMUNITY

Colonial Exposition Issue

People of French Empire
CD70

Women's Heads
CD71

France Showing Way to Civilization
CD72

"Colonial Commerce"
CD73

International Colonial Exposition, Paris 1931.

1931

Cameroun	213–216
Chad	60–63
Dahomey	97–100
Fr. Guiana	152–155
Fr. Guinea	116–119
Fr. India	100–103
Fr. Polynesia	76–79
Fr. Sudan	102–105
Gabon	120–123
Guadeloupe	138–141
Indo-China	140–142
Ivory Coast	92–95
Madagascar	169–172
Martinique	129–132
Mauritania	65–68
Middle Congo	61–64
New Caledonia	176–179
Niger	73–76
Reunion	122–125
St. Pierre & Miquelon	132–135
Senegal	138–141
Somali Coast	135–138
Togo	254–257
Ubangi-Shari	82–85
Upper Volta	66–69
Wallis & Futuna Isls.	85–88

Paris International Exposition Issue

Colonial Arts Exposition Issue

"Colonial Resources"
CD74 CD77

Overseas Commerce
CD75

Exposition Buildings and Women
CD76

"France and the Empire"
CD78

Cultural Treasures of the Colonies
CD79

Souvenir sheets contain one imperf. stamp.

1937

Cameroun	217–222A
Dahomey	101–107
Fr. Equatorial Africa	27–32, 73
Fr. Guiana	162–168
Fr. Guinea	120–126
Fr. India	104–110
Fr. Polynesia	117–123
Fr. Sudan	106–112
Guadeloupe	148–154
Indo-China	193–199
Inini	41
Ivory Coast	152–158
Kwangchowan	120
Madagascar	191–197
Martinique	179–185
Mauritania	69–75
New Caledonia	208–214
Niger	72–83
Reunion	167–173
St. Pierre & Miquelon	165–171
Senegal	172–178
Somali Coast	139–145
Togo	258–264
Wallis & Futuna Isls.	89

Curie Issue

Pierre and Marie Curie
CD80

40th anniversary of the discovery of radium. The surtax was for the benefit of the International Union for the Control of Cancer.

1938

Cameroun	B1
Dahomey	B2
France	B76
Fr. Equatorial Africa	B1
Fr. Guiana	B3
Fr. Guinea	B2
Fr. India	B6
Fr. Polynesia	B5
Fr. Sudan	B1
Guadeloupe	B3
Indo-China	B14
Ivory Coast	B2
Madagascar	B2
Martinique	B2
Mauritania	B3
New Caledonia	B4
Niger	B1
Reunion	B4
St. Pierre & Miquelon	B3
Senegal	B3
Somali Coast	B2
Togo	B1

Caillié Issue

René Caillié and Map of Northwestern Africa
CD81

Death centenary of René Caillié (1799–1838), French explorer.

All three denominations exist with colony name omitted.

1939

Dahomey	108–110
Fr. Guinea	161–163
Fr. Sudan	113–115
Ivory Coast	160–162
Mauritania	109–111
Niger	84–86
Senegal	188–190
Togo	265–267

New York World's Fair Issue

Natives and New York Skyline
CD82

1939

Cameroun	223–224
Dahomey	111–112
Fr. Equatorial Africa	78–79
Fr. Guiana	169–170
Fr. Guinea	164–165
Fr. India	111–112
Fr. Polynesia	124–125
Fr. Sudan	116–117
Guadeloupe	155–156
Indo-China	203–204
Inini	42–43
Ivory Coast	163–164
Kwangchowan	121–122
Madagascar	209–210
Martinque	186–187
Mauritania	112–113
New Caledonia	215–216
Niger	87–88
Reunion	174–175
St. Pierre & Miquelon	205–206
Senegal	191–192
Somali Coast	179–180
Togo	268–269
Wallis & Futuna Isls.	90–91

French Revolution Issue

Storming of the Bastille
CD83

150th anniversary of the French Revolution. The surtax was for the defense of the colonies.

1939

Cameroun	B2–B6
Dahomey	B3–B7
Fr. Equatorial Africa	B4–B8, CB1
Fr. Guiana	B4–B8, CB1
Fr. Guinea	B3–B7
Fr. India	B7–B11
Fr. Polynesia	B6–B10, CB1
Fr. Sudan	B2–B6
Guadeloupe	B4–B8
Indo-China	B15–B19, CB1
Inini	B1–B5
Ivory Coast	B3–B7
Kwangchowan	B1–B5
Madagascar	B3–B7, CB1
Martinique	B3–B7
Mauritania	B4–B8
New Caledonia	B5–B9, CB1
Niger	B2–B6
Reunion	B5–B9, CB1
St. Pierre & Miquelon	B4–B8
Senegal	B4–B8, CB1
Somali Coast	B3–B7
Togo	B2–B6
Wallis & Futuna Isls.	B1–B5

Plane over Coastal Area
CD85

All five denominations exist with colony name omitted.

1940

Dahomey	C1–C5
Fr. Guinea	C1–C5
Fr. Sudan	C1–C5
Ivory Coast	C1–C5
Mauritania	C1–C5
Niger	C1–C5
Senegal	C12–C16
Togo	C1–C5

Colonial Infantryman
CD86

1941

Cameroun	B13B
Dahomey	B13
Fr. Equatorial Africa	B8B
Fr. Guiana	B10
Fr. Guinea	B13
Fr. India	B13
Fr. Polynesia	B12
Fr. Sudan	B12
Guadeloupe	B10
Indo-China	B19B
Inini	B7
Ivory Coast	B13
Kwangchowan	B7
Madagascar	B9
Martinique	B9
Mauritania	B14
New Caledonia	B11
Niger	B12
Reunion	B11
St. Pierre & Miquelon	B8B
Senegal	B14
Somali Coast	B9
Togo	B10B
Wallis & Futuna Isls.	B7

Cross of Lorraine and Four-motor Plane
CD87

1941–5

Cameroun	C1–C7
Fr. Equatorial Africa	C17–C23
Fr. Guiana	C9–C10
Fr. India	C1–C6
Fr. Polynesia	C3–C9
Fr. West Africa	C1–C3
Guadeloupe	C1–C2
Madagascar	C37–C43
Martinique	C1–C2
New Caledonia	C7–C13
Reunion	C18–C24
St. Pierre & Miquelon	C1–C7
Somali Coast	C1–C7

Transport Plane
CD88

Caravan and Plane—CD89

1942

Dahomey C6–C13
Fr. Guinea C6–C13
Fr. Sudan C6–C13
Ivory Coast C6–C13
Mauritania C6–C13
Niger C6–C13
Senegal C17–C25
Togo C6–C13

Red Cross Issue

Marianne
CD90

The surtax was for the French Red Cross and national relief.

1944

Cameroun B28
Fr. Equatorial Africa B38
Fr. Guiana B12
Fr. India B14
Fr. Polynesia B13
Fr. West Africa B1
Guadeloupe B12
Madagascar B15
Martinique B11
New Caledonia B13
Reunion B15
St. Pierre & Miquelon B13
Somali Coast B13
Wallis & Futuna Isls. B9

Eboué Issue

Félix Eboué
CD91

Félix Eboué, first French colonial administrator to proclaim resistance to Germany after French surrender in World War II.

1945

Cameroun 296–297
Fr. Equatorial Africa 156–157
Fr. Guiana 171–172
Fr. India 210–211
Fr. Polynesia 150–151
Fr. West Africa 15–16
Guadeloupe 187–188
Madagascar 259–260
Martinique 196–197
New Caledonia 274–275
Reunion 238–239
St. Pierre & Miquelon 322–323
Somali Coast 238–239

Victory Issue

Victory
CD92

European victory of the Allied Nations in World War II.

1946, May 8

Cameroun C8
Fr. Equatorial Africa C24
Fr. Guiana C11
Fr. India C7
Fr. Polynesia C10
Fr. West Africa C4
Guadeloupe C3
Indo-China C19
Madagascar C44
Martinique C3
New Caledonia C14
Reunion C25
St. Pierre & Miquelon C8
Somali Coast C8
Wallis & Futuna Isls. C1

Chad to Rhine Issue

Leclerc's Departure from Chad
CD93

Battle at Cufra Oasis
CD94

Tanks in Action, Mareth
CD95

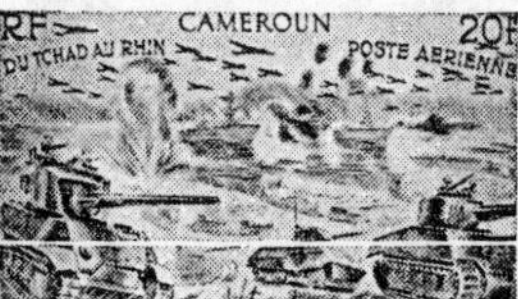

Normandy Invasion
CD96

Entering Paris
CD97

Liberation of Strasbourg
CD98

"Chad to the Rhine" march, 1942–44, by Gen. Jacques Leclere's column, later French 2nd Armored Division.

1946, June 6

Cameroun C9–C14
Fr. Equatorial Africa C25–C30
Fr. Guiana C12–C17
Fr. India C8–C13
Fr. Polynesia C11–C16
Fr. West Africa C5–C10
Guadeloupe C4–C9
Indo-China C20–C25
Madagascar C45–C50
Martinique C4–C9
New Caledonia C15–C20
Reunion C26–C31
St. Pierre & Miquelon C9–C14
Somali Coast C9–C14
Wallis & Futuna Isls. C2–C7

UPU Issue

French Colonials, Globe and Plane
CD99

75th anniversary of the Universal Postal Union.

1949, July 4

Cameroun C29
Fr. Equatorial Africa C34
Fr. India C17
Fr. Polynesia C20
Fr. West Africa C15
Indo-China C26
Madagascar C55
New Caledonia C24
St. Pierre & Miquelon C18
Somali Coast C18
Togo C18
Wallis & Futuna Isls. C10

Tropical Medicine Issue

Doctor Treating Infant
CD100

The surtax was for charitable work.

1950

Cameroun B29
Fr. Equatorial Africa B39
Fr. India B15
Fr. Polynesia B14
Fr. West Africa B3
Madagascar B17
New Caledonia B14
St. Pierre & Miquelon B14
Somali Coast B14
Togo B11

Military Medal Issue

Medal, Early Marine and Colonial Soldier
CD101

Centenary of the creation of the French Military Medal.

1952

Cameroun 332
Comoro Isls. 39
Fr. Equatorial Africa 186
Fr. India 233
Fr. Polynesia 179
Fr. West Africa 57
Madagascar 286
New Caledonia 295
St. Pierre & Miquelon 345
Somali Coast 267
Togo 327
Wallis & Futuna Isls. 149

Liberation Issue

Allied Landing, Victory Sign and Cross of Lorraine
CD102

10th anniversary of the liberation of France.

1954, June 6

Cameroun C32
Comoro Isls. C4
Fr. Equatorial Africa C38
Fr. India C18
Fr. Polynesia C23
Fr. West Africa C17
Madagascar C57
New Caledonia C25
St. Pierre & Miquelon C19
Somali Coast C19
Togo C19
Wallis & Futuna Isls. C11

FIDES Issue

Plowmen
CD103

Efforts of FIDES, the Economic and Social Development Fund for Overseas Possessions (Fonds d' Investissement pour le Developpement Economique et Social.)

Each stamp has a different design.

1956

Cameroun 326–329
Comoro Isls. 43
Fr. Polynesia 181
Madagascar 292–295
New Caledonia 303
Somali Coast 268
Togo 331

Flower Issue

Euadania
CD104

Each stamp shows a different flower.

1958–9

Cameroun 333
Comoro Isls. 45
Fr. Equatorial Africa 200–201
Fr. Polynesia 192
Fr. So. & Antarctic Terr. 11
Fr. West Africa 79–83
Madagascar 301–302
New Caledonia 304–305
St. Pierre & Miquelon 357

Somali Coast	270
Togo	348–349
Wallis & Futuna Isls.	152

Human Rights Issue

Sun, Dove and U. N. Emblem

CD105

10th anniversary of the signing of the Universal Declaration of Human Rights.

1958

Comoro Isls.	44
Fr. Equatorial Africa	202
Fr. Polynesia	191
Fr. West Africa	85
Madagascar	300
New Caledonia	306
St. Pierre & Miquelon	356
Somali Coast	274
Wallis & Futuna Isls.	153

C.C.T.A. Issue

Map of Africa and Cogwheels

CD106

10th anniversary of the Commission for Technical Cooperation in Africa south of the Sahara.

1960

Cameroun	335
Cent. African Rep.	3
Chad	66
Congo, P.R.	90
Dahomey	138
Gabon	150
Ivory Coast	180
Madagascar	9
Mali	117
Mauritania	104
Niger	89
Upper Volta	89

Air Afrique Issue, 1961

Modern and Ancient Africa, Map and Planes

CD107

Founding of Air Afrique (African Airlines).

1961–62

Cameroun	C37
Cent. African Rep.	C5
Chad	C7
Congo, P.R.	C5
Dahomey	C17
Gabon	C5
Ivory Coast	C18
Mauritania	C17
Niger	C22
Senegal	C31
Upper Volta	C4

Anti-Malaria Issue

Malaria Eradication Emblem

CD108

World Health Organization drive to eradicate malaria.

1962, Apr. 7

Cameroun	B36
Cent. African Rep.	B1
Chad	B1
Comoro Isls.	B1
Congo, P.R.	B3
Dahomey	B15
Gabon	B4
Ivory Coast	B15
Madagascar	B19
Mali	B1
Mauritania	B16
Niger	B14
Senegal	B16
Somali Coast	B15
Upper Volta	B1

Abidjan Games Issue

Relay Race

CD109

Abidjan Games, Ivory Coast, Dec. 24–31, 1961.

Each stamp shows a different sport.

1962

Chad	83–84
Cent. African Rep.	19–20
Congo, P.R.	103–104
Gabon	163–164
Niger	109–111
Upper Volta	103–105

African and Malagasy Union Issue

Flag of African and Malagasy Union

CD110

First anniversary of the Union.

1962, Sept. 8

Cameroun	373
Cent. African Rep.	21
Chad	85
Congo, P.R.	105
Dahomey	155
Gabon	165
Ivory Coast	198
Madagascar	332
Mauritania	170
Niger	112
Senegal	211
Upper Volta	106

Telstar Issue

Telstar and Globe Showing Andover and Pleumeur-Bodou

CD111

First television connection of the United States and Europe through the Telstar satellite, July 11–12, 1962.

1962–63

Andorra, French	154
Comoro Isls.	C7
Fr. Polynesia	C29
Fr. So. & Antarctic Terr.	C5
New Caledonia	C33
Somali Coast	C31
St. Pierre & Miquelon	C26
Wallis & Futuna Isls.	C17

Freedom From Hunger Issue

World Map and Wheat Emblem

CD112

United Nations Food and Agriculture Organization's "Freedom from Hunger" campaign.

1963, Mar. 21

Cameroun	B37–B38
Cent. African Rep.	B2
Chad	B2
Congo, P.R.	B4
Dahomey	B16
Gabon	B5
Ivory Coast	B16
Madagascar	B21
Mauritania	B17
Niger	B15
Senegal	B17
Upper Volta	B2

Red Cross Centenary Issue

Centenary Emblem

CD113

Centenary of the International Red Cross.

1963, Sept. 2

Comoro Isls.	55
Fr. Polynesia	205
New Caledonia	328
St. Pierre & Miquelon	367
Somali Coast	297
Wallis & Futuna Isls.	165

African Postal Union Issue

UAMPT Emblem, Radio Masts, Plane and Mail

CD114

Establishment of the African and Malagasy Posts and Telecommunications Union, UAMPT.

1963, Sept. 8

Cameroun	C47
Cent. African Rep.	C10
Chad	C9
Congo, P.R.	C13
Dahomey	C19
Gabon	C13
Ivory Coast	C25
Madagascar	C75
Mauritania	C22
Niger	C27
Rwanda	36
Senegal	C32
Upper Volta	C9

Air Afrique Issue, 1963

Symbols of Flight

CD115

First anniversary of Air Afrique and inauguration of DC-8 service.

1963, Nov. 19

Cameroun	C48
Chad	C10
Congo, P.R.	C14
Gabon	C18
Ivory Coast	C26
Mauritania	C26
Niger	C35
Senegal	C33

Europafrica Issue

Europe and Africa Linked Together

CD116

Signing of an economic agreement between the European Economic Community and the African and Malagasy Union, Yaoundé, Cameroun, July 20, 1963.

1963–64

Cameroun	402
Chad	C11
Cent. African Rep.	C12
Congo, P.R.	C16

Gabon	C19
Ivory Coast	217
Niger	C43
Upper Volta	C11

Human Rights Issue

Scales of Justice and Globe

CD117

15th anniversary of the Universal Declaration of Human Rights.

1963, Dec. 10

Comoro Isls.	58
Fr. Polynesia	206
New Caledonia	329
St. Pierre & Miquelon	368
Somali Coast	300
Wallis & Futuna Isls.	166

PHILATEC Issue

Stamp Album, Champs Elysées Palace and Horses of Marly

CD118

"PHILATEC," International Philatelic and Postal Techniques Exhibition, Paris, June 5-21, 1964.

1963–64

Comoro Isls.	60
France	1078
Fr. Polynesia	207
New Caledonia	341
St. Pierre & Miquelon	369
Somali Coast	301
Wallis & Futuna Isls.	167

Cooperation Issue

Maps of France and Africa and Clasped Hands

CD119

Cooperation between France and the French-speaking countries of Africa and Madagascar.

1964

Cameroun	409–410
Cent. African Rep.	39
Chad	103
Congo, P.R.	121
Dahomey	193
France	1111
Gabon	175
Ivory Coast	221
Madagascar	360
Mauritania	181
Niger	143
Senegal	236
Togo	495

ITU Issue

Telegraph, Syncom Satellite and ITU Emblem

CD120

Centenary of the International Telecommunication Union.

1965, May 17

Comoro Isls.	C14
Fr. Polynesia	C33
Fr. So. & Antarctic Terr.	C8
New Caledonia	C40
New Hebrides	124–125
St. Pierre & Miquelon	C29
Somali Coast	C36
Wallis & Futuna Isls.	C20

French Satellite A-1 Issue

Diamant Rocket and Launching Installations

CD121

Launching of France's first satellite, Nov. 26, 1965.

1965–66

Comoro Isls.	C15–C16
France	1137–1138
Fr. Polynesia	C40–C41
Fr. So. & Antarctic Terr.	C9–C10
New Caledonia	C44–C45
St. Pierre & Miquelon	C30–C31
Somali Coast	C39–C40
Wallis & Futuna Isls.	C22–C23

French Satellite D-1 Issue

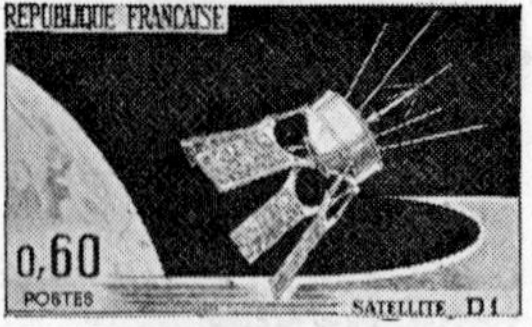

D-1 Satellite in Orbit

CD122

Launching of the D-1 satellite at Hammaguir, Algeria, Feb. 17, 1966.

1966

Comoro Isls.	C17
France	1148
Fr. Polynesia	C42
Fr. So. & Antarctic Terr.	C11
New Caledonia	C46
St. Pierre & Miquelon	C32
Somali Coast	C49
Wallis & Futuna Isls.	C24

Air Afrique Issue, 1966

Planes and Air Afrique Emblem

CD123

Introduction of DC-8F planes by Air Afrique.

1966

Cameroun	C79
Cent. African Rep.	C35
Chad	C26
Congo, P.R.	C42
Dahomey	C42
Gabon	C47
Ivory Coast	C32
Mauritania	C57
Niger	C63
Senegal	C47
Togo	C54
Upper Volta	C31

African Postal Union Issue, 1967

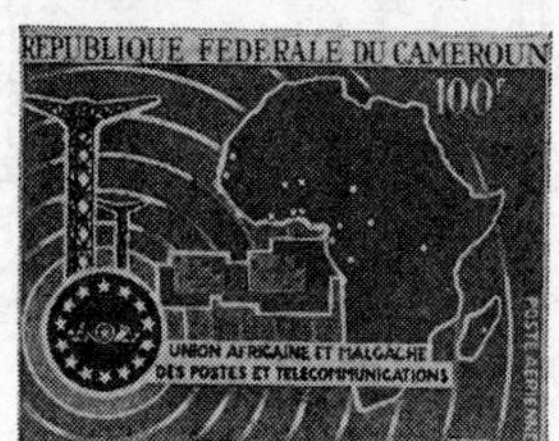

Telecommunications Symbols and Map of Africa

CD124

Fifth anniversary of the establishment of the African and Malagasy Union of Posts and Telecommunications, UAMPT.

1967

Cameroun	C90
Cent. African Rep.	C46
Chad	C37
Congo, P.R.	C57
Dahomey	C61
Gabon	C58
Ivory Coast	C34
Madagascar	C85
Mauritania	C65
Niger	C75
Rwanda	C1–C3
Senegal	C60
Togo	C81
Upper Volta	C50

Monetary Union Issue

Gold Token of the Ashantis, 17–18th Centuries

CD125

Fifth anniversary of the West African Monetary Union.

1967, Nov. 4

Dahomey	244
Ivory Coast	259
Mauritania	238
Niger	204
Senegal	294
Togo	623
Upper Volta	181

WHO Anniversary Issue

Sun, Flowers and WHO Emblem

CD126

20th anniversary of the World Health Organization.

1968, May 4

Afars & Issas	317
Comoro Isls.	73
Fr. Polynesia	241–242
Fr. So. & Antarctic Terr.	31
New Caledonia	367
St. Pierre & Miquelon	377
Wallis & Futuna Isls.	169

Human Rights Year Issue

Human Rights Flame

CD127

International Human Rights Year.

1968, Aug. 10

Afars & Issas	322–323
Comoro Isls.	76
Fr. Polynesia	243–244
Fr. So. & Antarctic Terr.	32
New Caledonia	369
St. Pierre & Miquelon	382
Wallis & Futuna Isls.	170

2nd PHILEXAFRIQUE Issue

Gabon No. 131 and Industrial Plant

CD128

Opening of PHILEXAFRIQUE, Abidjan, Feb. 14.

Each stamp shows a local scene and stamp.

1969, Feb. 14

Cameroun	C118
Cent. African Rep.	C65
Chad	C48
Congo, P.R.	C77
Dahomey	C94
Gabon	C82
Ivory Coast	C38–C40
Madagascar	C92
Mali	C65
Mauritania	C80
Niger	C104
Senegal	C68
Togo	C104
Upper Volta	C62

Concorde Issue

Concorde in Flight
CD129

First flight of the prototype Concorde super-sonic plane at Toulouse, Mar. 1, 1969.

1969

Afars & Issas	C56
Comoro Isls.	C29
France	C42
Fr. Polynesia	C50
Fr. So. & Antarctic Terr.	C18
New Caledonia	C63
St. Pierre & Miquelon	C40
Wallis & Futuna Isls.	C30

Development Bank Issue

Bank Emblem—CD130

Fifth anniversary of the African Development Bank.

1969

Cameroun	499
Chad	217
Congo, P.R.	181–182
Ivory Coast	281
Mali	127–128
Mauritania	267
Niger	220
Senegal	317–318
Upper Volta	201

ILO Issue

ILO Headquarters, Geneva, and Emblem
CD131

50th anniversary of the International Labor Organization.

1969–70

Afars & Issas	337
Comoro Isls.	83
Fr. Polynesia	251–252
Fr. So. & Antarctic Terr.	35
New Caledonia	379
St. Pierre & Miquelon	396
Wallis & Futuna Isls.	172

ASECNA Issue

Map of Africa, Plane and Airport
CD132

10th anniversary of the Agency for the Security of Aerial Navigation in Africa and Madagascar (ASECNA, Agence pour la Sécurité de la Navigation Aérienne en Afrique et à Madagascar).

1969–70

Cameroun	500
Cent. African Rep.	119
Chad	222
Congo, P.R.	197
Dahomey	269
Gabon	260
Ivory Coast	287
Mali	130
Niger	221
Senegal	321
Upper Volta	204

U.P.U. Headquarters Issue

U.P.U. Headquarters and Emblem
CD133

New Universal Postal Union headquarters, Bern, Switzerland.

1970

Afars & Issas	342
Algeria	443
Cameroun	503–504
Cent. African Rep.	125
Chad	225
Comoro Isls.	84
Congo, P.R.	216
Fr. Polynesia	261–262
Fr. So. & Antarctic Terr.	36
Gabon	258
Ivory Coast	295
Madagascar	444
Mali	134–135
Mauritania	283
New Caledonia	382
Niger	231–232
St. Pierre & Miquelon	397–398
Senegal	328–329
Tunisia	535
Wallis & Futuna Isls.	173

De Gaulle Issue

General de Gaulle, 1940
CD134

First anniversary of the death of Charles de Gaulle, (1890-1970), President of France.

1971–72

Afars & Issas	356–357
Comoro Isls.	104–105
France	1322–1325
Fr. Polynesia	270–271
Fr. So. & Antarctic Terr.	52–53
New Caledonia	393–394
Reunion	377, 380
St. Pierre & Miquelon	417–418
Wallis & Futuna Isls.	177–178

African Postal Union Issue, 1971

Carved Stool, UAMPT Building, Brazzaville, Congo
CD135

10th anniversary of the establishment of the African and Malagasy Posts and Telecommunications Union, UAMPT.

Each stamp has a different native design.

1971, Nov. 13

Cameroun	C177
Cent. African Rep.	C89
Chad	C94
Congo, P.R.	C136
Dahomey	C146
Gabon	C120
Ivory Coast	C47
Mauritania	C113
Niger	C164
Rwanda	C8
Senegal	C105
Togo	C166
Upper Volta	C97

West African Monetary Union Issue

African Couple, City, Village and Commemorative Coin
CD136

10th anniversary of the West African Monetary Union.

1972, Nov. 2

Dahomey	300
Ivory Coast	331
Mauritania	299
Niger	258
Senegal	374
Togo	825
Upper Volta	280

African Postal Union Issue, 1973

Telecommunications Symbols and Map of Africa
CD137

11th anniversary of the African and Malagasy Posts and Telecommunications Union (UAMPT).

1973, Sept. 12

Cameroun	574
Cent. African Rep.	194
Chad	272
Congo, P.R.	289
Dahomey	311
Gabon	320
Ivory Coast	361
Madagascar	500
Mauritania	304
Niger	287
Rwanda	540
Senegal	393
Togo	849
Upper Volta	285

Philexafrique II—Essen Issue

II-349

Buffalo and Dahomey No. C33
CD138

II-350

Wild Ducks and Baden No. 1
CD139

Designs: Indigenous fauna, local and German stamps.

Types CD138–CD139 printed horizontally and vertically se-tenant in sheets of 10 (2x5). Label between horizontal pairs alternately commemorates Philexafrique II, Libreville, Gabon, June 1978, and 2nd International Stamp Fair, Essen, Germany, Nov. 1–5.

SCOTT'S STANDARD POSTAGE STAMP CATALOGUE

ABYSSINIA

(See Ethiopia.)

AFARS AND ISSAS, French Territory of the

(ä-färz′ and ī-säz′)

LOCATION—East Africa.
GOVT.—French Overseas Territory.
AREA—8,880 sq. mi.
POP.—150,000 (est. 1974).
CAPITAL—Djibouti (Jibuti).

The French overseas territory of Somali Coast was renamed the French Territory of the Afars and Issas in 1967. It became the Djibouti Republic (which see) on June 27, 1977.

100 Centimes = 1 Franc

Imperforates

Most stamps of Afars and Issas exist imperforate in issued and trial colors, and also in small presentation sheets in issued colors.

Gray-headed Kingfisher
A48

Designs: 15fr, Oystercatcher. 50fr, Greenshanks. 55fr, Abyssinian roller. 60fr, Ground squirrel (vert.).

Unwmkd.

1967 Engraved *Perf. 13*

No.	Type	Description	Unused	Used
310	A48	10fr brt. blue, gray green & black	60	60
311	"	15fr dk. brown, blue, olive & ocher	1.00	75
312	"	50fr black, slate grn. & brown	1.85	1.50
313	"	55fr violet, brt. blue & gray green	2.50	1.85
314	"	60fr ocher, brt. green & slate green	3.25	2.75
		Nos. 310-314 (5)	9.20	7.45

Dates of Issue: 10fr, 55fr, Aug. 21; 15fr, 50fr, 60fr, Sept. 25. See No. C50.

Soccer
A49

Design: 30fr, Basketball.

1967, Dec. 18 Engraved *Perf. 13*

No.	Type	Description	Unused	Used
315	A49	25fr blue, brown & emerald	1.00	80
316	"	30fr red lilac, Prus. bl. & brown	1.20	1.00

WHO Anniversary Issue

Common Design Type

1968, May 4 Engraved *Perf. 13*

No.	Type	Description	Unused	Used
317	CD126	15fr multicolored	50	45

Issued to commemorate the 20th anniversary of the World Health Organization.

Common Design Types pictured in section at front of book.

Damer-djog Fortress
A50

Administration Buildings: 25fr, Ali Addé. 30fr, Dorra. 40fr, Assamo.

1968, May 17 Engraved *Perf. 13*

No.	Type	Description	Unused	Used
318	A50	20fr slate, brown & emerald	40	25
319	"	25fr brt. green, blue & brown	50	25
320	"	30fr brn. olive, brn. orange & slate	65	40
321	"	40fr brn. olive, slate & brt. green	1.00	50

Human Rights Year Issue

Common Design Type

1968, Aug. 10 Engraved *Perf. 13*

No.	Type	Description	Unused	Used
322	CD127	10fr purple, verm. & orange	45	30
323	"	70fr green, purple & orange	1.20	85

International Human Rights Year.

Radio-television Station, Djibouti
A52

High Commission Palace, Djibouti
A53

Designs: 2fr, Justice Building. 5fr, Chamber of Deputies. 8fr, Great Mosque. 15fr, Monument of Free French Forces (vert.). 40fr, Djibouti Post Office. 70fr, Residence of Gov. Léonce Lagarde at Obock. No. 332, Djibouti Harbormaster's Building. No. 333, Control tower, Djibouti Airport.

1968–70 Engraved *Perf. 13*

No.	Type	Description	Unused	Used
324	A52	1fr dk. red, sky blue & indigo ('69)	8	5
325	"	2fr green blue & indigo ('69)	10	8
326	"	5fr brown, sky blue & green ('69)	15	12
327	"	8fr chocolate, emerald & gray ('69)	22	15
328	"	15fr grn., sky bl. & yel. brn. ('69)	55	38
329	"	40fr green, brown & slate ('70)	65	40
330	A53	60fr multicolored	1.00	75
331	"	70fr dull grn., gray & olive bister ('69)	1.25	1.00
332	"	85fr multi. ('69)	1.50	1.00
333	A52	85fr dk. green, blue & gray ('70)	1.50	60
		Nos. 324-333 (10)	7.00	4.53

Locust
A54

Designs: 50fr, Pest control by helicopter. 55fr, Pest control by plane.

1969, Oct. 6 Engraved *Perf. 13*

No.	Type	Description	Unused	Used
334	A54	15fr brn., grn. & slate	30	18
335	"	50fr dark green, blue & olive brown	75	45
336	"	55fr red brown, blue & brown	85	55

Campaign against locusts.

ILO Issue

Common Design Type

1969, Nov. 24 Engraved *Perf. 13*

No.	Type	Description	Unused	Used
337	CD131	30fr orange, gray & lilac	75	60

Afar Dagger in Ornamental Scabbard
A56

1970, Apr. 3 Engraved *Perf. 13*

No.	Type	Description	Unused	Used
338	A56	10fr yel. grn., dk. grn. & org. brown	18	15
339	"	15fr yel. grn., blue & orange brown	22	15
340	"	20fr yel. grn., red & orange brown	30	22
341	"	25fr yel. grn., plum & orange brown	50	22

See No. 364.

U.P.U. Headquarters Issue

Common Design Type

1970, May 20 Engr. *Perf. 13*

No.	Type	Description	Unused	Used
342	CD133	25fr brn., brt. green & chocolate	50	30

Trap-shooting
A57

Motorboats
A58

Designs: 50fr, Steeplechase. 55fr, Sailboat (vert.). 60fr, Equestrians.

1970 Engraved *Perf. 13*

No.	Type	Description	Unused	Used
343	A57	30fr dp. brown, yellow green & brt. bl.	45	38
344	A58	48fr blue & multi.	70	38
345	"	50fr copper red, blue & purple	75	45
346	"	55fr red brown, blue & olive	90	55
347	"	60fr olive, black & red brown	90	55
		Nos. 343-347 (5)	3.70	2.31

Issue dates: 30fr, June 5; 48fr, Oct. 9; 50fr, 60fr, Nov. 6.

Automatic Ferry, Tadjourah
A59

1970, Nov. 25

No.	Type	Description	Unused	Used
348	A59	48fr blue, brn. & grn.	80	45

Volcanic Geode
A60

Diabase and Chrysolite
A61

Designs: 10fr, Doleritic basalt. 15fr, Olivine basalt.

1971 Photogravure *Perf. 13*

No.	Type	Description	Unused	Used
349	A61	10fr black & multi.	18	12
350	"	15fr " "	22	15
351	A60	25fr black, crimson & brown	40	25
352	A61	40fr black & multi.	65	38

Issue dates: 10fr, Nov. 22; 15fr, Oct. 8; 25fr, Apr. 26; 40fr, Jan. 25.

Manta Ray
A62

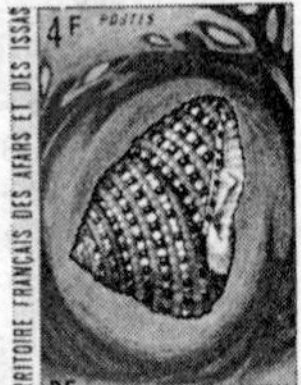

Strawberry Top
A63

Fishes: 5fr, Dolphinfish. 9fr, Smalltooth sawfish.

1971, July 1 Photo. *Perf. 12x12½*

No.	Type	Description	Unused	Used
353	A62	4fr green & multi.	18	15
354	"	5fr blue & multi.	25	22
355	"	9fr red & multi.	38	30

See No. C60.

De Gaulle Issue

Common Design Type

Designs: 60fr, Gen. Charles de Gaulle, 1940. 85fr, Pres. de Gaulle, 1970.

1971, Nov. 9 Engraved *Perf. 13*

No.	Type	Description	Unused	Used
356	CD134	60fr dk. violet blue & black	90	75
357	"	85fr dk. violet blue & black	1.35	1.10

1972, Mar. 8 Photo. *Perf. 12½x13*

Shells: 9fr, Cypraea pantherina. 20fr, Bull-mouth helmet. 50fr, Ethiopian volute.

No.	Type	Description	Unused	Used
358	A63	4fr olive & multi.	15	10
359	"	9fr dk. blue & multi.	20	10
360	"	20fr dp. green & multi.	40	20
361	"	50fr dp. claret & multi.	80	40

Shepherd—A64

Design: 10fr, Dromedary breeding.

1973, Apr. 11 Photo. *Perf. 13*

362	A64	9fr blue & multi.	22	12
363	"	10fr " "	22	12

Afar Dagger A65

1974, Jan. 29 Engraved *Perf. 13*

364	A65	30fr slate green & dark brown	55	45

Flamingos, Lake Abbé—A66

Designs: Flamingos and different views of Lake Abbé.

1974, Feb. 22 Photogravure *Perf. 13*

370	A66	5fr multicolored	10	8
371	"	15fr "	17	12
372	"	50fr "	75	45

Soccer Ball—A67

1974, May 24 Engr. *Perf. 13*

373	A67	25fr black & emerald	45	30

World Cup Soccer Championship, Munich, June 13–July 7.

Letters Around UPU Emblem A68

Oleo Chrysophylla A69

1974, Oct. 9 Engraved *Perf. 13*

374	A68	20fr multicolored	30	22
375	"	100fr "	1.75	1.25

Centenary of Universal Postal Union.

1974, Nov. 22 Photogravure

Multicolored

376	A69	10fr *shown*	22	20
377	A69	15fr *Ficus species*	32	30
378	"	20fr *Solanum adoense*	45	40

Day Primary Forest.

No. 364 Surcharged with New Value and Two Bars in Red

1975, Jan. 1 Engr. *Perf. 13*

379	A65	40fr on 30fr multi.	50	30

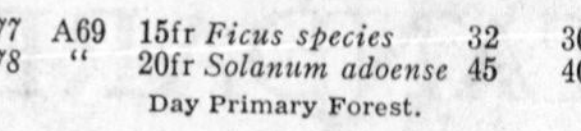

Treasury—A70

Design: 25fr, Government buildings.

1975, Jan. 7 Engr. *Perf. 13*

380	A70	8fr bl., gray & red	12	8
381	"	25fr red, bl. & indigo	30	25

Ranella Spinosa—A71

Sea Shells: No. 382, Darioconus textile. No. 383, Murex palmarosa. 10fr, Conus sumatrensis. 15fr, Cypraea pulchra. No. 386, 45fr, Murex scolopax. No. 387, Cypraea exhusta. 55fr, Cypraea erythraensis. 60fr, Conus taeniatus.

1975–76 Engraved *Perf. 13*

382	A71	5fr bl. grn. & brown	12	10
383	"	5fr bl. & multi. ('76)	12	10
384	"	10fr lilac, black & brown	18	12
385	"	15fr blue, indigo & brown	25	18
386	"	20fr pur. & lt. brn.	30	25
387	"	20fr bright green & multi. ('76)	35	25
388	"	40fr green & brown	65	55
389	"	45fr grn., bl. & bis.	70	45
390	"	55fr turquoise & multi. ('76)	70	50
391	"	60fr buff & sepia ('76)	80	60
		Nos. 382–391 (10)	4.17	3.10

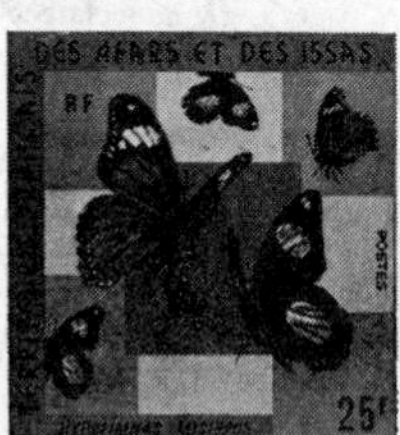

Hypolimnas Misippus A72

Butterflies: 40fr, Papilio nireus. 50fr, Acraea anemosa. 65fr, Holocerina smilax menieri. 70fr, Papilio demodocus. No. 397, Papilio dardanus. No. 398, Balachowsky gonimbrasca. 150fr, Vanessa cardui.

1975–76 Photogravure *Perf. 13*

392	A72	25fr emerald & multi.	32	22
393	"	40fr yellow & multi.	45	38
394	"	50fr ultramarine & multi. ('76)	60	38
395	"	65fr olive & multi. ('76)	70	50
396	"	70fr violet & multi.	90	60
397	"	100fr blue & multi.	1.50	1.00
398	"	100fr Prussian blue & multi. ('76)	1.10	90
399	"	150fr green & multi. ('76)	1.60	1.20
		Nos. 392–399 (8)	7.17	5.18

Mongoose—A73

Animals: 10fr, Hyena. No. 401, Catarrhine monkeys (vert.). No. 402, Wild ass (vert.). 30fr, Antelope. 60fr, Porcupines (vert.). 70fr, Skunks. 200fr, Aardvarks.

Perf. 13x12½, 12½x13

1975–76 Photogravure

400	A73	10fr light violet & multi. ('76)	15	8
401	"	15fr yellow green & multicolored	22	18
402	"	15fr green & multi. ('76)	20	15
403	"	30fr blue & multi. ('76)	40	30
404	"	50fr dp. orange & multicolored	60	45
405	"	60fr yel. brown & multicolored	75	60
406	"	70fr blk. & brown	1.00	75
407	"	200fr blue gray & multicolored	2.75	2.00
		Nos. 400–407 (8)	6.07	4.51

Pin-tailed Whydah A74

Palms A75

Birds: 25fr, Rose-ringed parakeet. 50fr, Variable sunbird. 60fr, Purple heron. No. 417, Hammerhead. No. 418, Turtle dove. 300fr, African spoonbill.

1975–76 Photo. *Perf. 12½x13*

413	A74	20fr lilac, black & orange	22	15
414	"	25fr carmine rose & multi. ('76)	30	20
415	"	50fr blue & multi.	55	40
416	"	60fr multicolored	60	45
417	"	100fr light green & multicolored	90	75
418	"	100fr light yellow & multi. ('76)	1.10	75
419	"	300fr multi. ('76)	3.50	2.00
		Nos. 413–419 (7)	7.17	4.70

1975, Dec. 19 Engr. *Perf. 13*

421	A75	20fr brt. bl. & multi.	30	15

Satellite and Alexander Graham Bell A76

1976, Mar. 10 Engr. *Perf. 13*

422	A76	200fr dp. bl., org. & slate green	2.25	1.50

Centenary of the first telephone call by Alexander Graham Bell, Mar. 10, 1876.

Basketball A77

Designs: 15fr, Bicycling. 40fr, Soccer. 60fr, Running.

1976, July 7 Litho. *Perf. 12½*

423	A77	10fr lt. blue & multi.	12	10
424	"	15fr yel. & multi.	18	15
425	"	40fr org. red & multi.	50	35
426	"	60fr lt. grn. & multi.	75	50

21st Olympic Games, Montreal, Canada, July 17–Aug. 1.

Turkeyfish—A78

1976, Aug. 10 Photo. *Perf. 13x13½*

428	A78	45fr blue & multi.	70	40

Psammophis Elegans—A79

Design: 70fr, Naja nigricollis (vert.).

Perf. 13x13½, 13½x13

1976, Sept. 27 Photogravure

430	A79	70fr ocher & multi.	85	50
431	"	80fr emerald & multicolored	1.10	60

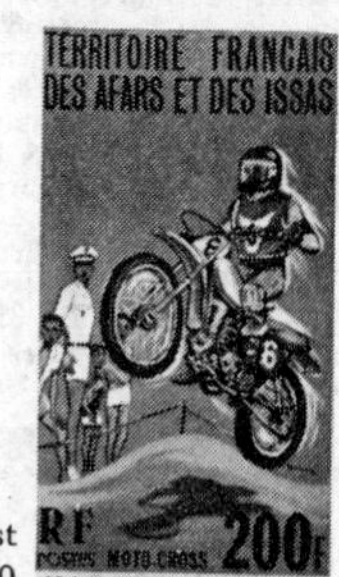

Motorcyclist A80

1977, Jan. 27 Litho. *Perf. 12x12½*

432	A80	200fr multicolored	2.50	1.65

Moto-Cross motorcycle race.

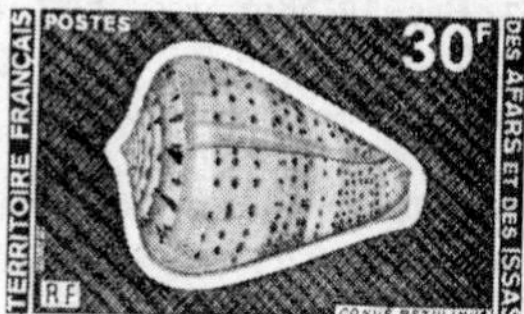

Conus Betulinus—A81

Sea Shells: 5fr, Cyprea tigris. 70fr, Conus striatus. 85fr, Cyprea mauritiana.

1977 Engr. *Perf. 13*

433	A81	5fr multicolored	10	4
434	"	30fr "	40	22

435 A81 70fr multicolored 90 60
436 " 85fr " 1.10 75

Gaterin Gaterinus
A82

Design: 65fr, Barracudas.

1977, Apr. 15 Photo. *Perf. 13x12½*

437 A82 15fr multicolored 20 12
438 " 65fr " 75 50

Stamps of the French Territory of the Afars and Issas were replaced in 1977 by those of the Republic of Djibouti.

AIR POST STAMPS

Tawny Eagles AP16 — Parachutists AP17

1967, Aug. 21 Engraved *Perf. 13*

C50 AP16 200fr multi. 5.50 2.25

1968 Engraved *Perf. 13*

Design: 85fr, Water skier and skin diver.

C51 AP17 48fr brn. olive, Prus. bl. & brn. 1.10 75
C52 " 85fr dk. brn., olive & Prus. bl. 1.75 1.25

Issue dates: 48fr, Jan. 5; 85fr, Mar. 15.

Aerial Map of the Territory
AP18

1968, Nov. 15 Engraved *Perf. 13*

C53 AP18 500fr blue, dk. brn. & ocher 7.50 3.50

Buildings Type of Regular Issue

Designs: 100fr, Cathedral (vert.). 200fr, Sayed Hassan Mosque (vert.).

1969 Engraved *Perf. 13*

C54 A53 100fr grn., sky bl. & bis. brown 1.50 75
C55 " 200fr lilac, blue, brn. & black 3.25 1.50

Issue dates: 100fr, Apr. 4; 200fr, May 8.

Concorde Issue
Common Design Type

1969, Apr. 17

C56 CD129 100fr orange red & olive 5.00 3.50

Arta Ionospheric Station—AP19 — Japanese Sword Guard, Fish Design—AP20

1970, May 8 Engraved *Perf. 13*

C57 AP19 70fr multicolored 1.35 90

Gold Embossed

1970, Sept. 29 *Perf. 12½*

Design: 200fr, Japanese sword guard, horse design.

C58 AP20 100fr gold, yel. grn., ultra. & brown 2.25 1.85
C59 " 200fr gold, car., yel. green & brown 3.75 2.50

EXPO '70 International Exposition, Osaka, Japan, Mar. 15–Sept. 13.

Parrot-fish
AP21

1971, July 1 Photo. *Perf. 12½*

C60 AP21 30fr black & multi. 90 75

Djibouti Harbor—AP22

1971, Nov. 26

C61 AP22 100fr blue & multi. 1.75 75

New Djibouti harbor.

Lichtenstein's Sandgrouse AP23 — Running, Olympic Rings AP24

Birds: 49fr, Hoopoe. 66fr, Great snipe. 500fr, Tawny-breasted francolin.

1972 Photogravure *Perf. 12½x13*

C62 AP23 30fr multicolored 60 45
C63 " 49fr " 90 60
C64 " 66fr blue & multi. 1.30 90
C65 " 500fr multicolored 7.50 3.00

Issue dates: No. C65, Nov. 3, others Apr. 21.

1972, June 8 Engr. *Perf. 13*

Designs (Olympic Rings and): 10fr, Basketball. 55fr, Swimming (horiz.). 60fr, Olympic torch and Greek frieze (horiz.).

C66 AP24 5fr pur., bl. green & dk. brown 22 15
C67 " 10fr dk. red, slate grn. & dk. brn. 32 20
C68 " 55fr grn., brn. & bl. 1.00 50
C69 " 60fr bl. grn., dk. red & purple 1.35 65

20th Olympic Games, Munich, Aug. 26–Sept. 11.

Louis Pasteur—AP25

Design: 100fr, Albert Calmette and C. Guérin.

1972, Oct. 5 Engraved *Perf. 13*

C70 AP25 20fr rose car., olive bister & brt. green 45 30
C71 " 100fr dk. brown, brt. green & dull red 1.50 90

Pasteur, Calmette, Guérin, chemists and bacteriologists, benefactors of mankind.

Map and Views of Territory—AP26

Design: 200fr, Woman and Mosque of Djibouti (vert.).

1973, Jan. 15 Photo. *Perf. 13*

C72 AP26 30fr brn. & multi. 1.00 90
C73 " 200fr multicolored 4.00 3.00

Visit of Pres. Georges Pompidou of France, Jan. 15–17.

Oryx—AP27

Animals: 50fr, Dik-dik. 66fr, Caracal.

1973, Feb. 26 Photo. *Perf. 13x12½*

C74 AP27 30fr green & multi. 55 30
C75 " 50fr rose & multi. 90 60
C76 " 66fr lilac & multi. 1.10 75

See also Nos. C94–C96.

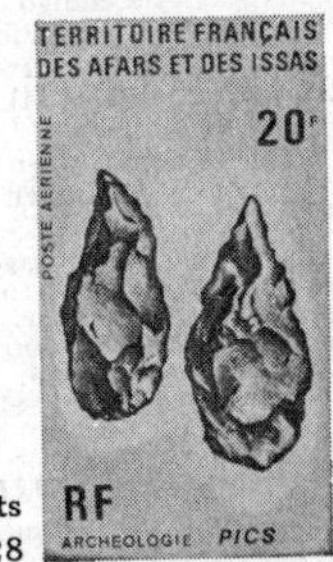

Celts
AP28

Designs: Various pre-historic flint tools. 40fr, 60fr, horizontal.

1973 Photographed *Perf. 13*

C77 AP28 20fr yel. grn., blk. & brown 50 30
C78 " 40fr yellow & multi. 60 45
C79 " 49fr lilac & multi. 90 65
C80 " 60fr blue & multi. 1.00 65

Issue dates: 20fr, 49fr, Mar. 16; 40fr, 60fr, Sept. 7.

Octopus—AP29

Design: 60fr, Dugong.

1973, Mar. 16

C81 AP29 40fr multicolored 65 45
C82 " 60fr brn. & multi. 1.00 75

Copernicus
AP30

Baboons
AP31

Designs: 8fr, Nicolaus Copernicus (1473–1534), Polish astronomer. 9fr, William C. Roentgen (1845–1923), physicist, X-ray discoverer. C85, Edward Jenner (1749–1823), physician, discoverer of vaccination. No. C86, Marie Curie (1867–1934), discoverer of radium and polonium. 49fr, Robert Koch (1843–1910), physician and bacteriologist. 50fr, Clément Ader (1841–1925), French aviation pioneer. 55fr, Guglielmo Marconi (1874–1937), Italian electrical engineer, inventor. 85fr, Molière (1622–1673), French playwright. 100fr, Henri Farman (1874–1937), French aviation pioneer. 150fr, André-Marie Ampère (1775–1836), French physicist. 250fr, Michelangelo Buonarroti (1475–1564), Italian sculptor, painter and architect.

1973–75 Engraved *Perf. 13*

C83	AP30	8fr blk., dk. bis. & maroon	22	15
C84	"	9fr brown, ocher & vio. brown	18	12
C85	"	10fr car., brown & vio. brown	22	15
C86	"	10fr red lilac, dp. claret & blue	22	20
C87	"	49fr slate grn., yel. grn. & vio. brown	75	55
C88	"	50fr ol. brn., slate grn. & bl.	55	45
C89	"	55fr multi. ('74)	90	65
C90	"	85fr blue, violet & indigo	1.50	1.00
C91	"	100fr yel. grn., vio. brown & blue ('74)	1.75	1.20
C92	"	150fr multi.	1.50	75
C93	"	250fr black, green & brown	2.75	1.75
		Nos. C83–C93 (11)	10.54	6.97

Issue dates: 8fr, 85fr, May 9, 1973. 9fr, C85, 49fr, Oct. 12, 1973. 100fr, Jan. 29, 1974. 55fr, Mar. 22, 1974. C86, Aug. 23, 1974. 150fr, July 24, 1975. 250fr, June 26, 1975. 50fr, Sept. 25, 1975.

Perf. 12½x13, 13x12½

1973, Dec. 12 Photogravure

Designs: 50fr, Genets (horiz.). 66fr, Hares.

C94	AP31	20fr org. & multi.	35	25
C95	"	50fr multicolored	90	65
C96	"	66fr blue & multi.	1.25	90

Spearfishing—AP32

1974, Apr. 14 Engr. ***Perf. 13***

C97	AP32	200fr multicolored	3.00	1.75

No. C97 was prepared for release in Nov. 1972, to commemorate the 3rd Underwater Spearfishing Contest in the Red Sea. Dates have been obliterated with a rectangle and the stamp was not issued without this obliteration.

Rock Carvings, Balho—AP33

1974, Apr. 26

C98	AP33	200fr car. & slate	2.75	2.25

Lake Assal—AP34

Designs (Lake Assal): 50fr, Rock formations on shore. 85fr, Crystallized wood.

1974, Oct. 25 Photogravure *Perf. 13*

C99	AP34	49fr multicolored	65	45
C100	"	50fr "	90	60
C101	"	85fr "	1.50	1.00

Guinea Dove
AP35

1975, May 23 Photo. ***Perf. 13***

C102	AP35	500fr multi.	5.50	2.75

Djibouti Airport—AP36

1977, Mar. 1 Litho. ***Perf. 12***

C103	AP36	500fr multi.	6.00	3.75

Opening of new Djibouti Airport.

Thomas A. Edison and Phonograph—AP37

Design: 75fr, Alexander Volta, electric train, lines and light bulb.

1977, May 5 Engr. ***Perf. 13***

C104	AP37	55fr multicolored	80	60
C105	"	75fr "	1.15	90

Famous inventors: Thomas Alva Edison (1847–1931) and Alexander Volta (1745–1827).

POSTAGE DUE STAMPS

Nomad's Milk Jug
D3

Unwmkd.

1969, Dec. 15 Engr. ***Perf. 14x13***

J49	D3	1fr red brown, red lilac & slate	5	5
J50	"	2fr red brn., emerald & slate	5	5
J51	"	5fr red brown, blue & slate	10	10
J52	"	10fr red brown, brown & slate	22	22

AFGHANISTAN

(ăf·găn′ĭ·stăn ; ăf·găn′ĭs·tän′)

LOCATION—Central Asia, bounded by Persia, Russian Turkestan, Pakistan, Baluchistan and China.
GOVT.—Republic.
AREA—253,861 sq. mi.
POP.—19,800,000 (est. 1976).
CAPITAL—Kabul.

Afghanistan changed from a constitutional monarchy to a republic in July, 1973.

12 Shahi = 6 Sanar = 3 Abasi = 2 Krans = 1 Rupee Kabuli

60 Paisas = 1 Rupee (1921)

100 Pouls = 1 Rupee Afghani (1927)

CHARACTERS OF VALUE.

Shahi.

1871-78 A7 A8

Sanar. Abasi. 6 Shahi.

1871-78 1871 1872

1 Rupee. ½ Rupee.

1874 1876(A8) 1876 (A7)

1 Rupee. Rupee.

1872 1874 1876 (A8) 1877-78

From 1871 to 1892 and 1898 the Moslem year date appears on the stamp. Numerals as follows:

۱	۲	۳	۴	۵
1	2	3	4	5
۶	۷	۸	۹	۰
6	7	8	9	0

Until 1891 cancellation consisted of cutting or tearing a piece from the stamps. Such copies should not be considered as damaged.

Prices are for cut square examples of good color. Cut to shape or faded copies sell for much less, particularly Nos. 2–10.

Nos. 2–108 are on laid paper of varying thickness except where wove is noted.

Until 1907 all stamps were issued ungummed.

The tiger's head on types A2 to A11 symbolizes the name of the contemporary amir, Sher (Tiger) Ali.

Kingdom of Kabul

Tiger's Head—A2
(Both circles dotted.)

Dated "1288".
Lithographed

1871 ***Imperf.*** **Unwmkd.**

No.	Type	Value	Unused	Used
2	A2	1sh black	60.00	22.50
3	"	1sa "	32.50	17.50
4	"	1ab "	22.50	17.50

Thirty varieties of the shahi, 10 of the sanar and 5 of the abasi.

Similar designs without the tiger's head in the center are revenues.

A3
(Outer circle dotted.)

Dated "1288".

No.	Type	Value	Unused	Used
5	A3	1sh black	135.00	25.00
6	"	1sa "	60.00	22.50
7	"	1ab "	32.50	27.50

Five varieties of each.

A4

Dated "1289".
Toned Wove Paper

1872

No.	Type	Value	Unused	Used
8	A4	6sh violet	425.00	275.00
9	"	1rup "	550.00	375.00

Two varieties of each. Date varies in location. Printed in sheets of 4 (2x2) containing two of each denomination.

Most used copies are smeared with a greasy ink cancel.

A4a

Dated "1290"

1873 White Laid Paper

No.	Type	Value	Unused	Used
10	A4a	1sh black	5.50	3.50
		a. Corner ornament missing	350.00	275.00
		b. Corner ornament retouched	40.00	17.50

15 varieties. Nos. 10a, 10b are the sixth stamp on the sheet.

A5

1873

No.	Type	Value	Unused	Used
11	A5	1sh black	2.00	1.50
11A	"	1sh violet	325.00	

Sixty varieties of each.

1874 Dated "1291".

No.	Type	Value	Unused	Used
12	A5	1ab black	32.50	22.50
13	"	½rup "	16.50	13.50
14	"	1rup "	20.00	16.50

Five varieties of each.

Nos. 12–14 were printed on the same sheet. Se-tenant varieties exist.

A6 A7

1875 Dated "1292".

No.	Type	Value	Unused	Used
15	A6	1sa black	135.00	90.00
		a. Wide outer circle	325.00	
16	A6	1ab black	185.00	140.00
17	"	1sa brown violet	20.00	20.00
		a. Wide outer circle	110.00	
18	A6	1ab brown violet	30.00	22.50

Ten varieties of the sanar, five of the abasi.

Nos. 15–16 and 17–18 were printed in the same sheets. Se-tenant pairs exist.

1876 Dated "1293"

No.	Type	Value	Unused	Used
19	A7	1sh black	225.00	125.00
20	"	1sa "	250.00	125.00
21	"	1ab "	325.00	125.00
22	"	½rup "	225.00	140.00
23	"	1rup "	300.00	140.00
24	"	1sh violet	325.00	160.00
25	"	1sa "	240.00	125.00
26	"	1ab "	375.00	160.00
27	"	½rup "	72.50	50.00
28	"	1rup "	72.50	55.00

12 varieties of the shahi and 3 each of the other values.

A8

1876 Dated "1293".

No.	Type	Value	Unused	Used
29	A8	1sh gray	5.50	3.25
30	"	1sa "	7.50	3.50
31	"	1ab "	15.00	7.00
32	"	½rup "	18.00	9.00
33	"	1rup "	18.00	9.00
34	"	1sh olive black	110.00	
35	"	1sa "	150.00	
36	"	1ab "	375.00	
37	"	½rup "	250.00	
38	"	1rup "	300.00	
39	"	1sh green	25.00	4.50
40	"	1sa "	37.50	17.50
41	"	1ab "	55.00	40.00
42	"	½rup "	95.00	45.00
43	"	1rup "	95.00	85.00
44	"	1sh ochre	22.50	8.50
45	"	1sa "	37.50	18.50
46	"	1ab "	60.00	32.50
47	"	½rup "	72.50	50.00
48	"	1rup "	125.00	110.00
49	"	1sh violet	18.00	3.25
50	"	1sa "	25.00	6.00
51	"	1ab "	35.00	12.00
52	"	½rup "	60.00	25.00
53	"	1rup "	72.50	30.00

24 varieties of the shahi, 4 of which show denomination written

12 varieties of the sanar, 6 of the abasi and 3 each of the ½ rupee and rupee.

A9

1877 Dated "1294".

No.	Type	Value	Unused	Used
54	A9	1sh gray	2.50	1.75
55	"	1sa "	4.50	2.00
56	"	1ab "	8.50	4.50
57	"	½rup "	12.00	12.00
58	"	1rup "	12.00	12.00
59	"	1sh black	7.50	
60	"	1sa "	18.50	
61	"	1ab "	42.50	
62	"	½rup "	50.00	
63	"	1rup "	50.00	
64	"	1sh green	3.25	2.50
		a. Wove paper	8.50	
65	"	1sa green	5.50	2.50
		a. Wove paper	15.00	11.00
66	"	1ab green	7.50	7.50
		a. Wove paper	25.00	
67	"	½rup green	13.50	13.50
		a. Wove paper	27.50	27.50
68	"	1rup green	13.50	13.50
		a. Wove paper	27.50	
69	"	1sh ochre	2.50	2.00
70	"	1sa "	8.00	3.25
71	"	1ab "	18.50	13.50
72	"	½rup "	27.50	22.50
73	"	1rup "	27.50	22.50
74	"	1sh violet	2.50	2.00
75	"	1sa "	5.50	2.00
76	"	1ab "	12.00	6.00
77	"	½rup "	18.50	12.00
78	"	1rup "	18.50	12.00

25 varieties of the shahi, 8 of the sanar, 3 of the abasi and 2 each of the ½ rupee and rupee.

A10 A11

1878 Dated "1295"

No.	Type	Value	Unused	Used
79	A10	1sh gray	1.50	1.50
80	"	1sa "	1.75	1.75
81	"	1ab "	3.25	3.25
82	"	½rup "	8.50	7.50
83	"	1rup "	8.50	7.50
84	"	1sh black	2.50	
85	"	1sa "	3.25	
86	"	1ab "	11.00	
87	"	½rup "	20.00	
88	"	1rup "	22.50	
89	"	1sh green	25.00	22.50
90	"	1sa "	2.50	2.50
91	"	1ab "	12.00	10.00
92	"	½rup "	25.00	18.50
93	"	1rup "	25.00	18.50
94	"	1sh ochre	8.50	2.50
95	"	1sa "	2.50	2.10
96	"	1ab "	5.50	5.50
97	"	½rup "	18.50	18.50
98	"	1rup "	18.50	18.50
99	"	1sh violet	1.50	1.50
100	"	1sa "	1.50	1.50
101	"	1ab "	4.25	4.25
102	"	½rup "	22.50	16.50
103	"	1rup "	22.50	16.50
104	A11	1sh gray	2.10	1.85
105	"	1sh black	*100.00*	
106	"	1sh green	1.75	1.25
107	"	1sh ochre	1.25	1.25
108	"	1sh violet	2.10	2.00

40 varieties of the shahi, 30 of the sanar, 6 of the abasi and 2 each of the ½ rupee and 1 rupee.

The 1876, 1877 and 1878 issues were printed in separate colors for each main post office on the Peshawar-Kabul-Khulm (Tashkurghan) postal route. Some specialists consider the black printings to be proofs or trial colors.

There are many shades of these colors.

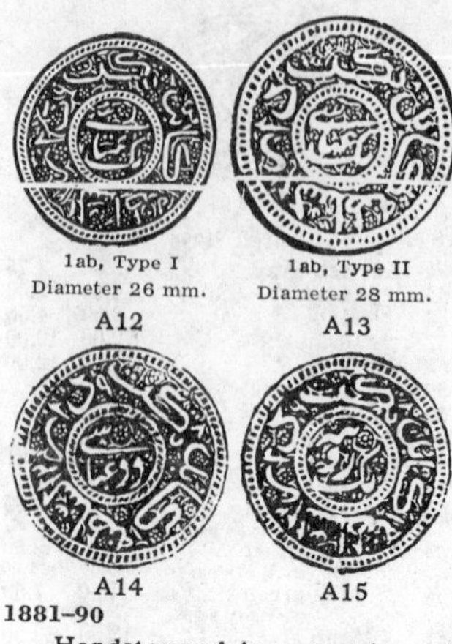

1ab, Type I Diameter 26 mm. A12 — 1ab, Type II Diameter 28 mm. A13

A14 — A15

1881–90

Handstamped, in watercolor.
Dated "1298", numerals scattered through design.

Thin White Laid Batonné Paper

109	A12	1ab violet	1.50	1.00
109A	A13	1ab violet	2.00	2.00
110	A12	1ab black brown	4.00	2.00
111	"	1ab rose	2.00	1.50
		b. Se-tenant with No. 111A	12.00	
111A	A13	1ab rose	2.00	2.00
112	A14	2ab violet	2.00	1.50
113	"	2ab black brown	7.50	6.00
114	"	2ab rose	3.00	2.50
115	A15	1rup violet	2.50	1.25
116	"	1rup black brown	10.00	10.00
117	"	1rup rose	3.50	3.50

Thin White Wove Batonné Paper

118	A12	1ab violet	10.00	6.00
119	"	1ab vermilion	5.00	
120	"	1ab rose		
121	A14	2ab violet		
122	"	2ab vermilion	7.50	
122A	"	2ab black brown		
123	A15	1rup violet	10.00	
124	"	1rup vermilion	5.00	
125	"	1rup black brown	5.00	

Thin White Laid Batonné Paper

126	A12	1ab brown orange	3.00	2.50
126A	A13	1ab brn. org. (II)	5.00	5.00
127	A12	1ab car. lake	3.00	2.50
		a. Laid paper		
128	A14	2ab brown orange	3.00	3.00
129	"	2ab car. lake	3.00	3.00
130	A15	1rup brown org.	5.00	4.00
131	"	1rup car. lake	3.00	3.00

Yellowish Laid Batonné Paper

132	A12	1ab purple		5.00
133	"	1ab red	10.00	5.00

1884

Colored Wove Paper

133A	A13	1ab pur., *yel.* (II)	22.50	22.50
134	A12	1ab purple, *green*	22.50	
135	"	1ab purple, *blue*	16.50	14.00
136	"	1ab red, *green*	40.00	
137	"	1ab red, *yellow*	2.00	
139	"	1ab red, *rose*	8.00	
140	A14	2ab red, *yellow*	7.00	
142	"	2ab red, *rose*	6.00	
143	A15	1rup red, *yellow*	5.00	4.00
145	"	1rup red, *rose*	7.00	7.00

Thin Colored Ribbed Paper

146	A14	2ab red, *yellow*	3.50	
147	A15	1rup " "	10.00	
148	A12	1ab lake, *lilac*	5.00	
149	A14	2ab " "	6.00	
150	A15	1rup " "	5.00	
151	A12	1ab lake, *green*	2.50	
152	A14	2ab " "	5.00	
153	A15	1rup " "	5.00	

1886–88

Colored Wove Paper.

155	A12	1ab *magenta*	12.50	
156	"	1ab claret brown, *orange*	6.00	
156A	"	1ab red, *orange*	3.00	
156B	A14	2ab red, *orange*	7.00	
156C	A15	1rup red, *orange*	5.00	

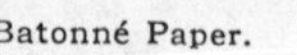

Laid Batonné Paper.

157	A12	1ab *lavender*	3.00	
158	"	1ab claret brown, *green*	7.00	
159	"	1ab *pink*	22.50	
160	A14	2ab "	40.00	
161	A15	1rup "		

Laid Paper.

162	A12	1ab *pink*	11.00	
163	A14	2ab "	11.00	
164	A15	1rup "	11.00	
165	A12	1ab brown, *yellow*	16.50	
166	A14	2ab " "	16.50	
167	A15	1rup " "	16.50	
168	A12	1ab blue, *green*	22.50	
169	A14	2ab " "	22.50	
170	A15	1rup " "	22.50	

1891

Colored Wove Paper.

175	A12	1ab green, *rose*	25.00	
176	A15	1rup purple, *green batonné*	27.50	

Nos. 109–176 fall into three categories:
1. Those regularly issued and in normal postal use from 1881 on, handstamped on thin white laid or wove paper in strip sheets containing 12 or more impressions of the same denomination arranged in two irregular rows, with the impressions often touching or overlappng.
2. The 1884 postal issues provisionally printed on smooth or ribbed colored wove paper as needed to supplement low stocks of the normal white paper stamps.
3. The "special" printings made in a range of colors on several types of laid or wove colored papers, most of which were never used for normal printings. These were produced periodically from 1886 to 1891 to meet philatelic demands. Although nominally valid for postage, most of the special printings were exported directly to fill dealers' orders, and few were ever postally used. Many of the sheets contained all three denominations with impressions separated by ruled lines. Sometimes different colors were used, so se-tenant multiples of denomination or color exist. Many combinations of stamp and paper colors exist besides those listed.

Various shades of each color exist.

Type A12 is known dated "1297".

Counterfeits, lithographed or typographed, are plentiful.

Kingdom of Afghanistan

A16

A17 — A18

Dated "1309".

1891 Pelure Paper Lithographed

177	A16	1ab slate blue	1.25	1.00
		a. Tête bêche pair	10.00	
178	A17	2ab slate blue	7.50	6.00
179	A18	1rup "	15.00	12.50

Revenue stamps of similar design exist in various colors.

Nos. 177–179 were printed in panes on the same sheet, so se-tenant gutter pairs exist. Examples in black or red are proofs.

A Mosque Gate and Crossed Cannons (National Seal)

A19

Dated "1310" in Upper Right Corner.

1892 Flimsy Wove Paper

180	A19	1ab *green*	2.50	1.50
181	"	1ab *orange*	3.50	3.00
182	"	1ab *yellow*	2.50	1.50
183	"	1ab *pink*	3.00	2.00
184	"	1ab *lilac rose*	2.75	2.25
185	"	1ab *blue*	5.00	4.00
186	"	1ab *salmon*	3.00	2.25
187	"	1ab *magenta*	3.00	3.00
188	"	1ab *violet*	2.75	2.75
188A	"	1ab *scarlet*	3.00	1.75

Many shades exist.

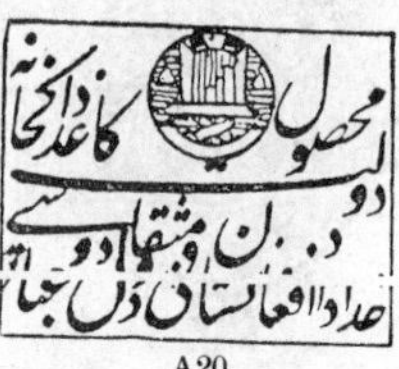

A20

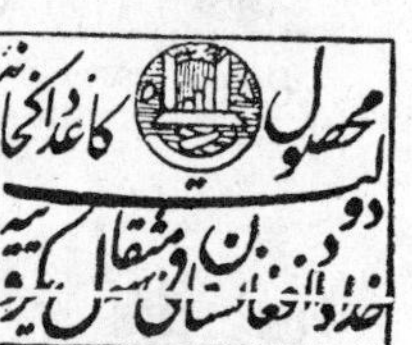

A21

Undated

1894 Flimsy Wove Paper

189	A20	2ab *green*	7.50	6.00
190	A21	1rup *green*	10.00	7.50

24 varieties of the 2 abasi and 12 varieties of the rupee.

Nos. 189–190 and F3 were printed se-tenant in the same sheet. Pairs exist.

A21a

Dated "1316"

1898 Flimsy Wove Paper

191	A21a	2ab *pink*	3.75	
192	"	2ab *magenta*	2.50	
193	"	2ab *yellow*	1.50	
193A	"	2ab *salmon*	3.75	
194	"	2ab *green*	1.75	
195	"	2ab *purple*	2.00	
195A	"	2ab *blue*	30.00	

Nos. 191–195A were not regularly issued. Genuinely used copies are scarce. No. 195A was found in remainder stocks and probably was never released.

National Coat of Arms

A22 — A23

A24

1907 Engraved *Imperf*

Medium Wove Paper

196	A22	1ab blue green	3.00	2.00
		a. 1ab emerald	7.50	4.00
197	"	1ab bright blue	6.00	1.75
198	A23	2ab deep blue	1.50	1.00
199	A24	1rup green	2.50	2.00
		a. 1rup blue green	5.00	5.00

Zigzag Roulette 10

200	A22	1ab green	27.50	20.00
201	A23	2ab blue	40.00	32.50
201A	A24	1rup blue green	50.00	42.50

1908 *Perf. 12*

202	A22	1ab green	5.00	5.00
203	A23	2ab deep blue	1.00	1.00
204	A24	1rup blue green	2.50	2.50

Twelve varieties of the 1 abasi, 6 of the 2 abasi, 4 of the 1 rupee.

Nos. 196–204 were issued in small sheets containing 3 or 4 panes. Gutter pairs, normal and tête bêche, exist.

A25 — A26

A27

1909–19 Typo. *Perf. 12*

205	A25	1ab ultramarine	50	35
		a. Imperf., pair	3.00	
206	"	1ab red ('16)	35	25
		a. Imperf.		
207	"	1ab rose ('18)	35	25
208	A26	2ab green	75	75
		a. Imperf., pair	7.00	
		b. Horizontal pair, imperf. between		
208C	"	2ab yellow ('16)	1.00	1.00
209	"	2ab bistre ('18–'19)	90	90
210	A27	1rup lilac brown	1.25	1.25
		a. 1rup red brown	1.25	1.25
211	"	1rup olive bis. ('16)	1.25	1.25
		Nos. 205–211 (8)	6.35	6.00

A28

1913

212	A28	2pa drab brown	1.00	1.00
		a. 2pa red brown	1.00	1.00

No. 212 is inscribed "Tiket waraq dak" (Postal card stamps). It was usable only on postcards and not accepted for postage on letters.

Nos. 196–212 sometimes show letters of a papermaker's watermark, "Howard & Jones, London."

Royal Star
A29

1920, Aug. 24 *Perf. 12*

Size: 39x47mm.

214	A29	10pa rose	18.50	10.00
215	"	20pa red brown	42.50	25.00
216	"	30pa green	75.00	70.00

Issued in sheets of two.

1921, Mar.

Size: 22½x28¼mm.

217	A29	10pa rose	25	25
		a. Perf. 11 ('27)	1.00	1.50
218	A29	20pa red brown	50	50
219	"	30pa yellow green	50	50
		a. Tête bêche pair	3.75	3.75
		b. 30pa green	50	50
		c. As "b," tête bêche pair	3.75	3.75

Two types of the 10pa, three of the 20pa.

Crest of King Amanullah
A30

1924, Feb. 26 *Perf. 12*

220	A30	10pa chocolate	13.50	9.00
		a. Tête bêche pair	27.50	25.00

Issued to commemorate the 6th Independence Day.

Printed in sheets of four consisting of two tête bêche pairs, and in sheets of two. Two types exist.

Some authorities believe that Nos. Q15-Q16 were issued as regular postage stamps.

Crest of King Amanullah
A32

1925, Feb. 26 *Perf. 12*

Size: 29x37mm.

222	A32	10pa light brown	10.00	7.00

Issued to commemorate the 7th Independence Day.

Printed in sheets of 8 (two panes of 4).

1926, Feb. 28 Wove Paper

Size: 26x33mm.

224	A32	10pa dark blue	1.25	1.25
		a. Imperf., pair	10.00	10.00
		b. Horizontal pair, imperf. between	12.00	
		c. Vertical pair, imperf. between	10.00	
		d. Laid paper	7.50	5.00

Issued for the 7th anniversary of Independence. Printed in sheets of 4, and in sheets of 8 (two panes of 4). Tête bêche gutter pairs exist.

Tughra and Crest of Amanullah—A33

1927, Feb.

225	A33	10pa magenta	4.00	3.25
		a. Vertical pair, imperf. between	20.00	

Dotted Background.

226	A33	10pa magenta	4.00	3.75
		a. Horizontal pair, imperf. between	15.00	

The surface of No. 226 is covered by a net of fine dots.

Nos. 225 and 226 were issued to commemorate the eighth anniversary of Independence. Printed in sheets of 8 (two panes of 4). Tête bêche gutter pairs exist.

National Seal
A34

A35 A35a

A36

1927, Oct. *Imperf.*

227	A34	15p pink	35	35
228	A35	30p Prussian green	50	40
229	A36	60p light blue	1.25	1.00
		a. Tête bêche pair	3.75	5.00

1927-30 *Perf. 11, 12*

230	A34	15p pink	35	25
231	"	15p ultra. ('29)	40	35
232	A35	30p Prussian green	50	25
233	A35a	30p deep green ('30)	60	60
234	A36	60p bright blue	1.25	1.00
		a. Tête bêche pair	3.50	3.50
235	"	60p black ('29)	1.00	75
		Nos. 230-235 (6)	4.10	3.20

Nos. 230, 232 and 234 are usually imperforate on one or two sides.

No. 233 has been redrawn. A narrow border of pearls has been added and "30", in European and Arabic numerals, inserted in the upper spandrels.

Tughra and Crest of Amanullah
A37

1928, Feb. 27

236	A37	15p pink	1.25	1.00
		a. Tête bêche pair	3.75	3.00
		b. Imperf. vertically, pair	4.00	
		c. Same as "a", imperf. vertically		

Issued to commemorate the ninth anniversary of Independence. This stamp is always imperforate on one or two sides.

A 15p blue of somewhat similar design was prepared for the 10th anniversary, but was not issued due to Amanullah's dethronement. Price, $5.

National Seal—A38

A39

A40

A41 A42

1928-30 *Perf. 11, 12*

237	A38	2p dull blue	3.00	2.00
		a. Vertical pair, imperf. between		
238	"	2p light rose ('30)	25	25
239	A39	10p gray green	25	15
		a. Tête bêche pair	6.00	6.00
		b. Imperf. horizontally, pair	1.00	
		c. Vertical pair, imperf. between	75	
240	"	10p chocolate ('30)	40	25
		a. 10p brn. pur. ('29)	2.50	1.50
241	A40	25p carmine rose	30	25
242	"	25p Prussian green ('29)	75	50
243	A41	40p ultramarine	40	30
		a. Tête bêche pair	6.00	6.00
244	"	40p rose ('29)	75	60
		a. Tête bêche pair	6.00	6.00
		b. Imperf. horizontally, pair	2.50	
245	A42	50p red	40	40
246	"	50p dark blue ('29)	1.00	75
		Nos. 237-246 (10)	7.50	5.45

The sheets of these stamps are often imperforate at the outer margins.

Nos. 237-238 are newspaper stamps.

Revolutionary Gov't. Issue

Stamps of 1927-28 Handstamped

On Stamps of 1927.

1929 *Imperf.*

252	A34	15p pink	3.00
253	A35	30p Prussian green	3.75
253A	A36	60p light blue	6.00

Perf. 11

254	A34	15p pink	3.00
255	A35	30p Prussian green	3.75
256	A36	60p bright blue	6.00

On Stamps of 1928.

257	A38	2p dull blue	2.50
258	A39	10p gray green	2.50
		a. Vertical pair, imperf. between	
259	A40	25p carmine rose	3.75
260	A41	40p ultramarine	5.00
		a. Tête bêche pair	60.00
261	A42	50p red	7.50
		Nos. 257-261 (5)	21.25

Impressions of the overprint vary greatly. It reads: "Khadim Din Mohammed Rasul Ullah Amir Habib Ullah, 1347." (The Servant of the Faith of Mohammed, Prophet of God, Amir Habibullah). Genuinely used copies are extremely rare. Counterfeit overprints and bogus cancellations are plentiful.

Independence Monument
A46

Lithographed.

Wmkd. Large Seal in the Sheet.

1931, Aug. Laid Paper *Perf. 12*

262	A46	20p red	75	50

Issued to commemorate the 13th Independence Day. Issued without gum.

National Assembly Chamber
A47

National Assembly Chamber
A48 A50

National Assembly Building
A49

National Assembly Chamber
A51

National Assembly Building
A52

Typographed
Wove Paper

1932 *Perf. 12* **Unwmkd.**

263	A47	40p olive	60	40
264	A48	60p violet	1.00	75
265	A49	80p dark red	1.50	1.25
266	A50	1af black	10.00	4.00
267	A51	2af ultramarine	3.75	2.50
268	A52	3af gray green	4.00	3.50
		Nos. 263-268 (6)	20.85	12.40

Issued to commemorate the formation of the National Council. Imperforate or perforated examples of Nos. 263-268 on ungummed chalky paper are proofs.

See also Nos. 304-305.

Mosque at Balkh A53 — Kabul Fortress A54

Parliament House, Darul Funun A55

Parliament House, Darul Funun A56 — Arch of Qalai Bist A57

Memorial Pillar of Knowledge and Ignorance A58

Independence Monument A59 — Minaret at Herat A60

Arch of Paghman A61

Ruins at Balkh A62

Minarets of Herat A63 — Great Buddha at Bamian A64

1932		Typographed		*Perf. 12*
269	A53	10p brown	18	15
270	A54	15p dark brown	30	15
271	A55	20p red	40	25
272	A56	25p dark green	40	20
273	A57	30p red	40	25
274	A58	40p orange	50	35
275	A59	50p blue	1.25	40
		a. Tête bêche pair	8.00	
276	A60	60p blue	85	50
277	A61	80p violet	1.75	1.50
278	A62	1af dark blue	2.50	70
279	A63	2af dark red violet	3.50	2.50
280	A64	3af claret	3.75	3.00
		Nos. 269-280 (12)	15.78	9.95

Counterfeits of types A53—A65 exist.

See also Nos. 290-295, 298-299, 302-303.

Entwined 2's A65

Two types:
Type I. Numerals shaded. Size about 21x29mm.
Type II. Numerals unshaded. Size about 21¾x30mm.

1931-38			*Perf. 12, 11x12*	
281	A65	2p red brown (I)	8	8
282	"	2p olive blk. (I) ('34)	8	8
283	"	2p greenish gray (I) ('34)	8	8
283A	"	2p black (II) ('36)	8	8
284	"	2p salmon (II) ('38)	8	8
284A	"	2p rose (I) ('38)	10	10
		b. Imperf., pair	75	
		Imperf.		
285	A65	2p black (II) ('37)	10	10
286	"	2p salmon (II) ('38)	10	10
		Nos. 281-286 (8)	70	70

The newspaper rate was 2 pouls.

Independence Monument A66

1932, Aug.			*Perf. 12*	
287	A66	1af deep rose	2.00	1.75

Issued to commemorate the 14th Independence Day.

1929 Liberation Monument, Kabul A67

1932, Oct.			Typographed	
288	A67	80p red brown	1.25	75

Arch of Paghman A68

1933, Aug.				
289	A68	50p lt. ultramarine	1.10	1.10

Issued to commemorate the 15th Independence Day.

Types of 1932 and

Royal Palace, Kabul A69 — Darrah-Shikari Pass, Hindu Kush A70

1934-38		Typographed		*Perf. 12*
290	A53	10p deep violet	15	12
291	A54	15p turquoise green	18	15
292	A55	20p magenta	25	15
293	A56	25p deep rose	30	25
294	A57	30p orange	35	30
295	A58	40p blue black	50	40
296	A69	45p dark blue	1.50	1.25
297	"	45p red ('38)	25	25
298	A59	50p orange	35	25
299	A60	60p purple	50	50
300	A70	75p red	2.25	1.75
301	"	75p dk. blue ('38)	75	60
302	A61	80p brown violet	1.10	75
303	A62	1af red violet	1.50	1.25
304	A51	2af gray black	3.25	2.75
305	A52	3af ultramarine	5.00	4.50
		Nos. 290-305 (16)	18.18	15.22

Independence Monument A71

1934, Aug.		Litho.	Without Gum	
306	A71	50p pale green	1.00	1.00
		a. Tête bêche pair	3.75	3.75

Issued to commemorate the 16th year of Independence. Each sheet of 40 (4x10) included 4 tête bêche pairs as lower half of sheet was inverted.

Independence Monument A74 — Fireworks Display A75

1935, Aug.		Laid Paper		
309	A74	50p dark blue	1.25	1.00

Issued in commemoration of the 17th year of Independence.

Wove Paper

1936, Aug.				*Perf. 12*
310	A75	50p red violet	1.25	1.00

Issued in commemoration of the 18th year of Independence.

Independence Monument and Nadir Shah—A76

311	A76	50p violet & bistre brown	1.25	75
		a. Imperf., pair	2.75	

Issued in commemoration of the 19th year of Independence.

Mohammed Nadir Shah A77 A78

1938				*Perf. 11x12*
315	A77	50p bright blue & sepia	75	75
		a. Imperf., pair	5.00	3.00

Issued in commemoration of the 20th year of Independence. Issued without gum.

1939				*Perf. 11*
317	A78	50p deep salmon	90	60

Issued in commemoration of the 21st year of Independence.

National Arms A79

Parliament House, Darul Funun A80

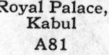

Royal Palace, Kabul A81 — Independence Monument A82

Independence Monument and Nadir Shah A83

Mohammed Zahir Shah
A84

Mohammed Zahir Shah
A85

Perf. 11, 11x12, 12x11, 12

1939-61 Typographed

No.	Type	Description	Unused	Used
318	A79	2p intense black	10	10
318A	"	2p bright pink ('61)	7	7
319	A80	10p bright purple	10	10
320	"	15p bright green	12	10
321	"	20p red lilac	15	10
322	A81	25p rose red	30	15
322A	"	25p green ('41)	12	8
323	"	30p orange	20	15
324	"	40p dark gray	20	15
325	A82	45p bright carmine	20	15
326	"	50p deep orange	30	20
327	"	60p violet	30	20
328	A83	75p ultramarine	2.00	60
328A	"	75p red violet ('41)	50	30
328C	"	75p bright red ('44)	1.35	1.35
328D	"	75p chestnut brown ('49)	1.65	1.65
329	"	80p chocolate	40	30
a.		80p dull red violet (error)		
330	A84	1af bright red violet	1.35	1.00
330A	A85	1af bright red violet ('44)	1.35	1.35
331	"	2af dp. rose car.	2.35	1.35
a.		2af copper red	1.60	50
332	A84	3af deep blue	3.25	1.65
		Nos. 318-332 (21)	16.36	11.10

On No. 332 the King faces slightly left.
No. 318A is without gum.
See Nos. 795A-795B.

Mohammed Nadir Shah
A86

1940, Aug. 23 *Perf. 11*

No.	Type	Description	Unused	Used
333	A86	50p gray green	85	60

Issued in commemoration of the 22nd year of Independence.

Independence Monument
A87

Arch of Paghman
A88

1941, Aug. 23 *Perf. 12*

No.	Type	Description	Unused	Used
334	A87	15p gray green	4.25	2.25
335	A88	50p red brown	75	60

Issued in commemoration of the 23rd year of Independence.

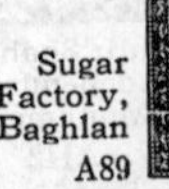

Sugar Factory, Baghlan
A89

1942, April *Perf. 12*

No.	Type	Description	Unused	Used
336	A89	1.25af ultramarine	2.00	1.75
a.		1.25af blue (shades)	1.50	50

In 1949, a 1.50af brown, type A89, was sold for 3af by the Philatelic Office, Kabul. It was not valid for postage. Price $3.50.

Independence Monument
A90

Mohammed Nadir Shah and Arch of Paghman
A91

1942, Aug. 23 *Perf. 12*

No.	Type	Description	Unused	Used
337	A90	35p bright green	3.50	3.00
338	A91	125p chalky blue	1.75	1.75

Issued in commemoration of the 24th year of Independence.

Independence Monument and Nadir Shah
A92

Mohammed Nadir Shah
A93

Perf. 11x12, 12x11

1943, Aug. 25 Typo. Unwmkd.

No.	Type	Description	Unused	Used
339	A92	35p carmine	12.00	9.00
340	A93	1.25af dark blue	2.10	1.75

Issued to commemorate the 24th year of Independence.

Tomb of Gohar Shad, Herat
A94

Ruins of Qalai Bist
A95

1944, May 1 *Perf. 12, 11x12*

No.	Type	Description	Unused	Used
341	A94	35p orange	60	40
342	A95	70p violet	1.20	75
a.		70p rose lilac	2.50	1.00

Arch of Paghman
A96

Independence Monument and Mohammed Nadir Shah
A97

1944, Aug. *Perf. 12*

No.	Type	Description	Unused	Used
343	A96	35p crimson	1.00	75
344	A97	1.25af ultramarine	1.75	1.50

Issued to commemorate the 26th year of Independence.

Independence Monument
A98

Mohammed Nadir Shah and Arch of Paghman
A99

1945, July

No.	Type	Description	Unused	Used
345	A98	35p deep red lilac	1.00	90
346	A99	1.25af blue	2.50	2.00

Issued to commemorate the 27th year of Independence.

Mohammed Zahir Shah
A100

Independence Monument
A101

Mohammed Nadir Shah
A102

1946, July

No.	Type	Description	Unused	Used
347	A100	15p emerald	60	45
348	A101	20p deep red lilac	90	70
349	A102	125p blue	2.25	2.25

Issued to commemorate the 28th year of Independence.

Zahir Shah and Ruins of Qalai Bist—A103

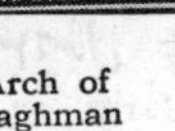
Arch of Paghman
A104

Nadir Shah and Independence Monument
A105

1947, Aug.

No.	Type	Description	Unused	Used
350	A103	15p yellow green	40	20
351	A104	35p plum	50	30
352	A105	125p deep blue	1.85	1.85

Issued to commemorate the 29th year of Independence.

Begging Child
A106

A107

Typographed.

1948, May *Perf. 12* Unwmkd.

No.	Type	Description	Unused	Used
353	A106	35p yellow green	2.25	1.75
354	A107	125p gray blue	2.75	2.25

Issued to commemorate Children's Day, May 29, 1948, and valid only on that day. Proceeds were used for Child Welfare.

Arch of Paghman
A108

Independence Monument
A109

Mohammed Nadir Shah
A110

1948, Aug.

No.	Type	Description	Unused	Used
355	A108	15p green	30	20
356	A109	20p magenta	50	25
357	A110	125p dark blue	1.10	90

Issued to commemorate the 30th year of Independence.

United Nations Emblem
A111

1948, Oct. 24

No.	Type	Description	Unused	Used
358	A111	125p dark violet blue	8.50	7.50

Issued to commemorate the third anniversary of the formation of the United Nations. Valid one day only. Sheets of 9.

Maiwand Victory Column, Kandahar
A112

Zahir Shah and Ruins of Qalai Bist
A113

Independence Monument and Nadir Shah
A114

1949, Aug. Typo. *Perf. 12*

359	A112	25p green	35	25
360	A113	35p magenta	50	35
361	A114	1.25af blue	1.25	1.00

Issued to commemorate the 31st year of Independence.

Nadir Shah
A117

1950, Aug.

364	A117	35p red brown	40	40
365	"	125p blue	1.00	75

Issued to commemorate the 32nd year of Independence.

Medical School and Nadir Shah
A119

1950, Dec. 22 Typo. *Perf. 12*

Size: 38x25mm.

367	A119	35p emerald	75	75

Size: 46x30mm.

368	A119	1.25af deep blue	2.50	2.00
	a.	1.25af black (error)	6.00	

Issued to commemorate the 19th anniversary of the founding of Afghanistan's Faculty of Medicine. On sale and valid for use on Dec. 22–23, 1950.

Minaret, Herat
A120

Zahir Shah
A121

Mosque of Khodja Abu Parsar, Balkh
A122

Zahir Shah
A123 A124

Designs: 20p, Buddha at Bamian. 40p, Ruined arch. 45p, Maiwand Victory Monument. 50p, View of Kandahar. 60p, Ancient tower. 70p, Afghanistan flag. 80p, 1af, Profile of Zahir Shah in uniform.

Photogravure, Engraved, Engraved and Lithographed.
Perf. 12, 12½, 13x12½, 13½.

1951, Mar. 21 Unwmkd.

Imprint:
"Waterlow & Sons Limited, London."

369	A120	10p yellow & brown	10	8
370	"	15p blue & brown	15	8
371	"	20p black	7.00	3.50
372	A121	25p green	18	10
373	A122	30p cerise	25	12
374	A121	35p violet	25	12
375	A122	40p chestnut brown	30	12
376	A120	45p deep blue	25	15
377	A122	50p olive black	60	18
378	A120	60p black	60	20
379	A122	70p dk. grn., blk., red & green	35	20
380	A123	75p cerise	80	25
381	"	80p car. & black	85	50
382	"	1af deep green & violet	60	50
383	A124	1.25af rose lilac & black	75	50
384	"	2af ultramarine	1.40	50
385	"	3af ultra. & blk.	3.25	1.25
		Nos. 369-385 (17)	17.68	8.35

Nos. 372, 374 and 381 to 385 are engraved, No. 379 is engraved and lithographed.

See also Nos. 445–451, 453, 552A–552D.

Arch of Paghman
A125

Nadir Shah and Independence Monument
A126

Overprint in Violet سال ۳۳ استقلال

Perf. 13½x13, 13

1951, Aug. 25 Engraved

386	A125	35p dark green & black	85	50
387	A126	1.25af deep blue	2.10	1.25

Overprint reads "Sol 33 Istiqlal" or "33rd Year of Independence." Overprint measures about 11 mm. wide.

See also Nos. 398–399B, 441–442.

Proposed Flag of Pashtunistan
A127

Design: 1.25af, Flag and Pashtunistan warrior.

1951, Sept. 2 Litho. *Perf. 11½*

388	A127	35p dull chocolate	1.25	1.00
389	"	125p blue	3.00	2.75

Issued to publicize "Free Pashtunistan" Day.

Imperforates

From 1951 to 1958, quantities of nearly all locally-printed stamps were left imperforate and sold by the government at double face. From 1959 until March, 1964, many of the imperforates were sold for more than face value.

Avicenna—A128

1951, Nov. 4 Typo. *Perf. 11½*

390	A128	35p deep claret	75	50
391	"	125p blue	2.10	1.65

Issued to commemorate the 20th anniversary of the founding of the national Graduate School of Medicine.

A129

Dove and U. N. Symbols
A130

1951, Oct. 24

392	A129	35p magenta	2.00	1.50
393	A130	125p blue	5.00	4.00

Issued to commemorate the 7th anniversary of the formation of the United Nations.

Amir Sher Ali Khan and Tiger Head Stamp
A131

Design: Nos. 395 and 397, Zahir Shah and stamp.

1951, Dec. 23 Lithographed

394	A131	35p chocolate	50	50
395	"	35p rose lilac	50	50
396	"	125p ultramarine	1.00	90
	a.	Cliché of 35p in plate of 125p	125.00	125.00
397	A131	125p aquamarine	1.00	90

Issued to commemorate the 76th anniversary of the formation of the Universal Postal Union.

Types of 1951
Without Overprint.
Perf. 13½x13, 13

1952, Aug. 24 Engraved

398	A125	35p dark green & black	2.50	2.50
399	A126	1.25af deep blue	2.50	2.50

Same Overprinted in Violet

۳۴ استقلال

399A	A125	35p dk. grn. & blk.	90	60
399B	A126	1.25af deep blue	2.50	1.50

Nos. 398–399B were issued to commemorate the 34th Independence Day.

Globe—A132

Lithographed

1952, Oct. 25 *Perf. 11½* Unwmkd.

400	A132	35p rose	80	70
401	"	125p aquamarine	1.75	1.50

Issued to honor the United Nations.

Symbol of Medicine
A134

Tribal Warrior and National Flag
A135

1952, Nov. *Perf. 11½*

403	A134	35p chocolate	60	50
404	"	125p violet blue	1.75	1.75

Issued to commemorate the 21st anniversary of the national Graduate School of Medicine.

No. 404 is inscribed in French with white letters on a colored background.

1952, Sept. 1 *Perf. 11*

405	A135	35p red	40	40
406	"	125p dark blue	85	85

No. 406 is inscribed in French "Pashtunistan Day, 1952."

Flags of Afghanistan and Pashtunistan
A139

Badge of Pashtunistan
A140

Perf. 10½x11, 11

1953, Sept. 1 Unwmkd.

411	A139	35p vermilion	30	25
412	A140	125p blue	85	65

Issued to publicize "Free Pashtunistan" Day.

Nadir Shah and Flag Bearer
A141

Nadir Shah and Independence Monument
A142

1953, Aug. 24 ***Perf. 11***

413 A141 35p green 25 20

414 A142 125p violet 1.00 75

Issued to commemorate the 35th anniversary of Independence.

United Nations Emblem
A143

1953, Oct. 24

415 A143 35p lilac 75 75

416 " 125p violet blue 1.85 1.50

Issued to publicize United Nations Day, 1953.

Nadir Shah
A144 A145

1953, Nov. 29

417 A144 35p orange 1.00 1.00

418 A145 125p chalky blue 2.25 2.25

Issued to commemorate the 22nd anniversary of the founding of the national Graduate School of Medicine.

Redrawn.

35p. Original - Right character in second line of Persian inscription: ٣

Redrawn - Persian character: ٢

125p. Original - Inscribed "XXIII," "MADECINE" and "ANNIVERAIRE"
Redrawn - Inscribed "XXII," "MEDECINE" and "ANNIVERSAIRE"

1953

419 A144 35p deep orange 5.00

420 A145 125p chalky blue 6.50

Nadir Shah and
Symbols of Independence
A146

1954, Aug. Typo. ***Perf. 11***

421 A146 35p carmine rose 50 40

422 " 125p violet blue 1.50 1.25

Issued to commemorate the 36th year of Independence.

Raising Flag of Pashtunistan
A147

1954, Sept. ***Perf. 11½***

423 A147 35p chocolate 50 40

424 " 125p blue 1.50 1.25

Issued to publicize "Free Pashtunistan" Day.

U.N. Flag and Map
A148

1954, Oct. 24 ***Perf. 11***

425 A148 35p carmine rose 1.00 1.00

426 " 125p dk. violet blue 3.00 3.00

Issued to commemorate the 9th anniversary of the United Nations.

U. N. Symbols
A149

Design: 125p, U. N. emblem & flags.

1955, June 26 Litho. ***Perf. 11***

Size: 26½x36mm.

427 A149 35p dark green 60 50

Size: 28½x36mm.

428 A149 125p aquamarine 1.50 1.25

Issued to commemorate the 10th anniversary of the signing of the United Nations charter.

Nadir Shah (center) and Brothers
A150

1929 Civil War Scene and Zahir Shah
A151

Tribal Elders' Council and Pashtun Flag
A152

1955, Aug. ***Perf. 11*** **Unwmkd.**

429 A150 35p bright pink 40 40

430 " 35p violet blue 40 40

431 A151 125p rose lilac 1.25 1.00

432 " 125p light violet 1.25 1.00

Issued to commemorate the 37th anniversary of Independence.

1955, Sept. 5

433 A152 35p orange brown 35 35

434 " 125p yellow green 1.25 1.00

Issued for "Free Pashtunistan" Day.

United Nations Flag
A153

Nadir Shah and Independence Monument
A154

1955, Oct. 24 ***Perf. 11*** **Unwmkd.**

435 A153 35p orange brown 90 75

436 " 125p brt. ultra. 1.85 1.50

Issued to commemorate the tenth anniversary of the United Nations, Oct. 24, 1955.

1956, Aug. **Lithographed**

437 A154 35p light green 35 30

438 " 140p lt. violet blue 1.35 1.10

Issued to commemorate the 38th year of Independence.

Jesh'n Exhibition Hall
A155

1956, Aug. 25

439 A155 50p chocolate 45 30

440 " 50p light violet blue 45 30

International Exposition at Kabul.
Of the 50p face value, only 35p paid postage. The remaining 15p went to the Exposition.

Nos. 398-399 Handstamped in Violet

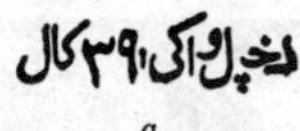

a

39 em Anv

b

Perf. 13½x13, 13

1957, Aug. **Engraved**

441 A125 (*a*) 35p dk. green & black 60 30

442 A126 (*b*) 1.25af deep blue 90 75

Arabic overprint on No. 441 measures 19mm. No. 442 overprinted: "39 em Anv". Issued to commemorate the 39th year of independence.

Pashtunistan Flag
A156

1957, Sept. 1 Litho. ***Perf. 11***

443 A156 50p pale lilac rose 75 50

444 " 155p light violet 1.25 1.00

Issued for "Free Pashtunistan" Day. French inscription on No. 444.

Types of 1951 and

Game of Buzkashi—A157

Photogravure, Engraved, Engraved and Lithographed.

Perf. 12, 12½, 12½x13, 13, 13x12, 13x12½, 13½x14

1957, Nov. 23 **Unwmkd.**

Imprint: "Waterlow & Sons Limited, London."

445 A122 30p brown 15 6

446 " 40p rose red 22 6

447 " 50p yellow 32 8

448 A120 60p ultramarine 38 10

449 A123 75p bright violet 45 10

450 " 80p violet & brn. 50 10

451 " 1af car. & ultra. 75 20

452 A157 140p olive & deep claret 1.50 75

453 A124 3af org. & blk. 1.85 75

Nos. 445-453 (9) 6.12 2.20

No. 452 lacks imprint.

Nadir Shah and Flag-bearer
A158

1958, Aug. 25 ***Perf. 13½x14***

454 A158 35p dp. yel. green 25 20

455 " 140p brown 60 50

Issued to commemorate the 40th year of Independence.

Exposition Buildings
A159

1958, Aug. 23 **Litho.** ***Perf. 11***

456 A159 35p bright blue green 25 20

457 " 140p vermilion 70 60

Issued for the International Exposition at Kabul.

Pres. Celal Bayar of Turkey
A160

Flags of U.N. and Afghanistan
A161

1958, Sept. 13 **Unwmkd.**

458 A160 50p light blue 30 20

459 " 100p brown 50 40

Issued to commemorate the visit of President Celal Bayar of Turkey.

Perf. 14x13½

1958, Oct. 24 **Photogravure**

Flags in Original Colors.

460 A161 50p dark gray 75 75

461 " 100p green 1.50 1.25

Issued for United Nations Day, Oct. 24.

Atomic Energy Encircling the Hemispheres—A162

1958, Oct. 20 ***Perf. 13½x14***

462 A162 50p blue 50 50

463 " 100p deep red lilac 85 85

Issued to promote Atoms for Peace.

UNESCO Building, Paris
A163

1958, Nov. 3

464 A163 50p dp. yel. green 75 60

465 " 100p brown olive 1.10 90

Issued to commemorate the opening of UNESCO (U.N. Educational, Scientific and Cultural Organization) Headquarters in Paris, Nov. 3.

Globe and Torch
A164

Perf. 13½x14

1958, Dec. 10 **Unwmkd.**

466 A164 50p lilac rose 50 50
467 " 100p maroon 1.00 1.00

Issued to commemorate the tenth anniversary of the signing of the Universal Declaration of Human Rights.

Nadir Shah and Flags
A165

1959, Aug. Litho. *Perf. 11 Rough*

468 A165 35p light vermilion 30 30
469 " 165p light violet 1.00 60

Issued to commemorate the 41st year of Independence.

Uprooted Oak Emblem
A166

1960, Apr. 7 *Perf. 11*

470 A166 50p deep orange 20 15
471 " 165p blue 50 40

Issued to publicize World Refugee Year, July 1, 1959–June 30, 1960.

Two imperf. souvenir sheets exist. Both contain a 50p and a 165p, type A166, with marginal inscriptions and WRY emblem in maroon. On one sheet the stamps are in the colors of Nos. 470–471 (size 108x81 mm.). On the other, the 50p is blue and the 165p is deep orange (size 107x80 mm.). Price $6 each.

Buzkashi—A167

1960, May 4 *Perf. 11, Imperf.*

472 A167 25p rose red 35 20
473 " 50p bluish green 75 50
a. Cliché of 25p in plate of 50p 20.00 20.00

See also Nos. 549–550A.

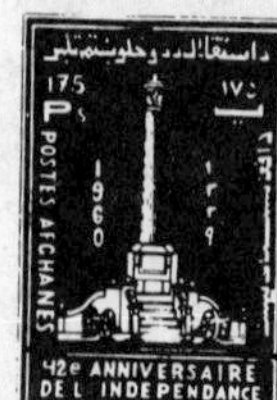

Independence Monument
A168

1960, Aug.

474 A168 50p light blue 15 15
475 " 175p bright pink 50 50

Issued to commemorate the 42nd Independence Day.

Globe and Flags
A169

1960, Oct. 24 Litho. *Perf. 11*

476 A169 50p rose lilac 30 25
477 " 175p ultramarine 1.00 85

Issued to commemorate United Nations Day.

An imperf. souvenir sheet contains one each of Nos. 476–477 with marginal inscriptions ("La Journée des Nations Unies 1960" in French and Persian) and UN emblem in light blue. Size: 127x85½mm. Price $5.

This sheet was surcharged "+20ps" in 1962. Price $8.50.

Teacher Pointing to Globe
A170

1960, Oct. 23 *Perf. 11*

478 A170 50p bright pink 25 18
479 " 100p bright green 90 60

Issued to publicize Teacher's Day.

Mohammed Zahir Shah
A171

1960, Oct. 15

480 A171 50p red brown 40 20
481 " 150p dk. car. rose 1.25 40

Issued to honor the King on his 46th birthday.

Buzkashi
A172

1960, Nov. 9 *Perf. 11*

482 A172 175p light red brown 1.50 60

See also Nos. 551–552.

No. 482 Overprinted "1960" and Olympic Rings in Bright Green.

1960, Dec. 24

483 A172 175p red brown 3.25 3.00
a. Souvenir sheet 12.00

Issued to commemorate the 17th Olympic Games, Rome, Aug. 25–Sept. 11.

No. 483a contains one of No. 483, imperf. Bright green marginal inscription. Size: 86x61mm.

Mir Wais
A173

1961, Jan. 5 *Perf. 10½* **Unwmkd.**

484 A173 50p bright rose lilac 30 20
485 " 175p ultramarine 75 50
a. Souv. sheet of 2 2.25 2.25

Issued to honor Mir Wais (1665–1708), national leader.

No. 485a contains one each of Nos. 484–485, imperf. Emerald marginal inscription. Size: 108x78mm.

No Postal Need

existed for the 1p to 15p denominations released with commemorative or semipostal sets of 1961–63 (between Nos. 486 and 649, B37 and B65). The lowest denomination actually used for non-philatelic postage in that period was 25p (except for the 2p newspaper rate for which separate stamps were provided).

Horse, Sheep and Camel
A174

Designs: No. 487, 175p, Rock partridge. 10p, 100p, Afghan hound. 15p, 150p, Grain and grasshopper (vert.).

1961, Mar. 29 Photo. *Perf. 13½x14*

486 A174 2p maroon & buff
487 " 2p ultra. & orange
488 " 5p brown & yel.
489 " 10p blk. & salmon
490 " 15p blue green & yellow
491 " 25p black & pink
492 " 50p black & citron
493 " 100p black & pink
494 " 150p green & yellow
495 " 175p ultra. & pink
Nos. 486–495 (10) 3.00

Two souvenir sheets, perf. and imperf., contain two stamps, one each of Nos. 492–493. Black marginal inscriptions, "Journee d'Agriculture 1961" in Persian and French. Size: 111x64mm. Price $2 each.

Afghan Fencing
A175

Designs: No. 497, 5p, 25p, 50p, Wrestlers. 10p, 100p, Man with Indian clubs. 15p, 150p, Afghan fencing. 175p, Children skating.

1961, July 6 *Perf. 13½x14*

496 A175 2p green & rose lilac
497 " 2p brn. & citron
498 " 5p gray & rose
499 " 10p blue & bistre
500 " 15p slate blue & dull lilac
501 " 25p black & dull blue
502 " 50p slate green & bistre brn.
503 A175 100p brown & blue green
504 " 150p brown & orange yel.
505 " 175p black & blue
Nos. 496–505 (10) 1.75

Issued for Children's Day.

A souvenir sheet exists containing one each of Nos. 502–503, with slate green marginal inscription and black control number. Size: 111x65mm. Price $3.50.

Bandé Amir Lakes
A176

1961, Aug. 7 Photo. *Perf. 13½x14*

506 A176 3af bright blue 50 40
507 " 10af rose claret 1.75 1.50

Nadir Shah
A177

Girl Scout
A178

1961, Aug. 23 *Perf. 14x13½*

508 A177 50p rose red & black 50 40
509 " 175p br. green & org. brn. 1.00 80

Issued to commemorate the 43rd Independence Day.

Two souvenir sheets, perf. and imperf., contain one each of Nos. 508–509. Black marginal inscription and control number, flag in black, red & green. Size: 104x74mm. Price, each $2.50.

Perf. 14x13½

1961, July 23 **Unwmkd.**

510 A178 50p deep carmine & dk. gray 40 20
511 " 175p deep green & rose brown 90 60

Issued for Women's Day.

Two souvenir sheets exist, perf. and imperf., containing one each of Nos. 510–511. Black marginal inscription. Size: 105x75mm. Price $4 each.

Exhibition Hall, Kabul
A179

1961, Aug. 23 *Perf. 13½x14*

512 A179 50p yellow brown & yel. grn. 25 20
513 " 175p blue & brown 60 40

International Exhibition at Kabul.

Pathan with Pashtunistan Flag
A180

Photogravure

1961, Aug. 31 *Perf. 14x13½*

514 A180 50p black, lilac & red 20 18
515 " 175p brown, greenish blue & red 50 40

Issued for "Free Pashtunistan Day."
Souvenir sheets exist perf. and imperf. containing one each of Nos. 514–515 with black marginal inscription and flag in red and black. Size: 104x75mm. Price $2 each.

Assembly Building—A181

1961, Sept. 10 *Perf. 12*

516 A181 50p dark gray & br. green 25 18
517 " 175p ultra. & brn. 65 45

Issued to commemorate the anniversary of the founding of the National Assembly.
Souvenir sheets exist, perf. and imperf., containing one each of Nos. 516–517 with black marginal inscription and flower in ultramarine and green. Size: 106x70mm. Price $1 each.

Exterminating Anopheles Mosquito
A182

1961, Oct. 5 *Perf. 13½x14*

518 A182 50p black & br. lilac 70 40
519 " 175p maroon & br. green 1.50 75

Issued to publicize the Anti-Malaria campaign. Souvenir sheets exist, perf. and imperf., containing one each of Nos. 518–519 with black marginal inscription and mosquito. Size: 110x65mm. Price $5 each.

Zahir Shah
A183

1961, Oct. 15 *Perf. 13½*

520 A183 50p lilac & blue 25 20
521 " 175p emerald & red brown 60 50

Issued to honor King Mohammed Zahir Shah on his 47th birthday.
See also Nos. 609–612.

Pomegranates—A184

Fruit: No. 523, 5p, 25p, 50p, Grapes. 10p, 150p, Apples. 15p, 175p, Pomegranates. 100p, Melons.

1961, Oct. 16 *Perf. 13½x14*

Fruit in Natural Colors.

522 A184 2p black
523 " 2p green
524 " 5p lilac rose
525 " 10p lilac
526 " 15p dark blue
527 " 25p dull red
528 " 50p purple
529 " 100p bright blue
530 " 150p brown
531 " 175p olive gray
Nos. 522-531 (10) 2.00

For Afghan Red Crescent Society.
Souvenir sheets exist, perf. and imperf., containing one each of Nos. 528–529 with black marginal inscription and red crescent. Size: 110x65mm. Price $1.75 each.

U.N. Headquarters, N.Y.—A185

1961, Oct. 24 *Perf. 13½x14*

Vertical Borders in Emerald, Red and Black.

532 A185 1p rose lilac
533 " 2p slate
534 " 3p brown
535 " 4p ultramarine
536 " 50p rose red
537 " 75p gray
538 " 175p bright green
Nos. 532-538 (7) 1.25

Issued to commemorate the 16th anniversary of the United Nations. Souvenir sheets exist, perf. and imperf., containing one each of Nos. 536–538. Black marginal inscription with U.N. emblem and control number. Size: 114x95mm. Price $2.25 each.

Children Giving Flowers to Teacher
A186

People Raising UNESCO Symbol
A187

Designs: No. 540, 5p, 25p, 50p, Tulips. 10p, 100p, Narcissus. 15p, 150p, Children giving flowers to teacher. 175p, Teacher with children in front of school.

1961, Oct. 26 Photo. *Perf. 12*

539 A186 2p multicolored
540 " 2p "
541 " 5p "
542 " 10p "
543 " 15p "
544 " 25p "
545 " 50p "
546 " 100p "
547 " 150p "
548 " 175p "
Nos. 539-548 (10) 2.00

Issued for Teacher's Day.
Souvenir sheets exist, perf. and imperf. containing one each of Nos. 545–546. Gray marginal inscription and black control number. Size: 104x78mm. Price, 2 sheets, $3.

Buzkashi Types of 1960.

1961–72 Lithographed *Perf. 10½*

549 A167 25p violet 10 5
b. 25p bright violet, typo. ('72) 5 5
549A A167 25p citron ('63) 15 5
550 " 50p blue 30 5
550A " 50p yel. orange ('69) 10 5
b. 50p orange yellow, typo. ('73) 10 5
551 A172 100p citron 40 10
551A A172 150p orange ('64) 30 15
552 " 2af light green 1.00 60
Nos. 549-552 (7) 2.35 1.05

Zahir Shah Types of 1951
Imprint: "Thomas De La Rue & Co. Ltd."

Photo., Engr., Engr. & Litho.

1962 *Perf. 13x12, 13*

552A A123 75p bright purple 1.00 25
552B " 1af car. & ultra. 1.25 30
552C A124 2af blue 1.50 60
552D " 3af orange & blk. 3.50 1.00

1962, July 2 Photo. *Perf. 14x13½*

553 A187 2p rose lilac & brn.
554 " 2p olive bis. & brn.
555 " 5p deep orange & dark green
556 " 10p gray & magenta
557 " 15p blue & brown
558 " 25p org. yel. & pur.
559 " 50p lt. grn. & purple
560 " 75p br. citron & brn.
561 " 100p dp. orge. & brn.
Nos. 553-561 (9) 1.40

Issued to commemorate the 15th anniversary of UNESCO (U.N. Educational, Scientific and Cultural Organization). Souvenir sheets exist, perf. and imperf. One contains Nos. 558–559 with purple marginal inscription; the other contains one each of Nos. 560–561 with brown marginal inscription and black control numbers. Size: 99x80mm. Price, $4 each.

Ahmad Shah
A188

Afghan Hound
A189

1962, Feb. 24 Photo. *Perf. 13½*

562 A188 50p red brown & gray 15 10
563 " 75p green & salmon 25 20
564 " 100p claret & bister 40 30

Issued to honor Ahmad Shah (1724–1773), who founded the Afghan kingdom in 1747 and ruled until 1773.

1962, Apr. 21 *Perf. 14x13½*

Designs: 5p, 75p, Afghan cock. 10p, 100p, Kondjid plant. 15p, 125p, Astrakhan skins.

565 A189 2p rose & brown
566 " 2p lt. grn. & brn.
567 " 5p dp. rose & claret
568 " 10p light green & slate green
569 " 15p blue grn. & blk.
570 " 25p blue & brown
571 " 50p gray & brown
572 " 75p rose lilac & lilac
573 " 100p gray & dull grn.
574 " 125p rose brn. & blk.
Nos. 565-574 (10) 2.00

Issued for Agriculture Day. Perf. and imperf. souvenir sheets exist. Set of 4 sheets, price $4.

Athletes with Flag and Nadir Shah
A190

Woman in National Costume
A191

1962, Aug. 23 *Perf. 12*

575 A190 25p multicolored 12 4
576 " 50p " 18 6
577 " 150p " 25 8

44th Independence Day.

1962, Aug. 30 *Perf. 11½x12*

578 A191 25p lilac & brown 12 6
579 " 50p green & brown 25 15

Issued for Women's Day. For souvenir sheet see note after No. C16.

Man and Woman with Flag
A192

Malaria Eradication Emblem and Swamp
A193

1962, Aug. 31 Photogravure

580 A192 25p black, pale blue & red 12 6
581 " 50p black, green & red 25 12
582 " 150p black, pink & red 60 20

Issued for "Free Pashtunistan Day."

1962, Sept. 5 *Perf. 14x13½*

583 A193 2p dark green & olive gray
584 " 2p dark green & salmon
585 " 5p red brn. & olive
586 " 10p red brown & bright green
587 " 15p red brown & gray
588 " 25p bright blue & bluish green
589 " 50p bright blue & rose lilac
590 " 75p black & blue
591 " 100p black & brt. pink
592 " 150p black & bister brown
593 " 175p black & orange
Nos. 583-593 (11) 2.25

Issued for the World Health Organization drive to eradicate malaria. Perf. and imperf. souvenir sheets exist. Set of 4 sheets, price $6.50.

National Assembly Building
A194

Lithographed

1962, Sept. 10 *Perf. 10½* **Unwmkd.**

594 A194 25p light green 8 6
595 " 50p blue 12 8
596 " 75p rose 15 12
597 " 100p violet 25 20
598 " 125p ultramarine 28 25
Nos. 594-598 (5) 88 71

Establishment of the National Assembly.

Stamps not listed in this Catalogue or mentioned in "For the Record" (unless recent issues) usually are revenues, locals or labels.

Horse Racing
A195

Designs: 3p, Wrestling. 4p, Weight lifting. 5p, Soccer.

1962, Sept. 22 Photo. *Perf. 12*

Black Inscriptions

599 A195 1p light olive & red brown
600 " 2p lt. grn. & red brn.
601 " 3p yellow & dk. pur.
602 " 4p pale blue & grn.
603 " 5p bluish green & dark brown
Nos. 599-603, C17-C22 (11) 2.50

Issued to commemorate the 4th Asian Games, Djakarta, Indonesia. Two souvenir sheets exist. A perforated one contains a 125p blue, dark blue and brown stamp in horse racing design. An imperf. one contains a 2af buff, purple and black stamp in soccer design. Both sheets have black control number. Size: 64x90mm. Price, $4.50 each.

Runners
A196

Designs: 1p, 2p, Diver (vert.). 4p, Peaches. 5p, Iris (vert.).

Perf. 11½x12, 12x11½

1962, Oct. 2 Unwmkd.

604 A196 1p rose lilac & brn.
605 " 2p blue & brown
606 " 3p brt. bl. & lilac
607 " 4p olive gray & multicolored
608 " 5p gray & multi.
Nos. 604-608, C23-C25 (8) 2.00

Issued for Children's Day.

King Type of 1961, Dated "1962"

Various Frames

1962, Oct. 15 *Perf. 13½*

609 A183 25p lilac rose & brn. 8 8
610 " 50p orge. brn. & grn. 15 15
611 " 75p blue & lake 22 22
612 " 100p green & red brn. 30 30

Issued to honor King Mohammed Zahir Shah on his 48th birthday.

Grapes
A197

Designs: 3p, Pears. 4p, Wistaria. 5p, Blossoms.

1962, Oct. 16 *Perf. 12*

Fruit and Flowers in Natural Colors; Carmine Crescent

613 A197 1p deep rose
614 " 2p blue
615 " 3p lilac
616 " 4p gray brown
617 " 5p gray
Nos. 613-617, C26-C28 (8) 1.20

For the Afghan Red Crescent Society.

U.N. Headquarters, N.Y. and Flags of U.N. and Afghanistan
A198

1962, Oct. 24 Unwmkd.

Flags in Original Colors, Black Inscriptions

618 A198 1p olive bister
619 " 2p lilac rose
620 " 3p dull violet
621 " 4p green
622 " 5p reddish brown
Nos. 618-622, C29-C31 (8) 1.50

Issued for United Nations Day. Souvenir sheets exist. One contains a single 4af ultramarine stamp, perforated; the other, a 4af ocher stamp, imperf. Both sheets have a black marginal inscription and control number. Size: 89x65mm. Price, 2 sheets, $6.50.

Boy Scout A199 — Pole Vault A200

1962, Oct. 18 Photo. *Perf. 12*

623 A199 1p yel., dk. green & salmon
624 " 2p dull yel., slate & salmon
625 " 3p rose, black & salmon
626 " 4p multicolored
Nos. 623-626, C32-C35 (8) 1.75

Issued to honor the Boy Scouts.

1962, Oct. 25 *Perf. 12* Unwmkd.

Designs: 3p, High jump. 4p, 5p, Different blossoms.

627 A200 1p lilac & dk. grn.
628 " 2p yel. grn. & brn.
629 " 3p bister & violet
630 " 4p salmon pink, grn. & ultra.
631 " 5p yel., green & blue
Nos. 627-631, C36-C37 (7) 1.40

Issued for Teacher's Day.

Rockets—A201

1962, Nov. 29

632 A201 50p pale lilac & dk. bl. 60
633 " 100p lt. bl. & red brn. 1.25

Issued to commemorate the United Nations World Meteorological Day. A souvenir sheet contains one 5af pink and green stamp, green marginal inscription and black control number. Size: 89x65mm. Price $8.

Ansari Mausoleum, Herat
A202

Photogravure

1963, Jan. 3 *Perf. 13½* Unwmkd.

634 A202 50p purple & green 12 12
635 " 75p gray & magenta 18 18
636 " 100p org. brn. & brn. 30 30

Issued to honor Khwaja Abdullah Ansari, Sufi, religious leader and poet, on the 900th anniversary of his death.

Sheep—A203

Silkworm, Cocoons, Moth and Mulberry Branch
A204

1963, March 1 *Perf. 12*

637 A203 1p greenish bl. & blk.
638 " 2p yel. grn. & black
639 " 3p lilac rose & black
640 A204 4p gray, grn. & brn.
641 " 5p red lilac, green & brown
Nos. 637-641, C42-C44 (8) 1.75

Issued for the Day of Agriculture.

Rice—A205

Designs: 3p, Corn. 300p, Wheat emblem.

1963, March 27 *Perf. 14* Unwmkd.

642 A205 2p gray, claret & grn. 8 8
643 " 3p grn., yel. & ocher 12 12
644 " 300p dark blue & yel. 45 45

Issued for the "Freedom from Hunger" campaign of the U.N. Food and Agriculture Organization.

Meteorological Measuring Instrument
A206

Designs: 3p, 10p, Weather station. 4p, 5p, Rockets in space.

1963, May 23 Photo. *Perf. 13½x1*

645 A206 1p deep magenta & brown
646 " 2p brt. bl. & brn.
647 " 3p red & brown
648 " 4p orange & lilac
649 " 5p grn. & dull vio.

Imperf.

650 A206 10p red brn. & grn.
Nos. 645-650, C46-C50 (11) 9.50

Issued to commemorate the United N tions Third World Meteorological Da Mar. 23.

Independence Monument
A207

1963, Aug. 23 Litho. *Perf. 10½*

651 A207 25p light green 10
652 " 50p orange 20
653 " 150p rose carmine 50

Issued to commemorate the 45th Inde pendence Day.

Pathans in Forest
A208

1963, Aug. 31 *Perf. 10½* Unwmk

654 A208 25p pale violet 10
655 " 50p sky blue 20
656 " 150p dull red brown 60

Issued for "Free Pashtunistan Day."

Certain unlisted stamps of 1963-64 a mentioned and briefly described in "Fo the Record" at the back of this volume.

National Assembly Building
A209

1963, Sept. 10 Litho

657 A209 25p gray 6
658 " 50p dull red 12
659 " 75p brown 20
660 " 100p olive 30
661 " 125p lilac 40
Nos. 657-661 (5) 1.08

Issued to honor the National Assembly.

Balkh Gate
A210

1963, Oct. 8

662 A210 3af chocolate (screened margins) 60 40
a. White margins 1.50 50

In the original printing (No. 662), a halftone screen extended across the plate, covering the space between the stamps. A retouch removed the screen between the stamps (No. 662a).

Zahir Shah A211 — Kemal Ataturk A212

963, Oct. 15 *Perf. 10½*

63 A211 25p green 10 4
64 " 50p gray 20 8
65 " 75p carmine rose 30 15
66 " 100p dull reddish brn. 40 18

Issued to honor King Mohammed Zahir hah on his 49th birthday.

963, Oct. 10 *Perf. 10½*

67 A212 1af blue 15 12
68 " 3af rose lilac 60 50

Issued to commemorate the 25th anniversary of the death of Kemal Ataturk, president of Turkey.

"Tiger's Head" of 1878—A214

964, March 22 Photo. *Perf. 12*

75 A214 1.25af gold, green & black 20 10
76 " 5af gold, rose car. & black 50 35

Issued to honor philately.

Unisphere and Flags—A215

1964, May 3 *Perf. 13½x14*

677 A215 6af crimson, gray & green 40 30

New York World's Fair, 1964–65.

Hand Holding Torch
A216

Photogravure

1964, May 12 *Perf. 14x13½*

678 A216 3.75af brt. bl., orge., yel., bl. & blk. 25 25

Issued to commemorate the first United Nations Seminar on Human Rights in Kabul, May 1964. The denomination in Persian at right erroneously reads "3.25" but the stamp was sold and used as 3.75af.

Kandahar Airport
A217

1964 Lithographed *Perf. 10½*

679 A217 7.75af dark red brn. 60 30
680 " 9.25af light blue 75 35
681 " 10.50af light green 75 40
682 " 13.75af carmine rose 90 50

Inauguration of Kandahar Airport.

Snow Leopard
A218

Designs: 50p, Ibex (vert.). 75p, Head of argali. 5af, Yak.

1964, June 25 Photogravure *Perf. 12*

683 A218 25p yellow & blue 8 8
684 " 50p dull red & green 8 8
685 " 75p Prus. bl. & lilac 8 8
686 " 5af bright green & dark brown 30 30

View of Herat
A219

Flag and Map of Afghanistan
A220

Design: 75p, Tomb of Queen Gowhar Shad (vert.).

Perf. 13½x14, 14x13½

1964, July 12

687 A219 25p sepia & blue 5 5
688 " 75p deep blue & buff 5 5
689 A220 3af red, black & grn. 30 10

Issued for tourist publicity.

Wrestling
A221

Designs: 25p, Hurdling (vert.). 1af, Diving (vert.). 5af, Soccer.

1964, July 26 *Perf. 12*

690 A221 25p olive bister, black & car. 5 5
691 " 1af blue green, black & car. 8 8
692 " 3.75af yellow green, black & car. 35 35
693 A221 5af brown, black & carmine 45 45
a. Souv. sheet of 4 1.10 1.10

Issued to commemorate the 18th Olympic Games, Tokyo, Oct. 10–25, 1964. No. 693a contains 4 imperf. stamps similar to Nos. 690–693, black inscription. Size: 95x95mm. Sold for 15af. The additional 5af went to the Afghanistan Olympic Committee.

Flag and Outline of Nadir Shah's Tomb
A222

1964, Aug. 24 Photogravure

695 A222 25p gold, blue, black, red & green 7 7
696 " 75p gold, blue, black, red & green 10 10

Issued to commemorate Independence Day. The stamps were printed with an erroneous inscription in upper left corner: "33rd year of independence." This was locally obliterated with a typographed gold bar.

Pashtunistan Flag A223 — Zahir Shah A225

1964, Sept. 1 Unwmkd.

697 A223 100p gold, blk., red, blue & green 7 7

Issued for "Free Pashtunistan Day."

1964, Oct. 17 *Perf. 14x13½*

699 A225 1.25af gold & yellow green 10 5
700 " 3.75af gold & rose 20 15
701 " 50af gold & gray 3.00 2.50

Issued to honor King Mohammed Zahir Shah on his 50th birthday.

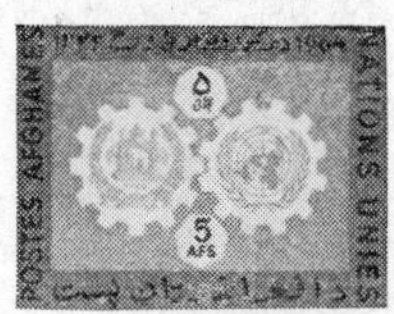

Coat of Arms of Afghanistan and U.N. Emblem
A226

1964, Oct. 24 *Perf. 13½x14*

702 A226 5af gold, black & dull blue 30 20

Issued for United Nations Day.

Emblem of Afghanistan Women's Association
A227

1964, Nov. 9 Photo. Unwmkd.

703 A227 25p pink, dk. blue & emerald 5 3
704 " 75p aquamarine, dk. blue & emerald 5 4
705 A227 1af silver, dark blue & emerald 10 5

Issued for Women's Day.

Abdul Rahman Jami
A228

Lithographed

1964, Nov. 23 *Perf. 11 Rough*

706 A228 1.50af blk., emerald & yellow 1.25

Issued to commemorate the 550th anniversary of the birth of the poet Mowlana Nooruddin Abdul Rahman Jami (1414–1492).

Woodpecker
A229

Birds: 3.75af, Black-throated jay (vert.). 5af, Impeyan pheasant (vert.).

Perf. 13½x14, 14x13½

1965, Apr. 20 Photo. Unwmkd.

707 A229 1.25af multicolored 12 6
708 " 3.75af " 30 20
709 " 5af " 40 20

ITU Emblem, Old and New Communication Equipment
A230

1965, May 17 *Perf. 13½x14*

710 A230 5af lt. blue, black & red 35 35

Issued to commemorate the centenary of the International Telecommunication Union.

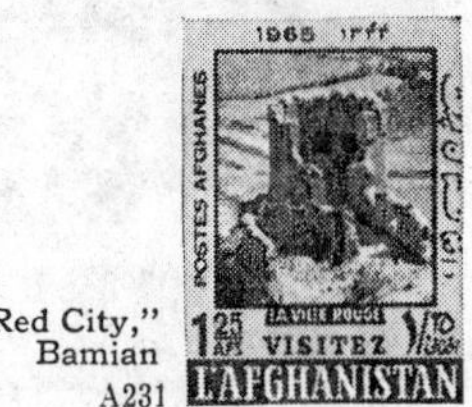

"Red City," Bamian
A231

Designs: 3.75af, Ruins of ancient Bamian city. 5af, Bandé Amir, mountain lakes.

1965, May 30 *Perf. 13x13½*

711 A231 1.25af pink & multi. 10 10
712 " 3.75af light blue & multi. 25 25
713 " 5af yel. & multi. 40 40

Issued for tourist publicity.

ICY Emblem
A232

1965, June 25 *Perf. 13½x13*

714 A232 5af grn., yel., blk. red & vio. blue 25 25

International Cooperation Year, 1965.

ARIANA Air Lines Emblem and DC-3
A233

Designs: 5af, DC-6 at right. 10af, DC-3 on top.

Perf. 13½x14

1965, July 15 Photo. **Unwmkd.**

715 A233 1.25af brt. bl., gray, & black 10 10
716 " 5af red lilac, black & bl. 30 30
717 " 10af bister, blk., bl. gray & grn. 75 75
a. Souv. sheet of 3 1.25 1.25

Issued to commemorate the 10th anniversary of Afghan Air Lines, ARIANA. No. 717a contains 3 imperf. stamps similar to Nos. 715–717; blue marginal inscription, black control number. Size: 90x90mm.

Nadir Shah
A234

1965, Aug. 23 *Perf. 14x13½*

718 A234 1af dull green, black & red brown 12 12

For the 47th Independence Day.

Flag of Pashtunistan
A235

Perf. 13½x14

1965, Aug. 31 Photo. **Unwmkd.**

719 A235 1af ultra., blk., gold, carm. & grn. 10 10

Issued for "Free Pashtunistan Day."

Zahir Shah Signing Constitution
A236

1965, Sept. 11 *Perf. 13x13½*

720 A236 1.50af bright green & black 25 25

Promulgation of the new Constitution.

Zahir Shah and Oak Leaves
A237

1965, Oct. 14 *Perf. 14x13½*

721 A237 1.25af black, ultra. & salmon 20 15
722 " 6af black, lt. blue & rose lilac 60 50

Issued to honor King Mohammed Zahir Shah on his 51st birthday.

Flags of UN and Afghanistan
A238

1965, Oct. 24 *Perf. 13½x14*

723 A238 5af multicolored 30 30

Issued for United Nations Day.

Dappled Ground Gecko
A239

Designs: 4af, Caucasian agamid (lizard). 8af, Horsfield's tortoise.

Perf. 13½x14

1966, May 10 Photo. **Unwmkd.**

724 A239 3af tan & multi. 30 30
725 " 4af brt. grn. & multi. 30 30
726 " 8af violet & multi. 50 50

Soccer Player and Globe
A240

1966, July 31 Litho. *Perf. 14x13½*

727 A240 2af rose red & black 30 25
728 " 6af violet bl. & blk. 60 35
729 " 12af bis. brn. & blk. 1.20 75

Issued to commemorate the World Cup Soccer Championship, Wembley, England, July 11–30.

Cotton Flower and Boll
A241

Designs: 5af, Silkworm. 7af, Farmer plowing with oxen.

1966, July 31 *Perf. 13½x14*

730 A241 1af multicolored 15 10
731 " 5af " 40 30
732 " 7af " 60 40

Issued for the Day of Agriculture.

Independence Monument
A242

1966, Aug. 23 Photo. *Perf. 13½x14*

733 A242 1af multicolored 10 10
734 " 3af " 35 25

Issued to commemorate Independence Day.

Flag of Pashtunistan
A243

1966, Aug. 31 Litho. *Perf. 11 rough*

735 A243 1af bright blue 25 10

Issued for "Free Pashtunistan Day."

Bagh-i-Bala Park Casino
A244

Designs: 2af, Map of Afghanistan. 8af, Tomb of Abd-er-Rahman. The casino on 4af is the former summer palace of Abd-er-Rahman near Kabul.

1966, Oct. 3 Photo. *Perf. 13½x14*

736 A244 2af red & multi. 18 15
737 " 4af multicolored 40 30
738 " 8af " 65 60
a. Souvenir sheet of 3 1.50 1.50

Issued for tourist publicity. No. 738a contains 3 imperf. stamps similar to Nos. 736–738: light yellow margin with black inscription and control number. Size: 110x 80mm.

Zahir Shah
A245

UNESCO Emblem
A246

1966, Oct. 14 *Perf. 14x13½*

739 A245 1af dk. slate green 20 10
740 " 5af red brown 50 25

Issued to honor King Mohammed Zahir Shah on his 52nd birthday. See Nos. 760–761.

1967 Litho. *Perf. 12*

741 A246 2af multicolored 30 20
742 " 6af " 50 20
743 " 12af " 1.00 40

Issued to commemorate the 20th anniversary of UNESCO (United Nations Educational, Scientific and Cultural Organization).

Zahir Shah and U.N. Emblem
A247

1967 Photogravure

744 A247 5af multicolored 50 20
745 " 10af " 1.00 40

Issued to commemorate the 20th anniversary of the U.N. International Organization for Refugees.

New Power Station
A248

Designs: 5af, Carpet (vert.). 8af, Cement factory.

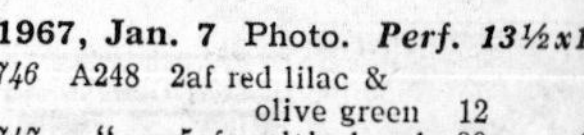

1967, Jan. 7 Photo. *Perf. 13½x1*

746 A248 2af red lilac & olive green 12
747 " 5af multicolored 30 2
748 " 8af black, dark blue & tan 50 3

Issued to publicize industrial develo ment.

International Tourist Year Emblem
A249

Designs: 6af, International Tourist Yea emblem and map of Afghanistan.

1967, May 11 Photo. *Perf. 1*

749 A249 2af yel., blk. & lt. bl.15 1
750 " 6af bister brn., blk. & lt. blue 50 3
a. Souv. sheet of 2 1.00 1.

Issued for International Tourist Yea 1967. No. 750a contains 2 imperf. stamp similar to Nos. 749–750 with black mar ginal inscription. Size: 110x70mm. Sol for 10af.

Power Dam, Dorunta
A250

Macaque
A251

Designs: 6af, Sirobi Dam (vert.). 8af Reservoir at Jalalabad.

1967, July 2 Photo. *Perf. 1*

751 A250 1af dk. grn. & lilac 6
752 " 6af red brown & greenish bl. 35 3
753 " 8af plum & dk. bl. 50 5

Issued to publicize progress in agri culture through electricity.

1967, July 28 Photo. *Perf. 12*

Designs: 6af, Striped hyena (horiz.) 12af, Persian gazelles (horiz.).

754 A251 2af dull yel. & indigo 12 1
755 " 6af lt. grn. & sepia 35 3
756 " 12af lt. bl. & red brn. 75 7

Pashtun Dancers
A252

1967, Sept. 1 Photo. *Perf. 12*

757 A252 2af magenta & violet 12 12

Issued for "Free Pashtunistan Day."

Horse Artillery in Action
A253

Fireworks and U.N. Emblem
A254

1967, Aug. 24

758 A253 1af dark brown & orange verm. 7 7
759 " 2af dark brown & bright pink 12 12

Issued to commemorate Independence Day.

King Type of 1966.

1967, Oct. 15 Photo. ***Perf. 14x13½***
760 A245 2af brown red 12 10
761 " 8af dark blue 50 25

Issued to honor King Mohammed Zahir Shah on his 53rd birthday.

1967, Oct. 24 Litho. ***Perf. 12***
762 A254 10af vio. bl. & multi. 65 35

Issued for United Nations Day.

Greco-Roman Wrestlers
A255

Said Jamalluddin Afghan
A256

Design: 6af, Wrestlers (free style).

1967, Nov. 20 Photogravure
763 A255 4af olive green & rose lilac 25 12
764 " 6af dp. car. & brn. 40 20
a. Souv. sheet of 2 1.10 1.10

Issued to publicize the 1968 Olympic Games. No. 764a contains 2 imperf. stamps similar to Nos. 763–764. Rose lilac marginal inscription and black control number. Size: 100x65mm.

1967, Nov. 27
765 A256 1af magenta 7 7
766 " 5af brown 35 20

Issued to honor Said Jamalluddin Afghan, politician (1839–1897).

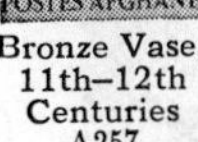

Bronze Vase, 11th–12th Centuries
A257

WHO Emblem
A258

Design: 7af, Bronze vase, Ghasnavide era, 11th–12th centuries.

1967, Dec. 23 Photo. ***Perf. 12***
767 A257 3af lt. green & brn. 18 15
768 " 7af yel. & slate grn. 42 30
a. Souv. sheet of 2 1.25 1.25

No. 768a contains 2 imperf. stamps similar to Nos. 767–768. Slate green marginal inscription and black control number. Size: 65x100mm.

1968, Apr. 7 Photo. ***Perf. 12***
769 A258 2af citron & brt. bl. 8 8
770 " 7af rose & brt. blue 28 22

Issued to commemorate the 20th anniversary of the World Health Organization.

Karakul
A259

1968, May 20 Photo. ***Perf. 12***
771 A259 1af yellow & black 6 3
772 " 6af lt. blue & black 35 20
773 " 12af lt. ultramarine & dark brown 70 40

Issued for the Day of Agriculture.

Map of Afghanistan
A260

Victory Tower, Ghazni
A261

Cinereous Vulture
A262

Design: 16af, Mausoleum, Ghazni.

1968, June 3 ***Perf. 13½x14, 12***
774 A260 2af red, black, lt. blue & green 12 8
775 A261 3af yel., dk. brown & light blue 18 10
776 " 16af pink & multi. 95 50

Issued for tourist publicity.

1968, July 3 ***Perf. 12***

Birds: 6af, Eagle owl. 7af, Greater flamingoes.

777 A262 1af sky blue & multi. 7 3
778 " 6af yellow & multi. 45 20
779 " 7af multicolored 50 30

Game of "Peg-sticking"
A263

Designs: 2af, Olympic flame and rings (vert.). 12af, Buzkashi.

1968, July 20 Photo. ***Perf. 12***
780 A263 2af multicolored 12 7
781 " 8af orange & multi. 50 30
782 " 12af multicolored 75 45

19th Olympic Games, Mexico City, Oct. 12–27.

Flower-decked Armored Car
A264

1968, Aug. 23
783 A264 6af multicolored 40 20

Issued to commemorate Independence Day.

Flag of Pashtunistan
A265

1968, Aug. 31 Photo. ***Perf. 12***
784 A265 3af multicolored 25 10

Issued for "Free Pashtunistan Day."

Zahir Shah
A266

Human Rights Flame
A267

1968, Oct. 14 Photo. ***Perf. 12***
785 A266 2af ultramarine 12 6
786 " 8af brown 45 28

Issued to honor King Mohammed Zahir Shah on his 54th birthday.

1968, Oct. 24
787 A267 1af multicolored 10 3
788 " 2af violet, bister & black 25 6
789 " 6af violet black, bister & vio. 50 20

Souvenir Sheet

Imperf.

790 A267 10af plum, bister & red org. 1.00 1.00

Issued for International Human Rights Year. No. 790 contains one stamp. Bister margin with plum inscription and black control number. Size: 100x65mm.

Maolana Djalalodine Balkhi
A268

Kushan Mural
A269

1968, Nov. 26 Photo. ***Perf. 12***
791 A268 4af dark green & magenta 27 12

Maolana Djalalodine Balkhi (1207–1273), historian.

1969, Jan. 2 ***Perf. 12***

Design: 3af, Jug shaped like female torso.

792 A269 1af dark green, maroon & yel. 10 4
793 " 3af violet, gray & maroon 25 10
a. Souv. sheet of 2 40 40

Issued to publicize the archaeological finds at Bagram, 1st century B.C. to 2nd century A.D.

No. 793a contains 2 imperf. stamps similar to Nos. 792–793. Maroon marginal inscription and black control number. Size: 100x65mm.

ILO Emblem
A270

1969, Mar. 23 Photo. ***Perf. 12***
794 A270 5af lt. yellow, lemon & black 30 18
795 " 8af lt. blue, greenish blue & black 50 30

Issued for the 50th anniversary of the International Labor Organization.

Arms Type of 1939

1969, May (?) Typographed
795A A79 100p dark green 8 4
795B " 150p deep brown 10 6

Nos. 795A–795B were normally used as newspaper stamps.

Badakhshan Scene
A271

Designs: 2af, Map of Afghanistan. 7af, Three men on mules ascending the Pamir Mountains.

1969, July 6 Photo. ***Perf. 13½x14***
796 A271 2af ocher & multi. 15 6
797 " 4af multicolored 25 12
798 " 7af " 55 22
a. Souv. sheet of 3 1.10 1.10

Issued for tourist publicity. No. 798a contains 3 imperf. stamps similar to Nos. 796–798. Black marginal inscription and control number. Size: 136x90½mm. Sold for 15af.

Bust, from Hadda Treasure, 3rd–5th Centuries
A272

Zahir Shah and Queen Humeira
A273

Designs: 5af, Vase and jug. 10af, Statue of crowned woman. 5af and 10af from Bagram treasure, 1st–2nd centuries.

1969, Aug. 3 Photo. ***Perf. 14x13½***
799 A272 1af olive grn. & gold 4 3
800 " 5af purple & gold 20 16
801 " 10af dp. blue & gold 40 32

1969, Aug. 23 ***Perf. 12***
802 A273 5af gold, dk. blue & red brown 35 20
803 " 10af gold, dp. lilac & blue green 65 35

Issued to commemorate Independence Day.

Map of Pashtunistan and Rising Sun
A274

1969, Aug. 31 Typo. ***Perf. 10½***
804 A274 2af light blue & red 12 6

Issued for "Free Pashtunistan Day."

Zahir Shah
A275

1969, Oct. 14 Photo. ***Perf. 12***

Portrait in Natural Colors

805 A275 2af dk. brown & gold 15 6
806 " 6af brown & gold 45 20

Issued to honor King Mohammed Zahir Shah on his 55th birthday.

U.N. Emblem and Flag of Afghanistan—A276

1969, Oct. 24 Litho. *Perf. 13½*

807 A276 5af blue & multi. 27 16

Issued for United Nations Day.

ITU Emblem A277 — Wild Boar A278

1969, Nov. 12

808 A277 6af ultra. & multi. 30 20
809 " 12af rose & multi. 60 35

Issued for World Telecommunications Day.

1969, Dec. 7 Photo. *Perf. 12*

Designs: 1af, Long-tailed porcupine. 8af, Red deer.

810 A278 1af yellow & multi. 6 3
811 " 3af blue & multi. 18 10
812 " 8af pink & multi. 50 25

Man's First Footprints on Moon, and Earth A279

1969, Dec. 28 *Perf. 13½x14*

813 A279 1af yel. grn. & multi. 6 3
814 " 3af yellow & multi. 17 10
815 " 6af blue & multi. 30 20
816 " 10af rose & multi. 50 32

Moon landing. See note after Algeria No. 427.

Anti-cancer Symbol A280 — Mirza Abdul Quader Bedel A281

1970, Apr. 7 Photogravure *Perf. 14*

817 A280 2af dark green & rose carmine 15 6
818 " 6af dark blue & rose claret 40 20

Issued to publicize the fight against cancer.

1970, May 6 *Perf. 14x13½*

819 A281 5af multicolored 27 15

Issued for the 250th anniversary of the death of Mirza Abdul Quader Bedel (1643–1720), poet.

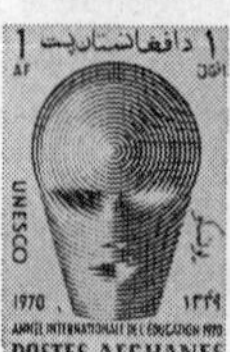

Education Year Emblem A282 — Mother and Child A283

1970, June 7 Photo. *Perf. 12*

820 A282 1af black 6 3
821 " 6af deep rose 35 20
822 " 12af green 75 35

International Education Year 1970.

1970, June 15 *Perf. 13½*

823 A283 6af yellow & multi. 27 20

Issued for Mother's Day.

U.N. Emblem, Scales of Justice, Spacecraft A284

1970, June 26

824 A284 4af yellow, dk. blue & deep blue 20 12
825 " 6af salmon pink, dk. bl. & brt. blue 35 20

25th anniversary of United Nations.

Mosque of the Amir of the two Swords, Kabul—A285

Designs: 2af, Map of Afghanistan. 7af, Arch of Paghman.

1970, July 6 *Perf. 12*

Size: 30½x30½mm.

826 A285 2af lt. blue, black & citron 12 6

Size: 36x26mm.

827 A285 3af pink & multi. 18 10
828 " 7af yellow & multi. 42 22

Issued for tourist publicity.

Zahir Shah Reviewing Troops A286

1970, Aug. 23 Photo. *Perf. 13½*

829 A286 8af multicolored 60 25

Issued to commemorate Independence Day.

Pathans A287

1970, Aug. 31 Typo. *Perf. 10½*

830 A287 2af ultra. & red 12 6

Issued for "Free Pashtunistan Day."

Quail A288

Dsigns: 4af, Golden eagle. 6af, Ring-necked pheasant.

1970, Sept. Photo. *Perf. 12*

831 A288 2af multicolored 8 6
832 " 4af " 16 12
833 " 6af " 24 20

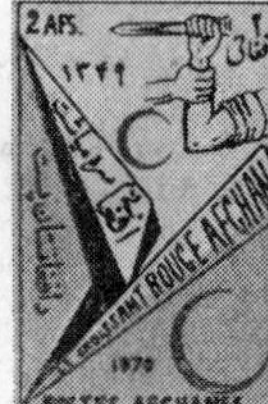

Zahir Shah A289 — Red Crescents A290

1970, Oct. 14 Photo. *Perf. 14x13½*

834 A289 3af green & violet 20 10
835 " 7af dark blue & violet brown 60 22

Issued to honor King Mohammed Zahir Shah on his 56th birthday.

1970, Oct. 16 Typo. *Perf. 10½*

836 A290 2af blk., gold & red 12 6

Issued for the Red Crescent Society.

U. N. Emblem and Charter A291

1970, Oct. 24 Photo. *Perf. 14*

837 A291 1af gold & multi. 10 5
838 " 5af " " 20 16

United Nations Day.

Tiger Heads of 1871 A292

1970, Nov. 10 *Perf. 12*

839 A292 1af sal., lt. greenish blue & black 4 3
840 " 4af lt. ultra., yellow & black 16 12
841 " 12af lilac, lt. bl. & blk. 48 35

Issued to commemorate the centenary of the first Afghan postage stamps. The postal service was established in 1870, but the first stamps were issued in May, 1871.

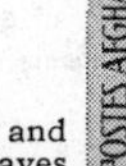

Globe and Waves A293

1971, May 17 Photo. *Perf. 13½*

842 A293 12af grn., blk. & blue 60 35

3rd World Telecommunications Day.

Callimorpha Principalis A294

Designs: 3af, Epizygaenella species. 5af, Parnassius autocrator.

1971, May 30 *Perf. 13½x14*

843 A294 1af verm. & multi. 4 3
844 " 3af yellow & multi. 12 10
845 " 5af ultra. & multi. 20 15

"UNESCO" and Half of Ancient Kushan Statue A295

1971, June 26 Photo. *Perf. 13½*

846 A295 6af ocher & violet 40 20
847 " 10af lt. blue & maroon 65 30

UNESCO-sponsored International Kushani Seminar.

Tughra and Independence Monument A296

1971, Aug. 23

848 A296 7af rose red & multi. 40 22
849 " 9af red org. & multi. 65 28

Independence Day.

Pashtunistan Square, Kabul A297

1971, Aug. 31 Typo. *Perf. 10½*

850 A297 5af deep rose lilac 27 15

"Free Pashtunistan Day."

Zahir Shah
A298

1971, Oct. 14 Photo. *Perf. 12½x12*

851 A298 9af lt. grn. & multi. 40 28
852 " 17af yellow & multi. 75 55

57th birthday of King Mohammed Zahir Shah.

Map of Afghanistan, Red Crescent, Various Activities
A299

1971, Oct. 16 *Perf. 14x13½*

853 A299 8af light blue, red, green & black 45 25

For Afghan Red Crescent Society.

Equality Year Emblem
A300

1971, Oct. 24 *Perf. 12*

854 A300 24af bright blue 1.25 70

International Year Against Racial Discrimination and United Nations Day.

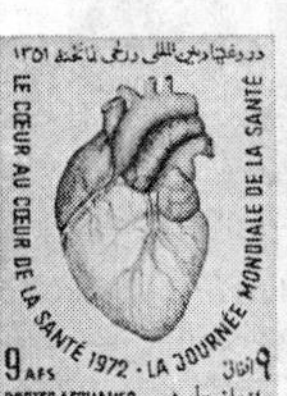

"Your Heart is your Health"
A301

Tulip
A302

1972, Apr. 7 Photo. *Perf. 14*

855 A301 9af pale yel. & multi. 36 28
856 " 12af gray & multi. 48 35

World Health Day.

1972, June 5 Photo. *Perf. 14*

Designs: 10af, Rock partridge (horiz.). 12af, Lynx (horiz.). 18af, Allium stipitatum (flower).

857 A302 7af green & multi. 28 22
858 " 10af blue & multi. 40 32
859 " 12af lt. grn. & multi. 48 35
860 " 18af bl. grn. & multi. 72 60

Buddhist Shrine, Hadda
A302a

Designs: 7af, Greco-Bactrian animal seal, 250 B.C. 9af, Greco-Oriental temple, Ai-Khanoum, 3rd–2nd centuries B.C.

1972, July 16 Photo. *Perf. 12*

861 A302a 3af brn. & dull blue 12 9
862 " 7af rose claret & dull green 28 22
863 " 9af green & lilac 36 30

Tourist publicity.

King and Queen Reviewing Parade
A303

1972, Aug. 23 Photo. *Perf. 13½*

864 A303 25af gold & multi. 1.35 85

Independence Day.

Wrestling
A304

Designs: 8af, Like 4af. 10af, 19af, 21af, Wrestling, different hold.

1972, Aug. 26

865 A304 4af ol. bis. & multi. 20 12
866 " 8af lt. blue & multi. 40 25
867 " 10af yel. grn. & multi. 50 32
868 " 19af multicolored 90 40
869 " 21af lilac & multi. 1.00 45
a. Souv. sheet of 5 3.25 3.25
Nos. 865–869 (5) 3.00 1.54

20th Olympic Games, Munich, Aug. 26–Sept. 11. No. 869a contains 5 imperf. stamps similar to Nos. 865–869. Olive bister marginal inscription and ornament, black control number. Size: 159x110mm. Sold for 60af.

Pathan and View of Tribal Territory
A305

Zahir Shah
A306

1972, Aug. 31 *Perf. 12½x12*

870 A305 5af ultra. & multi. 27 15

Pashtunistan day.

1972, Oct. 14 Photo. *Perf. 14x13½*

871 A306 7af gold, black & Prussian blue 50 22
872 " 14af gold, black & light brown 1.00 45

58th birthday of King Mohammed Zahir Shah.

City Destroyed by Earthquake, Refugees—A307

1972, Oct. 16 *Perf. 13½*

873 A307 7af lt. blue, red & black 40 22

For Afghan Red Crescent Society.

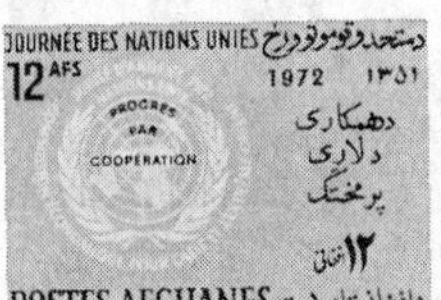

U.N. Emblem
A308

1972, Oct. 24

874 A308 12af lt. ultra. & blk. 65 35

United Nations Economic Commission for Asia and the Far East (ECAFE), 25th anniversary.

Ceramics
A309

Designs: 9af, Leather coat (vert.). 12af, Metal ware (vert.). 16af, Inlaid artifacts.

1972, Dec. 10 Photo. *Perf. 12*

875 A309 7af gold & multi. 42 22
876 " 9af " " 55 28
877 " 12af " " 70 35
878 " 16af " " 1.00 50
a. Souvenir sheet of 4 2.75 2.75

Handicraft industries. No. 878a contains 4 imperf. stamps similar to Nos. 875–878. Gold marginal inscription and black control number. Size: 109x109mm. Sold for 45af.

WMO and National Emblems—A310

1973, Apr. 3 Photo. *Perf. 14*

879 A310 7af light lilac & dark green 42 22
880 " 14af lt. blue & deep claret 85 45

Centenary of international meteorological cooperation.

abu-al-Rayhan al-Biruni
A311

Family
A312

1973, June 16 Photo. *Perf. 13½*

881 A311 10af multicolored 55 32

Millennium of the birth of abu-al-Rayhan al-Biruni (973–1048), philosopher and mathematician.

1973, June 30 Photo. *Perf. 13½*

882 A312 9af org. & red lilac 50 30

International Family Planning Federation, 21st anniversary.

Republic

Impeyan Pheasant
A313

Birds: 9af, Great crested grebe. 12af, Himalayan snow cock.

1973, July 29 Photo. *Perf. 12x12½*

883 A313 8af yellow & multi. 32 25
884 " 9af blue & multi. 36 30
885 " 12af multicolored 48 35

Stylized Buzkashi Horseman
A314

1973, Aug. *Perf. 13½*

886 A314 8af black 32 25

Tourist publicity.

Fireworks
A315

1973, Aug. 23 Photo. *Perf. 12*

887 A315 12af multicolored 48 35

55th Independence Day.

Lake Abassine, Pashtunistan Flag
A316

1973, Aug. 31 *Perf. 14x13½*

888 A316 9af multicolored 50 30

Pashtunistan Day.

Red Crescent
A317

1973, Oct. 16 *Perf. 13½*

889 A317 10af red, blk. & gold 60 32

Red Crescent Society.

Kemal Ataturk
A318

1973, Oct. 28 Litho. *Perf. 10½*

890	A318	1af blue	6	3
891	"	7af reddish brown	42	22

50th anniversary of the Turkish Republic.

Human Rights Flame, Arms of Afghanistan
A319

1973, Dec. 10 Photo. *Perf. 12*

892	A319	12af silver, black & light blue	45	35

25th anniversary of the Universal Declaration of Human Rights.

Asiatic Black Bears
A320

1974, Mar. 26 Lithographed *Perf. 12*

Multicolored

893	A320	5af *shown*	15	12
894	"	7af *Afghan hound*	22	20
895	"	10af *Persian goat*	30	25
896	"	12af *Leopard*	40	30
		a. Souvenir sheet of 4	1.25	1.25

No. 896a contains 4 imperf. stamps similar to Nos. 893–896. Magenta border and black marginal inscription. Size: 120x100mm.

Worker and Farmer
A321

1974, May 1 Photo. *Perf. 13½x12½*

897	A321	9af rose red & multi.	40	25

International Labor Day, May 1.

Independence Monument and Arch
A322

1974, May 27 Photo. *Perf. 12*

898	A322	4af blue & multi.	12	10
899	"	11af gold & multi.	35	30

56th Independence Day.

Arms of Afghanistan and Symbol of Cooperation—A323

Pres. Mohammad Daoud Khan
A324

Designs: 5af, Flag of Republic of Afghanistan. 15af, Soldiers and coat of arms of the Republic.

1974, July 25 *Perf. 13½x12½, 14*

Sizes: 4af, 15af, 36x22mm.; 5af, 7af, 36x26, 26x36mm.

900	A323	4af multicolored	18	10
901	"	5af "	22	12
902	A324	7af grn., brn. & blk.	32	18
		a. Souvenir sheet of 2	70	70
903	A323	15af multicolored	65	40
		a. Souvenir sheet of 2	1.00	1.00

First anniversary of the Republic of Afghanistan. No. 902a contains 2 imperf. stamps similar to Nos. 901–902, No. 903a contains 2 imperf. stamps similar to Nos. 900 and 903. Both sheets have yellow margins, black inscriptions and control numbers. Sizes: No. 902a, 99x99mm., No. 903a, 120x80mm.

Lesser Spotted Eagle
A325

Birds: 6af, White-fronted goose, ruddy shelduck and gray-lag goose. 11af, European coots and European crane.

1974, Aug. 6 Photo. *Perf. 13½x13*

904	A325	1af car. rose & multi.	6	3
905	"	6af blue & multi.	35	15
906	"	11af yellow & multi.	70	30

Nos. 904–906 printed se-tenant.

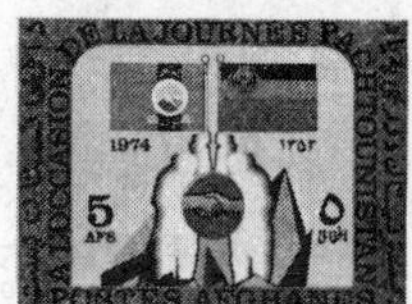

Flags of Pashtunistan and Afghanistan—A326

1974, Aug. 31 Photo. *Perf. 14*

907	A326	5af multicolored	27	12

Pashtunistan Day.

Coat of Arms
A327

1974, Oct. 9

908	A327	7af gold, grn. & blk.	22	18

Centenary of Universal Postal Union.

"UN" and UN Emblem
A328

1974, Oct. 24 Photo. *Perf. 14*

909	A328	5af lt. ultramarine & dark blue	27	12

United Nations Day.

Minaret of Jam A329 — Buddha, Hadda A330

Design: 14af, Lady riding griffin, 2nd century, Bagram.

1975, May 5 Photo. *Perf. 13½*

910	A329	7af multicolored	22	15
911	A330	14af "	44	30
912	"	15af "	48	30
		a. Souvenir sheet of 3	1.50	1.50

South Asia Tourism Year 1975.

No. 912a contains 3 imperf. stamps similar to Nos. 910–912. Tourism Year emblem in margin and black control number. Size: 130x90mm.

New Flag of Afghanistan
A331

1975, May 27 Photo. *Perf. 12*

913	A331	16af multicolored	75	35

57th Independence Day.

Celebrating Crowd
A332

1975, July 17 Photo. *Perf. 13½*

914	A332	9af blue & multi.	42	20
915	"	12af car. & multi.	55	28

Second anniversary of the Republic.

Women's Year Emblems
A333

1975, Aug. 24 Photo. *Perf. 12*

916	A333	9af car., lt. bl. & blk.	28	22

International Women's Year 1975.

Pashtunistan Flag, Sun Rising Over Mountains
A334

Mohammed Akbar Khan
A335

1975, Aug. 31 *Perf. 13½*

917	A334	10af multicolored	30	25

Pashtunistan Day.

1976, Feb. 4 Photo. *Perf. 14*

918	A335	15af lt. brn. & multi.	45	35

Mohammed Akbar Khan (1816–1846), warrior son of Amir Dost Mohammed Khan.

Pres. Mohammad Daoud Khan
A336 A337

1975–78 Photo. *Perf. 14*

919	A336	10af multi.	('76)	30	25
920	"	16af "	('78)	48	
921	"	19af "	('76)	58	48
922	"	21af "	('76)	62	50
923	"	22af "	('78)	65	
924	"	30af "	('78)	90	
925	A337	50af "	('75)	1.50	1.25
926	"	100af "	('75)	3.00	2.50
		Nos. 919–926 (8)		8.03	

Arms of Republic, Independence Monument
A338

1976, June 1 Photo. *Perf. 14*

927	A338	22af blue & multi.	65	45

58th Independence Day.

Flag Raising
A339

1976, July 17 Photo. *Perf. 14*

928	A339	30af multicolored	90	75

Republic Day.

Mountain Peaks and Flag of Pashtunistan
A340

1976, Aug. 31 Photo. *Perf. 14*

929	A340	16af multicolored	48	38

Pashtunistan Day.

Coat of Arms—A340a

1977 Litho. ***Roulette 11, Rough***

930	A340a	50p light green	3	3
931	"	1af ultramarine	3	3

Flag and Views on Open Book
A341

1977, May 27 Photo. ***Perf. 14***

937	A341	20af grn. & multi.	60	50

59th Independence Day.

Pres. Daoud and National Assembly
A342

President Taking Oath of Office
A343

Designs: 10af, Inaugural address. 18af, Promulgation of Constitution.

1977, June 22

938	A342	7af multicolored	22	16
939	A343	8af "	24	20
940	"	10af "	30	25
941	A342	18af "	55	45
		a. Souvenir sheet of 4	1.50	1.50

Election of first President and promulgation of Constitution. No. 941a contains 4 imperf. stamps similar to Nos. 938–941. Black marginal inscription and control number. Size: 135x105mm.

Jamalluddin Medal
A344

1977, July 6 Photo. ***Perf. 14***

942	A344	12af blue, black & gold	35	30

Sajo Jamalluddin Afghani, reformer, 80th death anniversary.

Afghanistan Flag over Crowd
A345

1977, July 17

943	A345	22af multicolored	65	55

Republic Day.

Dancers, Fountain, Pashtunistan Flag
A346

1977, Aug. 31

944	A346	30af multicolored	90	75

Pashtunistan Day.

Members of Parliament Congratulating Pres. Daoud—A347

1978, Feb. 5 Litho. ***Perf. 14***

945	A347	20af multicolored	60	

Election of first president, first anniversary.

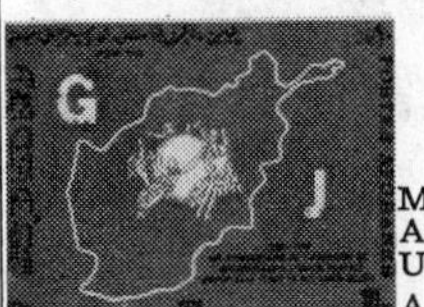

Map of Afghanistan, UPU Emblem
A348

1978, Apr. 1 Photo. ***Perf. 14***

946	A348	10af green, black & gold	30	25

50th anniversary of Afghanistan's membership in Universal Postal Union.

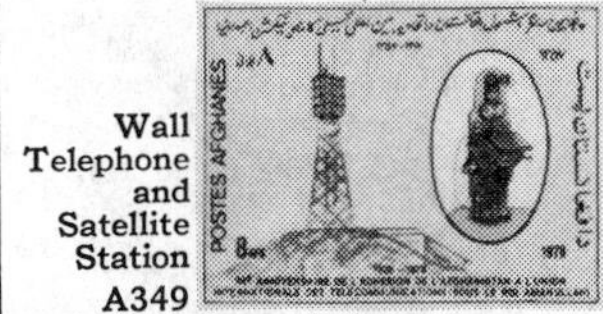

Wall Telephone and Satellite Station
A349

1978, Apr. 12

947	A349	8af multicolored	24	20

50th anniversary of Afghanistan's membership in International Telecommunications Union.

Arrows Pointing to Crescent, Cross and Lion
A350

1978, July 6 Litho. ***Perf. 11 Rough***

948	A350	3af black	10	6

50th anniversary of Afghani Red Crescent Society.

Arch
A351

1978, Aug. 19 ***Perf. 14***

949	A351	22af silver & multi.	65	55

Democratic Republic of Afghanistan.

Men with Pashtunistan Flag
A352

Coat of Arms and Emblems
A353

1978, Aug. 31 ***Perf. 11 Rough***

950	A352	7af ultra. & red	22	16

Pashtunistan Day.

1978, Sept. 8 ***Perf. 11***

951	A353	20af rose red	60	50

World Literacy Day.

A354

1978 Litho. ***Perf. 11½ Rough***

952	A354	18af light green	55	45

Hero of Afghanistan.

Flag
A355

1978 Photogravure ***Perf. 11½***

953	A355	8af blk., red & gold	24	20
954	"	9af " " "	30	22

"The mail serving the people."

SEMI-POSTAL STAMPS.

No. 373 Surcharged in Violet

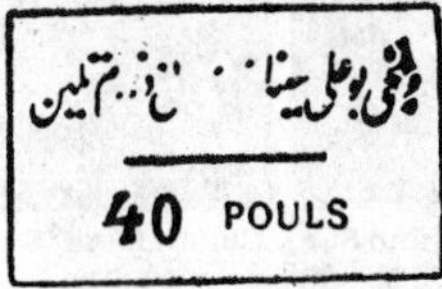

a

b

1952, July 12 ***Perf. 12½*** **Unwmkd.**

B1	A122 (*a*)	40p+30p cerise	1.50	1.00
B2	" (*b*)	125p+30p "	2.50	2.00

Issued to commemorate the 1000th anniversary of the birth of Avicenna.

Children at Play
SP1

1955, July 3 Typo. ***Perf. 11***

B3	SP1	35p+15p dark green	60	40
B4	"	125p+25p purple	1.25	1.00

The surtax was for child welfare.

Amir Sher Ali Khan, Tiger Head Stamp and Zahir Shah
SP2

Children at Play
SP3

1955, July 2 **Lithographed**

B5	SP2	35p+15p carmine	60	40
B6	"	125p+25p pale violet blue	1.25	80

Issued to commemorate the 85th anniversary of the Afghan post.

1956, June 20 **Typographed**

B7	SP3	35p+15p bright violet blue	40	40
B8	"	140p+15p dark orange brown	1.00	1.00

Issued for Children's Day. The surtax was for child welfare. No. B8 inscribed in French.

Pashtunistan Monument, Kabul
SP4

1956, Sept. 1 **Lithographed**

B9	SP4	35p+15p deep violet	25	25
B10	"	140p+15p dark brown	75	75

Issued for "Free Pashtunistan" Day. The surtax aided the "Free Pashtunistan" movement.

No. B9 measures 30½x19½mm.; No. B10, 29x19mm. On sale and valid for use only on Sept. 1–2.

Globe and Sun SP5 Children on Seesaw SP6

1956, Oct. 24 *Perf. 11*

B11	SP5	35p+15p ultra.	1.00	85
B12	"	140p+15p red brown	1.85	1.50

Issued for the tenth anniversary of Afghanistan's admission to the United Nations.

1957, June 20 **Unwmkd.**

B13	SP6	35p+15p bright rose	50	30
B14	"	140p+15p ultra.	1.25	90

Issued for Children's Day. The surtax was for child welfare.

U. N. Headquarters and Emblems SP7

1957, Oct. 24 *Perf. 11 Rough*

B15	SP7	35p+15p red brown	50	30
B16	"	140p+15p light ultramarine	1.00	90

Issued for United Nations Day.

Swimming Pool and Children SP8

1958, June 22 *Perf. 11*

B17	SP8	35p+15p rose	40	30
B18	"	140p+15p dull red brown	1.00	75

Issued for Children's Day. The surtax was for child welfare.

Pashtunistan Flag SP9

1958, Aug. 31

B19	SP9	35p+15p light blue	25	25
B20	"	140p+15p red brown	75	75

Issued for "Free Pashtunistan Day."

Children Playing Tug of War SP10

1959, June 23 **Litho.** *Perf. 11*

B21	SP10	35p+15p brn. vio.	35	25
B22	"	165p+15p brt. pink	1.10	75

Issued for Children's Day. The surtax was for child welfare.

Pathans in Tribal Dance—SP11

Perf. 11 Rough

1959, Sept. **Unwmkd.**

B23	SP11	35p+15p green	20	20
B24	"	165p+15p orange	75	75

Issued for "Free Pashtunistan Day."

Afghan Cavalryman with U.N. Flag SP12

1959, Oct. 24 *Perf. 11 Rough*

B25	SP12	35p+15p orange	30	25
B26	"	165p+15p light blue green	65	60

Issued for United Nations Day.

Children SP13

1960, Oct. 23 **Lithographed**

B27	SP13	75p+25p lt. ultra.	35	30
B28	"	175p+25p lt. grn.	60	45

Issued for Children's Day. The surtax was for child welfare.

Man with Spray Gun—SP14

1960, Sept. 6 *Perf. 11 Rough*

B29	SP14	50p+50p orange	1.25	1.00
B30	"	175p+50p red brown	3.00	2.00

11th anniversary of the WHO malaria control program in Afghanistan.

SP15

1960, Sept. 1 **Unwmkd.**

B31	SP15	50p+50p rose	35	30
B32	"	175p+50p dk. blue	85	60

Issued for "Free Pashtunistan Day."

Ambulance—SP16

Crescent in Red

1960, Oct. 16 *Perf. 11*

B33	SP16	50p+50p violet	50	25
B34	"	175p+50p blue	1.10	90

Issued for the Red Crescent Society.

Nos. 470–471 Surcharged in Blue or Orange.

1960, Dec. 31 **Litho.** *Perf. 11*

B35	A166	50p+25p deep orange (Bl)	3.00	3.00
B36	"	165p+25p blue (O)	3.00	3.00

The imperf. souvenir sheet with 50p in blue and 1.65af in deep orange, described in note below Nos. 470–471, was surcharged in carmine like Nos. B35–B36 ("+25 Ps" on each stamp). Price $5. See note after No. 485.

Nos. 496–500 Surcharged UNICEF يونيسف +25PS

Photogravure

1961 *Perf. 13½x14* **Unwmkd.**

B37	A175	2p+25p green & rose lilac		
B38	"	2p+25p brown & citron		
B39	"	5p+25p gray & rose		
B40	"	10p+25p blue & bistre		
B41	"	15p+25p slate blue & dull lilac		
		Nos. B37–B41 (5)	2.25	

Issued for the United Nations Children's Fund, UNICEF. The same surcharge was applied to an imperf. souvenir sheet like that noted after No. 505. Price $4.50.

Nos. 522–526 Surcharged "+25PS" and Crescent in Red.

1961, Oct. 16 *Perf. 13½x14*

Fruit in Natural Colors.

B42	A184	2p+25p black		
B43	"	2p+25p green		
B44	"	5p+25p lilac rose		
B45	"	10p+25p lilac		
B46	"	15p+25p dk. blue		
		Nos. B42–B46 (5)	2.50	

Issued for the Red Crescent Society.

Nos. 539–543 Surcharged in Red: "UNESCO + 25PS"

1962 *Perf. 12*

B47	A186	2p+25p multi.		
B48	"	2p+25p "		
B49	"	5p+25p "		
B50	"	10p+25p "		
B51	"	15p+25p "		
		Nos. B47–B51 (5)	1.50	

Issued for the United Nations Educational, Scientific and Cultural Organization. The same surcharge was also applied to the souvenir sheets mentioned after No. 548. Price, 2 sheets, $3.50.

Nos. 553–561 Surcharged: "Dag Hammarskjöld + 20PS"

1962, Sept. 17 *Perf. 14x13½*

B52	A187	2p+20p rose lilac & brown		
B53	"	2p+20p olive bister & brown		
B54	"	5p+20p dp. orange & dk. green		
B55	"	10p+20p gray & magenta		
B56	"	15p+20p bl. & brn.		
B57	"	25p+20p org. yel. & purple		
B58	"	50p+20p lt. green & purple		
B59	"	75p+20p brt. citron & brown		
B60	"	100p+20p dp. orange & brown		
		Nos. B52–B60 (9)	2.25	

Issued in memory of Dag Hammarskjold, Secretary General of the United Nations, 1953–61. Perf. and imperf. souvenir sheets exist. Price, 2 sheets, $3.

Nos. 583–593 Surcharged "+15PS"

1963, Mar. 15 *Perf. 14x13½*

B61	A193	2p+15p dark grn. & olive gray		
B62	"	2p+15p dark green & salmon		
B63	"	5p+15p red brown & olive		
B64	"	10p+15p red brn. & brt. grn.		
B65	"	15p+15p red brown & gray		
B66	"	25p+15p bright blue & bluish green		
B67	"	50p+15p bt. blue & rose lilac		
B68	"	75p+15p blk. & bl.		
B69	"	100p+15p black & bright pink		
B70	"	150p+15p black & bister brown		
B71	"	175p+15p black & orange		
		Nos. B61–B71 (11)	10.00	

Issued for the World Health Organization drive to eradicate malaria.

Postally used copies of Nos. B35–B71 are uncommon and command a considerable premium over the prices for unused copies.

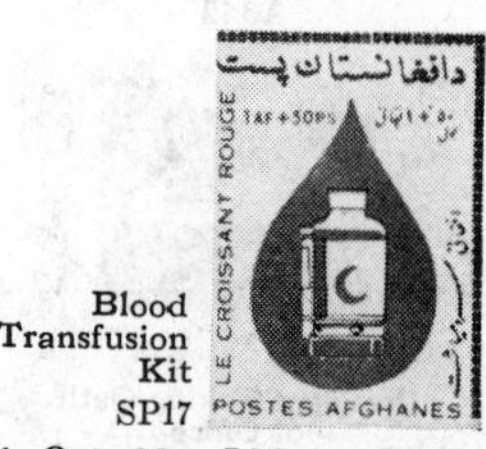

Blood Transfusion Kit SP17

1964, Oct. 18 **Litho.** *Perf. 10½*

B72	SP17	1af+50p blk. & rose	15	10

Issued for the Red Crescent Society and Red Crescent Week, Oct. 18–24.

First Aid Station SP18

1965, Oct. **Photo.** *Perf. 13½x14*

B73	SP18	1.50af+50p green, choc. & red	25	10

Issued for the Red Crescent Society.

Children Playing SP19

1966, Nov. 28 **Photo.** *Perf. 13½x14*

B74	SP19	1af+1af yel. green & claret	18	12
B75	"	3af+2af yel. & brn.	40	30
B76	"	7af+3af rose lilac & green	85	60

Children's Day.

Nadir Shah Presenting Society Charter—SP20

967 Photogravure *Perf. 13x14*

77 SP20 2af+1af red & dark green 25 15
78 " 5af+1af lilac rose & brown 50 25

Issued for the Red Crescent Society.

Vaccination SP21 — Red Crescent SP22

967, June 6 Photo. *Perf. 12*

79 SP21 2af+1af yel. & blk. 25 10
80 " 5af+2af pink & brn. 50 25

The surtax was for anti-tuberculosis ork.

967, Oct. 18 Photo. *Perf. 12*

Crescent in Red

81 SP22 3af+1af gray olive & black 25 15
82 " 5af+1af dull blue & black 35 20

Issued for the Red Crescent Society.

Queen Humeira SP23 — Red Crescent SP24

968, June 14 Photo. *Perf. 12*

83 SP23 2af+2af red brown 25 20
84 " 7af+2af slate green 75 50

Issued for Mother's Day.

968, Oct. 16 Photo. *Perf. 12*

385 SP24 4af+1af yellow, black & red 45 27

Issued for the Red Crescent Society.

Red Cross, Crescent, Lion and Sun Emblems SP25 — Mother and Child SP26

1969, May 5 Litho. *Perf. 14x13½*

B86 SP25 3af+1af multi. 30 18
B87 " 5af+1af " 50 30

Issued to commemorate the 50th anniversary of the League of Red Cross Societies.

1969, June 14 Photo. *Perf. 12*

B88 SP26 1af+1af yel. orange & brown 18 12
B89 " 4af+1af rose lilac & purple 40 27
a. Souv. sheet of 2 1.10 1.10

Issued for Mother's Day. No. B89a contains 2 imperf. stamps similar to Nos. B88–B89. Brown marginal inscription and black control number. Size: 120x80mm. Sold for 10af.

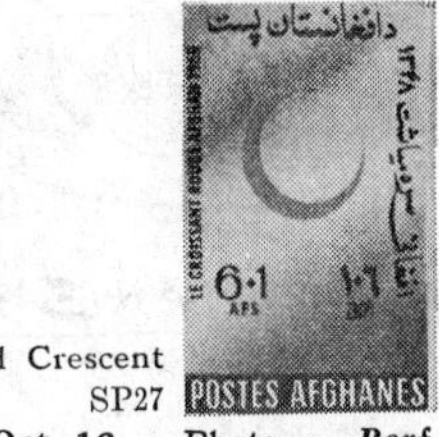

Red Crescent SP27

1969, Oct. 16 Photo. *Perf. 12*

B90 SP27 6af+1af multi. 55 30

Issued for the Red Crescent Society.

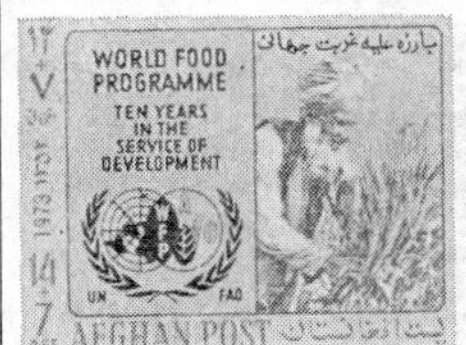

UN and FAO Emblems, Farmer SP28

1973, May 24 Photo. *Perf. 13½*

B91 SP28 14af+7af greenish blue & lilac 1.10 75

World Food Program, 10th anniversary.

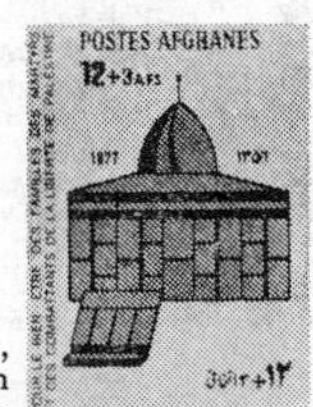

Dome of the Rock, Jerusalem SP29

1977, Sept. 11 Photo. *Perf. 14*

B92 SP29 12af+3af multi. 45 36

The surtax was for Palestinian families and soldiers.

AIR POST STAMPS

Plane over Kabul—AP1

Perf. 12, 12x11, 11

1939, Oct. 1 Typographed. Unwmkd.

C1 AP1 5af orange 1.25 1.25
a. Imperf., pair ('47) 20.00 20.00
b. Imperf. vertically, pair 15.00
C2 " 10af blue 2.00 1.75
a. 10af light blue 3.00 3.00
b. Imperf., pair ('47) 20.00
c. Imperf. vertically, pair 15.00
C3 " 20af emerald 4.00 3.00
a. Imperf., pair ('47) 20.00
b. Imperf. vertically, pair 15.00
c. Imperf. horiz., pair 20.00

These stamps come with clean-cut or rough perforations. Counterfeits exist.

1948, June 14 *Perf. 12x11½.*

C4 AP1 5af emerald 17.50 17.50
C5 " 10af red orange 17.50 17.50
C6 " 20af blue 17.50 17.50

Imperforates exist.

Plane over Palace Grounds, Kabul—AP2

Imprint: "Waterlow & Sons, Limited, London"

1951-54 Engraved. *Perf. 13½.*

C7 AP2 5af henna brown 2.00 80
C8 " 5af deep green('54) 1.50 70
C9 " 10af gray 5.00 1.75
C10 " 20af dark blue 7.00 3.50

1957

C11 AP2 5af ultramarine 1.25 75
C12 " 10af dark violet 2.50 1.50

See also No. C38.

Ariana DC-3 Plane over Hindu Kush AP3

Perf. 11, Imperf.

1960-63 Lithographed Unwmkd.

C13 AP3 75p light violet 30 30
C14 " 125p blue 40 45

Perf. 10½

C14A AP3 5af citron ('63) 1.10 1.10

Girl Scout AP4

1962, Aug. 30 Photo. *Perf. 11½x12*

C15 AP4 100p ocher & brn. 60 60
C16 " 175p brt. yel. grn. & brown 85 85

Issued for Women's Day. A souvenir sheet exists containing one each of Nos. 578–579 and C15–C16. Brown inscription. Size: 109x105mm. Price $3.

Sports Type of Regular Issue, 1962

Designs: 25p, 50p, Horse racing. 75p, 100p, Wrestling. 150p, Weight lifting. 175p, Soccer.

1962, Sept. 25 *Perf. 12* Unwmkd.

Black Inscriptions.

C17 A195 25p rose & red brn.
C18 " 50p gray & red brn.
C19 " 75p pale violet & dark green
C20 " 100p gray olive & dark purple
C21 " 150p rose lilac & grn.
C22 " 175p salmon & brn.
Nos. C17-C22 (6) 2.25

4th Asian Games, Djakarta, Indonesia.

Children's Day Type of Regular Issue

Designs: 75p, Runners. 150p, Peaches. 200p, Iris (vert.).

Perf. 11½x12, 12x11½

1962, Oct. 14 Unwmkd.

C23 A196 75p lt. green & lilac
C24 " 150p blue & multi.
C25 " 200p olive & multi.

Issued for Children's Day. A souvenir sheet contains one each of Nos. C23–C25. Lilac marginal inscription and black control number. Size: 119x90mm. Price $2.50.

Red Crescent Type of Regular Issue

Designs: 25p, Grapes. 50p, Pears. 100p, Wistaria.

1962, Oct. 16 *Perf. 12*

Fruit and Flowers in Natural Colors; Carmine Crescent

C26 A197 25p brown
C27 " 50p dull green
C28 " 100p dk. bl. gray

Issued for the Afghan Red Crescent Society. Two souvenir sheets exist. One contains a 150p gray brown stamp in blossom design, the other a 200p gray stamp in wistaria design, imperf. Each sheet has marginal inscriptions in color of stamp, and black control number. Size: 89x65mm. Price, each $5.

U.N. Type of Regular Issue

1962, Oct. 24 Photogravure

Flags in Original Colors, Black Inscriptions

C29 A198 75p blue
C30 " 100p lt. brown

C31 A198 125p brt. green

Issued for United Nations Day.

Boy Scout Type of Regular Issue

1962, Oct. 25 ***Perf. 12*** **Unwmkd.**

C32 A199 25p gray, black, dull green & salmon
C33 " 50p green, brown & salmon
C34 " 75p blue grn., red brown & sal.
C35 " 100p blue, slate & salmon

Issued to honor the Boy Scouts.

Teacher's Day Type of Regular Issue

Designs: 100p, Pole vault. 150p, High jump.

1962, Oct. 25

C36 A200 100p yellow & black
C37 " 150p bluish green & brown

Issued for Teacher's Day. A souvenir sheet contains one 250p pink and slate green stamp in design of 150p. Slate green marginal inscription and black control number. Size: 65x89mm. Price $2.50.

Type of 1951–54

1962 **Engraved** ***Perf. 13½***

Imprint: "Thomas De La Rue & Co. Ltd."

C38 AP2 5af ultramarine 6.50 1.00

Agriculture Types of Regular Issue

Photogravure

1963, March 1 ***Perf. 12*** **Unwmkd.**

C42 A204 100p dark carmine, grn. & brn.
C43 A203 150p ocher & blk.
C44 A204 200p ultramarine, green & brn.

Issued for the Day of Agriculture.

Hands Holding Wheat Emblem
AP5

1963, Mar. 27 **Photo.** ***Perf. 14***

C45 AP5 500p lilac, light brown & brown 85 85

Issued for the "Freedom from Hunger" campaign of the U.N. Food and Agriculture Organization.

Two souvenir sheets exist. One contains a 1000p blue green, light brown and brown, type AP5, imperf. Claret marginal inscription. Size: 76x100mm. The other contains a 200p brown and green and 300p ultramarine, yellow and ocher in rice and corn designs, type A205. Green marginal inscription. Size: 100x75mm. Both sheets have black control number. Prices $6 and $2.50.

Meteorological Day Type of Regular Issue

Designs: 100p, 500p, Meteorological measuring instrument. 200p, 400p, Weather station. 300p, Rockets in space.

1963, May 23 ***Imperf.***

C46 A206 100p brown & blue

Perf. 13½x14

C47 A206 200p bright green & lilac
C48 " 300p dk. bl. & rose
C49 " 400p blue & dull red brown
C50 A206 500p carmine rose & gray grn.

Issued to commemorate the United Nations Third World Meteorological Day, March 23. Nos. C47 and C50 printed se-tenant.

Two souvenir sheets exist. One contains a 125p red and brown stamp in rocket design. Red marginal inscription. The other contains a 100p blue and dull red brown in "rockets in space" design. Blue marginal inscription. Both sheets have black control number, and measure 100x75mm. Prices $5 and $7.50.

Kabul International Airport
AP8

Photogravure

1964, Apr. ***Perf. 12x11*** **Unwmkd.**

C57 AP8 10af red lilac & grn. 80 35
C58 " 20af dark green & red lilac 1.20 60
C59 " 50af dark blue & greenish bl. 3.25 1.50

Inauguration of Kabul Airport Terminal.

Zahir Shah and Ariana Plane—AP9

Design: 50af, Zahir Shah and Kabul Airport.

1971 **Photo.** ***Perf. 12½x13½***

C60 AP9 50af multicolored 2.00
C61 " 100af black, red & green 5.00

REGISTRATION STAMPS.

R1

Lithographed

Dated "1309"

1891 ***Imperf.*** **Unwmkd.**

Pelure Paper.

F1 R1 1r slate blue 1.25
a. Tête bêche pair 10.00

R2

Thin Wove Paper.

Dated "1311".

1893

F2 R2 1r *green* 1.25

Genuinely used copies of Nos. F1–F2 are rare. Counterfeit cancellations exist.

R3

1894 **Undated.**

F3 R3 2ab *green* 7.50 10.00

12 varieties. See note below Nos. 189–190.

R4

1898–1900 **Undated**

F4 R4 2ab *deep rose* 4.00 5.00
F5 " 2ab *lilac rose* 4.00 5.00
F6 " 2ab *magenta* 4.00 5.00
F7 " 2ab *salmon* 4.00 5.00
F8 " 2ab *orange* 4.00 5.00
F9 " 2ab *yellow* 4.00 5.00
F10 " 2ab *green* 4.00 5.00
Nos. F4–F10 (7) 28.00 35.00

Many shades of paper.

Nos. F4–F10 come in two sizes, measured between outer frame lines: 52x36 mm., first printing; 46x33mm., second printing. The outer frame line (not pictured) is 3–6mm. from inner frame line.

OFFICIAL STAMPS.

(Used only on interior mail.)

Coat of Arms
O1

Typographed

1909 ***Perf. 12*** **Unwmkd.**

Wove Paper.

O1 O1 red 75 75
a. carmine ('19) 1.00 1.00

Later printings of No. O1 in scarlet, vermilion, claret, etc., on various types of paper, were issued until 1927.

Official Stamp of 1909 Handstamped like Regular Issues of 1929.

1929

O2 O1 red 10.00

See note after No. 261.

Coat of Arms
O2

1939–68? **Typo.** ***Perf. 11, 1***

O3 O2 15p emerald 25
O4 " 30p ochre ('40) 50
O5 " 45p dark carmine 35
O6 " 50p brt. carmine ('68?) 25
a. 50p carmine rose ('55) 50
O7 O2 1af bright red violet 75
Nos. O3-O7 (5) 2.10 1.

Size of 50p, 24x31mm. Others 22½ 28mm.

1964-65 **Lithographed** ***Perf. 1***

O8 O2 50p rose 50
a. 50p salmon ('65) 1.00 1.

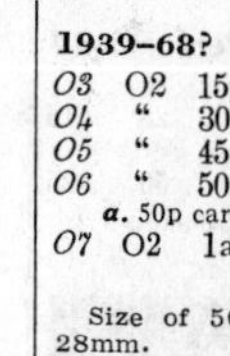

Stamps of this type are revenues.

PARCEL POST STAMPS.

Coat of Arms
PP1

PP2

PP3

PP4

Typographed.

1909 ***Perf. 12.*** **Unwmkd**

Q1 PP1 3sh bistre 50 6
a. Imperf., pair 1.25
Q2 PP2 1kr olive gray 75 1.0
a. Imperf., pair 2.00
Q3 PP3 1r orange 2.50 1.5
Q4 " 1r olive green 1.00 2.7
Q5 PP4 2r red 3.00 2.0
Nos. Q1-Q5 (5) 7.75 7.8

1916–18

Q6 PP1 3sh green 75 5
Q7 PP2 1kr pale red 1.25 9
a. 1kr rose red ('18) 1.50 2.0
Q8 PP3 1r brown orange 1.25 9
a. 1r dp. brn. ('18) 2.00 2.5
Q9 PP4 2r blue 2.50 2.50

Nos. Q1–Q9 sometimes show letters of the papermaker's watermark "HOWARD & JONES LONDON."

Ungummed copies are remainders. They sell for one-third the price of mint examples.

The indexes in each volume of the Scott Catalogue contain many listings which help to identify stamps.

Old Habibia College, near Kabul

PP5

1921 **Wove Paper.**

Q10 PP5 10pa chocolate 1.25 1.25
a. Tête bêche pair 5.00 4.50
Q11 " 15pa light brown 1.75 1.50
a. Tête bêche pair 5.00 4.50
Q12 " 30pa red violet 2.50 2.00
a. Tête bêche pair 7.50
b. Laid paper 7.50 7.50
Q13 " 1r bright blue 4.00 3.50
a. Tête bêche pair 15.00

Stamps of this issue are usually perforated on one or two sides only.

The laid paper of No. Q12b has a papermaker's watermark in the sheet.

PP6

1924-26 **Wove Paper**

Q15 PP6 5kr ultramarine ('26) 15.00 10.00
Q16 " 5r lilac 7.50 7.50

A 15r rose exists, but is not known to have been placed in use.

PP7

PP8

1928-29 ***Perf. 11, 11xImperf.***

Q17 PP7 2r yellow orange 2.50 2.50
Q18 " 2r green ('29) 2.50 2.50
Q19 PP8 3r deep green 4.50 4.00
Q20 " 3r brown ('29) 4.50 4.00

Nos. Q17 and Q19 Handstamped

1929

Q21 PP7 2r yellow orange 12.50
Q22 PP8 3r deep green 15.00

See note after No. 261.

POSTAL TAX STAMPS.

Aliabad Hospital near Kabul

PT1

Pierre and Marie Curie

PT2

Perf. 12x11½, 12

1938, Dec. 22 **Typo.** **Unwmkd.**

RA1 PT1 10p peacock grn. 7.00 6.00
RA2 PT2 15p dull blue 7.00 6.00

Obligatory on all mail Dec. 22-28, 1938. The money was used for the Aliabad Hospital. See note after France No. B76.

Begging Child

PT3 PT4

1949, May 28 **Typo.** ***Perf. 12***

RA3 PT3 35p red orange 2.00 2.00
RA4 PT4 125p ultramarine 3.00 2.00

United Nations Children's Day, May 28. Obligatory on all foreign mail on that date. Proceeds were used for child welfare.

Paghman Arch and U. N. Emblem

PT5

1949, Oct. 24

RA5 PT5 125p dk. bl. grn. 12.50 11.00

Issued to commemorate the fourth anniversary of the formation of the United Nations. Valid one day only. Issued in sheets of 9 (3x3).

Zahir Shah and Map of Afghanistan

PT6

1950, Mar. 30 **Typographed**

RA6 PT6 125p blue green 2.50 1.25

Issued to celebrate the return of Zahir Shah from a trip to Europe for his health. Valid for two weeks. The tax was used for public health purposes.

Hazara Youth

PT7

1950, May 28 **Typo.** ***Perf. 11½***

RA7 PT7 125p dark blue green 3.00 2.00

The tax was for Child Welfare. Obligatory and valid only on May 28, 1950, on foreign mail.

Ruins of Qalai Bist and Globe

PT8

1950, Oct. 24

RA8 PT8 1.25af ultramarine 6.50 5.00

Issued to commemorate the 5th anniversary of the formation of the United Nations. Proceeds went to Afghanistan's U.N. Projects Committee.

Zahir Shah and Medical Center

PT9

Typographed.

1950, Dec. 22 ***Perf. 11½***

Size: 38x25mm.

RA9 PT9 35p carmine 50 50

Size: 46x30mm.

RA10 PT9 1.25af black 6.00 3.00

The tax was for the national Graduate School of Medicine.

Koochi Girl with Lamb

PT10

Kohistani Boy and Sheep

PT11

1951, May 28

RA11 PT10 35p emerald 1.25 1.00
RA12 PT11 1.25af ultra. 1.25 1.00

The tax was for Child Welfare.

Distributing Gifts to Children

PT12

Qandahari Boys Dancing the 'Attan'

PT13

1952, May 28 **Lithographed**

RA13 PT12 35p chocolate 40 40
RA14 PT13 125p violet 1.10 1.10

The tax was for Child Welfare.

Soldier Receiving First Aid

PT14

1952, Oct.

RA15 PT14 10p light green 50 45

Stretcher-bearers and Wounded
PT15

Soldier Assisting Wounded
PT16

1953, Oct.

RA16 PT15 10p yel. green & orange red 60 50
RA17 PT16 10p violet brn. & orange red 60 50

Prince Mohammed Nadir
PT17

Map and Young Musicians
PT18

1953, May 28

RA18 PT17 35p orange yel. 25 20
RA19 " 125p chalky bl. 75 75

No. RA19 is inscribed in French "Children's Day." The tax was for child welfare.

1954, May 28 *Perf. 11* **Unwmkd.**

RA20 PT18 35p purple 40 20
RA21 " 125p ultramarine 1.50 1.50

No. RA21 is inscribed in French. The tax was for child welfare.

Red Crescent
PT19 PT20

1954, Oct. 17 *Perf. 11½*

RA22 PT19 20p blue & red 35 30

1955, Oct. 18 *Perf. 11*

RA23 PT20 20p dull green & carmine 30 25

Zahir Shah and Red Crescent
PT21

1956, Oct. 18

RA24 PT21 20p light green & rose carmine 35 25

Red Crescent Headquarters, Kabul
PT22

1957, Oct. 17

RA25 PT22 20p light ultra. & carmine 35 25

Map and Crescent
PT23

1958, Oct. *Perf. 11* **Unwmkd.**

RA26 PT23 25p yellow green & red 25 20

PT24

1959, Oct. 17 Lithographed *Perf. 11*

RA27 PT24 25p light violet & red 25 15

The tax on Nos. RA15–RA17, RA22–RA27 was for the Red Crescent Society. Use of these stamps was required for one week.

AGUERA, LA

(ä·gwā'rä)

LOCATION—An administrative district in southern Rio de Oro on the northwest coast of Africa.

GOVT.—Spanish possession.

AREA—Because of indefinite political boundaries, figures for area and population are not available.

See Spanish Sahara.

100 Centimos = 1 Peseta

Type of 1920 Issue of Rio de Oro Overprinted **LA AGÜERA**

1920 *Perf. 13* **Unwmkd.**

1 A8 1c blue green 3.00 3.00
2 " 2c olive brown 3.00 3.00
3 " 5c deep green 3.00 3.00
4 " 10c light red 3.00 3.00
5 " 15c yellow 3.00 3.00
6 " 20c lilac 3.00 3.00
7 " 25c deep blue 3.00 3.00
8 " 30c dark brown 3.00 3.00
9 " 40c pink 3.00 3.00
10 " 50c bright blue 6.00 6.00
11 " 1p red brown 10.00 10.00
12 " 4p dark violet 30.00 30.00
13 " 10p orange 60.00 60.00
Nos. 1-13 (13) 133.00 133.00

King Alfonso XIII
A2

1922 **Typographed**

14 A2 1c turquoise blue 1.35 1.35
15 " 2c dark green 1.35 1.35
16 " 5c blue green 1.35 1.35
17 " 10c red 1.35 1.35
18 " 15c red brown 1.35 1.35
19 " 20c yellow 1.35 1.35
20 " 25c deep blue 1.35 1.35
21 " 30c dark brown 1.35 1.35
22 " 40c rose red 1.50 1.50
23 " 50c red violet 4.50 4.50
24 " 1p rose 8.50 8.50
25 " 4p violet 20.00 20.00
26 " 10p orange 27.50 27.50
Nos. 14-26 (13) 72.80 72.80

For later issues see Spanish Sahara in Vol. IV.

ALAOUITES

(à·lä'wēt')

LOCATION—A division of Syria, in Western Asia.

GOVT.—Under French Mandate.

AREA—2,500 sq. mi.

POP.—278,000 (approx. 1930).

CAPITAL—Latakia.

This territory became an independent state in 1924, although still administered under the French Mandate. In 1930 it was renamed Latakia and Syrian stamps overprinted "Lattaquie" superseded the stamps of Alaouites. For these and subsequent issues see Latakia and Syria.

100 Centimes = 1 Piastre

Issued under French Mandate.

Stamps of France Surcharged:

ALAOUITES
0 P. 25
العلويين
١/٤ الغرش
a

ALAOUITES
2 PIASTRES
العلويين
غروش ٢
b

1925 *Perf. 14x13½* **Unwmkd.**

1 A16 (*a*) 10c on 2c violet brown 80 80
2 A22 (") 25c on 5c orange 50 50
3 A20 (") 75c on 15c gray green 1.00 1.00
4 A22 (") 1p on 20c red brown 80 80
5 " (") 1.25p on 25c blue 1.20 1.20
6 " (") 1.50p on 30c red 3.00 3.00
7 " (*b*) 2p on 35c violet 80 80
8 A18 (") 2p on 40c red & pale blue 1.20 1.20
9 " (") 2p on 45c green & blue 3.00 3.00
10 " (") 3p on 60c violet & ultra. 1.65 1.65
11 A20 (") 3p on 60c light violet 3.00 3.00
12 " (") 4p on 85c vermilion 30 30
13 A18 (") 5p on 1fr claret & olive grn. 1.65 1.65
14 " (") 10p on 2fr org. & pale blue 2.25 2.25
15 " (") 25p on 5fr blue & buff 3.00 3.00
Nos. 1-15 (15) 24.15 24.15

Same Surcharges on Stamps of France, 1923-24 (Pasteur)

16 A23 (*a*) 50c on 10c green 60 60
17 " (") 75c on 15c green 60 60
18 " (") 1.50p on 30c red 60 60
19 " (*b*) 2p on 45c red 70 70
20 " (") 2.50p on 50c blue 85 85
21 " (") 4p on 75c blue 90 90
Nos. 16-21 (6) 4.25 4.25

Stamps of Syria, 1925, Overprinted in Red, Black or Blue:

ALAOUITES
العلويين
c

ALAOUITES
العلويين
d

1925, Mar. 1 *Perf. 12½, 13½*

25 A3 (*c*) 10c dk. vio. (R) 20 20
a. Dbl. ovpt. 7.00 7.00
26 A4 (*d*) 25c olive black (R) 50 50
a. Inverted overprint 4.00 4.00
b. Blue ovpt. 7.00 7.00
27 " (") 50c yellow green 30 30
a. Inverted overprint 4.00 4.00
b. Blue ovpt. 7.00 7.00
c. Red ovpt. 8.50 8.50
28 " (") 75c brn. orange 30 30
a. Inverted overprint 4.00 4.00
29 A5 (*c*) 1p magenta 50 50
30 A4 (*d*) 1.25p deep green 40 40
a. Red ovpt. 6.00 6.00
31 " (") 1.50p rose red (Bl) 40 40
a. Inv. ovpt. 4.00 4.00
b. Black ovpt. 6.00 6.00
32 " (") 2p dk. brn. (R) 40 40
a. Blue ovpt. 1.50 1.50
33 " (") 2.50p peacock blue (R) 50 50
a. Black ovpt. 3.00 3.00
34 " (") 3p org. brown 40 40
a. Inverted overprint 4.00 4.00
b. Blue ovpt. 10.00 10.00
35 " (") 5p violet 40 40
a. Red ovpt. 10.00 10.00
36 " (") 10p violet brown 60 60
37 " (") 25p ultra. (R) 1.25 1.25
Nos. 25-37 (13) 6.15 6.15

Stamps of Syria, 1925, Surcharged in Black or Red:

4P.
غ ٤
ALAOUITES
العلويين
e

4P. 50 غ ٤ ١/٢
Alaouites
العلويين
f

1926

38 A4 (*e*) 3.50p on 75c brown orange 50 50
a. Surcharged on face and back 4.00 4.00
39 " (") 4p on 25c olive black (R) 50 50
40 " (") 6p on 2.50p peacock blue (R) 45 45
41 " (") 12p on 1.25p deep green 45 45
a. Inverted surch. 3.00 3.00
42 " (") 20p on 1.25p deep green 60 60
43 " (*f*) 4.50p on 75c brn. orange 1.00 1.00
a. Invtd. surch. 2.50
44 " (") 7.50p on 2.50p peacock blue 85 65
45 " (") 15p on 25p ultramarine 2.00 2.00
Nos. 38-45 (8) 6.35 6.15

Syria No. 199 Overprinted Type "c" in Red.

1928

46 A3 (*c*) 5c on 10c dk. vio. 20 20
a. Double surcharge 5.00

Syria Nos. 178 and 174
Surcharged in Red.

47 A4 (*f*) 2p on 1.25p deep green 3.50 3.50
48 " (") 4p on 25c olive black 2.50 2.00

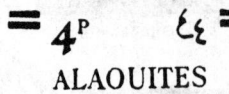

= 4P ٤ق =

ALAOUITES

العلويين

g

49 A4 (*g*) 4p on 25c olive black 17.50 15.00
 a. Double impression

AIR POST STAMPS.

Nos. 8, 10, 13 & 14 with
Additional Overprint in Black

Perf. 14x13½.

1925, Jan. 1 Unwmkd.

C1 A18 2p on 40c red & pale blue 2.50 2.50
 a. Overprint reversed 15.00
C2 " 3p on 60c violet & ultramarine 3.00 3.00
 a. Overprint reversed 22.50 22.50
C3 " 5p on 1fr claret & olive green 2.00 2.00
C4 " 10p on 2fr orange & pale blue 2.50 2.50

Nos. 32, 34, 35 & 36
With Additional Overprint in Green

AVION

1925, Mar. 1 *Perf. 13½*

C5 A4 2p dark brown 60 60
C6 " 3p orange brown 60 60
C7 " 5p violet 60 60
C8 " 10p violet brown 60 60

Nos. 32, 34, 35 & 36
With Additional Overprint in Red

k

1926, May 1

C9 A4 2p dark brown 90 90
C10 " 3p orange brown 90 90
C11 " 5p violet 90 90
C12 " 10p violet brown 90 90

No. C9 has the type "d" overprint in black.

Double or inverted overprints, types "d" or "k," are known on most of Nos. C9–C12. Price, $8–$10.

The red plane overprint, "k," was also applied to Nos. C5–C8. These are believed to have been essays, and were not regularly issued.

Nos. 27, 29, and 37
With Additional Overprint of Airplane
(k) in Red or Black.

1929, June-July

C17 A4 50c yellow green (R) 50 50
 a. Red overprint (k) double 7.00
 b. Red overprint (k) on face and back 7.00
 c. Pair with overprint (k) tête bêche 13.00
C18 A5 1p magenta (Bk) 1.50 1.50
C19 A4 25p ultramarine (R) 10.00 9.00
 a. Overprint (k) inverted 22.50 22.50

Nos. 47 and 45
With Additional Overprint of
Airplane (k) in Red.

1929-30

C20 A4 2p on 1.25p deep green ('30) 85 75
 a. Surcharge inverted 5.00
 b. Double surch. 4.00
C21 " 15p on 25p ultramarine (Bk+R) 13.50 9.00
 a. Overprint (k) inverted 20.00 20.00

POSTAGE DUE STAMPS.

Postage Due Stamps of France,
1893-1920, Surcharged in Black.

1925 *Perf. 14x13½.* Unwmkd.

J1 D2 (*a*) 50c on 10c chocolate 1.35 1.35
J2 " (") 1p on 20c olive green 1.35 1.35
J3 " (*b*) 2p on 30c red 1.35 1.35
J4 " (") 3p on 50c violet brown 1.35 1.35
J5 " (") 5p on 1fr red brown, *straw* 1.35 1.35
 Nos. J1–J5 (5) 6.75 6.75

Postage Due Stamps of Syria, 1925,
Overprinted in Black, Blue or Red.

1925 *Perf. 13½*

J6 D5 (*d*) 50c brown, *yellow* 45 45
J7 D6 (*c*) 1p vio., *rose* (Bl) 45 45
 a. Blk. overprint 6.00 6.00
 b. Double overprint (Bk+Bl) 12.00 12.00
J8 D5 (*d*) 2p *blue* 60 60
J9 " (") 3p *red orange* 1.00 1.00
J10 " (") 5p *blue green* 1.25 1.25
 Nos. J6–J10 (5) 3.75 3.75

The stamps of Alaouites were superseded in 1930 by those of Latakia.

ALBANIA

(ăl·bā′nĭ·ȧ)

LOCATION—Southeastern Europe.

GOVT.—Republic.

AREA—11,100 sq. mi.

POP.—2,550,000 (estimated 1976).

CAPITAL—Tirana.

After the outbreak of World War I, the country fell into a state of anarchy when the Prince and all members of the International Commission left Albania. Subsequently General Ferrero in command of Italian troops declared Albania an independent country. A constitution was adopted and a republican form of government was instituted which continued until 1928 when, by constitutional amendment, Albania was declared to be a monarchy. The President of the republic, Ahmed Zogu, became king of the new state. Many unlisted varieties of surcharges and lithographed labels are said to have done postal duty in Albania and Epirus during this unsettled period.

In March 1939, Italy invaded Albania. King Zog fled but did not abdicate. The King of Italy acquired the crown.

Germany occupied Albania from September, 1943, until late 1944 when it became an independent state. The People's Republic began in January, 1946.

40 Paras = 1 Piastre = 1 Grossion
100 Centimes = 1 Franc (1917)
100 Qintar = 1 Franc
100 Qintar (Qindarka) = 1 Lek (1947)

Stamps of Turkey
Handstamped

1913, June Unwmkd.
Perf. 12, 13½ and Compound.

Handstamped on Issue of 1908.

1 A19 2½pi violet brown 175.00 125.00

With Additional Overprint
in Carmine ب

2 A19 10pa blue green 175.00 175.00

The eagle handstamp was applied to other Turkish stamps of 1908: 25pi green (price $1,500) and 50pi red brown (price $3,000). The 5pa ocher, Albania No. 4, was surcharged "2 paras" (price $350). These three stamps were not placed on sale to the public, but were retained by officials.

Handstamped on Issue of 1909.

4 A21 5pa ochre 62.50 62.50
5 " 10pa blue green 47.50 42.50
6 " 20pa carmine rose 35.00 25.00
7 " 1pi ultramarine 50.00 50.00
8 " 2pi blue black 75.00 67.50
10 " 5pi dark violet 200.00 175.00
11 " 10pi dull red 625.00 600.00

With Additional Overprint
in Blue or Carmine ب

14 A21 20pa carmine rose (Bl) 95.00 95.00
15 " 1pi brt. blue (C) 275.00 275.00

Handstamped on Newspaper Stamp of 1911

17 A21 2pa olive green 60.00 55.00

Handstamped on
Postage Due Stamp of 1908.

18 A19 1pi *deep rose* 475.00 425.00

No. 18 was used for regular postage.

No. 6 Surcharged With New Value.

19 A21 10pa on 20pa carmine rose 180.00 180.00

The overprint on Nos. 1 to 19 was handstamped and, as usual, is found inverted, double, etc.

Nos. 6, 7 and 8 exist with the handstamp in red, blue or violet, but these varieties are not known to have been regularly issued.

Excellent counterfeits exist of Nos. 1 to 19.

A1

1913, July *Imperf.*

Handstamped on White Laid Paper
Without Eagle or Value.

20 A1 (1pi) black 125.00 110.00
 Cut to shape 60.00 60.00
 a. Sewing machine perf. 175.00 175.00

1913, Aug. With Eagle.
Value Typewritten in Violet

21 A1 10pa violet 3.00 1.85
22 " 20pa red & black 3.50 2.25
23 " 1gr black 3.50 2.25
24 " 2gr blue & violet 4.00 3.00
25 " 5gr violet & blue 6.00 4.00
26 " 10gr blue 6.00 4.25
 Nos. 21-26 (6) 26.00 17.60

Nos. 21-26 exist with the eagle inverted or omitted and with numerous errors in the figures of value and the spelling of the word "grosh".

A2

Skanderbeg
(George Castriota)
A3

1913, Nov. *Perf. 11½*

Handstamped on White Laid Paper
Eagle and Value in Black.

27 A2 10pa green 1.25 1.00
 a. Imperf. 5.00
 b. Eagle and value in green 15.00
 c. 10pa red (error) 10.00 10.00
 d. 10pa violet (error) 10.00 10.00
29 " 20pa red 1.50 1.00
 a. Imperf. 5.00
 b. 20pa green (error) 10.00 10.00
30 " 30pa violet 1.50 1.00
 a. 30p ultramarine (error) 10.00 10.00
 b. 30pa red (error) 10.00 10.00
31 " 1gr ultramarine 2.00 1.50
 a. 1gr green (error) 12.50 12.50
 b. 1gr black (error) 12.50 12.50
 c. 1gr violet (error) 10.00 10.00
33 " 2gr black 3.00 1.85
 a. 2gr violet (error) 15.00 15.00
 b. 2gr blue (error) 15.00 15.00
 Nos. 27–33 (5) 9.25 6.35

The stamps of this issue are known with eagle or value inverted or omitted.

The stamps were issued in commemoration of the first anniversary of Albanian independence.

1913, Dec. Typographed *Perf. 14*

35 A3 2q orange brown & buff 40 40
36 " 5q green & blue grn. 40 40
37 " 10q rose red 35 35
38 " 25q dark blue 40 40
39 " 50q violet & red 80 80
40 " 1fr deep brown 2.75 2.75
 Nos. 35–40 (6) 5.10 5.10

Nos. 35–40
Handstamped in
Black or Violet

7.Mars
1467.RROFTË MBRETI.1914

1914, Mar. 7

41 A3 2q org. brn. & buff 7.50 6.00
42 " 5q grn. & bl. grn. (V) 7.50 6.00
43 " 10q rose red 7.50 6.00
44 " 25q dark blue (V) 7.50 6.00
45 " 50q violet & red 7.50 6.00
46 " 1fr deep brown 7.50 6.00
 Nos. 41-46 (6) 45.00 36.00

Issued to celebrate the arrival of Prince Wilhelm zu Wied on Mar. 7, 1914.

Nos. 35–40 Surcharged in Black:

5 • PARA • (*a*)   1 GROSH (*b*)

1914, Apr. 2

47 A3 (*a*) 5pa on 2q orange brown & buff 60 60
 a. Inverted surcharge 2.00 2.00
48 " (") 10pa on 5q grn. & blue green 60 60
 a. Inverted surcharge 2.00 2.00
49 " (") 20pa on 10q rose red 90 70
 a. Inverted surcharge 2.00 2.00
50 " (*b*) 1gr on 25q blue 90 90
 a. Inverted surcharge 2.50 2.50
51 " (") 2gr on 50q violet & red 1.25 1.10
 a. Inverted surcharge 3.50 3.50
52 " (") 5gr on 1fr deep brown 4.00 2.75
 b. Invtd. surch. 7.50 7.50
 Nos. 47-52 (6) 8.25 6.65

Korce (Korytsa) Issues

A4

1914 Handstamped *Imperf.*

No.	Type	Description	Unused	Used
52A	A4	10pa violet & red	60.00	50.00
		c. 10pa black & red	60.00	50.00
53	"	25pa violet & red	60.00	50.00
		a. 25pa black & red	100.00	95.00

Nos. 52A–53a originally were handstamped directly on the cover, so the paper varies. Later they were also produced in sheets; these are rarely found. Nos. 52A–53a were issued by Albanian military authorities.

A5

A6

1917 Typo. & Litho. *Perf. 11½*

No.	Type	Description	Unused	Used
54	A5	1c dark brown & green	6.00	4.00
55	"	2c red & green	6.00	4.00
56	"	3c gray green & green	6.00	4.00
57	"	5c green & black	4.75	2.50
58	"	10c rose red & black	4.75	2.50
59	"	25c blue & black	4.75	2.50
60	"	50c violet & black	4.75	3.00
61	"	1fr brown & black	6.00	3.00
		Nos. 54–61 (8)	43.00	25.50

1917-18

No.	Type	Description	Unused	Used
62	A6	1c dark brown & green	1.10	1.00
63	"	2c red brown & green	1.10	1.00
		a. "CTM" for "CTS"	5.00	5.00
64	"	3c black & green	1.10	1.00
		a. "CTM" for "CTS"	5.00	5.00
65	"	5c green & black	1.60	1.60
66	"	10c dull red & black	1.60	1.60
67	"	50c violet & black	3.00	2.50
68	"	1fr red brown & black	9.00	4.00
		Nos. 62–68 (7)	18.50	12.70

Counterfeits exist of Nos. 54–68, 80–81.

No. 65 Surcharged in Red

QARKU
I
KORÇËS
25 CTS

1918

No.	Type	Description	Unused	Used
80	A6	25c on 5c green & black	25.00	20.00

A7

1918

No.	Type	Description	Unused	Used
81	A7	25c blue & black	11.00	10.00

General Issue

A8

A9

Handstamped in Rose or Blue

XV I MCMXIX

1919 *Perf. 12½*

No.	Type	Description	Unused	Used
84	A8	(2)q on 2h brown	2.50	2.25
85	"	5q on 16h green	2.50	2.25
86	"	10q on 8h rose (Bl)	2.50	2.25
87	"	25q on 64h blue	2.50	2.25
88	A9	25q on 64h blue	125.00	100.00
89	A8	50q on 32h violet	2.50	2.25
90	"	1fr on 1.28k org., *bl.*	2.75	2.25
		Nos. 84–90 (7)	140.25	113.50

Handstamped in Rose or Blue

1919, Jan. 16

No.	Type	Description	Unused	Used
91	A8	(2)q on 2h brown	4.25	4.25
92	"	5q on 16h green	4.25	4.25
93	"	10q on 8h rose (Bl)	4.25	4.25
94	"	25q on 64h blue	17.50	17.50
95	A9	25q on 64h blue	15.00	15.00
96	A8	50q on 32h violet	5.00	5.00
97	"	1fr on 1.28k org., *bl.*	5.00	5.00
		Nos. 91–97 (7)	55.25	55.25

Handstamped in Violet

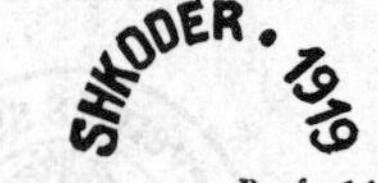

1919

No.	Type	Description	Unused	Used
98	A8	(2)q on 2h brown	6.00	6.00
99	"	5q on 16h green	6.00	6.00
100	"	10q on 8h rose	6.00	6.00
101	"	25q on 64h blue	6.00	6.00
102	A9	25q on 64h blue	11.00	11.00
103	A8	50q on 32h violet	6.00	6.00
104	"	1fr on 1.28k org., *bl.*	6.00	6.00
		Nos. 98–104 (7)	47.00	47.00

No. 50 Overprinted in Violet

SHKODER. 1919

1919 *Perf. 14*

No.	Type	Description	Unused	Used
105	A3	1gr on 25q blue	1.25	1.50

A10

A11

1919, June 5 *Perf. 11½, 12½*

No.	Type	Description	Unused	Used
106	A10	10q on 2h brown	1.75	1.75
107	A11	15q on 8h rose	1.75	1.75
108	"	20q on 16h green	1.75	1.75
109	A10	25q on 64h blue	1.75	1.75
110	A11	50q on 32h violet	1.75	1.75
111	"	1fr on 96h orange	1.75	1.75
112	A10	2fr on 1.60k violet, *buff*	4.25	4.25
		Nos. 106–112 (7)	14.75	14.75

Nos. 106–108, 110 exist with inverted surcharge. Price $10 each.

A12

A13

Black or Violet Surcharge

1919

No.	Type	Description	Unused	Used
113	A12	10q on 8h carmine	2.00	2.00
114	"	15q on 8h car. (V)	2.00	2.00
115	A13	20q on 16h green	2.00	2.00
116	"	25q on 32h violet	2.00	2.00
117	"	50q on 64h blue	5.00	5.00
118	"	1fr on 96h orange	2.50	2.50
119	A12	2fr on 1.60k violet, *buff*	2.50	2.50
		Nos. 113–119 (7)	18.00	18.00

A14

A15

Overprinted in Blue or Black. Without New Value.

1920 *Perf. 12½.*

No.	Type	Description	Unused	Used
120	A14	1q gray (Bl)	20.00	22.50
121	"	10q rose (Bk)	3.50	4.00
		a. Double overprint	17.50	17.50
122	"	20q brown (Bl)	13.00	16.00
123	"	25q blue (Bk)	110.00	*175.00*
124	"	50q brn. violet (Bk)	13.00	16.00
		Nos. 120–124 (5)	159.50	*233.50*

Counterfeit overprints exist.

Surcharged with New Value.

No.	Type	Description	Unused	Used
125	A14	2q on 10q rose (R)	3.50	4.00
126	"	5q on 10q rose (G)	3.50	4.00
127	"	25q on 10q rose (Bl)	3.50	4.00
128	"	50q on 10q rose (Br)	3.50	4.00

Stamps of type A14 (Portrait of the Prince zu Wied) were not placed in use without overprint or surcharge.

Post Horn Overprinted in Black.

1920 *Perf. 14x13*

No.	Type	Description	Unused	Used
129	A15	2q orange	1.30	1.30
130	"	5q deep green	2.00	2.00
131	"	10q red	4.00	4.00
132	"	25q light blue	4.25	4.25
133	"	50q gray green	1.40	1.40
134	"	1fr claret	1.40	1.40
		Nos. 129–134 (6)	14.35	14.35

Type A15 was never placed in use without post horn or "Besa" overprint.

Stamps of Type A15 (No Post Horn) Overprinted

BESA

1921

No.	Type	Description	Unused	Used
135	A15	2q orange	1.00	1.00
136	"	5q deep green	1.00	1.00
137	"	10q red	2.00	2.00
138	"	25q light blue	2.50	2.50
139	"	50q gray green	1.40	1.40
140	"	1fr claret	1.40	1.40
		Nos. 135–140 (6)	9.30	9.30

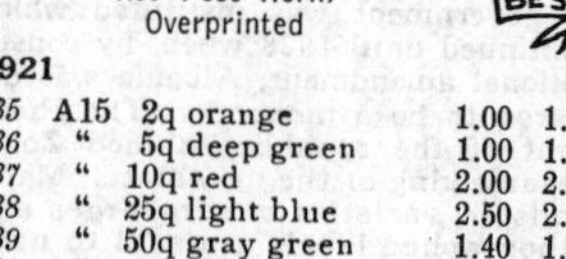

Stamps of these types, and with "TAKSE" overprint, were unauthorized and never placed in use.

Gjinokaster
A18

Korcha
A19

Designs: 5q, Kanina. 10q, Berati. 25q, Bridge at Vezirit. 50q, Rozafat. 2fr, Dursit.

1922 Typographed. *Perf. 12½.*

No.	Type	Description	Unused	Used
147	A18	2q orange	45	35
148	"	5q yellow green	25	17
149	"	10q carmine	25	17
150	"	25q dark blue	25	17
151	"	50q dark green	25	18
152	A19	1fr dark violet	45	45
153	"	2fr olive green	1.00	80
		Nos. 147–153 (7)	2.90	2.29

No. 135 Surcharged

Q 1

1922 *Perf. 14x13*

No.	Type	Description	Unused	Used
154	A15	1q on 2q orange	60	60

Stamps of Type A15 (No Post Horn) Overprinted

1922

No.	Type	Description	Unused	Used
156	A15	5q deep green	1.25	1.25
157	"	10q red	1.25	1.25

Nos. 147–151 Overprinted (top line in Black; diamond in Violet)

Mbledhje Kushtetuese
TIRANE
KALLNUER
1924

1924, Jan *Perf. 12½*

No.	Type	Description	Unused	Used
158	A18	2q red orange	1.50	1.50
159	"	5q yellow green	1.50	1.50
160	"	10q carmine	1.50	1.50
161	"	25q dark blue	1.50	1.50
162	"	50q dark green	1.50	1.50
		Nos. 158–162 (5)	7.50	7.50

The words "Mbledhje Kushtetuese" are in taller letters on the 25q than on the other values. This issue was to commemorate the opening of the Constituent Assembly.

No. 147 Surcharged

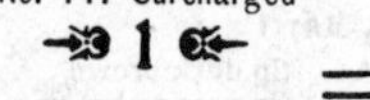

1924

No.	Type	Description	Unused	Used
163	A18	1q on 2q red orange	60	60

Nos. 163, 147–152 Overprinted

Triumf' i legalitetit
24 Dhetuer 1924

1924

No.	Type	Description	Unused	Used
164	A18	1q on 2q orange	75	75
165	"	2q orange	75	75
166	"	5q yellow green	75	75
167	"	10q carmine	75	75
168	"	25q dark blue	75	75
169	"	50q dark green	75	75
170	A19	1fr dark violet	75	75
		Nos. 164–170 (7)	5.25	5.25

Issued to celebrate the return of the Government to the Capital after a revolution.

Nos. 163, 147–152 Overprinted

Republika Shqiptare

21 Kallnduer 1925

1925

171 A18 1q on 2q orange 75 75
172 " 2q orange 75 75
173 " 5q yellow green 75 75
174 " 10q carmine 75 75
175 " 25q dark blue 75 75
176 " 50q dark green 75 75
177 A19 1fr dark violet 75 75
Nos. 171–177 (7) 5.25 5.25

Issued in honor of the proclamation of the Republic, Jan. 21, 1925. The date "1921" instead of "1925" occurs once in each sheet of 50.

Nos. 163, 147–153 Overprinted

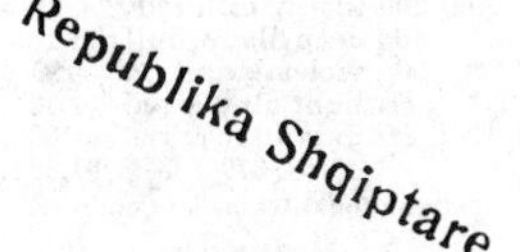

1925

178 A18 1q on 2q orange 30 30
a. Inverted overprint 2.50 2.50
179 " 2q orange 30 30
180 " 5q yellow green 30 30
181 " 10q carmine 30 30
182 " 25q dark blue 30 30
183 " 50q dark green 30 30
184 A19 1fr dark violet 45 45
185 " 2fr olive green 45 45
Nos. 178–185 (8) 2.70 2.70

President Ahmed Zogu
A25 A26

1925 ***Perf. 13½, 13½x13***

186 A25 1q orange 7 7
187 " 2q red brown 7 7
188 " 5q green 7 7
189 " 10q rose red 7 7
190 " 15q gray brown 35 35
191 " 25q dark blue 5 5
192 " 50q blue green 35 35
193 A26 1fr red & ultramarine 70 70
194 " 2fr green & orange 70 70
195 " 3fr brown & violet 85 85
196 " 5fr violet & black 1.85 1.85
Nos. 186–196 (11) 5.13 5.13

No. 193 in ultramarine and brown, and No. 194 in gray and brown were not regularly issued. Price (both), $6.

Nos. 186–196 Overprinted in Various Colors

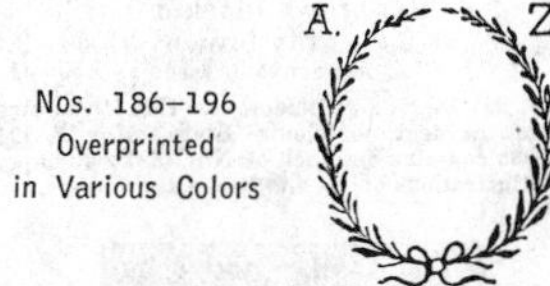

1927 ***Perf. 11½, 13½, 13½x13***

197 A25 1q orange (V) 25 20
198 " 2q red brown (G) 12 10
199 " 5q green (R) 60 10
200 " 10q rose red (Bl) 7 5
201 " 15q gray brown (G) 3.00 2.25
202 " 25q dark blue (R) 10 6
203 " 50q blue green (Bl) 10 8
204 A26 1fr red & ultra. (Bk) 9 8
205 " 2fr grn. & org. (Bk) 12 12
206 " 3fr brn. & vio. (Bk) 25 25
207 " 5fr violet & black (Bk) 50 50
Nos. 197–207 (11) 5.20 3.79

The letters "A. Z." are the initials of the President's name, Ahmed Zogu.

Nos. 200, 202 Surcharged **= 5 =** in Black or Red.

1928

208 A25 1q on 10q rose red 20 15
a. Inverted surcharge 1.25 1.25
b. Double surcharge, one inverted
209 " 5q on 25q dark blue (R) 20 15
a. Inverted surcharge 1.25 1.25
b. Double surcharge, one inverted

King Zog I
A27 A28

Black Overprint.

1928 ***Perf. 14x13½.***

210 A27 1q orange brown 1.75 1.75
211 " 2q slate 1.75 1.75
212 " 5q blue green 1.85 1.85
213 " 10q rose red 1.75 1.75
214 " 15q bistre 5.00 5.00
215 " 25q deep blue 1.25 1.25
216 " 50q lilac rose 1.75 1.75

Red Overprint.

Perf. 13½x14.

217 A28 1fr blue & slate 1.25 1.25
Nos. 210–217 (8) 16.35 16.35

A29 A30

Black or Red Overprint.

1928 ***Perf. 14x13½.***

218 A29 1q orange brown 4.50 4.50
219 " 2q slate (R) 4.00 4.00
220 " 5q blue green 3.50 3.50
221 " 10q rose red 1.75 1.75
222 " 15q bistre 2.25 2.25
223 " 25q deep blue (R) 2.25 2.25
224 " 50q lilac rose 3.50 3.50

Perf. 13½x14.

225 A30 1fr blue & slate (R) 3.50 3.50
226 " 2fr green & slate (R) 4.00 4.00
Nos. 218–226 (9) 29.25 29.25

Issued in commemoration of the proclamation of Ahmed Zogu as King of Albania.

A31 A32

Black Overprint.

1928 ***Perf. 14x13½.***

227 A31 1q orange brown 30 20
228 " 2q slate 15 10
229 " 5q blue green 75 15
230 " 10q rose red 15 10
231 A31 15q bistre 5.00 3.00
232 " 25q deep blue 15 10
233 " 50q lilac rose 15 10

Perf. 13½x14.

234 A32 1fr blue & slate 30 60
235 " 2fr green & slate 40 70
236 " 3fr dark red & olive bistre 60 80
237 " 5fr dull violet & gray 1.00 2.00
Nos. 227–237 (11) 8.95 7.85

The overprint reads "Kingdom of Albania".

Mbr. Shqiptare

Nos. 203, 202, 200 Surcharged in Black

■ 5 ■

1929 ***Perf. 13½x13, 11½***

238 A25 1(q) on 50q bl. green 20 20
239 " 5(q) on 25q dark blue 20 20
240 " 15(q) on 10q rose red 50 25

RROFT-MBRETI

Nos. 186–189, 191–194 Overprinted in Black or Red

8X1929.

1929 ***Perf. 11½, 13½.***

241 A25 1q orange 1.80 1.80
242 " 2q red brown 1.80 1.80
243 " 5q green 1.80 1.80
244 " 10q rose red 1.80 1.80
245 " 25q dark blue 1.80 1.80
246 " 50q blue green (R) 1.80 1.80
247 A26 1fr red & ultramarine 3.00 3.00
248 " 2fr green & orange 3.75 3.75
Nos. 241–248 (8) 17.55 17.55

Issued to commemorate the 34th birthday of King Zog. The overprint reads "Long live the King."

Lake Butrinto
A33

King Zog I
A34

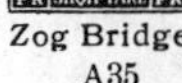

Zog Bridge
A35

Ruin at Zog Manor
A36

Wmk. 220

Wmkd.

Double Headed Eagle. (220)

1930, Sept. 1 Photo. *Perf. 14, 14½*

250 A33 1q slate 15 8
251 " 2q orange red 15 8
252 A34 5q yellow green 15 8
253 " 10q carmine 20 8
254 " 15q dark brown 24 16
255 " 25q dark ultramarine 24 20
256 A33 50q slate green 40 24
257 A35 1fr violet 95 55
258 " 2fr indigo 95 65
259 A36 3fr gray green 2.25 1.00
260 " 5fr orange brown 3.25 2.10
Nos. 250–260 (11) 8.93 5.22

2nd anniversary of accession of King Zog I.

Nos. 250–259 Overprinted in Black

1 1
9 9
2 3
4-24Dhetuer-4

1934, Dec. 24

261 A33 1q slate 1.75 1.75
262 " 2q orange red 1.75 1.75
263 A34 5q yellow green 1.75 1.75
264 " 10q carmine 1.75 1.75
265 " 15q dark brown 1.75 1.75
266 " 25q dark ultra. 1.75 1.75
267 A33 50q slate green 1.75 1.75
268 A35 1fr violet 4.50 4.50
269 " 2fr indigo 9.00 9.00
270 A36 3fr gray green 11.00 12.00
Nos. 261–270 (10) 36.75 37.75

Tenth anniversary of the Constitution.

Allegory of Death of Skanderbeg
A37

Albanian Eagle in Turkish Shackles
A38

Designs: 5q, 25q, 40q, 2fr, Eagle with wings spread.

1937 ***Perf. 14*** **Unwmkd.**

271 A37 1q brown violet 20 20
272 A38 2q brown 20 20
273 " 5q light green 35 35
274 A37 10q olive brown 45 45
275 A38 15q rose red 55 55
276 " 25q blue 1.00 1.00
277 A37 50q deep green 1.65 1.65
278 A38 1fr violet 3.00 3.00
279 " 2fr orange brown 4.75 4.75
Nos. 271–279 (9) 12.15 12.15

Souvenir Sheet.

280 Sheet of three 9.00 12.00
a. 20q red violet (A37) 2.50 3.00
b. 30q olive brn. (A38) 2.50 3.00
c. 40q red (A38) 2.50 3.00

Nos. 271–280 commemorate the 25th anniversary of independence from Turkey, proclaimed Nov. 26, 1912. No. 280 measures 138x140mm.

Queen Geraldine and King Zog
A40

1938 ***Perf. 14***

281 A40 1q slate violet 18 18
282 " 2q red brown 18 18
283 " 5q green 18 18
284 " 10q olive brown 27 33
285 " 15q rose red 40 60
286 " 25q blue 75 1.00
287 " 50q Prussian green 1.50 2.25
288 " 1fr purple 2.75 3.25
Nos. 281–288 (8) 6.21 7.97

Souvenir Sheet.

289 A40 Sheet of four 7.50 7.50
a. 20q dark red violet 1.25 1.25
b. 30q brn. olive 1.25 1.25

Nos. 281–289 were issued to commemorate the wedding of King Zog and Countess Geraldine Apponyi, April 27, 1938. Souvenir sheet measures 110½x139mm.

Queen Geraldine
A42

National Emblems
A43

King Zog I
A44

1938

290 A42 1q deep red violet 30 40
291 A43 2q red orange 30 40
292 A42 5q deep green 40 40
293 A44 10q red brown 60 65
294 A42 15q deep rose 80 80
295 A44 25q deep blue 85 1.00
296 A43 50q gray black 1.65 2.00
297 A44 1fr slate green 4.00 4.25
Nos. 290–297 (8) 8.90 9.90

Souvenir Sheet.

298 Sheet of three 7.50 7.50
b. 20q Prussian grn. (A43) 1.75 1.75
c. 30q deep violet (A44) 1.75 1.75

Nos. 290–298 were issued to commemorate the 10th anniversary of royal rule. They were on sale for three days (Aug. 30–31, Sept. 1) only, during which their use was required on all mail.

No. 298 has marginal inscriptions in Prussian green. Size: 110x65mm. The 15q deep rose (type A42) is identical with No. 294.

Issued under Italian Dominion.

Nos. 250–260 Overprinted in Black **Mbledhja Kushtetuëse 12-IV-1939 XVII**

1939 *Perf. 14* **Wmk 220**

299 A33 1q slate 7 6
300 " 2q orange red 14 7
301 A34 5q yellow green 14 12
302 " 10q carmine 12 6
303 " 15q dark brown 12 12
304 " 25q dark ultramarine 24 22
305 A33 50q slate green 35 30
306 A35 1fr violet 55 60
307 " 2fr indigo 70 70
308 A36 3fr gray green 1.75 1.75
309 " 5fr orange brown 2.75 3.00
Nos. 299–309 (11) 6.93 7.00

Issued in commemoration of the resolution adopted by the National Assembly, April 12, 1939, offering the Albanian Crown to Italy.

Native Costumes
A46 A47 A48

King Victor Emmanuel III A49 A50 — Native Costume A51

Monastery
A52

Designs: 2fr, Bridge at Vezirit. 3fr, Ancient Columns. 5fr, Amphitheater.

Photogravure

1939 *Perf. 14* **Unwmkd.**

310 A46 1q blue gray 8 6
311 A47 2q olive green 6 6
312 A48 3q golden brown 6 6
313 A49 5q green 15 3
314 A50 10q brown 15 5
315 " 15q crimson 20 6
316 " 25q sapphire 30 10
317 " 30q bright violet 40 10
318 A51 50q dull purple 50 10
319 A49 65q red brown 85 75
320 A52 1fr myrtle green 85 85
321 " 2fr brown lake 1.85 1.35
322 " 3fr brown black 4.00 4.00
323 " 5fr gray violet 4.75 4.75
Nos. 310–323 (14) 14.20 12.32

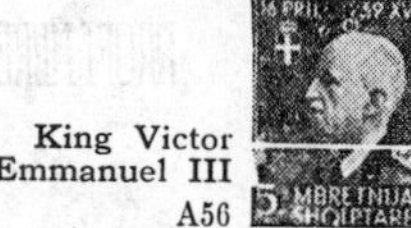

King Victor Emmanuel III
A56

1942 **Photogravure**

324 A56 5q green 9 9
325 " 10q brown 12 12
326 " 15q rose red 12 12
327 " 25q blue 20 20
328 " 65q red brown 30 30
329 " 1fr myrtle green 60 60
330 " 2fr gray violet 1.50 1.50
Nos. 324–330 (7) 2.93 2.93

Issued to commemorate the third anniversary of the conquest of Albania by Italy.

No. 311 Surcharged in Black **1 QIND**

331 A47 1q on 2q olive green 25 25

Issued under German Administration

Stamps of 1939 Overprinted in Carmine or Brown **14 Shtator 1943**

1943

332 A47 2q olive green 75 1.50
333 A48 3q golden brown 75 1.50
334 A49 5q green 75 1.50
335 A50 10q brown 75 1.50
336 " 15q crimson (Br) 75 1.50
337 " 25q sapphire 75 1.50
338 " 30q bright violet 75 1.50
339 A49 65q red brown 1.00 2.50
340 A52 1fr myrtle green 4.00 8.50
341 " 2fr brown lake 8.25 *22.50*
342 " 3fr brown black 27.50 *55.00*

Surcharged with New Values.

343 A48 1q on 3q golden brown 75 1.50
344 A49 50q on 65q red brn. 1.00 2.50
Nos. 332–344 (13) 47.75 *103.00*

Proclamation of Albanian independence.

The overprint "14 Shtator 1943" on Nos. 324 to 328 is private and fraudulent.

Independent State

Nos. 312 to 317 and 319 to 321 Surcharged with New Value and Bars in Black or Carmine, and **QEVERIJA DEMOKRAT. E SHQIPERISE 22-X-1944**

1945

345 A48 30q on 3q golden brown 1.25 75
346 A49 40q on 5q green 1.25 75
347 A50 50q on 10q brown 1.25 75
348 A50 60q on 15q crimson 1.25 75
349 " 80q on 25q sapphire (C) 1.25 75
350 " 1fr on 30q bright violet (C) 1.25 75
351 A49 2fr on 65q red brn. 1.25 75
352 A52 3fr on 1fr myrtle green 1.25 75
353 " 5fr on 2fr brown lake 1.25 75
Nos. 345–353 (9) 11.25 6.75

"DEMOKRATIKE" is not abbreviated on Nos. 352 and 353.

Nos. 250, 251, 256 and 258 Surcharged in Black or Carmine, and **1943 U.N.Ç.L.SHQ. 1945 10 FRRIK. FR.SHQ. 5**

1945 **Wmk. 220**

354 A33 30q on 1q slate 22 22
355 " 60q on 1q " 22 25
356 " 80q on 1q " 30 35
357 " 1fr on 1q " 45 45
358 " 2fr on 2q orange red 60 65
359 " 3fr on 50q slate green 1.20 1.60
360 A35 5fr on 2fr indigo 1.75 2.25
Nos. 354–360 (7) 4.74 5.77

Albanian National Army of Liberation, second anniversary.

The surcharge on No. 360 is condensed to fit the size of the stamp.

Country House, Labinot
A57

Designs: 40q, 60q, Bridge at Berat. 1fr, 3fr, Permet.

Typographed.

1945, Nov. 28 *Perf. 11* **Unwmkd.**

361 A57 20q bluish green 10 20
362 " 30q deep orange 20 30
363 " 40q brown 20 30
364 " 60q red violet 30 60
365 " 1fr rose red 60 80
366 " 3fr dark blue 3.00 3.25
Nos. 361–366 (6) 4.40 5.45

Counterfeits exist. See note after No. B33.

Nos. 361 to 366 Overprinted in Black **ASAMBLEJA KUSHTETUESE 10 KALLHUER 1946**

1946

367 A57 20q bluish green 18 18
368 " 30q deep orange 20 20
369 " 40q brown 30 30
370 " 60q red violet 40 40
371 " 1fr rose red 1.50 1.50
372 " 3fr dark blue 2.00 2.00
Nos. 367–372 (6) 4.58 4.58

Issued to commemorate the convocation of the Constitutional Assembly, January 10, 1946.

People's Republic

Nos. 361 to 366 Overprinted in Black **REPUBLIKA POPULLORE E SHQIPERISE**

1946

373 A57 20q bluish green 18 25
374 " 30q deep orange 25 27
375 " 40q brown 30 40
376 " 60q red violet 85 1.10
377 " 1fr rose red 90 1.25
378 " 3fr dark blue 2.25 2.40
Nos. 373–378 (6) 4.73 5.67

Issued to commemorate the proclamation of the Albanian People's Republic.

Globe, Dove and Olive Branch
A60

Typographed

1946, Mar. 8 *Perf. 11½, Imperf.*

Denomination in Black.

379 A60 20q lilac & dull red 10 10
380 " 40q deep lilac & dull red 15 15
381 " 50q violet & dull red 25 25
382 " 1fr light blue & red 30 30
383 " 2fr dark blue & red 65 65
Nos. 379–383 (5) 1.45 1.45

International Women's Congress.

Athletes with Shot and Indian Club
A61

Perf. 11½

1946, Oct. 6 **Litho.** **Unwmkd.**

384 A61 1q greenish black 3.50 2.25
385 " 2q green 3.50 2.25
386 " 5q brown 3.50 2.25
387 " 10q crimson 3.50 2.25
388 " 20q ultramarine 3.50 2.25
389 " 40q rose violet 3.50 2.25
390 " 1fr deep orange 7.00 5.50
Nos. 384–390 (7) 28.00 19.00

Balkan Games, Tirana, Oct. 6–13.

Qemal Stafa
A62

1947, May 5 *Perf. 12½x11½*

391 A62 20q brn. & yel. brn. 1.20 1.20
392 " 28q dark blue & blue 1.60 1.60
393 " 40q brown black & gray brown 2.50 2.50
a. Souvenir sheet 5.50 5.50

Nos. 391 to 393a commemorate the 5th anniversary of the death of Qemal Stafa, May 5, 1942. No. 393a contains one each of Nos. 391-393 imperf. with illustrations above and below the stamps.

Young Railway Laborers
A64

1947, May 16 *Perf. 11½*

395 A64 1q brown black & gray brown 80 22
396 " 4q dark green & green 80 22
397 " 10q black brown & bistre brown 90 30
398 " 15q dark red & red 90 30

399	A64	20q indigo & bl. gray	1.30	45
400	"	28q dark blue & blue	2.00	60
401	"	40q brown violet & rose violet	3.50	90
402	"	68q dark brown & orange brown	6.00	2.00
		Nos. 395-402 (8)	16.20	4.99

Issued to publicize the construction of the Durrës Elbasan Railway by Albanian youths.

Citizens Led by Hasim Zeneli

A65

Enver Hoxha and Vasil Shanto

A66

Vojo Kushi

A68

Inauguration of Vithkuq Brigade

A67

1947, July 10 Lithographed

403	A65	16q brown orange & red brown	1.00	70
404	A66	20q orange brown & dark brown	1.00	70
405	A67	28q blue & dark blue	1.25	1.10
406	A68	40q lilac & dk. brn.	2.00	1.75

Issued to commemorate the 4th anniversary of the formation of Albania's army, July 10, 1943.

Conference Building Ruins, Peza

A69

Disabled Soldiers

A70

1947, Sept. 16

407	A69	2 l red violet	2.25	50
408	"	2.50 l deep blue	2.25	70

Issued to commemorate the 5th anniversary of the Peza Conference, September 16, 1942.

1947, Nov. 17 ***Perf. 12½x11½***

408A	A70	1 l red	2.00	1.40

Issued to publicize the Disabled War Veterans Congress, November 14-20, 1947.

A71

A73

Designs: 2 l, Banquet. 2.50 l, Peasants rejoicing.

Perf. 11½x12½, 12½x11½

1947, Nov. 17 **Unwmkd.**

409	A71	1.50 l dull violet	2.00	1.25
410	"	2 l brown	2.00	1.25
411	"	2.50 l blue	2.00	1.25
412	A73	3 l rose red	2.00	1.25

Issued to commemorate the 1st anniversary of the agrarian reform law of November 17, 1946.

Burning Farm Buildings

A74

Designs: 2.50 l, Trench scene. 5 l, Firing line. 8 l, Winter advance. 12 l, Infantry column.

1947, Nov. 29 ***Perf. 11½x12½***

Inscribed: "29-XI-1944-1947 Pervjetori I IIIte Iclirimit."

413	A74	1.50 l red	75	75
414	"	2.50 l rose brown	1.00	1.00
415	"	5 l blue	1.50	1.50
416	"	8 l purple	3.00	3.00
417	"	12 l brown	6.00	6.00
		Nos. 413-417 (5)	12.25	12.25

Issued to commemorate the third anniversary of Albania's liberation.

Nos. 373 to 378 Surcharged with New Value and Bars in Black.

1948, Feb. 22 ***Perf. 11***

418	A57	50q on 30q deep org.	22	22
419	"	1 l on 20q bluish green	35	35
420	"	2.50 l on 60q red violet	60	60
421	"	3 l on 1fr rose red	80	80
422	"	5 l on 3fr dark blue	2.00	2.00
423	"	12 l on 40q brown	3.50	3.50
		Nos. 418-423 (6)	7.47	7.47

The two bars consist of four type squares each set close together.

Map, Train and Construction Workers

A75

1948, June 1 **Litho.** ***Perf. 11½***

424	A75	50q dark carmine rose	17	10
425	"	1 l light green & black	23	10
426	"	1.50 l deep rose	30	12
427	"	2.50 l orange brown & dark brown	35	20
428	"	5 l dull blue	70	25
429	A75	8 l salmon & dark brown	1.20	50
430	"	12 l red violet & dark violet	1.40	75
431	"	20 l olive gray	2.75	1.40
		Nos. 424-431 (8)	7.10	3.42

Issued to publicize the construction of the Durrës-Tirana Railway.

Marching Soldiers

A76

Design: 8 l, Battle scene.

1948, July 10

432	A76	2.50 l yellow brown	50	50
433	"	5 l dark blue	90	90
434	"	8 l violet gray	1.20	1.20

Issued to commemorate the 5th anniversary of the formation of Albania's army.

Bricklayer, Flag, Globe and "Industry"

A77

Map and Soldier

A78

1949, May 1 **Photo.** ***Perf. 12½x12***

435	A77	2.50 l olive brown	30	30
436	"	5 l blue	60	60
437	"	8 l violet brown	90	90

Issued to publicize Labor Day, May 1, 1949.

1949, July 10 **Unwmkd.**

438	A78	2.50 l brown	35	35
439	"	5 l lt. ultramarine	50	50
440	"	8 l brown orange	1.00	1.00

Issued to commemorate the 6th anniversary of the formation of Albania's army.

Enver Hoxha

A79

Albanian Citizen and Spasski Tower, Kremlin

A80

1949, Oct. 16 **Engr.** ***Perf. 12½***

441	A79	50q purple	3	3
442	"	1 l dull green	7	3
443	"	1.50 l carmine lake	10	3
444	"	2.50 l brown	20	3
445	"	5 l violet blue	45	10
446	"	8 l sepia	75	70
447	"	12 l rose lilac	1.25	75
448	"	20 l gray blue	2.25	1.25
		Nos. 441-448 (8)	5.10	2.92

Photogravure.

1949, Sept. 10 ***Perf. 12½x12***

449	A80	2.50 l orange brown	18	22
450	"	5 l deep ultramarine	45	55

Albanian-Soviet friendship.

Albanian Soldier and Flag

A81

Battle Scene

A82

1949, Nov. 29 ***Perf. 12*** **Unwmkd.**

451	A81	2.50 l brown	20	20
452	A82	3 l dark red	25	40
453	A81	5 l violet	40	50
454	A82	8 l black	75	1.00

Fifth anniversary of Albania's liberation.

Joseph V Stalin

A83

Symbols of UPU and Postal Transport

A84

1949, Dec. 21

455	A83	2.50 l dark brown	25	30
456	"	5 l violet blue	50	60
457	"	8 l rose brown	85	1.00

Issued to commemorate the 70th anniversary of the birth of Joseph V. Stalin.

Canceled to Order

Beginning in 1950, Albania sold some issues in sheets canceled to order. Prices in second column when much less than unused are for "CTO" copies. Postally used stamps are valued at slightly less than, or the same as, unused.

1950, July 1 **Photo.** ***Perf. 12x12½***

458	A84	5 l blue	45	50
459	"	8 l rose brown	75	75
460	"	12 l sepia	1.00	1.25

Issued to commemorate the 75th anniversary (in 1949) of the formation of the Universal Postal Union.

Sami Frasheri

A85

Arms and Albanian Flags

A86

Authors: 2.50 l, Andon Zako. 3 l, Naim Frashëri. 5 l, Kostandin Kristoforidhi.

1950, Nov. 5 ***Perf. 14***

461	A85	2 l dark green	20	12
462	"	2.50 l red brown	24	15
463	"	3 l brown carmine	36	20
464	"	5 l deep blue	50	30

Issued to commemorate the "Jubilee of the Writers of the Renaissance."

1951, Jan. 11 **Engr.** ***Perf. 14x13½***

465	A86	2.50 l brown carmine	20	15
466	"	5 l deep blue	40	30
467	"	8 l sepia	80	45

Issued to commemorate the 5th anniversary of the formation of the Albanian People's Republic.

Skanderberg A87

Enver Hoxha and Congress of Permet A88

1951, Mar. 1

468	A87	2.50 l brown	25	15
469	"	5 l violet	45	30
470	"	8 l olive bistre	70	45

Issued to commemorate the 483rd anniversary of the death of George Castriota (Skanderberg).

1951, May 24 Photo. ***Perf. 12***

471	A88	2.50 l dark brown	25	20
472	"	3 l rose brown	25	25
473	"	5 l violet blue	40	40
474	"	8 l rose lilac	75	60

Congress of Permet, 7th anniversary.

Child and Globe A89

Weighing Baby A90

1951, July 16

475	A89	2 l green	40	20
476	A90	2.50 l brown	50	35
477	"	3 l red	50	40
478	A89	5 l blue	1.00	65

Issued to publicize International Children's Day, June 1, 1951.

Enver Hoxha and Birthplace of Albanian Communist Party A91

1951, Nov. 8 Photo. ***Perf. 14***

479	A91	2.50 l olive brown	25	25
480	"	3 l rose brown	35	35
481	"	5 l dark slate blue	60	60
482	"	8 l black	85	85

Issued to commemorate the 10th anniversary of the founding of Albania's Communist Party.

Battle Scene A92

Designs: 5 l, Schoolgirl, "Agriculture and Industry." 8 l, Four portraits.

1951, Nov. 28 ***Perf. 12x12½***

483	A92	2.50 l brown	20	15
484	"	5 l blue	25	40
485	"	8 l brown carmine	75	75

Issued to commemorate the 10th anniversary of the formation of the Albanian Communist Youth Organization.

Albanian Heroes (Haxhija, Lezhe, Giyebegej, Mezi and Dedej) A93

1950, Dec. 25 ***Perf. 14*** **Unwmkd.**

Various Portraits

486	A93	2 l dark green	20	20
487	"	2.50 l purple	25	25
488	"	3 l scarlet	35	35
489	"	5 l bright blue	45	45
490	"	8 l olive brown	85	1.00
		Nos. 486-490 (5)	2.10	2.25

Isssued to commemorate the 6th anniversary of Albania's liberation. Nos. 486–489 each show five "Heroes of the People"; No. 490 shows two (Stafa and Shanto).

Tobacco Factory, Shkoder A94

Composite, Lenin Hydro-electric Plant A95

Designs: 1 l, Canal. 2.50 l, Textile factory. 3 l, "8 November" Cannery. 5 l, Motion Picture Studio, Tirana. 8 l, Stalin Textile Mill, Tirana. 20 l, Central Hydroelectric Dam.

Perf. 12x12½, 12½x12

1953, Aug. 1

491	A94	50q red brown	3	3
492	"	1 l dull green	7	3
493	"	2.50 l brown	15	4
494	"	3 l rose brown	18	5
495	"	5 l blue	30	8
496	"	8 l brown olive	45	12
497	A95	12 l deep plum	70	18
498	A94	20 l slate blue	1.15	50
		Nos. 491-498 (8)	3.03	1.03

Liberation Scene A96

1954, Nov. 29 ***Perf. 12x12½***

499	A96	50q brown violet	5	3
500	"	1 l olive green	7	3
501	"	2.50 l yellow brown	22	8
502	"	3 l carmine rose	25	17
503	"	5 l gray blue	45	17
504	"	8 l rose brown	70	35
		Nos. 499-504 (6)	1.74	83

10th anniversary of Albania's liberation.

School A97

Pandeli Sotiri, Petro Nini Luarasi, Nuci Naci A98

1956, Feb. 23 **Unwmkd.**

505	A97	2 l rose violet	10	6
506	A98	2.50 l light green	20	12
507	"	5 l ultramarine	30	20
508	A97	10 l bright greenish blue	60	35

Issued to commemorate the 70th anniversary of the opening of the first Albanian school.

Flags A99

Designs: 5 l, Labor Party headquarters, Tirana. 8 l, Marx and Lenin.

1957, June 1 Engr. ***Perf. 11½x11***

509	A99	2.50 l brown	15	8
510	"	5 l light violet blue	35	20
511	"	8 l rose lilac	60	30

Issued to commemorate the 15th anniversary of the founding of Albania's Labor Party.

Congress Emblem A100

1957, Oct. 4 ***Perf. 11½*** **Unwmkd.**

512	A100	2.50 l gray brown	10	8
513	"	3 l rose red	12	10
514	"	5 l dark blue	20	15
515	"	8 l green	45	30

Issued to publicize the fourth International Trade Union Congress, Leipzig, Oct. 4-15.

Lenin and Cruiser "Aurora" A101

1957, Nov. 7 Litho. ***Perf. 10½***

516	A101	2.50 l violet brown	15	12
517	"	5 l violet blue	30	22
518	"	8 l gray	60	40

Issued to commemorate the 40th anniversary of the Russian Revolution.

Albanian Fighter Holding Flag A102

Naum Veqilharxhj A103

1957, Nov. 28 ***Perf. 10½***

519	A102	1.50 l magenta	10	6
520	"	2.50 l brown	18	10
521	"	5 l blue	35	25
522	"	8 l green	75	40

Issued to commemorate the 45th anniversary of the proclamation of independence.

1958, Feb. 1 **Unwmkd.**

523	A103	2.50 l dark brown	20	12
524	"	5 l violet blue	40	20
525	"	8 l rose lilac	70	40

Issued to commemorate the 160th anniversary of the birth of Naum Veqilharxhj, patriot and writer.

Luigi Gurakuqi A104

Soldiers A105

1958, Apr. 15 Photo. ***Perf. 10½***

526	A104	1.50 l dark green	8	5
527	"	2.50 l brown	13	10
528	"	5 l blue	25	20
529	"	8 l sepia	60	30

Issued to commemorate the transfer of the ashes of Luigi Gurakuqi.

1958, July 10 **Lithographed**

Design: 2.50 l, 11 l, Airman, sailor, soldier and tank.

530	A105	1.50 l blue green	8	5
531	"	2.50 l dark red brown	12	6
532	"	8 l rose red	40	20
533	"	11 l bright blue	60	30

15th anniversary of Albanian army.

Cerciz Topulli and Mihal Grameno A106

Buildings and Tree A107

1958, July 1

534	A106	2.50 l dark olive bistre	12	8
535	A107	3 l green	15	10
536	A106	5 l blue	25	18
537	A107	8 l red brown	40	30

50th anniversary, Battle of Mashkullore.

Ancient Amphitheater and Goddess of Butrinto A108

1959, Jan. 25 Litho. ***Perf. 10½***

538	A108	2.50 l reddish brown	12	6
539	"	6.50 l light blue green	40	25
540	"	11 l dark blue	80	35

Cultural Monuments Week.

Frederic Joliot-Curie and World Peace Congress Emblem A109

Basketball A110

1959, July 1 **Unwmkd.**

541	A109	1.50 l carmine rose	35	8
542	"	2.50 l rose violet	60	15
543	"	11 l blue	2.00	65

Issued to commemorate the 10th anniversary of the World Peace Movement.

1959, Nov. 20 ***Perf. 10½***

Sports: 2 l, Soccer. 5 l, Runner. 11 l, Man and woman runners with torch and flags.

544	A110	1.50 l bright violet	15	8

545 A110 2 l emerald 25 15
546 " 5 l carmine rose 40 25
547 " 11 l ultramarine 75 45

Issued to publicize the first Albanian Spartacist Games.

Fighter and Flags
A111

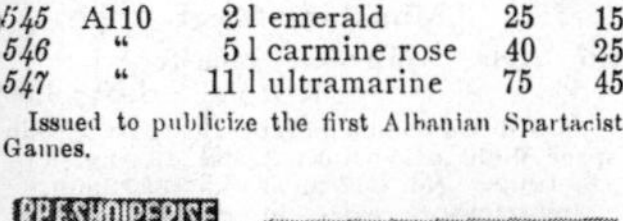

Mother and Child, U.N. Emblem
A112

1959, Nov. 29

Designs: 2.50 l, Miner with drill standing guard. 3 l, Farm woman with sheaf of grain. 6.50 l, Man and woman in laboratory.

548 A111 1.50 l bright carmine 5 3
549 " 2.50 l red brown 10 5
550 " 3 l bright blue green 15 5
551 " 6.50 l bright red 35 10
a. Souvenir sheet 1.50 1.50

15th anniversary of Albania's liberation.

No. 551a contains one each of Nos. 548–551, imperf. and all in bright carmine. Inscribed ribbon frame of sheet and frame lines for each stamp are blue green. Size: 144x97mm.

1959, Dec. 5 **Unwmkd.**

552 A112 5 l light greenish blue 85 15
a. Miniature sheet 1.25 1.25

Issued to commemorate the 10th anniversary (in 1958) of the signing of the Universal Declaration of Human Rights.

No. 552a contains one imperf. stamp similar to No. 552; ornamental border. Size: 74½x66mm.

Woman with Olive Branch
A113

Alexander Moissi
A114

1960, Mar. 8 **Litho.** ***Perf. 10½***

553 A113 2.50 l chocolate 15 12
554 " 11 l rose carmine 60 25

Issued to commemorate the 50th anniversary of International Women's Day, March 8.

1960, Apr. 20

555 A114 3 l deep brown 15 8
556 " 11 l Prussian green 60 25

80th anniversary of the birth of Alexander Moissi (Moisiu) (1880–1935), German actor.

Lenin
A115

School Building
A116

1960, Apr. 22

557 A115 4 l Prussian blue 20 8
558 " 11 l lake 60 20

90th anniversary of birth of Lenin.

1960, May 30 **Litho.** ***Perf. 10½***

559 A116 5 l green 25 12
560 " 6.50 l plum 45 20

Issued to commemorate the 50th anniversary of the first Albanian secondary school.

Soldier on Guard Duty
A117

Liberation Monument, Tirana, Family and Policeman
A118

1960, May 12 ***Perf. 10½*** **Unwmkd.**

561 A117 1.50 l carmine rose 8 5
562 " 11 l Prussian blue 40 20

15th anniversary of the Frontier Guards.

1960, May 14

563 A118 1.50 l green 10 5
564 " 8.50 l brown 50 15

15th anniversary of the People's Police.

Congress Site
A119

Pashko Vasa
A120

1960, Mar. 25

565 A119 2.50 l sepia 20 6
566 " 7.50 l dull blue 50 20

40th anniversary, Congress of Louchnia.

1960, May 5

Designs: 1.50 l, Jani Vreto. 6.50 l, Sami Frasheri. 11 l, Page of statutes of association.

567 A120 1 l gray olive 5 3
568 " 1.50 l brown 10 3
569 " 6.50 l blue 30 12
570 " 11 l rose red 55 25

Issued to commemorate the 80th anniversary (in 1959) of the Association of Albanian Authors.

Albanian Fighter and Cannon
A121

TU-104 Plane, Clock Tower, Tirana, and Kremlin, Moscow
A122

1960, Aug. 2 **Litho.** ***Perf. 10½***

571 A121 1.50 l olive brown 12 5
572 " 2.50 l maroon 15 8
573 " 5 l dark blue 30 12

Issued to commemorate the 40th anniversary of the Battle of Viona (against Italian troops.)

1960, Aug. 18

574 A122 1 l reddish brown 6 6
575 " 7.50 l brt. greenish blue 35 18
576 " 11.50 l gray 60 35

Issued to commemorate the 2nd anniversary of TU-104 flights, Moscow-Tirana.

Rising Sun and Federation Emblem
A123

Ali Kelmendi
A124

1960, Nov. 10 ***Perf. 10½*** **Unwmkd.**

577 A123 1.50 l ultramarine 12 6
578 " 8.50 l red 50 20

Issued to commemorate the 15th anniversary of the International Youth Federation.

1960, Dec. 5 **Litho.** ***Perf. 10½***

579 A124 1.50 l pale gray green 10 6
580 " 11 l dull rose lake 60 20

Issued to honor Ali Kelmendi, communist leader, on his 60th birthday.

Flags of Russia and Albania and Clasped Hands
A125

Marx and Lenin
A126

1961, Jan. 10 ***Perf. 10½*** **Unwmkd.**

581 A125 2 l violet 10 6
582 " 8 l dull red brown 50 20

Issued to commemorate the 15th anniversary of the Albanian-Soviet Friendship Society.

1961, Feb. 13 **Lithographed**

583 A126 2 l rose red 8 6
584 " 8 l violet blue 45 20

Fourth Communist Party Congress.

Man from Shkoder
A127

Otter
A128

1961, Apr. 28 ***Perf. 10½***

Costumes: 1.50 l, Woman from Shkoder. 6.50 l, Man from Lume. 11 l, Woman from Mirdite.

585 A127 1 l slate 10 5
586 " 1.50 l dull claret 15 6
587 " 6.50 l ultramarine 55 25
588 " 11 l red 1.00 50

1961, June 25 ***Perf. 10½*** **Unwmkd.**

Designs: 6.50 l, Badger. 11 l, Brown bear.

589 A128 2.50 l grayish blue 55 18
590 " 6.50 l blue green 1.25 45
591 " 11 l dk. red brn. 2.00 50

Dalmatian Pelicans
A129

Cyclamen
A130

Birds: 7.50 l, Gray herons. 11 l, Little egret.

1961, Sept. 30 ***Perf. 14***

592 A129 1.50 l rose carmine, *pinkish* 35 20
593 " 7.50 l violet, *bluish* 70 20
594 " 11 l red brown, *pinkish* 95 25

1961, Oct. 27 **Lithographed**

Designs: 8 l, Forsythia. 11 l, Lily.

595 A130 1.50 l bright blue & lilac rose 10 10
596 " 8 l red lilac & orange 50 35
597 " 11 l bright green & carmine rose 65 25

Milosh G. Nikolla
A131

Flag with Marx and Lenin
A132

1961, Oct. 30 ***Perf. 14***

598 A131 50q violet brown 8 6
599 " 8.50 l Pruss. green 50 25

Issued to commemorate the 50th anniversary of the birth of Milosh Gjergi Nikolla, poet.

1961, Nov. 8

600 A132 2.50 l vermilion 18 6
601 " 7.50 l dull red brn. 50 20

Issued to commemorate the 20th anniversary of the founding of Albania's Communist Party.

Worker, Farm Woman and Emblem
A133

Yuri Gagarin and Vostok 1
A134

1961, Nov. 23 ***Perf. 14*** **Unwmkd.**

602 A133 2.50 l violet blue 18 12
603 " 7.50 l rose claret 50 35

Issued to commemorate the 20th anniversary of the Albanian Workers' Party.

1962, Feb. 15 ***Perf. 14*** **Unwmkd.**

604 A134 50q blue 6 3
605 " 4 l red lilac 25 15
606 " 11 l dk. slate green 75 40

Issued to commemorate the first manned space flight, made by Yuri A. Gagarin, Soviet astronaut, Apr. 12, 1961.

Nos. 604–606 were overprinted with an over-all yellow tint and with "POSTA AJRORE" (Air Mail) in maroon in 1962. Price, set $10.

Petro Nini Luarasi

A135

Malaria Eradication Emblem

A136

1962, Feb. 28 **Lithographed**

607 A135 50q Prussian blue 5 4
608 " 8.50 l olive gray 70 20

Issued to commemorate the 50th anniversary (in 1961) of the death of Petro Nini Luarasi, Albanian patriot.

1962, Apr. 30 ***Perf. 14*** **Unwmkd.**

609 A136 1.50 l bright green 8 6
610 " 2.50 l brown red 12 8
611 " 10 l red lilac 50 30
612 " 11 l blue 60 30

Issued for the World Health Organization drive to eradicate malaria.

A souvenir sheet, issued both perf. and imperf., contains one each of Nos. 609–612, with blue marginal inscription and U.N. emblem. Size: 88x106½mm. Price $4 each.

Nos. 609–612 exist imperf. Price, set $8.

Camomile

A137

Woman Diver

A138

1962, May 10

Medicinal Plants: 8 l, Linden. 11.50 l, Garden sage.

613 A137 50q gray violet, yel. & green 3 3
614 " 8 l gray, yellow & green 45 25
615 " 11.50 l bistre, green & purple 65 30

Nos. 613–615 exist imperforate. Price, set $5.

1962, May 31 ***Perf. 14***

Designs: 2.50 l, Pole vault. 3 l, Mt. Fuji and torch (horiz.). 9 l, Woman javelin thrower. 10 l, Shot putting.

616 A138 50q bright greenish blue & blk. 5 3
617 " 2.50 l golden brown & sepia 15 7
618 " 3 l blue & gray 18 8
619 " 9 l rose car. & dark brown 55 20
620 " 10 l olive & black 60 22
Nos. 616–620 (5) 1.53 60

1964 Olympic Games, Tokyo.

Nos. 616–620 exist imperf. Price, set $9.

Globe and Orbits

A139

Dog Laika and Sputnik 2

A140

Designs: 1.50 l, Rocket to the sun. 20 l, Lunik 3 photographing far side of the moon.

1962, June ***Perf. 14*** **Unwmkd.**

621 A139 50q violet & orge. 4 3
622 A140 1 l bl. grn. & brn. 6 3
623 " 1.50 l yel. & verm. 10 4
624 A139 20 l magenta & blue 1.10 35

Russian space explorations.

Nos. 621–624 exist imperforate in changed colors. Price, set $5.

Two miniature sheets exist (101x77mm.), each containing one 14-lek picturing Sputnik 1. The perforated 14-lek is yellow and brown; the imperf. red and brown. Marginal design in blue and black. Price, each $4.

Soccer Game, Map of South America

A141

Design: 2.50 l, 15 l, Soccer game and globe as ball.

1962, July **Lithographed**

625 A141 1 l orange & dk. purple 8 3
626 " 2.50 l emerald & bluish grn. 17 5
627 " 6.50 l light brown & pink 40 15
628 " 15 l bluish green & maroon 85 30

Issued to commemorate the World Soccer Championships, Chile, May 30–June 17.

Nos. 625–628 exist imperforate in changed colors. Price $7 for set.

Two miniature sheets exist (67x49mm.), each containing a single 20-lek in design similar to A141. The perforated sheet is brown and green; the imperforate sheet, brown and orange. Price $4 each.

Map of Europe and Albania

A142

Woman of Dardhë

A143

Designs: 1 l, 2.50 l, Map of Adriatic Sea and Albania and Roman statue.

1962, Aug.

630 A142 50q multicolored 6 4
631 " 1 l ultra. & red 8 5
632 " 2.50 l blue & red 20 10
633 " 11 l multicolored 1.00 25

Issued for tourist propaganda. Imperforates in changed colors exist. Price $5. Miniature sheets containing a 7 l and 8 l stamp, perf. and imperf., exist. Price $4 each.

1962, Sept.

Regional Costumes: 1 l, Man from Devoll. 2.50 l, Woman from Lunxheri. 14 l, Man from Gjirokastër.

635 A143 50q carmine, blue & purple 4 3
636 " 1 l red brown & ochre 6 4
637 " 2.50 l violet, yellow grn. & blk. 15 6
638 " 14 l red brown & pale green 75 35

Imperforates exist. Price, set $8.

Chamois

A144

Ismail Qemali

A145

Animals: 1 l, Lynx (horiz.). 1.50 l, Wild boar (horiz.). 15 l, 20 l, Roe deer.

1962, Oct. 24 ***Perf. 14*** **Unwmkd.**

639 A144 50q slate green & dark purple 5 3
640 " 1 l orange & black 7 5
641 " 1.50 l red brn. & blk. 13 10
642 " 15 l yellow olive & red brown 1.10 65

Miniature Sheet

643 A144 20 l yellow olive & red brown 3.00 3.00

No. 643 measures 71½x89mm.

Nos. 639–643 exist imperforate in changed colors. Price, Nos. 639–642 imperf., $4; No. 643, $4.

1962, Dec. 28 **Lithographed**

Designs: 1 l, Albanian eagle. 16 l, Eagle over fortress formed by "RPSH."

644 A145 1 l red & red brn. 5 3
645 " 3 l org. brn. & blk. 13 7
646 " 16 l dark carmine rose & blk. 70 35

Issued to commemorate the 50th anniversary of independence. Imperforates in changed colors exist. Price, $5.

Monument of October Revolution

A146

Henri Dunant, Cross, Globe and Nurse

A147

Design: 10 l, Lenin statue.

1963, Jan. 5 ***Perf. 14*** **Unwmkd.**

647 A146 5 l yel. & dull vio. 22 10
648 " 10 l red orge. & blk. 50 25

Issued to commemorate the 45th anniversary of the October Revolution (Russia, 1917).

1963, Jan 25 ***Perf. 14*** **Unwmkd.**

649 A147 1.50 l rose lake, red & black 8 5
650 " 2.50 l light blue, red & black 12 8
651 " 6 l emerald, red & black 35 25
652 " 10 l dull yellow, red & black 80 45

Issued to commemorate the centenary of the Geneva Conference, which led to the establishment of the International Red Cross in 1864.

Nos. 649–652 exist imperforate in changed colors. Price $5.

Stalin and Battle of Stalingrad

A148

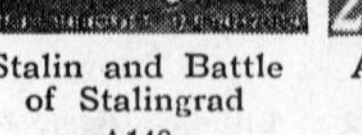

Andrian G. Nikolayev

A149

1963, Feb. 2

653 A148 8 l dk. green & slate 25 10

Issued to commemorate the 20th anniversary of the Battle of Stalingrad. See No. C67.

1963, Feb. 28 **Lithographed**

Designs: 7.50 l, Vostoks 3 and 4 and globe (horiz.). 20 l, Pavel R. Popovich. 25 l, Nikolayev, Popovich and globe with trajectories.

654 A149 2.50 l violet blue & sepia 12 5
655 " 7.50 l lt. blue & blk. 35 15
656 " 20 l vio. & sepia 1.10 40

Miniature Sheet

657 A149 25 l violet blue & & sepia 4.00 4.00

Issued to commemorate the first group space flight of Vostoks 3 and 4, Aug. 11–15, 1962. No. 657 measures 88x73mm.

Imperforates exist in changed colors. Price, Nos. 654–656 imperf., $5; No. 657, $5.

"Albania" Decorating Police Officer

A150

Polyphylla Fullo

A151

1963, Mar. 20 ***Perf. 14*** **Unwmkd.**

658 A150 2.50 l crimson magenta & black 12 15
659 " 7.50 l org. verm., dk. red & blk. 35 22

20th anniversary of the security police.

1963, Mar. 20

Beetles: 1.50 l, Lucanus cervus. 8 l, Procerus gigas. 10 l, Cicindela Albanica.

660 A151 50q olive grn & brown 5 3
661 " 1.50 l blue & brown 20 5
662 " 8 l dull rose & black violet 65 17
663 " 10 l bright citron & black 1.00 25

1913 Stamp and Postmark

A152

Design: 10 l, Stamps of 1913, 1937 and 1962.

1963, May 5

664 A152 5 l yellow, buff, blue & black 30 20
665 " 10 l carm. rose, green & black 70 30

50th anniversary of Albanian stamps.

Boxer

A153

Crested Grebe

A154

Designs: 3 l, Basketball baskets. 5 l, Athletes and umpire. 6 l, Bicyclists. 9 l, Gymnast. 15 l, Hands holding torch, and map of Japan.

1963, May 25 ***Perf. 13½***

666 A153 2 l yellow, black & red brown 10 3
667 " 3 l ocher, brn. & bl. 12 5
668 " 5 l gray blue, red brn. & brown 25 12
669 " 6 l gray, dark gray & green 50 20
670 " 9 l rose, red brown & blue 80 30
Nos. 666–670 (5) 1.77 70

Miniature Sheet

671 A153 15 l lt. blue, carm., black & brn. 2.75 2.75

Issued to publicize the 1964 Olympic Games in Tokyo. No. 671 contains one stamp (31x49mm.) with ocher border. Size: 60x80mm. Imperfs. of Nos. 666–671 exist. Price, set $6.

1963, Apr. 20 Litho. *Perf. 14*

Birds: 3 l, Golden eagle. 6.50 l, Gray partridges. 11 l, Capercaillie.

672 A154 50q multicolored 3 3
673 " 3 l " 15 8
674 " 6.50 l " 40 22
675 " 11 l " 70 35

Soldier and Building
A155

Designs: 2.50 l, Soldier with pack, ship and plane. 5 l, Soldier in battle. 6 l, Soldier and bulldozer.

1963, July 10 *Perf. 12* Unwmkd.

676 A155 1.50 l brick red, yel. & blk. 9 3
677 " 2.50 l blue, ocher & brown 15 6
678 " 5 l bluish green, gray & blk. 27 10
679 " 6 l red brown, buff & blue 35 13

Albanian army, 20th anniversary.

Maj. Yuri A. Gagarin
A156

Designs: 5 l, Maj. Gherman Titov. 7 l, Maj. Andrian G. Nikolayev. 11 l, Lt. Col. Pavel R. Popovich. 14 l, Lt. Col. Valeri Bykovski. 20 l, Lt. Valentina Tereshkova.

1963, July 30

Portraits in Yellow and Black

680 A156 3 l bright purple 18 5
681 " 5 l dull blue 28 10
682 " 7 l gray 40 15
683 " 11 l deep claret 60 22
684 " 14 l blue green 80 28
685 " 20 l ultramarine 1.25 45
Nos. 680-685 (6) 3.51 1.25

Man's conquest of space.
Exist imperf. Price, set $7.

Volleyball
A157

Sports: 3 l, Weight lifting. 5 l, Soccer. 7 l, Boxing. 8 l, Rowing.

1963, Aug. 31 *Perf. 12x12½*

686 A157 2 l citron, red & blk. 9 5
687 " 3 l dark red, bister & black 13 8
688 " 5 l emerald, orange & black 22 10
689 " 7 l deep pink, emerald & black 35 15
690 " 8 l deep blue, deep pink & black 40 20
Nos. 686-690 (5) 1.19 58

Issued to commemorate various European championships. Imperforates in changed colors exist. Price, set $5.

Papilio Podalirius
A158

Various Butterflies and Moths in Natural Colors

1963, Sept. 29 Lithographed

691 A158 1 l red 10 3
692 " 2 l blue 15 4
693 " 4 l dull lilac 30 9
694 " 5 l pale green 45 10
695 " 8 l bister 70 20
696 " 10 l light blue 1.00 25
Nos. 691-696 (6) 2.70 71

Oil Refinery, Cerrik
A159

Flag and Shield
A160

Designs: 2.50 l, Food processing plant, Tirana (horiz.). 30 l, Fruit canning plant. 50 l, Tannery (horiz.).

1963, Nov. 15 *Perf. 14* Unwmkd.

697 A159 2.50 l rose red, *pinkish* 10 8
698 " 20 l slate green, *greenish* 75 35
699 " 30 l dull purple, *grayish* 1.00 50
700 " 50 l ocher, *yellow* 1.50 75

Industrial development in Albania.

1963, Nov. 24 *Perf. 12½x12*

701 A160 2 l greenish bl., blk., ocher & red 25 6
702 " 8 l blue, black, ocher & red 60 25

1st Congress of Army Aid Assn.

Chinese, Caucasian and Negro Men
A161

1963, Dec. 10 *Perf. 12x11½*

703 A161 3 l bister & black 15 8
704 " 5 l bister & ultra. 25 12
705 " 7 l bister & violet 45 20

Issued to commemorate the 15th anniversary of the Universal Declaration of Human Rights.

Slalom Ascent
A162

Lenin
A163

Designs: 50q, Bobsled (horiz.). 6.50 l, Ice hockey (horiz.). 12.50 l, Women's figure skating. No. 709A, Ski jumper.

1963, Dec. 25 *Perf. 14*

706 A162 50q greenish blue & black 5 3
707 " 2.50 l red, gray & blk. 15 6
708 " 6.50 l yellow, black & gray 40 15
709 " 12.50 l red, blk., yel. green & red 85 35

Miniature Sheet

709A A162 12.50 l multi. 2.00 2.00

Issued to publicize the 9th Winter Olympic Games, Innsbruck, Jan. 29–Feb. 9, 1964. Size of No. 709A: 56x75mm.

Nos. 706–709A exist imperforate in slightly changed colors. Price, Nos. 706–709A imperf., $20.

1964, Jan. 21 *Perf. 12½x12*

710 A163 5 l gray & bister 25 12
711 " 10 l gray & ocher 50 30

40th anniversary, death of Lenin.

Hurdling
A164

Sturgeon
A165

Designs: 3 l, Track (horiz.). 6.50 l, Rifle shooting (horiz.). 8 l, Basketball.

Perf. 12½x12, 12x12½

1964, Jan. 30 Lithographed

712 A164 2.50 l pale violet & ultra. 12 6
713 " 3 l light green & red brown 15 8
714 " 6.50 l blue & claret 30 15
715 " 8 l lt. bl. & ocher 42 20

Issued to commemorate the 1st Games of the New Emerging Forces, GANEFO, Jakarta, Indonesia, Nov. 10–22, 1963.

1964, Feb. 26 *Perf. 14* Unwmkd.

Designs: Various fish.

Multicolored

716 A165 50q *shown* 5 3
717 " 1 l *Gilthead* 10 3
718 " 1.50 l *Striped mullet* 15 3
719 " 2.50 l *Carp* 25 5
720 " 6.50 l *Mackerel* 40 15
721 " 10 l *Lake Ohrid trout* 75 20
Nos. 716-721 (6) 1.70 49

Red Squirrel
A166

Designs: Wild animals.

1964, March 28 *Perf. 12½x12*

Multicolored

722 A166 1 l *shown* 6 3
723 " 1.50 l *Beech marten* 9 4
724 " 2 l *Red fox* 12 5
725 " 2.50 l *Hedgehog* 15 6
726 " 3 l *Hare* 20 6
727 " 5 l *Jackal* 35 12
728 " 7 l *Wildcat* 50 17
729 " 8 l *Wolf* 85 17
Nos. 722-729 (8) 2.32 70

Scott's editorial staff cannot undertake to identify, authenticate or appraise stamps and postal markings.

Lighting Olympic Torch
A167

Designs: 5 l, Torch and globes. 7 l, 15 l, Olympic flag and Mt. Fuji. 10 l, National Stadium, Tokyo.

1964, May 18 *Perf. 12x12½*

730 A167 3 l lt. yellow green, yellow & buff 15 6
731 " 5 l red & vio. blue 27 10
732 " 7 l lt. blue, ultra. & yellow 35 15
733 " 10 l orge., bl. & vio. 50 25

Miniature Sheet

734 A167 15 l light blue, ultra. & org. 2.50 2.50

Issued to publicize the 18th Olympic Games, Tokyo, October 10–25, 1964. No. 734 contains one stamp (49x62mm.) with orange border. Size: 80x90mm.

Imperfs. of Nos. 730–734 in changed colors exist. Price of imperfs., Nos. 730–733, $5; No. 734, $6.

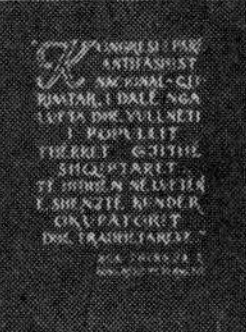

Partisans—A168

Designs: 5 l, Arms of Albania. 8 l, Enver Hoxha.

Perf. 12½x12

1964, May 24 Litho. Unwmkd.

735 A168 2 l orge., red, & blk. 12 6
736 " 5 l multicolored 30 18
737 " 8 l red brown, black & red 50 27

Issued to commemorate the 20th anniversary of the National Anti-Fascist Congress of Liberation, Permet, May 24, 1944. The label attached to each stamp, without perforations between, carries a quotation from the 1944 Congress.

Albanian Flag and Revolutionists
A169

Full Moon
A170

Perf. 12½x12

1964, June 10 Litho. Unwmkd.

738 A169 2.50 l red & gray 15 10
739 " 7.50 l lilac rose & gray 50 30

Issued to commemorate the 40th anniversary of the Albanian revolution of 1924.

1964, June 27 *Perf. 12x12½*

Designs: 5 l, New moon. 8 l, Half moon. 11 l, Waning moon. 15 l, Far side of moon.

740 A170 1 l purple & yel. 6 3
741 " 5 l violet & yellow 25 10
742 " 8 l blue & yellow 45 15
743 " 11 l green & yellow 70 25

Miniature Sheet
Perf. 12 on 2 sides

744 A170 15 l ultra. & yel. 1.75 1.75

No. 744 contains one stamp (35x36mm.) with bister border, perforated at top and bottom. Size: 66½x79mm.

Imperfs. exist in changed colors. Price of imperfs., Nos. 740–743, $4.25; No. 744, $3.

No. 733 with Added Inscription: "Rimini 25-VI-64"

1964 ***Perf. 12x12½***

745 A167 10 l orge., bl. & vio. 60 50

Issued to commemorate the "Toward Tokyo 1964" Philatelic Exhibition at Rimini, Italy, June 25–July 6.

Wren
A171

Birds: 1 l, Penduline titmouse. 2.50 l, Green woodpecker. 3 l, Tree creeper. 4 l, Nuthatch. 5 l, Great titmouse. 6 l, Goldfinch. 18 l, Oriole.

1964, July 31 ***Perf. 12x12½***

746 A171 50q multicolored 3 3
747 " 1 l orge. & multi. 5 3
748 " 2.50 l multicolored 10 4
749 " 3 l blue & multi. 15 7
750 " 4 l yel. & multi. 20 7
751 " 5 l blue & multi. 25 10
752 " 6 l lt. vio. & multi. 30 15
753 " 18 l pink & multi. 85 40
Nos. 746-753 (8) 1.93 89

Running and Gymnastics
A172

Sport: 2 l, Weight lifting—judo. 3 l, Equestrian—bicycling. 4 l, Soccer—water polo. 5 l, Wrestling—boxing. 6 l, Pentathlon—hockey. 7 l, Swimming—sailing. 8 l, Basketball—netball. 9 l, Rowing—canoeing. 10 l, Fencing—pistol shooting. 20 l, Three winners.

Perf. 12x12½

1964, Sept. 25 Litho. Unwmkd.

754 A172 1 l lt. blue, rose & emerald 5 3
755 " 2 l bister brown, bluish green & violet 10 3
756 " 3 l violet, red orge. & olive bister 15 5
757 " 4 l greenish blue, olive & ultra. 18 7
758 " 5 l greenish blue, carm. & pale lilac 25 10
759 " 6 l dk. bl., orge. & light blue 27 12
760 " 7 l dark blue, light olive & orange 38 17
761 " 8 l emerald, gray & yellow 42 18
762 " 9 l blue, yellow & lilac rose 45 22
763 " 10 l brt. grn., orge. brn. & yel. grn. 55 25
Nos. 754-763 (10) 2.80 1.22

Miniature Sheet
Perf. 12

764 A172 20 l violet & lemon 2.75 2.75

Issued to commemorate the 18th Olympic Games, Tokyo, Oct. 10–25. No. 764 contains one stamp (41x68mm.) with violet border. Size: 55x82mm.

Imperfs. exist; all in changed colors except 20 l. Price of imperfs., Nos. 754–763, $5.50; No. 764, $5.50.

Arms of Republic of China
A173

Mao Tse-tung and Flag
A174

Perf. 11½x12, 12x11½

1964, Oct. 1

765 A173 7 l blk., red & yel. 40 22
766 A174 8 l blk., red & yel. 50 30

Issued to commemorate the 15th anniversary of the People's Republic of China.

Karl Marx
A175

Jeronim de Rada
A176

Designs: 5 l, St. Martin's Hall, London. 8 l, Friedrich Engels.

1964, Nov. 5 ***Perf. 12x11½***

767 A175 2 l red, lt. vio. & blk. 15 6
768 " 5 l gray blue 35 9
769 " 8 l ocher, blk. & red 55 15

Centenary of First Socialist International.

1964, Nov. 15 ***Perf. 12½x11½***

770 A176 7 l slate green 35 15
771 " 8 l dull violet 45 18

Issued to commemorate the 150th anniversary of the birth of Jeronim de Rada, poet.

Arms of Albania
A177

Factories
A178

Designs: 3 l, Combine harvester. 4 l, Woman chemist. 10 l, Hands holding Constitution, hammer and sickle.

Perf. 11½x12, 12x11½

1964, Nov. 29

772 A177 1 l multicolored 5 3
773 A178 2 l red, yellow & violet blue 12 6
774 " 3 l red, yel. & brn. 18 8
775 " 4 l red, yel. & gray green 25 12
776 A177 10 l red, bl. & blk. 60 25
Nos. 772-776 (5) 1.20 54

20th anniversary of liberation.

Planet Mercury
A179

Planets: 2 l, Venus and rocket. 3 l, Earth, moon and rocket. 4 l, Mars and rocket. 5 l, Jupiter. 6 l, Saturn. 7 l, Uranus. 8 l, Neptune. 9 l, Pluto. 15 l, Solar system and rocket.

1964, Dec. 15 ***Perf. 12x12½***

777 A179 1 l yellow & purple 4 3
778 " 2 l multicolored 8 3
779 " 3 l " 14 3
780 " 4 l " 18 5
781 " 5 l yel., dk. purple & brown 22 8
782 " 6 l lt. grn., vio. brn. & yellow 40 10
783 " 7 l yellow & green 45 12
784 " 8 l yellow & violet 50 18
785 " 9 l lt. grn., yel. & black 55 25
Nos. 777-785 (9) 2.56 87

Miniature Sheet
Perf. 12 on 2 sides

786 A179 15 l car., blue, yel. & green 2.75 2.75

No. 786 contains one stamp (62x51mm.) with yellow marginal inscription, perforated at top and bottom. Size: 87x72mm.

Imperfs. exist in changed colors. Price of imperfs., Nos. 777–785, $6; No. 786, $3.50.

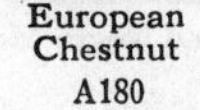

European Chestnut
A180

Symbols of Industry
A181

1965, Jan. 25 ***Perf. 11½x12***

Multicolored

787 A180 1 l *shown* 5 3
788 " 2 l *Medlars* 9 4
789 " 3 l *Persimmon* 15 6
790 " 4 l *Pomegranate* 18 9
791 " 5 l *Quince* 25 10
792 " 10 l *Orange* 45 20
Nos. 787-792 (6) 1.17 52

1965, Feb. 20

Designs: 5 l, Books, triangle and compass. 8 l, Beach, trees and hotel.

793 A181 2 l black, carmine rose & pink 20 17
794 " 5 l yel., gray & blk. 50 45
795 " 8 l black, violet blue & light blue 85 70

Issued to commemorate the 20th anniversary of professional trade associations.

Water Buffalo
A182

Various designs: Water buffalo.

1965, Mar. ***Perf. 12x11½***

796 A182 1 l lt. yel. grn., yel. & brown black 5
797 " 2 l light blue, dark gray & black 15
798 " 3 l yel., brn. & grn. 20
799 " 7 l bright grn., yel. & brown black 45 1
800 " 12 l pale lilac, dark brown & indigo 75 2
Nos. 796-800 (5) 1.60 5

Mountain View, Valbona
A183

Views: 1.50 l, Seashore. 3 l, Glacier and peak (vert.). 4 l, Gorge (vert.). 5 l, Mountain peaks. 9 l, Lake and hills.

1965, Mar. Lithographed ***Perf. 12***

801 A183 1.50 l multicolored 10
802 " 2.50 l " 16 1
803 " 3 l " 18 1
804 " 4 l " 25 2
805 " 5 l " 33 3
806 " 9 l " 50 4
Nos. 801-806 (6) 1.52 1.3

Frontier Guard
A184

Small-bore Rifle Shooting, Prone
A185

1965, Apr. 25 Unwmkd.

807 A184 2.50 l lt. bl. & multi. 15
808 " 12.50 l ultra. & multi. 75 4

20th anniversary of the Frontier Guards.

1965, May 10

Designs: 2 l, Rifle shooting, standing. 3 l, Target over map of Europe, showing Bucharest. 4 l, Pistol shooting. 15 l, Rifle shooting, kneeling.

809 A185 1 l lilac, carm. rose, black & brown 5
810 " 2 l blue, black, brn. & violet blue 10
811 " 3 l pink. & carmine rose 15
812 " 4 l bister, black & violet brown 20 1
813 " 15 l bright green, brn. & vio. brn. 70 3
Nos. 809-813 (5) 1.20 5

Issued to commemorate the European Shooting Championships, Bucharest.

TU Emblem, Old and New Communications Equipment
A186

Col. Pavel Belyayev
A187

965, May 17 *Perf. 12½x12*

14 A186 2.50 l brt. green, blk. & lilac rose 12 5
15 " 12.50 l violet, black & brt. blue 80 40

Issued to commemorate the centenary of he International Telecommunication Union.

965, June 15 *Perf. 12*

Designs: 2 l, Voskhod II. 6.50 l, Lt. ol. Alexei Leonov. 20 l, Leonov floating n space.

16 A187 1.50 l lt. bl. & brown 8 3
17 " 2 l dk. bl., lt. vio. & lt. ultra. 9 3
18 " 6.50 l lilac & brown 30 10
19 " 20 l chalky blue, yel. & blk. 90 35

Miniature Sheet
Perf. 12 on 2 sides

20 A187 20 l bright blue, org. & blk. 3.00 3.00

Issued to commemorate the space flight of Voskhod II and the first man walking in space, Lt. Col. Alexei Leonov. No. 820 contains one stamp (size: 51x59½mm.), orange border, perforated at top and bottom; size: 72x85mm. Exists imperf. with bright green background. Price, $3.

Marx and Lenin
A188

1965, June 21 *Perf. 12*

821 A188 2.50 l dark brown, red & yel. 20 5
822 " 7.50 l slate grn., org. verm. & buff 60 20

Issued to commemorate the 6th Conference of Postal Ministers of Communist Countries, Peking, June 21–July 15.

Mother and Child
A189

Designs: 2 l, Pioneers. 3 l, Boy and girl at play (horiz.). 4 l, Child on beach. 15 l, Girl with book.

Perf. 12½x12, 12x12½

1965, June 29 Litho. Unwmkd.

823 A189 1 l brt. blue, rose lilac & black 4 3
824 " 2 l salmon, violet & black 8 3
825 " 3 l grn., org. & vio. 12 5
826 " 4 l multicolored 15 5
827 " 15 l lilac rose, brn. & ocher 75 18
Nos. 823-827 (5) 1.14 34

Issued for International Children's Day.

Statue of Magistrate
A190

Fuchsia
A191

1965, July 20 *Perf. 12*

Designs: 1 l, Amphora. 2 l, Illyrian armor. 3 l, Mosaic (horiz.). 15 l, Torso, Apollo statue.

828 A190 1 l lt. olive, orange & brown 4 3
829 " 2 l gray grn., green & brown 8 4
830 " 3 l tan, brn., carm. & lilac 12 5
831 " 4 l green, bister & brown 18 8
832 " 15 l gray & pale claret 85 25
Nos. 828-832 (5) 1.27 45

1965, Aug. 11 *Perf. 12½x12*

Flowers: 2 l, Cyclamen. 3 l, Tiger lily. 3.50 l, Iris. 4 l, Dahlia. 4.50 l, Hydrangea. 5 l, Rose. 7 l, Tulips.

833 A191 1 l multicolored 4 3
834 " 2 l " 8 3
835 " 3 l " 15 4
836 " 3.50 l " 20 5
837 " 4 l " 20 8
838 " 4.50 l " 25 7
839 " 5 l " 30 10
840 " 7 l " 40 12
Nos. 833-840 (8) 1.62 52

Nos. 698-700 Surcharged New Value and Two Bars

1965, Aug. 16 *Perf. 14*

841 A159 5q on 30 l dull pur., *grayish* 4 3
842 " 15q on 30 l dull pur., *grayish* 8 3
843 " 25q on 50 l ocher, *yellow* 14 3
844 " 80q on 50 l ocher, *yellow* 32 10
845 " 1.10 l on 20 l slate grn., *greenish* 40 12
846 " 2 l on 20 l slate grn., *greenish* 75 22
Nos. 841-846 (6) 1.73 53

White Stork
A192

"Homecoming," by Bukurosh Sejdini
A193

Migratory Birds: 20q, Cuckoo. 30q, Hoopoe. 40q, European bee-eater. 50q, European nightjar. 1.50 l, Quail.

1965, Aug. 31 *Perf. 12*

847 A192 10q yel., black & gray 5 3
848 " 20q brt. pink, blk. & dark blue 10 4
849 " 30q vio., black & bister 15 7
850 " 40q emerald, black yel. & orange 22 8
851 A192 50q ultra., brn. & red brown 25 10
852 " 1.50 l bister, red brn. & deep org. 80 30
Nos. 847-852 (6) 1.57 62

1965, Sept. 26 Litho. *Perf. 12x12½*

853 A193 25q olive black 14 5
854 " 65q blue black 35 10
855 " 1.10 l black 60 17

Second war veterans' meeting.

Hunter and Capercaillie
A194

Oleander
A195

Hunting: 20q, Deer. 30q, Pheasant. 40q, Mallards. 50q, Boar. 1 l, Rabbit.

1965, Oct. 6 Litho. Unwmkd.

856 A194 10q gray & multi. 6 3
857 " 20q lt. green, red brn. & dk. brown 10 3
858 " 30q blue & multi. 16 7
859 " 40q rose lilac & grn. 22 8
860 " 50q lt. violet blue, blk. & brown 27 10
861 " 1 l citron, olive & brown 55 25
Nos. 856-861 (6) 1.36 56

1965, Oct. 26 *Perf. 12½x12*

Flowers: 20q, Forget-me-nots. 30q, Pink. 40q, White water lily. 50q, Bird's foot. 1 l, Corn poppy.

862 A195 10q brt. blue, green & carm. rose 4 3
863 " 20q org. red, blue, brn. & green 8 5
864 " 30q violet, carm. rose & green 12 5
865 " 40q emerald, yellow & black 16 10
866 " 50q orange brn., yel. & green 30 12
867 " 1 l yel. green, blk. & rose red 60 20
Nos. 862-867 (6) 1.30 55

Hotel Turizmi, Fier
A196

Freighter "Teuta"
A197

Buildings: 10q, Hotel, Peshkopi. 15q, Sanatorium, Tirana. 25q, Rest home, Pogradec. 65q, Partisan Sports Arena, Tirana. 80q, Rest home, Mali Dajt. 1.10 l, Culture House, Tirana. 1.60 l, Hotel Adriatik, Durrës. 2 l, Migjeni Theater, Shkoder. 3 l, Alexander Moissi House of Culture, Durrës.

1965, Oct. *Perf. 12x12½*

868 A196 5q blue & black 3 3
869 " 10q ocher & black 4 3
870 " 15q dull grn. & blk. 6 3
871 " 25q violet & black 10 5
872 " 65q lt. brn. & blk. 26 10
873 " 80q yel. grn. & blk. 32 12
874 " 1.10 l lilac & black 42 15
875 " 1.60 l lt. violet blue & black 65 30
876 " 2 l dull rose & blk. 80 35
877 " 3 l gray & black 1.15 60
Nos. 868-877 (10) 3.83 1.76

1965, Nov. 16

Ships: 20q, Raft. 30q, Sailing ship, 19th century. 40q, Sailing ship, 18th century. 50q, Freighter "Vlora." 1 l, Illyric galleys.

878 A197 10q bright green & dk. green 5 3
879 " 20q olive bister & dark green 10 3
880 " 30q lt. & dp. ultra. 15 6
881 " 40q violet & dp. vio. 20 8
882 " 50q pink & dk. red 25 8
883 " 1 l bister & brown 55 20
Nos. 878-883 (6) 1.30 48

Brown Bear
A198

Basketball and Players
A199

Designs: Various Albanian bears. 50q, 55q, 60q, horizontal.

1965, Dec. 7 *Perf. 11½x12*

884 A198 10q bister & dk. brn. 4 3
885 " 20q pale brown & dark brown 8 3
886 " 30q bister, dark brown & car. 12 4
887 " 35q pale brown & dark brown 15 4
888 " 40q bister & dk. brn. 20 5
889 " 50q bister & dk. brn. 25 10
890 " 55q bister & dk. brn. 40 10
891 " 60q pale brown, dk. brown & car. 42 20
Nos. 884-891 (8) 1.66 59

1965, Dec. 15 Litho. *Perf. 12½x12*

Designs: 10q, Games' emblem (map of Albania and basket). 30q, 50q, Players with ball (diff. designs). 1.40 l, Basketball medal on ribbon.

892 A199 10q bl., yel. & car. 5 3
893 " 20q rose lilac, lt. brn. & black 10 3
894 " 30q bister, lt. brn., red & black 15 5
895 " 50q lt. grn., lt brn. & black 30 6
896 " 1.40 l rose, blk., brn. & yellow 75 30
Nos. 892-896 (5) 1.35 47

Issued to commemorate the Seventh Balkan Basketball Championships, Tirana, Dec. 15–19.

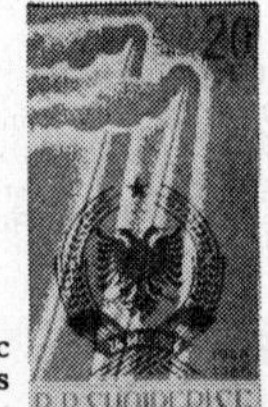

Arms of Republic and Smokestacks
A200

Designs (Arms and): 10q, Book. 30q, Wheat. 60q, Book, hammer and sickle. 80q, Factories.

1966, Jan. 11 Litho. *Perf. 11½x12*

Coat of Arms in Gold

897 A200 10q crimson & brown 5 3
898 " 20q blue & vio. blue 10 3
899 " 30q org. yel. & brn. 15 7
900 " 60q yellow green & bright green 27 12
901 " 80q crimson & brown 37 15
Nos. 897-901 (5) 94 40

Issued to commemorate the 20th anniversary of the Albanian People's Republic.

Cow
A201

Perf. 12½x12, 12x12½

1966, Feb. 25

Multicolored

902 A201 10q *shown* 5 3
903 " 20q *Pig* 10 3
904 " 30q *Ewe & lamb* 15 6
905 " 35q *Ram* 15 6
906 " 40q *Dog* 20 8
907 " 50q *Cat*, vert. 22 8
908 " 55q *Horse*, vert. 27 9
909 " 60q *Ass*, vert. 33 10
Nos. 902-909 (8) 1.47 53

Soccer Player and Map of Uruguay
A202

Andon Zako Cajupi
A203

Designs: 5q, Globe in form of soccer ball. 15q, Player and map of Italy. 20q, Goalkeeper and map of France. 25q, Player and map of Brazil. 30q, Player and map of Switzerland. 35q, Player and map of Sweden. 40q, Player and map of Chile. 50q, Player and map of Great Britain. 70q, World Championship cup and ball.

1966, March 20 Litho. ***Perf. 12***

Buff Background

910 A202 5q gray, & dp. org. 3 3
911 " 10q lt. brn., bl. & vio. 6 3
912 " 15q citron, dk. blue & brt. blue 9 3
913 " 20q org., violet blue & brt. blue 12 3
914 " 25q salmon & sepia 15 3
915 " 30q lt. yellow green & brown 18 5
916 " 35q lt. ultramarine & emerald 20 7
917 " 40q pink & brown 23 8
918 " 50q pale grn., magenta & rose red 30 10
919 " 70q gray, brn., yel. & black 40 15
Nos. 910-919 (10) 1.76 60

Issued to publicize the World Cup Soccer Championship, Wembley, England, July 11-30.

1966, March 27 **Unwmkd.**

920 A203 40q bluish black 25 7
921 " 1.10 l dark green 60 20

Issued to commemorate the centenary of the birth of the poet Andon Zako Cajupi.

Painted Lady
A204

WHO Headquarters, Geneva, and Emblem
A205

Designs: 20q, Blue dragonfly. 30q, Cloudless sulphur butterfly. 35q, 40q, Splendid dragonfly. 50q, Machaon swallowtail. 55q, Sulphur butterfly. 60q, White-marbled butterfly.

1966, Apr. 21 Litho. ***Perf. 11½x12***

922 A204 10q multicolored 5 3
923 " 20q yellow & multi. 10 3
924 " 30q multicolored 15 5
925 " 35q sky bl. & multi. 15 6
926 " 40q multicolored 18 7
927 " 50q rose & multi. 25 8
928 " 55q multicolored 25 10
929 " 60q " 30 12
Nos. 922-929 (8) 1.43 54

Perf. 12x12½, 12½x12

1966, May 3 **Lithographed**

Designs (WHO Emblem and): 35q, Ambulance and stretcher bearers (vert.). 60q, Albanian mother and nurse weighing infant (vert.). 80q, X-ray machine and hospital.

930 A205 25q lt. bl. & black 12 4
931 " 35q salmon & ultra. 25 6
932 " 60q light green, blue & red 35 10
933 " 80q yel., blue, green & light brown 55 18

Issued to commemorate the inauguration of the World Health Organization Headquarters, Geneva.

Bird's Foot Starfish
A206

Designs: 25q, Starfish. 35q, Brittle star. 45q, But-thorn starfish. 50q, Starfish. 60q, Sea cucumber. 70q, Sea urchin.

1966, May 10 ***Perf. 12x12½***

934 A206 15q multicolored 8 3
935 " 25q " 15 4
936 " 35q " 20 6
937 " 45q " 25 7
938 " 50q " 30 8
939 " 60q " 35 10
940 " 70q " 40 12
Nos. 934-940 (7) 1.73 50

Luna 10
A207

Designs: 30q, 80q, Trajectory of Luna 10, earth and moon.

1966, June 10 ***Perf. 12x12½***

941 A207 20q blue, yel. & blk. 10 4
942 " 30q yellow green, black & blue 15 5
943 " 70q vio., yel. & blk. 30 10
944 " 80q yellow, violet, green & black 45 15

Issued to commemorate the launching of the first artificial moon satellite, Luna 10, April 3, 1966.

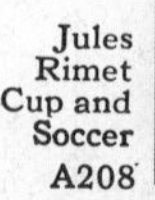

Jules Rimet Cup and Soccer
A208

Designs: Various scenes of soccer play.

1966, July 12 Litho. ***Perf. 12x12½***

Black Inscriptions

945 A208 10q ocher & lilac 5 3
946 " 20q lt. bl. & citron 10 3
947 A208 30q brick red & Prus. blue 15 4
948 " 35q lt. ultra. & rose 17 5
949 " 40q yel. grn. & lt. red brown 20 7
950 " 50q lt. red brown & yellow grn. 25 8
951 " 55q rose lilac & yellow green 27 10
952 " 60q dp. rose & ocher 30 15
Nos. 945-952 (8) 1.49 55

Issued to commemorate the World Cup Soccer Championship, Wembley, England, July 11-30.

Water Level Map of Albania
A209

Designs: 30q, Water measure and fields. 70q, Turbine and pylon. 80q, Hydrological decade emblem.

1966, July ***Perf. 12½x12***

953 A209 20q brick red, black & orange 12 8
954 " 30q emerald, black & light brown 18 9
955 " 70q brt. vio. & black 40 23
956 " 80q brt. blue, org., yellow & black 50 35

Issued to publicize the Hydrological Decade (UNESCO), 1965-74.

Greek Turtle—A210

Designs: 15q, Grass snake. 25q, European pond turtle. 30q, Wall lizard. 35q, Wall gecko. 45q, Emerald lizard. 50q, Slowworm. 90q, Horned viper (or sand viper).

1966, Aug. 10 Litho. ***Perf. 12½x12***

957 A210 10q gray & multi. 5 3
958 " 15q yellow & multi. 6 3
959 " 25q ultra. & multi. 10 3
960 " 30q multicolored 15 5
961 " 35q " 20 6
962 " 45q " 30 7
963 " 50q orange & multi. 30 12
964 " 90q lilac & multi. 70 25
Nos. 957-964 (8) 1.86 64

Persian Cat
A211

Cats: 10q, Siamese (vert.). 15q, European tabby (vert.). 25q, Black kitten. 60q, 65q, 80q, Various Persians.

Perf. 12x12½, 12½x12

1966, Sept. 20 **Lithographed**

965 A211 10q multicolored 6 3
966 " 15q blk., sepia & car. 8 3
967 " 25q black, dark & light brown 12 4
968 " 45q blk., org. & yel. 22 7
969 " 60q blk., brn. & yel. 32 9
970 A211 65q multicolored 45
971 " 80q blk., gray & yel. 55
Nos. 965-971 (7) 1.80

Pjeter Budi
A212

1966, Oct. 5 ***Perf. 12x12½***

972 A212 25q buff & slate grn. 12
973 " 1.75 l gray & dull claret 90

Issued to honor Pjeter Budi, writer.

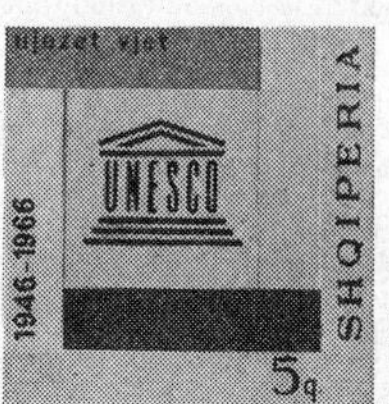

UNESCO Emblem
A213

Designs (UNESCO Emblem and): 15q, Open book, rose and school. 25q, Male folk dancers. 1.55 l, Jug, column and old building.

1966, Oct. 20 Litho. ***Perf. 1***

974 A213 5q lt. gray & multi. 5
975 " 15q dp. bl. & multi. 12
976 " 25q gray & multi. 20
977 " 1.55 l multicolored 1.10

Issued to commemorate the 20th anniversary of UNESCO (United Nations Educational, Scientific and Cultural Organization).

Hand Holding Book with Pictures of Marx, Engels, Lenin and Stalin
A214

Hammer and Sickle, Party Emblem in Sunburst
A215

Designs: 25q, Map of Albania, hammer and sickle, symbols of agriculture and industry. 65q, Symbolic grain and factories. 95q, Fists holding rifle, spade, axe, sickle and book.

1966, Nov. 1 Litho. ***Perf. 11½x12***

978 A214 15q verm. & gold 10
979 " 25q multicolored 15
980 " 65q brown, brown org. & gold 42 14
981 " 95q yel. & multi. 60 20

Issued to commemorate the 5th Congress of the Albanian Communist Party.

1966, Nov. 8

Designs: 25q, Partisan and sunburst. 65q, Steel worker and blast furnace. 95q, Combine harvester, factories, and pylon.

982 A215 15q org. & multi. 8 3
983 " 25q red & multi. 15 3
984 " 65q multicolored 42 12
985 " 95q blue & multi. 60 18

Issued to commemorate the 25th anniversary of the founding of the Albanian Workers Party.

Russian Wolfhound—A216

Dogs: 15q, Sheep dog. 25q, English setter. 45q, English springer spaniel. 60q, Bulldog. 65q, Saint Bernard. 80q, Dachshund.

1966 Litho. *Perf. 12½x12*

No.	Type	Description	Unused	Used
986	A216	10q green & multi.	6	3
987	"	15q multicolored	10	3
988	"	25q lilac & multi.	18	4
989	"	45q rose & multi.	27	8
990	"	60q brown & multi.	30	10
991	"	65q ultra. & multi.	40	15
992	"	80q bl. grn. & multi.	50	20
		Nos. 986-992 (7)	1.81	63

Ndre Mjeda
A217

Proclamation
A218

1966 *Perf. 12½x12*

No.	Type	Description	Unused	Used
993	A217	25q brt. blue & dark brown	15	6
994	"	1.75 l brt. green & dark brown	1.10	30

Birth Centenary of the priest Ndre Mjeda.

1966 *Perf. 11½x12, 12x11½*

Designs: 10q, Banner, man and woman holding gun and axe (horiz.). 1.85 l, man with axe and banner and partisan with gun.

No.	Type	Description	Unused	Used
995	A218	5q lt. brown, red & black	5	3
996	"	10q red, black, gray & blue	7	4
997	"	1.85 l red, blk. & sal.	90	30

Issued to commemorate the 25th anniversary of the Albanian Communist Party.

Golden Eagle
A219

Birds of Prey: 15q, European sea eagle. 25q, Griffon vulture. 40q, Common sparrowhawk. 50q, Osprey. 70q, Egyptian vulture. 90q, Kestrel.

1966, Dec. 20 Litho. *Perf. 11½x12*

No.	Type	Description	Unused	Used
998	A219	10q gray & multi.	6	3
999	"	15q multicolored	10	3
1000	"	25q citron & multi.	20	3
1001	"	40q multicolored	30	7
1002	"	50q "	35	12
1003	"	70q yellow & multi.	42	20
1004	"	90q multicolored	55	28
		Nos. 998-1004 (7)	1.98	76

Hake
A220

Fish: 15q, Red mullet. 25q, Opah. 40q, Atlantic wolf fish. 65q, Lumpfish. 80q, Swordfish. 1.15 l, Shorthorn sculpin.

1967, Jan. Photo. *Perf. 12x11½*

Fish in Natural Colors

No.	Type	Description	Unused	Used
1005	A220	10q blue	4	3
1006	"	15q lt. yel. green	6	3
1007	"	25q Prussian blue	12	4
1008	"	40q emerald	22	7
1009	"	65q brt. bl. green	35	15
1010	"	80q blue	52	22
1011	"	1.15 l bright green	90	25
		Nos. 1005-1011 (7)	2.21	79

White Pelican
A221

Designs: Various groups of pelicans.

1967, Feb. 22 Litho. *Perf. 12*

No.	Type	Description	Unused	Used
1012	A221	10q pink & multi.	4	3
1013	"	15q " "	8	6
1014	"	25q " "	22	8
1015	"	50q " "	55	12
1016	"	2 l " "	1.25	55
		Nos. 1012-1016 (5)	2.14	84

Camellia
A222

Flowers: 10q, Chrysanthemum. 15q, Hollyhock. 25q, Flowering Maple. 35q, Peony. 65q, Gladiolus. 80q, Freesia. 1.15 l, Carnation.

Lithographed

1967, Apr. 12 *Perf. 12* Unwmkd.

Flowers in Natural Colors

No.	Type	Description	Unused	Used
1017	A222	5q pale brown	3	3
1018	"	10q light lilac	5	3
1019	"	15q gray	6	3
1020	"	25q lt. ultramarine	15	4
1021	"	35q light blue	25	6
1022	"	65q lt. blue green	35	12
1023	"	80q lt. bluish gray	45	17
1024	"	1.15 l dull yellow	55	30
		Nos. 1017-1024 (8)	1.89	78

Congress Emblem and Power Station
A223

1967, Apr. 24 Litho. *Perf. 12*

No.	Type	Description	Unused	Used
1025	A223	25q gray lilac, sepia & brt. rose	20	4
1026	"	1.75 l gray, black & brt. rose	90	27

Issued to commemorate the Congress of the Union of Professional Workers, Tirana, Apr. 24.

Rose
A224

Various Roses in Natural Colors

1967, May 15 *Perf. 12x12½*

No.	Type	Description	Unused	Used
1027	A224	5q blue gray	3	3
1028	"	10q bright blue	7	3
1029	"	15q rose violet	8	3
1030	"	25q lemon	15	4
1031	"	35q brt. greenish blue	20	6
1032	"	65q gray	35	12
1033	"	80q brown	45	13
1034	"	1.65 l gray green	90	28
		Nos. 1027-1034 (8)	2.23	72

Seashore, Bregdet Borsh
A225

Views: 15q, Buthrotum (vert.). 25q, Shore, Fshati Piqeras. 45q, Shore, Bregdet. 50q, Shore, Bregdet Himare. 65q, Ship, Sarande (Santi Quaranta). 80q, Shore, Dhermi. 1 l, Sunset, Bregdet (vert.).

Perf. 12x12½, 12½x12

1967, June 10

No.	Type	Description	Unused	Used
1035	A225	15q multicolored	8	3
1036	"	20q "	12	3
1037	"	25q "	15	4
1038	"	45q "	25	8
1039	"	50q "	30	8
1040	"	65q "	40	12
1041	"	80q "	45	18
1042	"	1 l "	55	22
		Nos. 1035-1042 (8)	2.30	78

Fawn
A226

Roe Deer: 20q, Stag (vert.). 25q, Doe (vert.). 30q, Young stag and doe. 35q, Doe and fawn. 40q, Young stag (vert.). 65q, Stag and doe (vert.). 70q, Running stag and does.

Perf. 12½x12, 12x12½

1967, July 20 Lithographed

No.	Type	Description	Unused	Used
1043	A226	15q yel. grn., golden brn. & black	6	3
1044	"	20q lt. blue, orange brown & blk.	8	3
1045	"	25q yellow, orange brown & blk.	10	3
1046	"	30q vio. bl., olive bister & blk.	12	5
1047	"	35q pink, dk. red brown & blk.	14	6
1048	"	40q lt. vio., bister brown & blk.	17	5
1049	"	65q yellow, orange brown & blk.	28	10
1050	A226	70q greenish blue, org. brown & black	30	12
		Nos. 1043-1050 (8)	1.25	47

Man and Woman from Madhe
A227

Fighters and Newspaper
A228

Regional Costumes: 20q, Woman from Zadrimës. 25q, Dancer and drummer, Kukesit. 45q, Woman spinner, Dardhës. 50q, Farm couple, Myseqesë. 65q, Dancer with tambourine, Tirana. 80q, Man and woman, Dropullit. 1 l, Piper, Labërisë.

1967, Aug. 25 *Perf. 12*

No.	Type	Description	Unused	Used
1051	A227	15q tan & multi.	6	3
1052	"	20q lt. yellow green	8	3
1053	"	25q multicolored	10	4
1054	"	45q sky bl. & multi.	18	8
1055	"	50q lemon & multi.	20	8
1056	"	65q pink & multi.	26	10
1057	"	80q multicolored	32	13
1058	"	1 l gray & multi.	40	16
		Nos. 1051-1058 (8)	1.60	65

1967, Aug. 25 *Perf. 12½x12*

Designs: 75q, Printing plant, newspapers and microphone. 2 l, People holding newspaper.

No.	Type	Description	Unused	Used
1059	A228	25q multicolored	10	4
1060	"	75q pink & multi.	30	14
1061	"	2 l multicolored	80	35

Issued for the Day of the Press.

Street Scene, by Kolé Idromeno
A229

Hakmarrja Battalion, by Sali Shijaku
A230

Designs: 20q, David, fresco by Onufri, 16th century (vert.). 45q, Woman's head, ancient mosaic (vert.). 50q, Men on horseback from 16th century icon (vert.). 65q, Farm Women, by Zef Shoshi. 80q, Street Scene, by Vangjush Mio. 1 l, Bride, by Kolé Idromeno (vert.).

Perf. 12, 12x12½, (A230)

1967, Oct. 25 Lithographed

No.	Type	Description	Unused	Used
1062	A229	15q multicolored	8	3
1063	"	20q "	10	5
1064	A230	25q "	14	4
1065	A229	45q "	27	8
1066	"	50q "	30	8
1067	A230	65q "	45	14
1068	"	80q "	50	15
1069	"	1 l "	60	20
		Nos. 1062-1069 (8)	2.44	77

Lenin at Storming of Winter Palace
A231

Rabbit
A232

Designs: 15q, Lenin and Stalin (horiz.). 50q, Lenin and Stalin addressing meeting. 1.10 l, Storming of the Winter Palace (horiz.).

1967, Nov. 7 *Perf. 12*

1070	A231	15q red & multi.	6	3
1071	"	25q slate green & black	10	4
1072	"	50q brown, black & brn. vio.	20	8
1073	"	1.10 l lilac, gray & black	44	20

Issued to commemorate the 50th anniversary of the Russian October Revolution.

1967, Nov. 25

Designs: Various hares and rabbits. The 15q, 25q, 35q, 40q and 1 l are horizontal.

1074	A232	15q orange & multi.	6	3
1075	"	20q brt. yel. & multi.	8	3
1076	"	25q lt. brn. & multi.	12	4
1077	"	35q multicolored	14	6
1078	"	40q yellow & multi.	20	7
1079	"	50q pink & multi.	25	10
1080	"	65q multicolored	30	12
1081	"	1 l lilac & multi.	50	18
		Nos. 1074-1081 (8)	1.65	63

University, Torch and Book
A233

1967 Lithographed *Perf. 12*

1082	A233	25q multicolored	15	4
1083	"	1.75 l "	1.10	30

Issued to commemorate the 10th anniversary of the founding of the State University, Tirana.

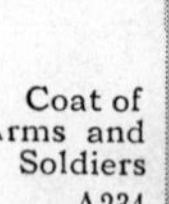

Coat of Arms and Soldiers
A234

Designs: 65q, Arms, Factory, grain, flag, gun and radio tower. 1.20 l, Arms and hand holding torch.

1967 *Perf. 12x11½*

1084	A234	15q multicolored	9	3
1085	"	65q "	33	10
1086	"	1.20 l "	60	20

25th anniversary of the Democratic Front.

Turkey
A235

Designs: 20q, Duck. 25q, Hen. 45q, Rooster. 50q, Guinea fowl. 65q, Goose (horiz.). 80q, Mallard (horiz.). 1 l, Chicks (horiz.).

Perf. 12x12½, 12½x12

1967, Nov. 25 Photogravure

1087	A235	15q gold & multi.	8	3
1088	"	20q " "	10	5
1089	"	25q " "	13	5
1090	"	45q " "	25	10
1091	"	50q " "	27	10
1092	"	65q " "	35	15
1093	"	80q " "	42	18
1094	"	1 l " "	55	25
		Nos. 1087-1094 (8)	2.15	91

Skanderbeg
A236

Designs: 10q, Arms of Skanderbeg. 25q, Helmet and sword. 30q, Kruje Castle. 35q, Petreles Castle. 65q, Berati Castle. 80q, Skanderbeg addressing national chiefs. 90q, Battle of Albulenes.

1967, Dec. 10 Litho. *Perf. 12x12½*

Medallion in Bister and Dark Brown

1095	A236	10q gold & violet	6	3
1096	"	15q gold & rose carmine	8	3
1097	"	25q gold & vio. bl.	13	6
1098	"	30q gold & dk. bl.	15	9
1099	"	35q gold & maroon	17	9
1100	"	65q gold & green	35	15
1101	"	80q gold & gray brown	45	18
1102	"	90q gold & ultra.	50	20
		Nos. 1095-1102 (8)	1.89	83

Issued to commemorate the 500th anniversary of the death of Skanderbeg (George Castriota), national hero.

Ice Hockey
A237

Designs: 15q, 2 l, Winter Olympics emblem. 30q, Women's figure skating. 50q, Slalom. 80q, Downhill skiing. 1 l, Ski jump.

1967-68

1103	A237	15q multicolored	6	3
1104	"	25q "	10	4
1105	"	30q "	12	5
1106	"	50q "	22	8
1107	"	80q "	37	13
1108	"	1 l "	45	16
		Nos. 1103-1108 (6)	1.32	49

Miniature Sheet

Imperf.

1109	A237	2 l red, gray & brt. bl. ('68)	2.00	2.00

Issued to publicize the 10th Winter Olympic Games, Grenoble, France, Feb. 6-18. Size of No. 1109: 55x66mm.
Nos. 1103-1108 issued Dec. 29, 1967.

Skanderbeg Monument, Kruje
A238

Designs: 10q, Skanderbeg monument, Tirana. 15q, Skanderbeg portrait, Uffizi Galleries, Florence. 25q, Engraved portrait of Gen. Tanush Topia. 35q, Portrait of Gen. Gjergj Arianti (horiz.). 65q, Portrait bust of Skanderbeg by O. Paskali. 80q, Title page of "The Life of Skanderbeg." 90q, Skanderbeg battling the Turks, painting by S. Rrota (horiz.).

Perf. 12x12½, 12½x12

1968, Jan 17 Lithographed

1110	A238	10q multicolored	6	3
1111	"	15q "	8	3
1112	"	25q black, yellow & light blue	12	5
1113	"	30q multicolored	15	5
1114	"	35q lt. violet, pink & black	17	6
1115	"	65q multicolored	30	12
1116	"	80q pink, black & yellow	35	13
1117	"	90q beige & multi.	42	17
		Nos. 1110-1117 (8)	1.65	64

Issued to commemorate the 500th anniversary of the death of Skanderbeg (George Castriota), national hero.

Carnation
A239

1968, Feb. 15 *Perf. 12*

Various Carnations in Natural Colors

1118	A239	15q green	8	3
1119	"	20q dark brown	10	3
1120	"	25q bright blue	12	4
1121	"	50q gray olive	25	8
1122	"	80q bluish gray	40	12
1123	"	1.10 l violet gray	55	20
		Nos. 1118-1123 (6)	1.50	50

"Electrification"
A240

Designs: 65q, Farm tractor (horiz.). 1.10 l, Cow and herd.

1968, Mar. 5 Litho. *Perf. 12*

1124	A240	25q multicolored	10	4
1125	"	65q "	26	10
1126	"	1.10 l "	44	20

Fifth Farm Cooperatives Congress.

Goat
A241

Designs: Various goats. 15q, 20q and 25q are vertical.

Perf. 12x12½, 12½x12

1968, Mar. 25

1127	A241	15q multicolored	8	3
1128	"	20q "	8	3
1129	"	25q "	12	4
1130	"	30q "	14	5
1131	"	40q "	20	7
1132	"	50q "	22	8
1133	"	80q "	38	15
1134	"	1.40 l "	60	25
		Nos. 1127-1134 (8)	1.82	70

Zee N. Jubani
A242

Physician and Hospital
A243

1968, Mar. 30 *Perf. 12*

1135	A242	25q yellow & chocolate	15	4
1136	"	1.75 l lt. vio. & blk.	85	35

Issued to commemorate the sesquicentennial of the birth of Zee N. Jubani, writer and scholar.

Perf. 12½x12, 12x12½

1968, Apr. 7 Lithographed

Designs (World Health Organization Emblem and): 65q, Hospital and microscope (horiz.). 1.10 l, Mother feeding child.

1137	A243	25q grn. & claret	18	6
1138	"	65q black, yellow & blue	45	15
1139	"	1.10 l blk. & dp. org.	70	25

Issued to commemorate the 20th anniversary of the World Health Organization.

Scientist
A244

Women: 15q, Militia member. 60q, Farm worker. 1 l, Factory worker.

1968, Apr. 14 *Perf. 12*

1140	A244	15q verm. & dk. red	6	3
1141	"	25q bl. grn. & grn.	12	4
1142	"	60q dull yel. & brn.	30	9
1143	"	1 l lt. vio. & vio.	50	16

Issued to commemorate the 25th anniversary of the Albanian Women's Organization.

Karl Marx
A245

Designs: 25q, Marx lecturing to students. 65q, "Das Kapital," "Communist Manifesto" and marching crowd. 95q, Full-face portrait.

1968, May 5 Litho. *Perf. 12*

1144 A245 15q gray, dk. blue & bister 8 3
1145 " 25q brown violet, dk. brown & dull yellow 13 4
1146 " 65q gray, blk., brn. & carmine 26 12
1147 " 95q gray, ocher & black 50 15

Karl Marx, 150th birth anniversary.

Heliopsis
A246

Flowers: 20q, Red flax. 25q, Orchid. 30q, Gloxinia. 40q, Turk's-cap lily. 80q, Amaryllis. 1.40 l, Red magnolia.

1968, May 10 *Perf. 12x12½*

1148 A246 15q gold & multi. 6 3
1149 " 20q " " 8 3
1150 " 25q " " 10 4
1151 " 30q " " 12 5
1152 " 40q " " 16 7
1153 " 80q " " 32 13
1154 " 1.40 l " " 56 25
Nos. 1148-1154 (7) 1.40 60

Proclamation of Prizren
A247

Designs: 25q, Abdyl Frasheri. 40q, House in Prizren.

1968, June 10 Litho. *Perf. 12*

1155 A247 25q emerald & blk. 15 4
1156 " 40q multicolored 22 7
1157 " 85q yel. & multi. 50 14

Issued to commemorate the 90th anniversary of the League of Prizren against the Turks.

Shepherd, by A. Kushi
A248

Paintings from Tirana Art Gallery: 20q, View of Tirana, by V. Mio (horiz.). 25q, Mountaineer, by G. Madhi. 40q, Refugees, by A. Buza. 80q, Guerrillas of Shahin Matrakut, by S. Xega. 1.50 l, Portrait of an Old Man, by S. Papadhimitri. 1.70 l, View of Scutari, by S. Rrota. 2.50 l, Woman in Scutari Costume, by Z. Colombi.

1968, June 20 *Perf. 12x12½*

1158 A248 15q gold & multi. 10 3
1159 " 20q " " 12 3
1160 " 25q " " 15 4
1161 " 40q " " 27 7
1162 " 80q " " 50 18
1163 " 1.50 l " " 95 30
1164 " 1.70 l " " 1.10 35
Nos. 1158-1164 (7) 3.19 1.00

Miniature Sheet
Perf. 12½xImperf.

1165 A248 2.50 l multicolored 1.75 75

No. 1165 contains one stamp with picture frame in margin. Size of stamp: 50x71mm.; size of sheet: 89x113mm.

Soldier and Guns—A249

Designs: 25q, Sailor and warships. 65q, Aviator and planes (vert.). 95q, Militiamen and woman.

1968, July 10 Litho. *Perf. 12*

1166 A249 15q multicolored 10 3
1167 " 25q " 18 4
1168 " 65q " 50 9
1169 " 95q " 75 13

25th anniversary of the People's Army.

Squid
A250

Designs: 20q, Crayfish. 25q, Whelk. 50q, Crab. 70q, Spiny lobster. 80q, Shore crab. 90q, Norway lobster.

1968, Aug. 20

1170 A250 15q multicolored 6 3
1171 " 20q " 8 4
1172 " 25q " 10 4
1173 " 50q " 20 8
1174 " 70q " 30 12
1175 " 80q " 35 14
1176 " 90q " 40 15
Nos. 1170-1176 (7) 1.49 60

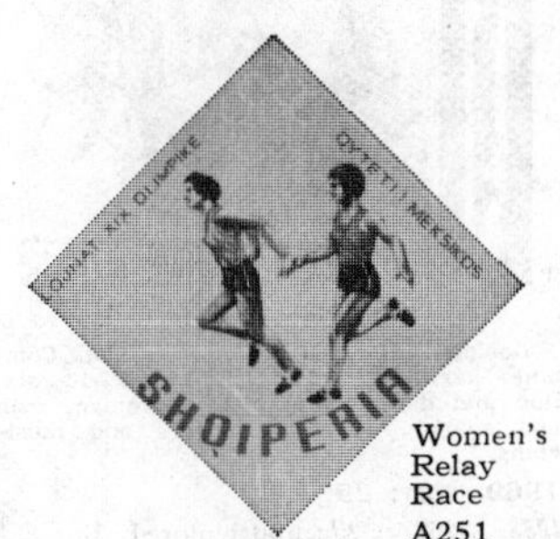

Women's Relay Race
A251

Sport: 20q, Running. 25q, Women's discus. 30q, Equestrian. 40q, High jump. 50q, Women's hurdling. 80q, Soccer. 1.40 l, Woman diver. 2 l, Olympic stadium.

1968, Sept. 23 Photo. *Perf. 12*

1177 A251 15q multicolored 8 3
1178 " 20q " 10 3
1179 " 25q " 12 4
1180 " 30q " 15 5
1181 " 40q " 20 6
1182 " 50q " 25 8
1183 " 80q " 40 12
1184 " 1.40 l " 70 24
Nos. 1177-1184 (8) 2.00 65

Souvenir Sheet
Perf. 12½ Horizontally

1185 A251 2 l multicolored 1.00 60

Issued to publicize the 19th Olympic Games, Mexico City, Oct. 12-27. No. 1185 contains one rectangular stamp, size: 64x54mm. Sheet has ocher marginal inscription. Size: 90x82mm.

Imperfs. exist. Price of Nos. 1177-1184, $5; No. 1185, $2.

Enver Hoxha
A252

1968, Oct. 16 Litho. *Perf. 12*

1186 A252 25q blue gray 18 12
1187 " 35q rose brown 25 14
1188 " 80q violet 55 30
1189 " 1.10 l brown 70 45

Souvenir Sheet
Imperf.

1190 A252 1.50 l rose red, blue vio. & gold 3.00 2.75

Issued for the 60th birthday of Enver Hoxha, First Secretary of the Central Committee of the Communist Party of Albania. No. 1190 contains portrait (size: 45x55mm.) with name of country, denomination and commemorative inscription in margin. Size: 79x90mm.

Book and Pupils
A253

1968, Nov. 14 Photogravure

1191 A253 15q maroon & slate green 14 3
1192 " 85q gray olive & sepia 90 15

Issued to commemorate the 60th anniversary of the Congress of Monastir, Nov. 14-22, 1908, which adopted a unified Albanian alphabet.

Wax-wing
A254

Birds: 20q, Rose-colored starling. 25q, Kingfishers. 50q, Long-tailed tits. 80q, Wallcreeper. 1.10 l, Bearded tit.

1968, Nov. 15 Lithographed
Birds in Natural Colors

1193 A254 15q lt. blue & black 8 3
1194 " 20q bister & black 10 3
1195 " 25q pink & black 12 4
1196 " 50q lt. yel. green & black 25 8
1197 " 80q bister brown & black 40 12
1198 " 1.10 l pale green & black 55 20
Nos. 1193-1198 (6) 1.50 50

Mao Tse-tung—A255

1968, Dec. 26 Litho. *Perf. 12½x12*

1199 A255 25q gold, red & black 15 4
1200 " 1.75 l gold, red & black 1.00 30

Issued to commemorate the 75th birthday of Mao Tse-tung, Chairman of the Communist Party of the People's Republic of China.

Adem Reka and Crane
A256

Portraits: 10q, Pjeter Lleshi and power lines. 15q, Mohammed Shehu and Myrteza Kepi. 25q, Shkurte Vata and women railroad workers. 65q, Agron Elezi, frontier guard. 80q, Ismet Bruçaj and mountain road. 1.30 l, Fuat Cela, blind revolutionary.

1969, Feb. 10 Litho. *Perf. 12x12½*

1201 A256 5q multicolored 3 3
1202 " 10q " 6 3
1203 " 15q " 10 3
1204 " 25q " 15 6
1205 " 65q " 40 10
1206 " 80q " 50 15
1207 " 1.30 l " 75 22
Nos. 1201-1207 (7) 1.99 62

Issued to honor a contemporary heroine and heroes.

Meteorological Instruments
A257

Designs: 25q, Water gauge. 1.60 l, Radar, balloon and isobars.

1969, Feb. 25 *Perf. 12*

1208 A257 15q multicolored 9 5
1209 " 25q ultra., orange & black 12 6
1210 " 1.60 l rose vio., yel. & black 1.05 30

Issued to commemorate the 20th anniversary of Albanian hydrometeorology.

Partisans, 1944, by F. Haxmiu
A258

Paintings: 5q, Student Revolutionists, by P. Mele (vert.). 65q, Steel Mill, by C. Ceka. 80q, Reconstruction, by V. Kilica. 1.10 l, Harvest, by N. Jonuzi. 1.15 l, Terraced Landscape, by S. Kaceli. 2 l, Partisans' Meeting.

Perf. 12x12½, 12½x12

1969, Apr. 25 Lithographed

Size: 31½x41½mm.

1211 A258 5q buff & multi. 3 3

Size: 51½x30½mm.

1212 A258 25q buff & multi. 10 4

Size: 40½x32mm.

1213 A258 65q buff & multi. 28 10

Size: 51½x30½mm.

1214	A258	80q buff & multi.	35	12
1215	"	1.10q " "	50	18
1216	"	1.15q " "	55	20
		Nos. 1211-1216 (6)	1.81	67

Miniature Sheet

Imperf.

Size: 111x90mm.

1217	A258	2 l ocher & multi.	1.10	50

Leonardo da Vinci, Self-portrait
A259

Designs (after Leonardo da Vinci): 35q, Lilies. 40q, Design for a flying machine (horiz.). 1 l, Portrait of Beatrice. No. 1222, Portrait of a Noblewoman. No. 1223, Mona Lisa.

Perf. 12x12½, 12½x12

1969, May 2 Lithographed

1218	A259	25q gold & sepia	13	4
1219	"	35q " "	20	4
1220	"	40q " "	20	6
1221	"	1 l gold & multi.	60	20
1222	"	2 l gold & sepia	1.10	60
		Nos. 1218-1222 (5)	2.23	94

Miniature Sheet

Imperf.

1223	A259	2 l gold & multi.	1.75	1.25

Issued to commemorate the 450th anniversary of the death of Leonardo da Vinci (1452-1519), painter, sculptor, architect and engineer. Size of No. 1223: 64x95 mm.

First Congress Meeting Place
A260

Designs: 1 l, Albanian coat of arms. 2.25 l, Two partisans with guns and flag.

1969, May 24 ***Perf. 12***

1224	A260	25q lt. green, black & red	15	4
1225	"	2.25 l multicolored	1.00	65

Souvenir Sheet

1226	A260	1 l gold, blue, blk. & red	1.00	1.00

25th anniversary of the First Anti-Fascist Congress of Permet, May 24, 1944.

No. 1226 contains one stamp; blue, black and red decorative margin. Size: 94½x100mm.

Albanian Violet
A261

Designs: Violets and Pansies.

1969, June 30 Litho. ***Perf. 12x12½***

1227	A261	5q gold & multi.	3	3
1228	"	10q " "	4	3
1229	"	15q " "	8	3
1230	"	20q " "	10	8
1231	"	25q " "	13	12
1232	"	80q " "	50	25
1233	"	1.95 l " "	1.15	45
		Nos. 1227-1233 (7)	2.03	99

Plum, Fruit and Blossoms
A262

Designs: Blossoms and Fruits.

1969, Aug. 10 Litho. ***Perf. 12***

Multicolored

1234	A262	10q *shown*	4	3
1235	"	15q *Lemon*	8	3
1236	"	25q *Pomegranate*	14	3
1237	"	50q *Cherry*	28	10
1238	"	80q *Peach*	50	20
1239	"	1.20 l *Apple*	70	27
		Nos. 1234-1239 (6)	1.74	66

Basketball
A263

Designs: 10q, 80q, 2.20 l, Various views of basketball game. 25q, Hand aiming ball at basket and map of Europe (horiz.).

1969, Sept. 15 Litho. ***Perf. 12***

1240	A263	10q multicolored	7	3
1241	"	15q buff & multi.	9	3
1242	"	25q blue & multi.	14	7
1243	"	80q multicolored	40	12
1244	"	2.20 l "	1.20	40
		Nos. 1240-1244 (5)	1.90	65

Issued to publicize the 16th European Basketball Championships, Naples, Italy, Sept. 27-Oct. 5.

Runner
A264

Designs: 5q, Games' emblem. 10q, Woman gymnast. 20q, Pistol shooting. 25q, Swimmer at start. 80q, Bicyclist. 95q, Soccer.

1969, Sept. 30

1245	A264	5q multicolored	3	3
1246	"	10q "	8	3
1247	"	15q "	10	3
1248	"	20q "	12	6
1249	"	25q "	14	8
1250	"	80q "	40	20
1251	"	95q "	55	25
		Nos. 1245-1251 (7)	1.42	68

Second National Spartakiad.

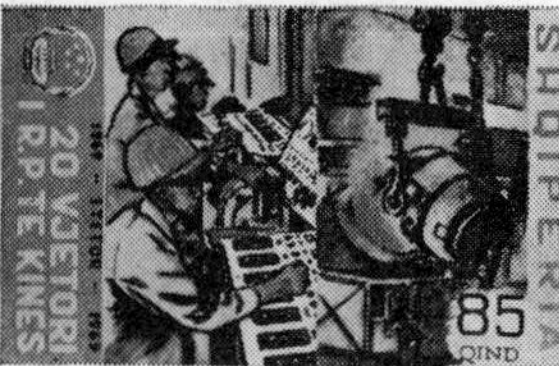

Electronic Technicians, Steel Ladle
A265

Designs: 25q, Mao Tse-tung with microphones (vert.). 1.40 l, Children holding Mao's red book (vert.).

1969, Oct. 1 Litho. ***Perf. 12***

1252	A265	25q multicolored	10	3
1253	"	85q "	38	10
1254	"	1.40 l "	60	22

Issued to commemorate the 20th anniversary of the People's Republic of China.

Enver Hoxha
A266

Designs: 80q, Pages from Berat resolution. 1.45 l, Partisans with flag.

1969, Oct. 20 Litho. ***Perf. 12***

1255	A266	25q multicolored	12	4
1256	"	80q gray & multi.	40	12
1257	"	1.45 l ocher & multi.	80	27

Issued to commemorate the 25th anniversary of the second reunion of the National Antifascist Liberation Council, Berat.

Soldiers—A267

Designs: 30q, Oil refinery. 35q, Combine harvester. 45q, Hydroelectric station and dam. 55q, Militia woman, man and soldier. 1.10 l, Dancers and musicians.

1969, Nov. 29

1258	A267	25q multicolored	13	3
1259	"	30q "	17	3
1260	"	35q "	20	4
1261	"	45q "	23	7
1262	"	55q "	30	11
1263	"	1.10 l "	65	25
		Nos. 1258-1263 (6)	1.68	53

Issued to commemorate the 25th anniversary of the socialist republic.

Joseph V. Stalin
A268

1969, Dec. 21 Litho. ***Perf. 12***

1264	A268	15q lilac	6	3
1265	"	25q slate blue	10	4
1266	"	1 l brown	55	20
1267	"	1.10 l violet blue	60	25

Issued to commemorate the 90th anniversary of the birth of Joseph V. Stalin (1879-1953), Russian political leader.

Head of Woman
A269

1969, Dec. 25 ***Perf. 12½x12***

Greco-Roman Mosaics: 25q, Geometrical floor design (horiz.). 80q, Bird and tree (horiz.). 1.10 l, Floor with birds and grapes (horiz.). 1.20 l, Fragment with corn within oval design.

1268	A269	15q gold & multi.	4	3
1269	"	25q " "	8	3
1270	"	80q " "	42	8
1271	"	1.10 l " "	60	14
1272	"	1.20 l " "	70	15
		Nos. 1268-1272 (5)	1.84	43

Cancellation of 1920
A270

Design: 25q, Proclamation and congress site.

1970, Jan. 21 Litho. ***Perf. 12***

1273	A270	25q red, gray & black	12	6
1274	"	1.25 l dk. green, yel. & black	70	25

Congress of Louchnia, 50th anniversary.

Worker, Student and Flag
A271

1970, Feb. 11 ***Perf. 12½x12***

1275	A271	25q red & multi.	15	4
1276	"	1.75 l " "	1.05	35

Issued to commemorate the 25th anniversary of vocational organizations in Albania.

Turk's-cap Lily
A272

Lilies: 5q, Cernum (vert.). 15q, Madonna (vert.). 25q, Royal (vert.). 1.10 l, Tiger. 1.15 l, Albanian.

Perf. 11½x12, 12x11½

1970, Mar. 10 Lithographed

1277	A272	5q multicolored	5	3

1278 A272 15q multicolored 8 3
1279 " 25q " 12 4
1280 " 80q " 40 12
1281 " 1.10 l " 55 25
1282 " 1.15 l " 65 28
Nos. 1277-1282 (6) 1.85 75

Lenin
A273

Designs (Lenin): 5q, Portrait (vert.). 25q, As volunteer construction worker. 95q, Addressing crowd. 1.10 l, Saluting (vert.).

1970, Apr. 22 Litho. ***Perf. 12***
Red, Black & Silver
1283 A273 5q 3 3
1284 " 15q 7 3
1285 " 25q 14 4
1286 " 95q 55 10
1287 " 1.10 l 65 25
Nos. 1283-1287 (5) 1.44 45

Centenary of birth of Lenin (1870-1924).

Frontier Guard
A274

1970, Apr. 25
1288 A274 25q multicolored 14 4
1289 " 1.25 l " 65 25

25th anniversary of Frontier Guards.

Soccer Players
A275

Designs: 5q, Jules Rimet Cup and globes. 10q, Aztec Stadium, Mexico City. 25q, Defending goal. 65q, 80q, No. 1296, Two soccer players in various plays. No. 1297, Mexican horseman and volcano Popocatepetl.

1970, May 15 Litho. ***Perf. 12½x12***
1290 A275 5q multicolored 3 3
1291 " 10q multicolored 3 3
1292 " 15q multicolored 3 3
1293 " 25q lt. grn. & multi. 8 6
1294 " 65q pink & multi. 32 13
1295 " 80q lt. bl. & multi. 40 18
1296 " 2 l yel. & multi. 1.20 28
Nos. 1290-1296 (7) 2.09 74

Souvenir Sheet
Perf. 12x Imperf.
1297 A275 2 l multicolored 1.25 50

Issued to publicize the World Soccer Championships for the Jules Rimet Cup, Mexico City, May 31-June 21, 1970. No. 1297 contains one large horizontal stamp, decorative border and inscription. Size: 81x74mm.

U.P.U. Headquarters and Monument, Bern
A276

1970, May 30 Litho. ***Perf. 12½x12***
1298 A276 25q ultra., gray & black 10 3
1299 " 1.10 l orange, buff & black 60 20
1300 " 1.15 l green, gray & black 65 22

Issued to commemorate the inauguration of the new Universal Postal Union Headquarters in Bern.

Bird and Grapes Mosaic
A277

Mosaics, 5th-6th centuries, excavated near Pogradec: 10q, Waterfowl and grapes. 20q, Bird and tree stump. 25q, Bird and leaves. 65q, Fish. 2.25 l, Peacock (vert.).

Perf. 12½x12, 12x12½
1970, July 10
1301 A277 5q multicolored 3 3
1302 " 10q " 6 3
1303 " 20q " 10 3
1304 " 25q " 12 8
1305 " 65q " 32 12
1306 " 2.25 l " 1.10 35
Nos. 1301-1306 (6) 1.73 64

Fruit Harvest and Dancers
A278

Designs: 25q, Contour-plowed fields and conference table. 80q, Cattle and newspapers. 1.30 l, Wheat harvest.

1970, Aug. 28 Litho. ***Perf. 12x11½***
1307 A278 15q brt. vio. & blk. 10 3
1308 " 25q dp. bl. & black 15 4
1309 " 80q dp. brn. & blk. 40 8
1310 " 1.30 l org. brn. & blk. 75 30

Issued to commemorate the 25th anniversary of the agrarian reform law.

Attacking Partisans
A279

Designs: 25q, Partisans with horses and flag. 1.60 l, Partisans.

1970, Sept. 3 ***Perf. 12***
1311 A279 15q org. brn. & blk. 10 3
1312 " 25q brn., yel. & blk. 13 3
1313 " 1.60 l dp. grn. & blk. 75 30

50th anniversary of liberation of Vlona.

Miners, by Nexhmedin Zajmi
A280

Paintings from the National Gallery, Tirana: 5q, Bringing in the Harvest, by Isuf Sulovari (vert.). 15q, The Activists, by Dhimitraq Trebicka (vert.). 65q, Instruction of Partisans, by Hasan Nallbani. 95q, Architectural Planning, by Vilson Kilica. No. 1319, Woman Machinist, by Zef Shoshi (vert.). No. 1320, Partisan Destroying Tank, by Sali Shijaku (vert.).

Perf. 12½x12, 12x12½
1970, Sept. 25 Lithographed
1314 A280 5q multicolored 3 3
1315 " 15q " 4 3
1316 " 25q " 6 4
1317 " 65q " 26 8
1318 " 95q " 40 15
1319 " 2 l " 1.20 45
Nos. 1314-1319 (6) 1.99 78

Miniature Sheet
Imperf.
1320 A280 2 l multicolored 1.25 60

Size of No. 1320: 66x93½mm.

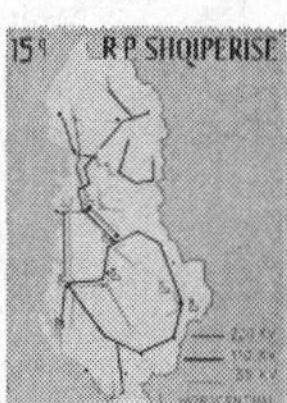

Electrification Map of Albania
A281

Designs: 25q, Light bulb, hammer and sickle emblem, map of Albania and power graph. 80q, Linemen at work. 1.10 l, Use of electricity on the farm, in home and business.

1970, Oct. 25 Litho. ***Perf. 12***
1321 A281 15q multicolored 10 3
1322 " 25q " 13 4
1323 " 80q " 40 10
1324 " 1.10 l " 60 25

Issued to publicize the completion of Albanian village electrification.

Friedrich Engels
A282

Designs: 1.10 l, Engels as young man. 1.15 l, Engels addressing crowd.

1970, Nov. 28 Litho. ***Perf. 12x12½***
1325 A282 25q bister & dk. bl. 13 4
1326 " 1.10 l bister & deep claret 60 20
1327 " 1.15 l bister & dark olive green 65 25

Issued to commemorate the 150th anniversary of the birth of Friedrich Engels (1820-1895), German socialist, collaborator with Karl Marx.

Ludwig van Beethoven
A283

Designs: 5q, Birthplace, Bonn. 25q, 65q, 1.10 l, various portraits. 1.80 l, Scene from Fidelio (horiz.).

1970, Dec. 16 Litho. ***Perf. 12***
1328 A283 5q dp. plum & gold 3 3
1329 " 15q brt. rose lilac & silver 4 3
1330 A283 25q green & gold 8 4
1331 " 65q magenta & silver 23 10
1332 " 1.10 l dk. blue & gold 55 22
1333 " 1.80 l black & silver 90 35
Nos. 1328-1333 (6) 1.83 77

Bicentenary of the birth of Ludwig van Beethoven (1770-1827), composer.

Coat of Arms
A284

Designs: 25q, Proclamation. 80q, Enver Hoxha reading proclamation. 1.30 l, Young people and proclamation.

1971, Jan. 11 Litho. ***Perf. 12***
1334 A284 15q lt. blue, gold, black & red 4 3
1335 " 25q rose lilac, blk., gold & gray 8 4
1336 " 80q emerald, black & gold 45 12
1337 " 1.30 l yel. org., blk. & gold 70 22

Declaration of the Republic, 25th anniversary.

"Liberty" A285 — Black Men A286

Designs: 50q, Women's brigade. 65q, Street battle (horiz.). 1.10 l, Execution (horiz.).

Perf. 12x11½, 11½x12
1971, March 18 Lithographed
1338 A285 25q dk. blue & blue 13 4
1339 " 50q slate green 22 7
1340 " 65q dk. brown & chestnut 28 12
1341 " 1.10 l purple 65 15

Centenary of the Paris Commune.

1971, March 21 ***Perf. 12x12½***
Designs: 1.10 l, Men of 3 races. 1.15 l, Black protest.
1342 A286 25q black & bister brown 12 4
1343 " 1.10 l black & rose carmine 60 15
1344 " 1.15 l blk. & verm. 65 20

International year against racial discrimination.

Tulip A287 — Horseman, by Dürer A288

Designs: Various tulips.

1971, March 25

1345 A287 5q multicolored 3 3
1346 " 10q yellow & multi. 4 3
1347 " 15q pink & multi. 6 3
1348 " 20q lt. bl. & multi. 8 3
1349 " 25q multicolored 12 6
1350 " 80q " 35 12
1351 " 1 l " 45 14
1352 " 1.45 l citron&multi. 1.00 30
Nos. 1345-1352 (8) 2.13 74

Perf. 11½x12, 12x11½

1971, May 15 **Lithographed**

Art Works by Dürer: 15q, Three peasants. 25q, Dancing peasant couple. 45q, The bagpiper. 65q, View of Kalkreut (horiz.). 2.40 l, View of Trent (horiz.). 2.50 l, Self-portrait.

1353 A288 10q blk. & pale grn. 4 3
1354 " 15q blk. & pale lilac 6 3
1355 " 25q blk. & pale bl. 10 4
1356 " 45q black & pale rose 18 7
1357 " 65q blk. & multi. 32 10
1358 " 2.40 l " " 1.40 45
Nos. 1353-1358 (6) 2.10 72

Miniature Sheet

Imperf.

1359 A288 2.50 l multicolored 1.50 60

500th anniversary of the birth of Albrecht Dürer (1471–1528), German painter and engraver. Size of No. 1359: 93x90 mm.

Satellite Orbiting Globe—289

Designs: 1.20 l, Government Building, Tirana, and Red Star emblem. 2.20 l, like 60q, 2.50 l, Flag of People's Republic of China forming trajectory around globe.

1971, June 10 Litho. *Perf. 12x12½*

1360 A289 60q pur. & multi. 32 8
1361 " 1.20 l vermilion & multi. 65 15
1362 " 2.20 l grn. & multi. 1.20 35

Miniature Sheet

Imperf.

1363 A289 2.50 l violet black & multi. 1.50 50

Space developments of People's Republic of China. Size of No. 1363: 64x112mm.

Mao Tse-tung A290

Designs: 1.05 l, House where Communist Party was founded (horiz.). 1.20 l, Peking crowd with placards (horiz.).

Perf. 12x12½, 12½x12

1971, July 1

1364 A290 25q silver & multi. 18 4
1365 A290 1.05 l silver & multi. 70 14
1366 " 1.20 l silver & multi. 80 18

50th anniversary of Chinese Communist Party.

Crested Titmouse—A291

1971, Aug. 15 Litho. *Perf. 12½x12*

Multicolored

1367 A291 5q *shown* 3 3
1368 " 10q *European serin* 6 3
1369 " 15q *Linnet* 8 3
1370 " 25q *Firecrest* 12 4
1371 " 45q *Rock thrush* 25 7
1372 " 60q *Blue tit* 33 10
1373 " 2.40 l *Chaffinch* 1.35 40
Nos. 1367-1373 (7) 2.22 70

Printed se-tenant in blocks of 8 (2x4) including a label showing bird's nest. The label is se-tenant horizontally with the 5q, and vertically with the 10q.

Olympic Rings and Running—A292

Designs (Olympic Rings and): 10q, Hurdles. 15q, Canoeing. 25q, Gymnastics. 80q, Fencing. 1.05 l, Soccer. 2 l, Runner at finish line. 3.60 l, Diving, women's.

1971, Sept. 15

1374 A292 5q green & multi. 3 3
1375 " 10q multicolored 6 3
1376 " 15q blue & multi. 8 3
1377 " 25q violet & multi. 12 4
1378 " 80q lilac & multi. 35 8
1379 " 1.05 l multicolored 60 12
1380 " 3.60 l " 2.00 65
Nos. 1374-1380 (7) 3.24 98

Souvenir Sheet

Imperf.

1381 A292 2 l brt. bl. & multi. 1.25 45

20th Olympic Games, Munich, Aug. 26–Sept. 10, 1972. No. 1381 contains one stamp, gray margin with brown inscription. Olympic rings and deep orange and silver flame emblem. Size: 68x82mm.

Workers with Flags A293

Designs: 1.05 l, Party Headquarters, Tirana, and Red Star. 1.20 l, Rifle, star, flag and "VI" (vert.).

1971, Nov. 1 ***Perf. 12***

1382 A293 25q gold, silver, red & blue 8 3
1383 " 1.05 l gold, silver, red & blue 60 14
1384 " 1.20 l gold, silver, red & black 65 20

6th Congress of Workers' Party.

Factories and Workers A294

Designs: 80q, "XXX" and flag (vert.). 1.55 l, Enver Hoxha and flags.

1971, Nov. 8

1385 A294 15q gold, silver, lilac & yel. 6 3
1386 " 80q gold, silver & red 50 10
1387 " 1.55 l gold, silver, red & brn. 1.00 35

30th anniversary of Workers' Party.

Construction Work, by M. Fushekati A295

Albanian Paintings: 5q, Young Man, by R. Kuci (vert.). 25q, Partisan, by D. Jukniu (vert.). 80q, Fliers, by S. Kristo. 1.20 l, Girl in Forest, by A. Sadikaj. 1.55 l, Warriors with Spears and Shields, by S. Kamberi. 2 l, Freedom Fighter, by I. Lulani.

Perf. 12x12½, 12½x12

1971, Nov. 20

1388 A295 5q gold & multi. 3 3
1389 " 15q " " 7 3
1390 " 25q " " 11 5
1391 " 80q " " 35 10
1392 " 1.20 l " " 55 15
1393 " 1.55 l " " 1.00 28
Nos. 1388-1393 (6) 2.11 64

Miniature Sheet

Imperf.

1394 A295 2 l gold & multi. 1.25 45

Contemporary Albanian paintings. Size of No. 1394: 87x67½mm.

Young Workers Emblem A296

1971, Nov. 23 ***Perf. 12x12½***

1395 A296 15q lt. bl. & multi. 7 3
1396 " 1.35 l greenish gray & multi. 85 25

30th anniversary of the Albanian Young Workers' Union.

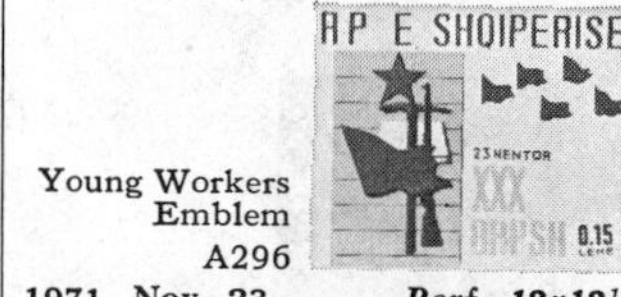

"Halili and Hajria" Ballet—A297

Scenes from "Halili and Hajria" Ballet: 10q, Brother and sister. 15q, Hajria before Sultan Suleiman. 50q, Hajria and husband. 80q, Execution of Halili. 1.40 l, Hajria killing her husband.

1971, Dec. 27 ***Perf. 12½x12***

1397 A297 5q silver & multi. 4 3
1398 " 10q " " 6 3
1399 " 15q " " 7 3
1400 " 50q " " 27 10
1401 A297 80q silver & multi. 45 12
1402 " 1.40 l " " 65 27
Nos. 1397-1402 (6) 1.54 58

Albanian ballet Halili and Hajria after drama by Kol Jakova.

Biathlon and Olympic Rings—A298

Designs (Olympic Rings and): 10q, Sledding. 15q, Ice hockey. 20q, Bobsledding. 50q, Speed skating. 1 l, Slalom. 2 l, Ski jump. 2.50 l, Figure skating, pairs.

1972, Feb. 10

1403 A298 5q lt. olive & multi. 3 3
1404 " 10q lt. vio. & multi. 6 3
1405 " 15q multicolored 7 3
1406 " 20q pink & multi. 12 3
1407 " 50q lt. blue & multi. 25 8
1408 " 1 l ocher & multi. 52 15
1409 " 2 l lilac & multi. 1.10 30
Nos. 1403-1409 (7) 2.15 65

Souvenir Sheet

Imperf.

1410 A298 2.50 l bl. & multi. 1.35 50

11th Winter Olympic Games, Sapporo, Japan, Feb. 3–13. No. 1410 contains one stamp. Blue, ultramarine and silver margin with inscription. Size: 71x90mm.

Wild Strawberries A299

Wild Fruits and Nuts: 10q, Blackberries. 15q, Hazelnuts. 20q, Walnuts. 25q, Strawberry-tree fruit. 30q, Dogwood berries. 2.40 l, Rowan berries.

1972, Mar. 20 **Litho.** ***Perf. 12***

1411 A299 5q lt. grn. & multi. 3 3
1412 " 10q yel. & multi. 6 3
1413 " 15q lt. vio. & multi. 7 3
1414 " 20q pink & multi. 12 3
1415 " 25q multicolored 17 5
1416 " 30q " 18 4
1417 " 2.40 l " 1.20 30
Nos. 1411-1417 (7) 1.83 51

"Your Heart is your Health" A300

Worker and Student A301

Design: 1.20 l, Cardiac patient and electrocardiogram.

1972, Apr. 7 ***Perf. 12x12½***

1418 A300 1.10 l multicolored 65 14
1419 " 1.20 l rose & multi. 75 18

World Health Day 1972.

1972, Apr. 24 Litho. *Perf. 11½x12½*

Design: 2.05 l, Assembly Hall, dancers and emblem.

1420	A301	25q multicolored	11	5
1421	"	2.05 l bl. & multi.	1.25	35

7th Trade Union Congress, May 8.

Qemal Stafa A302

Designs: 15q, Memorial flame. 25q, Monument "Spirit of Defiance" (vert.).

Perf. 12½x12, 12x12½

1972, May 5

1422	A302	15q gray & multi.	7	3
1423	"	25q sal. rose, blk. & gray	11	5
1424	"	1.90 l dull yellow & black	1.05	40

30th anniversary of the murder of Qemal Stafa and of Martyrs' Day.

Camellia A303

Designs: Various camellias.

1972, May 10 *Perf. 12x12½*

Flowers in Natural Colors

1425	A303	5q lt. bl. & blk.	3	3
1426	"	10q citron & blk.	6	3
1427	"	15q greenish gray & blk.	7	3
1428	"	25q pale salmon & black	15	5
1429	"	45q gray & black	25	6
1430	"	50q salmon pink & black	27	8
1431	"	2.50 l bluish gray & black	1.20	30
		Nos. 1425-1431 (7)	2.03	58

High Jump—A304

Designs (Olympic and Motion Emblems and): 10q, Running. 15q, Shot put. 20q, Bicycling. 25q, Pole vault. 50q, Hurdles, women's. 75q, Hockey. 2 l, Swimming. 2.50 l, Diving, women's.

1972, June 30 Litho. *Perf. 12½x12*

1432	A304	5q multicolored	3	3
1433	"	10q lt. brn. & multi.	5	3
1434	"	15q lt. lilac & multi.	7	3
1435	"	20q multicolored	12	3
1436	"	25q lt. vio. & multi.	14	3
1437	"	50q lt. grn. & multi.	27	4
1438	"	75q multicolored	40	8
1439	"	2 l multicolored	1.10	40
		Nos. 1432-1439 (8)	2.18	67

Miniature Sheet

Imperf.

1440	A304	2.50 l multi.	1.35	45

20th Olympic Games, Munich, Aug. 26–Sept. 11. Nos. 1432–1439 each issued in sheets of 8 stamps and one label (3x3) showing Olympic rings in gold. Size of No. 1440: 70x87mm.

Autobus A305

Designs: 25q, Electric train. 80q, Ocean liner Tirana. 1.05 l, Automobile. 1.20 l, Trailer truck.

1972, July 25 Litho. *Perf. 12*

1441	A305	15q org. brn. & multi.	10	3
1442	"	25q gray & multi.	11	5
1443	"	80q dp. grn. & multi.	40	8
1444	"	1.05 l multicolored	52	14
1445	"	1.20 l "	70	25
		Nos. 1441-1445 (5)	1.83	55

Arm Wrestling A306

Folk Games: 10q, Piggyback ball game. 15q, Women's jumping. 25q, Rope game (srum). 90q, Leapfrog. 2 l, Women throwing pitchers.

1972, Aug. 18

1446	A306	5q multicolored	3	3
1447	"	10q lt. bl. & multi.	5	3
1448	"	15q rose & multi.	10	3
1449	"	25q lt. bl. & multi.	15	5
1450	"	90q ocher & multi.	60	8
1451	"	2 l lt. grn. & multi.	1.25	32
		Nos. 1446-1451 (6)	2.18	54

1st National Festival of People's Games.

Mastheads—A307

Designs: 25q, Printing press. 1.90 l, Workers reading paper.

1972, Aug. 25

1452	A307	15q lt. bl. & black	7	3
1453	"	25q red, green & black	11	5
1454	"	1.90 l lt. vio. & blk.	1.05	27

30th Press Day.

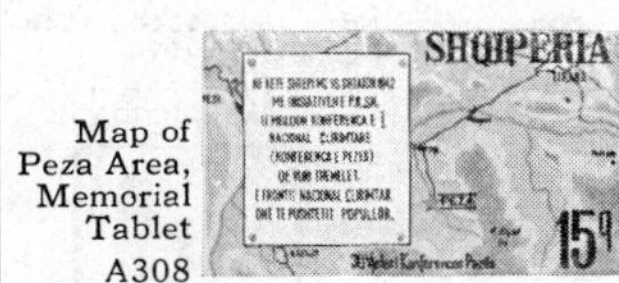

Map of Peza Area, Memorial Tablet A308

1972, Sept. 16 Multicolored

1455	A308	15q *shown*	7	3
1456	"	25q *Guerrillas with flag*	11	5
1457	"	1.90 l *Peza Conference memorial*	1.00	27

30th anniversary, Conference of Peza.

Partisans, by Sotir Capo—A309

Paintings: 10q, Woman, by Ismail Lulani (vert.). 15q, "Communists," by Lec Shkreli (vert.). 20q, View of Nendorit, 1941, by Sali Shijaku (vert.). 50q, Woman with Sheaf, by Zef Shoshi (vert.). 1 l, Landscape with Children, by Dhimitraq Trebicka. 2 l, Women on Bicycles, by Vilson Kilica. 2.30 l, Folk Dance, by Abdurrahim Buza.

Perf. 12½x12, 12x12½

1972, Sept. 25 Lithographed

1458	A309	5q gold & multi.	3	3
1459	"	10q " "	5	3
1460	"	15q " "	7	3
1461	"	20q " "	12	4
1462	"	50q " "	27	8
1463	"	1 l " "	65	15
1464	"	2 l " "	1.25	27
		Nos. 1458-1464 (7)	2.44	63

Miniature Sheet

Imperf.

1465	A309	2.30 l gold & multi.	1.50	45

No. 1465 contains one stamp (41x68 mm.); silver margin. Size: 55x82mm.

Congress Emblem A310

Design: 2.05 l, Young worker with banner.

1972, Oct. 23 Litho. *Perf. 12*

1466	A310	25q silver, red & gold	11	5
1467	"	2.05 l silver & multi.	1.10	30

Union of Working Youth, 6th Congress.

55 VJETORI I REVOLUCIONIT SOCIALIST TE TETORIT
1917 1972
SHQIPERIA 1.10 LEKE

Hammer and Sickle A311

60 VJETORI I PAVARESISE
1912 1972
25q
SHQIPERIA

Ismail Qemali A312

Design: 1.20 l, Lenin as orator.

1972, Nov. 7 Litho. *Perf. 11½x12*

1468	A311	1.10 l multicolored	55	15
1469	"	1.20 l "	60	18

55th anniversary of the Russian October Revolution.

Perf. 12x11½, 11½x12

1972, Nov. 29

Designs: 15q, Albanian fighters (horiz.). 65q, Rally (horiz.). 1.25 l, Coat of arms.

1470	A312	15q red, bright blue & black	7	3
1471	"	25q yellow, black & red	15	5
1472	"	65q red, salmon & black	35	10
1473	A312	1.25 l dull red & black	65	20

60th anniversary of independence.

Cock, Mosaic A313

Mosaics, 2nd–5th centuries, excavated near Buthrotium and Apollonia: 10q, Bird (vert.). 15q, Partridges (vert.). 25q, Warrior's legs. 45q, Nymph riding dolphin (vert.). 50q, Fish (vert.). 2.50 l, Warrior with helmet.

1972, Dec. 10 *Perf. 12½x12, 12x12½*

1474	A313	5q silver & multi.	3	3
1475	"	10q " "	5	3
1476	"	15q " "	10	6
1477	"	25q " "	14	8
1478	"	45q " "	25	9
1479	"	50q " "	27	10
1480	"	2.50 l " "	1.35	30
		Nos. 1474-1480 (7)	2.19	69

Nicolaus Copernicus A314

Designs: 10q, 25q, 80q, 1.20 l, Various portraits of Copernicus. 1.60 l, Heliocentric solar system.

1973, Feb. 19 Litho. *Perf. 12x12½*

1481	A314	5q lilac rose & multi.	4	3
1482	"	10q dull olive & multi.	5	3
1483	"	25q multicolored	15	5
1484	"	80q lt. vio. & multi.	42	14
1485	"	1.20 l blue & multi.	65	20
1486	"	1.60 l gray & multi.	85	27
		Nos. 1481-1486 (6)	2.16	72

500th anniversary of the birth of Nicolaus Copernicus (1473–1543), Polish astronomer.

Flowering Cactus—A315

Designs: Various flowering cacti.

1973, Mar. 25 Litho. *Perf. 12*

1487	A315	10q multicolored	5	3
1488	"	15q "	7	3
1489	"	20q beige & multi.	10	4
1490	"	25q gray & multi.	15	5
1491	"	30q beige & multi.	20	6
1492	"	65q gray & multi.	40	12
1493	"	80q multicolored	50	17
1494	"	2 l "	1.25	35
		Nos. 1487-1494 (8)	2.72	85

Nos. 1487–1494 printed se-tenant.

Guard and Factories A316

Design: 1.80 l, Guard and guards with prisoner.

1973, Mar. 20 Litho. *Perf. 12½x12*

1495 A316 25q ultra. & black 14 5
1496 " 1.80 l dk. red & multi. 95 35

30th anniversary of the State Security Branch.

Common Tern A317

Sea Birds: 15q, White-winged black terns (vert.). 25q, Black-headed gull (vert.). 45q, Great black-headed gull. 80q, Slender-billed gull (vert.). 2.40 l, Sandwich terns.

Perf. 12½x12, 12x12½

1973, Apr. 30

1497 A317 5q gold & multi. 3 3
1498 " 15q " " 8 3
1499 " 25q " " 14 5
1500 " 45q " " 25 9
1501 " 80q " " 45 17
1502 " 2.40 l " " 1.20 38
Nos. 1497-1502 (6) 2.15 75

Letters, 1913 Cancellation and Post Horn A318

Design: 1.80 l, Mailman and 1913 cancelation.

1973, May. 5 Litho. *Perf. 12x11½*

1503 A318 25q red & multi. 20 5
1504 " 1.80 l " " 1.25 35

60th anniversary of Albanian stamps.

Farmer, Worker, Soldier A319

Design: 25q, Woman and factory (vert.).

1973, June 4 *Perf.12*

1505 A319 25q carmine rose 20 5
1506 " 1.80 l yel., dp. orange & black 1.00 35

7th Congress of Albanian Women's Union.

Creation of General Staff, by G. Madhi—A320

Designs: 40q, "August 1949," sculpture by Sh. Haderi (vert.). 60q, "Generation after Generation," sculpture by H. Dule (vert.). 80q, "Defend Revolutionary Victories," by M. Fushekati.

1973, July 10 Litho. *Perf. 12½x12*

1507 A320 25q gold & multi. 11 5
1508 " 40q " " 20 8
1509 " 60q " " 28 12
1510 " 80q " " 36 17

30th anniversary of the People's Army.

"Electrification," by S. Hysa—A321

Albanian Paintings: 10q, Woman Textile Worker, by N. Nallbani. 15q, Gymnasts, by M. Fushekati. 50q, Aviator, by F. Stamo. 80q, Fascist Prisoner, by A. Lakuriqi. 1.20 l, Workers with Banner, by P. Mele. 1.30 l, Farm Woman, by Zef Shoshi. 2.05 l, Battle of Tenda, by F. Haxhiu. 10q, 50q, 80q, 1.20 l, 1.30 l, vertical.

Perf. 12½x12, 12x12½

1973, Aug. 10

1511 A321 5q gold & multi. 3 3
1512 " 10q " " 5 3
1513 " 15q " " 13 3
1514 " 50q " " 30 10
1515 " 80q " " 55 17
1516 " 1.20 l " " 75 25
1517 " 1.30 l " " 95 27
Nos. 1511-1517 (7) 2.76 88

Souvenir Sheet

Imperf.

1518 A321 2.05 l multi. 1.50 75

No. 1518 contains one stamp; light yellow margin. Size: 98x62mm.

Mary Magdalene, by Caravaggio A322

Paintings by Michelangelo da Caravaggio: 10q, The Lute Player (horiz.). 15q, Self-portrait. 50q, Boy Carrying Fruit and Flowers. 80q, Still Life (horiz.). 1.20 l, Narcissus. 1.30 l, Boy Peeling Apple. 2.05 l, Man with Feathered Hat.

Perf. 12x12½, 12½x12

1973, Sept. 28

1519 A322 5q gold & multi. 3 3
1520 " 10q " " 5 3
1521 " 15q gold, blk. & gray 7 3
1522 " 50q gold & multi. 25 10
1523 " 80q " " 40 17
1524 " 1.20 l " " 65 25
1525 " 1.30 l " " 75 27
Nos. 1519-1525 (7) 2.20 88

Souvenir Sheet

Imperf.

1526 A322 2.05 l multi. 1.25 75

400th anniversary of the birth of Michelangelo da Caravaggio (Merisi; 1573?-1609), Italian painter. No. 1526 contains one stamp (63x73mm.); gray marginal inscription. Size: 81x99mm.

Soccer—A323

Designs: 5q-1.25 l, Various soccer scenes. 2.05 l, Ball in goal and list of cities where championships were held.

1973, Oct. 30 Litho. *Perf. 12½x12*

1527 A323 5q multicolored 3 3
1528 " 10q " 5 3
1529 " 15q " 7 3
1530 " 20q " 10 3
1531 " 25q " 11 5
1532 " 90q " 40 18
1533 " 1.20 l " 54 25
1534 " 1.25 l " 55 25
Nos. 1527-1534 (8) 1.85 85

Minature Sheet

Imperf.

1535 A323 2.05 l multicolored 95 50

World Soccer Cup, Munich 1974. Size of No. 1535: 82x54mm.

Weight Lifter A324

Designs: Various stages of weight lifting. 1.20 l, 1.60 l, horizontal.

1973, Oct. 30 Litho. *Perf. 12*

1536 A324 5q multicolored 3 3
1537 " 10q " 5 3
1538 " 25q " 11 5
1539 " 90q " 40 18
1540 " 1.20 l " 54 25
1541 " 1.60 l " 75 33
Nos. 1536-1541 (6) 1.88 87

Weight Lifting Championships, Havana, Cuba.

Ballet A325 Harvester Combine A326

Perf. 12½x12, 12x12½

1973-74 Lithographed

Designs: 5q, Cement factory, Kavaje. 10q, Ali Kelmendi truck factory and tank cars (horiz.). 25q, "Communication." 35q, Skiers and hotel (horiz.). 60q, Resort (horiz.). 80q, Mountain lake. 1 l, Mao Tse-tung textile mill. 1.20 l, Steel workers. 2.40 l, Welder and pipe. 3 l, Skanderbeg Monument, Tirana. 5 l, Roman arches, Durrës.

1543 A325 5q gold & multi. 3 3
1544 " 10q " " 5 3
1545 " 15q " " 7 3
1545A A326 20q " " 10 3
1546 " 25q " " 11 5
1547 " 35q " " 16 7
1548 " 60q " " 27 12
1549 " 80q " " 36 17
1549A " 1 l " " 45 20
1549B " 1.20 l " " 54 25
1549C " 2.40 l " " 1.10 50
1550 " 3 l " " 1.35 60
1551 " 5 l " " 2.25 1.00
Nos. 1543-1551 (13) 6.84 3.08

Issue dates: Nos. 1545-1546, 1549-1550, Dec. 5, 1973; others in 1974.

Mao Tse-tung A327

Design: 1.20 l, Mao Tse-tung addressing crowd.

1973, Dec. 26 *Perf. 12*

1552 A327 85q gold, red & sepia 38 17
1553 " 1.20 l gold, red & sepia 54 25

80th birthday of Mao Tse-tung.

Old Man and Dog, by Gericault A328

Paintings by Jean Louis André Theodore Gericault: 10q, Horse's Head. 15q, Male Model. 25q, Head of Black Man. 1.20 l, Self-portrait. 2.05 l, Raft of the Medusa (horiz.). 2.20 l, Battle of the Giants.

Perf. 12x12½, 12½x12

1974, Jan. 18 Lithographed

1554 A328 10q gold & multi. 5 3
1555 " 15q " " 7 3
1556 " 20q " " 10 3
1557 " 25q gold & black 11 5
1558 " 1.20 l gold & multi. 54 25
1559 " 2.20 l " " 1.00 40
Nos. 1554-1559 (6) 1.87 79

Souvenir Sheet

Imperf.

1560 A328 2.05 l gold & multi. 95 50

No. 1560 contains one stamp (87x78 mm.). Sheet has gold margin and inscription. Size: 100x78mm.

Lenin, by Pandi Mele A329

Designs: 25q, Lenin with Sailors on Cruiser Aurora, by Dhimitraq Trebicka (horiz.). 1.20 l, Lenin, by Vilson Kilica.

Perf. 12½x12, 12x12½

1974, Jan. 21

1561 A329 25q gold & multi. 11 5
1562 " 60q " " 30 15
1563 " 1.20 l " " 54 25

50th anniversary of the death of Lenin (1870-1924).

Swimming Duck, Mosaic—A330

Designs: Mosaics from the 5th-6th Centuries A.D., excavated near Buthrotium, Pogradec and Apollonia.

1974, Feb. 20 Litho. *Perf. 12½x12*

Multicolored

1564 A330 5q *shown* 3 3
1565 " 10q *Bird and flower* 5 3
1566 " 15q *Vase and grapes* 7 3
1567 " 25q *Duck* 11 5
1568 " 40q *Donkey and bird* 20 6
1569 " 2.50 l *Sea horse* 1.10 42
Nos. 1564-1569 (6) 1.56 62

Soccer—A331

Designs: Various scenes from soccer. 2.05 l, World Soccer Cup and names of participating countries.

1974, Apr. 25 Litho. *Perf. 12½x12*

1570 A331 10q gold & multi. 5 3
1571 " 15q " " 7 3
1572 " 20q " " 10 3
1573 " 25q " " 11 5
1574 " 40q " " 20 6
1575 " 80q " " 40 12
1576 " 1 l " " 50 20
1577 " 1.20 l " " 54 25
Nos. 1570-1577 (8) 1.97 77

Souvenir Sheet

Imperf.

1578 A331 2.05 l gold & multi. 95 50

World Cup Soccer Championship, Munich, June 13–July 7. No. 1578 contains one stamp (60x60mm.) with simulated perforations. Size: 72x75mm.

Arms of Albania, Soldier
A332

Design: 1.80 l, Soldier and front page of 1944 Congress Book.

1974, May 24 Litho. *Perf. 12*

1579 A332 25q multicolored 11 5
1580 " 1.80 l " 90 35

30th anniversary of the First Anti-Fascist Liberation Congress of Permet.

Bittersweet
A333

Designs: Medicinal Plants. 40q, 80q, 2.20 l, horizontal.

1974, May 5 *Perf. 12x12½*

Multicolored

1581 A333 10q *shown* 5 3
1582 " 15q *Arbutus* 7 3
1583 " 20q *Lilies of the valley* 10 3
1584 " 25q *Autumn crocus* 11 5
1585 " 40q *Borage* 20 6
1586 " 80q *Soapwort* 40 12
1587 " 2.20 l *Gentian* 95 45
Nos. 1581-1587 (7) 1.88 77

Revolutionaries with Albanian Flag
A334

Design: 1.80 l, Portraits of 5 revolutionaries (vert.).

Perf. 12½x12, 12x12½

1974, June 10

1588 A334 25q red, blk. & lilac 11 5
1589 " 1.80 l yel., red & blk. 90 35

50th anniversary Albanian Bourgeois Democratic Revolution.

European Redwing—A335

Designs: Songbirds; Nos. 1597-1600 vertical.

Perf. 12½x12, 12x12½

1974, July 15 Lithographed

Multicolored

1594 A335 10q *shown* 5 3
1595 " 15q *European robin* 7 3
1596 " 20q *Greenfinch* 10 3
1597 " 25q *Bullfinch* 11 5
1598 " 40q *Hawfinch* 20 6
1599 " 80q *Blackcap* 40 12
1600 " 2.20 l *Nightingale* 95 45
Nos. 1594-1600 (7) 1.88 77

Globe
A336

Designs: 1.20 l, UPU emblem. 2.05 l, Jet over globe.

1974, Aug. 25 Litho. *Perf. 12x12½*

1601 A336 85q grn. & multi. 42 12
1602 " 1.20 l vio. & olive green 54 25

Miniature Sheet

Imperf.

1603 A336 2.05 l blue & multi. 95 50

Centenary of Universal Postal Union. No. 1603 contains one stamp, gold margin. Size: 77x78mm.

Widows, by Sali Shijaku—A337

Albanian Paintings: 15q, Drillers, by Danish Jukniu (vert.). 20q, Workers with Blueprints, by Clirim Ceka. 25q, Call to Action, by Spiro Kristo (vert.). 40q, Winter Battle, by Sabaudin Xhaferi. 80q, Comrades, by Clirim Ceka (vert.). 1 l, Aiding the Partisans, by Guri Madhi. 1.20 l, Teacher with Pupils, by Kleo Nini Brezat. 2.05 l, Comrades in Arms, by Guri Madhi.

Perf. 12½x12, 12x12½

1974, Sept. 25

1604 A337 10q silver & multi. 5 3
1605 " 15q " " 7 3
1606 " 20q " " 10 5
1607 " 25q " " 11 5
1608 " 40q " " 20 6
1609 " 80q " " 40 12
1610 " 1 l " " 50 20
1611 " 1.20 l " " 65 25
Nos. 1604-1611 (8) 2.08 79

Miniature Sheet

Imperf.

1612 A337 2.05 l silver & multi. 1.25 50

No. 1612 contains one stamp. Size: 86x77mm.

Crowd on Tien An Men Square
A338

Design: 1.20 l, Mao Tse-tung (vert.).

1974, Oct. 1 *Perf. 12*

1613 A338 85q gold & multi. 42 12
1614 " 1.20 l " " 54 25

25th anniversary of the proclamation of the People's Republic of China.

Women's Volleyball
A339

Designs (Spartakiad Medal and): 15q, Women hurdlers. 20q, Women gymnasts. 25q, Mass exercises in Stadium. 40q, Weight lifter. 80q, Wrestlers. 1 l, Military rifle drill. 1.20 l, Soccer.

1974, Oct. 9 *Perf. 12x12½*

1615 A339 10q multicolored 5 3
1616 " 15q " 7 3
1617 " 20q " 10 3
1618 " 25q gray & multi. 11 5
1619 " 40q multicolored 20 6
1620 " 80q lilac & multi. 40 12
1621 " 1 l multicolored 45 20
1622 " 1.20 l tan & multi. 54 25
Nos. 1615-1622 (8) 1.92 77

National Spartakiad, Oct. 9-17.

View of Berat
A340

Designs: 80q, Enver Hoxha addressing Congress, bas-relief (horiz.). 1 l, Hoxha and leaders leaving Congress Hall.

Perf. 12x12½, 12½x12

1974, Oct. 20 Lithographed

1623 A340 25q rose car. & blk. 11 5
1624 " 80q yel., brn. & blk. 40 12
1625 " 1 l dp. lilac & blk. 45 20

30th anniversary of 2nd Congress of Berat.

Anniversary Emblem, Factory Guards
A341

Designs (Anniversary Emblem and): 35q, Chemical industry. 50q, Agriculture. 80q, Arts. 1 l, Atomic diagram and computer. 1.20 l, Youth education. 2.05 l, Anniversary emblem: Crowd and History Book.

1974, Nov. 29 Litho. *Perf. 12½x12*

1626 A341 25q grn. & multi. 11 5
1627 " 35q ultra. & multi. 16 7
1628 " 50q brn. & multi. 22 10
1629 " 80q multicolored 40 12
1630 " 1 l violet & multi. 45 20
1631 " 1.20 l multicolored 54 25
Nos. 1626-1631 (6) 1.88 79

Miniature Sheet

Imperf.

1632 A341 2.05 l gold & multi. 95 50

30th anniversary of liberation from Fascism. No. 1632 contains one stamp. Size: 80x69mm.

Artemis, from Apolloni
A342

1974, Dec. 25 Photo. *Perf. 12x12½*

Silver & Multicolored

1633 A342 10q *shown* 5 3
1634 " 15q *Zeus statue* 7 3
1635 " 20q *Poseidon statue* 10 3
1636 " 25q *Illyrian helmet* 11 5
1637 " 40q *Amphora* 20 6
1638 " 80q *Agrippa* 40 12
1639 " 1 l *Demosthenes* 45 20
1640 " 1.20 l *Head of Bilia* 54 25
Nos. 1633-1640 (8) 1.92 77

Miniature Sheet

Imperf.

1641 A342 2.05 l *Artemis and amphora* 95 50

Archaeological discoveries in Albania. No. 1641 contains one stamp. Size: 95x95 mm.

Workers and Factories
A343

Design: 25q, Handshake, tools and book (vert.).

1975, Feb. 11 Litho. *Perf. 12*

1642 A343 25q brn. & multi. 11 5
1643 " 1.80 l yel. & multi. 85 32

Albanian Trade Unions, 30th anniversary.

Chicory
A344

1975, Feb. 15

Gray and Multicolored

1644 A344 5q *shown* 3 3
1645 " 10q *Houseleek* 5 3
1646 " 15q *Columbine* 7 3
1647 " 20q *Anemone* 10 3
1648 " 25q *Hibiscus* 11 5
1649 " 30q *Gentian* 14 6
1650 " 35q *Hollyhock* 17 6
1651 " 2.70 l *Iris* 1.20 50
Nos. 1644–1651 (8) 1.87 79

Protected flowers.

Jesus, from Doni Madonna
A345

Works by Michelangelo: 10q, Slave, sculpture. 15q, Head of Dawn, sculpture. 20q, Awakening Giant, sculpture. 25q, Cumaenian Sybil, Sistine Chapel. 30q, Lorenzo di Medici, sculpture. 1.20 l, David, sculpture. 2.05 l, Self-portrait. 3.90 l, Delphic Sybil, Sistine Chapel.

1975, Mar. 20 Litho. ***Perf. 12x12½***

1652 A345 5q gold & multi. 3 3
1653 " 10q " " 5 3
1654 " 15q " " 7 3
1655 " 20q " " 10 3
1656 " 25q " " 11 5
1657 " 30q " " 14 6
1658 " 1.20 l " " 54 25
1659 " 3.90 l " " 1.75 80
Nos. 1652–1659 (8) 2.79 1.28

Miniature Sheet

Imperf.

1660 A345 2.05 l gold & multi. 95 50

500th birth anniversary of Michelangelo Buonarroti (1475–1564), Italian sculptor, painter and architect. Size of No. 1660: 76x85mm.

Two-wheeled Cart—A346

Albanian Transportation of the Past: 5q, Horseback rider. 15q, Lake ferry. 20q, Coastal three-master. 25q, Phaeton. 3.35 l, Early automobile on bridge.

1975, Apr. 15 Litho. ***Perf. 12½x12***

1661 A346 5q bl. grn. & multi. 3 3
1662 " 10q olive & multi. 5 3
1663 " 15q lilac & multi. 7 3
1664 " 20q multicolored 10 3
1665 " 25q " 11 5
1666 " 3.35 l ocher & multi. 1.50 65
Nos. 1661–1666 (6) 1.86 82

Guard at Frontier Stone
A347

Guardsman and Militia
A348

1975, Apr. 25 ***Perf. 12***

1667 A347 25q multicolored 11 5
1668 A348 1.80 l " 86 32

30th anniversary of Frontier Guards.

Posting Illegal Poster—A349

Designs: 60q, Partisans in battle. 1.20 l, Partisan killing German soldier, and Albanian coat of arms.

1975, May 9 ***Perf. 12½x12***

1669 A349 25q multicolored 11 5
1670 " 60q " 30 12
1671 " 1.20 l red & multi. 60 24

30th anniversary of victory over Fascism.

European Widgeons
A350

Waterfowl: 10q, Red-crested pochards. 15q, White-fronted goose. 20q, Northern pintails. 25q, Red-breasted merganser. 30q, Eider ducks. 35q, Whooper swan. 2.70 l, Shovelers.

1975, June 15 Litho. ***Perf. 12***

1672 A350 5q brt. bl. & multi. 3 3
1673 " 10q yel. grn. & multi. 5 3
1674 " 15q brt. rose lilac & multi. 7 3
1675 " 20q bl. grn. & multi. 10 3
1676 " 25q multicolored 12 5
1677 " 30q " 14 6
1678 " 35q org. & multi. 18 6
1679 " 2.70 l multicolored 1.20 50
Nos. 1672–1679 (8) 1.89 79

Shyqyri Kanapari, by Musa Qarri
A351

Albanian Paintings: 10q, Woman Saving Children in Sea, by Agim Faja. 15q, "November 28, 1912" (revolution), by Petrit Ceno (horiz.). 20q, "Workers Unite," by Sali Shijaku. 25q, The Partisan Shota Galica, by Ismail Lulani. 30q, Victorious Resistance Fighters, 1943, by Nestor Jonuzi. 80q, Partisan Couple in Front of Red Flag, by Vilson Halimi. 2.05 l, Dancing Procession, by Abdurahim Buza. 2.25 l, Republic Day Celebration, by Fatmir Haxhiu (horiz.).

Perf. 12x12½, 12½x12

1975, July 15 **Lithographed**

1680 A351 5q gold & multi. 3 3
1681 " 10q " " 5 3
1682 " 15q " " 7 3
1683 " 20q " " 12 4
1684 " 25q " " 14 5
1685 " 30q " " 17 6
1686 " 80q " " 50 12
1687 " 2.25 l " " 1.15 45
Nos. 1680–1687 (8) 2.23 81

Miniature Sheet

Imperf.

1688 A351 2.05 l gold & multi. 1.10 50

No. 1688 contains one stamp. Size: 67x98mm. Nos. 1680–1687 issued in sheets of 8 stamps and gold center label showing palette and easel.

Farmer Holding Reform Law
A352

Design: 2 l, Produce and farm machinery.

1975, Aug. 28 ***Perf. 12***

1689 A352 15q multicolored 7 3
1690 " 2 l " 90 40

Agrarian reform, 30th anniversary.

Alcynonium Palmatum
A353

Corals: 10q, Paramuricea chamaeleon. 20q, Coralium rubrum. 25q, Eunicella covalini. 3.70 l, Cladocora cespitosa.

1975, Sept. 25 Litho. ***Perf. 12***

1691 A353 5q blue, olive & black 3 3
1692 " 10q blue & multi. 5 3
1693 " 20q " " 10 4
1694 " 25q blue & black 11 5
1695 " 3.70 l blue & black 1.65 70
Nos. 1691–1695 (5) 1.94 85

Bicycling
A354

Designs (Montreal Olympic Games Emblem and): 10q, Canoeing. 15q, Fieldball. 20q, Basketball. 25q, Water polo. 30q, Hockey. 1.20 l, Pole vault. 2.05 l, Fencing. 2.15 l, Montreal Olympic Games emblem and various sports.

1975, Oct. 20 Litho. ***Perf. 12½***

1696 A354 5q multicolored 3 3
1697 " 10q " 5 3
1698 " 15q " 7 3
1699 " 20q " 10 4
1700 " 25q " 11 5
1701 " 30q " 14 6
1702 " 1.20 l " 54 25
1703 " 2.05 l " 95 50
Nos. 1696–1703 (8) 1.99 99

Miniature Sheet

Imperf.

1704 A354 2.15 l org. & multi. 1.10 90

21st Olympic Games, Montreal, July 18–Aug. 8, 1976. Size of No. 1704: 72x76mm.

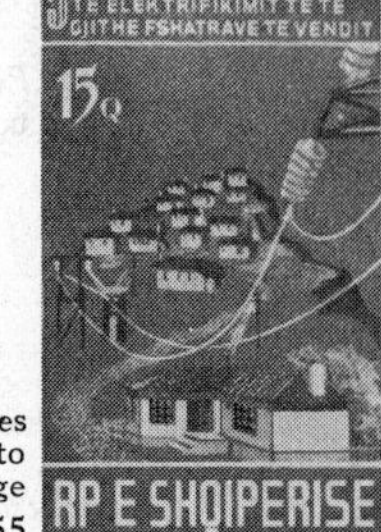

Power Lines Leading to Village
A355

Designs: 25q, Transformers and insulators. 80q, Dam and power station. 85q, Television set, power lines, grain and cogwheel.

1975, Oct. 25 ***Perf. 12x12½***

1705 A355 15q ultra. & yel. 7 3
1706 " 25q brt. vio. & pink 11 5
1707 " 80q lt. green & gray 40 12
1708 " 85q ocher & brown 42 12

General electrification, 5th anniversary.

Child, Rabbit and Teddy Bear Planting Tree—A356

Fairy Tales: 10q, Mother fox. 15q, Ducks in school. 20q, Little pigs building house. 25q, Animals watching television. 30q, Rabbit and bear at work. 35q, Working and playing ants. 2.70 l, Wolf in sheep's clothes.

1975, Dec. 25 Litho. ***Perf. 12½x12***

1709 A356 5q blk. & multi. 3 3
1710 " 10q " " 5 3
1711 " 15q " " 7 3
1712 " 20q " " 12 4
1713 " 25q " " 14 5
1714 " 30q " " 16 6
1715 " 35q " " 20 6
1716 " 2.70 l " " 1.40 50
Nos. 1709–1716 (8) 2.17 80

Arms, People, Factories
A357

Design: 1.90 l, Arms, government building, celebrating crowd.

1976, Jan. 11 Litho. ***Perf. 12***

1717 A357 25q gold & multi. 12 5
1718 " 1.90 l " " 88 34

30th anniversary of proclamation of Albanian People's Republic.

Ice Hockey, Olympic Games' Emblem
A358

Designs: 10q, Speed skating. 15q, Biathlon. 50q, Ski jump. 1.20 l, Slalom. 2.15 l, Figure skating, pairs. 2.30 l, One-man bobsled.

1976, Feb. 4

1719 A358 5q silver & multi. 3 3
1720 " 10q " " 5 3
1721 " 15q " " 7 3
1722 " 50q " " 22 10
1723 " 1.20 l " " 54 25
1724 " 2.30 l " " 1.05 48
Nos. 1719–1724 (6) 1.96 92

Miniature Sheet

Perf. 12 on 2 sides x imperf.

1725 A358 2.15 l silv. & multi. 1.10 90

12th Winter Olympic Games, Innsbruck, Austria, Feb. 4–15. Size of No. 1725 66x79mm.

Meadow Saffron
A359

Medicinal Plants: 10q, Deadly nightshade. 15q, Yellow gentian. 20q, Horse chestnut. 70q, Shield fern. 80q, Marsh mallow. 2.30 l, Thorn apple.

1976, Apr. 10 Litho. ***Perf. 12x12½***

1726 A359 5q black & multi. 3 3
1727 " 10q " " 5 3
1728 " 15q " " 7 3
1729 " 20q " " 10 4
1730 " 70q " " 32 12
1731 " 80q " " 40 12
1732 " 2.30 l " " 1.00 55
Nos. 1726–1732 (7) 1.97 92

Bowl and Spoon—A360

Designs: 15q, Flask (vert.). 20q, Carved handles (vert.). 25q, Pistol and dagger. 80q, Wall hanging (vert.). 1.20 l, Earrings and belt buckle. 1.40 l, Jugs (vert.).

1976 Litho. ***Perf. 12½x12, 12x12½***

1733 A360 10q lilac & multi. 5 3
1734 " 15q gray & multi. 7 3
1735 " 20q multicolored 10 4
1736 " 25q car. & multi. 11 5
1737 " 80q yel. & multi. 40 12
1738 " 1.20 l multicolored 54 25
1739 A360 1.40 l tan & multi. 60 28
Nos. 1733–1739 (7) 1.87 80

National Ethnographic Conference, Tirana, June 28.

Founding of Cooperatives, by Zef Shoshi
A361

Paintings: 10q, Going to Work, by Agim Zajmi (vert.). 25q, Crowd Listening to Loudspeaker, by Vilson Kilica. 40q, Woman Welder, by Sabaudin Xhaferi (vert.). 50q, Factory, by Isuf Sulovari (vert.). 1.20 l, 1942 Revolt, by Lec Shkreli (vert.). 1.60 l, Coming Home from Work, by Agron Dine. 2.05 l, Honoring a Young Pioneer, by Andon Lakuriqi.

Perf. 12½x12, 12x12½

1976, Aug. 8 Lithographed

1740 A361 5q gold & multi. 3 3
1741 " 10q " " 5 3
1742 " 25q " " 11 5
1743 " 40q " " 20 8
1744 " 50q " " 22 10
1745 " 1.20 l " " 54 25
1746 " 1.60 l " " 80 30
Nos. 1740–1746 (7) 1.95 84

Miniature Sheet

Perf. 12 on 2 sides x imperf.

1747 A361 2.05 l gold & multi. 1.00 50

Size of No. 1747: 92x79mm.

Red Flag, Agricultural Symbols
A362

Enver Hoxha, Partisans and Albanian Flag
A363

Design: 1.20 l, Red flag and raised pickax.

1976, Nov. 1

1748 A362 25q multicolored 12 5
1749 " 1.20 l " 60 25

7th Workers Party Congress.

1976, Oct. 28 ***Perf. 12x12½***

Design: 1.90 l, Demonstrators with Albanian flag.

1750 A363 25q multicolored 12 5
1751 " 1.90 l " 88 34

35th anniversary of anti-Fascist demonstrations.

Attacking Partisans, Meeting House
A364

Designs (Red Flag and): 25q, Partisans, pickax and gun. 80q, Workers, soldiers, pickax and gun. 1.20 l, Agriculture and industry. 1.70 l, Dancers, symbols of science and art.

1976, Nov. 8 Litho. ***Perf. 12x12½***

1752 A364 15q gold & multi. 8 3
1753 " 25q " " 12 5
1754 " 80q " " 40 12
1755 " 1.20 l " " 60 25
1756 " 1.70 l " " 85 28
Nos. 1752–1756 (5) 2.05 73

35th anniversary of 1st Workers Party Congress.

Young Workers and Track
A365

Design: 1.25 l, Young soldiers and Albanian flag.

1976, Nov. 23 ***Perf. 12***

1757 A365 80q yel. & multi. 40 12
1758 " 1.25 l car. & multi. 60 25

Union of Young Communists, 35th anniversary.

"Cuca e Maleve" Ballet
A366

Designs: Scenes from ballet "Mountain Girl."

1976, Dec. 14 ***Perf. 12***

1759 A366 10q gold & multi. 5 3
1760 " 15q " " 8 3
1761 " 20q " " 10 4
1762 " 25q " " 12 5
1763 " 80q " " 40 12
1764 " 1.20 l " " 60 25
1765 " 1.40 l " " 70 30
Nos. 1759–1765 (7) 2.05 82

Miniature Sheet

Perf. 12 on 2 sides x imperf.

1766 A366 2.05 l gold & multi. 1.10 40

Size of No. 1766: 77x68mm.

Bashtoves Castle
A367

Albanian Castles: 15q, Gjirokastres. 20q, Ali Pash Tepelenes. 25q, Petreles. 80q, Beratit. 1.20 l, Durresit. 1.40 l, Krujes.

1976, Dec. 30 Litho. ***Perf. 12***

1767 A367 10q black & dull blue 5 3
1768 " 15q black & green 8 3
1769 " 20q black & gray 10 4
1770 " 25q blk. & brn. 12 5
1771 " 80q black & rose 40 12
1772 " 1.20 l blk. & violet 60 25
1773 " 1.40 l blk. & brown red 70 30
Nos. 1767–1773 (7) 2.05 82

Skanderbeg's Shield and Spear
A368

Skanderbeg's Weapons: 80q, Helmet, sword and scabbard. 1 l, Halberd, quiver with arrows, crossbow and spear.

1977, Jan. 28 Litho. ***Perf. 12***

1774 A368 15q silver & multi. 8 3
1775 " 80q " " 40 12
1776 " 1 l " " 50 20

Skanderbeg (1403–1468), national hero.

Ilia Oiqi, Messenger in Storm
A369

Polyvinylchloride Plant, Vlore
A370

Modern Heroes: 10q, Ilia Dashi, sailor in battle. 25q, Fran Ndue Ivanaj, fisherman in storm. 80q, Zeliha Allmetaj, woman rescuing child. 1 l, Ylli Zaimi, rescuing goats from flood. 1.90 l, Isuf Plloci, fighting forest fire.

1977, Feb. 28 Litho. ***Perf. 12x12½***

1777 A369 5q brn. & multi. 3 3
1778 " 10q ultra. & multi. 5 3
1779 " 25q blue & multi. 12 5
1780 " 80q ocher & multi. 40 12
1781 " 1 l brn. & multi. 45 20
1782 " 1.90 l " " 85 38
Nos. 1777–1782 (6) 1.90 81

1977, Mar. 29 Litho. ***Perf. 12½x12***

Designs: 25q, Naphtha fractioning plant, Ballsh. 65q, Hydroelectric station and dam, Fjerzes. 1 l, Metallurgical plant and blast furance, Elbasan.

1783 A370 15q silver & multi. 8 3
1784 " 25q " " 12 5
1785 " 65q " " 32 12
1786 " 1 l " " 45 20

6th Five-year plan.

Qerime Halil Galica
A371

Victory Monument, Tirana
A372

Design: 1.25 l, Qerime Halil Galica "Shota" and father Azem Galica.

1977, Apr. 20 Litho. ***Perf. 12***

1787 A371 80q dark red 40 12
1788 " 1.25 l gray blue 60 25

"Shota" Galica, communist fighter.

1977, May 5 Litho. ***Perf. 12***

Designs (Red Star and): 80q, Clenched fist, Albanian flag. 1.20 l, Bust of Qemal Stafa and poppies.

1789 A372 25q multicolored 12 5
1790 " 80q " 40 12
1791 " 1.20 l " 60 25

35th anniversary of Martyrs' Day.

Physician Visiting Farm, Mobile Clinic
A373

Designs: 10q, Cowherd and cattle ranch. 20q, Militia woman helping with harvest, rifle and combine. 80q, Modern village, highway and power lines. 2.95 l, Tractor and greenhouses.

1977, June 18

1792	A373	5q	multicolored	3	3
1793	"	10q	"	5	3
1794	"	20q	"	10	4
1795	"	80q	"	40	12
1796	"	2.95 l	"	1.50	58
	Nos. 1792–1796 (5)			2.08	80

"Socialist transformation of the villages."

Armed Workers, Flag and Factory A374

Design: 1.80 l, Workers with proclamation and flags.

1977, June 20

1797	A374	25q	multicolored	12	5
1798	"	1.80 l	"	85	22

9th Labor Unions Congress.

Kerchief Dance A375

Designs: Various folk dances.

1977, Aug. 20 Litho. *Perf. 12*

1799	A375	5q	multicolored	3	3
1800	"	10q	"	5	3
1801	"	15q	"	8	3
1802	"	25q	"	12	5
1803	"	80q	"	40	12
1804	"	1.20 l	"	60	25
1805	"	1.55 l	"	75	30
	Nos. 1799–1805 (7)			2.03	81

Miniature Sheet

Perf. 12 on 2 sides x imperf.

1806	A375	2.05 l	multi.	1.10	40

Size of No. 1806: 56x74mm.
See Nos. 1836–1840.

Attack A376

Designs: 25q, Enver Hoxha addressing Army. 80q, Volunteers and riflemen. 1 l, Volunteers, hydrofoil patrolboat and MiG planes. 1.90 l, Volunteers and Albanian flag.

1977, July 10 Litho. *Perf. 12*

1807	A376	15q	gold & multi.	8	3
1808	"	25q	" "	12	5
1809	"	80q	" "	40	12
1810	"	1 l	" "	45	20
1811	"	1.90 l	" "	85	38
	Nos. 1807–1811 (5)			1.90	78

"One People—One Army."

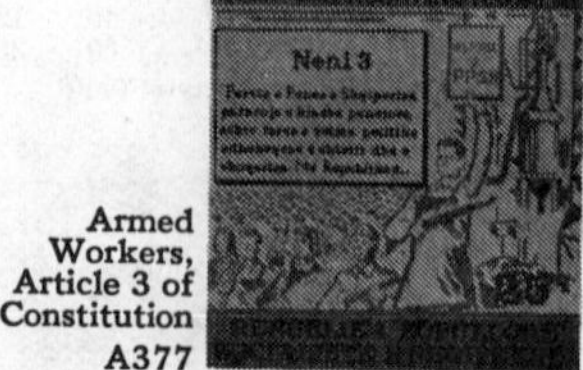

Armed Workers, Article 3 of Constitution A377

Design: 1.20 l, Symbols of farming and fertilizer industry, Article 25 of Constitution.

1977, Oct.

1812	A377	25q	red, gold & black	12	5
1813	A377	1.20 l	red, gold & black	60	25

New Constitution.

Picnic A378

Film Frames: 15q, Telephone lineman in winter. 25q, Two men and a woman. 80q, Workers. 1.20 l, Boys playing in street. 1.60 l, Harvest.

1977, Oct. 25 Litho. *Perf. 12½x12*

1814	A378	10q	blue green	5	3
1815	"	15q	multicolored	8	3
1816	"	25q	black	12	5
1817	"	80q	multicolored	40	12
1818	"	1.20 l	deep claret	60	25
1819	"	1.60 l	multicolored	80	25
	Nos. 1814–1819 (6)			2.05	73

Albanian films.

Farm Workers in Field, by V. Mio A379

Paintings by V. Mio: 10q, Landscape in Snow. 15q, Grazing Sheep under Walnut Tree in Spring. 25q, Street in Korce. 80q, Horseback Riders on Mountain Pass. 1 l, Boats on Shore. 1.75 l, Tractors Plowing Fields. 2.05 l, Self-portrait.

1977, Dec. 25 Litho. *Perf. 12½x12*

1820	A379	5q	gold & multi.	3	3
1821	"	10q	" "	5	3
1822	"	15q	" "	8	3
1823	"	25q	" "	12	5
1824	"	80q	" "	40	12
1825	"	1 l	" "	50	20
1826	"	1.75 l	" "	85	35
	Nos. 1820–1826 (7)			2.03	81

Miniature Sheet

Imperf.; Perf. 12 Horiz. between Vignette and Value Panel.

1827	A379	2.05 l	gold & multi.	1.00	50

Size of No. 1827: 66x101mm.

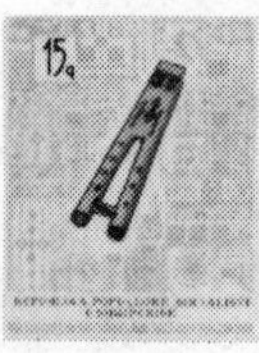

Pan Flute A380 **Albanian Flag, Monument and People A381**

Folk Musical Instruments: 25q, Single-string goat's-head fiddle. 80q, Woodwind. 1.20 l, Drum. 1.70 l, Bagpipe. Background shows various woven folk patterns.

1978, Jan. 20 *Perf. 12x12½*

1828	A380	15q	multicolored	8	3
1829	"	25q	"	12	5
1830	"	80q	"	40	12
1831	"	1.20 l	"	60	25
1832	"	1.70 l	"	85	32
	Nos. 1828–1832 (5)			2.05	77

1978 *Perf. 12½x12, 12x12½*

Designs: 25q, Ismail Qemali and fighters (horiz.). 1.65 l, People dancing around Albanian flag (horiz.).

1833	A381	15q	multicolored	8	3
1834	"	25q	"	12	5
1835	"	1.65 l	"	82	25

65th anniversary of independence.

Folk Dancing Type of 1977

Designs: Various dances.

1978, Feb. 15 Litho. *Perf. 12*

1836	A375	5q	multicolored	3	3
1837	"	25q	"	12	5
1838	"	80q	"	40	12
1839	"	1 l	"	50	20
1840	"	2.30 l	"	1.10	45
	Nos. 1836–1840 (5)			2.15	85

Nos. 1836–1840 have white background around dancers, Nos. 1799–1805 have pinkish shadows.

Tractor Drivers, by Dhimitraq Trebicka A382

Working Class Paintings: 80q, Steeplejack, by Spiro Kristo. 85q, "A Point in the Discussion," by Skender Milori. 90q, Oil rig crew, by Anesti Cini (vert.). 1.60 l, Metal workers, by Ramadan Karanxha. 2.20 l, Political discussion, by Sotiraq Sholla.

1978, Mar. 25 Litho. *Perf. 12*

1841	A382	25q	multicolored	12	5
1842	"	80q	"	40	12
1843	"	85q	"	42	14
1844	"	90q	"	45	16
1845	"	1.60 l	"	80	25
	Nos. 1841–1845 (5)			2.19	72

Miniature Sheet

Perf. 12 on 2 sides x imperf.

1846	A382	2.20 l	multi.	*2.00*	*75*

Size of No. 1846: 72x98mm.

Woman with Rifle and Pickax—A383

Design: 1.95 l, Farm and Militia women, industrial plant.

1978, June 1 Litho. *Perf. 12*

1847	A383	25q	gold & red	12	5
1848	"	1.95 l	" "	95	38

8th Congress of Women's Union.

Children and Flowers A384

Designs: 10q, Children with rifle, ax, book and flags. 25q, Dancing children in folk costume. 1.80 l, Children in school.

1978, June 1 Lithographed

1849	A384	5q	multicolored	3	3
1850	"	10q	"	5	3
1851	"	25q	"	12	5
1852	"	1.80 l	"	90	35

International Children's Day.

Spirit of Skanderbeg as Conqueror A385

Designs: 10q, Battle at Mostar Bridge 80q, Marchers and Albanian flag. 1.20 l Riflemen in winter battle. 1.65 l, Abdy Frasheri (1839–1892). 2.20 l, Rifles scroll and pen, League building. 2.60 l League headquarters, Prizren.

1978, June 10 Litho. *Perf. 12*

1853	A385	10q	multicolored	5	[illegible]
1854	"	25q	"	12	[illegible]
1855	"	80q	"	40	1[illegible]
1856	"	1.20 l	"	60	2[illegible]
1857	"	1.65 l	"	82	2[illegible]
1858	"	2.60 l	"	1.25	4[illegible]
	Nos. 1853–1858 (6)			3.24	1.1[illegible]

Miniature Sheet

Perf. 12 on 2 sides x imperf.

1859	A385	2.20 l	multi.	1.20	

Centenary of League of Prizren. Size of No. 1859: 74x69mm.

Guerrillas and Flag, 1943 A386

Designs: 25q, Soldier, sailor, airman, militiaman (horiz.). 1.90 l, Members of armed forces, civil guards, and Young Pioneers.

1978, July 10 *Perf. 11½x12½*

1860	A386	5q	multicolored	3	[illegible]
1861	"	25q	"	12	[illegible]
1862	"	1.90 l	"	95	3[illegible]

35th anniversary of People's Army.

Woman with Machine Carbine A387 **Kerchief Dance A388**

Designs: 25q, Man with target rifle (horiz.). 95q, Man shooting with telescopic sights (horiz.). 2.40 l, Woman target shooting with pistol.

Perf. 12½x12, 12x12½

1978, Sept. 20 Lithographed

1863	A387	25q	blk. & yellow	12	5
1864	"	80q	org. & black	40	12
1865	"	95q	red & black	42	14
1866	"	2.40 l	car. & blk.	1.15	45

32nd National Rifle-shooting Championships, Sept. 20.

1978, Oct. 6 *Perf. 12*

Designs: 15q, Musicians. 25q, Fiddler with single-stringed instrument. 80q, Dancers, men. 1.20 l, Saber dance. 1.90 l, Singers, women.

1867	A388	10q	multicolored	5	3
1868	"	15q	"	8	3
1869	"	25q	"	12	5
1870	"	80q	"	40	12
1871	"	1.20 l	"	60	25
1872	"	1.90 l	"	90	38
	Nos. 1867–1872 (6)			2.15	86

National Folklore Festival.

No. 1736 Surcharged with New Value, 2 Bars and "RICCIONE 78"

1978 Litho. *Perf. 12½x12*

1873	A360	3.30 l on 25q	multi.	1.55	65

Riccione 78 Philatelic Exhibition.

SEMI-POSTAL STAMPS.

Nos. 148-151 Surcharged in Red and Black

+ 5 qind.

1924 *Perf. 12½, 12* **Unwmkd.**

B1 A18 5q+5q yellow green 1.75 1.75
B2 " 10q+5q carmine 1.75 1.75
B3 " 25q+5q dark blue 1.75 1.75
B4 " 50q+5q dark green 1.75 1.75

Nos. B1 to B4 with Additional Surcharge in Red and Black

+ 5 qind.

1924 *Perf. 12½x11½, 12½.*

B5 A18 5q+5q+5q yel. grn. 1.75 1.75
B6 " 10q+5q+5q carmine 1.75 1.75
B7 " 25q+5q+5q dk. blue 1.75 1.75
B8 " 50q+5q+5q dk. grn. 1.75 1.75

Issued under Italian Dominion.

Nurse and Child
SP1
Photogravure

1943 *Perf. 14* **Unwmkd.**

B9 SP1 5q+5q dark green 10 13
B10 " 10q+10q olive brown 10 13
B11 " 15q+10q rose red 15 18
B12 " 25q+15q sapphire 20 25
B13 " 30q+20q violet 25 30
B14 " 50q+25q dark orange 30 35
B15 " 65q+30q greenish black 35 40
B16 " 1fr+40q chestnut 45 50
Nos. B9-B16 (8) 1.90 2.24

The surtax was for the control of tuberculosis.

Issued under German Administration.

War Victims
SP2

1944

B17 SP2 5q+5(q) dp. green 2.25 2.25
B18 " 10q+5(q) dp. brown 2.25 2.25
B19 " 15q+5(q) car. lake 2.25 2.25
B20 " 25q+10(q) dp. blue 2.25 2.25
B21 " 1fr+50q dark olive 2.25 2.25
B22 " 2fr+1(fr) purple 2.25 2.25
B23 " 3fr+1.50(fr) dark orange 2.25 2.25
Nos. B17-B23 (7) 15.75 15.75

The surtax was for victims of World War II.

Independent State

Nos. B9 to B12 Surcharged in Carmine

1945 *Perf. 14.* **Unwmkd.**

B24 SP1 30q+15q on 5q+5q dark green 70 70
B25 " 50q+25q on 10q+10q olive brown 70 70
B26 " 1fr+50q on 15q+10q rose red 2.75 2.75
B27 " 2fr+1fr on 25q+15q sapphire 3.50 3.50

The surtax was for the Albanian Red Cross.

People's Republic

Nos. 361 to 366 Overprinted in Red (cross) and Surcharged in Black

KONGRESI
K.K.SH.
24-25-11-46
+0.10

1946 **Lithographed** *Perf. 11*

B28 A57 20q+10q bluish green 3.00 2.50
B29 " 30q+15q dp. org. 3.00 2.50
B30 " 40q+20q brown 3.00 2.50
B31 " 60q+30q red violet 3.00 2.50
B32 " 1fr+50q rose red 3.00 2.50
B33 " 3fr+1.50fr dk. blue 3.00 2.50
Nos. B28-B33 (6) 18.00 15.00

Issued to commemorate the Congress of the Albanian Red Cross, with surtax for the benefit of that institution.

Excellent counterfeits exist. Genuine: lithographed, dull gum. Counterfeits: typographed, shiny gum.

First Aid and Red Cross
SP3

Designs: 25q+5q, Nurse carrying child on stretcher. 65q+25q, Symbolic blood transfusion. 80q+40q, Mother and child.

1967, Dec. 1 **Litho.** *Perf. 11½x12*

B34 SP3 15q+5q black, red & brown 35 18
B35 " 25q+5q multicolored 55 30
B36 " 65q+25q black, gray & red 1.50 80
B37 " 80q+40q multi. 2.50 1.20

6th congress of the Albanian Red Cross.

AIR POST STAMPS.

Airplane Crossing Mountains
AP1

Wmk. 125

Wmkd. Lozenges. (125)

1925, May 30 **Typo.** *Perf. 14*

C1 AP1 5q green 35 35
C2 " 10q rose red 35 35
C3 " 25q deep blue 35 35
C4 " 50q dark green 35 35
C5 " 1fr dark violet & black 1.00 1.00
C6 " 2fr olive green & violet 1.50 1.50
C7 " 3fr brown orange & dark green 2.00 2.00
Nos. C1-C7 (7) 5.90 5.90

Nos. C1-C7 exist imperforate but are not known to have been regularly issued in that condition.

Nos. C1-C7 Overprinted

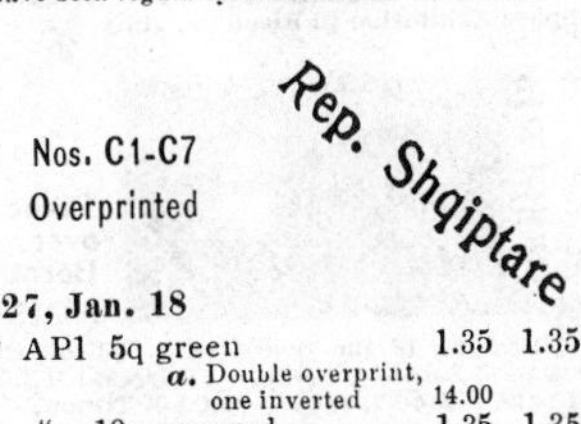

1927, Jan. 18

C8 AP1 5q green 1.35 1.35
a. Double overprint, one inverted 14.00
C9 " 10q rose red 1.35 1.35
a. Inverted overprint 12.00
b. Double overprint, one inverted 14.00
C10 " 25q deep blue 50 50
C11 " 50q dark green 50 50
a. Inverted overprint 12.00
C12 " 1fr dark violet & black 55 55
a. Inverted overprint 18.00
b. Double overprint 30.00
C13 " 2fr olive green & violet 55 55
C14 " 3fr brown orange & dark green 1.25 1.25
Nos. C8-C14 (7) 6.05 6.05

Nos. C1-C7 Overprinted

REP. SHQYPTARE
Fluturim' i I-ar
Vlonë--Brindisi
21. IV. 1928

1928, Apr. 21

C15 AP1 5q green 1.00 1.00
a. Inverted overprint 6.00
C16 " 10q rose red 1.00 1.00
C17 " 25q deep blue 1.00 1.00
C18 " 50q dark green 1.00 1.00
C19 " 1fr dark violet & black 10.00 10.00
C20 " 2fr olive green & violet 10.00 10.00
C21 " 3fr brown orange & dark green 10.00 10.00
Nos. C15-C21 (7) 34.00 34.00

First flight across the Adriatic, Valona to Brindisi, Apr. 21, 1928.

The variety "SHQYRTARE" occurs once in the sheet for each value. Price 3 times normal.

Nos. C1-C7 Overprinted in Red Brown

Mbr. Shqiptare

1929, Dec. 1

C22 AP1 5q green 3.00 3.00
C23 " 10q rose red 3.00 3.00
C24 " 25q deep blue 3.00 3.00
C25 " 50q dark green 10.00 10.00
C26 " 1fr dark violet & black 125.00 125.00
C27 AP1 2fr olive green & violet 125.00 125.00
C28 " 3fr brown orange & dk. green 125.00 125.00
Nos. C22-C28 (7) 394.00 394.00

Excellent counterfeits exist of Nos. C22 to C28.

King Zog and Airplane over Tirana
AP2

MBRETNIA SHQYPTARE
1 Fr. POSTA AJRORE

AP3

1930, Oct. 8 **Photo.** **Unwmkd.**

C29 AP2 5q yellow green 20 20
C30 " 15q rose red 40 40
C31 " 20q slate blue 50 50
C32 " 50q olive green 70 70
C33 AP3 1fr dark blue 1.20 1.20
C34 " 2fr olive brown 4.00 4.00
C35 " 3fr purple 5.00 5.00
Nos. C29-C35 (7) 12.00 12.00

Nos. C29-C35 Overprinted

TIRANE-ROME
6 KORRIK 1931

1931, July 6

C36 AP2 5q yellow green 1.50 1.50
a. Double overprint 20.00
C37 " 15q rose red 1.50 1.50
C38 " 20q slate blue 1.50 1.50
C39 " 50q olive green 1.50 1.50
C40 AP3 1fr dark blue 9.00 9.00
C41 " 2fr olive brown 9.00 9.00
C42 " 3fr purple 9.00 9.00
a. Inverted overprint 50.00
Nos. C36-C42 (7) 33.00 33.00

Issued in connection with the first air post flight from Tirana to Rome.

Only a very small part of this issue was sold to the public. Most of the stamps were given to the Aviation Company to help provide funds for conducting the service.

Issued under Italian Dominion.

Nos. C29-C30 Overprinted in Black

Mbledhja
Kushtetuëse
12-IV-1939
XVII

1939, Apr. 19 *Perf. 14.* **Unwmkd.**

C43 AP2 5q yellow green 40 30
C44 " 15q rose red 20 20

No. C32 With Additional Surcharge of New Value

C45 AP2 20q on 50q olive grn. 1.00 85
a. Inverted ovpt. 70.00 55.00

See note after No. 309.

King Victor Emmanuel III and Plane over Mountains
AP4

1939, Aug. 4 **Photogravure.**

C46 AP4 20q brown 7.00 2.00

Shepherds
AP5

Map of Albania Showing Air Routes
AP6

Designs: 20q, Victor Emmanuel III and harbor view. 50q, Woman and river valley. 1fr, Bridge at Vezirit. 2fr, Ruins. 3fr, Women waving to plane.

1940, Mar. **Unwmkd.**

C47	AP5	5q green	10	4
C48	AP6	15q rose red	15	5
C49	AP5	20q deep blue	15	6
C50	AP6	50q brown	20	25
C51	AP5	1fr myrtle green	75	85
C52	AP6	2fr brown black	1.75	1.85
C53	"	3fr rose violet	6.00	6.50
		Nos. C47-C53 (7)	9.10	9.60

People's Republic

Vuno-Himare
AP12

Designs (Albanian towns): 1 l and 10 l, Rozafat-Shkoder. 2 l and 20 l, Keshtjelle-Butrinto.

1950, Dec. 15 **Engr.** ***Perf. 12½x12***

C54	AP12	50q gray black	10	5
C55	"	1 l red brown	15	7
C56	"	2 l ultramarine	20	12
C57	"	5 l deep green	60	25
C58	"	10 l deep blue	1.10	65
C59	"	20 l purple	2.25	1.25
		Nos. C54-C59 (6)	4.40	2.39

Nos. C56-C58 Surcharged with New Value and Bars in Red or Black

1952-53

C60	AP12	50q on 2 l (R)	60.00	50.00
C61	"	50q on 5 l ('53)	10.00	6.00
C62	"	2.50 l on 5 l (R)	80.00	60.00
C63	"	2.50 l on 10 l ('53)	12.00	6.00

Banner with Lenin, Map of Stalingrad and Tanks
AP13

1963, Feb. 2 **Litho.** ***Perf. 14***

C67	AP13	7 l grn. & dp. car.	40	40

20th anniversary, Battle of Stalingrad.

Sputnik and Sun
AP14

Designs: 3 l, Lunik 4. 5 l, Lunik 3 photographing far side of the Moon. 8 l, Venus space probe. 12 l, Mars 1.

1963, Oct. 31 ***Perf. 12*** **Unwmkd.**

C68	AP14	2 l org., yel. & blk.	8	3
C69	"	3 l multicolored	12	4
C70	"	5 l rose lilac, yel. & black	40	10
C71	"	8 l dull viol., yel. & dp. car.	55	15
C72	"	12 l blue & orange	75	30
		Nos. C68-C72 (5)	1.90	62

Russian interplanetary explorations.

Nos. C68 and C71 Overprinted: "Riccione 23-8-1964"

1964, Aug. 23

C73	AP14	2 l org., yel. & blk.	1.25	1.25
C74	"	8 l dull violet, yel. & dp. car.	1.85	1.85

Issued to commemorate the International Space Exhibition in Riccione, Italy.

Plane over Berat
AP15

Designs (Plane over): 40q, Gjirokaster. 60q, Sarande. 90q, Dürres. 1.20 l, Kruje. 2.40 l, Boga. 4.05 l, Tirana.

1975, Nov. 25 **Litho.** ***Perf. 12***

C75	AP15	20q multicolored	10	4
C76	"	40q "	20	8
C77	"	60q "	28	12
C78	"	90q "	42	18
C79	"	1.20 l "	56	24
C80	"	2.40 l "	1.12	48
C81	"	4.05 l "	1.90	1.00
		Nos. C75-C81 (7)	4.58	2.14

SPECIAL DELIVERY STAMPS.

Issued under Italian Dominion.

King Victor Emmanuel III
SD1

Photogravure.

1940 ***Perf. 14.*** **Unwmkd.**

E1	SD1	25q bright violet	25	12
E2	"	50q red orange	1.35	1.60

Issued under German Administration.

No. E1 Overprinted in Carmine

14 Shtator 1943

1943

E3	SD1	25q bright violet	6.25	11.00

Proclamation of Albanian independence.

POSTAGE DUE STAMPS.

Nos. 35-39 Handstamped in Various Colors

1914 ***Perf. 14.*** **Unwmkd.**

J1	A3	2q org. brown & buff	1.75	1.20
J2	A3	5q green	1.75	1.50
J3	"	10q rose red	2.25	1.20
J4	"	25q dark blue	3.00	1.20
J5	"	50q violet & red	3.25	3.00
		Nos. J1-J5 (5)	12.00	8.10

The two parts of the overprint are handstamped separately. Stamps exist with one or both handstamps inverted, double, omitted or in wrong color.

Nos. 48-51 Overprinted in Black **TAKSË**

1914

J6	A3	(*a*) 10pa on 5q green	1.75	1.50
J7	"	(") 20pa on 10q rose red	1.75	1.50
J8	"	(*b*) 1gr on 25q blue	1.75	1.50
J9	"	(") 2gr on 50q violet & red	1.75	1.50

Same Design as Regular Issue of 1919, Overprinted

1919 ***Perf. 11½, 12½***

J10	A8	(4)q on 4k rose	4.00	4.00
J11	"	(10)q on 10k red, *green*	4.00	4.00
J12	"	20q on 2k orange, *gray*	4.00	4.00
J13	"	50q on 5k brown, *yellow*	4.00	4.00

Fortress at Scutari
D3

D5

Post Horn Overprinted in Black.

1920 ***Perf. 14x13.***

J14	D3	4q olive green	25	25
J15	"	10q rose red	28	55
J16	"	20q bistre brown	32	32
J17	"	50q black	40	50

1922 ***Perf. 12½.***

Background of Red Wavy Lines.

J23	D5	4q *red*	60	70
J24	"	10q "	60	70
J25	"	20q "	60	70
J26	"	50q "	60	70

Same Overprinted in White

1925

J27	D5	4q *red*	60	70
J28	"	10q "	60	70
J29	"	20q "	60	70
J30	"	50q "	60	70

The 10q with overprint in gold was a trial printing. It was not put in use.

D7

Coat of Arms
D8

Overprinted "QINDAR" in Red.

1926 ***Perf. 13½x13***

J31	D7	10q dark blue	15	20
J32	"	20q green	25	30
J33	"	30q red brown	40	50
		a. Double overprint		
J34	"	50q dark brown	60	75

Wmkd. Double Headed Eagle. (220)

1930 **Photogravure** ***Perf. 14, 14½***

J35	D8	10q dark blue	3.00	3.00
J36	"	20q rose red	80	80
J37	"	30q violet	80	80
J38	"	50q dark green	90	90

Nos. J36-J38 exist with overprint "14 Shtator 1943" (see Nos. 332-344) which is private and fraudulent on these stamps.

No. 253 Overprinted **Taksë**

1936 ***Perf. 14***

J39	A34	10q carmine	4.50	6.00

Issued under Italian Dominion.

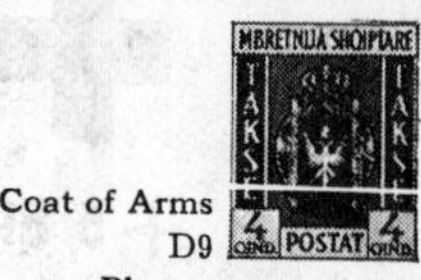

Coat of Arms
D9

Photogravure.

1940 ***Perf. 14.*** **Unwmkd.**

J40	D9	4q red orange	4.00	4.00
J41	"	10q bright violet	2.50	2.50
J42	"	20q brown	2.50	2.50
J43	"	30q dark blue	3.00	3.00
J44	"	50q carmine rose	4.00	4.00
		Nos. J40-J44 (5)	16.00	16.00

Prices of premium quality never hinged stamps will be in excess of catalogue price.

ALEXANDRETTA

(ăl'ĕg-zăn-drĕt'ȧ)

LOCATION—A political territory in northern Syria, bordering on Turkey.

GOVT.—A former French mandate.

AREA—10,000 sq. mi. (approx.).

POP.—270,000 (approx.).

Included in the Syrian territory mandated to France under the Versailles Treaty, the name was changed to Hatay in 1938. The following year France returned the territory to Turkey in exchange for certain concessions. See Hatay.

100 Centimes = 1 Piastre

Stamps of Syria, 1930-36, Overprinted or Surcharged in Black or Red:

Sandjak d'Alexandrette
a

SANDJAK D'ALEXANDRETTE
b

Sandjak d'Alexandrette
c

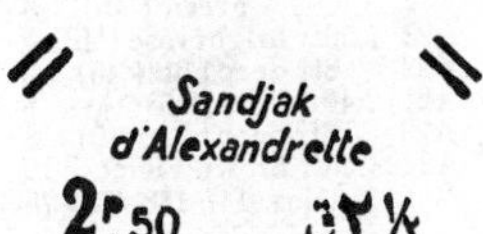

d

POSTES Sandjak d'Alexandrette 12P50

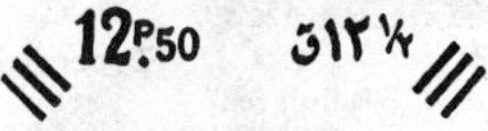
e

1938 *Perf. 12x12½, 13½.* **Unwmkd.**

1	A6	(a)	10c violet brown	15	15
2	A7	(")	20c brn. orange	15	15
3	A9	(b)	50c violet (R)	25	25
4	A10	(")	1p bis. brown	40	40
5	A12	(")	2p dk. vio. (R)	50	50
6	A13	(")	3p yellow green (R)	1.00	1.00
7	A14	(")	4p yel. orange	1.25	1.25
8	A16	(")	6p greenish black (R)	1.25	1.25
9	A20	(")	25p vio. brown	3.75	3.75
			Perf. 13½		
10	A15	(c)	75c orange red	35	35
11	A14	(d)	2.50p on 4p yellow orange	80	80
12	AP2	(e)	12.50p on 15p orange red	1.75	1.75
			Nos. 1-12 (12)	11.60	11.60

Nos. 4, 7, 10-12 Overprinted in Black

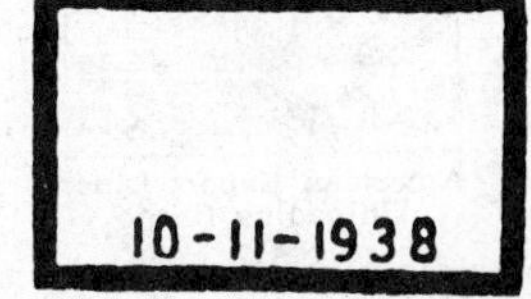

1938, Dec.

13	A15	75c orange red	20.00	14.00
14	A10	1p bistre brown	14.00	10.00
15	A14	2.50p on 4p yellow orange	8.00	6.00
16	"	4p yel. orange	11.00	8.00
17	AP2	12.50p on 15p orange red	22.50	22.50
		Nos. 13-17 (5)	75.50	60.50

Death of Kemal Atatürk, president of Turkey.

AIR POST STAMPS.

Air Post Stamps of Syria, 1937, Overprinted Type "b" in Red or Black

1938 *Perf. 13.* **Unwmkd.**

C1	AP14	½p dark violet (R)	27	27
C2	AP15	1p black (R)	27	27
C3	AP14	2p blue green (R)	1.00	1.00
C4	AP15	3p dp. ultra.	1.15	1.15
C5	AP14	5p rose lake	3.25	3.25
C6	AP15	10p red brown	3.75	3.75
C7	AP14	15p lake brown	3.75	3.75
C8	AP15	25p dark blue (R)	5.00	5.00
		Nos. C1-C8 (8)	18.44	18.44

POSTAGE DUE STAMPS.

Postage Due Stamps of Syria, 1925-31, Overprinted Type "b" in Black or Red

1938 *Perf. 13½.* **Unwmkd.**

J1	D5	50c brown, *yellow*	70	70
J2	D6	1p violet, *rose*	1.10	1.10
J3	D5	2p *blue* (R)	1.50	1.50
J4	"	3p *red orange*	2.25	2.25
J5	"	5p *blue green* (R)	3.50	3.50
J6	D7	8p *gray blue* (R)	3.50	3.50
		Nos. J1-J6 (6)	12.55	12.55

On No. J2, the overprint is vertical, reading up. On the other denominations, it is horizontal.

Stamps of Alexandretta were discontinued in 1938 and replaced by those of Hatay.

ALGERIA

(ăl-jēr'ĭ-ȧ)

LOCATION—North Africa.

GOVT.—Republic.

AREA—919,591 sq. mi.

POP.—17,300,000 (est. 1976).

CAPITAL—Algiers.

The former French colony of Algeria became an integral part of France on Sept. 1, 1958, when French stamps replaced Algerian stamps. Algeria became an independent country July 3, 1962.

100 Centimes = 1 Franc
100 Centimes = 1 Dinar (1964)

Stamps of France Overprinted in Red, Blue or Black:

ALGÉRIE
a

ALGÉRIE
b

ALGÉRIE
c

ALGÉRIE
d

1924-26 *Perf. 14x13½* **Unwmkd.**

1	A16	(a)	1c dark gray (R)	5	5
2	"	(")	2c violet brown	5	5
3	A16	(a)	3c orange	5	5
4	"	(")	4c yellow brown (Bl)	5	5
5	A22	(")	5c orange (Bl)	5	5
6	A16	(")	5c green ('25)	8	5
7	A23	(")	10c green	8	6
			a. Double ovpt.		
			b. Booklet pane of 10	2.50	
8	A22	(")	10c green ('25)	7	6
			a. Double ovpt.		
9	A20	(")	15c slate green	8	6
10	A23	(")	15c green ('25)	8	4
11	A22	(")	15c red brown (Bl) ('26)	10	8
12	"	(")	20c red brown (Bl)	6	5
13	"	(")	25c blue (R)	6	4
			a. Booklet pane of 10	5.00	
14	A23	(")	30c red (Bl)	12	8
15	A22	(")	30c cerise ('25)	15	5
16	"	(")	30c light blue (R) ('25)	6	5
			a. Booklet pane of 10	3.50	
17	"	(")	35c violet	12	12
18	A18	(b)	40c red & pale blue	12	12
			a. Inverted overprint		
19	A22	(a)	40c olive brown (R) ('25)	15	15
20	A18	(b)	45c green & blue (R)	15	15
			a. Inverted overprint		
21	A23	(a)	45c red (Bl) ('25)	12	10
22	"	(")	50c blue (R)	12	8
23	A20	(")	60c light violet	12	8
			a. Inverted overprint	250.00	
24	"	(")	65c rose (Bl)	12	6
25	A23	(")	75c blue (R)	25	10
			a. Double overprint	35.00	
26	A20	(")	80c vermilion ('26)	30	12
27	"	(")	85c vermilion (Bl)	25	6
28	A18	(b)	1fr claret & olive green	55	8
29	A22	(a)	1.05fr vermilion ('26)	45	25
30	A18	(c)	2fr orange & pale blue	40	22
31	"	(b)	3fr violet & blue ('26)	1.20	40
32	"	(d)	5fr blue & buff (R)	6.00	4.50
			Nos. 1-32 (32)	11.61	7.46

No. 15 was issued precanceled only. Prices for precanceled stamps in first column are for those which have not been through the post and have original gum. Prices in second column are for postally used, gumless stamps.

Street in Kasbah, Algiers
A1

Mosque of Sidi Abd-er-Rahman
A2

La Pêcherie Mosque
A3

1c POSTES ALGERIE RF
Marabout of Sidi Yacoub
A4

1926-39 Typo. *Perf. 14x13½*

33	A1	1c olive	4	4
34	"	2c red brown	6	5
35	"	3c orange	5	5
36	"	5c blue green	5	3
37	"	10c bright violet	5	3
		a. Booklet pane of 10	4.00	
38	A2	15c orange brown	8	6
39	"	20c green	7	3
40	A2	20c deep rose	7	3
41	"	25c blue green	10	10
42	"	25c blue ('27)	25	4
43	"	25c violet blue ('39)	5	3
44	"	30c blue	20	12
45	"	30c blue green ('27)	50	30
46	"	35c deep violet	60	55
47	"	40c olive green	5	3
		a. Booklet pane of 10	3.50	
48	A3	45c violet brown	20	12
49	"	50c blue	10	3
		a. Booklet pane of 10	3.50	
50	"	50c dark red ('30)	5	3
		a. Booklet pane of 10	5.00	
51	"	60c yellow green	8	5
52	"	65c black brown ('27)	1.25	90
53	A1	65c ultramarine ('38)	10	3
		a. Booklet pane of 10	1.50	
54	A3	75c carmine	25	18
55	"	75c blue ('29)	1.75	12
56	"	80c orange red	25	25
57	"	90c red ('27)	4.50	1.65
58	A4	1fr gray green & red brown	35	6
59	A3	1.05fr light brown	20	20
60	"	1.10fr magenta ('27)	3.75	90
61	A4	1.25fr dk. bl. & ultra.	50	50
62	"	1.50fr dark blue & ultra. ('27)	1.25	8
63	"	2fr Prussian blue & black brown	1.50	9
64	"	3fr violet & orange	2.50	75
65	"	5fr red & violet	5.00	1.65
66	"	10fr olive brown & rose ('27)	30.00	20.00
67	"	20fr violet & green ('27)	2.25	2.00
		Nos. 33-67 (35)	58.05	31.08

Type A4, 50c blue and rose red, inscribed "CENTENAIRE-ALGERIE" is France No. 255.

Stamps of 1926 Surcharged with New Values.

1927

68	A2	10c on 35c deep violet	6	6
69	"	25c on 30c blue	7	6
70	"	30c on 25c blue green	10	8
71	A3	65c on 60c yel. green	60	55
72	"	90c on 80c orange red	20	10
73	"	1.10fr on 1.05fr light brown	20	10
74	A4	1.50fr on 1.25fr dark blue & ultramarine	1.40	55
		Nos. 68-74 (7)	2.63	1.50

Bars cancel the old value on Nos. 68, 69, 73 and 74.

No. 4 Surcharged 5c

1927

75	A16	5c on 4c yellow brown	8	8

Bay of Algiers
A5

1930, May 4 **Engr.** *Perf. 11, 12½*

78	A5	10fr red brown	9.00	9.00
		a. Imperf. (pair)	32.50	

Centenary of Algeria and for International Philatelic Exhibition of North Africa, May, 1930.

One copy of No. 78 was sold with each 10fr admission.

Travel across the Sahara
A6

Arch of Triumph, Lambese
A7

Admiralty Building, Algiers
A8

Kings' Tombs near Touggourt
A9

El-Kebir Mosque, Algiers
A10

Oued River at Colomb-Béchar
A11

Sidi Bon Medine Cemetery at Tlemcen
A13

View of Ghardaia
A12

1936–41 Engraved *Perf. 13*

No.	Type	Description	Unused	Used
79	A6	1c ultramarine	5	5
80	A11	2c dark violet	5	5
81	A7	3c dark blue green	6	6
82	A12	5c red violet	6	6
83	A8	10c emerald	6	5
84	A9	15c red	6	5
85	A13	20c dark blue green	6	5
86	A10	25c rose violet	30	5
87	A12	30c yellow green	20	5
88	A9	40c brown violet	8	6
89	A13	45c deep ultra.	60	40
90	A8	50c red	40	5
91	A6	65c red brown	1.50	1.35
92	"	65c rose car. ('37)	25	5
93	"	70c red brn. ('39)	10	7
94	A11	75c slate blue	12	6
95	A7	90c henna brown	60	55
96	A10	1fr brown	15	5
97	A8	1.25fr light violet	30	20
98	"	1.25fr car. rose ('39)	6	7
99	A11	1.50fr turquoise blue	85	18
99A	"	1.50fr rose ('40)	22	10
100	A12	1.75fr henna brown	10	6
101	A7	2fr dark brown	10	8
102	A6	2.25fr yellow green	7.00	5.75
103	A12	2.50fr dk. ultra. ('41)	20	18
104	A13	3fr magenta	10	6
105	A10	3.50fr peacock blue	1.40	1.35
106	A8	5fr slate blue	10	6
107	A11	10fr henna brown	12	10
108	A9	20fr turquoise blue	35	35
		Nos. 79–108 (31)	15.60	11.65

See also Nos. 124–125, 162.

Nos. 82 and 100 with surcharge "E. F. M. 30frs" (Emergency Field Message) were used in 1943 to pay cable tolls for U. S. and Canadian servicemen.

Algerian Pavilion
A14

1937 *Perf. 13*

No.	Type	Description	Unused	Used
109	A14	40c bright green	50	35
110	"	50c rose carmine	15	6
111	"	1.50fr blue	75	30
112	"	1.75fr brown black	85	70

Paris International Exposition.

Constantine in 1837
A15

1937

No.	Type	Description	Unused	Used
113	A15	65c deep rose	35	8
114	"	1fr brown	3.00	35
115	"	1.75fr blue green	15	12
116	"	2.15fr red violet	15	5

Issued in commemoration of the centenary of the taking of Constantine by the French.

Ruins of a Roman Villa
A16

1938

No.	Type	Description	Unused	Used
117	A16	30c green	40	35
118	"	65c ultramarine	5	5
119	"	75c rose violet	45	40
120	"	3fr carmine rose	1.75	1.75
121	"	5fr yellow brown	2.25	1.50
		Nos. 117–121 (5)	4.90	4.05

Centenary of Philippeville.

No. 90 Surcharged in Black

0,25

1938

No.	Type	Description	Unused	Used
122	A8	25c on 50c red	6	4
		a. Dbl. surch.	20.00	15.00
		b. Invtd. surch.	15.00	11.00

1939 Types of 1936.
Numerals of Value on Colorless Background.

No.	Type	Description	Unused	Used
124	A7	90c henna brown	10	5
125	A10	2.25fr blue green	10	10

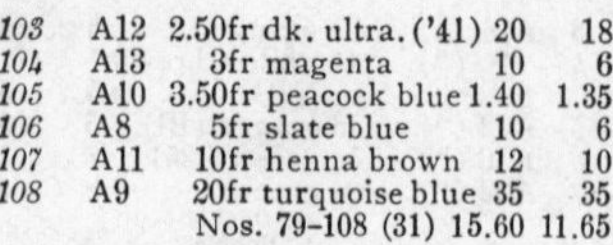

American Export Liner Unloading Cargo
A17

1939

No.	Type	Description	Unused	Used
126	A17	20c green	60	50
127	"	40c red violet	60	50
128	"	90c brown black	20	10
129	"	1.25fr rose	2.50	75
130	"	2.25fr ultramarine	60	60
		Nos. 126–130 (5)	4.50	2.45

New York World's Fair.

Type of 1926, Surcharged in Black

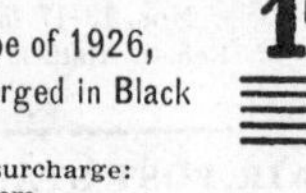

Two types of surcharge:
I. Bars 6mm.
II. Bars 7mm.

1939–40 *Perf. 14x13½*

No.	Type	Description	Unused	Used
131	A1	1fr on 90c crimson (I)	5	5
		a. Booklet pane of 10		
		b. Dbl. surcharge (I)	22.50	
		c. Invtd. surcharge (I)	13.50	
		d. Pair, one without surch. (I)	*400.00*	
		e. Type II ('40)	1.25	8
		f. Invtd. surcharge (II)	12.00	
		g. Pair, one without surch. (II)	*400.00*	

View of Algiers
A18

1941 Typographed

No.	Type	Description	Unused	Used
132	A18	30c ultramarine	6	5
133	"	70c sepia	6	5
134	"	1fr carmine rose	8	5

See also No. 163.

Marshal Pétain
A19 A20

1941 Engraved *Perf. 13*

No.	Type	Description	Unused	Used
135	A19	1fr dark blue	8	8

No. 53 Surcharged in Black with New Value and Bars.

1941 *Perf. 14x13½*

No.	Type	Description	Unused	Used
136	A1	50c on 65c ultramarine	15	6
		a. Booklet pane of 10		
		b. Inverted surch.	12.50	
		c. Pair, one without surch.	37.50	

1942 *Perf. 14x13*

No.	Type	Description	Unused	Used
137	A20	1.50fr orange red	15	15

Four other denominations of type A20 exist (4fr, 5fr, 10fr, 20fr), but were not placed in use.

Constantine A21 · Arms of Oran A22 · Algiers A23

Engraver's Name at Lower Left.

1942-43 Photogravure. *Perf. 12.*

No.	Type	Description	Unused	Used
138	A21	40c dark violet ('43)	7	5
139	A22	60c rose ('43)	8	6
140	A21	1.20fr yel. grn. ('43)	8	8
141	A23	1.50fr carmine rose	6	6
142	A22	2fr sapphire	7	6
143	A21	2.40fr rose ('43)	10	10
144	A23	3fr sapphire	8	8
145	A21	4fr blue ('43)	8	8
146	A22	5fr yel. grn. ('43)	8	8
		Nos. 138–146 (9)	70	65

Imperforates

Nearly all of Algeria Nos. 138–285, B39–B96, C1–C12 and CB1–CB3 exist imperforate. See note after France No. 395.

Without Engraver's Name.

1942–45 Typo. *Perf. 14x13½*

No.	Type	Description	Unused	Used
147	A23	10c dull brown violet ('45)	5	5
148	A22	30c deep blue green ('45)	4	4
149	A21	40c dull brown violet ('45)	5	4
150	A22	60c rose ('45)	5	4
151	A21	70c deep blue('45)	6	5
152	A23	80c dark blue green ('43)	5	5
153	A21	1.20fr deep blue green ('45)	6	6
154	A23	1.50fr bright rose ('43)	5	4
155	A22	2fr deep blue('45)	6	4
156	A21	2.40fr rose ('45)	8	8
157	A23	3fr deep blue('45)	8	5
158	A22	4.50fr brown violet	12	6
		Nos. 147–158 (12)	75	60

La Pêcherie Mosque
A24

1942 Typographed

No.	Type	Description	Unused	Used
159	A24	50c dull red	4	4
		a. Booklet pane of 10	3.50	

1942 Photogravure *Perf. 12*

No.	Type	Description	Unused	Used
160	A24	40c gray green	8	8
161	"	50c red	7	7

Types of 1936–41, Without "RF"

1942 Engraved *Perf. 13*

No.	Type	Description	Unused	Used
162	A11	1.50fr rose	6	4

Typographed.
Perf. 14x13½.

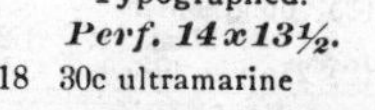

No.	Type	Description	Unused	Used
163	A18	30c ultramarine	6	6

"One Aim Alone—Victory"
A25 A26

1943 Lithographed *Perf. 12*

No.	Type	Description	Unused	Used
164	A25	1.50fr deep rose	5	5
165	A26	1.50fr dark blue	5	5

Type of 1942–3
Surcharged with New Value in Black.

1943 Photogravure

No.	Type	Description	Unused	Used
166	A22	2fr on 5fr red orange	8	8
		a. Surcharge omitted	125.00	

Summer Palace, Algiers
A27

1944, Dec. 1 **Lithographed**

167 A27 15fr slate 90 85
168 " 20fr light blue green 60 20
169 " 50fr dark carmine 35 30
170 " 100fr deep blue 1.20 1.00
171 " 200fr dull bistre brown 2.00 1.00
Nos. 167-171 (5) 5.05 3.35

Marianne A28 — Gallic Cock A29

1944-45

172 A28 10c gray 5 5
173 " 30c red violet 4 4
174 A29 40c rose carmine ('45) 6 6
175 A28 50c red 6 5
176 " 80c emerald 6 6
177 A29 1fr green ('45) 6 5
178 A28 1.20fr rose lilac 6 6
179 " 1.50fr dark blue 5 5
a. Dbl. impression 25.00
180 A29 2fr red 6 5
181 " 2fr dark brown ('45) 8 5
182 A28 2.40fr rose red 7 6
183 " 3fr purple 10 8
184 A29 4fr ultramarine ('45) 10 6
185 A28 4.50fr olive black 15 5
186 A29 10fr greenish black ('45) 30 18
Nos. 172-186 (15) 1.30 95

No. 38 Surcharged in Black **0f.30**

1944 ***Perf. 14 x 13½.***

187 A2 30c on 15c orange brown 5 4
a. Inverted surch. 5.00 4.00

This stamp exists precanceled only. See note below No. 32.

No. 154 Surcharged "RF" and New Value.

1945

190 A23 50c on 1.50fr bright rose 6 5
a. Inverted surch. 12.00

Stamps of France, 1944, Overprinted in Black **ALGÉRIE** *a*

1945-46

191 A99 80c yellow green 7 4
192 " 1fr greenish blue 7 4
193 " 1.20fr violet 7 4
194 " 2fr violet brown 8 5
195 " 2.40fr carmine rose 8 7
196 " 3fr orange 8 6
Nos. 191-196 (6) 45 30

Same Overprint on Stamps of France, 1945-47, in Black, Red or Carmine.

1945-47

197 A145 40c lilac rose 6 4
198 " 50c violet blue (R) 6 4
199 A146 60c brt. ultra. (R) 10 6
200 " 1fr rose red ('47) 6 5
201 " 1.50fr rose lilac ('47) 6 5
202 A147 2fr myrtle green (R) ('46) 6 4
203 " 3fr deep rose 7 4
204 " 4.50fr ultramarine (C) ('47) 35 5
205 " 5fr light green ('46) 12 8
206 " 10fr ultramarine 30 20
Nos. 197-206 (10) 1.24 65

Same Overprint on France No. 383 and New Value Surcharged in Black

1946

207 A99 2fr on 1.50fr henna brown 6 3
a. Without "2F" 110.00

Same Overprint on France Nos. 562 and 564, in Carmine or Blue.

1947

208 A153 10c deep ultramarine & black (C) 5 5
209 A155 50c brown, yellow & red (Bl) 15 10

Arms of: Constantine A30 — Algiers A31 — Oran A32

Typographed

1947-49 ***Perf. 14x13½*** **Unwmkd.**

210 A30 10c dark green & bright red 3 3
211 A31 50c black & orange 4 3
212 A32 1fr ultra. & yel. 5 3
213 A30 1.30fr black & greenish blue 25 25
214 A31 1.50fr purple & orange yellow 5 3
215 A32 2fr black & bright green 6 3
216 A30 2.50fr black & bright red 25 18
217 A31 3fr violet brown & green 7 5
218 A32 3.50fr light green & rose lilac 5 5
219 A30 4fr dark brown & bright green 6 5
220 A31 4.50fr ultramarine & scarlet 6 4
221 " 5fr black & greenish blue ('48) 5 4
222 A32 6fr brown & scarlet 8 6
223 " 8fr chocolate & ultra. ('48) 8 6
224 A30 10fr carmine & choc. ('48) 28 5
225 A31 15fr black & red ('49) 30 3
Nos. 210-225 (16) 1.76 1.01

See also Nos. 274-280, 285.

Peoples of the World
A33

1949, Oct. 24 **Engr.** ***Perf. 13***

226 A33 5fr green 70 70
227 " 15fr scarlet 80 80
228 " 25fr ultramarine 2.50 1.50

Issued to commemorate the 75th anniversary of the formation of the Universal Postal Union.

Grapes A34 — Apollo of Cherchell A35

Designs: 25fr, Dates. 40fr, Oranges and lemons.

1950, Feb. 25

229 A34 20fr violet brown, green & claret 85 15
230 " 25fr dark brown, dark green & brown orange 90 20
231 " 40fr brown, green, red orange & orange 1.50 30

1952 ***Perf. 13*** **Unwmkd.**

Designs: 12fr, 18fr, Isis statue, Cherchell. 15fr, 20fr, Child with eagle.

240 A35 10fr gray black 20 5
241 " 12fr orange brown 30 6
242 " 15fr deep blue 15 4
243 " 18fr rose red 35 15
244 " 20fr deep green 20 5
245 " 30fr deep blue 50 20
Nos. 240-245 (6) 1.70 55

War Memorial, Algiers A38 — Fossilized Nautilus A39

Phonolite Dike
A40

1952, Apr. 11

246 A38 12fr dark green 30 25

Issued to honor the French Africa Army.

1952, Aug. 11

247 A39 15fr bright crimson 50 40
248 A40 30fr deep ultramarine 60 50

Issued to publicize the 19th International Geological Congress, Algiers, Sept. 8-15, 1952.

French and Algerian Soldiers and Camel
A41

1952, Nov. 30

249 A41 12fr chestnut brown 50 35

Issued to commemorate the 50th anniversary of the establishment of the Sahara Companies.

Eugène Millon
A42

François C. Maillot A43 — Oranges A44

Portrait: 50fr, Alphonse Laveran.

Engraved.

1954, Jan. 4 ***Perf. 13*** **Unwmkd.**

250 A42 25fr dark green & chocolate 85 10
251 A43 40fr orange brown & brn. carmine 1.00 35
252 A42 50fr ultramarine & indigo 1.00 8

Military Health Service.

1954, May 8

253 A44 15fr indigo & blue 30 25

Issued to publicize the third International Congress on Agronomy, Algiers, 1954.

Type of France, 1954 Overprinted type "a" in Black.

Engraved.

1954, June 6 ***Perf. 13*** **Unwmkd.**

254 A240 15fr rose carmine 25 25

Liberation of France, 10th anniversary.

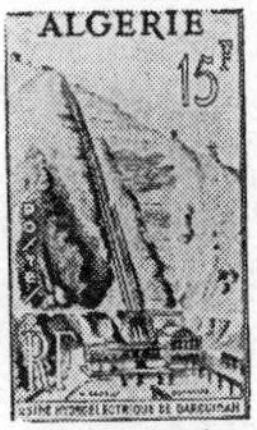

Darguinah Hydroelectric Works A45 — Patio of Bardo Museum A46

1954, June 19

255 A45 15fr lilac rose 40 30

Issued to commemorate the opening of Darguinah hydroelectric works.

1954 **Typographed** ***Perf. 14x13½***

257 A46 12fr red brown & brown orange 15 5
258 " 15fr dark blue & blue 15 5

See also Nos. 267-271.

Type of France, 1954, Overprinted type "a" in Carmine.

1954 **Engraved** ***Perf. 13***

260 A247 12fr dark green 45 40

Issued to commemorate the 150th anniversary of the first Legion of Honor awards at Camp de Boulogne.

St. Augustine—A47

1954, Nov. 11

261 A47 15fr chocolate 35 35

Issued to commemorate the 1600th anniversary of the birth of St. Augustine.

Aesculapius Statue and El Kattar Hospital, Algiers
A48

1955, Apr. 3 ***Perf. 13*** **Unwmkd.**
262 A48 15fr red 30 25

Issued to publicize the 30th French Congress of Medicine, Algiers, April 3-6, 1955.

Chenua Mountain and View of Tipasa
A49

1955, May 31
263 A49 50fr brown carmine 50 5

Issued to commemorate the 2000th anniversary of the founding of Tipasa.

Type of France, 1955
Overprinted type "a" in Red

1955, June 13
264 A251 30fr deep ultramarine 50 35

Issued to commemorate the 50th anniversary of the founding of Rotary International.

Marianne A50 **Great Kabylia Mountains** A51

Perf. 14x13½
1955, Oct. 3 **Typo.** **Unwmkd.**
265 A50 15fr carmine 15 5

See also No. 284.

1955, Dec. 17 **Engraved** ***Perf. 13***
266 A51 100fr indigo & ultra. 1.35 10

Bardo Type of 1954, "Postes" and "Algerie" in White. Typographed.

1955-57 ***Perf. 14x13½*** **Unwmkd.**
267 A46 10fr dark brown & light brown 12 5
268 " 12fr red brown & brown orange ('56) 15 5
269 " 18fr crimson & vermilion ('57) 35 8
270 " 20fr green & yellow green ('57) 20 20
271 " 25fr purple & bright purple 30 7
Nos. 267-271 (5) 1.12 45

Marshal Franchet d'Esperey
A52

1956, May 25 **Engraved** ***Perf. 13***
272 A52 15fr sapphire & indigo 40 40

Birth centenary of Marshal Franchet d'Esperey.

Marshal Jacques Leclerc
A53

1956, Nov. 29
273 A53 15fr red brown & sepia 35 35

Issued to commemorate the death of Marshal Leclerc.

Type of 1947-49 and

Arms of Bône
A54

Designs: 2fr, Arms of Tizi-Ouzou. 3fr, Arms of Mostaganem. 5fr, Arms of Tlemcen. 10fr, Arms of Setif. 12fr, Arms of Orleansville.

1956-58 **Typographed.** ***Perf. 14x13½***
274 A54 1fr green & vermilion 5 5
275 " 2fr vermilion & ultramarine ('58) 25 25
276 " 3fr ultramarine & emerald ('58) 30 10
277 " 5fr ultra. & yellow 10 5
278 A31 6fr red & green ('57) 30 25
279 A54 10fr deep claret & emerald ('58) 30 25
280 " 12fr ultramarine & red ('58) 30 27
Nos. 274-280 (7) 1.60 1.22

Nos. 275 and 279 are inscribed "Republique Francaise." See also No. 285.

View of Oran
A55

1956-58 **Engraved.** ***Perf. 13.***
281 A55 30fr dull purple 25 10
282 " 35fr carmine rose ('58) 55 30

Electric Train Crossing Bridge
A56

1957, Mar. 25
283 A56 40fr dark blue green & emerald 25 8

Marianne Type of 1955 Inscribed "Algerie" Vertically.

Perf. 14x13½
1957, Dec. 2 **Typo.** **Unwmkd.**
284 A50 20fr ultramarine 20 7

Arms Type of 1947-49 Inscribed "Republique Francaise"

1958, July
285 A31 6fr red & green 7.50 7.50

Independent State

France Nos. 939, 968, 945-946 and 1013 Overprinted "EA" and Bars, Handstamped or Typographed, in Black or Red

1962, July 2
286 A336 10c bright green 15 15
a. Typographed ovpt. 35 25
287 A349 25c lake & gray 25 10
a. Handstamped ovpt. 25 10
288 A339 45c bright violet & olive gray 3.00 2.75
a. Handstamped ovpt. 13.50 10.00
289 A339 50c slate green & light claret 3.00 2.75
a. Handstamped ovpt. 13.50 10.00
290 A372 1fr dark blue, slate & bistre 1.40 1.00
a. Handstamped ovpt. 1.60 1.00
Nos. 286-290 (5) 7.80 6.75

Post offices were authorized to overprint their stock of these 5 French stamps. The size of the letters was specified as 3x6mm. each, but various sizes were used. The post offices had permission to make their own rubber stamps. Typography, pen or pencil were also used. Many types exist. Colors of handstamped overprints include black, red, blue, violet. "EA" stands for Etat Algérien.

Mosque, Tlemcen
A57

Roman Gates of Lodi, Médéa
A58

Designs: 5c, Kerrata Gorge. 10c, Dam at Foum el Gherza. 95c, Oil field, Hassi Messaoud.

1962, Nov. 1 **Engr.** ***Perf. 13***
291 A57 5c Prussian green, grn. & choc. 12 10
292 A58 10c olive black & dark blue 12 10
293 A57 25c slate green, brn. & vermilion 45 7
294 " 95c dark blue, black & bistre 1.25 40
295 A58 1fr green & black 1.60 1.25
Nos. 291-295 (5) 3.54 1.92

The designs of Nos. 291-295 are similar to French issues of 1959-61 with "Republique Algeriénne" replacing "Republique Francaise."

Flag, Rifle, Olive Branch
A59

Design: Nos. 300-303, Broken chain and rifle added to design A59.

1963, Jan. 6 **Litho.** ***Perf. 12½***
Flag in Green and Red
296 A59 5c bister brown 20 6
297 " 10c blue 20 10
298 " 25c vermilion 1.40 5
299 " 95c violet 1.20 55
300 " 1fr green 85 15
301 " 2fr brown 2.50 50
302 " 5fr lilac 3.25 1.40
303 " 10fr gray 12.50 9.00
Nos. 296-303 (8) 22.10 11.81

Nos. 296-299 commemorate the successful revolution and Nos. 300-303 commemorate the return of peace.

Men of Various Races, Wheat Emblem and Globe
A60

1963, Mar. 21 **Engraved** ***Perf. 13***
304 A60 25c maroon, dull green & yellow 25 10

Issued for the "Freedom from Hunger" campaign of the U.N. Food and Agriculture Organization.

Map of Algeria and Emblems A61 **Physicians from 13th Century Manuscript** A62

1963, July 5 ***Perf. 13*** **Unwmkd.**
305 A61 25c blue, dk. brown, green & red 50 30

Issued to commemorate the first anniversary of Algeria's independence.

1963, July 29 **Engraved**
306 A62 25c brown red, grn. & bister 1.00 30

Issued to commemorate the Second Congress of the Union of Arab physicians.

Orange and Blossom A63 **Scales and Scroll** A64

1963 ***Perf. 14x13***
307 A63 8c gray grn. & org. 12 12
308 " 20c slate & org. red 18 18
309 " 40c greenish blue & orange 35 35
310 " 55c olive green & orange red 50 50

Nos. 307-310 issued precanceled only. See note below No. 32.

1963, Oct. 13 ***Perf. 13*** **Unwmkd.**
311 A64 25c black, green & rose red 60 30

Issued to honor the new constitution.

Guerrilla Fighters A65 **Centenary Emblem** A66

1963, Nov. 1
312 A65 25c dk. brown, yel. grn. & carmine 60 30

9th anniversary of Algerian revolution.

1963, Dec. 8 Photo. *Perf. 12*

313 A66 25c lt. vio. bl., yel. & dark red 60 30

Centenary of International Red Cross.

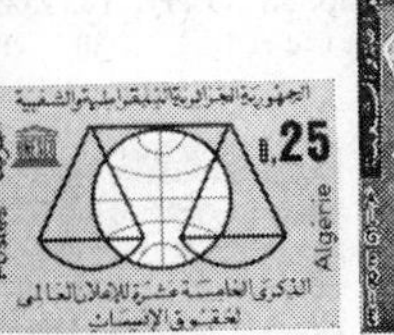

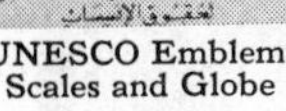

UNESCO Emblem, Scales and Globe
A67

Workers
A68

1963, Dec. 16 *Perf. 12* Unwmkd.

314 A67 25c lt. blue & black 50 25

Issued to commemorate the 15th anniversary of the Universal Declaration of Human Rights.

1964, May 1 Engraved *Perf. 13*

315 A68 50c dull red, red orange & blue 90 35

Issued for the Labor Festival.

Map of Africa and Flags
A69

1964, May 25 *Perf. 13* Unwmkd.

316 A69 45c blue, orge. & car. 70 30

Issued for Africa Day on the first anniversary of the Addis Ababa charter on African unity.

Ramses II Battling the Hittites (from Abu Simbel)—A70

Design: 30c, Two statues of Ramses II.

1964, June 28 Engraved *Perf. 13*

317 A70 20c chocolate, red & violet blue 50 35

318 " 30c brown, red & greenish blue 70 45

Issued to publicize the UNESCO world campaign to save historic monuments in Nubia.

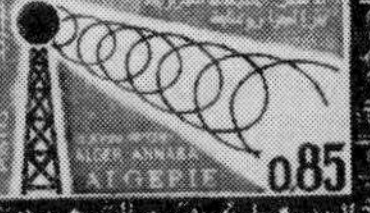

Tractors
A71

Communications Tower
A72

Designs: 5c, 25c, 85c, Tractors. 10c, 30c, 65c, Men working with lathe. 12c, 15c, 45c, Electronics center and atom symbol. 20c, 50c, 95c, Draftsman and bricklayer.

1964-65 Typographed *Perf. 14x13½*

319	A71	5c red lilac	5	3
320	"	10c brown	8	3
321	"	12c emerald ('65)	20	8
322	"	15c dark blue ('65)	12	3
323	"	20c yellow	15	6
324	"	25c red	40	3
325	"	30c purple ('65)	25	3
326	"	45c rose carmine	30	12
327	A71	50c ultramarine	35	3
328	"	65c orange	55	13
329	"	85c green	70	15
330	"	95c carmine rose	85	20
		Nos. 319-330 (12)	4.00	92

1964, Aug. 30 Engraved *Perf. 13*

331 A72 85c bl., blk. & red brn. 1.50 60

Inauguration of the Hertzian cable telephone line Algiers-Annaba.

Industrial and Agricultural Symbols
A73

Gas Flames and Pipes
A74

1964, Sept. 26 Typo. *Perf. 13½x14*

332 A73 25c light ultra., yellow & red 25 20

Issued to publicize the first International Fair at Algiers, Sept. 26–Oct. 11.

1964, Sept. 27

333 A74 30c vio., blue & yel. 35 25

Issued to commemorate the opening of the Arzew natural gas liquification plant.

Planting Trees
A75

Children and UNICEF Emblem
A76

1964, Nov. 29 Unwmkd.

334 A75 25c slate green, yel. & carmine 25 20

National reforestation campaign.

1964, Dec. 13 *Perf. 13½x14*

335 A76 15c pink, vio. blue & lt. green 18 15

Issued for Children's Day.

Decorated Camel Saddle
A77

1965, May 29 Typo. *Perf. 13½x14*

336 A77 20c blk. red, emerald & brown 20 17

Handicrafts of Sahara.

ICY Emblem
A78

1965, Aug. 29 Engraved *Perf. 13*

337 A78 30c black, maroon & blue green 50 30

338 " 60c black, bright blue & blue green 1.00 35

International Cooperation Year, 1965.

ITU Emblem
A79

1965, Sept. 19

339 A79 60c purple, emerald & buff 50 30

340 " 95c dark brown, maroon & buff 85 45

Issued to commemorate the centenary of the International Telecommunication Union.

Musicians
A80

Miniatures by Mohammed Racim: 60c, Two female musicians. 5d, Algerian princess and antelope.

1965, Dec. 27 Photo. *Perf. 11½*

341 A80 30c multicolored 60 25

342 " 60c " 90 55

343 " 5d " 7.00 3.75

Bulls, Painted in 6000 B.C.
A81

Wall Paintings from Tassili-N-Ajjer, c. 6000 B.C.: No. 345, Shepherd (vert.). 2d, Fleeing ostriches. 3d, Two girls (vert.).

1966, Jan. 29 Photo. *Perf. 11½*

344 A81 1d brn., bister & red brown 1.75 1.25

345 " 1d gray, blk., ocher & dk. brown 1.75 1.25

346 " 2d brn., ocher & red brown 3.50 1.75

347 " 3d buff, black, ocher & brown red 5.25 2.50

See also Nos. 365–368.

Pottery
A82

Handicrafts from Great Kabylia: 50c, Weaving, woman at loom (horiz.). 70c, Jewelry.

1966, Feb. 26 Engraved *Perf. 13*

348 A82 40c Prus. bl., brown red & black 30 20

349 " 50c dk. red, olive & ocher 40 25

350 " 70c vio. bl., blk. & red 75 35

Weather Balloon, Compass Rose and Anemometer
A83

1966, Mar. 23 Engr. Unwmkd.

351 A83 1d claret, brt. blue & green 85 40

World Meteorological Day.

Book, Grain, Cogwheel and UNESCO Emblem
A84

Design: 60c, Grain, cogwheel, book and UNESCO emblem.

1966, May 2 Typo. *Perf. 13x14*

352 A84 30c yel. bister & blk. 20 15

353 " 60c dk. red, gray & black 40 20

Literacy as basis for development.

WHO Headquarters, Geneva
A85

1966, May 30 Engraved *Perf. 13*

354 A85 30c multicolored 32 18

355 " 60c " 65 32

Issued to commemorate the inauguration of the World Health Organization Headquarters, Geneva.

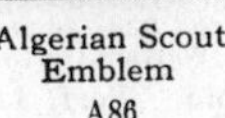

Algerian Scout Emblem
A86

Arab Jamboree Emblem
A87

1966, July 23 Photo. *Perf. 12x12½*

356 A86 30c multicolored 30 20

357 A87 1d " 85 40

No. 356 commemorates the 30th anniversary of the Algerian Mohammedan Boy Scouts. No. 357, the 7th Arab Boy Scout Jamboree, held at Good Daim, Libya, Aug. 12.

Map of Palestine and Victims

A88

Abd-el-Kader

A89

1966, Sept. 26 Typo. *Perf. 10½*

358 A88 30c red & black 22 12

Deir Yassin Massacre, Apr. 9, 1948.

1966, Nov. 2 Photo. *Perf. 11½*

359 A89 30c multicolored 25 10
360 " 95c " 75 20

Issued to commemorate the transfer from Damascus to Algiers of the ashes of Abd-el-Kader (1807?–1883), Emir of Mascara. See also Nos. 382–387.

UNESCO Emblem

A90

1966, Nov. 19 Typo. *Perf. 10½*

361 A90 1d multicolored 85 40

Issued to commemorate the 20th anniversary of UNESCO (United Nations Educational, Scientific and Cultural Organization).

Horseman

A91

Miniatures by Mohammed Racim: 1.50d, Woman at her toilette. 2d, The pirate Barbarossa in front of the Admiralty.

1966, Dec. 17 Photo. *Perf. 11½*

Granite Paper

362 A91 1d multicolored 1.65 1.00
363 " 1.50d " 2.75 1.40
364 " 2d " 3.75 1.85

Wall Paintings Type of 1966

Wall Paintings from Tassili-N-Ajjer, c.6000 B.C.: 1d, Cow. No. 366, Antelope. No. 367, Archers. 3d, Warrior (vert.).

1967, Jan. 28 Photo. *Perf. 11½*

365 A81 1d brown, bister & dull violet 2.00 1.20
366 " 2d brown, ocher & red brown 3.50 2.25
367 " 2d brown, yellow & red brown 3.50 2.25
368 " 3d blk., gray, yellow & red brown 6.00 3.50

Bardo Museum

A92

La Kalaa Minaret

A93

Design: 1.30d, Ruins at Sedrata.

1967, Feb. 27 Photo. *Perf. 13*

369 A92 35c multicolored 25 12
370 A93 95c " 80 60
371 A92 1.30d " 1.25 75

Moretti and International Tourist Year Emblem

A94

Design: 70c, Tuareg riding camel, Tassili, and Tourist Year Emblem (vert.).

1967, Apr. 29 Litho. *Perf. 14*

372 A94 40c multicolored 50 25
373 " 70c " 85 40

International Tourist Year, 1967.

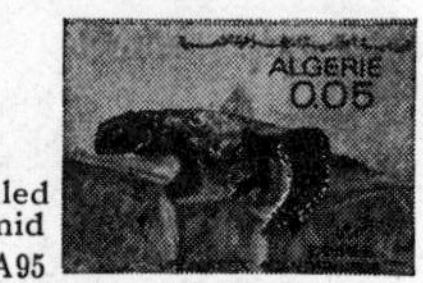

Spiny-tailed Agamid

A95

Designs: 20c, Ostrich (vert.). 40c, Slender-horned gazelle (vert.). 70c, Fennec.

1967, June 24 Photo. *Perf. 11½*

374 A95 5c bister & black 15 10
375 " 20c ocher, blk. & pink 35 25
376 " 40c olive bister, black & red brown 60 40
377 " 70c gray, black & deep orange 1.10 65

Dancers

A96

Typographed and Engraved

1967, July 4 *Perf. 10½*

378 A96 50c gray violet, yellow & black 50 30

National Youth Festival.

Map of the Mediterranean and Sport Scenes—A97

1967, Sept. 2 Typo. *Perf. 10½*

379 A97 30c black, red & blue 30 20

Issued to publicize the 5th Mediterranean Games, Tunis, Sept. 8–17.

Skiers

A98

Olympic Emblem and Sports

A99

1967, Oct. 21 Engraved *Perf. 13*

380 A98 30c brt. blue & ultra. 40 30
381 A99 95c brn. orange, pur. & bright green 1.20 65

Issued to publicize the 10th Winter Olympic Games, Grenoble, Feb. 6–18, 1968.

Abd-el-Kader Type of 1966

Lithographed, Photogravure

1967–71 *Perf. 13½, 11½*

382 A89 5c dull purple ('68) 5 5
383 " 10c green 12 8
383A " 10c slate green (litho., '69) 12 5
383B " 25c orange ('71) 18 8
384 " 30c black ('68) 25 10
385 " 30c light violet ('68) 25 10
386 " 50c rose claret 50 30
387 " 70c violet blue 75 40
Nos. 382–387 (8) 2.22 1.16

The 10c (No. 383), 50c and 70c are on granite paper, photogravure, and were issued Nov. 13, 1967. The 5c, 10c (No. 383A), 25c and both 30c are lithographed and perf. 13½; others, perf. 11½.

The three 1967 stamps (No. 383, 50c, 70c) have numerals thin, narrow and close together; the Arabic inscription at lower right is 2mm. high. The five lithographed stamps are redrawn, with numerals thicker and spaced more widely; Arabic at lower right 3mm. high.

Boy Scouts Holding Jamboree Emblem

A100

1967, Dec. 23 Engraved *Perf. 13*

388 A100 1d multicolored 1.00 60

Issued to commemorate the 12th Boy Scout World Jamboree, Farragut State Park, Idaho, Aug. 1–9.

No. 324 Surcharged

1967 Typographed *Perf. 14x13½*

389 A71 30c on 25c red 30 12

Mandolin

A101

Musical Instruments: 40c, Lute. 1.30d, Rebec.

1968, Feb. 17 Photo. *Perf. 12½x13*

390 A101 30c dk. brn., ocher & light blue 30 20
391 " 40c multicolored 35 25
392 " 1.30d " 1.25 85

Nememcha Rug

A102

Algerian Rugs: 70c, Guergour. 95c, Djebel-Amour. 1.30d, Kalaa.

1968, Apr. 13 Photo. *Perf. 11½*

393 A102 30c multicolored 40 25
394 " 70c " 80 35
395 " 95c " 1.00 60
396 " 1.30d " 1.25 75

Human Rights Flame

A103

1968, May 18 Typo. *Perf. 10½*

397 A103 40c blue, red & yel. 35 20

International Human Rights Year, 1968.

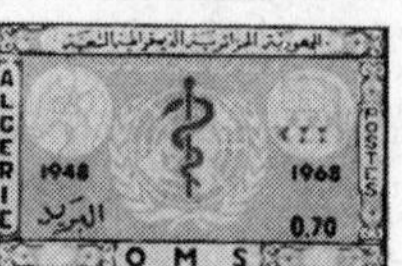

WHO Emblem

A104

1968, May 18

398 A104 70c blk., lt. bl. & yel. 55 30

Issued for the 20th anniversary of the World Health Organization.

Welder
A105

Athletes, Olympic Flame and Rings
A106

1968, June 15 Engr. ***Perf. 13***

399 A105 30c gray, brown & ultramarine 25 20

Algerian emigration to Europe.

Perf. 12½x13, 13x12½

1968, July 4 Photogravure

Designs: 50c, Soccer player. 1d, Mexican pyramid, emblem, Olympic flame, rings and athletes (horiz.).

400 A106 30c green, red & yel. 35 30
401 " 50c rose carmine & multicolored 55 35
402 " 1d dk. green, org., brown & red 1.10 75

Issued to publicize the 19th Olympic Games, Mexico City, Oct. 12–27.

Scouts and Emblem
A107

Barbary Sheep
A108

1968, July 4 ***Perf. 13***

403 A107 30c multicolored 30 20

Issued to publicize the 8th Arab Boy Scout Jamboree, Algiers, 1968.

1968, Oct. 19 Photo. ***Perf. 11½***

Design: 1d, Red deer.

404 A108 40c red brown, bister & black 40 30
405 " 1d lt. & dk. olive grn. & brown 1.00 60

Hunting Scenes, Djemila
A109

"Industry"
A110

Design: 95c, Neptune's chariot, Timgad (horiz.). Both designs are from Roman mosaics.

Perf. 12½x13, 13x12½

1968, Nov. 23 Photogravure

406 A109 40c gray & multi. 35 20
407 " 95c " " 90 50

1968, Dec. 14 ***Perf. 11½***

Designs: No. 409, Miner with drill. 95c, "Energy" (circle and rays).

408 A110 30c dp. org. & silver 25 10
409 " 30c brown & multi. 25 20
410 " 95c silver, red & blk. 80 30

Issued to publicize industrial development.

Opuntia Ficus Indica
A111

Flowers: 40c, Carnations. 70c, Roses. 95c, Bird-of-paradise flower.

1969, Jan. Photo. ***Perf. 11½***

Flowers in Natural Colors

411 A111 25c pink & black 25 20
412 " 40c yellow & black 45 35
413 " 70c gray & black 70 45
414 " 95c brt. bl. & blk. 1.10 70

See also Nos. 496–499.

Irrigation Dam at Djorf Torba-Oued Guir
A112

Design: 1.50d, Truck on Highway No. 51 and camel caravan.

1969, Feb. 22 Photo. ***Perf. 11½***

415 A112 30c multicolored 20 18
416 " 1.50d " 1.20 60

Public works in the Sahara.

Mail Coach
A113

1969, Mar. 22 Photo. ***Perf. 11½***

417 A113 1d multicolored 1.25 60

Issued for Stamp Day, 1969.

Capitol, Timgad
A114

Design: 1d, Septimius Temple, Djemila (horiz.).

1969, Apr. 5 Photo. ***Perf. 13x12½***

418 A114 30c gray & multi. 25 15
419 " 1d " " 90 25

Second Timgad Festival, Apr. 4–8.

ILO Emblem
A115

Arabian Saddle
A116

1969, May 24 Photo. ***Perf. 11½***

420 A115 95c deep carmine, yel. & black 1.00 40

50th anniversary of the International Labor Organization.

1969, June 28 Photo. ***Perf. 12x12½***

Algerian Handicrafts: 30c, Bookcase. 60c, Decorated copper plate.

Granite Paper

421 A116 30c multicolored 30 12
422 " 60c " 50 18
423 " 1d " 1.00 40

No. 321 Surcharged **0,20**

1969 Typographed ***Perf. 14x13½***

424 A71 20c on 12c emerald 18 6

Pan-African Culture Festival Emblem
A117

African Development Bank Emblem
A118

1969, July 19 Photo. ***Perf. 12½***

425 A117 30c multicolored 28 20

Issued to commemorate the First Pan-African Culture Festival, Algiers, July 21–Aug. 1.

1969, Aug. 23 Typo. ***Perf. 10½***

426 A118 30c dull blue, yellow & black 25 18

Issued to commemorate the 5th anniversary of the African Development Bank.

Astronauts and Landing Module on Moon
A119

Photogravure

1969, Aug. 23 ***Perf. 12½x11½***

427 A119 50c gold & multi. 50 35

Issued to commemorate man's first landing on the moon, July 20, 1969. U.S. astronauts Neil A. Armstrong and Col. Edwin E. Aldrin, Jr., with Lieut. Col. Michael Collins piloting Apollo 11.

Algerian Women, by Dinet
A120

Design: 1.50d, The Watchmen, by Etienne Dinet.

1969, Nov. 29 Photo. ***Perf. 14½***

428 A120 1d multicolored 1.00 70
429 " 1.50d " 1.40 90

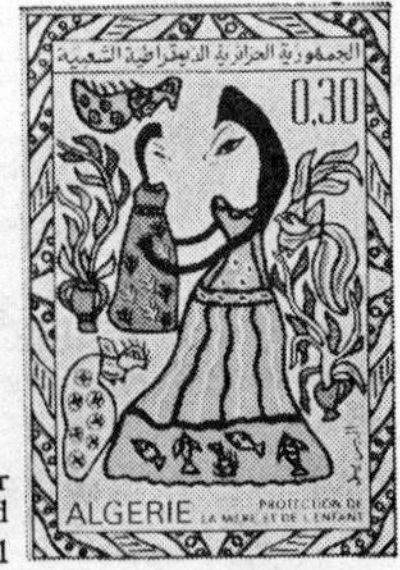

Mother and Child
A121

1969, Dec. 27 Photo. ***Perf. 11½***

430 A121 30c multicolored 30 20

Issued to promote mother and child protection.

Agricultural Growth Chart, Tractor and Dam
A122

Designs: 30c, Transportation and development. 50c, Abstract symbols of industrialization.

1970, Jan. 31 Photo. ***Perf. 12½***

Size: 37x23mm.

431 A122 25c dk. brown, yellow & orange 20 15

Lithographed *Perf. 14*

Size: 49x23mm.

432 A122 30c blue & multi. 25 20

Photogravure *Perf. 12½*

Size: 37x23mm.

433 A122 50c rose lilac & black 35 20

Issued to publicize the Four-Year Development Plan.

Old and New Mail Delivery
A123

Spiny Lobster
A124

1970, Feb. 28 Photo. ***Perf. 11½***

Granite Paper

434 A123 30c multicolored 25 18

Issued for Stamp Day.

1970, Mar. 28

Designs: 40c, Mollusks. 75c, Retepora cellulosa. 1d, Red coral.

435 A124 30c ocher & multi. 25 18
436 " 40c multicolored 35 25
437 " 75c ultra. & multi. 60 35
438 " 1d lt. blue & multi. 80 50

Oranges, EXPO '70 Emblem
A125

Designs (EXPO '70 Emblem and): 60c, Algerian pavilion. 70c, Grapes.

1970, Apr. 25 Photo. ***Perf. 12½x12***

439 A125 30c lt. blue, green & orange 25 17
440 " 60c multicolored 50 35

441 125A 70c multicolored 55 40

EXPO '70 International Exhibition, Osaka, Japan, Mar. 15–Sept. 13, 1970.

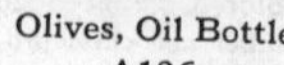

Olives, Oil Bottle A126 — Saber A127

1970, May 16 Photo. *Perf. 12½x12*

442 A126 1d yellow & multi. 80 50

Olive Year, 1969–1970.

U.P.U. Headquarters Issue

Common Design Type

1970, May 30 *Perf. 13*

Size: 36x26mm.

443 CD133 75c multicolored 60 40

1970, June 27 Photo. *Perf. 12½*

Designs: 40c, Guns, 18th century (horiz.). 1d, Pistol, 18th century (horiz.).

444 A127 40c yellow & multi. 40 20
445 " 75c red & multi. 60 40
446 " 1d multicolored 80 45

Map of Arab Countries and Arab League Flag A128

Typographed and Engraved

1970, July 25 *Perf. 10½*

447 A128 30c green, ocher & light blue 25 15

25th anniversary of the Arab League.

Lenin A129

1970, Aug. 29 Litho. *Perf. 11½x12*

448 A129 30c brown & buff 25 15

Issued to commemorate the centenary of the birth of Lenin (1870–1924), Russian communist leader.

Exhibition Hall and Algiers Fair Emblem—A130

1970, Sept. 11 Engr. *Perf. 14x13½*

449 A130 60c lt. olive green 50 30

New Exhibition Hall for Algiers International Fair.

Common Design Types pictured in section at front of book.

Education Year Emblem, Blackboard, Atom Symbol—A131

Koran Page A132

1970, Oct. 24 Photo. *Perf. 14*

450 A131 30c pink, black, gold & light blue 25 15
451 A132 3d multicolored 2.50 1.50

Issued for International Education Year.

Great Mosque, Tlemcen A133

Design: 40c, Ketchaoua Mosque, Algiers (vert.). 1d, Mosque, Sidi-Okba (vert.).

1970–71 Lithographed *Perf. 14*

456 A133 30c multicolored 25 17
457 " 40c sepia & lemon ('71) 28 16
458 " 1d multicolored 70 45

Symbols of the Arts A134

1970, Dec. 26 Photo. *Perf. 13x12½*

459 A134 1d green, lt. green & orange 80 45

Main Post Office, Algiers A135

1971, Jan. 23 *Perf. 11½*

460 A135 30c multicolored 25 20

Stamp Day, 1971.

Hurdling A136

Designs: 40c, Vaulting (vert.). 75c, Basketball (vert.).

1971, Mar. 7 Photo. *Perf. 11½*

461 A136 20c lt. blue & slate 18 12
462 A136 40c lt. olive green & slate 35 27
463 " 75c sal. pink & slate 55 35

Mediterranean Games, Izmir, Turkey, Oct. 1971.

Symbolic Head A137

1971, March 27 *Perf. 12½*

464 A137 60c carmine rose, black & silver 45 20

International year against racial discrimination.

Emblem and Technicians A138

1971, Apr. 24 Photo. *Perf. 12½x12*

465 A138 70c claret, orange & bluish black 50 20

Founding of the Institute of Technology.

Woman from Aurès A139

Regional Costumes: 70c, Man from Oran. 80c, Man from Algiers. 90c, Woman from Amour Mountains.

1971, Oct. 16 *Perf. 11½*

466 A139 50c gold & multi. 50 40
467 " 70c " " 50 50
468 " 80c " " 85 65
469 " 90c " " 1.00 85

See Nos. 485–488, 534–537.

UNICEF Emblem, Birds and Plants A140

1971, Dec. 6 *Perf. 11½*

470 A140 60c multicolored 50 40

25th anniversary of United Nations International Children's Fund (UNICEF).

Lion of St. Mark—A141

Design: 1.15d, Bridge of Sighs, Venice (vert.).

1972, Jan. 24 Litho. *Perf. 12*

471 A141 80c multicolored 85 60
472 " 1.15d " 1.10 85

UNESCO campaign to save Venice.

Javelin A142 — Book and Book Year Emblem A143

Designs: 25c, Bicycling (horiz.). 60c, Wrestling. 1d, Gymnast on rings.

1972, Mar. 25 Photo. *Perf. 11½*

473 A142 25c maroon & multi. 25 18
474 " 40c ocher & multi. 35 25
475 " 60c ultra. & multi. 50 35
476 " 1d rose & multi. 75 55

20th Olympic Games, Munich, Aug. 26–Sept. 11.

1972, Apr. 15

477 A143 1.15d bister, brown & red 85 60

International Book Year 1972.

Mailmen A144 — Jasmine A145

1972, Apr. 22

478 A144 40c gray & multi. 30 18

Stamp Day 1972.

1972, May 27

Flowers: 60c, Violets. 1.15d, Tuberose.

Flowers in Natural Colors

479 A145 50c brn. & pale sal. 40 30
480 " 60c violet & gray 50 35
481 " 1.15d lt. blue & Prus. blue 85 45

Olympic Stadium, Chéraga A146

1972, June 10

482 A146 50c gray, chocolate & green 40 25

New Day, Algerian Flag A147

1972, July 5

483 A147 1d green & multi. 85 60

10th anniversary of independence.

Festival Emblem
A148

Mailing a Letter
A149

1972, July 5 Litho. *Perf. 10½*

484 A148 40c green, dk. brown & orange 30 18

First Arab Youth Festival, Algiers, July 5–11.

Costume Type of 1971

Regional Costumes: 50c, Woman from Hoggar. 60c, Kabyle woman. 70c, Man from Mzab. 90c, Woman from Tlemcen.

1972, Nov. 18 Photo. *Perf. 11½*

485 A139 50c gold & multi. 60 40
486 " 60c " " 60 45
487 " 70c " " 70 50
488 " 90c " " 85 60

1973, Jan. 20 Photo. *Perf. 11*

489 A149 40c org. & multi. 35 15

Stamp Day.

Ho Chi Minh, Map of Viet Nam
A150

1973, Feb. 17 Photo. *Perf. 11½*

490 A150 40c multicolored 35 15

To honor the people of Viet Nam.

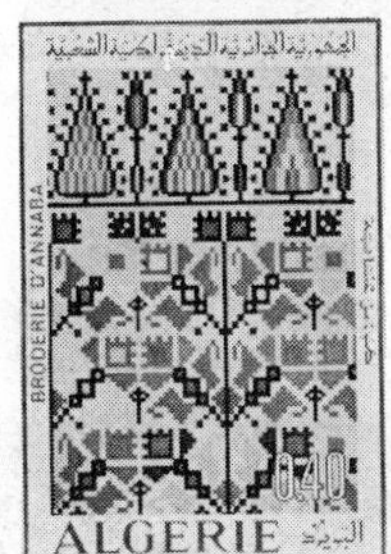

Embroidery from Annaba
A151

Designs: 60c, Tree of Life pattern from Algiers. 80c, Constantine embroidery.

1973, Feb. 24

491 A151 40c gray & multi. 40 30
492 " 60c blue and multi. 55 45
493 " 80c dk. red, gold & black 65 45

Scott's editorial staff cannot undertake to identify, authenticate or appraise stamps and postal markings.

Stylized Globe and Wheat
A152

1973, Mar. 26 Photo. *Perf. 11½*

494 A152 1.15d brt. rose lilac, org. & grn. 75 50

World Food Program, 10th anniversary.

Soldier and Flag—A153

1973, Apr. 23 Photo. *Perf. 14x13½*

495 A153 40c multicolored 30 15

Honoring the National Service.

Flower Type of 1969

Flowers: 30c, Opuntia ficus indica. 40c, Roses. 1d, Carnations. 1.15d, Bird-of-paradise flower.

1973, May 21 Photo. *Perf. 11½*

Flowers in Natural Colors

496 A111 30c pink & black 25 20
497 " 40c gray & black 35 25
498 " 1d yellow & multi. 85 55
499 " 1.15d multicolored 90 60

OAU Emblem
A154

1973, May 28 Photo. *Perf. 12½x13*

500 A154 40c multicolored 35 20

Organization for African Unity, 10th anniversary.

Desert and Fruitful Land, Farmer and Family—A155

1973, June 18 *Perf. 11½*

501 A155 40c gold & multi. 30 20

Agricultural revolution.

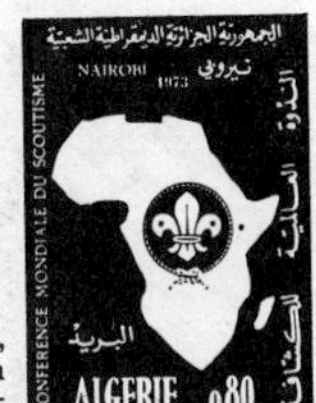

Map of Africa, Scout Emblem
A156

1973, July 16 Litho. *Perf. 10½*

502 A156 80c purple 60 40

24th Boy Scout World Conference (1st in Africa), Nairobi, Kenya, July 16–21.

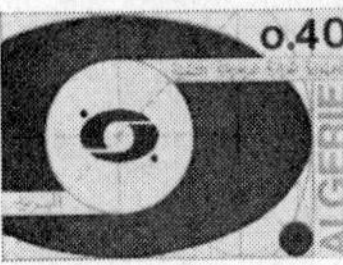

Algerian PTT Emblem
A157

1973, Aug. 6 *Perf. 14*

503 A157 40c blue & orange 30 15

Adoption of new emblem for Post, Telegraph and Telephone System.

Conference Emblem
A158

1973, Sept. 5 Photo. *Perf. 13½x12½*

504 A158 40c dp. rose & multi. 25 20
505 " 80c bl. grn. & multi. 50 30

4th Summit Conference of Non-aligned Nations, Algiers, Sept. 5–9.

Port of Skikda
A159

1973, Sept. 29 Photo. *Perf. 11½*

506 A159 80c ocher, black & ultramarine 60 40

New port of Skikda.

Young Workers
A160

1973, Oct. 22 Photo. *Perf. 13*

507 A160 40c multicolored 25 20

Voluntary work service.

Arms of Algiers
A161

1973, Dec. 22 Photo. *Perf. 13*

508 A161 2d gold & multi. 1.50 1.00

Millennium of Algiers.

Infant
A162

1974, Jan. 7 Litho. *Perf. 10½x11*

509 A162 80c orange & multi. 60 40

Fight against tuberculosis.

Man and Woman, Industry and Transportation
A163

1974, Feb. 18 Photo. *Perf. 11½*

510 A163 80c multicolored 50 30

Four-year plan.

A164

1974, Feb. 25 Photo. *Perf. 11½*

511 A164 1.50d multicolored 90 60

Millennium of the birth of abu-al-Rayhan al-Biruni (973–1048), philosopher and mathematician.

Map and Colors of Algeria, Tunisia, Morocco
A165

1974, Mar. 4 Photo. *Perf. 13*

512 A165 40c gold & multi. 20 15

Maghreb Committee for Coordination of Posts and Telecommunications.

Hand Holding Rifle
A166

Mother and Children
A167

1974, Mar. 25 *Perf. 11½*

513 A166 80c red & black 40 25

Solidarity with the struggle of the people of South Africa.

1974, Apr. 8 *Perf. 13½*

514 A167 85c multicolored 40 30

Honoring Algerian mothers.

Village—A168

Designs: 80c, Harvest. 90c, Tractor and sun. Designs after children's drawings.

1974, June 15 Size: 45x26mm.

515 A168 70c multicolored 45 35

Size: 48x33mm.

516 A168 80c multicolored 50 40
517 " 90c " 55 45

Nos. 498–499 Overprinted "FLORALIES/1974"

1974, June 22 Photo. *Perf. 11½*

518 A111 1d multicolored 55 30
519 " 1.15d " 65 40

1974 Flower Show.

Stamp Vending Machine A169

1974, Oct. 7 Photogravure *Perf. 13*

520 A169 80c multicolored 45 30

Stamp Day 1974.

UPU Emblem and Globe A170

1974, Oct. 14 *Perf. 14*

521 A170 80c multicolored 50 30

Centenary of Universal Postal Union.

"Revolution" A171

Soldiers and Mountains A172

Raising New Flag A173

Design: 1d, Algerian struggle for independence (people, sun and fields).

1974, Nov. 4 Photogravure *Perf. 14*

522 A171 40c multicolored 20 10
523 A172 70c " 25 15
524 A173 95c " 48 18
525 A171 1d " 50 25

20th anniversary of the start of the revolution.

"Horizon 1980" A174

Ewer and Basin A175

1974, Nov. 23 Photo. *Perf. 13*

526 A174 95c ocher, dk. red & black 50 22

10-year development plan, 1971–1980.

1974, Dec. 21 *Perf. 11½*

Designs: 60c, Coffee pot. 95c, Sugar bowl. 1d, Bath tub.

527 A175 50c pink & multi. 25 10
528 " 60c pale yel. & multi. 35 20
529 " 95c citron & multi. 50 25
530 " 1d ultra. & multi. 55 35

17th century Algerian copperware.

No. 497 Surcharged with New Value and Heavy Bar

1975, Jan. 4

531 A111 50c on 40c multi. 25 15

Mediterranean Games' Emblem—A176

1975, Jan. 27 *Perf. 13½*

532 A176 50c pur., yel. & grn. 25 15
533 " 1d orange, blue & maroon 50 25

Mediterranean Games, Algiers, 1975.

Costume Type of 1971

Regional Costumes: No. 534, Woman from Hoggar. No. 535, Woman from Algiers. No. 536, Woman from Oran. No. 537, Man from Tlemcen.

1975, Feb. 22 Photo. *Perf. 11½*

534 A139 1d gold & multi. 65 40
535 " 1d " " 65 40
536 " 1d " " 65 40
537 " 1d " " 65 40

Map of Arab Countries, ALO Emblem A177

1975, Mar. 10 Litho. *Perf. 10½x11*

538 A177 50c red brown 25 15

Arab Labor Organization, 10th anniversary.

Blood Transfusion A178

1975, Mar. 15 *Perf. 14*

539 A178 50c car. rose & multi. 30 20

Blood donations and transfusions.

Post Office, Al-Kantara A179

Policeman and Map of Algeria A180

1975, May 10 Photo. *Perf. 11½*

Granite Paper

540 A179 50c multicolored 30 12

Stamp Day 1975.

1975, June 1 Photo. *Perf. 13*

541 A180 50c multicolored 25 12

National Security and 10th National Police Day.

Ground Receiving Station A181

Designs: 1d, Map of Algeria with locations of radar sites, transmission mast and satellite. 1.20d, Main and subsidiary stations.

1975, June 28 Photo. *Perf. 13*

542 A181 50c blue & multi. 25 12
543 " 1d " " 50 25
544 " 1.20d " " 55 30

National satellite telecommunications network.

Revolutionary with Flag A182

1975, Aug. 20 Photo. *Perf. 11½*

545 A182 1d multicolored 50 30

August 20th Revolutionary Movement (Skikda), 20th anniversary.

Swimming and Games' Emblem A183

Perf. 13x13½, 13½x13

1975, Aug. 23 Photogravure

Multicolored

546 A183 25c *shown* 12 6
547 " 50c *Wrestling and map* 25 12
548 A183 70c *Soccer* (vert.) 35 22
549 " 1d *Running* (vert.) 55 30
550 " 1.20d *Handball* (vert.) 60 30
a. Souvenir sheet of 5 2.50 2.50
Nos. 546–550 (5) 1.87 1.00

7th Mediterranean Games, Algiers, Aug. 23–Sept. 6.

No. 550a contains one each of Nos. 546–550, perf. 13, buff margin with marginal inscription and ornament in blue and maroon. Size: 135x135mm. Sold for 4.50d. Exists imperf.; same price.

Setif, Guelma, Kherrata A184

1975 Litho. *Perf. 13½x14*

551 A184 5c orange & black 5 3
552 " 10c emerald & brn. 5 3
553 " 25c dull blue & blk. 12 6
554 " 30c lemon & black 15 7
555 " 50c brt. grn. & blk. 25 12
556 " 70c fawn & black 30 18
557 " 1d verm. & black 50 25
Nos. 551–557 (7) 1.42 74

30th anniversary of victory in World War II.

Issue dates: 50c, 1d, Nov. 3; others, Dec. 17.

Map of Maghreb and APU Emblem A185

1975 Nov. 20 Photo. *Perf. 11½*

558 A185 1d multicolored 50 30

10th Congress of Arab Postal Union, Algiers.

Mosaic, Bey Constantine's Palace A186

Dey-Alger Palace—A187

Design: 2d, Prayer niche, Medersa Sidi—Boumediene, Tlemcen.

1975, Dec. 22

559 A186 1d lt. bl. & multi. 50 25
560 " 2d buff & multi. 1.00 60
561 A187 2.50d buff & black 1.25 75

Famous buildings.

Al-Azhar University
A188

Lithographed

1975, Dec. 29 *Perf. 11½x12½*

562 A188 2d multicolored 1.10 60

Millennium of Al-Azhar University.

Red-billed Firefinch
A189

Birds: 1.40d, Black-headed bush shrike (horiz.). 2d, Blue tit. 2.50d, Black-bellied sandgrouse (horiz.).

1976, Jan. 24 Photo. *Perf. 11½*

563	A189	50c multicolored	24	15
564	"	1.40d "	65	50
565	"	2d "	1.00	65
566	"	2.50d "	1.20	90

See Nos. 595–598.

Telephones 1876 and 1976
A190

Map of Africa with Angola and its Flag
A191

1976, Feb. 23 Photo. *Perf. 13½x13*

567 A190 1.40d rose, dark & light blue 65 40

Centenary of first telephone call by Alexander Graham Bell, Mar. 10, 1876.

1976, Feb. 23 *Perf. 11½*

568 A191 50c brn. & multi. 24 12

Algeria's solidarity with the People's Republic of Angola.

Sahraoui Flag and Child, Map of former Spanish Sahara
A192

1976, Mar. 15 Photo. *Perf. 11½*

569 A192 50c multicolored 24 12

Algeria's solidarity with Sahraoui Arab Democratic Republic, former Spanish Sahara.

Mailman
A193

1976, Mar. 22

570 A193 1.40d multicolored 70 40

Stamp Day 1976.

Microscope, Slide with TB Bacilli, Patients
A194

1976, Apr. 26 *Perf. 13x13½*

571 A194 50c multicolored 24 12

Fight against tuberculosis.

"Setif, Guelma, Kherrata"
A195

1976, May 24 Photo. *Perf. 13½x13*

572 A195 50c blue & yellow 22 6
a. Booklet pane of 6 1.50
b. Booklet pane of 10 2.50

No. 572 was issued in booklets only.

Ram's Head over Landscape
A196

1976, June 17 Photo. *Perf. 11½*

573 A196 50c multicolored 24 12

Livestock breeding.

People Holding Torch, Map of Algeria
A197

Palestine Map and Flag
A198

1976, June 29 Photo. *Perf. 14x13½*

574 A197 50c multicolored 24 12

National Charter.

1976, July 12 *Perf. 11½*

Granite Paper

575 A198 50c multicolored 24 12

Solidarity with the Palestinians.

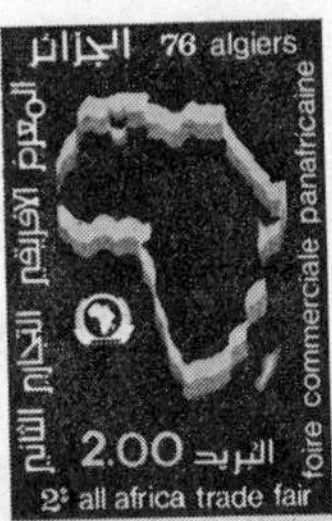

Map of Africa
A199

1976, Oct. 3 Litho. *Perf. 10½x11*

576 A199 2d dk. bl. & multi. 1.00 60

2nd Pan-African Commercial Fair, Algiers.

Blind Brushmaker
A200

The Blind, by Dinet
A201

1976, Oct. 23 Photo. *Perf. 14½*

577 A200 1.20d blue & multi. 58 35
578 A201 1.40d gold & multi. 70 45

Rehabilitation of the blind.

"Constitution 1976"—A202

1976, Nov. 19 Photo. *Perf. 11½*

579 A202 2d multicolored 1.00 55

New Constitution.

Soldiers Planting Seedlings
A203

1976, Nov. 25 Litho. *Perf. 12*

580 A203 1.40d multicolored 70 35

Green barrier against the Sahara.

Ornamental Border and Inscription
A204

1976, Dec. 18 Photo. *Perf. 11½*

Granite Paper

581 A204 2d multicolored 1.00 50

Re-election of Pres. Houari Boumediene.

Map with Charge Zones and Dials
A205

People and Buildings
A206

1977, Jan. 22 *Perf. 13*

582 A205 40c silver & multi. 20 10

Inauguration of automatic national and international telephone service.

1977, Jan. 29 Photo. *Perf. 11½*

583 A206 60c on 50c multi. 30 15

2nd General Population and Buildings Census. No. 583 was not issued without the typographed red brown surcharge, date, and bars.

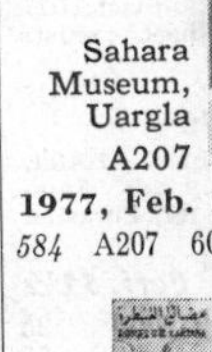

Sahara Museum, Uargla
A207

1977, Feb. 12 Litho. *Perf. 14*

584 A207 60c multicolored 30 15

El-Kantara Gorge
A208

1977, Feb. 19 Photo. *Perf. 12½x13½*

585 A208 20c green & yellow 10 6
a. Booklet pane of 7 (3 #585, 4 #586 + label) 1.50
b. Booklet pane of 7 (5 #585, 2 #587 + label) 1.50
586 A208 60c brt. lilac & yel. 30 10
587 " 1d brown & yellow 50 15

Nos. 585–587 issued only in booklets.

National Assembly—A209

1977, Feb. 27 ***Perf. 11½***

588 A209 2d multicolored 1.00 45

People and Flag A210 Soldier and Flag A211

Perf. 13½, 11½ (3d)

1977, Mar. 12 **Photogravure**

589 A210 2d multicolored 1.00 60
590 A211 3d " 1.50 1.25

Solidarity with the peoples of Zimbabwe (Rhodesia), 2d; Namibia, 3d.

Winter, Roman Mosaic A212

The Seasons from Roman Villa, 2nd century A.D.: 1.40d, Fall. 2d, Summer. 3d, Spring.

1977, Apr. 21 **Photo.** ***Perf. 11½***

Granite Paper

591 A212 1.20d multicolored 60 25
592 " 1.40d " 70 25
593 " 2d " 1.00 50
594 " 3d " 1.50 60
a. Souvenir sheet of 4 4.50 4.50

No. 594a contains one each of Nos. 591–594; gray marginal inscription. Size: 101x145mm. Sold for 8d. Sheet exists imperf.

Bird Type of 1976

Birds: 60c, Tristram's warbler. 1.40d, Moussier's redstart (horiz.). 2d, Temminck's horned lark (horiz.). 3d, Eurasian hoopoe.

1977, May 21 **Photo.** ***Perf. 11½***

595 A189 60c multicolored 30 25
596 " 1.40d " 70 55
597 " 2d " 1.00 60
598 " 3d " 1.50 1.00

Horseman A213

Design: 5d, Attacking horsemen (horiz.).

1977, June 25 **Photo.** ***Perf. 11½***

599 A213 2d multicolored 1.00 60
600 " 5d " 2.50 1.40

Helpful notes abound in the "Information for Collectors" section at the front of this volume.

Flag Colors, Games Emblem A214

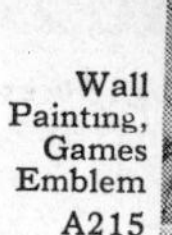

Wall Painting, Games Emblem A215

1977, Sept. 24 **Photo.** ***Perf. 11½***

601 A214 60c multicolored 30 25
602 A215 1.40d " 70 55

3rd African Games, Algiers 1978.

Village and Tractor A216

1977, Nov. 12 ***Perf. 14x13***

603 A216 1.40d multicolored 70 40

Socialist agricultural village.

Almohades Dirham, 12th Century—A217

Ancient Coins: 1.40d, Almohades coin, 12th century. 2d, Almoravides dinar, 11th century.

1977, Dec. 17 **Photo.** ***Perf. 11½***

604 A217 60c ultra., silver & black 30 20
605 " 1.40d green, gold & brown 70 40
606 " 2d red brn., gold & brown 1.00 60

Cherry Blossoms A218

Flowering Trees: 1.20d, Peach. 1.30d, Almond. 1.40d, Apple.

1978, Feb. 11 **Photo.** ***Perf. 11½***

607 A218 60c multicolored 30 20
608 " 1.20d " 60 40
609 " 1.30d " 65 40
610 " 1.40d " 70 50

No. 555 Surcharged with New Value and Bar

1978, Feb. 11 **Litho.** ***Perf. 13½x14***

611 A184 60c on 50c 30 6

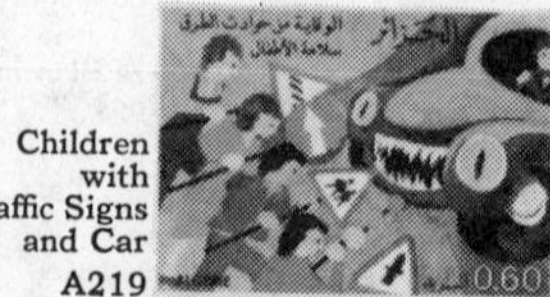

Children with Traffic Signs and Car A219

1978, Apr. 29 **Photo.** ***Perf. 11½***

612 A219 60c multicolored 30 10

Road safety and protection of children.

Sports and Games Emblems A220

Designs (Games Emblem and): 60c, Rower (vert.). 1.20d, Flag colors. 1.30d, Fireworks (vert.). 1.40d, Map of Africa and dancers (vert.).

1978, July 13 **Photo.** ***Perf. 11½***

613 A220 40c multicolored 20 10
614 " 60c " 30 15
615 " 1.20d " 60 30
616 " 1.30d " 65 32
617 " 1.40d " 70 35
Nos. 613–618 (5) 2.45 1.22

3rd African Games, Algiers, July 13–28.

TB Patient Returning to Family A221

1978, Oct. 5 **Photo.** ***Perf. 13½x14***

618 A221 60c multicolored 30 15

Anti-tuberculosis campaign.

Holy Kaaba A222

1978, Oct. 28 **Photo.** ***Perf. 11½***

619 A222 60c multicolored 30 15

Pilgrimage to Mecca.

National Servicemen Building Road A223

1978, Nov. 4

620 A223 60c multicolored 30 15

African Unity Road from El Goleah to In Salah, inauguration.

Fibula A224

Jewelry: 1.35d, Pendant. 1.40d, Ankle ring.

1978, Dec. 21 **Photo.** ***Perf. 12x11½***

621 A224 1.20d multicolored 60 30
622 " 1.35d " 68 35
623 " 1.40d " 70 35

SEMI-POSTAL STAMPS.

Regular Issue of 1926 Surcharged in Black or Red

+10c ★

1927 *Perf. 14x13½.* **Unwmkd.**

B1	A1	5c+5c blue green	20	20
B2	"	10c+10c lilac	20	20
B3	A2	15c+15c orange brown	20	20
B4	"	20c+20c carmine rose	20	20
B5	"	25c+25c blue green	20	20
B6	"	30c+30c light blue	20	20
B7	"	35c+35c deep violet	20	20
B8	"	40c+40c olive green	20	20
B9	A3	50c+50c deep blue (R)	20	20
		a. Dbl. surch.	100.00	100.00
B10	"	80c+80c red orange	20	20
B11	A4	1fr+1fr gray green & red brown	20	20
B12	"	2fr+2fr Prussian blue & blk. brown	11.00	11.00
B13	"	5fr+5fr red & violet	11.00	11.00
		Nos. B1-B13 (13)	24.20	24.20

The surtax was for the benefit of wounded soldiers. Government officials speculated in this issue.

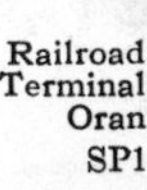

Railroad Terminal, Oran SP1

Ruins at Djemila SP2

Mosque of Sidi Abd-er-Rahman SP3

Designs: 10c+10c, Rummel Gorge, Constantine. 15c+15c, Admiralty Buildings, Algiers. 25c+25c, View of Algiers. 30c+30c, Trajan's Arch, Timgad. 40c+40c, Temple of the North, Djemila. 75c+75c Mansourah Minaret, Tlemcen. 1f+1f, View of Ghardaia. 1.50f+1.50f, View of Tolga. 2f+2f, Tuareg warriors. 3f+3f, Kasbah, Algiers.

1930 **Engraved.** *Perf. 12½.*

B14	SP1	5c+5c orange	3.75	3.75
B15	"	10c+10c olive green	3.75	3.75
B16	"	15c+15c dark brown	3.75	3.75
B17	"	25c+25c black	3.75	3.75
B18	"	30c+30c dark red	3.75	3.75
B19	"	40c+40c apple green	3.75	3.75
B20	SP2	50c+50c ultra.	3.75	3.75
B21	"	75c+75c red purple	3.75	3.75
B22	"	1fr+1fr org. red	3.75	3.75
B23	"	1.50fr+1.50fr deep ultramarine	3.75	3.75
B24	"	2fr+2fr dark carmine	3.75	3.75
B25	"	3fr+3fr dk. grn.	3.75	3.75
B26	SP3	5fr+5fr green & carmine	5.50	5.50
		a. Center inverted	225.00	
		Nos. B14-B26 (13)	50.50	50.50

Issued in connection with the celebration of the centenary of the French occupation of Algeria. The surtax on the stamps was given to the funds for the celebration.

Nos. B14-B26 exist imperf. Price, set in pairs, $250.

No. 102 Surcharged in Red

1918-11 Nov.-1938
0.65 + 0.35

1938 *Perf. 13.*

B27	A6	65c+35c on 2.25fr yellow green	30	30

20th anniversary of Armistice.

René Caillié, Charles Lavigerie and Henri Duveyrier—SP14

1939 **Engraved.**

B28	SP14	30c+20c dark blue green	50	50
B29	"	90c+60c carmine rose	50	50
B30	"	2.25fr+75c ultra.	5.50	5.50
B31	"	5fr+5fr brn. blk.	12.00	12.00

Pioneers of the Sahara.

French and Algerian Soldiers SP15

1940 **Photogravure** *Perf. 12*

B32	SP15	1fr+1fr bl. & car.	40	40
B33	"	1fr+2fr brown rose & black	40	40
B34	"	1fr+4fr deep green & red	50	50
B35	"	1fr+9fr brn. & car.	60	60

The surtax was used to assist the families of mobilized men.

Type of Regular Issue, 1941 Surcharged in Carmine

+ 4f

1941 **Engraved.** *Perf. 13.*

B36	A19	1fr+4fr black	12	12

No. 135 Surcharged in Carmine

SECOURS NATIONAL +4f

B37	A19	1fr+4fr dark blue	12	12

The surtax was for National Relief.

No. 124 Surcharged in Black "+60c"

1942

B38	A7	90c+60c henna brown	4	4
		a. Double surch.	35.00	

The surtax was used for National Relief. The stamp could also be used as 1.50 francs for postage.

Mother and Child SP16

1943, Dec. 1 **Litho.** *Perf. 12*

B39	SP16	50c+4.50fr bright pink	30	30
B40	"	1.50fr+8.50fr lt. grn.	30	30
B41	"	3fr+12fr deep blue	30	30
B42	"	5fr+15fr vio. brn.	30	30

The surtax was for the benefit of soldiers and prisoners of war.

Planes over Fields SP17

Engraved.

1945, July 2 *Perf. 13* **Unwmkd.**

B43	SP17	1.50fr+3.50fr light ultramarine, red orange & black	8	8

The surtax was for the benefit of Algerian airmen and their families.

France No. B192 Overprinted in Black

ALGÉRIE
a

1945

B44	SP146	4fr+6fr dark violet brown	12	10

The surtax was for war victims of the P. T. T.

Overprinted in Blue on Type of France, 1945.

1945, Oct. 15

B45	SP150	2fr+3fr dark brown	25	25

For Stamp Day.

Overprinted in Blue on Type of France, 1946.

1946, June 29

B46	SP160	3fr+2fr red	40	40

For Stamp Day.

Children Playing by Stream SP18

Girl SP19

Athlete SP20

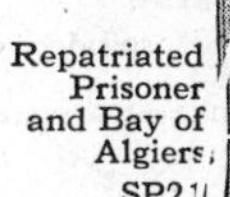

Repatriated Prisoner and Bay of Algiers SP21

1946, Oct. 2 **Engraved** *Perf. 13*

B47	SP18	3fr+17fr dk. green	75	75
B48	SP19	4fr+21fr red	75	75
B49	SP20	8fr+27fr rose lilac	2.00	2.00
B50	SP21	10fr+35fr dark blue	75	75

The surtax was for Algerian works of solidarity.

Type of France, 1947, Overprinted type "a" in Carmine.

1947, Mar. 15

B51	SP172	4.50fr+5.50fr deep ultramarine	35	35

For Stamp Day.

Same on Type of France, 1947, Surcharged Like No. B36 in Carmine.

1947, Nov. 13

B52	A173	5fr+10fr dark Prussian green	35	35

Type of France, 1948, Overprinted in Dark Green

ALGÉRIE
f

1948, Mar. 6

B53	SP176	6fr+4fr dark green	45	40

For Stamp Day.

Type of France, 1948, Overprinted type "a" in Blue and New Value.

1948, May

B54	A176	6fr+4fr red	30	30

Battleship Richelieu and the Admiralty, Algiers SP22

Aircraft Carrier Arromanches SP23

Engraved.

1949, Jan. 15 *Perf. 13* **Unwmkd.**

B55	SP22	10fr+15fr deep blue	3.00	3.00
B56	SP23	18fr+22fr red	3.00	3.00

The surtax was for naval charities.

Type of France, 1949, Overprinted in Blue

ALGÉRIE
g

1949, Mar. 26

B57	SP180	15fr+5fr lilac rose	90	90

For Stamp Day, Mar. 26–27.

Type of France, 1950, Overprinted type "f" in Green.

1950, Mar. 11

B58	SP183	12fr+3fr blk. brn.	75	75

For Stamp Day, Mar. 11–12.

Foreign Legionary SP24

1950, Apr. 30

B59	SP24	15fr+5fr dark green	80	80

Charles de Foucauld and Gen. J. F. H. Laperrine SP25

1950, Aug. 21 *Perf. 13* **Unwmkd.**

B60	SP25	25fr+5fr brown olive & brown black	2.50	2.50

50th anniversary of the presence of the French in the Sahara.

Emir Abd-el-Kader and Marshal T. R. Bugeaud
SP26

1950, Aug. 21

B61 SP26 40fr+10fr dark brown & black brown 2.50 2.50

Unveiling of a monument to Emir Abd-el-Kader at Cacheron.

Col. Colonna d'Ornano and Fine Arts Museum, Algiers
SP27

1951, Jan. 11

B62 SP27 15fr+5fr black brown, violet brown & red brown 50 50

Issued to commemorate the tenth anniversary of the death of Col. Colonna d'Ornano.

Type of France, 1951, Overprinted type "a" in Black.

1951, Mar. 10

B63 SP186 12fr+3fr brown 70 70

For Stamp Day.

Type of France, 1952, Overprinted type "g" in Dark Blue.

1952, Mar. 8 ***Perf. 13*** **Unwmkd.**

B64 SP190 12fr+3fr dk. bl. 1.25 1.25

For Stamp Day.

French Military Medal
SP28

Engraved.

1952, July 5 ***Perf. 13*** **Unwmkd.**

B65 SP28 15fr+5fr green, yel. & brown 1.00 1.00

Issued to commemorate the centenary of the creation of the French Military Medal.

Type of France 1952, Surcharged type "g" and Surtax in Black

1952, Sept. 15

B66 A222 30fr+5fr dp. ultra. 90 90

Issued to commemorate the 10th anniversary of the defense of Bir-Hakeim.

View of El Oued
SP29

Design: 12fr+3fr, View of Bou-Noura.

1952, Nov. 15 **Engraved**

B67 SP29 8fr+2fr ultra. & red 1.00 1.00
B68 " 12fr+3fr red 1.35 1.35

The surtax was for the Red Cross.

Type of France, 1953, Overprinted type "a" in Black.

1953, Mar. 14 **Engraved**

B69 SP193 12fr+3fr purple 75 75

For Stamp Day. Surtax for Red Cross.

Victory of Cythera
SP30

Engraved.

1953, Dec. 18 ***Perf. 13*** **Unwmkd.**

B70 SP30 15fr+5fr black brown & brown 50 50

The surtax was for army welfare work.

Type of France, 1954, Overprinted type "a" in Black.

1954, Mar. 20 ***Perf. 13*** **Unwmkd.**

B71 SP196 12fr+3fr scarlet 60 60

For Stamp Day.

Soldiers and Flags
SP31

Foreign Legionary
SP32

1954, Mar. 27

B72 SP31 15fr+5fr dark brown 30 25

The surtax was for old soldiers.

1954, Apr. 30

B73 SP32 15fr+5fr dk. green 60 60

The surtax was for the welfare fund of the Foreign Legion.

Nurses and Verdun Hospital, Algiers—SP33

Design: 15fr+5fr, J. H. Dunant & ruins at Djemila.

1954, Oct. 30

B74 SP33 12fr+3fr indigo & red 1.65 1.65
B75 " 15fr+5fr pur. & red 1.65 1.65

The surtax was for the Red Cross.

Earthquake Victims and Ruins
SP34

First Aid
SP35

Designs: 15fr+5fr, As No. B75. 20fr+7fr, As No. B77. 25fr+8fr & 30fr+10fr, Removing wounded.

1954, Dec. 5

B76 SP34 12fr+4fr dark violet brown 1.25 1.25
B77 " 15fr+5fr dp. blue 1.25 1.25
B78 SP35 18fr+6fr lilac rose 1.25 1.25
B79 " 20fr+7fr violet 1.25 1.25
B80 " 25fr+8fr rose brn. 1.25 1.25
B81 " 30fr+10fr bright blue green 1.25 1.25
Nos. B76-B81 (6) 7.50 7.50

The surtax was for victims of the Orleansville earthquake disaster of September 1954.

Type of France, 1955, Overprinted type "a" in Black.

1955, Mar. 19

B82 SP199 12fr + 3fr deep ultramarine 50 50

For Stamp Day, Mar. 19–20.

Women and Children
SP36

Cancer Victim
SP37

1955, Nov. 5

B83 SP36 15fr+5fr blue & indigo 40 40

The tax was for war victims.

1956, Mar. 3 ***Perf. 13*** **Unwmkd.**

B84 SP37 15fr+5fr dark brown 35 35

The surtax was for the Algerian Cancer Society. The male figure in the design is Rodin's "Age of Bronze."

Type of France, 1956, Overprinted type "a" in Black.

1956, Mar.

B85 SP202 12fr+3fr red 35 35

For Stamp Day, Mar. 17–18.

Foreign Legion Rest Home
SP38

1956, Apr. 29

B86 SP38 15fr+5fr dark blue green 60 60

Issued in honor of the French Foreign Legion.

Type of France, 1957, Overprinted type "f" in Black

1957, Mar. 16 **Engraved** ***Perf. 13***

B87 SP204 12fr+3fr dull purple 65 65

For Stamp Day and to honor the Maritime Postal Service.

Fennec
SP39

Design: 15fr+5fr, Stork flying over roofs.

1957, Apr. 6

B88 SP39 12fr+3fr red brown & red 2.50 2.50
B89 " 15fr+5fr sepia & red 2.50 2.50

The surtax was for the Red Cross.

Type of Regular Issue, 1956 Surcharged in Dark Blue

18 JUIN 1940
+ 5F

1957, June 18

B90 A53 15fr+5fr scarlet & rose red 40 40

Issued to commemorate the 17th anniversary of General de Gaulle's appeal for a Free France.

The Giaour, by Delacroix
SP40

On the Banks of the Oued, by Fromentin
SP41

Design: 35fr+10fr, Dancer, by Chasseriau.

Engraved.

1957, Nov. 30 ***Perf. 13*** **Unwmkd.**

B91 SP40 15fr+5fr dk. car. 2.50 2.50
B92 SP41 20fr+5fr green 2.50 2.50
B93 SP40 35fr+10fr dark blue 2.50 2.50

The surtax was for army welfare organizations.

Type of France Overprinted type "f" in Blue.

1958, Mar. 15 ***Perf. 13*** **Unwmkd.**

B94 SP206 15fr + 5fr orange brown 60 60

For Stamp Day.

Bird-of-Paradise Flower
SP42

Arms and Marshal's Baton
SP43

1958, June 14 **Engr.** ***Perf. 13***

B95 SP42 20fr+5fr green, orange & violet 1.35 1.35

The surtax was for Child Welfare.

1958, July 20

B96 SP43 20fr+5fr ultra., carmine & green 65 65

Issued for the Marshal de Lattre Foundation.

Independent State

Clasped Hands, Wheat and Olive Branch
SP44

Burning Books
SP45

1963, May 27 ***Perf. 13*** **Unwmkd.**

B97	SP44	50c+20c slate grn., brt. grn. & carmine	1.00	65

The surtax was for the National Solidarity Fund.

1965, June 7 **Engraved** ***Perf. 13***

B98	SP45	20c+5c olive green, red & black	35	25

Issued to commemorate the burning of the Library of Algiers, June 7, 1962.

Soldiers and Woman Comforting Wounded Soldier
SP46

1966, Aug. 20 **Photo.** ***Perf. 11½***

B99	SP46	30c+10c multi.	65	65
B100	"	95c+10c "	1.50	1.25

Issued for the Day of the Moudjahid (Moslem volunteers).

Red Crescent, Boy and Girl
SP47

1967, May 27 **Litho.** ***Perf. 14***

B101	SP47	30c+10c brt. grn., brn. & carmine	40	30

Algerian Red Crescent Society.

Flood Victims
SP48

Design: 95c+25c, Rescuing flood victims.

1969, Nov. 15 **Typo.** ***Perf. 10½***

B102	SP48	30c+10c dull blue, salmon & black	40	20

Lithographed

B103	SP48	95c+25c multi.	90	50

The surtax was for flood victims.

Red Crescent Flag
SP49

1971, May 17 **Engraved** ***Perf. 10½***

B104	SP49	30c+10c slate grn. & carmine	35	35

Algerian Red Crescent Society.

AIR POST STAMPS.

Plane over Algiers Harbor
AP1

Two types of 20fr:

Type I. Monogram "F" without serifs. "POSTE" indented 3mm.

Type II. Monogram "F" with serifs. "POSTE" indented 4½mm.

Engraved.

1946, June 20 ***Perf. 13.*** **Unwmkd.**

C1	AP1	5fr red	6	5
C2	"	10fr deep blue	8	5
C3	"	15fr deep green	25	5
C4	"	20fr brown (II)	15	5
C4A	"	20fr brown (I)	55.00	50.00
C5	"	25fr violet	25	10
C6	"	40fr gray black	45	10
		Nos. C1-C4, C5-C6 (6)	1.24	40

No. C1 Surcharged in Black — **—10 %**

1947, Jan. 18

C7	AP1	(4.50fr) on 5fr red	8	7

Storks over Mosque
AP2

Plane over Village
AP3

1949–53

C8	AP2	50fr green	1.75	25
C9	AP3	100fr brown	1.20	20
C10	AP2	200fr bright red	3.50	2.50
C11	AP3	500fr ultramarine ('53)	12.50	10.00

Beni Bahdel Dam
AP4

1957, July 1 ***Perf. 13*** **Unwmkd.**

C12	AP4	200fr dark red	3.50	65

Caravelle over Ghardaia
AP5

Designs: 2d, Caravelle over El Oued. 5d, Caravelle over Tipasa.

1967–68 **Engraved** ***Perf. 13***

C13	AP5	1d lilac, org. brown & emerald	1.00	55
C14	"	2d brt. bl., org. brn. & emerald	1.75	1.20
C15	"	5d brt. bl., green & org. brn. ('68)	4.00	2.50

Plane over Casbah, Algiers
AP6

Designs: 3d, Plane over Oran. 4d, Plane over Rhumel Gorge.

1971–72 **Photogravure** ***Perf. 12½***

C16	AP6	2d grayish black & multi.	1.00	60
C17	"	3d vio. & blk. ('72)	2.00	1.35
C18	"	4d black & multi. ('72)	2.75	1.75

Issue dates: 2d, June 12, 1971; 3d, 4d, Feb. 28, 1972.

AIR POST SEMI-POSTAL STAMPS.

No. C2 Surcharged in Carmine

‡
18 Juin 1940
+10Fr.

1947, June 18 ***Perf. 13.***

CB1	AP1	10fr+10fr deep blue	45	45

Issued to commemorate the 7th anniversary of Gen. Charles de Gaulle's speech in London, June 18, 1940.

No. C1 Surcharged in Blue

‡
18 JUIN 1940
+10 Fr.

1948, June 18

CB2	AP1	5fr+10fr red	45	45

Issued to commemorate the 8th anniversary of Gen. Charles de Gaulle's speech in London, June 18, 1940.

Monument, Clock Tower and Plane
SPAP1

1949, Nov. 10 **Engraved** **Unwmkd.**

CB3	SPAP1	15fr+20fr dark brown	2.25	2.25

Issued to commemorate the 25th anniversary of Algeria's first postage stamps.

POSTAGE DUE STAMPS.

D1

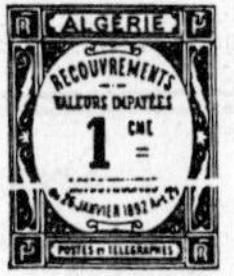

D2

Perf. 14x13½.

1926-27 **Typographed.** **Unwmkd.**

J1	D1	5c light blue	7	7
J2	"	10c dark brown	7	7
J3	"	20c olive green	15	15
J4	"	25c carmine rose	30	30
J5	"	30c rose red	15	10
J6	"	45c blue green	30	30
J7	"	50c brown violet	5	5
J8	"	60c green ('27)	1.00	35
J9	"	1fr red brown, *straw*	10	10
J10	"	2fr lilac rose ('27)	17	17
J11	"	3fr deep blue ('27)	10	10
		Nos. J1-J11 (11)	2.46	1.76

1926-27

J12	D2	1c olive green	5	5
J13	"	10c violet	30	20
J14	"	30c bistre	20	12
J15	"	60c dull red	15	12
J16	"	1fr brt. vio. ('27)	6.75	1.65
J17	"	2fr light blue ('27)	6.00	60
		Nos. J12-J17 (6)	13.45	2.74

See note below France No. J51.

Stamps of 1926 Surcharged with New Values.

1927

J18	D1	60c on 20c olive green	60	20
J19	"	2fr on 45c blue green	85	60
J20	"	3fr on 25c carmine rose	25	20

Recouvrement Stamps of 1926 Surcharged — **10c**

1927-32

J21	D2	10c on 30c bis. ('32)	1.15	1.15
J22	"	1fr on 1c olive green	50	30
J23	"	1fr on 60c dull red ('32)	8.00	10
J24	"	2fr on 10c violet	4.50	4.50

Type of 1926, Without "R F".

1942 **Typographed** ***Perf. 14x13½***

J25	D1	30c dark red	8	8
J26	"	2fr magenta	15	15

Type of 1926 Surcharged in Red — **T 0.50**

1944 ***Perf. 14x13½.***

J27	A2	50c on 20c yel. green	5	5
		a. Inverted surch.	2.00	
		b. Double surch.	7.50	

No. J27 was issued precanceled only. See note after No. 32.

Type of 1926.

1944 **Lithographed.** ***Perf. 12.***

J28	D1	1.50fr bright rose lilac	25	18
J29	"	2fr greenish blue	25	18
J30	"	5fr rose carmine	18	18

Type of 1926.

1947 **Typographed** ***Perf. 14x13½***

J32	D1	5fr green	50	50

France Nos. J80–J81 Overprinted in Carmine or Black — **ALGÉRIE**

1947

J33	D5	10c sepia (C)	4	4
J34	"	30c bright red violet	8	8

D3

Engraved.

1947–55 ***Perf. 14x13*** **Unwmkd.**

J35	D3	20c red	12	10
J36	"	60c ultramarine	30	25
J37	"	1fr dark orange brown	5	5
J38	"	1.50fr dull green	40	35
J39	"	2fr red	5	4

J40 D3 3fr violet 6 6
J41 " 5fr ultramarine ('49) 9 8
J42 " 6fr black 12 12
J43 " 10fr lilac rose 12 10
J44 " 15fr olive green ('55) 50 50
J45 " 20fr bright green 18 15
J46 " 30fr red orange ('55) 40 35
J47 " 50fr indigo ('51) 90 70
J48 " 100fr bright blue ('53) 3.25 2.50
Nos. J35-J48 (14) 6.54 5.35

Independent State

France Nos. J93-J97 Overprinted "EA" in Black like Nos. 286-290

Perf. 14x13½

1962, July 2 Typo. Unwmkd.

Handstamped Overprint

J49 D6 5c bright pink 1.35 1.00
J50 " 10c red orange 1.35 85
J51 " 20c olive bister 1.35 85
J52 " 50c dark green 2.50 1.85
J53 " 1fr deep green 3.75 3.75
Nos. J49-J53 (5) 10.30 8.30

Typographed Overprint

J49a D6 5c bright pink 3.50 3.50
J50a " 10c red orange 3.50 3.50
J51a " 20c olive bister 2.50 2.50
J52a " 50c dark green 9.00 9.00
J53a " 1fr deep green 13.50 13.50
Nos. J49a-J53a (5) 32.00 32.00

See note after No. 290.

Scales—D4

Grain—D5

1963, June 25 ***Perf. 14x13½***

J54 D4 5c car. rose & blk. 7 5
J55 " 10c olive & carmine 13 8
J56 " 20c ultra. & black 20 15
J57 " 50c bister brn. & grn. 50 40
J58 " 1fr lilac & orange 1.10 80
Nos. J54-J58 (5) 2.00 1.48

No. J58 Surcharged with New Value and 3 Bars

1968, Mar. 28 Typo. ***Perf. 14x13½***

J59 D4 60c on 1fr lilac & org. 30 15

1972, Oct. 21 Litho. ***Perf. 13½x14***

J60 D5 10c bister 4 3
J61 " 20c deep brown 10 6
J62 " 40c orange 20 7
J63 " 50c dk. violet blue 25 12
J64 " 80c dk. olive gray 40 18
J65 " 1d green 50 25
J66 " 2d blue 1.00 45
Nos. J60-J66 (7) 2.49 1.16

NEWSPAPER STAMPS.

No. 1 Surcharged in Red **½ centime**

1924 ***Perf. 14x13½*** **Unwmkd.**

P1 A16 ½c on 1c dark gray 5 5
a. Triple surcharge 35.00

1926

Same Surcharge in Red on No. 33

P2 A1 ½c on 1c olive 5 5

ALLENSTEIN

(äl'ĕn-shtīn)

LOCATION—In East Prussia.

AREA—4,457 sq. mi.

POP.—540,000 (estimated 1920).

CAPITAL—Allenstein.

Allenstein, a district of East Prussia, held a plebiscite in 1920 under the Versailles Treaty, voting to join Germany rather than Poland. Later that year, Allenstein became part of the German Republic.

100 Pfennig = 1 Mark

Stamps of Germany, 1906-20, Overprinted **PLÉBISCITE OLSZTYN ALLENSTEIN**

Perf. 14, 14½, 14x14½, 14½x14

1920 Wmkd. Lozenges. (125)

1 A16 5pf green 22 22
2 " 10pf carmine 22 22
3 A22 15pf dark violet 22 22
4 " 15pf violet brown 3.50 4.25
5 A16 20pf blue violet 22 22
6 " 30pf orange & black, *buff* 22 22
7 " 40pf lake & black 25 30
8 " 50pf purple & black, *buff* 25 30
9 " 75pf green & black 25 30
10 A17 1m carmine rose 1.10 1.10
a. Double ovpt.
11 " 1.25m green 55 60
a. Double ovpt.
12 " 1.50m yellow brown 55 60
13 A21 2.50m lilac rose 1.20 1.10
14 A19 3m black violet 1.90 1.90
a. Double ovpt.
b. Inverted overprint
Nos. 1-14 (14) 10.65 11.55

Overprinted

15 A16 5pf green 22 33
16 " 10pf carmine 22 22
17 A22 15pf dark violet 22 22
18 " 15pf violet brown 21.00 32.50
19 A16 20pf blue violet 20 22
20 " 30pf orange & black, *buff* 25 27
21 " 40pf lake & black 25 27
22 " 50pf purple & black, *buff* 22 22
23 " 75pf green & black 22 22
24 A17 1m carmine rose 70 85
a. Inverted overprint 650.00 550.00
25 " 1.25m green 70 85
26 " 1.50m yellow brown 70 85
27 A21 2.50m lilac rose 80 1.10
28 A19 3m black violet 1.10 1.35
a. Inverted overprint 525.00 800.00
b. Double ovpt. 500.00 650.00
Nos. 15-28 (14) 26.80 39.47

The 40pf carmine rose (Germany No. 124) exists with this oval overprint, but it is doubtful whether it was regularly issued. Price $350.

ANATOLIA

(ăn'ȧ-tō'lĭ-ȧ)

See Turkey in Asia, Vol. IV.

ANDORRA

(ăn-dŏr'ȧ)

LOCATION—On the southern slope of the Pyrenees Mountains between France and Spain.

GOVT.—Co-principality.

AREA—179 sq. mi.

POP.—26,500 (1976).

CAPITAL—Andorre-la-Vieille.

Andorra is subject to the joint control of France and the Spanish Bishop of Urgel and pays annual tribute to both. The country has no monetary unit of its own, the peseta and franc both being in general use.

100 Centimos = 1 Peseta
100 Centimes = 1 Franc

Spanish Administration.

Stamps of Spain, 1922-26, Overprinted in Red or Black :-: CORREOS :-: ANDORRA

Perf. 14, 13½x12½, 12½x11½.

1928 Unwmkd.

1 A49 2c olive green 38 30

Control Numbers on Back

2 A49 5c carmine rose (Bk) 45 45
3 " 10c green 45 45
4 " 15c slate blue 2.25 2.25
5 " 20c violet 2.25 2.25
6 " 25c rose red (Bk) 2.25 2.25
7 " 30c black brown 10.00 6.75
8 " 40c deep blue 10.00 4.50
9 " 50c orange (Bk) 10.00 6.75
10 A49a 1p blue black 12.50 9.00
11 " 4p lake (Bk) 85.00 65.00
12 " 10p brown (Bk) 140.00 90.00
Nos. 1-12 (12) 275.53 189.95

Counterfeit overprints exist.

La Vall
A1

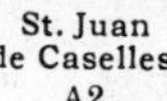
St. Juan de Caselles
A2

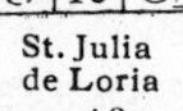
St. Julia de Loria
A3

St. Coloma
A4

General Council
A5

1929 Engraved ***Perf. 14, 11½***

13 A1 2c olive green 1.50 38

Control Numbers on Back

14 A2 5c carmine lake 2.50 45
a. Perf. 11½ 50.00 1.50
15 A3 10c yellow green 2.50 75
16 A4 15c slate green 2.50 75
17 A3 20c violet 2.50 90
18 A4 25c carmine rose 6.25 1.50
19 A1 30c olive brown 90.00 30.00
a. Perf. 11½ 60.00 22.50
20 A2 40c dark blue 4.75 75
21 A3 50c deep orange 4.75 90
a. Perf. 11½ 225.00 150.00
22 A5 1p slate 8.00 3.00
23 " 4p deep rose 65.00 18.50
a. Perf. 11½ 175.00
24 A5 10p bistre brown 72.50 25.00
Nos. 13-24 (12) 262.75 82.88

Both perforations were used for all values through 4p. The 10p is perf. 14.
Nos. 13-24, 26, 28, 32 exist imperforate.

Without Control Numbers.

1936-43 ***Perf. 11½x11***

25 A1 2c red brown ('37) 1.50 60
26 A2 5c dark brown 1.50 60
27 A3 10c blue green 3.00 1.10
a. 10c yel. green 100.00 15.00
28 A4 15c green ('37) 4.50 1.20
29 A3 20c violet 4.50 1.20
30 A4 25c deep rose ('37) 1.85 1.10
31 A1 30c carmine 3.00 1.10
31A A2 40c dark blue *300.00* 15.00
32 A1 45c rose red ('37) 1.50 60
33 A3 50c deep orange 6.75 1.85
34 A1 60c deep blue ('37) 4.50 1.10
34A A5 1p slate *1750.00*
35 " 4p deep rose ('43) 24.00 15.00
36 " 10p bis. brn. ('43) 32.50 15.00
Nos. 25-34, 35-36 (13) *389.10* 55.45

Edelweiss
A6

Provost
A7

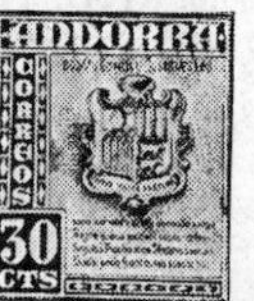
Coat of Arms
A8

Plaza of Ordino
A9

Chapel of Meritxell
A10

Map
A11

Photogravure.

1948-53 ***Perf. 12½*** **Unwmkd.**

37 A6 2c dark olive green ('51) 50 30
38 " 5c deep orange ('53) 50 30
39 " 10c deep blue ('53) 50 30

Engraved

Perf. 9½x10

40 A7 20c brown violet 9.00 75
41 " 25c orange, perf. 12½ ('53) 6.00 45
42 A8 30c dark slate green 10.00 1.10
43 A9 50c deep green 12.00 1.50
44 A10 75c dark blue 15.00 1.50
45 A9 90c dp. carmine rose 7.50 1.50
46 A10 1p brt. org. verm. 12.00 1.50
47 A8 1.35p dark blue violet 7.50 1.85

Perf. 10.

48 A11 4p ultra. ('53) 12.00 3.50
49 " 10p dark violet brown ('51) 22.50 6.00
Nos. 37-49 (13) 115.00 20.55

Bridge of St. Anthony
A12

Madonna of Meritxell, 8th Century
A13

Designs: 70c, Aynos pasture. 1p, View of Canillo. 2p, St. Coloma. 2.50p, Arms of Andorra. 3p, Old Andorra (horiz.). 5p, View of Ordino (horiz.).

Engraved

1963-64 ***Perf. 13*** **Unwmkd.**

50 A12 25c dark gray & sepia 8 8
51 " 70c dk. slate green & brown black 8 8
52 " 1p slate & dull purple 22 8
53 " 2p vio. & dull purple 22 8
54 " 2.50p rose claret ('64) 75 22
55 " 3p black & greenish gray ('64) 1.10 22
56 " 5p dark brown & chocolate ('64) 2.25 75
57 A13 6p sepia & car. ('64) 3.00 75
Nos. 50-57 (8) 7.70 2.26

Narcissus
A14

Encamp Valley
A15

Flowers: 1p, Pinks. 5p, Jonquils. 10p, Hellebore.

1966, June 10 Engraved ***Perf. 13***

58 A14 50c slate bl. & vio. bl. 15 8
59 " 1p brown & claret 22 8
60 " 5p brt. grn. & slate bl. 1.10 45
61 " 10p dk. violet & blk. 2.50 50

Europa Issue 1972
Common Design Type

1972, May 2 **Photo.** ***Perf. 13***
Size: 25½x38mm.

62 CD15 8p dk. grn. & multi. 100.00 80.00

1972, July 4 **Photo.** ***Perf. 13***

Designs: 1.50p, Massana (village). 2p, Skiing on De La Casa Pass. 5p, Pessons Lake (horiz.).

63 A15 1p multicolored 15 8
64 " 1.50p " 45 30
65 " 2p " 1.00 30
66 " 5p " 1.20 50

Tourist publicity.

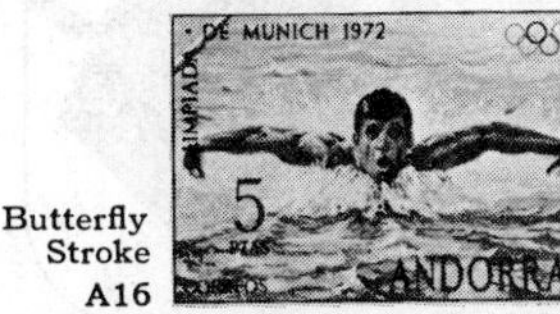

Butterfly Stroke
A16

Design: 2p, Volleyball (vert.).

1972, Oct. **Photo.** ***Perf. 13***

67 A16 2p lt. blue & multi. 45 30
68 " 5p multicolored 50 30

20th Olympic Games, Munich, Aug. 26-Sept. 11.

Common Design Types
pictured in section at front of book.

St. Anthony Singers
A17

1972, Dec. 5 **Photo.** ***Perf. 13***
Multicolored

69 A17 1p *shown* 8 8
70 " 1.50p *Les Caramelles (boys' choir)* 8 8
71 " 2p *Nativity scene* 18 8
72 " 5p *Man holding giant cigar* (vert.) 45 8
73 " 8p *Hermit of Meritxell* (vert.) 60 30
74 " 15p *Marratxa dancers* 1.50 50
Nos. 69-74 (6) 2.89 1.12

Andorran customs. No. 71 is for Christmas 1972.

Europa Issue 1973
Common Design Type and

Symbol of Unity
A18

1973, Apr. 30 **Photo.** ***Perf. 13***

75 A18 2p ultra., red & blk. 22 22

Size: 37x25mm.

76 CD16 8p tan, red & blk. 65 50

Nativity
A19

Virgin of Ordino
A20

Design: 5p, Adoration of the Kings. Designs are from altar panels of Meritxell Parish Church.

1973, Dec. 14 **Photo.** ***Perf. 13***

77 A19 2p multicolored 15 8
78 " 5p " 50 22

Christmas 1973.

Europa Issue 1974

1974, Apr. 29 **Photo.** ***Perf. 13***

Design: 8p, Les Banyes Cross.

79 A20 2p multicolored 15 7
80 " 8p slate & bt. blue 50 22

Cupboard
A21

Crowns of Virgin and Child of Roser
A22

1974, July 30 **Photo.** ***Perf. 13***

81 A21 10p multicolored 50 22
82 A22 25p dk. red & multi. 1.25 50

UPU Monument, Bern
A23

1974, Oct. **Photogravure** ***Perf. 13***

83 A23 15p multicolored 90 45

Centenary of Universal Postal Union.

Nativity
A24

Design: 5p, Adoration of the Kings.

1974, Dec. 4 **Photo.** ***Perf. 13***

84 A24 2p multicolored 8 8
85 " 5p " 30 15

Christmas 1974.

Mail Delivery, Andorra, 19th Century
A25

12th Century Painting, Ordino Church
A26

1975, Apr. 4 **Photo.** ***Perf. 13***

86 A25 3p multicolored 30 15

España 75 International Philatelic Exhibition, Madrid, Apr. 4-13.

1975, Apr. 28 **Photo.** ***Perf. 13***

Design: 12p, Christ in Glory, 12th century Romanesque painting, Ordino church.

87 A26 3p multicolored 22 15
88 " 12p " 50 30

Urgel Cathedral and Document
A27

1975, Oct. 4 **Photo.** ***Perf. 13***

89 A27 7p multicolored 1.50 1.10

Millennium of consecration of Urgel Cathedral, and Literary Festival 1975.

Nativity, Ordino
A28

Design: 7p, Adoration of the Kings, Ordino.

1975, Dec. 3 **Photo.** ***Perf. 13***

90 A28 3p multicolored 30 15
91 " 7p " 45 30

Christmas 1975.

Caldron and CEPT Emblem
A29

Slalom and Montreal Olympic Emblem
A30

Europa Issue 1976

Design: 12p, Chest and CEPT emblem (horiz.).

1976, May 3 **Photo.** ***Perf. 13***

92 A29 3p bister & multi. 22 10
93 " 12p yellow & multi. 45 22

1976, July 9 **Photo.** ***Perf. 13***

Design: 15p, One-man canoe and Montreal Olympic emblem (horiz.).

94 A30 7p multicolored 30 15
95 " 15p " 70 30

21st Olympic Games, Montreal, Canada, July 17-Aug. 1.

Nativity
A31

Design: 25p, Adoration of the Kings. Wall paintings in La Massana Church.

1976, Dec. 7 **Photo.** ***Perf. 13***

96 A31 3p multicolored 22 15
97 " 25p " 90 38

Christmas 1976.

Europa Issue 1977

View of Ansalonge
A32

Design: 12p, Xuclar, valley and mountains.

1977, May 2 **Litho.** ***Perf. 13***

98 A32 3p multicolored 9 8
99 " 12p " 45 22

Cross of Terme
A33

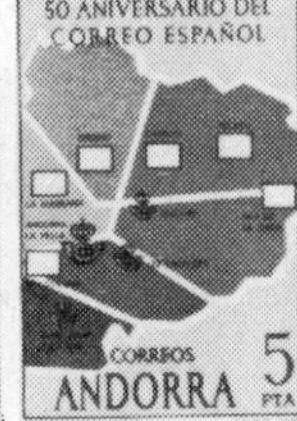

Map of Post Offices
A34

Design: 12p, Church of St. Miguel d'Engolasters.

1977, Dec. 2 **Photo.** ***Perf. 13x12½***

100 A33 5p multicolored 15 8
101 " 12p " 36 22

Christmas 1977.

Souvenir Sheet

Designs: 10p, Mail delivery. 20p, Post Office, 1928. 25p, Andorran coat of arms.

1978, Mar. 31 Photo. *Perf. 13x13½*

102	Sheet of 4	2.00	2.00
	a. A34 5p multicolored	15	
	b. " 10p "	30	
	c. " 20p "	60	
	d. " 25p "	75	

Spanish postal service in Andorra, 50th anniversary. No. 102 has black marginal inscription. Size: 105x149mm.

Europa Issue 1978

La Vall A35

Design: 12p, St. Juan de Caselles.

1978, May 2 *Perf. 13*

103	A35	5p multicolored	15	10
104	"	12p "	36	22

Crown, Bishop's Mitre and Staff A36

1978, Sept. 24 Photo. *Perf. 13*

105	A36	5p brn., car. & yel.	*45*	24

700th anniversary of the signing of treaty establishing Co-Principality of Andorra.

Holy Family A37

Design: 25p, Adoration of the Kings. Both designs after frescoes in the Church of St. Mary d'Encamp.

1978, Dec. 5 Photo. *Perf. 13*

106	A37	5p multicolored	15	10
107	"	25p "	75	30

Christmas 1978.

AIR POST STAMP

AP1

Engraved.

1951, June 27 *Perf. 11.* **Unwmkd.**

C1 AP1 1p dk. vio. brown 21.00 2.25

SPECIAL DELIVERY STAMPS.

Special Delivery Stamp of Spain, 1905 Overprinted

CORREOS

ANDORRA

1928 *Perf. 14.* **Unwmkd.**

Without Control Number on Back.

E1 SD1 20c red 52.50 35.00

With Control Number on Back.

E2 SD1 20c pale red 21.00 11.00

Eagle over Mountain Pass SD2 — Arms and Squirrel SD3

1929 *Perf. 14*

With Control Number on Back.

E3 SD2 20c scarlet 18.50 4.50
a. Perf. 11½ 110.00

Without Control Number on Back.

1937 *Perf. 11½x11.*

E4 SD2 20c red 6.75 3.00

Engraved.

1949 *Perf. 10x9½.* **Unwmkd.**

E5 SD3 25c red 5.25 2.50

French Administration.

Stamps and Types of France, 1900-1929, Overprinted ANDORRE

1931 *Perf. 14x13½* **Unwmkd.**

1 A16 1c gray 50 50
a. Double ovpt. 425.00 425.00
2 " 2c red brown 75 75
3 " 3c orange 75 75
4 " 5c green 1.00 1.00
5 " 10c lilac 1.50 1.50
6 A22 15c red brown 3.25 3.25
7 " 20c red violet 5.50 5.50
8 " 25c yellow brown 5.50 5.50
9 " 30c green 4.25 4.25
10 " 40c ultramarine 8.50 8.50
11 A20 45c light violet 12.50 12.50
12 " 50c vermilion 8.50 8.50
13 " 65c gray green 12.50 12.50
14 " 75c rose lilac 16.50 16.50
15 A22 90c red 17.50 17.50
16 A20 1fr dull blue 22.50 22.50
17 A22 1.50fr light blue 27.50 27.50

Overprinted ANDORRE

18 A18 2fr orange & pale blue 30.00 30.00
19 " 3fr bright violet & rose 85.00 85.00
20 " 5fr dk. bl. & buff 130.00 130.00
21 A18 10fr green & red 235.00 235.00
22 " 20fr magenta & green 300.00 300.00
Nos. 1-22 (22) 929.00 929.00

Nos. 9, 15 and 17 were not issued in France without overprint.

Chapel of Meritxell
A50

Bridge of St. Anthony
A51

St. Miguel d'Engolasters A52 — Gorge of St. Julia A53

Old Andorra
A54

1932-43 Engraved *Perf. 13*

23 A50 1c gray black 30 25
24 " 2c violet 60 50
25 " 3c brown 30 25
26 " 5c blue green 60 40
27 A51 10c dull lilac 1.00 65
28 A50 15c deep red 1.25 1.25
29 A51 20c light rose 10.00 6.75
30 A52 25c brown 4.25 2.50
31 A51 25c brn. car. ('37) 8.50 5.00
32 " 30c emerald 1.75 1.25
33 " 40c ultramarine 7.50 6.25
34 " 40c brn. blk. ('39) 1.00 1.00
35 " 45c light red 8.50 6.25
36 " 45c blue grn. ('39) 5.00 3.00
37 A52 50c lilac rose 11.00 8.50
38 A51 50c lt. violet ('39) 5.00 3.00
38A " 50c green ('40) 2.25 1.50
39 " 55c lt. vio. ('38) 15.00 10.00
40 " 60c yel. brn. ('38) 65 55
41 A52 65c blue green 40.00 30.00
42 A51 65c blue ('38) 10.00 7.25
43 " 70c red ('39) 2.00 1.25
44 A52 75c violet 4.00 2.75
45 A51 75c ultra. ('39) 3.75 2.50
46 " 80c green ('38) 18.50 13.50
46A A53 80c blue green ('40) 30 25
47 " 90c deep rose 4.50 3.25
48 " 90c dk. green('39) 3.75 1.85
49 " 1fr blue green 18.50 11.00
50 " 1fr scarlet ('38) 20.00 16.50
51 " 1fr dp. ultra. ('39) 30 25
51A " 1.20fr brt. vio. ('42) 30 25
52 A50 1.25fr rose carmine ('33) 13.50 8.50
52A " 1.25fr rose ('38) 5.25 2.25
52B A53 1.30fr sepia ('40) 30 25
53 A54 1.50fr ultramarine 17.00 15.00
53A A53 1.50fr crimson ('40) 30 25
54 " 1.75fr violet ('33) 95.00 75.00
55 " 1.75fr dk. blue('38) 32.50 25.00
56 " 2fr red violet 4.00 2.50
56A A50 2fr rose red ('40) 1.50 1.10
56B " 2fr dark blue green ('42) 30 25
57 " 2.15fr dk. vio. ('38) 40.00 32.50
58 " 2.25fr ultra. ('39) 7.50 5.00
58A " 2.40fr red ('42) 30 25
59 " 2.50fr gray blk. ('39) 7.50 5.00
59A " 2.50fr dp. ultra. ('40) 2.25 1.50
60 A53 3fr orange brown 4.00 2.50
60A A50 3fr red brown ('40) 30 25
60B " 4fr slate blue ('42) 30 25
60C " 4.50fr dp. violet('42) 1.00 40
61 A54 5fr brown 50 30
62 " 10fr violet 65 45
62B " 15fr dp. ultra. ('42) 75 40
63 " 20fr rose lake 65 45
63A A51 50fr turquoise blue ('43) 1.50 90
Nos. 23-63A (56) 447.70 329.70

A 20c ultramarine exists. Price $7,500.

No. 37 Surcharged with Bars and New Value in Black.

1935

64 A52 20c on 50c lilac rose 2.25 1.85
a. Double surcharge 300.00

Coat of Arms
A55 A56

1936-42 *Perf. 14x13*

65 A55 1c black ('37) 5 5
66 " 2c blue 6 6
67 " 3c brown 5 5
68 " 5c rose lilac 6 6
69 " 10c ultramarine ('37) 5 5
70 " 15c red violet 30 30
71 " 20c emerald ('37) 10 10
72 " 30c copper red ('38) 25 25
72A " 30c black brown ('42) 18 18
73 " 35c Prus. grn. ('38) 32.50 32.50
74 " 40c copper red ('42) 12 12
75 " 50c Prussian grn. ('42) 12 12
76 " 60c turquoise blue ('42) 12 12
77 " 70c violet ('42) 12 12
Nos. 65-77 (14) 34.08 34.08

1944

78 A56 10c violet 4 4
79 " 30c deep magenta 5 5
80 " 40c dull blue 5 5
81 " 50c orange red 6 6
82 " 60c black 8 8
83 " 70c bright red violet 10 8
84 " 80c blue green 6 6
Nos. 78-84 (7) 44 42

See also No. 114.

St. Jean de Caselles
A57

La Maison des Vallees
A58

Old Andorra
A59

Provost
A60

1944-47 *Perf. 13*

85 A57 1fr brown violet 18 10
86 " 1.20fr blue 15 8
87 " 1.50fr red 18 7
88 " 2fr dark blue green 10 7
89 A58 2.40fr rose red 25 15
90 " 2.50fr rose red ('46) 38 18
91 " 3fr sepia 12 8
92 " 4fr ultramarine 18 12
93 A59 4.50fr brown black 20 15
94 A58 4.50fr dark blue green ('47) 1.85 1.75
95 A59 5fr ultramarine 15 12
96 " 5fr Prussian green ('46) 38 22
97 " 6fr rose car. ('45) 38 17
98 " 10fr Prussian green 8 10
99 " 10fr ultra. ('46) 15 12
100 A60 15fr rose lilac 38 22
101 " 20fr deep blue 38 38
102 " 25fr light rose red ('46) 90 80
103 " 40fr dark green('46) 90 90
104 " 50fr sepia 85 80
Nos. 85-104 (20) 8.14 6.58

1948-49

105 A58 4fr light blue green 85 85
106 A59 6fr violet brown 25 25
107 " 8fr indigo 1.10 80
108 " 12fr bright red 75 75
109 " 12fr blue green ('49) 85 85
110 " 15fr crimson ('49) 50 50
111 A60 18fr deep blue 1.75 1.00
112 " 20fr dark violet 1.50 1.25
113 " 25fr ultra. ('49) 1.10 1.10
Nos. 105-113 (9) 8.65 7.35

1949-51 *Perf. 14x13, 13*

114 A56 1fr deep blue 65 50
115 A57 3fr red ('51) 3.25 2.75
116 " 4fr sepia 2.00 1.65
117 A58 5fr emerald 1.85 1.75
118 " 5fr purple('51) 1.65 1.00
119 " 6fr blue green ('51) 1.65 1.10
120 " 8fr red brown 60 60
121 A59 15fr blk. brown ('51) 1.50 1.25
122 " 18fr rose red ('51) 6.75 5.50
123 A60 30fr ultra. ('51) 8.50 5.00
Nos. 114-123 (10) 28.40 21.10

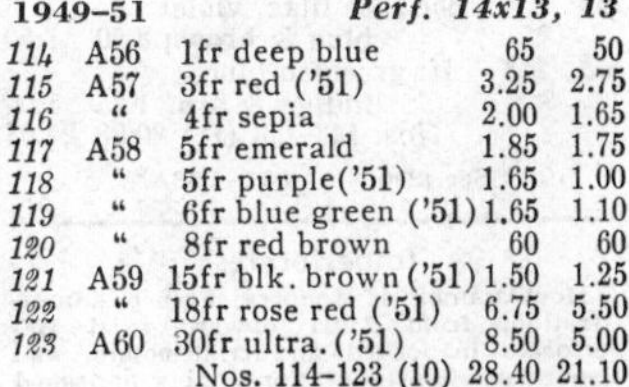

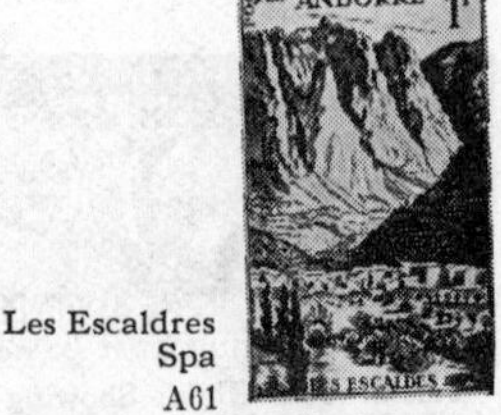

Les Escaldres Spa
A61

St. Coloma Belfry
A62

Designs: 15fr, 18fr, 20fr, 25fr, Gothic cross. 30fr, 35fr, 40fr 50fr, 65fr, 70fr, 75fr, Village of Les Bons.

Engraved.

1955-58 ***Perf. 13*** **Unwmkd.**

124 A61 1fr dark gray blue 5 5
125 " 2fr deep green 7 7
126 " 3fr red 7 7
127 " 5fr chocolate 6 6
128 A62 6fr dark blue green 30 25
129 " 8fr rose brown 30 28
130 " 10fr bright violet 65 38
131 " 12fr indigo 75 45
132 A61 15fr red 85 50
133 " 18fr blue green 85 50
134 " 20fr deep purple 1.00 50
135 " 25fr sepia 1.25 65
136 A62 30fr deep blue 22.50 11.00
137 " 35fr Prussian blue ('57) 10.00 7.00
138 " 40fr dark green 25.00 21.00
139 " 50fr cerise 2.50 1.75
140 " 65fr purple ('58) 5.50 5.50
141 " 70fr chestnut ('57) 5.50 5.50
142 " 75fr violet blue 35.00 27.50
Nos. 124-142 (19) 112.20 83.01

Coat of Arms
A63

Gothic Cross, Meritxell
A64

Designs: 65c, 85c, 1fr, Pond of Engolasters. 30c, 45c, 50c, as 25c.

1961, June 19 **Typo.** ***Perf. 14x13***

143 A63 5c bright green & black 5 5
144 " 10c red, pink & black 5 5
145 " 15c blue & black 6 6
146 " 20c yellow & brown 10 10

Engraved ***Perf. 13***

147 A64 25c violet, blue & green 22 22
148 " 30c maroon, olive green & brown 30 30
149 " 45c indigo, blue & green 8.50 5.00
150 " 50c purple, lt. brown & olive green 1.25 1.25
151 " 65c blue, olive & brown 10.00 8.50
152 " 85c rose lilac, violet blue & brown 8.50 7.50
153 " 1fr greenish blue, indigo & brn. 1.25 1.00
Nos. 143-153 (11) 30.28 24.03

See also Nos. 161-166A.

Imperforates

Most stamps of Andorra, French Administration, from 1961 onward exist imperforate in issued and trial colors, and also in small presentation sheets in issued colors.

Telstar and Globe Showing Andover and Pleumeur-Bodou
A65

1962, Sept. 29 **Engraved**

154 A65 50c ultra. & purple 1.75 1.75

Issued to commemorate the first television connection of the United States and Europe through the Telstar satellite, July 11-12.

"La Sardane"
A66

Charlemagne Crossing Andorra
A67

Design: 1fr, Louis le Debonnaire giving founding charter.

1963, June 22 ***Perf. 13*** **Unwmkd.**

155 A66 20c lilac rose, claret & olive grn. 3.00 3.00
156 A67 50c slate green & dk. car. rose 4.50 4.50
157 " 1fr red brn., ultra. & dk. green 6.25 6.25

Old Andorra Church and Champs-Elysées Palace
A68

1964, Jan. 20 **Engraved**

158 A68 25c black, green & violet brown 1.10 60

Issued to publicize "PHILATEC," International Philatelic and Postal Techniques Exhibition, Paris, June 5-21, 1964.

Bishop of Urgel and Seigneur of Caboët Confirming Co-Principality, 1288
A69

Design: 60c, Napoleon re-establishing Co-principality, 1806.

1964, Apr. 25 **Engraved** ***Perf. 13***

159 A69 60c dk. brn., red brn. & slate green 6.25 6.25
160 " 1fr brt. blue, orge. brown & black 7.50 7.50

Arms Type of 1961

1964, May 16 **Typo.** ***Perf. 14x13***

161 A63 1c dk. blue & gray 5 5
162 " 2c black & orange 5 5
163 " 12c purple, emerald & yellow 6 6
164 " 18c blk., lilac & pink 10 10

Scenic Type of 1961

Designs: 40c, 45c, Gothic Cross, Meritxell. 60c, 90c, Pond of Engolasters.

1965-71 **Engraved** ***Perf. 13***

165 A64 40c dark brn., orge. brn. & slate grn. 55 55
165A " 45c vio. blue, olive bister & slate ('70) 65 50
166 " 60c orange brown & dark brown 65 65
166A " 90c ultra., blue grn. & bister ('71) 65 50

Syncom Satellite over Pleumeur-Bodou Station
A70

Andorra House, Paris
A71

1965, May 17 **Unwmkd.**

167 A70 60c deep carmine, lilac & blue 3.75 3.00

Issued to commemorate the centenary of the International Telecommunication Union.

1965, June 5

168 A71 25c dk. bl., org. brn. & olive gray 70 55

Ski Lift
A72

Design: 25c, Chair lift (vert.).

1966, Apr. 2 **Engraved** ***Perf. 13***

169 A72 25c brt. blue, green & dk. brown 55 55
170 " 40c magenta, bright ultra. & sepia 85 75

Winter sports in Andorra.

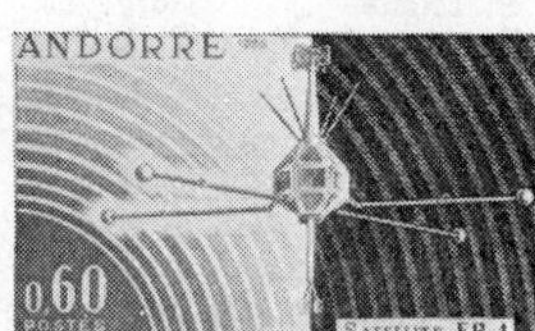

FR-1 Satellite
A73

1966, May 7 ***Perf. 13***

171 A73 60c brt. blue, green & dk. green 1.10 1.10

Issued to commemorate the launching of the scientific satellite FR-1, Dec. 6, 1965.

Europa Issue, 1966
Common Design Type

1966, Sept. 24 **Engraved** ***Perf. 13***

Size: 21½x35½mm.

172 CD9 60c brown 1.35 85

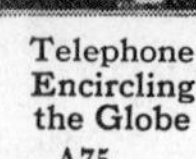

Folk Dancers, Sculpture by Josep Viladomat
A74

Telephone Encircling the Globe
A75

1967, Apr. 29 **Engraved** ***Perf. 13***

173 A74 30c olive green, deep green & slate 50 45

Issued to commemorate the centenary (in 1966) of the New Reform, which reaffirmed and strengthened political freedom in Andorra.

Europa Issue, 1967
Common Design Type

1967, Apr. 29

Size: 22x36mm.

174 CD10 30c bluish black & light blue 85 75
175 " 60c dark red & bright pink 1.65 1.25

1967, Apr. 29

176 A75 60c dark carmine, violet & black 85 75

Automatic telephone service.

Injured Father at Home
A76

1967, Sept. 23 **Engraved** ***Perf. 13***

177 A76 2.30fr ocher, dk. red brown & brown red 4.00 3.00

Introduction of Social Security System.

Jesus in Garden of Gethsemane
A77

Designs (from 16th century frescoes in La Maison des Vallees): 30c, The Kiss of Judas. 60c, The Descent from the Cross (Pieta).

1967, Sept. 23

178 A77 25c blk. & red brown 60 50
179 " 30c pur. & red lilac 85 55
180 " 60c indigo & Prus. blue 1.00 50

See also Nos. 185-187.

Downhill Skier
A78

1968, Jan. 27 **Engraved** ***Perf. 13***

181 A78 40c orange, vermilion & red lilac 75 60

Issued to publicize the 10th Winter Olympic Games, Grenoble, France, Feb. 6-18.

Europa Issue, 1968
Common Design Type

1968, Apr. 27 **Engraved** ***Perf. 13***

Size: 36x22mm.

182 CD11 30c gray & brt. bl. 1.10 75
183 " 60c brown & lilac 2.25 1.75

High Jump
A79

1968, Oct. 12 Engraved *Perf. 13*

184 A79 40c brt. blue & brown 85 75

Issued to commemorate the 19th Olympic Games, Mexico City, Oct. 12–27.

Fresco Type of 1967

Designs (from 16th century frescoes in La Maison des Vallees): 25c, The Scourging of Christ. 30c, Christ Carrying the Cross. 60c, The Crucifixion. (All horizontal.)

1968, Oct. 12

185 A77 25c dark green & gray green 60 60
186 " 30c dk. brown & lilac 75 75
187 " 60c dk. carmine & violet brown 1.35 1.35

Europa Issue, 1969
Common Design Type

1969, Apr. 26 Engraved *Perf. 13*

188 CD12 40c rose car., gray & dull blue 1.35 1.25
189 " 70c indigo, dull red & olive 2.25 2.00

Issued to commemorate the 10th anniversary of the Conference of European Postal and Telecommunications Administrations.

Kayak on Isère River A80 — Drops of Water and Diamond A80a

1969, Aug. 2 Engraved *Perf. 13*

190 A80 70c dk. slate green, ultra. & indigo 1.10 1.10

Issued to commemorate the International Canoe and Kayak Championships, Bourg-Saint-Maurice, Savoy, July 31–Aug. 6.

1969, Sept. 27 Engraved *Perf. 13*

191 A80a 70c blk., dp. ultra. & greenish blue 1.25 1.25

European Water Charter.

St. John, the Woman and the Dragon
A81

The Revelation (From the Altar of St. John, Caselles): 40c, St. John Hearing Voice from Heaven on Patmos. 70c, St. John and the Seven Candlesticks.

1969, Oct. 18

192 A81 30c brown, dp. purple & brown red 55 55
193 " 40c gray, dk. brown & brown olive 65 65
194 " 70c dk. red, maroon & brt. rose lilac 1.00 1.00

See also Nos. 199–201, 207–209, 214–216.

Field Ball A82 — Shot Put A83

1970, Feb. 21 Engraved *Perf. 13*

195 A82 80c multi. 1.25 1.10

Issued to publicize the 7th International Field Ball Games, France, Feb. 26–Mar. 8.

Europa Issue, 1970
Common Design Type

1970, May 2 Engraved *Perf. 13*

Size: 36x22mm.

196 CD13 40c orange 85 50
197 " 80c violet blue 1.25 80

1970, Sept. 11 Engraved *Perf. 13*

198 A83 80c bl. & dk. brn. 1.00 75

Issued to publicize the First European Junior Athletic Championships, Colombes, France, Sept. 11–13.

Altar Type of 1969

The Revelation (from the Altar of St. John, Caselles): 30c, St. John recording angel's message. 40c, Angel erecting column symbolizing faithful in heaven. 80c, St. John's trial in kettle of boiling oil.

1970, Oct. 24

199 A81 30c dp. carmine, dark brown & bright purple 60 60
200 " 40c vio. & slate grn. 75 75
201 " 80c olive, dk. blue & carmine rose 1.10 1.10

Ice Skating
A84

1971, Feb. 20 Engraved *Perf. 13*

202 A84 80c dk. red, red lilac & purple 1.10 75

World Figure Skating Championships, Lyons, France, Feb. 23–28.

Capercaillie
A85

Design: No. 204, Brown bear.

1971, Apr. 24 Photo. *Perf. 13*

203 A85 80c multicolored 1.25 85

Engraved

204 A85 80c bl. grn. & brown 1.25 85

Nature Protection.

Europa Issue, 1971
Common Design Type

1971, May 8 Engraved *Perf. 13*

Size: 35½x22mm.

205 CD14 50c rose red 75 60
206 " 80c light blue green 1.35 1.10

Altar Type of 1969

The Revelation (from the Altar of St. John, Caselles): 30c, St. John preaching, Rev. 1:3. 50c, "The Sign of the Beast . . ." Rev. 16:1–2. 90c, The Woman, Rev. 17:1.

1971, Sept. 18

207 A81 30c dull grn., olive & bright green 55 55
208 " 50c rose car., org. & olive brown 80 80
209 " 90c black, dk. purple & blue 1.10 1.10

Europa Issue 1972
Common Design Type

1972, Apr. 29 Photo. *Perf. 13*

Size: 21½x37mm.

210 CD15 50c brt. magenta & multicolored 75 60
211 " 90c multi. 1.35 1.10

Golden Eagle
A86

1972, May 27 Engraved

212 A86 60c dk. green, olive & plum 1.00 75

Nature protection.

Shooting
A87

1972, July 8

213 A87 1fr dark purple 1.25 1.00

20th Olympic Games, Munich, Aug. 26–Sept. 11.

Altar Type of 1969

The Revelation (from the Altar of St. John, Caselles): 30c, St. John, bishop and servant. 50c, Resurrection of Lazarus. 90c, Angel with lance and nails.

1972, Sept. 16 Engraved *Perf. 13*

214 A81 30c dk. olive, gray & red lilac 55 55
215 " 50c vio. blue & slate 80 80
216 " 90c dk. Prus. blue & slate green 1.10 1.10

De Gaulle as Co-prince of Andorra
A88

Design: 90c, De Gaulle in front of Maison des Vallées.

1972, Oct. 23 Engr. *Perf. 13*

217 A88 50c violet blue 1.10 1.10
218 " 90c dark carmine 1.35 1.35

5th anniversary of the visit of Charles de Gaulle to Andorra. Nos. 217–218 printed se-tenant in sheets of 10 stamps and 5 labels showing Andorran coat of arms and commemorative inscription.

Europa Issue 1973
Common Design Type

1973, Apr. 28 Photo. *Perf. 13*

Size: 36x22mm.

219 CD16 50c violet & multi. 60 60
220 " 90c dk. red & multi. 90 90

Virgin of Canòlich
A89

1973, June 16 Engraved *Perf. 13*

221 A89 1fr olive, Prus. blue & violet 1.35 1.35

Lily
A90

Designs: 45c, Iris. 50c, Columbine. 65c, Tobacco. No. 226, Pinks. No. 227, Narcissuses.

1973–74 Photo. *Perf. 13*

222 A90 30c car. rose & multi. 45 45
223 " 45c yel. grn. & multi. 38 38
224 " 50c buff & multi. 55 55
225 " 65c gray & multi. 60 60
226 " 90c ultra. & multi. 1.10 1.10
227 " 90c greenish blue & multicolored 85 85
Nos. 222–227 (6) 3.93 3.93

See Nos. 238–240.

Blue Titmouse
A91

Designs: 60c, Citril finch and mistletoe. 80c, Eurasian bullfinch. 1fr, Lesser spotted woodpecker.

1973–74 Photo. *Perf. 13*

228 A91 60c buff & multi. 70 70
229 " 80c gray & multi. 70 70
230 " 90c gray & multi. 75 75
231 " 1fr yel. grn. & multi. 85 85

Nature protection.

Europa Issue 1974

Virgin of Pal
A92

Design: 90c, Virgin of Santa Coloma. Statues are polychrome 12th century carvings by rural artists.

1974, Apr. 27 Engr. *Perf. 13*

232 A92 50c multicolored 55 50
233 " 90c " 1.00 75

Arms of Andorra and Cahors Bridge
A93

Mail Box, Chutes and Globe
A94

1974, Aug. 24 Engr. ***Perf. 13***
234 A93 1fr bl., vio. & orange 75 75

First anniversary of meeting of the co-princes of Andorra: Pres. Georges Pompidou of France and Msgr. Juan Marti Alanis, Bishop of Urgel.

1974, Oct. 5 Engraved ***Perf. 13***
235 A94 1.20fr multicolored 1.00 1.00

Centenary of Universal Postal Union.

Europa Issue 1975

Coronation of St. Marti, 16th Century—A95

Design: 80c, Crucifixion, 16th century (vert.).

Perf. 11½x13, 13x11½

1975, Apr. 26 Photogravure
236 A95 80c gold & multi. 75 75
237 " 1.20fr " " 1.10 1.10

Flower Type of 1973

Designs: 60c, Gentian. 80c, Anemone. 1.20fr, Autumn crocus.

1975, May 10 Photo. ***Perf. 13***
238 A90 60c olive & multi. 45 45
239 " 80c brt. rose & multi. 60 60
240 " 1.20fr green & multi. 80 80

Abstract Design—A96

1975, June 7 Engr. ***Perf. 13***
241 A96 2fr blue, magenta & emerald 1.25 1.25

ARPHILA 75 International Philatelic Exhibition, Paris, June 6–16.

Pres. Georges Pompidou
A97

1975, Aug. 23 Engr. ***Perf. 13***
242 A97 80c vio. blue & blk. 55 55

Georges Pompidou (1911–1974), president of France and co-prince of Andorra (1969–1974).

Costume and IWY Emblem
A98

1975, Nov. 8 Engr. ***Perf. 13***
243 A98 1.20fr multicolored 75 75

International Women's Year.

Skier and Snowflake
A99

1976, Jan. 31 Engr. ***Perf. 13***
244 A99 1.20fr multicolored 75 75

12th Winter Olympic Games, Innsbruck, Austria, Feb. 4–15.

Telephone and Satellite
A100

1976, Mar. 20 Engr. ***Perf. 13***
245 A100 1fr multicolored 60 60

Centenary of first telephone call by Alexander Graham Bell, Mar. 10, 1976.

Europa Issue 1976

Catalan Forge
A101

Design: 1.20fr, Lacemaker.

1976, May 8 Engr. ***Perf. 13***
246 A101 80c multicolored 50 50
247 " 1.20fr " 75 75

Thomas Jefferson
A102

Trapshooting
A103

1976, July 3 Engr. ***Perf. 13***
248 A102 1.20fr multicolored 75 75

American Bicentennial.

1976, July 17 Engr. ***Perf. 13***
249 A103 2fr multicolored 1.25 1.25

21st Olympic Games, Montreal, Canada, July 17–Aug. 1.

Meritxell Sanctuary and Old Chapel—A104

1976, Sept. 4 Engr. ***Perf. 13***
250 A104 1fr multicolored 60 60

Dedication of rebuilt Meritxell Church, Sept. 8, 1976.

Apollo
A105

Ermine
A106

Design: 1.40fr, Morio butterfly.

1976, Oct. 16 Photo. ***Perf. 13***
251 A105 80c blk. & multi. 50 50
252 " 1.40fr sal. & multi. 80 80

Nature protection.

1977, Apr. 2 Photo. ***Perf. 13***
253 A106 1fr violet blue, gray & black 60 60

Nature protection.

St. Jean de Caselles
A107

Manual Digest, 1748, Arms of Andorra
A108

Europa Issue 1977

Design: 1.40fr, Sant Vicens Castle.

1977, Apr. 30 Engr. ***Perf. 13***
254 A107 1fr multicolored 50 50
255 " 1.40fr " 75 75

1977, June 11 Engr. ***Perf. 13***
256 A108 80c grn., blue & brn. 40 35

Establishment of Institute of Andorran Studies.

St. Romanus of Caesarea
A109

1977, July 23 Engr. ***Perf. 12½x13***
257 A109 2fr multicolored 1.00 80

Design from altarpiece in Church of St. Roma de les Bons.

General Council Chamber
A110

Guillem d'Arény Plandolit
A111

1977, Sept. 24 Engr. ***Perf. 13***
258 A110 1.10fr multicolored 55 50
259 A111 2fr carmine & dk. brown 1.00 80

Andorran heritage. Guillem d'Arény Plandolit started Andorran reform movement in 1866.

Squirrel
A112

Flag and Valira River Bridge
A113

1978, Mar. 18 Engr. ***Perf. 13***
260 A112 1fr multicolored 50 40

1978, Apr. 8
261 A113 80c multicolored 40 33

700th anniversary of the signing of the treaty establishing the Co-Principality of Andorra.

Europa Issue 1978

Pal Church
A114

Design: 1.40fr, Charlemagne's Castle, Charlemagne on horseback (vert.).

1978, Apr. 29 Engr. ***Perf. 13***
262 A114 1fr multicolored 50 40
263 " 1.40fr " 70 55

Virgin of Sispony
A115

1978, May 20 Engr. ***Perf. 12x13***
264 A115 2fr multicolored 1.00 1.00

Visura Tribunal A116

1978, June 24 **Engr.** ***Perf. 13***

265	A116	1.20fr multicolored	60	45

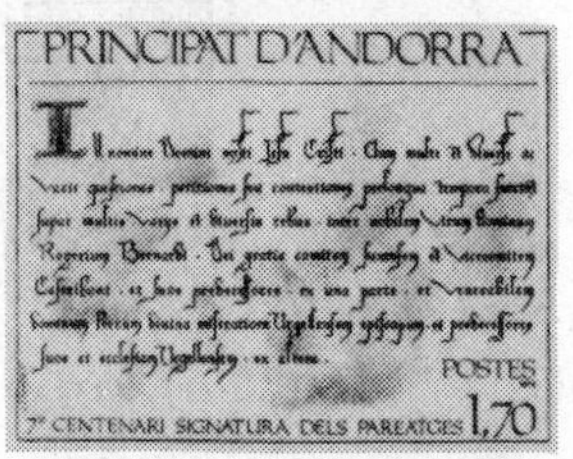

Preamble of 1278 Treaty—A117

1978, Sept. 2 **Engr.** ***Perf. 13x12½***

266	A117	1.70fr multicolored	85	65

700th anniversary of the signing of treaty establishing Co-Principality of Andorra.

SEMI-POSTAL STAMP

Virgin of St. Coloma SP1

Engraved

1964, July 25 ***Perf. 13*** **Unwmkd.**

B1	SP1	25c+10c multi.	17.50	17.50

The surtax was for the Red Cross.

AIR POST STAMPS.

Chamois—AP1

Engraved.

1950, Feb. 20 ***Perf. 13*** **Unwmkd.**

C1	AP1	100fr indigo	30.00	30.00

East Branch of Valira River AP2

1955–57

C2	AP2	100fr dark green	5.00	4.25
C3	"	200fr cerise	11.00	7.50
C4	"	500fr dp. blue ('57)	55.00	42.50

D'Inclès Valley AP3

1961, June 19 ***Perf. 13*** **Unwmkd.**

C5	AP3	2fr red, olive gray & claret	1.50	1.00
C6	"	3fr blue, maroon & slate green	2.25	1.50
C7	"	5fr rose lilac & red orange	3.25	2.50

1964, Apr. 25

C8	AP3	10fr blue green & slate green	6.75	5.00

POSTAGE DUE STAMPS.

Postage Due Stamps of France, 1893-1931, Overprinted **ANDORRE**

On Stamps of 1893-1926.

1931–33 ***Perf. 14x13½*** **Unwmkd.**

J1	D2	5c blue	1.25	1.25
J2	"	10c brown	1.25	1.25
J3	"	30c rose red	30	30
J4	"	50c violet brown	1.25	1.25
J5	"	60c green	7.50	7.50
J6	"	1fr red brn., *straw*	55	55
J7	"	2fr bright violet	6.50	6.50
J8	D2	3fr magenta	1.25	1.25
		Nos. J1–J8 (8)	19.85	14.85

On Stamps of 1927-31.

J9	D4	1c olive green	60	60
J10	"	10c rose	1.85	1.85
J11	"	60c red	22.50	17.50
J12	"	1fr Prus. grn. ('32)	42.50	30.00
J13	"	1.20fr on 2fr blue	18.50	15.00
J14	"	2fr olive brn. ('33)	62.50	52.50
J15	"	5fr on 1fr violet	50.00	42.50
		Nos. J9–J15 (7)	198.45	159.95

D5 **D6**

1935 **Typographed.**

J16	D5	1c gray green	75	50

1937

J17	D6	5c light blue	4.25	3.75

1941

J18	D6	10c brown	4.25	3.75
J19	"	2fr violet	2.50	1.25
J20	"	5fr red orange	1.85	1.25

Wheat Sheaves D7

1943–46 ***Perf. 14x13½***

J21	D7	10c sepia	12	12
J22	"	30c bright red violet	50	50
J23	"	50c blue green	75	75
J24	"	1fr brt. ultramarine	30	30
J25	"	1.50fr rose red	1.25	1.25
J26	"	2fr turquoise blue	55	55
J27	"	3fr brown orange	1.00	1.00
J28	"	4fr deep violet ('45)	1.50	1.50
J29	"	5fr bright pink	1.50	1.50
J30	"	10fr red orange ('45)	1.50	1.50
J31	"	20fr olive brown ('46)	2.25	2.25
		Nos. J21–J31 (11)	11.22	11.22

Inscribed: "Timbre Taxe."

1946-53

J32	D7	10c sepia ('46)	75	75
J33	"	1fr ultramarine	30	30
J34	"	2fr turquoise blue	30	30
J35	"	3fr orange brown	1.25	1.25
J36	"	4fr violet	1.85	1.85
J37	"	5fr bright pink	1.00	1.00
J38	"	10fr red orange	1.75	1.75
J39	"	20fr olive brown	2.75	2.75
J40	"	50fr dark green ('50)	12.50	12.50
J41	"	100fr deep green ('53)	32.50	32.50
		Nos. J32–J41 (10)	54.95	54.95

Inscribed: "Timbre Taxe."

1961, June 19 ***Perf. 14x13½***

J42	D7	5c rose pink	1.50	1.50
J43	"	10c red orange	2.25	2.25
J44	"	20c olive	3.75	3.75
J45	"	50c dk. slate green	5.00	5.00

Flower Type of France, 1964.

Designs: 5c, Centaury. 10c, Gentian. 15c, Corn poppy. 20c, Violets. 30c, Forget-me-not. 40c, Columbine. 50c, Clover.

1964–71 **Typo.** ***Perf. 14x13½***

J46	D7	5c carmine rose, red & green ('65)	5	5
J47	"	10c carmine rose, brt. bl. & green ('65)	10	10
J48	"	15c brn., green & red	12	12
J49	"	20c dk. green, green & violet ('71)	15	15
J50	"	30c brn., ultra. & grn.	18	18
J51	"	40c dk. green, scarlet & yellow ('71)	25	25
J52	D7	50c violet blue, car. & grn. ('65)	38	38
		Nos. J46–J52 (7)	1.23	1.23

NEWSPAPER STAMP.

Newspaper Stamp of France, 1919, Overprinted in Red **ANDORRE**

1931 ***Perf. 14x13½.*** **Unwmkd.**

P1	A16	½c on 1c gray	50	50

ANGOLA

(ăng·gō'lȧ)

LOCATION—Southwestern Africa between Congo and South-West Africa.

GOVT.—Republic.

AREA—481,351 sq. mi.

POP.—5,800,000 (est. 1972).

CAPITAL—Luanda.

Angola was a Portuguese overseas territory until it became independent Nov. 11, 1975, as the People's Republic of Angola.

1000 Reis = 1 Milreis
100 Centavos = 1 Escudo (1913, 1954)
100 Centavos = 1 Angolar (1932)
10 Lweys = 1 Kwanza (1977)

Portuguese Crown
A1

Perf. 12½, 13½.

1870-77 Typographed Unwmkd.

1 A1 5r black 2.25 1.90
a. Perf. 13½ 4.50 3.75
2 " 10r yellow 11.00 6.00
3 " 20r bistre 3.00 1.90
a. Perf. 13½ 18.00
4 " 25r red 6.75 3.50
a. 25r rose 6.75 3.50
b. Laid paper
c. 25r rose, perf. 14 100.00 35.00
d. Perf. 13½ 16.50 11.00
5 " 40r blue ('77) 100.00 60.00
6 " 50r green 20.00 8.25
a. Perf. 13½ 100.00 35.00
7 " 100r lilac 3.50 2.25
a. Perf. 12½ 12.00 6.00
8 " 200r orange ('77) 3.00 2.00
a. Perf. 12½ 5.50 2.75
9 " 300r chocolate ('77) 3.75 2.75
a. Perf. 12½ 7.25 4.50

1881-85

10 A1 10r green ('83) 2.50 1.40
a. Perf. 12½ 5.50 1.90
11 " 20r carmine rose ('85) 3.50 2.75
a. Cliché of 40r in plate of 20r 750.00
12 " 25r violet ('85) 1.40 90
a. Perf. 13½ 3.50 2.75
13 " 40r buff ('82) 2.75 1.50
a. Perf. 12½ 4.75 2.50
15 " 50r blue 8.75 1.40
a. Perf. 13½ 14.50 1.50

Two types of numerals are found on No. 2 and Nos. 11 to 15.

The error, No. 11a, was discovered before the stamps were issued. All copies were cancelled by a blue pencil mark.

In perf. 12½, Nos. 1-4, 4a and 6, as well as 7a, were printed in 1870 on thicker paper and 1875 on normal paper. Stamps of the earlier printing sell for 2 to 15 times more than those of the 1875 printing.

Some reprints of the 1870-85 issues are on a smooth white chalky paper, ungummed and perf. 13½. Price each, 50 cents.

Other reprints of these issues are on thin white paper with shiny white gum and clear-cut perf. 13½. Price each, $2.50.

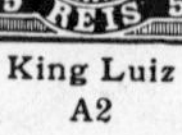

King Luiz
A2

King Carlos
A3

1886 Embossed Perf. 12½

16 A2 5r black 5.75 3.50
a. Perf. 13½ 9.25 7.25
17 " 10r green 6.00 3.75
a. Perf. 13½ 12.00 7.25
18 " 20r rose 9.00 7.25
a. Perf. 13½ 8.25 5.75
19 " 25r red violet 7.25 1.90
20 " 40r chocolate 7.25 3.25
21 " 50r blue 8.25 1.90
22 " 100r yellow brown 10.00 4.75
23 " 200r gray violet 14.00 7.00
24 " 300r orange 14.00 7.00

Reprints of 5r, 20r and 100r have clean-cut perf. 13½. Price each $2.

Typographed.

1893-94 Perf. 11½, 12½, 13½.

25 A3 5r yellow 1.10 90
26 " 10r reddish violet 1.90 1.25
27 " 15r chocolate 2.75 2.10
28 " 20r lavender 2.25 1.75
29 " 25r green 1.40 1.10
a. Perf. 12½ 3.25 1.40
30 " 50r light blue 2.00 1.10
a. Perf. 13½ 3.50 2.10
31 " 75r carmine 3.50 3.00
a. Perf. 11½ 8.00 6.00
32 " 80r light green 6.75 4.50
33 " 100r brown, *buff* 6.00 4.50
a. Perf. 11½ 11.00 7.25
34 " 150r carmine, *rose* 11.00 7.25
35 " 200r dark blue, *light blue* 11.00 7.25
36 " 300r dk. blue, *salmon* 11.00 7.25

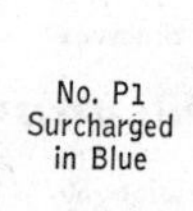

No. P1 Surcharged in Blue

1894, Aug.

37 N1 25r on 2½r brown 40.00 27.50

King Carlos
A5

1898-1903 Perf. 11½

Name and Value in Black except 500r

38 A5 2½r gray 20 15
39 " 5r orange 20 15
40 " 10r yellow green 20 15
41 " 15r violet brown 1.10 85
42 " 15r gray green ('03) 90 55
43 " 20r gray violet 40 30
44 " 25r sea green 1.10 60
45 " 25r carmine ('03) 50 20
46 " 50r blue 1.25 60
47 " 50r brown ('03) 4.75 3.00
48 " 65r dull blue ('03) 7.25 5.25
49 " 75r rose 3.75 2.00
50 " 75r red violet ('03) 1.65 1.10
51 " 80r violet 4.75 2.75
52 " 100r dark blue, *blue* 85 75
53 " 115r orange brown, *pink* ('03) 6.50 4.50
54 " 130r brown, *straw* ('03) 6.50 4.50
55 " 150r brown, *straw* 4.75 3.00
56 " 200r red violet, *pink* 3.00 1.00
57 " 300r dark blue, *rose* 2.25 1.90
58 " 400r dull blue, *straw* ('03) 2.75 2.50
59 " 500r black & red, *blue* ('01) 2.75 2.25
60 " 700r violet, *yellowish* ('01) 10.00 10.00
Nos. 38-60 (23) 67.35 48.05

Stamps of 1886-94 Surcharged in Black or Red

Two types of surcharge:
I. 3mm. between numeral and REIS.
II. 4½mm. spacing.

1902 Perf. 12½

61 A2 65r on 40r chocolate 3.50 2.25
62 " 65r on 300r orange, I 3.50 2.75
a. Type II 20.00 9.00
63 " 115r on 10r green 4.50 3.50
a. Inverted surcharge
b. Perf. 13½ 15.00 9.00
64 " 115r on 200r gray violet 3.50 3.00
65 " 130r on 50r blue 6.00 4.50
66 " 130r on 100r brown 3.50 3.00
67 " 400r on 20r rose 30.00 22.50
a. Perf. 13½ 30.00 22.50
68 " 400r on 25r violet 6.75 6.00
69 " 400r on 5r black (R) 9.00 8.00
a. Double surcharge
Nos. 61-69 (9) 70.25 55.50

Perf. 11½, 12½, 13½.

70 A3 65r on 5r yellow, I 4.25 3.50
a. Type II 9.00 9.00
71 " 65r on 10r red vio., I 4.25 3.50
a. Type II 13.50 7.00
b. Perf. 11½, type I 9.00 7.00
c. Perf. 11½, type II 3.00 2.50
72 " 65r on 20r lavender 4.25 3.50
a. Type II 9.00 8.00
73 " 65r on 25r green 4.25 3.50
a. Perf. 11½ 14.00 11.00
74 " 115r on 80r light green 8.00 6.25
75 " 115r on 100r brown, *buff* 13.00 10.00
a. Perf. 12½ 6.75 4.50
76 " 115r on 150r carmine, *rose* 14.00 7.75
a. Perf. 11½ 6.75 4.50
77 " 130r on 15r chocolate 2.75 2.50
78 " 130r on 75r carmine 5.00 3.50
a. Perf. 13½ 19.00 16.00
79 " 130r on 300r dark blue, *salmon* 11.00 7.25
80 " 400r on 50r light blue 2.50 2.00
81 " 400r on 200r blue, *blue* 1.00 75
a. Perf. 13½ 25.00 13.50
82 N1 400r on 2½r brown 1.25 1.00
a. Type II 3.75 3.50
Nos. 70-82 (13) 70.50 55.00

Reprints of Nos. 65, 67, 68 and 69 have clean-cut perforation 13½. Price $2 each.

Stamps of 1898 Overprinted PROVISORIO
a

1902 Perf. 11½

83 A5 15r brown 1.40 85
84 " 25r sea green 1.10 60
85 " 50r blue 1.40 85
86 " 75r rose 3.00 2.25

No. 48 Surcharged in Black 50 RÉIS

1905

87 A5 50r on 65r dull blue 2.50 1.65

Stamps of 1898-1903 Overprinted in Carmine or Green REPUBLICA
b

1911

88 A5 2½r gray 30 20
89 " 5r orange yellow 30 20
90 " 10r light green 35 30
a. Inverted overprint 5.75 5.75
91 " 15r gray green 40 30
92 " 20r gray violet 40 30
93 A5 25r carmine (G) 40 25
a. Inverted overprint 5.00 4.00
94 " 50r brown 1.65 1.10
95 " 75r lilac 3.25 3.25
96 " 100r dark blue, *blue* 3.25 2.25
97 " 115r orange brown, *pink* 90 80
98 " 130r brown, *straw* 1.10 90
99 " 200r red lilac, *pinkish* 1.10 90
100 " 400r dull blue, *straw* 1.40 90
101 " 500r black & red, *blue* 1.40 90
102 " 700r violet, *yellowish* 1.65 90
Nos. 88-102 (15) 17.85 13.45

King Manuel II
A6

Ceres
A7

1912 Perf. 11½x12.

Overprinted in Carmine or Green.

103 A6 2½r violet 35 50
104 " 5r black 45 60
105 " 10r gray green 55 45
106 " 20r carmine (G) 55 45
107 " 25r violet brown 55 45
108 " 50r dark blue 90 75
109 " 75r bistre brown 90 1.00
110 " 100r brown, *light green* 2.50 90
111 " 200r dark green, *salmon* 1.40 85
112 " 300r *azure* 1.40 85
Nos. 103-112 (10) 9.55 6.80

No. 91 Surcharged with New Values as 5 ■

1912, June Perf. 11½

113 A5 2½r on 15r gray green 2.25 2.25
114 " 5r on 15r gray green 1.65 1.10
115 " 10r on 15r gray green 1.65 1.10

Inverted and double surcharges of Nos. 113-115 were made intentionally.

Nos. 86 and 50 Surcharged "25" in Black and Overprinted in Violet REPUBLICA
c

1912

116 A5 25r on 75r rose 30.00 25.00
117 " 25r on 75r red violet 1.40 85
a. "REUPBLICA" 25.00 25.00
b. "25" omitted 25.00 25.00
c. "REPUBLICA" omitted 25.00 25.00

Typographed.

Name and Value in Black.

1914-26 Perf. 12x11½, 15x14.

118 A7 ¼c olive brown 12 25
a. Inscriptions inverted 3.00
119 " ½c black 12 25
120 " 1c blue green 12 25
121 " 1c yellow green ('22) 12 12
122 " 1½c lilac brown 12 12
123 " 2c carmine 12 12
124 " 2c gray ('25) 40 1.00
125 " 2½c light violet 12 12
126 " 3c orange ('22) 12 1.00
127 " 4c dull rose ('22) 12 12
128 " 4½c gray ('22) 12 1.00
130 " 5c blue 12 12
131 " 6c lilac ('22) 12 12
132 " 7c ultramarine ('22) 12 12
133 " 7½c yellow brown 12 12
134 " 8c slate 12 12
135 " 10c orange brown 40 12
136 " 12c olive brown ('22) 65 35
137 " 12c deep green ('25) 35 15
138 " 15c plum 65 35
139 " 15c brown rose ('22) 17 15
140 " 20c yellow green 15 10
141 " 24c ultramarine ('25) 1.75 50
142 " 25c chocolate ('25) 1.75 50
143 " 30c brown, *green* 1.50 1.50
144 " 30c gray green ('22) 1.00 10

145 A7 40c brown, *pink* 3.00 1.75
146 " 40c turquoise bl.('22) 90 12
147 " 50c orange, *salmon* 8.00 4.00
148 " 50c light violet ('25) 1.50 15
149 " 60c dark blue ('22) 75 15
150 " 60c deep rose ('26) 40.00 32.50
151 " 80c pink ('22) 2.00 15
152 " 1e green, *blue* 4.50 3.50
153 " 1e rose ('22) 2.25 15
154 " 1e deep blue ('25) 2.00 1.50
155 " 2e dark violet ('22) 2.25 60
156 " 5e buff ('25) 2.75 2.25
157 " 10e pink ('25) 7.50 5.00
158 " 20e pale turquoise ('25) 32.50 17.50
Nos. 118-158 (40) 120.47 *78.09*

Two kinds of chalky-surfaced paper, ordinary and coated, were used for Nos. 118-120, 122-123, 130, 133-135, 138 and 140. Those on coated paper sell unused for 10 to 40 times the prices listed; used for about 5 to 20 times.

Stamps of 1898-1903 Overprinted type "c" in Red or Green

On Stamps of 1898-1903.

1914 ***Perf. 11½, 12.***

159 A5 10r yellow green (R) 3.75 3.00
160 " 15r gray green (R) 3.75 3.00
161 " 20r gray violet (G) 55 45
163 " 75r red violet (G) 85 45
164 " 100r blue, *blue* (R) 85 50
165 " 115r orange brown, *pink* (R) 32.50
167 " 200r red violet, *pinkish* (G) 85 45
169 " 400r dull blue, *straw* (R) 15.00 12.00
170 " 500r black & red, *blue* (R) 2.25 1.40
171 " 700r violet, *yellowish* (G) 8.50 7.25

Inverted and double surcharges were made intentionally. No. 165 was not regularly issued.

On Provisional Stamps of 1902.

Perf. 11½, 12½, 13½.

172 A2 115r on 10r green (R) 11.00 8.25
a. Perf. 13½ 11.00 11.00
173 A2 115r on 200r gray violet (R) 10.00 8.25
174 " 130r on 50r blue (R) 13.00 10.00
175 A3 115r on 80r light green (R) 100.00 95.00
176 " 115r on 100r brown, *buff* (R) 160.00 160.00
177 " 115r on 150r carmine, *rose* (G) 130.00 120.00
178 " 130r on 75r carmine (G) 2.10 1.75
179 " 130r on 300r dark blue, *salmon* (R) 3.25 2.75
a. Perf. 12½ 7.25 5.00
180 N1 400r on 2½r brown (R) 30 30
a. Perf. 11½ 1.90 1.65
Nos. 172-180 (9) 429.65 406.30

On Stamps of 1902.

Overprinted PROVISORIO

Perf. 11½, 12.

181 A5 50r blue (R) 55 45
a. "Republica" double 3.00
182 " 75r rose (G) 1.90 1.65
a. "Republica" inverted 6.00

On Stamp of 1905.

183 A5 50r on 65r dull bl. (R) 2.25 1.90
a. "Republica" inverted 5.00 5.00
b. "Republica" double 4.00 4.00

Vasco da Gama Issue of Various Portuguese Colonies

Common Design Types CD20-CD27 Surcharged

REPUBLICA
ANGOLA
¼ C.

On Stamps of Macao.

1913 ***Perf. 12½ to 16.***

184 ¼c on ½a bl. green 2.00 1.90
185 ½c on 1a red 1.65 1.20
186 1c on 2a red violet 1.65 1.20
187 2½c on 4a yel. grn. 1.40 1.10
188 5c on 8a dark blue 1.40 1.10
189 7½c on 12a vio. brn. 3.25 3.00
190 10c on 16a bis. brn. 1.90 1.65
191 15c on 24a bistre 1.90 1.65
Nos. 184-191 (8) 15.15 12.80

On Stamps of Portuguese Africa.

Perf. 14 to 15.

192 ¼c on 2½r bl. green 1.00 90
193 ½c on 5r red 1.00 90
194 1c on 10r red violet 1.00 90
195 2½c on 25r yel. grn. 1.00 90
196 5c on 50r dark blue 1.00 90
197 7½c on 75r violet brown 3.75 3.25
198 10c on 100r bistre brown 1.40 1.10
199 15c on 150r bistre 2.25 1.85
Nos. 192-199 (8) 12.40 10.70

On Stamps of Timor

200 ¼c on ½a bl. green 2.00 1.75
201 ½c on 1a red 2.00 1.75
202 1c on 2a red violet 2.00 1.75
203 2½c on 4a yellow green 1.90 1.65
204 5c on 8a dark blue 1.90 1.65
205 7½c on 12a violet brown 3.25 3.00
206 10c on 16a bistre brown 2.25 1.65
207 15c on 24a bistre 2.25 1.65
Nos. 200-207 (8) 17.55 14.85

Provisional Issue of 1902 Overprinted in Carmine

REPUBLICA

1915 ***Perf. 11½, 12½, 13½.***

208 A2 115r on 10r green 1.65 *2.00*
209 " 115r on 200r gray vio. 1.40 *1.75*
210 " 130r on 100r brown 1.20 *1.75*
211 A3 115r on 80r lt. green 1.65 *2.00*
212 " 115r on 100r brown, *buff* 1.40 *1.75*
a. Perf. 11½ 16.50 *20.00*
213 " 115r on 150r carmine, *rose* 2.25 *3.00*
214 " 130r on 15r chocolate 1.10 *1.75*
a. Perf. 12½ 5.50 3.75
215 " 130r on 75r carmine 2.25 *2.75*
216 " 130r on 300r dark blue, *salmon* 1.75 *2.75*
Nos. 208-216 (9) 14.65 *19.50*

Stamps of 1911-14 Surcharged in Black:

1/2 C.

1/2 C. = = =
d *e*

On Stamps of 1911.

1919 ***Perf. 11½***

217 A5 (*d*) ½c on 75r red lilac 1.40 *2.00*
218 " (") 2½c on 100r blue, *grayish* 1.50 *2.25*

On Stamps of 1912.

Perf. 11½x12.

219 A6 (*e*) ½c on 75r bistre brown 85 *1.00*
220 " (") 2½c on 100r brown, *light green* 85 60

On Stamps of 1914.

221 A5 (*d*) ½c on 75r red lilac 85 60
222 A5 (*d*) 2½c on 100r blue, *grayish* 85 60

Inverted and double surcharges were made for sale to collectors.

Nos. 163, 98 and Type of 1914 Surcharged with New Values and Bars in Black.

1921

223 A5 (*c*) 00.5c on 75r red violet 90.00 90.00
224 " (*b*) 4c on 130r brown, *straw* (#98) 85 *1.00*
225 " (*c*) 4c on 130r brown, *straw* 2.25 1.65
a. Surch. omitted 100.00

Nos. 109 and 108 Surcharged with New Values and Bars in Black.

226 A6 00.5c on 75r bistre brown 85 60
227 " 1c on 50r dark blue 85 55

Nos. 133 and 138 Surcharged with New Values and Bars in Black.

228 A7 00.5c on 7½c yellow brown 85 55
229 " 04c on 15c plum 85 55

Nos. 81-82 Surcharged

República
40 C.

1925 ***Perf. 12½***

234 A3 40c on 400r on 200r blue, *blue* 85 55
a. Perf. 13½ 3.00 2.50
235 N1 40c on 400r on 2½r brown 55 45
a. Perf. 13½ 55 45

Nos. 150-151, 154-155 Surcharged

70 C.

1931 ***Perf. 11½.***

236 A7 50c on 60c deep rose 90 65
237 " 70c on 80c pink 2.40 90
238 " 70c on 1e deep blue 1.65 1.10
239 " 1.40e on 2e dk. violet 1.65 90

PORTUGAL-CORREIO 15 C. ANGOLA

Ceres
A14

Wmk. 232

Wmkd. Maltese Cross. (232)

1932-46 Typo. ***Perf. 12x11½***

243 A14 1c bistre brown 12 12
244 " 5c dark brown 12 12
245 " 10c deep violet 12 12
246 " 15c black 12 12
247 " 20c gray 12 12
248 " 30c myrtle green 12 12
249 " 35c yel. green ('46) 1.40 55
250 " 40c deep orange 12 12
251 " 45c light blue 45 30
252 " 50c light brown 12 12
253 " 60c olive green 25 12
254 " 70c orange brown 28 12
255 " 80c emerald 25 12
256 " 85c rose 1.65 1.25
257 " 1a claret 50 18
258 " 1.40a dark blue 2.75 1.20
258A " 1.75a dark blue ('46) 2.25 90
259 " 2a dull violet 1.90 30
260 " 5a pale yellow green 2.50 60
261 " 10a olive bistre 6.75 90
262 " 20a orange 15.00 1.65
Nos. 243-262 (21) 36.89 9.15

Stamps of 1932

Surcharged with New Value and Bars.

5½mm. between bars and new value.

1934

263 A14 10c on 45c light blue 85 65
264 " 20c on 85c rose 85 65
265 " 30c on 1.40a dark blue 85 65
266 " 70c on 2a dull violet 1.65 1.40
267 " 80c on 5a pale yellow green 1.90 1.40

See also Nos. 294A-300.

Nos. J26, J30 Surcharged in Black

CORREIOS
= 5
CENTAVOS

1935 ***Perf. 11½*** **Unwmkd.**

268 D2 5c on 6c light brown 85 45
269 " 30c on 50c gray 85 45
270 " 40c on 50c gray 85 45

No. 255 Surcharged in Black

0,15 Cent.

1938 ***Perf. 12x11½*** **Wmk. 232**

271 A14 5c on 80c emerald 25 *1.00*
272 " 10c on 80c " 55 *2.00*
273 " 15c on 80c " 90 *3.50*

Vasco da Gama Issue
Common Design Types
Engraved; Name and Value Typographed in Black.
Perf. 13½x13

1938, July 26 **Unwmkd.**

274 CD34 1c gray green 12 12
275 " 5c orange brown 12 12
276 " 10c dark carmine 12 12
277 " 15c dk. violet brown 25 12
278 " 20c slate 28 12
279 CD35 30c rose violet 40 12
280 " 35c bright green 55 30
281 " 40c brown 40 25
282 " 50c bright red violet 40 25
283 CD36 60c gray black 45 25
284 " 70c brown violet 40 25
285 " 80c orange 40 25
286 " 1a red 40 25
287 CD37 1.75a blue 95 40
288 " 2a brown carmine 1.40 40
289 " 5a olive green 3.25 40
290 CD38 10a blue violet 9.00 90
291 " 20a red brown 15.00 1.40
Nos. 274-291 (18) 33.89 6.02

Common Design Types

pictured in section at front of book.

Marble Column and Portuguese Arms with Cross
A20

1938, July 29 *Perf. 12½*

No.	Type	Description	Unused	Used
292	A20	80c blue green	2.10	1.90
293	"	1.75a deep blue	10.00	2.75
294	"	20a dark red brown	32.50	13.50

Issued to commemorate the visit of the President of Portugal to this colony in 1938.

Stamps of 1932 Surcharged with New Value and Bars.

8mm. between bars and new value.

1941-45 *Perf. 12x11½.* **Wmk. 232**

No.	Type	Description	Unused	Used
294A	A14	5c on 80c emerald ('45)	40	33
295	"	10c on 45c light blue	60	45
296	"	15c on 45c light blue	1.10	45
297	"	20c on 85c rose	60	45
298	"	35c on 85c rose	60	45
299	"	50c on 1.40a dark blue	60	45
300	"	60c on 1a claret	5.00	2.50
		Nos. 294A-300 (7)	8.90	5.08

Nos. 285 to 287 Surcharged with New Values and Bars in Black or Red.

1945 *Perf. 13½x13.* **Unwmkd.**

No.	Type	Description	Unused	Used
301	CD36	5c on 80c orange	40	33
302	"	50c on 1a red	60	33
303	CD37	50c on 1.75a blue (R)	40	33
304	"	50c on 1.75a blue	60	33

São Miguel Fort, Luanda
A21

John IV
A22

Designs: 10c, Our Lady of Nazareth Church, Luanda. 50c, Salvador Correia de Sa e Benevides. 1a, Surrender of Luanda. 1.75a, Diogo Cao. 2a, Manuel Cerveira Pereira. 5a, Stone Cliffs, Yelala. 10a, Paulo Dias de Novais. 20a, Massangano Fort.

Lithographed.

1948, May *Perf. 14½* **Unwmkd.**

No.	Type	Description	Unused	Used
305	A21	5c dark violet	12	12
306	"	10c dark brown	60	35
307	A22	30c blue green	30	25
308	"	50c violet brown	25	12
309	A21	1a carmine	55	20
310	A22	1.75a slate blue	1.10	40
311	"	2a green	1.10	30
312	A21	5a gray black	3.75	65
313	A22	10a rose lilac	5.75	65
314	A21	20a gray blue	13.00	1.90
		a. Sheet of ten	45.00	45.00
		Nos. 305-314 (10)	26.52	4.94

Issued to commemorate the 300th anniversary of the restoration of Angola to Portugal.

No. 314a measures 225x162mm. and contains one each of Nos. 305-314 with marginal inscriptions in gray. The sheet sold for 42.50 angolars.

Lady of Fatima Issue

Common Design Type

1948, Dec.

No.	Type	Description	Unused	Used
315	CD40	50c carmine	1.50	1.00
316	"	3a ultramarine	4.00	2.75
317	"	6a red orange	20.00	8.50
318	"	9a deep claret	45.00	10.00

Issued to honor Our Lady of the Rosary at Fatima, Portugal.

Chiumbe River
A24

Black Rocks
A25

Designs: 50c, View of Luanda. 2.50a, Sa da Bandeira. 3.50a, Mocamedes. 15a, Cubal River. 50a, Duke of Bragança Falls.

1949 *Perf. 13½* **Unwmkd.**

No.	Type	Description	Unused	Used
319	A24	20c dark slate blue	40	20
320	A25	40c black brown	45	15
321	A24	50c rose brown	45	20
322	"	2.50a blue violet	1.90	30
323	"	3.50a slate gray	2.25	55
323A	"	15a dark green	13.00	1.90
324	"	50a deep green	87.50	5.50
		Nos. 319-324 (7)	105.95	8.80

Sailing Vessel
A26

U.P.U. Symbols
A27

1949, Aug. *Perf. 14*

No.	Type	Description	Unused	Used
325	A26	1a chocolate	3.50	30
326	"	4a dk. Prussian grn.	8.25	90

Centenary of founding of Mocamedes.

1949, Oct.

No.	Type	Description	Unused	Used
327	A27	4a dark green & light green	3.50	1.20

Issued to commemorate the 75th anniversary of the formation of the Universal Postal Union.

Stamp of 1870
A28

1950, Apr. 2 *Perf. 11½x12*

No.	Type	Description	Unused	Used
328	A28	50c yellow green	90	35
329	"	1a terra cotta	70	35
330	"	4a black	1.90	90
		a. Sheet of three, perf. 11½		11.00

Issued for Angola's first philatelic exhibition, marking the 80th anniversary of Angola's first stamps.

No. 330a contains one each of Nos. 328, 329 (inverted) and 330, and sold for 6.50 angolars. Size: 119x80 mm. All copies carry an oval exhibition cancellation.

Holy Year Issue

Common Design Types

1950, May *Perf. 13x13½*

No.	Type	Description	Unused	Used
331	CD41	1a dull rose violet	1.10	20
332	CD42	4a black	4.25	55

Issued to commemorate the Holy Year, 1950.

Dark Chanting Goshawk
A31

European Bee Eater
A32

Designs: 10c, Racquet-tailed roller. 15c, Bataleur eagle. 50c, Giant kingfisher. 1a, Yellow-fronted barbet. 1.50a, Openbill (stork). 2a, Southern ground hornbill. 2.50a, African skimmer. 3a, Shikra. 3.50a, Denham's bustard. 4a, African golden oriole. 4.50a, Long-tailed shrike. 5a, Red-shouldered glossy starling. 6a, Sharp-tailed glossy starling. 7a, Red-shouldered widow bird. 10a, Half-colored kingfisher. 12.50a, White-crowned shrike. 15a, White-winged babbling starling. 20a, Yellow-billed hornbill. 25a, Amethyst starling. 30a, Orange-breasted shrike. 40a, Secretary bird. 50a, Rosy-faced lovebird.

Photogravure and Lithographed.

1951 *Perf. 11½* **Unwmkd.**

Birds in Natural Colors.

No.	Type	Description	Unused	Used
333	A31	5c light blue	25	*1.00*
334	A32	10c aquamarine	25	20
335	"	15c salmon pink	40	*2.00*
336	"	20c pale yellow	55	45
337	A31	50c gray blue	45	20
338	"	1a lilac	45	20
339	"	1.50a gray buff	75	20
340	"	2a cream	80	20
341	A32	2.50a gray	1.10	35
342	"	3a lemon yellow	90	35
343	A31	3.50a light gray	90	35
344	"	4a rose buff	1.00	35
345	A32	4.50a rose lilac	3.00	2.50
346	A31	5a green	4.50	60
347	"	6a blue	5.50	1.20
348	"	7a orange	5.50	1.50
349	"	10a lilac rose	37.50	2.75
350	A32	12.50a slate gray	7.25	4.50
351	A31	15a pale olive	7.25	4.50
352	"	20a pale bistre brown	75.00	15.00
353	"	25a lilac rose	20.00	8.25
354	A32	30a pale salmon	22.50	10.00
355	A31	40a yellow	30.00	12.50
356	"	50a turquoise	100.00	32.50
		Nos. 333-356 (24)	325.80	*101.65*

Holy Year Extension Issue.

Common Design Type

1951, Oct. **Litho.** *Perf. 14*

No.	Type	Description	Unused	Used
357	CD43	4a orange	2.25	90

Issued to publicize the extension of the Holy Year into 1951.

Sheets contain alternate vertical rows of stamps and labels bearing quotations from Pope Pius XII or the Patriarch Cardinal of Lisbon.

Medical Congress Issue.

Common Design Type

Design: Medical examination

1952, June *Perf. 13½*

No.	Type	Description	Unused	Used
358	CD44	1a violet blue & brown black	40	20

Issued to publicize the first National Congress of Tropical Medicine, Lisbon, 1952.

Head of Christ
A35

1952, Oct. *Perf. 13* **Unwmkd.**

No.	Type	Description	Unused	Used
359	A35	10c dark blue & buff	15	5
360	"	50c dark olive green & olive gray	25	10
361	"	2a rose vio. & cream	1.65	20

Issued to commemorate the Exhibition of Sacred Missionary Art held at Lisbon in 1951.

Leopard
A36

Sable Antelope
A37

Animals: 20c, Elephant. 30c, Eland. 40c, African crocodile. 50c, Impala. 1a, Mountain zebra. 1.50a, Sitatunga. 2a, Black rhinoceros. 2.30a, Gemsbok. 2.50a, Lion. 3a, Buffalo. 3.50a, Springbok. 4a, Brindled gnu. 5a, Hartebeest. 7a, Wart hog. 10a, Defassa waterbuck. 12.50a, Hippopotamus. 15a, Greater kudu. 20a, Giraffe.

1953, Aug. 15 *Perf. 12½*

No.	Type	Description		Unused	Used
362	A36	5c	multicolored	10	10
363	A37	10c	"	10	10
364	"	20c	"	10	10
365	"	30c	"	10	10
366	A36	40c	"	10	10
367	A37	50c	"	10	10
368	"	1a	"	35	10
369	"	1.50a	"	25	10
370	A36	2a	"	30	15
371	A37	2.30a	"	40	15
372	"	2.50a	"	1.00	12
373	A36	3a	"	1.20	12
374	A37	3.50a	"	30	12
375	"	4a	"	14.50	60
376	"	5a	"	55	20
377	"	7a	"	1.90	55
378	"	10a	"	3.00	35
379	"	12.50a	"	6.50	*7.50*
380	"	15a	"	6.50	*7.50*
381	"	20a	"	7.50	1.00
		Nos. 362-381 (20)		44.85	*19.16*

Stamp of Portugal and Arms of Colonies
A38

1953, Nov. **Photo.** *Perf. 13*

Stamp and Arms Multicolored.

No.	Type	Description	Unused	Used
382	A38	50c gray & dark gray	85	55

Issued to commemorate the centenary of Portugal's first postage stamps.

Map and Plane
A39

Typographed and Lithographed.

1954, May 27 *Perf. 13½*

No.	Type	Description	Unused	Used
383	A39	35c dark green, olive, blue green & red	15	15
384	"	4.50e black, dull violet, aqua. & red	1.10	30

Issued to publicize the visit of Pres. Francisco H. C. Lopes.

Sao Paulo Issue

Common Design Type

1954 **Lithographed**

No.	Type	Description	Unused	Used
385	CD46	1e bistre & gray	35	20

Issued to commemorate the 400th anniversary of the founding of Sao Paulo.

Map of Angola A41 — Artur de Paiva A42

1955, Aug. *Perf. 13½* **Unwmkd.**

Blue Outline, Red Highways, Black Inscriptions

386	A41	5c gray & pale green	6	6
387	"	20c gray, light blue & salmon	7	6
388	"	50c brown buff, pale green & light blue	15	6
389	"	1e gray, light blue green & orange yellow	25	6
390	"	2.30e brown buff, aquamarine & yellow	55	12
391	"	4e bistre, pale green & light blue	1.65	20
392	"	10e lilac, aquamarine & citron	1.65	20
393	"	20e olive green & pale green	3.00	40
		Nos. 386-393 (8)	7.38	1.16

1956, Oct. 9 *Perf. 13½x12½*

394	A42	1e black, dark blue & ochre	30	20

Issued to commemorate the centenary of the birth of Col. Artur de Paiva.

Man of Malange A43 — José M. Antunes A44

Various Costumes in Multicolor; Inscriptions in Black Brown.

1957, Jan. 1 Photo. *Perf. 11½*

Granite Paper.

395	A43	5c gray	5	4
396	"	10c orange yellow	7	6
397	"	15c light blue green	12	8
398	"	20c pale rose violet	12	8
399	"	30c bright rose	12	8
400	"	40c blue gray	12	8
401	"	50c pale olive	12	8
402	"	80c light violet	28	18
403	"	1.50e buff	2.50	18
404	"	2.50e lt. yellow green	2.75	18
405	"	4e salmon	1.25	18
406	"	10e salmon pink	1.90	45
		Nos. 395-406 (12)	9.40	1.67

1957, April *Perf. 13½*

407	A44	1e aquamarine & brown	95	55

Issued to commemorate the centenary of the birth of Father José Maria Antunes.

Fair Emblem, Globe and Arms A45

1958, July Litho. *Perf. 12x11½*

408	A45	1.50e multicolored	40	25

World's Fair, Brussels, Apr. 17–Oct. 19.

Tropical Medicine Congress Issue

Common Design Type

Design: Securidaca longipedunculata.

1958, Dec. 15 *Perf. 13½*

409	CD47	2.50e multicolored	1.90	1.10

Issued to publicize the 6th International Congress for Tropical Medicine and Malaria, Lisbon, Sept. 1958.

Medicine Man A47 — Welwitschia Mirabilis A48

Designs: 1.50e, Early government doctor. 2.50e, Modern medical team.

1958, Dec. 18 *Perf. 11½x12*

410	A47	1e bl., blk. & brn.	30	15
411	"	1.50e gray, black & brown	55	25
412	"	2.50e multicolored	90	20

Issued to commemorate the 75th anniversary of the Maria Pia Hospital, Luanda.

1959, Oct. 1 Litho. *Perf. 14½*

Various Views of Plant and Various Frames.

413	A48	1.50e light brown, green & black	60	40
414	"	2.50e multicolored	1.30	55
415	"	5e "	1.90	80
416	"	10e "	5.25	1.65

Centenary of discovery of Welwitschia mirabilis, desert plant.

Map of West Africa, c. 1540, by Jorge Reinel—A49

1960, June 25 *Perf. 13½*

417	A49	2.50e multicolored	45	30

Issued to commemorate the 500th anniversary of the death of Prince Henry the Navigator.

Distributing Medicines A50 — Girl of Angola A51

1960, Oct. Litho. *Perf. 14½*

418	A50	2.50e multicolored	45	25

Issued to commemorate the 10th anniversary of the Commission for Technical Co-operation in Africa South of the Sahara (C.C.T.A.).

1961, Nov. 30 *Perf. 13* **Unwmkd.**

Portraits of Angolese Women in Natural Colors

419	A51	10c black, yellow green & green	8	4
420	"	15c black, gray blue & lilac	8	8
421	"	30c black, yellow & dk. blue	10	10
422	"	40c black, gray & dark red	5	5
423	"	60c black, salmon & olive	8	8
424	A51	1.50e blk., blue & red	18	5
425	"	2e black, lilac & bistre	1.00	12
426	"	2.50e black, yellow & brown	1.00	12
427	"	3e black, pink & olive	2.50	30
428	"	4e black, gray grn. & brn.	1.85	40
429	"	5e black, lt. blue & carmine	1.20	30
430	"	7.50e black, dull yel. & brn.	1.50	1.40
431	"	10e black, ochre & green	1.65	60
432	"	15e black, beige & green	1.75	1.50
432A	"	25e black, rose & red brown	3.25	1.80
432B	"	50e black, gray & violet blue	6.75	3.25
		Nos. 419-432B (16)	23.02	10.19

Sports Issue

Common Design Type

Sports: 50c, Flying. 1e, Rowing. 1.50e, Water polo. 2.50e, Hammer throwing. 4.50e, High jump. 15e, Weight lifting.

1962, Jan. 18 *Perf. 13½*

Multicolored Design

433	CD48	50c light blue	15	10
434	"	1e olive bistre	95	35
435	"	1.50e salmon	45	15
436	"	2.50e light green	35	15
437	"	4.50e pale blue	60	60
438	"	15e yellow	2.00	1.75
		Nos. 433-438 (6)	4.50	3.10

Anti-Malaria Issue

Common Design Type

Design: Anopheles funestus.

1962, April Litho. *Perf. 13½*

439	CD49	2.50e multicolored	45	20

Issued for the World Health Organization drive to eradicate malaria.

Gen. Norton de Matos A54

1962, Aug. 8 *Perf. 14½* **Unwmkd.**

440	A54	2.50e multicolored	45	20

Issued to commemorate the 50th anniversary of the founding of Nova Lisboa.

Locusts A56

1963, June 2 Litho. *Perf. 14*

447	A56	2.50e multicolored	55	30

Issued to commemorate the 15th anniversary of the International Anti-Locust Organization.

Arms of Luanda A57

Vila de Santo Antonio do Zaire A58

Coats of Arms (Provinces and Cities): 10c, Massangano. 15c, Sanza-Pombo. 25c, Ambriz. 30c, Muxima. 40c, Ambrizete. 50c, Carmona. 60c, Catete. 70c, Quibaxe. No. 458, Maquelo do Zombo. 1e, Salazar. 1.20e, Bembe. No. 461, Caxito. 1.50e, Malanje. 1.80e, Dondo. No. 465, Damba. 2e, Henrique de Carvalho. 2.50e, Moçâmedes. 3e, Novo Redondo. 3.50e, S. Salvador do Congo. 4e, Cuimba. 5e, Luso. 6.50e, Negage. 7e, Quitexe. 7.50e, S. Filipe de Benguela. 8e, Mucaba. 9e, 31 de Janeiro. 10e, Lobito. 11e, Nova Caipemba. 12.50e, Gabela. 14e, Songo. 15e Sa' da Bandeira. 17e, Quimbele. 17.50e, Silva Porto. 20e, Nova Lisboa. 22.50e, Cabinda. 25e, Noqui. 30e, Serpa Pinto. 35e, Santa Cruz. 50e, General Freire.

1963 *Perf. 13½*

Arms in Original Colors; Red and Violet Blue Inscriptions.

448	A57	5c tan	10	10
449	"	10c light blue	10	10
450	A58	15c salmon	10	10
451	"	20c olive	10	10
452	"	25c light blue	12	10
453	A57	30c buff	10	10
454	A58	40c gray	12	10
455	A57	50c light green	10	10
456	A58	60c bright yellow	18	12
457	"	70c dull rose	18	12
458	A57	1e pale lilac	25	10
459	A58	1e dull yellow	30	10
460	"	1.20e rose	12	10
461	A57	1.50e pale salmon	50	10
462	A58	1.50e light green	55	12
463	"	1.80e yellow olive	30	18
464	A57	2e light yellow grn.	45	10
465	"	2.50e light gray	1.50	15
466	A58	2.50e dull blue	1.50	18
467	A57	3e yellow olive	65	12
468	"	3.50e gray	75	15
469	A58	4e citron	55	35
470	A57	5e citron	60	35
471	A58	6.50e tan	70	45
472	"	7e rose lilac	65	45
473	A57	7.50e pale lilac	85	55
474	A58	8e lt. aquamarine	85	55
475	"	9e yellow	90	55
476	A57	10e deep salmon	1.10	55
477	A58	11e dull yel. grn.	1.10	85
478	A57	12.50e pale blue	1.40	85
479	A58	14e light gray	1.40	85
480	A57	15e light blue	1.65	85
481	A58	17e pale blue	1.65	1.10
482	A57	17.50e dull yellow	2.25	1.25
483	"	20e lt. aquamarine	2.40	1.20
484	"	22.50e gray	2.25	1.50
485	A58	25e citron	3.00	2.25
486	A57	30e yellow	3.25	2.75
487	A58	35e grayish blue	3.75	3.00
488	"	50e deep yellow	5.50	4.00
		Nos. 448-488 (41)	43.87	26.69

Pres. Américo Rodrigues Thomaz A59

1963, Sept. 16 Lithographed

489	A59	2.50e multicolored	60	25

Visit of the President of Portugal.

Airline Anniversary Issue

Common Design Type

1963, Oct. 5 *Perf. 14½* **Unwmkd.**

490	CD50	1e lt. blue & multi.	40	20

Issued to commemorate the 10th anniversary of Transportes Aéreos Portugueses.

Cathedral of Sá da Bandeira — A61

Malange Cathedral — A62

Churches: 20c, Landana. 30c, Luanda Cathedral. 40c, Gabela. 50c, St. Martin's Chapel, Baia dos Tigres. 1.50e, St. Peter, Chibia. 2e, Church of Our Lady, Benguela. 2.50e, Church of Jesus, Luanda. 3e, Camabatela. 3.50e, Mission, Cabinda. 4e, Vila Folgares. 4.50e, Church of Our Lady, Lobito. 5e, Church of Cabinda. 7.50e, Cacuso Church, Malange. 10e, Lubango Mission. 12.50e, Huila Mission. 15e, Church of Our Lady, Luanda Island.

1963, Nov. 1 Lithographed

Multicolored Design and Inscription

No.	Type	Denomination / Color	Unused	Used
491	A61	10c gray blue	10	10
492	"	20c pink	10	10
493	"	30c light blue	10	10
494	"	40c tan	10	10
495	"	50c light green	10	10
496	A62	1e buff	12	10
497	A61	1.50e lt. violet blue	15	10
498	A62	2e pale rose	18	10
499	A61	2.50e gray	25	10
500	A62	3e buff	28	10
501	A61	3.50e olive	33	12
502	A62	4e buff	35	30
503	"	4.50e pale blue	42	35
504	A61	5e tan	45	35
505	A62	7.50e gray	70	60
506	A61	10e dull yellow	90	75
507	A62	12.50e bister	1.20	90
508	"	15e pale gray vio.	2.00	1.10
		Nos. 491-508 (18)	7.83	5.47

National Overseas Bank Issue

Common Design Type

Design: Antonio Teixeira de Sousa.

1964, May 16 *Perf. 13½*

No.	Type	Denomination / Color	Unused	Used
509	CD51	2.50e multicolored	40	15

Issued to commemorate the centenary of the National Overseas Bank of Portugal.

Commerce Building and Arms of Chamber of Commerce—A64

1964, Nov. Litho. *Perf. 12*

No.	Type	Denomination / Color	Unused	Used
510	A64	1e multicolored	30	20

Luanda Chamber of Commerce centenary.

ITU Issue

Common Design Type

1965, May 17 *Perf. 14½* **Unwmkd.**

No.	Type	Denomination / Color	Unused	Used
511	CD52	2.50e gray & multi.	1.00	30

Issued to commemorate the centenary of the International Telecommunication Union.

Plane over Luanda Airport — A65

Harquebusier, 1539 — A66

1965, Dec. 3 Litho. *Perf. 13*

No.	Type	Denomination / Color	Unused	Used
512	A65	2.50e multicolored	35	20

Issued to commemorate the 25th anniversary of DTA, Direcção dos Transportes Aéreos.

1966, Feb. 25 Litho. *Perf. 14½*

Designs: 50c, Harquebusier, 1539. 1e, Harquebusier, 1640. 1.50e, Infantry officer, 1777. 2e, Standard bearer, infantry, 1777. 2.50e, Infantry soldier, 1777. 3e, Cavalry officer, 1783. 4e, Cavalry soldier, 1783. 4.50e, Infantry officer, 1807. 5e, Infantry soldier, 1807. 6e, Cavalry officer, 1807. 8e, Cavalry soldier, 1807. 9e, Infantry soldier, 1873.

No.	Type	Denomination / Color	Unused	Used
513	A66	50c multicolored	15	15
514	"	1e "	18	18
515	"	1.50e "	15	15
516	"	2e "	18	18
517	"	2.50e "	50	30
518	"	3e "	55	12
519	"	4e "	75	40
520	"	4.50e "	85	30
521	"	5e "	1.00	40
522	"	6e "	1.00	45
523	"	8e "	1.50	55
524	"	9e "	1.50	55
		Nos. 513-524 (12)	8.31	3.73

National Revolution Issue

Common Design Type

Design: St. Paul's Hospital and Commercial and Industrial School.

1966, May 28 Litho. *Perf. 12*

No.	Type	Denomination / Color	Unused	Used
525	CD53	1e multicolored	25	15

40th anniversary, National Revolution.

Emblem of Holy Ghost Society — A68

1966 Lithographed *Perf. 13*

No.	Type	Denomination / Color	Unused	Used
526	A68	1e blue & multi.	25	10

Centenary of the Holy Ghost Society.

Navy Club Issue

Common Design Type

Designs: 1e, Mendes Barata and cruiser Dom Carlos I. 2.50e, Capt. Augusto de Castilho and corvette Mindelo.

1967, Jan. 31 Litho. *Perf. 13*

No.	Type	Denomination / Color	Unused	Used
527	CD54	1e multicolored	30	15
528	"	2.50e "	50	20

Centenary of Portugal's Navy Club.

Fatima Basilica — A70

Angola Map, Manuel Cerveira Pereira — A71

1967, May 13 Litho. *Perf. 12½x13*

No.	Type	Denomination / Color	Unused	Used
529	A70	50c multicolored	10	10

Issued to commemorate the 50th anniversary of the apparition of the Virgin Mary to three shepherd children at Fatima.

1967, Aug. 15 Litho. *Perf. 12½x13*

No.	Type	Denomination / Color	Unused	Used
530	A71	50c multicolored	18	15

Issued to commemorate the 350th anniversary of the founding of Benguela.

Administration Building, Carmona—A72

1967 Lithographed *Perf. 12*

No.	Type	Denomination / Color	Unused	Used
531	A72	1e multicolored	15	15

Issued to commemorate the 50th anniversary of the founding of Carmona.

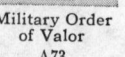

Military Order of Valor — A73

Our Lady of Hope — A74

Designs: 50c, Ribbon of the Three Orders. 1.50e, Military Order of Avis. 2e, Military Order of Christ. 2.50e, Military Order of St. John of Espada. 3e, Order of the Empire. 4e, Order of Prince Henry. 5e, Order of Benemerencia. 10e, Order of Public Instruction. 20e, Order for Industrial and Agricultural Merit.

1967, Oct. 31 *Perf. 14*

No.	Type	Denomination / Color	Unused	Used
532	A73	50c lt. gray & multi.	10	6
533	"	1e lt. grn. & multi.	10	6
534	"	1.50e yellow & multi.	12	6
535	"	2e multicolored	18	6
536	"	2.50e "	25	15
537	"	3e lt. olive & multi.	28	10
538	"	4e gray & multi.	35	15
539	"	5e multicolored	55	30
540	"	10e lilac & multi.	1.10	55
541	"	20e lt. bl. & multi.	1.85	1.10
		Nos. 532-541 (10)	4.88	2.59

Cabral Issue

Designs: 1e, Belmonte Castle (horiz.). 1.50e, St. Jerome's Convent. 2.50e, Cabral's Armada.

1968, Apr. 22 Litho. *Perf. 14*

No.	Type	Denomination / Color	Unused	Used
542	A74	50c yellow & multi.	10	10
543	"	1e gray & multi.	45	15
544	"	1.50e lt. blue & multi.	70	20
545	"	2.50e buff & multi.	95	20

Issued to commemorate the 500th anniversary of the birth of Pedro Alvares Cabral, navigator who took possession of Brazil for Portugal.

Francisco Inocencio de Souza Coutinho — A75

1969, Jan. 7 Litho. *Perf. 14*

No.	Type	Denomination / Color	Unused	Used
546	A75	2e multicolored	25	25

Issued to commemorate the 200th anniversary of the founding of Novo Redondo.

Admiral Coutinho Issue

Common Design Type

Design: Adm. Gago Coutinho and his first ship.

1969, Feb. 17 Litho. *Perf. 14*

No.	Type	Denomination / Color	Unused	Used
547	CD55	2.50e multicolored	45	20

Compass Rose — A77

Portal of St. Jeronimo's Monastery — A79

1969, Aug. 29 Litho. *Perf. 14*

No.	Type	Denomination / Color	Unused	Used
548	A77	1e multicolored	20	20

Issued to commemorate the 500th anniversary of the birth of Vasco da Gama (1469–1524), navigator.

Administration Reform Issue

Common Design Type

1969, Sept. 25 Litho. *Perf. 14*

No.	Type	Denomination / Color	Unused	Used
549	CD56	1.50e multicolored	20	20

Issued to commemorate the centenary of the administration reforms of the overseas territories.

1969, Dec. 1 Litho. *Perf. 14*

No.	Type	Denomination / Color	Unused	Used
550	A79	3e multicolored	35	25

Issued to commemorate the 500th anniversary of the birth of King Manuel I.

Angolasaurus Bocagei — A80

Fossils and Minerals: 1c, Ferrometeorite. 1.50e, Dioptase crystals. 2e, Gondwanidium. 2.50e, Diamonds. 3e, Estromatolite. 3.50e, Procarcharodon megalodon. 4e, Microceratodus angolensis. 4.50e, Moscovite. 5e, Barite. 6e, Nostoceras. 10e, Rotula orbiculus angolensis.

1970, Oct. 31 Litho. *Perf. 13*

No.	Type	Denomination / Color	Unused	Used
551	A80	50c tan & multi.	15	10
552	"	1e multicolored	25	15
553	"	1.50e "	25	10
554	"	2e "	30	10
555	"	2.50e lt. gray & multi.	40	15
556	"	3e multicolored	45	25
557	"	3.50e blue & multi.	60	30
558	"	4e lt. gray & multi.	65	30
559	"	4.50e gray & multi.	70	35
560	"	5e gray & multi.	70	40
561	"	6e pink & multi.	1.00	45
562	"	10e lt. bl. & multi.	1.50	90
		Nos. 551-562 (12)	6.95	3.55

Marshal Carmona Issue

Common Design Type

1970, Nov. 15 *Perf. 14*

No.	Type	Denomination / Color	Unused	Used
563	CD57	2.50e multicolored	25	10

Birth centenary of Marshal Antonio Oscar Carmona de Fragoso (1869–1951), President of Portugal.

Arms of Malanje, Cotton Boll and Field — A82

1970, Nov. 20 *Perf. 13*

No.	Type	Denomination / Color	Unused	Used
564	A82	2.50e multicolored	35	30

Centenary of the municipality of Malanje.

Mail Ships and Angola No. 1 — A83

Designs: 4.50e, Steam locomotive and Angola No. 4.

1970, Dec. 1 *Perf. 13½*

No.	Type	Denomination / Color	Unused	Used
565	A83	1.50e multicolored	30	20
566	"	4.50e "	75	35

Centenary of stamps of Angola. See No. C36.

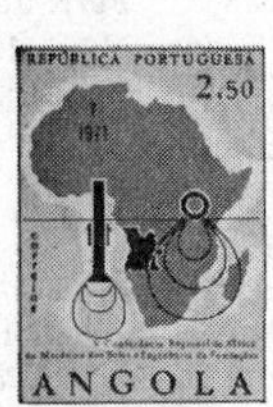

Map of Africa, Diagram of Seismic Tests
A84

Galleon on Congo River
A85

1971, Aug. 22 Litho. *Perf. 13*

567 A84 2.50e multicolored 35 20

5th Regional Conference of Soil and Foundation Engineers, Luanda, Aug. 22–Sept. 5.

1972, May 25 Litho. *Perf. 13*

568 A85 1e emerald & multi. 20 15

4th centenary of the publication of The Lusiads by Luiz Camoëns.

Olympic Games Issue
Common Design Type

1972, June 20 *Perf. 14x13½*

569 CD59 50c multicolored 20 15

20th Olympic Games, Munich, Aug. 26–Sept. 11.

Lisbon-Rio de Janeiro Flight Issue
Common Design Type

1972, Sept. 20 Litho. *Perf. 13½*

570 CD60 1e multicolored 25 15

WMO Centenary Issue
Common Design Type

1973, Dec. 15 Litho. *Perf. 13*

571 CD61 1e dk. gray & multi. 25 15

Centenary of international meteorological cooperation.

Radar Station
A89

1974, June 25 Litho. *Perf. 13*

572 A89 2e multicolored 35 20

Establishment of satellite communications network via Intelsat among Portugal, Angola and Mozambique.

Harpa Doris
A90

Designs: Sea shells.

1974, Oct. 25 Litho. *Perf. 12x12½*
Multicolored

573 A90 25c *shown* 12 12
574 " 30c *Murex melanamathos* 12 12
575 " 50c *Venus foliaceo lamellosa* 12 12
576 " 70c *Lathyrus filosus* 12 12
577 " 1e *Cymbium cisium* 12 12
578 " 1.50e *Cassis tesselata* 20 15
579 " 2e *Cypraea stercoraria* 25 12
580 " 2.50e *Conus prometheus* 35 20
581 " 3e *Strombus latus* 40 25
582 " 3.50e *Tympanotonus fuscatus* 45 25
583 " 4e *Cardium costatum* 50 35
584 A90 5e *Natica fulminea* 60 45
585 " 6e *Lyropecten nodosus* 85 45
586 " 7e *Tonna galea* 85 50
587 " 10e *Donax rugosus* 1.20 75
588 " 25e *Cymatium trigonum* 3.00 1.90
589 " 30e *Olivancilaria acuminata* 3.75 2.25
590 " 35e *Semifusus morio* 4.25 2.50
591 " 40e *Clavatula lineata* 4.75 3.00
592 " 50e *Solarium granulatum* 6.50 4.50
Nos. 573-592 (20) 28.50 18.22

No. 386 Overprinted in Blue:
"1974 / FILATELIA / JUVENIL"

1974, Dec. 21 Litho. *Perf. 13½*

593 A41 5c multicolored 50 50

Youth philately.

Republic

Star and Hand Holding Rifle
A91

1975, Nov. 11 Litho. *Perf. 13x13½*

594 A91 1.50e red & multi. 50 50

Independence in 1975.

Diquiche Mask
A92

Design: 3e, Bui ou Congolo mask.

1976, Feb. 6 *Perf. 13½*

595 A92 50c lt. blue & multi. 15 15
596 " 3e multicolored 75 75

Workers
A93

President Agostinho Neto
A94

1976, May 1 Litho. *Perf. 12*

597 A93 1e red & multi. 35 25

International Workers' Day.

No. 392 Overprinted Bar and:
"DIA DO SELO / 15 Junho 1976 / REP. POPULAR / DE"

1976, June 15 Litho. *Perf. 13½*

598 A41 10e multicolored 85 85

Stamp Day.

1976, Nov. 11 Litho. *Perf. 13*

599 A94 50c yel. & dk. brown 10
600 " 2e lt. gray & plum 40
601 " 3e gray & indigo 50
602 " 5e buff & brown 85
603 " 10e tan & sepia 1.50
a. Souvenir sheet 2.25
Nos. 599-603 (5) 3.35

First anniversary of independence. No. 603a contains one imperf. stamp. Gold margin with brown inscription. Size: 60x75mm.

Nos. 393, 588–589, 592 Overprinted with Bar over Republica Portuguesa and: "REPUBLICA POPULAR DE"

1977, Feb. 9 *Perf. 13½, 12x12½*

604 A41 20e multicolored
605 A90 25e "
606 " 30e "
607 " 50e "
Nos. 604-607 (4) 10.00

Overprint in 3 lines on No. 604, in 2 lines on others.

No. 438 Overprinted with Bar over Republica Portuguesa and: "S. Silvestre / 1976 / Rep. Popular / de"

1976, Dec. 31 *Perf. 13½*

608 CD48 15e multicolored

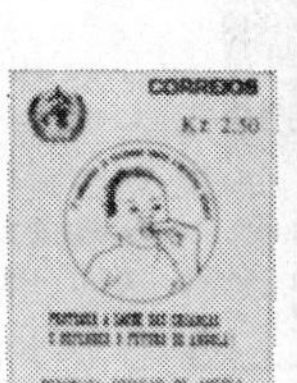

Child and WHO Emblem
A95

Map of Africa, Flag of Angola
A96

1977 Litho. *Perf. 10½*

609 A95 2.50k blk. & lt. bl. 25

Campaign for vaccination against poliomyelitis.

1977 Photogravure

610 A96 6k blk., red & blue 60

First congress of Popular Movement for the Liberation of Angola.

AIR POST STAMPS.

Common Design Type
Perf. 13½x13.

1938, July 26 Engraved Unwmkd.
Name and Value in Black.

C1 CD39 10c scarlet 40 35
C2 " 20c purple 50 35
C3 " 50c orange 55 35
C4 " 1a ultramarine 60 30
C5 " 2a lilac brown 1.00 40
C6 " 3a dark green 1.40 45
C7 " 5a red brown 2.75 55
C8 " 9a rose carmine 4.50 1.40
C9 " 10a magenta 5.50 1.40
Nos. C1-C9 (9) 17.20 5.55

No. C7 exists with overprint "Exposicao Internacional de Nova York, 1939–1940" and Trylon and Perisphere.

AP2

1947, Aug. Litho. *Perf. 10½*

C10 AP2 1a red brown 6.25 2.25
C11 " 2a yellow green 6.25 2.25
C12 " 3a orange 9.00 1.15
C13 " 3.50a orange 11.50 2.75
C14 " 5a olive green 50.00 4.25
C15 " 6a rose 30.00 9.00
C16 " 9a red 165.00 75.00
C17 " 10a green 87.50 25.00
C18 " 20a blue 105.00 25.00
C19 " 50a black 235.00 70.00
C20 " 100a yellow 475.00 250.00
Nos. C10-C20 (11) 1180.50 466.65

Planes Circling Globe
AP3

1949, May 1 Photo. *Perf. 11½*

C21 AP3 1a henna brown 45 25
C22 " 2a red brown 90 25
C23 " 3a plum 1.65 30
C24 " 6a dull green 3.75 85
C25 " 9a violet brown 5.75 1.90
Nos. C21-C25 (5) 12.50 3.55

Cambambe Dam
AP4

Designs: 1.50e, Oil refinery (vert.). 3e, Salazar Dam. 4e, Capt. Teófilo Duarte Dam. 4.50e, Craveiro Lopes Dam. 5e, Cuango Dam. 6e, Quanza River Bridge. 7e, Capt. Teófilo Duarte Bridge. 8.50e, Oliveira Salazar Bridge. 12.50e, Capt. Silva Carvalho Bridge.

Perf. 11½x12, 12x11½

1965, July 12 Litho. Unwmkd.

C26 AP4 1.50e multicolored 1.65 15
C27 " 2.50e " 1.00 20
C28 " 3e " 1.40 30
C29 " 4e " 1.00 30
C30 " 4.50e " 1.00 35
C31 " 5e " 1.40 40
C32 " 6e " 1.40 55
C33 " 7e " 1.90 55
C34 " 8.50e " 2.75 85
C35 " 12.50e " 3.00 85
Nos. C26-C35 (10) 16.50 4.50

Stamp Centenary Type of Regular Issue

Design: 2.50e, Boeing 707 jet and Angola No. 2.

1970, Dec. 1 Litho. *Perf. 13½*

C36 A83 2.50e multicolored 55 40
a. Souvenir sheet of 3 3.75 3.75

Centenary of stamps of Angola.

No. C36a contains one each of No. 565–566, C36. Margin shows Duke of Bragança Waterfall, with commemorative inscription. Size: 150x105mm. Sold for 15e.

POSTAGE DUE STAMPS.

D1

D2

Typographed.

1904 *Perf. 11½x12.* Unwmkd.

J1 D1 5r yellow green 40 30
J2 " 10r slate 40 30
J3 " 20r yellow brown 45 45
J4 " 30r orange 55 55
J5 " 50r gray brown 55 55
J6 " 60r red brown 3.25 3.00
J7 " 100r lilac 3.00 2.75
J8 " 130r dull blue 3.00 2.75
J9 " 200r carmine 4.50 4.00
J10 " 500r gray violet 3.75 3.50
Nos. J1–J10 (10) 19.85 18.15

Postage Due Stamps of 1904 Overprinted in Carmine or Green

REPUBLICA

1911

J11 D1 5r yellow green 30 30
J12 " 10r slate 30 30
J13 " 20r yellow brown 30 30
J14 " 30r orange 45 45
J15 " 50r gray brown 45 45
J16 " 60r red brown 55 55
J17 " 100r lilac 55 55
J18 " 130r dull blue 55 55
J19 " 200r carmine (G) 55 55
J20 " 500r gray violet 1.10 1.10
Nos. J11–J20 (10) 5.10 5.10

1921 *Perf. 11½.*

J21 D2 ½c yellow green 12 12
J22 " 1c slate 12 12
J23 " 2c orange brown 12 12
J24 " 3c orange 12 12
J25 " 5c gray brown 12 12
J26 " 6c light brown 12 12
J27 " 10c red violet 12 12
J28 " 13c dull blue 25 25
J29 " 20c carmine 25 25
J30 " 50c gray 25 25
Nos. J21–J30 (10) 1.59 1.59

Stamps of 1932 Surcharged in Black

PORTEADO
10
Centavos

1948 *Perf. 12x11½.* Wmk. 232

J31 A14 10c on 20c gray 40 30
J32 " 20c on 30c myrtle green 40 30
J33 " 30c on 50c light brown 40 30
J34 " 40c on 1a claret 40 30
J35 " 50c on 2a dull violet 40 30
J36 " 1a on 5a pale yellow green 1.10 45
Nos. J31–J36 (6) 3.10 1.95

Common Design Type

Photogravure and Typographed.

1952 *Perf. 14.* Unwmkd.

Numeral in Red, Frame Multicolored.

J37 CD45 10c red brown 15 15
J38 " 30c olive green 15 15
J39 " 50c chocolate 15 15
J40 " 1a dark violet blue 15 15
J41 " 2a red brown 30 30
J42 " 5a black brown 70 70
Nos. J37–J42 (6) 1.60 1.60

NEWSPAPER STAMP.

N1

Perf. 11½, 12½, 13½.

1893 Typographed Unwmkd.

P1 N1 2½r brown 1.40 90

No. P1 was also used for ordinary postage.

POSTAL TAX STAMPS.

Pombal Issue.

Common Design Types

1925 *Perf. 12½.* Unwmkd.

RA1 CD28 15c lilac & black 40 30
RA2 CD29 15c " " 40 30
RA3 CD30 15c " " 40 30

"Charity"
PT1

Coat of Arms
PT2

Without Gum

1929 Lithographed. *Perf. 11.*

RA4 PT1 50c dark blue 2.25 1.10

1939 Without Gum. *Perf. 10½.*

RA5 PT2 50c turquoise grn. 3.25 20
RA6 " 1a red 5.50 4.50

A 1.50a, type PT2, was issued for fiscal use.

Old Man
PT3

Mother and Child
PT4

Designs: 1e, Boy. 1.50e, Girl.

Imprint: "Foto-Lito—E.G.A.—Luanda"

1955 *Perf. 13* Unwmkd.

Heads in dark brown.

RA7 PT3 50c dark ochre 20 15
RA8 " 1e orange vermilion 90 30
RA9 " 1.50e bright yellow green 55 25

A 2.50e, type PT3 showing an old woman, was issued for revenue use.

See also Nos. RA16, RA19–RA21, RA25–RA27.

No. RA7 Surcharged with New Values and two Bars in Red or Black.

1957-58 Head in dark brown.

RA11 PT3 10c on 50c dark ochre (R) 40 25
RA12 " 10c on 50c dark ochre('58) 30 20
RA13 " 30c on 50c dark ochre 35 25

1959 Lithographed. *Perf. 13*

Design: 30c, Boy and girl.

RA14 PT4 10c orange & black 15 15
RA15 " 30c slate & black 15 15

Type of 1955 Redrawn

Design: 1e, Boy.

1961, Nov. *Perf. 13*

RA16 PT3 1e salmon pink & dk. brown 30 30

Denomination in italics.

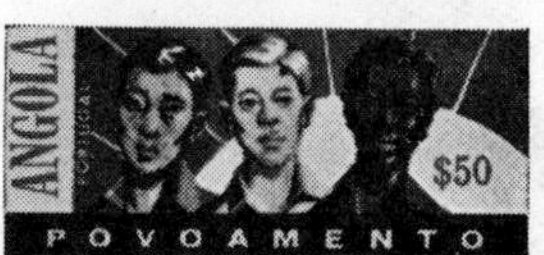

Yellow, White and Black Men
PT5

1962 Typographed *Perf. 10½*

Without Gum

RA17 PT5 50c multicolored 50 50
RA18 " 1e " 60 60

Issued for the Provincial Settlement Committee (Junta Provincial do Povoamento). The tax was used to promote Portuguese settlement in Angola, and to raise educational and living standards of recent immigrants.

See also No. RAJ4. Denominations higher than 2e were used for revenue purposes.

Head Type of 1955 Without Imprint

Designs: 50c, Old man. 1e, Boy. 1.50e, Girl.

1964-65 Litho. *Perf. 11½*

Heads in dark bown

RA19 PT3 50c orange 22 15
RA20 " 1e dull red org. ('65) 30 15
RA21 " 1.50e yel. green ('65) 40 25

No. RA20 is second redrawing of 1e, with bolder lettering and denomination in gothic. Space between "Assistencia" and denomination on RA19–RA21 is ½mm.; on 1955 issue space is 2mm.

Map of Angola, Industrial and Farm Workers
PT6

1965 Lithographed *Perf. 13*

RA22 PT6 50c multicolored 30 30
RA23 " 1e " 45 45

See also No. RAJ5.

Head Type of 1955

1966

Imprint: "I.N.A." or "INA" (1e)

Heads in dark brown

RA25 PT3 50c dull orange 15 15
RA26 " 1e dull brick red 25 15
RA27 " 1.50e lt. yel. green 25 20

Woman Planting Tree
PT7

Designs: 1e, Workers. 2e, Produce.

1972 Lithographed *Perf. 13*

RA28 PT7 50c gray & pink 10 10
RA29 " 1e green & black 20 20
RA30 " 2e brn. & black 30 30

POSTAL TAX DUE STAMPS.

Pombal Issue.

Common Design Types

1925 *Perf. 12½.* Unwmkd.

RAJ1 CD31 30c lilac & black 75 *1.25*
RAJ2 CD32 30c " " 75 *1.25*
RAJ3 CD33 30c " " 75 *1.25*

See note after Portugal No. RAJ4.

Three-Men Type of Postal Tax Stamps, 1962.

1962 Typographed *Perf. 10½*

Without Gum

RAJ4 PT5 2e multicolored 45 *1.00*

See note after Nos. RA17–RA18.

Type of Postal Tax Stamps, 1965

1965 Lithographed *Perf. 13*

RAJ5 PT6 2e multicolored 35 *1.00*

ANGRA

(äng′grȧ)

LOCATION — An administrative district of the Azores, consisting of the islands of Terceira, São Jorge and Graciosa.

GOVT.—A district of Portugal.

AREA—275 sq. mi.

POP.—70,000 (approx.).

CAPITAL—Angra do Heroismo.

1000 Reis = 1 Milreis

King Carlos
A1 A2

Perf. 11½, 12½, 13½.

1892-93 Typographed. **Unwmkd.**

No.	Type	Description	Unused	Used
1	A1	5r yellow	2.00	1.25
		a. Perf. 11½	4.50	2.50
2	"	10r reddish violet	2.75	1.75
3	"	15r chocolate	3.25	2.25
4	"	20r lavender	3.50	2.25
		a. Perf. 13½	6.75	2.50
5	"	25r green	1.40	35
		a. Perf. 12½	6.00	60
7	"	50r blue	4.50	1.65
		a. Perf. 13½	8.00	4.75
8	"	75r carmine	8.50	4.00
9	"	80r yellow green	9.50	5.00
10	"	100r brn., *yellow*, perf. 13½ ('93)	27.50	12.50
		a. Perf. 12½	95.00	65.00
11	"	150r car., *rose* ('93)	35.00	27.50
12	"	200r dark blue, *blue* ('93)	35.00	27.50
13	"	300r dk. blue, *salmon* ('93)	35.00	27.50

Reprints of 50r, 150r, 200r and 300r, made in 1900, are perf. 11½ and ungummed. Price, each $7.50. Reprints of all values, made in 1905, have shiny white gum and clean-cut perf. 13½. Price, each $1.

1897–1905 ***Perf. 11½***

Name and Value in Black except Nos. 26 and 35.

No.	Type	Description	Unused	Used
14	A2	2½r gray	30	25
15	"	5r orange	30	25
		a. Diagonal half used as 2½r on cover		4.00
16	"	10r yellow green	30	25
17	"	15r brown	3.00	1.65
18	"	15r gray green ('99)	1.10	70
19	"	20r gray violet	1.25	45
20	"	25r sea green	1.40	35
		a. Imperf., pair	10.00	
21	"	25r carmine rose ('99)	70	20
22	"	50r dark blue	1.90	90
23	"	50r ultramarine ('05)	7.75	7.00
24	"	65r slate blue ('98)	35	30
25	"	75r rose	1.10	60
26	"	75r gray brown & carmine, *straw* ('05)	8.50	7.50
27	"	80r violet	55	40
28	"	100r dark blue, *blue*	1.30	55
29	"	115r orange brown, *pink* ('98)	60	55
30	"	130r gray brown, *straw* ('98)	60	50
31	"	150r light brown, *straw*	60	55
32	"	180r slate, *pinkish* ('98)	1.40	1.10
33	"	200r red vio., *pinkish*	2.25	1.65
34	"	300r blue, *rose*	4.75	3.75
35	"	500r black & red, *blue*	8.25	5.50
		a. Perf. 12½	16.50	11.00
		Nos. 14-35 (22)	48.25	34.95

Azores stamps were used in Angra from 1906 to 1931, when they were superseded by those of Portugal.

ANJOUAN

(än′jōō·än′)

LOCATION—One of the Comoro Islands in the Mozambique Channel between Madagascar and Mozambique.

GOVT.—Former French colony.

AREA—89 sq. mi.

POP.—20,000 (approx. 1912).

CAPITAL—Mossamondu.

See Comoro Islands.

100 Centimes = 1 Franc

Navigation and Commerce

A1

Perf. 14x13½.

1892–1907 Typographed **Unwmkd.**

Name of Colony in Blue or Carmine.

No.	Type	Description	Unused	Used
1	A1	1c *blue*	60	60
2	"	2c brown, *buff*	75	75
3	"	4c claret, *lavender*	1.25	1.00
4	"	5c green, *greenish*	2.25	2.00
5	"	10c *lavender*	2.40	2.00
6	"	10c red ('00)	7.00	5.00
7	"	15c blue, quadrille paper	3.00	2.75
8	"	15c gray, *light gray* ('00)	4.50	3.75
9	"	20c red, *green*	3.25	2.75
10	"	25c *rose*	3.50	3.00
11	"	25c blue ('00)	5.50	5.00
12	"	30c brown, *bistre*	7.00	5.00
13	"	35c *yellow* ('06)	3.50	2.50
14	"	40c red, *straw*	11.00	10.00
15	"	45c *gray green* ('07)	52.50	45.00
16	"	50c carmine, *rose*	12.00	10.00
17	"	50c brn., *azure* ('00)	7.50	6.00
18	"	75c violet, *orange*	11.00	8.00
19	"	1fr bronze green, *straw*	22.50	22.50
		Nos. 1-19 (19)	161.00	137.60

Issues of 1892-1907 Surcharged in Black or Carmine **05** **10**

1912

No.	Type	Description	Unused	Used
20	A1	5c on 2c brown, *buff*	20	20
21	"	5c on 4c claret, *lavender* (C)	20	20
		a. Pair, one without surcharge		
22	"	5c on 15c blue (C)	20	20
		a. Pair, one without surcharge		
23	"	5c on 20c red, *green*	20	20
24	"	5c on 25c *rose* (C)	20	20
25	"	5c on 30c brown, *bistre* (C)	25	25
26	"	10c on 40c red, *straw*	25	25
27	"	10c on 45c *gray green* (C)	30	30
28	"	10c on 50c carmine, *rose*	70	70
29	"	10c on 75c violet, *orange*	50	50
30	"	10c on 1fr bronze green, *straw*	50	50
		Nos. 20-30 (11)	3.50	3.50

Two spacings between the surcharged numerals are found on Nos. 20 to 30.

Nos. 20 to 30 were available for use in Madagascar and the entire Comoro archipelago.

The stamps of Anjouan were superseded by those of Madagascar, and in 1950 by those of Comoro Islands.

ANNAM AND TONKIN

(ă·năm′ & tŏn′kĭn′)

LOCATION — In French Indo-China bordering on the China Sea on the east and Siam on the west.

GOVT.—French Protectorate.

AREA—97,503 sq. mi.

POP.—14,124,000 (approx. 1890).

CAPITALS—Annam: Hué.
Tonkin: Hanoi.

For administrative purposes, the Protectorates of Annam, Tonkin, Cambodia, Laos and the Colony of Cochin-China were grouped together and were known as French Indo-China.

100 Centimes = 1 Franc

Stamps of French Colonies, 1881-86 Surcharged in Black:

A&T 1 or **A&T 5**

1888 ***Perf. 14x13½.*** **Unwmkd.**

No.	Type	Description	Unused	Used
1	A9	1c on 2c brown, *buff*	12.00	12.00
		a. Inverted surch.	30.00	30.00
2	"	1c on 4c claret, *lavender*	10.00	9.00
		a. Inverted surch.	30.00	30.00
3	"	5c on 10c *lavender*	10.00	9.00
		a. Inverted surch.	30.00	30.00

A 5c on 2c was prepared but not issued.

Hyphen between "A" and "T"

No.	Type	Description	Unused	Used
7	A9	1c on 2c brown, *buff*	110.00	100.00
8	"	1c on 4c claret, *lavender*	150.00	140.00
9	"	5c on 10c *lavender*	80.00	70.00

In these surcharges there are different types of numerals and letters.

These stamps were superseded in 1892 by those of Indo-China.

ARABIA

See Saudi Arabia, Vol. IV.

ARGENTINA

(är′jĕn·tē′nȧ)

LOCATION—In South America.

GOVT.—Republic.

AREA—1,072,700 sq. mi.

POP.—26,060,000 (est. 1977).

CAPITAL—Buenos Aires.

100 Centavos = 1 Peso

Argentine Confederation.

Symbolical of the Argentine Confederation
A1 A2

Lithographed

1858, May 1 ***Imperf.*** **Unwmkd.**

No.	Type	Description	Unused	Used
1	A1	5c red	65	*7.00*
		a. Colon after "5"	75	*8.00*
		b. Colon after "V"	75	*8.00*
2	A1	10c green	1.75	*32.50*
		a. Half used as 5c on cover		*225.00*
3	"	15c blue	10.00	*70.00*
		a. One-third used as 5c on cover		*1500.00*

1860, Jan.

No.	Type	Description	Unused	Used
4	A2	5c red	2.00	*50.00*
4A	"	10c green	3.50	
4B	"	15c blue	12.50	

Nos. 4A and 4B were never placed in use. There are nine varieties of Nos. 1, 2 and 3, sixteen of No. 4 and eight of Nos. 4A and 4B. Forged cancellations are plentiful.

> Prices of Argentina Nos. 5–17 vary according to condition. Quotations are for fine copies. Very fine to superb specimens sell at much higher prices, and inferior or poor copies sell at reduced prices, depending on the condition of the individual specimen.

Argentine Republic.

Seal of the Republic
A3

Broad "C" in "CENTAVOS", Accent on "U" of "REPUBLICA".

1862, Jan. 11

No.	Type	Description	Unused	Used
5	A3	5c rose	25.00	20.00
		a. 5c red	30.00	20.00
6	"	10c green	100.00	55.00
		b. Diagonal half used as 5c on cover		1200.00
7	"	15c blue	175.00	135.00
		a. Without accent on "U"	*2500.00*	*1500.00*
		b. Tête bêche pair	*30,000.00*	*18,000.00*
		i. 15c ultramarine		325.00

Broad "C" in "CENTAVOS", No Accent on "U"

1863

No.	Type	Description	Unused	Used
7C	A3	5c rose	11.00	8.00
		d. 5c rose lilac	110.00	30.00
		e. Worn plate	50.00	15.00
7F	"	10c yellow green	175.00	135.00
		g. 10c olive green	325.00	150.00

Narrow "C" in "CENTAVOS", No Accent on "U"

1864

No.	Type	Description	Unused	Used
7H	A3	5c rose red	150.00	15.00

The so-called reprints of 10c and 15c are counterfeits. They have narrow "C" and straight lines in shield. Nos. 7C and 7H have been extensively counterfeited.

Rivadavia Issue.

Bernardino Rivadavia
A4 A5

Rivadavia
A6

Wmk. 84

Wmkd. RA in Italics (84)

1864-67 **Engraved** ***Imperf.***

Clear Impressions.

8	A4	5c brown rose	*1000.00*	*140.00*
		a. 5c orange red ('67)	*1000.00*	*140.00*
9	A5	10c green	*2000.00*	*900.00*
10	A6	15c blue	*4250.00*	*2600.00*

Perf. 11½.

Dull to Worn Impressions.

11	A4	5c brown rose ('65)	27.50	7.50
11B	"	5c lake	27.50	10.00
12	A5	10c green	60.00	30.00
		a. Diagonal half used as 5c on cover		225.00
13	A6	15c blue	135.00	55.00

1867-72 ***Imperf.*** **Unwmkd.**

14	A4	5c car. ('72)	100.00	32.50
15	"	5c rose	150.00	70.00
15A	A5	10c green	*2400.00*	*2400.00*
16	A6	15c blue	*2000.00*	*1750.00*

1867 ***Perf. 11½.***

17	A4	5c carmine	200.00	70.00

Rivadavia
A7

Manuel Belgrano
A8

José de San Martín
A9

Groundwork of Horizontal Lines.

1867-68 ***Perf. 12.***

18	A7	5c vermilion	75.00	5.00
18A	A8	10c green	15.00	2.50
		b. Diagonal half used as 5c on cover		200.00
19	A9	15c blue	50.00	7.50

Groundwork of Crossed Lines.

20	A7	5c vermilion	4.00	30
21	A9	15c blue	65.00	7.50

See also Nos. 27, 33-34, 39 and types A19, A33, A34, A37.

Gen. Antonio G. Balcarce
A10

Mariano Moreno
A11

Carlos Maria de Alvear
A12

Gervasio Antonio Posadas
A13

Cornelio Saavedra
A14

1873

22	A10	1c purple	3.00	1.50
		a. 1c gray violet	3.50	1.50
23	A11	4c brown	4.00	30
		a. 4c red brown	11.00	2.25
24	A12	30c orange	70.00	7.00
25	A13	60c black	70.00	2.75
26	A14	90c blue	11.00	1.25

1873 **Laid Paper.**

27	A8	10c green	75.00	10.00

A15

A16

Surcharged in Black.

1877, Feb. **Wove Paper**

30	A15	1c on 5c vermilion	27.50	8.00
		a. Inverted surcharge	135.00	65.00
31	"	2c on 5c vermilion	70.00	22.50
		a. Inverted surcharge	425.00	235.00
		b. Double surch.	475.00	
32	A16	8c on 10c green	37.50	8.00
		a. Laid paper	525.00	160.00
		b. Inverted surcharge	275.00	160.00
		c. Double surcharge	325.00	

Forgeries of these surcharges include the inverted and double varieties.

1876-77 ***Rouletted***

33	A7	5c vermilion	90.00	25.00
34	"	8c lake ('77)	9.00	25

Belgrano
A17

Dalmacio Vélez Sarsfield
A18

San Martín
A19

1878 ***Rouletted***

35	A17	16c green	3.50	75
36	A18	20c blue	4.00	1.10
37	A19	24c blue	22.50	1.75

See also No. 56.

Vicente López
A20

Alvear
A21

1877-80 ***Perf. 12.***

38	A20	2c yellow green	2.75	50
39	A7	8c lake ('80)	2.75	30
		a. 8c brown lake	3.75	30
40	A21	25c lake ('78)	22.50	4.50

A22

A23

1882 **Surcharged in Black.**

41	A22	½c on 5c vermilion	75	50
		a. Double surcharge	25.00	15.00
		b. Inverted surcharge	12.50	10.00
		c. "PROVISORIO" omitted	17.50	15.00
		d. Fraction omitted	25.00	
		e. "PROVISOBIO"	10.00	7.50
		f. Pair, one without surcharge	50.00	

Perforated across Middle of Stamp.

42	A22	½c on 5c vermilion	1.00	75
		a. "PROVISORIQ"	10.00	7.50
		b. Inverted surch.	25.00	
		c. Pair, one without perforation across the stamp	15.00	

The "½ (PROVISORIO)" surcharge on Nos. 41-42 is found in two types: I. Small "P" and narrow "V." II. Large "P" and wider "V."

1882 **Typographed** ***Perf. 12***

43	A23	½c brown	1.25	50
		a. Imperf., pair	25.00	25.00
44	"	1c red, perf. 14	2.75	50
		a. Perf. 12	3.50	1.50
45	"	12c ultramarine	27.50	6.00
		a. Perf. 14	35.00	7.00

Engraved

Perf. 14

46	A23	12c greenish blue	55.00	6.00

No. 21 Surcharged in Red:

1884
½
a

b

1884 ***Perf. 12.***

47	A9 (*a*)	½c on 15c blue	1.25	75
		a. Groundwork of horizontal lines	25.00	20.00
		b. Inverted surcharge	10.00	10.00
48	" (*b*)	1c on 15c blue	3.00	1.75
		a. Groundwork of horizontal lines	10.00	6.00
		b. Inverted surcharge	35.00	20.00
		c. Double surcharge	15.00	12.50
		d. Triple surch.	25.00	20.00

Nos. 20-21 Surcharged in Black

CUATRO
Centavos
1884
c

49	A7 (*a*)	½c on 5c vermilion	1.25	75
		a. Inverted surcharge	50.00	40.00
		b. Date omitted	35.00	
		c. Pair, one without surcharge	125.00	
50	A9 (")	½c on 15c blue	5.00	2.50
		a. Groundwork of horizontal lines	10.00	6.00
		b. Inverted surcharge	10.00	6.00
51	A7 (*c*)	4c on 5c vermilion	4.00	1.75
		a. Inverted surcharge	10.00	7.50
		b. Double surcharge	100.00	75.00
		c. Pair, one without surcharge but with "4" in manuscript	200.00	100.00

A29

1884-85 **Engraved** ***Perf. 12***

52	A29	½c red brown	75	25
		a. Imperf., pair	50.00	
53	"	1c rose red	2.00	25
		a. Imperf., pair	50.00	
54	"	12c greenish blue ('85)	10.00	75
		a. 12c deep blue	10.00	75

San Martin Type of 1878

1887 **Engraved**

56	A19	24c blue	17.50	1.00

Justo José de Urquiza
A30

López
A31

Miguel Juárez Celman
A32

Rivadavia
A33

Rivadavia
A34

Domingo F. Sarmiento
A35

Nicolás Avellaneda
A36

San Martin
A37

Julio A. Roca
A37a

Belgrano
A37b

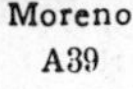

Manuel Dorrego A38 — Moreno A39

Bartolomé Mitre A40

CINCO CENTAVOS.

Type I. A33. Shows collar on left side only.
Type II. A34. Shows collar on both sides. Lozenges in background larger and clearer than in type I.

1888–90 Lithographed *Perf. 11½*

No.	Type	Description	Unused	Used
57	A30	½c blue	40	20
		a. Imperf., pair	17.50	17.50
58	A31	2c yellow green	10.00	5.00
		a. Imperf., pair	35.00	
59	A32	3c blue green	1.25	40
		a. Imperf., pair	17.50	10.00
		b. Imperf. vert., pair	25.00	
		c. Horizontal pair, imperf. between	25.00	
		d. Vertical pair, imperf. between	25.00	
60	A33	5c carmine, type I	6.00	1.00
61	A34	5c carmine, type II	3.50	50
		a. Imperf., pair		65.00
		b. Vertical pair, imperf. between	40.00	
62	A35	6c red	14.00	6.00
		a. Imperf., pair	25.00	
		b. Vertical pair, imperf. between	30.00	
		c. Perf. 12	17.50	10.00
63	A36	10c brown	6.50	45
		a. Imperf., pair	15.00	
64	A37	15c orange	2.25	1.25
		c. Imperf., pair		125.00
64A	A37a	20c green	5.00	70
64B	A37b	25c purple	5.00	60
65	A38	30c chocolate	7.00	1.25
		a. Imperf., pair	100.00	85.00
66	A39	40c slate, perf. 12	22.50	2.50
		a. Perf. 11½	30.00	6.00
67	A40	50c blue	45.00	5.00
		Nos. 57-67 (13)	128.40	24.85

In this issue there are several varieties of each value, the difference between them being in the relative position of the head to the frame.

Urquiza A41 — Vélez Sarsfield A42

Miguel Juárez Celman A43 — Rivadavia (Large head) A44

Sarmiento A45 — Juan Bautista Alberdi A46

1888–89 Engr. *Perf. 11½, 11½x12*

No.	Type	Description	Unused	Used
68	A41	½c ultramarine	25	10
		a. Imperf. horiz. pair	12.50	7.50
		b. Imperf., pair	12.50	7.00
69	A42	1c brown	50	20
		a. Imperf. horiz., pair	17.50	
		b. Vertical pair, imperf. between	17.50	
		c. Imperf., pair	15.50	
70	A43	3c blue green	75	35
71	A44	5c rose	1.50	15
		a. Imperf., pair	17.50	10.00
72	A45	6c blue black	1.50	60
		a. Imperf., pair	40.00	40.00
		b. Perf. 11½x12	5.00	1.25
73	A46	12c blue	3.00	60
		a. Imperf., pair	10.00	
		b. Bluish paper	3.00	1.00
		c. Perf. 11½	4.00	1.25
		Nos. 68-73 (6)	7.50	2.00

See also Nos. 77 and 89.

José Maria Paz A48 — Santiago Derqui A49

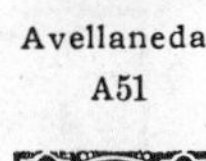

Rivadavia (Small head) A50 — Avellaneda A51

Moreno A53 — Mitre A54

Posadas—A55 — A56

1890 Engraved *Perf. 11½*

No.	Type	Description	Unused	Used
75	A48	¼c green	15	7
76	A49	2c violet	40	8
		a. 2c purple	50	10
		b. 2c slate	1.00	20
		c. Horizontal pair, imperf. between	15.00	
		d. Imperf., pair	20.00	
		e. Perf. 11½x12	1.00	15
77	A50	5c carmine	1.25	7
		a. Imperf., pair	25.00	20.00
		b. Perf. 11½x12	2.50	50
78	A51	10c brown	2.00	35
		a. Vertical pair, imperf. between	20.00	
80	A53	40c olive green	4.00	1.00
		a. Imperf., pair	20.00	
81	A54	50c orange	3.00	50
		a. Imperf., pair	30.00	
		b. Perf. 11½x12	5.00	50
82	A55	60c black	8.00	2.00
		a. Imperf., pair	35.00	35.00
		Nos. 75-82 (7)	18.80	4.07

Type A50 differs from type A44 in having the head smaller, the letters of "Cinco Centavos" not as tall, and the curved ornaments at sides close to the first and last letters of "Republica Argentina".

1890 *Perf. 11½x12*

Black or Red Lithographed Surcharge.

No.	Type	Description	Unused	Used
83	A56	¼c on 12c blue (Bk)	25	20
		a. Perf. 11½	2.00	1.75
84	"	¼c on 12c blue (R)	25	20
		a. Double surcharge	15.00	15.00
		b. Perf. 11½	50	30

Rivadavia A57 — José de San Martin A58

Gregorio Araoz de Lamadrid A59 — Admiral Guillermo Brown A60

1891 Engraved. *Perf. 11½*

No.	Type	Description	Unused	Used
85	A57	8c carmine rose	1.50	25
		a. Imperf., pair	40.00	
86	A58	1p deep blue	22.50	3.00
87	A59	5p ultramarine	110.00	17.50
88	A60	20p green	110.00	60.00

A 10p brown and a 50p red were prepared but not issued. Price $550 each.

Vélez Sarsfield A61

1890 *Perf. 11½*

No.	Type	Description	Unused	Used
89	A61	1c brown	1.00	25

Type A61 is a re-engraving of A42. The figure "1" in each upper corner has a short horizontal serif instead of a long one pointing downward. In type A61 the first and last letters of "Correos y Telegrafos" are closer to the curved ornaments below than in type A42. Background is of horizontal lines (crosshatching on No. 69).

"Santa Maria," "Niña" and "Pinta"—A62

Wmk. 85

Wmk. 86

The Small Sun (85) is 4½mm. in diameter and the Large Sun (86) 6mm.

Wmkd. Small Sun. (85)

1892, Oct. 12 *Perf. 11½*

No.	Type	Description	Unused	Used
90	A62	2c light blue	2.50	2.00
		a. Dbl. impression	50.00	
91	"	5c dark blue	3.00	2.50

Discovery of America, 400th anniversary.

Rivadavia A63 — Belgrano A64

San Martín A65

Perf. 11½, 12 and Compound.

1892–95 Wmk. 85

No.	Type	Description	Unused	Used
92	A63	½c dull blue	25	8
		a. ½c bright ultra.	8.00	1.25
		b. Imperf., pair	25.00	
93	"	1c brown	35	6
		a. Imperf., pair	17.50	
94	"	2c green	50	6
		a. Imperf., pair	10.00	
95	"	3c orange ('95)	60	7
96	"	5c carmine	85	4
		a. Imperf., pair	10.00	10.00
		b. 5c green (error)	200.00	200.00
98	A64	10c carmine rose	4.50	10
		a. Imperf., pair	30.00	
99	"	12c deep blue ('93)	5.00	15
		a. Imperf., pair	25.00	
100	"	16c gray	7.00	35
		a. Imperf., pair	25.00	
101	"	24c gray brown	6.00	40
		a. Imperf., pair	25.00	
		b. Perf. 12	10.00	1.00
102	"	50c blue green	7.00	40
		a. Imperf., pair	20.00	
		b. Perf. 12	10.00	1.00
103	A65	1p lake ('93)	7.00	65
		a. 1p red brown	7.50	3.00
		b. Imperf., pair	20.00	
104	"	2p dark green	17.50	2.00
		a. Perf. 12	25.00	4.00
105	"	5p dark blue	27.50	2.00
		a. Imperf., pair	50.00	
		Nos. 92-105 (13)	84.05	6.36

Part-perforate varieties of Nos. 92–98 include vert. or horiz. pairs imperf. between and pairs imperf. vert. or horiz. Price $6–$35.

The high values of this and succeeding issues are frequently punched with the word "INUTILIZADO," parts of the letters showing on each stamp. These punched stamps sell for only a small fraction of the catalogue prices.

Reprints of No. 96b have white gum. The original stamp has yellowish gum. Price $25.

1896–97 Wmkd. Large Sun. (86)

No.	Type	Description	Unused	Used
106	A63	½c slate	25	8
		a. ½c gray blue	25	8
		b. ½c indigo	25	8
107	"	1c brown	35	5
108	"	2c yellow green	30	5
109	"	3c orange	40	8
110	"	5c carmine	40	4
		a. Imperf., pair	25.00	
111	A64	10c carmine rose	4.00	10
112	"	12c deep blue	1.75	10
		a. Imperf., pair	25.00	
113	"	16c gray	5.00	35
114	"	24c gray brown	6.00	75
		a. Imperf., pair	25.00	
115	"	30c orange ('97)	8.00	35
116	"	50c blue green	8.00	35
117	"	80c dull violet	7.00	1.00
118	A65	1p lake	13.00	60
119	"	1p 20c black ('97)	11.00	1.50
120	"	2p dark green	11.00	3.00
121	"	5p dark blue	32.50	2.25
		a. Perf. 12	45.00	6.50
		Nos. 106-121 (16)	108.95	10.65

Allegory, Liberty Seated
A66 A67

Perf. 11½, 12 and Compound

1899-1903

No.	Type	Description	Unused	Used
122	A66	½c yellow brown	10	4
		a. Imperf., pair	15.00	
123	"	1c green	20	4
		a. Imperf., pair	15.00	
124	"	2c slate	20	4
		a. Imperf., pair	5.00	2.50
125	"	3c orange ('01)	50	10
		a. Imperf., pair	40.00	25.00
126	"	4c yellow ('03)	75	12
127	"	5c carmine rose	20	5
		a. Imperf., pair	5.00	4.00
128	"	6c black ('03)	60	15
		a. Imperf., pair	20.00	
129	"	10c dark green	1.25	5
		a. Imperf., pair	20.00	
130	"	12c dull blue	1.25	50
131	"	12c olive green ('01)	1.25	25
132	"	15c sea green ('01)	1.50	10
		a. Imperf., pair	20.00	
132B	"	15c dull blue ('01)	2.00	50
133	"	16c orange	9.00	4.00
134	"	20c claret	1.50	10
135	"	24c violet	2.50	65
136	"	30c rose	6.00	40
137	"	30c vermilion ('01)	1.75	10
		a. 30c scarlet	22.50	1.00
138	"	50c bright blue	4.00	10
139	A67	1p blue & black, perf. 11½	7.00	40
		a. Center inverted	*850.00*	*425.00*
		b. Perf. 12	25.00	5.00
140	"	5p orange & black	20.00	6.00
		Punch cancellation		60
		a. Center inverted	*850.00*	
141	"	10p green & black	55.00	8.50
		Punch cancellation		50
		a. Center invtd.	*3000.00*	
142	"	20p red & black	135.00	75.00
		Punch cancellation		50
		a. Center inverted (punch canc.)		*1250.00*
		Nos. 122-142 (22)	251.55	97.19

Part-perforate varieties of Nos. 122-129 include vert. or horiz. pairs imperf. between and pairs imperf. vert. or horiz. Price 50 cents to $10.

River Port of Rosario
A68

1902, Oct. 26 *Perf. 11½, 11½x12*

No.	Type	Description	Unused	Used
143	A68	5c deep blue	3.00	1.25
		a. Imperf., pair	60.00	

Completion of port facilities at Rosario.

San Martín
A69 A70

Perf. 13½, 13½x12½.

1908-09 Typographed.

No.	Type	Description	Unused	Used
144	A69	½c violet	15	10
145	"	1c brownish buff	15	10
146	"	2c chocolate	50	10
147	"	3c green	75	15
148	"	4c reddish violet	1.75	35
149	"	5c carmine	35	10
150	"	6c olive bistre	1.00	25
151	"	10c gray green	1.25	15
152	A69	12c yellow buff	1.00	50
153	"	12c dark blue ('09)	50	15
154	"	15c apple green	50	15
155	"	20c ultramarine	75	12
156	"	24c red brown	2.50	40
157	"	30c dull rose	3.00	40
158	"	50c black	3.00	30
159	A70	1p slate bl. & pink	6.00	1.00
		Nos. 144-159 (16)	23.15	4.32

No. 145 is known printed in blue, but was not issued. Price $250.

Stamps of 1908-09 issue without watermark are due to sheets having been misplaced on the printing press, so that the impression was printed on the unwatermarked margin.

Centenary of the Republic Issue.

Pyramid of May
A71

Nicolás Rodríguez Peña and Hipólito Vieytes
A72

Meeting at Peña's Home
A73

Designs: 3c, Miguel de Azcuénaga (1754-1833) and Father Manuel M. Alberti (1763-1811). 4c, Viceroy's house and Fort Buenos Aires. 5c, Cornelio Saavedra (1759-1829). 10c, Antonio Luis Beruti (1772-1842) and French distributing badges. 12c, Congress building. 20c, Juan José Castelli (1764-1812) and Domingo Matheu (1765-1831). 24c, First council. 30c, Manuel Belgrano (1770-1820) and Juan Larrea (1782-1847). 50c, First meeting of republican government, May 25, 1810. 1p, Mariano Moreno (1778-1811) and Juan José Paso (1758-1833). 5p, Oath of the Junta. 10p, Centenary Monument. 20p, José Francisco de San Martin (1778-1850).

Inscribed "1810 1910"
Various Frames

1910, May 1 Engraved *Perf. 11½*

No.	Type	Description	Unused	Used
160	A71	½c blue & gray blue	50	10
		a. Center inverted	*300.00*	
161	A72	1c blue grn. & blk.	75	20
		a. Center inverted	*300.00*	
		b. Horiz. pair, imperf. between	50.00	
162	A73	2c olive & gray	30	10
		a. Center inverted	150.00	
163	A72	3c green	1.25	20
164	A73	4c dark blue & green	1.25	30
		a. Center inverted	*300.00*	
165	A71	5c carmine	75	5
166	A73	10c yellow brown & black	1.75	30
167	"	12c bright blue	1.50	25
		a. Center inverted	*300.00*	
168	A72	20c gray brown & black	1.75	30
169	A73	24c orange brown & blue	1.75	50
170	A72	30c lilac & black	1.75	50
171	A71	50c carmine & black	4.00	60
		a. Center inverted	*300.00*	
172	A72	1p bright blue	8.50	2.25
173	A73	5p orange & vio.	55.00	20.00
		a. Center inverted	*300.00*	
		Punch cancel		1.50
174	A71	10p org. & black	110.00	40.00
		Punch cancel		1.75
175	A71	20p deep blue & indigo	175.00	85.00
		Punch cancel		3.00
		Nos. 160-175 (16)	365.80	150.65

Domingo F. Sarmiento — A87
Agriculture — A88

1911, May 15 Typo. *Perf. 13½*

No.	Type	Description	Unused	Used
176	A87	5c gray brown & black	75	50

Issued to commemorate the centenary of the birth of Domingo Faustino Sarmiento (1811-88), president of Argentina, 1868-74.

Wmkd. Large Sun. (86)

1911 Engraved. *Perf. 12.*

Size: 19x25mm.

No.	Type	Description	Unused	Used
177	A88	5c vermilion	25	10
		a. Booklet pane of 4		
		b. Booklet pane of 6		
178	"	12c deep blue	1.75	15

1911 Typographed *Perf. 13½x12½*

Size: 18x23mm.

No.	Type	Description	Unused	Used
179	A88	½c violet	12	8
180	"	1c brown ochre	12	8
181	"	2c chocolate	12	6
		a. Perf. 13½	3.00	40
		b. Imperf., pair	25.00	
182	"	3c green	50	12
183	"	4c brown violet	30	20
184	"	10c gray green	50	8
185	"	20c ultramarine	2.50	50
186	"	24c red brown	3.00	1.25
187	"	30c claret	1.00	25
188	"	50c black	3.00	50
		Nos. 179-188 (10)	11.16	3.12

The 5c dull red is a proof.

Wmk. 87

Wmkd. Honeycomb. (87) (Horizontal or Vertical)

1912-14 *Perf. 13½x12½*

No.	Type	Description	Unused	Used
189	A88	½c violet	25	8
		a. Perf. 13½	75	12
190	"	1c ochre	25	8
		a. Perf. 13½	75	12
191	"	2c chocolate	35	6
		a. Perf. 13½	1.00	10
192	"	3c green	85	15
		a. Perf. 13½	10.00	5.00
193	"	4c brown violet	85	20
		a. Perf. 13½	2.00	50
194	"	5c red	25	3
		a. Perf. 13½	50	10
195	"	10c deep green	60	5
196	"	12c deep blue	60	4
		a. Perf. 13½	8.00	1.50
197	"	20c ultramarine	1.75	25
		a. Perf. 13½	3.50	30
198	"	24c red brown	3.00	85
199	"	30c claret	2.25	50
200	"	50c black	11.00	1.00
		Nos. 189-200 (12)	22.00	3.29

See also Nos. 208-212.

A89

1912-13 *Perf. 13½.*

No.	Type	Description	Unused	Used
201	A89	1p dull blue & rose	6.00	60
		Punch cancel		10
202	"	5p slate & olive green	22.50	3.00
		Punch cancel		30
203	"	10p violet & blue	95.00	10.00
		Punch cancel		50
204	"	20p blue & claret	200.00	50.00
		Punch cancel		75

1915 *Perf. 13½x12½.* **Unwmkd.**

No.	Type	Description	Unused	Used
208	A88	1c ochre	60	8
209	"	2c chocolate	60	8
212	"	5c red	50	7

Only these denominations were printed on paper without watermark.

Other stamps of the series are known unwatermarked but they are from the outer rows of sheets the other parts of which are watermarked.

Francisco Narciso de Laprida — A90
Declaration of Independence — A91

José de San Martín
A92 A92a

Perf. 13½, 13½x12½.

1916, July 9 Lithographed **Wmk. 87**

No.	Type	Description	Unused	Used
215	A90	½c violet	25	6
216	"	1c buff	25	8

Perf. 13½x12½

No.	Type	Description	Unused	Used
217	A90	2c chocolate	25	10
218	"	3c green	60	15
219	"	4c red violet	90	15

Perf. 13½

No.	Type	Description	Unused	Used
220	A91	5c red	40	5
		a. Imperf., pair	40.00	
221	"	10c gray green	90	15
222	A92	12c blue	90	10
223	"	20c ultramarine	90	25
224	"	24c red brown	1.25	35
225	"	30c claret	1.50	25
226	"	50c gray black	2.25	30
227	A92a	1p slate bl. & red	9.00	2.25
		Punch cancel		30
		a. Imperf., pair	160.00	
228	"	5p black & gray green	120.00	40.00
		Punch cancel		3.00
229	"	10p violet & blue	150.00	65.00
		Punch cancel		2.00
230	"	20p dull blue & claret	175.00	65.00
		Punch cancel		75
		a. Imperf., pair	325.00	
		Nos. 215-230 (16)	464.35	174.24

Issued to commemorate the centenary of Argentina's declaration of independence of Spain, July 9, 1816.

The watermark is either vertical or horizontal on Nos. 215-220, 222; only vertical on No. 221, and only horizontal on Nos. 223-230.

A93

A94 A94a

1917 *Perf. 13½, 13½x12½*

No.	Type	Description	Unused	Used
231	A93	½c violet	25	6
232	"	1c buff	25	6
233	"	2c brown	25	4
234	"	3c light green	25	7
235	"	4c red violet	1.50	15
236	"	5c red	25	3
		a. Imperf., pair	10.00	
237	"	10c gray green	1.00	8

Perf. 13½

No.	Type	Description	Unused	Used
238	A94	12c blue	50	7
239	"	20c ultramarine	1.00	10
240	"	24c red brown	2.00	1.00
241	"	30c claret	2.50	60
242	"	50c gray black	2.50	50
243	A94a	1p slate bl. & red	2.00	15
244	"	5p black & gray green	12.50	1.50
		Punch cancel		20
245	"	10p violet & blue	40.00	6.00
		Punch cancel		25
246	"	20p dull blue & claret	55.00	15.00
		Punch cancel		25
		a. Center inverted	600.00	600.00
		Nos. 231-246 (16)	121.75	25.41

The watermark is either vertical or horizontal on Nos. 231–236, 238; only vertical on No. 237, and only horizontal on Nos. 239–246.

Juan Gregorio Pujol

A95

1918, June 15 **Litho.** *Perf. 13½*

No.	Type	Description	Unused	Used
247	A95	5c bistre & gray	35	25

Issued to commemorate the centenary of the birth of Juan G. Pujol (1817–61), lawyer and legislator.

Perf. 13½, 13½x12½

1918–19 **Unwmkd.**

No.	Type	Description	Unused	Used
248	A93	½c violet	15	8
249	"	1c buff	15	6
		a. Imperf., pair	15.00	
250	"	2c brown	20	5
251	"	3c light green	25	10
252	"	4c red violet	25	12
253	"	5c red	25	3
254	"	10c gray green	50	5

Perf. 13½

No.	Type	Description	Unused	Used
255	A94	12c blue	60	8
256	"	20c ultramarine	1.25	8
257	"	24c red brown	1.75	50
258	"	30c claret	1.50	25
259	"	50c gray black	2.75	25
		Nos. 248-259 (12)	9.60	1.65

The stamps of this issue sometimes show letters of papermakers' watermarks.

There were two printings, in 1918 and 1923, using different ink and paper.

Wmk. 88

Wmkd. Multiple Suns. (88)

1920 *Perf. 13½, 13½x12½*

No.	Type	Description	Unused	Used
264	A93	½c violet	25	10
265	"	1c buff	25	6
266	"	2c brown	25	6
267	"	3c green	1.00	12
268	"	4c red violet	1.25	30
269	"	5c red	75	5
270	"	10c gray green	1.75	8

Perf. 13½

No.	Type	Description	Unused	Used
271	A94	12c blue	1.25	10
272	"	20c ultramarine	2.50	10
274	"	30c claret	4.00	50
275	"	50c gray black	5.00	50
		Nos. 264-275 (11)	18.25	1.97

See also Nos. 292–300, 304–307A, 310–314, 318, 322.

Belgrano's Mausoleum A96 — Gen. Manuel Belgrano A98

Creation of Argentine Flag

A97

1920, June 18 *Perf. 13½*

No.	Type	Description	Unused	Used
280	A96	2c red	35	25
		a. Perf. 13½x12½	35	25
281	A97	5c rose & blue	40	25
282	A98	12c green & blue	90	60

Issued to commemorate the centenary of the death of Manuel Belgrano (1770–1820), Argentine general, patriot and diplomat.

Gen. Justo José de Urquiza A99 — Bartolomé Mitre A100

1920, Nov. 11

No.	Type	Description	Unused	Used
283	A99	5c gray blue	35	15

Issued to honor Gen. Justo José de Urquiza (1801–1870), president of Argentina, 1854–1860. See also No. 303.

1921, June 26 **Unwmkd.**

No.	Type	Description	Unused	Used
284	A100	2c violet brown	35	20
285	"	5c light blue	35	20

Issued to commemorate the centenary of the birth of Bartolomé Mitre (1821–1906), president of Argentina, 1862–65.

Allegory, Pan-America

A101

1921, Aug. 25 *Perf. 13½*

No.	Type	Description	Unused	Used
286	A101	3c violet	80	35
287	"	5c blue	75	15
288	"	10c violet brown	1.00	35
289	"	12c rose	1.00	35

Inscribed "Buenos Aires—Agosto de 1921" A102 — Inscribed "Republica Argentina" A103

1921, Oct. *Perf. 13½x12½*

No.	Type	Description	Unused	Used
290	A102	5c rose	85	8
		a. Perf. 13½	85	8
291	A103	5c rose	1.00	6
		a. Perf. 13½	1.00	6

Issued to commemorate the first Pan-American Postal Congress, held at Buenos Aires, August, 1921.

See also Nos. 308–309, 319.

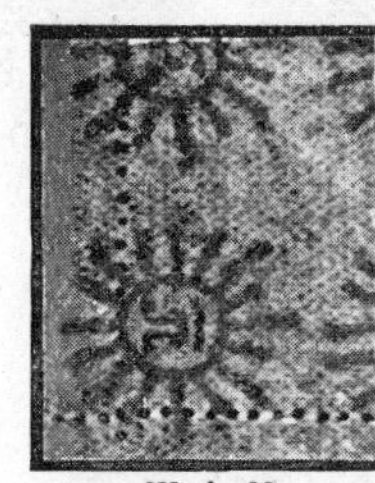

Wmk. 89

In this watermark the face of the sun is 7 mm. in diameter, the rays are heavier than in the large sun watermark of 1896-1911 and the watermarks are placed close together, so that parts of several frequently appear on one stamp. This paper was intended to be used for fiscal stamps and is usually referred to as "fiscal sun paper".

Wmkd. Large Sun. (89)

1920 *Perf. 13½, 13½x12½*

No.	Type	Description	Unused	Used
292	A93	½c violet	2.00	1.00
293	"	1c buff	4.00	1.00
294	"	2c brown	2.00	40
297	"	5c red	2.00	50
298	"	10c gray green	2.50	50

Perf. 13½

No.	Type	Description	Unused	Used
299	A94	12c blue	*600.00*	*60.00*
300	"	20c ultramarine	10.00	1.00
		Nos. 292-298, 300 (6)	22.50	4.40

1920

No.	Type	Description	Unused	Used
303	A99	5c gray blue	200.00	135.00

Wmk. 90

In 1928 the watermark R. A. in Sun (90) was slightly modified, making the diameter of the Sun 9 mm. instead of 10 mm. Several types of this watermark exist.

Wmkd. RA in Sun. (90)

1922–23 *Perf. 13½, 13½x12½*

No.	Type	Description	Unused	Used
304	A93	½c violet	25	8
305	"	1c buff	20	5
306	"	2c brown	15	5
307	"	3c green	50	20
307A	"	4c red violet	5.00	1.00
308	A102	5c rose	1.25	25
309	A103	5c red	25	5
310	A93	10c gray green	1.50	8

Perf. 13½

No.	Type	Description	Unused	Used
311	A94	12c blue	75	8
312	"	20c ultramarine	1.00	8
313	"	24c red brown	9.00	5.00
314	"	30c claret	5.00	35
		Nos. 304-314 (12)	24.85	7.27

Paper with Gray Overprint RA in Sun.

Perf. 13½, 13½x12½

1922-23 **Unwmkd.**

No.	Type	Description	Unused	Used
318	A93	2c brown	1.00	25
319	A103	5c red	50	12

Perf. 13½

No.	Type	Description	Unused	Used
322	A94	20c ultra.	5.00	50

San Martín

A104 A105

With Period after Value.

1923, May **Litho.** **Wmk. 90**

No.	Type	Description	Unused	Used
323	A104	½c red violet	30	8
324	"	1c buff	25	8
325	"	2c dark brown	15	6
326	"	3c light green	30	10
327	"	4c red brown	25	8
328	"	5c red	20	5
329	"	10c dull green	1.50	8
330	"	12c deep blue	25	8
331	"	20c ultramarine	1.00	8
332	"	24c light brown	2.75	50
333	"	30c claret	4.50	30
334	"	50c black	5.00	40

Without Period after Value.

Wmkd. Honeycomb. (87) *Perf. 13½*

No.	Type	Description	Unused	Used
335	A105	1p blue & red	2.75	8
336	"	5p gray lilac & green	17.50	2.75
		Punch cancel		30
337	"	10p claret & blue	40.00	7.50
		Punch cancel		50
338	"	20p slate & brown lake	60.00	14.00
		Punch cancel		30
		a. Center inverted		
		Nos. 323-338 (16)	136.70	26.22

Nos. 335 to 338 and 353 to 356 cancelled with round or oval killers in purple (revenue cancellations) sell for one-fifth to one-half the price of postally used copies.

Design of 1923.

Without Period after Value.

Wmkd. RA in Sun. (90)

1923–31 *Perf. 13½, 13½x12½*

No.	Type	Description	Unused	Used
340	A104	½c red violet	10	4
341	"	1c buff	10	4
342	"	2c dark brown	10	4
343	"	3c green	10	4
		a. Imperf., pair	8.00	
		b. Typographed	1.00	8
344	"	4c red brown	20	5
345	"	5c red	10	3
		a. Typographed	1.00	6
346	"	10c dull green	25	3
		a. Typographed	2.50	8
347	"	12c deep blue	40	5
		a. Typographed	3.00	25
348	"	20c ultramarine	40	5
		a. Typographed	10.00	40
349	"	24c light brown	90	60
350	"	25c purple	30	5
		a. Typographed	5.00	18
351	"	30c claret	90	5
		a. Typographed	3.00	20
352	"	50c black	90	10
353	A105	1p blue & red	1.50	5

354 A105 5p dark violet & green 11.00 50
Punch cancel 20
355 " 10p claret & blue 25.00 2.50
Punch cancel 20
356 " 20p slate & lake 40.00 9.00
Punch cancel 15
Nos. 340–356 (17) 82.25 13.22

There were two printings of many of the stamps of type A104: lithographed (1923–24), clear impression, and typographed (1931–33), rough impression with heavy shading about the eyes and nose. The typographed sheets were often torn into strips and rolled to form coils. Nos. 343 and 346 are known without watermark.

The 1c through 5c and 12c through 30c may be found in vertical pairs, one without period.

See note after No. 338. See also Nos. 362–368.

Rivadavia
A106

1926, Feb. 8 ***Perf. 13½***

357 A106 5c rose 35 25

Issued in commemoration of the centenary of the Presidency of Bernardino Rivadavia.

Rivadavia
A108

San Martín
A109

General Post Office, 1926
A110

General Post Office, 1826
A111

1926, July 1 ***Perf. 13½x12½***

358 A108 3c gray green 30 12
359 A109 5c red 20 5

Perf. 13½

360 A110 12c deep blue 50 15
361 A111 25c chocolate 75 12
a. "1326" for "1826" 2.00 1.00

Centenary of the Post Office.

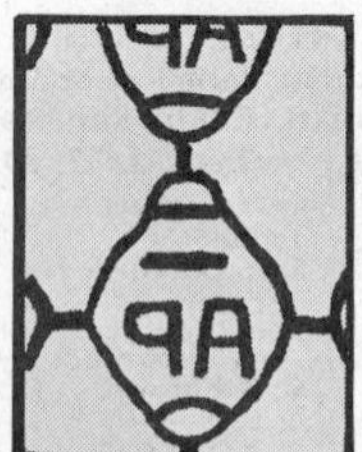

Wmk. 205

The letters "A. P." in the watermark are the initials of "AHORRO POSTAL". This paper was formerly used exclusively for Postal Savings stamps.

Type of 1923-31 Issue.
Without Period after Value.
Wmkd. AP in Oval. (205)

1927 ***Perf. 13½x12½***

362 A104 ½c red violet 25 20
a. Pelure paper 75 25
363 A104 1c buff 25 12
364 " 2c dark brown 30 12
a. Pelure paper 50 15
365 " 5c red 30 8
a. Period after value 4.00 1.75
b. Pelure paper 50 12
366 " 10c dull green 2.50 35
367 " 20c ultramarine 9.00 2.25

Perf. 13½

368 A105 1p blue & red 17.50 3.00
Nos. 362–368 (7) 30.10 6.12

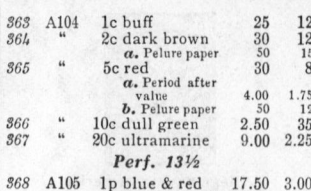

Arms of Argentina and Brazil
A112

Wmkd. RA in Sun. (90)

1928, Aug. 27 ***Perf. 12½x13***

369 A112 5c rose red 1.25 40
370 " 12c deep blue 1.75 60

Commemorative of the centenary of peace between the Empire of Brazil and the United Provinces of the Rio de la Plata.

Allegory, Discovery of the New World
A113

"Spain" and "Argentina"
A114

"America" Offering Laurels to Columbus
A115

1929, Oct. 12 Litho. ***Perf. 13½***

371 A113 2c lilac brown 75 25
372 A114 5c light red 1.00 15
373 A115 12c dull blue 1.25 30

Issued to commemorate the 437th anniversary of the discovery of America by Columbus.

Spirit of Victory Attending Insurgents
A116

March of the Victorious Insurgents
A117

Perf. 13½x12½ **(A116),**
12½x13 **(A117)**

1930

374 A116 ½c violet gray 30 15
375 " 1c myrtle green 50 25
376 A117 2c dull violet 35 15
377 A116 3c green 60 30
378 " 4c violet 50 30
379 " 5c rose red 25 5
380 " 10c gray black 1.50 30
381 A117 12c dull blue 1.00 20
382 " 20c ochre 75 25
383 " 24c red brown 2.25 1.00
384 " 25c green 3.00 1.25
385 " 30c deep violet 4.00 1.25
386 " 50c black 7.00 2.00
387 " 1p slate bl. & red 13.50 6.00
388 " 2p blk. & orange 22.50 6.00
389 A117 5p dull green & black 55.00 27.50
390 " 10p dp. red brown & dull blue 65.00 22.50
391 " 20p yellow green & dull blue 250.00 75.00
392 " 50p dark green & violet 650.00 400.00
Nos. 374–392 (19) 1078.00 544.45

Issued to commemorate the Revolution of 1930.

Nos. 387 to 392 with oval (parcel post) cancellation sell for one-fifth of above prices.

1931 ***Perf. 12½x13***

393 A117 ½c red violet 12 12
394 " 1c gray black 30 30
395 " 3c green 25 20
396 " 4c red brown 25 15
397 " 5c red 15 5
a. Plane omitted, top left corner 1.75 1.00
398 A117 10c dull green 50 25
Nos. 393–398 (6) 1.57 1.07

Issued to commemorate the Revolution of 1930.

Stamps of 1924-25 Overprinted in Red or Green — **-6- Septiembre 1930 - 1931**

Perf. 13½, 13½x12½

1931, Sept. 6

399 A104 3c green (R) 25 25
400 " 10c dull green (R) 30 30
401 " 30c claret (G) 3.50 2.00
402 " 50c black (R) 3.50 2.00

Overprinted in Blue — **1930 Septiembre 6 1931**

403 A105 1p blue & red 4.00 2.00
404 " 5p dark violet & green 27.50 12.50

No. 388 Overprinted in Blue
6 Septiembre 1931

Perf. 12½x13

405 A117 2p black & orange 9.00 4.00
Nos. 399–405 (7) 48.05 23.05

Issued in commemoration of the first anniversary of the Revolution of 1930.

Refrigeration Compressor
A118

Lithographed.

1932, Aug. 29 ***Perf. 13½x12½***

406 A118 3c green 1.00 20
407 " 10c scarlet 1.00 15
408 " 12c gray blue 1.50 30

Issued to commemorate the sixth International Refrigeration Congress.

Port of La Plata
A119

President Julio A. Roca
A120

Municipal Palace
A121

Cathedral of La Plata
A122

Dardo Rocha
A123

Perf. 13½x13, 13x13½ **(10c)**

1933, Jan.

409 A119 3c green & dark brown 75 25
410 A120 10c org. & dk. vio. 75 25
411 A121 15c dark blue & deep blue 5.00 1.50
412 A122 20c violet & yellow brown 2.50 75
413 A123 30c dark green & vio. brown 12.50 4.00
Nos. 409–413 (5) 21.50 6.75

Issued in commemoration of the 50th anniversary of the founding of the city of La Plata, November 19th, 1882.

Christ of the Andes
A124

Buenos Aires Cathedral
A125

Perf. 13x13½, 13½x13

1934, Oct. 1

414 A124 10c rose & brown 1.00 30
415 A125 15c dark blue 1.00 30

Issued to commemorate the 32nd International Eucharistic Congress, Oct. 10–14, 1934.

"Liberty" with Arms of Brazil and Argentina
A126

Symbolical of "Peace" and "Friendship"
A127

1935, May 15 *Perf. 13x13½*

416 A126 10c red 1.00 25
417 A127 15c blue 1.50 35

Visit of Pres. Getulio Vargas of Brazil.

Belgrano
A128

Sarmiento
A129

Urquiza
A130

Louis Braille
A131

San Martín
A132

Brown
A133

Moreno
A134

Alberdi
A135

Nicolás Avellaneda
A136

Rivadavia
A137

Mitre
A138

Bull (Cattle Breeding)
A139

Martín Güemes
A140

Agriculture
A141

Oil Well (Petroleum)
A144

Merino Sheep (Wool)
A142

Sugar Cane
A143

Map of South America
A145 A146

Fruit
A147

Iguassú Falls (Scenic Wonders)
A148

Grapes (Vineyards)
A149

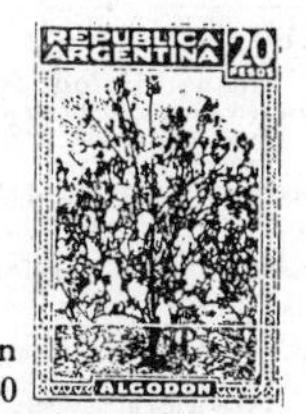

Cotton
A150

Two types of the 20c.
Type I—Inscribed Juan Martín Guemes.
Type II—Inscribed Martin Güemes.

Lithographed

Wmkd. RA in Sun. (90)

1935-51 *Perf. 13, 13½x13, 13x13½*

418 A128 ½c red violet 10 3
419 A129 1c buff 10 3
a. Typographed 10 3
420 A130 2c darkbrown 10 3
421 A131 2½c black ('39) 25 6
422 A132 3c green 15 4
423 " 3c light gray ('39) 15 3
424 A134 3c light gray ('46) 35 6
425 A133 4c light gray 20 3
426 " 4c sage green ('39) 20 3
427 A134 5c yellow brown 20 3
a. Tête bêche pair 1.00 40
b. Booklet pane of 8
c. Booklet pane of
d. Typographed 15 4
428 A135 6c olive green 30 4
429 A136 8c orange ('39) 20 9
430 A137 10c carmine 40 3
a. Typographed 50 4
431 " 10c brown ('42) 30 3
a. Typographed 25 4
432 A138 12c brown 20 8
433 " 12c red ('39) 20 5
434 A139 15c slate blue ('36) 50 5
435 " 15c pale ultra. ('39) 60 4
436 A140 15c light gray blue (II) ('42) 10.00 2.00
437 " 20c light ultra. (I) 50 6
438 " 20c light ultramarine (II) ('36) 30 4
439 " 20c blue gray (II) ('39) 50 4
439A A139 20c dark blue & pale blue, 22x33mm ('42) 50 3
440 " 20c blue ('51) 15 3
a. Typographed 15 3
441 A141 25c carmine ('36) 30 3
442 A142 30c orange brown ('36) 1.00 4
443 A143 40c dark violet ('36) 75 5
444 A144 50c red & orange ('36) 50 3
445 A145 1p brown black & lt. blue ('36) 10.00 40
446 A146 1p brown black & lt. blue ('37) 1.25 6
a. Chalky paper 7.50 12
447 A147 2p brown lake & dk. ultra. ('36) 2.00 8
448 A148 5p indigo & olive green ('36) 5.00 12
449 A149 10p brown lake & black 20.00 25
450 A150 20p blue green & brown ('36) 40.00 80
Nos. 418-450 (34) 97.25 4.84

No. 439A exists with label, showing medallion, attached. The pair sells for 10 times the price of the single stamp.

See also Nos. 485-500, 523-540, 659 and 668.

Souvenir Sheet.

A151

Without Period after Value.

1935, Oct. 17 **Litho.** ***Imperf.***

452 A151 10c dull green, sheet of four 40.00 25.00
a. Single stamp 6.50 4.00

Issued in commemoration of the Philatelic Exhibition at Buenos Aires, October 17–24, 1935. The stamps were on sale during the eight days of the exhibition only. Sheets measure 83x101mm.

Plaque
A152

1936, Dec. 1 *Perf. 13x13½*

453 A152 10c rose 50 20

Issued in commemoration of the Inter-American Conference for Peace.

Domingo Faustino Sarmiento
A153

"Presidente Sarmiento"
A154

1938, Sept. 5

454 A153 3c sage green 25 15
455 " 5c red 35 5
456 " 15c deep blue 50 25
457 " 50c orange 1.00 50

Issued in commemoration of the 50th anniversary of the death of Domingo Faustino Sarmiento, president, educator and author.

1939, Mar. 16

458 A154 5c greenish blue 25 18

Issued in commemoration of the final voyage of the training ship "Presidente Sarmiento."

Allegory of the Universal Postal Union
A155

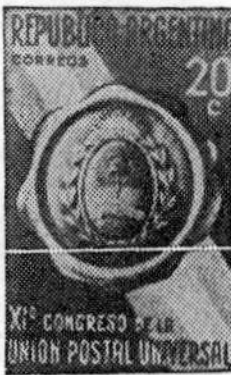

Coat of Arms
A157

Post Office, Buenos Aires
A156

Iguassú Falls
A158

Bonete Hill, Nahuel Huapi Park
A159

Allegory of Modern Communications
A160

Argentina, Land of Promise
A161

Lake Frias, Nahuel Huapi Park
A162

Perf. 13x13½, 13½x13

1939, Apr. 1 **Photogravure**

459	A155	5c rose carmine	50	10
460	A156	15c greenish black	50	20
461	A157	20c bright blue	50	20
462	A158	25c dp. blue green	1.50	50
463	A159	50c brown	1.50	50
464	A160	1p brown violet	2.50	75
465	A161	2p magenta	12.50	5.00
466	A162	5p purple	30.00	12.50
		Nos. 459-466 (8)	49.50	19.75

Universal Postal Union, 11th Congress.

Souvenir Sheets.

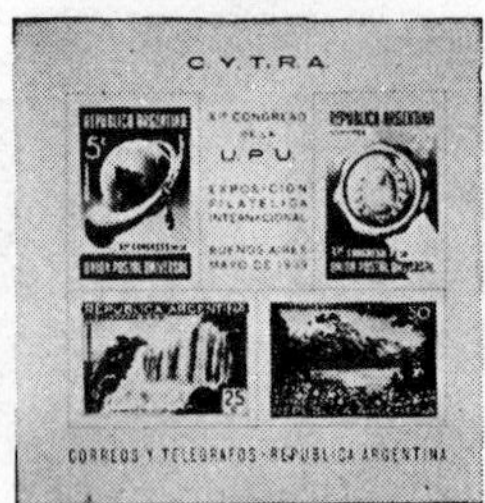

A163

A164

1939, May 12 ***Imperf.*** **Wmk. 90**

467 A163 Sheet of four 6.00 6.00
- *a.* 5c rose carmine (A155) 1.00 1.00
- *b.* 20c bright blue (A157) 1.00 1.00
- *c.* 25c deep blue green (A158) 1.00 1.00
- *d.* 50c brown (A159) 1.00 1.00

468 A164 Sheet of four 6.00 6.00

Issued in four forms:
- *a.* Unsevered horizontal pair of sheets
  Type A163 at left
  Type A164 at right 12.50 12.50
- *b.* Unsevered vertical pair of sheets
  Type A163 at top
  Type A164 at bottom 12.50 12.50
- *c.* Unsevered block of four sheets
  Type A163 at left
  Type A164 at right 70.00 70.00
- *d.* Unsevered block of four sheets
  Type A163 at top
  Type A164 at bottom 70.00 70.00

Issued in commemoration of the 11th Congress of the Universal Postal Union and the Argentina International Philatelic Exposition (C.Y.T.R.A.).

No. 468 contains one each of Nos. 467a-467d.

Size: No. 468a, 190x95mm. No. 468b, 95x190mm.

Family and New House
A165

Perf. 13½x13

1939, Oct. 2 **Litho.** **Wmk. 90**

469 A165 5c bluish green 25 6

Issued to commemorate the first Pan-American Housing Congress.

Bird Carrying Record
A166

Head of Liberty and Arms of Argentina
A167

Record and Winged Letter
A168

1939, Dec. 11 **Photo.** ***Perf. 13***

470	A166	1.18p indigo	12.50	6.00
471	A167	1.32p bright blue	12.50	6.00
472	A168	1.50p dark brown	30.00	10.00

These stamps were issued for the recording and mailing of flexible phonograph records.

Map of the Americas
A169

1940, Apr. 14 ***Perf. 13x13½***

473 A169 15c ultramarine 30 20

Issued to commemorate the 50th anniversary of the Pan American Union.

Souvenir Sheet.

Reproductions of Early Argentine Stamps
A170

Wmkd. RA in Sun. (90)

1940, May 25 **Litho.** ***Imperf.***

474 A170 Sheet of five 12.50 7.50
- *a.* 5c dk. bl. (*Corrientes*) 1.50 1.00
- *b.* 5c red (*Argentine Republic*) 1.50 1.00
- *c.* 5c dark blue (*Cordoba*) 1.50 1.00
- *d.* 5c red (*Argentine Republic*) 1.50 1.00
- *e.* 10c dark blue (*Buenos Aires*) 1.50 1.00

Issued in sheets measuring 111x116mm., in commemoration of the 100th anniversary of the first postage stamp.

General Domingo French and Colonel Antonio Beruti
A171

1941, Feb. 20 ***Perf. 13½x13***

475 A171 5c dark gray blue & light blue 15 6

Issued in honor of General French and Colonel Beruti, patriots.

Marco M. de Avellaneda
A172

Statue of Gen. Julio Roca
A173

1941, Oct. 3 ***Perf. 13x13½***

476 A172 5c dull slate blue 12 5

Issued in commemoration of the centenary of the death of Marco M. de Avellaneda, (1814-41), Army leader and martyr.

1941, Oct. 19 **Photo.** **Wmk. 90**

477 A173 5c dark olive green 15 6

Issued to commemorate the dedication of a monument to Lt. Gen. Julio Argentino Roca (1843-1914).

Carlos Pellegrini and Bank of the Nation
A174

1941, Oct. 26 ***Perf. 13½x13***

478 A174 5c brown carmine 12 5

Issued to commemorate the 50th anniversary of the founding of the Bank of the Nation.

Gen. Juan Lavalle
A175

1941, Dec. 5 ***Perf. 13x13½***

479 A175 5c bright blue 18 6

Issued to commemorate the centenary of the death of Gen. Juan Galo de Lavalle (1797-1841).

National Postal Savings Bank
A176

1942, Apr. 5 **Litho.** ***Perf. 13½x13***

480 A176 1c pale olive 8 5

José Manuel Estrada
A177

1942, July 13 ***Perf. 13x13½***

481 A177 5c brown violet 20 6

Issued to commemorate the centenary of the birth of José Estrada (1842-1894), writer and diplomat.

No. 481 exists with label, showing medallion, attached. The pair sells for 15 times the price of the single stamp.

Wmk. 288

Types of 1935-51.

Wmkd. RA in Sun with Straight Rays. (288)

Perf. 13, 13x13½, 13½x13.

1942-50 **Lithographed.**

485	A128	½c brown violet	4.00	40
486	A129	1c buff ('50)	10	4
487	A130	2c dark brown ('50)	10	4
488	A132	3c light gray	10.00	50
489	A134	3c light gray ('49)	15	5
490	A137	10c red brown ('49)	20	5
491	A138	12c red	50	10
492	A140	15c light gray blue (II)	25	5
493	A139	20c dark slate blue & pale blue	35	3
494	A141	25c dull rose ('49)	75	3
495	A142	30c orange brown ('49)	75	6
496	A143	40c violet ('49)	1.75	8
497	A144	50c red & orange ('49)	1.75	8
498	A146	1p brown black & light blue	3.00	6
499	A147	2p brown lake & blue ('49)	5.00	40

500 A148 5p indigo & olive green ('49) 25.00 1.10
Nos. 485-500 (16) 53.65 3.07

No. 493 measures 22x33mm.

Post Office, Buenos Aires
A178

Proposed Columbus Lighthouse
A179

Inscribed: "Correos y Telegrafos".

1942, Oct. 5 Litho. *Perf. 13*

503 A178 35c light ultramarine 25 6

See also Nos. 541-543.

1942, Oct. 12 **Wmk. 288**

504 A179 15c dull blue 20 10

Wmk. 90

505 A179 15c dull blue 30.00 3.00

Nos. 504-505 were issued to commemorate the 450th anniversary of the discovery of America by Columbus.

José C. Paz
A180

Books and Argentine Flag
A181

1942, Dec. 15 **Wmk. 288**

506 A180 5c dark gray 12 5

Issued in commemoration of the centenary of the birth of José C. Paz, statesman and founder of the newspaper La Prensa.

1943, Apr. 1 Litho. *Perf. 13*

507 A181 5c dull blue 10 5

Issued to commemorate the first Book Fair of Argentina.

Arms of Argentina Inscribed "Honesty, Justice, Duty"
A182

1943-50 *Perf. 13* **Wmk. 288**

Size: 20x26mm.

508 A182 5c red ('50) 35 4

Wmk. 90

509 A182 5c red 25 4
a. 5c dull red, unsurfaced paper 1.00 8
510 " 15c green 35 15

Perf. 13x13½

Size: 22x33mm.

511 A182 20c dark blue 35 15

Issued to commemorate the change of political organization on June 4, 1943.

Independence House, Tucuman
A183

Liberty Head and Savings Bank
A184

1943-51 *Perf. 13* **Wmk. 90**

512 A183 5c blue green 50 8

Wmk. 288

513 A183 5c blue green ('51) 50 8

Issued to commemorate the restoration of Independence House.

1943, Oct. 25 **Wmk. 90**

514 A184 5c violet brown 10 5

Wmk. 288

515 A184 5c violet brown 12.00 2.00

Issued to commemorate the first conference of National Postal Savings.

Port of Buenos Aires in 1800
A185

1943, Dec. 11 **Wmk. 90**

516 A185 5c gray black 10 5

Day of Exports.

Warship, Merchant Ship and Sailboat
A186

Arms of Argentine Republic
A187

1944, Jan. 31 *Perf. 13*

517 A186 5c blue 12 6

Issued to commemorate Sea Week.

1944, June 4

518 A187 5c dull blue 12 6

Issued to commemorate the first anniversary of the change of political organization in Argentina.

St. Gabriel
A188

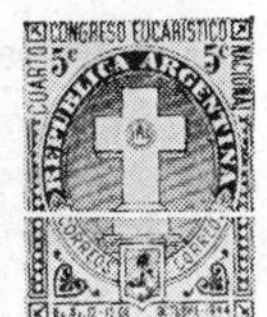

Cross at Palermo
A189

1944, Oct. 11

519 A188 3c yellow green 15 8
520 A189 5c deep rose 15 8

Fourth national Eucharistic Congress.

Allegory of Savings
A190

Reservists
A191

1944, Oct. 24

521 A190 5c gray 10 5

Issued to commemorate the 20th anniversary of the National Savings Bank.

1944, Dec. 1

522 A191 5c blue 10 5

Day of the Reservists.

Types of 1935-51.

Perf. 13x13½, 13½x13.

1945-47 Lithographed. **Unwmkd.**

523 A128 ½c brn. vio. ('46) 10 3
524 A129 1c yellow brown 10 3
525 A130 2c sepia 10 3
526 A132 3c light gray (*San Martin*) 15 5
527 A134 3c light gray (*Moreno*) ('46) 10 4
528 A135 6c olive green ('47) 25 10
529 A137 10c brown ('46) 40 5
530 A140 15c light gray blue (II) 30 3
531 A139 20c dark slate blue & pale blue 35 3
532 A141 25c dull rose 40 3
533 A142 30c orange brown 50 3
534 A143 40c violet 1.25 4
535 A144 50c red & orange 1.00 4
536 A146 1p brown black & light blue 1.25 6
537 A147 2p brn. lake & bl. 3.00 12
538 A148 5p indigo & olive green ('46) 30.00 1.00
539 A149 10p deep claret & intense black 6.00 1.00
540 A150 20p blue green & brown ('46) 9.00 1.00
Nos. 523-540 (18) 54.25 3.71

No. 531 measures 22x33mm.

Post Office Type

Inscribed: "Correos y Telecommunicaciones".

1945 *Perf. 13x13½* **Unwmkd.**

541 A178 35c light ultramarine 50 5

Wmk. 90

542 A178 35c light ultramarine 40 5

Wmk. 288

543 A178 35c light ultramarine 25 5

Bernardino Rivadavia
A192 A193

Mausoleum of Rivadavia
A194

Perf. 13½x13.

1945, Sept. 1 Litho. **Unwmkd.**

544 A192 3c blue green 15 6
545 A193 5c rose 20 5
546 A194 20c blue 25 6

Issued to commemorate the centenary of the death of Bernardino Rivadavia, Argentina's first president.

No. 546 exists with mute label attached. The pair sells for four times the price of the single stamp.

General José de San Martin
A195

Monument to Army of the Andes, Mendoza
A196

Lithographed or Typographed.

1945-46 **Wmk. 90**

547 A195 5c carmine, typo. 12 6
a. Lithographed ('46) 15 6

Wmk. 288

548 A195 5c carmine, litho. 60.00 15.00

Unwmkd.

549 A195 5c car., typo. ('46) 15 5
a. Lithographed ('46) 15 5

1946, Jan. 14 Litho. *Perf. 13½x13*

550 A196 5c violet brown 10 5

Issued to honor the Unknown Soldier of the War for Independence.

Franklin D. Roosevelt
A197

Liberty Administering Presidential Oath—A198

1946, Apr. 12

551 A197 5c slate black 12 8

Issued in memory of Franklin D. Roosevelt.

1946, June 4 *Perf. 13x13½*

552 A198 5c blue 10 5

Issued to commemorate the inauguration of President Juan D. Perón, June 4, 1946.

Argentina Receiving Popular Acclaim
A199

1946, Oct. 17 *Perf. 13½x13*

553 A199 5c rose violet 25 10
554 " 10c blue green 35 15
555 " 15c dark blue 75 20
556 " 50c red brown 1.00 35
557 " 1p carmine rose 2.00 1.00
Nos. 553-557 (5) 4.35 1.80

First anniversary of the political organization change of Oct. 17, 1945.

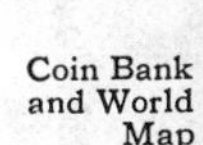

Coin Bank and World Map
A200

1946, Oct. 31 **Unwmkd.**

558 A200 30c dark rose carmine & pink 40 15

Issued to commemorate the Universal Day of Savings, October 31, 1946.

Argentine Industry
A201

International Bridge Connecting Argentina and Brazil
A202

1946, Dec. 6 ***Perf. 13x13½***
559 A201 5c violet brown 10 5
Day of Argentine Industry, Dec. 6.

1947, May 21 Litho. ***Perf. 13½x13***
560 A202 5c green 10 5
Issued to commemorate the opening of the Argentina-Brazil International Bridge, May 21, 1947.

Map of Argentine Antarctic Claims
A203

Justice
A204

1947–49 ***Perf. 13x13½*** **Unwmkd.**
561 A203 5c violet & lilac 10 6
562 " 20c dark carmine rose & rose 30 6

Wmk. 90
563 A203 20c dark carmine rose & rose 60 10

Wmk. 288
564 A203 20c dark carmine rose & rose ('49) 75 15
Issued to note the 43rd anniversary of the first Argentine Antarctic mail.

1947, June 4 **Unwmkd.**
565 A204 5c brown violet & pale yellow 10 5
Issued to commemorate the 1st anniversary of the Perón government.

Icarus Falling
A205

1947, Sept. 25 ***Perf. 13½x13***
566 A205 15c red violet 15 8
Aviation Week.

Training Ship Presidente Sarmiento
A206

1947, Oct. 5 ***Perf. 13x13½***
567 A206 5c blue 15 7
Issued to commemorate the 50th anniversary of the launching of the Argentine training frigate "Presidente Sarmiento".

Cervantes and Characters from Don Quixote—A207

Perf. 13½x13
1947, Oct. 12 Photo. **Wmk. 90**
568 A207 5c olive green 10 5
Issued to commemorate the 400th anniversary of the birth of Miguel de Cervantes Saavedra, playwright and poet.

Gen. José de San Martín
A208

Lithographed.
1947–49 ***Perf. 13½x13*** **Unwmkd.**
569 A208 5c dull green 12 6

Wmk. 288
570 A208 5c dull green ('49) 16 4
Issued to commemorate the transfer of the remains of Gen. José de San Martín's parents.

School Children
A209

Statue of Araucanian Indian
A210

1947–49 ***Perf. 13x13½*** **Unwmkd.**
571 A209 5c green 8 4

Wmk. 90
574 A209 20c brown 16 8

Wmk. 288
575 A209 5c green 15 5
Argentine School Crusade for World Peace.

1948, May 21 **Wmk. 90**
576 A210 25c yellow brown 20 12
American Indian Day, Apr. 19.

Cap of Liberty
A211

Manual Stop Signal
A212

1948, July 16
577 A211 5c ultramarine 10 5
Issued to commemorate the 5th anniversary of the Revolution of June 4, 1943.

1948, July 22
578 A212 5c choc. & yellow 10 5
Traffic Safety Day, June 10.

Post Horn and Oak Leaves
A213

Argentine Farmers
A214

1948, July 22 **Unwmkd.**
579 A213 5c lilac rose 12 5
Issued to commemorate the 200th anniversary of the establishment of regular postal service on the Plata River.

Perf. 13x13½
1948, Sept. 20 **Wmk. 288**
580 A214 10c red brown 12 6
Agriculture Day, Sept. 8, 1948.

Liberty and Symbols of Progress
A215

Wmk. 287
Wmkd. Double Circle and Letters in Sheet. (287)

1948, Nov. 23 Photo. ***Perf. 13x13½***
581 A215 25c red brown 15 6
Issued to commemorate the third anniversary of President Juan D. Peron's return to power, October 17, 1945.

Souvenir Sheets.

A216

Designs: 15c, Mail coach. 45c, Buenos Aires in 18th century. 55c, First train, 1857. 85c, Sailing ship, 1767.

1948, Dec. 21 ***Imperf.*** **Unwmkd.**
582 A216 Sheet of four 2.50 2.50
a. 15c dark green 50 50
b. 45c orange brown 50 50
c. 55c lilac brown 50 50
d. 85c ultramarine 50 50

A217

Designs: 85c, Domingo de Basavilibaso (1709–75). 1.05p, Postrider. 1.20p, Sailing ship, 1798. 1.90p, Courier in the Andes, 1772.

583 A217 Sheet of four 7.00 7.00
a. 85c brown 1.50 1.50
b. 1.05p dark green 1.50 1.50
c. 1.20p dark blue 1.50 1.50
d. 1.90p red brown 1.50 1.50

Issued in sheets measuring 143x101mm. (No. 582) and 101x143mm. (No. 583) to commemorate the 200th anniversary of the establishment of regular postal service on the Plata River.

Winged Wheel
A218

Perf. 13½x13
1949, Mar. 1 **Wmk. 288**
584 A218 10c blue 15 5
Nationalization of the railroads, first anniversary.

Liberty
A219

1949, June 20 Engraved Wmk. 90
585 A219 1p red & red violet 50 15
Ratification of the Constitution of 1949.

Allegory of the U.P.U.
A220

1949, Nov. 19
586 A220 25c dark green & yellow green 30 10
Issued to commemorate the 75th anniversary of the formation of the Universal Postal Union.

Gen. José de San Martín
A221

Mausoleum of San Martín
A223

San Martín at Boulogne sur Mer
A222

Designs: 20c, 50c, 75c, Different Portraits of San Martin. 1p, House where San Martin died.

Inscribed:
"Centenario de la Muerte del General Don José de San Martin 1850-1950."

Engraved, Photogravure (25c, 1p, 2p)

1950, Aug. 17 ***Perf. 13½*** **Wmk. 90**

587	A221	10c indigo & dark purple	15	5
588	"	20c red brown & dark brown	15	6
589	A222	25c brown	20	8
590	A221	50c dark green & indigo	30	10
591	"	75c choc. & dk. grn.	40	15
		a. Souv. sheet of 4	1.50	1.00
592	A222	1p dark green	75	20
593	A223	2p deep red lilac	1.00	25
		Nos. 587-593 (7)	2.95	89

Issued to commemorate the centenary of the death of General José de San Martin. No. 591a measures 120x150mm. and contains one each of Nos. 587, 588, 590 and 591, imperf., with marginal inscriptions and ornamental border in brown.

Map Showing Antarctic Claims
A224

1951, May 21 **Litho.** ***Perf. 13x13½***

594	A224	1p chocolate & light blue	30	3

Pegasus and Train
A225

Communications Symbols
A226

Design: 25c, Ship and dolphin.

1951, Oct. 17 **Photo.** ***Perf. 13½***

595	A225	5c dark brown	15	5
596	"	25c Prussian green	30	12
597	A226	40c rose brown	35	15

Close of Argentine Five Year Plan.

Woman Voter and "Argentina"
A227

1951, Dec. 14 ***Perf. 13½x13***

598	A227	10c brown violet	12	6

Granting of women's suffrage.

Eva Perón
A228 A229

Lithographed
or Engraved (#605).

1952, Aug. 26 ***Perf. 13*** **Wmk. 90**

599	A228	1c orange brown	10	5
600	"	5c gray	10	5
601	"	10c rose lilac	10	5
602	"	20c rose pink	10	5
603	"	25c dull green	10	8
604	"	40c dull violet	15	5
605	"	45c deep blue	20	10
606	"	50c dull brown	15	5

Photogravure

607	A229	1p dark brown	35	10
608	"	1.50p deep green	1.00	15
609	"	2p bright carmine	60	15
610	"	3p indigo	1.00	50
		Nos. 599-610 (12)	3.95	1.38

Inscribed: "Eva Perón."

1952-53 ***Perf. 13x13½***

611	A229	1p dark brown	60	5
612	"	1.50p deep green	75	5
613	"	2p brt. car. ('53)	1.50	15
614	"	3p indigo	2.25	20

Engraved

Size: 30x40mm.

Perf. 13½x13.

615	A229	5p red brown	2.25	75
616	A228	10p red	5.00	1.00
617	A229	20p green	12.50	5.00
618	A228	50p ultramarine	22.50	10.00
		Nos. 611-618 (8)	47.35	17.20

Indian Funeral Urn
A230

1953, Aug. 28 **Photo.** ***Perf. 13x13½***

619	A230	50c blue green	15	10

Issued to commemorate the 400th anniversary of the founding of Santiago del Estero.

Rescue Ship "Uruguay"
A231

1953, Oct. 8 ***Perf. 13½***

620	A231	50c ultramarine	35	12

Issued to commemorate the 50th anniversary of the rescue of the Antarctic expedition of Otto C. Nordenskjold.

Planting Argentine Flag in the Antarctic
A232

Engraved

1954, Jan. 20 ***Perf. 13½x13***

621	A232	1.45p blue	60	15

Issued to commemorate the 50th anniversary of Argentina's first antarctic post office and the establishing of the La Hoy radio post office in the South Orkneys.

Wired Communications
A233

Television
A234

Design: 3p, Radio.

Perf. 13x13½, 13½x13.

1954, Apr. **Photo.** **Wmk. 90**

622	A233	1.50p violet brown	50	25
623	"	3p violet blue	1.00	50
624	A234	5p carmine	2.00	1.00

Issued to publicize the International Plenipotentiary Conference of Telecommunications, Buenos Aires, 1952.

Pediment,
Buenos Aires Stock Exchange
A235

1954, July 13 ***Perf. 13½x13***

625	A235	1p dark green	35	10

Issued to commemorate the centenary of the establishment of the Buenos Aires Stock Exchange.

Eva Perón
A236

1954 **Wmk. 90**

626	A236	3p deep car. rose	1.50	60

Wmk. 288

627	A236	3p deep carmine rose	80.00	25.00

Issued to commemorate the second anniversary of the death of Eva Perón.

José de San Martin
A237

Eva Perón Foundation Building
A239

Wheat
A238

Industry
A238a

Cliffs of Humahuaca
A240

Gen. José de San Martin
A241

Designs: 50c, Buenos Aires harbor. 1p, Cattle ranch (Ganaderia). 3p, Nihuil Dam. 5p, Iguassu Falls (vert.). 20p, Mt. Fitz Roy (vert.).

Typographed.

1954-59 ***Perf. 13½*** **Wmk. 90**

628 A237 20c bright red 5 3

Lithographed.

629 A237 20c red ('55) 50 10
630 " 40c red ('56) 12 3

Typographed.

631 A237 40c bright red ('55) 10 3

Engraved.

632 A239 50c blue ('56) 6 3

Lithographed.

633 A239 50c blue ('59) 15 3

Photogravure.

Perf. 13x13½, 13½x13, 13½

634 A238 80c brown 10 4
635 A239 1p brown ('58) 30 3
636 A238a 1.50p ultra. ('58) 25 7
637 A239 2p dark rose lake 30 6

Engraved.

Perf. 13½

638 A239 3p violet brown ('56) 35 6
639 A240 5p gray green ('55) 1.50 6
640 " 10p yel. green ('55) 2.50 8

Perf. 13½x13, 13½

641 A240 20p dull violet ('55) 3.50 15
642 A241 50p ultramarine & indigo ('55) 4.50 50
Nos. 628-642 (15) 14.28 1.30

See Nos. 699-700. For similar designs inscribed "Republica Argentina" see Nos. 823-827, 890, 935, 937, 940, 990, 995, 1039, 1044, 1048.

Allegory
A242

1954, Aug. 26 **Typo.** ***Perf. 13½***

643 A242 1.50p slate black 40 10

Issued to commemorate the centenary of the establishment of the Buenos Aires Grain Exchange.

Clasped Hands and Congress Medal
A243

1955, Mar. 21 **Photo.** ***Perf. 13½x13***

644 A243 3p red brown 75 15

Issued to publicize the National Productivity and Social Welfare Congress.

Allegory of Aviation
A244

Argentina Breaking Chains
A245

Perf. 13½.

1955, June 18 **Wmk. 90**

645 A244 1.50p olive gray 40 8

Issued to commemorate the 25th anniversary of commercial aviation in Argentina.

1955, Oct. 16 **Lithographed**

647 A245 1.50p olive green 30 6

Liberation Revolution of Sept. 16, 1955.

Army Navy and Air Force Emblems—A246

Perf. 13½x13

1955, Dec. 31 **Photo.** **Wmk. 90**

648 A246 3p blue 40 10

"Brotherhood of the Armed Forces."

Justo José de Urquiza
A247

1956, Feb. 3 ***Perf. 13½***

649 A247 1.50p green 35 6

Battle of Caseros, 104th anniversary.

Coin and Die
A248

Engraved.

1956, July 28 ***Perf. 13½x13***

650 A248 2p gray brown & reddish brown 35 15

75th anniversary of the Argentine Mint.

1856 Stamp of Corrientes
A249

Juan G. Pujol
A250

Design: 2.40p, Stamp of 1860-78.

1956, Aug. 21

651 A249 40c dark green & blue 20 10
652 " 2.40p brown & lilac rose 40 12

Photogravure.

653 A250 4.40p bright blue 90 30
a. Souvenir sheet 1.75 1.75

Centenary of Argentine postage stamps.
No. 653a commemorates both the Argentine stamp centenary and the Philatelic Exhibition for the Centenary of Corrientes Stamps, Oct. 12-21. It is imperf. and contains one each of Nos. 651-653, with the 4.40p in photogravure and the other two stamps and border lithographed. Colors of 40c and 2.40p differ slightly from engraved stamps. Marginal inscriptions, coats of arms and scroll work in dull purple. Size: 146x170mm.

Felling Trees, La Pampa
A251

Maté Herb and Gourd, Misiones
A252

Design: 1p, Cotton plant and harvest, Chaco.

1956, Sept. 1 ***Perf. 13½***

654 A251 50c ultramarine 8 5
655 " 1p magenta 16 6
656 A252 1.50p green 30 8

Issued to commemorate the elevation of the territories of La Pampa, Chaco and Misiones to provinces.

"Liberty"
A253

Florentino Ameghino
A254

Photogravure.

1956, Sept. 15 ***Perf. 13½*** **Wmk. 90**

657 A253 2.40p lilac rose 40 20

Issued to commemorate the first anniversary of the Revolution of Liberation.

1956, Nov. 30

658 A254 2.40p brown 30 5

Issued to honor Florentino Ameghino (1854-1911), anthropologist.

Adm. Brown Type of 1935-51.

1956 **Lithographed** ***Perf. 13***

Two types:
I. Bust touches upper frame line of name panel at bottom.
II. White line separates bust from frame line.

Size: 19½-20½x26-27mm.

659 A133 20c dull purple (I) 20 3
a. Type II 20 3
b. Size 19¾x25¼ mm. (I) 15

Benjamin Franklin
A255

1956, Dec. 22 **Photo.** ***Perf. 13½***

660 A255 40c intense blue 30 8

Issued to commemorate the 250th anniversary of the birth of Benjamin Franklin.

Frigate "Hercules"
A256

Guillermo Brown
A257

1957, Mar. 2

661 A256 40c bright blue 12 6
662 A257 2.40p gray black 30 12

Issued to commemorate the centenary of the death of Admiral Guillermo (William) Brown (1777-1857), founder of the Argentine navy.

Roque Saenz Peña
A258

Church of Santo Domingo, 1807
A259

1957, Apr. 1

663 A258 4.40p greenish gray 40 12

Issued to honor Roque Saenz Peña (1851-1914), president in 1910-1914.

1957, July 6 **Wmk. 90**

664 A259 40c bright blue green 12 7

Issued to commemorate the 150th anniversary of the defense of Buenos Aires.

"La Portena"
A260

1957, Aug. 31 ***Perf. 13½*** **Wmk. 90**

665 A260 40c pale brown 12 7

Centenary of Argentine railroads.

Esteban Echeverria
A261

"Liberty"
A262

1957, Sept. 2 ***Perf. 13x13½***

666 A261 2p claret 20 5

Esteban Echeverria (1805-1851), poet.

1957, Sept. 28 *Perf. 13½*
667 A262 40c carmine rose 10 6
Constitutional reform convention.

Portrait Type of 1935-51.
Portrait: 5c, Jose Hernandez.

1957, Oct. 28 Litho. *Perf. 13½*
Size: 16½x22mm.
668 A128 5c buff 6 3

Oil Derrick and Hands Holding Oil

A263

Photogravure.
1957, Dec. 21 *Perf. 13½* **Wmk. 90**
669 A263 40c bright blue 10 6
Issued to commemorate the 50th anniversary of the national oil industry.

Museum, La Plata
A264

1958, Jan. 11
670 A264 40c dark gray 10 6
City of La Plata, 75th anniversary.

Locomotive and Arms of Argentina and Bolivia
A265

Map of Argentine-Bolivian Boundary and Plane
A266

1958, Apr. 19 *Perf. 13½* **Wmk. 90**
671 A265 40c slate & dp. car. 15 8
672 A266 1p dark brown 15 8
Issued to celebrate Argentine-Bolivian friendship. No. 671 commemorates the opening of the Jacuiba-Santa Cruz railroad; No. 672, the exchange of presidential visits.

Symbols of the Republic
A267

Flag Monument
A268

Engraved and Photogravure
1958, Apr. 30 **Wmk. 90**
673 A267 40c multicolored 12 4
674 " 1p " 18 6
675 " 2p " 30 12
Transmission of Presidential power.

1958, June 21 Litho. Wmk. 90
676 A268 40c blue & violet blue 12 6
Issued to commemorate the first anniversary of the Flag Monument of Rosario.

Map of Antarctica
A269

Stamp of Cordoba and Mail Coach
A270

1958, July 12 *Perf. 13½*
677 A269 40c carmine rose & black 12 6
International Geophysical Year, 1957-58.

1958, Oct. 18
678 A270 40c pale blue & slate 16 8
Centenary of Cordoba postage stamps.
See also Nos. C72-C73.

"Slave" by Michelangelo and U. N. Emblem
A271

Engraved and Lithographed
1959, Mar. 14 *Perf. 13½* **Wmk. 90**
679 A271 40c violet brown & gray 12 8
Issued to commemorate the tenth anniversary (in 1958) of the signing of the Universal Declaration of Human Rights.

Orchids and Globe
A272

1959, May 23 Photo. *Perf. 13½*
680 A272 1p dull claret 16 6
1st International Horticulture Exposition.

Pope Pius XII
A273

William Harvey
A274

1959, June 20 Engraved *Perf. 13½*
681 A273 1p yellow & black 15 6
Issued in memory of Pope Pius XII, 1876-1958.

1959, Aug. 8 Litho. Wmk. 90
Portraits: 1p, Claude Bernard. 1.50p, Ivan P. Pavlov.
682 A274 50c green 6 5
683 " 1p dark red 12 6
684 " 1.50p brown 18 8
Issued to publicize the 21st International Congress of Physiological Sciences, Buenos Aires.

Type of 1958 and

Domestic Horse
A275

José de San Martin
A276

Tierra del Fuego
A277

Inca Bridge, Mendoza
A278

Ski Jumper
A279

Mar del Plata
A280

Designs: 10c, Cayman. 20c, Llama. 50c, Puma. No. 690, Sunflower. 3p, Zapata Slope, Catamarca. 12p, 23p, 25p, Red quebracho tree. 20p, Nahuel Huapi Lake. 22p, "Industry" (cogwheel and factory).
Two overall paper sizes for 1p, 5p:
I. 27x37½mm. or 37½x27mm.
II. 27x39mm. or 39x27mm.

Perf. 13x13½
1959-70 Lithographed Wmk. 90
685 A275 10c slate green 3 3
686 " 20c dull red brown ('61) 3 3
687 " 50c bis., litho. ('60) 5 3
688 " 50c bister, typo. ('60) 4 3
689 " 1p rose red 4 3

Perf. 13½
690 A278 1p brown, photo., paper I ('61) 5 3
a. Paper II ('69) 5 3
690B A278 1p brown, litho., paper I 5 3
691 A276 2p rose red, litho. ('61) 25 6
692 A276 2p red, typo. (19½X26mm.) ('61) 1.00 3
a. Redrawn (19¾x25mm.) 10 3
693 A277 3p dk. blue, photo. ('60) 20 3
694 A276 4p red, typo. ('62) 25 3
694A " 4p red, litho. ('62) 50 3
695 A277 5p gray brn., photo., paper I 25 4
e. 5p dk. brn., paper II ('70) 12 4
695A A276 8p verm., litho. ('65) 50 6
695B " 8p red, typo. ('65) 35 5
695C " 10p verm., litho. ('66) 50 8
695D " 10p red, typo. ('66?) 40 6

Photogravure
696 A278 10p light red brown ('60) 40 9
697 " 12p dk. brn. violet ('62) 30 5
697A " 12p dark brown, litho. ('64) 6.00 6
698 " 20p Prussian green ('60) 1.50 8
698A A276 20p red, typo. ('67) 25 5
699 A238a 22p ultra. ('62) 1.00 8
700 " 22p ultra., litho. ('62) 17.50 10
701 A278 23p green ('65) 2.00 6
702 " 25p dp. vio. ('66) 1.00 6
703 " 25p purple, litho. ('66?) 4.00 6
704 A279 100p blue ('61) 4.00 15
705 A280 300p dp. vio. ('62) 2.00 40
Nos. 685-705 (28) 44.44 1.92
See Nos. 882-887, 889, 892, 923-925, 928-930, 938, 987-989, 991.
The 300p remained on sale as a 3p stamp after the 1970 currency exchange.

Symbolic Sailboat
A281

Child Playing with Doll
A282

1959, Oct. 3 Litho. *Perf. 13½*
706 A281 1p black, red & blue 10 5
Red Cross sanitary education campaign.

1959, Oct. 17
707 A282 1p red & black 10 5
Issued for Mother's Day, 1959.

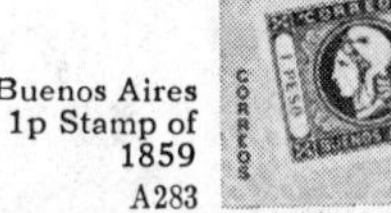

Buenos Aires 1p Stamp of 1859
A283

1959, Nov. 21 *Perf. 13½* **Wmk. 90**
708 A283 1p gray & dark blue 12 6
Issued for the Day of Philately.

Bartolomé Mitre and Justo José de Urquiza
A284

1959, Dec. 12 Photo. *Perf. 13½*
709 A284 1p purple 10 5
Treaty of San Jose de Flores, centenary.

WRY Emblem A285 — Abraham Lincoln A286

1960, Apr. 7 Litho. **Wmk. 90**

710 A285 1p bistre & carmine 8 6
711 " 4.20p apple green & deep claret 25 18

World Refugee Year, July 1, 1959–June 30, 1960. See also No. B25.

1960, Apr. 14 Photo. ***Perf. 13½***

712 A286 5p ultramarine 30 15

Issued to commemorate the sesquicentennial (in 1959) of the birth of Abraham Lincoln.

Cornelio Saavedra and Cabildo, Buenos Aires—A287

"Cabildo" and: 2p, Juan José Paso. 4.20p, Manuel Alberti and Miguel Azcuénaga. 10.70p, Juan Larrea and Domingo Matheu.

Photogravure

1960, May 28 *Perf. 13½* Wmk. 90

713 A287 1p rose lilac 8 5
714 " 2p bluish green 10 6
715 " 4.20p gray & green 25 12
716 " 10.70p gray & ultra. 50 25
Nos. 713-716, C75-C76 (6) 1.30 73

150th anniversary of the May Revolution. Souvenir sheets are Nos. C75a and C76a.

Luis Maria Drago A288 — Juan Bautista Alberdi A289

1960, July 8

717 A288 4.20p brown 15 8

Issued to commemorate the centenary of the birth of Dr. Luis Maria Drago, statesman and jurist.

1960, Sept. 10 *Perf. 13½* Wmk. 90

718 A289 1p green 8 6

Issued to commemorate the 150th anniversary of the birth of Juan Bautista Alberdi, statesman and philosopher.

Map of Argentina and Antarctic Sector A290 — Caravel and Emblem A291

1960, Sept. 24 Litho. ***Perf. 13½***

719 A290 5p violet 35 12

National census of 1960.

1960, Oct. 1 Photogravure

720 A291 1p dark olive green 10 6
721 " 5p brown 40 18

Issued to commemorate the 8th Congress of the Postal Union of the Americas and Spain. See also Nos. C78-C79.

Virgin of Luján, Patroness of Argentina—A292 — Argentine Boy Scout Emblem—A293

1960, Nov. 12 *Perf. 13½* Wmk. 90

722 A292 1p dark blue 12 8

First Inter-American Marian Congress.

1961, Jan. 17 Lithographed

723 A293 1p carmine rose & black 12 8

International Patrol Encampment of the Boy Scouts, Buenos Aires.

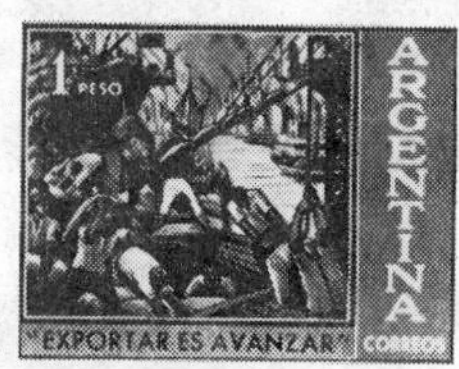

"Shipment of Cereals," by Quinquela Martin—A294

Photogravure

1961, Feb. 11 *Perf. 13½* Wmk. 90

724 A294 1p red brown 18 8

Export drive: "To export is to advance."

Naval Battle of San Nicolás A295 — Mariano Moreno by Juan de Dios Rivera A296

1961, Mar. 2 ***Perf. 13½***

725 A295 2p gray 15 8

Issued to commemorate the 150th anniversary of the naval battle of San Nicolás.

1961, Mar. 25 *Perf. 13½* Wmk. 90

726 A296 2p blue 15 6

Issued to commemorate the 150th anniversary of the death of Mariano Moreno (1778-1811), writer, politician, member of the 1810 Junta.

Emperor Trajan Statue A297

1961, Apr. 11

727 A297 2p slate green 15 8

Issued to commemorate the visit of Pres. Giovanni Gronchi of Italy to Argentina, April 1961.

Rabindranath Tagore A298

1961, May 13 Photo. ***Perf. 13½***

728 A298 2p purple, *grayish* 15 6

Issued to commemorate the centenary of the birth of Rabindranath Tagore, Indian poet.

San Martin Statue, Madrid—A299

1961, May 24 **Wmk. 90**

729 A299 1p olive gray 15 6

Issued to commemorate the unveiling of a statue of General José de San Martin in Madrid.

Manuel Belgrano A300

1961, June 17 ***Perf. 13½***

730 A300 2p violet blue 15 6

Issued to commemorate the erection of a monument by Hector Rocha, to General Manuel Belgrano in Buenos Aires.

Explorers, Sledge and Dog Team A301

1961, Aug. 19 Photo. **Wmk. 90**

731 A301 2p black 24 8

Issued to commemorate the 10th anniversary of the General San Martin Base, Argentine Antarctic.

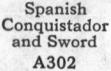

Spanish Conquistador and Sword A302 — Sarmiento Statue by Rodin, Buenos Aires A303

1961, Aug. 19 Lithographed

732 A302 2p red & black 15 8

First city of Jujuy, 400th anniversary.

1961, Sept. 9 Photogravure

733 A303 2p violet 15

Issued to commemorate the 150th anniversary of the birth of Domingo Faustino Sarmiento (1811-1888), political leader and writer.

Symbol of World Town Planning A304

Lithographed

1961, Nov. 25 *Perf. 13½* Wmk. 90

734 A304 2p ultra. & yellow 15 [8]

World Town Planning Day, Nov. 8.

Manuel Belgrano Statue, Buenos Aires A305 — Grenadier, Flag and Regimental Emblem A306

1962, Feb. 24 Photogravure

735 A305 2p Prussian blue 15 10

150th anniversary of the Argentine flag.

Perf. 13½

1962, March 31 **Wmk. 90**

736 A306 2p carmine rose 15 10

Issued to commemorate the 150th anniversary of the San Martin Grenadier Guards regiment.

Mosquito and Malaria Eradication Emblem A307

1962, Apr. 7 Lithographed

737 A307 2p verm. & black 15 10

Issued for the World Health Organization drive to eradicate malaria.

Church of the Virgin of Lujàn A308 — Bust of Juan Jufrè A309

1962, May 12 *Perf. 13½* Wmk. 90

738 A308 2p orange brown & black 15 8

Issued to commemorate the 75th anniversary of the pontifical coronation of the Virgin of Lujan.

1962, June 23 Photogravure

739 A309 2p Prussian blue 15 8

Issued to commemorate the fourth centenary of the founding of San Juan.

"Soaring into Space"
A310

Juan Vucetich
A311

1962, Aug. 18 Litho. *Perf. 13½*

740 A310 2p maroon, black & blue 15 8

Argentine Air Force, 50th anniversary.

1962, Oct. 6 Photo. Wmk. 90

741 A311 2p green 15 8

Issued to honor Juan Vucetich (1864-1925), inventor of the Argentine system of fingerprinting.

Domingo F. Sarmiento
A312

February 20th Monument, Salta
A313

Design: 4p, José Hernandez.

1962-66 Photogravure *Perf. 13½*

742 A312 2p deep green 20 5

Lithographed

742A A312 2p lt. green ('64) 40 4

Photogravure

742B A312 4p dull red ('65) 30 4

Lithographed

742C A312 4p rose red ('66) 30 4

See also No. 817-819.

1963, Feb. 23 Photo. Wmk. 90

743 A313 2p dark green 15 8

Issued to commemorate the 150th anniversary of the Battle of Salta, War of Independence.

Gear Wheels
A314

1963, Mar. 16 Litho. *Perf. 13½*

744 A314 4p gray, black & bright rose 15 8

Issued to commemorate the 75th anniversary of the Argentine Industrial Union.

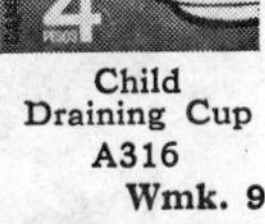

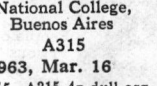

National College, Buenos Aires
A315

Child Draining Cup
A316

1963, Mar. 16 Wmk. 90

745 A315 4p dull org. & blk. 20 8

Issued to commemorate the centenary of the National College of Buenos Aires.

1963, Apr. 6

746 A316 4p multicolored 15 8

Issued for the "Freedom from Hunger" campaign of the U.N. Food and Agriculture Organization.

Frigate "La Argentina," 1817, by Emilio Biggeri
A317

1963, May 18 Photogravure

747 A317 4p bluish green 25 6

Issued for Navy Day, May 17.

Seat of 1813 Assembly and Official Seal
A318

Lithographed

1963, July 13 *Perf. 13½* Wmk. 90

748 A318 4p lt. blue & black 15 8

150th anniversary of the 1813 Assembly.

Battle of San Lorenzo, 1813
A319

1963, Aug. 24

749 A319 4p green & black, *greenish* 18 8

Issued to commemorate the sesquicentennial of the Battle of San Lorenzo.

Queen Nefertari Offering Papyrus Flowers, Abu Simbel
A320

1963, Sept. 14 *Perf. 13½* Wmk. 90

750 A320 4p ocher, black & blue green 15 8

Campaign to save the historic monuments in Nubia.

Government House, Buenos Aires
A321

1963, Oct. 12 *Perf. 13½* Wmk. 90

751 A321 5p rose & brown 15 8

Inauguration of President Arturo Illia.

"Science"
A322

Francisco de las Carreras, Supreme Court Justice—A323

1963, Oct. 16 Lithographed

752 A322 4p orange brown, blue & black 15 8

Issued to publicize the 10th Latin-American Neurosurgery Congress.

Photogravure

1963, Nov. 23 *Perf. 13½* Wmk. 90

753 A323 5p bluish green 15 8

Centenary of judicial power.

Blackboards
A324

1963, Nov. 23 Lithographed

754 A324 5p red, black & blue 15 8

Issued to publicize "Teachers for America" through the Alliance for Progress program.

Kemal Atatürk
A325

"Payador" by Juan Carlos Castagnino
A326

1963, Dec. 28 Photo. *Perf. 13½*

755 A325 12p dark gray 30 15

Issued to commemorate the 25th anniversary of the death of Kemal Atatürk, president of Turkey.

1964, Jan. 25 Lithographed

756 A326 4p ultra., black & light blue 15 8

Fourth National Folklore Festival.

Maps of South Georgia, South Orkney and South Sandwich Islands
A327

Design: 4p, Map of Argentina and Antarctic claims (vert.).

1964, Feb. 22 *Perf. 13½* Wmk. 90

Size: 33x22mm.

757 A327 2p light & dark blue & bister 50 20

Size: 30x40mm.

758 A327 4p light & dark blue & olive green 65 25

Issued to commemorate the 60th anniversary of Argentina's claim to Antarctic territories. See also No. C92.

Jorge Newbery in Cockpit
A328

1964, Feb. 23 Photogravure

759 A328 4p deep green 15 8

Issued to commemorate the 50th anniversary of the death of Jorge Newbery, aviator.

John F. Kennedy
A329

José Brochero by José Cuello
A330

1964, Apr. 14 Engraved Wmk. 90

760 A329 4p claret & dark blue 25 10

Issued in memory of President John F. Kennedy (1917-63).

1964, May 9 Photo. *Perf. 13½*

761 A330 4p light sepia 15 8

Issued to commemorate the 50th anniversary of the death of Father José Gabriel Brochero.

Soldier of Patricios Regiment
A331

Pope John XXIII
A332

1964, May 29 Litho. Wmk. 90

762 A331 4p blk., ultra. & red 35 12

Issued for Army Day. Later Army Day stamps, inscribed "Republica Argentina," are of type A340a.

1964, June 27 Engraved

763 A332 4p orange & black 15 10

Issued in memory of Pope John XXIII.

University of Cordoba Arms
A333

Pigeons and U.N. Building, N.Y.
A334

1964, Aug. 22 Litho. Wmk. 90

764 A333 4p blk., ultra. & yel. 15 10

Issued to commemorate the 350th anniversary of the University of Cordoba.

1964, Oct. 24 ***Perf. 13½***

765 A334 4p dk. blue & lt. bl. 15 10

Issued for United Nations Day.

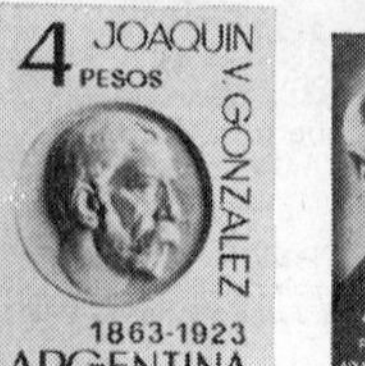

Joaquin V. Gonzalez
A335

Julio Argentino Roca
A336

1964, Nov. 14 **Photogravure**

766 A335 4p dk. rose carmine 15 10

Issued to commemorate the centenary (in 1963) of the birth of Joaquin V. Gonzalez, writer.

1964, Dec. 12 ***Perf. 13½*** **Wmk. 90**

767 A336 4p violet blue 15 10

Issued to commemorate the 50th anniversary of the death of General Julio A. Roca, (1843–1914), president of Argentina, (1880–86, 1898–1904).

Market at Montserrat Square, by Carlos Morel
A337

1964, Dec. 19 **Photogravure**

768 A337 4p sepia 28 12

Issued to honor the 19th century Argentine painter Carlos Morel.

Icebreaker General San Martin
A338

Girl with Piggy Bank
A339

Design: 2p, General Belgrano Base, Antarctica.

1965 ***Perf. 13½*** **Wmk. 90**

769 A338 2p dull purple 15 10
770 " 4p ultramarine 18 10

Issued to publicize the national territory of Tierra del Fuego, Antarctic and South Atlantic Isles.

Issue dates: 4p, Feb. 27; 2p, June 5.

1965, Apr. 3 **Lithographed**

771 A339 4p red orge. & blk. 12 10

Issued to commemorate the 50th anniversary of the National Postal Savings Bank.

Sun and Globe
A340

1965, May 29

772 A340 4p black, orange & dull blue 25 10

Issued for the International Quiet Sun Year, 1964–65. See also Nos. C98–C99.

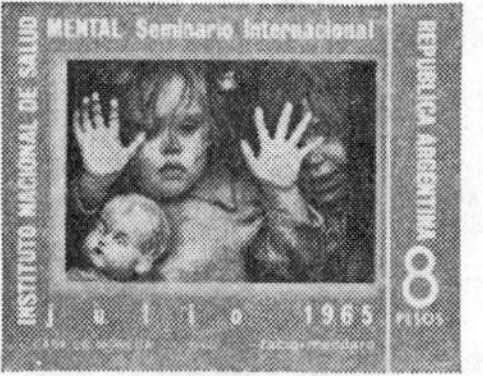

Hussar of Pueyrredon Regiment
A340a

Ricardo Rojas (1882–1957)
A341

1965, June 5 ***Perf. 13½*** **Wmk. 90**

773 A340a 8p deep ultramarine, black & red 40 12

Issued for Army Day. See also Nos. 796, 838, 857, 893, 944, 958, 974, 1145.

1965, June 26 **Photogravure**

Portraits: No. 775, Ricardo Guiraldes (1886–1927). No. 776, Enrique Larreta (1873–1961). No. 777, Leopoldo Lugones (1874–1938). No. 778, Roberto J. Payro (1867–1928).

774	A341	8p brown	25	10
775	"	8p "	25	10
776	"	8p "	25	10
777	"	8p "	25	10
778	"	8p "	25	10
	Nos. 774–778 (5)		1.25	50

Issued to honor Argentine writers. Printed se-tenant in sheets of 100 (10x10); 2 horizontal rows of each design with Guiraldes in top rows and Rojas in bottom rows.

Hipolito Yrigoyen
A342

1965, July 3 **Lithographed**

779 A342 8p pink & black 15 10

Issued in memory of Hipolito Yrigoyen (1852–1933), president of Argentina 1916–22 and 1928–30.

Children Looking Through Window
A343

1965, July 24 **Photogravure**

780 A343 8p salmon & black 18 10

International Seminar on Mental Health.

Child's Funerary Urn and 16th Century Map
A344

1965, Aug. 7 **Lithographed**

781 A344 8p lt. grn., dk. red, brown & ocher 18 10

City of San Miguel de Tucuman, 400th anniversary.

Cardinal Cagliero
A345

Dante Alighieri
A346

1965, Aug. 21 **Photogravure**

782 A345 8p violet 18 10

Issued to honor Juan Cardinal Cagliero (1839–1926), missionary to Argentina and Bishop of Magida.

1965, Sept. 16 ***Perf. 13½*** **Wmk. 90**

783 A346 8p light ultramarine 20 10

Issued to commemorate the 700th anniversary of the birth of Dante Alighieri (1265–1321), Italian poet.

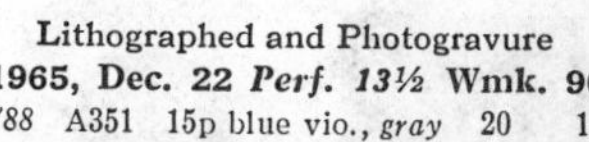

Clipper "Mimosa" and Map of Patagonia—A347

1965, Sept. 25 **Lithographed**

784 A347 8p red & black 18 10

Issued to commemorate the centenary of Welsh colonization of Chubut, and the founding of the city of Rawson.

Map of Buenos Aires, Cock and Compass Emblem of Federal Police
A348

1965, Oct. 30 **Photo.** ***Perf. 13½***

785 A348 8p carmine rose 15 10

Issued for Federal Police Day.

Child's Drawing of Children
A349

1965, Nov. 6 **Litho.** **Wmk. 90**

786 A349 8p lt. yel. grn. & blk. 18 10

Public education law, 81st anniversary.

Church of St. Francis, Catamarca
A350

Ruben Dario
A351

1965, Dec. 8

787 A350 8p orange yellow & red brown 18 10

Issued to honor Brother Mamerto de la Asuncion Esquiu, preacher, teacher and official of 1885 Provincial Constitutional Convention.

Lithographed and Photogravure

1965, Dec. 22 ***Perf. 13½*** **Wmk. 9**

788 A351 15p blue vio., *gray* 20 1

Issued to honor Ruben Dario (pen name of Felix Ruben Garcia Sarmiento, 1867–1916), Nicaraguan poet, newspaper correspondent and diplomat.

"The Orange Seller"
A352

Pueyrredon Paintings: No. 790, "Stop at the Grocery Store." No. 791, "Landscape at San Fernando" (sailboats). No. 792, "Bathing Horses at River Plata."

1966, Jan. 29 **Photo.** ***Perf. 13½***

789	A352	8p bluish green	55	25
790	"	8p " "	55	25
791	"	8p " "	55	25
792	"	8p " "	55	25

Issued to honor Prilidiano Pueyrredon (1823–1870), painter. Nos. 789–792 are printed in one sheet of 40 stamps and 20 labels.

Sun Yat-sen, Flags of Argentina and China
A353

1966, March 12 ***Perf. 13½*** **Wmk. 90**

793 A353 8p dark red brown 15 8

Issued to commemorate the centenary of the birth of Dr. Sun Yat-sen (1866–1925), founder of the Republic of China.

Souvenir Sheet

Rivadavia Issue of 1864
A354

Lithographed

1966, Apr. 20 ***Imperf.*** **Wmk. 90**

794 A354 Sheet of three 50
a. 4p gray & red brown 10
b. 5p gray & green 14
c. 8p gray & dark blue 16

Issued to commemorate the Second Rio de la Plata Stamp Show, Buenos Aires, March 16–24. No. 794 shows flags of Argentina and Uruguay in margin. Marginal inscriptions in gray and red brown, flags in blue and border in green. Size of stamps: 33x43mm. Size of sheet: 140x99mm.

People of Various Races and WHO Emblem
A355

1966, Apr. 23 ***Perf. 13½***

795 A355 8p brown & black 18 9

Issued to commemorate the opening of the World Health Organization Headquarters, Geneva.

Soldier Type of 1965

Design: 8p, Cavalryman, Guëmes Infernal Regiment.

1966, May 28 Lithographed

796 A340a 8p multicolored 40 12

Issued for Army Day.

Coat of Arms
A356

Designs (all 10p): Arms of Buenos Aires, Federal Capital, Catamarca, Cordoba, Corrientes, Chaco, Chubut, Entre Rios, Formosa, Jujuy, La Pampa, La Rioja, Mendoza, Misiones, Neuquen, Salta, San Juan, San Luis, Santa Cruz, Santa Fe, Santiago del Estero, Tucuman; maps of Rio Negro, and of Tierra del Fuego, Antarctica and South Atlantic Islands.

1966, July 30 ***Perf. 13½*** **Wmk. 90**

797 A356 10p blk. & multi. 35 10
a. Sheet of 25 15.00

Issued to commemorate the 150th anniversary of Argentina's Declaration of Independence.

Sheets of 25 (5x5) contain 25 different designs with commemorative inscription and border in sheet margin.

Three Crosses, Caritas Emblem
A357

1966, Sept. 10 Litho. ***Perf. 13½***

798 A357 10p olive green, blk. & light blue 18 8

Caritas, charity organization.

Hilario Ascasubi (1807–75)
A358

Portraits: No. 800, Estanislao del Campo (1834–80). No. 801, Miguel Cane (1851–1905). No. 802, Lucio V. Lopez (1848–94). No. 803, Rafael Obligado (1851–1920). No. 804, Luis Agote (1868–1954), M.D. No. 805, Juan B. Ambrosetti (1865–1917), naturalist and archaeologist. No. 806, Miguel Lillo (1862–1931), botanist and chemist. No. 807, Francisco P. Moreno (1852–1919), naturalist and paleontologist. No. 808, Francisco J. Muñiz (1795–1871), physician.

1966 Photogravure **Wmk. 90**

799 A358 10p dk. bl. green (*Ascasubi*) 30 5
800 " 10p dk. bl. green (*del Campo*) 30 5
801 " 10p dk. bl. green (*Cane*) 30 5
802 " 10p dk. bl. green (*Lopez*) 30 5
803 " 10p dk. bl. green (*Obligado*) 30 5
804 " 10p dp. vio. (*Agote*) 30 5
805 " 10p " " (*Ambrosetti*) 30 5
806 " 10p dp. vio. (*Lillo*) 30 5
807 A358 10p deep violet (*Moreno*) 30 5
808 " 10p dp. vio. (*Muñiz*) 30 5
Nos. 799–808 (10) 3.00 50

Nos. 799–803 issued Sept. 17 to honor Argentine writers. Printed se-tenant in sheets of 100 (10x10); 2 horizontal rows of each portrait with Ascasubi in top two rows and Obligado in bottom rows. Nos. 804–808 issued Oct. 22 to honor Argentine scientists; 2 horizontal rows of each portrait with Agote in top two rows and Muñiz in bottom rows. Scientists set has value at upper left, frame line with rounded corners.

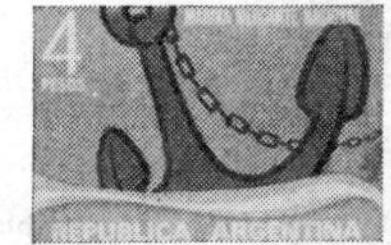

Anchor
A359

1966, Oct. 8 Lithographed

809 A359 4p multicolored 15 10

Argentine merchant marine.

Flags and Map of the Americas
A360

Argentine National Bank
A361

1966, Oct. 29 ***Perf. 13½*** **Wmk. 90**

810 A360 10p gray & multi. 18 10

7th Conference of American Armies.

1966, Nov. 5 Photogravure

811 A361 10p brt. bl. green 18 8

Issued to commemorate the 75th anniversary of the Argentine National Bank.

La Salle Monument and College, Buenos Aires
A362

1966, Nov. 26 Litho. ***Perf. 13½***

812 A362 10p brn. org. & blk. 18 8

Issued to commemorate the 75th anniversary of the Colegio de la Salle, Buenos Aires, and to honor Saint Jean Baptiste de la Salle (1651–1719), educator.

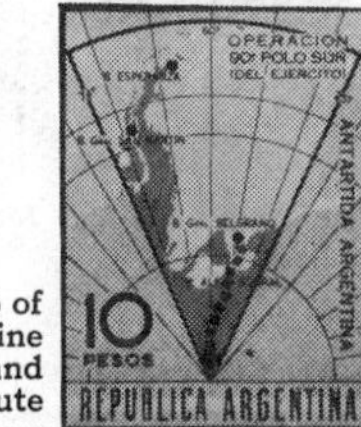

Map of Argentine Antarctica and Expedition Route
A363

1966, Dec. 10 **Wmk. 90**

813 A363 10p multicolored 25 10

Issued to commemorate the 1965 Argentine Antarctic expedition, which planted the Argentine flag on the South Pole. See also No. 851.

Juan Martin de Pueyrredon
A364

Gen. Juan de Las Heras
A365

1966, Dec. 17 Photo. ***Perf. 13½***

814 A364 10p dull red brown 15 10

Issued to honor Juan Martin de Pueyrredon (1777–1850), Governor of Cordoba and of the United Provinces of the River Plata.

1966, Dec. 17 Engraved

815 A365 10p black 15 10

Issued to honor Gen. Juan Gregorio de Las Heras (1780–1866), Peruvian field marshal and aide-de-camp to San Martin.

Inscribed "Republica Argentina"
Types of 1955–61 and

Guillermo Brown
A366

Trout Leaping in National Park
A366a

Designs: 6p, José Hernandez. 50p, Gen. José de San Martin. 500p, Red deer in forest.

Two overall paper sizes for 6p, 50p (No. 827) and 90p:
I. 27x37½mm.
II. 27x39mm.

Photogravure

1965–68 ***Perf. 13½*** **Wmk. 90**

817 A366 6p rose red, litho., paper I ('67) 1.00 8
818 " 6p rose red, photo. ('67) 1.50 8
819 " 6p brown, 15x22mm., ('68) 1.00 6
823 A238a 43p dk. car. rose 3.00 10
824 " 45p brown, photo. ('66) 2.50 10
825 " 45p brown, litho. ('67) 4.00 20
826 A241 50p dark blue, 29x40 mm. 2.50 18
827 " 50p dk. bl., 22x31½ mm., paper I ('67) 2.50 8
a. Paper II 1.50 8
828 A366 90p olive bister, paper I ('67) 2.25 15
a. Paper II 3.50 15

Engraved

829 A495 500p yel. green ('66) 2.00 25
829A A366a 1,000p vio. blue ('68) 3.00 1.25
Nos. 817–829A (11) 25.25 2.53

The 500p and 1,000p remained on sale as 5p and 10p stamps after the 1970 currency exchange.

See also Nos. 888, 891, 939, 941, 992, 1031, 1040, 1045–1047.

Pre-Columbian Pottery
A367

1967, Feb. 18 Litho. ***Perf. 13½***

830 A367 10p multicolored 15 10

Issued to commemorate the 20th anniversary of UNESCO (United Nations Educational, Scientific and Cultural Organization).

"The Meal" by Fernando Fader
A368

1967, Feb. 25 Photo. **Wmk. 90**

831 A368 10p red brown 20 10

Issued in memory of the Argentine painter Fernando Fader (1882–1935).

Col. Juana Azurduy de Padilla (1781–1862), Soldier
A369

Schooner "Invencible," 1811
A370

Famous Women: No. 833, Juana Manuela Gorriti, writer. No. 834, Cecilia Grierson (1858–1934), physician. No. 835, Juana Paula Manso (1819–75), writer and educator. No. 836, Alfonsina Storni (1892–1938), writer and educator.

1967, May 13 Photo. ***Perf. 13½***

832 A369 6p dk. brn. 25 10
833 " 6p " " 25 10
834 " 6p " " 25 10
835 " 6p " " 25 10
836 " 6p " " 25 10
Nos. 832–836 (5) 1.25 50

Issued to honor famous Argentine women. Printed se-tenant in sheets of 100 (10x10); 2 horizontal rows of each portrait with Azurduy in two top rows and Storni in bottom rows.

1967, May 20 Lithographed

837 A370 20p multicolored 40 10

Issued for Navy Day.

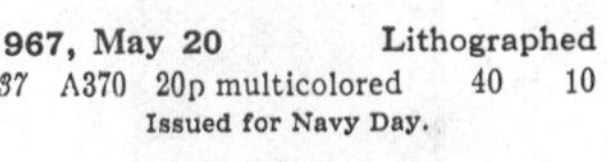

Soldier Type of 1965

Design: 20p, Highlander (Arribeños Corps).

1967, May 27

838 A340a 20p multicolored 35 10

Issued for Army Day.

Souvenir Sheet

Manuel Belgrano and José Artigas
A371

1967, June 22 ***Imperf.***

839 A371 Souv. sheet of 2 30
a. 6p gray & brown 5
b. 22p brown & gray 20

Third Rio de la Plata Stamp Show, Montevideo, Uruguay, June 18–25. Gray marginal inscription. Size: 56x42mm.

Peace Dove and Valise
A372

PADELAI Emblem
A373

1967, Aug. 5 Litho. ***Perf. 13½***

840 A372 20p multicolored 18 10

Issued for International Tourist Year 1967.

1967, Aug. 12 **Lithographed**

841 A373 20p multicolored 18 10

Issued to commemorate the 75th anniversary of the Children's Welfare Association (Patronato de la Infancia—PADELAI).

Stagecoach and Modern City
A374

1967, Sept. 23 ***Perf. 13½*** **Wmk. 90**

842 A374 20p rose, yel. & blk. 25 10

Centenary of Villa Maria, Córdoba.

San Martin by Ibarra
A375

"Battle of Chacabuco" by P. Subercaseaux
A376

1967, Sept. 30 **Lithographed**

843 A375 20p black brown & pale yellow 40 10

Engraved

844 A376 40p blue black 60 24

Battle of Chacabuco, 150th anniversary.

Exhibition Rooms
A377

1967, Oct. 11 **Photogravure**

845 A377 20p blue gray 18 10

Issued to commemorate the 10th anniversary of the Government House Museum.

Pedro L. Zanni, Fokker and 1924 Flight Route
A378

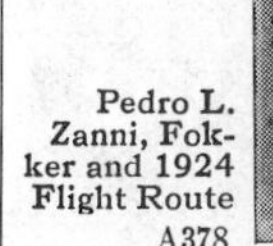

1967, Oct. 21 Litho. ***Perf. 13½***

846 A378 20p multicolored 18 10

Issued for Aviation Week and to commemorate the 1924 flight of the Fokker seaplane "Province of Buenos Aires" from Amsterdam, Netherlands, to Osaka, Japan.

Training Ship General Brown, by Emilio Biggeri
A379

1967, Oct. 28 **Wmk. 90**

847 A379 20p multicolored 60 10

Issued to honor the Military Naval School.

Ovidio Lagos and Front Page
A380

St. Barbara
A381

1967, Nov. 11 **Photogravure**

848 A380 20p sepia 15 10

Centenary of La Capital, Rosario newspaper.

1967, Dec. 2 ***Perf. 13½*** **Wmk. 90**

849 A381 20p rose red 20 10

Issued to honor St. Barbara, patron saint of artillerymen.

Portrait of his Wife, by Eduardo Sivori
A382

1968, Jan. 27 Photo. ***Perf. 13½***

850 A382 20p blue green 24 10

Issued to commemorate the 50th anniversary of the death of Eduardo Sivori (1847–1918), painter.

Antarctic Type of 1966 and

Admiral Brown Scientific Station
A383

Planes over Map of Antarctica
A384

Design: 6p, Map showing radio-postal stations 1966–67.

1968, Feb. 17 **Litho.** **Wmk. 90**

851 A363 6p multicolored 15 10
852 A383 20p " 25 10
853 A384 40p " 50 25

Issued to publicize Argentine research projects in Argentine Antarctica.

The Annunciation, by Leonardo da Vinci
A385

Man in Wheelchair and Factory
A386

1968, Mar. 23 Photo. ***Perf. 13½***

854 A385 20p lilac rose 20 10

Issued for the Day of the Army Communications System and its patron saint, Gabriel.

1968, Mar. 23 **Lithographed**

855 A386 20p green & black 20 10

Day of Rehabilitation of the Handicapped.

Children and WHO Emblem
A387

1968, May 11 ***Perf. 13½*** **Wmk. 90**

856 A387 20p dk. violet blue & vermilion 20 10

Issued for the 20th anniversary of the World Health Organization.

Soldier Type of 1965

Design: 20p, Uniform of First Artillery Regiment "General Iriarte."

1968, June 8 **Lithographed**

857 A340a 20p multicolored 60 10

Issued for Army Day.

Frigate "Libertad," Painting by Emilio Biggeri
A388

1968, June 15 **Wmk. 90**

858 A388 20p multicolored 60 10

Issued for Navy Day.

Guillermo Rawson and Old Hospital
A389

1968, July 20 Photo. ***Perf. 13½***

859 A389 6p olive bister 12 10

Issued to commemorate the centenary of Rawson Hospital, Buenos Aires.

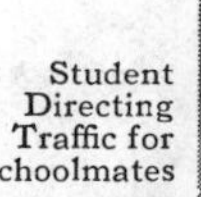

Student Directing Traffic for Schoolmates
A390

1968, Aug. 10 Litho. ***Perf. 13½***

860 A390 20p lt. blue, black, buff & carmine 15 10

Traffic safety and education.

O'Higgins Joining San Martin at Battle of Maipu, by P. Subercaseaux
A391

1968, Aug. 15 **Engraved**

861 A391 40p bluish black 45 20

Sesquicentennial of the Battle of Maipu.

Osvaldo Magnasco
A392

1968, Sept. 7 Photo. *Perf. 13½*

862 A392 20p brown 20 10

Issued to honor Osvaldo Magnasco (1864–1920), lawyer, Professor of Law and Minister of Justice.

Grandmother's Birthday, by Patricia Lynch
A393

The Sea, by Edgardo Gomez
A394

1968, Sept. 21 Lithographed

863 A393 20p multicolored 20 10
864 A394 20p " 20 10

The designs were chosen in a competition among kindergarten and elementary school children.

Mar del Plata at Night
A395

1968, Oct. 19 Litho. *Perf. 13½*

865 A395 20p blk., ocher & bl. 25 10

Issued to publicize the 4th Plenary Assembly of the International Telegraph and Telephone Consultative Committee, Mar del Plata, Sept. 23–Oct. 25. See Nos. C113–C114.

Frontier Gendarme
A396

Patrol Boat
A397

1968, Oct. 26

866 A396 20p multicolored 20 10
867 A397 20p blue, violet blue & black 20 10

No. 866 honors the Gendarmery; No. 867 the Coast Guard.

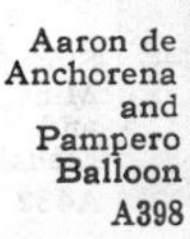

Aaron de Anchorena and Pampero Balloon
A398

1968, Nov. 2 Photogravure

868 A398 20p blue & multi. 20 10

22nd Aeronautics and Space Week.

St. Martin of Tours, by Alfredo Guido
A399

1968, Nov. 9 Lithographed

869 A399 20p lilac & dk. brown 20 10

Issued to honor St. Martin of Tours, patron saint of Buenos Aires.

Municipal Bank Emblem
A400

1968, Nov. 16

870 A400 20p multicolored 20 10

Issued to commemorate the 90th anniversary of the Buenos Aires Municipal Bank.

Anniversary Emblem
A401

1968, Dec. 14 *Perf. 13½* Wmk. 90

871 A401 20p carmine rose & dark green 20 10

Issued to commemorate the 25th anniversary of ALPI (Fight Against Polio Association).

Shovel and State Coal Fields Emblem
A402

Pouring Ladle and Army Manufacturing Emblem
A403

1968, Dec. 21 Lithographed

872 A402 20p org., bl. & blk. 20 10
873 A403 20p dull vio., dull yellow & blk. 20 10

Issued to publicize the National Coal and Steel industry at the Rio Turbio coal fields and the Zapla blast furnaces.

Woman Potter, by Ramon Gomez Cornet
A404

1968, Dec. 21 Photo. *Perf. 13½*

874 A404 20p carmine rose 25 10

Centenary of the Witcomb Gallery.

View of Buenos Aires and Rio de la Plata by Ulrico Schmidl—A405

1969, Feb. 8 Litho. Wmk. 90

875 A405 20p yellow, black & vermilion 25 10

Issued to honor Ulrico Schmidl (c. 1462–1554) who wrote "Journey to the Rio de la Plata and Paraguay."

Types of 1955–67

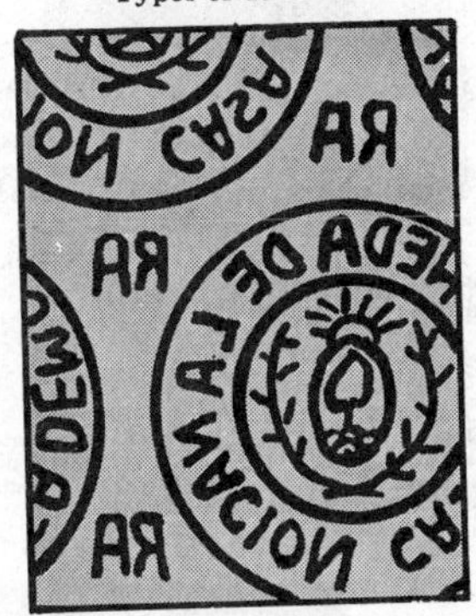

Wmk. 365

Designs: 50c, Puma. 1p, Sunflower. 3p, Zapata Slope, Catamarca. 5p, Tierra del Fuego. 6p, José Hernandez. 10p, Inca Bridge, Mendoza. 50p, José de San Martin. 90p, Guillermo Brown. 100p, Ski jumper.

Wmkd. Argentine Arms, 'Casa de Moneda de la Nacion' & 'RA' Mult. (365)

Photo.; Litho. (50c, 3p, 10p)

1969–70 *Perf. 13½*

882 A275 50c bister ('70) 50 8
883 A277 5p brown 75 12
884 A279 100p blue 12.50 50

Unwmkd.

885 A278 1p brown ('70) 40 8
886 A277 3p dark blue ('70) 40 8
a. Wmk. 90 4.00 40
887 A277 5p brown ('70) 60 8
888 A366 6p red brown, 15x22mm. ('70) 50 12
889 A278 10p dull red ('70) 50 8
a. Wmk. 90 125.00 5.00
890 A241 50p dark blue, 22x31½mm. ('70) 1.50 15
891 A366 90p olive brown, 22x32mm. ('70) 1.50 22
892 A279 100p blue ('70) 3.00 30
Nos. 882-892 (11) 22.15 1.81

Soldier Type of 1965

Design: 20p, Sapper (gastador) of Buenos Aires Province, 1856.

Lithographed

1969, May 31 *Perf. 13½* Wmk. 365

893 A340a 20p multicolored 60 12

Issued for Army Day.

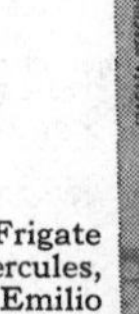

Frigate Hercules, by Emilio Biggeri
A406

1969, May 31

894 A406 20p multicolored 60 12

Issued for Navy Day.

"All Men are Equal"
A407

ILO Emblem
A408

1969, June 28 Wmk. 90

895 A407 20p black & ocher 20 10

International Human Rights Year.

1969, June 28 Litho. Wmk. 365

896 A408 20p lt. grn. & multi. 20 10

Issued to commemorate the 50th anniversary of the International Labor Organization.

Pedro N. Arata (1849–1922), Chemist
A409

Radar Antenna, Balcarce Station and Satellite
A410

Portraits: No. 898, Miguel Fernandez (1883–1950), zoologist. No. 899, Angel P. Gallardo (1867–1934), biologist. No. 900, Cristobal M. Hicken (1875–1933), botanist. No. 901, Eduardo Ladislao Holmberg, M.D. (1852–1937), natural scientist.

1969, Aug. 9 *Perf. 13½* Wmk. 365

Red Brown Design on Orange Yellow Background

897 A409 6p (*Arata*) 25 10
898 " 6p (*Fernandez*) 25 10
899 " 6p (*Gallardo*) 25 10
900 " 6p (*Hicken*) 25 10
901 " 6p (*Holmberg*) 25 10
Nos. 897-901 (5) 1.25 50

Issued to honor Argentine scientists.

1969, Aug. 23 Wmk. 90

902 A410 20p yellow & black 25 10

Issued to publicize communications by satellite through International Telecommunications Satellite Consortium (INTELSAT). See No. C115.

Nieuport 28, Flight Route and Map of Buenos Aires Province
A411

1969, Sept. 13 Litho. Wmk. 90

903	A411	20p multicolored	25	10

Issued to commemorate the 50th anniversary of the first Argentine airmail service from El Palomar to Mar del Plata, flown Feb. 23–24, 1919, by Capt. Pedro L. Zanni.

Military College Gate and Emblem
A412

1969, Oct. 4 *Perf. 13½* Wmk. 365

904	A412	20p multicolored	25	10

Issued to commemorate the centenary of the National Military College, El Palomar (Greater Buenos Aires).

Gen. Angel Pacheco
A413

La Farola, Logotype of La Prensa
A414

1969, Nov. 8 Photo. Wmk. 365

905	A413	20p deep green	20	10

Issued to commemorate the centenary of the death of Gen. Angel Pacheco (1795–1869).

1969, Nov. 8 Litho. *Perf. 13½*

Design: No. 907, Bartolomé Mitre and La Nacion logotype.

906	A414	20p org., yel. & blk.	45	12
907	"	20p brt. grn. & black	45	12

Centenary of newspapers La Prensa and La Nacion.

Julian Aguirre
A415

Musicians: No. 909, Felipe Boero. No. 910, Constantino Gaito. No. 911, Carlos Lopez Buchardo. No. 912, Alberto Williams.

Photogravure

1969, Dec. 6 *Perf. 13½* Wmk. 365

Dark Green Design on Light Blue Background

908	A415	6p (*Aguirre*)	40	8
909	"	6p (*Boero*)	40	8
910	"	6p (*Gaito*)	40	8
911	"	6p (*Buchardo*)	40	8
912	"	6p (*Williams*)	40	8
		Nos. 908-912 (5)	2.00	40

Issued to honor Argentine musicians.

Lt. Benjamin Matienzo and Nieuport Plane
A416

1969, Dec. 13 Lithographed

913	A416	20p multicolored	50	12

23rd Aeronautics and Space Week.

High Power Lines and Map
A417

Design: 20p, Map of Santa Fe Province and schematic view of tunnel.

1969, Dec. 13

914	A417	6p multicolored	30	10
915	"	20p "	60	20

Issued to publicize the completion of development projects. The 6p commemorates the hydroelectric dams on the Limay and Neuquen Rivers, the 20p the tunnel under the Rio Grande from Sante Fe to Parana.

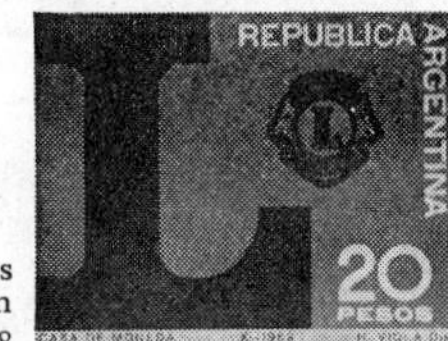

Lions Emblem
A418

1969, Dec. 20 *Perf. 13½* Wmk. 365

916	A418	20p black, emerald & orange	50	12

Issued to commemorate the 50th anniversary of the Argentine Lions International Club.

Madonna and Child, by Raul Soldi
A419

1969, Dec. 27 Lithographed

917	A419	20p multicolored	50	12

Christmas 1969.

Manuel Belgrano, by Jean Gericault
A420

The Creation of the Flag, Bas-relief by José Fioravanti
A421

Photogravure

1970, July 4 *Perf. 13½* Unwmkd.

918	A420	20c deep brown	30	12

Lithographed
Perf. 12½

919	A421	50c bis., blk. & blue	65	20

Issued to commemorate the sesquicentennial of the death of Gen. Manuel Belgrano (1770–1820), Argentine patriot.

San José Palace
A422

1970, Aug. 9 Litho. *Perf. 13½*

920	A422	20c yel. grn. & multi.	20	10

Issued to commemorate the centenary of the death of Gen. Justo José de Urquiza (1801–1870), president of Argentina, 1854–60.

Schooner "Juliet"
A423

1970, Aug. 8 Unwmkd.

921	A423	20c multicolored	75	25

Issued for Navy Day.

Receiver of 1920 and Waves—A424

1970, Aug. 29

922	A424	20c lt. blue & multi.	15	10

Issued to commemorate the 50th anniversary of Argentine broadcasting.

Types of 1955–67 Inscribed "Republica Argentina" and Types A425, A426

Manuel Belgrano
A425

Lujan Basilica
A426

Designs: 1c, Sunflower. 3c, Zapata Slope, Catamarca. 5c, Tierra del Fuego. 8c, No. 931, Belgrano. 10c, Inca Bridge, Mendoza. 25c, 50c, 70c, Jose de San Martin. 65c, 90c, 1.20p, San Martin. 1p, Ski jumper. 1.15p, 1.80p, Adm. Brown.

Unwmkd.

1970–73 Photogravure *Perf. 13½*

923	A278	1c dark green ('71)	5	4
924	A277	3c car. rose ('71)	6	5
925	"	5c blue ('71)	6	5
926	A425	6c deep blue	6	5
927	"	8c green ('72)	6	5
928	A278	10c dull red ('71)	20	6
929	"	10c brn., litho. ('71)	35	6
930	"	10c org. brn. ('72)	20	4
931	A425	10c brown ('73)	15	4
932	A426	18c yel. & dk. brown, litho. ('73)	15	3
933	A425	25c brown ('71)	20	4
934	"	50c scarlet ('72)	75	4
935	A241	65c brown, 22x31½ mm., paper II ('71)	50	4
936	A425	70c dk. blue ('73)	25	4
937	A241	90c emerald, 22x31½ mm. ('72)	2.00	4
938	A279	1p brn., 22½x29½ mm. ('71)	75	4
939	A366	1.15p dark blue, 22½x32 mm. ('71)	75	4
940	A241	1.20p orange, 22x31½ mm. ('73)	75	4
941	A366	1.80p brown ('73)	75	4
		Nos. 923-941 (19)	8.04	83

The imprint "Casa de Moneda de la Nacion" (in capitals) appears on 3c, 5c, Nos. 928–929; 65c, 90c, 1p, 1.20p.

On type A425 only the 6c is inscribed "Ley 18.188" below denomination.

Fluorescent paper was used in printing the 25c, 50c, and 70c. The 3c, 8c, No. 931 and 65c were issued on both ordinary and fluorescent paper.

See also Nos. 987–996, 1032–1038, 1042–1043, 1087–1103.

Soldier Type of 1965

Design: 20c, Galloping messenger of Field Army, 1879.

1970, Oct. 17 Litho. *Perf. 13½*

944	A340a	20c multicolored	75	25

Dome of Cathedral of Cordoba
A430

1970, Nov. 7 Unwmkd.

945	A430	50c gray & black	75	20

Bishopric of Tucuman, 400th anniversary. See No. C131.

People Around U.N. Emblem
A431

1970, Nov. 7

946	A431	20c tan & multi.	20	10

25th anniversary of the United Nations.

State Mint and Medal
A432

1970, Nov. 28 ***Perf. 13½*** **Unwmkd.**

947 A432 20c gold, grn. & blk. 20 10

Inauguration of the State Mint Building, 25th anniversary.

St. John Bosco and Dean Funes College
A433

1970, Dec. 19 **Lithographed**

948 A433 20c olive & black 20 10

Honoring the work of the Salesian Order in Patagonia.

Nativity, by Horacio Gramajo Gutierrez—A434

1970, Dec. 19

949 A434 20c multicolored 40 15

Christmas 1970.

Argentine Flag, Map of Argentine Antarctica
A435

1971, Feb. 20 **Litho.** ***Perf. 13½***

950 A435 20c multicolored 45 12

Fifth anniversary of Argentine South Pole Expedition.

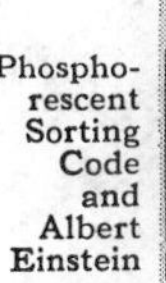

Phosphorescent Sorting Code and Albert Einstein
A436

1971, Apr. 30 ***Perf. 13½*** **Unwmkd.**

951 A436 25c multicolored 20 10

Electronics in postal development.

Symbolic Road Crossing
A437

1971, May 29 **Lithographed**

952 A437 25c blue & black 25 10

Inter-American Regional Meeting of the International Federation of Roads, Buenos Aires, March 28–31.

Elias Alippi
A438

Actors: No. 954, Juan Aurelio Casacuberta. No. 955, Angelina Pagano. No. 956, Roberto Casaux. No. 957, Florencio Parravicini.

1971, May 29 **Lithographed**

Black Design on Pale Rose Background

953 A438 15c (*Alippi*) 35 10
954 " 15c (*Casacuberta*) 35 10
955 " 15c (*Pagano*) 35 10
956 " 15c (*Casaux*) 35 10
957 " 15c (*Parravicini*) 35 10
Nos. 953–957 (5) 1.75 50

Soldier Type of 1965

Design: 25c, Artilleryman, 1826.

1971, July 3 ***Perf. 13½*** **Unwmkd.**

958 A340a 25c multicolored 1.00 20

Army Day, May 29.

Bilander "Carmen," by Emilio Biggeri
A439

1971, July 3

959 A439 25c multicolored 1.00 20

Navy Day

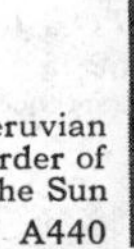

Peruvian Order of the Sun
A440

1971, Aug. 28

960 A440 31c multicolored 35 10

Sesquicentennial of Peru's independence.

Güemes in Battle, by Lorenzo Gigli
A441

Design: No. 962, Death of Güemes, by Antonio Alice.

1971, Aug. 28 Size: 39x29mm.

961 A441 25c multicolored 40 10

Size: 84x29mm.

962 A441 25c multicolored 40 10

Sesquicentennial of the death of Martin Miguel de Güemes, leader in Gaucho War, Governor and Captain General of Salta Province.

Stylized Tulip
A442

1971, Sept. 18

963 A442 25c tan & multi. 25 10

3rd International and 8th National Horticultural Exhibition.

Father Antonio Saenz, by Juan Gut
A443

1971, Sept. 18

964 A443 25c gray & multi. 25 10

Sesquicentennial of University of Buenos Aires, and to honor Father Antonio Saenz, first Chancellor and Rector.

Fabricaciones Militares Emblem
A444

1971, Oct. 16 ***Perf. 13½*** **Unwmkd.**

965 A444 25c brown, gold, blue & black 25 10

30th anniversary of military armament works.

Cars and Trucks
A445

Design: 65c, Tree converted into paper.

1971, Oct. 16

966 A445 25c dull bl. & multi. 40 10
967 " 65c green & multi. 80 20

Nationalized industries. See No. C134.

Luis C. Candelaria and his Plane, 1918
A446

1971, Nov. 27

968 A446 25c multicolored 25 10

25th Aeronautics and Space Week.

Observatory and Nebula of Magellan
A447

1971, Nov. 27

969 A447 25c multicolored 25 10

Centenary of Cordoba Astronomical Observatory.

Christ in Majesty
A448

1971, Dec. 18 **Lithographed**

970 A448 25c black & multi. 25 10

Christmas 1971. Design is from a tapestry by Horacio Butler in Basilica of St. Francis, Buenos Aires.

Mother and Child, by J. C. Castagnino
A449

1972, May 6 ***Perf. 13½*** **Unwmkd.**

971 A449 25c fawn & black 25 10

25th anniversary (in 1971) of the International United Nations Children's Fund (UNICEF).

Mailman's Bag
A450

1972, Sept. 2 **Litho.** ***Perf. 13½***

972 A450 25c lemon & multi. 15 8

Bicentenary of appointment of first Argentine mailman.

Adm. Brown Station, Map of Antarctica
A451

1972, Sept. 2

973 A451 25c blue & multi. 20 10

10th anniversary (in 1971) of Antarctic Treaty.

Soldier Type of 1965

Design: 25c, Sergeant, Negro and Mulatto Corps, 1806–1807.

1972, Sept. 23

974 A340a 25c multicolored 50 10

Army Day, May 29.

Brigantine "Santisima Trinidad"
A452

1972, Sept. 23

975 A452 25c multicolored 50 10

Navy Day. See also No. 1006.

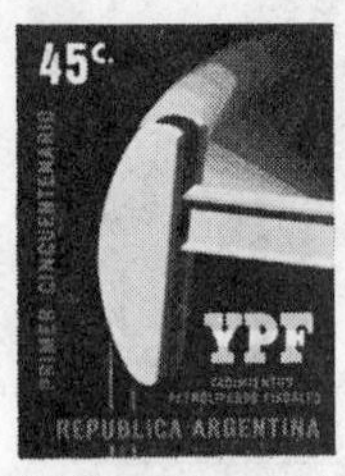

Oil Pump
A453

1972, Sept. 30 Litho. ***Perf. 13½***

976 A453 45c blk. & multi. 85 15

50th anniversary of the organization of the state oil fields (Yacimientos Petroliferos Fiscales).

Sounding Balloon
A454

1972, Sept. 30

977 A454 25c black, blue & ocher 25 10

Centenary of National Meteorological Service.

Trees and Globe—A455

1972, Oct. 14 ***Perf. 13x13½***

978 A455 25c blue, black & light blue 60 10

7th World Forestry Congress, Buenos Aires, Oct. 4–18.

Arms of Naval School, Frigate "Presidente Sarmiento"—A456

1972, Oct. 14

979 A456 25c gold & multi. 60 10

Centenary of Military Naval School.

Early Balloon and Plane, Antonio de Marchi—A457

25c BARTOLOME MITRE 1821-1906
REPUBLICA ARGENTINA

Bartolomé Mitre
A458

1972, Nov. 4 ***Perf. 13½***

980 A457 25c multicolored 25 10

Aeronautics and Space Week, and in honor of Baron Antonio de Marchi (1875–1934), aviation pioneer.

1972, Nov. 4 **Engraved**

981 A458 25c dark blue 15 8

Pres. Bartolomé Mitre (1821–1906), writer, historian, soldier.

Flower and Heart
A459

1972, Dec. 2 Litho. ***Perf. 13½***

982 A459 90c lt. blue, ultra. & black 40 15

"Your heart is your health," World Health Day.

"Martin Fierro," by Juan C. Castignano
A460

"Spirit of the Gaucho," by Vicente Forte
A461

1972, Dec. 2 Litho. ***Perf. 13½***

983 A460 50c multicolored 25 15
984 A461 90c " 50 25

International Book Year 1972, and to commemorate the centenary of publication of the poem, Martin Fierro, by José Hernandez (1834–1886).

Iguassu Falls and Tourist Year Emblem—A462

1972, Dec. 16 ***Perf. 13x13½***

985 A462 45c multicolored 30 12

Tourism Year of the Americas.

King, Wood Carving, 18th Century
A463

1972, Dec. 16 ***Perf. 13½***

986 A463 50c multicolored 40 12

Christmas 1972.

Types of 1955–73 Inscribed "Republica Argentina" and

Moon Valley, San Juan Province
A463a

Designs: 1c, Sunflower. 5c, Tierra del Fuego. 10c, Inca Bridge, Mendoza. 50c, Lujan Basilica. 65c, 22.50p, San Martin. 1p, Ski jumper. 1.15p, 4.50p, Guillermo Brown. 1.80p, Manuel Belgrano.

Perf. 13½, 12½ (1.80p)

Litho.; Photo. (1c, 65c, 1p)

1972–75 **Wmk. 365**

987	A278	1c dark green	12	3
988	A277	5c dark blue	12	3
989	A278	10c bister brown	12	3
989A	A426	50c dull purple ('75)	15	3
990	A241	65c gray brown	1.50	3
991	A279	1p brown	65	6
992	A366	1.15p dk. gray bl.	45	6
993	A425	1.80p blue ('75)	10	3
994	A366	4.50p green ('75)	40	6
995	A241	22.50p vio. bl. ('75)	90	10
996	A463a	50p multi. ('75)	2.00	50
		Nos. 987-996 (11)	6.51	96

Paper size of 1c is 27½x39mm.; others of 1972, 37x27, 27x37mm.

Size of 22.50p, 50p: 26½x38½mm.

See No. 1050.

Cock (Symbolic of Police)
A464

REPUBLICA ARGENTINA
50c.

First Coin of Bank of Buenos Aires
A465

1973, Feb. 3 Litho. **Unwmkd.**

997 A464 50c lt. grn. & multi. 15 10

Sesquicentennial of Federal Police of Argentina.

1973, Feb. 3 ***Perf. 13½***

998 A465 50c pur., yel. & brn. 15 10

Sesquicentennial of the Bank of Buenos Aires Province.

DC-3 Planes Over Antarctica
A466

1973, Apr. 28 Litho. ***Perf. 13½***

999 A466 50c lt. bl. & multi. 35 15

10th anniversary of Argentina's first flight to the South Pole.

Rivadavia's Chair, Argentine Arms and Colors
A467

1973, May 19 Litho. ***Perf. 13½***

1000 A467 50c multicolored 25 12

Inauguration of Pres. Hector J. Cámpora, May 25, 1973.

San Martin, by Gil de Castro
A468

San Martin and Bolívar
A469

1973, July 7 Litho. ***Perf 13½***

1001 A468 50c lt. grn. & multi. 30 10
1002 A469 50c yellow & multi. 30 10

Gen. San Martin's farewell to the people of Peru and his meeting with Simon Bolívar at Guayaquil July 26–27, 1822.

Eva Perón
A470

1973, July 26 Litho. ***Perf. 13½***

1003 A470 70c blk., org. & bl. 20 10

Maria Eva Duarte de Perón (1919–1952), political leader.

House of Viceroy Sobremonte, by Hortensia de Virgilion—A471

1973, July 28 ***Perf. 13x13½***

1004 A471 50c blue & multi. 20 10

400th anniversary of the city of Córdoba.

Woman, by Lino Spilimbergo
A472

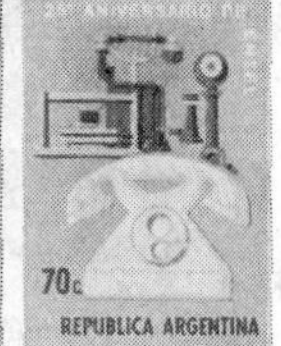

New and Old Telephones
A473

1973, Aug. 28 Litho. ***Perf. 13½***

1005 A472 70c multicolored 30 10

Philatelists' Day. See Nos. B60–B61.

Ship Type of 1972

Design: 70c, Frigate "La Argentina."

1973, Oct. 27 Litho. ***Perf. 13½***

1006 A452 70c multicolored 35 15

Navy Day.

1973, Oct. 27

1007 A473 70c brt. bl. & multi. 25 10

25th anniversary of national telecommunications system.

Plume Made of Flags of Participants
A474

1973, Nov. 3 *Perf. 13½*

1008 A474 70c yel. bis. & multi. 25 10

12th Congress of Latin Notaries, Buenos Aires.

No. 940 Overprinted

TRANSMISION DEL MANDO PRESIDENCIAL
12 OCTUBRE 1973

1973, Nov. 30 Photogravure

1010 A241 1.20p orange 65 20

Assumption of presidency by Juan Peron, Oct. 12.

Virgin and Child, Window, La Plata Cathedral
A476

Design: 1.20p, Nativity, by Bruno Venier, b. 1914.

1973, Dec. 15 Litho. *Perf. 13½*

1011 A476 70c gray & multi. 25 12
1012 " 1.20p blk. & multi. 40 20

Christmas 1973.

The Lama, by Juan Batlle Planas
A477

Paintings: 50c, Houses in Boca District, by Eugenio Daneri (horiz.). 90c, The Blue Grotto, by Emilio Pettoruti (horiz.).

1974, Feb. 9 Litho. *Perf. 13½*

1013 A477 50c multicolored 20 10
1014 " 70c " 25 15
1015 " 90c " 50 20

Argentine painters. See No. B64.

Mar del Plata
A478

1974, Feb. 9

1016 A478 70c multicolored 25 12

Centenary of Mar del Plata.

Weather Symbols
A479

Justo Santa Maria de Oro
A480

1974, Mar. 23 Litho. *Perf. 13½*

1017 A479 1.20p multicolored 30 15

Centenary of international meteorological cooperation.

1974, Mar. 23

1018 A480 70c multicolored 20 10

Bicentenary of the birth of Brother Justo Santa Maria de Oro (1772–1836), theologian, patriot, first Argentine bishop.

Belisario Roldan
A481

1974, June 29 Photo. **Unwmkd.**

1019 A481 70c blue & brown 15 10

Birth centenary of Belisario Roldan (1873–1922), writer.

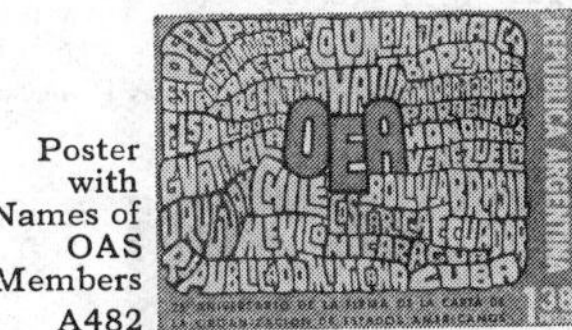

Poster with Names of OAS Members
A482

1974, June 29 Lithographed

1020 A482 1.38p multicolored 30 15

25th anniversary of the Organization of American States.

ENCOTEL Emblem—A483

1974, Aug. 10 Litho. *Perf. 13*

1021 A483 1.20p blue, gold & black 40 15

ENCOTEL, National Post and Telegraph Press.

Flags of Argentina, Bolivia, Brazil, Paraguay, Uruguay
A484

1974, Aug. 16 *Perf. 13½*

1022 A484 1.38p multicolored 50 15

6th Meeting of Foreign Ministers of Rio de la Plata Basin Countries.

El Chocon Hydro-electric Complex, Limay River
A485

Somisa Steel Mill, San Nicolas
A486

Gen. Belgrano Bridge, Chaco-Corrientes—A487

Perf. 13½, 13x13½ (4.50p)

1974, Sept. 14

1023 A485 70c multicolored 15 10
1024 A486 1.20p " 40 15
1025 A487 4.50p " 1.90 30

Development projects.

Brigantine Belgrano, by Emilio Biggeri
A488

1974, Oct. 26 Litho. *Perf. 13½*

1026 A488 1.20p multicolored 40 15

Departure into exile in Chile of General San Martin, Sept. 22, 1822.

Alberto R. Mascias and Bleriot Plane
A489

1974, Oct. 26

1027 A489 1.20p multicolored 40 15

Air Force Day, Aug. 10, and to honor Alberto Roque Garcias (1878–1951), aviation pioneer.

Hussar, 1812, by Eleodoro Marenco
A490

1974, Oct. 26

1028 A490 1.20p multicolored 40 15

Army Day.

Post Horn and Flags
A491

1974, Nov. 23 *Perf. 13½* **Unwmkd.**

1029 A491 2.65p multicolored 80 15

Centenary of Universal Postal Union.

Franciscan Monastery
A492

1974, Nov. 23 Lithographed

1030 A492 1.20p multicolored 40 15

400th anniversary, city of Santa Fe.

Trout Type of 1968.

1974 Engraved **Unwmkd.**

1031 A366a 1,000p vio. blue 2.50 1.25

Due to a shortage of 10p stamps a quantity of this 1,000p was released for use as 10p.

Types of 1954–73
Inscribed "Republica Argentina" and

Red Deer in Forest
A495

Congress Building
A497

Designs: 30c, 60c, 1.80p, Manuel Belgrano. 50c, Lujan Basilica. No. 1036, 2p, 6p, San Martin (16x22½mm.). 2.70p, 7.50p, 22.50p, San Martin (22x31½mm.). 4.50p, 13.50p, Guillermo Brown. 10p, Leaping trout.

Photogravure

1974–75 *Perf. 13½* **Unwmkd.**

1032 A425 30c brown violet 10 3
1033 A426 50c blk. & brown red ('75) 10 3
1034 " 50c bis. & blue ('75) 10 3
1035 A425 60c ocher ('75) 10 3
1036 " 1.20p red 25 3
1037 " 1.80p dp. blue ('75) 15 3
1038 " 2p dk. pur. ('75) 20 3
1039 A241 2.70p dark blue, 22x31½mm. 20 3
1040 A366 4.50p green 60 4
1041 A495 5p yellow green 25 4
1042 A425 6p red orange ('75) 20 4
1043 " 6p emerald ('75) 20 4
1044 A241 7.50p green, 22x31½ mm. ('75) 75 6
1045 A366a 10p violet blue 90 6

1046 A366 13.50p scarlet, 16x22½ mm. ('75) 75 6
1047 " 13.50p scarlet, 22x31½ mm. ('75) 50 8
1048 A241 22.50p dp. bl., 22x31½ mm. ('75) 75 10
1049 A497 30p yellow & dk. red brown 1.00 12
1050 A463a 50p multi. ('76) 1.10 15
Nos. 1032-1050 (19) 8.20 1.03

Fluorescent paper was used in printing No. 1036, 2p, Nos. 1044 and 1047. The 30p was issued on both ordinary and fluorescent paper.

See also No. 829.

Miniature Sheet

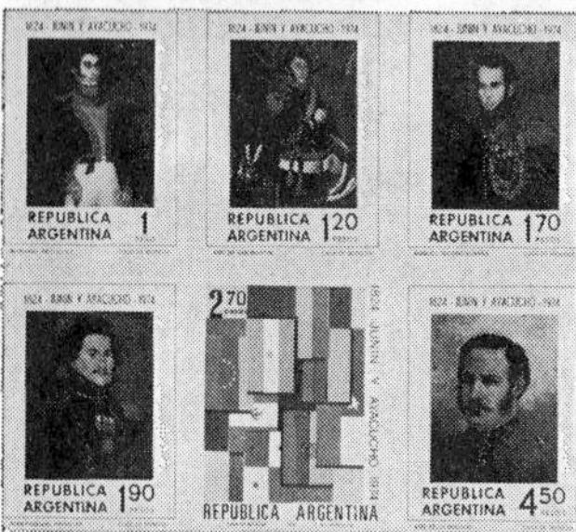

A498

1974, Dec. 7 Litho. *Perf. 13½*

1052 A498 Sheet of 6, multi. 3.25 2.50
a. 1p *Mariano Necochea* 22
b. 1.20p *José de San Martin* 25
c. 1.70p *Manuel Isidoro Suarez* 38
d. 1.90p *Juan Pascual Pringles* 40
e. 2.70p *Latin American flags* 60
f. 4.50p *José Felix Bogado* 1.00

Sesquicentennial of Battles of Junin and Ayacucho. No. 1052 has black control number. Size: 140x132mm.

Dove, by Vito Campanella
A499

St. Anne, by Raul Soldi
A500

1974, Dec. 21 Litho. *Perf. 13½*

1053 A499 1.20p multicolored 30 8
1054 A500 2.65p " 60 15

Christmas 1974.

Boy Looking at Stamp
A501

1974, Dec. 21

1055 A501 1.70p blk. & yellow 38 18

World Youth Philately Year.

Space Monsters, by Raquel Forner
A502

Design: 4.50p, Dream, by Emilio Centurion.

1975, Feb. 22 Litho. *Perf. 13½*

1056 A502 2.70p multicolored 75 25
1057 " 4.50p " 1.00 35

Argentine modern art.

Indian Woman and Cathedral, Catamarca—A503

Designs: No. 1059, Carved chancel and street scene. No. 1060, Grazing cattle and monastery yard. No. 1061, Painted pottery and power station. No. 1062, Farm cart and colonial mansion. No. 1063, Perito Moreno glacier and spinning mill. No. 1064, Lake Lapataia and scientific surveyor. No. 1065, Los Alerces National Park and oil derrick.

1975 Lithographed *Perf. 13½*

Multicolored

1058 A503 1.20p *shown* 25 10
1059 " 1.20p *Jujuy* 25 10
1060 " 1.20p *Salta* 25 10
1061 " 1.20p *Santiago del Estero* 25 10
1062 " 1.20p *Tucuman* 25 10
1063 " 6p *Santa Cruz* 25 10
1064 " 6p *Tierra del Fuego* 25 10
1065 " 6p *Chubut* 25 10
Nos. 1058-1065 (8) 2.00 80

Tourist publicity.
Issue dates: 1.20p, Mar. 8; 6p, Dec. 20.

"We Have Been Inoculated"
A504

1975, Apr. 26 Litho. *Perf. 13½*

1066 A504 2p multicolored 40 24

Children's inoculation campaign (child's painting).

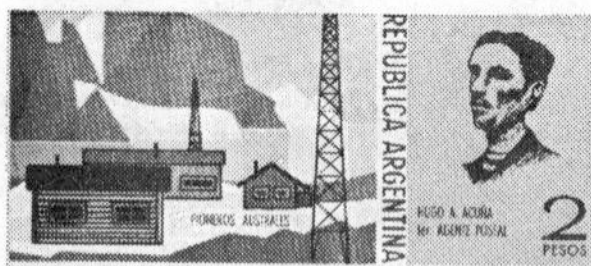

Hugo A. Acuña and South Orkney Station—A505

Designs: No. 1068, Francisco P. Moreno and Lake Nahuel Huapi. No. 1069, Lt. Col. Luis Piedra Buena and cutter, Luisito. No. 1070, Ensign José M. Sobral and Snow Hill House. No. 1071, Capt. Carlos M. Moyano and Cerro del Toro (mountain).

1975, June 28 Litho. *Perf. 13*

1067 A505 2p grnish. bl. & multi. 15 10
1068 " 2p yel. grn. & multi 15 10
1069 " 2p lt. vio. & multi. 15 10
1070 " 2p gray bl. & multi. 15 10
1071 " 2p pale green & multicolored 15 10
Nos. 1067-1071 (5) 75 50

Pioneers of Antarctica.

Frigate "25 de Mayo"
A506

1975, Sept. 27 *Perf. 13½* Unwmkd.

1072 A506 6p multicolored 30 12

Navy Day 1975.

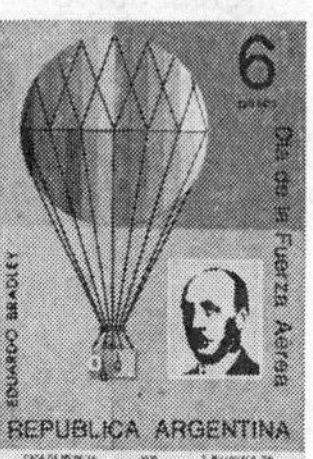

Eduardo Bradley and Balloon
A507

1975, Sept. 27 Wmk. 365

1073 A507 6p multicolored 30 12

Air Force Day.

Declaration of Independence, by Juan M. Blanes
A508

1975, Sept. 27 Unwmkd.

1074 A508 6p multicolored 30 12

Sesquicentennial of Uruguay's declaration of independence.

Flame
A509

1975, Oct. 17

1075 A509 6p gray & multi. 30 12

Loyalty Day, 30th anniversary of Pres. Peron's accession to power.

Nos. 886, 828a and 932 Surcharged

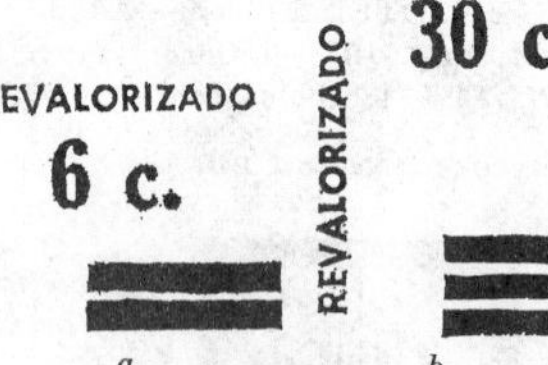

REVALORIZADO
5 pesos
c

Wmks. 365, 90, Unwmkd.

1975 Litho., Photo.

1076 A277 (*a*) 6c on 3p 10 5
1077 A366 (*b*) 30c on 90p 10 5
1078 A426 (*c*) 5p on 18c 35 20

Issue dates: 6c, Oct. 30; 30c, Nov. 20; 5p, Oct. 24.

International Bridge, Flags of Argentina and Uruguay
A510

1975, Oct. 25 Litho. Unwmkd

1081 A510 6p multicolored 30 1

Opening of bridge connecting Colon Argentina, and Paysandu, Uruguay.

Post Horn, Surcharged
A511

1975, Nov. 8

1082 A511 10p on 20c multi. 50 2

Introduction of postal code. Not issued without surcharge.

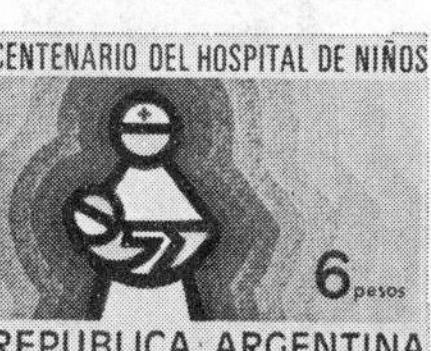

Nurse Holding Infant
A512

1975, Dec. 13 Litho. *Perf. 13½*

1083 A512 6p multicolored 50 20

Children's Hospital, centenary.

Nativity, Nueva Pompeya Church
A513

1975, Dec. 13 Litho. *Perf. 13½*

1084 A513 6p multicolored 25 10

Christmas 1975.

Types of 1970-75 and

Church of St. Francis, Salta
A515

Designs: 3p, No. 1099, 60p, 90p, Manuel Belgrano. 12p, 15p, 20p, 30p, No. 1100, 100p, 110p, 120p, 130p, San Martin. 15p, 70p, Guillermo Brown. 300p, Moon Valley (lower inscriptions italic). 500p, Adm. Brown Station, Antarctica.

Photo.; *Perf. 13½;* Unwmkd.

Litho.; *Perf. 12½x13;* Wmk. 365

1976-78

1089 A425 3p slate 3 3
1090 " 12p rose red 12 6

1091 A425 12p rose red, litho. 12 6
1092 " 12p emerald, litho. 12 6
1093 " 12p emerald ('77) 12 6
1094 " 15p rose red 15 8
1095 " 15p vio. blue ('77) 15 8
1097 " 20p rose red ('77) 20 10
1098 " 30p " " ('77) 30 14
1099 " 40p deep green 40 20
1100 " 40p rose red ('77) 25 15
1101 " 60p dk. blue ('77) 60 28
1102 " 70p " 70 30
1103 " 90p emerald ('77) 90 40
1104 " 100p red 78 35
1105 " 110p rose red ('78) 45 25
1106 " 120p " " ('78) 50 30
1107 " 130p " " ('78) 60 35

Litho.; *Perf. 13½;* Unwmkd.

1108 A463a 300p multi. 3.00 2.25
1109 A515 500p multi. ('77) 4.00 2.00
1110 " 1000p multi. ('77) 8.00 3.00
Nos. 1089-1110 (21) 21.49 10.50

Fluorescent paper was used in printing both 12p rose red, 15p rose red, 20p, 30p, 40p rose red, 100p, 110p, 120p, 130p. No. 1099 and the 300p were issued on both ordinary and fluorescent paper.
300p and 500p exist with wmk. 365.

Numeral
A516

Photo.; *Perf. 13½;* Unwmkd.
Litho.; *Perf. 13x12½;* Wmk. 365

1976

1112 A516 12c gray & black 3 3
1113 " 50c gray & green 3 3
1114 " 1p red & black 3 3
1115 " 4p blue & black 4 3
1116 " 5p org. & black 5 3
1117 " 5p org. & black, litho. 5 3
1118 " 6p deep brown & black 6 3
1119 " 10p gray & violet blue 10 4
1120 " 27p light green & black 26 8
1121 " 27p light green & blk., litho. 26 8
1122 " 30p lt. bl. & blk. 30 10
1123 " 45p yel. & black 45 15
1124 " 45p yel. & black, litho. 45 15
1125 " 50p dull green & black 50 18
1126 " 100p bright green & red 1.00 35
Nos. 1112-1126 (15) 3.61 1.34

Fluorescent paper was used in printing the 50p. The 1p, 6p, 10p and No. 1116 were issued on both ordinary and fluorescent paper.

Jet and Airlines Emblem
A517

1976, Apr. 24 Litho. *Perf. 13x13½*

1130 A517 30p blue, lt. blue & dark blue 75 20

Argentine Airlines, 25th anniversary.

Frigate Heroina and Map of Falkland Islands—A518

1976, Apr. 26

1131 A518 6p multicolored 20 12

Argentina's claim to Falkland Islands.

Louis Braille
A519

1976, May 22 Engr. *Perf. 13½*

1132 A519 19.70p deep blue 30 15

Sesquicentennial of the invention of the Braille system of writing for the blind by Louis Braille (1809-1852).

Private, 7th Infantry Regiment
A520

1976, May 29 Lithographed

1133 A520 12p multicolored 20 10

Army Day.

Schooner Rio de la Plata, by Emilio Biggeri
A521

1976, June 19

1134 A521 12p multicolored 25 10

Navy Day.

Dr. Bernardo Houssay
A522

Nobel Prize Winners: 15p, Luis F. Leloir, chemistry, 1970. 20p, Carlos Saavedra Lamas, peace, 1936. Bernardo Houssay, medicine and physiology, 1947.

1976, Aug. 14 Litho. *Perf. 13½*

1135 A522 10p org. & black 15 10
1136 " 15p yellow & black 25 15
1137 " 20p ocher & black 35 20

Argentine Nobel Prize winners.

Rio de la Plata International Bridge—A523

1976, Sept. 18 Litho. *Perf. 13½*

1138 A523 12p multicolored 15 10

Inauguration of International Bridge connecting Puerte Unzue, Argentina, and Fray Bentos, Uruguay.

Pipelines and Cooling Tower, Gen. Mosconi Plant—A524

1976, Nov. 20 Litho. *Perf. 13½*

1139 A524 28p multicolored 30 20

Pablo Teodoro Fels and Bleriot Monoplane, 1910—A525

1976, Nov. 20

1140 A525 15p multicolored 20 10

Air Force Day.

Nativity
A526

1976, Dec. 18 Litho. *Perf. 13½*

1141 A526 20p multicolored 30 15

Christmas 1976. Painting by Edith Chiapetto.

Water Conference Emblem
A527

1977, Mar. 19 Litho. *Perf. 13½*

1142 A527 70p multicolored 70 35

U.N. Water Conference, Mar del Plata, Mar. 14-25.

Dalmacio Vélez Sarsfield
A528

1977, Mar. 19 Engraved

1143 A528 50p blk. & red brn. 50 25

Dalmacio Vélez Sarsfield (1800-1875), author of Argentine civil code.

100
PESOS

Red Deer Type of 1974 Surcharged

150º ANIV.
DEL CORREO
NACIONAL DEL
URUGUAY

1977, July 30 Photo. *Perf. 13½*

1144 A495 100p on 5p brown 75 30

Sesquicentennial of Uruguayan postal service. Not issued without surcharge.

Soldier, 16th Lancers
A529

1977, July 30

1145 A529 30p multicolored 30 15

Army Day.

Schooner Sarandi, by Emilio Biggeri
A530

1977, July 30

1146 A530 30p multicolored 30 15

Navy Day.

Soccer Games' Emblem
A531

Design: 70p, Argentina '78 emblem, flags and soccer field.

1977, May 14

1147 A531 30p multicolored 40 15
1148 " 70p " 85 35

11th World Cup Soccer Championship, Argentina, June 1-25, 1978.

The Visit, by Horacio Butler
A532

Consecration, by Miguel P. Caride
A533

1977, Mar. 26 **Lithographed**

1149 A532 50p multicolored 50 25
1150 A533 70p " 70 35

Argentine artists.

Sierra de la Ventana—A534

Views: No. 1152, Civic Center, Santa Rosa. No. 1153, Skiers, San Martin de los Andes. No. 1154, Boat on Lake Fonck, Rio Negro.

1977, Oct. 8 **Litho.** ***Perf. 13x13½***

1151 A534 30p multicolored 30 15
1152 " 30p " 30 15
1153 " 30p " 30 15
1154 " 30p " 30 15

Guillermo Brown, by R. del Villar
A535

1977, Oct. 8 ***Perf. 13½***

1155 A535 30p multicolored 30 15

Adm. Guillermo Brown (1777–1857), leader in fight for independence, bicentenary of birth.

Jet
A536

Double-decker, 1926
A537

1977 **Litho.** ***Perf. 13½***

1156 A536 30p multicolored 25 15
1157 A537 40p " 30 20

50th anniversary of military plane production (30p); Air Force Day (40p).
Issue dates: 30p, Dec. 3; 40p, Nov. 26.

Adoration of the Kings
A538

1977, Dec. 17

1158 A538 100p multicolored 75 20

Christmas 1977.

Historic City Hall, Buenos Aires
A539

Chapel of Rio Grande Museum, Tierra del Fuego
A540

Designs: 5p, 20p, La Plata Museum. 10p, Independence Hall, Tucuman. 100p, Teatro Colon, Buenos Aires. 300p, like 280p. 480p, 520p, Ruins of Jesuit Mission. 500p, Candonga Chapel, Cordoba. 1000p, Post Office, Buenos Aires.

Unwmkd.

1977–78 **Photogravure** ***Perf. 13½***

Size: 32x21mm., 21x32mm.

1159 A540 5p gray & black ('78) 3 3
1160 " 10p lt. bl. & blk. litho. ('78) 3 3
1161 " 20p citron & blk. ('78) 3 3
1162 A539 50p yel. & black 25 15
1163 " 50p lt. yel. & blk., litho. ('78) 15 10
1164 A540 100p pale org. & blk., litho. ('78) 30 10
1165 " 280p rose & black, litho. 1.00 20
1166 " 300p lemon & blk. ('78) 90 15
1167 " 480p org. & black ('78) 1.50 30
1168 " 500p yel. grn. & black ('78) 1.50 25
1169 " 520p org. & black ('78) 1.50 30

Size: 40x29mm.

1175 A540 1000p gold & blk. ('78) 3.50 50
Nos. 1159–1175 (12) 10.69 2.14

Soccer Games' Emblem
A544

1978, Feb. 10 **Photo.** ***Perf. 13½***

1179 A544 200p yel. grn. & bl. 65 20

11th World Cup Soccer Championship, Argentina, June 1–25.

The indexes in each volume of the Scott Catalogue contain many listings which help to identify stamps.

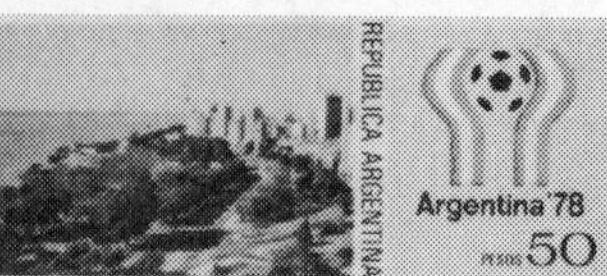

View of El Rio, Rosario—A545

Designs (Argentina '78 Emblem and): 100p, Rio Tercero Dam, Cordoba. 150p, Cordillera Mountains, Mendoza. 200p, City Center, Mar del Plata. 300p, View of Buenos Aires.

1978, May 6 **Litho.** ***Perf. 13***

1180 A545 50p multicolored 15 10
1181 " 100p " 30 10
1182 " 150p " 45 15
1183 " 200p " 60 20
1184 " 300p " 90 25
Nos. 1180–1184 (5) 2.40 80

Sites of 11th World Cup Soccer Championship, June 1–25.

Children—A546

1978, May 20

1185 A546 100p multicolored 30 15

50th anniversary of Children's Institute.

Labor Day, by B. Quinquela Martin
A547

Design: No. 1187, Woman's torso, sculpture by Orlando Pierri.

1978, May 20 ***Perf. 13½***

1186 A547 100p multicolored 30 10
1187 " 100p " 30 10

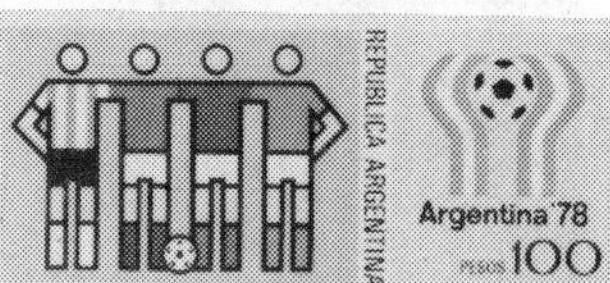

Argentina, Hungary, France, Italy and Emblem—A548

Stadium
A549

Teams and Argentina '78 Emblem: 200p, Poland, Fed. Rep. of Germany, Tunisia, Mexico. 300p, Austria, Spain, Sweden, Brazil. 400p, Netherlands, Iran, Peru, Scotland.

1978 **Litho.** ***Perf. 13***

1188 A548 100p multicolored 30 10
1189 " 200p " 60 10
1190 " 300p " 90 15
1191 " 400p " 1.20 25

Souvenir Sheet

Litho. and Engr. ***Perf. 13½***

1192 A549 700p buff & black 2.25 2.00

11th World Cup Soccer Championship, Argentina, June 1–25. No. 1192 contains one stamp; blue and black margin shows sports and communications emblems. Size: 89x60mm. Issue dates, Nos. 1188–1191, June 6, No. 1192, June 3.

Stadium Type of 1978 Inscribed in Red: "ARGENTINA / CAMPEON"

Lithographed and Engraved

1978, Sept. 2 ***Perf. 13½***

1193 A549 1000p buff, black & red 3.50 2.00

Argentina's victory in 1978 Soccer Championship. No. 1193 has margin similar to No. 1192 with Rimet Cup emblem added in red. Size: 89x60mm.

Young Tree Nourished by Old Trunk, U.N. Emblem—A550

1978, Sept. 2 **Lithographed**

1194 A550 100p multicolored 30 15

Technical Cooperation among Developing Countries Conference, Buenos Aires, Sept. 1978.

Emblems of Buenos Aires and Bank
A551

1978, Sept. 16

1195 A551 100p multicolored 30 15

Bank of City of Buenos Aires, centenary.

General Savio and Steel Production
A552

1978, Sept. 16

1196 A552 100p multicolored 30 15

Gen. Manuel N. Savio (1892–1948), general manager of military heavy industry, 30th death anniversary.

San Martin
A553

1978, Oct. **Engraved**

1197 A553 2000p greenish black 6.00 1.50

Gen. José de San Martin (1778–1850), soldier and statesman, 200th birth anniversary.

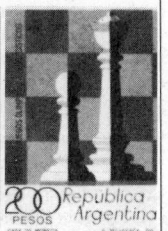

Globe and Argentine Flag
A554

Chessboard, Queen and Pawn
A555

1978, Oct. 7 Litho. ***Perf. 13½***

1199 A554 200p multicolored 60

12th International Cancer Congress, Buenos Aires, Oct. 5–11.

1978, Oct. 7

1200 A555 200p multicolored 60

23rd National Chess Olympics, Buenos Aires, Oct. 25–Nov. 12.

Correct Positioning of Stamps
A557

Design: 50p, Use correct postal code number.

1978 Photogravure ***Perf. 13½***

1201 A557 20p ultramarine 6

1203 " 50p carmine 15

Numeral
A558

1978 Photogravure ***Perf. 13½***

1206 A558 150p blue & ultra. 45

No. 1206 issued on fluorescent and ordinary paper.

Balsa "24"
A561

Ships: 200p, Tug Legador. 300p, River Parana tug No. 34. 400p, Passenger ship Ciudad de Parana.

1978, Nov. 4 Litho. ***Perf. 13½***

1220 A561 100p multicolored 30

1221 " 200p " 60

1222 " 300p " 90

1223 " 400p " 1.20

20th anniversary of national river fleet. Nos. 1220 and 1223, 1221–1222 printed se-tenant in sheets of 50. Issued on fluorescent paper.

View and Arms of Bahia Blanca
A562

1978, Nov. 25 Litho. ***Perf. 13½***

1224 A562 200p multicolored 60

Sesquicentennial of Bahia Blanca.

"Spain," (Queen Isabella and Columbus) by Arturo Dresco—A563

1978, Nov. 25

1225 A563 300p multicolored 90

Visit of King Juan Carlos and Queen Sofia of Spain to Argentina, Nov. 26.

Virgin and Child, San Isidro Cathedral
A564

1978, Dec. 16

1226 A564 200p gold & multi. 60

Christmas 1978.

SEMI-POSTAL STAMPS.

Samuel F. B. Morse
SP1

Globe
SP2

Landing of Columbus
SP5

Designs: 10c+5c, Alexander Graham Bell. 25c+15c, Rowland Hill.

Wmkd. RA in Sun. (90)

1944, Jan. 5 Lithographed ***Perf. 13***

B1	SP1	3c+2c light violet & slate blue	50	25
B2	SP2	5c+5c dull red & slate blue	1.00	25
B3	SP1	10c+5c orange & slate blue	2.00	75
B4	"	25c+15c red brown & slate blue	2.50	1.25
B5	SP5	1p+50c light green & slate blue	12.50	4.00
		Nos. B1–B5 (5)	18.50	6.50

The surtax was for the Postal Employees Benefit Association.

Map of Argentina
SP6

1944, Feb. 17 ***Perf. 13*** **Wmk. 90**

B6	SP6	5c+10c olive yellow & slate	1.00	60
B7	"	5c+50c violet brown & slate	3.00	1.50
B8	"	5c+1p dull orange & slate	10.00	6.00
B9	"	5c+20p deep blue & slate	25.00	15.00

The surtax was for the victims of the San Juan earthquake.

Souvenir Sheets

National Anthem and Flag
SP7

1944, July 17 ***Imperf.***

B10	SP7	5c+1p violet brown & light blue	2.00	2.00
B11	"	5c+50p blue black & light blue	200.00	200.00

The sheets measure 75x110mm. The surtax was for the needy in the provinces of La Rioja and Catamarca.

Stamp Designing
SP8

1950, Aug. 26 Photo. *Perf. 13½*

B12 SP8 10c+10c violet 15 15

Issued to publicize the Argentine International Philatelic Exhibition, 1950.

See also Nos. CB1–CB5 and note after No. CB5.

Poliomyelitis Victim
SP9

1956, Apr. 14 *Perf. 13½x13*

B13 SP9 20c+30c slate 30 10

The surtax was for the poliomyelitis fund. Head in design is from Correggio's "Antiope," Louvre.

Stamp of 1858 and Mail Coach on Raft
SP10

Designs: 2.40p+1.20p, Album, magnifying glass and stamp of 1858. 4.40p+2.20p, Government seat of Confederation, Parana.

Lithographed

1958, Mar. 29 *Perf. 13½* Wmk. 90

B14 SP10 40c+20c bright green & dull purple 40 30
B15 " 2.40p+1.20p olive gray & blue 50 35
B16 " 4.40p+2.20p light blue & deep claret 75 55
Nos. B14-B16, CB8-CB12 (8) 7.30 5.85

The surtax was for the International Centennial Philatelic Exhibition, Paraná, Entre Rios, April 19–27.

View of Flooded Land
SP11

1958, Oct. 4 Photo. *Perf. 13½*

B17 SP11 40c+20c brown 12 8

The surtax was for flood victims in the Buenos Aires district. See Nos. CB13–CB14.

Child Receiving Blood
SP12

Runner
SP13

1958, Dec. 20 Litho. Wmk. 90

B18 SP12 1p+50c black & rose red 15 12

The surtax went to the Anti-Leukemia Foundation.

1959, Sept. 5 *Perf. 13½*

Designs: 50c+20c, Basketball players (vert.). 1p+50c, Boxers (vert.).

B19 SP13 20c+10c emerald & black 10 10
B20 " 50c+20c yellow & black 15 15
B21 " 1p+50c maroon & black 20 20
Nos. B19-B21, CB15-CB16 (5) 1.70 1.40

Issued to commemorate the third Pan American Games, Chicago, Aug. 27-Sept. 7, 1959.

Condor
SP14

Birds: 50c+20c, Fork-tailed flycatchers. 1p+50c, Magellanic woodpecker.

1960, Feb. 6

B22 SP14 20c+10c dark blue 10 8
B23 " 50c+20c deep violet blue 15 10
B24 " 1p+50c brown & buff 25 12
Nos. B22-B24, CB17-CB18 (5) 1.30 90

The surtax was for child welfare work. See also No. B30, CB29.

Souvenir Sheet

Uprooted Oak Emblem—SP15

1960, Apr. 7 *Imperf.* Wmk. 90

B25 SP15 Sheet of two 1.50 1.50
a. 1p+50c bistre & carmine 70 70
b. 4.20p+2.10p apple green & deep claret 70 70

Issued to publicize World Refugee Year, July 1, 1959—June 30, 1960. No. B25 measures 112x84mm. with deep claret marginal inscription.

The surtax was for aid to refugees.

Jacaranda
SP16

Flowers: 1p+1p, Passionflower. 3p+3p, Orchid. 5p+5p, Tabebuia.

1960, Dec. 3 Photo. *Perf. 13½*

B26 SP16 50c+50c deep blue 10 6
B27 " 1p+1p bluish green 15 10
B28 " 3p+3p henna brn. 35 25
B29 " 3p+5p dark brown 60 45

Issued to publicize "TEMEX 61" (International Thematic Exposition).

Type of 1960

Bird: 4.20p+2.10p, Blue-eyed shag.

1961, Feb. 25 *Perf. 13½* Wmk. 90

B30 SP14 4.20p+2.10p chestnut brown 60 40

The surtax was for child welfare work. See also No. CB29.

Nos. B26–B29 Overprinted in Black, Brown, Blue or Red:
"14 DE ABRIL DIA DE LAS AMERICAS"

1961, Apr. 15

B31 SP16 50c+50c deep blue 10 10
B32 " 1p+1p bluish green (Br) 15 12
B33 " 3p+3p henna brown (Bl) 35 30
B34 " 5p+5p dark brown (R) 60 50

Day of the Americas, Apr. 14.

Cathedral, Cordoba
SP17

Stamp of 1862
SP18

Flight into Egypt, by Ana Maria Moncalvo
SP19

Design: 10p+10p, Cathedral, Buenos Aires.

Photogravure

1961, Oct. 21 *Perf. 13½* Wmk. 90

B35 SP17 2p+ 2p rose claret 25 15
B36 SP18 3p+ 3p green 35 20
B37 SP17 10p+10p br. blue 1.00 60
a. Souvenir sheet of 3 1.75 1.25

Issued to publicize the 1962 International Stamp Exhibition.

No. B37a contains three imperf. stamps similar to Nos. B35–B37 in dark blue. Violet brown marginal inscription. Size: 85x86mm.

1961, Dec. 16 Lithographed

B38 SP19 2p+1p lilac & black brown 15 10
B39 " 10p+5p lt. claret & deep claret 60 15

The surtax was for child welfare.

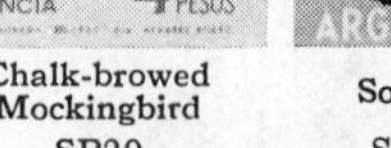

Chalk-browed Mockingbird
SP20

Soccer
SP21

Design: 12p+6p, Rufous-collared sparrow.

1962, Dec. 29 *Perf. 13½* Wmk. 90

B40 SP20 4p+2p bistre, brn. & blue grn 60 50
B41 " 12p+6p gray, yel., green & brown 1.00 90

The surtax was for child welfare. See also Nos. B44, B47, B48–B50, CB32, CB35–CB36.

1963, May 18 *Perf. 13½* Wmk. 90

Design: 12p+6p, Horsemanship.

B42 SP21 4p+2p brt. pink, grn. & black 25 12
B43 " 12p+6p sal., dark carm. & black 55 45
a. Dark carmine (jacket) omitted

Issued to commemorate the 4th Pan American Games, Sao Paulo. See also No. CB31.

Bird Type of 1962.

Design: Vermilion flycatcher.

1963, Dec. 21 Lithographed

B44 SP20 4p+2p black, red, orange & green 40 30

The surtax was for child welfare. See also No. CB32.

Fencers
SP22

Design: 4p+2p, National Stadium, Tokyo (horiz.).

1964, July 18 *Perf. 13½* Wmk. 90

B45 SP22 4p+2p red, ocher & brown 20 15
B46 " 12p+6p blue green & black 50 45

Issued to publicize the 18th Olympic Games, Tokyo, Oct. 10–25, 1964. See also No. CB33.

Bird Type of 1962

Design: Red-crested cardinal.

1964, Dec. 23 Lithographed

B47 SP20 4p+2p dk. bl., red & green 30 20

The surtax was for child welfare. See also No. CB35.

Bird Type of 1962
Inscribed "R. ARGENTINA"

Designs: 8p+4p, Lapwing. 10p+5p, Scarlet-headed marshbird (horiz.). 20p+10p, Amazon kingfisher.

1966–67 *Perf. 13½* Wmk. 90

B48 SP20 8p+4p blk., olive, brt. grn. & red 30 25
B49 " 10p+5p blk., blue, org. & grn. ('67) 30 25
B50 " 20p+10p blk., yel., bl. & pink ('67) 40 30

The surtax was for child welfare.

Issue dates: 8p+4p, Mar. 26, 1966. 10p+5p, Jan. 14, 1967. 20p+10p, Dec. 23, 1967.

See also Nos. CB36, CB38–CB39.

Grandmother's Birthday, by Patricia Lynch; Lions Emblem—SP23

Perf. 12½x13½

1968, Dec. 14 Litho. Wmk. 90

B51	SP23	40p+20p multi.	50	40

Issued to publicize the First Lions International Benevolent Philatelic Exhibition. The surtax was for the Children's Hospital Benevolent Fund.

White-faced Tree Duck
SP24

1969, Sept. 20 *Perf. 13½* Wmk. 365

B52	SP24	20p+10p multi.	30	25

The surtax was for child welfare. See No. CB40.

Slender-tailed Woodstar (Hummingbird)
SP25

1970, May 9 *Perf. 13½* Wmk. 365

B53	SP25	20c+10c multi.	30	25

The surtax was for child welfare. See Nos. CB41, B56–B59, B62–B63.

Dolphinfish—SP26

1971, Feb. 20 *Perf. 12½* Unwmkd.

Size: 75x15mm.

B54	SP26	20c+10c multi.	45	40

The surtax was for child welfare. See No. CB42.

Children with Stamps, by Mariette Lydis
SP27

1971, Dec. 18 Litho. *Perf. 13½*

B55	SP27	1p+50c multi.	80	60

2nd Lions International Solidarity Stamp Exhibition.

Bird Type of 1970

Birds: 25c+10c, Saffron finch. 65c+30c, Rufous-bellied thrush (horiz.).

1972, May 6 *Perf. 13½* Unwmkd.

B56	SP25	25c+10c multi.	30	20
B57	"	65c+30c "	50	40

Surtax was for child welfare.

Bird Type of 1970

Birds: 50c+25c, Southern screamer (chaja). 90c+45c, Saffron-cowled blackbird (horiz.).

1973, Apr. 28

B58	SP25	50c+25c multi.	40	40
B59	"	90c+45c "	60	60

Surtax was for child welfare.

Painting Type of Regular Issue

Designs: 15c+15c, Still Life, by Alfredo Guttero (horiz.). 90c+90c, Nude, by Miguel C. Victorica (horiz.).

1973, Aug. 28 Litho. *Perf. 13½*

B60	A472	15c+15c multi.	25	20
B61	"	90c+90c "	90	80

Philatelists' Day.

Bird Type of 1970

Birds: 70c+30c, Blue seed-eater. 1.20p +60c, Hooded siskin.

1974, May 11 Litho. *Perf. 13½*

B62	AP25	70c+30c multi.	22	10
B63	"	1.20p+60c "	40	20

Surtax was for child welfare.

Painting Type of 1974

Design: 70c+30c, The Lama, by Juan Batlle Planas.

1974, May 11 Litho. *Perf. 13½*

B64	A477	70c+30c multi.	22	10

PRENFIL-74 UPU, International Exhibition of Philatelic Periodicals, Buenos Aires, Oct. 1–12.

Plush-crested Jay
SP28

Designs: 13p+6.50p, Golden-collared macaw. 20p+10p, Begonia. 40p+20p, Teasel.

1976, June 12 Litho. *Perf. 13½*

B65	SP28	7p+3.50p multi.	20	15
B66	"	13p+6.50p "	30	25
B67	"	20p+10p "	50	40
B68	"	40p+20p "	75	60

Argentine philately.

Telegraph, Communications Satellite
SP29

Designs: 20p+10p, Old and new mail trucks. 60p+30p, Old, new packet boats. 70p+35p, Biplane and jet.

1977, July 16 Litho. *Perf. 13½*

B69	SP29	10p+5p multi.	15	10
B70	"	20p+10p "	30	20
B71	"	60p+30p "	90	60
B72	"	70p+35p "	1.05	70

Surtax was for Argentine philately.

Church of St. Francis Type, 1977, Inscribed: "EXPOSICION ARGENTINA '77"

1977, Aug. 27

B73	A515	160p+80p multi.	2.40	1.60

Surtax was for Argentina '77 Philatelic Exhibition. Issued in sheets of 4.

No. B73 Overprinted with Soccer Cup Emblem

1978, Feb. 4 Litho. *Perf. 13½*

B74	A515	160p+80p multi.	2.40	
		a. Souvenir sheet of 4	10.00	

11th World Cup Soccer Championship, Argentina, June 1–25.

No. B74a contains 4 No. B74, light blue margin with black inscription. Size: 103x133mm.

Spinus Magellanicus
SP30

Birds: 100p+100p, Variable seedeater. 150p+150p, Yellow thrush. 200p+200p, Pyrocephalus rubineus. 500p+500p, Great kiskadee.

1978, Aug. 5 Litho. *Perf. 13½*

B75	SP30	50p+ 50p multi.	75	50
B76	"	100p+100p "	1.50	1.00
B77	"	150p+150p "	2.25	1.50
B78	"	200p+200p "	3.00	2.00
B79	"	500p+500p "	7.50	5.00
		Nos. B75–B79 (5)	15.00	10.00

ARGENTINA '78, Inter-American Philatelic Exhibition, Buenos Aires, Oct. 27–Nov. 5. Nos. B75–B79 issued in sheets of 4 with marginal inscriptions commemorating Exhibition and 1978 Soccer Championship.

AIR POST STAMPS.

Airplane Circles the Globe
AP1

Eagle
AP2

Wings Cross the Sea
AP3

Condor on Mountain Crag
AP4

Perforations of Nos. C1–C37 vary from clean-cut to rough and uneven, with many skipped perfs.

Lithographed

Wmkd. RA in Sun. (90)

1928, Mar. 1 *Perf. 13x13½, 13½x13*

C1	AP1	5c light red	1.25	60
C2	"	10c Prussian blue	2.00	80
C3	AP2	15c light brown	2.00	80
C4	AP1	18c lilac gray	7.00	3.00
		a. 18c brown lilac	8.00	4.00
		b. Double impression	300.00	
C5	AP2	20c ultramarine	3.00	1.00
C6	"	24c deep blue	4.00	2.00
C7	AP3	25c bright violet	4.00	1.25
C8	"	30c rose red	3.50	1.25
C9	AP4	35c rose	2.50	1.00
C10	AP1	36c bistre brown	3.50	1.75
C11	AP4	50c gray black	4.00	75
C12	AP2	54c chocolate	4.00	2.00
C13	"	72c yellow green	4.00	1.75
		a. Double impression	275.00	
C14	AP3	90c dark brown	8.00	1.50
C15	"	1p slate blue & red	8.00	60
C16	"	1.08p rose & dark blue	12.00	3.00
C17	AP4	1.26p dull violet & green	18.00	7.00
C18	"	1.80p blue & lilac rose	16.00	7.50
C19	"	3.60p gray & blue	40.00	12.50
		Nos. C1–C19 (19)	146.75	50.05

The watermark on No. C4a is larger than on the other stamps of this set, measuring 10 mm. across Sun.

Zeppelin First Flight.

Air Post Stamps of 1928 Overprinted in Blue

"ZEPPELIN" 1er VUELO 1930

1930, May

C20	AP2	20c ultramarine	15.00	10.00
C21	AP4	50c gray black	20.00	10.00
		a. Invtd. ovpt.	*500.00*	
C22	AP3	1p slate blue & red	20.00	12.50
		a. Invtd. ovpt.	*600.00*	
C23	AP4	1.80p blue & lilac rose	50.00	25.00
C24	"	3.60p gray & blue	125.00	75.00
		Nos. C20–C24 (5)	230.00	132.50

Overprinted in Green.

C25	AP2	20c ultramarine	10.00	7.00
C26	AP4	50c gray black	10.00	8.00

C27 AP3 90c dark brown 10.00 8.00
C28 " 1p slate blue & red 15.00 9.00
C29 AP4 1.80p blue & lilac rose 550.00 400.00
a. Thick paper 1100.00
Nos. C25-C29 (5) 595.00 432.00

Air Post Stamps of 1928 Overprinted in Red

1930
6
Septiembre
-1931-

1931
C30 AP1 18c lilac gray 4.00 3.50
C31 AP2 72c yellow green 5.00 3.50

Overprinted in Red or Blue

6 de Septiembre
1930 — 1931

C32 AP3 90c dk. brown 6.00 3.50
C33 AP4 1.80p blue & lilac rose (Bl) 15.00 8.00
C34 " 3.60p gray & blue 35.00 17.50
Nos. C30-C34 (5) 65.00 36.00

Issued in commemoration of the first anniversary of the Revolution of 1930.

Zeppelin Issue.

Air Post Stamps of 1928 Overprinted in Blue or Red

GRAF
ZEPPELIN
1932

1932, Aug. 4
C35 AP1 5c light red (Bl) 8.00 5.00
C36 " 18c lilac gray (R) 15.00 10.00
a. 18c brown lilac (R) 75.00 75.00

Overprinted

GRAF ZEPPELIN
1932

C37 AP3 90c dk. brown (R) 20.00 12.50

Plane and Letter
AP5

Mercury
AP6

Plane in Flight
AP7

Photogravure
Wmkd. RA in Sun. (90)

1940, Oct. 23 ***Perf. 13½x13, 13x13½***
C38 AP5 30c deep orange 3.00 10
C39 AP6 50c dark brown 4.00 10
C40 AP5 1p carmine 1.25 10
C41 AP7 1.25p deep green 1.25 15
C42 AP5 2.50p bright blue 2.25 35
Nos. C38-C42 (5) 11.75 80

Perf. 13½x13, 13x13½
1942, Oct. 6 Lithographed Wmk. 90
C43 AP8 30c orange 50 10
C44 AP9 50c dull brown & buff 75 15

See also Nos. C49-C52, C57, C61.

Plane and Letter
AP8

Mercury and Plane
AP9

Plane over Iguaçu Falls
AP10

Plane over the Andes
AP11

Perf. 13½x13
1946, June 10 Unwmkd.
C45 AP10 15c dull red brown 16 8
C46 AP11 25c gray green 40 8

See also Nos. C53-C54.

Allegory of Flight
AP12

Astrolabe
AP13

Surface-Tinted Paper.
Perf. 13½x13, 13x13½.
1946, Sept. 25 Litho. Unwmkd.
C47 AP12 15c slate green, *pale green* 60 35
C48 AP13 60c violet brown, *ochre* 1.00 65

Types of 1942.
1946-48 ***Perf. 13½x13*** **Unwmkd.**
C49 AP8 30c orange 1.00 8
C50 AP9 50c dull brn.& buff 1.00 20
C51 AP8 1p carmine ('47) 1.00 15
C52 " 2.50p bright blue ('48) 4.00 85

Types of 1946.
1948 Wmk. 90
C53 AP10 15c dull red brown 15 10
C54 AP11 25c gray green 30 10

Atlas (National Museum, Naples)
AP14

Map of Argentine Republic, Globe and Caliper—AP15

Perf. 13½x13, 13x13½.
1948-49 Photogravure. Wmk. 288
C55 AP14 45c dp. brn. ('49) 40 20
C56 AP15 70c dark green 45 20

Issued to commemorate the 4th Pan-American Reunion of Cartographers, Buenos Aires, October-November, 1948.

Mercury Type of 1942.
Lithographed
1949 ***Perf. 13x13½*** **Wmk. 288**
C57 AP9 50c dull brown & buff 60 18

Marksmanship Trophy
AP16

1949, Nov. 4 Photogravure.
C58 AP16 75c brown 1.00 30

World Rifle Championship, 1949.

Douglas DC-3 and Condor
AP17

Perf. 13x13½.
1951, June 20 Wmk. 90
C59 AP17 20c dark olive green 15 8

10th anniversary of the State air lines.

Douglas DC-6 and Condor
AP18

1951, Oct. 17 ***Perf. 13½.***
C60 AP18 20c blue 15 9

End of Argentine 5-year Plan.

Plane-Letter Type of 1942.
Lithographed
1951 ***Perf. 13½x13*** **Wmk. 90**
C61 AP8 1p carmine 45 18

Jesus by Leonardo da Vinci (detail, "Virgin of the Rocks")
AP19

Perf. 13½x13
1956, Sept. 29 Photo. Wmk. 90
C62 AP19 1p dull purple 40 20

Issued to express the gratitude of the children of Argentina to the people of the world for their help against poliomyelitis.

Battle of Montevideo
AP20

Leonardo Rosales and Tomas Espora
AP21

Guillermo Brown
AP22

Map of Americas and Arms of Buenos Aires
AP23

1957, March 2 ***Perf. 13½***
C63 AP20 60c blue gray 15 8
C64 AP21 1p bright pink 15 8
C65 AP22 2p brown 25 15

Issued to commemorate the centenary of the death of Admiral Guillermo Brown, founder of the Argentine navy.

1957, Aug. 16
C66 AP23 2p rose violet 25 15

Issued to publicize the Inter-American Economic Conference in Buenos Aires.

Modern Locomotive
AP24

1957, Aug. 31 ***Perf. 13½*** **Wmk. 90**
C67 AP24 60c gray 12 8

Centenary of Argentine railroads.

Globe, Flag and Compass Rose
AP25

Design: 2p, Key.

1957, Sept. 14

C68 AP25 1p reddish brown 15 10
C69 " 2p Prussian blue 30 12

Issued to publicize the 1957 International Congress for Tourism.

Birds Carrying Letters
AP26

1957, Nov. 6

C70 AP26 1p bright blue 15 8

Issued for Letter Writing Week, Oct. 6–12.

Early Plane
AP27

1958, May 31 ***Perf. 13½*** **Wmk. 90**

C71 AP27 2p maroon 20 18

Issued to commemorate the 50th anniversary of the Argentine Aviation Club.

Stamp of 1858 and
"The Post of Santa Fe"
AP28

Design: 80c, Stamp of Buenos Aires and view of the Plaza de la Aduana.

1958 **Lithographed** ***Perf. 13½***

C72 AP28 80c pale bistre & slate blue 20 10
C73 " 1p red orange & dark blue 25 18

Issued to commemorate the centenary of the first postage stamps of Buenos Aires and the Argentine Confederation.
Issue dates: 80c, Oct. 18; 1p, Aug. 23.

Comet Jet over World Map
AP29

1959, May 16 ***Perf. 13½*** **Wmk. 90**

C74 AP29 5p black & olive 30 10

Issued to commemorate the inauguration of jet flights by Argentine Airlines.

Type of Regular Issue, 1960.

"Cabildo" and: 1.80p, Mariano Moreno. 5p, Manuel Belgrano and Juan José Castelli.

Photogravure

1960, May 28 ***Perf. 13½*** **Wmk. 90**

C75 A287 1.80p red brown 15 10
a. Souvenir sheet of 3 75 60
C76 " 5p buff & purple 35 15
a. Souvenir sheet of 3 1.50 1.25

Issued to commemorate the 150th anniversary of the May Revolution.
Souvenir sheets are imperf. No. C75a contains one No. C75 and 1p and 2p resembling Nos. 713–714; stamps in reddish brown, marginal inscriptions in green. No. C76a contains one No. C76 and 4.20p and 10.70p resembling Nos. 715–716; stamps are in green, marginal inscriptions in reddish brown. Sheet size: 152x106mm.

Symbolic of New Provinces
AP30

1960, July 8 **Lithographed**

C77 AP30 1.80p deep carmine & blue 15 10

Issued to commemorate the elevation of the territories of Chubut, Formosa, Neuquen, Rio Negro and Santa Cruz to provinces.

Type of Regular Issue, 1960
Photogravure

1960, Oct. 1 ***Perf. 13½*** **Wmk. 90**

C78 A291 1.80p rose lilac 20 10
C79 " 10.70p brt. greenish blue 50 25

Issued to commemorate the 8th Congress of the Postal Union of the Americas and Spain.

UNESCO Emblem
AP31

1962, July 14 **Lithographed**

C80 AP31 13p ochre & brown 50 40

Issued to commemorate the 15th anniversary of UNESCO (U.N. Educational, Scientific and Cultural Organization).

Mail Coach
AP32

1962, Oct. 6 ***Perf. 13½*** **Wmk. 90**

C81 AP32 5.60p gray brown & black 25 15

Mailman's Day, Sept. 14, 1962.

No. 695 and Type of 1959 Surcharged in Green

AEREO
5.60 PESOS

1962, Oct. 31 **Photogravure**

C82 A277 5.60p on 5p brown 30 20
C83 " 18p on 5p brown, *greenish* 1.00 30

UPAE Emblem
AP33

Skylark
AP34

Photogravure

1962, Nov. 24 ***Perf. 13½*** **Wmk. 90**

C84 AP33 5.60p dark blue 20 15

Issued to commemorate the 50th anniversary of the founding of the Postal Union of the Americas and Spain, UPAE.

1963, Feb. 9 **Lithographed**

Design: 11p, Super Albatros.

C85 AP34 5.60p blue & black 20 15
C86 " 11p bl., blk. & red 30 20

9th World Gliding Championships.

Symbolic Plane
AP35

1963–65 ***Perf. 13½*** **Wmk. 90**

C87 AP35 5.60p dk. pur., car. & brt. grn. 25 12
C88 " 7p blk. & bister ('64) 50 12
C88A " 7p blk. & bister ('65) 5.00 50
C89 " 11p blk., dk. pur. & green 50 25
C90 " 18p dk. pur., red & vio. blue 1.00 35
C91 " 21p brown, red & gray 1.00 50
Nos. C87-C91 (6) 8.25 1.84

"Argentina" reads down on No. C88, up on No. C88A. See also Nos. C101–C104, C108–C111, C123–C126, C135–C141.

Type of Regular Issue, 1964

Design: 18p, Map of Falkland Islands (Islas Malvinas).

1964, Feb. 22 ***Perf. 13½*** **Wmk. 90**

Size: 33x22mm.

C92 A327 18p lt. & dk. blue & olive green 75 50

Issued to commemorate the 60th anniversary of Argentina's claim to Antarctic territories.

U.P.U. Monument, Bern, and U.N. Emblem
AP36

Engraved

1964, May 23 ***Perf. 13½*** **Wmk. 90**

C93 AP36 18p red & dk. brn. 60 30

Issued to commemorate the 15th Universal Postal Union Congress, Vienna, Austria, May–June 1964.

Discovery of America, Florentine Woodcut
AP37

1964, Oct. 10 **Lithographed**

C94 AP37 13p tan & black 35 25

Issued for the Day of the Race, Columbus Day.

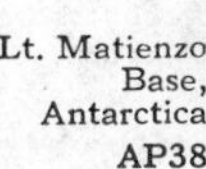

Lt. Matienzo Base, Antarctica
AP38

1965, Feb. 27 **Photo.** ***Perf. 13½***

C95 AP38 11p salmon pink 30 20

Issued to publicize the national territory of Tierra del Fuego, Antarctic and South Atlantic Isles.

No. C88A Overprinted in Silver:
"PRIMERAS / JORNADAS FILATELICAS / RIOPLATENSES"

1965, Mar. 17 **Lithographed**

C96 AP35 7p black & bister 25 20

Issued to commemorate the First Rio de la Plata Stamp Show, sponsored jointly by the Argentine and Uruguayan Philatelic Associations, Montevideo, March 19–28.

ITU Emblem
AP39

Ascending Rocket
AP40

1965, May 11 ***Perf. 13½*** **Wmk. 90**

C97 AP39 18p slate, blk. & red 50 30

Issued to commemorate the centenary of the International Telecommunication Union.

1965, May 29 **Photo.** ***Perf. 13½***

Design: 50p, Earth with trajectories and magnetic field (horiz.).

C98 AP40 18p vermilion 50 30
C99 " 50p dp. vio. blue 1.25 65

Issued to commemorate the 6th Symposium on Space Research, held in Buenos Aires, and to honor the National Commission of Space Research.

Type of 1963–65 Inscribed
"Republica Argentina" Reading
Down

1965, Oct. 13 **Litho.** **Wmk. 90**

C101 AP35 12p dk. carmine rose & brown 50 20
C102 " 15p vio. blue & dark red 75 25
C103 " 27.50p dk. bl. green & gray 1.00 40
C104 " 30.50p dk. brown & dk. blue 1.50 50

Argentine Antarctica Map and Centaur Rocket
AP41

1966, Feb. 19 ***Perf. 13½*** **Wmk. 90**

C105 AP41 27.50p bl., blk. & dp. org. 55 35

Issued to commemorate the launchings of sounding balloons and of a Gamma Centaur rocket in Antarctica during February, 1965.

Sea Gull and Southern Cross
AP42

1966, May 14 *Perf. 13½* Wmk. 90

C106 AP42 12p Prus. blue, black & red 20 15

Issued to commemorate the 50th anniversary of the Naval Aviation School.

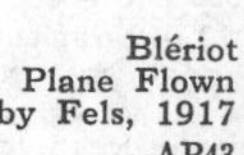

Blériot Plane Flown by Fels, 1917
AP43

1967, Sept. 2 Litho. *Perf. 13½*

C107 AP43 26p olive, blue & black 30 15

Issued to commemorate the flight by Theodore Fels from Buenos Aires to Montevideo, Sept. 2, 1917, allegedly the first International airmail flight.

Type of 1963–65 Inscribed "Republica Argentina" Reading Down

1967, Dec. 20 *Perf. 13½* Wmk. 90

C108	AP35	26p brown	60	20
C109	"	40p violet	90	30
C110	"	68p blue green	1.50	40
C111	"	78p ultramarine	2.50	50

Vito Dumas and Ketch "Legh II"
AP44

1968, July 27 Litho. Wmk. 90

C112 AP44 68p blue, blk., red & vio. blue 50 30

Issued to commemorate Vito Dumas's one-man voyage around the world in 1943.

Type of Regular Issue and

Assembly Emblem
AP45

Design: 40p, Globe and map of South America.

1968, Oct. 19 Litho. *Perf. 13½*

C113 A395 40p brt. pink, lt. blue & black 40 25
C114 AP45 68p blue, lt. blue, gold & black 60 40

Issued to publicize the 4th Plenary Assembly of the International Telegraph and Telephone Consultative Committee, Mar del Plata, Sept. 23–Oct. 25.

Radar Antenna, Balcarce Station
AP46

Photogravure

1969, Aug. 23 *Perf. 13½* Wmk. 90

C115 AP46 40p blue gray 50 25

Issued to publicize communications by satellite through International Telecommunications Consortium (INTELSAT).

Atucha Nuclear Center
AP47

1969, Dec. 13 Litho. Wmk. 365

C116 AP47 26p bl. & multi. 1.00 30

Completion of Atucha Nuclear Center.

Type of 1963–65 Inscribed "Republica Argentina" Reading Down

1969–71 *Perf. 13½* Wmk. 365

C123	AP35	40p violet	3.00	20
C124	"	68p dark blue green ('70)	1.50	25

Unwmkd.

C125	AP35	26p yel. brn. ('71)	25	10
C126	"	40p violet ('71)	2.50	16

Old Fire Engine and Fire Brigade Emblem
AP48

1970, Aug. 8 Litho. Unwmkd.

C128 AP48 40c green & multi. 45 15

Centenary of the Fire Brigade.

Education Year Emblem
AP49

1970, Aug. 29 *Perf. 13½*

C129 AP49 68c blue & black 45 25

Issued for International Education Year.

Fleet Leaving Valparaiso, by Antonio Abel
AP50

1970, Oct. 17 Litho. *Perf. 13½*

C130 AP50 26c multicolored 60 10

Issued to commemorate the 150th anniversary of the departure for Peru of the liberation fleet from Valparaiso, Chile.

Sumampa Chapel
AP51

1970, Nov. 7 Photogravure

C131 AP51 40c multicolored 1.00 25

Bishopric of Tucuman, 400th anniversary.

Buenos Aires Planetarium
AP52

1970, Nov. 28 Litho. *Perf. 13½*

C132 AP52 40c multicolored 60 25

Jorge Newbery and Morane Saulnier Plane
AP53

1970, Dec. 19

C133 AP53 26c bl., blk., yel. & green 30 10

24th Aeronautics and Space Week.

Industries Type of Regular Issue

Design: 31c, Refinery.

1971, Oct. 16 Litho. *Perf. 13½*

C134 A445 31c red, blk. & yel. 50 15

Nationalized industries.

Type of 1963–65 Inscribed "Republica Argentina" Reading Down

1971–74 Unwmkd.

C135	AP35	45c brown	1.25	6
C136	"	68c red	35	8
C137	"	70c vio. blue ('73)	35	8
C138	"	90c emerald ('73)	1.25	10
C139	"	1.70p blue ('74)	75	20
C140	"	1.95p emerald ('74)	75	22
C141	"	2.65p deep claret ('74)	80	25
		Nos. C135–C141 (7)	5.50	99

Fluorescent paper was used for Nos. C135–C136, C138–C141. The 70c was issued on both ordinary and fluorescent paper.

Don Quixote, Drawing by Ignacio Zuloaga
AP54

1975, Apr. 26 Photo. *Perf. 13½*

C145 AP54 2.75p yellow, black & red 60 24

Day of the Race and for España 75 International Philatelic Exhibition, Madrid, Apr. 4–13.

No. C87 Surcharged

100 ● PESOS

1975, Sept. 15 Litho. Wmk. 90

C146	AP35	9.20p on 5.60p	50	15
C147	"	19.70p on 5.60p	1.00	30
C148	"	100p on 5.60p	5.00	1.75

No. C87 Surcharged

REVALORIZADO 920 PESOS

1975, Oct. 15

C149	AP35	9.20p on 5.60p	75	15
C150	"	19.70p on 5.60p	1.25	35

AIR POST SEMI-POSTAL STAMPS.

Stamp Engraving
SPAP1

Designs: 70c+70c, Proofing stamp die. 1p+1p, Sheet of stamps. 2.50p+2.50p, The letter. 5p+5p, Gen. San Martín.

Photogravure.

1950, Aug. 26 ***Perf. 13½.*** **Wmk. 90**

CB1 SPAP1 45c+45c violet blue 50 40
CB2 " 70c+70c dark brown 75 60
a. Souvenir sheet of 3 3.75 3.75
CB3 " 1p+1p cerise 2.00 2.00
CB4 " 2.50p+2.50p olive gray 9.00 8.00
CB5 " 5p+5p dull green 12.50 10.00
Nos. CB1-CB5 (5) 24.75 21.00

Issued to publicize the Argentine International Philatelic Exhibition, 1950.

No. CB2a measures 120x150mm., and contains one each of Nos. B12, CB1 and CB2, imperf., with marginal inscriptions and ornamental border in olive green.

Pieta by Michelangelo
SPAP2

1951, Dec. 22 ***Perf. 13½x13.***

CB6 SPAP2 2.45p+7.55p greenish blk. 27.50 17.50

The surtax was for the Eva Perón Foundation.

Flower and Child's Head
SPAP3

Stamp of 1858
SPAP4

1958, Mar. 15 ***Perf. 13½***

CB7 SPAP3 1p+50c deep claret 25 25

Surtax for National Council for Children.

1958, Mar. 29 **Litho.** **Wmk. 90**

CB8 SPAP4 1p+50c gray olive & blue 50 40
CB9 " 2p+1p rose lilac & violet 65 55
CB10 " 3p+1.50p green & brown 75 70
CB11 " 5p+2.50p gray olive & carmine rose 1.25 1.00
CB12 " 10p+5p gray olive & brown 2.50 2.00
Nos. CB8-CB12 (5) 5.65 4.65

The surtax was for the International Centennial Philatelic Exhibition, Buenos Aires, April 19-27.

Type of Semi-Postal Issue, 1958.

Designs: 1p+50c, Flooded area. 5p+2.50p, House and truck under water.

Photogravure.

1958, Oct. 4 ***Perf. 13½*** **Wmk. 90**

CB13 SP11 1p+50c dull purple 25 20
CB14 " 5p+2.50p greenish blue 80 75

The surtax was for victims of a flood in the Buenos Aires district.

Type of Semi-Postal Issue, 1959.

Designs: 2p+1p, Rowing. 3p+1.50p, Woman diver.

1959, Sept. 5 **Litho.** ***Perf. 13½***

CB15 SP13 2p+1p bright blue & black 50 35
CB16 " 3p+1.50p olive & black 75 60

Issued to commemorate the third Pan American Games, Chicago, Aug. 27-Sept. 7, 1959.

Type of Semi-Postal Issue, 1960.

Birds: 2p+1p, Rufous tinamou. 3p+1.50p, Rhea.

1960, Feb. 6 ***Perf. 13½***

CB17 SP14 2p+1p rose carmine & salmon 30 20
CB18 " 3p+1.50p slate green 50 40

The surtax was for child welfare work. See also No. CB29.

Buenos Aires Market Place, 1810
SPAP5

Seibo, National Flower
SPAP6

Designs: 6p+3p, Oxcart water carrier. 10.70p+5.30p, Settlers landing. 20p+10p, The Fort.

1960, Aug. 20 **Photo.** **Wmk. 90**

CB19 SPAP5 2p+1p rose brown 18 10
CB20 " 6p+3p gray 40 30
CB21 " 10.70p+5.30p blue 75 45
CB22 " 20p+10p bluish green 1.25 1.00

Issued to publicize the Inter-American Philatelic Exhibition EFIMAYO 1960, Buenos Aires, Oct. 12-24, held to commemorate the sesquicentennial of the May Revolution of 1910.

1960, Sept. 10 ***Perf. 13½***

Design: 10.70p+5.30p, Copihue, Chile's national flower.

CB23 SPAP6 6p+3p lilac rose 40 30
CB24 " 10.70p+5.30p vermilion 60 55

The surtax was for earthquake victims in Chile.

Nos. CB19-CB22 Overprinted:
"DIA DE LAS NACIONES UNIDAS
24 DE OCTUBRE"

1960, Oct. 8

CB25 SPAP5 2p+1p rose brown 25 20
CB26 " 6p+3p gray 45 40
CB27 " 10.70p+5.30p blue 65 60
CB28 " 20p+10p bluish green 1.25 1.20

United Nations Day, Oct. 24, 1960.

Type of Semi-Postal Issue, 1960

Design: Emperor penguins.

1961, Feb. 25 **Photo.** **Wmk. 90**

CB29 SP14 1.80p+90c gray 30 25

The surtax was for child welfare work.

Stamp of 1862
SPAP7

Crutch, Olympic Torch and Rings
SPAP8

1962, May 19 **Lithographed**

CB30 SPAP7 6.50p+6.50p Pruss. bl. & greenish blue 70 70

Issued to publicize the opening of the "Argentina 62" Philatelic Exhibition, Buenos Aires, May 19-29.

Type of Semi-Postal Issue, 1963

Design: 11p+5p, Bicycling.

1963, May 18 ***Perf. 13½*** **Wmk. 90**

CB31 SP21 11p+5p grn., red & black 55 50

Issued to commemorate the 4th Pan American Games, Sao Paulo, Brazil.

Type of Semi-Postal Issue, 1962.

Design: 11p+5p, Great kiskadee.

1963, Dec. 21 ***Perf. 13½*** **Wmk. 90**

CB32 SP20 11p+5p dk. brn., brown, yellow & green 65 65

The surtax was for child welfare.

Type of Semi-Postal Issue, 1964.

Design: 11p+5p, Sailboat.

1964, July 18 **Lithographed**

CB33 SP22 11p+5p brt. blue & black 60 60

Issued to publicize the 18th Olympic Games, Tokyo, Oct. 10-25, 1964.

1964, Sept. 19 **Litho.** ***Perf. 13½***

CB34 SPAP8 18p+9p bluish grn., black, red & yel. 65 65

Issued to publicize the 13th "Olympic" games for the handicapped, Tokyo, 1964.

Bird Type of Semi-Postal Issue, 1962

Design: Chilean swallow.

1964, Dec. 23 **Litho.** **Wmk. 90**

CB35 SP20 18p+9p brn, dk. blue & grn. 1.00 85

The surtax was for child welfare.

Bird Type of Semi-Postal Issue, 1962, Inscribed "R. ARGENTINA"

Design: Rufous ovenbird.

1966, Mar. 26 ***Perf. 13½*** **Wmk. 90**

CB36 SP20 27.50p+12.50p bl., ocher, yel. & green 60 55

The surtax was for child welfare.

Coat of Arms—SPAP9

1966, June 25 **Litho.** ***Perf. 13½***

CB37 SPAP9 10p+10p yellow & multi. 1.75 1.50

Issued to publicize the ARGENTINA '66 Philatelic Exhibition held in connection with the sesquicentennial celebration of the Declaration of Independence, Buenos Aires, July 16-23. The surtax was for the Exhibition. Issued in sheets of 4.

Bird Type of Semi-Postal Issue, 1962, Inscribed "R. ARGENTINA"

Designs: 15p+7p, Blue and yellow tanager. 26p+13p, Toco toucan.

1967 **Lithographed** **Wmk. 90**

CB38 SP20 15p+7p blk., blue, green & yellow 50 40
CB39 " 26p+13p blk., org., yel. & blue 50 40

The surtax was for child welfare.
Issue dates: 15p+7p, Jan. 14. 26p+13p, Dec. 23.

Bird Type of Semi-Postal Issue, 1969

Design: 26p+13p, Lineated woodpecker.

1969, Sept. 20 ***Perf. 13½*** **Wmk. 365**

CB40 SP24 26p+13p multi. 30 25

The surtax was for child welfare.

Bird Type of Semi-Postal Issue, 1970

Design: 40c+20c, Chilean flamingo.

1970, May 9 **Litho.** **Wmk. 365**

CB41 SP25 40c+20c multi. 50 40

The surtax was for child welfare.

Fish Type of Semi-Postal Issue, 1971

Design: Pejerrey (atherinidae family).

1971, Feb. 20 ***Perf. 12½*** **Unwmkd.**

Size: 75x15mm.

CB42 SP26 40c+20c light blue & multicolored 40 35

The surtax was for child welfare.

OFFICIAL STAMPS.

Regular Issues Overprinted in Black

1884–87 *Perf. 12, 14.* **Unwmkd.**

O1 A29 ½c brown 5.00 5.00
a. Inverted overprint 5.00 5.00
O2 A23 1c red 2.50 2.00
a. Invtd. ovpt., perf. 14 8.50 8.50
b. Perf. 12 13.50 13.50
c. As "a," perf. 12 10.00 10.00
O3 A29 1c red 40 35
a. Inverted overprint 60 50
b. Double overprint 10.00 7.50
O4 A20 2c green 45 35
a. Inverted overprint 20.00 17.50
b. Double overprint 17.50 17.50
O5 A11 4c brown 35 35
a. Inverted overprint 15.00 15.00
O6 A7 8c lake 30 25
a. Inverted overprint 20.00 17.50
O7 A8 10c green 25.00 12.50
O8 A23 12c ultra. (#45) 1.75 1.50
a. Perf. 14 75.00 17.50
O9 A29 12c greenish blue 60 50
a. Inverted overprint 20.00 15.00
O10 A19 24c blue 75 75
a. Inverted overprint 1.75 1.50
O11 A21 25c lake 6.00 4.00
O12 A12 30c orange 11.00 8.00
O13 A13 60c black 6.00 4.00
a. Inverted overprint 20.00 12.50
O14 A14 90c blue 4.50 3.50
a. Inverted overprint 12.00 10.00
b. Double overprint 13.50
Nos. O1-O14 (14) 64.60 43.05

1884 ***Rouletted.***

O15 A17 16c green 60 50
a. Double overprint 8.00 8.00
b. Inverted overprint 22.50
O16 A18 20c blue 2.25 1.75
a. Inverted overprint 17.50 15.00
O17 A19 24c blue 75 60
a. Inverted overprint 1.50 1.25
b. Double ovpt., one inverted 22.50

Overprinted Diagonally in Red.

1885 ***Perf. 12.***

O18 A20 2c green 1.00 90
a. Inverted overprint 10.00 8.00
O19 A11 4c brown 1.25 1.00
a. Inverted overprint 9.00 9.00
b. Double overprint 9.00 9.00
O20 A13 60c black 10.00 6.00
O21 A14 90c blue 110.00 75.00

1885 ***Rouletted***

O22 A19 24c blue 9.00 4.00

On all of these stamps, the overprint is found reading both upwards and downwards.

Regular Issues Handstamped Horizontally in Black **OFICIAL**

1884 ***Perf. 12, 14.***

O23 A23 1c red 27.50 15.00
a. Perf. 12 50.00 50.00
O24 A20 2c green 75.00 60.00
a. Diagonal ovpt. 20.00 15.00
O25 A11 4c brown 10.00 8.00
O26 A7 8c lake 15.00 9.00
O27 A23 12c ultramarine 17.50 10.00

Overprinted Diagonally.

O28 A19 24c blue, rouletted 15.00 12.00
O29 A13 60c black 12.50 9.00

Liberty Head
O1

OFFICIAL STAMPS.

FOR DEPARTMENTS.

1913–37

Regular Issues of 1911–37 Overprinted in Black.

M. A. or **M. A.** (Ministry of Agriculture).
M. C. or **M. G.** (Ministry of War).
M. H. or **M. H.** (Ministry of Finance).
M. I. or **M. I.** (Ministry of the Interior).

Asterisk (*) indicates that the stamp is known.

The number in the first column is the catalogue number of the stamp overprinted.

Cat. No.	M. A. (Type I)		M. A. (Type II)		M. C. (Type I)		M. G. (Type II)		M. H. (Type I)		M. H. (Type II)		M. I. (Type I)		M. I. (Type II)	
181	10	5			25	5			25	10			50	15		
190	10	5			15	5			10	5			25	6		
191	25	6			50	5			25	5			1.00	35		
194	10	5			15	5			15	5			15	5		
196	15	5			30	5			15	5			40	5		
208	10	6			2.50	1.00										
209	10	6			25	10			10	6			1.00	50		
212	10	6			50	5			5	5			35	15		
220	15	5			3.50	50			15	15			75	25		
222					2.50	1.00										
232					10	5										
233					15	5			10	5						
236					10	5			75	25			1.00	10		
238	50	25			20	5			10	5						
249	5	5			5	5										
250	5	5			5	5			*	7.50			15	5		
253	15	5			10	5			25	5			15	5		
255	15	10			30	10			50	5						
256	15	10			25	5			1.00	25						
265	50	50							1.00	25			5.00	2.50		
266	50	50			75	5			1.00	50						
269	10	5			15	5			50	15			1.00	50		
271					75	25			1.00	35						
299					2.50	50										
305					50	15										
306					2.50	50							12.50	12.50		
309					2.50	20							5.00	5.00		
311	1.25	35											2.50	1.50		
312	25.00	*			50	10			10.00	10.00			2.50	1.50		
318					3.50	50										
324	5	5			10	5			30	15			5	5		
325	25	10			10	5			10	5			5	5		
328	5	5			10	5			10	5			10	5		
330	5	5			50	25			10	5			1.50	1.50		
331	5	5			75	5			15	5			50	5		
341	5	5			50	25							10	5		
342	5	5	3.50	3.50	20	5							15	5		
343			10	5	15	5	50	15			2.50	2.50	1.00	1.00	15	5
345	10	5	5	5	15	5	10	3	35	5			10	5	15	5
346	10	5	5	5	15	5	10	3			15	3			10	5
347	10	5							10.00	10.00			40	10		
348	15	5	15	5	50	5	15	3	50	5	50	3	25	5	15	5
351			15	5	1.00	25	25	5			25	3			35	15
353							1.25	75			75	15				
359					50	5										
360	15	10							10.00	10.00						
419			5	5			3	5			5	5			5	5
420			5	5			3	5			5	5			5	5
422			5	5			3	5			25	25			5	5
427			5	5			6	5			10	5			15	5
430			5	5			5	5			10	5			5	5
434			30	5			15	10			25	25			10	5
437			20	6			25	5			25	5			25	6
438			10	5			20	5			10	5			10	5
441			20	5			15	5								
442			15	5			15	5			15	5			15	5
444							35	15								
445			2.50	1.50			2.50	75			1.00	35			2.50	1.50
446			1.00	50			1.00	35			40	10			75	50

OFFICIAL STAMPS.

FOR DEPARTMENTS. (Continued)

1913-37

Regular Issues of 1911-37 Overprinted in Black.

M. J. I. or **M. J. I.** (Ministry of Justice and Instruction).

M. M. or **M. M.** (Ministry of Marine).

M. O. P. or **M. O. P.** (Ministry of Public Works).

M. R. C. or **M. R. C.** (Ministry of Foreign Affairs and Religion).

Asterisk (*) indicates that the stamp is known

The number in the first column is the catalogue number of the stamp overprinted.

Cat. No.	M. J. I. (Type I)		M. J. I. (Type II)		M. M. (Type I)		M. M. (Type II)		M. O. P. (Type I)		M. O. P. (Type II)		M. R. C. (Type I)		M. R. C. (Type II)	
181	1.00	25			15	5			25	10			6.00	2.00		
190	50	10			15	5			50	15			15	5		
191	50	10			50	25							25	10		
194	50	5			25	5			40	5			1.00	50		
196	40	5			30	5			2.00	50			30	10		
208	25	10														
209	25	10			50	15										
212	1.50	25			15	5							1.00	35		
220	20	10							10.00	75			50	20		
222	75	15														
232	10	5			25	6										
233	50	25			20	5										
236	50	5			20	5										
238	17.50	10.00							35.00	*						
249	10	5			5	5										
250	15	5			5	5										
253	15	5			10	5										
255	20	5			15	10										
256	2.50	50			2.50	1.00			35.00	*			2.50	1.50		
265	50	15			25	15							1.25	35		
266	15	5			10	5			7.50	3.50						
269	10	5			20	5			3.50	15			50	15		
271	50	15							20.00	*						
305	50	25														
306	1.25	75											12.50	7.50		
309	30	5			1.50	25							25.00	*		
311	7.50	3.50			7.50	7.50							25.00	*		
312	1.25	15			7.50	7.50										
318	2.50	3.50														
324	10	5			5	5			30	10			5	5		
325	5	5			10	5			30	5			5	5		
328	10	5			25	5			30	5			5	5		
330	10	5			50	15			50	10			10	5		
331	30	5			50	5			75	10			15	5		
340			2.50	2.50											1.50	1.50
341	5	5	50	50	1.50	1.50			15	5			6	5		
342	6	5			25	10			15	5			6	5		
343	10	5	6	5			75	35			10	5	20	10		
345	10	5	15	5	25	5	20	3	15	5	15	5	15	5		
346	1.00	25	5	5			25	3			10	5	2.50	25	25	10
347	15	5	75	50					10.00	3.50			25	10		
348	15	5	10	5	75	5	50	5	30	5	2.50	50	15	5	25	10
351			10	5			1.50	50			25	5	1.00	50	35	15
353			75	50			7.50	3.50			10.00	7.50			35	20
359	20	5			75	10			75	5						
360	50	50											15	10		
419			5	5			5	5			5	5			5	5
420			5	5			5	5			5	5			5	5
422			5	5			5	5			6	5			15	15
427			6	5			6	3			6	5			6	5
430			5	5			6	3			10	5			10	5
434			50	50			35	15			20	6			25	25
437			15	5			35	15			25	6			25	15
438			15	5			15	3			15	5			25	15
441			15	5												
442			15	5			25	3			15	6			15	5
444											25	6				
445			75	35			3.50	1.50			2.50	1.50			2.00	1.00
446			50	25			2.50	1.50			1.00	50			75	35

1901, Dec. 1 Engraved *Perf. 11½*

O31	O1	1c gray	25	15
O32	"	2c orange brown	35	20
O33	"	5c red	50	20
O34	"	10c dark green	50	25
O35	"	30c dark blue	1.50	75
O36	"	50c orange	1.00	35
		Nos. O31-O36 (6)	4.10	1.90

Regular Stamps of 1935-51 Overprinted in Black **SERVICIO OFICIAL** *c*

Wmkd. RA in Sun. (90)

Perf. 13x13½, 13½x13, 13.

1938-54

O37	A129	1c buff ('40)	7	5
O38	A130	2c dk. brn. ('40)	7	5
O39	A132	3c green ('39)	9	8
O40	"	3c light gray ('39)	8	5
O41	A134	5c yellow brown	7	5
O42	A195	5c carmine ('53)	9	5
O43	A137	10c carmine	8	4
O44	"	10c brown ('39)	7	3
O45	A140	15c light gray blue, type II ('47)	7	3
O46	A139	15c slate blue	9	8
O47	"	15c pale ultra. ('39)	8	3
O48	"	20c blue ('53)	1.00	3
O49	A141	25c carmine	10	3
		a. Overprint 11mm.	15	4
O49B	A143	40c dark violet	20	8
O50	A144	50c red & orange	8	3
		a. Overprint 11mm.	20	4
O51	A146	1p brown black & light blue ('40)	8	4
		a. Overprint 11mm.		
O52	A224	1p chocolate & light blue ('51)	30	8
		a. Overprint 11mm.	40	
O53	A147	2p brown lake & dk. ultra. (ovpt. 11mm.) ('54)	50	8
		Nos. O37-O53 (18)	3.12	91

Overprinted in Black on Stamps and Types of 1945-47

Perf. 13x13½, 13½x13.

1945-46 **Unwmkd.**

O54	A130	2c sepia	50	25
O55	A134	3c light gray	45	15
O56	"	5c yellow brown	25	5
O57	A195	5c deep carmine	5	5
O58	A137	10c brown	5	5
		a. Double overprint		
O59	A140	15c light gray blue, type II	9	5
O61	A141	25c dull rose	9	5
O62	A144	50c red & orange	45	5
O63	A146	1p brown black & light blue	25	5
O64	A147	2p brown lake & blue	20	5
O65	A148	5p indigo & olive green	30	12
O66	A149	10p deep claret & intense black	55	20
O67	A150	20p bl. grn. & brn.	85	40
		Nos. O54-O67 (13)	4.08	1.52

Overprinted in Black on Stamps and Types of 1942-50

Perf. 13, 13x13½.

1944-51 **Wmk. 288**

O73	A134	3c light gray	1.00	50
O74	"	5c yellow brown	20	6
O75	A137	10c red brown	8	3
O76	A140	15c light gray blue, type II	8	3
O77	A144	50c red & orange (overprint 11 mm.)	50	5
O78	A146	1p brown black & light blue (overprint 11mm.)	1.10	5
		Nos. O73-O78 (6)	2.96	72

Regular Issue of 1952

Overprinted in Black SERVICIO OFICIAL *d*

1953 ***Perf. 13.*** **Wmk. 90**

O79	A228	5c gray	5	3
O80	"	10c rose lilac	5	3
O81	"	20c rose pink	5	3

O82	A228	25c dull green	5	3
O83	"	40c dull violet	6	3
O84	"	45c deep blue	15	5
O85	"	50c dull brown	8	4

Nos. 611–617 Overprinted Type "e" in Blue

SERVICIO OFICIAL *e* SERVICIO OFICIAL *f*

Perf. 13x13½, 13½x13

O86	A229	1p dark brown	12	6
O87	"	1.50p deep green	25	8
O88	"	2p bright carmine	35	20
O89	"	3p indigo	70	30

Size: 30x40mm.

O90	A229	5p red brown	90	35
O91	A228	10p red	2.50	1.50
O92	A229	20p green	6.00	4.00
		Nos. O79–O92 (14)	11.31	6.73

No. 612 Overprinted Type "f" in Blue.

O93	A229	1.50p deep green	35	8

Regular Issue of 1954–59 Variously Overprinted in Black or Blue

S. OFICIAL *g* SERVICIO OFICIAL *h*

Perf. 13½, 13x13½, 13½x13

1955–61 Lithographed Wmk. 90

O94	A237	(*c*)	20c red (#629)	10	4
O95	"	(*d*)	20c red (#629)	8	4
O96	"	(")	40c red, ovpt. 15mm. (#630)	10	4

Engraved

O97	A239	(*g*)	50c blue (#632) ('58)	7	5

Photogravure

O98	A239	(*h*)	1p brown (#635) ('59)	8	5
O99	"	(*e*)	1p brown (Bl) (#635) ('59)	8	5
O100	"	(")	1p brown (Bk) (#635) ('60)	8	5

Engraved

O101	A239	(*h*)	3p vio. brown (#638) ('58)	8	5
O102	A240	(")	5p gray green (#639) ('57)	10	8
O103	"	(*e*)	10p yel. green (#640) ('58)	40	15
O104	"	(*f*)	20p dull violet (#641) ('59)	75	30
O105	"	(*h*)	20p dull violet (#641) ('58)	75	25
O106	A241	(*e*)	50p ultra. & ind. (#642) ('61)	1.75	75
			Nos. O94–O106 (13)	4.42	1.90

The overprints on Nos. O99–O100 and O103–O104 are horizontal; that on No. O109 is vertical. On No. O106 overprint measures 23mm.

No. 659 Overprinted Type "d".

Lithographed.

1957 *Perf. 13* Wmk. 90

O108	A133	20c dull pur. (ovpt. 15mm.)	8	5

Nos. 666, 658 and 663 Variously Overprinted

1957 Photo. *Perf. 13x13½, 13½*

O109	A261	(*g*)	2p claret	25	5
O110	A254	(*e*)	2.40p brown	25	5
O111	A258	(*c*)	4.40p greenish gray	45	8

Nos. 668, 685–687, 690–691, 693–705, 742, 742C and Types of 1959–65 Overprinted in Black, Blue or Red Types "e," "g" or

S. OFICIAL *i* S. OFICIAL *j*

S. OFICIAL *k* S. OFICIAL *m* S. OFICIAL *n*

Lithographed; Photogravure

1960–68 *Perf. 13x13½, 13½*

O112	A128	(*g*)	5c buff (vert. ovpt.) ('62)	7	3
O113	A275	(*j*)	10c slate green ('62)	5	3
O114	"	(")	20c dull red brown ('62)	5	3
O115	"	(*i*)	50c bister	5	3
O116	A278	(*k*)	1p brown ('62)	5	4
O117	"	(*j*)	1p brown, photo. (vert. ovpt.) ('65)	7	5
O117A	"	(")	1p brn., litho., (vert. ovpt., down, '68)	10	7
O118	A276	(")	2p rose red ('62)	10	5
O119	A312	(*m*)	2p dp. green (vert. ovpt., down) ('64)	25	8
O120	"	(*j*)	2p brt. green (vert. ovpt., up) ('66)	10	5
O121	"	(")	2p green litho. (vert. ovpt., down) ('67)	20	8
O122	A277	(*e*)	3p dark blue (horiz.) ('61)	15	7
O123	"	(*j*)	3p dk. blue ('67)	30	15
O124	A276	(")	4p red, litho. ('63?)	20	5
O125	A312	(")	4p rose red, litho. (vert. ovpt., down) ('65)	5	3
O126	A277	(*e*)	5p brown (Bl) (horiz.)	25	8
O127	"	(")	5p brown (Bk) (horiz.) ('61)	30	8
O128	"	(*j*)	5p sepia ('66)	12	3
O129	"	(*e*)	5p sepia (horiz. ovpt.) ('67)	12	4
O130	A276	(*j*)	8p red ('65)	15	8
O131	A278	(*i*)	10p lt. red brn.	40	10
O132	A276	(*j*)	10p verm. ('66)	18	5
O133	A278	(")	10p brn. carmine (vert. ovpt. up) ('66)	18	5
O134	"	(*m*)	12p dk. brown violet ('64)	30	5
O135	"	(*k*)	20p Pruss. grn. ('61)	80	20
O136	"	(*j*)	20p Pruss. grn. (vert. ovpt., up) ('66)	18	6
O137	A276	(")	20p red, litho. ('67)	30	6
O138	"	(*m*)	20p red, litho. ('67)	20	5
O139	A278	(*j*)	23p grn. (vert. ovpt.) ('65)	25	10
O140	"	(")	25p dp. violet, photo. (R) (vert. ovpt., up) ('66)	30	6
O141	"	(")	25p pur., litho. (R) (vert. ovpt., down) ('67)	40	15
O142	A241	(*n*)	50p dark blue ('66)	40	10
O143	A279	(*m*)	100p blue (horiz. ovpt.) ('64)	2.00	30
O144	"	(")	100p blue (vert. ovpt., up) ('65)	1.25	30
O145	A280	(*m*)	300p dp. violet ('66)	3.50	1.00

The "m" overprint measures 15½mm. on 2p; 14½mm. on 12p, 100p and 300p; 13mm. on 20p.

Nos. 699, 818, 823–825, 827–829, and Type of 1962 Overprinted in Black or Red Types "j," "m" or "o"

SERVICIO OFICIAL *o*

Inscribed: "Republica Argentina"

Litho., Photo., Engraved

1964–67 *Perf. 13½* Wmk. 90

O149	A312	(*j*)	6p rose red (vert. ovpt. down) ('67)	25	4
O153	A238a	(*m*)	22p ultra. ('64)	50	6
O154	"	(*j*)	43p dk. carmine rose (vert. ovpt., down)	65	6
O155	"	(")	45p brn., photo. (vert. ovpt., up) ('66)	45	6
O156	"	(")	45p brown, litho. (vert. ovpt., up) ('67)	45	6
O157	A241	(")	50p dk. blue (vert. ovpt., up) (R) ('67)	30	6
O158	A366	(")	90p olive bister (vert. ovpt., up) ('67)	1.00	10
O162	A279	(*o*)	500p yel. grn. ('67)	4.50	1.25

Type of 1959–67 Overprinted Type "j"

Perf. 13½

1969 Lithographed Wmk. 365

O163	A276	20p vermilion	20	10

Buenos Aires

(bwā'nos ī'rās)

The central point of the Argentine struggle for independence. At intervals Buenos Aires maintained an independent government but after 1862 became a province of the Argentine Republic.

8 REALES=1 PESO

Prices of Buenos Aires Nos. 1–8 vary according to condition. Quotations are for fine copies. Very fine to superb specimens sell at much higher prices, and inferior or poor copies sell at reduced prices, depending on the condition of the individual specimen.

CORREOS DOS-PS FRANCO BUENOS AIRES

Steamship

A1

Typographed.

1858 *Imperf.* Unwmkd.

1	A1	1 (in) pesos light brown	80.00	50.00
2	"	2 (dos) pesos blue	75.00	50.00
3	"	3 (tres) pesos green	500.00	*250.00*
		a. 3p dark green	600.00	*300.00*
4	"	4 (cuato) pesos vermilion	*2250.00*	*1300.00*
5	"	5 (cinco) pesos orange	*2250.00*	
		a. 5p ochre	*2250.00*	*1300.00*
		b. 5p olive yellow	*2250.00*	*1300.00*

Issue dates: Nos. 2–5, Apr. 29, 1858. No. 1, Oct. 26, 1858.

1858, Oct. 26

6	A1	4 (cuato) reales brown	75.00	60.00
		a. 4r gray brown	75.00	50.00
		b. 4r yellow brown	75.00	50.00

1859, Jan. 1

7	A1	1 (in) pesos blue	45.00	30.00
		a. 1p indigo	75.00	40.00
		b. Impression on reverse of stamp in blue	*1250.00*	
		c. Double impression		
		d. Tête bêche pair		*12,000.00*
8	"	1 (to) pesos blue	100.00	75.00

Nos. 1, 2, 3 and 7 have been reprinted on very thick, hand-made paper. The same four stamps and No. 8 have been reprinted on thin, hard, white wove paper.

Counterfeits of Nos. 1–8 are plentiful.

Liberty Head

A2

1859, Sept. 3

9	A2	4r green, *bluish*	75.00	40.00
10	"	1p blue	10.00	7.50
11	"	2p vermilion	75.00	45.00
		a. 2p red	75.00	45.00

Both clear and rough impressions of these stamps may be found. They have generally been called Paris and Local prints, respectively, but the opinion now obtains that the differences are due to the impression and that they do not represent separate issues.

Many shades exist of Nos. 1–11.

1862, Oct. 4

12	A2	1p rose	27.50	15.00
13	"	2p blue	35.00	25.00

All three values have been reprinted in black, brownish black, blue and red brown on thin hard white paper. The 4r has also been reprinted in green on bluish paper.

Cordoba

(kôr'dô·bä)

A province in the central part of the Argentine Republic.

100 CENTAVOS=1 PESO

Arms of Cordoba

A1

Lithographed

Laid Paper.

1858, Oct. 28 *Imperf.* Unwmkd.

1	A1	5c blue	40.00
2	"	10c black	*1200.00*

Cordoba stamps were printed on laid paper, but stamps from edges of the sheets sometimes do not show any laid lines and appear to be on wove paper. Counterfeits are plentiful.

Corrientes

(kŏr'rē·ĕn'tĕs)

The northeast province of the Argentine Republic.

1 REAL M(ONEDA) C(ORRIENTE)=12½ CENTAVOS M. C.=50 CENTAVOS

100 CENTAVOS FUERTES=1 PESO FUERTE

CORRIENTES UN REAL M.C. CORRIENTES

Ceres

A1 A2

1856, Aug. 21 *Imperf.* Unwmkd.
1 A1 1r *blue* 30.00 60.00

1860, Feb. 8

Value Cancelled by Pen Stroke.
2 A1 (3c) *blue* 80.00 80.00

1860-78
3 A2 (3c) *blue* 3.00 3.00
4 " (2c) *yellow green* ('64) 10.00 10.00
a. (2c) blue green 12.00 12.00
5 " (2c) *yellow* ('67) 3.50 3.50
6 " (3c) *dark blue* ('71) 3.50 3.50
7 " (3c) *lilac rose* ('73) 7.50 7.50
a. (3c) rose red ('76) 12.00 10.00
8 " (3c) *red violet* ('78) 15.00 10.00

Printed from settings of eight varieties, three or four impressions constituting a sheet. Some impressions were printed inverted and tête bêche pairs may be cut from adjacent impressions.

From Jan. 1st to Feb. 24th, 1864, No. 4 was used as a 5 centavos stamp but copies so used can only be distinguished when they bear dated cancellations.

The reprints show numerous spots and small defects which are not found on the originals. They are printed on gray blue, dull blue, gray green, dull orange and light magenta papers

ARMENIA

(är·mē'nĭ·ȧ)

LOCATION—In southern Russia bounded by Georgia, Azerbaijan, Persia and Turkey.
GOVT.—A Soviet Socialist Republic.
AREA—11,945 sq. mi.
POP.—1,214,391 (1923).
CAPITAL—Erevan.

With Azerbaijan and Georgia, Armenia made up the Transcaucasian Federation of Soviet Republics. Stamps of Armenia were replaced in 1923 by those of Transcaucasian Federated Republics.

100 Kopecks = 1 Ruble

Counterfeits abound of all overprinted and surcharged stamps.

National Republic.

Russian Stamps of 1902–19

Handstamped

Thirteen types exist of both framed and unframed overprints. The device is the Armenian "H," initial of Hayasdan (Armenia). Inverted and double overprints are found.

Surcharged K 60 K

Type I. Without periods.
Type II. Periods after first "K" and "60".

Black Surcharge.

1919 *Perf. 14, 14½x15.* Unwmkd.
1 A14 60k on 1k orange (II) 30 30
a. Imperf. (I) 20 20
b. Imperf. (II) 20 20

Violet Surcharge.
2 A14 60k on 1k orange (II) 40 40

Handstamped in Violet

a

Perf. 14, 14½x15, 13½.
6 A15 4k carmine 75 75
7 A14 5k claret 3.00 3.00
a. Imperf. 2.00 2.00
9 " 10k on 7k light blue 1.50 1.50
10 A11 15k red brown & blue 40 40
11 A8 20k blue & carmine 1.00 1.00
13 A11 35k red brown & green 75 75
14 A8 50k violet & green 60 60
15 A14 60k on 1k org. (II) 2.50 2.50
a. Imperf. (I) 2.25 2.25
b. Imperf. (II) 12.50 12.50
18 A13 5r dark blue, green & pale blue 5.00 5.00
a. Imperf. 1.50 1.50
19 A12 7r dark green & pink 1.75 1.75
20 A13 10r scarlet, yellow & gray 2.00 2.00

Handstamped in Black.

Perf. 14, 14½x15, 13½.
31 A14 2k green 6.00 6.00
a. Imperf. 25 25
32 " 3k red 3.50 3.50
a. Imperf. 25 25
33 A15 4k carmine 15 15
34 A14 5k claret 25 25
a. Imperf. 2.00 2.00
36 A15 10k dark blue 1.00 1.00
37 A14 10k on 7k light blue 10 10
38 A11 15k red brown & blue 10 10
a. Imperf. 2.00 2.00
39 A8 20k blue & carmine 15 15
40 A11 25k green & gray violet 15 15
41 " 35k red brown & green 10 10
42 A8 50k violet & green 10 10
43 A14 60k on 1k orange (II) 3.00 3.00
43A A11 70k brown & orange 30 30
b. Imperf. 25 25
44 A9 1r pale brown, dark brown & orange 70 70
a. Imperf. 40 40
45 A12 3½r maroon & light green 1.20 1.20
a. Imperf. 75 75
46 A13 5r dark blue, green & pale blue 75 75
a. Imperf. 1.25 1.25
47 A12 7r dark green & pink 1.75 1.75
48 A13 10r scarlet, yellow & gray 1.50 1.50

Vertically Laid Paper.

Wmkd. Wavy Lines. (168)

1920 *Imperf.*
60 A13 5r dark blue, green & pale blue 30.00

Handstamped in Violet

c

Unwmkd.

Perf. 14, 14½x15, 13½.

Wove Paper.
62 A14 2k green 7.00 7.00
a. Imperf. 50 50
63 " 3k red 4.50 4.50
a. Imperf. 25 25
64 A15 4k carmine 60 60
65 A14 5k claret 60 60
a. Imperf. 1.00 1.00
67 A15 10k dark blue 1.25 1.25
68 A14 10k on 7k light blue 1.00 1.00
69 A11 15k red brown & blue 50 50
70 A8 20k blue & carmine 60 60
71 A11 25k green & gray violet 50 50
72 " 35k red brown & green 40 40
73 A8 50k violet & green 30 30
74 A14 60k on 1k orange (II) 3.00 3.00
a. Imperf. (I) 2.50 2.50
b. Imperf. (II) 3.00 3.00
75 A9 1r pale brown, dark brown & orange 1.00 1.00
a. Imperf. 75 75
76 A12 3½r maroon & light green 1.50 1.50
a. Imperf. 1.00 1.00
77 A13 5r dark blue, green & pale blue 3.00 3.00
a. Imperf. 1.50 1.50
78 A12 7r dark green & pink 2.50 2.50
79 A13 10r scarlet, yellow & gray 2.50 2.50

Imperf.
85 A11 70k brown & orange 2.00 2.00

Handstamped in Black.

Perf. 14, 14½x15, 13½.
90 A14 1k orange 6.50 6.50
a. Imperf. 9.00 9.00
91 " 2k green 5.00 5.00
a. Imperf. 10 10
92 " 3k red 5.00 5.00
a. Imperf. 25 25
93 A15 4k carmine 20 20
94 A14 5k claret 10 10
a. Imperf. 1.00 1.00
95 " 7k light blue 6.00 6.00
96 A15 10k dark blue 1.25 1.25
97 " 10k on 7k light blue 10 10
98 A11 15k red brown & blue 12 12
99 A8 20k blue & carmine 12 12
100 A11 25k green & gray violet 25 25
101 " 35k red brown & green 15 15
102 A8 50k violet & green 12 12
102A A14 60k on 1k orange (II) 2.00 2.00
b. Imperf. (I) 40 40
c. Imperf. (II) 60 60
103 A9 1r pale brown, dark brown & orange 50 50
a. Imperf. 35 35
104 A12 3½r maroon & light green 75 75
a. Imperf. 50 50
105 A13 5r dark blue, green & pale blue 1.00 1.00
a. Imperf. 1.25 1.25
106 A12 7r dark green & pink 1.00 1.00
107 A13 10r scarlet, yellow & gray 1.00 1.00

Imperf.
113 A11 70k brown & orange 40 40

Handstamped in Violet or Black:

5r f 10r g

Violet Surcharge.

1920 *Perf. 14, 14½x15*
120 A14 (*f*) 3r on 3k red 3.00 3.00
a. Imperf. 1.25 1.25
121 " (") 5r on 3k red 5.00 5.00
122 A15 (") 5r on 4k carmine 3.50 3.50
123 A14 (") 5r on 5k claret 3.00 3.00
a. Imperf. 2.50 2.50
124 A15 (") 5r on 10k dark blue 3.50 3.50
125 A14 (") 5r on 10k on 7k light blue 3.00 3.00
126 A8 (") 5r on 20k blue & carmine

Imperf.
127 A14 (*f*) 5r on 2k green 12.50 12.50
128 A11 (") 5r on 35k red brown & green 12.50 12.50

Black Surcharge.

Perf. 14 to 15 and Compound, 13½
130 A14 (*g*) 1r on 1k orange 15 15
a. Imperf. 25 25
131 " (*f*) 3r on 3k red 8 8
a. Imperf. 8 8
132 A15 (") 3r on 4k carmine 5.00 5.00
133 A14 (") 5r on 2k grn. 1.00 1.00
a. Imperf. 12 12
134 " (") 5r on 3k red 2.50 2.50
a. Imperf. 2.50 2.50
135 A15 (") 5r on 4k carmine 60 60
a. Imperf. 7.50 7.50
136 A14 (") 5r on 5k claret 12 12
a. Imperf. 25 25
137 " (") 5r on 7k light blue 1.00 1.00
138 A15 (") 5r on 10k dark blue 12 12
139 A14 (*f*) 5r on 10k on 7k light blue 12 12
140 A11 (") 5r on 14k blue & rose 3.50 3.50
141 " (") 5r on 15k red brown & blue 20 20
a. Imperf. 4.00 4.00
142 A8 (") 5r on 20k blue & carmine 20 20
a. Imperf. 4.00 4.00
143 A11 (") 5r on 20k on 14k blue & rose 5.00 5.00
144 " (") 5r on 25k green & gray violet 5.00 5.00
145 A14 (*g*) 10r on 1k orange 175.00 175.00
a. Imperf. 1.25 1.25
146 " (") 10r on 3k red 90.00 90.00
147 " (") 10r on 5k claret 6.00 6.00
a. Imperf. 8.00
148 A8 (") 10r on 20k blue & car. 6.00 6.00
148A A11 (*f*) 10r on 25k green & gray violet 2.50 2.50
149 " (*g*) 10r on 25k green & gray violet 2.00 2.00
a. Imperf. 12.00 12.00
150 " (") 10r on 35k red brown & green 25 25
151 A8 (*f*) 10r on 50k brown violet & green 2.50 2.50
152 " (*g*) 10r on 50k brown violet & green 65 65
152A A11 (") 10r on 70k brown & orange 100.00 100.00
b. Imperf. 4.50 4.50
152C A8 (") 25r on 20k blue & car. 1.50 1.50
153 A11 (") 25r on 25k green & gray violet 1.25 1.25
154 " (") 25r on 35k red brown & green 1.25 1.25
a. Imperf. 6.00 6.00
155 A8 (") 25r on 50k violet & green 1.75 1.75
a. Imperf. 3.00 3.00
156 A11 (") 25r on 70k brown & orange 3.00 3.00
a. Imperf. 3.00 3.00
157 A9 (") 50r on 1r pale brown, dark brown & orange 2.00 2.00
a. Imperf. 50 50
158 A13 (") 50r on 5r dark blue, green & light blue 4.00 4.00
a. Imperf. 4.00 4.00
159 A12 (") 100r on 3½r maroon & light green 3.50 3.50
a. Imperf. 3.50 3.50
160 A13 (") 100r on 5r dark blue, green & pale blue 3.50 3.50
a. Imperf. 3.50 3.50
161 A12 (") 100r on 7r dark green & pink 4.00 4.00
a. Imperf. 16.00 16.00
162 A13 (") 100r on 10r scarlet, yellow & gray 3.50 3.50

Wmkd. Wavy Lines. (168)

Perf. 11½.

Vertically Laid Paper.
163 A12 (*g*) 100r on 3½r black & gray 15.00 15.00
164 " (") 100r on 7r black & yellow 12.50 12.50

1920 *Imperf.* **Unwmkd.**

Wove Paper.

166 A14 (*g*) 1r on 60k on 1k orange (I) 4.00 4.00
168 " (*f*) 5r on 1k orange 12.50 12.50
173 A11 (") 5r on 35k red brown & green 4.00 4.00
177 " (*g*) 50r on 70k brown & orange 4.00 4.00
179 A12 (") 50r on 3½r maroon & light green 3.00 3.00
181 A9 (") 100r on 1r pale brown, dark brown & orange 6.00 6.00

Romanov Issues Surcharged Types "f" or "g".

On Stamps of 1913.

1920 *Perf. 13½*

184 A16 (*g*) 1r on 1k brown orange 3.50 3.50
185 A18 (*f*) 3r on 3k rose red 3.00 3.00
186 A19 (") 5r on 4k dull red 3.00 3.00
187 A22 (") 5r on 14k blue green 18.00 18.00
187A A19 (*g*) 10r on 4k dull red 20.00
187B A26 (") 10r on 35k gray violet & dark green
187C A19 (") 25r on 4k dull red 4.00 4.00
188 A26 (") 25r on 35k gray violet & dark green 4.00 4.00
189 A28 (") 25r on 70k yellow green & brown 4.00 4.00
190 A31 (*f*) 50r on 3r dark violet 3.00 3.00
190A A16 (*g*) 100r on 1k brown orange 75.00 75.00
190B A17 (") 100r on 2k green 75.00 75.00
191 A30 (") 100r on 2r red brown 16.00 16.00
192 A31 (") 100r on 3r dark violet 16.00 16.00

On Stamps of 1915.

Thin Cardboard.

Inscriptions on Back.

Perf. 12.

193 A21 (*g*) 100r on 10k blue 4.00
194 A23 (") 100r on 15k brown 4.00
195 A24 (") 100r on 20k olive green 4.00

On Stamps of 1916.

Perf. 13½.

196 A20 (*f*) 5r on 10k on 7k brown 3.00 3.00
197 A22 (") 5r on 20k on 14k blue green 5.00 5.00

Surcharged

Type "f" or "g" over type "c",

Type "c" in Violet.

Perf. 14, 14½x15, 13½.

200 A15 (*f*) 5r on 4k carmine 1.75 1.75
201 " (") 5r on 10k dark blue 1.75 1.75
202 A11(*f*) 5r on 15k red brown & blue 3.00 3.00
203 A8 (") 5r on 20k blue & carmine 2.50 2.50
204 A11 (*g*) 10r on 25k green & gray violet 2.50 2.50
205 " (") 10r on 35k red brown & green 4.50 4.50
205A A8 (*g*) 10r on 50k brown violet & green 5.50 5.50
206 " (*f*) 25r on 50k brown violet & green *75.00 75.00*
207 A9 (*g*) 50r on 1r pale brown, dk. brown & orange 45.00 45.00
a. Imperf. 5.00 5.00
207B A12 (") 100r on 3½r maroon & lt. green 12.00
207C " (") 100r on 7r dark green & pink 12.00

Imperf.

208 A14 (*f*) 5r on 2k green 8.00 8.00
209 " (") 5r on 5k claret 2.50 2.50
210 A11 (*g*) 25r on 70k brown & orange 8.00 8.00
211 A13 (") 100r on 5r dark blue, green & pale blue 1.25 1.25

Type "c" in Black.

Perf. 14, 14½x15, 13½.

212 A14 (*f*) 5r on 7k light blue *100.00 100.00*
213 " (") 5r on 10k on 7k light blue 1.75 1.75
214 A11 (*g*) 5r on 15k red brn. & blue 70 70
215 A8 (*f*) 5r on 20k blue & carmine 50 50
215A A11 (*g*) 10r on 5r on 25k green & gray violet 7.50 7.50
216 " (") 10r on 35k red brown & green 75 75
217 A8 (") 10r on 50k brown violet & green 1.25 1.25
217A A9 (") 50r on 1r pale brn., dk. brn. & orange 1.50 1.50
b. Imperf. 1.75 1.75
217C A12 (") 100r on 3½r maroon & lt. green 2.50 2.50
218 A13 (") 100r on 5r dark blue, green & pale blue 3.50 3.50
a. Imperf. 3.00 3.00
219 A12 (*f*) 100r on 7r dark green & pink 5.00 5.00
219A A13 (") 100r on 10r scarlet, yellow & gray 5.00 5.00

Imperf.

220 A14 (*g*) 1r on 60k on 1k orange (I) 7.00 7.00
221 " (*f*) 5r on 2k green 1.00 1.00
222 " (") 5r on 5k claret 4.00 4.00
223 A11 (*g*) 10r on 70k brown & orange 3.00 3.00
224 " (") 25r on 70k brown & orange 2.50 2.50

Surcharged

Type "f" or "g" over type "a".

Type "a" in Violet.

Imperf.

231 A9 (*g*) 50r on 1r pale brn., dk. brn. & orange *60.00 60.00*
232 A13 (") 100r on 5r dark blue, green & pale blue 16.00

Type "a" in Black.

Perf. 14, 14½x15, 13½.

233 A8 (*f*) 5r on 20k blue & carmine 1.00 1.00
233A A11(*g*) 10r on 25k green & gray violet *75.00 75.00*
234 " (") 10r on 35k red brown & green 1.25 1.25
235 A12 (*g*) 100r on 3½r maroon & light green 2.00 2.00
a. Imperf. 2.50 2.50

Imperf.

237 A14 (*g*) 5r on 2k green 75.00 75.00
237A A11 (") 10r on 70k brn. & org.

Surcharged Type "a" and New Value.

Type "a" in Violet.

Perf. 14, 14½x15.

238 A11 10r on 15k red brown & blue 1.00 1.00

Type "a" in Black.

239 A8 5r on 20k blue & carmine 1.75 1.75
239A " 10r on 20k blue & carmine 5.00 5.00
239B " 10r on 50k brown red & green 10.00

Imperf.

240 A12 100r on 3½r maroon & light green 3.00 3.00

Surcharged Type "c" and New Value.

Type "c" in Black.

1920 *Perf. 14, 14½x15, 13½*

241 A15 5r on 4k red 3.00 3.00
242 A11 5r on 15k red brown & blue 1.75 1.75
243 A8 10r on 20k blue & carmine 3.00 3.00
243A A11 10r on 25k green & gray violet 1.25 1.25
244 " 10r on 35k red brown & green 1.00 1.00
a. With additional surcharge "5r" 2.00 2.00
245 A12 100r on 3½r maroon & light green 2.00 2.00

Imperf.

247 A14 3r on 3k red 8.00 8.00
248 " 5r on 2k green 50 50
249 A9 50r on 1r pale brown, dark brown & orange 1.50 1.50

Type "c" in Violet.

249A A14 5r on 2k green 10.00

Postal Savings Stamps Surcharged.

A1 A2

A3 Wmk. 171

Wmkd. Diamonds. (171)

Perf. 14½x15.

250 A1 60k on 1k red & buff 15.00 15.00
251 A2 1r on 1k red & buff 8.00 8.00
252 A3 5r on 5k green & buff 10.00 10.00
253 " 5r on 10k brown & buff 10.00 10.00

Russian Semi-Postal Stamps of 1914-18 Surcharged with Armenian Monogram and New Values like Regular Issues.

Unwmkd.

Perf. 11½, 12½, 13½.

On Stamps of 1914.

255 SP5 25r on 1k red brown & dark green, *straw* 90.00 90.00
256 SP6 25r on 3k maroon & gray green, *pink* 75.00 75.00
257 SP7 50r on 7k dark brown & dark green, *buff* 12.00 12.00
258 SP5 100r on 1k red brown & dark green, *straw* 5.00 5.00
259 SP6 100r on 3k maroon & gray green, *pink* 5.00 5.00
260 SP7 100r on 7k dark brown & dark green, *buff* 5.00 5.00

On Stamps of 1915-19.

261 SP5 25r on 1k orange brown & gray 90.00 90.00
262 SP6 25r on 3k carmine & gray 60.00 60.00
263 SP8 50r on 10k dark blue & brown 15.00 15.00
264 SP5 100r on 1k orange brown & gray 5.00 5.00
265 SP8 100r on 10k dark blue & brown 5.00 5.00

These surcharged semi-postal stamps were used for ordinary postage.

A set of 10 stamps in the above designs, and in a third design showing a woman quilling, was prepared in 1920, but not issued. Price of set, $2. Exist with "SPECIMEN" overprint and imperf. Counterfeits exist.

Soviet Socialist Republic.

Hammer and Sickle
A7

Mythological Monster
A8

Symbols of Soviet Republics on Designs from old Armenian Manuscripts
A9

Ruined City of Ani
A10

Mythological Monster
A11

Armenian Soldier
A12

Fisherman on River Aras
A16

Mythological Monster
A13

Soviet Symbols, Armenian Designs
A14

Mt. Alagöz and Plain of Shirak
A15

Post Office in Erevan and Mt. Ararat
A17

Ruin in City of Ani
A18

Street in Erevan
A19

Lake Gökcha and Sevan Monastery
A20

Mythological Subject from old Armenian Monument
A21

Mt. Ararat
A22

Perf. 11½, Imperf.

1921 Unwmkd.

No.	Type	Description	Unused	Used
278	A7	1r gray green	6	
279	A8	2r slate gray	6	
280	A9	3r carmine	6	
281	A10	5r dark brown	6	
282	A11	25r gray	7	7
283	A12	50r red	8	
284	A13	100r orange	8	
285	A14	250r dark blue	8	
286	A15	500r brown violet	8	
287	A16	1000r sea green	10	
288	A17	2000r bistre	10	
289	A18	5000r dark brown	10	
290	A19	10,000r dull red	20	
291	A20	15,000r slate blue	20	
292	A21	20,000r lake	20	
293	A22	25,000r gray blue	30	
294	"	25,000r brown olive	2.00	
		Nos. 278-294 (17)	3.83	

Except the 25r, Nos. 278-294 were not regulary issued and used. Counterfeits exist.

Russian Stamps of 1909-17 Surcharged

Wove Paper

Lozenges of Varnish on Face

1921, August *Perf. 13½*

No.	Type	Description	Unused	Used
295	A9	5000r on 1r pale brown, dark brown & orange	3.00	
296	A12	5000r on 3½r maroon & light green	3.00	
297	A13	5000r on 5r dark blue, green & pale blue	3.00	
298	A12	5000r on 7r dark green & pink	3.00	
299	A13	5000r on 10r scarlet, yellow & gray	3.00	
		Nos. 295-299 (5)	15.00	

Nos. 295-299 were not officially issued. Counterfeits abound.

Mt. Ararat and Soviet Star
A23 A24

Soviet Symbols
A25

Crane
A26

Peasant
A27

Harpy
A28

Peasant Sowing
A29

Soviet Symbols
A30

Forging
A31

Plowing
A32

1922 *Perf. 11½.*

No.	Type	Description	Unused	Used
300	A23	50r green & red	8	
301	A24	300r slate blue & buff	12	
302	A25	400r blue & pink	12	
303	A26	500r violet & pale lilac	6	
304	A27	1000r dull blue & pale blue	6	
305	A28	2000r black & gray	15	
306	A29	3000r black & green	10	
307	A30	4000r black & light brown	20	
308	A31	5000r black & dull red	10	
309	A32	10,000r black & pale rose	10	
		a. Tête bêche pair	15.00	
		Nos. 300-309 (10)	1.09	

Nos. 300 to 309 were not placed in use without surcharge.

Stamps of types A23 to A32, printed in other colors than Nos. 300 to 309, are essays.

1922-23

Stamps of Preceding Issue with Handstamped Surcharge of New Values in Rose, Violet or Black

No.	Type	Description	Unused	Used
310	A23	10,000(r) on 50r green & red (R)	7.50	7.50
311	"	10,000(r) on 50r green & red (V)	2.00	2.00
312	"	10,000(r) on 50r green & red (Bk)	75	75
313	A24	15,000(r) on 300r slate blue & buff (R)	10.00	10.00
314	"	15,000(r) on 300r slate blue & buff (V)	2.00	2.00
315	"	15,000(r) on 300r slate blue & buff (Bk)	1.00	1.00
316	A25	25,000(r) on 400r blue & pink (V)	2.00	2.00
317	"	25,000(r) on 400r blue & pink (Bk)	50	50
318	A26	30,000(r) on 500r violet & pale lilac (R)	15.00	15.00
319	"	30,000(r) on 500r violet & pale lilac (V)	1.00	1.00
320	"	30,000(r) on 500r violet & pale lilac (Bk)	60	60
321	A27	50,000(r) on 1000r dull blue & pale blue (R)	10.00	10.00
322	"	50,000(r) on 1000r dull blue & pale blue (V)	4.00	4.00
323	"	50,000(r) on 1000r dull blue & pale blue (Bk)	1.00	1.00
324	A29	75,000(r) on 3000r black & green (Bk)	1.25	1.25
325	A28	100,000(r) on 2000r black & gray (R)	15.00	15.00
326	"	100,000(r) on 2000r black & gray (V)	4.00	4.00
327	"	100,000(r) on 2000r black & gray (Bk)	1.00	1.00
328	A30	200,000(r) on 4000r black & light brown (V)	1.00	1.00
329	"	200,000(r) on 4000r black & light brown (Bk)	1.00	1.00
330	A31	300,000(r) on 5000r black & dull red (V)	8.00	8.00
331	"	300,000(r) on 5000r black & dull red (Bk)	75	75
332	A32	500,000(r) on 10,000r black & pale rose (V)	4.00	4.00
333	"	500,000(r) on 10,000r black & pale rose (Bk)	75	75
		Nos. 310-333 (24)	94.10	94.10

Goose
A33

Armenian Woman at Well
A35

Armenian Village Scene
A34

Mt. Ararat
A36

Mt. Ararat
A37

New Values in Gold Kopecks, Handstamped Surcharge in Black.

1922 *Imperf.*

334 A33 1(k) on 250r rose 2.50 2.50
335 " 1(k) on 250r gray 5.00 5.00
336 A34 2(k) on 500r rose 2.00 2.00
337 " 3(k) on 500r gray 1.50 1.50
338 A35 4(k) on 1000r rose 1.50 1.50
339 " 4(k) on 1000r gray 3.00 3.00
340 A36 5(k) on 2000r gray 1.50 1.50
341 " 10(k) on 2000r rose 1.50 1.50
342 A37 15(k) on 5000r rose 10.00 10.00
343 " 20(k) on 5000r gray 1.75 1.75
Nos. 334-343 (10) 30.25 30.25

Nos. 334-343 were issued for postal tax purposes.

Nos. 334 to 343 exist without surcharge but are not known to have been issued in that condition. Counterfeits exist of both sets.

Regular Issue of 1921 Handstamped with New Values in Black or Red.
Short, Thick Numerals.

1922-23 *Imperf.*

347 A8 2(k) on 2r slate gray (R) 17.50 17.50
350 A11 4(k) on 25r gray (R) 6.00 6.00
353 A13 10(k) on 100r orange (R) 12.50 12.50
354 A14 15(k) on 250r dark blue 1.00 1.00
355 A15 20(k) on 500r brown violet 1.50 1.50
a. With "k" written in red 2.00 2.00
357 A22 50(k) on 25,000r blue (R) 20.00 20.00
358 " 50(k) on 25,000r brown olive (R) 15.00 15.00
359 " 50(k) on 25,000r brown olive
Nos. 347-359 (8) 73.50 73.50

Perf. 11½.

360 A7 1(k) on 1r gray green 10.00 10.00
a. Imperf. 3.00 3.00
361 " 1(k) on 1r gray green (R) 6.00 6.00
a. Imperf. 10.00 10.00
362 A8 2(k) on 2r slate gray 15.00 15.00
a. Imperf. 6.00 6.00
363 A15 2(k) on 500r brown violet 3.50 3.50
a. Imperf. 3.00 3.00
364 " 2(k) on 500r brown violet (R) 15.00 15.00
365 A11 4(k) on 25r gray 12.00 12.00
a. Imperf. 6.00 6.00
366 A12 5(k) on 50r red 4.00 4.00
a. Imperf. 3.00 3.00
367 A13 10(k) on 100r orange 3.50 3.50
a. Imperf. 3.50 3.50
368 A21 35(k) on 20,000r claret 15.00 15.00
a. With "k" written in violet 15.00 15.00
b. Imperf. 6.00 6.00
c. As "a," imperf. 6.00 6.00
d. With "kop" written in violet, imperf.
Nos. 360-368 (9) 84.00 84.00

Manuscript Surcharge in Red.
Perf. 11½.

371 A14 1k on 250r dark blue 4.00 4.00
a. Surcharged "1" only
b. Imperf. 75.00

Handstamped in Black or Red.
Tall, Thin Numerals.
Imperf.

377 A11 4(k) on 25r gray (R) 7.00 7.00
379 A13 10(k) on 100r org. 4.00 4.00
380 A15 20(k) on 500r brown violet 10.00 10.00
381 A22 50k on 25,000r blue 1.50 1.50
a. Surcharged "50" only 25.00 25.00
382 " 50k on 25,000r blue (R) 20.00 20.00
382A " 50k on 25,000r brown olive 40.00 40.00
Nos. 377-382A (6) 82.50 82.50

On Nos. 381, 382 and 382A the letter "k" forms part of the surcharge.

Perf. 11½.

383 A7 1(k) on 1r gray green (R) 5.00 5.00
a. Imperf.
384 A14 1(k) on 250r dk. bl. 3.00 3.00
385 A15 2(k) on 500r brown violet 3.75 3.75
a. Imperf. 4.00 4.00
386 " 2(k) on 500r brown violet (R) 8.00 8.00
387 A9 3(k) on 3r rose 10.00 10.00
a. Imperf. 10.00 10.00
388 A21 3(k) on 20,000r claret 30.00 30.00
a. Imperf. 5.00 5.00
389 A11 4(k) on 25r gray 4.00 4.00
a. Imperf. 7.00 7.00
390 A12 5(k) on 50r red 3.00 3.00
a. Imperf. 2.00 2.00
Nos. 383-390 (8) 66.75 66.75

Foreign postal stationery (stamped envelopes, postal cards and air letter sheets) lies beyond the scope of this Catalogue which is limited to adhesive postage stamps.

AUSTRIA

(ôs′tri·*á*)

LOCATION—In Central Europe.
GOVT.—Republic.
AREA—32,376 sq. mi.
POP.—7,520,000 (est. 1977).
CAPITAL—Vienna.

Before 1867 Austria was an absolute monarchy which included Hungary and Lombardy-Venetia. In 1867 the Austro-Hungarian Monarchy was established, with Austria and Hungary as equal partners. After the first World War, in 1918, the different nationalities established their own states and only the German-speaking parts remained, forming a republic under the name "Deutschösterreich" (German Austria), which name was shortly again changed to Austria. In 1938 German forces occupied Austria, which became part of the German Reich. After the liberation by Allied troops in 1945, an independent republic was re-established.

60 Kreuzer = 1 Gulden
100 Neu-Kreuzer = 1 Gulden (1858)
100 Heller = 1 Krone (1899)
100 Groschen = 1 Schilling (1925)

Prices of early Austrian stamps vary according to condition. Quotations for Nos. 1-5, P1-P7 and PR1-PR4 are for fine copies. Very fine to superb specimens sell at much higher prices, and inferior or poor copies sell at reduced prices, depending on the condition of the individual specimen.

Prices for unused stamps of 1850-80 issues are for copies in fine condition with original gum. Specimens without gum sell for about one-third of the figures quoted.

Issues of the Austrian Monarchy (including Hungary).

Coat of Arms
A1

Wmkd. K. K. H. M. in Sheet or Unwmkd.

1850 Typographed *Imperf.*

Thin to Thick Paper.

The stamps of this issue were at first printed on a rough hand-made paper, varying in thickness and having a watermark in script letters K. K. H. M., the initials of Kaiserlich Königliches Handels-Ministerium (Imperial and Royal Ministry of Commerce), vertically in the gutter between the panes. Parts of these letters show on margin stamps in the sheet. From 1854 a thick, smooth machine-made paper without watermark was used.

NINE KREUZER.

Type I. The top of "9" is about on a level with "Kreuzer" and not near the top of the label.

Type IA. Similar to type I but with 1¼mm. instead of ½mm. space between "9" and "Kreuzer."

Type II. The top of "9" is much higher than the top of the word "Kreuzer" and nearly touches the top of the label.

1 A1 1kr yellow 850.00 65.00
a. Printed on both sides 1400.00 110.00
b. 1kr orange 1100.00 100.00
c. 1kr brn. org. 2100.00 350.00
2 " 2kr black 800.00 60.00
a. Ribbed paper *1500.00*
b. 2kr gray blk. 1350.00 65.00
3 " 3kr red 300.00 2.25
a. Ribbed paper *1850.00* 65.00
b. Laid paper *9000.00*
c. Printed on both sides *7500.00*
4 " 6kr brown 450.00 2.75
a. Ribbed paper *1250.00*
5 A1 9kr blue, type II 650.00 2.25
a. 9kr blue, type I 1200.00 8.00
b. 9kr blue, type IA *1300.00*
c. Laid paper, type II *10,000.00*
d. Printed on both sides, type II *7500.00*

In 1852-54, Nos. 1 to 5, rouletted 14, were used in Tokay. A 12kr blue exists, but was not issued.

The reprints are printed in brighter colors, some on paper watermarked "Briefmarken" in the sheet.

Emperor Franz Josef
A2 A3 A4

A5

A6

1858-59 Embossed. ***Perf. 14½.***

Two Types of Each Value.

Type I. Loops of the bow at the back of the head broken, except the 2kr. In the 2kr, the "2" has a flat foot, thinning to the right.

Type II. Loops complete. Wreath projects further at top of head. In the 2kr, the "2" has a more curved foot of uniform thickness, with a shading line in the upper and lower curves.

6 A2 2kr yellow, type II 650.00 30.00
a. 2kr yellow, type I 1500.00 275.00
b. 2kr orange, type II 1500.00 300.00
7 A3 3kr blk., type II 2250.00 225.00
a. 3kr black, type I 800.00 225.00
8 " 3kr green, type II ('59) 725.00 100.00
9 A4 5kr red, type II 235.00 1.00
a. 5kr red, type I 300.00 8.00
10 A5 10kr brn., type II 550.00 2.50
a. 10kr brown, type I 550.00 19.00
11 A6 15kr blue, type II 475.00 1.65
a. Type I 825.00 11.00

The reprints are of type II and are perforated 10½, 11, 12, 12½ and 13. There are also imperforate reprints of Nos. 6 to 8.

Emperor Franz Josef
A7

Coat of Arms
A8

1860-61 Embossed ***Perf. 14***

12 A7 2kr yellow 350.00 25.00
13 " 3kr green 325.00 19.00
a. Printed on both sides
14 " 5kr red 200.00 80
15 " 10kr brown 275.00 1.65
16 " 15kr blue 235.00 95

The reprints are perforated 9, 9½, 10, 10½, 11, 11½, 12, 12½, 13 and 13½. There are also imperforate reprints of the 2 and 3kr.

1863

17 A8 2kr yellow 500.00 100.00
18 " 3kr green 375.00 80.00
19 " 5kr rose 235.00 5.50
20 " 10kr blue 800.00 7.25
21 " 15kr yel. brown 1000.00 9.00

Wmk. 91

Unwmkd. or, after June 1864, Wmkd. "BRIEF-MARKEN" in Double-lined Capitals Across the Middle of the Sheet (91).

1863-64 *Perf. 9½.*

No.	Type	Description	Unused	Used
22	A8	2kr yellow ('64)	140.00	10.00
23	"	3kr green ('64)	140.00	9.50
24	"	5kr rose	55.00	30
25	"	10kr blue	125.00	2.40
26	"	15kr yellow brown	135.00	1.40

The reprints are perforated 10½, 11½, 13 and 13½. There are also imperforate reprints of the 2 and 3kr.

Issues of Austro-Hungarian Monarchy

From 1867 to 1871 the independent postal administrations of Austria and Hungary used the same stamps.

Emperor Franz Josef

A9 A10

5 kr:

Type I. In arabesques in lower left corner, the small ornament at left of the curve nearest the figure "5" is short and has three points at bottom.

Type II. The ornament is prolonged within the curve and has two points at bottom. The corresponding ornament at top of the lower left corner does not touch the curve (1872).

Type III. Similar to type II but the top ornament is joined to the curve (1881).

Two different printing methods were used for the 1867–74 issues. The first produced stamps on which the hair and whiskers were coarse and thick, from the second they were fine and clear.

Typographed

1867–72 *Perf. 9½* **Wmk. 91**

Coarse Print.

No.	Type	Description	Unused	Used
27	A9	2kr yellow	120.00	2.00
28	"	3kr green	115.00	1.30
29	"	5kr rose, type I	65.00	10
		a. 5kr rose, type II	75.00	10
		b. Perf. 10½, type II	120.00	
		c. Cliché of 3kr in plate of 5kr	*10,000.00*	
30	"	10kr blue	135.00	45
31	"	15kr brown	150.00	4.00
32	"	25kr lilac	21.00	16.50
		a. 25kr gray lilac	20.00	13.50
		b. 25kr brown violet	110.00	32.50

Perf. 12.

No.	Type	Description	Unused	Used
33	A10	50kr light brown	27.50	*65.00*
		a. 50kr pale red brown	120.00	90.00
		b. 50kr brownish rose	400.00	175.00
		c. Pair, imperf. btwn., vert. or horizontal	550.00	*1350.00*

Issues for Austria only.

1874–80 *Perf. 9½*

Fine Print.

No.	Type	Description	Unused	Used
34	A9	2kr yellow ('76)	11.00	65
		a. Perf. 9	190.00	25.00
		b. Perf. 10½	50.00	4.50
		c. Perf. 12	275.00	100.00
		d. Perf. 13	210.00	165.00
35	A9	3kr green ('76)	32.50	45
		a. Perf. 9	175.00	21.00
		b. Perf. 10½	50.00	2.50
		c. Perf. 12	210.00	9.50
		d. Perf. 13	165.00	25.00
36	"	5kr rose, type III	2.75	6
		a. Perf. 9	80.00	3.50
		b. Perf. 10½	12.00	70
		c. Perf. 12	65.00	2.50
		d. Perf. 13	100.00	10.00
37	"	10kr blue ('75)	80.00	20
		a. Perf. 9	325.00	25.00
		b. Perf. 10½	90.00	2.50
		c. Perf. 12	425.00	110.00
		d. Perf. 13	210.00	85.00
38	"	15kr brown ('77)	6.50	3.75
		a. Perf. 9	425.00	75.00
		b. Perf. 10½	210.00	22.50
		c. Perf. 12	650.00	125.00
		d. Perf. 13	385.00	225.00
39	"	25kr gray lilac ('78)	1.65	*55.00*
40	A10	50kr brown, perf. 12 ('80)	13.50	*75.00*
		a. Perf. 13	15.00	*80.00*
		b. Perf. 10½x12	300.00	

Various compound perforations exist.

A11

Inscriptions in Black

Perf. 9, 9½, 10, 10½, 11½, 12, 12½

1883

No.	Type	Description	Unused	Used
41	A11	2kr brown	5.50	28
42	"	3kr green	6.50	15
43	"	5kr rose	13.50	5
		a. Vertical pair, imperf. between	275.00	
44	"	10kr blue	6.00	8
45	"	20kr gray	65.00	2.25
46	"	50kr red lilac	400.00	45.00

The last printings of Nos. 41 to 46 are watermarked "ZEITUNGS-MARKEN" instead of "BRIEF-MARKEN."

The 5kr has been reprinted in a dull red rose, perforated 10½.

Emperor Franz Josef

A12 A13

Granite Paper.

Perf. 9 to 13½, also Compound.

1890–96 **Unwmkd.**

Numerals in black, Nos. 51 to 61.

No.	Type	Description	Unused	Used
51	A12	1kr dark gray	2.50	10
		a. Pair, imperf. between	250.00	500.00
52	"	2kr light brown	40	5
53	"	3kr gray green	55	5
		a. Pair, imperf. between	300.00	450.00
54	"	5kr rose	50	5
		a. Pair, imperf. between	250.00	350.00
55	"	10kr ultramarine	75	4
		a. Pair, imperf. between	325.00	500.00
56	"	12kr claret	3.25	25
57	"	15kr lilac	1.90	25
		a. Pair, imperf. between	350.00	500.00
58	"	20kr olive green	47.50	1.90
59	"	24kr gray blue	3.85	95
		a. Pair, imperf. between	350.00	525.00
60	"	30kr dark brown	1.90	32
61	"	50kr violet	11.00	7.50

Engraved

No.	Type	Description	Unused	Used
62	A13	1gld dark blue	1.50	1.90
63	"	1gld pale lilac ('96)	55.00	3.25
64	"	2gld carmine	5.50	9.00
65	"	2gld gray grn. ('96)	32.50	27.50

Nearly all values of the 1890-1907 issues are found with numerals missing in one or more corners, some with numerals printed on the back.

A14

1891 **Typographed.**

Numerals in black.

Perf. 9 to 13½, also Compound.

No.	Type	Description	Unused	Used
66	A14	20kr olive green	1.65	10
67	"	24kr gray blue	3.25	55
68	"	30kr brown	1.80	10
		a. Pair, imperf. between	450.00	650.00
		b. Perf. 9	180.00	37.50
69	A14	50kr violet	2.25	32

A15 A16

A17 A18

Perf. 10½ to 13½ and Compound.

Numerals in black, Nos. 70 to 82.

1899 **Without Varnish Bars.**

No.	Type	Description	Unused	Used
70	A15	1h lilac	1.25	7
		b. Imperf.	45.00	55.00
		c. Perf. 10½	22.50	5.50
		d. Numerals inverted	350.00	300.00
71	A15	2h dark gray	4.00	18
72	"	3h bistre brown	6.50	4
		b. "3" in lower right corner sideways		
73	A15	5h blue green	11.00	5
		c. Perf. 10½	19.00	5.00
74	A15	6h orange	65	5
75	A16	10h rose	9.00	5
		b. Perf. 10½	450.00	110.00
76	A16	20h brown	1.10	10
77	"	25h ultramarine	75.00	12
78	"	30h red violet	27.50	2.25
		b. Horizontal pair, imperf. between	400.00	
80	A17	40h green	47.50	2.75
81	"	50h gray blue	35.00	3.25
		b. All four "50's" parallel		*750.00*
82	A17	60h brown	55.00	90
		b. Horizontal pair, imperf. between	425.00	
		c. Perf. 10½	65.00	85

Engraved

No.	Type	Description	Unused	Used
83	A18	1k carmine rose	2.25	13
		a. 1k carmine	8.00	13
		b. Vertical pair, imperf. between	400.00	425.00
84	A18	2k gray lilac	70.00	38
		a. Vertical pair, imperf. between	550.00	575.00
85	A18	4k gray green	8.00	5.50

1901 **With Varnish Bars.**

No.	Type	Description	Unused	Used
70a	A15	1h lilac	2.00	25
71a	"	2h dark gray	2.00	17
72a	"	3h bistre brown	65	5
73a	"	5h blue green	33	5
74a	"	6h orange	33	5
75a	A16	10h rose	45	5
76a	"	20h brown	1.35	4
77a	"	25h ultramarine	1.65	15
78a	"	30h red violet	3.50	90
79	A17	35h green	1.65	15
80a	"	40h green	3.00	3.75
81a	"	50h gray blue	7.50	6.50
82a	"	60h brown	3.50	55
		Nos. 70a-78a, 79, 80a-82a (13)	27.91	12.66

The diagonal yellow bars of varnish were printed across the face to prevent cleaning.

A19

A20

A21

Perf. 12½ to 13½ and Compound.

Colored Numerals.

1904-07 **Typographed.**

Without Varnish Bars.

No.	Type	Description	Unused	Used
86	A19	1h lilac	18	15
87	"	2h dark gray	27	10
88	"	3h bistre brown	30	7
89	"	5h dk. blue green	13.00	7
90	"	5h yel. grn. ('06)	50	5
91	"	6h deep orange	55	7
92	A20	10h carmine ('06)	75	5
93	"	12h violet ('07)	1.30	55
94	"	20h brown ('06)	3.25	10
95	"	25h ultra. ('06)	4.50	33
96	"	30h red violet ('06)	6.50	28

Black Numerals.

No.	Type	Description	Unused	Used
97	A20	10h carmine	13.00	7
98	"	20h brown	55.00	1.20
99	"	25h ultramarine	55.00	2.25
100	"	30h red violet	65.00	3.25

White Numerals.

No.	Type	Description	Unused	Used
101	A21	35h green	3.00	25
102	"	40h deep violet	3.00	1.00
103	"	50h dull blue	3.25	3.00
104	"	60h yellow brown	3.25	50
105	"	72h rose	3.50	1.35
		Nos. 86-105 (20)	235.10	14.69

1905 **With Varnish Bars.**

No.	Type	Description	Unused	Used
86a	A19	1h lilac	80	45
87a	"	2h dark gray	3.00	50
88a	"	3h bistre brown	3.00	6
89a	"	5h dark blue green	7.00	4
91a	"	6h deep orange	13.00	27
97a	A20	10h carmine	4.00	5
98a	"	20h brown	55.00	60
99a	"	25h ultramarine	60.00	60
100a	"	30h red violet	65.00	1.20
101a	A21	35h green	55.00	50
102a	"	40h deep violet	55.00	3.75
103a	"	50h dull blue	60.00	5.50
104a	"	60h yellow brown	60.00	80
105a	"	72h rose	1.65	65
		Nos. 86a-105a (14)	442.45	14.97

Stamps of the 1901, 1904 and 1905 issues perf. 9 or 10½, also compound with 12½, were not sold at any post office, but were supplied only to some high-ranking officials. This applies also to the contemporary issues of Austrian Offices Abroad.

1905

Emperor Karl VI

A22

Emperor Franz Josef

A23

Schönbrunn Castle
A24

Emperor Franz Josef
A25

Designs: 2h, Empress Maria Theresa. 3h, Emperor Joseph II. 5h, 10h, 25h, Emperor Franz Josef. 6h, Emperor Leopold II. 12h, Emperor Franz I. 20h, Emperor Ferdinand I. 30h, Franz Josef as youth. 35h, Franz Josef in middle age. 60h, Franz Josef on horseback. 1k, Franz Josef in royal robes. 5k, Hofburg, Vienna.

1908-13 Typographed. *Perf. 12½.*

No.	Type	Description	Unused	Used
110	A22	1h gray black	33	8
111	"	2h blue violet ('13)	38	33
		a. 2h violet	60	8
112	A22	3h magenta	17	10
113	"	5h yellow green	17	5
		a. Booklet pane of 6	8.50	
114	A22	6h org. brn. ('13)	2.10	1.10
		a. 6h ochre ('13)	2.10	1.10
		b. 6h buff	1.15	55
115	A22	10h rose	15	5
		a. Booklet pane of 6	22.50	
116	A22	12h scarlet	2.25	45
117	"	20h chocolate	3.50	18
118	"	25h ultra. ('13)	1.40	22
		a. 25h deep blue	3.75	15
119	A22	30h olive green	6.50	27
120	"	35h slate	5.00	17

Engraved.

No.	Type	Description	Unused	Used
121	A23	50h dark green	1.10	22
		a. Pair, imperf. btwn., vert. or horizontal	325.00	325.00
122	A23	60h deep carmine	65	5
		a. Pair, imperf. btwn., vert. or horizontal	450.00	450.00
123	A23	72h dark brown ('13)	3.25	22
124	"	1k purple	21.00	9
		a. Pair, imperf. btwn., vert. or horizontal	325.00	325.00
125	A24	2k lake & olive green	32.50	38
126	"	5k bistre & dark violet	60.00	5.50
127	A25	10k blue, bistre & deep brn.	300.00	67.50
		Nos. 110-127 (18)	440.45	76.96

Issued in commemoration of the 60th year of the reign of Emperor Franz Josef for permanent use.

The 1 to 35h inclusive exist on both ordinary and chalk-surfaced paper.

All values exist imperforate. They were not sold at any post office, but presented to a number of high government officials. This applies also to all imperforate stamps of later issues, including semi-postals, etc., and those of the Austrian Offices Abroad.

Forgeries of No. 127 exist.

Birthday Jubilee Issue.

Similar to 1908 Issue, but designs enlarged by labels at top and bottom bearing dates "1830" and "1910".

1910 Typographed.

No.	Type	Description	Unused	Used
128	A22	1h gray black	10.00	6.50
129	"	2h violet	11.00	8.00
130	"	3h magenta	11.00	8.00
131	"	5h yellow green	27	17
132	"	6h buff	4.50	3.25
133	"	10h rose	27	17
134	"	12h scarlet	5.50	4.50
135	"	20h chocolate	8.00	6.50
136	"	25h deep blue	1.10	80
137	"	30h olive green	7.00	5.50
138		35h slate	7.00	5.50

Engraved

No.	Type	Description	Unused	Used
139	A23	50h dark green	8.00	8.00
140	"	60h deep carmine	8.00	8.00
141	"	1k purple	11.00	8.50
142	A24	2k lake & ol. grn.	250.00	250.00
143	"	5k bistre & dk. vio.	200.00	200.00

No.	Type	Description	Unused	Used
144	A25	10k blue, bistre & deep brown	375.00	350.00
		Nos. 128-144 (17)	917.64	873.39

Issued in celebration of the eightieth birthday of Emperor Franz Josef.

All values exist imperforate.

Forgeries of Nos. 142 to 144 exist.

Austrian Crown
A37

Emperor Franz Josef
A38

Coat of Arms
A39 A40

1916-18 Typographed.

No.	Type	Description	Unused	Used
145	A37	3h bright violet	4	4
146	"	5h light green	3	3
		a. Bklt. pane of 6	11.00	
		b. Booklet pane of 4+2 labels	22.50	
147	"	6h deep orange	33	80
148	"	10h magenta	5	5
		a. Bklt. pane of 6	11.00	
149	"	12h light blue	33	80
150	A38	15h rose red	75	8
		a. Booklet pane of 6	16.50	
151	"	20h chocolate	6.50	17
152	"	25h blue	12.50	55
153	"	30h slate	11.00	80
154	A39	40h olive green	18	4
155	"	50h blue green	33	4
156	"	60h deep blue	27	5
157	"	80h orange brown	22	5
158	"	90h red violet	22	8
159	"	1k carmine, *yellow* ('18)	40	10

Engraved.

No.	Type	Description	Unused	Used
160	A40	2k dark blue	1.10	17
161	"	3k claret	13.50	90
162	"	4k deep green	2.25	1.65
163	"	10k deep violet	40.00	40.00
		Nos. 145-163 (19)	90.00	46.40

Stamps of type A38 have two varieties of the frame. Stamps of type A40 have various decorations about the shield.

Nos. 145-163 exist imperf. Price, set $425.

1917 Ordinary Paper

No.	Type	Description	Unused	Used
164	A40	2k light blue	90	12
165	"	3k carmine rose	8.25	32
166	"	4k yellow green	1.10	75
167	"	10k violet	120.00	57.50

Nos. 164-167 exist imperf. Price, set $325.

See Nos. 172-175 (granite paper).

Emperor Karl I
A42

1917-18 Typographed

No.	Type	Description	Unused	Used
168	A42	15h dull red	9	5
		a. Booklet pane of 6	11.00	
169	"	20h dark green ('18)	17	5
		a. 20h green ('17)	80	10
170	"	25h blue	33	5
171	"	30h dull violet	22	5

Nos. 168-171 exist imperf. Price, set $50.

Engraved.

1918-19 Granite Paper.

No.	Type	Description	Unused	Used
172	A40	2k light blue	16	16
		a. Perf. 11½	550.00	400.00
173	"	3k carmine rose	40	30
174	"	4k yellow green ('19)	7.00	9.50
175	"	10k deep violet ('19)	9.50	13.00

Issues of the Republic.

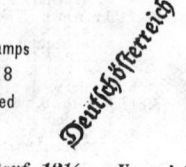

Austrian Stamps of 1916-18 Overprinted

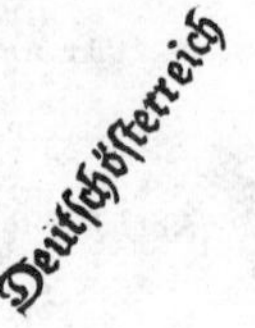

1918-19 *Perf. 12½.* Unwmkd.

No.	Type	Description	Unused	Used
181	A37	3h bright violet	5	5
182	"	5h light green	5	5
183	"	6h deep orange	12	45
184	"	10h magenta	5	5
185	"	12h light blue	25	60
186	A42	15h dull red	12	30
187	"	20h deep green	9	5
188	"	25h blue	20	10
189	"	30h dull violet	17	10
190	A39	40h olive green	17	15
191	"	50h deep green	75	70
192	"	60h deep blue	75	65
193	"	80h orange brown	18	18
		a. Inverted overprint	300.00	300.00
194	"	90h red violet	20	20
195	"	1k carmine, *yellow*	25	25

Granite Paper.

No.	Type	Description	Unused	Used
196	A40	2k light blue	9	5
		a. Pair, imperf. between	425.00	425.00
		b. Perf. 11½	14.00	8.25
197	"	3k carmine rose	28	35
198	"	4k yellow green	90	1.65
		a. Perf. 11½	15.00	13.50
199	"	10k deep violet	12.00	17.50
		Nos. 181-199 (19)	16.67	23.43

Nos. 181, 182, 184, 187 to 191, 194, 197 and 199 exist imperforate.

Post Horn A43 — Coat of Arms A44 — Allegory of New Republic A45

Ordinary Paper.

1919-20 Typographed. *Perf. 12½.*

No.	Type	Description	Unused	Used
200	A43	3h gray	3	3
201	A44	5h yellow green	3	3
202	"	5h gray ('20)	3	3
203	A43	6h orange	8	30
204	A44	10h deep rose	3	3
205	"	10h red ('20)	3	3
		a. Thick grayish paper ('20)	5	5
206	A43	12h greenish blue	8	40
207	"	15h bistre ('20)	33	40
		a. Thick grayish paper ('20)	5	5
208	A45	20h dark green	3	3
		a. 20h yellow green	3	3
		b. As "a," thick grayish paper ('20)	55	1.00
209	A44	25h blue	4	4
210	A43	25h violet ('20)	3	3
211	A45	30h dark brown	4	4
212	"	40h violet	6	4
213	"	40h lake ('20)	3	3
214	A44	45h olive green	22	42
215	A45	50h dark blue	6	5
		a. Thick grayish paper ('20)	15	15
216	A43	60h olive green ('20)	3	3
217	A44	1k carmine, *yellow*	3	5
218	"	1k light blue ('20)	3	3
		Nos. 200-218 (19)	1.24	2.04

All values exist imperf. (For regularly issued imperfs, see Nos. 227-235).

Parliament Building
A46

Granite Paper.

1919-20 Engraved *Perf. 12½, 11½*

No.	Type	Description	Unused	Used
219	A46	2k vermilion & black	32	35
		a. Center inverted	*2250.00*	
220	"	2½k olive bistre ('20)	17	17
221	"	3k blue & black brown	15	10
222	"	4k carmine & black	15	10
		a. Center invrt.	*1200.00*	*1000.00*
223	"	5k black ('20)	15	10
		a. Perf. 11½x12½	37.50	30.00
224	"	7½k plum ('20)	15	12
		a. Perf. 11½	90.00	70.00
		b. Perf. 11½x12½	55.00	55.00
225	"	10k olive green & black brown	40	40
		a. Perf. 11½x12½	65.00	70.00
		b. Perf. 11½	16.50	10.00
226	"	20k lilac & red ('20)	15	15
		a. Center invert.	*7500.00*	*6000.00*
		b. Perf. 11½	65.00	65.00
		Nos. 219-226 (8)	1.64	1.49

A number of values exist in pairs, imperforate between. Price $350 to $450 a pair.

See also No. 248.

Ordinary Paper.

1920 Typographed. *Imperf.*

No.	Type	Description	Unused	Used
227	A44	5h yellow green	18	35
228	"	5h gray	3	3
229	"	10h deep rose	3	3
230	"	10h red	3	3
231	A43	15h bistre	7	4
232	"	25h violet	3	3
233	A45	30h dark brown	7	7
234	"	40h violet	10	7
235	A43	60h olive green	3	7
		Nos. 227-235 (9)	57	72

Arms
A47 A48

Ordinary Paper.

1920-21 Typo. *Perf. 12½*

No.	Type	Description	Unused	Used
238	A47	80h rose	5	3
239	"	1k black brown	5	3
241	"	1½k green ('21)	6	5
242	"	2k blue	3	3
243	A48	3k yellow green & dark green ('21)	5	3
244	"	4k red & claret ('21)	6	5
245	"	5k violet & claret ('21)	6	4
246	"	7½k yel. & brn. ('21)	9	9
247	"	10k ultramarine & blue ('21)	15	12
		Nos. 238-247 (9)	60	47

Nos. 238-245, 247 exist on white paper of good quality and on thick grayish paper of inferior quality; No. 246 only on white paper.

1921 Engraved

No.	Type	Description	Unused	Used
248	A46	50k dark violet, *yellow*	45	55
		a. Perf. 11½	55.00	60.00

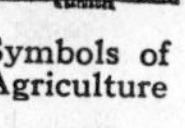

Symbols of Agriculture
A49

Symbols of Labor and Industry
A50

1922–24 Typographed *Perf. 12½*

250	A49	½k olive bistre	5	40
251	A50	1k brown	3	3
252	"	2k cobalt blue	3	3
253	A49	2½k orange brown	3	3
254	A50	4k dull violet	5	50
255	"	5k gray green	3	3
256	A49	7½k gray violet	3	3
257	A50	10k claret	3	3
258	A49	12½k gray green	5	3
259	"	15k bluish green	3	3
260	"	20k dark blue	3	3
261	"	25k claret	3	3
262	A50	30k pale gray	3	3
263	"	45k pale red	3	3
264	"	50k orange brown	3	3
265	"	60k yellow green	3	3
266	"	75k ultramarine	3	3
267	"	80k yellow	3	3
268	A49	100k gray	3	3
269	"	120k brown	5	3
270	"	150k orange	3	3
271	"	160k light green	3	3
272	"	180k red	3	3
273	"	200k pink	3	3
274	"	240k dark violet	3	3
275	"	300k light blue	6	3
276	"	400k deep green	60	10
		a. 400k gray green	65	15
277	"	500k yellow	3	3
278	"	600k slate	3	3
279	"	700k brown ('24)	30	3
280	"	800k violet ('24)	55	1.10
281	A50	1.000k violet ('23)	32	3
282	"	1.200k car. rose ('23)	25	12
283	"	1.500k orange ('24)	80	10
284	"	1.600k slate ('23)	1.00	1.00
285	"	2.000k dp. blue('23)	2.75	80
286	"	3.000k light bl. ('23)	8.00	1.60
287	"	4.000k dark blue, *blue* ('24)	3.25	1.60
		Nos. 250–287 (38)	18.77	8.16

Nos. 250–287 exist imperf. Price, set $750.

Symbols of Art and Science
A51

1922–24 Engraved *Perf. 12½*

288	A51	20k dark brown	9	8
		a. Perf. 11½	60	55
289	"	25k blue	9	6
		a. Perf. 11½	55	50
290	"	50k brown red	6	4
		a. Perf. 11½	1.75	1.85
291	"	100k deep green	12	9
		a. Perf. 11½	3.50	3.50
292	"	200k dark violet	6	3
		a. Perf. 11½	4.25	4.25
293	"	500k deep orange	18	32
294	"	1.000k black violet, *yellow*	5	3
		a. Perf. 11½	150.00	150.00
295	"	2.000k olive green, *yellow*	18	8
296	"	3.000k claret brown ('23)	12.50	35
297	"	5.000k gray blk. ('23)	2.50	1.25

Granite Paper.

298	A51	10.000k red brown ('24)	3.75	3.75
		Nos. 288–298 (11)	19.58	6.08

On Nos. 281 to 287 and Nos. 291 to 298 "kronen" is abbreviated to "k" and transposed with the numerals.

Nos. 288–298 exist imperf. Price, set $425.

Numeral
A52

Fields Crossed by Telegraph Wires
A53

White-Shouldered Eagle
A54

Church of Minorite Friars
A55

1925–27 Typographed *Perf. 12*

303	A52	1g dark gray	50	3
304	"	2g claret	75	3
305	"	3g scarlet	80	3
306	"	4g greenish bl. ('27)	1.75	5
307	"	5g brown orange	3.25	3
308	"	6g ultramarine	2.25	3
309	"	7g chocolate	2.50	3
310	"	8g yellow green	10.00	3
311	A53	10g orange	60	3
313	"	15g red lilac	60	3
314	"	16g dark blue	60	3
315	"	18g olive green	1.35	45
316	A54	20g dark violet	75	3
317	"	24g carmine	1.10	45
318	"	30g dark brown	80	3
319	"	40g ultramarine	1.50	3
320	"	45g yellow brown	2.00	3
321	"	50g gray	2.25	23
322	"	80g turquoise blue	5.50	4.50

Engraved.

Perf. 12½

323	A55	1s deep green	20.00	50
		a. 1s light green	125.00	2.00
324	A55	2s brown rose	11.00	10.00
		Nos. 303–324 (21)	69.85	11.60

Nos. 303–305 and 307–324 exist imperf. Price, set $450.

Güssing
A56

National Library, Vienna
A57

Designs: 15g, Hochosterwitz. 16g, 20g, Durnstein. 18g, Traunsee. 24g, Salzburg. 30g, Seewiesen. 40g, Innsbruck. 50g, Worthersee. 60g, Hohenems. 2s, St. Stephen's Cathedral, Vienna.

1929–30 Typo. *Perf. 12½*

Size: 25½x21½mm

326	A56	10g brown orange	2.00	3
327	"	10g bistre ('30)	1.75	3
328	"	15g violet brown	1.10	90
329	"	16g dark gray	40	5
330	"	18g blue green	80	70
331	"	20g dark gray ('30)	90	3
332	"	24g maroon	11.50	7.50
333	"	24g lake ('30)	11.50	75
334	"	30g dark violet	7.50	10
335	"	40g dark blue	13.50	15
336	"	50g gray violet('30)	57.50	13
337	"	60g olive green	45.00	32

Engraved.

Size: 21x26mm.

338	A57	1s black brown	13.50	30
339	"	2s dark green	19.50	9.00
		Nos. 326–339 (14)	186.45	19.99

Type of 1929–30 Issue.

Designs: 12g, Traunsee. 64g, Hohenems.

1932 *Perf. 12*

Size: 21 x 16½ mm.

340	A56	10g olive brown	1.50	3
341	"	12g blue green	3.00	3
342	"	18g blue green	2.75	2.00
343	"	20g dark gray	2.00	3
344	"	24g carmine rose	9.50	3
345	"	24g dull violet	6.50	3
346	"	30g dark violet	30.00	8
347	"	30g carmine rose	6.25	11
348	"	40g dark blue	37.50	1.00
349	"	40g dark violet	20.00	32
350	"	50g gray violet	40.00	32
351	A56	50g dull blue	11.00	32
352	"	60g gray green	100.00	1.85
353	"	64g gray green	12.50	15
		Nos. 340–353 (14)	282.50	6.30

Nos. 340–353 exist imperf. Price, set $550.

Burgenland
A67

Tyrol
A68

Designs (costumes of various districts): 3g, Burgenland. 4g, 5g, Carinthia. 6g, 8g, Lower Austria. 12g, 20g, Upper Austria. 24g, 25g, Salzburg. 30g, 35g, Styria. 45g, Tyrol. 60g, Vorarlberg bridal couple. 64g, Vorarlberg. 1s, Viennese family. 2s, Military.

1934–35 Typographed *Perf. 12*

354	A67	1g dark violet	5	3
355	"	3g scarlet	5	3
356	"	4g olive green	10	7
357	"	5g red violet	10	3
358	"	6g ultramarine	35	18
359	"	8g green	12	3
360	"	12g dark brown	12	3
361	"	20g yellow brown	15	3
362	"	24g greenish blue	15	3
363	"	25g violet	30	18
364	"	30g maroon	22	3
365	"	35g rose carmine	45	38

Perf. 12½

366	A68	40g slate gray	55	12
367	"	45g brown red	42	12
368	"	60g ultramarine	85	25
369	"	64g brown	1.00	13
370	"	1s deep violet	95	45
371	"	2s dull green	55.00	65.00

Designs Redrawn

Perf. 12 (6g), 12½ (2s)

372	A67	6g ultramarine ('35)	25	12
373	A68	2s emerald ('35)	3.25	5.00
		Nos. 354–373 (20)	64.23	72.24

The design of No. 358 looks as though the man's ears were on backwards, while No. 372 appears correctly.

On No. 373 there are seven feathers on each side of the eagle instead of five.

Nos. 354–373 exist imperf. Price, set $550.

Dollfuss Mourning Issue.

Engelbert Dollfuss
A85

1934 Engraved *Perf. 12½*

374	A85	24g greenish black	80	32

Exists imperf. Price $175.

1935

375	A85	24g indigo	1.65	1.10

First anniversary of death of Engelbert Dollfuss, chancellor. Exists imperf. Price $200.

"Mother and Child" by Joseph Danhauser
A86

"Madonna and Child", after Painting by Albrecht Dürer
A87

1935, May 1

376	A86	24g dark blue	70	28

Issued for Mother's Day.

Nos. 376–377 exist imperf. Price, each $200.

1936, May 5 Photogravure

377	A87	24g violet blue	40	30

Issued for Mother's Day.

Farm Workers
A88

Design: 5s, Factory workers.

1936, June Engraved *Perf. 12½*

378	A88	3s red orange	19.50	19.50
379	"	5s brown black	40.00	50.00

Nos. 378–379 exist imperf. Price, set $350.

Engelbert Dollfuss
A90

Mother and Child
A91

1936, July 25

380	A90	10s dark blue	1250.00	1250.00

Second anniversary of death of Engelbert Dollfuss, chancellor. Exists imperf. Price, $2,500.

1937, May 5 Photo. *Perf. 12*

381	A91	24g henna brown	40	30

Issued for Mother's Day. Exists imperf. Price, $225.

S. S. Maria Anna
A92

Steamships: 24g, Uranus, 64g, Oesterreich.

1937, June 9

382	A92	12g red brown	1.25	50
383	"	24g deep blue	1.25	45
384	"	64g dark green	1.25	1.00

Centenary of steamship service on Danube River.

Exist imperf. Price, set $175.

First Locomotive, "Austria"
A95

Designs: 25g, Modern steam locomotive. 35g, Modern electric train.

1937, Nov. 22

385	A95	12g black brown	16	7
386	"	25g dark violet	60	45
387	"	35g brown red	1.85	2.10

Centenary of Austrian railways. Exist imperf. Price, set $150.

Rose and Zodiac Signs
A98

1937 Engraved. *Perf. 13x12½.*

388 A98 12g dark green 15 8
389 " 24g dark carmine 15 8

Exist imperf. Price, set $80.

For Use in Vienna, Lower Austria and Burgenland.

Germany Nos. 509-511 and 511B Overprinted in Black

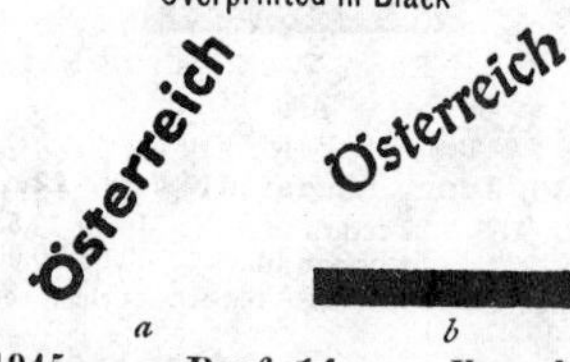

a b

1945 *Perf. 14.* **Unwmkd.**

390 A115 (*a*) 5(pf) deep yellow green 3 8
391 " (*b*) 6(pf) purple 10 18
392 " (*a*) 8(pf) red 5 8
393 " (*b*) 12(pf) carmine 6 12

Nos. 390–393 exist with overprint inverted or double.

Germany No. 507, the 3pf, with overprint "a" was prepared, not issued, but sold to collectors after the definitive Republic issue had been placed in use. Price $50.

German Semi-Postal Stamps, Nos. B207, B209, B210 and B283 Surcharged in Black

ÖSTERREICH
5 Pf.
c

ÖSTERREICH
8 Pf.
d

1945 *Perf. 14, 14x13½, 13½x14*

394 SP181 (*c*) 5pf on 12(pf) +88(pf) green 1.00 1.50
395 SP184 (*d*) 6pf on 6(pf) +14(pf) ultra. & dp. brown 8.00 11.00
396 SP242 (") 8pf on 42(pf) +108(pf) brown 1.25 1.85
397 SP183 (") 12pf on 3(pf) +7(pf) dull blue 1.00 1.50

The surcharges are spaced to fit the stamps.

Stamps not listed in this Catalogue or mentioned in "For the Record" (unless recent issues) usually are revenues, locals or labels.

Stamps of Germany, Nos. 509 to 511, 511B, 519 and 529 Overprinted

e f

1945 **Typo.** *Perf. 14*

Size: 18½x22½mm.

398 A115 (*e*) 5(pf) dp. yellow green 40 75
399 " (*f*) 5(pf) dp. yellow green 8.50 11.50
400 " (*e*) 6(pf) purple 25 50
401 " (") 8(pf) red 20 40
402 " (") 12(pf) carmine 40 75

Engraved.

Size: 21½x26mm.

403 A115 (*e*) 30 (pf) olive green 8.50 12.00
a. Thin bar at bottom 25.00 27.50
404 A118 (") 42(pf) bright green 32.50 42.50
a. Thin bar at bottom 22.50 30.00
Nos. 398-404 (7) 50.75 68.40

On Nos. 403a and 404a, the bottom bar of the overprint is 2½mm. wide, and, as the overprint was applied in two operations, "Osterreich" is usually not exactly centered in its diagonal slot. On Nos. 403 and 404, the bottom bar is 3mm. wide, and "Osterreich" is always well centered.

Germany Nos. 524–527 (the 1m, 2m, 3m and 5m), overprinted with vertical bars and "Osterreich" similar to "e" and "f", were prepared, not issued, but sold to collectors after the definitive Republic issue had been placed in use. Price for set $140.

For Use in Styria.

Stamps of Germany Nos. 506 to 511, 511A, 511B, 514 to 523 and 529 Overprinted in Black

Typographed

1945 *Perf. 14* **Unwmkd.**

Size: 18½x22½mm.

405 A115 1(pf) gray black 2.75 4.00
406 " 3(pf) light brown 2.40 3.50
407 " 4(pf) slate 10.50 15.00
408 " 5(pf) dp. yel. grn. 2.10 2.50
409 " 6(pf) purple 35 42
410 " 8(pf) red 1.40 1.90
411 " 10(pf) dark brown 2.75 4.00
412 " 12(pf) carmine 35 65

Engraved.

413 A115 15(pf) brown lake 1.40 2.10
414 " 16(pf) peacock green 19.00 27.50
415 " 20(pf) blue 5.25 9.00
416 " 24(pf) org. brown 19.00 27.50

Size: 22½x26mm.

417 A115 25(pf) bright ultra. 2.00 3.00
418 " 30(pf) olive green 2.00 3.00
419 " 40(pf) bright red violet 2.50 4.50
420 A118 42(pf) bright grn. 5.00 7.00
421 A115 50(pf) myrtle grn. 4.25 6.25
422 " 60(pf) dark red brown 5.25 7.50
423 " 80(pf) indigo 4.25 6.25
Nos. 405–423 (19) 92.50 135.57

Overprinted on Nos. 524 to 527.
Perf. 12½, 14.

424 A116 1m dk. slate grn. 13.50 25.00
a. Perf. 12½ 235.00
425 " 2m violet 14.00 24.50
a. Perf. 14 27.50 50.00
426 " 3m copper red 30.00 60.00
a. Perf. 14 325.00
427 " 5m dark blue 350.00 650.00
a. Perf. 14 800.00

On the preceding four stamps the innermost vertical lines are 10½ mm. apart; on the pfennig values 6½ mm. apart.

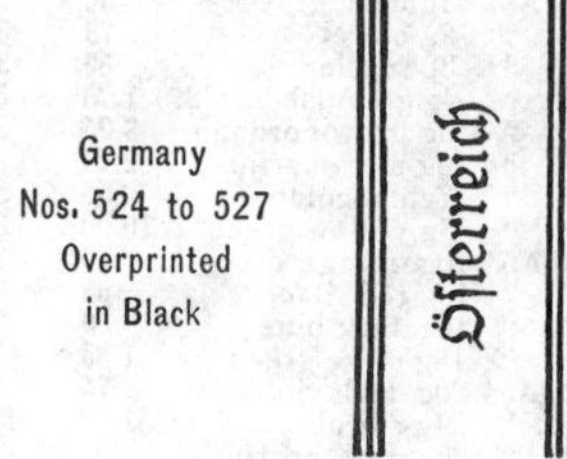

Germany Nos. 524 to 527 Overprinted in Black

Perf. 14

428 A116 1m dk. slate grn. 15.00 24.00
429 " 2m violet 16.00 30.00

Perf. 12½

430 A116 3m copper red 32.50 52.50
431 " 5m dark blue 250.00 375.00
a. Perf. 14 800.00

On the preceding four stamps, "Osterreich" is thinner, measuring 16 mm. On the previous set of 23 values it measures 18 mm.

Counterfeits exist of Nos. 424–431 overprints.

For Use in Vienna, Lower Austria and Burgenland.

Coat of Arms
A99 A100

Typographed or Lithographed.
Perf. 14x13½

1945, July 3 **Unwmkd.**

Size: 21x25mm.

432 A99 3(pf) brown 3 3
433 " 4(pf) slate 4 4
434 " 5(pf) dark green 3 3
435 " 6(pf) deep violet 3 3
436 " 8(pf) orange brown 3 3
437 " 10(pf) deep brown 3 3
438 " 12(pf) rose carmine 3 3
439 " 15(pf) orange red 3 3
440 " 16(pf) dull blue green 3 5

Perf. 14.

Size: 24x28½mm.

441 A99 20(pf) light blue 5 4
442 " 24(pf) orange 5 5
443 " 25(pf) dark blue 5 3
444 " 30(pf) dp. gray green 5 3
445 " 38(pf) ultramarine 5 5
446 " 40(pf) bright red violet 5 5
447 " 42(pf) sage green 5 5
448 " 50(pf) blue green 5 7
449 " 60(pf) maroon 5 7
450 " 80(pf) dull lilac 6 12

Engraved
Perf. 14x13½

451 A100 1(m) dark green 10 28
452 " 2(m) dark purple 12 32
453 " 3(m) dark violet 15 40
454 A100 5(m) brown red 18 65
Nos. 432–454 (23) 1.34 2.51

Nos. 432, 433, 437, 439, 440, 443, 446, 448 and 449 are typographed. Nos. 434, 435, 441 and 442 are lithographed; the other values exist both ways.

For General Use.

Lermoos, Winter Scene
A101

The Prater Woods, Vienna
A105

Hochosterwitz, Carinthia
A106

Lake Constance
A110

Dürnstein, Lower Austria
A124

Designs: 4g, Eisenerz surface mine. 5g, Leopoldsberg, near Vienna. 6g, Hohensalzburg, Salzburg Province. 12g, Wolfgang See, near Salzburg. 15g, Forchtenstein Castle, Burgenland. 16g, Gesäuse Valley. 24g, Höldrichs Mill, Lower Austria. 25g, Oetz Valley Outlet, Tyrol. 30g, Neusiedler Lake, Burgenland. 35g, Belvedere Palace, Vienna. 38g, Langbath Lake. 40g, Mariazell, Styria. 42g, Traunkirchen. 45g, Hartenstein Castle. 50g, Silvretta Mountains, Vorarlberg. 60g, Railroad viaducts near Semmering. 70g, Waterfall of Bad-Gastein, Salzburg. 80g, Kaiser Mountains, Tyrol. 90g, Wayside Shrine, Tragöss, Styria. 2s, St. Christof am Arlberg, Tyrol. 3s, Heiligenblut, Carinthia. 5s, Schönbrunn, Vienna.

Perf. 14x13½

1945–46 **Photogravure** **Unwmkd.**

455 A101 3g sapphire 3 3
456 " 4g deep orange ('46) 3 3
457 " 5g dark carmine rose 3 3
458 " 6g dark slate green 3 3
459 A105 8g golden brown 3 3
460 A106 10g dark green 3 3
461 " 12g dark brown 3 3
462 " 15g dk. slate bl. ('46) 3 3
463 " 16g chestnut brown ('46) 3 3

Perf. 13½x14

464 A110 20g deep ultra. ('46) 3 3
465 " 24g deep yellow green ('46) 3 3
466 " 25g gray black ('46) 3 3
467 " 30g dark red 3 3
468 " 35g brown red ('46) 3 3
469 " 38g brn. olive ('46) 5 5
470 " 40g gray 3 3
471 " 42g brn. orange ('46) 3 3
472 " 45g dark blue ('46) 25 35
473 " 50g dark blue 3 3
474 " 60g dark violet 8 6
a. Imperf. (pair) 57.50
475 " 70g Pruss. blue ('46) 12 15
476 " 80g brown 20 22
477 " 90g Prussian green 90 1.30
478 A124 1s dk. red brn. ('46) 55 50
479 " 2s blue gray ('46) 2.25 2.75
480 " 3s dark slate green ('46) 60 65
481 " 5s dark red ('46) 1.10 1.40
Nos. 455–481 (27) 6.61 7.94

See also Nos. 486–488, 496–515.

No. 461 Overprinted in Carmine

1946, Sept. 26
482 A106 12g dark brown 18 27

Issued to commemorate the meeting of the Society for Cultural and Economic Relations with the Soviet Union, Vienna, September 26 to 29, 1946.

City Hall Park, Vienna
A128

Hochosterwitz, Carinthia
A129

Perf. 14x13½

1946-47 Photogravure. Unwmkd.
483 A128 8g deep plum 3 3
484 " 8g olive brown 7 3
a. 8g dark olive green 3 3
485 A129 10g dark brown violet ('47) 6 3

Perf. 13½x14
486 A110 30g blue gray ('47) 10 12
487 " 50g brn. vio. ('47) 27 18
488 " 60g violet bl. ('47) 1.65 2.25
Nos. 483-488 (6) 2.18 2.64

See also No. 502.

Franz Grillparzer
A130

Franz Schubert
A131

1947 Engraved. *Perf. 14x13½.*
489 A130 18g chocolate 10 10

Photogravure.
490 A130 18g dark violet brn. 12 12

Issued to commemorate the 75th anniversary of the death of Franz Grillparzer, dramatic poet.

A second printing of No. 490 on thicker paper has a darker frame and clearer delineation of the portrait.

1947, Mar. 31 Engraved
491 A131 12g dark green 8 7

Issued to commemorate the 150th anniversary of the birth of Franz Schubert, musician and composer.

Nos. 469 and 463 Surcharged in Brown

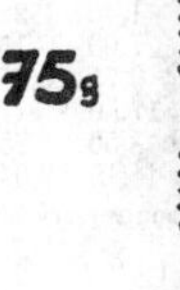

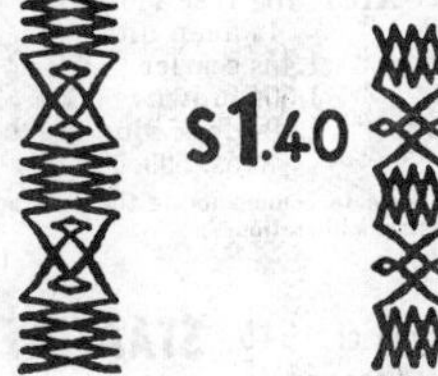

1947, Sept. 1 Photo. *Perf. 14*
492 A110 75g on 38g brown olive 27 32
493 A106 1.40s on 16g chestnut brown 7 8

The surcharge on No. 493 varies from brown to black brown.

Symbols of Global Telegraphic Communication
A132

Engraved

1947, Nov. 5 *Perf. 14x13½*
495 A132 40g dark violet 8 10

Centenary of the telegraph in Austria.

Scenic Type of 1946.

1946, Aug. Photo. *Perf. 13½x14*
496 A124 1s dark brown 50 42
497 " 2s dark blue 3.50 3.25
498 " 3s dark slate green 90 90
499 " 5s dark red 27.50 9.00

On Nos. 478 to 481 the upper and lower panels show a screen effect. On Nos. 496 to 499 the panels appear to be solid color.

Scenic Types of 1945-46.

1947-48 Photo. *Perf. 14x13½*
500 A101 3g bright red 3 3
501 " 5g " 4 3
502 A129 10g " 8 3
503 A106 15g " ('48) 1.00 1.00

Perf. 13½x14
504 A110 20g bright red 28 3
505 " 30g " 50 12
506 " 40g " 50 3
507 " 50g " 80 4
508 " 60g " ('48) 6.50 1.15
509 " 70g " ('48) 3.00 6
510 " 80g " ('48) 3.00 12
511 " 90g " ('48) 3.75 50
512 A124 1s dk. violet 40 4
513 " 2s " 65 15
514 " 3s " ('48) 7.75 1.10
515 " 5s " ('48) 9.50 1.10
Nos. 500-515 (16) 37.78 5.53

Carl Michael Ziehrer
A133

Designs: No. 517, Adalbert Stifter. No. 518, Anton Bruckner. 60g, Friedrich von Amerling.

1948-49 Engraved
516 A133 20g dull green 20 13
517 " 40g chocolate 4.00 3.00
518 " 40g dark green ('49) 6.25 6.25
519 " 60g rose brown 30 20

Issued to commemorate anniversaries of the death of Carl Michael Ziehrer (1843-1922), composer; Adalbert Stifter (1805-1868), novelist; Friedrich von Amerling (1803-1887), painter, and the birth of Anton Bruckner (1824-1896), composer.

Vorarlberg, Montafon Valley
A134

Costume of Vienna, 1850
A135

Designs (Austrian Costumes): 3g, Tyrol, Inn Valley. 5g, Salzburg, Pinzgau. 10g, Styria, Salzkammergut. 15g, Burgenland, Lutzmannsburg. 25g, Vienna, 1850. 30g, Salzburg, Pongau. 40g, Vienna, 1840. 45g, Carinthia, Lesach Valley. 50g, Vorarlberg, Bregenzer Forest. 60g, Carinthia, Lavant Valley. 70g, Lower Austria, Wachau. 75g, Styria, Salzkammergut. 80g, Styria, Enns Valley. 90g, Central Styria. 1s, Tyrol, Puster Valley. 1.20s, Lower Austria, Vienna Woods. 1.40s, Upper Austria, Inn District. 1.45s, Wilten. 1.50s, Vienna, 1853. 1.60s, Vienna, 1830. 1.70s, East Tyrol, Kals. 2s, Upper Austria. 2.20s, Ischl, 1820. 2.40s, Kitzbuhel. 2.50s, Upper Steiermark, 1850. 2.70s, Little Walser Valley. 3s, Burgenland. 3.50s, Lower Austria, 1850. 4.50s, Gail Valley. 5s, Ziller Valley. 7s, Steiermark, Sulm Valley.

Photogravure

1948-52 *Perf. 14x13½* Unwmkd.
520 A134 3g gray ('50) 40 45
521 " 5g dark green ('49) 4 3
522 " 10g deep blue 5 3
523 " 15g brown 45 3
524 " 20g yellow green 7 3
525 " 25g brown ('49) 10 4
526 " 30g dk. car. rose 2.10 3
527 " 30g dk. vio. ('50) 40 3
528 " 40g violet 2.10 3
529 " 40g green ('49) 20 3
530 " 45g violet blue 1.85 30
531 " 50g orge. brn. ('49) 45 3
532 " 60g scarlet 20 3
533 " 70g brt. bl. grn ('49) 18 3
534 " 75g blue 3.00 30
535 " 80g car. rose ('49) 30 3
536 " 90g brn. vio. ('49) 21.50 27
537 " 1s ultramarine 4.00 4
538 " 1s rose red ('50) 52.50 6
539 " 1s dk. green ('51) 18 3
540 " 1.20s violet ('49) 25 6
541 " 1.40s brown 2.25 12
542 " 1.45s dark car. ('51) 80 6
543 " 1.50s ultra. ('51) 45 3
544 " 1.60s orge. red ('49) 22 4
545 " 1.70s vio. blue ('50) 2.10 35
546 " 2s blue green 30 4
547 " 2.20s slate ('52) 2.00 4
548 " 2.40s blue ('51) 75 10
549 " 2.50s brown ('52) 1.50 50
550 " 2.70s dk. brown ('51) 35 35
551 " 3s brn. car. ('49) 1.25 3
552 " 3.50s dull green ('51) 5.50 4
553 " 4.50s brn. violet ('51) 45 40
554 " 5s dark red violet 45 4
555 " 7s olive ('52) 1.00 6

Engraved
556 A135 10s gray ('50) 27.50 5.50
Nos. 520-556 (37) 137.69 9.61

In 1958-59, 21 denominations of this set were printed on white paper, differing from the previous grayish paper with yellowish gum.

Pres. Karl Renner
A136

1948, Nov. 12 *Perf. 14x13½*
557 A136 1sh deep blue 2.75 1.60

Issued to commemorate the 30th anniversary of the founding of the Austrian Republic. See also Nos. 573, 636.

Franz Gruber and Josef Mohr
A137

1948, Dec. 18 *Perf. 13½x14*
558 A137 60g red brown 6.25 6.00

Issued to commemorate the 130th anniversary of the hymn "Silent Night, Holy Night."

Symbolical of Child Welfare
A138

Johann Strauss, the Younger
A139

Photogravure

1949, May 14 *Perf. 14x13½*
559 A138 1s bright blue 3.65 1.50

Issued to commemorate the first year of activity of the United Nations International Children's Emergency Fund in Austria.

1949 Engraved

Designs: 30g, Johann Strauss, the elder. No. 561, Johann Strauss, the younger. No. 562, Karl Millöcker.

560 A139 30g violet brown 3.50 3.50
561 " 1s dark blue 3.65 1.50
562 " 1s dark blue 12.25 10.00

Issued to commemorate the centenary of the death of Johann Strauss, the elder (1804-1849), and the 50th anniversary of the deaths of Johann Strauss, the younger (1825-1899), and Karl Millöcker (1842-1899), composers. See also No. 574.

Esperanto Star, Olive Branches
A140

St. Gebhard
A141

1949, June 25 Photogravure
563 A140 20g blue green 2.10 85

Austrian Esperanto Congress at Graz.

1949, Aug. 6 Engraved
564 A141 30g dark violet 2.40 1.60

Issued to commemorate the millenary of the birth of St. Gebhard (949-995), Bishop of Vorarlberg.

Letter, Roses and Post Horn
A142

Designs: 60g, Plaque. 1s, "Austria," wings and monogram.

1949, Oct. 8 *Perf. 13½x14*
565 A142 40g dark green 3.25 2.25
566 " 60g dark carmine 3.25 2.75
567 " 1s dk. violet blue 8.00 7.50

Issued to commemorate the 75th anniversary of the formation of the Universal Postal Union.

Moritz Michael Daffinger
A143

Andreas Hofer
A144

Designs: 30g, Alexander Girardi. No. 569, Daffinger. No. 570, Hofer. No. 571, Josef Madersperger.

1950 ***Perf. 14x13½*** **Unwmkd.**

568 A144 30g dark blue 2.00 85
569 A143 60g red brown 7.75 5.50
570 A144 60g dark violet 11.00 10.00
571 " 60g purple 5.50 3.00

Issued to commemorate the centenary of the birth of Alexander Girardi (1850–1918), actor; the death centenary of Moritz Michael Daffinger (1790–1849), painter; the 140th anniversary of the death of Andreas Hofer (1767–1810), patriot, and the death centenary of Josef Madersperger (1768–1850), inventor.

Austrian Stamp of 1850
A146

1950, May 20 ***Perf. 14½***

572 A146 1s *straw* 3.00 1.75

Centenary of Austrian postage stamps.

Renner Type of 1948, Frame and Inscriptions Altered.

1951, Mar. 3

573 A136 1s *straw* 2.25 30

Issued in memory of Pres. Karl Renner, 1870–1950.

Strauss Type of 1949.

Portrait: 60g, Joseph Lanner.

1951, Apr. 12

574 A139 60g dark blue green 4.25 1.35

Issued to commemorate the 150th anniversary of the birth of Joseph Lanner, composer.

Martin Johann Schmidt
A147

Boy Scout Emblem
A148

Engraved.

1951, June 28 ***Perf. 14x13½***

575 A147 1sh brown red 5.00 3.00

Issued to commemorate the 150th anniversary of the death of Martin Johann Schmidt, painter.

1951, Aug. 3 **Engr. & Litho.**

576 A148 1sh dark green, ochre & pink 5.00 4.00

Issued in connection with the 7th World Scout Jamboree, Bad Ischl-St. Wolfgang, Aug. 3–13, 1951.

Wilhelm Kienzl
A149

Josef Schrammel
A150

Design: 1s, Karl von Ghega.

1951-52 **Engraved** **Unwmkd.**

577 A149 1s deep grn. ('52) 5.25 1.65
578 " 1.50s indigo 4.00 1.10
579 A150 1.50s vio. blue ('52) 5.25 1.60

Issued to commemorate the 150th anniversary of the birth of Karl von Ghega (1802–1860), civil engineer; the 10th anniversary of the death of Wilhelm Kienzl (1857–1941), composer, and the birth centenary of Josef Schrammel (1852–1895), composer. See also No. 582.

Breakfast Pavilion, Schönbrunn
A151

1952, May 24 ***Perf. 13½x14***

580 A151 1.50s dark green 5.25 1.50

Issued to commemorate the 200th anniversary of the founding of the Vienna Zoological Gardens.

Globe as Dot Over "i"
A152

School Girl
A153

1952, July 1 ***Perf. 14x13½***

581 A152 1.50s dark blue 6.00 1.00

Issued to publicize the formation of the International Union of Socialist Youth Camp, Vienna, July 1-10, 1952.

Type Similar to A150.

Portrait: 1s, Nikolaus Lenau.

1952, Aug. 13

582 A150 1s deep green 5.75 1.65

Issued to commemorate the 150th anniversary of the birth of Nikolaus Lenau, pseudonym of Nikolaus Franz Niembsch von Strehlenau (1802–1850), poet.

1952, Sept. 6

583 A153 2.40s dp. vio. blue 11.00 3.50

Issued to stimulate letter-writing between Austrian and foreign school children.

Hugo Wolf
A154

Pres. Theodor Körner
A155

Engraved.

1953, Feb. 21 ***Perf. 14x13½***

587 A154 1.50s dark blue 6.50 1.00

Issued to commemorate the 50th anniversary of the death of Hugo Wolf, composer.

1953, Apr. 24

588 A155 1.50s dk. vio. blue 6.00 1.00

Issued to commemorate the 80th birthday of Pres. Theodor Körner. See also Nos. 591, 614.

State Theater, Linz, and Masks
A156

1953, Oct. 17 ***Perf. 13½x14***

589 A156 1.50s dark gray 7.00 1.60

Issued to commemorate the 150th anniversary of the founding of the State Theater at Linz.

Child and Christmas Tree
A157

Karl von Rokitansky
A158

1953, Nov. 30 ***Perf. 14x13½***

590 A157 1s dark green 1.90 28

See also No. 597.

Type Similar to A155.

Portrait: 1.50s, Moritz von Schwind.

1954, Jan. 21 ***Perf. 14x13½***

591 A155 1.50s purple 9.00 2.10

Issued to commemorate the 150th anniversary of the birth of Moritz von Schwind, painter.

1954, Feb. 19

592 A158 1.50s purple 9.50 2.25

Issued to commemorate the 150th anniversary of the birth of Karl von Rokitansky, physician. See also No. 595.

Esperanto Star and Wreath
A159

Engraved and Photogravure

1954, June 5 ***Perf. 13½14***

593 A159 1s dark brown & emerald 7.00 28

Issued to commemorate the 50th anniversary of the Esperanto movement in Austria.

Johann Michael Rottmayr
A160

Engraved

1954, Aug. 4 ***Perf. 14x13½***

594 A160 1s dark blue green 10.50 2.40

300th birth anniversary of Johann Michael Rottmayr von Rosenbrunn, painter.

Type Similar to A158

Portrait: 1.50s, Carl Auer von Welsbach.

595 A158 1.50s violet blue 18.50 2.10

25th death anniversary of Carl Auer von Welsbach (1858–1929), chemist.

Organ, St. Florian Monastery and Cherub
A161

1954, Oct. 2 **Unwmkd.**

596 A161 1s brown 3.25 28

Issued to publicize the second International Congress for Catholic Church Music, Vienna, October 4-10, 1954.

Christmas Type of 1953

1954, Nov. 30

597 A157 1s dark blue 3.75 50

Arms of Austria and Official Publication
A162

1954, Dec. 18 **Engraved**

598 A162 1s salmon & black 2.75 28

Issued to commemorate the 150th anniversary of the founding of Austria's State Printing Plant and the 250th year of publication of the government newspaper, Wiener Zeitung.

Parliament Building
A163

Designs: 1s, Western railroad station, Vienna. 1.45s, Letters forming flag. 1.50s, Public housing, Vienna. 2.40s, Limberg dam.

1955, Apr. 27 ***Perf. 13½x14***

599 A163 70g rose violet 1.40 22
600 " 1s deep ultra. 7.00 15
601 " 1.45s scarlet 9.75 2.75
602 " 1.50s brown 17.50 17
603 " 2.40s dark blue green 8.50 4.75
Nos. 599-603 (5) 44.15 8.04

Issued to commemorate the 10th anniversary of Austria's liberation.

Type of 1945 Overprinted in Blue **STAATSVERTRAG 1955**

1955, May 15 ***Perf. 14x13½***

604 A100 2(s) blue gray 2.50 42

Issued to commemorate the signing of the state treaty with the United States, France, Great Britain and Russia, May 15, 1955.

Workers of Three Races Climbing Globe
A164

1955, May 20 *Perf. 13½x14*

605 A164 1s indigo 2.60 2.50

Issued to publicize the 4th congress of the International Confederation of Free Trade Unions, Vienna, May 1955.

Burgtheater, Vienna
A165

Design: 2.40s, Opera House, Vienna.

1955, July 25

606 A165 1.50s light sepia 3.75 12
607 " 2.40s dark blue 4.25 2.25

Issued to celebrate the re-opening of the Burgtheater and Opera House in Vienna.

Symbolic of Austria's Desire to Join the U. N.
A166

1955, Oct. 24 **Unwmkd.**

608 A166 2.40s green 7.25 2.75

Tenth anniversary of United Nations.

Wolfgang Amadeus Mozart
A167

Symbolic of Austria's Joining the U. N.
A168

1956, Jan. 21 *Perf. 14x13½*

609 A167 2.40s slate blue 3.50 85

Issued to commemorate the 200th anniversary of the birth of Wolfgang Amadeus Mozart, composer.

1956, Feb. 20

610 A168 2.40s chocolate 7.50 2.10

Issued to commemorate Austria's admission to the United Nations Organization.

Globe Showing Energy of the Earth
A169

1956, May 8 *Perf. 13½14*

611 A169 2.40s deep blue 10.00 3.50

Issued to publicize the Fifth International Power Conference, Vienna, June 17-23, 1956.

Map of Europe and City Maps
A170

J. B. Fischer von Erlach
A171

Photogravure and Typographed

1956, June 8 *Perf. 14x13½*

612 A170 1.45s light green, black & red 4.25 1.00

Issued to publicize the 23rd International Housing and Town Planning Congress, Vienna, July 22–28.

1956, July 20 **Engraved**

613 A171 1.50s brown 3.00 2.10

Issued to commemorate the 300th anniversary of the birth of Johann Bernhard Fischer von Erlach, architect.

Körner Type of 1953.

1957, Jan. 11

614 A155 1.50s gray black 3.00 2.10

Issued to commemorate the death of Pres. Theodor Körner.

Dr. Julius Wagner-Jauregg
A172

Anton Wildgans
A173

1957, Mar. 7 *Perf. 14x13½*

615 A172 2.40s brown violet 4.25 2.10

Issued to commemorate the centenary of the birth of Dr. Julius Wagner-Jauregg, psychiatrist.

1957, May 3 **Unwmkd.**

616 A173 1s violet blue 75 22

Issued to commemorate the 25th anniversary of the death of Anton Wildgans, poet.

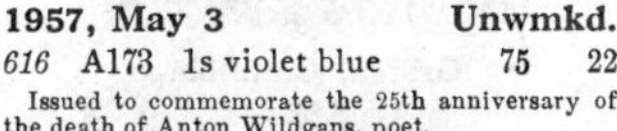

Old and New Postal Motor Coach
A174

1957, June 14 *Perf. 13½x14*

617 A174 1s *yellow* 55 22

Issued to commemorate the 50th anniversary of Austrian Postal Motor Coach Service.

Gasherbrum II and Glacier
A175

1957, July 27

618 A175 1.50s gray blue 80 20

Issued in honor of the Austrian Karakorum Expedition, which climbed Mount Gasherbrum II on July 7, 1956.

Mariazell
A176

Heidenreichstein Castle
A177

Designs: 20g, Farmhouse at Mörbisch. 50g, Heiligenstadt, Vienna. 1.40s, County seat, Klagenfurt. 1.50s, Rabenhof Building, Erdberg, Vienna. 1.80s, The Mint, Hall, Tyrol. 2s, Christkindl Church. 3.40s, Steiner Gate, Krems. 4s, Vienna Gate, Hainburg. 4.50s, Schwechat Airport, Vienna. 5.50s, Chur Gate, Feldkirch. 6s, County seat, Graz. 6.40s, "Golden Roof," Innsbruck.

1957-61 *Perf. 14x13½*

Lithographed.

Size: 20x25mm.

618A A176 20g violet black ('61) 3 3
619 " 50g bluish black ('59) 7 3

Engraved.

620 A176 1s chocolate 1.75 6

Typographed.

621 A176 1s chocolate 2.00 3

Lithographed.

622 A176 1s chocolate ('59) 50 3
622A " 1.40s bright greenish blue ('60) 18 6
623 " 1.50s rose lake ('58) 50 3
624 " 1.80s brt. ultra. ('60) 20 5
625 " 2s dull blue ('58) 5.00 3
626 " 3.40s yel. green ('60) 50 40
627 " 4s bright red lilac ('60) 85 3
627A " 4.50s dull green ('60) 60 35
628 " 5.50s greenish gray ('60) 70 25
629 " 6s brt. violet ('60) 1.30 3
629A " 6.40s bright blue ('60) 90 75

Engraved.

Size: 22x28mm.

630 A177 10s dark blue green 2.25 27
Nos. 618A-630 (16) 17.33 2.43

Of the three 1s stamps above, Nos. 620 and 621 have two names in imprint (designer H. Strohofer, engraver G. Wimmer). No. 622 has only Strohofer's name.

Prices for Nos. 618A–624, 626–630 are for stamps on white paper. Most denominations also come on grayish paper with yellowish gum.

See also Nos. 688–702.

1960-65 Photogravure *Perf. 14½x14*

Size: 17x21mm.

630A A176 50g slate ('64) 6 3

Size: 18x21½ mm.

630B A176 1s chocolate 15 5

Size: 17x21mm.

630C A176 1.50s dk. car. ('65) 21 18

Nos. 630A–630C issued in sheets and coils.

Graukogel, Badgastein
A180

1958, Feb. 1 Engr. *Perf. 14x13½*

631 A180 1.50s dark blue 40 15

Alpine championships of the International Ski Federation, Badgastein, Feb. 2–7.

Plane over Map of Austria
A181

1958, Mar. 27 *Perf. 13½x14*

632 A181 4s red 85 28

Re-opening of Austrian Airlines.

Mother and Daughter
A182

Walther von der Vogelweide
A183

Perf. 14x13½

1958, May 8 **Unwmkd.**

633 A182 1.50s dark blue 40 15

Issued for Mother's Day, 1958.

1958, July 17 **Litho. & Engr.**

634 A183 1.50s multicolored 40 15

Issued to commemorate the 3rd Austrian Song Festival, Vienna, July 17-20.

Oswald Redlich
A184

Giant "E" on Map
A185

1958, Sept. 17 **Engraved**

635 A184 2.40s ultramarine 75 35

Issued to commemorate the centenary of the birth of Prof. Oswald Redlich (1858–1944), historian.

Renner Type of 1948.

1958, Nov. 12

636 A136 1.50s deep green 65 45

Issued to commemorate the 40th anniversary of the founding of the Austrian Republic.

1959, Mar. 9

637 A185 2.40s emerald 55 50

Issued to promote the idea of a United Europe.

Cigarette Machine and Trademark of Tobacco Monopoly
A186

Archduke Johann
A187

1959, May 8 ***Perf. 13½*** **Unwmkd.**

638 A186 2.40s dk. olive bis. 50 30

Issued to commemorate the 175th anniversary of the establishment of the Austrian tobacco monopoly.

1959, May 11 ***Perf. 14x13½***

639 A187 1.50s deep green 45 15

Issued to commemorate the centenary of the death of Archduke Johann of Austria, military leader and humanitarian.

Capercaillie
A188

Joseph Haydn
A189

Animals: 1.50s, Roe buck. 2.40s, Wild boar. 3.50s, Red deer, doe and fawn.

1959, May 20 **Engraved**

640 A188 1s rose violet 42 15
641 " 1.50s blue violet 90 17
642 " 2.40s dark blue green 75 75
643 " 3.50s dark brown 65 32

Issued to publicize the Congress of the International Hunting Council, Vienna, May 20-24.

1959, May 30 **Unwmkd.**

644 A189 1.50s violet brown 75 15

Issued to commemorate the sesquicentennial of the death of Joseph Haydn, composer.

Coat of Arms, Tyrol
A190

Antenna, Zugspitze
A191

1959, June 13 ***Perf. 14x13½***

645 A190 1.50s rose red 40 15

Issued to commemorate the 150th anniversary of the fight for the liberation of Tyrol.

1959, June 19 ***Perf. 13½***

646 A191 2.40s dk. blue green 45 27

Inauguration of Austria's relay system.

Field Ball Player
A192

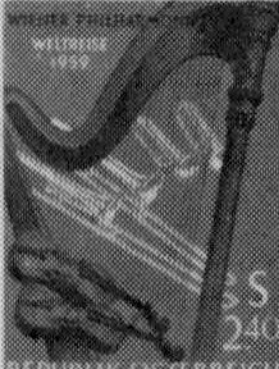

Orchestral Instruments
A193

Designs: 1s, Runner. 1.80s, Gymnast on vaulting horse. 2s, Woman hurdler. 2.20s, Hammer thrower.

1959–70 **Engr.** ***Perf. 14x13½***

647 A192 1s lilac 30 18
648 " 1.50s blue green 85 22
648A " 1.80s carmine ('62) 42 40
648B " 2s rose lake ('70) 27 20
648C " 2.20s bluish blk. ('67) 35 27
Nos. 647-648C (5) 2.19 1.27

Lithographed and Engraved

1959, Aug. 19 ***Perf. 14x13½***

649 A193 2.40s dull blue & black 50 32

Issued to publicize the 1959 world tour of the Vienna Philharmonic Orchestra.

Family Fleeing over Mountains
A194

Engraved

1960, Apr. 7 ***Perf. 13½x14***

650 A194 3s Prussian green 1.05 50

Issued to publicize World Refugee Year, July 1, 1959–June 30, 1960.

President Adolf Schärf
A195

1960, Apr. 20 ***Perf. 14x13½***

651 A195 1.50s gray olive 90 22

Issued to honor President Adolf Schärf on his 70th birthday.

Young Hikers and Hostel
A196

1960, May 20 ***Perf. 13½x14***

652 A196 1s carmine rose 33 15

Issued to publicize youth hiking and the youth hostel movement.

Anton Eiselsberg
A197

Gustav Mahler
A198

Lithographed and Engraved

1960, June 20 ***Perf. 14x13½***

653 A197 1.50s buff & dark brown 90 28

Issued to commemorate the centenary of the birth of Dr. Anton Eiselsberg, surgeon.

1960, July 7 **Engraved**

654 A198 1.50s chocolate 90 25

Issued to commemorate the centenary of the birth of Gustav Mahler, composer.

Jakob Prandtauer, Melk Abbey
A199

Gross Glockner Mountain Road
A200

1960, July 16 **Unwmkd.**

655 A199 1.50s red brown 90 25

Issued to commemorate the 300th anniversary of the birth of Jakob Prandtauer, architect.

1960, Aug. 3

656 A200 1.80s dark blue 90 90

Issued to commemorate the 25th anniversary of the opening of the Gross Glockner Mountain Road.

Europa Issue, 1960

Ionic Capital
A201

1960, Aug. 29 ***Perf. 14x13½***

657 A201 3s black 2.00 1.30

Issued to promote the idea of a united Europe.

Griffen, Carinthia
A202

Engraved

1960, Oct. 10 ***Perf. 13½x14***

658 A202 1.50s slate green 55 25

Issued to commemorate the 40th anniversary of the plebiscite which kept Carinthia with Austria.

Flame and Broken Chain
A203

Perf. 14x13½

1961, May 8 **Unwmkd.**

659 A203 1.50s scarlet 45 18

Issued to honor the victims in Austria's fight for freedom.

First Austrian Mail Plane, 1918
A204

1961, May 15 ***Perf. 13½x14***

660 A204 5s violet blue 90 55

Issued to publicize the Airmail Philatelic Exhibition, LUPOSTA 1961, Vienna, May, 1961.

Transportation by Road, Rail and Waterway
A205

Mountain Mower, by Albin Egger-Lienz
A206

Engraved and Typographed

1961, May 29 ***Perf. 13½***

661 A205 3s rose red & olive 70 65

Issued to commemorate the 13th European Conference of Transportation ministers, Vienna, May 29–31.

Engraved

1961, June 12 ***Perf. 13½x14***

Designs: 1.50s, The Kiss, by August von Pettenkofen. 3s, Girl, by Anton Romako. 5s, Ariadne's Triumph, by Hans Makart.

Inscriptions in Red Brown

662 A206 1s rose lake 23 15
663 " 1.50s dull violet 30 18
664 " 3s olive green 1.35 1.50
665 " 5s blue violet 90 85

Issued to commemorate the centenary of the Society of Creative Artists, Künstlerhaus, Vienna.

Sonnblick Mountain and Observatory
A207

Mercury and Globe
A208

1961, Sept. 1 ***Perf. 14x13½***

666 A207 1.80s violet blue 50 45

Issued to commemorate the 75th anniversary of the establishment of the Sonnblick meteorological observatory.

1961, Sept. 18

667 A208 3s black 90 70

Issued to publicize the International Banking Congress, Vienna, Sept. 1961. English inscription listing United Nations financial groups.

Coal Mine Shaft
A209

Designs: 1.50s, Generator. 1.80s, Iron blast furnace. 3s, Pouring steel. 5s, Oil refinery.

Engraved

1961, Sept. 15 ***Perf. 14x13½***

668	A209	1s black	18	12
669	"	1.50s green	25	20
670	"	1.80s dark carmine rose	85	85
671	"	3s bright lilac	1.05	1.10
672	"	5s blue	1.10	90
		Nos. 668-672 (5)	3.43	3.17

15th anniversary of nationalized industry.

Arms of Burgenland A210 — Franz Liszt A211

Engraved and Lithographed

1961, Oct. 9

673	A210	1.50s black, yellow & dark red	45	20

Issued to commemorate the 40th anniversary of Burgenland's joining the Austrian Republic.

1961, Oct. 20 Engraved

674	A211	3s dark brown	85	65

Issued to commemorate the 150th anniversary of the birth of Franz Liszt, composer.

Parliament
A212

1961, Dec. 18 ***Perf. 13½x14***

675	A212	1s brown	27	15

Issued to commemorate the 200th anniversary of the Austrian Bureau of Budget.

Kaprun-Mooserboden Reservoir
A213

Hydroelectric Power Plants: 1.50s, Ybbs-Persenbeug dam and locks. 1.80s, Lünersee dam and reservoir. 3s, Grossraming dam. 4s, Bisamberg transformer plant. 6.40s, St. Andrä power plant.

1962, March 26 **Unwmkd.**

676	A213	1s violet blue	25	15
677	"	1.50s red lilac	30	20
678	"	1.80s green	90	95
679	"	3s brown	65	65
680	"	4s rose red	70	32
681	"	6.40s gray	1.60	1.75
		Nos. 676-681 (6)	4.40	4.02

Issued to commemorate the 15th anniversary of the nationalization of the electric power industry.

Johann Nestroy A214 — Friedrich Gauermann A215

1962, May 25 ***Perf. 14x13½***

682	A214	1s violet	27	20

Issued to commemorate the centenary of the death of Johann Nepomuk Nestroy, Viennese playwright, author and actor.

1962, July 6 **Engraved**

683	A215	1.50s intense blue	32	20

Issued to commemorate the centenary of the death of Friedrich Gauermann (1807-1862), landscape painter.

Scout Emblem and Handshake
A216

1962, Oct. 5

684	A216	1.50s dark green	45	25

Issued to commemorate the 50th anniversary of Austria's Boy Scouts.

Lowlands Forest
A217

Designs: 1.50s, Deciduous forest. 3s, Fir and larch forest.

1962, Oct. 12 ***Perf. 13½x14***

685	A217	1s greenish gray	25	18
686	"	1.50s reddish brn.	35	32
687	"	3s dk. slate grn.	1.35	1.40

Buildings Types of 1957-61

Designs: 30g, City Hall, Vienna. 40g, Porcia Castle, Spittal on the Drau. 60g, Tanners' Tower, Wels. 70g, Residenz Fountain, Salzburg. 80g, Old farmhouse, Pinzgau. 1s, Romanesque columns, Millstatt Abbey. 1.20s, Kornmesser House, Bruck on the Mur. 1.30s, Schatten Castle, Feldkirch, Vorarlberg. 2s, Dragon Fountain, Klagenfurt. 2.20s, Beethoven House, Vienna. 2.50s, Danube Bridge, Linz. 3s, Swiss Gate, Vienna. 3.50s, Esterhazy Palace, Eisenstadt. 8s, City Hall, Steyr. 20s, Melk Abbey

1962-70 **Litho.** ***Perf. 14x13½***

Size: 20x25mm.

688	A176	30g greenish gray	5	3
689	A176	40g rose red	5	3
690	"	60g violet brown	10	4
691	"	70g dark blue	90	3
692	"	80g yellow brown	90	3
693	"	1s brown ('70)	18	3
694	"	1.20s red lilac	16	3
695	"	1.30s green ('67)	18	3
696	"	2s dk. blue ('68)	35	3
697	"	2.20s green	30	3
698	"	2.50s violet	48	12
699	"	3s bright blue	42	3
700	"	3.50s rose carmine	55	4
701	"	8s claret ('65)	1.10	15

Engraved

Perf. 13½

Size: 28x36½mm.

702	A177	20s rose claret ('63)	2.40	50
		Nos. 688-702 (15)	8.12	1.15

Prices for Nos. 688-702 are for stamps on white paper. Some denominations also come on grayish paper with yellowish gum.

Electric Locomotive and Train of 1837
A218

Lithographed and Engraved

1962, Nov. 9 ***Perf. 13½x14***

703	A218	3s buff & black	90	65

125th anniversary of Austrian railroads.

Postilions and Postal Clerk, 1863 A219 — Hermann Bahr A220

1963, May 7 **Photo.** ***Perf. 14x13½***

704	A219	3s dk. brn. & citron	90	65

Issued to commemorate the centenary of the first International Postal Conference, Paris, 1863.

Lithographed and Engraved

1963, July 19 ***Perf. 14x13½***

705	A220	1.50s blue & black	40	22

Centenary of birth of Hermann Bahr, poet.

St. Florian Statue, Kefermarkt, Contemporary and Old Fire Engines
A221

1963, Aug. 30 **Unwmkd.**

706	A221	1.50s brt. rose & blk.	40	22

Issued to commemorate the centenary of the Austrian volunteer fire brigades.

Factory, Flag and "ÖGB" on Map of Austria
A222

Lithographed

1963, Sept. 23 ***Perf. 13½x14***

707	A222	1.50s gray, red & dark brown	40	22

Issued to commemorate the 5th Congress of the Austrian Trade Union Federation (ÖGB), Sept. 23-28.

Arms of Austria and Tyrol
A223

1963, Sept. 27 **Unwmkd.**

708	A223	1.50s tan, black, red & yellow	40	22

Issued to commemorate the 600th anniversary of Tyrol's union with Austria.

Prince Eugene of Savoy A224 — Centenary Emblem A225

Engraved

1963, Oct. 18 ***Perf. 14x13½***

709	A224	1.50s violet	40	22

Issued to commemorate the 300th anniversary of the birth of Prince Eugene of Savoy (1663-1736), Austrian general.

Engraved and Photogravure

1963, Oct. 25 **Unwmkd.**

710	A225	3s blk., silver & red	70	65

Issued to commemorate the centenary of the founding of the International Red Cross.

Slalom
A226

Sports: 1.20s, Biathlon (skier with rifle). 1.50s, Ski jump. 1.80s, Women's figure skating. 2.20s, Ice hockey. 3s, Tobogganing. 4s, Bobsledding.

Photogravure and Engraved

1963, Nov. 11 ***Perf. 13½x14***

Inscriptions in Gold; Athletes in Black

711	A226	1s light gray	12	10
712	"	1.20s light blue	18	20
713	"	1.50s gray	20	13
714	"	1.80s pale lilac	28	27
715	"	2.20s light green	85	95
716	"	3s gray	55	50

717 A226 4s grayish blue 1.20 1.30
Nos. 711-717 (7) 3.38 3.45

Issued to publicize the 9th Winter Olympic Games, Innsbruck, Jan. 29-Feb. 9, 1964.

Baroque Crèche by Josef Thaddäus Stammel
A227

Engraved

1963, Nov. 29 ***Perf. 14x13½***

718 A227 2s dark Prussian grn. 35 12

Nasturtium
A228

Flowers: 1.50s, Peony. 1.80s, Clematis. 2.20s, Dahlia. 3s, Morning glory. 4s, Hollyhock.

Lithographed

1964, Apr. 17 ***Perf. 14*** **Unwmkd.**

Gray Background

719 A228 1s yellow, green & dark red 12 10
720 " 1.50s pink, grn. & yel. 18 13
721 " 1.80s lilac, grn. & yel. 42 45
722 " 2.20s car., grn. & yel. 45 50
723 " 3s blue, grn. & yel. 65 70
724 " 4s grn., yel. & pink 50 35
Nos. 719-724 (6) 2.32 2.23

Issued to publicize the Vienna International Garden Show, Apr. 16-Oct. 11.

St. Mary Magdalene and Apostle
A229

Pallas Athena and National Council Chamber
A230

1964, May 21 **Engraved** ***Perf. 13½***

725 A229 1.50s bluish black 32 30

Issued to publicize Romanesque art in Austria. The 12th century stained-glass window is from the Weitensfeld Church, the bust of the Apostle from the portal of St. Stephen's Cathedral, Vienna.

Engraved and Lithographed

1964, May 25 ***Perf. 14x13½***

726 A230 1.80s blk. & emerald 42 40

Issued to commemorate the second Parliamentary and Scientific Conference, Vienna.

The Kiss, by Gustav Klimt
A231

1964, June 5 **Litho.** ***Perf. 13½***

727 A231 3s multicolored 80 70

Issued to commemorate the re-opening of the Vienna Secession, a museum devoted to early 20th century art (art nouveau).

Brother of Mercy and Patient
A232

Perf. 14x13½

1964, June 11 **Engr.** **Unwmkd.**

728 A232 1.50s dark blue 32 20

Issued to commemorate the 350th anniversary of the Brothers of Mercy in Austria.

"Bringing the News of Victory at Kunersdorf" by Bernardo Bellotto
A233

"The Post in Art": 1.20s, Changing Horses at Relay Station, by Julius Hörmann. 1.50s, The Honeymoon Trip, by Moritz von Schwind. 1.80s, After the Rain, by Ignaz Raffalt. 2.20s, Mailcoach in the Mountains, by Adam Klein. 3s, Changing Horses at Bavarian Border, by Friedrich Gauermann. 4s, Postal Sleigh (Truck) in the Mountains, by Adalbert Pilch. 6.40s, Saalbach Post Office, by Adalbert Pilch.

1964, June 15 ***Perf. 13½x14***

729 A233 1s rose claret 13 10
730 " 1.20s sepia 22 22
731 " 1.50s violet blue 18 12
732 " 1.80s bright violet 35 38
733 " 2.20s black 28 27
734 " 3s dull car. rose 38 38
735 " 4s slate green 42 32
736 " 6.40s dull claret 1.25 1.25
Nos. 729-736 (8) 3.21 3.04

Issued to commemorate the 15th Universal Postal Union Congress, Vienna, May-June 1964.

Workers
A234

1964, Sept. 4 ***Perf. 14x13½***

737 A234 1s black 23 17

Centenary of Austrian Labor Movement.

Europa Issue, 1964

Common Design Type

Lithographed

1964, Sept. 14 ***Perf. 12*** **Unwmkd.**

Size: 21x36mm.

738 CD7 3s dark blue 45 38

Emblem of Radio Austria and Transistor Radio Panel
A235

1964, Oct. 1 **Photogravure** ***Perf. 13½***

739 A235 1s blk. brn. & red 22 17

Forty years of Radio Austria.

Old Printing Press
A236

Lithographed and Engraved

1964, Oct. 12 ***Perf. 14x13½***

740 A236 1.50s tan & black 22 17

Issued to publicize the 6th Congress of the International Graphic Federation, Vienna, Oct. 12-17.

Pres. Adolf Schärf and Schärf Student Center
A237

Ruins and New Buildings
A238

Typographed and Engraved

1965, Apr. 20 ***Perf. 12***

741 A237 1.50s bluish black 40 40

Issued in memory of Dr. Adolf Schärf (1890-1965), President of Austria (1957-65).

Engraved

1965, Apr. 27 ***Perf. 14x13½***

742 A238 1.80s carmine lake 30 25

Twenty years of reconstruction.

Oldest Seal of Vienna University
A239

St. George, 16th Century Wood Sculpture
A240

Photogravure and Engraved

1965, May 10 ***Perf. 14x13½***

743 A239 3s gold & red 45 42

Issued to commemorate the 600th anniversary of the founding of the University of Vienna.

1965, May 17 **Engraved**

744 A240 1.80s bluish black 35 32

Issued to publicize the art of the Danube Art School, 1490-1540, in connection with an art exhibition, May-Oct. 1965. The stamp background shows an engraving by Albrecht Altdorfer.

ITU Emblem, Telegraph Key and TV Antenna
A241

Ferdinand Raimund
A242

1965, May 17 **Unwmkd.**

745 A241 3s violet blue 45 35

Issued to commemorate the centenary of the International Telecommunication Union.

1965 **Engraved** ***Perf. 14x13½***

Portraits: No. 746, Ignaz Philipp Semmelweis. No. 747, Bertha von Suttner. No. 749, Ferdinand Georg Waldmüller.

746 A242 1.50s violet 25 15
747 " 1.50s bluish black 23 15
748 " 3s dark brown 45 32
749 " 3s greenish black 45 32

No. 746 commemorates the centenary of the death of Dr. Ignaz Philipp Semmelweis (1818-65), who discovered the cause of puerperal fever and introduced antisepsis into obstetrics. No. 747, the 60th anniversary of the awarding of the Nobel Prize for Peace to Bertha von Suttner (1843-1914), pacifist and author. No. 748, the 175th anniversary of the birth of Ferdinand Raimund (1790-1836), actor and playwright. No. 749, the centenary of the death of Ferdinand Georg Waldmüller (1793-1865), painter.

Issue dates: No. 746, Aug. 13; No. 747, Dec. 1; No. 748, June 1; No. 749, Aug. 23.

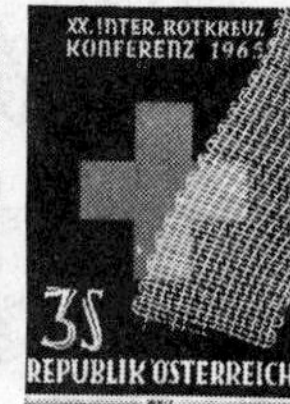

Dancers with Tambourines
A243

Red Cross and Strip of Gauze
A244

Design: 1.50s, Male gymnasts with practice bars.

1965, July 20 **Photo. and Engraved**

750 A243 1.50s gray & black 22 17
751 " 3s bister & black 45 45

Issued to commemorate the Fourth Gymnaestrada, international athletic meet, Vienna, July 20-24.

1965, Oct. 1 **Litho.** ***Perf. 14x13½***

752 A244 3s black & red 45 32

Issued to publicize the 20th International Red Cross Conference, Vienna.

Austrian Flag and Eagle with Mural Crown
A245

Austrian Flag, U.N. Headquarters and Emblem
A246

1965, Oct. 7 Photo. and Engraved
753 A245 1.50s gold, red & blk. 27 20

Issued to commemorate the 50th anniversary of the Union of Austrian Towns.

Lithographed and Engraved
1965, Oct. 25 *Perf. 12* Unwmkd.
754 A246 3s blk., brt. bl. & red 45 32

Issued to commemorate the 10th anniversary of Austria's admission to the United Nations.

University of Technology, Vienna
A247

1965, Nov. 8 Engraved *Perf. 13½x14*
755 A247 1.50s violet 25 17

Issued to commemorate the 150th anniversary of the founding of the Vienna University of Technology.

Map of Austria with Postal Zone Numbers—A248

1966, Jan. 14 Photo. *Perf. 12*
756 A248 1.50s yel., red & blk. 25 7

Issued to publicize the introduction of postal zone numbers, Jan. 1, 1966.

PTT Building, Emblem and Churches of Sts. Maria Rotunda and Barbara
A249

Maria von Ebner Eschenbach
A250

Lithographed and Engraved
1966, March 4 *Perf. 14x13½*
757 A249 1.50s *dull yellow* 23 14

Issued to commemorate the centenary of the headquarters of the Post and Telegraph Administration.

1966, March 11 Engraved
758 A250 3s plum 40 28

Issued to commemorate the 50th anniversary of the death of Maria von Ebner Eschenbach (1830–1916), novelist and poet.

Ferris Wheel, Prater
A251

1966, Apr. 19 Engr. *Perf. 14x13½*
759 A251 1.50s slate green 25 18

Issued to commemorate the 200th anniversary of the opening of the Prater (park), Vienna, to the public by Emperor Joseph II.

Josef Hoffmann
A252

Unwmkd.
1966, May 6 Engraved *Perf. 12*
760 A252 3s dark brown 40 27

Issued to commemorate the tenth anniversary of the death of Josef Hoffmann (1870–1956), architect.

Arms of Wiener Neustadt
A253

Photogravure and Engraved
1966, May 27 *Perf. 14*
761 A253 1.50s gray & multi. 25 17

Issued to publicize the Wiener Neustadt Art Exhibition, centered around the time and person of Emperor Frederick III (1440–1493).

Austrian Eagle and Emblem of National Bank
A254

1966, May 27 *Perf. 14*
762 A254 3s gray grn., dk. brn. & dk. green 40 32

Issued to commemorate the 150th anniversary of the Austrian National Bank.

Puppy
A255

Lithographed and Engraved
1966, June 16 *Perf. 12*
763 A255 1.80s yellow & black 27 22

Issued to commemorate the 120th anniversary of the Vienna Humane Society.

Columbine
A256

Alpine Flowers: 1.80s, Turk's cap. 2.20s, Wulfenia carinthiaca. 3s, Globeflowers. 4s, Fire lily. 5s, Pasqueflower.

Lithographed
1966, Aug. 17 *Perf. 13½* Unwmkd.
Flowers in Natural Colors

764 A256 1.50s dark blue 22 15
765 " 1.80s " " 25 25
766 " 2.20s " " 50 50
767 " 3s " " 55 60
768 " 4s " " 60 32
769 " 5s " " 65 70
Nos. 764-769 (6) 2.77 2.52

Fair Building
A257

1966, Aug. 26 Engr. *Perf. 13½x13*
770 A257 3s violet blue 40 30

First International Fair at Wels.

Peter Anich, Map, Globe and Books
A258

Sick Worker and Health Emblem
A259

1966, Sept. 1 *Perf. 14x13½*
771 A258 1.80s black 27 18

Issued to commemorate the 200th anniversary of the death of Peter Anich (1723–1766), Tirolean cartographer and farmer.

1966, Sept. 19 Engr. and Litho.
772 A259 3s black & verm. 40 28

Issued to publicize the 15th Occupational Medicine Congress, Vienna, Sept. 19–24.

Theater Collection: "Eunuchus" by Terence from a 1496 Edition
A260

Designs: 1.80s, Map Collection: Title page of Geographia Blavania (Cronus, Hercules and celestial sphere). 2.20s, Picture Archive and Portrait Collection: View of Old Vienna after a watercolor by Anton Stutzinger. 3s, Manuscript Collection: Illustration from the 15th century "Livre du Cuer d'Amours Espris" of the Duke René d'Anjou.

Photogravure and Engraved
1966, Sept. 28 *Perf. 13½x14*
773 A260 1.50s multicolored 22 17
774 " 1.80s " 25 25
775 " 2.20s " 35 32
776 " 3s " 42 40

Austrian National Library.

Young Girl
A261

Lithographed and Engraved
1966, Oct. 3 *Perf. 14x13½*
777 A261 3s lt. blue & black 40 28

Issued to commemorate the 10th anniversary of the "Save the Child" society.

Strawberries
A262

Coat of Arms of University of Linz
A263

Fruit: 1s, Grapes. 1.50s, Apple. 1.80s, Blackberries. 2.20s, Apricots. 3s, Cherries.

1966, Nov. 25 Photo. *Perf. 13½x13*
778 A262 50g multicolored 28 28
779 " 1s " 25 25
780 " 1.50s " 25 23
781 " 1.80s " 33 28
782 " 2.20s " 33 28
783 " 3s " 40 35
Nos. 778-783 (6) 1.84 1.67

Photogravure and Engraved
1966, Dec. 9 *Perf. 14x13½*
784 A263 3s gray, blk., red, silver & gold 40 30

Issued to commemorate the inauguration of the Universary of Linz, Oct. 8, 1966.

Ice Skater, 1866
A264

Ballet Dancer
A265

Photogravure and Engraved
1967, Feb. 3 *Perf. 14x13½*
785 A264 3s pale bl. & dk. bl. 40 30

Centenary of Vienna Ice Skating Club.

1967, Feb. 15 Engr. *Perf. 11½x12*
786 A265 3s deep claret 55 45
a. Perf. 12 1.75 1.60

Issued to commemorate the centenary of the "Blue Danube" waltz by Johann Strauss.

Karl Schönherr
A266

1967, Feb. 24 Engr. *Perf. 14x13½*
787 A266 3s gray brown 40 28

Issued to commemorate the centenary of the birth of Dr. Karl Schönherr (1867–1943), poet, playwright and physician.

Ice Hockey Goalkeeper
A267

Photogravure and Engraved

1967, March 17 *Perf. 13½x14*

788 A267 3s pale grn. & dk. bl. 40 30

Issued to publicize the Ice Hockey Championships, Vienna, March 18–29.

Violin, Organ and Laurel
A268

1967, Mar. 28 Engr. *Perf. 13½*

789 A268 3.50s indigo 45 35

Issued to commemorate the 125th anniversary of the Vienna Philharmonic Orchestra.

Motherhood, Watercolor by Peter Fendi
A269

Lithographed

1967, Apr. 28 *Perf. 14* **Unwmkd.**

790 A269 2s multicolored 35 28

Issued for Mother's Day, 1967.

Gothic Mantle Madonna
A270

1967, May 19 Engr. *Perf. 13½x14*

791 A270 3s slate 40 30

Issued to publicize the art exhibition "Austrian Gothic," Krems, 1967. The Gothic wood carving is from Frauenstein in Upper Austria.

Medieval Gold Cross
A271

Swan, Tapestry by Oscar Kokoschka
A272

Lithographed and Engraved

1967, June 9 *Perf. 13½*

792 A271 3.50s Prus. green & multi. 45 38

Issued to publicize the Salzburg Treasure Chamber in connection with an exhibition at Salzburg Cathedral, June 12–Sept. 15.

1967, June 9 Photogravure

793 A272 2s multicolored 30 25

Issued to publicize the Nibelungen District Art Exhibition, Pöchlarn, celebrating the 700th anniversary of Pöchlarn as a city. The design is from the border of the Amor and Psyche tapestry at the Salzburg Festival Theater.

View and Arms of Vienna
A273

Engraved and Photogravure

1967, June 12 *Perf. 13x13½*

794 A273 3s black & red 40 32

Issued to publicize the 10th Europa Talks, "Science and Society in Europe," Vienna, June 13–17.

Prize Bull "Mucki"
A274

1967, Aug. 28 Engr. *Perf. 13½*

795 A274 2s deep claret 30 23

Issued to commemorate the centenary of the Ried Festival and the Agricultural Fair.

Potato Beetle
A275

Engraved and Photogravure

1967, Aug. 29 *Perf. 13½x14*

796 A275 3s black & multi. 40 30

Issued to publicize the 6th International Congress for Plant Protection, Vienna.

First Locomotive Used on Brenner Pass—A276

1967, Sept. 23 Photo. *Perf. 12*

797 A276 3.50s tan & slate green 50 40

Centenary of railroad over Brenner Pass.

Christ in Glory
A277

1967, Oct. 9 *Perf. 13½*

798 A277 2s multicolored 30 28

Issued to commemorate the restoration of the Romanesque (11th century) frescoes in the Lambach monastery church.

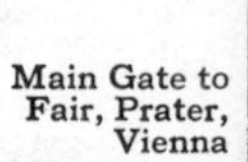

Main Gate to Fair, Prater, Vienna
A278

1967, Oct. 24 Photo. *Perf. 13½x14*

799 A278 2s chocolate & buff 30 25

Issued to publicize the Congress of International Trade Fairs, Vienna, Oct., 1967.

Medal Showing Minerva and Art Symbols
A279

Frankfurt Medal for Reformation, 1717
A280

Lithographed and Engraved

1967, Oct. 25 *Perf. 13½*

800 A279 2s dark brown, dark blue & yellow 32 25

Issued to commemorate the 275th anniversary of the Vienna Academy of Fine Arts. The medal was designed by Georg Raphael Donner (1693–1741) and is awarded as an artist's prize.

1967, Oct. 31 Engr. *Perf. 14x13½*

801 A280 3.50s blue black 45 38

450th anniversary of the Reformation.

Mountain Range and Stone Pines
A281

1967, Nov. 7 *Perf. 13½*

802 A281 3.50s green 50 42

Centenary of academic study of forestry.

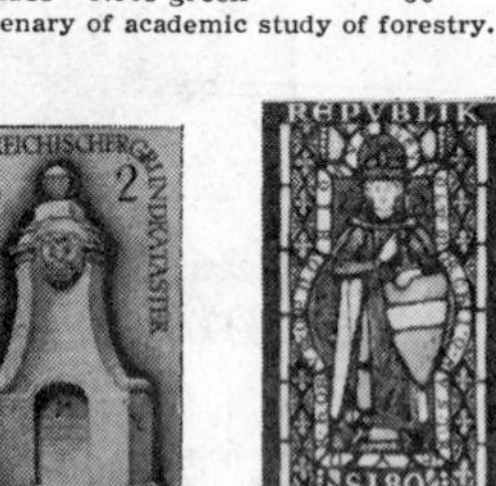

Land Survey Monument, 1770
A282

St. Leopold, Window, Heiligenkreuz Abbey
A283

1967, Nov. 7 Photogravure

803 A282 2s olive black 30 25

150th anniversary of official land records.

1967, Nov. 15 Engr. & Photo.

804 A283 1.80s multicolored 30 28

Issued in memory of Margrave Leopold III (1075–1136), patron saint of Austria.

Tragic Mask and Violin
A284

Nativity from 15th Century Altar
A285

1967, Nov. 17 *Perf. 13½*

805 A284 3.50s bluish lilac & black 50 38

Issued to commemorate the 150th anniversary of the Academy of Music and Dramatic Art.

1967, Nov. 27 Engr. *Perf. 14x13½*

806 A285 2s green 30 22

Christmas 1967.

The design shows the late Gothic carved center panel of the altar in St. John's Chapel in Nonnberg Convent, Salzburg.

Innsbruck Stadium, Alps and FISU Emblem
A286

Camillo Sitte
A287

1968, Jan. 22 Engraved *Perf. 13½*

807 A286 2s dark blue 33 27

Issued to publicize the Winter University Games under the auspices of FISU (Fédération Internationale du Sport Universitaire), Innsbruck, Jan. 21–28.

1968, Apr. 17 *Perf. 13½*

808 A287 2s black brown 32 27

Issued to commemorate the 125th anniversary of the birth of Camillo Sitte (1843–1903), architect and city planner.

Mother and Child
A288

Cup and Serpent Emblem
A289

1968, May 7 *Perf. 13½*

809 A288 2s slate green 32 27

Issued for Mother's Day, 1968.

1968, May 7 Photogravure

810 A289 3.50s dp. plum, gray & gold 50 40

Bicentenary of the Veterinary College.

Bride with Lace Veil
A290

1968, May 24 Engraved *Perf. 12*
811 A290 3.50s blue black 55 45

Issued to commemorate the centenary of the embroidery industry of Vorarlberg.

Horse Race
A291

1968, June 4 *Perf. 13½*
812 A291 3.50s sepia 55 50

Issued to commemorate the centenary of horse racing at Freudenau, Vienna.

Dr. Karl Landsteiner
A292

Peter Rosegger
A293

1968, June 14 *Perf. 14x13½*
813 A292 3.50s dark blue 55 45

Issued to commemorate the centenary of the birth of Dr. Karl Landsteiner (1868–1943), pathologist, discoverer of the four main human blood types.

1968, June 26
814 A293 2s slate green 35 25

Issued to commemorate the 50th anniversary of the death of Peter Rosegger (1843–1918), poet and writer.

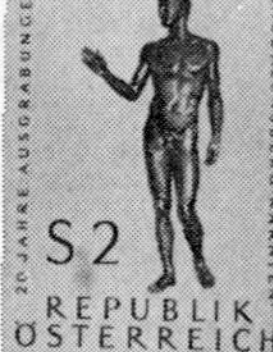

Angelica Kauffmann, Self-portrait
A294

Bronze Statue of Young Man, 1st Century B.C.
A295

1968, July 15 Engr. *Perf. 14x13½*
815 A294 2s intense black 35 25

Issued to publicize the art exhibitions "Angelica Kauffmann and her Contemporaries," Bregenz, July 28–Oct. 13, 1968, and Vienna, Oct. 22, 1968–January 6, 1969.

1968, July 15 Litho. and Engr.
816 A295 2s greenish gray & black 35 25

Issued to publicize 20 years of excavations on Magdalene Mountain, Carinthia.

Bishop, Romanesque Bas-relief
A296

1968, Sept. 20 Engr. *Perf. 14x13½*
817 A296 2s blue gray 35 25

Issued to commemorate the 750th anniversary of the Graz-Seckau Bishopric.

Koloman Moser
A297

Human Rights Flame—A298

Engraved and Photogravure

1968, Oct. 18 *Perf. 12*
818 A297 2s black brown & vermilion 35 25

Issued to commemorate the 50th anniversary of the death of Koloman Moser (1868–1918), stamp designer and painter.

1968, Oct. 18 Photo. *Perf. 14x13½*
819 A298 1.50s gray, deep car. & dk. green 32 25

International Human Rights Year.

Pres. Karl Renner and States' Arms
A299

Designs: No. 821, Coats of arms of Austria and Austrian states. No. 822, Article I of Austrian Constitution and States' coats of arms.

Engraved and Photogravure

1968 Nov. 11 *Perf. 13½*
820 A299 2s black & multi. 55 50
821 " 2s " " 55 50
822 " 2s " " 55 50

50th anniversary of Republic of Austria.

Crèche, Memorial Chapel, Oberndorf-Salzburg
A300

Perf. 14x13½

1968, Nov. 29 Engraved
823 A300 2s slate green 32 18

Christmas 1968.
150th anniversary of "Silent Night, Holy Night."

Angels, from Last Judgment by Troger (Röhrenbach-Greillenstein Chapel)—A301

Baroque Frescoes: No. 825, Vanquished Demons, by Paul Troger, Altenburg Abbey. No. 826, Sts. Peter and Paul, by Troger, Melk Abbey. No. 827, The Glorification of Mary, by Franz Anton Maulpertsch, Maria Treu Church, Vienna. No. 828, St. Leopold Carried into Heaven, by Maulpertsch, Ebenfurth Castle Chapel. No. 829, Symbolic figures from The Triumph of Apollo, by Maulpertsch, Halbthurn Castle.

Engraved and Photogravure

1968, Dec. 11 *Perf. 13½x14*
824 A301 2s multicolored 55 50
825 " 2s " 55 50
826 " 2s " 55 50
827 " 2s " 55 50
828 " 2s " 55 50
829 " 2s " 55 50
Nos. 824-829 (6) 3.30 3.00

St. Stephen
A302

Statues in St. Stephen's Cathedral, Vienna: No. 831, St. Paul. No. 832, Mantle Madonna. No. 833, St. Christopher. No. 834, St. George and the Dragon. No. 835, St. Sebastian.

1969, Jan. 28 Engraved *Perf. 13½*
830 A302 2s black 50 50
831 " 2s rose claret 50 50
832 " 2s gray violet 50 50
833 " 2s slate blue 50 50
834 " 2s slate green 50 50
835 " 2s dark red brown 50 50
Nos. 830-835 (6) 3.00 3.00

500th anniversary of Diocese of Vienna.

Parliament and Pallas Athena Fountain, Vienna
A303

1969, Apr. 8 Engraved *Perf. 13½*
836 A303 2s greenish black 32 25

Issued to publicize the Interparliamentary Union Conference, Vienna, Apr. 7–13.

Europa Issue, 1969
Common Design Type

1969, Apr. 28 Photo. *Perf. 12*
837 CD12 2s gray green, brick red & blue 40 30

Council of Europe Emblem
A304

1969, May 5
838 A304 3.50s gray, ultra., blk. & yellow 65 50

20th anniversary of Council of Europe.

Frontier Guards
A305

Engraved and Photogravure

1969, May 14 *Perf. 12*
839 A305 2s sepia & red 32 25

Honor to Austrian Federal Army.

Don Giovanni, by Mozart
A306

Gothic Armor of Maximilian I
A307

1969, May 23 *Perf. 13½*
840 A306 Sheet of 8, gold, red & brown black 5.25 5.25
a. 2s *Don Giovanni, Mozart* 60 60
b. 2s *Magic Flute, Mozart* 60 60
c. 2s *Fidelio, Beethoven* 60 60
d. 2s *Lohengrin, Wagner* 60 60
e. 2s *Don Carlos, Verdi* 60 60
f. 2s *Carmen, Bizet* 60 60
g. 2s *Rosencavalier, Richard Strauss* 60 60
h. 2s *Swan Lake, Ballet by Tchaikovsky* 60 60

Centenary of Vienna Opera House.

No. 840 contains 8 stamps arranged around gold and red center label showing Opera House. Printed in sheets containing 4 Nos. 840 with wide gutters between.

1969, June 4 Engraved
841 A307 2s bluish black 32 25

Issued to publicize the Emperor Maximilian I Exhibition, Innsbruck, May 30–Oct. 5.

Oldest Municipal Seal of Vienna
A308

Girl's Head and Village House
A309

1969, June 16 Photo. *Perf. 13½*
842 A308 2s tan, red & black 32 25

Issued to publicize the 19th Congress of the International Organization of Municipalities, Vienna, June 1969.

Engraved and Photogravure

1969, June 16 *Perf. 13½x14*
843 A309 2s yel. grn. & sepia 32 25

Issued to publicize the 20th anniversary of the Children's Village Movement in Austria (SOS Villages).

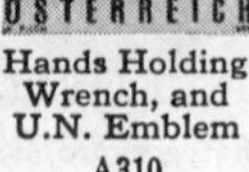

Hands Holding Wrench, and U.N. Emblem
A310

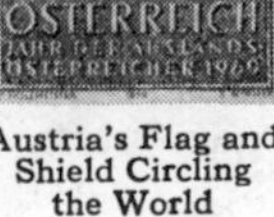

Austria's Flag and Shield Circling the World
A311

1969, Aug. 22 Photo. *Perf. 13x13½*

844 A310 2s deep green 32 25

Issued to commemorate the 50th anniversary of the International Labor Organization.

Engraved and Lithographed

1969, Aug. 22 *Perf. 14x13½*

845 A311 3.50s slate & red 50 40

Issued to publicize 1969 as the Year of Austrians Living Abroad.

Young Hare, by Dürer
A312

Etchings: No. 847, El Cid Killing a Bull, by Francisco de Goya. No. 848, Madonna with the Pomegranate, by Raphael. No. 849, The Painter, by Peter Brueghel. No. 850, Rubens' Son Nicolas, by Rubens. No. 851, Self-portrait, by Rembrandt. No. 852, Lady Reading, by Francois Guerin. No. 853, Wife of the Artist, by Egon Schiele.

Engraved and Photogravure

1969, Sept. 26 *Perf. 13½*

Gray Frame, Buff Background

846	A312	2s black & brown	45	45
847	"	2s black	45	45
848	"	2s black	45	45
849	"	2s black	45	45
850	"	2s black & salmon	45	45
851	"	2s black	45	45
852	"	2s black & salmon	45	45
853	"	2s black	45	45
		Nos. 846-853 (8)	3.60	3.60

Bicentenary of the etching collection in the Albertina, Vienna.

President Franz Jonas
A313

1969, Oct. 3

854 A313 2s gray & violet blue 32 25

Issued to commemorate the 70th birthday of Franz Jonas, president of Austria.

Post Horn, Globe and Lightning
A314

1969, Oct. 17 *Perf. 13½x14*

855 A314 2s multicolored 32 25

Issued to commemorate the 50th anniversary of the Union of Postal and Telegraph employees.

Savings Box, about 1450
A315

Madonna, by Albin Egger-Lienz
A316

1969, Oct. 31 Photo. *Perf. 13x13½*

856 A315 2s silver & slate grn. 32 25

Issued to publicize the importance of savings.

Engraved and Photogravure

1969, Nov. 24 *Perf. 12*

857 A316 2s deep claret & pale yellow 32 20

Christmas 1969.

Josef Schöffel
A317

St. Klemens M. Hofbauer
A318

1970, Feb. 6 Engr. *Perf. 14x13½*

858 A317 2s dull purple 35 25

Issued to commemorate the 60th anniversary of the death of Josef Schöffel, (1832–1910), who saved the Vienna Woods.

Engraved and Photogravure

1970, Mar. 13 *Perf. 14x13½*

859 A318 2s dk. brn. & lt. tan 35 25

Issued to commemorate the 150th anniversary of the death of St. Klemens Maria Hofbauer (1751–1820); Redemptorist preacher in Poland and Austria, canonized in 1909.

Chancellor Leopold Figl
A319

Belvedere Palace, Vienna
A320

1970, Apr. 27 Engraved *Perf. 13½*

860 A319 2s dark olive gray 38 27
861 A320 2s dark rose brown 38 27

25th anniversary of Second Republic.

Krimml Waterfalls
A321

1970, May 19 Engraved *Perf. 13½*

862 A321 2s slate green 35 25

Issued for the European Nature Conservation Year, 1970.

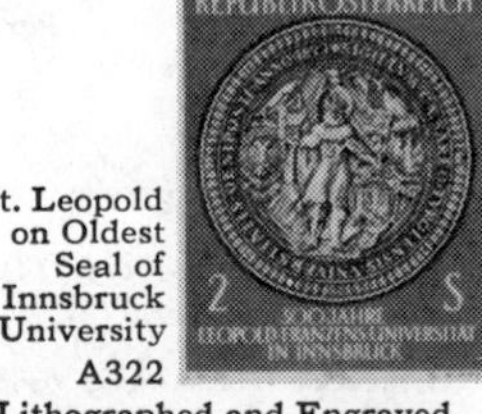

St. Leopold on Oldest Seal of Innsbruck University
A322

Lithographed and Engraved

1970, June 5 *Perf. 13½*

863 A322 2s red & black 35 25

Issued to commemorate the 300th anniversary of the founding of the Leopold Franzens University in Innsbruck.

Organ, Great Hall, Music Academy
A323

Photogravure and Engraved

1970, June 5 *Perf. 14*

864 A323 2s gold & dp. claret 35 25

Issued to commemorate the centenary of the Vienna Music Academy Building.

Tower Clock, 1450–1550
A324

The Beggar Student, by Carl Millöcker
A325

Old Clocks from Vienna Horological Museum: No. 866, Lyre clock, 1790–1815. No. 867, Pendant clock 1600–1650. No. 868, Pendant watch, 1800–1830. No. 869, Bracket clock, 1720–1760. No. 870, French column clock, 1820–1850.

1970

865	A324	1.50s buff & sepia	40	40
866	"	1.50s greenish & grn.	40	40
867	"	2s pale & dk. blue	48	45
868	"	2s pale rose & lake	48	45
869	"	3.50s buff & brown	75	60
870	"	3.50s pale lilac & brn. violet	75	60
		Nos. 865-870 (6)	3.26	2.90

Issue dates: Nos. 865, 867, 869, June 22. Others, Oct. 23.

1970 Photo. and Engr. *Perf. 13½*

Operettas: No. 872, Fledermaus, by Johann Strauss. No. 873, The Dream Waltz, by Oscar Strauss. No. 874, The Bird Seller, by Carl Zeller. No. 875, The Merry Widow, by Franz Lehar. No. 876, Two Hearts in Three-quarter Time, by Robert Stolz.

871	A325	1.50s pale green & green	40	40
872	"	1.50s yel. & vio. blue	40	40
873	"	2s pale rose & violet brown	48	45
874	"	2s pale grn. & sepia	48	45
875	"	3.50s pale blue & indigo	75	60
876	"	3.50s beige & slate	75	60
		Nos. 871-876 (6)	3.26	2.90

Issue dates: Nos. 871, 873, 875, July 3. Others Sept. 11.

Bregenz Festival Stage
A326

1970, July 23 Photogravure

877 A326 3.50s dk. blue & buff 55 42

25th anniversary of Bregenz Festival.

Salzburg Festival Emblem
A327

1970, July 27 *Perf. 14*

878 A327 3.50s black, red, gold & gray 50 45

50th anniversary of Salzburg Festival.

St. John, by Thomas Schwanthaler
A328

1970, Aug. 31 Engraved

879 A328 3.50s dark gray 50 42

Issued to publicize the 13th General Assembly of the World Veterans Federation, Aug. 28–Sept. 4. The head of St. John is from a sculpture showing the Agony in the Garden in the chapel of the Parish Church in Ried. It is attributed to Thomas Schwanthaler (1634–1702).

Thomas Koschat
A329

1970, Sept. 16 *Perf. 14x13½*

880 A329 2s chocolate 32 20

Issued to commemorate the 125th anniversary of the birth of Thomas Koschat (1845–1914), Carinthian composer of songs.

Mountain Scene
A330

1970, Sept. 16 Photo. *Perf. 14x13½*

881 A330 2s violet blue & pink 32 22

Issued to publicize hiking and mountaineering in Austria.

Alfred Cossmann
A331

Arms of Carinthia
A332

1970, Oct. 2 Engraved *Perf. 14x13½*

882 A331 2s dark brown 32 22

Issued to commemorate the centenary of the birth of Alfred Cossmann (1870–1951), engraver.

Photogravure and Engraved

1970, Oct. 2 *Perf. 14*

883 A332 2s olive, red, gold, black & silver 32 22

Carinthian plebiscite, 50th anniversary.

U.N. Emblem
A333

1970, Oct. 23 Litho. *Perf. 14x13½*

884 A333 3.50s lt. bl. & black 55 42

25th anniversary of the United Nations.

Adoration of the Shepherds, Carving from Garsten Vicarage
A334

1970, Nov. 27 Engr. *Perf. 13½x14*

85 A334 2s dk. violet blue 32 20

Christmas 1970.

Karl Renner
A335

Beethoven, by Georg Waldmüller
A336

1970, Dec. 14 Engr. *Perf. 14x13½*

886 A335 2s deep claret 32 22

Centenary of the birth of Karl Renner (1870–1950), President of Austria.

Photogravure and Engraved

1970, Dec. 16 *Perf. 13½*

887 A336 3.50s black & buff 50 45

Bicentenary of the birth of Ludwig van Beethoven (1770–1827), composer.

Enrica Handel-Mazzetti
A337

1971, Jan. 11 Engr. *Perf. 14x13½*

888 A337 2s sepia 35 25

Centenary of the birth of Enrica von Handel-Mazzetti (1871–1955), novelist and poet.

"Watch Out for Children!"
A338

1971, Feb. 18 Photo. *Perf. 13½*

889 A338 2s black, red brown & brt. green 45 30

Traffic safety.

Saltcellar, by Benvenuto Cellini
A339

Art Treasures: 1.50s, Covered vessel, made of prase, gold and precious stones, Florentine, 1580. 2s, Emperor Joseph I, ivory statue by Matthias Steinle, 1693.

Photogravure and Engraved

1971, March 22 *Perf. 14*

890 A339 1.50s gray & slate green 40 40

891 " 2s gray & deep plum 45 45

892 " 3.50s gray, black & bister 75 60

Emblem of Austrian Wholesalers' Organization
A340

1971, Apr. 16 Photo. *Perf. 13½*

893 A340 3.50s multicolored 55 45

International Chamber of Commerce, 23rd Congress, Vienna, Apr. 17–23.

Jacopo de Strada, by Titian
A341

Seal of Paulus of Franchenfordia, 1380—A342

Paintings in Vienna Museum: 2s, Village Feast, by Peter Brueghel, the Elder. 3.50s, Young Venetian Woman, by Albrecht Dürer.

1971, May 6 Engraved *Perf. 13½*

894 A341 1.50s rose lake 40 40

895 " 2s greenish black 45 45

896 " 3.50s deep brown 75 60

Photogravure and Engraved

1971, May 6 *Perf. 13½x14*

897 A342 3.50s dark brown & bister 55 45

Congress commemorating the centenary of the Austrian Notaries' Statute, May 5–8.

St. Matthew
A343

August Neilreich
A344

1971, May 27 *Perf. 12½x13½*

898 A343 2s bright rose lilac & brown 35 25

Exhibition of "1000 Years of Art in Krems." The statue of St. Matthew is from the Lentl Altar, created about 1520 by the Master of the Pulkau Altar.

1971, June 1 Engr. *Perf. 14x13½*

899 A344 2s brown 35 25

Centenary of the death of August Neilreich (1803–1871), botanist.

Singer with Lyre
A345

Photogravure and Engraved

1971, July 1 *Perf. 13½x14*

900 A345 4s light blue, violet blue & gold 75 60

International Choir Festival, Vienna, July 1–4.

Coat of Arms of Kitzbuhel
A346

1971, Aug. 23 *Perf. 14*

901 A346 2.50s gold & multi. 38 27

700th anniversary of the town of Kitzbuhel.

Vienna Stock Exchange—A347

1971, Sept. 1 Engr. *Perf. 13½x14*

902 A347 4s reddish brown 60 40

Bicentenary of the Vienna Stock Exchange.

First and Latest Exhibition Halls
A348

1971, Sept. 6 Photo. *Perf. 13½x13*

903 A348 2.50s deep rose lilac 38 25

50th anniversary of Vienna International Fair.

Trade Union Emblem
A349

Arms of Burgenland
A350

1971, Sept. 20 *Perf. 14x13½*

904 A349 2s gray, buff & red 30 20

25th anniversary of Austrian Trade Union Association.

1971, Oct. 1

905 A350 2s dark blue, gold, red & black 30 20

50th anniversary of Burgenland's joining Austria.

Marcus Car
A351

Photogravure and Engraved

1971, Oct. 1 *Perf. 14*

906 A351 4s pale grn. & black 55 42

75th anniversary of the Austrian Automobile, Motorcycle and Touring Club.

Europa Bridge
A352

1971, Oct. 8 Engr. *Perf. 14x13½*

907 A352 4s violet blue 55 42

Opening of highway over Brenner Pass.

Styria's Iron Mountain
A353

Designs: 2s, Austrian Nitrogen Products, Ltd., Linz. 4s, United Austrian Iron and Steel Works, Ltd. (VÖEST), Linz Harbor.

1971, Oct. 15 *Perf. 13½*

908	A353	1.50s reddish brown	27	27
909	"	2s bluish black	33	33
910	"	4s dk. slate green	60	50

25 years of nationalized industry.

High-speed Train on Semmering Pass—A354

Trout Fisherman
A355

1971, Oct. 21 *Perf. 14*

911 A354 2s claret 30 22

Inter-city rapid train service.

1971, Nov. 15 *Perf. 13½*

912 A355 2s dark red brown 30 22

Erich Tschermak-Seysenegg
A356

Infant Jesus as Savior, by Dürer
A357

Photogravure and Engraved

1971, Nov. 15 *Perf. 14x13½*

913 A356 2s pale olive & dark purple 30 22

Centenary of the birth of Dr. Erich Tschermak-Seysenegg (1871–1962), botanist.

1971, Nov. 26 *Perf. 13½*

914 A357 2s gold & multi. 30 20

Christmas 1971.

Franz Grillparzer, by Moritz Daffinger
A358

Fountain, Main Square, Friesach
A359

Lithographed and Engraved

1972, Jan. 21 *Perf. 14x13½*

915 A358 2s buff, gold & black 30 22

Death centenary of Franz Grillparzer (1791–1872), dramatic poet.

1972, Feb. 23 Engr. *Perf. 14x13½*

Designs: 2s, Fountain, Heiligenkreuz Abbey. 2.50s, Leopold Fountain, Innsbruck.

916	A359	1.50s rose lilac	30	28
917	"	2s brown	32	30
918	"	2.50s olive	45	42

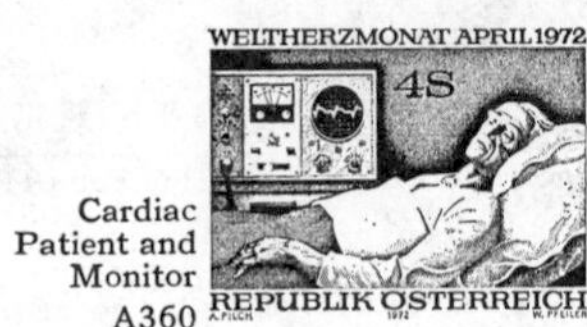

Cardiac Patient and Monitor
A360

1972, Apr. 11 *Perf. 13½x14*

919 A360 4s violet brown 55 45

World Health Day 1972.

St. Michael's Gate, Royal Palace, Vienna
A361

1972, Apr. 11 *Perf. 14x13½*

920 A361 4s violet blue 60 50

Conference of European Post and Telecommunications Ministers, Vienna, Apr. 11–14.

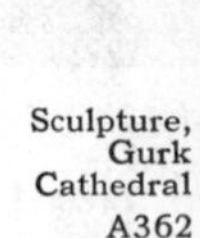

Sculpture, Gurk Cathedral
A362

Photogravure and Engraved

1972, May 5 *Perf. 14*

921 A362 2s gold & dark brown violet 30 22

900th anniversary of Gurk (Carinthia) Diocese. The design is after the central column supporting the sarcophagus of St. Hemma in Gurk Cathedral.

City Hall, Congress Emblem
A363

1972, May 23 Litho. and Engr.

922 A363 4s red, blk. & yellow 55 45

9th International Congress of Public and Cooperative Economy, Vienna, May 23–25.

Power Line in Carnic Alps
A364

Designs: 2.50s, Power Station, Simmering. 4s, Zemm Power Station (lake in Zillertaler Alps).

1972, June 28 *Perf. 13½x14*

923	A364	70g gray & violet	15	12
924	"	2.50s gray & red brn.	38	32
925	"	4s gray & slate	60	50

25 years of nationalization of the power industry.

Runner with Olympic Torch
A365

St. Hermes, by Conrad Laib
A366

Engraved and Photogravure

1972, Aug. 21 *Perf. 14x13½*

926 A365 2s sepia & red 30 22

Olympic torch relay from Olympia, Greece, to Munich, Germany, passing through Austria.

1972, Aug. 21 Engraved

927 A366 2s violet brown 30 22

Exhibition of Late Gothic Art, Salzburg.

Pears
A367

1972, Sept. *Perf. 14*

928 A367 2.50s dk. bl. & multi. 35 28

World Congress of small plot Gardeners, Vienna, Sept. 7–10.

Souvenir Sheet

Spanish Walk
A368

1972, Sept. 12 *Perf. 13½*

929 A368 Sheet of 6, gold, car., dk. brown 2.75 2.75

a.	2s *Spanish walk*	30	30
b.	2s *Piaffe*	30	30
c.	2.50s *Levade*	35	35
d.	2.50s *On long rein*	35	35
e.	4s *Capriole*	60	60
f.	4s *Courbette*	60	60

400th anniversary of the Spanish Riding School in Vienna. Gold and carmine margin. Size: 135x180mm.

Arms of University of Agriculture
A369

Church and Old University
A370

Photogravure and Engraved

1972, Oct. 17 *Perf. 14x13½*

930 A369 2s black & multi. 30 22

Centenary of the University of Agriculture, Vienna.

1972, Nov. 7 Engraved

931 A370 4s red brown 55 40

350th anniversary of the Paris Lodron University, Salzburg.

Carl Michael Ziehrer
A371

1972, Nov. 14

932 A371 2s rose claret 30 22

50th anniversary of the death of Carl Michael Ziehrer (1843–1922), composer.

Virgin and Child, Wood, 1420–30
A372

Photogravure and Engraved

1972, Dec. 1 *Perf. 13½*

933 A372 2s olive & chocolate 30 20

Christmas 1972.

Racing Sleigh, 1750
A373

Designs: 2s, Coronation landau, 1824. 2.50s, Imperial state coach, 1763.

1972, Dec. 12

934	A373	1.50s pale gray & brown	27	25
935	"	2s pale gray & slate green	32	30
936	"	2.50s pale gray & plum	40	38

Collection of historic state coaches and carriages in Schönbrunn Palace.

Map of Austrian Telephone System
A374

1972, Dec. 14 Photo. *Perf. 14*

937 A374 2s yellow & black 30 22

Completion of automation of Austrian telephone system.

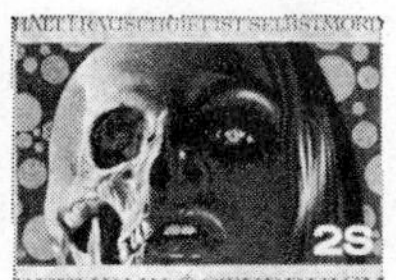

"Drugs are Death"
A375

1973, Jan. 26 Photo. ***Perf. 13½x14***

938 A375 2s scarlet & multi. 3.25 1.25

Fight against drug abuse.

REPUBLIK ÖSTERREICH 2S THEODOR KÖRNER 1873-1957.

Alfons Petzold A376 — Theodor Körner A377

1973, Jan. 26 Engr. ***Perf. 14x13½***

939 A376 2s reddish brown 30 22

50th anniversary of the death of Alfons Petzold (1882–1923), poet.

Photogravure and Engraved

1973, Apr. 24 ***Perf. 14x13½***

940 A377 2s gray & dp. claret 30 22

Centenary of the birth of Theodor Körner (1873–1957), President of Austria.

Douglas DC-9
A378

1973, May 14 ***Perf. 13½x14***

941 A378 2s vio. bl. & rose red 30 22

Austrian aviation anniversaries: First international airmail service Vienna to Kiev, Mar. 31, 1918, 55th anniversary; Austrian Aviation Corporation, 50th anniversary; Austrian Airlines, 15th anniversary.

25 JAHRE HAUPTVERBAND DER ÖSTERREICHISCHEN SOZIALVERSICHERUNGSTRÄGER S2 REPUBLIK ÖSTERREICH

Otto Loewi A379 — "Support" A380

1973, June 4 Engr. ***Perf. 14x13½***

942 A379 4s deep violet 55 40

Centenary of the birth of Otto Loewi (1873–1961), pharmacologist, winner of 1936 Nobel prize.

1973, June 25

943 A380 2s dark blue 30 22

Federation of Austrian Social Insurance Institutes, 25th anniversary.

Europa Issue 1973

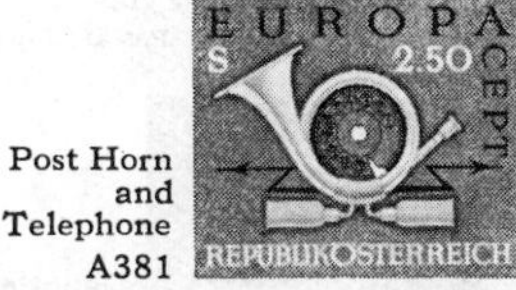

Post Horn and Telephone
A381

1973, July 9 Photo. ***Perf. 14***

944 A381 2.50s ocher, black & yellow 35 27

Dornbirn Fair Emblem
A382

1973, July 27 ***Perf. 13½x14***

945 A382 2s multicolored 30 22

Dornbirn Trade Fair, 25th anniversary.

Hurdles A383 — Leo Slezak A384

1973, Aug. 13 Engr. ***Perf. 14x13½***

946 A383 4s gray olive 55 40

23rd International Military Pentathlon Championships, Wiener Neustadt, Aug. 13–18.

1973, Aug. 17 ***Perf. 14***

947 A384 4s dark brown 55 40

Centenary of the birth of Leo Slezak (1873–1946), operatic tenor.

Gate, Vienna Hofburg, and ISI Emblem
A385

Photogravure and Engraved

1973, Aug. 20 ***Perf. 14x13½***

948 A385 2s gray, dk. brown & vermilion 30 22

39th Congress of International Statistical Institute, Vienna, Aug. 20–30.

Tegetthoff off Franz Josef Land, by Julius Prayer
A386

1973, Aug. 30 Engr. ***Perf. 13½x14***

949 A386 2.50s Prussian green 35 27

Centenary of the discovery of Franz Josef Land by an Austrian North Pole expedition.

Academy of Science, by Canaletto
A387

1973, Sept. 4

950 A387 2.50s violet 35 27

Centenary of international meteorological cooperation.

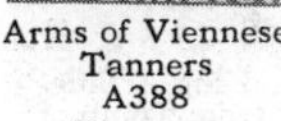

MAX REINHARDT 1873-1973 S 2 REPUBLIK ÖSTERREICH

Arms of Viennese Tanners A388 — Max Reinhardt A389

Photogravure and Engraved

1973, Sept. 4 ***Perf. 14***

951 A388 4s red & multi. 55 40

13th Congress of the International Union of Leather Chemists' Societies, Vienna, Sept. 1–7.

1973, Sept. 7 Engr. ***Perf. 13x13½***

952 A389 2s rose magenta 30 22

Centenary of the birth of Max Reinhardt (1873–1943), theatrical director and stage manager.

Trotter
A390

1973, Sept. 28 ***Perf. 13½***

953 A390 2s green 30 22

Centenary of Vienna Trotting Association.

Ferdinand Hanusch
A391

1973, Sept. 28 ***Perf. 14x13½***

954 A391 2s rose brown 30 22

50th anniversary of the death of Ferdinand Hanusch (1866–1923), secretary of state.

Police Radio Operator
A392

1973, Oct. 2 ***Perf. 13½x14***

955 A392 4s violet blue 55 40

50th anniversary of International Criminal Police Organization (INTERPOL).

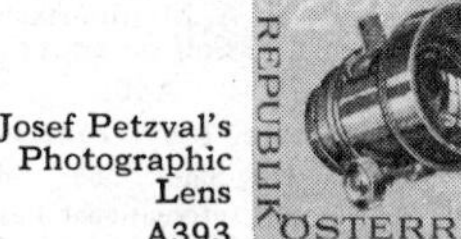

Josef Petzval's Photographic Lens
A393

Lithographed and Engraved

1973, Oct. 8 ***Perf. 14***

956 A393 2.50s blue & multi. 35 27

EUROPHOT Photographic Congress, Vienna.

Emperor's Spring, Hell Valley
A394

Photogravure and Engraved

1973, Oct. 23 ***Perf. 13½x14***

957 A394 2s sepia, blue & red 30 22

Centenary of Vienna's first mountain spring water supply system.

Almsee, Upper Austria A395 — Hofburg and Prince Eugene Statue, Vienna A395a

Designs: 50g, Farmhouses, Zillertal, Tirol. 1s, Kahlenbergerdorf. 1.50s, Bludenz, Vorarlberg. 2s, Inn Bridge, Alt Finstermunz. 2.50s, Murau, Styria. 3s, Bischofsmütze, Salzburg. 3.50s, Easter Church, Oberwart. 4.50s, Windmill, Retz. 5s, Aggstein Castle, Lower Austria. 6s, Lindauer Hut, Vorarlberg. 6.50s, Holy Cross Church, Villach, Carinthia. 7s, Falkenstein Castle, Carinthia. 7.50s, Hohensalzburg. 8s, Votive column, Reiteregg, Styria. 10s, Lake Neusiedl, Burgenland. 11s, Old Town, Enns. 16s, Open-air Museum, Bad Tatzmannsdorf. 20s, Myra waterfalls.

Photogravure and Engraved

1973–78 ***Perf. 13½x14***

Size: 23x29mm.

No.	Type	Description	Unused	Used
958	A395	50g gray & slate green ('75)	6	3
959	"	1s brown & dark brown ('75)	12	3
960	"	1.50s rose & brn. ('74)	20	3
961	"	2s gray blue & dk. blue ('74)	25	3
962	"	2.50s violet & deep violet ('74)	32	3
963	"	3s lt. ultra. & vio. blue ('74)	37	3
963A	"	3.50s dull orange & brown ('78)	40	3
964	"	4s brt. lilac & pur.	52	3
965	"	4.50s brt. green & bl. green ('76)	60	18
966	"	5s lilac & violet	65	6
967	"	6s deep rose & dk. vio. ('75)	77	13
968	"	6.50s blue green & indigo ('77)	85	15
969	"	7s sage green & slate green	90	13
970	"	7.50s lilac rose & claret ('77)	95	20
971	"	8s dull red & deep brown ('76)	1.05	27
972	"	10s gray green & dark green	1.30	13
973	"	11s vermilion & dk. car. ('76)	1.45	40
974	"	16s ocher & black ('77)	2.00	*60*
975	"	20s olive bister & ol. grn. ('77)	2.50	*75*
976	A395a	50s gray violet & vio. bl. ('75)	6.50	*1.00*
		Nos. 958-976 (20)	21.76	*4.24*

See No. 1102.

Nativity A396 — Fritz Pregl A397

1973, Nov. 30 ***Perf. 14***

977 A396 2s multicolored 30 20

Christmas 1973. Design from 14th century stained-glass window.

1973, Dec. 12 Engr. *Perf. 14x13½*

978 A397 4s deep blue 55 40

50th anniversary of the awarding of the Nobel prize for chemistry to Fritz Pregl (1869–1930).

Telex Machine A398 — Hugo Hofmannsthal A399

1974, Jan. 14 Photo. *Perf. 14x13½*

979 A398 2.50s ultramarine 35 27

50th anniversary of Radio Austria.

1974, Feb. 1 Engraved *Perf. 14*

980 A399 4s violet blue 55 40

Centenary of the birth of Hugo Hofmannsthal (1874–1929), poet and playwright.

Anton Bruckner and Bruckner House—A400

1974, Mar. 22 Engraved *Perf. 14*

981 A400 4s brown 55 40

Founding of Anton Bruckner House (concert hall), Linz, and sesquicentennial of the birth of Anton Bruckner (1824–1896), composer.

Vegetables A401

Photogravure and Engraved

1974, Apr. 18 *Perf. 14*

Multicolored

982 A401 2s *shown* 35 27
983 " 2.50s *Fruits* 42 35
984 " 4s *Flowers* 60 45

International Garden Show, Vienna, Apr. 18–Oct. 14.

Seal of Judenburg A402 — Karl Kraus A403

1974, Apr. 24 Photo. *Perf. 14x13½*

985 A402 2s plum & multi. 30 22

750th anniversary of Judenburg.

1974, Apr. 6 Engraved

986 A403 4s dark red 55 40

Centenary of the birth of Karl Kraus (1874–1936), poet and satirist.

St. Michael, by Thomas Schwanthaler A404 — King Arthur, from Tomb of Maximilian I A405

1974, May 3

987 A404 2.50s slate green 35 27

Exhibition of the works by the Schwanthaler Family of sculptors, (1633–1848), Reichersberg am Inn, May 3–Oct. 13.

Europa Issue 1974

1974, May 8 *Perf. 13½*

988 A405 2.50s ocher & slate bl. 38 27

De-Dion-Bouton Motor Tricycle A406

Photogravure and Engraved

1974, May 17 *Perf. 14x13½*

989 A406 2s gray & vio. brown 30 22

75th anniversary of the Austrian Automobile Association.

Satyr's Head, Terracotta A407

1974, May 22 *Perf. 13½x14*

990 A407 2s org. brn., gold & black 30 22

Exhibition, "Renaissance in Austria," Schallaburg Castle, May 22–Nov. 14.

Road Transport Union Emblem A408 — F. A. Maulbertsch, Self-portrait A409

1974, May 24 Photo. *Perf. 14x13½*

991 A408 4s dp. org. & black 55 40

14th Congress of the International Road Transport Union, Innsbruck.

1974, June 7 Engr. *Perf. 14x13½*

992 A409 2s violet brown 30 22

250th anniversary of the birth of Franz Anton Maulbertsch (1724–1796), painter.

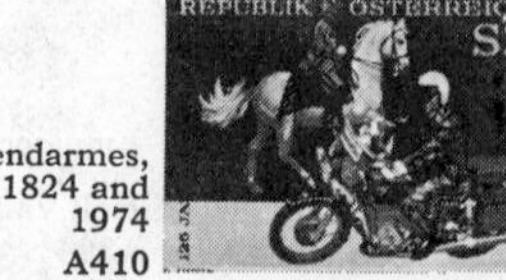

Gendarmes, 1824 and 1974 A410

1974, June 7 Photo. *Perf. 13½x14*

993 A410 2s red & multi. 30 22

125th anniversary of Austrian gendarmery.

Fencing A411

Photogravure and Engraved

1974, June 14 *Perf. 13½*

994 A411 2.50s red org. & blk. 35 27

Transportation Symbols A412 — St. Virgil, Sculpture from Nonntal Church A413

1974, June 18 Photo. *Perf. 14x13½*

995 A412 4s lt. ultra. & multi. 60 45

European Conference of Transportation Ministers, Vienna, June 18–21.

1974, June 28 Engr. *Perf. 13½x14*

996 A413 2s violet blue 30 22

1200th anniversary of the consecration of the Cathedral of Salzburg by Scotch-Irish Bishop Feirgil (St. Virgil). Salzburg was a center of Christianization in the 8th century.

Franz Jonas and Austrian Eagle A414

1974, June 28

997 A414 2s black 30 22

Franz Jonas (1899–1974), President of Austria 1965–1974.

Franz Stelzhamer A415 — Diver A416

1974, July 12 Engr. *Perf. 14x13½*

998 A415 2s indigo 30 22

Death centenary of Franz Stelzhamer (1802–1874), poet who wrote in Upper Austrian vernacular.

Perf. 13x13½

1974, Aug. 16 Photo. and Engr.

999 A416 4s lt. blue & sepia 50 35

13th European Swimming, Diving and Water Polo Championships, Vienna, Aug. 18–25.

Ferdinand Ritter von Hebra A417

1974, Sept. 10 Engr. *Perf. 14x13½*

1000 A417 4s brown 50 35

30th Meeting of the Association of German-speaking Dermatologists, Graz, Sept. 10–14. Dr. von Hebra (1816–1880) was a founder of modern dermatology.

Arnold Schönberg A418

1974, Sept. 13 *Perf. 13½x14*

1001 A418 2.50s purple 35 22

Centenary of the birth of Arnold Schönberg (1874–1951), composer.

Radio Station, Salzburg A419

1974, Oct. 1 Photo. *Perf. 13½x14*

1002 A419 2s multicolored 30 22

50th anniversary of Austrian broadcasting.

Edmund Eysler A420

1974, Oct. 4 Engr. *Perf. 14x13½*

1003 A420 2s dark olive 30 22

25th death anniversary of Edmund Eysler (1874–1949), composer.

Mailman, Mail Coach and Train, UPU Emblem—A421

Design: 4s, Mailman, jet, truck, 1974, and UPU emblem.

1974, Oct. 9 Photo. *Perf. 13½*

1004 A421 2s dp. claret & lilac 30 22
1005 " 4s dk. blue & gray 55 42

Centenary of Universal Postal Union.

Gauntlet Protecting Rose A422

1974, Oct. 23 Photo. ***Perf. 13½x14***

1006 A422 2s multicolored 30 22

Environment protection.

Austrian Sports Pool Emblem
A423

1974, Oct. 23 Photo. ***Perf. 13½x14***

1007 A423 70g multicolored 13 7

Austrian Sports Pool (lottery), 25th anniversary.

Carl Ditters von Dittersdorf
A424

Virgin and Child, Wood, c. 1600
A425

1974, Oct. 24 Engr. ***Perf. 14x13½***

1008 A424 2s.Prussian green 30 22

175th death anniversary of Carl Ditters von Dittersdorf (1739–1799), composer.

1974, Nov. 29 **Photo. & Engr.**

1009 A425 2s brown & gold 30 18

Christmas 1974.

Franz Schmidt
A426

St. Christopher
A427

1974, Dec. 18

1010 A426 4s gray & black 50 37

Birth centenary of Franz Schmidt (1874–1939), composer.

Photogravure and Engraved

1975, Jan. 24 ***Perf. 13½***

1011 A427 2.50s gray & brown 45 32

European Architectural Heritage Year. The design shows part of a wooden figure from central panel of the retable in the Kefermarkt Church, 1490–1497.

Safety Belt and Skeleton Arms
A428

Stained Glass Window, Vienna City Hall
A429

1975, Apr. 1 Photo. ***Perf. 14x13½***

1012 A428 70g vio. & multi. 12 6

Introduction of obligatory use of automobile safety belts.

1975, Apr. 2 ***Perf. 14***

1013 A429 2.50s multicolored 35 25

11th meeting of the Council of European Municipalities, Vienna, Apr. 2–5.

Austria as Mediator
A430

Forest
A431

1975, May 2 Litho. ***Perf. 14***

1014 A430 2s black & bister 30 20

30th anniversary of the Second Republic of Austria.

1975, May 6 **Engraved**

1015 A431 2s green 30 20

National forests, 50th anniversary.

High Priest, by Michael Pacher
A432

Gosaukamm Funicular
A433

Europa Issue 1975

Photogravure and Engraved

1975, May 27 ***Perf. 14x13½***

1016 A432 2.50s blk. & multi. 40 28

Design is detail from painting "The Marriage of Joseph and Mary," by Michael Pacher (c. 1450–1500).

1975, June 23 ***Perf. 14x13½***

1017 A433 2s slate & red 30 20

4th International Funicular Congress, Vienna, June 23–27.

Josef Misson and Mühlbach am Manhartsberg
A434

1975, June 27 ***Perf. 13½x14***

1018 A434 2s choc. & reddish brown 30 20

Death centenary of Josef Misson (1803–1875), poet who wrote in Lower Austrian vernacular.

Setting Sun and "P"
A435

1975, Aug. 27 Litho. ***Perf. 14x13½***

1019 A435 1.50s org., blk. & bl. 20 15

Austrian Association of Pensioners 25th anniversary meeting, Vienna, Aug. 1975.

Ferdinand Porsche
A436

Photogravure and Engraved

1975, Sept. 3 ***Perf. 13½x14***

1020 A436 1.50s gray & purple 20 15

Ferdinand Porsche (1875–1951), engineer, developer of Porsche and Volkswagen cars, birth centenary.

Leo Fall
A437

1975, Sept. 16 Engr. ***Perf. 14x13½***

1021 A437 2s violet 30 20

Leo Fall (1873–1925), composer, 50th death anniversary.

Judo Throw
A438

Heinrich Angeli
A439

1975, Oct. 20 Photo. ***Perf. 14x13½***

1022 A438 2.50s gold & multi. 37 25

10th World Judo Championships, Vienna, Oct. 20–26.

1975, Oct. 21 Engr. ***Perf. 14x13½***

1023 A439 2s rose lake 30 20

Heinrich Angeli (1840–1925), painter, 50th death anniversary.

Johann Strauss and Dancers
A440

Photogravure and Engraved

1975, Oct. 24 ***Perf. 13½x14***

1024 A440 4s ocher & sepia 50 40

Johann Strauss (1825–1899), composer, 150th birth anniversary.

Stylized Musician Playing a Viol
A441

Symbolic House
A442

1975, Oct. 30 ***Perf. 14x13½***

1025 A441 2.50s silver & violet blue 40 28

Vienna Symphony Orchestra, 75th anniversary.

1975, Oct. 31 **Photogravure**

1026 A442 2s multicolored 28 20

Austrian building savings societies, 50th anniversary.

Fan with "Hanswurst" Scene, 18th Century
A443

1975, Nov. 14 Photo. ***Perf. 13½x14***

1027 A443 1.50s grn. & multi. 30 17

Salzburg Theater bicentenary.

Virgin and Child, from 15th Century Altar
A444

"The Spiral Tree," by Hundertwasser
A445

Photogravure and Engraved

1975, Nov. 28 ***Perf. 13x13½***

1028 A444 2s gold & dull purple 32 17

Christmas 1975.

Photo., Engr. and Typo.

1975, Dec. 11 ***Perf. 13½x14***

1029 A445 4s multicolored 60 45

Austrian modern art. Friedensreich Hundertwasser is the pseudonym of Friedrich Stowasser (b. 1928).

Old Burgtheater—A446

Design: No. 1030b, Grand staircase, new Burgtheater.

Perf. 14 (pane), 13½x14 (stamps)

1976, Apr. 8 **Engraved**

1030 A446 Pane of 2 + label 95 95
- ***a.*** 3s violet blue 45 45
- ***b.*** 3s deep brown 45 45

Bicentenary of Vienna Burgtheater. Printed in sheets of 5 panes. Label (head of Pan) and commemorative inscription in vermilion. Size: 130x60mm.

Dr. Robert Barany
A447

Photogravure and Engraved

1976, Apr. 22 ***Perf. 14x13½***

1031 A447 3s blue & brown 38 30

Robert Barany (1876–1936), winner of Nobel Prize for Medicine, 1914, birth centenary.

Ammonite
A448

1976, Apr. 30 Photo. ***Perf. 13½x14***

1032 A448 3s red & multi. 38 30

Vienna Museum of Natural History, Centenary Exhibition.

Carinthian Dukes' Coronation Chair
A449

Siege of Linz, 17th Century Etching
A450

Photogravure and Engraved

1976, May 6 ***Perf. 14x13½***

1033 A449 3s greenish black & orange 38 30

Millennium of Carinthia.

1976, May 14

1034 A450 4s blk. & gray grn. 50 38

Upper Austrian Peasants' War, 350th anniversary.

Skittles
A451

1976, May 14 ***Perf. 13½x14***

1035 A451 4s black & orange 50 38

11th World Skittles Championships, Vienna.

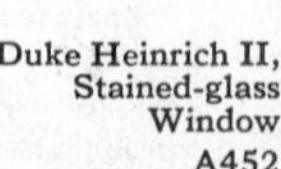

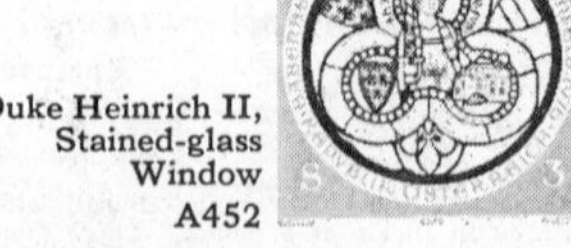

Duke Heinrich II, Stained-glass Window
A452

1976, May 14 ***Perf. 14***

1036 A452 3s multicolored 38 30

Babenberg Exhibition, Lilienfeld.

St. Wolfgang, from Pacher Altar
A453

1976, May 26 **Engr.** ***Perf. 13½***

1037 A453 6s bright violet 72 55

International Art Exhibition at St. Wolfgang.

Europa Issue 1976

Tassilo Cup, Kremsmunster, 777
A454

Photogravure & Engraved

1976, Aug. 13 ***Perf. 14x13½***

1038 A454 4s ultra. & multi. 50 42

Timber Fair Emblem
A455

Constantin Economo, M.D.
A456

1976, Aug. 13 Photogravure

1039 A455 3s green & multi. 38 30

25 years of Austrian Timber Fair, Klagenfurt.

1976, Aug. 23 Engraved

1040 A456 3s dk. red brown 38 30

Dr. Constantin Economo (1876–1931); neurologist.

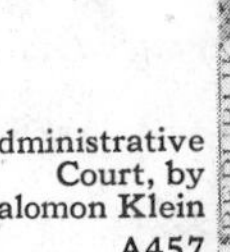

Administrative Court, by Salomon Klein
A457

1976, Oct. 25 **Engr.** ***Perf. 13½x14***

1041 A457 6s deep brown 72 55

Austrian Central Administrative Court, centenary.

Souvenir Sheet

Arms of Lower Austria
A458

Designs: Coats of Arms of Austrian Provinces.

Photogravure and Engraved

1976, Oct. 25 ***Perf. 14***

1042	A458	Sheet of 9, multi.	2.50	2.50
	a.	2s *shown*	27	27
	b.	2s *Upper Austria*	27	27
	c.	2s *Styria*	27	27
	d.	2s *Carinthia*	27	27
	e.	2s *Tyrol*	27	27
	f.	2s *Vorarlberg*	27	27
	g.	2s *Salzburg*	27	27
	h.	2s *Burgenland*	27	27
	i.	2s *Vienna*	27	27

Millennium of Austria. Austrian coat of arms, red border and black inscription in margin. Size: 135x180mm.

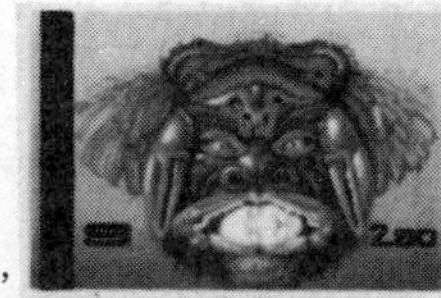

"Cancer"
A459

1976, Nov. 17 Photo. ***Perf. 14x13½***

1043 A459 2.50s multicolored 32 28

Fight against cancer.

UN Emblem and Bridge
A460

1976, Nov. 17

1044 A460 3s blue & gold 38 30

UN Industrial Development Organization (UNIDO), 10th anniversary.

Punched Tape, Map of Europe
A461

1976, Nov. 17 ***Perf. 14***

1045 A461 1.50s multicolored 18 15

Austrian Press Agency (APA), 30th anniversary.

Viktor Kaplan, Kaplan Turbine
A462

Photogravure and Engraved

1976, Nov. 26 ***Perf. 13½x14***

1046 A462 2.50s multicolored 32 28

Viktor Kaplan (1876–1934), inventor of Kaplan turbine, birth centenary.

Nativity, by Konrad von Friesach c. 1450
A463

1976, Nov. 26 ***Perf. 13½***

1047 A463 3s multicolored 38 25

Christmas 1976.

Augustin, the Piper
A464

Photogravure and Engraved

1976, Dec. 29 ***Perf. 13½***

1048 A464 6s multicolored 75 60

Modern Austrian art.

Rainer Maria Rilke
A465

Vienna City Synagogue
A466

1976, Dec. 29 **Engr.** ***Perf. 14x13½***

1049 A465 3s deep violet 34 30

Rainer Maria Rilke (1875–1926), poet.

1976, Dec. 29 **Photo.** ***Perf. 13½***

1050 A466 1.50s multicolored 18 15

Sesquicentennial of Vienna City Synagogue.

Nikolaus Joseph Jacquin
A467

1977, Feb. 16 **Engr.** ***Perf. 14x13½***

1051 A467 4s chocolate 45 38

Nikolaus Joseph von Jacquin (1727–1817), botanist.

Oswald von Wolkenstein
A468

Photogravure and Engraved

1977, Feb. 16 ***Perf. 14***

1052 A468 3s multicolored 34 30

Oswald von Wolkenstein (1377–1445), poet, 600th birth anniversary.

Handball
A469

1977, Feb. 25 Photo. ***Perf. 13½x14***

1053 A469 1.50s multicolored 18 15

World Indoor Handball Championships, Austria, Feb. 5–Mar. 6.

Alfred Kubin
A470

1977, Apr. 12 Engr. *Perf. 14x13½*

1054 A470 6s dark violet blue 70 55

Alfred Kubin (1877–1959), illustrator and writer, birth centenary.

Great Spire, St. Stephen's Cathedral
A471

Designs: 3s, Heathen Tower and Frederick's Gable. 4s, Interior view with Albertinian Choir.

1977, Apr. 22 Engr. *Perf. 13½*

1055	A471	2.50s dark brown	32	32
1056	"	3s dark blue	40	40
1057	"	4s rose lake	52	50

Restoration and re-opening of St. Stephen's Cathedral, Vienna, 25th anniversary.

Fritz Hermanovsky-Orlando
A472

Photogravure and Engraved

1977, Apr. 29 *Perf. 13½x14*

1058 A472 6s Prussian green & gold 68 55

Fritz Hermanovsky-Orlando (1877–1954), poet and artist, birth centenary.

IAEA Emblem
A473

Arms of Schwanenstadt
A474

1977, May 2 Photo. *Perf. 14*

1059 A473 3s brt. blue, light blue & gold 40 30

International Atomic Energy Agency (IAEA), 20th anniversary.

1977, June 10 Photo. *Perf. 14x13½*

1060 A474 3s dk. brn. & multi. 40 30

350th anniversary of the town Schwanenstadt.

Europa Issue 1977

Attersee, Upper Austria—A475

1977, June 10 Engr. *Perf. 14*

1061 A475 6s olive green 78 55

Globe, by Vincenzo Coronelli, 1688
A476

Photogravure and Engraved

1977, June 29 *Perf. 14*

1062 A476 3s black & buff 40 30

5th International Symposium of the Coronelli World Federation of Friends of the Globe, Austria, June 29–July 3.

Kayak Race
A477

1977, July 15 Photo. *Perf. 13½x14*

1063 A477 4s multicolored 45 30

3rd Kayak Slalom White Water Race on Lieser River, Spittal.

The Good Samaritan, by Francesco Bassano
A478

Photogravure and Engraved

1977, Sept. 16

1064 A478 1.50s brown & red 18 12

Workers' Good Samaritan Organization, 50th anniversary.

Papermakers' Coat of Arms
A479

Man with Austrian Flag Lifting Barbed Wire
A480

1977, Oct. 10 *Perf. 14x13½*

1065 A479 3s multicolored 40 15

17th Conference of the European Committee of Pulp and Paper Technology (EUCEPA), Vienna.

1977, Nov. 3 *Perf. 14*

1066 A480 2.50s slate & red 32 25

Honoring the martyrs for Austria's freedom.

"Austria," First Steam Locomotive in Austria—A481

Designs: 2.50s, Steam locomotive 214. 3s, Electric locomotive 1044.

Photogravure and Engraved

1977, Nov. 17 *Perf. 13½*

1067	A481	1.50s multicolored	20	15
1068	"	2.50s "	32	28
1069	"	3s "	40	30

140th anniversary of Austrian railroads.

Virgin and Child, Wood Statue, Mariastein, Tyrol
A482

1977, Nov. 25 *Perf. 14x13½*

1070 A482 3s multicolored 40 20

Christmas 1977.

The Danube Maiden, by Wolfgang Hutter
A483

1977, Dec. 2 *Perf. 13½x14*

1071 A483 6s multicolored 78 45

Modern Austrian art.

Egon Friedell
A484

Photogravure and Engraved

1978, Jan. 23

1072 A484 3s lt. blue & black 35 22

Egon Friedell (1878–1938), writer and historian.

Subway Train
A485

1978, Feb. 24 Photo. *Perf. 13½x14*

1073 A485 3s multicolored 35 22

New Vienna subway system.

Biathlon Competition
A486

1978, Feb. 28 Photo. & Engr.

1074 A486 4s multicolored 45 30

Biathlon World Championships, Hochfilzen, Tyrol, Feb. 28–Mar. 5.

Leopold Kunschak
A487

1978, Mar. 13 Engr. *Perf. 14x13½*

1075 A487 3s violet blue 35 22

Leopold Kunschak (1871–1953), political leader, 25th death anniversary.

Coyote, Aztec Feather Shield
A488

1978, Mar. 13 Photo. *Perf. 13½x14*

1076 A488 3s multicolored 35 22

Ethnographical Museum, 50th anniversary exhibition.

Alpine Farm, Woodcut by Suitbert Lobisser
A489

1978, Mar. 23 Engr. *Perf. 13½*

1077 A489 3s dk. brown, *buff* 35 22

Suitbert Lobisser (1878–1943), graphic artist, birth centenary.

Capercaillie, Hunting Bag, 1730, and Rifle, 1655
A490

Photogravure and Engraved

1978, Apr. 28 *Perf. 13½*

1078 A490 6s multicolored 70 45

International Hunting Exhibition, Marchegg.

Europa Issue 1978

Riegersburg, Styria—A491

1978, May 3 Engraved

1079 A491 6s dp. rose lilac 70 45

Parliament, Vienna, and Map of Europe
A492

Admont Pietà, c. 1410
A493

1978, May 3 Photo. ***Perf. 14x13½***

1080 A492 4s multicolored 45 30

3rd Interparliamentary Conference for European Cooperation and Security, Vienna.

Photogravure and Engraved

1978, May 26

1081 A493 2.50s ocher & blk. 28 18

Gothic Art in Styria Exhibition, St. Lambrecht, 1978.

Ort Castle, Gmunden
A494

1978, June 9

1082 A494 3s multicolored 35 22

700th anniversary of Gmunden City.

Child with Flowers and Fruit
A495

Lehar and his Home, Bad Ischl
A496

Photogravure and Engraved

1978, June 30 ***Perf. 14x13½***

1083 A495 6s gold & multi. 70 45

25 years of Social Tourism.

1978, July 14 Engr. ***Perf. 14x13½***

1084 A496 6s slate 70 45

International Lehar Congress, Bad Ischl. Franz Lehar (1870–1948), operetta composer.

Congress Emblem
A497

1978, Aug. 21 Photo. ***Perf. 13½x14***

1085 A497 1.50s black, red & yellow 18 10

Congress of International Federation of Building Construction and Wood Workers, Vienna, Aug. 20–24.

Ottokar of Bohemia and Rudolf of Hapsburg—A498

Photogravure and Engraved

1978, Aug. 25

1086 A498 3s multicolored 35 22

Battle of Durnkrut and Jedenspeigen (Marchfeld), which established Hapsburg rule in Austria, 700th anniversary.

First Documentary Reference to Villach, "ad pontem uillah"
A499

1978, Sept. 8 Litho. ***Perf. 13½x14***

1087 A499 3s multicolored 35 22

1100th anniversary of Villach, Carinthia.

Seal of Graz, 1440
A500

Emperor Maximilian Fishing
A501

Photogravure and Engraved

1978, Sept. 13 ***Perf. 14x13½***

1088 A500 4s multicolored 45 30

850th anniversary of Graz.

1978, Sept. 15 ***Perf. 14x13½***

1089 501 4s multicolored 45 30

World Fishing Championships, Vienna, Sept. 1978.

"Aid to the Handi-capped"
A502

1978, Oct. 2 Photo. ***Perf. 13½x14***

1090 A502 6s org. brn. & blk. 70 45

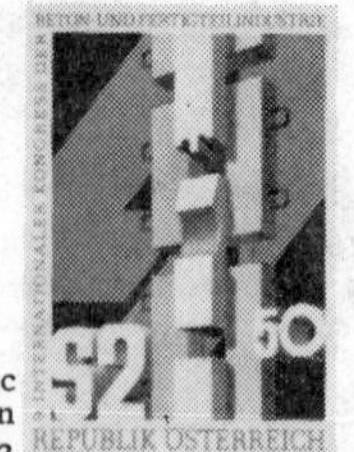

Symbolic Column
A503

1978, Oct. 9 Photo. ***Perf. 13½***

1091 A503 2.50s orange, black & gray 28 18

9th International Congress of Concrete and Prefabrication Industries, Vienna, Oct. 8–13.

Grace, by Albin Egger-Lienz
A504

1978, Oct. 27 ***Perf. 13½x14***

1092 A504 6s multicolored 70 45

European Family Congress, Vienna, Oct. 26–29.

Lise Meitner and Atom Symbol
A505

1978, Nov. 7 Engr. ***Perf. 14x13½***

1093 A505 6s dark violet 70 45

Lise Meitner (1878–1968), physicist.

Viktor Adler, by Anton Hanak
A506

Photogravure and Engraved

1978, Nov. 10 ***Perf. 13½x14***

1094 A506 3s vermilion & black 35 22

Viktor Adler (1852–1918), leader of Social Democratic Party, 60th death anniversary.

Franz Schubert, by Josef Kriehuber
A507

Virgin and Child, Wilhering Church
A508

1978, Nov. 17 Engr. ***Perf. 14***

1095 A507 6s reddish brown 70 45

Franz Schubert (1797–1828), composer.

Photogravure and Engraved

1978, Dec. 1 ***Perf. 12½x13½***

1096 A508 3s multicolored 35 22

Christmas 1978.

Archduke Johann Shelter, Grossglockner—A509

1978, Dec. 6 ***Perf. 13½x14***

1097 A509 1.50s gold & dark violet blue 18 15

Austrian Alpine Club, centenary.

Adam, by Rudolf Hausner
A510

Bound Hands
A511

1978, Dec. 6 Photo. ***Perf. 13½x14***

1098 A510 6s multicolored 70 45

Modern Austrian art.

1978, Dec. 6 ***Perf. 14x13½***

1099 A511 6s deep claret 70 45

30th anniversary of Universal Declaration of Human Rights.

Type of 1973

Design: 3s, Bishofsmütze, Salzburg.

1978, Dec. 7 Photo. ***Perf. 14½x14***

Size: 17x21mm.

1102 A395 3s lt. ultra. & violet blue 35 3

Issued in sheets and coils.

Child and IYC Emblem
A512

Photogravure and Engraved

1979, Jan. 16 ***Perf. 14***

1110 A512 2.50s dk. bl., blk. & brown 28 18

International Year of the Child.

CCIR Emblem
A513

1979, Jan. 16 Photo. ***Perf. 13½x14***

1111 A513 6s multicolored 70 45

International Radio Consultative Committee (CCIR) of the International Telecommunications Union, 50th anniversary.

Air Rifle, Air Pistol and Club Emblem—A514

Photogravure and Engraved

1979, Mar. 7 ***Perf. 13½***

1112 A514 6s multicolored 70 45

Centenary of Austrian Shooting Club, and European Air Rifle and Air Pistol Championships, Graz.

SEMI-POSTAL STAMPS.

Issues of the Monarchy.

Emperor Franz Josef
SP1

Perf. 12½

1914, Oct. 4 Typo. Unwmkd.

B1	SP1	5h green	22	16
B2	"	10h rose	27	18

Nos. B1–B2 were sold at an advance of 2h each over face value. Exist imperf.; price, set $90.

The Firing Step
SP2

Designs: 5h+2h, Cavalry. 10h+2h, Siege gun. 20h+3h, Battleship. 35h+3h, Airplane.

1915, May 1

B3	SP2	3h+1h violet brown	22	40
B4	"	5h+2h green	3	3
B5	"	10h+2h deep rose	3	3
B6	"	20h+3h Prussian blue	65	80
B7	"	35h+3h ultramarine	5.50	3.00
		Nos. B3–B7 (5)	6.43	4.26

Nos. B3–B7 exist imperf. Price, set $110.

Issues of the Republic.

Kärnten

Types of Austria, 1919-20, Overprinted in Black

Abstimmung

1920, Sept. 16 *Perf. 12½*

B11	A44	5h gray, *yellow*	50	50
B12	"	10h red, *pink*	85	85
B13	A43	15h bistre, *yellow*	50	50
B14	A45	20h dark green, *blue*	50	50
B15	A43	25h violet, *pink*	50	50
B16	A45	30h brown, *buff*	1.40	1.40
B17	"	40h carmine, *yellow*	50	50
B18	"	50h dark blue, *blue*	50	50
B19	A43	60h olive grn., *azure*	1.75	1.75
B20	A47	80h red	50	50
B21	"	1k orange brown	55	55
B22	"	2k pale blue	50	50

Granite Paper.

Imperf.

B23	A46	2½k brown red	65	65
B24	"	3k dark blue & green	65	65
B25	"	4k carmine & violet	90	90
B26	"	5k blue	1.15	1.15
B27	"	7½k yellow green	1.05	1.05
B28	"	10k gray grn. & red	1.00	1.00
B29	"	20k lilac & orange	1.00	1.00
		Nos. B11–B29 (19)	14.95	14.95

Carinthia Plebiscite. Sold at three times face value for the benefit of the Plebiscite Propaganda Fund.

Nos. B11–B22 exist imperf. Price, set $175.

Hochwasser

Types of Regular Issues of 1919-21 Overprinted

1920

1921, Mar. 1 *Perf. 12½*

B30	A44	5h gray, *yellow*	35	40
B31	"	10h orange brown	35	40
B32	A43	15h gray	35	40
B33	A45	20h green, *yellow*	35	40
B34	A43	25h blue, *yellow*	35	40
B35	A45	30h violet, *blue*	35	40
B36	"	40h orange brown, *pink*	50	55
B37	"	50h green, *blue*	1.40	1.50
B38	A43	60h lilac, *yellow*	35	40
B39	A47	80h pale blue	35	40
B40	"	1k red orange, *blue*	85	90
B41	"	1½k green, *yellow*	35	45
B42	"	2k lilac brown	35	45

Overprinted

Hochwasser

1920

B43	A46	2½k light blue	40	45
B44	"	3k olive green & brown red	40	45
B45	"	4k lilac & orange	1.10	1.15
B46	"	5k olive green	55	60
B47	"	7½k brown red	55	60
B48	"	10k blue & olive green	55	60
B49	"	20k carmine rose & violet	85	90
		Nos. B30–B49 (20)	10.65	11.80

Nos. B30–B49 were sold at three times face value, the excess going to help flood victims. Set exists imperf. Price $250.

Franz Joseph Haydn
SP9

View of Bregenz
SP16

Musicians: 5k, Mozart. 7½k, Beethoven. 10k, Schubert. 25k, Anton Bruckner. 50k, Johann Strauss (son). 100k, Hugo Wolf.

Engraved

1922, Apr. 24 *Perf. 11½, 12½*

B50	SP9	2½k brown	10.00	10.00
B51	"	5k dark blue	1.90	1.90
B52	"	7½k black	2.90	2.90
		a. Perf. 11½	65.00	62.50
B53	"	10k dark violet	3.85	3.85
B54	"	25k dark green	5.25	5.25
B55	"	50k claret	3.85	3.85
B56	"	100k brown olive	11.00	11.00
		Nos. B50–B56 (7)	38.75	38.75

These stamps were sold at 10 times face value, the excess being given to needy musicians.

All values exist imperf. on both regular and handmade papers. Price, set $500.

A 1969 souvenir sheet without postal validity contains reprints of the 5k in black, 7½k in claret and 50k in dark blue, each overprinted "NEUDRUCK" in black at top. It was issued for the Vienna State Opera Centenary Exhibition.

1923, May 22 *Perf. 12½*

Designs: 120k, Mirabelle Gardens, Salzburg. 160k, Church at Eisenstadt. 180k, Assembly House, Klagenfurt. 200k, "Golden Roof," Innsbruck. 240k, Main Square, Linz. 400k, Castle Hill, Graz. 600k, Abbey at Melk. 1000k, Upper Belvedere, Vienna.

Various Frames.

B57	SP16	100k dark green	4.75	4.25
B58	"	120k deep blue	4.50	4.00
B59	"	160k dark violet	4.50	4.00
B60	"	180k red violet	4.50	4.00
B61	"	200k lake	4.50	4.00
B62	"	240k red brown	4.50	4.00
B63	"	400k dark brown	4.50	4.25
B64	"	600k olive brown	4.50	4.25
B65	"	1000k black	6.75	6.25
		Nos. B57–B65 (9)	43.00	39.00

Nos. B57–B65 were sold at five times face value, the excess going to needy artists.

All values exist imperf. on both regular and handmade papers. Price, set $400.

Feebleness
SP25

Siegfried Slays the Dragon
SP30

Designs: 300k+900k, Aid to industry. 500k+1500k, Orphans and widow. 600k+1800k, Indigent old man. 1000k+3000k, Alleviation of hunger.

1924, Sept. 6 Photogravure

B66	SP25	100k+300k yellow green	6.50	6.50
B67	"	300k+900k red brown	8.25	8.25
B68	"	500k+1500k brown violet	8.25	3.25
B69	"	600k+1800k peacock blue	8.25	8.25
B70	"	1000k+3000k orange brown	15.00	15.00
		Nos. B66–B70 (5)	46.25	46.25

The surtax was for child welfare and anti-tuberculosis work. Set exists imperf. Price, $375.

1926, Mar. 8 Engraved

Designs: 8g+2g, Gunther's voyage to Iceland. 15g+5g, Brunhild accusing Kriemhild. 20g+5g, Nymphs telling Hagen the future. 24g+6g, Rudiger von Bechelaren welcomes the Nibelungen. 40g+10g, Dietrich von Bern vanquishes Hagen.

B71	SP30	3g+2g olive black	1.50	90
B72	"	8g+2g indigo	27	27
B73	"	15g+5g dark claret	27	27
B74	"	20g+5g olive green	40	40
B75	"	24g+6g dark violet	40	40
B76	"	40g+10g red brown	9.50	5.50
		Nos. B71–B76 (6)	12.34	7.74

Nibelungen issue.

The surtax was for child welfare. Set exists imperf. Price, $350.

President Michael Hainisch
SP36

President Wilhelm Miklas
SP37

1928, Nov. 5

B77	SP36	10g dark brown	7.50	7.50
B78	"	15g red brown	7.50	7.50
B79	"	30g black	7.50	7.50
B80	"	40g indigo	7.50	7.50

Tenth anniversary of Austrian Republic. Sold at double face value, the premium aiding war orphans and children of war invalids.

Set exists imperf. Price, $375.

1930, Oct. 4

B81	SP37	10(g) light brown	14.00	14.00
B82	"	20(g) red	14.00	14.00
B83	"	30(g) brn. violet	14.00	14.00
B84	"	40(g) indigo	14.00	14.00
B85	"	50(g) dark green	14.00	14.00
B86	"	1s blk. brown	14.00	14.00
		Nos. B81–B86 (6)	84.00	84.00

Nos. B81–B86 were sold at double face value. The excess aided the anti-tuberculosis campaign and the building of sanatoria in Carinthia.

Set exists imperf. Price, $450.

Regular Issue of 1929-30 Overprinted in Various Colors

CONVENTION
WIEN 1931

1931, June 20

B87	A56	10g bistre (Bl)	50.00	50.00
B88	"	20g dark gray (R)	50.00	50.00
B89	A56	30g dk. violet (Gl)	50.00	50.00
B90	"	40g dark blue (Gl)	50.00	50.00
B91	"	50g gray violet (O)	50.00	50.00
B92	A57	1s blk. brown (Bk)	50.00	50.00
		Nos. B87–B92 (6)	300.00	300.00

Rotary convention, Vienna.

Nos. B87 to B92 were sold at double their face values. The excess was added to the beneficent funds of Rotary International.

Set exists imperf. Price, $900.

Ferdinand Raimund
SP38

Poets: 20g, Franz Grillparzer. 30g, Johann Nestroy. 40g, Adalbert Stifter. 50g, Ludwig Anzengruber. 1s, Peter Rosegger.

1931, Sept. 12

B93	SP38	10(g) dark violet	22.50	22.50
B94	"	20(g) gray black	22.50	22.50
B95	"	30(g) orange red	22.50	22.50
B96	"	40(g) dull blue	22.50	22.50
B97	"	50(g) gray green	22.50	22.50
B98	"	1s yel. brn.	22.50	22.50
		Nos. B93–B98 (6)	135.00	135.00

Nos. B93–B98 were sold at double face value. The surtax aided unemployed young people.

Sets exists imperf. Price, $600.

Chancellor Ignaz Seipel
SP44

Ferdinand Georg Waldmüller
SP45

1932, Oct. 12 *Perf. 13*

B99	SP44	50g ultramarine	22.50	22.50

Msgr. Ignaz Seipel, Chancellor of Austria, 1922–29. Sold at double face value, the excess aiding wounded veterans of World War I.

Exists imperf. Price, $225.

1932, Nov. 21

Artists: 24g, Moritz von Schwind. 30g, Rudolf von Alt. 40g, Hans Makart. 64g, Gustav Klimt. 1s, Albin Egger-Lienz.

B100	SP45	12(g) slate grn.	30.00	30.00
B101	"	24(g) dp. violet	30.00	30.00
B102	"	30(g) dark red	30.00	30.00
B103	"	40(g) dark gray	30.00	30.00
B104	"	64(g) dk. brown	30.00	30.00
B105	"	1s claret	30.00	30.00
		Nos. B100–B105 (6)	180.00	180.00

Nos. B100 to B105 were sold at double their face values. The surtax was for the assistance of charitable institutions.

Set exists imperf. Price, $750.

Mountain Climbing
SP51

Designs: 24g, Ski gliding. 30g, Walking on skis. 50g, Ski jumping.

1933, Jan. 9 Photo. *Perf. 12½*

B106	SP51	12(g) dk. green	13.75	11.00
B107	"	24(g) dk. vio.	125.00	110.00

B108 SP51 30(g) brn. red 22.50 22.50
B109 " 50(g) dk. blue 125.00 110.00

Issued in connection with a meeting of the International Ski Federation at Innsbruck, Feb. 8–13, 1933.

These stamps were sold at double their face value. The surtax was for the benefit of "Youth in Distress."

Nos. B106–B109 exist imperf. Price $1,500.

Vienna Philatelic Exhibition Issue.

Stagecoach, after Painting by Moritz von Schwind
SP55

Ordinary Paper.

1933, June 23 Engraved *Perf. 12½*

B110 SP55 50g deep ultra. 275.00 275.00
a. Granite paper 550.00 600.00

Sheets of 25.

Nos. B110 and B110a exist imperf. Prices four times those of perf. stamps.

Souvenir Sheet

SP55a

Perf. 12.

Granite Paper.

B111 SP55a 50g dp. ultra., sheet of 4 3500.00 3750.00
a. Single stamp 750.00 750.00

Issued in connection with the International Philatelic Exhibition at Vienna in 1933. In addition to the postal value of 50g the stamp was sold at a premium of 50g for charity and of 1s60g for the admission fee to the exhibition.

Size of No. B111: 126x103mm.

The 50g dark red in souvenir sheet, with dark blue overprint ("NEUDRUCK WIPA 1965"), had no postal validity.

St. Stephen's Cathedral in 1683
SP56

Marco d'Aviano, Papal Legate
SP57

Designs: 30g, Count Ernst Rudiger von Starhemberg. 40g, John III Sobieski, King of Poland. 50g, Karl V, Duke of Lorraine. 64g, Burgomaster Johann Andreas von Liebenberg.

1933, Sept. 6 Photo. *Perf. 12½*

B112 SP56 12(g) dark green 45.00 45.00
B113 SP57 24(g) dk. violet 37.50 37.50
B114 " 30(g) brown red 37.50 37.50
B115 " 40(g) blue black 55.00 55.00
B116 " 50(g) dark blue 37.50 37.50
B117 SP57 64(g) olive brn. 45.00 45.00
Nos. B112–B117 (6) 257.50 257.50

Issued in commemoration of the 250th anniversary of the deliverance of Vienna from the Turks and in connection with the Pan-German Catholic Congress on September 6th, 1933.

The stamps were sold at double their face value, the excess being for the aid of Catholic works of charity.

Sets exists imperf. Price, $1,000.

Types of Regular Issue of 1925-30 Surcharged:

+2g Winterhilfe
a

WINTERHILFE +6g
b

+50g

WINTERHILFE
c

1933, Dec. 15

B118 A52 (*a*) 5g+2g olive green 55 45
B119 A56 (*b*) 12g+3g light blue 55 45
B120 " (") 24g+6g brown orange 55 45
B121 A57 (*c*) 1s+50g orange red 47.50 47.50

Winterhelp. Set exists imperf. Price, $200.

Anton Pilgram
SP62

Architects: 24g, J. B. Fischer von Erlach. 30g, Jakob Prandtauer. 40g, A. von Siccardsburg & E. van der Null. 60g, Heinrich von Ferstel. 64g, Otto Wagner.

Thick Yellowish Paper.

1934, Dec. 2 Engr. *Perf. 12½*

B122 SP62 12gr(+12gr) blk. 15.00 15.00
B123 " 24gr(+24gr) dull violet 15.00 15.00
B124 " 30gr(+30gr) car. 15.00 15.00
B125 " 40gr(+40gr) brn. 15.00 15.00
B126 " 60gr(+60gr) blue 15.00 15.00
a. Horizontal pair, imperf. between 275.00
B127 " 64gr(+64gr) dull green 15.00 15.00
Nos. B122–B127 (6) 90.00 90.00

The surtax on this and the following issues was devoted to general charity.

Nos. B122–B127 exist imperf. Price, set $650.

Types of Regular Issue of 1934 Surcharged in Black:

+50g

Winterhilfe +2g
a

WINTERHILFE
b

1935, Nov. 11 *Perf. 12, 12½*

B128 A67 (*a*) 5g+2g emerald 55 45
B129 " (") 12g+3g blue 1.35 75
B130 " (") 24g+6g lt. brn. 65 50
B131 A68 (*b*) 1s+50g verm. 42.50 42.50

Winterhelp. Set exists imperf. Price, $180.

Prince Eugene of Savoy
SP68

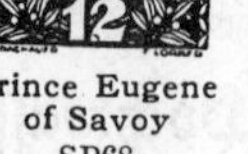

Slalom Turn
SP74

Military Leaders: 24g, Field Marshal Laudon. 30g, Archduke Karl. 40g, Field Marshal Josef Radetzky. 60g, Admiral Wilhelm Tegetthoff. 64g, Field Marshal Franz Conrad Hotzendorff.

1935, Dec. 1 *Perf. 12½*

B132 SP68 12g(+12g) brn. 15.00 15.00
B133 " 24g(+24g) dark green 15.00 15.00
B134 " 30g(+30g) claret 15.00 15.00
B135 " 40g(+40g) slate 15.00 15.00
B136 " 60g(+60g) deep ultra. 15.00 15.00
B137 " 64g(+64g) dark violet 15.00 15.00
Nos. B132–B137 (6) 90.00 90.00

Set exists imperf. Price, $650.

1936, Feb. 20 Photogravure

Designs: 24g, Jumper taking off. 35g, Slalom turn. 60g, Innsbruck view.

B138 SP74 12g(+12g) Pruss. green 3.50 3.50
B139 " 24g(+24g) deep violet 5.50 5.50
B140 " 35g(+35g) rose carmine 42.50 42.50
B141 " 60g(+60g) sapphire 42.50 42.50

Ski concourse issue. Set exists imperf. Price, $500.

St. Martin of Tours
SP78

Designs: 12g+3g, Medical clinic. 24g+6g, St. Elizabeth of Hungary. 1s+1s, "Flame of Charity."

1936, Nov. 2

B142 SP78 5g+2g deep green 55 55
B143 " 12g+3g deep violet 55 55
B144 " 24g+6g deep blue 55 55
B145 " 1s+1s dark carmine 14.00 15.00

Winterhelp. Set exists imperf. Price, $175.

Josef Ressel
SP82

Nurse and Infant
SP88

Inventors: 24g, Karl von Ghega. 30g, Josef Werndl. 40g, Carl Auer von Welsbach. 60g, Robert von Lieben. 64g, Viktor Kaplan.

1936, Dec. 6 Engraved

B146 SP82 12g(+12g) dark brown 5.00 5.00
B147 " 24g(+24g) dark violet 5.00 5.00
B148 " 30g(+30g) deep claret 5.00 5.00
B149 SP82 40g(+40g) gray violet 5.00 5.00
B150 " 60g(+60g) violet blue 5.00 5.00
B151 " 64g(+64g) dark slate green 5.00 5.00
Nos. B146–B151 (6) 30.00 30.00

Set exists imperf. Price, $400.

1937, Oct. 18 Photogravure

Designs: 12g+3g, Mother and child. 24g+6g, Nursing the aged. 1s+1s, Sister of Mercy with patient.

B152 SP88 5g+2g dark green 27 27
B153 " 12g+3g dark brown 30 30
B154 " 24g+6g dark blue 30 30
B155 " 1s+1s dk. car. 6.75 7.00

Winterhelp. Set exists imperf. Price, $175.

Gerhard van Swieten
SP92

The Dawn of Peace
SP101

Physicians: 8g, Leopold Auenbrugger von Auenbrugg. 12g, Karl von Rokitansky. 20g, Joseph Skoda. 24g, Ferdinand von Hebra. 30g, Ferdinand von Arlt. 40g, Joseph Hyrtl. 60g, Theodor Billroth. 64g, Theodor Meynert.

1937, Dec. 5 Engr. *Perf. 12½*

B156 SP92 5g+(5g) choc. 3.75 3.75
B157 " 8g+(8g) dark red 3.75 3.75
B158 " 12g+(12g) brown black 3.75 3.75
B159 " 20g+(20g) dark green 3.75 3.75
B160 " 24g+(24g) dark violet 3.75 3.75
B161 " 30g+(30g) brown carmine 3.75 3.75
B162 " 40g+(40g) deep olive green 3.75 3.75
B163 " 60g+(60g) indigo 3.75 3.75
B164 " 64g+(64g) brown violet 3.75 3.75
Nos. B156–B164 (9) 33.75 33.75

Set exists imperf. Price, $525.

Photogravure.

1945, Sept. 10 *Perf. 14* Unwmkd.

B165 SP101 1s+10s dk. green 90 1.10

No. 467 Surcharged in Black

1946, June 25

B166 A110 30g+20g dk. red 1.10 1.35

First anniversary of United Nations.

Pres. Karl Renner
SP102

1946 Engraved. *Perf. 13½x14.*

B167 SP102 1s+1s dark slate green 2.85 3.65

B168 SP102 2s+2s dark blue violet 2.85 3.65
B169 " 3s+3s dk. pur. 2.85 3.65
B170 " 5s+5s dark vio. brown 2.85 3.65

See also Nos. B185–B188.

Nazi Sword Piercing Austria SP103 — Sweeping Away Fascist Symbols SP104

Designs: 8g + 6g, St. Stephen's Cathedral in Flames. 12g+12g, Pleading hand in concentration camp. 30g + 30g, Hand choking Nazi serpent. 42g + 42g, Hammer breaking Nazi pillar. 1s + 1s, Oath of allegiance. 2s + 2s, Austrian eagle and burning swastika.

Photogravure

1946, Sept. 16 *Perf. 14* Unwmkd.

B171 SP103 5(g)+3(g) dark brown 60 80
B172 SP104 6(g)+4(g) dark slate green 45 60
B173 " 8(g)+6(g) orange red 45 60
B174 " 12(g)+12(g) slate black 45 60
B175 " 30(g)+30(g) violet 45 60
B176 " 42(g)+42(g) dull brown 45 60
B177 " 1s+1s dark red 55 75
B178 " 2s+2s dark carmine rose 65 90
Nos. B171-B178 (8) 4.05 5.45

Issued as anti-fascist propaganda.

Race Horse with Foal—SP111

Engraved.

1946, Oct. 20 *Perf. 13½x14*

Various Race Horses.

B179 SP111 16g+16g rose brn. 2.90 3.50
B180 " 24g+24g dk. pur. 2.50 3.00
B181 " 60g+60g dk. green 2.50 3.00
B182 " 1s+1s dark blue gray 2.50 3.00
B183 " 2s+2s yel. brn. 3.85 5.00
Nos. B179-B183 (5) 14.25 17.50

Austria Prize race, Vienna.

St. Ruprecht's Church, Vienna
SP116

1946, Oct. 30 *Perf. 14x13½*

B184 SP116 30g+70g dark red 45 60

Issued to commemorate the 950th anniversary of the founding of Austria. The surtax aided the Stamp Day celebration.

Souvenir Sheets.

President Karl Renner
SP117

1946, Sept. 5 *Imperf.*

B185 SP117 1s+1s dark slate green 800.00 900.00
a. Single stamp 75.00 85.00
B186 " 2s+2s dark blue violet 800.00 900.00
a. Single stamp 75.00 85.00
B187 " 3s+3s dark purple 800.00 900.00
a. Single stamp 75.00 85.00
B188 " 5s+5s dark violet brown 800.00 900.00
a. Single stamp 75.00 85.00

First anniversary of Austria's liberation. Sheets of 8. Size: 180x153mm.

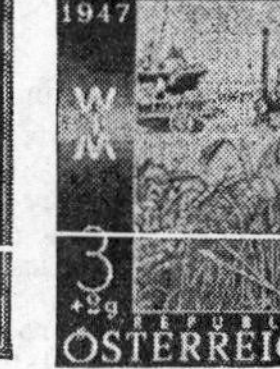

Statue of Rudolf IV the Founder SP118 — Reaping Wheat SP128

Designs: 5g+20g, Tomb of Frederick III. 6g+24g, Main pulpit. 8g+32g, Statue of St. Stephen. 10g+40g, Madonna of the Domestics statue. 12g+48g, High altar. 30g+1.20s, Organ, destroyed in 1945. 50g+1.80s, Anton Pilgram statue. 1s+5s, Cathedral from northeast. 2s+10s, Southwest corner of cathedral.

Engraved.

1946, Dec. 12 *Perf. 14x13½*

B189 SP118 3g+12g brown 25 32
B190 " 5g+20g dark violet brown 25 32
B191 " 6g+24g dark bl. 25 32
B192 " 8g+32g dk. grn. 25 32
B193 " 10g+40g deep bl. 35 45
B194 " 12g+48g dk. vio. 45 65
B195 " 30g+1.20s car. 1.60 2.10
B196 " 50g+1.80s dark blue 2.00 2.65
B197 " 1s+5s brown violet 2.85 3.50
B198 " 2s+10s violet brown 4.75 5.75
Nos. B189-B198 (10) 13.00 16.38

The surtax aided reconstruction of St. Stephen's Cathedral, Vienna.

1947, Mar. 23 *Perf. 14x13½*

Designs: 8g+2g, Log raft. 10g+5g, Cement factory. 12g+8g, Coal mine. 18g+12g, Oil derricks. 30g+10g, Textile machinery. 35g+15g, Iron furnace. 60g+20g, Electric power lines.

B199 SP128 3g+2g yel. brn. 45 55
B200 " 8g+2g dark blue green 45 55
B201 " 10g+5g slate black 45 55
B202 " 12g+8g dk. purple 45 55
B203 " 18g+12g olive grn. 45 55
B204 " 30g+10g dp. claret 45 55
B205 " 35g+15g crimson 45 55
B206 " 60g+20g dark blue 45 55
Nos. B199-B206 (8) 3.60 4.40

Vienna International Sample Fair, 1947.

Race Horse and Jockey
SP136

1947, June 29 *Perf. 13½x14*

B207 SP136 60g+20g dp. blue, *pale pink* 17 22

Cup of Corvinus SP137 — Prisoner of War SP147

Designs: 8g+2g, Statue of Providence, Vienna. 10g+5g, Abbey at Melk. 12g+8g, Picture of a Woman, by Kriehuber. 18g+12g, Children at the Window, by Waldmuller. 20g+10g, Entrance, Upper Belvedere Palace. 30g+10g, Nymph Egeria, Schönbrunn Castle. 35g+15g, National Library, Vienna. 48g+12g, "Workshop of a Printer of Engravings," by Schmutzer. 60g+20g, Girl with Straw Hat, by Amerling.

1947, June 20 *Perf. 14x13½*

B208 SP137 3g+2g brown .35 45
B209 " 8g+2g dark blue green 35 45
B210 " 10g+5g dp. claret 35 45
B211 " 12g+8g dark pur. 35 45
B212 " 18g+12g golden brown 35 45
B213 " 20g+10g sepia 35 45
B214 " 30g+10g dark yellow green 35 45
B215 " 35g+15g deep carmine 35 45
B216 " 48g+12g dark brown violet 35 45
B217 " 60g+20g dp. blue 50 65
Nos. B208-B217 (10) 3.65 4.70

1947, Aug. 30

Desigus: 12g+8g, Prisoners' Mail, 18g+12g, Prison camp visitor. 35g + 15g, Family reunion. 60g+20g, "Industry" beckoning. 1s+40g, Sower.

B218 SP147 8g+2(g) dark green 18 22
B219 " 12g+8(g) dark violet brown 28 32
B220 " 18g+12(g) black brown 18 22
B221 " 35g+15(g) rose brown 18 22
B222 " 60g+20(g) deep blue 18 22
B223 " 1s+40(g) reddish brown 20 30
Nos. B218-B223 (6) 1.20 1.50

Olympic Flame and Emblem SP153 — Laabenbach Bridge Neulengbach SP154

1948, Jan. 16 Engraved.

B224 SP153 1s+50g dark blue 45 35

The surtax was used to help defray expenses of Austria's 1948 Olympics team.

1948, Feb. 18 *Perf. 14x13½*

Designs: 20g+10g, Dam, Vermunt Lake. 30g+10g, Danube Port, Vienna. 40g+20g, Mining, Erzberg. 45g+20g, Tracks, Southern Railway Station, Vienna. 60g + 30g, Communal housing project, Vienna. 75g+35g, Gas Works, Vienna. 80g+40g, Oil refinery. 1s+50g, Gesäuse Highway, Styria. 1.40s+70g, Parliament Building, Vienna.

B225 SP154 10g+5g slate blk. 30 27
B226 " 20g+10g lilac 30 30
B227 " 30g+10g dull grn. 45 50
B228 " 40g+20g olive brn. 22 20
B229 " 45g+20g dark blue 9 9
B230 " 60g+30g dark red 10 8
B231 " 75g+35g dark violet brown 12 12
B232 " 80g+40g vio. brn. 12 15
B233 " 1s+50g dp. blue 15 15
B234 " 1.40s+70g dp. car. 38 45
Nos. B225-B234 (10) 2.23 2.31

The surtax was for the Reconstruction Fund.

Violet
SP155

Designs: 20g+10g, Anemone. 30g+10g, Crocus. 40g+20g, Yellow primrose. 45g+20g, Pasqueflower. 60g + 30g, Rhododendron. 75g + 35g, Dogrose. 80g + 40g, Cyclamen. 1s + 50g, Alpine Gentian. 1.40s + 70g, Edelweiss.

Engraved and Typographed.

1948, May 14 Unwmkd.

B235 SP155 10g+5g multi. 33 16
B236 " 20g+10g " 13 10
B237 " 30g+10g " 4.50 2.75
B238 " 40g+20g " 65 50
B239 " 45g+20g " 15 15
B240 " 60g+30g " 20 18
B241 " 75g+35g " 20 18
B242 " 80g+40g " 40 35
B243 " 1s+50g " 32 32
B244 " 1.40s+70g " 1.15 1.05
Nos. B235-B244 (10) 8.03 5.74

Hans Makart SP156 — St. Rupert SP157

Designs: 20g+10g, Künstlerhaus, Vienna. 40g+20g, Carl Kundmann. 50g+25g, A. S. von Siccardsburg. 60g+30g, Hans Cannon. 1s+50g, William Unger. 1.40s+70g, Friedrich von Schmidt.

1948, June 15 Engraved

B245 SP156 20g+10g deep yellow green 5.50 5.25
B246 " 30g+15g dk. brn. 2.10 2.10
B247 " 40g+20g indigo 2.10 2.10
B248 " 50g+25g dark violet 5.50 5.25
B249 " 60g+30g dark red 5.50 5.25
B250 " 1s+50g dk. blue 5.50 5.25
B251 " 1.40s+70g red brn. 13.50 13.50
Nos. B245-B251 (7) 39.70 38.70

Issued to commemorate the 80th anniversary of the Kunstlerhaus, home of the leading Austrian Artists Association.

1948, Aug. 6 *Perf. 14x13½*

Designs: 30g + 15g, Cathedral and Fountain. 40g+20g, Facade of Cathedral. 50g+25g, Cathedral from South. 60g+30g, Abbey of St. Peter. 80g + 40g, Inside Cathedral. 1s + 50g, Salzburg Cathedral and Castle. 1.40s + 70g, Madonna by Michael Pacher.

B252 SP157 20g+10g dp. grn. 6.25 5.25
B253 " 30g+15g red brn. 3.25 3.00

B254 SP157 40g+20g slate blk. 3.25 3.25
B255 " 50g+25g chocolate 55 60
B256 " 60g+30g dark red 55 60
B257 " 80g+40g dark brown violet 55 60
B258 " 1s+50g deep blue 85 85
B259 " 1.40s+70g dk. green 1.40 1.50
Nos. B252–B259 (8) 16.65 15.65

The surtax was to aid in the reconstruction of Salzburg Cathedral.

Easter SP158 — Arms of Austria, 1230 SP159

Designs: 60g + 20g, St. Nicholas Day. 1s+25g, Birthday. 1.40s+35g, Christmas.

1949, Apr. 13 **Unwmkd.**

Inscribed: "Glückliche Kindheit".

B260 SP158 40g+10g brown violet 14.00 13.50
B261 " 60g+20g brn. red 14.00 13.50
B262 " 1s+25g deep ultramarine 14.00 13.50
B263 " 1.40s+35g dk. grn. 15.00 13.50

The surtax was for Child Welfare.

1949, Aug. 17

Designs: 60g+15g, Arms, 1450. 1s+25g, Arms, 1600. 1.60s+40g, Arms, 1945.

Engraved and Photogravure.

B264 SP159 40g+10g yellow brown & yellow 7.50 7.50

Engraved and Typographed.

B265 SP159 60g+15g brn. car. & salmon 6.75 6.50
B266 " 1s+25g dp. blue & vermilion 6.75 6.50
B267 " 1.60s+40g deep green & salmon 7.25 6.75

The surtax was for returned prisoners of war.

Laurel Branch, Stamps and Magnifier
SP160

1949, Dec. 3 Engraved

B268 SP160 60g+15g dk. red 2.75 2.50

Stamp Day, Dec. 3–4.

Arms of Austria and Carinthia SP161 — Carinthian with Austrian Flag SP162

Design: 1.70s+40g, Casting ballot.

Photogravure.

1950, Oct. 10 ***Perf. 14x13½***

B269 SP161 60g+15g blue grn. & chocolate 32.50 28.50
B270 SP162 1s+25g red orange & red 35.00 29.00
B271 " 1.70s+40g dp. blue & greenish bl. 37.50 32.50

Issued to mark the 30th anniversary of the plebiscite in Carinthia.

Collector Examining Cover SP163 — Miner and Mine SP164

1950, Dec. 2 **Engraved**

B272 SP163 60g+15g blue green 9.50 8.00

Stamp Day.

1951, Mar. 10 **Unwmkd.**

Designs: 60g + 15g, Mason holding brick and trowel. 1s + 25g, Bridge builder with hook and chain. 1.70s+40g, Electrician, pole and insulators.

B273 SP164 40g+10g dark brown 14.00 13.50
B274 " 60g+15g dark green 14.00 13.50
B275 " 1s+25g red brn. 14.00 14.50
B276 " 1.70s+40g violet blue 14.00 14.50

Issued to publicize Austrian reconstruction.

Laurel Branch and Olympic Circles
SP165

1952, Jan. 26 ***Perf. 13½x14***

B277 SP165 2.40s+60g greenish black 18.50 18.00

The surtax was used to help defray expenses of Austria's athletes in the 1952 Olympic Games.

Cupid as Postman
SP166

1952, Mar. 10 ***Perf. 14x13½***

B278 SP166 1.50s+35g dark brn. carmine 20.00 20.00

Stamp Day.

Sculpture, "Christ, The Almighty"
SP167

1952, Sept. 6 ***Perf. 13½x14***

B279 SP167 1s+25g greenish gray 11.50 11.00

Issued to publicize the Austrian Catholic Convention, Vienna, Sept. 11-14, 1952.

Type of 1945-46 Overprinted in Gold

1953, Aug. 29 **Unwmkd.**

B280 A124 1s+25g on 5s dull blue 4.25 4.25

Issued to commemorate the 60th anniversary of labor unions in Austria.

Bummerlhaus Steyr SP168 — Globe and Philatelic Accessories SP169

Designs: 1s+25g, Johannes Kepler. 1.50s+40g, Lutheran Bible, 1st edition. 2.40s+60g, Theophil von Hansen. 3s+75g, Reconstructed Lutheran School, Vienna.

1953, Nov. 5 **Engr.** ***Perf. 14x13½***

B281 SP168 70g+15g vio. brn. 35 28
B282 " 1s+25g dark gray blue 35 35
B283 " 1.50s+40g chocolate 1.00 45
B284 " 2.40s+60g dk. grn. 3.75 4.00
B285 " 3s+75g dark purple 8.00 8.50
Nos. B281–B285 (5) 13.45 13.58

The surtax was used toward reconstruction of the Lutheran School, Vienna.

1953, Dec. 5

B286 SP169 1s+25g choc. 5.75 5.75

Stamp Day.

Type of 1945-46 with Denomination Replaced by Asterisks

Surcharged in Brown — LAWINENOPFER 1954 1s + 20g

1954, Feb. 19 ***Perf. 13½x14***

B287 A124 1s+20g blue gray 32 12

The surtax was used for aid to avalanche victims.

Patient Under Sun Lamp
SP170

Designs: 70g+15g, Physician using microscope. 1s+25g, Mother and children. 1.45s+35g, Operating room. 1.50s+35g, Baby on scale. 2.40s+60g, Nurse.

1954 **Engraved.** ***Perf. 14x13½.***

B288 SP170 30g+10g purple 1.50 1.10
B289 " 70g+15g dk. brn. 20 14
B290 " 1s+25g dk. blue 27 20
B291 " 1.45s+35g dark blue green 33 27
B292 " 1.50s+35g dk. red 5.25 5.50
B293 SP170 2.40s+60g dark red brown 6.25 6.50
Nos. B288–B293 (6) 13.80 13.71

The surtax was for social welfare.

Early Vienna-Ulm Ferryboat
SP171

1954, Dec. 4 ***Perf. 13½x14***

B294 SP171 1s+25g dark gray green 5.75 5.75

Stamp Day.

"Industry" Welcoming Returned Prisoner of War
SP172

1955, June 29

B295 SP172 1s+25g red brn. 2.75 2.50

The surtax was for returned prisoners of war and relatives of prisoners not yet released.

Collector Looking at Album SP173 — Ornamental Shield and Letter SP174

1955, Dec. 3 ***Perf. 14x13½***

B296 SP173 1s+25g violet brown 4.25 4.00

Issued for the Day of the Stamp. The surtax was for the promotion of Austrian philately.

1956, Dec. 1 **Engraved**

B297 SP174 1s+25g scarlet 4.25 3.50

Stamp Day. See note after No. B296.

Arms of Austria, 1945
SP175

Engraved and Typographed

1956, Dec. 21 ***Perf. 14x13½***

B298 SP175 1.50s+50g on 1.60s+40g gray & red 45 32

The surtax was for Hungarian refugees.

New Post Office, Linz 2
SP176

1957, Nov. 30 Engr. *Perf. 13½x14*
B299 SP176 1s+25g dark slate green 4.35 4.25

Stamp Day. See note after No. B296.

1958, Dec. 6
Design: 2.40s+60g, Post office, Kitzbuhel.
B300 SP176 2.40s+60g blue 1.40 1.35

Stamp Day. See note after B296. See also No. B303.

Roman Carriage from Tomb at Maria Saal
SP177

Lithographed and Engraved
1959, Dec. 5 *Perf. 13½x14*
B301 SP177 2.40s+60g pale lilac & black 1.00 1.00

Stamp Day.

Progressive Die Proof under Magnifying Glass
SP178

1960, Dec. 2 Engr. *Perf. 13½x14*
B302 SP178 3s+70g violet brown 1.30 1.30

Stamp Day.

P. O. Type of 1957
Design: 3s+70g, Post Office, Rust.
1961, Dec. 1 *Perf. 13½*
B303 SP176 3s+70g dark blue green 1.25 1.25

Stamp Day. See note after No. B296.

Hands of Stamp Engraver at Work—SP179

1962, Nov. 30 *Perf. 13½x14*
B304 SP179 3s+70g dull pur. 1.90 1.90

Stamp Day.

Railroad Exit, Post Office Vienna 101—SP180

Lithographed and Engraved
1963, Nov. 29 Unwmkd.
B305 SP180 3s+70g tan & blk. 1.00 1.00

Stamp Day.

View of Vienna, North
SP181

Designs: Various views of Vienna with compass indicating direction.

1964, July 20 Litho. *Perf. 13½x14*
Multicolored

B306	SP181	1.50s+30g ("N")	25	25
B307	"	1.50s+30g ("NO")	25	25
B308	"	1.50s+30g ("O")	25	25
B309	"	1.50s+30g ("SO")	25	25
B310	"	1.50s+30g ("S")	25	25
B311	"	1.50s+30g ("SW")	25	25
B312	"	1.50s+30g ("W")	25	25
B313	"	1.50s+30g ("NW")	25	25
		Nos. B306-B313 (8)	2.00	2.00

Issued to publicize the Vienna International Philatelic Exhibition (WIPA 1965).

Post Bus Terminal, St. Gilgen, Wolfgangsee—SP182

1964, Dec. 4 *Perf. 13½* Unwmkd.
B314 SP182 3s+70g multi. 55 55

Stamp Day.

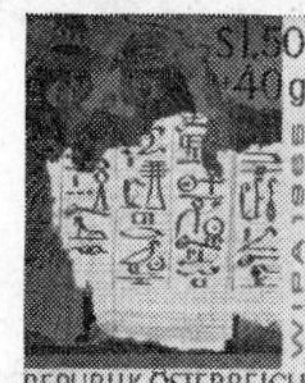

Wall Painting, Tomb at Thebes
SP183

Development of Writing: 1.80s+50g, Cuneiform writing on stone tablet and man's head from Assyrian palace. 2.20s+60g, Wax tablet with Latin writing, Corinthian column. 3s+80g, Gothic writing on sealed letter, Gothic window from Munster Cathedral. 4s+1s, Letter with seal and postmark and upright desk. 5s+1.20s, Typewriter.

Lithographed and Engraved
1965, June 4 *Perf. 14x13½*

B315	SP183	1.50s+40g deep rose & black	18	18
B316	"	1.80s+50g yellow & black	25	25
B317	"	2.20s+60g pale violet & black	90	90
B318	"	3s+80g apple grn. & black	35	35
B319	"	4s+1s light blue & black	1.20	1.20
B320	"	5s+1.20s bright green & blk.	1.35	1.35
		Nos. B315-B320 (6)	4.23	4.23

Issued to commemorate the Vienna International Philatelic Exhibition, WIPA, June 4-13.

Mailman Distributing Mail
SP184

Perf. 13½x14
1965, Dec. 3 Engraved Unwmkd.
B321 SP184 3s+70g blue grn. 50 50

Stamp Day.

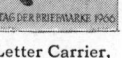

Letter Carrier, 16th Century
SP185

Letter Carrier, 16th Century Playing Card
SP186

Lithographed and Engraved
1966, Dec. 2 *Perf. 13½* Unwmkd.
B322 SP185 3s+70g multi. 50 50

Stamp Day. Design is from Ambras Heroes' Book, Austrian National Library.

Engraved and Photogravure
1967, Dec. 1 *Perf. 13x13½*
B323 SP186 3.50s+80g multi. 65 60

Stamp Day.

Mercury, Bas-relief from Purkersdorf
SP187

Unken Post Station Sign, 1710
SP188

1968, Nov. 29 Engr. *Perf. 13½*
B324 SP187 3.50s+80g slate green 65 65

Stamp Day.

Engraved and Photogravure
1969, Dec. 5 *Perf. 12*
B325 SP188 3.50s+80g tan, red & black 60 55

Stamp Day. Design is from a watercolor by Friedrich Zeller.

Saddle, Bag, Harness and Post Horn
SP189

Engraved and Lithographed
1970, Dec. 4 *Perf. 13½x14*
B326 SP189 3.50s+80g gray, black & yel. 60 55

Stamp Day.

"50 Years"
SP190

Engraved and Photogravure
1971, Dec. 3 *Perf. 13½*
B327 SP190 4s+1.50s gold & red brown 80 75

50th anniversary of the Federation of Austrian Philatelic Societies.

Local Post Carrier
SP191

Gabriel, by Lorenz Luchsperger, 15th Century
SP192

1972, Dec. 1 Engraved *Perf. 14x13½*
B328 SP191 4s+1s olive green 70 65

Stamp Day.

1973, Nov. 30
B329 SP192 4s+1s maroon 70 65

Stamp Day.

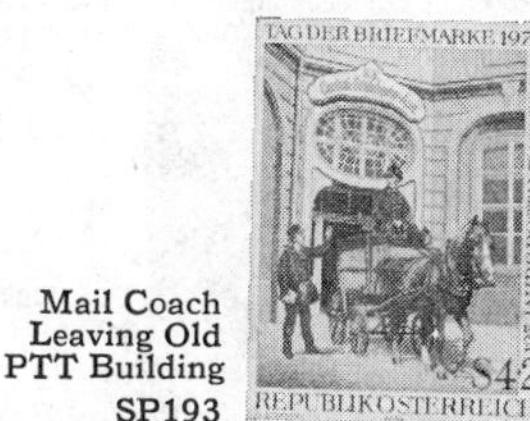

Mail Coach Leaving Old PTT Building
SP193

1974, Nov. 29 Engr. *Perf. 14x13½*
B330 SP193 4s+2s vio. blue 80 75

Stamp Day.

Alpine Skiing, Women's
SP194

Designs (Innsbruck Winter Olympic Games Emblem and): 1.50s+70g, Ice hockey. 2s+90g, Ski jump. 4s+1.90s, Bobsledding.

1975, Mar. 14 Photo. *Perf. 13½x14*

B331	SP194	1s+50g	multi.	27	27
B332	"	1.50s+70g	"	35	35
B333	"	2s+90g	"	45	45
B334	"	4s+1.90s	"	85	85

1975, Nov. 14

Designs (Innsbruck Winter Olympic Games Emblem and): 70g+30g, Figure skating, pair. 2s+1s, Cross-country skiing. 2.50s+1s, Luge. 4s+2s, Biathlon.

B335	SP194	70g+30g	multi.	20	20
B336	"	2s+1s	"	45	45
B337	"	2.50s+1s	"	52	52
B338	"	4s+2s	"	85	85

12th Winter Olympic Games, Innsbruck, Feb. 4-15, 1976.

Austria Nos. 5, 250, 455
SP195

Photogravure and Engraved
1975, Nov. 28 *Perf. 14*
B339 SP195 4s+2s multi. 80 75

Stamp Day and 125th anniversary of Austrian stamps.

Postilion's Gala Hat and Horn
SP196

1976, Dec. 3 ***Perf. 13½x14***

B340 SP196 6s+2s black & lt. vio. 1.00 1.00

Stamp Day 1976.

Emanuel Herrmann
SP197

1977, Dec. 2 ***Perf. 14x13½***

B341 SP197 6s+2s multi. 1.00 1.00

Stamp Day 1977. Emanuel Herrmann (1839–1902), economist, invented postal card. Austria issued first postal card in 1869.

Post Bus, 1913
SP198

1978, Dec. 1 Photo. ***Perf. 13½x14***

B342 SP198 10s+5s multi. 1.80 1.80

Stamp Day 1978.

AIR POST STAMPS.
Issues of the Monarchy.

FLUGPOST

Types of Regular Issue of 1916 Surcharged

2·50 K 2·50

Perf. 12½.

1918, Mar. 30 Unwmkd.

C1 A40 1.50k on 2k lilac 3.50 4.00
C2 " 2.50k on 3k ochre 13.75 20.00
a. Inverted surch. 1500.00
b. Perf. 11½ 400.00 250.00
c. Perf. 12½x11½ 35.00 30.00

Overprinted FLUGPOST

C3 A40 4k gray 8.25 10.00

Set exists imperf. Price, $500.

Nos. C1–C3 also exist without surcharge or overprint. Price, set perf., $900; imperf., $750.

Nos. C1–C3 were printed on grayish and on white paper.

A 7k on 10k red brown was prepared but not regularly issued. Price, perf. or imperf., $600.

Issues of the Republic.

Hawk AP1 — Wilhelm Kress AP2

1922–24 Typographed *Perf. 12½*

C4 AP1 300k claret 25 40
C5 " 400k green ('24) 5.50 7.00
C6 " 600k bistre 15 27
C7 " 900k brown orange 15 27

Engraved

C8 AP2 1200k brown violet 15 30
C9 " 2400k slate 15 30
C10 " 3000k dp. brn. ('23) 2.50 3.50
C11 " 4800k dk. blue ('23) 2.75 3.75
Nos. C4–C11 (8) 11.60 15.79

Set exists imperf. Price, $900.

Plane and Pilot's Head AP3 — Airplane Passing Crane AP4

1925–30 Typographed *Perf. 12½*

C12 AP3 2g gray brown 75 75
C13 " 5g red 33 20
a. Horizontal pair, imperf. between 350.00
C14 " 6g dark blue 1.75 1.25
C15 " 8g yellow green 1.60 1.00
C16 " 10g dp. orange ('26) 2.50 1.15
a. Horiz. pair, imperf. between 350.00
C17 " 15g red violet ('26) 70 50
a. Horiz. pair, imperf. between 450.00
C18 " 20g orange brown ('30) 15.00 6.00
C19 " 25g black violet ('30) 5.00 4.75
C20 " 30g bistre ('26) 11.00 7.50
C21 " 50g blue gray ('26) 25.00 13.50
C22 " 80g dark green ('30) 3.25 2.75

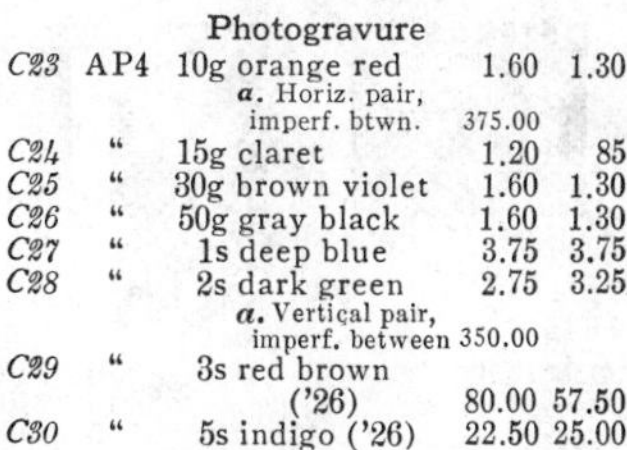

Photogravure

C23 AP4 10g orange red 1.60 1.30
a. Horiz. pair, imperf. btwn. 375.00
C24 " 15g claret 1.20 85
C25 " 30g brown violet 1.60 1.30
C26 " 50g gray black 1.60 1.30
C27 " 1s deep blue 3.75 3.75
C28 " 2s dark green 2.75 3.25
a. Vertical pair, imperf. between 350.00
C29 " 3s red brown ('26) 80.00 57.50
C30 " 5s indigo ('26) 22.50 25.00

Size: 25½x32mm.

C31 AP4 10s black brown, *gray* ('26) 16.50 18.50
Nos. C12–C31 (20) 198.38 152.10

Set exists imperf. Price, $1,250.

Airplane over Güssing Castle AP5 — Airplane over the Danube AP6

Designs (each includes plane): 10g, Maria-Worth. 15g, Durnstein. 20g, Hallstatt. 25g, Salzburg. 30g, Upper Dachstein and Schladminger Glacier. 40g, Lake Wetter. 50g, Arlberg. 60g, St. Stephen's Cathedral. 80g, Church of the Minorites. 2s, Railroad viaduct, Carinthia. 3s, Gross Glockner mountain. 5s, Aerial railway. 10s, Seaplane and yachts.

1935, Aug. 16 Engraved. *Perf. 12½.*

C32 AP5 5g rose violet 28 20
C33 " 10g red orange 15 15
C34 " 15g yellow green 1.65 1.65
C35 " 20g gray blue 25 25
C36 " 25g violet brown 25 25
C37 " 30g brown orange 25 25
C38 " 40g gray green 25 27
C39 " 50g light slate blue 28 30
C40 " 60g black brown 65 60
C41 " 80g light brown 60 45
C42 AP6 1s rose red 65 50
C43 " 2s olive green 4.00 4.25
C44 " 3s yel. brown 19.00 20.00
C45 " 5s dark green 6.50 7.00
C46 " 10s slate blue 82.50 100.00
Nos. C32–C46 (15) 117.26 136.12

Set exists imperf. Price, $425.

Windmill, Neusiedler Lake Shore AP20

Designs: 1s, Roman arch, Carnuntum. 2s, Town Hall, Gmund. 3s, Schieder Lake, Hinterstoder. 4s, Praegraten, Eastern Tyrol. 5s, Torsäule, Salzburg. 10s, St. Charles Church, Vienna.

1947 *Perf. 14x13½* Unwmkd.

C47 AP20 50g black brown 25 32
C48 " 1s dk. brn. violet 30 40
C49 " 2s dark green 50 60
C50 " 3s chocolate 2.65 3.00
C51 " 4s dark green 1.50 1.85
C52 " 5s dark blue 1.50 1.85
C53 " 10s dark blue 90 1.15
Nos. C47–C53 (7) 7.60 9.17

Rooks AP27

Birds: 1s, Barn swallows. 2s, Black-headed gulls. 3s, Great cormorants. 5s, Buzzard. 10s, Gray heron. 20s, Golden eagle.

1950–53 *Perf. 13½x14*

C54 AP27 60g dark blue violet 2.75 2.75
C55 " 1s dark violet blue ('53) 30.00 26.50
C56 " 2s dark blue 12.00 8.00
C57 " 3s dark slate green ('53) 120.00 110.00
C58 " 5s red brn. ('53) 115.00 115.00
C59 " 10s gray vio. ('53) 47.50 35.00
C60 " 20s brn. black ('52) 8.25 4.00
Nos. C54–C60 (7) 335.50 301.25

Value at lower left on Nos. C59 and C60.
No. C60 exists imperf.

Etrich "Dove" AP28

Designs: 3.50s, Twin-engine jet airliner. 5s, Four-engine jet airliner.

1968, May 31 Engr. *Perf. 13½x14*

C61 AP28 2s olive bister 42 55
C62 " 3.50s slate green 72 85
C63 " 5s dark blue 95 1.10

Issued to publicize IFA WIEN 1968 (International Air Post Exhibition), Vienna, May 30–June 4.

POSTAGE DUE STAMPS.
Issues of the Monarchy.

D1 — D2

Wmkd.
ZEITUNGS-MARKEN. (91)

1894–95 Typo. *Perf. 10 to 13½*

J1 D1 1kr brown 2.75 1.10
a. Perf. 13½ 27.50 8.00
J2 " 2kr brown ('95) 5.00 1.10
a. Vert. pair, imperf. btwn. 225.00 250.00
J3 " 3kr brown 4.50 38
J4 " 5kr brown 4.25 38
a. Perf. 13½ 19.00 8.00
b. Vertical pair, imperf. between 200.00 225.00
J5 " 6kr brown ('95) 4.25 3.50
J6 " 7kr brown ('95) 1.00 1.50
a. Vertical pair, imperf. between 250.00 275.00
J7 " 10kr brown 7.50 38
J8 " 20kr " 1.10 2.25
J9 " 50kr " 55.00 45.00
Nos. J1–J9 (9) 85.35 55.59

See also Nos. J204–J231.

1899–1900 *Imperf.*

J10 D2 1h brown 32 35
J11 " 2h " 32 35
J12 " 3h " ('00) 27 22
J13 " 4h " 4.50 1.40
J14 " 5h " ('00) 3.85 30
J15 " 6h " 38 1.00
J16 " 10h " 38 33
J17 " 12h " 65 3.00
J18 " 15h " 65 1.50
J19 " 20h " 30.00 2.85
J20 " 40h " 1.40 3.00
J21 " 100h " 5.75 2.25
Nos. J10–J21 (12) 48.47 16.55

Perf. 10½, 12½, 13½ and Compound.

J22 D2 1h brown 85 22
J23 " 2h " 70 17
J24 " 3h " ('00) 60 9
J25 " 4h " 60 9
J26 " 5h " ('00) 45 9
J27 " 6h " 45 12
J28 " 10h " 65 8
J29 " 12h " 70 55
J30 " 15h " 70 38
J31 D2 20h brown 80 33
J32 " 40h " 1.20 55
J33 " 100h " 26.50 1.50
Nos. J22–J33 (12) 34.20 4.17

Nos. J10 to J33 exist on unwatermarked paper.

D3

1908–13 *Perf. 12½* Unwmkd.

J34 D3 1h carmine 1.50 90
J35 " 2h " 50 33
J36 " 4h " 30 10
J37 " 6h " 30 10
J38 " 10h " 60 10
J39 " 14h " ('13) 5.00 1.35
J40 " 20h " 7.50 10
J41 " 25h " ('10) 13.00 2.75
J42 " 30h " 9.00 10
J43 " 50h " 13.50 17
J44 " 100h " 19.00 22
Nos. J34–J44 (11) 70.20 6.22

All values exist on ordinary paper, Nos. J34 to J38, J40 and J42 to J44 on chalky paper and Nos. J34 to J38, J40 and J44 on thin ordinary paper. All values exist imperforate.

1911

J45 D3 5k violet 60.00 11.00
J46 " 10k violet 325.00 3.85

Regular Issue of 1908 Overprinted or Surcharged in Carmine or Black:

a — b

1916

J47 A22 (*a*) 1h gray (C) 17 4
a. Pair, one without overprint 165.00
J48 " (*b*) 15h on 2h violet (Bk) 50 27

D4 — D5

1916

J49 D4 5h rose red 7 5
J50 " 10h " 7 5
J51 " 15h " 7 5
J52 " 20h " 6 4
J53 " 25h " 40 38
J54 " 30h " 10 8
J55 " 40h " 13 8
J56 " 50h " 1.10 1.35
J57 D5 1k ultramarine 27 5
a. Horizontal pair, imperf. btwn. 550.00 550.00
J58 " 5k ultramarine 2.25 2.25
J59 " 10k " 2.25 1.10
Nos. J49–J59 (11) 6.77 5.48

Set exists imperf. Price $135.

PORTO

Type of Regular Issue of 1916 Surcharged

15 ✻ 15

1917

J60 A38 10h on 24h blue 3.25 27
J61 " 15h on 36h violet 60 10

No.	Type	Description	Unused	Used
J62	A38	20h on 54h orange	55	17
J63	"	50h on 42h chocolate	55	10

All values of this issue are known imperforate, also without surcharge, perforated and imperforate.

Issues of the Republic.

Postage Due Stamps of 1916 Overprinted

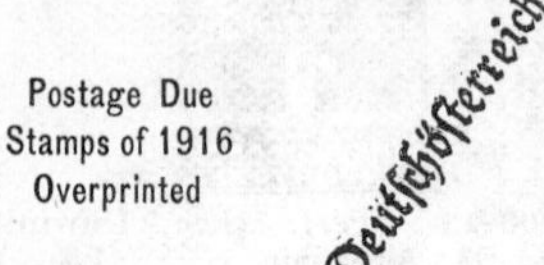

1919

No.	Type	Description	Unused	Used
J64	D4	5h rose red	22	27
		a. Inverted ovpt.	275.00	275.00
J65	"	10h rose red	22	27
J66	"	15h "	27	40
J67	"	20h "	50	75
J68	"	25h "	11.00	16.50
J69	"	30h "	27	40
J70	"	40h "	27	40
J71	"	50h "	42	75
J72	D5	1k ultramarine	9.00	8.00
J73	D3	5k "	10.50	8.00
J74	"	10k "	13.50	4.25
		Nos. J64-J74 (11)	46.17	39.99

Nos. J64, J65, J67 and J70 exist imperforate.

D6

D7

1920-21 *Perf. 12½.*

No.	Type	Description	Date	Unused	Used
J75	D6	5h bright red		9	27
J76	"	10h "		3	8
J77	"	15h "		5	55
J78	"	20h "		3	10
J79	"	25h "		11	55
J80	"	30h "		5	17
J81	"	40h "		3	5
J82	"	50h "		3	5
J83	"	80h "		3	5
J84	D7	1k ultramarine		5	6
J85	"	1½k "	('21)	5	6
J86	"	2k "	('21)	5	6
J87	"	3k "	('21)	5	27
J88	"	4k "	('21)	5	27
J89	"	5k "		5	17
J90	"	8k "	('21)	3	27
J91	"	10k "		5	17
J92	"	20k "	('21)	30	65
		Nos. J75-J92 (18)		1.13	3.85

Nos. J84 to J92 exist on white paper and on grayish white paper. They also exist imperf.; price, set $80.

Imperf.

No.	Type	Description	Unused	Used
J93	D6	5h bright red	8	12
J94	"	10h "	6	8
J95	"	15h "	7	8
J96	"	20h "	6	8
J97	"	25h "	7	8
J98	"	30h "	6	8
J99	"	40h "	6	8
J100	"	50h "	6	8
J101	"	80h "	6	8
		Nos. J93-J101 (9)	58	76

No. 237 Surcharged in Dark Blue

Nachmarke

7½K

Thin, Grayish Cardboard.

1921 *Perf. 12½*

No.	Type	Description	Unused	Used
J102	A447	7½k on 15h bistre	5	7
		a. Inverted surch.	300.00	300.00

D8

1922

No.	Type	Description	Unused	Used
J103	D8	1k reddish buff	5	7
J104	"	2k "	5	7
J105	"	4k "	5	7
J106	"	5k "	5	7
J107	"	7½k "	5	7
J108	"	10k blue green	5	9
J109	"	15k "	6	7
J110	"	20k "	9	9
J111	"	25k "	7	9
J112	"	40k "	7	9
J113	"	50k "	7	9
		Nos. J103-J113 (11)	66	87

Nos. J103 to J113 exist imperforate.

D9

D10

1922-24

No.	Type	Description	Date	Unused	Used
J114	D9	10k cobalt blue		9	10
J115	"	15k "		7	9
J116	"	20k "		10	10
J117	"	50k "		6	9
J118	D10	100k plum		3	3
J119	"	150k "		3	3
J120	"	200k "		3	3
J121	"	400k "		4	4
J122	"	600k "	('23)	7	7
J123	"	800k "		6	5
J124	"	1.000k "	('23)	10	5
J125	"	1.200k "	('23)	45	60
J126	"	1.500k "	('24)	15	13
J127	"	1.800k "	('24)	1.80	2.35
J128	"	2.000k "	('23)	30	32
J129	"	3.000k "	('24)	4.50	5.25
J130	"	4.000k "	('24)	3.85	4.50
J131	"	6.000k "	('24)	3.85	4.50
		Nos. J114-J131 (18)		15.58	18.33

Set exists imperf. Price, $375.

D11

D12

1925-34 *Perf. 12½*

No.	Type	Description	Date	Unused	Used
J132	D11	1g red		8	6
J133	"	2g "		8	6
J134	"	3g "		9	8
J135	"	4g "		12	8
J136	"	5g "	('27)	8	6
J137	"	6g "		30	33
J138	"	8g "		25	17
J139	"	10g dark blue		12	6
J140	"	12g "		12	6
J141	"	14g "	('27)	25	8
J142	"	15g "		15	6
J143	"	16g "	('29)	42	10
J144	"	18g "	('34)	1.35	3.25
J145	"	20g "		15	6
J146	"	23g "		1.20	6
J147	"	24g "	('32)	2.00	6
J148	"	28g "	('27)	45	12
J149	"	30g "		30	8
J150	"	31g "	('29)	1.10	10
J151	"	35g "	('30)	85	7
J152	"	39g "	('32)	2.25	5
J153	"	40g "		1.35	1.35
J154	"	60g "		1.20	80
J155	D12	1s dark green		5.25	55
J156	"	2s "		40.00	3.25
J157	"	5s "		130.00	30.00
J158	"	10s "		65.00	3.25
		Nos. J132-J158 (27)		254.51	44.25

Issues of 1925-27 (21 values) exist imperf. Price, set $500.

Coat of Arms

D13 D14

1935

No.	Type	Description	Unused	Used
J159	D13	1g red	10	10
J160	"	2g "	10	10
J161	"	3g "	10	10
J162	"	5g "	8	5
J163	"	10g blue	8	5
J164	"	12g "	8	5
J165	"	15g "	20	80
J166	"	20g "	10	5
J167	"	24g "	13	5
J168	"	30g "	20	6
J169	"	39g "	22	3
J170	"	60g "	45	1.35
J171	D14	1s green	70	33
J172	"	2s "	1.35	80
J173	"	5s "	2.65	1.35
J174	"	10s "	3.85	65
		Nos. J159-J174 (16)	10.39	5.92

On Nos. J163-J170, background lines are horizontal.

Nos. J159-J174 exist imperf. Price, set $125.

Coat of Arms

D15 D16

Typographed.

1945 *Perf. 10½* **Unwmkd.**

No.	Type	Description	Unused	Used
J175	D15	1g vermilion	3	3
J176	"	2g "	3	3
J177	"	3g "	3	3
J178	"	5g "	3	3
J179	"	10g "	3	3
J180	"	12g "	7	10
J181	"	20g "	3	7
J182	"	24g "	9	10
J183	"	30g "	4	7
J184	"	60g "	4	7
J185	"	1s violet	5	7
J186	"	2s "	6	7
J187	"	5s "	8	14
J188	"	10s "	12	15
		Nos. J175-J188 (14)	73	99

Occupation Stamps of the Allied Military Government Overprinted in Black

PORTO

1946 *Perf. 11.*

No.	Type	Description	Unused	Used
J189	OS1	3g deep orange	5	5
J190	"	5g bright green	5	5
J191	"	6g red violet	8	8
J192	"	8g rose pink	5	5
J193	"	10g light gray	5	5
J194	"	12g pale buff brown	5	5
J195	"	15g rose red	8	8
J196	"	20g copper brown	5	5
J197	"	25g deep blue	8	8
J198	"	30g bright violet	5	5
J199	"	40g light ultramarine	7	7
J200	"	60g light olive green	5	5
J201	"	1s dark violet	10	10
J202	"	2s yellow	28	28
J203	"	5s deep ultramarine	28	28
		Nos. J189-J203 (15)	1.37	1.37

Nos. J189-J203 were issued by the Renner Government. Inverted overprints exist on about half of the denominations.

Type of 1894-95.

Inscribed "Republik Osterreich".

1947 Typographed *Perf. 14*

No.	Type	Description	Unused	Used
J204	D1	1g chocolate	3	3
J205	"	2g "	3	3
J206	"	3g "	3	3
J207	"	5g "	3	3
J208	"	8g "	3	3
J209	"	10g "	4	4
J210	"	12g "	3	3
J211	D1	15g chocolate	3	3
J212	"	16g "	18	20
J213	"	17g "	18	20
J214	"	18g "	18	20
J215	"	20g "	35	3
J216	"	24g "	25	27
J217	"	30g "	15	15
J218	"	36g "	42	42
J219	"	40g "	3	3
J220	"	42g "	40	40
J221	"	48g "	40	40
J222	"	50g "	48	6
J223	"	60g "	12	12
J224	"	70g "	7	7
J225	"	80g "	4.25	3.75
J226	"	1s blue	10	3
J227	"	1.15s "	2.10	20
J228	"	1.20s "	2.35	65
J229	"	2s "	18	12
J230	"	5s "	25	12
J231	"	10s "	30	15
		Nos. J204-J231 (28)	12.99	7.82

1949-57

No.	Type	Description	Date	Unused	Used
J232	D16	1g carmine		12	6
J233	"	2g "		12	6
J234	"	4g "	('51)	42	15
J235	"	5g "		1.10	20
J236	"	8g "	('51)	1.30	1.10
J237	"	10g "		3	3
J238	"	20g "		3	3
J239	"	30g "		4	3
J240	"	40g "		6	3
J241	"	50g "		6	3
J242	"	60g "	('50)	6.00	20
J243	"	63g "	('57)	1.80	1.30
J244	"	70g "		8	3
J245	"	80g "		10	10
J246	"	90g "	('50)	12	12
J247	"	1s purple		12	3
J248	"	1.20s "		15	10
J249	"	1.35s "		18	7
J250	"	1.40s "	('51)	25	15
J251	"	1.50s "	('53)	18	3
J252	"	1.65s "	('50)	18	18
J253	"	1.70s "		18	18
J254	"	2s "		27	5
J255	"	2.50s "	('51)	30	5
J256	"	3s "	('51)	35	6
J257	"	4s "	('51)	50	30
J258	"	5s "		60	10
J259	"	10s "		1.25	15
		Nos. J232-J259 (28)		15.89	4.92

MILITARY STAMPS.

Issues of the Austro-Hungarian Military Authorities for the Occupied Territories in World War I.

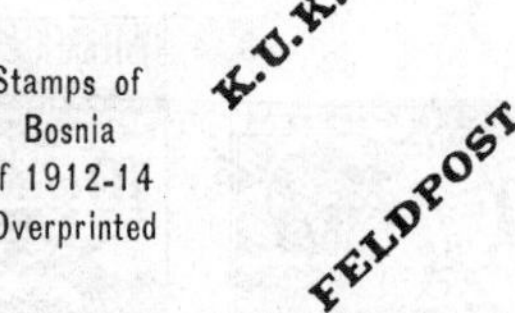

Stamps of Bosnia of 1912-14 Overprinted

1915 *Perf. 12½* **Unwmkd.**

No.	Type	Description	Unused	Used
M1	A23	1h olive green	25	22
M2	"	2h bright blue	25	22
M3	"	3h claret	25	22
M4	"	5h green	15	17
M5	"	6h dark gray	25	22
M6	"	10h rose carmine	15	17
M7	"	12h deep olive green	35	33
M8	"	20h orange brown	55	38
M9	"	25h ultramarine	55	33
M10	"	30h orange red	4.25	4.50
M11	A24	35h myrtle green	3.75	3.75
M12	"	40h dark violet	3.75	3.75
M13	"	45h olive brown	4.00	4.00
M14	"	50h slate blue	3.75	3.75
M15	"	60h brown violet	55	55
M16	"	72h dark blue	3.75	3.75
M17	A25	1k brown violet, *straw*	4.25	4.50
M18	"	2k dark gray, *blue*	4.25	3.75
M19	A26	3k carmine, *green*	37.50	40.00
M20	"	5k dark violet, *gray*	37.50	40.00

M21 A25 10k dark ultramarine, *gray* 250.00 250.00
Nos. M1-M21 (21) 360.05 364.56

Set exists imperf. Price, $450.

Nos. M1–M21 also exist with overprint double, inverted and in red. These varieties were made by order of an official but were not regularly issued.

Emperor Franz Josef
M1 M2

1915-17 Engraved.

Perf. 11½, 12½ and Compound.

M22 M1 1h olive green 11 9
M23 " 2h dull blue 17 13
M24 " 3h claret 11 9
M25 " 5h green 11 9
  a. Perf. 11½ 27.50 11.50
  b. Perf. 11½x12½ 40.00 19.00
  c. Perf. 12½x11½ 65.00 32.50
M26 " 6h dark gray 11 9
M27 " 10h rose carmine 17 9
M28 " 10h gray blue ('17) 17 13
M29 " 12h deep olive green 17 18
M30 " 15h carmine rose ('17) 6 5
  a. Perf. 11½ 11.00 8.00
M31 " 20h orange brown 45 22
M32 " 20h olive green ('17) 45 22
M33 " 25h ultramarine 22 17
M34 " 30h vermilion 22 18
M35 " 35h dark green 40 45
M36 " 40h dark violet 40 45
M37 " 45h olive brown 38 45
M38 " 50h myrtle green 38 27
M39 " 60h brown violet 38 38
M40 " 72h dark blue 38 38
M41 " 80h orange brown ('17) 22 17
M42 " 90h magenta ('17) 1.10 1.10
M43 M2 1k brown violet, *straw* 2.75 1.65
M44 " 2k dark gray, *blue* 1.80 75
M45 " 3k carmine, *green* 1.25 1.20
M46 " 4k dark violet, *gray* ('17) 1.25 1.20
M47 " 5k dk violet, *gray* 37.50 32.50
M48 " 10k dark ultramarine, *gray* 4.25 5.50
Nos. M22-M48 (27) 54.96 48.18

Nos. M22–M48 exist imperf. Price, set $80.

Emperor Karl I
M3 M4

1917–18 ***Perf. 12½***

M49 M3 1h greenish blue ('18) 6 5
  a. Perf. 11½ 4.50 3.25
M50 " 2h red orange ('18) 8 5
M51 " 3h olive gray 8 5
  a. Perf. 11½, 11½x12½ 13.50 11.00
M52 " 5h olive green 8 5
M53 " 6h violet 12 5
M54 " 10h orange brown 8 5
M55 " 12h blue 8 8
  a. Perf. 11½ 3.75 3.25
M56 " 15h bright rose 8 5
M57 " 20h red brown 7 5
M58 " 25h ultramarine 50 22
M59 " 30h slate 12 7
M60 " 40h olive bistre 12 7
  a. Perf. 11½ 2.25 1.75
M61 " 50h deep green 12 7
  a. Perf. 11½ 6.50 5.50
M62 " 60h carmine rose 12 12
M63 " 80h dull blue 10 5
M64 " 90h dark violet 55 38
M65 M4 2k rose, *straw* 12 5
  a. Perf. 11½ 2.50 2.25
M66 M4 3k green, *blue* 1.35 1.10
M67 " 4k rose, *green* 27.50 16.50
  a. Perf. 11½ 47.50 37.50
M68 " 10k dull violet, *gray* 3.50 3.75
  a. Perf. 11½ 16.50 15.00
Nos. M49-M68 (20) 34.83 22.86

Nos. M49–M68 exist imperf. Price, set $27.50.

Emperor Karl I
M5

1918 Typographed ***Perf. 12½***

M69 M5 1h greenish blue 50.00
M70 " 2h orange 22.50
M71 " 3h olive gray 22.50
M72 " 5h yellow green 27
M73 " 10h dark brown 27
M74 " 20h red 1.65
M75 " 25h blue 1.65
M76 " 30h bistre 110.00
M77 " 45h dark slate 165.00
M78 " 50h deep green 110.00
M79 " 60h violet 165.00
M80 " 80h rose 110.00
M81 " 90h brown violet 3.25

Engraved.

M82 M4 1k olive bistre, *blue* 27
M69-82 (14) 762.36

Nos. M69–M82 were on sale at the Vienna post office for a few days before the Armistice signing. They were never issued at the Army Post Offices. They exist imperf.; price, set $950.

MILITARY SEMI-POSTAL STAMPS.

Emperor Karl I Empress Zita
MSP7 MSP8

Typographed

1918 ***Perf. 12½x13*** **Unwmkd.**

MB1 MSP7 10h gray green 55 32
MB2 MSP8 20h magenta 55 32
MB3 MSP7 45h blue 55 32

These stamps were sold at a premium of 10h each over face value. The surtax was for "Karl's Fund."

Nos. MB1–MB3 exist imperf. Price, set $11.

MILITARY NEWSPAPER STAMPS.

Mercury
MN1

Typographed

1916 ***Perf. 12½*** **Unwmkd.**

MP1 MN1 2h blue 9 7
  a. Perf. 11½ 1.65 1.35
  b. Perf. 12½x11½ 65.00 32.50
MP2 " 6h orange 1.10 55
MP3 " 10h carmine 1.35 55
MP4 " 20h brown 90 45
  a. Perf. 11½ 2.25 1.65

Set exists imperf. Price, $42.50.

NEWSPAPER STAMPS.

From 1851 to 1866, the Austrian Newspaper Stamps were also used in Lombardy-Venetia.

Prices for unused stamps 1851–67 are for fine copies with original gum. Specimens without gum sell for about a third of the figures quoted.

Issues of the Monarchy.

Mercury
N1

Typographed.

Machine-made Paper.

Two Types.

Type I. The "G" of "Zeitungs" has no crossbar.
Type II. The "G" of "Zeitungs" has a crossbar.

1851–56 ***Imperf.*** **Unwmkd.**

P1 N1 (0.6kr) bl., type II 175.00 90.00
  a. blue, type I 200.00 135.00
  b. Ribbed paper 450.00 200.00
P2 N1 (6kr) yellow, type I *12,000.00 6000.00*
P3 " (30kr) rose, type I *17,500.00 8500.00*
P4 " (6kr) scarlet, type II ('56) *30,000.00 35,000.00*

From 1852 No. P3 and from 1856 No. P2 were used as 0.6 kreuzer values.

Pale shades of Nos. P2 and P3 sell at considerably lower prices.

Originals of Nos. P2 and P3 are usually in pale colors and poorly printed. Prices are for stamps clearly printed and in bright colors. Numerous reprints of Nos. P1 to P4 were made between 1866 and 1904. Those of Nos. P2 and P3 are always well printed and in much deeper colors. All reprints are in type I, but occasionally show faint traces of a crossbar on "G" of "ZEITUNGS."

N2 N3

Two Types of the 1858–59 Issue

Type I. Loops of the bow at the back of the head broken.

Type II. Loops complete. Wreath projects further at top of head.

1858–59 Embossed

P5 N2 (1kr) bl., type I 550.00 650.00
P6 " (1kr) lilac, type II ('59) 800.00 325.00

1861

P7 N3 (1kr) gray 175.00 150.00
  a. (1kr) gray lilac 500.00 225.00
  b. (1kr) dp. lilac 2250.00 800.00

The embossing on the reprints of the 1858–59 and 1861 issues is not as sharp as on the originals.

N4

1863

Unwmkd., or, after June 1864, Wmkd. "ZEITUNGS-MARKEN" in Double-lined Capitals across the Sheet. (91)

P8 N4 (1.05kr) gray 32.50 13.00
  a. Tête bêche pair *20,000.00*
  b. (1.05kr) gray lilac 65.00 22.50

The embossing of the reprints is not as sharp as on the originals.

Mercury
N5 N6

Typographed.

Wmkd. "ZEITUNGS-MARKEN" in Double-lined Capitals across the Sheet. (91)

Three Types.

Type I. Helmet not defined at back, more or less blurred. Two thick short lines in front of wing of helmet. Shadow on front of face not separated from hair.

Type II. Helmet distinctly defined. Four thin short lines in front of wing. Shadow on front of face clearly defined from hair.

Type III. Outer white circle around head is open at top (closed on types I and II). Greek border at top and bottom is wider than on types I and II.

1867-73 Coarse Print.

P9 N5 (1kr) violet, type I 55.00 2.25
  a. (1kr) violet, type II ('73) 225.00 15.00

1874-76 Fine Print.

P9B N5 (1kr) violet, type III ('76) 2.25 17
  c. (1kr) gray lilac, type I ('76) 165.00 22.50
  d. (1kr) violet, type II 45.00 3.75
  e. Double impression, type III 225.00

Stamps of this issue, except No. P9Bc, exist in many shades, from gray to lilac brown and deep violet. Stamps in type III exist also privately perforated or rouletted.

1880

P10 N6 ½kr green 7.00 75

Nos. P9B and P10 also exist on thicker paper without sheet watermark and No. P10 exists with unofficial perforation.

N7

1899 ***Imperf.*** **Unwmkd.**

Without Varnish Bars.

P11 N7 2h dark blue 27 5
P12 " 6h orange 4.25 1.35
P13 " 10h brown 1.60 80
P14 " 20h rose 2.50 1.30

1901 With Varnish Bars

P11a N7 2h dark blue 1.10 17
P12a " 6h orange 13.50 10.00
P13a " 10h brown 12.50 7.50
P14a " 20h rose 25.00 21.00

Nos. P11 to P14 were re-issued in 1905.

Mercury
N8 N9

1908 ***Imperf.***

P15 N8 2h dark blue 75 5
  a. Tête bêche pair 400.00 400.00
P16 " 6h orange 2.75 27
P17 " 10h carmine 2.75 27
P18 " 20h brown 2.75 22

All values are found on chalky, regular and thin ordinary paper. They exist privately perforated.

1916 ***Imperf.***

P19 N9 2h brown 5 5
P20 " 4h green 40 60
P21 " 6h dark blue 38 90
P22 " 10h orange 45 55
P23 " 30h claret 45 80
Nos. P19-P23 (5) 1.73 2.90

Issues of the Republic.

Newspaper Stamps of 1916 Overprinted

1919

P24	N9	2h brown	5	5
P25	"	4h green	27	60
P26	"	6h dark blue	20	90
P27	"	10h orange	42	60
P28	"	30h claret	23	90
		Nos. P24-P28 (5)	1.17	3.05

Mercury

N10 N11

1920-21 *Imperf.*

P29	N10	2h violet	3	5
P30	"	4h brown	3	6
P31	"	5h slate	3	6
P32	"	6h turquoise blue	3	6
P33	"	8h green	3	7
P34	"	9h yellow ('21)	3	6
P35	"	10h red	3	7
P36	"	12h blue	3	12
P37	"	15h lilac ('21)	3	5
P38	"	18h blue green ('21)	8	12
P39	"	20h orange	12	10
P40	"	30h yel. brown ('21)	12	12
P41	"	45h green ('21)	7	12
P42	"	60h claret	12	10
P43	"	72h chocolate ('21)	7	17
P44	"	90h violet ('21)	15	20
P45	"	1.20k red ('21)	7	20
P46	"	2.40k yel. green ('21)	7	20
P47	"	3k gray ('21)	11	23
		Nos. P29-P47 (19)	1.25	2.16

Nos. P37-P40, P42, P44 and P47 exist also on thick gray paper.

1921-22

P48	N11	45h gray	5	9
P49	"	75h brown orange ('22)	5	15
P50	"	1.50k olive bistre ('22)	5	15
P51	"	1.80k gray blue ('22)	5	15
P52	"	2.25k light brown	5	15
P53	"	3k dull green ('22)	5	15
P54	"	6k claret ('22)	5	15
P55	"	7.50k bistre	9	15
		Nos. P48-P55 (8)	44	1.14

Nos. P24-P55 exist privately perforated.

NEWSPAPER TAX STAMPS.

Prices for unused stamps 1853-59 are for copies in fine condition with gum. Specimens without gum sell for about one-third of the figures quoted.

Issues of the Monarchy.

NT1 NT2

Typographed

1853 *Imperf.* **Unwmkd.**

PR1	NT1	2kr green	1500.00	55.00

The reprints are in finer print than the more coarsely printed originals, and on a smooth toned paper.

Unwmkd. or, after June 1864, Wmkd. ZEITUNGS-MARKEN. (91)

1858-59

Two Types.

Type I. The banderol on the Crown of the left eagle touches the beak of the eagle.

Type II. The banderol does not touch the beak.

PR2	NT2	1kr blue, type II ('59)	27.50	5.50
		a. 1kr blue, type I	675.00	130.00
		b. Printed on both sides, type II		
PR3	"	2kr brown, type II ('59)	22.50	6.00
		a. 2kr red brown, type II	375.00	115.00
PR4	"	4kr brn., type I	450.00	*1000.00*

Nos. PR2a, PR3a, and PR4 were printed only on unwatermarked paper. Nos. PR2 and PR3 exist on unwatermarked and watermarked paper.

Nos. PR2 and PR3 exist in coarse and (after 1874) in fine print, like the contemporary postage stamps.

The reprints of the 4kr brown are of type II and on a smooth toned paper.

NT3 NT4

1877 **Redrawn.**

PR5	NT3	1kr blue	16.50	90
		a. 1kr pale ultramarine		*1100.00*
PR6	"	2kr brown	13.50	1.00

In the redrawn stamps the shield is larger and the vertical bar has eight lines above the white square and nine below, instead of five.

Nos. PR5 and PR6 exist also watermarked "WECHSEL" instead of "ZEITUNGS-MARKEN".

1890

PR7	NT4	1kr brown	13.50	85
PR8	"	2kr green	15.00	1.65

Nos. PR5 to PR8 exist with private perforation.

NT5

Wmkd. "STEMPEL-MARKEN" in Double-lined Capitals, across the Sheet. (91)

Perf. 13, 12½

PR9	NT5	25kr carmine	140.00	165.00

Nos. PR1 to PR9 did not pay postage, but were a fiscal tax, collected by the postal authorities on newspapers.

SPECIAL HANDLING STAMPS (For Printed Matter Only.)

Issues of the Monarchy.

Mercury

SH1

1916 ***Perf. 12½*** **Unwmkd.**

QE1	SH1	2h claret, *yellow*	60	1.10
QE2	"	5h deep green, *yellow*	60	1.10

SH2

1917 ***Perf. 12½***

QE3	SH2	2h claret, *yellow*	18	18
		a. Pair, imperf. between	375.00	375.00
		b. Perf. 11½x12½	75.00	75.00
		c. Perf. 12½x11½	110.00	110.00
		d. Perf. 11½	1.60	1.60
QE4	"	5h deep green, *yellow*	18	18
		a. Pair, imperf. between	350.00	350.00
		b. Perf. 11½x12½	75.00	75.00
		c. Perf. 12½x11½	110.00	110.00
		d. Perf. 11½	1.60	1.60

Nos. QE1-QE4 exist imperforate.

Issues of the Republic.

Nos. QE3 and QE4 Overprinted

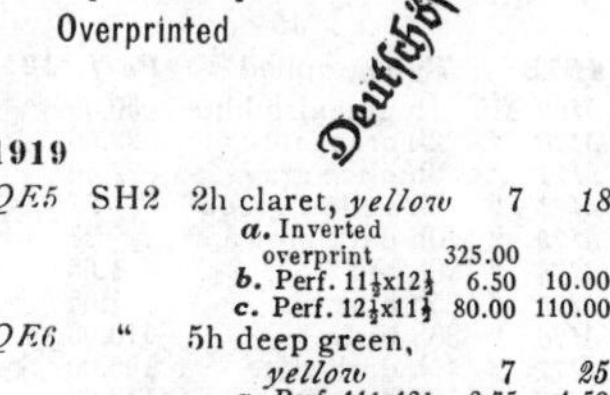

1919

QE5	SH2	2h claret, *yellow*	7	*18*
		a. Inverted overprint	325.00	
		b. Perf. 11½x12½	6.50	10.00
		c. Perf. 12½x11½	80.00	110.00
QE6	"	5h deep green, *yellow*	7	*25*
		a. Perf. 11½x12½	2.75	4.50
		b. Perf. 12½x11½	32.50	47.50

Nos. QE5 and QE6 exist imperforate.

SH3

1921 **Dark Blue Surcharge.**

QE7	SH3	50h on 2h claret, *yellow*	6	9

SH4

1922 ***Perf. 12½***

QE8	SH4	50h lilac, *yellow*	6	*1.00*

Nos. QE5 to QE8 exist in vertical pairs, imperforate between. No. QE8 exists imperforate.

OCCUPATION STAMPS.

Issued under Italian Occupation.

Issued in Trieste.

Austrian Stamps of 1916-18 Overprinted

Regno d'Italia
Venezia Giulia
3. XI. 18.

1918 ***Perf. 12½.*** **Unwmkd.**

N1	A37	3h bright violet	20	20
		a. Double overprint	15.00	15.00
		b. Inverted ovpt.	15.00	15.00
N2	"	5h light green	10	10
		a. Inverted ovpt.	15.00	15.00
		b. "3.XI." omitted	12.00	12.00
		c. Double overprint		15.00
N3	"	6h deep orange	50	50
N4	"	10h magenta	10	10
		a. Inverted overprint	9.00	9.00
N5	"	12h light blue	1.20	1.20
		a. Double overprint	15.00	15.00
N6	A42	15h dull red	10	10
		a. Inverted ovpt.	15.00	15.00
		b. Double overprint	15.00	15.00
		c. "3.XI." omitted	12.00	12.00
N7	"	20h dark green	10	10
		a. Inverted ovpt.	9.00	3.00
		b. "3.XI." omitted	12.00	12.00
		c. Double overprint	40.00	
N8	"	25h deep blue	3.25	3.25
		a. Inverted ovpt.	35.00	35.00
		b. "3.XI." omitted	60.00	60.00
N9	"	30h dull violet	60	60
N10	A39	40h olive green	40.00	40.00
N11	A39	50h dark green	1.10	1.10
N12	"	60h deep blue	2.00	2.00
N13	"	80h orange brown	1.10	1.10
		a. Inverted overprint		
N14	"	1k carmine, *yellow*	1.10	1.10
		a. Double ovpt.	25.00	25.00
N15	A40	2k light blue	85.00	75.00
N16	"	4k yellow green	150.00	140.00

Handstamped.

N17	A40	10k dp. violet	*13,000.00*	*13,000.00*

Granite Paper.

N18	A40	2k light blue		
N19	"	3k carmine rose	100.00	90.00

Some authorities question the authenticity of No. N18. Counterfeits of Nos. N10, N15-N19 are plentiful.

Italian Stamps of 1901-18 Overprinted

Venezia
Giulia

Wmkd. Crown. (140) ***Perf. 14.***

N20	A42	1c brown	18	18
		a. Inverted overprint	2.50	2.50
N21	A43	2c orange brown	18	18
		a. Inverted overprint	1.50	1.50
N22	A48	5c green	10	10
		a. Inverted overprint	3.00	3.00
		b. Double overprint	15.00	
N23	"	10c claret	10	10
		a. Inverted overprint	7.50	7.50
		b. Double overprint	15.00	
N24	A50	20c brown orange	10	10
		a. Inverted overprint	9.00	9.00
		b. Double overprint	15.00	15.00
N25	A49	25c blue	10	10
		a. Double overprint	50.00	
		b. Invtd. overprint	13.50	13.50
N26	"	40c brown	1.10	75
		a. Inverted overprint	40.00	
N27	A45	45c olive green	10	10
		a. Inverted overprint	13.50	13.50
N28	A49	50c violet	30	30
N29	"	60c brown carmine	5.50	4.50
N30	A46	1 l brown & green	2.25	1.50
		Nos. N20-N30 (11)	10.01	7.91

Italian Stamps of 1901-18 Surcharged

Venezia
Giulia
5 Heller

N31	A48	5h on 5c green	15	15
		a. "5" omitted	2.50	2.50
		b. Inverted surch.	7.00	7.00
N32	A50	20h on 20c brown orange	15	15
		a. Double surcharge	7.00	7.00

Issued in the Trentino.

Austrian Stamps of 1916-18 Overprinted

Regno d Italia
Trentino
3 nov 1918

1918 ***Perf. 12½*** **Unwmkd.**

N33	A37	3h bright violet	1.50	1.65
		a. Double ovpt.	25.00	25.00
		b. Inverted ovpt.	27.50	17.50
N34	"	5h light green	1.00	1.00
		a. "8 nov. 1918"	*250.00*	
		b. Inverted ovpt.	27.50	17.50
N35	"	6h deep orange	55.00	55.00
N36	"	10h magenta	1.00	1.25
		a. "8 nov. 1918"	30.00	25.00
N37	"	12h light blue	175.00	175.00
N38	A42	15h dull red	4.00	4.00
N39	"	20h dark green	35	35
		a. "8 nov. 1918"	40.00	35.00
		b. Double ovpt.	25.00	25.00
		c. Inverted ovpt.	12.50	12.50
N40	"	25h deep blue	30.00	30.00
N41	"	30h dull violet	6.00	6.00
N42	A39	40h olive green	55.00	55.00
N43	"	50h dark green	12.50	12.50
		a. Inverted ovpt.	50.00	50.00
N44	"	60h deep blue	35.00	35.00
		a. Double ovpt.	60.00	60.00
N45	"	80h orange brown	55.00	55.00
N46	"	90h red violet	*750.00*	*750.00*
N47	"	1k car., *yellow*	55.00	55.00
N48	A40	2k light blue	275.00	275.00
N49	"	4k yellow green	*1100.00*	*1100.00*
N50	"	10k deep violet	*32,500.00*	

Granite Paper.
N51 A40 2k light blue 275.00 300.00
Counterfeits of Nos. N33–N51 are plentiful.

Italian Stamps of 1901-18 Overprinted
Venezia Tridentina

Wmkd. Crown. (140) Perf. 14.
N52 A42 1c brown 15 18
a. Inverted overprint 6.00 6.00
N53 A43 2c orange brown 15 18
a. Inverted overprint 6.00 6.00
N54 A48 5c green 15 18
a. Inverted overprint 6.00 6.00
b. Double overprint 8.00 8.00
N55 " 10c claret 15 18
a. Inverted overprint 8.00 8.00
b. Double overprint 8.00 8.00
N56 A50 20c brown orange 15 18
a. Inverted overprint 8.00 8.00
N57 A49 40c brown 8.00 9.00
N58 A45 45c olive green 5.50 6.50
a. Double overprint 25.00 25.00
N59 A49 50c violet 5.50 6.50
N60 A46 1 l brown & green 6.00 7.00
a. Double overprint 25.00 25.00
Nos. N52-N60 (9) 25.75 29.90

Italian Stamps of 1906-18 Surcharged
Venezia Tridentina
5 Heller

N61 A48 5h on 5c green 15 18
N62 " 10h on 10c claret 15 18
a. Inverted overprint 10.00 10.00
N63 A50 20h on 20c brn. orange 15 18
a. Double surcharge 8.00 8.00

General Issue.

Italian Stamps of 1901-18 Surcharged
5 centesimi di corona

1919
N64 A42 1c on 1c brown 15 15
a. Inverted surcharge 1.25 1.25
N65 A43 2c on 2c orange brown 15 15
a. Double surcharge 25.00
b. Inverted surcharge 25 25
N66 A48 5c on 5c green 15 15
a. Inverted surcharge 2.25 2.25
b. Double surcharge 10.00 10.00
N67 " 10c on 10c claret 15 15
a. Inverted surcharge 2.25 2.25
b. Double surcharge 10.00 10.00
N68 A50 20c on 20c brown orange 15 15
a. Double surcharge 15.00 15.00
N69 A49 25c on 25c blue 15 15
a. Double surcharge 12.50 12.50
N70 " 40c on 40c brown 15 15
a. "ccrona" 4.00 4.00
N71 A45 45c on 45c olive green 15 15
a. Inverted surcharge 7.50 7.50
N72 A49 50c on 50c violet 15 15
N73 " 60c on 60c brown carmine 15 15
a. "00" for "60" 3.00 3.00

Surcharged:
1 corona

N74 A46 1 cor on 1 l brown & green 15 15
Nos. N64-N74 (11) 1.65 1.65
Surcharges similar to these but differing in style or arrangement of type were used in Dalmatia.

SPECIAL DELIVERY STAMPS.
Issued in Trieste.

Special Delivery Stamp of Italy of 1903 Overprinted
Venezia Giulia

Wmkd. Crown. (140)
1918 Perf. 14.
NE1 SD1 25c rose red 5.00 4.50
a. Invtd. ovpt. 25.00 25.00

General Issue.

Special Delivery Stamps of Italy of 1903-09 Surcharged
1919 25 centesimi di corona

NE2 SD1 25c on 25c rose 15 15
a. Double surcharge 6.00 6.00
NE3 SD2 30c on 30c blue & rose 15 15

POSTAGE DUE STAMPS.
Issued in Trieste.

Postage Due Stamps of Italy, 1870-94, Overprinted
Venezia Giulia

Wmkd. Crown. (140)
1918 Perf. 14.
NJ1 D3 5c buff & magenta 15 15
a. Inverted overprint 1.00 1.00
b. Double overprint 30.00
NJ2 D3 10c buff & magenta 15 15
a. Inverted overprint 6.00 5.00
NJ3 D3 20c buff & magenta 15 15
a. Double overprint 30.00
b. Inverted overprint 6.00 5.00
NJ4 D3 30c buff & magenta 30 30
NJ5 " 40c buff & magenta 1.65 1.65
a. Inverted overprint 30.00 30.00
NJ6 D3 50c buff & magenta 12.50 12.50
a. Inverted overprint 30.00 30.00
NJ7 D3 1 l blue & magenta 47.50 47.50
Nos. NJ1-NJ7 (7) 62.40 62.40

General Issue.

Postage Due Stamps of Italy, 1870–1903 Surcharged
5 centesimi di corona

1919
NJ8 D3 5c on 5c buff & magenta 15 15
a. Inverted overprint 65 65
NJ9 D3 10c on 10c buff & magenta 15 15
a. Center and surcharge invtd. 10.00 10.00
NJ10 D3 20c on 20c buff & magenta 15 15
a. Double overprint 16.50 16.50
NJ11 D3 30c on 30c buff & magenta 15 15
NJ12 " 40c on 40c buff & magenta 15 15
NJ13 " 50c on 50c buff & magenta 15 15

una
Surcharged
corona

NJ14 D3 1 cor on 1 l blue & magenta 15 15
NJ15 " 2 cor on 2 l blue & magenta 13.50 16.50
NJ16 " 5 cor on 5 l blue & magenta 13.50 16.50
Nos. NJ8-NJ16 (9) 28.05 34.05

A. M. G. Issue for Austria.

Issued jointly by the Allied Military Government of the United States and Great Britain, for civilian use in areas under American, British and French occupation. (Upper Austria, Salzburg, Tyrol, Vorarlberg, Styria and Carinthia).

OS1

Lithographed.
1945 Perf. 11. Unwmkd.
4N1 OS1 1g aquamarine 6 12
4N2 " 3g deep orange 3 3
4N3 " 4g buff 3 3
4N4 " 5g bright green 3 3
4N5 " 6g red violet 3 3
4N6 " 8g rose pink 3 3
4N7 " 10g light gray 3 3
4N8 " 12g pale buff brown 3 3
4N9 " 15g rose red 3 5
4N10 " 20g copper brown 3 5
4N11 " 25g deep blue 3 6
4N12 " 30g bright violet 3 3
4N13 " 40g light ultramarine 3 5
4N14 " 60g light olive green 3 8
4N15 " 1s dark violet 7 15
4N16 " 2s yellow 25 42
4N17 " 5s deep ultramarine 30 48
Nos. 4N1-4N17 (17) 1.07 1.70

AUSTRIAN OFFICES ABROAD
Offices in Crete.

100 CENTIMES=1 FRANC

These stamps were on sale and usable at all Austrian post-offices in Crete and in the Turkish Empire.

Used prices are italicized for stamps often found with false cancellations.

Stamps of Austria of 1899–1901 Issue, Surcharged in Black:

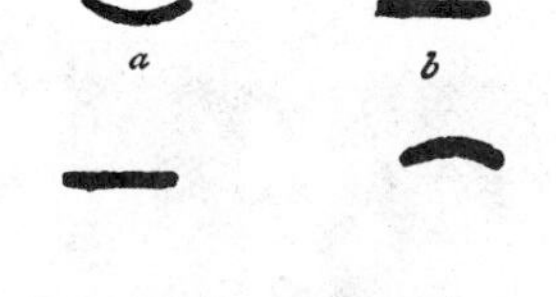

a b

FRANC
c d

Granite Paper.
1903–04 Perf. 12½, 13½ Unwmkd.
With Varnish Bars
(On Nos. 73a, 75a, 77a, 81a)
1 A15 (a) 5c on 5h blue green 2.25 3.25
2 A16 (b) 10c on 10h rose 1.10 3.75
3 " (") 25c on 25h ultra. 45.00 27.50
4 A17 (c) 50c on 50h gray blue 7.50 70.00

Without Varnish Bars
(On Nos. 83, 83a, 84, 85)
5 A18 (d) 1fr on 1k carmine rose 2.75 65.00
a. 1fr on 1k carmine 5.50
b. Horiz. or vert. pair, imperf. between 275.00
6 " (") 2fr on 2k gray lilac ('04) 13.50 160.00
7 " (") 4fr on 4k gray grn. ('04) 16.50 225.00

Surcharged on Austrian Stamps of 1904–05.
1905 Without Varnish Bars
(On Nos. 89, 97)
8 A19 (a) 5c on 5h bl. grn. 55.00 30.00
9 A20 (b) 10c on 10h car. 1.10 8.00

With Varnish Bars.
(On Nos. 89a, 97a, 99a, 103a)
8a A19 (a) 5c on 5h blue green 5.50 6.50
9a A20 (b) 10c on 10h carmine 22.50 22.50
10 A20 (b) 25c on 25h ultra. 80 65.00
11 A21 (") 50c on 50h dull blue 1.60 210.00

Surcharged on Austrian Stamps and Type of 1906-07.
1907 Perf. 12½, 13½.
Without Varnish Bars
12 A19 (a) 5c on 5h yellow green (#90) 1.10 5.50
13 A20 (b) 10c on 10h carmine (#92) 1.35 18.00
14 " (") 15c on 15h violet 1.65 20.00

A5

A6

1908 Typographed Perf. 12½
15 A5 5c green, *yellow* 55 45
16 " 10c scarlet, *rose* 65 65
17 " 15c brown, *buff* 75 4.25
18 " 25c deep blue, *blue* 16.50 4.25

Engraved.
19 A6 50c lake, *yellow* 2.75 27.50
20 " 1fr brown, *gray* 3.50 40.00
a. Vertical pair, imperf. between 225.00
Nos. 15-20 (6) 24.70 77.10

Nos. 15 to 18 are on paper colored on the surface only. All values exist imperforate.
Issued to commemorate the sixtieth year of the reign of Emperor Franz Josef, for permanent use.

Paper Colored Through.
1914 Typographed.
21 A5 10c rose, *rose* 2.75 1000.00
22 " 25c ultra., *blue* 1.10 110.00
Nos. 21 and 22 exist imperforate.

Offices in the Turkish Empire.

From 1863 to 1867 the stamps of Lombardy-Venetia (Nos. 15 to 24) were used at the Austrian Offices in the Turkish Empire.

Prices for unused stamps are for copies with gum. Specimens without gum sell for about one-third the figures quoted.
Used prices are italicized for stamps often found with false cancellations.

100 SOLDI=1 FLORIN
40 PARAS=1 PIASTRE

A1

A2

Typographed
Wmkd.
"BRIEF-MARKEN" in Double-lined Capitals, across the Sheet.
(91)

Two different printing methods were used, as in the 1867-74 issues of Austria. They may be distinguished by the coarse or fine lines of the hair and whiskers.

1867 Coarse Print. Perf. 9½.
1 A1 2sld orange 2.10 22.50
a. 2sld yellow 75.00 35.00
2 " 3sld green 110.00 38.50
a. 3sld dark green 130.00 47.50

3 A1 5sld red 110.00 13.50
a. 5sld carmine 120.00 22.50
4 " 10sld blue 110.00 1.60
a. 10sld light blue 120.00 2.75
b. 10sld dark blue 120.00 3.25
5 " 15sld brown 13.50 5.50
a. 15sld dark brown 55.00 16.00
b. 15sld reddish brn. 16.00 11.00
6 " 25sld gray lilac 11.00 *30.00*
a. 25sld brown violet 13.50 *35.00*
7 A2 50sld brown, perf. 10½ 1.10 *55.00*
a. Perf. 12 120.00 80.00
b. Perf. 13 375.00
k. Perf. 9 or 10½x9 35.00 65.00
l. 50sld pale red brown, perf. 12 90.00 70.00
m. Vertical pair, imperf. between 375.00 *1000.00*
n. Horiz. pair, imperf. btwn. 325.00 *800.00*

Fine Print.

Perf. 9, 9½, 10½ and Compound.

1876-83

7C A1 2sld yellow ('83) 32 *1650.00*
7D " 3sld green ('78) 1.65 *22.50*
7E " 5sld red ('78) 55 *16.50*
7F " 10sld blue 80.00 1.10
7I " 15sld orange brown ('81) 8.00 *135.00*
7J " 25sld gray lilac ('83) 80 *250.00*

The 10 soldi has been reprinted in deep dull blue, perforated 10½.

A3

1883 ***Perf. 9½, 10, 10½.***

8 A3 2sld brown 27 *110.00*
9 " 3sld green 1.35 *13.50*
10 " 5sld rose 27 *8.00*
11 " 10sld blue 1.10 55
12 " 20sld gray 1.65 *5.50*
13 " 50sld red lilac 1.65 *13.50*

A4

A5

10 PARAS ON 3 SOLDI:

Type I. Surcharge 16½mm. across. "PARA" about ½mm. above bottom of "10". 2mm. space between "10" and "P"; 1½mm. between "A" and "10". Perf. 9½ only.

Type II. Surcharge 15¼ to 16mm. across. "PARA" on same line with figures or slightly higher or lower. 1½mm. space between "10" and "P"; 1mm. between "A" and "10". Perf. 9½ and 10.

1886 ***Perf. 9½ and 10***

14 A4 10pa on 3sld green, type II 45 *5.50*
a. 10pa on 3sld green, type I 350.00 425.00
b. Inverted surcharge, type I *4000.00*

1888

15 A5 10pa on 3kr green 4.50 *5.50*
a. "01 PARA 10" *450.00*
16 " 20pa on 5kr rose 80 *6.50*
17 " 1pi on 10kr blue 65.00 1.10
a. Perf. 13½ 225.00
b. Double surcharge 225.00
18 " 2pi on 20kr gray 1.90 2.25
19 " 5pi on 50kr violet 2.75 *13.50*

A6

Granite Paper.

1890–92 ***Perf. 9 to 13½*** **Unwmkd.**

20 A6 8pa on 2kr brown ('92) 27 33
a. Perf. 9½ 5.50 3.25
21 A6 10pa on 3kr green 1.10 27
a. Pair, imperf. between 100.00
22 " 20pa on 5kr rose 27 27
23 " 1pi on 10kr ultra. 60 10
24 " 2pi on 20kr olive green 11.00 *27.50*
25 " 5pi on 50kr violet 17.50 *65.00*

See note after Austria No. 65 on missing numerals, etc.

A7

A8

1891 ***Perf. 9 to 13½***

26 A7 2pi on 20kr olive green 5.50 65
a. Perf. 9½ 135.00 22.50
27 A7 5pi on 50kr violet 4.50 2.25

There are two types of the surcharge on No. 26.

1892 ***Perf. 10½, 11½***

28 A8 10pi on 1gld blue 16.50 22.50
29 " 20pi on 2gld car. 17.50 *32.50*
a. Double surcharge

1896 ***Perf. 10½, 11½, 12½***

30 A8 10pi on 1gld pale lilac 16.50 22.50
31 " 20pi on 2gld gray green 55.00 55.00

A9

A10

A11

A12

Perf. 10½, 12½, 13½ and Compound.

1900 Without Varnish Bars

32 A9 10pa on 5h blue green 6.50 1.10
33 A10 20pa on 10h rose 6.50 1.10
a. Perf. 12½x10½ 375.00 50.00
34 A10 1pi on 25h ultra. 5.50 27
35 A11 2pi on 50h gray blue 11.00 2.25
36 A12 5pi on 1k carmine rose 1.35 27
a. 5pi on 1k carmine 1.65 1.10
b. Horiz. or vert. pair, imperf. between 175.00
37 " 10pi on 2k gray lilac 3.75 2.75
a. Horizontal pair, imperf. between
38 " 20pi on 4k gray green 2.75 *6.50*
Nos. 32-38 (7) 37.35 *14.24*

In the surcharge on Nos. 37 and 38 "piaster" is printed "PIAST."

1901 With Varnish Bars.

32a A9 10pa on 5h blue green 2.75 2.25
33a A10 20pa on 10h rose 2.75 *110.00*
34a " 1pi on 25h ultramarine 1.65 55
35a A11 2pi on 50h gray blue 3.50 2.25

A13

A14

A15

1906 ***Perf. 12½ to 13½***

Without Varnish Bars.

39 A13 10pa dark green 22.50 1.65
40 A14 20pa rose 1.35 55
41 " 1pi ultramarine 60 27
42 A15 2pi gray blue 1.65 80

1903 With Varnish Bars.

39a A13 10pa dark green 5.50 1.35
40a A14 20pa rose 3.50 55
41a " 1pi ultramarine 2.25 27
42a A15 2pi gray blue 165.00 1.65

1907 Without Varnish Bars.

43 A13 10pa yellow green 55 *2.25*
45 A14 30pa violet 1.00 *3.75*

A16

A17

1908 Typographed. ***Perf. 12½.***

46 A16 10pa green, *yellow* 17 17
47 " 20pa scarlet, *rose* 27 22
48 " 30pa brown, *buff* 38 80
49 " 1pi dp. blue, *blue* 20.00 6
50 " 60pa violet, *bluish* 55 *4.25*

Engraved

51 A17 2pi lake, *yellow* 42 17
52 " 5pi brown, *gray* 55 80
53 " 10pi green, *yellow* 1.10 *2.25*
54 " 20pi blue, *gray* 2.85 4.25
Nos. 46-54 (9) 26.29 *12.97*

Nos. 46 to 50 are on paper colored on the surface only. Issued in commemoration of the sixtieth year of the reign of Emperor Franz Josef I for permanent use. All values exist imperforate.

1913-14 Typographed

Paper Colored Through.

57 A16 20pa rose, *rose* ('14) 1.65 *325.00*
58 " 1pi ultramarine, *blue* 80 55

Nos. 57 and 58 exist imperforate.

POSTAGE DUE STAMPS.

D1

D2

Black Surcharge.

1902 ***Perf. 12½, 13½*** **Unwmkd.**

J1 D1 10pa on 5h green 1.65 *4.25*
J2 " 20pa on 10h " 1.65 *3.75*
J3 " 1pi on 20h " 2.75 *4.50*
J4 " 2pi on 40h " 2.75 4.25
J5 " 5pi on 100h green 3.50 2.25
Nos. J1-J5 (5) 12.30 19.00

Shades of Nos. J1 to J5 exist, varying from yellowish green to dark green.

1908 **Typographed.** ***Perf. 12½.***

J6 D2 ¼pi green 5.50 8.00
J7 " ½pi " 2.50 5.50
J8 " 1pi " 2.75 *8.00*
J9 " 1½pi " 1.10 *11.00*
J10 " 2pi " 3.85 *13.50*
J11 " 5pi " 3.85 *8.00*
J12 " 10pi " 27.50 *135.00*
J13 " 20pi " 22.50 *165.00*
J14 D2 30pi green 16.50 12.00
Nos. J6-J14 (9) 86.05

Nos. J6 to J14 exist in distinct shades of green and on thick chalky, regular and thin ordinary paper. All values exist imperforate.

LOMBARDY-VENETIA

(lŏm'bẽr·dĭ; lŭm'-·;
vẻ·nē'shĭ·ȧ;- shȧ)

Formerly a kingdom in the north of Italy forming part of the Austrian Empire. Milan and Venice were the two principal cities. Lombardy was annexed to Sardinia in 1859, and Venetia to the kingdom of Italy in 1866.

100 CENTESIMI = 1 LIRA
100 SOLDI = 1 FLORIN (1858)

Prices of the earliest Lombardy-Venetia stamps vary according to condition. Quotations for Nos. 1-6, PR1-PR3 are for fine copies. Very fine to superb specimens sell at much higher prices, and inferior or poor copies sell at reduced prices, depending on the condition of the individual specimen.

Prices for unused stamps are for fine copies with gum. Specimens without gum sell for about one-quarter of the prices quoted.

Coat of Arms
A1

15 CENTESIMI:

Type I. "5" of "15" is on a level with the "1."

Type II. "5" is a trifle sideways and is higher than the "1."

45 CENTESIMI:

Type I. Lower part of "45" is lower than "Centes."

Type II. Lower part of "45" is on a level with lower part of "Centes."

Wmkd. K. K. H. M. in Sheet or Unwmkd.

1850 Typographed ***Imperf.***

Thick to Thin Paper.

1 A1 5c buff 800.00 65.00
a. Printed on both sides *6750.00* 100.00
b. 5c yellow *4000.00* 425.00
c. 5c orange 1000.00 70.00
d. 5c lemon yellow *1000.00*
3 " 10c black 1100.00 50.00
a. 10c gray black 1400.00 65.00
4 " 15c pale red, type II 350.00 1.65
b. 15c red, type I *1500.00* 10.00
c. Ribbed paper, type II *10,000.00* 200.00
d. Ribbed paper, type I *4750.00* 55.00
e. Laid paper, type II *3750.00*
5 " 30c brown 1250.00 3.75
a. Ribbed paper 3000.00 35.00
6 " 45c blue, type II *3250.00* 11.00
a. 45c blue, type I *4500.00* 20.00
b. Ribbed paper, type I *13,000.00* 135.00

The note about the paper of the 1850 issue of Austria will also apply here. No. 1 and its minor varieties exist only on hand-made paper.

The reprints are in brighter colors.

A2

A3

A4

A5

A6

Two Types of Each Value.

Type I. Loops of the bow at the back of the head broken.

Type II. Loops complete. Wreath projects further at top of head.

1858-62 Embossed. ***Perf. 14½.***

7 A2 2s yellow, type II 325.00 60.00
- *a.* 2s yel., type I 950.00 300.00

8 A3 3s black, type II 1 450.00 100.00
- *a.* 3s black, type I 675.00 190.00
- *b.* Perf. 16, type I 650.00
- *c.* Perf. 15x16 or 16x15, type I *1350.00* 425.00

9 " 3s green, type II ('62) 275.00 55.00

10 A4 5s red, type II 140.00 3.75
- *a.* 5s red, type I 225.00 8.50
- *b.* Printed on both sides, type II *2000.00*

11 A5 10s brown, type II 650.00 8.50
- *a.* 10s brn., type I 190.00 35.00

12 A6 15s blue, type II 550.00 14.00
- *a.* 15s blue, type I 900.00 60.00

The reprints are of type II and are perforated 10½, 11, 11½, 12, 12½ and 13. There are also imperforate reprints of Nos. 7, 8 and 9.

A7

A8

1861-62 ***Perf. 14.***

13 A7 5s red 950.00 1.90
14 " 10s brown ('62) 850.00 20.00

The reprints are perforated 9, 9½, 10½, 11, 12, 12½ and 13. There are also imperforate reprints of the 2 and 3s.

The 2, 3 and 15s of this type exist only as reprints.

1863

15 A8 2s yellow 90.00 110.00
16 " 3s green 550.00 65.00
17 " 5s rose 600.00 11.00
18 " 10s blue *1650.00* 55.00
19 " 15s yellow brown 1150.00 90.00

Wmkd. "BRIEF-MARKEN" in Double-lined Capitals across the Sheet. (91)

1864-65 ***Perf. 9½.***

20 A8 2s yellow ('65) 85.00 *300.00*
21 " 3s green 15.00 13.00
22 " 5s rose 2.25 1.65
23 " 10s blue 15.00 5.50
24 " 15s yellow brown 27.50 26.00

The reprints are perforated 10½ and 13. There are also imperforate reprints of the 2s and 3s.

NEWSPAPER TAX STAMPS.

From 1853 to 1858 the Austrian Newspaper Tax Stamp 2kr green (No. PR1) was also used in Lombardy-Venetia, at the value of 10 centesimi.

NT1

Type I. The banderol of the left eagle touches the beak of the eagle.

Type II. The banderol does not touch the beak.

Typographed

1858-59 ***Imperf.*** **Unwmkd.**

PR1 NT1 1kr black, type I ('59) 1250.00 *3500.00*
PR2 " 2kr red, type II ('59) 200.00 60.00
PR3 NT1 4kr red, type I *40,000.00 3250.00*

No. PR2 exists also with watermark "ZEITUNGS-MARKEN" (91).

The reprints are on a smooth toned paper and are all of type II.

AZERBAIJAN

(ä'zĕr·bī'jan'; äz'ĕr-)

(Azerbaidjan)

LOCATION—Southernmost part of Russia in Eastern Europe. Bounded by Georgia, Dagestan, Caspian Sea, Persia and Armenia.

GOVT.—A Soviet Socialist Republic.

AREA—32,686 sq. mi.

POP.—2,096,973 (1923).

CAPITAL—Baku.

100 Kopecks = 1 Ruble

National Republic.

Standard Bearer
A1

Farmer at Sunset
A2

Baku
A3

Temple of Eternal Fires
A4

Lithographed

1919 ***Imperf.*** **Unwmkd.**

1 A1 10k multicolored 8 10
2 " 20k " 8 10
3 A2 40k grn., yel. & black 8 10
4 " 60k red, yellow & black 8 10
5 " 1r blue, yellow & blk. 12 20
6 A3 2r red, bistre & black 12 20
7 " 5r blue, bistre & black 20 35
8 " 10r olive green, bistre & black 25 40
9 A4 25r blue, red & black 50 70
10 " 50r olive green, red & black 60 90
Nos. 1-10 (10) 2.11 3.15

The two printings of Nos. 1-10 are distinguished by the grayish or thin white paper. Both have yellowish gum.

Soviet Socialist Republic.

Symbols of Labor
A5

Oil Well
A6

Bibi Eibatt Oil Field
A7

Khan's Palace, Baku
A8

Globe and Workers
A9

Maiden's Tower, Baku
A10

Blacksmiths
A12

Goukasoff House
A11

Hall of Judgment, Baku
A13

1922

15 A5 1r gray green 10 25
16 A6 2r olive black 10 25
17 A7 5r gray brown 10 25
18 A8 10r gray 25 30
19 A9 25r orange brown 10 30
20 A10 50r violet 10 30
21 A11 100r dull red 20 30
22 A12 150r blue 20 30
23 A9 250r violet & buff 20 30
24 A13 400r dark blue 20 30
25 A12 500r gray violet & black 12 30
26 A13 1000r dark blue & rose 15 30
27 A8 2000r blue & black 15 30
28 A7 3000r brown & blue 15 30
- *a.* Tête bêche pair 10.00 10.00

29 A11 5000r *olive green* 25 30
Nos. 15-29 (15) 2.37 4.35

Counterfeits exist of Nos. 1-29.

Stamps of 1922 Handstamped from Metal Dies in a Numbering Machine

15000

1922

32 A5 10.000r on 1r gray green 6.00 6.00
33 A7 15.000r on 5r gray brown 8.00 8.00
34 A9 33.000r on 250r violet & buff 3.00 3.00
35 A7 50.000r on 3.000r brown & blue 4.00 4.00
36 A8 66.000r on 2.000r blue & black 8.00 7.00
Nos. 32-36 (5) 29.00 28.00

Same Surcharges on Regular Issue and Semi-Postal Stamps of 1922.

1922-23

36A A7 500r on 5r gray brown 60.00 60.00
37 A6 1.000r on 2r olive black 10.00 10.00
38 A8 2.000r on 10r gray 3.50 3.50
39 " 5.000r on 2.000r blue & black 2.00 2.00
40 A11 15.000r on 5.000r *olive green* 7.50 7.50
41 A5 20.000r on 1r gray green 8.00 8.00
42 SP1 25.000r on 500r blue & pale blue 25.00
43 A7 50.000r on 5r gray brown 12.50 12.50
44 SP2 50.000r on 1.000r brown & bistre 25.00
45 A11 50.000r on 5.000r *olive green* 4.00 3.00
45A A8 60.000r on 2.000r blue & black 12.50 15.00
46 A11 70.000r on 5.000r *olive green* 20.00 20.00
47 A6 100.000r on 2r olive black 12.50 10.00
48 A8 200.000r on 10r gray 4.00 4.00
49 A9 200.000r on 25r orange brown 16.50 16.50
50 A7 300.000r on 3.000r brown & blue 4.00 4.00
51 A8 500.000r on 2.000r blue & black 8.50 7.50

Revalued.

52 A7 500r on 15.000r on 5r gray brown 30.00 *60.00*
53 A11 15.000r on 70.000r on 5.000r *olive green* 30.00 *60.00*
54 A7 300.000r on 50.000r on 3.000r brown & blue 50.00 *100.00*
55 A8 500.000r on 66.000r on 2.000r blue & black 60.00 *120.00*

The surcharged semi-postal stamps were used for regular postage.

Same Surcharges on Stamps of 1919.

57 A1 25.000r on 10k green, blue, red & black 50 75
58 " 50.000r on 20k blue, red, green & black 50 75
59 A2 75.000r on 40k green, yellow & black 1.35 2.00
60 " 100.000r on 60k red, yellow & black 50 75
61 " 200.000r on 1r blue, yellow & black 50 75
62 A3 300.000r on 2r red, bistre & black 60 1.00
63 " 500.000r on 5r blue, bistre & black 75 1.00
64 A2 750.000r on 40k green, yellow & black 2.50 2.50
Nos. 57-64 (8) 7.20 9.50

Handstamped from Settings of Rubber Type in Black or Violet

100000 *b*   **200.000** *c*

On Stamps of 1922.

65 A6 (*b*) 100.000r on 2r olive black 10.00 10.00
66 A8 (") 200.000r on 10r gray 17.50 15.00
67 " (") 200.000r on 10r gray (V) 12.00 12.00

68 A9 (*b*) 200.000r on 25r orange brown (V) 10.00 10.00
a. Black surch. 30.00 30.00
69 A7 (*c*) 300.000r on 3.000r brown & blue (V) 25.00 25.00
70 A8 (") 500.000r on 2.000r blue & black (V) 20.00 20.00
a. Black surch. 30.00 30.00
71 A11 (*b*) 1.500.000r on 5.000r *olive green* 12.50 12.50
72 " (") 1.500.000r on 5.000r *olive green* (V) 12.50 12.50

On Stamps of 1919.

75 A1 (*b*) 50.000r on 20k blue, red, green & black 30
76 A2 (") 75.000r on 40k green, yellow & black 20
77 " (") 100.000r on 60k red, yellow & black 50
78 " (") 200.000r on 1r blue, yellow & black 10 10
79 A3 (") 300.000r on 2r red, bistre & black 30
80 " (") 500,000r on 5r blue, bistre & black 50

Inverted and double surcharges of Nos. 32-80 sell for twice the normal price.
Counterfeits exist of Nos. 32-80.

Baku Province.

Regular Issue and Semi-Postal Stamps of 1922 Handstamped in Violet

БАКИНСКОИ П. К.

The overprint reads "Bakinskoi P(ochtovoy) K(ontory)," meaning Baku Post Office.

1922 *Imperf.* **Unwmkd.**

300	A5	1r gray green	12.00
301	A7	5r gray brown	12.00
302	A12	150r blue	3.00
303	A9	250r violet & buff	5.00
304	A13	400r dark blue	4.00
305	SP1	500r blue & pale blue	5.00
306	SP2	1000r brown & bistre	6.00
307	A8	2000r blue & black	6.00
308	A7	3000r brown & blue	12.00
309	A11	5000r *olive green*	12.00
		Nos. 300-309 (10)	77.00

Stamps of 1922 Handstamped in Violet

БАКИНСКАГО Г-П-Т.О.№1

Overprint reads: Baku Post, Telegraph Office No. 1.

1924

Overprint 24x2mm.

312	A12	150r blue	5.00
313	A9	250r violet & buff	5.00
314	A13	400r dark blue	5.00
317	A8	2000r blue & black	6.00
318	A7	3000r brown & blue	6.00
319	A11	5000r *olive green*	6.00

Overprint 30x3½mm.

323	A12	150r blue	5.00
324	A9	250r violet & buff	5.00
325	A13	400r dark blue	5.00
328	A8	2000r blue & black	5.00
329	A7	3000r brown & blue	6.00
330	A11	5000r *olive green*	5.00

Overprinted on Nos. 32-33, 35.

331	A5	10,000r on 1r gray green	25.00
332	A7	15,000r on 5r gray brown	25.00
333	"	50,000r on 3000r brown & blue	30.00
		Nos. 312-333 (15)	144.00

The overprinted semipostal stamps were used for regular postage.

This handstamp on Nos. 17, B1-B2 in size 24x2mm., and on Nos. 15, 17, B1-B2 in size 30x3½mm., was of private origin and not officially issued.

SEMI-POSTAL STAMPS.

Carrying Food to Sufferers
SP1

1922 *Imperf.* **Unwmkd.**

B1 SP1 500r blue & pale blue 30 50

Widow and Orphans
SP2

B2 SP2 1000r brown & bistre 45 75

Counterfeits exist.

OCCUPATION AZIRBAYEDJAN

Russian stamps of 1909-18 were privately overprinted as above in red, blue or black by a group of Entente officers working with Russian soldiers returning from Persia. Azerbaijan was not occupied by the Allies. There is evidence that existing covers (some seemingly postmarked at Baku, dated Oct. 19, 1917, and at Tabriz, Russian Consulate, Apr. 25, 1917) are fakes.

AZORES

(á-zōrz')

LOCATION—A group of islands in the North Atlantic Ocean, due west of Portugal.

GOVT.—Integral part of Portugal, former colony.

AREA—922 sq. mi.

POP.—253,935 (1930).

CAPITAL—Ponta Delgada.

Azores stamps were supplanted by those of Portugal in 1931.

1000 Reis = 1 Milreis

100 Centavos = 1 Escudo (1912)

Prices of early Azores stamps vary according to condition. Quotations for Nos. 1-37 are for fine copies. Very fine to superb specimens sell at much higher prices, and inferior or poor copies sell at reduced prices, depending on the condition of the individual specimen.

Stamps of Portugal Overprinted in Black or Carmine — **AÇORES** *a*

A second type of this overprint has a broad "O" and open "S".

1868 *Imperf.* **Unwmkd.**

1 A14	5r black	*1250.00*	*900.00*
2 "	10r yellow	*2750.00*	*2200.00*
3 "	20r bistre	125.00	100.00
4 "	50r green	175.00	115.00
5 "	80r orange	175.00	100.00
6 "	100r lilac	175.00	100.00

The reprints are on thick chalky white wove paper, ungummed, and on thin white paper with shiny white gum. Price $7.50 each.

1868-70 ***Perf. 12½.***

5 REIS:

Type I. The "5" at the right is 1mm. from end of label.
Type II. The "5" is 1½mm. from end of label.

7 A14	5r black (C)	22.50	17.50
8 "	10r yellow	50.00	35.00
	a. Inverted overprint	*100.00*	*100.00*
9 "	20r bistre	35.00	22.50
10 "	25r rose	27.50	2.50
	a. Inverted overprint	*75.00*	*75.00*
11 "	50r green	100.00	60.00
12 "	80r orange	110.00	70.00
13 "	100r lilac	125.00	75.00
14 "	120r blue	55.00	30.00
15 "	240r violet	275.00	175.00

The reprints are on thick chalky white paper ungummed and perforated 13, and on thin white paper with shiny white gum and perforated 13½. Price $6 each.

1871-75 ***Perf. 12½, 13½***

21 A15	5r black (C)	6.50	4.00
	a. Inverted overprint	35.00	35.00
23 "	10r yellow	9.00	7.50
	a. Inverted overprint	27.50	20.00
24 "	20r bistre	11.50	8.25
25 "	25r rose	6.50	1.75
	a. Inverted overprint	25.00	11.00
	b. Double overprint	25.00	
	c. Perf. 14	100.00	22.50
	d. Double impression of stamp		
26 "	50r green	18.00	9.00
27 "	80r orange	32.50	15.00
28 "	100r lilac	18.00	8.00
	a. Perf. 14	150.00	60.00
29 "	120r blue	60.00	30.00
	a. Inverted overprint	*125.00*	*110.00*
30 "	240r violet	325.00	200.00

The reprints are of the second type. They are on thick chalky white paper ungummed and perforated 13, also on thin white paper with shiny white gum and perforated 13½. Price $4 each.

Overprinted in Black — **AÇORES** *b*

1875-80

15 REIS:

Type I. The figures of value, 1 and 5, at the right in upper label are close together.
Type II. The figures of value at the right in upper label are spaced.

31 A15	10r blue green	25.00	16.50
32 "	10r yel. green	22.50	13.00
33 "	15r lilac brown	8.25	7.00
	a. Inverted overprint	25.00	18.50
34 "	50r blue	32.50	15.00
35 "	150r blue	65.00	40.00
36 "	150r yellow	72.50	60.00
37 "	300r violet	27.50	20.00

The reprints have the same papers, gum and perforations as those of the preceding issue. Price $4 each.

1880 Black Overprint.

Perf. 11½, 12½ and 13½.

38 A17	25r gray	20.00	6.50
39 A18	25r red lilac	6.50	3.25
	a. 25r gray	6.50	3.25
	b. Dbl. ovpt.		

Overprinted in Carmine or Black

1881-82

40 A16	5r black (C)	6.50	3.50
41 A23	25r brown ('82)	5.00	1.65
	a. Double overprint		
42 A19	50r blue	27.50	15.00

Reprints of Nos. 38, 39, 39a, 40 and 42 have the same papers, gum and perforations as those of preceding issues. Price $1.50 each.

Overprinted in Red or Black — **AÇORES** *c*

1882-85

15, 20 REIS

Type I. The figures of value are some distance apart and close to the end of the label.
Type II. The figures are closer together and farther from the end of the label. On the 15 reis this is particularly apparent in the upper right figures.

43 A16	5r black (R)	8.50	5.50
44 A21	5r slate	3.00	1.40
	a. Dbl. ovpt.		
	c. Inverted overprint		
45 A15	10r green	22.50	15.00
	a. Inverted overprint		
46 A22	10r green	4.00	2.25
	a. Dbl. ovpt.	6.00	4.00
47 A15	15r lilac brown	11.00	7.00
	a. 15r red brown	11.00	7.00
	b. Inverted overprint	22.50	
48 "	20r bister	15.00	10.00
	a. Inverted overprint	25.00	
49 "	20r carmine	25.00	15.00
	a. Double overprint	30.00	30.00
50 A23	25r brown	3.25	1.50
51 A15	50r blue	325.00	275.00
52 A24	50r blue	6.00	1.50
	a. Double overprint	18.50	13.50
53 A15	80r orange	10.00	4.00
	a. 80r yellow	10.00	4.00
	b. Double overprint	32.50	
54 "	100r lilac	10.00	4.50
55 "	150r blue	325.00	275.00
56 "	150r yellow	15.00	9.50
57 "	300r violet	25.00	20.00

Reprints of the 1882-85 issues have the same papers, gum and perforations as those of preceding issues. Price $3 each.

Red Overprint.

58 A21	5r slate	2.50	1.00
59 A24a	500r black	75.00	50.00
60 A15	1000r black	32.50	27.50

1887 Black Overprint.

61 A25	20r pink	6.00	3.00
	a. Inverted overprint	25.00	
	b. Dbl. ovpt.	25.00	
62 A26	25r lilac rose	4.00	50
	a. Inverted overprint	10.00	10.00
	b. Double overprint, one inverted		17.50
63 "	25r red violet	4.50	50
	a. Dbl. ovpt.		
64 A24a	500r red violet	40.00	30.00
	a. Perf. 13½	50.00	40.00

Nos. 58 to 64 inclusive have been reprinted on thin white paper with shiny white gum and perforated 13½. Price $2 each.

Prince Henry the Navigator Issue.

Portugal Nos. 97-109 Overprinted — AÇORES

1894 ***Perf. 14.***

65 A46	5r orange yellow	1.25	1.00
	a. Inverted overprint	13.50	11.00
66 "	10r violet rose	1.25	1.10
	a. Dbl. ovpt.	18.50	
	b. Inverted overprint	15.00	11.00
67 "	15r brown	2.75	1.25
68 "	20r violet	2.75	1.75
	a. Double overprint		16.50
69 A47	25r green	2.50	1.50
	a. Double overprint	13.50	13.50
	b. Inverted overprint	13.50	13.50
70 "	50r blue	4.00	2.50
71 "	75r deep carmine	8.50	5.75
72 "	80r yellow green	8.50	5.75
73 "	100r light brown, *pale buff*	8.00	5.25
	a. Dbl. ovpt.	22.50	

74 A48 150r light carmine, *pale rose* 12.00 10.00
75 " 300r dark blue, *salmon buff* 13.00 10.00
76 " 500r brown violet, *pale lilac* 17.50 12.50
77 " 1000r gray black, *yellowish* 30.00 20.00
a. Double overprint
Nos. 65-77 (13) 112.00 78.35

St. Anthony of Padua Issue.

Portugal Nos. 132-146 Overprinted in Red or Black — AÇORES

1895 *Perf. 12*
78 A50 2½r black (R) 1.75 1.75
79 A51 5r brown yellow 3.25 2.00
80 " 10r red lilac 4.00 3.25
81 " 15r red brown 6.00 4.50
82 " 20r gray lilac 6.00 4.50
83 " 25r grn. & violet 4.00 2.75
84 A52 50r bl. & brown 13.00 9.75
85 " 75r rose & brn. 22.50 20.00
86 " 80r light green & brown 27.50 22.50
87 " 100r choc. & blk. 25.00 18.00
88 A53 150r violet rose & bistre 50.00 32.50
89 " 200r bl. & bistre 55.00 40.00
90 " 300r slate & bistre 80.00 60.00
91 " 500r violet brown & green 100.00 75.00
92 " 1000r vio. & grn. 200.00 135.00
Nos. 78-92 (15) 598.00 431.50

Issued in commemoration of the seventh centenary of the birth of Saint Anthony of Padua.

Vasco da Gama Issue.

Common Design Types

1898 *Perf. 14, 15.*
93 CD20 2½r blue green 75 50
94 CD21 5r red 1.00 60
a. Horizontal pair, imperf. between
95 CD22 10r gray lilac 2.25 1.50
96 CD23 25r yellow green 1.25 85
97 CD24 50r dark blue 2.75 2.50
98 CD25 75r violet brown 5.00 4.75
99 CD26 100r bistre brown 5.00 4.25
100 CD27 150r bistre 8.50 7.50
Nos. 93-100 (8) 26.50 22.45

King Carlos A28 — King Manuel II A29

1906 Typographed *Perf. 11½x12*
101 A28 2½r gray 20 15
a. Inverted overprint 13.50 13.50
102 " 5r orange yellow 20 15
a. Inverted overprint 13.50 13.50
103 " 10r yellow green 20 15
104 " 20r gray violet 45 25
105 " 25r carmine 25 15
106 " 50r ultramarine 2.50 1.00
107 " 75r brown, *straw* 60 *1.00*
108 " 100r dark blue, *blue* 75 *1.25*
109 " 200r red lilac, *pinkish* 90 *1.50*
110 " 300r dark blue, *rose* 1.20 *1.75*
111 " 500r black, *blue* 2.00 1.25
Nos. 101-111 (11) 9.25 *8.60*

"Acores" and letters and figures in the corners are in red on the 2½, 10, 20, 75 and 500r and in black on the other values.

1910 *Perf. 14x15*
112 A29 2½r violet 25 20
113 " 5r black 35 30
114 " 10r dark green 40 35
115 " 15r lilac brown 65 60
116 " 20r carmine 65 60
117 " 25r violet brown 35 20
a. Perf. 11½ 1.50 1.00
118 A29 50r blue 75 50
a. Booklet pane of 6
119 " 75r bistre brown 2.00 1.75
120 " 80r slate 1.00 1.00
121 " 100r brn., *lt. green* 2.75 2.50
122 " 200r green, *salmon* 3.00 2.50
123 " 300r *blue* 3.00 3.00
124 " 500r olive & brown 4.75 4.25
125 " 1000r blue & black 7.50 7.50
Nos. 112-125 (14) 27.40 25.25

The errors of color 10r black, 15r dark green, 25r black and 50r carmine were not regularly issued.

Stamps of 1910 Overprinted in Carmine or Green — REPUBLICA

1910
126 A29 2½r violet 15 10
a. Inverted overprint 2.00 2.00
127 " 5r black 25 15
a. Inverted overprint 2.00 2.00
128 " 10r dark green 15 12
a. Inverted overprint 2.00 2.00
129 " 15r lilac brown 35 30
a. Inverted overprint 2.00 2.00
130 " 20r carmine (G) 65 55
a. Inverted overprint 3.00 3.00
b. Double overprint 3.00 3.00
131 " 25r violet brown 20 15
a. Perf. 11½ 25.00 20.00
132 " 50r blue 65 50
133 " 75r bistre brown 35 20
a. Double overprint 2.00 2.00
134 " 80r slate 65 30
135 " 100r brown, *green* 30 25
136 " 200r green, *salmon* 50 *1.00*
137 " 300r *blue* 1.00 1.00
138 " 500r olive & brown 75 *1.50*
139 " 1000r blue & black 1.00 *2.00*
Nos. 126-139 (14) 6.95 *8.12*

Vasco da Gama Issue Overprinted or Surcharged in Black:

REPUBLICA
d

REPUBLICA — REPUBLICA

REIS 15 REIS — 1$000
e — *f*

1911 *Perf. 14, 15*
141 CD20 (*d*) 2½r blue green 35 30
142 CD21 (*e*) 15r on 5r red 30 25
143 CD23 (*d*) 25r yel. green 50 30
144 CD24 (") 50r dark blue 75 50
145 CD25 (") 75r vio. brn. 50 75
146 CD27 (*e*) 80r on 150r bis. 50 75
147 CD26 (*d*) 100r yel. brn. 50 75
a. Dbl. surch. 6.00 6.00
148 CD22 (*f*) 1000r on 10r lilac 10.00 10.00
Nos. 141-148 (8) 13.40 13.60

Postage Due Stamps of Portugal Overprinted or Surcharged in Black "ACORES" and

REPUBLICA

REPUBLICA — Rs 300 Rs
g — *h*

1911 *Perf. 12*
149 D1 (*g*) 5r black 50 40
a. Half used as 2½r on cover
150 " (") 10r magenta 1.15 75
a. "Acores" double 7.50 7.50
151 D1 (*g*) 20r orange 1.00 75
152 " (") 200r brown, *buff* 5.75 4.00
a. "Acores" inverted
153 " (*h*) 300r on 50r slate 5.75 4.00
154 " (") 500r on 100r carmine, *pink* 5.75 4.00
Nos. 149-154 (6) 19.90 13.90

Ceres A30

Ceres Issue of Portugal Overprinted "ACORES" in Black or Carmine

With Imprint.

1912-31 *Perf. 12x11½, 15x14*
155 A30 ¼c olive brown 10 10
a. Inverted overprint 2.00
156 " ½c black (C) 10 10
157 " 1c deep green 50 20
a. Inverted overprint 4.50
158 " 1c deep brown ('18) 12 5
a. Inverted overprint
159 " 1½c chocolate ('13) 60 50
a. Inverted overprint 3.00
160 " 1½c deep green ('18) 25 15
a. Inverted overprint
161 " 2c carmine 30 25
a. Inverted overprint 4.50
162 " 2c orange ('18) 20 10
a. Inverted overprint 11.00
163 " 2½c violet 27 15
164 " 3c rose ('18) 20 10
165 " 3c dull ultra. ('25) 20 15
166 " 3½c light green ('18) 20 10
167 " 4c light green ('19) 15 6
168 " 4c orange ('30) 40 30
169 " 5c deep blue 40 12
170 " 5c yellow brown ('18) 25 15
171 " 5c olive brown ('23) 12 8
172 " 5c black brown ('30) 2.50 1.50
173 " 6c dull rose ('20) 25 15
174 " 6c chocolate ('25) 25 15
175 " 6c red brown ('31) 25 *1.00*
176 " 7½c yellow brown 4.00 1.25
177 " 7½c deep blue ('18) 85 50
178 " 8c slate ('13) 35 25
179 " 8c blue green ('22) 25 20
180 " 8c orange ('25) 65 35
181 " 10c orange brown 25 10
182 " 12c blue gray ('20) 65 50
183 " 12c deep green ('22) 65 35
184 " 13½c chalky blue ('20) 65 *3.00*
185 " 14c dark blue, *yellow* ('20) 4.00 *5.00*
186 " 15c plum ('13) 75 25
187 " 15c black (R) ('23) 50 50
188 " 16c brt. ultra. ('24) 1.00 30
189 " 16c deep blue ('30) 1.00 *2.00*
190 " 20c violet brown, *green* ('13) 9.00 4.00
191 " 20c chocolate('20) 75 25
192 " 20c deep green ('23) 1.00 1.00
a. Double overprint
193 " 20c gray ('24) 75 25
194 " 24c greenish blue ('21) 75 25
195 " 25c salmon ('23) 35 20
196 " 30c brn., *pink* ('13) 40.00 27.50
197 " 30c brn., *yellow* ('19) 2.75 2.75
198 " 30c gray brown ('21) 1.00 45
199 " 32c deep green ('25) 1.50 1.00
200 " 36c red ('21) 50 25
201 " 40c deep blue ('23) 50 50
202 " 40c black brown ('24) 25 10
203 " 40c bright green ('30) 1.75 35
204 " 48c bright rose ('24) 1.50 1.00
205 " 48c dull pink ('31) 2.00 85
206 " 50c orange, *salmon* ('13) 5.00 1.25
207 " 50c yellow ('23) 1.50 1.25
208 " 50c bistre ('30) 3.00 2.25
209 " 50c red brown ('31) 2.50 1.50
210 " 60c blue ('21) 1.00 50
211 " 64c pale ultra. ('24) 1.50 1.00
212 " 64c brown rose ('31) 15.00 10.00
213 " 75c dull rose ('23) 6.00 4.00
214 " 75c carmine rose ('30) 1.50 1.00
215 " 80c dull rose ('21) 1.50 65
216 " 80c violet ('24) 1.50 75
217 " 80c dark green ('31) 1.50 1.00
218 " 90c chalky blue ('21) 1.50 65
219 " 96c deep rose ('26) 8.50 4.00
220 " 1e deep green, *blue* 6.00 2.50
221 " 1e violet ('21) 1.50 65
222 A30 1e gray violet ('24) 2.00 1.25
223 " 1e brown lake ('30) 25.00 20.00
224 " 1.10e yellow brown ('21) 1.50 1.50
225 " 1.20e yellow green ('21) 1.50 65
226 " 1.20e buff ('24) 4.00 2.25
227 " 1.25e dark blue ('30) 1.75 50
228 " 1.50e black violet ('23) 2.25 1.50
229 " 1.50e lilac ('25) 3.25 2.00
230 " 1.60e deep blue ('25) 3.00 1.50
231 " 2e slate green ('21) 5.00 2.00
232 " 2.40e apple grn. ('26) 30.00 17.50
233 " 3e lilac pink ('26) 30.00 17.50
234 " 3.20e gray green ('25) 10.00 5.00
235 " 5e emerald ('24) 12.50 6.00
236 " 10e pink ('24) 25.00 10.00
237 " 20e pale turquoise ('25) 75.00 50.00
Nos. 155-237 (83) 378.21 232.81

Castello-Branco Issue.

Stamps of Portugal, 1925, Overprinted in Black or Red — AÇORES

1925 *Perf. 12½.*
238 A73 2c orange 20 20
239 " 3c green 20 20
240 " 4c ultramarine (R) 20 20
241 " 5c scarlet 20 20
242 A74 10c pale blue 20 20
243 " 16c red orange 30 30
244 A75 25c carmine rose 30 30
245 A74 32c green 35 35
246 A75 40c green & black (R) 30 30
247 A74 48c red brown 75 75
248 A76 50c blue green 75 75
249 " 64c orange brown 75 75
250 " 75c gray black (R) 90 90
251 A75 80c brown 90 90
252 A76 96c carmine rose 1.00 1.00
253 A77 1.50e dark blue, *blue* (R) 1.00 90
254 A75 1.60e indigo (R) 1.00 90
255 A77 2e dark green, *green* (R) 1.65 1.50
256 " 2.40e red, *orange* 2.00 1.75
257 " 3.20e *green* (R) 3.25 2.50
Nos. 238-257 (20) 16.20 14.85

First Independence Issue.

Stamps of Portugal, 1926, Overprinted in Red — AÇÔRES

1926 *Perf. 14, 14½*

Center in Black.
258 A79 2c orange 40 40
259 A80 3c ultramarine 40 40
260 A79 4c yellow green 40 40
261 A80 5c black brown 40 40
262 A79 6c ochre 40 40
263 A80 15c dark green 60 60
264 A81 20c dull violet 60 60
265 A82 25c scarlet 60 60
266 A81 32c deep green 60 60
267 A82 40c yellow brown 60 60
268 " 50c olive bistre 1.65 1.65
269 " 75c red brown 1.65 1.65
270 A83 1e black violet 2.00 2.00
271 A84 4.50e olive green 4.00 4.00
Nos. 258-271 (14) 14.30 14.30

The use of these stamps instead of those of the regular issue was obligatory on Aug. 13th and 14th Nov. 30th and Dec. 1st, 1926.

Second Independence Issue.

Stamps of Portugal, 1927, Overprinted in Red — AÇÔRES

1927 Center in Black.
272 A86 2c light brown 30 30
273 A87 3c ultramarine 30 30
274 A86 4c orange 30 30
275 A88 5c dark brown 30 30
276 A89 6c orange brown 30 30
277 A87 15c black brown 30 30
278 A86 25c gray 75 75
279 A89 32c blue green 75 75
280 A90 40c yellow green 75 75
281 " 96c red 1.75 1.75
282 A88 1.60e myrtle green 2.00 2.00
283 A91 4.50e bistre 4.00 4.00
Nos. 272-283 (12) 11.80 11.80

Third Independence Issue.

Stamps of Portugal, 1928, Overprinted in Red **AÇÔRES**

1928 Center in Black.

284	A93	2c light blue	30	30
285	A94	3c light green	30	30
286	A95	4c lake	30	30
287	A96	5c olive green	30	30
288	A97	6c orange brown	30	30
289	A94	15c slate	30	30
290	A95	16c dark violet	50	50
291	A93	25c ultramarine	50	50
292	A97	32c dark green	50	50
293	A96	40c olive brown	50	50
294	A95	50c red orange	90	90
295	A94	80c light gray	90	90
296	A97	96c carmine	1.25	1.25
297	A96	1e claret	1.25	1.25
298	A93	1.60e dark blue	1.25	1.25
299	A98	4.50e yellow	2.50	2.50
		Nos. 284-299 (15)	11.85	11.85

A31

A32

1929-30 *Perf. 12x11½, 15x14*

300	A31	4c on 25c pink ('30)	35	35
301	"	4c on 60c deep blue	35	35
302	"	10c on 25c pink	45	40
303	"	12c on 25c pink	45	40
304	"	15c on 25c pink	60	50
305	"	20c on 25c pink	75	60
306	"	40c on 1.10e yel. brn.	2.00	1.75
		Nos. 300-306 (7)	4.95	4.35

Black or Red Overprint.

1930 *Perf. 14.*

Without Imprint at Foot.

307	A32	4c orange	60	40
308	"	5c deep brown	1.00	75
309	"	10c vermilion	60	50
310	"	15c black (R)	60	50
311	"	40c bright green	60	45
312	"	80c violet	9.00	7.50
313	"	1.60e dark blue	60	50
		Nos. 307-313 (7)	13.00	10.60

POSTAGE DUE STAMPS.

D2

D3

Portugal Nos. J7-J13 Overprinted in Black

1904 *Perf. 12* Unwmkd.

J1	D2	5r brown	60	60
J2	"	10r orange	60	60
J3	"	20r lilac	90	90
J4	"	30r gray green	90	90
		a. Double overprint		
J5	"	40r gray violet	1.25	1.25
J6	"	50r carmine	1.75	1.75
J7	"	100r dull blue	2.25	2.25
		Nos. J1-J7 (7)	8.25	8.25

Same Overprinted in Carmine or Green (Portugal Nos. J14-J20) **REPUBLICA**

1911

J8	D2	5r brown	30	30
J9	"	10r orange	30	30
J10	"	20r lilac	30	30
J11	D2	30r gray green	30	30
J12	"	40r gray violet	40	40
J13	"	50r carmine (G)	2.50	2.50
J14	"	100r dull blue	1.00	1.00
		Nos. J8-J14 (7)	5.10	5.10

Portugal Nos. J21-J27 Overprinted in Black

1918

J15	D3	½c brown	15	15
		a. Inverted overprint	50	50
		b. Double overprint	50	50
J16	"	1c orange	15	15
		a. Inverted overprint	50	50
		b. Double overprint	50	50
J17	"	2c red lilac	15	15
		a. Inverted overprint	1.00	1.00
		b. Double overprint	1.00	1.00
J18	"	3c green	15	15
		a. Inverted overprint	1.00	1.00
		b. Double overprint	1.00	1.00
J19	"	4c gray	15	15
		a. Inverted overprint	1.00	1.00
		b. Double overprint	1.00	1.00
J20	"	5c rose	15	15
		b. Double overprint	1.00	1.00
J21	"	10c dark blue	25	25
		Nos. J15-J21 (7)	1.15	1.15

Stamps and Type of Portugal Postage Dues, 1921-27, Overprinted in Black

1922-24 *Perf. 11½x12.*

J30	D3	½c gray green ('23)	15	15
J31	"	1c " ('23)	15	15
J32	"	2c " ('23)	15	15
J33	"	3c " ('24)	25	25
J34	"	8c " ('24)	25	25
J35	"	10c " ('24)	30	30
J36	"	12c " ('24)	25	25
J37	"	16c " ('24)	25	25
J38	"	20c "	40	40
J39	"	24c "	25	25
J40	"	32c " ('24)	25	25
J41	"	36c "	25	25
J42	"	40c " ('24)	50	50
J43	"	48c " ('24)	35	35
J44	"	50c "	35	35
J45	"	60c "	35	35
J46	"	72c "	30	30
J47	"	80c " ('24)	60	60
J48	"	1.20e "	1.00	1.00
		Nos. J30-J48 (19)	6.35	6.35

NEWSPAPER STAMPS.

N1

N2

N3

Newspaper Stamps of Portugal Overprinted in Black or Red

Perf. 11½, 12½ and 13½.

1876-88 Unwmkd.

P1	N1	2½r olive	2.25	1.25
		a. Inverted overprint	12.00	
P2	N2	2½r olive ('82)	1.75	1.25
		a. Inverted overprint	6.00	
		b. Double overprint		
P3	N3	2r black ('85)	90	75
		a. Inverted overprint	3.00	3.00
		b. Double overprint, one inverted	7.00	5.00
P4	N2	2½r bistre ('82)	1.75	75
		a. Double overprint	2.50	2.50
P5	N3	2r black (R) ('88)	3.00	1.75

Reprints of the newspaper stamps have the same papers, gum and perforations as reprints of the regular issues. Price $2 each.

PARCEL POST STAMPS.

Mercury and Commerce
PP1

Portugal Nos. Q1-Q17 Overprinted in Black or Red.

1921-22 *Perf. 12.* Unwmkd.

Q1	PP1	1c lilac brown	20	18
		a. Inverted overprint	50	50
Q2	"	2c orange	20	18
		a. Inverted overprint	50	50
Q3	"	5c light brown	20	18
		a. Inverted overprint	1.00	1.00
		b. Double overprint	1.00	1.00
Q4	"	10c red brown	25	22
		a. Inverted overprint	1.00	1.00
		b. Double overprint	1.00	1.00
Q5	"	20c gray blue	25	22
		a. Inverted overprint	1.00	1.00
		b. Double overprint	1.00	1.00
Q6	"	40c carmine	25	25
		a. Double overprint	1.50	1.50
Q7	"	50c black (R)	35	30
Q8	"	60c dark blue (R)	35	35
Q9	"	70c gray brown	1.25	1.00
		a. Double overprint	2.00	2.00
Q10	"	80c ultramarine	1.25	1.00
Q11	"	90c light violet	1.25	1.00
Q12	"	1e light green	1.25	1.00
Q13	"	2e pale lilac	2.00	2.00
Q14	"	3e olive	2.50	2.50
Q15	"	4e ultramarine	3.25	3.25
Q16	"	5e gray	3.25	3.25
Q17	"	10e chocolate	8.50	8.50
		Nos. Q1-Q17 (17)	26.55	25.38

POSTAL TAX STAMPS.

These stamps represent a special fee for the delivery of postal matter on certain days in the year. The money derived from their sale is applied to works of public charity.

Nos. 114 and 157 Overprinted in Carmine **ASSISTENCIA**

1911-13 *Perf. 14x15* Unwmkd.

RA1	A29	10r dark green	60	50

The 20r of this type was for use on telegrams.

Perf. 15x14

RA2	A30	1c deep green	1.10	1.10

The 2c of this type was for use on telegrams.

Charity Sheltering Poor
PT1

Postal Tax Stamp of Portugal Overprinted in Black.

1915 *Perf. 12.*

RA3	PT1	1c carmine	15	12

The 2c of this type was for use on telegrams.

Postal Tax Stamp of 1915 Surcharged **15 ctvs.**

1924

RA4	PT1	15c on 1c rose	35	1.00

Comrades of the Great War Issue.

Postal Tax Stamps of Portugal, 1925, Overprinted AÇORES

1925 *Perf. 11.*

RA5	PT3	10c brown	40	40
RA6	"	10c green	40	40
RA7	"	10c rose	40	40
RA8	"	10c ultramarine	40	40

The use of Nos. RA5-RA11 in addition to the regular postage was compulsory on certain days. If the tax represented by these stamps was not prepaid, it was collected by means of Postal Tax Due Stamps.

Pombal Issue.

Common Design Types

1925 *Perf. 12½.*

RA9	CD28	20c deep green & black	40	35
RA10	CD29	20c deep green & black	40	35
RA11	CD30	20c deep green & black	40	35

POSTAL TAX DUE STAMPS.

Postal Tax Due Stamp of Portugal Overprinted AÇORES

1925 *Perf. 11x11½.* Unwmkd.

RAJ1	PTD1	20c brown orange	50	50

See note after No. RA8.

Pombal Issue.

Common Design Types

1925 *Perf. 12½.*

RAJ2	CD31	40c deep green & black	75	1.25
RAJ3	CD32	40c deep green & black	75	1.25
RAJ4	CD33	40c deep green & black	75	1.25

See note after No. RA8.

Azores stamps were superseded in 1931 by those of Portugal.

BADEN

See Vol. III, Early German States group preceding Germany.

BATUM

See Vol. I, British section.

BAVARIA

See Vol. III, Early German States group preceding Germany.

BELGIAN CONGO

LOCATION—Central Africa.
GOVT.—Belgian colony.
AREA—902,082 sq. mi. (estimated).
POP.—12,660,000 (1956).
CAPITAL—Léopoldville.

Congo was an independent state, founded by Leopold II of Belgium, until 1908 when it was annexed to Belgium as a colony. In 1960 it became the independent Republic of the Congo. See Congo Democratic Republic and Zaire.

100 Centimes = 1 Franc

Independent State

King Leopold II

A1 A2 A3

Typographed.

1886 ***Perf. 15.*** **Unwmkd.**

No.	Type	Description	Unused	Used
1	A1	5c green	11.50	11.50
2	"	10c rose	4.50	4.50
3	A2	25c blue	52.50	42.50
4	A3	50c olive green	5.25	4.50
5	A1	5fr lilac	350.00	265.00
		a. Perf. 14	475.00	

King Leopold II
A4

1887-94

No.	Type	Description	Unused	Used
6	A4	5c green ('89)	75	75
7	"	10c rose ('89)	1.50	1.35
8	"	25c blue ('89)	90	1.10
9	"	50c brown	50.00	17.50
10	"	50c gray ('94)	2.75	4.75
11	"	5fr violet	550.00	300.00
12	"	5fr gray ('92)	110.00	72.50
13	"	10fr buff ('91)	350.00	215.00

In 1890 stamps of 25fr and 50fr of type A4 were printed in gray but were not issued. Price $16 and $15 respectively.

Port Matadi
A5

River Scene on the Congo, Stanley Falls
A6

Inkissi Falls
A7

Railroad Bridge on M'pozo River
A8

Hunting Elephants
A9

Bangala Chief and Wife
A10

Engraved.

1894–1901 ***Perf. 12½ to 15***

No.	Type	Description	Unused	Used
14	A5	5c pale blue & black	12.50	13.50
15	"	5c red brown & black ('95)	4.00	1.75
16	"	5c grn. & blk. ('00)	2.25	60
17	A6	10c red brn. & blk.	12.50	13.50
18	"	10c greenish blue & black ('95)	1.35	1.35
		a. Center invtd.	1000.00	1600.00
19	"	10c carmine & black ('00)	2.25	60
20	A7	25c yellow orange & black	5.00	2.75
21	"	25c light blue & black ('00)	4.00	1.50
22	A8	50c green & black	1.75	1.50
23	"	50c olive & blk.('00)	4.00	75
24	A9	1fr lilac & black	27.50	12.00
		a. 1fr rose lilac & black	175.00	16.50
25	"	1fr carmine & black ('01)	150.00	2.25
26	A10	5fr lake & black	45.00	14.50
		Nos. 14–26 (13)	272.10	66.55

Climbing Oil Palms
A11

Congo Canoe
A12

1896

No.	Type	Description	Unused	Used
27	A11	15c ochre & black	4.75	60
28	A12	40c bluish green & black	5.50	3.50

Congo Village—A13

River Steamer on the Congo
A14

1898

No.	Type	Description	Unused	Used
29	A13	3.50fr red & black	125.00	50.00
30	A14	10fr yellow green & black	90.00	14.00
		a. Center invtd.	*3500.00*	
		b. Perf. 12	550.00	14.00
		c. Perf. 12x14	425.00	125.00

Belgian Congo

Overprinted **CONGO BELGE**

1908

No.	Type	Description	Unused	Used
31	A5	5c green & black	6.75	6.50
		a. Handstamped	2.50	2.00
32	A6	10c car. & black	12.50	12.50
		a. Handstamped	2.50	2.00
33	A11	15c ochre & black	7.50	3.75
		a. Handstamped	5.50	3.25
34	A7	25c lt. blue & black	4.25	3.75
		a. Handstamped	5.50	4.00
35	A12	40c bluish green & black	2.35	2.25
		a. Handstamped	8.25	6.75
36	A8	50c olive & black	5.00	2.75
		a. Handstamped	4.50	3.00
37	A9	1fr car. & black	24.00	2.75
		a. Handstamped	22.50	2.50
38	A13	3.50fr red & black	22.50	13.00
		a. Handstamped	125.00	90.00
39	A10	5fr car. & black	40.00	19.00
		a. Handstamped	45.00	30.00
40	A14	10fr yellow green & black	80.00	17.00
		a. Perf. 14	225.00	165.00
		b. Handstamped	100.00	35.00
		c. Handstamped, perf. 14	225.00	165.00
		Nos. 31–40 (10)	204.85	83.25

Most of the above handstamps are also found inverted and double.

Port Matadi—A15

River Scene on the Congo, Stanley Falls
A16

Climbing Oil Palms
A17

Railroad Bridge on M'pozo River
A18

1909 ***Perf. 14***

No.	Type	Description	Unused	Used
41	A15	5c green & black	1.00	1.00
42	A16	10c carmine & black	75	60
43	A17	15c ochre & black	18.50	11.00
44	A18	50c olive & black	3.25	2.50

Port Matadi
A19

River Scene on the Congo, Stanley Falls
A20

Climbing Oil Palms
A21

Bangala Chief and Wife
A27

Inkissi Falls
A22

Congo Canoe
A23

Railroad Bridge on M'pozo River
A24

Hunting Elephants
A25

Congo Village
A26

River Steamer on the Congo
A28

1910-15 Engraved. ***Perf. 14, 15.***

No.	Type	Description	Unused	Used
45	A19	5c green & black	1.60	30
46	A20	10c carmine & black	85	25
47	A21	15c ochre & black	85	25
48	"	15c green & black ('15)	30	25
		a. Bklt. pane of 10	8.50	
49	A22	25c blue & black	1.85	30
50	A23	40c bluish green & black	2.50	2.25
51	"	40c brown red & black ('15)	5.00	2.50
52	A24	50c olive & black	3.00	2.25
53	"	50c brown lake & black ('15)	6.75	2.10
54	A25	1fr carmine & black	4.00	3.00
55	"	1fr olive bistre & black ('15)	2.50	85
56	A26	3fr red & black	19.00	14.00
57	A27	5fr car. & black	23.50	19.00
58	"	5fr ochre & black ('15)	2.25	85
59	A28	10fr green & black	21.00	18.00
		Nos. 45-59 (15)	94.95	66.15

Nos. 48, 51, 53, 55 and 58 exist imperforate.

Port Matadi
A29

Stanley Falls, Congo River
A30

Inkissi Falls—A31

TEN CENTIMES.

Type I. Large white space at top of picture and two small white spots at lower edge. Vignette does not fill frame.

Type II. Vignette completely fills frame.

1915

No.	Type	Description	Unused	Used
60	A29	5c green & black	30	25
		a. Booklet pane of 10	8.00	
61	A30	10c car. & black (II)	35	25
		a. 10c carmine & black (I)	35	25
		b. Vertical pair, imperf. between	15.00	
		d. Booklet pane of 10, (II)	10.00	
62	A31	25c blue & black	1.75	45
		a. Booklet pane of 10	20.00	

Nos. 60 to 62 exist imperforate.

Stamps of 1910 Issue
Surcharged in Red or Black

10c ≡ 10c ≡

1921

No.	Type	Description	Unused	Used
64	A23	5c on 40c bluish grn. & black (R)	35	35
65	A19	10c on 5c green & black (R)	35	35
66	A24	15c on 50c olive & black (R)	35	35
67	A21	25c on 15c ochre & black (R)	2.35	1.65
68	A20	30c on 10c carmine & black	35	35
		a. Inverted surcharge	25.00	
69	A22	50c on 25c blue & black (R)	2.25	1.65
		Nos. 64-69 (6)	6.00	4.70

The position of the new value and the bars varies on Nos. 64 to 69.

Overprinted **1921**

1921

No.	Type	Description	Unused	Used
70	A25	1fr carmine & black	1.35	1.15
		a. Double overprint	17.50	
71	A26	3fr red & black	3.50	3.00
72	A27	5fr carmine & black	5.50	4.75
73	A28	10fr grn. & black (R)	7.00	4.25

Belgian Surcharges.

Stamps of 1915 Surcharged
in Black or Red

·10c·

1922

No.	Type	Description	Unused	Used
74	A24	5c on 50c brown lake & black	65	55
75	A29	10c on 5c green & black (R)	65	45
76	A23	25c on 40c brown red & blk. (R)	2.10	55
77	A30	30c on 10c carmine & black (II)	35	30
		a. 30c on 10c carmine & black (I)	35	30
		b. Double surcharge	6.00	6.00
78	A31	50c on 25c blue & black (R)	65	45
		Nos. 74-78 (5)	4.40	2.30

No. 74 has the surcharge at each side.

Nos. 74-78 were issued only in sheets of 50. Blocks of 10 (5x2), so-called "booklet panes," are believed to be from the sheets of 50.

Congo Surcharges.

Nos. 60, 51 Surcharged in Red or Black:

10 c.

═ ═
a
═ ═

b

1922

No.	Type	Description	Unused	Used
80	A29 (*a*)	10c on 5c green & black (R)	70	60
		a. Invtd. surch.	24.00	24.00
		b. Double surcharge	6.00	
		c. Double surcharge, one inverted	40.00	
		d. Pair, one without surcharge	45.00	
		e. On No. 45	140.00	140.00
81	A23 (*b*)	25c on 40c brown red & black	85	35
		a. Inverted surcharge	24.00	24.00
		b. Double surcharge	7.00	
		c. "25c" double		
		d. 25c on 5c, No. 60	130.00	130.00

Nos. 55, 58
Surcharged **10 c.**
and vertical bars over original values.

1922

No.	Type	Description	Unused	Used
84	A25	10c on 1fr olive bistre & black (R)	60	55
		a. Double surcharge	15.00	
		b. Inverted surcharge	25.00	25.00
85	A27	25c on 5fr ochre & black	2.00	2.00

Nos. 68, 77
Handstamped **0,25**

No.	Type	Description	Unused	Used
86	A20	25c on 30c on 10c car. & black	10.00	10.00
87	A30	25c on 30c on 10c carmine & black (II)	10.00	10.00

Nos. 86-87 exist with handstamp surcharge inverted.

Ubangi Woman A32 — Watusi Cattle A44

Designs: 10c, Baluba woman. 15c, Babuende woman. No. 91, 40c, 1.25fr, 1.50fr, 1.75fr, Ubangi man. 25c, Basket making. 30c, 35c, 75c, Carving wood. 50c, Archer. No. 92, 75c, Weaving. 1fr, Making pottery. 3fr, Working rubber. 5fr, Making palm oil. 10fr, African elephant.

1923-27 Engraved ***Perf. 12***

No.	Type	Description	Unused	Used
88	A32	5c yellow	25	15
89	"	10c green	25	15
90	"	15c olive brown	25	15
91	"	20c olive green ('24)	20	15
92	"	20c green ('26)	25	18
93	"	25c red brown	35	15
94	"	30c rose red ('24)	35	30
95	"	30c olive green('25)	25	18
96	"	35c green ('27)	65	50
97	"	40c violet ('25)	25	18
98	"	50c gray blue	35	25
99	"	50c buff ('25)	45	10
100	"	75c red orange	55	45
101	"	75c gray blue ('25)	55	30
102	"	75c salmon red ('26)	30	18
103	"	1fr bistre brown	70	25
104	"	1fr dull blue ('25)	55	15
105	"	1fr rose red ('27)	1.00	18
106	"	1.25fr dull blue ('26)	50	30
107	"	1.50fr dull blue ('26)	50	25
108	"	1.75fr dull blue ('27)	5.00	3.50
109	"	3fr gray brn.('24)	4.75	1.35
110	"	5fr gray ('24)	9.50	4.00
111	"	10fr gray black ('24)	20.00	5.75
		Nos. 88-111 (24)	47.75	19.10

1925-26 ***Perf. 12***

No.	Type	Description	Unused	Used
112	A44	45c dark violet ('26)	55	35
113	"	60c carmine rose	55	25

No. 107
Surcharged

═
1.75

1927, June 14

No.	Type	Description	Unused	Used
114	A32	1.75fr on 1.50fr dull blue	65	45

Sir Henry Morton Stanley
A45

1928, June 30 ***Perf. 14***

No.	Type	Description	Unused	Used
115	A45	5c gray black	10	10
116	"	10c deep violet	12	12
117	"	20c orange red	30	25
118	"	35c green	1.00	75
119	"	40c red brown	40	25
120	"	60c black brown	40	25
121	"	1fr carmine	40	12
122	"	1.60fr dark gray	3.25	2.75
123	"	1.75fr deep blue	1.75	1.00
124	"	2fr dark brown	1.25	40
125	"	2.75fr red violet	4.00	50
126	"	3.50fr rose lake	1.65	80
127	"	5fr slate green	1.25	35
128	"	10fr violet blue	1.85	80
129	"	20fr claret	5.00	3.25
		Nos. 115-129 (15)	22.72	11.69

Issued in memory of Sir Henry M. Stanley (1841-1904), explorer.

═ ═

Stamps of 1928
Surcharged in
Red, Blue or Black

1F25

1931, Jan. 15

No.	Type	Description	Unused	Used
130	A45	40c on 35c green (R)	90	65
131	"	1.25fr on 1fr carmine (Bl)	70	18
132	"	2fr on 1.60fr dark gray (R)	1.50	40
133	"	2fr on 1.75fr dp. blue (R)	1.25	35
134	"	3.25fr on 2.75fr red violet (Bk)	3.25	2.10
135	"	3.25fr on 3.50fr rose lake (Bk)	4.25	2.50

Stamps of 1923-27 Surcharged in Red

═ ═

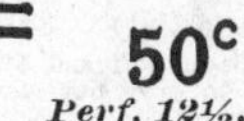

Perf. 12½, 12.

No.	Type	Description	Unused	Used
136	A32	40c on 35c green	5.00	4.00
137	A44	50c on 45c dark vio.	3.25	1.50

Surcharged **2**

No.	Type	Description	Unused	Used
138	A32	2(fr) on 1.75fr dull blue	11.00	9.00
		Nos. 130-138 (9)	31.10	20.68

View of Sankuru River
A46

Flute Players
A50

Designs: 15c, Kivu Kraal. 20c, Sankuru River rapids. 25c, Uele hut. 50c, Musicians of Lake Leopold II. 60c, Batetelas drummers. 75c, Mangbetu woman. 1fr, Domesticated elephant of Api. 1.25fr, Mangbetu chief. 1.50fr, 2fr, Village of Mondimbi. 2.50fr, 3.25fr, Okapi. 4fr, Canoes at Stanleyville. 5fr, Woman preparing cassava. 10fr, Baluba chief. 20fr, Young woman of Irumu.

1931-37 Engraved. *Perf. 11½.*

139 A46 10c gray brown ('32) 10 10
140 " 15c gray ('32) 10 10
141 " 20c brown lilac ('32) 10 10
142 " 25c deep blue ('32) 10 10
143 A50 40c deep green ('32) 35 30
144 A46 50c violet ('32) 10 10
a. Imperf. 20.00
b. Booklet pane of 8 7.50
145 A50 60c violet brown ('32) 18 15
146 " 75c rose ('32) 15 10
a. Imperf. 20.00
b. Booklet pane of 8 1.65
147 " 1fr rose red ('32) 25 12
148 " 1.25fr red brown 20 10
a. Imperf. 20.00
b. Booklet pane of 8 1.65
149 A46 1.50fr dark olive gray ('37) 25 18
a. Imperf. 20.00
b. Booklet pane of 8 7.50
150 " 2fr ultra. ('32) 30 18
151 " 2.50fr deep blue ('37) 55 20
a. Imperf., pair 50.00
b. Bklt. pane of 8 11.00
152 " 3.25fr gray black ('32) 90 50
153 " 4fr dull violet ('32) 35 25
154 A50 5fr deep violet ('32) 90 35
155 " 10fr red ('32) 70 60
156 " 20fr black brown ('32) 2.50 1.85
Nos. 139-156 (18) 8.08 5.38

No. 109 Surcharged in Red

3F25

= **=**

1932, Mar. 15 ***Perf. 12***

157 A32 3.25fr on 3fr gray brown 3.75 2.50

King Albert Memorial Issue.

King Albert
A62

1934, May 7 Photo. *Perf. 11½*

158 A62 1.50fr black 1.10 30

Leopold I, Leopold II, Albert I, Leopold III
A63

1935, Aug. 15 Engr. *Perf. 12½x12*

159 A63 50c green 1.10 70
160 " 1.25fr dark carmine 1.10 25
161 " 1.50fr brown violet 1.10 20
162 " 2.40fr brown orange 3.50 2.75
163 " 2.50fr light blue 3.00 1.10
164 " 4fr bright violet 3.50 1.65
165 " 5fr black brown 3.50 1.85
Nos. 159-165 (7) 16.80 8.50

Issued to commemorate the 50th anniversary of the founding of Congo Free State.

Molindi River
A64

Bamboos
A65

Suza River
A66

Rutshuru River
A67

Karisimbi
A68

Mitumba Forest
A69

1937-38 Photo. *Perf. 11½*

166 A64 5c purple & black 10 10
167 A65 90c carmine & brn. 85 65
168 A66 1.50fr deep red brown & black 22 15
169 A67 2.40fr olive black & brown 38 25
170 A68 2.50fr deep ultramarine & black 60 28
171 A69 4.50fr dark green & brown 60 25
172 " 4.50fr carmine & sepia 40 45
Nos. 166-172 (7) 3.15 2.13

National Parks.
No. 172 was issued in sheets of four measuring 140x111mm. It was sold by subscription, the subscription closing Oct. 20, 1937. Price, $1.60.
Nos. 166-171 were issued Mar. 1, 1938.

King Albert Memorial, Leopoldville
A70

1941, Feb. 7 Litho. *Perf. 11*

173 A70 10c light gray 35 30
174 " 15c brown violet 35 30
175 " 25c light blue 35 30
176 " 50c light violet 35 30
177 " 75c rose pink 1.50 45
178 " 1.25fr gray 35 30
179 " 1.75fr orange 1.10 1.00
180 " 2.50fr carmine 90 18
181 " 2.75fr violet blue 1.25 1.10
182 " 5fr light olive green 2.00 1.65
183 A70 10fr rose red 3.50 3.25
Nos. 173-183 (11) 12.00 9.13

Exist imperforate.

Stamps of 1938-41 Surcharged in Blue or Black

5 c. **75 c.**

a b

1941-42 *Perf. 11½, 11.*

184 A66 (*a*) 5c on 1.50fr deep red brown & black (Bl) 15 15
a. Inverted surcharge 20.00 20.00
185 A70 (*b*) 75c on 1.75fr orange (Bk) ('42) 65 60
a. Inverted surcharge 20.00 20.00
186 A67 (*a*) 2.50(fr) on 2.40fr olive black & brown (Bk) ('42) 1.25 90
a. Double surcharge 30.00 30.00
b. Inverted surcharge 20.00 20.00

Oil Palms
A71 A72

Congo Woman
A73

Askari
A75

Leopard
A74

Okapi
A76

1942, May 23 Engr. *Perf. 12½*

Inscribed "Congo Belge Belgisch Congo".

187 A71 5c red 6 6
188 A72 10c olive green 10 6
189 " 15c brown carmine 10 6
190 " 20c deep ultra. 10 6
191 " 25c brown violet 10 6
192 " 30c blue 10 10
193 A72 50c deep green 10 10
194 " 60c chestnut 12 12
195 A73 75c dull lilac & black 18 12
196 " 1fr dk. brn. & blk. 25 12
197 " 1.25fr rose red & black 25 18
198 A74 1.75fr dk. gray brn. 90 70
199 " 2fr ochre 90 22
200 " 2.50fr carmine 90 10
201 A75 3.50fr dark olive grn. 35 15
202 " 5fr orange 70 25
203 " 6fr bright ultra. 60 15
204 " 7fr black 60 15
205 " 10fr deep brown 80 15
206 A76 20fr plum & black 4.00 1.10
Nos. 187-206 (20) 11.21 4.01

Same
Inscribed "Belgisch Congo Congo Belge".

207 A72 10c olive green 10 6
208 " 15c brown carmine 10 6
209 " 20c deep ultra. 10 6
210 " 25c brown violet 10 6
211 " 30c blue 10 10
212 " 50c deep green 10 10
213 " 60c chestnut 12 12
214 A73 75c dull lilac & black 18 12
215 " 1fr dk. brn. & blk. 25 12
216 " 1.25fr rose red & black 25 18
217 A74 1.75fr dk. gray brn. 90 70
218 " 2fr ochre 90 22
219 " 2.50fr carmine 90 10
220 A75 3.50fr dk. olive green 35 15
221 " 5fr orange 70 25
222 " 6fr bright ultra. 60 15
223 " 7fr black 60 15
224 " 10fr deep brown 80 15
225 A76 20fr plum & black 4.00 1.10
Nos. 207-225 (19) 11.15 3.95

Miniature sheets of Nos. 193, 194, 197, 200, 211, 214, 217 and 219 were printed in 1944 by the Belgian Government in London and given to the Belgian political review, Message, which distributed them to its subscribers, one a month. Price per sheet, about $12.50.

Remainders of these eight miniature sheets received marginal overprints in various colors in 1950, specifying a surtax of 100fr per sheet and paying tribute to the Universal Postal Union. These sheets, together with four of Ruanda-Urundi, were sold by the Committee of Cultural Works (and not at post offices) in sets of 12 for 1,217.15 francs. Set price, about $150.

Nos. 187 to 227 exist imperforate but had no franking value.

Congo Woman
A77

Askari
A78

1943, Jan. 1

226 A77 50fr ultra. & black 4.25 75
227 A78 100fr car. & black 7.50 1.25

Slaves and Arab Guards
A79

Auguste Lambermont
A80

Design: 10fr, Leopold II.

Perf. 13x11½, 12½x12.

1947 Engraved. Unwmkd.

228	A79	1.25fr black brown	30	12
229	A80	3.50fr dark blue	45	15
230	"	10fr red orange	1.00	28

Issued to commemorate the 50th anniversary of the abolition of slavery in Belgian Congo. See also Nos. 261-262.

Baluba Carving of Former King

A82

Carved Figures and Masks of Baluba Tribe: 10c, 50c, 2fr, "Ndoha," figure of tribal king. 15c, 70c, 1.20fr, 2.50fr, "Tshimanyi," an idol. 20c, 75c, 1.60fr, 3.50fr, "Buangakokoma," statue of kneeling beggar. 25c, 1fr, 2.40fr, 5fr, "Mbuta," sacred double cup, carved with two faces, Man and Woman. 40c, 1.25fr, 6fr, 8fr, "Ngadimuashi," female mask. 1.50fr, 3fr, 10fr, 50fr, "Buadi-Muadi," mask with squared features. 6.50fr, 20fr, 100fr, "Mbowa," executioner's mask with buffalo horns.

1947-50 ***Perf. 12½.***

231	A82	10c dp. orange ('48)	10	10
232	"	15c ultra. ('48)	10	10
233	"	20c brt. blue ('48)	15	15
234	"	25c rose car. ('48)	30	18
235	"	40c violet ('48)	18	10
236	"	50c olive brown	18	10
237	"	70c yel. green ('48)	12	12
238	"	75c magenta ('48)	18	15
239	"	1fr yellow orange & dark violet	1.25	8
240	"	1.20fr gray & brown ('50)	18	18
241	"	1.25fr lt. blue green & magenta ('48)	32	28
242	"	1.50fr olive & magenta ('50)	7.25	1.50
243	"	1.60fr blue gray & bright blue ('50)	25	25
244	"	2fr orange & magenta ('48)	20	12
245	"	2.40fr blue green & dark green ('50)	32	28
246	"	2.50fr brown red & blue green	20	10
247	"	3fr light ultra. & indigo ('49)	3.50	8
248	"	3.50fr light blue & black ('48)	3.00	35
249	"	5fr bistre & magenta ('48)	50	12
250	"	6fr brown orange & indigo ('48)	70	10
251	"	6.50fr red orange & red brn. ('49)	1.50	10
252	"	8fr gray blue & dark green ('50)	55	35
253	"	10fr pale violet & red brn. ('48)	2.10	15
254	"	20fr red orange & vio. brn. ('48)	1.10	15
255	"	50fr deep orange & black ('48)	3.25	45
256	"	100fr crimson & blk. brown ('48)	5.00	90
		Nos. 231-256 (26)	32.48	6.54

Railroad Train and Map

A83

1948, July 1 ***Perf. 13½*** **Unwmkd.**

257	A83	2.50fr deep blue & green	80	22

50th anniversary of railway service in the Congo.

Globe and Ship—A84

1949, Nov. 21 ***Perf. 11½***

Granite Paper

258	A84	4fr violet blue	80	28

Issued to commemorate the 75th anniversary of the formation of the Universal Postal Union.

Allegorical Figure and Map

A85

1950, Aug. 12 ***Perf. 12x12½***

259	A85	3fr blue & indigo	1.60	18
260	"	6.50fr carmine rose & black brown	1.90	28

Issued to commemorate the 50th anniversary of the establishment of Katanga Province.

Portrait Type of 1947.

Designs: 1.50fr, Cardinal Lavigerie. 3fr, Baron Dhanis.

Perf. 12½x12

1951, June 25 Unwmkd.

261	A80	1.50fr purple	2.15	35
262	"	3fr black brown	2.15	10

Littonia

A86

Flowers: 10c, Dissotis. 15c, Protea. 20c, Vellozia. 40c, Ipomoea. 50c, Angraecum. 60c, Euphorbia. 75c, Ochna. 1fr, Hibiscus. 1.25fr, Protea. 1.50fr, Schizoglossum. 2fr, Ansellia. 3fr, Costus. 4fr, Nymphaea. 5fr, Thunbergia. 6.50fr, Thonningia. 7fr, Gerbera. 8fr, Gloriosa. 10fr, Silene. 20fr, Aristolochia. 50fr, Eulophia. 100fr, Cryptosepalum.

Granite Paper.

1952-53 Photogravure. ***Perf. 11½.***

Flowers in Natural Colors.

Size: 21x25½mm.

263	A86	10c deep plum & ochre	5	5
264	"	15c red & yellow green	5	5
265	"	20c green & gray	5	5
266	"	25c dark green & dull orange	5	5
267	"	40c green & salmon	7	5
268	"	50c dark carmine & aquamarine	7	5
269	"	60c blue green & pink	7	5
270	"	75c deep plum & gray	7	5
271	"	1fr carmine & yellow	12	5
272	"	1.25fr dark green & blue ('53)	1.00	60
273	"	1.50fr violet & apple green	15	5
274	"	2fr olive green & buff	30	5
275	"	3fr olive green & pink	30	5
276	"	4fr chocolate & lilac	38	5
277	"	5fr deep plum & light blue green	55	7
278	"	6.50fr dk. car. & lilac	70	5
279	"	7fr dark green & fawn	70	10
280	A86	8fr green & light yellow ('53)	1.00	20
281	"	10fr deep plum & pale olive ('53)	2.00	5
282	"	20fr violet blue & dull salmon	1.60	10

Size: 22x32mm.

283	A86	50fr deep plum & gray blue ('53)	8.00	60
284	"	100fr green & buff ('53)	12.00	1.50
		Nos. 263-284 (22)	29.28	3.92

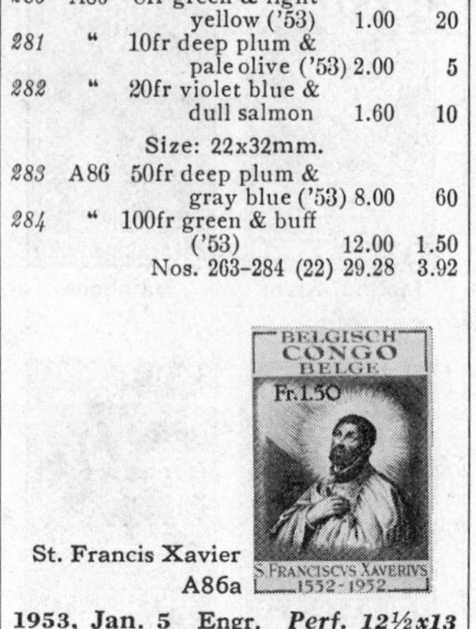

St. Francis Xavier

A86a

1953, Jan. 5 Engr. ***Perf. 12½x13***

285	A86a	1.50fr ultramarine & gray black	1.00	70

Issued to commemorate the 400th anniversary of the death of St. Francis Xavier.

Canoe on Lake Kivu

A87

1953, Jan. 5 ***Perf. 14***

286	A87	3fr carmine & black	1.65	35
287	"	7fr deep blue & brown orange	1.80	55

Issued to publicize the Kivu Festival, 1953.

Royal Colonial Institute Jubilee Medal

A88

Design: 6.50fr, Same with altered background and transposed inscriptions.

1954, Dec. 27 Photo. ***Perf. 13½***

288	A88	4.50fr indigo & gray	1.75	55
289	"	6.50fr dark green & brown	1.50	20

Issued to commemorate the 25th anniversary of the founding of the Belgian Royal Colonial Institute.

King Baudouin and Tropical Scene

A89

Designs: King and various views.

Engraved; Portrait Photogravure.

1955, Feb. 15 ***Perf. 11½*** **Unwmkd.**

Portrait in Black.

Inscribed "Congo Belge - Belgisch Congo."

290	A89	1.50fr rose carmine	1.00	35
291	"	3fr green	35	10
292	"	4.50fr ultramarine	45	18
293	"	6.50fr deep claret	70	15

Inscribed "Belgisch Congo - Congo Belge."

294	A89	1.50fr rose carmine	50	30
295	"	3fr green	35	10
296	"	4.50fr ultramarine	45	18
297	"	6.50fr deep claret	70	15
		Nos. 290-297 (8)	4.50	1.51

Map of Africa and Emblem of Royal Touring Club

A90

1955, July 26 Engr. ***Perf. 11½***

Inscription in French.

298	A90	6.50fr violet blue	4.00	45

Inscription in Flemish.

299	A90	6.50fr violet blue	4.00	45

Issued to publicize the fifth International Congress for African Tourism at Elizabethville, July 26 - Aug. 4, 1955.

Kings of Belgium—A91

1958, July 1 ***Perf. 12½*** **Unwmkd.**

300	A91	1fr rose violet	30	8
301	"	1.50fr ultramarine	30	6
302	"	3fr rose carmine	30	8
303	"	5fr green	1.00	70
304	"	6.50fr brown red	60	12
305	"	10fr dull violet	90	18
		Nos. 300-305 (6)	3.40	1.22

Issued to commemorate the 50th anniversary of Belgium's annexation of Congo.

Roan Antelope

A92

Black Buffaloes

A93

Animals: 20c, White rhinoceros. 40c, Giraffe. 50c, Thick-tailed bushbaby. 1fr, Gorilla. 2fr, Black-and-white colobus (monkey). 3fr, Elephants. 5fr, Okapis. 6.50fr, Impala. 8fr, Giant pangolin. 10fr, Eland and zebras.

1959 Photogravure. ***Perf. 11½***

Granite Paper.

306	A92	10c blue & brown	4	3
307	A93	20c red orange & slate	6	4
308	A92	40c brown & blue	6	6
309	A93	50c bright ultra., red & sepia	6	6

310 A92 1fr brown, green & black 8 6
311 A93 1.50fr black & orange yellow 10 8
312 A92 2fr crimson, black & brown 15 7
313 A93 3fr black, gray & lilac rose 20 15
314 A92 5fr brown, dark brown & bright green 45 10
315 A93 6.50fr blue, brown & orange yellow 60 10
316 A92 8fr orange brown, olive bistre & lilac 60 35
317 A93 10fr multicolored 60 15
Nos. 306–317 (12) 3.00 1.25

Madonna and Child
A94

1959, Dec. 1 *Perf. 11½* **Unwmkd.**

318 A94 50c golden brown, ochre & red brn. 10 6
319 " 1fr dark blue, purple & red brown 10 8
320 " 2fr gray, bright blue & red brown 20 15

Map of Africa
and Symbolic Honeycomb
A95

1960, Feb. 19 *Perf. 11½* **Unwmkd.**

Inscription in French.

321 A95 3fr gray & red 30 18

Inscription in Flemish.

322 A95 3fr gray & red 30 18

Issued to commemorate the 10th anniversary of the Commission for Technical Co-operation in Africa South of the Sahara. (C. C. T. A.)

Succeeding issues are listed under Congo Democratic Republic.

SEMI-POSTAL STAMPS.

Types of 1910-15 Issues
Surcharged in Red **+ 10c**

Perf. 14, 15

1918, May 15 **Unwmkd.**

B1 A29 5c+10c green & blue 35 50
B2 A30 10c+15c carmine & blue (I) 35 50
B3 A21 15c+20c blue green & blue 35 50
B4 A31 25c+25c deep blue & pale blue 50 50
B5 A23 40c+40c brown red & blue 60 75
B6 A24 50c+50c brown lake & blue 60 75
B7 A25 1fr+1fr olive bistre & blue 2.50 3.00
B8 A27 5fr+5fr ochre & blue 12.50 13.50
B9 A28 10fr+10fr green & blue 90.00 90.00
Nos. B1–B9 (9) 107.75 110.00

The position of the cross and the added value varies on the different stamps.
Nos. B1 to B9 exist imperforate.

SP1

Design: No. B11 inscribed "Belgisch Congo."

1925 *Perf. 12½.*

B10 SP1 25c+25c carmine & black 30 30
B11 " 25c+25c carmine & black 30 30

Colonial campaigns in 1914–1918.
The stamps with French and Flemish inscriptions alternate in the sheet.
The surtax helped erect at Kinshasa a monument to those who died in World War I.

Nurse Weighing Child
SP3

First Aid Station
SP5

Designs: 20c+10c, Missionary and Child. 60c+30c, Congo hospital. 1fr+50c, Dispensary service. 1.75fr+75c, Convalescent area. 3.50fr+1.50fr, Instruction on bathing infant. 5fr+2.50fr, Operating room. 10fr+5fr, Students.

1930, Jan. 16 **Engr.** *Perf. 11½*

B12 SP3 10c+5c vermilion 65 65
B13 " 20c+10c deep brown 85 85
B14 SP5 35c+15c dp. green 1.50 1.50
B15 " 60c+30c dull vio. 1.75 1.75
B16 SP3 1fr+50c dark carmine 2.50 2.50
B17 SP5 1.75fr+75c deep blue 3.50 3.50
B18 " 3.50fr+1.50fr rose lake 7.00 7.00
B19 " 5fr+2.50fr red brown 6.00 6.00
B20 " 10fr+5fr gray black 6.25 6.25
Nos. B12–B20 (9) 30.00 30.00

The surtax on these stamps was intended to aid welfare work among the natives, especially the children.

Nos. 161, 163
Surcharged "+50c" in Blue or Red.

1936, May 15 *Perf. 12½x12*

B21 A63 1.50fr+50c brown violet (Bl) 2.50 2.50
B22 " 2.50fr+50c light blue (R) 2.50 2.50

The surtax was for the benefit of the King Albert Memorial Fund.

Queen Astrid
with Congolese
Children
SP12

1936, Aug. 29 **Photo.** *Perf. 12½*

B23 SP12 1.25fr+5c dark brown 90 90
B24 " 1.50fr+10c dull rose 90 90
B25 " 2.50fr+25c dk. blue 1.00 1.00

Issued in memory of Queen Astrid. The surtax was for the aid of the National League for Protection of Native Children.

Souvenir Sheet.

SP13

1938, Oct. 3 *Perf. 11½*

B26 SP13 Sheet of six 12.00 12.00
a. 5c ultramarine & light brown (A64) 1.85 1.85
b. 90c ultramarine & light brown (A65) 1.85 1.85
c. 1.50fr ultramarine & light brown (A66) 1.85 1.85
d. 2.40fr ultramarine & light brown (A67) 1.85 1.85
e. 2.50fr ultramarine & light brown (A68) 1.85 1.85
f. 4.50fr ultramarine & light brown (A69) 1.85 1.85

Issued in sheets measuring 139x122mm. The star is printed in yellow. Issued in commemoration of the International Tourist Congress. A surtax of 3.15fr was for the benefit of the Congo Tourist Service.

Marabou Storks
and Vultures
SP14

Buffon's
Kob
SP15

Designs: 1.50fr+1.50fr, Pygmy chimpanzees. 4.50fr+4.50fr, Dwarf crocodiles. 5fr+5fr, Lioness.

1939 **Photogravure** *Perf. 14*

B27 SP14 1fr+1fr deep claret 5.25 4.75
B28 SP15 1.25fr+1.25fr car. 5.25 4.75
B29 " 1.50fr+1.50fr bright purple 8.50 8.25
B30 SP14 4.50fr+4.50fr slate green 5.25 4.75
B31 SP15 5fr+5fr brown 5.25 5.25
Nos. B27–B31 (5) 29.50 27.75

The surtax was for the Leopoldville Zoological Gardens.
Nos. B27–B31 were sold in full sets by subscription.

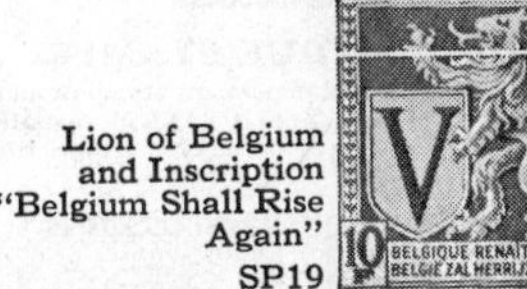

Lion of Belgium
and Inscription
"Belgium Shall Rise
Again"
SP19

1942, Feb. 17 **Engr.** *Perf. 12½*

B32 SP19 10fr+40fr bright green 1.75 1.75
B33 " 10fr+40fr violet blue 1.75 1.75

Nos. 193, 216, 198 and 220
Surcharged in Red

Au profit
de la
Croix Rouge
+ 50 Fr.
Ten voordeele
van het
Roode Kruis
a

Ten voordeele
van het
Roode Kruis
+ 100 Fr.
Au profit
de la
Croix Rouge
b

Au profit de la
Croix Rouge
+ 100 Fr.
Ten voordeele van het
Roode Kruis
c

1945

B34 A72 (a) 50c+50fr deep green 3.25 3.50
B35 A73 (b) 1.25fr+100fr rose red & black 3.25 3.50
B36 A74 (c) 1.75fr+100fr dark gray brown 3.25 3.75
B37 A75 (b) 3.50fr+100fr dark olive green 3.25 3.75

The surtax was for the Red Cross.
Nos. B34–B37 were sold in full sets by subscription.

Mozart at Age 7
SP20

Queen Elisabeth and Sonata
by Mozart
SP21

Engraved.

1956, Oct. 10 *Perf. 11½* **Unwmkd.**

B38 SP20 4.50fr+1.50fr bright lilac 2.00 1.50
B39 SP21 6.50fr+2.50fr ultramarine 2.65 2.50

Issued to commemorate the 200th anniversary of the birth of Wolfgang Amadeus Mozart.
The surtax was for the Pro-Mozart Committee.

Nurse and
Children
SP22

Designs: 4.50fr+50c, Patient receiving injection. 6.50fr+40c, Patient being bandaged.

1957, Dec. 10 Photo. *Perf. 13x10½*

Cross in Carmine.

B40	SP22	3fr+50c dark blue	1.50	1.50
B41	"	4.50fr+50c dk. green	1.25	1.25
B42	"	6.50fr+50c red brn.	1.75	1.75

The surtax was for the Red Cross.

High Jumper
SP23

Sports: 1.50fr+50c, Hurdlers. 2fr+1fr, Soccer. 3fr+1.25fr, Javelin thrower. 6.50fr+3.50fr, Discus thrower.

1960, May 2 *Perf. 13½* Unwmkd.

B43	SP23	50c+25c ultramarine & red	15	15
B44	"	1.50fr+50c carmine & green	20	20
B45	"	2fr+1fr green & vermilion	35	35
B46	"	3fr+1.25fr rose claret & blue	1.25	1.25
B47	"	6.50fr+3.50fr red brown & car.	1.50	1.50
		Nos. B43-B47 (5)	3.45	3.45

Issued to commemorate the 17th Olympic Games, Rome, Aug. 25–Sept. 11. The surtax was for the youth of Congo.

AIR POST STAMPS.

Wharf on Congo River
AP1

Congo "Country Store"
AP2

View of Congo River
AP3

Stronghold in the Interior
AP4

Engraved.

1920, July 1 *Perf. 12* Unwmkd.

C1	AP1	50c orange & black	30	15
		a. Booklet pane of 10		
C2	AP2	1fr dull violet & black	30	15
		a. Booklet pane of 10		
C3	AP3	2fr blue & black	1.00	35
C4	AP4	5fr green & black	1.85	85

Kraal
AP5

Porters on Safari
AP6

1930, Apr. 2

C5	AP5	15fr dk. brn. & blk.	4.00	1.50
C6	AP6	30fr brown violet & black	5.00	1.50

Fokker F VII over Congo
AP7

1934, Jan. 22 *Perf. 13½x14*

C7	AP7	50c gray black	20	15
C8	"	1fr dark carmine	30	20
		a. Bklt. pane of 8	7.00	
C9	"	1.50fr green	20	15
C10	"	3fr brown	35	20
C11	"	4.50fr bright ultra.	55	15
		a. Bklt. pane of 8	13.00	
C12	"	5fr red brown	45	20
C13	"	15fr brown violet	85	55
C14	"	30fr red orange	1.65	1.35
C15	"	50fr violet	5.00	2.10
		Nos. C7-C15 (9)	9.55	5.05

The 1fr, 3fr, 4.50fr, 5fr and 15fr exist imperf.

No. C10 Surcharged in Blue with New Value and Bars.

1936, Mar. 25

C16	AP7	3.50fr on 3fr brown	25	15

No. C9 Surcharged in Black

50 c.

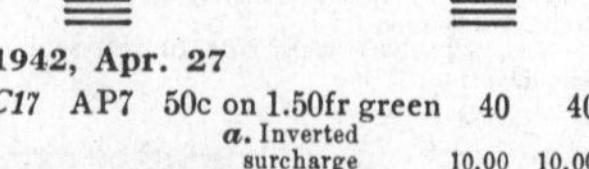

1942, Apr. 27

C17	AP7	50c on 1.50fr green	40	40
		a. Inverted surcharge	10.00	10.00

POSTAGE DUE STAMPS.

In 1908–23 regular postage stamps handstamped "TAXES" or "TAXE," usually boxed, were used in lieu of postage due stamps.

D1

D2

Perf. 14, 14½.

1923-29 Typographed. Unwmkd.

J1	D1	5c black brown	20	15
J2	"	10c rose red	20	15
J3	"	15c violet	30	20
J4	"	30c green	50	45
J5	"	50c ultramarine	70	60
J6	"	50c blue ('29)	70	60
J7	"	1fr gray	80	55
		Nos. J1-J7 (7)	3.40	2.70

1943 *Perf. 14x14½*

J8	D2	10c olive green	10	10
J9	"	20c dark ultramarine	10	10
J10	"	50c green	18	18
J11	"	1fr dark brown	22	22
J12	"	2fr yellow orange	30	30
		Nos. J8-J12 (5)	90	90

1943 *Perf. 12½*

J8a	D2	10c olive green	30	30
J9a	"	20c dark ultramarine	30	30
J10a	"	50c green	30	30
J11a	"	1fr dark brown	50	50
J12a	"	2fr yellow orange	50	50
		Nos. J8a-J12a (5)	1.90	1.90

D3

1957 Engraved. *Perf. 11½*

J13	D3	10c olive brown	10	10
J14	"	20c claret	12	12
J15	"	50c green	18	18
J16	"	1fr light blue	35	35
J17	"	2fr vermilion	55	50
J18	"	4fr purple	75	70
J19	"	6fr violet blue	1.10	90
		Nos. J13-J19 (7)	3.15	2.85

PARCEL POST STAMPS.

PP1

PP2 PP3

Handstamped Surcharges on Nos. 5, 11–12

1887–1893 *Perf. 15* Unwmkd.

Blue-Black Surcharge

Q1	PP1	3.50fr on 5fr lilac	500.00	400.00

Black Surcharge

Q3	PP2	3.50fr on 5fr violet	525.00	300.00
Q4	PP3	3.50fr on 5fr violet ('88)	400.00	250.00
		a. Blue surcharge	325.00	225.00
Q6	PP3	3.50fr on 5fr gray ('93)	100.00	65.00

Nos. Q1, Q3–Q4, Q4a and Q6 are known with inverted surcharge, No. Q1 with double surcharge and No. Q6 in pair with unsurcharged stamp. Most of these handstamp varieties sell for more than the normal surcharges.

BELGIAN EAST AFRICA

(See Ruanda-Urundi in Vol. IV.)

BELGIUM

(bĕl'jĭ·ŭm)

LOCATION — In western Europe, bordering on the North Sea.

GOVT.—Constitutional Monarchy.

AREA—11,781 sq. mi.

POP.—9,830,000 (est. 1977).

CAPITAL—Brussels.

100 Centimes = 1 Franc

Prices of early Belgian stamps vary according to condition. Quotations for Nos. 1–12 are for fine copies. Very fine to superb specimens sell at much higher prices, and inferior or poor copies sell at reduced prices, depending on the condition of the individual specimen.

Prices for unused stamps of 1849–1863 issues are for copies with original gum. Copies without gum sell for one third of the figures quoted, or less.

King Leopold I
A1 A2

Wmk. 96

Wmkd. Two "L"s Framed. (96)

1849 Engraved. *Imperf.*

1	A1	10c brown	2000.00	72.50
		a. 10c red brown	4500.00	250.00
2	"	20c blue	2850.00	57.50
		a. 20c milky blue	4000.00	165.00

The reprints are on thick and thin wove and thick laid paper unwatermarked.

A souvenir sheet containing reproductions of the 10c, 20c and 40c of 1849–51 with black burelage on back was issued Oct. 17, 1949, for the centenary of the first Belgian stamps. It was sold at BEPITEC 1949, an international stamp exhibition at Brussels, and was not valid. Size: 139x90mm.

1849-50

3	A2	10c brown ('50)	1750.00	62.50
4	"	20c blue ('50)	1850.00	52.50
5	"	40c carmine rose	1800.00	250.00

Nos. 3–5 on thin paper are as priced. Copies on thick paper sell for 5 to 12 per cent more.

Wmkd.
Two "L"s Without Frame. (96)

1851–54

6	A2	10c brown	475.00	7.50
		a. Ribbed paper ('54)	525.00	50.00
7	A2	20c blue	475.00	7.50
		a. Ribbed paper ('54)	525.00	50.00
8	A2	40c carmine rose	2400.00	70.00
		a. Ribbed paper ('54)	2500.00	275.00

Nos. 6–8 were printed on thin and thick paper. Nos. 6–7 on thick paper, unused, sell for 7 to 10 percent more.

1858–61 Unwmkd.

9	A2	1c green ('61)	225.00	165.00
		a. Laid paper		
10	"	10c brown	375.00	6.75
11	"	20c blue	375.00	6.75

12 A2 40c carmine rose 2250.00 67.50

Nos. 9 and 13 were valid for postage on newspapers and printed matter only.

Reprints of Nos. 9 to 12 are on thin wove paper. The colors are brighter than those of the originals. They were made from the dies and show lines outside the stamps.

1863

Perf. 12½, 12½x13, 12½x13½, 14½

13 A2 1c green 42.50 27.50
14 " 10c brown 65.00 1.35
15 " 20c blue 72.50 1.10
16 " 40c carmine rose 400.00 20.00

King Leopold I

A3 A3a

A4 A4a

A5

London Print.

1865 **Typographed** ***Perf. 14***

17 A5 1fr pale violet 850.00 110.00

Brussels Print.

Thick or Thin Paper.

1865-66 ***Perf. 15, 14½x14***

18 A3 10c slate ('66) 100.00 85
a. Pair, imperf. between 175.00
19 A3a 20c blue ('66) 115.00 85
a. 20c lilac blue 125.00 90
20 A4 30c brown 225.00 4.75
a. Pair, imperf. between 750.00
21 A4a 40c rose ('66) 350.00 13.50
22 A5 1fr violet 850.00 100.00

Nos. 18 to 22 on thin paper are perf. 14½x14; on thick paper, perf. 15.

The reprints are on thin paper, imperforate and ungummed.

Coat of Arms

A6

1866-67 ***Imperf.***

23 A6 1c gray 200.00 140.00

Perf. 15, 14½x14

24 A6 1c gray 35.00 14.00
25 " 2c blue ('67) 130.00 70.00
a. 2c ultramarine 140.00 70.00
26 " 5c brown 130.00 70.00

Nos. 23-26 were valid for postage on newspapers and printed matter only.

Nos. 24 to 26 on thin paper are perf. 14½ x 14; on thick paper, perf. 15.

Reprints of Nos. 24 to 26 are on thin paper, imperforate and ungummed.

King Leopold II

A7 A8

A9 A10

A11 A12

1869-70 ***Perf. 15***

28 A7 1c green 9.00 18
a. Imperf., pair 200.00
29 " 2c ultra. ('70) 12.50 35
a. Imperf., pair 150.00
30 " 5c buff ('70) 52.50 55
a. Imperf., pair 300.00
31 " 8c lilac ('70) 90.00 57.50
32 A8 10c green 30.00 18
a. Imperf., pair 225.00
33 A9 20c lt. ultra. ('70) 100.00 75
34 A10 30c buff ('70) 85.00 4.00
a. Imperf., pair 600.00
35 A11 40c brt. rose('70) 115.00 4.00
a. Imperf., pair 2250.00
36 A12 1fr dull lilac ('70) 225.00 17.50
a. 1fr rose lilac 225.00 21.00
b. Imperf., pair 1750.00

The frames and inscriptions of Nos. 30, 31 and 42 differ slightly from the illustration.

Minor "broken letter" varieties exist on several values.

Imperf. varieties of 1869-1912 (between Nos. 28-105) are without gum.

See also Nos. 40-43, 49-51, 55.

A13 A14 A15

1875-78

37 A13 25c olive bistre 65.00 1.35
a. 25c ochre 65.00 1.35
b. Imperf., pair 120.00
38 A14 50c gray 225.00 6.50
a. 50c gray black 450.00 45.00
39 A15 5fr pale brown ('78) 3500.00 850.00
a. 5fr deep red brown 1850.00 850.00
Roller cancel 300.00

Printed in Aniline Colors.

1881 ***Perf. 14, 15***

40 A7 1c gray green 8.50 60
41 " 2c light ultra. 10.00 75
a. Imperf., pair 225.00
42 " 5c orange buff 42.50 85
a. 5c red orange 42.50 85
b. Imperf., pair 300.00
43 A8 10c gray green 30.00 65
a. Imperf., pair 225.00
44 A13 25c olive bistre 45.00 1.50
a. Imperf., pair 120.00
Nos. 40-44 (5) 136.00 4.35

King Leopold II

A16 A17

A18 A19

1883

45 A16 10c carmine 32.50 60
a. Imperf., pair 90.00
46 A17 20c gray 135.00 3.00
a. Imperf., pair 90.00
47 A18 25c blue 240.00 27.50
a. Imperf., pair 90.00
Roller cancel 7.50
48 A19 50c violet 210.00 25.00
a. Imperf., pair 90.00
Roller cancel 6.50

A20 A21

A22

1884-85 ***Perf. 14***

49 A7 1c olive green 10.00 40
50 " 1c gray 5.25 6
a. Imperf., pair 75.00
51 " 5c green 13.50 10
a. Imperf., pair 125.00
52 A20 10c rose, *bluish* 8.25 6
a. Grayish paper 10.00 35
b. Imperf., pair 100.00
c. Yellowish paper 110.00 30.00
53 A21 25c blue, *pink* ('85) 12.00 45
a. Imperf., pair 400.00
54 A22 1fr brn., *greenish* 600.00 8.50
a. Imperf., pair 350.00

The frame and inscription of No. 51 differ slightly from the illustration. See note after No. 36.

A23 A24

A25 A26

1886-91

55 A7 2c purple brown ('88) 11.00 40
56 A23 20c olive, *greenish* 140.00 55
a. Imperf., pair 525.00
57 A24 35c violet brown, *brownish* ('91) 21.00 2.10
a. Imperf., pair 140.00
58 A25 50c bister, *yellowish* 11.00 1.50
59 A26 2fr violet, *pale lilac* 150.00 20.00
Roller cancel 6.00

Coat of Arms **King Leopold**

A27 A28

1893-1900

60 A27 1c gray 1.25 10
61 " 2c yellow 1.65 1.25
a. Wmkd. coat of arms in sheet ('95)
62 " 2c violet brown ('94) 3.25 22
63 " 2c red brown ('98) 3.25 22
64 " 5c yellow green 4.75 12
65 A28 10c orange brown 5.50 10
a. Imperf., pair 225.00
66 " 10c bright rose ('00) 5.50 10
67 " 20c olive green 32.50 45
a. Imperf., pair 225.00
68 " 25c ultramarine 27.50 45
a. No ball to "5" in upper left corner 45.00 16.50
69 " 35c violet brown 47.50 1.00
a. 35c brown 62.50 1.25
70 " 50c bistre 85.00 8.50
71 " 50c gray ('97) 85.00 1.85
72 " 1fr carmine, *light green* 90.00 14.00
73 " 1fr orange ('00) 150.00 4.75
a. Imperf., pair 175.00
74 " 2fr lilac, *rose* 140.00 115.00
75 " 2fr lilac ('00) 235.00 15.00

Prices quoted for Nos. 60-107, B1-B24 are for stamps with label attached. Stamps without label sell for about half.

Antwerp Exhibition Issue.

Arms of Antwerp

A29

1894

76 A29 5c green, *rose* 9.00 3.25
77 " 10c carmine, *bluish* 8.50 1.25
78 " 25c blue, *rose* 50 45

Brussels Exhibition Issue.

St. Michael and Satan

A30 A31

1896-97 ***Perf. 14x14½.***

79 A30 5c deep violet 1.25 75
80 A31 10c orange brown 16.50 3.25
81 " 10c lilac brown 75 60

Coat of Arms **King Leopold II**

A32 A33

King Leopold II

A34 A35

A36 A37

A38 A39

Two types of 1c:

I. Periods after "Dimanche" and "Zondag" in label.

II. No period after "Dimanche". Period often missing after "Zondag".

1905-07 ***Perf. 14.***

82	A32	1c gray (I) ('07)	2.50	15
		a. Type II ('08)	2.50	18
83	"	2c red brn. ('07)	10.00	2.00
84	"	5c green ('07)	11.00	15
		a. Booklet pane of 5		
		b. Booklet pane of 10		
85	A33	10c dull rose	4.00	12
		a. Imperf., pair	250.00	
		b. Booklet pane of 10		
		c. Booklet pane of 5		
86	A34	20c olive green	27.50	60
		a. Imperf., pair	175.00	
87	A35	25c ultramarine	22.50	55
		a. 25c dull blue	22.50	55
		b. Imperf., pair	125.00	
88	A36	35c purple brown	42.50	1.25
		a. Imperf., pair	500.00	
89	A37	50c bluish gray	110.00	1.35
90	A38	1fr yellow	140.00	5.50
		a. Imperf., pair	325.00	
91	A39	2fr violet	140.00	15.00
		Bar cancellation		4.00
		Nos. 82-91 (10)	510.00	26.67

Numeral

A40

Coat of Arms

A41

Lion of Belgium

A42

King Albert I

A43

A44

1912

92	A40	1c orange	10	10
		a. Imperf., pair	4.00	
93	A41	2c orange brown	25	25
94	A42	5c green	10	10
		a. Booklet pane of 10		
		b. Booklet pane of 5		
95	A43	10c red	1.65	25
		a. Booklet pane of 5		
		b. Booklet pane of 10		
96	"	20c olive green	22.50	1.25
97	"	35c bistre brown	2.00	75
98	"	40c green	32.50	20.00
99	"	50c gray	2.00	75
100	"	1fr orange	13.00	4.25
101	"	2fr violet	35.00	22.50
102	A44	5fr plum	250.00	40.00
		Nos. 92-102 (11)	359.10	90.20

A45

1912-13 **Larger Head**

103	A45	10c red	30	15
		a. Without engraver's name	10	10
		b. Imperf., pair	3.50	
		c. Booklet pane of 5		
		d. Booklet pane of 10		
		e. As "a", booklet pane of 5		
		f. As "a", booklet pane of 10		
104	"	20c olive green ('13)	50	30
		a. Without engraver's name	90	85
105	"	25c ultramarine	5.00	1.25
		a. Without engraver's name	.30	30
107	"	40c green ('13)	50	45

King Albert I

A46

Cloth Hall of Ypres

A47

Bridge of Dinant

A48

Library of Louvain

A49

Scheldt River at Antwerp

A50

Anti-slavery Campaign in the Congo

A51

King Albert I at Furnes

A52

Kings of Belgium

Leopold I, Albert I, Leopold II

A53

1915-20 **Typographed.** ***Perf. 14, 14½***

108	A46	1c orange	6	5
109	"	2c chocolate	6	5
110	"	3c gray black ('20)	18	6
111	"	5c green	45	5
112	"	10c carmine	85	5
113	"	15c purple	1.00	6
114	"	20c red violet	85	5
115	"	25c blue	1.15	18
		Engraved.		
116	A47	35c brown orange & black	1.00	30
117	A48	40c green & black	1.50	30
		a. Vertical pair, imperf. between		
118	A49	50c carmine rose & black	7.25	25
119	A50	1fr violet	37.50	45
120	A51	2fr slate	55.00	2.00
121	A52	5fr deep blue	425.00	135.00
		Telegraph or railroad cancel		100.00
122	A53	10fr brown	62.50	37.50
		Nos. 108-122 (15)	594.35	176.35

Two types each of the 1c, 10c and 20c; three of the 2c and 15c; four of the 5c, differing in the top left corner.

Nos. 108 to 120 and 122 exist imperforate. See also No. 138.

Perron of Liége (Fountain)

A54

King Albert in Trench Helmet

A55

1919 ***Perf. 11½***

123	A54	25c deep blue	3.25	15
		a. Sheet of ten	6000.00	6000.00

1919 ***Perf. 11, 11½, 11½x11, 11x11½.***

		Size: 18½x22mm.		
124	A55	1c lilac brown	10	10
125	"	2c olive	10	10
		Size: 23x26mm.		
126	A55	5c green	60	25
127	"	10c carmine	25	15
128	"	15c gray violet	30	15
129	"	20c olive black	1.65	1.50
130	"	25c deep blue	1.85	1.75
131	"	35c bistre brown	2.75	3.00
132	"	40c red	4.50	4.00
133	"	50c red brown	11.00	9.00
134	"	1fr light orange	62.50	47.50
135	"	2fr violet	675.00	525.00
		Size: 28x33⅛mm.		
136	A55	5fr car. lake	200.00	185.00
137	"	10fr claret	240.00	225.00
		Nos. 124-137 (14)	1200.60	1002.50

Type of 1915 Inscribed: "FRANK" instead of "FRANKEN"

1919, Dec. ***Perf. 14, 15***

138	A52	5fr deep blue	5.25	2.00
		a. Vert. pair, imperf. between		

Town Hall at Termonde

A56 A57

1920 ***Perf. 11½***

139	A56	65c claret & black	1.85	20
		a. Center inverted	10,000.00	10,000.00

Semi-Postal Stamps of 1920 Surcharged in Red or Black

20c X 20c X

1921 ***Perf. 12***

140	SP6	20c on 5c dp. grn. (R)	2.25	35
		a. Invtd. surcharge	300.00	300.00
141	SP7	20c on 10c carmine	1.75	35
		a. Surcharged on back instead of face		
		b. Invtd. surcharge	300.00	300.00
142	SP8	20c on 15c dark brown (R)	2.25	85
		a. Invtd. surcharge	300.00	300.00
		Red Surcharge.		
143	A57	55c on 65c claret & black	2.75	45
		a. Pair, one without surcharge	5.00	1.25

A58 A59

1922-27 **Typographed** ***Perf. 14***

144	A58	1c orange	8	5
145	"	2c olive ('26)	18	8
146	"	3c terra cotta	10	3
147	"	5c gray	12	3
		a. Booklet pane of 6	9.00	
148	"	10c blue green	30	3
149	"	15c plum ('23)	40	5
		a. Booklet pane of 6	10.00	
150	"	20c black brown	85	5
151	"	25c dull violet	50	8
152	"	30c vermilion	1.25	10
153	"	30c rose ('25)	1.25	5
154	"	35c red brown	70	10
		a. Booklet pane of 6	7.50	
155	"	35c blue green ('27)	4.00	30

156 A58 40c rose 1.35 8
157 " 50c bistre ('25) 1.25 8
158 " 60c olive brown ('27) 6.50 3
a. Booklet pane of 6 15.00
159 " 1.25fr deep blue ('26) 2.00 85
160 " 1.50fr bright blue ('26) 6.00 18
161 " 1.75fr ultra. ('27) 5.50 12
a. Tête bêche pair 18.00 9.00
b. Bklt. pane of 6 47.50
c. Bklt. pane 4 + 2 labels 57.50
Nos. 144-161 (18) 32.33 2.29

See also Nos. 185-190.

Perf. 11½, 11½x11, 11½x12, 11½x12½.

1921-25 **Engraved**

162 A59 50c dull blue 60 5
163 " 75c scarlet ('22) 45 15
164 " 75c ultramarine ('24) 90 15
165 " 1fr blk. brown ('22) 1.90 12
166 " 1fr dark blue ('25) 1.35 12
167 " 2fr dark green ('22) 1.90 30
168 " 5fr brn. vio. ('23) 27.50 27.50
169 " 10fr magenta ('22) 27.50 3.25
Nos. 162-169 (8) 62.10 31.64

No. 162 measures 18x20¾mm. and was printed in sheets of 100.

Philatelic Exhibition Issue.

1921, May 26 ***Perf. 11½***

170 A59 50c dark blue 10.00 7.00
a. Sheet of 25 275.00 225.00

No. 170 measures 17½x21¼mm., was printed in sheets of 25 and sold at the Philatelic Exhibition at Brussels.

Philatelic Exhibition Issue.

Souvenir Sheet.

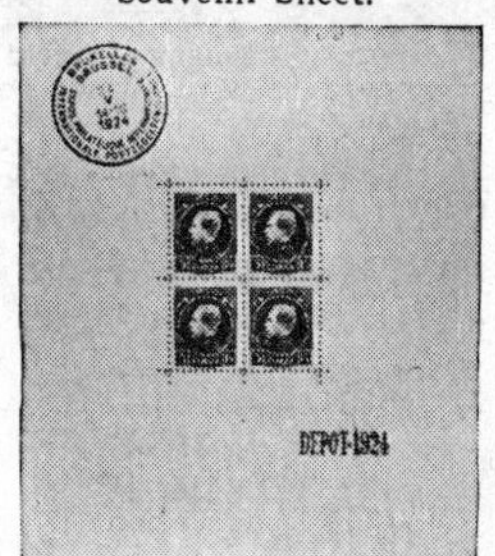

A59a

1924, May 24 ***Perf. 11½***

171 A59a 5fr red brown, sheet of 4 85.00 90.00
a. Single stamp (A59) 18.50 18.50

Sold only at the International Philatelic Exhibition, Brussels. Sheet size: 130x145 mm.

Kings Leopold I and Albert I

A60

1925 ***Perf. 14***

172 A60 10c deep green 16.00 12.50
173 " 15c dull violet 10.00 9.50
174 " 20c red brown 10.00 9.50
175 " 25c greenish black 10.00 9.50
176 " 30c vermilion 10.00 9.50
177 " 35c light blue 10.00 9.50
178 " 40c brownish blk. 10.00 9.50
179 " 50c yellow brown 10.00 9.50
180 " 75c dark blue 10.00 9.50
181 " 1fr dark violet 16.00 12.50
182 " 2fr ultramarine 10.00 9.50
183 " 5fr blue black 11.50 11.00
184 " 10fr deep rose 16.50 13.50
Nos. 172-184 (13) 150.00 135.00

75th anniversary of Belgian postage stamps.

Nos. 172-184 were sold only in sets and only by The Administration of Posts, not at post offices.

A61

1926-27 **Typographed.**

185 A61 75c dark violet 1.65 65
186 " 1fr pale yellow 1.15 25
187 " 1fr rose red ('27) 3.75 15
a. Tête bêche pair 10.00 6.00
b. Bklt. pane of 6 27.50
c. Bklt. pane 4 + 2 labels 30.00
188 " 2fr Prussian blue 6.25 12
189 " 5fr emerald ('27) 45.00 75
190 " 10fr dark brn. ('27) 90.00 2.00
Nos. 185-190 (6) 147.80 3.92

Stamps of 1921-27 Surcharged in Carmine, Red or Blue

≡ 1F75 ≡

1927

191 A58 3c on 2c olive (C) 12 12
192 " 10c on 15c plum (R) 25 10
193 " 35c on 40c rose (Bl) 75 12
194 " 1.75fr on 1.50fr bright blue (C) 4.25 1.00

Nos. 153, 185 and 159 Surcharged in Black

BRUXELLES
1929
BRUSSEL
=5c=

1929, Jan. 1

195 A58 5c on 30c rose 18 10
196 A61 5c on 75c dk. violet 55 35
197 A58 5c on 1.25fr dp. blue 25 15

The surcharge on Nos. 195 to 197 is a precancelation which alters the value of the stamp to which it is applied.

Prices for precanceled stamps in first column are for those which have not been through the post and have original gum. Prices in second column are for postally used, gumless stamps.

A63

A64

1929-32 **Typographed** ***Perf. 14***

198 A63 1c orange 12 12
199 " 2c emerald ('31) 45 45
200 " 3c red brown 12 5
201 " 5c slate 18 3
a. Tête bêche pair 1.65 1.35
b. Bklt. pane of 6 11.50
c. Bklt. pane 4 + 2 labels 11.00
202 " 10c olive green 18 3
a. Tête bêche pair 75 60
b. Bklt. pane of 6 6.00
c. Bklt. pane 4 + 2 labels 6.00
203 " 20c bright violet 2.25 12
204 " 25c rose red 1.35 5
a. Tête bêche pair 4.25 3.25
b. Bklt. pane of 6 12.00
c. Bklt. pane 4 + 2 labels 11.00
205 " 35c green 1.90 12
a. Tête bêche pair 6.25 5.00
b. Bklt. pane of 6 14.00
c. Bklt. pane 4 + 2 labels 13.00
206 " 40c red violet ('30) 1.90 5
a. Tête bêche pair 6.00 4.25
b. Bklt. pane of 6 14.00
c. Bklt. pane 4 + 2 labels 13.00
207 A63 50c deep blue 1.50 5
a. Tête bêche pair 4.75 2.50
b. Bklt. pane of 6 11.00
c. Bklt. pane 4 + 2 labels 11.00
208 " 60c rose ('30) 6.00 15
a. Tête bêche pair 16.00 13.00
b. Bklt. pane of 6 40.00
c. Bklt. pane 4 + 2 labels 40.00
209 " 70c orange brown ('30) 4.25 5
a. Tête bêche pair 11.00 9.50
b. Bklt. pane of 6 30.00
c. Booklet pane 4 + 2 labels 30.00
210 " 75c dark blue ('30) 6.25 8
a. Tête bêche pair 16.50 15.00
211 " 75c dp. brown ('32) 27.50 5
a. Tête bêche pair 60.00 40.00
b. Booklet pane of 4 + 2 labels 135.00
c. Bklt. pane of 6 185.00
Nos. 198-211 (14) 53.95 1.40

Nos. 198 and 199 exist se-tenant in booklets.

1929, Jan. 25 **Engr.** ***Perf. 14½, 14***

212 A64 10fr dark brown 42.50 9.50
213 " 20fr dark green 215.00 9.50
214 " 50fr red violet 8.00 6.75
a. Perf. 14½ 42.50 32.50
215 A64 100fr rose lake 19.00 16.50
a. Perf. 14½ 42.50 32.50

Nos. 212 to 215 exist imperforate.

Peter Paul Rubens

A65

Zenobe Gramme

A66

1930, Apr. 26 **Photo.** ***Perf. 12½x12***

216 A65 35c blue green 1.50 30
217 A66 35c blue green 1.50 30

No. 216 issued for the Antwerp Exhibition, No. 217 the Liege Exhibition.

King Leopold I, by Jacques de Winne

A67

King Leopold II, by Joseph Lempoels

A68

Design: 1.75fr, King Albert I.

1930, July 1 **Engraved** ***Perf. 11½***

218 A67 60c brown violet 35 15
219 A68 1fr carmine 5.50 3.00
220 " 1.75fr dark blue 13.50 2.00

Centenary of Belgian independence.

Antwerp Exhibition Issue.

Souvenir Sheet.

Arms of Antwerp

A70

1930, Aug. 9 ***Perf. 11½***

221 A70 Sheet of one 185.00 185.00
a. 4fr dark green & gray green 120.00 120.00

Issued in sheets of one stamp measuring 142x141 mm. Inscription in lower margin "ATELIER DU TIMBRE—1930—ZEGELFABRIEK." Each purchaser of a ticket to the Antwerp Philatelic Exhibition, August 9th to 15th, 1930, was allowed to purchase one of the exhibition stamps. The ticket cost 6 francs.

Nos. 218-220 Overprinted in Blue or Red

B.I.T.
OCT. 1930

1930, Oct.

222 A67 60c brn. vio. (Bl) 3.25 2.75
223 A68 1fr carmine (Bl) 15.00 12.00
224 " 1.75fr dk. blue (R) 37.50 25.00

Issued to commemorate the 50th meeting of the administrative council of the International Labor Bureau at Brussels.

The names of the painters and the initials of the engraver have been added at the foot of these stamps.

Stamps of 1929-30 Surcharged in Blue or Black:

≡ 2c ≡

a

BELGIQUE
1931
BELGIË
≡ 10c ≡

b

1931, Feb. 20 ***Perf. 14***

225 A63 (*a*) 2c on 3c red brown (Bl) 15 10
226 " (*b*) 10c on 60c rose (Bk) 1.85 22

The surcharge on No. 226 is a precancelation which alters the denomination. See note after No. 197.

A71

A71a

King Albert

1931, June 15 **Photogravure**

227 A71 1fr brown carmine 1.35 12

1932, June 1

228 A71a 75c bistre brown 1.50 4
a. Tête bêche pair 22.50 18.50
b. Booklet pane of 6 27.50
c. Bklt. pane 4 + 2 labels 27.50

See also No. 257.

A72

1931-32 **Engraved**

229 A72 1.25fr gray black 1.50 35
230 " 1.50fr brown violet 2.50 30
231 " 1.75fr deep blue 2.00 12
232 " 2fr red brown 3.00 12
233 " 2.45fr deep violet 4.75 30
234 " 2.50fr black brown ('32) 42.50 35
235 " 5fr deep green 37.50 60
236 " 10fr claret 110.00 9.00
Nos. 229-236 (8) 203.75 11.14

Nos. 206 and 209 Surcharged as No. 226, but dated "1932."

1932, Jan. 1

240 A63 10c on 40c red vio. 8.25 45
241 " 10c on 70c org. brn. 6.00 30

The surcharge on Nos. 240 and 241 is a precancelation which alters the value of the stamps. See note after No. 197.

Gleaner A73 — Mercury A74

1932, June 1 Typo. *Perf. 13½x14*

245 A73 2c pale green 55 55
246 A74 5c deep orange 45 8
247 A73 10c olive green 1.00 5
 a. Tête bêche pair 8.50 6.75
 b. Booklet pane of 6 15.00
 c. Bklt. pane 4 + 2 labels 15.00
248 A74 20c bright violet 2.00 15
249 A73 25c deep red 1.85 5
 a. Tête bêche pair 7.00 6.00
 b. Bklt. pane of 6 15.00
 c. Bklt. pane 4 + 2 labels 15.00
250 A74 35c deep green 12.50 8
 Nos. 245-250 (6) 18.35 96

Auguste Piccard's Balloon
A75

1932, Nov. 26 Engraved *Perf. 11½*

251 A75 75c red brown 13.50 18
252 " 1.75fr dark blue 30.00 1.85
253 " 2.50fr dark violet 27.50 9.00

Issued in commemoration of Prof. Auguste Piccard's two ascents to the stratosphere.
Nos. 251 to 253 are known imperforate.

Nos. 206 and 209 Surcharged as No. 226, but dated "1933."

1933, Nov. *Perf. 14*

254 A63 10c on 40c red vio. 32.50 4.00
255 " 10c on 70c org brn. 17.50 1.00

No. 206 Surcharged as No. 226, but dated "1934."

1934, Feb.

256 A63 10c on 40c red vio. 16.00 50

The surcharge on Nos. 254 to 256 is a precancelation which alters the value of the stamps. See note after No. 197.
Regummed copies of Nos. 254-256 abound.

King Albert Memorial Issue.

Type of 1932 with Black Margins.

1934, Mar. 10 Photogravure

257 A71a 75c black 1.00 7
 a. Imperf., pair 62.50

Brussels International Exhibition of 1935.

Congo Pavilion
A76

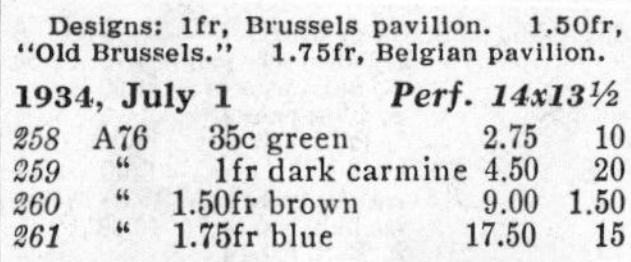

Designs: 1fr, Brussels pavilion. 1.50fr, "Old Brussels." 1.75fr, Belgian pavilion.

1934, July 1 *Perf. 14x13½*

258 A76 35c green 2.75 10
259 " 1fr dark carmine 4.50 20
260 " 1.50fr brown 9.00 1.50
261 " 1.75fr blue 17.50 15

King Leopold III
A80 — A81

1934-35 *Perf. 13½x14.*

262 A80 70c olive black ('35) 1.00 3
 a. Tête bêche pair 2.75 1.10
 b. Booklet pane of 6 7.50
 c. Bklt. pane 4 + 2 labels 7.50
263 " 75c brown 2.85 15

Perf. 14x13½

264 A81 1fr rose car. ('35) 22.00 45

Coat of Arms
A82

1935-46 Typographed. *Perf. 14.*

265 A82 2c green ('37) 5 3
266 " 5c orange 5 3
267 " 10c olive bistre 8 3
 a. Tête bêche pair 40 30
 b. Bklt. pane 4 + 2 labels 6.00
 c. Booklet pane of 6 6.00
268 " 15c dark violet 8 3
269 " 20c lilac 18 5
270 " 25c carmine rose 30 3
 a. Tête bêche pair 1.00 60
 c. Bklt. pane 4 + 2 labels 6.00
 d. Booklet pane of 6 6.00
270B " 25c yellow orange ('46) 15 5
271 " 30c brown 65 5
272 " 35c green 12 3
 a. Tête bêche pair 40 30
 b. Booklet pane of 6 4.00
 c. Bklt. pane 4 + 2 labels 4.00
273 " 40c red violet ('38) 65 5
274 " 50c blue 80 3
274A " 60c slate ('41) 30 5
274B " 70c lt. blue green ('45) 40 5
274C " 75c lilac rose ('45) 1.50 5
274D " 1fr red brown ('45) 90 5
 Nos. 265-274D (15) 6.21 61

Several stamps of type A82 exist in various shades.
See also Nos. 352, 352A and 353.
Nos. 265 and 345 were privately overprinted, and surcharged "+10FR.", by the Association Belgo-Américaine for the dedication of the Bastogne Memorial, July 16, 1950. The overprint is in four types.

King Leopold III
A83 — A83a

1936-43 Photo. *Perf. 14, 14x13½*

Size: 17½x21¾ mm.

275 A83 70c brown 1.35 5
 a. Tête bêche pair 3.75 2.00
 b. Bklt. pane of 6 10.00
 c. Bklt. pane 4 + 2 labels 10.00

Size: 20¾x24 mm.

276 A83a 1fr rose carmine 1.35 8
277 " 1.50fr bright red violet ('43) 1.00 12
278 " 1.75fr deep ultra. ('43) 28 18
279 " 2fr dk. purple ('43) 1.60 65
280 A83a 2.25fr greenish black ('43) 65 8
281 " 3.25fr chestnut ('43) 65 5
282 " 5fr dp. green ('43) 5.75 45
 Nos. 275-282 (8) 12.63 1.66

Nos. 278, 280 and 282 inscribed "Belgie-Belgique."
See also Nos. 400-402.

King Leopold III
A84 — A85

1936-41 Engraved *Perf. 14x13½*

283 A84 1.50fr rose lilac 1.00 10
284 " 1.75fr dull blue 35 5
285 " 2fr dull violet 1.50 10
286 " 2.25fr gray vio. ('41) 85 12
287 " 2.45fr black 110.00 30
288 " 2.50fr olive blk. ('40) 10.00 15
289 " 3.25fr org. brn. ('41) 85 12
290 " 5fr dull green 5.00 30
291 " 10fr dk. vio. brown 2.75 5
292 " 20fr vermilion 4.75 15
 Nos. 283-292 (10) 137.05 1.44

See also Nos. 403-406A.

No. 206 Surcharged as No. 226, but dated "1937."

1937 *Perf. 14.* Unwmkd.

293 A63 10c on 40c red vio. 1.00 50

The surcharge on No. 293 is a precancelation which alters the value of the stamp. See note after No. 197.

1938-41 Photo. *Perf. 13½x14*

294 A85 75c olive gray 1.15 5
 a. Tête bêche pair 3.00 1.65
 b. Booklet pane of 6 9.00
 c. Bklt. pane 4 + 2 labels 9.00
295 " 1fr rose pink ('41) 18 3
 a. Tete beche pair 65 30
 b. Booklet pane of 6 3.00
 c. Bklt. pane 4 + 2 labels 3.00

No. 287 Surcharged In Red ≡ 2F50

1938, Oct. 31 *Perf. 14*

296 A84 2.50fr on 2.45fr blk. 52.50 30

Basilica and Bell Tower A86 — Water Exhibition Buildings A87

Designs: 1.50fr, Albert Canal and Park. 1.75fr, Eygenbilsen Cut in Albert Canal.

Perf. 14x13½, 13½x14

1938, Oct. 31

297 A86 35c dark blue green 30 15
298 A87 1fr rose red 2.50 15
299 " 1.50fr violet brown 6.00 75
300 " 1.75fr ultramarine 6.00 18

Publicity for the International Water Exhibition, Liège, 1939.

See "Special Notices" at the front of this volume for data on the listing methods of this Catalogue, abbreviations, condition, prices and examination.

Nos. 271, 273, 275, 294 and 288 Surcharged in Blue, Black or Carmine:

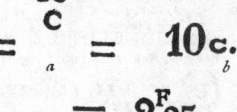

= 10 c = *a* = 10c. *b* ≡ 2F25 *c*

1941-42 *Perf. 14, 14x13½*

301 A82 (*a*) 10c on 30c brown (Bl) 15 12
302 " (") 10c on 40c red violet (Bl) 15 12
303 A83 (*b*) 10c on 70c brown (Bk) 15 12
304 A85 (") 50c on 75c olive gray (C) 1.00 12
305 A84 (*c*) 2.25fr on 2.50fr olive black (C) 1.75 85
 Nos. 301-305 (5) 3.20 1.33

Lion Rampant A90 — King Leopold III with Crown and V A91

Photogravure.

1944 *Perf. 12½.* Unwmkd.

Inscribed: "Belgique-Belgie".

306 A90 5c chocolate 5 5
307 " 10c green 5 5
308 " 25c light blue 8 5
309 " 35c brown 5 5
310 " 50c light blue green 22 5
310A " 75c purple 15 10
311 " 1fr vermilion 15 3
312 " 1.25fr chestnut 30 22
313 " 1.50fr orange 70 30
314 " 1.75fr bright ultra. 18 5
314A " 2fr aquamarine 4.75 1.50
315 " 2.75fr deep magenta 30 15
316 " 3fr claret 1.10 85
317 " 3.50fr slate black 1.15 85
318 " 5fr dark olive 11.50 6.75
319 " 10fr black 1.75 1.10
 Nos. 306-319 (16) 22.48 12.15

Inscribed: "Belgie-Belgique".

320 A90 5c chocolate 5 5
321 " 10c green 5 5
322 " 25c light blue 8 5
323 " 35c brown 5 5
324 " 50c light blue green 18 5
324A " 75c purple 15 10
325 " 1fr vermilion 15 3
326 " 1.25fr chestnut 30 22
327 " 1.50fr orange 70 30
328 " 1.75fr bright ultra. 18 5
329 " 2fr aquamarine 2.65 1.00
329A " 2.75fr deep magenta 30 15
330 " 3fr claret 1.10 85
331 " 3.50fr slate black 1.10 85
332 " 5fr dark olive 10.00 6.50
333 " 10fr black 1.75 1.10
 Nos. 320-333 (16) 18.79 11.40

1944-57 *Perf. 14x13½*

334 A91 1fr bright rose red 30 3
335 " 1.50fr magenta 60 4
336 " 1.75fr deep ultramarine 60 50
337 " 2fr deep violet 3.25 8
338 " 2.25fr greenish black 1.00 30
339 " 3.25fr chestnut brown 85 5
340 " 5fr dk. blue green 4.50 5
 a. Perf. 11½ ('57) 140.00 15
 Nos. 334-340 (7) 11.10 1.05

Nos. 335, 337 and 339 are inscribed "Belgique Belgie".

Stamps of 1935-41 Overprinted in Red **V**

1944 ***Perf. 14.***

345	A82	2c pale green	5	5
346	"	15c indigo	10	7
347	"	20c bright violet	10	7
348	"	60c slate	25	15

See note following No. 274D regarding Bastogne overprint on No. 345.

Nos. 335, 337 and 340 Surcharged Typographically in Black or Carmine **—10%**

1946 ***Perf. 14x13½.***

348A	A91	On 1.50fr magenta	1.10	10
348B	"	On 2fr dp. vio. (C)	3.25	50
348C	"	On 5fr dark blue green (C)	3.25	10

To provide denominations created by a reduction in postal rates, the Government produced Nos. 348A-348C by surcharging typographically. Also, each post office was authorized on May 20, 1946, to surcharge its stock of 1.50fr, 2fr and 5fr stamps "—10 percent." Hundreds of types and sizes of this surcharge exist, both hand-stamped and typographed. These include the "1,35", "1,80" and "4,50" applied at Ghislenghien.

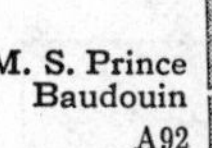

M. S. Prince Baudouin
A92

Designs: 2.25fr, S. S. Marie Henriette. 3.15fr, S. S. Diamant.

Perf. 14x13½, 13½x14.

1946, June 15 Photo. Unwmkd.

349	A92	1.35fr bright bluish green	18	7
350	"	2.25fr slate green	80	15
351	"	3.15fr slate black	65	25

Issued to commemorate the centenary of the steamship line between Ostend and Dover.

No. 349 exists in two sizes: 21¼ x 18¼ mm. and 21 x 17 mm. Nos. 350-351 measure 24½ x 20 mm.

Arms Type of 1935-46.

1946-48 Typographed *Perf. 14*

352	A82	65c red lilac	1.25	5
352A	"	80c green ('48)	16.00	50
353	"	90c dull violet	65	5

Capt. Adrien de Gerlache
A95

Belgica and Explorers
A96

1947, June ***Perf. 14x13½, 11½***

354	A95	1.35fr crimson rose	30	7
355	A96	2.25fr gray black	2.65	1.10

Issued to commemorate the 50th anniversary of Capt. Adrien de Gerlache's Antarctic Expedition.

Joseph A. F. Plateau
A97

1947, June ***Perf. 14x13½***

356	A97	3.15fr deep blue	85	15

Issued to mark the World Film and Fine Arts Festival, Brussels, June, 1947.

Sheets of thin cardboard, containing one each of Nos. 354 to 356, bearing commemorative inscriptions in French and Flemish, were also issued in 1947. Size: 180x150 mm.

Chemical Industry
A98

Industrial Arts
A99

Agriculture
A100

Communications Center
A101

Textile Industry
A102

Iron Manufacture
A103

Photogravure (# 357-359, 361), Typographed (# 360, 363), Engraved.

1948 ***Perf. 11½*** **Unwmkd.**

357	A98	60c blue green	45	15
358	"	1.20fr brown	4.50	10
359	A99	1.35fr red brown	50	5
360	A100	1.75fr bright red	1.15	7
361	A99	1.75fr dk. gray grn.	1.00	5
362	A101	2.25fr gray blue	2.65	60
363	A100	2.50fr dk. car. rose	14.50	12
364	A101	3fr brt. red vio.	17.50	18
365	A102	3.15fr deep blue	4.50	15
366	"	4fr brt. ultra.	17.00	12
367	A103	6fr blue green	27.50	12
368	"	6.30fr brt. red vio.	7.50	3.00
		Nos. 357-368 (12)	98.75	4.71

King Leopold I
A104

Engraved

1949, July 1 ***Perf. 14x13½***

369	A104	90c dark green	1.00	60
370	"	1.75fr brown	85	15
371	"	3fr red	6.25	3.75
372	"	4fr deep blue	11.00	1.10

Issued to commemorate the centenary of Belgium's first postage stamps.

See note on souvenir sheet below No. 2.

Stamps of 1935-45 Precanceled and Surcharged in Black

= 20c =

1949 ***Perf. 14***

373	A82	5c on 15c dark violet	15	10
374	"	5c on 30c brown	15	10
375	"	5c on 40c red violet	15	10
376	"	20c on 70c lt. bl. green	25	25
377	"	20c on 75c lilac rose	12	10

Similar Surcharge and Precancelation in Black on Nos. B455-B458.

Perf. 14x13½.

378	SP251	10c on 65c+35c rose red	6.75	5.25
379	"	40c on 90c+60c gray	2.00	1.50
380	"	80c on 1.35fr+1.15fr henna brown	90	65
381	"	1.20fr on 3.15fr+1.85fr bright blue	3.50	3.00
		Nos. 373-381 (9)	13.97	11.05

The surcharges on Nos. 373 to 381 are combined with the precancelations. See note after No. 197.

St. Mary Magdalene, from Painting by Gerard David
A105

1949, July 15 Photo. *Perf. 11*

382	A105	1.75fr dark brown	1.50	30

Issued to publicize the Gerard David Exhibition at Bruges, 1949.

Allegory of U.P.U.—A106

1949, Oct. 1 Engr. *Perf. 11½*

383	A106	4fr deep blue	7.25	3.00

Issued to commemorate the 75th anniversary of the formation of the Universal Postal Union.

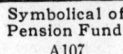

Symbolical of Pension Fund
A107

Lion Rampant
A108

Photogravure.

1950, May 1 *Perf. 11½* Unwmkd.

385	A107	1.75fr dark brown	1.00	15

Issued to commemorate the centenary of the foundation of the General Pension Fund.

1951, Feb. 15 Engr. *Perf. 11½*

388	A108	20c blue	40	8

1951 Typographed *Perf. 13½x14*

Size: 17½x21mm.

389	A108	5c pale violet	18	5
390	"	10c red orange	5	3
391	"	20c claret	5	3
392	"	25c green	2.65	15
393	"	40c brown olive	60	3
394	"	50c ultramarine	5	3
		a. 50c light blue	30	3
395	A108	60c lilac rose	5	5
396	"	65c violet brown	30.00	35
397	"	80c emerald	1.85	5
398	"	90c deep blue	1.85	8
399	"	1fr rose	15	3
		Nos. 389-399 (11)	37.48	88

On every other denomination, the order of "Belgique Belgie" is changed. See also Nos. 462, 500-503, 612-614B, 680, 680D, 681b, 714A-716, 878-884, 923.

Counterfeits exist of No. 396.

Leopold Types of 1936.

Photogravure.

1950-51 ***Perf. 14x13½, 11½.***

400	A83a	1.20fr dark brown	5.75	5
401	"	1.75fr dark carmine ('50)	1.15	3
402	"	2.50fr orange red	22.50	10

Engraved.

Perf. 11½.

403	A84	3fr yellow brown	4.00	5
404	"	4fr bl., *bluish* ('50)	19.00	10
		a. White paper	45.00	5
405	A84	6fr brt. rose carmine	23.50	8
406	"	10fr brown violet	3.50	4
406A	"	20fr red	5.75	6
		Nos. 400-406A (8)	85.15	51

Nos. 401 and 402 are inscribed "Belgie-Belgique."

Francois de Tassis (Franz von Taxis)
A109

Portraits: 1.75fr, Jean-Baptiste of Thurn & Taxis. 2fr, Baron Leonard I. 2.50fr, Count Lamoral I. 3fr, Count Leonard II. 4fr, Count Lamoral II. 5fr, Prince Eugene Alexander. 5.75fr, Prince Anselme Francois. 8fr, Prince Alexander Ferdinand. 10fr, Prince Charles Anselme. 20fr, Prince Charles Alexander.

Laid Paper.

Inscribed: "Congres 1952 U.P.U." etc.

1952, May 14 Engraved

407	A109	80c olive green	30	30
408	"	1.75fr red orange	30	10
409	"	2fr violet brown	1.35	18
410	"	2.50fr carmine	2.25	55
411	"	3fr olive bistre	2.00	25
412	"	4fr ultramarine	2.00	15
413	"	5fr red brown	4.25	75
414	"	5.75fr blue violet	8.75	1.50
415	"	8fr gray	19.00	1.85
416	"	10fr rose violet	27.50	3.75
417	"	20fr brown	65.00	35.00
		Nos. 407-417 (11)	132.70	44.38

Issued on the occasion of the 13th Universal Postal Union Congress, Brussels, 1952. See No. B514.

King Baudouin
A110 A111

1952 Size: 21x24mm.

418 A110 1.50fr gray 1.10 8
419 " 2fr crimson 90 5
420 " 4fr ultra. 10.00 30

Size: 24½x35mm.

421 A110 50fr gray brown 4.00 30
a. 50fr violet brown 52.50 60

See also No. 489.

1953 Photogravure.

Size: 21x24mm.

422 A111 1.50fr gray 30 3
423 " 2fr rose car. 30.00 3
424 " 4fr bright ultra. 1.00 3

See also Nos. 463-464, 480-488, 615, 680A-681D, 738A-738C.

No. 422 was also issued in coils with black control number on back of every 5th stamp.

Luminescent Paper

Stamps issued on both luminescent and ordinary paper include: Nos. 406, 406A, 421, 422, 424, 463-464, 480-482, 482A, 483, 483B, 485, 488-489, 503, 613, 615, 629-630, 646-647, 680A, 780, Q385, Q410.

Stamps issued only on luminescent paper include: Nos. 463a, 616-622, 633-636, 641-643, 650-652, 655-656, 659-662, 664-665, 668-673, 675-680, 680c, 680G, 681, 681C, 682-693, 696-710, 713-714, 717-717A, 718-728, 730-732, 734, 736-738, 740-746, 748-754, 757-761, 763-777, 779, 781-791. See note after No. 793.

Nos. 396 and 398 Surcharged and Precanceled in Black

20c
I-I-54
31-XII-54

Perf. 13½x14

1954, Jan. 1 Unwmkd.

425 A108 20c on 65c vio. brown 3.25 60
426 " 20c on 90c deep blue 3.25 45

The surcharges on Nos. 425-426 are combined with the precancellations. See note after No. 197.

Map and Rotary Emblem
A112

Designs: 80c, Mermaid and Mercury holding emblem. 4fr, Rotary emblem and two globes.

1954, Sept. 10 Engr. *Perf. 11½*

427 A112 20c red 15 15
428 " 80c dark green 60 45
429 " 4fr ultramarine 3.50 75

Nos. 427-428 were issued to publicize the fifth regional conference of Rotary International at Ostend; No. 429 to commemorate the 50th anniversary (in 1955) of the founding of Rotary.

A souvenir sheet containing one each of Nos. 427-429, imperforate, together with typographed inscriptions in black was sold for 500 francs. It was not valid for postage.

The Rabot and Begonia
A113

Designs: 2.50fr, The Oudeburg and azalea. 4fr, "Three Towers" and orchid.

1955, Feb. 15 Photogravure

430 A113 80c bright carmine 60 25
431 A113 2.50fr black brown 9.00 5.00
432 " 4fr dk. rose brn. 7.50 1.10

Issued to publicize the Ghent International Flower Exhibition, 1955.

Homage to Charles V as a Child, by Albrecht de Vriendt
A114

Charles V, by Titian
A115

Design: 4fr, Abdication of Charles V, by Louis Gallait.

1955, Mar. 25 *Perf. 11½* Unwmkd.

433 A114 20c rose red 15 15
434 A115 2fr dark gray green 3.25 10
435 A114 4fr blue 8.25 1.25

Issued to publicize the Charles V Exhibition, Ghent, 1955.

Emile Verhaeren, by Montald Constant
A116

1955, May 11 Engraved

436 A116 20c dark gray 12 7

Issued to commemorate the centenary of the birth of Emile Verhaeren, poet.

Allegory of Textile Manufacture
A117

1955, May 11

437 A117 2fr violet brown 2.25 15

Issued to publicize the second International Textile Exhibition, Brussels, June 1955.

"The Foolish Virgin" by Rik Wouters
A118

"Departure of Volunteers from Liege, 1830" by Charles Soubre
A119

1955, June 10

438 A118 1.20fr olive green 2.00 1.25
439 " 2fr violet 3.25 15

Issued to publicize the third biennial exhibition of sculpture, Antwerp, June 11-Sept. 10, 1955.

1955, Sept. 10 Photogravure

440 A119 20c greenish slate 25 25
441 " 2fr chocolate 1.85 22

Issued to publicize the exhibition "The Romantic Movement in Liege Province," Sept. 10 - Oct. 31, 1955; and to mark the 125th anniversary of Belgium's independence from the Netherlands.

Pelican Giving Blood to Young
A120

Buildings of Tournai, Ghent and Antwerp
A121

1956, Jan. 14 Engraved

442 A120 2fr bright carmine 1.10 15

Issued in honor of the blood donor service of the Belgian Red Cross.

1956, July 14 Photogravure

443 A121 2fr bright ultra. 85 15

Issued to publicize the Scheldt exhibition (Scaldis) at Tournai, Ghent and Antwerp, July-Sept. 1956.

Europa Issue.

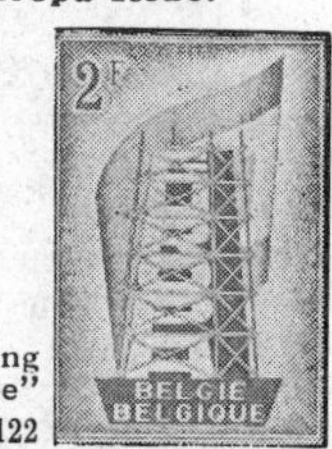

"Rebuilding Europe"
A122

1956, Sept. 15 Engraved

444 A122 2fr light green 5.00 12
445 " 4fr purple 6.75 1.00

Issued to symbolize the cooperation among the six countries comprising the Coal and Steel Community.

Train on Map of Belgium and Luxembourg—A123

1956, Sept. 29

446 A123 2fr dark blue 1.15 18

Issued to mark the electrification of the Brussels-Luxembourg railroad.

Edouard Anseele
A124

"The Atom" and Exposition Emblem
A125

1956, Oct. 27

447 A124 20c violet brown 10 6

Issued to commemorate the centenary of the birth of Edouard Anseele, statesman, and in connection with an exhibition held in his honor at Ghent.

1957-58 Unwmkd.

448 A125 2fr carmine rose 45 10
449 " 2.50fr green ('58) 85 12
450 " 4fr bright violet blue 85 25
451 " 5fr claret ('58) 2.25 1.10

Issued to publicize the 1958 World's Fair at Brussels.

Emperor Maximilian I Receiving Letter
A126

1957, May 19

452 A126 2fr claret 1.00 15

Issued for the Day of the Stamp, May 19, 1957.

Sikorsky S-58 Helicopter
A127

1957, June 15

453 A127 4fr gray green & bright blue 2.00 1.00

Issued to publicize the 100,000th passenger carried by Sabena helicopter service, June 15, 1957.

Zeebrugge Harbor
A128

1957, July 6

454 A128 2fr dark blue 85 10

Issued to commemorate the 50th anniversary of the completion of the port of Zeebrugge-Bruges.

Leopold I Entering Brussels, 1831
A129

Leopold I Arriving at Belgian Border
A130

1957, July 17 Photogravure

455 A129 20c dark gray green 12 12
456 A130 2fr lilac 1.50 35

Issued to commemorate the 126th anniversary of the arrival in Belgium of King Leopold I.

Boy Scout and Girl Scout Emblems
A131

Design: 4fr, Robert Lord Baden-Powell, painted by David Jaggers (vert.).

Engraved.

1957, July 29 *Perf. 11½* Unwmkd.

457 A131 80c gray 65 25
458 " 4fr light green 3.25 1.00

Issued to commemorate the centenary of the birth of Lord Baden-Powell, founder of the Boy Scout movement.

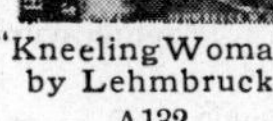

"Kneeling Woman" by Lehmbruck
A132

"United Europe"
A133

1957, Aug. 20 Photogravure

459 A132 2.50fr dark blue green 3.25 2.50

Issued to commemorate the fourth Biennial Exposition of Sculpture, Antwerp, May 25–Sept. 15.

Europa Issue, 1957.

1957, Sept. 16 Engr. *Perf. 11½*

460 A133 2fr dk. vio. brown 1.15 18
461 " 4fr dark blue 2.75 75

Issued to publicize a united Europe for peace and prosperity.

Types of 1951 (Lion) and 1953 (Baudouin).

Typographed.

1957–70 *Perf. 13½x14* Unwmkd.

462 A108 30c gray green 5 3

Photogravure.

Perf. 11½

463 A111 2.50fr red brown 65 3
a. 2.50fr org. brn. ('70) 2.00 3
464 A111 5fr violet 3.25 3

No. 463a was also issued in coils with black control number on back of every 5th stamp. The coil is on luminescent paper.

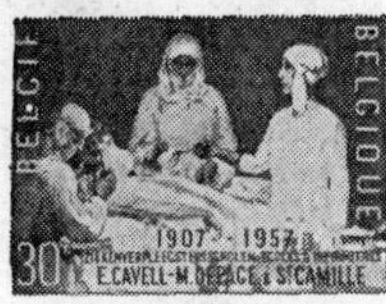

Queen Elisabeth Assisting at Operation, by Allard L'Olivier
A134

Engraved.

1957, Nov. 23 *Perf. 11½* Unwmkd.

465 A134 30c rose lilac 10 10

Issued to commemorate the 50th anniversary of the founding of the Edith Cavell-Marie Depage and St. Camille schools of nursing.

Post Horn and Historic Postal Insignia
A135

1958, Mar. 16 Photo. *Perf. 11½*

466 A135 2.50fr gray 65 10

Postal Museum Day.

United Nations Issue

International Labor Organization
A136

Allegory of U. N.
A137

Designs: 1fr, Food and Agriculture Organization. 2fr, World Bank. 2.50fr, UNESCO. 3fr, U. N. Pavilion. 5fr, International Telecommunication Union. 8fr, International Monetary Fund. 11fr, World Health Organization. 20fr, U. P. U.

Engraved.

1958, Apr. 17 *Perf. 11½* Unwmkd.

467 A136 50c gray 2.00 2.00
468 " 1fr claret 20 20
469 A137 1.50fr deep ultra. 20 20
470 " 2fr gray brown 1.35 1.35
471 A136 2.50fr olive green 30 30
472 " 3fr greenish blue 1.35 1.35
473 A137 5fr rose lilac 45 45
474 A136 8fr red brown 1.85 1.85
475 " 11fr dull lilac 2.50 2.50
476 " 20fr carmine rose 3.25 3.25
Nos. 467-476 (10) 13.45 13.45

World's Fair, Brussels, Apr. 17–Oct. 19. See Nos. C15–C20.

Nos. 467–476 were postally valid only at the United Nations Pavilion at the Brussels Fair. Proceeds from the sale of these stamps went toward financing the U. N. exhibits.

Eugène Ysaye
A138

1958, Sept. 1

477 A138 30c dark blue & plum 10 7

Issued to commemorate the centenary of the birth of Eugène Ysaye (1858–1931), violinist and composer.

Europa Issue, 1958

Common Design Type

1958, Sept. 13 Photogravure

Size: 24½x35mm.

478 CD1 2.50fr bright red & blue 30 6
479 " 5fr bright blue & red 65 40

Issued to show the European Postal Union at the service of European integration.

Baudouin Types of 1952–53

1958–62 Photogravure *Perf. 11½*

Size: 21x24mm.

480 A111 2fr green 25 3
481 " 3fr rose lilac 50 3
482 " 3.50fr brt. yel. green 35 5
482A " 4.50fr dk. red brown ('62) 65 5
483 " 6fr deep pink 1.00 5
483A " 6.50fr gray ('60) 110.00 12.50
483B " 7fr blue ('60) 1.00 5
484 " 7.50fr grayish brn. 110.00 20.00
485 " 8fr bluish gray 1.35 8
486 A111 8.50fr claret 37.50 35
487 " 9fr gray 115.00 1.00
488 " 30fr red orange 4.25 15

Engraved.

Size: 24½x35mm.

489 A110 100fr rose red 8.50 1.00
Nos. 480-489 (13) 390.35 35.34

Nos. 480–482A were also issued in coils with black control number on back of every fifth stamp. These coils are on luminescent paper.

No. 482A is inscribed 1962.

Infant and U. N. Emblem
A140

Charles V and Jean-Baptiste of Thurn and Taxis
A141

1958, Dec. 10 Engraved

490 A140 2.50fr blue gray 85 10

Issued to commemorate the tenth anniversary of the signing of the Universal Declaration of Human Rights.

1959, Mar. 15 Unwmkd.

491 A141 2.50fr green 1.15 15

Issued for the Day of the Stamp. Design from painting by J.-E. van den Bussche.

NATO Emblem
A142

City Hall, Audenarde
A143

1959, Apr. 3 Photo. *Perf. 11½*

492 A142 2.50fr deep red & dark blue 1.15 12
493 " 5fr emerald & dark blue 3.00 1.35

Issued to commemorate the 10th anniversary of the North Atlantic Treaty Organization.

1959, Aug. 17 Engraved

494 A143 2.50fr deep claret 50 6

Pope Adrian VI, by Jan van Scorel
A144

1959, Aug. 31 *Perf. 11½*

495 A144 2.50fr dark red 55 10
496 " 5fr Prussian bl. 1.60 90

Issued to commemorate the 500th anniversary of the birth of Pope Adrian VI.

Common Design Types

pictured in section at front of book.

Europa Issue, 1959

Common Design Type

1959, Sept. 19 Photogravure

Size: 24 x 35½mm.

497 CD2 2.50fr dark red 35 12
498 " 5fr bright greenish blue 85 70

No. 497 inscribed Belgie-Belgique.

Boeing 707
A146

Engraved and Photogravure

1959, Dec. 1 *Perf. 11½*

499 A146 6fr dark blue gray & carmine 3.75 1.65

Issued to commemorate the inauguration of jet flights by Sabena Airlines.

Lion Type of 1951

1959–60 Typographed. *Perf. 13½x14*

Size: 17½x21mm.

500 A108 2c orange brown ('60) 3 3
501 " 3c bright lilac ('60) 3 3
502 " 15c bright pink 5 3

Photogravure

Perf. 11½

Size: 20½x24½mm.

502A A108 50c lt. blue ('61) 1.35 15
503 " 1fr carmine rose 12 3
Nos. 500-503 (5) 1.58 27

No. 502A–503 were also issued in coils with black control number on back of every fifth stamp.

Countess of Taxis
A147

Indian Azalea
A148

Engraved

1960, Mar. 21 *Perf. 11½*

504 A147 3fr dark blue 2.10 18

Issued to honor Alexandrine de Rye, Countess of Taxis, Grand Mistress of the Netherlands Posts, 1628–1645, and to publicize the day of the stamp, March 21, 1960. The painting of the Countess is by Nicholas van der Eggermans.

1960, Mar. 28 Unwmkd.

Flowers: 3fr, Begonia. 6fr, Anthurium and bromelia.

505 A148 40c dull violet & deep carmine 15 12
506 " 3fr emerald, red & org. yellow 1.65 12
507 " 6fr dark blue, green & bright red 2.75 1.60

Issued to publicize the 24th Ghent International Flower Exhibition, Apr. 23–May 2, 1960.

Steel Workers, by Constantin Meunier
A149

Design: 3fr, The sower, field and dock workers, from "Monument to Labor," Brussels, by Constantin Meunier (horiz.).

Engraved and Photogravure

1960, Apr. 30 *Perf. 11½*

508 A149 40c claret & bright red 25 25
509 " 3fr brown & bright red 2.00 70

Issued to commemorate the 75th anniversary of the Socialist Party of Belgium.

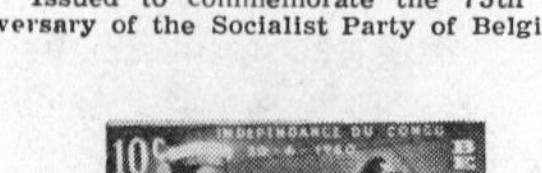

Congo River Boat Pilot
A150

Designs: 40c, Medical team. 1fr, Planting tree. 2fr, Sculptors. 2.50fr, Shot put. 3fr, Congolese officials. 6fr, Congolese and Belgian girls playing with doll. 8fr, Boy pointing on globe to independent Congo.

1960, June 30 Photo. *Perf. 11½*

Size: 35x24mm.

510 A150 10c bright red 12 10
511 " 40c rose claret 20 15
512 " 1fr bright lilac 2.25 85
513 " 2fr gray green 1.85 90
514 " 2.50fr blue 1.50 70
515 " 3fr dark blue gray 2.25 15

Size: 51x35mm.

516 A150 6fr violet blue 4.00 2.00
517 " 8fr dark brown 13.50 13.50
Nos. 510-517 (8) 25.67 18.35

Independence of Congo.

Europa Issue, 1960

Common Design Type

1960, Sept. 17

Size: 35x24½mm.

518 CD3 3fr claret 35 8
519 " 6fr gray 90 45

Children Examining Stamp and Globe
A152

H. J. W. Frère-Orban
A153

1960, Oct. 1 Photo. *Perf. 11½*

520 A152 40c bistre & black + label 15 15

Issued to promote stamp collecting among children. Issued in sheets of 30 with alternating label. Label shows post horn and inscription in Flemish and French.

Photogravure and Engraved

1960, Oct. 17 **Unwmkd.**

Portrait in Brown

521 A153 10c orange yellow 15 10
522 " 40c blue green 25 12
523 " 1.50fr bright violet 1.60 1.25
524 " 3fr red 2.75 10

Centenary of Communal Credit Society.

King Baudouin and Queen Fabiola—A154

1960, Dec. 13 Photo. *Perf. 11½*

Portraits in Dark Brown

525 A154 40c green 15 10
526 " 3fr red lilac 1.40 7
527 " 6fr dull blue 2.65 1.10

Issued to commemorate the wedding of King Baudouin and Dona Fabiola de Mora y Aragon, Dec. 15, 1960.

No. 462 Surcharged

15c

1961 Typographed *Perf. 13½x14*

528 A108 15c on 30c gray green 50 7
529 " 20c on 30c gray green 50 18

See also No. 657.

No. 462 Surcharged and Precanceled

1961

530 A108 15c on 30c gray green 1.85 12
531 " 20c on 30c gray green 3.00 90

The surcharges on Nos. 530-531 are combined with the precancellations. See note after No. 197.

Nicolaus Rockox, by Anthony Van Dyck
A155

Seal of Jan Bode, Alderman of Antwerp, 1264
A156

Engraved and Photogravure

1961, Mar. 18 *Perf. 11½*

532 A155 3fr bistre, black & brown 85 15

Issued to commemorate the 400th anniversary of the birth of Nicolaus Rockox, mayor of Antwerp.

1961, Apr. 16 Photogravure

533 A156 3fr buff & brown 85 15

Issued for Stamp Day, April 16.

Senate Building, Brussels, Laurel and Sword
A157

Engraved and Photogravure

1961, Sept. 14 *Perf. 11½* **Unwmkd.**

534 A157 3fr brown & Prussian grn. 60 12
535 " 6fr dark brown & dark carmine 1.35 1.00

Issued to commemorate the 50th Conference of the Interparliamentary Union, Brussels, Sept. 14-22.

Europa Issue, 1961

Common Design Type

1961, Sept. 16 Photogravure

Size: 35x25½mm.

536 CD4 3fr yellow green & dark green 25 10
537 " 6fr orange brown & black 55 35

Atomic Reactor Plant, BR2, Mol
A159

Designs: 3fr, Atomic Reactor BR3 (vert.). 6fr, Atomic Reactor plant BR3.

1961, Nov. 8 *Perf. 11½* **Unwmkd.**

538 A159 40c dk. blue green 10 10
539 " 3fr red lilac 40 6
540 " 6fr bright blue 85 1.00

Issued to publicize the atomic nuclear research center at Mol.

Horta Museum
A160

1962, Feb. 15 Engraved

541 A160 3fr red brown 65 10

Issued to honor Baron Victor Horta (1861-1947), architect.

Postrider, 16th Century
A161

Engraved and Photogravure

1962, March 25 *Perf. 11½*

Chalky Paper

542 A161 3fr brown & slate green 70 12

Stamp Day. See No. 631.

Gerard Mercator
A162

Bro. Alexis-Marie Gochet
A163

Engraved and Photogravure

1962, Apr. 14 **Unwmkd.**

543 A162 3fr sepia & gray 85 15

Issued to commemorate the 450th anniversary of the birth of Mercator (Gerhard Kremer, 1512-1594), geographer and map maker.

1962, May 19 Engr. *Perf. 11½*

Portrait: 3fr, Canon Pierre-Joseph Triest.

544 A163 2fr dark blue 45 10
545 " 3fr golden brown 85 10

Issued to honor Brother Alexis-Marie Gochet (1835-1910), geographer and educator, and Canon Pierre-Joseph Triest (1760-1836), educator and founder of hospitals and orphanages.

Europa Issue, 1962

Common Design Type

1962, Sept. 15 Photogravure

Size: 35x24mm.

546 CD5 3fr deep carmine, citron & black 40 10
547 " 6fr olive, citron & black 75 30

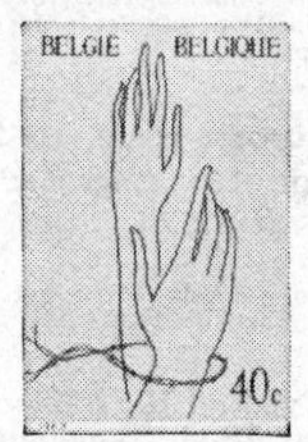

Hand with Barbed Wire and Freed Hand
A165

Engraved and Photogravure

1962, Sept. 16

548 A165 40c lt. blue & black 10 6

Issued in memory of concentration camp victims.

Adam, by Michelangelo, Broken Chain and U.N. Emblem
A166

1962, Nov. 24 *Perf. 11½*

549 A166 3fr gray & black 55 15
550 " 6fr lt. reddish brn. & dk. brown 80 40

Issued to publicize the U.N. Declaration of Human Rights.

Henri Pirenne
A167

1963, Jan. 15 Engraved

551 A167 3fr ultramarine 85 12

Issued to commemorate the centenary of the birth of Henri Pirenne (1862-1935), historian.

Swordsmen and Ghent Belfry
A168

Designs: 3fr, Modern fencers. 6fr, Arms of the Royal and Knightly Guild of St. Michael (vert.).

Engraved and Photogravure

1963, Mar. 23 *Perf. 11½* Unwmkd.

552 A168 1fr brown red & pale blue 18 18
553 " 3fr dark violet & yellow green 35 10
554 " 6fr gray, black, red, blue & gold 80 50

Issued to commemorate the 350th anniversary of the granting of a charter to the Ghent guild of fencers.

Stagecoach
A169

1963, Apr. 7

555 A169 3fr gray & ocher 60 10

Stamp Day. See No. 632.

Hotel des Postes, Paris, Stagecoach and Stamp, 1863
A170

Engraved

1963, May 7 *Perf. 11½* Unwmkd.

556 A170 6fr dark brown, gray, & yel. green 1.15 80

Issued to commemorate the centenary of the first International Postal Conference, Paris, 1863.

"Peace," Child in Rye Field
A171

Engraved and Photogravure

1963, May 8

557 A171 3fr green, black, yellow & brown 55 12
558 " 6fr buff, black, brown & orange 80 45

Issued to publicize the May 8th Movement for Peace. (On May 8, 1945, World War II ended in Europe).

Allegory and Shields of 17 Member Nations
A172

1963, June 13 *Perf. 11½* Unwmkd.

559 A172 6fr blue & black 1.00 45

10th anniversary of the Conference of European Transport Ministers.

Seal of Union of Belgian Towns
A173

1963, June 17

560 A173 6fr green, red, blk. & gold 90 45

50th anniversary of the International Union of Municipalities.

Caravelle over Brussels National Airport
A174

Photogravure and Engraved

1963, Sept. 1 *Perf. 11½* Unwmkd.

561 A174 3fr green & gray 65 10

40th anniversary of SABENA airline.

Europa Issue, 1963
Common Design Type

1963, Sept. 14 Photogravure

Size: 35x24mm.

562 CD6 3fr black, dull red & light brown 65 10
563 " 6fr blk., lt. blue & light brown 1.00 30

Jules Destrée
A176

Design: No. 565, Henry Van de Velde.

Engraved

1963, Nov. 16 *Perf. 11½* Unwmkd.

564 A176 1fr rose lilac 20 15
565 " 1fr green 20 15

Issued to commemorate the centenary of the birth of Jules Destrée (1863–1936), statesman and founder of the Royal Academy of French Language and Literature (No. 564), and of Henry Van de Velde (1863–1957), architect (No. 565).

No. 564 incorrectly inscribed "1864."

Development of the Mail, Bas-relief
A177

Engraved and Photogravure

1963, Nov. 23

566 A177 50c dull red, slate & black 10 7

50th anniversary of the establishment of postal checking service.

Dr. Armauer G. Hansen
A178

Designs: 2fr, Leprosarium. 5fr, Father Joseph Damien.

1964, Jan. 25 *Perf. 11½* Unwmkd.

567 A178 1fr brn. org. & blk. 15 10
568 " 2fr " " " 60 15
569 " 5fr " " " 1.25 35
a. Souvenir sheet of 3 2.00 2.00

Issued to publicize the fight against leprosy. No. 569a contains one each of Nos. 567–569; brown inscription and orange and brown emblem in margin. Size: 137x97 mm. Sold for 12fr.

Andreas Vesalius
A179

Jules Boulvin
A180

Design: 2fr, Henri Jaspar.

Engraved and Photogravure

1964, March 2 *Perf. 11½* Unwmkd.

570 A179 50c pale grn. & blk. 12 7
571 A180 1fr " " " 18 10
572 " 2fr " " " 40 18

Issued to commemorate 400th anniversary of the death of Andreas Vesalius (1514–64), anatomist (50c); honor Jules Boulvin (1855–1920), mechanical engineer (1fr) and to commemorate the 25th anniversary of the death of Henri Jaspar (1870–1939), satesman and lawyer (2fr).

Postilion of Liège, 1830–40
A181

1964, Apr. 5 Engraved *Perf. 11½*

573 A181 3fr black 50 6

Issued for Stamp Day 1964.

Arms of Ostend
A182

1964, May 16 Photogravure

574 A182 3fr ultra., vermilion, gold & black 35 6

Millennium of Ostend.

Flame, Hammer and Globe
A183

Designs: 1fr, "SI" and globe. 2fr, Flame over wavy lines.

1964, July 18 *Perf. 11½* Unwmkd.

575 A183 50c dark blue & red 12 10
576 " 1fr " " " 20 12
577 " 2fr " " " 35 25

Issued to commemorate the centenary of the First Socialist International, founded in London, Sept. 28, 1864.

Europa Issue, 1964
Common Design Type

1964, Sept. 12 Photo. *Perf. 11½*

Size: 24x35½mm.

578 CD7 3fr yel. green, dark carmine & gray 30 10
579 " 6fr car. rose, yel. green & blue 65 35

Benelux Issue

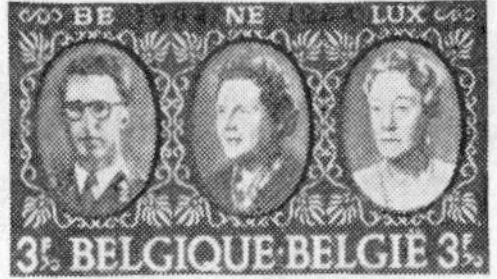

King Baudouin, Queen Juliana and Grand Duchess Charlotte
A185

1964, Oct. 12

580 A185 3fr olive, lt. green & maroon 35 10

Issued to commemorate the 20th anniversary of the customs union of Belgium, Netherlands and Luxembourg.

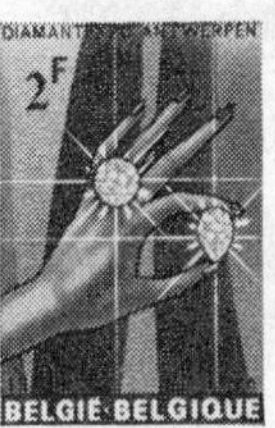

Hand, Round and Pear-shaped Diamonds
A186

Symbols of Textile Industry
A187

1965, Jan. 23 *Perf. 11½* Unwmkd.

581 A186 2fr ultra., dp. carmine & black 40 30

Issued to publicize the Diamond Exhibition "Diamantexpo," Antwerp, July 10–28, 1965.

1965, Jan. 25 Photogravure

582 A187 1fr blue, red & black 10 10

Issued to publicize the eighth textile industry exhibition "Textirama," Ghent, Jan. 29–Feb. 2, 1965.

Vriesia
A188

Paul Hymans
A189

Designs: 2fr, Echinocactus. 3fr, Stapelia.

Engraved and Photogravure

1965, Feb. 13

583 A188 1fr multicolored 15 10
584 " 2fr " 35 30
585 " 3fr " 22 7
a. Souv. sheet of 3 3.00 3.00

Issued to publicize the 25th Ghent International Flower Exhibition, Apr. 24–May 3, 1965.

No. 585a contains one each of Nos. 583–585, and was issued Apr. 26. It carries the UNRWA and Belgian Postal emblems in the margin. Sold for 20fr.

1965, Feb. 24 Engraved *Perf. 11½*

586 A189 1fr dull purple 10 7

Issued to commemorate the centenary of the birth of Paul Hymans (1865–1941), Belgian Foreign Minister and first president of the League of Nations.

Peter Paul Rubens
A190

Sir Rowland Hill as Philatelist
A191

Portraits: 2fr, Frans Snyders. 3fr, Adam van Noort. 6fr, Anthony Van Dyck. 8fr, Jacob Jordaens.

Photogravure and Engraved

1965, Mar. 15

Portraits in Sepia

587 A190 1fr carmine rose 15 10
588 " 2fr blue green 30 30
589 " 3fr plum 35 10
590 " 6fr deep carmine 55 15
591 " 8fr dark blue 90 80
Nos. 587-591 (5) 2.25 1.45

Issued to commemorate the founding of the General Savings and Pensions Bank.

1965, Mar. 27 Engraved *Perf. 11½*

592 A191 50c blue green 10 7

Issued to publicize youth philately. The design is from a mural by J. E. Van den Bussche in the General Post Office, Brussels.

Postmaster, c. 1833
A192

Staircase, Affligem Abbey
A194

Telephone, Globe and Teletype Paper
A193

1965, Apr. 26 *Perf. 11½* Unwmkd.

593 A192 3fr emerald 40 7

Issued for Stamp Day.

1965, May 8 Photogravure

594 A193 2fr dull pur. & blk. 32 18

Issued to commemorate the centenary of the International Telecommunication Union.

1965, May 27 Engraved

595 A194 1fr gray blue 15 10

St. Jean Berchmans and his Birthplace
A195

Engraved and Photogravure

1965, May 27

596 A195 2fr dark brown & red brown 32 12

Issued to honor St. Jean Berchmans (1599–1621), Jesuit "Saint of the Daily Life."

TOC H Lamp and Arms of Poperinge
A196

Farmer with Tractor
A197

1965, June 19 Photo. *Perf. 11½*

597 A196 3fr olive bister, blk. & carmine 25 7

Issued to commemorate the 50th anniversary of the founding of Talbot House in Poperinge, which served British soldiers in World War I, and where the TOC H Movement began (Christian Social Service; TOC H is army code for Poperinge Center).

Engraved and Photogravure

1965, July 17 *Perf. 11½* Unwmkd.

Design: 3fr, Farmer with horse-drawn roller.

598 A197 50c bl., olive, bister brown & black 10 10
599 " 3fr bl., olive green, olive & black 25 10

Issued to commemorate the 75th anniversary of the Belgian Farmers' Association (Boerenbond).

Europa Issue, 1965
Common Design Type

1965, Sept. 25 *Perf. 11½*

Size: 35½x24mm.

600 CD8 1fr dull rose & blk. 10 10
601 " 3fr greenish gray & black 30 10

King Leopold I
A199

Joseph Lebeau
A200

1965, Nov. 13 Engraved

602 A199 3fr sepia 32 10
603 " 6fr bright violet 70 55

Issued to commemorate the centenary of the death of King Leopold I (1790–1865). The designs of the vignettes are similar to the 30c and 1fr of 1865.

1965, Nov. 13 Photogravure

604 A200 1fr multicolored 18 12

Issued to commemorate the centenary of the death of Joseph Lebeau (1794–1865), Foreign Minister.

Tourist Issue

Grapes and Houses, Hoeilaart
A201

Bridge and Castle, Huy
A202

1965, Nov. 13 Engraved *Perf. 11½*

605 A201 50c vio. blue, lt. blue & yellow green 15 7
606 A202 50c slate green, lt. bl. & red brn. 15 7

See also Nos. 666, 669.

Queen Elisabeth Type of Semi-Postal Issue, 1956

1965, Dec. 23 Photo. *Perf. 11½*

607 SP305 3fr dark gray 32 7

Issued in memory of Queen Elisabeth (1876–1965).

A dark frame has been added in design of No. 607; "1956" date has been changed to "1965;" inscription in bottom panel "Koningin Elisabeth Reine Elisabeth 3F."

"Peace on Earth"
A203

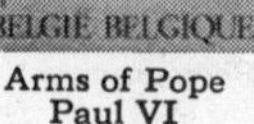

Arms of Pope Paul VI
A204

Rural Mailman, 19th Century
A205

Design: 1fr, "Looking toward a Better Future" (family, new buildings, sun and landscape).

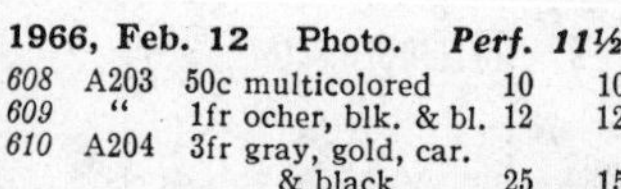

1966, Feb. 12 Photo. *Perf. 11½*

608 A203 50c multicolored 10 10
609 " 1fr ocher, blk. & bl. 12 12
610 A204 3fr gray, gold, car. & black 25 15

Issued to commemorate the 75th anniversary of the encyclical by Pope Leo XIII "Rerum Novarum," which proclaimed the general principles for the organization of modern industrial society.

1966, Apr. 17 Photo. Unwmkd.

611 A205 3fr blk., dull yellow & pale lilac 30 7

Issued for Stamp Day 1966.

Lion Type of 1951 and Baudouin Type of 1953
Perf. 13½x14 (25c, 75c, 1.50fr); 11½ (60c, 12fr); 13½x13 (2fr)
Typo. (25c, 75c, 1.50fr, 2fr); Photo. (60c, 12fr)

1966–69

Size: 17½x21mm. (25c, 75c); 20½x24½mm. (60c); 17x20½mm. (1.50fr, 2fr)

612 A108 25c light blue green 3 3
613 " 60c lilac rose 8.00 2.25
614 " 75c bluish lilac 50 5
614A " 1.50fr dark slate green ('69) 8 3
614B " 2fr emerald ('68) 50 5
615 A111 12fr lt. blue green 1.75 12
Nos. 612-615 (6) 10.86 2.53

Iguanodon, Natural Science Institute
A206

Arend-Roland Comet, Observatory
A207

Designs: No. 617, Ancestral head and spiral pattern, Kasai; Central Africa Museum. No. 618, Snowflakes, Meteorological Institute. No. 619, Seal of Charles V, Royal Archives. No. 620, Medieval scholar, Royal Library. 8fr, Satellite and rocket, Space Aeronautics Institute.

1966, May 28 Engr. and Photo.

616 A206 1fr green & black 12 10
617 " 2fr gray, black & brown orange 15 12
618 " 2fr blue, blk. & yel. 22 12
619 A207 3fr deep rose, black & gold 30 7
620 " 3fr multicolored 30 7
621 " 6fr ultra., yellow & black 50 18
622 " 8fr multicolored 1.00 75
Nos. 616-622 (7) 2.59 1.41

Issued to publicize the national scientific heritage.

Atom Symbol and Retort
A208

August Kekulé, Benzene Ring
A209

Engraved and Photogravure

1966, July 9 *Perf. 11½* **Unwmkd.**

623 A208 6fr gray, blk. & red 75 35

Issued to publicize the European chemical plant, EUROCHEMIC, at Mol.

1966, July 9

624 A209 3fr brt. bl. & black 30 7

Issued to honor August Friedrich Kekulé (1829–96), chemistry professor at University of Ghent (1858–67).

No. 611 Overprinted with Red and Blue Emblem

1966, July 11 Photogravure

625 A205 3fr multicolored 30 7

Issued to commemorate the 19th International P.T.T. Congress (Postal, Telegraph and Telephone Administrations), Brussels, July 11–15.

Rik Wouters, Self-portrait
A210

1966, Sept. 6 Photo. *Perf. 11½*

626 A210 60c multicolored 15 12

Issued to commemorate the 50th anniversary of the death of Rik Wouters (1882–1916), painter.

Europa Issue, 1966
Common Design Type

1966, Sept. 24 Engraved *Perf. 11½*

Size: 24x34mm.

627 CD9 3fr bright green 35 10
628 " 6fr bright rose lilac 75 35

Tourist Issue

Town Hall, Lier A212 | Castle Bouillon A213

1966, Nov. 11 Engraved *Perf. 11½*

629 A212 2fr brown, lt. blue & indigo 45 10
630 A213 2fr dk. brn., green & ocher 45 10

See also Nos. 646–647, 667–668, 691.

Types of 1962–1963 Overprinted in Black and Red

1966, Nov. 11 Engraved and Photo.

631 A161 60c sepia & greenish gray 12 10
632 A160 3fr sepia & pale bister 35 10

75th anniversary, Royal Federation of Philatelic Circles of Belgium. Overprint shows emblem of International Philatelic Federation (F.I.P.).

Lions Emblem
A214

Engraved and Photogravure

1967, Jan. 14 *Perf. 11½*

633 A214 3fr gray, blk. & bl. 30 7
634 " 6fr lt. green, blk. & violet 55 25

Issued to commemorate the 50th anniversary of the founding of the International Association of Lions Clubs.

Pistol by Leonhard Cleuter
A215

1967, Feb. 11 Photogravure

635 A215 2fr deep car., black & cream 20 10

Fire Arms Museum in Liège.

International Tourist Year Emblem
A216

1967, Feb. 11

636 A216 6fr verm., ultra. & black 50 18

International Tourist Year, 1967.

Birches and Trientalis
A217

Design: No. 638, Dunes, beach grass, privet and blue thistles.

1967, Mar. 11 Photo. *Perf. 11½*

637 A217 1fr multicolored 10 8
638 " 1fr " 10 8

Issued to publicize the nature preserves at Hautes Fagnes and Westhoek.

Paul E. Janson
A218

1967, Apr. 15 Engraved *Perf. 11½*

639 A218 10fr blue 1.00 45

Issued in memory of Paul Emile Janson (1872–1944), lawyer and statesman.

Postilion
A219

1967, Apr. 16 Photo. and Engr.

640 A219 3fr rose red & claret 30 10

Issued for Stamp Day, 1967.

See also No. 645.

Europa Issue, 1967
Common Design Type

1967, May 2 Photogravure

Size: 24x35mm.

641 CD10 3fr black, lt. blue & red 35 5
642 " 6fr black, greenish gray & yellow 50 25

Flax, Shuttle and Mills
A221

1967, June 3 Photo. *Perf. 11½*

643 A221 6fr tan & multi. 40 18

Belgian linen industry.

Old Kursaal, Ostend
A222

1967, June 3 Engraved and Photo.

644 A222 2fr dk. brown, lt. blue & yellow 30 10

700th anniversary of Ostend as a city.

Type of 1967 Inscribed: "FITCE"
Engraved and Photogravure

1967, June 24 *Perf. 11½*

645 A219 10fr ultra., sepia & emerald 1.15 50

Issued to commemorate the meeting of the Federation of Common Market Telecommunications Engineers, Brussels, July 3–8.

Tourist Issue
Type of 1966

Designs: No. 646, British War Memorial, Ypres. No. 647, Castle, Spontin.

1967, July 15 Engraved

646 A213 1fr grn., lt. blue, salmon & brn. 20 5
647 " 1fr indigo, lt. blue & olive 20 5

Caesar Crossing Rubicon, 15th Century Tapestry
A223

Design: No. 649, Emperor Maximilian Killing a Boar, 16th century tapestry.

1967, Sept. 2 Photo. *Perf. 11½*

648 A223 1fr multicolored 12 10
649 " 1fr " 12 10

Issued for the Charles Plisnier and Lodewijk de Raet Foundations.

Arms of University of Ghent A224 | Princess Margaret of York A225

Design: No. 651, Arms of University of Liège.

Engraved and Photogravure

1967, Sept. 30 *Perf. 11½*

650 A224 3fr gray & multi. 30 10
651 " 3fr " " 30 10

Issued to commemorate the 150th anniversaries of the Universities of Ghent and Liège.

1967, Sept. 30 Photogravure

652 A225 6fr multicolored 65 30

British Week, Sept. 28–Oct. 2.

"Virga Jesse," Hasselt
A226

1967, Nov. 11 Engraved *Perf. 11½*

653 A226 1fr slate blue 12 7

Christmas, 1967.

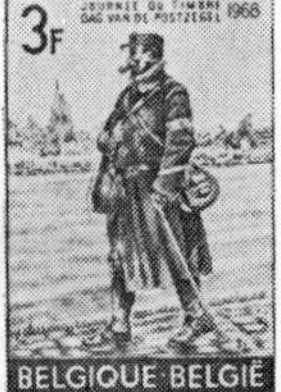

Hand Guarding Worker A227 | Military Mailman, 1916, by James Thiriar A228

1968, Feb. 3 Photo. *Perf. 11½*

655 A227 3fr multicolored 30 7

Issued to publicize industrial safety.

Engraved and Photogravure

1968, Mar. 17 *Perf. 11½*

656 A228 3fr sepia, light blue & brown 35 7

Issued for Stamp Day, 1968.

No. 394 Surcharged Like Nos. 528–529.

1968 Typographed *Perf. 13½x14*

657 A108 15c on 50c blue 8 5

View of Grammont and Seal of Baudouin VI
A229

Stamp of 1866, No. 23
A230

Historic Sites: 3fr, Theux-Franchimont fortress, sword and seal. 6fr, Neolithic cave and artifacts, Spiennes. 10fr, Roman oil lamp and St. Medard's Church, Wervik.

1968, Apr. 13 Photo. *Perf. 11½*

659 A229 2fr blue, blk., lilac & rose 32 22
660 " 3fr orange, black & carmine 32 10
661 " 6fr ultra., indigo & bister 50 25
662 " 10fr tan, blk., yellow & gray 85 55

1968, Apr. 13 Engr. *Perf. 13*

663 A230 1fr black 10 7

Centenary of the Malines Stamp Printery.

Europa Issue, 1968
Common Design Type

1968, Apr. 27 Photo. *Perf. 11½*
Size: 35x24mm.

664 CD11 3fr dull green, gold & black 30 12
665 " 6fr car., silver & blk. 65 35

Tourist Issue
Types of 1965–66

Designs: No. 666, City Hall, Louvain. No. 667, Ourthe Valley. No. 668, Fountain and Kursaal, Spa. No. 669, Windmill at Bokrijk.

1968 Engraved *Perf. 11½*

666 A201 1fr brt. rose lilac, lt. bl. & black 25 7
667 A213 1fr black, greenish blue & olive 28 10
668 " 2fr blue, brt. green & black 32 10
669 A202 2fr blk., lt. bl. & yel. 32 10

Issue dates: 2fr values, June 24. 1fr values, Dec. 16.

St. Laurent Abbey, Liège
A232

Designs: 3fr, Gothic Church, Lissweghe. 6fr, Barges in Zandvliet locks. 10fr, Ronquieres canal ship lift.

Engraved and Photogravure

1968, Sept. 7 *Perf. 11½*

670 A232 2fr ultra., gray olive & sepia 60 25
671 " 3fr olive bister, gray & sepia 65 10
672 " 6fr indigo, bright blue & sepia 75 25
673 " 10fr bister, bright blue & sepia 1.15 70

See also No. 675.

Christmas Candle
A233

Engraved and Photogravure

1968, Dec. 7 *Perf. 11½*

674 A233 1fr multicolored 12 7

Christmas, 1968.

Type of 1968

Design: 6fr, Ship in Neuzen Lock, Ghent Canal.

1968, Dec. 14

675 A232 6fr black, greenish blue & olive 60 18

Opening of lock at Neuzen, Netherlands.

St. Albertus Magnus—A234

1969, Feb. 15 Engraved *Perf. 11½*

676 A234 2fr sepia 25 12

The Church of St. Paul in Antwerp (16th century) was destroyed by fire in Apr. 1968.

Ruins of Aulne Abbey, Gozee
A235

1969, Feb. 15 Engr. and Photo.

677 A235 3fr brt. pink & black 28 7

Aulne Abbey was destroyed in 1794 during the French Revolution.

The Travelers, Roman Sculpture
A236

Broodjes Chapel, Antwerp
A237

1969, Mar. 15 Engraved *Perf. 11½*

678 A236 2fr violet brown 20 10

2,000th anniversary of city of Arlon.

1969, Mar. 15 Engraved & Photo.

679 A237 3fr gray & black 25 7

Issued to commemorate the 150th anniversary of public education in Antwerp.

Lion Type of 1951 and Baudouin Type of 1953

1969–72 Photo. *Perf. 13½x12½*
Size: 17½x22mm.

680 A108 1fr rose 7.50 2.25
680A A111 1.50fr gray ('70) 50 30
b. Bklt. pane of 10 7.00
c. Bklt. pane of 6 (3 # 680A+3 # 681C) 16.50
680D A108 2fr emerald ('72) 55 7
e. Booklet pane of 6 (4 #680D + 2 #681C) 5.00
f. Booklet pane of 5 (#680D, 4 #681D + label) 7.25
680G A111 2.50fr orange brn. ('70) 11.00 9.00
h. Bklt. pane of 6 (#680G+ 5 #681C) 20.00
681 A111 3fr lilac rose 85 15
a. Bklt. pane of 5 + label 35.00
b. Bklt. pane of 8 (2#680 + 6#681) 25.00
681C A111 3.50fr brt. yellow grn. ('70) 1.25 10
681D " 4.50fr dull red brn. ('72) 1.50 7
Nos. 680–681D (7) 23.15 11.94

Nos. 680–681D were issued in booklet panes only and have 1 or 2 straight edges. All panes have a large selvage, the size of 2, 4 or 6 stamps, with inscription or map of Belgium showing postal zones.

Post Office Train
A238

1969, Apr. 13 Photo. *Perf. 11½*

682 A238 3fr multicolored 30 7

Issued for Stamp Day.

Europa Issue, 1969
Common Design Type

1969, Apr. 26
Size: 35x24mm.

683 CD12 3fr lt. grn., brown & black 35 10
684 " 6fr salmon, rose carmine & blk. 75 38

NATO Type of 1959 Redrawn and Dated "1949–1969"

1969, May 31 Photo. *Perf. 11½*

685 A142 6fr org. brn. & ultra. 60 30

Issued to commemorate the 20th anniversary of the North Atlantic Treaty Organization.

No. 685 inscribed Belgique-Belgie and OTAN-NAVO.

Construction Workers, by F. Leger
A240

Bicyclist
A241

1969, May 31

686 A240 3fr multicolored 32 7

Issued to commemorate the 50th anniversary of the International Labor Organization.

1969, July 5 Photo. *Perf. 11½*

687 A241 6fr rose & multi. 65 30

Issued to publicize the World Bicycling Road Championships, Terlaemen to Zolder, Aug. 10.

Ribbon in Benelux Colors
A242

1969, Sept. 6 Photo. *Perf. 11½*

688 A242 3fr black, red, ultra. & yellow 38 7

Issued to commemorate the 25th anniversary of the signing of the customs union of Belgium, Netherlands and Luxembourg.

Annevoie Garden and Pascali Rose
A243

Design: No. 690, Lochristi Garden and begonia.

1969, Sept. 6

689 A243 2fr multicolored 32 15
690 " 2fr " 32 15

Tourist Issue
Type of 1966 and

View of Furnes
A244

Design: No. 691, Mountain Road, Vielsalm.

1969, Sept. 6 Engraved

691 A213 2fr black, lt. blue & yellow green 30 12
692 A244 2fr carmine, lt. blue & dark brown 35 12

See Nos. 711–712.

Armstrong, Collins, Aldrin and Map Showing Tranquillity Base
A245

1969, Sept. 20 Photogravure

693 A245 6fr black 65 32

See note after Algeria No. 427. See also No. B846.

Wounded Veteran
A246

Mailman
A247

1969, Oct. 11 Engr. *Perf. 11½*

694 A246 1fr blue gray 12 7

Issued to publicize the national war veterans' aid organization (O.N.I.G.). The design is similar to type SP10.

1969, Oct. 18 Photogravure

695 A247 1fr dp. rose & multi. 12 7

Issued to publicize youth philately. Design by Danielle Saintenoy, 14.

Kennedy Tunnel Under the Schelde, Antwerp
A248

Design: 6fr, Three highways crossing near Loncin.

1969, Nov. 8 Engraved *Perf. 11½*

696 A248 3fr multicolored 65 12
697 " 6fr " 85 50

Issued to publicize the John F. Kennedy Tunnel under the Schelde and the Walloon auto route and interchange near Loncin.

Henry Carton de Wiart, by Gaston Geleyn
A249

1969, Nov. 8

698 A249 6fr sepia 60 18

Issued to commemorate the centenary of the birth of Count Henry Carton de Wiart (1869–1951), statesman.

The Census at Bethlehem (detail), by Peter Brueghel
A250

1969, Dec. 13 Photogravure

699 A250 1.50fr multicolored 15 7

Christmas, 1969.

Symbols of Bank's Activity, 100fr Coin
A251

1969, Dec. 13

Engraved and Photogravure

700 A251 3.50fr lt. ultra., blk. & silver 30 7

Issued to commemorate the 50th anniversary of the Industrial Credit Bank (Société nationale de crédit à l'industrie).

Camellia
A252

Beeches in Botanical Garden
A253

Flowers: 2.50fr, Water lily. 3.50fr, Azalea.

1970, Jan. 31 Photo. *Perf. 11½*

701 A252 1.50fr multicolored 18 12
702 " 2.50fr " 40 20
703 " 3.50fr " 40 10
a. Souvenir sheet of 3 3.25 3.25

Ghent International Flower Exhibition.

No. 703a contains one each of Nos. 701–703, and was issued Apr. 25. It carries gray United Nations and U.N. Refugee emblems in margin. Size: 121x90mm. Sold for 25fr.

Engraved and Photogravure

1970, Mar. 7 *Perf. 11½*

Design: 7fr, Birches.

704 A253 3.50fr yel. & multi 60 10
705 " 7fr green & multi. 75 40

European Nature Conservation Year.

Mailman
A254

1970, Apr. 4 Photogravure

706 A254 1.50fr multicolored 12 7

Issued for Youth Stamp Day.

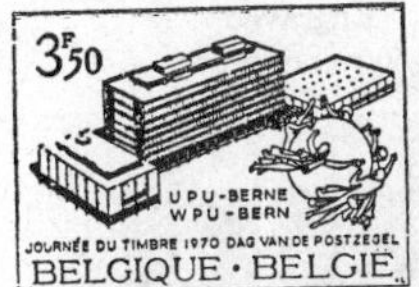

New UPU Headquarters and Monument, Bern
A255

1970, Apr. 12 Engr. and Photo.

707 A255 3.50fr grn. & lt. grn. 60 8

Issued to commemorate the opening of the new Universal Postal Union Headquarters, Bern.

Europa Issue, 1970

Common Design Type

1970, May 1 Photo. *Perf. 11½*

Size: 35x24mm.

708 CD13 3.50fr rose claret, yel. & black 45 10
709 " 7fr ultra., pink & black 70 40

Cooperative Alliance Emblem
A257

1970, June 27 Photo. *Perf. 11½*

710 A257 7fr black & orange 65 18

Issued to commemorate the 75th anniversary of the International Cooperative Alliance.

Tourist Type of 1969 and

Ship in Ghent Terneuzen Lock, Zelzate
A258

Designs: No. 711, Romanesque Cathedral and Gothic fountain, Nivelles (vert.). No. 712, Water mill, Kasterlee. No. 714, Clock Tower, Virton (vert.).

1970 Engr. & Photo.

711 A244 1.50fr slate, sky blue & bister 25 10
712 " 1.50fr blk., bl. & olive 25 10
713 A258 2.50fr indigo & lt. bl. 35 15
714 " 2.50fr dark purple & ocher 35 15

Issue dates: Nos. 711–712, July 6. Nos. 713–714, June 27.

Lion Type of 1951

1970–73 Typo. *Perf. 13½x14*

Size: 17½x21mm.

714A A108 2fr emerald ('73) 12 5
715 " 2.50fr brown 15 5
716 " 3fr bright pink 18 5

No. 714A differs from No. 614B in size and in some design details. On No. 714A, the "2" has a thicker base and the dash below "F" is thinner.

King Baudouin
A259

1970–73 Engraved *Perf. 11½*

Size: 24x21mm.

717 A259 1.75fr green ('71) 1.35 10
717A " 2.25fr gray grn. ('72) 1.35 6
717B " 3fr emerald ('73) 25 3
718 " 3.50fr orange brown 1.00 5
719 " 3.50fr brown ('71) 85 5
720 " 4fr blue ('72) 1.15 5
720A " 4.50fr brown ('72) 60 5
720B " 5fr lilac ('72) 30 5
720C " 6fr rose car. ('72) 35 5
721 " 7fr verm. ('71) 40 5
722 " 8fr black ('72) 50 6
723 " 9fr olive bis. ('71) 1.65 6
724 " 10fr rose car. ('71) 60 10
724A " 12fr Prus. blue ('72) 90 7
725 " 15fr lt. vio. ('71) 90 10
726 " 18fr steel bl. ('71) 4.50 12
727 " 20fr vio. bl. ('71) 1.20 10
727A " 30fr ocher ('72) 1.50 15
Nos. 717-727A (18) 19.35 1.30

No. 718 was issued Sept. 7, 1970, King Baudouin's 40th birthday, and is inscribed "1930–1970." Dates are omitted on other stamps of type A259.

Nos. 720 and 720B were also issued in coils in 1973 and Nos. 720C and 722 in 1978, with black control number on back of every fifth stamp.

See Nos. 802–804, 890–902, 924–925, 980–981.

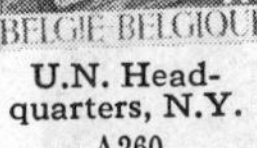

U.N. Headquarters, N.Y.
A260

Fair Emblem
A261

1970, Sept. 12 Engr. and Photo.

728 A260 7fr dark brown & Prus. blue 65 25

25th anniversary of the United Nations.

1970, Sept. 19

729 A261 1.50fr bister, orange & brown 12 7

Issued to publicize the 25th International Fair at Ghent, Sept. 12–27.

Queen Fabiola
A262

The Mason, by Georges Minne
A263

1970, Sept. 19

730 A262 3.50fr lt. bl. & black 35 7

Issued to publicize the Queen Fabiola Foundation for Mental Health.

Engraved and Photogravure

1970, Oct. 17 *Perf. 11½*

731 A263 3.50fr dull yellow & sepia 28 7

Issued to commemorate the 50th anniversary of the National Housing Society.

Man, Woman and City—A264

1970, Oct. 17 Photogravure

732 A264 2.50fr blk. & multi. 32 18

Issued to commemorate the 25th anniversary of the Social Security System.

Madonna with the Grapes, by Jean Gossaert
A265

1970, Nov. 14 Engraved *Perf. 11½*

733 A265 1.50fr dark brown 15 7

Christmas 1970.

Arms of Eupen, Malmédy and Saint-Vith
A266

Engraved and Photogravure

1970, Dec. 12 *Perf. 11½*

734 A266 7fr sepia & dk. brn. 70 18

The 50th anniversary of the return of the districts of Eupen, Malmédy and Saint-Vith.

Automatic Telephone
A267

Touring Club Emblem
A269

"Auto"
A268

1971, Jan. 16 Photo. *Perf. 11½*

735 A267 1.50fr multicolored 16 7

Automatization of Belgian telephone system.

1971, Jan. 16

736 A268 2.50fr carmine & blk. 30 18

Fiftieth Automobile Show, Brussels, Jan. 19–31.

1971, Feb. 13

737 A269 3.50fr ultra. & multi. 25 7

Belgian Touring Club, 75th anniversary.

Tournai Cathedral
A270

1971, Feb. 13 Engraved

738 A270 7fr bright blue 85 32

Cathedral of Tournai, 8th centenary.

Redrawn
Baudouin Type of 1953

1971–72 Photo. *Perf. 11½*

Size: 21x24mm.

738A A111 2.50fr org. brown 85 7
738B " 4.50fr brown ('72) 2.50 1.25
738C " 7fr blue 1.00 12

On Nos. 738A–738C the 2, 4 and 7 are 3mm high. The background around the head is white. On Nos. 463, 482A and 483B the 2, 4 and 7 are 2½mm high, tinted background.

"The Letter Box," by T. Lobrichon
A271

1971, March 13 Engr. *Perf. 11½*

739 A271 1.50fr dark brown 15 8

Youth philately.

Albert I, Jules Destrée and Academy—A272

Engraved and Photogravure

1971, Apr. 17 *Perf. 11½*

740 A272 7fr gray & black 85 30

50th anniversary of the founding of the Royal Academy of Language and French Literature.

Mailman
A273

1971, Apr. 25

741 A273 3.50fr multicolored 30 7

Stamp Day.

Europa Issue, 1971
Common Design Type

1971, May 1 Photogravure

Size: 35x24mm.

742 CD14 3.50fr olive & black 50 10
743 " 7fr dark olive grn. & blk. 65 30

Radar Ground Station
A275

1971, May 15 Photo. *Perf. 11½*

744 A275 7fr multicolored 65 18

3rd World Telecommunications Day.

Antarctic Explorer, Ship and Penguins—A276

1971, June 19 Photo. *Perf. 11½*

745 A276 10fr multicolored 1.50 65

Tenth anniversary of the Antarctic Treaty pledging peaceful uses of and scientific cooperation in Antarctica.

Orval Abbey
A277

1971, June 26 Engraved *Perf. 11½*

746 A277 2.50fr chocolate 25 12

9th centenary of the Abbey of Notre Dame, Orval.

Georges Hubin
A278

1971, June 26 Engr. and Photo.

747 A278 1.50fr vio. bl. & blk. 15 5

Georges Hubin (1863–1947), socialist leader and Minister of State.

Mr. and Mrs. Goliath, the Giants of Ath
A279

View of Ghent—A280

1971, Aug. 7 Photogravure

748 A279 2.50fr multicolored 25 12

Engraved

749 A280 2.50fr gray brown 30 12

Test Tubes and Insulin Molecular Diagram—A281

1971, Aug. 7 Photogravure

750 A281 10fr lt. gray & multi. 1.00 45

50th anniversary of the discovery of insulin.

City Hall and Belfry, Mons—A282

Family and "50"—A283

1971 Engraved *Perf. 11½*

Designs: 1.50fr, City Hall, Cloth Guild and statue of Margarethe of Austria, Malines (horiz.). No. 753, St. Martin's Church, Aalst. No. 754, Abbey and fountain, St. Hubert.

751 A282 1.50fr dk. bl. & buff 40 8
752 " 2.50fr violet, buff & black 40 6
753 A282 2.50fr vio., lt. blue, blk. & olive 40 8
754 " 2.50fr vio. bl. & yel. 40 8

Tourist issue.

1971, Sept. 11 Photogravure

755 A283 1.50fr green & multi. 10 5

50th anniversary of the Belgian Large Families League.

Achaemenidaen Tomb, Buzpar, and Persian Coat of Arms—A284

Engraved and Photogravure

1971, Oct. 2 *Perf. 11½*

756 A284 7fr multicolored 65 18

2500th anniversary of the founding of the Persian empire by Cyrus the Great.

Dr. Jules Bordet
A285

Flight into Egypt, Anonymous
A286

Portrait: No. 758, Stijn Streuvels.

1971, Oct. 2 Engraved

757 A285 3.50fr slate green 30 8
758 " 3.50fr dark brown 30 8

No. 757 honors Dr. Jules Bordet (1870–1945), serologist and immunologist; No. 758, Stijn Streuvels (1871–1945), novelist whose pen name was Frank Lateur.

1971, Nov. 13 Photogravure

759 A286 1.50fr multicolored 15 5

Christmas 1971.

Federation Emblem
A287

Book Year Emblem
A288

1971, Nov. 13

760 A287 3.50fr black, ultra. & gold 30 7

25th anniversary of the Federation of Belgian Industries (FIB).

1972, Feb. 19

761 A288 7fr bister, blk. & bl. 65 30

International Book Year 1972.

Coins of Belgium and Luxembourg
A289

1972, Feb. 19 **Engr. & Photo.**

762 A289 1.50fr org. black & silver 18 8

Economic Union of Belgium and Luxembourg, 50th anniversary.

Traffic Signal and Road Signs
A290

1972, Feb. 19 **Photogravure**

763 A290 3.50fr blue & multi. 28 7

Via Secura (road safety), 25th anniversary.

Belgica '72 Emblem
A291

1972, Mar. 27

764 A291 3.50fr chocolate, bl. & lilac 30 7

International Philatelic Exhibition, Brussels, June 24–July 9.

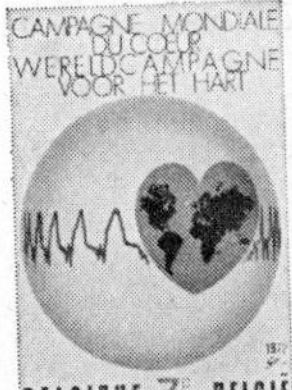

"Your Heart is your Health"
A292

Auguste Vermeylen
A293

1972, Mar. 27

765 A292 7fr black, gray, red & blue 65 30

World Health Day.

1972, Mar. 27

766 A293 2.50fr multicolored 30 15

Centenary of the birth of Auguste Vermeylen (1872–1945), Flemish writer and educator. Portrait by Isidore Opsomer.

Astronaut on Moon
A294

1972, Apr. 23

767 A294 3.50fr multicolored 30 7

Stamp Day 1972.

Europa Issue 1972
Common Design Type

1972, Apr. 29

Size: 24x35mm.

768 CD16 3.50fr lt. bl. & multi. 50 10
769 " 7fr rose & multi. 85 40

"Freedom of the Press"
A296

1972, May 13 **Photo.** ***Perf. 11½***

770 A296 2.50fr org. brn., buff & black 30 10

50th anniversary of the BELGA news information agency and 25th Congress of the International Federation of Newspaper Editors (F.I.E.J.), Brussels, May 15–19.

Freight Cars with Automatic Coupling
A297

1972, June 3

771 A297 7fr bl. & multi. 65 30

International Railroad Union, 50th anniversary.

View of Couvin
A298

Design: No. 773, Aldeneik Church, Maaseik (vert.).

1972, June 24 **Engr.** ***Perf. 13½x14***

772 A298 2.50fr bl., vio. brn. & slate grn. 55 25
773 " 2.50fr dk. brn. & bl. 55 25

Beatrice, by Gustave de Smet
A299

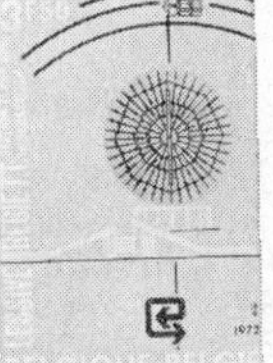

Radar Station, Intelsat 4
A300

1972, Sept. 9 **Photo.** ***Perf. 11½***

774 A299 3fr multicolored 25 12

Youth philately.

1972, Sept. 16

775 A300 3.50fr lt. blue, silver & black 40 16

Opening of the Lessive satellite earth station.

Frans Masereel, Self-portrait
A301

Adoration of the Kings, by Felix Timmermans
A302

1972, Oct. 21

776 A301 4.50fr lt. olive & blk. 45 6

Frans Masereel (1889–1972), wood engraver.

1972, Nov. 11 **Photo.** ***Perf. 11½***

777 A302 3.50fr blk. & multi. 30 8

Christmas 1972.

Maria Theresa, Anonymous
A303

1972, Dec. 16 **Photo.** ***Perf. 11½***

778 A303 2fr multicolored 30 15

200th anniversary of the Belgian Academy of Science, Literature and Art, founded by Empress Maria Theresa.

WMO Emblem, Meterological Institute, Ukkel
A304

1973, Mar. 24 **Photo.** ***Perf. 11½***

779 A304 9fr blue & multi. 85 25

Centenary of international meteorological cooperation.

"Fire"
A305

Man and WHO Emblem
A306

1973, Mar. 24

780 A305 2fr multicolored 45 18

National industrial fire prevention campaign.

1973, Apr. 7

781 A306 8fr dark red, ocher & black 85 35

25th anniversary of World Health Organization.

Europa Issue 1973
Common Design Type

1973, Apr. 28

Size: 35x24mm.

782 CD16 4.50fr org. brn. violet blue & yel. 45 10
783 " 8fr olive, dk. blue & yellow 85 40

Thurn and Taxis Courier
A308

Arrows Circling Globe
A309

1973, Apr. 28 ***Perf. 11½***

Engraved and Photogravure

784 A308 4.50fr blk. & red brn. 32 7

Stamp Day.

1973, May 12 **Photogravure**

785 A309 3.50fr dp. ocher & multi. 32 7

5th International Telecommunications Day.

Workers' Sports Exhibition Poster, Ghent, 1913
A310

1973, May 12

786 A310 4.50fr multicolored 45 15

60th anniversary of the International Workers' Sports Movement.

Fair Emblem
A311

1973, May 12 **Photo.** ***Perf. 11½***

787 A311 4.50fr multicolored 30 7

25th International Fair, Liège, May 12–27.

DC-10 and 1923 Biplane over Brussels Airport—A312

Design: 10fr, Tips biplane, 1908.

1973, May 19 **Engr. & Photo.**

788 A312 8fr gray blue, blk. & ultramarine 75 40
789 " 10fr green, lt. blue & black 2.00 50

50th anniversary of SABENA, Belgian airline (No. 788) and 25th anniversary of the "Vieilles Tiges" Belgian flying pioneers' society (No. 789).

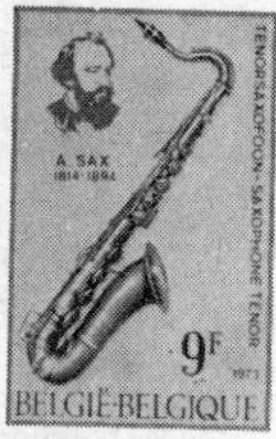

Adolphe Sax and Tenor Saxophone
A313

Fresco from Bathhouse, Ostend
A314

1973, Sept. 15 Photogravure

790 A313 9fr grn., blk. & blue 65 25

Adolphe Sax (1814–1894), inventor of saxophone.

1973, Sept. 15

791 A314 4.50fr multicolored 32 10

Year of the Spa.

St. Nicholas Church, Eupen
A315

Charley, by Henri Evenepoel
A316

1973, Oct. 1 Engraved *Perf. 13*

792 A315 2fr plum, sepia & light violet 25 7

1973, Oct. 13 Photo. *Perf. 11½*

793 A316 3fr multicolored 32 7

Youth philately.

Luminescent Paper

Starting with No. 794, all stamps are on luminescent paper unless otherwise noted.

Jean-Baptiste Moens
A317

1973, Oct. 13 Photo. & Engr.

794 A317 10fr gray & multi. 1.15 30

50th anniversary of the Belgian Stamp Dealers' Association. Printed in sheets of 12 stamps and 12 labels showing association emblem.

Adoration of the Shepherds, by Hugo van der Goes
A318

Louis Pierard, by M. I. Ianchelevici
A319

1973, Nov. 17 Engr. *Perf. 11½*

795 A318 4fr blue 30 7

Christmas 1973.

1973, Nov. 17 Photo. & Engr.

796 A319 4fr vermilion & buff 35 7

Louis Pierard (1886–1952), journalist, member of Parliament.

Highway, Automobile Club Emblem
A320

1973, Nov. 17 Photogravure

797 A320 5fr yellow & multi. 40 6

50th anniversary of the Vlaamse Automobile Club.

Early Microphone, Emblem of Radio Belgium
A321

1973, Nov. 24 Photo. & Engr.

798 A321 4fr blue & black 30 7

50th anniversary of Radio Belgium.

Town Hall, Léau
A322

Design: 4fr, Chimay Castle.

1973, Nov. 26 Engraved *Perf. 13*

799 A322 3fr black, lt. blue & maroon 70 7

800 " 4fr greenish black & greenish blue 45 10

Felicien Rops, Self-portrait
A323

Photogravure and Engraved

1973, Dec. 8 *Perf. 11½*

801 A323 7fr tan & black 60 18

Felicien Rops (1833–1898), painter and engraver.

King Type of 1970–73

1973 Photogravure *Perf. 12½x13½*

Size: 22x17mm.

802 A259 3fr emerald 3.00 15

a. Booklet pane of 4 (# 802 and 3 # 803)+labels 10.00

803 A259 4fr blue 2.00 5

804 " 5fr lilac 65 5

a. Booklet pane of 4+labels 2.75

Nos. 802–804 were issued in booklet panes only and have 1 or 2 straight edges, except No. 802 which has only one. Stamps within the panes are tête bêche and each pane has 2 labels showing Belgian postal emblem, also a large selvage, the size of 6 stamps, with zip code instruction.

See No. 923a.

King Albert
A324

Sun, Bird, Flowers and Girl
A325

1974, Feb. 16 Photo. *Perf. 11½*

805 A324 4fr Prus. grn. & blk. 40 18

King Albert, 1875–1934.

1974, Mar. 25 Photo. *Perf. 11½*

806 A325 3fr violet & multi. 45 10

Protection of the environment.

NATO Emblem
A326

1974, Apr. 20 Photo. *Perf. 11½*

807 A326 10fr deep to lt. blue 85 25

25th anniversary of the signing of the North Atlantic Treaty.

Hubert Krains
A327

"Destroyed City," by Ossip Zadkine
A328

Engraved and Photogravure

1974, Apr. 27 *Perf. 11½*

808 A327 5fr black & gray 35 6

Stamp Day.

Europa Issue 1974

1974, May 4

Design: 10fr, Solidarity, by Georges Minne.

809 A328 5fr black & red 65 10

810 " 10fr black & ultra. 85 40

Children
A329

1974, May 18 Photo. *Perf. 11½*

811 A329 4fr lt. bl. & multi. 32 12

10th Lay Youth Festival.

Planetarium, Brussels
A330

Soleilmont Abbey Ruins—A331

Engraved and Photogravure

1974, June 22 *Perf. 11½*

Designs: 4fr, Pillory, Braine-le-Chateau. 7fr, Fountain, Ghent (procession symbolic of Chamber of Rhetoric). 10fr, Belfry, Bruges (vert.).

812 A330 3fr sky blue & blk. 30 10

813 " 4fr lilac rose & blk. 45 10

814 A331 5fr lt. green & black 65 12

815 " 7fr dull yel. & blk. 65 35

816 A330 10fr blk., bl. & brn. 90 25

Nos. 812–816 (5) 2.95 92

Historic buildings and monuments.

"BENELUX"
A332

1974, Sept. 7 Photo. *Perf. 11½*

865 A332 5fr bl. grn., dk. grn. & light blue 40 6

30th anniversary of the signing of the customs union of Belgium, Netherlands and Luxembourg.

Jan Vekemans, by Cornelis de Vos
A333

1974, Sept. 14

866 A333 3fr multicolored 35 10

Youth philately.

Leon Tresignies, Willebroek Canal Bridge
A334

1974, Sept. 28 Engr. & Photo.

867 A334 4fr brn. & olive grn. 25 10

60th death anniversary of Corporal Leon Tresignies (1886–1914), hero of World War I.

Montgomery Blair, UPU Emblem
A335

Design: 10fr, Heinrich von Stephan and UPU emblem.

Engraved and Photogravure

1974, Oct. 5 *Perf. 11½*

868 A335 5fr green & black 60 12

869 " 10fr brick red & blk. 90 35

Centenary of Universal Postal Union.

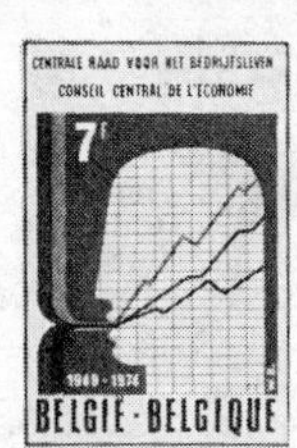

Symbolic Chart
A336

1974, Oct. 12 Photo. *Perf. 11½*

870 A336 7fr multicolored 85 22

Central Economic Council, 25th anniversary.

Rotary
Emblem
A337

1974, Oct. 19

871 A337 10fr multicolored 85 40

Rotary International of Belgium.

Wild Boar
(Regiment's
Emblem)
A338

1974, Oct. 26

872 A338 3fr multicolored 30 12

Granting of the colors to the Ardennes Chasseurs Regiment, 40th anniversary.

Aarshot
Church
A339

Gemmenich Border: Belgium, Germany, Netherlands
A340

Design: No. 875, St. Monan and Church, Nassogne.

1974, Nov. 4 Engraved *Perf. 13*

873 A339 3fr brn. blk. & yel. 35 12
874 A340 4fr greenish black & blue 45 12
875 " 4fr greenish black & blue 40 12

Tourist issue. 3fr is not luminescent.

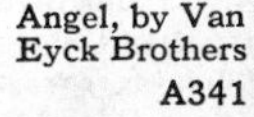

Angel, by Van
Eyck Brothers
A341

1974, Nov. 16 *Perf. 11½*

876 A341 4fr rose lilac 25 12

Christmas 1974. The Angel shown is from the triptyque "The Mystical Lamb" in the Saint-Bavon Cathedral, Ghent.

Adolphe Quetelet,
by J. Odevaere
A342

1974, Dec. 14 Engr. & Photo.

877 A342 10fr black & buff 65 30

Death centenary of Adolphe Quetelet (1796–1874), statistician, astronomer and Secretary of Royal Academy of Brussels.

Lion Type of 1951

1974–75 Typo. *Perf. 13½x14*

Size: 17½x21mm.

878 A108 5c bright pink 3 3
882 " 4fr brt. rose lilac 20 5
883 " 4.50fr blue 30 3
884 " 5fr brt. lilac ('75) 32 5

The 5fr is not luminescent.

Baudouin Type of 1970–73

1974–77 Engraved *Perf. 11½*

Size: 24x21mm.

890 A259 2.50fr gray green 20 3
891 " 3.25fr vio. brn. ('75) 16 3
893 " 4.50fr greenish blue 30 3
895 " 6.50fr violet black 45 3
896 " 7.50fr brt. pink ('75) 38 3
897 " 11fr gray ('76) 55 4
898 " 13fr slate ('75) 65 6
899 " 14fr gray green ('76) 70 6
900 " 16fr green ('77) 80 6
901 " 17fr dull magenta ('75) 85 8
902 " 22fr black 7.50 4.00
903 " 25fr lilac ('75) 1.25 14
910 " 40fr dk. blue ('77) 2.00 30
Nos. 890–910 (13) 15.79 4.89

No. 895 also issued in coils (in 1975) with black control number on back of every fifth stamp.

Nos. 890–892, 897, 899–900, 910 are not luminescent.

Themabelga
Emblem
A343

Neoregelia
Carolinae
A344

1975, Feb. 15 Photo. *Perf. 11½*

912 A343 6.50fr green, black & orange 45 10

Themabelga, International Thematic Stamp Exhibition, Brussels, Dec. 13–21, 1975.

1975, Feb. 22

Flowers: 5fr, Coltsfoot. 6.50fr, Azalea.

913 A344 4.50fr multicolored 35 10

Photogravure and Engraved

914 A344 5fr multicolored 45 10
915 " 6.50fr " 65 10

Ghent International Flower Exhibition, Apr. 26–May 5.

School Emblem,
Man Leading Boy
A345

Engraved and Photogravure

1975, Mar. 15 *Perf. 11½*

916 A345 4.50fr blk. & multi. 38 8

Centenary of the founding of the Charles Buls Normal School for Boys, Brussels.

Davids
Foundation
Emblem
A346

1975, Mar. 22 Photogravure

917 A346 5fr yellow & multi. 35 6

Centenary of the Davids Foundation, a Catholic organization for the promotion of Flemish through education and books.

King Albert
A347

Mailman, 1840,
by James Thiriar
A348

1975, Apr. 5 Engr. & Photo.

918 A347 10fr blk. & maroon 75 30

King Albert (1875–1934), birth centenary.

1975, Apr. 19 Engr. *Perf. 11½*

919 A348 6.50fr dull magenta 45 8

Stamp Day 1975.

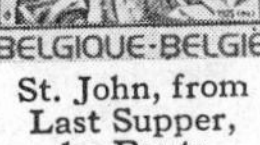

St. John, from
Last Supper,
by Bouts
A349

Concentration
Camp
Symbols
A350

Europa Issue 1975

Design: 10fr, Woman's Head, detail from "Trial by Fire," by Dirk Bouts.

1975, Apr. 26 Engr. & Photo.

920 A349 6.50fr blk., grn. & bl. 65 15
921 " 10fr black, ocher & red 90 30

1975, May 3 Photogravure

Design: "B" denoted political prisoners, "KG" prisoners of war.

922 A350 4.50fr multicolored 32 7

Liberation of concentration camps, 30th anniversary.

Lion Type of 1951 and King Type of 1970–73

Perf. 13½x12½, 12½x13½

1975 Photogravure

Size: 17x22mm., 22x17mm.

923 A108 50c light blue 10 3
a. Booklet pane of 4 (#923, 924 and 2#804) + labels 1.00
b. Booklet pane of 4 (#923 and 3#925) + labels 1.35
924 A259 4.50fr greenish blue 40 5
925 " 6.50fr dull purple 50 6

Nos. 923–925 were issued in booklet panes only. Nos. 923–924 have 1 straight edge, No. 925 has 1 or 2. Stamps within the panes are tete-beche and each pane has 2 labels showing Belgian postal emblem, also a large selvage, the size of 6 stamps, with zip code instructions.

Hospice of
St. John,
Bruges
A351

Church of
St. Loup, Namur
A352

Design: 10fr, Martyrs' Square, Brussels.

1975, May 12 Engr. *Perf. 11½*

926 A351 4.50fr deep rose lilac 45 22
927 A352 5fr slate green 45 15
928 A351 10fr bright blue 75 25

European Architectural Heritage Year.

Church Tower,
Dottignies
A353

Grand-Place, Sint-Truiden—A354

1975, May 24

929 A353 4.50fr multicolored 50 12
930 A354 5fr " 30 6

Tourism. No. 929 is not luminescent.

Library,
Louvain
University,
Ryckmans
and
Cerfaux
A355

1975, June 7 Photo. *Perf. 11½*

931 A355 10fr dull bl. & sepia 75 20

25th anniversary of Louvain Bible Colloquium, founded by Professors Gonzague Ryckmans (1887–1969) and Lucien Cerfaux (1883–1968).

"Metamorphose" by Pol Mara A356

Marie Popelin, Palace of Justice, Brussels A357

1975, June 14

932 A356 7fr multicolored 55 25

Queen Fabiola Mental Health Foundation.

1975, June 21 Engr. & Photo.

933 A357 6.50fr green & claret 55 10

International Women's Year 1975. Marie Popelin (1846–1913), first Belgian woman doctor of law.

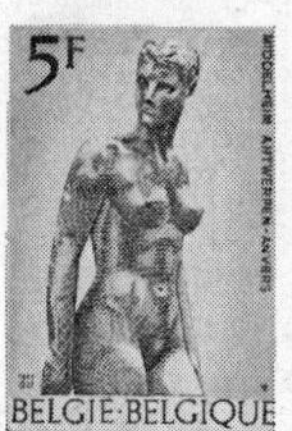

Assia, by Charles Despiau A358

Cornelia Vekemans, by Cornelis de Vos A359

Engraved & Photogravure

1975, Sept. 6 *Perf. 11½*

934 A358 5fr yel. grn. & blk. 40 15

Middelheim Outdoor Museum, 25th anniversary.

1975, Sept. 20 Photogravure

935 A359 4.50fr multicolored 35 15

Youth philately.

Map of Schelde-Rhine Canal A360

1975, Sept. 20

936 A360 10fr multicolored 65 25

Opening of connection between the Schelde and Rhine, Sept. 23, 1975.

National Bank, W. F. Orban, Founder A361

Photogravure and Engraved

1975, Oct. 11 *Perf. 12½x13*

937 A361 25fr multicolored 1.75 45

National Bank of Belgium, 125th anniversary.

Edmond Thieffry and Plane, 1925 A362

1975, Oct. 18 *Perf. 11½*

938 A362 7fr black & lilac 45 25

First flight Brussels to Kinshasa, Congo, 50th anniversary.

"Seat of Wisdom" St. Peter's, Louvain A363

Photogravure and Engraved

1975, Nov. 8 *Perf. 11½*

939 A363 6.50fr bl., black & green 50 20

University of Louvain, 550th anniversary.

Angels, by Rogier van der Weyden A364

1975, Nov. 15

940 A364 5fr multicolored 45 15

Christmas 1975.

Willemsfonds Emblem A365

American Bicentennial Emblem A366

1976, Feb. 21 Photo. *Perf. 11½*

941 A365 5fr multicolored 32 10

125th anniversary of the Willems Foundation, which supports Flemish language and literature.

1976, Mar. 13 Photo. *Perf. 11½*

942 A366 14fr gold, red, blue & black 1.00 50

American Bicentennial.

No. 942 printed checkerwise in sheets of 30 stamps and 30 gold and black labels which show medal with 1626 seal of New York. Black engraved inscription on labels commemorates arrival of first Walloon settlers in Nieu Nederland.

Cardinal Mercier A367

Symbolic of V.E.V. A368

1976, Mar. 20 Engraved

943 A367 4.50fr brt. rose lilac 35 10

Désiré Joseph Cardinal Mercier (1851–1926), professor at Louvain University, spiritual and patriotic leader during World War I, 50th death anniversary.

1976, Apr. 3 Photo. *Perf. 11½*

944 A368 6.50fr multicolored 45 6

Flemish Economic Organization (Vlaams Ekonomisch Verbond), 50th anniversary.

General Post Office, Brussels A369

1976, Apr. 24 Engr. *Perf. 11½*

945 A369 6.50fr sepia 45 6

Stamp Day.

Europa Issue 1976

Potter's Hands A370

Design: 6.50fr, Basket maker (vert.).

1976, May 8 Photogravure

946 A370 6.50fr multicolored 55 10

947 " 14fr " 1.00 30

Truck on Road A371

1976, May 8

948 A371 14fr blk., yel. & red 1.00 30

15th International Road Union Congress, Brussels, May 9–13.

Queen Elisabeth A372

1976, May 24 *Perf. 11½*

949 A372 14fr green 1.00 30

Queen Elisabeth (1876–1965), birth centenary.

Ardennes Draft Horses A373

1976, June 19

950 A373 5fr multicolored 45 12

Ardennes Draft Horses Association, 50th anniversary.

Souvenir Sheets

King Baudouin—A374

1976, June 26

951	A374	Sheet of 3	6.00	6.00
		a. 4.50fr gray	1.75	1.75
		b. 6.50fr ocher	1.75	1.75
		c. 10fr brick red	1.75	1.75
952	A374	Sheet of 2	7.00	7.00
		a. 20fr yellow green	3.00	3.00
		b. 30fr Prussian blue	3.00	3.00

25th anniversary of the reign of King Baudouin. Nos. 951–952 have silver marginal inscriptions. Size: 110x82mm. No. 951 sold for 30fr, No. 952 for 70fr. The surtax went to a new foundation for the improvement of living conditions in honor of the King.

Electric Train and Society Emblem A375

1976, Sept. 11 Photo. *Perf. 11½*

953 A375 6.50fr multicolored 50 6

National Belgian Railroad Society, 50th anniversary.

William of Nassau, Prince of Orange A376

1976, Sept. 11 Engraved

954 A376 10fr slate green 75 18

400th anniversary of the pacification of Ghent.

New Subway Train A377

1976, Sept. 18 Photogravure

955 A377 6.50fr multicolored 50 6

Opening of first line of Brussels subway.

Young Musician, by W. C. Duyster
A378

1976, Oct. 2 Photo. ***Perf. 11½***

956	A378	4.50fr multicolored	60	18

Young musicians and youth philately.

Charles Bernard
A379

St. Jerome in the Mountains, by Le Patinier
A380

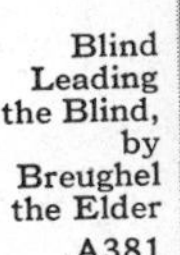

Blind Leading the Blind, by Breughel the Elder
A381

Design: No. 958, Fernand Victor Toussaint van Boelaere.

1976, Oct. 16 Engraved

957	A379	5fr violet	35	18
958	"	5fr red brown & sepia	35	18
959	A380	6.50fr dark brown	50	6
960	A381	6.50fr slate green	50	6

Charles Bernard (1875–1961), French-speaking journalist; Toussaint van Boelaere (1875–1947), Flemish journalist; No. 950, Charles Plisnier Belgian-French Cultural Society. No. 960, Association for Language Promotion.

Remouchamps Caves
A382

Hunnegem Priory, Gramont, and Madonna
A383

Designs: No. 963, River Lys and St. Martin's Church. No. 964, Ham-sur-Heure Castle.

1976, Oct. 23 Engr. ***Perf. 13***

961	A382	4.50fr multicolored	35	10
962	A383	4.50fr "	35	10
963	"	5fr "	40	10
964	"	5fr "	40	10

Tourism. Nos. 961–962 are not luminescent.

Nativity, by Master of Flemalle
A384

1976, Nov. 20 ***Perf. 11½***

965	A384	5fr violet	35	10

Christmas 1976.

Rubens' Monogram—A385

Photogravure and Engraved

1977, Feb. 12 ***Perf. 11½***

966	A385	6.50fr lilac & black	55	6

Peter Paul Rubens (1577–1640), painter, 400th birth anniversary.

King Type of 1970–73 and

Heraldic Lion
A386

1977–78 Typo. ***Perf. 13½x14***

Size: 17x20mm.

968	A386	1fr bright lilac	6	3
969	"	1.50fr gray ('78)	10	3
970	"	2fr yellow ('78)	14	3
971	"	3fr violet ('78)	22	3
972	"	4.50fr light ultra.	30	5

Nos. 968–972 are not luminescent.

Perf. 13½x12½, 12½x13½

1978, Aug. Photogravure

Size: 17x22mm., 22x17mm.

977	A386	1fr bright lilac	7	3
		a. Booklet pane of 4 (#977-978 and 2 #980)	1.10	
		b. Booklet pane of 4 (#977, 979 and 2 #981)	1.45	
978	A386	2fr yellow	14	3
979	"	3fr violet	22	3
980	A259	6fr carmine	42	5
981	"	8fr gray	56	8

Nos. 977–981 were issued in booklets only. Nos. 977–979 have one straight edge, Nos. 980–981 have 2. Nos. 980 and 981 are tete-beche within the panes. Each pane has 2 labels showing Belgian postal emblem, also a large selvage, the size of 6 stamps, with zip code instructions. Nos. 977–981 are not luminescent.

Anniversary Emblem
A387

1977, Mar. 14 Photo. ***Perf. 11½***

982	A387	6.50fr silv. & multi.	50	6

Royal Belgian Association of Civil and Agricultural Engineers, 50th anniversary.

Examination

The Catalogue editors cannot undertake to appraise, identify or pass upon genuineness or condition of stamps.

Birds and Lions Emblem
A388

1977, Mar. 28

983	A388	14fr multicolored	90	18

Belgian District No. 112 of Lions International, 25th anniversary.

Pillar Box, 1852
A389

1977, Apr. 23 Engraved

984	A389	6.50fr slate green	50	6

Stamp Day 1977.

Europa Issue 1977

Gileppe Dam, Jalhay
A390

Design: 14fr, War Memorial, Yser at Nieuport.

1977, May 7 Photo. ***Perf. 11½***

985	A390	6.50fr multicolored	50	6
986	"	14fr "	1.00	35

Mars and Mercury Association Emblem
A391

1977, May 14

987	A391	5fr multicolored	35	6

Mars and Mercury Association of Reserve and Retired Officers, 50th anniversary.

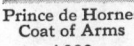

Prince de Hornes Coat of Arms
A392

Conversion of St. Hubertus
A394

Battle of the Golden Spur, from Oxford Chest—A393

Design: 6.50fr, Froissart writing book.

1977, June 11 Engr. ***Perf. 11½***

988	A392	4.50fr violet	35	5
989	A393	5fr red	40	6
990	A394	6.50fr dark brown	50	6
991	"	14fr slate green	1.00	20

300th anniversary of the Principality of Overijse (4.50fr); 675th anniversary of the Battle of the Golden Spur (5fr); 600th anniversary of publication of first volume of the Chronicles of Jehan Froissart (6.50fr); 1250th anniversary of the death of St. Hubertus (14fr).

Rubens, Self-portrait
A395

1977, June 25 Photogravure

992	A395	5fr multicolored	60	60
		a. Souvenir sheet of 3	2.00	2.00

Peter Paul Rubens (1577–1640), painter, 400th birth anniversary. No. 992a contains 3 No. 992; decorative margin. Size: 100x152mm. Sold for 20fr.

Open Book, from The Lamb of God, by Van Eyck Brothers—A396

1977, Sept. 3 Photo. ***Perf. 11½***

993	A396	10fr multicolored	65	15

International Federation of Library Associations (IFLA), 50th Anniversary Congress, Brussels, Sept. 5–10.

Gymnast and Soccer Player
A397

Designs: 6.50fr, Fencers in wheelchairs (horiz.). 10fr, Basketball players. 14fr, Hockey players.

1977, Sept. 10

994	A397	4.50fr multicolored	30	10
995	"	6.50fr "	50	6
996	"	10fr "	65	15
997	"	14fr "	90	22

Workers' Gymnastics and Sports Center, 50th anniversary (4.50fr); sport for the Handicapped (6.50fr); 20th European Basketball Championships (10fr); First World Hockey Cup (14fr).

Europalia 77 Emblem—A398

1977, Sept. 17

998	A398	5fr gray & multi.	35	6

5th Europalia Arts Festival, featuring German Federal Republic, Belgium, Oct.–Nov. 1977.

The Egg Farmer, by Gustave De Smet
A399

1977, Oct. 8 Engr. & Photo.

999 A399 4.50fr bis. & black 32 5

Publicity for Belgian eggs.

Mother and Daughter with Album, by Constant Cap
A400

1977, Oct. 15 Engraved

1000 A400 4.50fr dark brown 32 5

Youth Philately.

Bailiff's House, Gembloux
A401

Market Square, St. Nicholas
A402

Designs: No. 1002, St. Aldegonde Church and Cultural Center. No. 1004, Statue and bridge, Liège.

1977, Oct. 22

1001	A401	4.50fr multicolored		30	8
1002	"	4.50fr	"	30	8
1003	A402	5fr	"	35	6
1004	"	5fr	"	35	6

Tourism. Nos. 1001-1004 are not luminescent.

See Nos. 1017-1018.

Nativity, by Rogier van der Weyden
A403

1977, Nov. 11 Engraved

1005 A403 5fr rose red 35 6

Christmas 1977.

Symbols of Transportation and Map
A404

Parliament of Europe, Strasbourg, and Emblem
A405

Campidoglio Palace, Rome, and Map
A406

Design: No. 1009, Paul-Henri Spaak and map of 19 European member countries.

1978, Mar. 18 Photo. *Perf. 11½*

1006	A404	10fr blue & multi.		70	6
1007	A405	10fr "	"	70	6
1008	A406	14fr "	"	95	20
1009	"	14fr "	"	95	20

European Action: 25th anniversary of the European Transport Ministers' Conference; 1st general elections for European Parliament; 20th anniversary of the signing of the Treaty of Rome; Paul-Henri Spaak (1899-1972), Belgian statesman who worked for the establishment of European Community.

Grimbergen Abbey—A407

1978, Apr. 1 Engraved

1010 A407 4.50fr red brown 32 5

850th anniversary of the Premonstratensian Abbey at Grimbergen.

Emblem
A408

No. 39 with First Day Cancel
A409

1978, Apr. 8 Photogravure

1011 A408 8fr multicolored 55 10

Ostend Chamber of Commerce and Industry, 175th anniversary.

1978, Apr. 15

1012 A409 8fr multicolored 55 10

Stamp Day.

Europa Issue

Pont des Trous, Tournai
A410

Design: 8fr, Antwerp Cathedral, by Vaclav Hollar (vert.).

Photogravure and Engraved

1978, May 6 *Perf. 11½*

1013	A410	8fr multicolored		55	10
1014	"	14fr	"	95	20

Virgin of Ghent, Porcelain Plaque
A411

Paul Pastur Workers' University, Charleroi
A412

1978, Sept. 16 Photo. *Perf. 11½*

1015	A411	6fr multicolored		42	8
1016	A412	8fr	"	48	10

Municipal education in Ghent, 150th anniversary; Paul Pastur Workers' University, Charleroi, 75th anniversary. Nos. 1015-1016 are not luminescent.

Types of 1977 and

Tourist Guide, Brussels
A413

Designs: No. 1017, Jonathas House, Enghien. No. 1018, View of Wetteren and couple in local costume. No. 1020, Prince Carnival, Eupen-St. Vith.

1978, Sept. 25 Photo. & Engr.

1017	A401	4.50fr multicolored		32	6
1018	A402	4.50fr	"	32	6
1019	A413	6fr	"	42	8
1020	"	6fr	"	42	8

Tourism. Nos. 1017-1020 are not luminescent.

Emblem
A414

1978, Oct. 7 Photogravure

1021 A414 8fr red & black 48 10

Royal Flemish Engineer's Organization, 50th anniversary.

Young Philatelist
A415

1978, Oct. 14 Engr. *Perf. 11½*

1022 A415 4.50fr dark violet 32 6

Youth philately.

Nativity, Notre Dame, Huy
A416

1978, Nov. 18 Engr. *Perf. 11½*

1023 A416 6fr black 42 8

Christmas 1978.

SEMI-POSTAL STAMPS.

St. Martin of Tours Dividing His Cloak with a Beggar
SP1 SP2

Perf. 14

1910, June 1 Typo. Unwmkd.

B1	SP1	1c gray	2.25	1.35
B2	"	2c purple brown	18.50	16.00
B3	"	5c peacock blue	5.50	4.00
B4	"	10c brown red	5.00	4.00
B5	SP2	1c gray green	5.50	2.50
B6	"	2c violet brown	14.00	11.00
B7	"	5c peacock blue	5.50	3.50
B8	"	10c carmine	5.00	3.50
		Nos. B1-B8 (8)	61.25	45.85

Overprinted "1911" in Black.

1911, Apr. 1

B9	SP1	1c gray	27.50	20.00
B10	"	2c purple brown	60.00	50.00
B11	"	5c peacock blue	7.25	5.50
B12	"	10c brown red	7.25	5.25
		a. Double overprint		
B13	SP2	1c gray green	47.50	37.50
		a. Inverted overprint		
B14	"	2c violet brown	42.50	35.00
B15	"	5c peacock blue	7.25	5.25
		a. Double overprint		
B16	"	10c carmine	7.25	5.25
		Nos. B9-B16 (8)	206.50	163.75

Overprinted "CHARLEROI—1911".

1911, June

B17	SP1	1c gray	6.75	2.25
B18	"	2c purple brown	20.00	20.00
B19	"	5c peacock blue	11.00	10.00
B20	"	10c brown red	8.00	7.00
B21	SP2	1c gray green	8.00	3.75
B22	"	2c violet brown	16.00	15.00
B23	"	5c peacock blue	9.00	7.25
B24	"	10c carmine	8.00	7.25
		Nos. B17-B24 (8)	86.75	72.50

Nos. B1–B24 were sold at double face value, except the 10c denominations which were sold for 15c. The surtax benefited the national anti-tuberculosis organization.

SP3

Mérode Monument SP4 King Albert I SP5

1914, Oct. 3 Lithographed

B25	SP3	5c green & red	1.35	85
B26	"	10c red	40	40
B27	"	20c violet & red	17.50	16.50

1914, Oct. 3

B28	SP4	5c green & red	6.00	3.25
B29	"	10c red	6.00	3.25
B30	"	20c violet & red	70.00	60.00

Counterfeits of Nos. B25–B30 abound.

1915, Jan. 1 *Perf. 12, 14*

B31	SP5	5c green & red	13.50	3.75
		a. Perf. 12x14	22.50	14.00
B32	"	10c rose & red	25.00	6.50
B33	"	20c violet & red	70.00	15.00
		a. Perf. 14x12	400.00	325.00
		b. Perf. 12	82.50	45.00

Nos. B25–B33 were sold at double face value. The surtax benefited the Red Cross.

Types of Regular Issue of 1915 Surcharged in Red:

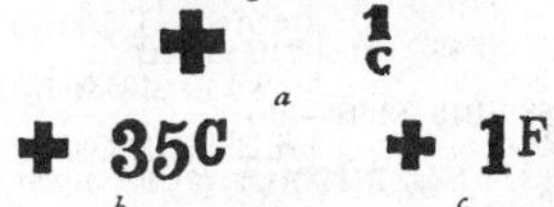

1918, Jan. 15 Typographed *Perf. 14*

B34	A46 (*a*)	1c+1c dp. orge.	55	55
B35	" (")	2c+2c brown	60	60
B36	" (")	5c+5c bl. green	2.65	2.25
B37	" (")	10c+10c red	4.50	4.00
B38	" (")	15c+15c brt. vio.	7.00	5.75
B39	" (")	20c+20c plum	15.00	12.00
B40	" (")	25c+25c ultra.	16.50	13.00

Engraved.

B41	A47 (*b*)	35c+35c light violet & black	22.00	20.00
B42	A48 (")	40c+40c dull red & black	22.00	20.00
B43	A49 (")	50c+50c turquoise blue & black	25.00	21.00
B44	A50 (*c*)	1f+1f bluish slate	72.50	60.00
B45	A51 (")	2f+2f deep gray green	185.00	160.00
B46	A52 (")	5f+5f brown	450.00	425.00
B47	A53 (")	10f+10f deep blue	800.00	750.00
		Nos. B34-B47 (14)	1623.30	1494.15

Discus Thrower
SP6

Runner
SP8

Racing Chariot
SP7

1920, May 20 Engraved *Perf. 12*

B48	SP6	5c+5c deep green	6.50	4.00
B49	SP7	10c+5c carmine	6.00	4.00
B50	SP8	15c+5c dk. brown	13.00	2.25

Issued to commemorate the 7th International Olympic Games of 1920. The surtax was to benefit wounded soldiers. Imperforates exist.

Allegory: Asking Alms from the Crown
SP9

Wounded Veteran
SP10

1922, May 20

B51	SP9	20c+20c brown	4.50	3.25

1923, July 5

B52	SP10	20c+20c slate gray	6.75	4.00

The surtax on Nos. B51–B52 was to aid wounded veterans.

SP11

SP12

St. Martin, by Van Dyck
SP13 SP14

1925, Dec. 15 Typo. *Perf. 14*

B53	SP11	15c+5c dull violet & red	75	60
B54	"	30c+5c gray & red	40	15
B55	"	1fr+10c chalky blue & red	2.50	2.25

The surtax on Nos. B53–B55 benefited the National Anti-Tuberculosis League.

1926, Feb. 10

B56	SP12	30c+30c bluish green (red surch.)	1.50	1.25
B57	SP13	1fr+1fr light blue	18.00	15.00
B58	SP14	1fr+1fr light blue	3.25	2.50

The surtax on Nos. B56–B58 aided victims of the Meuse flood.

Lion and Cross of Lorraine
SP15

Queen Elisabeth and King Albert
SP16

1926, Dec. 6 Typographed *Perf. 14*

B59	SP15	5c+5c dark brown	25	25
B60	"	20c+5c red brown	1.00	85
B61	"	50c+5c dull violet	50	15

Engraved

Perf. 11½.

B62	SP16	1.50fr+25c dk. blue	2.00	1.65
B63	"	5fr+1fr rose red	17.00	14.00
		Nos. B59-B63 (5)	20.75	16.90

The surtax on Nos. B59–B63 was used to benefit tubercular war veterans.

Boat Adrift
SP17

1927, Dec. 15 Engr. *Perf. 11½, 14*

B64	SP17	25c+10c dk. brown	1.65	1.65
B65	"	35c+10c yel. green	1.65	1.35
B66	"	60c+10c deep violet	1.35	45
B67	"	1.75fr+25c dark blue	3.50	3.00
B68	"	5fr+1fr plum	14.00	11.50
		Nos. B64-B68 (5)	22.15	17.95

The surtax on these stamps was divided among several charitable associations.

Ogives of Orval Abbey
SP18

Monk Carving Capital of Column
SP19

Ruins of Orval Abbey
SP20

Design: 60c+15c, 1.75fr+25c, 3fr+1fr, Countess Matilda recovering her ring.

1928, Sept. 15 Photo. *Perf. 11½*

B69	SP18	5c+5c red & gold	30	30
B70	"	25c+5c dark violet & gold	75	75

Engraved.

B71	SP19	35c+10c dp. green	3.00	2.25
B72	"	60c+15c red brown	4.25	30
B73	"	1.75fr+25c dk. blue	10.00	5.00
B74	"	2fr+40c dp. vio.	35.00	24.00
B75	"	3fr+1fr red	37.50	30.00

Perf. 14.

B76	SP20	5fr+5fr rose lake	52.50	42.50
B77	"	10fr+10fr olive brown	52.50	45.00
		Nos. B69-B77 (9)	195.80	150.10

The surtax on these stamps was to be used toward the restoration of the ruined Abbey of Orval.

St. Waudru, Mons
SP22

St. Rombaut, Malines
SP23

Designs: 25c + 15c, Cathedral of Tournai. 60c + 15c, St. Bavon, Ghent. 1.75fr + 25c, St. Gudule, Brussels. 5fr + 5fr, Louvain Library.

1928, Dec. 1 Photo. *Perf. 14, 11½*

B78	SP22	5c+5c carmine	30	25
		a. Booklet pane of 9		
B79	"	25c+15c olive brown	65	50
		a. Booklet pane of 9		

Engraved.

B80	SP23	35c+10c dp. green	2.75	1.85
		a. Booklet pane of 4		
B81	"	60c+15c red brown	85	30
		a. Booklet pane of 4		
B82	"	1.75fr+25c violet blue	24.00	15.00
B83	"	5fr+5fr red vio.	42.50	32.50
		Nos. B78-B83 (6)	71.05	50.40

The surtax was for anti-tuberculosis work.

Orval Abbey Stamps of 1928 Overprinted in Blue or Red

1929, Aug. 19

B84	SP18	5c+5c red & gold	150.00	150.00

B85 SP18 25c+5c dark violet & gold (R) 150.00 150.00
B86 SP19 35c+10c deep green (R) 150.00 150.00
B87 " 60c+15c red brown 150.00 150.00
B88 " 1.75fr+25c dark blue (R) 150.00 150.00
B89 " 2fr+40c deep violet (R) 150.00 150.00
B90 " 3fr+1fr red 150.00 150.00
B91 SP20 5fr+5fr rose lake 150.00 150.00
B92 " 10fr+10fr dark brown (R) 150.00 150.00
Nos. B84-B92 (9) 1350.00 1350.00

Issued in commemoration of the laying of the first stone toward the restoration of the ruined Abbey of Orval. Forgeries of the overprint exist.

Waterfall at Coo
SP28

Bayard Rock, Dinant
SP29

Designs: 35c+10c, Menin Gate, Ypres. 60c+15c, Promenade d'Orleans, Spa. 1.75fr+25c, Antwerp Harbor. 5fr+5fr, Quai Vert, Bruges.

1929, Dec. 2 Engr. *Perf. 11½, 14*
B93 SP28 5c+5c red brown 30 30
B94 SP29 25c+15c gray blk. 1.25 1.10
B95 SP28 35c+10c green 2.00 1.75
B96 " 60c+15c rose lake 75 20
B97 " 1.75fr+25c dp. blue 11.00 8.50
B98 SP29 5fr+5fr dull violet 65.00 52.50
Nos. B93-B98 (6) 80.30 64.35

Bornhem
SP34

Beloeil
SP35

Gaesbeek
SP36

Designs: 25c + 15c, Wynendaele. 70c + 15c, Oydonck. 1fr+25c, Ghent. 1.75fr+25c, Bouillon.

1930, Dec. 1 Photo. *Perf. 14*
B99 SP34 10c+5c red violet 30 15
B100 " 25c+15c olive brown 90 50

Engraved.
B101 SP35 40c+10c brown violet 1.35 75
B102 " 70c+15c gray black 60 15
B103 " 1fr+25c rose lake 7.00 4.75
B104 SP35 1.75fr+25c deep blue 8.25 3.75
B105 SP36 5fr+5fr gray green 60.00 55.00
Nos. B99-B105 (7) 78.40 65.05

Prince Leopold
SP41

Queen Elisabeth
SP42

Philatelic Exhibition Issue.
Souvenir Sheet.

1931, July 18 Photo. *Perf. 14*
B106 SP41 2.45fr+55c carmine brown 165.00 165.00

Issued in sheets measuring 122x159mm. Sold exclusively at the Brussels Philatelic Exhibition, July 18th to 21st, 1931. The surtax was for the Veterans' Relief Fund.

1931, Dec. 1 Engraved
B107 SP42 10c+5c red browr 40 35
B108 " 25c+15c dk. violet 2.35 2.00
B109 " 50c+10c dk. green 2.25 1.25
B110 " 75c+15c blk. brown 1.25 20
B111 " 1fr+25c rose lake 15.00 12.00
B112 " 1.75fr+25c ultra. 12.00 5.75
B113 " 5fr+5fr brown violet 125.00 110.00
Nos. B107-B113 (7) 158.25 131.55

The surtax was for the National Anti-Tuberculosis League.

Désiré Cardinal Mercier
SP43

Mercier Protecting Children and Aged at Malines
SP44

Mercier as Professor at Louvain University
SP45

Mercier in Full Canonicals, Giving His Blessing
SP46

1932, June 10 Photo. *Perf. 14½x14*
B114 SP43 10c+10c dark violet 45 45
B115 " 50c+30c brt. violet 4.50 3.50
B116 " 75c+25c olive brn. 4.25 1.00
B117 " 1fr+2fr brn. red 13.50 12.50

Engraved.
Perf. 11½.
B118 SP44 1.75fr+75c deep blue 135.00 125.00
B119 SP45 2.50fr+2.50fr dark brown 135.00 125.00
B120 SP44 3fr+4.50fr dull green 135.00 125.00
B121 SP45 5fr+20fr violet brown 135.00 125.00
B122 SP46 10fr+40fr brn. lake 375.00 350.00
Nos. B114-B122 (9) 937.70 867.45

Issued in commemoration of Cardinal Mercier and to obtain funds to erect a monument to his memory.

Belgian Infantryman
SP47

Sanatorium at Waterloo
SP48

1932, Aug. 4 *Perf. 14½x14*
B123 SP47 75c+3.25fr red brown 100.00 90.00
B124 " 1.75fr+4.25fr dark blue 100.00 90.00

Issued in commemoration of the Belgian soldiers who fought in World War I and to obtain funds to erect a national monument to their glory.

1932, Dec. 1 Photo. *Perf. 13½x14*
B125 SP48 10c+5c dark violet 30 30
B126 " 25c+15c red violet 2.65 1.90
B127 " 50c+10c red brown 2.25 1.50
B128 " 75c+15c olive brn. 2.25 35
B129 " 1fr+25c deep red 25.00 18.00
B130 " 1.75fr+25c dp. blue 20.00 16.00
B131 " 5fr+5fr gray green 190.00 175.00
Nos. B125-B131 (7) 242.45 213.05

The surtax was for the assistance of the National Anti-Tuberculosis Society at Waterloo.

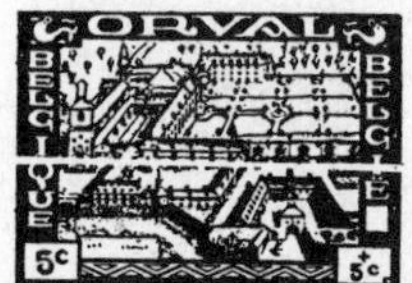

View of Old Abbey—SP49

Ruins of Old Abbey
SP50

Count de Chiny Presenting First Abbey to Countess Matilda
SP56

Restoration of Abbey in XVI and XVII Centuries
SP57

Abbey in XVIII Century, Maria Theresa and Charles V
SP58

Madonna and Arms of Seven Abbeys
SP60

Designs: 25c + 15c, Guests, courtyard. 50c + 25c, Transept. 75c + 50c, Bell Tower. 1fr + 1.25fr, Fountain. 1.25fr + 1.75fr, Cloisters. 5fr + 20fr, Duke of Brabant placing first stone of new abbey.

1933, Oct. 15 *Perf. 14*
B132 SP49 5c+5c dull green 100.00 90.00
B133 SP50 10c+15c olive green 85.00 80.00
B134 SP49 25c+15c dark brown 85.00 80.00
B135 SP50 50c+25c red brown 85.00 80.00
B136 " 75c+50c deep green 85.00 80.00
B137 " 1fr+1.25fr copper red 85.00 80.00
B138 SP49 1.25fr+1.75fr gray black 85.00 80.00
B139 SP56 1.75fr+2.75fr bl. 100.00 100.00
B140 SP57 2fr+3fr magenta 100.00 85.00
B141 SP58 2.50fr+5fr dull brown 100.00 85.00
B142 SP56 5fr+20fr vio. 100.00 85.00

Perf. 11½.
B143 SP60 10fr+40fr bl. 400.00 400.00
Nos. B132-B143 (12) 1410.00 1325.00

The surtax was for a fund to aid in the restoration of Orval Abbey. Counterfeits exist.

"Tuberculosis Society"
SP61

Peter Benoit
SP62

1933, Dec. 1 Engr. *Perf. 14x13½*
B144 SP61 10c+5c black 1.00 90
B145 " 25c+15c violet 5.00 3.50

B146 SP61 50c+10c red brn. 4.25 2.25
B147 " 75c+15c black brown 22.50 25
B148 " 1fr+25c claret 25.00 17.50
B149 " 1.75fr+25c violet blue 20.00 15.00
B150 " 5fr+5fr lilac 300.00 275.00
Nos. B144-B150 (7) 377.75 314.40

The surtax was for anti-tuberculosis work.

1934, June 1 Photogravure

B151 SP62 75c+25c olive brown 20.00 12.50

The surtax was to raise funds for the Peter Benoit Memorial.

King Leopold III
SP63 SP64

1934, Sept. 15

B152 SP63 75c+25c olive black 52.50 37.50
a. Sheet of 20 1200.00 1200.00
B153 SP64 1fr+25c red vio. 45.00 35.00
a. Sheet of 20 1200.00 1200.00

The surtax aided the National War Veterans' Fund. Sold for 4.50fr a set at the Exhibition of War Postmarks 1914–18, held at Brussels by the Royal Philatelic Club of Veterans. The price included an exhibition ticket. Sold at Brussels post office Sept. 18–22. No. B152 printed in sheets of 20 (4x5) and 100 (10x10). No. B153 printed in sheets of 20 (4x5) and 150 (10x15).

1934, Sept. 24

B154 SP63 75c+25c violet 4.00 2.25
B155 SP64 1fr+25c red brn. 22.50 16.50

The surtax aided the National War Veterans' Fund. No. B154 printed in sheets of 100 (10x10); No. B155 in sheets of 150 (10x15). These stamps remained in use one year.

Crusader
SP65

1934, Nov. 17 Engr. ***Perf. 13½x14***

B156 SP65 10c+5c black & red 50 50
B157 " 25c+15c brown & red 2.85 1.85
B158 " 50c+10c dull green & red 2.85 1.85
B159 " 75c+15c violet brown & red 1.60 25
B160 " 1fr+25c rose & red 20.00 16.00
B161 " 1.75fr+25c ultra. & red 16.50 13.50
B162 " 5fr+5fr brown vio. & red 250.00 225.00
Nos. B156-B162 (7) 294.30 258.95

The surtax was for anti-tuberculosis work.

Prince Baudouin, Princess Josephine and Prince Albert
SP66

1935, Apr. 10 Photogravure

B163 SP66 35c+15c dk. green 1.50 75
B164 " 70c+30c red brn. 1.50 75
B165 " 1.75fr+50c dark blue 18.00 8.50

Surtax was for Child Welfare Society.

Brussels Exhibition Issue.

Stagecoach—SP67

1935, Apr. 27

B166 SP67 10c+10c olive blk. 1.75 1.60
B167 " 25c+25c bis. brown 7.00 5.00
B168 " 35c+25c dark grn. 8.00 5.00

Nos. B166–B168 were printed in sheets of 10. Price, set of 3, $175.

Franz von Taxis
SP68

Queen Astrid
SP69

Souvenir Sheet.

1935, May 25 Engr. ***Perf. 14***

B169 SP68 5fr+5fr greenish black 225.00 210.00

Issued in sheets measuring 91½x117 mm., containing one stamp.

Nos. B166–B169 were issued for the Brussels Philatelic Exhibition (SITEB).

Queen Astrid Memorial Issue.

1935, Dec. 1 Photo. ***Perf. 11½***

Borders in Black.

B170 SP69 10c+5c olive black 15 15
B171 " 25c+15c brown 55 35
B172 " 35c+5c dark green 40 30
B173 " 50c+10c rose lilac 1.00 60
B174 " 70c+5c gray black 18 15
B175 " 1fr+25c red 3.00 2.25
B176 " 1.75fr+25c blue 8.00 4.50
B177 " 2.45fr+55c dk. violet 9.50 6.25
Nos. B170-B177 (8) 22.78 14.55

The surtax was divided among several charitable organizations.

Borgerhout Philatelic Exhibition Issue.

Souvenir Sheet.

Town Hall, Borgerhout
SP70

1936, Oct. 3

B178 SP70 70c+30c purple brown 67.50 55.00

Issued in sheets, measuring 115x126 mm., containing one stamp.

Town Hall and Belfry of Charleroi
SP71

Prince Baudouin
SP72

Charleroi Youth Exhibition.

Souvenir Sheet.

1936, Oct. 18 Engraved

B179 SP71 2.45fr+55c gray blue 45.00 50.00

Issued in sheets, measuring 95x120 mm., containing one stamp.

1936, Dec. 1 Photo. ***Perf. 14x13½***

B180 SP72 10c+5c dark brown 15 15
B181 " 25c+5c violet 45 30
B182 " 35c+5c dark green 45 30
B183 " 50c+5c violet brown 75 45
B184 " 70c+5c olive green 30 15
B185 " 1fr+25c cerise 2.25 1.10
B186 " 1.75fr+25c ultra. 3.25 1.60
B187 " 2.45fr+2.55fr violet rose 12.50 10.00
Nos. B180-B187 (8) 20.10 14.05

The surtax was for the assistance of the National Anti-Tuberculosis Society.

1937, Jan. 10

B188 SP72 2.45fr+2.55fr slate 4.25 3.25

Issued in commemoration of International Stamp Day. The surtax was for the benefit of the Brussels Postal Museum, the Royal Belgian Philatelic Federation and the Anti-Tuberculosis Society.

Queen Astrid and Prince Baudouin
SP73

Queen Mother Elisabeth
SP74

1937, Apr. 15 ***Perf. 11½***

B189 SP73 10c+5c magenta 15 15
B190 " 25c+5c olive black 50 30
B191 " 35c+5c dark green 50 30
B192 " 50c+5c violet 1.15 70
B193 " 70c+5c slate 50 15
B194 " 1fr+25c dk. car. 2.50 1.50
B195 " 1.75fr+25c dp. ultra. 4.25 2.10
B196 " 2.45fr+1.55fr dark brown 11.50 6.25
Nos. B189-B196 (8) 21.05 11.45

The surtax was to raise funds for Public Utility Works.

SP74a

1937, Sept. 15 ***Perf. 14x13½***

B197 SP74 70c+5c intense black 65 30
B198 " 1.75fr+25c bright ultramarine 1.50 1.15

Souvenir Sheet.

Perf. 11½.

B199 SP74a Sheet of four 47.50 30.00
a. 1.50fr+2.50fr red brown 11.00 7.50
b. 2.45fr+3.55fr red violet 9.25 6.00

Nos. B197–B199 were issued for the benefit of the Queen Elisabeth Music Foundation in connection with the Eugene Ysaye international competition.

No. B199 contains two se-tenant pairs of Nos. B199a and B199b. Size: 111x145mm. On sale one day, Sept. 15, at Brussels.

Princess Josephine-Charlotte
SP75

1937, Dec. 1 ***Perf. 14x13½***

B200 SP75 10c+5c slate green 15 15
B201 " 25c+5c lt. brown 45 30
B202 " 35c+5c yel. green 45 30
B203 " 50c+5c olive gray 70 45
B204 " 70c+5c brown red 55 15
B205 " 1fr+25c red 2.65 1.10
B206 " 1.75fr+25c vio. blue 3.00 1.50
B207 " 2.45fr+2.55fr mag. 13.00 8.50
Nos. B200-B207 (8) 20.95 12.45

King Albert Memorial Issue

Souvenir Sheet

King Albert Memorial—SP76

1938, Feb. 17 ***Perf. 11½***

B208 SP76 2.45fr+7.55fr brn. violet 21.00 18.50

Issued in connection with the dedication of the monument to King Albert. Sheet size: 143x115mm.

King Leopold III in Military Plane
SP77

1938, Mar. 15

B209 SP77 10c+5c car. brown 18 18
B210 " 35c+5c deep green 50 45
B211 " 70c+5c gray blk. 1.85 40
B212 " 1.75fr+25c ultra. 5.00 3.75
B213 " 2.45fr+2.55fr pur. 17.00 9.00
Nos. B209-B213 (5) 24.53 13.78

The surtax was for the benefit of the National Fund for Aeronautical Propaganda.

Basilica of Koekelberg
SP78

Interior View of the Basilica of Koekelberg
SP79

1938, June 1 **Photogravure**

B214	SP78	10c+5c light brown	15	15
B215	"	35c+5c green	25	18
B216	"	70c+5c gray green	35	15
B217	"	1fr+25c carmine	2.00	1.10
B218	"	1.75fr+25c ultra.	2.25	1.25
B219	"	2.45fr+2.55fr brown violet	8.00	6.50

Engraved.

B220	SP79	5fr+5fr dull grn.	45.00	27.50
		Nos. B214-B220 (7)	58.00	36.83

The surtax was for a fund to aid in completing the National Basilica of the Sacred Heart at Koekelberg.

Nos. B214, B216 and B218 are different views of the exterior of the Basilica.

Souvenir Sheet

Interior of Koekelberg Basilica
SP80

1938, July 21 **Engr.** ***Perf. 14***

B221	SP80	5fr+5fr lt. violet	21.00	18.50

Sheet size 94x120mm.

Stamps of 1938 Surcharged in Black:

40c (a) — 2.50 Fr (b) — 2.50 Fr

1938, Nov. 10 ***Perf. 11½***

B222	SP78 (a)	40c on 35c+5c green	60	30
B223	" (")	75c on 70c+5c gray grn.	1.00	50
B224	" (b)	2.50fr+2.50fr on 2.45fr+2.55fr brn. violet	15.00	13.50

Prince Albert of Liège
SP81

1938, Dec. 10 **Photo.** ***Perf. 14x13½***

B225	SP81	10c+5c brown	18	18
B226	"	30c+5c magenta	35	35
B227	"	40c+5c olive gray	50	35
B228	"	75c+5c slate green	30	15
B229	"	1fr+25c dk. car.	2.50	1.50
B230	"	1.75fr+25c ultra.	2.50	1.50
B231	"	2.50fr+2.50fr deep green	13.00	11.00
B232	"	5fr+5fr brown lake	42.50	20.00
		Nos. B225-B232 (8)	61.83	35.03

Henri Dunant
SP82

Florence Nightingale
SP83

King Leopold and Royal Children
SP85

Queen Mother Elisabeth and Royal Children
SP84

Queen Astrid
SP86

Queen Mother Elisabeth and Wounded Soldier
SP87

1939, Apr. 1 **Photo.** ***Perf. 11½***

The Cross is Printed in Carmine.

B233	SP82	10c+5c brown	15	15
B234	SP83	30c+5c brn. car.	60	45
B235	SP84	40c+5c olive gray	50	30
B236	SP85	75c+5c slate blk.	1.50	18
B237	SP84	1fr+25c bright rose	6.25	2.50
B238	SP85	1.75fr+25c bright ultramarine	2.50	2.00
B239	SP86	2.50fr+2.50fr dull violet	4.25	3.50
B240	SP87	5fr+5fr gray green	16.00	11.00
		Nos. B233-B240 (8)	31.75	20.08

75th anniversary of the founding of the International Red Cross Society.

Rubens' House, Antwerp
SP88

"Albert and Nicolas Rubens"
SP89

Arcade, Rubens' House
SP90

"Helena Fourment and Her Children"
SP91

Rubens and Isabelle Brandt
SP92

Peter Paul Rubens
SP93

"The Velvet Hat"
SP94

"Descent from the Cross"
SP95

1939, July 1

B241	SP88	10c+5c brown	15	15
B242	SP89	40c+5c brn. car.	60	45
B243	SP90	75c+5c olive bk.	2.35	60
B244	SP91	1fr+25c rose	6.75	3.50
B245	SP92	1.50fr+25c sepia	7.25	3.75
B246	SP93	1.75fr+25c deep ultra.	8.50	4.50
B247	SP94	2.50fr+2.50fr bright red violet	42.50	27.50
B248	SP95	5fr+5fr slate gray	52.50	35.00
		Nos. B241-B248 (8)	120.60	75.45

Issued to honor Peter Paul Rubens. The surtax was used to restore Rubens' home in Antwerp.

"Martin van Nieuwenhove" by Hans Memling
SP96

1939, July 1

B249	SP96	75c+75c olive blk	7.50	5.25

Issued in honor of Hans Memling, (1430?-1495), Flemish painter.

Twelfth Century Monks at Work
SP97

Reconstructed Tower Seen through Cloister
SP98

Monks Laboring in the Fields
SP99

Orval Abbey, Aerial View
SP100

Bishop Heylen of Namur, Madonna and Abbot General Smets of the Trappists
SP101

King Albert I and King Leopold III and Shrine—SP102

1939, July 20

B250 SP97 75c+75c olive black 7.00 6.75
B251 SP98 1fr+1fr rose red 5.00 4.25
B252 SP99 1.50fr+1.50fr dull brown 5.00 4.25
B253 SP100 1.75fr+1.75fr sapphire 5.00 4.25
B254 SP101 2.50fr+2.50fr brt. red violet 25.00 17.50
B255 SP102 5fr+5fr brown carmine 25.00 17.50
Nos. B250-B255 (6) 72.00 54.50

The surtax was used for the restoration of the Abbey of Orval.

Belfry at Bruges
SP103

Belfry at Furnes
SP104

Designs (Belfries): 30c + 5c, Thuin. 40c + 5c, Lierre. 75c + 5c, Mons. 1.75fr+25c, Namur. 2.50fr + 2.50fr, Alost. 5fr + 5fr, Tournai.

1939, Dec. 1 Photo. *Perf. 14x13½*

B256 SP103 10c+5c olive gray 15 15
B257 " 30c+5c brn. org. 35 30
B258 " 40c+5c bright red violet 40 35
B259 " 75c+5c olive black 30 15

Engraved

B260 SP104 1fr+25c rose carmine 2.65 1.85
B261 " 1.75fr+25c dark blue 2.65 1.85
B262 " 2.50fr+2.50fr deep red brown 21.50 17.00
B263 " 5fr+5fr purple 32.50 24.00
Nos. B256-B263 (8) 60.50 45.65

Arms of Mons
SP111

Arms of Ghent
SP112

Designs (Coats of Arms): 40c + 10c, Arel. 50c + 10c, Bruges. 75c + 15c, Namur. 1fr + 25c, Hasselt. 1.75fr. + 50c, Brussels. 2.50fr + 2.50fr, Antwerp. 5fr + 5fr, Liege.

1940-41 Typographed *Perf. 14x13½*

B264 SP111 10c+5c multi. ('41) 15 15
B265 SP112 30c+5c " 35 25
B266 SP111 40c+10c " 28 22
B267 SP112 50c+10c " 28 22
B268 SP111 75c+15c " 20 15
B269 SP112 1fr+25c multi. ('41) 90 75
B270 SP111 1.75fr+50c multi. ('41) 1.10 1.00
B271 SP112 2.50fr+2.50fr multi. ('41) 4.25 3.75
B272 SP111 5fr+5fr multi. ('41) 4.75 4.25
Nos. B264-B272 (9) 12.26 10.74

The surtax was used for winter relief.

Queen Elisabeth Music Chapel
SP120

Bust of Prince Albert of Liège
SP121

1940, Nov. Photo. *Perf. 11½*

B273 SP120 75c+75c slate 4.00 3.00
B274 " 1fr+1fr rose red 1.25 90
B275 SP121 1.50fr+1.50fr Pruss. green 1.25 90
B276 " 1.75fr+1.75fr ultra. 1.25 90
B277 SP120 2.50fr+2.50fr brn. orange 12.00 4.75
B278 SP121 5fr+5fr red violet 12.00 4.75
Nos. B273-B278 (6) 31.75 15.20

The surtax was for the Queen Elisabeth Music Foundation. Nos. B273-B278 were not authorized for postal use, but were sold to advance subscribers either mint or cancelled to order. See also Nos. B317-B318.

Souvenir Sheets.

Arms of Various Cities
SP122

Typographed.

1941, May *Perf. 14x13½, Imperf.*

Cross and City Name in Carmine.

B279 SP122 Sheet of nine 19.00 19.00
a. 10c+5c slate 1.50 1.50
b. 30c+5c emerald 1.50 1.50
c. 40c+10c chocolate 1.50 1.50
d. 50c+10c lt. violet 1.50 1.50
e. 75c+15c dull pur. 1.50 1.50
f. 1fr +25c carmine 1.50 1.50
g. 1.75fr+50c dull bl. 1.50 1.50
h. 2.50fr+2.50fr olive gray 1.50 1.50
i. 5fr+5fr dull violet 5.00 5.00

The sheets measure 106x148 mm. The surtax was used for relief work.

Painting
SP123

Sculpture
SP124

Monks Studying Plans of Orval Abbey
SP128

Designs: 40c+60c, 2fr+3.50fr, Monk carrying candle. 50c+65c, 1.75fr+2.50fr, Monk praying. 75c+1fr, 3fr+5fr, Two monks singing.

1941, June Photo. *Perf. 11½*

B281 SP123 10c+15c brown orange 1.35 90
B282 SP124 30c+30c olive gray 1.35 90
B283 " 40c+60c deep brown 1.35 90
B284 " 50c+65c violet 1.35 90
B285 " 75c+1fr bright red violet 1.35 90
B286 " 1fr+1.50fr rose red 1.35 90
B287 SP123 1.25fr+1.75fr deep yellow grn. 1.35 90
B288 " 1.75fr+2.50fr deep ultramarine 1.35 90
B289 " 2fr+3.50fr red violet 1.35 90
B290 SP124 2.50fr+4.50fr dull red brown 1.35 90
B291 " 3fr+5fr dark olive green 1.35 90
B292 SP128 5fr+10fr greenish black 4.50 3.25
Nos. B281-B292 (12) 19.35 13.15

The surtax was used for the restoration of the Abbey of Orval.

Maria Theresa
SP129

Charles the Bold
SP130

Portraits (in various frames): 35c+5c, Charles of Lorraine. 50c+10c, Margaret of Parma. 60c+10c, Charles V. 1fr+15c, Johanna of Castile. 1.50fr+1fr, Philip the Good. 1.75fr+1.75fr, Margaret of Austria. 3.25fr+3.25fr, Archduke Albert. 5fr+5fr, Archduchess Isabella.

1941-42 Photogravure.

B293 SP129 10c+5c olive blk. 10 10
B294 " 35c+5c dull grn. 15 15
B295 " 50c+10c brown 15 15
B296 " 60c+10c purple 15 15
B297 " 1fr+15c bright carmine rose 15 15
B298 " 1.50fr+1fr red vio. 60 60
B299 " 1.75fr+1.75fr royal blue 65 65
B300 SP130 2.25fr+2.25fr dull red brown 80 70
B301 SP129 3.25fr+3.25fr light brown 1.35 1.15
B302 " 5fr+5fr slate green 1.35 1.15
Nos. B293-B302 (10) 5.45 4.95

Souvenir Sheet.

Archduke Albert and Archduchess Isabella
SP139

B302A SP139 Sheet of two ('42) 7.25 6.75
b. 3.25fr+6.75fr turquoise blue 3.25 3.25
c. 5fr+10fr dark carmine 3.25 3.25

The sheets measure 77x59mm.
The surtax was for the benefit of National Social Service Work among soldiers' families.

Souvenir Sheets.

Monks Studying Plans of Orval Abbey
SP140

1941, Oct. Photo. *Perf. 11½*

Inscribed "Belgie-Belgique".

B303 SP140 5fr+15fr ultra. 15.00 15.00

Imperf.

Inscribed "Belgique-Belgie".

B304 SP140 5fr+15fr ultra. 15.00 15.00

The sheets measure 185x165 mm. and are inscribed in black, gold and ultramarine.
The surtax was for the restoration of Orval Abbey.
No. B304 exists perforated.
In 1942 these sheets were privately trimmed and overprinted "1142 1942" and ornament.

St. Martin Statue, Church of Dinant
SP141

Lennik, Saint-Quentin
SP142

St. Martin's Church, Saint-Trond
SP146

Designs (Statues of St. Martin): 50c+10c, 3.25fr +3.25fr, Beck, Limburg. 60c+10c, 2.25fr+2.25fr, Dave on the Meuse. 1.75fr+50c, Hal, Brabant.

1941-42 Photogravure *Perf. 11½*

B305 SP141 10c+5c chestnut 10 10
B306 SP142 35c+5c dark blue green 18 18
B307 " 50c+10c violet 18 18
B308 " 60c+10c deep brown 18 18
B309 " 1fr+15c carmine 18 18
B310 SP141 1.50fr+25c slate green 80 60
B311 SP142 1.75fr+50c dark ultramarine 85 65
B312 " 2.25fr+2.25fr red violet 85 75
B313 " 3.25fr+3.25fr brown violet 85 85
B314 SP146 5fr+5fr dark olive green 1.20 1.00
Nos. B305-B314 (10) 5.37 4.67

Souvenir Sheets.

Inscribed "Belgie-Belgique".

B315 SP146 5fr+20fr violet brown ('42) 18.50 18.50

Imperf.

Inscribed "Belgique-Belgie"

B316 SP146 5fr+20fr violet brown ('42) 18.50 18.50

Nos. B315–B316 contain one stamp each. Size: 105x139mm.

In 1956, the Bureau Européen de la Jeunesse et de l'Enfance privately overprinted Nos. B315–B316: "Congrès Européen de l'education 7–12 Mai 1956," in dark red and dark green respectively. A black bar obliterates "Winterhulp-Secours d'Hiver."

Souvenir Sheets.

Queen Elisabeth Music Chapel
SP147

1941, Dec. 1 Photo. ***Perf. 11½***

Inscribed "Belgique-Belgie".

B317 SP147 10fr+15fr olive black 5.00 5.00

Imperf.

Inscribed "Belgie-Belgique".

B318 SP147 10fr+15fr olive black 5.00 5.00

Issued in sheets measuring 105x139mm. The surtax was for the Queen Elisabeth Music Foundation. These sheets were perforated with the monogram of Queen Elisabeth in 1942.

In 1954 Nos. B317–B318 were overprinted to commemorate the birth centenary of Edgar Tinel, composer. Inscriptions in French, border in brown on No. B317; inscriptions in Flemish, border in green on No. B318. These overprinted sheets were not postally valid.

Jean Bollandus
SP148

Christophe Plantin
SP156

Designs: 35c+5c, Andreas Vesalius. 50c+10c, Simon Stevinus. 60c+10c, Jean Van Helmont. 1fr+15c, Rembert Dodoens. 1.75fr+50c, Gerardus Mercator. 3.25fr+3.25fr, Abraham Ortelius. 5fr+5fr, Justus Lipsius.

Photogravure.

1942, May 15 ***Perf. 14x13½***

B319 SP148 10c+5c dull brn. 7 7
B320 " 35c+5c gray grn. 12 12
B321 " 50c+10c fawn 12 12
B322 " 60c+10c greenish black 12 12

Engraved.

B323 SP148 1fr+15c bright rose 15 12
B324 " 1.75fr+50c dull blue 60 60
B325 " 3.25fr+3.25fr lilac rose 35 35
B326 " 5fr+5fr violet 55 55

Perf. 13½x14.

B327 SP156 10fr+30fr red orange 3.25 3.00
Nos. B319–B327 (9) 5.33 5.05

The surtax was used to help fight tuberculosis.

No. B327 was sold by subscription at the Brussels Post Office, July 1–10, 1942.

Belgian Prisoner
SP158

1942, Oct. 1 ***Perf. 11½***

B331 SP158 5fr+45fr olive gray, with label 13.50 13.50

The surtax was for prisoners of war. A brown label, inscribed "1942 POUR NOS PRISONNIERS/ VOOR ONZE GEVANGENEN," alternates with the stamps in the sheet.

SP159

SP164

SP162

SP168

Various Statues of St. Martin

1942–43

B332 SP159 10c+5c orange 10 10
B333 " 35c+5c dark blue green 15 15
B334 " 50c+10c dp. brn. 15 15
B335 SP162 60c+10c black 18 18
B336 SP159 1fr+15c bright rose 18 18
B337 SP164 1.50fr+25c greenish black 75 65
B338 " 1.75fr+50c dk. blue 85 75
B339 SP162 2.25fr+2.25fr brown 85 75
B340 " 3.25fr+3.25fr bright red violet 85 85
B341 SP168 5fr+10fr henna brown 1.25 1.10
B342 SP168 10fr+20fr rose brown & vio. brn. ('43) 2.50 2.50

Inscribed "Belgique-Belgie".

B343 SP168 10fr+20fr golden brown & vio. brn. ('43) 2.50 2.50
Nos. B332–B343 (12) 10.31 9.86

The surtax was for winter relief.

Issue dates: Nos. B332–B341, Nov. 12, 1942. Nos. B342–B343, Apr. 3, 1943.

Prisoners of War—SP170

Design: No. B345, Two prisoners with package from home.

1943, May Photo. ***Perf. 11½***

B344 SP170 1fr+30fr vermilion 6.00 6.00
B345 " 1fr+30fr brown rose 6.00 6.00

The surtax was used for prisoners of war.

Roof Tiler
SP172

Coppersmith
SP173

Designs: (Statues in Petit Sablon Park, Brussels). 35c+5c, Blacksmith. 60c+10c, Gunsmith. 1fr+15c, Armsmith. 1.75fr+75c, Goldsmith. 3.25fr+3.25fr, Fishdealer. 5fr+25fr, Watchmaker.

1943, June 1

B346 SP172 10c+5c chestnut brown 10 10
B347 " 35c+5c green 15 12
B348 SP173 50c+10c dk. brn. 15 12
B349 " 60c+10c slate 15 15
B350 " 1fr+15c dull rose brown 60 35
B351 " 1.75fr+75c ultra. 1.35 85
B352 " 3.25fr+3.25fr bright red violet 1.50 1.15
B353 " 5fr+25fr dark purple 1.50 1.40
Nos. B346–B353 (8) 5.50 4.24

The surtax was for the control of tuberculosis.

"O"
SP180

"ORVAL"
SP185

Designs: 60c+1.90fr, "R." 1fr+3fr, "V." 1.75fr+5.25fr, "A." 3.25fr+16.75fr, "L."

1943, Oct. 9

B354 SP180 50c+1fr ol. blk. 1.50 1.40
B355 " 60c+1.90fr dull violet 50 45
B356 " 1fr+3fr rose brown 50 45
B357 " 1.75fr+5.25fr dark blue 50 45
B358 SP180 3.25fr+16.75fr dark blue green 1.00 80
B359 SP185 5fr+30fr deep brown 2.10 1.65
Nos. B354–B359 (6) 6.10 5.20

The surtax aided restoration of Orval Abbey.

St. Léonard Church, Léau
SP186

St. Martin Church, Courtrai
SP190

Basilica of St. Martin, Angre
SP191

Notre Dame, Hal
SP193

St. Martin—SP194

Designs: 35c+5c, St. Martin Church, Dion-le-Val. 50c+15c, St. Martin Church, Alost. 60c+20c, St. Martin Church, Liege. 3.25fr+11.75fr, St. Martin Church, Loppem. No. B369, St. Martin, beggar and Meuse landscape.

1943-44

B360 SP186 10c+5c dp. brn. 12 12
B361 " 35c+5c dark blue green 22 18
B362 " 50c+15c olive black 22 18
B363 " 60c+20c bright red violet 25 22
B364 SP190 1fr+1fr rose brown 45 22
B365 SP191 1.75fr+4.25fr deep ultramarine 3.25 2.50
B366 SP186 3.25fr+11.75fr red lilac 3.25 2.50
B367 SP193 5fr+25fr dark blue 4.50 4.00
B368 SP194 10fr+30fr gray green ('44) 2.75 2.75

B369 SP194 10fr+30fr black brown ('44) 2.75 2.75
Nos. B360–B369 (10) 17.76 15.42

The surtax was for winter relief.

"Daedalus and Icarus"
SP196

Sir Anthony Van Dyck, Self-portrait
SP200

Paintings by Van Dyck: 50c+2.50fr. "The Good Samaritan." 60c+3.40fr, Detail of "Christ Healing the Paralytic." 1fr+5fr, "Madonna and Child." 5fr+30fr, "St. Sebastian."

1944, Apr. 16 Photo. *Perf. 11½*
Crosses in Carmine.

B370 SP196 35c+1.65fr dark slate green 90 80
B371 " 50c+2.50fr greenish black 90 80
B372 " 60c+3.40fr black brown 90 80
B373 " 1fr+5fr dk. car. 1.00 90
B374 SP200 1.75fr+8.25fr intense blue 90 90
B375 SP196 5fr+30fr copper brown 90 80
Nos. B370–B375 (6) 5.50 5.00

The surtax was for the Belgian Red Cross.

Jan van Eyck
SP202

Godfrey of Bouillon
SP203

Designs: 50c+25c, Jacob van Maerlant. 60c+40c, Jean Joses de Dinant. 1fr+50c, Jacob van Artevelde. 1.75fr+4.25fr, Charles Joseph de Ligne. 2.25fr+8.25fr, Andre Gretry. 3.25fr+11.25fr, Jan Moretus-Plantin. 5fr+35fr, Jan van Ruysbroeck.

1944, May 31

B376 SP202 10c+15c dark purple 75 55
B377 SP203 35c+15c green 65 55
B378 " 50c+25c chestnut brown 65 55
B379 " 60c+40c olive black 65 55
B380 " 1fr+50c rose brown 65 55
B381 " 1.75fr+4.25fr ultramarine 65 55
B382 " 2.25fr+8.25fr greenish black 1.85 1.35
B383 " 3.25fr+11.25fr dark brown 65 55
B384 " 5fr+35fr slate blue 1.35 1.35
Nos. B376–B384 (9) 7.85 6.55

The surtax was for prisoners of war.

Sons of Aymon Astride Bayard
SP211

Brabo Slaying the Giant Antigoon
SP212

Till Eulenspiegel Singing to Nele
SP214

Designs: 50c+10c, St. Hubert converted by stag with crucifix. 1fr+15fr, St. George slaying the dragon. 1.75fr+5.25fr, Genevieve of Brabant with son and roe-deer. 3.25fr+11.75fr, Tchantches wrestling with the Saracen. 5fr+25fr, St. Gertrude rescuing the knight with the cards.

1944, June 25

B385 SP211 10c+5c choc. 10 10
B386 SP212 35c+5c dark blue green 10 10
B387 SP211 50c+10c dull violet 10 10
B388 SP214 60c+10c black brown 10 10
B389 " 1fr+15c rose brown 10 10
B390 " 1.75fr+5.25fr ultra. 70 65
B391 SP211 3.25fr+11.75fr greenish black 85 70
B392 " 5fr+25fr dark blue 1.00 85
Nos. B385–B392 (8) 3.05 2.70

The surtax was for the control of tuberculosis.

Nos. B385–B389 were overprinted "Breendonk+10fr." in 1946 by the Union Royale Philatelique for an exhibition at Brussels. They had no postal validity.

Union of the Flemish and Walloon Peoples in their Sorrow
SP219

Union in Reconstruction
SP220

Photogravure

1945, May 1 *Perf. 11½* Unwmkd.

B395 SP219 1fr+30fr car. 2.00 2.00
B396 SP220 1¾fr+30fr bright ultramarine 2.00 2.00

1945, July 21

Size: 34½x23½mm.

B397 SP219 1fr+9fr scarlet 45 45
B398 SP220 1fr+9fr carmine rose 45 45

The surtax was for the postal employees' relief fund.

Prisoner of War
SP221

Reunion
SP222

Awaiting Execution
SP223

Symbolical Figures "Recovery of Freedom"
SP225

Design: 70c+30c, 3.50fr+3.50fr, Member of Resistance Movement.

1945, Sept. 10

B399 SP221 10c+15c orange 10 10
B400 SP222 20c+20c deep purple 12 12
B401 SP223 60c+25c sepia 15 15
B402 SP221 70c+30c deep yellow green 18 15
B403 " 75c+50c orange brown 22 22
B404 SP222 1fr+75c bright blue green 30 25
B405 SP223 1.50fr+1fr bright red 30 25
B406 SP221 3.50fr+3.50fr bright blue 2.35 2.10
B407 SP225 5fr+40fr brn. 2.50 2.10
Nos. B399–B407 (9) 6.22 5.44

The inscriptions are transposed on Nos. B403–B406.

The surtax was for the benefit of prisoners of war, displaced persons, families of executed victims and members of the Resistance Movement.

Arms of West Flanders
SP226

Arms of Provinces: 20c+20c, Luxembourg. 60c+25c, East Flanders. 70c+30c, Namur. 75c+50c, Limburg. 1fr+75c, Hainaut. 1.50fr+1fr, Antwerp. 3.50fr+1.50fr, Liege. 5fr+45fr, Brabant.

1945, Dec. 1

B408 SP226 10c+15c slate black & slate gray 10 10
B409 " 20c+20c rose carmine & rose 18 18

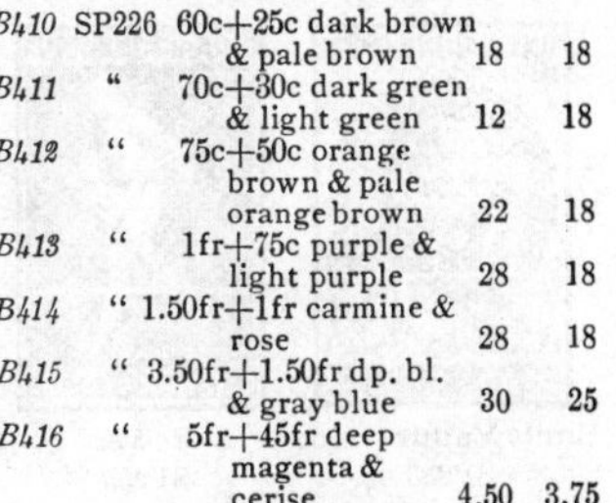

B410 SP226 60c+25c dark brown & pale brown 18 18
B411 " 70c+30c dark green & light green 12 18
B412 " 75c+50c orange brown & pale orange brown 22 18
B413 " 1fr+75c purple & light purple 28 18
B414 " 1.50fr+1fr carmine & rose 28 18
B415 " 3.50fr+1.50fr dp. bl. & gray blue 30 25
B416 " 5fr+45fr deep magenta & cerise 4.50 3.75
Nos. B408–B416 (9) 6.16 5.18

The surtax was for tuberculosis prevention.

Father Joseph Damien
SP227

Father Damien Comforting Leper
SP229

Leper Colony, Molokai Island, Hawaii
SP228

Photogravure.

1946, July 15 *Perf. 11½* Unwmkd.

B417 SP227 65c+75c dark blue 1.65 1.50
B418 SP228 1.35fr+2fr brn. 1.65 1.50
B419 SP229 1.75fr+18fr rose brown 1.85 1.65

The surtax was for the erection of a museum in Louvain.

Symbols of Wisdom and Patriotism
SP230

"In Memoriam"
SP232

François Bovesse
SP231

1946, July 15

B420 SP230 65c+75c violet 1.65 1.50
B421 SP231 1.35fr+2fr dark orange brn. 1.65 1.50
B422 SP232 1.75fr+18fr carmine rose 1.85 1.65

The surtax was for the erection of a "House of the Fine Arts" at Namur.

Emile Vandervelde
SP233

Sower
SP235

Vandervelde, Laborer and Family
SP234

1946, July 15

B423 SP233 65c+75c dark slate green 2.00 1.65
B424 SP234 1.35fr+2fr dark violet blue 2.00 1.65
B425 SP235 1.75fr+18fr deep carmine 2.10 2.00
Nos. B417-B425 (9) 16.40 14.60

The surtax was for the Emile Vandervelde Institute, to promote social, economic and cultural activities.

Pepin of Herstal
SP236

Arms of Malines
SP241

Designs: 1fr+50c, Charlemagne. 1.50fr +1fr, Godfrey of Bouillon. 3.50fr+1.50fr, Robert of Jerusalem. Nos. B430-B431, Baldwin of Constantinople.

1946, Sept. 15 Engr. *Perf. 11½x11*

B426 SP236 75c+25c green 55 35
B427 " 1fr+50c violet 1.00 85
B428 " 1.50fr+1fr plum 75 75
B429 " 3.50fr+1.50fr brt. blue 1.10 1.00
B430 " 5fr+45fr red violet 23.50 22.50
B431 " 5fr+45fr red orange 22.50 22.50
Nos. B426-B431 (6) 49.40 47.95

The surtax on Nos. B426-B429 was for the benefit of former prisoners of war, displaced persons, the families of executed patriots, and former members of the Resistance Movement.

The surtax on Nos. B430-B431 was divided among several welfare, national celebration and educational organizations.

Issue dates: Nos. B426-B429, Apr. 15; No. B430, Sept. 15; No. B431, Nov. 15.

See also Nos. B437-B441, B465-B466, B472-B476.

1946, Dec. 2 *Perf. 11½*

Designs (Coats of Arms): 90c+60c, Dinant. 1.35fr+1.15fr, Ostend. 3.15fr+1.85fr, Verviers. 4.50fr+45.50fr, Louvain.

B432 SP241 65c+35c rose carmine 75 55
B433 " 90c+60c lemon 75 55
B434 " 1.35fr+1.15fr deep green 75 55
B435 " 3.15fr+1.85fr bl. 1.50 1.10
B436 SP241 4.50fr+45.50fr dark violet brn. 27.50 24.00
Nos. B432-B436 (5) 31.25 26.75

The surtax was for anti-tuberculosis work
See also Nos. B442-B446.

Type of 1946.

Designs: 65c+35c, John II, Duke of Brabant. 90c+60c, Count Philip of Alsace. 1.35fr+1.15fr, William the Good. 3.15fr+1.85fr, Bishop Notger of Liege. 20fr+20fr, Philip the Noble.

1947, Sept. 25 Engr. *Perf. 11½x11*

B437 SP236 65c+35c Prussian green 1.00 1.00
B438 " 90c+60c yel. grn. 1.50 1.50
B439 " 1.35fr+1.15fr car. 2.35 2.35
B440 " 3.15fr+1.85fr ultramarine 2.75 2.75
B441 " 20fr+20fr red violet 75.00 75.00
Nos. B437-B441 (5) 82.60 82.60

The surtax was for victims of World War II.

Arms Type of 1946 Dated "1947"

Coats of Arms: 65c+35c, Nivelles. 90c+60c, St. Trond. 1.35fr+1.15fr, Charleroi. 3.15fr+1.85fr, St. Nicolas. 20fr+20fr, Bouillon.

1947, Dec. 15 *Perf. 11½*

B442 SP241 65c+35c orange 70 50
B443 " 90c+60c dp. claret 70 50
B444 " 1.35fr+1.15fr dark brown 70 50
B445 " 3.15fr+1.85fr deep blue 1.50 1.35
B446 " 20fr+20fr dark green 35.00 35.00
Nos. B442-B446 (5) 38.60 37.85

The surtax was for anti-tuberculosis work.

St. Benedict and King Totila
SP247

Achel Abbey
SP248

Designs: 3.15fr+2.85fr, St. Benedict, legislator and builder. 10fr+10fr, Death of St. Benedict.

1948, Apr. 5 Photogravure

B447 SP247 65c+65c red brown 1.50 1.15
B448 SP248 1.35fr+1.35fr gray 2.00 1.50
B449 SP247 3.15fr+2.85fr deep ultramarine 6.50 5.00
B450 " 10fr+10fr brt. red violet 27.50 22.50

The surtax was to aid the Abbey of the Trappist Fathers at Achel.

St. Begga and Chèvremont Castle
SP249

Chèvremont Basilica and Convent
SP250

Designs: 3.15fr+2.85fr, Madonna of Chevremont and Chapel. 10fr+10fr, Madonna of Mt. Carmel.

1948, Apr. 5 Unwmkd.

B451 SP249 65c+65c blue green 1.50 1.10
B452 SP250 1.35fr+1.35fr dark carmine rose 1.85 1.25
B453 SP249 3.15fr+2.85fr deep blue 5.50 4.25
B454 " 10fr+10fr deep brown 27.50 22.50

The surtax was to aid the Basilica of the Carmelite Fathers of Chèvremont.

Anseele Monument Showing French Inscription
SP251

Designs: 90c + 60c, View of Ghent. 1.35fr+1.15fr, Van Artevelde monument, Ghent. 3.15fr+1.85fr. Anseele Monument, Flemish inscription.

1948, June 21 *Perf. 14x13½*

B455 SP251 65c+35c rose red 2.75 1.75
B456 " 90c+60c gray 5.75 4.50
B457 " 1.35fr+1.15fr henna brown 3.50 2.50
B458 " 3.15fr+1.85fr bright blue 12.00 11.00
a. Souvenir sheet of 4 85.00 65.00

Issued to honor Edouard Anseele, statesman, founder of the Belgian Socialist Party.

No. B458a contains one each of Nos. B455-B458. Size: 144x81mm. Sold for 50fr.

Statue "The Unloader"
SP252

Underground Fighter
SP253

1948, Sept. 4 *Perf. 11½x11*

B460 SP252 10fr+10fr gray grn. 40.00 37.50
B461 SP253 10fr+10fr red brown 25.00 22.50

The surtax was used toward erection of monuments at Antwerp and Liège.

Double Barred Cross
SP254

Designs: 4fr+3.25fr, Isabella of Austria. 20fr+20fr, Archduke Albert of Austria.

Portrait Type of 1946 and SP255

1948, Dec. 15 Photo. *Perf. 13½x14*

B462 SP254 20c+5c dark slate green 30 30
B463 " 1.20fr+30c magenta 1.50 1.15
B464 " 1.75fr+25c red 2.25 1.75

Engraved

Perf. 11½x11

B465 SP236 4fr+3.25fr ultramarine 14.00 12.00
B466 " 20fr+20fr Prussian green 62.50 62.50
Nos. B462-B466 (5) 80.55 77.70

The surtax was divided among several charities.

Souvenir Sheets

Rogier van der Weyden Paintings—SP255

Paintings by van der Weyden (No. B466A): 90c, Virgin and Child. 1.75fr, Christ on the Cross. 4fr, Mary Magdalene.

Paintings by Jordaens (No. B466B): 90c, Woman Reading. 1.75fr, The Flutist. 4fr, Old Woman Reading Letter.

1949, Apr. 1 Photo. *Perf. 11½*

B466A SP255 Sheet of 3 160.00
c. 90c deep brown 40.00
d. 1.75fr deep rose lilac 40.00
e. 4fr dark violet blue 40.00
B466B SP255 Sheet of 3 160.00
f. 90c dark violet 40.00
g. 1.75fr red 40.00
h. 4fr blue 40.00

The surtax went to various cultural and philanthropic organizations. Nos. B466A and B466B have dark brown and orange decorative border. Size: 140x90½mm. Sheets sold for 50fr each.

Guido Gezelle
SP256

1949, Nov. 15 Photo. *Perf. 14x13½*

B467 SP256 1.75fr+75c dark Prussian grn. 4.25 3.75

Issued to commemorate the 50th anniversary of the death of Guido Gezelle, poet. The surtax was for the Guido Gezelle Museum, Bruges.

Portrait Type of 1946 and

Arnica
SP257

Designs: 65c+10c, Sand grass. 90c+10c, Wood myrtle. 1.20fr+30c, Field poppy. 1.75fr+25c, Philip the Good. 3fr+1.50fr, Charles V. 4fr+2fr, Maria-Christina. 6fr+3fr, Charles of Lorraine. 8fr+4fr, Maria-Theresa.

1949, Dec. 20 Typo. *Perf. 13½x14*

B468 SP257 20c+5c multi. 35 35
B469 " 65c+10c " 1.75 1.50
B470 " 90c+10c " 2.75 2.00
B471 " 1.20fr+30c " 3.25 2.50

Engraved

Perf. 11½x11

B472 SP236 1.75fr+25c red orange 1.25 45
B473 " 3fr+1.50fr deep claret 12.00 11.50
B474 " 4fr+2fr ultra. 14.00 13.00
B475 " 6fr+3fr chocolate 24.00 22.50
B476 " 8fr+4fr dull green 24.00 22.50
Nos. B468-B476 (9) 83.35 76.30

The surtax was apportioned among several welfare organizations.

Arms of Belgium and Great Britain
SP258

British Memorial
SP260

Design: 2.50fr+50c, British tanks at Hertain.

Engraved.

1950, Mar. 15 *Perf. 13½x14, 11½*

B477 SP258 80c+20c grn. 2.25 2.00
B478 " 2.50fr+50c red 7.50 5.75
B479 SP260 4fr+2fr deep blue 11.00 9.00

Issued to commemorate the 6th anniversary of the liberation of Belgian territory by the British army.

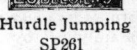

Hurdle Jumping
SP261

Relay Race
SP262

Designs: 90c+10c, Javelin throwing. 4fr+2fr, Pole vault. 8fr+4fr, Foot race.

Inscribed: "Heysel 1950."

Perf. 14x13½, 13½x14.

1950, July 1 Engr. Unwmkd.

B480 SP261 20c+5c bright green 45 45
B481 " 90c+10c violet brown 3.75 3.50
B482 SP262 1.75fr+25c car. 4.25 4.00
a. Souvenir sheet 52.50 52.50
B483 SP261 4fr+2fr light blue 42.50 40.00
B484 SP261 8fr+4fr deep green 50.00 50.00
Nos. B480-B484 (5) 100.95 97.95

Issued to publicize the European Athletic Games, Brussels, August 1950.

No. B482a measures 89 x 68½ mm., and contains a single copy of No. B482 with inscriptions typographed in black in upper and lower margins.

The margins of No. B482a were trimmed in April, 1951, and an overprint ("25 Francs pour le Fonds Sportif—25e Fofre Internationale Bruxelles") was added in red in French and in black in Flemish by a private committee. These pairs of altered sheets were sold at the Brussels Fair.

Gentian
SP263

Tombeek Sanatorium
SP265

Sijsele Sanatorium
SP264

Designs: 65c+10c, Cotton Grass. 90c+10c, Foxglove. 1.20fr+30c, Limonia. 4fr+2fr, Jauche Sanatorium.

Typographed.

1950, Dec. 20 *Perf. 14x13½*

Cross in Red.

B485 SP263 20c+5c maroon, blue & emerald 25 25
B486 " 65c+10c brown, buff & emerald 1.65 1.35
B487 " 90c+10c bluish green, deep magenta & yel. green 2.25 2.25
B488 " 1.20fr+30c vio. blue, blue & green 2.25 2.00

Engraved.

Perf. 11½.

B489 SP264 1.75fr+25c car. 2.25 2.25
B490 " 4fr+2fr blue 21.00 18.00
B491 SP265 8fr+4fr blue green 27.50 26.50
Nos. B485-B491 (7) 57.15 52.60

The surtax was for tuberculosis prevention and other charitable purposes.

Chemist
SP266

Allegory of Peace
SP268

Colonial Instructor and Class
SP267

1951, Mar. 27 Unwmkd.

B492 SP266 80c+20c green 2.10 1.85
B493 SP267 2.50fr+50c violet brown 15.00 15.00
B494 SP268 4fr+2fr deep blue 18.50 13.50

The surtax was for the reconstruction fund of the United Nations Educational, Scientific and Cultural Organization.

Monument to Political Prisoners
SP269

Fort of Breendonk
SP270

Design: 8fr+4fr, Monument: profile of figure on pedestal.

1951, Aug. 20 Photo. *Perf. 11½*

B495 SP269 1.75fr+25c black brown 2.00 1.65
B496 SP270 4fr+2fr blue & slate gray 32.50 32.50
B497 SP269 8fr+4fr dark blue green 35.00 35.00

The surtax was for the erection of a national monument.

Queen Elisabeth
SP271

1951, Sept. 22

B498 SP271 90c+10c greenish gray 2.00 1.50
B499 " 1.75fr+25c plum 3.75 1.85
B500 " 3fr+1fr green 26.00 24.00
B501 " 4fr+2fr gray bl. 35.00 30.00
B502 " 8fr+4fr sepia 37.50 35.00
Nos. B498-B502 (5) 104.25 92.35

The surtax was for the Queen Elisabeth Medical Foundation.

Cross, Sun Rays and Dragon
SP272

Beersel Castle
SP273

Horst Castle
SP274

Castles: 4fr+2fr, Lavaux St. Anne. 8fr+4fr, Veves.

1951, Dec. 17 Engr. Unwmkd.

B503 SP272 20c+5c red 10 10
B504 " 65c+10c deep ultramarine 55 45
B505 " 90c+10c sepia 70 60
B506 " 1.20fr+30c rose violet 1.25 1.00
B507 SP273 1.75fr+75c red brown 1.25 18
B508 SP274 3fr+1fr yellow green 16.00 14.00
B509 SP273 4fr+2fr blue 21.00 19.00
B510 SP274 8fr+4fr gray 25.00 24.00
Nos. B503-B510 (8) 65.85 59.33

The surtax was for anti-tuberculosis work.
See also Nos. B523-B526, B547-B550.

Main Altar
SP275

Basilica of the Sacred Heart Koekelberg
SP276

Procession Bearing Relics of St. Albert of Louvain
SP277

1952, Mar. 1 Photo. *Perf. 11½*

B511 SP275 1.75fr+25c black brown 1.35 45
B512 SP276 4fr+2fr indigo 19.00 17.50

Engraved.

B513 SP277 8fr+4fr violet brown 27.50 24.00
a. Souv. sheet 165.00 165.00

No. B513a measures 122x72mm., and contains one each of Nos. B511-B513, with inscriptions in indigo and black brown. Sold for 30 fr.

Issued to commemorate the 25th anniversary of the Cardinalate of J. E. Van Roey, Primate of Belgium. The surtax was for the Basilica.

Beaulieu Castle, Malines
SP278

August Vermeylen
SP279

1952, May 14 Engraved

Laid Paper.

B514 SP278 40fr+10fr light greenish bl. 300.00 275.00

Issued on the occasion of the 13th Universal Postal Union Congress, Brussels, 1952.

1952, Oct. 24 *Perf. 11½* Unwmkd.

Portraits: 80c+40c, Karel Van de Woestijne. 90c+45c, Charles de Coster. 1.75fr+75c, M. Maeterlinck. 4fr+2fr, Emile Verhaeren. 8fr+4fr, Hendrik Conscience.

Photogravure.

B515 SP279 65c+30c purple 2.75 2.25

B516	SP279	80c+40c dk. grn.	4.75	4.00
B517	"	90c+45c sepia	3.00	2.25
B518	"	1.75fr+75c cerise	4.50	3.00
B519	"	4fr+2fr bl. vio.	40.00	37.50
B520	"	8fr+4fr dark brown	40.00	37.50
		Nos. B515-B520 (6)	95.00	86.50

1952, Nov. 15

Portraits: 4fr, Emile Verhaeren. 8fr, Hendrik Conscience.

B521	SP279	4fr (+9fr) bl.	100.00	90.00
B522	"	8fr (+9fr) dark car. rose	100.00	90.00

On Nos. B521-B522, the denomination is repeated at either side of the stamp. The surtax is expressed on se-tenant labels bearing quotations of Verhaeren (in French) and Conscience (in Flemish).

A 9-line black overprint was privately applied to these labels: "Conference Internationale de la Musique Bruxelles UNESCO International Music Conference Brussels 1953*"

Type of 1951 Dated "1952," and

Arms of Malmédy
SP281

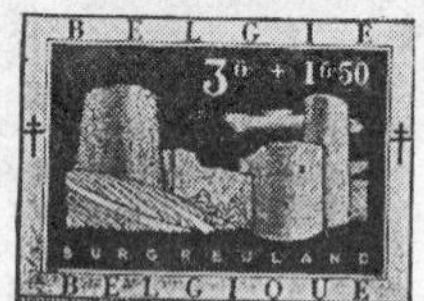

Castle Ruins, Burgreuland
SP282

Designs: 4fr+2fr, Vesdre Dam, Eupen. 8fr+4fr, St. Vitus, patron saint of Saint-Vith.

1952, Dec. 15 **Engraved**

B523	SP272	20c+5c red brown	15	15
B524	"	80c+20c green	60	45
B525	"	1.20fr+30c lilac rose	1.35	90
B526	"	1.50fr+50c olive brown	1.25	90
B527	SP281	2fr+75c carm.	2.50	1.50
B528	SP282	3fr+1.50fr chocolate	25.00	22.50
B529	SP281	4fr+2fr blue	22.50	19.00
B530	"	8fr+4fr violet brown	25.00	23.50
		Nos. B523-B530 (8)	78.35	68.90

The surtax on Nos. B523-B530 was for anti-tuberculosis and other charitable works.

Walthère Dewé
SP283

Princess Josephine-Charlotte
SP284

1953, Feb. 16 **Photogravure**

B531	SP283	2fr+1fr brown carmine	4.50	3.50

The surtax was for the construction of a memorial to Walthère Dewé, Underground leader in World War II.

1953, Mar. 14 **Cross in Red**

B532	SP284	80c+20c olive grn.	1.65	1.50
B533	"	1.20fr+30c brown	1.65	1.50
B534	"	2fr+50c rose lake	1.65	1.50
		a. Bklt. pane of 8	80.00	80.00
B535	"	2.50fr+50c crimson	22.00	22.00
B536	"	4fr+1fr bright blue	14.00	12.00
B537	"	5fr+2fr slate green	17.00	15.00
		Nos. B532-B537 (6)	57.95	53.50

The surtax was for the Belgian Red Cross.

The selvage of No. B534a is inscribed in French or Dutch. The price is for the French.

Boats at Dock
SP285

Bridge and Citadel, Namur
SP286

Allegory
SP287

Designs: 1.20fr+30c, Bridge at Bouillon. 2fr+50c, Antwerp waterfront. 4fr+2fr, Wharf at Ghent. 8fr+4fr, Meuse River at Freyr.

1953, June 22 ***Perf. 11½*** **Unwmkd.**

B538	SP285	80c+20c green	1.35	90
B539	"	1.20fr+30c reddish brown	2.25	1.65
B540	"	2fr+50c sepia	2.25	1.65
B541	SP286	2.50fr+50c deep magenta	16.00	15.00
B542	"	4fr+2fr violet blue	28.00	24.00
B543	"	8fr+4fr gray black	32.50	29.00
		Nos. B538-B543 (6)	82.35	72.20

The surtax was used to promote tourism in the Ardenne-Meuse region and for various cultural works.

1953, Oct. 26 **Engraved**

B544	SP287	80c+20c green	4.50	3.25
B545	"	2.50fr+1fr rose carmine	52.50	42.50
B546	"	4fr+1.50fr blue	57.50	50.00

The surtax was for the European Bureau of Childhood and Youth.

Type of 1951 Dated "1953," and

Ernest Malvoz
SP288

Robert Koch
SP289

Portraits: 3fr+1.50fr, Carlo Forlanini. 4fr+2fr, Leon Charles Albert Calmette.

1953, Dec. 15

B547	SP272	20c+5c blue	15	15
B548	"	80c+20c rose violet	80	60
B549	"	1.20fr+30c choc.	1.00	80
B550	"	1.50fr+50c dk. gray	1.25	1.00
B551	SP288	2fr+75c dk. grn.	2.00	1.60
B552	"	3fr+1.50fr dark red	22.00	18.00
B553	"	4fr+2fr ultra.	20.00	18.00
B554	SP289	8fr+4fr choc.	24.00	22.50
		Nos. B547-B554 (8)	71.20	62.65

The surtax was for anti-tuberculosis and other charitable works.

King Albert I Statue
SP290

Albert I Monument, Namur
SP291

Design: 9fr+4.50fr, Cliffs of Marche-les-Dames.

1954, Feb. 17 **Photogravure**

B555	SP290	2fr+50c chestnut brown	4.50	2.25
B556	SP291	4fr+2fr blue	24.00	21.00
B557	SP290	9fr+4.50fr olive black	29.00	25.00

Issued to commemorate the 20th anniversary of the death of King Albert I. The surtax aided in the erection of the monument pictured on B556.

Political Prisoners' Monument
SP292

Camp and Fort, Breendonk
SP293

Design: 9fr+4.50fr, Political prisoners' monument (profile).

1954, Apr. 1 ***Perf. 11½*** **Unwmkd.**

B558	SP292	2fr+1fr red	18.50	14.50
B559	SP293	4fr+2fr dark brown	40.00	25.00
B560	SP292	9fr+4.50fr olive green	42.50	37.50

The surtax was used toward the creation of a monument to political prisoners.

Gatehouse and Gateway
SP294

Nuns in Courtyard
SP295

Our Lady of the Vine
SP296

Designs: 2fr+1fr, Swans in stream. 7fr+3.50fr Nuns at well. 8fr+4fr, Statue above door.

1954, May 15

B561	SP294	80c+20c dark blue green	1.50	1.25
B562	"	2fr+1fr crimson	21.00	12.50
B563	SP295	4fr+2fr violet	30.00	21.00
B564	"	7fr+3.50fr lilac rose	57.50	42.50
B565	"	8fr+4fr brown	52.50	42.50
B566	SP296	9fr+4.50fr gray blue	70.00	52.50
		Nos. B561-B566 (6)	232.50	172.25

The surtax was for the Friends of the Beguinage of Bruges.

Child's Head
SP297

"The Blind Man and the Paralytic," by Antoine Carte
SP298

1954, Dec. 1 **Engraved**

B567	SP297	20c+5c dark green	25	25
B568	"	80c+20c dark gray	60	55
B569	"	1.20fr+30c orange brown	1.30	75
B570	"	1.50fr+50c purple	1.85	1.00
B571	SP298	2fr+75c rose carmine	11.00	8.00
B572	"	4fr+1fr bright blue	32.50	27.50
		Nos. B567-B572 (6)	47.50	38.05

The surtax was for anti-tuberculosis work.

Ernest Solvay
SP299

Jean-Jacques Dony
SP300

Portraits: 1.20fr+30c, Egide Walschaerts. 25fr+50c, Leo H. Baekeland. 3fr+1fr, Jean-Etienne Lenoir. 4fr+2fr, Emile Fourcault and Emile Gobbe.

Photogravure.

1955, Oct. 22 *Perf. 11½* Unwmkd.

B573 SP299 20c+5c brown & dark brown 20 15
B574 SP300 80c+20c violet 1.10 85
B575 SP299 1.20fr+30c indigo 1.50 1.20
B576 SP300 2fr+50c deep carmine 6.75 5.00
B577 " 3fr+1fr dark green 19.00 16.00
B578 SP299 4fr+2fr brn. 19.00 16.00
Nos. B573-B578 (6) 47.55 39.20

Issued in honor of Belgian scientists.
The surtax was for the benefit of various cultural organizations.

"The Joys of Spring" by E. Canneel
SP301

Einar Holböll
SP302

Portraits: 4fr+2fr, John D. Rockefeller. 8fr+4fr, Sir Robert W. Philip.

1955, Dec. 5 *Perf. 11½* Unwmkd.

B579 SP301 20c+5c red lilac 15 15
B580 " 80c+20c green 1.00 75
B581 " 1.20fr+30c reddish brown 1.15 90
B582 " 1.50fr+50c violet blue 2.00 1.40
B583 SP302 2fr+50c car. 13.00 8.00
B584 " 4fr+2fr ultra. 26.00 22.50
B585 " 8fr+4fr olive gray 32.50 30.00
Nos. B579-B585 (7) 75.80 63.70

The surtax was for anti-tuberculosis work.

Palace of Charles of Lorraine
SP303

Queen Elisabeth and Sonata by Mozart
SP304

Design: 2fr+1 fr, Mozart at age 7.

1956, Mar. 5 Engraved

B586 SP303 80c+20c steel blue 75 45
B587 " 2fr+1fr rose lake 7.00 5.25
B588 SP304 4fr+2fr dull purple 13.50 11.00

Issued to commemorate the 200th anniversary of the birth of Wolfgang Amadeus Mozart, composer.
The surtax was for the benefit of the Pro-Mozart Committee in Belgium.

Queen Elisabeth
SP305

1956, Aug. 16 Photogravure

B589 SP305 80c+20c slate grn. 1.10 75
B590 " 2fr+1fr dp. plum 5.00 3.50
B591 " 4fr+2fr brown 9.00 6.25

Issued in honor of the 80th birthday of Queen Elisabeth. The surtax went to the Queen Elisabeth Foundation.
See also No. 607.

Ship with Cross
SP306

Rehabilitation
SP308

Infant on Scales
SP307

Design: 4fr+2fr, X-Ray examination.

1956, Dec. 17 Engraved

B592 SP306 20c+5c reddish brown 15 12
B593 " 80c+20c green 1.35 1.00
B594 " 1.20fr+30c dull lilac 1.20 85
B595 " 1.50fr+50c light slate blue 1.20 85
B596 SP307 2fr+50c olive green 3.50 1.50
B597 " 4fr+2fr dull purple 20.00 16.00
B598 SP308 8fr+4fr deep carmine 18.50 17.50
Nos. B592-B598 (7) 45.90 37.82

The surtax was for anti-tuberculosis work.

Charles Plisnier and Albrecht Rodenbach
SP309

Portraits: 80c+20c, Emiel Vliebergh and Maurice Wilmotte. 1.20fr+30c, Paul Pastur and Julius Hoste. 2fr+50c, Lodewijk de Raet and Jules Destree. 3fr+1fr, Constantin Meunier and Constant Permeke. 4fr+2fr, Lieven Gevaert and Edouard Empain.

Photogravure.

1957, June 8 *Perf. 11½* Unwmkd.

B599 SP309 20c+5c brt. violet 22 18
B600 " 80c+20c light red brown 65 50
B601 " 1.20f+30c black brown 80 70
B602 " 2fr+50c claret 2.85 2.00
B603 " 3fr+1fr dark olive green 6.25 5.25
B604 " 4fr+2fr vio. blue 7.50 6.75
Nos. B599-B604 (6) 18.27 15.38

The surtax was for the benefit of various cultural organizations.

Dogs and Antarctic Camp
SP310

1957, Oct. 18 Engr. *Perf. 11½*

B605 SP310 5fr+2.50fr gray, orange & violet brown 5.00 5.00
a. Sheet of four 165.00 165.00
b. Blue, slate and red brown 40.00 40.00

Surtax for Belgian Antarctic Expedition, 1957–58.
No. B605a contains 4 No. B605b. Inscribed "Expedition Antarctique Belge 1957–1958" in French and Flemish. Size: 115x83mm.

Gen. Patton's Grave and Flag
SP311

Gen. George S. Patton, Jr.
SP312

Designs: 2.50fr+50c, Memorial, Bastogne. 3fr+1fr, Gen. Patton decorating Brig. Gen. Anthony C. McAuliffe. 6fr+3fr, Tanks of 1918 and 1944.

1957, Oct. 28 Photogravure

Size: 36x25mm., 25x36mm.

B606 SP311 1fr+50c dk. gray 1.50 1.25
B607 " 2.50fr+50c olive green 2.00 1.50
B608 " 3fr+1fr red brn. 5.25 4.00
B609 SP312 5fr+2.50fr grayish bl. 11.50 10.00

Size: 53x35mm.

B610 SP311 6fr+3fr pale brown carmine 18.50 15.00
Nos. B606-B610 (5) 38.75 31.75

The surtax was for the General Patton Memorial Committee and Patriotic Societies.

Adolphe Max
SP313

1957, Nov. 10 Engraved

B611 SP313 2.50fr+1fr ultra. 3.50 3.00

18th anniversary of the death of Adolphe Max, mayor of Brussels. The surtax was for the national "Adolphe Max" fund.

"Chinels," Fosses
SP314

"Op Signoorken," Malines
SP315

Infanta Isabella Shooting Crossbow
SP316

Legends: 1.50fr+50c, St. Remacle and the wolf. 2fr+1fr, Longman and the pea soup. 5fr+2fr, The Virgin with Inkwell (vert.). 6fr+2.50fr, "Gilles" (clowns), Binche.

Engraved and Photogravure.

1957, Dec. 14

B612 SP314 30c+20c purple & org. yellow 15 15
B613 SP315 1fr+50c brown & light blue 65 50
B614 SP314 1.50fr+50c gray & red 85 65
B615 SP315 2fr+1fr gray & bright grn. 1.15 85
B616 SP316 2.50fr+1fr blue grn. & lilac 2.50 1.75
B617 " 5fr+2fr blue & dark gray 8.00 7.00
B618 " 6fr+2.50fr violet brown & red org. 9.00 9.00
Nos. B612-B618 (7) 22.30 19.90

The surtax was for anti-tuberculosis work.
See also Nos. B631–B637.

Benelux Gate—SP317

Designs: 1fr+50c, Civil Engineering Pavilion. 1.50fr+50c, Ruanda-Urundi Pavilion. 2.50fr+1fr, Belgium 1900. 3fr+1.50fr, Atomium. 5fr+3fr, Telexpo Pavilion.

Engraved.

1958, Apr. 15 ***Perf. 11½*** **Unwmkd.**

Size: 35½x24½mm.

B619 SP317 30c+20c brown red, violet blue & sepia 15 15
B620 " 1fr+50c gray blue, dark brown & emerald 30 25
B621 " 1.50fr+50c greenish blue, purple & citron 45 35
B622 " 2.50fr+1fr ultramarine, red & brown red 60 55
B623 " 3fr+1.50fr gray, carmine & light ultramarine 2.50 2.10

Size: 49x33mm.

B624 SP317 5fr+3fr gray, ultramarine & red lilac 3.25 2.75
Nos. B619-B624 (6) 7.25 6.15

World's Fair, Brussels, Apr. 17–Oct. 19.

Marguerite van Eyck by Jan van Eyck
SP318

Christ Carrying Cross, by Hieronymus Bosch
SP319

Paintings: 1.50fr+50c, St. Donatien, Jan Gossart. 2.50fr+1fr, Self-portrait, Lambert Lombard. 3fr + 150fr, The Rower, James Ensor. 5fr + 3fr, Henriette, Henri Evenepoel.

1958, Oct. 30 Photo. ***Perf. 11½***

Various Frames in Ochre and Brown.

B625 SP318 30c+20c dark olive green 30 30
B626 SP319 1fr+50c maroon 1.85 1.00
B627 SP318 1.50fr+50c violet blue 2.25 1.50
B628 " 2.50fr+1fr dark brown 5.75 4.50
B629 SP319 3fr+1.50fr dull red 8.50 7.50
B630 SP318 5fr+3fr bright blue 16.00 15.00
Nos. B625-B630 (6) 34.65 29.80

The surtax was for the benefit of various cultural organizations.

Type of 1957.

Legends: 40c+10c, Elizabeth, Countess of Hoogstraten. 1fr+50c, Jean de Nivelles. 1.50fr+50c, St. Evermare play, Russon. 2fr+1fr, The Penitents of Furnes. 2.50fr+1fr, Manger and "Pax." 5fr+2fr, Sambre-Meuse procession. 6fr+2.50fr, Our Lady of Peace and "Pax" (vert.).

Engraved and Photogravure

1958, Dec. 6 ***Perf. 11½*** **Unwmkd.**

B631 SP314 40c+10c ultra. & bright green 15 15
B632 SP315 1fr+50c gray brn. & orange 75 55
B633 " 1.50fr+50c claret & bright green 1.00 85
B634 SP314 2fr+1fr brown & red 1.35 1.10
B635 SP316 2.50fr+1fr vio. brn. & blue green 4.25 4.00
B636 SP316 5fr+2fr claret & blue 6.50 6.25
B637 " 6fr+2.50fr blue & rose red 9.50 9.00
Nos. B631-B637 (7) 23.50 21.90

The surtax was for anti-tuberculosis work.

"Europe of the Heart"
SP320

1959, Feb. 25 Photo. **Unwmkd.**

B638 SP320 1fr+50c red lilac 1.00 75
B639 " 2.50fr+1fr dark green 2.50 2.00
B640 " 5fr+2.50fr deep brown 4.50 3.75

The surtax was for aid for displaced persons.

Allegory of Blood Transfusion
SP321

Henri Dunant and Battlefield at Solferino—SP322

Design: 2.50fr+1fr, 3fr+1.50fr, Red Cross, broken sword and drop of blood (horiz.).

1959, June 10 Photo. ***Perf. 11½***

B641 SP321 40c+10c blue gray & car. 30 30
B642 " 1fr+50c brown & carmine 1.15 90
B643 " 1.50fr+50c dull vio. & carmine 2.25 1.85
B644 " 2.50fr+1fr slate grn. & car. 4.00 3.25
B645 " 3fr+1.50fr violet blue & car. 7.50 6.25
B646 SP322 5fr+3fr dark brn. & car. 9.50 9.00
Nos. B641-B646 (6) 24.70 21.55

Issued to commemorate the centenary of the International Red Cross idea. The surtax was for the Red Cross and patriotic organizations.

Philip the Good
SP323

Arms of Philip the Good
SP324

Designs: 1fr+50c, Charles the Bold. 1.50fr+50c, Emperor Maximilian of Austria. 2.50fr+1fr, Philip the Fair. 3fr+1.50fr, Charles V. Portraits from miniatures by Simon Bening (c. 1483–1561).

1959, July 4 **Engraved**

B647 SP323 40c+10c multi. 25 25
B648 " 1fr+50c " 1.10 90
B649 " 1.50fr+50c " 2.25 1.85
B650 " 2.50fr+1fr " 4.00 3.00
B651 " 3fr+1.50fr " 7.50 6.50
B652 SP324 5fr+3fr " 9.50 8.00
Nos. B647-B652 (6) 24.60 20.50

The surtax was for the Royal Library, Brussels.

Portraits show Grand Masters of the Order of the Golden Fleece.

Whale, Antwerp
SP325

Carnival, Stavelot
SP326

Designs: 1fr+50c, Dragon, Mons. 2fr+50c, Prince Carnival, Eupen. 3fr+1fr, Jester and cats, Ypres. 6fr+2fr, Holy Family (horiz.). 7fr+3fr, Madonna, Liége (horiz.).

Engraved and Photogravure

1959, Dec. 5 ***Perf. 11½***

B653 SP325 40c+10c citron, Prussian blue & red 15 15
B654 " 1fr+50c olive & green 85 50
B655 " 2fr+50c light brown, orange & claret 1.10 75
B656 SP326 2.50fr+1fr gray, pur. & ultra. 1.75 1.35
B657 " 3fr+1fr gray, maroon & yel. 3.50 2.75
B658 " 6fr+2fr olive, bright blue & henna brown 5.75 4.50
B659 " 7fr+3fr chalky blue & orange yellow 9.00 8.50
Nos. B653-B659 (7) 22.10 18.50

The surtax was for anti-tuberculosis work.

Child Refugee
SP327

Designs: 3fr+1.50fr, Man. 6fr+3fr, Woman.

1960, Apr. 7 **Engraved**

B660 SP327 40c+10c rose claret 18 18
B661 " 3fr+1.50fr gray brown 2.75 2.25
B662 " 6fr+3fr dark blue 2.75 2.25
a. Souv. sheet of 3 70.00 70.00

Issued to publicize World Refugee Year, July 1, 1959–June 30, 1960.

No. B662a contains one each of Nos. B660–B662 with colors changed: 40c+10c, dull purple; 3fr+1.50fr, red brown; 6fr+3fr, henna brown. Black marginal inscription and uprooted oak emblem. Size: 121x92mm.

Parachutists and Plane
SP328

Designs: 2fr+50c, 2.50fr+1fr, Parachutists coming in for landing (vert.) 3fr+1fr, 6fr+2fr, Parachutist walking with parachute.

Photogravure and Engraved

1960, June 13 ***Perf. 11½***

B663 SP328 40c+10c light ultra. & blk. 30 30
B664 " 1fr+50c blue & black 1.65 1.50
B665 " 2fr+50c blue, blk. & olive 2.75 2.00
B666 " 2.50fr+1fr greenish blue, black & gray olive 4.00 3.00
B667 " 3fr+1fr blue, black & slate green 6.00 5.00
B668 " 6fr+2fr light violet blue, black & olive 7.00 5.75
Nos. B663-B668 (6) 21.70 17.55

The surtax was for various patriotic and cultural organizations.

Mother and Child, Planes and Rainbow
SP329

Designs: 40c+10c, Brussels Airport, planes and rainbow. 6fr+3fr, Rainbow connecting Congo and Belgium, and planes (vert.)

Photogravure

1960, Aug. 3 ***Perf. 11½*** **Unwmkd.**

Size: 35x24mm.

B669 SP329 40c+10c greenish blue 18 18
B670 " 3fr+1.50fr bright red 5.25 4.25

Size: 35x52mm.

B671 SP329 6fr+3fr violet 8.50 7.50

The surtax was for refugees from Congo.

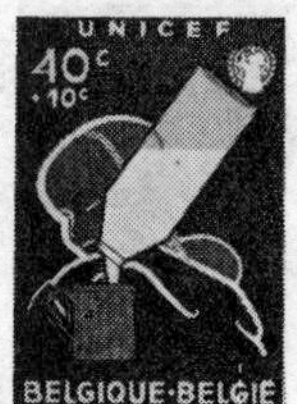

Infant, Milk Bottle and Mug
SP330

Designs: 1fr+50c, Nurse and children of 3 races. 2fr+50c, Refugee woman carrying gift clothes. 2.50fr+1fr, Negro nurse weighing infant. 3fr+1fr, Children of various races dancing. 6fr+2fr, Refugee boys.

Photogravure and Engraved

1960, Oct. 8 ***Perf. 11½***

B672 SP330 40c+10c golden brown, yellow & blue green 15 15
B673 " 1fr+50c olive gray, maroon & slate 2.15 1.75
B674 " 2fr+50c violet, pale brown & brt. green 2.25 1.85
B675 " 2.50fr+1fr dark red, sepia & light blue 3.25 3.00
B676 " 3fr+1fr blue green, red orange & dull violet 3.50 3.25
B677 " 6fr+2fr ultra. emerald & brown 5.25 4.75
Nos. B672-B677 (6) 16.55 14.75

Issued for the United Nations Children's Fund, UNICEF.

Tapestry
SP331

Belgian handicrafts: 1fr+50c, Cut crystal vases (vert.). 2fr+50c, Lace (vert.). 2.50fr+1fr, Metal plate & jug. 3fr+1fr, Diamonds. 6fr+2fr, Ceramics.

Photogravure and Engraved

1960, Dec. 5 ***Perf. 11½***

B678 SP331 40c+10c blue, bister & brn. 15 15
B679 " 1fr+50c indigo & org. brn. 2.00 1.65
B680 " 2fr+50c dark red brown, black & citron 2.75 2.25
B681 " 2.50fr+1fr choc. & yellow 4.50 3.75
B682 " 3fr+1fr orange brown, black & ultra. 5.50 4.50
B683 " 6fr+2fr deep blk. & yel. 7.50 7.00
Nos. B678-B683 (6) 22.40 19.30

The surtax was for anti-tuberculosis work.

Jacob Kats and Abbe Nicolas Pietkin
SP332

Portraits: 1fr+50c, Albert Mockel and J. F. Willems. 2fr+50c, Jan van Rijswijck and Xavier M. Neujean. 2.50fr+1fr, Joseph Demarteau and A. Van de Perre. 3fr+1fr, Canon Jan-Baptist David and Albert du Bois. 6fr+2fr, Henri Vieuxtemps and Willem de Mol.

Photogravure and Engraved

1961, Apr. 22 ***Perf. 11½*** **Unwmkd.**

Portraits in Gray Brown

B684 SP332 40c+10c verm. & maroon 15 15
B685 " 1fr+50c bistre brown & maroon 2.00 1.65
B686 " 2fr+50c yellow & crimson 3.25 2.75
B687 SP332 2.50fr+1fr pale citron & dark green 4.25 3.25
B688 " 3fr+1fr light & dk. blue 6.75 5.00
B689 " 6fr+2fr lilac & ultra. 7.00 5.75
Nos. B684-B689 (6) 23.40 18.55

The surtax was for the benefit of various cultural organizations.

White Rhinoceros
SP333

Antonius Cardinal Perrenot de Granvelle
SP334

Animals: 1fr+50c, Przewalski horses. 2fr+50c, Okapi. 2.50fr+1fr, Giraffe (horiz.). 3fr+1fr, Lesser panda (horiz.). 6fr+2fr, European elk (horiz.).

Photogravure

1961, June 5 ***Perf. 11½*** **Unwmkd.**

B690 SP333 40c+10c bistre brown & dk. brown 18 15
B691 " 1fr+50c gray & brown 2.25 1.65
B692 " 2fr+50c deep rose & blk. 3.25 2.25
B693 " 2.50fr+1fr red org. & brn. 2.25 1.85
B694 " 3fr+1fr org. & brown 3.00 2.10
B695 " 6fr+2fr blue & bistre brown 4.25 3.25
Nos. B690-B695 (6) 15.18 11.25

The surtax was for various philanthropic organizations.

1961, July 29 **Engraved**

Designs: 3fr+1.50fr, Arms of Cardinal de Granvelle. 6fr+3fr, Tower and crosier, symbolic of collaboration between Malines and the Archbishopric.

B696 SP334 40c+10c magenta, car. & brown 15 15
B697 " 3fr+1.50fr multi. 1.65 1.25
B698 " 6fr+3fr magenta pur. & bister 3.50 2.75

Issued to commemorate the 400th anniversary of Malines as an Archbishopric.

Mother and Child by Pierre Paulus
SP335

Castle of the Counts of Male
SP336

Paintings: 1fr+50c, Mother Love, Francois-Joseph Navez. 2fr+50c, Motherhood, Constant Permeke. 2.50fr+1fr, Madonna and Child, Rogier van der Weyden. 3fr+1fr, Madonna with Apple, Hans Memling. 6fr+2fr, Madonna of the Forget-me-not, Peter Paul Rubens.

1961, Dec. 2 Photo. ***Perf. 11½***

Gold Frame

B699 SP335 40c+10c deep brown 15 15
B700 " 1fr+50c bright blue 95 85
B701 SP335 2fr+50c rose red 1.50 1.25
B702 " 2.50fr+1fr magenta 2.50 2.10
B703 " 3fr+1fr violet blue 2.75 2.50
B704 " 6fr+2fr dark slate green 3.50 3.25
Nos. B699-B704 (6) 11.35 10.10

The surtax was for anti-tuberculosis work.

1962, Mar. 12 **Engr.** ***Perf. 11½***

Designs: 90c+10c, Royal library (horiz.). 1fr+50c, Church of Our Lady, Tongres. 2fr+50c, Collegiate Church, Soignies (horiz.). 2.50fr+1fr, Church of Our Lady, Malines. 3fr+1fr, St. Denis Abbey, Broqueroi. 6fr+2fr, Cloth Hall, Ypres (horiz.).

B705 SP336 40c+10c bright green 15 10
B706 " 90c+10c lilac rose 40 30
B707 " 1fr+50c dull violet 75 60
B708 " 2fr+50c violet 1.75 1.35
B709 " 2.50fr+1fr red brown 2.25 1.85
B710 " 3fr+1fr blue green 2.50 2.00
B711 " 6fr+2fr carmine rose 3.25 3.00
Nos. B705-B711 (7) 11.05 9.20

The surtax was for various cultural and philanthropic organizations.

Andean Cock of the Rock
SP337

Handicapped Child
SP338

Birds: 1fr+50c, Red lory. 2fr+50c, Guinea touraco. 2.50fr+1fr, Keel-billed toucan. 3fr+1fr, Great bird of paradise. 6fr+2fr, Congolese peacock.

Engraved and Photogravure

1962, June 23 ***Perf. 11½*** **Unwmkd.**

Birds in Natural Colors

B712 SP337 40c+10c blue 15 10
B713 " 1fr+50c ultra. & carmine 70 60
B714 " 2fr+50c blk. & car. rose 1.50 1.25
B715 " 2.50fr+1fr greenish bl. & verm. 1.75 1.35
B716 " 3fr+1fr red brn. & grn. 2.65 2.10
B717 " 6fr+2fr red & ultra. 3.25 2.50
Nos. B712-B717 (6) 10.00 7.90

The surtax was for various philanthropic organizations.

Photogravure

1962, Sept. 22 ***Perf. 11½*** **Unwmkd.**

Handicapped Children: 40c+10c, Reading Braille. 2fr+50c, Deaf-mute girl with earphones and electronic equipment (horiz.). 2.50fr+1fr, Child with ball (cerebral palsy). 3fr+1fr, Girl with crutches (polio). 6fr+2fr, Sitting boys playing ball (horiz.).

B718 SP338 40c+10c choc. 15 15
B719 " 1fr+50c rose red 65 60
B720 " 2fr+50c brt. lilac 1.50 1.35
B721 " 2.50fr+1fr dull green 1.75 1.60
B722 " 3fr+1fr dk. bl. 2.10 1.85
B723 " 6fr+2fr dk. brn. 3.25 3.00
Nos. B718-B723 (6) 9.40 8.55

The surtax was for various institutions for handicapped children.

Queen Louise-Marie
SP339

Belgian Queens: No. B725, like No. B724 with "ML" initials. 1fr+50c, Marie-Henriette. 2fr+1fr, Elisabeth. 3fr+1.50fr, Astrid. 8fr+2.50fr, Fabiola.

Photogravure and Engraved

1962, Dec. 8 ***Perf. 11½***

B724 SP339 40c+10c gray, black & gold ("L") 15 12
B725 " 40c+10c gray, black & gold ("ML") 15 12
B726 " 1fr+50c gray, black & gold 1.00 85
B727 " 2fr+1fr gray, black & gold 2.00 1.50
B728 " 3fr+1.50fr gray, black & gold 2.25 1.75
B729 " 8fr+2.50fr gray, black & gold 3.75 3.50
Nos. B724-B729 (6) 9.30 7.84

The surtax was for anti-tuberculosis work.

British War Memorial (Porte de Menin), Ypres
SP340

1962, Dec. 26 **Engr.** ***Perf. 11½***

B730 SP340 1fr+50c black, green, blue & red brown 1.00 1.00

Millennium of the city of Ypres. Issued in sheets of eight.

Peace Bell Ringing over Globe
SP341

The Sower by Brueghel
SP342

Engraved and Photogravure

1963, Feb. 18 ***Perf. 11½*** **Unwmkd.**

B731 SP341 3fr+1.50fr black, bl., org. & grn. 3.00 3.00
a. Sheet of 4 13.50 13.50
B732 " 6fr+3fr black, brown & org. 2.50 2.50

The surtax was for the installation of the Peace Bell (Bourdon de la Paix) at Koekelberg Basilica and for the benefit of various cultural organizations.

No. B731 was issued in sheets of 4. The sheet is inscribed "Bourdon de la Paix," repeated in Flemish, and measures 85x115 mm. No. B732 was issued in sheets of 30.

1963, Mar. 21 ***Perf. 11½***

Designs: 3fr+1fr, The Harvest, by Brueghel (horiz.). 6fr+2fr, "Bread," by Anton Carte (horiz.).

B733 SP342 2fr+1fr green, ocher & black 65 60

B734 SP342 3fr+1fr red lilac, ocher & black 1.35 90
B735 " 6fr+2fr red brown, citron & black 2.00 1.85

Issued for the "Freedom from Hunger" campaign of the U.N. Food and Agriculture Organization.

Speed Racing
SP343

Designs: 2fr+1fr, Bicyclists at check point (horiz.). 3fr+1.50fr, Team racing (horiz.). 6fr+3fr, Pace setters.

Engraved

1963, July 13 *Perf. 11½* Unwmkd.

B736 SP343 1fr+50c multi. 50 45
B737 " 2fr+1fr bl., car., blk. & olive gray 65 60
B738 " 3fr+1.50fr multi. 1.00 90
B739 " 6fr+3fr " 1.75 1.50

Issued to commemorate the 80th anniversary of the founding of the Belgian Bicycle League. The surtax was for athletes at the 1964 Olympic Games.

Princess Paola with Princess Astrid
SP344

Prince Albert and Family
SP345

Designs: 40c+10c, Prince Philippe. 2fr+50c, Princess Astrid. 2.50fr+1fr, Princess Paola. 6fr+2fr, Prince Albert.

1963, Sept. 28 Photogravure

Cross in Red

B740 SP344 40c+10c dark carmine rose & buff 15 15
B741 " 1fr+50c slate & buff 70 50
B742 " 2fr+50c dark carmine rose & buff 90 60
B743 " 2.50fr+1fr bright blue & buff 1.25 90
B744 SP345 3fr+1fr gray brn. & buff 1.25 90
B745 " 3fr+1fr slate grn. & buff 5.25 5.25
a. Bklt. pane of 8 42.50 42.50
B746 SP344 6fr+2fr slate & buff 2.25 2.25
Nos. B740-B746 (7) 11.75 10.55

Issued to commemorate the centenary of the International Red Cross. No. B745 issued only in booklet panes of 8, which are in two forms: French and Flemish inscriptions in top and bottom margins transposed.

Daughter of Balthazar Gerbier, Painted by Rubens
SP346

Jesus, St. John and Cherubs by Rubens
SP347

Portraits (Rubens' sons): 1fr+40c, Nicolas, 2 yrs. old. 2fr+50c, Franz. 2.50fr+1fr, Nicolas, 6 yrs. old. 3fr+1fr, Albert.

Photogravure and Engraved

1963, Dec. 7 *Perf. 11½* Unwmkd.

B747 SP346 50c+10c buff, gray & dark brown 15 15
B748 " 1fr+40c buff, red brown & dark brn. 30 30
B749 " 2fr+50c buff, violet brown & dark brn. 50 50
B750 " 2.50fr+1fr buff, green & dark brown 1.00 1.00
B751 " 3fr+1fr buff, red brown & dark brn. 1.00 1.00
B752 SP347 6fr+2fr buff & gray 1.65 1.65
Nos. B747-B752 (6) 4.60 4.60

The surtax was for anti-tuberculosis work.
See also No. B771.

John Quincy Adams and Lord Gambier Signing Treaty of Ghent, by Amédée Forestier—SP348

1964, May 16 Photo. *Perf. 11½*

B753 SP348 6fr+3fr dk. blue 3.00 2.75

Issued to commemorate the 150th anniversary of the signing of the Treaty of Ghent between the United States and Great Britain, Dec. 24, 1814.

Philip van Marnix
SP349

Portraits: 3fr+1.50fr, Ida de Bure Calvin. 6fr+3fr, Jacob Jordaens.

1964, May 30 Engraved

B754 SP349 1fr+50c blue gray 50 45
B755 " 3fr+1.50fr rose pink 85 85
B756 " 6fr+3fr reddish brown 1.65 1.50

Issued to honor Protestantism in Belgium. The surtax was for the erection of a Protestant church.

Foot Soldier, 1918
SP350

Battle of Bastogne
SP351

Designs: 2fr+1fr, Flag bearer, Guides Regiment, 1914. 3fr+1.50fr, Trumpeter of the Grenadiers and drummers, 1914.

1964, Aug. 1 Photo. *Perf. 11½*

B757 SP350 1fr+50c multi. 30 28
B758 " 2fr+1fr " 45 40
B759 " 3fr+1.50fr " 65 60

Issued to commemorate the 50th anniversary of the German aggression against Belgium in 1914. The surtax aided patriotic undertakings.

1964, Aug. 1 Unwmkd.

Design: 6fr+3fr, Liberation of the estuary of the Escaut.

B760 SP351 3fr+1fr multi. 50 45
B761 " 6fr+3fr " 90 80

Issued to commemorate Belgium's Resistance and liberation of World War II. The surtax was to help found an International Student Center at Antwerp and to aid cultural undertakings.

Souvenir Sheets

Rogier van der Weyden Paintings
SP352

Descent From the Cross
SP353

Designs: 1fr, Philip the Good. 2fr, Portrait of a Lady. 3fr, Man with Arrow.

1964, Sept. 19 Photo. *Perf. 11½*

B762 SP352 Sheet of 3 4.75 4.75
a. 1fr multi. 1.50 1.50
b. 2fr " 1.50 1.50
c. 3fr " 1.50 1.50

Engraved

B763 SP353 8fr red brown, sheet of 1 4.75 4.75

Issued to commemorate the 5th centenary of the death of the painter Rogier van der Weyden (Roger de La Pasture, 1400–1464). The surtax went to various cultural organizations. Sheets have gray brown frames and marginal inscriptions. Size of sheets: 153x114mm. Size of stamps: 24x36mm. (Nos. B762a,b,c); 54x35mm. (No. B763). No. B762 sold for 14fr, No. B763 for 16fr.

Ancient View of the Pand
SP354

Design: 3fr+1fr, Present view of the Pand from Lys River.

1964, Oct. 10 Photogravure

B764 SP354 2fr+1fr black, greenish blue & ultra. 65 60
B765 " 3fr+1fr lilac rose, bl. & dk. brn. 85 65

The surtax was for the restoration of the Pand Dominican Abbey in Ghent.

Type of 1963 and

Child of Charles I, Painted by Van Dyck
SP355

Designs: 1fr+40c, William of Orange with his bride, by Van Dyck. 2fr+1fr, Portrait of a small boy with dogs by Erasmus Quellin and Jan Fyt. 3fr+1fr, Alexander Farnese by Antonio Moro. 4fr+2fr, William II, Prince of Orange by Van Dyck. 6fr+3fr, Artist's children by Cornelis De Vos.

1964, Dec. 5 Engraved *Perf. 11½*

B766 SP355 50c+10c rose claret 15 15
B767 " 1fr+40c car. rose 28 25
B768 " 2fr+1fr vio. brn. 50 45
B769 " 3fr+1fr gray 60 55
B770 " 4fr+2fr violet bl. 65 60
B771 SP347 6fr+3fr brt. pur. 1.15 1.00
Nos. B766-B771 (6) 3.33 3.00

The surtax was for anti-tuberculosis work.

Liberator, Shaking Prisoner's Hand, Concentration Camp
SP356

Designs: 1fr+50c, Prisoner's hand reaching for the sun. 3fr+1.50fr, Searchlights and tank breaking down barbed wire (horiz.). 8fr+5fr, Rose growing amid the ruins (horiz.).

Engraved and Photogravure

1965, May 8 *Perf. 11½* Unwmkd.

B772 SP356 50c+50c tan, black & buff 15 15
B773 " 1fr+50c multi. 20 20

B774 SP356 3fr+1.50fr dull lilac & black 50 50
B775 " 8fr+5fr multi. 1.10 1.10

Issued to commemorate the 20th anniversary of the liberation of the concentration camps for political prisoners and prisoners of war.

Stoclet House, Brussels
SP357

Stoclet House: 6fr+3fr, Hall with marble foundation (vert.). 8fr+4fr, View of house from garden.

1965, June 21

B776 SP357 3fr+1fr slate & tan 40 35
B777 " 6fr+3fr sepia 70 60
B778 " 8fr+4fr vio. brn. & tan 1.00 1.00

Issued to commemorate the 95th anniversary of the birth of the Austrian architect Josef Hoffmann (1870–1956), builder of the art nouveau residence of Adolphe Stoclet, engineer and financier.

Jackson's Chameleon
SP358

Animals from Antwerp Zoo: 2fr+1fr, Common iguanas. 3fr+1.50fr, African monitor. 6fr+3fr, Komodo monitor. 8fr+4fr, Nile softshell turtle.

1965, Oct. 16 Photo. *Perf. 11½*

B779 SP358 1fr+50c multi. 15 15
B780 " 2fr+1fr " 30 25
B781 " 3fr+1.50fr " 40 35
B782 " 6fr+3fr " 80 80

Miniature Sheet

B783 SP358 8fr+4fr multi. 2.50 2.50

The surtax was for various cultural and philanthropic organizations. No. B783 contains one stamp (52x35mm.) and has gray animal border. Size: 117x95mm.

Boatmen's and Archers' Guild Halls
SP359

Buildings on Grand-Place, Brussels: 1fr+40c, Brewers' Hall. 2fr+1fr, "King of Spain." 3fr+1.50fr, "Dukes of Brabant." 10fr+4.50fr, Tower of City Hall and St. Michael.

1965, Dec. 4 Engraved *Perf. 11½*

Size: 35x24mm.

B784 SP359 50c+10c ultra. 15 15
B785 " 1fr+40c bl. grn. 18 18
B786 " 2fr+1fr rose claret 25 25
B787 " 3fr+1.50fr violet 50 50

Size: 24x44mm.

B788 SP359 10fr+4.50fr sepia & gray 1.00 1.00
Nos. B784-B788 (5) 2.08 2.08

The surtax was for anti-tuberculosis work.

Souvenir Sheets

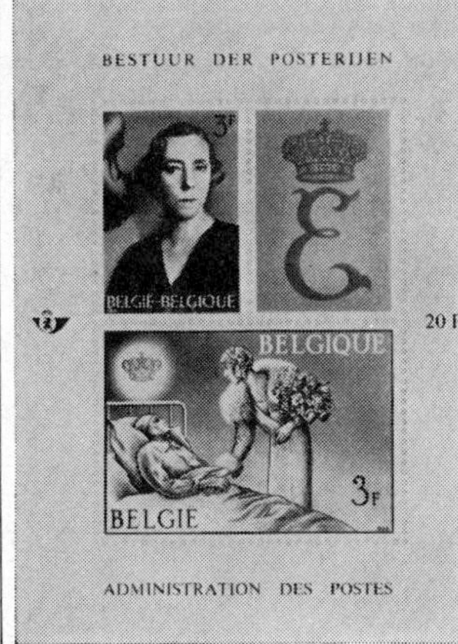

Queen Elisabeth
SP360

Design: No. B790, Types of 1931 and 1956.

1966, Apr. 16 Photo. *Perf. 11½*

B789 SP360 Sheet of 2 3.00 3.00
a. SP74 3fr dk. brn. & gray green 1.50 1.50
b. SP87 3fr dk. brn., yel. grn. & gold 1.50 1.50
B790 " Sheet of 2 3.00 3.00
a. SP42 3fr dk. brn. & dull blue 1.50 1.50
b. SP304 3fr dk. brn. & gray 1.50 1.50

The surtax went to various cultural organizations.

Each sheet contains two stamps plus label with the Queen's initial; sold for 20fr. Dark brown marginal inscription. Size: 81½x115mm.

Luminescent Paper

was used in printing Nos. B789-B790, B801-B806, B808-B809, B811-B823, B825-B831, B833-B835, B837-B840, B842-B846, B848-B850, B852-B854, B856-B863, and from B865 onward unless otherwise noted.

Diver
SP361

Design: 10fr+4fr, Swimmer at start.

1966, May 9 Engraved

B791 SP361 60c+40c Prus. green, olive & org. brown 12 10
B792 " 10fr+4fr olive grn., org. brn. & magenta 1.00 95

Issued to publicize the importance of swimming instruction.

Minorites' Convent, Liège
SP362

Designs: 1fr+50c, Val-Dieu Abbey, Aubel. 2fr+1fr, View and seal of Huy. 10fr+4.50fr, Statue of Ambiorix by Jules Bertin, and tower, Tongeren.

1966, Aug. 27 Engr. *Perf. 11½*

B793 SP362 60c+40c bl., vio. brn. & org. brn. 10 10
B794 " 1fr+50c vio. brn., bl. & greenish blue 18 18
B795 " 2fr+1fr car. rose, vio. brn. & orange brown 20 20
B796 " 10fr+4.50fr brt. grn., vio. brn. & slate blue 90 90

The surtax was for various patriotic and cultural organizations.

Surveyor and Dog Team
SP363

Designs: 3fr+1.50fr, Adrien de Gerlache and "Belgica." 6fr+3fr, Surveyor, weather balloon and ship. 10fr+5fr, Penguins and "Magga Dan" (ship used for 1964, 1965 and 1966 expeditions).

1966, Oct. 8 Engraved *Perf. 11½*

B797 SP363 1fr+50c bl. green 10 10
B798 " 3fr+1.50fr pale violet 30 25
B799 " 6fr+3fr dk. car. 55 55

Souvenir Sheet

Engraved and Photogravure

B800 SP363 10fr+5fr dk. gray, sky blue & dark red 1.00 1.00

Issued to publicize Belgian Antarctic expeditions. No. B800 contains one stamp (52x35mm.); inscriptions, map of Antarctica and observation post in margin. Size: 130x95mm.

Boy with Ball and Dog
SP364

Designs: 2fr+1fr, Girl skipping rope. 3fr+1.50fr, Girl and boy blowing soap bubbles. 6fr+3fr, Girl and boy rolling hoops (horiz.). 8fr+3.50fr, Four children at play and cat (horiz.).

Engraved and Photogravure

1966, Dec. 3 *Perf. 11½*

B801 SP364 1fr+1fr pink & black 12 12
B802 " 2fr+1fr lt. bluish grn. & black 30 30
B803 " 3fr+1.50fr lt. vio. & black 35 35
B804 " 6fr+3fr pale sal. & dk. brown 60 60
B805 " 8fr+3.50fr lt. yel. grn. & dk. brn. 70 70
Nos. B801-B805 (5) 2.07 2.07

The surtax was for anti-tuberculosis work.

Souvenir Sheet

Refugees
SP365

Designs: 1fr, Boy receiving clothes. 2fr, Tibetan children. 3fr, African mother and children.

1967, Mar. 11 Photo. *Perf. 11½*

B806 SP365 Sheet of 3 2.10 2.10
a. 1fr blk. & yel. 65 65
b. 2fr blk. & blue 65 65
c. 3fr blk. & org. 65 65

Issued to help refugees around the world. Sheet has black border with Belgian P.T.T. and U.N. Refugee emblems. Size: 110x76 mm. Sold for 20fr.

Robert Schuman
SP366

Colonial Brotherhood Emblem
SP368

Kongolo Memorial, Gentinnes
SP367

1967, June 24 Engraved *Perf. 11½*

B807 SP366 2fr+1fr gray bl. 60 60

Engraved and Photogravure

B808 SP367 5fr+2fr brown & olive 55 55
B809 SP368 10fr+5fr multi. 1.00 90

Issued to commemorate respectively: Robert Schuman (1886–1963), French statesman, one of the founders of European Steel and Coal Community, first president of European Parliament (2fr+1fr); Kongolo Memorial, erected in memory of missionary and civilian victims in the Congo (5fr+2fr); a memorial for African Troops, Brussels (10fr+5fr).

Preaching Fool from "Praise of Folly" by Erasmus
SP369

Erasmus, by Quentin Massys
SP370

Designs: 2fr+1fr, Exhorting Fool from Praise of Folly. 5fr+2fr, Thomas More's Family, by Hans Holbein (horiz.). 6fr+3fr, Pierre Gilles (Aegidius), by Quentin Massys.

Photogravure and Engraved (SP369); Photogravure (SP370)

1967, Sept. 2 *Perf. 11* Unwmkd.

B810 SP369 1fr+50c tan, blk., blue & carmine 15 15
B811 " 2fr+1fr tan, blk. & carmine 25 25
B812 SP370 3fr+1.50fr multi. 35 35
B813 SP369 5fr+2fr tan, blk. & carmine 45 45
B814 SP370 6fr+3fr multi. 60 60
Nos. B810-B814 (5) 1.80 1.80

Issued to commemorate Erasmus (1466(?)–1536), Dutch scholar and his era.

Souvenir Sheet

Pro-Post Association Emblem
SP371

Engraved and Photogravure

1967, Oct. 21 ***Perf. 11½***

B815 SP371 10fr+5fr multi. 1.75 1.75

Issued to publicize the POSTPHILA Philatelic Exhibition, Brussels, Oct. 21–29. No. B815 has black marginal inscription and ornaments. Size: 112x77mm.

Detail from Brueghel's "Children's Games"
SP372

Designs: Various Children's Games. Singles of Nos. B816–B821 arranged in 2 rows of 3 show complete painting by Pieter Brueghel.

1967, Dec. 9 Photo. ***Perf. 11½***

B816	SP372	1fr+50c multi.	25	25
B817	"	2fr+50c "	35	35
B818	"	3fr+1fr "	45	45
B819	"	6fr+3fr "	75	75
B820	"	10fr+4fr "	90	90
B821	"	13fr+6fr "	1.50	1.50
		Nos. B816–B821 (6)	4.20	4.20

Queen Fabiola Holding Refugee Child from Congo
SP373

Design: 6fr+3fr, Queen Elisabeth and Dr. Depage.

1968, Apr. 27 Photo. ***Perf. 11½***

Cross in Red

B822	SP373	6fr+3fr sepia & gray	75	75
B823	"	10fr+5fr sepia & gray	1.10	1.10

The surtax was for the Red Cross.

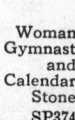

Woman Gymnast and Calendar Stone
SP374

Yachting and "The Swimmer" by Andrien
SP375

"Explosion"
SP376

Designs: 2fr+1fr, Weight lifter and Mayan motif. 3fr+1.50fr, Hurdler, colossus of Tula and animal head from Kukulkan. 6fr+2fr, Bicyclists and Chichen Itza Temple.

Engraved and Photogravure

1968, May 27 ***Perf. 11½***

B824	SP374	1fr+50c multi.	18	18
B825	"	2fr+1fr "	30	30
B826	"	3fr+1.50fr "	35	35
B827	"	6fr+2fr "	60	60

Photogravure

B828	SP375	13fr+5fr multi.	1.60	1.60
		Nos. B824–B828 (5)	3.03	3.03

Issued to publicize the 19th Olympic Games, Mexico City, Oct. 12–27.

1968, June 22 Photogravure

Designs (Paintings by Pol Mara): 12fr+5fr, "Fire." 13fr+5fr, "Tornado."

B829	SP376	10fr+5fr multi.	1.25	1.25
B830	"	12fr+5fr "	1.50	1.50
B831	"	13fr+5fr "	1.65	1.65

The surtax was for disaster victims.

Undulate Triggerfish
SP377

Tropical Fish: 3fr+1.50fr, Angelfish. 6fr+3fr, Turkeyfish (Pterois volitans). 10fr+5fr, Orange butterflyfish.

Engraved and Photogravure

1968, Oct. 19 ***Perf. 11½***

B832	SP377	1fr+50c multi.	30	30
B833	"	3fr+1.50fr "	50	50
B834	"	6fr+3fr "	1.00	90
B835	"	10fr+5fr "	1.25	1.15

King Albert and Queen Elisabeth Entering Brussels—SP378

Tomb of the Unknown Soldier and Eternal Flame, Brussels
SP379

Designs: 1fr+50c, King Albert, Queen Elisabeth and Crown Prince Leopold on balcony, Bruges (vert.). 6fr+3fr, King and Queen entering Liège.

1968, Nov. 9 Photo. ***Perf. 11½***

B836	SP378	1fr+50c multi.	30	30
B837	"	3fr+1.50fr multi.	50	50
B838	"	6fr+3fr multi.	1.00	95

Engraved and Photogravure

B839	SP379	10fr+5fr multi.	1.25	1.15

Issued to commemorate the 50th anniversary of the victory in World War I.

Souvenir Sheet

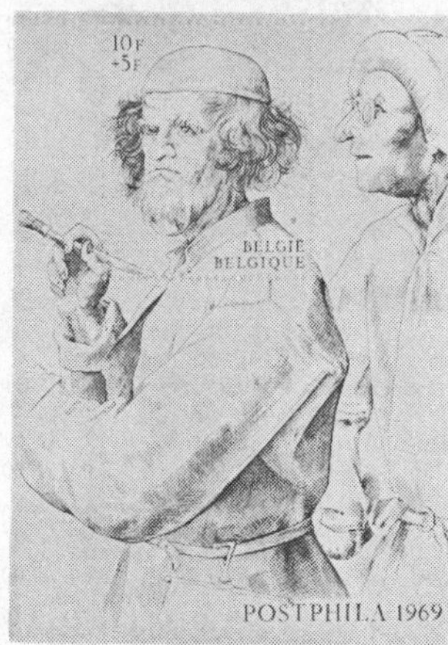

The Painter and the Amateur, by Peter Brueghel
SP380

1969, May 10 Engraved ***Perf. 11½***

B840 SP380 10fr+5fr sepia 2.65 2.65

Issued to publicize the POSTPHILA 1969 Philatelic Exhibition, Brussels, May 10–18. Size of stamp: 40x47mm.; size of sheet: 90x123mm.

Huts, by Ivanka D. Pancheva, Bulgaria
SP381

Msgr. Victor Scheppers
SP382

Children's Drawings and UNICEF Emblem: 3fr+1.50fr, "My Art" (Santa Claus), by Claes Patric, Belgium. 6fr+3fr, "In the Sun" (young boy), by Helena Rejchlova, Czechoslovakia. 10fr+5fr, "Out for a Walk" by Phillis Sporn, USA (horiz.).

1969, May 31 Photo. ***Perf. 11½***

B841	SP381	1fr+50c multi.	25	25
B842	"	3fr+1.50fr multi.	50	50
B843	"	6fr+3fr "	1.00	1.00
B844	"	10fr+5fr "	1.35	1.35

The surtax was for philanthropic purposes.

1969, July 5 Engraved

B845	SP382	6fr+3fr rose claret	1.35	1.35

Issued to commemorate Msgr. Victor Scheppers (1802–77), prison reformer and founder of the Brothers of Mechlin (Scheppers).

Souvenir Sheet

Moon Landing Type of 1969

Design: 20fr+10fr, Armstrong, Collins and Aldrin and moon with Tranquillity Base (vert.).

1969, Sept. 20 Photo. ***Perf. 11½***

B846 A245 20fr+10fr indigo 7.50 7.50

See note after No. 693. No. B846 contains one stamp. Margin has commemorative inscription and picture of Armstrong stepping on moon. Size: 94x129mm.

Heads from Alexander the Great Tapestry, 15th Century
SP383

Designs from Tapestries: 3fr+1.50fr, Fiddler from "The Feast," c. 1700. 10fr+4fr, Head of beggar from "The Healing of the Paralytic," 16th century.

1969, Sept. 20

B847	SP383	1fr+50c multi.	20	20
B848	"	3fr+1.50fr "	50	50
B849	"	10fr+4fr "	1.40	1.40

The surtax was for philanthropic purposes.

Bearded Antwerp Bantam
SP384

Engraved and Photogravure

1969, Nov. 8 ***Perf. 11½***

B850 SP384 10fr+5fr multi. 2.15 2.15

Angel Playing Lute
SP385

Designs from Stained Glass Windows: 1.50fr+50c, Angel with trumpet, St. Waudru's, Mons. 7fr+3fr, Angel with viol, St. Jacques', Liege. 9fr+4fr, King with bagpipes, Royal Art Museum, Brussels.

1969, Dec. 13 Photogravure

Size: 24x35mm.

B851	SP385	1.50fr+50c multi.	30	30
B852	"	3.50fr+1.50fr multi.	60	55
B853	"	7fr+3fr multi.	1.00	90

Size: 35x52mm.

B854	SP386	9fr+4fr multi.	1.35	1.25

The surtax was for philanthropic purposes.

Farm and Windmill, Open-air Museum, Bokrijk
SP386

Belgian Museums: 3.50fr+1.50fr, Stage Coach Inn, Courcelles. 7fr+3fr, "The Thresher of Trevires," Gallo-Roman sculpture, Gaumais Museum, Virton. 9fr+4fr, "The Sovereigns," by Henry Moore, Middelheim Museum, Antwerp.

Engraved and Photogravure

1970, May 30 ***Perf. 11½***

B855	SP386	1.50fr+50c multi.	50	50
B856	"	3.50fr+1.50fr multicolored	75	75
B857	"	7fr+3fr multi.	1.00	1.00
B858	"	9fr+4fr "	1.25	1.25

The surtax went to various culture organizations.

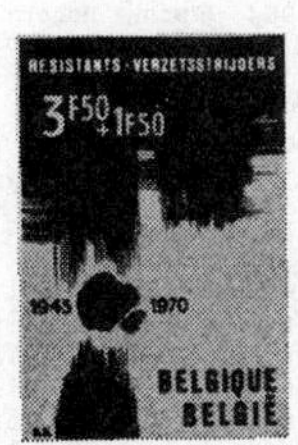

"Resistance" SP387

Design: 7fr+3fr, "Liberation of Camps." The designs were originally used as book covers.

1970, July 4 **Photo.** ***Perf. 11½***

B859	SP387	3.50fr+1.50fr blk., gray grn. & dp. carmine	50	50
B860	"	7fr+3fr black, lilac & deep carmine	1.00	1.00

Issued to honor the Resistance Movement and to commemorate the 25th anniversary of the liberation of concentration camps.

Fishing Rod and Reel
SP388

Design: 9fr+4fr, Hockey stick and puck (vert.).

Engraved and Photogravure

1970, Sept. 19 ***Perf. 11½***

B861	SP388	3.50fr+1.50fr multi.	65	60
B862	"	9fr+4fr brt. grn. & multi.	2.00	2.00

Souvenir Sheet

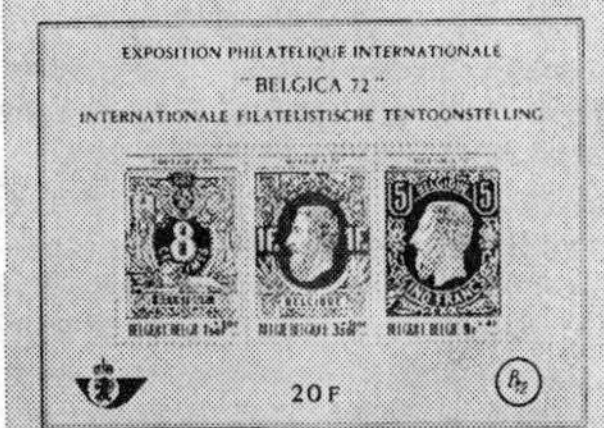

Belgium Nos. 31, 36 and 39
SP389

Engraved and Photogravure

1970, Oct. 10 ***Perf. 11½***

B863	SP389	20fr sheet of 3	6.50	6.50
	a.	1.50fr+50c black & dull lilac	2.00	2.00
	b.	3.50fr+1.50fr black & lilac	2.00	2.00
	c.	9fr+4fr black & red brown	2.00	2.00

Issued to publicize BELGICA 72 International Philatelic Exhibition, Brussels, June 24–July 9. No. B863 has black marginal inscription and lilac frame. Size: 130x97mm.

Camille Huysmans (1871–1968)
SP390

"Anxious City" (Detail) by Paul Delvaux
SP391

Portraits: 3.50fr+1.50fr, Joseph Cardinal Cardijn (1882–1967). 7fr+3fr, Maria Baers (1883–1959). 9fr+4fr, Paul Pastur (1866–1938).

Engraved and Photogravure

1970, Nov. 14 ***Perf. 11½***

Portraits in Sepia

B864	SP390	1.50fr+50c car. rose	35	35
B865	"	3.50fr+1.50fr lilac	55	55
B866	"	7fr+3fr green	1.00	1.00
B867	"	9fr+4fr blue	1.35	1.35

1970, Dec. 12 **Photogravure**

Design: 7fr+3fr, "The Memory," by René Magritte.

B868	SP391	3.50fr+1.50fr multi.	50	50
B869	"	7fr+3fr multi.	90	90

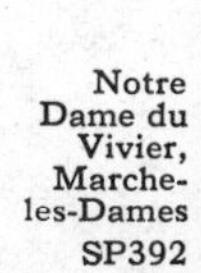

Notre Dame du Vivier, Marche-les-Dames
SP392

Design: 7fr+3fr, Turnhout Beguinage and Beguine.

1971, March 13 ***Perf. 11½***

B870	SP392	3.50fr+1.50fr multi.	65	65
B871	"	7fr+3fr multi.	1.10	1.10

The surtax was for philanthropic purposes.

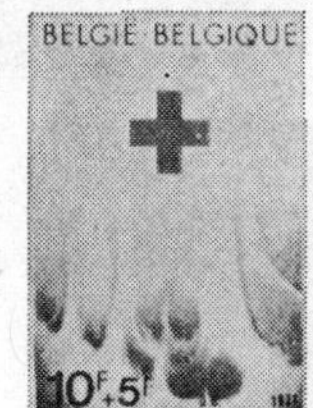

Red Cross
SP393

1971, May 22 **Photo.** ***Perf. 11½***

B872	SP393	10fr+5fr crimson & black	2.00	2.00

Belgian Red Cross.

Discobolus and Munich Cathedral
SP394

Festival of Flanders
SP395

Engraved and Photogravure

1971, June 19 ***Perf. 11½***

B873	SP394	7fr+3fr blue & black	2.25	2.25

Publicity for the 20th Summer Olympic Games, Munich 1972.

1971, Sept. 11 **Photo.** ***Perf. 11½***

Design: 7fr+3fr, Wallonia Festival.

B874	SP395	3.50fr+1.50fr multi.	55	55
B875	"	7fr+3fr multi.	1.00	90

Attre Palace—SP396

Steen Palace, Elewijt
SP397

Design: 10fr+5fr, Royal Palace, Brussels.

1971, Oct. 23 **Engraved**

B876	SP396	3.50fr+1.50fr slate green	1.35	1.35
B877	SP397	7fr+3fr red brown	1.65	1.65
B878	SP396	10fr+5fr vio. bl.	2.25	2.25

Surtax was for BELGICA 72, International Philatelic Exposition.

Ox Fly
SP398

Insects: 1.50fr+50c, Luna moth (vert.). 7fr+3fr, Wasp, polistes gallicus. 9fr+4fr, Tiger beetle (vert.).

1971, Dec. 11 **Photo.** ***Perf. 11½***

B879	SP398	1.50fr+50c multi.	45	45
B880	"	3.50fr+1.50fr multi.	60	60
B881	"	7fr+3fr multi.	1.00	1.00
B882	"	9fr+4fr multi.	1.50	1.50

Surtax was for philanthropic purposes.

Leopold I on No. 1
SP399

Epilepsy Emblem
SP400

Designs: 2fr+1fr, Leopold I on No. 5. 2.50fr+1fr, Leopold II on No. 45. 3.50fr+1.50fr, Leopold II on No. 48. 6fr+3fr, Albert I on No. 135. 7fr+3fr, Albert I on No. 214. 10fr+5fr, Albert I on No. 231. 15fr+7.50fr, Leopold III on No. 290. 20fr+10fr, King Baudouin on No. 718.

Engraved and Photogravure

1972, June 24 ***Perf. 11½***

"B" in Gold

B883	SP399	1.50fr+50c brown & black	45	45
B884	"	2fr+1fr brick red & brown	65	65
B885	"	2.50fr+1fr car. & black	1.00	1.00
B886	"	3.50fr+1.50fr vio. & black	1.50	1.50
B887	"	6fr+3fr rose lilac & blk.	2.40	2.40
B888	"	7fr+3fr rose car. & blk.	3.25	3.25
B889	"	10fr+5fr slate bl. & black	3.75	3.75
B890	"	15fr+7fr gray grn. & blue green	5.75	5.75
B891	"	20fr+10fr red brn. & brn.	7.50	7.50
		Nos. B883-B891 (9)	26.25	26.25

Belgica 72, International Philatelic Exhibition, Brussels, June 24–July 9. Nos. B883–B891 issued in sheets of 10 and of 20 (2 tête bêche sheets with gutter between). Belgica 72 emblem in stamp color and gray blue border and inscription in margin. Sold in complete sets.

1972, Sept. 9 **Photo.** ***Perf. 11½***

B892	SP400	10fr+5fr multi.	1.60	1.60

The surtax was for the William Lennox Center for epilepsy research and treatment.

Gray Lag Goose
SP401

Designs: 4.50fr+2fr, Lapwing. 8fr+4fr, Stork. 9fr+4.50fr, Kestrel (horiz.).

1972, Dec. 16 **Photo.** ***Perf. 11½***

B893	SP401	2fr+1fr multi.	50	50
B894	"	4.50fr+2fr "	90	90
B895	"	8fr+4fr "	1.25	1.25
B896	"	9fr+4.50fr "	1.75	1.75

Bijloke Abbey, Ghent—SP402

Designs: 4.50fr+2fr, St. Ursmer Collegiate Church, Lobbes. 8fr+4fr, Park Abbey, Heverle. 9fr+4.50fr, Abbey, Floreffe.

1973, Mar. 24 **Engr.** ***Perf. 11½***

B897	SP402	2fr+1fr slate grn.	60	60
B898	"	4.50fr+2fr brown	1.25	1.25
B899	"	8fr+4fr rose lilac	1.85	1.85
B900	"	9fr+4.50fr brt. blue	2.50	2.50

Basketball
SP403

1973, Apr. 7 **Photo. & Engr.**

B901	SP403	10fr+5fr multi.	2.00	2.00

First World Basketball Championships of the Handicapped, Bruges, Apr. 16–21.

Dirk Martens' Printing Press
SP404

Lady Talbot, by Petrus Christus
SP405

Hadrian and Marcus Aurelius Coins
SP406

Council of Malines, by Coussaert—SP407

Designs: 3.50fr+1.50fr, Head of Amon and Tutankhamen's cartouche. 10fr+5fr, Three-master of Ostend Merchant Company.

Photo. & Engr.; Photo. (B906)

1973, June 23 *Perf. 11½*

B902	SP404	2fr+1fr	multi.	1.00	1.00
B903	"	3.50fr+1.50fr	"	1.50	1.50
B904	SP405	4.50fr+2fr	"	2.00	2.00
B905	SP406	8fr+4fr	"	3.00	3.00
B906	SP407	9fr+4.50fr	"	3.50	3.50
B907	"	10fr+5fr	"	4.50	4.50
	Nos. B902-B907 (6)			15.50	15.50

Historical Anniversaries: 500th anniversary of first book printed in Belgium (B902); 50th anniversary of Queen Elisabeth Egyptological Foundation (B903); 500th anniversary of death of painter Petrus Christus (B904); Discovery of Roman treasure at Luttre-Liberchies (B905); 500th anniversary of Great Council of Malines (B906); 250th anniversary of the Ostend Merchant Company (B907).

No. B902 is not luminescent.

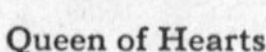

Queen of Hearts

Symbol of Blood Donations

SP408 SP409

Old Playing Cards: No. B909, King of Clubs. No. B910, Jack of Diamonds. No. B911, King of Spades.

1973, Dec. 8 Photo. *Perf. 11½*

B908	SP408	5+2.50fr	multi.	1.50	1.50
B909	"	5+2.50fr	"	1.50	1.50
B910	"	5+2.50fr	"	1.50	1.50
B911	"	5+2.50fr	"	1.50	1.50

Surtax was for philanthropic purposes. Nos. B908-B911 printed se-tenant in sheets of 24 (4x6).

1974, Feb. 23 Photo. *Perf. 11½*

Design: 10fr+5fr, Traffic lights, Red Cross (symbolic of road accidents).

B912	SP409	4fr+2fr	multi.	80	80
B913	"	10fr+5fr	"	1.50	1.50

The Red Cross as blood collector and aid to accident victims.

Armand Jamar, Self-portrait
SP410

Van Gogh, Self-portrait and House at Cuesmes
SP411

Designs: 5fr+2.50fr, Anton Bergmann and view of Lierre. 7fr+3.50fr, Henri Vieuxtemps and view of Verviers. 10fr+5fr, James Ensor, self-portrait, and masks.

1974, Apr. 6 Photo. *Perf. 11½*

Size: 24x35mm.

B914	SP410	4fr+2fr	multi.	80	80
B915	"	5fr+2.50fr	"	1.00	1.00
B916	"	7fr+3.50fr	"	1.35	1.35

Size: 35x52mm.

B917	SP410	10fr+5fr	multi.	2.00	2.00

1974, Sept. 21 Photo. *Perf. 11½*

B918	SP411	10fr+5fr	multi.	2.00	2.00

Opening of Vincent van Gogh House at Cuesmes, where he worked as teacher.

Gentian
SP412

Spotted Cat's Ear
SP414

Badger
SP413

Design: 7fr+3.50fr, Beetle.

1974, Dec. 8 Photo. *Perf. 11½*

B919	SP412	4fr+2fr	multi.	55	55
B920	SP413	5fr+2.50fr	"	85	85
B921	"	7fr+3.50fr	"	1.25	1.25
B922	SP414	10fr+5fr	"	1.75	1.75

Pesaro Palace, Venice
SP415

St. Bavon Abbey, Ghent
SP416

Virgin and Child, by Michelangelo
SP417

1975, Apr. 12 Engr. *Perf. 11½*

B923	SP415	6.50fr+2.50fr brown	1.10	1.10
B924	SP416	10fr+4.50 violet brown	1.85	1.85
B925	SP417	15fr+6.50fr brt. blue	2.25	2.25

Surtax was for various cultural organizations.

Frans Hemerijckx and Leprosarium, Kasai
SP418

1975, Sept. 13 Photo. *Perf. 11½*

B926	SP418	20fr+10fr	multi.	3.00	3.00

Dr. Frans Hemerijckx (1902-1969), tropical medicine and leprosy expert.

Emile Moyson
SP419

Hand Reading Braille
SP420

Beheading of St. Dympna
SP421

Design: 6.50fr+3fr, Dr. Ferdinand Augustin Snellaert.

1975, Nov. 22 Engr. *Perf. 11½*

B927	SP419	4.50fr+2fr lilac	85	85
B928	"	6.50fr+3fr green	1.00	1.00

Engraved and Photogravure

B929	SP420	10fr+5fr	multi.	1.50	1.50

Photogravure

B930	SP421	13fr+6fr	multi.	2.25	2.25

Emile Moyson (1838-1868), freedom fighter for the rights of Flemings and Walloons; Dr. Snellaert (1809-1872), physician and Flemish patriot; Louis Braille (1809-1852), sesquicentennial of invention of Braille system of writing for the blind; St. Dympna, patron saint of Geel, famous for treatment of mentally ill.

The Cheese Vendor
SP421

Designs (THEMABELGA Emblem and): No. B932, Potato vendor. No. B933, Basket carrier. No. B934, Shrimp fisherman with horse (horiz.). No. B935, Knife grinder (horiz.). No. B936, Milk vendor with dog cart (horiz.).

Engraved and Photogravure

1975, Dec. 13 *Perf. 11½*

B931	SP421	4.50fr+1.50fr	multicolored	75	75
B932	"	6.50fr+3fr	multi.	1.10	1.10
B933	"	6.50fr+3fr	"	1.10	1.10
B934	"	10fr+5fr	"	1.75	1.75
B935	"	10fr+5fr	"	1.75	1.75
B936	"	30fr+15fr	"	5.00	5.00
	Nos. B931-B936 (6)			11.45	11.45

THEMABELGA International Topical Philatelic Exhibition, Brussels, Dec. 13-21. Issued in sheets of 10 (5x2).

Blackface Fund Collector
SP422

1976, Feb. 14 Photo. *Perf. 11½*

B937	SP422	10fr+5fr	multi.	1.60	1.60

Centenary of the "Conservatoire Africain" philanthropic society, and to publicize the Princess Paola crèches.

Swimming and Olympic Emblem
SP423

Designs (Montreal Olympic Games Emblem and): 5fr+2fr, Running (vert.). 6.50fr+2.50fr, Equestrian.

1976, Apr. 10 Photo. *Perf. 11½*

B938	SP423	4.50f+1.50fr multi.	45	45
B939	"	5fr+2fr multi.	60	60
B940	"	6.50fr+2.50fr multi.	75	75

21st Olympic Games, Montreal, Canada, July 17-Aug. 1.

Queen Elisabeth Playing Violin
SP424

Engraved and Photogravure

1976, May 1 *Perf. 11½*

B941	SP424	14fr+6fr black & claret	2.00	2.00

Queen Elisabeth International Music Competition, 25th anniversary.

Souvenir Sheet

Jan Olieslagers, Bleriot Monoplane, Aero Club Emblem—SP425

Engraved and Photogravure

1976, June 12 *Perf. 11½*

B942 SP425 25fr+10fr multi. 4.50 4.50

Royal Belgian Aero Club, 75th anniversary, and Jan Olieslagers (1883–1942), aviation pioneer. No. B942 has blue marginal decorations and black inscription. Size: 83x116mm.

Adoration of the Shepherds (detail), by Rubens
SP426

Dwarf, by Velazquez
SP427

Rubens Paintings (Details): 4.50fr, Descent from the Cross. No. B945, The Virgin with the Parrot. No. B946, Adoration of the Kings. No. B947, Last Communion of St. Francis. 30fr+15fr, Virgin and Child.

1976, Sept. 4 Photo. *Perf. 11½*

Size: 30x52mm.

B943 SP426 4.50fr+1.50fr multi. 60 60

Size: 24x35mm.

B944 SP426 6.50fr+3fr multi. 1.00 1.00
B945 " 6.50fr+3fr multi. 1.00 1.00
B946 " 10fr+5fr multi. 1.75 1.75
B947 " 10fr+5fr multi. 1.75 1.75

Size: 30x52mm.

B948 SP426 30fr+15fr multi. 5.00 5.00
Nos. B943-B948 (6) 11.10 11.10

Peter Paul Rubens (1577–1640), Flemish painter, 400th birth anniversary.

1976, Nov. 6 Photo. *Perf. 11½*

B949 SP427 14fr+6fr multi. 1.25 1.25

Surtax was for the National Association for the Mentally Handicapped.

Dr. Albert Hustin
SP428

Red Cross and Rheumatism Year Emblem
SP429

1977, Feb. 19 Photo. *Perf. 11½*

B950 SP428 6.50fr+2.50fr multicolored 75 75
B951 SP429 14fr+7fr multi. 1.65 1.65

Belgian Red Cross.

Bordet Atheneum, Empress Maria Theresa
SP430

Conductor and Orchestra, by E. Tytgat
SP431

Lucien Van Obbergh, Stage
SP432

Humanistic Society Emblem
SP433

Camille Lemonnier
SP434

Design: No. B953, Marie-Therese College, Herve, and coat of arms.

1977, Mar. 21 Photo. *Perf. 11½*

B952 SP430 4.50fr+1fr multi. 60 60
B953 " 4.50fr+1fr " 60 60
B954 SP431 5fr+2fr " 60 60
B955 SP432 6.50fr+2fr " 90 90
B956 SP433 6.50fr+2fr black & red 70 70

Engraved

B957 SP434 10fr+5fr slate bl. 1.65 1.65
Nos. B952-B957 (6) 5.05 5.05

Bicentenaries of the Jules Bordet Atheneum, Brussels, and the Marie-Therese College, Herve (Nos. B952–B953); 50th anniversaries of the Brussels Philharmonic Society, and Artists' Union (Nos. B954–B955); 25th anniversary of the Flemish Humanistic Organization (No. B956); 75th anniversary of the French-speaking Belgian writers' organization (No. B957).

Young Soccer Players
SP435

1977, Apr. 18 Photogravure

B958 SP435 10fr+5fr multi. 1.50 1.50

30th International Junior Soccer Tournament.

Albert-Edouard Janssen, Financier
SP436

Famous Men: No. B960, Joseph Wauters (1875–1929), editor of Le Peuple, and newspaper. No. B961, Jean Capart (1877–1947), Egyptologist, and hieroglyph. No. B962, August de Boeck (1865–1937), composer, and score.

1977, Dec. 3 Engr. *Perf. 11½*

B959 SP436 5fr+2.50fr brn. 60 60
B960 " 5fr+2.50fr red 60 60
B961 " 10fr+5fr magenta 1.50 1.50
B962 " 10fr+5fr blue gray 1.50 1.50

Abandoned Child
SP437

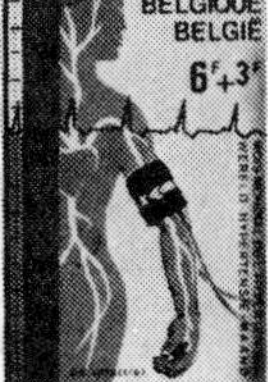

Checking Blood Pressure
SP438

De Mick Sanatorium, Brasschaat—SP439

1978, Feb. 18 Photo. *Perf. 11½*

B963 SP437 4.50fr+1.50fr multi. 36 36
B964 SP438 6fr+3fr multi. 55 55
B965 SP439 10fr+5fr " 90 90

Help for abandoned children (No. B963); fight against hypertension (No. B964); fight against tuberculosis (No. B965).

Actors and Theater
SP440

Karel van de Woestijne
SP441

Designs: No. B967, Harquebusier, Harquebusier Palace and coat of arms. 10fr+5fr, John of Austria and his signature.

Engraved and Photogravure

1978, June 17 *Perf. 11½*

B966 SP440 6fr+3fr multi. 55 55
B967 " 6fr+3fr " 55 55

Engraved

B968 SP441 8fr+4fr black 72 72
B969 " 10fr+5fr " 90 90

Centenary of Royal Flemish Theater, Brussels (No. B966); 400th anniversary of Harquebusiers' Guild of Visé, Liège (No. B967); Karel van de Woestijne (1878–1929), poet (No. B968); 400th anniversary of signing of Perpetual Edict by John of Austria (No. B969).

Lake Placid '80 and Belgian Olympic Emblems
SP442

Designs (Moscow '80 Emblem and): 8fr+3.50fr, Kremlin Towers and Belgian Olympic Committee emblem. 7fr+3fr, Runners from Greek vase, Lake Placid '80 emblem and Olympic rings. 14fr+6fr, Olympic flame, Lake Placid '80 and Belgian emblems, Olympic rings.

1978, Nov. 4 Photo. *Perf. 11½*

B970 SP442 6fr+2.50fr multi. 60 60
B971 " 8fr+3.50fr " 80 80

Souvenir Sheet

B972 Sheet of 2 2.25
a. SP442 7fr+3fr multicolored 70
b. " 14fr+6fr " 1.40

Surtax was for 1980 Olympic Games. No. B972 has marginal inscription, Olympic Flame and Rings in blue and brown. Size: 150x100mm.

Great Synagogue, Brussels
SP443

Dancers
SP444

Father Pire, African Village
SP445

1978, Dec. 2 Engr. *Perf. 11½*

B973 SP443 6fr+2fr sepia 56 56

Photogravure

B974 SP444 8fr+3fr multi. 78 78
B975 SP445 14fr+7fr " 1.50 1.50

Centenary of Great Synagogue of Brussels; Flemish Catholic Youth Action Organization, 50th anniversary; Nobel Peace Prize awarded to Father Dominique Pire for his "Heart Open to the World" movement, 20th anniversary.

AIR POST STAMPS.

Fokker FVII/3m over Ostend
AP1

Designs: 1.50fr, Plane over St. Hubert. 2fr, over Namur. 5fr, over Brussels.

Photogravure.

1930, Apr. 30 *Perf. 11½* Unwmkd.

C1	AP1	50c blue	75	20
C2	"	1.50fr black brown	6.50	4.25
C3	"	2fr deep green	6.50	75
C4	"	5fr brown lake	6.50	1.00

1930, Dec. 5

C5	AP1	5fr dark violet	65.00	50.00

Issued for use on a mail carrying flight from Brussels to Leopoldville, Belgian Congo, starting Dec. 7.

Nos. C1–C5 exist imperforate.

Nos. C2 and C4
Surcharged in Carmine or Blue

1935, May 23

C6	AP1	1fr on 1.50fr black brown (C)	50	50
C7	"	4fr on 5fr brown lake (Bl)	22.50	4.75

DC-4 Skymaster, Sabena Airline
AP5

1946–54 Engraved *Perf. 11½*

C8	AP5	6fr blue	60	12
C9	"	8.50fr violet brown	1.00	65
C10	"	50fr yellow green	9.50	65
		a. Perf. 12 x 11½ ('54)	85.00	75
C11	AP5	100fr gray	16.00	1.00
		a. Perf. 12 x 11½ ('54)	60.00	75

The French and Flemish inscriptions are transposed on Nos. C9 and C11.

Evolution of Postal Transportation
AP6

1949, July 1

C12	AP6	50fr dark brown	30.00	14.00

Centenary of Belgian postage stamps.

Glider—AP7

Design: 7fr, "Tipsy" plane.

1951, June 18 Photo. *Perf. 13½*

C12A	AP7	Strip of 2 + label	60.00	60.00
		b. 6fr dark blue	25.00	25.00
		c. 7fr carmine rose	25.00	25.00

For the 50th anniversary of the Aero Club of Belgium. The label is inscribed "1901 — 1951 + 37FR. BELGIE BELGIQUE" and carries the club emblem. The strip sold for 50fr.

1951, July 25 *Perf. 13½*

C13	AP7	6fr sepia	6.25	10
C14	"	7fr Prussian green	6.25	90

United Nations Issue

Types of Regular Issue, 1958

Designs: 5fr, International Civil Aviation Organization. 6fr, World Meteorological Organization. 7.50fr, Protection of Refugees. 8fr, General Agreement on Tariffs and Trade. 9fr, UNICEF. 10fr, Atomic Energy Agency.

Engraved.

1958, Apr. 17 *Perf. 11½* Unwmkd.

C15	A137	5fr dull blue	40	40
C16	A136	6fr yellow green	1.20	1.20
C17	A137	7.50fr lilac	40	40
C18	A136	8fr sepia	40	40
C19	A137	9fr carmine	60	60
C20	A136	10fr reddish brn.	1.75	1.75
		Nos. C15–C20 (6)	4.75	4.75

World's Fair, Brussels, Apr. 17–Oct. 19. See note after No. 476.

AIR POST SEMI-POSTAL STAMPS.

American Soldier in Combat
SPAP1

Engraved.

Perf. 11x11½

1946, June 15 Unwmkd.

CB1	SPAP1	17.50fr+62.50fr dull brown	2.00	2.00
CB2	"	17.50fr+62.50fr dull gray green	2.00	2.00

The French and Flemish inscriptions are transposed on No. CB2. The surtax was to erect an American memorial at Bastogne.

An overprint, "Hommage a Roosevelt", was privately applied to Nos. CB1 and CB2 in 1947 by the Association Belgo-Americaine.

In 1950 another private overprint was applied, in red, to Nos. CB1-2. It consists of "16-12-1944, 25-1-1945, Dedication July 16, 1950" and outlines of the American eagle emblem and the Bastogne Memorial. Similar overprints were applied to Nos. 265 and 345.

Flight Allegory
SPAP2

1946, Sept. 7 *Perf. 11½*

CB3	SPAP2	2fr+8fr bright violet	1.25	1.25

The surtax was for the benefit of aviation.

A particular stamp may be scarce, but if few want it, its market potential may remain relatively low.

Nos. B417–B425 Surcharged in Various Arrangements in Red or Dark Blue

POSTE AERIENNE
LUCHTPOST
1F + 2F

LUCHTPOST
POSTE AERIENNE
1F +2F

Type I. Top line "POSTE AERIENNE."
Type II. Top line "LUCHTPOST."

1947, May 18 Photo. *Perf. 11½*

CB4	SP227	1fr+2fr on 65c+75c dk. bl. (R)(I)	2.00	1.50
		a. Type II	2.00	1.50
CB5	SP228	1.50fr+2.50fr on 1.35fr+2fr brown (Bl) (I)	2.00	1.50
		a. Type II	2.00	1.50
CB6	SP229	2fr+45fr on 1.75fr+18fr rose brn. (Bl) (I)	2.00	1.50
		a. Type II	2.00	1.50
CB7	SP230	1fr+2fr on 65c+75c violet (R) (I)	2.00	1.50
		a. Type II	2.00	1.50
CB8	SP231	1.50fr+2.50fr on 1.35fr+2fr dark orge. brown (Bl) (I)	2.00	1.50
		a. Type II	2.00	1.50
CB9	SP232	2fr+45fr on 1.75fr+18fr carm. rose (Bl) (I)	2.00	1.50
		a. Type II	2.00	1.50
CB10	SP233	1fr+2fr on 65c+ 75c dk. slate grn. (R) (I)	2.00	1.50
		a. Type II	2.00	1.50
CB11	SP234	1.50fr+2.50fr on 1.35fr+2fr dk. vio. bl. (R) (I)	2.00	1.50
		a. Type II	2.00	1.50
CB12	SP235	2fr+45fr on 1.75fr+18fr deep carmine (Bl) (I)	2.00	1.50
		a. Type II	2.00	1.50
		Nos. CB4–CB12, CB4a–CB12a (18)	36.00	27.00

In 1948 Nos. CB4–CB12 and CB4a–CB12a were punched with the letters "IMABA," and the inscription "Imaba du 21 au 29 aout 1948" was applied to the backs. Price $20.

Helicopter Leaving Airport
SPAP3

1950, Aug. 7

CB13	SPAP3	7fr+3fr blue	5.25	5.25

The surtax was for the National Aeronautical Committee.

SPECIAL DELIVERY STAMPS

From 1874 to 1903 certain hexagonal telegraph stamps were used as special delivery stamps.

Town Hall, Brussels
SD1

Eupen
SD2

Designs: 2.35fr, Street in Ghent. 3.50fr, Bishop's Palace, Liege. 5.25fr, Notre Dame Cathedral, Antwerp.

Photogravure.

1929 *Perf. 11½.* Unwmkd.

E1	SD1	1.75fr dark blue	1.75	20
E2	"	2.35fr carmine	5.00	35
E3	"	3.50fr dark violet	10.00	7.50
E4	"	5.25fr olive green	10.00	7.50

1931

E5	SD2	2.45fr dark green	30.00	2.00
		Nos. E1–E5 (5)	56.75	17.55

No. E5
Surcharged in Red

2 Fr 50

1932

E6	SD2	2.50fr on 2.45fr dark green	22.50	1.50

POSTAGE DUE STAMPS.

D1 D2

Typographed.

1870 *Perf. 15.* Unwmkd.

J1	D1	10c green	5.50	2.50
		a. Half used as 5c on piece		5.00
J2	D1	20c ultramarine	27.50	3.50

1895-09 *Perf. 14.*

J3	D2	5c yellow green	25	20
J4	"	10c orange brown	7.00	1.25
J5	"	10c carmine ('00)	20	12
J6	"	20c olive green	20	12
J7	"	30c pale blue ('09)	40	30
J8	"	50c yellow brown	13.50	5.25
J9	"	50c gray ('00)	90	65
J10	"	1fr carmine	32.50	21.00
J11	"	1fr ochre ('00)	10.00	6.75
		Nos. J3–J11 (9)	64.95	35.64

1916 Redrawn

J12	D2	5c blue green	7.50	4.00
J13	"	10c carmine	10.00	2.75
J14	"	20c deep gray green	15.00	8.25
J15	"	30c bright blue	3.75	2.10
J16	"	50c gray	47.50	45.00
		Nos. J12–J16 (5)	83.75	62.10

In the redrawn stamps the lions have a heavy, colored outline. There is a thick vertical line at the outer edge of the design on each side.

D3 D4

1919 *Perf. 14*

J17	D3	5c green	45	30
J18	"	10c carmine	1.00	25
J19	"	20c gray green	7.50	40
J20	"	30c bright blue	2.25	25
J21	"	50c gray	3.25	25
		Nos. J17–J21 (5)	14.45	1.45

1922–32

J22	D4	5c dark gray	10	10
J23	"	10c green	8	5
J24	"	20c deep brown	20	10
J25	"	30c vermilion ('24)	45	10
		a. 30c rose red	1.35	45
J26	D4	40c red brown ('25)	50	10
J27	"	50c ultramarine	2.25	10
J28	"	70c red brown ('29)	60	10
J29	"	1fr violet ('25)	85	10
J30	"	1fr rose lilac ('32)	85	10
J31	"	1.20fr olive grn. ('29)	1.15	35
J32	"	1.50fr olive grn. ('32)	1.15	35
J33	"	2fr violet ('29)	1.25	10
J34	"	3.50fr deep blue ('29)	1.65	10
		Nos. J22–J34 (13)	11.08	1.75

1934-46 *Perf. 14x13½.*

J35	D4	35c green ('35)	60	60
J36	"	50c slate	50	10
J37	"	60c carmine ('38)	60	25
J38	"	80c slate ('38)	60	10
J39	"	1.40fr gray ('35)	1.15	22
J39A	"	3fr org. brown ('46)	2.00	25
J39B	"	7fr bright red violet ('46)	3.75	3.25
		Nos. J35-J39B (7)	9.20	4.77

See also Nos. J54-J61.

D5 D6

1945 Typographed *Perf. 12½*

Inscribed "TE BETALEN" at Top.

J40	D5	10c gray olive	10	10
J41	"	20c ultramarine	10	10
J42	"	30c carmine	10	10
J43	"	40c black violet	10	10
J44	"	50c dull blue green	10	10
J45	"	1fr sepia	10	10
J46	"	2fr red orange	15	15

Inscribed "A PAYER" at Top.

J47	D5	10c gray olive	10	10
J48	"	20c ultramarine	10	10
J49	"	30c carmine	10	10
J50	"	40c black violet	10	10
J51	"	50c dull blue green	10	10
J52	"	1fr sepia	10	10
J53	"	2fr red orange	15	15
		Nos. J40-J53 (14)	1.50	1.50

Type of 1922-32.

1949 Typographed. *Perf. 14x13½.*

J54	D4	65c emerald	7.50	7.00
J55	"	1.80fr red	15.00	7.75
J56	"	5fr red brown	3.25	25
J57	"	8fr lilac rose	7.25	6.75
J58	"	10fr dark violet	7.25	6.75
		Nos. J54-J58 (5)	40.25	28.50

1953

J59	D4	1.60fr lilac rose	9.50	8.00
J60	"	2.40fr gray lilac	8.50	2.50
J61	"	4fr deep blue	9.50	25

1966-70 Photogravure

J62	D6	1fr bright pink	5	5
J63	"	2fr blue green	10	8
J64	"	3fr blue	15	10
J65	"	5fr purple	25	12
J66	"	6fr bister brown	30	15
J67	"	7fr red orange ('70)	35	35
J68	"	20fr slate green	1.00	85
		Nos. J62-J68 (7)	2.20	1.70

MILITARY STAMPS

King Baudouin

M1 M2

Photogravure

1967, July 17 *Perf. 11* Unwmkd.

M1	M1	1.50fr greenish gray	1.75	25

1971-75 Engraved *Perf. 11½*

M2	M2	1.75fr green	6.75	1.15
M3	"	2.25fr gray grn. ('73)	3.50	1.15
M4	"	2.50fr gray green ('74)	90	50
M5	"	3.25fr vio. brn. ('75)	75	35

Nos. M1-M3 are luminescent, Nos. M4-M5 are not.

MILITARY PARCEL POST STAMP.

Type of Parcel Post Stamp of 1938 Surcharged with New Value and "M" in Blue.

1939 *Perf. 13½* Unwmkd.

MQ1	PP19	3fr on 5.50fr copper red	30	10

OFFICIAL STAMPS.

For franking the official correspondence of the Administration of the Belgian National Railways.

Regular Issue of 1921-27 Overprinted in Black

1929-30 *Perf. 14.* Unwmkd.

O1	A58	5c gray	12	12
O2	"	10c blue green	30	20
O3	"	35c blue green	35	10
O4	"	60c olive green	25	10
O5	"	1.50fr bright blue	8.00	2.25
O6	"	1.75fr ultra. ('30)	1.50	1.25
		Nos. O1-O6 (6)	10.52	4.02

Same Overprint, in Red or Black, on Regular Issues of 1929-30.

1929-31

O7	A63	5c slate (R)	12	12
O8	"	10c olive green (R)	35	20
O9	"	25c rose red (Bk)	1.35	40
O10	"	35c deep green (R)	1.65	40
O11	"	40c red violet (Bk)	1.35	15
O12	"	50c deep blue (R) ('31)	75	10
O13	"	60c rose (Bk)	5.00	1.35
O14	"	70c org. brown (Bk)	5.00	75
O15	"	75c black violet (R) ('31)	3.75	50
		Nos. O7-O15 (9)	19.32	3.97

Overprinted on Regular Issue of 1932.

1932

O16	A73	10c olive green (R)	75	75
O17	A74	35c deep green	15.00	40
O18	A71a	75c bis. brown (R)	2.25	25

Overprinted on No. 262 in Red.

1935 *Perf. 13½x14*

O19	A80	70c olive black	4.25	10

Regular Stamps of 1935-36 Overprinted in Red.

1936-38 *Perf. 13½, 13½x14, 14.*

O20	A82	10c olive bistre	30	12
O21	"	35c green	40	12
O22	"	50c dark blue	1.00	12
O23	A83	70c brown	3.00	45

Overprinted in Black or Red on Regular Issue of 1938.

Perf. 13½x14.

O24	A82	40c red violet (Bk)	60	12
O25	A85	75c olive gray (R)	1.00	12
		Nos. O20-O25 (6)	6.30	1.05

Regular Issues of 1935-41 Overprinted in Red or Dark Blue

1941-44 *Perf. 14, 14x13½, 13½x14.*

O26	A82	10c olive bistre	8	5
		a. Inverted overprint		
O27	"	40c red violet	30	25
O28	"	50c dark blue	8	8
		a. Inverted overprint		
O29	A83a	1fr rose car. (Bl)	60	10
O30	A85	1fr rose pink (Bl)	8	5
O31	A83a	2.25fr greenish black ('44)	60	50
O32	A84	2.25fr gray violet	45	40
		Nos. O26-O32 (7)	2.19	1.43

Nos. O21, O23 and O25 Surcharged with New Values in Black or Red.

1942

O33	A82	10c on 35c green	25	25
O34	A83	50c on 70c brown	15	15
O35	A85	50c on 75c olive gray (R)	15	15

O1 O2

1946-48 *Perf. 14.* Unwmkd.

O36	O1	10c olive bistre	10	8
O37	"	20c bright violet	2.00	20
O38	"	50c dark blue	10	8
O39	"	65c red lilac ('48)	3.00	28
O40	"	75c lilac rose	10	8
O41	"	90c brown violet	4.00	15
		Nos. O36-O41 (6)	9.30	87

Types A99, A101 and A102 with "B" Emblem Added to Design.

1948 *Perf. 11½.*

O42	A99	1.35fr red brown	3.25	80
O43	"	1.75fr dark gray green	4.25	25
O44	A101	3fr bright red violet	16.50	4.00
O45	A102	3.15fr deep blue	8.00	8.00
O46	"	4fr brt. ultra.	15.00	15.00
		Nos. O42-O46 (5)	47.00	28.05

1953-66 Typo. *Perf. 13½x14*

O47	O2	10c orange	40	10
O48	"	20c red lilac	40	10
O49	"	30c gray green ('58)	1.00	75
O50	"	40c olive gray	40	10
O51	"	50c light blue	55	15
O51A	"	60c lilac rose ('66)	1.00	60
O52	"	65c red lilac	30.00	30.00
O53	"	80c emerald	2.00	25
O54	"	90c deep blue	4.25	25
O55	"	1fr rose	60	10
		Nos. O47-O55 (10)	40.60	32.40

King Baudouin

O3 O4

1954-70 Photogravure *Perf. 11½*

O56	O3	1.50fr gray	60	10
O57	"	2fr rose red	50.00	10
O58	"	2fr blue green ('59)	60	10
O59	"	2.50fr red brn. ('58)	37.50	25
O60	"	3fr red lilac ('58)	2.50	10
O61	"	3.50fr yel. green ('70)	75	12
O62	"	4fr bright blue	2.50	20
O63	"	6fr car. rose ('58)	7.50	75
		Nos. O56-O63 (8)	101.95	1.72

Type of 1953-66 Redrawn

1970-75 Typo. *Perf. 13½x14*

O66	O2	1.50fr greenish gray ('75)	8	3
O68	"	2.50fr brown	14	10

1971-73 Engraved *Perf. 11½*

O71	O4	3.50fr org. brn. ('73)	1.35	60
O72	"	4.50fr brown ('73)	1.00	45
O73	"	7fr red	16.50	10.00
O74	"	15fr violet	1.65	75

Nos. O71-O74 are on luminescent paper.

1974-78

O75	O4	3fr yellow green	6.00	1.00
O76	"	4fr blue	2.00	60
O77	"	4.50fr greenish bl. ('75)	30	10
O78	O4	5fr lilac	20	35
O79	"	6fr carmine ('78)	35	30
O80	"	6.50fr black ('76)	50	28
O81	"	8fr bluish blk. ('78)	48	40
O82	"	10fr rose carmine	60	40
O83	"	25fr lilac ('76)	1.65	1.00
O84	"	30fr org. brn. ('78)	1.80	1.50
		Nos. O75-O84 (10)	13.88	5.93

Nos. O75-O76, O78, O82 are on luminescent paper.

Heraldic Lion

O5

1977 Typographed *Perf. 13½x14*

O85	O5	4fr red brown	25	15

NEWSPAPER STAMPS.

Parcel Post Stamps of 1923-27 Overprinted JOURNAUX DAGBLADEN 1928

Perf. 14½x14, 14x14½.

1928 Unwmkd.

P1	PP12	10c vermilion	25	20
P2	"	20c turquoise blue	25	20
P3	"	40c olive green	25	15
P4	"	60c orange	60	20
P5	"	70c dark brown	20	10
P6	"	80c violet	60	15
P7	"	90c slate	2.75	1.00
		a. Inverted overprint		
P8	PP13	1fr bright blue	1.00	15
		a. 1fr ultramarine	6.00	2.75
P10	"	2fr olive green	2.00	25
P11	"	3fr orange red	2.25	35
P12	"	4fr rose	2.25	35
		a. Inverted overprint		
P13	"	5fr violet	2.25	25
P14	"	6fr bistre brown	2.75	85
P15	"	7fr orange	4.75	85
P16	"	8fr dark brown	4.25	90
P17	"	9fr red violet	7.00	1.50
P18	"	10fr blue green	4.50	1.00
P19	"	20fr magenta	11.00	2.75
		Nos. P1-P8, P10-P19 (18)	48.90	11.20

Parcel Post Stamps of 1923-28 Overprinted JOURNAUX DAGBLADEN

1929-31

P20	PP12	10c vermilion	20	10
P21	"	20c turquoise blue	20	10
P22	"	40c olive green	20	12
		a. Inverted overprint		
P23	"	60c orange	60	20
P24	"	70c dark brown	28	10
P25	"	80c violet	70	15
P26	"	90c gray	2.50	90
		a. Inverted overprint		
P27	PP13	1fr ultramarine	1.00	10
		a. 1fr bright blue	1.50	30
P28	"	1.10fr orange brown ('31)	7.00	1.25
P29	"	1.50fr gray violet ('31)	7.00	1.65
P30	"	2fr olive green	1.85	22
P31	"	2.10fr slate gray ('31)	30.00	10.00
P32	"	3fr orange red	2.25	30
P33	"	4fr rose	2.25	30
P34	"	5fr violet	2.25	30
P35	"	6fr bistre brown	3.25	85
P36	"	7fr orange	4.75	85
P37	"	8fr dark brown	4.75	85
P38	"	9fr red violet	6.00	1.50
P39	"	10fr blue green	3.50	90
P40	"	20fr magenta	12.50	2.75
		Nos. P20-P40 (21)	93.03	23.49

PARCEL POST AND RAILWAY STAMPS.

Prices for used stamps are for copies with railway cancellations. Stamps with postal cancellations sell for twice as much.

Coat of Arms
PP1

Typographed.

1879–82 *Perf. 14* **Unwmkd.**

No.	Type	Description	Unused	Used
Q1	PP1	10c violet brown	32.50	2.00
Q2	"	20c blue	110.00	11.00
Q3	"	25c green ('81)	135.00	4.50
Q4	"	50c carmine	900.00	3.25
Q5	"	80c yellow	1000.00	30.00
Q6	"	1fr gray ('82)	100.00	9.00

Used copies of Nos. Q1–Q6 with pinholes, a normal state, sell for half price.

PP2

Most of the stamps of 1882-1902 (Nos. Q7 to Q28) are without watermark. Twice in each sheet of 100 stamps they have one of three watermarks: (1) A winged wheel and "Chemins de Fer de l'Etat Belge", (2) Coat of Arms of Belgium and "Royaume de Belgique", (3) Larger Coat of Arms, without inscription.

1882–94 *Perf. 15x14½.*

No.	Type	Description	Unused	Used
Q7	PP2	10c brown ('86)	12.50	60
Q8	"	15c gray ('94)	7.50	7.00
Q9	"	20c blue ('86)	40.00	2.50
		a. 20c ultra ('90)	40.00	2.50
Q10	"	25c yel. green ('91)	40.00	3.00
		a. 25c bl. green ('87)	50.00	3.00
Q11	"	50c carmine	40.00	25
Q12	"	80c brownish buff	40.00	40
Q13	"	80c lemon	50.00	1.75
Q14	"	1fr lavender	200.00	2.00
Q15	"	2fr yel. buff ('94)	175.00	40.00

Counterfeits exist.

PP3

Name of engraver below frame.

1895–97

Numerals in Black, except 1fr, 2fr.

No.	Type	Description	Unused	Used
Q16	PP3	10c red brown ('96)	6.25	25
Q17	"	15c gray	5.00	3.75
Q18	"	20c blue	14.00	60
Q19	"	25c green	14.00	80
Q20	"	50c carmine	16.00	20
Q21	"	60c violet ('96)	30.00	25
Q22	"	80c olive yel. ('96)	22.50	25
Q23	"	1fr lilac brown	100.00	70
Q24	"	2fr yel. buff ('97)	110.00	2.00

Counterfeits exist.

1902 Numerals in Black.

No.	Type	Description	Unused	Used
Q25	PP3	30c orange	17.50	1.00
Q26	"	40c green	19.00	1.00
Q27	"	70c blue	30.00	25
		a. Numerals omitted	400.00	
Q28	"	90c red	40.00	45

Winged Wheel
PP4

Without engraver's name.

1902–14 *Perf. 15*

No.	Type	Description	Unused	Used
Q29	PP3	10c yel. brown & slate	10	10
Q30	"	15c slate & violet	15	15
Q31	"	20c ultra. & yel. brn.	15	10
Q32	"	25c yellow green & red	25	15
Q33	"	30c orange & bl. green	15	10
Q34	"	35c bistre & blue green ('12)	15	15
Q35	"	40c blue green & vio.	25	15
Q36	"	50c pale rose & violet	10	10
Q37	"	55c lilac brown & ultra. ('14)	25	25
Q38	"	60c violet & red	10	10
Q39	"	70c blue & red	10	10
Q40	"	80c lemon & violet brown	10	10
Q41	"	90c red & yel. green	10	10
Q42	PP4	1fr violet brown & orange	10	10
Q43	"	1.10fr rose & black ('06)	10	10
Q44	"	2fr ocher & bl. green	15	10
Q45	"	3fr blk. & ultramarine	20	10
Q46	"	4fr yellow green & red ('13)	1.10	70
Q47	"	5fr orange & blue green ('13)	80	80
Q48	"	10fr olive yellow & brown violet ('13)	60	60
		Nos. Q29-Q48 (20)	5.00	4.15

Exist imperforate.

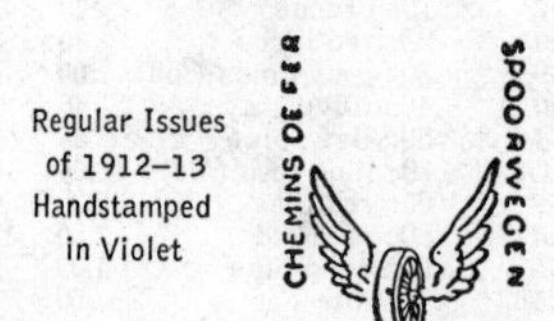

Regular Issues of 1912–13 Handstamped in Violet

1915 *Perf. 14*

No.	Type	Description	Unused	Used
Q49	A42	5c green	100.00	
Q50	A43	10c red	*500.00*	
Q51	A45	10c red	100.00	
		a. With engraver's name	275.00	
Q52	A43	20c olive green	*750.00*	
Q53	A45	20c olive green	*775.00*	
		a. With engraver's name	275.00	
Q54	"	25c ultramarine	115.00	
		a. With engraver's name	275.00	
Q55	A43	35c bis. brown	165.00	
Q55A	"	40c green	*1100.00*	
Q56	A45	40c green	115.00	
Q57	A43	50c gray	125.00	
Q58	"	1fr orange	175.00	
Q59	"	2fr violet	*900.00*	
Q60	A44	5fr plum	*1750.00*	

Excellent forgeries of this overprint exist.

PP5

Locomotive
PP6

1916 Lithographed *Perf. 13½*

No.	Type	Description	Unused	Used
Q61	PP5	10c pale blue	75	12
Q62	"	15c olive green	1.00	35
Q63	"	20c red	1.50	35
Q64	"	25c light brown	1.50	40
Q65	"	30c lilac	1.20	15
Q66	"	35c gray	1.00	15
Q67	"	40c orange yellow	2.25	90
Q68	"	50c bistre	1.85	15
Q69	"	55c brown	2.10	1.65
Q70	PP5	60c gray violet	1.75	15
Q71	"	70c green	1.35	15
Q72	"	80c red brown	1.65	15
Q73	"	90c blue	1.75	15
Q74	PP6	1fr gray	1.35	15
Q75	"	1.10fr ultramarine (*Franken*)	16.00	12.50
Q76	"	2fr red	17.50	20
Q77	"	3fr violet	17.50	20
Q78	"	4fr emerald	25.00	70
Q79	"	5fr brown	27.50	85
Q80	"	10fr orange	27.50	65
		Nos. Q61-Q80 (20)	152.00	20.07

Type of 1916 Inscribed "FRANK" instead of "FRANKEN."

1920

No.	Type	Description	Unused	Used
Q81	PP6	1.10fr ultramarine	2.10	20

PP7

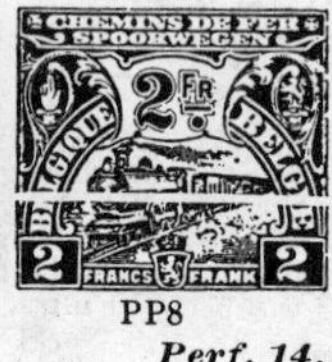

PP8

1920 *Perf. 14.*

No.	Type	Description	Unused	Used
Q82	PP7	10c blue green	1.25	20
Q83	"	15c olive green	1.65	60
Q84	"	20c red	1.50	20
Q85	"	25c gray brown	2.10	40
Q86	"	30c red violet	13.50	11.00
Q87	"	40c pale orange	8.00	40
Q88	"	50c bistre	5.25	25
Q89	"	55c pale brown	4.00	2.00
Q90	"	60c dark violet	7.50	35
Q91	"	70c green	13.50	35
Q92	"	80c red brown	32.50	40
Q93	"	90c dull blue	7.50	25
Q94	PP8	1fr gray	55.00	85
Q95	"	1.10fr ultramarine	14.00	85
Q96	"	1.20fr dark green	5.25	15
Q97	"	1.40fr black brown	5.25	15
Q98	"	2fr vermilion	60.00	30
Q99	"	3fr red violet	65.00	30
Q100	"	4fr yellow green	65.00	60
Q101	"	5fr bistre brown	85.00	50
Q102	"	10fr brown orange	65.00	25
		Nos. Q82-Q102 (21)	517.75	20.35

PP9

PP10

Types PP7 and PP9 differ in the position of the wheel and the tablet above it.

Types PP8 and PP10 differ in the bars below "FR".

There are many other variations in the designs.

1920-21 Typographed.

No.	Type	Description	Unused	Used
Q103	PP9	10c carmine	25	10
Q104	"	15c yellow green	12	10
Q105	"	20c blue green	60	10
Q106	"	25c ultramarine	60	12
Q107	"	30c chocolate	75	12
Q108	"	35c orange brown	75	16
Q109	"	40c orange	75	10
Q110	"	50c rose	75	10
Q111	"	55c yellow ('21)	1.75	1.50
Q112	"	60c dull rose	75	10
Q113	"	70c emerald	2.50	12
Q114	"	80c violet	2.00	10
Q115	"	90c lemon	13.00	9.50
Q116	"	90c claret	5.00	15
Q117	PP10	1fr buff	5.00	15
Q118	"	1fr red brown	5.00	10
Q119	"	1.10fr ultramarine	1.50	15
Q120	PP10	1.20fr orange	2.10	10
Q121	"	1.40fr yellow	10.00	60
Q122	"	1.60fr turq. blue	18.00	35
Q123	"	1.60fr emerald	45.00	35
Q124	"	2fr pale rose	21.00	18
Q125	"	3fr deep rose	21.00	18
Q126	"	4fr emerald	21.00	18
Q127	"	5fr lt. violet	17.50	18
Q128	"	10fr lemon	90.00	2.25
Q129	"	10fr dk. brown	17.50	20
Q130	"	15fr deep rose ('21)	17.50	20
Q131	"	20fr dark blue ('21)	210.00	1.25
		Nos. Q103-Q131 (29)	531.67	18.97

PP11

1922 Engraved. *Perf. 11½.*

No.	Type	Description	Unused	Used
Q132	PP11	2fr black	3.50	12
Q133	"	3fr brown	47.50	20
Q134	"	4fr green	10.00	12
Q135	"	5fr claret	10.00	12
Q136	"	10fr yel. brown	10.00	12
Q137	"	15fr rose red	11.00	25
Q138	"	20fr blue	65.00	25
		Nos. Q132-Q138 (7)	157.00	1.18

PP12

PP13

Perf. 14x13½, 13½x14.

1923–40 Typographed

No.	Type	Description	Unused	Used
Q139	PP12	5c red brown	25	20
Q140	"	10c vermilion	5	5
Q141	"	15c ultramarine	20	20
Q142	"	20c turq. blue	10	5
Q143	"	30c brown violet ('27)	8	5
Q144	"	40c olive green	8	5
Q145	"	50c magenta ('27)	8	5
Q146	"	60c orange	15	5
Q147	"	70c dark brown ('24)	8	5
Q148	"	80c violet	12	8
Q149	"	90c slate ('27)	1.75	15
Q150	PP13	1fr ultramarine	25	5
Q151	"	1fr bright blue ('28)	55	8
Q152	"	1.10fr orange	4.00	20
Q153	"	1.50fr turq. blue	4.00	20
Q154	"	1.70fr deep brown ('31)	75	20
Q155	"	1.80fr claret	5.25	35
Q156	"	2fr olive green ('24)	40	5
Q157	"	2.10fr gray green	13.50	35
Q158	"	2.40fr deep violet	6.00	55
Q159	"	2.70fr gray ('24)	22.50	20
Q160	"	3fr orange red	60	5
Q161	"	3.30fr brown ('24)	25.00	50
Q162	"	4fr rose ('24)	60	5
Q163	"	5fr violet ('24)	1.00	5
Q163A	"	5fr brown violet ('40)	45	45

No.	Type	Description	Unused	Used
Q164	PP13	6fr bistre brown ('27)	60	5
Q165	"	7fr orange ('27)	1.25	5
Q166	"	8fr deep brown ('27)	1.10	5
Q167	"	9fr red vio. ('27)	3.75	15
Q168	"	10fr blue green ('27)	1.50	5
Q168A	"	10fr black ('40)	2.75	2.75
Q169	"	20fr magenta ('27)	2.00	5
Q170	"	30fr turquoise green ('31)	8.00	15
Q171	"	40fr gray ('31)	60.00	45
Q172	"	50fr bistre ('27)	12.50	15
		Nos. Q139-Q172 (36)	181.24	8.21

See also Nos. Q239-Q262.

Stamps of this and later issues overprinted "Bagages Reisgod" are revenues used on baggage.

PP14

1924 Green Surcharge.

No.	Type	Description	Unused	Used
Q173	PP14	2.30fr on 2.40fr violet	4.25	45
		a. Inverted surcharge	150.00	

Type of Regular Issue of 1926-27 Overprinted

1928 *Perf. 14.*

No.	Type	Description	Unused	Used
Q174	A61	4fr buff	5.50	60
Q175	"	5fr bistre	5.50	75

Central P.O., Brussels

PP15

1929-30 Engraved *Perf. 11½*

No.	Type	Description	Unused	Used
Q176	PP15	3fr black brown	1.85	12
Q177	"	4fr gray	1.85	8
Q178	"	5fr carmine	1.85	10
Q179	"	6fr violet brown ('30)	32.50	25.00

No. Q179 Surcharged in Blue

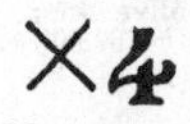

1933

No.	Type	Description	Unused	Used
Q180	PP15	4(fr) on 6fr violet brown	35.00	25

Modern Locomotive

PP16

1934 Photogravure *Perf. 13½x14*

No.	Type	Description	Unused	Used
Q181	PP16	3fr dark green	5.00	1.75
Q182	"	4fr red violet	2.50	5
Q183	"	5fr deep rose	5.00	10

Modern Railroad Train

PP17

Old Railroad Train

PP18

Perf. 14x13½, 13½x14.

1935 Engraved.

No.	Type	Description	Unused	Used
Q184	PP17	10c rose carmine	40	10
Q185	"	20c violet	40	10
Q186	"	30c black brown	60	25
Q187	"	40c dark blue	65	10
Q188	"	50c orange red	65	10
Q189	"	60c green	1.00	10
Q190	"	70c ultramarine	1.25	10
Q191	"	80c olive black	1.00	12
Q192	"	90c rose lake	1.25	45
Q193	PP18	1fr brown violet	1.25	10
Q194	"	2fr gray black	2.75	10
Q195	"	3fr red orange	3.25	10
Q196	"	4fr violet brown	3.50	10
Q197	"	5fr plum	4.00	10
Q198	"	6fr deep green	4.50	10
Q199	"	7fr deep violet	5.25	10
Q200	"	8fr olive black	7.00	10
Q201	"	9fr dark blue	7.50	10
Q202	"	10fr carmine lake	7.50	10
Q203	"	20fr green	27.50	10
Q204	"	30fr violet	110.00	75
Q205	"	40fr black brown	110.00	1.75
Q206	"	50fr rose carmine	110.00	1.00
Q207	"	100fr ultramarine	200.00	25.00
		Nos. Q184-Q207 (24)	611.20	31.02

Centenary of Belgian State Railway.

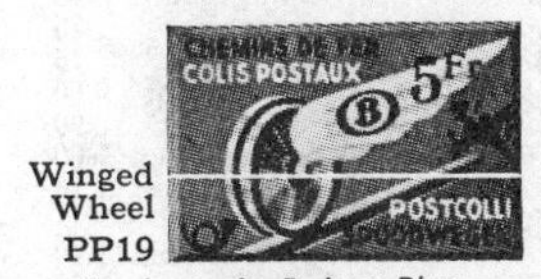

Winged Wheel

PP19

Surcharge in Red or Blue.

1938 Photogravure *Perf. 13½*

No.	Type	Description	Unused	Used
Q208	PP19	5fr on 3.50fr dark green (R)	11.50	40
Q209	"	5fr on 4.50fr rose violet (Bl)	25	5
Q210	"	6fr on 5.50fr copper red (Bl)	35	10
		a. Half used as 3fr on piece		75

See also Nos. MQ1, Q297-Q299.

Symbolizing Unity Achieved Through Railroads

PP20

1939 Engraved *Perf. 13½x14*

No.	Type	Description	Unused	Used
Q211	PP20	20c reddish brn.	4.75	4.75
Q212	"	50c violet blue	4.75	4.75
Q213	"	2fr rose red	4.75	4.75
Q214	"	9fr slate green	4.75	4.75
Q215	"	10fr dark violet	4.75	4.75
		Nos. Q211-Q215 (5)	23.75	23.75

Issued in commemoration of the Railroad Exposition and Congress held at Brussels.

Parcel Post Stamps of 1925-27 Overprinted in Blue or Carmine

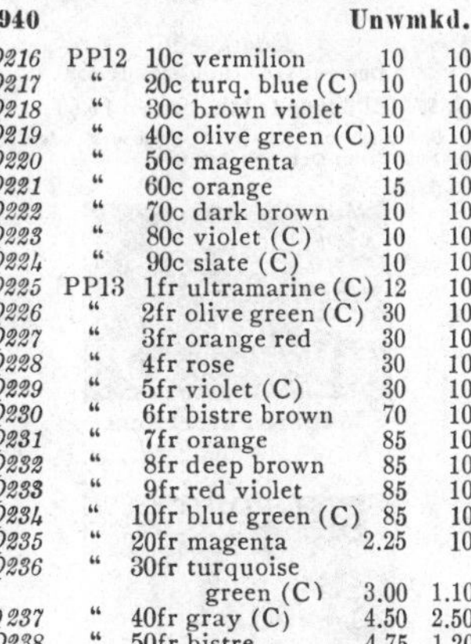

Perf. 14½x14, 14x14½.

1940 Unwmkd.

No.	Type	Description	Unused	Used
Q216	PP12	10c vermilion	10	10
Q217	"	20c turq. blue (C)	10	10
Q218	"	30c brown violet	10	10
Q219	"	40c olive green (C)	10	10
Q220	"	50c magenta	10	10
Q221	"	60c orange	15	10
Q222	"	70c dark brown	10	10
Q223	"	80c violet (C)	10	10
Q224	"	90c slate (C)	10	10
Q225	PP13	1fr ultramarine (C)	12	10
Q226	"	2fr olive green (C)	30	10
Q227	"	3fr orange red	30	10
Q228	"	4fr rose	30	10
Q229	"	5fr violet (C)	30	10
Q230	"	6fr bistre brown	70	10
Q231	"	7fr orange	85	10
Q232	"	8fr deep brown	85	10
Q233	"	9fr red violet	85	10
Q234	"	10fr blue green (C)	85	10
Q235	"	20fr magenta	2.25	10
Q236	"	30fr turquoise green (C)	3.00	1.10
Q237	"	40fr gray (C)	4.50	2.50
Q238	"	50fr bistre	4.75	1.20
		Nos. Q216-Q238 (23)	20.87	6.80

1941 Types of 1923-40.

No.	Type	Description	Unused	Used
Q239	PP12	10c dull olive	15	5
Q240	"	20c light violet	15	5
Q241	"	30c fawn	15	5
Q242	"	40c dull blue	15	15
Q243	"	50c light green	15	5
Q244	"	60c gray	15	10
Q245	"	70c chalky green	15	15
Q246	"	80c orange	25	15
Q247	"	90c rose lilac	25	15
Q248	PP13	1fr lt. yel. green	25	5
Q249	"	2fr violet brown	40	5
Q250	"	3fr slate	45	5
Q251	"	4fr dull olive	60	5
Q252	"	5fr rose lilac	75	5
Q253	"	5fr black	1.00	30
Q254	"	6fr orange verm.	1.00	5
Q255	"	7fr lilac	1.00	5
Q256	"	8fr chalky green	1.00	5
Q257	"	9fr blue	1.25	5
Q258	"	10fr rose lilac	1.25	5
Q259	"	20fr milky blue	3.00	5
Q260	"	30fr orange	6.25	35
Q261	"	40fr rose	7.25	30
Q262	"	50fr brt. red vio.	9.50	15
		Nos. Q239-Q262 (24)	36.50	2.55

Adjusting Tie Plates

PP21

Engineer at Throttle

PP22

Freight Station Interior

PP23

Signal and Electric Train

PP24

1942 Engraved *Perf. 14x13½*

No.	Type	Description	Unused	Used
Q263	PP21	9.20fr red orange	65	65
Q264	PP22	12.30fr deep green	65	65
Q265	PP23	14.30fr dark car.	65	65

Perf. 11½.

No.	Type	Description	Unused	Used
Q266	PP24	100fr ultra.	13.50	13.50

Engineer at Throttle

PP25

Adjusting Tie Plates

PP26

Freight Station Interior

PP27

1945-46 Photogravure Unwmkd.

Nos. Q268, Q270, Q272, Q274, Q287 and Q289 are inscribed "Belgique-Belgie", Nos. Q277, Q279, Q281 and Q283 are inscribed "Belgie-Belgique".

No.	Type	Description	Unused	Used
Q267	PP25	10c olive black ('46)	5	4
Q268	"	20c deep violet	5	4
Q269	"	30c chestnut brown ('46)	15	10
Q270	"	40c deep blue ('46)	6	10
Q271	"	50c peacock green	5	6
Q272	"	60c black ('46)	10	15
Q273	"	70c emerald ('46)	25	25
Q274	"	80c orange	25	25
Q275	"	90c brn. vio. ('46)	25	25
Q276	PP26	1fr blue green ('46)	8	3
Q277	"	2fr black brown	8	3
Q278	"	3fr greenish black ('46)	1.65	18
Q279	"	4fr dark blue	12	4
Q280	"	5fr sepia	15	8
Q281	"	6fr dark olive green ('46)	1.75	18
Q282	"	7fr dk. vio. ('46)	30	4
Q283	"	8fr red orange	25	4
Q284	"	9fr deep blue ('46)	60	7
Q285	PP27	10fr dk. red ('46)	3.00	4
Q286	"	10fr sepia ('46)	1.65	18
Q287	"	20fr dark yellow green ('46)	75	4
Q288	"	30fr deep violet	1.10	4
Q289	"	40fr rose pink	75	5
Q290	"	50fr bright blue ('46)	12.50	8
		Nos. Q267-Q290 (24)	25.94	2.36

Mercury

PP28

1945-46 *Perf. 13½x13*

No.	Type	Description	Unused	Used
Q291	PP28	3fr emerald ('46)	30	15
Q292	"	5fr ultramarine	12	10
Q293	"	6fr red	15	10

Inscribed "Belgique-Belgie".

No.	Type	Description	Unused	Used
Q294	PP28	3fr emerald ('46)	30	15
Q295	"	5fr ultramarine	12	10
Q296	"	6fr red	15	10
		Nos. Q291-Q296 (6)	1.14	70

Winged Wheel Type of 1938.
Carmine Surcharge.

1946 *Perf. 13½x14*

Q297 PP19 8fr on 5.50fr brown 1.00 20
Q298 " 10fr on 5.50fr dark blue 1.00 20
Q299 " 12fr on 5.50fr violet 1.00 20

Railway Crossing
PP29

1947 **Engraved** *Perf. 12½*

Q300 PP29 100fr dk. green 11.50 25

Crossbowman with Train
PP30

1947 **Photogravure** *Perf. 11½*

Q301 PP30 8fr dk. olive brown 1.50 20
Q302 " 10fr gray & blue 1.50 20
Q303 " 12fr dark violet 1.50 20

Surcharged with
New Value and Bars in Carmine.

1948

Q304 PP30 9fr on 8fr dark olive brn. 1.50 20
Q305 " 11fr on 10fr gray & blue 1.50 20
Q306 " 13.50fr on 12fr dark violet 1.50 20

Delivery of Parcel
PP31

1948

Q307 PP31 9fr chocolate 6.00 10
Q308 " 11fr brn. carmine 6.00 10
Q309 " 13.50fr gray 8.00 10

Locomotive of 1835
PP32

Various Locomotives.
Lathe Work in Frame Differs.

1949 **Engraved** *Perf. 12½*

Q310 PP32 ½fr dark brown 30 8
Q311 " 1fr carmine rose 45 8
Q312 " 2fr dp. ultra. 1.25 8
Q313 " 3fr deep magenta 65 8
Q314 " 4fr blue green 1.65 8
Q315 " 5fr orange red 1.65 8
Q316 " 6fr brown violet 1.75 8
Q317 " 7fr yellow green 2.50 8
Q318 " 8fr greenish blue 2.50 8
Q319 " 9fr yellow brown 3.50 8
Q320 " 10fr citron 4.00 8
Q321 " 20fr orange 5.50 8
Q322 " 30fr blue 11.00 8
Q323 " 40fr lilac rose 14.00 12
Q324 " 50fr violet 17.50 12
Q325 PP32 100fr red 32.50 10
Nos. Q310-Q325 (16) 100.70 1.38

See also No. Q337.

Engraved; Center Typographed.

Q326 PP32 10fr carmine rose & black 4.50 60

1949 **Engraved**

Design: Electric locomotive.

Q327 PP32 60fr blk. brown 17.50 30

Opening of Charleroi-Brussels electric railway line, Oct. 15, 1949.

Mailing Parcel Post
PP33

Sorting
PP34

Loading
PP35

1950-52 *Perf. 12, 12½*

Q328 PP33 11fr red orange 4.75 20
Q329 " 12fr red violet ('51) 12.00 1.75
Q330 PP34 13fr dk. bl. grn. 4.75 20
Q331 " 15fr ultra. ('51) 10.00 50
Q332 PP35 16fr gray 4.75 20
Q333 PP33 17fr brown ('52) 5.75 15
Q334 PP35 18fr brt. carmine ('51) 10.00 50
Q335 " 20fr brn. orange ('52) 5.75 15
Nos. Q328-Q335 (8) 57.75 3.65

Mercury and Winged Wheel
PP36

1951

Q336 PP36 25fr dark blue 9.00 6.75

Issued to commemorate the 25th anniversary of the founding of the National Society of Belgian Railroads.

Type of 1949.

1952 *Perf. 11½* **Unwmkd.**

Design: Electric locomotive.

Q337 PP32 300fr red violet 70.00 55

Nos. Q331, Q328 and Q334
Surcharged with New Value and "X"
in Red, Blue or Green.

1953 *Perf. 12.*

Q338 PP34 13fr on 15fr ultra. (R) 37.50 50
Q339 PP33 17fr on 11fr red orange (Bl) 22.50 40
Q340 PP35 20fr on 18fr brt. carmine (G) 16.00 1.00

Electric Train, 1952
PP37

1953 **Engraved**

Q341 PP37 200fr dark yellow green & violet brn. 160.00 5.00
Q342 " 200fr dark grn. 150.00 1.35

No. Q341 was issued to commemorate the opening of the railway link connecting Brussels North and South Stations, Oct. 4, 1952.

New North Station, Brussels
PP38

Chapelle Station, Brussels—PP39

Designs: No. Q348, 15fr, Congress Station. 10fr, 20fr, 30fr, 40fr, 50fr, South Station. 100fr, 200fr, 300fr, Central Station.

1953-57 *Perf. 11½* **Unwmkd.**

Q343 PP38 1fr bistre 25 3
Q344 " 2fr slate 35 3
Q345 " 3fr blue green 45 3
Q346 " 4fr orange 75 3
Q347 " 5fr red brown 75 3
Q348 " 5fr dk. red brn. 6.00 18
Q349 " 6fr rose violet 90 4
Q350 " 7fr bright green 90 4
Q351 " 8fr rose red 1.10 4
Q352 " 9fr bright greenish blue 1.10 4
Q353 " 10fr light green 1.50 4
Q354 " 15fr dull red 7.00 16
Q355 " 20fr blue 2.50 3
Q356 " 30fr purple 4.25 3
Q357 " 40fr brt. purple 5.50 3
Q358 " 50fr lilac rose 7.00 3
Q359 PP39 60fr brt. purple 10.00 15
Q360 " 80fr brn. violet 15.00 12
Q361 " 100fr emerald 13.00 16
Q361A " 200fr brt. vio. bl. 35.00 80
Q361B " 300fr lilac rose 50.00 80
Nos. Q343-Q361B (21) 163.30 2.84

Issue dates: No. Q347, 20fr and 30fr, 1953; 80fr, 1955; 200fr, 1956; 300fr, 1957. Rest of set, 1954.

See Nos. Q407, Q431-Q432.

Electric Train
PP40

Mercury and Winged Wheel
PP41

1954

Q362 PP40 13fr chocolate 12.00 10
Q363 " 18fr dark blue 12.00 8
Q364 " 21fr lilac rose 12.00 35

Nos. Q362-Q364 Surcharged with
New Value and "X" in Blue, Red
or Green.

1956

Q365 PP40 14fr on 13fr chocolate (B) 10.00 15
Q366 " 19fr on 18fr dark blue (R) 10.00 6
Q367 " 22fr on 21fr lilac rose (G) 10.00 20

1957 **Engraved.** *Perf. 11½*

Q368 PP41 14fr bright green 9.00 20
Q369 " 19fr olive gray 9.00 20
Q370 " 22fr carmine rose 9.00 40

Nos. Q369-Q370 Surcharged with
New Value and "X" in Pink or Green.

1959

Q371 PP41 20fr on 19fr olive gray (P) 27.50 30
Q372 " 20fr on 22fr car. rose (G) 27.50 75

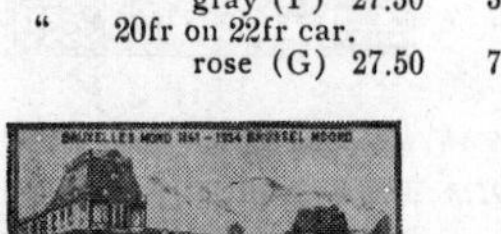

Old North Station, Brussels
PP42

1959 **Engraved** *Perf. 11½*

Q373 PP42 20fr olive green 21.00 10

See also No. Q381.

Diesel and Electric Locomotives and Association Emblem
PP43

1960 *Perf. 11½* **Unwmkd.**

Q374 PP43 20fr red 62.50 50.00
Q375 " 50fr dark blue 62.50 50.00
Q376 " 60fr red lilac 62.50 50.00
Q377 " 70fr emerald 62.50 50.00

Issued to commemorate the 75th anniversary of the International Association of Railway Congresses.

No. Q373 Surcharged with New Value
and "X" in Red.

1961

Q378 PP42 24fr on 20fr olive green 60.00 12

South Station, Brussels
PP44

1962 *Perf. 11½* **Unwmkd.**

Q379 PP44 24fr dull red 7.25 15

No. Q379 Surcharged with New Value
and "X" in Light Green

1963

Q380 PP44 26fr on 24fr dull red 8.00 12

Type of 1959

Design: 26fr, Central Station, Antwerp.

1963 Engraved *Perf. 11½*

Q381 PP42 26fr blue 7.50 60

No. Q381 Surcharged in Red

1964, Apr. 20

Q382 PP42 28fr on 26fr blue 7.50 12

Type of 1959.

Design: 28fr, St. Peter's Station, Ghent.

1965 Engraved *Perf. 11½*

Q383 PP42 28fr red lilac 7.50 45

Nos. Q383 Surcharged with New Value and "X" in Green

1966

Q384 PP42 35fr on 28fr red lilac 7.50 12

Arlon Railroad Station PP45

Engraved

1967, Aug. *Perf. 11½* Unwmkd.

Q385 PP45 25fr bister 14.00 10
Q386 " 30fr blue green 3.75 10
Q387 " 35fr deep blue 4.50 30

Electric Train PP46

Designs: 2fr, 3fr, 4fr, 5fr, 6fr, 7fr, 8fr, 9fr, like 1fr. 10fr, 20fr, 30fr, 40fr, Train going right. 50fr, 60fr, 70fr, 80fr, 90fr, Train going left. 100fr, 200fr, 300fr, Diesel train.

1968–73 Engraved *Perf. 11½*

Q388 PP46 1fr olive bister 5 4
Q389 " 2fr slate 10 5
Q390 " 3fr blue green 15 4
Q391 " 4fr orange 25 4
Q392 " 5fr brown 30 4
Q393 " 6fr plum 40 4
Q394 " 7fr bright green 45 4
Q395 " 8fr carmine 50 4
Q396 " 9fr blue 55 4
Q397 " 10fr green 65 4
Q398 " 20fr dark blue 1.25 4
Q399 " 30fr dark purple 2.00 4
Q400 " 40fr bright lilac 2.50 4
Q401 " 50fr bright pink 3.25 8
Q402 " 60fr bright violet 4.00 8
Q402A " 70fr dp. bis. ('73) 4.50 12
Q403 " 80fr dark brown 5.25 15
Q403A " 90fr yellow green ('73) 6.00 20
Q404 " 100fr emerald 6.50 4
Q405 " 200fr violet blue 13.00 1.10
Q406 " 300fr lilac rose 20.00 2.60
Nos. Q388–Q406 (21) 71.65 4.90

Types of 1953–68

Designs: 10fr, Congress Station, Brussels. 40fr, Arlon Station. 500fr, Electric train going left.

1968, June Engraved *Perf. 11½*

Q407 PP38 10fr gray 65 12
Q408 PP45 40fr vermilion 20.00 12
Q409 PP46 500fr yellow 32.50 1.25

Nos. Q385, Q387 and Q408 Surcharged with New Value and "X"

1970, Dec.

Q410 PP45 37fr on 25fr bis. 70.00
Q411 " 48fr on 35fr deep blue 14.00
Q412 " 53fr on 40fr vermilion 14.00

Ostend Station PP47

1971, March Engraved *Perf. 11½*

Q413 PP47 32fr bister & blk. 1.60 65
Q414 " 37fr gray & blk. 1.85 1.85
Q415 " 42fr blue & blk. 2.10 65
Q416 " 44fr bright rose & black 2.25 65
Q417 " 46fr violet & blk. 2.25 30
Q418 " 50fr brick red & black 2.50 30
Q419 " 52fr sepia & blk. 2.60 2.60
Q420 " 54fr yellow green & black 2.75 65
Q421 " 61fr greenish blue & black 3.00 1.00
Nos. Q413–Q421 (9) 20.90 8.65

Nos. Q413–Q416, Q419–Q421 Surcharged wth New Value and "X"

1971, Dec. 15

Denomination in Black

Q422 PP47 34fr on 32fr bister 1.70 65
Q423 " 40fr on 37fr gray 2.00 65
Q424 " 47fr on 44fr brt. rose 2.35 65
Q425 " 53fr on 42 fr blue 2.65 30
Q426 " 56fr on 52fr sepia 2.75 65
Q427 " 59fr on 54fr yel. green 3.00 65
Q428 " 66fr on 61fr greenish blue 3.25 30
Nos. Q422–Q428 (7) 17.70 3.85

Track, Underpinning of Railroad Car and Emblems—PP48

1972, Mar. Photogravure

Q429 PP48 100fr emerald, red & black 18.00 2.25

Centenary of International Railroad Union.

Congress Emblem PP49 100F

1974, Apr. Photo. *Perf. 11½*

Q430 PP49 100fr yellow, black & red 14.00 1.25

4th International Symposium on Railroad Cybernetics, Washington, D.C., Apr. 1974.

Type of 1953–1957

1975, June 1 Engr. *Perf. 11½*

Q431 PP38 20fr emerald 1.25
Q432 " 50fr blue 3.25

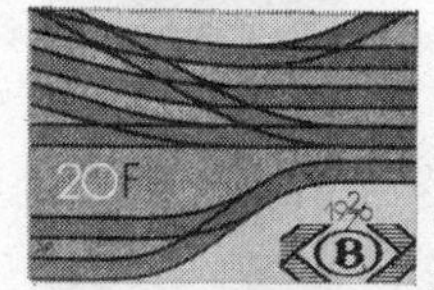

Railroad Tracks PP50

1976, June 10 Photo. *Perf. 11½*

Q433 PP50 20fr ultra. & multi. 1.25
Q434 " 50fr brt. green & multi. 3.25
Q435 " 100fr dp. org. & multi. 6.50
Q436 " 150fr brt. lilac & multi. 10.00

Railroad Station PP51

1977 Photo. *Perf. 11½*

Q437 PP51 1000fr multi. 50.00

OCCUPATION STAMPS.

Issued under German Occupation.

German Stamps of 1906-11 Surcharged

Belgien
3 Centimes
a

* 1Fr.25C. *

Belgien
b

Wmkd. Lozenges. (125)

1914-15 *Perf. 14, 14½.*

N1 A16 (*a*) 3c on 3pf brown 10 10
N2 " (") 5c on 5pf green 12 8
N3 " (") 10c on 10pf car. 10 8
N4 " (") 25c on 20pf ultramarine 10 10
N5 " (") 50c on 40pf lake & black 2.75 30
N6 " (") 75c on 60pf magenta 1.00 30
N7 " (") 1fr on 80pf lake & blk., *rose* 1.75 1.00
N8 A17 (*b*) 1fr 25c on 1m carmine 16.50 14.00
N9 A21 (") 2fr 50c on 2m gray blue 16.50 14.00
Nos. N1–N9 (9) 38.92 29.96

German Stamps of 1906-18 Surcharged

Belgien
3 Cent.
c

Belgien
1F.
d

* 1F.25Cent. *

Belgien
e

1916–18

N10 A22 (*c*) 2c on 2pf drab 18 10
N11 A16 (") 3c on 3pf brown 6 6
N12 " (") 5c on 5pf green 6 6
N13 A22 (") 8c on 7½pf orange 10 6
N14 A16 (") 10c on 10pf car. 10 6
N15 A22 (") 15c on 15pf yellow brown 25 6
N16 " (") 15c on 15pf dark violet 6 6
N17 A16 (") 20c on 25pf orange & black, *yellow* 15 6
N18 " (") 25c on 20pf ultra. 20 6
a. 25c on 20pf blue 15 6
N19 " (") 40c on 30pf orange & black, *buff* 18 6
N20 " (") 50c on 40pf lake & black 25 15
N21 " (") 75c on 60pf magenta 2.50 2.00
N22 " (*d*) 1f on 80pf lake & blk., *rose* 2.50 2.00
N23 A17 (*e*) 1f 25c on 1m carmine 3.75 2.00
N24 A21 (") 2f 50c on 2m gray blue 37.50 25.00
a. 2f50c on 1m carmine (error) *3500.00*
N25 A20 (") 6f 25c on 5m slate & carmine 45.00 42.50
Nos. N10–N25 (16) 92.84 74.29

A similar series of stamps without "Belgien" was used in parts of Belgium and France while occupied by German forces. See France Nos. N15–N26.

BENADIR

(See Vol. IV, Somalia.)

BENIN

(bĕ·nēn′)

French Colony

LOCATION—On the western coast of Africa, bordering on the Gulf of Guinea.

GOVT.—French Possession.

AREA—8,627 sq. mi.

POP.—493,000 (approx.).

CAPITAL—Benin.

In 1895 the French possessions known as Benin were incorporated into the colony of Dahomey and postage stamps of Dahomey superseded those of Benin. Dahomey took the name Benin when it became a republic in 1975.

100 Centimes = 1 Franc

Handstamped on Stamps of French Colonies **BÉNIN**

Black Overprint.

1892 *Perf. 14x13½.* **Unwmkd.**

1 A9 1c *bluish* 70.00 60.00
2 " 2c brown, *buff* 55.00 50.00
3 " 4c claret, *lavender* 18.50 18.50
4 " 5c green, *greenish* 7.00 5.00
5 " 10c *lavender* 30.00 20.00
6 " 15c blue 11.00 5.00
7 " 20c red, *green* 100.00 90.00
8 " 25c *rose* 35.00 18.00
9 " 30c brn., *yellowish* 70.00 60.00
10 " 35c *orange* 65.00 55.00
11 " 40c red, *straw* 60.00 55.00
12 " 75c carmine, *rose* 135.00 125.00
13 " 1f bronze green, *straw* 140.00 135.00

Red Overprint.

14 A9 15c blue 32.50 20.00

Blue Overprint.

15 A9 5c green, *greenish* 750.00 200.00
15A " 15c blue 750.00 185.00

Nos. 1–13 all exist with overprint inverted, and several with it double. These sell for slightly more than normal stamps. The overprints of Nos. 1–15A are of four types, three without accent mark on "E." They exist diagonal.

Counterfeits exist of Nos. 1–19.

Additional Surcharge Red or Black **40**

1892

16 A9 01c on 5c green, *greenish* 100.00 75.00
17 " 40c on 15c blue 80.00 27.50
18 " 75c on 15c blue 300.00 200.00
19 " 75c on 15c blue (Bk) 1000.00 800.00

Navigation and Commerce
A3 A4

1893 **Typographed.**

Name of Colony in Blue or Carmine.

20 A3 1c *bluish* 1.25 1.00
21 " 2c brown, *buff* 1.65 1.65
22 " 4c claret, *lavender* 1.65 1.00
23 " 5c green, *greenish* 2.00 1.65
24 " 10c *lavender* 2.00 1.85
25 " 15c blue, quadrille paper 10.00 6.00
26 " 20c red, *green* 6.00 3.25
27 A3 25c *rose* 13.50 8.00
28 " 30c brown, *bistre* 7.00 6.00
29 " 40c red, *straw* 1.40 1.25
30 " 50c carmine, *rose* 1.25 1.25
31 " 75c violet, *orange* 3.00 2.35
32 " 1fr bronze green, *straw* 20.00 15.00
Nos. 20-32 (13) 70.70 50.25

1894

33 A4 1c *bluish* 1.00 75
34 " 2c brown, *buff* 1.00 75
35 " 4c claret, *lavender* 1.00 75
36 " 5c green, *greenish* 1.00 60
37 " 10c *lavender* 1.85 1.50
38 " 15c blue, quadrille paper 3.00 1.00
39 " 20c red, *green* 3.00 2.00
40 " 25c *rose* 3.75 1.50
41 " 30c brown, *bistre* 2.00 1.50
42 " 40c red, *straw* 6.50 3.00
43 " 50c carmine, *rose* 8.00 5.00
44 " 75c violet, *orange* 4.50 3.00
45 " 1fr bronze green, *straw* 1.00 1.00
Nos. 33-45 (13) 37.60 22.35

People's Republic

LOCATION—West Coast of Africa.

GOVT.—Republic.

AREA—43,483 sq. mi.

POP.—3,290,000 (est. 1977).

CAPITAL—Porto-Novo.

The Republic of Dahomey proclaimed itself the People's Republic of Benin on Nov. 30, 1975. See Dahomey for stamps issued before then.

Allamanda Cathartica A83 — Flag Bearers, Arms of Benin A84

Photogravure

1975, Dec. 8 *Perf. 13* **Unwmkd.**

Flowers: 35fr, Ixora coccinea. 45fr, Hibiscus. 60fr, Phaemeria magnifica.

342 A83 10fr lilac & multi. 15 10
343 " 35fr gray & multi. 35 20
344 " 45fr multicolored 50 35
345 " 60fr blue & multi. 60 45

1976, Apr. 30 Litho. *Perf. 12*

Designs: 60fr, Speaker, wall with "PRPB," flag and arms of Benin. 100fr, Flag and arms of Benin.

346 A84 50fr ocher & multi. 40 30
347 " 60fr " " 45 30
348 " 100fr multicolored 80 60

Proclamation of the People's Republic of Benin, Nov. 30, 1975.

A. G. Bell, Satellite and 1876 Telephone—A85

1976, July 9 Litho. *Perf. 13*

349 A85 200fr lilac, red & brown 1.65 70

Centenary of first telephone call by Alexander Graham Bell, Mar. 10, 1876.

Dahomey Nos. 277–278 Surcharged

1976, July 19 Photo. *Perf. 12½x13*

350 A57 50fr on 1fr multi. 40 18
351 " 60fr on 2fr " 50 20

Scouts Cooking—A86

Design: 70fr, Three Scouts.

1976, Aug. 16 Litho. *Perf. 12½x13*

352 A86 50fr black, lilac & brown 40 30
353 " 70fr black, olive & red brown 55 40

African Jamboree, Nigeria 1976.

Blood Bank, Cotonou—A87

Designs: 50fr, Accident and first aid station. 60fr, Blood donation.

1976, Sept. 24 Litho. *Perf. 13*

354 A87 5fr multicolored 5 3
355 " 50fr " 40 30
356 " 60fr " 50 35

National Blood Donors Day.

Manioc A88

Designs: 50fr, Corn. 60fr, Cacao. 150fr, Cotton.

1976, Oct. 4 Litho. *Perf. 13x12½*

357 A88 20fr multicolored 15 10
358 " 50fr " 40 30
359 " 60fr " 45 30
360 " 150fr " 1.25 90

National Agricultural production campaign.

Classroom A89

1976, Oct. 25

361 A89 50fr multicolored 40 30

Third anniversary of KPARO newspaper, used in local language studies.

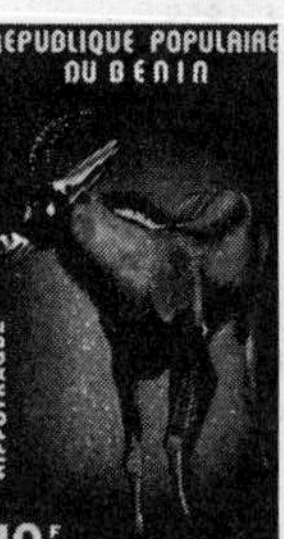

Roan Antelope A90 — Flags, Wall, Broken Chains A91

Designs: 30fr, Buffalo. 50fr, Hippopotamus (horiz.). 70fr, Lion.

1976, Nov. 8 Photogravure

362 A90 10fr multicolored 10 6
363 " 30fr " 25 18
364 " 50fr " 40 30
365 " 70fr " 55 35

Penjari National Park.

1976, Nov. 30 Litho. *Perf. 12½*

Design: 150fr, Corn, raised hands with weapons.

366 A91 40fr multicolored 30 20
367 " 150fr " 1.20 90

First anniversary of proclamation of the People's Republic of Benin.

Table Tennis, Map of Africa (Games' Emblem)—A92

Design: 50fr, Stadium, Cotonou.

1976, Dec. 26 Litho. *Perf. 13*

368 A92 10fr multicolored 10 6
369 " 50fr " 40 30

West African University Games, Cotonou, Dec. 26–31.

Europafrica Issue

Planes over Africa and Europe A93

1977, May 13 Litho. *Perf. 13*

370 A93 200fr multicolored 1.60 1.20

Snake A94

Designs: 3fr, Tortoise. 5fr, Zebus. 10fr, Cats.

1977, June 13 Litho. *Perf. 13x13½*

371 A94 2fr multicolored 3 3
372 " 3fr " 3 3
373 " 5fr " 5 3
374 " 10fr " 10 6

Patients at Clinic
A95

1977, Aug. 2 Litho. *Perf. 12½*

375 A95 100fr multicolored 85 60

World Rheumatism Year.

Karate, Map of Africa
A96

Designs: 100fr, Javelin, map of Africa, Benin flag (horiz.). 150fr, Hurdles.

1977, Aug. 30 Litho. *Perf. 12½*

376 A96 90fr multicolored 70 55
377 " 100fr " 85 60
378 " 150fr " 1.25 90
a. Souvenir sheet of 3 2.75 2.75

2nd West African Games, Lagos, Nigeria. No. 378a contains one each of Nos. 376–378; black marginal inscription. Size: 143x92mm.

Chairman Mao
A97

Lister and Vaporizer
A98

1977, Sept. 9 Litho. *Perf. 13x12½*

379 A97 100fr multicolored 85 60

Chairman Mao Tse-tung (1893–1976), Chinese communist leader, first death anniversary.

1977, Sept. 20 Engr. *Perf. 13*

Design: 150fr, Scalpels and flames, symbols of antisepsis, and Red Cross.

380 A98 150fr multicolored 1.20 90
381 " 210fr " 1.75 1.25

Joseph Lister (1827–1912), surgeon, founder of antiseptic surgery, birth sesquicentennial.

Guelede Mask, Ethnographic Museum, Porto Novo—A99

Designs: 50fr, Jar, symbol of unity, emblem of King Ghezo, Historical Museum, Abomey (vert.). 210fr, Abomey Museum.

1977, Oct. 17 *Perf. 13*

382 A99 50fr red & multi. 40 30
383 " 60fr black, blue & bister 50 35
384 " 210fr multicolored 1.75 1.25

Atacora Falls
A100

Mother and Child, Owl of Wisdom
A101

Designs: 60fr, Pile houses, Ganvie (horiz.). 150fr, Round huts, Savalou.

1977, Oct. 24 Litho. *Perf. 12½*

385 A100 50fr multicolored 40 30
386 " 60fr " 50 35
387 " 150fr " 1.25 90
a. Souvenir sheet of 3 2.80 2.80

Tourist publicity. No. 387a contains one each of Nos. 385–387; black marginal inscription. Size: 143x91mm.

Perf. 12½x13, 13x12½

1977, Dec. 3 Photogravure

Design: 150fr, Chopping down magical tree (horiz.).

388 A101 60fr multicolored 50 35
389 " 150fr " 1.25 90

Campaign against witchcraft.

Battle Scene—A102

1978, Jan. 16 Litho *Perf. 12½*

390 A102 50fr multicolored 50 28

Victory of people of Benin over imperialist forces.

Map, People and Houses of Benin
A103

1978, Feb. 1

391 A103 50fr multicolored 50 28

General population and dwellings census.

Alexander Fleming, Microscope and Penicillin—A104

1978, Mar. 12 Litho. *Perf. 13*

392 A104 300fr multicolored 3.00 1.65

Alexander Fleming (1881–1955), 50th anniversary of discovery of penicillin.

Abdoulaye Issa, Weapons and Fighters
A105

1978, Apr. 1 *Perf. 12½x13*

393 A105 100fr red, black & gold 1.00 55

First anniversary of death of Abdoulaye Issa and National Day of Benin's Youth.

El Hadj Omar and Horseback Rider
A106

Design: 90fr, L'Almamy Samory Toure (1830–1900) and horseback riders.

1978, Apr. 10 *Perf. 13x12½*

394 A106 90fr red & multi. 90 50
395 " 100fr multicolored 1.00 55

African heroes of resistance against colonialism.

ITU Emblem, Satellite, Landscape
A107

1978, May 17 Litho. *Perf. 13*

396 A107 100fr multicolored 1.00 55

10th World Telecommunications Day.

Soccer Player, Stadium, Argentina '78 Emblem—A108

Designs (Argentina '78 Emblem and): 300fr, Soccer players and ball (vert.). 500fr, Soccer player, globe with ball on map.

1978, June 1 Litho. *Perf. 12½*

397 A108 200fr multicolored 2.00 1.10
398 " 300fr " 3.00 1.65
399 " 500fr " 5.00 2.75
a. Souvenir sheet of 3 11.00 11.00

11th World Cup Soccer Championship, Argentina, June 1–25. No. 399a contains 3 stamps similar to Nos. 397–399 in changed colors; red marginal inscription and blue border. Size: 190x120mm.

Nos. 397–399a Overprinted in Red Brown:
a. FINALE / ARGENTINE: 3 / HOLLANDE: 1
b. CHAMPION / 1978 / ARGENTINE
c. 3e BRESIL / 4e ITALIE

1978, June 25 Litho. *Perf. 12½*

400 A108 (a) 200fr multi. 2.00 1.10
401 " (b) 300fr " 3.00 1.65
402 " (c) 500fr " 5.00 2.75
a. Souvenir sheet of 3 11.00 11.00

Argentina's victory in 1978 Soccer Championship.

Games' Flag over Africa, Basketball Players—A109

Designs (Games' Emblem and): 60fr, Map of Africa and volleyball players. 80fr, Map of Benin and bicyclists.

1978, July 13 *Perf. 13x12½*

403 A109 50fr lt. bl. & multi. 50 28
404 " 60fr ultra. & multi. 60 35
405 " 80fr multicolored 80 50
a. Souvenir sheet of 3 2.00 2.00

3rd African Games, Algiers, July 13–28. No. 405a contains 3 stamps in changed colors similar to Nos. 403–405; rose lilac and black margin. Size: 208–80mm.

Martin Luther King, Jr.
A110

1978, July 30 *Perf. 12½*

406 A110 300fr multicolored 3.00 1.65

Martin Luther King, Jr. (1929–1968), American civil rights leader.

Kanna Taxi, Oueme
A111

Designs: 60fr, Leatherworker and goods. 70fr, Drummer and tom-toms. 100fr, Metalworker and calabashes.

1978, Aug. 26

407 A111 50fr multicolored 50 28
408 " 60fr " 60 35
409 " 70fr " 70 42
410 " 100fr " 1.00 55

Getting to know Benin through its provinces.

Map of Italy and Exhibition Poster—A112

1978, Aug. 26 Litho. ***Perf. 13***

411 A112 200fr multicolored 2.00 1.10

Riccione 1978 Philatelic Exhibition.

Turkeys A113

Poultry: 20fr, Ducks. 50fr, Chicken. 60fr, Guinea fowl.

1978, Oct. 5 Photo. ***Perf. 12½x13***

412 A113 10fr multicolored 10 10
413 " 20fr " 20 20
414 " 50fr " 50 50
415 " 60fr " 60 60

Poultry breeding.

Royal Messenger, UPU Emblem A114

Designs (UPU Emblem and): 60fr, Boatsman, ship and car (vert.). 90fr, Special messenger and plane (vert.).

Perf. 13x12½, 12½x13

1978, Oct. 16

416 A114 50fr multicolored 50 50
417 " 60fr " 60 60
418 " 90fr " 90 90

Centenary of change of "General Postal Union" to "Universal Postal Union."

Raoul Follereau A115

1978, Dec. 17 Litho. ***Perf. 12½***

419 A115 200fr multicolored 2.00 2.00

Raoul Follereau (1903–1977), apostle to the lepers and educator of the blind.

AIR POST STAMPS

People's Republic

Nativity, by Aert van Leyden AP84

Paintings: 85fr, Adoration of the Kings, by Rubens (vert.). 140fr, Adoration of the Shepherds, by Charles Lebrun. 300fr, The Virgin with the Blue Diadem, by Raphael (vert.).

1975, Dec. 19 Litho. ***Perf. 13***

C240 AP84 40fr gold & multi. 40 15
C241 " 85fr " " 85 30
C242 " 140fr " " 1.20 50
C243 " 300fr " " 2.75 1.25

Christmas 1975.

Slalom, Innsbruck Olympic Emblem—AP85

Designs (Innsbruck Olympic Games Emblem and): 150fr, Bobsledding (vert.). 300fr, Figure skating, pairs.

1976, June 28 Litho. ***Perf. 12½***

C244 AP85 60fr multicolored 50 20
C245 " 150fr " 1.25 50
C246 " 300fr " 2.50 1.10

12th Winter Olympic Games, Innsbruck, Austria, Feb. 4–15.

Dahomey Nos. C235–C237 Overprinted: "POPULAIRE / DU BENIN" and Bars, with Surcharge Added on Nos. C236—C237

1976, July 4 Engr. ***Perf. 13***

C247 AP82 135fr multi. 1.10 50
C248 " 210fr on 300fr multi. 1.75 70
C249 " 380fr on 500fr multi. 3.00 1.30

The overprint includes a bar covering "DU DAHOMEY" in shades of brown; "POPULAIRE DU BENIN" is blue on Nos. C247–C248, red on No. C249. The surcharge and bars over old value are blue on No. C248, red, brown on No. C249.

Long Jump—AP86

Designs (Olympic Rings and): 150fr, Basketball (vert.). 200fr, Hurdles.

1976, July 16 Photo. ***Perf. 13***

C250 AP86 60fr multicolored 50 20
C251 " 150fr " 1.25 50
C252 " 200fr " 1.65 70
a. Souvenir sheet of 3 3.50 3.50

21st Olympic Games, Montreal, Canada, July 17–Aug 1. No. C252a contains one each of Nos. C250–C252; brown marginal inscription. Size:150x120mm.

Konrad Adenauer and Cologne Cathedral—AP87

Design: 90fr, Konrad Adenauer (vert.).

1976, Aug. 27 Engr. ***Perf. 13***

C253 AP87 90fr multicolored 70 30
C254 " 250fr " 2.00 80

Konrad Adenauer (1876–1967), German Chancellor, birth centenary.

Children's Heads and Flying Fish (Dahomey Type A32)—AP88

Design: 210fr, Lion cub's head and Benin type A3 (vert.).

1976, Sept. 13

C255 AP88 60fr Prus. blue & vio. blue 50 20
C256 " 210fr multi. 1.65 70

JUVAROUEN 76, International Youth Philatelic Exhibition, Rouen, France, Apr. 25–May 2.

Apollo 14 Emblem and Blast-off AP89

Design: 270fr, Landing craft and man on moon.

1976, Oct. 18 Engr. ***Perf. 13***

C257 AP89 130fr multi. 1.00 45
C258 " 270fr " 2.25 95

Apollo 14 Moon Mission, 5th anniversary.

Annunciation, by Master of Jativa AP90

Paintings: 60fr, Nativity, by Gerard David. 270fr, Adoration of the Kings, Dutch School. 300fr, Flight into Egypt, by Gentile Fabriano (horiz.).

1976, Dec. 20 Litho. ***Perf. 12½***

C259 AP90 50fr gold & multi. 40 25

C260	AP90	60fr gold & multi.	50	35
C261	"	270fr gold & multi.	2.25	95
C262	"	300fr gold & multi.	2.50	1.50

Christmas 1976.

Gamblers and Lottery Emblem
AP91

1977, Mar. 13 Litho. *Perf. 13*

C263	AP91	50fr multicolored	40	30

National lottery, 10th anniversary.

Sassenage Castle, Grenoble—AP92

1977, May 16 *Perf. 12½*

C264	AP92	200fr multi.	1.65	1.20

10th anniversary of International French Language Council.

Concorde, Supersonic Plane—AP93

Designs: 150fr, Zeppelin. 300fr, Charles A. Lindbergh and Spirit of St. Louis. 500fr, Charles Nungesser and François Coli, French aviators lost over Atlantic, 1927.

1977, July 25 Engr. *Perf. 13*

C265	AP93	80fr ultra. & red	65	50
C266	"	150fr multi.	1.25	90
C267	"	300fr "	2.50	1.80
C268	"	500fr "	4.00	3.00

Aviation history.

Soccer Player
AP94

Design: 200fr, Soccer players and Games' emblem.

1977, July 28 Litho. *Perf. 12½x12*

C269	AP94	60fr multicolored	50	30
C270	"	200fr "	1.65	1.20

World Soccer Cup elimination games.

Miss Haverfield, by Gainsborough
AP95

Designs: 150fr, Self-portrait, by Rubens. 200fr, Anguish, man's head by Da Vinci.

1977, Oct. 3 Engr. *Perf. 13*

C271	AP95	100fr slate green & maroon	80	60
C272	"	150fr red brn. & dk. brn.	1.25	90
C273	"	200fr brn. & red	1.65	1.20

Birth anniversaries: Thomas Gainsborough (1727–1788); Peter Paul Rubens (1577–1640); Leonardo da Vinci (1452–1519).

No. C265 Overprinted:
"1er VOL COMMERCIAL / 22.11.77
PARIS NEW-YORK"

1977, Nov. 22 Engr. *Perf. 13*

C274	AP93	80fr ultra. & red	65	50

Concorde, first commercial flight, Paris to New York.

Viking on Mars—AP96

Designs: 150fr, Isaac Newton, apple globe, stars. 200fr, Vladimir M. Komarov, spacecraft and earth. 500fr, Dog Laika, rocket and space.

1977, Nov. 28 Engr. *Perf. 13*

C275	AP96	100fr multi.	80	60
C276	"	150fr "	1.25	90
C277	"	200fr "	1.65	1.20
C278	"	500fr "	4.00	3.00

Operation Viking on Mars; 250th death anniversary of Isaac Newton (1642–1727); 10th death anniversary of Russian cosmonaut Vladimir M. Komarov; 20th anniversary of first living creature in space.

Monument, Red Star Place, Cotonou—AP97

Litho.; Gold Embossed

1977 Nov. 30 *Perf. 12½*

C279	AP97	500fr multi.	4.00	2.50

Common Design Types
pictured in section at front of book.

Suzanne Fourment, by Rubens
AP98

Design: 380fr, Albert Rubens, by Rubens.

1977, Dec. 12 Engr. *Perf. 13*

C280	AP98	200fr multi.	1.65	1.20
C281	"	380fr claret & ocher	3.00	2.10

Peter Paul Rubens (1577–1640), 400th birth anniversary.

Parthenon and UNESCO Emblem
AP99

Designs: 70fr, Acropolis and frieze showing Pan-Athenaic procession (vert.). 250fr, Parthenon and frieze showing horsemen (vert.).

1978, Sept. 22 Litho. *Perf. 12½x12*

C282	AP99	70fr multicolored	70	40
C233	"	250fr "	2.50	1.50
C284	"	500fr "	5.00	3.00

Save the Parthenon in Athens campaign.

Philexafrique II—Essen Issue
Common Design Types

Designs: No. C285, Buffalo and Dahomey No. C33. No. C286, Wild ducks and Baden No. 1.

1978, Nov. 1 Litho. *Perf. 12½*

C285	CD138	100fr multi.	1.00	60
C286	CD139	100fr "	1.00	60

Nos. C285–C286 printed se-tenant.

Wilbur and Orville Wright and Flyer—AP100

1978, Dec. 28 Engr. *Perf. 13*

C287	AP100	500fr multi.	5.00	3.00

75th anniversary of 1st powered flight.

POSTAGE DUE STAMPS.

French Colony

Handstamped in Black on Postage Due Stamps of French Colonies **BÉNIN**

1894 *Imperf.* Unwmkd.

J1	D1	5c black	60.00	27.50
J2	"	10c black	60.00	27.50
J3	"	20c black	60.00	27.50
J4	"	30c black	60.00	27.50

Nos. J1–J4 exist with overprint in various positions.

People's Republic

Pineapples
D6

Mail Delivery
D7

Designs: 20fr, Cashew (vert.). 40fr, Oranges. 50fr, Akee. 80fr, Mail delivery by boat.

1978, Sept. 5 Photo. *Perf. 13*

J44	D6	10fr multicolored	10	10
J45	"	20fr "	20	20
J46	"	40fr "	40	40
J47	"	50fr "	50	50

Engraved

J48	D7	60fr multicolored	60	60
J49	"	80fr "	80	80
		Nos. J44–J49 (6)	2.60	2.60

BERGEDORF

See Early German States group preceding Germany.

BHUTAN

(boot·än'; boo·tăn')

LOCATION—Eastern Himalayas.
GOVT.—Kingdom.
AREA—18,147 sq. mi.
POP.—1,035,000 (est. 1974).
CAPITAL—Thimphu.

100 Chetrum = 1 Ngultrum or Rupee.

Postal Runner
A1

Designs: 3ch, 70ch, Archer. 5ch, 1.30nu, Yak. 15ch, Map of Bhutan, portrait of Druk Gyalpo (Dragon King) Ugyen Wangchuk (1867–1902) and Paro Dzong (fortress-monastery). 33ch, Postal runner. All horiz. except 2ch and 33ch.

Perf. 14x14½, 14½x14

1962, Oct. 10 Litho. Unwmkd.

1 A1 2ch red & gray 5 5
2 " 3ch red & ultra. 5 5
3 " 5ch green & brown 30 30
4 " 15ch red, black & orange yellow 8 8
5 " 33ch blue green & lilac 15 15
6 " 70ch deep ultra. & light blue 35 35
7 " 1.30nu blue & black 75 75
Nos. 1–7 (7) 1.73 1.73

Nos. 1–7 were issued for inland use in April, 1962, and became valid for international mail on Oct. 10, 1962.

Refugee Year Emblem and Arms of Bhutan
A2

1962, Oct. 10 *Perf. 14½x14*

8 A2 1nu dark blue & dark carmine rose 80 80
9 " 2nu yellow green & red lilac 1.40 1.40

World Refugee Year.

Equipment of Ancient Warrior
A3

Boy Filling Grain Box and Wheat Emblem
A4

1963 *Perf. 14x14½* Unwmkd.

10 A3 33ch multicolored 35 35
11 " 70ch " 35 35
12 " 1.30nu " 80 80

Bhutan's membership in Colombo Plan.

1963, Sept. 17 *Perf. 13½x14*

13 A4 20ch light blue, yellow & red brown 20 20
14 " 1.50nu rose lilac, blue & red brown 75 75

Issued for the "Freedom from Hunger" Campaign of the U.N. Food and Agriculture Organization.

Masked Dancer—A5

Various Bhutanese Dancers (Five Designs; 2ch, 5ch, 20ch, 1nu, 1.30nu vertical)

1964, Mar. *Perf. 14½x14, 14x14½*

Dancers Multicolored

15 A5 2ch blue grn. & brn. 5 5
16 " 3ch light violet & blk. 7 7
17 " 5ch lt. ultra. & dk. bl. 7 7
18 " 20ch yellow & red 8 8
19 " 33ch gray & black 10 10
20 " 70ch emerald & black 30 30
21 " 1nu citron & red 45 45
22 " 1.30nu bister & dk. blue 45 45
23 " 2nu orange & black 45 45
Nos. 15–23 (9) 2.02 2.02

Stone Throwing
A6

Sport: 5ch, 33ch, Boxing. 1nu, 3nu, Archery. 2nu, Soccer.

1964, Oct. 10 Litho. *Perf. 14½*

24 A6 2ch emerald & multi. 5 5
25 " 5ch orange & multi. 7 7
26 " 15ch brt. citron & multi. 8 8
27 " 33ch rose lilac & multi. 20 20
28 " 1nu multicolored 60 60
29 " 2nu rose lilac & multi. 60 60
30 " 3nu lt. blue & multi. 90 90
Nos. 24–30 (7) 2.50 2.50

Issued to commemorate the 18th Olympic Games, Tokyo, Oct. 10–25. See No. B4.
Nos. 24–30 exist imperf. Price $4.

Flags of the World at Half-mast
A7

1964, Nov. 22 *Perf. 14½* Unwmkd.

Flags in Original Colors

31 A7 33ch steel gray 16 16
32 " 1nu silver 75 75
33 " 3nu gold 1.50 1.50
a. Souv. sheet of 2, perf. 13½ 2.00 2.00

Issued in memory of those who died in the service of their country. Nos. 31–33 exist imperf.
No. 33a contains 2 stamps similar to Nos. 32–33 with flag of Bhutan and gold inscription in margin. Size: 83x118mm. Sheet exists imperf.; price $2.

Primrose
A8

Flowers: 5ch, 33ch, Gentian. 50ch, 1nu, Rhododendron. 75ch, 2nu, Peony.

1964, Dec. Lithographed *Perf. 13*

34 A8 2ch lt. blue, violet blue & green 3 3
35 " 5ch vio., grn. & yellow 4 4
36 " 15ch yel., vio. & green 10 10
37 " 33ch gray, violet blue & green 15 15
38 " 50ch light gray, green & carmine 25 25
39 " 75ch lt. grn., yel. & brn. 35 35
40 " 1nu pink, green & dark gray 40 40
41 " 2nu sepia, yel. & grn. 60 60
Nos. 34–41 (8) 1.92 1.92

Nos. 5, 40, 32, 41 and 33 Overprinted: "WINSTON CHURCHILL 1874–1965"

1965, Feb. 27

42 A1 33ch blue green & lilac 40 20
43 A8 1nu pink, green & dark gray 50 40
44 A7 1nu silver & multi. 50 40
45 A8 2nu sepia, yel. & grn. 1.00 85
46 A7 3nu gold & multi. 1.35 1.25
Nos. 42–46 (5) 3.75 3.10

Issued in memory of Sir Winston Churchill (1874–1965), British statesman. The overprint is in three lines on Nos. 42–43 and 45; in two lines on Nos. 43 and 46.
Nos. 44 and 46 exist imperf. Price, both, $4.50.

Skyscraper, Pagoda and World's Fair Emblem—A9

Designs: 10ch, 2nu, Pieta by Michelangelo and statue of Khmer Buddha. 20ch, Skyline of New York and Bhutanese village. 33ch, George Washington Bridge, N. Y., and foot bridge, Bhutan.

1965, Apr. 21 Litho. *Perf. 14½*

47 A9 1ch blue & multi. 5 5
48 " 10ch green & multi. 8 8
49 " 20ch rose lilac & multi. 12 12
50 " 33ch bister & multi. 18 18
51 " 1.50nu bister & multi. 75 75
52 " 2nu multicolored 1.00 1.00
a. Souv. sheet of 2, perf. 13½ 2.00 2.00
Nos. 47–52 (6) 2.18 2.18

Issued to commemorate the New York World's Fair, 1964–65.
Nos. 47–52 exist imperf.; price $3.50.
No. 52a contains two stamps similar to Nos. 51–52. World's Fair emblems in margin in bister and inscription in black. Size: 118½x86½mm. Exists imperf.; price $2.

Telstar, Short-wave Radio and ITU Emblem—A10

Designs (ITU Emblem and): 2nu, Telstar and Morse key. 3nu, Syncom and ear phones.

1966, March 2 Litho. *Perf. 14½*

53 A10 35ch multicolored 15 15
54 " 2nu " 75 75
55 " 3nu " 1.10 1.10

Issued to commemorate the centenary (in 1965) of the International Telecommunication Union. Souvenir sheets exist containing two stamps similar to Nos. 54–55, perf. 13½ and imperf. Dark blue margin with white inscription and pictures of satellites in space. Size: 119x78mm. Price, 2 sheets, $5.

Leopard
A11

Animals: 1ch, 4nu, Asiatic black bear. 4ch, 2nu, Pigmy hog. 8ch, 75ch, Tiger. 10ch, 1.50nu, Dhole (Asiatic hunting dog). 1nu, 5nu, Takin (goat).

1966 Lithographed *Perf. 13*

Animals in Natural Colors

56 A11 1ch yellow & black 10 10
57 " 2ch pale grn. & blk. 10 10
58 " 4ch lt. citron & blk. 10 10
59 " 8ch lt. blue & blk. 10 10
60 " 10ch lt. lilac & blk. 10 10
61 " 75ch lt. yel. green & black 30 30
62 " 1nu lt. green & blk. 75 75
63 " 1.50nu lt. blue green & black 60 60
64 " 2nu dull orange & black 75 75
65 " 3nu bluish lilac & black 1.10 1.10
66 " 4nu lt. grn. & blk. 1.50 1.50
67 " 5nu pink & black 2.00 2.00
Nos. 56–67 (12) 7.50 7.50

Issue dates: Nos. 56–60, 62, March 28; Nos. 61, 63–67, Apr. 26.

Nos. 6–9, 20–23 Surcharged

10 CH

1965(?) *Perf. 14½x14, 14x14½*

68 A2 5ch on 1nu dark blue & dark carmine rose
69 " 5ch on 2nu yel. green & red lilac
70 A5 10ch on 70ch multi.
71 " 10ch on 2nu multi.
72 A1 15ch on 70ch dp. ultra. & lt. blue
73 " 15ch on 1.30nu blue & black
74 A5 20ch on 1nu multi.
75 " 20ch on 1.30nu multi.
Nos. 68–75 (8) *100.00*

The surcharges on Nos. 68–69 contain two bars at left and right obliterating the denomination on both sides of the design. Four bars on Nos. 72–73.

Simtokha Dzong
A12

Tashichho Dzong—A13

Daga Dzong
A14

Designs: 5ch, Rinpung Dzong. 50ch, Tongsa Dzong. 1nu, Lhuntsi Dzong.

Perf. 14½x14 (A12), 13½ (A13, A14)

1966–70 Photogravure

76	A12	5ch orange brown ('67)	4	4
77	A13	10ch dark green & rose violet ('68)	6	6
78	A12	15ch brown	10	8
79	"	20ch green	15	12
80	A13	50ch blue green ('68)	20	20
81	A14	75ch dark blue & olive gray ('70)	30	30
82	"	1nu dk. violet & vio. blue ('70)	40	40
		Nos. 76-82 (7)	1.25	1.20

Sizes: 5ch, 15ch, 20ch, 37x20½mm. 10ch, 53½x28½mm. 50ch, 35½x25½ mm.

Certain unlisted issues of Bhutan, starting in 1966, are mentioned and briefly described in "For the Record" at the back of this volume.

Mahatma Gandhi—A14a

1969, Oct. 2 Litho. ***Perf. 13x13½***

83	A14a	20ch lt. bl. & brown	60	60
84	"	2nu lemon & brown olive	90	90

Mohandas K. Gandhi (1869–1948), leader in India's struggle for independence, birth centenary.

Various Forms of Mail Transport, UPU Headquarters, Bern—A14b

1970, Feb. 25 Photo. ***Perf. 13½***

85	A14b	3ch olive green & gold		
86	"	10ch red brown & gold		
87	"	20ch Prus. blue & gold		
88	"	2.50nu deep magenta & gold		
		Nos. 85-88 (4)	1.25	1.25

New Headquarters of Universal Postal Union, Bern, Switzerland.
Exist imperf. Price $4.

Wangdiphodrang Dzong and Bridge
A15

1971–73 Photogravure ***Perf. 13½***

89	A15	2ch gray ('73)	5	5
90	"	3ch dp. red lilac ('73)	5	5
91	"	4ch violet ('73)	5	5
92	"	5ch dark green	15	15
93	"	10ch orange brown	15	15
94	"	15ch deep blue	15	15
95	"	20ch deep plum	15	15
		Nos. 89-95 (7)	75	75

U.N. Emblem and Bhutan Flag
A16

Designs (Bhutan Flag and): 10ch, U.N. Headquarters, New York. 20ch, Security Council Chamber and mural by Per Krohg. 3nu, General Assembly Hall.

1971, Sept. 21 Photo. ***Perf. 13½***

96	A16	5ch gold, bl. & multi.	3	3
97	"	10ch gold & multi.	3	3
98	"	20ch " "	6	6
99	"	3nu " "	85	85
		Nos. 96-99, C1-3 (7)	5.02	5.02

Bhutan's admission to the United Nations. Exist imperf.

Boy Scout Crossing Stream in Rope Sling—A17

Designs (Emblem and Boy Scouts): 20ch, 2nu, mountaineering. 50ch, 6nu, reading map. 75ch, as 10ch.

1971, Nov. 30 Litho. ***Perf. 13½***

143	A17	10ch gold & multi.	5	5
144	"	20ch " "	7	7
145	"	50ch " "	17	17
146	"	75ch silver & multi.	25	25
147	"	2nu " "	65	65
148	"	6nu " "	2.00	2.00
		a. Souvenir sheet of 2	2.75	2.75
		Nos. 143-148 (6)	3.19	3.19

60th anniversary of the Boy Scouts. No. 148a contains one each of Nos. 147–148 and 2 labels. Silver fleur-de-lis pattern on labels and margin. Size: 92½x92½mm. Exist imperf.

UNHCR
UNRWA
1971

Nos. 87–90 Overprinted in Gold

1971, Dec. 23

149	A16	5ch gold & multi.	5	5
150	"	10ch " "	5	5
151	"	20ch " "	7	7
152	"	3nu " "	1.00	1.00
		Nos. 149-152, C4-C6 (7)	5.57	5.57

World Refugee Year. Exist imperf.

Book Year Emblem
A17a

1972, May 15 Photo. ***Perf. 13½x13***

153	A17a	2ch multicolored		
154	"	3ch "		
155	"	5ch "		
156	A17a	20ch multicolored		
		Nos. 153-156 (4)		50

International Book Year.

King Jigme Singye Wangchuk and Royal Crest—A18

Designs (King and): 25ch, 90ch, Flag of Bhutan. 1.25nu, Wheel with 8 good luck signs. 2nu, 4nu, Punakha Dzong, former winter capital. 3nu, 5nu, Crown. 5ch, same as 10ch.

1974, June 2 Litho. ***Perf. 13½***

157	A18	10ch maroon & multi.	5	5
158	"	25ch gold & multi.	10	10
159	"	1.25nu multicolored	45	45
160	"	2nu gold & multi.	70	70
161	"	3nu multicolored	1.00	1.00
		Nos. 157-161 (5)	2.30	2.30

Souvenir Sheets

Perf. 13½, Imperf.

162	A18	Sheet of 2	2.00	2.00
		a. 5ch maroon & multi.	5	
		b. 5nu red org. & multi.	1.70	
163	A18	Sheet of 2	2.15	2.15
		a. 90ch gold & multi.	45	
		b. 4nu " "	1.40	

Coronation of King Jigme Singye Wangchuk, June 2, 1974. Nos. 162–163 have maroon and multicolored borders with picture of the king wearing peacock crown. Size: 177x127mm.

Mailman on Horseback
A19

Old and New Locomotives
A20

Designs (UPU Emblem, Carrier Pigeon and): 3ch, Sailing and steam ships. 4ch, Old biplane and jet. 25ch, Mail runner and jeep.

1974, Oct. 9 Litho. ***Perf. 14½***

164	A19	1ch green & multi.	3	3
165	A20	2ch lilac & multi.	3	3
166	"	3ch ocher & multi.	3	3
167	"	4ch yel. grn. & multi.	3	3
168	"	25ch salmon & multi.	10	10
		Nos. 164-168, C7-C9 (8)	1.82	1.82

Centenary of Universal Postal Union. Issued in sheets of 50 and sheets of 5 plus label with multicolored margin. Exist imperf.

Family and WPY Emblem—A21

1974, Dec. 17 ***Perf. 13½***

169	A21	25ch blue & multi.	6	6
170	"	50ch org. & multi.	12	12
171	"	90ch verm. & multi.	22	22
172	"	2.50nu brn. & multi.	60	60

World Population Year.

Sephisa Chandra
A22

Designs: Indigenous butterflies.

1975, Sept. Lithographed ***Perf. 14½***

Multicolored

173	A22	1ch *shown*	3	3
174	"	2ch *Lethe kansa*	3	3
175	"	3ch *Neope bhadra*	3	3
176	"	4ch *Euthalia duda*	3	3
177	"	5ch *Vindula erota*	3	3
178	"	10ch *Bhutanitis lidderdalei*	5	5
179	"	3nu *Limenitis zayla*	1.25	1.25
180	"	5nu *Delias thysbe*	2.00	2.00
		Nos. 173-180 (8)	3.45	3.45

Souvenir Sheet

Perf. 13

181	A22	10nu *Dabasa gyas*	3.50	3.50

No. 181 contains one stamp; Bhutanese landscape in multicolored margin. Size: 115x90mm.

Apollo and Apollo-Soyuz Emblem—A23

Design: No. 183, Soyuz and emblem.

1975, Oct. Litho. ***Perf. 14x13½***

182	A23	10nu multicolored	3.00	3.00
183	"	10nu "	3.00	3.00
		a. Souvenir sheet of 2, 15nu	9.50	9.50

Apollo Soyuz link-up in space, July 17. Nos. 182–183 printed se-tenant in sheets of 10. No. 183a contains two 15nu stamps similar to Nos. 182–183; light green margin with U.S. and U.S.S.R. flags and Apollo-Soyuz emblem. Size: 130x90 mm. Exist imperf.

Jewelry
A24

Designs: 2ch, Coffee pot, bell and sugar cup. 3ch, Container and drinking horn. 4ch, Pendants and box cover. 5ch, Painter. 15ch, Silversmith. 20ch, Wood carver with tools. 1.50nu, Mat maker. 5nu, 10nu, Printer.

1975, Nov. ***Perf. 14½***

184	A24	1ch multicolored	3	3
185	"	2ch "	3	3
186	"	3ch "	3	3
187	"	4ch "	3	3
188	"	5ch "	3	3
189	"	15ch "	5	5
190	"	20ch "	6	6
191	"	1.50nu "	45	45
192	"	10nu "	3.00	3.00
		Nos. 184-192 (9)	3.71	3.71

Souvenir Sheet

Perf. 13

193	A24	5nu multicolored	1.50	1.50

Handicrafts and craftsmen. No. 193 contains one stamp; multicolored margin with black inscription. Size: 105x80mm.

King Jigme Singye Wangchuk
A25

Designs: 25ch, 90ch, 1nu, 2nu, 4nu, like 15ch. 1.30nu, 3nu, 5nu, Coat of arms. Sizes (Diameter): 15ch, 1nu, 1.30nu, 38mm. 25ch, 2nu, 3nu, 49mm. 90ch, 4nu, 5nu, 63mm.

Lithographed, Embossed on Gold Foil

1975, Nov. 11 ***Imperf.***

194	A25	15ch emerald	5	5
195	"	25ch "	8	8
196	"	90ch "	28	28
197	"	1nu brt. carmine	30	30
198	"	1.30nu " "	40	40
199	"	2nu " "	60	60
200	"	3nu " "	90	90
201	"	4nu " "	1.20	1.20
202	"	5nu " "	1.50	1.50
		Nos. 194-202 (9)	5.31	5.31

King Jigme Singye Wangchuk's 20th birthday.

Rhododendron Cinnabarinum
A28

Designs (Rhododendron): 2ch, Campanulatum. 3ch, Fortunei. 4ch, Red arboreum. 5ch, Pink arboreum. 1nu, Falconeri. 3nu, Hodgsonii. 5nu, Keysii. 10nu, Cinnabarinum.

1976, Feb. 15 **Litho.** ***Perf. 15***

203	A28	1ch rose & multi.	3	3
204	"	2ch lt. grn. & multi.	3	3
205	"	3ch gray & multi.	3	3
206	"	4ch lilac & multi.	3	3
207	"	5ch ol. gray & multi.	3	3
208	"	1nu brown orange & multicolored	30	24
209	"	3nu ultra. & multi.	90	72
210	"	5nu gray & multi.	1.50	1.20
		Nos. 203-210 (8)	2.85	2.31

Souvenir Sheet

Perf. 13½

211	A28	10nu multicolored	3.50	3.50

No. 211 contains one stamp; multicolored margin showing rhododendrons around pool. Size: 105x80mm.

Slalom and Olympic Games Emblem
A29

Designs (Olympic Games Emblem and): 2ch, 4-men bobsled. 3ch, Ice hockey. 4ch, Cross-country skiing. 5ch, Figure skating, women's. 2nu, Downhill skiing. 4nu, Speed skating. 6nu, Ski jump. 10nu, Figure skating, pairs.

1976, Mar. 29 **Litho.** ***Perf. 13½***

212	A29	1ch multicolored	3	3
213	"	2ch "	3	3
214	A29	3ch multicolored	3	3
215	"	4ch "	3	3
216	"	5ch "	3	3
217	"	2nu "	60	45
218	"	4nu "	1.20	90
219	"	10nu "	3.00	2.25
		Nos. 212-219 (8)	4.95	3.75

Souvenir Sheet

220	A29	6nu multicolored	2.00	2.00

12th Winter Olympic Games, Innsbruck, Austria, Feb. 4-15. No. 220 has orange and brown margin showing ski jump. Size: 78x104mm.

Orchid
A30

Designs: Various orchids.

1976, June **Litho.** ***Perf. 14½***

221	A30	1ch multicolored	3	3
222	"	2ch "	3	3
223	"	3ch "	3	3
224	"	4ch "	3	3
225	"	5ch "	3	3
226	"	2nu "	60	45
227	"	4nu "	1.20	90
228	"	6nu "	1.80	1.35
		Nos. 221-228 (8)	3.75	2.85

Souvenir Sheet

Perf. 13½

229	A30	10nu multicolored	3.25	1.65

No. 229 contains one stamp; multicolored margin with orchid design. Size: 106x 80mm.

Double Carp Design—A31

Designs: Various symbolic designs and Colombo Plan emblem.

1976, July 1 **Litho.** ***Perf. 14½***

230	A31	3ch red & multi.	3	3
231	"	4ch verm. & multi.	3	3
232	"	5ch multicolored	3	3
233	"	25ch blue & multi.	8	6
234	"	1.25nu multicolored	38	30
235	"	2nu yel. & multi.	60	48
236	"	2.50nu vio. & multi.	75	60
237	"	3nu multicolored	90	72
		Nos. 230-237 (8)	2.80	2.25

Colombo Plan, 25th anniversary.

Bandaranaike Conference Hall—A32

1976, Aug. 16 **Litho.** ***Perf. 13½***

238	A32	1.25nu multicolored	45	30
239	"	2.50nu "	85	60

5th Summit Conference of Non-aligned Countries, Colombo, Sri Lanka, Aug. 9-19.

Queen Elizabeth II
A33

Liberty Bell
A34

Spirit of St. Louis
A35

Bhutanese Archer, Olympic Rings
A36

Designs: No. 242, Alexander Graham Bell. No. 245, LZ 3 Zeppelin docking, 1907. No. 246, Alfred B. Nobel.

1978, Nov. 15 **Litho.** ***Perf. 14½***

240	A33	20nu multicolored	5.00	
241	A34	20nu "	5.00	
242	A33	20nu "	5.00	
243	A35	20nu "	5.00	
244	A36	20nu "	5.00	
245	A35	20nu "	5.00	
246	A33	20nu "	6.00	
		Nos. 240-246 (7)	35.00	

Commemoration: 25th anniversary of coronation of Queen Elizabeth II; American Bicentennial; centenary of first telephone call by Alexander Graham Bell; Charles A. Lindbergh crossing the Atlantic, 50th anniversary; Olympic Games; 70th anniversary of the Zeppelin; 75th anniversary of Nobel Prize. Seven souvenir sheets exist, each 25nu, commemorating same events with different designs. Size: 103x80mm.

SEMI-POSTAL STAMPS

Nos. 10-12 Surcharged

+ 50ch

Perf. 14x14½

1964, March **Litho.** **Unwmkd.**

B1	A3	33ch+50ch multi.	3.00	3.00
B2	"	70ch+50ch "	3.00	3.00
B3	"	1.30nu+50ch "	3.00	3.00

Issued to commemorate the 9th Winter Olympic Games, Innsbruck, Jan. 29-Feb. 9, 1964.

Olympic Games Type of Regular Issue, 1964

Souvenir Sheet

Designs: 1nu+50ch, Archery. 2nu+50ch, Soccer.

1964, Oct. 10 ***Perf. 13½, Imperf.***

B4	A6	Sheet of 2	3.00	3.00
		a. 1nu+50ch multi.	75	75
		b. 2nu+50ch "	1.75	1.75

18th Olympic Games, Tokyo, Oct. 10-25. No. B4 has multicolored border. Size: 86x117½mm.

AIR POST STAMPS

U.N. Type of Regular Issue

Designs (Bhutan Flag and): 2.50nu, U.N. Headquarters, New York. 5nu, Security Council Chamber and mural by Per Krohg. 6nu, General Assembly Hall.

1971, Sept. 21 **Photo.** ***Perf. 13½***

C1	A16	2.50nu silver & multi.	75	75
C2	"	5nu " "	1.50	1.50
C3	"	6nu " "	1.80	1.80

Bhutan's admission to the United Nations. Exist imperf.

Nos. C1-C3 Overprinted in Gold: "UNHCR / UNRWA / 1971" Like Nos. 153-156

1971, Dec. 23 **Litho.** ***Perf. 13½***

C4	A16	2.50nu silver & multi.	80	80
C5	"	5nu " "	1.60	1.60
C6	"	6nu " "	2.00	2.00

World Refugee Year. Exist imperf.

UPU Types of 1974

Designs (UPU Emblem, Carrier Pigeon and): 1nu, Mail runner and jeep. 1.40nu, 10nu, Old and new locomotives. 2nu, Old biplane and jet.

1974, Oct. 9 **Litho.** ***Perf. 14½***

C7	A19	1nu sal. & multi.	35	35
C8	A20	1.40nu lilac & multi.	55	55
C9	"	2nu multicolored	70	70

Souvenir Sheet

Perf. 13

C10	A20	10nu lilac & multi.	3.75	

Centenary of Universal Postal Union. No. C10 contains one stamp; yellow and multicolored margin with UPU emblem and black inscription. Size: 91x78mm. Nos. C7-C9 were issued in sheets of 50 and sheets of 5 plus label with multicolored margin. Exist imperf.

BOHEMIA AND MORAVIA

Listed under Czechoslovakia.

BOLIVIA

(bō·liv'i·ȧ)

LOCATION—In the central part of South America, separated from the Pacific Coast by Chile and Peru.

GOVT.—Republic.

AREA—424,160 sq. mi.

POP.—5,950,000 (est. 1977).

CAPITAL—Sucre. (La Paz is the actual seat of government.)

100 Centavos = 1 Boliviano

100 Centavos = 1 Peso Boliviano (1963)

On February 21st, 1863, the Bolivian Government decreed contracts for carrying the mails should be let to the highest bidder, the service to commence on the day the bid was accepted, and stamps used for the payment of postage. On March 18th, 1863, the contract was awarded to Sr. Justiniano Garcia and was in effect until April 29th, 1863, when it was rescinded by the government. Stamps in the form illustrated above were prepared in denominations of ½, 1, 2 and 4 reales. All values exist in black and in blue. It is said that used copies exist on covers, but the authenticity of these covers remains to be established.

Condor
A1

A2

A3

72 varieties of each of the 5c, 78 varieties of the 10c, 30 varieties of each of the 50c and 100c.

The plate of the 5c stamps was entirely re-engraved four times and retouched at least six times. Various states of the plate have distinguishing characteristics, each of which is typical of most, though not all the stamps in a sheet. These characteristics (usually termed types) are found in the shading lines at the right side of the globe. (a.): vertical and diagonal lines; (b.): diagonal lines only; (c.): diagonal and horizontal with traces of vertical lines; (d): diagonal and horizontal lines; (e.): horizontal lines only; (f.): no lines except the curved ones forming the outlines of the globe.

Engraved.

1867–68 *Imperf.* **Unwmkd.**

1 A1 5c blue green (b) 7.00 *20.00*
a. 5c blue green (a) 7.00 *20.00*
b. 5c deep green (a) 7.00 *20.00*
c. 5c olive green, thick paper (a) 50.00 40.00
d. 5c yel. green, thick paper (a) 125.00 125.00
e. 5c yel. green, thick paper (b) 125.00 125.00
f. 5c yel. grn., thin paper (a, b) 5.00 7.00
2 A1 5c green (d) 6.00 11.00
a. 5c green (c) 7.00 11.00
b. 5c green (e) 6.00 11.00
c. 5c green (f) 6.00 11.00
3 A1 5c violet ('68) 275.00 175.00
a. 5c rose lilac ('68) 275.00 175.00
4 A3 10c brown 350.00 200.00
5 A2 50c orange 20.00 35.00
6 " 50c blue ('68) *400.00 275.00*
a. 50c dark blue ('68) *400.00 275.00*
7 A3 100c blue 65.00 *100.00*
8 A3 100c green ('68) 150.00 150.00
a. 100c pale blue green ('68) 150.00 150.00

Used prices are for postally canceled copies. Pen cancellations usually indicate that the stamps have been used fiscally and such stamps sell for about one-fifth as much as those with postal cancellations.

Nos. 2–8 have been reprinted.

(9 stars)

(11 stars)

Coat of Arms
A4 A5

1868–69 *Perf. 12*

Nine Stars

10 A4 5c green 25.00 12.50
11 " 10c vermilion 35.00 12.50
12 " 50c blue 50.00 30.00
13 " 100c orange 50.00 35.00
14 " 500c black 600.00 600.00

Eleven Stars

15 A5 5c green 12.50 7.50
16 " 10c vermilion 17.50 12.50
a. Half used as 5c as cover 500.00
17 A5 50c blue 40.00 20.00
18 " 100c deep orange 35.00 20.00
19 " 500c black *1500.00 1750.00*

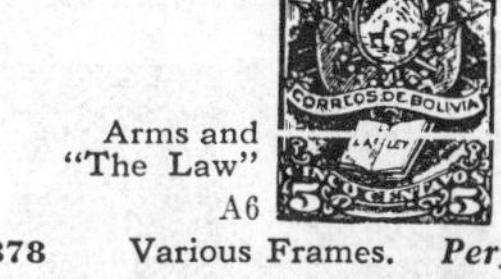

Arms and "The Law"
A6

1878 Various Frames. *Perf. 12*

20 A6 5c ultramarine 12.50 5.00
21 " 10c orange 10.00 4.00
a. Half used as 5c on cover 40.00
22 A6 20c green 30.00 5.00
a. Half used as 10c on cover 175.00
23 A6 50c dull carmine 125.00 15.00

(11 stars)

(9 stars)

Numerals Upright
A7 A8

1887 *Rouletted*

24 A7 1c rose 2.50 1.25
25 " 2c violet 2.50 1.25
26 A5 5c blue 9.00 2.00
27 " 10c orange 9.00 2.00

1890 *Perf. 12*

28 A8 1c rose 2.00 1.00
29 " 2c violet 4.00 1.55
30 A4 5c blue 2.50 1.00
31 " 10c orange 5.00 1.25
32 " 20c dark green 12.50 1.75
33 " 50c red 5.00 1.75
34 " 100c yellow 12.50 4.00
Nos. 28–34 (7) 43.50 12.25

1893 Lithographed. *Perf. 11.*

35 A8 1c rose 3.50 1.25
a. Imperf., pair 35.00
b. Imperf. vert., pair 17.50
c. Horizontal pair, imperf. between 35.00
36 " 2c violet 3.50 1.25
a. Block, of 4 imperf. vert. and horiz. through center 50.00
b. Horizontal pair, imperf. between 25.00
37 A7 5c blue 5.00 1.25
a. Imperf. horiz., pair 25.00
b. Horizontal pair imperf. between 35.00
38 A8 10c orange 15.00 2.00
a. Horizontal pair, imperf. between 60.00
39 " 20c dark green 50.00 15.00
a. Imperf. pair, vert. or horiz. 125.00
b. Pair, imperf. btwn., vert. or horiz. 125.00
Nos. 35–39 (5) 77.00 20.75

Coat of Arms
A9

Engraved.

Thin Paper.

1894 *Perf. 14, 14½.* **Unwmkd.**

40 A9 1c bistre 1.50 75
41 " 2c red orange 1.50 75
42 " 5c green 1.50 75
43 " 10c yellow brown 1.50 75
44 " 20c dark blue 4.00 1.50
45 " 50c claret 10.00 2.50
46 " 100c brown rose 25.00 10.00
Nos. 40–46 (7) 45.00 17.00

Stamps of type A9 on thick paper were surreptitiously printed in Paris on the order of an official and without government authorization. Some of these stamps were substituted for part of a shipment of stamps on thin paper, which had been printed in London on government order. When the thick paper stamps reached Bolivia they were at first repudiated but afterwards were allowed to do postal duty. A large quantity of the thick paper stamps were fraudulently cancelled in Paris with a cancellation of heavy bars forming an oval.

To be legitimate, copies of the thick paper stamps must have been bought at post offices in Bolivia, or must have genuine cancellations of Bolivia.

The 10c blue on thick paper is not known to have been issued.

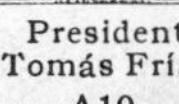

President Tomás Frías
A10

President José M. Linares
A11

Pedro Domingo Murillo
A12

Bernardo Monteagudo
A13

Gen. José Ballivián
A14

Gen. Antonio José de Sucre
A15

Simón Bolívar
A16

Coat of Arms
A17

1897 Lithographed. *Perf. 12.*

47 A10 1c pale yellow green 1.50 1.00
a. Imperf. horiz., pair 50.00
b. Vertical pair, imperf. between 50.00
48 A11 2c red 3.00 2.00
49 A12 5c dark green 3.00 1.00
a. Horizontal pair, imperf. between 50.00
50 A13 10c brown violet 3.00 1.00
a. Vertical pair, imperf. between 50.00
51 A14 20c lake & black 6.00 1.25
a. Imperf., pair 125.00
52 A15 50c orange 6.00 2.50
53 A16 1b Prussian blue 6.00 6.00
54 A17 2b red, yellow, green & black 30.00 40.00
Nos. 47–54 (8) 58.50 54.75

Excellent forgeries of No. 54 exist.

Nos. 40–44 Handstamped in Violet or Blue

E.F.
1899

1899 *Perf. 14½.*

55 A9 1c yellow bistre 15.00 15.00
56 " 2c red orange 20.00 20.00
57 " 5c green 12.50 12.50
58 " 10c yellow brown 15.00 12.50
59 " 20c dark blue 30.00 30.00
Nos. 55–59 (5) 92.50 90.00

The handstamp is found inverted, double, etc. Forgeries of this handstamp are plentiful. "E.F." stands for Estado Federal.

The 50c and 100c (Nos. 45–46) with similar handstamp are considered bogus.

Antonio José de Sucre
A18

Thin Paper.

1899 Engraved *Perf. 11½, 12*

62 A18 1c gray blue 1.50 75
63 " 2c brownish red 1.00 75
64 " 5c dark green 3.00 1.25
65 " 10c yellow orange 1.50 75
66 " 20c rose pink 2.00 75
67 " 50c bistre brown 3.50 1.25
68 " 1b gray violet 1.50 1.25
Nos. 62–68 (7) 14.00 6.75

1901

69 A18 5c dark red 2.00 80

Col. Adolfo Ballivián
A19

Eliodoro Camacho
A20

President Narciso Campero
A21

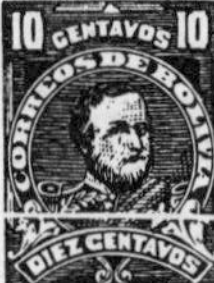

José Ballivián
A22

Gen. Andrés Santa Cruz
A23

Coat of Arms
A24

1901-02 **Engraved.**

No.	Type	Description	Unused	Used
70	A19	1c claret	50	25
71	A20	2c green	50	25
73	A21	5c scarlet	50	20
74	A22	10c blue	1.25	20
75	A23	20c violet & black	75	20
76	A24	2b brown	4.00	3.00
		Nos. 70–71, 73–76 (6)	7.50	4.10

1904 **Lithographed**

No.	Type	Description	Unused	Used
77	A19	1c claret	2.25	75

In No. 70 the panel above "CENTAVO" is shaded with continuous lines. In No. 77 the shading is of dots.

See also Nos. 103–105, 107, 110.

Coat of Arms of Dept. of La Paz
A25

Murillo
A26

José Miguel Lanza
A27

Ismael Montes
A28

1909 **Lithographed** ***Perf. 11***

No.	Type	Description	Unused	Used
78	A25	5c blue & black	10.00	5.00
79	A26	10c green & black	10.00	5.00
80	A27	20c orange & black	10.00	5.00
81	A28	2b red & black	10.00	5.00

Centenary of Revolution of July, 1809.

Nos. 78–81 exist imperf. and tête bêche. Nos. 79–81 exist with center inverted.

Miguel Betanzos
A29

Col. Ignacio Warnes
A30

Murillo
A31

Monteagudo
A32

Esteban Arce
A33

Antonio José de Sucre
A34

Simón Bolívar
A35

Manuel Belgrano
A36

Dated 1809–1825.

1909 ***Perf. 11½.***

No.	Type	Description	Unused	Used
82	A29	1c lt. brown & black	50	40
83	A30	2c green & black	60	50
84	A31	5c red & black	60	35
85	A32	10c dull blue & black	60	35
86	A33	20c violet & black	75	50
87	A34	50c olive bis. & blk.	1.00	75
88	A35	1b gray brn. & blk.	1.00	1.00
89	A36	2b chocolate & black	1.25	1.00
		Nos. 82-89 (8)	6.30	4.85

Issued in commemoration of the War of Independence, 1809-1825.

Warnes
A37

Betanzos—A38 Arce—A39

Dated 1910-1825.

1910 ***Perf. 13 x 13½.***

No.	Type	Description	Unused	Used
92	A37	5c green & black	40	20
		a. Imperf., pair	5.00	
93	A38	10c claret & indigo	40	20
		a. Imperf., pair	7.50	
94	A39	20c dull blue & indigo	85	50
		a. Imperf., pair	5.00	

Issued in commemoration of the War of Independence.

Nos. 92–94 may be found with parts of a papermaker's watermark: "A I & Co/ EXTRA STRONG/9303."

Nos. 71 and 75 Surcharged in Black

1911 ***Perf. 11½, 12.***

No.	Type	Description	Unused	Used
95	A20	5c on 2c green	60	30
		a. Inverted surcharge	7.00	7.00
		b. Double surcharge		
		c. Period after "1911"	5.00	1.25
		d. Blue surcharge	100.00	75.00
96	A23	5c on 20c violet & black	20.00	20.00
		a. Inverted surch.	45.00	45.00

No. 83 Handstamp Surcharged in Green

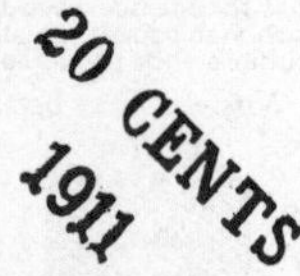

No.	Type	Description	Unused	Used
97	A30	20c on 2c green & black		*600.00*

This provisional was issued by local authorities at Villa Bella, a town on the Brazilian border. The 20c surcharge was applied after the stamp had been affixed to the cover. Excellent forgeries of No. 96–97 exist.

"Justice"
A40 A41

1912

Black or Dark Blue Overprint.

No.	Type	Description	Unused	Used
98	A40	2c green (Bk)	50	40
		a. Inverted overprint	6.00	
99	A41	10c vermilion (Bl)	1.00	70
		a. Inverted overprint	6.00	

A42

A43

Red or Black Overprint.

Engraved.

No.	Type	Description	Unused	Used
100	A42	5c orange (R)	50	50
		a. Inverted overprint	6.00	
		b. Pair, one without overprint	15.00	
		c. Black overprint	75.00	

Red or Black Surcharge.

No.	Type	Description	Unused	Used
101	A43	10c on 1c blue (R)	50	25
		a. Inverted surch.	7.50	
		b. Double surcharge	7.50	
		c. Double surcharge, one inverted	8.50	
102	"	10c on 1c bl. (Bk)	175.00	175.00

Revenue Stamp Surcharged "CORREOS / 10 Cts. / — 1917 —" in Red

1917 **Lithographed**

No.	Type	Description	Unused	Used
102D		10c on 1c blue	*1000.00*	*750.00*

Design similar to type A43.

Frías
A45

Sucre
A46

Bolívar
A47

1913 **Engraved.** ***Perf. 12.***

No.	Type	Description	Unused	Used
103	A19	1c carmine rose	25	20
104	A20	2c vermilion	25	15
105	A21	5c green	35	10
106	A45	8c yellow	75	50
107	A22	10c gray	75	20
108	A46	50c dull violet	1.25	50
109	A47	1b slate blue	2.00	1.00
110	A24	2b black	4.00	2.00
		Nos. 103–110 (8)	9.60	4.65

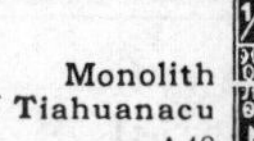

Monolith of Tiahuanacu
A48

Mt. Potosí
A49

Lake Titicaca
A50

Mt. Illimani
A51

Legislature Building
A53

FIVE CENTAVOS.

Type I. Numerals have background of vertical lines. Clouds formed of dots.

Type II. Numerals on white background. Clouds near the mountain formed of wavy lines.

1916-17 **Lithographed.** ***Perf. 11½.***

No.	Type	Description	Unused	Used
111	A48	½c brown	25	25
		a. Imperf. vert., pair	6.00	
112	A49	1c gray green	25	15
		a. Imperf., pair	2.00	
113	A50	2c carmine & black	25	15
		a. Imperf., pair	2.00	
		b. Imperf. horiz.		
		c. Center inverted	12.50	12.50
		d. Imperf., center inverted	15.00	
114	A51	5c dark blue (I)	65	25
		a. Imperf., pair	2.00	
		b. Imperf. horiz., pair	4.00	
		c. Imperf. vert., pair	4.00	
115	"	5c dark blue (II)	60	10
		a. Imperf., pair	2.50	
116	A53	10c orange & blue	1.00	10
		a. Imperf., pair	3.00	
		b. No period after "Legislativo"	1.00	15
		c. Center inverted	40.00	40.00
		d. Vertical pair, imperf. between	6.00	
		Nos. 111-116 (6)	3.00	1.00

Coat of Arms
A54 A55

Printed by the American Bank Note Co.

1919-20 **Engraved.** ***Perf. 12.***

No.	Type	Description	Unused	Used
118	A54	1c carmine	25	25
119	"	2c dark violet	5.00	3.00
120	"	5c dark green	40	10
121	"	10c vermilion	40	10
122	"	20c dark blue	1.50	35
123	"	22c light blue	75	75
124	"	24c purple	75	50
125	"	50c orange	4.00	65
126	A55	1b red brown	6.00	1.50
127	"	2b black brown	10.00	5.00
		Nos. 118-127 (10)	29.05	12.20

Printed by Perkins, Bacon & Co., Ltd.

Types of 1919–20 Issue.

Re-engraved.

1923-27 ***Perf. 13½.***

No.	Type	Description	Unused	Used
128	A54	1c carmine ('27)	15	10
129	"	2c dark violet	30	15

No.	Type	Description	Unused	Used
130	A54	5c deep green	75	10
131	"	10c vermilion	17.50	15.00
132	"	20c slate blue	1.50	25
135	"	50c orange	3.00	75
136	A55	1b red brown	75	40
137	"	2b black brown	50	35
		Nos. 128-137 (8)	24.45	17.10

The stamps of 1919–20 are perf. 12, those of 1923 are perf. 13½. The two issues may thus be readily distinguished. There are many differences in the designs of the two issues but they are too minute to be illustrated or described.

See also Nos. 144-146.

Stamps of 1919-20 Surcharged in Blue, Black or Red

Habilitada 15 cts.

1924 *Perf. 12.*

No.	Type	Description	Unused	Used
138	A54	5c on 1c carmine (Bl)	40	30
		a. Inverted surcharge	6.00	6.00
		b. Double surcharge	6.00	6.00
139	"	15c on 10c vermilion (Bk)	85	50
		a. Inverted surcharge	9.00	9.00
140	"	15c on 22c light blue (Bk)	75	35
		a. Inverted surcharge	7.50	7.50
		b. Double surcharge, one inverted		
		c. Red surcharge	30.00	

Same Surcharge on No. 131.

Perf. 13½

No.	Type	Description	Unused	Used
142	A54	15c on 10c vermilion (Bk)	40	30
		a. Inverted surch.	8.00	8.00

No. 121 Surcharged

Habilitada 15 cts.

Perf. 12.

No.	Type	Description	Unused	Used
143	A54	15c on 10c vermilion (Bk)	50	40
		a. Inverted surch.	8.00	8.00
		b. Double surcharge	7.00	7.00
		Nos. 138-143 (5)	2.90	1.85

Printed by Waterlow & Sons.

Type of 1919-20 Issue.

Second Re-engraving.

1925 *Perf. 12½* **Unwmkd.**

No.	Type	Description	Unused	Used
144	A54	5c deep green	75	35
145	"	15c ultramarine	75	20
146	"	20c dark blue	50	20

These stamps may be identified by the perforation.

Miner
A56

Condor Looking Toward the Sea
A57

Designs: 2c, Sower. 5c, Torch of Eternal Freedom. 10c, National flower (kantuta). 15c, Pres. Bautista Saavedra. 50c, Liberty head. 1b, Archer on horse. 2b, Mercury. 5b, Gen. A. J. de Sucre.

1925 Engraved. *Perf. 14.*

No.	Type	Description	Unused	Used
150	A56	1c dark green	1.25	75
151	"	2c rose	1.25	75
152	"	5c red, *green*	1.25	35
153	"	10c carmine, *yellow*	1.50	75
154	"	15c red brown	75	35
155	A57	25c ultramarine	1.00	50
156	A56	50c deep violet	1.00	50
157	"	1b red	1.75	1.25
158	A57	2b orange	2.75	2.00
159	A56	5b black brown	3.50	2.25
		Nos. 150-159 (10)	16.00	9.45

Issued to commemorate the centenary of the Republic.

Stamps of 1919-27 Surcharged in Blue, Black or Red

1927 5 CENTAVOS

1927

No.	Type	Description	Unused	Used
160	A54	5c on 1c carmine (Bl)	1.50	1.25
		a. Inverted surcharge	6.00	6.00
		b. Black surcharge	30.00	30.00

Perf. 12.

No.	Type	Description	Unused	Used
162	A54	10c on 24c purple (Bk)	1.50	1.25
		a. Inverted surcharge	40.00	40.00
		b. Red surcharge	30.00	30.00

Coat of Arms
A66

Printed by Waterlow & Sons.

1927 Lithographed. *Perf. 13½.*

No.	Type	Description	Unused	Used
165	A66	2c yellow	35	25
166	"	3c pink	50	40
167	"	4c red brown	50	35
168	"	20c light olive green	75	25
169	"	25c deep blue	75	35
170	"	30c violet	75	50
171	"	40c orange	1.75	50
172	"	50c deep brown	1.75	50
173	A55	1b red	2.00	50
174	"	2b plum	3.00	75
175	"	3b olive green	3.00	2.00
176	"	4b claret	4.00	2.50
177	"	5b bistre brown	5.00	1.50
		Nos. 165-177 (13)	22.10	10.35

Type of 1927 Issue Overprinted

Octubre 1927

1927

No.	Type	Description	Unused	Used
178	A66	5c dark green	35	25
179	"	10c slate	50	25
180	"	15c carmine	75	50

Stamps of 1919-27 Surcharged

15 cts. 1928

Perf. 12, 12½, 13½

1928 Red Surcharge.

No.	Type	Description	Unused	Used
181	A54	15c on 20c dark blue (No. 122)	10.00	10.00
182	"	15c on 20c slate blue (No. 132)	10.00	10.00
		a. Black surcharge	55.00	
183	"	15c on 20c dk. blue (No. 146)	200.00	200.00

Black Surcharge.

No.	Type	Description	Unused	Used
184	A54	15c on 24c purple (No. 124)	2.00	1.50
		a. Inverted surcharge	5.00	5.00
		b. Blue surcharge	55.00	
185	"	15c on 50c orange (No. 125)	50.00	50.00
186	"	15c on 50c orange (No. 135)	1.50	1.00
		Nos. 181-186 (6)	273.50	272.50

Forgeries of Nos. 181-186 exist.

Condor
A67

Hernando Siles
A68

Map of Bolivia
A69

Printed by Perkins, Bacon & Co., Ltd.

1928 Engraved. *Perf. 13½.*

No.	Type	Description	Unused	Used
189	A67	5c green	50	10
190	A68	10c slate	50	10
191	A69	15c carmine lake	1.00	15

Stamps of 1913-17 Surcharged in Various Colors

0.03 Centavos R. S. 21-4 1930

1930 *Perf. 12, 11½.*

No.	Type	Description	Unused	Used
193	A20	1c on 2c vermilion (Bl)	1.00	1.00
		a. "0.10" for "0.01"	15.00	15.00
194	A50	3c on 2c carmine & black (Br)	1.25	1.00
195	A48	25c on ½c brn. (Bk)	1.00	75
196	A50	25c on 2c carmine & black (V)	1.00	75

The lines of the surcharges were spaced to fit the various shapes of the stamps. The surcharges exist inverted, double, etc.

Trial printings were made of the surcharges on Nos. 193 and 194 in black and on No. 196 in brown.

Mt. Potosí
A70

Mt. Illimani
A71

Eduardo Abaroa
A72

Map of Bolivia
A73

Sucre
A74

Bolívar
A75

1931 Engraved. *Perf. 14.*

No.	Type	Description	Unused	Used
197	A70	2c green	50	40
198	A71	5c light blue	40	15
199	A72	10c red orange	50	15
200	A73	15c violet	75	20
201	"	35c carmine	1.50	75
202	"	45c orange	1.50	75
203	A74	50c gray	75	50
204	A75	1b brown	1.50	1.50
		Nos. 197-204 (8)	7.40	4.40

See also Nos. 207, 241.

Symbols of 1930 Revolution—A76

1931 Lithographed. *Perf. 11.*

No.	Type	Description	Unused	Used
205	A76	15c scarlet	3.00	50
		a. Pair, imperf. between		
206	A76	50c bright violet	1.00	75
		a. Pair, imperf. between	10.00	

Revolution of June 25, 1930.

Map Type of 1931.
Without Imprint.

1932 Lithographed.

No.	Type	Description	Unused	Used
207	A73	15c violet	1.50	40

Stamps of 1927-31 Surcharged

Habilitada A 15 Cts. D. S. 13-7.1933

1933 *Perf. 13½, 14.*

No.	Type	Description	Unused	Used
208	A66	5c on 1b red	50	25
		a. Without period after "Cts"	1.00	1.00
209	A73	15c on 35c carmine	25	25
210	"	15c on 45c orange	25	25
		a. Inverted surcharge	2.50	2.50
211	A66	15c on 50c deep brown	50	20
212	"	25c on 40c orange	50	15
		Nos. 208-212 (5)	2.00	1.10

The hyphens in "13-7-33" occur in three positions.

Coat of Arms
A77

1933 Engraved *Perf. 12*

No.	Type	Description	Unused	Used
213	A77	2c blue green	30	15
214	"	5c blue	20	10
215	"	10c red	50	35
216	"	15c deep violet	30	15
217	"	25c dark blue	75	50
		Nos. 213-217 (5)	2.05	1.25

Mariano Baptista
A78

Map of Bolivia
A79

1935

No.	Type	Description	Unused	Used
218	A78	15c dull violet	50	25

1935

No.	Type	Description	Unused	Used
219	A79	2c dark blue	25	15
220	"	3c yellow	25	15
221	"	5c vermilion	25	15
222	"	5c blue green	25	15
223	"	10c black brown	25	15
224	"	15c deep rose	30	15
225	"	15c ultramarine	30	15
226	"	20c yellow green	40	20

227	A79	25c light blue	40	15
228	"	30c deep rose	75	30
229	"	40c orange	75	25
230	"	50c gray violet	75	15
231	"	1b yellow	75	50
232	"	2b olive brown	1.50	1.00
		Nos. 219-232 (14)	7.15	3.60

Regular Stamps of 1925-33 Surcharged in Black

Comunicaciones
D. S.
25-2-37
0.05

1937 ***Perf. 11, 12, 13½.***

233	A77	5c on 2c blue green	25	25
234	"	15c on 25c dark blue	35	35
235	"	30c on 25c dark blue	50	50
236	A55	45c on 1b red brown	60	60
237	"	1b on 2b plum	75	75
		a. "1" missing	4.00	4.00
238	A77	2b on 25c dark blue	75	75

"Comunicaciones" on one line.

239	A76	3b on 50c bright violet	1.00	1.00
		a. "3" of value missing	5.00	5.00
240	"	5b on 50c bright violet	1.50	1.50
		Nos. 233-240 (8)	5.70	5.70

President Siles—A80

1937 ***Perf. 14*** **Unwmkd.**

241	A80	1c yellow brown	25	20

Native School
A81

Oil Wells
A82

Modern Factories
A83

Torch of Knowledge
A84

Map of the Sucre-Camiri R. R.
A85

Allegory of Free Education
A86

Allegorical Figure of Learning
A87

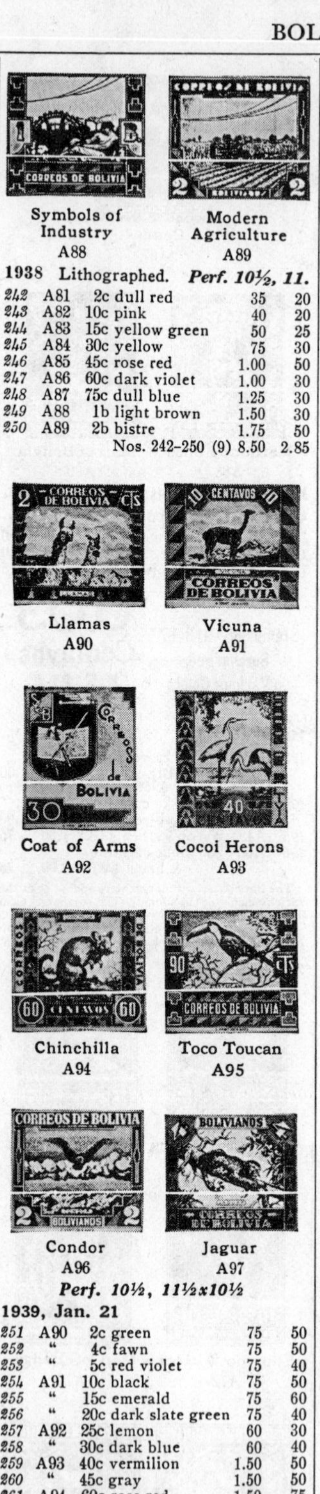

Symbols of Industry
A88

Modern Agriculture
A89

1938 Lithographed. ***Perf. 10½, 11.***

242	A81	2c dull red	35	20
243	A82	10c pink	40	20
244	A83	15c yellow green	50	25
245	A84	30c yellow	75	30
246	A85	45c rose red	1.00	50
247	A86	60c dark violet	1.00	30
248	A87	75c dull blue	1.25	30
249	A88	1b light brown	1.50	30
250	A89	2b bistre	1.75	50
		Nos. 242-250 (9)	8.50	2.85

Llamas
A90

Vicuna
A91

Coat of Arms
A92

Cocoi Herons
A93

Chinchilla
A94

Toco Toucan
A95

Condor
A96

Jaguar
A97

Perf. 10½, 11½x10½

1939, Jan. 21

251	A90	2c green	75	50
252	"	4c fawn	75	50
253	"	5c red violet	75	40
254	A91	10c black	75	50
255	"	15c emerald	75	60
256	"	20c dark slate green	75	40
257	A92	25c lemon	60	30
258	"	30c dark blue	60	40
259	A93	40c vermilion	1.50	50
260	"	45c gray	1.50	50
261	A94	60c rose red	1.50	75
262	"	75c slate blue	1.50	75
263	A95	90c orange	2.00	75
264	"	1b blue	2.50	75
265	A96	2b rose lake	3.00	75
266	"	3b dark violet	4.00	1.00
267	A97	4b brown orange	5.00	1.25
268	"	5b gray brown	6.00	1.25
		Nos. 251-268 (18)	34.20	11.85

Imperforate counterfeits of some values exist.

Flags of 21 American Republics
A98

1940, Apr. **Litho.** ***Perf. 10½***

269	A98	9b multicolored	2.75	2.00

Pan American Union, 150th anniversary.

Statue of Murillo
A99

Pedro Domingo Murillo
A102

Urns of Murillo and Sagarnaga
A100

Dream of Murillo
A101

1941, Apr. 15

270	A99	10c dull violet brn.	15	10
271	A100	15c light green	25	15
		a. Imperf. (pair)	5.00	
272	A101	45c carmine rose	25	20
		a. Double impression		
273	A102	1.05b dark ultra.	50	25

Issued to commemorate the 130th anniversary of the death (by execution) of Pedro Domingo Murillo (1759–1810), patriot.

First Stamp of Bolivia and 1941 Airmail Stamp—A103

1942, Oct. **Litho.** ***Perf. 13½***

274	A103	5c pink	1.00	75
275	"	10c orange	1.00	75
276	"	20c yellow green	1.50	75
277	"	40c carmine rose	2.00	1.00
278	"	90c ultramarine	4.00	1.25
279	"	1b violet	6.00	3.00
280	"	10b olive bistre	20.00	12.50
		Nos. 274-280 (7)	35.50	20.00

Issued in commemoration of the first School Philatelic Exposition held in La Paz, October, 1941.

Gen. Ballivian Leading Cavalry Charge, Battle of Ingavi
A104

1943 **Photogravure** ***Perf. 12½***

281	A104	2c light blue green	10	5
282	"	3c orange	10	5
283	A104	25c deep plum	15	10
284	"	45c ultramarine	20	15
285	"	3b scarlet	60	40
286	"	4b bright rose lilac	75	50
287	"	5b black brown	1.00	60
		Nos. 281-287 (7)	2.90	1.85

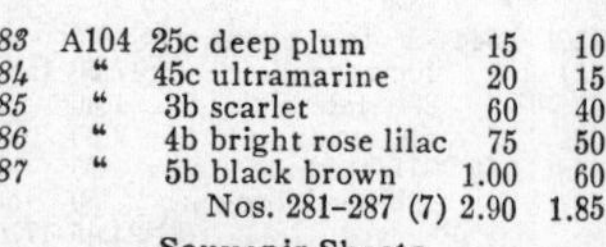

Souvenir Sheets.

Perf. 13, Imperf.

288	A104	Sheet of 4	2.50	2.50
289	"	Sheet of 3	7.50	7.50

Centenary of the Battle of Ingavi, 1841. No. 288 contains 4 stamps similar to Nos. 281–284, No. 289 three stamps similar to Nos. 285–287: black marginal inscriptions. Size: 139x100mm.

Potosí
A107

Quechisla
A108

Miner
A109

Dam
A110

Mine Interior
A111

Chaquiri Dam
A112

Entrance to Pulacayo Mine
A113

1943 Engraved. *Perf. 12½.*

290 A107 15c red brown 25 15
291 A108 45c violet blue 25 15
292 A109 1.25b bright rose violet 30 25
293 A110 1.50b emerald 35 25
294 A111 2b brown black 40 30
295 A112 2.10b light blue 50 35
296 A113 3b red orange 75 50
Nos. 290-296 (7) 2.80 1.95

General José Ballivián and Cathedral at Trinidad
A114

1943, Nov. 18

297 A114 5c dark green & brown 10 10
298 " 10c dull pur. & brown 15 15
299 " 30c rose red & brown 20 20
300 " 45c brt. ultra. & brown 30 30
301 " 2.10b deep orange & brown 35 35
Nos. 297-301, C91-C95 (10) 2.45 2.00

Department of Beni centenary.

"Honor—Work—Law"
A115

"United for the Country"
A116

1944 Lithographed *Perf. 13½*

302 A115 20c orange 10 10
303 " 90c ultramarine 15 10
304 A116 1b bright red violet 20 15
305 " 2.40b dull brown 30 20

1945

306 A115 20c green 5 5
307 " 90c deep rose 10 6
Nos. 302-307, C96-C99 (10) 2.00 1.21

Nos. 302-307 were issued to commemorate the Revolution of Dec. 20, 1943.

Leopold Benedetto Vincenti, Joseph Ignacio de Sanjines and Bars of Anthem
A117

1946, Aug. 21 Litho. *Perf. 10½*

308 A117 5c rose violet & black 10 10
309 " 10c ultra. & black 10 10
310 " 15c blue green & black 10 10
311 " 30c vermilion & brown 15 15
a. Souvenir sheet 75 75
312 " 90c dark blue & brown 15 15
313 " 2b black & brown 40 20
a. Souvenir sheet 1.50 1.50
Nos. 308-313 (6) 1.00 80

Issued to commemorate the centenary of the adoption of Bolivia's national anthem.

Nos. 311a and 313a measure 86x136½ mm., contain respectively one each of Nos. 311 and 313, and are imperforate. The price of each sheet included a surtax of 4 bolivianos.

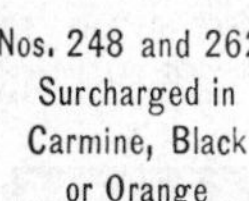

Nos. 248 and 262 Surcharged in Carmine, Black or Orange

1947, Mar. 12 *Perf. 10½, 11*

314 A87 1.40b on 75c dull blue (C) 15 8
315 A94 1.40b on 75c slate blue (Bk) 15 8
316 " 1.40b on 75c slate blue (C) 15 8
317 " 1.40b on 75c slate blue (O) 15 8
Nos. 314-317, C112 (5) 80 52

People Attacking Presidential Palace
A118

Arms of Bolivia and Argentina
A119

1947, Sept. Litho. *Perf. 13½*

318 A118 20c blue green 5 4
a. Imperf. (pair)
319 " 50c lilac rose 10 6
320 " 1.40b greenish blue 15 8
a. Imperf. (pair)
321 " 3.70b dull orange 25 12
322 " 4b violet 35 20
323 " 10b olive 75 45
Nos. 318-323, C113-C117 (11) 2.39 1.46

Issued to commemorate the first anniversary of the Revolution of July 21, 1946.

1947, Oct. 23

324 A119 1.40b deep orange 12 8

Issued to commemorate the meeting of Presidents Enrique Hertzog of Bolivia and Juan D. Peron of Argentina at Yacuiba on October 23, 1947. See also No. C118.

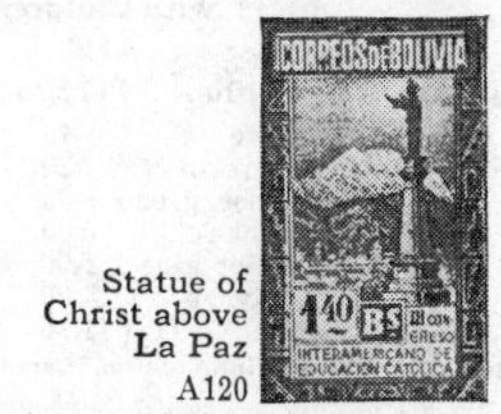

Statue of Christ above La Paz
A120

Designs: 2b, Child kneeling before cross of Golgotha. 3b, St. John Bosco. No. 328, Virgin of Copacabana. No. 329, Pope Pius XII blessing University of La Paz.

1948, Sept. 26 *Perf. 11½* Unwmkd.

325 A120 1.40b blue & yellow 40 18
326 " 2b yellow green & salmon 50 22
327 " 3b green & gray 1.00 30
328 " 5b vio. & salmon 1.50 35
329 " 5b red brown & light green 2.00 35
Nos. 325-329, C119-C123 (10) 10.40 2.88

Issued to publicize the 3rd Inter-American Congress of Catholic Education.

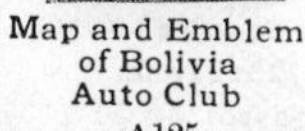

Map and Emblem of Bolivia Auto Club
A125

Pres. Gregorio Pacheco, Map and Post Horn
A126

1948, Oct. 20

330 A125 5b indigo & sal. 2.50 25

Issued to publicize the International Automobile Races of South America, September-October 1948. See also No. C124.

1950, Jan. 2 Litho. *Perf. 11½*

331 A126 1.40b violet blue 12 10
332 " 4.20b red 12 10
Nos. 331-332, C125-C127 (5) 64 60

Issued to commemorate the 75th anniversary of the formation of the Universal Postal Union.

No. 273 Surcharged in Black

Bs.2.-
Habilitada
D.S.6·VII·50

1950 *Perf. 10½*

333 A102 2b on 1.05b dark ultramarine 15 10

Crucifix and View of Potosí
A127

Symbols of United Nations
A128

Perf. 11½

1950, Sept. 14 Litho. Unwmkd.

334 A127 20c violet 6 6
335 " 30c deep orange 6 6
336 " 50c lilac rose 6 6
337 " 1b carmine 10 6
338 " 2b blue 15 6
339 " 6b chocolate 25 15
Nos. 334-339 (6) 68 45

Issued to commemorate the 400th anniversary of the appearance of a crucifix at Potosi.

1950, Oct. 24

340 A128 60c ultramarine 1.50 20
341 " 2b green 2.00 35

Issued to commemorate the 5th anniversary of the formation of the United Nations, October 24, 1945. See also Nos. C138-C139.

Gate of the Sun and Llama
A129

Church of San Francisco
A130

Designs: 40c, Avenue Camacho. 50c, Consistorial Palace. 1b, Legislative Palace. 1.40b, Communications Bldg. 2b, Arms. 3b, La Gasca ordering Mendoza to found La Paz. 5b, Capt. Alonso de Mendoza founding La Paz. 10b, Arms; portrait of Mendoza.

1951, Mar. Engraved *Perf. 12½*

Center in Black.

342 A129 20c green 8 8
343 A130 30c deep orange 8 8
344 A129 40c bistre brown 8 8
345 " 50c dark red 8 8
346 " 1b deep purple 10 10
347 " 1.40b dark violet blue 12 12
348 " 2b deep purple 12 12
349 A129 3b red lilac 18 12
a. Sheet, Nos. 345, 346, 348, 349 1.25 1.25
b. Sheet, imperf. 1.25 1.25
350 " 5b dark red 25 18
a. Sheet, Nos. 344, 347, 350 1.25 1.25
b. Sheet, imperf. 1.25 1.25
351 " 10b sepia 50 25
a. Sheet, Nos. 342, 343, 351 1.25 1.25
b. Sheet, imperf. 1.25 1.25
Nos. 342-351, C140-C149 (20) 3.98 3.60

Issued to commemorate the 400th anniversary of the founding of La Paz.

The souvenir sheets measure 150x100 mm., and contain marginal inscriptions in black.

Boxing
A131

Designs: 50c, Tennis. 1b, Diving. 1.40b, Soccer. 2b, Skiing. 3b, Handball. 4b, Cycling.

Engraved

1951, July 1 *Perf. 12½* Unwmkd.

Center in Black.

352 A131 20c deep blue 15 6
353 " 50c red 15 10
354 " 1b claret 20 10
355 " 1.40b yellow 20 12
356 " 2b bright carmine 50 18
357 " 3b yellow brown 75 40
a. Sheet, Nos. 352, 353, 356, 357 2.25 2.25
b. Sheet, imperf. 2.25 2.25
358 " 4b violet blue 1.00 50
a. Sheet, Nos. 354, 355, 358 1.75 1.75
b. Sheet, imperf. 1.75 1.75
Nos. 352-358, C150-C156 (14) 9.25 4.17

The stamps were intended to commemorate the 5th athletic championship matches held at La Paz, October 1948.

The sheets measure 150x100 mm., and contain marginal inscriptions in black.

Eagle and Flag of Bolivia
A132

1951, Nov. 5 Litho. *Perf. 11½*

Flag in Red, Yellow and Green.

359 A132 2b aquamarine 10 10
360 " 3.50b ultramarine 10 10
361 " 5b purple 20 15
362 " 7.50b gray 35 15
363 " 15b deep carmine 50 30
364 " 30b sepia 1.00 60
Nos. 359-364 (6) 2.25 1.40

Issued to commemorate the centenary of the adoption of Bolivia's national flag.

Eduardo Abaroa
A133

Queen Isabella I
A134

1952, Mar. *Perf. 11*

365 A133 80c dark carmine 10 5
366 " 1b red orange 10 10
367 " 2b emerald 15 10
368 " 5b ultramarine 20 15
369 " 10b lilac rose 40 20
370 " 20b dark brown 75 50
Nos. 365-370, C157-C162 (12) 5.55 2.80

Issued to commemorate the 73rd anniversary of the death of Eduardo Abaroa.

1952, July 16 ***Perf. 13½*** **Unwmkd.**

371 A134 2b violet blue 15 10
372 " 6.30b carmine 25 15

Issued to commemorate the 500th anniversary of the birth of Queen Isabella I of Spain. See also Nos. C163-C164.

Columbus Lighthouse
A135

1952, July 16 **Lithographed**

373 A135 2b violet blue, *blue* 15 10
374 " 5b carmine, *salmon* 35 20
375 " 9b emerald, *green* 50 35
Nos. 373-375, C165-C168 (7) 2.05 1.23

Miner
A136

1953, Apr. 9

376 A136 2.50b vermilion 10 8
377 " 8b violet 15 12

Issued to publicize the nationalization of the mines.

Gualberto Villarroel,
Victor Paz Estenssoro and
Hernan Siles Zuazo
A137

1953, Apr. 9 ***Perf. 11½***

378 A137 50c rose lilac 5 5
379 " 1b bright rose 5 5
380 " 2b violet blue 5 5
381 " 3b light green 10 10
382 " 4b yellow orange 10 10
383 " 5b dull violet 15 10
Nos. 378-383, C169-C175 (13) 1.50 1.20

Issued to commemorate the first anniversary of the Revolution of Apr. 9, 1952.

Map of
Bolivia and
Cow's Head
A138

Designs: 17b, Same as 5b.
25b, 85b, Map and ear of wheat.

1954, Aug. 2 ***Perf. 12x11½***

384 A138 5b carmine rose 5 4
385 " 17b aquamarine 10 7
386 " 25b chalky blue 15 8
387 " 85b black brown 35 25
Nos. 384-387, C176-C181 (10) 3.00 98

Nos. 384-385 were issued to commemorate the agrarian reform laws of 1953-54. Nos. 386-387 commemorate the 1st National Congress of Agronomy.

Oil Refinery
A139

Perf. 12x11½

1955, Oct. 9 **Unwmkd.**

388 A139 10b ultramarine & light ultramarine 5 4
389 " 35b rose car. & rose 10 5
390 " 40b dark & light yellow green 10 5
391 " 50b red violet & lilac rose 15 5
392 " 80b brown & bistre brown 25 8
Nos. 388-392, C182-C186 (10) 3.85 2.08

Nos. 342-351, Surcharged with
New Values and Bars in Ultramarine.

1957, Feb. 14 **Engr.** ***Perf. 12½***

Center in Black.

393 A129 50b on 3b red lilac 10 4
394 " 100b on 2b dp. pur. 10 4
395 " 200b on 1b dp. pur. 15 6
396 " 300b on 1.40b dark violet blue 20 6
397 " 350b on 20c green 25 8
398 " 400b on 40c bistre brown 25 8
399 A130 600b on 30c dp. org. 35 10
400 A129 800b on 50c dark red 50 12
401 " 1000b on 10b sepia 50 20
402 " 2000b on 5b dark red 85 30
Nos. 393-402 (10) 3.25 1.08

See also Nos. C187-C196.

CEPAL Building,
Santiago de Chile,
and Meeting Hall
in La Paz
A140

1957, May 15 **Litho.** ***Perf. 13***

403 A140 150b gray & ultra. 10 5
404 " 350b bistre brown & gray 20 8
405 " 550b chalky blue & brown 25 12
406 " 750b deep rose & green 30 15
407 " 900b green & brown black 50 20
Nos. 403-407, C197-C201 (10) 6.60 3.60

Issued to commemorate the seventh session of the C. E. P. A. L. (Comision Economica para la America Latina de las Naciones Unidas), La Paz.

Presidents
Siles Zuazo
and
Aramburu
A141

1957, Dec. 15 ***Perf. 11½*** **Unwmkd.**

408 A141 50b red orange 10 5
409 " 350b blue 25 10
410 " 1000b reddish brown 50 15
Nos. 408-410, C202-C204 (6) 1.95 70

Issued to commemorate the opening of the Santa Cruz-Yacuiba Railroad and the meeting of the Presidents of Bolivia and Argentina.

Flags of Bolivia and Mexico and
Presidents Hernan Siles Zuazo
and Adolfo Lopez Mateos
A142

1960, Jan. 30 **Litho.** ***Perf. 11½***

411 A142 350b olive 25 8
412 " 600b red brown 35 15
413 A147 1,500b black brown 75 25
Nos. 411-413, C205-C207 (6) 3.85 1.53

Issued for an expected visit of Mexico's President Adolfo Lopez Mateos. On sale Jan. 30-Feb. 1, 1960.

Indians and Mt. Illimani
A143

Refugee Children
A144

1960, Mar. 26 **Unwmkd.**

414 A143 500b olive bistre 25 10
415 " 1,000b blue 50 20
416 " 2,000b brown 1.00 50
417 " 4,000b green 2.00 75
Nos. 414-417, C208-C211 (8) 20.25 10.30

1960, Apr. 7 ***Perf. 11½***

418 A144 50b brown 10 5
419 " 350b claret 15 6
420 " 400b steel blue 20 8
421 " 1,000b gray brown 50 25
422 " 3,000b slate green 1.25 70
Nos. 418-422, C212-C216 (10) 5.20 3.24

Issued to publicize World Refugee Year, July 1, 1959-June 30, 1960.

Jaime Laredo
A145

Rotary Emblem
and Nurse
with Children
A146

1960, Aug. 15 **Litho.** ***Perf. 11½***

423 A145 100b olive 15 10
424 " 350b deep rose 20 10
425 " 500b Pruss. green 35 15
426 " 1,000b brown 60 25
427 " 1,500b violet blue 1.00 35
428 " 5,000b gray 3.00 1.25
Nos. 423-428, C217-C222 (12) 11.10 5.15

Issued to honor violinist Jaime Laredo.

1960, Nov. 19 ***Perf. 11½***

429 A146 350b green, yellow & deep blue 20 10
430 " 500b brown, yellow & deep blue 30 10
431 " 600b violet, yellow & deep blue 35 15
432 " 1,000b gray, yellow & deep blue 50 25
Nos. 429-432, C223-C226 (8) 6.60 3.65

Issued for the Children's Hospital, sponsored by the Rotary Club of La Paz.

Designs from Gate of the Sun
A147 A148

Designs: Various prehistoric gods and ornaments from Tiahuanacu excavations.

Lithographed

1960, Dec. 16 ***Perf. 13x12, 12x13***

Gold Background.

Surcharge in Black or Dark Red (#436)

Size: 21x23, 23x21mm.

433 A147 50b on ½c red 50 35
434 " 100b on 1c red 30 15
435 A147 200b on 2c black 1.00 10
436 " 300b on 5c green 25 12
437 " 350b on 10c green 25 1.00
438 A148 400b on 15c indigo 35 15
439 " 500b on 20c red 35 20
440 " 500b on 50c red 40 20
441 " 600b on 22½c green 50 30
442 " 600b on 60c violet 60 40
443 " 700b on 25c violet 80 25
444 " 700b on 1b green 1.25 75
445 " 800b on 30c red 50 25
446 " 900b on 40c green 50 30
447 " 1000b on 2b blue 60 35
448 " 1800b on 3b gray 5.00 4.00

Perf. 11

Size: 49½x23mm.

449 A148 4000b on 4b gray 45.00 40.00

Perf. 11x13½

Size: 49x53mm.

450 A147 5000b on 5b gray 9.00 9.00
Nos. 433-450 (18) 66.85 57.87

Nos. 433-450 were not regularly issued without surcharge. Price (set), $20.

The decree for Nos. 433-450 stipulated that seven were for air mail (500b on 50c, 600b on 60c, 700b on 1b, 1,000b, 1,800b, 4,000b and 5,000b), but the overprinting failed to include "Aereo."

The 800b surcharge also exists on the 1c red and gold. This was not listed in the decree.

Miguel
de Cervantes
A149

Nuflo de Chaves
A150

1961, Nov. Photo. ***Perf. 13x12½***

451 A149 600b ochre & dull violet 25 12

Issued to commemorate Cervantes' appointment as Chief Magistrate of La Paz. See also No. C230.

1961, Nov. **Unwmkd.**

452 A150 1500b dk. blue, *buff* 45 30

Issued to commemorate the 400th anniversary of the founding of Santa Cruz de la Sierra. See also Nos. 468, C246.

People below
Eucharist Symbol
A151

Hibiscus
A152

1962, Mar. 19 **Litho.** ***Perf. 10½***

453 A151 1000b gray green, red & yel. 75 35

Issued to commemorate the Fourth National Eucharistic Congress, Santa Cruz, 1961. See also No. C231.

Nos. 418-422 Surcharged Horizontally
with New Value and Bars or
Greek Key Border Segment

1962, June ***Perf. 11½***

454 A144 600b on 50b brn. 25 20
455 " 900b on 350b claret 35 20
456 " 1,000b on 400b steel blue 50 25
457 " 2,000b on 1,000b gray brown 65 40

458 A144 3,500b on 3,000b slate green 1.00 75
Nos. 454-458, C232-C236 (10) 6.75 4.80

Old value obliterated with two short bars on No. 454; four short bars on Nos. 455-456 and Greek key border on Nos. 457-458. The Greek key obliteration comes in two positions: two full "keys" on top, and one full and two half keys on top.

1962, June 28 Litho. ***Perf. 10½***

Flowers in Natural Colors

Flowers: 400b, Bicolored vanda. 600b, Lily. 1000b, Orchid.

459 A152 200b slate blue 25 10
460 " 400b brown 25 15
461 " 600b dark blue 50 20
462 " 1000b violet 75 35
Nos. 459-462, C237-C240 (8) 9.35 4.65

Infantry A153

Anti-Malaria Emblem A154

Designs: 500b, Cavalry. 600b, Artillery. 2000b, Engineers.

1962, Sept. 5 ***Perf. 11½***

Insigne in Red, Yellow & Green

463 A153 400b blk., maroon, & buff 10 8
464 " 500b blk., lt. & dk. green 15 10
465 " 600b black & pale bistre 20 15
466 " 2000b black & brn. 60 40
Nos. 463-466, C241-C244 (8) 3.40 2.73

Issued in honor of Bolivia's Armed Forces.

1962, Oct. 4

467 A154 600b dk. & lt. vio. & yellow 25 15

Issued for the World Health Organization drive to eradicate malaria. See No. C245.

Portrait Type of 1961.

Design: 600b, Alonso de Mendoza.

1962 Photogravure ***Perf. 13x12½***

468 A150 600b rose violet, *bluish* 25 15

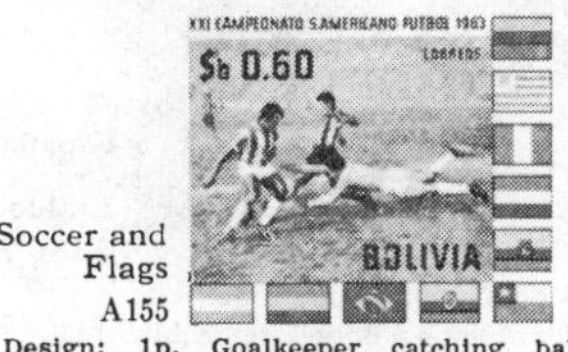

Soccer and Flags A155

Design: 1p, Goalkeeper catching ball (vert.).

1963, Mar. 21 Litho. ***Perf. 11½***

Flags in National Colors

469 A155 60c gray 35 15
470 " 1p gray 50 25

Issued to publicize the 21st South American Soccer Championships. See also Nos. C247-C248.

Globe and Wheat Emblem A156

1963, Aug. 1 ***Perf. 11½*** **Unwmkd.**

471 A156 60c dk. bl., bl. & yel. 25 15

Issued for the "Freedom from Hunger" campaign of the U.N. Food and Agriculture Organization. See also No. C249.

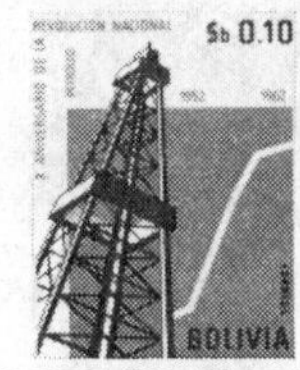

Oil Derrick and Chart A157

Designs: 60c, Map of Bolivia. 1p, Students.

1963, Dec. 21 Litho. ***Perf. 11½***

472 A157 10c grn. & dk. brn. 10 8
473 " 60c ocher & dk. brn. 30 12
474 " 1p dark blue, grn. & yellow 40 20
Nos. 472-474, C251-C253 (6) 3.15 1.85

Issued to commemorate the 10th anniversary of the Revolution of Apr. 9, 1952.

Flags of Bolivia and Peru A158

1966, Aug. 10 ***Perf. 13½*** **Wmk. 90**

Flags in National Colors

475 A158 10c black & tan 10 6
476 " 60c black & lt. green 20 10
477 " 1p black & gray 30 15
478 " 2p black & rose 50 25
Nos. 475-478, C254-C257 (8) 2.90 1.66

Issued to commemorate the centenary (in 1965) of the death of Marshal Andrés Santa Cruz (1792-1865), president of Bolivia and of Peru-Bolivian Confederation.

Children A159

Lithographed

1966, Dec. 16 ***Perf. 13½*** **Unwmkd.**

479 A159 30c ocher & sepia 10 8

Issued to help poor children. See No. C258.

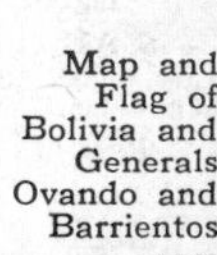

Map and Flag of Bolivia and Generals Ovando and Barrientos A160

1966, Dec. 16 Litho. ***Perf. 13½***

Flag in Red, Yellow and Green

480 A160 60c vio. brn. & tan 20 10
481 " 1p dull grn. & tan 25 15

Issued to honor Generals Rene Barrientos Ortuno and Alfredo Ovando C., co-Presidents, 1965-66. See also Nos. C259-C260.

A161

Various Issues 1957-60 and Type A161 Surcharged with New Values and Bars

1966, Dec. 21

On No. 403:
"Centenario de la / Cruz Roja / Internacional"

482 A140 20c on 150b gray & ultra. 10 5

On Nos. 405-406:
"Homenaje a la / Generala / J. Azurduy de / Padilla"

483 A140 30c on 550b chalky blue & brown 10 5
484 " 2.80p on 750b deep rose & green 75 50

On No. 424:
"CL Aniversario / Heroinas Coronilla"

485 A145 60c on 350b dp. rose 20 10

Nos. 429-430 Surcharged

486 A146 1.60p on 350b multi. 50 25
487 " 2.40p on 500b " 75 40

Revenue Stamps of 1946 surcharged with New Value, "X" and:
"XXV Aniversario / Gobierno Busch"

488 A161 20c on 5b red 10 5

Overprinted:
"XX Aniversario / Gob. Villaroel"

489 A161 60c on 2b green 20 10

Overprinted:
"Centenario do / Rurrenabaque"

490 A161 1p on 10b brown 30 15

Overprinted:
"XXV Aniversario / Dpto. Pando"

491 A161 1.60p on 50c violet 50 25
Nos. 482-491, C261-C272 (22) 11.20 6.15

Sower A162

"Macheteros" A163

1967, Sept. 20 Litho. ***Perf. 13½x13***

492 A162 70c multicolored 25 15

Issued to commemorate the 50th anniversary of Lions International. See Nos. C273-C273a.

1968, June 24 ***Perf. 13½x13***

Designs (Folklore characters): 60c, Chunchos. 1p, Wiphala. 2p, Diablada.

493 A163 30c gray & multi. 10 8
494 " 60c sky bl. & multi. 20 15
495 " 1b gray & multi. 30 20
496 " 2b gray olive & multi. 60 30
Nos. 493-496, C274-C277 (8) 3.50 2.43

Issued to publicize the 9th Congress of the Postal Union of the Americas and Spain.

A souvenir sheet exists containing 4 imperf. stamps similar to Nos. 493-496. Bister and gray marginal inscription. Size: 131x81½mm.

Arms of Tarija A164

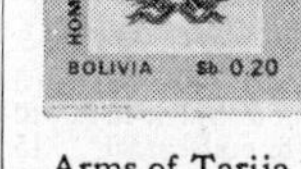

Pres. Gualberto Villaroël A165

1968, Oct. 29 Litho. ***Perf. 13½x13***

497 A164 20c pale sal. & multi. 10 6
498 " 30c gray & multi. 10 8
499 " 40c dull yel. & multi. 15 10
500 " 60c lt. yel. green & multi. 25 12
Nos. 497-500, C278-C281 (8) 3.50 2.11

Battle of Tablada sesquicentennial.

1968, Nov. 6 **Unwmkd.**

501 A165 20c sepia & orange 10 6
502 " 30c sepia & dull blue green 10 6
503 " 40c sepia & dull rose 10 8
504 " 50c sepia & yel. grn. 15 10
505 " 1b sepia & olive bister 25 15
Nos. 501-505 (5) 70 45

Issued to commemorate the 4th centenary of the founding of Cochabamba. See Nos. C282-C286.

ITU Emblem A166

1968, Dec. 3 Litho. ***Perf. 13x13½***

506 A166 10c gray, blk. & yel. 10 6
507 " 60c org., blk. & olive 20 10

Issued to commemorate the centenary (in 1965) of the International Telecommunication Union. See Nos. C287-C288.

Polychrome Painted Clay Cup, Inca Period A167

1968, Nov. 14 ***Perf. 13½x13***

508 A167 20c dk. blue green & multi. 10 6
509 " 60c vio. bl. & multi. 20 10

Issued to commemorate the 20th anniversary (in 1966) of UNESCO (United Nations Educational, Scientific and Cultural Organization). See Nos. C289-C290.

John F. Kennedy A168

Tennis Player A169

1968, Nov. 22 ***Perf. 13x13½***

510 A168 10c yel. green & blk. 10 10
511 " 4b violet & black 1.50 75

Issued in memory of Pres. John F. Kennedy (1917-1963).

A souvenir sheet contains one imperf. stamp similar to No. 511. Green marginal inscription. Size: 131x81½mm.

See Nos. C291-C292.

1968, Dec. 10 ***Perf. 13x13½***

512 A169 10c gray, black & light brown 10 10
513 " 20c yellow, black & light brown 10 10
514 " 30c ultra., black & light brown 10 10

Issued to commemorate the 32nd South American Tennis Championships, La Paz, 1965. See Nos. C293-C294.

A souvenir sheet exists containing 3 imperf. stamps similar to Nos. 512-514. Light brown marginal inscription. Size: 131x81½mm.

Issue of 1863
A170

1968, Dec. 23 Litho. *Perf. 13x13½*

515 A170 10c yellow green, brown & blk. 10 10
516 " 30c light blue, brown & blk. 10 10
517 " 2b gray, brown & black 25 20
Nos. 515-517, C295-C297 (6) 2.95 2.25

Issued to commemorate the centenary of Bolivian postage stamps. See Nos. C295-C297.

A souvenir sheet exists containing 3 imperf. stamps similar to Nos. 515-517. Yellow green marginal inscription. Size: 131x81½mm.

Rifle Shooting
A171

Sports: 50c, Equestrian. 60c, Canoeing.

1969, Oct. 29 Litho. *Perf. 13x13½*

518 A171 40c red brown, orange & black 15 10
519 " 50c emerald, red & black 15 10
520 " 60c blue, emerald & black 25 15
Nos. 518-520, C299-C301 (6) 3.55 2.10

Issued to commemorate the 19th Olympic Games, Mexico City, Oct. 12-27, 1968.

A souvenir sheet exists containing 3 imperf. stamps similar to Nos. 518-520. Marginal inscription in red brown, emerald and blue. Size: 130½x81mm.

Temenis Laothoe Violetta
A172

Butterflies: 10c, Papilio crassus. 20c, Catagramma cynosura. 30c, Eunica eurota flora. 80c, Ituna phenarete.

1970, Apr. 24 Litho. *Perf. 13x13½*

521 A172 5c pale lilac & multi. 10 5
522 " 10c pink & multi. 10 5
523 " 20c gray & multi. 10 5
524 " 30c yellow & multi. 10 5
525 " 80c multicolored 25 20
Nos. 521-525, C302-C306 (10) 5.35 3.35

A souvenir sheet exists containing 3 imperf. stamps similar to Nos. 521-523. Black marginal inscription. Size: 129½x80mm.

Boy Scout
A173

Design: 10c, Girl Scout planting rose bush.

1970, June 17 *Perf. 13½x13*

526 A173 5c multicolored 10 5
527 " 10c " 10 5

Issued to honor the Bolivian Scout movement. See Nos. C307-C308.

No. 437 Surcharged "EXFILCA 70 / $b. 0.30" and Two Bars in Red

1970, Dec. 6 Litho. *Perf. 13x12*

528 A147 30c on 350b on 10c gold & green 10 10

EXFILCA 70, 2nd Interamerican Philatelic Exhibition, Caracas, Venezuela, Nov. 27-Dec. 6.

Nos. 455 and 452 Surcharged in Black or Red

1970, Dec. Photo. *Perf. 11½*

529 A144 60c on 900b on 350b claret 20 12
533 A150 1.20b on 1500b dk. blue, *buff* (R) 40 20

Amaryllis Yungacensis
A174

Sica Sica Church, EXFILIMA Emblem
A175

Bolivian Flowers: 30c, Amaryllis escobar uriae (horiz.). 40c, Amaryllis evansae (horiz.). 2b, Gymnocalycium chiquitanum.

Perf. 13x13½, 13½x13

1971, Aug. 9 Litho. Unwmkd.

534 A174 30c gray & multi. 10 8
535 " 40c multicolored 10 8
536 " 50c " 15 10
537 " 2b " 60 30
Nos. 534-537, C310-C313 (8) 4.15 2.16

1971, Nov. 6 *Perf. 14x13½*

538 A175 20c red & multi. 15 10

EXFILIMA '71, 3rd Inter-American Philatelic Exhibition, Lima, Peru, Nov. 6-14.

Pres. Hugo Banzer Suarez
A176

1972, Jan. 24 Litho. *Perf. 13½*

539 A176 1.20b black & multi. 40 20

Bolivia's development, Aug. 19, 1971, to Jan. 24, 1972.

Chiriwano de Achocalla Dance
A177

Folk Dances: 40c, Rueda Chapaca. 60c, Kena-kena. 1b, Waca Thokori.

1972, Mar. 23 Litho. *Perf. 13½x13*

540 A177 20c red & multi. 5 5
541 " 40c rose lilac & multi. 15 10
542 " 60c cream & multi. 20 15
543 " 1b citron & multi. 35 20
Nos. 540-543, C314-C315 (6) 1.65 1.00

Madonna and Child by B. Bitti
A178

Tarija Cathedral, EXFILBRA Emblem
A179

Paintings: 10c, Nativity, by Melchor Perez de Holguín. 50c, Coronation of the Virgin, by G. M. Berrio. 70c, Harquebusier, anonymous. 80c, St. Peter of Alcantara, by Holguín.

1972 Lithographed *Perf. 14x13½*

544 A178 10c gray & multi. 10 10
545 " 50c salmon & multi. 20 10
546 " 70c lt. grn. & multi. 25 15
547 " 80c buff & multi. 30 20
548 " 1b multicolored 35 25
Nos. 544-548, C316-C319 (9) 3.45 1.95

Bolivian paintings. Issue dates: 1b, Aug. 17; others, Dec. 4.

1972, Aug. 26

549 A179 30c multicolored 15 10

4th Inter-American Philatelic Exhibition, EXFILBRA, Rio de Janeiro, Brazil, Aug. 26-Sept. 2.

Echinocactus Notocactus
A180

Designs: Various cacti.

1973, Aug. 6 Litho. *Perf. 13½*

550 A180 20c crimson & multi. 8 5
551 " 40c multicolored 12 8
552 " 50c " 15 10
553 " 70c " 20 12
Nos. 550-553, C321-C323 (7) 2.05 1.25

Power Station, Santa Isabel
A181

Designs: 20c, Tin industry. 90c, Bismuth industry. 1b, Natural gas plant.

1973, Nov. 26 Litho. *Perf. 13½*

554 A181 10c gray & multi. 5 5
555 " 20c tan & multi. 5 5
556 " 90c lt. grn. & multi. 20 12
557 " 1b yellow & multi. 20 15
Nos. 554-557, C324-C325 (6) 1.15 87

Bolivia's development.

Cattleya Nobilior
A182

Orchids: 50c, Zygopetalum bolivianum. 1b, Huntleya melagris.

1974, May 15 *Perf. 13½*

558 A182 20c gray & multi. 10 5
559 " 50c lt. blue & multi. 20 10
560 " 1b citron & multi. 30 15
Nos. 558-560, C327-C330 (7) 5.10 2.45

UPU and Philatelic Exposition Emblems—A183

1974, Oct. 9

561 A183 3.50s grn., blk. & bl. 1.00 60

Centenary of Universal Postal Union; PRENFIL-UPU Philatelic Exhibition, Buenos Aires, Oct. 1-12; EXPO-UPU Philatelic Exhibition, Montevideo, Oct. 20-27.

Gen. Sucre, by I. Wallpher
A184

1974, Dec. 9 Litho. *Perf. 13½*

562 A184 5b multicolored 1.25 75

Sesquicentennial of the Battle of Ayacucho.

Lions Emblem and Steles
A185

1975, Mar. Litho. *Perf. 13½*

563 A185 30c red & multi. 15 10

Lions International in Bolivia, 25th anniversary.

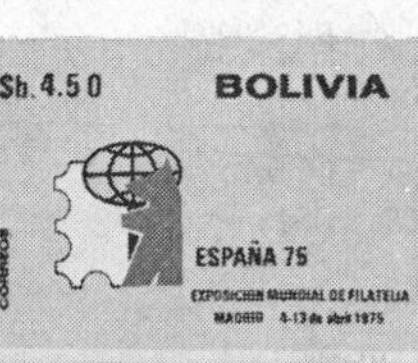

España 75 Emblem
A186

1975, Mar.

564 A186 4.50b yel., red & blk. 1.00 50

España 75 International Philatelic Exhibition, Madrid, Apr. 4-13.

Emblem
A187

1975 Lithographed *Perf. 13½*

565 A187 2.50b lilac, black & silver 75 40

First meeting of Postal Ministers, Quito, Ecuador, March 1974, and for the Cartagena Agreement.

CORREOS DE BOLIVIA
PANDO
Sb. 0.20
SESQUICENTENARIO DE LA REPUBLICA
1825-1975

Pando Coat of Arms
A188

Designs: Departmental coats of arms.

1975, July 16 Litho. *Perf. 13½*

Gold & Multicolored

566	A188	20c *shown*	5	5
567	"	2b *Chuquisaca*	50	30
568	"	3b *Cochabamba*	75	50
		Nos. 566-568, C336-C341 (9)	3.15	1.93

Sesquicentennial of Republic of Bolivia.

Simón Bolívar
A189

Presidents and Statesmen of Bolivia: 30c, Victor Paz Estenssoro. 60c, Tomas Frias. 1b, Ismael Montes. 2.50b, Aniceto Arce. 7b, Bautista Saavedra. 10b, José Manuel Pando. 15b, José Maria Linares. 50b, Simón Bolívar.

1975 Litho. *Perf. 13½*

Size: 24x32mm.

569	A189	30c	multicolored	10	5
569A	"	60c	"	15	10
570	"	1b	"	25	15
571	"	2.50b	"	60	35
572	"	7b	"	1.50	1.00
573	"	10b	"	2.50	1.50
574	"	15b	"	3.50	2.00

Size: 28x39mm.

575	A189	50b multicolored	12.50	
		Nos. 569-575, C346-C353 (16)	42.50	

Sesquicentennial of Republic of Bolivia.

"EXFIVIA 75"
A190

1975, Dec. 1 Litho. *Perf. 13½*

576	A190	3b multicolored	75	50
		a. Souvenir sheet	1.75	1.75

EXFIVIA 75, first Bolivian Philatelic Exposition. No. 576a contains one stamp similar to No. 576 with simulated perforations. Multicolored margin shows emblems of various international philatelic exhibitions. Size: 130x80mm. Sold for 5b.

Chiang Kai-shek, Flags of Bolivia and China
A191

1976, Apr. 4 Litho. *Perf. 13½*

577	A191	2.50b multicolored, red circle	60	40
578	"	2.50b multicolored, blue circle	60	40

Pres. Chiang Kai-shek of China (1887–1975), first death anniversary.

Erroneous red of sun's circle on Chinese flag of No. 577 was corrected on No. 578 with a dark blue overlay.

Naval Insignia
A192

1976, Apr. Litho. *Perf. 13½*

579	A192	50c blue & multi.	20	10

Navy anniversary.

Geological Map, Pickax and Lamp
A193

1976, May

580	A193	4b multicolored	1.00	75

Bolivian Geological Institute.

Lufthansa Jet, Bolivian and German Colors—A194

1976, May

581	A194	3b multicolored	75	50

Lufthansa, 50th anniversary.

Boy Scout and Scout Emblem
A195

1976, May Litho. *Perf. 13½*

582	A195	1b multicolored	25	20

Bolivian Boy Scouts, 60th anniversary.

Battle Scene, U.S. Bicentennial Emblem
A196

1976, May 25

583	A196	4.50b bis. & multi.	1.25	75

American Bicentennial.

A souvenir sheet contains one stamp similar to No. 583 with simulated perforations. Multicolored, inscribed margin shows U.S. flags of 1776 and 1976. Size: 130x80mm.

Family, Map of Bolivia
A197

Brother Vicente Bernedo
A198

1976 *Perf. 13½*

584	A197	2.50b multicolored	60	40

National Census 1976.

1976, Oct.

585	A198	1.50b multicolored	40	25

Brother Vicente Bernedo de Potosi (1544–1619), missionary to the Indians.

Policeman with Dog, Rainbow over La Paz
A199

1976, Oct.

586	A199	2.50b multicolored	60	40

Bolivian Police, 150 years of service.

Emblem, Bolivar and Sucre
A200

1976, Nov. 18 Litho. *Perf. 13½*

587	A200	1.50b multicolored	60	40

International Congress of Bolivarian Societies.

Pedro Poveda, View of La Paz
A201

1976, Dec.

588	A201	1.50b multicolored	40	25

Pedro Poveda (1874–1936), educator.

A202

1976, Dec. 17 *Perf. 10½*

589	A202	20c brown	5	5
595	"	1b ultramarine	25	10
596	"	1.50b green	35	10

Boy and Girl
A203

1977, Feb. 4 Litho. *Perf. 13½*

599	A203	50c multicolored	10	5

Christmas 1976, and for 50th anniversary of the Inter-American Children's Institute.

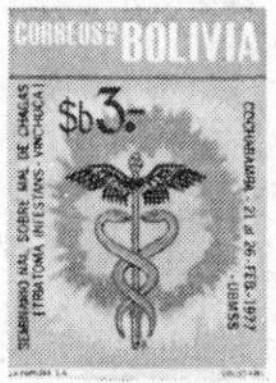

Staff of Aesculapius
A204

Supreme Court, La Paz
A205

1977, Mar. 18 Litho. *Perf. 13½x13*

600	A204	3b multicolored	65	15

National Seminar on Chagas' disease, Cochabamba, Feb. 21–26.

1977, May 3

Designs: 4b, Manuel Maria Urcullu, first President of Supreme Court. 4.50b, Pantaleon Dalence, President 1883–1889.

601	A205	2.50b	multicolored	45	12
602	"	4b	"	65	18
603	"	4.50b	"	75	20

Sesquicentennial of Bolivian Supreme Court.

Newspaper Mastheads
A206

Map of Bolivia, Tower and Flag
A207

Designs: 2.50b, Alfredo Alexander and Hoy (horiz.). 3b, José Carrasco and El Diario (horiz.). 4b, Demetrio Canelas and Los Tiempos. 5.50b, Frontpage of Presencia.

1977, June Lithographed *Perf. 13½*

604	A206	1.50b	multicolored	28	6
605	"	2.50b	"	45	12
606	"	3b	"	56	16
607	"	4b	"	65	18
608	"	5.50b	"	95	25
		Nos. 604-608 (5)		2.89	77

Bolivian newspapers and their founders.

1977, June

609	A207	3b multicolored	56	16

90th anniversary of Oruro Club.

Games' Poster
A208

Tin Miner and Emblem
A209

1977, Oct. 20 Litho. *Perf. 13½*

610	A208	5b blue & multi.	90	24

8th Bolivian Games, La Paz, Oct. 1977.

1977, Oct. 31 Litho. *Perf. 13*

611	A209	3b multicolored	56	16

Bolivian Mining Corporation, 25th anniversary.

Miners, Globe, Tin Symbol
A210

Map of Bolivia, Radio Masts
A211

1977, Nov. 3

612 A210 6b silver & multi. 1.10 32

International Tin Symposium, La Paz, Nov. 14–21.

1977, Nov. 11

613 A211 2.50b blue & multi. 45 12

Radio Bolivia, ASBORA, 50th anniversary.

No. 450 Surcharged with New Value, 3 Bars and "EXFIVIA–77"

1977, Nov. 25 Litho. ***Perf. 11x13½***

614 A147 5b on 5000b on 5b gold & gray 90 25

EXFIVIA '77 Philatelic Exhibition, Cochabamba.

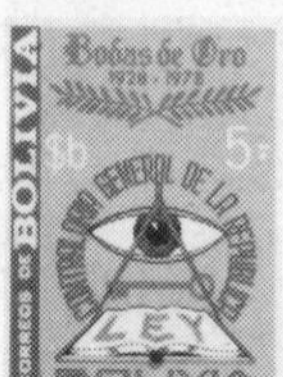

Eye, Compass, Book of Law
A212

1978, May 3 Litho. ***Perf. 13½x13***

615 A212 5b multicolored 90 25

Audit Department, 50th anniversary.

Mt. Illimani
A213

Pre-Columbian Monolith
A214

Design: 1.50b, Mt. Cerro de Potosi.

Perf. 11x10½, 10½x11

1978, June 1 Litho.

616 A213 50c blue & Prus. blue 10 3
617 A214 1b brn. & lemon 18 4
618 A213 1.50b red & bl. gray 28 6

Andean Countries, Staff of Aesculapius
A215

Map of Americas with Bolivia
A216

1978, June 1 ***Perf. 10½x11***

626 A215 2b orange & black 36 8

Health Ministers of Andean Countries, 5th meeting.

1978, June 1

627 A216 2.50b dp. ultra. & red 45 12

World Rheumatism Year.

Central Bank Building
A217

1978, July 26 Litho. ***Perf. 13½***

628 A217 7b multicolored 1.25 30

50th anniversary of Bank of Bolivia.

AIR POST STAMPS.

Aviation School
AP1 AP2

Engraved.

1924, Dec. *Perf. 14* **Unwmkd.**

C1 AP1 10c vermilion & blk. 25 25
a. Inverted center 850.00
C2 " 15c carmine & blk. 1.00 75
C3 " 25c dark blue & black 50 25
C4 " 50c orange & black 1.00 75
C5 AP2 1b red brown & blk. 1.00 90
C6 " 2b black brown & black 2.00 2.00
C7 " 5b dark violet & black 3.00 3.00
Nos. C1-C7 (7) 8.75 7.90

Issued to commemorate the establishing of the National Aviation School.

These stamps were available for ordinary postage. Nos. C1, C3, C5 and C6 exist imperforate. Proofs of the 2b with inverted center exist imperforate and privately perforated.

Emblem of Lloyd Aéreo Boliviano
AP3

1928 **Lithographed.** *Perf. 11.*

C8 AP3 15c green 1.00 85
a. Imperf. (pair) 25.00
C9 " 20c dark blue 20 15
C10 " 35c red brown 60 50

Graf Zeppelin Issues.

Nos. C1-C5 Surcharged or Overprinted in Various Colors:

CORREO AEREO
R. S. 6-V-1930
5 Cts.
a

CORREO AEREO
R. S.
6-V- 1930
b

1930, May 6 *Perf. 14.*

C11 AP1 (*a*) 5c on 10c vermilion & black (G) 11.00 11.00
C12 " (*b*) 10c vermilion & black (Bl) 11.00 11.00
C13 " (") 10c vermilion & black (Br) 550.00 750.00
C14 " (") 15c carmine & black (V) 11.00 11.00
C15 " (") 25c dark blue & black (R) 11.00 11.00
C16 " (") 50c orange & black (Br) 11.00 11.00
C17 " (") 50c orange & black (R) 625.00 750.00
C18 AP2 (") 1b red brown & black (Gold) 135.00 125.00

Experts consider the 50c with silver overprint to be a trial color proof.

Surcharged or Overprinted in Bronze Inks of Various Colors.

C19 AP1 (*a*) 5c on 10c vermilion & black (G) 60.00 60.00
C20 " (*b*) 10c vermilion & black (Bl) 50.00 50.00
C21 " (") 15c carmine & black (V) 60.00 60.00
C22 " (") 25c dark blue & black (Copper) 60.00 60.00
C23 AP2 (") 1b red brown & black (Gold) 135.00 135.00

Issued in commemoration of the flight of the airship Graf Zeppelin from Europe to Brazil and return via Lakehurst, N.J.

Nos. C11 to C18 exist with the surcharges inverted, double, or double with one inverted, but the regularity of these varieties is questioned.

Nos. C19 to C23 were intended for use on postal matter forwarded by the Graf Zeppelin.

No. C18 was overprinted with light gold or gilt bronze ink. No. C23 was overprinted with deep gold bronze ink. Nos. C13 and C17 were overprinted with trial colors but were sold with the regular printings. The 5c on 10c is known surcharged in black and in blue.

Air Post Stamps of 1928 Issue, Surcharged

Z 1930
Bs. 3.—

1930, May 6 *Perf. 11.*

C24 AP3 1.50b on 15c green 35.00 35.00
a. Inverted surcharge 65.00 65.00
b. Comma instead of period after "1" 45.00 45.00
C25 " 3b on 20c dark blue 35.00 35.00
a. Inverted surcharge 65.00 65.00
b. Comma instead of period after "3" 45.00 45.00
C26 " 6b on 35c red brown 50.00 55.00
a. Inverted surcharge 100.00 100.00
b. Comma instead of period after "6" 65.00 65.00

Airplane and Bullock Cart
AP6

Airplane and River Boat
AP7

1930, July 24 **Litho.** *Perf. 14*

C27 AP6 5c deep violet 50 40
C28 AP7 15c red 50 40
C29 " 20c yellow 50 40
C30 AP6 35c yellow green 50 20
C31 AP7 50c deep blue 50 20
C32 AP6 1b light brown 50 20
C33 AP7 2b deep rose 50 25
C34 AP6 3b slate 3.00 2.00
Nos. C27-C34 (8) 6.50 4.05

Nos. C27 to C34 exist imperforate.

Air Service Emblem
AP8

1932, Sept. 16 *Perf. 11.*

C35 AP8 5c ultramarine 1.00 60
C36 " 10c gray 50 25
C37 " 15c dark rose 1.00 75
C38 " 25c orange 1.00 75
C39 " 30c green 75 35
C40 " 50c violet 75 35
C41 " 1b dark brown 75 40
Nos. C35-C41 (7) 5.75 3.45

Map of Bolivia
AP9

1935, Feb. 1 **Engraved.** *Perf. 12.*

C42 AP9 5c brown red 20 15
C43 " 10c dark green 20 15
C44 " 20c dark violet 20 15
C45 " 30c ultramarine 20 15
C46 " 50c orange 30 15
C47 " 1b bistre brown 30 25
C48 " 1½b yellow 75 15
C49 " 2b carmine 75 30
C50 " 5b green 1.50 40
C51 " 10b dark brown 2.50 75
Nos. C42-C51 (10) 6.90 2.60

Air Post Stamps of 1924-30 Surcharged in Red or Green

Correo Aéreo
D. S. 25-2-37
0.05
c

1937, Oct. 6 *Perf. 11, 14.*

C52 AP6 5c on 35c yellow green (R) 40 30
a. "Carreo" 12.50
C53 AP3 20c on 35c red brown (R) 40 30
C54 " 50c on 35c red brown (R) 60 50
a. Inverted surcharge 20.00
C55 " 1b on 35c red brown (R) 1.00 60
C56 AP1 2b on 50c orange & black (R) 1.50 75
C57 " 12b on 10c vermilion & black (G) 5.00 4.00
a. Inverted surcharge 25.00
C58 " 15b on 10c verm. & black (G) 5.00 4.00

Regular Postage Stamps of 1925 Surcharged in Green or Red

Correo
Aéreo
D. S.
25-2-37
Bs. 4.—
d

Perf. 14.

C59 A56 (*d*) 3b on 50c deep violet (G) 1.50 1.25
C60 " (") 4b on 1b red (G) 2.00 1.75
C61 A57 (*c*) 5b on 2b orange (G) 2.50 2.00
C62 A56 (*d*) 10b on 5b black brown (R) 5.00 4.00
a. Double surcharge 40.00
Nos. C52-C62 (11) 24.90 19.45

Courtyard of Potosí Mint
AP10

Miner
AP11

Emancipated Woman
AP12

Pincers, Torch and Good Will Principles
AP15

Airplane over Field
AP13

Airplanes and Liberty Monument
AP14

Airplane over River
AP16

Emblem of New Government
AP17

Transport Planes over Map of Bolivia
AP18

1938, May **Lithographed.** *Perf. 10½.*

C63 AP10 20c deep rose 25 20
C64 AP11 30c gray 25 20
C65 AP12 40c yellow 25 20
C66 AP13 50c yellow green 35 20
C67 AP14 60c dull blue 35 20
C68 AP15 1b dull red 50 20
C69 AP16 2b bistre 1.25 20
C70 AP17 3b light brown 1.25 20
C71 AP18 5b dark violet 1.75 20
Nos. C63-C71 (9) 6.20 1.80

Chalice
AP19

Virgin of Copacabana
AP20

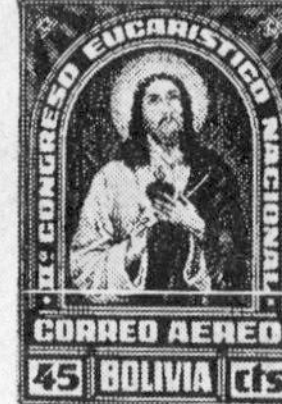

Jesus Christ
AP21

Church of San Francisco, La Paz
AP22

St. Anthony of Padua
AP23

Lithographed.

1939, July 19 *Perf. 13½, 10½.*

C72 AP19 5c dull violet 60 40
a. Pair, imperf. between 50.00
C73 AP20 30c lt. blue green 50 25
C74 AP21 45c violet blue 60 25
a. Vertical pair, imperf. between 75.00
C75 AP22 60c carmine 60 50
C76 AP23 75c vermilion 75 75
C77 " 90c deep blue 75 30
C78 AP22 2b dull brown 1.25 30
C79 AP21 4b deep plum 1.75 50
C80 AP20 5b light blue 3.50 30
C81 AP19 10b yellow 10.00 30
Nos. C72-C81 (10) 20.30 3.85

Issued to commemorate the second National Eucharistic Congress.

Plane over Lake Titicaca
AP24

Mt. Illimani and Condor
AP25

1941, Aug. 21 *Perf. 13½.*

C82 AP24 10b dull green 5.00 75
C83 " 20b light ultra. 6.00 1.25
C84 AP25 50b rose lilac 10.00 1.75
C85 " 100b olive bistre 25.00 6.00

Counterfeits exist.

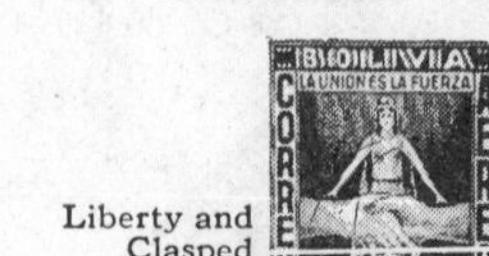

Liberty and Clasped Hands
AP26

1942, Nov. 12

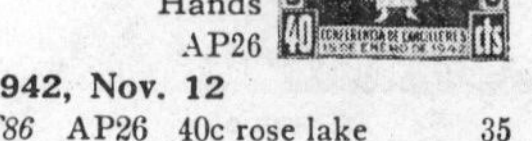

C86 AP26 40c rose lake 35 25
C87 " 50c ultramarine 40 25

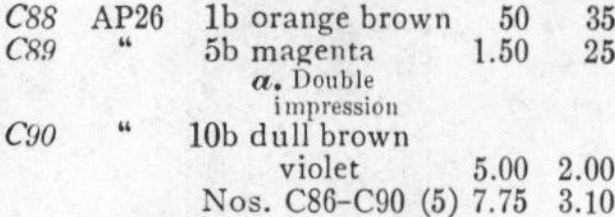

C88 AP26 1b orange brown 50 35
C89 " 5b magenta 1.50 25
a. Double impression
C90 " 10b dull brown violet 5.00 2.00
Nos. C86-C90 (5) 7.75 3.10

Issued to commemorate the Conference of Chancellors held January 15, 1942.

General José Ballivián; Old and Modern Transportation
AP27

1943, Nov. 18 Engr. *Perf. 12½*

C91 AP27 10c rose violet & brown 10 10
C92 " 20c emerald & brn. 15 10
C93 " 30c rose carmine & brown 20 15
C94 " 3b blue & brown 30 20
C95 " 5b black & brown 60 35
Nos. C91-C95 (5) 1.35 90

Department of Beni centenary.

Condor and Sun Rising
AP28

Plane
AP29

Lithographed.

1944, Sept. 19 *Perf. 13½.*

C96 AP28 40c red violet 15 10
C97 " 1b light violet 20 10
C98 AP29 1.50b yellow green 25 10
C99 " 2.50b dark gray blue 50 25

Revolution of Dec. 20, 1943.

Map of National Airways
AP30

Map of Bolivian Air Lines
AP31

1945, May 31 *Perf. 11*

C100 AP30 10c red 10 8
a. Imperf. (pair) 10.00
C101 " 50c yellow 15 8
a. Imperf. (pair) 17.50
C102 " 90c light green 20 8
C103 " 5b light ultra. 35 15
C104 " 20b deep brown 1.00 50
Nos. C100-C104 (5) 1.80 89

10th anniversary of first flight, La Paz to Tacna, Peru, by Panagra Airways.

Centers in Red and Blue.

1945, Sept. 15 *Perf. 13½.*

C105 AP31 20c violet 8 5
C106 " 30c orange brown 8 5
C107 " 50c brt. bl. green 8 8
C108 " 90c bright violet 8 8
C109 " 2b blue 15 10
C110 " 3b magenta 20 15
C111 " 4b olive bistre 30 20
Nos. C105-C111 (7) 97 71

Issued to commemorate the 20th anniversary of the founding of Lloyd Aéreo Boliviano.

No. C76 Surcharged in Blue

1947
Habilitada
Bs. 1.40

1947, Mar. 23

C112 AP23 1.40b on 75c vermilion 20 20

Mt. Illimani
AP32

Arms of Bolivia and Argentina
AP33

1947, Sept. 15 Litho. *Perf. 11½*

C113 AP32 1b rose carmine 6 6
C114 " 1.40b emerald 8 6
C115 " 2.50b blue 15 12
C116 " 3b deep orange 20 15
C117 " 4b rose lilac 25 12
Nos. C113-C117 (5) 74 51

Issued to commemorate the first anniversary of the Revolution of July 21, 1946.

1947, Oct. 23 *Perf. 13½*

C118 AP33 2.90b ultramarine 30 25
a. Imperf. (pair) 25.00
b. Perf. 10½ 6.00 5.00

Issued to commemorate the meeting of Presidents Enrique Hertzog of Bolivia and Juan D. Perón of Argentina at Yacuiba, Oct. 23, 1947.

Types of Regular Issue of 1948.

Designs: 2.50b, Statue of Christ above La Paz. 3.70b, Child kneeling before cross. No. C121, St. John Bosco. No. C122, Virgin of Copacabana. 13.60b, Pope Pius XII blessing University of La Paz.

1948, Sept. 26 *Perf. 11½.*

C119 A120 2.50b vermilion & yellow 75 35
C120 " 3.70b rose & cream 1.00 35
C121 " 4b rose lilac & gray 1.00 30
C122 " 4b light ultra. & salmon 1.00 18
C123 " 13.60b ultramarine & light green 1.25 30
Nos. C119-C123 (5) 5.00 1.48

Issued to publicize the 3rd Inter-American Congress of Catholic Education.

Type of Regular Issue of 1948

1948, Oct.

C124 A125 10b emerald & salmon 2.50 25

Issued to publicize the International Automobile Races of South America, September-October 1948.

Pres. Gregorio Pacheco, Map and Post Horn
AP34

L. A. B. Plane
AP35

1950, Jan. 2 **Unwmkd.**

C125 AP34 1.40b orange brn. 15 15
C126 " 2.50b orange 10 10
C127 " 3.30b rose violet 15 15

Issued to commemorate the 75th anniversary of the formation of the Universal Postal Union.

Nos. C100 and C104 Surcharged in Black

XV ANIVERSARIO
PANAGRA
Bs
4.-
1935-1950

1950, May 31 *Perf. 11.*

C128 AP30 4b on 10c red 15 15
C129 " 10b on 20b deep brown 40 30
a. Inverted surcharge 25.00 25.00

Issued to commemorate the 15th anniversary of Panagra air services in Bolivia.

1950, Sept. 15 Litho. *Perf. 13½*

C130 AP35 20c red orange 8 8
C131 " 30c purple 8 8
C132 " 50c green 8 8
C133 " 1b orange 8 8
C134 " 3b ultramarine 10 8
C135 " 15b carmine 30 10
C136 " 50b chocolate 1.00 15
Nos. C130-C136 (7) 1.72 65

Issued to commemorate the 25th anniversary of the founding of Lloyd Aéreo Boliviano. No. C132 exists imperforate.

No. C116 Surcharged in Black

Triunfo de la
Democracia
24 de Sept. 49
Bs. 1.40

1950, Sept. 24 *Perf. 11½*

C137 AP32 1.40b on 3b deep orange 15 15

Issued to commemorate the 1st anniversary of the ending of the Civil War of Aug. 24–Sept. 24, 1949.

Symbols of United Nations
AP36

1950, Oct. 24 **Unwmkd.**

C138 AP36 3.60b crimson rose 75 15
C139 " 4.70b blk. brown 1.00 15

Issued to commemorate the 5th anniversary of the formation of the United Nations, October 24, 1945.

Gate of the Sun and Llama
AP37

Church of San Francisco
AP38

Designs: 40c, Avenue Camacho. 50c, Consistorial Palace. 1b, Legislative Palace. 2b, Communications Bldg. 3b, Arms. 4b, La Gasca ordering Mendoza to found La Paz. 5b, Capt. Alonso de Mendoza founding La Paz. 10b, Arms; portrait of Mendoza.

1951, Mar. 1 Engr. *Perf. 12½.*

Center in Black.

C140 AP37 20c carmine 12 12
C141 AP38 30c dark violet blue 12 12
C142 AP37 40c dark blue 12 12
C143 " 50c blue green 15 15
C144 " 1b red 18 18
C145 " 2b red orange 25 25

C146 AP37 3b deep blue 25 25
C147 " 4b vermilion 30 30
a. Souv. sheet of 4 1.25 1.25
C148 " 5b dark green 35 35
a. Souv. sheet of 3 1.25 1.25
C149 " 10b red brown 55 55
a. Souv. sheet of 3 1.25 1.25
Nos. C140-C149 (10) 2.39 2.39

400th anniversary of the founding of La Paz.

No. C147a contains C143-C145, C147; No. C148a contains C142, C146, C148; No. C149a contains 140, C141, C149. Black marginal inscriptions. Perf. and imperf., size: 150x100mm.

Horsemanship
AP39

Designs: 30c, Basketball. 50c, Fencing. 1b, Hurdling. 2.50b, Javelin throwing. 3b, Relay race. 5b, La Paz stadium.

1951, Aug. 23 **Unwmkd.**

Center in Black.

C150 AP39 20c purple 25 6
C151 " 30c rose violet 35 10
C152 " 50c dp. red orange 60 10
C153 " 1b chocolate 60 10
C154 " 2.50b orange 75 50
C155 " 3b black brown 1.25 60
a. Souv. sheet of 3 5.00 4.50
C156 " 5b red 2.50 1.25
a. Souv. sheet of 4 6.00 5.50
Nos. C150-C156 (7) 6.30 2.71

The stamps were intended to commemorate the 5th South American Games and the 2nd National Sports Congress held at La Paz, October 1948.

No. C155a contains C153-C155; No. C156a contains C150-C152, C156. Black marginal inscriptions. Perf. and imperf., size: 150x100mm.

Eduardo Abaroa
AP40

Queen Isabella I
AP41

1952, Mar. 24 **Litho.** ***Perf. 11***

C157 AP40 70c rose red 10 10
C158 " 2b orange yellow 15 15
C159 " 3b yellow green 15 15
C160 " 5b blue 20 15
C161 " 50b rose lilac 1.50 40
C162 " 100b gray black 1.75 75
Nos. C157-C162 (6) 3.85 1.70

Issued to commemorate the 73rd anniversary of the death of Eduardo Abaroa.

1952, July 16 ***Perf. 13½***

C163 AP41 50b emerald 60 40
C164 " 100b brown 1.25 50

Issued to commemorate the 500th anniversary of the birth of Queen Isabella I of Spain. Exist imperforate.

Columbus Lighthouse
AP42

1952, July 16

C165 AP42 2b rose lilac, *salmon* 15 15
C166 " 3.70b blue green, *blue* 15 15
C167 AP42 4.40b org., *salmon* 25 10
C168 " 20b dk. brown, *cream* 50 18

No. C168 exists imperforate.

Soldiers
AP43

Gualberto Villarroel, Victor Paz Estenssoro and Hernan Siles Zuazo
AP44

Perf. 13½ (AP43), 11½ (AP44)

1953, Apr. 9 **Lithographed**

C169 AP44 3.70b chocolate 10 10
C170 AP43 6b red violet 10 10
C171 AP44 9b brown rose 10 10
C172 " 10b aquamarine 10 10
C173 " 16b vermilion 10 10
C174 AP43 22.50b dark brown 20 15
C175 AP44 40b gray 30 10
Nos. C169-C175 (7) 1.00 75

Issued to commemorate the first anniversary of the Revolution of Apr. 9, 1952. Nos. C170 and C174 exist imperf.

Pres. Victor Paz Estenssoro Embracing Indian
AP45

Map and Peasant
AP46

1954, Aug. 2 ***Perf. 12x11½.***

C176 AP45 20b orange brown 10 6
C177 AP46 27b bright pink 10 10
C178 " 30b red orange 15 8
C179 " 45b violet brown 25 6
C180 AP45 100b blue green 50 6
C181 AP46 300b yellow green 1.25 18
Nos. C176-C181 (6) 2.35 54

Nos. C176 and C180 were issued to commemorate the 3rd Inter-American Indian Congress. Nos. C177-C179 and C181 commemorate the agrarian reform laws of 1953-1954.

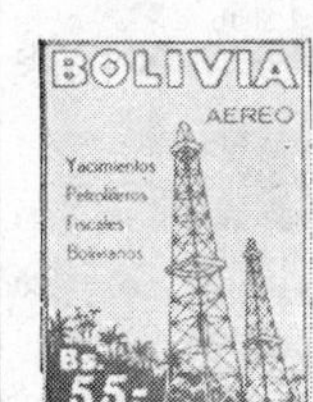

Oil Derricks
AP47

Map of South America and La Paz Arms
AP48

1955, Oct. 9 ***Perf. 10½***

C182 AP47 55b dark & light greenish blue 10 8
C183 " 70b dark gray & gray 15 8
C184 " 90b dark & light green 20 10

Perf. 13.

C185 AP47 500b red lilac 1.00 45
C186 " 1000b black brown & fawn 1.75 1.10
Nos. C182-C186 (5) 3.20 1.81

Nos. C140-C149 Surcharged with New Values and Bars in Black or Carmine.

1957 **Engraved.** ***Perf. 12½***

Center in Black

C187 AP37 100b on 3b dp.bl. (C) 10 6
C188 " 200b on 2b red org. 10 6
C189 " 500b on 4b verm. 20 12
C190 " 600b on 1b red 20 12
C191 " 700b on 20c carmine 30 18
C192 " 800b on 40c dark blue (C) 35 25
C193 AP38 900b on 30c dark violet blue (C) 40 10
C194 AP37 1800b on 50c blue green (C) 75 40
C195 " 3000b on 5b dark green (C) 1.25 75
C196 " 5000b on 10b red brown (C) 2.00 1.50
Nos. C187-C196 (10) 5.65 3.54

Lithographed.

1957, May 25 ***Perf. 12*** **Unwmkd.**

C197 AP48 700b lilac & violet 50 30
C198 " 1200b pale brown 60 40
C199 " 1350b rose carmine 65 55
C200 " 2700b blue green 1.50 70
C201 " 4000b violet blue 2.00 1.05
Nos. C197-C201 (5) 5.25 3.00

Issued to commemorate the seventh session of the C. E. P. A. L. (Comision Economica para la America Latina de las Naciones Unidas), La Paz.

Type of Regular Issue, 1957

1957, Dec. 19 ***Perf. 11½***

C202 A141 600b magenta 25 10
C203 " 700b violet blue 35 18
C204 " 900b pale green 50 12

Issued to commemorate the opening of the Santa Cruz-Yacuiba Railroad and the meeting of the Presidents of Bolivia and Argentina.

Type of Regular Issue, 1960.

1960, Jan. 30

C205 A142 400b rose claret 50 15
C206 " 800b slate blue 75 30
C207 " 2000b slate 1.25 60

Issued for an expected visit of Mexico's Pres. Adolfo Lopez Mateos. On sale Jan. 30-Feb. 1, 1960.

Gate of the Sun, Tiahuanacu
AP49

Uprooted Oak Emblem
AP50

1960, Mar. 26 **Litho.** ***Perf. 11½***

C208 AP49 3,000b gray 1.50 75
C209 " 5,000b orange 2.50 1.50
C210 " 10,000b rose claret 5.00 2.50
C211 " 15,000b bl. vio. 7.50 4.00

1960, Apr. 7 ***Perf. 11½***

C212 AP50 600b ultra. 35 25
C213 " 700b lt. red brn. 40 30
C214 " 900b dk. bl. grn. 50 25
C215 " 1,800b violet 75 65
C216 " 2,000b gray 1.00 65
Nos. C212-C216 (5) 3.00 2.10

Issued to publicize World Refugee Year, July 1, 1959-June 30, 1960.

No. C215 exists with "1961" overprint in dark carmine, but was not regularly issued in this form.

Jaime Laredo
AP51

Lithographed

1960, Aug. 15 ***Perf. 11½*** **Unwmkd.**

C217 AP51 600b rose violet 40 20
C218 " 700b olive gray 50 25
C219 " 800b violet brn. 60 25
C220 " 900b dark blue 80 25
C221 " 1,800b green 1.25 75
C222 " 4,000b dark gray 2.25 1.25
Nos. C217-C222 (6) 5.80 2.95

Issued to honor the violinist Jaime Laredo.

Type of Regular Issue, 1960.
(Children's Hospital)

1960, Nov. 21 ***Perf. 11½***

C223 A146 600b red brown, yellow & deep blue 50 35
C224 " 1,000b olive green, yellow & deep blue 75 35
C225 " 1,800b plum, yel. & dp. bl. 1.00 60
C226 " 5,000b blk., yel. & deep blue 3.00 1.75

Issued for the Children's Hospital, sponsored by the Rotary Club of La Paz.

Pres. Paz Estenssoro and Pres. Getulio Vargas of Brazil
AP52

1960, Dec. 14 **Litho.** ***Perf. 11½***

C227 AP52 1,200b on 10b org. & blk. 75 50

Exists with surcharge inverted.

No. C227 without surcharge was not regularly issued, although a decree authorizing its circulation was published. Counterfeits of surcharge exist.

Pres. Paz Estenssoro and Pres. Frondizi of Argentina
AP53

Design: 4,000b, Flags of Bolivia and Argentina.

1961, May 23 ***Perf. 10½***

C228 AP53 4,000b brown, red, yel., grn. & blue 1.00 90
C229 " 6,000b dark green & black 1.30 1.25

Issued to commemorate the visit of the President of Argentina, Dr. Arturo Frondizi, to Bolivia.

See "Special Notices" at the front of this volume for data on the listing methods of this Catalogue, abbreviations, condition, prices and examination.

Miguel de Cervantes
AP54

1961, Oct. Photogravure *Perf. 13*

C230 AP54 1400b pale grn. & dk. olive green 50 35

Issued to commemorate Cervantes' appointment as Chief Magistrate of La Paz.

Virgin of Cotoca and Symbol of Eucharist
AP55

Planes and Parachutes
AP56

1962, Mar. 19 Litho. *Perf. 10½*

C231 AP55 1400b brown, pink & yellow 75 50

Issued to commemorate the 4th National Eucharistic Congress, Santa Cruz, 1961.

Nos. C212-C216 Surcharged Vertically with New Value and Greek Key Border.

1962, June *Perf. 11½* **Unwmkd.**

C232 AP50 1,200b on 600b ultra. 65 50
C233 " 1,300b on 700b lt. red brn. 60 50
C234 " 1,400b on 900b dk. blue grn. 75 50
C235 " 2,800b on 1,800b violet 1.00 75
C236 " 3,000b on 2,000b gray 1.00 75
Nos. C232-C236 (5) 4.00 3.00

The overprinted segment of Greek key border on Nos. C232-C236 comes in two positions: two full "keys" on top, and one full and two half keys on top.

Flower Type of 1962

Flowers: 100b, 1,800b, Cantua buxifolia. 800b, 10,000b, Cantua bicolor.

1962, June 28 Litho. *Perf. 10½*

Flowers in Natural Colors

C237 A152 100b dark blue 10 10
C238 " 800b green 50 25
C239 " 1,800b violet 1.00 50
a. Souv. sheet of 3 5.00 5.00
C240 " 10,000b dark blue 6.00 3.00

No. C239a contains 3 imperf. stamps similar to Nos. C237-C239, but with the 1,800b background color changed to dark violet blue. Green marginal inscriptions. Size: 130x80mm.

1962, Sept. 5 Litho. *Perf. 11½*

Designs: 1,200b, 5,000b, Plane and oxcart. 2,000b, Aerial photography (plane over South America).

Emblem in Red, Yellow & Green

C241 AP56 600b blk. & blue 25 20
C242 " 1200b multi. 35 30
C243 " 2000b " 50 50
C244 " 5000b " 1.25 1.00

Armed Forces of Bolivia.

Malaria Type of 1962

Design: Inscription around mosquito, laurel around globe.

1962, Oct. 4

C245 A154 2000b indigo, grn. & yellow 1.00 75

Issued for the World Health Organization drive to eradicate malaria.

Type of Regular Issue, 1961

Design: 1,200b Pedro de la Gasca (1485-1567).

Photogravure

1962 *Perf. 13x12½* **Unwmkd.**

C246 A150 1,200b brn., *yellow* 50 30

Condor, Soccer Ball and Flags
AP57

Alliance for Progress Emblem
AP58

Design: 1.80p, Map of Bolivia, soccer ball, goal and flags.

1963, Mar. 21 Litho. *Perf. 11½*

Flags in National Colors

C247 AP57 1.40p blk., ocher & red 1.00 65
C248 " 1.80p black, red & ocher 1.00 75

Issued to publicize the 21st South American Soccer Championships.

Freedom from Hunger Issue

Type of Regular Issue

Design: 1.20p, Wheat, globe and wheat emblem.

1963, Aug. 1 *Perf. 11½* **Unwmkd.**

C249 A156 1.20p dark green, blue & yel. 75 50

Issued for the "Freedom from Hunger" campaign of the U.N. Food and Agriculture Organization.

1963, Nov. 15 *Perf. 11½*

C250 AP58 1.20p dull yellow, ultra. & grn. 1.00 50

Issued to commemorate the second anniversary of the Alliance for Progress, which aims to stimulate economic growth and raise living standards in Latin America.

Type of Regular Issue, 1963

Designs: 1.20p, Ballot box and voters. 1.40p, Map and farmer breaking chain. 2.80p, Miners.

1963, Dec. 21 *Perf. 11½*

C251 A157 1.20p gray, dark brn. & rose 50 30
C252 " 1.40p bister & grn. 60 40
C253 " 2.80p slate & buff 1.25 75

Issued to commemorate the 10th anniversary of the Revolution of Apr. 9, 1952.

Andrés Santa Cruz
AP59

Lithographed

1966, Aug. 10 *Perf. 13½* **Wmk. 90**

C254 AP59 20c deep blue 10 10
C255 " 60c deep green 20 15
C256 AP59 1.20p red brown 50 25
C257 " 2.80p black 1.00 60

Issued to commemorate the centenary (in 1965) of the death of Marshal Andrés Santa Cruz (1792-1865), president of Bolivia and of Peru-Bolivia Confederation.

Children Type of 1966

Design: 1.40p, Mother and children.

1966, Dec. 16 *Perf. 13½* **Unwmkd.**

C258 A159 1.40p gray blue & black 1.25 65

Issued to help poor children.

Co-Presidents Type of Regular Issue

1966, Dec. 16 Litho. *Perf. 12½*

Flag in Red, Yellow and Green

C259 A160 2.80p gray & tan 2.00 1.50
C260 " 10p sepia & tan 3.00 1.75
a. Souv. sheet of 4 7.50 7.50

Issued to honor Generals Rene Barrientos Ortuno and Alfredo Ovando C., Co-Presidents, 1965-66.

No. C260a contains 4 imperf. stamps similar to Nos. 480-481 and C259-C260. Dark green marginal inscription. Size: 135x82mm.

Various Issues 1954-62 Surcharged with New Values and Bars

1966, Dec. 21

On No. C177:
"XII Aniversario / Reforma / Agraria"

C261 AP46 10c on 27b brt. pink 10 10

On No. C182:
"XXV / Aniversario Paz / del Chaco"

C262 AP47 10c on 55b dk. & lt. greenish blue 10 10

On No. C199:
"Centenario de / Tupiza"

C263 AP48 60c on 1350b rose carmine 20 15

On No. C200:
"XXV / Aniversario / Automovil Club / Boliviano"

C264 AP48 2.80p on 2700b bl. green 2.50 1.25

On No. C201:
"Centenario de la / Cruz Roja / Internacional"

C265 AP48 4p on 4000b violet blue 1.50 75

On No. C219:
"CL Aniversario / Heroinas Coronilla"

C266 AP51 1.20p on 800b vio. brown 50 25

On No. C222:
"Centenario Himno / Paceño"

C267 AP51 1.40p on 4,000b dk. gray 50 25

Nos. C224-C225 Surcharged

C268 A146 1.40p on 1,000b multi. 50 35
C269 " 1.40p on 1,800b multi. 50 35

On Nos. C238-C239:
"Aniversario / Centro Filatelico / Cochabamba"

C270 A152 1.20p on 800b multi. 40 20
C271 " 1.20p on 1,800b multi. 40 20

Revenue Stamp of 1946 Surcharged with New Value "X" and:
"XXV Aniversario / Dpto. Pando / Aéreo"

C272 A161 1.20p on 1b dk. bl. 50 30
Nos. C261-C272 (12) 7.70 4.25

Lions Emblem and Pre-historic Sculptures
AP60

1967, Sept. 20 Litho. *Perf. 13x13½*

C273 AP60 2p red & multi. 75 50
a. Souv. sheet of 2 4.00 4.00

Issued to commemorate the 50th anniversary of Lions International. No. C273a contains 2 imperf. stamps similar to Nos. 492 and C273. Black marginal inscription. Size: 129x80mm.

Folklore Type of Regular Issue

Designs (Folklore characters): 1.20p, Pujllay. 1.40p, Ujusiris. 2p, Morenada. 3p, Auki-aukis.

1968, June 24 *Perf. 13½x13*

C274 A163 1.20b lt. yel. green & multi. 30 25
C275 " 1.40b gray & multi. 40 30
C276 " 2b dk. olive bis. & multi. 60 40
C277 " 3b sky blue & multi. 1.00 75

Issued to publicize the 9th Congress of the Postal Union of the Americas and Spain.

A souvenir sheet exists containing 4 imperf. stamps similar to Nos. C274-C277. Bister and gray marginal inscription. Size: 131x81½mm.

Moto Mendez
AP61

1968, Oct. 29 Litho. *Perf. 13½x13*

C278 AP61 1b deep orange & multi. 40 25
C279 " 1.20b lt. ultra. & multi. 50 25
C280 " 2b bister brown & multi. 75 50
C281 " 4b bluish lilac & multi. 1.25 75

Battle of Tablada sesquicentennial.

Pres. Guálberto Villaroël
AP62

1968, Nov. 6 *Perf. 13x13½*

C282 AP62 1.40b org. & black 40 25
C283 " 3b lt. bl. & blk. 75 50
C284 " 4b rose & blk. 1.00 60
C285 " 5b gray green & black 1.25 75
C286 " 10b pale purple & black 2.50 1.50
Nos. C282-C286 (5) 5.90 3.60

4th centenary of Cochabamba.

ITU Type of Regular Issue

1968, Dec. 3 Litho. *Perf. 13x13½*

C287 A166 1.20b gray, black & yellow 40 20
C288 " 1.40b blue, blk. & gray olive 50 30

Issued to commemorate the centenary (in 1965) of the International Telecommunication Union.

UNESCO Emblem
AP63

1968, Nov. 14 *Perf. 13½x13*

C289 AP63 1.20b pale violet & black 50 25
C290 " 2.80b yellow green & black 1.00 50

Issued to commemorate the 20th anniversary (in 1966) of UNESCO (United Nations Educational, Scientific and Cultural Organization).

Kennedy Type of Regular Issue

1968, Nov. 22 **Unwmkd.**

C291 A168 1b green & black 50 30
C292 " 10b scarlet & blk. 3.50 2.00

Issued in memory of Pres. John F. Kennedy, 1917–1963.

A souvenir sheet contains one imperf. stamp similar to No. C291. Dark violet marginal inscription. Size: 131x81½mm.

Tennis Type of Regular Issue

1968, Dec. 10 *Perf. 13x13½*

C293 A169 1.40b orange, black & lt. brown 50 35
C294 " 2.80b sky bl., blk. & lt. brn. 1.00 75

Issued to commemorate the 32nd South American Tennis Championships, La Paz, 1965.

A souvenir sheet exists containing one imperf. stamp similar to No. C293. Light brown marginal inscription. Size: 131x 81½mm.

Stamp Centenary Type of Regular Issue

Design: 1.40b, 2.80b, 3b, Bolivia No. 1.

1968, Dec. 23 Litho. *Perf. 13x13½*

C295 A170 1.40b orange, green & black 50 35
C296 " 2.80b pale rose, grn. & black 1.00 75
C297 " 3b light violet, green & black 1.00 75

Issued to commemorate the centenary of Bolivian postage stamps.

A souvenir sheet exists containing 3 imperf. stamps similar to Nos. C295–C297. Dark brown marginal inscription. Size: 131x81½mm.

Franklin D. Roosevelt
AP64

1969, Oct. 29 Litho. *Perf. 13½x13*

C298 AP64 5b brown, blk. & buff 1.50 1.00

Issued to honor Franklin D. Roosevelt (1882–1945), 32nd President of the United States.

Olympic Type of Regular Issue

Sports: 1.20b, Woman runner (vert.). 2.80b, Discus thrower (vert.). 5b, Hurdler.

Perf. 13½x13, 13x13½

1969, Oct. 29 **Lithographed**

C299 A171 1.20b yellow green, bister & black 50 25
C300 " 2.80b red, orange & black 1.00 50
C301 " 5b blue, lt. blue, red & blk. 1.50 1.00

Issued to commemorate the 19th Olympic Games, Mexico City, Oct. 12–27, 1968.

A souvenir sheet exists containing 3 imperf. stamps similar to Nos. C299–C301. Marginal inscription in blue, yellow green and red brown. Size: 130½x81mm.

Butterfly Type of Regular Issue

Butterflies: 1b, Metamorpha dido wernichei. 1.80b, Heliconius felix. 2.80b, Morpho casica. 3b, Papilio yuracares. 4b, Heliconius melitus.

1970, Apr. 24 Litho. *Perf. 13x13½*

C302 A172 1b sal. & multi. 35 20
C303 " 1.80b lt. bl. & multi. 60 40
C304 " 2.80b multicolored 1.00 75
C305 A172 3b multicolored 1.25 75
C306 " 4b " 1.50 85
Nos. C302-C306 (5) 4.70 2.95

A souvenir sheet exists containing 3 imperf. stamps similar to Nos. C302–C304. Black marginal inscription. Size: 129½x 80mm.

Scout Type of Regular Issue

Designs: 50c, Boy Scout building brick wall. 1.20b, Bolivian Boy Scout emblem.

1970, June 17 Litho. *Perf. 13½x13*

C307 A173 50c yel. & multi. 20 10
C308 " 1.20b multicolored 40 20

Issued to honor the Bolivian Boy Scout movement.

No. C228 Surcharged

1970, Dec. **Litho.** *Perf. 10½*

C309 AP53 1.20b on 4,000b multicolored 40 20

Flower Type of Regular Issue

Bolivian Flowers: 1.20b, Amaryllis pseudopardina (horiz.). 1.40b, Rebutia kruegeri. 2.80b, Lobivia pentlandii (horiz.). 4b, Rebutia tunariensis.

Perf. 13x13½, 13½x13

1971, Aug. 9 **Litho.** **Unwmkd.**

C310 A174 1.20b multicolored 40 20
C311 " 1.40b " 45 25
C312 " 2.80b " 85 40
C313 " 4b " 1.50 75

Two souvenir sheets of 4 exist. One contains imperf. stamps similar to Nos. 534–535 and C310, C312. The other contains imperf. stamps similar to Nos. 536–537, C311, C313. Black marginal inscriptions. Size: 130x80mm.

Dance Type of Regular Issue

Folk Dances: 1.20b, Kusillo. 1.40b, Taquirari.

1972, Mar. 23 Litho. *Perf. 13½x13*

C314 A177 1.20b yel. & multi. 40 25
C315 " 1.40b org. & multi. 50 25

Two souvenir sheets of 3 exist. One contains imperf. stamps similar to Nos. 542–543, C314. The other contains imperf. stamps similar to Nos. 540–541, C315. Sheets have Sapporo '72 Olympic Games emblem in multicolor and marginal inscriptions in yellow, green and orange. Size: 80x129mm.

Painting Type of Regular Issue

Bolivian Paintings: 1.40b, Portrait of Chola Paceña, by Cecilio Guzmán de Rojas. 1.50b, Adoration of the Kings, by G. Gamarra. 1.60b, Adoration of Pachamama (mountain), by A. Borda. 2b, The Kiss of the Idol, by Guzman de Rojas.

1972 **Lithographed** *Perf. 13½*

C316 A178 1.40b multicolored 50 25
C317 " 1.50b " 50 25
C318 " 1.60b " 50 25
C319 " 2b " 75 40

Two souvenir sheets of 2 exist. One contains imperf. stamps similar to Nos. 548 and C318. The other contains imperf. stamps similar to Nos. C317 and C319. Sheets have "Munich 1972," Olympic and Munich emblems in margins. Size: 129x80mm.

Issue dates: 1.40b, Dec. 4. Others, Aug. 17.

Bolivian Coat of Arms
AP65

1972, Dec. 4 *Perf. 13½x14*

C320 AP65 4b lt. bl. & multi. 1.50 1.00

Cactus Type of Regular Issue

Designs: Various cacti.

1973, Aug. 6 **Litho.** *Perf. 13½*

C321 A180 1.20b tan & multi. 35 20
C322 " 1.90b org. & multi. 50 30
C323 " 2b multicolored 65 40

Development Type of Regular Issue

Designs: 1.40b, Highway 1Y4. 2b, Bus crossing bridge.

1973, Nov. 26 **Litho.** *Perf. 13½*

C324 A181 1.40b sal. & multi. 25 20
C325 " 2b multicolored 40 30

Bolivia's development.

Santos-Dumont and 14-Bis Plane
AP66

1973, July 20

C326 AP66 1.40b yel. & black 50 25

Centenary of the birth of Alberto Santos-Dumont (1873–1932), Brazilian aviation pioneer.

Orchid Type of 1974

Orchids: 2.50b, Cattleya luteola (horiz.). 3.80b, Stanhopaea. 4b, Catasetum (horiz.). 5b, Maxillaria.

1974 **Lithographed** *Perf. 13½*

C327 A182 2.50b multicolored 75 35
C328 " 3.80b rose & multi. 1.00 50
C329 " 4b multi. 1.25 60
C330 " 5b sal. & multi. 1.50 70

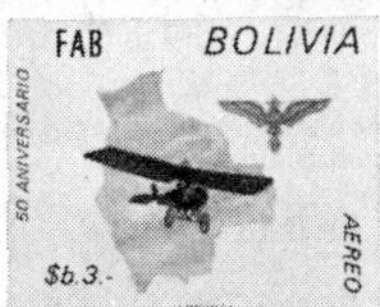

Air Force Emblem, Plane over Map of Bolivia
AP67

Designs: 3.80b, Plane over Andes. 4.50b, Triple decker and jet. 8b, Rafael Pabon and double decker. 15b, Jet and "50."

1974 **Lithographed** *Perf. 13x13½*

C331 AP67 3b multicolored 75 50
C332 " 3.80b " 85 60
C333 " 4.50b " 1.00 70
C334 " 8b " 1.75 1.25
C335 " 15b " 3.00 2.25
Nos. C331-C335 (5) 7.35 5.30

Bolivian Air Force, 50th anniversary.

Coat of Arms Type of 1975

Designs: Departmental coats of arms.

1975, July 16 **Litho.** *Perf. 13½*

Gold & Multicolored

C336 A188 20c *Beni* 5 5
C337 " 30c *Tarija* 10 5
C338 " 50c *Potosi* 10 8
C339 " 1b *Oruro* 25 15
C340 " 2.50b *Santa Cruz* 60 35
C341 " 3b *La Paz* 75 40
Nos. C336-C341 (6) 1.85 1.08

Sesquicentennial of Republic of Bolivia.

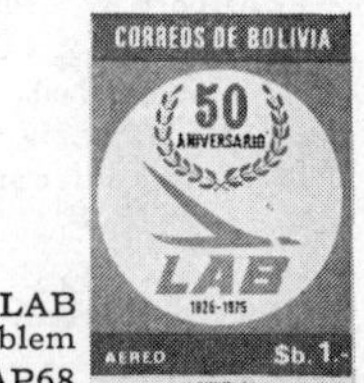

LAB Emblem
AP68

Bolivia on Map of Americas
AP69

Map of Bolivia, Plane and Kyllmann
AP70

1975 **Lithographed** *Perf. 13½*

C342 AP68 1b gold, blue & black 25 15
C343 AP69 1.50b multicolored 35 25
C344 AP70 2b " 50 35

Lloyd Aereo Boliviano, 50th anniversary, founded by Guillermo Kyllmann.

Bolivar, Presidents Perez and Banzer, and Flags
AP71

1975, Aug. 4 **Litho.** *Perf. 13½*

C345 AP71 3b gold & multi. 75 50

Visit of Pres. Carlos A. Perez of Venezuela.

Bolivar Type of 1975.

Presidents and Statesmen of Bolivia: 50c, Rene Barrientes O. 2b, Francisco B. O'Connor. 3.80b, Gualberto Villarroel. 4.20b, German Busch. 4.50b, Hugo Banzer Suarez. 20b, José Ballivian. 30b, Andres de Santa Cruz. 40b, Antonio Jose de Sucre.

1975 **Litho.** *Perf. 13½*

Size: 24x33mm.

C346 A189 50c multicolored 15 10
C347 " 2b " 50 30
C348 " 3.80b " 75 50
C349 " 4.20b " 1.00 60

Size: 28x39mm.

C350 A189 4.50b multi. 1.00 75

Size: 24x33mm.

C351 A189 20b multi. 4.00 3.00
C352 " 30b " 6.00 4.00
C353 " 40b " 8.00 5.00
Nos. C346-C353 (8) 21.40 14.25

Sesquicentennial of Republic of Bolivia.

UPU Emblem
AP72

1975, Dec. 7 **Litho.** *Perf. 13½*

C358 AP72 25b bl. & multi. 5.00 3.00

Centenary of Universal Postal Union (in 1974).

POSTAGE DUE STAMPS.

D1

Engraved.

1931 ***Perf. 14, 14½.*** **Unwmkd.**

No.	Type	Description	Unused	Used
J1	D1	5c ultramarine	1.00	1.00
J2	"	10c red	1.00	1.00
J3	"	15c yellow	1.00	1.00
J4	"	30c deep green	1.00	1.00
J5	"	40c deep violet	1.00	1.00
J6	"	50c black brown	1.00	1.00
		Nos. J1-J6 (6)	6.00	6.00

Symbol of Youth
D2

Torch of Knowledge
D3

Symbol of the Revolution of May 17, 1936
D4

1938 **Lithographed.** ***Perf. 11.***

No.	Type	Description	Unused	Used
J7	D2	5c deep rose	40	35
		a. Pair, imperf. between		
J8	D3	10c green	40	35
J9	D4	30c gray blue	40	35

POSTAL TAX STAMPS.

Worker
PT1

Symbols of Communications
PT2

Imprint: "LITO. UNIDAS LA PAZ."

Perf. 13½ x 10½, 10½, 13½.

1939 **Lithographed.** **Unwmkd.**

No.	Type	Description	Unused	Used
RA1	PT1	5c dull violet	20	15
		a. Double impression		

Redrawn

Imprint: "TALL. OFFSET LA PAZ."

1940 ***Perf. 12 x 11, 11.***

No.	Type	Description	Unused	Used
RA2	PT1	5c violet	20	15
		a. Horizontal pair, imperf. between	2.00	
		b. Imperf. horiz., pair		

Tax of Nos. RA1–RA2 was for the Workers' Home Building Fund.

1944–45 **Lithographed** ***Perf. 10½***

No.	Type	Description	Unused	Used
RA3	PT2	10c salmon	25	15
RA4	"	10c blue ('45)	25	15

A 30c orange inscribed "Centenario de la Creacion del Departmento del Beni" was issued in 1946 and required to be affixed to all air and surface mail to and from the Department of Beni in addition to regular postage. Five higher denominations in the same scenic design were used for local revenue purposes.

Type of 1944 Redrawn.

1947-48 ***Perf. 10½.*** **Unwmkd.**

No.	Type	Description	Unused	Used
RA5	PT2	10c carmine	20	5
RA6	"	10c orange yel. ('48)	15	5
RA7	"	10c yel. brn. ('48)	15	5
RA8	"	10c emerald ('48)	15	5

Post horn and envelope reduced in size.

Condor, Envelope and Post Horn
PT3

Communication Symbols
PT4

1951-52

No.	Type	Description	Unused	Used
RA9	PT3	20c deep orange	20	10
		a. Imperf., pair		
RA10	"	20c green ('52)	20	10
RA11	"	20c blue ('52)	20	10

1952–54 ***Perf. 13½, 10½, 10½x12***

No.	Type	Description	Unused	Used
RA12	PT4	50c green	25	10
RA13	"	50c carmine	25	10
RA14	"	3b green	25	10
RA15	"	3b olive bistre	40	30
RA16	"	5b violet ('54)	40	10
		Nos. RA12-RA16 (5)	1.55	70

No. RA10 and Type of 1951-52.
Surcharged with New Value in Black.

1953 ***Perf. 10½.***

No.	Type	Description	Unused	Used
RA17	PT3	50c on 20c green	25	10
RA18	"	50c on 20c red violet	25	10

Postman Blowing Horn
PT5

1954-55 ***Perf. 10½.*** **Unwmkd.**

No.	Type	Description	Unused	Used
RA19	PT5	1b brown	25	10
RA20	"	1b carmine rose ('55)	25	10

Nos. RA15 and RA14 Surcharged in Black
"Bs. 5.—/D. S./21-IV-55"

1955 ***Perf. 10½, 10½x12***

No.	Type	Description	Unused	Used
RA21	PT4	5b on 3b olive bistre	20	10
RA22	"	5b on 3b green	20	10

Tax of Nos. RA3–RA22 was for the Communications Employees Fund.

No. RA21 is known with surcharge in thin type of different font and with comma added after "55".

Plane over Airport
PT6

Planes
PT7

Lithographed.

1955 ***Perf. 10½, 12, 13½,*** **Unwmkd.**

No.	Type	Description	Unused	Used
RA23	PT6	5b deep ultramarine	20	10
		a. Vertical pair imperf. between		

Perf. 11½

No.	Type	Description	Unused	Used
RA24	PT7	10b light green	20	10

PT8

PT9

1955 **Lithographed** ***Perf. 10½***

No.	Type	Description	Unused	Used
RA25	PT8	5b red	20	10

Perf. 12

No.	Type	Description	Unused	Used
RA26	PT9	20b dark brown	20	10

Tax of Nos. RA23–RA26 was for the building of new airports.

General Alfredo Ovando and Three Men
PT10

1970, Sept. 26 Litho. ***Perf. 13x13½***

No.	Type	Description	Unused	Used
RA27	PT10	20c black & red	15	10

See No. RAC1.

Pres. German Busch
PT11

1971, May 13 Litho. ***Perf. 13x13½***

No.	Type	Description	Unused	Used
RA28	PT11	20c lilac & black	15	6

AIR POST POSTAL TAX STAMPS

Type of Postal Tax Issue

1970, Sept. 26 Litho. ***Perf. 13x13½***

Design: 30c, General Ovando and oil well.

No.	Type	Description	Unused	Used
RAC1	PT10	30c blk. & green	15	6

Pres. Gualberto Villarroel, Refinery
PTAP1

1971, May 25 Litho. ***Perf. 13x13½***

No.	Type	Description	Unused	Used
RAC2	PTAP1	30c light blue & black	15	6

Type of 1971 Inscribed:
"XXV ANIVERSARIO DE SU GOBIERNO"

1975 **Litho.** ***Perf. 13x13½***

No.	Type	Description	Unused	Used
RAC3	PTAP1	30c lt. bl. & blk.	15	6

BOSNIA AND HERZEGOVINA

(bŏz′ni·*ȧ* & hĕr′tsĕ·gô·vē′nä)

LOCATION—In what is now Jugoslavia, between Dalmatia and Serbia.

GOVT.—Provinces of Turkey under Austro-Hungarian occupation, 1879-1908; provinces of Austria-Hungary 1908-1918.

AREA—19,768 sq. mi.

POP.—2,000,000 (approx. 1918).

CAPITAL—Sarajevo.

Following World War I Bosnia and Herzegovina united with the kingdoms of Montenegro and Serbia, and Croatia, Dalmatia and Slovenia, to form the Kingdom of Jugoslavia (See Jugoslavia.)

100 Novcica (Neukreuzer) = 1 Florin (Gulden)

100 Heller = 1 Krone (1900)

Coat of Arms
A1

Type I. The heraldic eaglets on the right side of the escutcheon are entirely blank. The eye of the lion is indicated by a very small dot, which sometimes fails to print. All values except the ½n exist in this type.

Type II. There is a colored line across the lowest eaglet. A similar line sometimes appears on the middle eaglet. The eye of the lion is formed by a large dot which touches the outline of the head above it. All values are found in this type.

Type III. The eaglets and eye of the lion are similar to type I. Each tail feather of the large eagle has two lines of shading and the lowest feather does not touch the curved line below it. In types I and II there are several shading lines in these feathers, and the lowest feather touches the curved line. Only the 5n is found in type III.

Varieties of the Numerals.

2 NOVCICA:

A. The "2" has curved tail. All are type I.
B. The "2" has straight tail. All are type II.

15 NOVCICA:

C. The serif of the "1" is short and forms a wide angle with the vertical stroke.
D. The serif of the "1" forms an acute angle with the vertical stroke.

The numerals of the 5n were retouched several times and show minor differences, especially in the flag.

Other Varieties.

½ NOVCICA:

All printings of the ½n are type II.

There is a black dot between the curved ends of the ornaments near the lower spandrels.

G. This dot touches the curve at its right. Stamps of this (first) printing are lithographed.

H. This dot stands clear of the curved lines. Stamps of this (second) printing are typographed.

10 NOVCICA:

Ten stamps in each sheet of type II show a small cross in the upper section of the right side of the escutcheon.

Wmk. 91

Lithographed.

Wmkd. BRIEF-MARKEN or (from 1890) ZEITUNGS-MARKEN in Double-lined Capitals, Across the Sheet (91)

Perf. 9 to 13½ and Compound

1879–94 **Type 1.**

No.	Type	Description	Unused	Used
1	A1	½n black (type II) ('94)	11.00	15.00
2	"	1n gray	9.00	1.10
		c. 1n gray lilac		2.75
4	"	2n yellow	11.00	1.35
5	"	3n green	11.50	1.65
6	"	5n rose red	14.00	35
7	"	10n blue	50.00	50
8	"	15n brown	57.50	3.85
9	"	20n gray grn. ('93)	275.00	6.00
10	"	25n violet	60.00	6.75

No. 2c was never issued. It is usually cancelled by blue pencil marks and "mint" copies generally have been cleaned.

Typographed.

Perf. 10½ to 13 and Compound.

1894-98 **Type II.**

No.	Type	Description	Unused	Used
1a	A1	½n black	10.00	16.50
2a	"	1n gray	3.50	55
4a	"	2n yellow	2.10	50
5a	"	3n green	3.50	70
6a	"	5n rose red	55.00	32
7a	"	10n blue	4.25	50
8a	"	15n brown	3.50	2.10
9a	"	20n gray green	5.50	3.50
10a	"	25n violet	8.50	4.50

Type III.

No.	Type	Description	Unused	Used
6b	A1	5n rose red ('98)	2.25	32

All the preceding stamps exist in various shades.

Nos. 1a to 10a were reprinted in 1911 in lighter colors, on very white paper and perf. 12½. Price, set $18.

A2

A3

Perf. 10½, 12½ and Compound

1900 Typographed.

No.	Type	Description	Unused	Used
11	A2	1h gray black	35	7
12	"	2h gray	35	7
13	"	3h yellow	38	7
14	"	5h green	35	3
15	"	6h brown	70	10
16	"	10h red	35	3
17	"	20h rose	100.00	5.50
18	"	25h blue	1.10	20
19	"	30h bistre brown	120.00	6.00
20	"	40h orange	185.00	11.00
21	"	50h red lilac	1.20	42
22	A3	1k dark rose	1.40	55
23	"	2k ultramarine	2.10	1.60
24	"	5k dull blue green	4.50	4.25
		Nos. 11–24 (14)	417.78	29.89

All values of this issue except the 3h exist on ribbed paper.

Nos. 17, 19 and 20 were reprinted in 1911. The reprints are in lighter colors and on whiter paper than the originals. Reprints of Nos. 17 and 19 are perf. 10½ and those of No. 20 are perf. 12½. Price $2 each.

Numerals in Black.

1901-04 ***Perf. 12½.***

No.	Type	Description	Unused	Used
25	A2	20h pink ('02)	1.15	32
26	"	30h bistre brn. ('03)	1.15	38
27	"	35h blue	1.50	45
		a. 35h ultramarine	9.00	90
28	"	40h orange ('03)	1.75	70
29	"	45h grnsh. blue ('04)	1.40	50
		Nos. 25–29 (5)	6.95	2.35

Nos. 11 to 29 exist imperforate. Nearly all are known perf. 6½, also compound with perf. 12½, and part perf. or in pairs, imperf. between, but they were only supplied to some high-ranking officials and never sold at any post office.

View of Deboj
A4

The Carsija at Sarajevo
A17

Designs: 2h, View of Mostar. 3h, Pliva Gate, Jajce. 5h, Narenta Pass and Prenj River. 6h, Rama Valley. 10h, Vrbas Valley. 20h, Old Bridge, Mostar. 25h, Bey's Mosque, Sarajevo. 30h, Donkey post. 35h, Jezero and tourists' pavilion. 40h, Mail wagon. 45h, Bazaar at Sarajevo. 50h, Postal car. 2k, St. Luke's Campanile, Jajce. 5k, Emperor Franz Josef.

Perf. 6½, 9½, 10½ and 12½, also Compounds.

1906 Engraved. **Unwmkd.**

No.	Type	Description	Unused	Used
30	A4	1h black	15	7
31	"	2h violet	18	7
32	"	3h olive	20	7
33	"	5h dark green	22	3
34	"	6h brown	25	13
		a. Perf. 13½	19.00	17.50
35	"	10h carmine	30	3
36	"	20h dark brown	75	20
		a. Perf. 13½	55.00	32.50
37	A4	25h deep blue	2.10	1.10
38	"	30h green	2.25	32
39	"	35h myrtle green	2.25	35
40	"	40h orange red	2.25	32
41	"	45h brown red	2.25	1.10
42	"	50h dull violet	2.50	85
43	A17	1k maroon	5.75	2.50
44	"	2k gray green	9.00	9.00
45	"	5k dull blue	6.00	7.50
		Nos. 30–45 (16)	36.40	23.64

Nos. 30–45 exist imperf. Price, set $50 unused, $32.50 canceled.

Birthday Jubilee Issue.

Designs of 1906 Issue, with "1830-1910" in label at bottom.

1910 ***Perf. 12½.***

No.	Type	Description	Unused	Used
46	A4	1h black	55	20
47	"	2h violet	60	20
48	"	3h olive	65	27
49	"	5h dark green	75	13
50	"	6h orange brown	75	27
51	"	10h carmine	75	13
52	"	20h dark brown	1.90	1.65
53	"	25h deep blue	3.85	3.25
54	"	30h green	2.85	3.00
55	"	35h myrtle green	3.25	3.00
56	"	40h orange red	3.50	3.75
57	"	45h brown red	6.25	6.50
58	"	50h dull violet	6.50	7.00
59	A17	1k maroon	6.50	7.00
60	"	2k gray green	26.00	21.00
61	"	5k dull blue	3.00	4.75
		Nos. 46–61 (16)	67.65	62.10

80th birthday of Emperor Franz Josef.

Scenic Type of 1906.

Designs (Views): 12h, Jaice. 60h, Konjica. 72h, Vishegrad.

1912

No.	Type	Description	Unused	Used
62	A4	12h ultramarine	7.50	4.25
63	"	60h dull blue	3.85	4.25
64	"	72h carmine	14.00	14.00

Nos. 62–64 exist imperf. Price, set $60.

Emperor Franz Josef
A23 A24

A25 A26

1912-14 **Various Frames.**

No.	Type	Description	Unused	Used
65	A23	1h olive green	70	4
66	"	2h bright blue	70	4
67	"	3h claret	70	3
68	"	5h green	70	3
69	"	6h dark gray	70	7
70	"	10h rose carmine	70	3
71	"	12h deep olive green	1.75	27
72	"	20h orange brown	7.25	3
73	"	25h ultramarine	3.00	10
74	"	30h orange red	3.00	3
75	A24	35h myrtle green	3.25	4
76	"	40h dark violet	10.00	3
77	"	45h olive brown	4.00	20
78	"	50h slate blue	4.00	3
79	"	60h brown violet	4.00	10
80	"	72h dark blue	4.75	3.85
81	A25	1k brown violet, *straw*	19.00	42
82	"	2k dark gray, *blue*	8.50	27
83	A26	3k carmine, *green*	12.50	9.50
84	"	5k dark violet, *gray*	32.50	27.50
85	A25	10k dark ultra., *gray* ('14)	135.00	100.00
		Nos. 65–85 (21)	256.70	142.61

Nos. 65–85 exist imperf. Price, set $450.

A27

A28

1916-17 ***Perf. 12½***

No.	Type	Description	Unused	Used
86	A27	3h dark gray	27	25
87	"	5h olive green	42	45
88	"	6h violet	48	50
89	"	10h bistre	2.10	1.90
90	"	12h blue gray	55	60
91	"	15h carmine rose	10	3
92	"	20h brown	50	50
93	"	25h blue	38	42
94	"	30h dark green	38	42
95	"	40h vermilion	38	42
96	"	50h green	38	42
97	"	60h lake	42	50
98	"	80h orange brown	95	20
		a. Perf. 11½	3.75	3.50
99	"	90h dark violet	1.00	70
		a. Perf. 11½	350.00	385.00
101	A28	2k claret, *straw*	65	70
102	"	3k green, *blue*	2.00	2.25
103	"	4k carmine, *green*	9.00	9.00
104	"	10k dp. violet, *gray*	22.50	25.00
		Nos. 86–104 (18)	42.46	44.26

Nos. 86–104 exist imperf. Price, set $100.

Emperor Karl I
A29 A30

1917 ***Perf. 12½***

No.	Type	Description	Unused	Used
105	A29	3h olive gray	20	25
		a. Perf. 11½	57.50	47.50
		b. Perf. 12½x11½	15.00	15.00
106	"	5h olive green	15	17
107	"	6h violet	55	70
108	"	10h orange brown	20	7
		a. Perf. 11½x12½	50.00	42.50
		b. Perf. 11½		
109	"	12h blue	65	90
110	"	15h bright rose	15	7
111	"	20h red brown	15	15
112	"	25h ultramarine	1.00	55
113	"	30h gray green	33	20
114	"	40h olive bistre	33	17
115	"	50h deep green	1.20	55
116	"	60h carmine rose	1.00	50
		a. Perf. 11½	16.00	15.00
117	"	80h steel blue	38	25
118	"	90h dull violet	1.30	1.40
119	A30	2k carmine, *straw*	75	38
120	"	3k green, *blue*	21.00	22.00
121	"	4k carmine, *green*	7.50	8.50
122	"	10k deep violet, *gray*	4.50	6.00
		Nos. 105–122 (18)	41.34	42.81

Nos. 105–122 exist imperf. Price, set $85.

Nos. 47 and 66 Overprinted in Red **1918**

1918

No.	Type	Description	Unused	Used
126	A4	2h violet	75	1.10
		a. Overprinted "1913"	8.50	8.50
		b. Inverted overprint	20.00	20.00
		c. Same as "a" inverted	75.00	75.00
		d. Double overprint	17.50	17.50
		e. Same as "a" double	75.00	75.00
		f. Double overprint, one inverted	20.00	
		g. Same as "a", double, one inverted	40.00	
127	A23	2h bright blue	75	1.10
		a. Pair, one without overprint		
		b. Inverted overprint	20.00	20.00
		c. Double overprint	17.50	17.50
		d. Double overprint, one inverted	13.50	

Emperor Karl I
A31

1918 **Typo.** ***Perf. 12½, Imperf.***

No.	Type	Description	Unused	Used
128	A31	2h orange	9.00	
129	"	3h dark green	9.00	
130	"	5h light green	9.00	
131	"	6h blue green	9.00	
132	"	10h brown	9.00	
133	"	20h brick red	9.00	
134	"	25h ultramarine	9.00	
135	"	45h dark slate	9.00	
136	"	50h lt. bluish green	9.00	
137	"	60h blue violet	9.00	
138	"	70h ocher	9.00	
139	"	80h rose	9.00	
140	"	90h violet brown	9.00	

Engraved

No.	Type	Description	Unused	Used
141	A30	1k olive green, *greenish*	1850.00	
		Nos. 128–140 (13)	117.00	

Nos. 128–141 were prepared for use in Bosnia and Herzegovina, but were not issued there. They were sold after the Armistice at the Vienna post office for a few days.

SEMI-POSTAL STAMPS.

Nos. 33 and 35 Surcharged in Red **1914. 7 Heller**

1914 ***Perf. 12½.*** **Unwmkd.**

No.	Type	Description	Unused	Used
B1	A4	7h on 5h dark green	55	60
		a. Pair, one without surcharge		
B2	"	12h on 10h carmine	50	55

Various minor varieties of the surcharge include "4" with open top, narrow "4" and wide "4".

Nos. B1–B2 exist with double and inverted surcharges. Price about $20 each.

Nos. 33 and 35 Surcharged in Red or Blue **1915. 7 Heller**

1915 ***Perf. 12½***

No.	Type	Description	Unused	Used
B3	A4	7h on 5h dark green (R)	12.00	12.50
		a. Perf. 9½	120.00	110.00
B4	A4	12h on 10h carmine (Bl)	38	45

Nos. B3–B4 exist with double and inverted surcharges. Price about $18.50 each.

1915

Nos. 68 and 70 Surcharged in Red or Blue

7 Heller.

1915

No.	Type	Description	Unused	Used
B5	A23	7h on 5h green (R)	75	90
		a. "1915" at top and bottom	37.50	37.50
B6	"	12h on 10h rose car. (Bl)	1.65	1.30
		a. Surcharged "7 Heller."	37.50	37.50

Nos. B5–B6 are found in three types differing in length of surcharge lines: I, date 18mm., denomination 14mm. II, date 16mm., denomination 14mm. III, date 18mm., denomination 16mm.

Nos. B5–B6 exist with double and inverted surcharges. Price $15 each.

Nos. B5a and B6a exist double and inverted.

❖ 1916. ❖

Nos. 68 and 70 Surcharged in Red or Blue

7 Heller.

1916				
B7	A23	7h on 5h green (R)	55	50
B8	"	12h on 10h rose car. (Bl)	60	65

Nos. B7–B8 exist with double and inverted surcharges. Price $12.50 each.

Wounded Soldier
SP1

Blind Soldier
SP2

1916 Engraved.

B9	SP1	5h (+2h) green	1.25	85
B10	SP2	10h (+2h) magenta	1.75	1.20

Nos. B9–B10 exist imperf. Price, set $27.50.

Nos. 89, 91 Overprinted

WITWEN-UND WAISENWOCHE 1917

1917				
B11	A27	10h bistre	12	12
B12	"	15h carmine rose	12	12

Nos. B11–B12 exist imperf. Price, set $12.50.

Nos. B11–B12 exist with double and inverted overprint. Price $9 each.

Design for Memorial Church at Sarajevo—SP3

Archduke Francis Ferdinand
SP4

Duchess Sophia and Archduke Francis Ferdinand
SP5

1917 Typo. *Perf. 11½, 12½*

B13	SP3	10h violet black	20	27
B14	SP4	15h claret	20	27
B15	SP5	40h deep blue	20	27

Assassination of Archduke Ferdinand and Archduchess Sophia. Sold at a premium of 2h each which helped build a memorial church at Sarajevo.

Nos. B13–B15 exist imperf. Price, set $2.50.

Blind Soldier
SP6

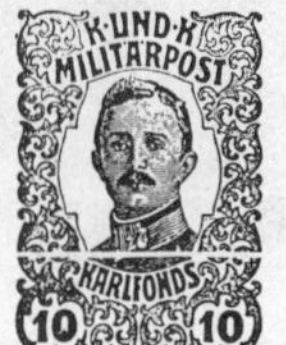

Emperor Karl I
SP8

Design: 15h, Wounded soldier.

1918 Engraved *Perf. 12½*

B16	SP6	10h (+10h) greenish blue	75	75
B17	"	15h (+10h) red brown	75	75

Nos. B16–B17 exist imperf. Price, set $18.50.

1918 Typographed. *Perf. 12½x13.*

Design: 15h, Empress Zita.

B18	SP8	10h gray green	50	60
B19	"	15h brown red	50	60
B20	"	40h violet	50	60

Sold at a premium of 10h each which went to the "Karl's Fund."

Nos. B18–B20 exist imperf. Price, set $22.50.

POSTAGE DUE STAMPS.

D1

D2

Perf. 9½, 10½, 12½ and Compound.

1904 Unwmkd.

J1	D1	1h black, red & yellow	65	7
J2	"	2h " "	70	20
J3	"	3h " "	70	7
J4	"	4h " "	70	7
J5	"	5h " "	70	7
J6	"	6h " "	48	7
J7	"	7h " "	4.25	3.25
J8	"	8h " "	4.25	1.10
J9	"	10h " "	1.00	7
J10	"	15h " "	90	10
J11	"	20h " "	4.75	20
J12	"	50h " "	3.50	17
J13	"	200h blk., red & green	16.50	1.25
		Nos. J1-J13 (13)	39.08	6.69

Nos. J1–J13 exist imperf. Price, set $75.

1916–18 *Perf. 12½*

J14	D2	2h red ('18)	55	60
J15	"	4h " ('18)	42	50
J16	"	5h "	55	42
J17	"	6h " ('18)	42	50
J18	"	10h "	48	50
J19	"	15h "	4.25	4.50
J20	"	20h "	48	50
J21	"	25h "	1.50	1.90
J22	"	30h "	1.20	1.50
J23	"	40h "	11.00	12.00
J24	"	50h "	37.50	42.50
J25	"	1k dark blue	4.50	5.50
J26	"	3k "	22.50	27.50
		Nos. J14-J26 (13)	85.35	98.42

Nos. J25 and J26 have colored numerals on a white tablet. Nos. J14–J26 exist imperf. Price, set $125.

NEWSPAPER STAMPS.

Bosnian Girl
N1

1913 *Imperf.* Unwmkd.

P1	N1	2h ultramarine	90	75
P2	"	6h violet	2.50	1.65
P3	"	10h rose	2.35	1.65
P4	"	20h green	3.50	1.90

After Bosnia and Herzegovina became part of Jugoslavia stamps of type N1 perforated, also imperforate copies surcharged with new values, were used as regular postage stamps.

SPECIAL HANDLING STAMPS.

"Lightning"
SH1

Engraved.

1916 *Perf. 12½.* Unwmkd.

QE1	SH1	2h vermilion	33	42
		a. Perf. 11½x12½	90.00	85.00
QE2	"	5h deep green	60	75
		a. Perf. 11½	17.50	17.50

BRAZIL

(brȧ·zĭl′)

Brasil (after 1918)

LOCATION—On the north and east coasts of South America, bordering on the Atlantic Ocean.

GOVT.—Republic.

AREA—3,287,000 sq. mi.

POP.—112,240,000 (est. 1977).

CAPITAL—Brasilia.

Brazil was an independent empire from 1822 to 1889 when a constitution was adopted and the country became officially known as The United States of Brazil.

1000 Reis = 1 Milreis

100 Centavos = 1 Cruzeiro (1942)

> Prices of Brazil Nos. 1–13 vary according to condition. Quotations are for fine copies. Very fine to superb specimens sell at much higher prices, and inferior or poor copies sell at reduced prices, depending on the condition of the individual specimen.

Issues of the Empire.

A1

Engraved

Grayish or Yellowish Paper.

1843, Aug. 1 *Imperf.* Unwmkd.

1	A1	30r black	1000.00	400.00
		a. In pair with No. 2		*35,000.00*
2	"	60r black	625.00	225.00
3	"	90r "	2250.00	900.00

Early impressions of Nos. 1 to 3 bring higher prices than quoted which are for copies from worn plates.

A2

A3

Grayish or Yellowish Paper.

1844-46

7	A2	10r black	60.00	30.00
8	"	30r "	65.00	37.50
9	"	60r "	60.00	30.00
10	"	90r "	375.00	150.00
11	"	180r "	2500.00	1500.00
12	"	300r "	4500.00	2000.00
13	"	600r "	4000.00	2250.00

Nos. 8, 9 and 10 exist on thick paper and are considerably scarcer.

Grayish or Yellowish Paper.

1850, Jan. 1

21	A3	10r black	30.00	17.50
22	"	20r "	70.00	90.00
23	"	30r "	7.50	1.25
24	"	60r "	7.50	1.00
25	"	90r "	80.00	10.00
26	"	180r "	80.00	50.00
27	"	300r "	240.00	75.00
28	"	600r "	275.00	75.00

All values except the 90r were reprinted in 1910 on very thick paper.

1854

37	A3	10r blue	12.50	12.50
38	"	30r "	35.00	40.00

A4

1861

39	A4	280r red	150.00	125.00
40	"	430r yellow	225.00	150.00

Nos. 39 and 40 have been reprinted on thick white paper with white gum. They are printed in aniline inks and the colors are brighter than those of the originals.

1866 *Perf. 13½.*

41	A3	10r black	22.50	17.50
42	"	10r blue	20.00	20.00
43	"	20r black	225.00	100.00
44	"	30r "	150.00	100.00
45	"	30r blue	50.00	50.00
46	"	60r black	60.00	12.50
47	"	90r "	300.00	200.00
48	"	180r "	300.00	150.00
49	A4	280r red	300.00	300.00
50	A3	300r black	600.00	350.00
51	A4	430r yellow	275.00	250.00
52	A3	600r black	300.00	175.00

Fraudulent perforations abound.

Emperor Dom Pedro
A5

A6

A7

A8 A8a

A9 A9a

Thick or Thin White Wove Paper.

1866, July 1 *Perf. 12*

53	A5	10r vermilion	8.00	3.00
		a. Bluish paper	110.00	80.00
54	A6	20r red lilac	10.00	2.25
		a. 20r dull violet	20.00	6.00
		b. Bluish paper	50.00	25.00
56	A7	50r blue	20.00	1.50
		a. Bluish paper	30.00	10.00
57	A8	80r slate violet	40.00	4.00
		a. Bluish paper	45.00	17.50
58	A8a	100r blue green	12.50	50
		a. 100r yel. green	12.50	50
		b. Bluish paper	120.00	30.00
59	A9	200r black	50.00	4.00
		a. Imperf. vert.	75.00	
60	A9a	500r orange	175.00	30.00
		Nos. 53-60 (7)	315.50	45.25

The 10r and 20r exist imperf. on both white and bluish paper. Some authorities consider them proofs.

Nos. 58 and 65 are found in two types.

1876-77 ***Rouletted.***

61	A5	10r verm. ('77)	30.00	25.00
62	A6	20r red lilac ('77)	35.00	20.00
63	A7	50r blue ('77)	35.00	4.50
64	A8	80r violet ('77)	90.00	12.50
65	A8a	100r green	17.50	75
66	A9	200r black ('77)	35.00	4.50
		a. Diagonal half used as 100r on cover		
67	A9a	500r orange	150.00	35.00
		Nos. 61-67 (7)	392.50	102.25

A10 A11

A12 A13

A14 A15

A16 A17

A18 A19

A20

1878-79 *Rouletted.*

68	A10	10r vermilion	5.00	2.50
69	A11	20r violet	5.50	1.75
70	A12	50r blue	12.50	1.25
71	A13	80r lake	12.50	6.00
72	A14	100r green	12.00	70
73	A15	200r black	80.00	10.00
		a. Diagonal half used as 100r on cover		
74	A16	260r dark brown	45.00	20.00
75	A18	300r bistre	45.00	5.00
76	A19	700r red brown	125.00	90.00
77	A20	1000r gray lilac	150.00	35.00
		Nos. 68-77 (10)	492.50	172.20

1878, Aug. 21 *Perf. 12*

78	A17	300r org. & green	50.00	15.00

Nos. 68-78 exist imperforate.

A21 A22 A23

Small Heads

1881, July 15 Laid Paper

Perf. 13, 13½ and Compound

79	A21	50r blue	70.00	15.00
80	A22	100r olive green	250.00	20.00
81	A23	200r pale red brn.	400.00	90.00

On Nos. 79 and 80 the hair above the ear curves forward. On Nos. 83 and 88 it is drawn backward. On the stamps of the 1881 issue the beard is smaller than in the 1882-85 issues and fills less of the space between the neck and the frame at the left.

See also No. 88.

A24 A25

A26 A27

Two types each of the 100 and 200 reis.

100 REIS:

Type I. Groundwork formed of diagonal crossed lines and horizontal lines.

Type II. Groundwork formed of diagonal crossed lines and vertical lines.

200 REIS:

Type I. Groundwork formed of diagonal and horizontal lines.

Type II. Groundwork formed of diagonal crossed lines.

Larger Heads.

Perf. 12½ to 14 and Compound.

1882-84 Laid Paper

82	A24	10r black	3.50	4.50
83	A25	100r olive green, type I	25.00	2.00
		a. 100r dark green, type I	25.00	2.00
		b. 100r dark green, type II	100.00	8.00
84	A26	200r pale red brown, type I	50.00	20.00
85	A27	200r pale rose, type II	30.00	3.50
		a. Diagonal half used as 100r on cover		20.00

See also No. 86.

A28 A29 A30

Three types of A29.

Type I. Groundwork formed of horizontal lines.

Type II. Groundwork formed of diagonal crossed lines.

Type III. Groundwork solid.

Perf. 13, 13½, 14 and Compound

1884-85

86	A24	10r orange	1.25	1.50
87	A28	20r slate green	5.00	1.25
		a. 20r olive green	2.50	2.50
88	A21	50r blue, head larger	15.00	2.50
89	A29	100r lilac, type III	200.00	15.00
		a. 100r lilac, type II	100.00	10.00
90	"	100r lilac, type I	50.00	1.75
91	A30	100r lilac	50.00	1.50

A31

Perf. 13, 13½, 14 and Compound.

1885

92	A31	100r lilac	25.00	85
		a. Imperf., pair	75.00	75.00

A32 — Southern Cross A33 — Crown A34

1887

93	A32	50r chalky blue	15.00	3.00
94	A33	300r gray blue	75.00	8.00
95	A34	500r olive	50.00	7.50

A35

A36

Entrance to Bay of Rio de Janeiro

A37

1888

96	A35	100r lilac	25.00	75
		a. Imperf., pair	60.00	60.00
97	A36	700r violet	15.00	*50.00*
98	A37	1000r dull blue	100.00	50.00

Issues of the Republic.

Southern Cross

A38

Wove Paper, Thin to Thick.

Perf. 12½ to 14, 11 to 11½, and 12½ to 14 x 11 to 11½, Rough or Clean-Cut.

1890-91 Engr.; Typo. (#102)

99	A38	20r gray green	1.50	1.25
		a. 20r blue green	1.50	1.25
		b. 20r emerald	10.00	5.00
100	"	50r gray green	2.50	1.00
		a. 50r olive green	10.00	1.00
		b. 50r yellow green	10.00	5.00
		c. 50r dark slate green	10.00	5.00
		d. Horizontal pair, imperf. between		
101	"	100r lilac rose	200.00	50.00
102	"	100r red lilac, redrawn	40.00	2.00
		a. Tête bêche pair	*10,000.00*	
103	"	200r purple	15.00	1.25
		a. 200r violet	15.00	2.25
		b. 200r violet blue	15.00	2.25
104	"	300r slate violet	50.00	2.50
		a. 300r gray	50.00	7.50
		b. 300r gray blue	100.00	10.00
		c. 300r dark violet	25.00	6.00
105	"	500r olive bistre	15.00	10.00
		a. 500r olive gray	15.00	10.00
106	"	500r slate	15.00	10.00
107	"	700r chocolate	20.00	20.00
		a. 700r fawn	22.50	22.50
108	"	1000r bistre	20.00	4.00
		a. 1000r yellow buff	25.00	7.50
		Nos. 99-108 (10)	379.00	107.00

The redrawn 100r may be distinguished by the absence of the curved lines of shading in the left side of the central oval. The pearls in the oval are not well aligned and there is less shading at right and left of "CORREIO" and "100 REIS."

A 100 reis stamp of type A38 but inscribed "BRAZIL" instead of "E. U. DO BRAZIL" was not placed in issue but postmarked copies are known. A reprint on thick paper was made in 1910.

No. 101 exists imperf., not regularly issued.

Liberty Head

A39

Liberty Head

A40

Perf. 12½ to 14, 11 to 11½ and 12½ to 14 x 11 to 11½

1891, May 1 Typographed

109	A39	100r blue & red	20.00	50
		a. Head inverted	100.00	75.00
		b. Tête bêche pair	600.00	500.00
		c. 100r ultra. & red	22.50	60

Perf. 11, 11½, 13, 13½, 14 and Compound.

1893, Jan. 18 **Lithographed**

111 A40 100r rose 35.00 50

Sugarloaf Mountain

A41 A41a

A42

Liberty Head A42a

Hermes A43

Perf. 11 to 11½, 12½ to 14 and 12½ to 14x11 to 11½.

1894–97 **Unwmkd.**

112 A41 10r rose & blue 2.00 50

113 A41a 10r rose & blue 1.25 25

114 " 20r orange & blue 1.75 30

115 " 50r dark blue & blue 7.50 1.50

116 A42 100r car. & black 10.00 25
 a. Vertical pair, imperf. between 80.00

118 A42a 200r orange & black 3.00 25
 a. Imperf. horiz., pair 60.00
 b. Vertical pair, imperf. between 60.00

119 " 300r green & black 25.00 50

120 " 500r blue & black 25.00 1.00

121 " 700r lilac & black 15.00 1.50

122 A43 1000r green & violet 70.00 1.50

124 " 2000r black & gray lilac 120.00 20.00

Nos. 112–124 (11) 280.50 27.55

The head of No. 116 exists in five types. See also Nos. 140–150A, 159–161, 166–171G.

Newspaper Stamps Surcharged:

100 200

1898 1898

100 200

a *b*

100

1898

100

c

Surcharged on 1889 Issue of type N1.

1898 ***Rouletted***

Green Surcharge.

125 (*b*) 700r on 500r yellow 10.00 10.00

126 (*c*) 1000r on 700r yellow 30.00 30.00
 a. Surcharged "700r" 400.00 400.00

127 (*c*) 2000r on 1000r yel. 17.50 12.50

128 (") 2000r on 1000r brown 15.00 6.00

Violet Surcharge.

129 (*a*) 100r on 50r brn. yel. 3.50 6.00

130 (*c*) 100r on 50r brn. yel. 40.00 40.00

131 (") 300r on 200r black 3.50 1.25
 a. Double surcharge 75.00 60.00

The surcharge on No. 130 is handstamped. The impression is blurred and lighter in color than on No. 129. The two surcharges differ most in the shapes and serifs of the figures "1."

Counterfeits exist of No. 126a.

Black Surcharge.

132 (*b*) 200r on 100r violet 2.50 1.25
 a. Double surcharge 75.00 60.00
 b. Inverted surcharge 75.00 65.00

132C (") 500r on 300r carmine 4.00 2.50

133 (") 700r on 500r green 6.00 2.00

Blue Surcharge.

134 (*b*) 500r on 300r carmine 6.00 2.25

Red Surcharge.

135 (*c*) 1000r on 700r ultra. 20.00 12.50
 a. Inverted surcharge 150.00 150.00

Surcharged on 1890-94 Issues:

200 1898

1898 50 RÉIS 50

d *e*

Perf. 11 to 14 and Compound.

Black Surcharge.

136 N3 (*e*) 20r on 10r blue 1.00 1.50

137 N2 (*d*) 200r on 100r red lilac 10.00 6.00
 a. Double surcharge 60.00 50.00

Blue Surcharge.

138 N3 (*e*) 50r on 20r green 2.00 4.00
 a. Double surcharge

138B N2 (*d*) 200r on 100r red lilac 7.50 5.00

Red Surcharge.

139 N3 (*e*) 100r on 50r green 7.50 10.00
 a. Blue surch. 15.00 15.00

The surcharge on Nos. 139 and 139a exists double, inverted, one missing, etc.

Types of 1894–97

Perf. 5½ to 7 and 11 to 11½x5½ to 7

140 A41a 10r rose & blue 5.00 3.00

141 " 20r orange & blue 7.00 1.50

142 " 50r dark blue & light blue 8.00 5.00

143 A42 100r car. & black 15.00 1.50

144 A42a 200r orange & black 9.00 2.00

145 " 300r green & black 30.00 3.00

Perf. 8½ to 9½ and 8½ to 9½x11 to 11½

146 A41a 10r rose & blue 4.00 1.75

147 " 20r org. & blue 10.00 1.75

147A " 50r dark blue & blue 100.00 27.50

148 A42 100r car. & black 15.00 1.00

149 A42a 200r orange & black 5.00 1.25

150 " 300r grn. & black 35.00 3.00

150A A43 1000r green & vio. 100.00 4.00

Issue of 1890-93 Surcharged in Violet or Magenta

1899

50 RÉIS

Perf. 11 to 11½, 12½ to 14 and Compound

1899, June 25

151 A38 50r on 20r gray grn. 1.25 1.25
 a. Double surcharge

152 A38 100r on 50r gray grn. 1.35 1.25
 a. Pair, one without surcharge
 b. Double surch. 30.00

153 " 300r on 200r purple 8.00 8.00
 a. Double surcharge

154 " 500r on 300r slate violet 20.00 10.00
 a. 500r on 300r gray lilac 16.00 8.00
 b. Pair, one without surcharge 250.00

155 " 700r on 500r olive bistre 20.00 5.00
 a. Pair, one without surcharge 250.00
 b. Double surcharge

156 " 1000r on 700r choc. 10.00 3.50

157 " 1000r on 700r fawn 12.50 5.00
 a. Pair, one without surcharge 250.00
 b. Double surcharge

158 " 2000r on 1000r yellow buff 20.00 5.00
 a. 2000r on 1000r bistre 20.00 5.00
 b. Pair, one without surcharge 250.00

Nos. 151–158 (8) 93.10 39.00

Types of 1894–97

Perf. 11, 11½, 13 and Compound.

1900

159 A41a 50r green 8.50 40

160 A42 100r rose 15.00 30
 a. Frame around inner oval 20.00 50

161 A42a 200r blue 20.00 30

Three types exist of No. 161, all of which have the frame around inner oval.

Cabral Arrives at Brazil

A44

Independence Proclaimed

A45

"Emancipation of Slaves"

A46

Allegory, Republic of Brazil

A47

1900, Jan. 1 **Litho.** ***Perf. 12½***

162 A44 100r red 6.00 6.00
 a. Imperf. (pair) 200.00 200.00

163 A45 200r green & yellow 6.00 6.00

164 A46 500r blue 6.00 6.00

165 A47 700r emerald 6.00 6.00

Discovery of Brazil, 400th anniversary.

Wmk. 97 Wmk. 98

Types of 1894–97.

Wmkd. (97? or 98?)

1905 ***Perf. 11, 11½***

166 A41a 10r rose & blue 3.00 1.50

167 " 20r orange & blue 6.00 40

168 " 50r green 15.00 40

169 A42 100r rose 15.00 25

170 A42a 200r dark blue 15.00 25

171 " 300r green & blk. 20.00 1.50

Nos. 166–171 (6) 74.00 4.30

Positive identification of Wmk. 97 or 98 places stamp in specific watermark groups below.

Wmkd.

"CORREIO FEDERAL REPUBLICA DOS ESTADOS UNIDOS DO BRAZIL"

in Sheet. (97)

166b A41a 10r rose & blue 35.00 12.00

167b " 20r orange & blue 20.00 4.00

168b " 50r green 40.00 5.00

169b A42 100r rose 200.00 5.00

170b A42a 200r dark blue 40.00 2.00

171b " 300r green & black 250.00 30.00

171A A43 1000r grn. & vio. 250.00 25.00

Nos. 166b–171A (7) 835.00 83.00

Wmkd.

"IMPOSTO DE CONSUMO REPUBLICA DOS ESTADOS UNIDOS DO BRAZIL"

in Sheet. (98)

166c A41a 10r rose & blue 50.00 20.00

167c " 20r orange & blue 45.00 10.00

168c " 50r green 100.00 20.00

169c A42 100r rose 40.00 2.00

170c A42a 200r dark blue 40.00 75

171d " 300r green & black 200.00 30.00

Nos. 166c–171d (6) 475.00 82.75

Allegory, Pan-American Congress

A48

1906, July 23 **Litho.** **Unwmkd.**

172 A48 100r carmine rose 30.00 15.00

173 " 200r blue 50.00 7.50

Third Pan-American Congress.

Aristides Lobo

A48a

Benjamin Constant

A49

Pedro Alvares Cabral

A50

Eduardo Wandenkolk

A51

Manuel Deodoro da Fonseca
A52

Floriano Peixoto
A53

Prudente de Moraes
A54

Manuel Ferraz de Campos Salles
A55

Francisco de Paula Rodrigues Alves
A56

Liberty Head
A57

A58

A59

1906–16 Engraved *Perf. 12*

No.	Type	Description	Unused	Used
174	A48a	10r bluish slate	35	6
175	A49	20r aniline violet	20	6
176	A50	50r green	40	8
		a. Booklet pane of 6 ('08)	15.00	20.00
177	A51	100r aniline rose	1.00	5
		a. Imperf. vert., coil ('16)	3.00	40
		b. Booklet pane of 6 ('08)	25.00	30.00
178	A52	200r blue	1.00	8
		a. Booklet pane of 6 ('08)	15.00	20.00
179	A52	200r ultra. ('15)	1.25	8
		a. Imperf. vert., coil ('16)	1.50	40
180	A53	300r gray black	3.00	15
181	A54	400r olive green	15.00	75
182	A55	500r dark violet	4.00	20
183	A54	600r olive green ('10)	1.25	50
184	A56	700r red brown	3.00	1.50
185	A57	1000r vermilion	30.00	50
186	A58	2000r yellow green	3.50	25
187	"	2000r Prussian blue ('15)	10.00	30
188	A59	5000r carmine rose	4.00	1.00
		Nos. 174–188 (15)	77.95	5.56

Allegorical Emblems: Liberty, Peace, Industry, etc.
A60

1908, July 14

No.	Type	Description	Unused	Used
189	A60	100r carmine	17.50	1.00

National Exhibition, Rio de Janeiro.

Emblems of Peace Between Brazil and Portugal
A61

1908, July 14

No.	Type	Description	Unused	Used
190	A61	100r red	6.00	60

Issued to commemorate the centenary of the opening of Brazilian ports to foreign commerce. Medallions picture King Carlos I of Portugal and Pres. Affonso Penna of Brazil.

Bonifacio, Bolívar, Hidalgo, O'Higgins, San Martin, Washington
A62

1909

No.	Type	Description	Unused	Used
191	A62	200r deep blue	3.50	50

Nilo Peçanha
A63

Baron of Rio Branco
A64

1910, Nov. 15

No.	Type	Description	Unused	Used
192	A63	10,000r brown	5.00	1.00

1913–16

No.	Type	Description	Unused	Used
193	A64	1000r deep green	1.25	30
194	"	1000r slate ('16)	10.00	30

Cabo Frio
A65

Wmk. 99

Wmkd. "CORREIO." (99)

1915, Nov. 13 Litho. *Perf. 11½*

No.	Type	Description	Unused	Used
195	A65	100r dark green, *yellowish*	3.00	1.75

Founding of the town of Cabo Frio, 300th anniversary.

Bay of Guajara
A66

1916, Jan. 5

No.	Type	Description	Unused	Used
196	A66	100r carmine	5.00	2.00

City of Belem, 300th anniversary.

Revolutionary Flag
A67

1917, Mar. 6

No.	Type	Description	Unused	Used
197	A67	100r deep blue	20.00	6.00

Centenary of Revolution of Pernambuco, Mar. 6, 1817.

Rodrígues Alves
A68

Engraved.

1917, Aug. 31 *Perf. 12* Unwmkd.

No.	Type	Description	Unused	Used
198	A68	5000r red brown	40.00	10.00

Liberty Head
A69 A70

Perf. 12½, 13, 13 x 13½.

1918-20 Typographed. Unwmkd.

No.	Type	Description	Unused	Used
200	A69	10r orange brown	25	15
201	"	20r slate	25	15
202	"	25r olive gray ('20)	25	15
203	"	50r green	15.00	1.00
204	A70	100r rose	75	15
		a. Imperf. (pair)		
205	"	300r red orange	12.50	1.00
206	"	500r dull violet	15.00	60
		Nos. 200–206 (7)	44.00	3.20

Wmk. 100

Because of the spacing of this watermark, a few stamps in each sheet may show no watermark.

Wmkd.

CASA DA MOEDA in Sheet. (100)

No.	Type	Description	Unused	Used
207	A69	10r red brown	2.50	80
		a. Imperf. (pair)		
207B	"	20r slate	80	60
		c. Imperf. (pair)		
208	"	25r olive gray ('20)	40	25
209	"	50r green	40	15
210	A70	100r rose	25.00	50
		a. Imperf. (pair)		
211	"	200r dull blue	3.50	50
212	"	300r orange	20.00	2.00
213	"	500r dull violet	20.00	5.00
214	"	600r orange	1.25	90
		Nos. 207–214 (9)	73.85	10.70

"Education"
A72

1918 Engraved. *Perf. 11½.*

No.	Type	Description	Unused	Used
215	A72	1000r blue	2.00	20
216	"	2000r red brown	20.00	4.00
217	"	5000r dark violet	6.00	5.00

Watermark note below No. 257 also applies to Nos. 215–217.

See also Nos. 233–234, 283–285, 404, 406, 458, 460.

Railroad
A73

"Industry"
A74

"Aviation"
A75

Mercury
A76

"Navigation"
A77

Perf. 13½x13, 13x13½

1920-22 Typographed. Unwmkd.

No.	Type	Description	Unused	Used
218	A73	10r red violet	40	10
219	"	20r olive green	40	10
220	A74	25r brown violet	30	10
221	"	50r blue green	50	10
222	"	50r org. brn. ('22)	80	20
223	A75	100r rose red	1.00	10
224	"	100 orange ('22)	2.50	20
225	"	150r violet ('21)	80	20
226	"	200r blue	1.50	15
227	"	200r rose red ('22)	1.50	15
228	A76	300r olive gray	8.00	25
229	"	400r dull blue ('22)	10.00	1.75
230	"	500r red brown	10.00	40
		Nos. 218–230 (13)	37.70	3.80

See also Nos. 236–257, 265–266, 268–271, 273–274, 276–281, 302–311, 316–322, 326–340, 357–358, 431–434, 436–441, 461–463B, 467–470, 472–474, 488–490, 492–494.

***Perf. 11, 11½* Engr. Wmk. 100**

No.	Type	Description	Unused	Used
231	A77	600r red orange	1.00	20
232	"	1000r claret	2.00	12
		a. Perf. 8½	15.00	2.00
233	A72	2000r dull violet	10.00	40
234	"	5000r brown	15.00	5.00

Nos. 233 and 234 are inscribed "BRASIL CORREIO". Watermark note below No. 257 also applies to Nos. 231–234.

See also No. 282.

King Albert of Belgium and President Epitacio Pessoa
A78

1920, Sept. 19 Engr. *Perf. 11½x11*

No.	Type	Description	Unused	Used
235	A78	100r dull red	1.00	75

This stamp was issued to commemorate the visit of the King and Queen of Belgium to Brazil.

Types of 1920–22 Issue.

Perf. 13 x 13½, 13 x 12½.

1922–29 Typographed Wmk. 100

No.	Type	Description	Unused	Used
236	A73	10r red violet	20	10
237	"	20r olive green	20	10
238	A75	20r gray violet ('29)	15	10

239 A74 25r brown violet 25 10
240 " 50r blue green 5.00 5.00
241 " 50r org. brn. ('23) 20 10
a. Booklet pane of 6
242 A75 100r rose red 12.00 30
243 " 100r orange ('26) 40 10
a. Booklet pane of 6
244 " 100r turq. grn. ('28) 30 15
245 " 150r violet 1.75 10
246 " 200r blue 200.00 3.00
247 " 200r rose red 30 10
a. Booklet pane of 6
248 " 200r olive grn. ('28) 1.75 75
249 A76 300r olive gray 1.00 20
a. Booklet pane of 6
250 " 300r rose red ('29) 25 20
251 " 400r blue 1.00 20
252 " 400r orange ('29) 60 60
253 " 500r red brown 5.00 30
a. Booklet pane of 6
254 " 500r ultra. ('29) 8.00 15
255 " 600r brn. org. ('29) 4.00 2.00
256 " 700r dull violet ('29) 6.00 30
257 " 1000r turq. blue ('29) 4.00 30
Nos. 236-257 (22) 252.35 14.25

Because of the spacing of the watermark, a few stamps in each sheet show no watermark.

"Agriculture"
A79

1922 *Perf. 13x13½.* Unwmkd.

258 A79 40r orange brown 40 10
259 " 80r greenish blue 30 20

See also Nos. 263, 267, 275.

Declaration of Ypiranga
A80

Dom Pedro I and José Bonifacio
A81

National Exposition and President Pessoa
A82

Engraved.

1922, Sept. 7 *Perf. 14* Unwmkd.

260 A80 100r ultramarine 1.50 40
261 A81 200r red 2.50 30
262 A82 300r green 4.50 30

Issued in commemoration of the centenary of independence and the National Exposition of 1922.

Agriculture Type of 1922
Typographed

1923 *Perf. 13½x12* Wmk. 100

263 A79 40r orange brown 25 15

Brazilian Army Entering Bahia
A83

Perf. 13

1923, July 12 Litho. Unwmkd.

264 A83 200r rose 8.00 4.00

Centenary of the taking of Bahia from the Portuguese.

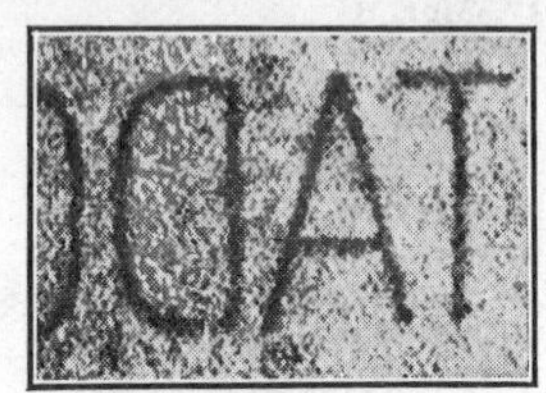

Wmk. 193

Types of 1920–22 Issues
Typographed
Wmkd.
ESTADOS UNIDOS DO BRASIL. (193)

1924 *Perf. 13x13½*

265 A73 10r red violet 3.50 1.50
266 " 20r olive green 3.50 1.50
267 A79 40r orange brown 3.00 40
268 A74 50r orange brown 3.50 3.50
269 A75 100r orange 3.00 35
270 " 200r rose 4.00 35
271 A76 400r blue 4.00 3.00
Nos. 265-271 (7) 24.50 10.60

Arms of Equatorial Confederation, 1824
A84

Perf. 11

1924, July 2 Litho. Unwmkd.

272 A84 200r blue, black, yellow & red 3.00 2.00
a. Red omitted 400.00 400.00

Centenary of the Equatorial Confederation.

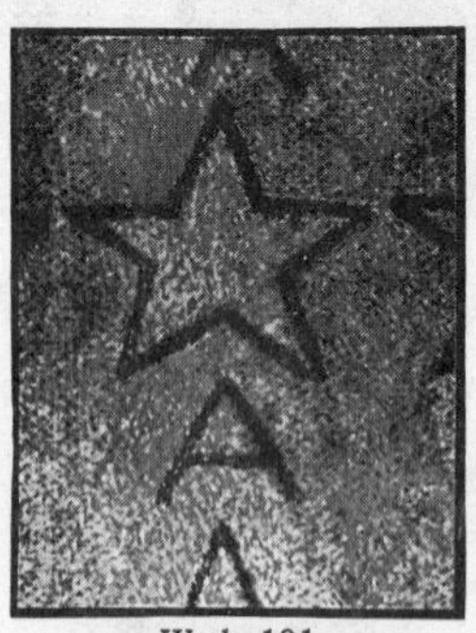

Wmk. 101

Types of 1920–22 Issues.
Wmkd. Stars and CASA DA MOEDA. (101)
Perf. 9½ to 13½ and Compound.

1924–28 Typographed

273 A73 10r red violet 20 8
274 " 20r olive gray 20 8
275 A79 40r orange brown 40 12
276 A74 50r orange brown 40 10
277 A75 100r red orange 50 10
278 " 200r rose 30 10
279 A76 300r olive gray ('25) 6.00 50
280 A76 400r blue 2.00 25
281 " 500r red brown 8.00 30

Engraved.

282 A77 600r red orange ('26) 50 15
283 A72 2000r dull vio ('26) 1.50 15
284 " 5000r brown ('26) 7.50 40
285 " 10,000r rose ('28) 7.50 40
Nos. 273-285 (13) 35.00 2.73

Nos. 283 to 285 are inscribed "BRASIL CORREIO".

Ruy Barbosa
A85

1925 *Perf. 11½* Wmk. 100

286 A85 1000r claret 3.00 1.50
a. Unwmkd. 12.00 6.00

1926 Wmk. 101

287 A85 1000r claret 1.50 20

"Justice"
A86

Scales of Justice and Map of Brazil
A87

Wmk. 206

Wmkd.
Star-framed CM, Multiple (206)

1927, Aug. 11 Typo. *Perf. 13½x13*

288 A86 100r deep blue 1.00 50
289 A87 200r rose 1.00 50

Issued in commemoration of the centenary of the founding of the law courses.

Liberty Holding Coffee Leaves
A88

1928, Mar. 5

290 A88 100r blue green 1.50 60
291 " 200r carmine 1.00 50
292 " 300r olive black 8.50 40

Issued to commemorate the bicentenary of the introduction of the coffee tree in Brazil.

Official Stamps of 1919 Surcharged in Red or Black **700 Réis**

Engraved.

1928 *Perf. 11, 11½* Wmk. 100

293 O3 700r on 500r orange (R) 4.00 2.50
a. Inverted surcharge 500.00 500.00
294 O3 1000r on 100r rose red (Bk) 2.75 30
295 " 2000r on 200r dull blue (R) 3.50 30
296 " 5000r on 50r green (R) 3.50 50
a. Inverted surcharge
297 " 10,000r on 10r olive green (R) 20.00 1.50
Nos. 293-297 (5) 33.75 5.10

Nos. 293 to 297 were used for ordinary postage.

Stamps in the outer rows of the sheets are often without watermark.

Ruy Barbosa
A89

Perf. 9, 9½x11, 11, and Compound.

1929 Wmk. 101

300 A89 5000r blue violet 7.50 30

For other stamps of type A89, see Nos. 323, 405 and 459.

Wmk. 218

Types of 1920-21 Issue.
Typographed.
Wmkd. E U BRASIL Multiple. (218) (Letters 8 mm. high.)

Wmk. 218 exists both in vertical alignment and in echelon.

1929 *Perf. 13½x12½.*

302 A75 20r gray violet 15 8
a. Wmk. in echelon 20 15
303 A75 50r red brown 15 8
a. Wmk. in echelon 65.00 30.00
304 A75 100r turquoise green 25 8
305 " 200r olive green 12.00 2.00
306 A76 300r rose red 40 8
a. Wmk. in echelon 40 20
307 A76 400r orange 40 20
308 " 500r ultramarine 5.00 30
a. Wmk. in echelon 120.00 15.00
309 A76 600r brown orange 8.00 50
310 " 700r deep violet 1.50 8
311 " 1000r turquoise blue 2.50 8
a. Wmk. in echelon 12.00 7.50
Nos. 302-311 (10) 30.35 3.48

Architectural Fantasies
A90 A91

Architectural Fantasy
A92

Perf. 13x13½

1930, June 20 Wmk. 206

312	A90	100r turquoise blue	1.75	1.00
313	A91	200r olive gray	3.00	75
314	A92	300r rose red	5.00	1.25

Issued in connection with the Fourth Pan-American Congress of Architects and Exposition of Architecture.

Wmk. 221

Types of 1920-21 Issues.

Wmkd. ESTADOS UNIDOS DO BRASIL, Multiple. (221)

(Letters 6 mm. high.)

1930 ***Perf. 13 x12½.***

316	A75	20r gray violet	15	10
317	"	50r red brown	15	8
318	"	100r turquoise blue	20	12
319	"	200r olive green	65	15
320	A76	300r rose red	30	10
321	"	500r ultramarine	75	12
322	"	1000r turquoise blue	3.50	1.50
		Nos. 316-322 (7)	5.70	2.17

Barbosa Type of 1929.

1930 Engraved *Perf. 11*

323	A89	5000r bl. violet	1000.00

Imperforates

Since 1930, imperforate or partly perforated sheets of nearly all commemorative and some definitive issues have become obtainable.

Wmk. 222

Types of 1920-29 Issue.

Wmkd. CORREIO BRASIL and 5 Stars in Squared Circle. (222)

Perf. 11, 13½x13, 13 x12½.

1931-34 Typographed

326	A75	10r deep brown	10	5
327	"	20r gray violet	10	5
328	A74	25r brown vio. ('34)	10	8
330	A75	50r blue green	10	5
331	"	50r red brown	15	8
332	"	100r orange	25	5
334	"	200r deep carmine	30	5
335	A76	300r olive green	35	5
336	"	400r ultramarine	40	5
337	"	500r red brown	2.00	5
338	"	600r brown orange	2.00	5
339	"	700r deep violet	5.00	5
340	"	1000r turquoise bl.	10.00	5
		Nos. 326-340 (13)	20.85	71

Getulio Vargas and João Pessoa

A93

Vargas and Pessoa—A94

Oswaldo Aranha

A95 A96

Antonio Carlos

A97

Pessoa A98 Vargas A99

Lithographed.

1931, Apr. 29 *Perf. 14* Unwmkd.

342	A93	10r+10r light blue	20	20
343	"	20r+20r yellow brown	20	20
344	A95	50r+50r dull green, red & yellow	20	20
		a. Red missing at left	1.25	1.25
345	A93	100r+50r orange	40	30
346	"	200r+100r green	40	35
347	A94	300r+150r multi.	40	35
348	A93	400r+200r dp. rose	1.25	75
349	"	500r+250r dk. bl.	1.00	60
350	"	600r+300r brn. vio.	70	70
351	A94	700r+350r multi.	1.25	75
352	A96	1000r+500r bright green, red & yellow	3.00	30
353	A97	2000r+1000r gray black & red	5.50	75
354	A98	5000r+2500r black & red	25.00	7.00
355	A99	10,000r+5000r brt. grn. & yellow	40.00	15.00
		Nos. 342-355 (14)	79.50	27.45

Issued to commemorate the Revolution of Oct. 3, 1930. Prepared as semipostal stamps, Nos. 342-355 were sold as ordinary postage stamps with stated surtax ignored.

Nos. 306, 320 and 250 Surcharged **1931 200 Réis**

Wmkd. E U BRASIL Multiple. (218)

1931, July 20 *Perf. 13½x12½*

356	A76	200r on 300r rose red	75	75
		a. Wmk. in echelon	25.00	25.00
		b. Inverted surcharge	25.00	

***Perf. 13x12½* Wmk. 221**

357	A76	200r on 300r rose red	30	15
		a. Inverted surcharge	40.00	40.00

***Perf. 13½x12½* Wmk. 100**

358	A76	200r on 300r rose red	40.00	40.00

Map of South America Showing Meridian of Tordesillas

A100

João Ramalho and Tibiriçá

A101

Martim Affonso de Souza

A102

King John III of Portugal

A103

Disembarkation of M. A. de Souza at São Vicente

A104

Typographed.

1932, June 3 *Perf. 13* Wmk. 222

359	A100	20r dark violet	20	20
360	A101	100r black	50	40
361	A102	200r purple	1.25	20
362	A103	600r red brown	2.50	1.00

Perf. 9½, 11, 9½x11.

Engraved Wmk. 101

363	A104	700r ultramarine	3.00	1.50
		Nos. 359-363 (5)	7.45	3.30

Nos. 359 to 363 commemorate the fourth century of the first colonization of Brazil at Sao Vicente, in 1532, under the hereditary captaincy of Martim Affonso de Souza.

Revolutionary Issue.

Map of Brazil

A105

Soldier and Flag

A106

Allegory: Freedom, Justice, Equality

A107

Soldier's Head

A108

"LEX" and Sword

A109

Symbolical of Law and Order

A110

Symbolical of Justice

A111

Perf. 11½

1932, Sept. 13 Litho. Unwmkd.

364	A105	100r brown orange	25	1.50
365	A106	200r dark carmine	50	75
366	A107	300r gray green	3.00	4.00
367	A108	400r dark blue	5.00	6.00
368	A105	500r black brown	5.00	7.50
369	A107	600r red	5.00	7.50
370	A106	700r violet	3.00	7.50
371	A108	1000r orange	2.50	7.50
372	A109	2000r dark brown	17.50	22.50
373	A110	5000r yel. green	22.50	40.00
374	A111	10,000r plum	25.00	50.00
		Nos. 364-374 (11)	89.75	154.75

Issued by the revolutionary forces in the state of Sao Paulo during the revolt of September, 1932. Subsequently the stamps were recognized by the Federal Government and placed in general use.

Excellent counterfeits of Nos. 373 and 374 exist.

Counterfeit cancellations abound.

City of Vassouras and Illuminated Memorial

A112

Typographed.

1933, Jan. 15 *Perf. 12* Wmk. 222

375	A112	200r rose red	1.25	75

Commemorative of the centenary of the founding of the city of Vassouras.

No. 306 Surcharged **200 RÉIS**

Perf. 13½x12½

1933, July 28 Wmk. 218

376	A76	200r on 300r rose red	75	75
		a. Wmk. 218 in echelon (No. 306a)	30.00	30.00
		b. Wmk. 100 (No. 250)	50.00	50.00

Same Surcharge on No. 320.

Perf. 13 x12½. **Wmk. 221**

377	A76	200r on 300r rose red	25	15
		a. Inverted surcharge	40.00	
		b. Double surcharge	40.00	

Religious Symbols and Inscriptions
A113

Typographed

1933, Sept. 3 *Perf. 13* **Wmk. 222**

378 A113 200r dark red 1.00 60

Issued in commemoration of the First National Eucharistic Congress in Brazil.

"Flag of the Race"
A114

1933, Aug. 18

379 A114 200r deep red 1.00 60

Commemorating the raising of the "Flag of the Race" and the 441st anniversary of the sailing of Columbus from Palos, Spain, August 3, 1492.

Republic Figure, Flags of Brazil and Argentina
A115

Wmk. 236

Engraved.

1933, Oct. 7 *Perf. 11½* **Wmk. 101**

380 A115 200r blue 60 35

Wmkd.

Coat of Arms in Sheet (236)

Watermark (reduced illustration) covers 22 stamps in sheet.

Thick Laid Paper.

Perf. 11, 11½.

381 A115 400r green 90 70
382 " 600r bright rose 3.50 3.50
383 " 1000r light violet 5.00 3.00

Issued in commemoration of the visit of President Justo of the Argentine Republic to Brazil, October 2nd to 7th, 1933.

Allegory: "Faith and Energy"
A116

Allegory of Flight
A117

1933 **Typographed.** **Wmk. 222**

384 A116 200r dark red 30 15
385 " 200r dark violet 35 10

See also Nos. 435, 471 and 491.

Wmk. 236

1934, Apr. 15 **Engraved** ***Perf. 12***

386 A117 200r blue 75 1.00

Issued in commemoration of the first National Aviation Congress at Sao Paulo.

A118

Perf. 11

1934, May 12 **Typo.** **Wmk. 222**

387 A118 200r dark olive 80 50
388 " 400r carmine 3.00 2.50
389 " 700r ultramarine 2.50 1.75
390 " 1000r orange 5.00 1.50

Issued in commemoration of the Seventh International Fair at Rio de Janeiro.

Christ of Corcovado
A119

1934, Oct. 20

392 A119 300r dark red 2.50 2.50
a. Tête bêche pair 7.50 7.50
393 " 700r ultramarine 10.00 7.50
a. Tête bêche pair 30.00 30.00

Visit of Eugenio Cardinal Pacelli, later Pope Pius XII, to Brazil.

The three printings of Nos. 392–393, distinguishable by shades, sell for different prices.

José de Anchieta
A120

Thick Laid Paper.

1934, Nov. 8 *Perf. 11, 12* **Wmk. 236**

394 A120 200r yellow brown 1.25 75
395 " 300r violet 1.00 45
396 " 700r blue 4.00 2.00
397 " 1000r light green 5.00 2.00

Issued in commemoration of the 400th anniversary of the birth of Jose de Anchieta, S.J. (1534–1597), Portuguese missionary and "father of Brazilian literature."

"Brazil" and "Uruguay"
A121 A122

Perf. 11

1935, Jan. 8 **Typo.** **Wmk. 222**

398 A121 200r orange 90 50
399 A122 300r yellow 1.25 75
400 A122 700r ultramarine 3.50 3.50
401 A121 1000r dark violet 10.00 5.00

Visit of President Terra of Uruguay.

View of Town of Igarassu
A123

1935, July 1

402 A123 200r maroon & brn. 1.50 75
403 " 300r violet & olive brown 1.50 75

Issued in commemoration of the 400th anniversary of the founding of the captaincy of Pernambuco.

Types of 1918-29.

Thick Laid Paper.

Perf. 9½, 11, 12, 12x11.

1934–36 **Engraved** **Wmk. 236**

404 A72 2000r violet 1.00 15
405 A89 5000r bl. vio. ('36) 10.00 40
406 A72 10,000r claret ('36) 9.00 75

No. 404 is inscribed "BRASIL CORREIO".

Revolutionist
A124

Bento Gonçalves da Silva
A125

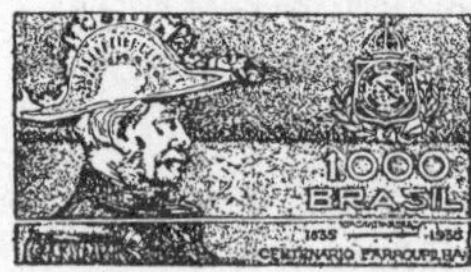

Duke of Caxias
A126

1935, Sept. 20 ***Perf. 11, 12***

407 A124 200r black 80 75
408 " 300r rose lake 80 60
409 A125 700r dull blue 4.00 3.00
410 A126 1000r light violet 4.00 2.50

Centenary of the "Ragged" Revolution.

Federal District Coat of Arms
A127

Perf. 11

1935, Oct. 19 **Typo.** **Wmk. 222**

411 A127 200r blue 4.00 3.00

Issued in commemoration of the Eighth International Sample Fair held at Rio de Janeiro.

Coutinho's Ship
A128

Arms of Fernandes Coutinho
A129

1935, Oct. 25

412 A128 300r maroon 3.00 1.00
413 A129 700r turquoise blue 4.00 2.50

Issued in commemoration of the 400th anniversary of the establishment of the first Portuguese colony at Espirito Santo by Vasco Fernandes Coutinho.

Gavea, Rock near Rio de Janeiro
A130

Wmk. 245

Wmkd. Multiple "CASA DA MOEDA DO BRASIL" and Small Formée Cross. (245)

1935, Oct. 12 ***Perf. 11***

414 A130 300r brown & violet 2.00 1.50
415 " 300r black & turquoise blue 2.00 1.50
416 " 300r Prussian blue & ultramarine 2.00 1.50
417 " 300r crimson & black 2.00 1.50

"Child's Day," Oct. 12.

Viscount of Cairú
A131

Perf. 11, 12x11

1936, Jan. 20 **Engraved** **Wmk. 236**

418 A131 1200r violet 8.50 5.00

Issued in commemoration of the centenary of the death of José da Silva Lisboa, Viscount of Cairú (1756-1835).

View of Cametá
A132

1936, Feb. 26 *Perf. 11, 12*

419 A132 200r brown orange 1.75 1.25
420 " 300r green 1.75 75

Issued in commemoration of the 300th anniversary of the founding of the city of Cameta, Dec. 24, 1635.

Coining Press
A133

Thick Laid Paper.

1936, Mar. 24 *Perf. 11*

421 A133 300r purple brown, *cream* 1.25 75

Issued in commemoration of the first Numismatic Congress at Sao Paulo, March, 1936.

Carlos Gomes—A134

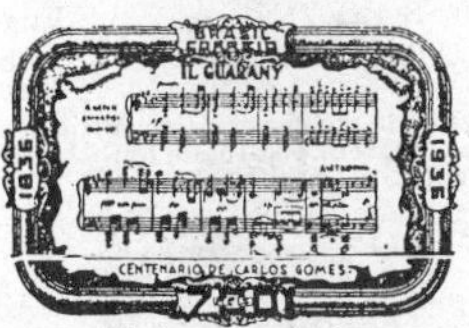

"Il Guarany"
A135

1936, July 11 *Perf. 11, 11x12*

Thick Laid Paper.

422 A134 300r dull rose 90 60
423 " 300r black brown 90 60
424 A135 700r ochre 3.50 1.75
425 " 700r blue 5.00 2.50

Issued in commemoration of the 100th anniversary of the birth of Antonio Carlos Gomes, who composed the opera "Il Guarany."

Scales of Justice
A136

Perf. 11

1936, July 4 Typo. Wmk. 222

426 A136 300r rose 1.00 45

First National Judicial Congress.

Federal District Coat of Arms
A137

Wmk. 249

Wmkd. "CORREIO BRASIL" Multiple. (249)

1936, Nov. 13 Typographed

427 A137 200r rose red 1.25 1.00

Issued in commemoration of the Ninth International Sample Fair held at Rio de Janeiro.

Eucharistic Congress Seal
A138

1936, Dec. 17 *Perf. 11½* **Wmk. 245**

428 A138 300r green, yellow, bl. & black 1.25 75

Issued in commemoration of the Second National Eucharistic Congress in Brazil.

Botafogo Bay
A139

Thick Laid Paper.

Engraved.

1937, Jan. 2 *Perf. 11* **Wmk. 236**

429 A139 700r blue 1.50 75
430 " 700r black 1.50 75

Issued to commemorate the birth centenary of Francisco Pereira Passos, engineer who planned the modern city of Rio de Janeiro.

Types of 1920-21, 1933.

Perf. 11, 11½ and Compound.

1936-37 Typographed. **Wmk. 249**

431 A75 10r deep brown 10 5
432 " 20r dull violet 10 5
433 " 50r blue green 10 5
434 " 100r orange 10 5
435 A116 200r dark violet 10 3
436 A76 300r olive green 20 5
437 " 400r ultramarine 15 5
438 " 500r light brown 30 5
439 " 600r brn. org. ('37) 1.00 5
440 " 700r deep violet 1.00 5
441 " 1000r turquoise blue 2.00 4
Nos. 431-441 (11) 5.15 52

Massed Flags and Star of Esperanto
A140

1937, Jan. 19

442 A140 300r green 1.75 75

Ninth Brazilian Esperanto Congress.

Bay of Rio de Janeiro
A141

Perf. 12½

1937, June 9 **Unwmkd.**

443 A141 300r orange red & black 75 75
444 " 700r bl. & dk. brn. 2.00 75

Issued in commemoration of the Second South American Radio Communication Conference held in Rio de Janeiro, June 7 to 19, 1937.

Globe
A142

1937, Sept. 4 *Perf. 11, 12* **Wmk. 249**

445 A142 300r green 1.50 75

50th anniversary of Esperanto.

Monroe Palace, Rio de Janeiro
A143

Botanical Garden, Rio de Janeiro
A144

1937, Sept. 30 *Perf. 12½* **Unwmkd.**

446 A143 200r lt. brn. & blue 75 50
447 A144 300r orange & olive green 75 50
448 A143 2000r grn. & cerise 6.00 6.00
449 A144 10,000r lake & indigo 50.00 30.00

Brig. Gen. José da Silva Paes
A145

Eagle and Shield
A146

1937, Oct. 11 *Perf. 11½* **Wmk. 249**

450 A145 300r blue 1.00 40

Bicentenary of Rio Grande do Sul.

1937, Dec. 2 Typo. *Perf. 11*

451 A146 400r dark blue 1.25 50

Issued in commemoration of the 150th anniversary of the Constitution of the United States of America.

Bags of Brazilian Coffee
A147

Frame Engr., Center Typo.

Center Typographed.

1938, Jan. 17 *Perf. 12½* **Unwmkd.**

452 A147 1200r multicolored 6.00 1.00

Arms of Olinda
A148

Perf. 11, 11x11½.

1938, Jan. 24 Engraved Wmk. 249

453 A148 400r violet 75 40

Issued in commemoration of the fourth centenary of the founding of the city of Olinda.

Independence Memorial, Ypiranga
A149

1938, Jan. 24 Typo. *Perf. 11*

454 A149 400r brown olive 1.00 40

Issued to commemorate the proclamation of Brazil's independence by Dom Pedro, Sept. 7, 1822.

Iguaçu Falls
A150

Engraved.

1938, Jan. 10 *Perf. 12½* **Unwmkd.**

455 A150 1000r sepia & yellow brown 2.00 1.25
456 " 5000r olive black & green 22.50 8.50

Couto de Magalhães
A151

Perf. 11, 11x11½

1938, Mar. 17 **Wmk. 249**

457 A151 400r dull green 75 30

Issued to commemorate the centenary of the birth of General Couto de Magalhaes (1837–1898), statesman, soldier, explorer, writer, developer.

Types of 1918–38

Perf. 11, 12x11, 12x11½, 12.

1938 Engraved **Wmk. 249**

458 A72 2000r blue violet 5.00 10
459 A89 5000r violet blue 5.00 20
a. 5000r deep blue 5.00 30
460 A72 10,000r rose lake 10.00 30

No. 458 is inscribed "BRASIL CORREIO".

Types of 1920-22.

Typographed.

1938 *Perf. 11.* **Wmk. 245**

461 A75 50r blue green 25 25
462 " 100r orange 25 25
463 A76 300r olive green 25 25

463A A76 400r ultramarine 75.00
463B " 500r red brown 75 75
Nos. 461-463B (5) 76.50

National Archives Building
A152

1938, May 20 **Wmk. 249**
464 A152 400r brown 75 30
Centenary of National Archives.

Souvenir Sheets.

Sir Rowland Hill
A153

1938, Oct. 22 ***Imperf.***
465 A153 400r dull green, sheet of 10 15.00 15.00
a. Single stamp 1.25 1.25

Issued in commemoration of the Brazilian International Philatelic Exposition (Brapex).
Issued in sheets measuring 106x118 mm. A few perforated sheets exist.

President Vargas
A154

1938, Nov. 10 ***Perf. 11***
Without Gum
466 A154 400r slate blue, sheet of 10 6.00 6.00
a. Single stamp 55 45

Issued in commemoration of the Constitution of Brazil, set up by President Vargas, Nov. 10, 1937. Size: 113x135½mm.

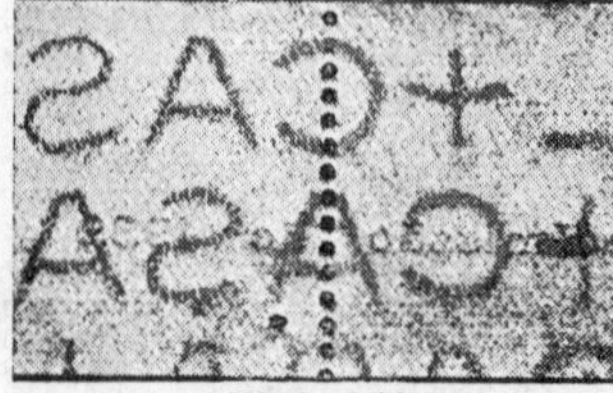
Wmk. 256

Types of 1920-33.
Wmkd.
"CASA+DA+MOEDA+DO+ BRAZIL" in 8mm. Letters (256)

1939 **Typographed.** ***Perf. 11.***
467 A75 10r red brown 30 30
468 " 20r dull violet 15 10
469 A75 50r blue green 15 8
470 " 100r yellow orange 15 8
471 A116 200r dark violet 25 8
472 A76 400r ultramarine 75 8
473 " 600r dull orange 60 8
474 " 1000r turquoise bl. 5.00 8
Nos. 467-474 (8) 7.35 88

View of Rio de Janeiro
A155

View of Santos
A156

1939, June 14 Engraved Wmk. 249
475 A155 1200r dull violet 2.50 20

1939, Aug. 23
476 A156 400r dull blue 60 30
Centenary of founding of Santos.

Chalice Vine and Blossoms
A157

Eucharistic Congress Seal
A158

1939, Aug. 23
477 A157 400r green 2.00 50
Issued in commemoration of the first South American Botanical Congress held in January, 1938.

1939, Sept. 3
478 A158 400r rose red 60 25
Third National Eucharistic Congress.

Duke of Caxias, Army Patron
A159

1939, Sept. 12 Photo. ***Rouletted***
479 A159 400r deep ultra. 60 40
Issued for Soldiers' Day.

George Washington
A159a

Grover Cleveland
A159c

Emperor Pedro II
A159b

Statue of Friendship, Given by U. S. A.
A159d

Engraved.
1939, Oct. 7 ***Perf. 12*** **Unwmkd.**
480 A159a 400r yellow orange 75 40
481 A159b 800r dark green 45 25
482 A159c 1200r rose carmine 1.00 25
483 A159d 1600r dark blue 1.00 40
New York World's Fair.

Benjamin Constant
A160

Fonseca on Horseback
A161

Manuel Deodoro da Fonseca and President Vargas
A162

Rouletted
1939, Nov. 15 Photo. **Wmk. 249**
484 A160 400r deep green 60 30
485 A162 1200r chocolate 1.50 40
Engraved ***Perf. 11***
486 A161 800r gray black 90 45
Issued in commemoration of the 50th anniversary of the Proclamation of the Republic.

President Roosevelt, President Vargas and Map of the Americas
A163

1940, Apr. 14
487 A163 400r slate blue 1.25 60
Pan American Union, 50th anniversary.

Wmk. 264

Types of 1920-33.
Wmkd.
"☆ CORREIO ☆ BRASIL ☆" Multiple. Letters 7mm. high. (264)

1940-41 **Typographed.** ***Perf. 11.***
488 A75 10r red brown 10 4
489 " 20r dull violet 18 4
489A " 50r blue green ('41) 1.50 60
490 " 100r yellow orange 60 4
491 A116 200r violet 60 4
492 A76 400r ultramarine 1.20 6
493 " 600r dull orange 1.20 6
494 " 1000r turquoise blue 7.50 6
Nos. 488-494 (8) 12.88 94

Map of Brazil
A164

1940, Sept. 7 **Engraved**
495 A164 400r carmine 60 40
a. Unwmkd. 20.00 15.00

Issued in commemoration of the 9th Brazilian Congress of Geography held at Florianopolis.

Victoria Regia Water Lily
A165

President Vargas
A166

Relief Map of Brazil
A167

1940, Oct. 30 ***Perf. 11*** **Wmk. 249**
Without Gum
496 A165 1000r dull violet 5.00 2.50
a. Sheet of ten 50.00 50.00
497 A166 5000r red 15.00 6.50
a. Sheet of ten 150.00 150.00
498 A167 10,000r slate blue 15.00 2.50
a. Sheet of ten 150.00 150.00

New York World's Fair.
All three sheets exist unwatermarked and also with papermaker's watermark of large globe and "AMERICA BANK" in sheet. A few imperforate sheets also exist.

Joaquim Machado de Assis
A168

Pioneers and Buildings of Porto Alegre
A169

1940, Nov. 1

499	A168	400r black	75	40

Birth centenary of Joaquim Maria Machado de Assis, poet and novelist.

1940, Nov. 2 **Wmk. 264**

500	A169	400r green	60	35

Issued to commemorate the bicentenary of the colonization of Porto Alegre.

Proclamation of King John IV of Portugal
A173

1940, Dec. 1 **Wmk. 249**

501	A173	1200r blue black	2.00	50

Issued in commemoration of the 800th anniversary of Portuguese independence and the 300th anniversary of the restoration of the monarchy.

No. 501 was also printed on paper with papermaker's watermark of large globe and "AMERICA BANK." Unwatermarked copies are from these sheets.

Brazilian Flags and Head of Liberty
A175

Calendar Sheet and Inscription "Day of the Fifth General Census of Brazil"
A176

Engraved.

1940, Dec. 18 ***Perf. 11*** **Wmk. 256**

502	A175	400r dull violet	75	40
		b. Unwmkd.	60.00	60.00

Wmk. 245

502A	A175	400r dull violet	30.00	30.00

Issued in commemoration of the 10th anniversary of the inauguration of President Vargas.

Typographed.

1941, Jan. 14 ***Perf. 11*** **Wmk. 256**

503	A176	400r blue & red	45	20

Wmk. 245

504	A176	400r blue & red	3.50	1.00

Fifth general census of Brazil.

The only foreign revenue stamps listed in this Catalogue are those authorized for prepayment of postage.

King Alfonso Henriques
A177

Father Antonio Vieira
A178

Salvador Corrêia de Sa e Benevides
A179

President Carmona of Portugal and President Vargas
A180

Photogravure.

1940–41 ***Rouletted*** **Wmk. 264**

504A	A177	200r pink	30	25
505	A178	400r ultramarine	35	20
506	A179	800r bright violet	40	25
506A	A180	5400r slate green	2.00	80

Wmk. 249

507	A177	200r pink	5.00	3.50
507A	A178	400r ultramarine	20.00	15.00
508	A180	5400r slate green	3.50	2.00
		Nos. 504A–508 (7)	31.55	22.00

Issued in commemoration of the 800th anniversary of Portuguese Independence.

José de Anchieta
A181

Amador Bueno
A182

Engraved

1941, Aug. 1 ***Perf. 11*** **Wmk. 264**

509	A181	1000r gray violet	1.75	1.00

Society of Jesus, 400th anniversary.

1941, Oct. 20 ***Perf. 11½***

510	A182	400r black	80	50

Issued in commemoration of the 300th anniversary of the acclamation of Amador Bueno (1572–1648) as king of Sao Paulo.

Air Force Emblem
A183

1941, Oct. 20 ***Perf. 11***

511	A183	5400r slate green	6.00	3.50

Issued in connection with Aviation Week, as propaganda for the Brazilian Air Force.

Petroleum
A184

Agriculture
A185

Steel Industry
A186

Commerce
A187

Marshal Peixoto
A188

Count of Porto Alegre
A189

Admiral J. A. C. Maurity
A190

"Armed Forces"
A191

Vargas
A192

Typographed

1941–42 ***Perf. 11*** **Wmk. 264**

512	A184	10r yellow brown	8	4
513	"	20r olive green	8	4
514	"	50r olive bistre	8	4
515	"	100r blue green	15	4
516	A185	200r brown orange	30	4
517	"	300r lilac rose	18	5
518	"	400r greenish blue	60	5
519	"	500r salmon	25	5
520	A186	600r violet	60	5
521	"	700r bright rose	30	10
522	"	1000r gray	1.50	4
523	"	1200r dull blue	1.25	4
524	A187	2000r gray violet	1.80	10

Engraved

525	A188	5000r blue	7.50	45
526	A189	10,000r rose red	5.00	35
527	A190	20,000r deep brown	4.50	75
528	A191	50,000r red ('42)	15.00	4.50
529	A192	100,000r blue ('42)	90	60
		Nos. 512–529 (18)	40.07	7.33

Nos. 512 to 527 and later issues come on thick or thin paper. The stamps on both papers also exist with three vertical green lines printed on the back, a control mark.

See also Nos. 541–587, 592–593, 656–670.

Bernardino de Campos
A193

Prudente de Morais
A194

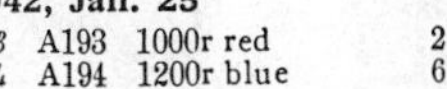

1942, Jan. 25

533	A193	1000r red	2.50	75
534	A194	1200r blue	6.00	50

Issued in commemoration of the 100th anniversary of the birth of Bernardino de Campos and Prudente de Morais, lawyers and statesmen of Brazil.

Head of Indo-Brazilian Bull
A195

1942, May 1 ***Perf. 11½*** **Wmk. 264**

535	A195	200r blue	75	40
536	"	400r orange brown	75	40
		a. Wmk. 267	40.00	40.00

Issued in commemoration of the second Agriculture and Livestock Show of Central Brazil held at Uberaba. Wmk. 267 is illustrated with Nos. 573–587.

Outline of Brazil and Torch of Knowledge
A196

Map of Brazil Showing Goiania
A197

Perf. 11

1942, July 5 **Typo.** **Wmk. 264**

537	A196	400r orange brown	70	35

8th Brazilian Congress of Education.

1942, July 5

538	A197	400r light violet	70	40

Founding of Goiania city.

Seal of Congress
A198

1942, Sept. 20 **Wmk. 264**

539	A198	400r olive bistre	50	25
		a. Wmk. 267	12.50	10.00

Issued to commemorate the 4th National Eucharistic Congress at Sao Paulo. Wmk. 267 is illustrated with Nos. 573–587.

Types of 1941-42.

1942-47 ***Perf. 11.*** **Wmk. 245**

541	A184	20r olive green	18	6
542	"	50r olive bistre	15	6
543	"	100r blue green	35	6
544	A185	200r brown orange	35	6
545	"	400r greenish blue	35	10
546	A186	600r light violet	1.50	10
547	"	700r bright rose	50	10
548	"	1200r dull blue	1.50	10
549	A187	2000r gray violet ('47)	5.00	3.00

Engraved

550 A188 5000r blue 5.00 30
551 A189 10,000r rose red 4.50 1.50
552 A190 20,000r deep brown ('47) 2.00 45
553 A192 100,000r blue 5.00 5.00
Nos. 541-553 (13) 26.38 10.89

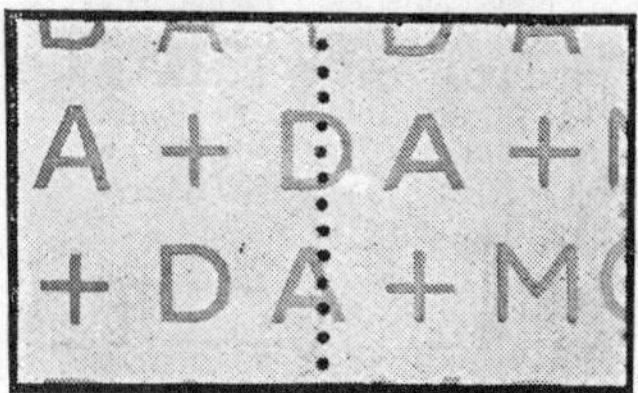

Wmk. 268

Types of 1941-42.
Wmkd.
"CASA+DA+MOEDA+DO+BRASIL" in 6mm. Letters. (268)

1941-47 Typographed. *Perf. 11.*

554 A184 20r olive green 12 6
555 " 50r olive bistre ('47) 45 45
556 " 100r blue green ('43) 18 8
557 A185 200r brn. org. ('43) 25 6
558 " 300r lilac rose ('43) 18 6
559 " 400r greenish blue ('42) 25 6
560 " 500r salmon ('43) 18 10
561 A186 600r violet 60 8
562 " 700r brt. rose ('45) 40 8
563 " 1000r gray 75 8
564 " 1200r dp. blue ('44) 1.20 8
565 A187 2000r gray vio. ('43) 1.75 8

Engraved

566 A188 5000r blue ('43) 2.50 12
567 A189 10,000r rose red ('43) 6.00 45
568 A190 20,000r deep brown ('42) 12.00 35
569 A191 50,000r red ('42) 15.00 2.50
a. 50,000r dark brown red ('47) 15.00 3.00
570 A192 100,000r blue 75 65
Nos. 554-570 (17) 42.56 5.34

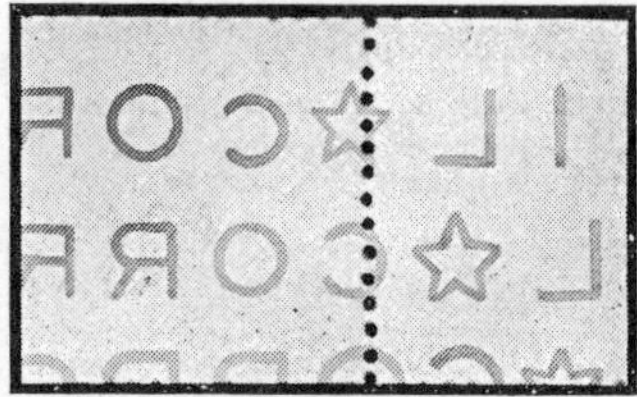

Wmk. 267
Wmkd.
"☆ CORREIO ☆ BRASIL ☆" Multiple in Small Letters (5 mm. high). (267)

Types of 1941-42.

1942-47 Typographed Wmk. 267

573 A184 20r olive green ('43) 12 10
574 " 50r olive bistre ('43) 12 10
575 " 100r blue grn. ('43) 18 10
576 A185 200r brn. org. ('43) 30 10
577 " 400r greenish blue 30 10
578 " 500r salmon ('43) 50.00 15.00
579 A186 600r violet ('43) 3.00 60
580 " 700r bright rose ('47) 90 90
581 " 1000r gray ('44) 1.75 15
582 " 1200r dull blue 1.50 12
583 A187 2000r gray violet 3.00 6

Engraved

584 A188 5000r blue 4.50 20
585 A189 10,000r rose red ('44) 7.50 2.40
586 A190 20,000r deep brown ('45) 10.00 45
587 A191 50,000r red ('43) 25.00 15.00
Nos. 573-587 (15) 108.17 35.38

1942 Typographed Wmk. 249

592 A184 100r blue green 3.50 3.50
593 A186 600r violet 3.00 75

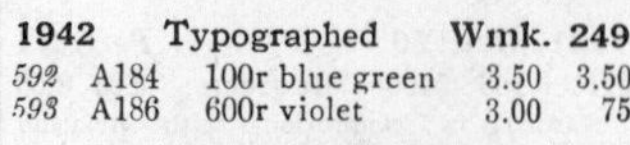

Map Showing Amazon River
A199

1943, Mar. 19 *Perf. 11* Wmk. 267

607 A199 40c orange brown 50 50

Issued in commemoration of the 400th anniversary of the discovery of the Amazon River.

Reproduction of Brazil Stamp of 1866
A200

Adaptation of 1843 "Bull's-eye"
A201

1943, Mar. 28 Wmk. 267

608 A200 40c violet 75 40
a. Wmk. 268 1000.00

Centenary of city of Petropolis.

1943, Aug. 1 Engraved *Imperf.*

609 A201 30c black 1.00 50
610 " 60c black 1.25 50
611 " 90c black 1.00 50

Centenary of the first postage stamp of Brazil. The 30c and 90c exist unwatermarked; prices $25 and $65.

Souvenir Sheet.

A202

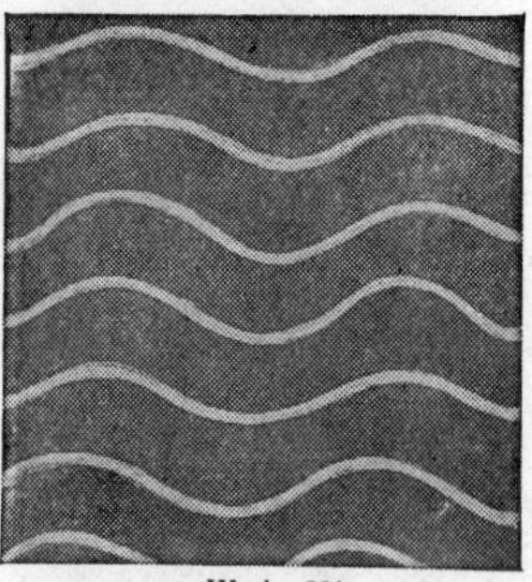

Wmk. 281

Wmkd. Wavy Lines. (281) Horizontally or Vertically.
Without Gum.

1943 Engraved *Imperf.*

612 A202 Sheet of three 8.00 8.00
a. 30c black 2.50 2.50
b. 60c black 2.50 2.50
c. 90c black 2.50 2.50

Sheet measures 125½x94½mm.

Ubaldino do Amaral
A203

"Justice"
A204

Perf. 11, 12

1943, Aug. 27 Typo. Wmk. 264

613 A203 40c dull slate green 50 25
a. Wmk. 267 17.50 17.50

Birth centenary of Ubaldino do Amaral, banker and statesman.

1943, Aug. 30 Wmk. 267

614 A204 2cr bright rose 1.00 75

Centenary of Institute of Brazilian Lawyers.

Indo-Brazilian Bull
A205

1943, Aug. 30 Engraved

615 A205 40c dk. red brown 1.25 75

9th Livestock Show at Bahia.

José Barbosa Rodrigues
A206

1943, Nov. 13 Typographed

616 A206 40c bluish green 60 25

Birth centenary of José Barbosa Rodrigues, botanist.

Charity Hospital, Santos
A207

1943, Nov. 7 Engraved

617 A207 1cr blue 75 40

400th anniversary of Charity Hospital, Santos.

Pedro Americo
A208

Perf. 11

1943, Dec. 16 Typo. Wmk. 267

618 A208 40c brown orange 50 30

Issued to commemorate the birth centenary of Pedro Americo de Figueirido e Melo (1843-1905), artist-hero and statesman.

Gen. A. E. Gomes Carneiro
A209

1944, Feb. 9 Engraved

619 A209 1.20cr rose 1.00 50

50th anniversary of the Lapa siege.

Statue of Baron of Rio Branco
A210

1944, May 13 Typographed

620 A210 1cr blue 75 40

Issued to commemorate the unveiling of a statue of the Baron of Rio Branco.

Duke of Caxias
A211

Granite Paper.

1944, May 13 *Perf. 12* Unwmkd.

621 A211 1.20cr blue green & pale orange 90 50

Centenary of pacification of Sao Paulo and Minas Gerais in an independence movement in 1842.

YMCA Seal
A212

1944, June 7 Litho. *Perf. 11*
Granite Paper.

622 A212 40c deep blue, carmine & yellow 40 30

Centenary of Young Men's Christian Assn.

Chamber of Commerce Rio Grande
A213

Engraved.

1944, Sept. 25 *Perf. 12* **Wmk. 268**

623 A213 40c light yellow brown 40 35

Issued to commemorate the centenary of the Chamber of Commerce of Rio Grande.

Martim F. R. de Andrada
A214

1945, Jan. 30 *Perf. 11*

624 A214 40c blue 40 35

Issued to commemorate the centenary of the death of Martim F. R. de Andrada, statesman.

Meeting of Duke of Caxias and David Canabarro
A215

1945, Mar. 19 **Photogravure**

625 A215 40c ultramarine 40 25

Centenary of the pacification of Rio Grande do Sul.

Globe and "Esperanto"
A216

1945, Apr. 16

626 A216 40c light blue green 60 30

10th Esperanto Congress, Rio de Janeiro, Apr. 14–22.

Baron of Rio Branco's Bookplate
A217

1945, Apr. 20 *Perf. 11* **Wmk. 268**

627 A217 40c violet 30 25

Issued to commemorate the centenary of the birth of José Maria da Silva Paranhos, Baron of Rio Branco.

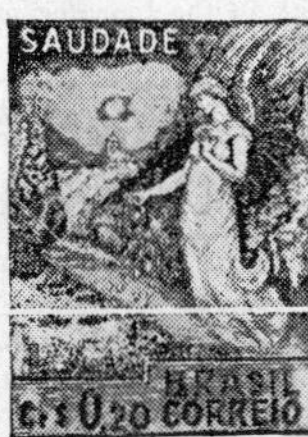

Tranquility
A218

Glory
A219

Victory
A220

Peace
A221

Cooperation
A222

Rouletted 7

1945, May 8 **Engraved** **Wmk. 268**

628	A218	20c dark rose violet	25	25
629	A219	40c dark carmine	28	25
630	A220	1cr dull orange	60	50
631	A221	2cr steel blue	1.50	75
632	A222	5cr green	3.00	1.00
		Nos. 628–632 (5)	5.63	2.75

Victory of the Allied Nations in Europe.

Nos. 628–632 exist on thin card, imperf. and unwatermarked.

Francisco Manoel da Silva
A223

Perf. 12

1945, May 30 **Typo.** **Wmk. 245**

633 A223 40c bright rose 75 40
 a. Wmk. 268 9.00 9.00

Issued to commemorate the 150th anniversary of the birth of Francisco Manoel da Silva (1795–1865), composer (in 1831) of the national anthem.

Bahia Institute of Geography and History
A224

1945, May 30 *Perf. 11* **Wmk. 268**

634 A224 40c light ultramarine 30 25

Issued to commemorate the 50th anniversary of the founding of the Institute of Geography and History at Bahia.

Emblems of 5th Army and B. E. F.
A225 A226

U.S. Flag and Shoulder Patches
A227

Brazilian Flag and Shoulder Patches—A228

Victory Symbol and Shoulder Patches
A229

1945, July 18 **Lithographed**

635	A225 20c	multicolored	25	25
636	A226 40c	"	25	25
637	A227 1cr	"	1.25	75
638	A228 2cr	"	1.75	1.00
639	A229 5cr	"	5.00	1.25
		Nos. 635–639 (5)	8.50	3.50

Issued in honor of the Brazilian Expeditionary Force and the United States Fifth Army Battle against the Axis in Italy.

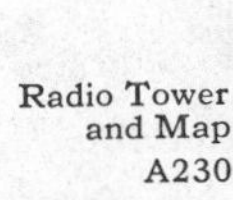

Radio Tower and Map
A230

1945, Sept. 3 **Engraved**

640 A230 1.20cr gray 60 25

Third Inter-American Conference on Radio Communications.

No. 640 was reproduced on a souvenir card with blue background and inscriptions. Size: 145x161mm.

A 40c lilac stamp, picturing the International Bridge between Argentina and Brazil and portraits of Presidents Justo and Vargas, was prepared late in 1945. It was not issued, but later was sold, without postal value, to collectors. Price, 15 cents.

Adm. Saldanha da Gama
A231

1946, Apr. 7

641 A231 40c gray black 25 25

Issued to commemorate the centenary of the birth of Admiral Luiz Felipe Saldanha da Gama (1846–1895).

Princess Isabel d'Orleans-Braganca
A232

1946, July 29 **Unwmkd.**

642 A232 40c black 30 30

Issued to commemorate the centenary of the birth of Princess Isabel d'Orleans-Braganca.

Post Horn, V and Envelope
A233

Post Office, Rio de Janeiro
A234

Bay of Rio de Janeiro and Plane
A235

Perf. 11

1946, Sept. 2 **Litho.** **Wmk. 268**

643 A233 40c black & pale orange 30 25

Perf. 12½ **Engraved** **Unwmkd.**

Center in Ultramarine.

644	A234	2cr slate	75	25
645	"	5cr orange brown	4.00	1.50
646	"	10cr dark violet	4.25	1.50

Center in Brown Orange.

647	A235	1.30cr dark green	50	50
648	"	1.70cr carmine rose	50	50
649	"	2.20cr dp. ultra.	75	75
		Nos. 643–649 (7)	11.05	5.25

Nos. 643 to 649 were issued to commemorate the 5th Postal Union Congress of the Americas and Spain.

No. 643 was reproduced on a souvenir card with inscriptions and marginal illustrations of the Palacio da Fazenda, Rio de Janeiro. Size: 188x239mm. Sold for 10 cruzeiros.

Liberty
A236

Perf. 11x11½

1946, Sept. 18 Wmk. 268

650 A236 40c black & gray 20 15
a. Unwmkd. 15.00

Adoption of the Constitution of 1946.

Columbus Lighthouse, Dominican Republic
A237

1946, Sept. 14 Litho. *Perf. 11*

651 A237 5cr Prussian green 6.00 2.50

Orchid
A238

Gen. A. E. Gomes Carneiro
A239

1946, Nov. 8 Wmk. 268

652 A238 40c ultra., red & yel. 55 30
a. Unwmkd. 27.50

Issued to publicize the 4th National Exhibition of Orchids, Rio de Janeiro, November, 1946.

Perf. 10½x12

1946, Dec. 6 Engraved Unwmkd.

653 A239 40c deep green 20 20

Issued to commemorate the centenary of the birth of General Antonio Ernesto Gomes Carneiro.

Brazilian Academy of Letters
240

1946, Dec. 14 *Perf. 11*

654 A240 40c blue 20 20

Issued to commemorate the 50th anniversary of the foundation of the Brazilian Academy of Letters, Rio de Janeiro.

Antonio de Castro Alves—A241

1947, Mar. 14 Litho. Wmk. 267

655 A241 40c bluish green 25 25

Issued to commemorate the birth centenary of Antonio de Castro Alves (1847–1871), poet.

Types of 1941–42,
Values in Centavos or Cruzeiros.
Typographed

1947–54 *Perf. 11* Wmk. 267

656 A184 2c olive 10 5
657 " 5c yellow brown 10 5
658 " 10c green 10 4
659 A185 20c brown orange 10 4
660 " 30c dark lilac rose 15 5
661 " 40c blue 15 4
b. Wmk. 268 500.00 50.00
661A " 50c salmon 20 5
662 A186 60c light violet 30 3
663 " 70c brt. rose ('54) 60 15
664 " 1cr gray 60 6
665 " 1.20cr dull blue 60 6
a. Wmk. 268 5.00 5.00
666 A187 2cr gray violet 1.20 4

Engraved

667 A188 5cr blue 6.00 10
668 A189 10cr rose red 6.00 15

Perf. 11, 13.

669 A190 20cr deep brown 7.50 15
670 A191 50cr red 20.00 50
Nos. 656-670 (16) 43.70 1.56

The 5cr, 20cr and 50cr also exist with perf. 12 to 13.

Pres. Gonzalez Videla of Chile
A242

1947, June 26 *Perf. 12x11* Unwmkd.

671 A242 40c dark brown orange 20 20

Issued to commemorate the visit of President Gabriel Gonzalez Videla of Chile, June 1947.

A souvenir folder contains four impressions of No. 671, measures 6½x8¼ inches and has marginal inscriptions, including a coat of arms, in blue.

"Peace" and Western Hemisphere
A243

1947, Aug. 15 *Perf. 11x12*

672 A243 1.20cr blue 35 25

Issued to commemorate the Inter-American Defense Conference at Rio de Janeiro, August–September, 1947.

Pres. Harry S Truman, Map and Statue of Liberty
A244

1947, Sept. 1 Typo. *Perf. 12x11*

673 A244 40c ultramarine 30 25

Visit of U.S. President Harry S Truman to Brazil, Sept. 1947.

Pres. Eurico Gaspar Dutra
A245

Mother and Child
A246

Engraved.

1947, Sept. 7 *Perf. 11* Wmk. 268

674 A245 20c green 20 20
675 " 40c rose carmine 25 15
676 " 1.20cr deep blue 50 22

The souvenir sheet containing Nos. 674–676 is listed as No. C73A. See also No. 679.

1947, Oct. 10 Typo. Unwmkd.

677 A246 40c bright ultra. 25 20

Issued to mark Child Care Week, 1947.

Arms of Belo Horizonte
A247

Globe
A248

1947, Dec. 12 Engraved Wmk. 267

678 A247 1.20cr rose carmine 50 25

Issued to commemorate the 50th anniversary of the founding of the city of Belo Horizonte.

Dutra Type of 1947.

1948 Engraved. Wmk. 267

679 A245 20c green 3.00 3.00

1948, July 10 Lithographed

680 A248 40c dull green & pale lilac 20 20

Issued to commemorate the International Exposition of Industry and Commerce, Petropolis, 1948.

Arms of Paranagua
A249

BRASIL
40 CORREIO CTS

Child Reading Book
A250

1948, July 29

681 A249 5cr bistre brown 3.00 1.00

Issued to commemorate the 300th anniversary of the founding of the city of Paranagua, July 29, 1648.

1948, Aug. 1

682 A250 40c green 30 20

National Education Campaign.

No. 682 was reproduced on a souvenir card with brown orange background and inscriptions. Size: 124x157mm.

Tiradentes
A251

Symbolical of Cancer Eradication
A252

1948, Nov. 12

683 A251 40c brown orange 20 20

Issued to commemorate the 200th anniversary of the birth of Joaquim José da Silva Xavier (Tiradentes).

1948, Dec. 14

684 A252 40c claret 25 20

Anti-cancer publicity.

Adult Student
A253

1949, Jan. 3 *Perf. 12x11* Wmk. 267

685 A253 60c red vio. & pink 25 15

Campaign for adult education.

"Battle of Guararapes," by Vitor Meireles—A254

1949, Feb. 15 *Perf. 11½x12*

686 A254 60c light blue 1.00 60

Issued to commemorate the 300th anniversary of the Second Battle of Guararapes.

Church of São Francisco de Paula
A255

Manuel de Nobrega
A256

Engraved.

1949, Mar. 8 *Perf. 11x12* Unwmkd.

687 A255 60c dark brown 30 25
a. Souvenir sheet 50.00 50.00

Bicentenary of city of Ouro Fino, state of Minas Gerais.

No. 687a contains one imperf. stamp similar to No. 687, with dates in lower margin. Size: 70x89mm.

1949, Mar. 29 *Imperf.*

688 A256 60c violet 20 20

Issued to commemorate the 400th anniversary of the founding of the City of Salvador.

Emblem of Brazilian Air Force and Plane—A257

1949, June 18

689 A257 60c blue violet 20 20

Issued to honor the Brazilian Air Force.

Star and Angel
A258

Lithographed.

1949 ***Perf. 11x12.*** **Wmk. 267**

690 A258 60c pink 20 20

Issued to publicize the first Ecclesiastical Congress, Salvador, Bahia.

"U. P. U." Encircling Globe
A259

1949, Oct. 22 Typo. ***Perf. 12x11***

691 A259 1.50cr blue 40 20

Issued to commemorate the 75th anniversary of the formation of the Universal Postal Union.

Ruy Barbosa
A260

Engraved.

1949, Dec. 14 ***Perf. 12*** **Unwmkd.**

692 A260 1.20cr rose carmine 75 40

Centenary of birth of Ruy Barbosa.

Joaquim Cardinal Arcoverde
A261

Perf. 11x12

1950, Feb. 27 Litho. Wmk. 267

693 A261 60c rose 30 25

Issued to commemorate the birth centenary of Joaquim Cardinal Arcoverde A. Cavalcanti.

Grapes and Factory
A262

1950, Mar. 15 ***Perf. 12x11***

694 A262 60c rose lake 20 20

Issued to commemorate the 75th anniversary of Italian immigration to the state of Rio Grande do Sul.

Virgin of the Globe
A263

Globe and Soccer Players
A264

1950, May 31 ***Perf. 11x12***

695 A263 60c black & light blue 30 20

Issued to commemorate the centenary of the establishment in Brazil of the Daughters of Charity of St. Vincent de Paul.

1950, June 24

696 A264 60c ultramarine, blue & gray 1.00 50

4th World Soccer Championship.

Symbolical of Brazilian Population Growth
A265

1950, July 10 Typo. ***Perf. 12x11***

697 A265 60c rose lake 20 20

Issued to publicize the 6th Brazilian census.

Dr. Oswaldo Cruz
A266

1950, Aug. 23 Litho. ***Perf. 11x12***

698 A266 60c orange brown 30 25

Issued to publicize the 5th International Congress of Microbiology.

View of Blumenau and Itajai River
A267

1950, Sept. 9 ***Perf. 12x11*** **Wmk. 267**

699 A267 60c bright pink 25 20

Centenary of the founding of Blumenau.

Amazonas Theater, Manaus
A268

1950, Sept. 27

700 A268 60c light brown red 20 20

Centenary of Amazonas Province.

Arms of Juiz de Fora
A269

1950, Oct. 24 ***Perf. 11x12***

701 A269 60c carmine 25 25

Centenary of the founding of Juiz de Fora.

Post Office at Recife
A270

1951, Jan. 10 Typo. ***Perf. 12x11***

702 A270 60c carmine 20 20
703 " 1.20cr carmine 30 20

Issued to commemorate the opening of the new building of the Pernambuco Post Office.

Arms of Joinville
A271

Jean-Baptiste de La Salle
A272

1951, Mar. 9 ***Perf. 11x12***

704 A271 60c orange brown 20 20

Centenary of the founding of Joinville.

1951, Apr. 30 **Lithographed**

705 A272 60c blue 30 25

Issued to commemorate the 300th anniversary of the birth of Jean-Baptiste de La Salle.

Heart and Flowers
A273

Sylvio Romero
A274

1951, May 13 **Engraved**

706 A273 60c deep plum 30 25

Issued to honor Mother's Day, May 14, 1951.

1951, Apr. 21 **Lithographed**

707 A274 60c dull violet brown 20 20

Issued to commemorate the centenary of the birth of Sylvio Romero (1851–1914), poet and author.

João Caetano, Stage and Masks
A275

1951, July 9 ***Perf. 12x11***

708 A275 60c light gray blue 25 20

Issued to publicize the first Brazilian Theater Congress, Rio de Janeiro, July 9–13, 1951.

Orville A. Derby
A276

First Mass Celebrated in Brazil
A277

1951, July 23 ***Perf. 11x12***

709 A276 2cr slate 40 40

Issued to commemorate the centenary of the birth (in New York State) of Orville A. Derby, geologist.

1951, July 25

710 A277 60c dull brown & buff 30 20

Issued to publicize the 4th Inter-American Congress on Catholic Education, Rio de Janeiro, 1951.

Euclides Pinto Martins
A278

1951, Aug. 16 ***Perf. 12x11***

711 A278 3.80cr brn. & citron 2.00 30

Issued to commemorate the 29th anniversary of the first flight from New York City to Rio de Janeiro.

Monastery of the Rock
A279

1951, Sept. 8

712 A279 60c dull brown & cream 25 25

Founding of Vitoria, 4th centenary.

Santos-Dumont and Model Plane Contest
A280

Dirigible and Eiffel Tower
A281

Lithographed.

1951, Oct. 19 ***Perf. 11x12*** **Wmk. 267**

713 A280 60c salmon & dark brown 50 50

Engraved
Unwmkd.

714 A281 3.80cr dark purple 2.00 50

Issued to publicize the Week of the Wing and to commemorate the 50th anniversary of Santos-Dumont's flight around the Eiffel Tower.

In December 1951, Nos. 713 and 714 were privately overprinted: "Exposicao Filatelica Regional Distrito Federal 15-XII-1951 23-XII-1951." These were attached to souvenir sheets bearing engraved facsimiles of Nos. 38, 49 and 51, which were sold by Clube Filatelico do Brasil to mark its 20th anniversary. The overprinted stamps on the sheets were cancelled, but 530 "unused" sets were sold by the club.

Farmers and Ear of Wheat
A282

1951, Nov. 10 Litho. Wmk. 267

715 A282 60c dp. grn. & gray 40 30

Issued to publicize Festival of Grain at Bagé, 1951.

Map and Open Bible
A283

1951, Dec. 9 ***Perf. 12x11***

716 A283 1.20cr brown orange 75 40

Issued to publicize the Day of the Bible.

Queen Isabella A284 — Henrique Oswald A285

1952, Mar. 10 ***Perf. 11x12***

717 A284 3.80cr light blue 1.00 30

Issued to commemorate the 500th anniversary of the birth of Queen Isabella I of Spain.

1952, Apr. 22

718 A285 60c brown 30 20

Issued to commemorate the centenary of the birth of Henrique Oswald (1852–1931), composer.

Vicente Licinio Cardoso A286 — Map and Symbol of Labor A287

1952, May 2

719 A286 60c gray blue 30 20

4th Brazilian Homeopathic Congress.

1952, Apr. 30

720 A287 1.50cr brownish pink 40 20

Issued to publicize the 5th International Labor Organization Conference for American Countries.

Gen. Polidoro da Fonseca A288 — Luiz de Albuquerque M. P. Caceres A289

Portraits: 5cr, Baron de Capanema. 10cr, Minister Eusebio de Queiros.

Engraved

1952, May 11 ***Perf. 11*** **Unwmkd.**

721 A288 2.40cr light carmine 50 30
722 " 5cr blue 3.50 40
723 " 10cr dk. blue grn. 3.50 40

Centenary of telegraph in Brazil.

Perf. 11x12

1952, June 8 Litho. Wmk. 267

724 A289 1.20cr violet blue 30 20

Issued to commemorate the 200th anniversary of the founding of the city of Mato Grosso.

Symbolizing the Glory of Sports
A290

1952, July 21 ***Perf. 12x11***

725 A290 1.20cr deep blue & blue 85 40

Fluminense Soccer Club, 50th anniversary.

José Antonio Saraiva A291 — Emperor Dom Pedro A292

1952, Aug. 16 ***Perf. 11x12***

726 A291 60c lilac rose 20 20

Issued to commemorate the centenary of the founding of Terezina, capital of Piaui State.

1952, Sept. 3 Wmk. 267

727 A292 60c light blue & black 25 20

Issued for Stamp Day and the 2nd Philatelic Exhibition of Sao Paulo.

Flag-encircled Globe
A293

1952, Oct. 24 ***Perf. 13½***

728 A293 3.80cr blue 1.50 50

Issued to publicize United Nations Day.

View of Sao Paulo, Sun and Compasses
A294

1952, Nov. 8 Litho. ***Perf. 12x11***

729 A294 60c dull blue, yellow & gray green 30 20

City Planning Day.

Father Diogo Antonio Feijo
A295

1952, Nov. 9 ***Perf. 11x12***

730 A295 60c terra cotta 20 20

Rodolpho Bernardelli and His "Christ and the Adultress"
A297

1952, Dec. 18 ***Perf. 12x11***

732 A297 60c gray blue 25 20

Issued to commemorate the centenary of the birth of Rodolpho Bernardelli, sculptor and painter.

Map of Western Hemisphere and View of Rio de Janeiro
A298

1952, Sept. 20

733 A298 3.80cr violet brown & light green 90 30

Issued to commemorate the 2nd Congress of American Industrial Medicine, Rio de Janeiro, 1952.

Arms and Head of Pioneer
A299

Coffee, Cotton and Sugar Cane
A300

Designs: 2.80cr, Jesuit monk planting tree. 3.80cr and 5.80cr, Spiral, symbolizing progress.

1953, Jan. 25 Litho. ***Perf. 11***

734 A299 1.20cr olive brown & black brown 75 50
735 A300 2cr olive green & yellow 2.50 50
736 " 2.80cr red brown & deep orange 1.75 30
737 " 3.80cr dark brown & yel. green 1.50 30
738 " 5.80cr intense blue & yel. green 1.00 30
Nos. 734-738 (5) 7.50 1.90

400th anniversary of Sao Paulo.

Ledger and Winged Cap
A301

1953, Feb. 22 ***Perf. 12x11***

739 A301 1.20cr dull brown & fawn 40 20

6th Brazilian Accounting Congress.

Joao Ramalho
A302

Engraved

1953, Apr. 8 ***Perf. 11½*** **Wmk. 264**

740 A302 60c blue 25 20

Issued to commemorate the fourth centenary of the founding of the city of Santo Andre.

Aarao Reis and Plan of Belo Horizonte
A303

1953, May 6 Photogravure

741 A303 1.20cr red brown 35 25

Issued to commemorate the centenary of the birth of Aarao Leal de Carvalho Reis (1853–1936), civil engineer.

Training Ship Almirante Saldanha
A304

1953, May 16

742 A304 1.50cr violet blue 50 30

Issued to commemorate the fourth globe-circling voyage of the training ship Almirante Saldanha.

Joaquim Jose Rodrigues Torres, Viscount of Itaborai
A305

1953, July 5 Photogravure

743 A305 1.20cr violet 30 20

Centenary of the Bank of Brazil.

Lamp and Rio-Petropolis Highway
A306

1953, July 14

744 A306 1.20cr gray 30 20

Issued to publicize the tenth International Congress of Nursing, Petropolis, 1953.

Bay of Rio de Janeiro
A307

1953, July 15

745 A307 3.80cr dark blue green 60 20

Issued to publicize the fourth World Congress of Baptist Youth, July 1953.

Arms of Jau and Map
A308

1953, Aug. 15 Engraved

746 A308 1.20cr purple 30 20

Centenary of the city of Jau.

Ministry of Health and Education Building, Rio
A309

Maria Quiteria de Jesus Medeiros
A310

1953, Aug. 1

747 A309 1.20cr deep green 30 20

Issued to publicize the Day of the Stamp and the first Philatelic Exhibition of National Education.

1953, Aug. 21 Photogravure

748 A310 60c violet blue 20 20

Issued to commemorate the centenary of the death of Maria Quiteria de Jesus Medeiros (1792–1848), independence heroine.

Pres. Odria of Peru
A311

Duke of Caxias Leading his Troops
A312

1953, Aug. 25

749 A311 1.40cr rose brown 30 20

Issued to publicize the visit of Gen. Manuel A. Odria, President of Peru, Aug. 25, 1953.

Engraved (60c, 5.80cr); Photo.
Identical Frames.

1953, Aug. 25

Designs: 1.20cr, Caxias' tomb. 1.70cr, 5.80cr, Portrait of Caxias. 3.80cr, Arms of Caxias.

750	A312	60c deep green	50	25
751	"	1.20cr deep claret	75	25
752	"	1.70cr slate green	75	25
753	"	3.80cr rose brown	1.25	25
754	"	5.80cr gray violet	1.25	25
		Nos. 750-754 (5)	4.50	1.25

Issued to commemorate the 150th anniversary of the birth of Luis Alves de Lima e Silva, Duke of Caxias.

Quill Pen, Map and Tree
A313

Horacio Hora
A314

1953, Sept. 12 Photogravure

755 A313 60c ultramarine 25 20

5th National Congress of Journalism.

1953, Sept. 17 Litho. Wmk. 267

756 A314 60c org. & dp. plum 25 20

Issued to commemorate the centenary of the birth of Horacio Pinto de Hora (1853–1890), painter.

Pres. Somoza of Nicaragua
A315

Auguste de Saint-Hilaire
A316

1953, Sept. 24 Photo. Wmk. 264

757 A315 1.40cr dk. vio. brown 30 20

Issued to publicize the visit of Gen. Anastasio Somoza, president of Nicaragua.

1953, Sept. 30

758 A316 1.20cr dark brown carmine 40 25

Issued to commemorate the centenary of the death of Auguste de Saint-Hilaire, explorer and botanist.

José Carlos do Patrocinio
A317

Clock Tower, Crato
A318

1953, Oct. 9 Photogravure

759 A317 60c dark slate gray 25 20

Issued to commemorate the centenary of the birth of José Carlos do Patrocinio, (1853–1905), journalist and abolitionist.

1953, Oct. 17

760 A318 60c blue green 25 20

Centenary of the city of Crato.

Joao Capistrano de Abreu
A319

Allegory: "Justice"
A320

1953, Oct. 23

761 A319 60c dull blue 30 30
762 " 5cr purple 2.00 30

Issued to commemorate the centenary of the birth of Joao Capistrano de Abreu (1853–1927), historian.

1953, Nov. 17

763 A320 60c indigo 25 20
764 " 1.20cr deep magenta 25 20

Issued to commemorate the 50th anniversary of the Treaty of Petropolis.

Farm Worker in Wheat Field
A321

Teacher and Pupils
A322

1953, Nov. 29 Photo. *Perf. 11½*

766 A321 60c dark green 30 20

Issued to publicize the Third National Wheat Festival, Erechim, 1953.

1953, Dec. 14

767 A322 60c red 25 25

Issued to publicize the First National Conference of Primary School Teachers, Salvador, 1953.

Zacarias de Gois e Vasconsellos
A323

Alexandre de Gusmão
A324

Design: 5cr, Porters with Trays of Coffee Beans.

1953-54 Photogravure.

Inscribed: "Centenario do Parana."

768 A323 2cr orange brown & black ('54) 1.00 40
 a. Buff paper 90 40
769 " 5cr dp. org. & blk. 2.00 40

Centenary of the state of Paraná.

1954, Jan. 13

770 A324 1.20cr brown violet 30 20

Issued to commemorate the 200th anniversary of the death of Alexandre de Gusmao (1695–1753), statesman, diplomat and writer.

Symbolical of Sao Paulo's Growth
A325

Arms and View of Sao Paulo
A326

Designs: 2cr, Priest, settler and Indian. 2.80cr, José de Anchieta.

1954, Jan. 25 ***Perf. 11½x11***

771	A325	1.20cr dark violet brown	1.25	50
		a. Buff paper	1.75	1.00
772	"	2cr lilac rose	1.75	60
773	"	2.80cr purple gray	1.75	1.00

Engraved.

Perf. 11x11½.

774	A326	3.80cr dull green	1.75	50
		a. Buff paper	2.00	1.00
775	"	5.80cr dull red	2.00	60
		a. Buff paper	6.00	1.00
		Nos. 771-775 (5)	8.50	3.20

400th anniversary of Sao Paulo.

J. Fernandes Vieira, A. Vidal de Negreiros, A. F. Camarao and H. Dias
A327

Perf. 11x11½

1954, Feb. 18 Photo. Unwmkd.

776 A327 1.20cr ultramarine 40 30

Issued to commemorate the 300th anniversary of the recovery of Pernambuco from the Dutch.

Sao Paulo and Minerva
A328

1954, Feb. 24

777 A328 1.50cr deep plum 30 25

Issued to publicize the 10th International Congress of Scientific Organizations, Sao Paulo, 1954.

Stylized Grapes, Jug and Map
A329

Monument of the Immigrants
A330

1954, Feb. 27 Photo. *Perf. 11½x11*

778 A329 40c deep claret 30 25

Grape Festival, Rio Grande do Sul.

1954, Feb. 28

779 A330 60c deep violet blue 30 25

Issued to commemorate the unveiling of the Monument to the Immigrants of Caxias do Sul.

First Brazilian Locomotive
A331

Perf. 11x11½

1954, Apr. 30 Unwmkd.

781 A331 40c carmine 50 25

Issued to commemorate the centenary of the first railroad engine built in Brazil.

Pres. Chamoun of Lebanon
A332

1954, May 12 Photo. *Perf. 11½x11*

782 A332 1.50cr maroon 35 30

Issued to commemorate the visit of Pres. Camille Chamonn of Lebanon, 1954.

Sao Jose College, Rio de Janeiro
A333

J. B. Champagnat Marcelin
A334

Apolonia Pinto
A335

1954, June 6 *Perf. 11x11½, 11½x11*

783 A333 60c purple 30 20
784 A334 1.20cr violet blue 35 25

Issued to commemorate the 50th anniversary of the founding of the Marist Brothers in Brazil.

1954, June 21 Photogravure

785 A335 1.20cr bright green 15 12

Issued to commemorate the centenary of the birth of Apolonia Pinto (1854–1937), actress.

Adm. Margues Tamandare
A336

Portraits: 2c, 5c, 10c, Admiral Margues Tamandare. 20c, 30c, 40c, Oswaldo Cruz. 50c, 60c, 90c, Joaquim Murtinho. 1cr, 1.50cr, 2cr, Duke of Caxias. 5cr, 10cr, Ruy Barbosa. 20cr, 50cr, José Bonifacio.

1954-60 *Perf. 11x11½* Wmk. 267

786	A336	2c violet blue	15	12
787	"	5c orange red	10	3
788	"	10c bright green	15	3
789	"	20c magenta	15	3
790	"	30c dark gray green	25	3
791	"	40c rose red	50	3
792	"	50c violet	30	3
793	"	60c gray green	15	3
794	"	90c orange ('55)	60	15
795	"	1cr brown	1.25	3
796	"	1.50cr blue	10	3
		a. Wmk. 264	17.50	9.00
797	"	2cr dark blue green ('56)	40	3
798	"	5cr rose lilac ('56)	25	5
799	"	10cr light green ('60)	50	5
800	"	20cr crimson rose ('59)	50	6
801	"	50cr ultra. ('59)	3.00	10
		Nos. 786-801 (16)	8.35	83

See also Nos. 890, 930–933.

Boy Scout Waving Flag (Statue)
A337

Baltasar Fernandes, Explorer
A338

Perf. 11½x11

1954, Aug. 2 Unwmkd.

802 A337 1.20cr violet blue 60 30

Issued to publicize the International Boy Scout Encampment, Sao Paulo, 1954.

1954, Aug. 15

803 A338 60c dark red 30 25

300th anniversary of city of Sorocaba.

Adeodato Giovanni Cardinal Piazza
A339

Our Lady of Aparecida, Map of Brazil
A340

1954, Sept. 2

804 A339 4.20cr red orange 75 35

Issued to commemorate the visit of Adeodato Cardinal Piazza, papal legate to Brazil.

1954

Design: 1.20cr, Virgin standing on globe.

805 A340 60c claret 75 35
806 " 1.20cr violet blue 1.00 30

No. 805 was issued to commemorate the 1st Congress of Brazil's Patron Saint (Our Lady of Aparecida); No. 806, the centenary of the proclamation of the dogma of the Immaculate Conception. Both stamps also commemorate the Marian Year.

Issue dates: 60c, Sept. 6; 1.20cr, Sept. 8.

Benjamin Constant and Hand Reading Braille
A341

1954, Sept. 27 Photo. Unwmkd.

807 A341 60c dark green 30 20

Issued to commemorate the centenary of the founding of the Benjamin Constant Institute.

River Battle of Riachuelo
A342

Admiral F. M. Barroso
A343

Dr. Christian F. S. Hahnemann
A344

1954, Oct. 6 *Perf. 11x11½, 11½x11*

808 A342 40c reddish brown 50 25
809 A343 60c purple 40 25

Issued to commemorate the 150th anniversary of the birth of Admiral Francisco Manoel Barroso da Silva (1804–82).

1954, Oct. 8 *Perf. 11½x11*

810 A344 2.70cr dark green 40 25

Issued to publicize the first World Congress of Homeopathic Medicine.

Nizia Floresta
A345

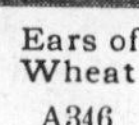
Ears of Wheat
A346

1954, Oct. 12

811 A345 60c lilac rose 30 25

Issued to commemorate the reburial of the remains of Nizia Floresta (Dio Nizia Pinto Lisboa), writer and educator.

1954, Oct. 22

812 A346 60c olive green 40 25

4th National Wheat Festival, Carazinho.

Basketball Player and Ball-Globe
A347

Allegory of the Spring Games
A348

1954, Oct. 23 Photogravure

813 A347 1.40cr orange red 50 30

Issued to publicize the second World Basketball Championship Matches, 1954.

Perf. 11½x11

1954, Nov. 6 Wmk. 267

814 A348 60c red brown 40 25

Issued to publicize the 6th Spring Games.

San Francisco Hydroelectric Plant
A349

1955, Jan. 15 *Perf. 11x11½*

815 A349 60c brown orange 20 15

Issued to publicize the inauguration of the San Francisco Hydroelectric Plant.

Itutinga Hydroelectric Plant
A350

1955, Feb. 3

816 A350 40c blue 20 15

Issued to publicize the inauguration of the Itutinga Hydroelectric Plant at Lavras.

Rotary Emblem and Bay of Rio de Janeiro
A351

1955, Feb. 23 ***Perf. 12x11½***

817 A351 2.70cr slate gray & black 75 20

Rotary International, 50th anniversary.

Fausto Cardoso Palace
A352

1955, Mar. 17 ***Perf. 11x11½***

818 A352 40c henna brown 25 25

Centenary of Aracaju.

Aviation Symbols
A353

1955, Mar. 13 Photo. ***Perf. 11½***

819 A353 60c dark gray green 20 15

Issued to publicize the third National Aviation Congress at Sao Paulo, Mar. 6–13.

Arms of Botucatu
A354

1955, Apr. 14

820 A354 60c orange brown 25 15
821 " 1.20cr bright green 35 15

Centenary of Botucatu.

Young Racers at Starting Line
A355

Perf. 11½

1955, Apr. 30 Photo. **Unwmkd.**

823 A355 60c orange brown 35 20

5th Children's Games.

Marshal Hermes da Fonseca
A356

Congress Altar, Sail and Sugar-loaf Mountain
A357

1955, May 12 **Wmk. 267**

824 A356 60c purple 25 15

Issued to commemorate the centenary of the birth of Marshal Hermes da Fonseca.

Engr.; Photo. (2.70cr)

1955, July 17 ***Perf. 11½*** **Unwmkd.**

Designs: 2.70cr, St. Pascoal. 4.20cr, Aloisi Benedetto Cardinal Masella.

825 A357 1.40cr green 25 25
826 " 2.70cr deep claret 50 40
827 " 4.20cr blue 60 25

Issued to commemorate the 36th World Eucharistic Congress in Rio de Janeiro.

Girl Gymnasts
A358
Granite Paper

1955, Nov. 12 **Engraved**

828 A358 60c rose lilac 35 20

Issued to publicize the 7th Spring Games.

José B. Monteiro Lobato
A359

1955, Dec. 8 **Granite Paper**

829 A359 40c dark green 20 15

Issued in honor of José B. Monteiro Lobato, author.

Adolfo Lutz
A360

Lt. Col. Vilagran Cabrita
A361

1955, Dec. 18 **Granite Paper**

830 A360 60c dark green 20 15

Issued to commemorate the centenary of the birth of Adolfo Lutz, public health pioneer.

1955, Dec. 22 Photo. **Wmk. 267**

831 A361 60c violet blue 20 15

Issued to commemorate the centenary of the First Battalion of Engineers.

Salto Grande Hydroelectric Dam
A362
Granite Paper.

1956, Jan. 15 ***Perf. 11½*** **Unwmkd.**

832 A362 60c brick red 20 15

Arms of Mococa
A363

"G" and Globe
A364

Photogravure

1956, Apr. 17 ***Perf. 11½*** **Wmk. 256**

833 A363 60c brick red 15 10

Centenary of Mococa, Sao Paulo.

Granite Paper

1956, Apr. 14 **Unwmkd.**

834 A364 1.20cr violet blue 30 20

18th International Geographic Congress, Rio de Janeiro, August 1956.

Girls' Foot Race
A365

1956, Apr. 28 **Photogravure**

Granite Paper.

835 A365 2.50cr bright blue 50 20

6th Children's Games.

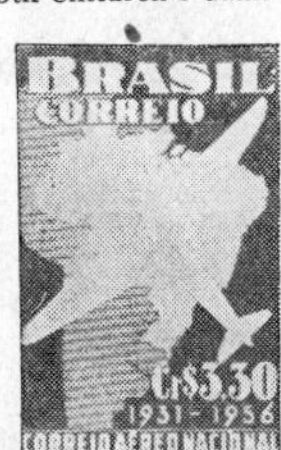

Plane over Map of Brazil
A366

1956, June 12 ***Perf. 11½*** **Wmk. 267**

836 A366 3.30cr brt. vio. blue 1.00 15

Issued to commemorate the 25th anniversary of the National Airmail Service.

Fireman Rescuing Child
A367

1956, July 2 **Wmk. 264**

837 A367 2.50cr crimson 60 20
a. Buff paper 1.50 50

Centenary of the Fire Brigade.

Map of Brazil and Open Book
A368

1956, Sept. 8 **Wmk. 267**

838 A368 2.50cr bright violet blue 40 15

Issued to commemorate the 50th anniversary of the arrival of the Marist Brothers in Northern Brazil.

Church and Monument, Franca
A369

1956, Sept. 7 **Engraved**

839 A369 2.50cr dark blue 40 15

Centenary of city of Franca, Sao Paulo.

Woman Hurdler
A370

1956, Sept. 22 Photo. **Unwmkd.**

Granite Paper.

840 A370 2.50cr dk. carmine 1.00 25

Issued to publicize the 8th Spring Games.

Forest and Map of Brazil
A371

1956, Sept. 30 ***Perf. 11½*** **Wmk. 267**

841 A371 2.50cr dark green 35 15

Issued to publicize education in forestry.

Baron da Bocaina
A372

1956, Oct. 8 Engraved **Wmk. 246**

842 A372 2.50cr reddish brown 35 15

Issued to commemorate the centenary of the birth of Baron da Bocaina, who introduced the special delivery mail system to Brazil.

Marbleized Paper

Paper with a distinct wavy-line or marbleized watermark (which Brazilians call *marmorizado* paper) has been found on many stamps of Brazil, 1956–68, including Nos. 843–845, 847, 851–854, 858–858A, 864, 878, 880, 882, 884, 886–887, 896, 909, 918, 920–921, 925–928, 936–939, 949, 955–958, 960, 962–964, 978–979, 983, 985–987, 997–998, 1002–1003, 1005, 1009–1012, 1017, 1024, 1026, 1055, 1075, 1078, 1082, C82, C82a, C83–C87, C96, C99, C109.

Quantities are much less than those of stamps on regular paper.

Panama Stamp Showing Pres. Juscelino Kubitschek
A373

1956, Oct. 12 Photo. Wmk. 267
843 A373 3.30cr green & black 1.00 20

Issued on America Day, Oct. 12, to commemorate the meeting of the Presidents and the Pan-American Conference at Panama City, July 21-22.

Symbolical of Steel Production
A374

Photogravure.

1957, Jan. 31 *Perf. 11½* Wmk. 267
844 A374 2.50cr chocolate 40 15

Issued to commemorate the second expansion of the National Steel Company at Volta Redonda.

Joaquim E. Gomes da Silva
A375

Granite Paper.

1957, Mar. 1 Photo. Unwmkd.
845 A375 2.50cr dark blue green 35 15

Issued to commemorate the centenary of the birth (in 1856) of Joaquim E. Gomes da Silva.

Allan Kardec
A376

Engraved.

1957, Apr. 18 *Perf. 11½* Wmk. 268
846 A376 2.50cr dark brown 35 15

Issued in honor of Allan Kardec, pen name of Leon Hippolyto Denizard Rivail, and for the centenary of the publication of his "Codification of Spiritism."

Boy Gymnast
A377

Granite Paper.

1957, Apr. 27 Photo. Unwmkd.
847 A377 2.50cr lake 75 20

7th Children's Games.

Pres. Craveiro Lopes
A378

Stamp of 1932
A379

1957, June 7 Engraved Wmk. 267
848 A378 6.50cr blue 75 15

Issued to commemorate the visit of Gen. Francisco Higino Craveiro Lopes, President of Portugal.

1957, July 9 Photogravure
849 A379 2.50cr rose 20 10

Issued to commemorate the 25th anniversary of the movement for a constitution.

St. Antonio Monastery, Pernambuco
A380

1957, Aug. 24 Engraved Wmk. 267
850 A380 2.50cr deep magenta 30 15

Issued to commemorate the 300th anniversary of the emancipation of the Franciscan province of St. Antonio in Pernambuco State.

Volleyball
A381

Basketball
A382

1957, Sept. 28 Photo. *Perf. 11½*
851 A381 2.50cr dull orange red 75 20

Issued for the 9th Spring Games.

1957, Oct. 12
852 A382 3.30cr orange & bright green 75 20

Issued to commemorate the second Women's International Basketball Championship, Rio de Janeiro.

Count of Pinhal and Sao Carlos
A383

1957, Nov. 4 *Perf. 11½* Wmk. 267
853 A383 2.50cr rose 60 20

Issued to commemorate the centenary of the city of Sao Carlos and to honor the Count of Pinhal, its founder.

Auguste Comte
A384

1957, Nov. 15
854 A384 2.50cr dark red brown 50 20

Issued to commemorate the centenary of the death of Auguste Comte, French mathematician and philosopher.

Radio Station
A385

1957, Dec. 10 Wmk. 268
855 A385 2.50cr dark green 35 15

Opening of Sarapui Central Radio Station.

Admiral Tamandare and Warship
A386

Design: 3.30cr, Aircraft carrier.

1957–58 Photogravure
856 A386 2.50cr light blue 45 15

Engraved
857 A386 3.30cr green ('58) 50 15

Issued to commemorate the 150th anniversary of the birth of Admiral Joaquin Marques de Tamandare, founder of the Brazilian navy.

Coffee Plant and Symbolic "R"
A387

Photogravure.

1957–58 *Perf. 11½* Wmk. 267
858 A387 2.50cr magenta 60 20

Unwmkd.

Granite Paper.

858A A387 2.50cr magenta ('58) 50 20

Issued to commemorate the centenary (in 1956) of the city of Ribeirao Preto in Sao Paulo state.

Dom John VI—A388

1958, Jan. 28 Engraved Wmk. 268
859 A388 2.50cr magenta 50 15

Issued to commemorate the 150th anniversary of the opening of the ports of Brazil to foreign trade.

Bugler
A389

1958, Mar. 18 Wmk. 267
860 A389 2.50cr red 60 20

Issued to commemorate the 150th anniversary of the Brazilian Marine Corps.

Station at Rio and Locomotive of 1858
A390

Court House
A391

Photogravure.

1958, Mar. 29 *Perf. 11½* Wmk. 267
861 A390 2.50cr red brown 50 15

Issued to commemorate the centenary of the Central Railroad of Brazil.

1958, Apr. 1 Engraved Wmk. 256
862 A391 2.50cr green 35 15

Issued to commemorate the 150th anniversary of the Military Superior Court.

Emblem and Brazilian Pavilion
A392

1958, Apr. 17 Wmk. 267
863 A392 2.50cr dark blue 25 25

World's Fair, Brussels, Apr. 17–Oct. 19.

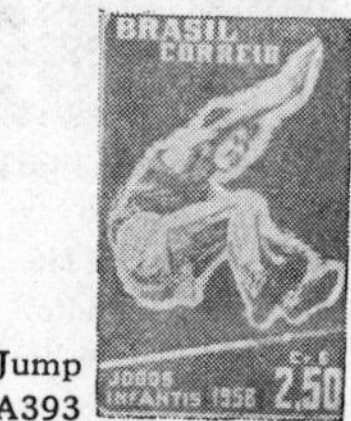

High Jump
A393

1958, Apr. 20 Photo. **Unwmkd.**
Granite Paper
864 A393 2.50cr crimson rose 45 15
8th Children's Games.

Marshal Mariano da Silva Rondon
A394

1958, Apr. 19 Engraved **Wmk. 267**
865 A394 2.50cr magenta 35 15
Issued to honor Marshal Mariano da Silva Rondon and the "Day of the Indian."

Hydroelectric Station
A395

1958, Apr. 28 ***Perf. 11½*** **Wmk. 267**
866 A395 2.50cr magenta 25 15
Opening of Sao Paulo State power plant.

National Printing Plant
A396

1958, May 22 **Photogravure**
867 A396 2.50cr reddish brown 25 15
Issued to commemorate the 150th anniversary of the founding of the National Printing Plant.

Marshal Osorio
A397

1958, May 24
868 A397 2.50cr bright violet 25 15
Issued to commemorate the 150th anniversary of the birth of Marshal Manoel Luiz Osorio.

Pres. Ramon Villeda Morales
A398

Fountain
A399

Engraved.
1958, June 7 ***Perf. 11½*** **Wmk. 267**
869 A398 6.50cr dark green 2.00 60
a. Wmk. 268 3.00 2.00
Issued to commemorate the visit of Pres. Ramon Villeda Morales of Honduras.

1958, June 13
870 A399 2.50cr dark green 35 15
Issued to commemorate the 150th anniversary of the Botanical Garden, Rio de Janeiro.

Symbols of Agriculture
A400

Prophet Joel
A401

1958, June 18 **Photogravure**
871 A400 2.50cr rose carmine 25 15
Issued to commemorate the 50th anniversary of Japanese immigration to Brazil.

1958, June 21 **Engraved**
872 A401 2.50cr dark blue 30 15
Issued to commemorate the bicentenary of the Cathedral of Bom Jesus at Matosinhos.

Stylized Globe
A402

1958, July 10 **Photogravure**
873 A402 2.50cr dark brown 25 15
Issued to publicize the International Investment Conference, Belo Horizonte.

Julio Bueno Brandao
A403

1958, Aug. 1 ***Perf. 11½*** **Wmk. 268**
874 A403 2.50cr red brown 25 15
Issued to commemorate the centenary of the birth of Julio Bueno Brandao, President of Minas Gerais.

Palacio Tiradentes
(House of Congress)
A404

1958, July 24 **Engraved**
875 A404 2.50cr sepia 25 15
Issued to honor the 47th Interparliamentary Conference, Rio de Janeiro, July 24–Aug. 1.

Presidential Palace, Brasilia
A405

1958, Aug. 8 Photo. **Wmk. 267**
876 A405 2.50cr ultramarine 35 15
Issued to publicize the construction of Brazil's new capital, Brasilia.

Freighters
A406

1958, Aug. 22
877 A406 2.50cr blue 45 15
Issued in honor of the Brazilian merchant marine.

Joaquim Caetano da Silva
A407

1958, Sept. 2 **Unwmkd.**
Granite Paper
878 A407 2.50cr reddish brown 35 15
Issued in honor of Joaquim Caetano da Silva, scientist and historian.

Giovanni Gronchi
A408

Archers
A409

1958, Sept. 4 Engraved **Wmk. 268**
879 A408 7cr dark blue 75 15
Issued to commemorate the visit of Italy's President Giovanni Gronchi to Brazil.

Perf. 11½
1958, Sept. 21 Photo. **Unwmkd.**
Granite Paper
880 A409 2.50cr red orange 60 20
Issued to publicize the 10th Spring Games.

Elderly Couple
A410

Machado de Assis
A411

1958, Sept. 27 **Wmk. 267**
881 A410 2.50cr magenta 40 15
Issued to publicize the Day of the Old People, Sept. 27.

1958, Sept. 28 **Unwmkd.**
882 A411 2.50cr red brown 35 15
Issued to commemorate the 50th anniversary of the death of Joaquim Maria Machado de Assis, writer.

Pres. Vargas and Oil Derrick
A412

1958, Oct. 6 **Wmk. 268**
883 A412 2.50cr blue 25 15
Issued to commemorate the 5th anniversary of Pres. Getulio D. Vargas' oil law.

Globe
A413

Gen. Lauro Sodré
A414

Perf. 11½
1958, Nov. 14 Photo. **Wmk. 267**
884 A413 2.50cr blue 50 15
Issued to commemorate the seventh Inter-American Congress of Municipalities.

1958, Nov. 15 **Engraved**
885 A414 3.30cr green 15 15
Issued to commemorate the centenary of the birth of Gen. Lauro Sodré.

U. N. Emblem
A415

Soccer Player
A416

1958, Dec. 26 Photo. ***Perf. 11½***
886 A415 2.50cr bright blue 35 15
Issued to commemorate the tenth anniversary of the signing of the Universal Declaration of Human Rights.

1959, Jan. 20
887 A416 3.30cr emerald & red brown 50 20
World Soccer Championships of 1958.

Railroad Track and Map
A417

Pres. Sukarno of Indonesia
A418

1959, Apr. ***Perf. 11½*** **Wmk. 267**

888 A417 2.50cr deep orange 30 20

Issued to commemorate the centenary of the linking of Patos and Campina Grande by railroad.

1959, May 20

889 A418 2.50cr blue 25 15

Visit of President Sukarno of Indonesia.

Dom John VI A419 — Boy Polo Players A420

Perf. 10½x11½

1959, June 12 **Wmk. 267**

890 A419 2.50cr crimson 30 10

1959, June 13 ***Perf. 11½***

891 A420 2.50cr orange brown 35 15

9th Children's Games.

Loading Freighter A421 — Organ and Emblem A422

1959, July 10

892 A421 2.50cr dark green 35 15

Issued to honor the merchant marine.

1959, July 16 Photogravure

893 A422 3.30cr magenta 20 15

Issued to commemorate the bicentenary of the Carmelite Order in Brazil.

Joachim Silverio de Souza A423 — Symbolic Road A424

1959, July 20 ***Perf. 11½***

894 A423 2.50cr red brown 20 15

Issued to commemorate the birth centenary of Joachim Silverio de Souza, first bishop of Diamantina, Minas Gerais.

1959, Sept. 27 **Wmk. 267**

895 A424 3.30cr blue green & ultra. 25 15

11th International Roadbuilding Congress.

Girl Athlete A425

1959, Oct. 4

896 A425 2.50cr lilac rose 40 20

11th Spring Games.

Map of Parana—A426

1959, Sept. 27

897 A426 2.50cr dark green 25 15

Issued to commemorate the 25th anniversary of the founding of Londrina, Parana.

Globe and Snipes A427 — Lusignan Cross A428

1959, Oct. 22 ***Perf. 11½***

898 A427 6.50cr dull green 15 15

Issued to commemorate the World Championship of Snipe Class Sailboats, Porto Alegre, won by Brazilian yachtsmen.

1959, Oct. 24 Engraved

899 A428 6.50cr dull blue 15 15

Issued to commemorate the 4th International Conference on Brazilian-Portuguese Studies, Univeristy of Bahia, Aug. 10–20.

Factory Entrance and Order of Southern Cross A429 — Corcovado Christ, Globe and Southern Cross A430

1959, Nov. 19 Photogravure

900 A429 3.30cr orange red 15 15

Issued to commemorate the 50th anniversary of the Pres. Vargas Gunpowder Factory.

1959, Nov. 26 ***Perf. 11½***

901 A430 2.50cr blue 40 15

Universal Thanksgiving Day.

Burning Bush—A431

1959, Dec. 24 **Wmk. 267**

902 A431 3.30cr light green 15 15

Centenary of Presbyterian work in Brazil.

Piraja da Silva and Schistosoma Mansoni A432

1959, Dec. 28

903 A432 2.50cr rose violet 35 15

Issued to commemorate the 25th anniversary of the discovery and identification of schistosoma mansoni, a parasite of the fluke family, by Dr. Piraja da Silva.

Luiz de Matos—A433

1960, Jan. 3 Photogravure

904 A433 3.30cr red brown 15 15

Birth centenary of Luiz de Matos.

L. L. Zamenhof A434 — Adél Pinto A435

Perf. 11½

1960, Mar. 10 **Wmk. 267**

905 A434 6.50cr emerald 15 15

Issued to commemorate the birth centenary of Lazarus Ludwig Zamenhof (1859–1917), Polish oculist who invented Esperanto in 1887.

1960, Mar. 19 **Engr.** **Wmk. 268**

906 A435 11.50cr rose red 15 15

Issued to commemorate the centenary of the birth of Adél Pinto, civil engineer and railroad expert.

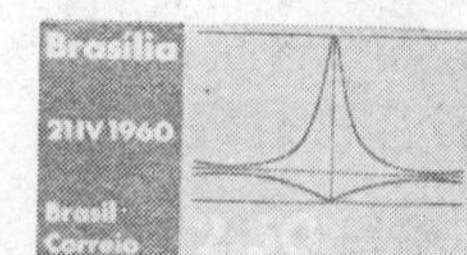

Presidential Palace, Colonnade A436

Design: 27cr, Plan of Brasilia (like No. C98).

Perf. 11x11½

1960 Photogravure **Wmk. 267**

907 A436 2.50cr bright green 40 15

908 A436 27cr salmon 1.00 1.00

Nos. 907-908, C95-C98 (6) 3.15 1.62

No. 907 issued Apr. 21 to commemorate the inauguration of Brazil's new capital, Brasilia, Apr. 21, 1960.

No. 908 issued Sept. 12 to commemorate the birthday of Pres. Juscelino Kubitschek. It measures 105x46½mm., carrying at center a 27cr in design of No. C98, flanked by the chief design features of Nos. 907, C95-C97, with Kubitschek signature below. Issued in sheets of 4 with wide horizontal gutter.

Grain, Coffee, Cotton and Cacao A437 — Paulo de Frontin A438

Perf. 11½x11

1960, July 28 **Wmk. 267**

909 A437 2.50cr brown 30 15

Centenary of Ministry of Agriculture.

1960, Oct. 12 **Wmk. 268**

910 A438 2.50cr orange red 20 15

Issued to commemorate the centenary of the birth of Paulo de Frontin, engineer.

Girl Athlete Holding Torch A439

1960, Oct. 18 ***Perf. 11½x11***

911 A439 2.50cr blue green 30 15

12th Spring Games.

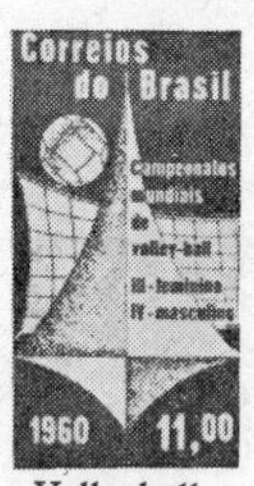

Volleyball and Net A440 — Locomotive Wheels A441

Perf. 11½x11

1960, Nov. 12 **Wmk. 268**

912 A440 11cr blue 50 20

International Volleyball Championships.

1960, Oct. 15 ***Perf. 11½x11***

913 A441 2.50cr ultramarine 20 10

10th Pan-American Railroad Congress.

Symbols of Flight A442

1960, Dec. 16 Photo. ***Perf. 11½***

914 A442 2.50cr brown & yel. 20 15

Issued to commemorate the International Fair of Industry and Commerce, Rio de Janeiro.

Emperor Haile Selassie I
A443

1961, Jan. 31 ***Perf. 11½x11***

915 A443 2.50cr dark brown 20 15

Issued to commemorate the visit of Emperor Haile Selassie I of Ethiopia to Brazil, Dec. 1960.

Map of Brazil, Open Book and Sacred Heart Emblem
A444

Perf. 11x11½

1961, Mar. 13 **Wmk. 268**

916 A444 2.50cr blue 30 15

The 50th anniversary of the operation in Brazil of the Order of the Blessed Heart of Mary.

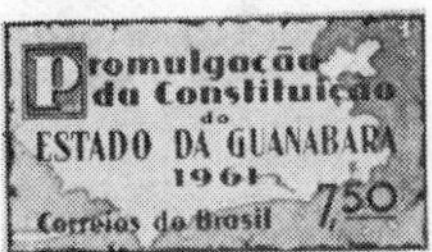

Map of Guanabara
A445

1961, March 27 **Wmk. 267**

917 A445 7.50cr orange brown 25 15

Issued to commemorate the promulgation of the constitution of the state of Guanabara.

Arms of Agulhas Negras
A446

Brazil and Senegal Linked on Map
A447

Design: 3.30cr, Dress helmet and sword.

Perf. 11½x11

1961, Apr. 23 **Wmk. 267**

918 A446 2.50cr green 35 15
919 " 3.30cr rose carmine 15 15

Issued to commemorate the sesquicentennial of the Agulhas Negras Military Academy.

1961, Apr. 28 **Photogravure**

920 A447 27cr ultramarine 50 20

Issued to commemorate the visit of Afonso Arinos, Brazilian foreign minister, to Senegal to attend its independence ceremonies.

View of Ouro Preto, 1711
A448

1961, June 6 ***Perf. 11x11½***

921 A448 1cr orange 20 20

250th anniversary of Ouro Preto.

War Arsenal
A449

1961, June 20 **Wmk. 256**

924 A449 5cr dk. red brown 40 15

Issued to commemorate the 150th anniversary of the War Arsenal, Rio de Janeiro.

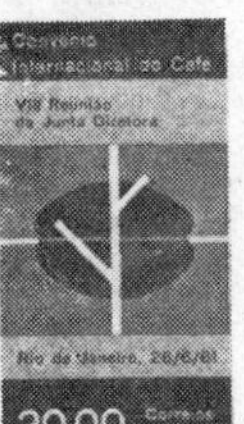

Coffee Bean and Branch
A450

Rabindranath Tagore
A451

Perf. 11½x11

1961, June 26 **Wmk. 267**

925 A450 20cr reddish brown 1.50 15

Issued to commemorate the 8th Directorial Committee meeting of the International Coffee Convention, Rio de Janeiro, June 26, 1961.

1961, July 28 Photo. **Wmk. 267**

926 A451 10cr rose carmine 30 15

Issued to commemorate the centenary of the birth of Rabindranath Tagore, Indian poet.

Stamp of 1861 and Map of English Channel
A452

Design: 20cr, 430r stamp of 1861 and map of Netherlands.

1961, Aug. 1 ***Perf. 11x11½***

927 A452 10cr rose 75 15
928 " 20cr salmon pink 1.75 18

Centenary of 1861 stamp issue.

Portrait Type of 1954–60

Designs as Before.

1961 ***Perf. 11x11½*** **Wmk. 268**

930 A336 1cr brown 1.00 50
931 " 2cr dk. blue green 1.50 50
932 " 5cr red lilac 3.50 25
933 " 10cr emerald 6.50 25

The 1cr, 5cr and 10cr have patterned background.

Sun, Clouds, Rain and Weather Symbols
A453

Dedo de Deus Peak
A454

1962, March 23 ***Perf. 11½x11***

936 A453 10cr red brown 1.25 15

World Meteorological Day, Mar. 23.

1962, Apr. 14 Photo. **Wmk. 267**

937 A454 8cr emerald 20 15

Issued to commemorate the 50th anniversary of the climbing of Dedo de Deus (Finger of God) peak.

Dr. Gaspar Vianna and Leishmania Protozoa
A455

1962, Apr. 24 ***Perf. 11x11½***

938 A455 8cr blue 25 15

Issued to commemorate the 50th anniversary of the discovery by Gaspar Oliveiro Vianna (1885–1914) of a cure for leishmaniasis.

Henrique Dias—A456

1962, June 18 **Wmk. 267**

939 A456 10cr dk. violet brn. 50 15

Issued to commemorate the 300th anniversary of the death of Henrique Dias, Negro military leader who fought against the Dutch and Spaniards.

Millimeter Gauge
A457

Sailboats, Snipe Class
A458

1962, June 26 ***Perf. 11½x11***

940 A457 100cr carmine rose 60 20

Issued to commemorate the centenary of the introduction of the metric system in Brazil.

1962, July 21 Photo. **Wmk. 267**

941 A458 8cr Prussian green 30 15

Issued to commemorate the 13th Brazilian championships for Snipe Class sailing.

Julio Mesquita—A459

1962, Aug. 18 ***Perf. 11x11½***

942 A459 8cr dull brown 30 15

Issued to commemorate the centenary of the birth of Julio Mesquita, journalist and founder of Sao Paulo.

Empress Leopoldina
A460

1962, Sept. 7 ***Perf. 11½x11***

943 A460 8cr rose claret 25 15

140th anniversary of independence.

Buildings, Brasilia—A461

Perf. 11x11½

1962, Oct. 24 **Wmk. 267**

944 A461 10cr orange 60 15

Issued to commemorate the 51st Interparliamentary Conference, Brasilia.

Pouring Ladle
A462

1962, Oct. 26 ***Perf. 11½x11***

945 A462 8cr orange 25 15

Issued to mark the inauguration of the Usiminas State Iron and Steel Foundry at Belo Horizonte, Minas Gerais.

UPAE Emblem
A463

1962, Nov. 19 ***Perf. 11x11½***

946 A463 8cr bright magenta 20 15

Issued to commemorate the 50th anniversary of the founding of the Postal Union of the Americas and Spain, UPAE.

Chimney and Cogwheel Forming "10"
A464

1962, Nov. 26 ***Perf. 11½x11***

947 A464 10cr lt. blue green 40 15

Issued to commemorate the 10th anniversary of the National Economic and Development Bank.

Quintino Bocaiuva
A465

Soccer Player and Globe
A466

Perf. 11½x11

1962, Dec. 27 Photo. **Wmk. 267**

948 A465 8cr brown orange 20 15

Issued to commemorate the 50th anniversary of the death of Quintino Bocaiuva, journalist.

1963, Jan. 14

949 A466 10cr blue green 12 7

World Soccer Championship of 1962.

Carrier Pigeon
A467

Lithographed

1963, Jan. ***Perf. 14*** **Unwmkd.**

950 A467 8cr yel., dk. blue, red & green 25 15

Souvenir Sheet

Imperf.

951 A467 100cr yel., dark blue, red & green 1.00 1.00

Issued to commemorate 300 years of Brazilian postal service. No. 951 contains one stamp. Black inscription and ultramarine border. Size: 145x57mm.

Issue dates: 8cr, Jan. 25; 100cr, Jan. 31.

Severino Neiva
A468

Perf. 10½x11½

1963, Jan. 31 Photo. **Wmk. 267**

952 A468 8cr bright violet 25 10

Radar Tracking Station and Rockets
A469

"Cross of Unity"
A470

Perf. 11½x11

1963, Mar. 15 **Wmk. 268**

953 A469 21cr lt. ultramarine 30 15

Issued to publicize the International Aeronautics and Space Exhibition, Sao Paulo.

1963 ***Perf. 11½x11*** **Wmk. 267**

954 A470 8cr red lilac 20 15

Issued to commemorate Vatican II, the 21st Ecumenical Council of the Roman Catholic Church.

"ABC" in Geometric Form
A471

Basketball Player
A472

1963, Apr. 22 Photo. **Wmk. 267**

955 A471 8cr bright blue & light blue 20 15

Issued for Education Week, Apr. 22–27, in connection with the 3-year alphabetization program.

1963, May 15

956 A472 8cr deep lilac rose 35 15

Issued to commemorate the 4th International Basketball Championships, Rio de Janeiro, May 10–25, 1963.

Games Emblem
A473

"OEA" and Map of the Americas
A474

1963, May 22 ***Perf. 11½x11***

957 A473 10cr carmine rose 60 15

4th Pan American Games, Sao Paulo.

1963, June 6

958 A474 10cr orange & deep orange 60 15

Issued to commemorate the 15th anniversary of the charter of the Organization of American States.

José Bonifacio de Andrada
A475

1963, June 13

959 A475 8cr dark brown 20 15

Issued to commemorate the bicentenary of the birth of José Bonifacio de Andrada de Silva, statesman.

Wheat
A476

Perf. 11x11½

1963, June 19 Photo. **Wmk. 267**

960 A476 10cr blue 50 15

Issued for the "Freedom from Hunger" campaign of the U.N. Food and Agriculture Organization.

Centenary Emblem
A477

João Caetano
A478

1963, Aug. 19 ***Perf. 11½x11***

961 A477 8cr yel. org. & red 30 15

Centenary of International Red Cross.

1963, Aug. 24 ***Perf. 11½x11***

962 A478 8cr slate 30 15

Death centenary of João Caetano, actor.

Symbols of Agriculture, Industry and Atomic Energy
A479

Hammer Thrower
A480

1963, Aug. 28

963 A479 10cr carmine rose 40 15

Issued to commemorate the first anniversary of the Atomic Development Law.

1963, Sept. 13

964 A480 10cr gray 75 10

International College Students' Games, Porto Alegre.

Marshal Tito
A481

Compass Rose, Map of Brazil and View of Rio de Janeiro
A482

1963, Sept. 19

965 A481 80cr sepia 60 30

Visit of Marshal Tito of Jugoslavia.

1963, Sept. 20

966 A482 8cr light blue green 20 15

8th International Leprology Congress.

Oil Derrick and Storage Tank
A483

1963, Oct. 3 ***Perf. 11x11½***

967 A483 8cr dark slate green 20 15

Issued to commemorate the 10th anniversary of Petrobras, the national oil company.

"Spring Games"—A484

1963, Nov. 5 Photo. **Wmk. 267**

968 A484 8cr yellow & orange 25 20

1963 Spring Games.

Borges de Medeiros
A485

1963, Nov. 29 ***Perf. 11½x11***

969 A485 8cr red brown 20 15

Issued to commemorate the centenary of the birth of Dr. Borges de Medeiros (1863–1962), Governor of Rio Grande do Sul.

São João del Rei
A486

1963, Dec. 8 ***Perf. 11x11½***

970 A486 8cr violet blue 20 15

250th anniversary of São João del Rei.

Dr. Alvaro Alvim
A487

1963, Dec. 19

971 A487 8cr dark gray 20 15

Issued to commemorate the centenary of the birth of Dr. Alvaro Alvim (1863–1928), X-ray specialist and martyr of science.

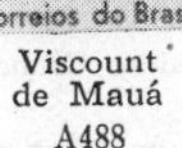

Viscount de Mauá A488 — Mandacaru Cactus and Emblem A489

1963, Dec. 28 *Perf. 11½x11*

972 A488 8cr rose carmine 20 15

Issued to commemorate the sesquicentennial of the birth of Viscount de Mauá, founder of first Brazilian railroad.

1964, Jan. 23 Photo. Wmk. 267

973 A489 8cr dull green 25 15

Issued to commemorate the 10th anniversary of the Bank of Northeast Brazil.

Coelho Netto A490 — Lauro Müller A491

1964, Feb. 21 *Perf. 11½x11*

974 A490 8cr brt. violet 20 15

Birth centenary of Coelho Netto, writer.

1964, March 8 Wmk. 267

975 A491 8cr deep orange 20 15

Issued to commemorate the centenary of the birth of Lauro Siverino Müller, politician and member of the Brazilian Academy of Letters.

Child Holding Spoon
A492

1964, March 25 *Perf. 11x11½*

976 A492 8cr yel. brn. & yel. 25 15

Issued for "School Meals Week."

Chalice Rock A493 — Allan Kardec A494

1964, Apr. 9 Engraved *Perf. 11½x11*

977 A493 80cr red orange 40 20

Issued for tourist publicity.

1964, Apr. 18 Photogravure

978 A494 30cr slate green 75 15

Issued to commemorate the centenary of "O Evangelho" (Gospel) of the codification of Spiritism.

Heinrich Lübke A495 — Pope John XXIII A496

Perf. 11½x11

1964, May 8 Photo. Wmk. 267

979 A495 100cr red brown 60 18

Issued to commemorate the visit of President Heinrich Lübke of Germany.

1964, June 29 Wmk. 267

980 A496 20cr dk. carm. rose 30 20
a. Unwmkd. 30 20

Issued in memory of Pope John XXIII.

Pres. Senghor of Senegal
A497

1964, Sept. 19 Wmk. 267

981 A497 20cr dark brown 40 15

Issued to commemorate the visit of Léopold Sédar Senghor, President of Senegal.

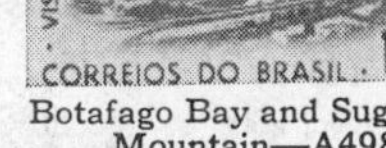

Botafago Bay and Sugarloaf Mountain—A498

Designs: 100cr, Church of Our Lady of the Rock (vert.). 200cr, Copacabana beach.

Perf. 11x11½, 11½x11

1964–65 Photogravure

983	A498	15cr orange & blue	40	25
984	"	100cr brt. grn. & red brn., *yellow*	50	18
985	"	200cr blk. & red	2.50	35
		a. Souv. sheet of 3 ('65)	1.50	1.50

Issued to commemorate the 4th centenary of Rio de Janeiro. See Nos. 993–995a.

No. 985a contains three imperf. stamps similar to Nos. 983–985, but printed in brown with marginal inscriptions and border in deep orange. Size: 129x79mm. Sold for 320cr. Issued Dec. 30, 1965.

A souvenir card containing one lithographed facsimile of No. 984, imperf., exists, but has no franking value. Marginal inscriptions in green. Size: 100x125mm. Sold by P.O. for 250cr.

Pres. Charles de Gaulle A499 — Pres. John F. Kennedy A500

1964, Oct. 13 *Perf. 11½x11*

986 A499 100cr orange brown 30 15

Issued to commemorate the visit of Charles de Gaulle, President of France, Oct. 13–15.

1964, Oct. 24 Photo. Wmk. 267

987 A500 100cr slate 30 15

Issued in memory of President John F. Kennedy (1917–63).

"Prophet" by A. F. Lisbao
A501

1964, Nov. 18 *Perf. 11½x11*

988 A501 10cr slate 10 6

Issued to commemorate the 150th anniversary of the death of the sculptor Antonio Francisco Lisbao, "O Aleijadinho" (The Cripple).

Antonio Goncalves Dias
A502

Designs: 30cr, Euclides da Cunha. 50cr, Prof. Angelo Moreira da Costa Lima. 200cr, Tiradentes. 500cr, Dom Pedro I. 1000cr, Dom Pedro II.

1965–66 *Perf. 11x11½* **Wmk. 267**

989	A502	30cr bright bluish green ('66)	1.25	20
989A	"	50cr dull brown ('66)	1.25	8
990	"	100cr blue	50	8
991	"	200cr brown orange	1.00	8
992	"	500cr red brown	4.00	30
992A	"	1000cr slate bl. ('66)	5.00	75
		Nos. 989-992A (6)	13.00	1.49

Statue of St. Sebastian, Guanatara Bay
A503

The Arches
A504

Design: 35cr, Estacio de Sá (1520–67), founder of Rio de Janeiro.

1965 Photogravure *Perf. 11½*

Size: 24x37mm.

993 A503 30cr blue & rose red 60 15

Lithographed and Engraved

Perf. 11x11½

994 A504 30cr lt. bl. & black 60 15

Photogravure

Perf. 11½

Size: 21x39mm.

995 A503 35cr black & orange 25 25
a. Souv. sheet of 3 1.50 1.50

Issued to commemorate the 4th centenary of Rio de Janeiro. Issue dates: No. 993, Mar. 5. No. 994, Nov. 30. No. 995, July 28. No. 995a, Dec. 30.

No. 995a contains three imperf. stamps similar to Nos. 993–995, but printed in deep orange with marginal inscriptions and border in brown. Size: 130x79mm. Sold for 100cr.

Sword and Cross
A505

1965, Apr. 15 *Perf. 11½* **Wmk. 267**

996 A505 120cr gray 40 15

Issued to commemorate the first anniversary of the democratic revolution.

Vital Brazil A506 — Shah of Iran A507

1965, Apr. 28 *Perf. 11½* **Wmk. 267**

997 A506 120cr deep orange 50 15

Centenary of birth of Vital Brazil, M.D.

A souvenir card containing one impression similar to No. 997, imperf., exists, printed in dull plum. Sold by P.O. for 250cr. Size: 114x180mm.

1965, May 5 Photogravure

998 A507 120cr rose claret 40 15

Issued to commemorate the visit of Shah Mohammed Riza Pahlavi of Iran.

Marshal Mariano da Silva Rondon
A508

Lions' Emblem
A509

1965, May 7 **Engraved**

999 A508 30cr claret 50 15

Issued to commemorate the centenary of the birth of Marshal Mariano da Silva Rondon (1865–1958), explorer and expert on Indians.

1965, May 14 **Photogravure**

1000 A509 35cr pale vio. & blk. 30 15

Issued to commemorate the 12th convention of the Lions Clubs of Brazil, Rio de Janeiro, May 11–16.

ITU Emblem, Old and New Communication Equipment
A510

1965, May 21 ***Perf. 11½*** **Wmk. 267**

1001 A510 120cr yel. & green 50 20

Issued to commemorate the centenary of the International Telecommunication Union.

Epitácio Pessoa
A511

Statue of Admiral Barroso
A512

1965, May 23 **Photogravure**

1002 A511 35cr blue gray 20 15

Issued to commemorate the centenary of the birth of Epitácio da Silva Pessoa (1865–1942), jurist, president of Brazil, 1919–22.

1965, June 11

1003 A512 30cr blue 40 15

Centenary of the naval battle of Riachuelo.

A souvenir card containing one lithographed facsimile of No. 1003, imperf., exists. Size: 100x139½mm.

José de Alencar and Indian Princess
A513

1965, June 24 ***Perf. 11½x11***

1004 A513 30cr deep plum 50 15

Issued to commemorate the centenary of the publication of "Iracema" by José de Alencar.

A souvenir card containing one lithographed facsimile of No. 1004, printed in rose red and imperf., exists. Size: 100x141½mm.

Winston Churchill
A514

1965, June 25 ***Perf. 11x11½***

1005 A514 200cr slate 1.00 25

Issued in memory of Sir Winston Spencer Churchill (1874–1965), statesman and World War II leader.

Scout Jamboree Emblem
A515

1965, July 17 **Photogravure**

1006 A515 30cr dull blue green 50 15

Issued to commemorate the First Pan-American Boy Scout Jamboree, Fundao Island, Rio de Janeiro, July 15–25.

ICY Emblem
A516

1965, Aug. 25 ***Perf. 11½*** **Wmk. 267**

1007 A516 120cr dull blue & black 40 15

International Cooperation Year, 1965.

Leoncio Correias
A517

Emblem
A518

1965, Sept. 1 ***Perf. 11½x11***

1008 A517 35cr slate green 20 15

Issued to commemorate the centenary of the birth of Leoncio Correias, poet.

1965, Sept. 4

1009 A518 30cr bright rose 30 15

Issued to publicize the Eighth Biennial Fine Arts Exhibition, Sao Paulo, Nov.–Dec., 1965.

Pres. Saragat of Italy
A519

1965, Sept. 11 **Photo.** **Wmk. 267**

1010 A519 100cr slate green, *pink* 25 12

Visit of Pres. Giuseppe Saragat of Italy.

Grand Duke and Duchess of Luxembourg
A520

1965, Sept. 17 ***Perf. 11x11½***

1011 A520 100cr brown olive 25 12

Issued to commemorate the visit of Grand Duke Jean and Grand Duchess Josephine Charlotte of Luxembourg.

Biplane
A521

1965, Oct. 8 **Photo.** ***Perf. 11½x11***

1012 A521 35cr ultramarine 25 15

Issued to publicize the 3rd Aviation Week Philatelic Exhibition, Rio de Janeiro.

A souvenir card carries one impression of this 35cr, imperf. Size: 102x140mm. Sold for 100cr.

Flags of OAS Members
A522

1965, Nov. 17 ***Perf. 11x11½***

1013 A522 100cr brt. bl. & blk. 40 20

Issued to commemorate the second meeting of Foreign Ministers of the Organization of American States, Rio de Janeiro.

King Baudouin and Queen Fabiola of Belgium—A523

1965, Nov. 18

1014 A523 100cr gray 40 20

Visit of King and Queen of Belgium.

"Coffee Beans"
A524

Perf. 11½x11

1965, Dec. 21 **Photo.** **Wmk. 267**

1015 A524 30cr brown 60 15

Brazilian coffee publicity.

Conveyor and Loading Crane
A525

1966, Apr. 1 ***Perf. 11x11½***

1016 A525 110cr tan & dark slate green 40 25

Issued to commemorate the opening of the new terminal of the Rio Doce Iron Ore Company at Tubarao.

Pouring Ladle and Steel Beam
A526

Prof. de Rocha Dissecting Cadaver
A527

Perf. 11½x11

1966, Apr. 16 **Photo.** **Wmk. 267**

1017 A526 30cr *deep orange* 35 15

Issued to commemorate the 25th anniversary of the National Steel Company (nationalization of the steel industry).

1966, Apr. 26

1018 A527 30cr brt. bluish grn. 60 15

Issued to commemorate the 50th anniversary of the discovery and description of Rickettsia prowazeki, the cause of typhus fever, by Prof. Henrique de Rocha Lima.

Battle of Tuiuti
A528

Perf. 11x11½

1966, May 24 **Photo.** **Wmk. 267**

1019 A528 30cr gray green 60 15

Centenary of the Battle of Tuiuti.

Symbolic Water Cycle
A529

Pres. Shazar of Israel
A530

1966, July 1 *Perf. 11½x11*

1020 A529 100cr lt. brn. & blue 45 20

Hydrological Decade (UNESCO), 1965–74.

1966, July 18 Photo. Wmk. 267

1021 A530 100cr ultramarine 50 20

Visit of Pres. Zalman Shazar of Israel.

Imperial Academy of Fine Arts
A531

Perf. 11x11½

1966, Aug. 12 Engr. Wmk. 267

1022 A531 100cr red brown 40 20

150th anniversary of French art mission.

Military Service Emblem
A532

1966, Sept. 6 Photo. *Perf. 11x11½*

1023 A532 30cr yellow, ultra. & green 40 15
  a. With commemorative border 1.50 1.50

Issued to publicize the new Military Service Law. No. 1023a, issued in sheets of four, measures 103½x47mm. It carries at left a single 30cr, type A532, in deeper tones of yellow and ultramarine, Wmk. 264. Top and bottom "frames" in ultramarine are inscribed "Departamento dos Correios e Telégrafos" and "100 Cruzeiros." Inscription at right: "Bloco Comemorativo da Nova Lei do Serviço Militar." Without gum. Sold for 100cr.

Rubén Dario
A533

Perf. 11½x11

1966, Sept. 20 Photo. Wmk. 267

1024 A533 100cr brt. rose lilac 40 15

Issued to commemorate the 50th anniversary of the death of Rubén Dario (pen name of Felix Rubén Garcia Sarmiento (1867–1916), Nicaraguan poet, newspaper correspondent and diplomat.

Ceramic Candlestick from Santarém
A534

1966, Oct. 6 *Perf. 11x11½*

1025 A534 30cr dk. brn., *salmon* 40 15

Centenary of Goeldi Museum at Belém.

Arms of Santa Cruz
A535

Perf. 11½x11

1966, Oct. 15 Photo. Wmk. 267

1026 A535 30cr slate green 45 15

Issued to publicize the First National Tobacco Exposition, Santa Cruz.

UNESCO Emblem
A536

1966, Oct. 24 Engraved *Perf. 11½*

1027 A536 120cr black 60 25
  a. With commemorative border 1.50 1.50

Issued to commemorate the 20th anniversary of UNESCO (United Nations Educational, Scientific and Cultural Organization). No. 1027a issued in sheets of 4 with red control number measures 102x48mm. It carries at right a design similar to No. 1027. Inscribed at left: "Bloco comemorativo do 20° aniversario da UNESCO," "Cr$150" and "Departamento dos Correios e Telegrafos". Unwatermarked granite paper, without gum. Sold for 150cr.

Captain Antonio Correia Pinto and Map of Lages
A537

Formée Cross and Southern Cross
A538

Perf. 11½x11

1966, Nov. 22 Photo. Wmk. 267

1028 A537 30cr salmon pink 35 15

Issued to commemorate the bicentenary of the arrival of Capt. Antonio Correia Pinto.

1966, Dec. 4 *Perf. 11½*

1029 A538 100cr blue green 45 15

Issued to commemorate LUBRAPEX 1966 philatelic exhibition at the National Museum of Fine Arts, Rio de Janeiro.

Madonna and Child
A539

Madonna and Child
A540

Perf. 11½x11

1966, Dec. Photo. Wmk. 267

1030 A539 30cr blue green 30 15

Perf. 11½

1031 A540 35cr sal. & ultra. 25 20
  a. 150cr sal. & ultra. 1.25 1.25

Christmas 1966.

No. 1031a measures 46x103mm. and is printed in sheets of 4. It is inscribed "Pax Hominibus" (but not "Brasil Correio") and carries the Madonna shown on No. 1031. Issued without gum.

Issue dates: 30cr, Dec. 8; 35cr, Dec. 22; 150cr, Dec. 28.

Arms of Laguna
A541

1967, Jan. 4 Engr. *Perf. 11x11½*

1032 A541 60cr sepia 25 15

Issued to commemorate the centenary of the Post and Telegraph Agency of Laguna, Santa Catarina.

Railroad Bridge
A542

1967, Feb. 16 Photo. Wmk. 267

1033 A542 50cr dp. orange 60 20

Centenary of the Santos-Jundiai railroad.

Black Madonna of Czestochowa, Polish Eagle and Cross
A543

1967, Mar. 12 *Perf. 11x11½*

1034 A543 50cr yellow, blue & rose red 60 20

Issued to commemorate the thousandth anniversary of the adoption of Christianity in Poland.

Research Rocket
A544

Anita Garibaldi
A545

1967, March 23 *Perf. 11½x11*

1035 A544 50cr blk. & brt. bl. 75 30

World Meteorological Day, March 23.

Perf. 11x11½

1967–69 Photo. Wmk. 267

Portraits: 1c, Mother Joana Angelica. 2c, Marilia de Dirceu. 3c, Dr. Rita Lobato. 6c, Ana Neri. 10c, Darcy Vargas.

1036	A545	1c deep ultra.	10	5
1037	"	2c red brown	10	5
1038	"	3c bright green	20	8
1039	"	5c black	30	8
1040	"	6c brown	30	8
1041	"	10c dark slate green ('69)	2.00	75
		Nos. 1036–1041 (6)	3.00	1.09

Issue dates: 1c, May 3; 2c, Aug. 14; 3c, June 7; 5c, Apr. 14; 6c, May 14, 1967; 10c, June 18, 1969.

VARIG Airlines
A546

Madonna and Child, by Robert Feruzzi
A548

Lions Emblem and Globes
A547

1967, May 8 *Perf. 11½x11*

1046 A546 6c brt. bl. & black 30 25

40th anniversary of VARIG Airlines.

1967, May 9 Engr. *Perf. 11x11½*

1047 A547 6c green 50 25
  a. Souv. sheet 1.00 1.00

Issued to commemorate the 50th anniversary of Lions International. No. 1047a contains one imperf. stamp similar to No. 1047. Green inscription and Lions emblem in margin. Size: 131x80mm. Sold for 15c.

1967, May 14 Photo. *Perf. 11½x11*

1048 A548 5c violet 30 25
  a. 15c, souv. sheet 1.00 1.00

Issued for Mother's Day. No. 1048a contains one 15c imperf. stamp in design of No. 1048. Violet marginal inscription. Size: 129x77mm.

Prince Akihito and Princess Michiko
A549

1967, May 25 *Perf. 11x11½*

1049	A549	10c black & pink	40	20

Issued to commemorate the visit to Brazil of Crown Prince Akihito and Princess Michiko of Japan.

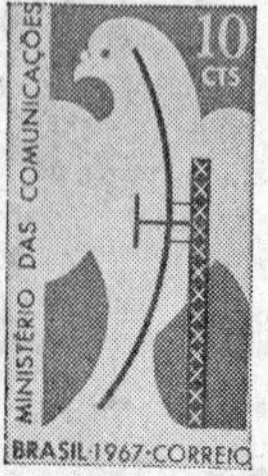

Carrier Pigeon and Radar Screen
A550

Brother Vicente do Salvador
A551

Perf. 11½x11

1967, June 20 Photo. **Wmk. 267**

1050	A550	10c slate & bright pink	40	20

Issued to commemorate the opening of the Communications Ministry in Brasilia.

1967, June 28 Engraved

1051	A551	5c brown	35	25

Issued to commemorate the 400th anniversary of the birth of Brother Vicente do Salvador (1564–1636), founder of Franciscan convent in Rio de Janeiro, and historian.

Boy, Girl and 4-S Emblem
A552

1967, July 12 Photo. *Perf. 11½*

1052	A552	5c green & black	30	20

National 4-S (4-H) Day.

Möbius Strip
A553

1967, July 21 *Perf. 11x11½*

1053	A553	5c brt. bl. & black	30	25

Issued to commemorate the 6th Brazilian Mathematical Congress.

Fish
A554

1967, Aug. 1 *Perf. 11½*

1054	A554	5c slate	50	25

Bicentenary of city of Piracicaba.

Golden Rose and Papal Arms
A555

1967, Aug. 15

1055	A555	20c magenta & yel.	1.25	50

Issued to commemorate the offering of a golden rose by Pope Paul VI to the Virgin Mary of Fatima (Our Lady of Peace), Patroness of Brazil.

General Sampaio
A556

King Olaf of Norway
A557

1967, Aug. 25 Engr. *Perf. 11½x11*

1056	A556	5c blue	30	25

Issued to honor General Antonio de Sampaio, hero of the Battle of Tutui.

1967, Sept. 8 Photogravure

1057	A557	10c brown orange	30	25

Visit of King Olaf of Norway.

Sun over Sugar Loaf, Botafogo Bay
A558

Nilo Peçanha
A559

Photogravure and Embossed

1967, Sept. 25 *Perf. 11½* **Wmk. 267**

1058	A558	10c blk. & dp. org.	30	20

Issued to commemorate the 22nd meeting of the International Monetary Fund, International Bank for Reconstruction and Development, International Financial Corporation and International Development Association.

Perf. 11½x11

1967, Oct. 1 Photo. **Wmk. 267**

1059	A559	5c brown violet	30	25

Issued to commemorate the centenary of the birth of Nilo Peçanha (1867–1924), President of Brazil 1909–1910.

Virgin of the Apparition and Basilica of Aparecida
A560

Cockerel, Festival Emblem
A561

1967, Oct. 11 *Perf. 11½*

1060	A560	5c ultra. & dull yel.	50	25
		a. Souv. sheet of 2	1.50	1.50

Issued to commemorate the 250th anniversary of the discovery of the statue of Our Lady of the Apparition, now in the National Basilica of the Apparition at Aparecida do Norte.

No. 1060a contains imperf. 5c and 10c stamps similar to No. 1060. Blue marginal inscriptions with pink and blue design. Issued Dec. 27, 1967, for Christmas. Size: 77½x129mm.

Engraved and Photogravure

1967, Oct. 16 *Perf. 11½x11*

1061	A561	20c blk. & multi.	75	40

Second International Folksong Festival.

Balloon, Plane and Rocket
A562

Perf. 11x11½

1967, Oct. 18 Photo. **Unwmkd.**

1062	A562	10c blue	60	35
		a. 15c, souv. sheet	1.25	1.25

Issued for the Week of the Wing, Oct. 18–23. No. 1062a contains one imperf. 15c stamp similar to No. 1062, blue marginal design and inscription; it was issued Oct. 23. Size: 130x75mm.

Pres. Arthur Bernardes
A563

Portraits of Brazilian Presidents: 20c, Campos Salles. 50c, Wenceslau Pereira Gomes Braz. 1cr, Washington Pereira de Souza Luiz. 2cr, Castello Branco.

Perf. 11x11½

1967–68 Photogravure **Wmk. 267**

1063	A563	10c blue	25	8
1064	"	20c dk. red brown	50	8
		Engraved		
1065	A563	50c black ('68)	2.00	12
1066	"	1cr lilac rose ('68)	3.00	15
1067	"	2cr emerald ('68)	75	15
		Nos. 1063–1067 (5)	6.50	58

Carnival of Rio
A564

Ships, Anchor and Sailor
A565

1967, Nov. 22 *Perf. 11½x11*

1070	A564	10c lemon, ultra. & pink	40	25
		a. 15c, souv. sheet	1.25	1.25

Issued for International Tourist Year, 1967. No. 1070a contains a 15c imperf. stamp in design of No. 1070. Pink marginal design and inscription. Size: 76x130mm. Issued Nov. 24.

1967, Dec. 6

1071	A565	10c ultramarine	40	30

Issued for Navy Week.

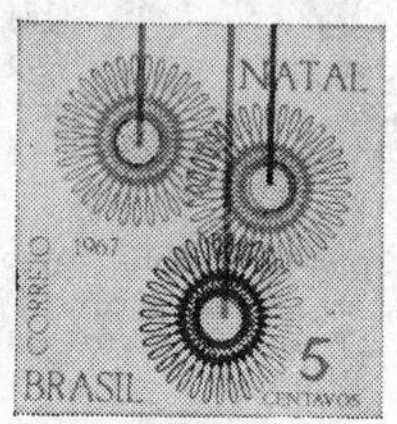

Christmas Decorations
A566

1967, Dec. 8 *Perf. 11½*

1072	A566	5c car., yel. & blue	40	25

Christmas 1967.

Olavo Bilac, Planes, Tank and Aircraft Carrier—A567

Perf. 11x11½

1967, Dec. 16 Photo. **Wmk. 267**

1073	A567	5c brt. blue & yel.	40	25

Issued for Reservists' Day and to honor Olavo Bilac, sponsor of compulsory military service.

Rodrigues de Carvalho
A568

1967, Dec. 18 Engr. *Perf. 11½x11*

1074	A568	10c green	30	25

Issued to commemorate the centenary of the birth of Rodrigues de Carvalho, poet and lawyer.

Orlando Rangel
A569

Photogravure

1968, Feb. 29 *Perf. 11x11½*

1075	A569	5c lt. greenish blue & black	60	35

Issued to commemorate the centenary of the birth of Orlando de Fonseca Rangel, pioneer of pharmaceutical industry in Brazil.

Virgin of Paranagua and Diver
A570

Map of Brazil Showing Manaus
A571

1968, Mar. 9 ***Perf. 11½x11***

1076 A570 10c dk. slate green & bright yellow green 50 30

Issued to commemorate the 250th anniversary of the first underwater explorations at Paranagua.

1968, Mar. 13 Photo. **Wmk. 267**

1077 A571 10c yellow, green & red 40 30

Issued to publicize the free port of Manaus on the Amazon River.

Human Rights Flame
A572

Paul Harris and Rotary Emblem
A573

1968, Mar. 21 ***Perf. 11½x11***

1078 A572 10c blue & salmon 40 30

International Human Rights Year.

1968, Apr. 19 Litho. **Unwmkd.**

Without Gum

1079 A573 20c green & orange brown 1.25 70

Issued to commemorate the centenary of the birth of Paul Percy Harris (1868–1947), founder of Rotary International.

Pedro Alvares Cabral and his Fleet—A574

Design: 20c, First Mass celebrated in Brazil.

1968 Without Gum ***Perf. 11½***

1080 A574 10c multicolored 75 50
1081 " 20c " 1.00 60

Issued to commemorate the 500th anniversary of the birth of Pedro Alvares Cabral, navigator, who took possession of Brazil for Portugal.

Issue dates: 10c, Apr. 22; 20c, July 11.

College Arms
A575

1968, Apr. 22 Photo. **Wmk. 267**

1082 A575 10c violet blue, red & gold 75 35

Centenary of St. Luiz College, São Paulo.

Motherhood, by Henrique Bernardeli
A576

1968, May 12 Litho. **Unwmkd.**

Without Gum

1083 A576 5c multicolored 40 30

Issued for Mother's Day.

Harpy Eagle
A577

Photogravure and Engraved

1968, May 28 **Wmk. 267**

1084 A577 20c brt. bl. & blk. 1.25 60

Sesquicentennial of National Museum.

Brazilian and Japanese Women
A578

1968, June 28 Litho. **Unwmkd.**

Without Gum

1085 A578 10c yellow & multi. 75 50

Issued to commemorate the inauguration of Varig's direct Brazil-Japan airline.

Horse Race
A579

Perf. 11x11½

1968, July 16 Litho. **Unwmkd.**

Without Gum

1086 A579 10c multicolored 50 30

Centenary of the Jockey Club of Brazil.

Musician Wren—A580

Designs: 10c, Red-crested cardinal (vert.). 50c, Royal flycatcher (vert.).

Perf. 11½x11, 11x11½

1968-69 Engraved **Sheet Wmk.**

Without Gum

1087 A580 10c multi. ('69) 75 30
1088 " 20c multicolored 1.25 30
1089 " 50c " 1.75 60

Some stamps in each sheet of Nos. 1087-1089 show parts of a two-line papermaker's watermark: "WESTERPOST / INDUSTRIA BRASILEIRA" with diamond-shaped emblem between last two words. Entire watermark appears in one sheet margin.

Issue dates: 10c, Aug. 20, 1969. 20c, July 19, 1968. 50c, Aug. 2, 1968.

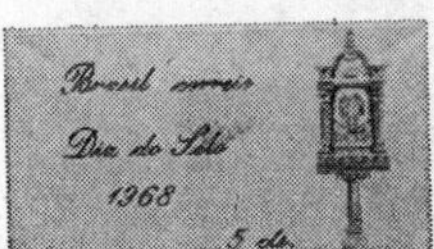

Mailbox and Envelope
A581

Photogravure and Engraved

1968, Aug. 1 ***Perf. 11*** **Wmk. 267**

1091 A581 5c citron, black & green 25 20

Issued for Stamp Day, 1968 and to commemorate the 125th anniversary of the first Brazilian postage stamps.

Emilio Luiz Mallet
A582

Map of South America
A583

Perf. 11½x11

1968, Aug. 25 Engraved **Wmk. 267**

1092 A582 10c pale purple 25 20

Issued to honor Marshal Emilio Luiz Mallet, Baron of Itapevi, patron of the marines.

1968, Sept. 5 Photogravure

1093 A583 10c deep orange 20 20

Visit of President Eduardo Frei of Chile.

Seal of Portuguese Literary School
A584

Photogravure and Engraved

1968, Sept. 10 ***Perf. 11½***

1094 A584 5c pink & green 25 20

Centenary of Portuguese Literary School.

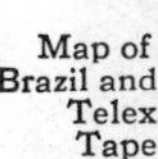

Map of Brazil and Telex Tape
A585

1968, Sept. Photo. ***Perf. 11x11½***

1095 A585 20c citron & bright green 60 25

Linking of 25 Brazilian cities by teletype.

Soldiers' Heads on Medal
A586

Perf. 11½x11

1968, Sept. 24 Litho. **Unwmkd.**

Without Gum

1096 A586 5c blue & gray 30 25

8th American Armed Forces Conference.

Clef, Notes and Sugarloaf Mountain
A587

1968, Sept. 30 ***Perf. 11½***

Without Gum

1097 A587 6c black, yel. & red 60 30

Third International Folksong Festival.

Catalytic Cracking Plant
A588

1968, Oct. 4 **Without Gum**

1098 A588 6c blue & multi. 60 40

Issued to commemorate the 15th anniversary of Petrobras, the national oil company.

Child Protection
A589

Whimsical Girl
A590

Design: 5c, School boy walking toward the sun.

Perf. 11½x11, 11x11½

1968, Oct. 16 Litho. Unwmkd.

Without Gum

1099 A590 5c gray & lt. blue 50 40
1100 A589 10c brt. blue, dark red & black 60 30
1101 A590 20c multicolored 75 30

Issued to commemorate the 22nd anniversary of the United Nations Children's Fund.

Children with Books
A591

1968, Oct. 23 *Perf. 11x11½*

Without Gum

1102 A591 5c multicolored 35 25

Issued to publicize Book Week.

U.N. Emblem and Flags
A592

Perf. 11½x11

1968, Oct. 24 Without Gum

1103 A592 20c black & multi. 75 35

Issued to commemorate the 20th anniversary of the World Health Organization.

Jean Baptiste Debret, Self-portrait
A593

Perf. 11x11½

1968, Oct. 30 Litho. Unwmkd.

Without Gum

1104 A593 10c dark gray & pale yellow 50 25

Issued to commemorate the bi-centenary of the birth of Jean Baptiste Debret, (1768–1848), French painter who worked in Brazil (1816–31). Design includes his "Burden Bearer."

Queen Elizabeth II
A594

1968, Nov. 4 *Perf. 11½*

Without Gum

1105 A594 70c lt. bl. & multi. 1.75 1.00

Issued to commemorate the visit of Queen Elizabeth II of Great Britain.

Francisco Braga
A595

Perf. 11½x11

1968, Nov. 19 Wmk. 267

1106 A595 5c dull red brown 40 25

Issued to commemorate the centenary of the birth of Antonio Francisco Braga, composer of the Hymn of the Flag.

Brazilian Flag
A596

1968, Nov. 19 *Perf. 11½* Unwmkd.

Without Gum

1107 A596 10c multicolored 50 30

Issued for Flag Day.

Clasped Hands and Globe
A597

Perf. 11x11½

1968, Nov. 25 Typo. Unwmkd.

Without Gum

1108 A597 5c multicolored 30 25

Issued for Voluntary Blood Donor's Day.

Old Locomotive—A598

1968, Nov. 28 Litho. *Perf. 11½*

Without Gum

1109 A598 5c multicolored 1.00 50

Centenary of the São Paulo Railroad.

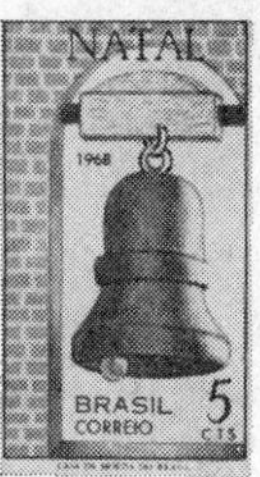

Bell
A599

Francisco Caldas, Jr.
A600

Design: 6c, Santa Claus and boy.

1968 Without Gum *Perf. 11½x11*

1110 A599 5c multicolored 50 25
1111 " 6c " 50 25

Christmas 1968.
Issue dates: 5c, Dec. 12; 6c, Dec. 20.

1968, Dec. 13 Without Gum

1112 A600 10c crimson & blk. 35 20

Issued to commemorate the centenary of the birth of Francisco Caldas, Jr., journalist and founder of Correio de Povo, newspaper.

Map of Brazil, War Memorial and Reservists' Emblem
A601

Perf. 11x11½

1968, Dec. 16 Photo. Wmk. 267

1113 A601 5c blue green & orange brown 50 25

Issued for Reservists' Day.

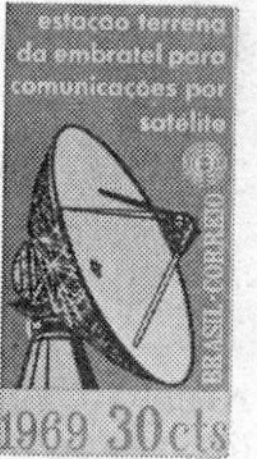

Radar Antenna
A602

Viscount of Rio Branco
A603

Perf. 11½x11

1969, Feb. 28 Litho. Unwmkd.

Without Gum

1114 A602 30c ultra., lt. blue & black 1.25 60

Issued to publicize the inauguration of EMBRATEL, satellite communications ground station bringing U.S. television to Brazil via Telstar.

1969, Mar. 16 Without Gum

1115 A603 5c black & buff 35 25

Issued to commemorate the 150th anniversary of the birth of José Maria da Silva Paranhos, Viscount of Rio Branco (1819–1880), statesman.

St. Gabriel
A604

1969, Mar. 24 Without Gum

1116 A604 5c multicolored 50 25

Issued to honor St. Gabriel as patron saint of telecommunications.

Shoemaker's Last and Globe
A605

Perf. 11x11½

1969, Mar. 29 Litho. Unwmkd.

Without Gum

1117 A605 5c multicolored 35 25

Issued to publicize the 4th International Shoe Fair, Novo Hamburgo.

Allan Kardec
A606

1969, Mar. 31 Photo. Wmk. 267

1118 A606 5c bright green & orange brown 40 25

Issued to commemorate the centenary of the death of Allan Kardec (pen name of Leon Hippolyto Denizard Rivail, 1803–1869), French physician and spiritist.

Men of 3 Races and Arms of Cuiabá
A607

1969, Apr. 8 Litho. Unwmkd.

Without Gum

1119 A607 5c black & multi. 30 25

Issued to commemorate the 250th anniversary of the founding of Cuiabá, capital of Matto Grosso.

State Mint—A608

1969, Apr. 11 *Perf. 11½*

Without Gum

1120 A608 5c olive bis & org. 60 40

Issued to commemorate the opening of the state money printing plant.

Brazilian Stamps and Emblem
A609

Perf. 11x11½

1969, Apr. 30 Litho. Unwmkd.

Without Gum

1121 A609 5c multicolored 40 25

Issued to commemorate the 50th anniversary of the São Paulo Philatelic Society.

St. Anne, Baroque Statue
A610

1969, May 8 *Perf. 11½*

Without Gum

1122 A610 5c lemon & multi. 60 40

Issued for Mother's Day.

ILO Emblem
A611

Perf. 11x11½

1969, May 13 Photo. Wmk. 267

1123 A611 5c deep rose red & gold 40 20

Issued to commemorate the 50th anniversary of the International Labor Organization.

Diving Platform and Swimming Pool A612 — Mother and Child at Window A613

Lithographed and Photogravure

Perf. 11½x11

1969, June 13 Unwmkd.

Without Gum

1124 A612 20c bister brown, blk.& bl. grn. 1.00 60

40th anniversary of the Cearense Water Sports Club, Fortaleza.

1969 Lithographed *Perf. 11½*

Designs: 20c, Modern sculpture by Felicia Leirner. 50c, "The Sun Sets in Brasilia," by Danilo di Prete. 1cr, Angelfish, painting by Aldemir Martins.

Size: 24x36mm.

1125 A613 10c orange & multi. 75 30

Size: 33x34mm.

1126 A613 20c red & multi. 75 60

Size: 33x53mm.

1127 A613 50c yel. & multi. 2.50 1.50

Without Gum

1128 A613 1cr gray & multi 3.00 1.50

Issued to publicize the 10th Biennial Art Exhibition, São Paulo, Sept.–Dec. 1969.

Angelfish
A614

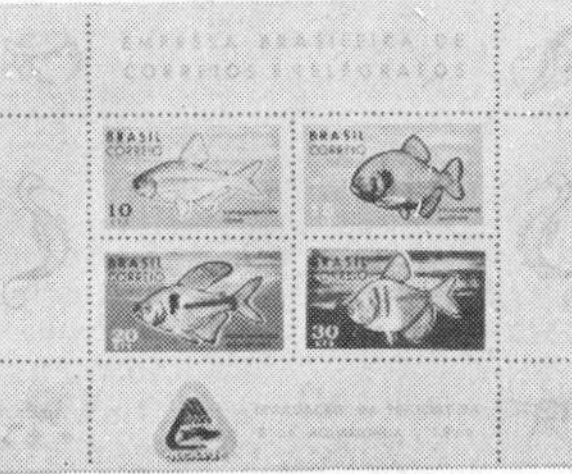

Fish
A615

Fish: 10c, Tetra. 15c, Piranha. No. 1130c, Megalamphodus megalopterus. 30c, Black tetra.

Perf. 11½

1969, July 21 Litho. Wmk. 267

1129 A614 20c multicolored 80 35

Souvenir Sheet

Perf. 10½x11½

1969, July 24 Unwmkd.

1130 A615 Sheet of four 3.50 3.50
- *a.* 10c yellow & multicolored 75 75
- *b.* 15c bright blue & multicolored 75 75
- *c.* 20c green & multicolored 75 75
- *d.* 30c orange & multicolored 75 75

Issued to publicize the work of ACAPI, an organization devoted to the preservation and development of fish in Brazil.

No. 1130 contains 4 stamps (size: 38½x21mm.). Greenish margin with commemorative inscription, marine life design and ACAPI emblem. Size: 132½x98½mm.

L. O. Teles de Menezes A616 — Mailman A617

Perf. 11½x11

1969, July 26 Photo. Wmk. 267

1131 A616 50c deep orange & blue green 2.00 1.00

Centenary of Spiritism press in Brazil.

1969, Aug. 1

1132 A617 30c blue 2.00 1.00

Issued for Stamp Day.

Map of Brazil A618 — Gen. Tasso Fragoso A620

Railroad Bridge
A619

Lithographed

1969, Aug. 25 *Perf. 11½* Unwmkd.

Without Gum

1133 A618 10c light ultra., grn. & yellow 50 25

Perf. 11x11½

1134 A619 20c multicolored 1.00 40

Engraved *Perf. 11½x11* Wmk. 267

With Gum

1135 A620 20c green 1.00 50

No. 1133 honors the Army as guardian of security; No. 1134, as promoter of development. No. 1135 commemorates the birth centenary of Gen. Tasso Fragoso.

Jupia Dam, Parana River
A621

Perf. 11½

1969, Sept. 10 Litho. Unwmkd.

Without Gum

1136 A621 20c lt. bl. & multi. 50 50

Issued to commemorate the inauguration of the Jupia Dam, part of the Urubupunga hydroelectric system serving Sao Paulo.

Gandhi and Spinning Wheel
A622

1969, Oct. 2 *Perf. 11x11½*

1137 A622 20c yellow & black 50 30

Issued to commemorate the centenary of the birth of Mohandas K. Gandhi (1869–1948), leader in India's fight for independence.

Santos Dumont, Eiffel Tower and Module Landing on Moon
A623

1969, Oct. 17 *Perf. 11½*

Without Gum

1138 A623 50c dk. bl. & multi. 2.00 1.25

Man's first landing on the moon, July 20, 1969. See note after U.S. No. C76.

Smelting Plant
A624

1969, Oct. 26 *Perf. 11½* Unwmkd.

Without Gum

1139 A624 20c multicolored 50 40

Expansion of Brazil's steel industry.

Steel Furnace
A625

1969, Oct. 31 Litho. Without Gum

1140 A625 10c yellow & multi. 50 40

25th anniversary of Acesita Steel Works.

Water Vendor, by J. B. Debret
A626

Design: 30c, Street Scene, by Debret.

1969–70 Without Gum

1141 A626 20c multi. 1.25 50

1141A " 30c " 1.25 1.00

Issued to commemorate the 200th anniversary of the birth of Jean Baptiste Debret (1768–1848), painter.

Issue dates: 20c, Nov. 5, 1969; 30c, May 19, 1970.

Exhibition Emblem
A627

1969, Nov. 15 ***Perf. 11½x11***

Without Gum

1142 A627 10c multicolored 50 25

Issued to publicize the ABUEXPO 69 Philatelic Exposition, Sao Paulo, Nov. 15–23.

Plane—A628

1969, Nov. 23 Without Gum

1143 A628 50c multicolored 2.50 1.50

Issued to publicize the year of the expansion of the national aviation industry.

Pelé Scoring
A629

1969–70 Without Gum

1144 A629 10c multicolored 75 75

Souvenir Sheet

Imperf.

1145 A629 75c multi. ('70) 5.00 5.00

Issued to commemorate the 1,000th goal scored by Pelé, Brazilian soccer player.

No. 1145 contains one imperf. stamp with simulated perforations, commemorative marginal inscription. Size: 80x119 mm.

Issued dates: 10c, Nov. 28, 1969. 75c, Jan. 23, 1970.

Madonna and Child from Villa Velha Monastery
A630

Lithographed

1969, Dec. ***Perf. 11½*** **Unwmkd.**

Without Gum

1146 A630 10c gold & multi. 50 25

Souvenir Sheet

Imperf.

1147 A630 75c gold & multi. 3.00 3.00

Christmas 1969.

No. 1147 has simulated perforations; commemorative inscription and Christmas decorations in margin. Size: 136x102mm.

Issue dates: 10c, Dec. 8; 75c, Dec. 18.

Destroyer and Submarine
A631

Perf. 11x11½

1969, Dec. 9 Engraved Wmk. 267

1148 A631 5c bluish gray 50 25

Issued for Navy Day.

Dr. Herman Blumenau
A632

1969, Dec. 26 ***Perf. 11½*** **Wmk. 267**

1149 A632 20c gray green 1.00 60

Issued to commemorate the 150th anniversary of the birth of Dr. Herman Blumenau (1819–1899), founder of Blumenau, Santa Catarina State.

Carnival Scene—A633

Sugarloaf Mountain, Mask, Confetti and Streamers
A634

Designs: 5c, Jumping boy and 2 women (vert.). 20c, Clowns. 50c, Drummer.

1969–70 Litho. Unwmkd.

Without Gum

1150	A633	5c multicolored	50	30
1151	"	10c "	50	30
1152	"	20c "	60	40
1153	A634	30c multi. ('70)	3.00	1.50
1154	"	50c " ('70)	2.50	1.50
		Nos. 1150–1154 (5)	7.10	4.00

Carico Carnival, Rio de Janeiro.

Issue dates: Nos. 1150–1152, Dec. 29, 1969. Nos. 1153–1154, Feb. 5, 1970.

Opening Bars of "Il Guarani" with Antonio Carlos Gomes Conducting
A635

1970, Mar. 19 Litho. ***Perf. 11½***

Without Gum

1155 A635 20c black, yellow, gray & brown 75 40

Issued to commemorate the centenary of the opera Il Guarani, by Antonio Carlos Gomes.

Church of Penha
A636

1970, Apr. 6 ***Perf. 11½*** **Unwmkd.**

Without Gum

1156 A636 20c black & multi. 40 20

Issued to commemorate the 400th anniversary of the Church of Penha, State of Esperito Santo.

Assembly Building
A637

Designs: 50c, Reflecting Pool. 1cr, Presidential Palace.

1970, Apr. 21 Without Gum

1157	A637	20c multicolored	1.00	60
1158	"	50c "	3.00	1.50
1159	"	1cr "	3.00	1.50

10th anniversary of Brasilia.

Symbolic Water Design
A638

1970, May 5 ***Perf. 11½*** **Unwmkd.**

Without Gum

1161 A638 50c multicolored 2.50 1.50

Issued to publicize the Rondon Project for the development of the Amazon River basin.

Marshal Manoel Luiz Osorio and Osorio Arms—A639

1970, May 8 Without Gum

1162 A639 20c multicolored 2.00 75

Issued to commemorate the inauguration of the Marshal Osorio Historical Park.

Madonna, from San Antonio Monastery, Rio de Janeiro
A640

Detail from Brasilia Cathedral
A641

1970, May 10 Without Gum

1163 A640 20c multicolored 60 50

Issued for Mother's Day.

1970, May 27 Engraved Wmk. 267

1164 A641 20c lt. yellow green 40 30

8th National Eucharistic Congress, Brasilia.

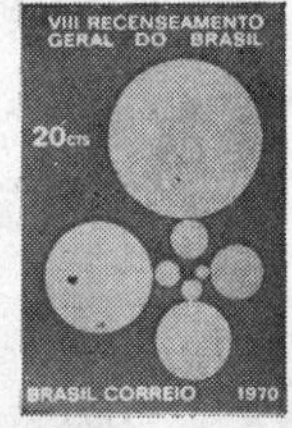

Census Symbol
A642

Lithographed

1970, June 22 ***Perf. 11½*** **Unwmkd.**

Without Gum

1165 A642 20c green & yellow 75 40

Issued to publicize the 8th general census.

Soccer Cup, Maps of Brazil and Mexico
A643

Swedish Flag and Player Holding Rimet Cup—A644

Designs: 2cr, Chilean flag and soccer. 3cr, Mexican flag and soccer.

1970 Without Gum

1166	A643	50c blk., lt. blue & gold	1.00	1.00
1167	A644	1cr pink & multi.	3.50	1.50
1168	"	2cr gray & multi.	5.00	1.50
1169	"	3cr multicolored	4.00	1.00

Issued to commemorate the 9th World Soccer Championships for the Jules Rimet Cup, Mexico City, May 30–June 21. No. 1166 commemorates Brazil's victory.

Issue dates: No. 1166, June 24; Nos. 1167–1169, Aug. 4.

Corcovado Christ and Map of South America
A645

1970, July 18 Without Gum

1170 A645 50c brown, dark red & blue 2.50 1.25

Issued to publicize the 6th World Congress of Marist Brothers' Alumni.

Pandiá Calógeras
A646

Perf. 11½x11

1970, Aug. 25 Photo. **Unwmkd.**

1171 A646 20c blue green 75 50

Issued to honor Pandiá Calógeras, Minister of War.

Brazilian Military Emblems and Map
A647

Perf. 11x11½

1970, Sept. 8 Litho. **Unwmkd.**

Without Gum

1172 A647 20c gray & multi. 60 50

25th anniversary of victory in World War II.

Annunciation (Brazilian Primitive Painting)
A648

1970, Sept. 29 ***Perf. 11½***

Without Gum

1173 A648 20c multicolored 1.75 1.00

Issued for St. Gabriel's (patron saint of communications) Day.

Boy in Library
A649

U.N. Emblem
A650

1970, Oct. 23 Without Gum

1174 A649 20c multicolored 1.75 1.00

Issued to publicize Book Week.

1970, Oct. 24 Without Gum

1175 A650 50c dk. blue, lt. blue & silver 2.00 1.50

25th anniversary of the United Nations.

Rio de Janeiro, 1820—A651

Designs: 50c, LUBRAPEX 70 emblem. 1 cr, Rio de Janeiro with Sugar Loaf Mountain, 1970. No. 1179, like 20c.

1970, Oct. Without Gum

1176 A651 20c multicolored 1.50 75
1177 " 50c yel. brn. & blk. 3.00 1.50
1178 " 1cr multicolored 2.50 2.00

Souvenir Sheet

Imperf.

1179 A651 1cr multicolored 5.00 5.00

Issued to commemorate LUBRAPEX 70, third Portuguese-Brazilian Philatelic Exhibition, Rio de Janeiro, Oct. 24–31. No. 1179 contains one stamp, black marginal inscription. Size: 60x80mm.

Issue dates: Nos. 1176–1178, Oct. 27. No. 1179, Oct. 31.

Holy Family by Candido Portinari
A652

1970, Dec. Litho. ***Perf. 11½***

Without Gum

1180 A652 50c multicolored 1.25 1.00

Souvenir Sheet

Imperf.

1181 A652 1cr multicolored 4.50 4.50

Christmas 1970. No. 1181 contains one stamp with simulated perforations. Light yellow green margin with red and black inscription. Size: 106x52mm. Issue dates: 50c, Dec. 1; 1cr, Dec. 8.

Battleship
A653

CIH Emblem
A654

1970, Dec. 11 Litho. ***Perf. 11½***

Without Gum

1182 A653 20c multicolored 1.25 1.00

Navy Day.

1971, Mar. 28 Litho. ***Perf. 11½***

Without Gum

1183 A654 50c black & red 2.00 1.25

Third Inter-American Housing Congress, Mar. 27–Apr. 3.

Links Around Globe
A655

1971, Mar. 31 Litho. ***Perf. 12½x11***

Without Gum

1184 A655 20c green, yellow, black & red 75 50

International year against racial discrimination.

Morpho Melacheilus
A656

Design: 1cr, Papilio thoas brasiliensis.

Perf. 11x11½

1971, Apr. 28 Litho. **Unwmkd.**

Without Gum

1185 A656 20c multicolored 1.50 40
1186 " 1cr " 6.00 3.50

Madonna and Child
A657

1971, May 9 Litho. ***Perf. 11½***

Without Gum

1187 A657 20c multicolored 75 40

Mother's Day, 1971.

Basketball
A658

1971, May 19 Without Gum

1188 A658 70c multicolored 2.25 1.25

6th World Women's Basketball Championship.

Map of Trans-Amazon Highway
A660 A659

Lithographed

1971, July 1 ***Perf. 11½*** **Unwmkd.**

Without Gum

1189 A659 40c multicolored 2.50 1.50
1190 A660 1cr " 2.50 2.00

Trans-Amazon Highway. Nos. 1189–1190 printed se-tenant in sheets of 28 (4x7). Horizontal rows contain 2 pairs of 1189–1190 with a label between. Each label carries different inscription.

Man's Head, by Victor Mairelles de Lima
A661

Design: 1cr, Arab Violinist, by Pedro Américo.

1971, Aug. 1 Without Gum

1191 A661 40c pink & multi. 2.50 1.25
1192 " 1cr gray & multi. 3.00 2.00

Stamp Day.

Duke of Caxias and Map of Brazil
A662

1971, Aug. 23 Photogravure

1193 A662 20c yellow green & red brown 75 40

Army Day.

Anita Garibaldi
A663

1971, Aug. 30 Litho. Without Gum

1194 A663 20c multicolored 75 50

Anita Garibaldi (1821–1849), heroine in liberation of Brazil.

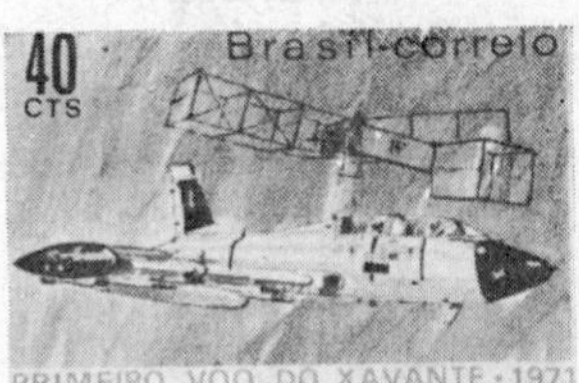

Xavante Jet and Santos Dumont's Plane, 1910—A664

1971, Sept. 6 Without Gum

1195 A664 40c yel. & multi. 1.75 75

First flight of Xavante jet plane.

Flags and Map of Central American Nations
A665

"71" in French Flag Colors
A666

1971, Sept. 15 **Without Gum**

1196 A665 40c ocher & multi. 1.25 60

Sesquicentennial of the independence of Central American nations.

1971, Sept. 16 **Without Gum**

1197 A666 1.30cr ultramarine & multi. 2.00 1.50

French Exhibition.

Black Mother, by Lucilio de Albuquerque
A667

Archangel Gabriel
A668

1971, Sept. 28 **Without Gum**

1198 A667 40c multicolored 1.00 60

Centenary of law guaranteeing personal freedom starting at birth.

Perf. 11½x11

1971, Sept. 29 **Without Gum**

1199 A668 40c multicolored 1.00 75

St. Gabriel's Day.

Bridge over River
A669

Children's Drawings: 35c, People crossing bridge. 60c, Woman with hat.

1971, Oct. 25 ***Perf. 11½***

Without Gum

1200 A669 35c pink, bl. & blk. 1.00 75
1201 " 45c blk. & multi. 1.25 75
1202 " 60c olive & multi. 1.25 75

Children's Day.

Werkhäuserii Superba
A670

1971, Nov. 16 **Without Gum**

1203 A670 40c blue & multi. 2.00 1.00

In memory of Carlos Werkhauser, botanist.

Greek Key Pattern "25"
A671

Design: 40c, like 20c but inscribed "sesc / servicio social / do comercio."

1971, Dec. 3

Without Gum

1204 A671 20c black & blue 1.50 75
1205 " 40c blk. & orange 1.50 75

25th anniversary of SENAC (national apprenticeship system) and SESC (commercial social service). Nos. 1204–1205 printed se-tenant.

Gunboat
A672

1971, Dec. 8 ***Perf. 11***

Without Gum

1206 A672 20c blue & multi. 1.00 40

Navy Day.

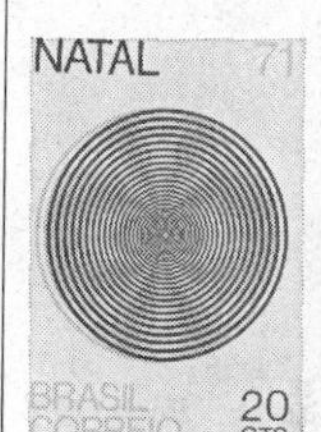

Cross and Circles
A673

Washing of Bonfim Church, Salvador, Bahia
A674

1971, Dec. 11

1207 A673 20c car. & blue 1.25 50
1208 " 75c silver & gray 60 50
1209 " 1.30cr blk., yel., grn. & blue 4.00 2.00

Christmas 1971.

1972, Feb. 18 Litho. ***Perf. 11½x11***

Designs: 40c, Grape Festival, Rio Grande do Sul. 75c, Festival of the Virgin of Nazareth, Belém. 1.30cr, Winter Arts Festival, Ouro Preto.

Without Gum

1210 A674 20c silver & multi. 2.00 75
1211 " 40c " " 2.00 75
1212 " 75c " " 2.50 1.75
1213 " 1.30cr " " 3.00 1.50

Pres. Lanusse and Flag of Argentina
A675

1972, Mar. 13 ***Perf. 11x11½***

Without Gum

1214 A675 40c blue & multi. 2.50 1.50

Visit of Lt. Gen. Alejandro Agustin Lanusse, president of Argentina.

Presidents Castello Branco, Costa e Silva and Garrastazu Medici—A676

1972, Mar. 29 **Without Gum**

1215 A676 20c emer. & multi. 1.50 75

Anniversary of 1964 revolution.

Post Office Emblem
A677

Perf. 11½x11

1972, Apr. 10 Photo. Unwmkd.

1216 A677 20c red brown 60 10

No. 1216 is luminescent.

Pres. Thomas and Portuguese Flag
A678

1972, Apr. 22 Litho. ***Perf. 11***

Without Gum

1217 A678 75c olive brown & multi. 2.50 1.50

Visit of Pres. Américo Thomas of Portugal to Brazil, Apr. 22–27.

Soil Research (CPRM)
A679

1972, May 3 ***Perf. 11½***

Without Gum; Multicolored

1218 A679 20c *shown* 2.00 50
1219 " 40c *Offshore oil rig* 2.00 1.00
1220 " 75c *Hydroelectric dam* 2.00 2.00
1221 " 1.30cr *Iron ore production* 2.50 1.50

Industrial development. Stamps are inscribed with names of industrial firms.

Souvenir Sheet

Poster for Modern Art Week 1922
A680

1972, May 5

1222 A680 1cr black & car. 6.00 4.00

50th anniversary of Modern Art Week. No. 1222 contains one stamp. Silver margin with black inscription. Size: 78x110 mm.

Mailman, Map of Brazil and Letters
A681

Designs: 45c, "Telecommunications" (vert.). 60c, Tropospheric scatter system. 70c, Road map of Brazil and worker.

1972, May 26 **Without Gum**

1223 A681 35c blue & multi. 2.50 75
1224 " 45c silver & multi. 1.75 1.25
1225 " 60c black & multi. 1.50 1.00
1226 " 70c multicolored 1.75 1.00

Unification of communications in Brazil.

Development Type and

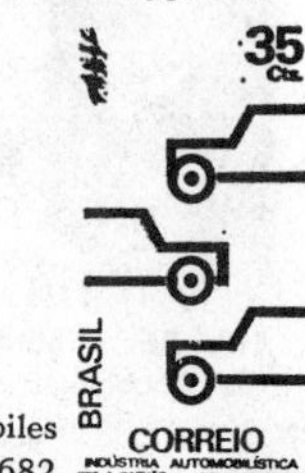

Automobiles
A682

Designs: 45c, Ships. 70c, Ingots.

Perf. 11x11½, 11½x11

1972, June 21 **Photogravure**

1227 A682 35c blk., magenta & orange 75 50

Lithographed

1228 A679 45c lilac & multi. 75 60
1229 " 70c vio. & multi. 1.25 50

Industrial development. The 35c is luminescent.

Soccer
A683

Designs: 75c, Folk music. 1.30cr, Plastic arts.

Perf. 11½x11

1972, July 7 Photo. Unwmkd.

1230 A683 20c blk. & yellow 1.25 75
1231 " 75c black & verm. 2.50 1.50
1232 " 1.30cr blk. & ultra. 2.50 1.25

150th anniversary of independence. No. 1230 publicizes the 1972 sports tournament, a part of independence celebrations.

Nos. 1230–1232 are luminescent.

Souvenir Sheet

Shout of Independence, by Pedro Américo de Figueiredo e Melo
A684

1972, July 19 Litho. *Perf. 11½*

Without Gum

1233 A684 1cr multicolored 3.50 3.50

4th Interamerican Philatelic Exhibition, EXFILBRA, Rio de Janeiro, Aug 26–Sept. 2. No. 1233 contains one stamp (55x 37mm.). Black and multicolored margin with white inscription. Size: 125x87mm.

Figurehead—A685

Designs: 60c, Gauchos dancing fandango. 75c, Acrobats (capoeira). 1.15cr, Karajá (ceramic) doll. 1.30cr, Mock bullfight (bumba meu boi).

1972, Aug. 6 Without Gum

1234 A685 45c multicolored 1.50 75
1235 " 60c org. & multi. 1.50 75
1236 " 75c gray & multi. 1.50 1.00
1237 " 1.15cr multicolored 75 1.00
1238 " 1.30cr yel. & multi. 4.50 1.75
Nos. 1234–1238 (5) 9.75 5.25

Brazilian folklore.

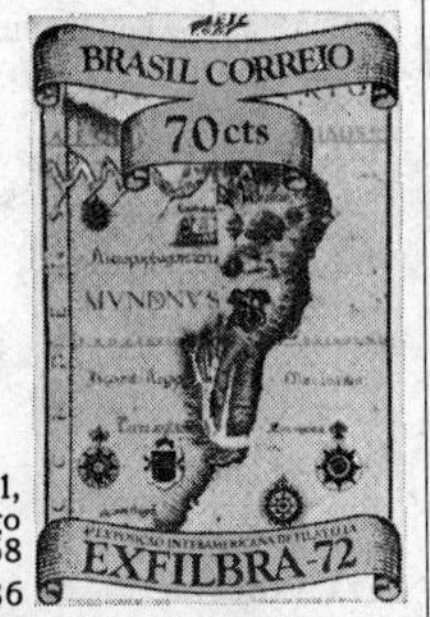

Map of Brazil, by Diego Homem, 1568
A686

Designs: 1cr, Map of Americas, by Nicholas Visscher, 1652. 2cr, Map of Americas, by Lopo Homem, 1519.

1972, Aug. 26 Litho. *Perf. 11½*

Without Gum

1239 A686 70c multicolored 2.25 1.25
1240 " 1cr " 4.00 2.00
1241 " 2cr " 2.25 1.75

4th Inter-American Philatelic Exhibition, EXFILBRA, Rio de Janeiro, Aug. 26–Sept. 2.

Dom Pedro Proclaimed Emperor, by Jean Baptiste Debret—A687

Designs: 30c, Founding of Brazil (people with imperial flag; vert.). 1cr, Coronation of Emperor Dom Pedro (vert.). 2cr, Dom Pedro commemorative medal. 3.50cr, Independence Monument, Ipiranga.

1972, Sept. 4 Litho. *Perf. 11½x11*

1242 A687 30c yel. & green 2.50 2.50
1243 " 70c pink & rose lilac 1.50 1.00
1244 " 1cr buff & red brown 10.00 2.50
1245 " 2cr pale yellow & black 5.00 2.50
1246 " 3.50cr gray & black 3.50 3.50
Nos. 1242–1246 (5) 22.50 12.00

Sesquicentennial of independence.

Souvenir Sheet

"Automobile Race"—A688

1972, Nov. 14 *Perf. 11½*

1247 A688 2cr multicolored 5.00 5.00

Emerson Fittipaldi, Brazilian world racing champion. No. 1247 contains one stamp. Multicolored margin with race car design and black inscription. Size: 120x 86½mm.

Numeral and Post Office Emblem
A689

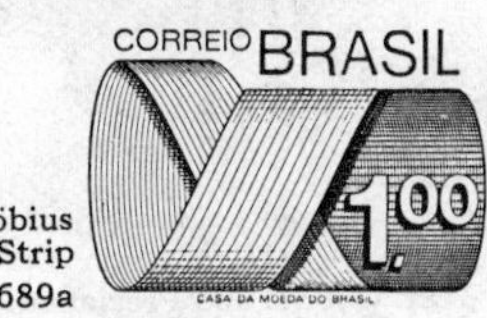

Möbius Strip
A689a

Photogravure

1972–75 *Perf. 11½x11* Unwmkd.

1248 A689 5c orange 10 5
a. Wmk. 267 50 8
1249 A689 10c brown ('73) 20 5
a. Wmk. 267 20 8
1250 A689 15c brt. bl. ('75) 10 5
1251 " 20c ultramarine 10 5
1252 " 25c sepia ('75) 10 5
1253 " 30c deep carmine 20 10
1254 " 40c dk. green ('73) 25 10
1255 " 50c olive ('74) 20 10
1256 " 70c red lilac ('75) 15 10

Engraved *Perf. 11½*

1257 A689a 1cr lilac ('74) 30 10
1258 " 2cr greenish blue ('74) 40 10
1259 " 4cr org. & violet ('75) 50 10
1260 " 5cr brn., car. & buff ('74) 60 10
1261 " 10cr grn., blk. & buff ('74) 1.00 25
Nos. 1248–1261 (14) 4.20 1.30

The 5cr and 10cr have beige lithographed multiple Post Office emblem underprint.

Nos. 1248–1261 are luminescent. Nos. 1248a and 1249a are not.

Hand Writing "Mobral"
A690

Designs: 20c, Multiracial group and population growth curve. 1cr, People and hands holding house. 2cr, People, industrial scene and upward arrow.

1972, Nov. 28 Litho. *Perf. 11½*

Without Gum

1262 A690 10c blk. & multi. 1.00 75
1263 " 20c " " 2.00 1.00
1264 " 1cr " " 5.00 75
1265 " 2cr " " 1.75 1.50

Publicity for: "Mobral" literacy campaign (10c); Centenary of census (20c); Housing and retirement fund (1cr); Growth of gross national product (2cr).

Congress Building, Brasilia, by Oscar Niemeyer, and "Os Guerreiros," by Bruno Giorgi—A691

1972, Dec. 4 Without Gum

1266 A691 1cr bl., blk. & org. 8.00 6.00

Meeting of National Congress, Brasilia, Dec. 4–8.

Holy Family (Clay Figurines)
A692

Retirement Plan
A693

1972, Dec. 13 Photo. *Perf. 11½x11*

1267 A692 20c ocher & black 75 50

Christmas 1972. Luminescent.

Perf. 11½x11, 11x11½

1972, Dec. 20 Lithographed

Designs: No. 1269, School children and traffic lights (horiz.). 70c, Dr. Oswaldo Cruz with Red Cross, caricature. 2cr, Produce, fish and cattle (horiz.).

Without Gum

1268 A693 10c black, blue & dull org. 75 50
1269 " 10c org. & multi. 1.25 1.00
1270 " 70c black, red & brown 7.50 1.50
1271 " 2cr grn. & multi. 12.50 8.50

Publicity for: Agricultural workers' assistance program (No. 1268); highway and transportation development (No. 1269); centenary of the birth of Dr. Oswaldo Cruz (1872–1917), Director of Public Health Institute (70c); agricultural and cattle export (2cr). Nos. 1268–1271 are luminescent.

Sailing Ship, Navy
A694

Designs: 10c, Monument, Brazilian Expeditionary Force. No. 1274, Plumed helmet, Army. No. 1275, Rocket, Air Force.

Lithographed and Engraved

1972, Dec. 28 *Perf. 11x11½*

Without Gum

1272 A694 10c brown, dk. brn. & black 60 60
1273 " 30c lt. ultra., green & black 60 60
1274 " 30c yel. green, blue green & blk. 60 60
1275 " 30c lilac, maroon & black 60 60
Block of 4 with label 2.50

Armed Forces Day. Nos. 1272–1275 are se-tenant in blocks of 4 with greenish blue label showing Navy, Army and Air Force insignia in black.

The first price column gives the catalogue value of an unused stamp, the second that of a used stamp.

Rotary Emblem and Cog-wheels
A695

1973, Mar. 21 Litho. Unwmkd.

Perf. 11½

1276 A695 1cr ultra., greenish blue & yellow 2.50 1.50

Rotary International serving Brazil 50 years.

Swimming
A696

Designs: No. 1278, Gymnastics. No. 1279, Volleyball (vert.).

1973 Photo. *Perf. 11x11½, 11½x11*

1277 A696 40c brt. blue & red brown 50 50
1278 " 40c grn. & org. brn. 2.50 1.00
1279 " 40c vio. & org. brown 1.00 50

Issue dates: No. 1277, Apr. 19; No. 1278, May 22; No. 1279, Oct. 15.

Flag of Paraguay
A697

Perf. 11½

1973, Apr. 27 Litho. Unwmkd.

1280 A697 70c multicolored 1.75 1.00

Visit of Pres. Alfredo Stroessner of Paraguay, Apr. 25–27.

"Communi-cations"
A698

Design: 1cr, Neptune, map of South America and Africa.

1973, May 5 *Perf. 11x11½*

1281 A698 70c multicolored 1.00 1.00
1282 " 1cr " 6.00 3.00

Inauguration of the Ministry of Communications Building, Brasilia (70c); and of the first underwater telephone cable between South America and Europe, Bracan 1 (1cr).

Congress Emblem
A699

1973, May 19 ***Perf. 11½x11***

1283 A699 1cr org. & purple 6.00 3.00

24th Congress of the International Chamber of Commerce, Rio de Janeiro, May 19–26.

Swallow-tailed Manakin
A700

Birds: No. 1285, Orange-backed oriole. No. 1286, Brazilian ruby (hummingbird).

1973 Lithographed ***Perf. 11x11½***

1284 A700 20c multicolored 50 30
1285 " 20c " 50 30
1286 " 20c " 50 30

Issue dates: No. 1284, May 26; No. 1285, June 6; No. 1286, June 19.

Tourists
A701

1973, June 28 Litho. ***Perf. 11x11½***

1287 A701 70c multicolored 1.50 1.00

National Tourism Year.

Conference at Itu
A702

Satellite and Multi-spectral Image
A703

1973 ***Perf. 11½x11***

1288 A702 20c *shown* 75 40
1289 " 20c *Decorated wagon* 1.00 40
1290 " 20c *Indian* 75 50
1291 " 20c *Graciosa Road* 75 50

Centenary of the Itu Convention (1288); sesquicentennial of the July 2 episode (1289); 400th anniversary of the founding of Niteroi (1290); centenary of Graciosa Road (1291).

Issue dates: No. 1291, July 29; others July 2.

1973, July 11 ***Perf. 11½***

Designs: 70c, Official opening of Engineering School, 1913. 1cr, Möbius strips and "IMPA."

1292 A703 20c black & multi. 75 75
1293 " 70c dk. bl. & multi. 3.00 1.00
1294 " 1cr lilac & multi. 3.50 1.00

Institute for Space Research (20c); School of Engineering, Itajubá, 60th anniversary (70c); Institute for Pure and Applied Mathematics (1cr).

Santos-Dumont and 14-Bis Plane
A704

Designs (Santos-Dumont and): 70c, No. 6 Balloon and Eiffel Tower. 2cr Demoiselle plane.

Lithographed and Engraved

1973, July 20 ***Perf. 11x11½***

1295 A704 20c lt. green, brt. grn. & brown 75 75
1296 " 70c yellow, rose red & brown 2.25 75
1297 A704 2cr blue, vio. blue & brown 2.50 1.50

Centenary of the birth of Alberto Santos-Dumont (1873–1932), aviation pioneer.

Mercator Map
A705

Design: No. 1299, Same, red border on top and at left.

Photogravure & Engraved

1973, Aug. 1 **Wmk. 267**

1298 A705 40c red & black 75 75
1299 " 40c " " 75 75
Block of 4 6.00 6.00

Stamp Day. Nos. 1298–1299 are printed se-tenant horizontally and tête bêche vertically in sheets of 55. Blocks of 4 have red border all around.

Gonçalves Dias
A706

Perf. 11½x11

1973, Aug. 10 **Wmk. 267**

1300 A706 40c violet & blk. 1.00 50

Sesquicentenary of the birth of Antonio Gonçalves Dias (1823–1864), poet.

Souvenir Sheet

Copernicus and Sun—A707

Perf. 11x11½

1973, Aug. 15 Litho. Unwmkd.

1301 A707 1cr multicolored 1.50 1.50

500th anniversary of the birth of Nicolaus Copernicus (1473–1543), Polish astronomer. No. 1301 contains one stamp; multicolored margin. Size: 124x86mm.

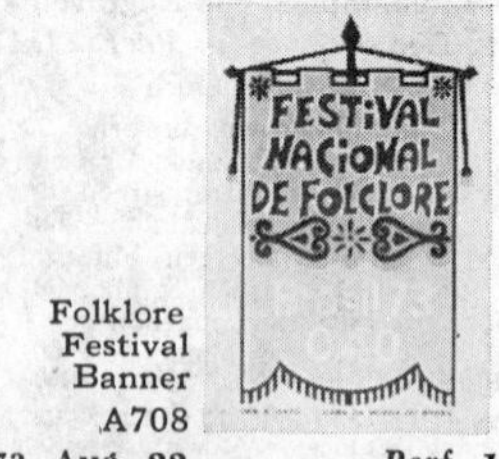

Folklore Festival Banner
A708

1973, Aug. 22 ***Perf. 11½***

1302 A708 40c ultra. & multi. 1.25 75

Folklore Day, Aug. 22.

Masonic Emblem
A709

1973, Aug. 24 Photo. ***Perf. 11x11½***

1303 A709 1cr Prussian blue 3.00 2.00

Free Masons of Brazil, 1822–1973.

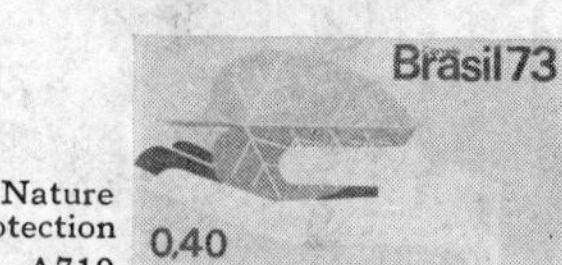

Nature Protection
A710

Designs: No. 1305, Fire protection. No. 1306, Aviation safety. No. 1307, Safeguarding cultural heritage.

1973, Sept. 20 Litho. ***Perf. 11x11½***

1304 A710 40c brt. green & multicolored 75 60
1305 " 40c dk. bl. & multi. 75 60
1306 " 40c lt. bl. & multi. 75 60
1307 " 40c pink & multi. 1.25 60

Souvenir Sheet

St. Gabriel and Proclamation of Pope Paul VI—A711

Lithographed and Engraved

1973, Sept. 29 ***Perf. 11½*** **Unwmkd.**

1308 A711 1cr bister & blk. 2.50 2.00

1st National Exhibition of Religious Philately, Rio de Janeiro, Sept. 29–Oct. 6. No. 1308 contains one stamp; bister margin and black inscription. Size: 123x87½mm.

St. Teresa
A712

Photogravure and Engraved

Perf. 11½x11

1973, Sept. 30 **Wmk. 267**

1309 A712 2cr dk. org. & brn. 5.00 2.50

Centenary of the birth of St. Teresa of Lisieux, the Little Flower (1873–1897), Carmelite nun.

Monteiro Lobato and Emily
A713

Perf. 11½

1973, Oct. 12 Litho. Unwmkd.

Multicolored

1310 A713 40c *shown* 60 50
1311 " 40c *Aunt Nastacia* 60 50
1312 " 40c *Snubnose, Peter and Rhino* 60 50
1313 " 40c *Viscount de Sabugosa* 60 50
1314 " 40c *Dona Benta* 60 50
Block of 5 + label 3.00 2.50

Monteiro Lobato, author of children's books. Nos. 1310–1314 printed in sheets of 30 stamps and 6 labels.

Soapstone Sculpture of Isaiah (detail)
A714

Baroque Art in Brazil: No. 1316, Arabesque, gilded wood carving (horiz.). 70c, Father José Mauricio Nuñes Garcia and music score. 1cr, Church door, Salvador, Bahia. 2cr, Angels, church ceiling painting by Manoel da Costa Athayde (horiz.).

1973, Nov. 5

1315 A714 40c multicolored 75 30
1316 " 40c " 75 30
1317 " 70c " 1.50 75
1318 " 1cr " 7.00 3.00
1319 " 2cr " 5.00 3.00
Nos. 1315–1319 (5) 15.00 7.35

Old and New Telephones
A715

1973, Nov. 28 ***Perf. 11x11½***

1320 A715 40c multicolored 50 40

50th anniversary of Brazilian Telephone Company.

Symbolic Angel
A716

1973, Nov. 30 ***Perf. 11½***

1321 A716 40c verm. & multi. 50 40

Christmas 1973.

"Gaiola"
A717

Designs: River boats.

1973, Nov. 30 Litho. ***Perf. 11x11½***

Multicolored

1322 A717 40c *shown* 50 35
1323 " 70c *"Regatao"* 1.00 40
1324 " 1cr *"Jangada"* 6.00 3.00
1325 " 2cr *"Saveiro"* 5.00 3.00

Nos. 1322–1325 are luminescent.

Scales of Justice
A718

1973, Dec. 5 ***Perf. 11½***

1326 A718 40c mag. & violet 75 35

To honor the High Federal Court, created in 1891. Luminescent.

José Placido de Castro
A719

Scarlet Ibis and Victoria Regia
A720

Lithographed and Engraved

Perf. 11½x11

1973, Dec. 12 **Wmk. 267**

1327 A719 40c lilac rose & black 1.00 35

Centenary of the birth of José Placido de Castro, liberator of the State of Acre.

Perf. 11½x11

1973, Dec. 28 **Litho.** **Unwmkd.**

Designs: 70c, Jaguar and spathodea campanulata. 1cr, Scarlet macaw and carnauba palm. 2cr, Rhea and coral tree.

1328 A720 40c brn. & multi. 1.00 35
1329 " 70c " " 2.50 1.00
1330 " 1cr bis. & multi. 1.50 1.00
1331 " 2cr " " 5.00 2.50

Nos. 1328–1331 are luminescent.

Saci Pereré, Mocking Goblin
A721

Characters from Brazilian Legends: 80c, Zumbi, last chief of rebellious slaves. 1cr, Chico Rei, African king. 1.30cr, Little Black Boy of the Pasture. 2.50cr, Iara, Queen of the Waters.

Perf. 11½x11

1974, Feb. 28 **Litho.** **Unwmkd.**

Size: 21x39mm.

1332 A721 40c multicolored 75 25
1333 " 80c " 1.00 75
1334 " 1cr " 1.50 50

Size: 32½x33mm.

Perf. 11½

1335 A721 1.30cr multi 4.50 1.75
1336 " 2.50cr " 4.50 2.50
Nos. 1332–1336 (5) 12.25 5.75

Nos. 1332–1336 are luminescent.

Pres. Costa e Silva Bridge
A722

1974, Mar. 11

1337 A722 40c multicolored 75 35

Inauguration of the Pres. Costa e Silva Bridge, Rio Niteroi, connecting Rio de Janeiro and Guanabara State.

"The Press"
A723

1974, Mar. 25 ***Perf. 11½***

Multicolored

1338 A723 40c *shown* 50 40
1339 " 40c "*Radio*" 50 40
1340 " 40c "*Television*" 75 40

Communications Commemorations: No. 1338, bicentenary of first Brazilian newspaper, published in London by Hipolito da Costa; No. 1339, founding of the Radio Sociedade do Rio de Janeiro by Roquette Pinto; No. 1340, installation of first Brazilian television station by Assis Chateaubriand. Luminescent.

"Reconstruction"
A724

1974, Mar. 31

1341 A724 40c multicolored 1.00 50

10 years of progress. Luminescent.

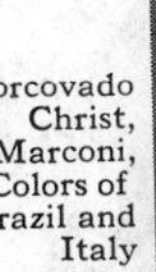

Corcovado Christ, Marconi, Colors of Brazil and Italy
A725

1974, Apr. 25 **Litho.** ***Perf. 11½***

1342 A725 2.50cr multi. 6.00 3.50

Centenary of the birth of Guglielmo Marconi (1874–1937), Italian physicist and inventor. Luminescent.

Stamp Printing Press, Stamp Designing
A726

1974, May 6

1343 A726 80c multicolored 50 35

Brazilian mint.

World Map, Indian, Caucasian and Black Men
A727

Designs (World Map and): No. 1345, Brazilians. No. 1346, Cabin and German horseback rider. No. 1347, Italian farm wagon. No. 1348, Japanese woman and torii.

1974, May 11 **Unwmkd.**

1344 A727 40c multicolored 50 35
1345 " 40c " 50 35
1346 " 2.50cr " 3.50 1.50
1347 " 2.50cr " 4.50 1.50
1348 " 2.50cr " 2.00 1.50
Nos. 1344–1348 (5) 11.00 5.20

Ethnic and migration influences in Brazil.

Sandstone Cliffs, Sete Cidades National Park—A728

Design: 80c, Ruins of Cathedral of São Miguel das Missões.

Lithographed and Engraved

1974, June 8 ***Perf. 11x11½***

1349 A728 40c multicolored 1.00 50
1350 " 80c " 1.00 50

Tourist publicity.

Souvenir Sheet

Soccer—A729

1974, June 20 **Litho.** ***Perf. 11½***

1351 A729 2.50cr multi. 2.00 1.50

World Cup Soccer Championship, Munich, June 13–July 7. No. 1351 has multicolored margin. Size: 130x95mm.

Church and College, Caraça
A730

1974, July 6 **Litho.** ***Perf. 11x11½***

1352 A730 40c multicolored 75 35

Bicentenary of the College (Seminary) of Caraça.

Wave on Television Screen
A731

1974, July 15 ***Perf. 11½***

1353 A731 40c black & blue 50 40

TELEBRAS, Third Brazilian Congress of Telecommunications, Brasilia, July 15–20.

Fernão Dias Paes
A732

1974, July 21 ***Perf. 11½***

1354 A732 20c green & multi. 50 30

3rd centenary of the expedition led by Fernão Dias Paes exploring Minas Gerais and the passage from South to North in Brazil.

Mexican Flag
A733

1974, July 24 **Litho.** ***Perf. 11½***

1355 A733 80c multi. 2.50 75

Visit of Pres. Luis Echeverria Alvares of Mexico, July 24–29.

Flags of Brazil and Germany
A734

1974, Aug. 5 ***Perf. 11x11½***

1356 A734 40c multicolored 1.00 50

World Cup Soccer Championship, 1974, victory of German Federal Republic.

Souvenir Sheet

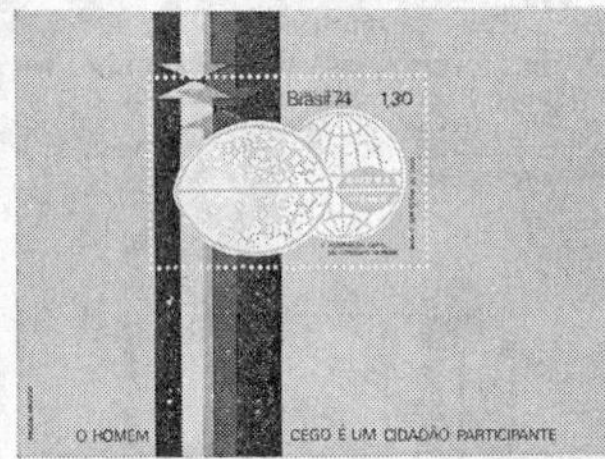

Congress Emblem—A735

1974, Aug. 7 ***Perf. 11½***

1357 A735 1.30cr multi. 1.00 75

5th World Assembly of the World Council for the Welfare of the Blind, São Paulo, Aug. 7–16. No. 1357 has ocher margin with black inscription. Stamp and margin inscribed in Braille with name of Assembly. Size: 126x88½mm.

Raul Pederneiras, Caricature by J. Carlos
A736

Lithographed and Engraved

1974, Aug. 15 ***Perf. 11½x11***

1358 A736 40c buff, black & ocher 50 40

Centenary of the birth of Raul Pederneiras (1874–1953), journalist, professor of law and fine arts.

Society Emblem and Landscape
A737

Perf. 11x11½

1974, Aug. 19 **Lithographed**

1359 A737 1.30cr multi. 1.75 75

13th Congress of the International Union of Building and Savings Societies.

Souvenir Sheet

Five Women, by Di Cavalcanti—A738

1974, Aug. 26 Litho. ***Perf. 11½***

1360 A738 2cr multicolored 2.00 1.50

LUBRAPEX 74, 5th Portuguese-Brazilian Philatelic Exhibition, São Paulo, Nov. 26–Dec. 4. No. 1360 has gray marginal inscription. Size of stamp: 37x55mm., size of sheet: 87x125mm.

"UPU" and World Map
A739

1974, Oct. 9 Litho. ***Perf. 11½***

1361 A739 2.50cr blk. & brt. blue 5.00 2.50

Centenary of Universal Postal Union.

Hammock (Antillean Arawak Culture)
A740

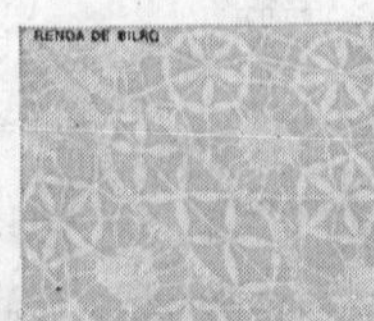

Bilro Lace
A741

Singer of "Cord" Verses
A742

Ceramic Figure by Master Vitalino
A743

1974, Oct. 16 Litho. ***Perf. 11½***

1362 A740 50c deep rose lilac 1.25 50
1363 A741 50c lt. & dk. blue 1.25 50
1364 A742 50c yel. & red brn. 1.25 50
1365 A743 50c bright yellow & dk. brown 1.25 50

Popular Brazilian crafts.

Branch of Coffee
A744

1974, Oct. 27 ***Perf. 11*** **Unwmkd.**

1366 A744 50c multicolored 1.75 75

Centenary of city of Campinas.

Hornless Tabapuã
A745

Animals of Brazil: 1.30cr, Creole horse. 2.50cr, Brazilian mastiff.

1974, Nov. 10 ***Perf. 11½***

1367 A745 80c multicolored 50 50
1368 " 1.30cr " 1.00 1.00
1369 " 2.50cr " 5.00 2.50

Angel
A746

1974, Nov. 18 ***Perf. 11½x11***

1370 A746 50c ultra. & multi. 75 35

Christmas 1974.

Solteira Island Hydroelectric Dam
A747

1974, Nov. 18 ***Perf. 11½***

1371 A747 50c black & yel. 2.50 75

Inauguration of the Solteira Island Hydroelectric Dam over Parana River.

The Girls, by Carlos Reis
A748

1974, Nov. 26

1372 A748 1.30cr multicolored 75 50

LUBRAPEX 74, 5th Portuguese-Brazilian Philatelic Exhibition, São Paulo, Nov. 26–Dec. 4.

Youths, Judge, Scales
A749

1974, Dec. 20 Litho. ***Perf. 11½***

1373 A749 90c yel., red & blue 50 50

Juvenile Court of Brazil, 50th anniversary.

Long Distance Runner
A750

1974, Dec. 23

1374 A750 3.30cr multi. 1.00 50

São Silvestre long distance running, 50th anniversary.

News Vendor, 1875, Masthead, 1975
A751

1975, Jan. 4

1375 A751 50c multicolored 1.75 75

Centenary of the newspaper "O Estado de S. Paulo."

São Paulo Industrial Park
A752

Designs: 1.40cr, Natural rubber industry, Acre. 4.50cr, Manganese mining, Amapá.

1975, Jan. 24 Litho. ***Perf. 11x11½***

1376 A752 50c vio. bl. & yel. 2.00 50
1377 " 1.40cr yel. & brn. 75 75
1378 " 4.50cr yel. & black 2.25 50

Economic development.

Fort of the Holy Cross
A753

Designs: No. 1380, Fort of the Three Kings. No. 1381, Fort of Montserrat. 90c, Fort of Our Lady of Help.

Lithographed, Engraved

1975, Mar. 14 ***Perf. 11½***

1379 A753 50c yel. & red brn. 75 40
1380 " 50c " " 75 40
1381 " 50c " " 75 40
1382 " 90c " " 75 60

Colonial forts.

House on Stilts, Amazon Region
A754

Designs: 50c, Modern houses and plan of Brasilia. 1.40cr, Indian hut, Rondonia. 3.30cr, German-style cottage (Enxaimel), Santa Catarina.

1975, Apr. 18 Litho. ***Perf. 11½***

1383 A754 50c yel. & multi. 1.50 75
1384 " 50c " " 3.00 1.50
1385 " 1cr " " 75 50
1386 " 1.40cr " " 2.00 1.00
1387 " 1.40cr " " 1.00 50
1388 " 3.30cr " " 1.00 50
1389 " 3.30cr " " 2.00 1.00
Nos. 1383–1389 (7) 11.25 5.75

Brazilian architecture. Nos. 1383–1384, 1386–1387, 1388–1389 printed se-tenant in sheets of 50. Nos. 1383, 1386, 1388 have yellow strip at right side, others at left; No. 1385 has yellow strip on both sides.

Astronotus Ocellatus
A755

Designs: Brazilian fresh-water fish.

1975, May 2 Litho. ***Perf. 11½***

Pale Green and Multicolored

1390 A755 50c *shown* 75 50
1391 " 50c *Colomesus psitacus* 75 50
1392 " 50c *Phallocerus caudimaculatus* 75 50
1393 " 50c *Symphysodon discus* 75 50

Soldier's Head in Brazil's Colors, Plane, Rifle and Ship
A756

Brazilian Otter
A757

1975, May 8 ***Perf. 11½x11***

1394 A756 50c vio. bl. & multi. 75 35

In honor of the veterans of World War II, on the 30th anniversary of victory.

1975, June 17 Litho. *Perf. 11½*

Designs: 70c, Brazilian pines (horiz.). 3.30cr, Marsh cayman.

1395	A757	70c bl.,grn.& blk.	1.25	35
1396	"	1cr multicolored	1.00	35
1397	"	3.30cr "	1.00	60

Nature protection.

Petroglyphs, Stone of Ingá
A758

Marjoara Vase, Pará
A759

Vinctifer Comptoni, Petrified Fish
A760

1975, July 8 Litho. *Perf. 11½*

1398	A758	70c multicolored	1.00	30
1399	A759	1cr "	60	30
1400	A760	1cr "	75	30

Archaeological discoveries.

Immaculate Conception, Franciscan Monastery, Vitoria
A761

Post and Telegraph Ministry
A762

1975, July 15

1401	A761	3.30cr bl. & multi.	1.50	50

Holy Year 1975 and 300th anniversary of establishment of the Franciscan Province in Southern Brazil.

1975, Aug. 8 Engr. *Perf. 11½*

1402	A762	70c dark carmine	1.25	30

Stamp Day 1975.

Sword Dance, Minas Gerais
A763

Folk Dances: No. 1404, Umbrella Dance, Pernambuco. No. 1405, Warrior's Dance, Alagoas.

1975, Aug. 22 Litho. *Perf. 11½*

1403	A763	70c gray & multi.	75	35
1404	"	70c pink & multi.	75	35
1405	"	70c yel. & multi.	75	35

Trees
A764

1975, Sept. 15 *Perf. 11x11½*

1406	A764	70c multicolored	60	25

Annual Tree Festival.

Globe, Radar and Satellite
A765

1975, Sept. 16 *Perf. 11½*

1407	A765	3.30cr multicolored	1.25	50

Inauguration of 2nd antenna of Tangua Earth Station, Rio de Janeiro State.

Woman Holding Flowers and Globe
A766

1975, Sept. 23

1408	A766	3.30cr multi.	1.50	60

International Women's Year 1975.

Tile, Railing and Column, Alcantara
A767

Cross and Monastery, São Cristovão
A768

Design: No. 1411, Jug and Clock Tower, Goiás (vert.).

1975, Sept. 27 Litho. *Perf. 11½*

1409	A767	70c multicolored	75	30
1410	A768	70c "	75	30
1411	"	70c "	75	30

Historic cities.

"Books teach how to live"
A769

1975, Oct. 23 Litho. *Perf. 11½*

1412	A769	70c multicolored	40	25

Day of the Book.

ASTA Congress Emblem
A770

1975, Oct. 27 *Perf. 11x11½*

1413	A770	70c multicolored	50	25

American Society of Travel Agents, 45th World Congress, Rio de Janeiro, Oct. 27–Nov. 1.

Angels
A771

1975, Nov. 11

1414	A771	70c red & brown	50	20

Christmas 1975.

Map of Americas, Waves
A772

Dom Pedro II
A773

1975, Nov. 19 *Perf. 11½x12*

1415	A772	5.20cr gray & multi.	2.25	75

2nd Interamerican Conference of Telecommunications (CITEL), Rio de Janeiro, Nov. 19–27.

1975, Dec. 2 Engr. *Perf. 12*

1416	A773	70c violet brown	1.25	25

Dom Pedro II (1825–1891), emperor of Brazil, birth sesquicentennial.

People and Cross
A774

1975, Dec. 4 Litho. *Perf. 11x11½*

1417	A774	70c light blue & deep blue	1.00	30

National Day of Thanksgiving.

Guarapari Beach, Espirito Santo
A775

Designs: No. 1419, Salt Stone beach, Piaui. No. 1420, Cliffs, Rio Grande Do Sul.

1975, Dec. 19 Litho. *Perf. 11½*

1418	A775	70c multicolored	50	25
1419	"	70c "	50	25
1420	"	70c "	50	25

Tourist publicity.

Triple Jump, Games Emblem
A776

1975, Dec. 22 *Perf. 11x11½*

1421	A776	1.60cr bl. green & black	35	25

Triple jump world record by Joao Carlos de Oliveira in 7th Pan-American Games, Mexico City, Oct. 12–26.

UN Emblem and Headquarters
A777

1975, Dec. 29 *Perf. 11½*

1422	A777	1.30cr dp. blue & vio. blue	30	20

United Nations, 30th anniversary.

Light Bulbs, House and Sun
A778

Design: No. 1424, Gasoline drops, car and sun.

1976, Jan. 16

1423	A778	70c multicolored	50	15
1424	"	70c "	50	15

Energy conservation.

Concorde—A779

1976, Jan. 21 Litho. *Perf. 11x11½*

1425	A779	5.20cr bluish blk.	1.00	50

First commercial flight of supersonic jet Concorde from Paris to Rio de Janeiro, Jan. 21.

Souvenir Sheet

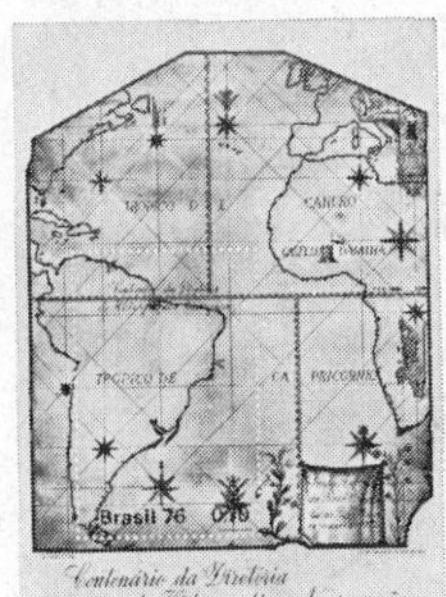

Nautical Map of South Atlantic, 1776—A780

1976, Feb. 2 *Perf. 11½*

1426	A780	70c sal. & multi.	75	50

Centenary of the Naval Hydrographic and Navigation Institute. Size: 88x123mm.

Telephone Lines, 1876 Telephone
A781

1976, Mar. 10 Litho. *Perf. 11x11½*

1427	A781	5.20cr org. & bl.	75	40

Centenary of first telephone call by Alexander Graham Bell, March 10, 1876.

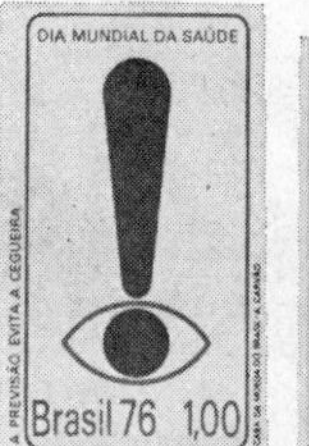

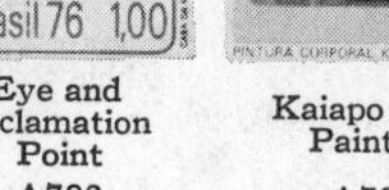

Eye and Exclamation Point
A782

Kaiapo Body Painting
A783

1976, Apr. 7 Litho. *Perf. 11½x11*

1428	A782	1cr violet, red brn. & brown	60	40

World Health Day: "Foresight prevents blindness."

1976, Apr. 19 Litho. *Perf. 11½*

Designs: No. 1430, Bakairi ceremonial mask. No. 1431, Karajá feather headdress.

1429	A783	1cr lt. vio. & multi.	25	20
1430	"	1cr " "	25	20
1431	"	1cr " "	25	20

Preservation of indigenous culture.

Itamaraty Palace, Brasilia
A784

1976, Apr. 20

1432	A784	1cr multicolored	1.00	75

Diplomats' Day. Itamaraty Palace, designed by Oscar Niemeyer, houses the Ministry of Foreign Affairs.

Watering Can over Stones, by José Tarcisio
A785

Fingers and Ribbons, by Pietrina Checcacci
A786

1976, May 14 Litho. *Perf. 11½*

1433	A785	1cr multicolored	30	20
1434	A786	1.60cr "	30	20

Modern Brazilian art.

Basketball
A787

Orchid
A788

Designs (Olympic Rings and): 1.40cr, Yachting. 5.20cr, Judo.

1976, May 21 Litho. *Perf. 11½*

1435	A787	1cr emerald & black	20	15
1436	"	1.40cr dark blue & black	25	15
1437	"	5.20cr org. & blk.	60	35

21st Olympic Games, Montreal, Canada, July 17–Aug. 1.

1976, June 4 *Perf. 11½x11*

Design: No. 1439, Golden-faced lion monkey.

1438	A788	1cr multicolored	20	10
1439	"	1cr "	20	10

Nature protection.

Film Camera, Brazilian Colors
A789

1976, June 19

1440	A789	1cr vio. bl., brt. grn. & yel.	20	10

Brazilian film industry.

Bahia Woman
A790

Designs: 10c, Oxcart driver (horiz.). 20c, Raft fishermen (horiz.). 30c, Rubber plantation worker. 40c, Cowboy (horiz.). 50c, Gaucho. 80c, Gold panner. 1cr, Banana plantation worker. 1.10cr, Grape harvester. 1.30cr, Coffee picker. 1.80cr, Farmer gathering wax palms. 2cr, Potter. 5cr, Sugar cane cutter. 7cr, Salt mine worker. 10cr, Fisherman. 15cr, Coconut seller. 20cr, Lacemaker.

Perf. 11½x11, 11x11½

1976–78 Photogravure

1441	A790	10c red brown ('77)	5	3
1442	"	15c brown	5	3
1443	"	20c violet blue	5	3
1444	"	30c lilac rose	5	3
1445	"	40c orange ('77)	10	3
1446	"	50c citron	10	3
1447	"	80c slate green	10	6
1448	"	1cr black	10	8
1449	"	1.10cr magneta ('77)	10	8
1450	"	1.30cr red ('77)	15	10
1451	"	1.80cr dark violet blue ('78)	20	15

Engraved

1454	A790	2cr brown ('77)	20	10
1455	"	5cr dk. pur. ('77)	45	10
1456	"	7cr violet	60	10
1457	"	10cr yel. grn. ('77)	85	15
1458	A790	15cr gray green ('78)	1.25	25
1459	"	20cr blue	1.75	25
		Nos. 1441–1459 (17)	6.15	1.60

Hyphessobrycon Innesi
A791

Designs: Brazilian fresh-water fish.

1976, July 12 Litho. *Perf. 11x11½*

Multicolored

1460	A791	1cr *shown*	20	10
1461	"	1cr *Copeina arnoldi*	20	10
1462	"	1cr *Prochilodus insignis*	20	10
1463	"	1cr *Crenicichla lepidota*	20	10
1464	"	1cr *Ageneiosus*	20	10
1465	"	1cr *Corydoras reticulatus*	20	10
		Nos. 1460–1465 (6)	1.20	60

Nos. 1460–1465 printed se-tenant in sheets of 36.

Santa Marta Lighthouse
A792

1976, July 29 Engr. *Perf. 12x11½*

1466	A792	1cr blue	50	20

300th anniversary of the city of Laguna.

Children on Magic Carpet
A793

1976, Aug. 1 Litho. *Perf. 11½x12*

1467	A793	1cr multicolored	20	10

Stamp Day.

Nurse's Lamp and Head
A794

1976, Aug. 12 Litho. *Perf. 11½*

1468	A794	1cr multicolored	40	10

Brazilian Nurses' Association, 50th anniversary.

Puppet, Soldier
A795

Winner's Medal
A796

Designs: 1.30cr, Girl's head. 1.60cr, Hand with puppet head on each finger (horiz.).

1976, Aug. 20

1469	A795	1cr multicolored	40	20
1470	"	1.30cr "	40	20
1471	"	1.60cr "	40	20

Mamulengo puppet show.

1976, Aug. 21

1472	A796	5.20cr multi.	75	30

27th International Military Athletic Championships, Rio de Janeiro, Aug. 21–28.

Family Protection
A797

1976, Sept. 12

1473	A797	1cr lt. & dk. blue	35	20

National organizations SENAC and SESC helping commercial employees to improve their living standard, both commercially and socially.

Dying Tree
A798

1976, Sept. 20 Litho. *Perf. 11½*

1474	A798	1cr gray & multi.	25	20

Protection of the environment.

Atom Symbol, Electron Orbits
A799

1976, Sept. 21

1475	A799	5.20cr multi.	75	30

20th General Conference of the International Atomic Energy Agency, Rio de Janeiro, Sept. 21–29.

Train in Tunnel
A800

1976, Sept. 26

1476 A800 1.60cr multicolored 25 12

Inauguration of Sao Paulo subway, first in Brazil.

St. Francis and Birds
A801

1976, Oct. 4

1477 A801 5.20cr multi. 75 30

St. Francis of Assisi, 750th death anniversary.

Ouro Preto School of Mining
A802

1976, Oct. 12 Engr. ***Perf. 12x11½***

1478 A802 1cr dark violet 50 50

Ouro Preto School of Mining, centenary.

Three Kings
A803

Designs: Children's drawings.

1976, Nov. 4 Litho. ***Perf. 11½***

Multicolored

1479 A803 80c *shown* 20 6
1480 " 80c *Santa Claus on donkey* 20 6
1481 " 80c *Virgin and Child and Angels* 20 6
1482 " 80c *Angels with candle* 20 6
1483 " 80c *Nativity* 20 6
Nos. 1479–1483 (5) 1.00 30

Christmas 1976. Nos. 1479–1483 printed se-tenant in sheets of 35.

Souvenir Sheet

30,000 Reis Banknote—A804

1976, Nov. 5 Litho. ***Perf. 11½***

1484 A804 80c multicolored 20 6

Opening of 1000th branch of Bank of Brazil, Barra do Bugres, Mato Grosso. No. 1484 contains one stamp. Size of stamp: 38x56½mm.; size of sheet: 125x87mm.

Virgin of Monte Serrat, by Friar Agostinho
A805

St. Joseph, 18th Century Wood Sculpture
A806

Designs: 5.60cr, The Dance, by Rodolfo Bernadelli, 19th century. 6.50cr, The Caravel, by Bruno Giorgi, 20th century abstract sculpture.

1976, Nov. 5

1485 A805 80c multicolored 20 6
1486 A806 5cr " 50 25
1487 A805 5.60cr " 60 25
1488 A806 6.50cr " 75 25

Development of Brazilian sculpture.

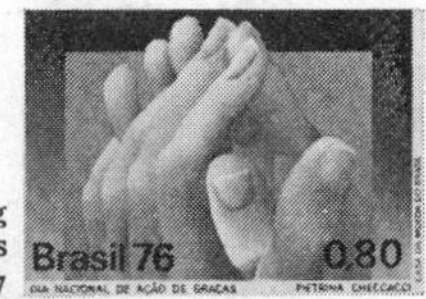

Praying Hands
A807

1976, Nov. 25

1489 A807 80c multicolored 50 10

National Day of Thanksgiving.

Sailor, 1840
A808

Design: 2cr, Marine's uniform, 1808.

1976, Dec. 13 Litho. ***Perf. 11½x11***

1490 A808 80c multicolored 30 10
1491 " 2cr " 30 10

Brazilian Navy.

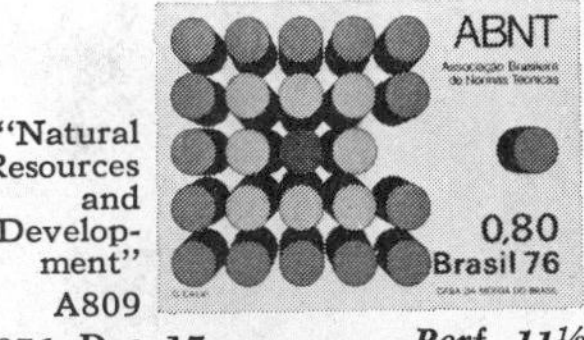

"Natural Resources and Development"
A809

1976, Dec. 17 ***Perf. 11½***

1492 A809 80c multicolored 35 10

Brazilian Bureau of Standards, founded 1940.

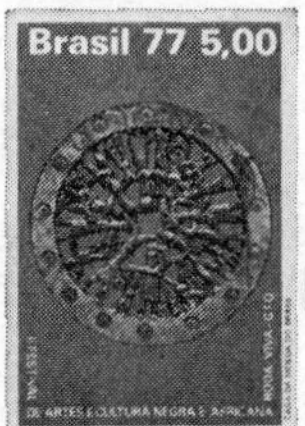

Wheel of Life
A810

Designs: 5.60cr, Beggar, sculpture by Agnaldo dos Santos. 6.50cr, Benin mask.

1977, Jan. 14

1493 A810 5cr multicolored 50 25
1494 " 5.60cr " 60 25
1495 " 6.50cr " 75 25

FESTAC '77, 2nd World Black and African Festival, Lagos, Nigeria, Jan. 15–Feb. 12.

A811

1977, Jan. 20 Litho. ***Perf. 11½***

1496 A811 6.50cr blue & yel. green 75 25

Rio de Janeiro International Airport.

Seminar Emblem with Map of Americas
A812

Salicylate, Microphoto
A813

1977, Feb. 6

1497 A812 1.10cr gray, vio. bl. & blue 50 10

6th Inter-American Budget Seminar.

1977, Apr. 10 Litho. ***Perf. 11½***

1498 A813 1.10cr multicolored 30 10

International Rheumatism Year.

Lions International Emblem
A814

1977, Apr. 16

1499 A814 1.10cr multicolored 25 10

25th anniversary of Brazilian Lions International.

Heitor Villa Lobos
A815

1977, Apr. 26 ***Perf. 11x11½***

Multicolored

1500 A815 1.10cr *shown* 30 10
1501 A815 1.10cr *Chiquinha Gonzaga* 20 10
1502 " 1.10cr *Noel Rosa* 20 10

Brazilian composers.

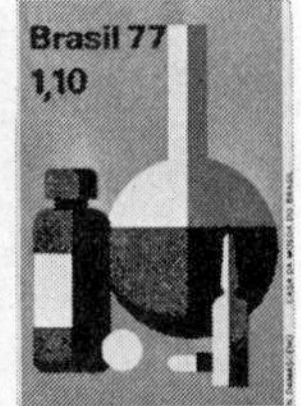

Farmer and Worker
A816

Medicine Bottles and Flask
A817

1977, May 8 Litho. ***Perf. 11½***

1503 A816 1.10cr grn. & multi. 15 10
1504 A817 1.10cr lt. & dk. grn. 15 10

Support and security for rural and urban workers (No. 1503) and establishment in 1971 of Medicine Distribution Center (CEME) for low-cost medicines (No. 1504).

Churchyard Cross, Porto Seguro
A818

Views, Porto Seguro: 5cr, Beach and boats. 5.60cr, Our Lady of Pena Chapel. 6.50cr, Town Hall.

1977, May 25 Litho. ***Perf. 11½***

1505 A818 1.10cr multicolored 15 10
1506 " 5cr " 50 25
1507 " 5.60cr " 55 30
1508 " 6.50cr " 65 35

Centenary of Brazil's membership in Universal Postal Union.

Diario de Porto Alegre
A819

1977, June 1

1509 A819 1.10cr multicolored 20 10

150th anniversary of Diario de Porto Alegre, newspaper.

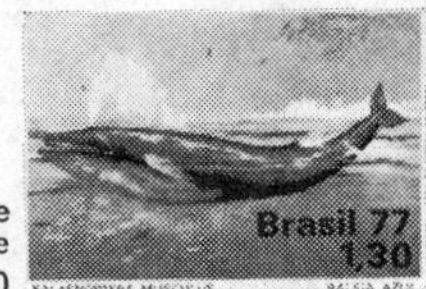

Blue Whale
A820

1977, June 3

1510 A820 1.30cr multicolored 15 10

Protection of marine life.

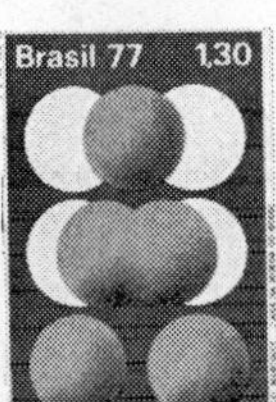

"Life and Development"
A821

1977, June 20

1511 A821 1.30cr multicolored 15 10

National Development Bank, 25th anniversary.

Train Leaving Tunnel
A822

1977, July 8 Engr. ***Perf. 11½***

1512 A822 1.30cr black 15 10

Centenary of São Paulo-Rio de Janeiro railroad.

Vasum Cassiforme
A823

Caduceus, Formulas for Water and Fluoride
A824

Sea Shells: No. 1514, Strombus goliath. No. 1515, Murex tenuivaricosus.

1977, July 14 Lithographed

1513 A823 1.30cr bl. & multi. 15 10
1514 " 1.30cr brown & multi. 15 10
1515 " 1.30cr green & multi. 15 10

1977, July 15 ***Perf. 11½x11***

1516 A824 1.30cr multicolored 15 10

3rd International Odontology Congress, Rio de Janeiro, July 15–21.

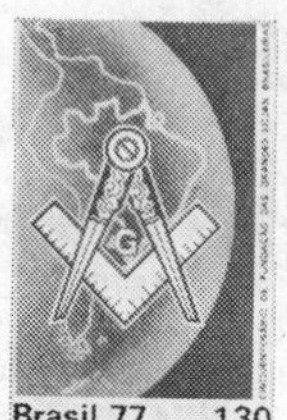

Masonic Emblem, Map of Brazil
A825

"Stamps Don't Sink or Lose their Way"
A826

1977, July 18 ***Perf. 11½***

1517 A825 1.30cr bl., lt bl. & black 15 10

50th anniversary of the founding of the Brazilian Grand Masonic Lodge.

1977, Aug. 1

1518 A826 1.30cr multicolored 15 10

Stamp Day 1977.

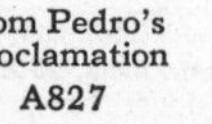

Dom Pedro's Proclamation
A827

Horses and Bulls
A828

1977, Aug. 11 Litho. ***Perf. 11½***

1519 A827 1.30cr multicolored 20 10

150th anniversary of Brazilian Law School.

Perf. 11½x11, 11x11½

1977, Aug. 20 Lithographed

Designs: No. 1521, King on horseback. No. 1522, Joust (horiz.).

1520 A828 1.30cr ocher & multi. 15 10
1521 " 1.30cr bl. & multi. 15 10
1522 " 1.30cr yellow & multi. 15 10

Brazilian folklore.

2000-reis Doubloon
A829

Brazilian Colonial Coins: No. 1524, 640r pataca. No. 1525, 20r copper "vintem."

1977, Aug. 31 ***Perf. 11½***

1523 A829 1.30cr violet blue & multi. 15 10
1524 " 1.30cr dark red & multi. 15 10
1525 " 1.30cr yellow & multi. 15 10

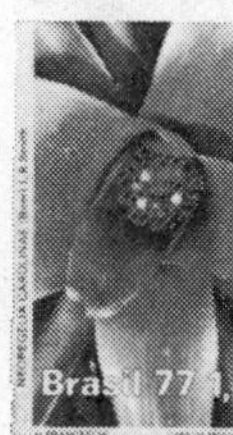

Pinwheel
A830

Neoregelia Carolinae
A831

1977, Sept. 1

1526 A830 1.30cr multicolored 20 10

National Week.

1977, Sept. 21 Litho. ***Perf. 11½***

1527 A831 1.30cr multicolored 15 10

Nature preservation.

Pen, Pencil, Letters
A832

1977, Oct. 15 Litho. ***Perf. 11½***

1528 A832 1.30cr multicolored 15 10

Primary education, sesquicentennial.

Dome and Telescope
A833

1977, Oct. 15

1529 A833 1.30cr multicolored 15 10

National Astrophysics Observatory, Brasópolis, sesquicentennial.

"Jahu" Hydroplane (Savoia Marchetti S-55)
A834

Design: No. 1531, PAX, dirigible.

1977, Oct. 17

1530 A834 1.30cr multicolored 15 10
1531 " 1.30cr " 15 10

50th anniversary of crossing of South Atlantic by Joao Ribeiro de Barros from Genoa to Sao Paulo (No. 1530) and 75th anniversary of the PAX airship (No. 1531).

O'Guarani
A835

1977, Oct. 24

1532 A835 1.30cr multicolored 15 10

Book Day and to honor José Martiniano de Alencar, writer, jurist.

Waves
A836

1977, Nov. 5 Litho. ***Perf. 11½***

1533 A836 1.30cr multicolored 15 10

Amateur Radio Operators' Day.

Nativity
A837

Designs (Folk Art): 2cr, Annunciation. 5cr, Nativity.

1977, Nov. 10

1534 A837 1.30cr bis. & multi. 15 10
1535 " 2cr " " 20 15
1536 " 5cr " " 50 25

Christmas 1977.

Emerald
A838

Designs: No. 1538, Topaz. No. 1539, Aquamarine.

1977, Nov. 19

1537 A838 1.30cr multicolored 15 10
1538 " 1.30cr " 15 10
1539 " 1.30cr " 15 10

PORTUCALE 77, 2nd International Topical Exhibition, Porto, Nov. 19–20.

Angel with Cornucopia
A839

1977, Nov. 24 Litho. ***Perf. 11½***

1540 A839 1.30cr multicolored 15 10

National Thanksgiving Day.

Army's Railroad Construction Battalion—A840

Designs: No. 1542, Navy's Amazon flotilla. No. 1543, Air Force's postal service (plane).

1977, Dec. 5

1541 A840 1.30cr multicolored 15 10
1542 " 1.30cr " 15 10
1543 " 1.30cr " 15 10

Civilian services of armed forces.

Varig Emblem, Jet
A841

1977, Dec. ***Perf. 11x11½***

1544 A841 1.30cr blue & black 15 10

50th anniversary of Varig Airline.

Sts. Cosme and Damiao Church, Igaracu
A842

Woman Holding Sheaf
A843

Brazilian Architecture: 7.50cr, St. Bento Monastery Church, Rio de Janeiro. 8.50cr, Church of St. Francis of Assisi, Ouro Preto. 9.50cr, St. Anthony Convent Church, Joao Pessoa.

1977, Dec. 8

1545 A842 2.70cr multicolored 25 15
1546 " 7.50cr " 70 35
1547 " 8.50cr " 80 40
1548 " 9.50cr " 90 45

1977, Dec. 19 ***Perf. 11½***

1549 A843 1.30cr multicolored 15 10

Brazilian diplomacy.

Soccer Ball and Foot
A844

Designs: No. 1551, Soccer ball in net. No. 1552, Symbolic soccer player.

1978, Mar. 1 Litho. *Perf. 11½*

1550 A844 1.80cr multicolored 20 15
1551 " 1.80cr " 20 15
1552 " 1.80cr " 20 15

11th World Cup Soccer Championship, Argentina, June 1–25.

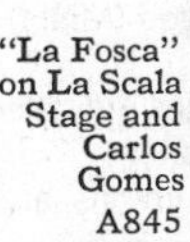

"La Fosca" on La Scala Stage and Carlos Gomes
A845

1978, Feb. 9

1553 A845 1.80cr multicolored 20 15

Bicentenary of La Scala in Milan, and to honor Carlos Gomes (1836–1893), Brazilian composer.

Symbols of Postal Mechanization
A846

1978, Mar. 15 Litho. *Perf. 11½*

1554 A846 1.80cr multicolored 20 15

Opening of Postal Staff College.

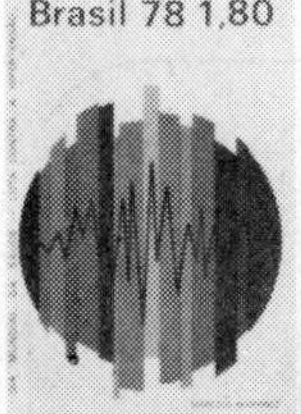

Hypertension Chart
A847

Waves from Antenna Uniting World
A848

1978, Apr. 4

1555 A847 1.80cr multicolored 20 15

World Health Day, fight against hypertension.

1978, May 17 Litho. *Perf. 12x11½*

1556 A848 1.80cr multicolored 20 10

10th World Telecommunications Day.

Brazilian Canary
A849

Birds: 8.50cr, Cotinga. 9.50cr, Tanager fastuosa.

1978, June 5 *Perf. 11½x12*

1557 A849 7.50cr multicolored 75 30
1558 " 8.50cr " 80 40
1559 " 9.50cr " 85 50

Inocencio Serzedelo Correa and Manuel Francisco Correa, 1893
A850

1978, June 20 Litho. *Perf. 11x11½*

1560 A850 1.80cr multicolored 20 10

85th anniversary of Union Court of Audit.

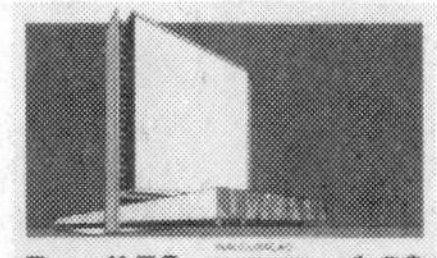

Post and Telegraph Building
A851

1978, June 22 *Perf. 11½*

1561 A851 1.80cr multicolored 20 10

Souvenir Sheet

Imperf.

1562 A851 7.50cr multi. 75 50

Inauguration of Post and Telegraph Building (ECT), Brasilia, and for BRAPEX, 3rd Brazilian Philatelic Exhibition, Brasilia, June 23–28 (No. 1562). No. 1562 has buff margin with black inscription. Size: 70x90mm.

Ernesto Geisel
A852

1978, June 22 Engr. *Perf. 11½*

1563 A852 1.80cr dull green 20 10

Ernesto Geisel, President of Brazil.

Savoia-Marchetti S-64, Map of South Atlantic
A853

1978, July 3 Lithographed

1564 A853 1.80cr multicolored 20 10

50th anniversary of first crossing of South Atlantic by Carlos del Prete and Arturo Ferrarin.

Symbolic of Smallpox Eradication
A854

Brazil No. 68
A855

1978, July 25

1565 A854 1.80cr multicolored 20 10

Eradication of smallpox.

1978, Aug. 1

1566 A855 1.80cr multicolored 20 10

Stamp Day, centenary of the "Barba Branca" (white beard) issue.

Stormy Sea, by Seelinger
A856

1978, Aug. 4

1567 A856 1.80cr multicolored 20 10

Helios Seelinger, painter, birth centenary.

Guitar Players
A857

Musicians and Instruments: No. 1569, Flutes. No. 1570, Percussion instruments.

1978, Aug. 22 Litho. *Perf. 11½*

1568 A857 1.80cr multicolored 20 10
1569 " 1.80cr " 20 10
1570 " 1.80cr " 20 10

Children at Play
A858

1978, Sept. 1 Litho. *Perf. 11½*

1571 A858 1.80cr multicolored 20 10

National Week.

Collegiate Church
A859

1978, Sept. 6 Engraved

1572 A859 1.80cr red brown 20 10

Restoration of patio of Collegiate Church, Sao Paulo.

Justice by A. Geschiatti
A860

1978, Sept. 18 Lithographed

1573 A860 1.80cr blk. & olive 20 10

Federal Supreme Court, sesquicentennial.

Iguacu Falls
A861

Design: No. 1575, Yellow ipecac.

1978, Sept. 21

1574 A861 1.80cr multicolored 20 10
1575 " 1.80cr " 20 10

Iguacu National Park.

Stages of Intelsat Satellite
A862

1978, Oct. 9 Litho. *Perf. 11½*

1576 A862 1.80cr multicolored 20 10

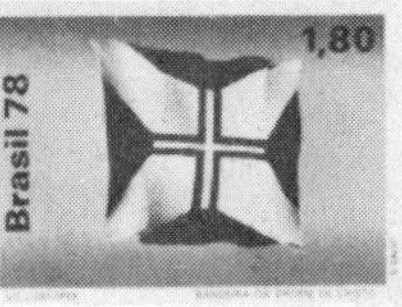

Flag of Order of Christ
A863

Brazilian Flags: No. 1578, Principality of Brazil. No. 1579, United Kingdom. No. 1580, Imperial Brazil. No. 1581, National flag (current).

1978, Oct. 13

1577 A863 1.80cr multicolored 20 10
1578 " 1.80cr " 20 10
1579 " 1.80cr " 20 10
1580 " 8.50cr " 1.00 50
1581 " 8.50cr " 1.00 50
a. Block of 5 + label 2.75

7th LUBRAPEX Philatelic Exhibition, Porto Alegre. Nos. 1577–1581 printed se-tenant in blocks of 5 plus label showing Acorianos monument.

Mail Street Car
A864

Mail Transportation: No. 1583, Overland mail truck. No. 1584, Mail delivery truck. 7.50cr. Railroad mail car. 8.50cr, Mail coach. 9.50cr, Post riders.

1978, Oct. 21 *Perf. 11x11½*

1582 A864 1.80cr multicolored 20 10
1583 " 1.80cr " 20 10
1584 " 1.80cr " 20 10
1585 " 7.50cr " 90 45
1586 " 8.50cr " 1.00 50
1587 " 9.50cr " 1.10 55
Nos. 1582–1587 (6) 3.60 1.80

18th Universal Postal Union Congress, Rio de Janeiro, 1979. Nos. 1582–1587 printed se-tenant.

Brasil 78 1,80

Gaucho Herding Cattle, and Cactus
A865

1978, Oct. 23 *Perf. 11½x11*

1588 A865 1.80cr multicolored 20 10

Joao Guimaraes Rosa, poet and diplomat, 70th birthday.

A little time given to study of the arrangement of the Scott Catalogue can make it easier to use effectively.

St. Anthony's Hill, by Nicholas A. Taunay
A866

Landscape Paintings: No. 1590, Castle Hill, by Victor Meirelles. No. 1591, View of Sabara, by Alberto da Veiga Guignard. No. 1592, View of Pernambuco, by Frans Post.

1978, Nov. 6 Litho. *Perf. 11½*

1589	A866	1.80cr multicolored		22	10
1590	"	1.80cr	"	22	10
1591	"	1.80cr	"	22	10
1592	"	1.80cr	"	22	10

Angel with Harp
A867

Designs: No. 1594, Angel with lute. No. 1595, Angel with oboe.

1978, Nov. 10

1593	A867	1.80cr multicolored		22	10
1594	"	1.80cr	"	22	10
1595	"	1.80cr	"	22	10

Christmas 1978.

Symbolic Candles
A868

1978, Nov. 23

1596	A868	1.80cr black, gold & carmine	22	10

National Thanksgiving Day.

Red Crosses and Activities—A869

1978, Dec. 5 Litho. *Perf. 11x11½*

1597	A869	1.80cr blk. & red	22	10

70th anniversary of Brazilian Red Cross.

Paz Theater, Belem
A870

Designs: 12cr, José de Alencar Theater, Portaleza. 12.50cr, Municipal Theater, Rio de Janeiro.

1978, Dec. 6 *Perf. 11½*

1598	A870	10.50cr multi.		1.25	60
1599	"	12cr	"	1.45	75
1600	"	12.50cr	"	1.50	78

SEMI-POSTAL STAMPS

National Philatelic Exhibition Issue.

SP1

Wmkd. Coat of Arms in Sheet. (236)

1934, Sept. 16 Engraved *Imperf.*
Thick Paper

B1 SP1 200r+100r deep claret 75 1.25
B2 " 300r+100r vermilion 75 1.25
B3 " 700r+100r brt. blue 6.00 7.50
B4 " 1000r+100r black 6.00 7.50

The surtax was to help defray the expenses of the exhibition. Issued in sheets of 60, inscribed "EXPOSICAO FILATELICA NACIONAL".

Red Cross Nurse and Soldier
SP2

Perf. 11

1935, Sept. 19 Typo. Wmk. 222

B5 SP2 200r+100r pur. & red 1.00 1.00
B6 " 300r+100r olive brown & red 1.00 75
B7 " 700r+100r turquoise blue and red 10.00 7.00

3rd Pan-American Red Cross Conference. Exist imperf.

Three Wise Men and Star of Bethlehem
SP3

Angel and Child
SP4

Southern Cross and Child
SP5

Mother and Child
SP6

Perf. 10½

1939, Dec. 20 Litho. Wmk. 249

B8 SP3 100r+100r chalky blue & blue black 50 50
a. Horiz. or vert. pair, imperf. between 45.00
B9 SP4 200r+100r bright greenish blue 1.00 1.00
a. Horizontal pair, imperf. between 45.00
B10 SP5 400r+200r olive green & olive 1.00 25
B11 SP6 1200r+400r crimson & brown red 4.00 1.50
a. Vertical pair, imperf. between 45.00

The surtax was distributed to charitable institutions.

AIR POST STAMPS.

Official Stamps of 1913 Surcharged

SERVIÇO
AEREO
200 Rs.

1927, Dec. 28 *Perf. 12* Unwmkd.
Center in Black.

C1 O2 50r on 10r gray 15 15
a. Inverted surcharge 200.00
b. Top ornaments missing 40.00
C2 " 200r on 1000r black brown 2.00 2.00
a. Double surch. 200.00
C3 " 200r on 2000r red brown 1.50 3.00
a. Double surcharge 40.00
C4 " 200r on 5000r brown 1.00 1.25
a. Double surch. 200.00
b. Double surcharge, one inverted 225.00
c. Triple surch. 250.00
C5 " 300r on 500r orange 1.00 1.50
C6 " 300r on 600r violet 60 50
b. Pair, one without surch.
C6A " 500r on 10r gray 250.00 250.00
C7 " 500r on 50r gray 1.25 45
a. Double surch. 200.00 200.00
C8 " 1000r on 20r olive grn. 1.00 15
a. Double surch. 200.00
C9 " 2000r on 100r verm. 2.25 1.50
a. Pair, one without surcharge 750.00
C10 " 2000r on 200r blue 3.00 1.50
C11 " 2000r on 10,000r black 2.25 50
C12 " 5000r on 20,000r blue 4.00 2.50
C13 " 5000r on 50,000r green 4.00 3.00
C14 " 5000r on 100,000r orange 15.00 20.00
C15 " 10,000r on 500,000r brown 17.50 17.50
C16 " 10,000r on 1,000,000r dark brown 16.00 19.00
Nos. C1-C6, C7-C16 (16) 72.50 74.50

Nos. C1, C1b, C7, C8 and C9 have small diamonds printed over the numerals in the upper corners.

Monument to de Gusmão
AP1

Santos-Dumont's Airship
AP2

Augusto Severo's Airship "Pax"
AP3

Santos-Dumont's Biplane "14 Bis"
AP4

Ribeiro de Barros's Seaplane "Jahu"
AP5

Perf. 11, 12½x13, 13x13½.

1929 Typographed. Wmk. 206

C17 AP1 50r blue green 25 20
C18 AP2 200r red 1.25 20
C19 AP3 300r bright blue 1.50 20
C20 AP4 500r red violet 2.00 20
C21 AP5 1000r orange brown 5.00 40
Nos. C17-C21 (5) 10.00 1.20

See also Nos. C32-C36.

Bartholomeu de Gusmão
AP6

Augusto Severo
AP7

Alberto Santos-Dumont
AP8

Perf. 9, 11 and Compound.

1929-30 Engraved. Wmk. 101

C22 AP6 2000r light green ('30) 10.00 25
C23 AP7 5000r carmine 10.00 1.00
C24 AP8 10,000r olive green 10.00 1.25

See also Nos. C37, C40.

Allegory: Airmail Service between Brazil and the United States
AP9

1929 Typographed Wmk. 206

C25 AP9 3000r violet 7.50 50

See also Nos. C38, C41. Nos. C23-C25 exist imperforate.

Air Post Stamps of 1929 Surcharged in Blue or Red

ZEPPELIN
2$500

1931, Aug. 16 *Perf. 12½x13½.*

C26 AP2 2500r on 200r red (Bl) 12.00 15.00
C27 AP3 5000r on 300r brt. blue (R) 13.00 15.00

No. C25 Surcharged

2.500 REIS

1931, Sept. 2 *Perf. 11*

C28 AP9 2500r on 3000r vio. 12.00 10.00
a. Inverted surcharge 150.00
b. Surcharged on front and back 100.00

Regular Issues of 1928-29 Surcharged

ZEPPELIN
3$500

Perf. 11, 11½.

1932, May Wmk. 101

C29 A89 3500r on 5000r gray lilac 10.00 12.50
C30 A72 7000r on 10,000r rose 10.00 12.50
a. Vert. pair, imperf. between 150.00
b. Horiz. pair, imperf. between 175.00

Imperforates

Since 1933, imperforate or partly perforated sheets of nearly all of the airmail issues have become available.

Flag and Airplane
AP10

Typographed

1933, June 7 *Perf. 11.* Wmk. 222

C31 AP10 3500r green, yellow & dark blue 5.00 1.00

See also Nos. C39, C42.

1934 Wmk. 222

C32 AP1 50r blue green 60 60
C33 AP2 200r red 1.25 60
C34 AP3 300r bright blue 2.50 1.25
C35 AP4 500r red violet 1.25 50
C36 AP5 1000r orange brown 3.00 40
Nos. C32-C36 (5) 8.60 3.35

Engraved.

1934 *Perf. 12x11.* Wmk. 236

Thick Laid Paper.

C37 AP6 2000r light green 4.00 1.00

Types of 1929, 1933.
Perf. 11, 11½, 12.

1937-40 Typographed Wmk. 249

C38 AP9 3000r violet 25.00 1.00
C39 AP10 3500r green, yellow & dark blue 1.25 1.00

Engraved.

C40 AP7 5000r verm. ('40) 4.00 60

Watermark note after No. 501 also applies to No. C40.

Types of 1929-33.
Perf. 11, 11½x12

1939-40 Typographed Wmk. 256

C41 AP9 3000r violet 75 50
C42 AP10 3500r blue, dull green & yellow ('40) 50 40

Map of the Western Hemisphere Showing Brazil
AP11

1941, Jan. 14 Engr. *Perf. 11*

C43 AP11 1200r dark brown 2.50 30

5th general census of Brazil.

Nos. 506A and 508 Overprinted in Carmine

AÉREO
"10 Nov."
937-941

Rouletted.

1941, Nov. 10 Wmk. 264

C45 A180 5400r slate green 2.00 1.00
a. Overprint inverted 150.00

Issued in commemoration of the fourth anniversary of President Vargas' new constitution.

Nos. 506A and 508 Surcharged in Black

AÉREO
"10 Nov."
937-942

Cr.$ 5,40

1942, Nov. 10 **Wmk. 264**

C47	A180	5.40cr on 5400r slate green	2.00	1.00
		a. Wmk. 249	50.00	50.00
		b. Surcharge inverted	75.00	75.00

Issued in commemoration of the fifth anniversary of President Vargas' new constitution.

The status of No. C47a is questioned.

Southern Cross and Arms of Paraguay
AP12

Wmk. 270

Wmkd.
Wavy Lines and Seal. (270)

1943, May 11 **Engr.** ***Perf. 12½***

C48	AP12	1.20cr lt. gray blue	1.00	50

Issued in commemoration of the visit of President Higinio Morinigo of Paraguay.

Map of South America
AP13

Wmk. 271

Wmkd. Wavy Lines. (271)

1943, June 30 ***Perf. 12½.***

C49	AP13	1.20cr multi.	1.00	50

Visit of President Penaranda of Bolivia.

Numeral of Value
AP14

1943, Aug. 7

C50	AP14	1cr black & dull yellow	3.00	2.00
		a. Double impression	50.00	
C51	"	2cr black & pale green	4.00	2.00
		a. Double impression	60.00	
C52	"	5cr black & pink	5.00	2.75

Centenary of Brazil's first postage stamps.

Souvenir Sheet.

AP15

Imperf.

Without Gum

C53	AP15	Sheet of three	35.00	35.00
		a. 1cr black & dull yellow	10.00	10.00
		b. 2cr blk. & pale grn.	10.00	10.00
		c. 5cr black & pink	10.00	10.00

Issued to commemorate the 100th anniversary of the first postage stamps of Brazil and the second Philatelic Exposition (Brapex). Printed in panes of 6 sheets, perforated 12½ between. Each sheet is perforated on two or three sides. Size approximately 155x155mm. Inscriptions are printed in light brown.

Law Book
AP16

1943, Aug. 13 ***Perf. 12½***

C54	AP16	1.20cr rose & lilac rose	60	25

Issued to commemorate the second Inter-American Conference of Lawyers.

Semi-Postal Stamps of 1939 Surcharged in Red, Carmine or Black

AÉREO
20
Cts.

1944, Jan. 3 ***Perf. 10½*** **Wmk. 249**

C55	SP5	20c on 400r+200r olive green & olive (R)	50	50
C56	"	40c on 400r+200r olive green & olive (Bk)	1.00	35
C57	SP5	60c on 400r+200r olive green & olive (C)	1.00	25
C58	"	1cr on 400r+200r olive green & olive (Bk)	1.25	30
C59	"	1.20cr on 400r+200r olive green & olive (C)	1.50	30
		Nos. C55-C59 (5)	5.25	1.70

No. C59 is known with surcharge in black but its status is questioned.

Bartholomeu de Gusmão and the "Aerostat"
AP17

Engraved

1944, Oct. 23 ***Perf. 12*** **Wmk. 268**

C60	AP17	1.20cr rose carmine	50	20

Week of the Wing.

L. L. Zamenhof
AP18

1945, Apr. 16 **Litho.** ***Perf. 11***

C61	AP18	1.20cr dull brown	60	30

Issued to commemorate the Esperanto Congress held in Rio de Janeiro, April 14-22, 1945.

Map of South America
AP19

Baron of Rio Branco
AP20

1945, Apr. 20

C62	AP19	1.20cr gray brown	50	25
C63	AP20	5cr rose lilac	1.50	40

Issued to commemorate the centenary of the birth of José Maria de Silva Paranhos, Baron of Rio Branco.

Dove and Flags of American Republics
AP21

Perf. 12x11

1947, Aug. 15 **Engr.** **Unwmkd.**

C64	AP21	2.20cr dark blue green	55	30

Issued to commemorate the Inter-American Defense Conference at Rio de Janeiro August-September, 1947.

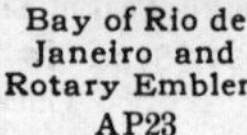

Santos-Dumont Monument, St. Cloud, France
AP22

Bay of Rio de Janeiro and Rotary Emblem
AP23

1947, Nov. 15 **Typo.** ***Perf. 11x12***

C65	AP22	1.20cr orange brown & olive	50	25

Issued to commemorate the Week of the Wing and to honor the Santos-Dumont monument which was destroyed in World War II.

1948, May 16 **Engraved.** ***Perf. 11.***

C66	AP23	1.20cr deep claret	60	35
C67	"	3.80cr dull violet	1.25	35

Issued in honor of the 39th convention of Rotary International, Rio de Janeiro, May 1948.

Hotel Quitandinha, Petropolis
AP24

1948, July 10 **Litho.** **Wmk. 267**

C68	AP24	1.20cr orange brown	35	25
C69	"	3.80cr violet	65	30

Issued to commemorate the International Exposition of Industry and Commerce, Petropolis, 1948.

Musician and Singers
AP25

1948, Aug. 13 **Engraved.** **Unwmkd.**

C70	AP25	1.20cr blue	50	20

Issued to commemorate the centenary of the establishment of the National School of Music.

Luis Batlle Berres
AP26

1948, Sept. 2 **Typographed.**

C71	AP26	1.70cr blue	35	25

Issued to commemorate the visit of President Luis Batlle Berres of Uruguay, September, 1948.

Merino Ram
AP27

Perf. 12x11.

1948, Oct. 10 Wmk. 267

C72 AP27 1.20cr deep orange 80 30

Issued to publicize the International Livestock Exposition at Bagé.

Eucharistic Congress Seal
AP28

Engraved.

1948, Oct. 23 *Perf. 11* Unwmkd.

C73 AP28 1.20cr dark carmine rose 40 30

Issued to commemorate the 5th National Eucharistic Congress, Porto Alegre, October 24 to 31.

Souvenir Sheet

AP28a
Without Gum

1948, Dec. 14 Engraved *Imperf.*

C73A AP28a Sheet of three 40.00 50.00

No. C73A contains one each of Nos. 674-676. Issued in honor of President Eurico Gaspar Dutra and the armed forces. Exists both with and without number on back. Measures 130x75mm. Marginal inscriptions typographed in black.

Church of Prazeres, Guararapes
AP29

Perf. 11½x12.

1949, Feb. 15 Litho. Wmk. 267

C74 AP29 1.20cr pink 1.50 75

Issued to commemorate the 300th anniversary of the Second Battle of Guararapes.

Thomé de Souza Meeting Indians
AP30

Perf. 11x12.

1949, Mar. 29 Engr. Unwmkd.

C75 AP30 1.20cr blue 35 25

Issued to commemorate the 400th anniversary of the founding of the City of Salvador.

A souvenir folder, issued with No. C75, has an engraved 20cr red brown postage stamp portraying John III printed on it, and a copy of No. C75 affixed to it and postmarked. Paper is laid, inscriptions are in red brown and size of folder front is 100x150mm. Price, $5.

Franklin D. Roosevelt
AP31

1949, May 20 *Imperf.* Unwmkd.

C76 AP31 3.80cr deep blue 1.00 80
a. Souvenir sheet 8.00 12.00

No. C76a measures 85x110mm., with deep blue inscriptions in upper and lower margins. It also exists with papermaker's watermark.

Joaquim Nabuco
AP32

1949, Aug. 30 *Perf. 12*

C77 AP32 3.80cr rose lilac 70 40
a. Wmk. 256, imperf. 25.00

Issued to commemorate the centenary of the birth of Joaquim Nabuco (1849–1910), lawyer and writer.

Maracanã Stadium
AP33

Soccer Player and Flag
AP34

Perf. 11x12, 12x11

1950, June 24 Litho. Wmk. 267

C78 AP33 1.20cr ultramarine & salmon 1.25 40

C79 AP34 5.80cr blue, yellow green & yellow 3.00 50

Issued to publicize the 4th World Soccer Championship at Rio de Janeiro.

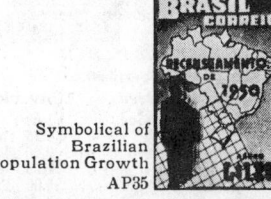

Symbolical of Brazilian Population Growth
AP35

1950, July 10 *Perf. 12x11*

C80 AP35 1.20cr red brown 40 15

Issued to publicize the 6th Brazilian census.

J. B. Marcelino Champagnat
AP36

Engraved.

1956, Sept. 8 *Perf. 11½* Wmk. 267

C81 AP36 3.30cr rose lilac 30 10

Issued to commemorate the 50th anniversary of the arrival of the Marist Brothers in Northern Brazil.

Santos-Dumont's 1906 Plane
AP37

1956, Oct. 16 Photogravure

C82 AP37 3cr dark blue green 1.25 30
a. Souvenir sheet of four 1.75 1.75
b. 3cr dk. car. 35 25

C83 " 3.30cr brt. ultra. 30 10

C84 " 4cr deep claret 60 10

C85 " 6.50cr red brown 20 10

C86 " 11.50cr orange red 1.25 35

Nos. C82–C86 (5) 3.60 95

Issued to commemorate the 50th anniversary of the first flight by Santos-Dumont.

No. C82a measures 123½x156mm. and contains four copies of No. C82b. Inscribed in dark carmine in four languages: "50TH ANNIVERSARY OF THE FIRST FLIGHT OF THE HEAVIER THAN THE AIR." Issued Oct. 14, 1956.

Lord Baden-Powell
AP38

1957, Aug. 1 Unwmkd.

Granite Paper

C87 AP38 3.30cr deep red lilac 40 10

Issued to commemorate the centenary of the birth of Lord Baden-Powell, founder of the Boy Scouts.

U.N. Emblem, Soldier and Map of Suez Canal Area
AP39

Engraved.

1957, Oct. 24 *Perf. 11½* Wmk. 267

C88 AP39 3.30cr dark blue 30 25

Issued to honor the Brazilian contingent of the United Nations Emergency Force.

Basketball Player
AP40

1959, May 30 Photo. *Perf. 11½*

C89 AP40 3.30cr bright red brown & blue 40 10

Brazil's victory in the World Basketball Championships of 1959.

Symbol of Flight
AP41

1959, Oct. 21 Wmk. 267

C90 AP41 3.30cr deep ultra. 20 10

Issued to publicize Week of the Wing.

Caravelle
AP42

1959, Dec. 18 *Perf. 11½*

C91 AP42 6.50cr ultramarine 15 10

Inauguration of Brazilian jet flights.

Pres. Adolfo Lopez Mateos
AP43

Pres. Dwight D. Eisenhower
AP44

1960, Jan. 19 Photo. Wmk. 267

C92 AP43 6.50cr brown 15 10

Issued to commemorate the visit of President Adolfo Lopez Mateos of Mexico.

1960, Feb. 23 *Perf. 11½*

C93 AP44 6.50cr deep orange 20 12

Visit of Pres. Dwight D. Eisenhower.

World Refugee Year Emblem
AP45

Tower at Brasilia
AP46

1960, Apr. 7 **Wmk. 268**

C94 AP45 6.50cr blue 15 10

Issued to publicize World Refugee Year, July 1, 1959–June 30, 1960.

Type of Regular Issue and AP46.

Designs: 3.30cr, Square of the Three Entities. 4cr, Cathedral. 11.50cr, Plan of Brasilia.

Perf. 11x11½, 11½x11

1960, Apr. 21 Photo. **Wmk. 267**

C95 A436 3.30cr violet 15 10
C96 " 4cr blue 1.25 15
C97 AP46 6.50cr rose car. 15 10
C98 A436 11.50cr brown 20 12

Issued to commemorate the inauguration of Brazil's new capital, Brasilia, Apr. 21, 1960.

Chrismon and Oil Lamp
AP47

1960, May 16 ***Perf. 11x11½***

C99 AP47 3.30cr lilac rose 15 10

Issued to publicize the Seventh National Eucharistic Congress at Curitiba.

Cross, Sugarloaf Mountain and Emblem—AP48

1960, July 1 **Wmk. 267**

C100 AP48 6.50cr bright blue 15 10

Issued to commemorate the 10th Congress of the World Baptist Alliance, Rio de Janeiro.

Boy Scout
AP49

Caravel
AP50

1960, July 23 ***Perf. 11½x11***

C101 AP49 3.30cr org. verm. 15 10

Boy Scouts of Brazil, 50th anniversary.

1960, Aug. 5 **Engraved** **Wmk. 268**

C102 AP50 6.50cr black 20 10

Issued to commemorate the 500th anniversary of the birth of Prince Henry the Navigator.

Maria E. Bueno
AP51

Photogravure

1960, Dec. 15 ***Perf. 11x11½***

C103 AP51 6cr pale brown 15 10

Issued to commemorate the victory at Wimbledon of Maria E. Bueno, women's singles tennis champion.

War Memorial, Sugarloaf Mountain and Allied Flags
AP52

1960, Dec. 22 **Wmk. 268**

C104 AP52 3.30cr lilac rose 15 10

Issued to commemorate the reburial of Brazilian servicemen of World War II.

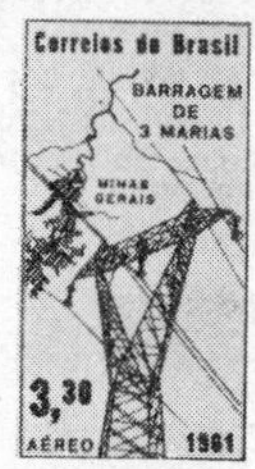

Power Line and Map
AP53

Malaria Eradication Emblem
AP54

1961, Jan. 20 ***Perf. 11½x11***

C105 AP53 3.30cr lilac rose 10 10

Issued to commemorate the inauguration of Three Marias Dam and hydroelectric station in Minas Gerais.

Engraved

1962, May 24 **Wmk. 267**

C106 AP54 21cr blue 10 7

Issued for the World Health Organization drive to eradicate malaria.

F. A. de Varnhagen
AP55

1966, Feb. 17 Photo. **Wmk. 267**

C107 AP55 45cr red brown 30 10

Issued to commemorate the 150th anniversary of the birth of Francisco Adolfo de Varnhagen, Viscount of Porto Seguro (1816–1878), historian and diplomat.

Map of the Americas and Alliance for Progress Emblem
AP56

1966, March 14 ***Perf. 11x11½***

C108 AP56 120cr greenish blue & vio. blue 40 15

Issued to commemorate the fifth anniversary of the Alliance for Progress.

A souvenir card contains one impression of No. C108, imperf. Black inscriptions. Size: 113x160mm.

Nun and Globe
AP57

Face of Jesus from Shroud of Turin
AP58

1966, Mar. 25 Photo. ***Perf. 11½x11***

C109 AP57 35cr violet 20 10

Issued to commemorate the centenary of the arrival of the teaching Sisters of St. Dorothea.

1966, June 3 Photo. **Wmk. 267**

C110 AP58 45cr brn. orange 25 10

Issued to commemorate Vatican II, the 21st Ecumenical Council of the Roman Catholic Church, Oct. 11, 1962–Dec. 8, 1965.

A souvenir card contains one impression of No. C110, imperf. Brown orange inscription and head of Jesus in margin. Size: 100x39mm.

Admiral Mariz e Barros
AP59

"Youth" by Eliseu Visconti
AP60

1966, June 13 Photo. **Wmk. 267**

C111 AP59 35cr red brown 20 10

Death centenary of Admiral Antonio Carlos Mariz e Barros, who died in the Battle of Itaperu.

1966, July 31 ***Perf. 11½x11***

C112 AP60 120cr red brown 50 12

Birth centenary of Eliseu Visconti, painter.

SPECIAL DELIVERY STAMP.

No. 191 Surcharged

1930 ***Perf. 12*** **Unwmkd.**

E1 A62 1000r on 200r dp. blue 2.50 1.25
a. Inverted surcharge 400.00

POSTAGE DUE STAMPS.

D1

D2

Typographed.

1889 ***Rouletted.*** **Unwmkd.**

J1 D1 10r carmine 1.00 60
J2 " 20r " 1.25 1.00
J3 " 50r " 3.00 1.50
J4 " 100r " 1.50 60
J5 " 200r " 25.00 7.50
J6 D1 300r carmine 3.50 4.00
J7 " 500r " 3.50 4.00
J8 " 700r " 5.00 6.00
J9 " 1000r " 5.00 7.00
Nos. J1–J9 (9) 48.75 31.20

1890

J10 D1 10r orange 40 20
J11 " 20r ultramarine 40 20
J12 " 50r olive 60 20
J13 " 200r magenta 2.00 30
J14 " 300r blue green 1.25 65
J15 " 500r slate 1.75 2.00
J16 " 700r purple 4.00 3.00
J17 " 1000r dark violet 3.50 4.00
Nos. J10–J17 (8) 13.90 12.55

Perf. 11 to 11½, 12½ to 14 and Compound.

1895-1901

J18 D2 10r dark blue ('01) 1.00 50
J19 " 20r yellow green 10.00 5.00
J20 " 50r yel. green ('01) 6.00 6.00
J21 " 100r brick red 7.00 40
J22 " 200r violet 4.00 25
a. 200r gray lilac ('98) 6.00 1.25
J23 D2 300r dull blue 3.00 1.25
J24 " 2000r brown 10.00 10.00
Nos. J18–J24 (7) 41.00 23.40

1906 **Wmk. 97**

J25 D2 100r brick red 6.00 2.00

Wmkd. (97? or 98?)

J26 D2 200r violet 4.00 75
a. Wmk. 97 75.00 50.00
b. Wmk. 98 10.00 10.00

D3

D4

Engraved

1906–10 ***Perf. 12*** **Unwmkd.**

J28 D3 10r slate 15 10
J29 " 20r bright violet 15 10
J30 " 50r dark green 20 10
J31 " 100r carmine 1.25 40
J32 " 200r deep blue 40 20
J33 " 300r gray black 25 40
J34 " 400r olive green 80 60
J35 " 500r dark violet 30.00 30.00
J36 " 600r violet ('10) 1.00 1.00
J37 " 700r red brown 25.00 25.00
J38 " 1000r red 1.00 1.00
J39 " 2000r green 3.50 3.50
J40 " 5000r chocolate ('10) 1.00 1.00
Nos. J28–J40 (13) 64.70 63.40

Typographed.

1919-23 ***Perf. 12½, 11, 11x10½.***

J41 D4 5r red brown 20 20
J42 " 10r violet 20 20
J43 " 20r olive gray 25 20
J44 " 50r green ('23) 25 25
J45 " 100r red 1.25 1.25
J46 " 200r blue 6.00 2.00
J47 " 400r brown ('23) 1.00 1.00
Nos. J41–J47 (7) 9.15 5.10

Perf. 12½, 12½x13½.

1924–35 **Wmk. 100**

J48 D4 5r red brown 40 40
J49 " 100r red 75 50
J50 " 200r slate blue ('29) 50 50
J51 " 400r dp. brown ('29) 1.00 1.00
J52 " 600r dark violet ('29) 1.00 1.00
J53 " 600r orange ('35) 50 50
Nos. J48–J53 (6) 4.15 3.90

1924 ***Perf. 11x10½.*** **Wmk. 193**

J54 D4 100r red 30.00 30.00
J55 " 200r slate blue 4.00 3.00

Perf. 11x10½, 13x13½.

1925-27 **Wmk. 101**

J56 D4 20r olive gray 20 20
J57 " 100r red 60 40
J58 " 200r slate blue 2.00 80

J59 D4 400r brown 1.75 1.75
J60 " 600r dark violet 5.00 5.00
Nos. J56–J60 (5) 9.55 8.15

Wmkd. E U BRASIL Multiple. (218)

1929-30 ***Perf. 12½x13½.***

J61 D4 100r light red 25 25
J62 " 200r blue black 40 40
J63 " 400r brown 40 40
J64 " 1000r myrtle green 75 75

Perf. 11, 12½x13, 13.

1931-36 **Wmk. 222**

J65 D4 10r light violet ('35) 15 10
J66 " 20r black ('33) 35 35
J67 " 50r blue green ('35) 40 40
J68 " 100r rose red ('35) 20 20
J69 " 200r slate blue ('35) 35 30
J70 " 400r blk. brown ('35) 1.75 1.50
J71 " 600r dark violet 30 25
J72 " 1000r myrtle green 50 40
J73 " 2000r brown ('36) 70 70
J74 " 5000r indigo ('36) 2.00 2.00
Nos. J65–J74 (10) 6.70 6.20

1938 ***Perf. 11.*** **Wmk. 249**

J75 D4 200r slate blue 70 70

1940 Typographed. **Wmk. 256**

J76 D4 10r light violet 60 60
J77 " 20r black 60 60
J79 " 100r rose red 60 60
J80 " 200r myrtle green 60 60

1942 **Wmk. 264**

J81 D4 10r light violet 15 10
J82 " 20r olive black 15 10
J83 " 50r light blue green 40 40
J84 " 100r vermilion 18 10
J85 " 200r gray blue 45 40
J86 " 400r claret 40 40
J87 " 600r rose violet 30 25
J88 " 1000r dark blue green 30 20
J89 " 2000r dp. yel. brown 45 40
J90 " 5000r indigo 80 75
Nos. J81–J90 (10) 3.58 3.10

1949 **Wmk. 268**

J91 D4 10c pale rose lilac 4.00 3.50
J92 " 20r black 40.00 35.00

No. J92 exists in shades of gray ranging to gray olive.

OFFICIAL STAMPS

Pres. Affonso Penna
O1

Pres. Hermes da Fonseca
O2

Engraved

1906, Nov. 15 ***Perf. 12*** **Unwmkd.**

O1 O1 10r orange & green 20 10
O2 " 20r " " 25 10
O3 " 50r " " 1.00 10
O4 " 100r " " 25 10
O5 " 200r " " 60 10
O6 " 300r " " 1.50 20
O7 " 400r " " 1.75 60
O8 " 500r " " 1.75 40
O9 " 700r " " 1.50 1.50
O10 " 1000r " " 1.25 60
O11 " 2000r " " 1.75 75
O12 " 5000r " " 6.00 90
O13 " 10,000r " " 8.00 50
Nos. O1–O13 (13) 25.80 5.95

The portrait is the same but the frame differs for each denomination of this issue.

1913, Nov. 15 **Center in Black**

O14 O2 10r gray 30 25
O15 " 20r olive green 30 25
O16 " 50r gray 30 25
O17 " 100r vermilion 60 10
O18 " 200r blue 80 20
O19 " 500r orange 2.00 40
O20 " 600r violet 2.25 80
O21 " 1000r blk. brown 2.50 50
O22 O2 2000r red brown 3.50 75
O23 " 5000r brown 4.00 1.00
O24 " 10,000r black 5.00 2.75
O25 " 20,000r blue 16.00 16.00
O26 " 50,000r green 20.00 20.00
O27 " 100,000r orange red 90.00 90.00
O28 " 500,000r brown 160.00 160.00
O29 " 1,000,000r dark brn. 175.00 175.00
Nos. O14–O29 (16) 482.55 468.25

The portrait is the same on all denominations of this series but there are eight types of the frame. Though all the stamps are inscribed "Correio" (postage) the higher values were used only for fiscal purposes.

Pres. Wenceslau Braz
O3

Perf. 11, 11½

1919, Apr. 11 **Wmk. 100**

O30 O3 10r olive green 50 40
O31 " 50r green 50 40
O32 " 100r rose red 75 40
O33 " 200r dull blue 1.00 40
O34 " 500r orange 6.00 6.50
Nos. O30–O34 (5) 8.75 8.10

The official decree called for eleven stamps in this series but only five were issued.

See Nos. 293–297.

NEWSPAPER STAMPS.

N1

Lithographed.

1889, Feb. 1 ***Rouletted*** **Unwmkd.**

P1 N1 10r yellow 2.50 2.75
a. Pair, imperf. between 60.00 80.00
P2 " 20r yellow 6.00 7.00
P3 " 50r " 10.00 6.00
P4 " 100r " 4.00 3.00
P5 " 200r " 2.50 1.25
P6 " 300r " 3.00 1.50
P7 " 500r " 17.50 8.00
P8 " 700r " 3.00 3.00
P9 " 1000r " 4.00 5.00
Nos. P1–P9 (9) 52.50 37.50

1889, May 1

P10 N1 10r olive 40 20
P11 " 20r green 40 25
P12 " 50r brown yellow 60 25
P13 " 100r violet 1.25 60
P14 " 200r black 1.25 80
P15 " 300r carmine 6.00 6.00
P16 " 500r green 32.50 32.50
P17 " 700r ultramarine 17.50 20.00
P18 " 1000r brown 9.00 9.00
Nos. P10–P18 (9) 68.90 69.60

N2

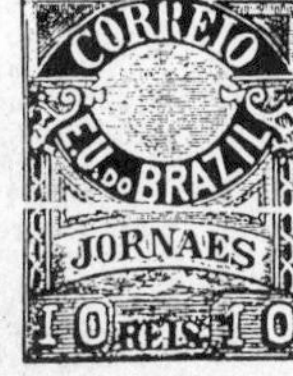

N3

White Wove Paper Thin to Thick

Perf. 11 to 11½, 12½ to 14 and 12½ to 14x11 to 11½

1890 **Typographed**

P19 N2 10r blue 4.00 3.00
a. 10r ultramarine 4.00 3.00
P20 " 20r emerald 12.50 4.00
P21 " 100r violet 5.00 4.00

1890-93

P22 N3 10r blue 40 25
a. 10r ultramarine 80 60
P23 " 10r ultramarine, *buff* 1.00 75
P24 " 20r green 80 50
a. 20r emerald 1.25 75
P25 " 50r yellow grn. ('93) 5.00 4.00

POSTAL TAX STAMPS.

Icarus from the Santos-Dumont Monument at St. Cloud, France
PT1

Perf. 13½x12½, 11.

1933, Oct. 1 **Typo.** **Wmk. 222**

RA1 PT1 100r deep brown 35 10

No. RA1 was issued in commemoration of the Brazilian aviator, Santos-Dumont. It did not pay postage but its use was obligatory as a tax on all correspondence sent to countries in South America, the United States and Spain. Its use on correspondence to other countries was optional. The money obtained from its sale was added to funds for the construction of airports throughout Brazil.

Father Joseph Damien and Children
PT2

Father Bento Dias Pacheco
PT3

Perf. 12x11

1952, Nov. 24 **Litho.** **Wmk. 267**

RA2 PT2 10c yellow brown 25 25

1953, Nov. 30

RA3 PT2 10c yellow green 15 15

1954, Nov. 22 **Photo.** ***Perf. 11½***

RA4 PT3 10c violet blue 20 20

1955, Nov. 24

RA5 PT3 10c dk. car. rose 20 20

1957, Nov. 24

RA6 PT3 10c orange red 15 10

1958, Nov. 24

RA7 PT3 10c deep emerald 15 10

1961, Nov. 24

RA8 PT3 10c red lilac 15 10

1962, Nov. 24

RA9 PT3 10c chocolate 15 10

1963, Nov. 24

RA10 PT3 10c slate 15 10

1964, Nov. 24

RA11 PT3 2cr deep magenta 15 10

1965, Nov. 24

RA12 PT3 2cr violet 15 10

1966, Nov. 24

RA13 PT3 2cr orange 15 10

1968, Nov. 25

RA14 PT3 5c brt. yel. green 80 60

1969, Nov. 28

RA15 PT3 5c deep plum 15 10

Eunice Weaver
PT4

Father Nicodemos
PT5

1971, Nov. 24

RA16 PT4 10c slate green 30 30

1973, Nov. 24

RA17 PT4 10c brt. rose lilac 15 10

1975, Nov. 24 **Litho.** **Unwmkd.**

RA18 PT5 10c sepia 15 10

Use of Nos. RA2–RA18 was required for one week. The tax was for the care and treatment of lepers.

POSTAL TAX SEMI-POSTAL STAMP.

Icarus
PTSP1

Typographed.

1947, Nov. 15 ***Perf. 11*** **Wmk. 267**

RAB1 PTSP1 40c+10c bright red 30 20
a. Pair, imperf. between 40.00

Issued to commemorate Aviation Week, November 15-22, 1947, and compulsory on all domestic correspondence during that week.

BREMEN BRUNSWICK

See Early German States group preceding Germany.

BULGARIA

(bŭl·gâr'ĭ·ȧ; bo͞ol·gâr'ĭ·ȧ)

LOCATION—In southeastern Europe bordering on the Black Sea in the east and the Danube River on the north.

GOVT.—Republic.

AREA—42,796 sq. mi.

POP.—8,760,000 (est. 1976).

CAPITAL—Sofia.

In 1885 Bulgaria, then a principality under the suzerainty of the Sultan of Turkey, was joined by Eastern Rumelia. Her independence of Turkey was established in 1908.

100 Centimes = 1 Franc

100 Stotinki = 1 Lev (1881)

Lion of Bulgaria

A1 A2 A3

Wmk. 168

Typographed.

Laid Paper.

Wmkd. ЭЗГБ & Wavy Lines (168)

1879, June 1 *Perf. 14½x15*

1 A1 5c black & yellow 35.00 12.50
2 " 10c black & green 110.00 25.00
3 " 25c black & violet 110.00 10.00
a. Imperf. 1500.00
4 " 50c black & blue 125.00 22.50
5 A2 1fr black & red 35.00 12.50

1881, June 10

6 A3 3s red & silver 11.50 2.25
7 " 5s black & orange 15.00 2.25
a. Background inverted 1500.00
8 " 10s black & green 55.00 4.50
9 " 15s red & green 75.00 5.00
10 " 25s black & violet 150.00 14.00
11 " 30s blue & fawn 25.00 6.50

1882, Dec. 4

12 A3 3s orange & yellow 75 30
a. Background inverted 1500.00
13 " 5s green & pale green 5.00 35
a. 5s rose & pale rose (error) 1250.00 1000.00
14 " 10s rose & pale rose 5.75 30
15 " 15s red violet & pale lilac 4.75 30
16 " 25s blue & pale blue 4.75 45
17 " 30s violet & green 5.75 40
18 " 50s blue & pink 5.50 40

See also Nos. 207–210, 286.

A4

A5

Surcharged in Black, Carmine or Vermilion

1884, May 1

Typographed Surcharge

19 A4 3s on 10s rose (Bk) 85.00 25.00
20 " 5s on 30s blue & fawn (C) 75.00 25.00
20A " 5s on 30s blue & fawn (Bk) 1500.00 1000.00
21 A5 15s on 25s bl. (C) 125.00 25.00

On some values the surcharge may be found inverted or double.

1885, June

Lithographed Surcharge

21B A4 3s on 10s rose (Bk) 35.00 25.00
21C " 5s on 30s blue & fawn (V) 35.00 30.00
21D A5 15s on 25s blue (V) 35.00 30.00
22 " 50s on 1fr black & red (Bk) 150.00 125.00

Forgeries of Nos. 19–22 are plentiful.

Word below left star in oval has 5 letters

A6

Third letter below left star is "A"

A7

1885, May 25

23 A6 1s gray violet & pale gray 9.00 3.00
24 A7 2s slate green & pale gray 9.00 2.50

Word below left star has 4 letters

A8

Third letter below left star is "b" with cross-bar in upper half

A9

A10

1886–87

25 A8 1s gray violet & pale gray 60 18
26 A9 2s slate green & pale gray 60 18
27 A10 1l black & red ('87) 25.00 5.00

A11

Perf. 10½, 11, 11½, 13, 13½.

1889 Wove Paper. Unwmkd.

28 A11 1s lilac 20 5
29 " 2s gray 75 10
30 " 3s bistre brown 50 10
31 " 5s yellow green 20 4
a. Vertical pair, imperf. between 50.00 50.00
32 " 10s rose 1.00 12
33 " 15s orange 60 5
34 " 25s blue 75 8
35 " 30s dark brown 3.00 8
36 " 50s green 60 10
37 " 1l orange red 50 20
Nos. 28–37 (10) 8.10 92

The 10s orange is a proof.
Nos. 28–34 are known imperforate. Price, set $225. See Nos. 39, 41–42.

No. 35 Surcharged in Black **15**

1892, Jan. 26

38 A11 15s on 30s brown 5.00 75
a. Inverted surcharge 60.00 40.00

1894 *Perf. 10½, 11, 11½.*

Pelure Paper.

39 A11 10s red 10.00 20
a. Imperf. 40.00

No. 26 Surcharged in Red **01**

Wmkd. Wavy Lines. (168)

1895, Oct. 25 *Perf. 14½x15*

Laid Paper.

40 A9 1s on 2s slate green & pale gray 40 15
a. Inverted surcharge 7.50 5.00
b. Double surcharge 60.00 60.00
c. Pair, one without surcharge 150.00 150.00

This surcharge on No. 24 is a proof.

Wmkd. Coat of Arms in the Sheet.

1896, Apr. 30 *Perf. 11½, 13*

Wove Paper.

41 A11 2l rose & pale rose 3.50 2.50
42 " 3l black & buff 3.50 2.50

Coat of Arms

A14

Cherry Wood Cannon

A15

1896, Feb. 2 *Perf. 13*

43 A14 1s blue green 25 15
44 " 5s dark blue 25 15
45 " 15s purple 75 30
46 " 25s red 4.00 1.00

Baptism of Prince Boris.
Examples of Nos. 41–46 from sheet edges show no watermark.
Nos. 43, 45–46 were also printed on rough unwatermarked paper.

1901, Apr. 20 Litho. **Unwmkd.**

53 A15 5s carmine 1.00 1.50
54 " 15s yellow green 1.00 1.50

Insurrection of Independence in April, 1876, 25th anniversary.
Exist imperf. Forgeries exist.

Nos. 30 and 36 Surcharged in Black

1901, Mar. 24 Typographed

55 A11 5s on 3s bistre brown 1.25 1.00
a. Inverted surcharge 30.00 30.00
b. Pair, one without surcharge 75.00 75.00
56 " 10s on 50s green 1.25 1.00
a. Inverted surcharge 30.00
b. Pair, one without surcharge 75.00 75.00

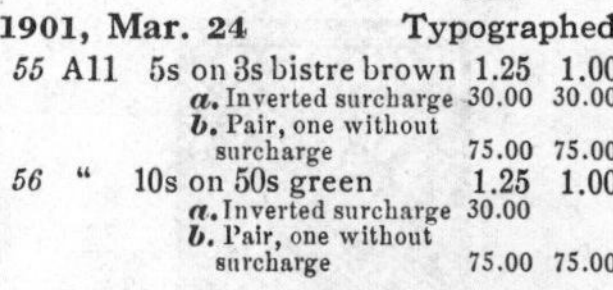

Tsar Ferdinand

A17

Fighting at Shipka Pass

A18

ONE LEVA:

Type I. The numerals in the upper corners have, at the top, a sloping serif on the left side and a short straight serif on the right.
Type II. The numerals in the upper corners are of ordinary shape without the serif at the right.

1901–05 Typo. *Perf. 12½*

57 A17 1s violet & gray black 5 4
58 " 2s bronze green & indigo 10 3
a. Imperf.
59 " 3s orange & indigo 15 6
60 " 5s emerald & brown 2.00 4
61 " 10s rose & black 90 4
62 " 15s claret & gray black 60 5
63 " 25s blue & black 60 5
64 " 30s bistre & gray black 10.00 12
65 " 50s dark blue & brown 90 9
66 " 1l red orange & bronze green, type I 2.50 18
67 " 1l brown red & bronze green, II ('05) 50.00 1.50
68 " 2l carmine & black 5.00 1.00
69 " 3l slate & red brown 6.50 2.75
Nos. 57–69 (13) 79.30 5.95

1902, Aug. 29 Litho. *Perf. 11½*

70 A18 5s lake 1.00 50
71 " 10s blue green 1.00 50
72 " 15s blue 3.00 1.50

Battle of Shipka Pass, 1877.
Imperf. copies are proofs.
Excellent forgeries of Nos. 70 to 72 exist.

No. 62 Surcharged in Black **10**

1903, Oct. 1 *Perf. 12½*

73 A17 10s on 15s claret & gray black 5.00 20
a. Invtd. surch. 50.00 35.00
b. Double surcharge 50.00 35.00
c. Pair, one without surcharge 85.00 85.00
d. 10s on 10s rose & black 250.00 150.00

Ferdinand in 1887 and 1907

A19

1907, Aug. 12 Litho. *Perf. 11½*

74 A19 5s deep green 4.00 85
75 " 10s red brown 7.00 1.00
76 " 25s deep blue 9.50 1.75

Accession to the throne of Ferdinand I, 20th anniversary.
Nos. 74–76 imperf. are proofs. Nos. 74–76 exist in pairs imperforate between.

Stamps of 1889 Overprinted **1909**

1909

77 A11 1s lilac 1.00 20
a. Inverted overprint 5.00 4.00
b. Double overprint, one inverted 12.50 7.50
78 " 5s yellow green 85 30
a. Inverted ovpt. 15.00 15.00
b. Double overprint 8.00 8.00

With Additional Surcharge **5** or **10**

79 A11 5s on 30s brn. (Bk) 1.25 30
a. "5" double 10.00 10.00
b. "1990" for "1909" 400.00 300.00
80 " 10s on 15s org. (Bk) 1.25 35
a. Inverted surcharge 7.50 7.50
b. "1909" omitted 15.00 15.00
81 " 10s on 50s dark green (R) 1.25 35
a. "1990" for "1909" 75.00 75.00
b. Black surcharge 40.00 40.00

Stamps of 1901 Surcharged with Value Only.

83 A17 5s on 15s claret & gray black (Bl) 1.25 30
a. Inverted surcharge 20.00 20.00
84 " 10s on 15s claret & gray black (Bl) 2.00 20
a. Inverted surcharge 20.00 20.00
85 " 25s on 30s brown bistre & gray black (R) 4.50 40
a. Double surcharge 15.00 15.00
b. "2" of "25" omitted 15.00 15.00
c. Blue surcharge 250.00 150.00

Surcharged in Blue **1910** **5**

1910, Oct.

87 A17 1s on 3s orange & indigo 2.25 50
a. "1910" omitted 10.00
88 " 5s on 15s claret & gray black 1.50 45

Tsar Assen's Tower (Crown over lion)
A20

Tsar Ferdinand
A21

City of Trnovo
A22

Tsar Ferdinand
A23

Tsar Ferdinand
A24

Isker River
A25

Ferdinand
A26

Rila Monastery (Crown at upper right)
A27

Tsar and Princes
A28

Ferdinand in Robes of Ancient Tsars
A29

Monastery of Holy Trinity
A30

View of Varna
A31

1911, Feb. 14 Engraved *Perf. 12*

89	A20	1s myrtle green	15	4
90	A21	2s carmine & black	15	5
91	A22	3s lake & black	40	8
92	A23	5s green & black	85	4
93	A24	10s deep red & black	1.25	4
94	A25	15s brown bistre	1.25	10
95	A26	25s ultra. & black	50	6
96	A27	30s blue & black	3.00	15
97	A28	50s ochre & black	10.00	20
		a. Center inverted	*1500.00*	
98	A29	1 l chocolate	6.00	25
99	A30	2 l dull purple & blk.	1.50	60
100	A31	3 l blue violet & black	7.00	1.75
		Nos. 89-100 (12)	32.05	3.36

See also Nos. 114–120, 161–162.

Tsar Ferdinand
A32

1912, Aug. 2 Typo. *Perf. 12½*

101	A32	5s olive green	1.75	70
		a. 5s pale green	*275.00*	*125.00*
102	"	10s claret	3.25	1.65
103	"	25s slate	4.00	1.65

25th year of reign of Tsar Ferdinand.

Nos. 89–95 Overprinted in Various Colors

ОСВОБ. ВОЙНА
1912-1913

1913, Aug. 6 Engr.

104	A20	1s myrtle green (C)	20	10
105	A21	2s carmine & black (Bl)	20	10
107	A22	3s lake & black (Bl Bk)	20	10
108	A23	5s green & black (R)	20	8
109	A24	10s deep red & black (Bk)	30	7
110	A25	15s brown bistre (G)	70	30
111	A26	25s ultramarine & black (R)	1.50	25
		Nos. 104-111 (7)	3.30	1.00

Victory over the Turks in Balkan War of 1912–1913.

No. 95 Surcharged in Red

10 СТ.

1915, July 6

112	A26	10s on 25s ultramarine & black	40	10

No. 28 Surcharged in Green

3 СТОТИНКИ

113	A11	3s on 1s lilac	3.00	3.00

Types of 1911 Re-engraved.

1915, Nov. 7 *Perf. 11½, 14*

114	A20	1s dark blue green	5	3
115	A23	5s green & brown violet	60	5
116	A24	10s red brown & brownish black	10	4
117	A25	15s olive green	20	4
118	A26	25s indigo & black	15	4
119	A27	30s olive green & red brown	15	4
120	A29	1 l dark brown	60	6
		Nos. 114-120 (7)	1.85	30

No. 114 is 19½mm. wide; No. 89, 18½mm. No. 118 is 19½mm. wide; No. 95, 18½mm. No. 120 is 20mm. wide; No. 98, 19mm. The re-engraved stamps also differ from the 1911 issue in many details of design. Nos. 114-120 exist imperforate.

The 5s and 10s exist perf. 14x11½.

For Nos. 114–116 and 118 overprinted with Cyrillic characters and "1916–1917," see Romania Nos. 2N1–2N4.

Coat of Arms
A33

Peasant and Bullock
A34

Soldier and Mt. Sonichka
A35

View of Nish
A36

Town and Lake Okhrida
A37

Demir-Kapiya (Iron Gate)
A37a

View of Gevgeli
A38

Perf. 11½, 12½x13, 13x12½.

1917–19 Typographed

122	A33	5s green	30	15
123	A34	15s slate	7	6
124	A35	25s blue	7	6
125	A36	30s orange	10	10
126	A37	50s violet	45	30
126A	A37a	2 l brn. orange ('19)	75	30
127	A38	3 l claret	90	45
		Nos. 122-127 (7)	2.64	1.42

Commemorative of the liberation of Macedonia. A 1 l dark green was prepared but not issued. Price $1.50.

View of Veles
A39

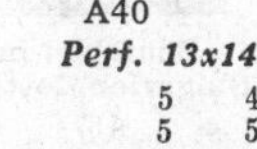

Monastery of St. Clement at Okhrida
A40

1918 *Perf. 13x14*

128	A39	1s gray	5	4
129	A40	5s green	5	5

Tsar Ferdinand
A41

Plowing with Oxen
A42

1918, July 1 *Perf. 12½x13*

130	A41	1s dark green	4	4
131	"	2s dark brown	4	4
132	"	3s indigo	20	10
133	"	10s brown red	20	10

30th anniversary of Tsar Ferdinand's accession to the throne.

1919 *Perf. 13½x13.*

134	A42	1s gray	4	4

Sobranye Palace
A43

Tsar Boris III
A44

1919 *Perf. 11½x12, 12x11½*

135	A43	1s black	3	3
137	A43	2s olive green	3	3

1919, Oct. 3

138	A44	3s org. brown	3	3
139	"	5s green	4	3
140	"	10s rose red	3	3
141	"	15s violet	3	3
142	"	25s deep blue	3	3
143	"	30s chocolate	5	4
144	"	50s yellow brown	5	3
		Nos. 138-144 (7)	26	22

First anniversary of enthronement of Tsar Boris III.

Nos. 135–144 exist imperforate.

Birthplace of Vazov at Sopot and Cherrywood Cannon
A47

"The Bear Fighter"—a Character from "Under the Yoke"
A48

Ivan Vazov in 1870 and 1920
A49

Vazov
A50

The Monk Paisii
A52

Homes of Vazov
at Plovdiv and Sofia
A51

1920, Oct. 20 Photo. *Perf. 11½*

No.	Type	Description	Unused	Used
147	A47	30s brown red	10	5
148	A48	50s dark green	15	7
149	A49	1 l drab	30	15
150	A50	2 l light brown	40	15
151	A51	3 l black violet	50	25
152	A52	5 l deep blue	60	40
		Nos. 147-152 (6)	2.05	1.07

Issued to commemorate the 70th birthday of Ivan Vazov (1850-1921), Bulgarian poet and novelist.

Several values of this series exist imperforate and in pairs imperforate between.

Tsar Ferdinand
A53 A54

Mt. Shar
A55

Bridge over Vardar River
A56

View of Ohrid
A57

Typographed.

1921, June 11 *Perf. 13x14, 14x13*

No.	Type	Description	Unused	Used
153	A53	10s claret	5	3
154	A54	10s claret	5	3
155	A55	10s claret	5	3
156	A56	10s rose lilac	5	3
157	A57	20s blue	15	8
		Nos. 153-157 (5)	35	20

Nos. 153-157 were intended to be issued in 1915 to commemorate the liberation of Macedonia. They were not put in use until 1921. A 50s violet was prepared but never placed in use. Price $1.

View of Sofia
A58

"The Liberator,"
Monument to Alexander II
A59

Monastery at Shipka Pass
A62

Tsar Boris III
A63

Harvesting Grain
A64

Tsar Assen's Tower
(No crown over lion)
A65

Rila Monastery
(Rosette at upper right)
A66

1921-23 Engraved *Perf. 12*

No.	Type	Description	Unused	Used
158	A58	10s blue gray	8	3
159	A59	20s deep green	8	3
160	A63	25s blue green ('22)	8	3
161	A22	50s orange	8	3
162	"	50s dark blue ('23)	1.50	1.50
163	A62	75s dull violet	15	4
164	"	75s deep blue ('23)	30	12
165	A63	1 l carmine	30	12
166	"	1 l deep blue ('22)	15	5
167	A64	2 l brown	30	6
168	A65	3 l brown violet	30	9
169	A66	5 l light blue	1.50	20
170	A63	10 l violet brown	3.00	50
		Nos. 158-170 (13)	7.82	2.80

Bourchier in Bulgarian Costume
A67

James David Bourchier
A68

View of Rila Monastery
A69

1921, Dec. 31

No.	Type	Description	Unused	Used
171	A67	10s red orange	5	5
172	"	20s orange	5	5
173	A68	30s deep gray	7	5
174	"	50s bluish gray	7	5
175	"	1 l dull violet	25	7
176	A69	1½ l olive green	12	8
177	"	2 l deep green	18	10
178	"	3 l Prussian blue	40	20
179	"	5 l red brown	85	45
		Nos. 171-179 (9)	2.04	1.10

Issued to commemorate the death of James D. Bourchier, Balkan correspondent of the London Times.

Postage Due Stamps of 1919-22 Surcharged

10
СТОТИНКИ
a

1924

No.	Type	Description	Unused	Used
182	D6	10s on 20s yellow	4	4
183	"	20s on 5s gray green	4	4
		a. 20s on 5s emerald	10.00	10.00
184	"	20s on 10s violet	4	4
185	"	20s on 30s orange	4	4

Nos. 182 to 185 were used for ordinary postage.

Regular Issues of 1919-23 Surcharged in Blue or Red:

1 ЛЕВЪ *b*

3 ЛЕВА *c*

No.	Type	Description	Unused	Used
186	A43 (*a*)	10s on 1s black (R)	4	4
187	A44 (*b*)	1 l on 5s emerald (Bl)	10	4
188	A22 (*c*)	3 l on 50s dark blue (R)	15	10
189	A63 (*b*)	6 l on 1 l carmine (Bl)	40	16
		Nos. 182-189 (8)	85	50

The surcharge of No. 188 comes in three types: normal, thick and thin.

Nos. 182, 184-189 exist with inverted surcharge. Price, each $5.

Lion of Bulgaria
A70 A71

Tsar Boris III
A72

New Sofia Cathedral
A73

Harvesting
A74

1925 Typo. *Perf. 13, 11½*

No.	Type	Description	Unused	Used
191	A70	10s red & blue, *pink*	4	3
192	"	15s carmine & orange, *blue*	4	3
193	"	30s black & buff	5	4
		a. Cliché of 15s in plate of 30s		
194	A71	50s chocolate, *green*	7	5
195	A72	1 l dull green	50	4
196	A73	2 l dark green & buff	75	5
197	A74	4 l lake & yellow	75	5
		Nos. 191-197 (7)	2.20	29

Several values of this series exist imperforate and in pairs imperforate between. See also Nos. 199, 201.

Cathedral of Sveta Nedelya, Sofia,
Ruined by Bomb—A75

1926 *Perf. 11½*

No.	Type	Description	Unused	Used
198	A75	50s gray black	20	10

A76

A77

Type A72 Re-engraved.
(Shoulder at left does not touch frame.)

1926

No.	Type	Description	Unused	Used
199	A76	1 l greenish gray	40	4
		a. 1 l green	40	4
201	A76	2 l olive brown	60	4
		Center Embossed.		
202	A77	6 l deep blue & pale lemon	1.50	10
203	"	10 l brown black & brown orange	4.00	50

Christo Botev
A78

Tsar Boris III
A79

1926, June 2

No.	Type	Description	Unused	Used
204	A78	1 l olive green	30	8
205	"	2 l slate violet	40	8
206	"	4 l red brown	50	12

Issued to commemorate the 50th anniversary of the death of Christo Botev (1847-1876), Bulgarian revolutionary and poet.

Lion Type of 1881.

1927-29 *Perf. 13.*

No.	Type	Description	Unused	Used
207	A3	10s dark red & drab	3	3
208	"	15s black & orange('29)	5	4
209	"	30s dark blue & bistre brown ('28)	5	4
		a. 30s indigo & buff	5	4
210	"	50s black & rose red ('28)	6	3

1928, Oct. 3 *Perf. 11½*

No.	Type	Description	Unused	Used
211	A79	1 l olive green	60	4
212	"	2 l deep brown	60	5

St. Clement

A80

Konstantin Miladinov

A81

George S. Rakovski

A82

Drenovo Monastery

A83

Paisii

A84

Tsar Simeon

A85

Lyuben Karavelov

A86

Vassil Levski

A87

Georgi Benkovski

A88

Tsar Alexander II

A89

1929, May 12

213	A80	10s dark violet	15	10
214	A81	15s violet brown	15	4
215	A82	30s red	15	4
216	A83	50s olive green	30	4
217	A84	1 l orange brown	60	4
218	A85	2 l dark blue	60	3
219	A86	3 l dull green	1.25	25
220	A87	4 l olive brown	2.00	10
221	A88	5 l brown	1.75	15
222	A89	6 l Prussian green	1.75	35
		Nos. 213-222 (10)	8.70	1.14

Issued to commemorate the millenary of Tsar Simeon and the 50th anniversary of the liberation of Bulgaria from the Turks.

Royal Wedding Issue.

Tsar Boris and Fiancée, Princess Giovanna

A90

Queen Ioanna and Tsar Boris

A91

1930, Nov. 12 ***Perf. 11½***

223	A90	1 l green	20	15
224	A91	2 l dull violet	30	15
225	A90	4 l rose red	30	20
226	A91	6 l dark blue	40	20

Fifty-five copies of a miniature sheet incorporating one each of Nos. 223-226 were printed and given to royal, governmental and diplomatic personages.

Tsar Boris III

A92 A93

Perf. 11½, 12x11½, 13.

1931-37 **Unwmkd.**

227	A92	1 l blue green	20	3
228	"	2 l carmine	35	3
229	"	4 l red orange ('34)	50	5
230	"	4 l yel. org. ('37)	70	4
231	"	6 l deep blue	70	5
232	"	7 l deep blue ('37)	25	6
233	"	10 l slate black	5.00	20
234	"	12 l light brown	35	15
235	"	14 l light brown ('37)	40	10
236	A93	20 l claret & orange brown	1.00	30
		Nos. 227-236 (10)	9.45	1.01

Nos. 230–233 and 235 have outer bars at top and bottom as shown on cut A92; Nos. 227–229 and 234 are without outer bars.

See also Nos. 251, 252, 279–280, 287.

Balkan Games Issues.

Gymnast

A95

Soccer

A96

Riding

A97

Swimmer

A100

"Victory"

A101

Designs: 6 l, Fencing. 10 l, Bicycle race.

1931, Sept. 18 ***Perf. 11½***

237	A95	1 l light green	1.25	50
238	A96	2 l garnet	1.25	50
239	A97	4 l carmine	2.50	75
240	A95	6 l Prussian blue	5.00	1.50
241	"	10 l red orange	12.00	3.50
242	A100	12 l dark blue	20.00	7.00
243	A101	50 l olive brown	45.00	32.50
		Nos. 237-243 (7)	87.00	46.25

1933, Jan. 5

244	A95	1 l blue green	90	70
245	A96	2 l blue	1.50	70
246	A97	4 l brown violet	3.25	1.50
247	A95	6 l bright rose	6.00	1.50
248	"	10 l olive brown	32.50	7.50
249	A100	12 l orange	55.00	20.00
250	A101	50 l red brown	125.00	110.00
		Nos. 244-250 (7)	224.15	141.90

Nos. 244–250 were sold only at the philatelic agency.

Boris Type of 1931.

Outer Bars at Top and Bottom Removed.

1933 ***Perf. 13.***

251	A92	6 l deep blue	65	4

Type of 1931 Surcharged in Blue **2**

1934

252	A92	2(1) on 3 l olive brn.	1.25	12

Soldier Defending Shipka Pass

A102

Shipka Battle Memorial

A103

Color-Bearer

A104

Widow and Orphans

A106

Veteran of the War of Liberation, 1878

A105

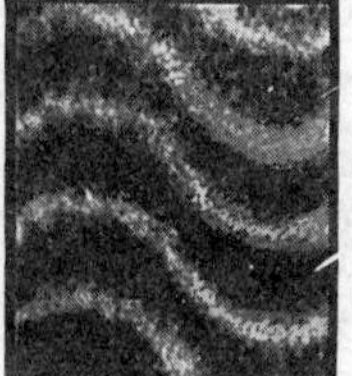

Wmk. 145

Wmkd. Wavy Lines. (145)

1934, Aug. 26 ***Perf. 10½, 11½***

253	A102	1 l green	50	40
254	A103	2 l pale red	25	12
255	A104	3 l bistre brown	1.25	75
256	A105	4 l dark carmine	75	25
257	A104	7 l dark blue	1.25	75
258	A106	14 l plum	6.25	5.50
		Nos. 253-258 (6)	10.25	7.77

Issued to commemorate the unveiling of the Shipka Pass Battle memorial.

An unwatermarked miniature sheet incorporating one each of Nos. 253-258 was put on sale in 1938 in five cities at a price of 8,000 leva. Printing: 100 sheets.

1934, Sept. 21

259	A102	1 l bright green	50	40
260	A103	2 l dull orange	25	12
261	A104	3 l yellow	1.25	75
262	A105	4 l rose	75	25
263	A104	7 l blue	1.25	75
264	A106	14 l olive bistre	6.25	5.50
		Nos. 259-264 (6)	10.25	7.77

An unwatermarked miniature sheet incorporating one each of Nos. 259–263 was issued.

Velcho A. Djamjiyata

A108

Capt. G. S. Mamarchev

A109

1935, May 5 ***Perf. 11½***

265	A108	1 l deep blue	50	20
266	A109	2 l maroon	70	35

Issued in commemoration of the centenary of a Bulgarian uprising against the Turks.

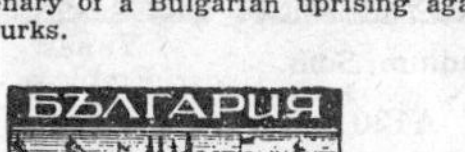

Soccer Game

A110

Cathedral of Alexander Nevski

A111

Symbolical of Victory

A113

Soccer Team

A112

Player and Trophy A114

The Trophy A115

1935, June 14

267	A110	1 l green	1.75	1.50
268	A111	2 l blue gray	2.50	2.00
269	A112	4 l crimson	5.00	3.75
270	A113	7 l bright blue	11.00	4.25
271	A114	14 l orange	11.00	4.25
272	A115	50 l lilac brown	95.00	80.00
		Nos. 267-272 (6)	126.25	95.75

5th Balkan Soccer Tournament.

Gymnast on Parallel Bars A116

Youth in "Yunak" Costume A117

Girl in "Yunak" Costume A118

Pole Vaulting A119

Stadium, Sofia A120

Yunak Emblem A121

1935, July 10

273	A116	1 l green	1.75	1.25
274	A117	2 l light blue	2.25	1.25
275	A118	4 l carmine	7.25	2.25
276	A119	7 l dark blue	7.25	3.50
277	A120	14 l dark brown	7.25	3.50
278	A121	50 l red	70.00	55.00
		Nos. 273-278 (6)	95.75	66.75

Issued to commemorate the 8th tournament of the Yunak Gymnastic Organization at Sofia, July 12-14.

Boris Type of 1931.
Wmkd. Wavy Lines. (145)

1935 *Perf. 12½, 13*

279	A92	1 l green	20	3
280	"	2 l carmine	15.00	5

Janos Hunyadi A122

King Ladislas Varnenchik A123

Varna Memorial A124

King Ladislas III A125

Battle of Varna, 1444 A126

1935, Aug. 4 *Perf. 10½, 11½*

281	A122	1 l brown orange	90	75
282	A123	2 l maroon	70	70
283	A124	4 l vermilion	4.50	1.00
284	A125	7 l dull blue	2.25	1.00
285	A126	14 l green	2.00	1.00
		Nos. 281-285 (5)	10.35	4.45

Issued to commemorate the Battle of Varna, and the death of the Polish King, Ladislas Varnenchik (1424-1444).

Lion Type of 1881.

1935 *Perf. 13.* **Wmk. 145**

286	A3	10s dark red & drab	45	15

Boris Type of 1933.
Outer Bars at Top and Bottom Removed.

287	A92	6 l gray blue	65	10

Dimitr Monument A127

Haji Dimitr A128

Haji Dimitr and Stefan Karaja A129

Taking the Oath A130

Birthplace of Dimitr A131

1935, Oct. 1 *Perf. 11½* **Unwmkd.**

288	A127	1 l green	75	35
289	A128	2 l brown	1.00	40
290	A129	4 l carmine rose	3.00	2.00
291	A130	7 l blue	3.50	2.25
292	A131	14 l orange	4.00	2.50
		Nos. 288-292 (5)	12.25	7.50

Issued to commemorate the 67th anniversary of the death of the Bulgarian patriots, Haji Dimitr and Stefan Karaja.

Numeral A132

Lion A133

1936-39 *Perf. 13x12½, 13*

293	A132	10s red orange ('37)	4	3
294	"	15s emerald	4	3
295	A133	30s maroon	8	3
296	"	30s yellow brown ('37)	8	3
297	"	30s Prussian bl. ('37)	10	3
298	"	50s ultramarine	8	3
299	"	50s dark carmine ('37)	12	3
300	"	50s slate green ('39)	6	3
		Nos. 293-300 (8)	60	24

Meteorological Station, Mt. Moussalla A134

Peasant Girl A135

Town of Nessebr A136

1936, Aug. 16 Photo. *Perf. 11½*

301	A134	1 l purple	1.10	60
302	A135	2 l ultramarine	1.10	40
303	A136	7 l dark blue	2.25	1.50

Issued to commemorate the fourth Geographical and Ethnographical Congress, Sofia, August, 1936.

Sts. Cyril and Methodius A137

Displaying the Bible to the People A138

1937, June 2

304	A137	1 l dark green	15	10
305	"	2 l dark plum	15	10
306	A138	4 l vermilion	25	15
307	A137	7 l dark blue	1.25	60
308	A138	14 l rose red	85	75
		Nos. 304-308 (5)	2.65	1.70

Millennium of Cyrillic alphabet.

Princess Marie Louise A139

Tsar Boris III A140

1937, Oct. 3

310	A139	1 l yellow green	25	8
311	"	2 l brown red	30	12
312	"	4 l scarlet	40	20

Issued in honor of Princess Marie Louise.

1937, Oct. 3

313	A140	2 l brown red	20	10

Issued to commemorate the 19th anniversary of the accession of Tsar Boris III to the throne. See No. B11.

National Products Issue.

Peasants Bundling Wheat A141

Sunflower A142

Wheat A143

Chickens and Eggs A144

Cluster of Grapes A145

Rose and Perfume Flask A146

Strawberries A147

Girl Carrying Grape Clusters A148

Rose A149 — Tobacco Leaves A150

1938 *Perf. 13.*

No.	Type	Value / Color	Unused	Used
316	A141	10s orange	4	4
317	"	10s red orange	4	4
318	A142	15s bright rose	30	6
319	"	15s deep plum	30	6
320	A143	30s golden brown	10	6
321	"	30s copper brown	10	6
322	A144	50s black	6	6
323	"	50s indigo	10	9
324	A145	1 l yellow green	60	7
325	"	1 l green	60	7
326	A146	2 l rose pink	40	8
327	"	2 l rose brown	40	6
328	A147	3 l deep red lilac	85	20
329	"	3 l brown lake	85	20
330	A148	4 l plum	60	20
331	"	4 l golden brown	80	20
332	A149	7 l violet blue	1.50	75
333	"	7 l deep blue	1.50	75
334	A150	14 l dark brown	1.75	90
335	"	14 l red brown	2.00	90
		Nos. 316-335 (20)	12.89	4.85

Several values of this series exist imperforate.

Crown Prince Simeon
A151 A153

Designs: 2 l, Same portrait as 1 l, value at lower left. 14 l, Similar to 4 l, but no wreath.

1938, June 16

No.	Type	Value / Color	Unused	Used
336	A151	1 l bright green	10	6
337	"	2 l rose pink	12	6
338	A153	4 l deep orange	13	8
339	A151	7 l ultramarine	50	25
340	"	14 l deep brown	50	25
		Nos. 336-340 (5)	1.35	70

First birthday of Prince Simeon.

Tsar Boris III
A155 A156

Various Portraits of Tsar.

1938, Oct. 3

No.	Type	Value / Color	Unused	Used
341	A155	1 l light green	10	6
342	A156	2 l rose brown	60	8
343	"	4 l golden brown	15	6
344	"	7 l bright ultramarine	30	20
345	"	14 l deep red lilac	35	25
		Nos. 341-345 (5)	1.50	65

20th anniversary, reign of Tsar Boris III.

Early Locomotive
A160

Designs: 2 l, Modern locomotive. 4 l, Train crossing bridge. 7 l, Tsar Boris in cab.

1939, Apr. 26

No.	Type	Value / Color	Unused	Used
346	A160	1 l yellow green	15	8
347	"	2 l copper brown	15	8
348	"	4 l red orange	50	15
349	"	7 l dark blue	1.00	65

Issued in commemoration of the 50th anniversary of Bulgarian State Railways.

Post Horns and Arrows
A164

Central Post Office, Sofia
A165

1939, May 14 Typographed

No.	Type	Value / Color	Unused	Used
350	A164	1 l yellow green	12	6
351	A165	2 l bright carmine	18	6

Issued in commemoration of the 60th anniversary of the establishment of the postal system.

Gymnast on Bar
A166

Yunak Emblem
A167

Discus Thrower
A168

Athletic Dancer A169 — Weight Lifter A170

1939, July 7 Photogravure

No.	Type	Value / Color	Unused	Used
352	A166	1 l yellow green & pale green	15	15
353	A167	2 l bright rose	20	15
354	A168	4 l brown & golden brown	20	25
355	A169	7 l dk. blue & blue	70	60
356	A170	14 l plum & rose vio.	3.00	2.00
		Nos. 352-356 (5)	4.25	3.15

Issued to commemorate the 9th tournament of the Yunak Gymnastic Organization at Sofia, July 4-8.

Tsar Boris III A171 — Bulgaria's First Stamp A172

1940-41 Typographed.

No.	Type	Value / Color	Unused	Used
356A	A171	1 l dull green ('41)	75	3
357	"	2 l bright crimson	20	4

1940, May 19 Photo. *Perf. 13*

Design: 20 l, Similar design, scroll dated "1840-1940."

No.	Type	Value / Color	Unused	Used
358	A172	10 l olive black	75	75
359	"	20 l indigo	75	75

Centenary of first postage stamp. Exist imperf.

Peasant Couple and Tsar Boris
A174

Flags over Wheat Field and Tsar Boris
A175

Tsar Boris and Map of Dobrudja
A176

1940, Sept. 20

No.	Type	Value / Color	Unused	Used
360	A174	1 l slate green	5	4
361	A175	2 l rose red	10	7
362	A176	4 l dark brown	15	8
363	"	7 l dark blue	50	30

Issued in commemoration of the return of Dobrudja from Romania.

Fruit A177 — Bees and Flowers A178

Plowing A179 — Shepherd and Sheep A180

Tsar Boris III
A181

Perf. 10, 10½x11½, 11½, 13.

1940-44 Typographed. Unwmkd.

No.	Type	Value / Color	Unused	Used
364	A177	10s red orange	3	3
365	A178	15s blue	4	3
366	A179	30s olive brown ('41)	4	3
367	A180	50s violet	15	4
368	A181	1 l bright green	5	3
369	"	2 l rose carmine	7	3
370	"	4 l red orange	10	3
371	"	6 l red violet ('44)	20	4
372	"	7 l blue	12	4
373	"	10 l blue green ('41)	20	10
		Nos. 364-373 (10)	1.00	40

See No. 440.

1940-41 *Perf. 13.* Wmk. 145

No.	Type	Value / Color	Unused	Used
373A	A180	50s violet ('41)	10	3
374	A181	1 l bright green	10	3
375	"	2 l rose carmine	15	3
376	"	7 l dull blue	20	8
377	"	10 l blue green	30	10
		Nos. 373A-377 (5)	85	27

Watermarked vertically or horizontally.

P. R. Slaveikov
A182

Sofronii, Bishop of Vratza
A183

Saint Ivan Rilski
A184

Martin S. Drinov
A185

Monk Khrabr
A186

Kolio Ficheto
A187

1940, Sept. 23 Photo. Unwmkd.

No.	Type	Value / Color	Unused	Used
378	A182	1 l bright blue green	7	4
379	A183	2 l bright carmine	8	5
380	A184	3 l deep red brown	15	8
381	A185	4 l red orange	12	8
382	A186	7 l deep blue	1.20	75
383	A187	10 l deep red brown	1.35	90
		Nos. 378-383 (6)	2.97	1.90

Issued in commemoration of the liberation of Bulgaria from the Turks in 1878.

Johannes Gutenberg
A188

N. Karastoyanov, First Bulgarian Printer
A189

1940, Dec. 16

384 A188 1 l slate green 10 8
385 A189 2 l orange brown 10 8

Issued in commemoration of the 500th anniversary of the invention of the printing press and the 100th anniversary of the first Bulgarian printing press.

Christo Botev
A190

Monument to Botev
A192

Botev with his Insurgent Band
A191

1941, May 3

386 A190 1 l dark blue green 10 5
387 A191 2 l crimson rose 15 5
388 A192 3 l dark brown 60 30

Issued in honor of Christo Botev, patriot and poet.

Palace of Justice, Sofia
A193

Designs: 20 l, Workers' hospital. 50 l, National Bank.

1941-43 Engraved *Perf. 11½*

389 A193 14 l lt. gray brn. ('43) 15 15
390 " 20 l gray green ('43) 25 25
391 " 50 l light blue gray 2.50 2.00

Macedonian Woman
A196

City of Okhrida
A200

Outline of Macedonia and Tsar Boris III
A197

View of Aegean Sea
A198

Poganovski Monastery
A199

1941, Oct. 3 Photo. *Perf. 13*

392 A196 1 l slate green 5 4
393 A197 2 l crimson 6 4
394 A198 2 l red orange 9 4
395 A199 4 l orange brown 10 8
396 A200 7 l deep gray blue 35 25
Nos. 392-396 (5) 65 45

Issued to commemorate the acquisition of Macedonian territory from neighboring countries.

Peasant Working in a Field
A201

Designs: 15s, Plowing. 30s, Apiary. 50s, Women harvesting fruit. 3 l, Shepherd and sheep. 5 l, Inspecting cattle.

1941-44

397 A201 10s dark violet 4 4
398 " 10s dark blue 4 4
399 " 15s Prussian blue 4 4
400 " 15s dark olive brown 4 4
401 " 30s red orange 5 4
402 " 30s dark slate green 5 3
403 " 50s blue violet 6 3
404 " 50s red lilac 8 3
405 " 3 l henna brown 30 10
406 " 3 l dk. brown ('44) 1.25 60
407 " 5 l sepia 70 30
408 " 5 l vio. blue ('44) 1.25 60
Nos. 397-408 (12) 3.90 1.89

Girls Singing
A207

Boys in Camp
A208

Raising Flag
A209

Folk Dancers
A211

Camp Scene
A210

1942, June 1 Photogravure

409 A207 1 l dark blue green 8 5
410 A208 2 l scarlet 10 6
411 A209 4 l olive gray 12 6
412 A210 7 l deep blue 15 8
413 A211 14 l fawn 20 15
Nos. 409-413 (5) 65 40

National "Work and Joy" movement.

Wounded Soldier
A212

Soldier's Farewell
A213

Designs: 4 l, Aiding wounded soldier. 7 l, Widow and orphans at grave. 14 l, Tomb of Unknown Soldier. 20 l, Queen Ioanna visiting wounded.

1942, Sept. 7

414 A212 1 l slate green 8 6
415 A213 2 l bright rose 8 6
416 " 4 l yellow orange 8 5
417 " 7 l dark blue 9 5
418 " 14 l brown 12 8
419 " 20 l olive black 20 10
Nos. 414-419 (6) 65 40

Issued to aid war victims. No. 419 was printed in sheets of 50, alternating with 50 labels.

Legend of Kubrat
A218

Cavalry Charge
A219

Designs: 30s, Rider of Madara. 50s, Christening of Boris I. 1 l, School, St. Naum. 2 l, Crowning of Tsar Simeon by Boris I. 3 l, Golden era of Bulgarian literature. 4 l, Sentencing of the Bogomil Basil. 5 l, Proclamation of 2nd Bulgarian Empire. 7 l, Ivan Assen II at Trebizond. 10 l, Deporting the Patriarch Jeftimi. 14 l, Wandering minstrel. 20 l, Monk Paisii. 30 l, Monument, Shipka Pass.

1942, Oct. 12

420 A218 10s bluish black 4 4
421 A219 15s Prussian green 4 4
422 " 30s dark rose violet 4 4
423 " 50s indigo 4 4
424 " 1 l slate green 5 5
425 " 2 l crimson 5 5
426 " 3 l brown 5 5
427 " 4 l orange 6 6
428 " 5 l greenish black 6 6
429 " 7 l dark blue 7 7
430 " 10 l brown black 15 15
431 " 14 l olive black 15 15
432 " 20 l henna brown 35 35
433 " 30 l black 50 50
Nos. 420-433 (14) 1.65 1.65

Tsar Boris III
A234

Wmk. 275

Designs: Various portraits of Tsar.

Wmkd. Entwined Curved Lines. (275)

Perf. 13, Imperf.

1944, Feb. 28 Photogravure

Frames in Black.

434 A234 1 l olive green 5 5
435 " 2 l red brown 12 12
436 " 4 l brown 14 14
437 " 5 l gray violet 18 18
438 " 7 l slate blue 18 18
Nos. 434-438 (5) 67 67

Issued in memory of Tsar Boris III (1894-1943).

Tsar Simeon II
A239

Perf. 11½, 13

1944, June 12 Typo. Unwmkd.

439 A239 3 l red orange 20 4

Shepherd Type of 1940

1944

440 A180 50s yellow green 15 5

Parcel Post Stamps of 1944 Overprinted in Black or Orange

ВСИЧКО ЗА ФРОНТА

1945, Jan. 25 *Perf. 11½*

448 PP5 1 l dark carmine 3 3
449 " 7 l rose lilac 5 3
450 " 20 l orange brown 7 3
451 " 30 l dk. brn. carmine 15 3
452 " 50 l red orange 30 15
453 " 100 l blue (O) 70 35

The overprint reads: "Everything for the Front".

No. 448 with Additional Surcharge of New Value in Black.

454 PP5 4 l on 1 l dark carmine 5 3
Nos. 448-454 (7) 1.35 65

Nos. 368 to 370 Overprinted in Black

СЪБИРАЙТЕ СТАРО ЖЕЛЪЗО

1945, Mar. 15 *Perf. 11½, 13*

455 A181 1 l bright green 5 3
456 " 2 l rose carmine 8 3
457 " 4 l red orange 12 4

The overprint reads: "Collect old iron."

Overprinted in Black

СЪБИРАЙТЕ ХАРТИЕНИ ОТПАДЪЦИ

458 A181 1 l bright green 5 3
459 " 2 l rose carmine 8 3
460 " 4 l red orange 12 4

The overprint reads: "Collect discarded paper."

Overprinted in Black

СЪБИРАЙТЕ ВСЪКАКВИ ПАРЦАЛИ

461 A181 1 l bright green 5 3
462 " 2 l rose carmine 8 3

463 A181 4 l red orange 12 4
Nos. 455-463 (9) 75 30

The overprint reads: "Collect all kinds of rags."

Oak Tree
A245

Imperf., Perf. 11½.

1945 Lithographed Unwmkd.

464 A245 4 l vermilion 8 6
465 " 10 l blue 8 6

Imperf.

466 A245 50 l brown lake 25 20

Slav Congress, Sofia, March, 1945.

A246 A247

Lion Rampant A248 — Arms of Bulgaria A249

A251 A252

Arms of Bulgaria
A253 A254

Two types of 2 l and 4 l: Type I: Large crown close to coat of arms. Type II: Smaller crown standing high.

1945–46 Photogravure *Perf. 13*

469 A246 30s yellow green 3 3
470 A247 50s peacock green 3 3
471 A248 1 l dark green 3 3
472 A249 2 l chocolate (I) 4 3
a. Type II 3 3
473 " 4 l dark blue (I) 8 3
a. Type II 5 3
475 A251 5 l red violet 5 3
476 " 9 l slate gray 6 3
477 A252 10 l Prussian blue 8 3
478 A253 15 l brown 10 4
479 A254 20 l carmine 15 6
480 " 20 l gray black 15 6
Nos. 469-480 (11) 80 40

Breaking Chain A255 — 1 Lev Coin A256

Water Wheel A257 — Coin and Symbols of Agriculture and Industry A258

Lithographed.

1945, June 4 *Imperf.* Unwmkd.

Laid Paper.

481 A255 50 l brown red, *pink* 10 8
482 " 50 l orange, *pink* 10 8
483 A256 100 l gray blue, *pink* 15 12
484 " 100 l brown, *pink* 15 12
485 A257 150 l dark olive gray, *pink* 30 15
486 " 150 l dull car., *pink* 30 15
487 A258 200 l deep blue, *pink* 45 25
488 " 200 l olive green, *pink* 45 25
Nos. 481-488 (8) 2.00 1.20

Souvenir Sheets.

489 Sheet of four 1.50 1.50
a. 50 l violet blue 25 25
b. 100 l " 25 25
c. 150 l " 25 25
d. 200 l " 25 25
490 Sheet of four 1.50 1.50
a. 50 l brown orange 25 25
b. 100 l " 25 25
c. 150 l " 25 25
d. 200 l " 25 25

Nos. 481 to 490 were issued to publicize Bulgaria's Liberty Loan.

Nos. 489 and 490 measure 90x122mm. and contain one each of types A255–A258. Margin inscription: "March 9, 1935, Sofia" in Bulgarian characters.

Olive Branch
A260

1945, Sept. 1 Typo. *Perf. 13*

491 A260 10 l orange brown & yellow green 7 5
492 " 50 l dull red & deep green 25 12

Victory of Allied Nations, World War II.

September 9, 1944 A261 — Numeral and Broken Chain A262

1945, Sept. 7

493 A261 1 l gray green 3 3
494 " 4 l deep blue 3 3
495 " 5 l rose lilac 3 3
496 A262 10 l light blue 5 3
497 " 20 l bright carmine 8 6
498 A261 50 l bright blue green 40 25
499 " 100 l orange brown 50 40
Nos. 493-499 (7) 1.12 83

Issued to commemorate the 1st anniversary of Bulgaria's liberation.

Old Postal Savings Emblem— A263

First Bulgarian Postal Savings Stamp
A264

Child Putting Coin in Bank A265 — Postal Savings Building, Sofia A266

1946, Apr. 12

500 A263 4 l brown orange 6 4
501 A264 10 l dark olive 8 5
502 A265 20 l ultramarine 10 6
503 A266 50 l slate gray 60 40

Issued to commemorate the 50th anniversary of Bulgarian Postal Savings.

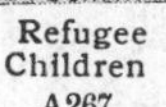

Refugee Children A267 — Nurse Assisting Wounded Soldier A269

Wounded Soldier
A268

Design: 35 l, 100 l, Red Cross hospital train.

1946, Apr. 4

Cross in Carmine

504 A267 2 l dark olive 5 5
505 A268 4 l violet 10 5
506 A267 10 l plum 10 6
507 A268 20 l ultramarine 10 6
508 A269 30 l brown orange 15 10
509 A268 35 l gray black 15 15
510 A269 50 l violet brown 25 20
511 A268 100 l gray brown 60 60
Nos. 504-511 (8) 1.50 1.27

See also Nos. 553 to 560.

Advancing Troops
A271

Grenade Thrower A272 — Attacking Planes A274

Designs: 5 l, Horse-drawn cannon. 9 l, Engineers building pontoon bridge. 10 l, 30 l, Cavalry charge. 40 l, Horse-drawn supply column. 50 l, Motor transport column. 60 l, Infantry, tanks and planes.

1946, Aug. 9 Typo. Unwmkd.

512 A271 2 l dark red violet 4 4
513 A272 4 l dark gray 4 4
514 A271 5 l dark orange red 4 4
515 A274 6 l black brown 5 4
516 A271 9 l rose lilac 5 4
517 " 10 l deep violet 5 4
518 " 20 l deep blue 18 7
519 " 30 l red orange 18 10
520 " 40 l dark olive bistre 25 15
521 " 50 l dark green 30 18
522 " 60 l red brown 40 25
Nos. 512-522 (11) 1.58 99

Bulgaria's participation in World War II.

Arms of Russia and Bulgaria A279 — Lion Rampant A280

1946, May 23

523 A279 4 l red orange 8 8
525 " 20 l turquoise green 20 15

Issued to commemorate the Congress of the Bulgarian-Soviet Association, May 1946.

No. 523 exists in dark carmine rose and No. 525 exists in blue. Price $8 for both.

1946, May 25 *Imperf.*

526 A280 20 l blue 25 12

Issued to commemorate the Day of the Postage Stamp, May 26, 1946.

Alexander Stambolisky A281 — Flags of Albania, Romania, Bulgaria and Jugoslavia A282

1946, June 13 ***Perf. 12***

527	A281	100 l red orange	3.00	3.00

Issued to commemorate the 23rd anniversary of the death of Alexander Stambolisky, agrarian leader.

1946, July 6 ***Perf. 11½***

528	A282	100 l black brown	75	60

Issued to publicize the 1946 Balkan Games.

Sheet of 100 arranged so that all stamps are tête bêche vertically and horizontally, except two center rows in left pane which provide 10 vertical pairs that are not tête bêche vertically.

St. Ivan Rilski
A283

Rila Monastery
A286

A284

A285

Views of Rila Monastery
A287

1946, Aug. 26

529	A283	1 l red brown	7	6
530	A284	4 l black brown	8	6
531	A285	10 l dark green	15	8
532	A286	20 l deep blue	20	10
533	A287	50 l dark red	75	45
		Nos. 529-533 (5)	1.25	75

Millenary of Rila Monastery.

People's Republic

A288

1946, Sept. 15 **Typographed**

534	A288	4 l brown lake	4	4
535	"	20 l dull blue	5	5
536	"	50 l olive bistre	15	15

No. 535 is inscribed "BULGARIA" in Latin characters.

Issued to commemorate the referendum of September 8, 1946, resulting in the establishment of the Bulgarian People's Republic.

Partisan Army
A289

Snipers
A290

Soldiers: Past and Present
A291

Design: 30 l, Partisans advancing.

1946, Dec. 2

537	A289	1 l violet brown	3	3
538	A290	4 l dull green	4	3
539	A291	5 l chocolate	5	3
540	A290	10 l crimson	5	4
541	A289	20 l ultramarine	12	12
542	A290	30 l olive bistre	20	13
543	A291	50 l black	30	22
		Nos. 537-543 (7)	79	60

Relief Worker and Children
A294

Child with Gift Parcels
A295

Waiting for Food Distribution
A296

Mother and Child
A297

1946, Dec. 30

545	A294	1 l dark violet brown	3	3
546	A295	4 l bright red	4	4
547	"	9 l olive bistre	5	4
548	A294	10 l slate gray	5	4
549	A296	20 l ultramarine	12	6
550	A297	30 l dp. brn. orange	15	10
551	A296	40 l maroon	20	15
552	A294	50 l peacock green	35	30
		Nos. 545-552 (8)	99	76

"Bulgaria" is in Latin characters on No. 548.

Red Cross Types of 1946

1947, Jan. 31

Cross in Carmine

553	A267	2 l olive bistre	5	5
554	A268	4 l olive black	5	5
555	A267	10 l blue green	10	10
556	A268	20 l bright blue	18	18
557	A269	30 l yellow green	25	25
558	A268	35 l greenish gray	30	30
559	A269	50 l henna brown	50	50
560	A268	100 l dark blue	65	65
		Nos. 553-560 (8)	2.08	2.08

Laurel Branch, Allied and Bulgarian Emblems
A298

Dove of Peace
A299

1947, Feb. 28

561	A298	4 l olive	5	5
562	A299	10 l brown red	6	6
563	"	20 l deep blue	20	20

Issued to commemorate the return to peace at the close of World War II. "Bulgaria" in Latin characters on No. 563.

A302

Guerrilla Fighters
A303 A304

1947, Jan. 21 ***Perf. 11½***

567	A302	10 l chocolate & brown orange	20	20
568	A303	20 l dark blue & blue	20	20
569	A304	70 l dp. claret & rose	11.50	11.50

Issued to honor the anti-fascists.

Hydroelectric Station
A305

Miner
A306

Symbols of Industry
A307

Tractor
A308

1947, Aug. 6

570	A305	4 l olive green	8	5
571	A306	9 l red brown	8	6
572	A307	20 l deep blue	17	17
573	A308	40 l olive brown	40	40

Exhibition Building
A309

Former Home of Alphonse de Lamartine
A310

Symbols of Agriculture and Horticulture
A311

Perf. 11x11½, 11½x11.

1947, Aug. 31 **Litho.** **Unwmkd.**

574	A309	4 l scarlet	7	3
575	A310	9 l brown lake	9	5
576	A311	20 l bright ultra.	35	12

Issued to publicize the Plovdiv International Fair, 1947. See No. C54.

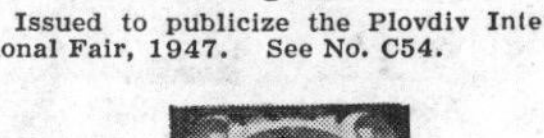

Basil Evstatiev Aprilov
A312

1947, Oct. 19 **Photo.** ***Perf. 11***

577	A312	40 l bright ultramarine	40	25

Issued to commemorate the centenary of the death of Basil Evstatiev Aprilov, educator and historian. See also No. 603.

Balkan Games Issue.

Bicycle Race
A313

Basketball
A314

Chess
A315

Designs: 20 l, Soccer players. 60 l, Four flags of participating nations.

1947, Sept. 29 **Typo.** ***Perf. 11½***

578	A313	2 l plum	25	15
579	A314	4 l dark olive green	25	15
580	A315	9 l orange brown	35	20
581	"	20 l bright ultra.	70	30
582	"	60 l violet brown	1.75	80
		Nos. 578-582 (5)	3.30	1.60

People's Theater, Sofia
A316

National Assembly
A317

Central Post Office, Sofia
A318

Presidential Mansion
A319

1947–48 Typographed *Perf. 12½*

583	A316	50s yellow green	4	3
584	A317	50s yellow green	4	3
585	A318	1 l green	4	3
586	A319	1 l green	4	3
587	A316	2 l brown lake	4	3
588	A317	2 l light brown	4	3
589	A316	4 l deep blue	6	4
590	A317	4 l deep blue	8	4
591	A316	9 l carmine	25	4
592	A317	20 l deep blue	45	15
		Nos. 583-592 (10)	1.08	45

On Nos. 583–592 inscription reads "Bulgarian Republic." No. 592 is inscribed in Latin characters.

Redrawn.

НАРОДНА

added to inscription.

593	A318	1 l green	6	3
594	"	2 l brown lake	8	3
595	"	4 l deep blue	10	4

Cyrillic inscription beneath design on Nos. 593–595 reads "Bulgarian People's Republic".

Geno Kirov
A320

Actors' Portraits: 1 l, Zlatina Nedeva. 2 l, Ivan Popov. 3 l, Athanas Kirchev. 4 l, Elena Snejina. 5 l, Stoyan Bachvarov.

Lithographed

1947, Dec. 8 *Perf. 10½* Unwmkd.

596	A320	50s bistre brown	5	4
597	"	1 l light blue green	5	4
598	"	2 l slate green	6	5
599	"	3 l deep blue	10	6
600	"	4 l scarlet	12	8
601	"	5 l red brown	12	8
		Nos. 596-601, B22-B26 (11)	1.54	1.39

National Theater, 50th anniversary.

Merchant Ship "Fatherland"
A321

1947, Dec. 19

602	A321	50 l Prussian blue *cream*	35	25

B. E. Aprilov
A322

Bulgarian Worker
A323

1948, Feb. 19 *Perf. 11*

603	A322	4 l brown carmine, *cream*	10	10

Issued to commemorate the centenary of the death of Basil Evstatiev Aprilov, educator and historian.

1948, Feb. 29 Photo. *Perf. 11½x12*

604	A323	4 l deep blue, *cream*	8	6

2nd Bulgarian Workers' Congress.

Self-education
A324

Accordion Player
A325

Factory Recess
A326

Girl Throwing Basketball
A327

1948, Mar. 31 Photogravure

605	A324	4 l red	6	6
606	A325	20 l deep blue	8	6
607	A326	40 l dull green	12	10
608	A327	60 l brown	30	20

Nicholas Vaptzarov
A328

Portraits: 9 l, P. K. Iavorov. 15 l, Christo Smirnenski. 20 l, Ivan Vazov. 45 l, P. R. Slaveikov.

1948, May 18 Litho. *Perf. 11*

Cream Paper.

611	A328	4 l bright vermilion	7	4
612	"	9 l light brown	8	5
613	"	15 l claret	10	6
614	"	20 l deep blue	10	8
615	"	45 l green	40	12
		Nos. 611-615 (5)	75	35

Soviet Soldier
A329

Civilians Offering Gifts to Soldiers
A330

Designs: 20 l, Soldiers, 1878 and 1944. 60 l, Stalin and Spasski Tower.

1948, July 5 Photogravure

Cream Paper.

616	A329	4 l brown orange	6	5
617	A330	10 l olive green	6	5
618	"	20 l deep blue	15	12
619	A329	60 l olive brown	45	40

Issued to honor the Soviet Army.

Demeter Blagoev
A331

Monument to Bishop Andrey
A332

Designs: 9 l, Gabriel Genov. 60 l, Marching youths.

1948, Sept. 6 Lithographed

Cream Paper.

620	A331	4 l dark brown	4	4
621	"	9 l brown orange	5	5
622	A332	20 l deep blue	12	9
623	"	60 l brown	50	35

No. 623 is inscribed in Cyrillic characters.
Issued to commemorate the 25th anniversary of the National Insurrection of 1923.

Christo Smirnenski
A333

Battle of Grivitza, 1877
A334

1948, Oct. 2 Photo. *Perf. 11½*

Cream Paper

624	A333	4 l blue	7	4
625	"	16 l red brown	15	6

Issued to commemorate the 25th anniversary of the death of Christo Smirnenski, poet, 1898–1923.

1948, Nov. 1

626	A334	20 l blue	15	8

Issued to publicize Romanian-Bulgarian friendship. See Nos. C56–C57.

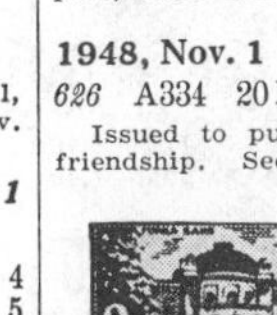

Bath, Gorna Banya
A335

Bath, Bankya
A336

Mineral Bath, Sofia
A337

Maliovitza
A338

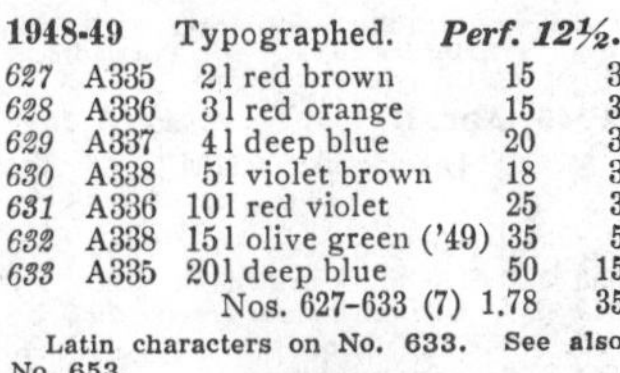
1948-49 Typographed. *Perf. 12½.*

627	A335	2 l red brown	15	3
628	A336	3 l red orange	15	3
629	A337	4 l deep blue	20	3
630	A338	5 l violet brown	18	3
631	A336	10 l red violet	25	3
632	A338	15 l olive green ('49)	35	5
633	A335	20 l deep blue	50	15
		Nos. 627-633 (7)	1.78	35

Latin characters on No. 633. See also No. 653.

Emblem of the Republic
A339

1948–50

634	A339	50s red orange	4	3
634A	"	50s org. brown ('50)	6	3
635	"	1 l green	6	3
636	"	9 l black	12	4

Botev's Birthplace, Kalofer
A340

Christo Botev
A341

Cyrillic Inscription:
"Chr. Botev 1848-1948."

Designs: 9 l, Steamer "Radetzky." 15 l, Kalofer village. 20 l, Botev in uniform. 40 l, Botev's mother. 50 l, Pen, pistol and wreath.

Photogravure.

1948, Dec. 21 *Perf. 11x11½, 11½*

Cream Paper.

638	A340	1 l dark green	3	3
639	A341	4 l violet brown	4	3
640	A340	9 l violet	5	3
641	"	15 l brown	8	6
642	A341	20 l blue	12	10
643	A340	40 l red brown	25	15
644	A341	50 l olive black	35	25
		Nos. 638-644 (7)	92	65

Issued to commemorate the centenary of the birth of Christo Botev, Bulgarian national poet.

Lenin
A342

Lenin Speaking
A343

1949, Jan. 24 *Perf. 11½* Unwmkd.

Cream Paper.

645	A342	4 l brown	6	
646	A343	20 l brown red	30	15

25th anniversary of the death of Lenin.

Road Construction
A344

Designs: 5 l, Tunnel construction. 9 l, Locomotive. 10 l, Textile worker. 20 l, Female tractor driver. 40 l, Workers in truck.

1949, Apr. 6 *Perf. 10½*

Inscribed: "CHM".

Cream Paper.

647	A344	4 l dark red	15	5
648	"	5 l dark brown	20	8
649	"	9 l dark slate green	25	8
650	"	10 l violet	40	15
651	"	20 l dull blue	75	25
652	"	40 l brown	1.25	40
		Nos. 647-652 (6)	3.00	1.01

Issued to honor the Workers' Cultural Brigade.

Type of 1948.

Redrawn.

Country Name and "POSTA" in Latin Characters.

1949 Typographed *Perf. 12½*

653	A337	20 l deep blue	60	10

Miner
A345

1949 *Perf. 11x11½.*

654	A345	4 l dark blue	20	5

George Dimitrov
A347

A348

1949, July 10 Photogravure

656	A347	4 l red brown	15	3
657	A348	20 l dark blue	50	15

Issued in tribute to Prime Minister George Dimitrov, 1882–1949.

Power Station
A349

Grain Towers
A350

Farm Machinery
A351

Tractor Parade
A352

Agriculture and Industry
A353

Perf. 11½x11, 11x11½.

1949, Aug. 5

658	A349	4 l olive green	6	3
659	A350	9 l dark red	15	5
660	A351	15 l purple	25	7
661	A352	20 l blue	60	22
662	A353	50 l orange brown	2.00	75
		Nos. 658-662 (5)	3.06	1.12

Issued to publicize Bulgaria's Five Year Plan.

Grenade and Javelin Throwers
A354

Boy and Girl Athletes
A357

Hurdlers
A355

Motorcycle and Tractor
A356

1949, Sept. 5

663	A354	4 l brown orange	35	13
664	A355	9 l olive green	60	18
665	A356	20 l violet blue	1.25	40
666	A357	50 l red brown	2.00	1.40

Frontier Guards
A358 A359

1949, Oct. 31

667	A358	4 l chestnut brown	10	5
668	A359	20 l gray blue	65	30

See also No. C60.

George Dimitrov
A360

Allegory of Labor
A361

Laborers of Both Sexes
A362

Workers and Flags of Bulgaria and Russia
A363

Perf. 11½

1949, Dec. 13 Photo. Unwmkd.

669	A360	4 l orange brown	10	5
670	A361	9 l purple	25	8
671	A362	20 l dull blue	40	15
672	A363	50 l red	1.00	45

Joseph V. Stalin
A364

Stalin and Dove
A365

1949, Dec. 21

673	A364	4 l deep orange	10	8
674	A365	40 l rose brown	80	40

Issued to commemorate the 70th anniversary of the birth of Joseph V. Stalin.

Kharalamby Stoyanov
A366

Communications Strikers
A368

Railway Strikers
A367

1950, Feb. 15

675	A366	4 l yellow brown	10	5
676	A367	20 l violet blue	25	10
677	A368	60 l brown olive	75	40

Issued to commemorate the 30th anniversary (in 1949) of the General Railway and Postal Employees' Strike of 1919.

Miner
A369

Shipbuilding
A371

Locomotive
A370

Tractor
A372

Farm Machinery
A373

Stalin Central Heating Plant
A374

Textile Worker
A375

1950-51 *Perf. 11½, 13.*

678	A369	1 l olive	12	4
679	A370	2 l gray black	20	4
680	A371	3 l gray blue	20	4
681	A372	4 l dark blue green	1.50	40
682	A373	5 l henna brown	50	6
682A	"	9 l gray black ('51)	25	6
683	A374	10 l deep plum ('51)	25	6
684	A375	15 l dk. carmine ('51)	60	6
685	"	20 l dark blue ('51)	60	10
		Nos. 678-685 (9)	4.22	86

No. 685 is inscribed in Latin characters.
See Nos. 750–751A.

Vassil Kolarov
A377

1950, Mar. 6 *Perf. 11½*

Size: 21½x31½ mm.

686	A377	4 l red brown	7	5

Size: 27x39½ mm.

687	A377	20 l violet blue	60	30

Issued in memory of Vassil Kolarov (1877–1950).

No. 687 has altered frame and is inscribed in Latin characters.

Stanislav Dospevski, Self-portrait
A378

King Kaloyan and Desislava
A379

Plowman Resting, by Christo Stanchev
A380

Statue of Dimtcho Debelianov, by Ivan Lazarov
A381

"Harvest," by V. Dimitrov
A382

Design: 9 l, Nikolai Pavlovich, self-portrait.

1950, Apr. 15 *Perf. 11½*

688	A378	1 l dark olive green	15	5
689	A379	4 l dark red	60	8
690	A378	9 l chocolate	60	8
691	A380	15 l brown	75	18
692	"	20 l deep blue	75	40
693	A381	40 l red brown	1.25	50
694	A382	60 l deep orange	2.25	85
		Nos. 688-694 (7)	6.35	2.14

Latin characters on No. 692.

Ivan Vazov and Birthplace
A383

1950, June 26

695	A383	4 l olive green	12	10

Issued to commemorate the centenary of the birth of Ivan Vazov (1850–1921), poet.

Road Building
A384

Men of Three Races and "Stalin" Flag
A385

Perf. 11½x11, 11x11½

1950, Sept. 19

696	A384	4 l brown red	5	4
697	A385	20 l violet blue	25	15

2nd National Peace Conference.

Molotov, Kolarov, Stalin and Dimitrov
A386

Spasski Tower and Flags
A387

Russian and Bulgarian Women
A388

Loading Russian Ship
A389

Photogravure.

1950, Oct. 10 *Perf. 11½* **Unwmkd.**

698	A386	4 l brown	10	4
699	A387	9 l rose carmine	12	6
700	A388	20 l gray blue	30	20
701	A389	50 l dark greenish blue	75	45

Issued to commemorate the 2nd anniversary of the Soviet-Bulgarian treaty of mutual assistance.

St. Constantine Sanatorium
A390

Children at Seashore
A391

Design: 5 l, Rest home.

1950 **Typographed**

702	A390	1 l dark green	6	3
703	A391	2 l carmine	6	3
704	"	5 l deep orange	15	4
705	"	10 l deep blue	40	10

Originally prepared in 1945 as "Sunday Delivery Stamps," this issue was released for ordinary postage in 1950.

Runners
A393

Designs: 9 l, Cycling. 20 l, Putting the Shot. 40 l, Volleyball.

1950, Aug. 21 Photo. *Perf. 11*

706	A393	4 l dark green	35	8
707	"	9 l red brown	45	12
708	"	20 l gray blue	65	30
709	"	40 l plum	1.35	65

Marshal Fedor I. Tolbukhin
A394

Natives Greeting Tolbukhin
A395

Perf. 11½x11, 11x11½.

1950, Dec. 10 Photo. **Unwmkd.**

710	A394	4 l claret	15	10
711	A395	20 l dark blue	50	25

Issued to publicize the return of Dobrich and part of the province of Dobruja from Romania to Bulgaria.

Dimitrov's Birthplace
A396

George Dimitrov
A397 A398

Various Portraits, Inscribed:

Г.ДИМИТРОВ

1950, July 2 *Perf. 10½*

712	A396	50s olive green	20	3
713	A397	50s brown	20	3
714	"	1 l reddish brown	30	3
715	A396	2 l gray (*Dimitrov Museum, Sofia*)	30	4
716	A397	4 l claret	55	4
717	"	9 l red brown	75	13
718	A398	10 l brown red	75	15
719	A396	15 l olive gray	75	25
720	"	20 l dark blue	1.00	45
		Nos. 712-720, C61 (10)	6.05	2.15

Issued to commemorate the first anniversary of the death of George Dimitrov, statesman. No. 720 is inscribed in Latin characters.

A. S. Popov
A400

1951, Feb. 10

722	A400	4 l red brown	25	18
723	"	20 l dark blue	50	35

No. 723 is inscribed in Latin characters.

Arms of Bulgaria
A401 A402

Typographed

1950 *Perf. 13* **Unwmkd.**

724	A401	2 l dark brown	6	3
725	"	3 l rose	7	3
726	A402	5 l carmine	7	4
727	"	9 l aquamarine	15	5

Nos. 724–727 were prepared in 1947 for official use but were issued as regular postage stamps Oct. 1, 1950.

Heroes Chankova, Antonov-Malchik, Dimitrov and Dimitrova
A403

Stanke Dimitrov-Marek
A404

George Kirkov
A405

George Dimitrov at Leipzig
A406

Natcho Ivanov and Avr. Stoyanov
A407

Portraits: 9 l, Anton Ivanov. 15 l, Christo Michailov.

1951, Mar. 25 Photo. *Perf. 11½*

728	A403	1 l red violet	20	6
729	A404	2 l dark red brown	20	8
730	A405	4 l carmine rose	20	10
731	"	9 l orange brown	60	15
732	"	15 l olive brown	90	25
733	A406	20 l dark blue	90	40
734	A407	50 l olive gray	1.75	1.00
		Nos. 728-734 (7)	4.75	2.04

First Bulgarian Tractor
A408

First Steam Roller
A409

First Truck
A410

Bulgarian Embroidery
A411

Designs: 15 l, Carpet. 20 l, Tobacco and roses. 40 l, Fruits.

Perf. 11x10½

1951, Mar. 30 Photo. **Unwmkd.**

735	A408	1 l olive brown	9	4
736	A409	2 l violet	20	4
737	A410	4 l red brown	30	6
738	A411	9 l purple	45	12
739	A409	15 l deep plum	65	20
740	A411	20 l violet blue	90	30
741	A410	40 l deep green	1.35	75

Perf. 13.

Size: 23x18½ mm.

742	A408	1 l purple	6	3
743	A409	2 l Prussian green	6	3
744	A410	4 l red brown	9	5
		Nos. 735-744 (10)	4.15	1.62

See also Nos. 894, 973.

Turkish Attack on Mt. Zlee Dol
A412

Designs: 4 l, Georgi Benkovski speaking to rebels. 9 l, Cherrywood cannon of 1876 and Russian cavalry, 1945. 20 l, Rebel, 1876 and partisan, 1944. 40 l, Benkovski and Dimitrov.

1951, May 3 *Perf. 10½*

Cream Paper.

745	A412	1 l reddish brown	20	5
746	"	4 l dark green	20	5
747	"	9 l violet brown	40	15
748	"	20 l deep blue	70	25
749	"	40 l dark red	95	50
		Nos. 745-749 (5)	2.45	1.00

Issued to commemorate the 75th anniversary of the "April" revolution.

Industrial Types of 1950.

1951 *Perf. 13*

750	A369	1 l violet	9	3
751	A370	2 l dark brown	12	3
751A	A372	4 l dk. yel. green	1.00	3

Demeter Blagoev Addressing 1891 Congress at Busludja
A413

1951 Photogravure *Perf. 11*

752	A413	1 l purple	9	6
753	"	4 l dark green	30	12
754	"	9 l deep claret	90	35

Issued to commemorate the 60th anniversary of the first Congress of the Bulgarian Social-Democratic Party.

See also Nos. 1174-1176.

Day Nursery
A414

Designs: 4 l, Model building construction. 9 l, Playground. 20 l, Children's town.

1951, Oct. 10 **Unwmkd.**

755	A414	1 l brown	15	6
756	"	4 l deep plum	35	10
757	"	9 l blue green	45	20
758	"	20 l deep blue	90	50

Issued to publicize Children's Day, Sept. 25, 1951.

Order of Labor
A415 A416

1952, Feb. 1 *Perf. 13*

Reverse of Medal

759	A415	1 l red brown	5	3
760	"	4 l blue green	10	3
761	"	9 l dark blue	35	10

Obverse of Medal

762	A416	1 l carmine	5	3
763	"	4 l green	10	3
764	"	9 l purple	35	10
		Nos. 759-764 (6)	1.00	32

No. 764 has numeral at lower left and different background.

Workers and Symbols of Industry
A417

Design: 4 l, Flags and heads of George Dimitrov and V. Tchervenkov.

1951, Dec. 29 *Perf. 11*

Inscribed: "16 XII 1951."

765	A417	1 l olive black	4	3
766	"	4 l chocolate	5	5

Issued to publicize the Third Congress of Bulgarian General Workers' Professional Union.

Dimitrov and Chemical Works
A418

George Dimitrov and V. Chervenkov
A419

Portrait: 80s, Dimitrov.

Photogravure.

1952, June 18 *Perf. 11* **Unwmkd.**

767	A418	16s brown	20	6
768	A419	44s brown carmine	45	8
769	A418	80s bright blue	65	30

Issued to commemorate the 70th anniversary of the birth of George Dimitrov.

Vassil Kolarov Dam
A420

Republika Power Station
A421

1952, May 16 *Perf. 13*

770	A420	4s dark green	6	4
771	"	12s purple	9	4
772	"	16s red brown	13	5
773	"	44s rose brown	50	10
774	"	80s bright blue	1.25	20
		Nos. 770-774 (5)	2.03	43

No. 774 is inscribed in Latin characters.

1952, June 30 *Perf. 13, Pin Perf.*

775	A421	16s dark brown	15	4
776	"	44s magenta	45	6

Nikolai I. Vapzarov
A422

Designs: Various portraits.

1952, July 23 *Perf. 10½*

777	A422	16s rose brown	25	10
778	"	44s dark red brown	65	15
779	"	80s dark olive brown	95	40

Issued to commemorate the 10th anniversary of the death of Nikolai I. Vapzarov, poet and revolutionary.

Dimitrov and Youth Conference
A423

Designs: 16s, Resistance movement incident. 44s, Frontier guards and industrial scene. 80s, George Dimitrov and young workers.

1952, Sept. 1 *Perf. 11x11½*

780	A423	2s brown carmine	7	4
781	"	16s purple	15	6
782	"	44s dark green	45	15
783	"	80s dark brown	75	35

Issued to commemorate the 40th anniversary of the founding conference of the Union of Social Democratic Youth.

Assault on the Winter Palace
A424

Designs: 8s, Volga-Don Canal. 16s, Symbols of world peace. 44s, Lenin and Stalin. 80s, Himlay hydroelectric station.

Photogravure.

1952, Nov. 6 *Perf. 11½* **Unwmkd.**

Dated: "1917-1952."

784	A424	4s red brown	6	4
785	"	8s dark green	9	4
786	"	16s dark blue	13	5
787	"	44s brown	30	10
788	"	80s olive brown	60	30
		Nos. 784-788 (5)	1.18	53

Issued to commemorate the 35th anniversary of the Russian revolution.

Vassil Levski
A425

Design: 44s, Levski and comrades.

1953, Feb. 19 Cream Paper *Perf. 11*

789	A425	16s brown	10	6
790	"	44s brown black	25	10

Issued to commemorate the 80th anniversary of the death of Vassil Levski, patriot.

Ferrying Artillery and Troops into Battle
A426

Soldier
A427

Mother and Children
A428

Designs: 44s, Victorious soldiers. 80s, Soldier welcomed. 1 l, Monuments.

1953, Mar. 3 *Perf. 10½*

791	A426	8s Prussian green	10	4
792	A427	16s deep brown	18	6
793	A426	44s dark slate green	40	15
794	"	80s dull red brown	80	18
795	"	1 l black	1.00	22
		Nos. 791-795 (5)	2.48	65

Issued to commemorate the 75th anniversary of Bulgaria's independence from Turkey.

1953, Mar. 9

796	A428	16s slate green	10	5
797	"	16s bright blue	10	5

Issued to commemorate Women's Day.

Certain countries cancel stamps in full sheets and sell them (usually with gum) for less than face value. Dealers generally sell "CTO" (canceled to order) stamps for much less than postally used copies.

Woodcarvings at Rila Monastery

A429 A430

Designs: 12s, 16s, 28s, Woodcarvings, Rila Monastery. 44s, Carved Ceilings, Trnovo. 80s, 1 l, 4 l, Carvings, Pasardjik.

Photogravure.

1953 *Perf. 13.* **Unwmkd.**

798	A429	2s gray brown	5	3
799	A430	8s dark slate green	7	3
800	"	12s brown	20	3
801	"	16s rose lake	50	3
802	A429	28s dark olive green	65	5
803	A430	44s dark brown	1.00	8
804	"	80s ultramarine	1.35	12
805	"	1 l violet blue	1.75	20
806	"	4 l rose lake	4.00	90
		Nos. 798-806 (9)	9.57	1.47

Karl Marx A431 "Capital" A432

1953, Apr. 30 *Perf. 10½*

807	A431	16s bright blue	10	8
808	A432	44s deep brown	30	15

70th anniversary of the death of Karl Marx.

Labor Day Parade A433 Joseph V. Stalin A434

1953, Apr. 30 *Perf. 13*

809	A433	16s brown red	12	5

Issued to publicize Labor Day, May 1, 1953.

1953, May 23 *Perf. 13x13½*

810	A434	16s dark gray	15	5
811	"	16s dark brown	15	5

Death of Joseph V. Stalin, Mar. 5, 1953.

Georgi Delchev A435 Battle Scene A436

Peasants Attacking Turkish Troops—A437

1953, Aug. 8 *Perf. 13*

812	A435	16s dark brown	8	4
813	A436	44s purple	30	20
814	A437	1 l deep claret	65	22

Issued to commemorate the 50th anniversary of the Ilinden Revolt (Nos. 812 and 814) and the Preobrazhene Revolt (No. 813).

Soldier and Rebels

A438

Design: 44s, Soldier guarding industrial construction.

1953, Sept. 18

815	A438	16s deep claret	10	5
816	"	44s greenish blue	25	15

Issued to publicize Army Day.

George Dimitrov and Vassil Kolarov A439 Demeter Blagoev A440

Designs: 16s, Citizens in revolt. 44s, Attack.

1953, Sept. 22

817	A439	8s olive gray	10	4
818	"	16s dark red brown	15	5
819	"	44s cerise	40	20

September Revolution, 30th anniversary.

1953, Sept. 21

Portraits: 44s, G. Dimitrov and D. Blagoev.

820	A440	16s brown	30	5
821	"	44s red brown	45	12

Issued to commemorate the 50th anniversary of the formation of the Social Democratic Party.

Railway Viaduct A441 Pouring Molten Metal A442

Designs: 16s, Welder and storage tanks. 80s, Harvesting machine.

1953, Oct. 17

826	A441	8s bright blue	7	4
827	"	16s greenish black	12	4
828	A442	44s brown red	35	18
829	A441	80s orange	60	30

Month of Bulgarian-Russian friendship.

Belladonna A443 Kolarov Library, Sofia A444

Medicinal Flowers: 4s, Jimson weed. 8s, Sage. 12s, Dog rose. 16s, Gentian. 20s, Poppy. 28s, Peppermint. 40s, Bear grass. 44s, Coltsfoot. 80s, Cowslip. 1 l, Dandelion. 2 l, Foxglove.

Photogravure.

1953 *Perf. 13.* **Unwmkd.**

White or Cream Paper

830	A443	2s dull blue	6	3
831	"	4s brown orange	6	3
832	"	8s blue green	10	6
833	"	12s brown orange	12	6
834	"	12s blue green	12	6
835	"	16s violet blue	25	8
836	"	16s deep red brown	25	8
837	"	20s carmine rose	35	8
838	"	28s dark gray green	50	8
839	"	40s dark blue	50	18
840	"	44s brown	50	18
841	"	80s yellow brown	95	30
842	"	1 l henna brown	1.50	40
843	"	2 l purple	2.50	80
		a. Souvenir sheet	15.00	15.00
		Nos. 830-843 (14)	7.76	2.42

No. 843a contains 12 stamps, one of each denomination above, printed in dark green, with floral border and frame of inscriptions. Size: 161x172mm. Sold for 6 leva.

1953, Dec. 16

854	A444	44s brown	30	15

Issued to commemorate the 75th anniversary of the founding of the Kolarov Library, Sofia.

Singer and Accordionist A445 Lenin and Stalin A446

Design: 44s, Dancers.

1953, Dec. 26

855	A445	16s red brown	10	4
856	"	44s dark green	22	10

1954, Mar. 13

Designs: 44s, Lenin statue. 80s, Lenin mausoleum, Moscow. 1 l, Lenin.

Cream Paper.

857	A446	16s brown	15	3
858	"	44s rose brown	30	5
859	"	80s blue	45	15
860	"	1 l deep olive green	60	25

30th anniversary of the death of Lenin.

Demeter Blagoev and Followers

A447

Design: 44s, Blagoev at desk.

1954, Apr. 28 **Cream Paper**

861	A447	16s deep red brown	10	4
862	"	44s black brown	30	8

Issued to commemorate the 30th anniversary of the death of Demeter Blagoev.

George Dimitrov A448 Dimitrov and Refinery A449

1954, June 11 **Cream Paper**

863	A448	44s lake	20	8
864	A449	80s brown	40	12

Issued to commemorate the 5th anniversary of the death of George Dimitrov.

Train Leaving Tunnel

A450

1954, July 30 **Cream Paper**

865	A450	44s dark green	45	10
866	"	44s black brown	45	10

Day of the Railroads, Aug. 1, 1954.

Miner at Work

A451

1954, Aug. 19 **Cream Paper**

867	A451	44s greenish black	30	10

Issued to publicize Miners' Day.

Academy of Science

A452

1954, Oct. 27 **Cream Paper**

868	A452	80s black	65	25

Issued to commemorate the 85th anniversary of the foundation of the Bulgarian Academy of Science.

Gymnastics A453 Horsemanship A454

Designs: 44s, Wrestling. 2 l, Skiing.

1954, Dec. 21

869	A453	16s dark gray green	60	20
870	"	44s brown red	90	30
871	A454	80s copper brown	1.50	65
872	A453	2 l violet blue	3.00	1.50

Welcoming Liberators A455 Soldier's Return A456

Designs: 28s, Refinery. 44s, Dimitrov and workers. 80s, Girl and boy. 1 l, George Dimitrov.

1954, Oct. 4 **Cream Paper**

873	A455	12s brown carmine	5	3
874	A456	16s deep carmine	5	3
875	A455	28s indigo	15	4
876	"	44s reddish brown	20	5
877	A456	80s deep blue	50	12
878	"	1 l dark green	60	18
		Nos. 873-878 (6)	1.55	45

10th anniversary of Bulgaria's liberation.

Recreation at Workers' Rest Home A457 — Metal Worker and Furnace A458

Portraits: 80s, Dimitrov, Blagoev, and Kirkov.

Photogravure.

1954, Dec. 28 *Perf. 13* Unwmkd.

Cream Paper

879	A457	16s dark green	10	4
880	A458	44s brown orange	20	6
881	A457	80s deep violet blue	60	25

Issued to commemorate the 50th anniversary of Bulgaria's trade union movement.

Geese
A459

Designs: 4s, Chickens. 12s, Hogs. 16s, Sheep. 28s, Telephone building. 44s, Communist party headquarters. 80s, Apartment buildings. 1 l, St. Kiradgieff Mills.

1955-56

882	A459	2s dark blue green	10	3
883	"	4s olive green	15	3
884	"	12s dark red brown	20	5
885	"	16s brown orange	20	8
886	"	28s violet blue	25	6
887	"	44s lilac red, *cream*	35	7
		a. 44s brown red	3.75	12
888	"	80s dark red brown	60	12
889	"	1 l dark blue green	65	18
		Nos. 882-889 (8)	2.50	62

Issue dates: No. 887, Apr. 20, 1956; others, Feb. 19, 1955.

Textile Worker A460 — Mother and Child A461

Design: 16s, Woman feeding calf.

1955, Mar. 5

890	A460	12s dark brown	6	3
891	"	16s dark green	12	3
892	A461	44s dark carmine rose	35	10
893	"	44s blue	45	10

Women's Day, Mar. 8, 1955.

No. 744 Surcharged in Blue.

1955, Mar. 8 *Perf. 13*

894	A410	16s on 4 l red brown	45	3

May Day Demonstration of Workers A462 — Sts. Cyril and Methodius A463

Design: 44s, Three workers and globe.

1955, Apr. 23 Photogravure

895	A462	16s carmine rose	9	5
896	"	44s blue	28	10

Labor Day, May 1, 1955.

1955, May 21 Cream Paper

Designs: 8s, Paisii Hilendarski. 16s, Nicolas Karastoyanov's printing press. 28s, Christo Botev. 44s, Ivan Vazov. 80s, Demeter Blagoev and socialist papers. 2 l, Blagoev printing plant, Sofia.

897	A463	4s deep blue	3	3
898	"	8s olive	4	3
899	"	16s black	8	5
900	"	28s henna brown	15	6
901	"	44s brown	20	8
902	"	80s rose red	45	18
903	"	2 l black	1.25	40
		Nos. 897-903 (7)	2.20	83

Issued to commemorate the 1100th anniversary of the creation of the Cyrillic alphabet. Latin lettering at bottom on Nos. 901-903.

Sergei Rumyantzev A464 — Mother and Children A465

Portraits: 16s, Christo Jassenov. 44s, Geo Milev.

Cream Paper

1955, June 30 *Perf. 13* Unwmkd.

904	A464	12s orange brown	15	4
905	"	16s light brown	20	4
906	"	44s greenish black	35	15

Issued to commemorate the 25th anniversary of the deaths of Sergei Rumyanchev, Christo Jassenov and Geo Milev. Latin lettering at bottom of No. 906.

1955, July 30 Cream Paper

907	A465	44s brown carmine	25	8

Issued to commemorate the World Congress of Mothers in Lausanne, 1955.

Young People of Three Races A466 — Friedrich Engels and Book A467

1955, July 30 Cream Paper

908	A466	44s blue	25	8

Issued to commemorate the fifth World Festival of Youth in Warsaw, July 31-Aug. 14, 1955.

1955, July 30

909	A467	44s brown	30	8

Issued to commemorate the 60th anniversary of the death of Friedrich Engels.

Entrance to Fair, 1892 A468 — Statuary Group at Fair, 1955 A469

Designs: 44s, "Fruit of our Land." 80s, Woman holding Fair emblem.

1955, Aug. 31 Cream Paper

910	A468	4s deep brown	3	3
911	A469	16s dark carmine rose	5	3
912	A468	44s olive black	25	12
913	A469	80s deep blue	40	15

Issued to commemorate the 16th International Plovdiv Fair. Latin lettering on Nos. 912-913.

Friedrich von Schiller
A470

Portraits: 44s, Adam Mickiewicz. 60s, Hans Christian Andersen. 80s, Baron de Montesquieu. 1 l, Miguel de Cervantes. 2 l, Walt Whitman.

1955, Oct. 31 Cream Paper

914	A470	16s brown	20	5
915	"	44s brown red	45	10
916	"	60s Prussian blue	60	10
917	"	80s black	75	15
918	"	1 l rose violet	1.25	25
919	"	2 l olive green	1.75	45
		Nos. 914-919 (6)	5.00	1.10

Issued in honor of various anniversaries of famous writers. Nos. 918 and 919 are issued in sheets alternating with labels without franking value. The labels show title pages for Leaves of Grass and Don Quixote in English and Spanish, respectively. Latin lettering on Nos. 915-919.

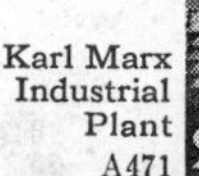

Karl Marx Industrial Plant
A471

Friendship Monument A472 — I. V. Michurin A473

Designs: 4s, Alexander Stambolisky Dam. 16s, Bridge over Danube. 1 l, Vladimir V. Mayakovsky.

1955, Dec. 1 Unwmkd.

920	A471	2s slate black	3	3
921	"	4s deep blue	3	3
922	"	16s dark blue green	6	4
923	A472	44s red brown	30	8
924	A473	80s dark green	40	12
925	"	1 l gray black	75	18
		Nos. 920-925 (6)	1.57	48

Issued to publicize Russian-Bulgarian friendship.

Library Seal A474 — Krusto Pishurka A475

Portrait: 44s, Bacho Kiro.

1956, Feb. 10 *Perf. 11x10½*

Cream Paper

926	A474	12s carmine lake	5	3
927	A475	16s deep brown	10	3
928	"	44s slate black	22	12

Issued to commemorate the 100th anniversary of the National Library. Latin lettering at bottom of No. 928.

Canceled to Order

Beginning about 1956, some issues were sold in sheets canceled to order. Prices in second column when much less than unused are for "CTO" copies. Postally used stamps are valued at slightly less than, or the same as, unused.

Quinces A476 — Cherrywood Cannon A477

Designs: 8s, Pears. 16s, Apples. 44s, Grapes.

1956 Photogravure *Perf. 13*

929	A476	4s carmine	1.10	8
930	"	8s blue green	50	10
931	"	16s lilac rose	60	5
932	"	44s deep violet	90	15

Latin lettering on No. 932. See also Nos. 964-967.

1956, Apr. 28 *Perf. 11x10½*

Design: 44s, Cavalry attack.

933	A477	16s dark claret	10	4
934	"	44s dark slate green	25	15

Issued to commemorate the 80th anniversary of the April (1876) Uprising against Turkish rule.

Demeter Blagoev and Birthplace A478 — Cherries A479

1956, May 30 *Perf. 11*

935	A478	44s Prussian blue	25	10

Issued to commemorate the centenary of the birth of Demeter Blagoev (1856-1924), writer.

1956 *Perf. 13* Unwmkd.

Designs: 12s, Plums. 28s, Peaches. 80s, Strawberries.

936	A479	2s rose carmine	7	3
937	"	12s blue	13	3
938	"	28s orange brown	27	5
939	"	80s deep carmine	60	20

Latin lettering on No. 939.

Gymnastics
A480

Pole Vaulting
A481

Designs: 12s, Discus throw. 44s, Soccer. 80s, Basketball. 1 l, Boxing.

Perf. 11x10½, 10½x11

1956, Aug. 29

940 A480 4s brt. ultramarine 15 5
941 " 12s brick red 20 6
942 A481 16s yellow brown 20 7
943 " 44s dark green 60 17
944 A480 80s dark red brown 90 35
945 A481 1 l deep magenta 1.50 45
Nos. 940-945 (6) 3.55 1.15

Latin lettering on Nos. 943–945.
Issued to publicize the forthcoming 16th Olympic Games at Melbourne, Nov. 22–Dec. 8, 1956.

Tobacco, Rose and Distillery A482 — People's Theater A483

1956, Sept. 1 ***Perf. 13***

946 A482 44s deep carmine 35 12
947 " 44s olive green 35 12

17th International Plovdiv Fair.

1956, Nov. 16 **Unwmkd.**

Design: 44s, Dobri Woinikoff and Sawa Dobroplodni, dramatists.

948 A483 16s dull red brown 10 6
949 " 44s dark blue green 25 8

Bulgarian Theater centenary.

Benjamin Franklin A484 — Cyclists, Palms and Pyramids A485

Portraits: 20s, Rembrandt. 40s, Mozart. 44s, Heinrich Heine. 60s, G. B. Shaw. 80s, Dostoevski. 1 l, Henrik Ibsen. 2 l, Pierre Curie.

1957, Dec. 29

950 A484 16s dark olive green 15 4
951 " 20s brown 20 4
952 " 40s dark carmine rose 30 6
953 " 44s dark violet brown 35 8
954 " 60s dark slate 45 8
955 " 80s dark brown 50 10
956 " 1 l bluish green 75 10
957 " 2 l Prussian green 1.25 15
Nos. 950-957 (8) 3.95 65

Issued in honor of great personalities of the world.

1957, Mar. 6 Photo. ***Perf. 10½***

958 A485 80s henna brown 60 15
959 " 80s Prussian green 60 15

Fourth Egyptian bicycle race.

Woman Technician A486 — "New Times" Review A487

Designs: 16s, Woman and children. 44s, Woman feeding chickens.

1957, Mar. 8

960 A486 12s deep blue 6 3
961 " 16s henna brown 8 3
962 " 44s slate green 25 12

Women's Day, Mar. 8, 1957. Latin lettering on 44s.

1957, Mar. 8 **Unwmkd.**

963 A487 16s deep carmine 15 7

Issued to commemorate the 60th anniversary of the founding of the "New Times" review.

Fruit Type of 1956.

Designs: 4s, Quinces. 8s, Pears. 16s, Apples. 44s, Grapes.

1957 Photogravure. ***Perf. 13***

964 A476 4s yellow green 4 3
965 " 8s brown orange 8 3
966 " 16s rose red 15 3
967 " 44s orange yellow 45 10

Latin lettering on No. 967.

Sts. Cyril and Methodius A488 — Basketball A489

1957, May 22 ***Perf. 11***

968 A488 44s olive green & buff 35 15

Issued for the centenary of the first public veneration of Sts. Cyril and Methodius, inventors of the Cyrillic alphabet.

1957, June 20 Photo. ***Perf. 10½x11***

969 A489 44s dark green 90 20

Issued to commemorate the 10th European Basketball Championship at Sofia.

Dancer and Spasski Tower, Moscow A490

1957, July 18 ***Perf. 13***

970 A490 44s blue 15 8

Issued to publicize the Sixth World Youth Festival in Moscow.

George Dimitrov—A491

1957, July 18

971 A491 44s deep carmine 20 8

75th anniversary of the birth of George Dimitrov (1882–1949).

Vassil Levski A492

1957, July 18 ***Perf. 11***

972 A492 44s greenish black 25 8

Issued to commemorate the 120th anniversary of the birth of Vassil Levski, patriot and national hero.

No. 742 Surcharged in Carmine.

1957 ***Perf. 13*** **Unwmkd.**

973 A408 16s on 1 l purple 12 3

Trnovo and Lazarus L. Zamenhof A493

1957, July 27

974 A493 44s slate green 45 15

Issued to commemorate the 50th anniversary of the Bulgarian Esperanto Society and the 70th anniversary of Esperanto.

Bulgarian Veteran of 1877 War and Russian Soldier A494

Design: 44s, Battle of Shipka Pass.

1957, Aug. 13

975 A494 16s dark blue green 8 3
976 " 44s brown 25 7

Issued to commemorate the 80th anniversary of Bulgaria's liberation from the Turks. Latin lettering on No. 976.

Woman Planting Tree A495 — Red Deer in Forest A496

Designs: 16s, Dam, lake and forest. 44s, Plane over forest. 80s, Fields on edge of forest.

1957, Sept. 16 Photo. ***Perf. 13***

977 A495 2s deep green 4 3
978 A496 12s dark brown 7 3
979 " 16s Prussian blue 8 3
980 " 44s Prussian green 20 8
981 " 80s yellow green 45 18
Nos. 977-981 (5) 84 35

Latin lettering on Nos. 980 and 981.

Lenin A497

Designs: 16s, Cruiser "Aurora." 44s, Dove over map of communist area. 60s, Revolutionaries and banners. 80s, Oil refinery.

1957, Oct. 29 ***Perf. 11***

982 A497 12s chocolate 5 3
983 " 16s Prussian green 7 4
984 " 44s deep blue 18 8
985 A497 60s dark carmine rose 35 10
986 " 80s dark green 50 25
Nos. 982-986 (5) 1.15 50

Issued to commemorate the 40th anniversary of the Communist Revolution.
Latin lettering on Nos. 984–985.

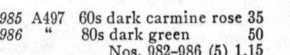

Globes A498

1957, Oct. 4 ***Perf. 13***

987 A498 44s Prussian blue 30 18

Issued to commemorate the fourth International Trade Union Congress, Leipzig, Oct. 4-15.

Vassil Kolarov Hotel A499

Health Resorts: 4s, Skis and Pirin Mountains. 8s, Old house at Koprivspitsa. 12s, Rest home at Velingrad. 44s, Momin-Prochod Hotel. 60s, Nesebr Hotel, shoreline and peninsula. 80s, Varna beach scene. 1 l, Hotel at Varna.

1958 Photogravure ***Perf. 13***

988 A499 4s blue 3 3
989 " 8s orange brown 6 3
990 " 12s dark green 6 5
991 " 16s green 10 3
992 " 44s dark blue green 18 8
993 " 60s deep blue 22 12
994 " 80s terra cotta 35 15
995 " 1 l dark red brown 40 20
Nos. 988-995 (8) 1.40 69

Issued to publicize various Bulgarian health resorts. Latin lettering on 44s, 60s, 80s, and 1 l.
Issue dates: Nos. 991-994, Jan. 20. Others, July 5.

Mikhail I. Glinka A500

Portraits: 16s, Jan A. Komensky (Comenius). 40s, Carl von Linné. 44s, William Blake. 60s, Carlo Goldoni. 80s, Auguste Comte.

1957, Dec. 30

996 A500 12s dark brown 25 3
997 " 16s dark green 25 3
998 " 40s Prussian blue 60 7
999 " 44s maroon 60 10
1000 " 60s orange brown 75 12
1001 " 90s deep plum 1.00 20
Nos. 996-1001 (6) 3.45 55

Issued to honor famous men of other countries. Latin lettering on Nos. 999–1001.

Young Couple, Flag, Dimitrov A501 — People's Front Salute A502

1958, Dec. 28 ***Perf. 11***

1002	A501	16s carmine rose	18	7

Issued to commemorate the 10th anniversary of Dimitrov's Union of the People's Youth.

1958, Dec. 28

1003	A502	16s dark vio. brown	18	7

15th anniversary of the People's Front.

Hare
A503

Animals: 12s, Red deer (doe) (vert.). 16s, Red deer (stag). 44s, Chamois. 80s, Brown bear. 1 l, Wild boar.

Photogravure.

1958, Apr. 5 ***Perf. 10½*** **Unwmkd.**

1004	A503	2s light & dark olive green	6	3
1005	"	12s slate green & red brown	10	3
1006	"	16s bluish green & dark red brown	18	3
1007	"	44s blue & brown	25	7
1008	"	80s bistre & dark brown	65	22
1009	"	1 l steel blue & dark brown	85	30
		Nos. 1004-1009 (6)	2.09	68

Latin lettering on Nos. 1007–1009. Nos. 1004–1009 exist imperf.; price $3.

Marx and Lenin—A504

Designs: 16s, Marchers and flags. 44s, Lenin blast furnaces.

1958, July 2 ***Perf. 11***

1010	A504	12s dark brown	8	3
1011	"	16s dark carmine	10	4
1012	"	44s dark blue	25	8

Issued to commemorate the 7th Congress of the Bulgarian Communist Party.

Wrestlers
A505

1958, June 20 ***Perf. 10½***

1013	A505	60s dk. carmine rose	65	25
1014	"	80s deep brown	90	40

World Wrestling Championship, Sofia.

Chessmen and Globe
A506

Photogravure

1958, July 18 ***Perf. 10½*** **Unwmkd.**

1015	A506	80s green & yellow green	1.50	35

5th World Students' Chess Games, Varna.

Conference Emblem
A507

1958, Sept. 24

1016	A507	44s blue	30	12

Issued to commemorate the World Trade Union Conference of Working Youth, Prague, July 14–20.

Swimmer
A508

Designs: 28s, Dancer (vertical). 44s, Volleyball (vertical).

1958, Sept. 19 ***Perf. 11x10½***

1017	A508	16s bright blue	15	7
1018	"	28s brown orange	25	10
1019	"	44s bright green	35	15

1958 Students' Games.

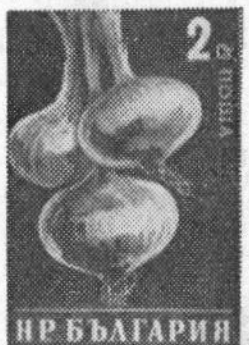

Onions
A509

Vegetables: 12s, Garlic. 16s, Peppers. 44s, Tomatoes. 80s, Cucumbers. 1 l, Eggplant.

1958, Sept. 20 ***Perf. 13***

1020	A509	2s orange brown	3	3
1021	"	12s Prussian blue	3	3
1022	"	16s dark green	6	5
1023	"	44s deep carmine	15	5
1024	"	80s deep green	35	12
1025	"	1 l bright purple	55	15
		Nos. 1020-1025 (6)	1.17	43

Latin lettering on Nos. 1023–1025. Nos. 1020–1025 exist imperf.; price $3. See also No. 1072.

Plovdiv Fair Building
A510

1958, Sept. 14 ***Perf. 11*** **Unwmkd.**

1026	A510	44s deep carmine	35	12

18th International Plovdiv Fair.

Attack
A511

Design: 44s, Fighter dragging wounded man.

1958, Sept. 23 **Photo.** ***Perf. 11***

1027	A511	16s orange vermilion	8	6
1028	"	44s lake	25	10

Issued to commemorate the 35th anniversary of the September Revolution.

Emblem, Brussels Fair
A512

1958, Oct. 13 ***Perf. 11***

1029	A512	1 l black & bright blue	1.50	1.50

World's Fair, Brussels, Apr. 17–Oct. 19. Exists imperf.; price $4.

Runner at Finish Line
A513

Woman Throwing Javelin
A514

Sports: 60s, High jumper. 80s, Hurdler. 4 l, Shot putter.

1958, Nov. 30

1030	A513	16s red brown, *pinkish*	30	13
1031	A514	44s olive, *yellowish*	30	17
1032	"	60s dark blue, *bluish*	40	20
1033	"	80s deep green, *greenish*	55	25
1034	A513	4 l deep rose claret, *pinkish*	3.50	1.25
		Nos. 1030-1034 (5)	5.05	2.00

1958 Balkan Games.
Latin lettering on Nos. 1032–1033.

Christo Smirnenski
A515

1958, Dec. 22

1035	A515	16s dark carmine	12	6

Issued to commemorate the 60th anniversary of the birth of Christo Smirnenski, poet, 1898–1923.

Girls Harvesting
A516

Girl Tending Calves
A517

Designs: 16s, Boy and girl laborers. 40s, Boy pushing wheelbarrow. 44s, Headquarters building.

1959, Nov. 29 **Photogravure**

1036	A516	8s dark olive green	5	3
1037	A517	12s reddish brown	7	3
1038	A516	16s violet brown	8	3
1039	A517	40s Prussian blue	15	5
1040	A516	44s deep carmine	45	12
		Nos. 1036-1040 (5)	80	26

Issued to commemorate the 4th Congress of Dimitrov's Union of People's Youth.

UNESCO Building, Paris
A518

1959, Mar. 28 ***Perf. 11*** **Unwmkd.**

1041	A518	2 l deep red lilac, *cream*	1.75	75

Issued to commemorate the opening of UNESCO (U. N. Educational, Scientific and Cultural Organization) Headquarters in Paris, Nov. 3, 1958. Exists imperf.; price $3.

Skier
A519

Soccer Players
A520

1959, Mar. 28 ***Perf. 11***

1042	A519	1 l blue, *cream*	85	40

Forty years of skiing in Bulgaria.

1959, Mar. 25

1043	A520	2 l chestnut, *cream*	1.50	65

Issued to commemorate the 1959 European Youth Soccer Championship.

Russian Soldiers Installing Telegraph Wires
A251

First Bulgarian Postal Coach
A522

Designs: 60s, Stamp of 1879. 80s, First Bulgarian automobile. 1 l, Television tower. 2 l, Strike of railroad and postal workers, 1919.

1959, May 4

No.	Type	Description	Unused	Used
1044	A521	12s dark green & citron	8	3
1045	A522	16s deep plum	12	3
1046	A521	60s dk. brn. & yel.	30	4
1047	A522	80s henna brown & salmon	40	15
1048	A521	1 l blue	50	25
1049	A522	2 l dark red brown	1.00	50
		Nos. 1044-1049 (6)	2.40	1.00

Issued to commemorate the 80th anniversary of the Bulgarian post. Latin lettering on Nos. 1046-1049.

Two imperf. souvenir sheets exist with olive borders and inscriptions. One contains one copy of No. 1046 in black & ochre, and measures 92x121mm. The other sheet contains one copy each of Nos. 1044-1045 and 1047-1048 in changed colors: 12s, olive green & ochre; 16s, deep claret & ochre; 80s, dark red & ochre; 1 l, olive & ochre. Each sheet sold for 5 leva. Price $15 each.

Great Tits—A523

Birds: 8s, Hoopoe. 16s, Great spotted woodpecker (vert.). 45s, Gray partridge (vert.). 60s, Rock partridge. 80s, Euro-$15 each.

1959, June 30 Photogravure

No.	Type	Description	Unused	Used
1050	A523	2s olive and slate green	5	3
1051	"	8s dp. orange & blk.	7	3
1052	"	16s chestnut & dark brown	10	5
1053	"	45s brown & black	20	7
1054	"	60s deep blue & gray	30	12
1055	"	80s deep blue green & gray	55	15
		Nos. 1050-1055 (6)	1.27	45

Bagpiper
A524

Designs: 12s, Acrobats. 16s, Girls exercising with hoops. 20s, Male dancers. 80s, Ballet dancers. 1 l, Ceramic pitcher. 16s, 20s, 80s are horizontal.

1959, Aug. 29 ***Perf. 11*** **Unwmkd.**

Surface-colored Paper.

No.	Type	Description	Unused	Used
1056	A524	4s dark olive	4	3
1057	"	12s scarlet	5	3
1058	"	16s maroon	7	4
1059	"	20s dark blue	10	5
1060	"	80s bright green	60	15
1061	"	1 l brown orange	80	30
		Nos. 1056-1061 (6)	1.66	60

Issued to publicize the 7th International Youth Festival, Vienna. Latin inscriptions on Nos. 1060-1061.

Partisans in Truck
A525

Designs: 16s, Partisans and soldiers shaking hands. 45s, Refinery. 60s, Tanks. 80s, Harvester. 1.25 l, Children with flag (vert.).

1959, Sept. 8

No.	Type	Description	Unused	Used
1062	A525	12s red & Pruss. grn.	3	3
1063	"	16s red & dark purple	6	3
1064	"	45s red & intense blue	12	5
1065	"	60s red & olive green	15	8
1066	"	80s red & brown	35	10
1067	"	1.25 l red & deep brown	75	25
		Nos. 1062-1067 (6)	1.46	54

15th anniversary of Bulgarian liberation.

Soccer—A526

1959, Oct. 10 ***Perf. 11.*** **Unwmkd.**

No.	Type	Description	Unused	Used
1068	A526	1.25 l deep green, *yellow*	3.75	2.25

Issued to commemorate 50 years of Bulgarian soccer. An imperf. 1.25 l lake, *yellow*, exists; sold for double face value. Price $7.50 unused, $4 used.

Batak Defenders
A527

1959, Aug. 8

No.	Type	Description	Unused	Used
1069	A527	16s deep claret	12	5

Issued to commemorate the 300th anniversary of the settlement of Batak.

Post Horn and Letter
A528

Bird-shaped Lyre
A529

Design: 1.25 l, Dove and letter.

1959, Nov. 23

No.	Type	Description	Unused	Used
1070	A528	45s emerald & blk.	25	10
1071	"	1.25 l light blue, red & black	40	20

Issued for International Letter Writing Week Oct. 5-11.

Type of 1958 Surcharged "45 CT." in Dark Blue.

Design: Tomatoes.

1959 Photogravure ***Perf. 13***

No.	Type	Description	Unused	Used
1072	A509	45s on 44s scarlet	28	8

1960, Feb. 23 ***Perf. 10½*** **Unwmkd.**

Design: 1.25 l, Lyre.

No.	Type	Description	Unused	Used
1073	A529	80s emerald & black	40	15
1074	A529	1.25 l bright red & black	55	15

Issued to commemorate the 50th anniversary of Bulgaria's State Opera.

N. I. Vapzarov
A530

Parachute and Radio Tower
A531

1959, Dec. 14 ***Perf. 11***

No.	Type	Description	Unused	Used
1075	A530	80s yellow green & red brown	40	12

Issued to commemorate the 50th anniversary of the birth of N. I. Vapzarov, poet and patriot.

1959, Dec. 3 Photogravure

No.	Type	Description	Unused	Used
1076	A531	1.25 l dp. greenish bl. & yellow	1.10	40

Issued to publicize the third Congress of Voluntary Participants in Defense.

Cotton Picker
A532

Harvester Combine
A533

Designs: 2s, Kindergarten. 4s, Woman doctor and child. 10s, Woman milking cow. 12s, Woman holding tobacco leaves. 15s, Woman working loom. 16s, Stalin textile mill, Dimitrovgrad. 25s, Rural electrification. 28s, Woman picking sunflowers. 40s, "Cold-well" hydroelectric dam. 45s, Miner. 60s, Foundry worker. 80s, Woman harvesting grapes. 1 l, Worker and peasant with cogwheel. 1.25 l, Industrial worker. 2 l, Party leader.

1959-61 Photogravure ***Perf. 13***

No.	Type	Description	Unused	Used
1077	A533	2s brn. org. ('60)	4	3
1077A	A532	4s golden brown ('61)	4	3
1078	"	5s dark green	4	3
1079	A533	10s red brown ('61)	4	3
1080	A532	12s red brown	5	3
1081	"	15s red lilac ('60)	6	3
1082	A533	16s deep violet ('60)	6	3
1083	"	20s orange	8	3
1084	A532	25s bright blue ('60)	8	3
1085	"	28s bright green	15	3
1086	A533	40s bright greenish blue	25	3
1087	A532	45s chocolate ('60)	20	3
1088	A533	60s scarlet	35	3
1089	A532	80s olive ('60)	35	3
1090	"	1 l maroon	50	3
1090A	A533	1.25 l dull blue ('61)	1.00	5
1091	A532	2 l dp. car. ('60)	1.00	5
		Nos. 1077-1091 (17)	4.29	55

Issued to commemorate the early completion of the 5-year plan (in 1959).

L. L. Zamenhof
A534

Path of Lunik 3
A535

1959, Dec. 5 ***Perf. 11*** **Unwmkd.**

No.	Type	Description	Unused	Used
1092	A534	1.25 l dark green & yellow green	55	25

Issued to commemorate the centenary of the birth (in 1859) of Lazarus Ludwig Zamenhof, inventor of Esperanto.

1960, Mar. 28 ***Perf. 11***

No.	Type	Description	Unused	Used
1093	A535	1.25 l Prussian blue & brt. yel.	2.50	1.00

Flight of Russia's Lunik 3 around moon. Exists imperf. Price $7.50 unused, $5 used.

Skier
A536

1960, Apr. 15 **Lithographed**

No.	Type	Description	Unused	Used
1094	A536	2 l ultra., black & brown	1.00	30

Issued to commemorate the 8th Olympic Winter Games, Squaw Valley, Calf., Feb. 18-29, 1960. Exists imperf.; price $2 unused, 75 cents used.

Vela Blagoeva
A537

Portraits: 28s, Anna Maimunkova. 45s, Vela Piskova. 60s, Rosa Luxemburg. 80s, Klara Zetkin. 1.25 l, N. K. Krupskaya.

1960, Apr. 27 Photo. ***Perf. 11***

No.	Type	Description	Unused	Used
1095	A537	16s rose & red brown	5	3
1096	"	28s citron & olive	8	3
1097	"	45s olive green & slate green	12	3
1098	"	60s light blue & Prus. blue	15	3
1099	"	80s red orange & deep brown	30	6
1100	"	1.25 l dull yellow & olive	50	7
		Nos. 1095-1100 (6)	1.20	25

International Women's Day, Mar. 8, 1960.

Lenin
A538

Design: 45s, Lenin sitting.

1960, May 12

No.	Type	Description	Unused	Used
1101	A538	16s red brown	15	5
1102	"	45s salmon pink & black	20	10

90th anniversary of the birth of Lenin.

Women Playing Basketball
A539

1960, June 3 ***Perf. 11***

1103 A539 1.25 l yellow & slate grn. 60 25

Issued to commemorate the seventh European Women's Basketball championships.

Parachutist
A541

Design: 1.25 l, Parachutes.

1960, June 29 Lithographed

1105 A541 16s lilac & dark blue 45 8
1106 " 1.25 l blue & claret 1.10 30

Issued to commemorate the 5th International Parachute Championships.

Yellow Gentian
A542

Flowers: 5s, Tulips. 25s, Turk's-cap lily. 45s, Rhododendron. 60s, Lady's-slipper. 80s, Violets.

1960, July 27 Photo. ***Perf. 11***

1107 A542 2s beige, green & yellow 12 3
1108 " 5s yellow green, green & carmine rose 12 3
1109 " 25s pink, green & orange 16 3
1110 " 45s pale lilac, green & rose lilac 16 3
1111 " 60s yellow, green & orange 30 5
1112 " 80s gray, green & violet blue 30 10
Nos. 1107-1112 (6) 1.16 27

Soccer
A543

Sports: 12s, Wrestling. 16s, Weight lifting. 45s, Woman gymnast. 80s, Canoeing. 2 l, Runner.

1960, Aug. 29 ***Perf. 11*** **Unwmkd.**

Athletes' Figures in Pink

1113 A543 8s brown 3 3
1114 " 12s violet 4 4
1115 " 16s Prussian blue 8 8
1116 " 45s deep plum 15 10
1117 " 80s blue 30 15
1118 " 2 l deep green 65 50
Nos. 1113-1118 (6) 1.25 90

Issued to commemorate the 17th Olympic Games, Rome, Aug. 25-Sept. 11.

Nos. 1113-1118 were also issued imperf. in changed colors, figures in yellow. Price $6 unused, $3.50 canceled.

Globes
A544
Photogravure

1960, Oct. 12 ***Perf. 11*** **Unwmkd.**

1125 A544 1.25 l blue & ultra. 45 17

Issued to commemorate the 15th anniversary of the World Federation of Trade Unions.

Alexander Popov
A545

1960, Oct. 12

1126 A545 90s blue & black 65 15

Issued to commemorate the centenary of the birth of Alexander Popov, radio pioneer.

Bicyclists
A546

1960, Sept. 22

1127 A546 1 l yellow, red org. & black 60 25

The 10th Tour of Bulgaria Bicycle Race.

Jaroslav Vésin
A547

1960, Nov. 22 ***Perf. 11*** **Unwmkd.**

1128 A547 1 l bright citron & olive green 1.10 60

Birth centenary of Jaroslav Vésin, painter.

U.N. Headquarters
A548

Costume of Kyustendil
A549

1961, Jan. 14 Photo. ***Perf. 11***

1129 A548 1 l brown & yellow 90 30
a. Souvenir sheet 3.75 2.25

Issued to commemorate the 15th anniversary of the United Nations. No. 1129 sold for 2 l. It exists imperf. Price, $2.50.

No. 1129a sold for 2.50 l and contains one copy of No. 1129, imperf. in dark olive and pink with orange marginal inscription. Size: 74x58mm.

1961, Jan. 28

Designs (Regional Costumes): 16s, Pleven. 28s, Sliven. 45s, Sofia. 60s, Rhodope. 80s, Karnobat.

1130 A549 12s salmon, slate green & yel. 4 3
1131 " 16s pale lilac, brown violet & buff 6 3
1132 " 28s pale green, slate green & rose 12 7
1133 " 45s blue & red 18 8
1134 " 60s greenish blue, Prussian blue & yellow 22 10
1135 " 80s yellow, slate green & pink 45 12
Nos. 1130-1135 (6) 1.07 43

Theodor Tiro (Fresco)
A550

Designs: 60s, Boyana Church. 1.25 l, Duchess of Dessislava (fresco).

1961, Jan. 28 Photogravure

1136 A550 60s yellow green, blk. & green 20 12
1137 " 80s yellow, slate grn. & org. 30 15
1138 " 1.25 l yellow green, henna brown & buff 45 20

700th anniversary of murals in Boyana Church.

Clock Tower, Vratsa
A551

Wooden Jug
A552

Designs: 12s, Clock tower, Bansko. 20s, Anguchev House, Mogilitsa. 28s, Oslekov House, Koprivspitsa (horiz.). 40s, Pasha's house, Melnik (horiz.). 45s, Lion sculpture. 60s, Man on horseback, Madara. 80s, Fresco, Bratchkovo monastery. 1 l, Tsar Assen coin.

1961, Feb. 25 ***Perf. 11*** **Unwmkd.**

Denomination and Stars in Vermilion.

1139 A551 8s olive green 3 3
1140 " 12s light violet 3 3
1141 A552 16s dark red brown 5 3
1142 A551 20s bright blue 5 3
1143 " 28s greenish blue 8 5
1144 " 40s red brown 12 7
1145 A552 45s olive gray 15 8
1146 " 60s slate 25 10
1147 " 80s dk. olive gray 35 12
1148 " 1 l green 50 15
Nos. 1139-1148 (10) 1.61 69

Capercaillie
A553

Birds: 4s, Dalmatian pelican. 16s, Ring-necked pheasant. 80s, Great bustard. 1 l, Lammergeier. 2 l, Hazel hen.

1961, March 31

1149 A553 2s black, salmon & Prus. green 4 3
1150 " 4s black, yellow grn. & orange 4 3
1151 " 16s brown, light grn. & orange 7 3
1152 " 80s brown, bluish grn. & yellow 35 5
1153 " 1 l black, light blue & yellow 40 18
1154 " 2 l brown, blue & yellow 1.00 20
Nos. 1149-1154 (6) 1.90 52

Radio Tower and Winged Anchor
A554

1961, Apr. 1 ***Perf. 11*** **Unwmkd.**

1155 A554 80s bright green & black 30 15

Issued to commemorate the 50th anniversary of the Transport Workers' Union.

T. G. Shevchenko
A555

Water Polo
A556

1961, Apr. 27

1156 A555 1 l olive & black 1.20 45

Issued to commemorate the centenary of the death of Taras G. Shevchenko, Ukrainian poet.

1961, May 15

Designs: 5s, Tennis. 16s, Fencing. 45s, Throwing the discus. 1.25 l, Sports Palace. 2 l, Basketball. 5 l, Sports Palace, different view. 5s, 16s, 45s and 1.25 l, are horizontal.

Black Inscriptions

1157 A556 4s light ultra. 4 3
1158 " 5s orange verm. 5 3
1159 " 16s olive green 6 3
1160 " 45s dull blue 15 6
1161 " 1.25 l yellow brown 45 15
1162 " 2 l lilac 60 25
Nos. 1157-1162 (6) 1.35 55

Souvenir Sheet

Imperf.

1163 A556 5 l yellow green, dull blue & yellow 4.00 3.00

Nos. 1157-1163 were issued to publicize the 1961 World University Games, Sofia, Aug. 26-Sept. 3.

No. 1163 measures 66x66mm.

Nos. 1157-1162 were issued imperf. and in changed colors: 4s, blue violet; 5s, orange brown; 16s, green; 45s, slate; 1.25 l, blue; 2 l, rose carmine. Price $5 unused, $3.50 used.

Monk Seal—A557

Black Sea Fauna: 12s, Jellyfish. 16s, Dolphin. 45s, Black Sea sea horse (vert.). 1 l, Starred sturgeon. 1.25 l, Thornback ray.

1961, June 19 *Perf. 11*

1164 A557 2s green & black 3 3
1165 " 12s Prus. green & pink 4 3
1166 " 16s ultramarine & violet blue 6 3
1167 " 45s lt. blue & brn. 18 5
1168 " 1 l yel. green & Prus. green 40 20
1169 " 1.25 l lt. violet blue & red brown 45 25
Nos. 1164-1169 (6) 1.16 59

Hikers
A558

Designs: 4s, "Sredetz" hostel (horiz.). 16s, Tents. 1.25 l, Mountain climber.

1961, Aug. 25 Litho. *Perf. 11*

1170 A558 4s yel. green, yel. & black 4 3
1171 " 12s lt. blue, cream & black 5 3
1172 " 16s green, cream & black 6 3
1173 " 1.25 l bistre, cream & black 55 12

"Know Your Country" campaign.

Demeter Blagoev Addressing 1891 Congress at Busludja
A559

1961, Aug. 5 Photogravure

1174 A559 45s dk. red & buff 20 4
1175 " 80s blue & pink 30 4
1176 " 2 l dk. brown & pale citron 75 6

Issued to commemorate the 70th anniversary of the first Congress of the Bulgarian Social-Democratic Party.

The Golden Girl
A560

Fairy Tales: 8s, The Living Water. 12s, The Golden Apple. 16s, Krali-Marko, hero. 45s, Samovila-Vila, Witch. 80s, Tom Thumb.

1961, Oct. 10 *Perf. 11* **Unwmkd.**

1177 A560 2s blue, blk. & org. 7 3
1178 " 8s rose lilac, black & gray 7 3
1179 " 12s bl. green, black & pink 10 3
1180 A560 16s red, black, blue & gray 15 6
1181 " 45s olive green, black & pink 30 15
1182 " 80s ochre, black & dark carmine 50 25
Nos. 1177-1182 (6) 1.19 55

Caesar's Mushroom
A561

Miladinov Brothers and Title Page
A562

Designs: Various mushrooms.

1961, Dec. 20 Photo. *Perf. 11*

Denominations in Black

1183 A561 2s lemon & red 5 3
1184 " 4s olive green & red brown 5 3
1185 " 12s bistre & red brown 5 3
1186 " 16s lilac & red brown 5 4
1187 " 45s carmine rose & yellow 20 7
1188 " 80s brown orange & sepia 35 15
1189 " 1.25 l violet & dk. brown 60 15
1190 " 2 l orange brown & brown 90 40
Nos. 1183-1190 (8) 2.25 90

The set was also issued imperf., with denominations in dark green. Price $4 unused, $2.50 canceled.

1961, Dec. 21 *Perf. 10½* **Unwmkd.**

1191 A562 1.25 l olive & black 50 15

Issued to commemorate the centenary of the publication of "Collected Folksongs" by the Brothers Miladinov, Dimitri and Konstantin.

Nos. 1079-85, 1087, 988, 1023, 1084, 1090-91 and 806 Surcharged with New Value in Black, Red or Violet.

1962, Jan. 1

1192 A533 1s on 10s red brown 3 3
1193 A532 1s on 12s red brown 3 3
1194 " 2s on 15s red lilac 7 3
1195 A533 2s on 16s deep violet (R) 7 3
1196 " 2s on 20s orange 7 3
a. "2 CT." on 2 lines 7 4
1197 A532 3s on 25s bright blue (R) 12 4
a. Black surch. 6.25 3.00
1198 A532 3s on 28s bright green (R) 12 3
1199 " 5s on 45s choc. 18 5
1200 A499 5s on 44s dark blue green (R) 18 5
1201 A509 5s on 44s deep car. (V) 18 5
1202 A532 10s on 1 l maroon 35 7
1203 " 20s on 2 l deep carmine 75 15
1204 A430 40s on 4 l rose lake (V) 1.50 30
Nos. 1192-1204 (13) 3.65 89

Freighter "Varna"
A563

Designs: 5s, Tanker "Komsomoletz." 20s, Liner "G. Dimitrov."

1962, Mar. 1 Photo. *Perf. 10½*

1205 A563 1s light green & bright blue 4 3
1206 " 5s lt. blue & green 15 6
1207 " 20s gray blue & greenish blue 75 15

Dimitrov working as Printer
A564

Roses
A565

Design: 13s, Griffin, emblem of state printing works.

1962, March 19 **Unwmkd.**

1208 A564 2s vermilion, black & yel. 5 3
1209 " 13s red orange, black & yel. 20 6

Issued to commemorate the 80th anniversary (in 1961) of the George Dimitrov state printing works.

1962, March 28

Various Roses in Natural Colors

1210 A565 1s deep violet 3 3
1211 " 2s salmon & dk. carmine 4 3
1212 " 3s gray & carmine 8 4
1213 " 4s dk. green 10 4
1214 " 5s ultramarine 15 4
1215 " 6s bluish green & dk. carmine 20 5
1216 " 8s citron & car. 1.25 21
1217 " 13s blue 1.75 30
Nos. 1210-1217 (8) 3.60 74

Malaria Eradication Emblem and Mosquito—A566

Design: 20s, Malaria eradication emblem.

1962, Apr. 19

1218 A566 5s orange brown, yel. & black 25 8
1219 " 20s emerald, yel. & black 70 25

Issued for the World Health Organization drive to eradicate malaria.

Exist imperf.; price $3 unused, 80 cents canceled.

Lenin and First Issue of Pravda
A567

1962, May 4 *Perf. 10* **Unwmkd.**

1220 A567 5s dp. rose & slate 35 8

Issued to commemorate the 50th anniversary of Pravda, Russian newspaper founded by Lenin.

Blackboard and Book
A568

1962, May 21 Photogravure

1221 A568 5s Prussian blue, blk. & yellow 15 6

The 1962 Teachers' Congress.

Soccer Player and Globe
A569

1962, May 26 *Perf. 10½*

1222 A569 13s br. grn., blk. & lt. brn. 1.00 25

Issued to commemorate the World Soccer Championships, Chile, May 30–June 17. Exists imperf. in changed colors. Price $3 unused, $1.25 canceled.

George Dimitrov
A570

1962, June 18 Photogravure

1223 A570 2s dark green 8 3
1224 " 5s turquoise blue 30 5

Issued to commemorate the 80th anniversary of the birth of George Dimitrov (1882–1949), communist leader and premier of the Bulgarian Peoples' Republic.

Bishop
A571

Chessmen: 2s, Rook. 3s, Queen. 13s, Knight. 20s, Pawn.

1962, July 7 *Perf. 10½* **Unwmkd.**

1225 A571 1s gray, emerald & black 3 3
1226 " 2s gray, lemon & black 5 3
1227 " 3s gray, lilac & blk. 10 3
1228 " 13s gray, dk. orange & black 40 13
1229 " 20s gray, bl. & blk. 70 20
Nos. 1225-1229 (5) 1.28 42

Issued to commemorate the 15th Chess Olympics, Varna. Nos. 1225–1229 were also issued imperf. in changed colors. Price $3 unused, $1 canceled.

An imperf. souvenir sheet contains one 20s horizontal stamp showing five chessmen. Lilac and gray border of sea horses and waves. Size: 75x66mm. Price $5 unused, $3 canceled.

Rila Mountain
A572

Designs: 2s, Pirin mountain. 6s, Nesebr, Black Sea. 8s, Danube. 13s, Vidin Castle. 1 l, Rhodope mountain.

1962-63 *Perf. 13*

1230	A572	1s dk. blue green	5	3
1231	"	2s blue	6	4
1232	"	6s greenish blue	15	4
1233	"	8s lilac	20	4
1234	"	13s yellow green	50	15
1234A	"	1 l deep grn. ('63)	3.00	55
		Nos. 1230-1234A (6)	3.96	85

XXXV КОНГРЕС
1962

No. 974 Surcharged in Red

13 =

1962, July 14 *Perf. 13*

1235 A493 13s on 44s slate green 1.45 70

Issued to commemorate the 25th Bulgarian Esperanto Congress, Burgas, July 14–16.

Girl and Festival Emblem
A573

Design: 5s, Festival emblem.

1962, Aug. 18 Photo. *Perf. 10½*

1236	A573	5s green, light blue & pink	15	6
1237	"	13s lilac, light blue & gray	40	10

Issued to commemorate the 8th Youth Festival for Peace and Friendship, Helsinki, July 28–Aug. 6, 1962.

Parnassius Apollo—A574

1962, Sept. 13

Various Butterflies in Natural Colors

1238	A574	1s pale citron & dark green	4	3
1239	"	2s rose & brown	7	3
1240	"	3s buff & red brown	10	3
1241	"	4s gray & brown	12	3
1242	"	5s lt. gray & brown	15	3
1243	"	6s gray & black	20	4
1244	"	10s pale grn. & blk.	55	9
1245	"	13s buff & red brn.	65	12
		Nos. 1238-1245 (8)	1.88	40

Planting Machine—A575

Designs: 2s, Electric locomotive. 3s, Blast furnace. 13s, Blagoev and Dimitrov and Communist flag.

1962, Nov. 1 *Perf. 11½*

1246	A575	1s blue green & dk. olive green	3	3
1247	"	2s blue & Prussian blue	7	3
1248	"	3s carmine & brn.	10	4
1249	"	13s plum, red & blk.	50	15

Bulgarian Communist Party, 8th Congress.

Title Page of "Slav-Bulgarian History" A576 — Paisii Hilendarski Writing History A577

1962, Dec. 8 *Perf. 10½* **Unwmkd.**

1250	A576	2s olive grn. & blk.	7	3
1251	A577	5s brn. org. & blk.	17	5

Issued to commemorate the 200th anniversary of "Slav-Bulgarian History" by Paisii.

Aleco Konstantinov
A578

1963, Mar. 5 Photo. *Perf. 11½*

1252 A578 5s red, grn. & black 22 5

Issued to commemorate the centenary of the birth of Aleco Konstantinov (1863–1897), writer. Printed with alternating red brown and black label showing Bai Ganu, hero from Konstantinov's books.

Arms of Bulgaria A579 — Sofia University A580

Designs: No. 1255, Levski Stadium, Sofia. No. 1256, Arch, Nissaria. No. 1257, Parachutist.

1963, Feb. 20 *Perf. 10* **Unwmkd.**

1253	A579	1s brown red	3	3
1254	A580	1s red brown	3	3
1255	"	1s blue green	3	3
1256	"	1s dark green	3	3
1257	"	1s bright blue	3	3
		Nos. 1253-1257 (5)	15	15

Vassil Levski A581 — Boy, Girl and Dimitrov A582

1963, Apr. 11 Photogravure

1258 A581 13s greenish blue & buff 60 15

Issued to commemorate the 90th anniversary of the death of Vassil Levski, revolutionary leader in the fight for liberation from the Turks.

1963, Apr. 25 *Perf. 11½* **Unwmkd.**

Design: 13s, Girl with book and boy with hammer.

1259	A582	2s orange, verm., red brn. & blk.	8	5
1260	"	13s bluish green, brown & black	40	12

Issued to commemorate the 10th Congress of Dimitrov's Union of the People's Youth.

Red Squirrel A583 — Sun Coast Promenade A584

Animals: 2s, Hedgehog. 3s, European polecat. 5s, Pine marten. 13s, Badger. 20s, Otter. (2s, 3s, 13s, horiz.)

1963, Apr. 30

Red Numerals

1261	A583	1s green & brown, *greenish*	3	3
1262	"	2s green & black, *yellow*	4	3
1263	"	3s green & brown, *bister*	7	3
1264	"	5s violet & red brown, *lilac*	15	6
1265	"	13s red brown & black, *pink*	50	20
1266	"	20s blk. & brn., *blue*	75	25
		Nos. 1261-1266 (6)	1.54	60

1963, Mar. 12 *Perf. 13* **Unwmkd.**

Black Sea Resorts: 2s, 3s, 13s, Views of Gold Sand. 5s, 20s, Sun Coast.

1267	A584	1s blue	5	3
1268	"	2s vermilion	10	3
1269	"	2s carmine rose	50	3
1270	"	3s ocher	10	3
1271	"	5s lilac	16	3
1272	"	13s blue green	50	12
1273	"	20s green	75	15
		Nos. 1267-1273 (7)	2.16	42

Freestyle Wrestling
A585

Design: 20s, Freestyle wrestling (horiz.).

1963, May 31 *Perf. 11½*

1274	A585	5s yellow bister & black	15	10
1275	"	20s orange brown & black	75	30

Issued to commemorate the 15th International Freestyle Wrestling Competitions, Sofia.

"Women for Peace"
A586

1963, June 24 *Perf. 11½* **Unwmkd.**

1276 A586 20s blue & black 65 20

Issued to commemorate the World Congress of Women, Moscow, June 24–29.

Esperanto Emblem and Arms of Sofia A587 — Moon, Earth and Lunik 4 A588

1963, June 29 Photogravure

1277 A587 13s multicolored 60 10

Issued to commemorate the 48th World Esperanto Congress, Sofia, Aug. 3–10.

1963, July 22

Designs: 2s, Radar equipment. 3s, Satellites and moon.

1278	A588	1s ultramarine	5	5
1279	"	2s red lilac	6	5
1280	"	3s greenish blue	8	5

Issued to commemorate Russia's rocket to the moon, Apr. 2, 1963.

MOSTRA EUROPEISTICA·1963 13 RICCIONE

Nos. 1211–1212 and 1215 Overprinted or Surcharged in Green, Ultramarine or Black

1963, Aug. 31 *Perf. 10½*

Roses in Natural Colors

1281	A565	2s salmon & dark carmine (G)	15	8
1282	"	5s on 3s gray & dk. carmine (U)	35	10
1283	"	13s on 6s bluish grn. & dk. car.	85	30

Issued to commemorate the International Stamp Fair, Riccione, Aug. 31.

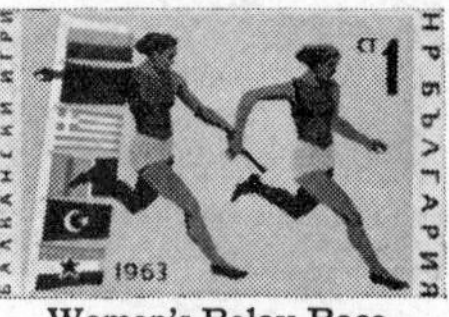

Women's Relay Race
A589

Designs: 2s, Hammer thrower. 3s, Women's long jump. 5s, Men's high jump. 13s, Discus thrower.

Perf. 11½

1963, Sept. 13 Photo. **Unwmkd.**

Flags in National Colors

1284	A589	1s slate green	5	3
1285	"	2s purple	6	3
1286	"	3s Prussian blue	10	5
1287	"	5s maroon	35	15
1288	"	13s chestnut brn.	1.45	50
		Nos. 1284-1288 (5)	2.01	76

Issued to publicize the Balkan Games. A multicolored, 50s, imperf. souvenir sheet shows design of women's relay race. Size: 74x70mm. Price $3.50 unused, $1.50 canceled.

"Slav-Bulgarian History"
A590

1963, Sept. 19 ***Perf. 10½***

1289	A590	5s salmon pink, slate & yel.	15	4

5th International Slavic Congress.

Revolutionists A591 — Christo Smirnenski A592

1963, Sept. 22 ***Perf. 11½***

1290	A591	2s brt. red & blk.	8	3

Issued to commemorate the 40th anniversary of the September Revolution.

1963, Oct. 28 ***Perf. 10½***

1291	A592	13s pale lilac & indigo	40	12

Issued to commemorate the 65th anniversary of the birth of Christo Smirnenski, poet.

Columbine A593 — Horses A594

1963, Oct. 9 Photo. ***Perf. 11½***

Multicolored

1292	A593	1s *shown*	4	3
1293	"	2s *Edelweiss*	5	5
1294	"	3s *Primrose*	10	5
1295	"	5s *Water lily*	15	6
1296	"	6s *Tulips*	20	8
1297	"	8s *Larkspur*	25	12
1298	"	10s *Alpine clematis*	60	15
1299	"	13s *Anemone*	60	20
		Nos. 1292-1299 (8)	1.99	74

1963, Dec. 28 ***Perf. 10½*** **Unwmkd.**

Designs: 2s, Charioteer and chariot. 3s, Trumpeters. 5s, Woman carrying tray with food. 13s, Man holding bowl. 20s, Woman in armchair. Designs are from a Thracian tomb at Kazanlik.

1300	A594	1s gray, orange & dark red	5	3
1301	"	2s gray, ocher & purple	5	3
1302	"	3s gray, dull yellow & slate green	8	5
1303	"	5s pale green, ocher & brown	15	6
1304	"	13s pale green, bister & black	50	15
1395	"	20s pale green, orge. & dk. car.	70	25
		Nos. 1300-1305 (6)	1.53	57

World Map and Emblem
A595

Designs: 2s, Blood transfusion. 3s, Nurse bandaging injured wrist. 5s, Red Cross nurse. 13s, Henri Dunant.

1964, Jan. 27 ***Perf. 10½***

1306	A595	1s lemon, black & red	4	3
1307	"	2s ultra., black & red	5	3
1308	"	3s gray, slate, black & red	6	3
1309	"	5s bright blue, black & red	15	6
1310	"	13s orge. yellow, black & red	45	18
		Nos. 1306-1310 (5)	75	33

Centenary of International Red Cross.

Speed Skating—A596

Sports: 2s, 50s, Women's figure skating. 3s, Cross-country skiing. 5s, Ski jump. 10s, Ice hockey goalkeeper. 13s, Ice hockey players.

1964, Feb. 21 ***Perf. 10½*** **Unwmkd.**

1311	A596	1s greenish blue, indigo & ocher	5	3
1312	"	2s brt. pink, olive green & dark slate green	5	3
1313	"	3s dull green, dk. green & brown	8	3
1314	"	5s blue, black & yellow brown	12	3
1315	"	10s gray, org. & blk.	25	8
1316	"	13s lilac, black & lilac rose	45	10
		Nos. 1311-1316 (6)	1.00	30

Miniature Sheet

Imperf.

1317	A596	50s gray, Prussian green & pink	2.50	1.00

Issued to commemorate 9th Winter Olympic Games, Innsbruck, Jan. 29-Feb. 9, 1964.

No. 1317 measures 64x67½mm.

Mask of Nobleman, 2nd Century
A597

Designs: 2s, Thracian horseman. 3s, Ceramic jug. 5s, Clasp and belt. 6s, Copper kettle. 8s, Angel. 10s, Lioness. 13s, Scrub woman, contemporary sculpture.

1964, Mar. 14 Photo. ***Perf. 10½***

Gray Frame

1318	A597	1s dp. green & red	4	3
1319	"	2s olive gray & red	5	3
1320	"	3s bister & red	10	6
1321	"	5s indigo & red	15	6
1322	"	6s orge. brn. & red	20	8
1323	"	8s brown red & red	30	10
1324	"	10s olive & red	40	12
1325	"	13s gray olive & red	45	20
		Nos. 1318-1325 (8)	1.69	68

2,500 years of Bulgarian art.

"The Unborn Maid"
A598

Fairy Tales: 2s, Grandfather's Glove. 3s, The Big Turnip. 5s, The Wolf and the Seven Kids. 8s, Cunning Peter. 13s, The Wheat Cake.

1964, Apr. 17 ***Perf. 10½*** **Unwmkd.**

1326	A598	1s blue green, red & orange brn.	4	3
1327	"	2s ultramarine, ocher & black	5	3
1328	"	3s citron, red & blk.	6	4
1329	"	5s deep rose, brown & black	15	4
1330	"	8s yellow green, red & black	30	9
1331	"	13s light violet blue, green & black	40	12
		Nos. 1326-1331 (6)	1.00	35

Ascalaphus Otomanus
A599

Insects: 2s, Nemoptera coa. (vert.). 3s, Saga natalia (grasshopper). 5s, Rosalia alpina (vert.). 13s, Anisoplia austriaca (vert.). 20s, Scolia flavitrons.

1964, May 16 Photo. ***Perf. 11½***

1332	A599	1s brown orange, yellow & blk.	5	3
1333	"	2s dull blue green, bister & black	6	5
1334	"	3s gray, grn. & blk.	10	8
1335	"	5s lt. olive green, black & violet	15	10
1336	"	13s violet, bister & black	40	18
1337	"	20s gray blue, yellow & blk.	60	25
		Nos. 1332-1337 (6)	1.36	69

Soccer
A600

Designs: 13s, Women's volleyball. 60s, Map of Europe and European Women's Volleyball Championship Cup (rectangular, size: 60x69mm.).

1964, June 8 ***Perf. 11½*** **Unwmkd.**

1338	A600	2s blue, dark blue, ocher & red	15	10
1339	"	13s blue, dark blue, ocher & red	50	30

Miniature Sheet

Imperf.

1340	A600	60s ultra., ocher, red & gray	1.75	1.75

Issued to commemorate the 50th anniversary of the Levski Physical Culture Association.

Peter Beron and Title Page of Primer—A601

1964, June 22 ***Perf. 11½***

1341	A601	20s red brn. & dark brown, *grayish*	60	45

Issued to commemorate the 140th anniversary of the publication of the first Bulgarian primer.

Robert Stephenson's "Rocket" Locomotive, 1825
A602

Designs: 2s, Modern steam locomotive. 3s, Diesel locomotive. 5s, Electric locomotive. 8s, Freight train on bridge. 13s, Diesel locomotive and tunnel.

1964, July 1 Photo. ***Perf. 11½***

1342	A602	1s org. brn., black, bister & gray	4	3
1343	"	2s org. brn., black, Prussian blue & olive	5	3
1344	"	3s org. brn., black, green & gray	6	3
1345	"	5s orange brown, black & blue	20	4
1346	"	8s org. brown, blk., blue & gray	25	5
1347	"	13s org. brn., black, yellow & gray	40	7
		Nos. 1342-1347 (6)	1.00	25

German Shepherd
A603

1964, Aug. 22 Photogravure

Multicolored

1348	A603	1s *shown*	3	3
1349	"	2s *Setter*	4	3
1350	"	3s *Poodle*	6	3
1351	"	4s *Pomeranian*	15	4
1352	"	5s *St. Bernard*	18	4
1353	"	6s *Terrier*	30	5
1354	"	10s *Pointer*	60	15
1355	"	13s *Dachshund*	90	35
		Nos. 1348-1355 (8)	2.26	72

Partisans—A604

Designs: 2s, People welcoming Soviet army. 3s, Russian aid to Bulgaria. 4s, Blast furnace, Kremikovski. 5s, Combine. 6s, Peace demonstration. 8s, Sentry. 13s, Demeter Blagoev and George Dimitrov.

1964, Sept. 9 ***Perf. 11½*** **Unwmkd.**

Flag in Red

1356	A604	1s lt. & dp. ultra.	4	3
1357	"	2s olive bister & deep olive	5	3

1358 A604 3s rose lilac & maroon 6 3
1359 " 4s lt. violet & vio. 6 3
1360 " 5s org. & red brn. 20 4
1361 " 6s blue & dp. blue 25 5
1362 " 8s lt. green & green 30 6
1363 " 13s terra cotta & red brown 55 12
Nos. 1356-1363 (8) 1.51 39

Issued to commemorate the 20th anniversary of People's Government of Bulgaria.

М М панаир
Пловдив - 1964
ST 20

No. 967 Surcharged

1964, Sept. 13 ***Perf. 13***

1364 A476 20s on 44s orge. yel. 60 20

International Plovdiv Fair.

Gymnast on Parallel Bars
A606

Vratcata Mountain Road
A607

Sports: 2s, Long jump. 3s, Woman diver. 5s, Soccer. 13s, Women's volleyball. 20s, Wrestling.

1964, Oct. 10 ***Perf. 11½***

1366 A606 1s pale green, green & red 4 3
1367 " 2s pale vio., violet blue & red 5 3
1368 " 3s blue green, brown & red 6 5
1369 " 5s pink, pur. & red 10 8
1370 " 13s blue, Prussian green & red 35 15
1371 " 20s yel., grn. & red 50 35
Nos. 1366-1371 (6) 1.10 69

Issued for the 18th Olympic Games, Tokyo. Oct. 10-25. See No. B27.

1964, Oct. 26 Photo. ***Perf. 12½x13***

Bulgarian Views: 2s, Ritlite mountain road. 3s, Pines, Malovica peak. 4s, Pobitite rocks. 5s, Erkupria. 6s, Rhodope mountain road.

1372 A607 1s dk. slate green 3 3
1373 " 2s brown 3 3
1374 " 3s greenish blue 8 3
1375 " 4s dk. red brown 12 3
1376 " 5s deep green 18 3
1377 " 6s blue violet 20 5
Nos. 1372-1377 (6) 64 20

Mail Coach, Plane and Rocket
A608

1964, Oct. 3 ***Perf. 11½*** **Unwmkd.**

1378 A608 20s greenish blue 75 30

Issued to commemorate the first national stamp exhibition, Sofia, Oct. 3-18. Issued in sheets of 12 stamps and 12 labels (woman's head and inscription, 5x5) arranged around one central label showing stylized bird design.

Students Holding Book
A609

1964, Dec. 30 Photogravure

1379 A609 13s lt.bl. & black 40 12

Issued to commemorate the 8th International Students' Congress, Sofia.

500-Year-Old Walnut Tree at Golemo Drenovo—A610

Designs: Various Old Trees.

1964, Dec. 28

1380 A610 1s black, buff & claret brown 3 3
1381 " 2s black, pink & deep claret 5 3
1382 " 3s black, yellow & dark brown 6 3
1383 " 4s blk., lt. blue & Prussian blue 8 3
1384 " 10s blk., pale grn. & green 28 10
1385 " 13s blk., pale bister & dk. olive green 50 14
Nos. 1380-1385 (6) 1.00 36

Soldiers' Monument
A611

1965, Jan. 1 **Unwmkd.**

1386 A611 2s red & black 25 5

Issued to honor Bulgarian-Soviet friendship.

Olympic Medal Inscribed "Olympic Glory"
A612

1965, Jan. 27 Photo. ***Perf. 11½***

1387 A612 20s orange brown, gold & black 55 20

Issued to commemorate Bulgarian victories in the 1964 Olympic Games.

"Victory Over Fascism"
A613

Design: 13s, "Fight for Peace" (dove and globe).

1965, Apr. 16 ***Perf. 11½***

1388 A613 5s gray, black & olive bister 15 5
1389 " 13s gray, blk. & bl. 40 13

Issued to commemorate the 20th anniversary of victory over Fascism, May 9, 1945.

Vladimir M. Komarov and Section of Globe
A614

Designs: 2s, Konstantin Feoktistov. 5s, Boris B. Yegorov. 13s, Komarov, Feoktistov and Yegorov. 20s, Spaceship Voskhod.

1965, Feb. 15 Photogravure

1390 A614 1s pale lilac & dark blue 3 3
1391 " 2s light blue, indigo & dull violet 3 3
1392 " 5s pale green, green & olive green 9 5
1393 " 13s pale pink, deep rose & maroon 25 9
1394 " 20s light blue, violet blue, greenish blue & yellow 60 20
Nos. 1390-1394 (5) 1.00 40

Russian three-man space flight, Oct. 12-13, 1964.

Exist imperf. in changed colors. Four lower values printed se-tenant. Price, set of 5, $2 unused, $1.50 canceled.

Bullfinch
A615

Birds: 2s, European golden oriole. 3s, Common rock thrush. 5s, Barn swallow. 8s, European roller. 10s, European goldfinch. 13s, Rosy pastor starling. 20s, Nightingale.

1965, Apr. 20 ***Perf. 11½*** **Unwmkd.**

Birds in Natural Colors

1395 A615 1s blue green 4 3
1396 " 2s rose lilac 10 3
1397 " 3s rose 15 3
1398 " 5s bright blue 20 5
1399 " 8s citron 30 6
1400 " 10s gray 60 8
1401 " 13s light violet blue 60 10
1402 " 20s emerald 75 22
Nos. 1395-1402 (8) 2.74 60

Sting Ray
A616

Black Sea Fish: 2s, Belted bonito. 3s, Hogfish. 5s, Gurnard. 10s, Scad. 13s, Turbot.

1965, June 10 Photo. ***Perf. 11½***

Gray Frames

1403 A616 1s orge., blk. & gold 3 3
1404 " 2s ultramarine, indigo & silver 4 3
1405 " 3s emerald, black & gold 10 3
1406 " 5s deep carmine, black & gold 15 6
1407 " 10s greenish blue, blk. & silver 60 15
1408 " 13s red brown, blk. & gold 1.00 40
Nos. 1403-1408 (6) 1.92 70

Plane, Bus, Train, Ship and Whale
A617

ITU Emblem and Communications Symbols
A618

1965, Apr. 30

1409 A617 13s multicolored 30 10

Issued to publicize the fourth International Conference of Transport, Dock and Fishery Workers, Sofia, May 10-14.

1965, May 17

1410 A618 20s multicolored 55 25

Issued to commemorate the centenary of the International Telecommunication Union.

Col. Pavel Belyayev and Lt. Col. Alexei Leonov
A619

Design: 20s, Leonov floating in space.

1965, May 20 **Unwmkd.**

1411 A619 2s gray, dull blue & dark brown 15 8
1412 " 20s multicolored 1.00 40

Space flight of Voskhod 2 and the first man floating in space, Lt. Col. Alexei Leonov.

ICY Emblem
A620

1965, May 15 Photogravure

1413 A620 20s orange, olive & black 50 20

International Cooperation Year, 1965.

Corn A621 — Marx and Lenin A622

Designs: 2s, Wheat. 3s, Sunflowers. 4s, Sugar beet. 5s, Clover. 10s, Cotton. 13s, Tobacco.

1965, Apr. 1 *Perf. 12½x13*

No.	Type	Description	Unused	Used
1414	A621	1s orange yellow	3	3
1415	"	2s bright green	5	3
1416	"	3s deep orange	8	3
1417	"	4s olive	10	3
1418	"	5s bright rose	15	3
1419	"	10s greenish blue	25	5
1420	"	13s bister	35	5
		Nos. 1414-1420 (7)	1.01	25

1965, June *Perf. 10½*

No.	Type	Description	Unused	Used
1421	A622	13s red & dk. brn.	32	12

Issued to commemorate the 6th Conference of Postal Ministers of Communist Countries, Peking, June 21–July 15.

Film and UNESCO Emblem A623

1965, June 30

No.	Type	Description	Unused	Used
1422	A623	13s dp. bl., black & light gray	32	12

Balkan Film Festival, Varna.

Ballerina A624

1965, July 10 Photogravure

No.	Type	Description	Unused	Used
1423	A624	5s deep lilac rose & black	45	22

Issued to publicize the Second International Ballet Competition, Varna.

Map of Balkan Peninsula and Dove with Letter—A625

Col. Pavel Belyayev and Lt. Col. Alexei Leonov—A626

Designs: 2s, Sailboat and modern buildings. 3s, Fish and plants. 13s, Symbolic sun and rocket. 40s, Map of Balkan Peninsula and dove with letter (like 1s).

1965, July 23–Aug. 7 *Perf. 10½*

No.	Type	Description	Unused	Used
1424	A625	1s silver, deep ultra. & yellow	5	3
1425	"	2s silver, purple & yellow	6	3
1426	A625	3s gold, grn. & yel.	10	8
1427	"	13s gold, henna brown & yel.	45	35
1428	A626	20s silver, bl. & brn.	60	45
		Nos. 1424-1428 (5)	1.26	94

Miniature Sheet

Imperf.

No.	Type	Description	Unused	Used
1429	A625	40s gold & bright blue	1.35	1.10

Issued to publicize "Balkanphila 1965," Philatelic Exhibition, Varna, Aug. 7–15, and the visit of the Russian astronauts Belyayev and Leonov. The 20s and 40s were issued Aug. 7. The 20s exists imperf. in changed colors. Price 60 cents.

No. 1429 has gold denomination and inscription in margin. Size: 69x61½mm.

Woman Gymnast A627

Designs: 2s, Woman gymnast on parallel bars. 3s, Weight lifter. 5s, Automobile and chart. 10s, Women basketball players. 13s, Automobile and map of rally.

1965, Aug. 14 *Perf. 10½*

No.	Type	Description	Unused	Used
1430	A627	1s crimson, brown & black	4	3
1431	"	2s rose violet, dp. claret & black	5	3
1432	"	3s deep carmine, brn. & black	6	3
1433	"	5s terra cotta, red brn. & black	10	3
1434	"	10s dp. lilac rose, dp. claret & black	30	12
1435	"	13s lilac, claret & black	45	16
		Nos. 1430-1435 (6)	1.00	40

Issued to commemorate various sports events in Bulgaria during May–June, 1965.

No. 989 Surcharged

2 Ст

ПЪРВИ НАЦИОНАЛЕН
СЪБОР НА НАРОДНО
10 ТВОРЧЕСТВО
12-15-VIII
1965

1965, Aug. 12 *Perf. 13*

No.	Type	Description	Unused	Used
1436	A499	2s on 8s orange brn.	40	15

Issued to publicize the First National Folklore Competition, Aug. 12–15.

Escaping Prisoners A628 — Apples A629

1965, July 23 *Perf. 10½*

No.	Type	Description	Unused	Used
1437	A628	2s slate	20	15

Issued to commemorate the 40th anniversary of the escape of political prisoners from Bolshevik Island.

1965, July 1 *Perf. 13*

Fruit: 2s, Grapes. 3s, Pears. 4s, Peaches. 5s, Strawberries. 6s, Walnuts.

No.	Type	Description	Unused	Used
1438	A629	1s deep orange	3	3
1439	"	2s light olive green	3	3
1440	"	3s bister	5	3
1441	A629	4s orange	6	3
1442	"	5s carmine rose	18	3
1443	"	6s yellow brown	20	10
		Nos. 1438-1443 (6)	55	25

Dressage—A630

Horsemanship: 2s, Three-day test. 3s, Jumping. 5s, Race. 10s, Steeplechase. 13s, Hurdle race.

1965, Sept. 30 *Perf. 10½* **Unwmkd.**

No.	Type	Description	Unused	Used
1444	A630	1s bluish gray, blk. & dk. violet	4	3
1445	"	2s buff, black & henna brown	4	3
1446	"	3s gray, black & dk. car. rose	5	3
1447	"	5s gray olive, dk. grn. & red brn.	8	5
1448	"	10s lt. gray, black & dk. red brown	27	13
1449	"	13s salmon, dk. grn. & dk. red brn.	80	30
		Nos. 1444-1449 (6)	1.28	57

See also No. B28.

Smiling Children A631

Designs: 2s, Two girl Pioneers. 3s, Bugler. 5s, Pioneer with model plane. 8s, Two singing girls in national costume. 13s, Running boy.

1965, Oct. 24 Photogravure

No.	Type	Description	Unused	Used
1450	A631	1s dk. blue green & yellow green	3	3
1451	"	2s vio. & dp. rose	3	3
1452	"	3s olive & lemon	5	3
1453	"	5s dp. bl. & bister	10	6
1454	"	8s oliver bister & orange	25	15
1455	"	13s rose car. & vio.	50	30
		Nos. 1450-1455 (6)	96	60

Issued to honor the Dimitrov Pioneer Organization.

U-52 Plane over Trnovo A632

Designs: 2c, 1L-14 over Plovdiv. 3s, Mi-4 Helicopter over Dimitrovgrad. 5s, Tu-104 over Ruse. 13s, IL-18 over Varna. 20s, Tu-114 over Sofia.

1965, Nov. 25 *Perf. 10½*

No.	Type	Description	Unused	Used
1456	A632	1s gray, blue & red	3	3
1457	"	2s gray, lilac & red	3	3
1458	"	3s gray, greenish blue & red	7	5
1459	"	5s gray, org. & red	12	8
1460	"	13s gray, bister & red	45	24
1461	"	20s gray, lt. green & red	50	30
		Nos. 1456-1461 (6)	1.20	73

Issued to publicize the development of Bulgarian Civil Air Transport.

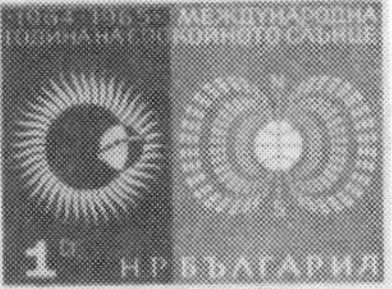

IQSY Emblem, and Earth Radiation Zones A633

Designs (IQSY Emblem and): 2s, Sun with corona. 13s, Solar eclipse.

1965, Dec. 15 Photo. *Perf. 10½*

No.	Type	Description	Unused	Used
1462	A633	1s grn., yel. & ultra.	3	3
1463	"	2s yel., red lilac & red	5	3
1464	"	13s blue, yel. & blk.	30	8

International Quiet Sun Year, 1964–65.

"North and South Bulgaria" A634 — "Martenitsa" Emblem A635

1965, Dec. 6

No.	Type	Description	Unused	Used
1465	A634	13s bright yellow green & black	30	15

Issued to commemorate the centenary of the Union of North and South Bulgaria.

1966, Jan. 10 Photo. *Perf. 10½*

"Spring" in Folklore: 2s, Drummer. 3s, Bird ornaments. 5s, Dancer "Lazarka." 8s, Vase with flowers. 13s, Bagpiper.

No.	Type	Description	Unused	Used
1466	A635	1s rose lilac, violet blue & gray	3	3
1467	"	2s gray, black & crimson	3	3
1468	"	3s red, vio. & gray	5	3
1469	"	5s lilac, black & crimson	9	3
1470	"	8s rose lilac, brn. & purple	15	7
1471	"	13s blue, black & rose lilac	40	8
		Nos. 1466-1471 (6)	75	27

Church of St. John the Baptist, Nessebr—A636

Designs: 1s, Christ, fresco from Bojana Church. 2s, Ikon "Destruction of Idols" (horiz.). 3s, Bratchkovo Monastery. 4s, Zemen Monastery (horiz.). 13s, Nativity, ikon from Arbanassi. 20s, Ikon "Virgin and Child," 1342.

1966, Feb. 25 Litho. *Perf. 11½*

No.	Type	Description	Unused	Used
1472	A636	1s gray & multi.	40	40
1473	"	2s " "	30	25
1474	"	3s multicolored	30	25
1475	"	4s "	30	25
1476	"	5s "	40	30
1477	"	13s gray & multi.	50	30
1478	"	20s multicolored	90	75
		Nos. 1472-1478 (7)	3.10	2.50

2,500 years of art in Bulgaria.

Georgi Benkovski and T. Kableshkov—A637

Designs: 1s, Proclamation of April Uprising, Koprivstitsa. 3s, Dedication of flag, Panaguriste. 5s, V. Petleshkov and Z. Dyustabanov. 10s, Botev landing at Kozlodui. 13s, P. Volov and Ilarion Dragostinov.

1966, March 3 Photo. *Perf. 10½*

Center in Black

1479 A637 1s red brn. & gold 3 3
1480 " 2s brt. red & gold 4 3
1481 " 3s olive grn. & gold 6 3
1482 " 5s steel bl. & gold 12 3
1483 " 10s brt. rose lilac & gold 20 4
1484 " 13s lt. violet & gold 30 4
Nos. 1479-1484 (6) 75 20

Issued to commemorate the 90th anniversary of the April Uprising against the Turks.

Elephant
A638

Animals from Sofia Zoo: 2s, Tiger. 3s, Chimpanzee. 4s, Siberian ibex. 5s, Polar bear. 8s, Lion. 13s, Bison. 20s, Kangaroo.

1966, May 23 Lithographed

1485 A638 1s yel., blk. & gray 4 3
1486 " 2s dull yel., orange yel. & black 4 3
1487 " 3s pale grn., bister & black 6 3
1488 " 4s tan, brn. & blk. 8 3
1489 " 5s lt. blue & blk. 10 4
1490 " 8s pale rose, bister & black 18 5
1491 " 13s citron, brown & black 55 13
1492 " 20s pale lilac, bister & black 70 16
Nos. 1485-1492 (8) 1.75 50

WHO Headquarters, Geneva
A639

1966, May 3 Photogravure

1493 A639 13s dp. bl. & silver 35 15

Issued to commemorate the inauguration of the World Health Organization Headquarters, Geneva.

Worker
A640

1966, May 9 Photo. *Perf. 10½*

1494 A640 20s gray & rose 60 20

Sixth Trade Union Congress.

Yantra River Bridge, Biela
A641

Designs: No. 1496, Maritsa River Bridge, Svilengrad. No. 1497, Fountain, Samokov. No. 1498, Ruins of Fort, Kaskovo. 8s, Old Fort, Ruse. 13s, House, Gabrovo.

1966, Feb. 10 Photo. *Perf. 13*

1495 A641 1s Prussian blue 3 3
1496 " 1s bright green 3 3
1497 " 2s olive green 5 3
1498 " 2s dark red brown 5 3
1499 " 8s red brown 18 3
1500 " 13s dark blue 35 5
Nos. 1495-1500 (6) 69 20

Souvenir Sheet

Moon Allegory—A642

1966, Apr. 29 *Imperf.*

1501 A642 60s black, plum & silver 2.00 1.50

Issued to commemorate the first Russian soft landing on the moon by Luna 9, Feb. 3, 1966. Size: 70x50mm.

Steamer Radetzky and Bugler—A643

1966, May 28 *Perf. 10½*

1502 A643 2s multicolored 8 5

Issued to commemorate the 90th anniversary of the participation of the Danube steamer Radetzky in the uprising against the Turks.

Standard Bearer Nicola Simov-Kuruto
A644

1966, May 30

1503 A644 5s bister, green & olive 15 12

Issued to honor Nicola Simov-Kuruto, hero of the Turkish War.

UNESCO Emblem
A645

1966, June 8

1504 A645 20s gold, black & vermilion 40 15

Issued to commemorate the 20th anniversary of UNESCO (United Nations Educational, Scientific and Cultural Organization).

Youth Federation Badge—A646

1966, June 6 Photo. *Perf. 10½*

1505 A646 13s silver, bl. & blk. 28 15

Issued to publicize the 7th Assembly of the International Youth Federation.

Soccer—A647

Designs: Various soccer scenes. 50s, Jules Rimet Cup.

1966, June 27

1506 A647 1s gray, yellow brown & black 3 3
1507 " 2s gray, crimson & black 4 3
1508 " 5s gray, olive bister & black 10 5
1509 " 13s gray, ultra. & black 30 13
1510 " 20s gray, Prussian blue & black 50 16
Nos. 1506-1510 (5) 97 40

Miniature Sheet

Imperf.

1511 A647 50s gray, deep lilac rose & gold 1.75 1.00

Issued to commemorate the World Soccer Cup Championship, Wembley, England, July 11–30. Size of No. 1511: 60x64mm.

Woman Javelin Thrower—A648

Designs: No. 1513, Runner. No. 1514, Young man and woman carrying banners (vert.).

1966 Photo. *Perf. 10½*

1512 A648 2s grn., yel. & verm. 5 3
1513 " 13s dp. green, yel. & salmon pink 35 10
1514 " 13s bl., lt. bl. & sal. 35 15

Nos. 1512–1513 commemorate the 3rd Spartacist Games; issued Aug. 10. No. 1514 commemorates the 3rd congress of the Bulgarian Youth Federation; issued May 25.

Wrestlers Nicolas Petrov and Dan Kolov—A649

1966, July 29

1515 A649 13s bister brown, dk. brn. & lt. olive green 25 15

3rd International Wrestling Championships.

Map of Balkan Countries, Globe and UNESCO Emblem
A650

1966, Aug. 26 *Perf. 10½x11½*

1516 A650 13s ultra., light green & pink 35 15

First Congress of Balkanologists.

Children with Building Blocks
A651

Designs: 2s, Bunny and teddy bear with book. 3s, Children as astronauts. 13s, Children with pails and shovel.

1966, Sept. 1 *Perf. 10½*

1517 A651 1s dark carmine, orange & black 3 3
1518 " 2s emerald, black & red brown 5 3
1519 " 3s ultra., org. & blk. 10 3
1520 " 13s bl., rose & black 30 15

Issued for Children's Day.

Yuri A. Gagarin and Vostok 1
A652

Designs: 2s, Gherman S. Titov and Vostok 2. 3s, Andrian G. Nikolayev, Pavel R. Popovich, and Vostoks 3 & 4. 5s, Valentina Tereshkova, Valeri Bykovski and Vostoks 5 and 6. 8s, Vladimir M. Komarov, Boris B. Yegorov, Konstantin Feoktistov and Voskhod 1. 13s, Pavel Belyayev, Alexei Leonov and Voskhod 2.

1966, Sept. 29 Photo. *Perf. 11½x11*

1521 A652 1s slate & gray 3 3
1522 " 2s plum & gray 3 3
1523 " 3s yel. brn. & gray 6 4
1524 " 5s brn. red & gray 8 6
1525 " 8s ultra. & gray 20 10
1526 " 13s Prus. bl. & gray 35 20
Nos. 1521-1526, B29 (7) 1.45 86

Russian space explorations.

St. Clement, 14th Century Wood Sculpture
A653

1966, Oct. 27 Photo. *Perf. 11½x11*

1527 A653 5s red, buff & brn. 15 5

Issued to commemorate the 1050th anniversary of the birth of St. Clement of Ochrida.

Metodi Shatorov
A654

Portraits: 3s, Vladimir Trichkov. 5s, Valcho Ivanov. 10s, Raiko Daskalov. 13s, General Vladimir Zaimov.

1966, Nov. 8 ***Perf. 11x11½***

Gold Frame, Black Denomination

1528 A654 2s crimson & blue violet 3 3
1529 " 3s magenta & black 5 3
1530 " 5s car. rose & dark blue 8 5
1531 " 10s orange & olive 25 10
1532 " 13s red & brown 40 15
Nos. 1528-1532 (5) 81 36

Issued to honor fighters against fascism.

George Dimitrov
A655

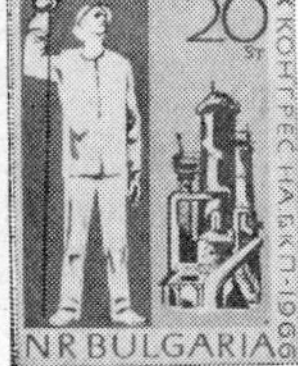

Steel Worker
A656

1966, Nov. 14 Photo. ***Perf. 11½x11***

1533 A655 2s magenta & blk. 5 3
1534 A656 20s fawn, gray & black 55 20

Bulgarian Communist Party, 9th Congress.

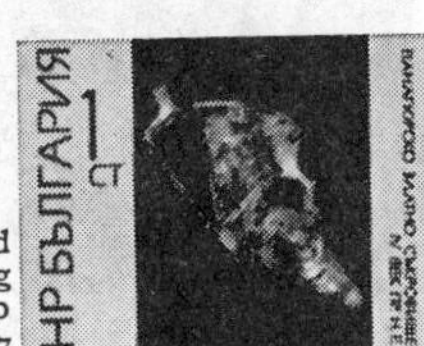

Deer's Head Drinking Cup
A667

Gold Treasure: 2s, 6s, 10s, Various Amazon's head jugs. 3s, Ram's head cup. 5s, Circular plate. 8s, Deer's head cup. 13s, Amphora. 20s, Ram drinking horn.

1966, Nov. 28 ***Perf. 12x11½***

Vessels in Gold and Brown; Black Inscriptions

1535 A667 1s gray & violet 3 3
1536 " 2s gray & green 7 3
1537 " 3s gray & dk. blue 10 3
1538 " 5s gray & red brn. 15 3
1539 " 6s gray & Prus. bl. 18 4
1540 " 8s gray & brn. olive 30 4
1541 " 10s gray & sepia 35 5
1542 " 13s gray & dark violet blue 60 7
1543 " 20s gray & vio. brn. 90 8
Nos. 1535-1543 (9) 2.68 40

The gold treasure from the 4th century B.C. was found near Panagyurishte in 1949.

Tourist House, Bansko
A668

Tourist Houses: No. 1545, Belogradchik. No. 1546, Triavna. 20s, Rila.

1966, Nov. 29 Photo. ***Perf. 11x11½***

1544 A668 1s dark blue 4 3
1545 " 2s dark green 4 3
1546 " 2s brown red 4 3
1547 " 20s lilac 45 12

Decorated Tree
A669

Design: 13s, Jug with bird design.

1966, Dec. 12 ***Perf. 11***

1548 A669 2s grn., pink & gold 3 3
1549 " 13s brown lake, rose, emerald & gold 35 7

Issued for New Year, 1967.

Pencho Slavikov, Author
A670

Dahlia
A671

Portraits: 2s, Dimcho Debeljanov, author. 3s, P. H. Todorov, author. 5s, Dimitri Dobrovich, painter. 8s, Ivan Markvichka, painter. 13s, Ilya Bezhkov, painter.

1966, Dec. 15 ***Perf. 10½x11***

1550 A670 1s bl., olive & org. 3 3
1551 " 2s org., brn. & gray 3 3
1552 " 3s olive, bl. & org. 5 3
1553 " 5s gray, red brown & orange 8 3
1554 " 8s lilac, dark gray & blue 20 8
1555 " 13s blue, vio. & lilac 40 15
Nos. 1550-1555 (6) 79 35

1966, Dec. 29

Flowers: No. 1557, Clematis. No. 1558, Foxglove. No. 1559, Narcissus. 3s, Snowdrop. 5s, Petunia. 13s, Tiger lily. 20s, Bellflower.

Flowers in Natural Colors

1556 A671 1s gray & lt. brown 5 5
1557 " 1s gray & dull blue 5 5
1558 " 2s gray & dull lilac 10 5
1559 " 2s gray & brown 10 5
1560 " 3s gray & dk. grn. 15 6
1561 " 5s gray & dp. ultra. 15 12
1562 " 13s gray & brown 40 25
1563 " 20s gray & ultra. 60 40
Nos. 1556-1563 (8) 1.60 1.03

Ring-necked Pheasant
A672

Game: 2s, Rock partridge. 3s, Gray partridge. 5s, Hare. 8s, Roe deer. 13s, Red deer.

1967, Jan. 28 ***Perf. 11x10½***

1564 A672 1s lt. ultra., dark brown & ocher 3 3
1565 " 2s pale yel. grn. & dark green 3 3
1566 " 3s lt. blue, black & cream 10 3
1567 " 5s lt. grn. & black 10 4
1568 " 8s pale blue, dark brn. & ocher 50 15
1569 " 13s blue & dk. brn. 70 22
Nos. 1564-1569 (6) 1.46 50

Bulgaria No. 1, 1879
A673

Thracian Coin, 6th Century, B.C.
A674

1967, Feb. 4 Photo. ***Perf. 10½***

1570 A673 10s emerald, black & yellow 60 20

Issued to publicize the 10th Congress of the Bulgarian Philatelic Union.

1967, March 30 ***Perf. 11½x11***

Coins: 2s, Macedonian tetradrachma, 2nd century, B.C. 3s, Tetradrachma of Odessus, 2nd century, B.C. 5s, Philip II of Macedonia, 4th century, B.C. 13s, Thracian King Seuthus VII, 4th century, B.C., obverse and reverse. 20s, Apollonian coin, 5th century, B.C., obverse and reverse.

Size: 25x25mm.

1571 A674 1s brown, black & silver 3 3
1572 " 2s red lilac, black & silver 3 3
1573 " 3s green, black & silver 5 3
1574 " 5s brn. org., black & silver 9 4

Size: 37½x25mm.

1575 A674 13s brt. blue, black & bronze 60 12
1576 " 20s violet, black & silver 95 20
Nos. 1571-1576 (6) 1.75 45

Partisans Listening to Radio
A675

Design: 20s, George Dimitrov addressing crowd and Bulgarian flag.

1967, Apr. 20 ***Perf. 11x11½***

1577 A675 1s red, gold, buff & slate green 5 3
1578 " 20s red, gold, dull red, grn. & black 50 20

Issued to commemorate the 25th anniversary of the Union of Patriotic Front Organizations.

Nikolas Kofardjiev
A676

Portraits: 2s, Petko Napetov. 5s, Petko D. Petkov. 10s, Emil Markov. 13s, Traitcho Kostov.

1967, Apr. 24 ***Perf. 11½x11***

1579 A676 1s brn. red, gray & black 3 3
1580 " 2s olive green, gray & black 5 3
1581 " 5s brn., gray & blk. 8 5
1582 " 10s dp. blue, gray & black 17 10
1583 " 13s magenta, gray & black 40 12
Nos. 1579-1583 (5) 73 33

Issued to honor fighters against fascism.

Symbolic Flower and Flame
A677

1967, May 18 Photo. ***Perf. 11x11½***

1584 A677 13s gold, yellow & lt. green 30 12

First Cultural Congress, May 18-19.

Gold Sand Beach and ITY Emblem
A678

Designs: 20s, Hotel, Pamporovo. 40s, Nessebr Church.

1967, June 12 Photo. ***Perf. 11x11½***

1585 A678 13s ultramarine, yel. & black 25 8
1586 " 20s Prus. blue, black & buff 40 10
1587 " 40s bright green, blk. & ocher 75 18

Issued for International Tourist Year, 1967.

Angora Cat
A679

Cats: 2s, Siamese (horiz.). 3s, Abyssinian. 5s, Black European. 13s, Persian (horiz.). 20s, Striped domestic.

Perf. 11½x11, 11x11½

1967, June 19

1588 A679 1s dull violet, dk. brn. & buff 3 3
1589 " 2s olive, slate & bright blue 10 3
1590 " 3s dull bl. & brn. 15 3
1591 " 5s grn., blk. & yel. 20 4
1592 " 13s dull red brn., slate & org. 35 7
1593 " 20s gray green, brown & buff 70 15
Nos. 1588-1593 (6) 1.53 35

Scene from Opera "The Master of Boyana" by K. Iliev
A680

Songbird on Keyboard
A681

1967, June 19

1594 A680 5s gray, vio. blue & dp. carmine 10 3
1595 A681 13s gray, dp. car. & dk. blue 25 12

Issued to commemorate the 3rd International Competition for Young Opera Singers.

George Kirkov
A682

1967, June 24 *Perf. 11x11½*

1596 A682 2s rose red & dark brown 5 3

Issued to commemorate the centenary of the birth of George Kirkov (1867–1919), revolutionist.

Symbolic Tree and Stars
A683

1967, July 28 Photo. *Perf. 11½x11*

1597 A683 13s deep blue, car. & black 30 20

Issued to commemorate the 11th Congress of Dimitrov's Union of the People's Youth.

Roses and Distillery
A684

Designs: No. 1599, Chick and incubator. No. 1600, Cucumbers and hothouse. No. 1601, Lamb and sheep farm. 3s, Sunflower and oil mill. 4s, Pigs and pig farm. 5s, Hops and hop farm. 6s, Corn and irrigation system. 8s, Grapes and Bolgar tractor. 10s, Apples and cultivated tree. 13s, Bees and honey. 20s, Bee, blossoms and beehives.

1967 *Perf. 11x11½*

1598 A684 1s multicolored 3 3
1599 " 1s dark carmine, yellow & black 3 3
1600 " 2s violet, light green & black 3 3
1601 " 2s bright green, gray & black 3 3
1602 " 3s yellow green, yellow & black 5 3
1603 " 4s bright purple, yellow & black 7 4
1604 " 5s olive bister, yel. green & black 10 8
1605 " 6s olive, bright green & black 15 10
1606 " 8s green, bister & black 20 12
1607 " 10s multicolored 25 15
1608 " 13s green, bister brown & black 32 24
1609 " 20s greenish bl., brt. pink & black 60 30
Nos. 1598-1609 (12) 1.86 1.18

Issue dates: Nos. 1598–1601, 1607 and 1609, July 15; Nos. 1602–1606 and 1608, July 24.

Map of Communist Countries, Spasski Tower
A685

Designs: 2s, Lenin speaking to soldiers. 3s, Fighting at Wlodaja, 1918. 5s, Marx, Engels and Lenin. 13s, Oil refinery. 20s, Molniya communication satellite.

1967, Aug. 25 *Perf. 11*

1610 A685 1s multicolored 3 3
1611 " 2s magenta & olive 3 3
1612 " 3s magenta & dull violet 5 3
1613 " 5s magenta & red 8 5
1614 A685 13s magenta & ultra. 25 12
1615 " 20s magenta & blue 55 20
Nos. 1610-1615 (6) 99 46

Issued to commemorate the 50th anniversary of the Russian October Revolution.

Rod, "Fish" and Varna
A686

1967, Aug. 29 Photo. *Perf. 11*

1616 A686 10s multicolored 20 15

7th World Angling Championships, Varna.

Skiers and Winter Olympics' Emblem—A687

Sports and Emblem: 2s, Ski jump. 3s, Biathlon. 5s, Ice hockey. 13s, Figure skating couple.

1967, Sept. 20 Photo. *Perf. 11*

1617 A687 1s dk. blue green, red & black 3 3
1618 " 2s ultra., black & olive 3 3
1619 " 3s violet brown, blue & black 5 3
1620 " 5s grn., yel. & blk. 8 5
1621 " 13s violet blue, black & buff 25 6
Nos. 1617-1621, B31 (6) 1.04 40

Issued to publicize the 10th Winter Olympic Games, Grenoble, France, Feb. 6–18, 1968.

Bogdan Mountain
A688

Mountain Peaks: 2s, Czerny. 3s, Ruen (vert.). 5s, Persenk. 10s, Botev. 13s, Rila (vert.). 20s, Vihren.

1967, Sept. 25 Engr. *Perf. 11½*

1622 A688 1s slate grn. & yel. 3 3
1623 " 2s sepia & pale blue 3 3
1624 " 3s indigo & lt. blue 5 3
1625 " 5s slate green & light blue 10 5
1626 " 10s deep claret & light blue 18 6
1627 " 13s dk. gray & lt. bl. 25 8
1628 " 20s indigo & rose 35 12
Nos. 1622-1628 (7) 99 40

George Rakovski
A689

1967, Oct. 20 Photo. *Perf. 11*

1629 A689 13s yel. grn. & blk. 25 12

Issued to commemorate the centenary of the death of George Rakovski, revolutionary against Turkish rule.

Yuri A. Gagarin, Valentina Tereshkova and Alexei Leonov
A690

Designs: 2s, Lt. Col. John H. Glenn, Jr., and Maj. Edward H. White. 5s, Earth and Molniya 1. 10s, Gemini 6 and 7. 13s, Luna 13 moon probe. 20s, Gemini 10 and Agena rocket.

1967, Nov. 25

1630 A690 1s Prus. blue, blk. & yellow 3 3
1631 " 2s dull blue, blk. & dull yellow 3 3
1632 " 5s vio. bl., greenish blue & black 8 5
1633 " 10s dk. bl., blk. & red 25 10
1634 " 13s greenish bl., brt. yel. & black 30 12
1635 " 20s dull blue, black & red 60 15
Nos. 1630-1635 (6) 1.29 48

Achievements in space exploration.

Ratchenitza Folk Dance, by Ivan Markvichka
A692

1967, Dec. 9

1642 A692 20s gold & gray green 80 40

Issued to commemorate the Belgo-Bulgarian Philatelic Exposition, Brussels, Dec. 9–10. Printed in sheets of 8 stamps and 8 labels.

View of Trnovo
A691

Various Views of Trnovo

1967, Dec. 5 Photogravure *Perf. 11*

1636 A691 1s multicolored 3 3
1637 " 2s " 3 3
1638 " 3s " 5 3
1639 " 5s " 8 5
1640 " 13s " 35 10
1641 " 20s " 55 20
Nos. 1636-1641 (6) 1.09 44

Issued to publicize the restoration of the ancient capital Veliko Trnovo.

Canceled-to-order stamps are often from remainders. Most collectors of canceled stamps prefer postally used specimens.

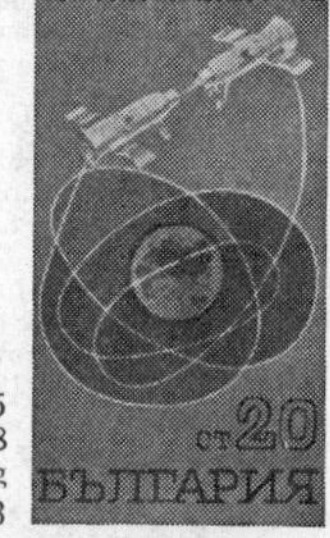

Cosmos 186 and 188 Docking
A693

Design: 40s, Venus 4 and orbits around Venus (horiz.).

1968, Jan.

1643 A693 20s violet, gray & pink 40 12
1644 " 40s rose car., gray, silver & blk. 80 25

Issued to commemorate the docking maneuvers of the Russian spaceships Cosmos 186 and Cosmos 188, Nov. 1, 1967, and the flight to Venus of Venus 4, June 12–Nov. 18, 1967.

Crossing the Danube, by Orenburgski
A694

Paintings: 2s, Flag of Samara, by J. Veschin (vert.). 3s, Battle of Pleven by Orenburgski. 13s, Battle of Orlovo Gnezdo, by N. Popov (vert.). 20s, Welcome for Russian Soldiers, by D. Gudienov.

1968, Jan. 25 Photo. *Perf. 11*

1645 A694 1s gold & dk. green 5 3
1646 " 2s gold & dk. blue 5 3
1647 " 3s gold & claret brown 5 3
1648 " 13s gold & dk. vio. 25 15
1649 " 20s gold & Prussian green 60 20
Nos. 1645-1649 (5) 1.00 44

Issued to commemorate the 90th anniversary of the liberation from Turkey.

Shepherds, by Zlatyn Boyadjiev
A695

Paintings: 2s, Wedding dance, by V. Dimitrov. (vert.). 3s, Partisans' Song, by Ilya Petrov. 5s, Portrait of Anna Penchovich, by Nikolai Pavlovich (vert.). 13s, Self-portrait, by Zachary Zograf (vert.). 20s, View of Old Plovdiv, by T. Lavrenov. 60s, St. Clement of Ochrida, by A. Mitov.

1967, Dec. Litho. *Perf. 11½*

Size: 45x38mm., 38x45mm.

1650 A695 1s gray & multi. 8 3
1651 " 2s " " 7 3

Size: 55x35mm.

1652 A695 3s gray & multi. 8 3

Size: 38x45mm., 45x38mm.

1653 A695 5s gray & multi. 30 15
1654 " 13s " " 55 25
1655 " 20s " " 75 25
Nos. 1650-1655 (6) 1.83 47

Miniature Sheet

Imperf.

Size: 65x84mm.

1656 A695 60s multicolored **3.50 3.50**

Marx Statue, Sofia — A696

Maxim Gorky — A697

1968, Feb. 20 Photo. ***Perf. 11***

1657 A696 13s black & red 30 10

150th anniversary of birth of Karl Marx.

1968, Feb. 20

1658 A697 13s vermilion & greenish blk. 30 10

Issued to commemorate the centenary of the birth of Maxim Gorky (1868–1936), Russian writer.

Folk Dancers—A698

Designs: 5s, Runners. 13s, Doves. 20s, Festival poster, (head, flowers and birds). 40s, Globe and Bulgaria No. 1 under magnifying glass.

1968, Mar. 20

1659 A698 2s multicolored 5 3
1660 " 5s " 10 5
1661 " 13s " 25 8
1662 " 20s " 40 12
1663 " 40s " 80 22
Nos. 1659-1663 (5) 1.60 50

Issued to publicize the 9th Youth Festival for Peace and Friendship, Sofia, July 28–Aug. 6.

Bellflower — A699

Flowers: 2s, Gentian. 3s, Crocus. 5s, Iris. 10s, Dog-tooth violet. 13s, Sempervivum. 20s, Dictamnus.

1968, Apr. 25 ***Perf. 11***

Flowers in Natural Colors

1664 A699 1s dull bl. & black 3 3
1665 " 2s yel. brn. & black 3 3
1666 " 3s gray grn. & blk. 5 3
1667 " 5s brn. org. & blk. 8 5
1668 " 10s ultra. & black 16 10
1669 " 13s rose lilac & blk. 25 12
1670 " 20s olive & black 50 20
Nos. 1664-1670 (7) 1.10 56

"The Unknown Hero," Tale by Ran Bosilek — A700

Design: 20s, The Witch and the Young Man (Hans Christian Andersen fairy tale.)

1968, Apr. 25 Photo. ***Perf. 10½***

1671 A700 13s blk. & multi. 20 10
1672 " 20s " " 40 15

Bulgarian-Danish Philatelic Exhibition.

Memorial Church, Shipka — A701

Steeplechase — A702

1968, May 3

1673 A701 13s multicolored 40 20

Bulgarian Stamp Exhibition in West Berlin.

1968, June 24 Photo. ***Perf. 10½***

Designs (Olympic Rings and): 1s, Gymnast on bar. 3s, Fencer. 10s, Boxer. 13s, Woman discus thrower.

1674 A702 1s red & black 3 3
1675 " 2s gray, black & rose brown 3 3
1676 " 3s magenta, gray & black 5 3
1677 " 10s greenish blue, black & lemon 16 5
1678 " 13s violet blue, gray & pink 30 7
Nos. 1674-1678, B33 (6) 1.17 41

Issued to publicize the 19th Olympic Games, Mexico City, Oct. 12–27.

Battle of Buzluja — A703

Design: 13s, Haji Dimitr and Stefan Karaja.

1968, July 1

1679 A703 2s silver & red brn. 5 3
1680 " 13s gold & slate grn. 25 10

Issued to commemorate the centenary of the death of the patriots Haji Dimitr and Stefan Karaja.

Lakes of Smolian — A704

Cinereous Vulture — A705

Bulgarian Scenes: 2s, Ropotamo Lake. 3s, Erma-Idreloto mountain pass. 8s, Isker River dam. 10s, Slanchev Breg (sailing ship). 13s, Cape Caliacra. 40s, Old houses, Sozopol. 2 1, Chudnite Skali ("Strange Mountains").

1968 Photogravure ***Perf. 13***

1681 A704 1s Prussian green 3 3
1682 " 2s dark green 3 3
1683 " 3s dark brown 5 3
1684 " 8s olive green 15 8
1685 " 10s reddish brown 18 10
1686 " 13s dark olive green 25 12
1687 " 40s Prussian blue 70 20
1688 " 2 l sepia 3.50 30
Nos. 1681-1688 (8) 4.89 89

1968, July 29 ***Perf. 10½***

Designs: 2s, Crowned crane. 3s, Zebra. 5s, Leopard. 13s, Indian python. 20s, African crocodile.

1689 A705 1s ultramarine, black & tan 3 3
1690 " 2s orange brown, blk. & yellow 3 3
1691 " 3s yellow green & black 10 5
1692 " 5s brn. red, black & yellow 15 6
1693 " 13s deep green, black & tan 30 18
1694 " 20s dull blue, black & gray green 50 25
Nos. 1689-1694 (6) 1.11 60

Centenary of the Sofia Zoo.

Human Rights Flame — A706

1968, July 8

1695 A706 20s dp. blue & gold 40 15

International Human Rights Year, 1968.

Congress Hall, Varna, and Emblem — A707

1968, Sept. 17 Photo. ***Perf. 10½***

1696 A707 20s bister, green & red 40 15

Issued to publicize the 56th International Dental Congress, Varna.

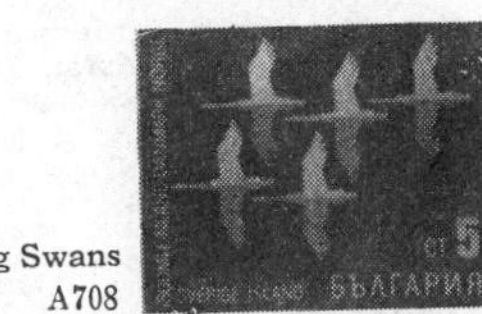

Flying Swans — A708

Rose — A709

Stag Beetle — A710

Designs: 2s, Jug. 20s, Five Viking ships.

1968 Photogravure ***Perf. 10½***

1697 A709 2s green & ocher 55 50
1698 A708 5s dp. blue & gray 50 50
1699 A709 13s deep plum & lilac rose 80 80
1700 A708 20s deep violet & gray 70 50

Issued to publicize cooperation with the Scandinavian countries. Nos. 1697 and 1700 are printed with connecting label showing bridge made of flags of Scandinavian countries.

Issue dates: 5s, 13s, Sept. 12. Others, Nov. 22.

Perf. 12½x13, 13x12½

1968, Aug. 26

Insects: No. 1702, Ground beetle (Procerus scabrosus). No. 1703, Ground beetle (Calosoma sycophania). No. 1704, Scarab beetle (horiz.). No. 1705, Saturnid moth (horiz.).

1701 A710 1s brown olive 3 3
1702 " 1s dark blue 3 3
1703 " 1s dark green 3 3
1704 " 1s orange brown 3 3
1705 " 1s magenta 3 3
Nos. 1701-1705 (5) 15 15

Turks Fighting Insurgents, 1688 — A711

1968, Aug. 22 ***Perf. 10½***

1706 A711 13s multicolored 30 10

Issued to commemorate the 280th anniversary of the Tchiprovtzi insurrection.

Christo Smirnenski—A712

1968, Sept. 28 Litho. ***Perf. 10½***

1707 A712 13s gold, red orange & black 25 12

Issued to commemorate the 70th birthday of Christo Smirnenski (1898–1923), poet.

Dalmatian Pelican — A713

Birds: 2s, Little egret. 3s, Crested grebe. 5s, Common tern. 13s, European spoonbill. 20s, Glossy ibis.

1968, Oct. 28 Photogravure

1708 A713 1s silver & multi. 5 3
1709 " 2s " " 5 3
1710 " 3s " " 8 5
1711 " 5s " " 10 8
1712 " 13s " " 30 20
1713 " 20s " " 70 50
Nos. 1708-1713 (6) 1.28 89

Issued to publicize the Srebirna wild life reservation.

Carrier Pigeon — A714

1968, Oct. 19

1714 A714 20s emerald 40 25
a. Sheet of 4 + labels 1.75 1.50

Issued to publicize the 2nd National Stamp Exhibition in Sofia, Oct. 25–Nov. 15. No. 1714a contains 4 No. 1714 and 5 decorative labels of two types with commemorative inscriptions. Gold frame. Size: 133x161½mm. No. 1714 was issued only as sheet No. 1714a.

Man and Woman from Lovetch
A715

Regional Costumes: 1s, Silistra. 3s, Jambol. 13s, Chirpan. 20s, Razgrad. 40s, Ihtiman.

1968, Nov. 20 Litho. ***Perf. 13½***

1715 A715 1s dp. org. & multi. 3 3
1716 " 2s Prus. bl. & multi. 6 3
1717 " 3s multicolored 7 3
1718 " 13s " 30 8
1719 " 20s " 35 13
1720 " 40s green & multi. 85 25
Nos. 1715–1720 (6) 1.66 55

St. Arsenius
A716

Designs (10th century Murals and Icons): 2s, Procession with relics of St. Ivan Rilsky (horiz.). 3s, St. Michael Torturing the Soul of the Rich Man. 13s, St. Ivan Rilsky. 20s, St. John. 40s, St. George. 1 l, Procession meeting relics of St. Ivan Rilsky (horiz.).

Perf. 11½x12½, 12½x11½

1968, Nov. 25 Photogravure

1721 A716 1s gold & multi. 3 3
1722 " 2s " " 3 3
1723 " 3s " " 10 3
1724 " 13s " " 50 8
1725 " 20s " " 60 13
1726 " 40s " " 1.25 25
Nos. 1721–1726 (6) 2.51 55

Souvenir Sheet
Imperf.

1727 A716 1 l gold & multi. 3.00 3.00

Issued to commemorate the millenium of Rila Monastery. No. 1727 also publicizes "Sofia 1969," International Philatelic Exhibition, May 31–June 8, 1969. No. 1727 contains one stamp (size: 57x51mm.), gray margin with emblems of Philatelic Exhibition. Size: 100x75mm.

Medlar
A717

Herbs: No. 1729, Camomile. 2s, Lily-of-the-valley. 3s, Belladonna. 5s, Mallow. 10s, Buttercup. 13s, Poppies. 20s, Thyme.

1969, Jan. 2 Litho. ***Perf. 10½***

1728 A717 1s black, green & orange red 3 3
1729 " 1s blk., grn. & yel. 3 3
1730 " 2s black, emerald & green 3 3
1731 " 3s black & multi. 5 3
1732 " 5s " " 7 4
1733 A717 10s black, green & yellow 16 8
1734 " 13s black & multi. 22 10
1735 " 20s black, lilac & green 45 15
Nos. 1728–1735 (8) 1.04 49

Silkworms and Spindles
A718

Designs: 2s, Silkworm, cocoons and pattern. 3s, Cocoons and spinning wheel. 5s, Cocoons, woof-and-warp diagram. 13s, Silk moth, cocoon and spinning frame. 20s, Silk moth, eggs and shuttle.

1969, Jan. 30 Photo. ***Perf. 10½***

1736 A718 1s blue, green, silver & black 3 3
1737 " 2s dp. car., silver & black 3 3
1738 " 3s Prus. blue, silver & black 5 3
1739 " 5s purple, vermilion, silver & black 8 6
1740 " 13s red lilac, ocher, silver & black 25 15
1741 " 20s green, orange, silver & black 45 25
Nos. 1736–1741 (6) 89 55

Bulgarian silk industry.

Attack and Capture of Emperor Nicephorus
A719

Sts. Cyril and Methodius, Mural, Troian Monastery
A720

Designs (Manasses Chronicle): No. 1742, Death of Ivan Asen. 3s, Khan Kroum feasting after victory. No. 1748, Invasion of Bulgaria by Prince Sviatoslav of Kiev. No. 1750, Russian invasion and campaigns of Emperor John I Zimisces, c. 972 A.D. 40s, Tsar Ivan Alexander, Jesus and Constantine Manasses.

Horizontal designs: No. 1743, Kings Nebuchadnezzar, Balthazar, Darius and Cyrus. No. 1745, Kings Cambyses, Gyges and Darius. 5s, King David and Tsar Ivan Alexander. No. 1749, Persecution of Byzantine army after battle of July 26, 811. No. 1751, Christening of Bulgarian Tsar Boris, 865. 60s, Arrival of Tsar Simeon in Constantinople and his succeeding surprise attack on that city.

1969 Photo. ***Perf. 14x13½, 13½x14***

Gold Frame

1742 A719 1s multicolored 3 3
1743 " 1s " 3 3
1744 " 2s " 3 3
1745 " 2s " 3 3
1746 " 3s " 5 3
1747 " 5s " 10 5
1748 " 13s " 25 8
1749 " 13s " 25 12
1750 " 20s " 35 12
1751 " 20s " 35 18
1752 " 40s " 75 25
1753 " 60s " 1.00 35
Nos. 1742–1753 (12) 3.22 1.30

1969, Mar. 23

1754 A720 28s gold & multi. 90 50

Post Horn
A721

Designs: 13s, Bulgaria Nos. 1 and 534. 20s, Street fighting at Stačkata, 1919.

1969, Apr. 15 Photo. ***Perf. 10½***

1755 A721 2s green & yellow 3 3
1756 " 13s multicolored 20 10
1757 " 20s dk. bl. & lt. blue 32 17

Issued to commemorate the 90th anniversary of the Bulgarian postal administration.

The Fox and the Rabbit
A722

Children's Drawings: 2s, Boy reading to wolf and fox. 13s, Two birds and cat. singing together.

1969, Apr. 21

1758 A722 1s emerald, orange & black 3 3
1759 " 2s orange, lt. blue & black 3 3
1760 " 13s lt. blue, olive & black 25 12

Issued for Children's Week.

ILO Emblem
A723

1969, Apr. 28

1761 A723 13s dull grn. & blk. 25 15

Issued to commemorate the 50th anniversary of the International Labor Organization.

St. George and SOPHIA 69 Emblem
A724

Designs: 2s, Virgin Mary and St. John Bogoslov. 3s, Archangel Michael. 5s, Three Saints. 8s, Jesus Christ. 13s, Sts. George and Dimitrie. 20s, Christ, the Almighty. 40s, St. Dimitrie. 60s, The 40 Martyrs. 80s, The Transfiguration.

1969, Apr. 30 ***Perf. 11x12***

1762 A724 1s gold & multi. 3 3
1763 " 2s " " 3 3
1764 " 3s " " 5 3
1765 " 5s " " 10 4
1766 " 8s " " 15 5
1767 " 13s " " 22 8
1768 " 20s " " 35 12
1769 " 40s " " 75 25
a. Sheet of four 3.25 3.25
1770 A724 60s gold & multi. 1.10 40
1771 " 80s " 1.50 50
Nos. 1762–1771 (10) 4.28 1.53

Issued to show old Bulgarian art from the National Art Gallery. No. 1769a contains 4 of No. 1769 with center label showing Alexander Nevski Shrine. See note on SOPHIA 69 after Nos. C112–C120.

St. Cyril Preaching
A725

St. Sophia Church
A726

Design: 28s, St. Cyril and followers.

1969, June 20 Litho. ***Perf. 10½***

1772 A725 2s silver, grn. & red 9 5
1773 " 28s silver, dark blue & red 45 20

Issued to commemorate the 1100th anniversary of the death of St. Cyril (827–869), apostle to the Slavs, inventor of Cyrillic alphabet. Issued in sheets of 25 with se-tenant labels; Cyrillic inscription on label of 2s, Glagolitic inscription on label of 28s.

1969, May 25 ***Perf. 13x12½***

Sofia Through the Ages: 1s, Roman coin with inscription "Ulpia Serdica." 2s, Roman coin with Aesculapius Temple. 4s, Bojana Church. 5s, Sobranie Parliament. 13s, Vasov National Theater. 20s, Alexander Nevski Shrine. 40s, Clement Ochrida University. 1 l, Coat of arms.

1774 A726 1s gold & blue 3 3
1775 " 2s gold & olive green 3 3
1776 " 3s gold & red brown 5 3
1777 " 4s gold & purple 7 3
1778 " 5s gold & plum 10 3
1779 " 13s gold & brt. green 22 8
1780 " 20s gold & vio. blue 35 13
1781 " 40s gold & dp. car. 70 26
Nos. 1774–1781 (8) 1.55 62

Souvenir Sheet
Imperf.

1782 A726 1 l grn., gold & red 1.60 1.60

Issued to show historic Sofia in connection with the International Philatelic Exhibition. Sofia, May 31–June 8.

No. 1782 contains one stamp (size: 43½x43½mm.). Emblems of 8 preceding philatelic exhibitions in metallic ink in margin; gold inscription. Size: 80x72mm.

No. 1782 was overprinted in green "IBRA '73" and various symbols, and released May 4, 1973, for the Munich Philatelic Exhibition. The overprint also exists in gray. Price, in green $25; gray $40.

St. George
A727

1969, June 9 Litho. ***Perf. 11½***

1783 A727 40s silver, black & pale rose 75 30

Issued to commemorate the 38th FIP (Féderation Internationale de Philatelie) Congress, June 9–11.

Hand Planting Sapling
A728

1969, Apr. 28 Photo. ***Perf. 11***

1784 A728 2s olive green, black & lilac 5 3

Issued to publicize 25 years of the reforestation campaign.

Partisans
A729

Designs: 2s, Combine harvester. 3s, Dam. 5s, Flutist and singers. 13s, Factory. 20s, Lenin, Dimitrov, Russian and Bulgarian flags.

1969, Sept. 9

1785 A729 1s blk., pur. & org. 3 3
1786 " 2s black, olive bister & orange 3 3
1787 " 3s black, blue green & orange 5 3
1788 " 5s black, brown red & orange 8 3
1789 " 13s blk., blue & org. 20 8
1790 " 20s blk., brn. & org. 40 15
Nos. 1785-1790 (6) 79 35

25th anniversary of People's Republic.

Women Gymnasts
A730

Design: 20s, Wrestlers.

1969, Sept. Photo. ***Perf. 11***

1791 A730 2s blue, black & pale brown 3 3
1792 " 20s red org. & multi. 50 22

Third National Spartakiad.

Tchanko Bakalov Tcherkovski
A731

1969, Sept.

1793 A731 13s multicolored 30 15

Birth centenary of Tchanko Bakalov Techerkovski, poet.

Woman Gymnast
A732

Designs: 2s, Two women with hoops. 3s, Woman with hoop. 5s, Two women with spheres.

1969, Oct.

Gymnasts in Light Gray

1794 A732 1s green & dk. blue 3 3
1795 " 2s blue & dark blue 3 3
1796 " 3s emerald & slate green 8 5
1797 A732 5s orange & purple 12 8
Nos. 1794-1797, B35-B36 (6) 1.11 76

Issued to publicize the World Championships for Artistic Gymnastics, Varna.

The Priest Rilski, by Zachary Zograf
A733

Paintings from the National Art Gallery. 2s, Woman at Window, by Vasil Stoilov. 3s, Workers at Rest, by Nenko Balkanski (horiz.). 4s, Woman Dressing (Nude), by Ivan Nenov. 5s, Portrait of a Woman, by N. Pavlovich. 13s, Falstaff, by Duzunov Kr. Sarafov. No. 1804, Portrait of a Woman, by N. Mihajlov (horiz.). No. 1805, Workers at Mealtime, by Stojan Sotirov (horiz.). 40s, Self-portrait, by Tcheno Togorov.

Perf. 11½x12, 12x11½

1969, Nov. 10

1798 A733 1s gold & multi. 3 3
1799 " 2s " " 3 3
1800 " 3s " " 5 3
1801 " 4s " " 7 3
1802 " 5s " " 10 3
1803 " 13s " " 22 8
1804 " 20s " " 35 13
1805 " 20s " " 35 13
1806 " 40s " " 75 26
Nos. 1798-1806 (9) 1.95 75

Roman Bronze Wolf—A734

Design: 2s, Roman statue of woman, found at Silistra (vert.).

1969, Oct. Photogravure ***Perf. 11***

1807 A734 2s silver, ultra. & gray 5 5
1808 " 13s silver, dark green & gray 25 12

City of Silistra's 1,800th anniversary.

Worker and Factory
A735

1969 ***Perf. 13***

1809 A735 6s ultra. & black 15 8

25th anniversary of the factory militia.

European Hake—A736

Designs: No. 1811, Deep-sea fishing trawler. Fish: 2s, Atlantic horse mackerel. 3s, Pilchard. 5s, Dentex macrophthalmus. 10s, Chub mackerel. 13s, Otolithes macrognathus. 20s, Lichia vadigo.

1969 ***Perf. 11***

1810 A736 1s olive grn. & blk. 3 3
1811 A736 1s ultramarine, indigo & gray 3 3
1812 " 2s lilac & black 3 3
1813 " 3s vio. blue & black 5 3
1814 " 5s rose claret, pink & black 10 6
1815 " 10s gray & black 18 10
1816 " 13s verm., sal. & blk. 24 12
1817 " 20s ocher & black 35 20
Nos. 1810-1817 (8) 1.01 60

Marin Drinov
A737

1969, Nov. 10 Litho. ***Perf. 11***

1818 A737 20s blk. & red org. 40 15

Issued to commemorate the centenary of the Bulgarian Academy of Science, founded by Marin Drinov.

Trapeze Artists
A738

Pavel Bania Sanatorium
A739

Circus Performers: 2s, Jugglers. 3s, Jugglers with loops. 5s, Juggler and bear on bicycle. 13s, Woman and performing horse. 20s, Musical clowns.

1969 Photogravure ***Perf. 11***

1819 A738 1s dk. bl. & multi. 5 3
1820 " 2s dk. grn. & multi. 5 3
1821 " 3s dk. vio. & multi. 8 3
1822 " 5s multicolored 12 8
1823 " 13s " 50 24
1824 " 20s " 75 36
Nos. 1819-1824 (6) 1.55 77

1969, Dec. Photogravure ***Perf. 10½***

Health Resorts: 5s, Chisar Sanatorium. 6s, Kotel Children's Sanatorium. 20s, Narechen Polyclinic.

1825 A739 2s blue 5 3
1826 " 5s ultramarine 9 6
1827 " 6s green 12 10
1828 " 20s emerald 45 18

G. S. Shonin, V. N. Kubasov and Spacecraft
A740

Designs: 2s, A. V. Filipchenko, V. N. Volkov, V. V. Gorbatko and spacecraft. 3s, Vladimir A. Shatalov, Alexei S. Yeliseyev and spacecraft. 28s, Three spacecraft in orbit.

1970, Jan. Photo. ***Perf. 11***

1829 A740 1s rose car., olive green & black 3 3
1830 " 2s blue, dull claret & black 3 3
1831 A740 3s greenish blue, violet & black 5 5
1832 " 28s vio. bl., lilac rose & light blue 60 30

Issued to commemorate the Russian space flights of Soyuz 6, 7 and 8, Oct. 11-13, 1969.

Khan Krum and Defeat of Emperor Nicephorus, 811
A741

Bulgarian History: 1s, Khan Asparuch and Bulgars crossing the Danube (679). 3s, Conversion of Prince Boris to Christianity, 865. 5s, Tsar Simeon and battle of Akhelo, 917. 8s, Tsar Samuel defeating the Byzantines, 976. 10s, Tsar Kaloyan defeating Emperor Baldwin, 1205. 13s, Tsar Ivan Assen II defeating Greek King Theodore Komnine, 1230. 20s, Coronation of Tsar Ivailo, 1277.

1970, Feb. ***Perf. 10½***

1833 A741 1s gold & multi. 3 3
1834 " 2s " " 5 3
1835 " 3s " " 5 3
1836 " 5s " " 10 6
1837 " 8s " " 14 6
1838 " 10s " " 20 10
1839 " 13s " " 25 12
1840 " 20s " " 55 18
Nos. 1833-1840 (8) 1.37 61

See also Nos. 2126-2133.

Bulgarian Pavilion, EXPO '70
A742

1970 ***Perf. 12½***

1841 A742 20s brown, silver & orange 40 15

Issued to publicize EXPO '70 International Exposition, Osaka, Japan, Mar. 15-Sept. 13, 1970.

Soccer
A743

Designs: Various views of soccer game.

1970, Mar. 4 Photo. ***Perf. 12½***

1842 A743 1s blue & multi. 5 4
1843 " 2s rose car. & multi. 5 4
1844 " 3s ultra. & multi. 7 5
1845 " 5s green & multi. 12 10
1846 " 20s emerald & multi. 50 35
1847 " 40s red & multi. 1.00 70
Nos. 1842-1847 (6) 1.79 1.28

Issued to publicize the 9th World Soccer Championships for the Jules Rimet Cup, Mexico City, May 30-June 21, 1970. See No. B37.

Lenin
A744

Designs: 13s, Lenin portrait. 20s, Lenin writing.

1970, Apr. 22

No.	Type	Description	Unused	Used
1848	A744	2s vio. bl. & multi.	3	3
1849	"	13s brown & multi.	25	10
1850	"	20s multicolored	45	15

Centenary of birth of Lenin (1870–1924).

Tephrocactus Alexanderi V. Bruchii
A745

Cacti: 2s, Opuntia drummondii. 3s, Hatiora cilindrica. 5s, Gymnocalycium vatteri. 8s, Heliantho cereus grandiflorus. 10s, Neochilenia andreaeana. 13s, Peireskia vargasii v. longispina. 20s, Neobesseya rosiflora.

1970 Photogravure *Perf. 12½*

No.	Type	Description	Unused	Used
1851	A745	1s multicolored	3	3
1852	"	2s dk. grn. & multi.	3	3
1853	"	3s multicolored	5	3
1854	"	5s blue & multi.	10	5
1855	"	8s brown & multi.	14	5
1856	"	10s vio. bl. & multi.	20	7
1857	"	13s brn. red & multi.	25	12
1858	"	20s purple & multi.	40	20
		Nos. 1851-1858 (8)	1.20	58

Rose
A746

Designs: Various Roses.

1970, June 8 Litho. *Perf. 13½*

No.	Type	Description	Unused	Used
1859	A746	1s gray & multi.	3	3
1860	"	2s " "	3	3
1861	"	3s " "	5	3
1862	"	4s " "	7	3
1863	"	5s " "	8	3
1864	"	13s " "	20	8
1865	"	20s " "	32	13
1866	"	28s " "	45	15
		Nos. 1859-1866 (8)	1.23	51

Gold Bowl
A747

Designs: Various bowls and art objects from Gold Treasure of Thrace.

1970, June 15 Photo. *Perf. 12½*

No.	Type	Description	Unused	Used
1867	A747	1s blk., bl. & gold	3	3
1868	"	2s black, lt. violet & gold	3	3
1869	"	3s blk., vermilion & gold	7	5
1870	"	5s black, yellow green & gold	10	6
1871	"	13s blk., org. & gold	25	15
1872	"	20s black, lilac & gold	40	25
		Nos. 1867-1872 (6)	88	57

EXPO Emblem, Rose and Bulgarian Woman
A748

Designs (EXPO Emblem and): 2s, Three women. 3s, Woman and fruit. 28s, Dancers. 40s, Mt. Fuji and pavilions.

1970, June 20

No.	Type	Description	Unused	Used
1873	A748	1s gold & multi.	10	5
1874	"	2s " "	10	5
1875	"	3s " "	12	5
1876	"	28s " "	80	40

Miniature Sheet

Imperf.

No.	Type	Description	Unused	Used
1877	A748	40s gold & multi.	1.20	80

Issued to publicize EXPO '70 International Exposition, Osaka, Japan, Mar. 15–Sept. 13. No. 1877 contains one stamp with simulated perforations; gray margin with blue border and roses. Size: 75½x90mm.

Ivan Vasov
A749

1970, Aug. 1 Photo. *Perf. 12½*

No.	Type	Description	Unused	Used
1878	A749	13s violet blue	30	15

Issued to commemorate the 120th anniversary of the birth of Ivan Vasov, author.

U.N. Emblem—A750

1970, Aug. 1

No.	Type	Description	Unused	Used
1879	A750	20s Prussian blue & gold	60	30

25th anniversary of the United Nations.

George Dimitrov
A751

Retriever
A752

1970, Aug.

No.	Type	Description	Unused	Used
1880	A751	20s blk., gold & org.	45	20

Issued to commemorate the 70th anniversary of BZNC (Bulgarian Communist Party).

1970 Photo. *Perf. 12½*

Dogs: 1s, Golden retriever (horiz.). 3s, Great Dane. 4s, Boxer. 5s, Cocker spaniel. 13s, Doberman pinscher. 20s, Scottish terrier. 28s, Russian greyhound (horiz).

No.	Type	Description	Unused	Used
1881	A752	1s multicolored	5	4
1882	"	2s "	5	4
1883	"	3s "	7	5
1884	A752	4s multicolored	10	6
1885	"	5s "	12	8
1886	"	13s "	28	15
1887	"	20s "	40	20
1888	"	28s "	60	30
		Nos. 1881-1888 (8)	1.67	92

Volleyball
A753

Designs: No. 1890, Two women players. No. 1891, Woman player. No. 1892, Man player.

1970, Sept. Photo. *Perf. 12½*

No.	Type	Description	Unused	Used
1889	A753	2s dk. red brown, blue & black	5	5
1890	"	2s ultra., orange & black	5	5
1891	"	20s Prus. blue, yel. & black	50	20
1892	"	20s green, yellow & black	50	20

World Volleyball Championships.

Enrico Caruso and "I Pagliacci" by Ruggiero Leoncavallo
A754

Opera Singers and Operas: 2s, Christina Morfova and "The Bartered Bride" by Bedrich Smetana. 3s, Peter Reitchev and "Tosca" by Giacomo Puccini. 10s, Svetana Tabakova and "The Flying Dutchman" by Richard Wagner. 13s, Katia Popova and "The Masters" by Paroshkev Hadjev. 20s, Feodor Chaliapin and "Boris Godunov" by Modest Musorgski.

1970, Oct. 15 Photo. *Perf. 14*

No.	Type	Description	Unused	Used
1893	A754	1s black & multi.	8	8
1894	"	2s " "	8	8
1895	"	3s " "	8	8
1896	"	10s " "	18	12
1897	"	13s " "	25	15
1898	"	20s " "	50	25
		Nos. 1893-1898 (6)	1.17	76

Issued to honor opera singers in their best roles.

Ivan Assen II Coin—A755

Coins from 14th Century with Ruler's Portrait: 2s, Theodor Svetoslav. 3s, Mikhail Chichman. 13s, Ivan Alexander and Mikhail Assen. 20s, Ivan Sratsimir. 28s, Ivan Chichman (initials).

1970, Nov. *Perf. 12½*

No.	Type	Description	Unused	Used
1899	A755	1s buff & multi.	5	5
1900	"	2s gray & multi.	5	5
1901	"	3s multicolored	8	5
1902	"	13s "	32	12
1903	"	20s lt. bl. & multi.	56	24
1904	"	28s multicolored	72	36
		Nos. 1899-1904 (6)	1.78	87

Fireman
A756

Design: 3s, Fire engine.

1970 Lithographed *Perf. 12½*

No.	Type	Description	Unused	Used
1905	A756	1s blk., gray & yel.	3	3
1906	"	3s blk., gray & red	5	3

Fire protection publicity.

Bicyclists
A757

Congress Emblem
A758

1970 Photogravure

No.	Type	Description	Unused	Used
1907	A757	20s grn., yel & pink	50	35

For the 20th Bulgarian bicycle race.

1970

No.	Type	Description	Unused	Used
1908	A758	13s gold & multi.	30	15

For the 7th World Congress of Sociology, Varna, Sept. 14–19.

Beethoven
A759

Friedrich Engels
A760

1970

No.	Type	Description	Unused	Used
1909	A759	28s lilac rose & dark blue	60	20

Bicentenary of the birth of Ludwig van Beethoven (1770–1827), composer.

1970 Photogravure *Perf. 12½*

No.	Type	Description	Unused	Used
1910	A760	13s vermilion, tan & brown	30	12

Sesquicentennial of the birth of Friedrich Engels (1820–1895), German socialist, collaborator of Karl Marx.

Miniature Sheets

Luna 16
A761

Design (Russian moon mission): 80s, Lunokhod 1, unmanned vehicle on moon (horiz.).

1970 Photogravure *Imperf.*

1911	A761	80s plum, silver, blk. & bl.	1.35	1.35
1912	"	1 l vio. blue, silver & red	1.75	1.50

No. 1911 commemorates Lunokhod 1, Nov. 10–17. Size: 60x72mm. No. 1912, Luna 16 mission, Sept. 12–24. Size: 50x 68mm.

Issue dates: 80s, Dec. 18; 1 lev, Nov. 10.

Snowflake
A762

1970, Dec. 15 Photo. *Perf. 12½x13*

1913	A762	2s ultra. & multi.	5	3

New Year 1971.

Birds and Flowers
A763

Folk Art: 2s, Bird and flowers. 3s, Flying birds. 5s, Birds and flowers. 13s, Sun. 20s, Tulips and pansies.

1971, Jan. 25 *Perf. 12½x13½*

1914	A763	1s multicolored	3	3
1915	"	2s "	3	3
1916	"	3s "	3	3
1917	"	5s "	10	6
1918	"	13s "	30	10
1919	"	20s "	50	20
		Nos. 1914–1919 (6)	99	45

Spring 1971.

Girl, by Zeko Spiridonov
A764

Modern Bulgarian Sculpture: 2s, Third Class (people looking through train window), by Ivan Funev. 3s, Bust of Elin Pelin, by Marko Markov. 13s, Bust of Nina, by Andrej Nikolov. 20s, Monument to P. K. Yavorov (kneeling woman), by Ivan Lazarov. 28s, Engineer, by Ivan Funev. 1 l, Refugees, by Sekul Krimov (horiz.).

1971, Feb. *Perf. 12½*

1920	A764	1s gold & violet	6	6
1921	"	2s gold & dark olive green	6	6
1922	"	3s gold & rose brn.	10	8
1923	"	13s gold & dk. green	32	20
1924	"	20s gold & red brn.	56	30
1925	"	28s gold & dk. brn.	72	48
		Nos. 1920–1925 (6)	1.82	1.18

Souvenir Sheet

Imperf.

1926	A764	1 l gold, dk. brown & buff	2.00	2.00

No. 1926 has green marginal inscription. Size: 60x72mm.

Runner
A765

Design: 20s, Woman putting the shot.

1971, Mar. 13 Photo. *Perf. 12½x13*

1927	A765	2s brown & multi.	5	5
1928	"	20s dp. green, orange & black	45	30

2nd European Indoor Track and Field Championships.

Bulgarian Secondary School, Bolgrad
A766

Educators: 20s, Dimiter Mitev, Prince Bogoridi and Sava Radoulov.

1971, March 16 *Perf. 12½*

1929	A766	2s silver, brown & green	3	3
1930	"	20s silver, brown & violet	45	18

First Bulgarian secondary school, 1858, in Bolgrad, USSR.

Communards
A767

1971, Mar. 18 Photo. *Perf. 12½x13*

1931	A767	20s rose magenta & black	45	20

Centenary of the Paris Commune.

Dimitrov Facing Goering, Quotation, FIR Emblem
A768

1971, Apr. 11 *Perf. 12½*

1932	A768	2s green, gold, black & red	3	3
1933	"	13s plum, gold, black & red	25	10

International Federation of Resistance Fighters (FIR), 20th anniversary.

George S. Rakovski
A769

1971, Apr. 14

1934	A769	13s olive & blk. brn.	25	10

150th anniversary of birth of George S. Rakovski (1821–1867), revolutionary against Turkish rule.

Edelweiss Hotel, Borovets
A770

Designs: 2s, Panorama Hotel, Pamporovo. 4s, Boats at Albena, Black Sea. 8s, Boats at Rousalka. 10s, Shtastlivetsa Hotel, Mt. Vitosha.

1971 *Perf. 13*

1935	A770	1s bright green	3	3
1936	"	2s olive gray	5	3
1937	"	4s bright blue	7	3
1938	"	8s blue	14	5
1939	"	10s bluish green	25	7
		Nos. 1935–1939 (5)	54	21

Technological Progress—A771

Designs: 1s, Mason with banner (vert.). 13s, Two men and doves (vert.).

1971, Apr. 20 Photo. *Perf. 12½*

1940	A771	1s gold & multi.	3	3
1941	"	2s gray bl. & multi.	3	3
1942	"	13s lt. grn. & multi.	30	12

Tenth Congress of Bulgarian Communist Party.

Panayot Pipkov and Anthem
A772

1971, May 20

1943	A772	13s silver, black & bright green	25	18

Birth centenary of Panayot Pipkov, composer.

Mammoth
A773

Prehistoric Animals: 2s, Bear (vert.). 3s, Hipparion (horse). 13s, Platybelodon. 20s, Dinotherium (vert.). 28s, Saber-tooth tiger.

1971, May 29 *Perf. 12½*

1944	A773	1s dull blue & multi.	6	5
1945	"	2s lilac & multi.	6	5
1946	"	3s multicolored	10	8
1947	"	13s "	30	14
1948	"	20s dp. grn. & multi.	45	20
1949	"	28s multicolored	75	35
		Nos. 1944–1949 (6)	1.72	87

Khan Asparuch Crossing Danube, 679 A.D., by Boris Angelushev—A774

Historical Paintings: 3s, Reception at Trnovo, by Ilya Petrov. 5s, Chevartov's Troops at Benkovsky, by P. Morozov. 8s, Russian Gen. Gurko and People in Sofia, 1878, by D. Gudjenko. 28s, People Greeting Red Army, by S. Venov.

1971, Mar. 6 *Perf. 13½x14*

1950	A774	2s gold & multi.	5	3
1951	"	3s " "	5	3
1952	"	5s " "	12	6
1953	"	8s " "	20	8
		a. Souv. sheet of 4	75	75
1954	A774	28s gold & multi.	65	25
		Nos. 1950–1954 (5)	1.07	45

No. 1953a contains one each of Nos. 1950–1953. Gold decoration in gutter between stamps. Size: 137½x130mm.

In 1973, No. 1953a was surcharged 1 lev and overprinted "Visitez la Bulgarie", airline initials and emblems, and, on the 5s stamp, "Par Avion".

Freed Black, White and Yellow Men
A775

1971, May 20 Photo. *Perf. 12½*

1955	A775	13s blue, black & yellow	25	10

International Year against Racial Discrimination.

Map of Europe, Championship Emblem
A776

"XXX" Supporting Barbell
A777

1971, June 19

1956	A776	2s lt. blue & multi.	3	3
1957	A777	13s yellow & multi.	25	14

30th European Weight Lifting Championships, Sofia, June 19–27.

Facade, Old House, Koprivnica
A778

Designs: Decorated facades of various old houses in Koprivnica.

1971, July 10 Photo. *Perf. 12½*

1958	A778	1s green & multi.	5	4
1959	"	2s brown & multi.	5	4
1960	"	6s violet & multi.	12	9
1961	"	13s dk. red & multi.	30	18

Frontier Guard and German Shepherd
A779

1971, July 31 *Perf. 13*

1962	A779	2s grn. & olive grn.	5	3

25th anniversary of the Frontier Guards.

Congress of Busludja, Bas-relief
A780

1971, July 31 *Perf. 12½*

1963 A780 2s dark red & olive green 5 3

80th anniversary of the first Congress of the Bulgarian Social Democratic party.

Young Woman, by Ivan Nenov
A781

Paintings: 2s, Lazarova in Evening Gown, by Stefan Ivanov. 3s, Performer in Dress Suit, by Kyril Zonev. 13s, Portrait of a Woman, by Detchko Uzunov. 20s, Woman from Kalotina, by Vladimir Dimitrov. 40s, Gorjanin (Mountain Man), by Stoyan Venev.

1971, Aug. 2 *Perf. 14x13½*

1964	A781	1s green & multi.	5	5
1965	"	2s " "	5	5
1966	"	3s " "	5	5
1967	"	13s " "	30	8
1968	"	20s " "	50	15
1969	"	40s " "	1.00	25
		Nos. 1964-1969 (6)	1.95	63

National Art Gallery.

Wrestlers
A782

Designs: 13s, Wrestlers.

1971, Aug. 27 *Perf. 12½*

1970 A782 2s green, black & bl. 5 3
1971 " 13s red orange, black & blue 35 8

European Wrestling Championships.

Young Workers
A783

Post Horn Emblem
A784

1971 **Photogravure** *Perf. 13*

1972 A783 2s dark blue 5 3

25th anniversary of the Young People's Brigade.

1971, Sept. 15 *Perf. 12½*

1973 A784 20s dp. grn. & gold 45 12

8th meeting of postal administrations of socialist countries, Varna.

FEBS Waves Emblem—A785

1971, Sept. 20

1974 A785 13s black, red & maroon 30 12

7th Congress of European Biochemical Association (FEBS), Varna.

Statue of Republic
A786

Design: 13s, Bulgarian flag.

1971, Sept. 20 *Perf. 13x12½*

1975 A786 2s gold, yellow & dark red 5 3
1976 " 13s gold, grn. & red 30 12

25th anniversary of the Bulgarian People's Republic.

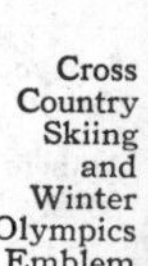

Cross Country Skiing and Winter Olympics Emblem
A787

Sport and Winter Olympics Emblem: 2s, Downhill skiing. 3s, Ski jump and skiing. 4s, Women's figure skating. 13s, Ice hockey. 28s, Slalom skiing. 1 l, Torch and stadium.

1971, Sept. 25 *Perf. 12½*

1977	A787	1s dk. grn. & multi.	6	5
1978	"	2s vio. bl. & multi.	6	5
1979	"	3s ultra. & multi.	6	5
1980	"	4s dp. plum & multi.	9	5
1981	"	13s dk. blue & multi.	24	10
1982	"	28s multicolored	55	25
		Nos. 1977-1982 (6)	1.06	55

Miniature Sheet

Imperf.

1983 A787 1 l multicolored 2.00 1.75

11th Winter Olympic Games, Sapporo, Japan, Feb. 3-13, 1972.
Size of No. 1983: 70x80mm.

Factory, Botevgrad
A788

Industrial Buildings: 2s, Petro-chemical works, Pleven (vert.). 10s, Chemical works, Vratsa. 13s, Maritsa-Istok Power Station, Dimitrovgrad. 40s, Electronics works, Sofia.

1971 **Photogravure** *Perf. 13*

1984	A788	1s violet	5	3
1985	"	2s orange	6	3
1986	"	10s deep purple	20	9
1987	"	13s lilac rose	25	12
1988	"	40s deep brown	85	25
		Nos. 1984-1988 (5)	1.41	52

UNESCO Emblem
A789

1971, Nov. 4 *Perf. 12½*

1989 A789 20s lt. blue, black, gold & red 45 18

25th anniversary of the United Nations Educational, Scientific and Cultural Organization (UNESCO).

Soccer Player, by Kyril Zonev (1896-1971)
A790

Paintings by Kyril Zonev: 2s, Landscape (horiz.). 3s, Self-portrait. 13s, Lilies. 20s, Landscape (horiz.). 40s, Portrait of a Young Woman.

1971, Nov. 10 *Perf. 11x12*

1990	A790	1s gold & multi.	8	8
1991	"	2s " "	8	8
1992	"	3s " "	8	8
1993	"	13s " "	32	18
1994	"	20s " "	54	30
1995	"	40s " "	1.05	48
		Nos. 1990-1995 (6)	2.15	1.20

Salyut Space Station—A791

Astronauts Dobrovolsky, Volkov and Patsayev—A792

Designs: 13s, Soyuz 11 space transport. 40s, Salyut and Soyuz 11 joined.

1971, Dec. 20 *Perf. 12½*

1996 A791 2s dk. green, yellow & red 5 5
1997 " 13s multicolored 30 20
1998 " 40s dk. bl. & multi. 1.20 60

Souvenir Sheet

Imperf.

1999 A792 80s multicolored 2.00 2.00

Salyut-Soyuz 11 space mission, and in memory of the Russian astronauts Lt. Col. Georgi T. Dobrovolsky, Vladislav N. Volkov and Victor I. Patsayev, who died during the Soyuz 11 space mission, June 6-30, 1971. Size of No. 1999: 70x73½mm.

Oil Tanker Vihren—A793

1972, Jan. 8 **Photo.** *Perf. 12½*

2000 A793 18s lilac rose, violet & black 40 20

Bulgarian shipbuilding industry.

Goce Delchev
A794

Portraits: 5s, Jan Sandanski. 13s, Damjan Gruev.

1972, Jan. 21 **Photo.** *Perf. 12½*

2001 A794 2s brick red & blk. 5 5
2002 " 5s green & black 11 6
2003 " 13s lemon & black 30 9

Centenary of the births of Bulgarian patriots Delchev (1872-1903) and Sandanski, and of Macedonian Gruev (1871-1906).

Gymnast with Ball, Medals—A795

Designs: 18s, Gymnast with hoop, and medals. 70s, Gymnasts with hoops, and medals.

1972, Feb. 10

2004 A795 13s green, brown, red & gold 21 9
2005 " 18s brown, green, red & gold 40 20

Miniature Sheet

Imperf.

2006 A795 70s gold, brown, green & red 1.25 1.00

5th World Women's Gymnastic Championships, Havana, Cuba.
Size of No. 2006: 61½x73mm.

View of Melnik, by Petar Mladenov
A796

Paintings from National Art Gallery: 2s, Plower, by Pencho Georgiev. 3s, Funeral, by Alexander Djendov. 13s, Husband and Wife, by Vladimir Dimitrov. 20s, Nursing Mother, by Nenko Balkanski. 40s, Paisii Hilendarski Writing History, by Koio Denchev.

1972, Feb. 20 *Perf. 13½x14*

2007	A796	1s green & multi.	6	5
2008	"	2s " "	6	5
2009	"	3s " "	10	8
2010	"	13s " "	35	12
2011	"	20s " "	60	20
2012	"	40s " "	1.20	30
		Nos. 2007-2012 (6)	2.37	80

Paintings from National Art Gallery.

Worker A797 — Singing Harvesters A798

1972, Mar. 7 *Perf. 12½*

2013 A797 13s silver & multi. 30 15

7th Bulgarian Trade Union Congress.

Perf. 11½x12, 12x11½

1972, Mar. 31

Designs: Paintings by Vladimir Dimitrov.

Olive Brown & Multicolored

2014 A798 1s *shown* 8 5
2015 " 2s *Harvester* 8 5
2016 " 3s *Women Diggers* 12 10
2017 " 13s *Fabric Dyers* 35 20
2018 " 20s *"My Mother"* 60 30
2019 " 40s *Self-portrait* 1.20 50
Nos. 2014-2019 (6) 2.43 1.20

90th anniversary of birth of Vladimir Dimitrov, painter.

"Your Heart is your Health" A799 — St. Mark's Basilica and Wave A800

1972, Apr. 30 *Perf. 12½*

2020 A799 13s red, blk. & grn. 30 15

World Health Day.

1972, May 6 *Perf. 13x12½*

Design: 13s, Ca' D'Oro and wave.

2021 A800 2s olive grn., bl. grn. & light blue 5 5
2022 " 13s red brown, violet & light green 30 15

UNESCO campaign to save Venice.

Dimitrov in Print Shop, 1901—A801

Designs: Life of George Dimitrov.

1972, May 8 Photo. *Perf. 12½*

Gold and Multicolored

2023 A801 1s *shown* 6 5
2024 " 2s *Dimitrov as leader of 1923 uprising* 6 5
2025 " 3s *Leipzig trial, 1933* 6 5
2026 " 5s *as Communist functionary, 1935* 9 6
2027 A801 13s *as leader and teacher, 1948* 21 9
2028 " 18s *addressing youth rally, 1948* 30 13
2029 " 28s *with Pioneers, 1948* 60 20
2030 " 40s *Mausoleum* 90 30
2031 " 80s *Portrait* 1.75 55
a. Souvenir sheet 1.75 1.60
Nos. 2023-2031 (9) 4.03 1.48

90th anniversary of the birth of George Dimitrov (1882-1949), communist leader.

No. 2031a contains one imperf. stamp similar to No. 2031, but in different colors. Gold marginal inscription. Size: 86x82mm.

No. 2031 exists imperf in slightly changed colors. Price, $3.

Paisii A802

Design: 2s, Flame and quotation.

1972, May 12

2032 A802 2s gold, grn. & brn. 3 3
2033 " 13s " " " 30 9

250th anniversary of the birth of the monk Paisii Hilendarski (1722-1798), writer of Bulgarian-Slavic history.

Canoeing, Motion and Olympic Emblems—A803

Designs (Motion and Olympic emblems and): 2s, Gymnastics. 3s, Swimming, women's. 13s, Volleyball. 18s, Jumping. 40s, Wrestling. 80s, Stadium and sports.

1972, June 25

Figures of Athletes in Silver & Black

2034 A803 1s lt. blue & multi. 5 5
2035 " 2s orange & multi. 8 8
2036 " 3s multicolored 10 10
2037 " 13s yellow & multi. 35 25
2038 " 18s multicolored 45 25
2039 " 40s pink & multi. 1.00 50
Nos. 2034-2039 (6) 2.03 1.23

Miniature Sheet

Imperf.

Size: 62x60mm.

2040 A803 80s gold, vermilion & yellow 1.40 1.20

20th Olympic Games, Munich, Aug. 26-Sept. 11.

Angel Kunchev A804

1972, June 30 Photo. *Perf. 12½*

2041 A804 2s magenta, dark purple & gold 5 3

Centenary of the death of Angel Kunchev, patriot and revolutionist.

Zlatni Pyassatsi A805

1972, Sept. 16 Multicolored

2042 A805 1s *shown* 5 3
2043 " 2s *Drouzhba* 5 3
2044 " 3s *Slunchev Bryag* 8 5
2045 " 13s *Primorsko* 30 18
2046 " 28s *Roussalka* 70 40
2047 " 40s *Albena* 90 50
Nos. 2042-2047 (6) 2.08 1.19

Bulgarian Black Sea resorts.

Bronze Medal, Olympic Emblems, Canoeing A806

Designs (Olympic Emblems and): 2s, Silver medal, broad jump. 3s, Gold medal, boxing. 18s, Gold medal, wrestling. 40s, Gold medal, weight lifting.

1972, Sept. 29

2048 A806 1s Prus. bl. & multi. 5 5
2049 " 2s dk. grn. & multi. 5 5
2050 " 3s org. brn. & multi. 5 5
2051 " 18s olive & multi. 28 20
2052 " 40s multicolored 80 40
Nos. 2048-2052 (5) 1.23 75

Bulgarian victories in 20th Olympic Games.

Stoj Dimitrov A807

Resistance Fighters: 2s, Cvetko Radoinov. 3s, Bogdan Stivrodski. 5s, Mirko Laiev. 13s, Nedelyo Nikolov.

1972, Oct. 30 Photo. *Perf. 12½x13*

2053 A807 1s olive & multi. 5 5
2054 " 2s multicolored 5 5
2055 " 3s " 6 6
2056 " 5s " 10 4
2057 " 13s " 30 9
Nos. 2053-2057 (5) 56 29

"50 Years USSR" A808

1972, Nov. 3 Photo. *Perf. 12½x13*

2058 A808 13s gold, red & yel. 25 12

50th anniversary of Soviet Union.

Turk's-cap Lily A809

Protected Plants: 2s, Gentian. 3s, Sea daffodil. 4s, Globe flower. 18s, Primrose. 23s, Pulsatilla vernalis. 40s, Snake's-head.

1972, Nov. 25 *Perf. 12½*

Flowers in Natural Colors

2059 A809 1s olive bister 5 5
2060 " 2s " " 5 5
2061 " 3s " " 8 5
2062 " 4s " " 10 8
2063 " 18s " " 40 25
2064 " 23s " " 55 40
2065 " 40s " " 1.00 70
Nos. 2059-2065 (7) 2.23 1.58

No. 2052 Overprinted in Red — СВЕТОВЕН ПЪРВЕНЕЦ

1972, Nov. 27

2066 A806 40s multicolored 80 30

Bulgarian weight lifting Olympic gold medalists.

Dobri Chintulov—A810

1972, Nov. 28 Photo. *Perf. 12½*

2067 A810 2s gray, dark & light green 6 3

Dobri Chintulov, writer, 150th birth anniversary.

Forehead Band—A811

Designs (14th-19th Century Jewelry): 2s, Belt buckles. 3s, Amulet. 8s, Pendant. 23s, Earrings. 40s, Necklace.

1972, Dec. 27 Engr. *Perf. 14x13½*

2068 A811 1s red brn. & black 5 3
2069 " 2s emerald & black 5 3
2070 " 3s Prus. bl. & black 7 5
2071 " 8s dk. red & black 16 12
2072 " 23s red org. & multi. 45 25
2073 " 40s violet & black 75 35
Nos. 2068-2073 (6) 1.53 83

Skin Divers—A812

Designs: 2s, Shelf-1 underwater house and divers. 18s, Diving bell and diver (vert.). 40s, Elevation balloon and divers (vert.).

1973, Jan. 24 Photo. *Perf. 12½*

2074 A812 1s lt. bl., blk. & yel. 3 3
2075 " 2s blk., bl. & orange yellow 3 3
2076 " 18s blk., Prus. bl. & dull orange 30 15
2077 " 40s black, ultra. & bister 75 35

Bulgarian deep-sea research in the Black Sea.

A souvenir sheet of four contains imperf. 20s stamps in designs of Nos. 2074-2077 with colors changed. Gray marginal inscriptions. Size: 118x99mm. Sold for 1 lev. Price $1.75.

Execution of Levski, by Boris Angelushev
A813

Design: 20s, Vassil Levski, by Georgi Danchev.

1973, Feb. 19 *Perf. 13x12½*

2078 A813 2s dull rose & Prus. green 3 3
2079 " 20s dull grn. & brn. 35 20

Centenary of the death of Vassil Levski (1837–1873), patriot, executed by the Turks.

Kukersky Mask, Elhovo Region
A814

Nicolaus Copernicus
A815

Kukersky Masks at pre-Spring Festival: 2s, Breznik. 3s, Hissar. 13s, Radomir. 20s, Karnobat. 40s, Pernik.

1973, Feb. 26 *Perf. 12½*

2080 A814 1s dp. rose & multi. 10 8
2081 " 2s emerald & multi. 10 8
2082 " 3s violet & multi. 10 8
2083 " 13s multicolored 35 18
2084 " 20s " 60 30
2085 " 40s " 1.00 45
Nos. 2080-2085 (6) 2.25 1.17

1973, Mar. 21 Photo. *Perf. 12½*

2086 A815 28s ocher, black & claret 55 35

500th anniversary of the birth of Nicolaus Copernicus (1473–1543), Polish astronomer.

Vietnamese Worker and Rainbow
A816

1973, Apr. 16

2087 A816 18s lt. bl. & multi. 30 15

Peace in Viet Nam.

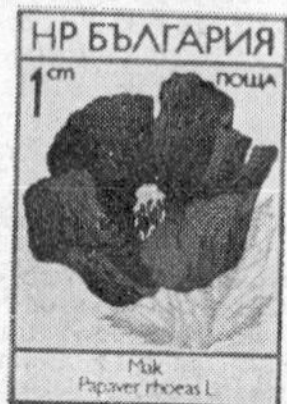

Poppy
A817

Designs: Wild flowers.

1973, May Photo. *Perf. 13*

Multicolored

2088 A817 1s *shown* 5 5
2089 " 2s *Daisy* 6 5
2090 " 3s *Peony* 7 5
2091 " 13s *Centaury* 25 15
2092 " 18s *Corn cockle* 35 20
2093 " 28s *Ranunculus* 55 32
Nos. 2088-2093 (6) 1.33 82

Christo Botev
A818

1973, June 2

2094 A818 2s pale grn., buff & brown 6 5
2095 " 18s pale brn., gray & green 32 15

125th anniversary of the birth of Christo Botev (1848–1876), poet.

"Suffering Worker"—A819

Design: 1s, Asen Halachev and revolutionists.

1973, June 6 Photo. *Perf. 13*

2096 A819 1s gold, red & blk. 3 3
2097 " 2s gold, orange & dark brown 5 5

50th anniversary of Pleven uprising.

Muskrat
A820

Perf. 12½x13, 13x12½

1973, June 29 Lithographed

Multicolored

2098 A820 1s *shown* 5 5
2099 " 2s *Raccoon* 5 5
2100 " 3s *Mouflon* (vert.) 7 5
2101 " 12s *Fallow deer* (vert.) 25 15
2102 " 18s *European bison* 35 20
2103 " 40s *Elk* 70 30
Nos. 2098-2103 (6) 1.47 80

Aleksandr Stamboliski—A821

1973, June 14 Photo. *Perf. 12½*

2104 A821 18s dp. brn. & org. 40 10
a. 18s orange 2.00

50th anniversary of the death of Aleksandr Stamboliski (1879–1923), leader of Peasants' Party and premier.

Trade Union Emblem
A822

Stylized Sun, Olympic Rings
A823

1973, Aug. 27 Photo. *Perf. 12½*

2105 A822 2s yellow & multi. 5 3

8th Congress of World Federation of Trade Unions, Varna, Oct. 15–22.

1973, Aug. 29 *Perf. 13*

Designs: 28s, Emblem of Bulgarian Olympic Committee and Olympic rings. 80s, Soccer, emblems of Innsbruck and Montreal 1976 Games (horiz.).

2106 A823 13s multicolored 23 15
2107 " 28s " 50 27

Souvenir Sheet

2108 A823 80s multicolored 3.00 2.00

Olympic Congress, Varna. No. 2108 contains one stamp. Blue and gray green margin shows emblems of various Olympic committees and games. Size: 60x77½ mm. It also exists imperf.; also with violet margin, imperf.

Revolutionists with Communist Flag
A824

Designs: 5s, Revolutionists on flatcar blocking train. 13s, Raising Communist flag (vert.). 18s, George Dimitrov and Vassil Kolarov.

1973, Sept. 22 Photo. *Perf. 12½*

2109 A824 2s magenta & multi. 5 3
2110 " 5s " " 9 6
2111 " 13s " " 23 15
2112 " 18s " " 30 20

50th anniversary of the September Revolution.

Warrior Saint
A825

Murals from Boyana Church: 1s, Tsar Kaloyan and 2s, his wife Dessislava. 5s, "St. Wystratti." 10s, Tsar Constantine Assen. 13s, Deacon Laurentius. 18s, Virgin Mary. 20s, St. Ephraim. 28s, Jesus. 80s, Jesus in the Temple (horiz.).

1973, Sept. 24

2113 A825 1s gold & multi. 10 8
2114 " 2s " " 10 8
2115 " 3s " " 12 8
2116 " 5s " " 15 12
2117 " 10s " " 25 12
2118 " 13s " " 30 20
2119 " 18s " " 40 25
2120 " 20s " " 50 30
2121 " 28s " " 75 40
Nos. 2113-2121 (9) 2.67 1.61

Miniature Sheet

Imperf.

2122 A825 80s gold & multi. 3.75 2.00

No. 2122 contains one stamp with simulated perforations. Gold margin with view of Boyana Church. Size: 56x76½mm.

Christo Smirnenski—A826

1973, Sept. 29 Photo. *Perf. 12½*

2123 A826 1s multicolored 3 3
2124 " 2s vio. bl. & multi. 5 5

75th anniversary of the birth of Christo Smirnenski (1898–1923), poet.

Human Rights Flame
A827

1973, Oct. 10

2125 A827 13s dark blue, red & gold 23 15

25th anniversary of the Universal Declaration of Human Rights.

Type of 1970

History of Bulgaria: 1s, Tsar Theodor Svetoslav receiving Byzantine envoys. 2s, Tsar Mihail Shishman's army in battle with Byzantines. 3s, Tsar Ivan Alexander's victory at Russocastro. 4s, Patriarch Euthimius at the defense of Turnovo. 5s, Tsar Ivan Shishman leading horsemen against the Turks. 13s, Momchil attacking Turks at Umour. 18s, Tsar Ivan Stratsimir meeting King Sigismund's crusaders. 28s, The Boyars Balik, Theodor and Dobrotitsa, meeting ship bringing envoys from Anne of Savoy.

1973, Oct. 23 *Perf. 13*

Silver and Black Vignettes

2126 A741 1s olive bister 8 8
2127 " 2s Prussian blue 8 8
2128 " 3s lilac 10 8
2129 " 4s green 12 8
2130 " 5s violet 15 10
2131 " 13s orange & brown 24 18
2132 " 18s olive green 34 24
2133 " 28s yel. brn. & brn. 50 40
Nos. 2126-2133 (8) 1.61 1.24

Fin Class
A828

1973, Oct. 29 Lithographed *Perf. 13*

Sailboats: 2s, Flying Dutchman. 3s, Soling class. 13s, Tempest class. 20s, Class 470. 40s, Tornado class.

2134 A828 1s ultra. & multi. 8 8
2135 " 2s green & multi. 8 8
2136 " 3s dk. blue & multi. 10 8
2137 " 13s dull vio. & multi. 28 20

2138 A828 20s gray bl. & multi. 60 28
2139 " 40s multicolored 1.25 50
Nos. 2134–2139 (6) 2.39 1.22

Nos. 2134–2139 exist imperf. in changed colors. Price, set, $3.50.

Village, by Bencho Obreshkov
A829

Paintings: 2s, Mother and Child, by Stoyan Venev. 3s, Rest (woman), by Tsenko Boyadjiev. 13s, Flowers in Vase, by Sirak Skitnik. 18s, Meri Kuneva (portrait), by Ilya Petrov. 40s, Winter in Plovdiv, by Zlatyu Boyadjiev. 13s, 18s, 40s, vertical.

Perf. 12½x12, 12x12½

1973, Nov. 10

2140 A829 1s gold & multi. 8 8
2141 " 2s " " 8 8
2142 " 3s " " 8 8
2143 " 13s " " 30 15
2144 " 18s " " 45 20
2145 " 40s " " 1.35 35
Nos. 2140–2145 (6) 2.34 94

Souvenir Sheet

Paintings by Stanislav Dospevski: No. 2146a, Domnica Lambreva. No. 2146b, Self-portrait. Both vertical.

2146 A829 Sheet of 2 3.00 1.75
a. 50s gold & multicolored 1.00 75
b. 50s " " 1.00 75

Bulgarian paintings. No. 2146 commemorates the centenary of the birth of Stanislav Dospevski; gold margin and brown inscription. Size: 100x96mm.

Souvenir Sheet

Soccer—A830

1973, Dec. 10 Photo. ***Perf. 13***
2147 A830 28s multicolored 3.00 2.00

World Soccer Championships, Munich 1974. No. 2147 has blue margin with carmine Championship emblem. Size: 65x 100mm. Sold for 1 l.

Angel and Ornaments
A831

Designs: 1s, Attendant facing right. 2s, Passover table and lamb. 3s, Attendant facing left. 8s, Abraham and ornaments. 13s, Adam and Eve. 28s, Expulsion from Garden of Eden.

1974, Jan. 21 Photo. ***Perf. 13***

2148 A831 1s fawn, yel. & brn. 10 8
2149 " 2s " " " 10 8
2150 " 3s " " " 12 10
2151 " 5s slate grn. & yel. 15 10
2152 " 8s " " " 25 12
2153 " 13s lt. brown, yel. & olive 40 24
2154 " 28s lt. brown, yel. & olive 90 50
Nos. 2148–2154 (7) 2.02 1.22

Woodcarvings from Rozhen Monastery, 19th century. Nos. 2148–2150, 2151–2152, 2153–2154 printed se-tenant.

Lenin, by N. Mirtchev—A832

Design: 18s, Lenin visiting Workers, by W. A. Serov.

1974, Jan. 28 Litho. ***Perf. 12½x12***
2155 A832 2s ocher & multi. 5 5
2156 " 18s " " 30 18

50th anniversary of the death of Lenin.

1974, Jan. 28

Design: Demeter Blagoev at Rally, by G. Kowachev.

2157 A832 2s multicolored 5 5

50th anniversary of the death of Demeter Blagoev, founder of Bulgarian Communist Party.

Sheep
A833

Designs: Domestic animals.

1974, Feb. 1 Photo. ***Perf. 13***

Multicolored

2158 A833 1s *shown* 8 8
2159 " 2s *Goat* 8 8
2160 " 3s *Pig* 8 8
2161 " 5s *Cow* 12 8
2162 " 13s *Buffalo cow* 25 18
2163 " 20s *Horse* 45 30
Nos. 2158–2163 (6) 1.06 80

Comecon Emblem
A834

1974, Feb. 11 Photo. ***Perf. 13***
2164 A834 13s silver & multi. 40 14

25th anniversary of the Council of Mutual Economic Assistance.

Soccer—A835

Designs: Various soccer action scenes.

1974, Mar. Photo. ***Perf. 13***
2165 A835 1s dull grn. & multi. 8 8
2166 " 2s brt. grn. & multi. 8 8
2167 " 3s slate grn. & multi. 10 8
2168 A835 13s olive & multi. 30 18
2169 " 28s bl. grn. & multi. 60 32
2170 " 40s emerald & multicolored 1.00 50
Nos. 2165–2170 (6) 2.16 1.24

Souvenir Sheet

2171 A835 1 l green & multi. 2.50 1.25

World Soccer Championship, Munich, June 13–July 7. No. 2171 contains one stamp. Red margin with emblem and inscription in white; soccer cup in yellow and gold. Size: 67x78½mm. No. 2171 exists imperf.

Salt Production
A836

Children's Paintings: 1s, Cosmic Research for Peaceful Purposes. 3s, Fire Dancers. 28s, Russian-Bulgarian Friendship (train and children). 60s, Spring (birds).

1974, Apr. 15 Photo. ***Perf. 13***
2172 A836 1s lilac & multi. 8 8
2173 " 2s lt. grn. & multi. 8 8
2174 " 3s blue & multi. 8 8
2175 " 28s slate & multi. 75 30

Souvenir Sheet

Imperf.

2176 A836 60s blue & multi. 1.25 1.00

Third World Youth Philatelic Exhibition, Sofia, May 23–30. No. 2176 contains one stamp with simulated perforations, rose and lilac border. Size: 70x70mm.

Folk Singers
A837

Designs: 2s, Folk dancers (men). 3s, Bagpiper and drummer. 5s, Wrestlers. 13s, Runners (women). 18s, Gymnast.

1974, Apr. 25 ***Perf. 13***
2178 A837 1s verm. & multi. 5 5
2179 " 2s org. brn. & multi. 5 5
2180 " 3s brn. red & multi. 5 5
2181 " 5s blue & multi. 9 5
2182 " 13s ultra. & multi. 21 9
2183 " 18s vio. bl. & multi. 28 10
Nos. 2178–2183 (6) 73 39

4th Amateur Arts and Sports Festival

Aster
A838

Flowers: 2s, Petunia. 3s, Fuchsia. 18s, Tulip. 20s, Carnation. 28s, Pansy. 80s, Sunflower.

1974, May Photogravure ***Perf. 13***
2184 A838 1s green & multi. 5 5
2185 " 2s vio. bl. & multi. 5 5
2186 " 3s olive & multi. 5 5
2187 " 18s brown & multi. 28 16
2188 " 20s multicolored 35 18
2189 " 28s dull bl. & multi. 46 30
Nos. 2184–2189 (6) 1.24 79

Souvenir Sheet

2190 A838 80s multicolored 1.75 1.20

No. 2190 contains one stamp. Deep ultramarine margin with white inscription and flower design. Size: 78x60mm.

Automobiles and Emblems
A839

1974, May 15 Photo. ***Perf. 13***
2191 A839 13s multicolored 21 9

International Automobile Federation (FIA) Spring Congress, Sofia, May 20–24.

Old and New Buildings, UNESCO Emblem
A840

1974, June 15
2192 A840 18s multicolored 28 10

UNESCO Executive Council, 94th Session, Varna.

Postrider
A841

Designs: 18s, First Bulgarian mail coach. 28s, UPU Monument, Bern.

1974, Aug. 5
2193 A841 2s ocher, blk. & vio. 3 3
2194 " 18s ocher, blk. & grn. 28 10

Souvenir Sheet

2195 A841 28s ocher, blb. & bl. 1.75 1.00

Centenary of Universal Postal Union. No. 2195 contains one stamp, multicolored marginal inscription. Size: 79x 58mm. Exists imperf.

Pioneer and Komsomol Girl
A842

"Bulgarian Communist Party"
A843

Designs: 2s, Pioneer and birds. 60s, Emblem with portrait of George Dimitrov.

1974, Aug. 12
2196 A842 1s green & multi. 3 3
2197 " 2s blue & multi. 3 3

Souvenir Sheet

2198 A842 60s red & multi. 1.25 1.00

30th anniversary of Dimitrov Pioneer Organization, Sepremvriiche. No. 2198 contains one stamp, gold margin with black inscription. Size: 60x83mm.

1974, Aug. 20

Symbolic Designs: 2s, Russian liberators. 5s, Industrialization. 13s, Advanced agriculture and husbandry. 18s, Scientific and technical progress.

2199 A843 1s bl. gray & multi. 3 3
2200 " 2s " " 3 3

2201 A843 5s bl. gray & multi. 9 3
2202 " 13s " " 21 9
2203 " 18s " " 28 10
Nos. 2199–2203 (5) 64 28

30th anniversary of the People's Republic.

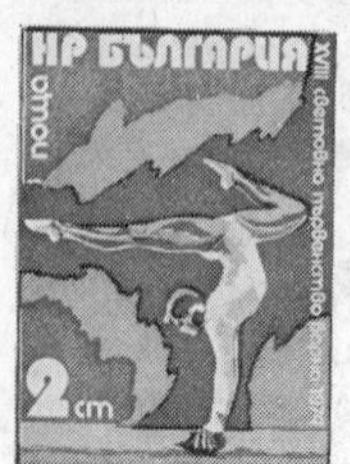

Gymnast on Parallel Bars
A844

Design: 13s, Gymnast on vaulting horse.

1974, Oct. 18 Photo. *Perf. 13*

2204 A844 2s multicolored 5 5
2205 " 13s " 25 16

18th Gymnastic Championships, Varna.

Souvenir Sheet

Symbols of Peace—A845

1974, Oct. 29 Photo. *Perf. 13*

2206 A845 Sheet of 4, multi. 2.25 1.50
a. 13s *Doves* 21 10
b. 13s *Map of Europe* 21 10
c. 13s *Olive Branch* 21 10
d. 13s *Inscription* 21 10

1974 European Peace Conference. "Peace" in various languages written on Nos. 2206a–2206c. No. 2206 has yellow, brown and lilac margin. Size: 97½x117 mm. Sold for 60s. Exists imperf.

Nib and Envelope
A846

1974, Nov. 20

2207 A846 2s yel., blk. & green 3 3

Introduction of postal zone numbers.

Flowers
A847

1974, Dec. 5

2208 A847 2s emerald & multi. 3 3

St. Todor, Ceramic Icon
A848

Apricot Blossoms
A849

Designs: 2s, Medallion, Veliko Turnovo. 3s, Carved capital. 5s, Silver bowl. 8s, Goblet. 13s, Lion's head finial. 18s, Gold plate with Cross. 28s, Breastplate with eagle.

1974, Dec. 18 Photogravure *Perf. 13*

2209 A848 1s org. & multi. 5 5
2210 " 2s pink & multi. 5 5
2211 " 3s blue & multi. 5 5
2212 " 5s lt. vio. & multi. 9 5
2213 " 8s brown & multi. 13 8
2214 " 13s multicolored 21 16
2215 " 18s red & multi. 28 22
2216 " 28s ultra. & multi. 46 36
Nos. 2209–2216 (8) 1.32 1.02

Art works from 9th–12th centuries.

1975, Jan. Photogravure *Perf. 13*

Fruit Tree Blossoms: 2s, Apple. 3s, Cherry. 19s, Pear. 28s, Peach.

2217 A849 1s org. & multi. 5 5
2218 " 2s multicolored 5 5
2219 " 3s car. & multi. 5 5
2220 " 19s lemon & multi. 30 15
2221 " 28s verm. & multi. 46 25
Nos. 2217–2221 (5) 91 55

Tree and Book
A850

1975, Mar. 25 Photo. *Perf. 13*

2222 A850 2s gold & multi. 3 3

Forestry High School, 50th anniversary.

Souvenir Sheet

Farmers' Activities (Woodcuts)—A851

1975, Mar. 25

2223 A851 Sheet of 4 multi. 75 60
a. 2s *Farmer with ax and flag*
b. 5s *Farmers on guard*
c. 13s *Dancing couple*
d. 18s *Woman picking fruit*

Bulgarian Agrarian Peoples' Union, 75th anniversary. No. 2223 has orange and green margin. Size: 102x95mm.

Michelangelo, Self-portrait
A852

Designs: 13s, Night (horiz.). 18s, Day (horiz.). Both designs after sculptures from Medici Tomb, Florence.

1975

2224 A852 2s plum & dk. blue 5 5
2225 " 13s vio. bl. & plum 21 9
2226 " 18s brown & green 28 10

Souvenir Sheet

2227 A852 2s olive & red 1.00 90

500th birth anniversary of Michelangelo Buonarotti (1475–1564), Italian sculptor, painter and architect. No. 2227 issued to publicize ARPHILA 75 International Philatelic Exhibition, Paris, June 6–16. Marginal inscriptions and border in gold, red and green. Sheet sold for 60s. Size: 69x83mm.

Issue dates: Nos. 2224–2226, Mar. 28. No. 2227, Mar. 31.

Souvenir Sheet

Spain No. 1 and España 75 Emblem—A853

1975, Apr. 4

2228 A853 40s multicolored 4.75 3.00

España 75 International Philatelic Exhibition, Madrid, Apr. 4–13. No. 2228 contains one stamp; bright ultramarine margin with white design and inscription, bister post horn. Size: 70x102mm.

Gabrov Costume
A854

Regional Costumes: 3s, Trnsk. 5s, Vidin. 13s, Gocedelchev. 18s, Risen.

1975, Apr. Photogravure *Perf. 13*

2229 A854 2s blue & multi. 5 5
2230 " 3s emerald & multi. 5 5
2231 " 5s orange & multi. 12 8
2232 " 13s olive & multi. 25 12
2233 " 18s multicolored 35 18
Nos. 2229–2233 (5) 82 48

Red Star and Arrow
A855

Standard Kilogram and Meter
A856

Design: 13s, Dove and broken sword.

1975, May 9

2234 A855 2s red, blk. & gold 3 3
2235 " 13s bl., blk. & gold 21 9

Victory over Fascism, 30th anniversary.

1975, May 9 *Perf. 13x13½*

2236 A856 13s silver, lilac & black 21 9

Centenary of International Meter Convention, Paris, 1875.

IWY Emblem, Woman's Head
A857

Ivan Vasov
A858

1975, May 20 Photo. *Perf. 13*

2237 A857 13s multicolored 21 9

International Women's Year 1975.

1975, May

Design: 13s, Ivan Vasov, seated.

2238 A858 2s buff & multi. 3 3
2239 " 13s gray & multi. 21 9

125th birth anniversary of Ivan Vasov.

Nikolov and Sava Kokarechkov
A859

Designs: 2s, Mitko Palaouzov and Ivan Vassilev. 5s, Nicolas Nakev and Stevtcho Kraychev. 13s, Ivanka Pachkoulova and Detelina Mintcheva.

1975, May 30

2240 A859 1s multicolored 5 5
2241 " 2s " 5 5
2242 " 5s " 9 5
2243 " 13s " 25 15

Teen-age resistance fighters, killed during World War II.

Aleksei A. Leonov and Soyuz
A860

Designs: 18s, Thomas P. Stafford and Apollo. 28s, Apollo and Soyuz over earth. 1 l, Apollo Soyuz link-up.

1975, July 15

2244 A860 13s blue & multi. 21 9
2245 " 18s pur. & multi. 28 10
2246 " 28s multicolored 46 18

Souvenir Sheet

2247 A860 1 l vio. & multi. 3.00 1.50

Apollo Soyuz space test project (Russo-American cooperation), launching July 15; link-up July 17. No. 2247 contains one stamp. Apollo-Soyuz emblem, Russian and American flags in margin. Size: 75x83mm.

Mother Feeding Child, by John E. Millais
A861

Etchings: 2s, The Dead Daughter, by Goya. 3s, Reunion, by Bemkov. 13s, Seated Nude, by Renoir. 20s, Man in a Fur Hat, by Rembrandt. 40s, The Dream, by Daumier (horiz.). 1 l, Temptation, by Dürer.

Photogravure and Engraved

1975, Aug. *Perf. 12x11½, 11½x12*

2248 A861 1s yellow green & multicolored 5 5
2249 " 2s orange & multi. 5 5
2250 " 3s lilac & multi. 5 5
2251 " 13s lt. bl. & multi. 21 9
2252 " 20s ocher & multi. 36 15
2253 " 40s rose & multi. 72 30
Nos. 2248-2253 (6) 1.44 69

Souvenir Sheet

2254 A861 1 l emerald & multi. 2.40 1.50

World Graphics Exhibition. No. 2254 contains one stamp; gray green marginal inscription and border. Size: 80x95mm.

Letter "Z" from 12th Century Manuscript
A862

Whimsical Globe
A863

Initials from Illuminated Manuscripts: 2s, "B" from 17th century prayerbook. 3s, "V" from 16th century Bouhovo Gospel. 8s, "B" from 14th century Turnovo collection. 13s, "V" from Dobreisho's Gospel, 13th century. 18s, "E" from 11th century Enina book of the Apostles.

1975, Aug. Litho. *Perf. 11½*

2255 A862 1s multicolored 3 3
2256 " 2s " 3 3
2257 A862 3s multicolored 3 3
2258 " 8s " 13 5
2259 " 13s " 21 9
2260 " 18s " 28 10
Nos. 2255-2260 (6) 71 33

Bulgarian art.

1975, Aug. Photo. *Perf. 13*

2261 A863 2s multicolored 3 3

Festival of Humor and Satire.

Lifeboat Dju IV and Gibraltar-Cuba Route
A864

1975, Aug. 5 Photo. *Perf. 13*

2262 A864 13s multicolored 21 15

Oceanexpo 75, First International Ocean Exhibition, Okinawa, July 20, 1975–Jan. 18, 1976.

Sts. Cyril and Methodius
A865

Sts. Constantine and Helena
A866

St. Sophia Church, Sofia, Woodcut by V. Zahriev—A867

1975, Aug. 21

2263 A865 2s verm., yellow & brown 5 5
2264 A866 13s grn., yel. & brn. 25 15

Souvenir Sheet

2265 A867 50s org. & multi. 1.25 90

Balkanphila V, philatelic exhibition, Sofia, Sept. 27–Oct. 5. No. 2265 has bluish gray and orange margin. Size: 89x85mm.

Peace Dove and Map of Europe
A868

1975, Nov. Photogravure *Perf. 13*

2266 A868 18s ultra., rose & yellow 28 10

European Security and Cooperation Conference, Helsinki, Finland, July 30–Aug. 1. No. 2266 printed in sheets of 5 stamps and 4 labels, arranged checkerwise.

Acherontia Atropos
A869

Designs: Moths.

1975 Photo. *Perf. 13*

2267 A869 1s *shown* 3 3
2268 " 2s *Daphnis nerii* 3 3
2269 " 3s *Smerinthus ocellata* 5 3
2270 " 10s *Deilephila nicea* 18 8
2271 " 13s *Choerocampa elpenor* 21 9
2272 " 18s *Macroglossum fuciformis* 28 10
Nos. 2267-2272 (6) 78 36

Soccer Player
A870

1975, Sept. 21

2273 A870 2s multicolored 3 3

8th Inter-Toto (soccer pool) Soccer Championships, Varna.

Constantine's Rebellion Against the Turks, 1403—A871

Designs (Woodcuts): 2s, Campaign of Vladislav III, 1443–1444. 3s, Battles of Turnovo, 1598 and 1686. 10s, Battle of Liprovsko, 1688. 13s, Guerrillas, 17th century. 18s, Return of exiled peasants.

1975, Nov. 27 Photo. *Perf. 13*

2274 A871 1s bis., grn. & blk. 5 5
2275 " 2s bl., car. & blk. 5 5
2276 " 3s yellow, lilac & black 8 6
2277 " 10s orange, green & black 24 8
2278 " 13s green, lilac & black 30 12
2279 " 18s pink, green & black 40 18
Nos. 2274-2279 (6) 1.12 54

Bulgarian history.

Red Cross and First Aid—A872

Design: 13s, Red Cross and dove.

1975, Dec. 1

2280 A872 2s red brown, red & black 3 3
2281 " 13s blue green, red & black 21 9

90th anniversary of Bulgarian Red Cross.

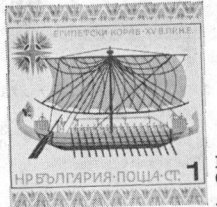

Egyptian Galley
A873

Historic Ships: 2s, Phoenician galley. 3s, Greek trireme. 5s, Roman galley. 13s, Viking longship. 18s, Venetian galley.

1975, Dec. 15 Photo. *Perf. 13*

2282 A873 1s multicolored 5 5
2283 " 2s " 5 5
2284 " 3s " 5 6
2285 " 5s " 12 6
2286 " 13s " 25 12
2287 " 18s " 40 18
Nos. 2282-2287 (6) 92 52

See Nos. 2431-2436.

Souvenir Sheet

Ethnographical Museum, Plovdiv
A874

1975, Dec. 17

2288 A874 Sheet of 3 4.50 3.00
a. 80s green, yellow, & dk. brown 1.40 90

European Architectural Heritage Year. No. 2288 contains 3 stamps and 3 labels showing stylized bird. Olive margin and inscription. Size: 160x96½mm.

Dobri Hristov
A875

1975, Dec. *Perf. 13*

2289 A875 5s bright green, yel. & brown 10 3

Dobri Hristov, musician, birth centenary.

United Nations Emblem
A876

1975, Dec.

2290 A876 13s gold, black & magenta 22 10

United Nations, 30th anniversary.

Glass Ornaments A877

Design: 13s, Peace dove, decorated ornament.

1975, Dec. 22 Photo. *Perf. 13*

2291 A877 2s bright violet & multicolored 3 3
2292 " 13s gray & multi. 22 10

New Year 1976.

Downhill Skiing—A878

Designs (Winter Olympic Games Emblem and): 2s, Cross country skier (vert.). 3s, Ski jump. 13s, Biathlon (vert.). 18s, Ice hockey (vert.). 23s, Speed skating (vert.). 80s, Figure skating, pair (vert.).

1976, Jan. 30 *Perf. 13½*

2293 A878 1s silver & multi. 3 3
2294 " 2s " " 3 3
2295 " 3s " " 3 3
2296 " 13s " " 21 9
2297 " 18s " " 28 10
2298 " 23s " " 36 12
Nos. 2293-2298 (6) 94 40

Souvenir Sheet

2299 A878 80s silver & multi. 2.25 1.50

12th Winter Olympic Games, Innsbruck, Austria, Feb. 4-15. No. 2299 has light blue margin with white inscription. Size: 71x80mm.

Electric Streetcar, Sofia, 1976 A879

Design: 13s, Streetcar and trailer, 1901.

1976, Jan. 12 Photo. *Perf. 13½x13*

2300 A879 2s gray & multi. 3 3
2301 " 13s " " 21 9

75th anniversary of Sofia streetcars.

Stylized Bird A880

Designs: 5s, Dates "1976" and "1956" and star. 13s, Hammer and sickle. 50s, George Dimitrov.

1976, Mar. 1 *Perf. 13*

2302 A880 2s gold & multi. 3 3
2303 " 5s " " 10 3
2304 " 13s " " 21 9

Souvenir Sheet

2305 A880 50s gold & multi. 90 75

11th Bulgarian Communist Party Congress. No. 2305 contains one stamp; crimson margin. Size: 56x64mm.

A. G. Bell and Telephone, 1876 A881

1976, Mar. 10

2306 A881 18s dk. brn., yellow & ocher 28 10

Centenary of first telephone call by Alexander Graham Bell, Mar. 10, 1876.

Mute Swan—A882

Waterfowl: 2s, Ruddy shelduck. 3s, Common shelduck. 5s, Garganey teal. 13s, Mallard. 18s, Red-crested pochard.

1976, Mar. 27 Litho. *Perf. 11½*

2307 A882 1s vio. blue & multi. 3 3
2308 " 2s yel. grn. & multi. 3 3
2309 " 3s blue & multi. 3 3
2310 " 5s multicolored 10 3
2311 " 13s purple & multi. 21 9
2312 " 18s green & multi. 28 10
Nos. 2307-2312 (6) 68 31

Guerrillas—A883

Designs (Woodcuts by Stoev): 2s, Peasants with rifle and proclamation. 5s, Raina Knaginia with horse and guerrilla. 13s, Insurgents with cherrywood cannon.

1976, Apr. 5 Photo. *Perf. 13*

2313 A883 1s multicolored 3 3
2314 " 2s " 3 3
2315 " 5s " 9 3
2316 " 13s " 21 9

Centenary of uprising against Turkey.

Guard and Dog A884

Design: 13s, Men on horseback, observation tower.

1976, May 15

2317 A884 2s multicolored 3 3
2318 " 13s " 21 9

30th anniversary of Border Guards.

Construction Worker A885

1976, May 20

2319 A885 2s multicolored 3 3

Young Workers Brigade, 30th anniversary.

Busludja, Bas-relief A886

AES Complex A887

Design: 5s, Memorial building.

1976, May 28 Photo. *Perf. 13*

2320 A886 2s green & multi. 3 3
2321 " 5s vio. bl. & multi. 10 3

First Congress of Bulgarian Social Democratic Party, 85th anniversary.

1976, Apr. 7

Designs: 8s, Factory. 10s, Apartment houses. 13s, Refinery. 20s, Hydroelectric station.

2322 A887 5s green 9 3
2323 " 8s maroon 13 5
2324 " 10s green 18 8
2325 " 13s violet 20 8
2326 " 20s bright green 36 16
Nos. 2322-2326 (5) 96 40

Five-year plan accomplishments.

Children Playing Around Table A888

Designs (Kindergarten Children): 2s, with doll carriage and hobby horse. 5s, playing ball. 23s, in costume.

1976, June 15

2327 A888 1s green & multi. 3 3
2328 " 2s yellow & multi. 3 3
2329 " 5s lilac & multi. 10 3
2330 " 23s rose & multi. 40 18

Demeter Blagoev A889

Christo Botev A890

1976, May 28

2331 A889 13s bluish blk., red & gold 20 8

Demeter Blagoev (1856-1924), writer, political leader, 120th birth anniversary.

1976, May 25

2332 A890 13s ocher & slate green 20 8

Christo Botev (1848-1876), poet, death centenary. Printed se-tenant with yellow green and ocher label, inscribed with poem.

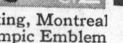

Boxing, Montreal Olympic Emblem A891

Belt Buckle A892

Designs (Montreal Olympic Emblem): 1s, Wrestling (horiz.). 3s, 1 l, Weight lifting. 13s, One-man kayak. 18s, Woman gymnast. 28s, Woman diver. 40s, Woman runner.

1976, June 25

2333 A891 1s orange & multi. 3 3
2334 " 2s multicolored 3 3
2335 " 3s lilac & multi. 3 3
2336 " 13s multicolored 20 8
2337 " 18s " 28 10
2338 " 28s blue & multi. 46 18
2339 " 40s lemon & multi. 72 30
Nos. 2333-2339 (7) 1.75 75

Souvenir Sheet

2340 A891 1 l orange & multi. 1.80

21st Olympic Games, Montreal, Canada, July 17-Aug. 1. No. 2340 contains one stamp; multicolored margin. Size: 69x79mm.

1976, July 30 Photo. *Perf. 13*

Thracian Art (8th-4th Centuries): 2s, Brooch. 3s, Mirror handle. 5s, Helmet cheek cover. 13s, Gold ornament. 18s, Lion's head (harness decoration). 20s, Knee guard. 28s, Jeweled pendant.

2341 A892 1s brn. & multi. 3 3
2342 " 2s blue & multi. 3 3
2343 " 3s multicolored 3 3
2344 " 5s claret & multi. 9 3
2345 " 13s pur. & multi. 21 9
2346 " 18s multicolored 28 10
2347 " 20s " 36 16
2348 " 28s " 46 18
Nos. 2341-2348 (8) 1.49 65

Composite of Bulgarian Stamp Designs—A893

1976, June 5

2349 A893 50s red & multi. 1.00 75

International Federation of Philately (F.I.P.), 50th anniversary and 12th Congress. No. 2349 has multicolored margin. Size: 73x102mm.

Partisans at Night, by Ilya Petrov—A894

Paintings: 5s, Old Town, by Stanko Davrelov. 13s, Seated Woman, by Petrov (vert.). 18s, Seated Boy, by Petrov (vert.). 28s, The Visit, by Davrelov (vert.). 80s, Ilya Petrov, self-portrait (vert.).

1976, Aug. 11 Photo. *Perf. 14*

No.	Type	Description	Unused	Used
2350	A894	2s multicolored	3	3
2351	"	5s "	9	3
2352	"	13s ultra. & multi.	21	9
2353	"	18s multicolored	28	10
2354	"	28s "	46	18
		Nos. 2350-2354 (5)	1.07	43

Souvenir Sheet

No.	Type	Description	Unused	Used
2354A	A894	80s multi.	1.60	1.20

No. 2354A has green border. Size: 60x83mm.

Souvenir Sheet

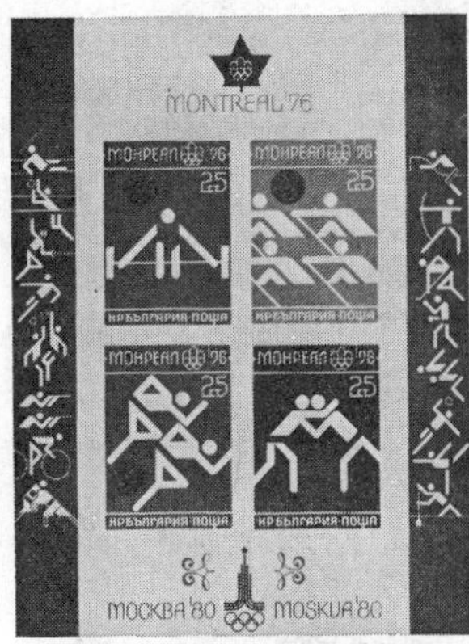

Olympic Sports and Emblems
A895

1976, Sept. 6 Photo. *Perf. 13*

Multicolored

No.	Type	Description	Unused	Used
2355	A895	Sheet of 4	1.80	1.25
		a. 25s *Weight Lifting*	40	25
		b. 25s *Rowing*	40	25
		c. 25s *Running*	40	25
		d. 25s *Wrestling*	40	25

Medalists, 21st Olympic Games, Montreal. No. 2355 has gold margin, green and red inscription. Size: 98x117mm.

Souvenir Sheet

Fresco and UNESCO Emblem—A896

1976, Dec. 3

No.	Type	Description	Unused	Used
2356	A896	50s red & multi.	1.00	75

U.N. Educational, Scientific and Cultural Organization, 30th anniversary. No. 2356 has brown and orange margin. Size: 71x80mm.

"The Pianist" by Jendov
A897

Fish and Hook
A898

Designs (Caricatures by Jendov): 5s, Imperialist "Trick or Treat." 13s, The Leader, 1931.

1976, Sept. 30 Photo. *Perf. 13*

No.	Type	Description	Unused	Used
2357	A897	2s green & multi.	3	3
2358	"	5s pur. & multi.	9	3
2359	"	13s magenta & multicolored	21	9

Alex Jendov (1901–1953), caricaturist.

1976, Sept. 21 Photo. *Perf. 13*

No.	Type	Description	Unused	Used
2360	A898	5s multicolored	9	3

World Sport Fishing Congress, Varna.

St. Theodore
A899

Frescoes: 3s, St. Paul. 5s, St. Joachim. 13s, Melchizedek. 19s, St. Porphyrius. 28s, Queen. 1 l, The Last Supper.

1976, Oct. 4 Litho. *Perf. 12x12½*

No.	Type	Description	Unused	Used
2361	A899	2s gold & multi.	3	3
2362	"	3s " "	3	3
2363	"	5s " "	9	3
2364	"	13s " "	21	9
2365	"	19s " "	32	14
2366	"	28s " "	46	18
		Nos. 2361-2366 (6)	1.14	50

Miniature Sheet
Perf. 12

No.	Type	Description	Unused	Used
2367	A899	1 l gold & multi.	2.00	1.35

Frescoes from Zemen Monastery, 14th century. No. 2367 has gold and vermilion border. Size: 60x75mm.

Document
A900

1976, Oct. 5

No.	Type	Description	Unused	Used
2368	A900	5s multicolored	9	3

State Archives, 25th anniversary.

Cinquefoil
A901

Designs: 1s, Chestnut. 5s, Holly. 8s, Yew. 13s, Daphne. 23s, Judas tree.

1976, Oct. 14 Photo. *Perf. 13*

No.	Type	Description	Unused	Used
2369	A901	1s car. & green	3	3
2370	"	2s green & multi.	3	3
2371	"	5s multicolored	9	3
2372	"	8s "	13	5
2373	"	13s brown & multi.	21	9
2374	"	23s multicolored	40	18
		Nos. 2369-2374 (6)	89	41

Dimitri Polianov
A902

1976, Nov. 19

No.	Type	Description	Unused	Used
2375	A902	2s dk. pur. & ocher	3	3

Dimitri Polianov (1876–1953), poet, birth centenary.

Christo Boteff, by Zlatyu Boyadjiev
A903

Paintings: 2s, Partisan Carrying Cherrywood Cannon, by Ilya Petrov. 3s, "Necklace of Immortality" (man's portrait), by Detchko Uzunov. 13s, "April 1876," by Georgi Popoff. 18s, Partisans, by Stoyan Venev. 60s, The Oath, by Svetlin Ruseff.

1976, Dec. 8

No.	Type	Description	Unused	Used
2376	A903	1s bister & multi.	3	3
2377	"	2s " "	3	3
2378	"	3s " "	3	3
2379	"	13s " "	21	9
2380	"	18s " "	28	10
		Nos. 2376-2380 (5)	58	28

Souvenir Sheet
Imperf.

No.	Type	Description	Unused	Used
2381	A903	60s gold & multi.	1.25	90

Uprising against Turkish rule, centenary. No. 2381 contains one stamp; gold border. Size: 44x82mm.

"Pollution" and Tree—A904

Design: 18s, "Pollution" obscuring sun.

1976, Nov. 10 *Perf. 13*

No.	Type	Description	Unused	Used
2382	A904	2s ultra. & multi.	3	3
2383	"	18s blue & multi.	28	10

Protection of the environment.

Congress Emblem
A904a

Flags
A904b

1976, Nov. 24 Photo. *Perf. 13*

No.	Type	Description	Unused	Used
2384	A904a	2s multicolored	3	3
2384A	A904b	13s "	22	10

33rd BSIS Congress (Bulgarian Socialist Party).

Tobacco Workers, by Stajkov
A905

Paintings by Stajkov: 2s, View of Melnik. 13s, Shipbuilder.

1976, Dec. 16 Photo. *Perf. 13*

No.	Type	Description	Unused	Used
2385	A905	1s multicolored	3	3
2386	"	2s "	3	3
2387	"	13s "	21	9

Veselin Stajkov (1906–1970), painter, 70th birth anniversary.

Snowflake
A906

1976, Dec. 20

No.	Type	Description	Unused	Used
2388	A906	2s silver & multi.	5	3

New Year 1977.

Zachary Stoyanov
A907

1976, Dec. 30

No.	Type	Description	Unused	Used
2389	A907	2s multicolored	3	3

Zachary Stoyanov (1851–1889), historian, 125th birth anniversary.

Bronze Coin of Septimus Severus
A908

Roman Coins: 2s, 13s, 18s, Bronze coins of Caracalla (diff.). 23s, Copper coin of Diocletian.

1977, Jan. 28 Photo. *Perf. 13½x13*

No.	Type	Description	Unused	Used
2390	A908	1s gold & multi.	3	3
2391	"	2s " "	3	3

2392 A908 13s gold & multi. 21 9
2393 " 18s " " 28 10
2394 " 23s " " 40 18
Nos. 2390–2394 (5) 95 43

Coins struck in Serdica (modern Sofia).

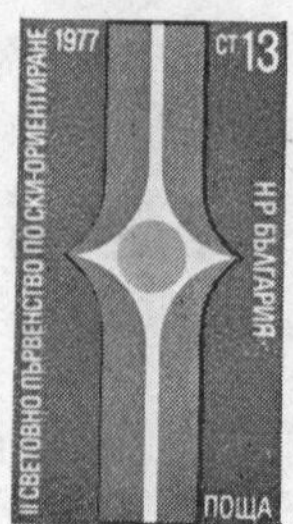

Skis and Compass A909

Tourist Congress Emblem A910

1977, Feb. 24 ***Perf. 13***

2395 A909 13s ultra., red & light blue 21 9

2nd World Ski Orienteering Championships.

1977, Feb. 24 **Photo.** ***Perf. 13***

2396 A910 2s multicolored 3 3

5th Congress of Bulgarian Tourist Organization.

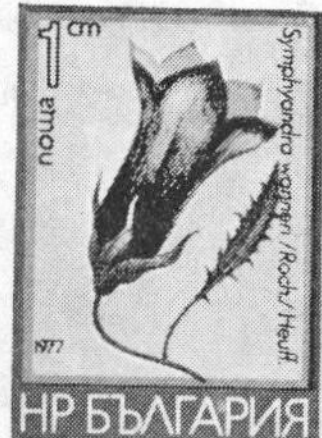

Bellflower
A911

Designs: Various bellflowers.

1977, Mar. 2

2397 A911 1s yellow & multi. 3 3
2398 " 2s rose & multi. 3 3
2399 " 3s lt. bl. & multi. 3 3
2400 " 13s multicolored 21 9
2401 " 43s yel. & multi. 75 20
Nos. 2397–2401 (5) 1.05 38

Vasil Kolarov
A912

Union Congress Emblem
A913

1977, Mar. 21 **Photo.** ***Perf. 13***

2402 A912 2s blue & black 3 3

Vasil Kolarov (1877–1950), politician.

1977, Mar. 25

2403 A913 2s multicolored 3 3

8th Bulgarian Trade Union Congress, Apr. 4–7.

Wolf—A914

Wild Animals: 2s, Red fox. 10s, Weasel. 13s, European wildcat. 23s, Jackal.

1977, May 16 **Litho.** ***Perf. 12½x12***

2404 A914 1s multicolored 3 3
2405 " 2s " 3 3
2406 " 10s " 18 6
2407 " 13s " 21 9
2408 " 23s " 40 18
Nos. 2404–2408 (5) 85 39

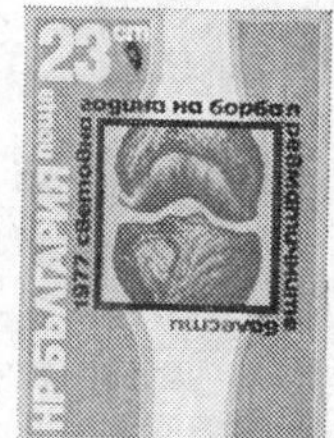

Diseased Knee
A915

1977, Mar. 25 **Photo.** ***Perf. 13***

2409 A915 23s multicolored 40 18

World Rheumatism Year.

Writers' Congress Emblem
A916

1977, Apr.

2410 A916 23s lt. bl. & yel. green 40 18

International Writers Congress: "Peace, the Hope of the Planet." No. 2410 printed in sheets of 8 stamps and 4 labels with signatures of participating writers.

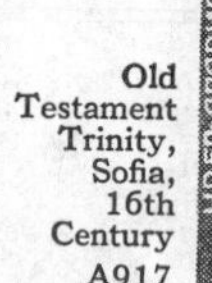

Old Testament Trinity, Sofia, 16th Century
A917

Icons: 1s, St. Nicholas, Nessebur, 13th century. 3s, Annunciation, Royal Gates, Veliko Turnovo, 16th century. 5s, Christ Enthroned, Nessebur, 17th century. 13s, St. Nicholas, Elena, 18th century. 23s, Presentation of the Virgin, Rila Monastery, 18th century. 35s, Virgin and Child, Tryavna, 19th century. 40s, St. Demetrius on Horseback, Provadia, 19th century. 1 l, The 12 Holidays, Rila Monastery, 18th century.

1977, May 10 **Photo.** ***Perf. 13***

2411 A917 1s black & multi. 3 3
2412 " 2s grn. & multi. 3 3
2413 " 3s brn. & multi. 3 3
2414 " 5s blue & multi. 10 3
2415 " 13s olive & multi. 21 9
2416 " 23s maroon & multicolored 40 18
2417 " 35s green & multi. 60 20
2418 " 40s dp. ultra. & multicolored 70 20
Nos. 2411–2418 (8) 2.10 79

Miniature Sheet

Imperf.

2419 A917 1 l gold & multi. 2.00 1.60

Bulgarian icons. No. 2419 has decorative orange border. Size: 101x100mm.

Souvenir Sheet

St. Cyril
A918

1977 **Photo.** ***Perf. 13***

2420 A918 1 l gold & multi. 2.00 1.60

1150th anniversary of the birth of St. Cyril (827–869), reputed inventor of Cyrillic alphabet. No. 2420 has violet blue and gold margin showing ancient Cyrillic writing. Size: 103x87mm.

Congress Emblem
A919

1977

2421 A919 2s red, gold & grn. 3 3

13th Komsomol Congress.

Newspaper Masthead—A920

1977, July **Photo.** ***Perf. 13***

2422 A920 2s multicolored 3 3

Centenary of Bulgarian daily press and 50th anniversary of Rabotnichesko Delo newspaper.

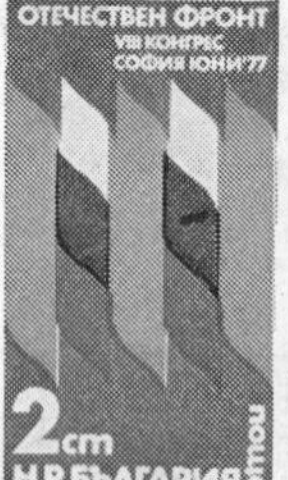

Patriotic Front Emblem
A921

Weight Lifting
A922

1977

2423 A921 2s gold & multi. 3 3

8th Congress of Patriotic Front.

1977

2424 A922 13s deep brown & multicolored 22 10

European Youth Weight Lifting Championships, Sofia, June.

Women Basketball Players
A923

1977 **Photo.** ***Perf. 13***

2425 A923 23s multicolored 40 18

7th European Women's Basketball Championships.

Wrestling—A924

Designs (Games' Emblem and): 13s, Running. 23s, Basketball. 43s, Women's gymnastics.

1977, Aug.

2426 A924 2s multicolored 3 3
2427 " 13s " 21 9
2428 " 23s " 40 18
2429 " 43s " 75 20

UNIVERSIADE '77, University Games, Sofia, Aug. 18–27.

TV Tower, Berlin
A925

1977, Aug. **Litho.** ***Perf. 13***

2430 A925 25s bl. & dk. blue 40 36

SOZPHILEX 77 Philatelic Exhibition, Berlin, Aug. 19–28.

Ship Type of 1975

Historic Ships: 1s, Hansa cog. 2s, Santa Maria, caravelle. 3s, Golden Hind, frigate. 12s, Santa Catherina, carrack. 13s, La Corone, galleon. 43s, Mediterranean galleass.

1977, Sept. **Photo.** ***Perf. 13***

2431 A873 1s multicolored 3 3
2432 " 2s " 3 3
2433 " 3s " 3 3
2434 " 12s " 20 6
2435 " 13s " 22 10
2436 " 43s " 75 20
Nos. 2431–2436 (6) 1.26 45

Ivan Vasov National Theater
A926

Buildings, Sofia: 13s, Party Headquarters. 23s, House of the People's Army. 30s, Clement Ochrida University. 80s, National Gallery. 1 l, National Assembly.

1977, Apr. 30 Photogravure *Perf. 13*

2437 A926 12s red, *gray* 20 8
2438 " 13s red brn., *gray* 21 9
2439 " 23s blue, *gray* 40 18
2440 " 30s olive, *gray* 55 20
2441 " 80s violet, *gray* 1.40 40
2442 " 1 l claret, *gray* 1.75 50
Nos. 2437-2442 (6) 4.51 1.45

Map of Europe
A927

1977

2443 A927 23s brn., bl. & grn. 40 18

21st Congress of the European Organization for Quality Control, Varna.

Union of Earth and Water, by Rubens
A928

Rubens Paintings: 23s, Venus and Adonis. 40s, Pastoral Scene (man and woman). 1 l, Portrait of a Lady in Waiting.

1977 Litho. *Perf. 12*

2444 A928 13s gold & multi. 21 9
2445 " 23s " " 40 18
2446 " 40s " " 70 20

Souvenir Sheet

2447 A928 1 l gold & multi. 2.00 1.60

Peter Paul Rubens (1577–1640), 400th birth anniversary. No. 2447 has gold border. Size: 72x88mm.

George Dimitrov
A929

1977 Photo. *Perf. 13*

2448 A929 13s red & deep claret 21 9

George Dimitrov (1882–1947), first Prime Minister of Bulgaria, 95th birth anniversary.

1977

2449 A930 13s gold & multi. 21 9

3rd Bulgarian Culture Congress.

1977

2450 A931 2s multicolored 3 3

11th National Festival of Humor and Satire, Grabovo.

Elin Pelin
A932

Portraits: 5s, Peju K. Jaworov. 13s, Boris Angelushev. 23s, Ceno Todorov.

1977 Photo. *Perf. 13*

2451 A932 2s gold & brown 3 3
2452 " 5s gold & gray green 10 3
2453 " 13s gold & claret 21 9
2454 " 23s gold & blue 40 18

Elin Pelin (Dimitur Ivanov Stojanov, 1877–1949), writer; Peju K. Jaworov (1878–1914), writer; Boris Angelushev (1902–1966), painter and graphic artist; Ceno Todorov (Ceno Todorov Dikov, 1877–1953), painter. Nos. 2451–2454 each printed with se-tenant label showing scenes from authors' works or illustrations by the artists.

Women's Kayak—A933

Design: 23s, 2-man canoe.

1977 Photo. *Perf. 13*

2455 A933 2s dk. bl. & yel. 3 3
2456 " 23s vio. & lt. grn. 40 18

13th Canoe World Championships.

Dr. Pirogov
A934

1977, Oct. 14 Photo. *Perf. 13*

2457 A934 13s olive, ocher & brown 21 9

Centenary of visit by Russian physician N. J. Pirogov during war of liberation from Turkey.

Designs: 13s, Lenin, 1917. 23s, "1917" as a flame.

1977, Oct. 21

2458 A935 2s blk., buff & red 3 3
2459 " 13s multicolored 21 9
2460 " 23s " 40 18

60th anniversary of Russian October Revolution.

1977, Nov.

Designs (Festival Posters): 13s, "The Bugler." 23s, Liberation Monument, Sofia (detail). 25s, Samara flag.

2461 A936 2s multicolored 3 3
2462 " 13s " 21 9
2463 " 23s " 40 18
2464 " 25s " 45 20

Liberation from Turkish rule, centenary.

Souvenir Sheet

Games' and Sports Emblems—A937

1977 Photo. *Perf. 13½x13*

2465 A937 1 l multicolored 2.00 1.60

University Games '77, Sofia. No. 2465 has multicolored margin. Size: 83x75mm.

Conference Building—A938

1977 *Perf. 13½*

2466 A938 23s multicolored 40 18

64th Interparliamentary Union Conference, Sofia.

Balloon over Plovdiv
A939

1977

2467 A939 25s yel., brn. & red 45 20

85th International Aviation Conference, PANAIR, Plovdiv.

Design: 13s, Different ornament.

1977, Nov.

2468 A940 2s gold & multi. 3 3
2469 " 13s silver & multi. 21 9

New Year 1978.

Railroad Bridge—A941

1977, Nov. 9

2470 A941 13s green, yellow & gray 21 9

Transport Organization, 50th anniversary.

Petko Ratchev Slaveikov
A942

1977, Nov. 15

2471 A942 8s gold & vio. brn. 14 5

Petko Ratchev Slaveikov (1827–95), poet, birth sesquicentennial. No. 2471 printed in sheets of 8 stamps and 8 labels in 4 alternating vertical rows. Pink and black label shows woman rocking cradle.

Soccer Player
A943

Design: 23s, Soccer player and Games' emblem. 50s, Soccer players.

1978, Feb. Photo. *Perf. 13*

2472 A943 13s multicolored 21 9
2473 " 23s " 40 18

Souvenir Sheet

2474 A943 50s ultra. & multicolored 1.00 80

11th World Cup Soccer Championship, Argentina, June 1–25.

No. 2474 contains one stamp; cup and Argentina '78 emblem in margin. Size: 75x62mm.

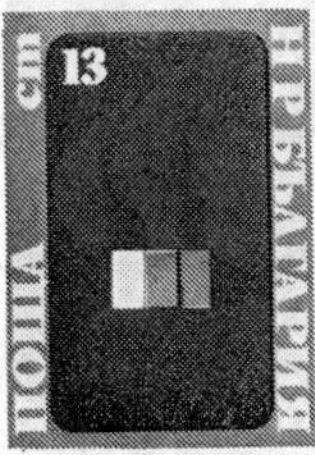

Flame with Star
A930

Smart Pete on Donkey, by Ilija Beskor
A931

Peace Decree, 1917
A935

Old Soldier with Grandchild
A936

Ornament
A940

Todor Zhivkov and Leonid I. Brezhnev
A944

Ostankino Tower, Moscow, Bulgarian Post Emblem
A945

1978 Photo. *Perf. 13*

2475 A944 18s gold, car. & brown 30 15

Bulgarian-Soviet Friendship. No. 2475 issued in sheets of 3 stamps and 3 labels.

1978, Mar.

2476 A945 13s multicolored 21 9

20th anniversary of the Comecon Postal Organization (Council of Mutual Economic Assistance).

Leo Tolstoy A946 **Shipka Pass Monument A947**

Portraits: 5s, Fedor Dostoevski. 13s, Ivan Sergeevich Turgenev. 23s, Vasili Vasilievich Vershchagin. 25s, Giuseppe Garibaldi. 35s, Victor Hugo.

1978, Mar. 3 Photo. *Perf. 13*

2477 A946 2s yel. & dk. grn. 3 3
2478 " 5s lemon & brn. 8 4
2479 " 13s tan & slate green 21 9
2480 " 23s gray & violet brown 40 18
2481 " 25s yel. grn. & blk. 45 20
2482 " 35s light blue & violet blue 60 28
Nos. 2477-2482 (6) 1.77 82

Souvenir Sheet

2483 A947 50s multicolored 95 40

Centenary of Bulgaria's liberation from Ottoman rule. No. 2483 has yellow ornaments in margin. Size: 55x73mm.

Bulgarian and Russian Colors A948

1978, Mar. 18

2484 A948 2s multicolored 3 3

30th anniversary of Russo-Bulgarian cooperation.

Heart and WHO Emblem A949

1978, Apr.

2485 A949 23s gray, red & orange 40 18

World Health Day, fight against hypertension.

Goddess A950

Ceramics (2nd–4th Centuries) and Exhibition Emblem: 5s, Mask of bearded man. 13s, Vase. 23s, Vase. 35s, Head of Silenus. 53s, Cock.

1978, Apr.

2486 A950 2s green & multi. 3 3
2487 " 5s multicolored 8 4
2488 " 13s " 21 9
2489 " 23s " 40 18
2490 " 35s " 60 28
2491 " 53s car. & multi. 95 45
Nos. 2486-2491 (6) 2.27 1.07

Philaserdica Philatelic Exhibition.

Nikolai Roerich, by Svyatoslav Roerich A951 **"Mind and Matter," by Andrei Nikolov A952**

1978, Apr.

2492 A951 8s multicolored 15 6
2493 A952 13s " 22 10

Nikolai K. Roerich (1874–1947) and Andrei Nikolov (1878–1959), artists.

Bulgarian Flag and Red Star—A953

1978, Apr.

2494 A953 2s vio. bl. & multi. 3 3

Bulgarian Communist Party Congress.

Young Man, by Albrecht Dürer A954

Paintings: 23s, Bathsheba at Fountain, by Rubens. 25s, Portrait of a Man, by Hans Holbein the Younger. 35s, Rembrandt and Saskia, by Rembrandt. 43s, Lady in Mourning, by Tintoretto. 60s, Old Man with Beard, by Rembrandt. 80s, Knight in Armor, by Van Dyck.

1978, May Photo. *Perf. 13*

2495 A954 13s multicolored 21 9
2496 " 23s " 40 18
2497 " 25s " 45 20
2498 " 35s " 60 28
2499 " 43s " 75 35
2500 " 60s " 1.10 40
2501 " 80s " 1.40 45
Nos. 2495-2501 (7) 4.91 1.95

Dresden Art Gallery paintings.

Doves and Festival Emblem—A955

1978, June

2502 A955 13s multicolored 21 9

11th World Youth Festival, Havana, July 28–Aug. 5.

Fritillaria Stribrnyi A956

Rare Flowers: 2s, Fritillaria drenovskyi. 3s, Lilium rhodopaeum. 13s, Tulipa urumoffii. 23s, Lilium jankae. 43s, Tulipa rhodopaea.

1978, June 27

2503 A956 1s multicolored 3 3
2504 " 2s " 3 3
2505 " 3s " 3 3
2506 " 13s " 21 9
2507 " 23s " 40 18
2508 " 43s " 75 35
Nos. 2503-2508 (6) 1.45 71

Yacht Cor Caroli and Map of Voyage A957

1978 Photo. *Perf. 13*

2509 A957 23s multicolored 40 18

First Bulgarian around-the-world voyage, Capt. Georgi Georgiev, Dec. 20, 1976–Dec. 20, 1977.

Market, by Naiden Petkov—A958

Views of Sofia: 5s, Street, by Emil Stoichev. 13s, Street, by Boris Ivanov. 23s, Tolbukhin Boulevard, by Nikola Tanev. 35s, National Theater, by Nikola Petrov. 53s, Market, by Anton Mitov.

1978, Aug. 28 Litho. *Perf. 12½x12*

2510 A958 2s multicolored 3 3
2511 " 5s " 10 3
2512 " 13s " 22 10
2513 " 23s " 40 18
2514 " 35s " 60 28
2515 " 53s " 95 45
Nos. 2510-2515 (6) 2.30 1.07

Miniature Sheet

Sleeping Venus, by Giorgione—A959

1978, Sept. 6 Photo. *Imperf.*

2516 A959 1 l multicolored 2.00

No. 2516 has light green decorative margin. Size: 71x71mm.

View of Varna—A960

1978, July 13 Photo. *Perf. 13*

2517 A960 13s multicolored 22 10

63rd Esperanto Congress, Varna, July 29–Aug. 5.

Dryocopus Martius A961

Woodpeckers: 2s, Dendrocopos syriacus. 3s, Picoides tridactylus. 13s, Dendrocopos medius. 23s, Dendrocopos minor. 43s, Picus viridis.

1978, Sept. 1

2518 A961 1s multicolored 3 3
2519 " 2s " 3 3
2520 " 3s " 5 3
2521 " 13s " 22 10
2522 " 23s " 40 18
2523 " 43s " 75 35
Nos. 2518-2523 (6) 1.48 72

Battle A962

1978, Sept. 5

2524 A962 2s red & brown 3 3

55th anniversary of September uprising.

Souvenir Sheet

National Theater, Sofia A963

Photogravure and Engraved

1978, Sept. 8 *Perf. 12x11½*

Multicolored

2525 Sheet of 4 3.00
a. A963 40s *shown* 70
b. " 40s *Festival Hall, Sofia* 70
c. " 40s *Charles Bridge, Prague* 70
d. " 40s *Belvedere Palace, Prague* 70

PRAGA '78 and PHILASERDICA '79 Philatelic Exhibitions. No. 2525 has pink marginal inscriptions and PRAGA and PHILASERDICA emblems. Size: 153x112mm.

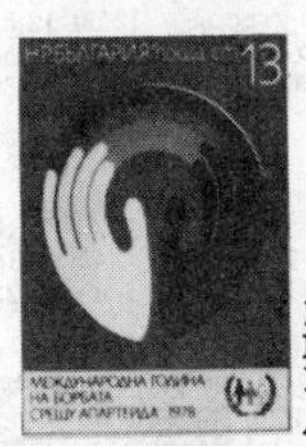

Black and White Hands, Human Rights Emblem
A964

1978, Oct. 3 Photo. ***Perf. 13x13½***

2526	A964	13s multicolored	22	10

Anti-Apartheid Year.

Gotse Deltchev
A965

Bulgarian Computer
A966

1978 Photo. ***Perf. 13***

2527	A965	13s multicolored	22	10

Gotse Deltchev (1872–1903), patriot.

1978

2528	A966	2s multicolored	3	3

International Sample Fair, Plovdiv.

Guerrillas—A967

1978

2529	A967	5s blk. & rose red	10	3

75th anniversary of the Ilinden and Preobrazhene revolts.

"Pipe Line" and Flags
A968

1978, Oct. 3

2530	A968	13s multicolored	22	10

Construction of gas pipe line from Orenburg to Russian border.

Human Pyramid
A969

1978, Oct. 4 ***Perf. 13x13½***

2531	A969	13s multicolored	22	10

3rd World Acrobatics Championships, Sofia.

SEMI-POSTAL STAMPS.

Regular Issues of 1911-20 Surcharged:

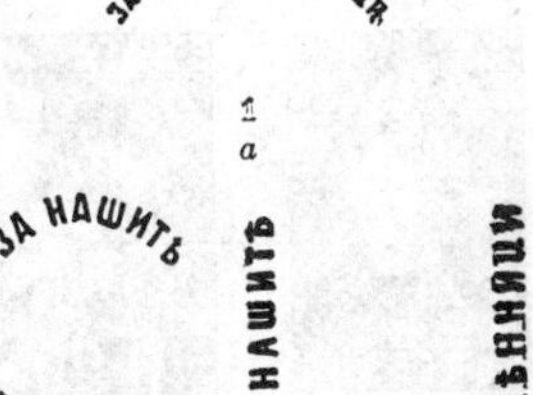

a b c

Perf. 11½x12, 12x11½.

1920, June 20 **Unwmkd.**

B1	A43	(*a*)	2s+1s olive green	3	3
B2	A44	(*b*)	5s+2½s green	4	4
B3	"	(")	10s+5s rose	4	4
B4	"	(")	15s+7½s violet	4	4
B5	"	(")	25s+12½s dp. bl.	5	5
B6	"	(")	30s+15s chocolate	5	5
B7	"	(")	50s+25s yel. brn.	5	5
B8	A29	(*c*)	1l+50s dk. brn.	10	10
B9	A37a	(*a*)	2l+1l brn. org.	15	15
B10	A38	(")	3l+1½l claret	30	30
			Nos. B1–B10 (10)	85	85

The surtax aided returned prisoners of war. Nos. B1–B7 exist imperf. Price $7.50.

Souvenir Sheet

SP1

1937, Nov. 22 Photo. ***Imperf.***

B11	SP1	2l+18l ultramarine	3.00	3.00

Issued to commemorate the 19th anniversary of the accession of Tsar Boris III to the throne. Size: 80x115mm.

Stamps of 1917-21 Surcharged in Black

Наводненнето
1939
1+1
лсва

1939, Oct. 22 ***Perf. 12½, 12***

B12	A34	1l+1l on 15s slate	8	8
B13	A69	2(l)+1(l) on 1½l olive green	10	10
B14	"	4(l)+2(l) on 2l deep green	12	12
B15	"	7(l)+4(l) on 3l Prussian blue	40	40
B16	"	14(l)+7(l) on 5l red brown	50	50
		Nos. B12–B16 (5)	1.20	1.20

The surtax aided victims of the Sevlievo flood.

The surcharge on Nos. B13–B16 omits "leva."

Map of Bulgaria
SP2

1947, June 6 Typo. *Perf. 11½*

B17 SP2 20l+10l dark brown red & green 50 40

Issued to commemorate the 30th Jubilee Esperanto Congress, Sofia, 1947.

Postman
SP3

Radio Towers
SP6

Designs: 10l+5l, Lineman. 20l+10l, Telephone operators.

1947, Nov. 5

B18	SP3	4l+ 2l olive brown	7	7
B19	"	10l+ 5l bright red	7	7
B20	"	20l+10l deep ultra.	15	15
B21	SP6	40l+20l chocolate	45	45

Christo Ganchev
SP7

Actors' Portraits: 10l+6l, Adriana Budevska. 15l+7l, Vasil Kirkov. 20l+15l, Sava Ognianov. 30l+20l, Krostyu Sarafov.

1947, Dec. 8 Litho. *Perf. 10½*

B22	SP7	9l+5l Prussian grn.	10	10
B23	"	10l+6l carmine lake	10	10
B24	"	15l+7l rose violet	12	12
B25	"	20l+15l ultramarine	22	22
B26	"	30l+20l violet brown	50	50
		Nos. B22-B26 (5)	1.04	1.04

National Theater, 50th anniversary.

Souvenir Sheet

Olympic Emblem—SP8

1964, Oct. 10 Litho. *Imperf.*

B27 SP8 40s+20s bister, red & blue 2.25 1.75

Issued to commemorate the 18th Olympic Games, Tokyo, Oct. 10-25. No. B27 measures 60x68mm.

Horsemanship Type of 1965
Miniature Sheet

Design: 40s+20s, Hurdle race.

1965, Sept. 30 Photo. *Imperf.*

B28 A630 40s+20s bluish gray, gold & violet black 1.75 1.25

No. B28 measures 80x79mm.

Space Exploration Type of 1966

Designs: 20s+10s, Yuri A. Gagarin, Alexei Leonov and Valentina Tereshkova. 30s+10s, Rocket and globe.

1966, Sept. 29 Photo. *Perf. 11½x11*

B29 A652 20s+10s purple & gray 70 40

Miniature Sheet
Imperf.

B30 A652 30s+10s gray, terra cotta & black 1.20 1.20

Issued to publicize Russian space explorations. No. B30 measures 59x51mm.

Winter Olympic Games Type of 1967

Sports and Emblem: 20s+10s, Slalom. 40s+10s, Figure skating couple.

1967, Sept. Photo. *Perf. 11*

B31 A687 20s+10s multi. 60 20

Souvenir Sheet
Imperf.

B32 A687 40s+10s multi. 1.20 1.00

Issued to publicize the 10th Winter Olympic Games, Grenoble, France, Feb. 6-8, 1968. No. B32 has silver and bister marginal design. Size: 68x68mm.

Type of Olympic Games Issue, 1968

Designs: 20s+10s, Rowing. 50s+10s, Stadium, Mexico City, and communications satellite.

1968, June 24 Photo. *Perf. 10½*

B33 A702 20s+10s vio. blue, gray & pink 60 20

Miniature Sheet
Imperf.

B34 A702 50s+10s gray, blk. & Prus. blue 1.25 1.00

Issued to publicize the 19th Olympic Games, Mexico City, Oct. 12-27. No. B34 measures 75x75mm.

Sports Type of Regular Issue, 1969

Designs: 13s+5s, Woman with ball. 20s+10s, Acrobatic jump.

1969, Oct. Photo. *Perf. 11*

Gymnasts in Light Gray

B35	A732	13s+5s bright rose & violet	25	10
B36	"	20s+10s citron & blue green	60	30

Issued to publicize the Championships for Artistic Gymnastics in Varna.

Miniature Sheet

Soccer Ball
SP9

1970, Mar. 4 Photo. *Imperf.*

B37 SP9 80s+20s org., black, silver & blue 2.00 2.00

Issued to publicize the 9th World Soccer Championships for the Jules Rimet Cup, Mexico City, May 30-June 21, 1970. No. B37 measures 55x73½mm.

Souvenir Sheet

Yuri A. Gagarin—SP10

1971, Apr. 12 Photo. *Imperf.*

B38 SP10 40s+20s multi. 1.30 1.00

10th anniversary of the first man in space. No. B38 measures 80x53mm.

Bulgarian Lion, Magnifying Glass, Stamp Tongs
SP11

1971, July 10 Photo. *Perf. 12½*

B39 SP11 20s+10s brn. org., black & gold 60 32

11th Congress of Bulgarian Philatelists, Sofia, July, 1971.

AIR POST STAMPS.

Regular Issues of 1925-26
Overprinted in Various Colors

1927-28 *Perf. 11½.* **Unwmkd.**

C1	A76	2l olive (R) ('28)	1.00	60
C2	A74	4l lake & yellow (Bl)	85	60
C3	A77	10l brown black & brown orange (G) ('28)	15.00	10.00

Overprinted Vertically and Surcharged with New Value.

C4	A77	1(l) on 6l deep blue & pale lemon (C)	1.00	60
		a. Inverted surcharge	*325.00*	*250.00*
		b. Pair, one without surcharge	*400.00*	

Nos. C2-C4 with overprint in changed colors were prepared but not issued. Price $12.50.

Dove Delivering Message
AP1

Junkers Plane, Rila Monastery
AP2

1931, Oct. 28 **Typographed.**

C5	AP1	1(l) dark green	25	10
C6	"	2(l) maroon	25	10
C7	"	6(l) deep blue	40	20
C8	"	12(l) carmine	40	30
C9	"	20(l) dark violet	65	50
C10	"	30(l) deep orange	1.00	65
C11	"	50(l) orange brown	2.00	1.25
		Nos. C5-C11 (7)	4.95	3.10

Counterfeits exist.

1932, May 9

C12	AP2	18l blue green	12.50	12.50
C13	"	24l deep red	12.50	12.50
C14	"	28l ultramarine	12.50	12.50

1938, Dec. 27

C15	AP1	1(l) violet brown	15	7
C16	"	2(l) green	20	10
C17	"	6(l) deep rose	45	18
C18	"	12(l) peacock blue	45	22

Counterfeits exist.

Mail Plane
AP3

Plane over Tsar Assen's Tower
AP4

Designs: 4 l, Plane over Bachkovski Monastery. 6 l, Bojurishte Airport, Sofia. 10 l, Plane, train and motorcycle. 12 l, Planes over Sofia Palace. 16 l, Plane over Pirin Valley. 19 l, Plane over Rila Monastery. 30 l, Plane and Swallow. 45 l, Plane over Sofia Cathedral. 70 l, Plane over Shipka Monument. 100 l, Plane and Royal Cipher.

Photogravure.

1940, Jan. 15 *Perf. 13.*

C19	AP3	1l dark green	8	6
C20	AP4	2l crimson	70	6
C21	"	4l red orange	15	8
C22	AP3	6l deep blue	25	10
C23	AP4	10l dark brown	40	20
C24	AP3	12l dull brown	35	17
C25	"	16l brt. blue violet	45	22
C26	"	19l sapphire	50	30
C27	AP4	30l rose lake	85	50
C28	"	45l gray violet	1.75	90
C29	"	70l rose pink	1.60	90
C30	"	100l dp. slate blue	4.00	2.75
		Nos. C19-C30 (12)	11.08	6.24

Nos. 368 and 370 Overprinted in Black

1945, Jan. 26

C31	A181	1l bright green	5	5
C32	"	4l red orange	5	5

A similar overprint on Nos. O4, O5, O7 and O8 was privately applied.

Type of Parcel Post Stamps of 1944 Surcharged or Overprinted in Various Colors

10 10

Imperf.

C37	PP5	10l on 100l dull yellow (Bl)	12	10
C38	"	45l on 100l dull yellow (C)	18	15
C39	"	75l on 100l dull yellow (G)	30	25
C40	"	100l dull yellow (V)	50	35

Plane and Sun
AP16

Pigeon with Letter
AP17

Plane and Letter
AP18

Wings and Posthorn
AP19

Winged Letter
AP20

Plane and Sun
AP21

Pigeon and Posthorn
AP22

Mail Plane
AP23

Conventionalized Figure Holding Pigeon
AP24

1946, July 15 Litho. *Perf. 13*

C41	AP16	1 l dull lilac	5	4
C42	"	2 l slate gray	5	4
C43	AP17	4 l violet black	6	5
C44	AP18	6 l blue	6	5
C45	AP19	10 l turquoise green	6	5
C46	"	12 l yellow brown	8	6
C47	AP20	16 l rose violet	8	6
C48	AP19	19 l carmine	12	6
C49	AP21	30 l orange	18	6
C50	AP22	45 l light olive green	25	18
C51	"	75 l red brown	35	10
C52	AP23	100 l slate black	65	20
C53	AP24	100 l red	65	35
		Nos. C41-C53 (13)	2.64	1.30

No. C47 exists imperf. Price $90.

People's Republic

Plane over Plovdiv
AP25

1947, Aug. 31 Photo. *Imperf.*

C54	AP25	40 l dull olive green	40	40

Plovdiv International Fair, 1947.

Baldwin's Tower
AP26

1948, May 23 Litho. *Perf. 11½*

C55	AP26	50 l olive brown, *cream*	75	50

Issued to commemorate Stamp Day and the 10th Congress of Bulgarian Philatelic Societies, June 1948.

Romanian and Bulgarian Parliament Buildings
AP27

Romanian and Bulgarian Flags, Bridge over Danube
AP28

1948, Nov. 3 Photogravure

Cream Paper

C56	AP27	40 l olive gray	15	12
C57	AP28	100 l red violet	45	30

Issued to publicize Romanian-Bulgarian friendship.

Mausoleum of Pleven
AP29

1949, June 26

C58	AP29	50 l brown	1.25	1.00

Issued to commemorate the 7th Congress of Bulgarian Philatelic Associations, June 26–27, 1949.

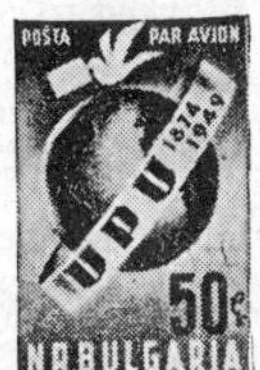

Symbols of the U.P.U.
AP30

Frontier Guard and Dog
AP31

1949, Oct. 10 *Perf. 11½*

C59	AP30	50 l violet blue	75	60

Issued to commemorate the 75th anniversary of the formation of the Universal Postal Union.

1949, Oct. 31

C60	AP31	60 l olive black	75	60

Dimitrov Mausoleum
AP32

1950, July 3 *Perf. 10½.*

C61	AP32	40 l olive brown	1.25	1.00

Issued to commemorate the first anniversary of the death of George Dimitrov, statesman.

Belogradchic Rocks
AP33

Air View of Plovdiv Fair
AP34

Designs: 16s, Beach, Varna. 20s, Harvesting grain. 28s, Rila monastery. 44s, Studena dam. 60s, View of Dimitrovgrad. 80s, View of Trnovo. 1 l, University building, Sofia. 4 l, Partisans' Monument.

1954, Apr. 1 *Perf. 13* Unwmkd.

C62	AP33	8s olive black	6	3
C63	AP34	12s rose brown	6	3
C64	AP33	16s brown	6	3
C65	"	20s brown red, *cream*	7	3
C66	"	28s deep blue, *cream*	15	3
C67	"	44s violet brown, *cream*	20	5
C68	"	60s red brown, *cream*	35	8
C69	AP34	80s dark green, *cream*	35	12
C70	AP33	1 l dk. blue green, *cream*	1.00	15
C71	AP34	4 l deep blue	2.00	55
		Nos. C62-C71 (10)	4.30	1.10

Glider on Mountainside
AP35

Designs:
60s, Glider over airport. 80s, Three gliders.

1956, Oct. 15 Photogravure

C72	AP35	44s bright blue	20	10
C73	"	60s purple	40	15
C74	"	80s dark blue green	50	20

Issued to commemorate the 30th anniversary of glider flights in Bulgaria.

Passenger Plane
AP36

1957, May 21 *Perf. 13* Unwmkd.

C75	AP36	80s deep blue	50	15

Issued to commemorate the tenth anniversary of civil aviation in Bulgaria.

Sputnik 3 over Earth
AP37

1958, Nov. 28 *Perf. 11*

C76	AP37	80s bright greenish blue	2.00	1.50

International Geophysical Year, 1957–58. Exists imperf.; price $4.50.

Lunik 1 Leaving Earth for Moon
AP38

1959, Feb. 28 *Perf. 10½*

C77	AP38	2 l bright blue & ochre	2.25	1.75

Issued to commemorate the launching of the first man-made satellite to orbit the moon. No. C77 exists imperf. in slightly different colors. Price $5 unused, $3.75 cancelled.

Statue of Liberty and Tu-110 Airliner
AP39

Perf. 10½

1959, Nov. 11 Photo. Unwmkd.

C78	AP39	1 l violet blue & pink	1.00	50

Issued to commemorate the visit of Prime Minister Khrushchev of Russia to the United States. Exists imperf. Price $4 unused, $2 cancelled.

Lunik 2 and Moon
AP40

1960, June 23 Litho. *Perf. 11*

C79	AP40	1.25 l blue, black & yellow	2.25	1.75

Russian rocket to the Moon, Sept. 12, 1959.

Sputnik 5 and Dogs Belka and Strelka
AP41

1961, Jan. 14 Photo. *Perf. 11*

C80	AP41	1.25 l bright greenish blue & orange	2.25	1.00

Russian rocket flight of Aug. 19, 1970.

Maj. Yuri A. Gagarin and Vostok 1—AP42

1961, Apr. 26 **Unwmkd.**

C81 AP42 4 l greenish blue, black & red 2.00 1.00

First manned space flight, Apr. 12, 1961.

Soviet Space Dogs AP43

1961, June 28 ***Perf. 11***

C82 AP43 2 l slate & dark carmine 1.25 75

Venus-bound Rocket AP44

1961, June 28

C83 AP44 2 l brt. blue, yel. & orange 2.00 1.00

Issued to commemorate the Soviet launching of the Venus space probe, Feb. 12, 1961.

Maj. Gherman Titov AP45

Design: 1.25 l, Spaceship Vostok 2.

1961, Nov. 20 Photo. ***Perf. 11x10½***

C84 AP45 75s dk. olive green & gray grn. 1.00 50
C85 " 1.25 l violet blue, lt. blue & pink 1.25 60

Issued to commemorate the first manned space flight around the world, Maj. Gherman Titov of Russia, Aug. 6–7, 1961.

Iskar River Narrows AP46

Designs: 2s, Varna and sailboat. 3s, Melnik. 10s, Trnovo. 40s, Pirin mountains.

1962, Feb. 3 ***Perf. 13*** **Unwmkd.**

C86 AP46 1s blue green & gray blue 3 3
C87 " 2s blue & pink 5 3
C88 " 3s brn. & ochre 7 3
C89 " 10s black & lemon 25 6
C90 " 40s dk. grn. & grn. 1.00 15
Nos. C86–C90 (5) 1.40 30

Ilyushin Turboprop Airliner AP47

1962, Aug. 18 ***Perf. 11***

C91 AP47 13s blue & black 50 15

15th anniversary of TABSO airline.

Konstantin E. Tsiolkovsky and Rocket Launching—AP48

Design: 13s, Earth, moon and rocket on future flight to the moon.

1962, Sept. 24 ***Perf. 11***

C92 AP48 5s dp. grn. & gray 75 20
C93 " 13s ultra. & yellow 75 15

Issued to commemorate the 13th meeting of the International Astronautical Federation.

Maj. Andrian G. Nikolayev AP49

Designs: 2s, Lt. Col. Pavel R. Popovich. 40s, Vostoks 3 and 4 in orbit.

1962, Dec. 9 **Photo.** **Unwmkd.**

C94 AP49 1s blue, slate green & black 5 3
C95 " 2s blue green, green & blk. 10 3
C96 " 40s dk. blue green, pink & black 1.50 10

First Russian group space flight of Vostoks 3 and 4, Aug. 12–15, 1962.

Spacecraft "Mars 1" Approaching Mars—AP50

Design: 13s, Rocket launching spacecraft, Earth, Moon and Mars.

1963, Feb. 25 ***Perf. 11*** **Unwmkd.**

C97 AP50 5s multicolored 35 10
C98 " 13s " 85 15

Issued to commemorate the launching of the Russian spacecraft "Mars 1," Nov. 1, 1962.

Lt. Col. Valeri F. Bykovski AP51

Designs: 2s, Lt. Valentina Tereshkova. 5s, Globe and trajectories.

1963, Aug. 26 ***Perf. 11½*** **Unwmkd.**

C99 AP51 1s pale violet & Prussian blue 5 4
C100 " 2s citron & red brown 8 5
C101 " 5s rose & dk. red 15 6

Issued to commemorate the space flights of Valeri Bykovski, June 14–19, and Valentina Tereshkova, first woman cosmonaut, June 16–19, 1963. An imperf. souvenir sheet contains one 50s stamp showing Spasski tower and globe in lilac and red brown. Light blue border with red brown inscription. Size: 77x67mm. Price $1.50.

See also No. CB3.

Nos. C99–C100 Surcharged in Magenta or Green

МЕЖДУНАРОДНА
КОСМИЧЕСКА
ИЗЛОЖБА
РИЧИОНЕ·1964
ST 10

1964, Aug. 22

C102 AP51 10s on 1s pale vio. & Prus. bl. (M) 25 10
C103 " 20s on 2s citron & red brown (G) 45 20

Issued to commemorate the International Space Exhibition in Riccione, Italy. Overprint in Italian on No. C103.

St. John's Monastery, Rila AP52

Design: 13s, Notre Dame, Paris; French inscription.

1964, Dec. 22 **Photo.** ***Perf. 11½***

C104 AP52 5s pale brown & black 20 5
C105 " 13s light ultra. & slate blue 40 15

Issued to commemorate the philatelic exhibition at St. Ouen (Seine) organized by the Franco-Russian Philatelic Circle and philatelic organizations in various People's Democracies.

Paper Mill, Bukijovtz AP53

Designs: 10s, Metal works, Plovdiv. 13s, Metal works, Kremikovtsi. 20s, Oil refinery, Stara-Zagora. 40s, Fertilizer plant, Stara-Zagora. 1 l, Rest home, Meded.

1964–68 ***Perf. 13*** **Unwmkd.**

C106 AP53 8s greenish blue 20 4
C107 " 10s red lilac 25 6
C108 " 13s bright violet 30 8
C109 " 20s slate blue 55 12
C110 " 40s dk. olive green 1.00 30
C111 " 1 l red ('68) 2.00 50
Nos. C106–C111 (6) 4.30 1.10

Three-master AP54 **Veliko Turnovo AP55**

Means of Communication: 2s, Postal coach. 3s, Old steam locomotive. 5s, Early cars. 10s, Montgolfier balloon. 13s, Early plane. 20s, Jet planes. 40s, Rocket and satellites. 1 l, Postrider.

1969, Mar. 31 Photo. ***Perf. 13x12½***

C112 AP54 1s gray & multi. 3 3
C113 " 2s " " 3 3
C114 " 3s " " 5 3
C115 AP54 5s gray & multi. 8 3
C116 " 10s " " 16 6
C117 " 13s " " 20 8
C118 " 20s " " 32 12
C119 " 40s " " 65 30
Nos. C112–C119 (8) 1.52 68

Miniature Sheet

Imperf.

C120 AP54 1 l gold & orange 1.60 1.60

Issued to publicize SOFIA 1969 Philatelic Exhibition, Sofia, May 31–June 8. No. C120 contains one stamp, silver marginal inscription. Size: 57x54mm.

1973, July 30 **Photo.** ***Perf. 13***

Designs: Historic buildings in various cities.

Multicolored

C121 AP55 2s *shown* 3 3
C122 " 13s *Roussalka* 35 15
C123 " 20s *Plovdiv* 1.00 25
C124 " 28s *Sofia* 75 30

Alexei Leonov Floating in Space—AP56

Designs: 25s, Mariner 6, US spacecraft. 35s, Venera 4, USSR Venus probe.

1977, Oct. 14 **Photo.** ***Perf. 13½***

C125 AP56 12s multicolored 20 8
C126 " 25s " 45 20
C127 " 35s " 62 28

Space era, 20 years.

TU-154, Balkanair Emblem AP57

1977 ***Perf. 13***

C128 AP57 35s ultra. & multi. 62 28

30th anniversary of Bulgarian airline, Balkanair. No. C128 issued in sheets of 6 stamps and 3 labels (in lilac) with commemorative inscription and Balkanair emblem.

Baba Vida Fortress AP58

Design: 35s, Peace Bridge, connecting Rousse, Bulgaria, with Giurgiu, Romania.

1978 **Photo.** ***Perf. 13***

C129 AP58 25s multicolored 45 20
C130 " 35s " 62 28

The Danube, European Intercontinental Waterway. Issued in sheets containing 5 each of Nos. C129–C130 and 2 labels, one showing course of Danube, the other hydrofoil and fish.

Red Cross AP59

1978, Mar. Photo. *Perf. 13*

C131 AP59 25s multicolored 45 20

Centenary of Bulgarian Red Cross.

AIR POST SEMI-POSTAL STAMPS.

Statue of Liberty, Plane and Bridge
SPAP1

Lithographed.

1947, May 24 *Perf. 11½.* **Unwmkd.**

CB1 SPAP1 70l+30l red brown 65 40

Issued to honor the 5th Philatelic Congress, Trnovo, and the Centenary International Philatelic Exhibition, New York, May, 1947.

Bulgarian Worker
SPAP2

Photogravure.

1948, Feb. 28 *Perf. 12x11½.*

CB2 SPAP2 60l (+16l) henna brown, *cream* 28 20

Issued to commemorate the 2nd Bulgarian Workers' Congress, and sold by subscription only, at a premium of 16 levas over face value.

Type of Air Post Stamps, 1963

Design: Valeri Bykovski and Valentina Tereshkova.

1963, Aug. 26 *Perf. 11½* **Unwmkd.**

CB3 AP51 20s+10s pale bluish grn. & dk. green 1.00 25

See note after No. C101.

SPECIAL DELIVERY STAMPS.

Postman on Bicycle
SD1

Postman on Motorcycle
SD3

Mail Car
SD2

Photogravure.

1939 *Perf. 13* **Unwmkd.**

E1	SD1	5l deep blue	50	20
E2	SD2	6l copper brown	25	20
E3	SD3	7l golden brown	40	20
E4	SD2	8l red orange	35	20
E5	SD1	20l bright rose	50	40
		Nos. E1–E5 (5)	2.00	1.20

POSTAGE DUE STAMPS.

D1 D2

Large Lozenge Perf. 5½ to 6½.

1884 Typographed. **Unwmkd.**

J1	D1	5s orange	150.00	17.50
J2	"	25s lake	55.00	10.00
J3	"	50s blue	7.50	7.50

1886 *Imperf.*

J4	D1	5s orange	70.00	2.50
J5	"	25s lake	90.00	2.50
J6	"	50s blue	4.00	2.50

1887 *Perf. 11½.*

J7	D1	5s orange	6.00	1.00
J8	"	25s lake	6.00	1.00
J9	"	50s blue	4.00	1.00

Same, Redrawn.
24 horizontal lines of shading in upper part instead of 30 lines.

1892 *Perf. 10½, 11½*

J10	D1	5s orange	8.50	1.00
J11	"	25s lake	8.50	1.00

1893 Pelure Paper.

J12	D2	5s orange	10.00	3.00

D3 D4

Imperf.

1895 Ordinary Paper

J13	D3	30s on 50s blue	5.00	2.50

Perf. 10½, 11½

J14	D3	30s on 50s blue	7.00	3.50

Wmkd. Coat of Arms in the Sheet.

1896 *Perf. 13*

J15	D4	5s orange	2.75	55
J16	"	10s purple	2.50	60
J17	"	30s green	2.50	40

Nos. J15–J17 are also known on unwatermarked paper from the edges of sheets.

In 1901 a cancellation, "T" in circle, was applied to Nos. 60–65 and used provisionally as postage dues.

D5

D6

1901–04 *Perf. 11½* **Unwmkd.**

J19	D5	5s dull rose	20	10
J20	"	10s yellow green	50	15
J21	"	20s dull blue ('04)	3.00	15
J22	"	30s violet brown	30	15
J23	"	50s orange ('02)	4.25	3.00
		Nos. J19–J23 (5)	8.25	3.55

Nos. J19–J23 exist imperf. and in pairs imperf. between. Price, imperf., $250.

Thin Semi-Transparent Paper.

1915 *Perf. 11½* **Unwmkd.**

J24	D6	5s green	10	5
J25	"	10s purple	12	5
J26	"	20s dull rose	15	8
J27	"	30s deep orange	45	25
J28	"	50s deep blue	25	10
		Nos. J24–J28 (5)	1.07	53

1919–21 *Perf. 11½, 12x11½*

J29	D6	5s emerald	10	6
		a. 5s gray green ('21)	20	20
J30	"	10s violet	10	6
J31	"	20s salmon	10	6
		a. 20s yellow	15	7
J32	"	30s orange	10	8
		a. 30s red org. ('21)	1.00	1.00
J33	"	50s blue	10	6
J34	"	1l emerald ('21)	6	4
J35	"	2l rose ('21)	10	4
J36	"	3l brown orange('21)	15	4
		Nos. J29–J36 (8)	81	44

Stotinki values of the above series surcharged 10s or 20s were used as ordinary postage stamps. See Nos. 182–185.

The 1919 printings are on thicker white paper with clean-cut perforations, the 1921 printings on thicker grayish paper with rough perforations.

Most of this series exist imperforate and in pairs imperforate between.

Heraldic Lion
D7

Lion of Trnovo
D8

National Arms
D9

1932, Aug. 15 Thin Paper

J37	D7	1l olive bistre	40	30
J38	"	2l rose brown	40	30
J39	"	6l brown violet	1.00	40

1933, Apr. 10

J40	D8	20s dark brown	3	3
J41	"	40s deep blue	4	3
J42	"	80s carmine rose	4	3
J43	D9	1l orange brown	20	4
J44	"	2l olive	25	6
J45	"	6l dull violet	15	12
J46	"	14l ultramarine	25	20
		Nos. J40–J46 (7)	96	51

National Arms
D10

Arms of the People's Republic
D11

1947, June Typo. *Perf. 10½*

J47	D10	1l chocolate	4	4
J48	"	2l deep claret	4	4
J49	"	8l deep orange	6	6
J50	"	20l blue	18	8

1951 *Perf. 11½x10½*

J51	D11	1l chocolate	3	3
J52	"	2l claret	3	3
J53	"	8l red orange	12	12
J54	"	20l deep blue	35	30

OFFICIAL STAMPS.

Bulgarian Coat of Arms
O1 O2

Typographed

1942 *Perf. 13* **Unwmkd.**

O1	O1	10s yellow green	3	3
O2	"	30s red	3	3
O3	"	50s bistre	3	3
O4	O2	1l violet blue	3	3
O5	"	2l dark green	4	3
O6	"	3l lilac	6	4
O7	"	4l rose	8	3
O8	"	5l carmine	10	4
		Nos. O1–O8 (8)	40	26

1944 *Perf. 10½x11½*

O9	O2	1l blue	10	4
O10	"	2l bright red	10	4

Lion Rampant
O3 O4

O5

1945 *Imperf.*

O11	O5	1l pink	3	3

Perf. 10½x11½, Imperf.

O12	O3	2l blue green	3	3
O13	O4	3l bistre brown	3	3
O14	"	4l light ultramarine	3	3
O15	O5	5l brown lake	4	3
		Nos. O11–O15 (5)	16	15

In 1950, four stamps prepared for official use were issued as regular postage stamps. See Nos. 724–727.

PARCEL POST STAMPS.

Weighing Packages
PP1

Parcel Post
PP2

Designs: 3l, 8l, 20l, Parcel post truck. 4l, 6l, 10l, Motorcycle.

Perf. 12½x13½, 13½x12½.

1941-42 Photogravure. **Unwmkd.**

Q1	PP1	1l slate green	3	3
Q2	PP2	2l crimson	4	3
Q3	"	3l dull brown	4	3
Q4	"	4l red orange	4	3
Q5	PP1	5l deep blue	4	3
Q6	"	5l slate green ('42)	4	3
Q7	PP2	6l red violet	4	3
Q8	"	6l henna brown ('42)	4	3
Q9	PP1	7l dark blue	4	3
Q10	"	7l dark brown ('42)	6	4
Q11	PP2	8l bright blue green	6	3
Q12	"	8l green ('42)	6	3
Q13	"	9l olive gray	6	4
Q14	"	9l deep olive ('42)	8	4
Q15	"	10l orange	6	3
Q16	"	20l gray violet	25	6
Q17	"	30l dull black	25	7
Q18	"	30l sepia ('42)	15	6
		Nos. Q1–Q18 (18)	1.38	67

Arms of Bulgaria
PP5

1944 Lithographed. *Imperf.*

Q21	PP5	1 l dark carmine	3	3
Q22	"	3 l blue green	3	3
Q23	"	5 l dull blue green	4	3
Q24	"	7 l rose lilac	6	3
Q25	"	10 l deep blue	6	3
Q26	"	20 l orange brown	8	3
Q27	"	30 l dk. brn. carmine	15	4
Q28	"	50 l red orange	25	5
Q29	"	100 l blue	50	8
		Nos. Q21–Q29 (9)	1.20	35

POSTAL TAX STAMPS.

The use of stamps Nos. RA1 to RA18 was compulsory on letters, etc., to be delivered on Sundays and holidays. The money received from their sale was used toward maintaining a sanatorium for employees of the post, telegraph and telephone services.

View of Sanatorium
PT1

Sanatorium, Peshtera
PT2

Typographed.

1925–29 *Perf. 11½* Unwmkd.

RA1	PT1	1 l *greenish blue*	2.25	6
RA2	"	1 l chocolate ('26)	1.25	6
RA3	"	1 l orange ('27)	2.25	7
RA4	"	1 l pink ('28)	3.50	8
RA5	"	1 l violet, *pinkish* ('29)	3.50	6
RA6	PT2	2 l blue green	25	6
RA7	"	2 l violet ('27)	25	6
RA8	"	5 l deep blue	3.00	50
RA9	"	5 l rose ('27)	3.00	35
		Nos. RA1–RA9 (9)	19.25	1.30

St. Constantine Sanatorium
PT3

1930–33

RA10	PT3	1 l red brown & olive green	3.50	6
RA11	"	1 l olive green & yellow ('31)	40	6
RA12	"	1 l red violet & olive brown ('33)	40	8

Trojan Rest Home
PT4

Sanatorium
PT5

Wmkd. Wavy Lines. (145)

1935 *Perf. 11, 11½.*

RA13	PT4	1 l chocolate & red orange	25	10
RA14	"	1 l emerald & indigo	25	10
RA15	PT5	5 l red brown & indigo	1.25	30

St. Constantine Sanatorium
PT6

Children at Seashore
PT7

Rest Home
PT8

Photogravure.

1941 *Perf. 13* Unwmkd.

RA16	PT6	1 l dark olive green	4	3
RA17	PT7	2 l red orange	6	4
RA18	PT8	5 l deep blue	20	15

BURMA

See British Commonwealth Section of Vol. I.

BURUNDI

(bo͞o·ro͞on'dē)

LOCATION—Central Africa, adjoining the ex-Belgian Congo Republic, Rwanda and Tanganyika.

GOVT.—Republic.

AREA—10,739 sq. mi.

POP.—3,970,000 (est. 1977).

CAPITAL—Bujumbura.

Burundi was established as an independent country on July 1, 1962. With Rwanda, it had been a United Nations trusteeship territory (Ruanda-Urundi) administered by Belgium. A military coup overthrew the monarchy Nov. 28, 1966.

100 Centimes = 1 Franc

Flower Issue of Ruanda-Urundi, 1953 Overprinted:

Royaume du

Burundi

Photogravure

1962, July 1 *Perf. 11½* Unwmkd.

Flowers in Natural Colors

1	A86	25c dark green & dull orange	20	20
2	"	40c green & salmon	20	20
3	"	60c blue grn. & pink	30	30
4	"	1.25fr dk. grn. & blue	15.00	15.00
5	"	1.50fr violet & apple green	75	75
6	A86	5fr deep plum & lt. blue green	90	90
7	"	7fr dk. grn. & fawn	1.50	1.50
8	"	10fr deep plum & pale olive	2.50	2.50
		Nos. 1–8 (8)	21.35	21.35

Animal Issue of Ruanda-Urundi, 1959–61 with Similar Overprint or Surcharge in Black or Violet Blue.

Size: 23x33mm., 33x23mm.

9	A28	10c brn., crimson & black brown	5	3
10	A29	20c gray, apple green & black	5	3
11	A28	40c magenta, black & gray green	5	3
12	A29	50c green, orange yellow & brn.	6	3
		a. Larger ovpt. and bar	10	10
13	A28	1fr brown, ultra. & black	15	10
14	A29	1.50fr black, gray & orange (VB)	15	10
15	A28	2fr greenish blue, indigo & brown	15	10
16	A29	3fr brown, deep carm. & black	18	5
17	"	3.50fr on 3fr brown, deep carmine & black	20	5
18	"	4fr on 10fr multi. ("XX" 6 mm. wide)	25	8
		a. "XX" 4mm. wide	90	90
19	"	5fr multicolored	35	20
20	"	6.50fr red, orange yellow & brn.	50	20
21	"	8fr blue, magenta & black	60	30
		a. Vio. blue ovpt.	4.00	4.00
22	"	10fr multicolored	60	35

Size: 45x26½mm.

23	A29	20fr multicolored	1.35	75
24	"	50fr red, orange, dp. blue & brown (ovpt. bars 2mm. wide)	2.50	2.00
		a. Ovpt. bars 4mm. wide	3.50	2.25
		Nos. 9–24 (16)	7.19	4.40

On No. 12a, "Burundi" is 13mm. long; bar is continuous line across sheet. On No. 12, "Burundi" is 10mm.; bar is 29mm. No. 12a was issued in 1963.

Two types of overprint exist on 10c, 40c, 1fr and 2fr: I, "du" is below "me"; bar 22½mm. II, "du" below "oy"; bar 20 mm.

The 50c and 3fr exist in two types, besides the larger 50c overprint listed as No. 12: I, "du" is closer to "Royaume" than to "Burundi"; bar is less than 29mm; wording is centered above bar. II, "du" is closer to "Burundi"; bar is more than 30mm.; wording is off-center leftward.

King Mwami Mwambutsa IV and Royal Drummers—A1

Flag and Arms of Burundi
A2

Design: 2fr, 8fr, 50fr, Map of Burundi and King.

Photogravure

1962, Sept. 27 *Perf. 14* Unwmkd.

25	A1	50c dull rose carmine & dark brown	5	3
26	A2	1fr dark green, red & emerald	10	3
27	A1	2fr brown olive & dark brown	18	3
28	"	3fr vermilion & dark brown	20	4
29	A2	4fr Prussian blue, red & emerald	30	5
30	A1	8fr violet & dk. brown	60	10
31	"	10fr brt. grn. & dk. brn.	75	15
32	A2	20fr brown, red & emerald	1.50	30
33	A1	50fr bright pink & dark brown	3.00	65
		Nos. 25–33 (9)	6.68	1.38

Issued to commemorate Burundi's independence, July 1, 1962.

Ruanda-Urundi Nos. 151–152 Surcharged:

HOMMAGE A
DAG HAMMARSKJÖLD
3.50F
ROYAUME DU BURUNDI

Photogravure, Surcharge Engraved

1962, Oct. 31 *Perf. 11½*

Inscription in French

34	A92	3.50fr on 3fr ultra. & red	30	20
35	"	6.50fr on 3fr ultra. & red	55	40
36	"	10fr on 3fr ultra. & red	85	65

Inscription in Flemish

37	A92	3.50fr on 3fr ultra. & red	30	20
38	"	6.50fr on 3fr ultra. & red	55	40
39	"	10fr on 3fr ultra. & red	85	65
		Nos. 34–39 (6)	3.40	2.50

Issued in memory of Dag Hammarskjold, Secretary General of the United Nations, 1953–61.

King Mwami Mwambutsa IV, Map of Burundi and Emblem—A3

1962, Dec. 10 Photo. *Perf. 14*

40	A3	8fr yellow, blue grn. & black brown	90	30
41	"	50fr gray green, blue grn. & blk. brn.	2.50	70

Issued for the World Health Organization drive to eradicate malaria.

Stamps of type A3 without anti-malaria emblem are listed as Nos. 27, 30 and 33.

Sowing Seed over Africa
A4

1963, Mar. 21 *Perf. 14x13*

42	A4	4fr olive & dull purple	20	10
43	"	8fr dp. org. & dull pur.	40	25

44 A4 15fr emer. & dull purple 60 40

Issued for the "Freedom from Hunger" campaign of the U.N. Food and Agriculture Organization.

Nos. 27 and 33 Overprinted in Dark Green

1963, June 19 *Perf. 14* Unwmkd.

45 A1 2fr brown olive & dark brown 3.75 2.50
46 " 50fr bright pink & dark brown 4.25 2.50

Conquest and peaceful use of outer space.

Types of 1962 Inscribed: "Premier Anniversaire" in Red or Magenta

1963, July 1 Photogravure

47 A2 4fr olive, red & emerald (R) 25 10
48 A1 8fr orange & dark brown (M) 40 20
49 " 10fr lilac & dk. brn. (M) 60 30
50 A2 20fr gray, red & emerald (R) 1.50 60

First anniversary of independence.

Nos. 26 and 32 Surcharged in Brown

1963, Sept. 24 *Perf. 14* Unwmkd.

51 A2 6.50fr on 1fr dark green red & emerald 75 20
52 " 15fr on 20fr brown, red & emerald 1.50 50

Red Cross Flag over Globe with Map of Africa
A5

1963, Sept. 26 *Perf. 14x13*

53 A5 4fr emerald, carmine & gray 25 10
54 " 8fr brown olive, carmine & gray 50 20
55 " 10fr blue, car. & gray 75 30
56 " 20fr lilac, car. & gray 1.50 50

Centenary of International Red Cross.

"1962", Arms of Burundi, U.N. and UNESCO Emblems
A6

U.N. Agency Emblems: 8fr, International Telecommunications Union. 10fr, World Meteorological Organization. 20fr, Universal Postal Union. 50fr, Food and Agriculture Organization.

1963, Nov. 4 *Perf. 14* Unwmkd.

57 A6 4fr yellow, olive green & black 25 10
58 A6 8fr pale lilac, Prus. blue & black 45 12
59 " 10fr blue, lilac & black 60 18
60 " 20fr yellow green, green & black 1.20 30
61 " 50fr yellow, red brn. & black 3.00 60
a. Souv. sheet of 2 6.00 6.00
Nos. 57-61 (5) 5.50 1.30

Issued to commemorate the first anniversary of Burundi's admission to the United Nations. No. 61a contains two imperf. stamps with simulated perforations similar to Nos. 60-61. The 20fr stamp shows the FAO and the 50fr the WMO emblems. Gray margin with black inscription. Size: 111x73½mm.

UNESCO Emblem, Scales and Map—A7

Designs: 3.50fr, 6.50fr, Scroll, scales and "UNESCO". 10fr, 20fr, Abraham Lincoln, broken chain and scales.

Lithographed

1963, Dec. 10 *Perf. 14x13½*

62 A7 50c pink, lt. bl. & blk. 3 3
63 " 1.50fr org., lt. bl. & blk. 5 5
64 " 3.50fr terra cotta, light green & black 12 15
65 " 6.50fr light violet, light green & black 25 18
66 " 10fr blue, bister & blk. 40 20
67 " 20fr pale brown, ocher, blue & black 80 35
Nos. 62-67 (6) 1.65 96

Issued to commemorate the 15th anniversary of the Universal Declaration of Human Rights and the centenary of the American Emancipation Proclamation (Nos. 66-67).

Ice Hockey A8 — Impala A9

Designs; 3.50 fr, Women's figure skating. 6.50fr, Torch. 10fr, Men's speed skating. 20fr, Slalom.

Photogravure

1964, Jan 25 *Perf. 14* Unwmkd.

68 A8 50c olive, black & gold 8 3
69 " 3.50fr light brown, black & gold 25 8
70 " 6.50fr pale gray, black & gold 50 15
71 " 10fr gray, blk. & gold 75 20
72 " 20fr tan, blk. & gold 1.50 50
Nos. 68-72 (5) 3.08 96

Issued to publicize the 9th Winter Olympic Games, Innsbruck, Jan. 29-Feb. 9, 1964.

A souvenir sheet contains two stamps (10fr+5fr and 20fr+5fr) in tan, black and gold. Size: 121x65mm.

Canceled to Order

Starting about 1964, prices in the used column are for "canceled to order" stamps. Postally used copies sell for much more.

1964 Lithographed

Animals: 1fr, 5fr, Hippopotamus (horiz.). 1.50fr, 10fr, Giraffe. 2fr, 8fr, Cape buffalo (horiz.). 3fr, 6.50fr, Zebra (horiz.). 3.50fr, 15fr, Defassa waterbuck. 20fr, Cheetah. 50fr, Elephant. 100fr, Lion.

Perf. 14x13, 13x14

Size: 21½x35mm., 35x21½mm.

73 A9 50c multicolored 8 3
74 " 1fr " 10 3
75 " 1.50fr " 12 4
76 " 2fr " 15 4
77 " 3fr " 24 6
78 " 3.50fr " 28 7

Size: 26x42mm., 42x26mm.

79 A9 4fr multicolored 30 8
80 " 5fr " 36 10
81 " 6.50fr " 45 10
82 " 8fr " 50 15
83 " 10fr " 65 15
84 " 15fr " 1.00 25

Perf. 14

Size: 53x33mm.

85 A9 20fr multicolored 1.25 30
86 " 50fr " 3.25 50
87 " 100fr " 6.00 1.00
Nos. 73-87 (15) 14.73 2.90

See also Nos. C1-C7.

Burundi Dancer
A10

Designs: Various Dancers and Drummers.

Lithographed

1964, Aug. 21 *Perf. 14* Unwmkd.

Dancers Multicolored

88 A10 50c gold & emerald 8 3
89 " 1fr gold & vio. blue 10 5
90 " 4fr gold & brt. blue 25 10
91 " 6.50fr gold & red 40 18
92 " 10fr gold & brt. blue 60 25
93 " 15fr gold & emerald 90 30
94 " 20fr gold & red 1.25 45
a. Souv. sheet of 3 5.00
Nos. 88-94 (7) 3.58 1.36

1965, Sept. 10

Dancers Multicolored

88a A10 50c silver & emerald 8 5
89a " 1fr silver & vio. bl. 8 5
90a " 4fr silver & brt. blue 20 10
91a " 6.50fr silver & red 30 15
92a " 10fr silver & brt. blue 50 20
93a " 15fr silver & emerald 60 35
94b " 20fr silver & red 90 60
c. Souv. sheet of 3 4.00
Nos. 88a-94b (7) 2.66 1.50

Issued to commemorate the New York World's Fair, 1964-65. No. 94a contains one each of Nos. 92-94, gold background and bright blue border. No. 94c, dated "1965" in yellow, contains one each of Nos. 92a-94b, silver background and bright blue border. Size of souvenir sheets: 120x100mm.

Pope Paul VI and King Mwami Mwambutsa IV—A11

22 Sainted Martyrs
A12

Designs: 4fr, 14fr, Pope John XXIII and King Mwami.

1964, Nov. 12 Photo. *Perf. 12*

95 A11 50c brt. bl., gold & red brown 5 3
96 A12 1fr magenta, gold & slate 5 5
97 A11 4fr pale rose lilac, gold & brown 20 8
98 A12 8fr red, gold & brn. 45 15
99 A11 14fr light green, gold & brown 90 30
100 " 20fr red brown, gold & green 1.50 50
Nos. 95-100 (6) 3.15 1.11

Issued to commemorate the canonization of 22 African martyrs, Oct. 18, 1964.

Shot Put
A13

African Purple Gallinule
A14

Sports: 1fr, Discus. 3fr, Swimming (horiz.). 4fr, Running. 6.50fr, Javelin, woman. 8fr, Hurdling (horiz.). 10fr, Broad jump (horiz.). 14fr, Diving, woman. 18fr, High jump (horiz.). 20fr, Vaulting (horiz.).

1964, Nov. 18 Litho. *Perf. 14*

101 A13 50c olive & multi. 4 3
102 " 1fr brt. pink & multi. 6 5
103 " 3fr multicolored 15 10
104 " 4fr " 18 12
105 " 6.50fr " 30 18
106 " 8fr lt. bl. & multi. 40 20
107 " 10fr multicolored 50 25
108 " 14fr " 75 30
109 " 18fr bister & multi. 90 40
110 " 20fr gray & multi. 1.00 50
Nos. 101-110 (10) 4.28 2.13

Issued to commemorate the 18th Olympic Games, Tokyo, Oct. 10-25, 1964. See also No. B8.

1965 *Perf. 14* Unwmkd.

Birds: 1fr, 5fr, Little bee eater. 1.50fr, 6.50fr, Secretary bird. 2fr, 8fr, Yellow-billed stork. 3fr, 10fr, Congo peacock. 3.50fr, 15fr, African anhinga. 20fr, Saddle-billed stork. 50fr, Abyssinian ground hornbill. 100fr, Crowned crane.

Birds in Natural Colors

Size: 21x35mm.

111 A14 50c tan, grn. & blk. 4 3

112 A14 1fr pink, magenta & black 5 3
113 " 1.50fr blue & black 6 3
114 " 2fr yel. grn., dk. grn. & black 8 3
115 " 3fr yel., brn. & blk. 10 5
116 " 3.50fr yel. grn., dk. grn. & blk. 10 6

Size: 26x43mm.

117 A14 4fr tan, grn. & blk. 12 8
118 " 5fr pink, magenta & black 15 8
119 " 6.50fr blue & black 20 10
120 " 8fr yel. grn., dk. grn. & black 25 12
121 " 10fr yel., brn. & blk. 35 14
122 " 15fr yel. green, dk. grn. & blk. 50 20

Size: 33x53mm.

123 A14 20fr rose lilac & black 65 25
124 " 50fr yellow, brown & black 1.75 50
125 " 100fr green, yellow & black 3.50 1.00
Nos. 111-125 (15) 7.90 2.70

Issue dates: Nos. 111-116, Mar. 31. Nos. 117-122, Apr. 16. Nos. 123-125, Apr. 30.

See also Nos. C8-C16.

Relay Satellite and Morse Key
A15

Designs: 3fr, Telstar and old telephone handpiece. 4fr, Relay satellite and old wall telephone. 6.50fr, Orbiting Geophysical Observatory and radar screen. 8fr, Telstar II and headphones. 10fr, Sputnik II and radar aerial. 14fr, Syncom and transmission aerial. 20fr, Interplanetary Explorer and tracking aerial.

1965, July 3 Litho. *Perf. 13*

126 A15 1fr multicolored 5 5
127 " 3fr " 10 5
128 " 4fr " 10 10
129 " 6.50fr " 20 15
130 " 8fr " 30 20
131 " 10fr " 35 22
132 " 14fr " 50 30
133 " 20fr " 60 40
Nos. 126-133 (8) 2.20 1.47

Issued to commemorate the centenary of the International Telecommunication Union. Perf. and imperf. souvenir sheets of two contain one each of Nos. 131 and 133. Bluish black margin and gold inscription. Size: 120x86mm. Price, both sheets, $7.50.

Globe and ICY Emblem—A16

Designs: 4fr, Map of Africa and U.N. development emblem. 8fr, Map of Asia and Colombo Plan emblem. 10fr, Globe and U.N. emblem. 18fr, Map of the Americas and Alliance for Progress emblem. 25fr, Map of Europe and EUROPA emblems. 40fr, Map of Outer Space and satellite with U.N. wreath.

1965, Oct. 1 Litho. *Perf. 13*

134 A16 1fr olive grn. & multi. 5 3
135 " 4fr dull blue & multi. 15 3
136 " 8fr pale yel. & multi. 30 10
137 " 10fr lilac & multi. 40 10
138 " 18fr salmon & multi. 60 15
139 " 25fr gray & multi. 85 15
140 " 40fr blue & multi. 1.40 20
a. Souv. sheet of 3 4.50
Nos. 134-140 (7) 3.75 76

Issued for the International Cooperation Year. No. 140a contains one each of Nos. 138-140. Gray margin with multicolored inscription. Size: 101½x100mm.

Protea
A17

Flowers: 1fr, 5fr, Crossandra. 1.50fr, 6.50fr, Ansellia. 2fr, 8fr, Thunbergia. 3fr, 10fr, Schizoglossum. 3.50fr, 15fr, Dissotis. 4fr, 20fr, Protea. 50fr, Gazania. 100fr, Hibiscus. 150fr, Markhamia.

1966 *Perf. 13½* Unwmkd.

Size: 26x26mm.

141 A17 50c multicolored 3 3
142 " 1fr " 3 3
143 " 1.50fr " 5 3
144 " 2fr " 7 3
145 " 3fr " 10 3
146 " 3.50fr " 10 3

Size: 31x31mm.

147 A17 4fr multicolored 12 5
148 " 5fr " 15 8
149 " 6.50fr " 20 10
150 " 8fr " 25 12
151 " 10fr " 30 15
152 " 15fr " 50 20

Size: 39x39mm.

153 A17 20fr multicolored 60 20
154 " 50fr " 1.50 60
155 " 100fr " 3.00 90
156 " 150fr " 4.50 1.25
Nos. 141-156 (16) 11.50 3.83

Issue dates: Nos. 141-147, Feb. 28; Nos. 148-153, May 18; Nos. 154-156, June 15.

See also Nos. C17-C25.

Souvenir Sheets

Allegory of Prosperity and Equality Tapestry by Peter Colfs—A18

1966, Nov. 4 Litho. *Perf. 13½*

157 A18 Sheet of 7 (1.50fr) 75 35
158 " " " " (4fr) 1.75 1.00

Issued to commemorate the 20th anniversary of UNESCO (United Nations Educational, Scientific and Cultural Organization). Each sheet contains 6 stamps showing a reproduction of the Colfs tapestry from the lobby of the General Assembly Building, New York, and one stamp with the UNESCO emblem plus a label. The labels on Nos. 157-158 and C26 are inscribed in French or English. The 3 sheets with French inscription have light blue marginal border. The 3 sheets with English inscription have pink border. Size: 203x124mm. See also No. C26.

Republic

Nos. 141-152, 154-156 Overprinted

REPUBLIQUE DU BURUNDI

1967 Lithographed *Perf. 13½*

Size: 26x26mm.

159 A17 50c multicolored 5 3
160 " 1fr " 5 3
161 " 1.50fr " 6 3
162 " 2fr " 8 3
163 " 3fr " 12 3
164 " 3.50fr " 15 3

Size: 31x31mm.

165 A17 4fr multicolored 1.00 60
166 " 5fr " 18 5
167 " 6.50fr " 20 5
168 " 8fr " 30 5
169 " 10fr " 35 7
170 " 15fr " 50 10

Size: 39x39mm.

171 A17 50fr multicolored 5.00 2.00
172 " 100fr " 9.50 4.00
173 " 150fr " 7.75 3.50
Nos. 159-173 (15) 25.29 10.60

Nos. 111, 113, 116, 118-125 Overprinted "REPUBLIQUE DU BURUNDI" and Horizontal Bar.

1967 Lithographed *Perf. 14*

Birds in Natural Colors

Size: 21x35mm.

174 A14 50c multicolored 1.25 1.00
175 " 1.50fr blue & black 10 3
176 " 3.50fr multicolored 20 3

Size: 26x43mm.

177 A14 5fr multicolored 25 5
178 " 6.50fr blue & black 30 5
179 " 8fr multicolored 40 5
180 " 10fr yellow, brown & black 50 7
181 " 15fr multicolored 80 10

Size: 33x53mm.

182 A14 20fr multicolored 3.00 1.00
183 " 50fr " 7.50 3.00
184 " 100fr " 15.00 6.00
Nos. 174-184 (11) 29.30 11.38

Haplochromis Multicolor
A19

Various Tropical Fish.

1967 Photogravure *Perf. 13½*

Size: 42x19mm.

186 A19 50c multicolored 6 3
187 " 1fr " 6 3
188 " 1.50fr " 8 3
189 " 2fr " 10 3
190 " 3fr " 14 3
191 " 3.50fr " 18 3

Size: 50x25mm.

192 A19 4fr multicolored 18 5
193 " 5fr " 20 5
194 " 6.50fr " 24 5
195 " 8fr " 30 5
196 " 10fr " 36 7
197 " 15fr " 55 10

Size: 59x30mm.

198 A19 20fr multicolored 75 20
199 " 50fr " 2.00 30
200 " 100fr " 4.00 50
201 " 150fr " 6.00 70
Nos. 186-201 (16) 15.20 2.25

Issue Dates: Nos. 186-191, Apr. 4; Nos. 192-197, Apr. 28; Nos. 198-201, May 18.

See also Nos. C46-C54.

Ancestor Figures, Ivory Coast
A20

African Art: 1fr, Seat of Honor, Southeast Congo. 1.50fr, Antelope head, Aribinda Region. 2fr, Buffalo mask, Upper Volta. 4fr, Funeral figures, Southwest Ethiopia.

1967, June 5 Photo. *Perf. 13½*

202 A20 50c silver & multi. 5 5
203 " 1fr " " 5 5
204 " 1.50fr " " 10 5
205 " 2fr " " 12 5
206 " 4fr " " 18 5
Nos. 202-206, C36-C40 (10) 3.50 2.00

Scouts on Hiking Trip
A21

Designs: 1fr, Cooking at campfire. 1.50fr, Lord Baden-Powell. 2fr, Boy Scout and Cub Scout giving Scout sign. 4fr, First aid.

1967, Aug. 9 Photo. *Perf. 13½*

207 A21 50c silver & multi. 5 6
208 " 1fr " " 8 6
209 " 1.50fr " " 10 6
210 " 2fr " " 12 8
211 " 4fr " " 18 8
Nos. 207-211, C41-C45 (10) 3.78 1.54

Issued to commemorate the 60th anniversary of the Boy Scouts and the 12th Boy Scout World Jamboree, Farragut State Park, Idaho, Aug. 1-9.

The Gleaners, by Francois Millet
A22

Paintings Exhibited at EXPO '67: 8fr, The Water Carrier of Seville, by Velazquez. 14fr, The Triumph of Neptune and Amphitrite, by Nicolas Poussin. 18fr, Acrobat Standing on a Ball, by Picasso. 25fr, Marguerite van Eyck, by Jan van Eyck. 40fr, St. Peter Denying Christ, by Rembrandt.

1967, Oct. 12 Photo. *Perf. 13½*

212	A22	4fr multicolored	25	8
213	"	8fr "	48	10
214	"	14fr "	80	14
215	"	18fr "	1.10	20
216	"	25fr "	1.60	35
217	"	40fr "	2.40	50
		a. Souv. sheet of 2	4.00	2.00
		Nos. 212-217 (6)	6.63	1.37

Issued to commemorate EXPO '67 International Exhibition, Montreal, Apr. 28–Oct. 27. Printed in sheets of 10 stamps and 2 labels inscribed in French or English. No. 217a contains one each of Nos. 216–217. Blue margin with black and red inscription. Size: 105x105mm. Exists imperf.

Place de la Revolution and Pres. Michel Micombero
A23

Designs: 5fr, President Michel Micombero and flag. 14fr, Formal garden and coat of arms. 20fr, Modern building and coat of arms.

1967, Nov. 23 *Perf. 13½*

218	A23	5fr multicolored	25	10
219	"	14fr "	60	20
220	"	20fr "	90	20
221	"	30fr "	1.20	45

First anniversary of the Republic.

Madonna by Carlo Crivelli
A24

Designs: 1fr, Adoration of the Shepherds by Juan Bautista Mayno. 4fr, Holy Family by Anthony Van Dyck. 14fr, Nativity by Maitre de Moulins.

1967, Dec. 7 Photo. *Perf. 13½*

222	A24	1fr multicolored	8	5
223	"	4fr "	20	10
224	"	14fr "	65	30
225	"	26fr "	1.50	50

Christmas 1967.
Printed in sheets of 25 and one corner label inscribed "Noel 1967" and giving name of painting and painter.

Slalom
A25

Designs: 10fr, Ice hockey. 14fr, Women's skating. 17fr, Bobsled. 26fr, Ski jump. 40fr, Speed skating. 60fr, Hand holding torch, and Winter Olympics emblem.

1968, Feb. 16 Photo. *Perf. 13½*

226	A25	5fr silver & multi.	20	4
227	"	10fr " "	35	5
228	"	14fr " "	50	10
229	"	17fr " "	55	10
230	"	26fr " "	90	15
231	"	40fr " "	1.40	25
232	"	60fr " "	2.10	40
		Nos. 226-232 (7)	6.00	1.09

Issued to publicize the 10th Winter Olympic Games, Grenoble, France, Feb. 6–18. Issued in sheets of 10 stamps and label.

The Lacemaker, by Vermeer
A26

Paintings: 1.50fr, Portrait of a Young Man, by Botticelli. 2fr, Maja Vestida, by Goya (horiz.).

1968, Mar. 29 Photo. *Perf. 13½*

233	A26	1.50fr gold & multi.	8	5
234	"	2fr " "	12	8
235	"	4fr " "	24	12
		Nos. 233-235, C59-C61 (6)	3.39	1.30

Issued in sheets of 6.

Moon Probe
A27

Designs: 6fr, Russian astronaut walking in space. 8fr, Weather satellite. 10fr, American astronaut walking in space.

1968, May 15 Photo. *Perf. 13½*

Size: 35x35mm.

236	A27	4fr silver & multi.	20	10
237	"	6fr " "	30	10
238	"	8fr " "	40	10
239	"	10fr " "	45	15
		Nos. 236-239, C62-C65 (8)	4.75	1.28

Issued to publicize peaceful space explorations.

A souvenir sheet contains one 25fr stamp in Moon Probe design and one 40fr in Weather Satellite design. Margin in silver and deep red lilac; black inscription. Stamp size: 41x41mm. Sheet size: 109x83mm. Price $2.

Sheet exists imperf. Price $3.

Salamis Aethiops
A28

Butterflies: 1fr, 5fr, Graphium ridleyanus. 1.50fr, 6.50fr, Cymothoe. 2fr, 8fr, Charaxes eupale. 3fr, 10fr, Papilio bromius. 3.50fr, 15fr, Teracolus annae. 20fr, Salamis aethiops. 50fr, Papilio zonobia. 100fr, Danais chrysippus. 150fr, Salamis temora.

1968

Size: 30x33½mm.

240	A28	50c gold & multi.	5	3
241	"	1fr " "	5	3
242	"	1.50fr " "	6	3
243	"	2fr " "	8	5
244	"	3fr " "	10	6
245	"	3.50fr " "	12	6

Size: 33½x37½mm.

246	A28	4fr gold & multi.	12	8
247	"	5fr " "	15	8
248	"	6.50fr " "	20	8
249	"	8fr " "	25	8
250	"	10fr " "	30	10
251	"	15fr " "	50	15

Size: 41x46mm.

252	A28	20fr gold & multi.	75	20
253	"	50fr " "	1.50	25
254	"	100fr " "	3.00	55
255	"	150fr " "	4.50	80
		Nos. 240-255 (16)	11.73	2.63

Issue dates: Nos. 240–245, June 7; Nos. 246–251, June 28. Nos. 252–255, July 19.

See also Nos. C66–C74.

Women, Along the Manzanares, by Goya
A29

Paintings: 7fr, The Letter, by Pieter de Hooch. 11fr, Woman Reading a Letter, by Gerard Terborch. 14fr, Man Writing a Letter, by Gabriel Metsu.

1968, Sept. 30 Photo. *Perf. 13½*

256	A29	4fr multicolored	15	8
257	"	7fr "	25	12
258	"	11fr "	35	18
259	"	14fr "	50	25
		Nos. 256-259, C84-C87 (8)	4.65	2.03

International Letter Writing Week.

Soccer
A30

Designs: 7fr, Basketball. 13fr, High jump. 24fr, Relay race. 40fr, Javelin.

1968, Oct. 24

260	A30	4fr gold & multi.	10	3
261	"	7fr " "	18	6
262	"	13fr " "	32	11
263	"	24fr " "	60	20
264	"	40fr " "	1.00	30
		Nos. 260-264, C88-C92 (10)	6.65	2.10

Issued to commemorate the 19th Olympic Games, Mexico City, Oct. 12–27. Printed in sheets of 8.

Virgin and Child, by Fra Filippo Lippi
A31

Paintings: 5fr, The Magnificat, by Sandro Botticelli. 6fr, Virgin and Child, by Albrecht Durer. 11fr, Madonna del Gran Duca, by Raphael.

1968, Nov. 26 Photo. *Perf. 13½*

265	A31	3fr multicolored	15	8
266	"	5fr "	20	10
267	"	6fr "	24	15
268	"	11fr "	45	24
		a. Souv. sheet of 4	1.50	
		Nos. 265-268, C93-C96 (8)	3.14	1.47

Christmas 1968.

No. 268a contains one each of Nos. 265–268, decorative border and inscription. Size: 120x120mm. See Nos. C93–C96.

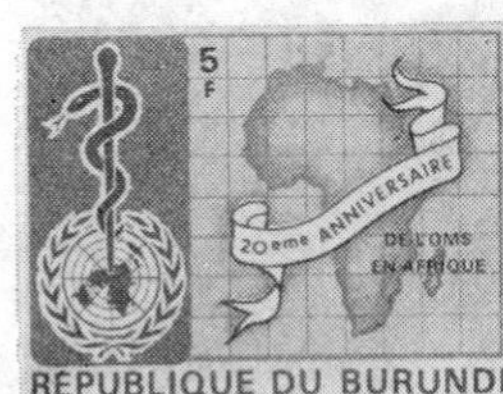

WHO Emblem and Map of Africa
A32

1969, Jan. 22

269	A32	5fr gold, dk. green & yellow	20	10
270	"	6fr gold, violet & vermilion	30	15
271	"	11fr gold, purple & red lilac	50	25

Issued to commemorate the 20th anniversary of the World Health Organization in Africa.

Nos. 265–268 Overprinted in Silver

1969, Feb. 17 Photo. *Perf. 13½*

272	A31	3fr multicolored	15	8
273	"	5fr "	20	10
274	"	6fr "	30	15
275	"	11fr "	50	25
		Nos. 272-275, C100-C103 (8)	4.50	1.98

Issued to commemorate man's first flight around the moon by the U.S.A. spacecraft Apollo 8, Dec. 21–27, 1968.

Map of Africa, and CEPT Emblem
A33

Designs: 14fr, Plowing with tractor. 17fr, Teacher and pupil. 26fr, Maps of Europe and Africa and CEPT (Conference of European Postal and Telecommunications Administrations) emblem (horiz.).

1969, Mar. 12 Photo. *Perf. 13*

276	A33	5fr multicolored	20	8
277	"	14fr "	60	24

278	A33	17fr multicolored	75	30
279	"	26fr "	1.00	40

Issued to commemorate the 5th anniversary of the Yaoundé (Cameroun) Agreement, creating the European and African-Malgache Economic Community.

Resurrection, by Gaspard Isenmann
A34

Paintings: 14fr, Resurrection by Antoine Caron. 17fr, Noli me Tangere, by Martin Schongauer. 26fr, Resurrection, by El Greco.

1969, Mar. 24

280	A34	11fr gold & multi.	45	15
281	"	14fr " "	55	20
282	"	17fr " "	75	25
283	"	26fr " "	1.10	30
		a. Souv. sheet of 4	3.00	

Easter 1969.
No. 283a contains one each of Nos. 280–283; gold and blue border and inscription. Size: 100½x125mm.

Potter
A35

Designs (BIT Emblem and): 5fr, Farm workers. 7fr, Foundry worker. 10fr, Woman testing corn crop.

1969, May 17 Photo. *Perf. 13½*

284	A35	3fr multicolored	12	4
285	"	5fr "	20	4
286	"	7fr "	30	6
287	"	10fr "	40	10

Issued to commemorate the 50th anniversary of the International Labor Organization.

Industry and Bank's Emblem
A36

Designs (African Development Bank Emblem and): 17fr, Communications. 30fr, Education. 50fr, Agriculture.

1969, July 29 Photo. *Perf. 13½*

288	A36	10fr gold & multi.	35	10
289	"	17fr " "	60	20
290	"	30fr " "	1.00	30
291	"	50fr " "	1.60	50
		a. Souv. sheet of 4	3.75	

Issued to publicize the 5th anniversary of the African Development Bank. No. 291a contains one each of Nos. 288–291, gold decorative border. Size: 103x124mm.

Girl Reading Letter, by Vermeer
A37

Paintings: 7fr, Graziella (young woman), by Auguste Renoir. 14fr, Woman writing a letter, by Gerard Terborch. 26fr, Galileo Galilei, painter unknown. 40fr, Ludwig van Beethoven, painter unknown.

1969, Oct. 24 Photo. *Perf. 13½*

292	A37	4fr multicolored	18	5
293	"	7fr "	30	10
294	"	14fr "	65	18
295	"	26fr "	1.10	30
296	"	40fr "	1.50	45
		a. Souv. sheet of 2	2.75	
		Nos. 292–296 (5)	3.73	1.08

Issued for International Letter Writing Week, Oct. 7–13.
No. 296a contains one each of Nos. 295–296. Buff decorative margin with commemorative inscription. Size: 133x75mm.

Moon Landing Issue

Rocket Launching
A38

Designs: 6.50fr, Rocket in space. 7fr, Separation of landing module from capsule. 14fr, 26fr, Landing module landing on moon. 17fr, Capsule in space. 40fr, Neil A. Armstrong leaving landing module. 50fr, Astronaut on moon.

1969, Nov. 6 Photo. *Perf. 13½*

297	A38	4fr blue & multi.	20	5
298	"	6.50fr vio. bl. & multi.	28	10
299	"	7fr vio. bl. & multi.	28	10
300	"	14fr black & multi.	48	15
301	"	17fr vio. bl. & multi.	72	20
		Nos. 297–301, C104–C106 (8)	4.81	1.45

Souvenir Sheet

302	A38	Souvenir sheet of 3	5.00	
		a. 26fr multicolored	1.00	
		b. 40fr "	1.50	
		c. 50fr "	2.00	

See note after Algeria No. 427.
On. No. 302 stamp designs extend into inscribed margin. Size: 140x88mm.

Madonna and Child, by Rubens
A39

Paintings: 6fr, Madonna and Child with St. John, by Giulio Romano. 10fr, Magnificat Madonna, by Botticelli.

1969, Dec. 2 Photogravure

303	A39	5fr gold & multi.	15	8
304	"	6fr " "	25	10
305	"	10fr " "	50	15
		a. Souvenir sheet of 3	1.00	
		Nos. 303–305, C107–C109 (6)	3.80	1.08

Christmas 1969.
No. 305a contains one each of Nos. 303–305. Gold frame with inscription. Size: 110x87mm.

Sternotomis Bohemani
A40

Designs: Various Beetles and Weevils.

1970 *Perf. 13½*

Size: 39x28mm.

306	A40	50c silver & multi.	3	3
307	"	1fr " "	3	3
308	"	1.50fr " "	4	3
309	"	2fr " "	5	3
310	"	3fr " "	8	3
311	"	3.50fr " "	9	3

Size: 46x32mm.

312	A40	4fr silver & multi.	10	3
313	"	5fr " "	13	3
314	"	6.50fr " "	17	3
315	"	8fr " "	20	3
316	"	10fr " "	25	3
317	"	15fr " "	40	4

Size: 52x36mm.

318	A40	20fr silver & multi.	50	6
319	"	50fr " "	1.20	25
320	"	100fr " "	2.40	50
321	"	150fr " "	3.60	75
		Nos. 306–321, C110–C118 (25)	17.12	3.35

Issue dates: Nos. 306–313, Jan. 20; Nos. 314–318, Feb. 17; Nos. 319–321, Apr. 3.

Jesus Condemned to Death
A41

Stations of the Cross, by Juan de Aranoa y Carredano: 1.50fr, Jesus carries His Cross. 2fr, Jesus falls the first time. 3fr, Jesus meets His mother. 3.50fr, Simon of Cyrene helps carry the cross. 4fr, Veronica wipes the face of Jesus. 5fr, Jesus falls the second time.

1970, Mar. 16 Photo. *Perf. 13½*

322	A41	1fr gold & multi.	5	5
323	"	1.50fr " "	6	6
324	"	2fr " "	8	6
325	"	3fr " "	12	6
326	"	3.50fr " "	14	8
327	"	4fr " "	18	10
328	"	5fr " "	24	10
		a. Souv. sheet of 7+label	90	
		Nos. 322–328, C119–C125 (14)	4.21	1.88

Easter 1970.
No. 328a contains one each of Nos. 322–328 and label showing three crosses. Gold decorative border. Size: 154x123mm.

Parade and EXPO '70 Emblem
A42

Designs (EXPO '70 Emblem and): 6.50fr, Aerial view. 7fr, African pavilions. 14fr, Pagoda (vert.). 26fr, Recording pavilion and pool. 40fr, Tower of the Sun (vert.). 50fr, Flags of participating nations.

1970, May 5 Photo. *Perf. 13½*

329	A42	4fr gold & multi.	15	3
330	"	6.50fr " "	25	5
331	"	7fr " "	30	6
332	"	14fr " "	50	12
333	"	26fr " "	80	18
334	"	40fr " "	1.25	30
335	"	50fr " "	1.75	40
		Nos. 329–335 (7)	5.00	1.14

Issued to publicize EXPO '70 International Exhibition, Osaka, Japan, March 15–Sept. 13, 1970. See No. C126.

White Rhinoceros—A43

Designs, FAUNA: Camel, dromedary, okapi, addax, Burundi cow (2 stamps of each animal in 2 different poses). MAP OF THE NILE: Delta and pyramids, dhow, cataract, Blue Nile and crowned crane, Victoria Nile and secretary bird, Lake Victoria and source of Nile on Mt. Gikizi.

1970, July 8 Photo. *Perf. 13½*

336	A43	7fr multicolored	28	10
		a. Sheet of 18	5.25	

Issued in sheets of 18 (3x6) stamps of different designs, to publicize the southernmost source of the Nile on Mt. Gikizi in Burundi. See No. C127.

Winter Wren, Firecrest, Skylark and Crested Lark—A44

Birds: 2fr, 3.50fr and 5fr, vertical; others horizontal.

1970, Sept. 30 Photo. *Perf. 13½*

Stamp Size: 44x33mm.

Gold Frame & Multicolored; Birds in Natural Colors

337	A44	2fr Block of four	36
		a. Northern shrike	9
		b. European starling	9
		c. Yellow wagtail	9
		d. Bank swallow	9
338	A44	3fr Block of four	60
		a. Winter wren	15
		b. Firecrest	15
		c. Skylark	15
		d. Crested lark	15
339	A44	3.50fr Block of four	64
		a. Woodchat shrike	16
		b. Common rock thrush	16
		c. Black redstart	16
		d. Ring ouzel	16
340	A44	4fr Block of four	72
		a. European redstart	18
		b. Hedge sparrow	18
		c. Gray wagtail	18
		d. Meadow pipit	18

341 A44 5fr Block of four 96
a. *Eurasian hoopoe* 24
b. *Pied flycatcher* 24
c. *Great reed warbler* 24
d. *Eurasian kingfisher* 24
342 A44 6.50fr Block of four 1.20
a. *House martin* 30
b. *Sedge warbler* 30
c. *Fieldfare* 30
d. *European golden oriole* 30
Nos. 337-342, C132-C137 (12 blocks of 4) 28.88 9.00

Nos. 337-342 are printed in sheets of 16 containing 4 blocks of 4.

Library, U.N. Emblem—A45

Designs: 5fr, Students taking test, and emblem of University of Bujumbura. 7fr, Students in laboratory and emblem of Ecole Normale Supérieure of Burundi. 10fr, Students with electron-microscope and Education Year emblem.

1970, Oct. 23

343 A45 3fr gold & multi. 12 4
344 " 5fr " " 20 5
345 " 7fr " " 30 8
346 " 10fr " " 40 10

Issued for International Education Year.

Pres. and Mrs. Michel Micombero A46

Designs: 7fr, Pres. Michel Micombero and Burundi flag. 11fr, Pres. Micombero and Revolution Memorial.

1970, Nov. 28 Photo. ***Perf. 13½***

347 A46 4fr gold & multi. 18 6
348 " 7fr " " 30 10
349 " 11fr " " 50 14
a. Souvenir sheet of 3 1.25

Issued to commemorate the 4th anniversary of independence. No. 349a contains 3 stamps similar to Nos. 347-349, but inscribed "Poste Aerienne." Dark gray and gold margin with commemorative inscription. Size: 125x143mm. Exists imperf.

See Nos. C140-C142.

Lenin with Delegates A47

Designs (Lenin, Paintings): 5fr, addressing crowd. 6.50fr, with soldier and sailor. 15fr, speaking from balcony. 50fr, Portrait.

1970, Dec. 31 Photo. ***Perf. 13½***
Gold Frame

350 A47 3.50fr dark red brown 14 6
351 " 5fr " " " 20 8
352 " 6.50fr " " " 28 12
353 " 15fr " " " 60 25
354 " 50fr " " " 2.00 35
Nos. 350-354 (5) 3.22 86

Lenin's birth centenary (1870-1924).

Lion A48

1971, March 19 Photo. ***Perf. 13½***
Multicolored
Size: 38x38mm.

355 A48 1fr Strip of four 20
a. *Lion* 5
b. *Cape buffalo* 5
c. *Hippopotamus* 5
d. *Giraffe* 5
356 A48 2fr Strip of four 32
a. *Hartebeest* 8
b. *Black rhinoceros* 8
c. *Zebra* 8
d. *Leopard* 8
357 A48 3fr Strip of four 48
a. *Grant's gazelles* 12
b. *Cheetah* 12
c. *African white-backed vultures* 12
d. *Johnston's okapi* 12
358 A48 5fr Strip of four 80
a. *Chimpanzee* 20
b. *Elephant* 20
c. *Spotted hyenas* 20
d. *Beisa* 20
359 A48 6fr Strip of four 96
a. *Gorilla* 24
b. *Gnu* 24
c. *Wart hog* 24
d. *Cape hunting dog* 24
360 A48 11fr Strip of four 1.80
a. *Sable antelope* 45
b. *Caracal lynx* 45
c. *Ostriches* 45
d. *Bongo* 45
Nos. 355-360, C146-C151 (12 strips of 4) 20.76 6.00

The Resurrection, by Il Sodoma A49

Paintings: 6fr, Resurrection, by Andrea del Castagno. 11fr, Noli me Tangere, by Correggio.

1971, Apr. 2

361 A49 3fr gold & multi. 15
362 " 6fr " " 30
363 " 11fr " " 55
a. Souvenir sheet of 3 1.10
Nos. 361-363, C143-C145 (6) 2.80 80

Easter 1971. No. 363a contains one each of Nos. 361-363. Red and gold margin. Size: 120x85mm. Sheet exists imperf.

Young Venetian Woman, by Dürer A50

Dürer Paintings: 11fr, Hieronymus Holzschuher. 14fr, Emperor Maximilian I. 17fr, Holy Family, from Paumgartner Altar. 26fr, Haller Madonna. 31fr, Self-portrait, 1498.

1971, Sept. 20

364 A50 6fr multicolored 30
365 " 11fr " 55
366 " 14fr " 70
367 " 17fr " 85
368 " 26fr " 1.30
369 " 31fr " 1.55
a. Souvenir sheet of 2 3.00
Nos. 364-369 (6) 5.25 1.00

International Letter Writing Week. Paintings by Dürer. 500th anniversary of the birth of Albrecht Dürer (1471-1528), German painter and engraver. No. 369a contains one each of Nos. 368-369. Tan margin with portrait of Erasmus. Size: 137x80mm. Exists imperf.

Nos. 364-369, 369a Overprinted in Black and Gold:
"VIème CONGRES / DE L'INSTITUT INTERNATIONAL / DE DROIT D'EXPRESSION FRANCAISE"

1971, Oct. 8

370 A50 6fr multicolored 30
371 " 11fr " 55
372 " 14fr " 70
373 " 17fr " 85
374 " 26fr " 1.30
375 " 31fr " 1.55
a. Souvenir sheet of 2 3.00
Nos. 370-375 (6) 5.25 1.00

6th Congress of the International Legal Institute of the French-speaking Area, Usumbura, Aug. 10-19.

Madonna and Child, by Il Perugino A51

Paintings of the Madonna and Child by: 5fr, Andrea del Sarto. 6fr, Luis de Morales.

1971, Nov. 2 Photo. ***Perf. 13½***

376 A51 3fr dk. green & multi. 12 4
377 " 5fr " " " 20 6
378 " 6fr " " " 24 8
a. Souvenir sheet of 3 60
Nos. 376-378, C153-C155 (6) 2.51 75

Christmas 1971. No. 378a contains one each of Nos. 376-378. Multicolored border. Size: 125x81mm. Sheet exists imperf.

Lunar Orbiter A52

Designs: 11fr, Vostok. 14fr, Luna 1. 17fr, Apollo 11 astronaut on moon. 26fr, Soyuz 11. 40fr, Lunar Rover (Apollo 15).

1972, Jan. 15

379 A52 6fr gold & multi. 30
380 " 11fr " " 55
381 " 14fr " " 70
382 " 17fr " " 85
383 " 26fr " " 1.30
384 " 40fr " " 2.00
a. Souvenir sheet of 6 6.00
Nos. 379-384 (6) 5.70 1.25

Conquest of space. See No. C156.

No. 384a contains one each of Nos. 379-384 inscribed "APOLLO 16." Multicolored margin inscribed "La Conquête de l'Espace." Size: 134x135mm.

Slalom and Sapporo '72 Emblem A53

Designs (Sapporo '72 Emblem and): 6fr, Figure skating, pairs. 11fr, Figure skating, women's. 14fr, Ski jump. 17fr, Ice hockey. 24fr, Speed skating, men's. 26fr, Snow scooter. 31fr, Downhill skiing. 50fr, Bobsledding.

1972, Feb. 3

385 A53 5fr silver & multi. 20
386 " 6fr " " 25
387 " 11fr " " 45
388 " 14fr " " 55
389 " 17fr " " 70
390 " 24fr " " 95
391 " 26fr " " 1.00
392 " 31fr " " 1.25
393 " 50fr " " 2.00
Nos. 385-393 (9) 7.35 1.50

11th Winter Olympic Games, Sapporo, Japan, Feb. 3-13. Printed in sheets of 12. See No. C157.

Issue dates: Nos. 385-390, Feb. 1; Nos. 391-393, Feb. 21.

Ecce Homo, by Quentin Massys A54

Paintings: 6.50fr, Crucifixion, by Rubens. 10fr, Descent from the Cross, by Jacopo da Pontormo. 18fr, Pietà, by Ferdinand Gallegos. 27fr, Trinity, by El Greco.

1972, Mar. 20 Photo. ***Perf. 13½***

394 A54 3.50fr gold & multi. 15 4
395 " 6.50fr " " 30 6
396 " 10fr " " 45 10
397 " 18fr " " 80 18

398 A54 27fr gold & multi. 1.20 27
a. Souvenir sheet of 5+label 3.00
Nos. 394-398 (5) 2.90 65

Easter 1972. Printed in sheets of 8 with label. No. 398a contains one each of Nos. 394-398 and decorative label. Dark brown and gold margin. Size: 120x 157mm. Exists imperf.

Gymnastics, Olympic Rings and "Motion"
A55

1972, May 19

Gold and Multicolored

399 A55 5fr *shown* 18
400 " 6fr *Javelin* 20
401 " 11fr *Fencing* 42
402 " 14fr *Bicycling* 52
403 " 17fr *Pole vault* 65
Nos. 399-403, C158-C161 (9) 5.62 1.00

Souvenir Sheet

404 A55 Souv. sheet of 2 2.50
a. 31fr *Discus* 90
b. 40fr *Soccer* 1.20

20th Olympic Games, Munich, Aug. 26-Sept. 11. No. 404 has multicolored margin with Olympic flag, "Motion" and commemorative inscription. Size: 126x80mm.

Prince Rwagasore, Pres. Micombero, Burundi Flag, Drummers
A56

Designs: 7fr, Rwagasore, Micombero, flag, map of Africa, globe. 13fr, Micombero, flag, globe.

1972, Aug. 24 Photo. ***Perf. 13½***

405 A56 5fr silver & multi. 15
406 " 7fr " " 25
407 " 13fr " " 45
a. Souvenir sheet of 3 1.00
Nos. 405-407, C162-C164 (6) 2.85 75

10th anniversary of independence.

No. 407a contains one each of Nos. 405-407. Silver and light blue margin with black inscription. Size: 146x80mm.

Madonna and Child, by Andrea Solario
A57

Paintings of the Madonna and Child by: 10fr, Raphael. 15fr, Botticelli.

1972, Nov. 2

408 A57 5fr lt. bl. & multi. 15
409 " 10fr " " " 30
410 A57 15fr lt. blue & multi. 45
a. Souvenir sheet of 3 1.00
Nos. 408-410, C165-C167 (6) 3.45 1.00

Christmas 1972. Sheets of 20 stamps and one label. No. 410a contains one each of Nos. 408-410. Deep carmine and gold border. Size: 128x81mm.

Platy-coryne Crocea
A58

1972 **Multicolored**

Size: 33x33mm.

411 A58 50c *shown* 3
412 " 1fr *Cattleya trianaei* 3
413 " 2fr *Eulophia cucullata* 5
414 " 3fr *Cymbidium hamsey* 8
415 " 4fr *Thelymitra pauciflora* 10
416 " 5fr *Miltassia* 13
417 " 6fr *Miltonia* 16

Size: 38x38mm.

418 A58 7fr Like 50c 18
419 " 8fr Like 1fr 20
420 " 9fr Like 2fr 23
421 " 10fr Like 3fr 26
Nos. 411-421, C168-C174 (18) 5.07 2.00

Orchids. Issue dates: Nos. 411-417, Nov. 6; Nos. 418-421, Nov. 29.

Henry Morton Stanley—A59

Designs: 7fr, Porters, Stanley's expedition. 13fr, Stanley entering Ujiji.

1973, Mar. 19 Photo. ***Perf. 13½***

422 A59 5fr gold & multi. 15
423 " 7fr " " 20
424 " 13fr " " 40
Nos. 422-424, C175-C177 (6) 2.55 90

Exploration of Africa by David Livingstone (1813-1873) and Henry Morton Stanley (John Rowlands; 1841-1904).

Crucifixion, by Roger van der Weyden
A60

Paintings: 5fr, Flagellation of Christ, by Caravaggio. 13fr, The Burial of Christ, by Raphael.

1973, Apr. 10

425 A60 5fr gold & multi. 15
426 " 7fr " " 20
427 " 13fr " " 40
a. Souvenir sheet of 3 90
Nos. 425-427, C178-C180 (6) 2.55 90

Easter 1973. No. 427a contains one each of Nos. 425-427. Multicolored margin. Size: 121x73mm.

INTERPOL Emblem, Flag—A61

Design: 10fr, INTERPOL flag and emblem. 18fr, INTERPOL Headquarters and emblem.

1973, May 19 Photo. ***Perf. 13½***

428 A61 5fr silver & multi. 15
429 " 10fr " " 30
430 " 18fr " " 55
Nos. 428-430, C181-C182 (5) 2.75 90

50th anniversary of International Criminal Police Organization (INTERPOL).

Signs of the Zodiac, Babylon—A62

Designs: 5fr, Greek and Roman gods representing planets. 7fr, Ptolemy (No. 433a) and Ptolemaic solar system. 13fr, Copernicus (No. 434a) and heliocentric system.

1973, July 27 Photo. ***Perf. 13½***

Gold and Multicolored

431 A62 3fr Block of four 32
a. 3fr in UL 8
b. 3fr in UR 8
c. 3fr in LL 8
d. 3fr in LR 8
432 A62 5fr Block of four 60
a. 5fr in UL 15
b. 5fr in UR 15
c. 5fr in LL 15
d. 5fr in LR 15
433 A62 7fr Block of four 80
a. 7fr in UL 20
b. 7fr in UR 20
c. 7fr in LL 20
d. 7fr in LR 20
434 A62 13fr Block of four 1.60
a. 13fr in UL 40
b. 13fr in UR 40
c. 13fr in LL 40
d. 13fr in LR 40
e. Souvenir sheet of 4 3.50
Nos. 431-434, C183-C186 (8 blocks of 4) 18.32 2.75

500th anniversary of the birth of Nicolaus Copernicus (1473-1543), Polish astronomer.

Nos. 431-434 are printed in sheets of 32 containing 8 blocks of 4. No. 434e contains one each of Nos. 431-434. Gold and multicolored margin. Size: 136x136mm.

Flowers and Butterflies—A63

Designs: Each block of 4 contains 2 flower and 2 butterfly designs. The 1fr, 2fr, 5fr and 11fr have flower designs listed as "a" and "d" numbers, butterflies as "b" and "c" numbers; the arrangement is reversed for the 3fr and 6fr.

1973, Sept. 3 Photo. ***Perf. 13***

Stamp Size: 34x41½mm.

Gold and Multicolored

435 A63 1fr Block of 4 16
a. *Protea cynaroides* 4
b. *Precis octavia* 4
c. *Epiphora bauhiniae* 4
d. *Gazania longiscapa* 4
436 A63 2fr Block of 4 32
a. *Kniphofia* 8
b. *Cymothoe coccinata* 8
c. *Nudaurelia zambesina* 8
d. *Freesia refracta* 8
437 A63 3fr Block of 4 48
a. *Calotis eupompe* 12
b. *Narcissus* 12
c. *Cineraria hybrida* 12
d. *Cyrestis camillus* 12
438 A63 5fr Block of 4 80
a. *Iris tingitana* 20
b. *Papilio demodocus* 20
c. *Catopsilia avelaneda* 20
d. *Nerine sarniensis* 20
439 A63 6fr Block of 4 96
a. *Hypolimnas dexithea* 24
b. *Zantedeschia tropicalis* 24
c. *Sandersonia aurantiaca* 24
d. *Drurya antimachus* 24
440 A63 11fr Block of 4 1.76
a. *Nymphaea capensis* 44
b. *Pandoriana pandora* 44
c. *Precis orythia* 44
d. *Pelargonium domestica* 44
Nos. 435-440, C187-C192 (12 blocks of 4) 24.32 2.75

Virgin and Child, by Giovanni Bellini
A64

Virgin and Child by: 10fr, Jan van Eyck. 15fr, Giovanni Boltraffio.

1973, Nov. 13 Photo. ***Perf. 13***

441 A64 5fr gold & multi. 15
442 " 10fr " " 30
443 " 15fr " " 45
a. Souvenir sheet of 3 1.00
Nos. 441-443, C193-C195 (6) 3.45 90

Christmas 1973. No. 443a contains one each of Nos. 441-443 with multicolored margin. Size: 143x79mm.

Pietá, by Paolo Veronese
A65

Paintings: 10fr, Virgin and St. John, by van der Weyden. 18fr, Crucifixion, by van der Weyden. 27fr, Burial of Christ, by Titian. 40fr, Pietá, by El Greco.

1974, Apr. 19 Photo. ***Perf. 14x13½***

444 A65 5fr gold & multi. 15
445 " 10fr " " 30
446 " 18fr " " 55
447 " 27fr " " 80
448 " 40fr " " 1.20
a. Souvenir sheet of 5 3.10
Nos. 444-448 (5) 3.00 75

Easter 1974. No. 448a contains one each of Nos. 444-448, rose brown and gold margin. Size: 145x120mm.

Fish—A66

Designs: Fish.

1974, May 30 Photo. *Perf. 13*

Stamp Size: 35x35mm.

Multicolored

449 A66 1fr Block of 4 12
- *a. Haplochromis multicolor* 3
- *b. Pantodon buchholzi* 3
- *c. Tropheus duboisi* 3
- *d. Distichodus sexfasciatus* 3

450 A66 2fr Block of 4 24
- *a. Pelmatochromis kribensis* 6
- *b. Nannaethiops tritaeniatus* 6
- *c. Polycentropsis abbreviata* 6
- *d. Hemichromis bimaculatus* 6

451 A66 3fr Block of 4 36
- *a. Ctenopoma acutirostre* 9
- *b. Synodontis angelicus* 9
- *c. Tilapia melanopleura* 9
- *d. Aphyosemion bivittatum* 9

452 A66 5fr Block of 4 60
- *a. Monodactylus argenteus* 15
- *b. Zanclus canescens* 15
- *c. Pygoplites diacanthus* 15
- *d. Cephalopholis argus* 15

453 A66 6fr Block of 4 72
- *a. Priacanthus arenatus* 18
- *b. Pomacanthus arcuatus* 18
- *c. Scarus guacamaia* 18
- *d. Zeus faber* 18

454 A66 11fr Block of 4 1.32
- *a. Lactophrys quadricornis* 33
- *b. Balistes vetula* 33
- *c. Acanthurus bahianus* 33
- *d. Holocanthus ciliaris* 33

Nos. 449-454, C207-C212 (12 blocks of 4) 18.04 3.00

Soccer and Cup A67

Designs: Various soccer scenes and cup.

1974, July 4 Photogravure *Perf. 13*

455 A67 5fr gold & multi. 15
456 " 6fr " " 18
457 " 11fr " " 33
458 " 14fr " " 42
459 " 17fr " " 50
- *a.* Souvenir sheet of 3 2.75

Nos. 455-459, C196-C198 (8) 4.16 75

World Soccer Championship, Munich, June 13-July 7. No. 459a contains 3 stamps similar to Nos. C196-C198 without "Poste Aerienne." Gold and multicolored margin with picture of Munich City Hall. Size: 88x142mm.

Nos. 455-459 and 459a exist imperf.

Flags over UPU Headquarters, Bern A68

Designs: No. 461, G.P.O., Usumbura. No. 462, Mailmen ("11F" in UR). No. 463, Mailmen ("11F" in UL). No. 464, UPU emblem. No. 465, Means of transportation. No. 466, Pigeon over globe showing Burundi. No. 467, Swiss flag, pigeon over map showing Bern.

1974, July 23

460 A68 6fr gold & multi. 24
461 " 6fr " " 24
462 " 11fr " " 45
463 " 11fr " " 45
464 " 14fr " " 55
465 " 14fr " " 55
466 " 17fr " " 70
467 " 17fr " " 70
- *a.* Souvenir sheet of 8 4.25

Nos. 460-467, C199-C206 (16) 13.48 2.00

Centenary of Universal Postal Union. Stamps of same denomination printed se-tenant (continuous design) in sheets of 40.

No. 467a contains one each of Nos. 460-467. Violet, gold and light blue margin. Size: 96x162mm.

St. Ildefonso Writing Letter, by El Greco A69

Paintings: 11fr, Lady Sealing Letter, by Chardin. 14fr, Titus at Desk, by Rembrandt. 17fr, The Love Letter, by Vermeer. 26fr, The Merchant G. Gisze, by Holbein. 31fr, Portrait of Alexandre Lenoir, by David.

1974, Oct. 1 Photo. *Perf. 13*

468 A69 6fr gold & multi. 18
469 " 11fr " " 33
470 " 14fr " " 42
471 " 17fr " " 50
472 " 26fr " " 78
473 " 31fr " " 93
- *a.* Souvenir sheet of 2 2.00

Nos. 468-473 (6) 3.14 75

International Letter Writing Week, Oct. 6-12. No. 473a contains one each of Nos. 472-473. Multicolored margin. Size: 95 x105mm. Sheet exists imperf.

Virgin and Child, by Bernaert van Orley A70

Paintings of the Virgin and Child: 10fr, by Hans Memling. 15fr, by Botticelli.

1974, Nov. 7 Photo. *Perf. 13*

474 A70 5fr gold & multi. 15
475 " 10fr " " 30
476 " 15fr " " 45
- *a.* Souvenir sheet of 3 1.00

Nos. 474-476, C213-C215 (6) 3.45 80

Christmas 1974. Sheets of 20 stamps and one label. No. 476a contains one each of Nos. 474-476, gold and multicolored margin. Size: 137x90mm. Sheet exists imperf.

Apollo-Soyuz Space Mission and Emblem—A71

1975, July 10 Photo. *Perf. 13*

Multicolored

477 A71 26fr Block of 4 4.00
- *a. A. A. Leonov, V. N. Kubasov, Soviet flag* 78
- *b. Soyuz and Soviet flag* 78
- *c. Apollo and American flag* 78
- *d. D. K. Slayton, V. D. Brand, T. P. Stafford, American flag* 78

478 A71 31fr Block of 4 5.00
- *a. Apollo-Soyuz link-up* 92
- *b. Apollo, blast-off* 92
- *c. Soyuz, blast-off* 92
- *d. Kubasov, Leonov, Slayton, Brand, Stafford* 92

Nos. 477-478, C216-C217 (4 blocks of 4) 19.50 2.00

Apollo Soyuz space test project (Russo-American cooperation), launching July 15; link-up, July 17. Nos. 477-478 are printed in sheets of 32 containing 8 blocks of 4.

Addax A72

1975, July 31 Photo. *Perf. 13½*

Multicolored

479 A72 1fr Strip of four 12
- *a. shown* 3
- *b. Roan antelope* 3
- *c. Nyala* 3
- *d. White rhinoceros* 3

480 A72 2fr Strip of four 24
- *a. Mandrill* 6
- *b. Oryx* 6
- *c. Dik-dik* 6
- *d. Thomson's gazelles* 6

481 A72 3fr Strip of four 36
- *a. African small-clawed civet* 9
- *b. Reed buck* 9
- *c. Indian civet* 9
- *d. Cape buffalo* 9

482 A72 5fr Strip of four 60
- *a. White-tailed gnu* 15
- *b. Donkeys* 15
- *c. Colobus monkey* 15
- *d. Gerenuk* 15

483 A72 6fr Strip of four 72
- *a. Dama gazelle* 18
- *b. Wild dog* 18
- *c. Sitatungas* 18
- *d. Striped duiker* 18

484 A72 11fr Strip of four 1.32
- *a. Fennec* 33
- *b. Lesser kudus* 33
- *c. Blesbok* 33
- *d. Serval* 33

Nos. 479-484, C218-C223 (12 strips of 4) 18.02 2.25

Jonah, by Michelangelo A73

Designs: Paintings from Sistine Chapel.

1975, Dec. 3 Photo. *Perf. 13*

Multicolored

485 A73 5fr *shown* 15
486 " 5fr *Libyan Sybil* 15
487 " 13fr *Prophet Isaiah* 40
488 " 13fr *Delphic Sybil* 40
489 " 27fr *Daniel* 80
490 " 27fr *Cumaean Sybil* 80
- *a.* Souvenir sheet of 6 3.00

Nos. 485-490, C228-C233 (12) 8.04 1.25

Michelangelo Buonarotti (1475-1564), Italian sculptor, painter and architect. Stamps of same denominations printed se-tenant in sheets of 18 stamps and 2 labels. No. 490a contains one each of Nos. 485-490; brown & gold margin, black inscription. Size: 137x111mm.

Speed Skating A74

Basketball A75

Designs (Innsbruck Games Emblem and): 24fr, Figure skating, women's. 26fr, Two-man bobsled. 31fr, Cross-country skiing.

1976, Jan. 23 Photo. *Perf. 14x13½*

491 A74 17fr dp. bl. & multi. 50
492 " 24fr multicolored 72
493 " 26fr " 76
494 " 31fr plum & multi. 93
- *a.* Souvenir sheet of 3 3.25

Nos. 491-494, C234-C236 (7) 6.03 75

12th Winter Olympic Games, Innsbruck, Austria, Feb. 4-15.

No. 494a contains 3 stamps similar to Nos. C234-C236, perf. 13½, without "POSTE AERIENNE." Multicolored margin with snowflakes and Games' emblem. Size: 130x62½mm.

1976, May 3 Litho. *Perf. 13½*

Designs (Montreal Games Emblem and): Nos. 496, 499, 503b, Pole vault. Nos. 497, 500, 503d, Running. Nos. 498, 501, 503a, Soccer. No. 502, 503c, Basketball.

495 A75 14fr blue & multi. 42
496 " 14fr olive & multi. 42
497 " 17fr magenta & multi. 50
498 " 17fr verm. & multi. 50
499 " 28fr olive & multi. 80
500 " 28fr magenta & multi. 80
501 " 40fr verm. & multi. 1.20
502 " 40fr blue & multi. 1.20

Nos. 495-502, C237-C242 (14) 12.26 1.75

Souvenir Sheet

503 A75 Sheet of 4 3.20 60
- *a.* 14fr red & multicolored 42
- *b.* 17fr olive & multicolored 50
- *c.* 28fr blue & multicolored 80
- *d.* 40fr magenta & multicolored 1.20

21st Olympic Games, Montreal, Canada, July 17-Aug. 1. Stamps of same denomination printed se-tenant in sheets of 20.

No. 503 has gold inscription, black Montreal Olympic emblem and multicolored band in margin. Size: 115x120mm.

Virgin and Child, by Dirk Bouts
A76

Virgin and Child by: 13fr, Giovanni Bellini. 27fr, Carlo Crivelli.

1976, Oct. 18 Photo. ***Perf. 13½***

504 A76 5fr gold & multi. 15
505 " 13fr " " 40
506 " 27fr " " 80
a. Souvenir sheet of 3 1.50
Nos. 504-506, C250-C252 (6) 4.03 80

Christmas 1976. Sheets of 20 stamps and descriptive label. No. 506a contains one each of Nos. 504-506; multicolored margin. Size: 123x80mm.

St. Veronica, by Rubens
A77

Paintings by Rubens: 21fr, Christ on the Cross. 27fr, Descent from the Cross. 35fr, The Deposition.

1977, Apr. 5 Photo. ***Perf. 13***

507 A77 10fr gold & multi. 30
508 " 21fr " " 62
509 " 27fr " " 80
510 " 35fr " " 1.05
a. Souvenir sheet of 4 3.00

Easter 1977. Sheets of 30 stamps and descriptive label. No. 510a contains 4 stamps similar to Nos. 507-510 inscribed "POSTE AERIENNE." Multicolored margin. Size: 111x85mm.

Alexander Graham Bell
A78

Intelsat Satellite, Modern and Old Telephones
A79

Designs: No. 513, Switchboard operator, c. 1910, and wall telephone. No. 514, Intelsat and radar. No. 515, A.G. Bell and first telephone. No. 516, Satellites around globe and videophone.

1977, May 17 Photo. ***Perf. 13***

511 A78 10fr multicolored 30
512 A79 10fr " 30
513 A78 17fr " 50
514 A79 17fr " 50
515 A78 26fr " 80
516 A79 26fr " 80
Nos. 511-516, C253-C256 (10) 6.38

Centenary of first telephone call by Alexander Graham Bell, Mar. 10, 1876. Stamps of same denomination printed se-tenant in sheets of 32.

Buffon's Kob
A80

1977, Aug. 22 Photo. ***Perf. 14x14½***
Multicolored

517 A80 2fr Strip of four 24
a. *shown* 6
b. *Marabous* 6
c. *Brindled gnu* 6
d. *River hog* 6
518 A80 5fr Strip of four 60
a. *Zebras* 15
b. *Shoebill* 15
c. *Striped hyenas* 15
d. *Chimpanzee* 15
519 A80 8fr Strip of four 96
a. *Flamingos* 24
b. *Nile crocodiles* 24
c. *Green mamba* 24
d. *Greater kudus* 24
520 A80 11fr Strip of four 1.36
a. *Hyrax* 34
b. *Cobra* 34
c. *Jackals* 34
d. *Verreaux's eagles* 34
521 A80 21fr Strip of four 2.56
a. *Honey badger* 64
b. *Harnessed antelopes* 64
c. *Secretary bird* 64
d. *Klipspringer* 64
522 A80 27fr Strip of four 2.80
a. *African big-eared fox* 70
b. *Elephants* 70
c. *Vulturine guineafowl* 70
d. *Impalas* 70
Nos. 517-522, C258-C263 (12 strips of 4) 33.92

The Goose Girl, by Grimm
A81

Fairy Tales: 5fr, by Grimm Brothers. 11fr, by Aesop. 14fr, by Hans Christian Andersen. 17fr, by Jean de La Fontaine. 26fr, English fairy tales.

1977, Sept. 14 ***Perf. 14***
Multicolored

523 A81 5fr Block of four 60
a. *shown* 15
b. *The Two Wanderers* 15
c. *The Man of Iron* 15
d. *Snow White and Rose Red* 15
524 A81 11fr Block of four 1.36
a. *The Quarreling Cats* 34
b. *The Blind and The Lame* 34
c. *The Hermit and the Bear* 34
d. *The Fox and the Stork* 34
525 A81 14fr Block of four 1.68
a *The Princess and the Pea* 42
b. *The Old Tree Mother* 42
c. *The Ice Maiden* 42
d. *The Old House* 42
526 A81 17fr Block of four 2.00
a. *The Oyster and the Suitors* 50
b. *The Wolf and the Lamb* 50
c. *Hen with the Golden Egg* 50
d. *The Wolf as Shepherd* 50
527 A81 26fr Block of four 3.20
a. *Three Heads in the Well* 80
b. *Mother Goose* 80
c. *Jack and the Beanstalk* 80
d. *Alice in Wonderland* 80
Nos. 523-527 (5 blocks of four) 8.84

Unused prices are for stamps that have been hinged.

Security Council Chamber, UN Nos. 28, 46, 37, C7—A82

Designs (UN Stamps and): 8fr, UN General Assembly, interior. 21fr, UN Meeting Hall.

1977, Oct. 10 Photo. ***Perf. 13½***

528 A82 8fr Block of four 96
a. No. 25 24
b. No. C5 24
c. No. 23 24
d. No. 2 24
529 A82 10fr Block of four 1.20
a. No. 28 30
b. No. 46 30
c. No. 37 30
d. No. C7 30
530 A82 21fr Block of four 2.48
a. No. 45 62
b. No. 42 62
c. No. 17 62
d. No. 13 62
e. Souvenir sheet of 3 1.30
Nos. 528-530, C264-C266 (6 blocks of 4) 14.92

25th anniversary (in 1976) of the United Nations Postal Administration. No. 530e contains 8fr in design of No. 529d, 10fr in design of No. 530b, 21fr in design of No. 528c; silver margin. Size: 128x76mm.

Virgin and Child
A83

Designs: Paintings of the Virgin and Child.

1977, Oct. 31 Photo. ***Perf. 14x13***

531 A83 5fr multicolored 15
532 " 13fr " 40
533 " 27fr " 80
a. Souvenir sheet of 3 1.50
Nos. 531-533, C267-C269 (6) 4.05

Christmas 1977. Sheets of 24 stamps with descriptive label. No. 533a contains one each of Nos. 531-533; gold and multicolored margin. Size: 130x72mm.

Cruiser Aurora, Russia Nos. 211, 303, 1252, 187—A84

Designs (Russian Stamps and): 8fr, Kremlin, Moscow. 11fr, Pokrovski Cathedral, Moscow. 13fr, Labor Day parade, 1977 and 1980 Olympic Games emblem.

1977, Nov. 14 Photo. ***Perf. 13***

534 A84 5fr Block of four 60
a. *No. 211* 15
b. *No. 303* 15
c. *No. 1252* 15
d. *No. 187* 15
535 A84 8fr Block of four 96
a. *No. 856* 24
b. *No. 1986* 24
c. *No. 908* 24
d. *No. 2551* 24
536 A84 11fr Block of four 1.36
a. *No. 3844b* 34
b. *No. 3452* 34
c. *No. 3382* 34
d. *No. 3837* 34
537 A84 13fr Block of four 1.60
a. *No. 4446* 40
b. *No. 3497* 40
c. *No. 2926* 40
d. *No. 2365* 40
Nos. 534-537 (4 blocks of 4) 4.52

60th anniversary of Russian October Revolution.

Ship at Dock, Arms and Flag—A85

Burundi Arms and Flag and: 5fr, Men at lathes. 11fr, Male leopard dance. 14fr, Coffee harvest. 17fr, Government Palace.

1977, Nov. 25 Photo. ***Perf. 13½***

538 A85 1fr silver & multi. 3
539 " 5fr " " 15
540 " 11fr " " 35
541 " 14fr " " 42
542 " 17fr " " 50
Nos. 538-542 (5) 1.45

15th anniversary of independence.

SEMI-POSTAL STAMPS

Prince Louis Rwagasore
SP1

Prince and Stadium—SP2

Design: 1.50fr+75c, 6.50fr+3fr, Prince and memorial monument.

Perf. 14x13, 13x14

1963, Feb. 15 Photo. Unwmkd.

B1 SP1 50c+25c brt. violet 4 4
B2 SP2 1fr+50c red orange & dark blue 6 6
B3 " 1.50fr+75c lemon & dark violet 10 10
B4 SP1 3.50fr+1.50fr lilac rose 20 16
B5 SP2 5fr+2fr rose pink & dark blue 30 18
B6 " 6.50fr+3fr gray olive & dk. violet 40 25
Nos. B1-B6 (6) 1.10 79

Issued in memory of Prince Louis Rwagasore (1932–61), son of King Mwami Mwambutsa IV and Prime Minister. The surtax was for the stadium and monument in his honor.

Red Cross Type of Regular Issue
Souvenir Sheet

1963, Sept. 26 Litho. *Imperf.*

B7 A5 Sheet of four 4.00 4.00
a. 4fr+2fr fawn, red & black 65 65
b. 8fr+2fr grn., red & black 75 75
c. 10fr+2fr gray, red & black 85 85
d. 20fr+2fr ultra., red & black 1.25 1.25

Issued to commemorate the centenary of the International Red Cross. The surtax was for Red Cross work in Burundi. Pale yellow margin with black and red inscription. Size: 90x140mm.

Olympic Type of Regular Issue
Souvenir Sheet

Designs: 18fr+2fr, Hurdling (horiz.). 20fr+5fr, Vaulting (horiz.).

1964, Nov. 18 *Perf. 13½*

B8 A13 Sheet of two 6.50 5.00
a. 18fr+2fr yellow grn. & multi. 2.50 2.50
b. 20fr+5fr bright pink & multi. 2.50 2.50

Issued to commemorate the 18th Olympic Games, Tokyo, Oct. 10–25, 1964. No. B8 has ornamental red brown border and black and blue marginal inscriptions. Size: 115x71mm.

Scientist with Microscope and Map of Burundi—SP3

Lithographed and Photogravure

1965, Jan. 28 *Perf. 14½* Unwmkd.

B9 SP3 2fr+50c tan, red & dark brown 15 8
B10 " 4fr+1.50fr pink, red & green 35 12
B11 " 5fr+2.50fr ocher, red & violet 50 16
B12 " 8fr+3fr gray, red & dark blue 60 24
B13 " 10fr+5fr greenish gray, red & red brown 90 32
Nos. B9-B13 (5) 2.50 92

Souvenir Sheet
Perf. 13x13½

B14 SP3 10fr+10fr pale olive, red & dk. brown 2.50 2.50

Issued for the fight against tuberculosis. No. B14 contains one stamp. Tan, red & dark brown margin. Size: 100x71mm.

Coat of Arms, 10fr Coin, Reverse
SP4

Designs (Coins of Various Denominations): 4fr+50c, 8fr+50c, 15fr+50c, 40fr+50c, King Mwambutsa IV, obverse.

Litho.; Embossed on Gilt Foil

1965, Aug. 9 *Imperf.*

Diameter: 39mm.

B15 SP4 2fr+50c crimson & orange 15 10
B16 " 4fr+50c ultra. & vermilion 25 15

Diameter: 45mm.

B17 SP4 6fr+50c org. & gray 35 25
B18 " 8fr+50c blue & magenta 45 30

Diameter: 56mm.

B19 SP4 12fr+50c lt. green & red lilac 70 50
B20 " 15fr+50c yel. green & light lilac 85 65

Diameter: 67mm.

B21 SP4 25fr+50c vio. blue & buff 1.40 1.00
B22 " 40fr+50c brt. pink & red brown 2.25 1.50
Nos. B15-B22 (8) 6.40 4.45

Stamps are backed with patterned paper in blue, orange and pink engine-turned design.

Prince Louis Rwagasore and Pres. John F. Kennedy
SP5

Designs: 4fr+1fr, 20fr+5fr, Prince Louis and memorial. 20fr+2fr, 40fr+5fr, Pres. John F. Kennedy and library shelves. 40fr+2fr, King Mwambutsa IV at Kennedy grave, Arlington (vert.).

1966, Jan. 21 Photo. *Perf 13½*

B23 SP5 4fr+1fr gray blue & dark brown 20 5
B24 " 10fr+1fr pale green, indigo & brown 40 10
B25 " 20fr+2fr lilac & deep green 85 15
B26 " 40fr+2fr gray green & dark brown 1.50 20

Souvenir Sheet

B27 SP5 Sheet of two 4.50 2.50
a. 20fr+5fr gray bl. & dk. brown 1.75
b. 40fr+5fr lilac & deep green 2.25

Issued in memory of Prince Louis Rwagasore and President John F. Kennedy. No. B27 has brown margin with picture of King Mwambutsa IV and inscription. Size: 75x90mm.

Republic

Winston Churchill and St. Paul's, London
SP6

Designs: 15fr+2fr, Tower of London and Churchill. 20fr+3fr, Big Ben and Churchill.

1967, March 23 Photo. *Perf.13½*

B28 SP6 4fr+1fr multi. 20 6
B29 " 15fr+2fr " 70 20
B30 " 20fr+3fr " 90 35

Issued in memory of Sir Winston Churchill (1874–1965), statesman and World War II leader.

A souvenir sheet contains one airmail stamp, 50fr+5fr, with Churchill portrait centered, marginal decorations and inscriptions. Size: 80x80mm. Exists perf. and imperf. Price, each sheet, $3.50.

Nos. B28–B30 Overprinted

1967, July 14 Photo. *Perf. 13½*

B31 SP6 4fr+1fr multi. 30 12
B32 " 15fr+2fr " 85 40
B33 " 20fr+3fr " 1.25 60

50th anniversary of Lions International. Exist with dates transposed.

The souvenir sheets described below No. B30 also received this Lions overprint. Price, each $3.50.

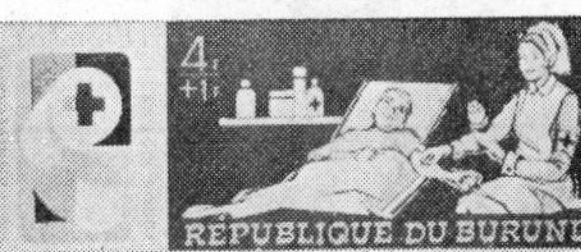

Blood Transfusion and Red Cross
SP7

Designs: 7fr+1fr, Stretcher bearers and wounded man. 11fr+1fr, Surgical team. 17fr+1fr, Nurses tending blood bank.

1969, June 26 Photo. *Perf. 13½*

B34 SP7 4fr+1fr multicolored 20 3
B35 " 7fr+1fr " 30 8
B36 " 11fr+1fr " 60 8
B37 " 17fr+1fr " 65 15
Nos. B34-B37, CB9-CB11 (7) 4.95 1.54

Issued to commemorate the 50th anniversary of the League of Red Cross Societies.

Pope Paul VI and Map of Africa—SP8

Designs: 3fr+2fr, 17fr+2fr, Pope Paul VI (vert.). 10fr+2fr, Flag made of flags of African Nations. 14fr+2fr, View of St. Peter's, Rome. 40fr+2fr, 40fr+5fr, Martyrs of Uganda. 50fr+2fr, 50fr+5fr, Pope on Throne. All designs include portrait of Pope Paul VI.

1969, Sept. 12 Photo. *Perf. 13½*

B38 SP8 3fr+2fr multi. 15 3
B39 " 5fr+2fr " 30 5
B40 " 10fr+2fr " 45 10
B41 " 14fr+2fr " 65 12
B42 " 17fr+2fr " 75 15
B43 " 40fr+2fr " 1.50 35
B44 " 50fr+2fr " 1.75 40
Nos. B38-B44 (7) 5.55 1.20

Souvenir Sheet

B45 SP8 Sheet of 2 4.00 3.50
a. 40fr+5fr multi. 1.75
b. 50fr+5fr " 2.00

Issued to commemorate the visit of Pope Paul VI to Uganda, July 31–Aug. 2. No. B45 contains 2 stamps, yellow margin with black inscription and church window design. Size: 80x102mm.

Virgin and Child, by Albrecht Dürer
SP9

Paintings: 11fr+1fr, Madonna of the Eucharist, by Sandro Botticelli. 20fr+1fr, Holy Family, by El Greco.

1970, Dec. 14 Photo. *Perf. 13½*

Gold Frame

B46 SP9 6.50fr+1fr multi. 30
B47 " 11fr+1fr " 45
B48 " 20fr+1fr " 85
a. Souvenir sheet of 3 1.50
Nos. B46-B48, CB12-CB14 (6) 4.30 1.25

Christmas 1970. No. B48a contains one each of Nos. B46–B48 with ornamental border and inscription. Size: 135x75mm.

Nos. 376–378 Surcharged in Gold and Black

1971, Nov. 27

B49 A51 3fr+1fr multicolored 18
B50 " 5fr+1fr " 24
B51 " 6fr+1fr " 30
a. Souvenir sheet of 3 80
Nos. B49-B51, CB19-CB21 (6) 2.40 1.10

25th anniversary of the United Nations International Children's Fund (UNICEF). No. B51a contains 3 stamps similar to Nos. B49–B51 with 2fr surtax each. Size: 125x81mm.

"La Polenta," by Pietro Longhi
SP10

Designs: 3fr+1fr, Archangel Michael, Byzantine icon from St. Mark's 6fr+1fr, "Gossip," by Pietro Longhi. 11fr+1fr, "Diana's Bath," by Giovanni Batista Pittoni. All stamps inscribed UNESCO.

1971, Dec. 27

B52 SP10 3fr+1fr gold & multicolored 15
B53 " 5fr+1fr gold & multicolored 24
B54 " 6fr+1fr gold & multicolored 28
B55 " 11fr+1fr gold & multicolored 48
a. Souvenir sheet of 4 1.20
Nos. B52-B55, CB22-CB25 (8) 3.67 1.25

The surtax was for the UNESCO campaign to save the treasures of Venice. No. B55a contains 4 stamps similar to Nos. B52-B55, but with 2fr surtax instead 1f. Gold and black ornamental margin. Size: 113x131½mm. Sheet exists imperf.

Nos. 408-410 Surcharged "+1F" in Silver

1972, Dec. 12 Photo. ***Perf. 13½***

B56 A57 5fr+1fr multi. 20
B57 " 10fr+1fr " 40
B58 " 15fr+1fr " 60
a. Souvenir sheet of 3 1.25
Nos. B56-B58, CB26-CB28 (6) 3.45 1.25

Christmas 1972. No. B58a contains 3 stamps similar to Nos. B56-B58, but with 2fr surtax. Deep carmine and gold border. Size: 128x81mm.

Nos. 441-443 Surcharged "+1F" in Silver

1973, Dec. 14 Photo. ***Perf. 13***

B59 A64 5fr+1fr multi. 20
B60 " 10fr+1fr " 40
B61 " 15fr+1fr " 60
a. Souvenir sheet of 3 1.25
Nos. B59-B61, CB29-CB31 (6) 3.81 1.30

Christmas 1973. No. B61a contains 3 stamps similar to Nos. B59-B61 with 2fr surtax each. Size: 143x79mm.

Christmas Type of 1974

1974, Dec. 2 Photogravure ***Perf. 13***

B62 A70 5fr+1fr multi. 20
B63 " 10fr+1fr " 33
B64 " 15fr+1fr " 50
a. Souvenir sheet of 3 1.25
Nos. B62-B64, CB32-CB34 (6) 3.69 1.35

No. B64a contains 3 stamps similar to Nos. B62-B64 with 2fr surtax each. Size: 137x90mm.

Nos. 485-490 Surcharged "+1 F" in Silver and Black

1975, Dec. 22 Photo. ***Perf. 13***

Multicolored

B65 A73 5fr+1fr #485 20
B66 " 5fr+1fr #486 20
B67 " 13fr+1fr #487 44
B68 " 13fr+1fr #488 44
B69 " 27fr+1fr #489 84
B70 " 27fr+1fr #490 84
a. Souvenir sheet of 6 3.50
Nos. B65-B70, CB35-CB40 (12) 8.52 1.75

Michelangelo Buonarroti (1475-1564), 500th birth anniversary. No. B70a contains 6 stamps similar to Nos. B65-B70 with 2fr surcharge each. Size: 132x106 mm.

Nos. 504-506 Surcharged "+1f" in Silver and Black

1976, Nov. 25 Photo. ***Perf. 13½***

B71 A76 5fr+1fr multi. 18
B72 " 13fr+1fr " 45
B73 " 27fr+1fr " 85
a. Souvenir sheet of 3 1.70
Nos. B71-B73, CB41-CB43 (6) 4.26 1.50

Christmas 1976. No. B73a contains 3 stamps similar to Nos. B71-B73 with 2fr surtax each. Size: 123x80mm.

Nos. 531-533 Surcharged "+1fr" in Silver and Black

1977 Photo. ***Perf. 14x13***

B74 A83 5fr+1fr multi. 18
B75 " 13fr+1fr " 45
B76 A83 27fr+1fr multi. 85
a. Souvenir sheet of 3 1.70
Nos. B74-B76, CB44-CB46 (6) 4.31

Christmas 1977. No. B76a contains 3 stamps similar to Nos. B74-B76 with 2fr surtax each. Size: 130x71mm.

AIR POST STAMPS

Animal Type of Regular Issue.

Animals: 6fr, Zebra. 8fr, Cape buffalo (bubalis). 10fr, Impala (vert.). 14fr, Hippopotamus. 15fr, Defassa waterbuck (vert.). 20fr, Cheetah. 50fr, Elephant.

Lithographed

1964, July 2 ***Perf. 14*** **Unwmkd.**

Border in Gold

Size: 42x21mm., 21x42mm.

C1 A9 6fr multicolored 40 5
C2 " 8fr " 50 8
C3 " 10fr " 65 10
C4 " 14fr " 90 15
C5 " 15fr " 1.00 18

Size: 53x32½mm.

C6 A9 20fr multicolored 1.35 25
C7 " 50fr " 3.50 65
Nos. C1-C7 (7) 8.30 1.46

Bird Type of Regular Issue

Birds: 6fr, Secretary bird. 8fr, African anhinga. 10fr, African peacock. 14fr, Bee eater. 15fr, Yellow-billed stork. 20fr, Saddle-billed stork. 50fr, Abyssinian ground hornbill. 75fr, Martial eagle. 130fr, Lesser flamingo.

1965, June 10 Litho. ***Perf. 14***

Birds in Natural Colors, Border in Gold.

Size: 26x43mm.

C8 A14 6fr multicolored 20 5
C9 " 8fr " 25 8
C10 " 10fr " 30 10
C11 " 14fr " 45 12
C12 " 15fr " 45 15

Size: 33x53mm.

C13 A14 20fr multicolored 60 18
C14 " 50fr " 1.50 35
C15 " 75fr " 2.20 45
C16 " 130fr " 4.00 65
Nos. C8-C16 (9) 9.95 2.13

Flower Type of Regular Issue

Flowers: 6fr, Dissotis. 8fr, Crossandra. 10fr, Ansellia. 14fr, Thunbergia. 15fr, Schizoglossum. 20fr, Gazania. 50fr, Protea. 75fr, Hibiscus. 130fr, Markhamia.

1966, Oct. 10 ***Perf. 13½*** **Unwmkd.**

Gold Background.

Size: 31x31mm.

C17 A17 6fr multicolored 15 5
C18 " 8fr " 20 8
C19 " 10fr " 25 10
C20 " 14fr " 35 12
C21 " 15fr " 35 15

Size: 39x39mm.

C22 A17 20fr multicolored 50 18
C23 " 50fr " 1.25 35
C24 " 75fr " 1.85 45
C25 " 130fr " 3.35 65
Nos. C17-C25 (9) 8.25 2.13

Souvenir Sheet

Tapestry Type of Regular Issue

1966, Nov. 4 ***Perf. 13½*** **Unwmkd.**

C26 A18 Sheet of 7 (14fr) 3.50 2.00

See note after No. 158.

Republic

Nos. C17-C25, Overprinted

REPUBLIQUE
DU
BURUNDI

1967 Lithographed ***Perf. 13½***

Size: 31x31mm.

Gold Background

C27 A17 6fr multicolored 20 8
C28 " 8fr " 25 10
C29 " 10fr " 30 10
C30 " 14fr " 45 12
C31 " 15fr " 45 15

Size: 39x39mm.

C32 A17 20fr multicolored 1.60
C33 " 50fr " 2.65
C34 " 75fr " 4.50
C35 " 130fr " 4.50
Nos. C27-C35 (9) 14.90 5.00

Nos. C8-C16 Overprinted "REPUBLIQUE / DU / BURUNDI" and Horizontal Bar

1967 **Lithographed** ***Perf. 14***

Birds in Natural Colors, Border in Gold

Size: 26x43mm.

C35A A14 6fr multicolored *30*
C35B " 8fr " *40*
C35C " 10fr " *40*
C35D " 14fr " *60*
C35E " 15fr " *60*

Size: 33x53mm

C35F A14 20fr multicolored *1.20*
C35G " 50fr " *3.00*
C35H " 75fr " *4.00*
C35I " 130fr " *6.50*
Nos. C35A-C35I (9) *17.00*

African Art Type of Regular Issue

African Art: 10fr, Spirit of Bakutu figurine, Equatorial Africa. 14fr, Pearl throne of Sultan of the Bamum, Cameroun. 17fr, Bronze head of Mother Queen of Benin, Nigeria. 24fr, Statue of 109th Bakouba king, Kata-Mbula, Central Congo. 26fr, Baskets and lances, Burundi.

1967, June 5 Photo. ***Perf. 13½***

C36 A20 10fr gold & multi. 30 20
C37 " 14fr " " 40 20
C38 " 17fr " " 45 20
C39 " 24fr " " 65 40
C40 " 26fr " " 1.20 75
Nos. C36-C40 (5) 3.00 1.75

Boy Scout Type of Regular Issue

Designs: 10fr, Scouts on hiking trip. 14fr, Cooking at campfire. 17fr, Lord Baden-Powell. 24fr, Boy Scout and Cub Scout giving Scout sign. 26fr, First aid.

1967, Aug. 9 ***Perf. 13½***

C41 A21 10fr gold & multi. 30 20
C42 " 14fr " " 45 20
C43 " 17fr " " 50 20
C44 " 24fr " " 75 30
C45 " 26fr " " 1.25 30
Nos. C41-C45 (5) 3.25 1.20

Issued to commemorate the 60th anniversary of the Boy Scouts and the 12th Boy Scout World Jamboree, Farragut State Park, Idaho, Aug. 1-9.

A souvenir sheet of 2 contains one each of Nos. C44-C45 and 2 labels in the designs of Nos. 208-209 with commemorative inscriptions was issued Jan. 8, 1968. Size: 100x100mm.

Fish Type of Regular Issue

Designs: Various Tropical Fish

1967, Sept. 8 Photo. ***Perf. 13½***

Size: 50x23mm.

C46 A19 6fr multicolored 20 5
C47 " 8fr " 25 6
C48 " 10fr " 30 8
C49 " 14fr " 45 10
C50 " 15fr " 45 12

Size: 58x27mm.

C51 A19 20fr multicolored 65 14
C52 " 50fr " 1.50 25
C53 " 75fr " 2.25 35
C54 " 130fr " 4.00 60
Nos. C46-C54 (9) 10.05 1.75

Boeing 707 of Air Congo and ITY Emblem
AP1

Designs: 14fr, Boeing 727 of Sabena over lake. 17fr, Vickers VC10 of East African Airways over lake. 26fr, Boeing 727 of Sabena over airport.

1967, Nov. 3 Photo. *Perf. 13*

C55 AP1 10fr black, yellow brn. & silver 25 10
C56 " 14fr black, orange & silver 40 15
C57 " 17fr black, bright blue & silver 50 20
C58 " 26fr blk., brt. rose lilac & silver 75 30

Issued to commemorate the opening of the jet airport at Bujumbura and for International Tourist Year, 1967.

Paintings Type of Regular Issue

Paintings: 17fr, Woman with Cat, by Renoir. 24fr, The Jewish Bride, by Rembrandt (horiz.). 26fr, Pope Innocent X, by Velazquez.

1968, Mar. 29 Photo. *Perf. 13½*

Light Green and Gold Frame

C59 A26 17fr multicolored 75 30
C60 " 24fr " 1.00 35
C61 " 26fr " 1.20 40

Issued in sheets of 6.

Space Type of Regular Issue

Designs: 14fr, Moon Probe. 18fr, Russian astronaut walking in space. 25fr, Weather satellite. 40fr, American astronaut walking in space.

1968, May 15 Photo. *Perf. 13½*

Size: 41x41mm.

C62 A27 14fr silver & multi. 50 10
C63 " 18fr " " 60 18
C64 " 25fr " " 90 20
C65 " 40fr " " 1.40 35

Issued to publicize peaceful space explorations.

Butterfly Type of Regular Issue

Butterflies: 6fr, Teracolus annae. 8fr, Graphium ridleyanus. 10fr, Cymothoe. 14fr, Charaxes eupale. 15fr, Papilio bromius. 20fr, Papilio zenobia. 50fr, Salamis aethiops. 75fr, Danais chrysippus. 130fr, Salamis temora.

1968, Sept. 9 Photo. *Perf. 13½*

Size: 38x42mm.

C66 A28 6fr gold & multi. 20 3
C67 " 8fr " " 25 4
C68 " 10fr " " 30 5
C69 " 14fr " " 45 5
C70 " 15fr " " 50 8

Size: 44x49mm.

C71 A28 20fr gold & multi. 65 10
C72 " 50fr " " 1.50 15
C73 " 75fr " " 2.25 20
C74 " 130fr " " 4.00 30
Nos. C66-C74 (9) 10.10 1.00

Painting Type of Regular Issue

Paintings: 17fr, The Letter, by Jean H. Fragonard. 26fr, Young Woman Reading Letter, by Jan Vermeer. 40fr, Lady Folding Letter, by Elisabeth Vigée-Lebrun. 50fr, Mademoiselle Lavergne, by Jean Etienne Liotard.

1968, Sept. 30 Photo. *Perf. 13½*

C84 A29 17fr multicolored 40 20
C85 " 26fr " 75 30
C86 " 40fr " 1.00 40
C87 " 50fr " 1.25 50

Issued for International Letter Writing Week, Oct. 7-13.

Olympic Games Type of 1968

Designs: 10fr, Shot put. 17fr, Running. 26fr, Hammer throw. 50fr, Hurdling. 75fr, Broad jump.

1968, Oct. 24

C88 A30 10fr gold & multi. 25 8
C89 " 17fr " " 40 12
C90 " 26fr " " 65 20
C91 " 50fr " " 1.25 40
C92 " 75fr " " 1.90 60
Nos. C88-C92 (5) 4.45 1.40

Issued to commemorate the 19th Olympic Games, Mexico City, Oct. 12-27.

Christmas Type of 1968

Paintings: 10fr, Virgin and Child, by Correggio. 14fr, Nativity, by Federigo Baroccio. 17fr, Holy Family, by El Greco. 26fr, Adoration of the Magi, by Maino.

1968, Nov. 26 Photo. *Perf. 13½*

C93 A31 10fr multicolored 30 15
C94 " 14fr " 45 20
C95 " 17fr " 55 25
C96 " 26fr " 80 30
a. Souv. sheet of 4 2.25

No. C96a contains one each of Nos. C93-C96, decorative border and inscriptions. Size: 120x120mm.

Human Rights Flame, Hand and Globe
AP2

1969, Jan. 22

C97 AP2 10fr multicolored 30 10
C98 " 14fr " 42 10
C99 " 26fr lilac & multi. 80 25

International Human Rights Year, 1968.

Nos. C93-C96 Overprinted in Silver

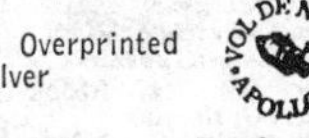

1969, Feb. 17 Photo. *Perf. 13½*

C100 A31 10fr multicolored 50 20
C101 " 14fr " 70 30
C102 " 17fr " 90 35
C103 " 26fr " 1.25 55

Issued to commemorate man's first flight around the moon by the U.S. spacecraft Apollo 8, Dec. 21-27, 1968.

Moon Landing Type of 1969

Designs: 26fr, Neil A. Armstrong leaving landing module. 40fr, Astronaut on moon. 50fr, Splashdown in the Pacific.

1969, Nov. 6 Photo. *Perf. 13½*

C104 A38 26fr gold & multi. 65 20
C105 " 40fr " " 1.00 30
C106 " 50fr " " 1.20 35

See note after Algeria No. 427.

Christmas Type of 1969

Paintings: 17fr, Madonna and Child, by Benvenuto da Garofalo. 26fr, Madonna and Child, by Jacopo Negretti. 50fr, Madonna and Child, by Il Giorgione. All horizontal.

1969, Dec. 2 Photogravure

C107 A39 17fr gold & multi. 60 15
C108 " 26fr " " 80 20
C109 " 50fr " " 1.50 40
a. Souvenir sheet of 3 3.00

No. C109a contains one each of Nos. C107-C109. Gold frame with black and red inscription. Size: 87x110mm.

Insect Type of Regular Issue

Designs: Various Beetles and Weevils.

1970 *Perf. 13½*

Size: 46x32mm.

C110 A40 6fr gold & multi. 15 3
C111 " 8fr " " 20 3
C112 " 10fr " " 25 3
C113 " 14fr " " 35 3
C114 " 15fr " " 40 4

Size: 52x36mm.

C115 A40 20fr gold & multi. 50 6
C116 " 50fr " " 1.20 25
C117 " 75fr " " 1.80 35
C118 " 130fr " " 3.00 60
Nos. C110-C118 (9) 7.85 1.42

Issue dates: Nos. C110-C115, Jan. 20. Nos. C116-C118, Feb. 27.

Easter Type of 1970

Stations of the Cross, by Juan de Aranoa y Carredano: 8fr, Jesus meets the women of Jerusalem. 10fr, Jesus falls a third time. 14fr, Jesus stripped. 15fr, Jesus nailed to the cross. 18fr, Jesus dies on the cross. 20fr, Descent from the cross. 50fr, Jesus laid in the tomb.

1970, Mar. 16 Photo. *Perf. 13½*

C119 A41 8fr gold & multi. 20 8
C120 " 10fr " " 25 10
C121 " 14fr " " 36 15
C122 " 15fr " " 40 16
C123 " 18fr " " 45 18
C124 " 20fr " " 48 20
C125 " 50fr " " 1.20 50
a. Souv. sheet of 7+label 3.40
Nos. C119-C125 (7) 3.34 1.37

No. C125a contains one each of Nos. C119-C125 and label showing Ascension. Gold decorative border. Size: 154x123mm.

EXPO '70 Type of Regular Issue

Souvenir Sheet

Designs: 40fr, Tower of the Sun (vert.). 50fr, Flags of participating nations (vert.).

1970, May 5 Photo. *Perf. 13½*

C126 A42 Souv. sheet of 2 2.50
a. 40fr multicolored 95
b. 50fr " 1.20

Issued to publicize EXPO '70 International Exhibition, Osaka, Japan, March 15-Sept. 13, 1970. No. C126 has gold and black decorative border. Size: 104½x80mm.

Rhinoceros Type of Regular Issue

Designs, FAUNA: Camel, dromedary, okapi, rhinoceros, addax, Burundi cow (2 stamps of each animal in 2 different poses). MAP OF THE NILE: Delta and pyramids, dhow, cataract, Blue Nile and crowned crane, Victoria Nile and secretary bird, Lake Victoria and source of Nile on Mt. Gikizi.

1970, July 8 Photo. *Perf. 13½*

C127 A43 14fr multicolored 56 20
a. Sheet of 18 10.50

Issued in sheets of 18 (3x6) stamps of different designs, to publicize the southernmost source of the Nile on Mt. Gikizi in Burundi.

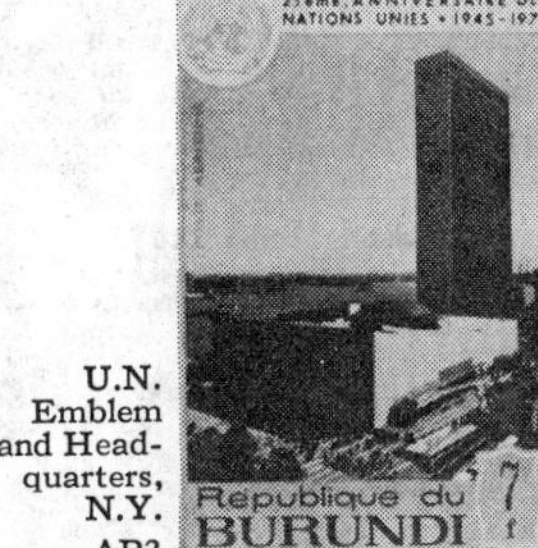

U.N. Emblem and Headquarters, N.Y.
AP3

Designs (U.N. Emblem and): 11fr, Security Council and mural by Per Krohg. 26fr, Pope Paul VI and U Thant. 40fr, Flags in front of U.N. Headquarters, N.Y.

1970, Oct. 23 Photo. *Perf. 13½*

C128 AP3 7fr gold & multi. 20 5
C129 " 11fr " " 35 8
C130 " 26fr " " 75 15
C131 " 40fr " " 1.20 25
a. Souvenir sheet of 2 2.00

Issued to commemorate the 25th anniversary of the United Nations. No. C131a contains 2 stamps similar to Nos. C130-C131 but without "Poste Aerienne"; blue margin with gold ornament, black inscription and U.N. emblem. Size: 123x80mm. Exists imperf.

Bird Type of Regular Issue

Birds: 8fr, 14fr, 30fr, vertical; 10fr, 20fr, 50fr, horizontal.

1970 Photogravure *Perf. 13½*

Gold Frame & Multicolored; Birds in Natural Colors

Stamp size: 52x44mm.

C132 A44 8fr Block of four 1.20
a. *Northern shrike* 30
b. *European starling* 30
c. *Yellow wagtail* 30
d. *Bank swallow* 30
C133 A44 10fr Block of four 1.80
a. *Winter wren* 45
b. *Firecrest* 45
c. *Skylark* 45
d. *Crested lark* 45
C134 A44 14fr Block of four 2.40
a. *Woodchat shrike* 60
b. *Common rock thrush* 60
c. *Black redstart* 60
d. *Ring ouzel* 60
C135 A44 20fr Block of four 3.80
a. *European redstart* 95
b. *Hedge sparrow* 95
c. *Gray wagtail* 95
d. *Meadow pipit* 95
C136 A44 30fr Block of four 5.60
a. *Eurasian hoopoe* 1.40
b. *Pied flycatcher* 1.40
c. *Great reed warbler* 1.40
d. *Eurasian kingfisher* 1.40
C137 A44 50fr Block of four 9.60
a. *House martin* 2.40
b. *Sedge warbler* 2.40
c. *Fieldfare* 2.40
d. *European golden oriole* 2.40
Nos. C132-C137 (6 blocks of 4) 24.40

Nos. C132-C137 are printed in sheets of 16 containing 4 blocks of 4.

Queen Fabiola and King Baudouin of Belgium
AP4

Designs: 20fr, Pres. Michel Micombero and King Baudouin. 40fr, Pres. Micombero and coats of arms of Burundi and Belgium.

1970, Nov. 28 Photo. *Perf. 13½*

C140 AP4 6fr gold, dp. brown & deep plum 20 6
C141 " 20fr gold, dp. brown & deep plum 60 20
C142 " 40fr gold, dp. brown & deep plum 1.25 40
a. Souvenir sheet of 3 2.25

Issued to commemorate the visit of the King and Queen of Belgium. No. C142a contains 3 stamps similar to Nos. C140-C142, but without "Poste Aerienne." Deep plum and gold margin with commemorative inscription. Size: 143½x108mm.

Easter Type of Regular Issue

Paintings of the Resurrection: 14fr, by Louis Borrassá. 17fr, Piero della Francesca. 26fr, Michel Wohlgemuth.

1971, Apr. 2 Photo. *Perf. 13½*

C143 A49 14fr gold & multi. 50
C144 " 17fr " " 55
C145 " 26fr " " 75
a. Souvenir sheet of 3 1.90

Easter 1971. No. C145a contains one each of Nos. C143-C145. Red and gold margin. Size: 120x85mm. Sheet exists imperf.

Animal Type of Regular Issue

1971 Photogravure *Perf. 13½*

Multicolored

Size: 44x44mm.

C146 A48 10fr Strip of four 1.20
a. *Lion* 30
b. *Cape buffalo* 30
c. *Hippopotamus* 30
d. *Giraffe* 30
C147 A48 14fr Strip of four 2.00
a. *Hartebeest* 50
b. *Black rhinoceros* 50
c. *Zebra* 50
d. *Leopard* 50
C148 A48 17fr Strip of four 2.40
a. *Grant's gazelles* 60
b. *Cheetah* 60
c. *African white-backed vultures* 60
d. *Johnston's okapi* 60
C149 A48 24fr Strip of four 3.00
a. *Chimpanzee* 75
b. *Elephant* 75
c. *Spotted Hyenas* 75
d. *Beisa* 75

C150 A48 26fr Strip of four 3.60
a. Gorilla 90
b. Gnu 90
c. Warthog 90
d. Cape hunting dog 90
C151 A48 31fr Strip of four 4.00
a. Sable antelope 1.00
b. Caracal lynx 1.00
c. Ostriches 1.00
d. Bongo 1.00
Nos. C146-C151 (6 strips of 4) 16.20

No. C146 Overprinted in Gold and Black

LUTTE CONTRE LE RACISME ET LA DISCRIMINATION RACIALE

1971, July 20 Photo. *Perf. 13½*

C152 A48 10fr Strip of four 1.20 24
a. Lion 30
b. Cape buffalo 30
c. Hippopotamus 30
d. Giraffe 30

International Year Against Racial Discrimination.

Christmas Type of Regular Issue

Paintings of the Madonna and Child by: 14fr, Cima de Conegliano. 17fr, Fra Filippo Lippi. 31fr, Leonardo da Vinci.

1971, Nov. 2 Photo. *Perf. 13½*

C153 A51 14fr red & multi. 50
C154 " 17fr " " 55
C155 " 31fr " " 90
a. Souvenir sheet of 3 2.00

Christmas 1971. No. C155a contains one each of Nos. C153-C155. Multicolored margin. Size: 125x81mm. Sheet exists imperf.

Spacecraft Type of Regular Issue
Souvenir Sheet

1972, Jan. 15 Photo. *Perf. 13½*

C156 A52 Sheet of 6, multicolored 3.00 2.00
a. 6fr *Lunar Orbiter* 16
b. 11fr *Vostok* 29
c. 14fr *Luna 1* 36
d. 17fr *Apollo 11 astronaut on moon* 43
e. 26fr *Soyuz 11* 68
f. 40fr *Lunar rover (Apollo 15)* 96

Conquest of space. No. C156 has dark blue and multicolored margin. Size: 134x 135mm.

Sapporo '72 Type of Regular Issue
Souvenir Sheet

Designs (Sapporo '72 Emblem and): 26fr, Snow scooter. 31fr, Downhill skiing. 50fr, Bobsledding.

1972, Feb. 3

C157 A53 Sheet of 3 2.80 1.75
a. 26fr silver & multi. 68
b. 31fr " " 78
c. 50fr " " 1.20

11th Winter Olympic Games, Sapporo, Japan, Feb. 3-13. No. C157 contains 3 stamps, arranged vertically. Silver decorative margin with blue and black inscription. Size: 106x125mm.

Olympic Games Type of 1972

1972, July 24 Photo. *Perf. 13½*
Gold and Multicolored

C158 A55 24fr *Weight lifting* 72
C159 " 26fr *Hurdles* 78
C160 " 31fr *Discus* 95
C161 " 40fr *Soccer* 1.20

20th Olympic Games, Munich, Aug. 26-Sept. 11.

Independence Type of 1972

Designs: 15fr, Prince Rwagasore, Pres. Micombero, Burundi flag, drummers. 18fr, Rwagasore, Micombero, flag, map of Africa, globe. 27fr, Micombero, flag, globe.

1972, Aug. 24 Photo. *Perf. 13½*

C162 A56 15fr gold & multi. 50
C163 " 18fr " " 60
C164 A56 27fr gold & multi. 90
a. Souvenir sheet of 3 2.25

10th anniversary of independence.
No. C164a contains one each of Nos. C162-C164. Gold and light blue margin with black inscription. Size: 146x80mm.

Christmas Type of 1972

Paintings of the Madonna and Child by: 18fr, Sebastiano Mainardi. 27fr, Hans Memling. 40fr, Lorenzo Lotto.

1972, Nov. 2 Photo. *Perf. 13½*

C165 A57 18fr dk. carmine & multicolored 55
C166 " 27fr dk. carmine & multicolored 80
C167 " 40fr dk. carmine & multi. 1.20
a. Souvenir sheet of 3 2.75

Christmas 1972. No. C167a contains one each of Nos. C165-C167, slate green and gold border. Size: 128x81mm.

Orchid Type of Regular Issue

1973, Jan. 18 Photo. *Perf. 13½*
Multicolored
Size: 38x38mm.

C168 A58 13fr *Thelymitra pauciflora* 34
C169 " 14fr *Miltassia* 36
C170 " 15fr *Miltonia* 39
C171 " 18fr *Platycoryne crocea* 45
C172 " 20fr *Cattleya trianaei* 48
C173 " 27fr *Eulophia cucullata* 70
C174 " 36fr *Cymbidium hamsey* 90
Nos. C168-C174 (7) 3.62

African Exploration Type of 1973

Designs: 15fr, Livingstone writing his diary. 18fr, "Dr. Livingstone, I presume." 27fr, Livingstone and Stanley discussing expedition.

1973, Mar. 19 Photo. *Perf. 13½*

C175 A59 15fr gold & multi. 45
C176 " 18fr " " 55
C177 " 27fr " " 80
a. Souvenir sheet of 3 2.00

Exploration of Africa by David Livingstone and Henry Morton Stanley. No. C177a contains 3 stamps similar to Nos. C175-C177, but without "Poste Aerienne." Gold and violet decorative margin. Size: 100x140mm.

Easter Type of 1973

Paintings: 15fr, Christ at the Pillar, by Guido Reni. 18fr, Crucifixion, by Mathias Grunewald. 27fr, Descent from the Cross, by Caravaggio.

1973, Apr. 10

C178 A60 15fr gold & multi. 45
C179 " 18fr " " 55
C180 " 27fr " " 80
a. Souvenir sheet of 3 2.00

Easter 1973. No. C180a contains one each of Nos. C178-C180. Multicolored margin. Size: 121x73mm.

INTERPOL Type of Regular Issue

Designs: 27fr, INTERPOL emblem and flag. 40fr, INTERPOL flag and emblem.

1973, May 19 Photo. *Perf. 13½*

C181 A61 27fr gold & multi. 80
C182 " 40fr " " 95

50th anniversary of International Criminal Police Organization (INTERPOL).

Copernicus Type of Regular Issue

Designs: 15fr, Copernicus (C183a), Earth, Pluto, and Jupiter. 18fr, Copernicus (No. C184a), Venus, Saturn, Mars. 27fr, Copernicus (No. C185a), Uranus, Neptune, Mercury. 36fr, Earth and various spacecrafts.

1973, July 27 Photo. *Perf. 13½*
Gold and Multicolored

C183 A62 15fr Block of four 2.40
a. 15fr in UL 60
b. 15fr in UR 60
c. 15fr in LL 60
d. 15fr in LR 60
C184 A62 18fr Block of four 2.80
a. 18fr in UL 70
b. 18fr in UR 70
c. 18fr in LL 70
d. 18fr in LR 70
C185 A62 27fr Block of four 4.20
a. 27fr in UL 1.05
b. 27fr in UR 1.05
c. 27fr in LL 1.05
d. 27fr in LR 1.05
C186 A62 36fr Block of four 5.60
a. 36fr in UL 1.40
b. 36fr in UR 1.40
c. 36fr in LL 1.40
d. 36fr in LR 1.40
e. Souvenir sheet of 4 15.00

500th anniversary of the birth of Nicolaus Copernicus (1473-1543), Polish astronomer. Nos. C183-C186 are printed in sheets of 32 containing 8 blocks of 4. No. C186e contains one each of Nos. C183-C186. Gold and multicolored margin. Size: 136x136mm.

Flower-Butterfly Type of 1973

Designs: Each block of 4 contains 2 flower and 2 butterfly designs. The 10fr, 14fr, 24fr and 31fr have flower designs listed as "a" and "d" numbers, butterflies as "b" and "c" numbers; the arrangement is reversed for the 17fr and 26fr.

1973, Sept. 28 Photo. *Perf. 13*
Stamp Size: 35x45mm.
Gold and Multicolored

C187 A63 10fr Block of 4 1.60
a. Protea cynaroides 40
b. Precis octavia 40
c. Epiphora bauhiniae 40
d. Gazania longiscapa 40
C188 A63 14fr Block of 4 2.24
a. Kniphofia 56
b. Cymothoe coccinata 56
c. Nudaurelia zambesina 56
d. Freesia refracta 56
C189 A63 17fr Block of 4 2.60
a. Calotis eupompe 65
b. Narcissus 65
c. Cineraria hybrida 65
d. Cyrestis camillus 65
C190 A63 24fr Block of 4 3.80
a. Iris tingitana 95
b. Papilio demodocus 95
c. Catopsilia avelaneda 95
d. Nerine sarniensis 95
C191 A63 26fr Block of 4 4.40
a. Hypolimnas dexithea 1.10
b. Zantedeschia tropicalis 1.10
c. Sandersonia aurantiaca 1.10
d. Drurya antimachus 1.10
C192 A63 31fr Block of 4 5.20
a. Nymphaea capensis 1.30
b. Pandoriana pandora 1.30
c. Precis orythia 1.30
d. Pelargonium domestica 1.30
Nos. C187-C192 (6 blocks of 4) 19.84

Christmas Type of 1973

Virgin and Child by: 18fr, Raphael. 27fr, Pietro Perugino. 40fr, Titian.

1973, Nov. 19

C193 A64 18fr gold & multi. 55
C194 " 27fr " " 80
C195 " 40fr " " 1.20
a. Souvenir sheet of 3 2.75

Christmas 1973. No. C195a contains one each of Nos. C193-C195 with multicolored margin. Size: 143x79mm.

Soccer Type of Regular Issue

Designs: Various soccer scenes and cup.

1974, July 4 Photogravure *Perf. 13*

C196 A67 20fr gold & multi. 60 12
C197 " 26fr " " 78 16
C198 " 40fr " " 1.20 24

World Cup Soccer Championships, Munich, June 13-July 7. For souvenir sheet see No. 459a.

UPU Type of 1974

Designs: No. C199, Flags over UPU Headquarters, Bern. No. C200, G.P.O., Usumbura. No. C201, Mailmen ("26F" in UR). No. C202, Mailmen ("26F" in UL). No. C203, UPU emblem. No. C204, Means of transportation. No. C205, Pigeon over globe showing Burundi. No. C206, Swiss flag, pigeon over map showing Bern.

1974, July 23

C199 A68 24fr gold & multi. 95
C200 " 24fr " " 95
C201 " 26fr " " 1.00
C202 " 26fr " " 1.00
C203 " 31fr " " 1.25
C204 " 31fr " " 1.25
C205 " 40fr " " 1.60
C206 A68 40fr gold & multi. 1.60
a. Souvenir sheet of 8 10.00
Nos. C199-C206 (8) 9.60

Centenary of Universal Postal Union. Stamps of same denomination printed se-tenant (continuous design) in sheets of 40. No. C206a contains one each of Nos. C199-C206. Violet, gold and light blue margin. Size: 96x162mm.

Fish Type of 1974

1974, Sept. 9 Photo. *Perf. 13*
Size: 35x35mm.
Multicolored

C207 A66 10fr Block of 4 1.20
a. Haplochromis multicolor 30
b. Pantodon buchholzi 30
c. Tropheus duboisi 30
d. Distichodus sexfasciatus 30
C208 A66 14fr Block of 4 1.68
a. Pelmatochromis kribensis 42
b. Nannaethiops tritaeniatus 42
c. Polycentropsis abbreviata 42
d. Hemichromis bimaculatus 42
C209 A66 17fr Block of 4 2.00
a. Ctenopoma acutirostre 50
b. Synodontis angelicus 50
c. Tilapia melanopleura 50
d. Aphyosemion bivittatum 50
C210 A66 24fr Block of 4 2.90
a. Monodactylus argenteus 72
b. Zanclus canescens 72
c. Pygoplites diacanthus 72
d. Cephalopholis argus 72
C211 A66 26fr Block of 4 3.15
a. Priacanthus arenatus 78
b. Pomacanthus arcuatus 78
c. Scarus guacamaia 78
d. Zeus faber 78
C212 A66 31fr Block of 4 3.75
a. Lactophrys quadricornis 93
b. Balistes vetula 93
c. Acanthurus bahianus 93
d. Holocanthus ciliaris 93
Nos. C207-C212 (6 blocks of 4) 14.68

Christmas Type of 1974

Paintings of the Virgin and Child: 18fr, by Hans Memling. 27fr, by Filippino Lippi. 40fr, by Lorenzo di Gredi.

1974, Nov. 7 Photo. *Perf. 13*

C213 A70 18fr gold & multi. 55
C214 " 27fr " " 80
C215 " 40fr " " 1.20
a. Souvenir sheet of 3 3.00

Christmas 1974. Sheets of 20 stamps and one label. No. C215a contains one each of Nos. C213-C215, gold and multicolored border. Size: 137x90mm. Sheet exists imperf.

Apollo-Soyuz Type of 1975.

1975, July 10 Photo. *Perf. 13*
Multicolored

C216 A71 27fr Block of 4 4.25
a. A. A. Leonov, V. N. Kubasov, Soviet flag 80
b. Soyuz and Soviet flag 80
c. Apollo and American flag 80
d. Slayton, Brand, Stafford, American flag 80
C217 A71 40fr Block of 4 6.25
a. Apollo-Soyuz link-up 1.20
b. Apollo, blast-off 1.20
c. Soyuz, blast-off 1.20
d. Kubasov, Leonov, Slayton, Brand, Stafford 1.20

Apollo Soyuz space test project (Russo-American cooperation), launching July 15; link-up, July 17. Nos. C216-C217 are printed in sheets of 32 containing 8 blocks of 4.

Animal Type of 1975

1975, Sept. 17 Photo. *Perf. 13½*
Multicolored

C218 A72 10fr Strip of four 1.20
a. Addax 30
b. Roan antelope 30
c. Nyala 30
d. White rhinoceros 30
C219 A72 14fr Strip of four 1.68
a. Mandrill 42
b. Oryx 42
c. Dik-dik 42
d. Thomson's gazelles 42
C220 A72 17fr Strip of four 2.00
a. African small-clawed civet 50
b. Reed buck 50
c. Indian civet 50
d. Cape buffalo 50

C221 A72 24fr Strip of four 2.88
a. *White-tailed gnu* 72
b. *Donkeys* 72
c. *Colobus monkey* 72
d. *Gerenuk* 72
C222 A72 26fr Strip of four 3.15
a. *Dama gazelle* 76
b. *Wild dog* 76
c. *Sitatungas* 76
d. *Striped duiker* 76
C223 A72 31fr Strip of four 3.75
a. *Fennec* 93
b. *Lesser kudus* 93
c. *Blesbok* 93
d. *Serval* 93
Nos. C218–C223 (6 strips of 4) 14.66

Nos. C218–C219 Overprinted in Black and Silver with IWY Emblem and: "ANNEE INTERNATIONALE / DE LA FEMME"

1975, Nov. 19 Photo. *Perf. 13½*

C224 A72 10fr Strip of four 1.20 24
a. *Addax* 30
b. *Roan antelope* 30
c. *Nyala* 30
d. *White rhinoceros* 30
C225 A72 14fr Strip of four 1.68 35
a. *Mandrill* 42
b. *Oryx* 42
c. *Dik-dik* 42
d. *Thomson's gazelles* 42

International Women's Year 1975.

Nos. C222–C223 Overprinted in Black and Silver with U.N. Emblem and: "30ème ANNIVERSAIRE DES/ NATIONS UNIES"

1975, Nov. 19

C226 A72 26fr Strip of four 3.15 60
a. *Dama gazelle* 76
b. *Wild dog* 76
c. *Sitatungas* 76
d. *Striped duiker* 76
C227 A72 31fr Strip of four 3.75 65
a. *Fennec* 93
b. *Lesser kudus* 93
c. *Blesbok* 93
d. *Serval* 93

United Nations, 30th anniversary.

Michelangelo Type of 1975

Designs: Paintings from Sistine Chapel.

1975, Dec. 3 Photo. *Perf. 13*

C228 A73 18fr *Zachariah* 54
C229 " 18fr *Joel* 54
C230 " 31fr *Erythrean Sybil* 93
C231 " 31fr *Prophet Ezekiel* 93
C232 " 40fr *Persian Sybil* 1.20
C233 " 40fr *Prophet Jeremiah* 1.20
a. Souvenir sheet of 6 5.50
Nos. C228–C233 (6) 5.34

Michelangelo Buonarotti (1475–1564), Italian sculptor, painter and architect. Stamps of same denominations printed se-tenant in sheets of 18 stamps and 2 labels. No. C233a contains one each of Nos. C228–C233, green & gold margin, black inscription. Size: 137x111mm.

Olympic Games Type, 1976

Designs (Olympic Games Emblem and): 18fr, Ski jump. 36fr, Slalom. 50fr, Ice hockey.

1976, Jan. 23 Photo. *Perf. 14x13½*

C234 A74 18fr olive brown & multicolored 54
C235 " 36fr grn. & multi. 1.08
C236 " 50fr pur. & multi. 1.50
a. Souvenir sheet of 4 3.10

12th Winter Olympic Games, Innsbruck, Austria, Feb. 4–15.

No. C236a contains 4 stamps similar to Nos. 491–494, perf. 13½, inscribed "POSTE AERIENNE." Multicolored margin with snowflakes and Games' emblem. Size: 100x103mm.

Hurdles—AP5

Designs (Montreal Games Emblem and): Nos. C238, C241, C243b, High jump. Nos. C239, C242, C243a, Athlete on rings. No. C240, C243c, Hurdles.

1976, May 3 Litho. *Perf. 13½*

C237 AP5 27fr grn. & multi. 78
C238 " 27fr dk. bl. & multi. 78
C239 " 31fr ocher & multi. 93
C240 " 31fr green & multi. 93
C241 " 50fr dark blue & multi. 1.50
C242 " 50fr ocher & multi. 1.50
Nos. C237–C242 (6) 6.42

Souvenir Sheet

C243 AP5 Sheet of 3 3.40 60
a. 27fr ocher & multicolored 78
b. 31fr dark blue & multicolored 95
c. 50fr green & multicolored 1.50

21st Olympic Games, Montreal, Canada, July 17–Aug. 1. Stamps of same denomination printed se-tenant in sheets of 20.

No. C243 has gold inscription, Montreal Olympic emblem and multicolored band in margin. Size: 100x120mm.

Battle of Bunker Hill, by John Trumbull

AP6 AP7

Paintings: 26fr, Franklin, Jefferson and John Adams. 36fr, Declaration of Independence, by John Trumbull.

1976, July 16 Photo. *Perf. 13*

C244 AP6 18fr gold & multi. 54
C245 AP7 18fr " " 54
C246 AP6 26fr " " 76
C247 AP7 26fr " " 76
C248 AP6 36fr " " 1.05
C249 AP7 36fr " " 1.05
a. Souvenir sheet of 6 5.00
Nos. C244–C249 (6) 4.70 90

American Bicentennial. Stamps of same denomination printed se-tenant in sheets of 50. No. C249a contains one each of Nos. C244–C249 with Bicentennial emblem in margin. Size: 102x148mm.

Christmas Type of 1976

Paintings: 18fr, Virgin and Child with St. Anne, by Leonardo da Vinci. 31fr, Holy Family with Lamb, by Raphael. 40fr, Madonna of the Basket, by Correggio.

1976, Oct. 18 Photo. *Perf. 13½*

C250 A76 18fr gold & multi. 54
C251 " 31fr " " 94
C252 " 40fr " " 1.20
a. Souvenir sheet of 3 2.80

Christmas 1976. Sheets of 20 stamps and descriptive label. No. C252a contains one each of Nos. C250–C252; multicolored margin. Size: 123x80mm.

A.G. Bell Type 1977

Designs: 10fr, A.G. Bell and first telephone. Nos. C253, 17fr, A.G. Bell speaking into microphone. Nos. C254, C257e, Satellites around globe and videophone. No. C255, Switchboard operator, c.1910, and wall telephone. Nos. C256, 26fr, Intelsat satellite, modern and old telephones. No. C257c, Intelsat and radar.

1977, May 17 Photo. *Perf. 13*

C253 A78 18fr multicolored 54
C254 A79 18fr " 54
C255 A78 36fr " 1.05
C256 A79 36fr " 1.05

Souvenir Sheet

C257 Sheet of 5 3.50
a. A78 10fr multicolored 30
b. " 17fr " 50
c. A79 18fr " 54
d. " 26fr " 80
e. " 36fr " 1.05

Centenary of first telephone call by Alexander Graham Bell, Mar. 10, 1876. No. C257 contains 3 postage (10fr, 17fr, 26fr) and 2 air post stamps (18fr, 36fr). Multicolored margin with ITU emblem and old telephone. Size: 120x135mm.

Animal Type of 1977

1977, Aug. 22 Photo. *Perf. 14x14½*

Multicolored

C258 A80 9fr Strip of four 1.10
a. *Buffon's kob* 26
b. *Marabous* 26
c. *Brindled gnu* 26
d. *River hog* 26
C259 A80 13fr Strip of four 1.60
a. *Zebras* 40
b. *Shoebill* 40
c. *Striped hyenas* 40
d. *Chimpanzee* 40
C260 A80 30fr Strip of four 3.60
a. *Flamingos* 90
b. *Nile Crocodiles* 90
c. *Green mamba* 90
d. *Greater kudus* 90
C261 A80 35fr Strip of four 4.20
a. *Hyrax* 1.05
b. *Cobra* 1.05
c. *Jackals* 1.05
d. *Verreaux's eagles* 1.05
C262 A80 54fr Strip of four 6.50
a. *Honey badger* 1.62
b. *Harnessed antelopes* 1.62
c. *Secretary bird* 1.62
d. *Klipspringer* 1.62
C263 A80 70fr Strip of four 8.40
a. *African big-eared fox* 2.10
b. *Elephants* 2.10
c. *Vulturine guineafowl* 2.10
d. *Impalas* 2.10
Nos. C258–C263 (6 strips of 4) 25.40

UN Type of 1977

Designs (UN Stamps and): 24fr, UN buildings by night. 27fr, UN buildings and view of Manhattan. 35fr, UN buildings by day.

1977, Oct. 10 Photo. *Perf. 13½*

C264 A82 24fr Block of four 2.88
a. No. 77 72
b. No. 78 72
c. No. 40 72
d. No. 32 72
C265 A82 27fr Block of four 3.20
a. No. 50 80
b. No. 21 80
c. No. 30 80
d. No. 44 80
C266 A82 35fr Block of four 4.20
a. No. C6 1.05
b. No. 105 1.05
c. No. 4 1.05
d. No. 1 1.05
e. Souvenir sheet of 3 2.75

25th anniversary (in 1976) of the United Nations Postal Administration. No. C266e contains 24fr in design of No. C265b, 27fr in design of No. C266a, 35fr in design of No. C264c; silver margin. Size: 128x76 mm.

Christmas Type of 1977

Designs: Paintings of the Virgin and Child.

1977, Oct. 31 Photo. *Perf. 14x13*

C267 A83 18fr multicolored 55
C268 " 31fr " 95
C269 " 40fr " 1.20
a. Souvenir sheet of 3 3.00

Christmas 1977. Sheets of 24 stamps and descriptive label. No. C269a contains one each of Nos. C267–C269; gold and multicolored margin. Size: 130x72mm.

AIR POST SEMI-POSTAL STAMPS

Coin Type of Semi-Postal Issue

Designs (Coins of Various Denominations): 3fr+1fr, 11fr+1fr, 20fr+1fr, 50fr+1fr, Coat of Arms, reverse. 5fr+1fr, 14fr+1fr, 30fr+1fr, 100fr+1fr, King Mwambutsa IV, obverse.

1965, Nov. 15 *Imperf.*

Lithographed; Embossed on Gilt Foil

Diameter: 39mm.

CB1 SP4 3fr+1fr lt. & dark violet 15 10
CB2 " 5fr+1fr pale green & red 20 15

Diameter: 45mm.

CB3 SP4 11fr+1fr orange & lilac 45 25
CB4 " 14fr+1fr red & emerald 60 40

Diameter: 56mm.

CB5 SP4 20fr+1fr ultra. & black 80 50
CB6 " 30fr+1fr dp. orange & maroon 1.15 80

Diameter: 67mm.

CB7 SP4 50fr+1fr blue & violet blue 2.00 1.25
CB8 " 100fr+1fr rose & deep claret 4.00 2.50
Nos. CB1–CB8 (8) 10.35 5.95

Stamps are backed with patterned paper in blue, orange, and pink engine-turned design.

Red Cross Type of Semi-Postal Issue

Designs: 26fr+3fr, Laboratory. 40fr+3fr, Ambulance and thatched huts. 50fr+3fr, Red Cross nurse with patient.

1969, June 26 Photo. *Perf. 13½*

CB9 SP7 26fr+3fr multi. 75 30
CB10 " 40fr+3fr " 1.10 40
CB11 " 50fr+3fr " 1.35 50

Issued to commemorate the 50th anniversary of the League of Red Cross Societies. Perf. and imperf. souvenir sheets exist containing 3 stamps similar to Nos. CB9–CB11, but without "Poste Aerienne." Gold frame with green commemorative inscription. Size: 90½x97mm.

Christmas Type of Semi-Postal Issue

Paintings: 14fr+3fr, Virgin and Child, by Velázquez. 26fr+3fr, Holy Family, by Joos van Cleve. 40fr+3fr, Virgin and Child, by Rogier van der Weyden.

1970, Dec. 14 Photo. *Perf. 13½*

CB12 SP9 14fr+3fr multi. 50
CB13 " 26fr+3fr " 90
CB14 " 40fr+3fr " 1.30
a. Souvenir sheet of 3 3.00

No. CB14a contains one each of Nos. CB12–CB14 with ornamental border and inscription. Size: 135x75mm.

No. C147 Surcharged in Gold and Black

LUTTE CONTRE
L'ANALPHABETISME

1971, Aug. 9 Photo. *Perf. 13½*

CB15 A48 14fr+2fr Strip of four 1.60 32
a. *Hartebeest* 40
b. *Black rhinoceros* 40
c. *Zebra* 40
d. *Leopard* 40

UNESCO campaign against illiteracy.

No. C148 Surcharged in Gold and Black

AIDE INTERNATIONALE AUX REFUGIES

1971, Aug. 9 **Multicolored**

CB16 A48 17fr+1fr Strip of four 1.84 36
- *a. Grant's gazelles* 46
- *b. Cheetah* 46
- *c. African white-backed vultures* 46
- *d. Johnston's okapi* 46

International help for refugees.

Nos. C150–C151 Surcharged in Black and Gold

+1F

75eme ANNIVERSAIRE DES JEUX OLYMPIQUES MODERNES (1896-1971)

a

+1F

JEUX PRE-OLYMPIQUES MUNICH 1972

b

1971, Aug. 16

CB17 A48 (*a*) 26fr+1fr Strip of four 4.50 90
- *a. Gorilla* 1.10
- *b. Gnu* 1.10
- *c. Warthog* 1.10
- *d. Cape hunting dog* 1.10

CB18 A48 (*b*) 31fr+1fr Strip of four 6.00 1.20
- *a. Sable antelope* 1.50
- *b. Caracal lynx* 1.50
- *c. Ostriches* 1.50
- *d. Bongo* 1.50

75th anniversary of modern Olympic Games (No. CB17); Olympic Games, Munich, 1972 (No. CB18).

Nos. C153–C155 Surcharged

1971, Nov. 27 **Photo.** ***Perf. 13½***

CB19 A51 14fr+1fr multi. 40
CB20 " 17fr+1fr " 48
CB21 " 31fr+1fr " 80

25th anniversary of the United Nations International Children's Fund (UNICEF).

Casa D'Oro, Venice
SPAP1

Views in Venice: 17fr+1fr, Doge's Palace. 24fr+1fr, Church of Sts. John and Paul. 31fr+1fr, Doge's Palace and Piazzetta at Feast of Ascension, by Canaletto.

1971, Dec. 27

CB22 SPAP1 10fr+1fr gold & multicolored 33
CB23 " 17fr+1fr gold & multicolored 54
CB24 " 24fr+1fr gold & multicolored 75
CB25 " 31fr+1fr gold & multicolored 90
- *a.* Souvenir sheet of 4 2.60

The surtax was for the UNESCO campaign to save the treasures of Venice. No. CB25a contains 4 stamps similar to Nos. CB22–CB25, but with 2fr surtax instead 1fr. Gold and black ornamental margin. Size: 113x131½mm. Sheet exists imperf.

Nos. C165–C167 Surcharged "+1F" in Silver

1972, Dec. 12 **Photo.** ***Perf. 13½***

CB26 A57 18fr+1fr multi. 50
CB27 " 27fr+1fr " 75
CB28 " 40fr+1fr " 1.00
- *a.* Souvenir sheet of 3 2.30

Christmas 1972. No. CB28a contains 3 stamps similar to Nos. CB26–CB28 but with 2fr surtax. Slate green and gold border. Size: 128x81mm.

Nos. C193–C195 Surcharged "+1F" in Silver

1973, Dec. 14 **Photo.** ***Perf. 13***

CB29 A64 18fr+1fr multi. 56
CB30 " 27fr+1fr " 80
CB31 " 40fr+1fr " 1.25
- *a.* Souvenir sheet of 3 3.00

Christmas 1973. No. CB31 contains 3 stamps similar to Nos. CB29–CB31 with 2fr surtax each. Size: 143x79mm.

Christmas Type of 1974

1974, Dec. 2 **Photogravure** ***Perf. 13***

CB32 A70 18fr+1fr multi. 56
CB33 " 27fr+1fr " 85
CB34 " 40fr+1fr " 1.25
- *a.* Souvenir sheet of 3 3.00

Christmas 1974. No. CB34a contains 3 stamps similar to Nos. CB32–CB34 with 2fr surtax. Size: 137x90mm.

Nos. C228–C233 Surcharged "+ 1 F" in Silver and Black

1975, Dec. 22 **Photo.** ***Perf. 13***

Multicolored

CB35 A73 18fr+1fr # C228 58
CB36 " 18fr+1fr # C229 58
CB37 " 31fr+1fr # C230 96
CB38 " 31fr+1fr # C231 96
CB39 " 40fr+1fr # C232 1.24
CB40 " 40fr+1fr # C233 1.24
- *a.* Souvenir sheet of 6 6.00

Nos. CB35–CB40 (6) 5.56

Michelangelo Buonarroti (1475–1564), 500th birth anniversary. No. CB40a contains 6 stamps similar to Nos. CB35–CB40 with 2fr surtax each. Size: 132x106mm.

Nos. C250–C252 Surcharged "+1f" in Silver and Black

1976, Nov. 25 **Photo.** ***Perf. 13½***

CB41 A76 18fr+1fr multi. 58
CB42 " 31fr+1fr " 1.00
CB43 " 40fr+1fr " 1.25
- *a.* Souvenir sheet of 3 3.00

Christmas 1976. No. CB43a contains 3 stamps similar to Nos. CB41–CB43 with 2fr surtax each. Size: 123x80mm.

Nos. C267–C269 Surcharged "+1fr" in Silver and Black

1977 **Photo.** ***Perf. 14x13***

CB44 A83 18fr+1fr multi. 58
CB45 " 31fr+1fr " 1.00
CB46 " 40fr+1fr " 1.25
- *a.* Souvenir sheet of 3 3.00

Christmas 1977. No. CB46a contains 3 stamps similar to Nos. CB44–CB46 with 2fr surtax each. Size: 130x71mm.

CAMBODIA

(kăm·bō'dĭ·ȧ)

Khmer Republic

LOCATION—Southern Indo-China.

GOVT.—Republic

AREA—69,866 sq. mi.

POP.—7,640,000 (est. 1974).

CAPITAL—Phnom Penh.

Before 1951, Cambodia used stamps of Indo-China. In October, 1970, the Kingdom of Cambodia became the Khmer Republic.

100 Cents = 1 Piaster

100 Cents = 1 Riel (1955)

Imperforates

Most Cambodia stamps exist imperforate in issued and trial colors, and also in small presentation sheets in issued colors.

Apsaras

A1

King Norodom Sihanouk

A3

Enthronement Hall

A2

Engraved.

1951-52 *Perf. 13* **Unwmkd.**

No.	Type	Description	Unused	Used
1	A1	10c dark blue green	55	55
2	"	20c claret & orange brown	35	20
3	"	30c purple & indigo	35	20
4	"	40c ultramarine & bright blue green	35	20
5	A2	50c dark green & dark olive green	35	20
6	A3	80c blue black & dark blue green	70	70
7	A2	1pi indigo & purple	90	90
8	A3	1.10pi deep carmine & bright red	90	90
9	"	1.50pi black brown & red brown	1.25	90
10	A1	1.50pi deep carmine & cerise	1.25	90
11	A2	1.50pi indigo & deep ultramarine	1.25	1.10
12	A3	1.90pi indigo & deep ultramarine	1.75	1.60
13	A2	2pi deep carmine & orange brown	1.60	1.00
14	A3	3pi deep carmine & orange brown	2.25	1.60
15	A1	5pi indigo & purple	7.25	3.50
		a. Souvenir sheet of 1 ('52)	20.00	
16	A2	10pi pur. & indigo	13.50	7.25
		a. Souvenir sheet of 1 ('52)	20.00	
17	A3	15pi dark purple & purple	17.50	10.00
		a. Souvenir sheet of 1 ('52)	25.00	
		Nos. 1-17 (17)	52.05	31.70

No. 9 issued in 1951, others in 1952.

Nos. 15a, 16a and 17a contain single copies respectively of the 5pi, 10pi and 15pi. They were sold in a booklet for 30pi. Size: 128x89mm.

Phnom Daun Penh

A4

East Gate, Angkor Thom

A5

Arms of Cambodia

A6

Methods of Mail Transport

A7

1954-55 *Perf. 13* **Unwmkd.**

No.	Type	Description	Unused	Used
18	A4	10c rose carmine	6	6
		a. Souvenir sheet of 5 ('55)	22.50	
19	"	20c dark green	6	6
20	"	30c indigo	6	6
21	"	40c dark purple	6	6
22	"	50c dark violet brown	6	6
23	A5	70c chocolate	20	20
		a. Souvenir sheet of 5 ('55)	22.50	
24	"	1pi red violet	20	20
25	"	1.50pi red	20	20
26	A6	2pi rose red	40	40
		a. Souvenir sheet of 5 ('55)	22.50	
27	"	2.50pi green	60	60
28	A7	2.50pi blue green	80	60
		a. Souvenir sheet of 5 ('55)	22.50	
29	A6	3pi ultramarine	90	75
30	A7	4pi black brown	1.00	1.00
31	A6	4.50pi purple	1.20	1.00
32	A7	5pi rose red	1.25	1.00
33	A6	6pi chocolate	1.50	1.00
34	A7	10pi purple	1.50	1.50
35	"	15pi deep blue	2.00	1.85
36	A5	20pi ultramarine	4.00	2.50
37	"	30pi blue green	6.00	5.00
		Nos. 18-37 (20)	22.05	18.10

The four souvenir sheets each contain five different stamps: No. 18a (10c, 20c, 30c, 40c, 50c); No. 23a (70c, 1pi, 1.50pi, 20pi, 30pi); No. 26a (2pi, 2.50pi green, 3pi, 4.50pi, 6pi); No. 28a (2.50pi blue green, 4pi, 5pi, 10pi, 15pi). Size of Nos. 18a, 26a and 28a: 120x120mm. Size of No. 23a: 160x92mm.

King Norodom Suramarit

A8

King Norodom Suramarit and Queen Kossamak Nearirat Serey Vathana

A9

Portraits: 50c (No. 39), 2.50r, 4r, 6r, 15r, Queen Kossamak Nearirat Serey Vathana.

Perf. 14x13(A8), 13(A9)

1955, Nov. 24 **Engr.** **Unwmkd.**

No.	Type	Description	Unused	Used
38	A8	50c violet	10	10
39	"	50c indigo	10	10
40	"	1r carmine lake	15	15
41	A9	1.50r dark brown	40	40
42	"	2r black & indigo	40	30
43	A8	2r deep ultramarine	25	40
44	"	2.50r dark violet brown	40	40
45	A9	3r brn. org. & car.	40	40
46	A8	4r dark green	60	60
47	A9	5r black & dark green	60	60
48	A8	6r deep plum	1.00	75
49	"	7r dark brown	1.25	75
50	A9	10r brown carmine & violet	1.00	1.00
51	A8	15r purple	1.75	1.25
52	"	20r deep green	2.25	2.00
		Nos. 38-52 (15)	10.65	9.20

Issued to commemorate the coronation of King Norodom Suramarit and Queen Kossamak Nearirat Serey Vathana.

See also Nos. 74-75.

King Norodom Suramarit

A10

Prince Sihanouk, Globe and Flags

A11

Portrait: 3r, 5r, 50r, Queen Kossamak Nearirat Serey Vathana.

1956, Mar. 8 *Perf. 13*

No.	Type	Description	Unused	Used
53	A10	2r dark red	1.00	1.00
54	"	3r dark blue	1.50	1.50
55	"	5r yellow green	2.25	2.25
56	"	10r dark green	5.75	5.75
57	"	30r dark violet	11.50	11.50
58	"	50r rose lilac	21.00	21.00
		Nos. 53-58 (6)	43.00	43.00

Issued to commemorate the coronation of King Norodom Suramarit and Queen Kossamak Nearirat Serey Vathana.

1957, Mar. 1

No.	Type	Description	Unused	Used
59	A11	2r green, ultramarine & carmine	60	45
60	"	4.50r ultramarine	60	45
61	"	8.50r carmine	60	45

Issued to commemorate the first anniversary of Cambodia's admission to the United Nations (in 1956).

Type of Semi-Postal Stamps, 1957.

1957, May 12 *Perf. 13* **Unwmkd.**

No.	Type	Description	Unused	Used
62	SP1	1.50r vermilion	55	55
63	"	6.50r bluish violet	70	70
64	"	8r dark green	70	70

Issued to commemorate the 2500th anniversary of the birth of Buddha.

King Ang Duong

A12

1958, Mar. 4

No.	Type	Description	Unused	Used
65	A12	1.50r purple & brown	20	20
66	"	5r olive gray & olive	40	40
67	"	10r claret & dull brown	80	60
		a. Souvenir sheet of 3	3.50	3.50

Issued to honor King Ang Duong (1795-1860).

No. 67a contains one each of Nos. 65-67. Sold for 25r. Size: 155x93mm.

King Norodom I

A13

1958-59 **Engraved** *Perf. 12½x13*

No.	Type	Description	Unused	Used
68	A13	2r ultramarine & olive	30	30
69	"	6r org. & slate green	60	60
70	"	15r green & olive gray	90	90
		a. Souvenir sheet of 3 ('59)	3.50	3.00

Issued in honor of King Norodom I (1835-1904).

No. 70a contains one each of Nos. 68-70. Sold for 32r. Size: 155x93mm.

Issue dates: Nos. 68-70, Nov. 3, 1958. No. 70a, Jan. 31, 1959.

Children of the World

A14

1959, Dec. 9 *Perf. 13* **Unwmkd.**

No.	Type	Description	Unused	Used
71	A14	20c rose violet	8	8
72	"	50c blue	20	20
73	"	80c rose carmine	32	32

Issued to promote friendship among the children of the world.

Nos. 49 and 52 with Black Border.

1960 *Perf. 14x13*

No.	Type	Description	Unused	Used
74	A8	7r dk. brn. & black	1.25	1.25
75	"	20r dp. grn. & black	1.25	1.25

Issued to commemorate the death of King Norodom Suramarit.

Port of Sihanoukville, Prince Sihanouk and Serpent Naga

A15

(double size) 20r

1960, Apr. *Perf. 13x12½*

No.	Type	Description	Unused	Used
76	A15	2r carmine & sepia	40	40
		a. Cambodian 20r	1.20	1.20
77	"	5r ultramarine & deep brown	40	40
		a. Cambodian 20r	1.60	1.60
78	"	20r lilac & dark blue	1.40	1.00

Issued to commemorate the opening of the port of Sihanoukville. By error the denomination in Cambodian on the 2r and 5r was engraved as 20r; it was corrected later.

Ceremonial Plow
A16

1960 ***Perf. 12***

79 A16 1r magenta 40 40
80 " 2r brown 40 40
81 " 3r bluish green 40 40

Feast of the Sacred Furrow.

Works of Sangkum Issue

Fight Against Illiteracy
A17

Water Conservation,
Dam at Chhouksar
A18

Dove, Factory
and Books
A19

Buddhist
Ceremony
A20

Designs: 6r, Workman and house. 10r, Woman in rice field.

1960, Sept. 1 **Engraved** ***Perf. 13***

82 A17 2r dark green, brown & dark blue 22 18
a. Souvenir sheet of 3 3.00 3.00
83 A18 3r brown & green 32 27
a. Souvenir sheet of 3 3.00 3.00
84 A19 4r rose carmine, violet & green 35 32
85 A17 6r brn., org. & green 45 40
86 " 10r ultramarine, green & bister 90 80
87 A20 25r dark carmine, red & magenta 2.25 1.65
Nos. 82-87 (6) 4.49 3.62

No. 82a contains one each of Nos. 82, 85 and 87, and sold for 42r. No. 83a contains one each of Nos. 83, 84 and 86, and sold for 23r. Marginal inscriptions in bister. Size: 149x100mm. Nos. 82a-83a were issued Dec. 5, 1960.

Cambodian Flag
and Dove
A21

Frangipani
A22

1960, Dec. 24 **Engraved** ***Perf. 13***

Flag in Ultramarine and Red.

88 A21 1.50r brown & green 25 25
89 " 5r orange red 35 35
90 " 7r green & ultra. 65 65
a. Souvenir sheet of 3 2.00 2.00
b. Souvenir sheet of 3 (colors changed) 5.00 5.00

Issued as peace propaganda.

No. 90a contains one each of Nos. 88-90 and sold for 16r. No. 90b contains one of each denomination with colors changed to: 1.50r orange red, 5r green & ultramarine, 7r brown & green. No. 90b sold for 20r. Marginal inscriptions in bistre. Size: 146½x93mm.

1961, July 1 ***Perf. 13*** **Unwmkd.**

Flowers: 5r, Oleander. 10r, Amaryllis.

91 A22 2r lilac rose, yellow & green 30 30
92 " 5r ultramarine, lilac rose & green 50 50
93 " 10r vio., car. & green 1.25 1.25
a. Souv. sheet of 3 2.75 2.75

No. 93a contains one each of Nos. 91-93. Gold marginal inscription. Size: 130x100mm. Sold for 20r.

Krishna
in Chariot,
Khmer
Frieze
A23

Independence
Monument
A24

1961-63 **Typo.** ***Perf. 14x13½***

94 A23 1r lilac 10 10
94A " 2r blue ('63) 1.25 75
95 " 3r emerald 25 25
96 " 6r orange 45 25
a. Souv. sheet of 3 3.50 3.50

Issued to honor Cambodian armed forces.

No. 94A issued in coils. No. 96a contains one each of Nos. 94, 95, 96. Orange marginal inscriptions. Size: 149x85mm. Sold for 12r.

1961, Nov. 9 **Engr.** ***Perf. 13x12½***

97 A24 2r green 30 30
98 " 4r gray brown 30 30
a. Souvenir sheet of 2 1.20 1.20
Nos. 97-98, C15-C17 (5) 6.70 5.10

Issued to commemorate the tenth anniversary of Independence. No. 98a contains one each of Nos. 97-98 with gold marginal inscription. Size: 150x85mm.

Nos. 27 and 31 Overprinted in Red:
"VIe CONFERENCE MONDIALE
BOUDDIQUE 12-11-1961"

1961, Nov. 11 ***Perf. 13***

99 A6 2.50pi (r) green 35 35
100 " 4.50pi (r) purple 50 50

Sixth World Conference of Buddhism.

Highway (American Aid)
A25

Foreign Aid: 2r, Power station (Czech aid). 4r, Textile factory (Chinese aid). 5r, Hospital (Russian aid). 6r, Airport (French aid).

1961, Dec. **Engraved** ***Perf. 13***

101 A25 2r orange & rose carmine 20 12
102 " 3r blue, green & orange brown 30 20
103 " 4r dull blue, orange brown & magenta 35 22
104 " 5r dull green & lilac rose 40 35
105 " 6r dark blue & orange brown 55 40
a. Souvenir sheet of 5 2.50 2.50
Nos. 101-105 (5) 1.80 1.29

Issued to publicize foreign aid to Cambodia. No. 105a contains one each of Nos. 101-105 with bistre marginal inscription. Size: 148x84mm.

Malaria Eradication Emblem
A26

1962, Apr. 7 ***Perf. 13*** **Unwmkd.**

106 A26 2r magenta & brown 25 18
107 " 4r green & dk. brown 38 32
108 " 6r violet & olive bistre 45 38

Issued for the World Health Organization drive to eradicate malaria.

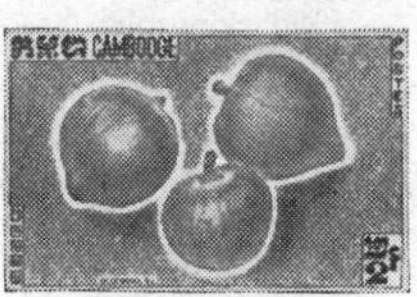

Turmeric—A27

Fruits: 4r, Cinnamon. 6r, Mangosteens.

1962, June 4 **Engraved**

109 A27 2r gray & bistre 45 40
110 " 4r dk. blue grn. & olive gray 45 40
111 " 6r dark blue, green & magenta 70 60
a. Souv. sheet of 3 2.00 2.00

Nos. 111a contains one each of Nos. 109-111 with marginal inscription in gray. Size: 149x84mm. Sold for 15r.

Pineapples
A28

Designs: 5r, Sugar cane. 9r, Sugar palms.

1962 ***Perf. 13*** **Unwmkd.**

112 A28 2r bluish grn. & brn. 40 35
113 " 5r brn. & green 50 40
114 " 9r Prussian green & brown 75 50

No. 73 Surcharged

1962, Nov. 9 ***Perf. 13***

115 A14 50c on 80c rose car. 25 25

No. 97 Surcharged with New Value in Red and Overprinted in Black with Two Bars and:
"INAUGURATION / DU / MONUMENT"

1962

116 A24 3r on 2r green 25 18

Dedication of Independence Monument.

Corn, Rice and FAO Emblem
A29

1963, Mar. 21 **Engraved** ***Perf. 13***

117 A29 3r multicolored 55 45
118 " 6r orange red, violet blue & ocher 55 45

Issued for the "Freedom from Hunger" campaign of the U.N. Food and Agriculture Organization.

Preah Vihear,
Ancient Temple
A30

Tonsay Lake
A31

1963, June 15 ***Perf. 12½x13***

119 A30 3r claret, brown & slate green 25 25
120 " 6r org., slate green & greenish blk. 50 38
121 " 15r blue, chocolate & green 1.00 85

Return by Thailand of Preah Vihear on the Mekong River.

No. 44 Surcharged with New Value and Bars

1963 **Engraved** ***Perf. 14x13***

122 A8 3r on 2½r dk. vio. brn. 35 35

Perf. 12x12½, 12½x12

1963, Aug. 1 **Photogravure**

Designs: 7r, Popokvil Falls. 20r, Beach (horiz.).

123 A31 3r multicolored 20 20
124 " 7r " 45 30
125 " 20r " 1.20 70

UNESCO Emblem, Scales
and Globe
A32

1963, Dec. 10 **Engraved** ***Perf. 13***

126 A32 1r violet blue, rose claret & green 20 20

127 A32 3r yellow green, violet bl. & rose claret 35 35
128 " 12r rose claret, yellow green & violet bl. 75 75

Issued to commemorate the 15th anniversary of the Universal Declaration of Human Rights.

Kouprey
A33

1964, March 3 ***Perf. 13*** **Unwmkd.**

129 A33 50c green, dark brn. & orge. brown 15 15
130 " 3r orge., brn., dk. brown & green 25 25
131 " 6r blue, dark brown & green 40 30

Black-billed Magpie
A34

Birds: 6r, Kingfisher. 12r, Gray heron.

1964, May 2 **Engraved** ***Perf. 13***

132 A34 3r dark blue, indigo & green 20 20
133 " 6r indigo, orange & brown 40 40
134 " 12r Prussian green, indigo & red brown 85 85

Emblem of Royal Cambodian Airline
A35

1964 ***Perf. 13x12½*** **Unwmkd.**

135 A35 1.50r rose car. & purple 20 20
136 " 3r verm. & dk. bl. 25 20
137 " 7.50r ultra. & car. 60 50

Issued to commemorate the 8th anniversary of the Royal Cambodian Airline.

Prince Norodom Sihanouk
A36

1964 **Engraved** ***Perf. 12½x13***

138 A36 2r purple 18 18
139 " 3r red brown 25 25
140 " 10r dark blue 70 60

Issued to commemorate the 10th anniversary of the Sangkum (political party).

Woman Weaver
A37

Khmer Handicrafts: 3r, Metal worker. 5r, Basket maker.

1965, Feb. 1 ***Perf. 13x12½***

141 A37 1r multicolored 15 15
142 " 3r red lilac, red brn. & gray olive 35 25
143 " 5r green, dark brown & carmine 40 30

Nos. 139–140 Overprinted in Black or Red:
"CONFERENCE / DES PEUPLES / INDOCHINOIS"

1965, Mar. 1 ***Perf. 12½x13***

144 A36 3r red brown 40 40
145 " 10r dark blue (R) 60 40

Conference of the people of Indo-China.

ITU Emblem, Old and New Communication Equipment
A38

1965, May 17 **Engraved** ***Perf. 13***

146 A38 3r grn. & olive bistre 30 30
147 " 4r red & blue 40 30
148 " 10r vio. & rose lilac 70 60

Issued to commemorate the centenary of the International Telecommunication Union.

Cotton Plant
A39

Designs: 3r, Peanut plant. 7.50r, Coconut palm.

1965, Aug. 2 ***Perf. 12½x13***

149 A39 1.50r org., slate grn. & purple 20 20
150 " 3r blue, yellow, grn. & brown 30 30
151 " 7.50r orange brn. & slate green 55 55

Preah Ko Temple, Rolouoh
A40

Temples at Angkor: 5r, Baksei Chamkrong, Rolouoh. 7r, Banteay Srei (Citadel of Women). 9r, Angkor Wat. 12r, Bayon, Angkor Thom.

1966, Feb. 1 **Engraved** ***Perf. 13***

152 A40 3r gray olive, salmon & dull green 32 28
153 A40 5r lilac, dk. green & reddish brown 45 40
154 " 7r dk. grn., reddish brn. & bister 50 45
155 " 9r vio. blue, purple & dark green 85 55
156 " 12r dk. green, rose car. & vermilion 1.10 75
Nos. 152–156 (5) 3.22 2.43

WHO Headquarters, Geneva
A41

1966, July 1 **Photo.** ***Perf. 12½x13***
WHO Emblem in Blue and Yellow

157 A41 2r black & pale rose 20 15
158 " 3r black & yel. green 25 20
159 " 5r black & light blue 35 25

Issued to commemorate the inauguration of World Health Headquarters, Geneva.

Tree Planting A42 UNESCO Emblem A43

1966, July 22 **Engr.** ***Perf. 12½x13***

160 A42 1r brown, dull brn. & bright green 15 10
161 " 3r orange, dull brn. & bright green 25 20
162 " 7r gray, dull brown & bright green 50 30

Issued for Arbor Day.

1966 **Photogravure** ***Perf. 13***

163 A43 3r multicolored 30 30
164 " 7r " 50 30

Issued to commemorate the 20th anniversary of UNESCO (United Nations Educational, Scientific and Cultural Organization).

Wrestlers and Games' Emblem
A44

Designs (Games Emblem and): 3r, Stadium, Phnom Penh. 7r, Swordsmen. 10r, Indian club swingers. Bas-reliefs from Angkor Wat.

1966, Nov. 25 **Engraved** ***Perf. 13***

165 A44 3r violet blue 25 20
166 " 4r green 30 20
167 " 7r dk. carmine rose 45 25
168 " 10r dark brown 60 40

Issued to commemorate the GANEFO Games.

Indian Wild Boar
A45

Designs: 5r, Muntjac (vert.). 7r, Elephant.

Perf. 13x12½, 12½x13

1967, Feb. 20 **Engraved**

169 A45 3r brt. blue, green & black 25 20
170 " 5r multicolored 35 20
171 " 7r " 50 30

Nos. 152–153, 155–156 and 121 Overprinted in Red:
"ANNEE INTERNATIONALE DU TOURISME 1967"

1967, Apr. 27 **Engr.** ***Perf. 13***

172 A40 3r multicolored 30 30
173 " 5r " 40 30
174 " 9r " 70 60
175 " 12r " 80 80
176 A30 15r " 1.00 1.00
Nos. 172–176 (5) 3.20 3.00

International Tourist Year, 1967.

No. 154 Overprinted in Red:
"MILLENAIRE / DE BANTEAY SREI / 967-1967"

1967, Apr. 27

177 A40 7r multicolored 65 35

Issued to commemorate the millennium of the Banteay Srei Temple at Angkor.

Royal Ballet Dancer
A46

Various Dancers

1967, June **Engraved** ***Perf. 13***

178 A46 1r orange 15 15
179 " 3r Prussian blue 30 25
180 " 5r ultramarine 45 35
181 " 7r carmine rose 60 55
182 " 10r multicolored 90 70
Nos. 178–182 (5) 2.40 2.00

Issued to publicize the Cambodian Royal Ballet.

Nos. 128 and 70 Surcharged in Red

Journée Internationale de l'Alphabétisation 8-9-67

6

1967, Sept. 8 **Engraved**

183 A32 6r on 12r multi. 50 40
184 A13 7r on 15r green & olive gray 60 45

Issued for International Literacy Day, Sept. 8. The surcharge on No. 184 is adapted to fit the shape of the stamp.

Symbolic Water Cycle
A47

1967, Nov. 1 **Typo.** ***Perf. 13x14***

185 A47 1r blk, blue & orange 18 18
186 " 6r lilac, lt. bl. & org. 50 30
187 " 10r dk. blue, emerald & orange 80 45

Hydrological Decade (UNESCO), 1965–74.

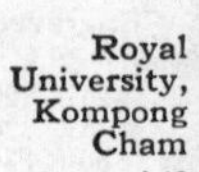

Royal University, Kompong Cham
A48

Designs: 6r, Engineering School, Pnompenh. 9r, University Center, Sangkum Reastr Niyum.

1968, Mar. 1 Engraved *Perf. 13*

188	A48	4r vio. blue & multi.	30	30
189	"	6r slate & multi.	45	45
190	"	9r Prus. blue & multi.	65	45

Vaccination and WHO Emblem
A49

Design: 7r, Malaria control and WHO emblem (man spraying DDT).

1968, July 8 Engraved *Perf. 13*

191	A49	3r ultramarine	20	18
192	"	7r deep blue	45	30

Issued for the 20th anniversary of the World Health Organization.

Stadium, Mexico City
A50

Designs: 2r, Wrestling. 3r, Bicycling. 5r, Boxing (vert.). 7.50r, Torch bearer (vert.).

1968, Oct. 12 Engraved *Perf. 13*

193	A50	1r brown olive, green & brown red	17	15
194	"	2r brown, dk. blue & rose claret	20	17
195	"	3r plum, Prussian blue & sepia	30	25
196	"	5r dark purple	38	30
197	"	7.50r multicolored	42	38
		Nos. 193-197 (5)	1.47	1.25

Issued to commemorate the 19th Olympic Games, Mexico City, Oct. 12–27.

Red Cross Team
A51

1968, Nov. 1 Engraved *Perf. 13*

198	A51	3r Prus. blue, green & red	20	12

Issued to honor the Cambodian Red Cross.

Prince Norodom Sihanouk
A52

Design: 8r, Soldiers wading through swamp.

1968, Nov. 9

199	A52	7r emerald, ultra. & purple	45	30
200	"	8r bl., grn. & dp. brn.	55	30

15th anniversary of independence.

Human Rights Flame and Prince Sihanouk
A53

1968, Dec. 10 Engraved *Perf. 13*

201	A53	3r blue	25	18
202	"	5r bright plum	40	25
203	"	7r multicolored	50	30

International Human Rights Year.

ILO Emblem
A54

1969, May 1 Engraved *Perf. 13*

204	A54	3r ultramarine	22	18
205	"	6r deep carmine	35	25
206	"	9r blue green	50	30

Issued to commemorate the 50th anniversary of the International Labor Organization.

Globe, Red Cross, Crescent, Lion and Sun Emblems
A55

1969, May 8

207	A55	1r blue, red & yellow	15	15
208	"	3r slate green, red & violet brown	22	20
209	"	10r bright lilac, red & brown	60	30

Issued to commemorate the 50th anniversary of the League of Red Cross Societies.

Papilio Oeacus—A56

Butterflies: 4r, Papilio agamenon. 8r, Danaus plexippus.

1969, Oct. 10 Engraved *Perf. 13*

210	A56	3r lilac, blk. & yellow	25	25
211	"	4r verm., blk. & grn.	35	35
212	"	8r yellow green, dk. brown & orange	60	45

Map of Cambodia and Diesel Engine
A57

Designs: Various railroad stations and trains.

1969, Nov. 27 Engraved *Perf. 13*

213	A57	3r multicolored	25	20
214	"	6r slate grn. & lt. brn.	35	28
215	A57	8r black	45	38
216	"	9r dk. green & blue	50	38

Issued to publicize the new rail link between Phnom Penh and Sihanoukville.

Tripletail
A58

Fish: 7r, Sleeper goby. 9r, Snakehead.

1970, Jan. 29 Photo. *Perf. 13*

217	A58	3r multicolored	18	12
218	"	7r "	35	27
219	"	9r "	45	35

Wat Maniratanaram
A59

Monasteries: 2r, Wat Tepthidaram (vert.). 6r, Wat Patumavati. 8r, Wat Unnalom.

1970, Apr. 29 Photo. *Perf. 13*

220	A59	2r multicolored	12	10
221	"	3r "	25	15
222	"	6r "	38	25
223	"	8r "	50	38

U.P.U. Headquarters and Monument, Bern—A60

1970, May 20

224	A60	1r green & multi.	7	5
225	"	3r scarlet & multi.	10	10
226	"	4r dp. blue & multi.	22	12
227	"	10r brown & multi.	30	20

Issued to commemorate the inauguration of the new Universal Postal Union Headquarters in Bern.

Open Book and Satellite Earth Receiving Station
A61

1970, May 17 Photo. *Perf. 13*

228	A61	3r dk. vio. bl. & multi.	10	5
229	"	4r slate grn. & multi.	13	8
230	"	9r brn. olive & multi.	27	18

World Telecommunications Day.

Nelumbium Speciosum
A62

Flowers: 4r, Eichhornia crassipes. 13r, Nymphea lotus.

1970, Aug. 17 Photo. *Perf. 13*

231	A62	3r multicolored	10	8
		a. Cambodian and Arabic 3's transposed	25	
232	A62	4r multicolord	14	12
233	"	13r "	32	25

Elephant God, Bas-relief at Banteay Srei
A63

1970, Sept. 21 Engraved *Perf. 13*

234	A63	3r lilac rose & dp. grn.	8	6
235	"	4r blue green, green & lilac rose	10	7
236	"	7r blue green, dark brown & green	18	10

Issued for World Meteorological Day.

Khmer Republic

Globe, Rocket, Dove and U.N. Emblem—A64

1970, Nov. 9 Photo. *Perf. 12½x12*

237	A64	3r black & multi.	10	7
238	"	5r brn. red & multi.	15	10
239	"	10r dp. violet & multi.	30	20

25th anniversary of the United Nations.

Education Year Emblem
A65

1970, Nov. 9 Engr. *Perf. 13x12½*

240	A65	1r blue	4	4
241	"	3r bright rose lilac	8	6
242	"	8r blue green	20	10

Issued for International Education Year.

Chuon-Nath—A66

1971, Jan. 27 Photo. *Perf. 13*

243	A66	3r olive green & multi.	7	5
244	"	8r purple & multi.	20	10
245	"	9r violet & multi.	22	12

In memory of Chuon-Nath (1883–1969), Cambodian language expert.

Soldiers in Battle
A67

1971, March 18 Photo. *Perf. 13*

246	A67	1r gray & multi.	4	4
247	"	3r bister & multi.	15	10
248	"	10r blue & multi.	50	25

National territorial defense.

U.N. Emblem, Men of Four Races
A68

1971, March 21

249	A68	3r blue & multi.	6	5
250	"	7r green & multi.	15	10
251	"	8r brt. rose & multi.	20	12

International year against racial discrimination.

General Post Office, Phnom Penh
A69

1971, Apr. 19

252	A69	3r blue & multi.	15	10
253	"	9r lilac rose & multi.	45	20
254	"	10r black & multi.	50	25

Symbolic Globe and Waves—A70

Design: 7r, 8r, ITU emblem and waves.

1971, May 17 Photo. *Perf. 13*

255	A70	3r grn., black & blue	5	5
256	"	4r yellow & multi.	13	5
257	"	7r lilac, black & red	8	8
258	"	8r salmon pink, black & red	15	10

3rd World Telecommunications Day.

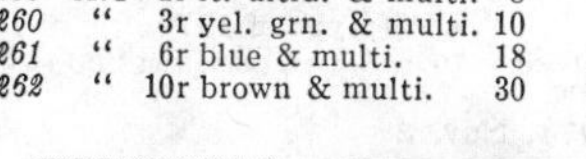

Erythrina Indica
A71

Wild Flowers: 3r, Bauhinia variegata. 6r, Butea frondosa. 10r, Lagerstroemia floribunda (vert.).

1971, July 5 *Perf. 13x12½, 12½x13*

259	A71	2r lt. ultra. & multi.	8	5
260	"	3r yel. grn. & multi.	10	8
261	"	6r blue & multi.	18	12
262	"	10r brown & multi.	30	25

Khmer Coat of Arms
A72

Flag and Square of the Republic
A73

1971, Oct. 9 Engraved *Perf. 13*

263	A72	3r brt. grn. & bister	6	5
264	A73	3r purple & multi.	6	5
265	"	4r dp. claret & multi.	6	5
266	A72	8r orange & bister	12	7
267	"	10r lt. brn. & bister	17	8
		a. Souvenir sheet of 3	1.00	1.00
268	A73	10r slate grn. & multi.	17	8
		a. Souvenir sheet of 3	85	85
		Nos. 263-268 (6)	64	38

First anniversary of the Republic. No. 267a contains one each of Nos. 263, 266-267 with olive marginal inscriptions. Sold for 25fr. No. 268a contains one each of Nos. 264-265 and 268 with purple marginal inscription. Sold for 20r. Size of sheets: 129x100mm.

UNICEF Emblem
A74

1971, Dec. 11

269	A74	3r black brown	6	5
270	"	5r ultramarine	10	6
271	"	9r dk. pur. & brn. red	18	10

25th anniversary of the United Nations International Children's Fund (UNICEF).

Book Year Emblem
A75

1972, Feb. 7

272	A75	3r bl., green & violet	6	5
273	"	8r vio., grn. & blue	15	8
274	"	9r emerald & multi.	18	10
		a. Souvenir sheet of 3	90	90

International Book Year 1972. No. 274a contains one each of Nos. 272-274 with emerald marginal inscription. Size: 159x99mm. Sold for 23r.

Lion of St. Mark
A76

Designs: 5r, Waves engulfing St. Mark's Basilica. 10r, Bridge of Sighs (vert.).

1972, Feb. 7 Engraved *Perf. 13*

275	A76	3r lilac rose & orange brown	8	5
276	"	5r yellow green & orange brown	13	7
277	"	10r org. brown, blue & yellow green	27	18
		a. Souvenir sheet of 3	85	85

UNESCO campaign to save Venice. No. 277a contains one each of Nos. 275-277. Yellow green marginal inscription. Size: 140x99mm. Sold for 23r.

U.N. Emblem
A77

1972, Mar. 28

278	A77	3r deep carmine	8	5
279	"	6r deep blue	17	12
280	"	9r deep orange	25	17
		a. Souvenir sheet of 3	90	90

25th anniversary. United Nations Economic Commission for Asia and the Far East (ECAFE), No. 280a contains one each of Nos. 278-280. Deep blue marginal inscription. Size: 138x100mm. Sold for 23r.

Dancing Apsarases
A78

"UIT"
A79

1972, May 5 Engraved *Perf. 13*

281	A78	1r golden brown	5	5
282	"	3r violet	8	6
283	"	7r rose claret	20	15
284	"	8r olive brown	22	15
285	"	9r blue green	25	18
286	"	10r ultramarine	28	20
287	"	12r purple	32	25
288	"	14r Prussian blue	40	28
		Nos. 281-288 (8)	1.80	1.32

1972, May 17 Lithographed

Size: 35½x22mm.

289	A79	3r black, yellow & greenish blue	7	5
290	"	9r blk., dp. lilac rose & blue green	20	13
291	"	14r black, brown & blue green	35	25

4th World Telecommunications Day.

"Human Environment"
A80

1972, June 5 Engraved

292	A80	3r org., plum & grn.	10	7
293	"	12r brt. grn. & plum	40	25
294	"	15r plum & brt. grn.	48	32
		a. Souv. sheet of 3	1.10	1.10

U.N. Conference on Human Environment, Stockholm, June 5-16. No. 294a contains one each of Nos. 292-294. Green marginal inscription. Size: 129x100mm. Sold for 35r.

Javan Rhinoceros
A81

1972, Aug. 1 Engraved *Perf. 13*

Multicolored

295	A81	3r *shown*	6	5
296	"	4r *Serow*	6	5
297	"	6r *Malayan sambar*	10	7
298	"	7r *Banteng*	12	8
299	"	8r *Water buffalo*	12	8
300	"	10r *Gaur*	15	10
		Nos. 295-300 (6)	61	43

Nos. 263, 267, 134, 293, 294 Overprinted in Red

XXe JEUX OLYMPIQUES MUNICH 1972

1972, Sept. 9 Engr. *Perf. 13*

301	A72	3r brt. grn. & bister	15	10
302	"	10r orange & bister	45	30
303	A34	12r multicolored	60	35
304	A80	12r brt. grn. & plum	60	35
305	"	15r plum & brt. green	80	50
		Nos. 301-305 (5)	2.60	1.60

20th Olympic Games, Munich, Aug. 26-Sept. 11.

Raising Khmer Flag
A82

1972, Oct. 9 Photo. *Perf. 12½x13*

306	A82	3r multicolored	8	5
307	"	5r brt. rose & multi.	10	8
308	"	9r yel. grn. & multi.	20	13

2nd anniversary of the establishment of the Khmer Republic.

Stupa and Crest
A83

Apsaras
A84

1973, May 12 Engraved *Perf. 13*

309	A83	3r ocher & multi.	7	5
310	"	12r yel. grn. & multi.	20	18
311	"	14r blue & multi.	25	23
		a. Souvenir sheet of 3	90	90

New Constitution. No. 311a contains one each of Nos. 309-311 with brown marginal inscription. Size: 128½x99mm. Sold for 34r.

1973, July 23 Engraved *Perf. 13*

Sculptures from Angkor Wat: 8r, 10r, Devata (different).

312	A84	3r brown black	7	5
313	"	8r Prussian green	13	13
314	"	10r olive bister	17	17
		a. Souvenir sheet of 3	75	75

No. 314a contains one each of Nos. 312-314 with black marginal inscription. Size: 130x100mm. Sold for 25r.

INTERPOL Emblem
A85

Marshal Lon Nol
A86

1973, Oct. 2 Engraved *Perf. 13*

315	A85	3r green & multi.	6	5
316	"	7r red brn. & multi.	15	13
317	"	10r olive & multi.	20	20
		a. Souvenir sheet of 3	70	70

50th anniversary of the International Criminal Police Organization. No. 317a contains one each of Nos. 315-317; black marginal inscription. Size: 123x100mm. Sold for 30r.

1973, Oct. 9

318	A86	3r lt. grn., blk. & brn.	10	7
319	"	8r brn., olive & blk.	20	15
320	"	14r black & brown	35	25
		a. Souvenir sheet of 3	1.10	1.10

Marshal Lon Nol, first president of the Republic. No. 320a contains stamps similar to Nos. 318-320 in changed colors; greenish black marginal inscription. Size: 129x99mm. Sold for 50r.

Nos. 248, 243 and 307 Surcharged with New Value, 2 Bars and Overprinted in Red or Silver: "4th ANNIVERSAIRE/DE LA REPUBLIQUE"

1974 Photo. *Perf. 13, 12½x13*

321 A67 10r multi. (R) 4 3
322 A66 50r on 3r " (S) 20 15
323 A82 100r on 5r " (S) 40 30

4th anniversary of independence.

Copernicus and "Nerva"—A87

Designs: Copernicus, various spacecraft and events.

1974, Sept. 10 Litho. *Perf. 13*

Multicolored

324 A87 1r *shown* 3 3
325 " 5r *Mariner II* 3 3
326 " 10r *Apollo* 4 3
327 " 25r *Telstar* 10 7
328 " 50r *Space walk* 20 14
329 " 100r *Moon landing* 40 28
330 " 150r *Separation of spaceship and module* 60 42
Nos. 324-330, C32-C33 (9) 3.20 2.26

500th anniversary of the birth of Nicolaus Copernicus (1473–1543), Polish astronomer.

Carrier Pigeon and UPU Emblem

A88

Design: 60r, Sailing ship and UPU emblem.

1974, Nov. 2

331 A88 10r multicolored 4 3
332 " 60r " 25 15

Centenary of Universal Postal Union. A souvenir sheet containing one No. 332 exists. See No. C34.

Importation Prohibited

The U.S. Treasury Department prohibited the importation of stamps of Cambodia (Khmer Republic) as of Apr. 17, 1975.

SEMI-POSTAL STAMPS.

Nos. 8, 12, 14 and 15 Surcharged in Black

+60c
AIDE A L'ÉTUDIANT

1952, Oct. 20 *Perf. 13* Unwmkd.

B1 A3 1.10pi+40c dp. carmine & bright red 3.75 3.75
B2 " 1.90pi+60c indigo & deep ultra. 3.75 3.75
B3 " 3pi+1pi dp. carmine & orange brown 3.75 3.75
B4 A1 5pi+2pi indigo & purple 3.75 3.75

Preah Stupa

SP1

1957, Mar. 15 Engraved *Perf. 13*

B5 SP1 1.50r+50c indigo, olive & red 60 60
B6 " 6.50r+1.50r red lilac, olive & red 1.00 1.00
B7 " 8r+2r blue, olive & red 1.50 1.50

Issued to commemorate the 2500th anniversary of the birth of Buddha. See Nos. 62–64.

Type of Regular Issue, 1959, with Red Typographed Surcharge

\+ 0,30

1959, Dec. 9

B8 A14 20c+20c rose violet 10 8
B9 " 50c+30c blue 20 18
B10 " 80c+50c rose carmine 25 20

The surtax was for the Red Cross.

Nos. 107–108 Surcharged and Overprinted in Red: "1863–1963 CENTENAIRE DE LA CROIX ROUGE"

1963, Oct. 1 *Perf. 13* Unwmkd.

B11 A26 4r+40c grn. & dk. brn. 60 60
B12 " 6r+60c violet & olive bister 75 75

Centenary of International Red Cross.

Nos. 263, 267, 293–294, 134 Surcharged in Red

SECOURS AUX VICTIMES DE GUERRE

1972, Nov. 15 Engr. *Perf. 13*

B13 A72 3r+2r multi. 13 10
B14 " 10r+6r " 45 30
B15 A80 12r+7r " 50 35
B16 A34 12r+7r " 50 35
B17 A80 15r+8r " 85 65
Nos. B13-B17 (5) 2.43 1.75

Surtax was for war victims. Surcharge arranged differently on Nos. B15–B17.

AIR POST STAMPS.

Kinnari

AP1

Engraved

1953, Apr. 16 *Perf. 13* Unwmkd.

C1 AP1 50c deep green 55 55
a. Souvenir sheet of 4 45.00
C2 " 3pi red brown 65 55
a. Souvenir sheet of 3 45.00
C3 AP1 3.30pi rose violet 90 65
C4 " 4pi dark brown & deep blue 1.10 65
C5 " 5.10pi brown, red & orange 1.35 90
C6 " 6.50pi dark brown & lilac rose 1.35 1.50
a. Souvenir sheet of 2 45.00
C7 " 9pi lilac rose & deep green 2.00 2.00
C8 " 11.50pi multicolored 3.75 3.00
C9 " 30pi dark brown, blue green & orange 5.75 3.50
Nos. C1-C9 (9) 17.40 13.30

No. C1a contains one each of the 50c, 3.30pi, 5.10pi and 30pi, and sold for 50pi. No. C2a contains one each of the 3pi, 4pi and 11.50pi, and sold for 25pi. No C6a contains one each of the 6.50pi and 9pi, and sold for 20pi. Marginal inscriptions in brown. Size: 129x100mm.

AP2

1957, Dec. 11

C10 AP2 50c maroon 12 8
C11 " 1r emerald 20 15
C12 " 4r ultramarine 90 55
C13 " 50r carmine rose 5.00 4.50
C14 " 100r green, blue & carmine 8.00 6.00
a. Souvenir sheet of 5 15.00 15.00
Nos. C10-C14 (5) 14.22 11.28

No. C14a contains one each of Nos. C10–C14, and sold for 160r. Size: 159x93mm.

Independence Type of 1961

1961, Nov. 9 *Perf. 13x12½*

C15 A24 7r multicolored 75 40
C16 " 30r green, carmine & ultra. 2.00 1.60
C17 " 50r indigo, green & olive 3.50 2.50
a. Souvenir sheet of 3 8.00 8.00

Issued to commemorate the tenth anniversary of Independence. No. C17a contains one each of Nos. C15–C17 with gold marginal inscription. Size: 150x85mm.

No. C15 Surcharged with New Value in Red and Overprinted in Black with Two Bars and: "INAUGURATION DU MONUMENT"

1962, Nov. 9

C18 A24 12r on 7r multi. 1.25 1.00

Dedication of Independence Monument.

Hanuman, Monkey God

AP3

1964, Sept. 1 Engraved *Perf. 13*

C19 AP3 5r multicolored 50 27
C20 " 10r olive bister, lilac rose & green 70 35
C21 " 20r violet, blue & olive bister 1.20 55
C22 " 40r bl., olive bister & dark blue 2.75 1.10
C23 " 80r multicolored 4.50 3.25
Nos. C19-C23 9.65 5.52

Nos. C19-C22 Surcharged in Red

12$
JEUX OLYMPIQUES TOKYO-1964

1964, Oct.

C24 AP3 3r on 5r multi. 40 32
C25 " 6r on 10r " 55 50
C26 " 9r on 20r " 80 70
C27 " 12r on 40r " 1.20 1.00

18th Olympic Games, Tokyo, Oct. 10–25.

Certain unlisted issues of Cambodia, starting in 1972, are mentioned and briefly described in "For the Record" at the back of this volume.

Garuda, 12th Century, Angkor Thom

AP4

1973, Jan. 18 Engraved *Perf. 13*

C28 AP4 3r carmine 8 6
C29 " 30r violet blue 60 50
C30 " 50r dull purple 1.00 80
C31 " 100r dull green 2.00 1.50

Copernicus Type of 1974

Designs: 200r, Copernicus and Skylab III. 250r, Copernicus, Concorde and solar eclipse.

1974, Sept. 10 Litho. *Perf. 13*

C32 A87 200r multicolored 80 56
C33 " 250r " 1.00 70

500th anniversary of the birth of Nicolaus Copernicus (1473–1543), Polish astronomer. A souvenir sheet containing No. C32 is perf., size 110x82mm. A souvenir sheet containing No. C33 is imperf., size 83x111 mm.

UPU Type of 1974

Design: 700r, Rocket, globe and UPU emblem.

1974, Nov. 2

C34 A88 700r gold & multi. 2.80 2.00

Centenary of Universal Postal Union. A souvenir sheet containing one No. C34 exists.

POSTAGE DUE STAMPS

D1

Frieze, Angkor Wat

D2

Typographed.

1957 ***Perf. 13½*** **Unwmkd.**

Denomination in Black.

J1 D1 10c vermilion & pale blue 12 12
J2 " 50c " " 18 18
J3 " 1r " " 22 22
J4 " 3r " " 33 33
J5 " 5r " " 60 60
Nos. J1-J5 (5) 1.45 1.45

1974, Feb. 18 Engr. ***Perf. 12½x13***

J6 D2 2r ocher 6 6
J7 " 6r green 10 10
J8 " 8r deep carmine 15 15
J9 " 10r violet blue 20 20

CAMEROUN

(kăm′ẽr·ōōn)

(Kamerun)

LOCATION—On the west coast of Africa, north of the equator.

GOVT.—Republic.

AREA—182,964 sq. mi.

POP.—6,670,000 (est. 1977).

CAPITAL—Yaoundé.

Before World War I, Cameroun (Kamerun) was a German Protectorate. It was occupied during the War by Great Britain and France and in 1922 was mandated to these countries by the League of Nations. The French mandated part became the independent State of Cameroun Jan. 1, 1960. The Southern Cameroons, a United Kingdom Trust Territory, joined this state to form the Federal Republic of Cameroun Oct. 1, 1961. The name was changed to United Republic of Cameroon on May 20, 1972.

Stamps of Southern Cameroons are listed under Cameroons in Vol. I.

100 Pfennig = 1 Mark
12 Pence = 1 Shilling
100 Centimes = 1 Franc

Issued under German Dominion.

A1 A2

Stamps of Germany, 1889-1900, Overprinted in Black.

1897 ***Perf. 13½x14½*** **Unwmkd.**

1 A1 3pf yellow brown 11.00 13.50
a. 3pf red brown 25.00 32.50
b. 3pf dark brown 9.50 *40.00*
2 " 5pf green 7.50 4.00
3 A2 10pf carmine 5.50 5.50
4 " 20pf ultramarine 6.50 7.50
5 " 25pf orange 27.50 38.50
6 " 50pf red brown 25.00 32.50
Nos. 1-6 (6) 83.00 101.50

Kaiser's Yacht "Hohenzollern"
A3 A4

Typographed.

1900 ***Perf. 14*** **Unwmkd.**

7 A3 3pf brown 1.65 1.65
8 " 5pf green 27.50 1.10
9 " 10pf carmine 75.00 1.65
10 " 20pf ultramarine 38.50 2.75
11 A3 25pf orange & black, *yellow* 1.65 *8.00*
12 " 30pf orange & black, *salmon* 2.25 *5.50*
13 " 40pf lake & black 2.25 *6.50*
14 " 50pf purple & black, *salmon* 2.75 *8.00*
15 " 80pf lake & black, *rose* 3.25 *11.00*

Engraved.

Perf. 14½x14

16 A4 1m carmine 100.00 72.50
17 " 2m blue 8.00 *55.00*
18 " 3m black violet 8.50 *110.00*
19 " 5m slate & car. 165.00 *550.00*
Nos. 7-19 (13) 436.30 *833.65*

Wmk. 125

Typographed.

1905-18 **Wmkd. Lozenges. (125)**

20 A3 3pf brown ('18) 1.10
21 " 5pf green ('06) 1.10 *2.25*
a. Booklet pane of 6 9.50
b. Booklet pane of 6, (2 No. 21+4 No. 22) 47.50
22 " 10pf carmine 1.10 1.10
a. Booklet pane of 6 9.50
23 " 20pf ultramarine ('14) 2.75 *190.00*
24 A4 1m carmine ('15) 3.25
25 " 5m slate & carmine ('13) 27.50 *2750.00*

The 3pf and 1m were not placed in use.

Issued under British Occupation.

Stamps of German Cameroun Surcharged

C. E. F.
½ d.

Wmkd. Lozenges (125) (#54-56, 65) Unwmkd. (Other Values.)

1915 ***Perf. 14, 14½***

Blue Surcharge.

53 A3 ½p on 3pf brown 2.25 3.00
54 " ½p on 5pf green 1.00 1.50
a. Double surcharge 200.00 115.00
b. Black surcharge 2.00 2.75
55 " 1p on 10pf carmine 1.00 1.50
a. "1" with thin serifs 11.00 13.50
b. Double surcharge 50.00 60.00
c. Black surcharge 4.50 6.00
d. "C.E.F." omitted *1100.00*
e. "1d" double *1000.00*

Black Surcharge.

56 A3 2p on 20pf ultra. 1.00 1.50
57 " 2½p on 25pf orange & black, *yellow* 2.00 3.00
a. Double surcharge *1350.00*
58 " 3p on 30pf orange & black, *salmon* 2.00 3.00
59 " 4p on 40pf lake & black 2.00 3.00
60 " 6p on 50pf purple & black, *salmon* 2.00 3.00
61 " 8p on 80pf lake & black, *rose* 2.00 3.00

Surcharged

C. E. F.
1s.

62 A4 1sh on 1m carmine 75.00 85.00
a. "S" inverted 325.00 350.00
63 A4 2sh on 2m blue 75.00 85.00
a. "S" inverted 325.00 350.00
64 " 3sh on 3m black violet 75.00 85.00
a. "S" inverted 325.00 350.00
b. Double surcharge *1800.00*
65 " 5sh on 5m slate & carmine 75.00 85.00
a. "S" inverted 325.00 350.00
Nos. 53-65 (13) 315.25 362.50

The letters "C. E. F." are the initials of "Cameroons Expeditionary Force."

Issued under French Occupation.

Stamps of Gabon, 1910, Overprinted

Corps Expéditionnaire
Franco-Anglais
CAMEROUN

1915 ***Perf. 13½x14.*** **Unwmkd.**

101 A10 10c red & car. 10.00 5.00
102 A13 1c choc. & org. 35.00 11.00
103 " 2c black & choc. 65.00 60.00
104 " 4c violet & deep blue 65.00 60.00
105 " 5c olive gray & green 10.00 5.00
105A " 10c red & car. *6500.00 6500.00*
106 " 20c olive brn. & dk. violet 70.00 65.00
107 A14 25c deep blue & chocolate 20.00 7.00
108 " 30c gray black & red 60.00 55.00
109 " 35c dk. vio. & grn. 15.00 7.00
a. Double ovpt. 575.00 575.00
110 " 40c choc. & ultra. 70.00 60.00
111 " 45c car. & violet 75.00 65.00
112 " 50c bl. grn. & gray 75.00 60.00
113 " 75c org. & choc. 100.00 60.00
114 A15 1fr dk. brn. & bis. 90.00 65.00
115 " 2fr car. & brown 90.00 65.00
Nos. 101-105, 106-115 (15) 850.00 650.00

The overprint is vertical, reading up, on Nos. 101-106, 114-115, and horizontal on Nos. 107-113.

Stamps of Middle Congo, Issue of 1907, Overprinted

Occupation
Francaise
du Cameroun

1916 **Unwmkd.**

116 A1 1c olive gray & brown 30.00 30.00
117 " 2c violet & brown 35.00 30.00
118 " 4c blue & brown 35.00 30.00
119 " 5c dk. grn. & blue 11.00 10.00
120 A2 35c violet brown & blue 45.00 30.00
121 " 45c violet & red 25.00 25.00

The overprint is horizontal on Nos. 116-119, and vertical, reading down, on Nos. 120-121.

Same Overprint
On Stamps of French Congo, 1900.

Wmkd. Branch of Thistle. (122)

122 A4 15c dull violet & olive green 25.00 25.00
a. Inverted overprint 40.00 40.00

Wmkd. Branch of Rose Tree. (123)

123 A5 20c yellow green & orange 60.00 30.00
124 " 30c carmine rose & orange 35.00 20.00
125 " 40c orange brown & bright green 25.00 25.00
126 " 50c gray violet & lilac 27.50 25.00
127 " 75c red violet & orange 27.50 20.00

Wmkd. Branch of Olive. (124)

128 A6 1fr gray lilac & olive 45.00 30.00
129 " 2fr carmine & brn. 45.00 30.00
Nos. 116-129 (14) 471.00 360.00

The overprint is horizontal on No. 122; vertical, reading down or up, on Nos. 123-129.

Counterfeits exist of Nos. 101-129.

Stamps of Middle Congo, Issue of 1907 Overprinted

CAMEROUN
Occupation
Française

1916-17 **Unwmkd.**

130 A1 1c olive gray & brown 6 6
131 " 2c violet & brown 7 6
132 " 4c blue & brown 7 6
133 " 5c dark green & blue 10 7
a. Booklet pane of 4
134 " 10c carmine & blue 35 25
135 " 15c brown violet & rose ('17) 40 20
a. Booklet pane of 4
136 " 20c brown & blue 13 12
137 A2 25c blue & green 20 15
a. Triple ovpt. 100.00
138 " 30c scarlet & green 18 15
a. Double ovpt. 40.00
139 " 35c violet brown & blue 20 18
140 " 40c dull grn. & brown 35 25
141 " 45c violet & red 40 30
142 " 50c blue green & red 40 35
143 " 75c brown & blue 60 40
144 A3 1fr dp. grn. & violet 40 30
145 " 2fr violet & gray green 2.75 1.75
146 " 5fr blue & rose 2.75 2.35
Nos. 130-146 (17) 9.41 7.00

Nos. 130 to 146 exist on ordinary paper and, with the exception of No. 132, on chalk surfaced paper. Nos. 137 to 146 are known with inverted "S" in "Francaise."

On Nos. 137 to 146 there is a space of 7mm. between "Cameroun" and "Occupation."

Provisional French Mandate.

Types of Middle Congo, 1907, Overprinted

CAMEROUN

1921

147 A1 1c olive green & orange 4 4
148 " 2c brown & rose 4 4
149 " 4c gray & light green 4 4
150 " 5c dull red & orange 6 6
a. Double overprint 225.00
151 " 10c blue green & light green 10 10
152 " 15c blue & orange 10 10
153 " 20c red brown & olive 10 10
154 A2 25c slate & orange 12 10
155 " 30c rose & vermilion 13 10
156 " 35c gray & ultramarine 20 20
157 " 40c olive grn. & org. 15 12
158 " 45c brown & rose 15 13
159 " 50c blue & ultra. 10 10
160 " 75c red brown & light green 15 15
161 A3 1fr slate & orange 50 45
162 " 2fr olive grn. & rose 1.85 1.50
163 " 5fr dull red & gray 2.25 2.00
Nos. 147-163 (17) 6.08 5.33

The 2c, 4c, 15c, 25c and 50c exist with overprint omitted.

Nos. 152, 162, 163, 158, 160 Surcharged with New Value and Bars.

1924-25

164 A1 25c on 15c blue & orange ('25) 20 20
165 A3 25c on 2fr olive green & rose 20 20
166 " 25c on 5fr red & gray 20 20
a. Pair, one without new value and bars
167 A2 65c on 45c brown & rose ('25) 55 55
168 " 85c on 75c red brown & light green ('25) 65 65
Nos. 164-168 (5) 1.80 1.80

French Mandate

Herder and Cattle Crossing Sanaga River—A5

Tapping Rubber Tree A6 — Rope Suspension Bridge A7

1925–38 Typo. ***Perf. 14x13½***

170 A5 1c olive green & brown violet, *lavender* 5 5
171 " 2c rose & green, *greenish* 5 5
172 " 4c blue & black 5 5
173 " 5c orange & red violet, *lavender* 6 5
174 " 10c red brown & orange, *yellow* 8 7
175 " 15c slate green & green 10 7
176 " 15c lilac & red ('27) 28 28

Perf. 13½x14.

177 A6 20c olive brown & red brown 6 5
178 " 20c green ('26) 6 6
179 " 20c brown red & olive brown ('27) 10 8
180 " 25c light green & black 15 8
181 " 30c bluish green & vermilion 6 6
182 " 30c dark green & green ('27) 10 8
183 " 35c brown & black 10 10
184 " 35c dull green & green ('38) 28 25
185 " 40c orange & violet 30 25
186 " 45c deep rose & cerise 8 7
187 " 45c violet & orange brown ('27) 85 60
188 " 50c light green & cerise 10 7
189 " 55c ultramarine & carmine ('38) 38 35
190 " 60c red violet & black 10 6
191 " 60c brown red ('26) 6 6
192 " 65c indigo & brown 6 6
193 " 75c indigo & deep blue 15 8
194 " 75c orange brown & red violet ('27) 13 10
195 " 80c car. & brown ('38) 35 35
196 " 85c deep rose & blue 15 10
197 " 90c brown red & cerise ('27) 85 30

Perf. 14x13½.

198 A7 1fr indigo & brown 25 20
199 " 1fr dull blue ('26) 15 10
200 " 1fr olive brown & red violet ('27) 18 18
201 " 1fr green & dark brown ('29) 50 30
202 " 1.10fr rose red & dark brown ('28) 1.40 1.20
203 " 1.25fr gray & deep blue ('33) 1.50 75
204 " 1.50fr dull blue ('27) 30 10
205 " 1.75fr brown & orange ('33) 40 30
206 " 1.75fr dark blue & light blue ('38) 35 25
207 " 2fr dull green & brown orange 70 20
208 " 3fr olive brown & red violet ('27) 2.35 40
209 " 5fr brown & black, *bluish* 1.00 40
a. Cliché of 2fr in plate of 5fr *700.00*
210 " 10fr orange & violet ('27) 4.00 2.00
211 " 20fr rose & olive green ('27) 7.00 3.25
Nos. 170–211 (42) 25.22 13.36

Common Design Types pictured in section at front of book.

No. 199 Surcharged with New Value and Bars in Red.

1926

212 A7 1.25fr on 1fr dull blue 12 12

Colonial Exposition Issue.
Common Design Types
Name of Country in Black.

1931 Engraved. ***Perf. 12½.***

213 CD70 40c deep green 1.00 85
214 CD71 50c violet 1.65 1.50
215 CD72 90c red orange 1.65 1.25
216 CD73 1.50fr dull blue 1.65 1.50

Paris International Exposition Issue.
Common Design Types

1937 ***Perf. 13.***

217 CD74 20c deep violet 40 40
218 CD75 30c dark green 30 30
219 CD76 40c carmine rose 35 35
220 CD77 50c dark brown 20 20
221 CD78 90c red 40 40
222 CD79 1.50f ultramarine 35 35
Nos. 217–222 (6) 2.00 2.00

French Colonial Art Exhibition.
Common Design Type
Souvenir Sheet.

1937 ***Imperf.***

222A CD77 3fr orange red & black 1.65 1.65
Size: 118x99mm.

New York World's Fair Issue.
Common Design Type

1939 ***Perf. 12½x12.***

223 CD82 1.25fr carmine lake 25 25
224 " 2.25fr ultramarine 25 25

Mandara Woman A19 — Falls on M'bam River near Banyo A20

Elephants
A21

Man in Yaré
A22

1939–40 Engraved ***Perf. 13***

225 A19 2c black brown 4 4
226 " 3c magenta 4 4
227 " 4c dp. ultramarine 6 6
228 A19 5c red brown 10 10
229 " 10c deep blue green 5 5
230 " 15c rose red 6 6
231 " 20c plum 6 6
232 A20 25c black brown 20 20
233 " 30c dark red 12 10
234 " 40c ultramarine 15 15
235 " 45c slate green 60 50
236 " 50c brown carmine 15 15
237 " 60c peacock blue 15 15
238 " 70c plum 85 85
239 A21 80c Prussian blue 60 55
240 " 90c Prussian blue 25 10
241 " 1fr carmine rose 35 35
242 " 1fr chocolate ('40) 35 20
243 " 1.25fr carmine rose 90 85
244 " 1.40fr orange red 40 35
245 " 1.50fr chocolate 20 20
246 " 1.60fr black brown 85 75
247 " 1.75fr dark blue 15 15
248 " 2fr dark green 10 10
249 " 2.25fr dark blue 25 25
250 " 2.50fr brt. red violet 40 33
251 " 3fr dark violet 15 10
252 A22 5fr black brown 30 25
253 " 10fr brt. red violet 50 40
254 " 20fr da:k green 70 60
Nos. 225–254 (30) 9.08 8.04

Stamps of 1925–40 Overprinted in Black or Orange "CAMEROUN FRANCAIS 27.8.40."

1940 ***Perf. 14x13½, 13½x14, 13.***

255 A19 2c black brown (O) 10 10
256 " 3c magenta (Bk) 10 10
257 " 4c deep ultra. (O) 15 15
258 " 5c red brown (Bk) 60 60
259 " 10c deep blue green (O) 8 8
260 " 15c rose red (Bk) 25 25
260A " 20c plum (O) 2.35 2.00
261 A20 25c black brown (Bk) 15 10
b. Inverted ovpt. 85.00 85.00
261A " 30c dark red (Bk) 2.00 1.25
262 " 40c ultra. (Bk) 85 40
263 " 45c slate green (Bk) 60 30
264 A6 50c light green & cerise (Bk) 20 10
a. Inverted ovpt. 75.00
265 A20 60c peacock blue (Bk) 1.00 60
266 " 70c plum (Bk) 20 20
267 A21 80c Prus. blue (O) 1.00 75
268 " 90c Prus. blue (O) 25 25
269 " 1.25fr carmine rose (Bk) 40 30
270 " 1.40fr orange red (Bk) 60 50
271 " 1.50fr chocolate (Bk) 25 25
272 " 1.60fr black brown (O) 40 40
273 " 1.75fr dark blue (O) 40 40
274 " 2.25fr dark blue (O) 25 20
275 " 2.50fr bright red violet (Bk) 25 20
276 A7 5fr brown & black, *bluish* (Bk) 4.00 3.25
277 A22 5fr black brown (Bk) 5.00 4.00
278 A7 10fr orange & violet (Bk) 6.00 5.00
278A A22 10fr bright red violet (Bk) 12.50 8.00
279 A7 20fr rose & olive green (Bk) 14.00 11.00
279A A22 20fr dark green 70.00 70.00

Same Overprint on Stamps of 1939.

Perf. 12½x12.

280 CD82 1.25fr carmine lake (Bk) 1.00 1.00
281 " 2.25fr ultra. (Bk) 1.00 1.00
Nos. 255–281 (31) 125.93 112.73

Issued to note Cameroun's affiliation with General de Gaulle's "Free France" movement.

Cattle Fording Sanaga River and Marshal Petain
A22a

1941 Engraved ***Perf. 12½x12***

281A A22a 1fr green 20
281B " 2.50fr dark blue 20

Nos. 281A–281B were issued by the Vichy government, and were not placed on sale in Cameroun.

Lorraine Cross and Joan of Arc Shield
A23

1941 Photo. ***Perf. 14x14½***

282 A23 5c brown 4 4
283 " 10c dark blue 4 4
284 " 25c emerald 6 6
285 " 30c deep orange 6 6
286 " 40c dark slate green 4 4
287 " 80c red brown 5 5
288 " 1fr deep red lilac 5 5
289 " 1.50fr bright red 5 5
290 " 2fr gray black 5 5
291 " 2.50fr bright ultra. 10 10
292 " 4fr dull violet 20 18
293 " 5fr bistre 30 27
294 " 10fr deep brown 40 20
295 " 20fr deep green 70 25
Nos. 282–295 (14) 2.14 1.44

Eboue Issue
Common Design Type
Engraved.

1945 ***Perf. 13.*** **Unwmkd.**

296 CD91 2fr black 5 5
297 " 25fr Prussian green 25 25
Nos. 296 and 297 exist imperforate.

Nos. 282, 284 and 291 Surcharged with New Values and Bars in Red, Carmine or Black.

1946 ***Perf. 14x14½.***

297A A23 50c on 5c brown (R) 7 7
298 " 60c on 5c brown (R) 7 7
a. Inverted surcharge 35.00
299 " 70c on 5c brown (R) 15 15
300 " 1.20fr on 5c brown (C) 7 7
301 " 2.40fr on 25c emerald 8 8
302 " 3fr on 25c emerald 22 22
302A " 4.50fr on 25c emerald 40 40
303 " 15fr on 2.50fr bright ultramarine (C) 40 40
Nos. 297A–303 (8) 1.46 1.46

Zebu and Herder
A25

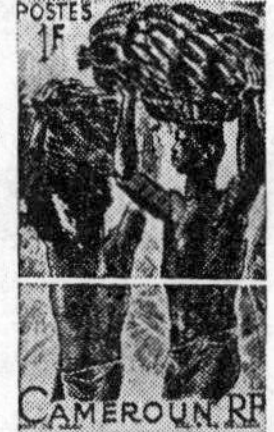

Tikar Women A26 — Porters Carrying Bananas A27

Bowman

A28

Lamido Horsemen

A29

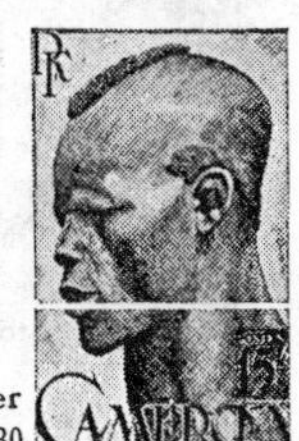

Farmer

A30

Perf. 12½x12, 12x12½.

1946 Engraved.

304 A25 10c blue green 3 3
305 " 30c brown orange 3 3
306 " 40c bright ultra. 4 4
307 A26 50c olive brown 4 4
308 " 60c deep plum 6 6
309 " 80c chestnut brown 10 8
310 A27 1fr orange red 6 6
311 " 1.20fr deep green 10 10
312 " 1.50fr dark carmine 50 45
313 A28 2fr black 6 6
314 " 3fr dark carmine 6 5
314A " 3.60fr red brown 25 20
315 " 4fr deep blue 10 6
316 A29 5fr brown carmine 20 6
317 " 6fr ultramarine 20 8
318 " 10fr slate green 20 4
319 A30 15fr greenish blue 60 6
320 " 20fr dark green 55 8
321 " 25fr black 85 15
Nos. 304-321 (19) 4.03 1.73

Imperforates

Most Cameroun stamps from 1952 onward exist imperforate in issued and trial colors, and also in small presentation sheets in issued colors.

Military Medal Issue.

Common Design Type

Engraved and Typographed.

1952 *Perf. 13.* Unwmkd.

322 CD101 15fr multicolored 1.40 90

Issued to commemorate the centenary of the creation of the French Military Medal.

Porters Carrying Bananas

A32

Picking Coffee Beans

A33

1954 Engraved

323 A32 8fr red violet, orange brown & violet blue 20 8
324 " 15fr brown red, yellow & black brown 50 12
325 A33 40fr black brown, orange brown & lilac rose 45 10

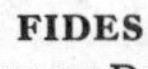

FIDES Issue

Common Design Type

Designs: 5fr, Plowmen. 15fr, Wouri bridge. 20fr, Technical instruction. 25fr, Mobile medical station.

1956 *Perf. 13* Unwmkd.

326 CD103 5fr orange brown & dark brown 25 15
327 " 15fr aquamarine, slate & black 30 10
328 " 20fr greenish blue & deep ultramarine 45 25
329 " 25fr deep ultramarine 65 40

Coffee Issue

Coffee—A35

1956 Engraved *Perf. 13*

330 A35 15fr car. & brt. red 25 12

Autonomous Government

Flag and Woman Holding Child

A36

1958

331 A36 20f multicolored 45 10

Issued to commemorate the anniversary of the installation of the first autonomous government of Cameroun.

Men Looking to the Sun

A37

1958

332 A37 20fr sepia & brown red 50 40

Issued to commemorate the tenth anniversary of the signing of the Universal Declaration of Human Rights.

Flower Issue

Common Design Type

Design: 20fr, Randia malleifera.

1959 Photogravure *Perf. 12½x12*

333 CD104 20fr deep green, yellow & rose 40 20

Loading Bananas

A38

Harvesting Bananas

A39

1959 Engraved. *Perf. 13*

334 A38 20fr dk. green & org. 30 8
335 A39 25fr maroon & slate green 40 10

Independent State

Map and Flag of Cameroun

A40

Prime Minister Ahmadou Ahidjo

A41

Engraved.

1960 *Perf. 13* Unwmkd.

336 A40 20fr multicolored 40 10
337 A41 25fr black, green & pale lemon 45 15

Declaration of independence, Jan. 1, 1960.

Uprooted Oak Emblem

A42

1960

338 A42 30fr red brown, ultra. & yel. green 60 55

Issued to publicize World Refugee Year, July 1, 1959–June 30, 1960.

C.C.T.A. Issue

Common Design Type

1960

339 CD106 50fr dull claret & slate 1.00 60

U.N. Headquarters, New York, and Flag—A43

1961, May 20 *Perf. 13*

Flag in Green, Red and Yellow

340 A43 15fr green, dk. blue & brown 40 35
341 " 25fr dk. blue & grn. 45 35
342 " 85fr red, dk. blue & violet brown 1.35 1.20

Issued to commemorate Cameroun's admission to the United Nations, Sept. 20, 1960.

Federal Republic

Stamps of 1946-60 Surcharged in Red or Black:

REPUBLIQUE FEDERALE 2d

Two types of 2sh6p:
I. Large figures. "2/6" measures 8x3¾mm.
II. Small figures. "2/6" measures 6x2½mm.

Engraved

1961, Oct. 1 *Perf. 12x12½, 13*

343 A27 ½p on 1fr orange red (#310) 25 25
344 A28 1p on 2fr black (#313) 35 25
345 A34 1½p on 5fr orange brown & dk. brown (#326) 35 25
346 A29 2p on 10fr slate green (#318) 40 30
347 A34 3p on 15fr aquamarine, slate & black (#327) 45 35
348 A35 4p on 15fr carmine & br. red (Bk) (#330) 60 45
349 A38 6p on 20fr dark green & org. (#334) 75 50
350 A41 1sh on 25fr black, green & pale lemon (#337) 1.50 1.25
351 A42 2sh6p on 30fr red brn., ultra. & yel. grn. (#338) (I) 2.50 2.50
a. Type II 6.50 6.50
Nos. 343-351 (9) 7.15 6.10

Issued for use in the former United Kingdom Trust Territory of Southern Cameroons.

The "Republique Federale" overprint is in one line on Nos. 345, 347-349, in two vertical lines on No. 350. See Nos. C38-C40.

President Ahidjo and Prime Minister Foncha

A45

Engraved

1962, Jan. 1 *Perf. 13* Unwmkd.

352 A45 20fr violet & choc. 4.50 4.00
353 " 25fr dk. grn. & brn. 6.50 6.00
354 " 60fr carmine & dull green 22.50 20.00

Same Surcharged for Use in Southern Cameroons

3 d

355 A45 3p on 20fr violet & chocolate 70.00 70.00
356 " 6p on 25fr dark grn. & brn. 70.00 70.00
357 " 2sh6p on 60fr carm. & dull grn. 70.00 70.00

Issued to commemorate the reunification of the former French and British Sections of Cameroun. It is reported that Nos. 352-357 were withdrawn after a few days and destroyed.

Mustache Monkey

A46

Designs: 1fr, 4fr, Elephant, Ntem Falls. 1.50fr, 3fr, Buffon's kob, Dschang. 2fr, 5fr, Hippopotamus. 6fr, 15fr, Mustache monkey. 8fr, 30fr, Manatee, Lake Ossa. 10fr, 25fr, Buffalo, Batouri. 20fr, 40fr, Giraffes, Waza Reservation (vert.).

Engraved

1962 *Perf. 12* Unwmkd.

358 A46 50c brn., brt. green & blue 10 3
359 " 1fr gray brn., blue grn. & orange 10 3
360 " 1.50fr brn., lt. green & slate green 10 4
361 " 2fr dark gray, greenish blue & green 10 4

362 A46 3fr brn., orange & lilac rose 10 6
363 " 4fr brn., yel. grn. & blue green 12 6
364 " 5fr gray brown, grn. & salmon 15 8
365 " 6fr brn., yel. & blue 18 10
366 " 8fr dk. blue, red & green 25 15
367 " 10fr olive blk., orange & br. blue 25 8
368 " 15fr brn., Prussian blue & blue 30 8
369 " 20fr brown & gray 40 12
370 " 25fr red brn., green & yellow 60 30
371 " 30fr blk., orge. & blue 85 40
372 " 40fr dp. claret, yel. green & black 1.20 60
Nos. 358-372 (15) 4.80 2.17

See also Nos. 396-397.

African and Malgasy Union Issue

Common Design Type

1962, Sept. 8 Photo. *Perf. 12½x12*

373 CD110 30fr multicolored 65 55

Issued to commemorate the first anniversary of the African and Malgasy Union.

Village and Map of Cameroun
A48

Designs: 20fr, 25fr, Sun rising over city. 50fr, Hands holding scroll.

1962, Oct. 1 Engr. *Perf. 13*

374 A48 9fr purple, olive & dark brown 20 20
375 " 18fr grn., org. brn. & dark blue 35 25
376 " 20fr lilac rose, olive bistre & indigo 35 25
377 " 25fr blue, red orange & sepia 50 30
378 " 50fr dark red, sepia & blue 1.00 75
Nos. 374-378 (5) 2.40 1.75

Issued to commemorate the first anniversary of the reunification of Cameroun.

"School under the Trees"
A49

1962, Nov. 5 Photo. *Perf. 12x12½*

379 A49 20fr verm., emerald & yellow 40 20

Literacy and popular education campaign.

Telstar and Globe
A50

1963, Feb. 9 Engraved *Perf. 13*

Size: 36x22mm.

380 A50 1fr dark blue, olive & purple 5 5
381 " 2fr dark blue, claret & green 8 8
382 " 3fr dark green, olive & deep claret 12 12
383 " 25fr green, dp. claret & brt. blue 70 60

Issued to commemorate the first television connection of the United States and Europe through the Telstar satellite, July 11-12, 1962. See No. C45.

High Frequency Transmission Station, Mt. Bankolo
A51

"Yaoundé—Regional Center of Textbook Production"
A52

Design: 20fr, Station and wiring plan.

1963, May 18 Photo. *Perf. 12x12½*

384 A51 15fr multicolored 25 20
385 " 20fr " 35 25

Issued to publicize the high frequency telegraph connection Douala-Yaounde. See No. C46.

1963, Aug. 10 *Perf. 12½* Unwmkd.

386 A52 20fr emerald, black & red 35 20
387 " 25fr orge., blk. & red 45 25
388 " 100fr gold, blk. & red 1.75 1.00

Issued to publicize the UNESCO regional center for the production of school books at Yaounde.

Pres. Ahmadou Ahidjo and Flag
A53

Design: 18fr, Flag and map of Cameroun.

1963, Oct. 1 *Perf. 12x12½*

Flag in Green, Red and Yellow

389 A53 9fr green, blue, & dark brown 15 15
390 " 18fr grn., bl. & lilac 30 25
391 " 20fr green, black & yellow green 35 30

Second anniversary of reunification.

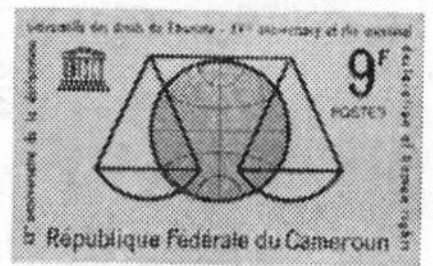

Scales, Globe, UNESCO Emblem
A54

1963, Dec. 10 Photo. *Perf. 12½x12*

392 A54 9fr ultra., blk. & sal. 15 12
393 " 18fr bright yellow green, black & rose red 30 20
394 " 25fr rose red, black & brt. yel. grn. 40 30
395 " 75fr yel., blk. & ultra. 1.35 75

Issued to commemorate the 15th anniversary of the Universal Declaration of Human Rights.

Animal Type of 1962

Design: 10fr, 25fr, Lion, Waza National Park, North Cameroun.

1964, June 20 Engr. *Perf. 13*

396 A46 10fr red brown, bister & green 25 10
397 " 25fr green & bister 50 25

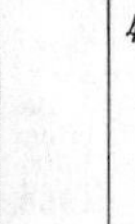

Soccer Game in Stadium
A55

Designs: 18fr, Pile of sports equipment. 30fr, Stadium (outside), flags and map of Africa.

1964, July 11 Engraved *Perf. 13*

398 A55 10fr green, blue & red brown 20 10
399 " 18fr car., grn. & vio. 30 20
400 " 30fr black, dark blue & orange brown 50 30

Tropics Cup Games, Yaounde, July 11-19.

Europafrica Issue, 1964

Common Design Type and

Palace of Justice, Yaounde
A56

Design: 40fr, Emblems of Science, Agriculture, Industry and Education and two sunbursts.

1964, July 20 Photo. *Perf. 12x13*

401 A56 15fr multicolored 50 40
402 CD116 40fr " 1.00 85

Issued to commemorate the first anniversary of the economic agreement between the European Economic Community and the African and Malgache Union.

Hurdling and Olympic Flame
A57

Design: 10fr, Runners (vert.).

1964, Oct. 10 Engraved *Perf. 13*

403 A57 9fr red, yellow green & black 85 60
404 " 10fr red, violet & olive gray 85 60

18th Olympic Games, Tokyo, Oct. 10-25. See Nos. C49, C49a.

Bamileke Dance Dress
A58

Ntem Falls, Ebolowa Region
A59

Designs: 18fr, Dance mask, Bamenda region. 25fr, Fulani horseman, North Cameroun (horiz.).

1964 *Perf. 13* Unwmkd.

405 A58 9fr red, yel. grn. & bl. 15 10
406 " 18fr blue, red & brn. 30 20
407 A59 20fr dark carmine, green & olive 35 20
408 A58 25fr dk. brown, orge. & carmine 45 30

See also No. C50.

Cooperation Issue

Common Design Type

1964, Nov. 7 Engraved

409 CD119 18fr dk. bl., yel. grn. & dk. brown 35 20
410 " 30fr red brn., blue green & dk. brown 60 25

Memorial Stone
A60

Diesel Train
A61

1965, Jan. 1 Engraved *Perf. 13*

411 A60 12fr blue, indigo & green 25 15

Typographed

Perf. 14x13

412 A61 20fr rose car., yellow & green 40 20

Issued to commemorate the laying of the first rail of the Mbanga-Kumba Railroad, March 28, 1964.

Red Cross Station and Ambulance
A62

Design: 50fr, Red Cross nurse and infant (vert.).

1965, May 8 Engraved *Perf. 13*

413 A62 25fr carmine, slate green & ocher 45 25
414 " 50fr gray, red & red brown 90 45

Issued for the Cameroun Red Cross.

Coins Inserted in Map of Cameroun, and Bankbook
A63

Savings Bank Building
A64

Design: 20fr, Bankbook and coins inserted in cacao pod-shaped bank (horiz.).

1965, June 10

Size: 22x37mm.

415 A63 9fr grn., red & org. 20 20

Size: 48x27mm., 27x48mm.

416 A64 15fr chocolate, ultra. & green 30 25
417 A63 20fr ocher, bright green & brown 35 30

Federal Postal Savings Banks.

Soccer Players and Africa Cup
A65

Engraved

1965, June 26 *Perf. 13* Unwmkd.

418 A65 9fr car., brn. & yel. 20 15
419 " 20fr car., slate blue & yellow 35 25

Issued to honor the Cameroun Oryx Club, winner of the club champions' Africa Cup, February 1965.

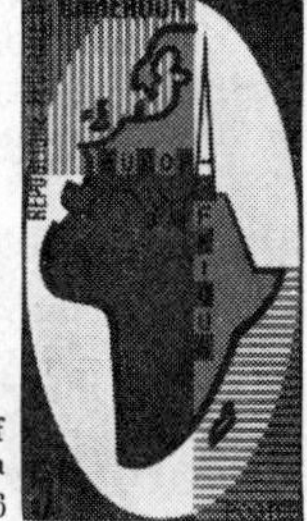

Symbolic Map of Europe and Africa
A66

Designs: 40fr, Delegates around conference table.

1965, July 20 Photo. *Perf. 12x12½*

420 A66 5fr car., blk. & lilac 10 10
421 " 40fr brn., buff, green & ultramarine 70 50

Issued to commemorate the second anniversary of the economic agreement between the European Economic Community and the African and Malgache Union.

UPU Monument, Bern
A67

1965, July 26 Engraved *Perf. 13*

422 A67 30fr black & red 55 40

Issued to commemorate the fifth anniversary of Cameroun's admission to the UPU.

ICY Emblem—A68

1965, Sept. 11 *Perf. 13* Unwmkd.

423 A68 10fr dark blue & carmine rose 25 25

Issued for the International Cooperation Year, 1964–65. See also No. C57.

Pres. Ahidjo and Government House
A69

Design: 9fr, 20fr, Pres. Ahidjo and Government House (vert.).

Perf. 12x12½, 12½x12

1965, Oct. 1 Photo. Unwmkd.

Portrait in Dark Brown; Building in Gray

424 A69 9fr dp. red, brt. pink, & bright blue 15 12
425 " 18fr brt. yellow & blk. 30 18
426 " 20fr violet blue, brt. blue & orange 35 20
427 " 25fr yel. grn. & black 45 25

Reelection of Pres. Ahmadou Ahidjo.

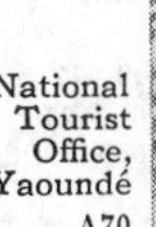

National Tourist Office, Yaoundé
A70

Designs: 9fr, Pouss Musgum houses. 18fr, Great Calao's dance (North Cameroun). 20fr, Gate of Sultan's Palace, Foumban (vert.).

1965 Engraved *Perf. 13*

428 A70 9fr brown, rose red & green 15 10
429 " 18fr brt. blue, brown & green 30 25
430 " 20fr blue, brown & chocolate 35 20
431 " 25fr maroon, emerald & gray 35 20

See also No. C58.

Mountain Hotel, Buea—A71

Designs: 20fr, Hotel of the Deputies, Yaoundé. 35fr, Dschang Health Center.

1966

432 A71 9fr slate grn., rose claret & brn. 20 15
433 " 20fr brt. blue, slate grn. & black 35 20
434 " 35fr brn., slate grn. & carmine 60 45
Nos. 432–434, C63–C69 (10) 8.55 4.75

Issue dates: Nos. 432–433, Apr. 6; No. 434, June 4.

Bas-relief, Foumban
A72

Designs: 18fr, Ekoi mask (vert.). 20fr, Mother and child, carving, Bamiléké (vert.). 25fr, Ceremonial stool, Bamoun.

1966, Apr. 15 Unwmkd.

435 A72 9fr red & black 25 15
436 " 18fr brt. green, org. brn. & choc. 35 25
437 " 20fr brt. blue, red brn. & purple 45 25
438 " 25fr pur. & dk. brown 50 30

Issued to commemorate the International Negro Arts Festival, Dakar, Senegal, Apr. 1–24.

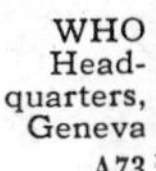

WHO Headquarters, Geneva
A73

1966, May 3 Photo. *Perf. 12½x13*

439 A73 50fr ultra., red brown & yellow 85 50

Issued to commemorate the inauguration of the World Health Organization Headquarters, Geneva.

ITU Headquarters, Geneva
A74

1966, May 3 Photo. *Perf. 12½x13*

440 A74 50fr ultra. & yellow 85 50

Issued to publicize the International Telecommunication Union Headquarters, Geneva.

Phaeomeria Magnifica
A75

"6" and Men Dancing around U.N. Emblem
A76

Flowers: 18fr, Hibiscus (rose of China). 20fr, Mountain rose.

1966, May 20 *Perf. 12x12½*

Flowers in Natural Colors

Size: 22x36mm.

441 A75 9fr red brown 15 10
442 " 18fr green 30 15
443 " 20fr dark green 35 15
Nos. 441-443, C70-C72 (6) 3.60 1.15

See also No. 469.

1966, Sept. 20 Engraved *Perf. 13*

Design: 50fr, U.N. General Assembly (horiz.).

444 A76 50fr ultra., green & violet brown 85 20
445 " 100fr red brown, green & ultra. 1.75 75

Issued to commemorate the 6th anniversary of Cameroun's admission to the United Nations.

Prime Minister's Residence, Buea
A77

Designs (Prime Minister's Residences): 18fr, at Yaoundé, front view. 20fr, at Yaoundé, side view. 25fr, at Buea, front view.

1966, Oct. 1 Photogravure

446 A77 9fr multicolored 15 12
447 " 18fr " 30 18
448 " 20fr " 35 15
449 " 25fr " 40 25

5th anniversary of re-unification.

Learning to Write and UNESCO Emblem
A78

Design: No. 451, Children's heads and UNICEF emblem.

1966, Nov. 24 Engraved *Perf. 13*

450 A78 50fr red lilac, blue & brown 85 45
451 " 50fr red lilac, black & brt. blue 85 45

No. 450 commemorates the 20th anniversary of UNESCO (United Nations Educational, Scientific and Cultural Organization), No. 451 commemorates the 20th anniversary of UNICEF (United Nations International Children's Emergency Fund).

Independence Proclamation
A79

1967, Jan. 1 Engraved *Perf. 13*

452 A79 20fr green, red & yel. 45 35

7th anniversary of independence.

Map of Africa and Madagascar, Railroad Tracks and Symbols
A80

Design: 25fr, Map of Africa and Madagascar and train.

1967, Feb. 21 Photo. *Perf. 13*

453 A80 20fr multicolored 35 25
454 " 25fr " 45 25

Issued to commemorate the 5th Conference of African and Madagascan Railroad Technicians.

Lions Emblem and Forest—A81

Design: 100fr, Lions emblem and palms.

1967, Mar. 3

455 A81 50fr multicolored 85 50
456 " 100fr " 1.75 1.00

Lions International, 50th anniversary.

Jet and I.C.A.O. Emblem
A82

Dove and I.A.E.A. Emblem
A83

Perf. 13x12½, 12½x13

1967, March 15 Photogravure

457 A82 50fr ultra., lt. blue, brown & gold 85 50
458 A83 50fr ultra. & emerald 85 50

Issued to honor United Nations agencies: No. 457, the International Civil Aviation Organization; No. 458, the International Atomic Energy Agency.

Rotary International Emblem
A84

1967, Apr. 17 Photo. *Perf. 12½*

459 A84 25fr crimson, violet blue & gold 45 25

Issued to commemorate the 10th anniversary of the Douala, Cameroun, branch of Rotary International.

Pomelo
A85

Bird-of-Paradise Flower
A86

Fruit: 2fr, Papaya. 3fr, Custard apple. 4fr, Breadfruit. 5fr, Coconut. 6fr, Mango. 8fr, Avocado. 10fr, Pineapple. 30fr, Bananas.

1967, May 10 Photo. *Perf. 12x12½*

460 A85 1fr multicolored 5 5
461 " 2fr " 5 5
462 " 3fr " 8 5
463 " 4fr " 8 5
464 " 5fr " 10 6
465 " 6fr " 15 6
466 " 8fr " 18 10
467 " 10fr " 20 12
468 " 30fr " 50 30
Nos. 460-468 (9) 1.39 84

1967, June 22 Photo. *Perf. 12x12½*
Size: 22x36mm.

469 A86 15fr lt. blue & multi. 25 10

Sanaga Falls and ITY Emblem
A87

1967, Aug. 14 Photo. *Perf. 13x12½*

470 A87 30fr multicolored 50 30

Issued for International Tourist Year 1967.

Art of Cameroun: Coconut Harvest
A88

Designs (Carved Bas-reliefs): 20fr, Lion hunt. 30fr, Women carrying baskets. 100fr, Carved chest.

1967, Sept. 22 *Perf. 12½x13*

471 A88 10fr brn., bl. & car. 15 10
472 " 20fr brn., yel. & grn. 35 20
473 " 30fr emerald, brown & carmine 50 20
474 " 100fr red orange, brn. & emerald 1.75 70

Coat of Arms
A89

1968, Jan. 1 Litho. *Perf. 12½x13*

475 A89 30fr gold & multi. 60 30

Spiny Lobster
A90

Designs (Fish and Crustaceans): 10fr, River crayfish. 15fr, Nile mouth-breeder. 20fr, Sole. 25fr, Common pike. 30fr, Crab. 40fr, Spadefish (vert.). 50fr, Shrimp (vert.). 55fr, African snakehead. 60fr, Threadfin.

1968, July 25 Engraved *Perf. 13*

476 A90 5fr brown, vio. blue & dull green 10 5
477 " 10fr ultra., brown olive & slate 15 6
478 " 15fr salmon, red lilac & sepia 20 10
479 " 20fr red brown, deep blue & sepia 25 12
480 " 25fr lt. brown, emerald & slate 40 15
481 " 30fr magenta, dk. blue & dark brown 50 15
482 " 40fr slate blue & org. 60 20
483 " 50fr emerald, gray & rose carmine 75 30
484 " 55fr lt. brn., Prus. blue & dark brown 85 40
485 " 60fr brown, blue green & indigo 1.00 50
Nos. 476-485 (10) 4.80 2.03

Tanker, Refinery and Map of Area Served—A91

1968, July 30 Photo. *Perf. 12½*

486 A91 30fr multicolored 45 20

Issued to commemorate the opening of the Port Gentil (Gabon) Refinery, June 12, 1968.

Human Rights Flame
A92

1968, Sept. 14 Photo. *Perf. 12½x13*

487 A92 15fr blue & salmon 25 12

Issued for International Human Rights Year. See also No. C110.

Pres. Ahmadou Ahidjo
A93

1969, Apr. 10 Photo. *Perf. 12½x12*

488 A93 30fr carmine & multi. 45 20

Chocolate Vat
A94

Designs: 30fr, Chocolate factory. 50fr, Candy making (vert.).

1969, Apr. 24 Engraved *Perf. 13*

489 A94 15fr red brn., indigo & chocolate 25 10
490 " 30fr green, black & red brown 45 20
491 " 50fr brown & multi. 75 30

Cameroun chocolate industry.

Fertility Symbol, Abbia
A95

Diesel Train on Bridge
A96

Art and Folklore from Abbia: 10fr, Two toucans (horiz.). 15fr, Forest symbol. 30fr, Vulture attacking monkey (horiz.). 70fr, Oliphant player.

1969, May 30 Engraved *Perf. 13*

492 A95 5fr ultra., Prus. blue & brt. rose lilac 10 6
493 " 10fr blue, olive gray & orange 18 8
494 " 15fr ultra., dark red & black 20 15
495 " 30fr bright blue, lemon & green 45 18
496 " 70fr brt. blue, dk. green & vermilion 1.10 50
Nos. 492-496 (5) 2.03 97

Perf. 12½x13, 13x12½

1969, July 11 Photogravure

Design: 30fr, Kumba Railroad station (horiz.).

497 A96 30fr blue & multi. 45 20
498 " 50fr black & multi. 85 40

Opening of Mbanga-Kumba Railroad.

Development Bank Issue
Common Design Type

1969, Sept. 10 Engraved *Perf. 13*

499 CD130 30fr violet blue, green & ocher 50 20

Issued to commemorate the 5th anniversary of the African Development Bank.

ASECNA Issue
Common Design Type

1969, Dec. 12 Engraved *Perf. 13*

500 CD132 100fr slate green 1.50 90

Red Sage
A99

Design: 30fr, Passionflower.

1970, Mar. 24 Photo. *Perf. 12x12½*
Size: 22x36½mm.

501 A99 15fr yel. grn. & multi. 25 15
502 " 30fr multicolored 40 15

See Nos. C140-C141.

U.P.U. Headquarters Issue
Common Design Type

1970, May 20 Engraved *Perf. 13*

50 CD133 30fr bl., pur. & green 45 18
504 " 50fr gray, red & blue 75 25

Brewery
A100

Design: 30fr, Cellar with barrels.

1970, July 9 Engraved *Perf. 13*

505 A100 15fr brown, gray & dark green 20 15
506 " 30fr bl. grn., dk. brn. & brown red 40 15

Cameroun brewing industry.

Ozila Dancers A101 — Cameroun Doll A102

Design: 50fr, Ozila dancer and drummer.

1970, Oct. 19 Engraved *Perf. 13*

507 A101 30fr multicolored 40 15
508 " 50fr red & multi. 75 30

1970, Nov. 2

Designs: 15fr, Doll in short skirt. 30fr, Doll with basket on back.

509 A102 10fr car. & multi. 20 12
510 " 15fr dk. grn. & multi. 28 15
511 " 30fr brn. red & multi. 50 20

Cogwheels and Grain A103

1970, Feb. 9 Photo. *Perf. 13*

512 A103 30fr multicolored 40 20

Europafrica Economic Conference.

Federal University, Yaoundé A104

1971, Jan. 19 Engraved

513 A104 50fr multicolored 60 20

Inauguration of Federal University at Yaoundé.

Presidents Ahidjo and Pompidou, Flags of Cameroun and France A105

1971, Feb. 9 Photogravure *Perf. 13*

514 A105 30fr multicolored 60 50

Visit of Georges Pompidou, President of France.

Young People, Globe, Map of Cameroun A106

1971, Feb. 11

515 A106 30fr blue & multi. 35 13

Fifth National Youth Festival, Feb. 11.

Gerbera Hybrida A107 — Men of Four Races—A108

Designs: 40fr, Opuntia polyantha (cactus). 50fr, Hemerocallis hybrida (lily).

1971, Mar. 14 Photogravure

516 A107 20fr multicolored 27 10
517 " 40fr green & multi. 45 22
518 " 50fr blue & multi. 60 20

1971, March 21 *Perf. 13x12½*

Design: 30fr, Hands and globe.

519 A108 20fr green & multi. 25 7
520 " 30fr ultra. & multi. 40 13

International year against racial discrimination.

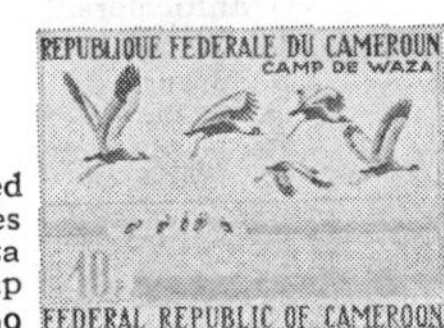

Crowned Cranes at Waza Camp A109

Designs: 20fr, Canoe on Sanaga River. 30fr, Sanaga River.

1971, Apr. 9. Engraved *Perf. 13*

521 A109 10fr red, grn. & blk. 12 8
522 " 20fr dk. green, brn. & red 27 8
523 " 30fr red, dk. green & brt. blue 35 12

International Court, The Hague A110

1971, June 14 Engr. *Perf. 13*

524 A110 50fr ultramarine, org. brown & slate green 60 25

25th anniversary of the International Court in The Hague, Netherlands.

Liana Bridge A111 — Bamoun Horseman A113

Local Market A112

1971, Aug. 16 Photo. *Perf. 13*

525 A111 40fr multicolored 50 20
526 A112 45fr " 55 20

1971, Sept. 18

African Art: 15fr, Animal fetish statuette.

527 A113 10fr brn. & yellow 12 5
528 " 15fr deep brown & orange yellow 18 8

Communications Satellite and Globe A114

1971, Oct. 14 *Perf. 13x12½*

529 A114 40fr Prus. bl., slate grn. & orange 45 18

Pan-African telecommunications system.

UNICEF Emblem A115

Design: 50fr, UNICEF emblem and grain (vert.).

1971, Dec. 11 Engraved *Perf. 13*

530 A115 40fr slate grn., blue green & plum 60 30
531 " 50fr dp. blue, dk. red & lt. green 85 40

25th anniversary of the United Nations International Children's Fund (UNICEF).

Giraffe A117

Houses from South-Central Region A116

Design: 15fr, Adamaua round houses.

1972, Jan. 15 Photo. *Perf. 13*

532 A116 10fr dk. bl. & multi. 10 8
533 " 15fr black & multi. 20 12

Designs: 5fr, Home industries. 10fr, Smith (horiz.). 15fr, Women carrying burdens.

Perf. 13x13½, 13½x13

1972, Feb. 18 Lithographed

534 A117 2fr multicolored 5 3
535 " 5fr black, org. & red 7 4
536 " 10fr multicolored 13 5
537 " 15fr " 15 10

Youth Day 1972.

Soccer Players and Field—A118

1972, Feb. 22 *Perf. 13½*

Designs: 20fr, African Soccer Cup (vert.). 45fr, Team captains shaking hands (vert.).

538 A118 20fr gray & multi. 25 15
539 " 40fr " " 50 30
540 " 45fr yellow & multi. 60 35

African Soccer Cup, Yaoundé, Feb. 23–Mar. 5.

Government Building, Yaoundé, and Laurel A119

1972, Apr. 6 Photo. *Perf. 12½x12*

541 A119 40fr multicolored 35 20

110th session of Inter-Parliamentary Council, Yaoundé, Apr. 1972.

"Fantasia," North Cameroun A120

Bororo Woman A121

Design: 40fr, Boat on Wouri River and Mt. Cameroun.

Perf. 13x12½, 12½x13

1972, Apr. 24

542 A120 15fr dk. vio. & multi. 20 10
543 A121 20fr multicolored 20 10
544 A120 40fr " 35 20

Chemical Apparatus A122

1972, May 15 Engraved *Perf. 13*

545 A122 40fr lilac, red & grn. 35 18

President Ahmadou Ahidjo Prize.

United Republic

Solanum Macranthum A123

Design: 45fr, Wax plant.

1972, July 20 Photo. *Perf. 13*

546 A123 40fr multicolored 40 18
547 " 45fr yellow & multi. 42 20

Charaxes Ameliae
A124

Design: 45fr, Papilio tynderaeus.

1972, Aug. 20 Photo. *Perf. 13*

548 A124 40fr bl., dk. blue & gold 50 25
549 " 45fr lt. green, black & gold 55 30

No. 468 Surcharged

=
40 F

1972, Aug. 30 Photo. *Perf. 12x12½*

550 A85 40fr on 30fr multi. 40 20

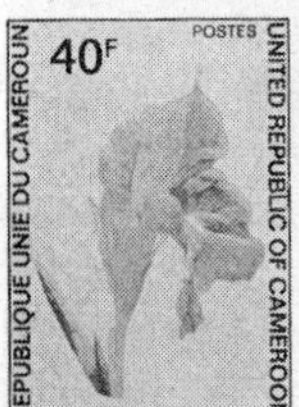

Resurrection Lily A125 **Great Blue Touraco A126**

Flowers: 45fr, Candlestick cassia. 50fr, Amaryllis.

1972, Sept. 16 *Perf. 13*

551 A125 40fr lt. grn. & multi. 40 20
552 " 45fr multicolored 45 25
553 " 50fr lt. blue & multi. 55 30

Perf. 12½x13, 13x12½

1972, Nov. 20 Lithographed

Design: 45fr, Red-faced lovebirds (horiz.).

554 A126 10fr yel. & multi. 10 7
555 " 45fr " " 45 20

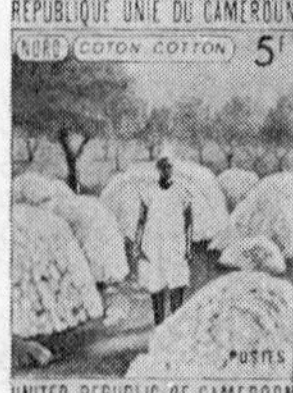

Cotton (North)
A127

Designs: 10fr, Cacao (south central). 15fr, Logging (southeast and southern coast). 20fr, Coffee (west). 45fr, Tea (northwest and southwest).

1973, Mar. 26 Photo. *Perf. 12½x13*

556 A127 5fr black & multi. 6 6
557 " 10fr " " 8 8
558 " 15fr " " 13 10
559 " 20fr " " 18 15
560 " 45fr " " 45 20
Nos. 556-560 (5) 90 59

Third 5-Year Plan.

Flag and Map of Cameroun, Pres. Ahidjo and No. 331—A128

Design: 20fr, Proclamation of independence, Pres. Ahidjo and No. 336.

1973, May 20 Engr. *Perf. 13*

561 A128 10fr ultra. & multi. 10 10
562 " 20fr multicolored 20 12

First anniversary of the United Republic of Cameroun. See Nos. C200–C201.

Bamoun Mask A129 **Dr. Hansen A130**

Designs: Various Bamoun masks.

1973, July 10 Engraved *Perf. 13*

563 A129 5fr grn., brn. & blk. 5 5
564 " 10fr lilac, brown & black 10 6
565 " 45fr red, brn. & blk. 35 20
566 " 100fr ultra., brown & black 80 50

1973, July 25 Engraved *Perf. 13*

567 A130 45fr multicolored 40 20

Centenary of the discovery by Dr. Armauer G. Hansen of the Hansen bacillus, the cause of leprosy.

No. 556 Surcharged with New Value, 2 Bars, and Overprinted in Ultramarine: "SECHERESSE/SOLIDARITE AFRICAINE"

1973, Aug. 16 Photo. *Perf. 12½x13*

568 A127 100fr on 5fr multi. 80 60

African solidarity in drought emergency.

Dancers, South West Africa A131 **WMO Emblem A132**

Designs: Southwest African dances.

1973, Aug. 17 *Perf. 13*

569 A131 10fr multicolored 8 6
570 " 25fr " 20 15
571 " 45fr " 45 20

1973, Sept. 1 Engraved *Perf. 13*

572 A132 45fr green & ultra. 40 25

Centenary of international meteorological cooperation.

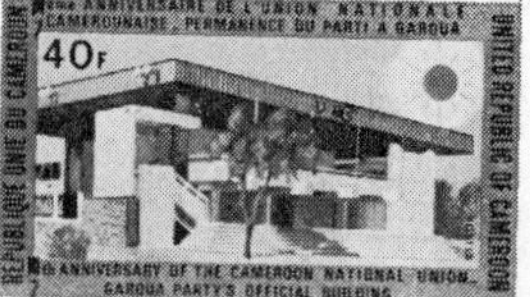

Garoua Party Headquarters—A133

1973, Sept. 1 Photogravure

573 A133 40fr multicolored 35 25

7th anniversary of Cameroun National Union.

African Postal Union Issue, 1973
Common Design Type

1973, Sept. 12 Engraved

574 CD137 100fr brt. bl., bl. & slate green 90 60

11th anniversary of African and Malagasy Posts and Telecommunications Union (UAMPT).

Avocados A135

1973, Sept. 20
Multicolored

575 A135 10fr *shown* 10 6
576 " 20fr *Mangos* 20 13
577 " 45fr *Plums* 40 20
578 " 50fr *Custard apple* 50 25

Kirdi Village A136

Views: 45fr, Mabas village. 50fr, Fishing village.

1973, Oct. 25 Engraved *Perf. 13*

579 A136 15fr black, bister & green 15 10
580 " 45fr magenta, brown & orange 40 25
581 " 50fr grn., blk. & org. 45 30

Handshake on Map of Africa A137

1974, May 15 Engr. *Perf. 12½x13*

582 A137 40fr car. & multi. 35 18
583 " 45fr indigo & multi. 40 20

10th anniversary of the Organization for African Unity.

Spinning Mill A138

1974, May 25 Engr. *Perf. 13x12½*

584 A138 45fr multicolored 40 25

CICAM Industrial Complex.

Carved Panel from Bilinga A139

Cameroun Art (Carvings): 40fr, Detail from Bubinga chair. 45fr, Detail Acajou Ngollon panel.

1974, May 30

585 A139 10fr brt. grn. & ocher 10 6
586 " 40fr red & brown 35 20
587 " 45fr blue & rose brn. 40 25

Zebu A140

1974, June 1 *Perf. 13½*

588 A140 40fr multicolored 35 23

North Cameroun cattle raising. See No. C210.

Laying Rail Section A141

Designs: 5fr, Map showing line Yaoundé to Ngaoundéré (vert.). 40fr, Welding rail joint (vert.). 100fr, Train on Djerem River Bridge.

Perf. 12½x13, 13x12½

1974, June 10 Engraved

589 A141 5fr multicolored 8 4
590 " 20fr " 18 10
591 " 40fr " 35 20
592 " 100fr " 85 65

Opening of Yaoundé-Ngaoundéré railroad line.

No. 466 Surcharged

1974, June 1 Photo. *Perf. 12x12½*

593 A85 40fr on 8fr multi. 35 20

UPU Emblem, Hands Holding Letters A142

1974, Oct. 8 Engraved *Perf. 13*

594 A142 40fr multicolored 35 20

Centenary of Universal Postal Union. See Nos. C218–C219.

Presidents and Flags of Cameroun, CAR, Congo, Gabon and Meeting Center—A143

1974, Dec. 8 Photogravure *Perf. 13*

595 A143 40fr gold & multi. 35 20

10th anniversary of Central African Customs and Economic Union (Union Douanière et Economique de l'Afrique Centrale, UDEAC). See also No. C223.

No. 589 Surcharged in Violet Blue

═ 100F

10 DECEMBRE 1974

1974, Dec. 10 Engr. *Perf. 12½x13*

596 A141 100fr on 5fr multi. 80 70

Virgin of Autun, 15th Century Sculpture
A144

Design: 45fr, Virgin and Child, by Luis de Morales (c. 1509–1586).

1974, Dec. 20 Photogravure *Perf. 13*

597 A144 40fr gold & multi. 35 25
598 " 45fr " " 40 30

Christmas 1974.

Cockscomb
A145

1975, Mar. 10 Photo. *Perf. 13*
Multicolored

599 A145 5fr *shown* 8 5
600 " 40fr *Costus spectabilis* 35 20
601 " 45fr *Mussaenda erythrophylla* 38 25

Tropical plants.

Fishing by Night—A146
Design: 45fr, Fishing by day.

1975, Apr. 1 Engr. *Perf. 13*

602 A146 40fr blue & multi. 35 20
603 " 45fr " " 40 25

Afo Akom Statue and Chief's Stool
A147

1975, Apr. 1 Photogravure

604 A147 40fr multicolored 30 20
605 " 45fr " 35 20
606 " 200fr " 1.60 1.10

Tree Fungus
A148
Design: 40fr, Chrysalis.

1975, Apr. 14

607 A148 15fr brown & multi. 12 10
608 " 40fr black & multi. 35 23

Ministry of Posts and Telecommunications
A149

1975, July 21 Engraved *Perf. 13*

609 A149 40fr brn., green & Prusian blue 35 25
610 " 45fr Prus. bl., brn. & green 40 30

Presbyterian Church, Elat
A150

Designs: No. 612, Foumban Mosque. 45fr, Catholic Church, Ngaoundere.

1975, Aug. 20 Engr. *Perf. 13*

611 A150 40fr multicolored 32 20
612 " 40fr " 32 20
613 " 45fr " 38 25

Plowing
A151
Design: No. 615, Corn harvest (vert.).

Perf. 13x12½, 12½x13

1975, Dec. 15 Photogravure

614 A151 40fr dp. grn. & multi. 32 20
615 " 40fr " " 32 20

Green revolution.

Zamengoe Satellite Monitoring Station—A152

Design: 100fr, Radar (vert.).

1976, May 20 Litho. *Perf. 13*

616 A152 40fr multicolored 30 25
617 " 100fr " 85 60

Porcelain Rose
A153

Design: 50fr, Flower of North Cameroun.

1976, July 20 Litho. *Perf. 12½*

618 A153 40fr multicolored 30 20
619 " 50fr " 40 25

Leopard Dance
A154

Telephone Exchange
A155

1976, Sept. 15 Litho. *Perf. 12*

620 A154 40fr gray & multi. 32 25

See Nos. C233–C234.

1976, Oct. 5 *Perf. 13*

621 A155 50fr multicolored 40 30

Centenary of first telephone call by Alexander Graham Bell, Mar. 10, 1876.

Young Men Building House—A156
Design: 45fr, Young women working in field.

1976, Oct. 10 Litho. *Perf. 12*

622 A156 40fr multicolored 32 25
623 " 45fr " 40 25

10th National Youth Day.

Konrad Adenauer, Cologne Cathedral
A157

1976, Oct. 20

624 A157 100fr multicolored 85 60

Konrad Adenauer (1876–1967), German chancellor, birth centenary.

Party Headquarters, Douala—A158
Design: No. 626, Party Headquarters, Yaoundé.

1976, Dec. 28 Litho. *Perf. 12*

625 A158 50fr org. & multi. 40 30
626 " 50fr blue & multi. 40 30

10th anniversary of the Cameroun National Union.

Bamoun Copper Pipe
A159

Ostrich
A160

1977, Feb. 4 Litho. *Perf. 12½*

627 A159 50fr multicolored 40 30

2nd World Black and African Festival, Lagos, Nigeria, Jan. 15–Feb. 12. See No. C239.

1977, Mar. 20 Litho. *Perf. 12*

Design: 50fr, Crowned cranes.

628 A160 30fr multicolored 25 15
629 " 50fr " 40 25

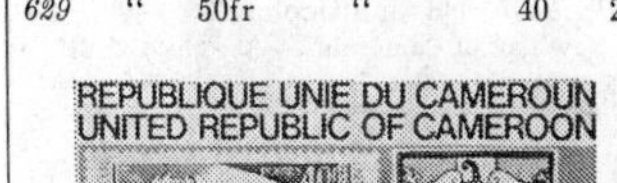

Cameroun No. 609 and Switzerland No. 3L1—A161

1977, June 5 Litho. *Perf. 12*

630 A161 50fr multicolored 40 30

Jufilex Philatelic Exhibition, Bern, Switzerland. See Nos. C252–C253.

No. 617 Overprinted in French and English in Red:

"To the Welfare of the / families of martyrs and / freedom fighters of Palestine."

1977, Aug. 22 Litho. *Perf. 13*

635 A152 100fr multicolored 85 60

Palestinian fighters and their families.

Chairman Mao and Great Wall
A164

1977, Sept. 9 Engr. *Perf. 13*

636 A164 100fr olive & brn. 85 60

Mao Tse-tung (1893–1976), Chinese communist leader, first death anniversary.

Nativity, by Albrecht Altdorfer
A165

Design: 50fr, Madonna of the Grand Duke, by Raphael.

1977, Dec. 15 Litho. *Perf. 12½x12*

637	A165	30fr multicolored	25	20
638	"	50fr "	40	30

Christmas 1977. See Nos. C264–C265.

Gazelle and Rotary Emblem
A166

Pres. Ahidjo, Flag and Map of Cameroun
A167

1978, Feb. 11 Litho. *Perf. 12*

639	A166	50fr org. & multi.	40	30

Rotary Club of Yaoundé, 20th anniversary.

1978, Apr. 3 Litho. *Perf. 12½*

640	A167	50fr multicolored	40	20

New flag of Cameroun. See No. C266.

Cardioglossa Escalerae
A168

Design: 60fr, Cardioglossa elegans.

1978, Apr. 5

641	A168	50fr multicolored	40	25
642	"	60fr "	50	35

See No. C267.

Jules Verne and "From Earth to Moon"
A169

1978, Oct. 10 Litho. *Perf. 12*

643	A169	250fr multicolored	2.50	2.00

Jules Verne (1828–1905), science fiction writer, birth sesquicentennial. See No. C276.

Hypolimnas Salmacis Drury—A170

Butterflies: 25fr, Euxanthe trajanus ward. 30fr, Euphaedra cyparissa cramer.

1978, Oct. 15

644	A170	20fr multicolored	20	15
645	"	25fr "	25	20
646	"	30fr "	30	20

Men Planting Seedlings
A171

1978, Oct. 30 *Perf. 12½*

647	A171	10fr multicolored	10	8
648	"	15fr "	15	10

Green barrier against the desert.

Carved Bamun Drum
A172

Designs: 60fr, String instrument (Guegerou; horiz.).

1978, Nov. 20 Litho. *Perf. 12½*

649	A172	50fr multicolored	50	30
650	"	60fr "	60	40

See No. C277.

SEMI-POSTAL STAMPS.

Curie Issue
Common Design Type

1938 *Perf. 13* **Unwmkd.**
B1 CD80 1.75fr+50c bright ultramarine 2.85 2.50

French Revolution Issue
Common Design Type

1939 Photogravure.
Name and Value Typo. in Black.
B2 CD83 45(c)+25(c) green 3.00 3.00
B3 " 70(c)+30(c) brown 3.00 3.00
B4 " 90(c)+35(c) red orange 3.00 3.00
B5 " 1.25fr+1fr rose pink 3.50 3.50
B6 " 2.25fr+2fr blue 3.50 3.50
Nos. B2-B6 (5) 16.00 16.00

Stamps of 1925–33 Surcharged in Black

OEUVRES DE GUERRE

+ 2 frs.

1940 *Perf. 14x13½.*
B7 A7 1.25fr+2fr gray & deep blue 4.50 4.50
B8 " 1.75fr+3fr brown & orange 4.50 4.50
B9 " 2fr+5fr dull green & brown orange 4.50 4.50

The surtax was used for war relief work.

Regular Stamps of 1939 Surcharged in Black **+ 5 Frs. SPITFIRE**

1940 *Perf. 13.*
B10 A20 25c+5fr black brown 40.00 35.00
B11 " 45c+5fr slate green 40.00 35.00
B12 " 60c+5fr peacock bl. 50.00 40.00
B13 " 70c+5fr plum 50.00 40.00

The surtax was used to purchase Spitfire planes for the Free French army.

Common Design Type and

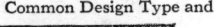

Military Doctor
SP2

Cameroun Militiaman
SP4

1941 Photogravure *Perf. 13½*
B13A SP2 1fr+1fr red 45
B13B CD86 1.50fr+3fr maroon 45
B13C SP4 2.50fr+1fr dk. bl. 45

Nos. B13A–B13C were issued by the Vichy government, and were not placed on sale in Cameroun.
Nos. 281A–281B were surcharged "OEUVRES COLONIALES" and surtax (including change of denomination of the 2.50fr to 50c). These were issued in 1944 by the Vichy government, and not placed on sale in Cameroun.

New York World's Fair Stamps, 1939 Surcharged in Black

+
SPITFIRE 10fr.
Général de GAULLE

1941 *Perf. 12½x12.*
B14 CD82 1.25fr+10fr car. lake 35.00 25.00
B15 " 2.25fr+10fr ultra. 35.00 25.00

New York World's Fair Stamps, 1939, Surcharged in Black or Blue

+ 10 Frs.
AMBULANCE
LAQUINTINIE

1941
B16 CD82 1.25fr+10fr car. lake (Bl) 6.00 4.50
B17 " 2.25fr+10fr ultramarine (Bk) 6.00 4.50

The surtax was used to purchase ambulances for the Free French army.

Regular Stamps of 1933–39 Surcharged in Black

Valmy
+ 100 frs.

1943
Perf. 14x13½, 13, 12½x12.
B21 A7 1.25fr+100fr gray & deep blue 3.50 3.50
B22 A21 1.25fr+100fr carmine rose 3.50 3.50
B23 CD82 1.25fr+100fr carmine lake 3.50 3.50
B24 A21 1.50fr+100fr choc. 3.50 3.50
B25 CD82 2.25fr+100fr ultra. 3.50 3.50
Nos. B21-B25 (5) 17.50 17.50

Red Cross Issue
Common Design Type

1944 Photogravure. *Perf. 14½x14.*
B28 CD90 5fr+20fr rose 70 70

The surtax was for the French Red Cross and national relief.

Tropical Medicine Issue
Common Design Type

1950 Engraved *Perf. 13*
B29 CD100 10fr+2fr dark blue green & dark green 1.25 1.25

The surtax was for charitable work.

Independent State

Map and Flag
SP7

Engraved

1961, Mar. 25 *Perf. 13* **Unwmkd.**
B30 SP7 20fr+5fr green, carmine & yellow 50 50
B31 " 25fr+10fr multi. 60 60
B32 " 30fr+15fr carmine, yellow & green 90 90

The surtax was for the Red Cross.

Federal Republic

Map of Cameroun, Lions Emblem and Physician Helping Leper
SP8

1962, Jan. 28
B33 SP8 20fr+5fr black, maroon & red brown 50 50
B34 " 25fr+10fr ultra., maroon & red brown 75 75
B35 SP8 50fr+15fr green, maroon & red brown 1.25 1.25

Issued for leprosy relief work.

Anti-Malaria Issue
Common Design Type

1962, Apr. 7 *Perf. 12½x12*
B36 CD108 25fr+5fr rose lilac 60 60

Issued for the World Health Organization drive to eradicate malaria.

Freedom from Hunger Issue
Common Design Type

1963, Mar. 21 Engraved *Perf. 13*
B37 CD112 18fr+5fr grn., dark ultra. & brown 45 35
B38 " 25fr+5fr red brown & green 65 45

AIR POST STAMPS.

Common Design Type
Photogravure.

1942 *Perf. 14½x14.* **Unwmkd.**
C1 CD87 1fr dark orange 10 10
C2 " 1.50fr bright red 10 10
C3 " 5fr brown red 10 10
C4 " 10fr black 20 20
C5 " 25fr ultramarine 30 30
C6 " 50fr dark green 40 40
C7 " 100fr plum 60 60
Nos. C1-C7 (7) 1.80 1.80

Victory Issue
Common Design Type

1946, May 8 Engraved *Perf. 12½*
C8 CD92 8fr dark violet brown 18 18

Issued to commemorate the European victory of the Allied Nations in World War II.

Chad to Rhine Issue
Common Design Types

1946, June 6
C9 CD93 5fr dark blue green 20 20
C10 CD94 10fr dark rose violet 25 25
C11 CD95 15fr red 30 30
C12 CD96 20fr bright blue 35 35
C13 CD97 25fr orange red 40 40
C14 CD98 50fr gray 50 50
Nos. C9-C14 (6) 2.00 2.00

Plane and Map
AP9

Seaplane Alighting
AP10

Plane and Freighters
AP11

1946 Photogravure *Perf. 13, 13½*
C15 AP9 25c brown red 5 5
C16 " 50c green 5 5
C17 " 1fr bright violet 7 7
C18 AP10 2fr olive green 7 7
C19 " 3fr chocolate 7 7
C20 " 4fr deep ultra. 7 7
C21 " 6fr blue green 10 10
C22 " 7fr bright violet 7 7
C23 " 12fr orange 2.00 2.00
C24 " 20fr crimson 35 35
C25 AP11 50fr dark ultra. 45 45
Nos. C15-C25 (11) 3.35 3.35

Nos. C15 to C25 were "issued" in 1941 in France by the Vichy Government, but were not sold in Cameroun until 1946.

V8

This 100fr stamp and eight denominations of types AP9, AP10 and AP11 without "RF" monogram were issued by the Vichy Government in 1943-44, but were not on sale in Cameroun.

Birds over Mountains
AP12

Cavalry and Plane
AP13

Warrior, Dance Mask and Nose of Plane
AP14

Engraved

1947, Feb. 10 *Perf. 12½.* **Unwmkd.**
C26 AP12 50fr dark green 70 45
C27 AP13 100fr brown red 1.50 20
C28 AP14 200fr black 2.75 65

U.P.U. Issue
Common Design Type

1949, July *Perf. 13.*
C29 CD99 25fr multicolored 1.85 1.65

Issued to commemorate the 75th anniversary of the Universal Postal Union.

Humsiki Peak
AP16

1953, Feb. 16

C30 AP16 500fr greenish black, dark violet & violet blue 7.00 1.50

Edéa Dam and Sacred Ibis
AP17

1953, Nov. 18

C31 AP17 15fr chocolate, brown lake & ultramarine 1.20 50

Issued to publicize the official dedication of Edea Dam on the Sanaga River.

Liberation Issue
Common Design Type

1954, June 6

C32 CD102 15fr dark greenish blue & blue green 1.50 1.25

10th anniversary of the liberation of France.

Dr. Eugene Jamot, Research Laboratory and Tsetse Flies
AP19

1954, Nov. 29

C33 AP19 15fr dark green, indigo & dark brown 1.40 1.25

Issued to commemorate the 75th anniversary of the birth of Dr. Eugene Jamot.

Logging—AP20

Designs: 100fr, Giraffes. 200fr, Port of Douala.

1955, Jan. 24

C34 AP20 50fr olive green, brown & violet brown 70 15
C35 " 100fr greenish blue, brown & dark brown 2.00 30
C36 " 200fr dark green, chocolate & deep ultramarine 2.75 50

Federal Republic

Air Afrique Issue
Common Design Type
Engraved

1962, Feb. 17 *Perf. 13* Unwmkd.

C37 CD107 25fr maroon, purple & lt. green 60 55

Founding of Air Afrique (African Airlines).

The lack of a price for a listed item does not necessarily indicate rarity.

Nos. C35-C36 and C30 Surcharged in Red with New Value, Bars and: "REPUBLIQUE FEDERALE"

Two types of 5sh:
I. "5/-" measures 6½x4mm.
II. "5/" measures 3¾x3mm. No dash after diagonal line.
Three types of 10sh:
I. "10/-" measures 9x3¾mm.
II. "10/-" measures 7x2½–3mm.
III. "1" of "10/" vertically in line with last "E" of "FEDERALE".
Two types of £1:
I. "REPUBLIQUE / FEDERALE" 17¼ mm. wide.
II. "REPUBLIQUE / FEDERALE" 22mm. wide.

1961, Oct. 1 Engraved *Perf. 13*

C38 AP20 5sh on 100fr (I) 4.00 4.00
a. Type II 10.00 10.00
C39 " 10sh on 200fr (I) 8.00 8.00
a. Type II 35.00 35.00
b. Type III 8.00 8.00
C40 AP16 £1 on 500fr (I) 15.00 15.00
a. Type II 22.50 22.50

Issued for use in the former United Kingdom Trust Territory of Southern Cameroons.

Kapsikis Mokolo—AP21

Designs: 50fr, Cocotieres Hotel, Douala. 100fr, Cymothoe sangaris butterflies. 200fr, Ostriches, Waza Reservation.

1962, June 15

C41 AP21 50fr slate green, blue & dull red 75 45
C42 " 100fr multicolored 1.65 60
C43 " 200fr dk. grn., blk. & bistre 3.50 1.00
C44 " 500fr violet brown, blue & ochre 7.50 2.50

Telstar Type of Regular Issue

1963, Feb. 9
Size: 48x27mm.

C45 A50 100fr dark green & red brown 1.75 1.00

See note after No. 383.

Edéa Relay Station
AP22

1963, May 18 Photo. *Perf. 12x12½*

C46 AP22 100fr multicolored 1.75 1.00

Issued to publicize the high frequency telegraph connection Douala-Yaounde.

African Postal Union Issue
Common Design Type

1963, Sept. 8 *Perf. 12½* Unwmkd.

C47 CD114 85fr ultra., ocher & red 1.75 1.50

Air Afrique Issue, 1963
Common Design Type

1963, Nov. 19 *Perf. 13x12*

C48 CD115 50fr pink, gray, black & green 85 60

Olympic Games Type of 1964

Design: 300fr, Greco-Roman wrestlers (ancient).

1964, Oct. 10 Engraved *Perf. 13*

C49 A57 300fr red, dk. brn. & dull grn. 5.00 3.00
a. Sheet of 3 6.50 6.50

Issued to commemorate the 18th Olympic Games, Tokyo, Oct. 10–25. No. C49a contains one each of Nos. 403-404 and C49. Size: 168x99mm.

Kribi Port—AP25

1964, Oct. 26 *Perf. 13* Unwmkd.

C50 AP25 50fr red brown, ultra. & grn. 85 50

Black Rhinoceros—AP26

1965, Dec. 15 Engraved *Perf. 13*

C51 AP26 250fr brn. red, grn. & dk. brn. 4.50 1.75

Pres. John F. Kennedy—AP27

1964, Dec. 8 Photogravure *Perf. 12½*

C52 AP27 100fr grn., yel. grn. & brown 1.75 1.75
a. Souv. sheet of 4 7.00 7.00

Issued in memory of Pres. John F. Kennedy (1917–63). No. C52a contains 4 No. C52; green marginal inscription. Size: 128x90mm.

Abraham Lincoln—AP28

1965, Apr. 20 *Perf. 13* Unwmkd.

C53 AP28 100fr multicolored 1.65 1.25

Abraham Lincoln, death centenary.

Syncom Satellite and ITU Emblem
AP29

1965, May 17 Engraved

C54 AP29 70fr red, dark blue, & black 1.25 90

Centenary of International Telecommunication Union.

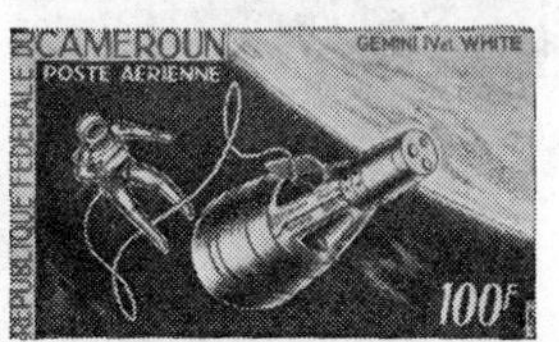

Winston Churchill
AP30

Design: 18fr, Churchill, battleship and oak leaves with acorns.

Perf. 13x12½

1965, May 28 Photo. Unwmkd.

C55 AP30 12fr orge., dk. brn. & ultra. 1.00 75
C56 " 18fr orge., dk. brn. & ultra. 1.00 75
a. Strip of 2 + label 2.50 2.00

Issued in memory of Sir Winston Spencer Churchill, statesman and World War II leader. No. C56a contains Nos. C55-C56 and label between inscribed "Sir Winston Churchill 1874 1965."

ICY Type of Regular Issue

1965, Sept. 11 Engraved *Perf. 13*

C57 A68 100fr dark red & dark blue 1.65 1.10

International Cooperation Year, 1964–65.

Racing Boat, Sanaga River, Edéa
AP31

1965, Oct. 27 *Perf. 13* Unwmkd.

C58 AP31 50fr brown, dark green & slate 90 50

Edward H. White Floating in Space and Gemini IV—AP32

Designs: 50fr, Vostok 6. 200fr, Gemini V and REP (rendezvous evaluation pod). 500fr, Gemini VI & VII rendezvous.

1966, March 30 Engraved *Perf. 13*

C59 AP32 50fr car. rose & dk. slate green 85 50
C60 " 100fr red lilac & violet blue 1.65 1.00
C61 " 200fr ultra. & dk. purple 3.00 2.00
C62 " 500fr bright blue & indigo 8.00 4.50

Man's conquest of space.

Hotel Type of Regular Issue

Designs: 18fr, Mountain Hotel, Buea. 25fr, Hotel Akwa Palace, Douala. 50fr, Terminus Hotel, Yaoundé. 60fr, Imperial Hotel, Yaoundé. 85fr, Independence Hotel, Yaoundé. 100fr, Hunting Lodge, Mora (vert.). 150fr, Boukarous (round huts), Waza Camp.

1966

C63 A71 18fr slate grn., brt. blue & black 25 20
C64 " 25fr carmine, ultra. & slate 40 25
C65 " 50fr chocolate, grn. & ocher 85 50

C66 A71 60fr choc., green & bright blue 90 50
C67 " 85fr dk. car. rose, dull bl. & grn. 1.25 75
C68 " 100fr brown, green & slate 1.65 75
C69 " 150fr brown, dull bl. & ocher 2.10 1.00
Nos. C63-C69 (7) 7.40 3.95

Issue dates: Nos. C63-C64, Apr. 6; Nos. C65-C69, June 4.

Flower Type of Regular Issue

Flowers: 25fr, Hibiscus mutabilis. 50fr, Delonix regia. 100fr, Bougainvillea.

1966, May 20 Photo. *Perf. 12½*

Flowers in Natural Colors

Size: 26x45mm.

C70 A75 25fr slate green 40 15
C71 " 50fr brt. greenish bl. 75 20
C72 " 100fr gold 1.65 40

Military Police—AP33

Design: 25fr, "Army," soldier, tanks and parachutes. 60fr, "Navy," and "Vigilante." 100fr, "Air Force," plane.

1966, June 21 Engraved *Perf. 13*

C73 AP33 20fr violet blue, org. brown & dull purple 30 20
C74 " 25fr dk. green, dull purple & brn. 40 25
C75 " 60fr blue green, blue & indigo 1.00 45
C76 " 100fr brown, Prus. bl. & car. rose 1.65 1.00

Issued to honor Cameroun's armed forces.

Wembley Stadium, London

AP34

Design: 200fr, Soccer.

1966, July 20

C77 AP34 50fr green, copper red & slate 85 40
C78 " 200fr red, bl. & grn. 3.00 1.75

Issued to commemorate the 8th World Cup Soccer Championship, Wembley, England, July 11-30.

Air Afrique Issue, 1966

Common Design Type

1966, Aug. 31 Photo. *Perf. 13*

C79 CD123 25fr red lilac, black & gray 40 20

Issued to commemorate the introduction of DC-8F planes by Air Afrique.

Yaoundé Cathedral—AP35

Designs: 18fr, Buea Cathedral. 30fr, Orthodox Church, Yaoundé. 60fr, Mosque, Garoua.

1966, Dec. 19 Engraved *Perf. 13*

C80 AP35 18fr chocolate, blue & green 30 25
C81 " 25fr brn., green & brt. violet 40 25
C82 " 30fr lilac, green & dull red 45 30
C83 " 60fr maroon, brt. grn. & green 1.00 50

Pioneer A and Moon—AP36

Designs: 50fr, Ranger 6. 100fr, Luna 9. 250fr, Luna 10.

1967, Apr. 30 Engraved *Perf. 13*

C84 AP36 25fr green, blue & bister 40 25
C85 " 50fr grn., dk. purple & brown 85 50
C86 " 100fr red brown, brt. blue & lilac 1.75 1.00
C87 " 250fr red brn., slate & brown 4.00 3.00

"Conquest of the Moon."

Flower Type of Regular Issue

Flowers: 200fr, Thevetia Peruviana. 250fr, Amaryllis.

1967, June 22 Photo. *Perf. 12½*

Size: 26x46mm.

C88 A86 200fr multicolored 3.00 1.35
C89 " 250fr " 4.00 1.75

African Postal Union Issue, 1967

Common Design Type

1967, Sept. 9 Engraved *Perf. 13*

C90 CD124 100fr red brown, Prus. blue & brt. lilac 1.60 1.00

Skis, Ice Skates, Olympic Flame and Emblem

AP38

1967, Oct. 11 Engr. *Perf. 13*

C91 AP38 30fr ultra. & sepia 55 30

Issued to publicize the 10th Winter Olympic Games, Grenoble, Feb. 6-8, 1968.

Cameroun Exhibit, EXPO '67

AP39

Designs: 100fr, Bangwa house poles carved with ancestor figures. 200fr, Canadian Pavilions.

1967, Oct. 18

C92 AP39 50fr magenta, olive & maroon 75 35
C93 " 100fr dark green, maroon & dark brown 1.75 80
C94 " 200fr brn., lilac rose & slate grn. 3.50 1.75

Issued to commemorate EXPO '70, International Exhibition, Montreal, Apr. 28-Oct. 27, 1967.

See note after No. C116 regarding 1969 moon overprint.

Konrad Adenauer and Cologne Cathedral

AP40

Design: 70fr, Adenauer and Chancellery, Bonn.

1967, Dec. 1 Photo. *Perf. 12½*

C95 AP40 30fr multicolored 50 30
C96 " 70fr " 1.25 60
a. Strip of 2 + label 1.80 1.00

Issued in memory of Konrad Adenauer (1876-1967), chancellor of West Germany (1949-63). No. C96a contains Nos. C95-C96 and label between showing the CEPT design of the 1967 Europa issues.

Pres. Ahidjo, King Faisal and View of Mecca—AP41

Design: 60fr, Pres. Ahidjo, Pope Paul VI and view of Rome.

1968, Feb. 18 Photo. *Perf. 12½*

C97 AP41 30fr multicolored 45 25
C98 " 60fr " 90 45

Issued to commemorate President Ahidjo's pilgrimage to Mecca and visit to Rome.

Earth on Television Transmitted by Explorer VI—AP42

Designs: 30fr, Molniya spacecraft. 40fr, Earth on television screen transmitted by Molniya.

1968, Apr. 20 Engraved *Perf. 13*

C99 AP42 20fr multicolored 30 15
C100 " 30fr " 45 25
C101 " 40fr " 60 30

Telecommunication by satellite.

Forge—AP43 Boxing—AP44

Designs: No. C103, Tea harvest. No. C104, Trans-Cameroun railroad (diesel train emerging from tunnel). 40fr, Rubber harvest. 60fr, Douala Harbor (horiz.).

1968, June 5 Engraved *Perf. 13*

C102 AP43 20fr red brown, dark green & indigo 30 15
C103 " 30fr dk. brn., grn. & ultra. 45 25
C104 " 30fr indigo, slate green & bister brn. 45 25
C105 " 40fr olive bister, dk. green & bl. green 50 30
C106 " 60fr ultra., dark brn. & slate 90 60
Nos. C102-C106 (5) 2.60 1.55

Issued to publicize the Second Economic Development Five-Year Plan.

1968, Aug. 19 Engraved *Perf. 13*

Design: 50fr, Broad jump. 60fr, Athlete on rings.

C107 AP44 30fr bright green, dk. green & chocolate 45 25
C108 " 50fr bright green, brown red & chocolate 75 45
C109 " 60fr bright green, ultra. & chocolate 90 50
a. Min. sheet of 3 2.25 2.25

Issued to commemorate the 19th Olympic Games, Mexico City, Oct. 12-27. No. C109a contains one each of Nos. C107-C109. Size: 128x99mm.

Human Rights Type of Regular Issue

1968, Sept. 14 Photo. *Perf. 12½x13*

C110 A92 30fr green & bright pink 40 22

International Human Rights Year, 1968.

Martin Luther King, Jr.

AP45

Portraits: No. C112, Mahatma Gandhi and map of India. 40fr, John F. Kennedy. 60fr, Robert F. Kennedy. No. C115, Rev. Martin Luther King, Jr. No. C116, Mahatma Gandhi.

1968, Dec. 5 Photo. *Perf. 12½*

C111 AP45 30fr blue & black 50 30
C112 " 30fr multicolored 50 30
C113 " 40fr pink & black 60 40
C114 " 60fr bluish lilac & black 90 60
C115 " 70fr yellow green & black 1.00 70
a. Souv. sheet of 4 3.00 3.00

C116 AP45 70fr multicolored 1.00 70
Nos. C111-C116 (6) 4.50 3.00

Issued to honor exponents of non-violence. The 2 King stamps (Nos. C111 and C115), the 2 Gandhi stamps (Nos. C112 and C116) and the 2 Kennedy stamps (Nos. C113-C114) are each printed as triptychs with a descriptive label between. No. C115a contains one each of Nos. C112-C115; black marginal inscription. Size: 122x160mm.

In 1969 Nos. C111-C116 and C94 were overprinted in carmine capitals: "Premier Homme / sur la Lune / 20 Juillet 1969" and "First Man / Landing on Moon / 20 July 1969".

PHILEXAFRIQUE Issue

The Letter, by Armand Cambon
AP46

1968, Dec. 10

C117 AP46 100fr multi. 1.65 1.25

Issued to publicize PHILEXAFRIQUE, Philatelic Exhibition in Abidjan, Feb. 14-23, 1969. Printed with alternating light green label.

2nd PHILEXAFRIQUE Issue

Common Design Type

Design: 50fr, Cameroun No. 199 and Wouri Bridge.

1969, Feb. 14 Engraved *Perf. 13*

C118 CD128 50fr slate grn., olive & dull blue 85 85

Issued to commemorate the opening of PHILEXAFRIQUE, Abidjan, Feb. 14.

Caladium Bicolor
AP47

Flowers: 50fr, Aristolochia elegans. 100fr, Gloriosa simplex.

1969, May 14 Photo. *Perf. 12½*

C119 AP47 30fr lilac & multi. 45 30
C120 " 50fr grn. & multi. 85 50
C121 " 100fr brn. & multi. 1.50 80

Issued to publicize the 3rd International Flower Show, Paris, Apr. 23-Oct. 5.

Douala Post Office—AP48

Designs: 50fr, Buèa Post Office. 100fr, Bafoussam Post Office.

1969, June 19 Engraved *Perf. 13*

C122 AP48 30fr green, violet blue & brn. 35 20
C123 " 50fr slate, emerald & red brn. 70 40
C124 " 100fr dk. brn., brt. grn. & brn. 1.40 75

Coronation of Napoleon I, by Jacques Louis David
AP49

Napoleon Crossing Saint Bernard, after J. L. David
AP50

1969, July 4 Photo. *Perf. 12x12½*

C125 AP49 30fr vio. blue & multi. 60 30

Embossed on Gold Foil
Die-cut Perf. 10

C126 AP50 1000fr gold 25.00 25.00

Bicentenary of birth of Napoleon I.

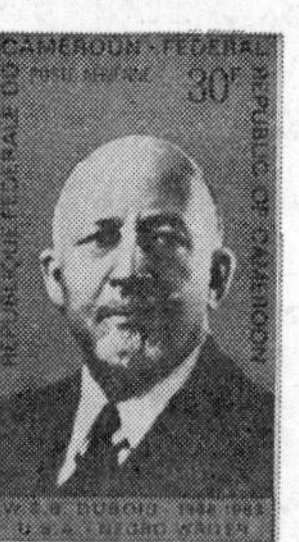

William E. B. Dubois (1868-1963), American Writer—AP51

Portraits: 15fr, Dr. Price Mars, Haiti (1876-1969). No. C128, Aimé Cesaire, Martinique (1913-). No. C130, Langston Hughes, U.S. (1902-1967). No. C131, Marcus Garvey, Jamaica (1887-1940). 100fr, René Maran, Martinique (1887-1960).

1969, Sept. 25 Photo. *Perf. 12½*

C127 AP51 15fr lt. bl. & black 20 10
C128 " 30fr lemon & black 40 20
C129 " 30fr rose brown & black 40 20
C130 " 50fr gray & black 65 35
C131 " 50fr emerald & black 65 35
C132 " 100fr yel. & black 1.35 85
a. Min. sheet of 6 4.00 4.00
Nos. C127-C132 (6) 3.65 2.05

Issued to honor Negro writers.

No. C132a contains one each of Nos. C127-C132. Size: 114x125mm.

ILO Emblem
AP52

1969, Oct. 29 Photo. *Perf. 13*

C133 AP52 30fr black, blue grn. & gray 45 20
C134 " 50fr black, dp. lilac rose & gray 75 40

Issued to commemorate the 50th anniversary of the International Labor Organization.

Armstrong, Collins and Aldrin Splashdown in the Pacific
AP53

Design: 500fr, Landing module and Neil A. Armstrong's first step on moon.

1969, Nov. 29 Photo. *Perf. 12½*

C135 AP53 200fr multi. 3.00 1.50
C136 " 500fr " 6.50 3.75

See note after Algeria No. 427.

Pres. Ahidjo, Arms and Map of Cameroun—AP54

Embossed on Gold Foil

1970, Jan. 1 *Die-cut Perf. 10*

C137 AP54 1000fr gold & multi. 12.50 12.50

10th anniversary of independence.

Hotel Mont Fébé, Yaoundé
AP55

1970, Jan. 15 Engraved *Perf. 13*

C138 AP55 30fr lt. brn., slate grn. & gray 40 20

Demand as well as supply determine a stamp's market value. The first is as important as the other.

Lenin
AP56

1970, Jan. 25 Photo. *Perf. 12½*

C139 AP56 50fr org. & black 65 40

Issued to commemorate the centenary of the birth of Nikolai Lenin (1870-1924), Russian Communist leader.

Plant Type of Regular Issue

Designs: 50fr, Cleome speciosa (caper). 100fr, Mussaenda erythrophylla (madder).

1970, Mar. 24 Photo. *Perf. 12½*

Size: 26x46mm.

C140 A99 50fr black & multi. 60 40
C141 " 100fr multicolored 1.20 60

Map of Africa and Lions Emblem Pinpointing Yaoundé—AP57

1970, May 2 Photo. *Perf. 12½*

C142 AP57 100fr multicolored 1.35 75

Issued to commemorate the 13th Lions International Congress of District 13, Yaoundé, May 2, 1970.

U.N. Emblem and Doves—AP58

Design: 50fr, U.N. emblem and dove (vert.).

1970, June 26 Engraved *Perf. 13*

C143 AP58 30fr brn. & orange 40 25
C144 " 50fr Prussian blue & slate blue 65 35

25th anniversary of the United Nations.

Japanese Pavilion and EXPO Emblem—AP59

Designs (EXPO Emblem and): 100fr, Map of Japan (vert.). 150fr, Australian pavilion.

1970, Aug. 1 Engraved *Perf. 13*

C145 AP59 50fr indigo, light grn. & verm. 65 35
C146 " 100fr blue, lt. green & red 1.35 65
C147 " 150fr choc., blue & gray 2.00 1.00

Issued to commemorate EXPO '70 International Exhibition, Osaka, Japan, Mar. 15-Sept. 13.

Charles de Gaulle AP60 — Pelé and Team AP61

Design: 200fr, de Gaulle in uniform.

1970, Aug. 27

C148	AP60	100fr green, violet blue & olive brown	1.50	75
C149	"	200fr olive brown, vio. blue & green	3.00	1.40
		a. Strip of 2 + label	5.00	2.50

Issued to commemorate the 30th anniversary of the rallying of the Free French.

Nos. C148–C149 were printed in same sheet flanking a label showing maps of Cameroun and France, and Cross of Lorraine.

1970, Oct. 14 Photo. *Perf. 12½*

Designs: 50fr, Aztec Stadium, Mexico City (horiz.). 100fr, Mexican soccer team (horiz.).

C150	AP61	50fr multi.	75	35
C151	"	100fr "	1.50	75
C152	"	200fr "	3.00	1.50

Issued to publicize the 9th World Soccer Championships for the Jules Rimet Cup, Mexico City, May 30–June 21, and the final victory of Brazil over Italy.

Ludwig van Beethoven AP62

1970, Nov. 23 Engraved *Perf. 13*

C153	AP62	250fr multi.	2.75	1.50

Issued to commemorate the bicentenary of the birth of Ludwig van Beethoven (1770–1827), composer.

Christ at Emmaus, by Rembrandt AP63

Design: 150fr, The Anatomy Lesson, by Rembrandt.

1970, Dec. 5 Photo. *Perf. 12x12½*

C154	AP63	70fr grn. & multi.	80	40
C155	"	150fr multi.	1.80	90

Charles Dickens AP64

Designs: 50fr, Scenes from David Copperfield. 100fr, Dickens holding quill.

1970, Dec. 22 *Perf. 13*

C156	AP64	40fr black & rose	50	25
C157	"	50fr bister & multi.	.60	30
C158	"	100fr rose & multi.	1.20	60

Death centenary of Charles Dickens (1812–1870), English novelist. Nos. C156–C158 printed se-tenant.

De Gaulle Type of 1970 Overprinted with Black Border and: "IN MEMORIAM / 1890–1970"

1971, Jan. 15 Engraved *Perf. 13*

C159	AP60	100fr violet blue, emerald & brown red	1.20	60
C160	"	200fr brown red, emerald & vio. blue	2.40	1.20
		a. Strip of 2+label	4.00	2.00

In memory of Gen. Charles de Gaulle (1890–1970), President of France.

Timber Storage, Douala—AP65

Designs (Industrialization): 70fr, ALUCAM aluminum plant, Edea (vert.). 100fr, Mbakaou Dam.

1971, Feb. 14 Engraved *Perf. 13*

C161	AP65	40fr dark red, blue green & olive brown	50	20
C162	"	70fr olive brown, slate green & brt. blue	80	40
C163	"	100fr Prussian blue, yel. grn. & red brown	1.20	60

Relay Race—AP66

Designs: 50fr, Torch bearer (vert.). 100fr, Discus.

1971, Apr. 24 Engraved *Perf. 13*

C164	AP66	30fr dk. brn., verm. & indigo	40	20
C165	"	50fr black, blue & chocolate	70	35
C166	"	100fr multicolored	1.25	50

75th anniversary of revival of Olympic Games.

Fishing Trawler—AP67

Designs: 40fr, Local fishermen, Northern Cameroun. 70fr, Fishing harbor, Douala. 150fr, Shrimp boats, Douala.

1971, May 14 Engraved *Perf. 13*

C167	AP67	30fr light brown, bl. & green	35	20
C168	"	40fr slate grn., bl. & dk. brn.	45	25
C169	"	70fr dk. brn., bl. & red org.	85	40
C170	"	150fr multi.	1.80	90

Cameroun fishing industry.

Cameroun No. 123 and War Memorial, Yaoundé—AP68

Designs (Cameroun Stamps): 25fr, No. C33 and Jamot memorial. 40fr, No. 431 and government buildings, Yaoundé. 50fr, No. 19 and Imperial German postal emblem. 100fr, No. 101 and World War II memorial.

1971, Aug. 1 Engraved *Perf. 13*

C171	AP68	20fr green, ocher & dk. brn.	25	10
C172	"	25fr dk. brn., vio. blue & slate green	30	15
C173	"	40fr grn., maroon & slate	45	25
C174	"	50fr dk. brn., blk. & vermilion	60	30
C175	"	100fr maroon, slate grn. & org.	1.20	60
		Nos. C171–C175 (5)	2.80	1.40

PHILATECAM 1971 Philatelic Exhibition.

Cameroun Flag, Pres. Ahidjo and Reunification Highway—AP69

Typo., Silk Screen, Embossed

1971, Oct. 1 *Perf. 12½*

C176	AP69	250fr gold & multi.	3.75	3.00

PHILATECAM Philatelic Exhibition, Yaoundé-Douala.

African Postal Union Issue, 1971

Common Design Type

1971, Nov. 13 Photo. *Perf. 13x13½*

C177	CD135	100fr bl. & multi.	1.35	65

Annunciation, by Fra Angelico AP71

Paintings: 45fr, Virgin and Child, by Andrea del Sarto. 150fr, Christ Child with Lamb, detail from Holy Family, by Raphael (vert.).

Perf. 13x13½, 13½x13

1971, Dec. 19

Brown Inscriptions

C178	AP71	40fr multicolored	40	20
C179	"	45fr "	60	30
C180	"	150fr "	2.00	90

Christmas 1971.

Cameroun Airlines Emblem AP72

1972, Feb. 2 Photo. *Perf. 12½x12*

C181	AP72	50fr lt. bl. & multi.	60	30

Inauguration of Cameroun Airlines.

Doge's Palace, by Ippolito Caffi AP73

Paintings: 100fr, 200fr, Details from "Regatta on the Grand Canal," by School of Canaletto.

1972 Photogravure *Perf. 13*

C182	AP73	40fr gold & multi.	50	25
C183	"	100fr " "	1.20	60
C184	"	200fr " "	2.50	1.20

UNESCO campaign to save Venice.

Astronauts Patsayev, Dobrovolsky and Volkov—AP74

1972, May 1 Photo. *Perf. 13x13½*

C185	AP74	50fr multicolored	50	25

Salute-Soyuz 11 space mission, and in memory of the Russian astronauts Victor I. Patsayev, Georgi T. Dobrovolsky and Vladislav N. Volkov, who died during Soyuz 11 space mission, June 6–30, 1971.

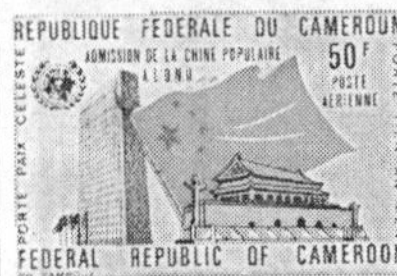

U.N. Headquarters, Chinese Flag and Gate of Heavenly Peace AP75

1972, May 19 *Perf. 13*

C186	AP75	50fr blk., scarlet & gold	50	25

Admission of People's Republic of China to United Nations.

United Republic

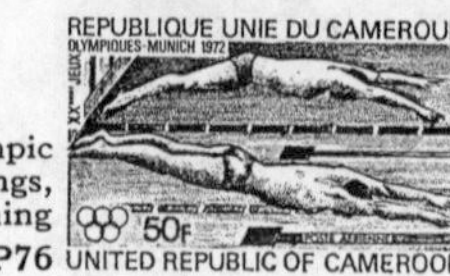

Olympic Rings, Swimming
AP76

Designs (Olympic Rings and): No. C188, Boxing (vert.). 200fr, Equestrian.

1972, Aug. 1 Engraved *Perf. 13*

C187 AP76 50fr lake & slate green 60 30
C188 " 50fr choc. & slate 60 30
C189 " 200fr claret, gray & dk. brn. 2.25 1.10
a. Min. sheet of 3 3.25 3.25

20th Olympic Games, Munich, Aug. 26–Sept. 11. No. C189a contains stamps similar to Nos. C187–C189, but in changed colors. The 50fr (swimming) is Prussian blue, violet & brown; the 50c (boxing) lilac, Prussian blue & brown; the 200fr, Prussian blue & brown. Size: 139x99mm.

Nos. C187–C189 Overprinted in Red or Black

NATATION MARK SPITZ
MEDAILLES D'OR
a

SUPER WELTER
KOTTYSCH
MEDAILLE D'OR
b

CONCOURS COMPLET
MEADE
MEDAILLE D'OR
c

1972, Oct. 23 Engraved *Perf. 13*

C190 AP76 (*a*) 50fr lake & slate green (R) 60 30
C191 " (*b*) 50fr chocolate & slate (B) 60 30
C192 " (*c*) 200fr claret, gray & dk. brn. (B) 2.50 1.20

Gold Medal Winners in 20th Olympic Games: Mark Spitz, USA, swimming (C190); Dieter Kottysch, West Germany, light middleweight boxing (C191); Richard Meade, Great Britain, 3-day equestrian (C192).

Madonna with Angels, by Cimabue
AP77

Design: 140fr, Madonna of the Rose Arbor, by Stefan Lochner.

1972, Dec. 21 Photo. *Perf. 13*

C193 AP77 45fr gold & multi. 60 30
C194 " 140fr gold & multi. 1.40 70

Christmas 1972.

St. Teresa, the Little Flower
AP78

Design: 100fr, Lisieux Cathedral and St. Teresa.

1973, Jan. 2 Engraved

C195 AP78 45fr vio. bl., pur. & maroon 50 25
C196 " 100fr mag., ultra. & brown 1.00 55

Centenary of the birth of St. Teresa of Lisieux (1873–1897), Carmelite nun.

African Unity Hall, Addis Ababa and Emperor Haile Selassie—AP79

1973, Mar. 14 Photo. *Perf. 13*

C197 AP79 45fr yel. & multi. 40 25

80th birthday of Emperor Haile Selassie of Ethiopia.

Corn, Grain, Healthy and Starving People—AP80

1973, Apr. 10 Typo. *Perf. 13*

C198 AP80 45fr multicolored 40 20

World Food Program, 10th anniversary.

Hearts and Blood Vessels
AP81

1973, May 5 Engraved

C199 AP81 50fr dk. car. rose & dk. vio. bl. 40 25

"Your Heart is Your Health" and for the 25th anniversary of the World Health Organization.

Type of Regular Issue

Designs: 45fr, Map of Cameroun, Pres. Ahidjo and No. C176. 70fr, National colors and commemorative inscriptions.

1973, May 20 Engr. *Perf. 13*

C200 A128 45fr grn. & multi. 40 25
C201 " 70fr red & multi. 60 40

First anniversary of the United Republic of Cameroun.

Scout Emblem and Flags
AP82

1973, July 31 Typo. *Perf. 13*

C202 AP82 40fr multicolored 40 25
C203 " 45fr " 45 30
C204 " 100fr " 85 65

Cameroun's admission to the World Scout Conference, Mar. 26, 1971.

African Weeks Issue

Head and City Hall, Brussels
AP83

1973, Sept. 17 Engraved *Perf. 13*

C205 AP83 40fr dp. brown & rose claret 40 25

African Weeks, Brussels, Sept. 15–30.

Map of Africa with Cameroun
AP84

1973, Sept. 29 Engraved *Perf. 13*

C206 AP84 40fr black, red & green 40 25

Help for handicapped children.

Zamengoe Radar Station
AP85

1973, Dec. 8 Engraved *Perf. 13*

C207 AP85 100fr blue, lt. brn. & green 85 60

Chancellor Rolin Madonna, by Van Eyck
AP86

Design: 140fr, Nativity, by Federigo Barocci.

1973, Dec. 11 Photo. *Perf. 13*

C208 AP86 45fr gold & multi. 45 30
C209 " 140fr " " 1.50 1.10

Christmas 1973.

Zebu Type of 1974

Design: Zebu herd.

1974, June 1 Lithographed *Perf. 13*

C210 A140 45fr multicolored 40 20

North Cameroun cattle raising.

Churchill and Union Jack
AP87

1974, July 10 Engraved *Perf. 13*

C211 AP87 100fr black, blue & red 90 60

Birth centenary of Winston Churchill (1874–1965).

Soccer, Arms of Frankfurt, Dortmund, Gelsenkirchen and Stuttgart—AP88

Designs: 100fr, Soccer and arms of Berlin, Hamburg, Hanover and Düsseldorf. 200fr, Soccer cup and game.

1974, Aug. 5 Photo. *Perf. 13*

C212 AP88 45fr gray, slate & orange 40 20
C213 " 100fr gray, slate & orange 85 60
C214 " 200fr orange, slate & blue 1.65 1.00
Strip of 3, Nos. C212–C214 3.25 2.00

World Cup Soccer Championship, Munich, June 13–July 7. Nos. C212–C214 printed se-tenant in sheets containing 5 triptychs.

Nos. C212–C214 Overprinted in Dark Blue:
"7th JULY 1974 / R.F.A. 2 HOLLANDE 1 / 7 JUILLET 1974"

1974, Sept. 16 Photo. *Perf. 13*

C215 AP88 45fr multicolored 40 25
C216 " 100fr " 85 65
C217 " 200fr " 1.65 1.20
Strip of 3, Nos. C215–C217 3.25 2.25

World Cup Soccer Championship, 1974, victory of German Federal Republic.

UPU Type of 1974

Designs: 100fr, Cameroun No. 503. 200fr, Cameroun No. C29.

1974, Oct. 8 Engraved *Perf. 13*

C218 A142 100fr blue & multi. 80 60
C219 " 200fr red & multi. 1.65 1.10

Centenary of Universal Postal Union.

Copernicus and Planets Circling Sun
AP89

1974, Oct. 15 Engraved *Perf. 13*

C220 AP89 250fr multi. 2.00 1.50

500th anniversary of the birth of Nicolaus Copernicus (1473–1543), Polish astronomer.

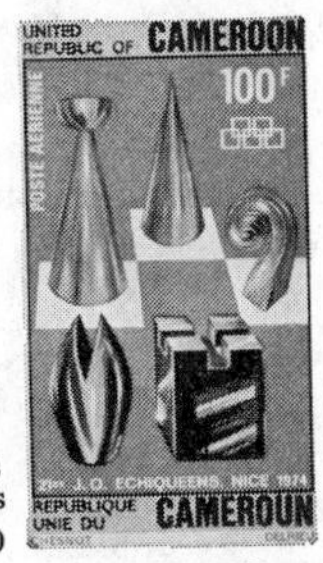

Chess Pieces
AP90

1974, Nov. 3 Photo. *Perf. 13x12½*

C221 AP90 100fr multi. 75 65

21st Chess Olympiad, Nice, France, June 6–30.

Mask and ARPHILA Emblem—AP91

1974, Nov. 30 Engraved *Perf. 13*

C222 AP91 50fr chocolate & magenta 40 25

ARPHILA 75, Paris, June 6–16, 1975.

Presidents and Flags of Cameroun, CAR, Gabon and Congo—AP92

1974, Dec. 8 Photogravure

C223 AP92 100fr gold & multi. 80 60

See note after No. 595.

Man Landing on Moon—AP93

1974, Dec. 15 Engraved

C224 AP93 200fr brown, blue & car. 1.60 1.20

5th anniversary of man's first landing on the moon.

Charles de Gaulle and Félix Eboué—AP94

1975, Feb. 24 Typo. *Perf. 13*

C225 AP94 45fr multicolored 40 25
C226 " 200fr " 1.60 1.20

Félix A. Eboué (1884–1944), Governor of Chad, first colonial governor to join Free French in WWII, 30th death anniversary.

Marquis de Lafayette
AP95

Designs: 140fr, George Washington and soldiers. 500fr, Benjamin Franklin and Independence Hall.

1975, Oct. 20 Engr. *Perf. 13*

C227 AP95 100fr vio. bl. & multi. 80 60
C228 " 140fr brown & multi. 1.10 90
C229 " 500fr green & multi. 4.00 2 50

American Bicentennial.

The Burning Bush, by Nicolas Froment
AP96

Painting: 500fr, Adoration of the Kings, by Gentile da Fabriano (horiz.).

1975, Dec. 25 Photo. *Perf. 13*

C230 AP96 50fr gold & multi. 40 25
C231 " 500fr gold & multi. 4.00 2.50

Christmas 1975.

Concorde and Route: Paris–Dakar–Rio de Janeiro—AP97

1976, July 20 Litho. *Perf. 13*

C232 AP97 500fr lt. blue & multi. 4.00 2.50
a. Souvenir sheet 5.00 5.00

First commercial flight of supersonic jet Concorde from Paris to Rio de Janeiro, Jan. 21. No. C232a contains one stamp; black marginal inscription giving specifications of Concorde. Size: 130x93mm. Sold for 600fr.

Dance Type of 1976

Designs: 50fr, Dancers and drummer. 100fr, Woman dancer.

1976, Sept. 15 Litho. *Perf. 12*

C233 A154 50fr gray & multi. 40 30
C234 " 100fr gray & multi. 80 50

Virgin and Child, by Giovanni Bellini—AP98

Paintings: 30fr, Adoration of the Shepherds, by Le Brun. 60fr, Adoration of the Kings, by Rubens. 500fr, The Newborn, by Georges de la Tour.

1976, Dec. 15 Litho. *Perf. 12½*

C235 AP98 30fr gold & multi. .25 15
C236 " 60fr " " .50 35
C237 " 70fr " " .55 40
C238 " 500fr " " 4.00 2.50
a. Souvenir sheet of 4 5.50 5.50

Christmas 1976. No. C238a contains one each of Nos. C235–C238; black and gold marginal inscription. Size: 150x120 mm.

Festival Type of 1977

Design: 60fr, Traditional Chief on his throne, sculpture.

1977, Feb. 4 Litho. *Perf. 12½*

C239 A159 60fr multicolored 50 35

2nd World Black and African Festival, Lagos, Nigeria, Jan. 15–Feb. 12.

Crucifixion, by Matthias Grunewald—AP99

Paintings: 125fr, Christ on the Cross, by Velazquez (vert.). 150fr, The Deposition, by Titian.

1977, Apr. 2 Litho. *Perf. 12½*

C240 AP99 50fr gold & multi. 40 30
C241 " 125fr " " 1.00 60
C242 " 150fr " " 1.25 80
a. Souvenir sheet of 3 2.75 2.75

Easter 1977. No. C242a contains one each of Nos. C240–C242, perf. 12; black and gold marginal inscription and black control number. Size: 210x115mm. Sold for 350fr.

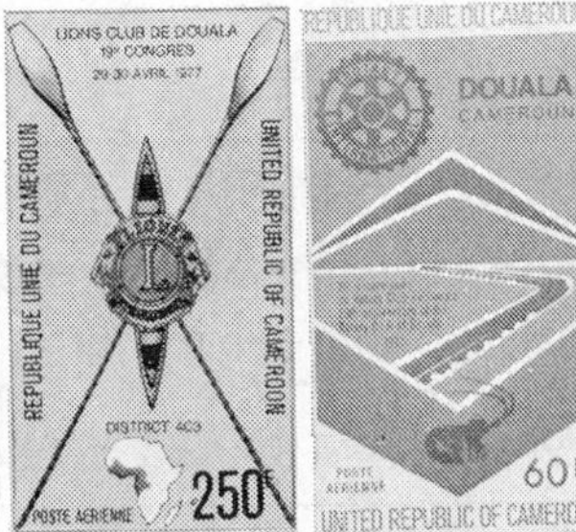

Lions Emblem, Map of Africa
AP100

Rotary Emblem
AP101

1977, Apr. 29 Litho. *Perf. 12½*

C243 AP100 250fr multi. 2.00 1.50

Lions Club of Douala, 19th Congress, Apr. 29–30.

1977, May 18

C244 AP101 60fr multicolored 50 35

Rotary Club of Douala, 20th anniversary.

Antoine de Saint-Exupéry
AP102

Charles Lindbergh and Spirit of St. Louis—AP103

Designs: 50fr, Jean Mermoz and his plane. 80fr, Maryse Bastié and her plane. 100fr, Sikorsky S-43. 300fr, Concorde.

1977, May 20 Engr. *Perf. 13*

C245 AP103 50fr org. & blue 40 30
C246 AP102 60fr magenta & orange 50 35
C247 AP103 80fr magenta & blue 60 45
a. Souvenir sheet of 3 1.75 1.75
C248 AP103 100fr grn. & yel. 80 60
C249 " 300fr multi. 2.50 1.85
C250 " 500fr " 4.00 2.75
a. Souvenir sheet of 3 8.50 8.50
Nos. C245–C250 (6) 8.80 6.30

Aviation pioneers and events. No. C247a contains one each of Nos. C245–C247; blue marginal inscription. Size: 170x100mm. Sold for 200fr. No. C250a contains one each of Nos. C248–C250; blue marginal inscription. Size: 190x100mm. Sold for 1000fr.

Sassenage Castle, Grenoble—AP104

1977, May 21 Litho. *Perf. 12½*

C251 AP104 70fr multicolored 55 40

10th anniversary of International French Language Council.

Jufilex Type of 1977

Designs: 70fr, Switzerland (Zurich) No. 1L1 and Cameroun No. 16. 100fr, Switzerland (Geneva) No. 2L1 and Cameroun No. 254.

1977, June 5 Litho. *Perf. 12*

C252 A161 70fr multicolored 55 40
C253 " 100fr " 80 60

Jufilex Philatelic Exhibition, Bern, Switzerland.

Diseased Knee, WHO Emblem
AP105

1977, Oct. 15 Engr. *Perf. 13*

C260 AP105 70fr multicolored 55 40

World Rheumatism Year.

Nos. C249 and C232 Overprinted in Red:
"PREMIER VOL PARIS – NEW YORK /
FIRST FLIGHT PARIS – NEW YORK /
22 Nov. 1977–22nd Nov. 1977"

Perf. 13

1977, Nov. 22 Engr., Litho.

C262 AP103 300fr multi. 2.50 1.85
C263 AP97 500fr " 4.00 3.00

Concorde, first commercial flight Paris to New York.

Christmas Type of 1977

Paintings: 60fr, Virgin and Child with 4 Saints, by Bellini (horiz.). 400fr, Adoration of the Shepherds, by George de la Tour (horiz.).

1977, Dec. 15 Litho. *Perf. 12x12½*

C264 A165 60fr multicolored 50 35
C265 " 400fr " 3.50 2.50

Christmas 1977.

Flag Type of 1978

Design: 60fr, New flag, Pres. Ahidjo and spear.

1978, Apr. 3 Litho. *Perf. 12½*

C266 A167 60fr multicolored 50 25

New flag of Cameroun.

Frog Type of 1978

Design: 100fr, Cardioglossa trifasciata.

1978, Apr. 5

C267 A168 100fr multi. 85 60

L'Arlesienne, by Van Gogh
AP106

Painting: No. C269, Burial of Christ, by Albrecht Dürer.

1978, May 15 Litho. *Perf. 12½*

C268 AP106 200fr multi. 2.00 1.60
C269 " 200fr " 2.00 1.60

Vincent Van Gogh (1853–1890), 125th birth anniversary and Albrecht Dürer (1471–1528), 450th death anniversary.

Leprosy Distribution on World Map, Raoul Follereau—AP107

1978, June 6 Litho. *Perf. 12*

C270 AP107 100fr multi. 1.00 80

25th World Leprosy Day.

Capt. Cook and Siege of Quebec
AP108

Design: 250fr, Capt. Cook, Adventure and Resolution, map of voyages.

1978, July 26 Engr. *Perf. 13*

C271 AP108 100fr multi. 1.00 80
C272 " 250fr " 2.50 2.00

Capt. James Cook (1728–1779), explorer.

Argentine Soccer Team, Coat of Arms and Rimet Cup—AP109

Designs: 200fr, Two soccer players (vert.). 1000fr, Soccer ball illuminating world map (vert.).

1978, Sept. 1 Litho. *Perf. 13*

C273 AP109 100fr multi. 1.00 80
C274 " 200fr " 2.00 1.60
C275 " 1000fr " 10.00 8.00

11th World Cup Soccer Championship, Argentina, June 1–25.

Jules Verne Type of 1978

Design: 400fr, Jules Verne and "20,000 Leagues Under the Sea" (horiz.).

1978, Oct. 10 Litho. *Perf. 12*

C276 A169 400fr multi. 4.00 3.20

Jules Verne (1828–1905), science fiction writer, birth sesquicentennial.

Musical Instrument Type of 1978

Design: 100fr, Man playing Mvet zither.

1978, Nov. 20 Litho. *Perf. 12½*

C277 A172 100fr multi. 1.00 60

AIR POST SEMI-POSTAL STAMPS.

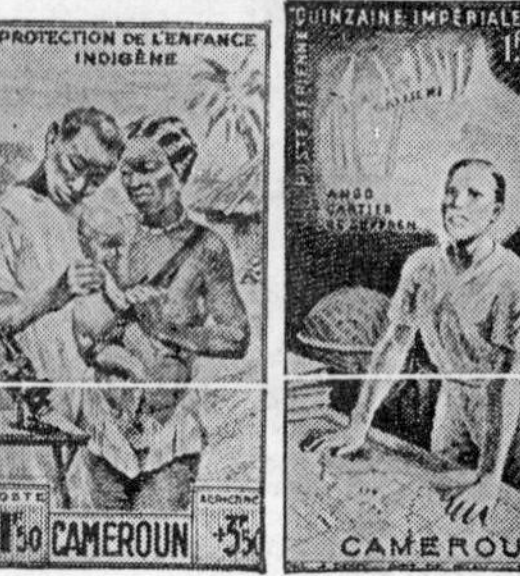

V9 V10

Stamps of the designs shown above were issued in 1942 by the Vichy Government, but were not placed on sale in Cameroun.

POSTAGE DUE STAMPS.

Man Felling Tree
D1

Typographed.

1925–27 *Perf. 14x13½* Unwmkd.

J1 D1 2c light blue & black 8 8
J2 " 4c olive bistre & red violet 10 10
J3 " 5c violet & black 13 13
J4 " 10c red & black 15 15
J5 " 15c gray & black 18 18
J6 " 20c olive green & black 25 25
J7 " 25c yellow & black 35 35
J8 " 30c blue & orange 40 40
J9 " 50c brown & black 45 45
J10 " 60c blue green & rose red 60 60
J11 " 1fr dull red & green, *greenish* 65 65
J12 " 2fr red & violet ('27) 1.00 1.00
J13 " 3fr orange brown & ultra. ('27) 1.40 1.40
Nos. J1–J13 (13) 5.74 5.74

Carved Figures
D2 D3

1939 Engraved *Perf. 14x13*

J14 D2 5c bright red violet 4 4
J15 " 10c Prussian blue 23 23
J16 " 15c carmine rose 6 6
J17 " 20c black brown 6 6
J18 " 30c ultramarine 8 8
J19 " 50c dark green 8 8
J20 " 60c brown violet 10 10
J21 " 1fr dark violet 23 23
J22 " 2fr orange red 35 35
J23 " 3fr dark blue 55 50
Nos. J14–J23 (10) 1.78 1.73

A 10c stamp, type D2, without "RF" was issued in 1944 by the Vichy Government, but was not placed on sale in Cameroun.

1947 *Perf. 13.* Unwmkd.

J24 D3 10c dark red 5 5
J25 " 30c deep orange 5 5
J26 " 50c greenish black 6 6
J27 " 1fr dark carmine 6 6
J28 " 2fr deep yellow green 8 8
J29 " 3fr deep red lilac 12 12
J30 " 4fr deep ultramarine 15 15
J31 " 5fr red brown 20 20
J32 D3 10fr peacock blue 35 35
J33 " 20fr sepia 55 55
Nos. J24–J33 (10) 1.67 1.67

Federal Republic

Hibiscus
D4

Flowers: No. J35, Erythrine. No. J36, Plumeria lutea. No. J37, Ipomoea. No. J38, Hoodia gordonii. No. J39, Grinum. No. J40, Ochna. No. J41, Gloriosa. No. J42, Costus spectabilis. No. J43, Bougainvillea spectabilis. No. J44, Delonix regia. No. J45, Haemanthus. No. J46, Ophthalmophyllum. No. J47, Titanopsis. No. J48, Amorphophallus. No. J49, Zingiberacee.

Engraved

1963, Apr. 10 *Perf. 11* Unwmkd.

J34 D4 50c carmine, blue, green & yel. 5 5
J35 " 50c carmine, blue, green & yel 5 5
J36 " 1fr magenta, green & yellow 6 6
J37 " 1fr magenta, green & yellow 6 6
J38 " 1.50fr dark green, lilac & yellow 7 7
J39 " 1.50fr dark green, lilac & yellow 7 7
J40 " 2fr orange verm., yellow & green 6 6
J41 " 2fr orange verm., yellow & green 6 6
J42 " 5fr magenta, green & yellow 7 7
J43 " 5fr magenta, green & yellow 7 7
J44 " 10fr crimson, green & yellow 18 18
J45 " 10fr crimson, green & yellow 18 18
J46 " 20fr green, yellow & lilac 45 45
J47 " 20fr green, yellow & lilac 45 45
J48 " 40fr lilac & yellow 80 80
J49 " 40fr lilac & yellow 80 80
Nos. J34–J49 (16) 3.48 3.48

The two types of each value in Nos. J34–J49 were printed tête bêche, se-tenant at the base.

MILITARY STAMP

M1

Typographed

1963, July 1 *Perf. 13* Unwmkd.

M1 M1 rose claret 1.50 1.50

CAMPIONE D'ITALIA

The 1944 issues of this Italian enclave within the borders of Switzerland are not listed because of their local nature. These stamps were valid only on mail going from Campione d'Italia to Switzerland. Letters going to other countries required Swiss stamps in addition.

CAPE JUBY

(kāp jōō'bĭ)

LOCATION — Northwest coast of Africa in Spanish Sahara.

GOVT.—Spanish administration.

AREA—12,700 sq. mi.

POP.—9,836.

CAPITAL—Villa Bens (Cape Juby).

By agreement with France, Spain's Sahara possessions were extended to include Cape Juby and in 1916 Spanish troops occupied the territory. It is attached for administrative purposes to Spanish Sahara.

100 Centimos = 1 Peseta

Stamps of Rio de Oro, 1914 Surcharged in Violet, Red or Green

CABO JUBI 5 CÉNTIMOS

1916 *Perf. 13.* **Unwmkd.**

1 A6 5c on 4p rose (V) 67.50 18.50
2 " 10c on 10p dull violet (R) 32.50 18.50
3 " 15c on 50c dark brown (G) 50.00 42.50
4 " 15c on 50c dark brown (R) 32.50 18.50
5 " 40c on 1p red violet (G) 75.00 60.00
6 " 40c on 1p red violet (R) 52.50 22.50
Nos. 1-6 (6) 310.00 180.50

Nos. 1-6 exist with inverted surcharge. Prices about twice those quoted.

Stamps of Spain, 1876-1917, Overprinted in Red or Black

CABO JUBY

1919 *Imperf.*

7 A21 ¼c blue green (R) 30 10

Perf. 13x12½, 14.

8 A46 2c dark brown (Bk) 30 10
a. Double overprint 7.50 3.00
9 " 5c green (R) 60 10
a. Double overprint 7.50 3.00
b. Inverted overprint 9.00 6.00
10 " 10c carmine (Bk) 75 25
a. Double overprint (Bk+R) 17.50 12.50
11 " 15c ochre (Bk) 3.50 40
b. Double overprint 7.50 3.00
c. Red control # 3.50 3.50
d. As "c," inverted ovpt. 12.00
12 " 20c olive green (R) 18.00 3.00
13 " 25c deep blue (R) 3.00 30
a. Double overprint 10.00 4.50
14 " 30c blue green (R) 3.00 50
15 " 40c rose (Bk) 3.00 50
16 " 50c slate blue (R) 3.75 50
17 " 1p lake (Bk) 10.00 3.00
18 " 4p deep violet (R) 40.00 13.50
19 " 10p orange (Bk) 50.00 15.00
Nos. 7-19 (13) 136.70 37.25

Nos. 8-19 have blue control number on back.

Nos. 8-13, 15, 17-19 exist imperf.

Same Overprint on Stamps of Spain, 1920-21.

1922 *Imperf.*

20 A47 1c blue green (R) 22.50 13.50

Perf. 13x12½.

Engraved.

Blue Control Number on Back.

23 A46 20c violet 150.00 67.50

A lithographed 2c of type A46 exists with this overprint. Price $250.

Same Overprint on Stamps of Spain, 1922-23.

1925 *Perf. 13½x13.*

25 A49 5c red violet 7.50 3.50
26 " 10c blue green 21.00 3.50
28 " 20c violet 45.00 11.50

The 2c olive green, Spain No. 331, exists with this overprint. Price $185 unused, $67.50 canceled.

Seville-Barcelona Exposition Issue.

Stamps of Spain, 1929, Overprinted CABO JUBY in Red or Blue.

1929 *Perf. 11.*

29 A52 5c rose lake (Bl) 38 30
30 A53 10c green (R) 38 30
31 A50 15c Pruss. blue (R) 38 30
32 A51 20c purple (R) 38 30
33 A50 25c bright rose (Bl) 38 30
34 A52 30c black brown (Bl) 45 50
35 A53 40c dark blue (R) 45 50
36 A51 50c dp. orange (Bl) 75 90
37 A52 1p blue black (R) 15.00 7.50
38 A53 4p deep rose (Bl) 18.50 16.50
39 " 10p brown (Bl) 18.50 12.00
Nos. 29-39 (11) 55.55 39.40

Stamps of Spanish Morocco, 1928-33, Overprinted in Black or Red

Cabo Juby

1934 *Perf. 14.*

40 A7 1c bright rose (Bk) 45 45
41 A2 2c dark violet (R) 3.50 50
42 " 5c deep blue (R) 3.50 65
43 " 10c dark green (Bk) 6.75 1.00
43A A10 10c dark green (R) 2.25 1.85
44 A2 15c org. brn. (Bk) 15.00 5.25
45 A7 20c slate green (R) 6.00 3.50
46 A3 25c copper red (Bk) 3.50 3.00
47 A10 30c red brown (Bk) 6.00 3.50
48 A13 40c deep blue (R) 21.00 12.00
49 " 50c red org. (Bk) 37.50 18.50
50 A4 1p yel. green (Bk) 25.00 11.00
51 A5 2.50p red vio. (Bk) 52.50 22.50
52 A6 4p ultramarine (R) 67.50 30.00

No. 43A and 1c, 20c, 30c, 40c, 50c, with control numbers.

Same Overprint in Black on Stamp of Spanish Morocco, 1932.

53 A2 1c car. rose ("Ct") 1.85 85
Nos. 40-53 (15) 252.30 114.55

Stamps of Spanish Morocco, 1933-35, Overprinted in Black, Blue or Red

CABO JUBY

1935-36

54 A8 2c green (R) 70 22
55 A9 5c magenta (Bk) 2.25 30
55A A10 10c dark green (R) ('36) 12.50 2.50
56 A11 15c yellow (Bl) 4.75 1.85
57 A12 25c crimson (Bk) 40.00 25.00
58 A8 1p slate black (R) 7.50 4.50
59 A9 2.50p brown (Bl) 30.00 16.50
60 A11 4p yel. grn. (R) 37.50 20.00
61 A12 5p black (R) 37.50 25.00
Nos. 54-61 (9) 172.70 95.87

Same Overprint in Black or Red on Stamps of Spanish Morocco, 1935.

1935 *Perf. 13½.*

62 A14 25c violet (R) 3.50 1.85
63 A15 30c crimson (Bk) 3.50 1.50
64 A14 40c orange (Bk) 4.50 1.85
65 A15 50c bright blue (R) 9.00 1.85
66 A14 60c dark blue green (R) 10.00 4.00
67 A15 2p brn. lake (Bk) 50.00 25.00

Same Overprint on Stamps of Spanish Morocco, 1933.

Perf. 13½, 14.

68 A7 1c bright rose (Bk) 30 15

Perf. 14

69 A7 20c slate green (R) 4.50 2.50
Nos. 62-69 (8) 85.30 38.70

Same Overprint on Stamps of Spanish Morocco, 1937.

1937 *Perf. 13½.*

70 A21 1c dark blue (Bk) 15 15
71 " 2c org. brn. (Bk) 15 15
72 " 5c cerise (Bk) 15 15
73 " 10c emerald (Bk) 15 15
74 " 15c bright blue (Bk) 22 22
75 " 20c red brown (Bk) 22 22
76 " 25c magenta (Bk) 22 22
77 " 30c red orange (Bk) 22 22
78 " 40c orange (Bk) 1.10 90
79 " 50c ultramarine (R) 1.10 90
80 " 60c yel. grn. (Bk) 1.10 90
81 " 1p blue violet (Bk) 1.10 90
82 " 2p Prussian blue (Bk) 30.00 30.00
83 " 2.50p gray black (R) 30.00 30.00
84 " 4p dk. brown (Bk) 30.00 30.00
85 A22 10p vio. black (R) 30.00 30.00
Nos. 70-85 (16) 125.88 125.08

Issued in commemoration of the First Year of the Revolution.

Same Overprint in Black on Types of Spanish Morocco, 1939.

Designs: 5c, Spanish quarter. 10c, Moroccan quarter. 15c, Street scene, Larache. 20c, Tetuan.

1939 **Photogravure.** *Perf. 13½.*

86 A25 5c vermilion 75 60
87 " 10c deep green 75 60
88 " 15c brown lake 75 75
89 " 20c bright blue 75 75

Same Overprint in Black or Red on Stamps of Spanish Morocco, 1940.

1940 *Perf. 11½x11.*

90 A26 1c dk. brown (Bk) 23 8
91 A27 2c olive green (R) 23 8
92 A28 5c dark blue (R) 23 8
93 A29 10c dark red lilac (Bk) 30 8
94 A30 15c dark green (R) 30 8
95 A31 20c purple (R) 30 8
96 A32 25c blk. brown (R) 30 23
97 A33 30c bright green (Bk) 30 23
98 A34 40c slate green (R) 75 30
99 A35 45c org. vermilion (Bk) 75 30
100 A36 50c brn. org. (Bk) 75 30
101 A37 70c sapphire (R) 1.85 45
102 A38 1p indigo & brown (Bk) 4.50 60
103 A39 2.50p chocolate & dark green (Bk) 9.00 3.75
104 A40 5p dark cerise & sepia (Bk) 9.00 3.75
105 A41 10p dk. olive grn. & brown org. (Bk) 25.00 13.50
Nos. 90-105 (16) 53.79 23.89

Stamps of Spanish Morocco, 1944, Overprinted in Black or Red

CABO JUBY

1944 *Perf. 12½.* **Unwmkd.**

106 A47 1c chocolate & light blue 10 10
107 A48 2c slate green & light green 10 10
108 A49 5c chocolate & greenish black (R) 10 10
109 A50 10c bright ultra. & red orange 10 10
110 A51 15c slate green & light green 10 10
111 A52 20c deep claret & black (R) 10 10
112 A53 25c light blue & chocolate 10 10
113 A47 30c yellow green & bright ultramarine (R) 10 10
114 A48 40c chocolate & red violet 10 10
115 A49 50c bright ultra. & red brown 10 10
116 A50 75c yellow green & bright ultramarine (R) 75 50
117 A51 1p bright ultra. & chocolate 75 50
118 A52 2.50p black & bright ultra. (R) 2.25 1.85
119 A53 10p salmon & gray black (R) 14.00 12.00
Nos. 106-119 (14) 18.75 15.85

Same Overprint on Stamps of Spanish Morocco, 1946.

1946 *Perf. 10½x10.*

120 A54 1c purple & brown 10 10
121 A55 2c dark Prussian green & violet black (R) 10 10
122 A54 10c deep orange & violet blue 10 10
123 A55 15c dark blue & blue green 10 10
124 A54 25c yellow green & ultramarine 10 10
125 A56 40c dark blue & brown (R) 10 10
126 A55 45c black & rose 30 30
127 A57 1p dark Prussian green & deep blue 75 45
128 A58 2.50p deep orange & greenish gray (R) 2.40 2.10
129 A59 10p dark blue & gray (R) 9.00 7.00
Nos. 120-129 (10) 13.05 10.45

Same Overprint in Carmine, Black or Brown on Stamps of Spanish Morocco, 1948.

1948 *Perf. 10, 10x10½*

130 A64 2c purple & brown 7 7
131 A65 5c deep claret & violet 7 7
132 A66 15c bright ultramarine & blue green (Bk) 7 7
133 A67 25c black & Prussian green 7 7
134 A65 35c bright ultra. & gray black 10 10
135 A68 50c red & violet (Br) 10 10
136 A66 70c dark gray green & ultramarine (Bk) 10 10
137 A67 90c cerise & dark gray green (Bk) 10 10
138 A68 1p bright ultra. & violet (Br) 38 38
139 A64 2.50p violet brown & slate green 1.15 75
140 A69 10p black & deep ultramarine 3.00 2.40
Nos. 130-140 (11) 5.21 4.21

SEMI-POSTAL STAMPS.

Types of Semi-Postal Stamps of Spain, 1926, Overprinted

CABO—JUBY

1926 *Perf. 12½, 13* **Unwmkd.**

B1 SP1 1c orange 6.75 3.75
B2 SP2 2c rose 6.75 3.75
B3 SP3 5c black brown 1.85 1.50
B4 SP4 10c dark green 1.35 90
B5 SP1 15c dark violet 75 75
B6 SP4 20c violet brown 75 75
B7 SP5 25c deep carmine 75 75
B8 SP1 30c olive green 75 75
B9 SP3 40c ultramarine 7 7
B10 SP2 50c red brown 7 7
B11 SP4 1p vermilion 7 7
B12 SP3 4p bistre 90 60
B13 SP5 10p light violet 1.15 90
Nos. B1-B13 (13) 21.96 14.61

AIR POST STAMPS.

Spanish Morocco, Nos. C1 to C10

Overprinted in Black CABO JUBY

1938, June 1 *Perf. 13½.* **Unwmkd.**

C1 AP1 5c brown 30 7
C2 " 10c bright green 30 7
C3 " 25c crimson 22 7
C4 " 40c light blue 3.00 1.50
C5 AP2 50c bright magenta 30 7
C6 " 75c dark blue 30 38
C7 AP1 1p sepia 30 38
C8 " 1.50p deep violet 1.85 75
C9 " 2p deep red brn. 3.75 1.85
C10 " 3p brown black 10.00 6.25
Nos. C1-C10 (10) 20.32 11.39

Strait of Gibraltar
AP3

Designs: 5c, Ketama landscape. 10c, Mosque, Tangier. 15c, Velez. 90c, Sanjurjo.

1942, Apr. 1 Photo. *Perf. 12½*

C11 AP3 5c deep blue 10 10
C12 " 10c orange brown 10 10
C13 " 15c greenish black 10 10
C14 " 90c dark rose 75 60
C15 " 5p black 3.00 2.25
Nos. C11-C15 (5) 4.05 3.15

SPECIAL DELIVERY STAMPS.

Special Delivery Stamp of Spain Overprinted "CABO JUBY" as on Nos. 7-28.

1919 *Perf. 14* **Unwmkd.**

E1 SD1 20c red (Bk) 1.85 1.15
a. Inverted overprint
b. Double overprint 12.00 6.00

Spanish Morocco No. E4 Overprinted in Red

Cabo Juby

1934

E2 SD2 20c black 6.75 6.00

Spanish Morocco No. E5 Overprinted in Black

CABO JUBY

1935

E3 SD3 20c vermilion 3.50 1.15

Same Overprint on Spanish Morocco, No. E6.

1937 *Perf. 13½.*

E4 SD4 20c bright carmine 1.15 90

Issued in commemoration of the First Year of the Revolution.

Same Overprint on Spanish Morocco, No. E8.

1940 *Perf. 11½x11.*

E5 SD5 25c scarlet 50 35

SEMI-POSTAL SPECIAL DELIVERY STAMP.

Type of Semi-Postal Special Delivery Stamp of Spain, 1926, Overprinted CABO-JUBY

1926 *Perf. 12½, 13.* **Unwmkd.**

EB1 SPSD1 20c ultramarine & black 1.85 1.15

CAPE VERDE

(kāp vûrd)

LOCATION—A group of ten islands and five islets in the Atlantic Ocean, lying about 500 miles due west of Senegal.
GOVT.—Republic.
AREA—1,557 sq. mi.
POP.—300,000 (1976).
CAPITAL—Praia.

The Portuguese territory of Cape Verde became independent July 5, 1975.

1000 Reis = 1 Milreis
100 Centavos = 1 Escudo (1913)

Crown of Portugal
A1

King Luiz
A2

Typographed.

1877 *Perf. 12½, 13½.* **Unwmkd.**

1 A1 5r black 2.50 2.00
2 " 10r yellow 11.00 10.00
3 " 20r bistre 2.00 1.75
4 " 25r rose 1.50 1.25
a. Perf. 13½ 8.00 5.25
5 " 40r blue 52.50 32.50
a. Cliché of Mozambique in Cape Verde plate, in pair with #5 800.00 750.00
b. As "a," perf. 13½ 1250.00 1250.00
6 " 50r green 50.00 30.00
7 " 100r lilac 6.00 2.75
8 " 200r orange 4.00 3.00
a. Perf. 13½ 12.50 8.50
9 " 300r brown 6.50 5.00

1881-85

10 A1 10r green 2.00 1.75
11 " 20r carmine ('85) 3.00 2.50
a. Perf. 13½ 30.00 22.50
12 " 25r violet ('85) 2.25 2.00
13 " 40r yellow buff 3.00 2.00
a. Imperf. 1.00
b. Cliché of Mozambique in Cape Verde plate, in pair with #13 60.00 60.00
c. As "b," imperf. 20.00
14 " 50r blue 5.00 3.00

Reprints of the 1877-85 issues are on smooth white chalky paper, ungummed, and on thin white paper with shiny white gum. They are perf. 13½. Price $1 each.

Embossed.
Chalk-Surfaced Paper.

1886 *Perf. 12½, 13½*

15 A2 5r black 2.75 2.00
16 " 10r green 3.25 2.25
17 " 20r carmine 4.00 3.00
a. Perf. 13½ 4.00 3.75
18 " 25r violet 4.00 2.00
19 " 40r chocolate 4.00 2.25
a. Perf. 13½ 7.50 3.00
20 " 50r blue 4.50 2.25
21 " 100r yellow brown 5.25 2.50
22 " 200r gray lilac 10.00 8.00
23 " 300r orange 12.50 10.00

The 25, 50 and 100r have been reprinted in aniline colors with clean-cut perf. 13½. Price $2 each.

King Carlos
A3 A4

Typographed.

1894-95 *Perf. 11½, 12½, 13½.*

24 A3 5r orange 1.00 75
25 " 10r reddish violet 1.15 1.00
26 " 15r chocolate 2.75 1.75
a. Perf. 12½ 75.00 50.00
27 " 20r lavender 2.75 1.75
28 " 25r deep green 3.00 2.00
a. Perf. 12½ 3.50 3.50
29 " 50r light blue 3.00 2.00
a. Perf. 13½ 6.00 3.00
30 " 75r carmine ('95) 6.50 5.50
a. Perf. 13½ 17.50 12.50
31 " 80r yellow green ('95) 8.50 7.00
a. Perf. 13½ 15.00 10.00
32 " 100r brown, *buff* ('95) 5.25 2.25
a. Perf. 12½ 30.00 10.00
33 " 150r carmine, *rose* ('95) 13.50 10.00
a. Perf. 12½ 95.00 80.00
b. Perf. 11½ 25.00 14.00
34 " 200r dark blue, *light blue* ('95) 12.50 10.00
a. Perf. 12½ 85.00 70.00
35 " 300r dark blue, *salmon* ('95) 14.00 10.00

1898-1903 *Perf. 11½.*

Name and Value in Black except 500r

36 A4 2½r gray 30 20
37 " 5r orange 30 20
38 " 10r light green 30 20
39 " 15r brown 2.25 1.25
40 " 15r gray green ('03) 1.25 90
41 " 20r gray violet 1.00 50
42 " 25r sea green 2.50 1.00
a. Perf. 12½ 45.00 18.50
43 " 25r carmine ('03) 1.25 20
44 " 50r dark blue 1.90 90
45 " 50r brown ('03) 2.50 1.25
46 " 65r slate blue ('03) *10.00 10.00*
47 " 75r rose 5.00 3.00
48 " 75r lilac ('03) 2.25 1.25
49 " 80r violet 5.00 3.50
50 " 100r dark blue, *blue* 1.75 75
51 " 115r orange brown, *pink* ('03) *10.00 10.00*
52 " 130r brown, *straw* ('03) *10.00 10.00*
53 " 150r brown, *straw* 6.00 4.00
54 " 200r red vio., *pinkish* 2.00 1.50
55 " 300r dark blue, *rose* 5.00 3.50
56 " 400r dull blue, *straw* ('03) 6.50 4.75
57 " 500r black & red, *blue* ('01) 5.00 3.50
58 " 700r violet, *yellowish* ('01) 15.00 12.50
Nos. 36-58 (23) *97.05 74.85*

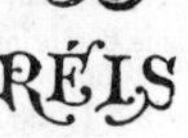

Regular Issues Surcharged in Red or Black

Two spacing types of surcharge. See note above Angola No. 61.

On Issue of 1886.

1902, Dec. 1 *Perf. 12½, 13½*

59 A2 65r on 5r black (R) 4.00 3.00
60 " 65r on 200r gray lilac 4.00 3.00
61 " 65r on 300r orange 4.00 3.00
62 " 115r on 10r green 4.00 3.00
63 " 115r on 20r rose 2.75 2.50
a. Perf. 13½ 20.00 15.00
64 " 130r on 50r blue 4.00 3.00
65 " 130r on 100r brown 4.00 3.00
66 " 400r on 25r violet 2.00 1.50
67 " 400r on 40r chocolate 2.75 2.75
a. Perf. 13½ 17.50 17.50

On Issue of 1894.

Perf. 11½, 12½, 13½.

68 A3 65r on 10r red violet 6.50 4.00
69 " 65r on 20r lavender 5.00 3.00
70 " 65r on 100r brown, *buff* 6.00 4.00
a. Perf. 12½ 12.50 8.50
71 " 115r on 5r orange 3.00 2.50
a. Inverted surcharge 15.00 15.00
72 " 115r on 25r blue green 2.50 2.00
a. Perf. 11½ 12.50 7.50
73 " 115r on 150r carmine, *rose* 6.00 5.00
a. Perf. 13½ 15.00 10.00
74 A3 130r on 75r carmine 3.25 2.75
a. Perf. 13½ 27.50 20.00
75 " 130r on 80r yel. green 2.50 2.00
76 " 130r on 200r dark blue, *blue* 4.00 3.00
77 " 400r on 50r light blue 4.50 3.00
a. Inverted surcharge 40.00 40.00
b. Perf. 13½ 37.50 30.00
78 " 400r on 300r dark blue, *salmon* 1.25 1.25

On Newspaper Stamp of 1893.

79 N1 400r on 2½r brown 1.25 1.25
a. Inverted surcharge 12.50
b. Perf. 12½ 22.50 20.00
Nos. 59-79 (21) 77.25 58.50

Reprints of Nos. 59, 66, 67, and 77 have shiny white gum and clean-cut perforation 13½. Price $1 each.

Overprinted in Black PROVISORIO
On Nos. 39, 42, 44, 47

1902-03 *Perf. 11½*

80 A4 15r brown 1.25 1.00
81 " 25r sea green 1.25 1.00
82 " 50r blue ('03) 1.50 1.25
83 " 75r rose ('03) 2.25 1.50
a. Invtd. ovpt. 20.00 20.00

No. 46 Surcharged in Black 50 RÉIS

1905, July 1

84 A4 50r on 65r slate blue 2.25 1.75

Stamps of 1898-1903 Overprinted in Carmine or Green

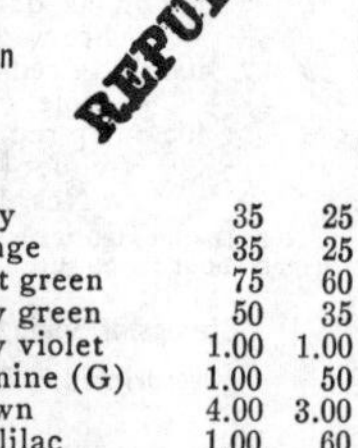

1911, Aug. 20

85 A4 2½r gray 35 25
86 " 5r orange 35 25
87 " 10r light green 75 60
88 " 15r gray green 50 35
89 " 20r gray violet 1.00 1.00
90 " 25r carmine (G) 1.00 50
91 " 50r brown 4.00 3.00
92 " 75r red lilac 1.00 60
93 " 100r dark blue, *blue* 1.00 1.00
94 " 115r org. brn., *pink* 65 *2.00*
95 " 130r brown, *straw* 65 *2.00*
96 " 200r red violet, *pinkish* 3.25 3.25
97 " 400r dull blue, *straw* 1.75 1.75
98 " 500r black & red, *blue* 1.75 1.50
99 " 700r violet, *straw* 1.75 1.50
Nos. 85-99 (15) 19.75 *19.55*

King Manuel II
A5

Overprinted in Carmine or Green.

1912 *Perf. 11½x12*

100 A5 2½r violet 20 *2.00*
101 " 5r black 20 18
102 " 10r gray green 35 25
103 " 20r carmine (G) 1.50 1.00
104 " 25r violet brown 50 30
105 " 50r dark blue 2.75 2.00
106 " 75r bistre brown 75 50
107 " 100r brown, *light green* 75 50
108 " 200r dark green, *salmon* 1.00 75
109 " 300r *azure* 1.00 75

Perf. 14½x15.

110 A5 400r black & blue 2.25 2.00
111 " 500r olive green & violet brown 2.25 2.00
Nos. 100-111 (12) 13.50 *12.23*

Vasco da Gama Issue of Various Portuguese Colonies. Common Design Types CD20–CD27 Surcharged

REPUBLICA
CABO VERDE
¼ C.

On Stamps of Macao.

1913, Feb. 13 *Perf. 12½ to 16*

112 ¼c on ½a bl. green 1.25 1.25
113 ½c on 1a red 1.25 1.25
114 1c on 2a red violet 1.25 1.25
115 2½c on 4a yellow green 1.25 1.25
116 5c on 8a dark blue 4.00 4.00
117 7½c on 12a violet brown 3.00 3.00
118 10c on 16a bistre brown 1.75 1.75
119 15c on 24a bistre 2.75 2.75
Nos. 112–119 (8) 16.50 16.50

On Stamps of Portuguese Africa.
Perf. 14 to 15.

120 ¼c on 2½r bl. green 1.00 1.00
121 ½c on 5r red 1.00 1.00
122 1c on 10r red violet 1.00 1.00
123 2½c on 25r yellow green 1.00 1.00
124 5c on 50r dark blue 2.00 1.50
125 7½c on 75r violet brown 2.25 1.75
126 10c on 100r bistre brown 1.50 1.25
127 15c on 150r bistre 2.00 2.00
Nos. 120–127 (8) 11.75 10.50

On Stamps of Timor.

128 ¼c on ½a bl. green 1.00 1.00
129 ½c on 1a red 1.00 1.00
130 1c on 2a red violet 1.00 1.00
131 2½c on 4a yellow green 1.00 1.00
132 5c on 8a dark blue 3.00 3.00
133 7½c on 12a violet brown 3.00 3.00
134 10c on 16a bistre brown 1.75 1.75
135 15c on 24a bistre 2.25 2.25
Nos. 128–135 (8) 14.00 14.00

No. 75 Overprinted in Red **REPUBLICA**

1913 *Perf. 11½, 12½, 13½.*

137 A3 130r on 80r yellow green 2.75 2.25

Nos. 73 and 76 were also overprinted but not issued. Prices $7 and $8 respectively.

Same Overprint on No. 83 in Green

1914 *Perf. 12*

139 A4 75r rose 3.00 2.75
a. "PROVISORIO" double (G and R) 30.00 20.00

Ceres
A6

Perf. 11½, 12x11½, 15x14.

1914-26 Typographed.

Name and Value in Black.

144 A6 ¼c olive brown 10 10
a. Imperf.
145 A6 ½c black 10 10
146 " 1c blue green 1.25 1.00
147 " 1c yellow green ('22) 10 10
148 " 1½c lilac brown 10 10
149 " 2c carmine 18 15
150 " 2c gray ('26) 25 3.00
151 " 2½c light violet 10 5
152 " 3c orange ('22) 35 25
153 " 4c rose ('22) 12 2.00
154 " 4½c gray ('22) 18 3.00
155 " 5c deep blue 1.00 60
156 " 5c bright blue ('22) 18 18
157 " 6c lilac ('22) 20 3.00
158 " 7c ultramarine ('22) 20 3.00
159 " 7½c yellow brown 20 3.00
160 " 8c slate 65 50
161 " 10c orange brown 20 15
162 " 12c blue green ('22) 30 25
163 " 15c plum 7.50 4.50
164 " 15c brown rose ('22) 25 15
165 " 20c yellow green 20 15
166 " 24c ultramarine ('26) 1.50 1.50
167 " 25c chocolate ('26) 1.50 1.50
168 " 30c brown, *green* 5.00 5.00
169 " 30c gray green ('22) 35 25
170 " 40c brown *pink* 5.00 5.00
171 " 40c turq. blue('22) 75 22
172 " 50c orange, *salmon* 5.00 5.00
173 " 50c violet ('26) 1.00 40
174 " 60c dark blue ('22) 75 50
175 " 60c rose ('26) 1.00 60
176 " 80c bright rose ('22) 2.00 90
177 " 1e green, *blue* 5.00 5.00
178 " 1e rose ('22) 5.00 3.00
179 " 1e deep blue ('26) 4.00 2.00
180 " 2e dark violet ('22) 5.00 3.00
181 " 5e buff ('26) 8.00 6.00
182 " 10e pink ('26) 15.00 10.00
183 " 20e pale turq. ('26) 27.50 22.50
Nos. 144–183 (40) 107.06 97.70

Provisional Issue of 1902 Overprinted in Carmine **REPUBLICA**

1915 *Perf. 11½, 12½, 13½*

184 A2 115r on 10r green 1.75 1.75
a. Perf. 13½ 15.00 15.00
185 " 115r on 20r rose 2.00 2.00
a. Perf. 13½ 15.00 15.00
186 " 130r on 50r blue 1.75 1.75
187 " 130r on 100r brown 1.00 1.00
188 A3 115r on 5r orange 75 50
a. Invtd. ovpt. 15.00
189 " 115r on 25r blue green 1.00 90
a. Perf. 11½ 14.50 14.50
190 " 115r on 150r carmine, *rose* 1.00 1.00
191 " 130r on 75r carmine 1.25 1.25
192 " 130r on 80r yel. grn. 1.25 1.25
a. Inverted overprint 15.00
193 " 130r on 200r blue, *blue* 1.25 1.25
a. Perf. 12½ 50.00 37.50
Nos. 184–193 (10) 13.00 12.65

War Tax Stamps of Portuguese Africa Surcharged

CABO VERDE
CORREIOS
½ C.

1921, Feb. 3 *Perf. 15x14, 11½*

194 WT1 ¼c on 1c green 25 25
195 " ½c on 1c green 30 25
a. "1/2" instead of "½" 7.50 7.50
196 WT1 1c green 35 35

Nos. 127 and 126 Surcharged

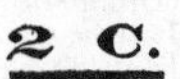

Perf. 14 to 15.

197 CD27 2c on 15c on 150r bis. 1.25 1.25
198 CD26 4c on 10c on 100r bistre brown 1.50 1.25
a. On No. 118 (error) 75.00 75.00

No. 50 Surcharged

6 C.
REPUBLICA

Perf. 12.

200 A4 6c on 100r dark blue, *blue* 1.25 75
a. Accent on "U" of surch. 7.50 7.50

Stamps of 1913-15 Surcharged

$04

1922, Apr. *Perf. 11½, 12½, 13½*

On No. 137

201 A3 4c on 130r on 80r yellow green 2.00 2.00

On Nos. 191–193

202 A3 4c on 130r on 75r carmine 2.50 2.50
203 " 4c on 130r on 80r yellow green 2.00 2.00
204 " 4c on 130r on 200r blue, *blue* 90 60
a. Perf. 12½ 12.50 12.50

Surcharge of Nos. 201–204 with smaller $ occurs once in sheet of 28. Price eight times normal.

Nos. 78–79 Surcharged

República
40 C.

1925 *Perf. 13½, 11½*

205 A3 40c on 400r on 300r blue, *salmon* 75 60
206 N1 40c on 400r on 2½r brown 65 60

No. 176 Surcharged

70 C.

1931, Nov. *Perf. 12x11½*

214 A6 70c on 80c light rose 1.50 1.40

Ceres
A7

Wmkd. Maltese Cross. (232)

1934, May 1 *Perf. 12x11½*

215 A7 1c bistre 10 1.00
216 " 5c olive brown 10 10
217 " 10c violet 10 10
218 " 15c black 10 10
219 " 20c gray 10 10
220 " 30c dark green 13 10
221 " 40c red orange 40 25
222 " 45c bright blue 75 50
223 " 50c brown 75 50
224 " 60c olive green 75 50
225 " 70c brown orange 1.00 1.00
226 " 80c emerald 1.00 40
227 " 85c deep rose 2.50 2.00
228 " 1e maroon 2.00 1.00
229 " 1.40e dark blue 3.00 2.50
230 " 2e dark violet 2.00 85
231 " 5e apple green 5.00 4.00
232 " 10e olive bistre 13.50 10.00
233 " 20e orange 25.00 17.50
Nos. 215–233 (19) 58.28 42.50

Vasco da Gama Issue
Common Design Types

1938 *Perf. 13½x13.* **Unwmkd.**

Name and Value in Black.

234 CD34 1c gray green 5 1.00
235 " 5c orange brown 10 1.00
236 " 10c dark carmine 10 10
237 " 15c dk. violet brown 75 45
238 " 20c slate 35 25
239 CD35 30c rose violet 30 25
240 " 35c bright green 50 30
241 " 40c brown 30 25
242 " 50c bright red violet 30 25
243 CD36 60c gray black 45 40
244 " 70c brown violet 45 30
245 " 80c orange 45 35
246 " 1e red 60 30
247 CD37 1.75e blue 1.50 80
248 " 2e dark blue green 2.00 1.00
249 " 5e olive green 5.00 2.00
250 CD38 10e blue violet 7.50 4.00
251 " 20e red brown 20.00 5.00
Nos. 234–251 (18) 40.70 18.00

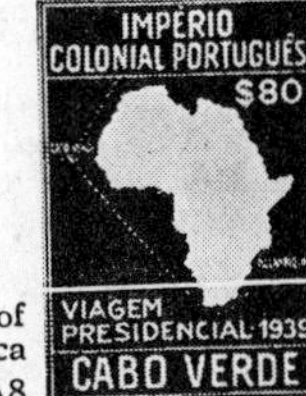

Outline Map of Africa
A8

1939, June 23 Litho. *Perf. 11½x12*

252 A8 80c violet, *pale rose* 5.00 3.50
253 " 1.75e blue, *pale blue* 12.50 8.50
254 " 20e brown, *buff* 50.00 22.50

Issued to commemorate the visit of the President of Portugal to this colony in 1939.

Nos. 239 and 221 Surcharged with New Value and Bars in Black.

1948 *Perf. 13½x13* **Unwmkd.**

255 CD35 10c on 30c rose vio. 1.00 1.50

Perf. 12x11½ **Wmk. 232**

256 A7 25c on 40c red org. 1.00 1.50

Machado Pt., Sao Vicente
A9

Brava Creek, Sao Nicoláo
A10

Designs: 10c, Ribeira Grande. 1e, Harbor, Sao Vicente. 1.75e, Mindelo, distant view. 2e, Joao de Evora Beach. 5e, Mindelo. 10e, Volcano, Fire Island. 20e, Mt. Paul.

Perf. 14½

1948, Oct. 1 Litho. Unwmkd.

257 A9 5c violet brown & bistre 40 40
258 " 10c olive green & pale green 40 25
259 A10 50c magenta & lilac rose 1.00 50
260 " 1e brown violet & rose lilac 2.50 1.50
261 " 1.75e ultramarine & greenish blue 3.00 2.50
262 " 2e dark brown & buff 7.50 3.75
263 " 5e olive green & yellow 15.00 7.50
264 " 10e red & cream 22.50 12.50
265 " 20e dk. vio. & bis. 45.00 25.00
Nos. 257–265 (9) 97.30 53.90

Common Design Types pictured in section at front of book

Lady of Fatima Issue.
Common Design Type

1948, Dec.
266 CD40 50c dark blue 10.00 7.50

U.P.U Symbols
A10a

1949, Oct. ***Perf. 14***
267 A10a 1e red violet & pink 5.50 4.25
U.P.U., 75th anniversary

Holy Year Issue
Common Design Types

1950, May ***Perf. 13x13½***
268 CD41 1e orange brown 75 50
269 CD42 2e slate 3.50 2.25

Holy Year Conclusion Issue
Common Design Type

1951, Oct. ***Perf. 14*** **Unwmkd.**
270 CD43 2e purple & lilac 75 75

Stamps of 1938 Surcharged with New Value and Bars in Black.
Perf. 13½x13

1951, May 21 **Unwmkd.**
271 CD35 10c on 35c brt. green 50 *1.50*
272 CD36 20c on 70c brn. violet 75 *1.50*
273 " 40c on 70c brn. vio. 1.50 *2.00*
274 " 50c on 80c orange 2.50 *3.00*
275 CD37 1e on 1.75e blue 3.00 *4.00*
276 CD38 2e on 10e bl. violet 5.00 *7.50*
a. 1e on 10e blue violet 75.00 75.00
Nos. 271-276 (6) 13.25 *19.50*

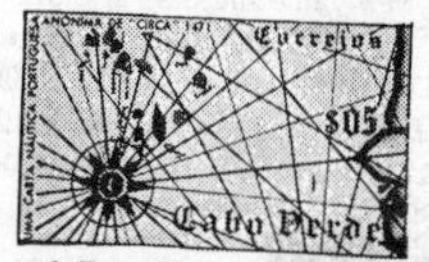

Map of Cape Verde Islands, 1502
A11

Vicente Dias and Gonçalo de Cintra
A12

Portraits: 30c, Diogo Alfonso and Alvaro Fernandes. 50c, Lançarote and Soeiro da Costa. 1e, Diogo Gomes and Antonio da Nola. 2e, Prince Fernando and Prince Henry the Navigator. 3e, Antao Gonçalves and Dinis Dias. 5e, Alfonso Goncalves Baldaia and Joao Fernandes. 10e, Dinis Eanes da Gra and Alvaro de Freitas. 20e, Map of Cape Verde Islands, 1502.

1952, Feb. 24 ***Perf. 14***
277 A11 5c multicolored 10 10
278 A12 10c " 10 10
279 " 30c " 10 10
280 " 50c " 13 10
281 " 1e " 20 13
282 " 2e " 1.25 20
283 " 3e " 3.00 40
284 " 5e " 2.00 50
285 " 10e " 6.00 1.50
286 A11 20e " 10.00 2.50
Nos. 277-286 (10) 22.88 5.63

Medical Congress Issue.
Common Design Type
Design: Hypodermic Injection.

1952, June ***Perf. 13½***
287 CD44 20c olive green & dark brown 50 40

No. 247 Surcharged with New Values and "X" in Black.

1952, Jan. 25 ***Perf. 13½x13***
288 CD37 10c on 1.75e blue 1.75 1.75
289 " 20c on 1.75e " 1.75 1.75
290 " 50c on 1.75e " 6.00 6.00
291 " 1e on 1.75e " 75 75
292 " 1.50e on 1.75e " 75 75
Nos. 288-292 (5) 11.00 11.00

Facade of Jeronymos Convent
A13

Lithographed.

1953, Jan. ***Perf. 13½*** **Unwmkd.**
293 A13 10c brown & pale olive 25 25
294 " 50c purple & fawn 25 25
295 " 1e dk. green & fawn 60 25

Issued to commemorate the Exhibition of Sacred Missionary Art held at Lisbon in 1951.

Stamp of Portugal and Arms of Colonies
A13a

1953 **Photogravure**
Stamp and Arms Multicolored.
296 A13a 50c lilac rose & gray 1.00 60
Centenary of Portuguese stamps.

Sao Paulo Issue
Common Design Type

1954 **Lithographed.** ***Perf. 13½***
297 CD46 1e green, cream & gray 25 15

Belem Tower, Lisbon, and Colonial Arms
A14

Arms of Praia
A15

1955, May 15 **Litho.** ***Perf. 13½***
298 A14 1e multicolored 25 15
299 " 1.60e buff & multicolored 40 20

Issued to publicize the visit of Pres. Francisco H. C. Lopes.

1958, June 14 ***Perf. 12x11½***
300 A15 1e multicolored 24 20
301 " 2.50e pink & multi. 50 24
Centenary of city of Praia.

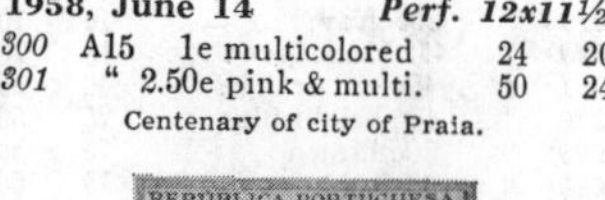

Fair Emblem, Globe and Arms
A15a

1958 ***Perf. 12x11½***
302 A45 2e multicolored 50 40
World's Fair, Brussels, Apr. 17-Oct. 19.

Tropical Medicine Congress Issue
Common Design Type
Design: Aloe vera.

1958, Sept. 5 ***Perf. 13½***
303 CD47 3e multicolored 3.00 2.00

Prince Henry
A16

Antonio da Nola
A17

1960, June 25 **Litho.** ***Perf. 13½***
304 A16 2e multicolored 50 40

Issued to commemorate the 500th anniversary of the death of Prince Henry the Navigator.

1960, Oct. ***Perf. 14½*** **Unwmkd.**
Design: 2.50e, Diogo Gomes.
305 A17 1e multicolored 25 20
306 " 2.50e multicolored 75 40
Discovery of Cape Verde, 500th anniversary.

School Children
A18

1960
307 A18 2.50e multicolored 60 50

Issued to commemorate the 10th anniversary of the Commission for Technical Co-operation in Africa South of the Sahara (C.C.T.A.).

Arms of Praia
A19

Designs: Arms of various cities and towns of Cape Verde.

1961, July **Litho.** ***Perf. 13½***
Multicolored
308 A19 5c *shown* 5 5
309 " 15c *Nova Sintra* 5 5
310 " 20c *Ribeira Brava* 5 5
311 " 30c *Assomada* 10 10
312 " 1e *Maio* 65 13
313 " 2e *Mindelo* 50 13
314 " 2.50e *Santa Maria* 90 18
315 " 3e *Pombas* 1.35 28
316 " 5e *Sal-Rei* 1.25 25
317 " 7.50e *Tarrafal* 1.00 28
318 " 15e *Maria Pia* 1.25 60
319 " 30e *San Felipe* 2.50 1.10
Nos. 308-319 (12) 9.65 3.20

Sports Issue
Common Design Type

Sports: 50c, Throwing javelin. 1e, Discus throwing. 1.50e, Cricket. 2.50e, Boxing. 4.50e, Hurding. 12.50e, Golf.

1962, Jan. 18 ***Perf. 13½***
Multicolored Design
320 CD48 50c light brown 10 10
321 " 1e light green 60 25
322 " 1.50e lt. blue green 25 20
323 " 2.50e pale vio. blue 40 20
324 " 4.50e orange 75 40
325 " 12.50e beige 2.00 1.25
Nos. 320-325 (6) 4.10 2.40

Anti-Malaria Issue
Common Design Type
Design: Anopheles pretoriensis.

1962 **Lithographed** ***Perf. 13½***
326 CD49 2.50e multicolored 75 45

Issued for the World Health Organization drive to eradicate malaria.

Airline Anniversary Issue
Common Design Type

1963, Oct. ***Perf. 14½*** **Unwmkd.**
327 CD50 2.50e gray & multi. 50 40

Issued to commemorate the 10th anniversary of Transportes Aéreos Portugueses.

National Overseas Bank Issue
Common Design Type
Design: 1.50e, José da Silva Mendes Leal.

1964, May 16 ***Perf. 13½***
328 CD51 1.50e multicolored 50 40

Issued to commemorate the centenary of the National Overseas Bank of Portugal.

ITU Issue
Common Design Type

1965, May 17 **Litho.** ***Perf. 14½***
329 CD52 2.50e buff & multi. 1.25 75

Issued to commemorate the centenary of the International Telecommunication Union.

Militia Drummer, 1806
A20

Designs: 1e, Soldier, Militia, 1806. 1.50e, Grenadier officer, 1833. 2.50e, Grenadier, 1833. 3e, Cavalry officer, 1834. 4e, Grenadier, 1835. 5e, Artillery officer, 1848. 10e, Drum major, infantry, 1856.

1965, Dec. 1 **Litho.** ***Perf. 14½***
330 A20 50c multicolored 12 12
331 " 1e " 27 18
332 " 1.50e " 45 18
333 " 2.50e " 1.00 35
334 " 3e " 1.50 50
335 " 4e " 1.00 50
336 " 5e " 1.00 65
337 " 10e " 2.50 1.60
Nos. 330-337 (8) 7.84 4.08

National Revolution Issue
Common Design Type
Design: 1e, Dr. Adriano Moreira School and Health Center.

1966, May 28 **Litho.** ***Perf. 12***
338 CD53 1e multicolored 25 20
National Revolution, 40th anniversary.

Navy Club Issue
Common Design Type

Designs: 1e, Capt. Fontoura da Costa and gunboat Mandovy. 1.50e, Capt. Carvalho Araujo and minesweeper Augusto Castilho.

1967, Jan. 31 **Litho.** ***Perf. 13***
339 CD54 1e multicolored 40 20
340 " 1.50e " 50 25
Centenary of Portugal's Navy Club.

Virgin Mary Statue
A21

Pres. Rodrigues Thomaz
A22

1967, May 13 Litho. *Perf. 12½x13*

341 A21 1e multicolored 20 15

Issued to commemorate the 50th anniversary of the apparition of the Virgin Mary to 3 shepherd children at Fatima.

1968, Feb. 9 Litho. *Perf. 13½*

342 A22 1e multicolored 25 20

Issued to commemorate the 1968 visit of Pres. Americo de Deus Rodrigues Thomaz.

Cabral Issue

Pedro Alvares Cabral
A23

Design: 1e, Cantino's world map, 1502 (horiz.).

1968, Apr. 22 Litho. *Perf. 14*

343 A23 1e multicolored 40 25
344 " 1.50e " 60 40

See note after Angola No. 545.

São Vicente Harbor
A24

Physic Nut
A25

Designs: 1.50e, Peanut plant. 2.50e, Castor-oil plant. 3.50e, Yams. 4e, Date palm. 4.50e, Guavas. 5e, Tamarind. 10e, Bitter cassava. 30e, Woman carrying fruit baskets.

1968, Oct. 15 Litho. *Perf. 14*

345	A24	50c	multicolored	6	3
346	A25	1e	"	10	5
347	"	1.50e	"	15	15
348	"	2.50e	"	25	12
349	"	3.50e	"	33	15
350	"	4e	"	35	18
351	"	4.50e	"	50	18
352	"	5e	"	60	18
353	"	10e	"	1.00	35
354	"	30e	"	3.00	1.25
		Nos. 345-354 (10)		6.34	2.64

Admiral Coutinho Issue

Common Design Type

Design: 30c, Adm. Coutinho and map showing route of first flight from Lisbon to Rio de Janeiro (vert.).

1969, Feb. 17 Litho. *Perf. 14*

355 CD55 30c multicolored 20 10

Issued to commemorate the centenary of the birth of Admiral Carlos Viegas Gago Coutinho (1869–1959), explorer and aviation pioneer.

Vasco da Gama
A26

King Manuel I
A27

Vasco da Gama Issue

1969, Aug. 29 Litho. *Perf. 14*

356 A26 1.50e multicolored 25 10

Issued to commemorate the 500th anniversary of the birth of Vasco da Gama (1469–1524), navigator.

Administration Reform Issue

Common Design Type

1969, Sept. 25 Litho. *Perf. 14*

357 CD56 2e multicolored 40 20

King Manuel I Issue

1969, Dec. 1 Litho. *Perf. 14*

358 A27 3e multicolored 60 30

Issued to commemorate the 500th anniversary of the birth of King Manuel I.

Marshal Carmona Issue

Common Design Type

Design: 2.50e, Antonio Oscar Carmona in marshal's uniform.

1970, Nov. 15 Litho. *Perf. 14*

359 CD57 2.50e multicolored 50 25

Galleons on Sanaga River
A28

1972, May 25 Litho. *Perf. 13*

360 A28 5e lilac rose & multi. 75 40

4th centenary of the publication of The Lusiads by Luiz Camoëns.

Olympic Games Issue

Common Design Type

Design: 4e, Basketball and boxing, Olympic emblem.

1972, June 20 *Perf. 14x13½*

361 CD59 4e multicolored 75 40

20th Olympic Games, Munich, Aug. 26–Sept. 11.

Lisbon-Rio de Janeiro Flight Issue

Common Design Type

Design: 3.50e, "Lusitania" landing at San Vicente.

1972, Sept. 20 Litho. *Perf. 13½*

362 CD60 3.50e multicolored 75 40

WMO Centenary Issue

Common Design Type

1973, Dec. 15 Litho. *Perf. 13*

363 CD61 2.50e ultra. & multi. 50 30

Centenary of international meteorological cooperation.

Mindelo Desalination Plant
A29

1974 Lithographed *Perf. 13½*

364 A29 4e multicolored 75 40

Opening of the Mindelo desalination plant.

Republic

No. 343 Overprinted:
"INDEPENDENCIA / 5-Julho-75"

1975, Dec. 19 Litho. *Perf. 14*

365 A23 1e multicolored 25 15

Proclamation of Independence.

Amilcar Cabral, Flag and Crowd
A30

1976, Jan. 20

366 A30 5e multicolored 1.00 75

3rd anniversary of the assassination of Amilcar Cabral (1924–1973), revolutionary leader.

Rising Sun, Coat of Arms, Liberated People—A31

1976, July 5 Litho. *Perf. 14*

367	A31	50c	multicolored	8	6
368	"	3e	"	32	25
369	"	15e	"	1.60	1.20
370	"	50e	"	6.50	4.00
	a.	Miniature sheet of 4		*15.00*	

First anniversary of independence. No. 370a contains one each of Nos. 367–370. Size: 154x110mm.

No. 351 Overprinted with Row of Stars and: "REPUBLICA / DE"

1976 Litho. *Perf. 14*

372 A25 4.50e multicolored 3.00

Amilcar Cabral, Map and Flag of Cape Verde—A32

1976, Sept. 19 *Perf. 14*

373 A32 1e multicolored 50

Party of International Action (PAICC), 20th anniversary.

Electronic Tree and ITU Emblem
A33

Ashtray
A34

1977, May 17 Litho. *Perf. 13½x13*

374 A33 5.50e multicolored 45

World Telecommunications Day.

1977, July 5 Litho. *Perf. 14*

Carved Coconut Shells: 30c, Bell on stand. 50c, Lamp with Adam and Eve. 1e, Hollow shell with Nativity. 1.50e, Desk lamp. 5e, Jar. 10e, Jar with hinged cover. 20e, Tobacco jar with palms. 30e, Stringed instrument.

375	A34	20c lilac & multi.		
376	"	30c rose & multi.		
377	"	50c salmon & multi.		
378	"	1e lt. grn. & multi.		
379	A34	1.50e org. yel. & multi.		
380	"	5e gray & multi.		
381	"	10e lt. bl. & multi.		
382	"	20e yel. & multi.		
383	"	30e rose lilac & multi.		
		Nos. 375-383 (9)	*5.00*	*2.75*

Cape Verde No. 1 and Coat of Arms
A35

Congress Emblem
A36

1977, Nov. Litho. *Perf. 13½*

384 A35 4e blue & multi. 42
385 " 8e lilac & multi. 85

Centenary of Cape Verde stamps.

1977, Nov. 15 *Perf. 14*

386 A36 3.50e multicolored 38

African Party of Independence of Guinea-Bissau and Cape Verde (PAIGC), 3rd congress, Nov. 15–20.

No. 363 Overprinted with Row of Stars and: "REPUBLICA / DE"

1978, May 1 *Perf. 12*

387 CD61 2.50e ultra. & multi. 25

No. 355 Surcharged with New Value and Bars

1978, May 1 *Perf. 14*

388 CD55 3e on 30c multi. 35

Antenna and ITU Emblem—A37

1978, May 17 Litho. *Perf. 14*

389 A37 3.50e silver & multi. 38

10th World Telecommunications Day.

AIR POST STAMPS.

Common Design Type
Name and Value in Black
Perf. 13½x13.

1938, July 26 **Unwmkd.**

C1	CD39	10c scarlet	50	45
C2	"	20c purple	50	45
C3	"	50c orange	50	45
C4	"	1e ultramarine	50	45
C5	"	2e lilac brown	1.50	1.00
C6	"	3e dark green	2.25	1.50
C7	"	5e red brown	3.00	1.25
C8	"	9e rose carmine	6.00	2.00
C9	"	10e magenta	7.50	3.75
		Nos. C1-C9 (9)	22.25	11.30

No. C7 exists with overprint "Exposicao Internacional de Nova York, 1939–1940" and Trylon and Perisphere.

POSTAGE DUE STAMPS.

D1

D2

Typographed.

1904 *Perf. 12.* **Unwmkd.**

J1	D1	5r yellow green	28	50
J2	"	10r slate	28	50
J3	"	20r yellow brown	50	60
J4	"	30r red orange	90	1.00
J5	"	50r gray brown	50	1.00
J6	"	60r red brown	3.00	3.00
J7	"	100r lilac	1.00	1.25
J8	"	130r dull blue	1.00	1.50
J9	"	200r carmine	1.25	1.50
J10	"	500r dull violet	2.50	3.00
		Nos. J1-J10 (10)	11.21	13.85

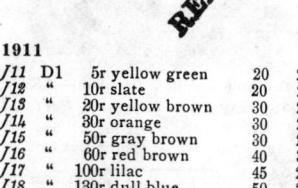

Overprinted in Carmine or Green **REPUBLICA**

1911

J11	D1	5r yellow green	20	20
J12	"	10r slate	20	20
J13	"	20r yellow brown	30	25
J14	"	30r orange	30	25
J15	"	50r gray brown	30	25
J16	"	60r red brown	40	35
J17	"	100r lilac	45	25
J18	"	130r dull blue	50	25
J19	"	200r carmine (G)	50	25
J20	"	500r dull violet	1.00	1.00
		Nos. J11-J20 (10)	4.15	3.25

1921 *Perf. 11½.*

J21	D2	½c yellow green	12	25
J22	"	1c slate	12	25
J23	"	2c red brown	12	25
J24	"	3c orange	12	25
J25	"	5c gray brown	12	25
J26	"	6c light brown	12	12
J27	"	10c red violet	12	12
J28	"	13c dull blue	25	50
J29	"	20c carmine	25	50
J30	"	50c gray	50	75
		Nos. J21-J30 (10)	1.84	3.24

Common Design Type
Photogravure and Typographed.

1952 *Perf. 14.* **Unwmkd.**

Numeral in Red, Frame Multicolored.

J31	CD45	10c chocolate	8	8
J32	"	30c black brown	12	12
J33	"	50c dark blue	8	8
J34	"	1e dark blue	25	25
J35	"	2e red brown	50	50
J36	"	5e olive green	1.00	1.00
		Nos. J31-J36 (6)	2.03	2.03

NEWSPAPER STAMP.

N1

1893 Typo. *Perf. 11½* **Unwmkd.**

P1	N1	2½r brown	75	60
		a. Perf. 12½	2.00	1.50
		b. Perf. 13½	4.50	3.00

POSTAL TAX STAMPS.

Pombal Issue
Common Design Types
Engraved.

1925 *Perf. 12½.* **Unwmkd.**

RA1	CD28	15c dull vio. & blk.	50	35
RA2	CD29	15c " " "	50	35
RA3	CD30	15c " " "	50	35

St. Isabel
PT1

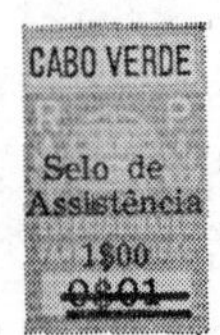

PT2

1948 Lithographed *Perf. 11*

RA4	PT1	50c dark green	2.25	2.00
RA5	"	1e henna brown	3.00	3.00

No. RA5 Surcharged with New Value and Bars

1959

RA6	PT1	50c on 1e henna brown	2.25	2.25

Perf. 14

RA7	PT1	50c carmine rose	1.00	75
RA8	"	1e blue	1.00	75

St. Isabel Type Redrawn

1967-72 Lithographed *Perf. 14*

Multicolored

RA9	PT1	30c (blue panel)	30	30
RA10	"	50c (lilac rose panel)	75	75
RA11	"	50c (red panel) ('72)	25	25
RA12	"	1e (brn. panel)	1.00	1.00
RA13	"	1e (red lilac panel) ('72)	50	50
		Nos. RA9-RA13 (5)	2.80	2.80

Nos. RA9–RA13 are inscribed "ASSISTENCIA" in large letters in bottom panel and "PORTUGAL" and "CABO VERDE" in small letters in upper left corner.

Revenue Stamps Surcharged in Green, Blue or Black

1967–72 Typographed *Perf. 12*

Black "CABO VERDE" & Value
Pale Green Burelage

RA14	PT2	50c on 1c orange (Bl) ('71)	1.50	35
		a. Black surcharge ('68?)	*8.50*	*4.50*
RA15	PT2	50c on 2c orange (G) ('69)	1.25	1.00
		a. Blue surcharge	1.25	1.00
		b. Black surcharge ('68?)	*8.50*	*4.50*
		c. Inverted surcharge (Bk)	15.00	
RA16	PT2	50c on 3c orange (G) ('72)	4.00	
RA17	"	50c on 5c orange (G) ('72)	4.00	
RA18	"	50c on 10c orange (G) ('71)	1.00	1.00
RA19	PT2	1e on 1c orange (Bk)	3.00	2.50
RA20	"	1e on 2c orange (G) ('71)	35	
		a. Blue surcharge ('71)	35	
		b. Black surcharge	3.00	2.50
		Nos. RA14-RA20 (7)	*10.60*	

POSTAL TAX DUE STAMPS.

Pombal Issue.
Common Design Types

1925 *Perf. 12½.* **Unwmkd.**

RAJ1	CD31	30c dull violet & black	35	33
RAJ2	CD32	30c dull violet & black	35	33
RAJ3	CD33	30c dull violet & black	35	33

CARINTHIA

See Austria and Jugoslavia.

CAROLINE ISLANDS

(kăr'ô·līn)

LOCATION—A group of about 549 small islands in the West Pacific Ocean, north of the Equator.

GOVT.—Former German colony.

AREA—550 sq. mi.

POP.—40,000 (approx. 1915.)

100 Pfennig = 1 Mark

Stamps of Germany 1889–90 Overprinted in Black **Karolinen**

Overprinted at 56° Angle.

1900 *Perf. 13½x14½.* **Unwmkd.**

1	A9	3pf dark brown	14.00	16.50
2	"	5pf green	19.00	16.50
3	A10	10pf carmine	27.50	27.50
4	"	20pf ultramarine	27.50	32.50
5	"	25pf orange	80.00	85.00
6	"	50pf red brown	80.00	85.00
		Nos. 1-6 (6)	248.00	263.00

1899 Overprinted at 48° Angle.

1a	A9	3pf light brown	500.00	550.00
2a	"	5pf green	550.00	550.00
3a	A10	10pf carmine	110.00	165.00
4a	"	20pf ultramarine	110.00	165.00
5a	"	25pf orange	*2750.00*	*3000.00*
6a	"	50pf red brown	1350.00	1650.00

Kaiser's Yacht "Hohenzollern"
A3 A4

1900-10 Typographed *Perf. 14*

7	A3	3pf brown	1.10	1.35
8	"	5pf green	1.10	*2.25*
9	"	10pf carmine	1.10	*6.50*
		a. Half used as 5pf on cover, backstamped ('05)		*300.00*
10	"	20pf ultramarine	1.75	*11.00*
		a. Half used as 10pf on cover ('10)		*3500.00*
11	"	25pf orange & black, *yellow*	2.25	*19.00*
12	"	30pf orange & black, *salmon*	2.25	*19.00*
13	"	40pf lake & black	2.25	*22.50*
14	"	50pf purple & black, *salmon*	2.75	*27.50*
15	"	80pf lake & blk., *rose*	3.75	*32.50*

Engraved.
Perf. 14½x14

16	A4	1m carmine	5.50	*65.00*
17	"	2m blue	9.00	*80.00*
18	"	3m black violet	13.50	*150.00*
19	"	5m slate & carmine	225.00	*600.00*
		Nos. 7-19 (13)	271.30	

No. 9a is known as the "typhoon provisional" the stock of 5pf stamps having been destroyed during a typhoon. Covers (cards) without backstamp, price about $90.

Forged cancellations are found on Nos. 7–19.

No. 7 Handstamp Surcharged **5 Pf**

1910, July 12

20	A3	5pf on 3pf brown		*4000.00*

Price is for stamp tied to cover. Stamps on piece sell for about one-third less.

Surcharge exists inverted, price $4,250; double, price $4,500.

Wmk. 125

Typographed

1915-19 **Wmkd. Lozenges. (125)**

21	A3	3pf brown ('19)	1.10
22	"	5pf green	19.00

Engraved.

23	A4	5m slate & carmine	27.50

Nos. 21–23 were never placed in use.

CARPATHO-UKRAINE

(Listed under Czechoslovakia).

CASTELLORIZO

(käs·tĕl'lō·rē'tsō)
(Castelrosso)

LOCATION—A Mediterranean island in the Dodecanese group lying close to the coast of Asia Minor and about 60 miles east of Rhodes.

GOVT.—Former Italian Colony.

AREA—4 sq. mi.

POP.—2,238 (1936).

Formerly a Turkish possession, Castellorizo was occupied by the French in 1915 and ceded to Italy after World War I.

Issued under French Occupation.

25 Centimes = 1 Piastre
100 Centimes = 1 Franc

Stamps of French Offices in Turkey Overprinted **B. N. F. CASTELLORIZO**

1920 *Perf. 14x13½* **Unwmkd.**

1	A2	1c gray	15.00	15.00
		a. Inverted ovpt.	40.00	40.00
		b. Double ovpt.	40.00	40.00
2	"	2c violet brown	15.00	15.00
3	"	3c red orange	15.00	15.00
		a. Inverted overprint	40.00	40.00
4	"	5c green	15.00	15.00
		a. Inverted overprint	40.00	40.00
5	A3	10c rose	20.00	20.00
6	"	15c pale red	25.00	25.00
		a. Inverted overprint	70.00	70.00
7	"	20c brown violet	30.00	30.00
8	A5	1pi on 25c blue	30.00	30.00

9 A3 30c lilac 30.00 30.00
10 A4 40c red & pale blue 60.00 60.00
a. Inverted ovpt. 250.00 250.00
11 A6 2pi on 50c bistre brn. & lavender 70.00 70.00
a. Inverted ovpt. 250.00 250.00
12 " 4pi on 1fr claret & olive green 75.00 75.00
a. Double ovpt. 300.00 300.00
b. Inverted ovpt. 300.00 300.00
13 " 20pi on 5fr dark blue & buff 200.00 200.00
a. Double overprint 500.00 500.00
Nos. 1-13 (13) 600.00 600.00

On Nos. 10-13 the overprint is placed vertically.

No. 1-9 were overprinted in blocks of 25. Position 4 had "CASTELLORIZO" inverted and Positions 8 and 18 had "CASTELLORISO". The later variety also occurred in the setting of the form for Nos. 10-13.

"B. N. F." are the initials of "Base Navale Francaise".

Overprinted in Black or Red **O. N. F. Castellorizo**

1920

On Stamps of French Offices in Turkey

14 A2 1c gray 7.00 7.00
15 " 2c violet brown 7.00 7.00
16 " 3c red orange 8.00 8.00
17 " 5c green (R) 8.00 8.00
19 A3 10c rose 8.00 8.00
20 " 15c pale red 10.00 10.00
21 " 20c brown violet 20.00 20.00
22 A5 1pi on 25c blue (R) 18.50 18.50
a. Inverted ovpt.
23 A3 30c lilac (R) 18.50 18.50
24 A4 40c red & pale blue 18.50 18.50
25 A6 2pi on 50c bistre brown & lavender 18.50 18.50
26 " 4pi on 1fr claret & olive green 20.00 20.00
28 " 20pi on 5fr dark blue & buff 110.00 110.00
Nos. 14-28 (13) 272.00 272.00

On Nos. 25, 26 and 28 the two lines of the overprint are set wider apart than on the lower values.

"O.N.F." are the initials of "Occupation Navale Francaise."

This overprint also exists on the 8pi on 2fr (No. 37). Price $275.

On Stamps of France.

30 A22 10c red 7.00 5.00
a. Inverted ovpt. 40.00
31 " 25c blue (R) 8.00 5.00
a. Inverted ovpt. 40.00

This overprint exists on 8 other 1900–1907 denominations of France (5c, 15c, 20c, 30c, 40c, 50c, 1fr, 5fr). These are believed not to have been issued or postally used.

Stamps of France, 1900-1907, Handstamped in Black or Violet **O F CASTELLORISO**

1920

33 A22 5c green 50.00 45.00
34 " 10c red 50.00 45.00
35 " 20c violet brown 50.00 45.00
36 " 25c blue 50.00 45.00
37 A18 50c bistre brn. & lavender 350.00 325.00
38 " 1fr claret & olive green (V) 350.00 325.00
Nos. 33-38 (6) 900.00 830.00

Nos. 1-38 are considered speculative.

Forgeries of overprints on Nos. 1-38 exist. They abound of Nos. 33-38.

Stamps of French Offices in Turkey handstamped "Occupation Francaise Castellorizo" were made privately.

Issued under Italian Dominion.

100 Centesimi = 1 Lira

Italian Stamps of 1906-20 Overprinted **CASTELROSSO**

Wmkd. Crown. (140)

1922 *Perf. 14*

51 A48 5c green 30 55
52 " 10c claret 30 55
53 " 15c slate 30 55
54 A50 20c brown orange 30 55
a. Double ovpt. 65.00
55 A49 25c blue 30 55
56 " 40c brown 3.75 3.75
57 " 50c violet 4.50 3.75
58 " 60c carmine 4.50 3.75
59 " 85c chocolate 75 1.15
Nos. 51-59 (9) 15.00 15.15

Map of Castellorizo; Flag of Italy
A1

1923

60 A1 5c gray green 45 75
61 " 10c dull rose 45 75
62 " 25c dull blue 45 75
63 " 50c gray lilac 45 75
64 " 1 l brown 45 75
Nos. 60-64 (5) 2.25 3.75

Italian Stamps of 1901-20 Overprinted

1924

65 A48 5c green 45 90
66 " 10c claret 45 90
67 " 15c slate 45 90
68 A50 20c brown orange 45 90
69 A49 25c blue 45 90
70 " 40c brown 45 90
71 " 50c violet 45 90
72 " 60c carmine 45 1.50
a. Double ovpt. 65.00
73 " 85c red brown 45 1.75
74 A46 1 l brown & green 45 2.50
Nos. 65-74 (10) 4.50 12.05

Ferrucci Issue.

Types of Italian Stamps of 1930, Overprinted in Red or Blue **CASTELROSSO**

1930 **Wmkd. Crowns. (140)**

75 A102 20c violet 45 45
76 A103 25c dark green 45 45
77 " 50c black 45 45
78 " 1.25 l deep blue 45 45
79 A104 5 l+2 l deep carmine (Bl) 2.00 2.00
Nos. 75-79 (5) 3.80 3.80

Garibaldi Issue.

Types of Italian Stamps of 1932, Overprinted in Red or Blue **CASTELROSSO**

1932

80 A138 10c brown 1.85 1.85
81 " 20c red brown (Bl) 1.85 1.85
82 " 25c deep green 1.85 1.85
83 " 30c bluish slate 1.85 1.85
84 " 50c red violet (Bl) 1.85 1.85
85 A141 75c copper red (Bl) 1.85 1.85
86 " 1.25 l dull blue 1.85 1.85
87 " 1.75 l+25c brown 1.85 1.85
88 A144 2.55 l+50c orge. (Bl) 1.85 1.85
89 A145 5 l+1 l dull violet 1.85 1.85
Nos. 80-89 (10) 18.50 18.50

CENTRAL AFRICA

LOCATION—Western Africa, north of equator.
GOVT.—Empire.
AREA—241,313 sq. mi.
POP.—2,610,000 (est. 1974).
CAPITAL—Bangui.

The former French colony of Ubangi-Shari, a unit in French Equatorial Africa, proclaimed itself the Central African Republic Dec. 1, 1958. It became the Central African Empire Dec. 4, 1976.

100 Centimes = 1 Franc

Central African Republic

Premier Barthélemy Boganda and Flag
A1

Design: 25fr, Barthélemy Boganda and flag (horiz.).

Engraved.

1959 *Perf. 13* **Unwmkd.**

1 A1 15fr multicolored 25 20
2 " 25fr " 40 20

Issued to commemorate the first anniversary of the establishment of the Republic and to honor Premier Barthélemy Boganda (1910-1959).

Imperforates

Most stamps of Central African Republic exist imperforate in issued and trial colors, and also in small presentation sheets in issued colors.

C.C.T.A. Issue

Common Design Type

1960 *Perf. 13* **Unwmkd.**

3 CD106 50fr light green & dark blue 1.15 85

Dactyloceras Widenmanni—A2

Designs: Various butterflies.

1960-61

4 A2 50c blue green & dark red ('61) 4 3
5 " 1fr multicolored 4 3
6 " 2fr dk. green & brown ('61) 6 5
7 " 3fr yellow green & dark red ('61) 6 6
8 " 5fr dark slate green, pale green & olive brown 8 8
9 " 10fr multicolored 20 10
10 " 20fr " 35 18
11 " 85fr " 1.35 80
Nos. 4-11 (8) 2.18 1.33

No. 2 Overprinted: "FETE NATIONALE 1-12-1960"

1960

12 A1 25fr multicolored 1.10 1.10

National Holiday, Dec. 1, 1960.

Common Design Types pictured in section at front of book.

Louis Pasteur and Pasteur Institute, Bangui
A3

1961, Feb. 25 *Perf. 13* **Unwmkd.**

13 A3 20fr multicolored 65 65

Opening of Pasteur Institute at Bangui.

Flag, Map, and U.N. Emblem
A4

1961, Mar. 4 **Engraved**

14 A4 15fr multicolored 30 20
15 " 25fr " 40 30
16 " 85fr " 1.35 1.10

Issued to commemorate the admission of Central African Republic to the United Nations.

No. 15 Overprinted in Green: "FETE NATIONALE 1-12-61" and Star

1961, Dec. 1

17 A4 25fr multicolored 1.40 1.40

National Holiday, Dec. 1.

No. 16 Surcharged in Red Brown: "U.A.M. CONFERENCE DE BANGUI 25-27 Mars 1962"

1962, March 25

18 A4 50fr on 85fr multi. 1.20 1.20

Issued to commemorate the conference of the African and Malgache Union at Bangui, March 25-27.

Abidjan Games Issue

Common Design Type

Designs: 20fr, Hurdling. 50fr, Bicycling.

1962, July 21 Photo. *Perf. 12½x12*

19 CD109 20fr multicolored 30 25
20 " 50fr " 80 55

See No. C6.

African-Malgache Union Issue

Common Design Type

1962, Sept. 8 **Unwmkd.**

21 CD110 30fr multicolored 55 45

Issued to commemorate the first anniversary of the African and Malgache Union.

President David Dacko—A5 Soldiers with Flag—A6

1962 *Perf. 12*

22 A5 20fr multicolored 30 12
23 " 25fr " 35 15

1963, Aug. 13 **Photogravure**

24 A6 20fr black & multi. 30 20

National Army, third anniversary.

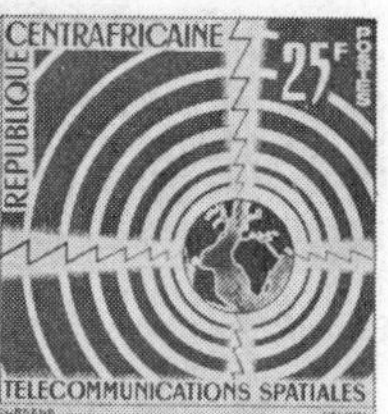

Waves Around Globe
A6a

Design: 100fr, Orbit patterns around globe.

1963, Sept. 19 *Perf. 12½* Unwmkd.

25 A6a 25fr plum & green 45 40
26 " 100fr org., blue & green 1.75 1.65

Issued to publicize space communications.

Young Pioneers
A7

1963, Oct. 14 Engr. *Perf. 12½*

27 A7 50fr greenish blue, vio. blue & brown 70 50

Issued to honor Young Pioneers.

Boali Falls
A8

1963, Oct. 28 *Perf. 13*

28 A8 30fr blue, green & red brown 45 30

Colotis Evippe
A9

Designs: Various butterflies.

1963, Nov. 18 Photo. *Perf. 12½x13*

29 A9 1fr multicolored 15 15
30 " 3fr " 20 20
31 " 4fr " 25 25
32 " 60fr " 1.00 1.00

UNESCO Emblem, Scales and Tree—A9a

1963, Dec. 10 *Perf. 13*

33 A9a 25fr green, olive & red brown 45 35

Issued to commemorate the 15th anniversary of the Universal Declaration of Human Rights.

Leaves and IQSY Emblem
A10

1964, Apr. 20 Engr. *Perf. 13*

34 A10 25fr orange, Prussian green & bister 1.10 1.00

International Quiet Sun Year, 1964–65.

Child
A11

"All Men Are Men"
A12

Designs: Heads of Children.

1964, Aug. 13 *Perf. 13* Unwmkd.

35 A11 20fr rose lilac, red brn. & lt. olive green 35 25
36 " 25fr brick red, red brown & blue 40 30
37 " 40fr light olive green, red brown & rose lilac 60 45
38 " 50fr dull claret, red brn. & lt. green 80 50
a. Min. sheet of 4 2.25 2.25

No. 38a contains one each of Nos. 35–38. Size: 144x99mm.

Cooperation Issue
Common Design Type

1964, Nov. 7 Engraved

39 CD119 25fr green, magenta & dk. brown 45 30

1964, Dec. 1 Litho. *Perf. 13x12½*

40 A12 25fr multicolored 42 20

Issued to publicize National Unity.

Putting Yoke on Oxen
A13

Designs: 50fr, Ox pulling harrow. 85fr, Team of oxen in field. 100fr, Hay wagon.

1965, Apr. 28 Engr. *Perf. 13*

41 A13 25fr slate green, sepia & rose 40 30
42 " 50fr slate green, lt. blue & brn. 75 45
43 " 85fr blue, green & red brown 1.25 75
44 " 100fr multicolored 1.50 1.00

Telegraph Receiver by Pouget-Maisonneuve—A14

Designs: 30fr, Chappe telegraph (vert.). 50fr, Doignon regulator (vert.). 85fr, Pouillet telegraph transcriber.

1965, May 17 Unwmkd.

45 A14 25fr red, grn. & ultra. 40 30
46 " 30fr lake & green 50 35
47 " 50fr carmine & violet 85 50
48 " 85fr red lilac & slate 1.25 80

Issued to commemorate the centenary of the International Telecommunication Union.

"Health"
A15

Designs: 25fr, "Clothes;" shuttle, cloth and women. 60fr, "Teaching;" student and school. 85fr, "Food;" mother feeding child, tractor in wheat field.

1965, June 10 Engr. *Perf. 13*

49 A15 25fr ultra., brt. green & brown 40 30
50 " 50fr ultra., brn. & grn. 75 50
51 " 60fr grn., ultra. & brn. 90 65
52 " 85fr multicolored 1.35 75

Issued to publicize the slogans and aims of "M.E.S.A.N." (Mouvement d'Evolution Sociale de l'Afrique Noire). See No. C30.

Caterpillars and Moth on Coffee Branch
A16

Designs: 3fr, Hawk moth and caterpillar on coffee leaves (horiz.). 30fr, Platyedra moth and larvae on cotton plant.

1965, Aug. 25 Engr. *Perf. 13*

53 A16 2fr dk. pur., dp. org. & slate green 5 5
54 " 3fr black, slate green & red 8 8
55 " 30fr red lilac, red & slate green 1.00 40

Issued to publicize plant protection.

Boy Scout, Tents and Animals
A17

Design: 25fr, Campfire and Scout emblem.

1965, Sept. 27 *Perf. 13* Unwmkd.

56 A17 25fr red orange, blue & red lilac 40 22
57 " 50fr brn. & Prus. blue 80 55

Issued to honor the Boy Scouts.

Nos. 30, 1 and 22 Surcharged in Black or Brown

5 F

Engraved; Photogravure
Perf. 13, 12, 12½x13

1965, Aug. 26 Unwmkd.

58 A9 2fr on 3fr multi. 1.75 1.75
59 A1 5fr on 15fr " 1.75 1.75
60 A5 10fr on 20fr " (Br) 2.00 2.00

The surcharges are adjusted to shape of stamps.

U.N. Emblem and Wheat
A18

1965, Oct. 16 Engraved *Perf. 13*

61 A18 50fr ocher, slate green & bright blue 90 60

Issued for the "Freedom from Hunger Campaign" of the United Nations Food and Agriculture Organization.

Diamond Cutter
A19

1966, March 14 Engraved *Perf. 13*

62 A19 25fr car. rose, dk. pur. & brown 40 25

Nos. 43–44 Surcharged

5 F

1966, Feb.

63 A13 5fr on 85fr multi. 25 25
64 " 10fr on 100fr multi. 45 45

Issue dates: No. 63, Feb. 17. No. 64, Feb. 15.

Statue of Mbaka Woman Porter
A20

WHO Headquarters, Geneva
A21

1966, Apr. 9 Photo. *Perf. 13x12½*

65 A20 25fr multicolored 40 25

Issued to commemorate the International Negro Arts Festival. Dakar, Senegal, Apr. 1–24.

1966, May 3 Photo. Unwmkd.

66 A21 25fr purple, bl. & yel. 40 25

Issued to commemorate the inauguration of the World Health Organization Headquarters, Geneva.

Eulophia Cucullata
A22

Orchids: 5fr, Lissochilus horsfalii. 10fr, Tridactyle bicaudata. 15fr, Polystachya. 20fr, Eulophia alta. 25fr, Microcelia macrorrhynchium.

1966, May 16 Photo. *Perf. 12x12½*

Orchids in Natural Colors

67 A22 2fr dark red 8 5
68 " 5fr brown org. & vio. 10 8
69 " 10fr blue green & black 15 10
70 " 15fr lt. green & dk. brn. 25 15
71 " 20fr dark green 35 20
72 " 25fr lt. ultra. & brown 45 20
Nos. 67-72 (6) 1.38 78

Congo Forest Mouse
A23

Rodents: 10fr, One-stripe mouse. 20fr, Dollman's tree mouse (vert.).

1966, Sept. 15 Photo. *Perf. 12½x12*

73 A23 5fr yellow & multi. 12 10
74 " 10fr tan & multi. 18 10
75 " 20fr lt. grn. & multi. 35 25

UNESCO Emblem
A24

Pres. Jean Bedel Bokassa
A25

1966, Dec. 5 Photo. *Perf. 13*
76 A24 30fr multicolored 45 25

Issued to commemorate the 20th anniversary of UNESCO (United Nations Educational, Scientific and Cultural Organization).

1967, Jan. 1 *Perf. 12x12½*
77 A25 30fr yel. grn., black & bister brown 50 25

No. 72 Surcharged with New Value and "XX"

1967, May 8 Photo. *Perf. 12x12½*
78 A22 10fr on 25fr multi. 20 10

See also No. C43.

Central Market, Bangui
A26

1967, Aug. 8 Photo. *Perf. 12½x13*
79 A26 30fr multicolored 50 30

Safari Hotel, Bangui
A27

1967, Sept. 26 Photo. *Perf. 12½x13*
80 A27 30fr multicolored 50 30

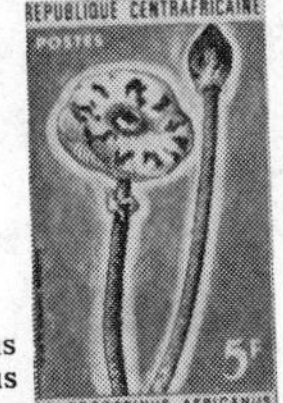

Leucocoprinus Africanus
A28

Various Mushrooms

1967, Oct. 3 Engraved *Perf. 13*
81 A28 5fr dark brown, olive & ocher 12 10
82 " 10fr dark brown, ultra. & yellow 18 13
83 " 15fr dark brown, slate green & yellow 25 17
84 " 30fr multicolored 60 25
85 " 50fr " 85 50
Nos. 81-85 (5) 2.00 1.15

Map, Radio Tower, Projector and People—A29

1967, Oct. 31
86 A29 30fr emerald, ocher & indigo 50 30

Radiovision service.

African Hair Style
A30

Various African Hair Styles.

1967, Nov. 7 Engraved *Perf. 13*
87 A30 5fr ultra., dk. brown & bister brown 10 8
88 " 10fr car., dk. brown & bister brown 20 12
89 " 15fr dp. grn., dk. brn. & bister brown 25 15
90 " 20fr org., dk. brown & bister brown 35 15
91 " 30fr red lilac, dk. brn. & bister brown 50 25
Nos. 87-91 (5) 1.40 75

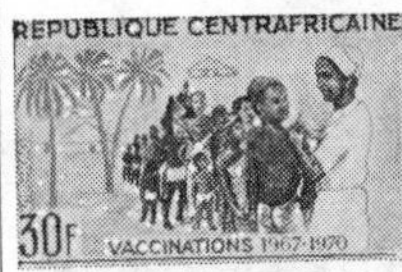

Nurse Vaccinating Children
A31

1967, Nov. 14
92 A31 30fr dark red brown & bright green 50 25

Vaccination campaign, 1967–70.

Douglas DC-3
A32

Designs: 2fr, Beechcraft Baron. 5fr, Douglas DC-4.

1967, Nov. 24
93 A32 1fr brown red, indigo & green 6 6
94 " 2fr bright blue, black & bright pink 6 6
95 " 5fr greenish blue, blk. & emerald 13 12
Nos. 93-95, C47-C49 (6) 11.85 6.14

Pierced Stone, Kwe Tribe
A33

Designs: 30fr, Primitive dwelling at Toulou (horiz.). 100fr, Megaliths, Bouar. 130fr, Rock painting (people), Toulou (horiz.).

1967, Dec. 26 Engraved *Perf. 13*
96 A33 30fr crimson, indigo & maroon 50 30
97 " 50fr olive brn., ocher & dark green 80 40
98 " 100fr dk. brown, brt. blue & brown 1.60 70
99 " 130fr dk. red, brown & dark green 2.00 90

Issued to publicize the 6th Pan-African Prehistoric Congress, Dakar.

Tanker, Refinery and Map of Area Served—A33a

1968, July 30 Photo. *Perf. 12½*
100 A33a 30fr multicolored 40 20

Issued to commemorate the opening of the Port Gentil (Gabon) Refinery, June 12, 1968.

Bulldozer Clearing Land
A34

Designs: 10fr, Baoule cattle. 20fr, 15,000-spindle spinning machine. No. 104, Automatic Diederichs looms. No. 105, Bulldozer.

1968, Oct. 1 Engraved *Perf. 13*
101 A34 5fr black, green & dark brown 7 5
102 " 10fr black, pale green & bister brown 18 15
103 " 20fr green, red brown & yellow 30 18
104 " 30fr brown, olive & ultramarine 50 20
105 " 30fr indigo, red brown & slate green 50 20
Nos. 101-105 (5) 1.55 78

Issued to publicize "Operation Bokassa."

Bangui Mosque
A35

1968, Oct. 14
106 A35 30fr green, blue & ocher 45 20

Hunting Knife of Baya and Boufi Tribes—A36

Designs: 20fr, Hunting knife of Nzakara tribe. 30fr, Crossbow of Babinga and Babenzele (pygmy) tribes.

1968, Nov. 19 Engraved *Perf. 13*
107 A36 10fr lemon, Prus. blue & ultramarine 15 12
108 " 20fr ultra., dk. olive & slate green 30 17
109 " 30fr slate green, ultra. & brn. orange 45 17

"Ville de Bangui," 1958
A37

River Boats: 30fr, "J. B. Gouandjia," 1968. 50fr, "Lamblin," 1944.

1968, Dec. 10 Engraved *Perf. 13*
Size: 36x22mm.
110 A37 10fr magenta, brt. grn. & violet blue 15 10
111 A37 30fr bl., green & brn. 50 20
112 " 50fr brown, slate & olive green 85 40
Nos. 110-112, C62-C63 (5) 5.00 2.40

Woman Javelin Thrower
A38

Sport Designs: 10fr, Women runners. 15fr, Soccer.

1969, Mar. 18 Photo. *Perf. 13x12½*
113 A38 5fr multicolored 10 6
114 " 10fr " 17 10
115 " 15fr " 25 12
Nos. 113-115, C71-C72 (5) 2.77 1.23

BIT and ILO Emblems and Worker
A39

1969, May 20 Photo. *Perf. 12½x13*
116 A39 30fr dp. blue, green & olive brown 40 15
117 " 50fr dp. carmine, grn. & olive brown 75 35

Issued to commemorate the 50th anniversary of the International Labor Organization.

Pres. Jean Bedel Bokassa
A40

Garayah
A41

1969, Dec. 1 Litho. *Perf. 13x13½*
118 A40 30fr verm. & multi. 40 20

ASECNA Issue

Common Design Type

1969, Dec. 12 Engraved *Perf. 13*
119 CD132 100fr deep blue 1.50 70

1970, Jan. 6 Engraved *Perf. 13*

Musical Instuments: 15fr, Ngombi (harp; horiz.). 30fr, Xylophone (horiz.). 50fr, Ndala (lute; horiz.). 130fr, Gatta and babyon (drums).

120 A41 10fr yel. green, dk. green & ocher 15 12
121 " 15fr bl. green, ocher & dk. brown 25 15
122 " 30fr maroon, ocher & dark brown 45 20
123 " 50fr rose carmine & indigo 75 45
124 " 130fr brt. blue, brown & olive 2.00 70
Nos. 120-124 (5) 3.60 1.62

U.P.U. Headquarters Issue

Common Design Type

1970, May 20 Engraved *Perf. 13*
125 CD133 100fr ultra., verm. & red brown 1.00 50

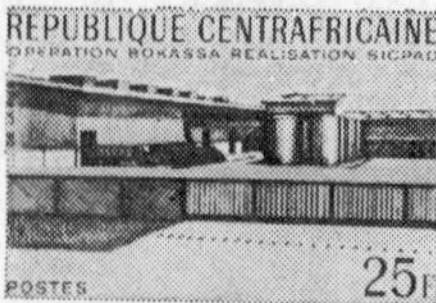

Loading Platform and Flour Storage Bins
A42

Designs: 50fr, Flour milling machinery. 100fr, View of mill.

1970, Feb. 24 Litho. ***Perf. 14***

126 A42 25fr slate & multi. 35 18
127 " 50fr lilac & multi. 70 32
128 " 100fr red & multi. 1.40 75

Inauguration of SICPAD (Société Industrielle Centrafricaine des Produits Alimentaires et Dérivés, a part of Operation Bokassa, Feb. 22, 1968.

Pres. Bokassa
A43

1970, Aug. 13 Litho. ***Perf. 14***

129 A43 30fr multicolored 3.25 2.75
130 " 40fr " 4.75 3.50

Cheese Factory, Sarki—A44

Silk Worm
A45

Designs: 10fr, M'Bali Ranch. 20fr, Zebu (vert.).

Perf. 13x13½, 13½x13

1970, Sept. 15

131 A44 5fr red & multi. 20 10
132 " 10fr " " 4.00 3.50
133 " 20fr " " 65 45
134 A45 40fr " " 1.10 75
Nos. 131-134, C83 (5) 7.95 5.90

Issued to publicize Operation Bokassa, a national development plan.

Gnathonemus Monteiri—A46

River Fish: 20fr, Mormyrus proboscirostris. 30fr, Marcusenius wilverthi. 40fr, Gnathonemus elephas. 50fr, Gnathonemus curvirostris.

1971, Apr. 6 Photo. ***Perf. 12½***

135 A46 10fr multicolored 15 10
136 " 20fr " 30 20
137 " 30fr " 50 25
138 " 40fr " 65 25
139 " 50fr " 80 40
Nos. 135-139 (5) 2.40 1.20

Berberati Cathedral
A47

1971, July 20 Litho. ***Perf. 13½***

140 A47 5fr green & multi. 10 8

New Roman Catholic Cathedral at Berberati.

Charles de Gaulle
A48

Gray Galago
A49

1971, Aug. 20 ***Perf. 13½x13***

141 A48 100fr brt. bl. & multi. 1.50 1.10

In memory of Gen. Charles de Gaulle (1890-1970), president of France.

1971, Oct. 25 Photo. ***Perf. 13***

Designs: 40fr, Elegant galago. 100fr, Calabar potto (horiz.). 150fr, Bosman's potto (horiz.). 200fr, Oustalet's colobo (horiz.).

142 A49 30fr pink & multi. 50 40
143 " 40fr lt. blue & multi. 70 50
144 " 100fr multicolored 1.40 1.00
145 " 150fr " 2.25 1.25
146 " 200fr " 3.25 1.50
Nos. 142-146 (5) 8.10 4.65

Alan B. Shepard
A50

Designs: No. 148, Yuri Gagarin. No. 149, Edwin E. Aldrin, Jr. No. 150, Alexei Leonov. No. 151, Neil A. Armstrong on moon. No. 152, Lunokhod I on moon.

1971, Nov. 19 Litho. ***Perf. 14***

147 A50 40fr violet & multi. 50 25
148 " 40fr " " 50 25
149 " 100fr multicolored 1.35 60
150 " 100fr " 1.35 60
151 A50 200fr red & multi. 2.50 1.00
152 " 200fr " " 2.50 1.00
Nos. 147-152 (6) 8.70 3.70

Space achievements of United States and Russia.

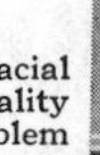

"Operation Bokassa" and Pres. Bokassa
A51

1971, Dec. 1 Photo. ***Perf. 13***

153 A51 40fr red & multi. 60 22

12th anniversary of independence.

Racial Equality Emblem
A52

1971, Dec. 6 Lithographed

154 A52 50fr multicolored 60 25

International Year Against Racial Discrimination.

Bokassa School Emblem and Cadets—A53

Book Year Emblem
A54

1972, Jan. 1 Photogravure

155 A53 30fr gold & multi. 45 20

J. B. Bokassa Military School.

1972, Mar. 11 Photo. ***Perf. 12½x13***

156 A54 100fr red brown, gold & orange 1.10 65

International Book Year 1972.

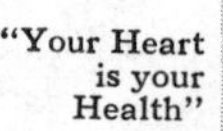

"Your Heart is your Health"
A55

1972, Apr. 7 Photo. ***Perf. 13x12½***

157 A55 100fr yellow, black & carmine 1.10 65

World Health Day.

Red Cross Workers in Village
A56

1972, May 8 ***Perf. 13***

158 A56 150fr multicolored 2.00 90

25th World Red Cross Day.

Globe
A57

1972, May 17 Lithographed

159 A57 50fr yellow, black & deep orange 60 30

4th World Telecommunications Day.

Pres. and Mrs. Bokassa and Family—A58

1972, May 28 ***Perf. 14***

160 A58 30fr yellow & multi. 40 15

Mother's Day. Mothers' gold medal awarded to Catherine Bokassa.

Pres. Bokassa Planting Cotton, Map of Africa
A59

1972, June 5 Photo. ***Perf. 13***

161 A59 40fr yellow & multi. 50 25

Operation Bokassa, a national development plan.

Postal Checking and Savings Center
A60

1972, June 21

162 A60 30fr yel. org. & multi. 40 18

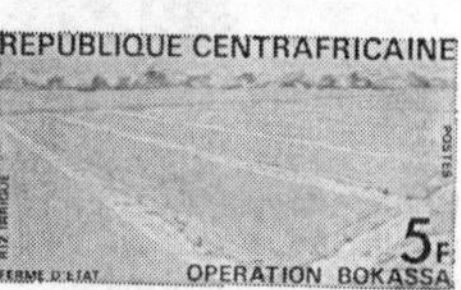

Irrigated Rice Fields—A61

"Le Pacifique" Apartment House
A62

Designs: 25fr, Plowing rice field. No. 166, Swimming pool, Hotel St. Sylvestre. No. 167, Entrance, Hotel St. Sylvestre. No. 168, J. B. Bokassa University.

1972 Lithographed ***Perf. 13x13½***

163 A61 5fr multicolored 7 6
164 " 25fr " 32 15

Engraved ***Perf. 13***

165 A62 30fr multicolored 35 15
166 " 30fr " 35 15
167 " 40fr " 45 25
168 " 40fr " 45 20
Nos. 163–168 (6) 1.99 96

Operation Bokassa. Issue dates: 5fr, 25fr, Nov. 10; No. 165, June 27; Nos. 166–167, Dec. 9; No. 168, Aug. 26.

Bull Chasing Woman on Clock Face
A63

Designs (Scenes Painted on Clock Faces): 10fr, Men and open cooking fire. 20fr, Fishermen. 30fr, Palms, monkeys and giraffe. 40fr, Warriors.

1972, July 31 Photo. ***Perf. 12½***

169 A63 5fr dk. red & multi. 8 4
170 " 10fr brt. bl. & multi. 10 6
171 " 20fr green & multi. 25 10
172 " 30fr yellow & multi. 45 20
173 " 40fr violet & multi. 50 30
Nos. 169–173 (5) 1.38 70

HORCEN Central African clock and watch factory.

Protestant Youth Center—A64

Design: 10fr, Postal runner carrying mail in cleft stick (vert.).

1972, Aug. 12 ***Perf. 13***

174 A64 10fr multicolored 15 8
175 " 20fr " 25 10
Nos. 174–175, C95–C98 (6) 5.50 2.48

Centraphilex 1972, Central African Philatelic Exhibition, Bangui.

Mail Truck
A65

1972, Oct. 23 Photo. ***Perf. 13***

176 A65 100fr ocher & multi. 1.35 50

Universal Postal Union Day.

Mother Teaching Child to Write
A66

Central African Mothers: 10fr, Caring for infant. 15fr, Combing child's hair. 20fr, Teaching to read. 180fr, Nursing. 190fr, Teaching to walk.

1972, Dec. 27 ***Perf. 13½x13***

177 A66 5fr multicolored 8 4
178 " 10fr lilac & multi. 12 7
179 " 15fr dull org. & multi. 20 8
180 " 20fr yel. grn. & multi. 25 12
181 " 180fr multicolored 2.25 75
182 " 190fr pink & multi. 2.25 1.10
Nos. 177–182 (6) 5.15 2.16

Farmer Carrying Sheaf—A67

1973, May 30 Photo. ***Perf. 13***

183 A67 50fr vio. bl. & multi. 55 35

10th anniversary of the World Food Program.

Garcinia Punctata
A68

African Flora: 20fr, Bertiera racemosa. 30fr, Corynanthe pachyceras. 40fr, Combretodendron africanum. 50fr, Xylopia Villosa (vert.).

1973, June 8

184 A68 10fr pale bl. & multi. 10 7
185 " 20fr multicolored 20 10
186 " 30fr lt. gray & multi. 40 15
187 " 40fr multicolored 40 30
188 " 50fr " 50 35
Nos. 184–188 (5) 1.60 97

Pygmy Chameleon
A69

1973, June 26 Photo. ***Perf. 13***

189 A69 15fr multicolored 20 10

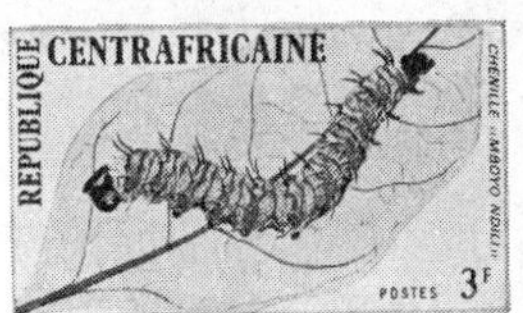

Caterpillar—A70

Designs: Various caterpillars.

1973, Aug. 6 Photo. ***Perf. 13***

190 A70 3fr multicolored 5 5
191 " 5fr " 8 5
192 " 25fr " 30 15

No. 184 Surcharged with New Value, 2 Bars, and Overprinted in Red: "SECHERESSE SOLIDARITE AFRICAINE"

1973, Aug. 16

193 A68 100fr on 10fr multi. 90 75

African solidarity in drought emergency.

African Postal Union Issue
Common Design Type

1973, Sept. 12 Engraved ***Perf. 13***

194 CD137 100fr dk. brn., red org. & olive 90 65

Pres. Bokassa and CAR Flag
A71

1973, Nov. 30 Photo. ***Perf. 12½***

195 A71 1fr brown & multi. 3 3
196 " 2fr purple & multi. 5 5
197 " 3fr vio. bl. & multi. 5 5
198 A71 5fr ocher & multi. 5 5
199 " 10fr multicolored 10 7
200 " 15fr orange & multi. 15 10
201 " 20fr multicolored 20 15
202 " 30fr dk. grn. & multi. 30 20
203 " 40fr dk. brn. & multi. 40 30
Nos. 195–203, C117–C118 (11) 2.83 2.05

INTERPOL Emblem
A72

1973, Dec. 20 ***Perf. 13x12½***

204 A72 50fr yellow & multi. 50 40

50th anniversary of the International Criminal Police Organization.

Catherine Bokassa Center
A73

Design: 40fr, Ambulance in front of Catherine Bokassa Center.

1974, Jan. 24 Engraved ***Perf. 13***

205 A73 30fr multicolored 25 18
206 " 40fr " 32 25

Catherine Bokassa Center for Mothers and Children.

Cigarette-making Machine
A74

Designs: 10fr, Cigarette in ashtray, and factory. 30fr, Hand lighting cigarette, and Administration Building.

1974, Jan. 29

207 A74 5fr slate grn. & multi. 7 5
208 " 10fr " " " 10 10
209 " 30fr " " " 25 15

Publicity for Centra cigarettes.

"Communications"
A75

1974, June 8 Photo. ***Perf. 12½x13***

210 A75 100fr multicolored 1.00 70

World Telecommunications Day.

People and WPY Emblem
A76

1974, June 20 Engraved ***Perf. 13***

211 A76 100fr red, slate green & brown 1.00 70

World Population Year.

Mother, Child, WHO Emblem
A77

1974, July 10

212 A77 100fr multicolored 1.00 45

26th anniversary of World Health Organization.

Hoeing—A78

Designs: 10fr, Battle scene ("yesterday"). 15fr, Pastoral scene ("today"). 20fr, Rice planting. 25fr, Storehouse. 40fr, Veterans Headquarters. Borders show tanks and tractors.

1974, Nov. 15 Litho. ***Perf. 13***

213 A78 10fr multicolored 10 7
214 " 15fr " 12 8
215 " 20fr " 18 10
216 " 25fr " 22 15
217 " 30fr " 25 15
218 " 40fr " 35 15
Nos. 213–218 (6) 1.22 70

Veterans' activities.

Presidents and Flags of Cameroun, CAR, Congo, Gabon and Meeting Center—A79

1974, Dec. 8 Photogravure ***Perf. 13***

219 A79 40fr gold & multi. 40 22

See No. C126 and note after Cameroun No. 595.

House in OCAM City
A80

Designs: Scenes in housing development, OCAM City.

1975, Feb. 1 Photo. ***Perf. 13***

220 A80 30fr multicolored 30 17
221 " 40fr " 40 22
222 " 50fr " 45 30
223 " 100fr " 90 65

1975, Feb. 22

Designs: Cottage scenes in J. B. Bokassa "pilot village."

224 A80 25fr multicolored 20 12
225 " 30fr " 25 15
226 " 40fr " 40 20

Foreign Ministry
A81

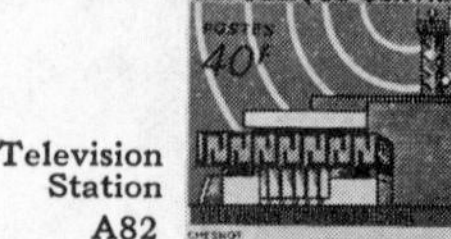

Television Station A82

1975, Feb. 28 ***Perf. 13x12½***
227 A81 40fr multicolored 40 18
Perf. 13
228 A82 40fr multicolored 40 18
Public buildings, Bangui.

Bokassa's Saber—A83

Design: 40fr, Bokassa's baton.

1975, Feb. 22 **Photo.** ***Perf. 13***
229 A83 30fr dp. blue & multi. 25 17
230 " 40fr vio. bl. & multi. 35 20
Jean Bedel Bokassa, President for Life and Marshal of the Republic. See Nos. C127–C128.

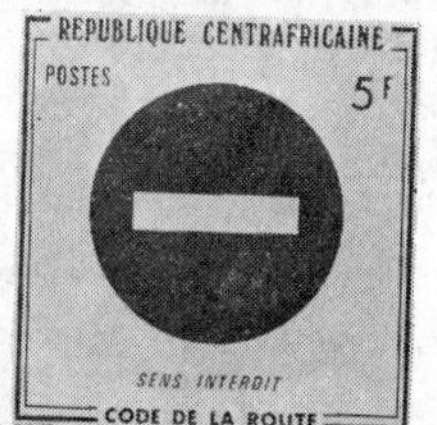

Do Not Enter A84

Traffic Signs: 10fr, Stop. 20fr, No parking. 30fr, School. 40fr, Intersection.

1975, Mar. 20
231 A84 5fr ultra. & red 5 5
232 " 10fr " " 10 8
233 " 20fr " " 15 10
234 " 30fr ultra. & multi. 20 17
235 " 40fr " " 40 20
Nos. 231–235 (5) 90 60

Buffon's Kob A85

Designs: 15fr, Wart hog. 20fr, Waterbuck. 30fr, Lion.

1975, June 24 **Photo.** ***Perf. 13***
236 A85 10fr dull grn. & multi. 10 7
237 " 15fr lemon & multi. 15 8
238 " 20fr yel. grn. & multi. 20 13
239 " 30fr lt. bl. & multi. 30 17

Crane Lifting Log onto Truck A86

Designs: 10fr, Forest (vert.). 15fr, Tree felling (vert.). 100fr, Log pile. 150fr, Logs transported by raft. 200fr, Lumber-yard.

1975, Nov. 28 **Engr.** ***Perf. 13***
240 A86 10fr multicolored 8 5
241 " 15fr " 12 8
242 " 50fr " 40 25
243 " 100fr " 75 55
244 " 150fr " 1.10 90
245 A86 200fr multicolored 1.50 1.10
Nos. 240–245 (6) 3.95 2.93
Promotion of Central African wood.

Women's Heads and Various Occupations—A87

1975, Dec. 10 **Photogravure**
246 A87 40fr multicolored 35 20
247 " 100fr " 75 55
International Women's Year 1975.

Alexander Graham Bell A88

1976, Mar. 25 **Litho.** ***Perf. 12½x13***
248 A88 100fr yel. & black 75 50
Centenary of first telephone call by Alexander Graham Bell, Mar. 10, 1876.

Satellite and ITU Emblem—A89

Design: No. 250, UPU emblem, various forms of mail transport.

1976 **Engr.** ***Perf. 13***
249 A89 100fr vio. bl., claret & green 75 50
250 " 100fr carmine, green & ocher 90 70
World Telecommunications Day (No. 249); Universal Postal Union Day (No. 250).

Soyuz on Launching Pad—A90

Design: 50fr, Apollo rocket.

1976, June 14 **Litho.** ***Perf. 14x13½***
251 A90 40fr multicolored 35 15
252 " 50fr " 45 20
Nos. 251–252, C135–C137 (5) 5.60 2.35
Apollo Soyuz space test project, Russo-American cooperation, launched July 15, link-up July 17, 1975.

Drurya Antimachus—A91

Butterfly: 40fr, Argema mittrei (vert.).

1976, Sept. 20 **Litho.** ***Perf. 12½***
253 A91 30fr ocher & multi. 25 15
254 " 40fr ultra. & multi. 35 20
See Nos. C145–C146.

Slalom, Piero Gros—A92

Design: 60fr, Karl Schnabel and Toni Innauer.

1976, Sept. 23 ***Perf. 13½***
255 A92 40fr multicolored 35 15
256 " 60fr " 55 25
Nos. 255–256, C147–C149 (5) 5.70 2.40
12th Winter Olympic Games winners, Innsbruck.

Viking Components A93

Design: 60fr, Viking take-off.

1976, Dec.
257 A93 40fr multicolored 35 15
258 " 60fr " 55 25
Nos. 257–258, C151–C153 (5) 5.70 2.40
Viking Mars project.

Empire

Stamps of 1973–76 Overprinted with Bars and "EMPIRE CENTRAFRICAIN" in Black, Green, Violet Blue, Silver, Carmine, Brown or Red

Printing and Perforations as Before

1977, March

Multicolored

259 A70 3fr (#190; B) 5 5
260 A78 10fr (#213;B) 12 10
261 A84 10fr (#232;VB) 12 10
262 A85 10fr (#236;C) 15 12
263 " 15fr (#237;C) 20 15
264 A86 15fr (#241;B) 17 12
265 A78 20fr (#215;B) 20 18
266 A85 20fr (#238;C) 20 18
267 A78 25fr (#216;B) 25 20
268 A80 25fr (#224;B) 25 20
269 " 30fr (#220;VB) 30 25
270 " 30fr (#225;B) 30 25
271 A85 30fr (#239;C) 30 25
272 A79 40fr (#219;B) 35 30
273 A80 40fr (#221;VB) 40 30
274 " 40fr (#226;B) 35 30
275 A81 40fr (#227;B & S) 35 30
276 A82 40fr (#228;B) 35 30
277 A84 40fr (#235; VB) 30 25
78 A91 40fr (#254; B) 30 25
279 A86 50fr (#242;Br) 45 35
280 A75 100fr (#210;B) 90 70
281 A76 100fr (#211;B) 90 70
282 A77 100fr (#212;G) 1.00 80
283 A88 100fr (#248;R) 1.00 80
284 A89 100fr (#249;B) 1.00 80
285 " 100fr (#250;B) 1.00 80
Nos. 259–285 (27) 11.26 9.10

Stamps of 1975–76 Overprinted "EMPIRE CENTRAFRICAIN" in Black on Silver Panel

1977, Apr. 1
286 A83 40fr multi. (#230) 30 25
287 A90 40fr " (#251) 40 30
288 A92 40fr " (#255) 30 25
289 A93 40fr " (#257) 30 25
290 A90 50fr " (#252) 50 35
291 A92 60fr " (#256) 50 35
292 A93 60fr " (#258) 50 35
Nos. 286–292 (7) 2.80 2.10

Pierre and Marie Curie—A94

Design: 60fr, Wilhelm C. Roentgen.

1977, Apr. 1 **Litho.** ***Perf. 13½***
293 A94 40fr multicolored 30 15
294 " 60fr " 50 25
Nos. 293–294, C180–C182 (5) 5.70 2.40
Nobel Prize winners.

Italy No. C42 and Faustine Temple, Rome—A95

Design: 60fr, Russia No. C12 and St. Basil's Cathedral, Moscow.

1977, Apr. 11 **Litho.** ***Perf. 11***
295 A95 40fr multicolored 30 15
296 " 50fr " 50 25
Nos. 295–296, C184–C186 (5) 5.60 2.40
75th anniversary of the Zeppelin.

Lindbergh over Paris—A96

Designs: 60fr, Santos Dumont and "14 bis." 100fr, Bleriot and monoplane. 200fr, Roald Amundsen and "N24." 300fr, Concorde. 500fr, Lindbergh and Spirit of St. Louis.

1977, Sept. 30 **Litho.** ***Perf. 13½***
297 A96 50fr multicolored 40 20
298 " 60fr " 50 25
299 " 100fr " 80 30
300 " 200fr " 1.60 65
301 " 300fr " 2.40 1.00
Nos. 297–301 (5) 5.70 2.40

Souvenir Sheet

302 A96 500fr multicolored 4.00 1.85
History of aviation, famous fliers. No. 302 has multicolored margin showing Spirit of St. Louis and Concorde. Size: 117x91½mm.

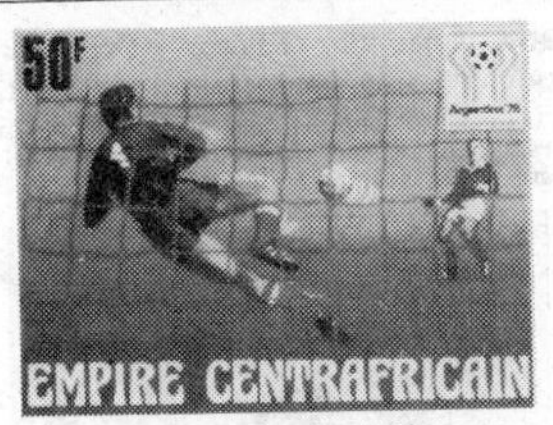

Shot on Goal—A97

Designs: 60fr, Heading ball in net. 100fr, Backfield defense. 200fr, Argentina '78 poster. 300fr, Mario Zagalo and stadium. 500fr, Ferenc Puskas.

1977, Nov. 18 Litho. *Perf. 13½*

303	A97	50fr multicolored	40	20
304	"	60fr "	50	25
305	"	100fr "	80	30
306	"	200fr "	1.60	65
307	"	300fr "	2.40	1.00
		Nos. 303-307 (5)	5.70	2.40

Souvenir Sheet

308	A97	500fr multicolored	4.00	1.85

World Soccer Championships, Argentina, June 1-25, 1978. No. 308 has multicolored margin showing Argentina '78 emblem, World Cup and Stadium. Size: 120x81mm.

Emperor Bokassa I, Central African Flag
A98

1977, Dec. 4 Litho. *Perf. 13½*

309	A98	40fr multicolored	30	25
310	"	60fr "	50	35
311	"	100fr "	80	60
312	"	150fr "	1.20	90
		Nos. 309-312, C188-C189 (6)	6.90	4.60

Coronation of Emperor Bokassa I, Dec. 4.

Lilium
A99

Electronic Tree, ITU Emblem
A100

Design: 10fr, Hibiscus.

1977 Litho. *Perf. 13½x14*

313	A99	5fr multicolored	5	3
314	"	10fr "	10	5

1977

315	A100	100fr blk., org. & brown	1.20	90

World Telecommunications Day.

Bible and People
A101

1977 Litho. *Perf. 14x13½*

316	A101	40fr multicolored	40	20

Bible Week.

People and Rotary Emblem
A102

1977

317	A102	60fr multicolored	60	30

Rotary Club of Bangui, 20th anniversary.

Holy Family, by Rubens
A103

Rubens Paintings: 150fr, Marie de Medicis. 200fr, Son of artist. 300fr, Neptune. 500fr, Marie de Medicis (different).

1978, Jan. 26

318	A103	60fr multicolored	50	25
319	"	150fr "	1.20	50
320	"	200fr "	1.60	65
321	"	300fr "	2.40	1.00

Souvenir Sheet

322	A103	500fr gold & multi.	5.00	1.85

Peter Paul Rubens (1577-1640), 400th birth anniversary. No. 322 contains one stamp; multicolored margin shows entire painting. Size: 89x116mm.

Rhinoceros—A104

Endangered Animals and Wildlife Fund Emblem: 50fr, Slender-nosed crocodile. 60fr, Leopard (vert.). 100fr, Giraffe (vert.). 200fr, Elephant. 300fr, Gorilla (vert.).

1978, Feb. 21 Litho. *Perf. 13½*

323	A104	40fr multicolored	30	15
324	"	50fr "	40	20
325	"	60fr "	50	25
326	"	100fr "	80	35
327	"	200fr "	1.60	65
328	"	300fr "	2.40	1.00
		Nos. 323-328 (6)	6.00	2.60

Bokassa Sports Palace
A105

Design: 60fr, Sports Palace, side view.

1978 *Perf. 14*

329	A105	40fr multicolored	32	25
330	"	60fr "	50	35

Automatic Telephone Exchange, Bangui—A106

1978

331	A106	40fr multicolored	40	20
332	"	60fr "	60	30

Diligence and Satellite—A107

Designs (UPU Emblem and): 50fr, Steam locomotive and communications via satellite. 60fr, Paddle-wheel steamer and ship-to-shore communication via satellite. 80fr, Old mail truck and satellite.

1978, May 17 *Perf. 13½*

333	A107	40fr multicolored	40	20
334	"	50fr "	50	25
335	"	60fr "	60	30
336	"	80fr "	80	40
		Nos. 333-336, C191-C192 (6)	5.30	2.65

Century of progress of posts and telecommunications.

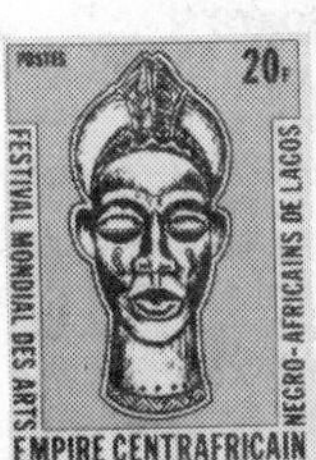

Mask
A108

Capt. Cook on "Endeavour"
A109

Designs: 30fr, Mask. 60fr, Women dancers (horiz.). 100fr, Men dancers (horiz.).

Perf. 13½x14, 14x13½

1978, July 11 Lithographed

337	A108	20fr blk. & yellow	20	10
338	"	30fr blk. & brt. bl.	30	15
339	"	60fr blk. & multi.	60	30
340	"	100fr " "	1.00	50

Black-African World Arts Festival, Lagos.

1978, Aug. 30 *Perf. 14½*

Designs: 60fr, Resolution off Hawaii (horiz.). 200fr, Hawaiians welcoming Capt. Cook (horiz.). 350fr, Masked rowers in Hawaiian boat (horiz.).

341	A109	60fr multicolored	60	30
342	"	80fr "	80	40
343	"	200fr "	2.00	1.00
344	"	350fr "	3.50	1.75

Capt. James Cook (1728-1779), explorer.

Dürer, Self-portrait
A110

Dürer Paintings: 80fr, The Four Apostles. 200fr, Virgin and Child. 350fr, Emperor Maximilian I.

1978, Oct. 24 Litho. *Perf. 13½*

345	A110	60fr multicolored	60	30
346	"	80fr "	80	40
347	"	200fr "	2.00	1.00
348	"	350fr "	3.50	1.75

Albrecht Dürer (1471-1528), German painter.

Tutankhamen's Gold Mask
A111

Treasures of Tutankhamen: 60fr, King and Queen, gold back panel of throne. 80fr, Gilt folding chair. 100fr, King wearing crowns of Upper and Lower Egypt, painted wood sculpture. 120fr, Lion's head. 150fr, Tutankhamen, wood stature. 180fr, Gold throne. 250fr, Gold miniature coffin.

1978, Nov. 22

349	A111	40fr multicolored	40	20
350	"	60fr "	60	30
351	"	80fr "	80	40
352	"	100fr "	1.00	50
353	"	120fr "	1.20	60
354	"	150fr "	1.50	75
355	"	180fr "	1.80	90
356	"	250fr "	2.50	1.25
		Nos. 349-356 (8)	9.80	4.90

Tutankhamen, c. 1358 B.C., King of Egypt.

Lenin at Smolny Institute
A112

Designs: 60fr, 200fr, 300fr, Various Lenin portraits. 100fr, Ulyanov family (horiz.). 150fr, Lenin, Cruiser "Aurora" and flag (horiz.). 500fr, "Aurora" and star.

1978, Nov. *Perf. 14*

357	A112	40fr multicolored	40	20
358	"	60fr "	60	30
359	"	100fr black & gold	1.00	50
360	"	150fr blk., gold & red	1.50	75
361	"	200fr multicolored	2.00	1.00
362	"	300fr "	3.00	1.50
		Nos. 357-362 (6)	8.50	4.25

Souvenir Sheet

363	A112	500fr multicolored	5.25	

60th anniversary of the Soviet Union. No. 363 has red marginal inscription and hammer and sickle emblem. Size: 78x110mm.

SEMI-POSTAL STAMPS

Central African Republic

Anti-Malaria Issue

Common Design Type

Perf. 12½x12

1962, Apr. 7 Engraved Unwmkd.

B1 CD108 25fr+5fr slate 70 70

Issued for the World Health Organization drive to eradicate malaria.

Freedom from Hunger Issue

Common Design Type

1963, Mar. 21 ***Perf. 13***

B2 CD112 25fr+5fr bister, Prus. green & brown 65 65

Guinea Fowl and Partridge
SP1

Designs: 10fr+5fr, Yellow-backed duiker and snail. 20fr+5fr, Elephant, tortoise and hippopotamus playing tug-of-war. 30fr+10fr, Cuckoo and tortoise. 50fr+20fr, Patas monkey and leopard.

1971, Feb. 9 Photo. ***Perf. 12½x12***

B3	SP1 5fr+5fr	multi.	1.20	60
B4	" 10fr+5fr	"	1.75	1.25
B5	" 20fr+5fr	"	2.50	1.75
B6	" 30fr+10fr	"	3.50	2.50
B7	" 50fr+20fr	"	7.00	5.00
	Nos. B3-B7 (5)		15.95	11.10

Lengué Dancer
SP2

Dancers: 40fr+10fr, Le Lengué. 100fr+40fr, Teke. 140fr+40fr, Englabolo.

1971 Lithographed ***Perf. 13***

B8	SP2 20fr+5fr	multi.	35	20
B9	" 40fr+10fr	"	65	40
B10	" 100fr+40fr	"	1.75	90
B11	" 140fr+40fr	"	2.25	1.20

AIR POST STAMPS

Central African Republic

Abyssinian Roller—AP1

Birds: 200fr, Gold Coast touraco. 500fr, African fish eagle.

Engraved

1960, Sept. 3 ***Perf. 13*** **Unwmkd.**

C1 AP1 100fr violet blue, orange brown & emerald 1.50 65
C2 " 200fr multicolored 3.00 1.25
C3 " 500fr Prussian blue, emerald & red brown 7.50 3.00

Olympic Games Issue

French Equatorial Africa No. C37 Surcharged in Red Like Chad No. C1.

1960, Dec. 15 ***Perf. 13***

C4 AP8 250fr on 500fr greenish black, black & slate 6.50 6.50

Issued to commemorate the 17th Olympic Games, Rome, Aug. 25–Sept. 11.

Air Afrique Issue

Common Design Type

1962, Feb. 17 ***Perf. 13*** **Unwmkd.**

C5 CD107 50fr violet, lt. green & red brown 75 70

Founding of Air Afrique airline.

Pole Vault
AP1a

1962, July 21 Photo. ***Perf. 12x12½***

C6 AP1a 100fr green, yellow, brn. & blk. 1.50 1.00

Abidjan games.

Red-faced Lovebirds—AP2

Bird: 50fr, Great blue touraco.

1962–63 Engraved ***Perf. 13***

C7 AP2 50fr slate green, blue green & orange 75 35
C8 " 250fr multi. ('63) 3.75 2.10

Issue dates: 50fr, Nov. 15, 1962; 250fr, Mar. 11, 1963.

Runner with Torch and Palm Branch
AP3

1962, Dec. 24

C9 AP3 100fr gray grn., brn. & carmine 1.50 1.00

Tropics Cup Games, Bangui, Dec. 24–31.

African Postal Union Issue

Common Design Type

1963, Sept. 8 Photo. ***Perf. 12½***

C10 CD114 85fr emerald, ocher & red 1.25 85

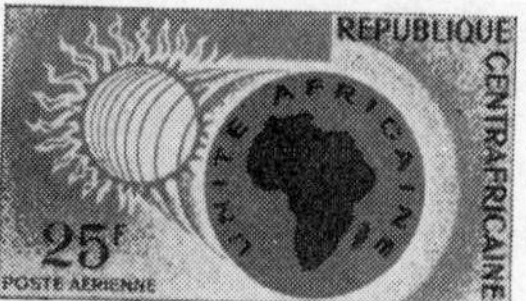

Sun Shining on Africa—AP4

1963, Nov. 9 ***Perf. 13x12***

C11 AP4 25fr blue, yellow & violet blue 40 30

Issued for African unity.

Europafrica Issue

Common Design Type

1963, Nov. 30 ***Perf. 12x13***

C12 CD116 50fr ultra., yellow & dk. brown 1.35 1.10

Diesel Engine—AP5

Designs: Various Locomotives; 25fr, 50fr, vertical.

1963, Dec. 1 Engraved ***Perf. 13***

C13 AP5 20fr brown, claret & dark green 30 30
C14 " 25fr brn., bl. & choc. 40 30
C15 " 50fr brown, red lilac & violet 80 60
C16 " 100fr brown, green & dull red brn. 1.65 1.20
a. Min. sheet of 4 3.25 3.25

Bangui-Douala railroad project.
No. C16a contains one each of Nos. C13–C16. Size: 189x99mm.

Bangui Cathedral—AP6

1964, Jan. 21 ***Perf. 13*** **Unwmkd.**

C17 AP6 100fr yel. grn., org. brown & bl. 1.50 90

Radar Tracking Station and WMO Emblem—AP7

1964, Mar. 23 Engr. ***Perf. 13***

C18 AP7 50fr orange brown, blue & purple 75 65

World Meteorological Day.

Map and Presidents of Chad, Congo, Gabon and Central African Republic
AP8

1964, June 23 Photo. ***Perf. 12½***

C19 AP8 100fr multicolored 1.50 1.00

Issued to commemorate the 5th anniversary of the Conference of Chiefs of State of Equatorial Africa.

Javelin Throwers—AP9

Designs: 50fr, Basketball game. 100fr, Four runners. 250fr, Swimmers, one in water.

1964, June 23 Engraved ***Perf. 13***

C20 AP9 25fr green, dk. brown & lt. vio. blue 40 20
C21 " 50fr blk., car. & grn. 75 40
C22 " 100fr green, violet bl. & dk. brn. 1.50 80
C23 " 250fr green, black & carmine 3.75 2.25
a. Min. sheet 6.50 6.50

Issued for the 18th Olympic Games, Tokyo, Oct. 10–25, 1964.
No. C23a contains one each of Nos. C20–C23. Size: 128½x99mm.

John F. Kennedy
AP10

1964, July 4 Photo. ***Perf. 12½***

C24 AP10 100fr lilac, brown & black 1.65 1.35
a. Min. sheet of 4 7.50 7.50

Issued in memory of President John F. Kennedy.

Industrial Symbols, Maps of Africa and Europe
AP11

1964, Dec. 19 ***Perf. 13x12*** **Unwmkd.**

C25 AP11 50fr yellow, org. & green 75 70

See note after Cameroun No. 402.

International Cooperation Year Emblem—AP12

1965, Jan. 2 ***Perf. 13***

C26 AP12 100fr red brn., yel. & blue 1.50 90

International Cooperation Year.

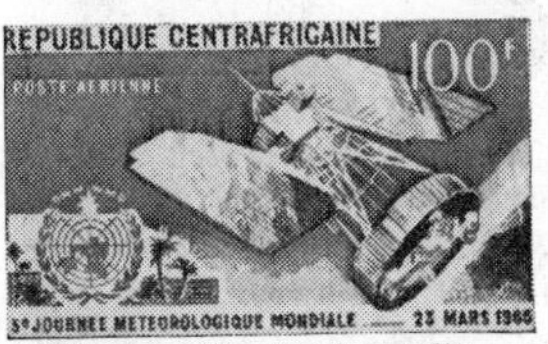

Nimbus Weather Satellite
AP13

1965, Mar. 23 Engraved *Perf. 13*

C27 AP13 100fr orange brn., ultra. & blk. 1.60 1.00

Fifth World Meteorological Day.

Lincoln and Statue of Liberty
AP14

1965, Apr. 15 Photo. *Perf. 13*

C28 AP14 100fr bluish green, indigo & bister 1.60 90

Centenary of death of Abraham Lincoln.

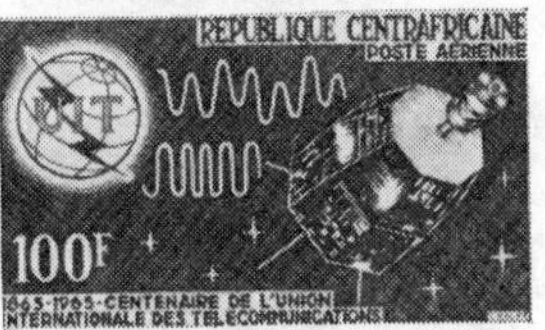

ITU Emblem and Relay Satellite
AP15

1965, May 17 Engr. *Perf. 13*

C29 AP15 100fr dk. grn., vio. blue & brn. 1.60 90

Issued to commemorate the centenary of the International Telecommunication Union.

"Housing," New Home in Village
AP16

1965, June 10 Unwmkd.

C30 AP16 100fr ultra., brn. & slate green 1.50 90

See note after No. 52.

Europafrica Issue

Tractor, Cotton Picker, Cotton, Sun and Emblem
AP17

1965, Nov. 7 Photo. *Perf. 12x13*

C31 AP17 50fr multicolored 70 50

See note after Chad No. C11.

Mercury by Antoine Coysevox AP18 — Father Holding Sick Child AP19

1965, Dec. 5 Engraved *Perf. 13*

C32 AP18 100fr red brown, bl. & blk. 1.60 1.00

Issued to commemorate the fifth anniversary of Central African Republic's admission to the Universal Postal Union.

1965, Dec. 12

Design: 100fr, Mother and child.

C33 AP19 50fr dk. blue, carm. & black 75 50

C34 " 100fr red brown, red & brt. grn. 1.50 1.00

Issued to honor the Red Cross.

Air Afrique Issue
Common Design Type

1966, Aug. 31 Photo. *Perf. 13*

C35 CD123 25fr blue, black & lemon 40 15

Issued to commemorate the introduction of DC-8F planes by Air Afrique.

Surveyor Spacecraft on Moon
AP20

Designs: No. C37, Luna 9 on Moon and Earth. 200fr, Rocket take-off, Jules Verne's "From the Earth to the Moon."

1966, Oct. 24 Photo. *Perf. 12x12½*

C36 AP20 130fr multi. 2.00 1.20

C37 " 130fr " 2.00 1.20

C38 " 200fr " 3.00 1.80

a. Souv. sheet of 3 8.00 8.00

Issued to commemorate the conquest of the Moon. No. C38a contains one each of Nos. C36–C38, black marginal inscription and control number. Size: 132x158mm.

Eugene A. Cernan, Gemini 9 and Agena Rocket
AP21

Design: No. C40, Pavel R. Popovich and rocket.

1966, Nov. 14 Photo. *Perf. 13*

C39 AP21 50fr multicolored 75 35

C40 " 50fr " 75 35

Issued to honor American and Russian astronauts.

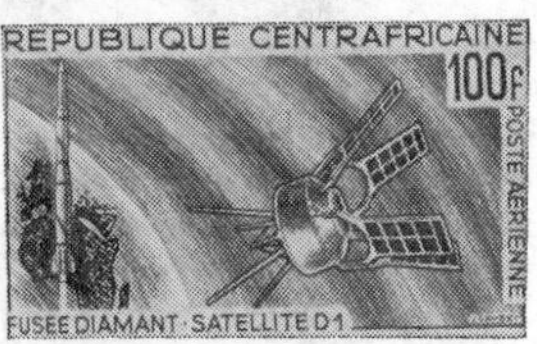

Diamant Rocket, D-1 Satellite and Globe with Map of Africa
AP22

1966, Nov. 14 Engraved

C41 AP22 100fr brt. rose lilac & brown 1.60 70

Issued to commemorate the launching of France's first satellite, Nov. 26, 1965, and the launching of the D-1 satellite, Feb. 17, 1966.

Exchange of Agricultural and Industrial Products between Africa and Europe
AP23

1966, Dec. 5 Photo. *Perf. 12x13*

C42 AP23 50fr multicolored 75 45

See note after Gabon No. C46.

No. C35 Surcharged

1967, May 8 *Perf. 13*

C43 CD123 5fr on 25fr multi. 15 10

The surcharge obliterates the "2" of the original 25fr denomination.

DC-8F Over M'Poko Airport, Bangui—AP24

1967, July 3 Engraved *Perf. 13*

C44 AP24 100fr slate, dk. grn. & brown 1.60 75

View of EXPO '67, Montreal
AP25

1967, July 17

C45 AP25 100fr vio. blue, dk. red brown & dk. grn. 1.50 70

Issued to commemorate the International Exposition, EXPO '67, Montreal, Apr. 28–Oct. 27.

African Postal Union Issue, 1967
Common Design Type

1967, Sept. 9 Engraved *Perf. 13*

C46 CD124 100fr brt. grn., dk. carm. rose & plum 1.50 70

Potez 25 TOE—AP26

Designs: 200fr, Junkers 52. 500fr, Caravelle 11R.

1967, Nov. 24 Engraved *Perf. 13*

C47 AP26 100fr brt. bl., brn. & gray grn. 1.60 65

C48 " 200fr dk. brn., grn. & indigo 2.75 1.25

C49 " 500fr blue, indigo & org. brn. 7.25 4.00

Presidents Boganda and Bokassa
AP27

1967, Dec. 1 Photo. *Perf. 12½*

C50 AP27 130fr org., red, lt. bl. & blk. 2.00 1.35

9th anniversary of the republic.

Pres. Jean Bedel Bokassa
AP28

1968, Jan. 1 *Perf. 12½x12*

C51 AP28 30fr multicolored 50 30

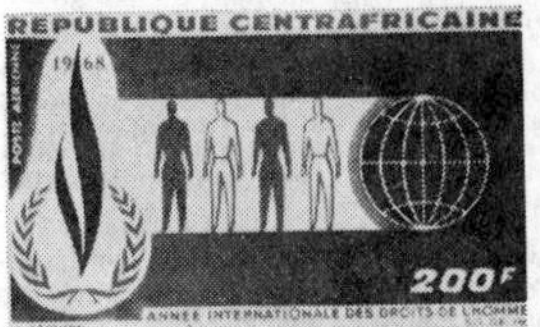

Human Rights Flame, Men and Globe—AP29

1968, Mar. 26 Photo. *Perf. 13*

C52 AP29 200fr brt. grn., vio. & verm. 3.00 1.50

International Human Rights Year.

Man, WHO Emblem and Tsetse Fly—AP30

1968, Apr. 8 Engraved

C53 AP30 200fr multicolored 3.00 1.50

Issued to commemorate the 20th anniversary of the World Health Organization.

Javelin Thrower

AP31

Space Probe Landing on Venus

AP32

Design: No. C55, Downhill skier.

1968, Apr. 16 Engraved *Perf. 13*

C54 AP31 200fr choc., dk. red & Prus. bl. 3.00 1.60
C55 " 200fr dk. red, choc. & Prus. bl. 3.00 1.60

The 1968 Olympic Games.

1968, Apr. 23

C56 AP32 100fr ultra., dk. & brt. green 1.50 70

Issued to commemorate the Venus exploration by Venus IV, Oct. 18, 1967.

Marie Curie and "Cancer Destroyed"—AP33

1968, Apr. 30

C57 AP33 100fr violet, brt. bl. & brn. 1.50 70

Issued to commemorate the centenary of the birth of Marie Curie (1867–1934), scientist.

Nos. C36–C37 and C47–C48 Surcharged with New Value

Photogravure; Engraved

1968, Sept. 16 *Perf. 12x12½, 13*

C58	AP20	5fr on 130fr multi.	10	8
C59	AP26	10fr on 100fr "	15	10
C60	"	20fr on 200fr "	30	12
C61	AP20	50fr on 130fr "	80	55

On No. C58 the old denomination has been obliterated with "XIX", on No. C61 the obliteration is a rectangular bar. On Nos. C59–C60 the last zero of the old denomination has been obliterated with a black square.

River Boat Type of Regular Issue

Craft: 100fr, "Pie X," Bangui, 1894. 130fr, "Ballay," Bangui, 1891.

1968, Dec. 10 Engraved *Perf. 13*

Size: 48x27mm.

C62 A37 100fr blue, dark brn. & olive 1.50 70
C63 " 130fr brt. pink, slate grn. & slate 2.00 1.00

PHILEXAFRIQUE Issue

Mme. de Sévigné, French School, 17th Century

AP34

1968, Dec. 17 Photo. *Perf. 12½*

C64 AP34 100fr brn. & multi. 1.60 1.40

Issued to publicize PHILEXAFRIQUE, Philatelic Exhibition in Abidjan, Feb. 14–23. Printed with alternating brown label.

2nd PHILEXAFRIQUE Issue

Common Design Type

Design: 50fr, Ubangi No. J16, cotton field and Pres. Bokassa.

1969, Feb. 14 Engraved *Perf. 13*

C65 CD128 50fr bister brn., blk. & dk. green 90 90

Issued to commemorate the opening of PHILEXAFRIQUE, Abidjan, Feb. 14.

Holocerina Angulata Aur.—AP35

Butterflies and Moths: 20fr, Nudaurelia dione fabr. 30fr, Eustera troglophylla hamp. (vert.). 50fr, Aurivillius aratus west. 100fr, Epiphora albida druce.

1969, Feb. 25 Photogravure

C66	AP35	10fr yellow & multi.	15	6
C67	"	20fr violet & multi.	30	15
C68	"	30fr multicolored	45	20
C69	"	50fr "	85	40
C70	"	100fr "	1.65	80
		Nos. C66–C70 (5)	3.40	1.61

Boxing—AP36

Sport Design: 100fr, Basketball.

1969, Mar. 18 Photo. *Perf. 13*

C71 AP36 50fr multicolored 75 35
C72 " 100fr yel. & multi. 1.50 60

Apollo 8 over Moonscape—AP37

1969, May 27 Photo. *Perf. 13*

C73 AP37 200fr dp. blue, gray & yellow 3.00 1.35

Issued to commemorate the U.S. Apollo 8 mission, the first men in orbit around the moon, Dec. 21–27, 1968.

Market Cross, Nuremberg, and Toys—AP38

1969, June 3

C74 AP38 100fr black, bright rose lilac & emerald 1.50 1.00

Issued to publicize the International Toy Fair in Nuremberg, Germany.

Napoleon as First Consul, by Anne-Louis Girodet-Trioson

AP39

Designs: 130fr, Napoleon meeting Emperor Francis II, by Antoine Jean Gros (horiz.). 200fr, The Wedding of Napoleon and Marie-Louise, by Georges Rouget (horiz.).

1969, Nov. 4 Photo. *Perf. 12½*

C75 AP39 100fr multicolored 1.75 1.25
C76 " 130fr brn. & multi. 2.50 1.50
C77 " 200fr multicolored 4.00 3.00

Issued to commemorate the bicentenary of the birth of Napoleon Bonaparte (1769–1821).

Pres. Bokassa, Map of Africa and Flag

AP40

Franklin Delano Roosevelt

AP41

1970, Jan. 1 *Die-cut Perf. 10½*

Embossed on Gold Foil

C78 AP40 2000fr gold 25.00 25.00

1970 Lithographed *Perf. 13½x14*

Design: No. C80, Lenin.

C79 AP41 100fr gold, yellow, black & bl. 1.35 80
C80 " 100fr gold, yellow, blk. & red 1.25 70

No. C79 issued to commemorate the 25th anniversary of the death of Pres. Franklin Delano Roosevelt (1882–1945); Nos. C80 commemorates the centenary of the birth of Lenin (1870–1924).

Issue dates: No. C79, Apr. 29; No. C80, Apr. 22.

No. C73 Overprinted in Red:

ATTERRISSAGE
d'APOLLO 12
19 novembre 1969

1970, June 1 Photogravure *Perf. 13*

C81 AP37 200fr multicolored 8.50 6.50

Issued to commemorate the moon landing mission of Apollo 12, Nov. 14–24, 1969.

AP42

1970, Sept. 15 Litho. *Perf. 10*

C82 AP42 200fr triptych 2.50 1.25
a. 100fr *Dancer* 1.25 50
b. 100fr *Still life* 1.25 50

Issued to publicize Knokphila 70, 6th International Philatelic Exhibition at Knokke, Belgium, July 4–10. The two stamps and violet blue label are printed se-tenant and imperf. between stamps and label.

Sericulture Type of Regular Issue

1970, Sept. 15 *Perf. 10*

C83 A45 140fr multicolored 2.00 1.10

Issued to publicize Operation Bokassa, a plan for the development of the country.

C.A.R. Flag, EXPO Emblem and Pavilion

AP43

1970, Dec. 18 Litho. *Perf. 13½x13*

C84 AP43 200fr red & multi. 2.75 1.35

International Exposition EXPO '70, Osaka, Japan.

Soccer

AP44

1970, Dec. 8 *Perf. 13x13½*

C85 AP44 200fr multi. 2.75 1.35

World Soccer Championships, Mexico, May 30–June 21, 1970.

Dove

AP45

1970, Dec. 31

C86 AP45 200fr blue, yellow & black 2.75 1.35

25th anniversary of the United Nations.

Presidents Mobutu, Bokassa, and Tombalbaye—AP46

1971, Jan. 10

C87 AP46 140fr multicolored 2.00 90

Return of Central African Republic to the United States of Central Africa which also includes Congo Democratic Republic and Chad.

Satellite over Globe—AP47

1971, May 17 Photo. *Perf. 12½*

C88 AP47 100fr multicolored 1.35 65

3rd World Telecommunications Day.

African Postal Union Issue, 1971

Common Design Type

Design: 100fr, Carved head and UAMPT building, Brazzaville, Congo.

1971, Nov. 13 Photo. *Perf. 13x13½*

C89 CD135 100fr blue & multi. 1.35 65

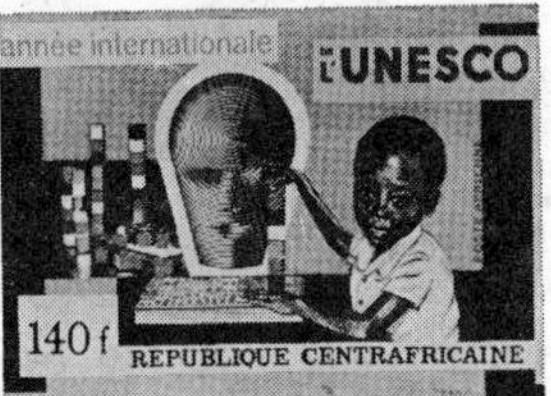

Child and Education Year Emblem—AP48

1971, Nov. 11 Litho. *Perf. 13x13½*

C90 AP48 140fr multicolored 1.75 75

25th anniversary of the United Nations Educational, Scientific and Cultural Organization (UNESCO).

Fight Against Cancer AP49

Gamal Abdel Nasser AP50

1971, Nov. 20 Photo. *Perf. 12½*

C91 AP49 100fr grn. & multi. 1.35 60

1972, Jan. 15

C92 AP50 100fr dk. red, black & bister 1.25 60

In memory of Gamal Abdel Nasser (1918–1970), president of Egypt.

Olympic Rings and Boxing—AP51

Design: No. C94, Track and Olympic rings (vert.).

1972, May 26 Engraved *Perf. 13*

C93 AP51 100fr brn. orange & sepia 1.50 60

C94 " 100fr green & vio. 1.50 60

a. Miniature sheet of 2 3.00 3.00

20th Olympic Games, Munich, Aug. 26–Sept. 10. No. C94a contains 2 stamps similar to Nos. C93–C94, but in changed colors. The boxing stamp is red lilac and green, the track stamp ocher and red lilac. Size: 129x98mm.

Tiling's Mail Rocket, 1931, and Mailman—AP52

Designs: 50fr, DC-3 and mailman riding camel (vert.). 150fr, Sirio satellite and rocket (vert.). 200fr, Intelsat 4 and rocket.

1972, Aug. 12

C95 AP52 40fr blue, orange & indigo 50 25

C96 " 50fr bl., brn. & org. 60 25

C97 " 150fr brown, orange & gray 1.75 80

C98 " 200fr brown, blue & orange 2.25 1.00

a. Souv. sheet of 4 5.25 5.25

Centraphilex 1972, Central African Philatelic Exhibition, Bangui. No. C98a contains one each of Nos. C95–C98. Brown marginal inscription. Size: 200x99½mm.

Europafrica Issue

Arrows with Symbols of Agriculture and Industry AP53

1972, Nov. 17 Litho. *Perf. 13*

C99 AP53 100fr multicolored 1.10 60

Nos. C93–C94, C94a Overprinted

a. POIDS-MOYEN / LEMECHEV MEDAILLE D'OR

b. LONGUER / WILLIAMS MEDAILLE D'OR

1972, Nov. 24 Engraved

C100 AP51 (*a*) 100fr brn. org. & sepia 1.35 60

C101 " (*b*) 100fr green & violet 1.35 60

a. Miniature sheet of 2 3.00 3.00

Gold Medal Winners in 20th Olympic Games: Viatschesiav Lemechev, USSR, middleweight boxing (C100); Randy Williams, USA, broad jump (C101).

Lunar Rover and Module—AP54

1972, Dec. 18 Engr. *Perf. 13*

C102 AP54 100fr slate green, blue & gray 1.20 65

Apollo 16 U.S. moon mission, Apr. 15–27, 1972.

Virgin and Child, by Francesco Pesellino AP55

Design: 150fr, Adoration of the Child with St. John the Baptist and St. Romuald, by Fra Filippo Lippi.

1972, Dec. 25 Photogravure

C103 AP55 100fr gold & multi. 1.25 65

C104 " 150fr gold & multi. 1.85 1.00

Christmas 1972.

Parthenon, Athens, Spyridon Louis, Marathon, 1896—AP56

Designs (Olympic Rings and): 40fr, Arc de Triomphe, Paris, H. Barrelet, single scull, 1900. 50fr, Old Courthouse and Western Arch, St. Louis, Myer Prinstein, triple jump, 1904. 100fr, Tower, London, Henry Taylor, swimming, 1908. 150fr, City Hall, Stockholm, Greco-Roman wrestling, 1912.

1972, Dec. 28 Engraved

C105 AP56 30fr brt. green, mag. & brn. 40 12

C106 " 40fr violet blue, emerald & brown 50 18

C107 " 50fr carmine rose, violet blue & Prus. bl. 60 25

C108 " 100fr slate, red lilac & brown 1.25 55

C109 " 150fr red lilac, blk. & Prus. bl. 1.85 90

Nos. C105–C109 (5) 4.60 2.00

Olympic Games 1896–1912.

WHO Emblem, Surgeon and Nurse—AP57

1973, Apr. 7 Photo. *Perf. 13*

C110 AP57 100fr multi. 1.25 70

World Health Organization, 25th anniversary.

World Map, Arrows, Waves AP58

1973, May 17 Litho. *Perf. 12½*

C111 AP58 200fr lt. blue, dp. orange & black 2.00 1.20

5th International Telecommunications Day.

Head and City Hall, Brussels AP58a

1973, Sept. 17 Engr. *Perf. 13*

C112 AP58a 100fr pur., ocher & brown 1.25 70

African Weeks, Brussels, Sept. 15–30, 1973.

Europafrica Issue

Map of Central African Republic with Industry and Agriculture, Young Man—AP59

1973, Sept. 28 Engraved *Perf. 13*

C113 AP59 100fr sepia, green & orange 1.10 70

Carrier Pigeon with Letter and UPU Emblem—AP60

1973, Oct. 9 Photogravure

C114 AP60 200fr multi. 2.25 1.40

Universal Postal Union Day.

WMO Emblem, Weather Map—AP61

1973, Oct. 20 Engraved *Perf. 13*

C115 AP61 150fr brt. ultra. & slate grn. 1.50 75

Centenary of international meteorological cooperation.

Copernicus, Heliocentric System
AP62

1973, Nov. 2 Photogravure

C116 AP62 100fr gold & multi. 1.15 70

500th anniversary of the birth of Nicolaus Copernicus (1473–1543), Polish astronomer.

Pres. Bokassa
AP63

Pres. Bokassa AP64 — Rocket Launch and Apollo 17 Badge AP65

1973, Nov. 30 Photo. *Perf. 12½*

C117 AP63 50fr multicolored 50 35
C118 AP64 100fr " 1.00 70

1973, Dec. 15 Engraved *Perf. 13*

Designs: 65fr, Capsule over moonscape (horiz.). 100fr, Moon landing (horiz.). 150fr, Astronauts on moon. 200fr, Splash-down with parachutes and badge.

C119 AP65 50fr verm., gray grn. & brn. 50 40
C120 " 65fr dk. brn., brn. red & slate green 60 50
C121 " 100fr verm., slate & choc. 1.00 70
C122 " 150fr brn., olive & slate grn. 1.40 1.00
C123 " 200fr red, blue & slate grn. 2.00 1.40
Nos. C119–C123 (5) 5.50 4.00

Apollo 17 U.S. moon mission, Dec. 7–19, 1972.

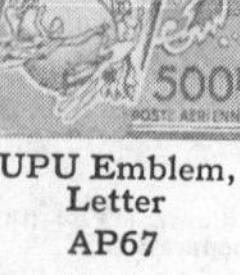

St. Teresa AP66 — UPU Emblem, Letter AP67

1973, Dec. 25

C124 AP66 500fr vio. blue & greenish blue 5.00 3.00

Centenary of the birth of St. Teresa of the Infant Jesus, the Little Flower (1873–1897), Carmelite nun.

1974, Oct. 9 Engraved *Perf. 13*

C125 AP67 500fr multi. 5.00 3.50

Centenary of Universal Postal Union.

Presidents and Flags of Cameroun, CAR, Gabon and Congo
AP68

1974, Dec. 8 Photogravure *Perf. 13*

C126 AP68 100fr gold & multi. 90 65

See note after Cameroun No. 595.

Marshal Bokassa
AP69

Design: 100fr, Bokassa in Marshal's uniform with cape.

1975, Feb. 22 Photo. *Perf. 13*

C127 AP69 50fr tan & multi. 40 30
C128 " 100fr " " 80 60

Jean Bedel Bokassa, President for Life and Marshal of the Republic.

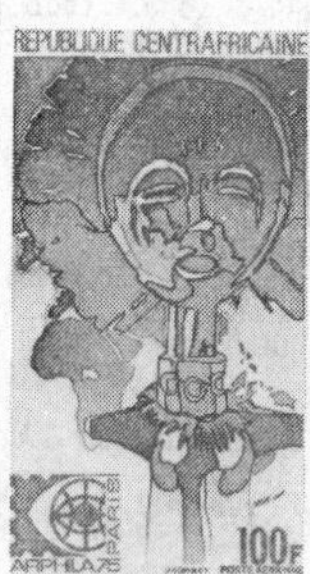

Mask, Map of Africa, Arphila Emblem AP70 — Albert Schweitzer and Dugout, Lambarene AP71

1975, Aug. 25 Engr. *Perf. 13*

C129 AP70 100fr brt. bl., red brn. & red. 1.00 50

ARPHILA 75 International Philatelic Exhibition, Paris, June 6–16.

1975, Sept. 30 Engr. *Perf. 13*

C130 AP71 200fr black, ultra. & olive 2.00 1.00

Dr. Albert Schweitzer (1875–1965), medical missionary and musician.

Pres. Bokassa's Houseboat, Bow—AP72

Design: 40fr, Pres. Bokassa's houseboat, stern.

1976, Feb. 22 Litho. *Perf. 13*

C131 AP72 30fr multicolored 25 15
C132 " 40fr " 35 20

Monument to Franco-CAR Cooperation
AP73

Presidents and Flags of France and CAR
AP74

1976, Mar. 5

C133 AP73 100fr multi. 80 50
C134 AP74 200fr " 1.60 1.00

Official visit of Pres. Valery Giscard d'Estaing to Central African Republic, Mar. 5–8.

Apollo Soyuz Type, 1976

Designs: 100fr, Soyuz space ship. 200fr, Apollo space ship. 300fr, Astronauts and cosmonauts in cabin. 500fr, Apollo and Soyuz after link-up.

1976, June 14 Litho. *Perf. 14x13½*

C135 A90 100fr multicolored 80 30
C136 " 200fr " 1.60 70
C137 " 300fr " 2.40 1.00

Souvenir Sheet

C138 A90 500fr multicolored 4.00 1.85

Apollo Soyuz space test project, Russo-American cooperation, launched July 15, link-up July 17. No. C138 has multicolored margin showing Apollo Soyuz insignia. Size: 103½x78mm.

French Hussar
AP75

Uniforms: 125fr, Scottish "Black Watch." 150fr, German dragoon. 200fr, British grenadier. 250fr, American ranger. 450fr, American dragoon.

1976, July 4 *Perf. 13½*

C139 AP75 100fr multi. 80 30
C140 " 125fr " 1.00 50
C141 " 150fr " 1.20 60
C142 " 200fr " 1.60 70
C143 " 250fr " 1.90 90
Nos. C139–C143 (5) 6.50 3.00

Souvenir Sheet

C144 AP75 450fr multi. 3.75 1.65

American Bicentennial. No. C144 has U.S. Bicentennial emblem in tri-color in margin, black inscription. Size: 118x80 mm.

Acherontia Atropos—AP76

Design: 100fr, Papilio nireus and heniocha marnois.

1976, Sept. 20 Litho. *Perf. 12½*

C145 AP76 50fr multicolored 40 25
C146 " 100fr " 80 50

Olympic Winners Type, 1976

Designs: 100fr, Women's figure skating, Dorothy Hamill (vert.). 200fr, Ice skating, Alexander Gorshkov and Ludmilla Pakhomova. 300fr, Men's figure skating, John Curry (vert.). 500fr, Down-hill skiing, Rosi Mittermaier (vert.).

1976, Sept. 23 Litho. *Perf. 13½*

C147 A92 100fr multicolored 80 30
C148 " 200fr " 1.60 70
C149 " 300fr " 2.40 1.00

Souvenir Sheet

C150 A92 500fr multicolored 4.00 1.85

12th Winter Olympic Games winners, Innsbruck. No. C150 has multicolored margin showing Olympic flags and eternal flame, black inscriptions. Size: 103x78 mm.

Viking Mars Type, 1976

Designs: 100fr, Phases of Mars landing. 200fr, Viking descending on Mars (horiz.). 300fr, Viking probe. 500fr, Viking flight to Mars (horiz.).

1976, Dec.

C151 A93 100fr multicolored 80 30
C152 " 200fr " 1.60 70
C153 " 300fr " 2.40 1.00

Souvenir Sheet

C154 A93 500fr multicolored 4.00 1.85

Viking Mars project. No. C154 has multicolored margin showing flight control room. Size: 102x77mm.

Empire

Stamps of 1973–76 Overprinted with Bars and "EMPIRE CENTRAFRICAIN" in Black, Violet Blue or Gold

Printing and Perforations as Before

1977, March

Multicolored

C155 AP68 100fr (#C126;B) 90 70
C156 AP70 100fr (#C129;VB) 90 70
C157 AP73 100fr (#C133;G) 90 70
C158 AP71 200fr (#C130; B) 2.00 1.50
C159 AP67 500fr (#C125;B) 5.50 4.00
Nos. C155–C159 (5) 10.20 7.60

No bar on No. C159.

Stamps of 1976 Overprinted "EMPIRE CENTRAFRICAIN" in Black on Silver Panel

1977, Apr. 1

C160 AP76 50fr multi. (#C145) 50 30
C161 A90 100fr " (#C135) 90 70
C162 AP75 100fr " (#C139) 80 60
C163 AP76 100fr " (#C146) 80 60

C164 A92 100fr multi. (⋇C147) 80 60
C165 A93 100fr " (⋇C151) 80 60
C166 AP75 125fr " (⋇C140) 1.00 80
C167 " 150fr " (⋇C141) 1.20 90
C168 A90 200fr " (⋇C136) 2.00 1.50
C169 AP75 200fr " (⋇C142) 1.60 1.20
C170 A92 200fr " (⋇C148) 1.60 1.20
C171 A93 200fr " (⋇C152) 1.60 1.20
C172 AP75 250fr " (⋇C143) 2.00 1.50
C173 A90 300fr " (⋇C137) 3.00 2.25
C174 A92 300fr " (⋇C149) 2.50 1.85
C175 A93 300fr " (⋇C153) 2.50 1.85
Nos. C160–C175 (16) 23.60 17.65

Souvenir Sheets

C176 AP75 450fr multi. (⋇C144) 3.75 3.75
C177 A90 500fr " (⋇C138) 4.00 4.00
C178 A92 500fr " (⋇C150) 4.00 4.00
C179 A93 500fr " (⋇C154) 4.00 4.00

Overprint on type AP75 is in upper and lower case letters.

Nobel Prize Type, 1977

Designs: 100fr, Rudyard Kipling. 200fr, Ernest Hemingway. 300fr, Luigi Pirandello. 500fr, Rabindranath Tagore.

1977, Apr. 1 Litho. *Perf. 13½*

C180 A94 100fr multicolored 80 30
C181 " 200fr " 1.60 70
C182 " 300fr " 2.50 1.00

Souvenir Sheet

C183 A94 500fr multicolored 4.00 1.85

Nobel Prize winners. No. C183 has multicolored margin with black inscription. Size: 118x80mm.

Zeppelin Type of 1977

Designs: 100fr, Germany No. C42 and North Pole. 200fr, Germany No. C44 and Science and Industry Building, Chicago. 300fr, Germany No. C35 and Brandenburg Gate, Berlin. 500fr, U.S. No. C14 and U.S. Capitol, Washington, D.C.

1977, Apr. 11 Litho. *Perf. 11*

C184 A95 100fr multicolored 80 30
C185 " 200fr " 1.60 70
C186 " 300fr " 2.40 1.00

Souvenir Sheet

C187 A95 500fr multicolored 4.00 1.85

75th anniversary of Zeppelin. No. C187 has multicolored margin showing early Zeppelin and 15 Zeppelin stamps from various countries. Size: 129x90mm.

Bokassa Type of 1977

1977, Dec. 4 Litho. *Perf. 13½*

C188 A98 200fr multicolored 1.60 1.00
C189 " 300fr " 2.50 1.50
a. Souvenir sheet, 500fr 4.00 3.00

Coronation of Emperor Bokassa I, Dec. 4. No. C189a contains a horizontal stamp in similar design; multicolored margin with eagle and government buildings. Size: 112x80mm. A 2500fr gold embossed horizontal stamp in similar design exists.

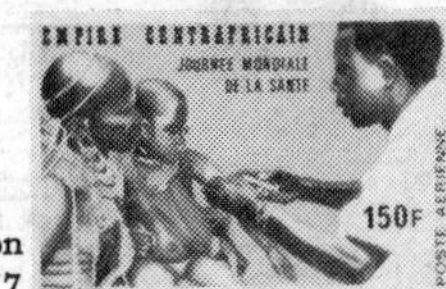

Vaccination AP77

1977 Litho. *Perf. 14x13½*

C190 AP77 150fr multi. 1.50 75

World Health Day.

Communications Type of 1978

Designs: 100fr, Balloon and spaceships docking in space. 200fr, Hydrofoil and Concorde. 500fr, Tom-tom and Zeppelin.

1978, May 17 Litho. *Perf. 13½*

C191 A107 100fr multi. 1.00 50
C192 " 200fr " 2.00 1.00

Souvenir Sheet

C193 A107 500fr multi. 5.50 3.50

Century of progress of posts and telecommunications. No. C193 contains one stamp (53x35mm.); multicolored margin shows allegory of posts. Size: 104x70mm.

Clement Ader and his Plane—AP78

Designs: 50fr, Wilbur and Orville Wright and plane. 60fr, John W. Alcock, Arthur W. Brown and plane. 100fr, Alan Cobham and plane 150fr, Claude Dornier and hydroplane. 500fr, Wilbur and Orville Wright and plane.

1978, Sept. 19 *Perf. 14*

C194 AP78 40fr multicolored 40 20
C195 " 50fr " 50 25
C196 " 60fr " 60 30
C197 " 100fr " 1.00 50
C198 " 150fr " 1.50 75
Nos. C194–C198 (5) 4.00 2.00

Souvenir Sheet

C199 AP78 500fr multi. 5.50

History of aviation. No. C199 has multicolored margin showing Concorde. Size: 116x80mm.

Philexafrique II—Essen Issue

Common Design Types

Designs: No. C200, Crocodile and Central African Rep. No. C3. No. C201, Birds and Mecklenburg-Schwerin No. 1.

1978, Nov. 1 Litho. *Perf. 12½*

C200 CD138 100fr multi. 1.00 50
C201 CD139 100fr " 1.00 50

Nos. C200–C201 printed se-tenant.

AIR POST SEMI-POSTAL STAMPS

Central African Republic

Isis of Kalabsha SPAP1

Engraved

1964, March 7 *Perf. 13* Unwmkd.

CB1 SPAP1 25fr+10fr olive, ultra. & brt. pink 1.00 1.00
CB2 " 50fr+10fr dk. bl. green, olive & red brown 1.50 1.50
CB3 " 100fr+10fr olive gray, lilac & maroon 2.50 2.50

Issued to publicize the UNESCO world campaign to save historic monuments in Nubia.

African Infants and Globe—SPAP2

1971, Dec. 11 Litho. *Perf. 13x13½*

CB4 SPAP2 140fr+50fr multi. 2.50 1.50

25th anniversary of the United Nations International Children's Fund (UNICEF), and Children's Day.

POSTAGE DUE STAMPS

Central African Republic

Sternotomis Virescens—D1

Beetles: No. J2, Sternotomis gama. No. J3, Augosoma centaurus. No. J4, Phosphorus virescens and ceroplesis carabarica. No. J5, Cetoine scaraboidae. No. J6, Ceroplesis S.P. No. J7, Macrorhina S.P. No. J8, Cetoine scaraboidae. No. J9, Phryneta leprosa. No. J10, Taurina longiceps. J11, Monohamus griseoplagiatus. J12, Jambonus trifasciatus.

Engraved

1962, Oct. 15 *Perf. 11* Unwmkd.

J1 D1 50c grn. & dp. org. 5 5
J2 " 50c grn. & dp. org. 5 5
J3 " 1fr black, brown & light green 10 10
J4 " 1fr black, brown & light green 10 10
J5 " 2fr black, orange & yellow green 10 10
J6 " 2fr blk. & red org. 10 10
J7 " 5fr brn., org. & grn. 10 10
J8 " 5fr brown, orange, green & red 10 10
J9 " 10fr blk., grn. & brn. 25 25
J10 " 10fr blk., brn. & grn. 25 25
J11 " 25fr black, blue green & brown 60 60
J12 " 25fr black, brown & blue green 60 60
Nos. J1–J12 (12) 2.40 2.40

Each two stamps of the same denomination are printed together in the sheet, se-tenant at the base.

MILITARY STAMPS

Central African Republic

No. 1 Overprinted **FM**

Engraved

1962, Jan. 1 *Perf. 13* Unwmkd.

M1 A1 bl., car., grn. & yel. 8.00 8.00

No. 1 Overprinted **FM**

1963

M2 A1 bl., car., grn. & yel. 7.00 7.00

OFFICIAL STAMPS

Central African Republic

Coat of Arms O1

Imprint: "d'après G. RICHER SO.GE.IM."

Perf. 13x12½

1965–69 Litho. Unwmkd.

Arms in Original Colors

O1 O1 1fr blk. & brn. org. 6 6
O2 " 2fr black & violet 7 6
O3 O1 5fr black & gray 10 6
O4 " 10fr black & green 20 12
O5 " 20fr black & red brn. 38 25
O6 " 30fr black & emerald ('69) 65 50
O7 " 50fr black & dk. blue 85 65
O8 " 100fr black & bister 1.85 1.00
O9 " 130fr blk. & vermilion ('69) 2.65 1.85
O10 " 200fr black & claret 3.25 2.50
Nos. O1–O10 (10) 10.06 7.05

Redrawn

Imprint: "d'après G. RICHER DELRIEU"

1971 Photo. *Perf. 12x12½*

Arms in Original Colors

O11 O1 5fr black & gray 10 10
O12 " 30fr black & emerald 40 25
O13 " 40fr black & deep claret 60 35
O14 " 100fr black & bister 1.40 70
O15 " 140fr black & light blue 2.00 80
O16 " 200fr black & claret 2.50 1.25
Nos. O11–O16 (6) 7.00 3.45

Empire

Nos. O11, O13–O16 Overprinted with Bar and "EMPIRE CENTRAFRICAIN"

1977 Lithographed *Perf. 12x12½*

O17 O1 5fr multicolored 15 15
O18 " 40fr " 30 25
O19 " 100fr " 80 55
O20 " 140fr " 1.10 85
O21 " 200fr " 1.65 1.25
Nos. O17–O21 (5) 4.00 3.05

Type of 1965 Inscribed: "EMPIRE CENTRAFRICAIN"

1978, July Litho. *Perf. 12½*

O22 O1 1fr multicolored 3
O23 " 2fr " 3
O24 " 5fr " 5
O25 " 10fr " 10
O26 " 15fr " 15
O27 " 20fr " 20
O28 " 30fr " 30
O29 " 40fr " 40
O30 " 50fr " 50
O31 " 60fr " 60
O32 " 100fr " 1.00
O33 " 130fr " 1.30
O34 " 140fr " 1.40
O35 " 200fr " 2.00
Nos. O22–O35 (14) 8.06

CENTRAL LITHUANIA

(lĭth'ů-ā'nĭ-ȧ)

LOCATION—North of Poland and east of Lithuania.

CAPITAL—Vilnius.

At one time Central Lithuania was a grand duchy of Lithuania but at the end of the 18th Century it fell under Russian rule. After World War I, Lithuania regained her sovereignty but certain areas were occupied by Poland. During the Russo-Polish war this territory was seized by Lithuania whose claim was promptly recognized by the Soviet Government. Under the leadership of the Polish General Zeligowski the territory was recaptured and it was during this occupation the stamps of Central Lithuania came into being. Subsequently the territory became a part of Poland.

100 Fennigi = 1 Markka

Coat of Arms
A1

Perf. 11½, Imperf.

1920-21 Typo. Unwmkd.

No.	Type	Description	Unused	Used
1	A1	25f red	12	20
2	"	25f dark green ('21)	12	20
3	"	1m blue	12	20
4	"	1m dark brown ('21)	12	20
5	"	2m violet	15	20
6	"	2m orange ('21)	15	20
		Nos. 1-6 (6)	78	1.20

Lithuanian Stamps of 1919 Surcharged in Blue or Black

Wmkd. Wavy Lines. (145)

Perf. 11½x12, 12½x11½, 14

1920, Nov. 23

No.	Type	Description	Unused	Used
13	A5	2m on 15sk lilac	6.00	6.00
		a. Invtd. surch.	150.00	
14	"	4m on 10sk red	6.00	6.00
		a. Invtd. surch.	150.00	
15	"	4m on 20sk dull blue (Bk)	6.00	6.00
		a. Invtd. surch.	150.00	
16	"	4m on 30sk buff	6.00	6.00
		a. Invtd. surch.	150.00	
17	A6	6m on 50sk lt. green	6.00	6.00
		a. 4m on 50sk light green (error)	150.00	
		b. 10m on 50sk light green (error)	150.00	
18	"	6m on 60sk violet & red	6.00	6.00
		a. 4m on 60sk vio. & red (error)	150.00	
		b. 10m on 60sk vio. & red (error)	150.00	
19	"	6m on 75sk bistre & red	6.00	6.00
		a. 4m on 75sk bis. & red (error)	150.00	
		b. 10m on 75sk bis. & red (error)	150.00	
20	A8	10m on 1auk gray & red	9.00	9.00
		a. Invtd. surch.	225.00	
21	"	10m on 3auk light brown & red	150.00	250.00
22	"	10m on 5auk blue green & red	150.00	250.00
		Nos. 13-22 (10)	351.00	551.00

Reprints of Nos. 17a, 17b, 18a, 18b, 19a and 19b. Price, each $65.

Counterfeits of Nos. 21-22 exist.

Lithuanian Girl
A2

Warrior
A3

Holy Gate of Vilnius
A4

Tower and Cathedral, Vilnius
A5

Rector's Insignia
A6

Gen. Lucien Zeligowski
A7

Perf. 11½, Imperf.

1920 Litho. Unwmkd.

No.	Type	Description	Unused	Used
23	A2	25f gray	15	15
24	A3	1m orange	15	15
25	A4	2m claret	15	15
26	A5	4m gray green & buff	25	25
27	A6	6m rose & gray	32	35
28	A7	10m brown & yellow	40	50
		Nos. 23-28 (6)	1.42	1.55

St. Anne's Church, Vilnius
A8

White Eagle and White Knight Vytis
A10

St. Stanislas Cathedral, Vilnius
A9

Queen Hedwig and King Ladislas II Jagello
A11

Coat of Arms of Vilnius
A12

Poczobut Astronomical Observatory
A13

Union of Lithuania and Poland
A14

Tadeusz Kosciuszko and Adam Mickiewicz
A15

1921 *Perf. 11½, 13½, 14, Imperf.*

No.	Type	Description	Unused	Used
35	A8	1(m) dk. gray & yel.	15	20
36	A9	2(m) rose & green	15	20
37	A10	3(m) dark green	15	20
38	A11	4(m) brown & buff	20	25
39	A12	5(m) red brown	20	25
40	A13	6(m) slate & buff	20	25
41	A14	10(m) red violet & buff	25	30
42	A15	20(m) blk. brown & buff	28	35
		Nos. 35-42 (8)	1.58	2.00

Peasant Girl Sowing
A16

Allegory: Peace and Industry
A19

White Eagle and Vytis
A17

Great Theater at Vilnius
A18

Gen. Zeligowski Entering Vilnius
A20

Gen. Zeligowski
A21

1921-22 *Perf. 11½, Imperf.*

No.	Type	Description	Unused	Used
53	A16	10m brown ('22)	80	1.00
54	A17	25m red & yellow ('22)	80	1.00
55	A18	50m dark blue ('22)	1.20	1.50
56	A19	75m violet ('22)	1.60	2.00
57	A20	100m blue & bistre	1.40	1.75
58	A21	150m olive green & brown	1.85	2.50
		Nos. 53-58 (6)	7.65	9.75

Nos. 53-56 commemorate the opening of the National Parliament; Nos. 57-58, the anniversary of the entry of General Zeligowski into Vilnius.

SEMI-POSTAL STAMPS.

Nos. 1-6 Surcharged in Black or Red

NA
ŚLĄSK
2 M.

1921 *Perf. 11½, Imperf.* Unwmkd.

No.	Type	Description	Unused	Used
B1	A1	25f+2m red (Bk)	32	40
B2	"	25f+2m dark green	32	40
B3	"	1m+2m blue	40	50
B4	"	1m+2m dark brown	40	50
B5	"	2m+2m violet	40	50
B6	"	2m+2m orange	40	50
		Nos. B1-B6 (6)	2.24	2.80

The surcharge means "For Silesia 2 marks." The stamps were intended to provide a fund to assist the plebiscite in Upper Silesia.

Nos. 25, 26 Surcharged:

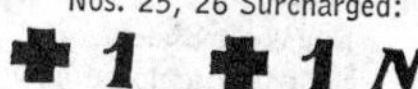

a b

Perf. 11½, Imperf.

No.	Type	Description	Unused	Used
B13	A4	(a) 2m+1(m) claret	40	70
B14	A5	(b) 4m+1m gray green & buff	40	70

Nos. 25-26, 28 with inset 10M

Perf. 11½, Imperf.

No.	Type	Description	Unused	Used
B17	A4	2m+1m claret	17	30
B18	A5	4m+1m gray green & buff	23	30
B19	A7	10m+2m brn. & yel.	23	30
		Nos. B13-B19 (5)	1.27	2.10

POSTAGE DUE STAMPS.

University, Vilnius
D1

Castle Ruins, Troki
D3

Castle Hill, Vilnius
D2

Holy Gate, Vilnius
D4

St. Stanislas Cathedral
D5

St. Anne's Church, Vilnius
D6

Perf. 11½, Imperf.

1920-21 Unwmkd.

No.	Type	Description	Unused	Used
J1	D1	50f red violet	15	20
J2	D2	1m green	15	20
J3	D3	2m red violet	15	20
J4	D4	3m red violet	30	35
J5	D5	5m red violet	30	35
J6	D6	20m scarlet	45	55
		Nos. J1-J6 (6)	1.50	1.85

CHAD

(chäd)

(Tchad)

LOCATION—In Central Africa south of Libya.

GOVT.—Republic.

AREA—495,752 sq. mi.

POP.—4,200,000 (est. 1977).

CAPITAL—N'djamena (formerly Fort Lamy).

A former dependency of Ubangi-Shari, Chad became a separate French colony in 1920. In 1934 the colonies of Chad, Gabon, Middle Congo and Ubangi-Shari were grouped in a single administrative unit known as French Equatorial Africa, with the capital at Brazzaville. The Republic of Chad was proclaimed Nov. 28, 1958.

100 Centimes = 1 Franc

Types of Middle Congo, 1907-17, Overprinted **TCHAD**

Perf. 14x13½, 13½x14.

1922 **Unwmkd.**

1 A1 1c red & violet 5 5
a. Overprint omitted 52.50
2 " 2c olive brown & salmon 8 8
a. Ovpt. omitted 85.00
3 " 4c indigo & violet 10 10
4 " 5c chocolate & green 25 25
5 " 10c deep green & gray green 40 40
6 " 15c violet & red 45 45
7 " 20c green & violet 1.50 1.50
8 A2 25c olive brown & brown 2.75 2.75
9 " 30c rose & pale rose 30 30
10 " 35c dull blue & dull rose 80 80
11 " 40c chocolate & green 80 80
12 " 45c violet & green 60 60
13 " 50c dark blue & pale blue 60 60
14 " 60c on 75c violet, *pinkish* 85 85
a. "TCHAD" omitted 70.00
b. "60" omitted 70.00
15 " 75c red & violet 50 50
16 A3 1fr indigo & salmon 3.50 3.50
17 " 2fr indigo & violet 5.00 5.00
18 " 5fr indigo & olive brown 3.75 3.75
Nos. 1-18 (18) 22.28 22.28

Stamps of 1922 Overprinted in Various Colors:

AFRIQUE EQUATORIALE FRANÇAISE *a*

AFRIQUE EQUATORIALE FRANÇAISE *b*

1924-33

19 A1 (*a*) 1c red & violet 5 5
a. "TCHAD" omitted 37.50
b. Dbl. ovpt. 32.50
20 " (") 2c olive brown & salmon 5 5
a. "TCHAD" omitted 37.50
b. Dbl. ovpt. 32.50
21 " (") 4c indigo & vio. 5 5
a. "TCHAD" omitted 225.00
22 " (") 5c chocolate & green (Bl) 25 25
a. "TCHAD" omitted 42.50
23 " (") 5c choc. & grn. 15 15
a. "TCHAD" omitted 52.50
24 " (") 10c deep green & gray gr. (Bl) 15 15
25 " (") 10c deep green & gray green 10 10
26 " (") 10c red orange & black ('25) 10 10
27 " (") 15c violet & red 15 15
28 " (") 20c green & violet 15 15
29 A2 (*b*) 25c olive brown & brown 15 15
30 A2 (*b*) 30c rose & pale rose 6 6
31 " (") 30c gray & blue (R) ('25) 7 7
32 " (") 30c dark green & green ('27) 25 25
a. "Afrique Equatoriale Francaise" omitted 60.00
33 " (") 35c indigo & dull rose 7 7
34 " (") 40c choc. & grn. 28 28
a. Dbl. overprint (R+Bk) 70.00
35 " (") 45c violet & green 15 15
a. Double ovpt. (R+Bk) 70.00
36 " (") 50c dark blue & pale blue 15 15
a. Inverted overprint 37.50
37 " (") 50c green & violet ('25) 25 25
38 " (") 65c orange brown & blue ('28) 50 50
39 " (") 75c red & violet 15 15
40 " (") 75c deep blue & light blue (R) ('25) 13 13
a. "TCHAD" omitted 37.50
41 " (") 75c rose & dark brown ('28) 70 70
42 " (") 90c brown red & pink ('30) 2.25 2.25
43 A3 (") 1fr indigo & salmon 40 40
44 " (")1.10fr dull green & blue ('28) 60 60
45 " (")1.25fr orange brown & light blue ('33) 2.25 2.25
46 " (")1.50fr ultramarine & blue ('30) 2.25 2.25
47 " (")1.75fr olive brown & violet ('33) 16.50 16.50
48 " (") 2fr indigo & vio. 65 65
49 " (") 3fr red vio. ('30) 2.50 2.50
50 " (") 5fr indigo & olive brown 65 65
Nos. 19-50 (32) 32.16 32.16

Types of 1922 Overprinted Type "b" and Surcharged with New Values.

1924-27

51 A2 60c on 75c dark violet, *pinkish* 10 10
a. "60" omitted 47.50
52 A3 65c on 1fr brown & olive green('25) 40 40
53 " 85c on 1fr brown & olive green('25) 40 40
54 A2 90c on 75c brown red & rose red ('27) 40 40
55 A3 1.25fr on 1fr dark blue & ultramarine (R) ('26) 10 10
a. "Afrique Equatoriale Francaise" omitted 42.50
56 " 1.50fr on 1fr ultramarine & blue ('27) 50 50
57 " 3fr on 5fr orange brown & dull red ('27) 1.35 1.35
58 " 10fr on 5fr olive green & cerise ('27) 4.00 4.00
59 " 20fr on 5fr violet & vermilion('27) 4.75 4.75
Nos. 51-59 (9) 12.00 12.00

Colonial Exposition Issue.

Common Design Types

Name of Country in Black.

1931 Engraved ***Perf. 12½***

60 CD70 40c deep green 1.40 1.40
61 CD71 50c violet 1.40 1.40
62 CD72 90c red orange 1.40 1.40
63 CD73 1.50fr dull blue 1.40 1.40

Common Design Types pictured in section at front of book.

Republic

"Birth of the Republic"

A1

"Solidarity of the Community"

A2

Engraved.

1959 ***Perf. 13*** **Unwmkd.**

64 A1 15fr ultramarine, green & maroon 27 15
65 A2 25fr dark green & deep claret 40 15

Issued to commemorate the first anniversary of the proclamation of the Republic.

Imperforates

Most Chad stamps from 1959 onward exist imperforate in issued and trial colors, and also in small presentation sheets in issued colors.

C.C.T.A. Issue

Common Design Type

1960

66 CD106 50fr rose lilac & dark purple 90 80

Flag and Map of Chad and U.N. Emblem

A3

Engraved

1961, Jan. 11 ***Perf. 13*** **Unwmkd.**

Flag in blue, yellow and carmine.

67 A3 15fr brown & dark blue 35 25
68 " 25fr orange brown & dark blue 45 25
69 " 85fr slate green & dark blue 1.50 85

Admission of Chad to United Nations.

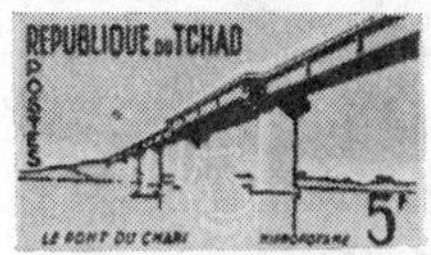

Chari Bridge and Hippopotamus

A4

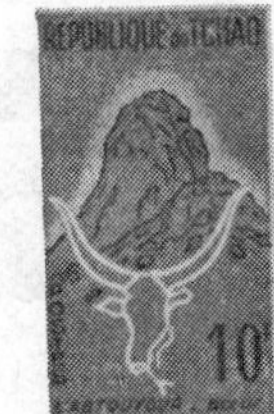

Abtouyoua Mountain and Ox

A5

Designs: 50c, Biltine and dorcas gazelle. 1fr, Logone and elephant. 2fr, Batha and lion. 3fr, Salamat and buffalo. 4fr, Ouaddai and Kudu. 15fr, Bessada and giant eland. 20fr, Tibesti mountains and mouflon. 25fr, Rocherg and antelope. 30fr, Kanem and cheetah. 60fr, Borkou and oryx. 85fr, Gorge of Archet and addax.

Typographed

1961-62 ***Perf. 13½x14, 14x13½***

70 A5 50c yellow green & dark green ('62) 3 3
71 " 1fr blue green & dk. blue green ('62) 4 3
72 " 2fr dark red brown & black ('62) 4 3
73 " 3fr ochre & dull green ('62) 6 6
74 " 4fr dark crimson & black ('62) 8 8
75 A4 5fr yellow & black 10 10
76 A5 10fr pink & black 15 10
77 " 15fr lilac & black ('62) 25 8
78 " 20fr red & black 30 15
79 " 25fr blue & black ('62) 40 15
80 " 30fr ultra. & black ('62) 50 20
81 " 60fr yellow & olive green ('62) 90 30
82 " 85fr orange & black 1.20 50
Nos. 70-82 (13) 4.05 1.81

First anniversary of Independence.

Abidjan Games Issue

Common Design Type

Designs: 20fr, Relay race. 50fr, High jump.

1962, July 21 Photo. ***Perf. 12½x12***

83 CD109 20fr brown, light green & black 35 20
84 " 50fr brown, light green & black 75 50

See No. C8.

African-Malgache Union Issue

Common Design Type

1962, Sept. 8 **Unwmkd.**

85 CD110 30fr dk. blue, bluish grn., red & gold 50 45

Issued to commemorate the first anniversary of the African and Malgache Union.

Pres. Ngarta Tombalbaye

A7

1963, Apr. 22 ***Perf. 12x12½***

86 A7 20fr multicolored 30 15
87 " 85fr " 1.20 45

Space Communciations Issue

Waves Around Globe

A8

Design: 100fr, Orbit patterns around globe.

Photogravure

1963, Sept. 19 ***Perf. 12½*** **Unwmkd.**

88 A8 25fr green & purple 40 35
89 " 100fr pink & ultra. 1.50 1.10

Ancestral Mask
A9

Excavated Sao Art: 5fr, Clay weight. 25fr, Ancestral clay statuette. 60fr, Gazelle, bronze. 80fr, Bronze pectoral.

1963, Dec. 2 Engraved *Perf. 13*

90 A9 5fr brt. grn. & red brn. 10 5
91 " 15fr gray, dull claret & red 25 15
92 " 25fr dk. bl. & orge. brn. 40 25
93 " 60fr orange brown & slate green 90 40
94 " 80fr orge. red & olive 1.20 40
Nos. 90-94 (5) 2.85 1.25

UNESCO Emblem, Scales and Tree—A10

1963, Dec. 10

95 A10 25fr green & maroon 40 30

Issued to commemorate the 15th anniversary of the Universal Declaration of Human Rights.

Potter
A11

Designs: 30fr, Boatmaker. 50fr, Weaver. 85fr, Smiths.

Engraved

1964, Feb. 5 *Perf. 12½* Unwmkd.

96 A11 10fr bl., blk. & org. 15 10
97 " 30fr yellow, black & carmine 45 20
98 " 50fr green, black & carmine 75 30
99 " 85fr pur., blk. & yel. 85 50

Barograph and WMO Emblem
A12

1964, March 23 *Perf. 13*

100 A12 50fr red lilac, purple & ultramarine 85 45

Fourth World Meteorological Day.

Cotton
A13

Design: 25fr, Royal poinciana.

1964, Apr. 6 Photo. *Perf. 12½x13*

101 A13 20fr multicolored 40 20
102 " 25fr " 40 20

Co-operation Issue
Common Design Type

1964, Nov. 7 Engraved *Perf. 13*

103 CD119 25fr verm., dk. bl. & dk. brown 40 30

National Guard and Map of Chad
A14

Design: 25fr, Infantry, flag and map (vert.).

Perf. 12½x13, 13x12½

1964, Dec. 11 Photogravure

104 A14 20fr multicolored 35 20
105 " 25fr lt. blue & multi. 40 20

Issued to honor the army of Chad.

Aoudad or Barbary Sheep
A15

Animals: 10fr, Addax. 20fr, Oryx. 25fr, Derby's eland (vert.). 30fr, Giraffe, buffalo and lion, Zakouma Park (vert.). 85fr, Great kudu at water hole.

Perf. 12½x12, 12x12½

1965, Jan. 11 Unwmkd.

106 A15 5fr dk. brn., ultra. & yellow 7 4
107 " 10fr ultra., orange & black 18 12
108 " 20fr multicolored 30 15
109 " 25fr " 40 20
110 " 30fr " 45 25
111 " 85fr " 1.25 65
Nos. 106-111 (6) 2.65 1.41

Olsen Perforator
A16

Designs: 60fr, Mildé telephone (vert.). 100fr, Distributor of Baudot telegraph.

1965, May 17 Engraved *Perf. 13*

112 A16 30fr chocolate, red, green & verm. 45 30
113 " 60fr red brown, slate green & verm. 90 60
114 " 100fr slate green, red brn. & verm. 1.40 1.00

Issued to commemorate the centenary of the International Telecommunication Union.

Motorized Police
A17

Perf. 12½x12

1965, June 22 Photo. Unwmkd.

115 A17 25fr olive, dk. green, gold & brown 40 25

Issued to honor the national police.

Guitar
A18

Musical Instruments from National Museum: 1fr, Drum and stool (vert.). 3fr, Shoulder drums (vert.). 15fr, Viol. 60fr, Harp (vert.).

1965, Oct. 26 Engraved *Perf. 13*

Size: 22x36, 36x22mm.

116 A18 1fr carmine, emerald & brown 6 3
117 " 2fr red, brt. lilac & brown 6 3
118 " 3fr red & sepia 6 6
119 " 15fr red, ocher & slate green 25 15
120 " 60fr maroon & slate green 90 40
Nos. 116-120, C23 (6) 2.68 1.12

Head and Bowl
A19

WHO Headquarters, Geneva
A20

Sao Art: 20fr, Head. 60fr, Head with crown. 80fr, Circlet with human head. From excavations at Bouta Kebira and Gawi.

1966, Apr. 1 Engr. *Perf. 13*

121 A19 15fr olive, chocolate & ultra. 20 15
122 " 20fr dk. red, brown & blue green 30 20
123 " 60fr brt. blue, choc. & vermilion 90 50
124 " 80fr brn. org., green & purple 1.20 60

Issued to publicize the International Negro Arts Festival, Dakar, Senegal, Apr. 1-24.

No. 86 Surcharged with New Value and Two Bars in Orange

1966, Apr. 15 Photo. *Perf. 12x12½*

125 A7 25fr on 20fr multi. 40 20

1966, May 3

126 A20 25fr car., lt. ultra. & yellow 40 30
127 " 32fr emerald, ultra. & yellow 45 35

Issued to commemorate the inauguration of the World Health Organization Headquarters, Geneva.

Staff of Mercury and Map of Africa
A21

1966, May 24 *Perf. 12½x12*

128 A21 30fr multicolored 45 20

Central African Customs and Economic Union (Union Douaniere et Economique de l'Afrique Centrale, UDEAC).

Soccer Player
A22

Design: 60fr, Soccer player facing left.

1966, July 12 Engraved *Perf. 13*

129 A22 30fr green, bl. green & maroon 45 25
130 " 60fr dark blue, gray & carmine 90 50

Issued to commemorate the 8th World Cup Soccer Championship, Wembley, England, July 11-30.

Young Men, Flag and Emblem
A23

Photogravure

1966, Aug. 11 *Perf. 12½x13*

131 A23 25fr dk. bl. & multi. 40 25

Chad Youth Movement.

Greek Columns and UNESCO Emblem
A24

1966, Aug. 23 Engr. *Perf. 13*

132 A24 32fr slate bl., vio. & carmine rose 50 30

Issued to commemorate the 20th anniversary of UNESCO (United Nations Educational, Scientific and Cultural Organization).

Reconstructed Skull of Chadanthropus
A25

1966, Sept. 20 Engraved *Perf. 13*

133 A25 30fr gray, red & ocher 45 20

Issued to commemorate Yves Coppens' discovery of Lake Chad man.

Stone Axe
A26

Prehistoric Tools: 30fr, Flint arrow head. 85fr, Bone harpoon. 100fr, Sandstone millstone with grinder.

1966, Dec. 11 Engraved *Perf. 13*

134 A26 25fr deep blue, red & dk. brown 32 18
135 " 30fr brown, dp. blue & black 45 22
136 " 85fr dark red, bright blue & brown 1.20 55
137 " 100fr Prus. green, dk. brown & bister brown 1.40 70
a. Min. sheet of 4 3.75 3.75

No. 137a contains one each of Nos. 134-137. Size: 128x99mm.

Map of Chad and Various Sports
A27

1967, Apr. 10 Photo. *Perf. 12x12½*

138 A27 25fr multicolored 40 25

Issued for Sports Day, Apr. 10, 1967.

Colotis Protomedia
A28

Various Butterflies.

1967, May 23 Photo. *Perf. 12½x12*

139 A28 5fr blue & multi. 10 8
140 " 10fr emerald & multi. 20 12
141 " 20fr orange & multi. 30 20
142 " 130fr red & multi. 1.75 90

WHO Headquarters, Brazzaville
A29

1967, Sept. 23 Photo. *Perf. 12½x13*

143 A29 30fr violet blue & multicolored 45 25

Issued to commemorate the opening of the Regional Office of the United Nations World Health Organization, Brazzaville.

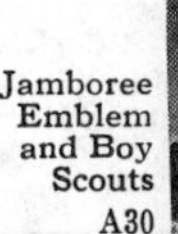

Jamboree Emblem and Boy Scouts
A30

Design: 32fr, Jamboree emblem and Boy Scout.

1967, Oct. 17 Photo. *Perf. 12½x13*

144 A30 25fr multicolored 35 15
145 " 32fr " 50 25

Issued to publicize the 12th Boy Scout World Jamboree, Farragut State Park, Idaho, Aug. 1–9.

Great Mills of Chad
A31

Design: 30fr, Lake reclamation project, grain fields.

1967, Nov. 14 Engraved *Perf. 13*

146 A31 25fr brt. bl., indigo & sepia 35 15
147 " 30fr ultra., emerald & olive brown 40 25

Economic development of Chad.

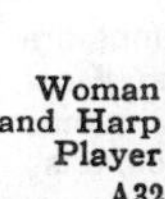

Woman and Harp Player
A32

Rock Paintings: 30fr, Giraffes. 50fr, Camel rider hunting ostrich.

1967, Dec. 19 Engraved *Perf. 13*

Size: 36x22mm.

148 A32 15fr blue, salmon & maroon 20 12
149 " 30fr greenish blue, sal. & maroon 45 25
150 " 50fr emerald, salmon & maroon 75 32
Nos. 148-150, C38-C39 (5) 4.75 2.24

Issued to commemorate the Balloud expedition in the Ennedi Mountains. See also Nos. 163–166.

Rotary Emblem
A33

Map of Chad, WHO Emblem, Well, Physicians, Mother and Child
A34

1968, Jan. 9 Photo. *Perf. 13x12½*

151 A33 50fr multicolored 75 35

Rotary Club of Chad, 10th anniversary.

1968, Apr. 6 *Perf. 13x12½*

152 A34 25fr multicolored 35 20
153 " 32fr " 50 30

Issued to commemorate the 20th anniversary of the World Health Organization.

"Water" Aiding Agriculture and Industry—A35

1968, Apr. 23 Engraved *Perf. 13*

154 A35 50fr greenish blue, brown & bright green 70 30

Hydrological Decade (UNESCO), 1965–74.

National Administration School
A36

1968, Aug. 20 Engraved *Perf. 13*

155 A36 25fr slate, brown red & rose violet 35 20

Boy Learning to Write
A37

1968, Sept. 10

156 A37 60fr dark blue, dark brown & black 75 35

Issued for National Literacy Day.

Cotton Harvest
A38

Loom, Fort Archambault Factory
A39

Tiger Moth
A40

1968, Sept. 24 Engraved *Perf. 13*

157 A38 25fr Prus. bl., choc. & dark green 35 13
158 A39 30fr bright green, olive & ultra. 45 20

Issued to publicize the cotton industry.

1968, Oct. 1 Photogravure

Designs (Moths): 30fr, Owlet. 50fr, Saturnid (Gynanisa maja). 100fr, Saturnid (Epiphora bauhiniae).

159 A40 25fr multicolored 30 15
160 " 30fr " 40 20
161 " 50fr " 70 35
162 " 100fr " 1.25 50

Rock Paintings Type of 1967

Rock Paintings: 2fr, Archers. 10fr, Costumes (4 women, 1 man). 20fr, Funeral vigil. 25fr, Dispute.

1968, Nov. 19 Engraved *Perf. 13*

Size: 36x22mm.

163 A32 2fr scarlet, salmon & brown 6 5
164 " 10fr purple, salmon & dark red 15 6
165 " 20fr green, salmon & maroon 30 15
166 " 25fr blue, salmon & maroon 40 20

Man and Human Rights Flame
A41

St. Paul
A42

1968, Dec. 10 Engraved *Perf. 13*

167 A41 32fr green, bright blue & red 50 30

International Human Rights Year.

1969, May 6 Litho. *Perf. 12½x13*

Apostles: 1fr, St. Peter. 2fr, St. Thomas. 5fr, St. John the Evangelist. 10fr, St. Bartholomew. 20fr, St. Matthew. 25fr, St. James the Less. 30fr, St. Andrew. 40fr, St. Jude. 50fr, St. James the Greater. 85fr, St. Philip. 100fr, St. Simon.

168 A42 50c multicolored 4 3
169 " 1fr " 5 3
170 " 2fr " 5 3
171 " 5fr " 6 3
172 " 10fr " 12 8
173 " 20fr " 23 15
174 A42 25fr multicolored 28 17
175 " 30fr " 35 20
176 " 40fr " 45 25
177 " 50fr " 50 30
178 " 85fr " 85 55
179 " 100fr " 1.00 60
Nos. 168-179 (12) 3.98 2.42

Issued to commemorate the Jubilee Year of the Catholic Church in Chad. Nos. 168–179 printed se-tenant in sheets of 12 (4x3).

Tractors and Trucks
A43

1969, June 19 Engraved *Perf. 13*

180 A43 32fr green, red brn. & indigo 40 25

Issued to commemorate the 50th anniversary of the International Labor Organization.

Deborah Meyer, U.S., 200 Meter Freestyle
A44

Woman with Flowers, by Veneto
A45

Winners of 1968 Olympic Games: No. 182, Roland Matthes, East Germany, 100 meter backstroke. No. 183, Klaus DiBiasi, Italy, springboard diving. No. 184, Bruno Cipolla, Primo Baran and Renzo Sambo, Italy, pair with coxswain. No. 185, Annemarie Zimmermann and Rosewitha Esser, West Germany, women's kayak tandem. No. 186, Sailing, Great Britain. No. 187, Pierre Trentin, France, 1000 meter bicycling. No. 188, Pier Franco Vianelli, Italy, 196 kilometer bicycle road race. No. 189, Daniel Morelon and Pierre Trentin, France, tandem. No. 190, Daniel R. Rebillard, France, 4000 meter pursuit (bicycle). No. 191, Ingrid Becker, West Germany, pentathlon. No. 192, Jean J. Guyon, France, equestrian. No. 193, Olympic dressage team, West Germany. No. 194, Bernd Klinger, West Germany, small bore rifle. No. 195, Manfred Wolke, East Germany, welterweight. No. 196, Randy Matson, U.S., shot put. No. 197, Colette Besson, France, 400 meter run. No. 198, Mohammed Gammoudi, Tunisia, 5,000 meter run. No. 199, Tommie Smith, U.S., 200 meter run. No. 200, David Hemery, Great Britain, 200 meter hurdles. No. 201, Willie Davenport, U.S., 110 meter hurdles. No. 202, Bob Beamon, U.S., broad jump. No. 203, Sawao Kato, Japan, all around gymnastics. No. 204, Dick Fosbury, U.S., high jump.

Paintings: No. 206, Holy Family, by Murillo (horiz.). No. 207, Adoration of the Kings, by Rubens. No. 208, Portrait of an African Woman, by Bezombes. No. 209, Three Negroes, by Rubens. No. 210, Mother and Child, by Gauguin.

Lithographed

1969, June 30 *Perf. 12½x13*

Multicolored

181 A44 1fr *Meyer* 35 35
182 " 1fr *Matthes* 35 35
183 " 1fr *DiBiasi* 35 35
184 " 1fr *Cipolla, Baran & Sambo* 35 35
185 " 1fr *Zimmermann & Esser* 35 35
186 " 1fr *Sailing, Great Britain* 35 35
187 " 1fr *Trentin* 35 35
188 " 1fr *Vianelli* 35 35
189 " 1fr *Morelon & Trentin* 35 35
190 " 1fr *Rebillard* 35 35
191 " 1fr *Becker* 35 35
192 " 1fr *Guyon* 35 35
193 " 1fr *Dressage, Germ.* 35 35
194 " 1fr *Klinger* 35 35
195 " 1fr *Wolke* 35 35
196 " 1fr *Matson* 35 35
197 " 1fr *Besson* 35 35
198 " 1fr *Gammoudi* 35 35
199 " 1fr *Smith* 35 35
200 " 1fr *Hemery* 35 35
201 " 1fr *Davenport* 35 35
202 " 1fr *Beamon* 35 35
203 " 1fr *Kato* 35 35
204 " 1fr *Fosbury* 35 35

Perf. 12½x13, 13x12½

205 A45 1fr *Veneto* 35 35
206 " 1fr *Murillo* 35 35
207 " 1fr *Rubens* 35 35
208 " 1fr *Bezombes* 35 35
209 " 1fr *Rubens* 35 35
210 " 1fr *Gauguin* 35 35
Nos. 181-210 (30) 10.50 10.50

Issued to stress the brotherhood of mankind.

Cochlospermum Tinctorium
A46

Flowers: 4fr, Parkia biglobosa. 10fr, Pancratium trianthum. 15fr, Morning glory.

1969, July 8 Photo. *Perf. 12½x13*

211 A46 1fr pink, yel. & blk. 5 5
212 " 4fr dk. grn., yel. & red 5 5
213 " 10fr dk. green, yellow & gray 15 8
214 " 15fr vio. bl. & multi. 20 10

Meat Freezer, Farcha
A47

Design: 30fr, Cattle at Farcha slaughterhouse.

1969, Aug. 19 Engraved *Perf. 13*

215 A47 25fr slate grn., ocher & red brown 32 18
216 " 30fr red brown, slate green & gray 38 25

Economic development in Chad.

Development Bank Issue

Common Design Type

1969, Sept. 10

217 CD130 30fr dull red, green & ocher 40 20

Issued to commemorate the 5th anniversary of the African Development Bank.

Tilapia Nilotica
A48

Fish: 3fr, Citharinus latus. 5fr, Tetraodon fahaka strigosus. 20fr, Hydrocyon forskali.

1969, Nov. 25 Engraved *Perf. 13*

218 A48 2fr choc., grn. & gray 5 3
219 " 3fr gray, red & blue 8 5
220 " 5fr ocher, black & yel. 10 8
221 " 20fr blk., red & green 32 18

ASECNA Issue

Common Design Type

1969, Dec. 12 Engraved *Perf. 13*

222 CD132 30fr orange 30 15

Pres. François Tombalbaye
A49

Lenin
A50

1970, Jan. 11 Litho. *Perf. 14*

223 A49 25fr multicolored 38 20

1970, Apr. 22 Photo. *Perf. 11½*

224 A50 150fr gold, black & buff 1.60 1.00

Issued to commemorate the centenary of the birth of Lenin (1870-1924), Russian communist leader.

U.P.U. Headquarters Issue

Common Design Type

1970, May 20 Engraved *Perf. 13*

225 CD133 30fr dark red, purple & brown 40 12

Adult Education Class and U.N. Emblem
A52

1970, June 16 Litho. *Perf. 14*

226 A52 100fr blue & multi. 1.20 30

Issued for International Education Year.

Bull's Head, Symbols of Weather and Agriculture—A53

Ahmed Mangue
A54

1970, July 22 Engr. *Perf. 13*

227 A53 50fr org., gray & grn. 55 15

Issued for World Meteorological Day.

Lithographed and Engraved

1970, Sept. 15 *Perf. 13*

228 A54 100fr gold, car. & blk. 1.10 25

Issued in memory of Ahmed Mangue, Minister of Education.

Tanner
A55

Designs: 2fr, Cloth dyer (vert.). 3fr, Camel turning oil press (horiz.). 4fr, Water carrier. 5fr, Copper worker (horiz.).

1970, Oct. 10 Engraved *Perf. 13*

229 A55 1fr olive brown, blue & brown 5 5
230 " 2fr dk. brown, olive & indigo 5 5
231 " 3fr purple, olive brn. & rose carmine 4 4
232 " 4fr chocolate, lemon & blue green 6 6
233 " 5fr red, chocolate & slate green 5 5
Nos. 229-233 (5) 25 25

U.N. Emblem, Grain and Dove
A56

1970, Oct. 24 Photo. *Perf. 12x12½*

234 A56 32fr dk. blue & multi. 40 25

25th anniversary of United Nations.

Certain unlisted issues of Chad, starting in 1970, are mentioned and briefly described in "For the Record" at the back of this volume.

OCAM Headquarters, Map of Africa, Stars
A57

1971, Jan. 23 Photo. *Perf. 12½x12*

235 A57 30fr dk. grn. & multi. 40 25

OCAM (Organisation Commune Africaine, Malgache et Mauricienne) Summit Conference, N'djamena, Jan. 22-30.

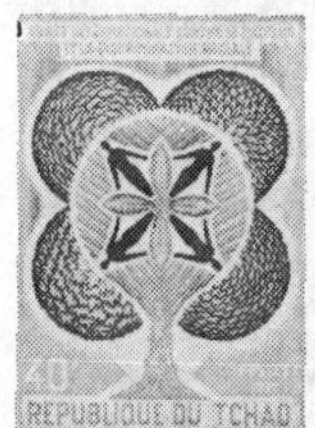

Symbolic Tree
A58

1971, March 21 Engraved *Perf. 13*

236 A58 40fr blue green, dark red & green 50 25

International year against racial discrimination.

Map of Africa, Radar Antenna
A59

Designs (Map of Africa and): 40fr, Communications tower. 50fr, Communications satellite.

1971, May 17 Engraved *Perf. 13*

237 A59 5fr ultra., orange & dark red 10 8
238 " 40fr purple, emerald & brown 40 20
239 " 50fr dark red, black & brown 60 30

3rd World Telecommunications Day.

UNICEF Emblem and Children
A60

1971, Dec. 11

240 A60 50fr Prussian blue, emerald & bright pink 60 30

25th anniversary of the United Nations International Children's Fund (UNICEF).

Gorane Nangara Dancers
A61

Dancers: 15fr, Girls' initiation dance, Yondo. 30fr, Women of M'Boum (vert.). 40fr, Men of Sara Kaba (vert.).

1971, Dec. 18 Litho. *Perf. 13*

241 A61 10fr black & multi. 15 5
242 " 15fr brn. org. & multi. 25 8
243 " 30fr blue & multi. 50 15
244 " 40fr yel. grn. & multi. 65 18

Presidents Pompidou and Tombalbaye, Map with Paris and Fort Lamy—A62

1972, Jan. 25 Photo. *Perf. 13*

245 A62 40fr blue & multi. 50 30

Visit of Pres. Georges Pompidou of France, Jan. 1972.

Examination

The Catalogue editors cannot undertake to appraise, identify or pass upon genuineness or condition of stamps.

Canceled-to-order stamps are often from remainders. Most collectors of canceled stamps prefer postally used specimens.

President Tombalbaye A63

1972, Apr. 13 Litho. *Perf. 13*

246 A63 30fr multicolored 30 15
247 " 40fr " 40 20

See Nos. C112–C113.

Downhill Skiing—A64

Designs: 75fr, Women's figure skating. 150fr, Luge.

1972, Apr. 13 *Perf. 13½*

248 A64 25fr multicolored 25 13
249 " 75fr " 75 38
250 " 150fr " 1.50 75
Nos. 248–250, C114–C115 (5) 5.80 2.91

11th Winter Olympic Games, Sapporo, Japan.

Heart A65

Gorrizia Dubiosa A66

1972, Apr. 25 Engraved *Perf. 13*

251 A65 100fr pur., bl. & car. 1.20 25

"Your heart is your health," World Health Month.

1972, May 6 Photogravure

Insects: 2fr, Spider (argiope sector). 3fr, Silk spider (nephila senegalense). 4fr, Beetle (oryctes boas). 5fr, Dragonfly (hemistigma albipunctata).

252 A66 1fr green & multi. 8 6
253 " 2fr blue & multi. 8 6
254 " 3fr car. rose & multi. 8 6
255 " 4fr yel. grn. & multi. 8 6
256 " 5fr dp. grn. & multi. 8 6
Nos. 252–256 (5) 40 30

Scout Greeting—A67

Designs: 70fr, Mountain climbing. 80fr, Canoeing.

1972, May 15

257 A67 30fr multicolored 30 15
258 " 70fr " 70 35
259 " 80fr " 80 40
Nos. 257–259, C118–C119 (5) 4.00 2.25

Scout Jamboree.

Hurdles, Motion and Olympic Emblems A68

Designs (Motion and Olympic Emblems and): 130fr, Gymnast on rings. 150fr, Swimming. 300fr, Bicycling.

1972, June 9 Litho. *Perf. 13½*

260 A68 50fr black & multi. 60 18
261 " 130fr " " 1.40 38
262 " 150fr " " 1.80 45

Souvenir Sheet

263 A68 300fr blk. & multi. 3.50 3.00

20th Olympic Games, Munich, Aug. 26–Sept. 10. No. 263 contains one stamp. Black marginal inscription and multicolored torch. Size: 101x86mm.

Ski Jump, Kasaya, Japan—A69

Designs: 75fr, Cross-country skiing, P. Tyldum, Sweden. 100fr, Figure-skating, pairs, L. Rodnina and A. Ulanov, USSR. 130fr, Men's speed skating, A. Schenk, Netherlands.

1972, June 15 *Perf. 14½*

264 A69 25fr gold & multi. 25 13
265 " 75fr " " 75 38
266 " 100fr " " 1.00 50
267 " 130fr " " 1.30 65
Nos. 264–267, C130–C131 (6) 6.80 3.41

11th Winter Olympic Games, gold-medal winners. Nos. 264–267 exist se-tenant with label showing earth satellite.

TV Tower and Weight-lifting—A70

Designs (TV Tower, Munich and): 40fr, Woman sprinter. 60fr, Soccer goalkeeper.

1972, Aug. 15 Litho. *Perf. 14½*

268 A70 20fr gold & multi. 20 10
269 " 40fr " " 40 20
270 " 60fr " " 60 30
Nos. 268–270, C135–C137 (6) 4.90 2.45

20th Summer Olympic Games, Munich. Nos. 268–270 exist se-tenant with label showing arms of Munich.

Dromedary A71

Domestic Animals: 30fr, Horse. 40fr, Dog. 45fr, Goat.

1972, Aug. 29 Engraved *Perf. 13*

271 A71 25fr purple & bister 35 12
272 " 30fr red lilac & indigo 40 15
273 " 40fr emerald & light brown 50 15
274 " 45fr dk. blue & brown 55 20

Tobacco Cultivation A72

Design: 50fr, Plowing.

1972, Oct. 24 Engraved *Perf. 13*

275 A72 40fr dk. brown, dk. carmine & slate green 40 20
276 " 50fr ultra., brn. & slate green 50 25

Massa Warrior A73

Design: 20fr, Moundang warrior.

1972, Nov. 15 Photo. *Perf. 14x13*

277 A73 15fr orange & multi. 25 20
278 " 20fr yellow & multi. 30 25

King Faisal and Pres. Tombalbaye A74

1972, Nov. 17 Litho. *Perf. 13*

279 A74 100fr gold & multi. 1.00 60

Visit of King Faisal of Saudi Arabia. See No. C143.

Gen. Gowon and Pres. Tombalbaye A75

1972, Dec. 7

280 A75 70fr multicolored 75 40

Visit of Gen. Yakubu Gowon of Nigeria.

Olympic Emblem and 100-meter Sprint, Valeri Borzov, USSR—A76

Designs (Olympic Emblem and): 20fr, Shotput, Komar, Poland. 40fr, Hammer throw, Bondartchuk, USSR. 60fr, Discus, Danek, Czechoslovakia.

1972, Dec. 22 *Perf. 11*

281 A76 10fr multicolored 10 5
282 " 20fr " 20 10
283 " 40fr " 40 20
284 " 60fr " 60 30
Nos. 281–284, C148–C149 (6) 5.30 2.65

20th Summer Olympic Games, winners.

Olympic Emblem and Fencing, Woyda, Poland—A77

Designs (Olympic Emblem and): 30fr, 3-day equestrian event, Richard Meade, Gt. Britain. 50fr, Two-man sculls, Brietzke-Mager, East Germany.

1972, Dec. 22

285 A77 20fr gold & multi. 20 10
286 " 30fr " " 30 15
287 " 50fr " " 50 25
Nos. 285–287, C151–C152 (5) 5.00 2.50

20th Summer Olympic Games, winners.

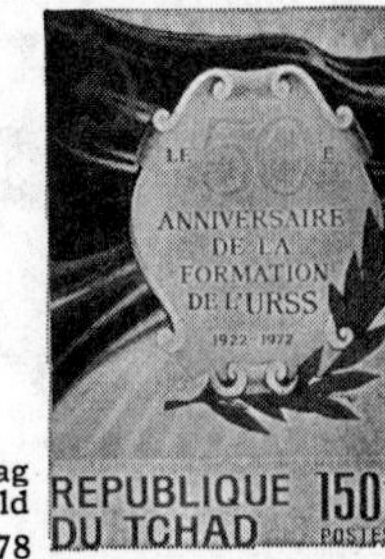

Soviet Flag and Shield A78

1972, Dec. 30 Lithographed *Perf. 12*

288 A78 150fr red & multi. 1.35 65

50th anniversary of the Soviet Union.

High Jump A79

Designs (Games Emblem and): 125fr, Running. 200fr, Shot put. 250fr, Discus.

1973, Jan. 17 Litho. *Perf. 13½x13*

289 A79 50fr vio. bl. & multi. 50 22
290 " 125fr olive & multi. 1.20 60
291 " 200fr lilac & multi. 2.00 1.00

Souvenir Sheet

292 A79 250fr brn. & multi. 3.00 3.00

2nd African Games, Lagos, Nigeria, Jan. 7–18. No. 292 contains one stamp. Ultramarine margin with inscription and black Games emblems. Size: 101½x 85mm.

No. 271 Surcharged with New Value, 2 Bars, and Overprinted in Red: "SECHERESSE SOLIDARITE AFRICAINE"

1973, Aug. 16 Engr. *Perf. 13*

293 A71 100fr on 25fr multi. 1.00 65

African solidarity in drought emergency.

African Postal Union Issue

Common Design Type

1973, Sept. 17 Engraved *Perf. 13*

294 CD137 100fr claret, slate grn. & brn. olive 1.00 60

Dinothrombium Tinctorium

A80

Rotary Emblem

A81

1974, Sept. 3 Photogravure *Perf. 13*

Multicolored

295 A80 25fr *shown* 22 12
296 " 30fr *Bupreste sternocera* 25 15
297 " 40fr *Diptere hyperechia* 35 20
298 " 50fr *Chrysis* 45 27
299 " 100fr *Longicorn beetle* 85 40
300 " 130fr *Spider* 1.10 50
Nos. 295–300 (6) 3.22 1.64

1975, Apr. 11 Typo. *Perf. 13*

301 A81 50fr multicolored 45 25

Rotary International, 70th anniversary.

Craterostigma Plantagineum

A82

Flowers: 10fr, Tapinanthus globiferus. 15fr, Commelina forskalaei (vert.). 20fr, Adenium obesum. 25fr, Yellow hibiscus. 30fr, Red hibiscus. 40fr, Kigelia africana.

1975, Sept. 25 Photo. *Perf. 13*

302 A82 5fr orange & multi. 5 5
303 " 10fr gray bl. & multi. 8 5
304 " 15fr yel. grn. & multi. 13 8
305 " 20fr lt. brn. & multi. 17 10
306 " 25fr lilac & multi. 20 12
307 " 30fr bister & multi. 25 13
308 " 40fr ultra. & multi. 32 18
Nos. 302–308 (7) 1.20 71

A. G. Bell, Satellite and Waves

A83

1976, June 10 Litho. *Perf. 12½*

309 A83 100fr blue, brown & ocher 80 50
310 " 125fr lt. grn., brown & ocher 1.00 60

Centenary of first telephone call by Alexander Graham Bell, Mar. 10, 1876.

Ice Hockey, USSR—A84

Design: 90fr, Ski jump, Karl Schnabl, Austria.

1976, June 21 *Perf. 14*

311 A84 60fr multicolored 50 25
312 " 90fr " 70 30

12th Winter Olympic Games, winners. See Nos. C178–C180.

High Hurdles—A85

1976, July 12 Litho. *Perf. 13½*

313 A85 45fr multicolored 40 20

21st Summer Olympic Games, Montreal, Canada. See Nos. C187—C190.

Mars Landing and Viking Rocket

A86

Design (Mars Landing and): 90fr, Viking trajectory, Earth to Mars.

1976, July 23 *Perf. 14*

314 A86 45fr multicolored 35 20
315 " 90fr " 70 35
Nos. 314–315, C191–C193 (5) 5.45 2.45

Viking Mars project.

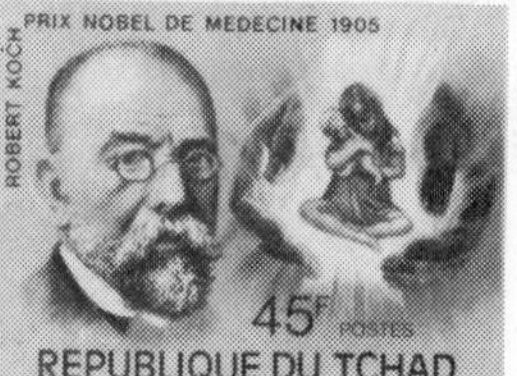

Robert Koch, Medicine—A87

Design: 90fr, Anatole France, literature.

1976, Dec. 15

316 A87 45fr multicolored 40 20
317 " 90fr " 70 35
Nos. 316–317, C196–C198 (5) 5.90 2.55

Nobel Prize winners.

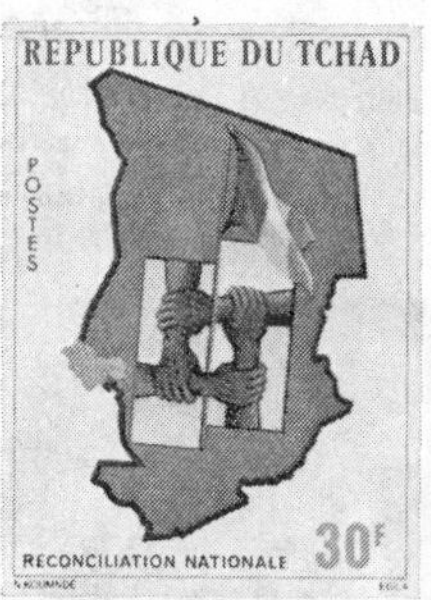

Map and Flag of Chad, Clasped Hands

A88

Designs: 60fr, like 30fr. 120fr, Map of Chad, people and various occupations.

1976, Sept. 15 Litho. *Perf. 12½x13*

318 A88 30fr multicolored 25 18
319 " 60fr org. & multi. 50 30
320 " 120fr brn. & multi. 1.00 65

National reconciliation.

Freed Political Prisoners—A89

Designs: 60fr, Parade of cadets. 120fr, like 30fr.

1976, Sept. 25 Litho. *Perf. 12½*

321 A89 30fr blue & multi. 25 18
322 " 60fr black & multi. 50 30
323 " 120fr red & multi. 1.00 65

Revolution of Apr. 13, 1975, first anniversary.

Decorated Calabashes—A90

Designs: Various pyrographed calabashes.

1976, Nov. Litho. *Perf. 12½x13*

324 A90 30fr multicolored 25 18
325 " 60fr " 50 30
326 " 120fr " 1.00 65

Germany No. C57 and Friedrichshafen, Germany—A91

1977, Mar. 30 *Perf. 14*

327 A91 100fr multicolored 80 35
Nos. 327, C206–C209 (5) 6.00 2.55

75th anniversary of the Zeppelin.

Elizabeth II in Coronation Regalia and Clergy—A92

Design: 450fr, Elizabeth II and Prince Philip.

1977, June 15 Litho. *Perf. 14x13½*

328 A92 250fr multicolored 2.00 70

Souvenir Sheet

329 A92 450fr multicolored 3.75 1.65

25th anniversary of the reign of Elizabeth II. No. 329 has multicolored margin showing Buckingham Palace and heraldic supporters. Size: 110x91mm.

Simon Bolivar—A93

Famous Personalities: 175fr, Joseph J. Roberts. No. 332, Queen Wihelmina of Netherlands. No. 333, Charles de Gaulle. 325fr, King Baudouin and Queen Fabiola of Belgium.

1977, June 15 *Perf. 13½x14*

330 A93 150fr multi. 1.20 50
331 " 175fr " 1.40 60
332 " 200fr " 1.60 65
333 " 200fr " 1.60 65
334 " 325fr " 2.65 1.00
Nos. 330–334 (5) 8.45 3.40

Post and Telecommunications Emblem—A94

Map of Chad and Waves
A95

Society Emblem
A96

Perf. 13 (A94); 12½ (A95); 13½x13 (A96)

1977, Aug. 15 **Lithographed**

335	A94	30fr yellow & black	25	18
336	A95	60fr multicolored	50	30
337	A96	120fr "	1.00	65

Telecommunications (30fr); National Telecommunications School, 10th anniversary (60fr); International Telecommunication Society of Chad (120fr).

WHO Emblem and Man (Back Pain)
A97

Designs (WHO Emblem and): 60fr, Woman's head (neck pain; horiz.). 120fr, Leg (knee pain).

Perf. 12½x13, 13x12½

1977, Nov. 10 **Engraved**

338	A97	30fr multicolored	25	18
339	"	60fr "	50	30
340	"	120fr "	1.00	65

World Rheumatism Year.

World Cup Emblems and Saving a Goal—A98

Designs (Argentina '78, World Cup Emblems and): 60fr, Heading the ball. 100fr, Referee whistling a goal. 200fr, World Cup poster. 300fr, Pelé. 500fr, Helmut Schoen and Munich stadium.

1977, Nov. 25 **Litho.** ***Perf. 13½***

341	A98	40fr multicolored	30	12
342	"	60fr "	50	20
343	"	100fr "	80	32
344	"	200fr "	1.60	55
345	"	300fr "	2.50	85
		Nos. 341-345 (5)	5.70	2.04

Souvenir Sheet

346	A98	500fr multicolored	4.00	1.85

World Cup Soccer Championship, Argentina '78. No. 346 has multicolored margin showing Argentina '78 emblem and stadium. Size: 119x80½mm.

Nos. 328-329 Overprinted in Silver:
"ANNIVERSAIRE DU COURONNEMENT 1953-1978"

1978, Sept. 13 ***Perf. 14x13½***

347	A92	250fr multicolored	2.00	1.00

Souvenir Sheet

348	A92	450fr multicolored	4.00	

25th anniversary of coronation of Queen Elizabeth II. Size of No. 348: 111x92mm.

Abraham and Melchisedek, by Rubens—A99

Rubens Paintings: 120fr, Helene Fourment (vert.). 200fr, David and the Elders of Israel. 300fr, Anne of Austria (vert.). 500fr, Marie de Medicis (vert.).

1978, Nov. 23 **Litho.** ***Perf. 13½***

349	A99	60fr multicolored	60	30
350	"	120fr "	1.20	60
351	"	200fr "	2.00	1.00
352	"	300fr "	3.00	1.50

Souvenir Sheet

353	A99	500fr multicolored	5.50	

Peter Paul Rubens (1577-1640). No. 353 has multicolored margin showing entire painting. Size: 78x103mm.

Dürer Portrait
A100

Dürer Paintings: 150fr, Jacob Muffel. 250fr, Young Woman. 350fr, Oswolt Krel.

1978, Nov. 23

354	A100	60fr multicolored	60	30
355	"	150fr "	1.50	75
356	"	250fr "	2.50	1.25
357	"	350fr "	3.50	1.75

Albrecht Dürer (1471-1528), German painter.

Head, Village and Fly
A101

1978, Nov. 28 ***Perf. 13***

358	A101	60fr multicolored	60	30

National Health Day.

Nos. 341-346 Overprinted in Silver:

a. 1962 BRESIL-TCHECOSLOVAQUIE / 3-1
b. 1966 / GRANDE BRETAGNE / - ALLEMAGNE (RFA) / 4-2
c. 1970 BRESIL-ITALIE 4-1
d. 1974 ALLEMAGNE (RFA)- / PAY BAS 2-1
e. 1978 / ARGENTINE -/ PAY BAS / 3-1
f. ARGENTINE -PAYS BAS / 3-1

1978, Dec. 30 **Litho.** ***Perf. 13½***

359	A98	(*a*) 40fr multi.	40	20
360	"	(*b*) 60fr "	60	30
361	A98	(*c*) 100fr multi.	1.00	50
362	"	(*d*) 200fr "	2.00	1.00
363	"	(*e*) 300fr "	3.00	1.50
		Nos. 359-363 (5)	7.00	3.50

Souvenir Sheet

364	A98	(*f*) 500fr multi.	5.00	2.50

World Soccer Championship winners. Size of No. 364: 119x80½mm.

SEMI-POSTAL STAMPS

Anti-Malaria Issue

Common Design Type

Perf. 12½x12

1962, Apr. 7 Engraved Unwmkd.

B1 CD108 25fr+5fr orange 60 60

Issued for the World Health Organization drive to eradicate malaria.

Freedom from Hunger Issue

Common Design Type

1963, Mar. 21 ***Perf. 13***

B2 CD112 25fr+5fr dark green, dark blue & brn. 60 60

Red Cross, Mother and Children
SP1

1974, Oct. 2 Photo. ***Perf. 12½x13***

B3 SP1 30fr+10fr multi. 35 30

Red Cross of Chad, first anniversary.

AIR POST STAMPS

Olympic Games Issue

French Equatorial Africa No. C37 Surcharged in Red

XVII• OLYMPIADE 1960 REPUBLIQUE DU TCHAD 250F

Engraved

1960, Dec. 15 ***Perf. 13*** **Unwmkd.**

C1 AP8 250fr on 500fr greenish blk., blk. & slate 6.50 6.50

Issued to commemorate the 17th Olympic Games, Rome, Aug. 25–Sept. 11. Surcharge 46mm. wide; illustration reduced.

Red Bishops AP1 Discus Thrower AP2

Designs (birds in pairs): 100fr, Scarlet-chested sunbird. 200fr, African paradise flycatcher. 250fr, Malachite kingfisher. 500fr, Nubian carmine bee-eater.

Engraved

1961-63 ***Perf. 13*** **Unwmkd.**

C2	AP1	50fr dark green, magenta & black	80	15
C3	"	100fr multicolored	1.50	70
C4	"	200fr "	3.00	1.25
C5	"	250fr dk. blue, grn. & dp. orange ('63)	3.75	1.85
C6	"	500fr multicolored	7.50	4.00
		Nos. C2-C6 (5)	16.55	7.95

Air Afrique Issue

Common Design Type

1962, Feb. 17 ***Perf. 13*** **Unwmkd.**

C7 CD107 25fr lt. blue, orange brown & black 45 25

Issued to commemorate the founding of Air Afrique (African Airlines).

Abidjan Games Issue

Photogravure

1962, July 21 ***Perf. 12x12½***

C8 AP2 100fr brown, light green & blk. 1.50 85

African Postal Union Issue

Common Design Type

1963, Sept. 8 ***Perf. 12½*** **Unwmkd.**

C9 CD114 85fr dk. blue, ocher & red 1.20 65

Air Afrique Issue, 1963

Common Design Type

1963, Nov. 19 ***Perf. 13x12***

C10 CD115 50fr multicolored 1.10 75

Europafrica Issue

Common Design Type

1963, Nov. 30 Photo. ***Perf. 12x13***

C11 CD116 50fr deep green, yel. & dk. brn. 75 55

Mail Truck and Broussard Plane
AP4

Engraved

1963, Dec. 16 ***Perf. 13*** **Unwmkd.**

C12 AP4 100fr slate green, ultra. & red brown 1.50 50

Chiefs of State Issue

Map and Presidents of Chad, Congo, Gabon and Central African Republic
AP4a

1964, June 23 Photo. ***Perf. 12½***

C13 AP4a 100fr multicolored 1.35 65

See note after Central African Republic No. C19.

Europafrica Issue, 1964

Globe and Emblems of Industry and Agriculture—AP5

1964, July 20 ***Perf. 13x12***

C14 AP5 50fr brown, purple & deep orange 65 45

See note after Cameroun No. 402.

Soccer—AP6

Designs: 50fr, Javelin throw (vert.). 100fr, High jump (vert.). 200fr, Runners.

1964, Aug. 12 Engr. ***Perf. 13***

C15	AP6	25fr yellow green, slate green & orange brown	35	25
C16	"	50fr orange brown, indigo & brt. bl.	75	50
C17	"	100fr black, red & bright green	1.50	1.00
C18	"	200fr bister, black & carmine	3.00	1.65
		a. Min. sheet of 4	6.00	6.00

Issued for the 18th Olympic Games, Tokyo, Oct. 10–25, 1964. No. C18a contains one each of Nos. C15–C18. Size: 191x99mm.

Communications Symbols
AP7

1964, Nov. 2 Litho. ***Perf. 12½x13***

C19 AP7 25fr lilac, dk. brn. & lt. red brn. 40 20

Issued to commemorate the Pan-African and Malagasy Posts and Telecommunications Congress, Cairo, Oct. 24–Nov. 6.

President John F. Kennedy
AP8

1964, Nov. 3 Photo. ***Perf. 12½***

C20 AP8 100fr multicolored 1.75 1.25
a. Souv. sheet of 4 7.00 7.00

Issued in memory of Pres. John F. Kennedy (1917–1963). No. C20a contains 4 No. C20; black marginal inscription. Size: 90x129mm.

ICY Emblem
AP9

1965, July 5 Photo. ***Perf. 13***

C21 AP9 100fr multicolored 1.50 85

International Cooperation Year, 1965.

Abraham Lincoln—AP10

1965, Sept. 7 ***Perf. 13*** **Unwmkd.**

C22 AP10 100fr multicolored 1.50 85

Centenary of death of Abraham Lincoln.

Musical Instrument Type of Regular Issue

Design: 100fr, Xylophone (marimba).

1965, Oct. 26 Engraved ***Perf. 13***

Size: 48x27mm.

C23 A18 100fr ocher, brt. blue & violet bl. 1.35 45

Winston Churchill
AP11

1965, Nov. 23 Engraved ***Perf. 13***

C24 AP11 50fr dk. grn. & blk. 75 35

Issued in memory of Sir Winston Spencer Churchill (1874–1965), statesman and World War II leader.

Dr. Albert Schweitzer and Outstretched Hands
AP12

1966, Feb. 15 Photo. ***Perf. 12½***

C25 AP12 100fr multicolored 1.50 75

Issued in memory of Dr. Albert Schweitzer (1875–1965), medical missionary, theologian and musician.

Air Afrique Issue, 1966

Common Design Type

1966, Aug. 31 Photo. ***Perf. 13***

C26 CD123 30fr yel. grn., blk. & gray 45 25

Issued to commemorate the introduction of DC-8F planes by Air Afrique.

White-throated Bee-eater—AP13

Birds: 50fr, Blue-eared glossy starling. 200fr, African pygmy kingfisher. 250fr, Red-throated bee-eater. 500fr, Little green bee-eater.

1966-67 Photo. *Perf. 13x12½*

C27 AP13 50fr gold & multi. 50 25
C28 " 100fr bluish gray & multi. 1.00 45
C29 " 200fr greenish gray & multi. 2.00 1.00
C30 " 250fr pale blue & multi. 2.50 1.20
C31 " 500fr pale salmon & multi. 5.00 2.50
Nos. C27-C31 (5) 11.00 5.40

Issue dates: 100fr, 200fr, 500fr, Oct. 18, 1966. Others, Mar. 21, 1967.

Congress Hall—AP14

1967, Jan. 5 Photo. *Perf. 12½*

C32 AP14 25fr multicolored 40 20

Opening of the new Congress Hall.

Breguet 19 Biplane—AP15

Planes: 30fr, Latécoère 631 hydroplane. 50fr, Douglas DC-3. 100fr, Piper Cherokee 6.

1967, Aug. 1 Engr. *Perf. 13*

C33 AP15 25fr sky blue, slate green & light brown 40 20
C34 " 30fr sky bl., indigo & green 45 25
C35 " 50fr sky blue, olive bister & slate green 75 40
C36 " 100fr dark blue, slate green & dark red 1.50 75

First anniversary of Air Chad.

African Postal Union Issue, 1967

Common Design Type

1967, Sept. 9 Engraved *Perf. 13*

C37 CD124 100fr olive, bright pink & red brown 1.35 70

Rock Painting Type of Regular Issue

Rock Paintings: 100fr, Masked dancers. 125fr, Rabbit hunt.

1967, Dec. 19 Engraved *Perf. 13*

Size: 48x27mm.

C38 A32 100fr brt. grn., sal. & maroon 1.50 65
C39 " 125fr ultra., salmon & maroon 1.85 90

Issued to commemorate the Balloud expedition in the Ennedi Mountains.

Downhill Skiing—AP16

Design: 100fr, Ski jump (vert.).

1968, Feb. 5 Engraved *Perf. 13*

C40 AP16 30fr red lilac, brt. green & dark olive 45 25
C41 AP16 100fr vio. bl., brt. bl. & slate grn. 1.50 85

Issued to commemorate the 10th Winter Olympic Games, Grenoble, France, Feb. 6-18.

Konrad Adenauer AP17

1968, Mar. 19 Photo. *Perf. 12½*

C42 AP17 52fr grn., dk. brn. & lt. lilac 80 45
a. Souv. sheet of 4 3.25 3.25

Issued in memory of Konrad Adenauer (1876-1967), chancellor of West Germany (1949-63). No. C42a contains four No. C42. Margin with black inscription and 1967 CEPT (Europa) emblem. Size: 120½x169mm.

The Snake Charmer, by Henri Rousseau—AP18

Design: 130fr, "War" by Henri Rousseau.

1968, May 14 Photo. *Perf. 13½*

Size: 41x41mm.

C43 AP18 100fr ultra. & multi. 1.50 60

Size: 48x35mm. ***Perf. 12½***

C44 AP18 130fr brn. & multi. 1.80 80

Hurdlers—AP19

Design: 80fr, Relay race.

1968, Oct. 16 Engraved *Perf. 13*

C45 AP19 32fr copper red, grn. & choc. 50 20
C46 " 80fr ultra., choc. & carmine 1.00 30

Issued to commemorate the 19th Olympic Games, Mexico City, Oct. 12-27.

PHILEXAFRIQUE Issue

The Actor Wolf (Bernard), by Jacques L. David AP20

1969, Jan. 15 Photo. *Perf. 12½*

C47 AP20 100fr multi. 1.50 90

Issued to publicize PHILEXAFRIQUE, Philatelic Exhibition in Abidjan, Feb. 14-23. Printed with alternating lilac rose label.

2nd PHILEXAFRIQUE Issue

Common Design Type

Design: 50fr, Chad No. J12 and Moundang Dancers.

1969, Feb. 14 Engraved *Perf. 13*

C48 CD128 50fr red, brt. blue, brn. & green 75 50

Issued to commemorate the opening of PHILEXAFRIQUE, Abidjan, Feb. 14.

Gustav Nachtigal and Tibesti Gorge, 1869 AP21

Design: No. C50, Heinrich Barth and Lake Chad, 1851.

1969, Feb. 17

C49 AP21 100fr vio. blue, dk. brn. & brn. 1.25 35
C50 " 100fr green, purple & blue 1.25 35

Issued to honor the German explorers Gustav Nachtigal (1834-1885) and Heinrich Barth (1821-1865), and to commemorate the state visit of the President of West Germany Heinrich Lubke.

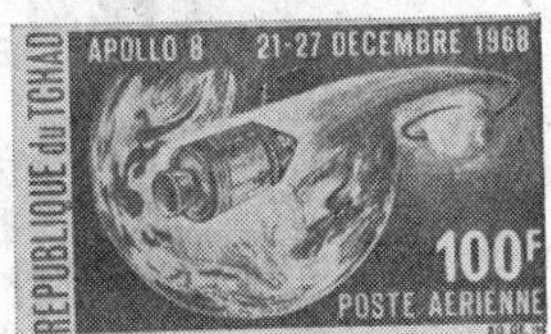

Apollo 8, Earth and Moon AP22

1969, Apr. 10 Photo. *Perf. 13*

C51 AP22 100fr multicolored 1.25 65

Issued to commemorate the U.S. Apollo 8 mission, the first men in orbit around the moon, Dec. 21-27, 1968.

Mahatma Gandhi AP23

Portraits: No. C53, John F. Kennedy. No. C54, Rev. Dr. Martin Luther King, Jr. No. C55, Robert F. Kennedy.

1969, May 20 Photo. *Perf. 12½*

C52 AP23 50fr blk. & lt. grn. 65 35
C53 " 50fr black & tan 65 35
C54 " 50fr black & pink 65 35
C55 " 50fr black & light violet blue 65 35
a. Souv. sheet of 4 3.00 3.00

Issued to honor exponents of non-violence. No. C55a contains one each of Nos. C52-C55. Black marginal inscription. Size: 120x159mm.

Presidents Tombalbaye and Mobutu, Map and Flags of Chad and Congo—AP24

Embossed on Gold Foil

1969 *Die-cut Perf. 13½*

C56 AP24 1000fr gold, dk. bl. & red 16.00 16.00

Issued to commemorate the first anniversary of the establishment of the Union of Central African States, comprising Chad, Congo Democratic Republic and Central African Republic.

Napoleon Visiting Hospital, by Alexandre Veron-Bellecourt AP25

Paintings: 85fr, Battle of Wagram, by Horace Vernet. 130fr, Battle of Austerlitz, by Francois Pascal Gerard.

1969, July 23 Photo. *Perf. 12x12½*

C57 AP25 30fr multicolored 60 45
C58 " 85fr " 1.50 1.10
C59 " 130fr " 2.50 1.75

Bicentenary of birth of Napoleon I.

Apollo 11 Issue

Astronaut on Moon—AP26

Embossed on Gold Foil

1969, Oct. 17 *Die-cut Perf. 13½*

C60 AP26 1000fr gold 16.00 16.00

See note after Algeria No. 427.

Village Life, by Goto Narcisse AP27

Designs: No. C62, Women at the Market, by Iba N'Diaye. No. C63, Woman with Flowers, by Iba N'Diaye (vert.).

Perf. 12x12½, 12½x12

1970 Photogravure

C61 AP27 100fr multicolored 1.10 30
C62 " 250fr grn. & multi. 3.00 70
C63 " 250fr brn. & multi. 3.00 70

Issue dates: Mar. 17, 100fr. Aug. 28, Nos. C62-C63.

EXPO Emblem and Osaka Print
AP28

Designs (EXPO Emblem and): 100fr, Tower of the Sun. 125fr, Osaka print (diff. design).

1970, June 30 Engraved *Perf. 13*

C64 AP28 50fr bl., red brown & slate grn. 55 18
C65 " 100fr red, yel. grn. & Prus. bl. 1.10 28
C66 " 125fr black, dk. red & bister 1.35 40

Issued to publicize EXPO '70 International Exhibition, Osaka, Japan, Mar. 15–Sept. 13.

Nos. C28–C30 Surcharged in Carmine with New Value and Bars and Overprinted:
a. "APOLLO XI / 1er débarquement sur la lune / 20 juillet 1969"
b. "APOLLO XII / Exploration de la lune / 19 novembre 1969"
c. "APOLLO XIII / Exploit spatial / 11–17 avril 1970"

1970, July 9 Photo. *Perf. 13x12½*

C67 AP13 (*a*) 50fr on 100fr multi. 55 40
C68 " (*b*) 100fr on 200fr multi. 1.10 60
C69 " (*c*) 125fr on 250fr multi. 1.35 80

Space missions of Apollo 11, 12 and 13.

DC-8 "Fort Lamy" over Airport
AP29

1970, Aug. 5 *Perf. 12½*

C70 AP29 30fr dk. slate green & multi. 40 15

The Visitation, Venetian School, 15th Century
AP30

Paintings, Venetian School: 25fr, Nativity, 15th century. 30fr, Virgin and Child, c. 1350.

1970, Dec. 15 Photo. *Perf. 12½x12*

C71 AP30 20fr gold & multi. 30 15
C72 " 25fr " " 32 20
C73 " 30fr " " 40 25

Christmas 1970. See Nos. C105–C108.

Post Office Mauritius and Emblem
AP31

Designs (PHILEXOCAM Emblem and): 20fr, Tuscany No. 23. 30fr, France No. 8. 60fr, United States No. 2. 80fr, Japan No. 8. 100fr, Saxony No. 1.

1971, Jan. 23 Engraved *Perf. 13*

C74 AP31 10fr lt. blue green, bister & dark blue 15 5
C75 " 20fr brt. green, blk. & bister 25 8
C76 " 30fr maroon, black & org. brown 40 15
C77 " 60fr car. lake, org. brn. & black 70 25
C78 " 80fr bl., bister brn. & dull blue 90 38
C79 " 100fr blue, dull bl. & bister brn. 1.35 45
a. Souvenir sheet of 6 4.00 4.00
Nos. C74–C79 (6) 3.75 1.36

Publicity for PHILEXOCAM, philatelic exhibition, Fort Lamy, Jan. 23–30. No. C79a contains one each of Nos. C74–C79 with orange brown marginal inscription. Size: 158x130mm.

Gamal Abdel Nasser
AP32

1971, Feb. 16 Photo. *Perf. 12½*

C80 AP32 75fr multicolored 75 20

In memory of Gamal Abdel Nasser (1918–1970), President of Egypt.

Presidents Mobutu, Bokassa and Tombalbaye—AP33

1971, Apr. 28 Photo. *Perf. 13*

C81 AP33 100fr multicolored 1.00 50

Return of Central African Republic to the United States of Central Africa which also includes Congo Democratic Republic and Chad.

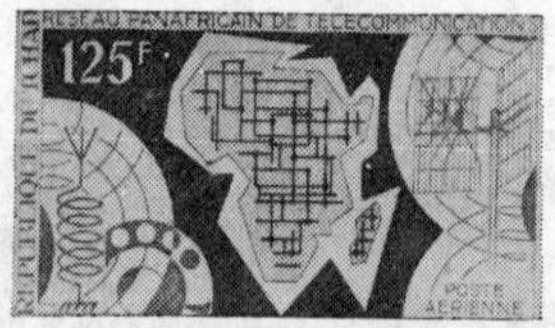

Map of Africa, Communications Network and Symbols—AP34

1971, May 17 Engraved *Perf. 13*

C82 AP34 125fr ultra., slate green & brown red 1.40 30

Pan-African telecommunications system.

Boys Around Campfire, Torii
AP35

1971, Aug. 24 Photo. *Perf. 12½*

C83 AP35 250fr multicolored 2.75 85

13th Boy Scout World Jamboree, Asagiri Plain, Japan, Aug. 2–10.

White Egret—AP36

1971, Sept. 28 Photo. *Perf. 13x12½*

C84 AP36 1000fr blk., dk. bl. & ocher 10.00 7.00

Greek Marathon Runners—AP37

Designs: 45fr, Ancient Olympic Stadium. 75fr, Greek wrestlers. 130fr, Olympic Stadium, Athens, 1896.

1971, Oct. 5 *Perf. 12½*

C85 AP37 40fr multicolored 50 25
C86 " 45fr " 55 35
C87 " 75fr " 85 40
C88 " 130fr " 1.40 75

75th anniversary of modern Olympic Games.

Duke Ellington
AP38

Portraits: 50fr, Sidney Bechet. 100fr, Louis Armstrong.

1971, Oct. 20 Lithographed *Perf. 13*

C89 AP38 50fr multicolored 55 18
C90 " 75fr lt. bl. & multi. 80 23
C91 " 100fr multicolored 1.10 35

Famous American jazz musicians.

Charles de Gaulle
AP39

Design: No. C93, Félix Eboué.

Lithographed and Embossed

1971, Nov. 9 *Perf. 12½*

C92 AP39 200fr grn., yel. grn. & gold 3.50 3.50
C93 " 200fr blue, lt. blue & gold 3.50 3.50
a. Souvenir sheet of 2 7.50 7.50

First anniversary of the death of Charles de Gaulle (1890–1970), president of France. No. C93a contains one each of Nos. C92–C93 with brown and ocher label carrying commemorative inscription and de Gaulle's signature. Size: 110x70mm.

African Postal Union Issue, 1971
Common Design Type

Design: 100fr, Sao antelope head and UAMPT building, Brazzaville, Congo.

1971, Nov. 13 Photo. *Perf. 13x13½*

C94 CD135 100fr bl. & multi. 1.10 50

Apollo 15 Rocket
AP40

Designs: 80fr, Apollo 15 capsule (horiz.). 150fr, Lunar module on Moon (horiz.). 250fr, Astronaut making tests. 300fr, Moon-buggy. No. C100, Successful splashdown (horiz.). No. C101, Apollo 15 insignia.

1972, Jan. 5 Litho. *Perf. 13½*

C95 AP40 40fr multi. 32 15
C96 " 80fr " 65 33
C97 " 150fr " 1.20 60
C98 " 250fr " 2.00 1.00
C99 " 300fr " 2.40 1.20
C100 " 500fr " 4.00 2.00
Nos. C95–C100 (6) 10.57 5.28

Souvenir Sheet

C101 AP40 500fr multi. 4.00 1.85

Apollo 15 moon landing. No. C101 has multicolored margin with American flag, and portraits of the families of astronauts Scott, Worden and Irwin. Size: 103x84 mm.

Soyuz 2 Link-up—AP41

Designs: 30fr, Soyuz 2 on launching pad (vert.). 50fr, No. C108, Cosmonauts in uniform. 200fr, V. I. Patzaev. No. C106, V. N. Volkov. 400fr, G. L. Dobrovolsky. No. C109, Three cosmonauts.

1972, Jan. 5 *Perf. 13½x13*

C102 AP41 30fr multi. 25 13
C103 " 50fr " 40 20
C104 " 100fr " 80 40
C105 " 200fr " 1.60 80
C106 " 300fr " 2.40 1.20
C107 " 400fr " 3.25 1.60
Nos. C102–C107 (6) 8.70 4.33

Souvenir Sheets

C108 AP41 300fr multi. 3.00 1.50
C109 " 400fr " 4.00 2.00

Soyuz 2 link-up project. No. C108 has multicolored margin depicting launching pad, No. C109, Moscow sky-line. Size: 100x79mm.

Bobsledding—AP42

Design: 100fr, Slalom.

1972, Feb. 24 Engraved *Perf. 13*

C110 AP42 50fr Prus. blue & rose red 60 20
C111 " 100fr red lilac & slate grn. 1.20 35

11th Winter Olympic Games, Sapporo, Japan, Feb. 3–13.

Pres. Tombalbaye Type, 1972

1972, Apr. 13 Litho. *Perf. 13*

C112 A63 70fr multicolored 70 35
C113 " 80fr " 80 40

11th Winter Olympic Type, 1972

Designs: 130fr, Speed skating. No. C115, Ice hockey. No. C116, Ski jumping. 250fr, 4-man bobsled.

1972, Apr. 13 *Perf. 13½*

C114 A64 130fr multi. 1.30 65
C115 " 200fr " 2.00 1.00

Souvenir Sheets

C116 A64 200fr multi. 2.00 1.00
C117 " 250fr " 2.50 1.25

11th Winter Olympic Games, Sapporo, Japan. Nos. C116 and C117 have multicolored margins showing Japanese religious figures. Size: 99x79mm.

Scout Jamboree Type, 1972

Designs: 100fr, Cooking preparation. 120fr, Lord Baden Powell. 250fr, Hiking.

1972, May 15

C118 A67 100fr multi. 1.00 60
C119 " 120fr " 1.20 75

Souvenir Sheet

C120 A67 250fr multi. 2.50 1.50

Scout Jamboree. No. C120 has multicolored margin showing African veldt and ostrich. Size: 102x81mm.

Zebras—AP43

Designs: 30fr, Mandrills. 100fr, African elephants. 130fr, Gazelles. 150fr, Hippopotamuses. 200fr, Lion cub.

1972, May 15 Litho. *Perf. 13*

C121 AP43 20fr multi. 20 10
C122 " 30fr " 30 15
C123 " 100fr " 1.00 50
C124 " 130fr " 1.30 65
C125 " 150fr " 1.50 75
Nos. C121-C125 (5) 4.30 2.15

Souvenir Sheet

C126 AP43 200fr multi. 2.00 1.00

African wild animals. No. C126 has multicolored margin showing map of Africa, sun and various animals. Size: 102½x79 mm.

See "Special Notices" at the front of this volume for data on the listing methods of this Catalogue, abbreviations, condition, prices and examination.

View of Venice, by Caffi—AP44

Paintings by Ippolito Caffi: 40fr, Sailing ship and Doge's Palace (vert.). 140fr, Grand Canal (vert.).

1972, May 23 Photo.

C127 AP44 40fr gold & multi. 50 15
C128 " 45fr " " 60 20
C129 " 140fr " " 1.50 1.00

UNESCO campaign to save Venice.

11th Winter Olympic Winners Type, 1972

Designs: 150fr, Slalom, B. Cochran, U.S. 200fr, Women's figure skating, B. Schuba, Austria. 250fr, Ice hockey, USSR. 300fr, 2-man bobsled. W. Zimmerer and P. Utzschneider, West Germany.

1972, June 15 *Perf. 14½*

C130 A69 150fr gold & multi. 1.50 75
C131 " 200fr gold & multi. 2.00 1.00

Souvenir Sheets

C132 A69 250fr gold & multi. 2.00 1.25
C133 " 300fr gold & multi. 3.00 1.75

11th Winter Olympic gold medal winners. Nos. C130–C131 exist se-tenant with label showing earth satellite. Nos. C132–C133 have multicolored margins showing satellite orbiting earth. Size: 127x89mm.

Daudet, "Tartarin de Tarascon," Book Year Emblem—AP45

1972, July 22 Engraved *Perf. 13*

C134 AP45 100fr dk. red, lilac & dk. brn. 1.20 30

International Book Year, 1972, and to honor Alphonse Daudet (1840–1897), French writer.

20th Summer Olympics Type, 1972

Designs (TV Tower, Munich and): 100fr, Gymnast. 120fr, Pole vault. 150fr, Fencing. 250fr, Hammer throw. 300fr, Boxing.

1972, Aug. 15

C135 A70 100fr gold & multi. 1.00 50
C136 " 120fr gold & multi. 1.20 60
C137 " 150fr gold & multi. 1.50 75

Souvenir Sheets

C138 A70 250fr gold & multi. 2.50 1.25
C139 " 300fr gold & multi. 3.00 1.50

20th Summer Olympic Games, Munich, Nos. C135–C137 exist se-tenant with label showing arms of Munich. Nos. C138–C139 have multicolored margin with Munich views. Size: 127x89mm.

Lunokhod on Moon—AP46

Design: 100fr, Luna 16 on moon and rocket in flight (vert.).

1972, Sept. 19

C140 AP46 100fr dk. bl., pur. & bister 1.00 50
C141 " 150fr slate, brn. & lilac 1.50 75

Russian moon missions.

Farcha Laboratory, Cattle, Scientist—AP47

1972, Nov. 11 Photo. *Perf. 13*

C142 AP47 75fr yel. & multi. 70 35

20th anniversary of the Farcha Laboratory for veterinary research.

King Faisal and Holy Kaaba, Mecca—AP48

1972, Nov. 17

C143 AP48 75fr multicolored 75 40

Visit of King Faisal of Saudi Arabia.

Christmas Type of 1970

Designs: 40fr, Virgin and Child, by Giovanni Bellini. 75fr, Virgin and Child, by Dall'Occhio. 80fr, Nativity, by Fra Angelico (horiz.). 95fr, Adoration of the Kings, by Il Perugino.

1972, Dec. 15 Photo. *Perf. 13*

C144 AP30 40fr gold & multi. 50 15
C145 " 75fr " " 85 25
C146 " 80fr " " 1.00 28
C147 " 95fr " " 1.10 38

Christmas 1972.

20th Summer Olympic Winners Type, 1972

Designs (Olympic Emblems and): 150fr, Pole vault, Nordwig, East Germany. 250fr, Hurdles, Milburn, U.S. 300fr, Javelin, Wolfermann, West Germany.

1972, Dec. 22

C148 A76 150fr multi. 1.50 75
C149 " 250fr " 2.50 1.25

Souvenir Sheet

C150 A76 300fr multi. 3.00 1.50

20th Summer Olympic Games winners. No. C150 has multicolored margin showing Olympic emblems. Size: 111½x82 mm.

Summer Olympic Winners Type, 1972

Designs (Olympic Emblem and): 150fr, Dressage, Mancinelli, Italy. No. C152; Finn class sailing, Serge Maury, France. No. C153, Swimming, Mark Spitz.

1972, Dec. 22 Litho. *Perf. 11*

C151 A77 150fr gold & multi. 1.50 75
C152 A77 250fr gold & multi. 2.50 1.25

Souvenir Sheet

C153 A77 250fr multi. 2.50 1.25

20th Summer Olympic Games, winners. No. C153 has gold and multicolored margin showing Olympic emblem and flame. Size: 111x82½mm.

Copernicus and Solar System AP49

1973, Mar. 31 Engraved *Perf. 13*

C154 AP49 250fr gray, magenta & brown 2.75 1.50

500th anniversary of the birth of Nicolaus Copernicus (1473–1543), Polish astronomer.

Skylab over Africa—AP50

Design: 150fr, Skylab.

1974, Aug. 6 Engraved *Perf. 13*

C155 AP50 100fr maroon, blue & olive 1.00 55
C156 " 150fr brown, blue & slate green 1.40 75

Exploits of Skylab, U.S. manned space station.

Soccer—AP51

Designs: 125fr, 150fr, Soccer players; 125fr, vertical.

1974, Oct. 22 Engraved *Perf. 13*

C157 AP51 50fr dull red & chocolate 45 25
C158 " 125fr red & deep green 1.10 65
C159 " 150fr green & rose red 1.35 75

World Cup Soccer Championship, Munich, June 13–July 7.

Family and WPY Emblem AP52

1974, Nov. 11

C160 AP52 250fr multi. 2.25 1.40

World Population Year.

Mail Delivery by Canoe—AP53

Designs (UPU Emblem and): 40fr, Diesel train. 100fr, Jet. 150fr, Spacecraft.

1974, Dec. 20 Engraved *Perf. 13*

C161 AP53 30fr car. & multi. 28 18
C162 " 40fr ultra. & blk. 35 20
C163 " 100fr brown, ultra. & black 90 55
C164 " 150fr green, lilac & olive 1.40 85

Centenary of Universal Postal Union.

Women of Different Races, IWY Emblem—AP54

1975, June 25 Photo. *Perf. 13*

C165 AP54 250fr bl. & multi. 2.10 1.25

International Women's Year 1975.

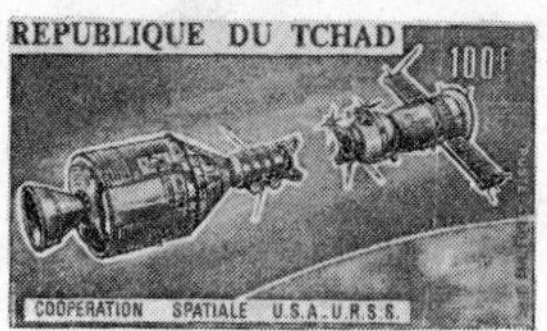

Apollo and Soyuz Before Link-up—AP55

Design: 130fr, Apollo and Soyuz after link-up.

1975, July 15 Engr. *Perf. 13*

C166 AP55 100fr ultra., choc. & green 1.00 50
C167 " 130fr vio. bl., brn. & green 1.20 75

Apollo Soyuz space test project (Russo-American space cooperation), launching July 15; link-up July 17.

Soccer Player, View of Montreal AP56

Designs (Olympic Rings, Montreal Skyline): 100fr, Discus thrower. 125fr, Runner.

1975, Oct. 14 Engr. *Perf. 13*

C168 AP56 75fr car. & slate green 70 38
C169 " 100fr car., choc. & bl. green 1.00 50
C170 " 125fr brn., bl. & carmine 1.25 75

Pre-Olympic Year 1975.

Nos. C166-C167 Overprinted: "JONCTION / 17 JUILLET 1975"

1975, Nov. 4 Engr. *Perf. 13*

C171 AP55 100fr multi. 1.00 50
C172 " 130fr " 1.20 70

Apollo-Soyuz link-up in space, July 17.

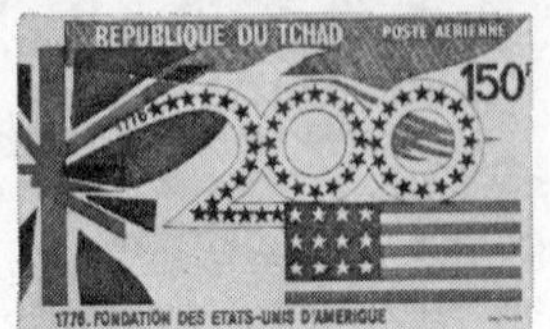

Stylized British and American Flags, "200"—AP57

1975, Dec. 5 Engr. *Perf. 13*

C173 AP57 150fr vio. bl., car. & ol. bis. 1.35 75

American Bicentennial.

Adoration of the Shepherds, by Murillo—AP58

Paintings: 75fr, Adoration of the Shepherds, by Georges de La Tour. 80fr, Virgin and Child with Bible, by Rogier van der Weyden (vert.). 100fr, Holy Family, by Raphael (vert.).

1975, Dec. 15 Litho. *Perf. 13x12½*

C174 AP58 40fr yel. & multi. 40 20
C175 " 75fr " " 70 38
C176 " 80fr " " 80 40
C177 " 100fr " " 1.00 45

Christmas 1975.

12th Winter Olympic Winners Type, 1976

Designs: 250fr, 4-man bobsled, West Germany. 300fr, Speed skating, J. E. Storholt, Norway. 500fr, Downhill skiing, F. Klammer, Austria.

1976, June 21 *Perf. 14*

C178 A84 250fr multi. 2.00 90
C179 " 300fr " 2.40 1.10

Souvenir Sheet

C180 A84 500fr multi. 4.00 2.00

12th Winter Olympic Games winners, Innsbruck. No. C180 has multicolored margin showing snowflakes. Size: 114x 78mm.

Paul Revere's Ride and Portrait by Copley—AP59

Designs: 125fr, George Washington crossing Delaware. 150fr, Lafayette offering his services to America. 200fr, Rochambeau at Yorktown with Washington. 250fr, Benjamin Franklin presenting Declaration of Independence. 400fr, Count de Grasse's victory at Cape Charles.

1976, July 4 Litho. *Perf. 14*

C181 AP59 100fr multi. 80 40
C182 " 125fr " 1.00 50
C183 " 150fr " 1.20 60
C184 AP59 200fr multi. 1.60 70
C185 " 250fr " 2.00 80
Nos. C181-C185 (5) 6.60 3.00

Souvenir Sheet

C186 AP59 400fr multi. 3.25 1.85

American Bicentennial. No. C186 has multicolored margin showing George Washington and his staff. Size: 113x 78mm.

Summer Olympics Type, 1976

Designs: 100fr, Boxing. 200fr, Pole vault. 300fr, Shot put. 500fr, Sprint.

1976, July 12

C187 A85 100fr multicolored 80 40
C188 " 200fr " 1.60 70
C189 " 300fr " 2.40 90

Souvenir Sheet

C190 A85 500fr multicolored 4.00 2.00

21st Summer Olympic Games, Montreal. No. C190 has multicolored margin showing Olympic stadium. Size: 103x77mm.

Viking Mars Project Type, 1976

Designs (Mars Lander and): 100fr, Viking landing on Mars. 200fr, Capsule over Mars. 250fr, Lander over Mars. 450fr, Lander and probe.

1976, July 23 Litho. *Perf. 14*

C191 A86 100fr multi. 80 40
C192 " 200fr " 1.60 70
C193 " 250fr " 2.00 80

Souvenir Sheet

C194 A86 450fr multi. 3.75 1.85

Viking Mars project, No. C194 has multicolored margin showing Viking probe. Size: 114x89mm.

Concorde—AP60

1976, Oct. 15 Litho. *Perf. 12½*

C195 AP60 250fr blue, black & verm. 2.00 75

First commercial flight of supersonic jet Concorde, Jan. 21.

Nobel Prize Type, 1976

Designs: 100fr, Albert Einstein, physics. 200fr, Dag Hammarskjold, peace. 300fr, Shinichiro Tomanaga, physics. 500fr, Alexander Fleming, medicine.

1976, Dec. 15

C196 A87 100fr multi. 80 40
C197 " 200fr " 1.60 70
C198 " 300fr " 2.40 90

Souvenir Sheet

C199 A87 500fr multi. 4.00 2.00

Nobel Prize winners. No. C199 has multicolored margin showing reverse and obverse of Nobel medal. Size: 116x79mm.

Adoration of the Shepherds, by Gerard van Honthorst—AP61

Paintings: 30fr, Nativity, by Albrecht Altdorfer (vert.). 60fr, Nativity, by Hans Holbein (vert.). 150fr, Adoration of the Kings, by Gerard David.

1976, Dec. 22 Litho. *Perf. 12½*

C200 AP61 30fr gold & multi. 25 15
C201 " 60fr " " 50 30
C202 AP61 120fr gold & blk. 1.00 60
C203 " 150fr " " 1.20 70

Christmas 1976.

Lesdiguières Bridge, by Jongkind—AP62

Design: 120fr, Sailing Ship and Boats, by Johan Barthold Jongkind (1819-1891).

1976, Dec. 27 Photo. *Perf. 13*

C204 AP62 100fr multi. 80 45
C205 " 120fr " 1.00 60

Centenary of impressionism.

Zeppelin Type of 1977

Designs: 125fr, Germany No. C40 and North Pole. 150fr, Germany No. C45 and Chicago department store. 175fr, Germany No. C38 and scenes of New York and London. 200fr, 500fr, U.S. No. C15 and New York.

1977, Mar. 30 *Perf. 11*

C206 A91 125fr multicolored 1.00 40
C207 " 150fr " 1.20 50
C208 " 175fr " 1.40 60
C209 " 200fr " 1.60 70

Souvenir Sheet

C210 A91 500fr multicolored 4.00 2.00

75th anniversary of the Zeppelin. No. C210 has multicolored margin showing world map with cancellations of Zeppelin flights. Size: 130x91mm.

Sassenage Castle, Grenoble—AP63

1977, May 21 Litho. *Perf. 12½*

C211 AP63 100fr multi. 80 45

10th anniversary of the International French Language Council.

Lafayette and Ships—AP64

Designs: 120fr, Abraham Lincoln, eagle and flags (vert.). 150fr, James Madison and family.

1977, July 30 Engr. *Perf. 13*

C212 AP64 100fr multi. 80 60
C213 " 120fr " 1.00 70
C214 " 150fr " 1.20 90

American Bicentennial.

Lindbergh and Spirit of St. Louis—AP65

Designs: 100fr, Concorde. 150fr, 200fr, 300fr, Various Lindbergh portraits and Spirit of St. Louis.

1977, Sept. 27

No.	Type	Description		
C215	AP65	100fr multi.	80	60
C216	"	120fr "	1.00	70
C217	"	150fr "	1.20	90
C218	"	200fr "	1.60	1.10
C219	"	300fr "	2.40	1.65
		Nos. C215-C219 (5)	7.00	4.95

Charles A. Lindbergh's solo transatlantic flight from New York to Paris, 50th anniversary, and first supersonic transatlantic flight of Concorde.

Mariner 10—AP66

Spacecraft: 200fr, Lunokhod on moon, Luna 21. 300fr, Viking on Mars.

1977, Oct. 10 Engr. *Perf. 13*

No.	Type	Description		
C220	AP66	100fr multi.	80	60
C221	"	200fr "	1.60	1.20
C222	"	300fr "	2.40	1.60

Running AP67

Designs: 60fr, Volleyball. 120fr, Soccer. 125fr, Basketball.

1977, Oct. 24 Engr. *Perf. 13*

No.	Type	Description		
C223	AP67	30fr multicolored	25	20
C224	"	60fr "	50	35
C225	"	120fr "	1.00	70
C226	"	125fr "	1.00	75

No. C215 Overprinted:

"PARIS NEW – YORK / 22.11.77"

1977, Nov. 22

No.	Type	Description		
C227	AP65	100fr multi.	80	60

Concorde, first commercial flight Paris to New York.

Virgin and Child, by Rubens AP68

Rubens Paintings: 60fr, Virgin and Child and Two Donors. 100fr, Adoration of the Shepherds. 125fr, Adoration of the Kings.

1977, Dec. 20 Litho. *Perf. 12½x12*

No.	Type	Description		
C228	AP68	30fr multicolored	25	20
C229	"	60fr "	50	35
C230	"	100fr "	80	60
C231	"	125fr "	1.00	75

Christmas 1977.

AIR POST SEMI-POSTAL STAMPS

Ramses II Battling the Hittites (from Abu Simbel)
SPAP1

Engraved

1964, March 9 *Perf. 13* Unwmkd.

No.	Type	Description		
CB1	SPAP1	10fr+5fr red, green & vio.	35	30
CB2	"	25fr+5fr red, grn. & vio. brn.	60	50
CB3	"	50fr+5fr red, grn. & slate grn.	1.00	90

Issued to publicize the UNESCO world campaign to save historic monuments in Nubia.

Lions Emblem
SPAP2

1967, July 5 Photo. *Perf. 13*

No.	Type	Description		
CB4	SPAP2	50fr+10fr multi.	90	35

Issued to commemorate the 50th anniversary of Lions International and to publicize the Lions work for the blind.

POSTAGE DUE STAMPS

Postage Due Stamps of France Overprinted

TCHAD

A. E. F.

1928 *Perf. 14x13½* Unwmkd.

No.	Type	Description		
J1	D2	5c light blue	7	7
J2	"	10c gray brown	10	10
J3	"	20c olive green	15	15
J4	"	25c bright rose	20	20
J5	"	30c light red	27	27
J6	"	45c blue green	30	30
J7	"	50c brown violet	50	50
J8	"	60c yellow brown	50	50
J9	"	1fr red brown	50	50
J10	"	2fr orange red	1.35	1.35
J11	"	3fr bright violet	85	85
		Nos. J1-J11 (11)	4.79	4.79

Huts
D3

Canoe
D4

Typographed.

1930 *Perf. 14x13½, 13½x14.*

No.	Type	Description		
J12	D3	5c deep blue & olive	10	10
J13	"	10c dark red & brown	15	15
J14	"	20c green & brown	35	35
J15	"	25c light blue & brown	40	40
J16	"	30c bistre brown & Prussian blue	40	40
J17	"	45c Prussian blue & olive	45	45
J18	"	50c red violet & brown	45	45
J19	"	60c gray lilac & blue black	80	80
J20	D4	1fr bistre brown & blue black	80	80
J21	"	2fr violet & brown	1.10	1.10
J22	"	3fr dp. red & brown	12.50	12.50
		Nos. J12-J22 (11)	17.50	17.50

In 1934 stamps of Chad were superseded by those of French Equatorial Africa.

Republic

Rhinoceros—D5

Tibesti Pictographs: No. J24, Kudu. No. J25, Two antelopes. No. J26, Three antelopes. No. J27, Ostrich. No. J28, Horned bull. No. J29, Bull. No. J30, Wild swine. No. J31, Elephant. No. J32, Rhinoceros. No. J33, Warrior with spear and shield. No. J34, Masked archer.

Engraved

1962, Apr. 20 *Perf. 13* Unwmkd.

No.	Type	Description		
J23	D5	50c olive bistre	4	3
J24	"	50c brown red	4	3
J25	"	1fr blue	5	5
J26	"	1fr green	5	5
J27	"	2fr vermilion	8	8
J28	"	2fr maroon	8	8
J29	"	5fr slate green	15	15
J30	"	5fr violet blue	15	15
J31	"	10fr brown	35	35
J32	"	10fr orange brown	35	35
J33	"	25fr carmine rose	85	85
J34	"	25fr violet	85	85
		Nos. J23-J34 (12)	3.04	3.02

The two designs of the same denomination are printed se-tenant.

Kanem Doll
D6

Dolls: 2fr, Kotoko. 5fr, Leather doll. 10fr, Kotoko. 25fr, Guera.

1969, Sept. 19 Engr. *Perf. 14x13*

No.	Type	Description		
J35	D6	1fr grn., verm. & brn.	5	5
J36	"	2fr verm., yel. green & brown	5	5
J37	"	5fr green, brown & slate green	7	5
J38	"	10fr grn., lilac & brown	13	7
J39	"	25fr rose, bl. & brown	32	20
		Nos. J35-J39 (5)	62	42

MILITARY STAMPS

Flag Bearer and Map of Chad
M1

1st Regiment Emblem
M2

Lithographed

1968 *Perf. 13x12½* Unwmkd.

No.	Type	Description		
M1	M1	tan & multicolored		

1972, Jan. 21 Photo. *Perf. 13*

No.	Type	Description		
M2	M2	blue & multi.	65	40

OFFICIAL STAMPS

Flag and Map of Chad
O1

Perf. 13½x14

1966-71 Typographed Unwmkd.

Flag in blue, yellow and carmine.

No.	Type	Description		
O1	O1	1fr light blue	6	3
O2	"	2fr gray	6	3
O3	"	5fr black	7	4
O4	"	10fr violet blue	12	8
O5	"	25fr orange	30	18
O6	"	30fr bright green	40	20
O7	"	40fr carmine ('71)	50	22
O8	"	50fr red lilac	60	25
O9	"	85fr green	1.00	50
O10	"	100fr brown	1.40	55
O11	"	200fr red	2.50	90
		Nos. O1-O11 (11)	7.01	2.98

CHILE

(chē'lā ; chil'ē)

LOCATION — Southwest coast of South America.
GOVT.—Republic.
AREA—286,397 sq. mi.
POP.—10,660,000 (est. 1977).
CAPITAL—Santiago.

100 Centavos = 1 Peso
1000 Milésimos = 100 Centésimos = 1 Escudo (1960)
100 Centavos = 1 Peso (1975)

> Prices of early Chile stamps vary according to condition. Quotations for Nos. 1–14 are for fine copies. Very fine to superb specimens sell at much higher prices, and inferior or poor copies sell at reduced prices, depending on the condition of the individual specimen.
>
> Pen cancellations are common on the 1862–67 issues. Such stamps sell for much less than the quoted prices which are for those with handstamped postal cancellations.

Christopher Columbus
A1

Wmkd.

1 5 5 5
a b c d

10 10 20
e f g

London Prints.
Engraved.

1853 *Imperf.* **Wmk. b.**
Blued Paper.

1 A1 5c brown red *450.00* 40.00
a. White paper 90.00

Wmk. e.
White Paper.

2 A1 10c deep bright blue *700.00* 90.00
a. Blued paper *650.00*
b. Diagonal half used as 5c on cover *500.00*

Santiago Prints.
Impressions Fine and Clear.
White Paper.

1854 **Wmks. b and e.**

3 A1 5c pale red brown 400.00 40.00
a. 5c deep red brown *450.00* 40.00
b. 5c chestnut *750.00* 150.00
4 " 5c burnt sienna *1250.00* 175.00
a. 5c dull chocolate *2000.00* 650.00
5 " 10c deep blue *1100.00* 125.00
a. 10c slate blue 125.00
b. 10c greenish blue 700.00
c. Half used as 5c on cover 375.00
6 " 10c light dull blue *1100.00* 125.00
a. 10c pale blue 125.00
b. Diagonal half used as 5c on cover 300.00

Lithographed.

7 A1 5c red brown *1800.00* 225.00
a. 5c pale brown *1600.00* 225.00

London Print.
Engraved.

1855 Blued Paper **Wmk. c.**

8 A1 5c brown red 150.00 9.00

Santiago Prints.
Impressions Worn and Blurred.
White Paper.

1856-62 **Wmks. b and e.**

9 A1 5c rose red ('58) 35.00 3.50
a. 5c carmine red ('62) 80.00 15.00
b. 5c orange red ('61) 150.00 85.00
c. 5c dull reddish brown ('57) 185.00 16.50
d. Printed on both sides *500.00*
e. Double impression
10 " 10c deep blue 185.00 20.00
a. 10c sky blue ('57) 185.00 20.00
b. 10c light blue 185.00 20.00
c. 10c indigo blue 185.00 27.50
d. Half used as 5c on cover 100.00

London Prints.

1862 **Wmks. a, f and g.**

11 A1 1c lemon yellow 25.00 30.00
a. Double impression *600.00*
12 " 10c bright blue 45.00 9.00
a. 10c deep blue 45.00 9.00
b. Blued paper 100.00 22.50
c. Wmkd. "20" (error) *4000.00* 2000.00
d. Half used as 5c on cover 125.00
13 " 20c green 65.00 45.00
a. 20c emerald

Santiago Print.

1865 **Wmk. d.**

14 A1 5c rose red 25.00 8.00
a. 5c carmine red 30.00 8.00
b. Printed on both sides *200.00*
c. Laid paper *200.00*
d. Double impression *200.00*

The 5c rose red (shades) on unwatermarked paper, either wove or ribbed, and on paper watermarked Chilean arms in the sheet are reprints made about 1870.

No. 13 has been reprinted in the color of issue and in fancy colors, both from the original engraved plate and from lithographic transfers. The reprints are on paper without watermark or with watermark CHILE and Star.

A2

A3

1867 *Perf. 12* **Unwmkd.**

15 A2 1c orange 7.50 2.00
Pen cancellation 10
16 " 2c black 10.00 3.00
Pen cancellation 10
17 " 5c red 6.00 50
Pen cancellation 5
18 " 10c blue 8.00 60
Pen cancellation 5
19 " 20c green 8.00 2.00
Pen cancellation 10

1877 *Rouletted*

20 A3 1c gray 1.50 30
21 " 2c orange 6.00 90
22 " 5c dull lake 6.00 20
23 " 10c blue 6.50 40
a. Diagonal half used as 5c on cover
24 " 20c green 6.50 1.50

The panel inscribed "CENTAVO" is straight on No. 22.

A4

A5

Columbus
A6

1878-99 *Rouletted*

25 A4 1c green ('81) 75 8
26 " 2c rose ('81) 1.25 8
27 A5 5c dull lake ('78) 5.00 35
28 " 5c ultramarine ('83) 1.25 5
29 " 10c orange ('85) 2.00 18
a. 10c yellow 8.00 25
30 " 15c dark green ('92) 75 25
31 " 20c gray ('86) 1.25 20
32 " 25c orange brown('92) 1.25 25
33 " 30c rose carmine ('99) 2.00 65
34 " 50c lilac ('78) 40.00 7.50
35 " 50c violet ('85) 1.00 50
36 A6 1p dark brown & black ('92) 9.00 35
a. Imperf. horiz. or vert., pair 60.00 60.00
Nos. 25-36 (12) 65.50 10.44

Columbus
A7 A8

1894 Re-engraved.

37 A7 1c blue green 30 10
38 " 2c carmine lake 30 10

In type A4 there is a small colorless ornament at each side of the base of the numeral, above the "E" and "V" of "CENTAVO". In type A7 these ornaments are missing, the figure "1" is broader than in type A4 and the head of the figure "2" is formed by a curved line instead of a ball.

1900-01

Type I. There is a heavy shading of short horizontal lines below "Chile" and the adjacent ornaments.

Type II. There is practically no shading below "Chile" and the ornaments.

Type I.

39 A8 1c yellow green 25 10
40 " 2c brown rose 50 10
41 " 5c deep blue 2.50 10
42 " 10c violet 2.50 12
a. Horizontal pair, imperf. between
43 " 20c gray 1.50 25
44 " 30c deep org. ('01) 2.00 40
45 " 50c red brown 2.50 45
a. Horizontal pair, imperf. between 50.00
Nos. 39-45 (7) 11.75 1.52

Type II.

46 A8 1c yellow green ('01) 20 8
47 " 2c rose ('01) 20 10
48 " 5c dull blue ('01) 1.50 15
a. Printed on both sides
49 " 10c violet ('01) 3.00 35

Columbus
A9 A10

1900 Black Surcharge

50 A9 5c on 30c rose carmine 25 15
a. Inverted surcharge 7.50 7.50
b. Double surcharge 25.00 25.00
c. Double surcharge, both inverted 25.00 25.00
d. Double surcharge, one inverted 25.00 25.00
e. Surcharged on front and back 50.00 50.00

Counterfeits exist of Nos. 50a-50e.

1901-02 *Perf. 12*

51 A10 1c green 20 10
52 " 2c carmine 20 10
53 " 5c ultramarine 35 10
54 " 10c red & black 75 30
55 " 30c violet & black 2.50 30
56 " 50c red org. & black 3.00 85
Nos. 51-56 (6) 7.00 1.75

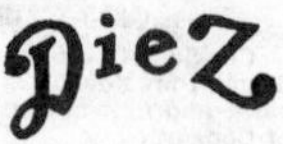

No. 44 Surcharged in Dark Blue

1903 *Rouletted.*

57 A8 10c on 30c orange 50 20
a. Inverted surcharge 15.00 15.00
b. Double surcharge 30.00 30.00
c. Double, one inverted 30.00 30.00
d. Double, both inverted 30.00 30.00
e. Stamp design printed on both sides

Pedro de Valdivia
A11

Coat of Arms
A12

A13

Telegraph Stamps Surcharged or Overprinted in Black

Type I. Animal at left has neither mane nor tail.
Type II. Animal at left has mane and tail.

1904 *Perf. 12.*

58 A11 1c on 20c ultramarine 10 8
a. Imperf. horiz., pair 40.00 40.00
b. Inverted surcharge 35.00 35.00
59 A13 2c yellow brown, I 18 8
a. Inverted overprint 15.00 15.00
b. Pair, one without overprint 50.00 50.00
60 " 5c red, I 25 10
a. Inverted overprint 15.00 15.00
c. Pair, one without overprint 25.00 25.00
61 " 10c olive green, I 1.25 25
a. Inverted overprint 50.00 50.00

Perf. 12½ to 16.

62 A13 2c yel. brown, II 4.00 3.50
63 A11 3c on 5c brown red 30.00 30.00
a. Inverted surcharge
64 A12 3c on 1p brown, II 15 15
a. Double surcharge 50.00 50.00
65 A13 5c red, II 10.00 7.50
a. Inverted overprint
66 " 10c olive green, II 15.00 9.00
67 A11 12c on 5c brown red 45 20
a. No star at left of "Centavos" 1.50 1.25
b. Inverted surcharge 40.00 40.00
c. Double surcharge 50.00 50.00
Nos. 62-67 (6) 59.60 50.35

Counterfeits exist of the overprint and surcharge varieties of Nos. 57–67.

Columbus
A14 A15

Columbus
A16

1905-09 ***Perf. 12.***

68	A14	1c green	15	10
69	"	2c carmine	10	10
70	"	3c yellow brown	25	20
71	"	5c ultramarine	20	10
72	A15	10c gray & black	60	10
73	"	12c lake & black	1.50	1.00
74	"	15c violet & black	60	20
75	"	20c org. brn. & blk.	1.25	20
76	"	30c bl. grn. & blk.	1.25	30
77	"	50c ultra. & black	1.25	25
78	A16	1p gold, green & gray	6.50	6.00
		Nos. 68–78 (11)	13.65	8.55

A 20c dull red and black, type A15, was prepared but not issued. Price $125. "Specimen" copies of Nos. 74, 76–78 exist, punched to prevent postal use.

Nos. 73, 78 Surcharged in Blue or Red

ISLAS DE
JUAN FERNANDEZ
5
a

ISLAS DE
JUAN FERNANDEZ
10 Cts.
b

1910

79	A15 (*a*)	5c on 12c lake & black (Bl)	15	15
80	A16 (*b*)	10c on 1p gold, green & gray (R)	35	30
81	" (")	20c on 1p gold, green & gray (R)	60	50
82	" (")	1p gold, green & gray (R)	2.00	1.50

The 1p is overprinted "ISLAS DE JUAN FERNANDEZ" only. The use of these stamps throughout Chile was authorized.

Independence Centenary Issue.

Oath of Independence
A17

Monument to O'Higgins
A26

Gen. Manuel Blanco Encalada
A29

Designs: 2c, Battle of Chacabuco. 3c, Battle of Roble. 5c, Battle of Maipú. 10c, Naval Engagement of "Lautaro" and "Esmeralda." 12c, Capturing the "Maria Isabel." 15c, First Sortie of Liberating Forces. 20c, Abdication of O'Higgins. 25c, Chile's First Congress. 50c, Monument to José M. Carrera. 1p, Monument to San Martin. 5p, Gen. José Ignacio Zenteno. 10p, Adm. Lord Thomas Cochrane.

1910 **Center in Black.**

83	A17	1c dark green	20	15
		a. Center inverted		5000.00
84	"	2c lake	20	15
85	"	3c red brown	20	20
86	A17	5c deep blue	20	10
87	"	10c gray brown	45	40
88	"	12c vermilion	1.00	85
89	"	15c slate	40	35
90	"	20c red orange	1.00	85
91	"	25c ultramarine	2.00	1.85
92	A26	30c violet	1.50	60
93	"	50c olive green	3.50	1.50
94	"	1p yellow orange	6.00	4.00
95	A29	2p red	4.00	2.50
96	"	5p yellow green	30.00	30.00
97	"	10p dark violet	22.50	20.00
		Nos. 83–97 (15)	73.15	63.50

Columbus
A32

De Valdivia
A33

Mateo de Toro Zambrano
A34

Bernardo O'Higgins
A35

Ramón Freire
A36

F. A. Pinto
A37

Joaquín Prieto
A38

Manuel Bulnes
A39

Manuel Montt
A40

José Joaquín Pérez
A41

Federico Errázuriz Zanartu
A42

Aníbal Pinto
A43

Designs: 2p, Domingo Santa María. 5p, José de Balmaceda. 10p, Federico Errázuriz Echaurren.

Outer backgrounds consist of horizontal and diagonal lines.

1911 **Engraved.** ***Perf. 12.***

98	A32	1c deep green	10	5
99	A33	2c scarlet	10	5
100	A34	3c sepia	30	25
101	A35	5c dark blue	10	4
102	A36	10c gray & black	30	8
		a. Center inverted	650.00	550.00
103	A37	12c carmine & black	15	10
104	A38	15c violet & black	30	5
		a. Center inverted		3500.00
105	A39	20c orange red & black	80	5
		a. Center inverted	35.00	35.00
106	A40	25c light blue & black	50	25
107	A41	30c bistre brn. & blk.	2.00	10
108	A42	50c myrtle green & black	2.00	15
109	A43	1p green & black	3.50	15
110	"	2p verm. & black	7.00	2.00
111	"	5p olive grn. & blk.	22.50	3.50
112	"	10p org. yel. & blk.	10.00	3.00
		Nos. 98–112 (15)	49.65	9.82

See also Nos. 117, 121, 123, 127–128, 133–141, 143, 155A, 157–161, 165–169, 171–172.

Columbus
A47

Toro Z.
A48

Freire
A49

O'Higgins
A50

1912-13 **Engraved.** ***Perf. 12.***

113	A47	2c scarlet	10	5
114	A48	4c black brown	10	5
115	A49	8c gray	15	6
116	A50	10c blue & black	40	3
		a. Center inverted	475.00	400.00
		b. Imperf. horizontally or vertically, pair	50.00	
117	A37	14c carmine & black	25	20
121	A38	40c violet & black	2.00	25
123	A40	60c light blue & black	3.00	85
		Nos. 113–123 (7)	6.00	1.49

See also Nos. 125–126, 131, 164, 170, 173.

Cochrane
A52

Columbus
A53

1915 **Engraved.** ***Perf. 13½x14.***

124	A52	5c slate blue	15	10
		a. Imperf., pair	10.00	

See also Nos. 155, 162–163.

1918

125	A49	8c slate	2.00	30

No. 125 is from a plate made in Chile to resemble No. 115. The top of the head is further from the oval, the spots of color enclosed in the figures "8" are oval instead of round, and there are many small differences in the design.

1921 **Worn Plate.**

126	A49	8c gray	17.50	4.50

No. 126 differs from No. 125 in not having diagonal lines in the frame and only a few diagonal lines above the shoulders (due to wear), while No. 125 has diagonal lines in the oval up to the level of the forehead.

1915–25 **Typo.** ***Perf. 13½x14½***

127	A32	1c gray green	10	5
128	A33	2c red	10	5
129	A53	4c brown ('18)	25	5

Frame Litho.; Head Engraved

131	A50	10c blue & black	45	4
		a. 10c dark blue & black	45	
		b. Imperf., pair	27.50	
		c. Center inverted	250.00	
133	A38	15c violet & black	60	6
134	A39	20c org. red & blk.	1.00	5
		a. 20c brown orange & black	1.00	5
135	A40	25c dull blue & black	20	6
136	A41	30c bistre brown & black	85	5
137	A42	50c deep green & black	60	6

Perf. 14

138	A43	1p green & black	4.00	15
139	"	2p red & black	4.00	18
		a. 2p vermilion & black	9.00	25
140	"	5p olive green & black ('20)	7.00	70
141	"	10p orange & black ('25)	8.50	2.50
		Nos. 127–141 (13)	27.65	4.00

The frames have crosshatching on the 15c, 20c, 30c, 2p, 5p and 10p. They have no crosshatching on the 10c, 25c, 50c and 1p.

Nos. 131a and 134a are printed from new head plates which give blacker and heavier impressions. No. 131a exists with; (a) frame lithographed and head engraved; (b) frame typographed and head engraved; (c) frame typographed and head lithographed. No. 134a is with frame typographed and head engraved.

A 4c stamp with portrait of Balmaceda and a 14c with portrait of Manuel de Salas were prepared but not placed in use. Both stamps were sent to the paper mill at Puente Alto for destruction. They were not all destroyed as some were privately preserved and sold. Price $7.50 each.

Columbus
A54

Manuel Rengifo
A55

Types of 1915-20 Re-drawn.

1918–20 ***Perf. 13½x14½***

143	A32	1c gray green ('20)	20	10
144	A54	4c brown	20	10

No. 143 has all the lines much finer and clearer than No. 127. The white shirt front is also much less shaded.

1921

145	A55	40c dk. violet & black	60	10

Pan-American Congress Building
A56

Admiral Juan José Latorre
A57

1923, Apr. 25 **Typo.** ***Perf. 14½x14***

146	A56	2c red	15	15
147	"	4c brown	15	15

Typographed; Center Engraved.

148	A56	10c blue & black	15	10
149	"	20c orange & black	25	12
150	"	40c dull violet & black	40	20
151	"	1p green & black	65	20
152	"	2p red & black	2.00	35
153	"	5p dk. green & blk.	5.00	3.00
		Nos. 146–153 (8)	8.75	4.27

Fifth Pan-American Congress.

Typographed; Head Engraved.

1927 ***Perf. 13½x14½***

154	A57	80c dark brown & black	75	65

Wmk. 215

Wmkd.
Small Star in Shield, Multiple. (215)

Types of 1915-25 Issues.
Inscribed: "Chile Correos".

1928–31 **Engr.** ***Perf. 13½x14½***

155	A52	5c slate blue	30	15

Frame Typo.; Center Engraved

155A	A38	15c violet & black	*325.00*	
156	A55	40c dark violet & black	40	10
157	A42	50c deep green & black	1.25	10

Perf. 14

158	A43	1p green & black	50	10
159	"	2p red & black	2.00	20
160	"	5p olive green & black	3.00	35
161	"	10p orange & black	2.50	1.00
		Nos. 155, 156-161 (7)	9.95	2.00

Paper of Nos. 155-161 varies from thin to thick.

Types of 1915-25 Issues.
Inscribed: "Correos de Chile"
Perf. 13½x14½

1928 **Engraved.**

162	A52	5c deep blue	20	10

1929 **Lithographed.**

163	A52	5c light green	10	4

Frame Litho.; Center Engraved

164	A50	10c blue & black	1.00	4
165	A38	15c violet & black	1.00	5
166	A39	20c orange red & black	2.50	12
167	A40	25c blue & black	35	5
168	A41	30c brown & black	30	6
169	A42	50c deep green & black	40	6
		Nos. 163-169 (7)	5.65	42

Redrawn.
Frame Typo.; Center Litho.

1929

170	A50	10c blue & black	30	6
171	A38	15c violet & black	30	8
172	A39	20c orange red & black	3.00	60

1931 **Unwmkd.**

173	A50	10c blue & black	20	8

In the redrawn stamps the lines behind the portraits are heavier and completely fill the ovals. There are strong diagonal lines above the shoulders. On No. 170 the head is larger than on Nos. 164 and 173.

A58

Prosperity of Saltpeter Trade
A59 A60

Perf. 13½x14
1930, July 21 **Litho.** **Wmk. 215**
Size: 20x25 mm.

175	A58	5c yellow green	25	8
176	"	10c red brown	25	8
177	"	15c violet	35	10
178	A59	25c deep gray	1.00	50
179	A60	70c dark blue	5.20	45

Perf. 14
Size: 24½x30 mm.

180	A60	1p dark gray grn.	1.85	20
		Nos. 175-180 (6)	5.20	1.41

Issued to commemorate the centenary of the first shipment of saltpeter from Chile, July 21, 1830.

Manuel Bulnes
A61

Bernardo O'Higgins
A62

1931 ***Perf. 13½, 14***

181	A61	20c dark brown	20	8

1932

182	A62	10c deep blue	15	8

Mariano Egana
A63

Joaquín Tocornal
A64

1934 ***Perf. 13½x14***

183	A63	30c magenta	25	6

Perf. 14

184	A64	1.20p bright blue	40	20

Centenary of the constitution.

José Joaquín Pérez
A65

1934 ***Perf. 13½x14***

185	A65	30c bright pink	20	8

Atacama Desert
A66

Fishing Boats
A67

Coquito Palms
A68

Sheep
A69

Mining
A70

Lonquimay Forest
A71

Colliery at Port Lota
A72

Shipping at Valparaiso
A73

Puntiagudo Volcano—A74

Diego de Almagro—A75

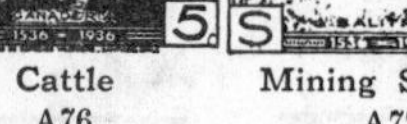
Cattle
A76

Mining Saltpeter
A77

Perf. 14
1936, Mar. 1 **Litho.** **Wmk. 215**

186	A66	5c vermilion	15	8
187	A67	10c violet	15	7
188	A68	20c magenta	20	8
189	A69	25c greenish blue	1.00	50
190	A70	30c light green	20	12
191	A71	40c black, *cream*	75	65
192	A72	50c blue, *bluish*	25	20

Engraved.

193	A73	1p dark green	1.00	20
194	A74	1.20p deep blue	1.00	40
195	A75	2p dark brown	1.25	85
196	A76	5p copper red	3.00	2.00
197	A77	10p dark violet	7.00	6.00
		Nos. 186-197 (12)	15.95	11.15

Issued in commemoration of the 400th anniversary of the discovery of Chile by Diego de Almagro.

Laja Waterfall
A78

Agriculture
A79

Boldo Tree
A79a

Nitrate Industry
A80

Mineral Spas
A81

Copper Mine
A82

Mining
A83

Fishing in Chiloé
A84

Osorno Volcano
A85

Mercantile Marine
A86

Lake Villarrica
A87

State Railways
A88

Perf. 13½x14
1938–40 **Lithographed** **Wmk. 215**

198	A78	5c brown car. ('39)	6	4
199	A79	10c salmon pink ('39)	6	4
200	A79a	15c brown orange ('40)	8	4
201	A80	20c light blue	6	4
202	A81	30c bright pink	10	4
203	A82	40c light green ('39)	10	4
204	A83	50c violet	10	4

Perf. 14
Engraved.

205	A84	1p orange brown	30	4
206	A85	1.80p deep blue	35	12
207	A86	2p carmine lake	10	5
208	A87	5p dark slate green	50	5
209	A88	10p rose violet ('40)	50	6
		Nos. 198-209 (12)	2.31	60

See also Nos. 217-227.

Map of the Americas
A89

Perf. 14

1940, Sept. 11 Litho. Unwmkd.

210 A89 40c dull green & yellow green 30 18

Pan American Union, 50th anniversary.

Camilo Henriquez
A90

Founding of Santiago
A93

Designs: 40c, Pedro de Valdivia. 1.10p, Benjamin Vicuna Mackenna. 3.60p, Diego Barros Arana.

Perf. 14½x14, 14½.

1941, Jan. 23 Engraved Wmk. 215

211 A90 10c carmine lake 10 10
212 " 40c green 20 10
213 " 1.10p red 50 50
214 A93 1.80p blue 50 50
215 A90 3.60p indigo 1.50 1.50
Nos. 211-215 (5) 2.80 2.70

400th anniversary of Santiago.

Types of 1938.
Lithographed.

1942-46 *Perf. 13½x14.* Unwmkd.

217 A79 10c salmon pink ('43) 5 5
218 A79a 15c brown orange ('43) 8 5
219 A80 20c light blue ('43) 12 5
220 A81 30c bright pink ('43) 15 5
221 A82 40c yellow green 25 5
222 A83 50c violet ('43) 6 5

Engraved.
Perf. 14.

223 A84 1p brown orange 35 5
225 A86 2p carmine lake ('43) 8 5
226 A87 5p dark slate green ('43) 20 5
227 A88 10p rose violet ('46) 40 8
Nos. 217-227 (10) 1.74 53

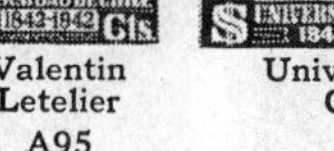

Valentin Letelier
A95

University of Chile
A98

Designs: 40c, Andrés Bello. 90c, Manuel Bulnes. 1.80p, Manuel Montt.

1942, Nov. 1 *Perf. 14x14½, 14 (1p)*

228 A95 30c rose red 8 8
229 " 40c deep green 8 8
230 " 90c rose violet 45 45
231 A98 1p deep brown 40 30
232 A95 1.80p dark blue 90 90
Nos. 228-232 (5) 1.91 1.81

University of Chile centenary. See also No. C89.

Manuel Bulnes
A100

Map Showing Strait of Magellan
A104

Designs: 30c, Juan Williams Wilson. 40c, Diego Duble Almeida. 1p, José Mardones.

1944, Mar. 2 Litho. *Perf. 14*

233 A100 15c black 5 5
234 " 30c deep rose 5 5
235 " 40c yellow green 5 5
236 " 1p brown carmine 75 8
237 A104 1.80p ultramarine 60 30
Nos. 233-237 (5) 1.50 53

Issued to commemorate the 100th anniversary of the occupation of the Strait of Magellan.

Red Cross and Lamp of Life
A105

Serpent and Cup
A106

1944, Oct. 18 Unwmkd.

238 A105 40c green, red & black 25 10
239 A106 1.80p ultra. & red 50 20

Issued to commemorate the 80th anniversary of the International Red Cross Society.

Bernardo O'Higgins
A107

"Embrace of Maipú"
(O'Higgins Joining San Martin)
A108

Designs: 40c, Abdication of O'Higgins. 1.80p, Battle of Rancagua.

1945 Engr. *Perf. 14 (15c), 14½*

Center in Black.

240 A107 15c carmine 5 5
241 A108 30c brown 5 5
242 " 40c deep green 5 5
243 " 1.80p dark blue 60 60

Issued to commemorate the centenary of the death of Bernardo O'Higgins in 1842.

Proposed Columbus Lighthouse
A111

Perf. 14

1945, Sept. 10 Litho. Wmk. 215

244 A111 40c light green 20 10

Issued in honor of the discovery of America by Columbus and the Memorial Lighthouse to be erected in his memory.

Andrés Bello
A112

1946 Engraved.

245 A112 40c dark green 15 8
246 " 1.80p dark blue 15 12

Issued to commemorate the 80th anniversary of the death of Andrés Bello, poet and educator.

Map Showing Chile's Claims of Antarctic Territory
A113

1947, May 12 Litho. *Perf. 14½*

247 A113 40c carmine 50 15
248 " 2.50p deep blue 70 15

Eusebio Lillo and Ramon Carnicer
A114

1947, Sept. 18 Engraved

249 A114 40c dark green 25 15

Centenary of national anthem.

Miguel de Cervantes Saavedra
A115

1947, Oct. 11 Wmk. 215

250 A115 40c dark carmine 15 10

Issued to commemorate the 400th anniversary of the birth of Miguel de Cervantes Saavedra, novelist, playwright and poet.

Arturo Prat Chacón and Iquique Naval Battle
A116

1948, Dec. 24 *Perf. 14½*

251 A116 40c deep blue 15 8

Issued to commemorate the centenary of the birth of Arturo Prat Chacon, Chilean naval hero.

Bernardo O'Higgins
A117

Lithographed.

1948 *Perf. 13½x14.* Wmk. 215

252 A117 60c black 12 10

See also No. 262.

No. 203 Surcharged in Black

VEINTE
CTS.

1948

253 A82 20c on 40c light green 12 10

Chilean Pigeons
A118

American Skunk
A119

Designs not illustrated, FAUNA: Chilean Otter. Southern sea lions. Sugar-cane borer moth. Emperor penguins. Bat. Chinchilla. Grant's stag beetle. Trevally (fish). Chilean slender lizard. Crested caracara. Red-gartered coot. Chilean guemal (deer). Spiny rock lobster. Tilefish. Praying mantis. Torrent duck. Red conger. FLORA: Araucarian pine (monkey puzzle tree). Evening primrose. Chilean red bell flower. Loxodon (flower). Boldo tree. Coquito palm trees.

Lithographed.

1948, Dec. 6 *Perf. 14* Wmk. 215

254 A118 60c ultramarine 60 30
a. Block of 25 22.50
255 A119 2.60p green 90 75
a. Block of 25 35.00

Issued in panes of 100 stamps, divisible into four blocks of 25 different designs.

The stamps commemorate the centenary (in 1944) of the publication of the first volume of Claudio Gay's Natural History of Chile. See also No. C124.

Benjamin Vicuna Mackenna
A121

1949, Mar. 22 Engr. *Perf. 13½x14*

257 A121 60c deep blue 10 8

See also No. C126.

Symbols of Arts and Crafts Education
A122

Heinrich von Stephan
A123

Design: 2.60p, Badge and book.

Lithographed.

1949, Nov. 11 ***Perf. 14*** **Unwmkd.**

258 A122 60c lilac rose 10 8
259 " 2.60p violet blue 30 25

Issued to commemorate the centenary of the foundation of Chile's School of Arts and Crafts. See also Nos. C127-C128.

1950, Jan. 6 **Engraved**

260 A123 60c deep carmine 10 8
261 " 2.50p deep blue 50 40

Issued to commemorate the 75th anniversary of the formation of the Universal Postal Union. See also Nos. C129-C130.

O'Higgins Type of 1948.

1950 **Lithographed** ***Perf. 13x14***

262 A117 60c black 12 8

Gen. José de San Martin
A124

Queen Isabella I
A125

Perf. 14

1951, Mar. 16 **Engr.** **Wmk. 215**

263 A124 60c deep blue 15 8

Issued to commemorate the centenary of the death of Gen. José de San Martin. See also No. C165.

1952, Mar. 20

264 A125 60c bright blue 15 8

Issued to commemorate the 500th anniversary of the birth of Queen Isabella I of Spain. See also No. C166.

Bernardo O'Higgins
A126

Mateo de Toro Zambrano
A127

Lithographed.

1952 ***Perf. 13½x14*** **Unwmkd.**

265 A126 1p dark blue green 10 8

See also No. 275.

Nos.252 and 262 Surcharged "40 Ctvs." in Red.

1952, Sept.

266 A117 40c on 60c black 12 8

Wmk. 215

267 A117 40c on 60c black 10 8

1953, Mar. 13 **Wmk. 215**

268 A127 80c green 10 8

See also No. 285.

Valdivia Arms
A128

Old Fort
A129

Designs: 3p, Modern Valdivia. 5p, Street in ancient Valdivia.

1953, May ***Perf. 14***

269 A128 1p bright ultra. 10 5
270 A129 2p dull rose violet 15 5
271 " 3p blue green 15 6
272 " 5p deep brown 25 10
Nos. 269-272, C167 (5) 1.05 66

Issued to commemorate the 4th centenary of the founding of Valdivia, capital of Valdivia province.

José Toribio Medina
A130

1953, June **Engraved** ***Perf. 14½***

273 A130 1p brown 12 8
274 " 2.50p deep blue 12 8

Issued to commemorate the centenary of the birth of Jose Toribio Medina (1852-1930), historian and bibliographer.

O'Higgins Type of 1952.
Lithographed.

1953, Oct. ***Perf. 13½x14*** **Wmk. 215**

275 A126 1p dark blue green 10 8

Stamp of 1853
A131

1953, Oct. 15 **Engr.** ***Perf. 14½***

276 A131 1p chocolate 40 25

Centenary of Chile's first postage stamps. Souvenir sheet including No. 276 is noted below No. C168.

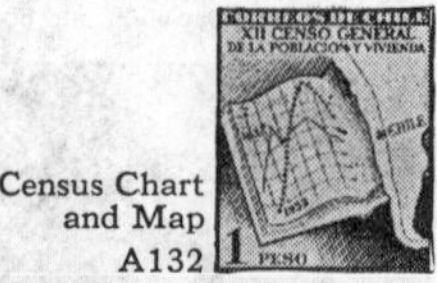

Census Chart and Map
A132

1953, Nov. 5 **Litho.** ***Perf. 13½x14***

277 A132 1p blue green 10 8
278 " 2.50p violet blue 20 10
279 " 3p chocolate 20 15
280 " 4p carmine 20 15

Issued to publicize the 12th general census of population and housing.

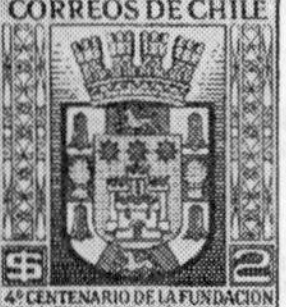

Arms of Angol
A133

Ignacio Domeyko
A134

1954, May 28 ***Perf. 14*** **Unwmkd.**

281 A133 2p deep carmine 15 8

Issued to commemorate the 400th anniversary of the founding of Angol, capital of Malleco province.

1954, Aug. 16 **Engr.** ***Perf. 13½x14***

282 A134 1p greenish blue 10 5

Issued to commemorate the 150th anniversary of the birth of Ignacio Domeyko (1802-1889), mineralogist and educator. See also No. C171.

Early Steam Locomotive—A135

Perf. 14½

1954, Sept. 10 **Wmk. 215**

283 A135 1p red 18 10

Issued to commemorate the centenary (in 1951) of the first South American railroad. See also No. C172.

Adm. Arturo Prat Chacón
A136

Arms of Viña del Mar
A137

Lithographed.

1954 ***Perf. 14*** **Unwmkd.**

284 A136 2p dark violet blue 12 8

Issued to commemorate the 75th anniversary of the naval Battle of Iquique.

Toro Zambrano Type of 1953

1954, Nov. 6 ***Perf. 13½x14***

285 A127 80c green 12 6

1955, Mar. 5 ***Perf. 14*** **Wmk. 215**

Design: 2p, Arms of Valparaiso.

286 A137 1p violet blue 10 8
287 " 2p carmine 15 8

Issued to publicize the first International Philatelic Exhibition, Valparaiso, March 1955.

Dr. Alejandro del Rio
A138

1955, May 24 ***Perf. 13½x14***

288 A138 2p violet blue 12 8

14th Pan-American Sanitary Conference.

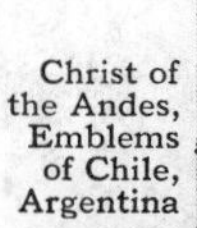

Christ of the Andes, Emblems of Chile, Argentina
A139

1955, Aug. 31 ***Perf. 14½*** **Unwmkd.**

289 A139 1p violet blue 25 20

Issued to publicize the reciprocal visits of Presidents Juan D. Peron and Carlos Ibanez del Campo. See also No. C173.

Manuel Rengifo
A140

Portraits: 5p, Mariano Egana. 50p, Diego Portales.

1955-56 ***Perf. 14x14½*** **Unwmkd.**

290 A140 3p violet blue 12 8
291 " 5p dk. carmine rose 12 8
292 " 50p rose lilac ('56) 60 20

Issued to commemorate the centenary of the death of Joaquin Prieto (1786-1854), soldier and political leader; president, 1831-41. See No. QRA1.

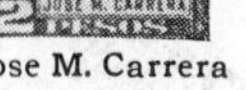

Jose M. Carrera
A141

Ramón Freire
A142

Portraits: 5p, Manuel Bulnes. 10p, Pres. Francisco A. Pinto. 50p, Manuel Montt.

Lithographed

1956-58 ***Perf. 14x14½*** **Unwmkd.**

293 A141 2p purple 8 6
293A A142 3p light violet blue 8 6
294 A141 5p reddish brown (19½x23mm.) 10 6
a. Size 19x22mm. 10 8
295 A142 10p violet (19x22¼mm.) 15 6
a. Perf. 13½x14 (19½x22½mm.) ('58) 60 8
296 A141 50p rose red 40 10
Nos. 293-296 (5) 81 34

No. 294 has yellow gum; No. 294a, white gum.

Wmk. 215

297 A141 2p dull purple 15 8
298 A142 3p violet blue 15 8

Federico Santa Maria
A143

Gabriela Mistral
A144

Engraved.

1957, Jan. 31 ***Perf. 14*** **Unwmkd.**

299 A143 5p dark red brown 12 8

Issued to commemorate the 25th anniversary of the Federico Santa Maria Technical University. See Nos. C190-C191.

Souvenir sheet including No. 299 is noted below No. C191.

1958, Jan. 10
300 A144 10p red brown 10 5

Issued in honor of Gabriela Mistral, poet and educator. See also No. C192.

Arms of Osorno A145 — Arms of Santiago A146

Design: 50p, Garcia Hdo. de Mendoza.

1958, Mar. 23 Lithographed *Perf. 14*
301 A145 10p carmine 20 10

Engraved
302 A145 50p green 30 15

Issued to commemorate the 400th anniversary of the founding of the city of Osorno, capital of Osorno province.
Souvenir sheet including No. 302 in red brown is noted below No. C193.

1958, Oct. 18 *Perf. 14* Unwmkd.
303 A146 10p dark violet 10 6

Issued to publicize the National Philatelic Exposition, Santiago, Oct. 18–26.
Souvenir sheet including No. 303 in deep red is noted below No. C194.

Symbolical Savings Bank A147 — Modern Map of Antarctica A148

1958, Dec. 18
304 A147 10p dark blue 10 6

Issued to commemorate the centenary of the Savings Bank for Public Employees.
Souvenir sheet including No. 304 in violet is noted below No. C195.

1958, Aug. 28 *Perf. 14* Unwmkd.
305 A148 40p rose carmine 50 15

Issued to commemorate the International Geophysical Year, 1957–1958. See No. C214.

Antarctic Map and 'La Araucana' A149 — Map of Strait of Magellan, 1588 A150

1958 Lithographed. *Perf. 14*
310 A149 10p violet blue 25 10

Engraved.
311 A150 200p dull purple 1.75 75

See also Nos. C199–C200.

Valdivia River Bridge A153

1959, Feb. 9 Engraved *Perf. 14*
319 A153 40p green 25 12

Issued to commemorate the centenary of the German School in Valdivia and to publicize the Valdivia Philatelic Exhibition, Feb. 9–18.
Souvenir sheet including No. 319 is noted below No. C213.

Strait of Magellan, Map by Pedro Sarmiento de Gamboa, c. 1582 A154

1959, Aug. 27 Lithographed
320 A154 10p dull purple 25 10

Issued to commemorate the 400th anniversary of the Juan Ladrillero expedition to explore the Strait of Magellan, 1557–1558. See also No. C215.

Diego Barros Arana A155 — Henri Dunant A156

1959, Aug. 27
321 A155 40p ultramarine 25 10

Issued to commemorate the 50th anniversary of the death of Diego Barros Arana (1830–1907), historian. See No. C216.

1959, Oct. 6 *Perf. 14* Unwmkd.
322 A156 20p red & red brown 20 6

Issued to commemorate the centenary of the Red Cross idea. See No. C217.

Manuel Bulnes A157 — Francisco A. Pinto A158

Choshuenco Volcano A159

Designs: No. 326, Choshuenco volcano, redrawn. 5c, Manuel Montt. 10c, Maule River Valley. 20c, 1e, Inca Lake.

1960–67 Lithographed *Perf. 13x14*
323 A157 5m bluish green 8 5
324 A158 1c carmine 8 5

Perf. 14
Size: 29x25mm.
325 A159 2c ultramarine ('61) 10 5

Perf. 14x13
Size: 23½x18mm.
326 A159 2c ultramarine ('62) 8 5

Perf. 13x14
327 A157 5c blue 12 5

Perf. 14
Size: 29x25mm.
328 A159 10c green ('62) 30 10
329 " 20c Prussian blue ('62) 50 15
329A A159 1e bluish green ('67) 60 25
Nos. 323-329A (8) 1.86 75

On No. 325 "Volcan Choshuenco" is at upper left, below "Correos." On No. 326, it is at bottom, above "Centesimos."

Refugee Family A160

1960, Apr. 7 *Perf. 14½*
330 A160 1c green 20 10

Issued to publicize World Refugee Year, July 1, 1959–June 30, 1960. A souvenir sheet is noted below No. C218.

Type of Air Post Issue, 1962, and

Arms of Chile A161

José M. Carrera A162

Designs: No. 332, Palace of Justice. 5c, National Memorial. 10c, Manuel de Toro y Zambrano and Martinez de Rozas. 20c, Manuel de Salas and Juan Egana. 50c, Manuel Rodriguez and Juan Mackenna.

Wmk. 215 (#331, 1e); Unwmkd.
1960–65 Engraved *Perf. 14½*
331 A161 1c maroon & sepia 15 10
332 " 1c brn. & claret ('62) 10 5
333 A162 5c green & Prussian green ('61) 20 5
334 AP54 10c brown & violet brown ('64) 20 5
334A " 20c indigo & blue green ('65) 25 6
335 " 50c red brown & maroon ('65) 40 15
336 A162 1e gray olive & brown 3.00 50
Nos. 331-336, C218A-C220D (14) 7.05 2.46

Issued to commemorate the 150th anniversary of the formation of the first National Government. A souvenir sheet is noted below No. C220B. See also No. C285.

Family A163

Design: 10c, Various buildings.

Lithographed
1960, Jan. 18 *Perf. 14* Unwmkd.
337 A163 5c green 25 8
338 " 10c bright violet 35 12

Issued to publicize the 13th population census (No. 337) and the second housing census (No. 338).

Chamber of Deputies A164

1961, Aug. 14 *Perf. 14½* Unwmkd.
339 A164 2c red brown 15 8

Issued to commemorate the 150th anniversary of the first National Congress. See also No. C245.

Soccer Players and Globe A165

Design: 5c, Goalkeeper and stadium (vert.).

1962, May 30 Engr. *Perf. 14½*
340 A165 2c blue 10 10
341 " 5c green 20 10

Issued to commemorate the World Soccer Championship, Chile, May 30–June 17.
Note on souvenir sheet follows No. C247.

Mother and Child A166 — Centenary Emblem A167

1963, Mar. 21 Litho. *Perf. 14*
342 A166 3c maroon 6 5

Issued for the "Freedom from Hunger" campaign of the U.N. Food and Agriculture Organization. See also No. C248.

1963, Aug. 23 *Perf. 14* Unwmkd.
343 A167 3c red & gray 10 8

Issued to commemorate the centenary of the International Red Cross. See No. C249.

Fireman Carrying Woman A168 — Enrique Molina A169

1963, Dec. 20 *Perf. 14* Unwmkd.
344 A168 3c violet 10 8

Issued to commemorate the centenary of the Santiago Fire Brigade. See No. C250.

1964, Nov. 14 Litho. *Perf. 14*

Design: No. 346, Msgr. Carlos Casanueva.

345 A169 4c bister brown 6 4
346 " 4c rose claret 6 4

Issued to honor Enrique Molina, founder of the University of Concepcion, and Msgr. Carlos Casanueva, rector of the Catholic University, 1920-53. See Nos. C257-C258.

Easter Island Statue A170

Copihue, National Flower A171

Design: 30c, Robinson Crusoe.

1965-69 Litho. *Perf. 14x14½*

347 A170 6c rose lilac 10 6
347A " 10c rose pink ('68) 10 6

Perf. 14

348 A171 15c yellow green & rose red 15 8
348A " 20c yellow green & rose red ('69) 10 6

Perf. 14x14½

349 A170 30c rose claret 25 15

Skier A172

Lorenzo Sazie A173

1965, Aug. 30 *Perf. 14*

350 A172 4c blue green 10 6

World Skiing Championships, Chile, 1966.

1966, Feb. 9 Litho. *Perf. 14x14½*

351 A173 1e green 1.00 30

Issued to commemorate the centenary of the death of Dr. Lorenzo Sazie, dean of the Faculty of Medicine, University of Santiago.

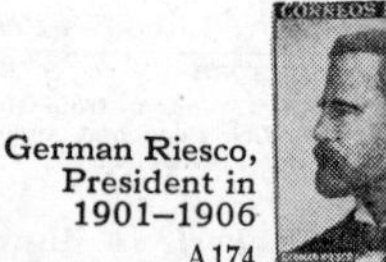

German Riesco, President in 1901-1906 A174

Portrait: 30c, Jorge Montt (1847-1922), president in 1891-1896.

1966 *Perf. 13x14* **Unwmkd.**

354 A174 30c violet 25 8
355 " 50c dull brown 35 10

William Wheelwright and S.S. Chile A175

1966, Aug. 2 *Perf. 14½*

358 A175 10c ultra. & lt. blue 10 8

Issued to commemorate the 125th anniversary (in 1965) of the arrival of the paddle steamers "Chile" and "Peru." See also No. C268.

Learning to Read A176

1966, Aug. 13 Litho. *Perf. 14*

359 A176 10c red brown 10 8

Literacy campaign.

U.N. and ICY Emblems A177

1966, Oct. 28 *Perf. 14½* **Unwmkd.**

360 A177 1e green & brown 1.00 75

International Cooperation Year, 1965. See No. C269.

Capt. Luis Pardo and Ship in Antarctica—A178

1967, Jan. Litho. *Perf. 14½*

361 A178 20c turquoise blue 15 10

Issued to commemorate the 50th anniversary of the rescue of the Shackleton South Pole expedition by Capt. Luis Pardo of Chile. See also No. C271.

Family A179

Trees and Mountains A180

1967, Apr. 13 *Perf. 14* **Unwmkd.**

362 A179 10c magenta & blk. 6 4

Issued to publicize the 8th International Conference for Family Planning, Santiago, April 1967. See also No. C272.

1967, June 9 Litho. *Perf. 14½*

363 A180 10c bl. green & lt. bl. 6 4

Reforestation Campaign. See No. C274.

Lions Emblem A181

1967, July 12 Litho. *Perf. 14*

364 A181 20c Prus. bl. & yel. 25 15

Issued to commemorate the 50th anniversary of Lions International. See also Nos. C275-C276.

Chilean Flag A182

1967, Oct. 20 *Perf. 14½* **Unwmkd.**

365 A182 80c crimson & ultra. 50 30

Issued to commemorate the sesquicentennial of the national flag. See No. C277.

José Maria Cardinal Caro A183

1967, Dec. 4 Engraved *Perf. 14½*

366 A183 20c deep carmine 20 10

Issued to commemorate the centenary of the birth of José Maria Cardinal Caro, the first Chilean cardinal. See No. C279.

San Martin and O'Higgins A184

1968, Apr. 23 Litho. **Unwmkd.**

367 A184 3e blue 1.25 60

Issued to commemorate the sesquicentennial of the Battles of Chacabuco and Maipu. See No. C280.

Farm Couple A185

1968, June 18 *Perf. 14½*

368 A185 20c blk., org. & grn. 25 15

Agrarian reforms. See No. C281.

Juan I. Molina A186

1968, Aug. 27 Litho. *Perf. 14½*

369 A186 2e red lilac 60 35

Issued to honor Juan I. Molina, educator and scientist. See also No. C282.

Hand Holding Cogwheel A187

1968, Sept. *Perf. 14x14½*

370 A187 30c deep carmine 15 10

Fourth census of manufacturers.

Map of Chiloé Province, Sailing Ship and Coastal Vessel A188

1968, Oct. 7 *Perf. 14½*

371 A188 30c ultramarine 15 10

Issued to commemorate the anniversaries of the founding of five towns in Chiloé Province. See also No. C283.

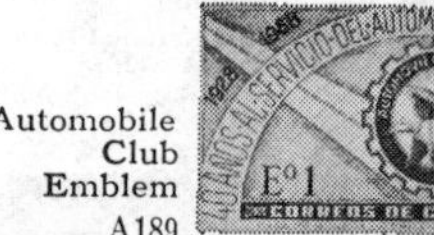

Automobile Club Emblem A189

1968, Nov. 10 Engr. *Perf. 14½x14*

372 A189 1e carmine rose 35 25

Issued to commemorate the 40th anniversary of the Automobile Club of Chile. See No. C284.

Francisco Garcia Huidobro A190

Design: 5e, King Philip V of Spain.

1968, Dec. 31 Litho. *Perf. 14½*

373 A190 2e pale rose & ultra. 50 35
374 " 5e brn. & yel. grn. 1.25 90

Issued to commemorate the 225th anniversary of the founding of the State Mint (Casa de Moneda de Chile). See Nos. C288-C289.

Satellite and Radar Station A191

1969, May 20 Litho. *Perf. 14½*

375 A191 30c blue 10 5

Issued to publicize the inauguration of ENTEL-Chile, the first commercial satellite communications ground station, Longovilo. See No. C290.

Red Cross, Crescent and Lion and Sun Emblems—A192

1969, Sept. Lithographed *Perf. 14½*

376 A192 2e violet blue & red 45 30

Issued to commemorate the 50th anniversary of the League of Red Cross Societies. See No. C291.

Rapel Hydro-electric Plant A193

1969, Nov. 18 Litho. *Perf. 14½*

377 A193 40c green 9 6

See No. C292.

Col. Rodriguez Monument A194

1969, Nov. 24

378 A194 2e rose claret 50 30

Issued to commemorate the 150th anniversary of the death of Col. Manuel Rodriguez. See No. C293.

EXPO '70 Emblem A195

1969, Dec. 2 Litho. *Perf. 14*

379 A195 3e blue 70 50

Issued to publicize EXPO '70 International Exhibition, Osaka, Japan, March 15–Sept. 13, 1970. See No. C294.

Open Book A196

1969, Dec. 3 *Perf. 14½*

380 A196 40c red brown 15 10

Issued to commemorate the 400th anniversary of the translation of the Bible into Spanish by Casiodoro de Reina. See No. C295.

Globes and ILO Emblem A197

1969, Dec. 17 *Perf. 14½*

381 A197 1e green & black 24 18

Issued to commemorate the 50th anniversary of the International Labor Organization. See No. C296.

Human Rights Flame A198

1969, Dec. 18

382 A198 4e blue & red 1.00 70

Human Rights Year, 1968. See No. C297.

Policarpo Toro and Easter Island A199

1970, Jan. 26 *Perf. 14½*

383 A199 5e lilac 1.20 90

Issued to commemorate the 80th anniversary of the acquisition of Easter Island. See No. C298.

Sailing Ship and Arms of Valdivia A200

1970, Feb. 4 Litho. *Perf. 14½*

384 A200 40c dark carmine 10 6

Issued to commemorate the 150th anniversary of the capture of Valdivia during Chile's war of independence by Thomas Cochrane (1775–1860), naval commander. See No. C299.

Paul Harris and Rotary Emblem A201

1970, Mar. 18 Lithographed *Perf. 14*

385 A201 10c violet blue 2.00 1.50

Issued to commemorate the centenary of the birth of Paul Harris (1868–1947), founder of Rotary International. See No. C300.

Mahatma Gandhi A202

Santo Domingo Church, Santiago, Chile A203

1970, Apr. 1 Litho. *Perf. 14½*

386 A202 40c blue green 10 4

Issued to commemorate the centenary of the birth of Mohandas K. Gandhi (1869–1948), leader in India's fight for independence. See No. C301.

1970, Apr. 30 Engraved

Designs: 2e, Casa de Moneda de Chile (horiz.). 3e, Pedro de Valdivia. 5e, Bridge (horiz.). 10e, Ambrosio O'Higgins.

387	A203	2e violet brown	40	20
388	"	3e dark red	60	30
389	"	4e dark blue	75	45
390	"	5e brown	1.00	60
391	"	10e green	1.75	1.10
		Nos. 387-391 (5)	4.50	2.65

Issued to commemorate the exploration and development of Chile by Spanish explorers.

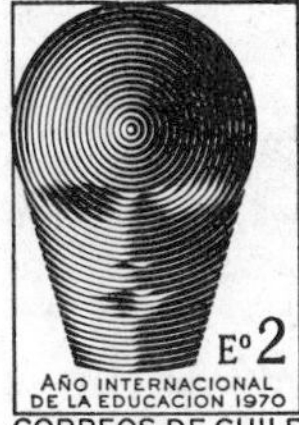

Education Year Emblem A204

Virgin and Child A205

1970, July 17 Litho. *Perf. 14½*

392 A204 2e claret 40 25

Issued for International Education Year. See No. C302.

1970, July 28

393 A205 40c green 8 6

Issued to publicize the O'Higgins National Shrine at Maipu. See No. C303.

Torch and Snake—A206

Copper Symbol, Chile Arms A207

1970, Aug. 11

394 A206 40c claret & lt. blue 6 4

Issued to commemorate the International Cancer Congress, Houston, Texas, May 22–29. See No. C304.

1970, Oct. 21 Litho. *Perf. 14½*

395 A207 40c car. & lt. red brn. 6 4

Issued to commemorate the nationalization of the copper industry. See No. C305.

Dove and World Map A208

1970, Oct. 22

396 A208 3e rose magenta & purple 60 25

Issued to commemorate the 25th anniversary of the United Nations. See No. C306.

No. 375 Surcharged in Red

1970, Dec. 24 Litho. *Perf. 14½*

397 A191 52c on 30c blue 10 8

Freighter and Ship's Wheel A209

1971, Jan. 18 Litho. *Perf. 14*

398 A209 52c deep carmine 10 8

National Maritime Commission. See No. C307.

Bernardo O'Higgins and Ship A210

1971, Feb. 3 *Perf. 14½*

399 A210 5e greenish blue & green 75 50

The 150th anniversary of the expedition to liberate Peru from Spanish rule. See No. C309.

Youth, Girl and U.N. Emblem A211

1971, Feb. 11 Litho. *Perf. 14½*

400 A211 52c dk. blue & brn. 10 8

First meeting in Latin America of the Executive Council of UNICEF (U.N. Children's Fund), Santiago, May 20–31, 1969. See No. C310.

Chilean Boy Scout Emblem A212

1971, Feb. 10 *Perf. 14*

401 A212 1e green & brown 15 12

Founding of Chilean Boy Scouts, 60th anniversary. See No. C311.

Satellite and Radar Station A213

1971, May 25 Litho. *Perf. 14½*

402 A213 40c dull green 10 6

First commercial Chilean satellite communications ground station, Longovilo. See No. C312.

Diver with Harpoon Gun A214

1971, Sept. 1

403	A214	1.15e lt. & dk. green	20	15
404	"	2.35e vio. blue & dp. violet blue	35	20

10th World Championship of Underwater Fishing.

Ferdinand Magellan and Sailing Ship A215

1971, Nov. 3

405 A215 35c light violet & brown violet 10 8

450th anniversary of first trip through and discovery of the Strait of Magellan, Oct. 21–Nov. 28, 1520.

Dagoberto Godoy and Plane over Andes
A216

1971, Nov. 4

406 A216 1.15e blue & green 25 15

First trans-Andean flight, Dec. 12, 1918.

Virgin of San Cristobal
A217

Chilean Flag and Congress Emblem
A218

Designs (Congress Emblem and): 4.35e, Church of San Francisco. 9.35e, Central post office (horiz.). 18.35e, La Posada (Inn) del Corregidor (horiz.).

1971

407 A217 1.15e dark blue 15 10
408 A218 2.35e ultra. & car. 30 15
409 A217 4.35e brown red 65 35
410 " 9.35e violet 1.50 1.00
411 " 18.35e lilac rose 3.00 2.00
Nos. 407-411 (5) 5.60 3.60

10th Congress of the Postal Union of the Americas and Spain, Santiago. Issue dates: 2.35e, 4.35e, Nov. 5; 1.15e, Nov. 11; 9.35e, Nov. 18; 18.35e, Nov. 19.

Observation Dome, Cerro el Tololo Observatory
A219

1971, Dec. 18

412 A219 1.95e lt. & dk. blue 20 10

Boeing 707 over Easter Island
A220

1971, Dec. 18

413 A220 2.35e dk. brn. & yel. 40 20

Inauguration of flights to Easter Island.

Alonso de Ercilla y Zuniga
A221

1972, Mar. 20 Engraved *Perf. 14*

414 A221 1e dark red 16 10

4th centenary (in 1969) of "La Araucana," by Alonso de Ercilla y Zuniga (1533–1596), Spanish author. See No. C313.

Map of Antarctica and Dog Sled
A222

1972, Mar. 20 Litho. *Perf. 14½x15*

415 A222 1.15e vio. bl. & blk. 25 10
416 " 3.50e bl. grn. & grn. 50 35

10th anniversary (in 1971) of the Antarctic Treaty pledging peaceful uses of and scientific cooperation in Antarctica.

"Your Heart is your Health"
A223

1972, Apr. 2 Litho. *Perf. 14½*

417 A223 1.15e black & car. 20 15

World Health Day.

People and Statement by Pres. Allende
A224

Conference Hall and U.N. Emblem
A225

1972, Apr. 13 Litho. *Perf. 14½*

418 A224 35c dull grn. & buff 10 5
419 A225 1.15e ultra. & purple 20 15
420 A224 4e dark purple & pale rose 75 40
421 A225 6e org. & vio. bl. 1.00 75

3rd United Nations Conference on Trade and Development (UNCTAD III), Santiago, Apr.–May 1972. Design A224 is perforated horizontally in the middle.

Soldier, 1822, Andes, Military College Emblem
A226

1972, June 9

422 A226 1.15e blue & yellow 20 15

Sesquicentennial of Bernardo O'Higgins Military College.

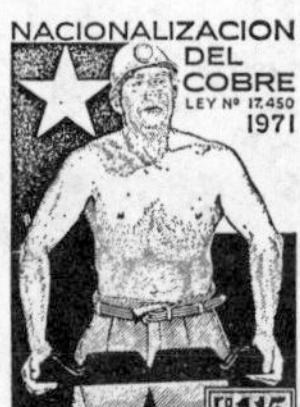

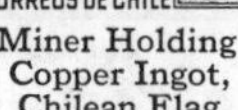

Miner Holding Copper Ingot, Chilean Flag
A227

Sailing Ship
A228

1972, July 11 Litho. *Perf. 15x14½*

423 A227 1.15e blue & rose red 25 15
424 " 5e blue, black & rose red 85 50

Nationalization of copper industry.

1972, Aug. 4

425 A228 1.15e violet brown 20 15

Sesquicentennial of the Arturo Pratt Naval Training School.

Mt. Calan Observatory
A229

1972, Aug. 31 Litho. *Perf. 14½*

426 A229 50c ultramarine 15 10

University of Chile Mt. Calan Observatory.

Carrier Pigeon
A230

1972, Oct. 9 Litho. *Perf. 14½*

427 A230 1.15e red lilac & vio. 20 15

International Letter Writing Week, Oct. 9–15.

René Schneider and Army Flag—A231

1972, Oct. 25 *Perf. 14*

428 A231 2.30e multicolored 40 30

2nd anniversary of the death of Gen. René Schneider. No. 428 is perforated vertically in the middle.

Book and Young People
A232

1972, Oct. 31 *Perf. 14½*

429 A232 50c blk. & dp. org. 12 8

International Book Year 1972.

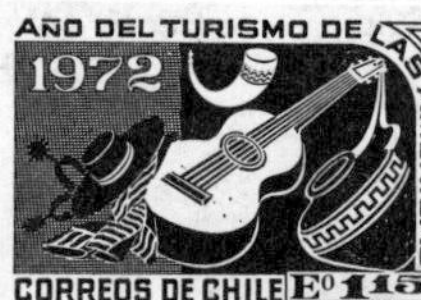

Guitar and Earthen Jar
A233

Designs: 2.65e, Fish and produce. 3.50e, Stove, pots and rug (vert.).

1972, Nov. 20 Litho. *Perf. 14½*

430 A233 1.15e red & black 25 15
431 " 2.65e ultramarine & rose lake 50 25
432 " 3.50e red & red brn. 75 40

Tourism Year of the Americas.

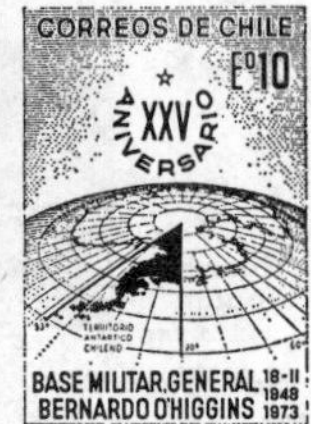

José M. Carrera Before Execution
A234

Map of Antarctica, Flag at O'Higgins Base
A235

1973, Feb. 1 Litho. *Perf. 14½*

433 A234 2.30e lt. ultramarine 15 10

Sesquicentennial of the death of José Miguel Carrera (1785–1821), Chilean revolutionist and dictator.

1973, Feb. 8

434 A235 10e ultra. & red 30 20

25th anniversary of the Bernardo O'Higgins Antarctic Base.

Naval Air Service Emblem, Destroyer
A236

La Silla Observatory
A237

1973, Mar. 16 Litho. *Perf. 14½*

435 A236 20e brt. bl. & ocher 30 12

Chilean Naval Aviation, 50th anniversary.

1973, Apr. 25 Litho. *Perf. 14½*

436 A237 2.30e ultra. & black 25 10

INTERPOL Emblem
A238

Designs: 50e, Fingerprint over globe.

1973, Sept. 23 Litho. *Perf. 14½*

437 A238 30e bister & ultra. 40 15
438 " 50e black & red 60 20

50th anniversary of International Criminal Police Organization.

Grapes
A239

Design: 100e, Globe inscribed "Chile Exporta Vino."

1973, Dec. 10 **Litho.** ***Perf. 14½***

439 A239 20e buff & lilac 25 10
440 " 100e blue & claret 1.25 40

Chilean wine export.

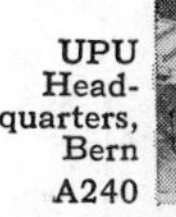

UPU Head-quarters, Bern
A240

1974, Apr. 4

441 A240 500e on 45c green 2.50 1.25

Centenary of Universal Postal Union. No. 441 was not issued without dark green surcharge and overprint.

Bernardo O'Higgins, Armed Forces Emblems—A241

1974, Apr. 11 **Litho.** ***Perf. 14½***

Multicolored

442 A241 30e *shown* 15 10
443 " 30e *Soldiers with mortar* 15 10
444 " 30e *Navy anti-aircraft gunners* 15 10
445 " 30e *Pilot in cockpit* 15 10
446 " 30e *Mounted policeman* 15 10
Nos. 442–446 (5) 75 50

Honoring the Armed Forces.

Soccer Ball and Globe
A242

Traffic Police
A243

Design: 1000e, Soccer ball and stadium (horiz.).

1974 **Lithographed** ***Perf. 14***

447 A242 500e dk. red & org. 2.50 75
448 " 1000e blue & indigo 5.00 1.25

World Cup Soccer Championship, Munich, June 13–July 7.

A souvenir sheet contains 2 imperf. stamps similar to Nos. 447–448, with blue marginal inscription. Printed on thin card. Size: 90x119mm.

Nos. 386, 355 Surcharged

1974, June **Litho.** ***Perf. 14½***

449 A202 100e on 40c bl. grn. 50 15

Perf. 13x14

450 A174 300e on 50c dull brown 1.50 40

1974, June 20 ***Perf. 14½***

451 A243 30e red brn. & grn. 15 8

Traffic safety.

Santiago-Fiji Air Service—A244

1974, Sept. 5 **Litho.** ***Perf. 14½x14***

Brown & Green

452 A244 Block of 4 2.50 1.50
a. 200e *Easter Island turtle* 50 30
b. 200e *Polynesian dancer* 50 30
c. 200e *Map of Fiji Islands* 50 30
d. 200e *Kangaroo* 50 30

Inauguration of air service by LAN (Chile's national airline) from Santiago to Easter Island, Tahiti, Fiji, Australia.

Globe Cut to Show Mantle and Core
A245

1974, Sept. 9 ***Perf. 14x14½***

453 A245 500e red brown & orange 1.75 55

International Volcanology Congress, Santiago, Sept. 9–14.

No. 393 Surcharged in Brown

E°100

24 OCTUBRE 1974

INAUGURACION TEMPLO VOTIVO

1974, Oct. 24 **Litho.** ***Perf. 14½***

454 A205 100e on 40c green 40 20

Inauguration of the O'Higgins National Shrine at Maipu, Oct. 24, 1974.

Juan Fernandez Archipelago—A246

1974, Nov. 22 **Litho.** ***Perf. 14½x14***

Blue & Brick Red

455 A246 Block of 4 2.00 1.10
a. 200e *Robinson Crusoe Island* 40 20
b. 200e *Chonta palms* 40 20
c. 200e *Mountain goat* 40 20
d. 200e *Crayfish* 40 20

400th anniversary of discovery of Juan Fernandez Archipelago.

O'Higgins and Bolivar
A247

1974, Dec. 9 ***Perf. 14½***

456 A247 100e red brn. & buff 60 40

Sesquicentennial of the Battles of Junin and Ayacucho.

F. Vidal Gormaz and Institute Seal
A248

Albert Schweitzer
A249

1975, Jan. 22 **Litho.** ***Perf. 14½***

457 A248 100e rose claret & bl. 30 15

Centenary of the Naval Hydrographic Institute; F. Vidal Gormaz was first commandant.

1975, Apr. 7 **Litho.** ***Perf. 14x14½***

458 A249 500e yel. & red brn. 1.00 50

Dr. Albert Schweitzer (1875–1965), medical missionary, birth centenary.

E° 70.-

No. 395 Surcharged in Red

Revalorizada
1975

1975, Apr. 7 ***Perf. 14½***

459 A207 70e on 40c car. & lt. red brown 15 8

Volunteer Lifeboat Service—A250

1975, Apr. 15 **Litho.** ***Perf. 14½x14***

Dark Blue & Gray Olive

460 A250 Block of 4 1.00 75
a. 150e *Lighthouse* 20 15
b. 150e *Shipwreck* 20 15
c. 150e *Lifeboat* 20 15
d. 150e *Sailor reaching for life preserver* 20 15

Valparaiso Volunteer Lifeboat service, 50th anniversary.

Frigate Lautaro
A251

1975, May 21 **Photo. & Engr.**

Emerald & Black

461 A251 500e *shown* 50 25
462 " 500e *Corvette Baquedano* 50 25
463 " 500e *Cruiser Chacabuco* 50 25
464 " 500e *Brigantine Goleta Esmeralda* 50 25

Orange & Black

465 A251 800e *Frigate Lautaro* 75 25
466 " 800e *Corvette Baquedano* 75 25
467 " 800e *Cruiser Chacabuco* 75 25
468 " 800e *Brigantine Goleta Esmeralda* 75 25

Ultramarine & Black

469 A251 1000e *Frigate Lautaro* 1.00 40
470 " 1000e *Corvette Baquedano* 1.00 40
471 " 1000e *Cruiser Chacabuco* 1.00 40
472 " 1000e *Brigantine Goleta Esmeralda* 1.00 40
Nos. 461–472 (12) 9.00 3.60

Shipwreck of training frigate Lautaro, 30th anniversary. Stamps of same denomination printed se-tenant in sheets of 25 (5x5) with 7 Lautaro stamps and 6 each of the others.

A souvenir card contains impressions of Nos. 469–472 with ultramarine and orange marginal inscription and decoration. Size: 118x150mm.

Happy Mother, by Alfredo Valenzuela P.
A252

Diego Portales, Finance Minister
A253

Paintings: No. 474, Young Girl, by Francisco Javier Mandiola. No. 475, Lucia Guzman, by Pedro Lira Rencoret. No. 476, Woman, by Magdalena Mira Mena.

1975, Oct. 13 **Litho.** ***Perf. 14½***

473 A252 50c multicolored 30 10
474 " 50c " 30 10
475 " 50c " 30 10
476 " 50c " 30 10

International Women's Year 1975. Gray inscription on back, printed beneath gum, gives details about painting shown.

A souvenir card contains impressions of Nos. 473–476 with black and blue marginal inscription and decoration. Size: 149x120 mm.

1975–78 **Litho.** ***Perf. 13x14***

477 A253 10c gray green 20 3
478 " 20c violet ('76) 20 3
479 " 30c orange ('76) 20 3
480 " 50c light brown 20 3
481 " 1p blue 30 4
482 " 1.50p ocher ('76) 40 15
483 " 2p gray ('77) 40 10
483A " 2.50p citron ('78) 75 10
484 " 5p rose claret 1.50 15
Nos. 477–484 (9) 4.15 66

Cochrane and Liberating Squadron, 1820—A254

Designs: No. 486, Capture of Valdivia, 1820. No. 487, Capture of Three-master Esmeralda, 1820. No. 488, Cruiser Cochrane, 1874. No. 489, Destroyer Cochrane, 1962.

1976, Jan. 6 ***Perf. 14½***

485	A254	1p	multicolored	35	15
486	"	1p	"	35	15
487	"	1p	"	35	15
488	"	1p	"	35	15
489	"	1p	"	35	15
	Nos. 485-489 (5)			1.75	75

Lord Thomas Cochrane, first commander of Chilean Navy, birth bicentenary. Nos. 485-489 printed se-tenant.

Flags of Chile and Bolivia A255

1976, May 25 **Litho.** ***Perf. 14½***

490	A255	1.50p	multicolored	50	20

Sesquicentennial of Bolivia's independence.

Lake of the Inca, OAS Emblem A256

1976, June 11

491	A256	1.50p	multicolored	50	20

6th General Assembly of the Organization of American States.

George Washington A257

1976, July

492	A257	5p	multicolored	2.25	50

American Bicentennial.

Minerva and Academy Emblem A258

1976, July

493	A258	2.50p	multicolored	1.00	20

Polytechnic Military Academy, 50th anniversary.

Araucan Indian A259

Designs: 2p, Condor with broken chain. 3p, Winged woman, symbolizing rebirth.

1976, Sept. 20 **Litho.** ***Perf. 14½***

494	A259	1p	blue & multi.	25	15
495	"	2p	" "	50	15
496	"	3p	yellow & multi.	75	25

3rd anniversary of the Military Junta. Nos. 494-496 printed se-tenant.

View, Antarctica A260

1977, Feb. 10 **Litho.** ***Perf. 14½***

497	A260	2p	multicolored	40	10

Visit of President Augusto Pinochet to Antarctica.

School Emblem, Planted Field A261 **Justice A262**

1977, Mar. 10 ***Perf. 14½***

498	A261	2p	multicolored	40	10

Centenary of advanced agricultural education.

1977, Mar. 30 **Litho.** ***Perf. 14½***

499	A262	2p	brown & slate	30	10

Supreme Court of Justice, sesquicentennial.

Eye with Globe, Caduceus A263

1977, Mar. 30 **Litho.** ***Perf. 14½***

500	A263	2p	multicolored	30	20

11th Pan-American Ophthalmological Congress.

Mounted Policeman A264

Designs: No. 502, Policewoman with children. No. 503, Paine Peaks and Osorno Volcano, crossed rifle emblem. No. 504, Crossed rifle emblem, mounted and motorcycle policemen, helicopter and automobile. (horiz.).

1977, Apr. 27

501	A264	2p	multicolored	30	20
502	"	2p	"	30	20
503	"	2p	"	30	20
504	"	2p	"	30	20

Chilean police organization, 50th anniversary.

Intelsat Satellite over Globe A265

1977, May 17 **Litho.** ***Perf. 14½***

505	A265	2p	multicolored	30	20

World Telecommunications Day.

El Mercurio's First Front Page, Press and Ship—A266

1977, July 5 **Litho.** ***Perf. 14½***

506	A266	2p	multicolored	30	20

El Mercurio de Valparaiso, first Chilean newspaper, 150th anniversary.

St. Francis, Birds and Cross A267 **Science and Technology A268**

1977, July 26 **Litho.** ***Perf. 14½***

507	A267	5p	multicolored	75	25

St. Francis of Assisi, 750th death anniversary.

1977, Aug. 26 **Litho.** ***Perf. 14½***

508	A268	4p	multicolored	60	25

Young Mother Weaving A269

Designs: No. 510, Handicapped boy in wheelchair and nurse. No. 511, Children dancing in circle (horiz.). No. 512, Old man and home (horiz.).

1977, Sept. 13 **Litho.** ***Perf. 14½***

509	A269	5p	multicolored	55	20
510	"	5p	"	55	20
511	A269	10p	multicolored	1.10	40
512	"	10p	"	1.10	40

4th anniversary of Government Junta and social services of armed forces.

Diego de Almagro A270

1977, Oct. 31 **Engr.** ***Perf. 14½***

513	A270	5p	rose & carmine	55	25

Diego de Almagro (1475-1538), leader of Spanish expedition to Chile.

Bell, Letters, Dove and Child A271

1977, Dec. 12 **Litho.** ***Perf. 14½***

514	A271	2.50p	multicolored	38	20

Christmas 1977.

Loading Timber A272

1978 **Litho.** ***Perf. 15***

515	A272	10p	multicolored	1.10	35
516	"	20p	"	1.60	40

No. 516 inscribed "CORREOS," ship is flying Chilean flag.

Papal Arms and Globe A273

University A274

1978 **Litho.** ***Perf. 14½***

521	A273	10p	multicolored	80	35
522	A274	25p	"	2.00	75

World Peace Day (10p); Catholic University of Valparaiso, 50th anniversary (25p). Issue dates: 10p, July 28; 25p, July 31.

O'Higgins, by Gil de Castro A275

1978, Aug. 20 Litho. *Perf. 15*

523 A275 10p multicolored 80 30

Bernardo O'Higgins (1778–1842), soldier and statesman.

Chacabuco Victory Monument
A276

1978, Sept. 11

524 A276 10p multicolored 80 30

160th anniversary of O'Higgins victory at Chacabuco, and 5th anniversary of military government.

Teacher Writing on Blackboard
A277

1978, Sept. 21

525 A277 15p multicolored 1.20 50

10th anniversary and 9th Reunion of Interamerican Council for Education, Science and Culture (C.I.E.C.C.), Sept. 21–29.

First National Fleet, by Thomas Somerscales—A278

Design: 30p, Last Moments of Rancagua Battle, by Pedro Subercaseaux.

1978 Litho. *Perf. 15*

526 A278 20p multicolored 1.60 40
527 " 30p " 2.40 50

Bernardo O'Higgins (1778–1842), soldier and statesman.

Issue dates: 20p, Oct. 9; 30p, Oct. 2.

San Martin-O'Higgins Medal, by Rene Thenot, 1942—A279

1978, Oct. 20

528 A279 7p multicolored 55 15

José de San Martin and Bernardo O'Higgins, 200th birth anniversaries.

A particular stamp may be scarce, but if few want it, its market potential may remain relatively low.

Council Emblem
A280

1978, Nov. 27 Litho. *Perf. 14½*

529 A280 50p multicolored 4.00

International Council of Military Sports, 30th anniversary.

Three Kings
A281

Virgin and Child
A282

1978, Dec. 14 Litho. *Perf. 14½*

530 A281 3p multicolored 18 8
531 A282 11p " 65 25

Christmas 1978.

Philippi Brothers
A283

1978, Dec. 29 Litho. *Perf. 14½x15*

532 A283 3.50p multicolored 22 8

Bernardo E. Philippi (1811–1852) and Rodulfo A. Philippi (1808–1904), scientists and travelers.

Questions?
Comment?
Corrections?
Help us serve you better. Let us know what you think by filling out our questionnaire at the front of this book.

SEMI-POSTAL STAMPS.

S. S. Abtao and Captain Policarpo Toro—SP1

S. S. Abtao and Brother Eugenio Eyraud SP2

Perf. 14½x15

1940, Mar. 1 Engr. Unwmkd.

B1 SP1 80c+2.20p dark green & lake 1.00 1.00
B2 SP2 3.60p+6.40p lake & dark green 1.00 1.00

Issued in commemoration of the 50th anniversary of Chilean ownership of Easter Island. The surtax was used for charitable institutions.

These stamps were printed together in a sheet containing fifteen of each value, of which nine pairs are se-tenant.

Pedro de Valdivia SP3

Portraits: 10c+10c, Jose Toribio Medina.

1961, Apr. 29 Photo. *Perf. 13x12½*

B3 SP3 5c+5c pale brown & slate green 60 25
B4 " 10c+10c buff & violet black 50 35

Printed without charge by the Spanish Mint as a gift to Chile. The surtax was to aid the 1960 earthquake victims and to increase teachers' salaries. See also Nos. CB1–CB2.

No. 402 Surcharged in Dark Green

Eº 27+3

"Centenario de la Organización Meteorológica Mundial IMO-W-MO 1973"

1974, Mar. 25 Litho. *Perf. 14½*

B5 A213 27e+3e on 40c dull green 25 15

Centenary of international meteorological cooperation.

The 3e surtax of Nos. B5–B10 was for modernization of the postal system.

Eº 27+3

No. 412 Surcharged in Dark Blue

"V Centenario del Nacimiento de Copérnico 1473 - 1973"

1974, Apr. 25 Litho. *Perf. 14½*

B6 A219 27e+3e on 1.95e lt. & dark blue 30 20

500th anniversary of the birth of Nicolaus Copernicus (1473–1534), Polish astronomer.

Eº 27+3

No. 329A Surcharged

" Centenario de la ciudad de Viña del Mar 1874 - 1974 "

1974, May 2 Litho. *Perf. 14*

B7 A159 27e+3e on 1e bluish green 25 15

Centenary of the city of Viña del Mar.

No. 377 Surcharged

1974, June 7 Litho. *Perf. 14½*

B8 A193 47e+3e on 40c grn. 35 25

Nos. 395 and 380 Surcharged in Red

1974

B9 A207 67e+3e on 40c multicolored 35 25
B10 A196 97e+3e on 40c red brown 50 25

Issue dates: No. B9, July 9; No. B10, June 20.

AIR POST STAMPS.

Bernardo O'Higgins AP1

Lithographed; Center Engraved

Black Surcharge.

1927 *Perf. 13½x14.* Unwmkd.

C1 AP1 40c on 10c black brown & blue 250.00 250.00
C2 " 80c on 10c black brown & blue 275.00 50.00
C3 " 1.20p on 10c black brown & blue 275.00 50.00
C4 " 1.60p on 10c black brown & blue 275.00 50.00
C5 " 2p on 10c black brown & blue 275.00 50.00
Nos. C1–C5 (5) 1350.00 250.00

Nos. C1 to C5 were issued for air post service between Santiago and Valparaiso, and are not known without surcharge.

Regular Issues of 1915–28 Overprinted or Surcharged in Black, Red or Blue

Inscribed: "Chile Correos".

1928–29 *Perf. 13½x14, 14*

C6 A39 20c brown orange & black (Bk) 50 40
C6A A55 40c dark violet & black (R) 50 50
C6B A43 1p green & black (Bl) 1.25 60
C6C " 2p red & blk. (Bl) 1.25 40
f. 2p vermilion & black (Bl) 200.00 40.00
C6D " 5p olive green & black (Bl) 3.00 1.00
C6E A50 6p on 10c dp. blue & black (R) 50.00 40.00
C7 A43 10p orange & black (Bk) ('29) 8.00 2.50
C8 " 10p orange & black (Bl) 45.00 45.00
Nos. C6–C8 (8) 109.50 90.40

On Nos. C6B to C6D, C7 and C8 the overprint is larger than on the other stamps of the issue.

Same Overprint or Surcharge on Nos. 155, 156, 158-161.

Inscribed: "Chile Correos".

1928–32 Wmk. 215

C9 A55 40c violet & black (R) 35 18
C10 A43 1p green & black (Bl) 75 50
C11 A43 2p red & black (Bl) 7.00 1.00
C12 A52 3p on 5c slate blue (R) 40.00 40.00
C13 A43 5p olive green & black (Bl) 3.50 1.25
C14 " 10p orange & black (Bk) 10.00 1.50
Nos. C9–C14 (6) 61.60 44.43

Same Overprint on Nos. 166-169, 172 and 158 in Black, Red or Blue.

Inscribed: "Correos de Chile"

1928–30

C15 A39 20c orange red & black (#166) (Bk) ('29) 1.75 1.00
C16 " 20c orange red & black (#172) (Bk) ('30) 25 8
C17 A40 25c blue & black (R) 15 12
C18 A41 30c brn. & blk. (Bk) 25 18
a. Double ovpt., one inverted 275.00 275.00
C19 A42 50c deep green & black (R) 20 12
Nos. C15–C19 (5) 2.60 1.50

Inscribed: "Chile Correos".

1932 *Perf. 13½x14, 14.*

C21 A43 1p yellow green & black (Bk) 2.00 1.50

Condor on Andes

AP1a

Airplane Crossing Andes

AP3

Los Cerrillos Airport

AP2

Lithographed.

1931 *Perf. 13½x14, 14½x14*

C22 AP1a 5c yellow green 10 6
C23 " 10c yellow brown 10 6
C24 " 20c rose 10 6
C25 AP2 50c dark blue 1.25 50
C26 AP3 50c black brown 30 8
C27 " 1p purple 60 12
C28 " 2p blue black 1.00 25
a. 2p bluish slate 2.50 1.50
C29 AP2 5p light red 1.25 50
Nos. C22–C29 (8) 4.70 1.63

Airplane over City

AP4

Wings over Chile

AP5

Condor

AP6

Airplane and Star of Chile

AP7

Condor and Statue of Capolican

AP8

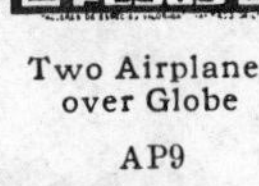

Two Airplanes over Globe

AP9

Seaplane

AP10

Airplane

AP11

Airplane and Southern Cross

AP12

Airplane and Symbols of Space

AP13

Perf. 13½x14

1934–39 Engraved Wmk. 215

Size: 21x25 mm.

C30 AP4 10c yellow green ('35) 5 4
C31 " 15c dark green ('35) 6 5
C32 " 20c deep blue ('36) 5 4
C33 AP5 30c black brown ('35) 6 4
C34 " 40c indigo ('38) 6 4
C35 " 50c dark brown ('36) 6 4
C36 AP6 60c violet black ('35) 6 4
C37 AP7 70c blue ('35) 10 10
C38 AP8 80c olive black ('35) 6 4

Perf. 14

Size: 24½x29 mm.

C39 AP9 1p slate black 8 4
C40 " 2p greenish blue 10 4
C41 AP10 3p org. brn. ('35) 15 4
C42 " 4p brown ('35) 15 5
C43 " 5p orange red 15 5
C44 AP11 6p yel. brn. ('35) 25 5
a. 6p brown ('39) 2.50 1.25
C45 " 8p green ('35) 30 6
C46 " 10p brown lake 35 5
C47 AP12 20p olive 75 5
C48 " 30p gray black 1.50 10
C49 AP13 40p gray violet 2.00 20
C50 " 50p brown violet 3.00 20
Nos. C30–C50 (21) 9.34 1.36

Nos. C30–C50 have been re-issued in slightly different colors, with white gum. The first printings are considerably scarcer. See also Nos. C90–C107B, C148–C154.

Types of 1931 Surcharged in Black or Red

Cts.80

Perf. 13½x14, 14½x14.

1940 Wmk. 215

C51 AP1a 80c on 20c light rose 25 8
C52 AP2 1.60p on 5p light red 1.50 40
C53 AP3 5.10p on 2p slate blue (R) 1.75 1.50

The surcharge on No. C52 measures 21½mm.

Plane and Weather Vane
AP14

Plane and Caravel
AP23

Designs (Plane and): 20c, Globe. 30c, Chilean flag. 40c, Star of Chile and Southern Cross. 50c, Mountains. 60c, Tree. 70c, Lakes. 80c, Shore. 90c, Sunrise. 2p, Compass. 3p, Telegraph lines. 4p, Rainbow. 5p, Factory. 10p, Snow-capped mountain.

Lithographed

1941-42 *Perf. 14.* Wmk. 215

No.	Type	Description	Unused	Used
C54	AP14	10c olive gray	8	8
C55	"	20c deep rose	10	8
C56	"	30c blue violet	10	8
C57	"	40c dull red brown	15	12
C58	"	50c red orange ('42)	10	8
C59	"	60c deep green	12	6
C60	"	70c rose	25	25
C61	"	80c ultra. ('42)	2.00	50
C62	"	90c dark brown	30	25
C63	AP23	1p bright blue	30	6
C64	"	2p rose lake	50	30
C65	"	3p dark blue green & yel. grn.	1.00	65
C66	"	4p blue violet & buff	1.25	85
C67	"	5p dark orange red ('42)	10.00	6.00
C68	"	10p gray green & blue green	5.00	3.00
		Nos. C54-C68 (15)	21.25	12.36

The 1p, dated "1541-1941", commemorates the 400th anniversary of Santiago.

1942-46 Unwmkd.

No.	Type	Description	Unused	Used
C69	AP14	10c ultra. ('43)	5	5
C70	"	10c rose lilac ('45)	10	8
C71	"	20c dull green ('43)	10	6
C72	"	20c copper brown ('45)	10	4
C73	"	30c dull violet ('44)	10	8
C74	"	30c olive black ('45)	10	8
C75	"	40c red brown ('44)	25	18
C76	"	40c ultra. ('45)	10	4
C77	"	50c rose ('43)	15	10
C78	"	50c orange red ('45)	15	6
C79	"	60c orange	15	10
C79B	"	60c deep green ('46)	15	8
C80	"	70c rose ('45)	25	25
C81	"	80c slate green	15	5
C82	"	90c brown ('45)	25	25
C83	AP23	1p gray green & light blue ('43)	15	5
C84	"	2p orange red ('43)	40	12
C85	"	3p dark purple & pale orange ('43)	40	12
C86	"	4p blue green & yellow green	25	12
C87	"	5p dk. rose carmine ('43)	75	25
		a. 5p dk. carmine rose ('44)	30	20
C88	"	10p sapphire ('43)	75	40
		Nos. C69-C88 (21)	4.85	2.56

No. C83 is without dates "1541-1941." See Nos. C109-C123, C145-C147.

Coat of Arms and Plane
AP29

1942, Nov. 5 Engr. *Perf. 14½*

No.	Type	Description	Unused	Used
C89	AP29	100p carmine lake	32.50	25.00

University of Chile centenary.

Types of 1934-39.
Engraved.

1944-55 *Perf. 13½x14.* Unwmkd.

No.	Type	Description	Unused	Used
C90	AP4	10c yel. grn. ('55)	25	25
C92	"	20c deep blue	6	6
C93	AP5	30c black brown	5	4
C94	"	40c indigo	8	4
C95	"	50c dark brown ('47)	8	5
C96	AP6	60c slate violet	8	5
C97	AP7	70c blue ('48)	10	6
C98	AP8	80c olive black	10	4

Perf. 14

No.	Type	Description	Unused	Used
C99	AP9	1p slate black	10	4
C100	"	2p greenish blue	12	8
C101	AP10	3p org. brn. ('45)	12	6
C102	"	4p brown	15	6
C103	"	5p orange red	30	5
C104	AP11	6p yel. brn. ('46)	35	20
C105	"	8p green	30	15
C106	"	10p brown lake	40	8
C107	AP12	20p olive gray ('45)	50	12
		a. Imperf., pair	100.00	
C107B	AP13	50p rose vio. ('50)	1.75	90
		Nos. C90-C107B (18)	4.89	2.33

Plane and Radio Tower
AP30

Lithographed.

1945 *Perf. 14* Unwmkd.

No.	Type	Description	Unused	Used
C108	AP30	1.60p bright violet	20	7

Types of 1941-42.

1946-48 Wmk. 215

No.	Type	Description	Unused	Used
C109	AP14	10c rose lilac('47)	6	5
C110	"	20c dark red brown ('48)	6	4
C111	"	20c dull green ('48)	85	15
C112	"	30c black ('48)	12	10
C113	"	40c ultra. ('48)	8	4
C114	"	60c olive green ('48)	10	8
C115	"	80c olive black ('48)	8	8
C116	"	90c choc. ('48)	10	6
C117	AP23	1p gray green & light blue ('48)	10	6
C118	AP30	1.60p bright violet	15	5
C119	"	1.80p bright violet ('48)	10	8
C119A	AP23	2p orange red	20	8
C120	"	3p dark purple & pale orange ('47)	1.10	25
C121	"	4p blue green & yellow green	35	30
C122	"	5p rose carmine ('47)	35	10
C123	"	10p sapphire ('47)	90	30
		Nos. C109-C123 (16)	4.70	1.82

No. C117 is without dates "1541-1941."

Araucarian Pine
AP31

1948

No.	Type	Description	Unused	Used
C124	AP31	3p carmine	90	90
		a. Block of 25	40.00	

Issued in panes of 100 stamps, divisible into four blocks of 25 different designs, the same animals, insects, birds, fish, flowers and trees of Chile as illustrated and described for Nos. 254-255.

The stamps commemorate the centenary (in 1944) of the publication of the first volume of Claudio Gay's Natural History of Chile.

Air Line Emblem and Planes
AP32

Lithographed.

1949 *Perf. 14.* Wmk. 215

No.	Type	Description	Unused	Used
C125	AP32	2p ultramarine	20	10

Issued to commemorate the 20th anniversary of the establishment of Chile's National Air Line.

Benjamin Vicuna Mackenna
AP33

Factory, Badge and Book
AP34

1949, Mar. 22 Engr. *Perf. 13½x14*

No.	Type	Description	Unused	Used
C126	AP33	3p dk. car. rose	30	25

Lithographed.

1949, Nov. 11 *Perf. 14* Unwmkd.

Design: 10p, Column and cogwheel.

No.	Type	Description	Unused	Used
C127	AP34	5p green	35	25
C128	"	10p red brown	60	30

Issued to commemorate the centenary of the founding of Chile's School of Arts and Crafts.

Plane and Globe—AP35

1950, Jan. Engraved

No.	Type	Description	Unused	Used
C129	AP35	5p green	30	20
C130	"	10p red brown	50	35

Issued to commemorate the 75th anniversary of the formation of the Universal Postal Union.

Plane over Snow-capped Mountain
AP36

Plane over Fishing Boat—AP37

Araucarian Pine and Plane
AP38

Plane Above River
AP39

Plane and: 40c, Coast and Sunrise. 2p, Chilean flag. 3p, Dock crane. 5p, Blast furnace. 10p, Mountain lake. 20p, Cable cars.

Imprint: "Especies Valoradas-Chile"
Lithographed.

1950-54 *Perf. 14* Wmk. 215

No.	Type	Description	Unused	Used
C135	AP36	20c yel. brown ('54)	6	5
C136	"	40c purple ('52)	6	5
C137	AP37	60c lt. blue ('53)	12	12
C138	AP38	1p dull green	8	4
C139	"	2p brown red	12	5
C140	"	3p violet blue	15	6
C141	AP39	4p red org. ('54)	18	8
C142	AP38	5p violet	18	5
C143	AP39	10p yel. green ('53)	35	10
C144	"	20p red brn. ('54)	70	15
		Nos. C135-C144 (10)	2.00	75

See also Nos. C155-C164, C207-C212.

Nos. C115, C81 and C116 Surcharged with New Value in Carmine or Black.

1951-52 Wmk. 215

No.	Type	Description	Unused	Used
C145	AP14	40c on 80c olive black (C) ('52)	15	10

Unwmkd.

No.	Type	Description	Unused	Used
C146	AP14	40c on 80c slate green (C) ('52)	8.00	8.00

Wmk. 215

No.	Type	Description	Unused	Used
C147	AP14	1p on 90c choc.	12	10

Types of 1934-39.
Engraved.

1951-53 *Perf. 14* Unwmkd.

No.	Type	Description	Unused	Used
C148	AP9	1p deep blue	8	6
C149	"	2p blue	15	5
C150	AP11	6p bistre brown ('52)	20	15
C151	AP12	30p dk. gray ('53)	90	75
C152	AP13	40p dk. pur. brn.	1.50	1.25
C153	"	50p dark purple	2.50	1.50
		Nos. C148-C153 (6)	5.33	3.76

Wmk. 215

No.	Type	Description	Unused	Used
C154	AP13	50p dk. pur. ('52)	1.00	20

Types of 1950-54.
Designs as Before.
Imprint: "Especies Valoradas-Chile"
Lithographed.

1951-55 *Perf. 14* Unwmkd.

No.	Type	Description	Unused	Used
C155	AP36	20c yel. brn. ('54)	6	5
C156	"	40c purple	5	5
C157	AP37	60c lt. bl. ('53)	60	60
C158	AP38	1p dk.bl.grn. ('55)	6	5
C159	"	2p brown red	6	5
C160	"	3p violet blue	8	6
C161	AP39	4p red org. ('52)	20	8
C162	AP38	5p violet	15	6
C163	AP39	10p emerald	35	12
C164	"	20p brown	50	18
		Nos. C155-C164 (10)	2.11	1.30

San Martin Crossing Andes—AP40

Engraved.

1951, Mar. 16 *Perf. 14½.* Wmk. 215

C165 AP40 5p red violet 40 15

Issued to commemorate the centenary of the death of Gen. José de San Martin.

Isabella Type of Regular Issue, 1952.

1952, Mar. 21 *Perf. 14*

C166 A125 10p carmine 45 35

Issued for the 500th anniversary of the birth of Queen Isabella I of Spain.

A souvenir card without franking value was issued for the Hispano-Chilean Philatelic Exhibition at Santiago, Oct. 12, 1969. It contains 2 imperf. stamps similar to Nos. 264 and C166—60c green and 10p rose red. Size: 115x137½mm. Price $12.50.

Ancient Fortress
AP42

1953, Apr. 28

C167 AP42 10p brown carmine 40 40

4th centenary of the founding of Valdivia.

Stamp Centenary Type of 1953.

1953, Oct. 15 Engraved *Perf. 14½*

C168 A131 100p deep greenish blue 6.00 3.50

Issued to commemorate the centenary of Chile's first postage stamps.

An imperf. souvenir sheet contains one each of Nos. 276 and C168, with inscriptions in black at top and bottom center. Sheet measures 178x229mm. It is stated that this sheet was not valid for postage. Price $425.

Early Plane and Stylized Modern Version
AP44

Engraved.

1954, May 26 *Perf. 14* Unwmkd.

C170 AP44 3p deep blue 12 8

Issued to commemorate the 25th anniversary of the founding of Chile's National Air Line.

Domeyko Type of Regular Issue, 1954.

1954, Aug. 16 *Perf. 13½x14*

C171 A134 5p orange brown 25 20

Issued to commemorate the 150th anniversary (in 1952) of the birth of Ignacio Domeyko.

Railroad Type of Regular Issue, 1954.

1954, Sept. 10 *Perf. 14½* Wmk. 215

C172 A135 10p dark purple 50 30

Issued to commemorate the centenary (in 1951) of the first South American railroad.

An imperforate souvenir sheet contains one each of Nos. 283 and C172. Size: 174x232mm. Price, $300.

Presidential Visits Type of 1955

1955, May 24

C173 A139 100p red 2.50 2.50

Issued to publicize the reciprocal visits of Presidents Juan D. Peron and Carlos Ibanez del Campo.

Jet Plane in Clouds
AP48

Comet Air Liner
AP49

Designs: 2p, Helicopter over bridge. 10p, Oil derricks and plane. 50p, Control tower and plane. 200p, Beechcraft monoplane. 500p, Douglas DC-6.

Perf. 14½x14, 14x13½ (AP49)

1955–56 Engraved. Wmk. 215

C174 AP48 1p deep red lilac ('56) 5 4
C175 " 2p pale brn. ('56) 5 4
C176 " 10p bluish green ('56) 8 5
C177 " 50p rose ('56) 30 8
C178 AP49 100p green 75 12
C179 " 200p deep ultra. 1.50 25
C180 " 500p dark carmine 3.00 50
Nos. C174–C180 (7) 5.73 1.08

Stamps similar to type AP49, but inscribed in escudo currency, are listed as type AP58.

1956-58 Unwmkd.

Designs: 5p, Train and plane. 20p, Jet plane and Easter Island statue.

C183 AP48 5p violet 10 5
C184 " 10p green ('57) 10 5
C185 " 20p ultramarine 15 5
C186 " 50p rose ('57) 35 10
C187 AP49 100p blue green ('57) 50 12
C188 " 200p deep ultra. ('57) 1.25 15
C189 " 500p carmine ('58) 2.50 40
Nos. C183–C189 (7) 4.95 92

Symbols of University Departments
AP50

Design: 100p, View of the University.

1956, Dec. 15 *Perf. 14½* Unwmkd.

C190 AP50 20p green 40 30
C191 " 100p dark violet blue 75 65

Issued to commemorate the 25th anniversary of the Federico Santa Maria Technical University, Valparaiso.

A souvenir sheet contains one each of Nos. 299, C190–C191, imperf. It was not issued for postal use, though some served postally. Size: 127x160mm. Price, $30.

Mistral Type of Regular Issue, 1958

1958, Jan. 10 Engraved *Perf. 14*

C192 A144 100p green 50 20

Issued in honor of Gabriela Mistral, poet and educator.

Ambrosio O'Higgins
AP51

1958, March 23

C193 AP51 100p light blue 60 30

Issued to commemorate the 400th anniversary of the founding of the city of Osorno.

A souvenir sheet contains one each of Nos. 302 and C193, imperf. and printed in red brown. It was not issued for postal use, though some served postally. Size: 155x138mm. Price, $20.

Exhibition Type of Regular Issue

1958, Oct. 18 Unwmkd.

C194 A146 50p dull green 40 20

Issued to publicize the National Philatelic Exhibition, Santiago, Oct. 18–26.

A souvenir sheet contains one each of Nos. 303 and C194, imperf. and printed in deep red. It was not issued for postal use, though some served postally. Size: 188x 220mm. Price, $20.

Bank Type of Regular Issue, 1958.

1958, Dec. 18 Engraved. *Perf. 14*

C195 A147 50p reddish brown 30 20

Issued to commemorate the centenary of the Savings Bank for Public Employees.

A souvenir sheet contains one each of Nos. 304 and C195, printed in dull violet, imperf. It was not issued for postal use, though some served postally. Price, $17.50.

Antarctic Types of Regular Issue

1958 Lithographed. *Perf. 14*

C199 A149 20p violet 50 10

Engraved.

C200 A150 500p dark blue 4.00 1.00

Symbols of Various Religions
AP52

Engraved.

1959, Jan. 23 *Perf. 14½* Unwmkd.

C206 AP52 50p dark carmine rose 55 45

Issued to commemorate the 10th anniversary of the Universal Declaration of Human Rights.

Types of 1950–54.

Imprint: "Casa de Moneda de Chile."

Designs: 1p, Araucarian pine and plane. 10p, Plane over mountain lake. 20p, Plane and cable cars. 50p, Plane silhouette over shore. 100p, Plane over map of Antarctica. 200p, Plane over natural arch rock.

1959 Lithographed. *Perf. 14*

C207 AP38 1p dk. blue grn. 2.00 50
a. Wmk. 215 40.00
C208 AP39 10p emerald 20 5
C209 " 20p red brown 25 8
C210 " 50p yellow green 30 15
C211 " 100p carmine rose 35 15
C212 " 200p bright blue 1.00 45
Nos. C207–C212 (6) 4.10 1.38

Carlos Anwandter
AP53

1959, June 18 Engraved. *Perf. 14*

C213 AP53 20p rose carmine 15 12

Issued to commemorate the centenary of the German School in Valdivia, founded by Carlos Anwandter.

A souvenir sheet contains one each of Nos. 319 and C213, imperf. It was not issued for postal use, though some served postally. Price, $25.

IGY Type of Regular Issue, 1958.

1959, Aug. 28 *Perf. 14* Unwmkd.

C214 A148 50p green 40 15

Issued to commemorate the International Geophysical Year, 1957-58.

Ladrillero Type of Regular Issue.

1959, Aug. 28 Lithographed.

C215 A154 50p green 35 25

Issued to commemorate the 400th anniversary (in 1957) of the Juan Ladrillero expedition.

Barros Arana Type of Regular Issue.

1959, Aug. 28

C216 A155 100p purple 50 40

Issued to commemorate the 50th anniversary of the death of Diego Barros Arana (1830–1907), historian.

Red Cross Type of Regular Issue.

1959, Oct. 6

C217 A156 50p red & black 30 20

Centenary of Red Cross idea.

WRY Type of Regular Issue, 1960.

1960, Apr. 7 *Perf. 14½* Unwmkd.

C218 A160 10c violet 35 30

Issued to publicize World Refugee Year, July 1, 1959–June 30, 1960.

A souvenir sheet contains two stamps similar to Nos. 330 and C218, the 1c printed in blue, the 10c airmail in maroon. The sheet is imperf., printed on thin cardboard and has border, inscriptions and WRY emblems in dark green with drab background. Size: 160x204mm. Price, $110.

Type of Regular Issue, 1960–62, and

José Agustin Eyzaguirre and José Miguel Infante—AP54

Designs: 2c, Palace of Justice. 5c, National memorial. No. C220, Arms of Chile. No. C220A, José Gaspar Marin and J. Gregorio Argomedo. 50c, Archbishop J. I. Cienfuegos and Brother Camilo Henriquez. 1e, Bernardo O'Higgins.

Engraved

1960–65 *Perf. 14½* Unwmkd.

C218A AP54 2c maroon & gray vio. ('62) 10 10
C219 A162 5c violet blue & dull purple ('61) 20 10

Wmk. 215

C220 A161 10c dark brown & red brown 30 15

Unwmkd.

C220A AP54 10c violet brown & brn. ('64) 15 10
C220B " 20c dk. bl. & dull purple ('64) 25 15
C220C " 50c blue green & indigo ('65) 50 30
C220D A162 1e dk. red & red brn. ('63) 1.25 60
Nos. C218A–C220D (7) 2.75 1.50

Issued to commemorate the 150th anniversary of the formation of the first National Government.

A souvenir sheet contains two airmail stamps: a 5c brown similar to No. C219 (National Memorial) and a 10c green, type A161. The sheet is imperf., printed on heavy paper with papermaker's watermark, and has green inscriptions. Size: 120x 168mm. Price, $40.

Map and Rotary Emblem
AP55

Lithographed

1960, Dec. 1 *Perf. 14* Unwmkd.

C221 AP55 10c blue 35 20

Issued to commemorate the South American Rotary Regional Conference, Santiago, 1960.

A souvenir sheet contains one 10c maroon, type AP55, with brown marginal inscription. Size: 118x158mm. Price, $17.50.

The souvenir sheet was overprinted in green "El Mundo Unida Contra la Malaria" and the outline of a mosquito, and released in October, 1962. Price, $35.

Plane over Mountain Lake
AP56

Designs: 1m, Araucarian pine and plane. 2m, Chilean flag and plane. 3m, Plane and dock crane. 4m, Plane above river (vignette like AP39). 5m, Blast furnace. 2c, Plane over cable cars. 5c, Plane silhouette over shore. 10c, Plane over map of Antarctica. 20c, Plane over natural arch rock.

Imprint: "Casa de Moneda de Chile."

1960–62 Lithographed *Perf. 14*

C222	AP56	1m orange	5	4
C223	"	2m yellow green	5	5
C224	"	3m violet	5	5
C225	"	4m gray olive	5	5
C226	"	5m brt. blue green	6	5
C227	"	1c ultramarine	8	5
C228	"	2c red brown ('61)	10	5
C229	"	5c yel. green ('61)	15	8
C230	"	10c car. rose ('62)	40	18
C231	"	20c brt. blue ('62)	60	40
		Nos. C222–C231 (10)	1.59	1.00

Oil Derricks and Douglas DC-6 AP57 **Beechcraft Monoplane** AP58

Designs: 5m, Train and plane. 2c, Jet plane and Easter Island statue. 5c, Control tower and plane. 10c, Comet airliner. 50c, Douglas DC-6.

Lithographed

1960–67 *Perf. 14x13½* Unwmkd.

C234	AP57	5m red brown	5	5
C235	"	1c dull blue	5	5
C236	"	2c ultra. ('62)	5	5
C237	"	5c rose red ('64)	8	5
C238	AP58	10c ultra. ('67)	8	6
C239	"	20c carmine ('62)	30	20
C240	"	50c green ('63)	35	20
		Nos. C234–C240 (7)	96	66

Stamps similar to type AP58, but inscribed in peso ($) currency, are listed as type AP49.

Congress Type of Regular Issue.

1961, Oct. 5 *Perf. 14½*

C245 A164 10c gray green 30 20

Issued to commemorate the 150th anniversary of the first National Congress.

Soccer Type of Regular Issue, 1962.

Designs: 5c, Goalkeeper and stadium (vert.). 10c, Soccer players and globe.

Engraved

1962, May 30 *Perf. 14½* Unwmkd.

C246	A165	5c rose lilac	25	10
C247	"	10c dark carmine	35	20

Issued to commemorate the World Soccer Championship, Chile, May 30–June 17.

A souvenir sheet of four contains one each of Nos. 340–341, C246–C247, imperf., with light brown marginal inscriptions. Size: 123x194mm. Sold for 7.50 escudos (face value, 22 centavos). Price, $7.50.

Hunger Type of Regular Issue.

Design: 20c, Mother with empty bowl (horiz.).

1963, Mar. 21 Litho. *Perf. 14*

C248 A166 20c green 40 35

Issued for the "Freedom from Hunger" campaign of the U.N. Food and Agriculture Organization.

Red Cross Type of Regular Issue.

Design: 20c, Centenary emblem and plane silhouette (horiz.).

1963, Sept. 6 *Perf. 14* Unwmkd.

C249 A167 20c gray & red 35 30

Centenary of International Red Cross.

Fire Engine of 1860's
AP59

1963, Dec. 20 Litho. *Perf. 14½*

C250 AP59 30c red 60 40

Centenary of the Santiago Fire Brigade.

Western Hemisphere
AP60

1964, Apr. 9 *Perf. 14½* Unwmkd.

C254 AP60 4c ultramarine 12 10

Issued in memory of President John F. Kennedy and to honor the Alliance for Progress.

Battle of Rancagua
AP61

1965, May 7 Engraved *Perf. 14½*

C255 AP61 5c dull grn. & sepia 10 8

Issued to commemorate the sesquicentennial of the Battle of Rancagua, Oct. 7, 1814.

ITU Emblem, Old and New Communication Equipment
AP62

1965, May 7 Litho. *Perf. 14½x14*

C256 AP62 40c red & maroon 30 20

Issued to commemorate the centenary of the International Telecommunication Union.

Portrait Type of 1964

Portraits: No. C257, Enrique Molina. No. C258, Msgr. Carlos Casanueva.

1965, June Litho. *Perf. 14*

C257	A169	60c bright violet	40	30
C258	"	60c green	40	30

See note after No. 346.

Skier Type of Regular Issue 1965

Design: 20c, Skier (horiz.).

1965, Aug. 30 *Perf. 14* Unwmkd.

C259 A172 20c ultramarine 25 20

World Skiing Championships, Chile, 1966.

Fishing Boats, Angelmo Harbor AP63 **Aviators' Monument** AP64

1965

C260 AP63 40c brown 25 8

Perf. 14x14½

C262 AP64 1e carmine rose 40 30

Andrés Bello
AP65

1965, Nov. 29 Engraved Unwmkd.

C263 AP65 10c dk. car. rose 10 10

Issued to commemorate the centenary of the death of Andrés Bello (1780?–1865), Venezuela-born writer and educator.

Skiers
AP66

Basketball
AP67

1966, Apr. 6 Litho. *Perf. 14*

C264 AP66 4e dk. blue & red brown 1.50 1.25

World Skiing Championships, Partillo, Aug. 1966.

1966, Apr. 28

C265 AP67 13c rose carmine 10 8

International Basketball Championships.

Slalom
AP68

Perf. 14½x15

1966, July 20 Litho. Unwmkd.

C266	AP68	75c rose carmine & lilac	35	20
C267	"	3e ultramarine & lt. blue	1.50	60

International Skiing Championships, Partillo, August 1966. A souvenir sheet of 2 contains imperf. stamps similar to Nos. C266–C267. Marginal inscription in ultramarine and rose carmine. No gum. Size: 109x140mm. Price $3.50.

Ship Type of Regular Issue

1966 Lithographed *Perf. 14½*

C268 A175 70c Prussian green & yel. green 30 20

See note below No. 358.

ICY Type of Regular Issue

1966, Oct. 28 *Perf. 14½* Unwmkd.

C269 A177 3e blue & car. 2.25 1.25

International Cooperation Year, 1965.

A souvenir sheet of 2 contains imperf. stamps similar to Nos. 360 and C269. Brown marginal inscription. No gum. Size: 111x140mm. Price $3.

Chilean Flag and Ships
AP69

1966, Nov. 21 Litho. *Perf. 14*

C270 AP69 13c dull red brn. 10 8

Centenary of the city of Antofagasta.

Pardo Type of Regular Issue

Design: 40c, Pardo and map of Chile's claim to Antarctica.

1967, Jan. 6 *Perf. 14½* Unwmkd.

C271 A178 40c ultramarine 25 20

See note below No. 361.

Family Type of Regular Issue

1967, Apr. 13 Litho. *Perf. 14*

C272 A179 80c brt. bl. & blk. 45 30

Issued to publicize the 8th International Conference for Family Planning, Santiago, April 1967.

Ruben Dario and Title Page of "Azul"
AP70

1967, May 15 Engr. *Perf. 14½*

C273 AP70 10c dark blue 10 8

Issued to commemorate the centenary of the birth of Ruben Dario (pen name of Felix Ruben Garcia Sarmiento, 1867–1916), Nicaraguan poet, newspaper correspondent and diplomat.

Tree Type of Regular Issue

1967, June 9 Lithographed

C274 A180 75c grn. & pale rose 40 35

Reforestation Campaign.

Lions Type of Regular Issue

1967 Lithographed *Perf. 14*

C275	A181	1e purple & yellow	50	40
C276	"	5e blue & yellow	2.00	1.00

Issued to commemorate the 50th anniversary of Lions International. A souvenir sheet without franking value contains 3 imperf. stamps, 20c, 1e and 5e, in violet blue and yellow. Marginal inscription and design in violet blue and yellow. Size: 110x140mm. Price, $10.

Issue dates: 1e, July 12; 5e, Aug. 11.

Flag Type of Regular Issue

1967, Oct. 20 *Perf. 14½* Unwmkd.

C277 A182 50c ultra. & crimson 30 25

Sesquicentennial of the national flag.

ITY Emblem
AP71

1967, Nov. 22 Litho. *Perf. 14½*

C278 AP71 30c lt. vio. blue & black 20 15

Issued for International Tourist Year, 1967.

Caro Type of Regular Issue, 1967.

1967, Dec. 4 Engraved *Perf. 14½*

C279 A183 40c violet 30 25

Issued to commemorate the centenary of the birth of José Maria Cardinal Caro.

Type of Regular Issue, 1968

1968, Apr. 23 Litho. *Perf. 14½*

C280 A184 2e bright violet 65 55

Issued to commemorate the sesquicentennial of the Battles of Chacabuco and Maipu. A souvenir sheet of 2 contains imperf. stamps similar to Nos. 367 and C280. Gold marginal inscription commemorates the battles and the First Trans-Andes Philatelic Week, Apr. 4–10. Price, $5. A second sheet exists with the 2e in green and the 3e in brown. Size: 139½x100mm. Price, $5.

Farm Type of Regular Issue

1968, June 18 Unwmkd.

C281 A185 50c black, orange & green 25 15

Issued to publicize the agrarian reforms.

Juan I. Molina
AP72

1968, Aug. 27 Litho. *Perf. 14½*

C282 AP72 1e bright green 30 25

Issued to honor Juan I. Molina, educator and scientist.

Map of Chiloé Province
AP73

British Crown and Map of Chile
AP74

Lithographed

1968, Oct. 7 *Perf. 14½* Unwmkd.

C283 AP73 1e rose claret 20 15

Issued to commemorate the anniversaries of the founding of five towns in Chiloé Province.

Auto Club Type of Regular Issue

1968, Nov. 10 Engr. *Perf. 14½x14*

C284 A189 5e ultramarine 1.25 60

Issued to commemorate the 40th anniversary of the Automobile Club of Chile.

1968, Nov. 12 Litho. *Perf. 14½*

Designs: 50c, Chilean coat of arms (horiz.; similar to type A161). 3e, British coat of arms (horiz.).

C285 AP74 50c green & brn. 10 8
C286 " 3e bl. & org. brn. 65 40

Engraved

C287 AP74 5e purple & magenta 1.00 60

Visit of Queen Elizabeth II of Great Britain, Nov. 11–18. A souvenir sheet of 3 contains imperf., lithographed stamps similar to Nos. C285–C287. Dark blue marginal inscription. Size: 124½x190mm. The souvenir sheet also publicizes the British-Chilean Philatelic Exhibition. Price, $10.

First Coin Minted in Chile and Coin Press
AP75

Design: 1e, Chile No. 128.

1968, Dec. 31 Litho. *Perf. 14½*

C288 AP75 50c ocher & violet brown 10 10
C289 " 1e light blue & deep orange 25 15

Issued to commemorate the 225th anniversary of the founding of the State Mint (Casa de Moneda de Chile).

A souvenir sheet of 4 contains imperf. stamps similar to Nos. 373–374, C288–C289. Brown marginal inscription. Size: 150x119mm. Price, $2.50.

Satellite Type of Regular Issue

1969, May 20 Litho. *Perf. 14½*

C290 A191 2e rose lilac 45 30

Issued to publicize the inauguration of ENTEL-Chile, the first commercial satellite communications ground station, Longovilo.

Red Cross Type of Regular Issue

1969, Sept. Litho. *Perf. 14½*

C291 A192 5e black & red 1.15 90

Issued for the 50th anniversary of the League of Red Cross Societies.

A souvenir card contains 2 imperf. stamps similar to Nos. 376 and C291, with red marginal inscription. Size: 109x140 mm. Price $4.

Dam Type of Regular Issue

1969, Nov. 18 Litho. *Perf. 14½*

C292 A193 3e blue 70 50

Rodriguez Type of Regular Issue

1969, Nov. 24

C293 A194 30c brown 10 5

Issued to commemorate the 150th anniversary of the death of Col. Manuel Rodriguez.

EXPO '70 Type of Regular Issue

1969, Dec. 1 Litho. *Perf. 14*

C294 A195 5e red 1.15 90

Issued to publicize EXPO '70 International Exposition, Osaka, Japan, March 15–Sept. 13, 1970.

Bible Type of 1969

1969, Dec. 2 *Perf. 14½*

C295 A196 1e green 20 15

Issued to commemorate the 400th anniversary of the translation of the Bible into Spanish by Casiodoro de Reina.

ILO Type of Regular Issue

1969, Dec. 17 *Perf. 14½*

C296 A197 2e rose lilac & blk. 45 30

Issued to commemorate the 50th anniversary of the International Labor Organization.

Human Rights Year Type of 1969

1969, Dec. 18

C297 A198 4e brown & red 90 75

Human Rights Year, 1968.

A souvenir sheet of 2 contains imperf. stamps similar to Nos. 382 and C297. Blue commemorative marginal inscription. Size: 110x140mm. Price, $4.50.

Easter Island Type of 1970

1970, Jan. 26

C298 A199 50c dull greenish blue 15 10

Issued to commemorate the 80th anniversary of the acquisition of Easter Island.

Ship Type of Regular Issue

1970, Feb. 4 Litho. *Perf. 14½*

C299 A200 2e deep ultra. 30 25

Issued to commemorate the 150th anniversary of the capture of Valdivia during Chile's war of independence by Thomas Cochrane (1775–1860), naval commander.

Rotary Type of Regular Issue

1970, Mar. 18 Lithographed *Perf. 14*

C300 A201 1e rose claret 20 12

Issued to commemorate the centenary of the birth of Paul Harris (1868–1947), founder of Rotary International.

Gandhi Type of Regular Issue

1970, Apr. 1 Litho. *Perf. 14½*

C301 A202 1e red brown 20 12

Issued to commemorate the centenary of the birth of Mohandas K. Gandhi (1869–1948), leader in India's fight for independence.

Education Year Type of 1970

1970, July 17 Litho. *Perf. 14½*

C302 A204 4e red brown 60 45

Issued for International Education Year.

National Shrine Type of 1970

1970, July 28 Litho. *Perf. 14½*

C303 A205 1e ultramarine 20 12

Issued to publicize the O'Higgins National Shrine at Maipu.

Cancer Type of Regular Issue

1970, Aug. 11

C304 A206 2e brn. & lt. olive 30 20

Issued to commemorate the International Cancer Congress, Houston, Texas, May 22–29.

Copper Type of Regular Issue

1970, Oct. 21 Litho. *Perf. 14½*

C305 A207 3e green & lt. red brown 50 35

Nationalization of the copper industry.

United Nations Type of 1970

1970, Oct. 22

C306 A208 5e dk. car. & grn. 75 40

United Nations, 25th anniversary.

Freighter Type of Regular Issue

1971, Jan. 18 Litho. *Perf. 14*

C307 A209 5e light red brown 75 50

National Maritime Commission.

No. C290 Surcharged in Red

1971, Jan. 21 Litho. *Perf. 14½*

C308 A191 52c on 2e rose lilac 10 8

Liberation Type of Regular Issue

1971, Feb. 3 *Perf. 14½*

C309 A210 1e gray bl. & brown 20 15

The 150th anniversary of the expedition to liberate Peru.

UNICEF Type of Regular Issue

1971, Feb. 11 Litho. *Perf. 14½*

C310 A211 2e blue & green 30 25

First meeting in Latin America of the Executive Council of UNICEF, Santiago, May 20–31, 1969.

Boy Scout Type of Regular Issue

1971, Feb. 10 *Perf. 14*

C311 A212 5c dk. car. & olive 10 8

Founding of Chilean Boy Scouts, 60th anniversary.

Satellite Type of Regular Issue

1971, May 25 Litho. *Perf. 14½*

C312 A213 2e brown 30 25

First commercial Chilean satellite communications ground station, Longovilo.

De Ercilla Type of Regular Issue

1972, Mar. 20 Engraved *Perf. 14*

C313 A221 2e Prussian blue 30 25

4th centenary (in 1969) of "La Araucana," by Alonso de Ercilla y Zuniga (1533–1596).

A souvenir card contains impressions of Nos. 414 and C313 with black marginal inscription commemorating España 75 Philatelic Exhibition. Size: 165x220mm.

AIR POST SEMI-POSTAL STAMPS

Type of Semi-Postal Stamps, 1961.

Portraits: 10c+10c, Alonso de Ercilla. 20c+20c, Gabriela Mistral.

Perf. 13x12½

1961, Apr. 29 Photo. Unwmkd.

CB1 SP3 10c+10c salmon & chocolate 80 35
CB2 " 20c+20c gray & deep claret 80 35

Printed without charge by the Spanish Mint as a gift to Chile. The surtax was to aid the 1960 earthquake victims and to increase teachers' salaries.

ACKNOWLEDGMENT OF RECEIPT STAMPS.

AR1

1894 *Perf. 11½.* Unwmkd.

H1 AR1 5c brown 1.00 1.10
a. Imperf., pair 8.50 8.50

The black stamp of design similar to AR1 inscribed "Avis de Paiement" was prepared for use on notices of payment of funds but was not regularly issued.

POSTAGE DUE STAMPS.

D1 D2

Handstamped

1894 *Perf. 13* Unwmkd.

J1	D1	2c black, *straw*	5.00	4.00
J2	"	4c " "	5.00	4.00
J3	"	6c " "	5.00	4.00
J4	"	8c " "	5.00	4.00
J5	D2	10c " "	5.00	4.00
J6	D1	16c " "	5.00	4.00
J7	"	20c " "	5.00	4.00
J8	"	30c " "	5.00	4.00
J9	"	40c " "	5.00	4.00
		Nos. J1–J9 (9)	45.00	36.00

J1a	D1	2c black, *yellow*	75.00	70.00
J2a	"	4c " "	35.00	30.00
J3a	"	6c " "	25.00	25.00
J4a	"	8c " "	12.50	12.50
J5a	D2	10c " "	12.50	12.50
J6a	D1	16c " "	12.50	12.50
J7a	"	20c " "	12.50	12.50
J8a	"	30c " "	12.50	12.50
J9a	"	40c " "	12.50	12.50
		Nos. J1a–J9a (9)	210.00	200.00

Counterfeits exist.

D3

1895 Lithographed. ***Perf. 11.***

J19 D3 1c red, *yellow* 6.00 1.25
J20 " 2c " 6.00 1.25
J21 " 4c " 6.00 1.25
J22 " 6c " 6.00 1.25
J23 " 8c " 3.50 1.25
J24 " 10c " 3.50 1.25
J25 " 20c " 1.25 1.25
J26 " 40c " 1.25 1.25
J27 " 50c " 1.25 1.25
J28 " 60c " 2.00 2.00
J29 " 80c " 3.50 3.50
J30 " 1p " 3.50 3.50
Nos. J19-J30 (12) 43.75 20.25

Nos. J19-J30 were printed in sheets of 100 (10x10) containing all 12 denominations.

Counterfeits of Nos. J19-J42 exist.

1896 ***Perf. 13½.***

J31 D3 1c red, *straw* 40 40
J32 " 2c " 40 40
J33 " 4c " 40 40
J34 " 6c " 75 75
J35 " 8c " 40 40
J36 " 10c " 40 40
J37 " 20c " 40 40
J38 " 40c " 8.00 7.50
J39 " 50c " 9.00 7.50
J40 " 60c " 10.00 7.50
J41 " 80c " 22.50 17.50
J42 " 100c " 22.50 17.50
Nos. J31-J42 (12) 75.15 60.65

D4

D5

1898 ***Perf. 13.***

J43 D4 1c scarlet 12 12
J44 " 2c " 40 40
J45 " 4c " 12 12
J46 " 10c " 12 12
J47 " 20c " 12 12
Nos. J43-J47 (5) 88 88

1924 ***Perf. 11½, 12½.***

J48 D5 2c blue & red 25 25
J49 " 4c " " 25 25
J50 " 8c " " 25 25
J51 " 10c " " 20 20
J52 " 20c " " 20 20
J53 " 40c " " 20 20
J54 " 60c " " 25 25
J55 " 80c " " 30 30
J56 " 1p " " 75 75
J57 " 2p " " 3.00 3.00
J58 " 5p " " 3.00 3.00
Nos. J48-J58 (11) 8.65 8.65

Nos. J48-J58 were printed in sheets of 150 containing all 11 denominations, and in sheets of 50 containing the five lower denominations, providing various se-tenants.

All values of this issue exist imperforate, also with center inverted, but are not believed to have been regularly issued. Those with inverted centers sell for about 10 times normal stamps.

OFFICIAL STAMPS.

For Domestic Postage.

O1

Single-lined frame.

Control number in violet.

1907 ***Imperf.*** **Unwmkd.**

O1 O1 dull blue, "CARTA" in orange 110.00 65.00
O2 " red, "OFICIO" in blue 110.00 65.00
O3 O1 violet, "PAQUETE" in red 110.00 65.00
O4 " orange, *blue*, "EP" in violet 110.00 65.00

The diagonal inscription in differing color indicates type of usage: CARTA for letters of ordinary weight; OFICIO, heavy letters to 100 grams; PAQUETE, parcels to 100 grams; E P (Encomienda Postal), heavier parcels; C (Certificado), as on No. O8, registration including postage.

Varieties include CARTA, PAQUETE and E P inverted, OFICIO omitted, etc.

Double-lined frame.

Large control number in black.

Perf. 11.

O5 O1 blue, "CARTA" in yellow 17.50 15.00
O6 " red, "OFICIO" in blue 30.00 17.50
O7 " brown, "PAQUETE" in green 30.00 17.50
O8 " green, "C" in red 375.00 200.00

Nos. O5-O8 exist in tête bêche pairs; with CARTA, OFICIO or PAQUETE double or inverted, and other varieties.

Counterfeits of Nos. O1-O8 exist.

For Foreign Postage.

Regular Issues of 1892-1909 Overprinted in Red

a

On Stamps of 1904-09.

1907 ***Perf. 12.***

O9 A14 1c green 13.00 13.00
a. Inverted ovpt. 65.00
O10 A12 3c on 1p brown 50.00 50.00
a. Inverted ovpt. 250.00
O11 A14 5c ultramarine 25.00 18.50
a. Inverted ovpt. 125.00
O12 A15 10c gray & black 30.00 25.00
O13 " 15c violet & black 50.00 40.00
O14 " 20c orange brown & black 50.00 40.00
O15 " 50c ultra. & blk. 150.00 125.00

On Stamp of 1892.

Rouletted.

O16 A6 1p dark brown & black 175.00 150.00

Counterfeits of Nos. O9-O16 exist.

Regular Issues of 1915-25 Overprinted in Red or Blue

b

1926 ***Perf. 13½x14, 14.***

O17 A52 5c slate blue (R) 1.50 30
O18 A50 10c blue & black (R) 2.50 30
O19 A39 20c orange red & black (Bl) 65 25
O20 A42 50c deep green & black (Bl) 75 20
O21 A43 1p grn. & blk. (R) 1.25 50
O22 " 2p vermilion & black (Bl) 2.50 60
Nos. O17-O22 (6) 9.15 2.15

Nos. O21 and O22 are overprinted vertically at each side.

Nos. O17 to O22 were for the use of the Biblioteca Nacional.

Regular Issue of 1915-25 Overprinted in Red

Servicio del
ESTADO
c

1928 ***Perf. 13½x14, 14.***

O23 A50 10c blue & black 5.00 60
O24 A39 20c brown orange & black 5.00 60
O25 A40 25c dull blue & black 6.00 60
O26 A42 50c deep green & black 6.00 80
O27 A43 1p green & black 6.50 60
Nos. O23-O27 (5) 28.50 3.20

The overprint on Nos. O23 to O26 is 16½mm. high; on No. O27 it is 20mm.

Regular Issues of 1928-30 Overprinted in Red

Servicio del
ESTADO
d

On Stamp Inscribed: "Correos de Chile".

1930-31

O28 A50 10c blue & black 90 75

Wmkd.

Small Star in Shield, Multiple. (215)

On Stamps Inscribed: "Correos de Chile".

O29 A50 10c blue & black 2.00 1.25
O30 A39 20c orange red & black 60 30
O31 A40 25c blue & black 60 20
O32 A42 50c dp. grn. & blk. 90 35

On Stamps Inscribed: "Chile Correos".

O33 A42 50c dp. green & black 90 25
O34 A43 1p green & black 90 20
Nos. O28-O34 (7) 6.80 3.30

Same Overprint on No. 181.

1933 ***Perf. 13½x14.***

O35 A61 20c dark brown 25 18

Same Overprint in Red on No. 182.

1935 **Wmk. 215**

O36 A62 10c deep blue 25 18

No. 163 Overprinted Type "b" in Red.

Inscribed: "Correos de Chile".

1934

O37 A52 5c light green 45 30

Overprint "b" on No. 182.

1935

O38 A62 10c deep blue 35 20

Same Overprint in Black on No. 181.

1936 ***Perf. 13½x14.*** **Wmk. 215**

O39 A61 20c dark brown 10.00 15

Overprint "b" in Red on No. 158.

1938 ***Perf. 14.***

O40 A43 1p green & black 1.75 1.25

Nos. 204 and 205 Overprinted Type "d" in Black.

1939 ***Perf. 13½x14, 14.***

O41 A83 50c violet 2.50 2.50
O42 A84 1p orange brown 7.50 1.00

Stamps of 1938-40 Overprinted Type "b" in Black, Red or Blue.

1940-46 ***Perf. 13½x14, 14.***

O43 A79 10c sal. pink ('45) 5.25 4.50
O44 A79a 15c brown orange 50 35
O45 A80 20c light blue (R) ('42) 50 18
O46 A81 30c bright pink (Bl) 50 18
O47 A82 40c light green 50 18
O48 A83 50c violet ('45) 2.25 1.50
O49 A84 1p orange brown ('42) 3.00 1.00
O50 A85 1.80p deep blue (R) ('45) 10.00 10.00
O51 A86 2p carmine lake ('42) 4.00 1.00
Nos. O43-O51 (9) 26.50 18.89

Overprint "b" in Black on Nos. 223, 225.

Unwmkd.

O58 A84 1p brown orange 3.00 1.00
O59 A86 2p carmine lake ('46) 4.00 1.00

Regular Issues of 1938-43 Overprinted Diagonally in Carmine, Black or Blue

e

1948-54 **Unwmkd., Wmk. 215**

Perf. 13½x14, 14.

O60 A80 20c light blue, #219 (C) 3.00 75
O61 A81 30c bright pink, #202 (Bl) ('54) 7.50 4.50
O62 A82 40c bright green, #203 ('54) 7.50 4.00
O63 A83 50c violet, #222 ('49) 3.00 75
O64 A84 1p org. brn., #205 4.50 1.00
O65 A86 2p carmine lake, #207 ('54) 8.00 75
O66 A87 5p dark slate green, #208 (C) ('51) 9.00 1.50
Nos. O60-O66 (7) 42.50 13.25

Overprint "e" Diagonally on Nos. 265 and 275 in Red or Black.

1953-55 **Unwmkd., Wmk. 215**

Perf. 13½x14, 13x14

O67 A126 1p dark blue green, #265 (R) 3.00 1.00
O68 " 1p dark blue green, #265 (Bk) ('55) 3.00 35
O69 " 1p dark blue green, #275 (R) ('55) 3.00 60

Overprint "e" Horizontally on Nos. 207, 209 in Black or Blue

1955-56 ***Perf. 14.*** **Wmk. 215**

O70 A86 2p carmine lake ('56) 5.00 2.00
O71 A88 10p rose violet (Bl) 8.00 3.00

Overprint "e" Horizontally on Nos. 293-295 and Types of 1956 Regular Issue in Black or Red.

1956 ***Perf. 14x14½.*** **Unwmkd.**

O72 A141 2p purple 3.00 2.00
O73 A142 3p light violet blue (R) 13.00 12.00
O74 A141 5p reddish brown 3.00 2.00
O75 A142 10p violet (19x22¼mm.) (R) 8.00 2.50
a. Perf. 13½x14 (19¼x22½mm.) ('58) 6.00 1.25
O76 A141 50p rose red 27.50 8.00

No. 310 Overprinted in Red Vertically, Reading Down, Similar to Type "e."

Size of Overprint: 21x2½mm.

1958 **Lithographed** ***Perf. 14***

O77 A149 10p violet blue *27.50* *17.50*

Overprint "e" Horizontally on No. 327 in Red.

1960 ***Perf. 13x14*** **Unwmkd.**

O79 A157 5c blue 8.50 2.75

Methods and style of listing are detailed in "Special Notices" at the front of this volume.

POSTAL TAX STAMPS

Talca Issue.

A 10c blue postal tax stamp, inscribed "Bicentenario de Talca" and picturing a coat of arms, was issued in 1942. It was sold only in Talca and was required for a time on all domestic letters sent from that city. The tax helped pay for Talca's bicentenary celebration. Price 10 cents.

Nos. 326 and 347 Surcharged

Eº 0,10
Art. 77
LEY
17272

Lithographed

1970 *Perf. 14x13* **Unwmkd.**

RA1 A159 10c on 2c ultra. 10 8

Perf. 14x14½

RA2 A170 10c on 6c rose lilac 10 8

Chilean Arms
PT1

Perf. 14½x14

1970, Apr. 23 Litho. **Unwmkd.**

RA3 PT1 10c blue 15 8

No. RA3 Surcharged in Red

Eº0,15 Eº0,15

a b

1971-72

RA4 PT1 (a) 15c on 10c blue 5 5
RA5 " (b) 15c on 10c " ('72) 10 8

Type of 1970

1972, July Litho. *Perf. 14½x14*

RA6 PT1 15c rose red 15 8

No. RA6 Surcharged in Ultramarine

Eº0,20

1972-73

RA7 PT1 20c on 15c rose red 12 6
RA8 " 50c on 15c rose red ('73) 15 8

No. RA8 has 9 bars instead of 8.

The surtax on Nos. RA1-RA8 was for modernization of postal system. Compulsory on all inland mail.

PARCEL POST POSTAL TAX STAMP

Pres. J. J. Prieto V.
PPT1

Lithographed

1957, Apr. 8 *Perf. 14* **Unwmkd.**

QRA1 PPT1 15p green 25 15

The surtax aided the Prieto Foundation. No. QRA1 was required on parcel post entering or leaving Chile.

CHINA

(chī'nȧ)

LOCATION—Eastern Asia.
GOVT.—Republic.
AREA—2,903,475 sq. mi.
POP.—462,798,093 (1948).

10 Candareen = 1 Mace
10 Mace = 1 Tael
100 Cents = 1 Dollar (Yuan) (1897)

Issues of the Imperial Maritime Customs Post.

Imperial Dragon
A1

Typographed

1878 *Perf. 12½* **Unwmkd.**

Thin Paper.

Stamps printed 2½ mm. apart.

1 A1 1c green 40.00 15.00
a. Imperf. (pair) 350.00
2 " 3c brown red 20.00 6.00
a. Imperf. (pair) 300.00
3 " 5c orange 20.00 7.50
a. Imperf. (pair) 350.00

Imperforate proofs of Nos. 1-3 have an extra circle near the dragon's lower left foot.

1882

Thin or Pelure Paper.

Stamps printed 4½ mm apart.

4 A1 1c green 65.00 27.50
5 " 3c brown red 110.00 10.00
6 " 5c orange yellow 1100.00 200.00

1883

Rough to smooth Perf. 12½.

Medium to Thick Opaque Paper.

Stamps printed 2 to 3¼ mm. apart.

7 A1 1c green 35.00 10.00
a. Vertical pair, imperf. between 1000.00
8 " 3c brown red 50.00 6.00
a. Vertical pair, imperf. between *1000.00*
9 " 5c yellow 65.00 7.50

Nos. 1 to 9 were printed from plates of 25, 20 or 15 individual copper dies, but only No. 5 exists in the 15-die setting. Many different printings and plate settings exist. All values occur in a wide variety of shades and papers. The effect of climate on certain papers has produced the varieties on so-called toned papers in Nos. 1 to 15.

Counterfeits, frequently with forged cancellations, occur in all early Chinese issues.

Imperial Dragon
A2

Wmk. 103

Wmkd. Yin-Yang Symbol. (103)

1885 *Perf. 12½*

10 A2 1c green 5.00 2.00
a. Vertical pair, Imperf. between 350.00
b. Horiz. pair, imperf. between
11 " 3c lilac 7.50 2.50
a. Horizontal pair, imperf. between 175.00
b. Vertical pair, imperf. between 400.00
12 A2 5c greenish yellow 12.50 4.00
a. 5c bistre brown 17.50 7.00
b. Vertical pair, imperf. between 450.00
c. Horizontal pair, imperf. between 400.00

1888 *Perf. 11½-12*

13 A2 1c green 1.50 75
14 " 3c lilac 3.00 1.00
b. Double impression
15 " 5c greenish yellow 2.50 1.00
b. Horiz. pair, imperf. vert. 300.00
c. Double impression 175.00 125.00

Nos. 10 to 15 were printed from plates made of 40 individual copper dies, arranged in two panes of 20 each. Several different settings exist of all values.

Imperforates of Nos. 13-15 are considered proofs by most authorities.

Stamps overprinted "Formosa" in English or Chinese are proofs.

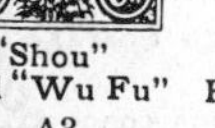

"Shou" and "Wu Fu"
A3

Dragon and Hydrangea Leaves
A4

"Pa Kua" Signs in Corners
A5

Dragon and Peony
A6

Carp, the Messenger Fish
A7

Dragon, "Pa Kua" and Immortelle
A8

Dragons and "Shou"
A9

Dragons and Giant Peony
A10

Junk on the Yangtse
A11

Lithographed in Shanghai.

1894

16 A3 1c orange red 2.50 1.50
a. Vertical pair, imperf. between 125.00 125.00
b. Horizontal pair, imperf. between 150.00 150.00
c. Imperf. horizontally (pair) 100.00 100.00
17 A4 2c green 2.50 1.50
a. Horizontal pair, imperf. between 150.00
18 A5 3c orange yellow 2.00 1.00
a. Vertical pair, imperf. between 100.00 100.00
b. Horizontal pair, imperf. between 100.00 100.00
19 A6 4c rose pink 10.00 5.00
a. Horizontal pair, imperf. between 150.00
20 A7 5c dull orange 15.00 7.50
a. Horizontal pair, imperf. between 150.00
21 A8 6c brown 4.00 2.00
a. Vertical pair, imperf. between 125.00
b. Horizontal pair, imperf. between 125.00
22 A9 9c dull green 10.00 4.00
a. Imperf., pair 125.00
b. Imperf. vert., pair 150.00
c. Imperf. horiz., pair 125.00
d. Vertical pair, imperf. between 125.00
e. Tête bêche pair 100.00 100.00
f. Tête bêche pair, imperf. horizontally 500.00
g. Tête bêche pair, imperf. vertically 400.00
h. Vert. strip of 3, imperf. between 150.00
23 A10 12c orange 20.00 7.50
24 A11 24c carmine 30.00 15.00
a. Vertical pair, imperf. between 350.00

Nos. 16 to 24 were issued to commemorate the 60th birthday of Tsz'e Hsi, the Empress Dowager. All values exist in several distinct shades.

On March 20, 1896, the Customs Post was changed, by Imperial Edict, to a National Post and the dollar was adopted as the unit of currency. The effective date of the Imperial Edict was January 1, 1897 and until that date the Customs Post continued operating.

Time was required to work out details of the Imperial Post and design new stamps. As a provisional measure, stocks of Nos. 16 to 24 were ordered surcharged with new values in dollars and cents. It is believed that only the Shanghai office stock of Nos. 16 to 24 (plus any reserve stock at the printer's) was surcharged with small figures of value. Other post offices throughout China were instructed to return all unoverprinted stocks on receipt of the new surcharges.

Early in the year it was apparent that all stamps would be exhausted before the new issues were ready (Nos. 86 to 97), and since the stones from which Nos. 16 to 24 had been printed no longer existed, new stones were made from the original transfers. A printing from the new stones was made early in 1897 and surcharged with large figures of value spaced 2½mm. below the Chinese characters. During the surcharging, sheets from the 1894 (original) printing were received from outlying post offices and surcharged as they arrived. A small quantity of the 1897 printing reached the public without surcharge (Nos. 16n to 24n).

Additional stamps were still required and another printing was made from the new stones and surcharged with large figures, but in a new setting with 1½mm. between the Chinese characters and the value. Additional sheets of the 1894 printing were received from the most distant post offices and were also surcharged with the 1½mm. setting. Thus there are four different sets of the large-figure surcharges. All these stamps were regularly issued but no attempt was made by the post office to separate printings. Some values are difficult to distinguish as to printing, particularly in used condition.

1897 Lithographed in Shanghai.

16n A3 1c red orange 110.00
17n A4 2c yellow green 65.00
18n A5 3c chrome yellow 45.00
p. 3c yel. buff 225.00
19n A6 4c pale rose 100.00
20n A7 5c yellow 55.00
21n A8 6c red brown 125.00
22n A9 9c yellowish green 175.00
23n A10 12c pale orange yellow 200.00
24n A11 24c rose red 185.00

Nos. 16n to 24n were new printings from new stones. These stamps were prepared solely for surcharging and were not regularly issued without surcharge. The colors of the 1897 printings are pale or dull; the gum is thin and white. The 1894 printing has a thicker, yellowish gum.

The set of nine values on thick unwatermarked paper is a special printing ordered by P. G. von Mollendorf, a Customs official, for presentation purposes. Price, set, $100.

Issues of the Chinese Government Post.

Preceding Issues Surcharged in Black

貳洋暫
分銀作
2
cents.

Small Numerals.

Surcharged on Nos. 13–15.

1897, Jan. 2 *Perf. 11½–12.*

25 A2 1c on 1c green 3.50 1.25
26 " 2c on 3c lilac 11.50 2.50
27 " 5c on 5c greenish yellow 3.50 1.25

Surcharged on Nos. 16–24.

28 A5 ½c on 3c orange yellow 60 55
a. "1" instead of "½" 75.00 75.00
b. Horizontal pair, imperf. between 150.00
c. Imperf. horizontally (pair) 85.00 85.00
d. Double surcharge 200.00
e. Vert. pair, imperf. between 200.00
29 A3 1c on 1c orange red 1.50 1.00
a. Inverted surcharge 500.00 400.00
30 A4 2c on 2c green 1.75 1.00
a. Imperf. vertically (pair) 150.00
b. Vertical pair, imperf. between 200.00
c. Double surcharge 250.00
d. Inverted surcharge 500.00
e. Horizontal pair, imperf. between 175.00
31 A6 4c on 4c rose pink 1.50 1.25
a. Double surch. 250.00 250.00
b. Vertical pair, imperf. between 175.00 175.00
c. Horizontal pair, imperf. between 175.00 175.00
32 A7 5c on 5c dull orange 2.00 1.00
a. Vertical pair, imperf. between 225.00
33 A8 8c on 6c brown 2.25 1.35
a. Vertical pair, imperf. between 125.00 125.00
b. Vertical strip of three, imperf. between 200.00 200.00
c. Horizontal pair, imperf. between 175.00 175.00
34 " 10c on 6c brown 6.00 4.50
a. 10c on 6c chocolate 6.00 4.50
b. Vertical pair, imperf. between 125.00 125.00
c. Imperf. vertically (pair) 175.00
35 A9 10c on 9c dull green 10.00 6.00
a. Double surcharge 300.00 300.00
b. Invtd. surch. 500.00 500.00
36 A10 10c on 12c orange 17.50 10.00
a. Imperf. horizontally (pair) 100.00
37 A11 30c on 24c carmine 25.00 20.00
a. Vert. pair, imperf. between 900.00

Preceding Issues Surcharged in Black

貳洋暫
分銀作
2
cents.

Large Numerals

Numerals 2½mm. below Chinese characters.

1897, March

Surcharged on Nos. 16 to 24.

38 A5 ½c on 3c org. yel. 225.00 60.00
b. Inverted surch. 325.00
39 A3 1c on 1c org. red 32.50 32.50
40 A4 2c on 2c green 60.00 50.00
41 A6 4c on 4c rose pink 65.00 35.00
b. Horiz. pair, imperf. between 1250.00
42 A7 5c on 5c dull org. 17.50 17.50
43 A8 8c on 6c brown 250.00 350.00
44 A9 10c on 9c dull green 85.00 50.00
45 A10 10c on 12c orange 900.00 175.00
46 A11 30c on 24c carmine 160.00 175.00
b. 2mm. spacing between "30" and "cents." 1000.00

Same Surcharge on Nos. 16n to 24n.

47 A5 ½c on 3c chrome yel. 75 60
a. "cen" for "cent" 110.00 110.00
b. Vertical pair, imperf. between 110.00 110.00
c. Imperf. horizontally (pair) 55.00 55.00
d. As "a," imperf. horiz. (pair) 550.00 550.00
48 A3 1c on 1c red orange 1.75 1.50
a. Horiz. pair, imperf. between 185.00
49 A4 2c on 2c yel. green 1.25 90
50 A6 4c on 4c pale rose 2.25 1.75
a. Horizontal pair, imperf. between 110.00 110.00
51 A7 5c on 5c yellow 2.75 2.25
52 A8 8c on 6c red brown 12.50 8.00
53 A9 10c on 9c yellowish green 13.50 8.25
a. 10c on 9c emerald 15.00 9.00
54 A10 10c on 12c pale orange yellow 13.50 9.00
55 A11 30c on 24c rose red 30.00 20.00
a. 2mm. spacing between "30" and "cents" 175.00 100.00
b. Vertical pair, imperf. between 1500.00

Numerals 1½mm. below Chinese characters.

1897, May

Surcharged on Nos. 16 to 24.

56 A5 ½c on 3c org. yel. 27.50 27.50
57 A3 1c on 1c org. red 37.50 37.50
58 A4 2c on 2c green 3250.00 75.00
59 A6 4c on 4c rose pink 22.50 22.50
60 A7 5c on 5c dull org. 20.00 20.00
61 A8 8c on 6c brown 135.00 135.00
62 A9 10c on 9c dull green 17.50 17.50
63 A10 10c on 12c orange 135.00 110.00
64 A11 30c on 24c car. 1500.00

Same Surcharge on Nos. 16n to 24n.

65 A5 ½c on 3c yellow 50 50
a. Invtd. surch. 125.00 125.00
b. ½mm. spacing 550.00 550.00
66 A3 1c on 1c red orange 1.00 75
67 A4 2c on 2c yellow green 1.75 1.00
a. Inverted surcharge 450.00
68 A6 4c on 4c pale rose 27.50 20.00
a. Inverted surcharge 100.00 90.00
69 A7 5c on 5c yellow 27.50 20.00
70 A9 10c on 9c gray green 20.00 9.00
a. Inverted surcharge 100.00 90.00
71 A10 10c on 12c brown orange 45.00 17.50
72 A11 30c on 24c pale rose 950.00 325.00

Same Surcharge (1½mm. Spacing) on Type A12, and

A12

A12a

Redrawn Designs.
Printed from New Stones.

1897

73 A12 ½c on 3c yellow 35.00 20.00
a. ½mm. spacing 225.00 200.00
74 A12a 2c on 2c yellow green 7.50 1.50
a. Horizontal pair, imperf. between 200.00

Nos. 73 and 74 were surcharged on stamps printed from new stones, which differ slightly from the originals. On No. 73 the numeral "3" and symbols in the four corner panels have been enlarged and strengthened. On No. 74, the numeral "2" has a thick, flat base.

Surcharged on 1888 Issue.

75 A2 1c on 1c green 50.00
76 " 2c on 3c lilac 100.00
77 " 5c on 5c greenish yellow 25.00

Nos. 75–77 were not regularly issued.

Type A13 Surcharged in Black:

A13

政郵清大
分 壹 當
one cent
a

政郵清大
貳洋暫
分銀作
2 cents
b

政郵清大
貳洋暫
分銀作
2
cents
c

政郵清大
肆洋暫
分銀作
4
cents.
d

政郵清大
肆洋暫
分銀作
4
cents.
e

政郵清大
當
壹
圓
1 dollar.
f

政郵清大
當
壹
圓
1 dollar
g

1897 *Perf. 12 to 15.* **Unwmkd.**

78 A13 (a) 1c on 3c red 3.00 1.25
a. No period after "cent" 15.00 15.00
b. Central character with large "box" 5.00 4.00
79 " (b) 2c on 3c red 12.50 6.00
a. Invtd. surch. 150.00 150.00
b. Inverted "S" in "CENTS" 20.00 20.00
c. No period after "CENTS" 20.00 20.00
d. Comma after "CENTS" 20.00 20.00
e. Double surch. 550.00
f. Double surcharge, both inverted 1100.00
g. Double surch. (blk. & grn.) 1000.00
80 " (c) 2c on 3c red 3.50 2.00
81 " (d) 4c on 3c red 850.00 700.00
a. Double surch. (blk. & vio.) 1350.00 1100.00
82 " (e) 4c on 3c red 22.50 10.00
83 " (f) $1 on 3c red 12,500.00 12,500.00
a. No period after "r"
84 " (g) $1 on 3c red 100.00 45.00
85 " (") $5 on 3c red 1100.00 900.00
a. Inverted surcharge 1250.00 1250.00

A few copies of the 3c red exist without surcharge; one cancelled. No. 79 with green surcharge is a trial printing.

Dragon
A14

Carp
A15

Wild Goose
A16

"Imperial Chinese Post".

Lithographed in Japan.
Perf. 11, 11½, 12.

1897, Aug. 16 **Wmk. 103**

86 A14 ½c purple brown 60 50
a. Horizontal pair, imperf. between 100.00
87 " 1c yellow 60 40
88 " 2c orange 50 25
a. Imperf. horizontally (pair) 135.00
89 " 4c brown 1.00 50
a. Horizontal pair, imperf. between 175.00
90 " 5c rose red 1.25 60
91 " 10c dark green 2.50 50
92 A15 20c maroon 5.00 2.50
93 " 30c red 7.50 3.50
94 " 50c yellow green 9.00 6.00
a. 50c black green 100.00
b. 50c blue green 175.00
95 A16 $1 carm. & rose 40.00 20.00
a. Imperf. vertically (pair) 600.00
96 " $2 orange & yel. 135.00 150.00
a. Imperf. vertically (pair) 600.00
97 " $5 yellow green & pink 85.00 100.00

The inner circular frames and outer frames of Nos. 86 to 91 differ for each denomination.

No. 97 imperforate was not regularly issued. Copies have been privately perforated and offered as No. 97. Shades occur in most values of this issue.

Dragon
A17

Carp
A18

Wild Goose
A19

Engraved in London.

"Chinese Imperial Post".

1898 *Perf. 12 to 16.* **Wmk. 103**

98 A17 ½c chocolate 20 8
a. Vertical pair, imperf. between 135.00
99 " 1c ochre 20 6
a. Vertical pair, imperf. between 30.00 30.00
b. Horizontal pair, imperf. between 60.00 60.00
100 " 2c scarlet 25 6
a. Vertical pair, imperf. between 17.50 17.50
b. Imperf. vertically (pair)
101 " 4c orange brown 60 8
a. Vertical pair, imperf. between 50.00
b. Imperf. vertically (pair) 25.00 25.00
c. Horiz. pair, imperf. between 75.00 75.00
d. Horiz. strip of 3, imperf. between 90.00 90.00
102 " 5c salmon 1.00 40
a. Vertical pair, imperf. between 35.00 35.00
b. Horizontal pair, imperf. between 40.00 40.00
103 " 10c dark blue green 90 15
a. Vert. or horiz. pair, imperf. between 40.00 40.00
104 A18 20c claret 3.00 60
a. Horizontal pair, imperf. between 90.00
b. Imperf. horiz. (pair) 60.00 60.00
105 " 30c dull rose 3.00 40
a. Horizontal pair, imperf. between 90.00
b. Imperf. horizontally (pair) 90.00
106 " 50c light green 6.00 1.25
a. Vertical pair, imperf. between 125.00
107 A19 $1 red & pale rose 15.00 2.50

108 A19 $2 brn. red & yel. 27.50 10.00
109 " $5 deep green & salmon 50.00 20.00
  a. Horizontal pair, imperf. between 700.00
  b. Vert. pair, imperf. between 750.00

No. 98 surcharged "B. R. A.—5—Five Cents" in three lines in black or green, was surcharged by British military authorities shortly after the Boxer riots for use from military posts in an occupied area along the Peking-Mukden railway. Usually canceled in violet.

1902–03 ***Perf. 12 to 16*** **Unwmkd.**

110 A17 ½c brown 15 5
  a. Horiz. or vert. pair, imperf. between 40.00 40.00
111 " 1c ochre 15 5
  a. Horizontal pair, imperf. between 17.50 17.50
  b. Vertical pair, imperf. between 22.50 22.50
  c. Vert. pair, imperf. horiz. 15.00 15.00
112 " 2c scarlet 30 5
  a. Horiz. or vert. pair, imperf. between 17.50 17.50
  c. Vert. pair, imperf. horiz. 15.00 15.00
  d. Horiz. pair, imperf. vert. 15.00 15.00
  e. Vert. strip of 3 imperf. between 25.00 25.00
113 " 4c orange brown 50 8
  a. Horiz. or vert. pair, imperf. between 27.50 27.50
114 " 5c rose red 3.50 75
  a. Vertical pair, imperf. between 60.00
  b. Vert. pair, imperf. horiz. 30.00
115 " 5c orange 3.50 75
  a. 5c yellow ('03) 40.00 8.00
  b. Vertical pair, imperf. between 45.00
  c. Horizontal pair, imperf. between 55.00
116 " 10c green 90 6
  a. Vertical pair, imperf. between 22.50
  b. Horizontal pair, imperf. between 27.50
  c. Vert. pair, imperf. horiz. 22.50
  d. Vert. strip of 3, imperf. between 55.00
117 A18 20c red brown 2.25 15
  a. Horizontal pair, imperf. between 55.00
  b. Vertical pair, imperf. between 45.00
118 " 30c dull red 3.50 25
  a. Vertical pair, imperf. between 85.00
119 " 50c yellow green 4.00 30
120 A19 $1 red & pale rose 15.00 75
121 " $2 brown red & yellow 30.00 3.00
122 " $5 deep green & salmon 45.00 20.00
Nos. 110–122 (13) 108.75 26.24

Diagonal Half of No. 112 Surcharged on Stamp and Envelope

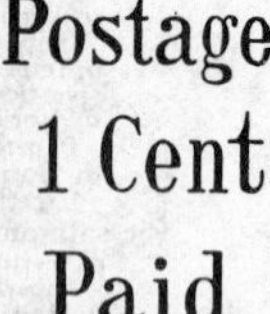

1903

123 A17 1c on half of 2c scarlet, on cover 200.00

Excellent forgeries of No. 123 are plentiful, particularly on pieces of cover.

1905-10

124 A17 2c green ('08) 30 3
  a. Horizontal pair, imperf. between 30.00 30.00
  b. Vertical pair, imperf. between 35.00 35.00
  c. Imperf. vertically (pair) 30.00
  d. Horiz. strip of 4, imperf. between 75.00
125 A17 3c slate green ('10) 50 5
  a. Horiz. or vert. pair, imperf. between 40.00
126 " 4c vermilion ('09) 60 10
127 " 5c violet 1.00 10
  a. 5c lilac 1.25 10
  b. Horiz. or vert. pair, imperf. between 40.00
  d. Vert. pair, imperf. horiz. 22.50
128 " 7c maroon ('10) 2.25 40
129 " 10c ultra. ('08) 1.75 7
  a. Horiz. or vert. pair, imperf. between 60.00
  c. Vert. pair, imperf. horiz. 40.00 30.00
130 A18 16c olive green ('07) 8.00 1.00
Nos. 124–130 (7) 14.40 1.75

Temple of Heaven, Peking
A20

1909 ***Perf. 14***

131 A20 2c orange & green 60 30
132 " 3c orange & blue 90 40
133 " 7c orange & brown violet 1.00 40

Issued to commemorate the first year of the reign of Hsuan T'ung, who later became Henry Pu-yi and then Emperor Kang Teh of Manchukuo.

Stamps of 1902-10 Overprinted with Chinese Characters.

1912 ***Perf. 12 to 16***

Foochow Issue.

Overprinted in Red or Black 立中時臨

134 A17 3c slate grn. (R) 30.00 17.50
135 A19 $1 red & pale rose (Bk) 275.00 275.00
136 " $2 brown red & yellow (Bk) 375.00 350.00
137 " $5 deep green & salmon (Bk) 300.00 300.00

The overprint "Ling Shih Chung Li" or "Provisional Neutrality," signified that the Post Office was conducted neutrally by agreement between the Manchu and opposing forces.

Nanking Issue

Overprinted in Red or Black 中華 立中時臨 民國

138 A17 1c ochre (R) 17.50 12.50
139 " 3c slate green (R) 15.00 12.50
140 " 7c maroon (Bk) 65.00 60.00
141 A18 16c olive grn. (R) 200.00 175.00
142 " 50c yellow green (R) 400.00 350.00
143 A19 $1 red & pale rose (Bk) 350.00 325.00
144 " $2 brown red & yellow (Bk) 600.00 600.00
145 " $5 deep green & sal. (Bk) 1000.00 900.00

Vertical overprint reads: "Chung Hwa Min Kuo" (Republic of China).
Stamps of this issue were also used in Shanghai and Hankow.
Additional values were overprinted but not issued. Excellent forgeries of the overprints of Nos. 134–145 exist.

Issues of the Republic

Overprinted in Black or Red 中華民國 *a*

Overprinted by the Maritime Customs Statistical Department, Shanghai.

146 A17 ½c brown (Bk) 15 5
  a. Inverted overprint 2.00 2.00
  b. Double overprint 22.50
147 " 1c ochre (R) 15 5
  a. Vert. pair, imperf. horiz. 27.50 27.50
  b. Invtd. ovpt. 22.50 17.50
  c. Double overprint 27.50 27.50
  d. Horizontal pair, imperf. between 27.50 27.50
  e. Horiz. pair, imperf. vert. 15.00
  f. Pair, one without overprint 50.00
148 " 2c green (R) 25 5
  a. Vertical pair, imperf. between 30.00 30.00
149 " 3c slate green (R) 35 4
  a. Inverted overprint 27.50 12.50
  b. Horiz. or vert. pair, imperf. between 35.00 35.00
  d. Horiz. pair, imperf. vert. 27.50
150 " 4c vermilion (Bk) 40 8
  a. Vertical pair, imperf. between 225.00
151 " 5c violet (R) 60 10
  a. Horizontal pair, imperf. between
152 " 7c maroon (Bk) 85 30
153 " 10c ultramarine (R) 85 8
  a. Double overprint 45.00
  b. Pair, one without overprint 190.00
  c. Brownish red overprint 3.50 2.50
  d. Inverted overprint 60.00 60.00
154 A18 16c olive green (R) 1.50 75
155 " 20c red brown (Bk) 1.75 20
156 " 30c rose red (Bk) 2.50 40
157 " 50c yellow green (R) 2.75 30
158 A19 $1 red & pale rose (Bk) 12.50 60
  a. Inverted overprint 1250.00
159 " $2 brown red & yellow (Bk) 17.50 3.50
  a. Inverted overprint 75.00 85.00
160 " $5 deep green & salmon (Bk) 45.00 50.00
Nos. 146–160 (15) 87.10 56.50

Stamps with blue overprint similar to the preceding were not an official issue but were privately made by a printer in Tientsin.

Overprinted in Red 中華民國 *b*

Overprinted by the Commercial Press, Shanghai

Type "b" differs from "a" in that the top character is shifted slightly to right and the bottom character is larger and has small "legs".

161 A17 1c ochre (R) 75 10
  a. Inverted overprint 27.50 27.50
  b. Vertical pair, imperf. between 37.50
  c. Double ovpt. 32.50
162 " 2c green (R) 8.00 20
  a. Inverted overprint 400.00 250.00
  b. Vertical pair, imperf. between 55.00
  e. Horizontal pair, imperf. between 65.00

Overprinted in Blue, Carmine or Black 中華民國

Overprinted by Waterlow & Sons, London.

163 A17 ½c brown (Bl) 10 4
  a. Vertical pair, imperf. between 225.00 225.00
164 " 1c ochre (C) 10 4
  a. Horizontal pair, imperf between 32.50
165 " 2c green (C) 15 4
166 " 3c slate green (C) 25 4
  a. Inverted overprint 275.00
167 " 4c vermilion (Bk) 30 8
168 " 5c violet (C) 40 12
169 " 7c maroon (Bk) 2.00 1.00
170 " 10c ultramarine (C) 60 6
  a. Vertical pair, imperf. between 85.00 70.00
171 A18 16c olive green (R) 2.00 75
172 " 20c red brown (Bk) 1.75 30
173 " 30c dull red (Bk) 2.25 40
174 " 50c yellow green (R) 3.50 90
175 A19 $1 red & pale rose (Bk) 10.00 1.25
176 " $2 brown red & yellow (Bk) 30.00 20.00
177 " $5 deep green & salmon (C) 45.00 45.00
Nos. 163–177 (15) 98.40 70.02

Due to instructions issued to postmasters throughout China at the time of the Revolution, a number of them prepared unauthorized overprints using the same characters as the overprints prepared by the government. While many were made in good faith, some, like the blue overprints from Tientsin, were bogus, and the status of certain others is extremely dubious.

Dr. Sun Yat-sen
A21

1912, Dec. 14 ***Perf. 14½***

178 A21 1c orange 50 40
179 " 2c yellow green 50 40
180 " 3c slate green 50 40
181 " 5c rose lilac 75 50
182 " 8c deep brown 1.00 75
183 " 10c dull blue 1.00 75
184 " 16c olive green 2.50 1.50
185 " 20c maroon 2.75 1.25
186 " 50c dark green 9.00 6.00
187 " $1 brown red 25.00 12.00
188 " $2 yellow brown 125.00 75.00
189 " $5 gray 50.00 35.00
Nos. 178–189 (12) 218.50 133.95

Issued in honor of the leader of the Revolution.

President Yuan Shih-kai
A22

1912, Dec. 14

190 A22 1c orange 40 35
191 " 2c yellow green 40 35
192 " 3c slate green 40 35
193 " 5c rose lilac 50 40
194 " 8c deep brown 1.50 1.00
195 " 10c dull blue 1.00 75
196 " 16c olive green 2.00 1.75
197 " 20c maroon 2.50 1.75
198 " 50c dark green 11.00 7.00
199 " $1 brown red 15.00 10.00
200 " $2 yellow brown 22.50 12.50

201 A22 $5 gray 50.00 40.00
Nos. 190-201 (12) 107.20 76.20

Issued in honor of the first president of the Republic.

Junk
A24

Reaping Rice
A25

Gateway, Hall of Classics, Peking
A26

DESIGN A24.

London Printing: Vertical shading lines under top panel fine, junk with clear diagonal shading lines on sails, right pennant of junk usually long, lines in water weak except directly under junk.

Peking Printing: Vertical shading lines under top panel and inner vertical frame line much heavier, water and sails of junk more evenly and strongly colored, white wave over "H" of "CHINA" pointed upward, touching the junk.

DESIGN A25.

London: Front hat brim thick and nearly straight, left foot touches shadow.

Peking: Front hat brim thin and strongly upturned, left foot and sickle clearly outlined in white, shadow of middle tree lighter than those of the right and left trees.

DESIGN A26.

London: Light colored walk clearly defined almost to the doorway, figure in right doorway "T" shaped with strong horizontal cross-bar, white panel in base of central tower rectangular, vertical stroke in top left character uniformly thick at its base, tree to right of doorway ends in minute dots.

Peking: Walk more heavily shaded near doorway, especially at right; figure in right doorway more like a "Y", white panel at base of central tower is a long oval, right vertical stroke in top left character incurved near its base, tree at right has five prominent dots at top.

London Printing: By Waterlow & Sons, London, perforated 14 to 15.

Peking Printing: By the Chinese Bureau of Engraving and Printing, Peking, perforated 14.

London Printing.

1913, May 5 *Perf. 14-15.*

202 A24 ½c black brown 10 4
a. Horiz. or vert. pair, imperf. btwn. 60.00
203 " 1c orange 10 4
a. Horizontal pair, imperf. between 60.00
b. Vertical pair, imperf. between 55.00
c. Horiz. strip of 5, imperf. between 150.00
204 " 2c yellow green 30 4
a. Horizontal pair, imperf. between 85.00
205 " 3c blue green 40 4
a. Horizontal pair, imperf. between 60.00
b. Vertical pair, imperf. between 150.00
206 " 4c scarlet 75 4
207 " 5c rose lilac 1.25 5
208 " 6c gray 85 8
209 " 7c violet 1.25 50
210 " 8c brown orange 1.50 12
211 " 10c dark blue 1.50 4
a. Horizontal pair, imperf. between 125.00 125.00
b. Vertical pair, imperf. between 140.00 110.00
212 A25 15c brown 6.00 40
213 " 16c olive green 1.75 35
214 " 20c brown red 2.50 10
215 " 30c brown violet 3.00 15
a. Horiz. pair, imperf. between 150.00 110.00
216 " 50c green 5.00 15
217 A26 $1 ochre & black 12.50 25
218 " $2 blue & black 20.00 1.50
219 " $5 scarlet & black 40.00 15.00
220 " $10 yellow green & black 175.00 175.00
Nos. 202-220 (19) 273.75 193.89

First Peking Printing.

1915 *Perf. 14.*

221 A24 ½c black brown 10 4
222 " 1c orange 10 4
a. Bklt. pane of 6 35.00
b. Bklt. pane of 4
223 " 2c yellow green 15 4
224 " 3c blue green 20 4
a. Bklt. pane of 6 40.00
225 " 4c scarlet 60 4
226 " 5c rose lilac 60 4
a. Bklt. pane of 4 35.00
227 " 6c gray 75 10
228 " 7c violet 1.00 40
229 " 8c brown orange 75 5
230 " 10c dark blue 75 4
a. Bklt. pane of 4 35.00
231 A25 15c brown 5.00 50
232 " 16c olive green 1.25 15
233 " 20c brown red 1.50 4
234 " 30c brown violet 1.50 6
235 " 50c green 2.00 4
236 A26 $1 ochre & black 6.00 15
237 " $2 blue & black 10.00 30
a. Center invtd. 2000.00 2250.00
238 " $5 scarlet & black 20.00 2.50
239 " $10 yellow green & black 80.00 40.00
Nos. 221-239 (19) 132.25 44.57

1919

240 A24 1½c violet 15 6
241 A25 13c brown 25 5
242 A26 $20 yellow & black 450.00 425.00

Nos. 226 and 230 overprinted in red with five characters in vertical column were for postal savings use.

The higher values of the 1913-19 issues are often overprinted with Chinese characters, which are the names of various postal districts. Stamps were frequently stolen while in transit to post offices. The overprints served to protect them, since the stamps could only be used in the districts for which they were overprinted.

Yeh Kung-cho, Hsu Shi-chang and Chin Yun-peng
A27

1921, Oct. 10

243 A27 1c orange 2.50 50
244 " 3c blue green 2.50 50
245 " 6c gray 2.50 50
246 " 10c blue 2.50 50

National Post Office, 25th anniversary.

A28

1923 Red Surcharge.

247 A28 2c on 3c blue green 50 5
a. Inverted surcharge 700.00 650.00

Second Peking Printing.

A29

A30

A31

Types of 1913-19 Issues.

Re-engraved.

Type A29: Most of the whitecaps in front of the junk have been removed and the water made darker. The shading lines have been removed from the arabesques and pearls above the top inscription. The inner shadings at the top and sides of the picture have been cut away.

Type A30: The heads of rice in the side panels have a background of crossed lines instead of horizontal lines. The Temple of Heaven is strongly shaded and has a door. There are rows of pearls below the Chinese characters in the upper corners. The arabesques above the top inscription have been altered and are without shading lines.

Type A31: The curved line under the inscription at top is single instead of double. There are four vertical lines, instead of eight, at each side of the picture. The trees at the sides of the temple had foliage in the 1913-19 issues, but now the branches are bare. There are numerous other alterations in the design.

1923 *Perf. 14.*

248 A29 ½c black brown 10 3
a. Horizontal pair, imperf. between 45.00 45.00
b. Horiz. pair, imperf. vert. 37.50 37.50
249 " 1c orange 10 3
a. Imperf., pair 22.50
b. Horiz. pair, imperf. vert. 32.50
c. Booklet pane of 6 32.50
d. Booklet pane of 4 15.00
250 " 1½c violet 15 4
251 " 2c yellow green 20 3
252 " 3c blue green 20 3
a. Bklt. pane of 6 25.00
253 " 4c gray 2.25 4
254 " 5c claret 35 3
a. Bklt. pane of 4 55.00
255 " 6c scarlet 50 4
256 " 7c violet 75 5
257 " 8c orange 50 4
258 " 10c blue 50 3
a. Bklt. pane of 6 37.50
b. Bklt. pane of 2 45.00
259 A30 13c brown 3.00 5
260 " 15c deep blue 1.25 3
261 " 16c olive green 1.50 6
262 " 20c brown red 1.25 3
263 " 30c purple 1.75 4
264 " 50c deep green 7.50 4
265 A31 $1 orange brown & sepia 6.00 6
266 " $2 blue & red brown 8.50 10
267 " $5 red & slate 17.50 25
268 " $10 green & claret 50.00 7.50
269 " $20 plum & blue 100.00 15.00
Nos. 248-269 (22) 198.85 23.55

To prevent speculation and theft, the dollar denominations were overprinted with single characters in red for use in Kwangsi ($1-$20) and Kweichow ($1-$5).

See also Nos. 275, 324.

Temple of Heaven, Peking
A32

1923, Oct. 17 *Perf. 14*

270 A32 1c orange 1.00 25
271 " 3c blue green 1.25 35
272 " 4c red 1.75 35
273 " 10c blue 3.50 1.00

Adoption of Constitution, October, 1923.

No. 253 Surcharged in Red

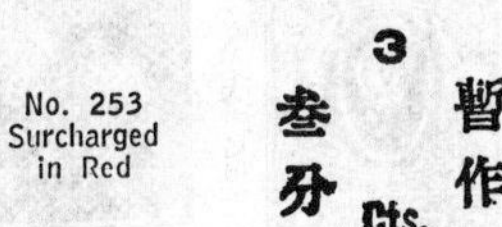

1925

274 A29 3c on 4c gray 75 6
a. Invtd. surch. 750.00 750.00
b. Vertical pair, imperf. between

Junk Type of 1923

1926

275 A29 4c olive green 35 3
a. Imperf. vertically (pair) 50.00
b. Horiz. pair, imperf. between 60.00
c. Horiz. strip of 3, imperf. between 70.00

Marshal Chang Tso-lin
A34

President Chiang Kai-shek
A35

1928, Mar. 1 *Perf. 14*

276 A34 1c brown orange 50 20
277 " 4c olive green 75 25
278 " 10c dull blue 3.50 1.00
279 " $1 red 20.00 14.00

Issued to commemorate the assumption of office by Marshal Chang Tso-lin. The stamps of this issue were only available for postage in the Provinces of Chihli and Shantung and at the Offices in Manchuria and Sinkiang.

1929, May

280 A35 1c brown orange 75 25
281 " 4c olive green 1.00 35
282 " 10c dark blue 10.00 1.00
283 " $1 dark red 35.00 20.00

Issued to commemorate the unification of China.

Sun Yat-sen Mausoleum, Nanking
A36

1929, May 30 *Perf. 14*

284 A36 1c brown orange 40 25
285 " 4c olive green 60 25
286 " 10c dark blue 3.00 1.00
287 " $1 dark red 25.00 15.00

Issued in commemoration of Dr. Sun Yat-sen on the occasion of the transfer of his remains from Peiping to the mausoleum at Nanking.

Nos. 224 and 252 Surcharged in Red

1
壹 暫
分 作
Ct.

1930

288 A24 1c on 3c blue green 85 25
289 A29 1c on 3c blue green 25 4
a. No period after "Ct" 6.00 5.00

See Nos. 311, 325, 330.

Dr. Sun Yat-sen—A37

Type I. Double-lined circle in the sun.
Type II. Heavy, single-lined circle in the sun.

Engraved

Perf.

11½x12½, 12½x13, 12½, 13½.

Printed by De la Rue & Co., Ltd., London.

1931 Type I.

290 A37 1c orange 10 4
291 " 2c olive green 10 5

292 A37 4c green 25 4
293 " 20c ultramarine 25 4
294 " $1 orange brown & dark brown 2.50 8
295 " $2 blue & orange brown 5.00 15
296 " $5 dull red & black 7.50 50
Nos. 290–296 (7) 15.70 90

Stamps issued prior to 1933 were printed by a wet-paper process, and owing to shrinkage such stamps are 1—1½ mm. narrower than the later dry-printed stamps. Early printings are perf. 12½x13. Nos. 304, 305 and 306 were later perf. 11½x12½.

1931-37 Type II.

297 A37 2c olive green 5 4
a. Bklt. pane of 6 22.50
b. Bklt. pane of 4 17.50
298 " 4c green 5 4
299 " 5c green ('33) 5 4
a. Bklt. pane of 6 20.00
b. Bklt. pane of 4 15.00
300 " 15c dark green 1.50 8
301 " 15c scarlet ('34) 10 4
302 " 20c ultramarine ('37) 15 4
303 " 25c ultramarine 15 4
a. Bklt. pane of 6 25.00
304 " $1 orange brown & dark brown 2.50 4
305 " $2 blue & orange brown 5.00 8
306 " $5 dull red & black 8.50 16
Nos. 297–306 (10) 18.05 60

See Nos. 631 to 635 for other stamps of type A37.

"Nomads in the Desert"
A38

1932 *Perf. 14* **Unwmkd.**

307 A38 1c deep orange 12.50 11.00
308 " 4c olive green 12.50 11.00
309 " 5c claret 12.50 11.00
310 " 10c deep blue 12.50 11.00

Issued to commemorate the Northwest Scientific Expedition of Sven Hedin. A small quantity of this issue was sold at face at Peking and several other cities. The bulk of the issue was given to Hedin and sold at $5 (Chinese) a set for funds to finance the expedition. Letters franked with these stamps were carried without additional charge.

No. 252 Surcharged in Black Like No. 288.

1932

311 A29 1c on 3c blue green 50 10

Martyrs Issue.

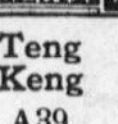

Teng Keng
A39

Ch'en Ying-shih
A40

Chu Chih-hsin
A45

Sung Chiao-jen
A46

Huang Hsing
A47

Liao Chung-kai
A48

1932–34 *Perf. 14*

312 A39 ½c black brown 5 5
313 A40 1c orange ('34) 5 5
a. Booklet pane of 6 25.00
b. Booklet pane of 4 25.00
314 A39 2½c rose lilac ('33) 5 5
315 A48 3c deep brown ('33) 5 5
316 A45 8c brown orange 15 5
317 A46 10c dull violet 20 5
318 A45 13c blue green 15 5
319 A46 17c brown olive 15 5
320 A47 20c brown red 15 5
321 A48 30c brown violet 15 5
322 A47 40c orange 15 5
323 A40 50c green ('34) 20 5
Nos. 312–323 (12) 1.50 60

Perfs. 12 to 13 and compound and with secret marks are listed as Nos. 402-439. No. 316 re-drawn is No. 485.

Junk Type of 1923 Issue.

1933 *Perf. 14.*

324 A29 6c brown 8.00 25

No. 275 Surcharged in Red Like No. 288.

325 A29 1c on 4c olive green 50 4
a. No period after "Ct"

Tan Yuan-chang
A49

1933, Jan. 9

326 A49 2c olive green 75 25
327 " 5c green 1.00 30
328 " 25c ultramarine 4.25 75
329 " $1 red 22.50 14.00

Issued in commemoration of Tan Yuan-chang more commonly known as Tan Yen-kai, a prominent statesman in China since the revolution of 1912 and President of the Executive Department of the National Government. The stamps were placed on sale January 9, 1933, the date of the ceremony in celebration of the completion of the Tan Yuan-chang Memorial Hall and Tomb at Mukden.

No. 251 Surcharged in Red Like No. 288.

1935 *Perf. 14*

330 A29 1c on 2c yellow green 35 6

Emblem of New Life Movement
A50

Four Virtues of New Life
A51

Lighthouse
A52

1936, Jan. 1

331 A50 2c olive green 50 25
332 " 5c green 75 25
333 A51 20c dark blue 4.00 75
334 A52 $1 rose red 12.50 3.00

"New Life" movement.

Methods of Mail Transportation
A53

Maritime Scene
A54

Shanghai General Post Office
A55

Ministry of Communications, Nanking
A56

1936, Oct. 10

335 A53 2c orange 40 20
336 A54 5c green 50 15
337 A55 25c blue 3.00 50
338 A56 $1 dark carmine 12.50 2.00

Issued in commemoration of the 40th anniversary of the founding of the Chinese Post Office.

Nos. 260 and 261 Surcharged in Red

暫 伍 5 作 分

339 A30 5c on 15c deep blue 50 5
340 " 5c on 16c olive green 50 5

No. 298 Surcharged in Red

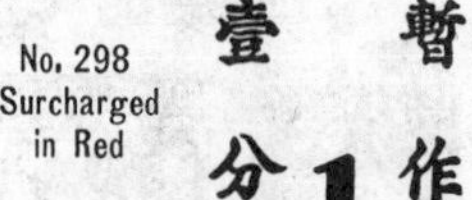

1937 Type II.

341 A37 1c on 4c green 25 5
a. Upper left character missing

Nos. 322 and 303 Surcharged in Black or Red

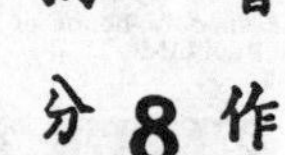

1938 *Perf. 12½, 14.*

342 A47 8c on 40c orange (Bk) 45 4
343 A37 10c on 25c ultra. (R) 40 4

Dr. Sun Yat-sen
A57

Type I. Coat button half circle. Six lines of shading above head. Top frame partially shaded with vertical lines.

Type II. Coat button complete circle. Nine lines of shading above head. Top frame partially shaded with vertical lines.

Type III. Coat button complete circle. Nine lines of shading above head. Top frame line fully shaded with vertical lines.

Engraved.

1938 *Perf. 12½* **Unwmkd.**

Printed by the Chung Hwa Book Co.

Type I.

344 A57 $1 henna & dark brown 16.00 1.75
345 " $2 deep blue & orange brown 2.50 25
346 " $5 red & greenish black 25.00 6.00

1939 Type II.

347 A57 $1 henna & dark brown 2.25 15
348 " $2 deep blue & orange brown 2.75 20

1939-41 Type III.

349 A57 2c olive green 4 4
350 " 3c dull claret 4 4
351 " 5c green 4 4
352 " 5c olive green 4 4
353 " 8c olive green 4 4
354 " 10c green 4 4
355 " 15c scarlet 8 4
356 " 15c dark violet brown ('41) 75 75
357 " 16c olive gray 15 4
358 " 25c dark blue 10 4
359 " $1 henna & dark brown 75 10
360 " $2 deep blue & orange brown 1.00 10
a. Imperf., pair 200.00
361 " $5 red & greenish black 50 10
362 " $10 dark green & dull purple 3.00 50
363 " $20 rose lake & dark blue 8.00 2.25
Nos. 349–363 (15) 14.57 4.16

Several values exist imperforate, but these were not regularly issued. No. 361 imperforate was sold as waste paper.

See also Nos. 368–401, 506–524.

Chinese and American Flags and Map of China
A58

Frame Engr., Center Litho.

1939, July 4 *Perf. 12* **Unwmkd.**

Printed by American Bank Note Co.

Flag in Deep Rose and Ultramarine.

No.	Type	Description	Unused	Used
364	A58	5c dark green	50	25
365	"	25c deep blue	1.00	50
366	"	50c brown	1.50	1.00
367	"	$1 rose carmine	3.00	2.00

Issued in commemoration of the 150th anniversary of the Constitution of the United States of America.

Type of 1939-41 Issue.
Re-engraved.

2c, 1939-41 — Re-engraved.

8c, 1939-41 — Re-engraved.

1940 *Perf. 12½.*

No.	Type	Description	Unused	Used
368	A57	2c olive green	10	5
369	"	8c olive green	10	5

Type of 1938-41 Issue.

1940 *Perf. 14* **Unwmkd.**

Type III.

No.	Type	Description	Unused	Used
370	A57	2c olive green	30	15
371	"	5c green	75	30
372	"	$1 henna & dark brown	17.50	3.50
373	"	$2 deep blue & orange brown	5.00	1.25
374	"	$5 red & greenish black	4.00	75
375	"	$10 dark green & dull purple	4.00	50
		Nos. 370-375 (6)	31.55	6.45

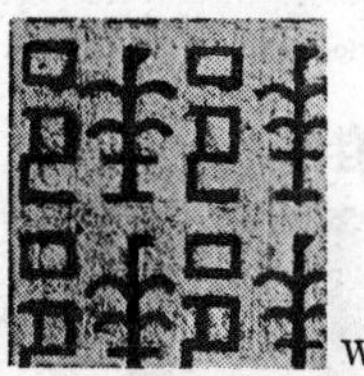

Wmk. 261

Type of 1939-41.
Wmkd.
Character Yu (Post) Multiple. (261)

1940 *Perf. 12½.*

Type III.

No.	Type	Description	Unused	Used
376	A57	$1 henna & dark brn.	35	15
377	"	$2 deep blue & orange brown	75	25
378	"	$5 red & greenish black	1.25	75
379	"	$10 dark green & dull purple	2.25	1.25
380	"	$20 rose lake & deep blue	3.75	2.00
		Nos. 376-380 (5)	8.35	4.40

Printed by the Dah Tung Book Co.

Type III with secret marks.

Five Cent.

Type III
Characters joined.

Secret Mark.
Characters not joined.

Eight Cent.

Type III
Characters not joined.

Secret Mark.
Characters joined.

Ten Cent.

Type III
Characters sharp and well-proportioned.

Secret Mark.
Characters coarse and varying in thickness.

Dollar Values.

Type III

Secret Mark.

1940 *Perf. 14.* **Unwmkd.**

No.	Type	Description	Unused	Used
381	A57	5c green	5	4
382	"	5c olive green	5	4
383	"	8c olive green	20	4
		a. Without "star" in uniform button	25	10
384	"	10c green	5	4
385	"	30c scarlet	5	4
386	"	50c dark blue	8	4
387	"	$1 org. brn. & sepia	12	4
388	"	$2 deep blue & yellow brown	20	4
389	"	$5 red & slate green	25	12
390	"	$10 dark green & dull purple	85	25
391	"	$20 rose lake & dark blue	1.75	50
		Nos. 381-391 (11)	3.65	1.19

Type III with secret marks.

1940 *Perf. 14.* **Wmk. 261**

No.	Type	Description	Unused	Used
392	A57	5c green	5	4
393	"	5c olive green	5	4
394	"	10c green	5	4
395	"	30c scarlet	5	4
396	"	50c dark blue	5	4
397	"	$1 org. brn. & sepia	15	4
398	"	$2 deep blue & yellow brown	60	4
399	"	$5 red & slate green	1.50	20
400	"	$10 dark green & dull purple	5.00	1.00
401	"	$20 rose lake & dark blue	6.00	1.50
		Nos. 392-401 (10)	13.50	2.98

Nos. 383, 384, 385, 397, 400 and 401 exist perf. 12½, but were not issued with this perforation.

Types of 1932-34.
Martyrs Issue with secret mark.

1932-34 Issue.
In the left Chinese character in bottom row, the two parts are not joined.

Secret Mark, 1940-41 Issue.
The two parts are joined.

Perf. 12½, 13 and Compound.

1940-41 **Wmk. 261**

No.	Type	Description	Unused	Used
402	A39	½c olive black	6	3
403	A40	1c orange	6	3
404	A46	2c deep blue ('41)	6	3
405	A39	2½c rose lilac	6	3
406	A48	3c deep yellow brown	6	3
407	A39	4c pale violet ('41)	6	3
408	A48	5c dull red orange ('41)	6	3
409	A45	8c deep orange	6	3
410	A46	10c dull violet	6	3
411	A45	13c deep yellow green	6	3
412	A48	15c brown carmine	6	3
413	A46	17c brown olive	6	3
414	A47	20c light blue	6	3
415	A45	21c olive brown ('41)	6	3
416	A40	25c red violet ('41)	6	3
417	A46	28c olive ('41)	6	3
418	A48	30c brown carmine	6	3
		a. Vert. pair, imperf. btwn.	75.00	
419	A47	40c orange	6	3
420	A40	50c green	6	3

Unwmkd.

No.	Type	Description	Unused	Used
421	A39	½c olive black	6	3
422	A40	1c orange	6	3
		a. Without secret mark	40	35
		b. Horiz. pair, imperf. vert.	17.50	
423	A46	2c deep blue	6	3
		a. Vert. pair, imperf. horiz.	4.00	
		b. Horiz. pair, imperf. between	100.00	
424	A39	2½c rose lilac	6	3
425	A48	3c dp. yel. brown	6	3
426	A39	4c pale violet	6	3
427	A48	5c dull red orange	6	3
428	A45	8c deep orange	6	3
429	A46	10c dull violet	6	3
430	A45	13c deep yellow green	6	3
431	A48	15c brown carmine	6	3
432	A46	17c brown olive	6	3
433	A47	20c light blue	6	3
		a. Vert. pair, imperf. horiz.	90.00	
		b. Horiz. pair, imperf. vert.	90.00	
434	A45	21c olive brown	6	3
435	A40	25c rose violet	6	3
436	A46	28c olive	6	3
437	A48	30c brown carmine	60	15
438	A47	40c orange	6	3
439	A40	50c green	6	3
		Nos. 402-439 (38)	2.82	1.26

Several values exist imperforate, but they were not regularly issued.

Regional Surcharges.

The regional surcharges, Nos. 440 to 448, 482 to 484, 486 to 491 and 525 to 549, have been given a general listing according to the basic stamps, with black or red surcharges. The surcharges of the individual provinces, plus Hong Kong and Shanghai, are noted in small type beneath each major listing. These surcharges are identified by the following italic letters:

a—Hong Kong	*i*—Kwangsi
b—Shanghai	*j*—Kwantung
bx—Anhwei	*k*—Western Szechwan
c—Hunan	*l*—Yunnan
d—Kansu	*m*—Honan
e—Kiangsi	*n*—Shensi
f—Eastern Szechwan	*o*—Kweichow
g—Chekiang	*p*—Hupeh
h—Fukien	

The numeral following each italic letter is the surcharge denomination.

In listings that include more than one region, the lowest price is used for the major.

Regional Surcharges on Stamps of 1939-40:

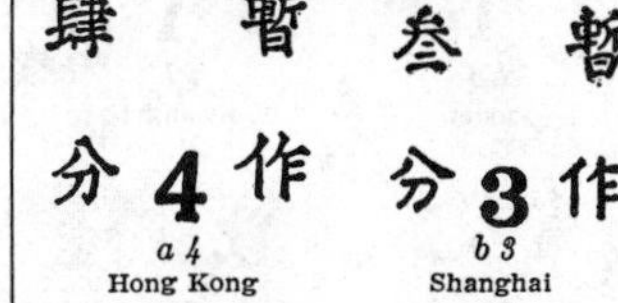

a 4 Hong Kong — *b 3* Shanghai

c 3 Hunan

d 3-I — *d 3*-II
Kansu

e 3 Kiangsi — *f 3* Eastern Szechwan

g 3 Chekiang

1940-41 *Perf. 12½, 14.* **Unwmkd.**

Parenthetical number indicates basic stamp.

Carmine Surcharge.

No.	Type	Description	Unused	Used
440	A57 (*a4*)	4c on 5c olive green (#382)	6	6
		a. Lower right character duplicated at left	10.00	10.00

Black Surcharge.

No.	Type	Description	Unused	Used
441	A57 (*b3*)	3c on 5c green (#351)	10	10
442	"	3c on 5c olive green (#352)	30	20
		(*c3*) Hunan	30	20
		(*d3*-I) Kansu	30	30
		(*d3*-II) Kansu	30	30
443	" (")	3c on 5c green (#381)	10	10
444	"	3c on 5c olive green (#382)	10	10
		(*b3*) Shanghai	10	10
		(*e3*) Kiangsi	10	10
		r. Lower left character duplicated at right (Kiangsi)	25.00	25.00
		(*f3*) Eastern Szechwan	10	10

1940-41 *Perf. 14.* **Wmk. 261**

No.	Type	Description	Unused	Used
445	A57	3c on 5c green (#392)	10	10
		(*b3*) Shanghai	10	10
		(*c3*) Hunan	20	20
		(*e3*) Kiangsi	10	10
		r. Lower left character duplicated at right (Kiangsi)	15.00	15.00
446	"	3c on 5c olive green (#393)	15	15
		(*b3*) Shanghai	15	15
		(*f3*) Eastern Szechwan	25	25
		r. Lower left character duplicated at right (Eastern Szechwan)	27.50	27.50

Red Surcharge.

No.	Type	Description	Unused	Used
447	A57 (*g3*)	3c on 5c grn. (#392)	25	10
448	" (")	3c on 5c olive green (#393)	1.50	75

Dr. Sun Yat-sen
A59

Engraved

1941 *Perf. 12* **Unwmkd.**

Printed by American Bank Note Co.

No.	Type	Description	Unused	Used
449	A59	½c sepia	4	4
450	"	1c orange	4	4
451	"	2c bright ultramarine	4	4
452	"	5c green	4	4
453	"	8c red orange	4	4
454	"	8c turquoise green	4	4
455	"	10c bright green	4	4
456	"	17c olive	75	25
457	"	25c rose violet	4	4
458	"	30c scarlet	4	4

459	A59	50c dark blue	6	5
460	"	$1 brown & black	10	4
461	"	$2 blue & black	10	7
		a. Center invert.	1750.00	
462	"	$5 scarlet & black	15	10
463	"	$10 green & black	25	20
464	"	$20 rose violet & black	50	40
		Nos. 449-464 (16)	2.27	1.47

Industry and Agriculture
A60

1941, June 21 *Perf. 12½*

Printed by Chung Hwa Book Co.

465	A60	8c green	5	5
466	"	21c red brown	10	10
467	"	28c dark olive green	12	12
468	"	33c vermilion	18	15
469	"	50c deep ultramarine	20	18
470	"	$1 dark violet	50	40
		Nos. 465-470 (6)	1.15	1.00

Issued to promote the Thrift Movement and its aim to "Save for Reconstruction."

Souvenir Sheet.

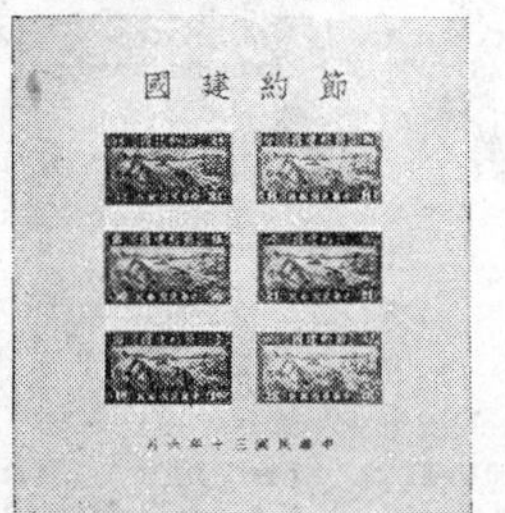

A61

Typographed
Imperf.

471	A61	Sheet of six	7.50	7.50
		a. 8c dull green	75	75
		b. 21c dark orange brown	75	75
		c. 28c dull yellow green	75	75
		d. 33c red	75	75
		e. 50c dull blue	75	75
		f. $1 dark violet	75	75

Issued in sheets measuring 155x171mm. without gum.

This sheet exists with additional blue marginal overprints in Russia, French and Chinese reading "Souvenir of the Exhibition of the Russian Philatelic Society in China, Shanghai, China, Feb. 28, 1943."

The overprinting was applied by the society, and when so overprinted this sheet had no franking power.

Stamps of 1939-41 Overprinted in Carmine or Blue

中華民國創立
三十週年紀念
日十月十年十三

1941, Oct. 10 *Perf. 12½, 14, 13*

472	A40	1c dull orange (Bl)	4	4
473	A57	2c olive green (C)	4	4
474	A39	4c pale violet (C)	4	4
475	A57	8c olive green (#369) (C)	5	5
476	"	10c green (#354) (C)	5	5
477	"	16c olive gray (#357) (C)	5	5
478	A45	21c olive brown (C)	7	7
479	A46	28c olive (C)	15	15
480	A57	30c scarlet (Bl)	25	25
481	"	$1 henna & dark brown (#359) (Bl)	40	40
		Nos. 472-481 (10)	1.14	1.14

Chinese Republic, 30th anniversary.

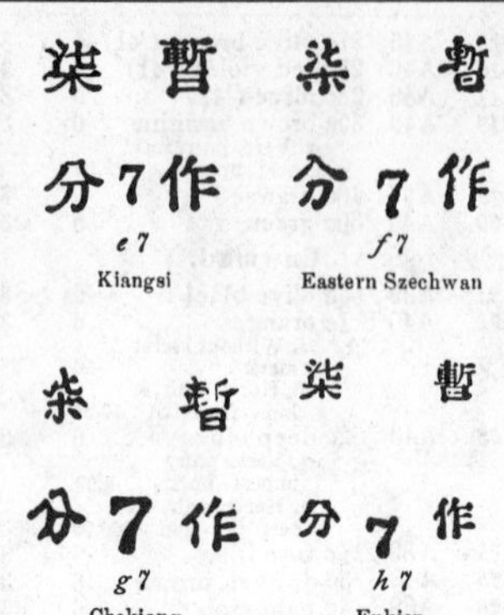

e7 Kiangsi — f7 Eastern Szechwan — g7 Chekiang — h7 Fukien

1941 *Perf. 12½, 14* **Unwmkd.**

482	A57	7c on 8c olive green (#353)	10	10
		(g7) Chekiang	10	10
		(h7) Fukien	10	10
483	" (f7)	7c on 8c olive green (#369)	8	8
484	"	7c on 8c olive green (#383)	10	10
		(e7) Kiangsi	10	10
		(g7) Chekiang	10	10
		(h7) Fukien	10	10
		a. Without "star" in uniform button	20.00	

Type of 1932-34 Re-engraved.

1941 *Perf. 14* **Unwmkd.**

485	A45	8c deep orange	1.25	1.50

The original stamps are 19½mm. wide, the re-engraved 21mm.

Eleven other values of the Martyrs Issue and types A37 and A57 exist re-engraved, but were not issued.

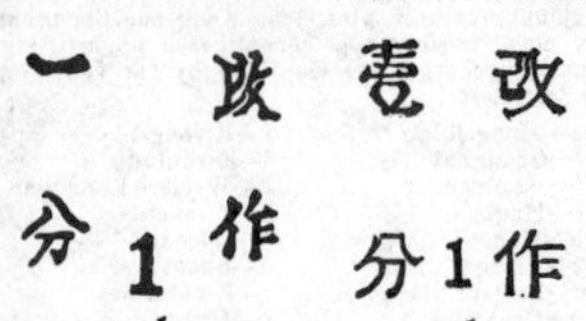

c1 Hunan — e1 Kiangsi

h1 Fukien — i1 Kwangsi

j1 Kwangtung

1942 **Red Surcharge.**

486	A39	1c on ½c black brown (#312)	10	10
		(c1) Hunan	10	10
		(i1) Kwangsi	10	10
487	"	1c on ½c olive black (#421)	6	6
		(c1) Hunan	10	6
		(e1) Kiangsi	10	6
		(h1) Fukien	7	7
		(i1) Kwangsi	7	6
488	A59	1c on ½c sepia (#449)	4	4
		(c1) Hunan	4	4
		(j1) Kwangtung	4	4

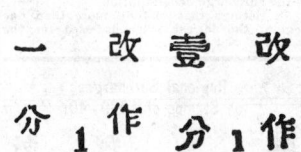

c40 Hunan — f40 Eastern Szechwan — k40 Western Szechwan — l40 Yunnan

Red Surcharge.

489	A57	40c on 50c dark blue (#386)	20	8
		(f40) Eastern Szechwan	20	8
		(k40) Western Szechwan	50	30
		(l40) Yunnan	20	8
		a. Inverted surcharge (Yunnan)	50.00	

Wmk. 261.

490	A40 (c40)	40c on 50c green (#420)	15	10

Unwmkd.

491	A59 (c40)	40c on 50c dark blue (#459)	10	5

Dr. Sun Yat-sen
A62

Central Trust Printing.
Perf. 10½-11, 11½-12½, 13 and Compounds

1942-43 **Typo.** **Without Gum**

492	A62	10c deep green ('43)	5	5
493	"	16c dull olive brn.	2.00	2.00
		a. Perf. 10½	75.00	50.00
494	"	20c dark olive green ('43)	5	5
		a. Perf. 11	60	40
495	"	25c brown violet	5	5
496	"	30c dull vermilion	5	5
		a. Perf. 11	75	35
497	"	40c dk. red brn. ('43)	5	5
		a. Perf. 11x13	25.00	
		b. Perf. 11	2.00	1.50
498	"	50c sage green	5	5
		a. Perf. 11	25	10
499	"	$1 rose lake	5	5
		a. Perf. 11	15.00	11.50
500	"	$1 dull green ('43)	5	5
501	"	$1.50 deep blue ('43)	5	5
		a. Perf. 11	175.00	
502	"	$2 dark blue green	5	5
503	"	$3 dark yellow ('43)	5	5
504	"	$4 red brown	5	5
505	"	$5 cerise ('43)	5	5
		Nos. 492-505 (14)	2.65	2.65

Many shades and part-perforate varieties exist. See Nos. 550 to 563 for other stamps of type A62 with secret mark and new values and colors.

Type of 1938.
Thin Paper Without Gum.
Engraved.

1942-44 ***Imperf.*** **Unwmkd.**

506	A57	$10 red brown	10	8
507	"	$20 blue green	15	10
508	"	$20 rose red ('44)	2.00	30
509	"	$30 dull violet ('43)	25	20
510	"	$40 rose red ('43)	10	5
511	"	$50 blue	25	17
512	"	$100 org. brown ('43)	75	50

Rouletted.

513	A57	$5 lilac gray ('44)	1.00	25
		a. Rouletted x perf. 12½	8.00	
514	"	$10 red brown	75	20
515	A57	$50 blue	1.25	50
		a. Rouletted x imperf.		
		Nos. 506-515 (10)	6.60	2.35

1942-45 ***Perf. 12½ to 15.***

516	A57	$4 deep blue ('43)	10	6
517	"	$5 lilac gray ('43)	10	7
518	"	$10 red brown	10	7
519	"	$20 blue green ('43)	10	10
520	"	$20 rose red ('45)	15.00	15.00
521	"	$30 dull violet ('43)	10	10
522	"	$40 rose ('43)	35	20
523	"	$50 blue	20	15
524	"	$100 orange brown ('45)	15.00	15.00
		Nos. 516-524 (9)	31.05	30.75

No. 493 Overprinted in Black or Red

國內平信
附加已付

1942

525	A62	16c dull olive brown (Bk)	12.50	12.50
		(c) Hunan	150.00	
		(i) Kwangsi	12.50	12.50
		r. Perf. 10½ (Kwangsi)	200.00	
		(k) Western Szechwan	30.00	30.00
		(m) Honan	250.00	250.00
		(n) Shensi	40.00	40.00
		s. Inverted ovpt. (Shensi)	70.00	
526	"	16c dull olive brown (R)	2.00	2.50
		(bx) Anhwei	75.00	75.00
		(d) Kansu	2.00	2.50
		(e) Kiangsi	4.00	4.00
		(f) Eastern Szechwan	4.50	4.50
		r. Perf. 10½ (E. Szechwan)	275.00	
		(h) Fukien	30.00	30.00
		(j) Kwangtung	200.00	225.00
		(l) Yunnan	4.50	4.50
		s. Horiz. pair, imperf. between (Yunnan)	125.00	
		(o) Kweichow	25.00	25.00
		(p) Hupeh, perf. 10½	250.00	250.00
		t. Perf. 13 (Hupeh)	500.00	350.0

This overprint means "Domestic Ordinary Letter Surcharge Paid." It was applied in various sizes and types by 14 districts, 9 using red ink, 5 using black. (The Anhwei overprint comes in two types.) These overprinted stamps were briefly sold for $1.16 before the government ordered their sale suspended. The vertical bars and 50c surcharge of Nos. 527-528 were then applied.

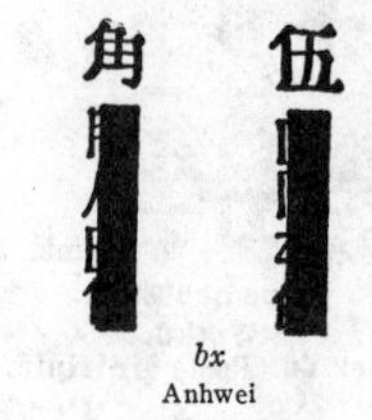

bx
Anhwei

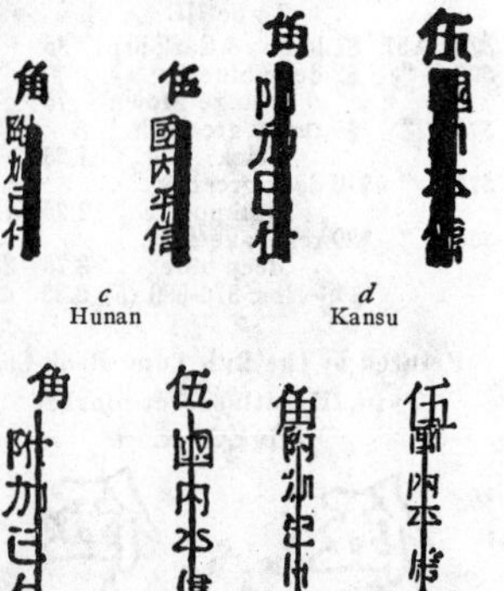

c Hunan — d Kansu — e Kiangsi — f Eastern Szechwan

h Fukien

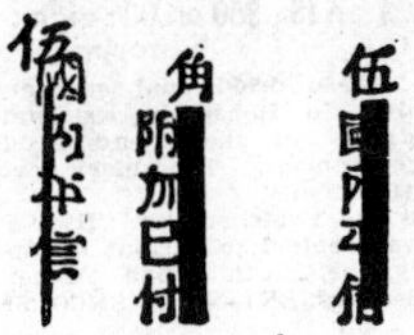

i Kwangsi

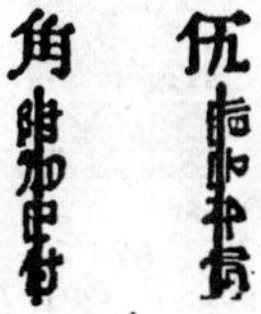

j Kwangtung

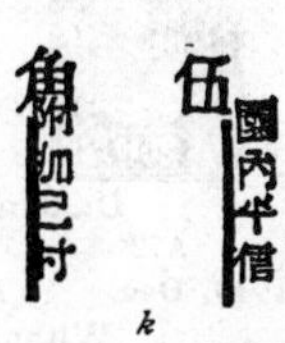

k Western Szechwan

l Yunnan

m Honan

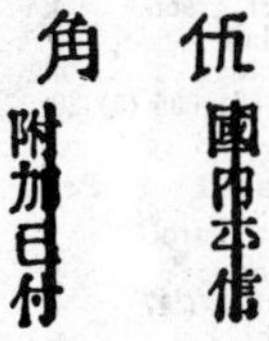

n Shensi

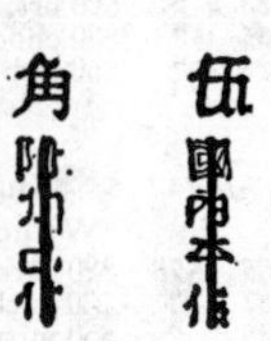

o Kweichow

p Hupeh

Nos. 525-526 Surcharged "50 cents" and 2 Vertical Bars in Black or Red.

1942 **Unwmkd.**

527 A62 50c on 16c dull olive brown (Bk) 75 75
- (*c*) Hunan 75 75
- (*f*) Eastern Szechwan (Bk on R) 75 75
- (*i*) Kwangsi 90 90
- (*k*) Western Szechwan 1.75 1.75
- *r.* Inverted surch. (W. Szech.) 35.00
- *s.* "k" surch. on #493 50.00
- (*m*) Honan 1.25 1.25
- (*n*) Shensi 1.25 1.25

528 " 50c on 16c dull olive brown (R) 50 50
- (*bx*) Anhwei 5.00 5.00
- (*d*) Kansu 50 50
- (*e*) Kiangsi 1.50 1.50
- (*h*) Fukien 2.00 2.00
- (*j*) Kwangtung 1.25 1.25
- (*l*) Yunnan 1.50 1.50
- (*o*) Kweichow 1.00 1.00
- *r.* Inverted surch. (Kweichow) 20.00
- (*p*) Hupeh 85 85
- *s.* "p" surch. on #526f 20.00 20.00

Many varieties of Nos. 527-528 exist, including narrow or wide spacing between the two top characters, or between the vertical bars, or both.

Surcharges on stamps perf. 10½ (basic No. 493a) usually sell at much higher prices."

General Issue

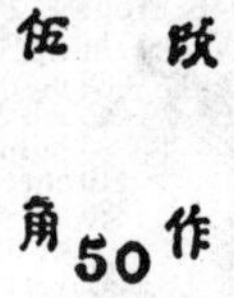

c 50 Hunan

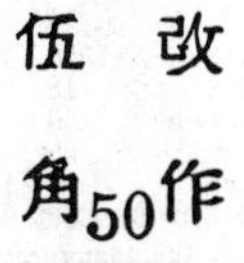

f 50 Eastern Szechwan

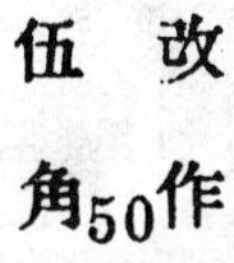

g 50 Chekiang

i 50 Kwangsi

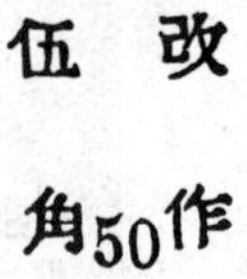

j 50 Kwangtung

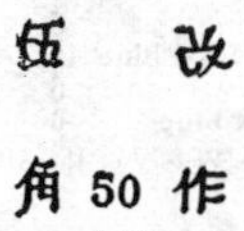

k 50 Western Szechwan

m 50 Honan

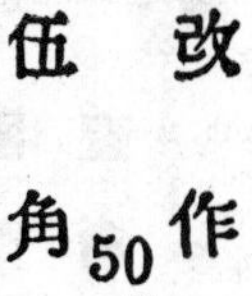

n 50 Shensi

o 50 Kweichow

No. 493 Surcharged in Black, Red or Carmine.

1943 **Unwmkd.**

529 A62 50c on 16c dull olive brown (Bk) 60 60
- (*m50*) Honan 90 90
- (*n50*) Shensi 60 60
- *r.* Perf. 11x13 (Shensi) 35.00

530 A62 50c on 16c dull olive brown (R, C) 15 15
- *a.* General Issue (C) 15 15
- (*c50*) Hunan 85 85
- *r.* Inverted surch. (Hunan) 30.00
- (*f50*) Eastern Szechwan 35 35
- (*g50*) Chekiang 6.00
- (*i50*) Kwangsi 75 75
- (*j50*) Kwangtung 75 75
- (*k50*) Western Szechwan 1.00 1.00
- (*m50*) Honan 1.50 1.25
- (*o50*) Kweichow 50 50
- *s.* "05" instead of "50" (Kweichow) 200.00

Many varieties of Nos. 529-530 exist, such as narrow or wide spacing horizontally or vertically between the overprinted Chinese characters.

Surcharges on No. 493a (perf. 10½) usually sell at much higher prices.

The General Issue type, No. 530a, was distributed to all head offices, which in turn supplied the post offices under their direction. It is surcharged in carmine; the other stamps listed under No. 530 are surcharged in red or carmine.

The lack of a price for a listed item does not necessarily indicate rarity.

c 20 Hunan

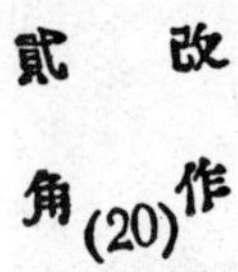

d 20 Kansu

e 20 Kiangsi

f 20 Eastern Szechwan

h 20 Fukien

i 20 Kwangsi

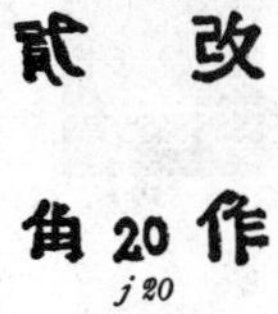

j 20 Kwangtung

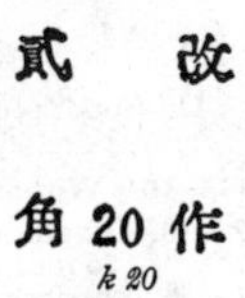

k 20 Western Szechwan

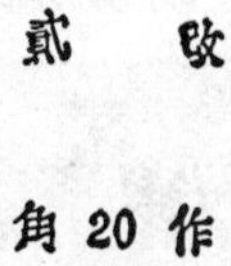

l 20 Yunnan

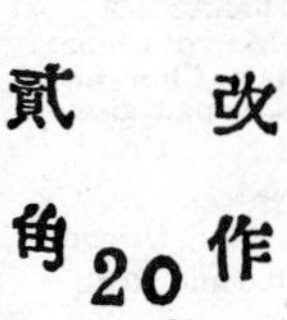

m 20 Honan

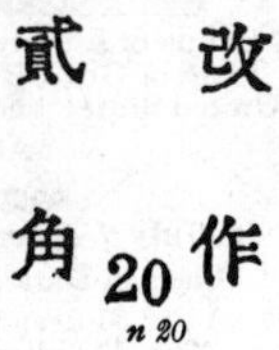

n 20 Shensi

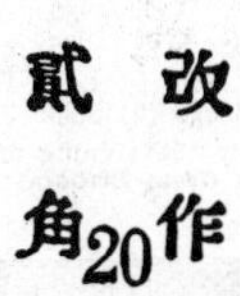

o 20 Kweichow

p 20 Hupeh

1943 **Unwmkd.**

531 A45 20c on 13c blue green (#318) (Bk) 6 6
- (*d20*) Kansu 20 20
- (*k20*) Western Szechwan 8 8
- (*n20*) Shensi 6 6

532 " 20c on 13c blue green (#318) (R) 7 7
- (*c20*) Hunan 300.00
- (*e20*) Kiangsi 22.50
- (*i20*) Kwangsi 7 7
- (*j20*) Kwangtung 6.00 6.00
- (*p20*) Hupeh 12 25

Wmk. 261

533 A45 20c on 13c deep yellow green (#411) (Bk) 8 8
- (*d20*) Kansu 18 18
- (*k20*) Western Szechwan 10 10
- (*l20*) Yunnan 30 30
- (*m20*) Honan 25.00
- (*n20*) Shensi 8 8

534 " 20c on 13c deep yellow green (#411) (R) 6 6
- (*c20*) Hunan 10 10
- (*e20*) Kiangsi 8 8
- (*f20*) Eastern Szechwan 6 6
- (*h20*) Fukien 15 15
- (*i20*) Kwangsi 12 12
- (*j20*) Kwangtung 4.00 4.00
- (*o20*) Kweichow 10 10
- (*p20*) Hupeh 8 8

Unwmkd.

535 A45 20c on 13c deep yellow green (#430) (Bk) 8 8
- (*d20*) Kansu 12 12
- (*k20*) Western Szechuan 4.00 4.00
- (*l20*) Yunnan 10 10
- (*m20*) Honan 15 15
- (*n20*) Shensi 8 8

536 " 20c on 13c deep yellow green (#430) (R) 8 8
- (*c20*) Hunan 75 75
- (*e20*) Kiangsi 12 12
- (*f20*) Eastern Szechwan 8 8
- (*i20*) Kwangsi 8 8
- (*j20*) Kwangtung 8 8
- (*o20*) Kweichow 10 10
- (*p20*) Hupeh 8 8

537 A57 20c on 16c olive gray (#357) (Bk) 6 6
- (*c20*) Hunan 6 8
- (*d20*) Kansu 8 8
- (*k20*) Western Szechwan 8 8
- (*m20*) Honan 40 40
- (*n20*) Shensi 6 6

538 " 20c on 16c olive gray (#357) (R) 12 12
- (*c20*) Hunan 40 40
- (*e20*) Kiangsi 12 12
- (*i20*) Kwangsi 12 12
- (*j20*) Kwangtung 9.00 9.00
- (*o20*) Kweichow 12 12

Wmk. 261.

539 A46 20c on 17c brown olive (#413) (R) 8 8
- (*c20*) Hunan 20 20
- (*i20*) Kwangsi 8 8
- (*j20*) Kwantung 5.00 5.00

Unwmkd.

540 A46 20c on 17c brown olive (#432) (Bk) 10 10
- (*d20*) Kansu 60 60
- (*k20*) Western Szechwan 10 10
- (*m20*) Honan 4.50 4.50

541 " 20c on 17c brown olive (#432) (R) 12 12
- (*e20*) Kiangsi 12 12
- (*j20*) Kwangtung 12 12
- (*o20*) Kweichow 12 12

542 A59 (*m20*) 20c on 17c olive (#456) (Bk) 50.00 50.00

543 " (*c20*) 20c on 17c olive (#456) (R) 60 60

Wmk. 261.

544 A45 (*e20*) 20c on 21c olive brown (#415) (R) 12 12

Unwmkd.

545 A45 20c on 21c olive brown (#434) (Bk) 5 5
- (*c20*) Hunan 5 5
- (*d20*) Kansu 12 12
- (*k20*) Western Szechwan 8 8
- (*l20*) Yunnan 8 8
- (*m20*) Honan 18 18

546 " 20c on 21c olive brown (#434) (R) 5 5
- (*e20*) Kiangsi 10 10
- (*f20*) Eastern Szechwan 5 5
- (*h20*) Fukien 10 10
- (*i20*) Kwangsi 6 6
- (*j20*) Kwangtung 5 5
- (*o20*) Kweichow 10 10
- (*p20*) Hupeh 8 8

Wmk. 261.

547 A46 (*e20*) 20c on 28c olive (#417) (R) 225.00 225.00

Unwmkd.

548 A46 20c on 28c olive (#436) (Bk) 8 8
(*d20*) Kansu 3.50 3.50
(*k20*) Western Szechwan 5.00 5.00
(*l20*) Yunnan 8 8
(*m20*) Honan 5.00 5.00

549 " 20c on 28c olive (#436) (R) 5 5
(*c20*) Hunan 5 5
(*e20*) Kiangsi 8 8
(*h20*) Fukien 5 5
(*i20*) Kwangsi 8 8
(*j20*) Kwangtung 8 8
(*k20*) Kweichow 12 12

Many varieties of Nos. 531-549 exist, such as narrow or wide spacing between the overprinted Chinese characters, and "20" higher or lower than illustrated.

Type of 1942-43.

Pacheng Printing.

1944-46 *Perf. 12* **Unwmkd.**

Without Gum

550 A62 30c chocolate 20 10
551 " $1 green 50 50
552 " $2 dark violet brown 4 5
a. Imperf., pair 1.75
553 " $2 dark blue green 6 5
a. Perf. 10½ 65.00 65.00
554 " $2 deep blue 10 10
555 " $3 light yellow 7 5
556 " $4 violet brown 4 6
a. Imperf., pair 40.00
557 " $5 carmine ('46) 4 3
a. Perf. 10½ 60.00 60.00
558 " $6 gray violet ('45) 4 3
559 " $10 red brown ('45) 4 4
a. Imperf., pair 40.00
560 " $20 deep ultra. ('46) 4 3
561 " $50 dark green ('46) 6 3
562 " $70 lilac ('46) 6 4
563 " $100 light brown ('46) 6 4
Nos. 550-563 (14) 1.35 1.15

In the Pacheng printing of the Central Trust type stamps, the secret mark "C" has been added below the lower left foliate ornament beneath the sun emblem. On the $3, it is below the right ornament. New values also include a "P" at right of sun emblem on the $6 and $10, and at right of necktie on the $20. Some values of Pacheng printing exist on paper with elephant watermark in sheet.

Dr. Sun Yat-sen
A63

Allegory of Savings
A64

Typographed

1944-46 *Perf. 12½* **Unwmkd.**

Without Gum.

565 A63 40c brown red 3 3
566 " $2 gray brown 3 3
567 " $3 red 3 3
568 " $3 lt. red brown ('45) 10 10
569 " $6 pale lilac gray ('45) 3 5
570 " $10 dull lake ('45) 3 5
571 " $20 rose ('45) 3 5
a. Perf. 15½ 25.00
572 A63 $50 light brown ('46) 3 3
573 " $70 rose violet ('46) 4 3
Nos. 565-573 (9) 35 40

1944-45 Engraved *Perf. 13*

Without Gum.

574 A64 $40 indigo ('45) 5 4
575 " $50 yellow green ('45) 5 4
576 " $100 yellow brown 5 4
577 " $200 dark green ('45) 8 7

All four values were printed on thick paper; the first three were also printed on thin paper.

Dr. Sun Yat-sen
A65 A66

Lithographed

1944, Dec. 25 Without Gum

578 A65 $2 deep green 10 10
579 " $5 fawn 15 15
580 " $6 dull rose violet 20 20
581 " $10 violet blue 35 35
582 " $20 carmine 60 60
Nos. 578-582 (5) 1.40 1.40

50th anniversary of the Kuomintang.

1945, Mar. 12 Without Gum

583 A66 $2 gray green 5 5
584 " $5 red brown 8 8
585 " $6 dark violet blue 12 12
586 " $10 light blue 20 20
587 " $20 rose 30 30
588 " $30 buff 40 40
Nos. 583-588 (6) 1.15 1.15

Issued to commemorate the 20th anniversary of the death of Dr. Sun Yat-sen.

Dr. Sun Yat-sen
A67

1945-46 Without Gum *Perf. 12½*

589 A67 $2 green 5 3
590 " $5 dull green 5 3
591 " $10 dark blue 5 3
a. Imperf., pair 20.00
592 " $20 carmine ('46) 5 3
a. Imperf., pair 40.00

Statue of Liberty, Map of China, Flags of Great Britain, China and United States, and Chiang Kai-shek
A68

Engraved

1945, July 7 *Perf. 12* **Unwmkd.**

Flags in Dark Blue and Red.

593 A68 $1 deep blue 10 10
594 " $2 dull green 20 20
595 " $5 olive gray 20 20
596 " $6 brown 50 50
597 " $10 rose lilac 75 75
598 " $20 carmine rose 1.50 1.50
Nos. 593-598 (6) 3.25 3.25

Issued to commemorate the signing of a Treaty in 1943 between Great Britain, the United States and China.

President Lin Sen
A69

President Chiang Kai-shek
A70

1945, Aug. *Perf. 12* **Unwmkd.**

599 A69 $1 dp. ultra. & black 5 5
600 " $2 myrtle green & black 5 5
601 " $5 red & black 10 10
602 " $6 purple & black 20 20
603 " $10 chocolate & black 30 30
604 " $20 olive green & black 55 55
Nos. 599-604 (6) 1.25 1.25

Issued in memory of President Lin Sen (1864-1943).

1945, Oct. 10

Flag in Rose Red and Violet Blue.

605 A70 $2 green 18 18
606 " $4 dark blue 18 18
607 " $5 olive gray 18 18
608 " $6 bistre brown 40 40
609 " $10 gray 65 65
610 " $20 red violet 1.00 1.00
Nos. 605-610 (6) 2.59 2.59

Issued to commemorate the inauguration of Chiang Kai-shek as president, October 10, 1943.

President Chiang Kai-shek
A71

1945, Oct. 10 Typo. *Perf. 13*

Without Gum.

Flag in Carmine and Blue.

611 A71 $20 green & blue 5 4
612 " $50 bistre brown & blue 12 10
613 " $100 blue 6 5
614 " $300 rose red & blue 6 5

Issued to commemorate the Victory of the Allied Nations over Japan.

C. N. C. Surcharges.

The green surcharges on Nos. 615 to 621, and the surcharges on Nos. 647 to 721, and 768 to 774 represent Chinese National Currency and were applied at Shanghai.

Stamps of 1938-41 Surcharged in Black with Chinese Characters and New Value in Checkered Rectangle at Bottom, Re-surcharged in Green

壹 國
角 幣

1945 *Perf. 12, 12½*

615 A57 10c on $20 on 3c dull claret (#350) 5 4
616 A46 15c on $30 on 2c deep blue (#423) 5 4
a. Horiz. pair, imperf. between 65.00
b. Vert. pair, imperf. between 57.50
617 A59 25c on $50 on 1c orange (#450) 5 4
618 A57 50c on $100 on 3c dull claret (#350) 5 4
619 A40 $1 on $200 on 1c orange (#422) 5 4
a. Horiz. pair, imperf. btwn. 75.00
620 A57 $2 on $400 on 3c dull claret (#350) 5 4
621 A59 $5 on $1000 on 1c orange (#450) 5 4

The black (first) surcharges on Nos. 615 to 621 represent Nanking puppet government currency.

In the green surcharge, the characters at the left express the new value and are either two or four in number.

Types of 1932-34, Re-engraved, Overprinted in Black 北 華 and Surcharged in Green with Horizontal Bar and Four or Five Chinese Characters.

Perf. 14.

622 A47 $10 on 20c brn. red 1.00 1.25
623 " $20 on 40c orange 3.50 4.00
a. Green surcharge inverted 15.00
624 A48 $50 on 30c violet brown 3.00 4.00

These provisional surcharges were applied in Honan in National currency to stamps of the Hwa Pei (North China) government. The black overprint reads: "Hwa Pei."

The two-character "Hwa Pei" overprint was applied to various stamps in 1941-43 by the North China puppet government. See Nos. 8N1-8N53, 8N60-8N84.

Dr. Sun Yat-sen
A72 A73

1945, Dec. Typo. *Perf. 12*

Without Gum.

625 A72 $20 deep carmine 4 4
626 " $30 deep blue 4 4
627 " $40 orange 4 4
628 " $50 green 4 3
629 " $100 dark brown 5 3
630 " $200 brown violet 6 4
Nos. 625-630 (6) 27 22

Type of 1931-37.

Perf. 12½, 13x12½, 13½.

1946 **Unwmkd.**

631 A37 $1 dark violet 4 3
632 " $2 olive green 4 3
633 " $20 brt. yel. green 4 3
634 " $30 chocolate 4 3
635 " $50 red orange 4 3
Nos. 631-635 (5) 20 15

1946-47 Engraved *Perf. 14*

Without Gum.

636 A73 $20 carmine 4 3
637 " $30 dark blue ('47) 4 3
638 " $50 purple 4 3
639 " $70 red org. ('47) 3.00 60
640 " $100 dark carmine 4 3
641 " $200 olive green ('47) 8 5
642 " $500 bright blue green ('47) 12 3
643 " $700 red brown ('47) 15 5
644 " $1000 rose lake 20 3
645 " $3000 blue 50 5
646 " $5000 deep green & vermilion 60 7
Nos. 636-646 (11) 4.81 1.00

Stamps of 1932-41 Surcharged in Black

Perf. 12½, 13, 13x12, 14.

Wmk. 261

647 A45 $20 on 8c deep orange (#409) 4 3
648 A39 $30 on ½c olive black (#402) 350.00 350.00
649 A45 $50 on 21c olive brown (#415) 4 3
650 " $70 on 13c deep yellow green (#411) 4 3
651 A46 $100 on 28c olive (#417) 4 3

Unwmkd.

652 A39 $3 on 2½c rose lilac (#424) 25 25
653 A48 $10 on 15c brown carmine (#431) 4 3
654 A45 $20 on 8c deep orange (#428) 4 3
655 A47 $20 on 20c light blue (#433) 4 8
656 A39 $30 on ½c olive black (#421) 4 3
657 A45 $50 on 21c olive brown (#434) 4 3

657A A45 $70 on 13c blue green (#318) 35.00 35.00
658 " $70 on 13c deep yellow green (#430) 4 3
659 A46 $100 on 28c olive (#436) 4 3

Stamps of 1931-1946 Surcharged in Black or Carmine

國幣 伍拾圓 50.00

Perf. 12½, 13, 14

1946-47 Wmk. 261

660 A57 $50 on 5c grn. (#392) 5 5
661 " $50 on 5c olive green (#393) 12.50 12.50
662 A48 $50 on 5c dull red orange (#408) 4 3
663 A40 $100 on 1c org. (#403) 4 3

Perf. 12, 12½, 12½x13, 13, 14.

1946-47 Unwmkd.

664 A57 $20 on 3c dull claret (#350) 4 3
665 A45 $20 on 8c deep orange (#428) 4 3
666 A57 $50 on 3c dull claret (#350) 5 5
667 " $50 on 5c olive green (#352) 4 3
668 " $50 on 5c olive green (#382) 5 5
669 A48 $50 on 5c dull red orange (#427) 4 3
670 A59 $50 on 5c green (#452) 5 5
671 A62 $50 on $1 dull green (#500) 4 3
672 A40 $100 on 1c orange (#422) 5 5
a. Without secret mark (No. 422a) 35.00
673 A57 $100 on 3c dull claret (#350) 5 5
674 " $100 on 8c olive green (#353) 5.00 5.00
675 " $100 on 8c olive green (#369) 5 4
676 " $100 on 8c olive green (#383) 5 3
a. Without "star" in uniform button (No. 383a) 10.00 10.00
677 A59 $100 on 8c turquoise green (#454) 5 4
678 A37 $100 on $1 dark violet (#631) 10 3
679 A73 $100 on $20 carmine (#636) 30 3
680 A57 $200 on 10c green (#354) 4 3
681 " $200 on 10c green (#384) 5 4
682 A37 $200 on $4 dull blue 4 3
a. Double surch. 10.00
683 A62 $250 on $1.50 deep blue (#501) 5 5
a. Perf. 11 150.00
684 A37 $250 on $2 olive green (#632) 5 5
685 " $250 on $5 carmine 4 3
686 A57 $300 on 10c green (#354) 4 3
687 A59 $300 on 10c bright green (#455) 4 3
688 A57 $500 on 3c dull claret (#350) 4 3
689 A37 $500 on $20 bright yellow green (#633) 4 3
690 " $800 on $30 chocolate (#634) 5 5
691 " $1000 on 2c olive green (#297) 5 5
692 A62 $1000 on $2 dk. vio. brown (#552) 8 8
a. Imperf., pair 8.50 8.50
693 " $1000 on $2 dark blue green (#553) 5 5
694 " $1000 on $2 deep blue (#554) 5 5
695 A67 $1000 on $2 green (#589) 8 8
696 A62 $2000 on $5 carmine (#557) 5 5
697 A67 $2000 on $5 dull green (C) (#590) 8 8
Nos. 664-697 (34) 6.92 6.41

Nos. 682 and 685 wer not issued without surcharge. No. 682 is perf. 13x13½; No. 685, perf. 12x12½.
The characters at the left express the new value and vary in number.

Stamps of 1938-41 Surcharged in Black

國幣 伍拾圓 50.00

Perf. 12, 12½, 13, 14.

1946 Wmk. 261

698 A45 $20 on 8c deep orange (#409) 65.00 65.00
699 A57 $50 on 5c green (#392) 5 5
700 " $50 on 5c olive green (#393) 5 5

1946-48 Unwmkd.

700A A57 $20 on 5c green (#381) 275.00
701 " $20 on 8c olive green (#353) 5 5
702 " $20 on 8c olive green (#369) 18 18
703 " $20 on 8c olive green (#383) 5 5
a. Without "star" in uniform button (No. 383a) 1.50 1.50
b. Inverted surch. 10.00
c. Double surcharge, one on back 12.00 12.00
d. Double surch. 15.00
704 A45 $20 on 8c deep orange (#428) 5 5
a. Double surch. 10.00
705 A59 $20 on 8c red orange (#453) 5 5
706 " $20 on 8c turquoise green (#454) 5 5
a. Inverted surch. 10.00
b. Double surcharge 10.00
707 A57 $50 on 5c green (#351) 15 15
708 " $50 on 5c olive green (#352) 5 5
a. Inverted surch. 15.00
709 " $50 on 5c green (#381) 5 5
710 " $50 on 5c olive green (#382) 5 5
711 A48 $50 on 5c dull red orange (#427) 5 5
a. Inverted surch. 20.00
712 A59 $50 on 5c green (#452) 5 5
a. Double surch. 15.00

Stamps of 1939-41 Surcharged in Blue or Red

國幣 拾圓 10.00

1946 *Perf. 12½.* Wmk. 261

713 A40 $10 on 1c orange (Bl) (#403) 5 5
a. Inverted surch. 25.00
714 A48 $20 on 3c deep yellow brown (#406) (Bl) 200.00 125.00

1946 *Perf. 12, 12½, 13* Unwmkd.

715 A40 $10 on 1c orange (Bl) (#422) 5 5
a. Without secret mark (No. 422a) 3.50 3.50
b. Inverted surcharge 6.00 6.00
716 A59 $10 on 1c orange (Bl) (#450) 5 5
a. Double surch. 15.00
717 A57 $20 on 2c olive green (R) (#368) 5 5
718 A59 $20 on 2c bright ultramarine (R) (#451) 4 3
a. Inverted surch. 10.00
b. Double surch. 10.00
719 A57 $20 on 3c dull claret (Bl) (#350) 4 3
a. Double surch. 15.00
720 A48 $20 on 3c deep yellow brown (Bl) (#425) 4 3
721 A39 $30 on 4c pale violet (R) (#426) 4 3
a. Inverted surch. 8.00

President Chiang Kai-shek
A74

Perf. 14, 10½-11½

1946, Oct. 31 Engraved Unwmkd.

722 A74 $20 carmine 10 4
723 " $30 green 10 4
724 " $50 vermilion 10 4
725 " $100 yellow green 10 4
726 " $200 yellow orange 10 4
727 " $300 magenta 10 5
Nos. 722-727 (6) 60 25

60th birthday of Chiang Kai-shek.
Perf. 14 stamps were printed by Dah Tung Book Co. and have no gum. Perf. 10½-11½ stamps were printed by Dah Yeh Printing Co.; the earlier ones are gumless, the later ones gummed.

Assembly House, Nanking—A75

1946, Nov. 15 Litho. *Perf. 14*

Without Gum

728 A75 $20 green 6 6
729 " $30 blue 6 6
730 " $50 dark brown 6 6
a. Horiz. pair, imperf. between 35.00 35.00
731 " $100 carmine 6 6

Convening of National Assembly.

Entrance to Dr. Sun Yat-sen Mausoleum
A76

Dr. Sun Yat-sen
A77

1947, May 1 Engraved

732 A76 $100 deep green 8 4
733 " $200 deep blue 8 4
734 " $250 carmine 8 4
735 " $350 light brown 8 4
736 " $400 deep claret 8 4
Nos. 732-736 (5) 40 20

First anniversary of return of Chinese National Government to Nanking.

1947 *Perf. 12½, 11½x12½*

737 A77 $500 olive green 10 4
738 " $1000 green & carmine 10 4
739 " $2000 deep blue & red brown 15 6
740 " $5000 orange red & black 15 6

Confucius
A78

Confucius' Lecturing School
A79

Tomb of Confucius
A80

Temple of Confucius
A81

1947, Aug. 27 Litho. *Perf. 14*

Without Gum

741 A78 $500 carmine rose 8 5

Engraved.

742 A79 $800 yellow brown 8 5
743 A80 $1250 blue green 8 5
744 A81 $1800 blue 8 6

Sun Yat-sen and Plum Blossoms
A82

Chinese Flag and Map of Taiwan
A83

1947-48 Engraved *Perf. 14*

Without Gum

745 A82 $150 dark blue 8 3
746 " $250 deep lilac 25 3
747 " $500 blue green 5 3
748 " $1000 red 6 3
749 " $2000 vermilion 12 3
750 " $3000 blue 5 3
751 " $4000 gray ('48) 12 3
752 " $5000 dark brown 6 3
753 " $6000 rose lilac ('48) 12 3
754 " $7000 light red brown ('48) 12 3
755 " $10,000 deep blue & carmine 40 3
756 " $20,000 carmine & yellow green 25 3
757 " $50,000 green & dark blue 25 4
758 " $100,000 dull yellow & olive green ('48) 25 15
759 " $200,000 violet brown & deep blue ('48) 60 15
760 " $300,000 sepia & orange brown ('48) 60 15
761 " $500,000 dark Prussian green & sepia ('48) 90 15
Nos. 745-761 (17) 4.28 1.00

See also Nos. 788-799.

1947, Oct. 25 With Gum

762 A83 $500 carmine 10 6
763 " $1250 deep green 10 7

Second anniversary, restoration of Taiwan to China.

Mobile Post Office A84

Street-Corner Branch Post Office A85

1947, Nov. 5

764 A84 $500 carmine 8 5
765 A85 $1000 lilac 8 5
766 " $1250 green 8 5
767 A84 $1800 deep blue 8 5

Stamps and Type of 1943-47 Surcharged in Black or Green [國幣 伍佰圓 500.00]

Perf. 12½, 13, 14.

1947-48 Unwmkd.

768 A37 $500 on $20 brt. yel. green (#633) 4 3
769 A73 $1250 on $70 red orange (#639) 4 3
770 A82 $1800 on $350 yellow orange 4 3
771 A62 $2000 on $3 dk. yel. ('48) (#503) 4 3
772 A63 $2000 on $3 red (#567) 4 3
773 A62 $3000 on $3 light yellow ('48) (#555) 4 3
774 A63 $3000 on $3 light red brown (G) ('48) (#568) 4 3
Nos. 768-774 (7) 28 21

The characters at the left express the new value and vary in number.

No. 640 Surcharged [國幣 伍千圓 5000]

1948, Aug. *Perf. 14*

775 A73 $5000 on $100 dark carmine 1.25 1.40

No. 775 received its surcharge in Kwangsi for use in that province.

Map of China and Mail-carrying Vehicles—A86

Rural Mail Delivery—A87

Early and Modern Mail Transportation A88

1947, Dec. 16 Engraved *Perf. 12*

776 A86 $100 violet 5 3
777 A87 $200 bright green 5 3
778 " $300 red brown 5 3
779 A88 $400 scarlet 5 3
780 " $500 brt. violet blue 5 3
Nos. 776-780 (5) 25 15

Issued to commemorate the 50th anniversary of the Chinese Postal Administration.

National Assembly Building and New Constitution A89

1947, Dec. 25 *Perf. 14*

Without Gum.

781 A89 $2000 bright red 8 5
782 " $3000 blue 8 5
783 " $5000 deep green 8 5

Issued to commemorate the first anniversary of the adoption of China's new constitution, Dec. 25, 1946.

Chinese Stamps of 1947 and 1912 A90

Lithographed

1948, Mar. 20 *Perf. 14, Imperf.*

Without Gum

784 A90 $5000 dark carmine rose 18 18
a. Vert. pair, imperf. between 25.00
785 " $5000 dark green 18 18
a. Vert. pair, imperf. btwn. 15.00

Issued to commemorate stamp exhibitions at Nanking, Mar. 20 (No. 784), and at Shanghai, May 19 (No. 785).

Sun Yat-sen Memorial Hall, Taipei A91

1948, Apr. 28 Engraved *Perf. 14*

786 A91 $5000 violet 12 8
787 " $10,000 red 12 8

Issued to commemorate the third anniversary of the restoration of Formosa to China.

Sun Yat-sen Type of 1947–48

1948 Without Gum

788 A82 $20,000 rose pink 4 4
789 " $30,000 chocolate 5 5
790 " $40,000 green 4 4
791 " $50,000 deep blue 4 4
792 " $100,000 dull green 10 4
793 " $200,000 brown violet 12 4
794 " $300,000 yellow green 12 4
795 " $500,000 lilac rose 25 8
796 " $1,000,000 claret 20 8
797 " $2,000,000 vermilion 40 15
798 " $3,000,000 olive bistre 65 20
799 " $5,000,000 ultra. 1.00 35
Nos. 788-799 (12) 3.01 1.15

Zeros for "cents" omitted.

Early Ship and Modern Hai Tien A92

Passenger Ship Kiang Ya A93

1948, Aug. 16 Without Gum

800 A92 $20,000 blue 6 4
801 " $30,000 rose lilac 6 4
802 A93 $40,000 yellow brown 6 4
803 " $60,000 vermilion 6 4

Issued to commemorate the 75th anniversary of the China Merchants' Steam Navigation Company.

Type of 1947-48 Surcharged in Black [改作伍仟圓 ☆☆ 5000.00 ☆☆]

1948 *Perf. 14* Unwmkd.

804 A82 $4000 on $100 carmine 6 6
805 " $5000 on $100 carmine 6 6
806 " $8000 on $700 red brown 6 6

Stamps of 1942-46 Surcharged in Black or Red [改作伍仟圓 5000.00]

1948 *Perf. 12½, 13*

807 A62 $5000 on $1 dull green (#500) 8 8
808 " $5000 on $1 green (#551) 1.50 1.50
809 " $5000 on $2 dark blue green (#502) 8 8
810 A72 $10,000 on $20 deep carmine (#625) 8 8
811 A62 $20,000 on 10c deep green (#492) 8 8
812 " $20,000 on 50c sage green (R) (#498) 8 8
813 " $30,000 on 30c dull vermilion (#496) 8 8
a. Perf. 10½ 12.50
Nos. 807-813 (7) 1.98 1.98

Nos. 492, 556 and 558 Surcharged in Black or Carmine [改作壹萬伍仟圓 15000]

1948

814 A62 $15,000 on 10c deep green 8 8
815 " $15,000 on $4 violet brown 8 8
816 " $15,000 on $6 gray violet (C) 8 8

No. 498, 494 and 504 Surcharged in Black [改作肆萬圓 40000]

1948 *Perf. 11½, 13.* Unwmkd.

817 A62 $15,000 on 50c sage green 8 8
818 " $40,000 on 20c dark olive green 8 8
a. Perf. 11 3.50 3.50
819 " $60,000 on $4 red brown 8 8

Gold Yuan Surcharges
(Nos. 820–885E)

Stamps of 1942-47 Surcharged in Black, Carmine or Red [金圓 ½分]

1948 *Perf. 14, 13, 11*

820 A62 ½c on 30c dull vermilion (#496) 5 5
821 A82 ½c on $500 blue grn. (Bk) (#747) 5 5
822 " ½c on $500 blue green (C) (#747) 5 5
823 A73 1c on $20 car. (#636) 5 5
824 A62 2c on $1.50 deep blue (R) (#501) 5 5
825 " 3c on $5 cerise (#505) 5 5
826 " 4c on $1 rose lake (#499) 5 5
827 " 5c on 50c sage green (#498) 5 5
a. Perf. 11 2.00 2.00
Nos. 820-827 (8) 40 40

On No. 820-827, the position of the surcharged denomination and "Gold Yuan" characters varies, the aim being to obliterate the original denomination.

Stamps of 1940-48 Surcharged in Black, Violet, Carmine, Blue or Green [壹角 金圓 10]

Perf. 12, 12½, 13, 14, 12½x13.

1948–49

828 A63 5c on $20 rose (#571) 5 5
829 A72 5c on $30 deep blue (C) (#626) 4 4
a. Double surch. 7.50
830 A57 10c on 2c olive green (#368) 4 4
831 A39 10c on 2½c rose lilac (#424) 6 6
832 A62 10c on 25c brown violet (V) (#495) 5 5
833 A63 10c on 40c brown red (#565) 5 5
834 A62 10c on $1 dull green (#500) 5 5
834A " 10c on $1 green (#551) 20.00 20.00
835 A63 10c on $2 gray brown (#566) 5 5
836 A62 10c on $20 ultramarine (C) (#560) 6 6
836A A63 10c on $20 rose (#571) 20.00 20.00
837 A67 10c on $20 car. (#592) 8 8
837A A73 10c on $20 car. (#636) 30 30
838 A72 10c on $30 deep blue (C) (#626) 5 5
839 A63 10c on $70 rose violet (#573) 5 5
a. Double surch. 6.50
840 A82 10c on $7000 light red brown (#754) 6 8
841 " 10c on $20,000 rose pink (#788) 6 6
842 A63 20c on $6 pale lilac gray (#569) 5 5
843 A37 20c on $30 choc. (#634) 6 6
844 A73 20c on $30 dark blue (C) (#637) 4 4
845 " 20c on $100 dark carmine (#640) 5 5
a. Inverted surch. 8.50
b. Double surch. 10.00
846 A39 50c on ½c black brown (#312) 8.50 8.50
847 " 50c on ½c olive black (#421) 5 5
a. Inverted surch. 15.00
848 A62 50c on 20c dark olive green (#494) 5 5
849 " 50c on 30c dull vermilion (Bl) (#496) 4 4
850 " 50c on 40c dark red brown (V) (#497) 4 4
a. Perf. 11 2.00 2.00
851 A63 50c on 40c brown red (V) (#565) 4 4
852 A62 50c on $4 violet brown (#556) 6 6
853 " 50c on $4 violet brown (Bl) (#556) 4 4
854 " 50c on $20 deep ultramarine (C) (#560) 5 5
855 A67 50c on $20 carmine (V) (#592) 4 4
856 A73 50c on $20 carmine (#636) 4 4
857 A62 50c on $70 lilac (C) (#562) 5 5

No.	Type	Description	Unused	Used
858	A82	50c on $6000 rose lilac (#753)	4	4
859	"	50c on $6000 rose lilac (Bl) (#753)	8	8
860	A62	$1 on 30c chocolate (#550)	6	6
		a. Perf. 11	25.00	
861	"	$1 on 40c dark red brown (#497)	6	6
		a. Perf. 11	2.00	2.00
862	"	$1 on $1 rose lake (#499)	4	4
863	"	$1 on $5 car. (#557)	5	5
864	A63	$2 on $2 gray brown (R) (#566)	5	5
865	A72	$2 on $20 deep carmine (#625)	5	5
866	A73	$2 on $100 dark carmine (#640)	5	5
867	A46	$5 on 17c brown olive (#432)	4	5
868	A63	$5 on $2 gray brown (#566)	8	8
869	A82	$5 on $3000 blue (C) (#750)	5	5
870	A47	$8 on 20c light blue (#433)	5	5
871	A82	$8 on $30,000 choc. (C) (#789)	8	8
872	A47	$10 on 40c orange (#438)	6	6
873	A63	$10 on $2 gray brown (G) (#566)	5	6
874	"	$10 on $2 gray brown (C) (#566)	8	8
875	"	$20 on $2 gray brown (C) (#566)	8	8
875A	A73	$20 on $20 carmine (#636)	25	25
876	A62	$50 on 30c dull vermilion (#496)	6	8
877	A63	$50 on $2 gray brown (Bl) (#566)	10	10
878	A73	$80 on $20 carmine (#636)	6	8
879	A62	$100 on $1 green (#551)	6	8
		a. Perf. 11	25.00	
880	A63	$100 on $2 gray brown (C) (#566)	10	10
880A	A82	$50,000 on $20,000 rose pink (#788)	18	18
880B	"	$100,000 on $30,000 chocolate (V) (#789)	18	18

Wmk. 261.

No.	Type	Description	Unused	Used
881	A39	10c on 2½c rose lilac (#405)	4	4
882	"	50c on ½c olive black (#402)	5	5
		Nos. 828-882 (61)	52.38	52.48

Characters at left express the new value. Style of characters and numerals varies.

Nos. Q7 to Q9 Surcharged in Black or Carmine

改作郵票
金圓伍佰圓
500⁰⁰

1948 *Perf. 12½* **Unwmkd.**

No.	Type	Description	Unused	Used
883	PP2	$200 on $3000 red orange	6	8
884	"	$500 on $5000 dark blue (C)	8	8
885	"	$1000 on $10,000 violet	10	15

Nos. 788-791 Surcharged in Gold Yuan in Red or Black at Foochow

金圓
念萬圓
200000

1949, Apr. 30 *Perf. 14* **Unwmkd.**

No.	Type	Description	Unused	Used
885A	A82	$20,000 on $40,000 green	2.25	2.25
885B	"	$50,000 on $30,000 chocolate (B)	2.25	2.25
885C	A82	$100,000 on $20,000 rose pink (B)	2.25	2.25
885D	"	$200,000 on $40,000 green	2.25	2.25
885E	"	$200,000 on $50,000 deep blue	2.25	2.25
		Nos. 885A-885E (5)	11.25	11.25

Nos. 885A-885E were issued in Fukien Postal District.

Dr. Sun Yat-sen
A94

Engraved.

1949 *Perf. 14* **Unwmkd.**

Without Gum.

No.	Type	Description	Unused	Used
886	A94	$1 orange	5	4
887	"	$10 green	5	4
888	"	$20 violet brown	5	4
889	"	$50 dk. Prus. green	8	8
890	"	$100 orange brown	5	4
891	"	$200 red orange	6	6
892	"	$500 rose lilac	5	4
893	"	$800 carmine rose	12	7
894	"	$1000 blue	5	4

Redrawn. Engraved.

Perf. 12½

No.	Type	Description	Unused	Used
894A	A94	$10 green	15	10
		b. Perf. 14	1.50	1.50
894C	"	$20 violet brown	10	10
		d. Perf. 14	25	15
		Nos. 886-894C (11)	81	65

Small "T" at left of necktie on Nos. 894A-894d.

Redrawn.

1949 Lithographed *Perf. 12½*

Without Gum

No.	Type	Description	Unused	Used
895	A94	$50 greenish gray	7	7
896	"	$100 dk. org. brown	5	5
897	"	$200 orange red	5	5
898	"	$1000 deep blue	6	6
899	"	$5000 light blue	6	6
900	"	$10,000 sepia	6	6
		Nos. 895-900 (6)	35	35

Diagonal lines have been added to the background of the redrawn design. See also Nos. 945-958, 973-981.

Plane, Train and Ship
A95

Two types, 50c on $20:
I. Thick numerals in "20." Vertical stroke in lower right corner of vignette. (Dah Tung Book Co.)
II. Thin "20." No vertical stroke in corner. (Central Trust.)

Two types, $2 on $50, $10 on $30, $100 on $50 and $300 on $50:
III. "Y" in lower right corner of vignette. (Dah Yeh Printing Co.)
IV. No "Y" in corner. (Dah Tung, Central Trust or Chung Ming.)

Two types, $50 on $300 and $1000 on $100:
V. Projection on left frame column below foliate ornament. (Dah Yeh Printing Co.)
VI. No projection. (Dah Tung Book Co.)

Gold Yuan Surcharge in Various Colors on Revenue Stamps.
Lithographed;
Nos. 923, 933, 935-936 Engraved.

1949 *Perf. 12½, 13, 14*

Without Gum.

No.	Type	Description	Unused	Used
915	A95	50c on $20 red brn., I (Bk)	5	4
		a. 50c on $20 brown, II (Bk)	8	5
916	"	$1 on $15 red orange (Bk)	5	4
917	A95	$2 on $50 dark blue, IV (C)	5	4
		d. Type III	15	10
917A	"	$3 on $50 dark blue (Bl)	7	6
917C	"	$3 on $50 dark blue (Bk)	5	4
918	"	$5 on $500 brown (Dk Br)	5	4
919	"	$10 on $30 dark violet, III (Bl)	6	4
		a. Type IV	12	12
		b. Dbl. surch., IV		
920	"	$15 on $20 orange brown (Bl)	5	4
921	"	$25 on $20 orange brown (G)	5	4
922	"	$50 on $50 dark blue (R O)	5	4
923	"	$50 on $300 grn., VI (C)	5	4
		a. $50 on $300 yel. green, V (C)	10	10
924	"	$80 on $50 dark blue (Dk Br)	6	4
925	"	$100 on $50 dark blue, IV (Bk)	6	4
		a. Type III	25	7
926	"	$200 on $50 dark blue (Bk)	6	4
927	"	$200 on $500 brn. (Bl)	12	8
928	"	$300 on $50 dark blue, III (C)	8	4
		a. Type IV	15	10
929	"	$300 on $50 dk. bl. (Br)	20	18
930	"	$500 on $15 red orange (Bl)	15	15
931	"	$500 on $30 dark violet (Bk)	15	15
932	"	$1000 on $50 dark blue (C)	20	20
933	"	$1000 on $100 olive grn., V (Bk)	20	20
		a. Type VI	1.50	1.50
934	"	$1500 on $50 dark blue (Bl)	25	20
935	"	$2000 on $300 grn. (Bl)	12	10
936	"	$5000 on $100 olive green (C)	50.00	
		Nos. 915-935 (23)	2.23	1.88

No. 936 was officially authorized, but never issued.

Key pattern of overprinted border inverted and in 2 or 3 detached sections at top and bottom.

Hankow Prints.
Lithographed.
Without Gum.

No.	Type	Description	Unused	Used
937	A95	$50 on $10 slate green (Bk)	75	50
938	"	$100 on $10 slate green (Bl)	2.50	1.40
939	"	$500 on $10 slate green (Bk)	2.50	1.50
940	"	$1000 on $10 slate green (Bl)	1.00	25
941	"	$5000 on $20 red brown (Bl)	1.50	35
942	"	$10,000 on $20 red brown (Bk)	1.25	50
943	"	$50,000 on $20 red brown (Bl)	1.25	50
944	"	$100,000 on $20 red brown (Bk)	1.25	60
944A	"	$500,000 on $20 red brn. (Bl)	100.00	30.00
944B	"	$2,000,000 on $20 red brn. (G)	175.00	75.00
944C	"	$5,000,000 on $20 red brn. (Bl)	350.00	150.00
		Nos. 937-944C (11)	637.00	260.60

The basic revenue stamps of Nos. 915-944C were the work of several printers. There are three main types, differing in the bottom label. Nos. 922 and 925 are in a second type: Nos. 923 and 930 in a third. Varieties of paper, color and overprint exist.

Counterfeits exist of Nos. 944A-944C.

Type of 1949 Redrawn.

1949 Without Gum *Perf. 12½*

No.	Type	Description	Unused	Used
945	A94	$500 rose lilac	7	7
946	"	$2000 violet	8	8
947	"	$20,000 apple green	8	8
948	"	$50,000 rose pink	12	12
949	"	$80,000 brown red	30	30
950	"	$100,000 blue green	15	15
		Nos. 945-950 (6)	80	80

Zeros for "cents" omitted on No. 950.

Redrawn Coarse Impression

1949 Litho. Without Gum

Size: 18¼x20¾ mm.

No.	Type	Description	Unused	Used
951	A94	$50 green	35	25
952	"	$1000 deep blue	30	15
953	"	$5000 carmine	30	20
954	"	$10,000 brown	25	15
955	"	$20,000 orange	30	25
956	"	$50,000 blue	30	25
957	"	$200,000 violet	30	25
958	"	$500,000 violet brown	35	25
		Nos. 951-958 (8)	2.45	1.75

Zeros for "cents" omitted on Nos. 957-958.

Locomotive and Ship
A96

1949, May 1 Litho. *Perf. 12½*

Without Gum

No.	Type	Description	Unused	Used
959	A96	orange	50	15
		a. Rouletted	60	60

Nos. 959, C62, E12 and F2 were printed without denomination and sold at the daily rate of the yuan. This was necessitated by the gold yuan inflation.

Revenue Stamps Overprinted in Black

1949, May *Perf. 12½, 13, 14*

Without Gum

No.	Type	Description	Unused	Used
960	A95	$30 dark violet	35.00	25.00

Engraved.

No.	Type	Description	Unused	Used
961	A95	$200 violet brown	5.00	4.00
962	"	$500 dark green	5.00	4.00

A similar overprint appears on Nos. C63, E13 and F3, differing in second and third characters of bottom row.

Silver Yuan Surcharge in Various Colors

1949 Lithographed

No.	Type	Description	Unused	Used
963	A95	1c on $5000 brown (G)	50	35
964	"	4c on $100 olive green (Bl)	20	25
965	"	4c on $3000 orange (Bk)	20	25
966	"	10c on $50 dark blue (RV)	20	25
967	"	10c on $1000 carmine (Bk)	30	20
		a. Inverted surch.	30.00	
968	"	20c on $1000 red (V)	25	30
		b. Inverted surch.	12.50	
968A	"	50c on $20 red violet (C)	20	40
969	"	50c on $50 dark blue (C)	1.00	40
970	"	$1 on $50 dark blue (Bk)	60	40
		Nos. 963-970 (9)	3.45	2.80

Nos. 963-965 and 967 are engraved.

Sun Type of 1949 Redrawn.
Coarse Impression.
Perf. 12½, 13 or Compound

1949

No.	Type	Description	Unused	Used
973	A94	1c apple green	15	15
974	"	2c orange	25	25
975	"	4c blue green	8	8
976	"	10c deep lilac	8	8
977	"	16c orange red	50	50
978	"	20c blue	20	20
979	"	50c dark brown	1.25	1.25

980 A94 100c deep blue 65.00 65.00

981 " 500c scarlet 85.00 85.00

Nos. 973-981 (9) 152.51 152.51

Flying Geese Over Globe A97

Pigeons, Globe and Wreath A98

1949, May Litho. *Perf. 12½*

Without Gum

984 A97 $1 brown orange 1.50 65

985 " $2 blue 3.50 1.00

986 " $5 carmine rose 5.00 2.50

987 " $10 blue green 10.00 3.50

Five other denominations—10c, 16c, 50c, $20 and $50—were also printed at Shanghai, but were not issued.

Engraved and Typographed.

1949, Aug. 1 Without Gum *Imperf.*

988 A98 $1 org. red & black 2.25 2.50

Issued to commemorate the 75th anniversary of the formation of the Universal Postal Union.

Exists with black denomination omitted.

Summer Palace, Peiping A99

Bronze Bull and Kunming Lake A100

Engraved and Typographed.

1949, Aug. *Rouletted*

Without Gum

989 A99 15c org. brn. & grn. 12 12

990 A100 40c dull green & carmine 15 15

a. 2nd and 3rd characters at top transposed 35.00 35.00

Silver Yuan Surcharge in Black on 1949 Sun Yat-sen Issues

1 壹分

1949 *Perf. 12½, 14*

991 A94 1c on $100 orange brown (890) 1.25 1.00

992 " 1c on $100 dark org. brn. (896) 1.50 1.25

993 " 2½c on $500 rose lilac (892) 1.75 1.50

a. Inverted surch. 10.00

994 A94 2½c on $500 rose lilac (945) 1.75 1.50

995 " 15c on $10 green (887) 4.00 3.25

a. Inverted surch. 10.00

996 A94 15c on $20 violet brown (894C) 5.00 4.00

Nos. 991-996 (6) 15.25 12.50

Silver Yuan Surcharge in Black or Carmine

5 伍分

997 A94 2½c on $50 green (951) 40 35

998 " 2½c on $50,000 blue (956) 40 35

999 " 5c on $1000 deep blue (952) (C) 65 50

1000 A94 5c on $20,000 orange (955) 65 50

1001 " 5c on $200,000 vio. (957) (C) 75 75

1002 " 5c on $500,000 violet brown (958) 75 75

1003 " 10c on $5000 carmine (953) 1.00 85

1004 " 10c on $10,000 brown (954) 1.00 75

1005 " 15c on $200 red orange (891) 1.50 1.50

1006 " 25c on $100 dk. org. brown (896) 2.50 2.50

Nos. 997-1006 (10) 9.60 8.80

Republic of China (Taiwan)

LOCATION (since 1949)—Taiwan (Formosa).

GOVT.—Republic.

AREA—13,892 sq. mi.

POP.—16,700,000 (est. 1978).

CAPITAL—Taipei.

Stamps issued and used in Taiwan after Communist forces occupied the Chinese mainland include Taiwan Nos. 91-96, 101-103, J10-J17.

Type of 1949 with Value Omitted Surcharged in Various Colors

壹 臺 圓 幣 1^{00}

1950, Jan. 1 *Perf. 12½* Unwmkd.

1007 A97 $1 green (Bk) 10.00 1.00

1008 " $2 " (C) 12.50 3.50

1009 " $5 " (V) 200.00 15.00

1010 " $10 " (Br) 250.00 50.00

1011 " $20 " (Dk Bl) 500.00 200.00

Nos. 1007-1011 (5) 972.50 269.50

Two printings of the $1 and $2 show minor differences.

Cheng Ch'eng-kung (Koxinga) A101

1950 Typographed *Rouletted*

Without Gum.

1012 A101 3c dark gray green 35 10

1013 " 10c orange brown 35 10

1014 " 15c orange yellow 35 10

1015 " 20c emerald 75 15

1016 " 30c claret 1.00 15

1017 " 40c red orange 1.25 15

1018 " 50c chocolate 1.50 25

1019 " 80c carmine 2.50 1.25

1020 " $1 ultramarine 3.00 15

1021 " $1.50 green 7.50 1.00

1022 " $1.60 blue 10.00 75

1023 " $2 red violet 12.50 75

1024 " $5 aquamarine 35.00 4.50

Nos. 1012-1024 (13) 76.05 9.40

Part perforate pairs exist of the 10c, 20c, and 80c.

Stamps of 1947-48 Surcharged in Carmine or Black

臺幣叁分 3

1950 *Perf. 14*

1025 A82 3c on $30,000 choc. 1.50 1.25

1026 " 3c on $40,000 grn. (C) 1.50 1.25

1027 " 3c on $50,000 deep blue (C) 2.00 1.25

1028 A82 5c on $200,000 brown violet 2.00 1.25

1029 " 10c on $4000 gray 4.00 2.00

a. Inverted surch. 40.00

1030 A82 10c on $6000 rose lilac 4.00 2.00

a. Inverted surch. 100.00

1031 A82 10c on $20,000 rose pink 6.00 3.00

1032 " 10c on $2,000,000 vermilion 6.00 3.00

a. Inverted surch. 60.00

1033 A82 20c on $500,000 lilac rose 6.50 3.50

a. Inverted surch. 75.00

1034 A82 20c on $1,000,000 claret 6.50 5.00

a. Inverted surch. 75.00

1035 A82 30c on $3,000,000 olive bistre 12.50 7.50

1036 " 50c on $5,000,000 ultramarine (C) 20.00 15.00

Nos. 1025-1036 (12) 72.50 46.00

Allegory of Election A102

Perf. 12x12½, Imperf.

1951, Mar. 20 Engraved Unwmkd.

Without Gum

1037 A102 40c carmine 2.50 25

a. Horiz. pair, imperf. btwn. 35.00

1038 " $1 deep blue 3.00 50

1039 " $1.60 purple 7.50 1.25

1040 " $2 brown 10.00 2.50

Adoption of local self-government in Taiwan.

Souvenir Sheet.

Imperf.

1041 A102 $2 dp. blue green 30.00 30.00

Marginal inscriptions publicize Postal Commemorative Day, Mar. 20, 1951. Size: 100x71 mm.

Type A97 Surcharged A103

Farmer and Scroll Announcing Tax Reduction A104

Surcharge in Various Colors.

1951, July 19 *Perf. 12½*

Without Gum

1042 A103 $5 green (RBr) 10.00 2.00

1043 " $10 " (Bk) 22.50 2.00

1044 " $20 " (R) 110.00 15.00

1045 " $50 " (P) 225.00 30.00

1952, Jan. 1 *Imperf., Perf. 14*

Without Gum

1046 A104 20c red orange 2.00 1.25

1047 " 40c dark green 4.00 2.00

1048 " $1 brown 6.00 4.00

1049 " $1.40 deep blue 10.00 6.00

1050 " $2 dark gray 12.50 6.00

1051 " $5 brown car. 22.50 8.00

Nos. 1046-1051 (6) 57.00 27.25

Land tax reduction of 37.5% in Taiwan.

Pres. Chiang Kai-shek, Flag and Followers A105

Imperf., Perf. 14

1952, Mar. 1 Unwmkd.

Without Gum

Flag in Violet Blue and Carmine.

1052 A105 40c rose carmine 2.50 50

a. Vert. pair, imperf. btwn. 25.00

1053 " $1 deep green 3.50 1.25

1054 " $1.60 brown orange 7.50 75

a. Horiz. pair, imperf. btwn. 65.00

1055 " $2 bright blue 12.50 2.50

1056 " $5 violet brown 17.50 2.50

Nos. 1052-1056 (5) 43.50 7.50

Issued to commemorate the 2nd anniversary of Chiang Kai-shek's return to the presidency.

See Nos. 1064 - 1069.

Nos. 975, 976, 978 and 979 Surcharged in Black

叁 臺 分 幣 3

1952 *Perf. 12½.*

1057 A94 3c on 4c bl. green 1.00 50

1058 " 3c on 10c dp. lilac 1.00 50

a. Inverted surch.

1059 " 3c on 20c blue 1.00 50

1060 " 3c on 50c dk. brn. 1.00 50

Geese Type of 1949 with Value Omitted Surcharged

臺幣壹拾圓 10^{00}

1952, Dec. 8

1061 A97 $10 green (P) 25.00 6.00

1062 " $20 " (R) 100.00 12.00

1063 " $50 " (Bk) 400.00 175.00

Chiang Type of 1952 Redrawn.

Perf. 12½

1953, Mar. 1 Engraved Unwmkd.

Without Gum

Flag in Dark Blue & Carmine.

1064 A105 10c red orange 2.50 20

1065 " 20c green 2.50 25

1066 " 40c rose pink 3.50 40

1067 " $1.40 blue 9.00 50

1068 " $2 brown 12.50 1.00

1069 " $5 rose violet 25.00 2.00

Nos. 1064-1069 (6) 55.00 4.35

Third anniversary of Chiang Kai-shek's return to presidency.

Many differences in redrawn design.

Nos. 1064-1069 exist imperf. Price, set $75.

Nos. 1020, 1014, 1016 and 1022 Surcharged in Various Colors

3 cts. 叁分

1953-54 *Rouletted.*

1070 A101 3c on $1 ultra. (C) 75 15

1070A " 10c on 15c orange yel. (G) ('54) 7.50 25

1071 " 10c on 30c claret (Bl) 75 15

1072 " 20c on $1.60 blue (Bk) 75 15

Chinese characters and ornamental device at bottom differ on each value.

Nurse and Patients A106

1953, July 1 Litho. *Perf. 12½*

Without Gum

Cross in Red, Burelage Color in Italics.

1073	A106	40c brown, *buff*	4.00	35
1074	"	$1.60 blue, *blue*	6.00	50
1075	"	$2 green, *yellow*	15.00	75
1076	"	$5 red orange, *orange*	22.50	2.50

Issued to honor the Chinese Anti-Tuberculosis Association.

Pres. Chiang Kai-shek
A107

1953, Oct. 31 Engraved

Without Gum

1077	A107	10c dark brown	75	7
1078	"	20c lilac	75	7
1079	"	40c deep green	75	10
1080	"	50c deep pink	60	7
1081	"	80c brown bistre	6.00	18
1082	"	$1 deep olive green	2.00	12
1083	"	$1.40 deep blue	4.00	45
1084	"	$1.60 deep carmine	6.00	40
1085	"	$1.70 apple green	2.50	1.35
1086	"	$2 brown	3.00	15
1087	"	$3 dark blue	15.00	60
1088	"	$4 aquamarine	7.50	70
1089	"	$5 red orange	5.00	1.15
1090	"	$10 dark green	7.50	1.50
1091	"	$20 dk. brown lake	20.00	3.25
		a. Souvenir folder	27.50	
		Nos. 1077-1091 (15)	81.35	10.16

67th birthday of Pres. Chiang Kai-shek.
No. 1091a contains Nos. 1077-1091 imperf., arranged in 3 sheets of 5 stamps each.

Silo Highway Bridge A108 — Forest of Evergreens A109

Design: $1.60 and $5, Silo bridge, side view.

Without Gum

1954, Jan. 28 *Perf. 12½* **Unwmkd.**

Various Frames.

1092	A108	40c vermilion	50	40
1093	"	$1.60 blue violet	20.00	50
1094	"	$3.60 sepia	7.50	1.25
1095	"	$5 magenta	25.00	1.75
		a. Souv. sheet	35.00	

Opening of Silo bridge, 1st anniversary.
No. 1095a contains one each of Nos. 1092-1095 imperforate.

1954, Mar. 12 *Perf. 12x12½*

Design: $10, Nursery.

Without Gum

1096	A109	40c blue green	7.50	50
1097	"	$10 red violet	20.00	3.00

Issued to publicize forest conservation.

Runner A110 — Globe, Bridge and Ship A111

1954, Mar. 29 Without Gum

1098	A110	40c deep ultra.	8.50	1.00
1099	"	$5 carmine	20.00	4.00

Issued to publicize 11th Youth Day, March 29, 1954.

1954, Oct. 21 *Perf. 12*

Without Gum

1100	A111	40c red orange	7.50	25
1101	"	$5 deep blue	4.00	1.25

Issued to publicize the second Overseas Chinese Day, October 21, 1954.

Ex-Prisoner with Broken Chains
A112

Designs: $1, Ex-prisoner with torch and flag, UN emblem. $1.60, Torch and date.

1955, Jan. 23

1102	A112	40c blue green	1.00	30
		a. Vert. pair, imperf. between	110.00	
1103	A112	$1 sepia	8.00	1.35
1104	"	$1.60 lake	10.00	1.20

Issued to honor anti-Communist Chinese prisoners who fought with the North Korean army, released January 23, 1955.

Nos. 1019-1021, 1017 Surcharged in Brown, Blue or Green:

分 叁 角 壹

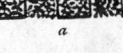

a — 0.10 *b*

角 貳

0.20 *c*

1955 *Rouletted*

1105	A101	(*a*)	3c on $1 ultra. (Br)	1.25	35
1106	"	(*b*)	10c on 80c car. (Bl)	1.25	35
1107	"	(")	10c on $1.50 green (Bl)	1.25	35
1108	"	(*c*)	20c on 40c red orange (G)	1.25	35

Hand Planting Evergreen Tree A113 — Chiang Kai-shek, Flags, Building A114

Design: $50, Seedling and map of Taiwan.

1955, Apr. 1 *Perf. 12*

Without Gum

1109	A113	$20 deep carmine	9.00	1.00
1110	"	$50 blue	16.00	4.00

Issued to publicize forest conservation.

1955, May 20 Engraved *Perf. 12*

Without Gum

1111	A114	20c olive	75	6
1112	"	40c blue green	1.25	8
1113	A114	$2 carmine rose	2.50	50
1114	"	$7 deep ultra.	5.00	1.00
		a. Souvenir sheet of 4	12.50	12.50

No. 1114a contains one each of Nos. 1111-1114, imperforate, with ornamental border typographed in red.
First anniversary of Pres. Chiang Kai-shek's re-election.

Armed Forces Emblem
A115

1955, Sept. 3 Without Gum

1115	A115	40c dark blue	1.00	15
1116	"	$2 org. verm.	7.50	50
1117	"	$7 blue green	6.50	1.00
		a. Sheet of three	25.00	25.00

Armed Forces Day, Sept. 3.
No. 1117a measures 147x104mm. and contains one each of Nos. 1115-1117.

Nos. 1017, 1018 and C64 Surcharged in Magenta

角 貳

0.20

1955 Typographed *Rouletted*

1118	A101	20c on 40c red orange	1.35	30
1119	"	20c on 50c choc.	1.35	30
1120	AP6	20c on 60c dp. blue	1.35	30

Flags of U.N. and China
A116

1955, Oct. 24 Engraved *Perf. 11½*

Without Gum.

1121	A116	40c dark blue	1.25	15
1122	"	$2 dark carmine rose	4.50	40
1123	"	$7 slate green	4.00	1.00

Issued to commemorate the tenth anniversary of the United Nations, Oct. 24, 1955.

Pres. Chiang Kai-shek A117 — Birthplace of Sun Yat-sen A118

1955, Oct. 31 Photo. *Perf. 13½*

1124	A117	40c dark blue, red & brown	1.00	15
1125	"	$2 green, red & dark blue	3.00	50
1126	"	$7 brown, red & green	4.00	1.00
		a. Souvenir sheet of 3	8.50	8.50

69th birthday of Pres. Chiang Kai-shek.
No. 1126a measures 147x105 mm. and contains one each of Nos. 1124-1126, imperf.

1955, Nov. 12 Engraved *Perf. 12*

Without Gum

1127	A118	40c blue	50	10
1128	"	$2 red brown	3.00	50
1129	"	$7 rose lake	4.00	90

90th anniversary, birth of Sun Yat-sen.

No. 959a Surcharged in Bright Green

角 貳

0.20

1956 Litho. *Rouletted*

1130	A96	20c on orange	20	10

See also No. 1213.

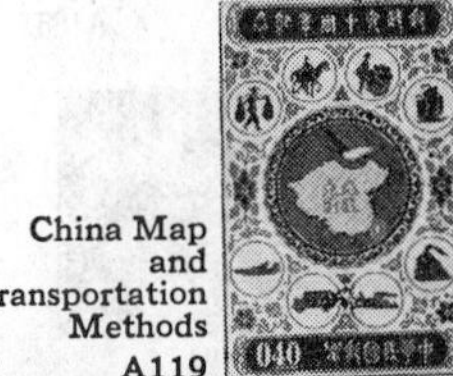

China Map and Transportation Methods
A119

Wmk. 281

Wmkd. Wavy Lines (281).

1956, Mar. 20 Engraved *Perf. 12*

Without Gum

1131	A119	40c dark carmine	35	10
1132	"	$1 intense black	65	30
1133	"	$1.60 chocolate	1.25	15
1134	"	$2 dark green	1.75	30

Issued to commemorate the 60th anniversary of the founding of the modern Chinese postal system.

Souvenir Sheets

Imperf.

1135	A119	$2 magenta	3.00	3.00
1136	"	$2 red	3.00	3.00

Issued for the exhibition for the 60th anniversary of the modern Chinese postal system, March 20, 1956.
Nos. 1135-36 measure 148x103mm. Marginal floral design and inscription in red and silver (No. 1135), and red and gold (No. 1136).

Children at Play A120 — Early and Modern Locomotives A121

1956, Apr. 4 *Perf. 12* **Unwmkd.**

Without Gum.

1137	A120	40c emerald	30	10
1138	"	$1.60 dark blue	80	15
1139	"	$2 dark carmine	1.00	50

Children's Day, Apr. 4, 1956.

1956, June 9 **Wmk. 281 (vert.)**

Without Gum

1140	A121	40c rose carmine	75	8
1141	"	$2 blue	75	10
1142	"	$8 green	2.50	70

75th anniversary of Chinese Railroads.

Pres. Chiang Kai-shek
A122 A123

A124
Various Portraits of Chiang

Perf. 14½x13½,
14½ **(A123),** ***13½x14½***

1956, Oct. 31 Photo. Unwmkd.

1143	A122	20c red orange	20	10
1144	"	40c carmine rose	35	10
1145	A123	$1 brt. ultra.	40	12
1146	"	$1.60 red lilac	75	15
1147	A124	$2 red brown	2.00	18
1148	"	$8 bright greenish bl.	5.00	80
		Nos. 1143-1148 (6)	8.70	1.45

Issued in honor of the 70th birthday of Pres. Chiang Kai-shek.

Types of Special Delivery, Air Post and Registration Stamps of 1949 Surcharged in Black or Maroon

分叁

3
a

分叁 角壹

3
b

$0.10
c

Lithographed.

1956 *Rouletted* Unwmkd.

Without Gum.

1150	SD2 (*a*)	3c red violet	75	20
	a.	Perf. 12½	1.00	50
1151	AP5 (*b*)	3c bl. green(M)	75	20
1152	R2	(*c*) 10c bright red	75	20

Telecommunications Emblem and Radio Tower
A125

Engraved.

1956, Dec. 28 *Perf. 12* Wmk. 281

Without Gum.

1153	A125	40c deep ultra.	15	5
1154	"	$1.40 carmine	25	8
1155	"	$1.60 dark green	35	10
1156	"	$2 chocolate	2.25	25

Issued to commemorate the 75th anniversary of the founding of the Chinese telegraph service.

Map of China
A126

Mother Instructing Mencius
A127

Pin Perf., Perf. 12x12½

1957 Lithographed. Wmk. 281

Without Gum.

1157	A126	3c bright blue	25	6
1158	"	10c violet	25	6
1159	"	20c red orange	25	6
1160	"	40c rose red	25	6

Unwmkd.

1161	A126	$1 orange brown	40	8
1162	"	$1.60 green	50	12
		Nos. 1157-1162 (6)	1.90	44

Map inscription reads: "Recovery of Mainland."

See also Nos. 1177-82.

Engraved

1957, May 12 *Perf. 12* Unwmkd.

Design: $3, Mother tattooing Yueh Fei.

Without Gum

1163	A127	40c green	35	12
1164	"	$3 reddish brown	90	30

Issued to honor Mother's Day, 1957.

Badge of Chinese Boy Scouts
A128

1957, Aug. 11 Without Gum

1165	A128	40c lilac	15	8
1166	"	$1 green	30	12
1167	"	$1.60 dark blue	50	18

Issued to commemorate the centenary of the birth of Lord Baden-Powell and to publicize the World Scout Jubilee Jamboree, England, Aug. 1-12.

Globe, Radio Tower and Microphone—A129

1957, Sept. 16 Without Gum

1168	A129	40c vermilion	15	6
1169	"	50c bright rose lilac	30	8
1170	"	$3.50 dark blue	80	30

Issued to commemorate the 30th anniversary of Chinese broadcasting.

Map of Taiwan
A130

1957, Oct. 26 Without Gum

1171	A130	40c blue green	35	5
1172	"	$1.40 light ultra.	75	30
1173	"	$2 gray	1.00	25

Issued to commemorate the start of construction on the Cross Island Highway, Taiwan.

Freighter "Hai Min" and River Boat "Kiang Foo"
A131

1957, Dec. 16 Engraved *Perf. 12*

Without Gum.

1174	A131	40c deep ultra.	12	5
1175	"	80c rose lake	40	12
1176	"	$2.80 vermilion	1.00	40

Issued to commemorate the 85th anniversary of the establishment of the China Merchants Steam Navigation Co.

Type of 1957.

1957, Dec. 25 Typo. Unwmkd.

Pin Perf., Perf. 12x12½

Without Gum.

Dark Blue Frames.

1177	A126	3c bright blue	20	5
1178	"	10c violet	20	5
1179	"	20c brick red	20	5
		a. Booklet pane of 6		
		b. Booklet pane of 4		
1180	"	40c rose red	50	8
		a. Booklet pane of 6		
		b. Booklet pane of 4		
1181	"	$1 dp. org. brn.	50	12
		a. Booklet pane of 6		
1182	"	$1.60 deep green	75	12
		Nos. 1177-1182 (6)	2.35	47

Butterfly
A132

Mme. Chiang Kai-shek Orchid
A133

Photogravure.

1958, Mar. 20 *Perf. 13½* Unwmkd.

Various Insects in Natural Colors

1183	A132	10c pale green, green & black	25	10
1184	"	40c lemon, pink, green & black	25	15
1185	"	$1 yellow green & maroon	35	15
1186	"	$1.40 yellow, orange & black	50	20
1187	"	$1.60 pale brown & dark purple	60	20
1188	"	$2 bright yellow, orange & black	75	30
		Nos. 1183-1188 (6)	2.70	1.10

1958, Mar. 20

Orchids: 20c, Formosan Wilson (horiz.). $1.40, Klotzsch. $3, Fitzgerald (horiz.).

Orchids in Natural Colors.

1189	A133	20c chocoate	25	12
1190	"	40c purple	35	12
1191	"	$1.40 dark violet brown	50	20
1192	"	$3 dark blue	75	40

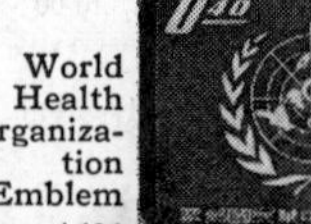

World Health Organization Emblem
A134

1958, May 28 Engraved *Perf. 12*

Without Gum.

1193	A134	40c dark blue	10	4
1194	"	$1.60 brick red	25	8
1195	"	$2 deep red lilac	45	30

Issued to commemorate the 10th anniversary of the World Health Organization.

President's Mansion, Taipei
A135

Wmk. 323
Wmk. 323 is found with "Yu" in various arrangements.

Wmkd.

Seal Character 'Yu' (323)

1958, Sept. 20 Engraved *Perf. 12*

Without Gum

1196	A135	$10 blue green	3.00	10
		a. Granite paper ('63)	3.00	5
1197	"	$20 carmine rose	4.00	25
		a. Granite paper ('63)	4.00	10
1198	"	$50 red brown	15.00	1.35
1199	"	$100 dark blue	25.00	3.00

See also Nos. 1349-1351.

Taiwan Farm Scene
A136

1958, Oct. 1 Unwmkd.

Without Gum

1200	A136	20c emerald	10	3
1201	"	40c black	10	3
1202	"	$1.40 bright magenta	40	10
1203	"	$3 ultramarine	90	30

Issued to commemorate the tenth anniversary of the Joint Commission on Rural Reconstruction.

Pres. Chiang Kai-shek
A137

1958, Oct. 31 Photo. *Perf. 13½*

Without Gum.

1204	A137	40c multicolor	30	12

Issued to honor Pres. Chiang Kai-shek on his 72nd birthday.

UNESCO Building, Paris
A138

1958, Nov. 3 Engraved *Perf. 12*
Without Gum.

1205	A138	20c dark blue	8	4
1206	"	40c green	12	5
1207	"	$1.40 orange verm.	40	10
1208	"	$3 red lilac	65	30

Issued to commemorate the opening of UNESCO (U. N. Educational, Scientific and Cultural Organization) Headquarters in Paris, Nov. 3.

Flame from Liberty Torch Encircling Globe
A139

1958, Dec. 10 Unwmkd.
Without Gum

1209	A139	40c green	6	4
1210	"	60c gray brown	15	5
1211	"	$1 carmine	30	12
1212	"	$3 ultramarine	70	35

Issued to commemorate the tenth anniversary of the signing of the Universal Declaration of Human Rights.

No. 959a Surcharged in Bright Green

0.20
角貳

Rouletted

1958, Dec. 11 Litho. Unwmkd.
Without Gum

1213	A96	20c on orange	25	7

Ballot Box, Scales and Constitution
A140

1958, Dec. 25 Engraved *Perf. 12*
Without Gum.

1214	A140	40c green	15	4
1215	"	50c dull purple	20	5
1216	"	$1.40 carmine rose	50	15
1217	"	$3.50 dark blue	1.00	40

Issued to commemorate the 10th anniversary of the adoption of the constitution.

Chu Kwang Tower, Quemoy
A141

Lithographed.

1959–60 *Perf. 12* Wmk. 323
Without Gum.

1218	A141	3c orange	10	3
1218A	"	5c light yellow green ('60)	10	6
1219	"	10c lilac	10	3
1220	"	20c ultramarine	10	3
1221	"	40c brown	15	3
1222	"	50c bluish green	25	4
1223	"	$1 rose red	40	4
1224	"	$1.40 yellow green	50	5
1225	"	$2 gray green	50	8
1226	"	$2.80 rose pink	1.00	8
1227	"	$3 slate blue	1.00	9
		Nos. 1218–1227 (11)	4.20	56

See also Nos. 1270–1283.

ILO Emblem and Headquarters, Geneva
A142

1959, June 15 Engraved *Perf. 12*
Without Gum

1228	A142	40c blue	6	4
1229	"	$1.60 dark brown	20	5
1230	"	$3 bright blue green	45	12
1231	"	$5 org. verm.	1.10	35

Issued to commemorate the 40th anniversary of the International Labor Organization.

Bugler and Tents
A143

1959, July 8 Unwmkd.
Without Gum

1232	A143	40c carmine	12	5
1233	"	50c dark blue	40	15
1234	"	$5 green	1.10	40

Issued to publicize the 10th World Boy Scout Jamboree, at Makiling National Park, Philippines, July 17–26.

Inscribed Stone, Mt. Tai-wu, Quemoy
A144

Map of Taiwan Straits
A145

1959, Sept. 3 Engraved *Perf. 12*
Without Gum.

1235	A144	40c brown	15	10
1236	A145	$1.40 ultramarine	30	10
1237	A145	$2 green	75	25
1238	A144	$3 dark blue	80	35

Defense of Quemoy and Matsu islands.

Pigeons Circling Globe
A146

1959, Oct. 4 Without Gum

1239	A146	40c blue	10	10
1240	"	$1 rose carmine	15	12
1241	"	$2 gray brown	30	10
1242	"	$3.50 red orange	80	35

Issued for International Letter Writing Week, Oct. 4–10.

National Taiwan Science Hall, Taipei—A147

Design: $3, Front view.

1959, Nov. 12 Photo. *Perf. 13x13½*

1243	A147	40c multicolored	50	15
1244	"	$3 "	1.25	45

Emblem
A148

1959, Dec. 7 Engraved *Perf. 12*
Without Gum

1245	A148	40c blue green	15	8
1246	"	$1.60 red lilac	40	12
1247	"	$3 orange	75	25

Issued to commemorate the 10th anniversary of the International Confederation of Free Trade Unions.

Sun Yat-sen, Lincoln and Flags
A149

Perf. 13½, 12

1959, Dec. 25 Photo. Unwmkd.

1248	A149	40c multicolored	15	5
1249	"	$3 "	90	18

Issued to honor Sun Yat-sen and Abraham Lincoln as "Leaders of Democracy."

Mailman on Motorcycle Delivering Night Mail
A150

Postal Launch
A151

1960, Mar. 20 Engraved *Perf. 11½*
Without Gum

1250	A150	$1.40 dark violet brown	45	10
1251	A151	$1.60 ultramarine	55	15

Issued to publicize the Prompt Delivery Service.

WRY Uprooted Oak Emblem
A152

1960, Apr. 7 Photo. *Perf. 13*

1252	A152	40c black, red brown & emerald	18	10
1253	"	$3 black, red orange & green	55	25

Issued to publicize World Refugee Year, July 1, 1959–June 30, 1960.

Cross Island Highway, Taiwan
A153

Design: $1, $2, Road through tunnel (vert.).

Perf. 11½

1960, May 9 Engr. Unwmkd.
Without Gum

1254	A153	40c green	15	8
1255	"	$1 dark blue	70	30
1256	"	$2 brown violet	25	15
1257	"	$3 brown	90	22
		a. Souv. sheet of 2, wmk. 323	20.00	20.00

Issued to commemorate the opening of the Cross Island Highway, Taiwan.

No. 1257a contains imperf. copies of Nos. 1255 and 1257, with multicolored pictorial background and marginal inscriptions in red. Size: 144x103mm.

Red Overprint on Nos. 1237–1238 Chinese and English: "Welcome U.S. President Dwight D. Eisenhower 1960"

1960, June 18 *Perf. 12* Unwmkd.

1258	A145	$2 green	35	12
		a. Invtd. ovpt.	125.00	125.00
1259	A144	$3 dark blue	70	35

Issued to commemorate President Eisenhower's visit to China, June 18, 1960.

Phonopost
A154

1960, June 27 Without Gum

1260	A154	$2 red orange	50	15

Issued to publicize the Phonopost Service of the Chinese armed forces.

Two Horses and Groom, by Han Kan
A155

Paintings from Palace Museum, Taichung: $1, Two Riders, by Wei Yen. $1.60, Flowers and Birds by Hsiao Yung (vert.). $2, Pair of Mandarin Ducks by Monk Hui Ch'ung.

1960, Aug. 4 Photo. *Perf. 13*

No.	Type	Description	Unused	Used
1261	A155	$1 olive gray, blk. & brn.	65	25
1262	"	$1.40 bistre brown, black & terra cotta	75	25
1263	"	$1.60 multicolored	1.00	35
1264	"	$2 beige, black & gray green	1.65	60

Chinese paintings, 7th–11th centuries.

Youth Corps Flag and Summer Activities **A156**

Reforestation **A157**

Design: $3, similar to 50c (horiz.).

1960, Aug. 20 Engraved *Perf. 12*
Without Gum

No.	Type	Description	Unused	Used
1265	A156	50c slate green	20	8
1266	"	$3 copper brown	90	35

Summer activities of China Youth Corps.

1960, Aug. 29 Photo. *Perf. 13½x13*

Designs: $2, Protection of forest. $3, Timber industry.

No.	Type	Description	Unused	Used
1267	A157	$1 multicolored	30	8
1268	"	$2 "	85	35
1269	"	$3 multicolored	85	35
		a. Souvenir sheet of three	1.25	1.25

Issued to commemorate the Fifth World Forestry Congress, Seattle, Washington, Aug. 29–Sept. 10.

No. 1269a contains Nos. 1267–1269 assembled as a triptych, 65½x40mm. and imperf., but with simulated black perforations. Marginal inscriptions in carmine. Size of sheet: 99x144½mm.

Chu Kwang Tower, Quemoy **A158**

Diver **A159**

Lithographed
1960–61 *Perf. 12* Wmk. 323
Without Gum

No.	Type	Description	Unused	Used
1270	A158	3c lt. red brown	15	5
1271	"	40c pale violet	15	5
1272	"	50c orange ('61)	15	5
1273	"	60c rose lilac	15	5
1274	A158	80c pale green	15	5
1275	"	$1 gray grn. ('61)	1.15	5
1276	"	$1.20 gray olive	50	5
1277	"	$1.50 ultramarine	50	6
1278	"	$2 car. rose ('61)	1.20	8
1279	"	$2.50 pale blue	1.20	8
1280	"	$3 bluish green	75	8
1281	"	$3.20 lt. red brown	2.00	8
1282	"	$3.60 vio. bl. ('61)	1.75	18
1283	"	$4.50 vermilion	3.00	25
		Nos. 1270–1283 (14)	12.80	1.16

1962–64 Granite Paper
Without Gum

No.	Type	Description	Unused	Used
1270a	A158	3c lt. red brown	25	4
1270B	A158	10c emerald ('63)	60	4
1271a	"	40c pale violet	25	4
1274a	"	80c pale green	40	4
1275a	"	$1 gray green ('63)	1.75	4
1278a	"	$2 carmine rose	2.00	7
1281a	"	$3.20 red brown ('64)	2.25	6
1282A	"	$4 brt. bl. green	3.50	15
1283a	"	$4.50 vermilion	2.00	20
		Nos. 1270a–1283a (9)	13.00	68

Two types of No. 1271a: I. Seven lines in "0" of "40." II. Eight lines in "0."

Perf. 12½
1960, Oct. 25 Photo. Unwmkd.

Sports: 80c, Discus thrower. $2, Basketball. $2.50, Soccer. $3, Hurdling. $3.20, Runner.

No.	Type	Description	Unused	Used
1284	A159	50c ultra., yel. & orange	25	8
1285	"	80c rose claret, pur. & yel.	25	12
1286	"	$2 black, red org. & yel.	40	20
1287	"	$2.50 org. & black	70	25
1288	"	$3 multicolored	80	40
1289	"	$3.20 "	1.20	50
		Nos. 1284–1289 (6)	3.60	1.55

Bronze Wine Container, 1751–1111 B.C.
A160

Flat Bowl, 1111–771 B.C.
A161

Designs: $1, Cauldron, 1111–771 B.C. $1.20, Porcelain vase, 960–1126 A.D. $1.50, Perforated tube, 1111–771 B.C. $2, Jug in shape of monk's cap, 1368–1661 A.D. $2.50, Jade flower vase, 1368–1661, A.D.

Art Series I
1961–62 Photo. *Perf. 13*

No.	Type	Description	Unused	Used
1290	A160	80c light olive, black & dark violet	50	12
1291	"	$1 salmon, blue & black	55	15
1292	"	$1.20 yellow, brn. & ultra.	75	30
1293	"	$1.50 lilac, blue & sepia	75	40
1294	"	$2 pale green, dark green & red brn.	1.00	30
1295	"	$2.50 greenish blue & dk. vio.	1.25	35
		Nos. 1290–1295 (6)	4.75	1.62

Art Series II

Designs: 80c, Palace perfumer, 1662–1911. $1, Corn vase, 770–221 B.C. $2, Jade tankard, 960–1126 A.D. $4, Glazed washer, 1127–1279 A.D. $4.50, Jade chimera, 8 B.C.–206 A.D.

No.	Type	Description	Unused	Used
1296	A160	80c pink, brown, blue & yellow	30	7
1297	A160	$1 citron, black & brown	75	15
1298	A161	$1.50 salmon & indigo	85	40
1299	A160	$2 blue, black & rose	85	28
1300	A161	$4 red, black & bluish gray	3.00	28
1301	"	$4.50 greenish blue, blk. & brown	2.75	80
		Nos. 1296–1301 (6)	8.50	1.98

Art Series III
(1962)

Designs: 80c, Topaz twin wine vessels, 1662–1911 A.D. $1, Squat pouring vase, 1751–1111 B.C. $2.40, Vase, 1368–1661 A.D. $3, Wine vase, 1751–1111 B.C. $3.20, Covered porcelain jar, 1662–1911 A.D. $3.60, Perforated disc, 206 B.C.–8 A.D.

No.	Type	Description	Unused	Used
1302	A160	80c crimson, black & ochre	30	10
1303	"	$1 blue & violet black	30	10
1304	"	$2.40 henna brown, blk. & bl.	1.15	30
1305	"	$3 blue, black & pink	2.50	90
1306	"	$3.20 ultra., light grn. & red	3.00	20
1307	"	$3.60 yellow, black & brown	2.50	60
		Nos. 1302–1307 (6)	9.75	2.20

Issued to publicize ancient Chinese art treasures.

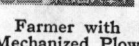

Farmer with Mechanized Plow
A162

Madame Chiang Kai-shek and League Emblem
A163

1961, Feb. 4 Engraved *Perf. 12*
Without Gum

No.	Type	Description	Unused	Used
1308	A162	80c rose violet	25	8
1309	"	$2 green	75	35
1310	"	$3.20 vermilion	75	15

Issued to publicize the 1961 agricultural census.

Photogravure
1961, March 8 *Perf. 13* Unwmkd.
Portrait in Black

No.	Type	Description	Unused	Used
1311	A163	80c light green & car. rose	25	8
1312	"	$1 yellow green & car. rose	1.00	22
1313	"	$2 orange brown & car. rose	1.00	20
1314	"	$3.20 lilac & car. rose	2.00	40

Issued to commemorate the 10th anniversary of the Chinese Women's Anti-Aggression League.

Spiny Lobster and Mail Order Service Emblem
A164

Jeme Tien-yow and Pataling Tunnel
A165

1961, Mar. 20 Engraved *Perf. 11½*
Without Gum

No.	Type	Description	Unused	Used
1315	A164	$3 slate green	90	20

Issued to publicize the mail order service for consumer goods.

1961, Apr. 26 *Perf. 11½*
Without Gum

Design: $2, Jeme Tien-yow and 1909 locomotive (horiz.).

No.	Type	Description	Unused	Used
1316	A165	80c lilac	20	8
1317	"	$2 black	90	35

Issued to commemorate the centenary of the birth of Jeme Tien-yow, builder of the Peking-Kalgan railroad.

Map of China inscribed: "Recovery of the Mainland"
A166

Pres. Chiang Kai-shek
A167

1961, May 20 Photo. *Perf. 13½*

No.	Type	Description	Unused	Used
1318	A166	80c multicolored	50	12
1319	A167	$2 "	1.75	60
		a. Souvenir sheet of two	1.25	1.25

Issued to commemorate the first anniversary of Pres. Chiang Kai-shek's 3rd term inauguration.

No. 1319a contains one each of Nos. 1318–1319, imperf. with simulated perforations and red marginal inscription. Without gum. Size: 135x100mm.

Convair 880-M, Biplane of 1921 and Flag
A168

1961, July 1 *Perf. 13x12½*

No.	Type	Description	Unused	Used
1320	A168	$10 multicolored	2.00	30

40th anniversary of civil air service.

Sun Yat-sen and Chiang Kai-shek
A169

Flag and Map of China
A170

Photogravure

1961, Oct. 10 *Perf. 13½* Unwmkd.

1321 A169 80c gray, lt. brown & slate 75 8
1322 A170 $5 gray, ultra., red & beige 2.25 70
a. Souvenir sheet of two 2.25 2.25

Issued to commemorate the 50th anniversary of the Republic of China. No. 1322a contains one each of Nos. 1321–1322, imperf. with simulated perforations and red marginal inscription. No gum. Size of sheet: 135x99mm.

Lotus Pond
A172

Green Lake
A171

Oil Refinery
A173

Taiwan Scenery: $2, Sun-Moon Lake. $3.20, Wulai waterfalls.

Perf. 13½x14, 14x13½

1961, Oct. 31 Unwmkd.

1323 A171 80c multicolored 45 12
1324 A172 $1 " 1.25 35
1325 " $2 " 1.25 25
1326 A171 $3.20 " 2.25 60

1961, Nov. 14 *Perf. 11½*

Designs: $1.50, Steel works. $2.50, Aluminum plant. $3.20, Fertilizer plant (horiz.).

1327 A173 80c multicolored 30 10
1328 " $1.50 " 1.00 70
1329 " $2.50 " 1.00 60
1330 " $3.20 " 1.75 35

Issued to publicize Chinese industrial development and in connection with the Golden Jubilee Convention of the Chinese Institute of Engineers, Nov. 13–16.

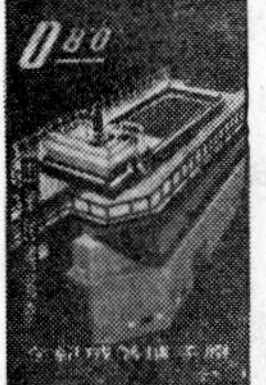

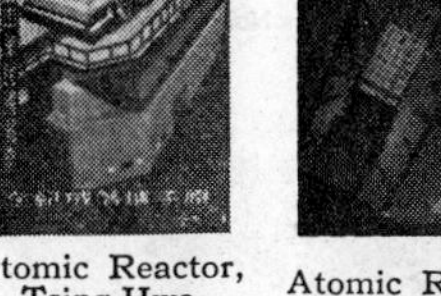

Atomic Reactor, Tsing-Hwa University
A174

Atomic Reactor in Operation
A175

Design: $3.20, Atomic symbol and laboratory, Tsing-Hwa (horiz.).

1961-62 Photogravure *Perf. 12½*

1331 A174 80c multicolored 75 10
1332 A175 $2 multi. ('62) 1.85 1.10
1333 " $3.20 multi. ('62) 2.50 65

Issued to commemorate the inauguration on Apr. 13, 1961, of the first Chinese atomic reactor at the National Tsing-Hwa University Institute of Nuclear Science.

Microwave Reflector and Telegraph Wires
A176

Design: $3.20, Microwave parabolic antenna and mountains (horiz.).

1961, Dec. 28 *Perf. 12½*

1334 A176 80c multicolored 35 12
1335 " $3.20 " 1.90 70

Issued to commemorate the 80th anniversary of Chinese telecommunications.

Mechanical Postal Equipment and Twine Tying Machine—A176a

Perf. 11½

1962, Mar. 20 Engraved Wmk. 323

Without Gum

1336 A176a 80c chocolate 50 10

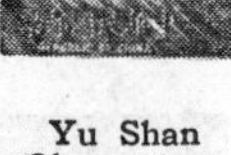

Yu Shan Observatory
A177

Observation Balloon, Earth and Cumulus Clouds
A178

Design: $1, Map showing route of typhoon Pamela, Sept. 1961 (horiz.).

1962 Without Gum

1337 A177 80c brown 15 8
1338 A178 $1 bluish black 1.50 30
1339 " $2 green 1.50 65

Issue dates: 80c, $2, Mar. 23; $1, May 7. World Meteorological Day, Mar. 23.

Child Receiving Milk, U.N. Emblem—A179

1962, Apr. 4 Without Gum

1340 A179 80c rose red 15 8
1341 " $3.20 green 1.25 65
a. Souvenir sheet of 2 75 75

Issued to commemorate the 15th anniversary of UNICEF (United Nations Children's Emergency Fund.) No. 1341a contains one each of Nos. 1340–1341 imperf. with simulated perforations and red marginal inscription. Size: 135x100mm.

Malaria Eradication Emblem
A180

Photogravure

1962, Apr. 7 *Perf. 12½* Unwmkd.

1342 A180 80c dk. blue, red & lt. green 40 8
1343 " $3.60 brown, pink & green 1.00 65

Issued for the World Health Organization drive to eradicate malaria.

Yu Yu-jen
A181

Cheng Ch'eng-kung (Koxinga)
A182

1962, Apr. 24 *Perf. 13*

1344 A181 80c gray, black & pink 50 10

Issued to honor Yu Yu-jen, newspaper reporter, revolutionary leader and co-worker of Sun Yat-sen, on his 84th birthday.

1962, Apr. 29

1345 A182 80c deep claret 50 8
1346 " $2 dark green 1.00 25

Issued to commemorate the 300th anniversary (in 1961) of the recovery of Taiwan from the Dutch by Koxinga.

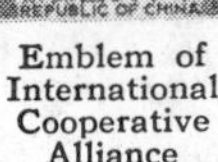

Emblem of International Cooperative Alliance
A183

Clasped Hands Across Globe
A184

Engraved

1962, July 7 *Perf. 12* Wmk. 323

Without Gum

1347 A183 80c brown 40 8
1348 A184 $2 violet 1.00 40

Issued to publicize the International Cooperative Movement and to commemorate the 40th International Cooperative Day, July 7, 1962.

Mansion Type of 1958

1962, July 20 Without Gum

1349 A135 $5 gray green 1.75 6
a. Granite paper ('63) 1.90 10
1350 " $5.60 violet 2.00 8
a. Granite paper ('63) 3.00 10
1351 " $6 orange 2.25 10
a. Granite paper ('63) 3.25 10

"Art and Science"
A185

Designs: $2, "Education," book and UNESCO emblem (horiz.). $3.20, "Communications," globes (horiz.).

1962, Aug. 28 *Perf. 12* Wmk. 323

Without Gum

1352 A185 80c lilac rose 25 12
1353 " $2 rose claret 50 40
1354 " $3.20 yellow green 75 30

Issued to publicize the activities of UNESCO in China.

Emperor T'ai Tsung, T'ang Dynasty, 627–649—A186

Emperors: $2, T'ai Tsu, Sung dynasty, 960–975. $3.20, T'ai Tsu, Yuan dynasty (Genghis Khan), 1206–27. $4, T'ai Tsu, Ming dynasty, 1368–98.

1962, Sept. 20 Photo. Unwmkd.

1355 A186 80c multicolored 1.00 18
1356 " $2 " 3.50 1.10
1357 " $3.20 " 4.00 85
1358 " $4 " 3.50 1.20

Lions International Emblem
A187

1962, Oct. 8 *Perf. 13*

1359 A187 80c multicolored 50 8
1360 " $3.60 " 1.50 65
a. Souvenir sheet of 2 1.50 1.50

Issued to commemorate the 45th anniversary of Lions International. No. 1360a contains one each of Nos. 1359–1360, imperf. with simulated perforations and gold marginal inscription. Size: 100x75mm.

Pole Vaulting
A188

Shooting
A189

1962, Oct. 25 *Perf. 13* Unwmkd.

1361 A188 80c multicolored 60 12
1362 A189 $3.20 " 1.25 35

Sports meet.

Young Farmers and 4-H Emblem — A190

Flag and Liner of China Merchants' Steam Navigation Co. — A191

Design: $3.20, 4-H emblem and rice.

Engraved

1962, Dec. 7 *Perf. 12* Wmk. 323

Without Gum

1363 A190 80c carmine 30 5
1364 " $3.20 green 70 38
a. Souvenir sheet of 2 75 75

Issued to commemorate the 10th anniversary of the 4-H Club in China. No. 1364a contains one each of Nos. 1363-1364, imperf. with simulated perforations and red lithographed marginal inscription. Size: 135x100mm.

Photogravure

1962, Dec. 16 *Perf. 13½* Unwmkd.

Design: $3.60, Company's Pacific navigation chart and freighter (horiz.).

1365 A191 80c multicolored 60 8
1366 " $3.60 " 2.00 65

Issued to commemorate the 90th anniversary of the China Merchants' Steam Navigation Co., Ltd.

Farm Woman, Tractor and Plane Dropping Food over Mainland — A192

Photogravure

1963, Mar. 21 *Perf. 12½* Unwmkd.

1367 A192 $10 multicolored 2.75 70

Issued for the "Freedom from Hunger" campaign of the U.N. Food and Agriculture Organization.

Torch, Young Couple and Martyrs' Monument, Canton — A193

Engraved

1963, Mar. 29 *Perf. 11½* Wmk. 323

Without Gum

1368 A193 80c purple 25 8
1369 " $3.20 green 75 30

Issued for the 20th Youth Day.

Swallows, Pagoda and AOPU Emblem — A194

Designs: $2, Northern gannet (horiz.). $6, Japanese crane and pine.

Photogravure

1963, Apr. 1 *Perf. 13* Unwmkd.

1370 A194 80c multicolored 1.50 12
1371 " $2 " 1.50 12
1372 " $6 " 4.00 1.40

Issued to commemorate the first anniversary of the formation of the Asian-Oceanic Postal Union, AOPU.

Refugee Girl (Li Ying) and Map of China — A195

Refugees Fleeing Mainland — A196

Engraved

1963, June 27 *Perf. 11½* Wmk. 323

Without Gum

1373 A195 80c bluish black 50 15
1374 A196 $3.20 deep claret 1.25 22

Issued to commemorate the first anniversary of the evacuation of Chinese mainland refugees from Hong Kong to Taiwan. Designs from photographs of refugees.

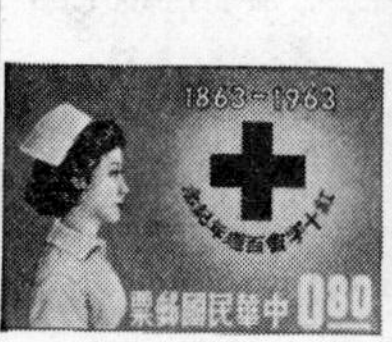

Nurse and Red Cross — A197

Basketball Player, Stadium and Asian Cup — A198

Design: $10, Globe and Red Cross.

Photogravure

1963, Sept. 1 *Perf. 12½* Unwmkd.

1375 A197 80c black & car. 1.00 15
1376 " $10 slate, gray & carmine 4.50 1.75

Centenary of International Red Cross.

Engraved

1963, Nov. 20 *Perf. 12* Wmk. 323

Without Gum

Design: $2, Hands reaching for ball and Asian cup.

1377 A198 80c lilac rose 30 5
1378 " $2 violet 1.50 60

Issued to commemorate the 2nd Asian Basketball Championship, Taipei, Nov. 20.

U.N. Emblem, Torch and Men — A199

Scales and Men of Various Races — A200

1963, Dec. 10 *Perf. 11½* Wmk. 323

Without Gum

1379 A199 80c bright green 25 4
1380 A200 $3.20 maroon 75 16

Universal Declaration of Human Rights, 15th anniversary.

Village and Orchids — A201

"Kindle the Fire of Conscience" — A202

Perf. 13½x13

1963, Dec. 17 Photo. Unwmkd.

1381 A201 40c multicolored 75 8
1382 A202 $4.50 " 2.50 60

Issued to commemorate the contribution of the Good-People-Good-Deeds campaign to improve ethical standards.

Sun Yat-sen and Book, "Three Principles of the People" — A203

1963, Dec. 25 *Perf. 13*

1383 A203 $5 blue & multi. 1.85 25

"Land-to-the-Tillers" program, 10th anniversary.

Torch — A204

Hands Unchained — A205

Engraved

1964, Jan. 23 *Perf. 11½* Wmk. 323

Without Gum

1384 A204 80c red orange 15 4
1385 A205 $3.20 indigo 75 12

Liberty Day, 10th anniversary.

Broadleaf Cactus — A206

Wu Chih-hwei — A207

Designs: $1, Crab cactus. $3.20, Nopalxochia. $5, Grizzly bear cactus.

Photogravure

1964, Feb. 27 *Perf. 12½* Unwmkd.

Plants in Original Colors

1386 A206 80c dp. plum & fawn 30 7
1387 " $1 dk. bl. & carm. 90 35
1388 " $3.20 green 1.10 10
1389 " $5 lilac & yellow 1.65 30

Perf. 11½

1964, Mar. 25 Engraved Wmk. 323

Without Gum

1390 A207 80c black brown 50 5

Issued to commemorate the centenary of the birth of Wu Chih-hwei (1865-1953), politician and leader of the Kuomintang.

Chu Kwang Tower, Quemoy — A208

Lithographed

1964-66 *Perf. 13x12½* Wmk. 323

Granite Paper; Without Gum

1391 A208 3c sepia 4 4
1392 " 5c brt. yel. grn. ('65) 5 4
1393 " 10c yellow green 5 4
1394 " 20c slate green ('65) 7 4
1395 " 40c rose red 7 4
1396 " 50c brown 10 4
1397 " 80c orange ('65) 12 4
1398 " $1 violet ('65) 15 4
1399 " $1.50 brt. lilac ('66) 25 12
1400 " $2 lilac rose 25 4
1401 " $2.50 ultra. ('65) 25 4
1402 " $3 slate 40 10
1403 " $3.20 bright blue 50 4
1404 " $4 bright green 60 4
Nos. 1391-1404 (14) 2.90 70

Nurses Holding Candles — A209

Florence Nightingale and Student Nurse — A210

1964, May 12 Engr. *Perf. 11½*

Without Gum

1406 A209 80c violet blue 35 5
1407 A210 $4 red 1.25 18

Issued for Nurses Day.

Shihmen Reservoir — A211

Designs: $1, Irrigation system. $3.20, Main dam and power plant. $5, Spillway.

Photogravure

1964, June 14 *Perf. 12½* Unwmkd.

1408 A211 80c multicolored 50 10
1409 " $1 " 50 10
1410 " $3.20 " 1.00 12
1411 " $5 " 2.50 60

Completion of Shihmen Reservoir.

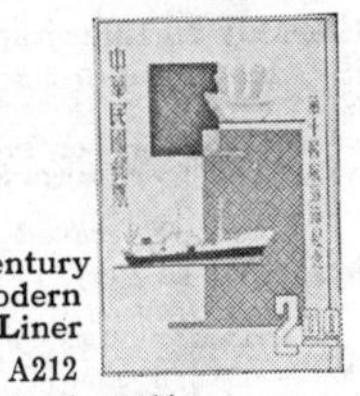
15th Century Ship, Modern Liner
A212

Perf. 11½

1964, July 11 Engr. Wmk. 323
Without Gum

1412	A212	$2 orange	30	5
1413	"	$3.60 bright green	60	15

China's 10th Navigation Day.

Bananas
A213

Photogravure
1964, July 25 *Perf. 14* Unwmkd.
Multicolored

1414	A213	80c *shown*	50	5
1415	"	$1 *Oranges*	1.00	35
1416	"	$3.20 *Pineapple*	1.25	18
1417	"	$4 *Watermelon*	2.00	55

Artillery, Warships, Jet Fighters
A214

Engraved
1964, Sept. 3 *Perf. 11½* Wmk. 323
Without Gum

1418	A214	80c dark blue	20	5
1419	"	$6 violet brown	1.30	28

Issued for the 10th Armed Forces Day.

Unisphere, Flags of China and U.S.
A215

Chinese Pavilion, N.Y. World's Fair
A216

1964, Sept. 10 Photo. Unwmkd.

1420	A215	80c violet & multi.	50	6
1421	A216	$5 blue & multi.	2.25	38

New York World's Fair, 1964–65.
See also Nos. 1450–1451.

Cowboy Carrying Calf, and Ranch
A217

Bicycling
A218

Engraved
1964, Sept. 24 *Perf. 11½* Wmk. 323
Without Gum

1422	A217	$2 brown lake	45	8
1423	"	$4 dk. violet blue	1.15	35

Animal Protection Week, Sept. 24–30.

1964, Oct. 10 Without Gum

Sports: $1, Runner. $3.20, Gymnast on rings. $10, High jump.

1424	A218	80c violet blue	20	5
1425	"	$1 rose red	40	8
1426	"	$3.20 dull blue grn.	90	8
1427	"	$10 lilac	2.50	1.20

18th Olympic Games, Tokyo, Oct. 10–25.

Hsü Kuang-chi
A219

Pharmaceutical Industry
A220

Textile Industry
A221

1964, Nov. 8 Engraved *Perf. 11½*
Without Gum

1428	A219	80c indigo	60	5

Issued to honor Hsü Kuang-chi (1562–1633), scholar and statesman.

1964, Nov. 11 Photo. Unwmkd.

Designs: $2, Chemical industry. $3.60, Cement industry.

1429	A220	40c multicolored	25	5
1430	A221	$1.50 "	85	35
1431	A220	$2 "	1.00	12
1432	A221	$3.60 "	1.65	22

Dr. Sun Yat-sen
A222

Eleanor Roosevelt and Scales of Justice
A223

1964, Nov. 24 Engraved Wmk. 323
Without Gum

1433	A222	80c green	50	5
1434	"	$3.60 purple	1.00	18

Founding of the Kuomintang by Sun Yat-sen, 70th anniversary.

Photogravure
1964, Dec. 10 *Perf. 13* Unwmkd.

1435	A223	$10 violet & brn.	1.10	30

Issued to honor Eleanor Roosevelt (1884–1962) on the 16th anniversary of the Universal Declaration of Human Rights.

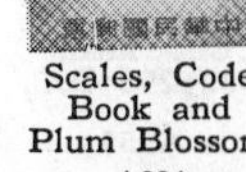
Scales, Code Book and Plum Blossom
A224

Rotary Emblem and Mainspring
A225

Engraved
1965, Jan. 11 *Perf. 11½* Wmk. 323
Without Gum

1436	A224	80c carmine rose	25	5
1437	"	$3.20 dull slate grn.	65	15

The 20th Judicial Day.

1965, Feb. 23 *Perf. 11½* Wmk. 323
Without Gum

1438	A225	$1.50 vermilion	25	5
1439	"	$2 emerald	75	12
1440	"	$2.50 blue	75	22

Rotary International, 60th anniversary.

Double Carp Design
A226

Madame Chiang Kai-shek
A227

Engraved
1965, Mar. 29 *Perf. 11½* Wmk. 323
Granite Paper; Without Gum

1441	A226	$5 purple	2.50	10
1442	"	$5.60 deep blue	1.50	30
1443	"	$6 brown	1.25	15
1444	"	$10 lilac rose	2.50	10
1445	"	$20 rose carmine	2.75	30
1446	"	$50 green	6.00	90
1447	"	$100 crimson rose	15.00	2.00
		Nos. 1441–1447 (7)	31.50	3.85

1965, Apr. 17 Photo. Unwmkd.

1448	A227	$2 multicolored	1.00	10
1449	"	$6 salmon & multi.	3.00	90

Chinese Women's Anti-Aggression League, 15th anniversary.

Unisphere and Chinese Pavilion
A228

"100 Birds Paying Homage to Queen Phoenix" and Unisphere
A229

1965, May 8

1450	A228	$2 blue & multi.	1.00	10
1451	A229	$10 red, ocher & bister	4.00	60

New York World's Fair, 1964–65.

ITU Emblem, Old and New Communication Equipment—A230

Design: $5, similar to 80c (vert.).

Perf. 13½x13, 13x13½
1965, May 17 Photo. Unwmkd.

1452	A230	80c multicolored	22	8
1453	"	$5 "	1.50	40

Issued to commemorate the centenary of the International Telecommunication Union.

Red Sea Bream
A231

Fish: 80c, White pomfret. $2, Skipjack (vert.). $4, Moonfish.

1965, July 1 *Perf. 13*

1454	A231	40c multicolored	25	3
1455	"	80c "	50	3
1456	"	$2 "	75	8
1457	"	$4 "	1.50	25

Issued for Fishermen's Day.

Confucius
A232

ICY Emblem
A233

Portraits: $2.50, Yueh Fei. $3.50, Wen Tien-hsiang. $3.60, Mencius.

Engraved
1965–66 *Perf. 11½* Wmk. 323
Without Gum

1458	A232	$1 deep carmine	50	4
1459	"	$2.50 blk. brn.	50	8
1460	"	$3.50 dark red	1.00	12
1461	"	$3.60 dark blue	1.50	15

Issue dates: Nos. 1458, 1461, Sept. 28, 1965. Nos. 1459–1460, Sept. 3, 1966.
The $2.50 and $3.50 have colored background.
See also Nos. 1507–1508.

Photogravure
1965, Oct. 24 *Perf. 13* Unwmkd.

Design: $6, ICY emblem (horiz.).

1462	A233	$2 brn., blk. & gold	45	8
1463	"	$6 bright green, red & gold	1.75	80

International Cooperation Year, 1965.

Street Crossing and Traffic Light
A234

Sun Yat-sen
A235

Engraved
1965, Nov. 1 *Perf. 11½* Wmk. 323
Without Gum

1464	A234	$1 brown violet	50	5
1465	"	$4 crimson rose	90	18

Issued to publicize traffic safety.

Photogravure
1965, Nov. 12 *Perf. 13½* Unwmkd.

Designs: $4, Dr. Sun Yat-sen, portrait at right. $5, Sun Yat-sen and flags (horiz.).

1466	A235	$1 multicolored	50	8
1467	"	$4 "	1.00	18
1468	"	$5 "	2.50	90

Children with New Year's Firecrackers
A236

Dragon Dance, "Dragon Playing Ball"
A237

1965, Dec. 1 Photo. *Perf. 13*

1469	A236	$1 multicolored	1.00	10
1470	A237	$4.50 "	1.00	60

Lien Po from "Marshal and Prime Minister Reconciled"
A238

Facial Paintings for Chinese Operas: $3, Kuan Yü from "Reunion at Ku City." $4, Gen. Chang Fei from "The Battle of Chang Pan Hill." $6, Buddha from "The Flower-Scattering Angel."

1966, Feb. 15 *Perf. 11½* Unwmkd.

1471	A238	$1 olive & multi.	2.00	25
1472	"	$3 multicolored	2.00	18
1473	"	$4 "	2.00	25
1474	"	$6 verm. & multi.	3.50	1.65

Postal Service Emblem Held by Carrier Pigeon
A239

Stone, Mt. Tai-wu, Quemoy, and Mailman
A240

Designs (postal service emblem and): $3, Postal Museum. $4, Mailman climbing symbolic slope.

1966, Mar. 20 Photo. *Perf. 12½*

1475	A239	$1 green & multi.	50	8
1476	A240	$2 multicolored	50	8
1477	"	$3 "	75	12
1478	A239	$4 "	1.50	38

China postal service, 70th anniversary.

Fishing on a Snowy Day, "Five Dynasties" (907–960)
A241

Paintings from Palace Museum: $3.50, Calves on the Plain, Sung artist (960–1126). $4.50, Winter landscape, Sung artist (960–1126). $5, Magpies, by Lin Ch'un, Southern Sung dynasty (1127–1279).

1966, May 20 Photo. *Perf. 13*

1479	A241	$2.50 blk., brown & red	1.00	8
1480	"	$3.50 bister brown, blk. & gray	75	10
1481	"	$4.50 black, buff & slate	75	30
1482	"	$5 multi.	2.00	40

Issued to commemorate the inauguration of Pres. Chiang Kai-shek for a fourth term.

Dragon Boat Race
A242

Lion Dance
A243

Design: $4, Lady Chang O flying to the Moon.

1966 Unwmkd.

1483	A242	$2.50 multicolored	1.50	8
1484	"	$4 "	1.00	8
1485	A243	$6 "	75	20

Issued for the Dragon Boat, Mid-Autumn and Lunar New Year Festivals. Issue dates: $2.50, June 23; $4, Sept. 29; $6, Nov. 26.

Flags of China and Argentina
A244

1966, July 9 Photogravure *Perf. 13*

1486	A244	$10 multicolored	1.20	22

Issued to commemorate the 150th anniversary of Argentina's Independence.

Lin Sen
A245

Flying Geese
A246

Engraved

1966, Aug. 1 *Perf. 11½* Wmk. 323

Without Gum

1487	A245	$1 dark brown	50	8

Issued to commemorate the centenary of the birth of Lin Sen (1867–1943), Chairman of the Nationalist Government of China (1931–43).

1966–67 *Perf. 11½ rough*

Granite Paper; Without Gum

1496	A246	$3.50 brown	25	5
1497	"	$4 vermilion	35	5
1498	"	$4.50 bright green	40	12
1499	"	$5 rose lilac	45	5
1500	"	$5.50 yel. grn. ('67)	40	12
1501	"	$6 bright blue	1.50	35
1502	"	$6.50 violet	55	25
1503	"	$7 black	55	5
1504	A246	$8 car. rose ('67)	1.00	12
		Nos. 1496-1504 (9)	5.45	1.16

The $4.50, $5, $6, $7 and $8 were reissued with gum in 1970–71.

Pres. Chiang Kai-shek in Chung San Robe
A247

Design: $5, Chiang Kai-shek in marshal's uniform.

Photogravure

1966, Oct. 31 *Perf. 13* Unwmkd.

1505	A247	$1 multicolored	35	10
1506	"	$5 "	1.60	45

Issued to commemorate Chiang Kai-shek's inauguration for a fourth term as president, May 20, 1966.

Famous Men Type of 1965–66 with Frame Line

Portraits: No. 1507, Tsai Yuan-pei (1868–1940), educator. No. 1508, Chiu Ching (1875–1907), woman educator and revolutionist.

Engraved

1967 *Perf. 11½* Wmk. 323

Without Gum

1507	A232	$1 violet blue	40	8
1508	"	$1 black	40	6

Issue dates: No. 1507, Jan. 11. No. 1508, July 15.
No. 1507 is on granite paper.

Motorized Mailman and Microwave Station
A248

"Transportation" and Radar Weather Station
A249

Photogravure

1967, Mar. 15 *Perf. 13* Unwmkd.

1511	A248	$1 multicolored	40	5
1512	A249	$5 "	90	18

Issued to publicize the progress in communication and transportation services.

Pres. Chiang Kai-shek and Chinese Flag
A250

Chu Yuan, 332–295 B.C.
A251

Design: $4, Different frame.

1967, May 20 Lithographed *Perf. 13*

1513	A250	$1 multicolored	75	8
1514	"	$4 "	1.50	15

First anniversary of President Chiang Kai-shek's 4th-term inauguration.

Engraved

1967, June 12 *Perf. 11½* Wmk. 323

Portraits: $2, Li Po (705–760). $2.50, Tu Fu (712–770). $3, Po Chu-i (772–846).

Granite Paper; Without Gum

1515	A251	$1 black	50	5
1516	"	$2 brown	75	8
1517	"	$2.50 brown black	75	15
1518	"	$3 greenish black	75	12

Issued for Poets' Day.

Hotei, Wood Carving
A252

World Map
A253

Handicrafts: $2.50, Vase and plate. $3, Dolls. $5, Palace lanterns.

Photogravure

1967, Aug. 12 *Perf. 11½* Unwmkd.

1519	A252	$1 gray & multi.	25	5
1520	"	$2.50 multicolored	50	8
1521	"	$3 "	75	12
1522	"	$5 "	1.25	40

Taiwan handicraft industry.

Engraved

1967, Sept. 25 *Perf. 11½* Wmk. 323

Granite Paper; Without Gum

1523	A253	$1 vermilion	10	6
1524	"	$5 blue	45	18

Issued to commemorate the first Conference of the World Anti-Communist League, WACL, Taipei, Sept. 25–29.

Players on Stilts: "The Fisherman and the Woodcutter"
A254

Photogravure

1967, Oct. 10 *Perf. 13* Unwmkd.

1525	A254	$4.50 multicolored	50	18

Issued for the 56th National Day.

Maroon Oriole—A255

Formosan Birds: $1, Formosan barbet (vert.). $2.50, Formosan green pigeon. $3, Formosan blue magpie. $5, Crested serpent eagle (vert.). $8, Mikado pheasants.

1967, Nov. 25 Photo. *Perf. 11*

Granite Paper

1526	A255	$1 multicolored	15	12
1527	"	$2 "	30	12
1528	"	$2.50 "	35	18
1529	"	$3 "	40	18
1530	"	$5 "	80	25
1531	"	$8 "	1.10	65
		Nos. 1526-1531 (6)	3.10	1.50

Chung Hsing Pagoda
A256

Buddha, Changhua
A257

Designs: $2.50, Seashore, Yeh Liu Park. $5, National Palace Museum, Taipei.

Photogravure

1967, Dec. 10 *Perf. 13* **Unwmkd.**

1532	A256	$1 multicolored	25	5
1533	A257	$2.50 "	75	25
1534	"	$4 "	1.00	15
1535	"	$5 "	1.50	38

Issued for International Tourist Year 1967.

China Park, Manila, and Flags
A258

1967, Dec. 30 *Perf. 13½*

1536	A258	$1 multicolored	20	4
1537	"	$5 "	70	18

Sino-Philippine Friendship Year 1966–67.

Sun Yat-sen Building, Yangmingshan
A259 A259a

Perf. 13x12½

1968–75 Lithographed Wmk. 323

Granite Paper

1538	A259	5c light brown	10	4
1539	"	10c greenish black	10	4
1540	"	50c brt. rose lilac	10	3
	a.	Booklet pane of 4	25	
1541	A259	$1 vermilion	15	3
	a.	Booklet pane of 4	75	
1542	A259	$1.50 emerald	25	5
1543	"	$2 plum	30	4
1544	"	$2.50 blue	30	4
	a.	Booklet pane of 4	1.25	
1545	A259	$3 greenish blue	50	5
		Nos. 1538–1545 (8)	1.80	32

Coil Stamps

Perf. 13 Horiz.

Photo. Unwmkd.

1546	A259a	$1 car. rose ('70)	20	12
1547	"	$1 verm. ('75)	15	5

Issue dates: 50c, $1, $2.50, Jan. 23, 1968; No. 1546, Mar. 20, 1970; No. 1547, Jan. 28, 1975; others July 11, 1968.

Inscription on No. 1546 is in color with white background. On No. 1547 it is white with colored background.

Harvesting Sugar Cane
A260

Jade Cabbage, 1662–1911
A261

Photogravure

1968, Mar. 1 *Perf. 13* **Unwmkd.**

1548	A260	$1 olive & multi.	35	10
1549	"	$4 multicolored	50	25

Taiwan sugar industry.

1968, Mar. 29 *Perf. 13* **Unwmkd.**

Ancient Art Treasures: $1.50, Jade battle axe. $2, Porcelain flower bowl, 960–1126 A.D. (horiz.). $2.50, Cloisonné enamel vase, 1723–1736 A.D. $4, Agate flower holder in shape of finger citrus, 1662–1911 A.D. (horiz.). $5, Sacrificial kettle, 1111–771 B.C.

1550	A261	$1 rose & multi.	25	8
1551	"	$1.50 blue & multi.	50	18
1552	"	$2 blue & multi.	50	10
1553	"	$2.50 dull rose & multi.	50	22
1554	"	$4 pink & multi.	50	25
1555	"	$5 blue & multi.	75	35
		Nos. 1550–1555 (6)	3.00	1.18

View of City in Cathay (1)—A262

Views: No. 1557, City and wall of Forbidden City (2). No. 1558, Wall at right, bridge at left (3). No. 1559, Queen's ship landing at left (4). No. 1560, Palace (5). $5, City wall and gate. $8, Suburb around Great Bridge. Design from scroll "A City in Cathay," painted 1736.

1968, June 18 Photo. *Perf. 13½*

Size: 50x29mm.

1556	A262	$1 multicolored	25	9
1557	"	$1 "	25	9
1558	"	$1 "	25	9
1559	"	$1 "	25	9
1560	"	$1 "	25	9

Size: 60x31mm. *Perf. 13x13½*

1561	A262	$5 multicolored	1.00	70
1562	"	$8 "	1.50	75
		Nos. 1556–1562 (7)	3.75	1.90

Nos. 1556–1560 printed se-tenant in sheet of 50 with horizontal strips of five containing one of each.

See also Nos. 1610–1614.

Entrance Gate, Taroko Gorge
A263

Design: $8, Sun Yat-sen Building, Yangmingshan.

1968, Feb. 12 Photo. *Perf. 13*

1563	A263	$5 multicolored	70	22
1564	"	$8 "	70	22

The 17th Annual Conference of the Pacific Area Travel Association.

Vice President Chen Cheng
A264

Flying Geese
A265

1968, Mar. 5

1565	A264	$1 brown & multi.	50	5

Issued in memory of Vice President Chen Cheng (1898–1965).

Lithographed

1968, Mar. 20 *Perf. 12* **Wmk. 323**

Granite Paper

1566	A265	$1 vermilion	28	12

Souvenir Sheet

Imperf.

1567	A265	$3 green	50	50

Issued to commemorate the 90th anniversary of Chinese postage stamps. No. 1567 contains one stamp with simulated perforations, yellow decorative margin with red inscription. Size: 75x100mm.

WHO Emblem and "20"
A266

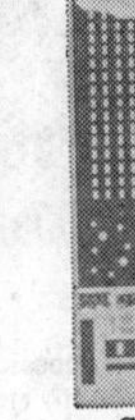

Symbolic Water Cycle
A267

1968, Apr. 7 Engraved *Perf. 12*

Granite Paper

1568	A266	$1 green	25	5
1569	"	$5 scarlet	50	30

Issued to commemorate the 20th anniversary of the World Health Organization.

Lithographed

1968, June 6 *Perf. 11½* **Wmk. 323**

Granite Paper

1570	A267	$1 green & orange	25	8
1571	"	$4 brt. blue & org.	50	8

Hydrological Decade (UNESCO) 1965–74.

Broadcasting to Mainland China
A268

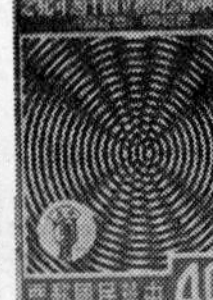

Dual Carriers for F.M. Broadcasting
A269

Lithographed

1968, Aug. 1 *Perf. 12* **Wmk. 323**

Granite Paper

1572	A268	$1 blue, violet blue & gray	20	6
1573	A269	$4 lt. ultramarine & vermilion	50	12

Issued to commemorate the 40th anniversary of the Broadcasting Corporation of China, and the inauguration of frequency modulation broadcasting.

Human Rights Flame
A270

Crop Improvement and Extension Work
A271

1968, Sept. 3 **Granite Paper**

1574	A270	$1 multicolored	25	12
1575	"	$5 "	50	15

International Human Rights Year 1968.

Lithographed

1968, Sept. 30 *Perf. 12* **Wmk. 323**

Granite Paper

1576	A271	$1 yellow, bister & dark brown	25	5
1577	"	$5 yellow, emerald & dark green	60	40

Joint Commission on Rural Reconstruction, 20th anniversary.

Javelin
A272

Designs: $2.50, Weight lifting. $5, Pole vault (horiz.). $8, Woman hurdling (horiz.).

Photogravure

1968, Oct. 12 *Perf. 13* **Unwmkd.**

1578	A272	$1 multicolored	20	5
1579	"	$2.50 "	30	12
1580	"	$5 "	50	10
1581	"	$8 pink & multi.	75	28

Issued to commemorate the 19th Olympic Games, Mexico City, Oct. 12–27.

Pres. Chiang Kai-shek and Whampoa Military Academy
A273

Designs: $2, Pres. Chiang Kai-shek reviewing forces of the Northern Expedition. $2.50, Suppression of bandits, reconstruction work and New Life Movement emblem. $3.50, Marco Polo Bridge near Peking and victory parade, Nanking. $4, Original copy of Constitution of Republic of China. $5, Nationalist Chinese flag flying over mainland China.

1968, Oct. 31 *Perf. 11½x12*

1582	A273	$1 multicolored	35	7
1583	"	$2 "	50	18
1584	"	$2.50 "	50	15
1585	"	$3.50 "	60	12
1586	"	$4 "	75	35
1587	"	$5 "	1.00	35
		Nos. 1582–1587 (6)	3.70	1.22

Chiang Kai-shek's achievements for China.

Cock
A274

1968, Nov. 12 Litho. *Perf. 12*

Granite Paper

1588	A274	$1 pink & multi.	4.00	10
1589	"	$4.50 lilac & multi.	4.00	2.00

Issued for use on New Year's greetings.

Flag
A275

1968, Dec. 25 *Perf. 12½* Wmk. 323

Granite Paper

1590	A275	$1 multicolored	25	4
1591	"	$5 lt. blue & multi.	60	18

Constitution of the Republic of China, 20th anniversary.

Jade Belt Buckle, 1662–1911
A276

Ancient Art Treasures: $1.50, Yellow jade vase, 960–1126 A.D. (vert.). $2, Cloisonné enamel square teapot, 1662–1911 A.D. $2.50, Kuei, sacrificial bronze vessel, 722–481 B.C. $4, Heavenly ball vase, 1368–1661 A.D. (vert.). $5, Gourd-shaped vase, 1662–1911 A.D. (vert.).

Photogravure

1969, Jan. 15 *Perf. 13* Unwmkd.

1592	A276	$1 dull rose & multi.	20	5
1593	"	$1.50 rose & multi.	25	12
1594	"	$2 bright rose & multi.	25	10
1595	"	$2.50 light blue & multi.	40	15
1596	"	$4 tan & multi.	55	15
1597	"	$5 pale blue & multi.	70	30
		Nos. 1592–1597 (6)	2.35	87

Servicemen and Savings Emblem
A277

Engraved

1969, Feb. 1 *Perf. 12* Wmk. 323

Granite Paper

1598	A277	$1 dull red brown	20	4
1599	"	$4 deep blue	60	12

Issued to commemorate the 10th anniversary of the Military Savings Program.

Ti (Flute)
A278

Musical Instruments: $2.50, Sheng (13 bamboo pipes connected at the base). $4, P'i p'a (lute). $5, Cheng (zither).

Photogravure

1969, Mar. 16 *Perf. 13* Unwmkd.

1600	A278	$1 buff & multi.	15	5
1601	"	$2.50 lt. apple green & multi.	30	10
1602	"	$4 pink & multi.	60	30
1603	"	$5 lt. greenish blue & multi.	60	15

Sun Yat-sen Building and Kuomintang Emblem—A279

Double Carp Design
A280

1969, Mar. 29 Litho. *Perf. 13½*

1604	A279	$1 multicolored	25	5

Issued to commemorate the 10th National Congress of the Chinese Nationalist Party (Kuomintang), Mar. 29. A $2.50 stamp portraying Sun Yat-sen and Chiang Kai-shek was prepared but not issued.

Perf. 13½x12½

1969–74 Engr. Wmk. 323

Granite Paper

1606	A280	$10 dk. blue ('74)	75	15
	a.	Perf. 11½	1.50	15
1607	A280	$20 dk. brn. ('74)	1.75	20
	a.	Perf. 11½	2.00	20
1608	A280	$50 green ('74)	4.00	65
	a.	Perf. 11½	5.00	65
1609	A280	$100 brt. red ('74)	8.00	2.00
	a.	Perf. 11½	8.00	2.00

The 1969 issue is 27mm. high; 1974, 28mm. See No. 1980.

Bridal Procession—A281

Designs: No. 1610, Musicians and standard bearer from bridal procession. $2.50, Emigrant farm family in oxcart. $5, Art gallery. $8, Roadside food stands. Designs from scroll "A City in Cathay," painted in 1736. Nos. 1610–1611 printed se-tenant in sheets of 30 (6x5).

Photogravure

1969, May 20 *Perf. 13½* Unwmkd.

1610	A281	$1 multicolored	20	10
1611	"	$1 "	20	10
1612	"	$2.50 "	50	32
1613	"	$5 "	60	42
1614	"	$8 "	1.00	65
		Nos. 1610–1614 (5)	2.50	1.59

ILO Emblem
A282

Perf. 11½

1969, June 15 Engr. Wmk. 323

Granite Paper

1615	A282	$1 dark blue	15	5
1616	"	$8 dark carmine	60	30

International Labor Organization, 50th anniversary.

Family at Dinner Table and Dressing
A283

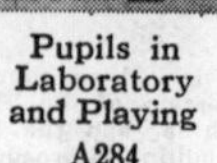

Pupils in Laboratory and Playing
A284

Designs: $2.50, Housecleaning and obeying traffic rules. $4, Recreation (music, fishing, basketball) and education.

Perf. 11½

1969, July 15 Engr. Wmk. 323

1617	A283	$1 brick red	12	5
1618	"	$2.50 blue	45	20
1619	"	$4 green	45	12

Model Citizen's Life Movement.

1969, Sept. 1 *Perf. 11½* Wmk. 323

Design: $1, $5, Pupils with book and various school activities (horiz.).

Granite Paper

1620	A284	$1 bright red	15	5
1621	"	$2.50 bright green	30	8
1622	"	$4 dark blue	40	12
1623	"	$5 brown	50	18

Issued to commemorate the first anniversary of the free 9-year education system.

Wild Flowers and Pheasants, by Lu Chih (Ming)
A285

Paintings: $2.50, Bamboo and birds, Sung dynasty. $5, Flowers and Birds, Sung dynasty. $8, Cranes and Flowers, by G. Castiglione, S.J. (1688–1766).

1969, Oct. 9 Photo. *Perf. 13½*

1624	A285	$1 multicolored	15	7
1625	"	$2.50 "	35	15
1626	"	$5 "	70	20
1627	"	$8 "	1.00	28

Golden Scepter Rose
A286

Rocket and Radar Station
A287

Roses: $1, "Charles Mollerin," called black rose. $5, Peace. $8, Josephine Bruce.

1969, Oct. 31 Litho. *Perf. 14*

1628	A286	$1 lt. vio. & multi.	20	8
1629	"	$2.50 lt. bl. & multi.	35	15
1630	"	$5 dull orange & multi.	65	45
1631	"	$8 apple green & multi.	65	30

Engraved

1969, Nov. 21 *Perf. 11½* Wmk. 323

1632	A287	$1 rose claret	25	5

The 30th Air Defense Day.

Symbol of International Cooperation
A288

Pekingese
A289

1969, Nov. 25

1633	A288	$1 rose claret	25	5
1634	"	$5 green	50	15

Issued to commemorate the 5th General Assembly of the Asian Parliamentary Union, Taipei, Nov. 24–28.

1969, Dec. 1 Lithographed *Perf. 12*

Granite Paper

1635	A289	50c red & multi.	20	5
1636	"	$4.50 grn. & multi.	1.85	50

Issued for use on New Year's greetings.

Satellite, Earth Station and Map of Taiwan
A290

Photogravure

1969, Dec. 28 *Perf. 13* Unwmkd.

1637	A290	$1 brown & multi.	15	8
1638	"	$5 vio. bl. & multi.	55	30
1639	"	$8 purple & multi.	75	40

Issued to commemorate the inauguration of the Communication Satellite Earth Station at Chin-Shan-Li, Dec. 28.

Agate Grinding Stone, 1662–1911
A291

Ancient Art Treasures: $1, Carved lacquer ware vase, 1662–1911 (vert.). $2, White jade Chin-li-chih melons, 1662–1911. $2.50, Black jade shepherd and ram, 206 B.C.–220 A.D. $4, Chien-lung twin porcelain vase, 1736–1796 (vert.). $5, Ju porcelain vase with 3 bulls, 960–1126 (vert.).

1970, Jan. 23

1640	A291	$1 lt. greenish bl. & multi.	12	7
1641	"	$1.50 pale blue & multicolored	18	12
1642	"	$2 green & multi.	20	12
1643	"	$2.50 pink & multi.	25	14
1644	"	$4 olive bister & multicolored	50	14
1645	"	$5 ultra. & multi.	65	28
		Nos. 1640–1645 (6)	1.90	87

Hsuan Chuang
A292

Chu Hsi
A293

Design: $2.50, Hua To.

Engraved

1970, Feb. 20 *Perf. 11½* Wmk. 323

Granite Paper

1646	A292	$1 carmine rose	22	8
1647	A293	$2.50 blue green	35	10
1648	"	$4 blue	40	18

Issued in memory of Hsuan Chuang (602–664), who propagated Buddhism in China; Chu Hsi (1130–1200), who developed Neo-Confucianism, and Hua To (3rd century A.D.) physician and surgeon.

EXPO '70 Pavilion, Emblem and Flags of Participants
A294

Design: $5, Chinese pavilion, EXPO '70 emblem, exhibition and Chinese flags.

Photogravure

1970, Mar. 13 *Perf. 13* Unwmkd.

1649	A294	$5 org. red & multi.	40	20
1650	"	$8 lt. blue & multi.	60	30

EXPO '70 International Exhibition, Osaka, Japan, Mar. 15–Sept. 13.

Nimbus III and WMO Emblem
A295

Design: $1, Agricultural meteorological station and tropical landscape (vert.).

Perf. 14x13½, 13½x14

1970, Mar. 23 Litho. Wmk. 323

Granite Paper

1651	A295	$1 green & multi.	25	8
1652	"	$8 blue & multi.	60	38

10th Annual World Meteorological Day.

Martyrs' Shrine, Taipei
A296

Shrine's Gate
A297

Photogravure

1970, Mar. 29 *Perf. 13* Unwmkd.

1653	A296	$1 multicolored	25	8
1654	A297	$8 "	60	32

Issued to commemorate the completion of the Martyrs' Shrine in Northern Taipei, dedicated to the memory of 72 young revolutionaries who died March 29, 1911.

Yueh Fei Fighting for Lost Territories
A298

Characters from Chinese Operas: $2.50, Emperor Shun and stepmother. $5, The Lady Warrior Chin Liang-yu. $8, Kuan Yu and groom.

1970, May 4 *Perf. 13½* Unwmkd.

1655	A298	$1 multicolored	20	10
1656	"	$2.50 "	35	20
1657	"	$5 "	55	30
1658	"	$8 "	75	40

"One Hundred Horses" (Detail), by Lang Shih-ning—A299

Three Horses Playing—A300

Designs (Horses): No. 1660, Trees in left background. No. 1661, Tree trunk in lower left corner. No. 1662, Group of trees at right. No. 1663, Barren tree at right. $8, Groom roping horses. Designs from scroll "One Hundred Horses" by Lang Shih-ning (Giuseppe Castiglione, 1688–1766). Nos. 1659–1663 printed se-tenant in sheets of 50 (5x10).

Photogravure

1970, June 18 *Perf. 13½* Unwmkd.

1659	A299	$1 multicolored	18	6
1660	"	$1 "	18	6
1661	"	$1 "	18	6
1662	"	$1 "	18	6
1663	"	$1 "	18	6
1664	A300	$5 bister & multi.	70	50
1665	"	$8 dull yel. & multi.	1.00	60
		Nos. 1659–1665 (7)	2.60	1.40

Lai-tsu Amusing his Old Parents
A301

Chinese Fairy Tales: No. 1667, Man disguised as deer, and hunters. No. 1668, Boy cooling his father's bed. No. 1669, Boy fishing through ice. No. 1670, Son reunited with old mother. No. 1671, Emperor tasting mother's medicine. No. 1672, Boy saving oranges for mother. No. 1673, Boy saving father from tiger.

Lithographed

1970, July 10 *Perf. 13½* Wmk. 323

Granite Paper

1666	A301	10c red & multi.	5	3
1667	"	10c carmine rose & multi.	5	3
1668	"	10c light violet & multi.	5	3
1669	"	10c gray & multi.	5	3
1670	"	10c emerald & multi.	5	3
1671	"	50c bister & multi.	10	3
1672	"	$1 sky bl. & multi.	20	3
1673	"	$1 dp. bl. & multi.	20	3
		Nos. 1666–1673 (8)	75	24

See also Nos. 1726–1733.

Man's First Step onto Moon
A302

Designs: $1, Pres. Chiang Kai-shek's message brought to the moon. $5, Neil A. Armstrong, Michael Collins, Edwin E. Aldrin, Jr., and moon (horiz.).

Perf. 13½x13, 13x13½

1970, July 21 Photo. Unwmkd.

1674	A302	$1 yellow & multi.	20	8
1675	"	$5 lt. yellow green & multi.	45	22
1676	"	$8 blue & multi.	70	45

Issued to commemorate the first anniversary of man's first landing on the moon.

Asian Productivity Year Symbol
A303

Lithographed

1970, Aug. 18 *Perf. 13½* Wmk. 323

Granite Paper

1677	A303	$1 emerald & multi.	25	5
1678	"	$5 blue & multi.	60	20

Issued to publicize Asian Productivity Year.

Flags of China and U.N.
A304

1970, Sept. 19 *Perf. 12* Wmk. 323

Granite Paper

1679	A304	$5 bl., car. & black	75	18

Issued to commemorate the 25th anniversary of the United Nations.

Postal Zone Map of Taiwan—A305

Postal Code Emblem—A306

1970, Oct. 8 Lithographed

1680	A305	$1 lt. bl. & multi.	20	8
1681	A306	$2.50 green & multi.	50	20

Issued to publicize the postal code system.

Eleventh Month Scroll
A307

Designs: A scroll series, "Activities of the 12 Months," painted on silk by a group of painters of the Ch'ien Lung court (1736–1796). Chinese number in parenthesis at right of denomination tells month.

Perf. 13½x13

1970–71 Photo. Unwmkd.

Jan., Feb., Mar. Scrolls

(一) (二) (三)

1682	A307	$1 multi.	15	12
1683	"	$2.50 "	40	28
1684	"	$5 "	55	40

Apr., May, June Scrolls

(四) (五) (六)

1685	A307	$1 multi.	15	8
1686	"	$2.50 "	40	17
1687	"	$5 "	55	32

July, Aug., Sept. Scrolls

(七) (八) (九)

1688	A307	$1 multi.	15	8
1689	"	$2.50 "	40	15
1690	"	$5 "	55	28

Oct., Nov., Dec. Scrolls

(十) (十一) (十二)

1691	A307	$1 multi.	15	8
1692	"	$2.50 "	40	15
1693	"	$5 "	55	28
		Nos. 1682–1693 (12)	4.40	2.39

Issue dates: Nos. 1691–1693, Oct. 21, 1970. Nos. 1682–1684, Jan. 14, 1971. Nos. 1685–1687, Apr. 26, 1971. Nos. 1688–1690, Aug. 27, 1971.

Family at Home
A308

Piggy Bank
A309

Design: $4, Family of 5 going on an excursion (vert.).

Perf. 13½x14, 14x13½

1970, Nov. 11 Litho. Wmk. 323

Granite Paper

1694	A308	$1 multicolored	15	5
1695	"	$4 yel. grn. & multi.	50	18

Issued to publicize family planning.

1970, Dec. 1 *Perf. 12½x12*

Granite Paper

1696	A309	50c multicolored	15	5
1697	"	$4.50 blue & multi.	1.00	35

Issued for use on New Year's greetings.

Tibia Fusus Shells
A310

Rare Taiwan Shells: $2.50, Harpeola kurodai. $5, Conus stupa kuroda. $8, Entemnotrochus rumphii.

1971, Feb. 25 *Perf. 13x13½*

1698 A310 $1 violet & multi. 15 7
1699 " $2.50 multicolored 20 18
1700 " $5 org. & multi. 50 20
1701 " $8 grn. & multi. 80 38

Sun Yat-sen Building, Yangmingshan
A311

Passbook and Postal Savings Certificate
A312

Perf. 13½x12½

1971 Lithographed **Wmk. 323**

Granite Paper

1702 A311 5c brown 4 3
1703 " 10c dark gray 4 3
1704 " 50c bright rose lilac 8 3
1705 " $1 vermilion 8 3
1706 " $1.50 ultramarine 12 5
1707 " $2 plum 18 3
1708 " $2.50 emerald 30 3
1709 " $3 aquamarine 35 5
Nos. 1702-1709 (8) 1.19 28

Perf. 13½x14

1971, Mar. 20 Litho. **Wmk. 323**

Design: $4, People and hand dropping coin into bank.

1712 A312 $1 yel. grn. & multi. 12 8
1713 " $4 verm. & multi. 50 16

Publicizing Chinese Postal Savings Service.

Cooperation Emblem, Farmers
A313

Rock Monkey
A314

Design: $8, Chinese teaching rice farming to Africans (horiz.).

Photogravure

1971, May 20 *Perf. 13* **Unwmkd.**

1714 A313 $1 multicolored 10 5
1715 " $8 " 70 30

Sino-African Technical Cooperation Committee, 10th anniversary.

1971, June 25 *Perf. 11½*

Taiwan Animals: $2, White-face flying squirrel. $3, Chinese pangolin. $5, Formosan sika deer. ($2, $3, $5 are horiz.).

1716 A314 $1 gold & multi. 25 10
1717 " $2 " " 25 15
1718 " $3 " " 50 15
1719 " $5 " " 50 30

Pitcher
A315

Designs: $2.50, Players at base (horiz.). $4, Hitter and catcher.

1971, July 29 Photo. *Perf. 13*

1720 A315 $1 multicolored 12 6
1721 " $2.50 " 25 12
1722 " $4 " 45 18

Pacific Regional competition for the 1971 Little League World Series.

中華少年棒球世界冠軍紀念

Nos. 1541, 1544-1545 Overprinted in Magenta or Red

Perf. 13x12½

1971, Sept. 9 Litho. **Wmk. 323**

Granite Paper

1723 A259 $1 vermilion (M) 12 8
1724 " $2.50 blue (R) 45 20
1725 " $3 greenish blue (R) 35 25

Chinese victory in 1971 Little League World Series, Williamsport, Pa., Aug. 24.

Fairy Tale Type of 1970

Chinese Fairy Tales (Filial Piety): No. 1726, Birds and elephant helping in rice field. No. 1727, Son gathering mulberries for mother. No. 1728, Son gathering firewood. No. 1729, Son, mother and bandits. No. 1730, Son carrying heavy burden. 50c, Son digging for bamboo shoots in winter. No. 1732, Man and wife working as slaves. No. 1733, Father, son and carriage.

1971, Sept. 22 *Perf. 13½*

Granite Paper

1726 A301 10c dp. org. & multi. 6 3
1727 " 10c lilac & multi. 6 3
1728 " 10c ocher & multi. 6 3
1729 " 10c dp. carmine & multi. 6 3
1730 " 10c lt. ultra & multi. 6 3
1731 " 50c multicolored 10 4
1732 " $1 emerald & multicolored 12 5
1733 " $1 lt. red brown & multi. 12 5
Nos. 1726-1733 (8) 64 29

Flag of China, "Double Ten" and Anniversary Emblems
A316

Designs (Flag of China and): $2.50, National anthem. $5, Gen. Chiang Kai-shek. $8, Sun Yat-sen.

1971, Oct. 10 Photo. *Perf. 13*

1734 A316 $1 org. & multi. 12 6
1735 " $2.50 multicolored 25 10
1736 " $5 grn. & multi. 55 35
1737 " $8 olive & multi. 65 30

60th National Day.

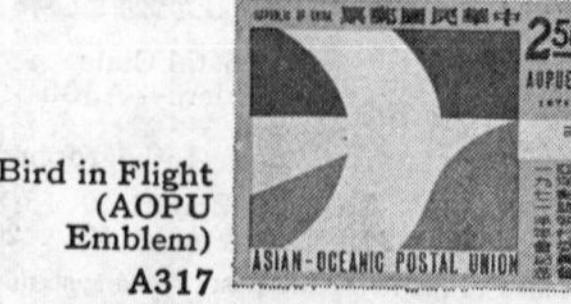

Bird in Flight (AOPU Emblem)
A317

Perf. 13½x14

1971, Nov. 8 Litho. **Wmk. 323**

1738 A317 $2.50 yel. & multi. 50 15
1739 " $5 org. & multi. 50 15

Asian-Oceanic Postal Union Executive Committee Session, Taipei, Nov. 8-15.

"White Frost Hawk," by Lang Shih-ning
A318

Dog Series I

Designs: $2, "Star-Glancing Wolf." $2.50, "Golden-Winged Face." $5, "Young Black Dragon." $8, "Young Gray Dragon."

Designs from painting series "Ten Prized Dogs," by Lang Shih-ning (Giuseppe Castiglione, 1688-1766).

Perf. 13½x13

1971, Nov. 16 Litho. **Unwmkd.**

Multicolored

1740 A318 $1 *Facing left* 15 8
1741 " $2 *Lying down* 20 10
1742 " $2.50 *Scratching* 25 12
1743 " $5 *Facing right* 50 25
1744 " $8 *Looking back* 80 50
Nos. 1740-1744 (5) 1.90 1.05

Dog Series II

Designs: $1, "Black with Snow-white Paws." $2, "Yellow Leopard." $2.50, "Flying Magpie." $5, "Heavenly Lion." $8, "Mottled Tiger."

1972, Jan. 12

1745 A318 $1 *Facing right* 15 10
1746 " $2 *Walking* 20 10
1747 " $2.50 *Sleeping* 30 15
1748 " $5 *Facing left* 50 20
1749 " $8 *Sitting* 75 40
Nos. 1745-1749 (5) 1.90 95

Squirrels—A319

Perf. 13½x12½

1971, Dec. 1 **Wmk. 323**

1750 A319 Block of 4, multi. 50 17
a. 50c in UL corner 8 4
b. 50c in UR corner 8 4
c. 50c in LL corner 8 4
d. 50c in LR corner 8 4
1751 A319 Block of 4, multi. 2.65 1.75
a. $4.50 in UL corner 50 25
b. $4.50 in UR corner 50 25
c. $4.50 in LL corner 50 25
d. $4.50 in LR corner 50 25

New Year 1972.

Flags of China and Jordan
A320

1971, Dec. 16 *Perf. 13½*

Granite Paper

1752 A320 $5 multicolored 50 12

50th anniversary of the founding of the Hashemite Kingdom of Jordan.

Cargo Ship "Hai King"
A321

Design: $7, Ocean liner and map of Pacific Ocean (vert.).

1971, Dec. 16 *Perf. 12½*

1753 A321 $4 green, dark blue & red 35 15
1754 " $7 ocher & multi. 50 15

Centenary of China Merchants Steam Navigation Co.

Downhill Skiing, Olympic Rings
A322

Designs: $5, Cross-country skiing. $8, Giant slalom.

1972, Feb. 3 *Perf. 13½*

1755 A322 $1 org., blk. & blue 10 5
1756 " $5 yel. green, deep orange & black 40 12
1757 " $8 red, gray & blk. 50 38

11th Winter Olympic Games, Sapporo, Japan, Feb. 3-13.

Vase, 18th Century
A323

Porcelain Series I

Porcelain Masterworks of Ching Dynasty: $2, Covered jar. $2.50, Pitcher. $5, Vase with 5 openings and dragon design. $8, Covered jar with children design.

Perf. 11½

1972, Mar. 20 Photo. **Unwmkd.**

1758 A323 $1 vio. & multi. 25 5
1759 " $2 plum & blue 25 10
1760 " $2.50 orange verm. & blue 25 10
1761 " $5 bister brown & blue 50 20
1762 " $8 slate green & multicolored 75 30
Nos. 1758-1762 (5) 2.00 75

See also Nos. 1812-1821, 1864-1868.

Nine Flying Doves
A324

Perf. 13½x14

1972, Apr. 1 Litho. Wmk. 323

1763 A324 $1 lt. blue & black 15 5
1764 " $5 lt. violet & black 55 18

Asian-Oceanic Postal Union, 10th anniversary.

"Dignity with Self-reliance"
A325

Perf. 13½x12½

1972–75 Litho. Wmk. 323

1765 A325 5c brn. & yellow 5 3
1766 " 10c blue & orange 5 3
1767 " 20c claret & yellow green ('75) 5 3
1768 " 50c lilac & lilac rose 5 3
1769 " $1 red & brt. bl. 10 3
1770 " $1.50 yel. & dk. bl. 15 4
1771 " $2 maroon & org. 15 6
1772 " $2.50 emerald & vermilion 20 7
1773 " $3 red & lt. grn. 20 8
Nos. 1765–1773 (9) 1.00 40

Souvenir Sheet

Imperf.

1775 A325 Sheet of 2 60 60

No. 1775 commemorates ROCPEX '72 Philatelic Exhibition, Taipei, Oct. 24–Nov. 2. It contains 2 stamps similar to Nos. 1771 and 1773 with simulated perforations. Orange brown margin with white inscriptions. Size: 69x100mm.

Issue dates: $1, $1.50, $2, $3, May 20, 1972; 5c, 10c, 50c, $2.50, No. 1775, Oct. 24, 1972; 20c, 1975.

Emperor Shih-tsung's Procession
A326

Messengers on Horseback—A327

Designs from scrolls depicting Emperor Shih-tsung's (reigned 1522–1566) journey to and from tombs at Cheng-tien. No. 1776 shows land journey and is designed from right to left. No. 1779 shows return trip by boat and is designed from left to right. The five stamps of Nos. 1776 and 1780 are numbered 1 to 5 in Chinese (see illustrations with Nos. 1682–1686 for numerals).

1972 Photo. Perf. 13½ Unwmkd.

Multicolored

1776 A326 Strip of 5, *Departure* 60 35
a. $1 *shown* (1) 8 5
b. $1 *Seven carriages* (2) 8 5
c. $1 *Carriage drawn by 23 horses* (3) 8 5
d. $1 *Procession* (4) 8 5
e. $1 *Emperor under 2 canopies* (5) 8 5
1777 A327 $2.50 *shown* 25 8
1778 " $5 *Guards with flags, fans & spears* 45 12
1779 A327 $8 *Sedan chair carried by 28 men* 65 35
1780 A326 Strip of 5, *Return trip* 60 35
a. $1 *Three barges* (1) 8 5
b. $1 *Procession, sedan chairs* (2) 8 5
c. $1 *Two barges with trunks* (3) 8 5
d. $1 *Procession on land* (4) 8 5
e. $1 *Procession, 2 sedan chairs* (5) 8 5
1781 A327 $2.50 *Courtiers at city welcoming Emperor* 25 8
1782 A327 $5 *Orchestra on horseback* 45 12
1783 " $8 *Barges* 65 35
Nos. 1776–1783 (8) 3.90 1.80

Issue dates: No. 1776–1779, June 14; Nos. 1780–1783, July 12.

First Day Covers
A328

Magnifying Glass, Tongs, Gauge
A329

Design: $2.50, Sun Yat-sen stamp of 1971 (type A311) under magnifying glass.

Wmk. 323

1972, Aug. 9 Engr. Perf. 12

1785 A328 $1 dk. violet blue 15 5
1784 " $2.50 bright green 20 8
1786 A329 $8 scarlet 60 40

Promotion of philately. Printed in sheets of 40. Each sheet contains 4 blocks of 10 stamps surrounded by margins with inscriptions.

Nos. 1768–1770, 1772 Overprinted in Dark Blue or Red

Perf. 13½x12½

1972, Sept. 9 Litho. Wmk. 323

1787 A325 $1 red & brt. blue (DB) 15 5
1788 " $1.50 yellow & dark blue (R) 30 15
1789 " $2 maroon & orange (R) 30 8
1790 " $3 red & light green (DB) 40 10

China's championship victories in the Little League World Series, Gary, Ind., and in the Senior League World Series, Williamsport, Pa., Aug. 1972.

Emperor Yao (2357–2258 B.C.)
A330

Mountain Climbing
A331

Rulers: $4, Emperor Shun (ruled 2255–2208 B.C.). $4.50, Yü, the Great (ruled 2205–2198 B.C.). $5, King T'ang (ruled 1783–1754 B.C.). $5.50, King Wen (ruled 1171–1122 B.C.). $6, King Wu (ruled 1121–1114 B.C.). $7, Chou Kung (died 1105 B.C.). $8, Confucius (551–479 B.C.).

1972–73 Engraved Perf. 12

Granite Paper

1791 A330 $3.50 dark blue 25 10
1792 " $4 rose red 25 12
1793 " $4.50 bluish lilac 30 14
1794 A330 $5 bright green 35 18
1795 " $5.50 dp. org. ('73) 50 18
1796 " $6.00 deep claret ('73) 50 20
1797 " $7 sepia ('73) 50 22
1798 " $8 indigo ('73) 75 25
Nos. 1791–1798 (8) 3.40 1.39

Issue dates: Nos. 1791–1794, Sept. 20, 1972; Nos. 1795–1798, Apr. 2, 1973.

Photogravure

1972, Oct. 31 Perf. 12 Unwmkd.

Designs (China Youth Corps emblem and): $2.50, Skiing (skiers forming circle). $4, Diving. $8, Parachute jumping.

1800 A331 $1 grn. & multi. 10 5
1801 " $2.50 bl. & multi. 25 8
1802 " $4 org. & multi. 35 16
1803 " $8 multicolored 75 30

China Youth Corps, 20th anniversary.

JCI Emblem
A332

1972, Nov. 12 Litho. Wmk. 323

1804 A332 $1 multicolored 15 5
1805 " $5 org. & multi. 45 15
1806 " $8 multicolored 60 35

27th Junior Chamber International (JCI) World Congress, Taipei, Nov. 12–19.

Electronic Mail Sorter
A333

Plane, Ship and Pier
A334

Design: $5, Highway overpass over railroad.

Engraved

1972, Nov. 12 Perf. 11½ Wmk. 323

1807 A333 $1 red 15 5
1808 A334 $2.50 blue 35 10
1809 " $5 dark violet & brown 75 25

Progress of communications system on Taiwan.

Cow and Calf (Parental Love)
A335

1972, Dec. 1 Litho. Perf. 12

1810 A335 50c red & black 25 5
1811 " $4.50 yellow, red & brown 75 25

New Year 1973. Printed in sheets of 80, divided into 4 panes of 20, separated by vertical and horizontal gutters 2 rows wide. 20 red chops meaning "Happy New Year" are printed in the gutters.

Porcelain Type of 1972 and

Stem Bowl with Dragons
A336

Porcelain Series II

1973 Photogravure Perf. 11½

Porcelain Masterworks of Ming Dynasty: $1, Covered vase with fruits and flowers. $2, Vase with ornamental and floral design. $2.50, Vase imitating ancient bronze. $5, Flask with flowers of 4 seasons. $8, Garlic head vase.

1812 A323 $1 gray & multi. 10 3
1813 " $2 lt. brn. & multi. 15 6
1814 " $2.50 brt. green & multicolored 25 8
1815 " $5 ultra. & multi. 40 20
1816 " $8 olive & multi. 60 28
Nos. 1812–1816 (5) 1.50 65

Porcelain Series III

Ming Porcelain: $2, Refuse container with dragons. $2.50, Covered jar with lotus. $5, Covered jar with horses. $8, Bowl with figures of immortals.

1817 A336 $1 gray & multi. 10 3
1818 " $2 light violet & multicolored 15 6
1819 " $2.50 dark red & multicolored 30 8
1820 " $5 blue & multi. 40 20
1821 " $8 deep orange & multicolored 60 28
Nos. 1817–1821 (5) 1.55 65

Issue dates: Nos. 1812–1816, Jan. 10; Nos. 1817–1821, Mar. 24.

See also Nos. 1865–1868.

Oyster Fairy and Fisherman's Dance—A337

1973, Feb. 7 Photo. Perf. 11½

Granite Paper

Multicolored

1822 A337 $1 *Kicking shuttlecock* (vert.) 25 3
1823 " $4 *shown* 50 15
1824 " $5 *Rowing boat over land* 50 18
1825 " $8 *Old man carrying young lady* (vert.) 75 28

Chinese folklore popular entertainment.

Bamboo Boat
A338

Taiwanese Handicrafts: $2.50, Painted marble vase (vert.). $5, Painted glass plate. $8, Doll, bridegroom carrying bride on back (vert.).

Perf. 13½x14½, 14½x13½

1973, Mar. 9 Photogravure

1826 A338 $1 multicolored 15 3
1827 " $2.50 " 30 9
1828 " $5 " 50 15
1829 " $8 " 75 28

Federation Emblem, Cargo Hook, Crane
A339

Emblem, Tractor, New Buildings
A340

Perf. 12½

1973, Apr. 2 Litho. Wmk. 323

1830 A339 $1 salmon & multi. 10 3
1831 A340 $5 blue & black 40 15

12th convention of International Federation of Asian and Western Pacific Contractors Association, Taipei, Apr. 2–10.

Pres. Chiang Kai-shek, Flag of China
A341

Lin Tse-hsü
A342

Design: $4, like $1 with different border.

Perf. 12

1973, May 20 Photo. Unwmkd.

1832 A341 $1 yel. & multi. 20 5
1833 " $4 dk. grn. & multi. 50 12

First anniversary of Pres. Chiang Kai-shek's inauguration for a fifth term.

Engraved

1973, June 3 *Perf. 12* Wmk. 323

1834 A342 $1 sepia 15 6

Lin Tse-hsü (1785–1850), Governor of Hunan and Kwantung, who destroyed large quantity of opium at Humen, Kwantung, June 3, 1839.

Willows and Palace Gate in the Morning—A343

Lady Watering Peonies, Stone Ornament
A344

Design from scroll "Spring Morning in the Han Palace," by Chiu Ying. The five stamps of No. 1835 are numbered 1 to 5 and the five stamps of No. 1838 are numbered 6–10 in Chinese (see illustrations with Nos. 1682–1691 for numerals). The stamps are numbered and listed from right to left.

Perf. 11½

1973 Photogravure Unwmkd.

Multicolored; Granite Paper

1835 A343 Strip of 5 45 20
a. $1 *shown* (1) 7 4
b. $1 *Ladies feeding peacocks* (2) 7 4
c. $1 *Lady watering peonies* (3) 7 4
d. $1 *Pear tree in bloom* (4) 7 4
e. $1 *Lady musicians* (5) 7 4
1836 A344 $5 *shown* 30 15
1837 " $8 *Lady musicians* 55 25
1838 A343 Strip of 5 45 20
a. $1 *Ladies playing go* (6) 7 4
b. $1 *Various games* (7) 7 4
c. $1 *Talking and playing music* (8) 7 4
d. $1 *Artist painting portrait* (9) 7 4
e. $1 *Sentries guarding wall* (10) 7 4
1839 A344 $5 *Ladies playing go* 30 15
1840 " $8 *Girl chasing butterfly* 55 25
Nos. 1835–1840 (6) 2.60 1.20

Issue dates: Nos. 1835–1837, June 20; Nos. 1838–1840, July 18.

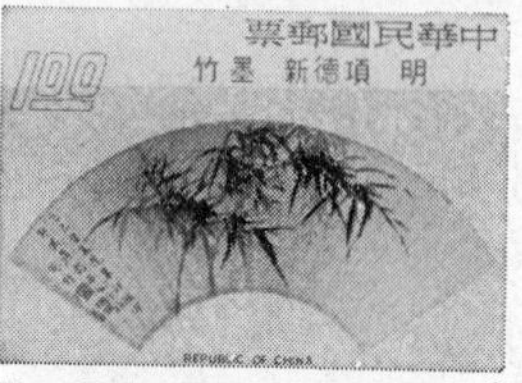

Fan, Bamboo Design, by Hsiang Te-hsin—A345

Wmk. 368

Wmkd. JEZ Multiple (368)

Designs: Painted fans, Ming dynasty.

1973, Aug. 15 Photo. *Perf. 12½x13*

1841 A345 $1 bister & multi. 10 4
1842 " $2.50 " " 25 8
1843 " $5 " " 40 15
1844 " $8 " " 70 25

See also Nos. 1934–1937.

Little League Emblem
A346

INTERPOL Emblem
A347

Wmk. 370

Wmkd. Geometrical Design (370)

1973, Sept. 9 Litho. *Perf. 13½*

1845 A346 $1 yel., carmine & dark blue 15 4
1846 " $4 yel., green & dark blue 35 15

Chinese victory in Little League Twin Championships, Gary, Ind., and Williamsport, Pa.

1973, Sept. 11 Litho. Wmk. 370

Perf. 12

1847 A347 $1 blue & orange 8 4
1848 " $5 green & orange 35 15
1849 A347 $8 magenta & org. 50 25

50th anniversary of International Criminal Police Organization.

Ch'iu Feng-chia
A348

Engraved

1973, Oct. 5 *Perf. 11½* Wmk. 323

1850 A348 $1 violet black 16 8

2nd meeting of overseas Hakkas, Taipei, Oct. 5–7, and to honor Ch'iu Feng-chia (1864–1912), Hakka scholar, poet and revolutionist.

Tseng-wen Reservoir
A349

Tsengwen Dam
A350

Perf. 13½

1973, Oct. 31 Photo. Unwmkd.

Multicolored

1851 A349 Strip of 3 30 10
a. $1 *Upper shore* 8 3
b. $1 *shown* 8 3
c. $1 *Lower shore* 8 3

Perf. 12x11½

1852 A350 $5 *shown* 30 15
1853 " $8 *Spillway* 50 25

Inauguration of Tsengwen Reservoir. No. 1851 printed se-tenant in sheets of 15.

Tiger
A351

Wmk. 370

1973, Dec. 1 Litho. *Perf. 12½*

1854 A351 50c multicolored 10 3
1855 " $4.50 " 42 15

New Year 1974.

"Snow-dotted Eagle," by Lang Shih-ning—A352

Designs: No. 1857, "Comfortable Ride." No. 1858, "Red Flower Eagle." No. 1859, "Cloud-running Steed." No. 1860, "Sky-running steed." $2.50, "Red Jade Seat." $5, "Thunderclap Steed." $8, "Arabian Champion." Designs from painting series "Ten Prized Horses," by Lang Shih-ning (Giuseppe Castiglione, 1688–1766).

Perf. 13

1973 Lithographed Unwmkd.

Multicolored; Without Gum

1856 A352 50c *shown* 5 3
1857 " $1 *Pinto, black tail* 10 3
1858 " $1 *Facing left* 10 3
1859 " $1 *Facing right* 10 3
1860 " $1 *Pinto, white tail* 10 3
1861 " $2.50 *Palomino* 25 8
1862 " $5 *Grazing* 40 15
a. Souvenir sheet of 4 70
1863 A352 $8 *Brown stallion* 80 25
Nos. 1856–1863 (8) 1.90 63

Nos. 1857–1860 printed se-tenant in sheets of 50. No. 1862a contains 4 stamps with simulated perforations similar to Nos. 1856–1857, 1861–1862. Bluish green ornamental margin, black inscription. Size: 150x120mm.

Issue dates: 50c, $2.50, $5, Nov. 21; others Dec. 21.

Porcelain Types of 1972–73

Porcelain Series IV

Porcelain Masterworks of Sung Dynasty: $1, Vase. $2, Three-tiered vase. $2.50, Lotus-shaped bowl. $5, Incense burner. $8, Incense burner on stand.

1974, Jan. 16 Photo. *Perf. 11½*

1864 A323 $1 ultra. & multi. 10 3
1865 A336 $2 multicolored 15 5
1866 " $2.50 red & multi. 20 7
1867 " $5 lilac & multi. 35 15
1868 " $8 green & multi. 55 25
Nos. 1864–1868 (5) 1.35 55

Juggler
A353

Taroko Gorge, Hualien
A354

Design: $8, Magician producing dishes from his robe (horiz.).

1974, Feb. 6 Photo. *Perf. 11½*

1869 A353 $1 yellow & multi. 15 3
1870 " $8 " " 55 25

1974, Mar. 22 Photo. *Perf. 12*

Designs: $2.50, Luce Chapel, Tunghai University. $5, Tzu En Pagoda, Sun Moon Lake. $8, Goddess of Mercy, Keelung.

1871 A354 $1 multicolored 10 3
1872 " $2.50 " 25 7
1873 " $5 " 50 15
1874 " $8 " 75 25

Taiwan landmarks.

Fighting Cocks (Brass)
A355

Designs: $2.50, Grapes and bowl with fruit (imitation jade). $5, Fisherman (wood carving; vert.). $8, Basket with plastic roses (vert.).

Perf. 13½x14½, 14½x13½

1974, Apr. 10

1875 A355 $1 bl. grn. & multi. 10 3
1876 " $2.50 brown & multi. 25 7
1877 " $5 crimson & multi. 50 15
1878 " $8 multicolored 75 25

Taiwanese handicraft products.

Sun Yat-sen Memorial Hall
A356

Designs: $2.50, Reaching-moon Tower, Cheng Ching Lake. $5, Orchid Island (boats). $8, Penghu Interisland Bridge.

1974, May 15 Photo. *Perf. 11½*
Granite Paper

1879 A356 $1 blue & multi. 10 3
1880 " $2.50 " " 25 7
1881 " $5 " " 50 15
1882 " $8 " " 75 25

Taiwan landmarks.

Pres. Chiang and Gate of Whampoa Military Academy
A357

Marching Cadets and Entrance Gate
A358

Perf. 11½
1974, June 16 Engraved Wmk. 323

1883 A357 $1 carmine rose 25 3
1884 A358 $14 violet blue 1.00 45

50th anniversary of the founding of the Whampoa Military Academy.

Long-distance Runner and Olympic Rings
A359

The Boy Wang Ch'i Fighting Invaders
A360

Design: $8, Women's relay race and Olympic rings.

1974, June 23 Litho. *Perf. 12½*

1885 A359 $1 blue, blk. & red 10 3
1886 " $8 pink, blk. & red 60 25

80th anniversary of International Olympic Committee.

1974, July 15 *Perf. 13½* Wmk. 370

Folk Tales: No. 1888, T'i Ying pleading for her father before the Emperor. No. 1889, Wen Yen-po flushing out ball caught in tree. No. 1890, Boy Wang Hua returning gold piece he found. No. 1891, Pu Shih, a rich sheep raiser and benefactor. No. 1892, K'ung Yung as a child choosing smallest pear. No. 1893, Tung Yu studying. No. 1894, Szu Ma-kuang saving playmate from drowning in water jar.

1887 A360 50c olive & multi. 5 3
1888 " 50c ultra. & multi. 5 3
1889 " 50c ocher & multi. 5 3
1890 " 50c red brn. & multi. 5 3
1891 " $1 green & multi. 10 3
1892 " $1 lilac & multi. 10 3
1893 " $1 blue & multi. 10 3
1894 " $1 car. & multi. 10 3
Nos. 1887-1894 (8) 60 24

Same denominations printed in blocks of four in sheets of 100.

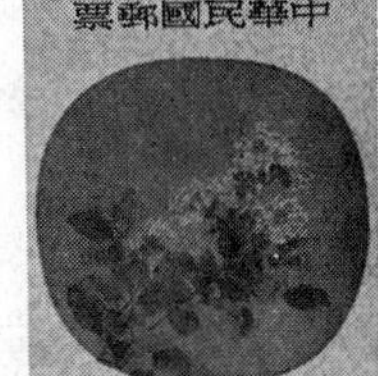

Myrtle, by Wei Sheng
A361

Silk Fan Paintings, Sung Dynasty (960-1279 A.D.): $2.50, Cabbage and Insects, by Hsu Ti. $5, Hibiscus, Cat and Dog, by Li Ti. $8, Pomegranate and Birds, by Wu Ping. Fans from National Palace Museum.

Perf. 13x12½
1974, Aug. 14 Photo. Wmk. 368

1895 A361 $1 multicolored 10 3
1896 " $2.50 " 25 7
1897 " $5 " 50 15
1898 " $8 " 75 25

See Nos. 1950-1953.

Battle at Marco Polo Bridge, July 7, 1937
A362

Perf. 13½
1974, Sept. 3 Litho. Wmk. 370

1899 A362 $1 multicolored 8 3

Souvenir Sheet
Wmk. 323
Without Gum; Granite Paper

1900 A362 $1 multi., sheet of 8 70
a. Single stamp 8

20th Armed Forces Day. No. 1900 commemorates Armed Forces Stamp Exhibition, Sun Yat-sen Memorial Hall, Sept. 3-9. Sheet has yellow ornamental margin with black inscription. Size: 106x146mm.

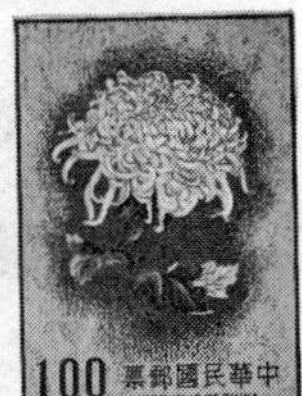

Chrysanthemum
A363

Designs: Various chrysanthemums.

Perf. 12
1974, Sept. 30 Photo. Unwmkd.
Granite Paper

1901 A363 $1 lilac & multi. 10 3
1902 " $2.50 multicolored 25 7
1903 " $5 org. & multi. 50 15
1904 " $8 multicolored 75 25

Rep. of China Pavilion, EXPO Emblem
A364

Map of Fair Grounds, Chinese Flag
A364a

Perf. 13
1974, Oct. 10 Litho. Wmk. 370

1905 A364 $1 multicolored 15 3
1906 A364a $8 " 60 25

EXPO '74, Spokane, Wash., May 4-Nov. 4. Theme, "Preserve the Environment."

Steel Mill, Kaohsiung
A365

Taichung Harbor
A366

Designs: $1, Taiwan North Link Railroad and map. $2, Oil refinery. $2.50, Electric train. $3.50, Taoyuan International Airport. $4, Taiwan North-South Highway and map. $4.50, Kaohsiung shipyard. $5, Su-ao Port.

Perf. 13x12½, 12½x13
1974, Oct. 31 Wmk. 323

1907 A365 50c lilac, yellow & brown 5 3
1908 " $1 green & org. 10 3
1909 " $2 blue & yellow 15 5
1910 " $2.50 emerald & orange 15 8
1911 A366 $3 ocher & ultra. 20 10
1912 " $3.50 slate green & yellow 25 12
1913 " $4 brown & yel. 25 14
1914 " $4.50 verm. & blue 30 15
1915 " $5 sepia & dk. bl. 35 16
Nos. 1907-1915 (9) 1.80 86

Major construction projects.
See Nos. 2009-2017, 2068-2076.

Agaricus Bisporus
A367

Edible Mushrooms: $2.50, Pleurotus ostreatus. $5, Dictyophora indusiata. $8, Flammulina velutipes.

Photogravure
1974, Nov. 15 *Perf. 11½* Unwmkd.

1916 A367 $1 multicolored 10 3
1917 " $2.50 " 25 8
1918 " $5 " 50 16
1919 " $8 " 75 25

9th International Scientific Congress on the Cultivation of Edible Fungi, Taipei, Nov. 1974.

Batters and World Map
A368

Pitcher and Championship Banners
A369

Lithographed
1974, Nov. 24 *Perf. 13½* Wmk. 323

1920 A368 $1 multicolored 15 3
1921 A369 $8 " 60 25

China's victory in 1974 Little League Baseball World Series Triple Championships.

Rabbit
A370

Acrobat with Iron Rod
A371

Perf. 12½
1974, Dec. 10 Photo. Wmk. 323

1922 A370 50c org. & multi. 10 3
1923 " $4.50 brn. & multi. 40 15

New Year 1975.

1975, Jan. 15 *Perf. 11½* Unwmkd.

Design: $5, Two acrobats spinning tops (horiz.).

Granite Paper

1924 A371 $4 yellow & multi. 30 14
1925 " $5 " " 45 16

Children Watching Puppet Show—A372

Ceremonial New Year Greetings—A373

Designs from scroll "Festivals for the New Year," by Ting Kuan-p'eng. Nos. 1926a-1926e are numbered 1-5 in Chinese.

1975, Feb. 25 Photo. *Perf. 11½*
Multicolored; Granite Paper

1926 A372 Strip of 5 40 20
a. $1 *Ceremonial New Year Greetings* (1) 7 4
b. $1 *Man with trained monkey* (2) 7 4
c. $1 *Crowd and musicians* (3) 7 4
d. $1 *Picnic under a tree* (4) 7 4
e. $1 *shown* (5) 7 4
1927 A373 $2.50 *shown* 25 8
1928 " $5 *Children buying firecrackers* 40 16
1929 " $8 *Children and man with trained monkey* 60 25

Sun Yat-sen Memorial Hall, Taipei
A374

Sun Yat-sen's Handwriting
A375

Sun Yat-sen, Bronze Statue in Memorial Hall
A376

Sun Yat-sen Memorial Hall, St. John's University, N.Y.
A377

Perf. 13½x14, 14x13½

1975, Mar. 12 Lithographed

No.	Type	Description	Unused	Used
1930	A374	$1 green & multi.	10	4
1931	A375	$4 yel. grn. & multi.	25	12
1932	A376	$5 yellow & multi.	50	16
1933	A377	$8 gray & multi.	75	24

Dr. Sun Yat-sen (1866–1925), statesman and revolutionary leader, 50th death anniversary.

Fan Type of 1973 Inscribed: "Landscape" (1st Characters, 水山 2nd Row)

Designs: Painted fans, Ming Dynasty. Second row of inscription gives design description.

Perf. 12½x13

1975, Apr. 16 Photo. Wmk. 368

No.	Type	Description	Unused	Used
1934	A345	$1 bister & multi.	10	4
1935	"	$2.50 " "	25	8
1936	"	$5 " "	50	16
1937	"	$8 " "	75	24

Yuan-chin coin, 1122–221 B.C.
A378

Ancient Chinese Coins: $4, Pan-liang, 221–207 B.C. $5, Five chu, 206 B.C.–220 A.D. $8, Five chu, 502–557 A.D.

Perf. 13

1975, May 20 Litho. Wmk. 323

No.	Type	Description	Unused	Used
1938	A378	$1 salmon & multi.	10	4
1939	"	$4 yellow & multi.	25	12
1940	"	$5 dull yel. & multi.	50	16
1941	"	8 lt. vio. & multi.	75	24

The Cloth-bag Monk, by Chang Hung (1577–1668)
A379

Chinese Paintings: $4, Lao-tzu Riding Buffalo, by Chao Pu-chih (1053–1110). $5, Portrait of Shih-te, by Wang Wen (1497–1576). $8, Splashed-ink Immortal, by Liang K'ai (early 13th century).

Perf. 11½

1975, June 18 Photo. Unwmkd.

Granite Paper

No.	Type	Description	Unused	Used
1942	A379	$2 black, buff & vermilion	10	6
1943	"	$4 black, gray & red	25	12
1944	"	$5 blk., yel. & verm.	50	16
1945	"	$8 tan, red & black	75	24

Chu Yin Reading by the Light of Fireflies
A380

Folk Tales: No. 1947, Hua Mu-lan going to war for her father. No. 1948, King Kou Chien tasting gall. $5, Chou Ch'u killing tiger.

Perf. 14x13½

1975, July 16 Litho. Wmk. 368

No.	Type	Description	Unused	Used
1946	A380	$1 olive & multi.	10	4
1947	"	$2 bister brown & multicolored	15	8
1948	"	$2 lt. grn. & multi.	15	8
1949	"	$5 blue & multi.	40	16

See Nos. 2108–2111.

Cherry-Apple Blossoms, by Lin Ch'un
A381

Silk Fan Paintings, Sung Dynasty: $2, Spring Blossoms and Butterfly, by Ma K'uei. $5, Monkeys and Deer, by I Yüan-chih. $8, Tame Sparrow among Bamboo.

Perf. 13x12½

1975, Aug. 15 Litho. Wmk. 323

No.	Type	Description	Unused	Used
1950	A381	$1 multicolored	10	4
1951	"	$2 "	20	8
1952	"	$5 "	40	16
1953	"	$8 "	60	25

See Nos. 2001–2004.

Gen. Chang Tzu-chung (1891–1940)
A382

Portraits: No. 1955, Maj. Gen. Kao Chih-hong (1908–1937). No. 1956, Capt. Sha Shih-chiun (1896–1938). No. 1957, Maj. Gen. Hsieh Chin-yuan (1905–1941). No. 1958, Lt. Yen Hai-wen (1916–1937). No. 1959, Lt. Gen. Tai An-lan (1905–1942).

Perf. 12

1975, Sept. 3 Engr. Wmk. 323

No.	Type	Description	Unused	Used
1954	A382	$2 carmine	20	8
1955	"	$2 sepia	20	8
1956	"	$2 dull green	20	8
1957	"	$5 violet black	50	16
1958	"	$5 violet blue	50	16
1959	"	$5 dark blue	50	16
		Nos. 1954–1959 (6)	2.10	72

Martyrs of the resistance fight against Japan.

Lotus Pond with Willows, by Madame Chiang—A383

Paintings by Madame Chiang Kai-shek: $5, Sun Breaks through Mountain Clouds. $8, A Pair of Pine Trees. $10, Fishing and Farming.

Perf. 13½

1975, Oct. 31 Litho. Unwmkd.

No.	Type	Description	Unused	Used
1960	A383	$2 multicolored	20	8
1961	"	$5 "	40	16
1962	"	$8 "	60	25
1963	"	$10 "	75	32

Cauldron with Phoenix Handles, 481-221 B.C.
A384

Ancient Bronzes: $2, Rectangular cauldron, 1122–722 B.C. (vert.). $8, Flat jar, 481–221 B.C. $10, 3-legged wine vessel, 1766–1122 B.C. (vert.).

1975, Nov. 12 Photo. *Perf. 12*

No.	Type	Description	Unused	Used
1964	A384	$2 pink & multi.	15	8
1965	"	$5 lt. bl. & multi.	40	16
1966	"	$8 yel. & multi.	60	25
1967	"	$10 lilac & multi.	75	32

Dragon, Nine-Dragon Wall, Peihai
A385

Techi Dam
A386

Perf. 12½

1975, Dec. 1 Litho. Wmk. 323

No.	Type	Description	Unused	Used
1968	A385	$1 orange & multi.	10	4
1969	"	$5 green & multi.	40	20

New Year 1976.

1975, Dec. 17 *Perf. 13½* Unwmkd.

Design: $10, Panoramic view of Techi Dam.

No.	Type	Description	Unused	Used
1970	A386	$2 green & multi.	25	8
1971	"	$10 blue & multi.	1.00	32

Completion of Techi Dam, Tachia River.

Biathlon and Olympic Rings
A387

Designs (Olympic Rings and): $5, Luge. $8, Skiing.

1976, Jan. 15 Litho. *Perf. 13½*

No.	Type	Description	Unused	Used
1972	A387	$2 blue & multi.	20	8
1973	"	$5 " "	40	16
1974	"	$8 " "	60	25

12th Winter Olympic Games, Innsbruck, Austria, Feb. 4–15.

Chin, Oldest Chinese Instrument
A388

Musical Instruments: $5, Se, c. 2900 B.C. $8, Standing kong-ho (harp). $10, Sleeping kong-ho.

1976, Feb. 11 *Perf. 14* Unwmkd.

No.	Type	Description	Unused	Used
1975	A388	$2 yel. & multi.	20	8
1976	"	$5 org. & multi.	40	16
1977	"	$8 greenish blue & multi.	60	25
1978	"	$10 multicolored	75	32

Double Carp Type of 1969.

Perf. 13½x12½

1976, Dec. 15 Engraved Unwmkd.

No.	Type	Description	Unused	Used
1980	A280	$14 carmine rose	1.00	20

Mail Collecting
A389

Mail Sorting
A390

Designs: $8, Mail transport. $10, Mail delivery.

Perf. 13½

1976, Mar. 20 Litho. Wmk. 323

No.	Type	Description	Unused	Used
1984	A389	$2 yel. & multi.	20	8
1985	A390	$5 grn. & multi.	40	16
1986	"	$8 blue & multi.	60	25
1987	A389	$10 org. & multi.	75	32
		a. Souvenir sheet of 4	2.00	2.00

80th anniversary of postal service. No. 1987a contains one each of Nos. 1984–1987; buff margin with red inscription. Size: 130x100mm.

Pres. Chiang Kai-shek
A391

People Paying Homage—A392

Designs: No. 1990, Pres. Chiang lying in state. No. 1991, Hearse leaving funeral chapel. $5, People along funeral route. $8, Spirit tablet in Tzuhu Guest House. $10, Tzuhu Guest House, Pres. Chiang's burial place.

1976, Apr. 4

1988	A391	$2 gray & multi.	15	8
1989	A392	$2 " "	15	8
1990	"	$2 " "	15	8
1991	"	$2 " "	15	8
1992	"	$5 " "	25	16
1993	"	$8 " "	50	25
1994	"	$10 " "	50	32
		Nos. 1988–1994 (7)	1.85	1.05

Pres. Chiang Kai-shek (1887–1975), first death anniversary.

Flags of China and USA
A393

Perf. 13½

1976, May 29 Litho. Wmk. 323

1995	A393	$2 multicolored	20	8
1996	"	$10 yel. & multi.	70	32

American Bicentennial.

Coin, 12th Century B.C.
A394

Cauldron, Shang Dynasty
A395

Bronze Shovel Coins (pu): $5, Pointed-feet coin, 481–221 B.C. $8, Round-feet coin, 722–481 B.C. $10, Square-feet coin, 3rd–2nd centuries B.C.

1976, June 16

1997	A394	$2 sal. & multi.	15	8
1998	"	$5 lt. bl. & multi.	40	16
1999	"	$8 gray & multi.	60	25
2000	"	$10 multicolored	75	32

Fan Painting Type of 1975

Silk Fan Paintings, Sung Dynasty: $2, Hibiscus, by Li Tung. $5, Lilies, by Lin Ch'un. $8, Deer and Pine, by Mou Chung-fu. $10, Quail and Wild Flowers, by Li An-chung.

Perf. 13x12½

1976, July 14 Litho. Wmk. 323

2001	A381	$2 multicolored	20	8
2002	"	$5 "	40	16
2003	"	$8 "	60	25
2004	"	$10 "	75	32

1976, Aug. 25 Photo. *Perf. 11½*

Granite Paper

Ancient Bronzes: $5, 3-legged cauldron, Chou Dynasty (1122–722 B.C.). $8, Wine container, Chou Dynasty. $10, Wine vessel with spout, Shang Dynasty (1766–1122 B.C.).

2005	A395	$2 rose & multi.	20	8
2006	"	$5 lt. bl. & multi.	40	16
2007	"	$8 yel. & multi.	60	25
2008	"	$10 lilac & multi.	75	32

Construction Types of 1974

Designs: $1, Taiwan North Link railroad and map. $2, Railroad electrification. $3, Taichung Harbor. $4, Taiwan North-South Highway and map. $5, Steel Mill, Kaohsiung. $6, Taoyuan International Airport. $7, Kao-hsiung shipyard. $8, Oil refinery. $9, Su-ao Port.

Perf. 13½x12½, 12½x13½

1976 Lithographed Wmk. 323

2009	A365	$1 carmine & green	10	4
2010	"	$2 orange & multi.	15	5
2011	A366	$3 violet & multi.	20	10
2012	"	$4 car. & multi.	25	14
2013	A365	$5 green & brown	30	16
2014	A366	$6 brown & multi.	35	20
2015	"	$7 " "	40	25
2016	A365	$8 carmine & green	50	30
2017	A366	$9 olive & blue	50	30
		Nos. 2009–2017 (9)	2.75	1.54

Chiang Kai-shek and Mother
A396

Sun Yat-sen and Chiang Kai-shek at Canton Station—A397

Design: $5, Chiang Kai-shek, portrait.

1976, Oct. 31 Litho. *Perf. 13½*

2023	A396	$2 multicolored	20	8
2024	"	$5 "	40	20
2025	A397	$10 "	75	40

Pres. Chiang Kai-shek, 90th anniversary of birth.

Flags of Kuomintang and China
A398

Sun Yat-sen and Chiang Kai-shek
A399

1976, Nov. 12 *Perf. 13½x14*

2026	A398	$2 multicolored	20	8
2027	A399	$10 "	75	40
		a. Souvenir sheet of 2	1.00	1.00

11th National Kuomintang Congress, Taipei.

No. 2027a contains one each of Nos. 2026–2027; yellow margin with red inscription. Size: 110x87mm.

Brazen Serpent
A400

1976, Dec. 15 Wmk. 323 *Perf. 12½*

2028	A400	$1 red, lilac & gold	10	4
2029	"	$5 plum, yellow & gold	40	16

New Year 1977.

Bird and Plum Blossoms, by Ch'en Hung-shou
A401

Chinese Paintings: $8, "Wintry Days" (pine), by Yang Wei-chen. $10, Rock and Bamboo, by Hsia Ch'ang.

Unwmkd.

1977, Jan. 12 Photo. *Perf. 11½*

Granite Paper

2030	A401	$2 multicolored	20	8
2031	"	$8 "	50	30
2032	"	$10 "	75	32

Black-naped Orioles—A402

Birds of Taiwan: $8, Common Kingfisher. $10, Chinese pheasant-tailed jacana.

1977, Feb. 16 Lithographed

2033	A402	$2 multicolored	20	8
2034	"	$8 "	50	30
2035	"	$10 "	75	32

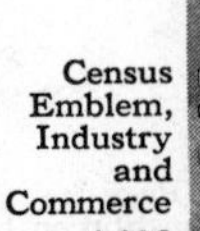

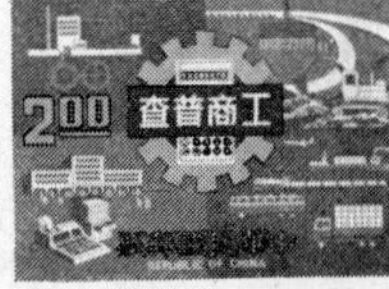

Census Emblem, Industry and Commerce
A403

Unwmkd.

1977, Mar. 16 Litho. *Perf. 13½*

2036	A403	$2 red & multi.	20	8
2037	"	$10 pur. & multi.	75	32

Industry and Commerce Census.

Green Mountains Rising into Clouds, by Madame Chiang—A404

Landscapes, by Madame Chiang Kai-shek: $5, Boat in the Beauty of Spring. $8, Scholar beside Waterfall. $10, Water Rises to Meet the Bridge.

Photogravure

1977, Mar. 31 *Perf. 11½* Unwmkd.

Granite Paper

2038	A404	$2 multicolored	20	5
2039	"	$5 "	40	12
2040	"	$8 "	60	20
2041	"	$10 "	75	25

League Emblem
A405

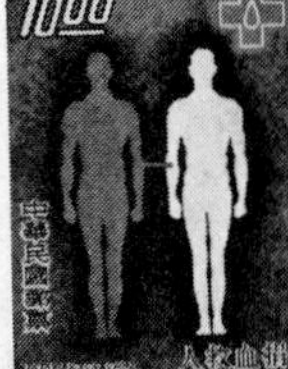

Blood Donation
A406

1977, Apr. 18 Litho. *Perf. 12½*

2042	A405	$2 car. & multi.	20	5
2043	"	$10 grn. & multi.	70	25

10th World Anti-Communist League Conference.

1977, May 5 *Perf. 13½* Wmk. 323

Design: $2, Donating blood (horiz).

2044	A406	$2 red & black	20	5
2045	"	$10 " "	70	25

Blood donation movement.

San-hsien
A407

Musical Instruments: $5, Tung-hsiao (bamboo flute). $8, Yang-chin (butterfly harpsichord). $10, Pai-hsiao (pipes). Background shows musician playing instrument.

Unwmkd.

1977, June 21 Photo. *Perf. 14*

2046	A407	$2 multicolored	20	5
2047	"	$5 "	40	12
2048	"	$8 "	60	20
2049	"	$10 "	75	25

Idea Leuconoe
A408

Protected Butterflies: $4, Hebomoia glaucippe formosana. $6, Stichophthalma howqua formosana. $10, Atrophaneura horishana.

1977, July 20 Litho. *Perf. 13½*

2050 A408 $2 verm. & multi. 20 5
2051 " $4 lt. green & multicolored 40 10
2052 " $6 lt. bl. & multi. 60 15
2053 " $10 yel. & multi. 75 25

National Palace Museum
A409

Temple
A410

Children's Drawings: $2, Sea Goddess Festival. $4, Boats on Shore of Lan-yu.

Perf. 13½

1977, Aug. 27 Litho. Wmk. 323

2054 A409 $1 multicolored 10 3
2055 " $2 " 20 5
2056 " $4 " 30 10
2057 A410 $5 " 40 12

8th Exhibition of World School Children's Art.

Carved Lacquer Plate, Wan-li Ware
A411

Ancient Carved Lacquer Ware: $5, Bowl, Ching dynasty. $8, Round box, Ming dynasty. $10, Four-tiered box, Ching dynasty.

Perf. 13x14

1977, Sept. 28 Photo. Wmk. 368

2058 A411 $2 multicolored 20 5
2059 " $5 " 40 12
2060 " $8 " 60 20
2061 " $10 " 75 25

Lions International, Emblem and Activities
A412

Unwmkd.

1977, Oct. 8 Litho. *Perf. 13*

2062 A412 $2 multicolored 20 5
2063 " $10 " 70 25

International Association of Lions Clubs, 60th anniversary.

Nos. 2010 and 2016 Overprinted in Carmine

1977
中華民國青年、青少年及少年棒球隊再獲世界三冠軍紀念

Perf. 13½x12½

1977, Sept. 9 Litho. Wmk. 323

2064 A365 $2 org. & multi. 20 5
2065 " $8 car. & green 60 20

Little League baseball championship.

Chinese Quality Mark
A413

Unwmkd.

1977, Oct. 14 Litho. *Perf. 13x12½*

2066 A413 $2 red & multi. 20 5
2067 " $10 blue & multi. 70 25

International Standardization Day.

Construction Types of 1974

Redrawn: Numerals Outlined

Designs as 1976 Issue.

Perf. 13½x12½, 12½x13½

1977 Lithographed Unwmkd.

Granite Paper

2068 A365 $1 car. & dp. grn. 10 3
2069 " $2 vermilion & multicolored 15 5
2070 A366 $3 vio. & multi. 20 7
2071 " $4 car. & multi. 25 10
2072 A365 $5 grn. & multi. 30 12
2073 A366 $6 sepia & multi. 35 15
2074 " $7 " " 40 18
2075 A365 $8 red lilac & multicolored 50 20
2076 A366 $9 olive & multi. 50 22
Nos. 2068-2076 (9) 2.75 1.12

Numerals are in solid color on Nos. 1907-1915, 2009-2017; in outline on Nos. 2068-2076.

Man and Heart
A414

Wmk. 323

1977, Nov. 12 Litho. *Perf. 13½x12½*

2077 A414 $2 multicolored 20 5
2078 " $10 " 70 25

Physical health, cardiac care.

White Stallion
A415

Design: $5, Two horses (horiz.). Designs from painting "100 Horses," by Lang Shih-ning.

Lithographed

1977, Dec. 1 *Perf. 12½* Unwmkd.

2079 A415 $1 red & multi. 10 3
2080 " $5 emerald & multicolored 40 15

New Year 1977.

First Page of Constitution
A416

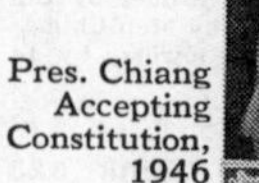

Pres. Chiang Accepting Constitution, 1946
A417

1977, Dec. 25 Litho. *Perf. 13½*

2081 A416 $2 multicolored 20 6
2082 A417 $10 " 70 30

30th anniversary of the Constitution.

Knife Coin with 3 Characters, 403-221 B.C.
A418

Designs: Ancient knife coins.

1978, Jan. 18 *Perf. 13½* Wmk. 323

2083 A418 $2 sal. & multi. 20 5
2084 " $5 lt. bl. & blk. 40 16
2085 " $8 light gray & multicolored 60 25
2086 " $10 tan & multi. 75 32

China No. 1 and Flag of China
A419

Designs: $5, No. 464 (Sun Yat-sen). $10, No. 1204 (Chiang Kai-shek).

1978, Feb. 21 Litho. *Perf. 13½*

2087 A419 $2 brn. & multi. 20 8
2088 " $5 blue & multi. 40 16
2089 " $10 org. & multi. 75 32
a. Souvenir sheet of 3 1.50

Centenary of Chinese postage stamps. No. 2089a contains one each of Nos. 2087-2089; orange and dark carmine margin. Size: 143x101mm.

Sun Yat-Sen Memorial Hall
A420

China Nos. 2079 and 2
A421

Perf. 14x12½, 12½x14

1978, Mar. 20 Wmk. 323

2090 A420 $2 multicolored 20 8
2091 A421 $10 " 70 32

ROCPEX '78 Philatelic Exhibition, Taipei, Mar. 20-29.

Chiang Kai-shek with Revolutionary Army—A422

Designs (Chiang Kai-shek); $2, as young man, 1912 (vert.). $8, Making speech at Mt. Lu, July 17, 1937. $10, Reviewing Armed Forces on National Day, 1956, and Chinese flags (vert.).

1978, Apr. 5 *Perf. 13½* Wmk. 323

2092 A422 $2 violet & multi. 20 8
2093 " $5 green & multi. 40 16
2094 " $8 blue & multi. 60 25
2095 " $10 violet blue & multicolored 75 32

Pres. Chiang Kai-shek (1887-1975).

Nuclear Reactor and Plant
A423

Poem by Wen Cheng-ming (1470-1559)
A424

Perf. 13½x12½

1978, Apr. 28 Unwmkd.

2096 A423 $10 multicolored 65 32

First nuclear power plant on Taiwan.

Lithographed

1978, May 20 *Perf. 13½* Wmk. 323

Chinese Calligraphy: $2, Letter by Wang Hsi-chih (307-365). $4, Eulogy by Chu Sui-liang (596-658). $8, From Autobiography of Huai-su, Tang Dynasty. $10, Poem by Ch'ang Piao, Sung Dynasty.

2097 A424 $2 multicolored 15 8
2098 " $4 " 25 16
2099 " $6 " 35 24
2100 " $8 " 50 32
2101 " $10 " 60 40
Nos. 2097-2101 (5) 1.85 1.20

Head and Dao Cancer Fund Emblem
A425

Carved Lacquer Vase, Ming Dynasty
A426

1978, June 15 Litho. *Perf. 13½*

2102 A425 $2 red, org. & ol. 15 8
2103 " $10 dark & light blue & green 60 40

Cancer prevention.

1978, July 12

Ancient Carved Lacquer Ware: $2, Box with dragon and cloud design, Ch'ing dynasty (horiz.). $5, Double box on legs, Ch'ing dynasty (horiz.). $8, Round box with peonies, Ming dynasty (horiz.).

2104 A426 $2 gray ol. & multi. 15 8
2105 " $5 " " 30 16
2106 " $8 " " 50 25
2107 " $10 " " 60 32

Tsu Ti Practicing with his Sword
A427

Folk Tales: No. 2109, Pan Ch'ao, diplomat and governor. No. 2110, Tien Tan's "Fire Bull Battle." $5, Liang Hung-yu, a general's wife, who served as drummer in battle.

Perf. 13½

1978, Aug. 16 Litho. Wmk. 323

2108 A427 $1 multicolored 10 4
2109 " $2 bister & multi. 15 8
2110 " $2 gray & multi. 15 8
2111 " $5 multicolored 30 16

Nos. 2012 and 2014 Overprinted in Red — 1978

1978, Sept. 9 *Perf. 12½x13*

2112 A366 $4 multicolored 25 16
2113 " $6 " 40 25

Triple championships won by Chinese teams in Little League World Series. "1978" overprint on $4 at left, on $6 at right.

Ixias Pyrene
A428

Protected Butterflies: $4, Euploea sylvestor swinhoei. $6, Cyrestis thyodamas formosana. $10, Byasa polyeuctes termessus.

1978, Sept. 20

2114 A428 $2 multicolored 15 8
2115 " $4 " 25 16
2116 " $6 " 35 25
2117 " $10 " 60 40

Scout Symbols
A429

Tropical Tomatoes
A430

1978, Oct. 5 Litho. *Perf. 13½*

2118 A429 $2 multicolored 25 8
2119 " $10 " 40 40

5th Chinese Boy Scout Jamboree, Cheng Ching Lake, Oct. 5–12.

1978, Oct. 23 Wmk. 323

Design: $10, Tropical tomatoes (horiz.).

2120 A430 $2 multicolored 10 8
2121 " $10 " 50 40

International Symposium on Tropical Tomatoes, Taiwan, Oct. 23–28.

Sino-Saudi Bridge
A431

Design: $6, Buttresses of bridge, flags of Taiwan and Saudi Arabia (horiz.).

1978, Oct. 31

2122 A431 $2 multicolored 10 8
2123 " $6 " 30 25

Completion of Sino-Saudi Bridge over Cho-Shui River.

National Flag
A432

1978–79

2124 A432 $1 multicolored 5 4
2125 " $2 " 10 8
2126 " $5 " 25 20
2127 " $6 " 30 24
2128 " $8 " 40 32
2129 " $10 " ('79) 50 40

Nos. 2124–2129 (6) 1.60 1.28

Three Rams, by Emperor Hsuan-tsung
A433

Taoyuan International Airport
A434

Wmk. 323

1978, Dec. 1 Litho. *Perf. 12½*

2135 A433 $1 multicolored 5 4
2136 " $5 " 25 20

New Year 1978.

1978, Dec. 31 *Perf. 13½*

Design: $10, Passenger terminal and control tower (horiz.).

2137 A434 $2 multicolored 10 8
2138 " $10 " 50 40

Completion of Taoyuan International Airport.

Oracle Bones and Inscription, 1766–1123 B.C.—A435

Antiquities and Inscriptions: $5, Lehchi cauldron, 722–481 B.C. $8, Small seal (turtle), 206 B.C.–8 A.D. $10, Inscribed stone tablet, 175–183 A.D.

1979, Jan. 17

2139 A435 $2 multicolored 10 8
2140 " $5 " 25 20
2141 A435 $8 multicolored 40 32
2142 " $10 " 50 40

Origin and development of Chinese characters.

Chihkan Tower, 1653
A436

Taiwan Scenery: $5, Shrine of Confucius, 1665. $8, Shrine of Koxinga, 1661. $10, Eternal Castle and moat.

1979, Feb. 11 Litho. *Perf. 13½*

2143 A436 $2 multicolored 10 8
2144 " $5 " 25 20
2145 " $8 " 40 32
2146 " $10 " 50 40

Children Playing on Winter Day, Sung Dynasty—A437

1979, Mar. 8

Multicolored

2147 A437 Block of four 1.00
a. $5 in UL corner 25
b. $5 in UR corner 25
c. $5 in LL corner 25
d. $5 in LR corner 25
e. Souvenir sheet of 4 1.25

No. 2147e contains No. 2147; pink and black margin. Size: 101x145mm.

SEMI-POSTAL STAMPS.

SP1

Red or Blue Surcharge.

1920, Dec. 1 *Perf. 14, 15* **Unwmkd.**

B1 SP1 1c on 2c green 3.50 1.00
B2 " 3c on 4c scarlet (B) 4.00 1.75
B3 " 5c on 6c gray 6.50 2.50

The surcharge represents the actual franking value. The extra cent helped victims of the 1919 Yellow River flood.

War Refugees
SP2

Black Surcharge.

1944, Oct. 10 **Engraved** *Perf. 12*

B4 SP2 $2+$2 on 50c+50c bright ultramarine 15 15
B5 " $4+$4 on 8c+8c bright green 15 15
B6 " $5+$5 on 21c+21c red brown 55 55
B7 " $6+$6 on 28c+28c olive green 85 85
B8 " $10+$10 on 33c+33c red 1.40 1.40
B9 " $20+$20 on $1+$1 violet 2.50 2.50
a. Sheet of six 10.00 10.00
Nos. B4-B9 (6) 5.60 5.60

The borders of each stamp differ slightly in design.

The surtax was for war refugees.

No. B9a measures 191x112mm. and contains one each of Nos. B4 to B9 with marginal inscriptions in olive green, red brown and bright green.

Nos. B4-B8 exist without surcharge, but were not regularly issued.

Great Wall of China
SP4

Chinese Refugee Family
SP5

Lithographed.

1948, July 5 *Perf. 14, Imperf.*

Without Gum.

Cross in Carmine.

B11 SP4 $5000+$2000 violet 12 12
B12 " $10,000+$2000 brown 12 12
B13 " $15,000+$2000 gray 12 12
a. Cross omitted 120.00

The surtax was for anti-tuberculosis work.

Republic of China (Taiwan)

1954, Oct. 1 **Engraved** *Perf. 12*

Without Gum

B14 SP5 40c+10c deep blue 5.00 65
B15 " $1.60+40c lilac rose 10.00 1.50
B16 " $5+$1 red 25.00 15.00

The surtax was used to aid in the evacuation of Chinese from North Viet Nam.

AIR POST STAMPS.

Curtiss "Jenny" over Great Wall
(Bars of Republic flag on tail.)
AP1

Engraved

1921, July 1 *Perf. 14* **Unwmkd.**

C1 AP1 15c blue green & black 14.00 7.50
C2 " 30c scarlet & black 11.00 6.00
C3 " 45c dull violet & black 11.00 6.00
C4 " 60c dark blue & black 14.00 7.00
C5 " 90c olive green & black 15.00 7.50
Nos. C1-C5 (5) 65.00 34.00

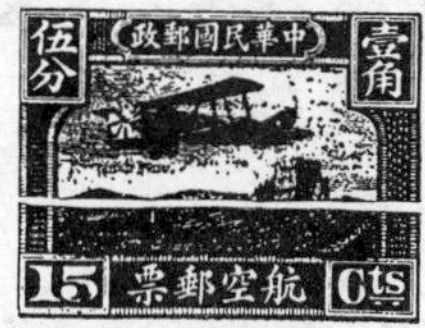

(Nationalist sun emblem on tail.)
AP2

1929, July 5

C6 AP2 15c bl. green & blk. 2.00 50
C7 " 30c dk. red & black 3.00 75
C8 " 45c dk. vio. & blk. 6.00 2.50
C9 " 60c dark blue & black 6.00 2.50
C10 " 90c olive green & black 7.00 3.00
Nos. C6-C10 (5) 24.00 9.25

Junkers F-13 over Great Wall
AP3

1932-37

C11 AP3 15c gray green 10 6
C12 " 25c orange ('33) 10 4
C13 " 30c red 15 8
C14 " 45c brown violet 10 8
C15 " 50c dark brown ('33) 10 8
C16 " 60c dark blue 10 8
C17 " 90c olive green 15 10
C18 " $1 yel. green ('33) 15 10
C19 " $2 brown ('37) 15 10
C20 " $5 brown carmine ('37) 75 60
Nos. C11-C20 (10) 1.85 1.32

Type of 1932-37, with secret mark

1932-37 Issue. Lower part of left character joined.

Secret Mark, 1940-41 Issue. Separated.

Wmkd. Character Yu (Post) Multiple. (261)

Perf. 12, 12½, 12½x13, 13.

1940-41

C21 AP3 15c gray green 10 6
C22 " 25c yellow orange 12 7
C23 " 30c red 10 6
a. Vert. pair, imperf. between 100.00
C24 AP3 45c dull rose violet ('41) 8 6
C25 AP3 50c brown 8 6
C26 " 60c deep blue ('41) 8 6
C27 " 90c olive ('41) 10 7
C28 " $1 apple green ('41) 12 10
C29 " $2 light brown ('41) 12 10
C30 " $5 lake 12 10
Nos. C21-C30 (10) 1.02 74

Unwmkd.

Perf. 12½, 13, 13½.

C31 AP3 15c gray green ('41) 6 6
C32 " 25c lt. orange ('41) 6 6
C33 " 30c light red ('41) 6 6
C34 " 45c dull rose violet ('41) 8 8
C35 " 50c brown 6 6
C36 " 60c blue ('41) 6 6
C37 " 90c light olive ('41) 6 6
C38 " $1 apple green ('41) 10 10
C39 " $2 light brown ('41) 15 15
C40 " $5 lake ('41) 12 12
Nos. C31-C40 (10) 81 81

Nos. C11 and C12 Surcharged in Black

圓叁拾伍幣國

1946, May 2 *Perf. 14* **Unwmkd.**

C41 AP3 $53 on 15c gray green 20 20
C42 " $73 on 25c org. 425.00 425.00

Forgeries of No. C42 exist.

On Nos. C23, C21, C22, C29 and C30.

Perf. 13, 13x12, 12½.

Wmk. 261

C43 AP3 $23 on 30c red 8 10
C44 " $53 on 15c gray green 4.00 4.00
C45 " $73 on 25c yel. org. 8 10
C46 " $100 on $2 light brown 8 10
C47 " $200 on $5 lake 8 10

On Nos. C33, C31, C32, C39 and C40.

Perf. 13, 13x12, 13x12½, 12½.

Unwmkd.

C48 AP3 $23 on 30c light red 5 5
a. Inverted surcharge 75.00
b. "23⁰⁰" omitted 35.00
c. Last character (kuo) of surch. omitted 30.00
C49 AP3 $53 on 15c gray green 5 5
a. Horiz. pair, imperf. between 400.00
C50 AP3 $73 on 25c light orange 5 5
a. Inverted surcharge 400.00
C51 AP3 $100 on $2 light brown 5 5
C52 AP3 $200 on $5 lake 5 5
a. Inverted surcharge 60.00

The surcharges on Nos. C41-C52 represent Chinese national currency and were applied at Shanghai.

Douglas DC-4 over Sun Yat-sen Mausoleum, Nanking
AP4

1946, Sept. 10 **Litho.** *Perf. 14*

Without Gum.

C53 AP4 $27 blue 15 10

No. C23 Surcharged in Black

圓萬壹作改

Perf. 13x12

1948, May 18 **Wmk. 261**

C54 AP3 $10,000 on 30c red 10 10

Same, in Black or Carmine, on Nos. C33, C32, C37, C36, C18 and C38.

Perf. 12½, 13x12½, 14

Unwmkd.

C55 AP3 $10,000 on 30c light red 7 7
C56 " $20,000 on 25c light orange 8 8
C57 " $30,000 on 90c light olive (C) 8 8
C58 " $50,000 on 60c blue (C) 7 7
C59 " $50,000 on $1 yellow grn. (C) 20.00 20.00
C60 " $50,000 on $1 apple green (C) 8 8

No. C53 Surcharged in Black

Perf. 14.

C61 AP4 $10,000 on $27 blue 8 8
Nos. C54-C61 (8) 18.06 20.56

Douglas DC-4 and Arrow
AP5

Lithographed

1949, May 2 *Perf. 12½* **Unwmkd.**

Without Gum.

C62 AP5 blue green 85 85
a. Rouletted 1.25 1.25

See note after No. 959.

Revenue Stamp Overprinted in Blue

政郵國民華中

費空航內國

1949, May **Engraved** *Perf. 14*

C63 A95 $100 olive green 11.00 11.00

See note after No. 962.

Republic of China (Taiwan)

Cheng Ch'eng-kung (Koxinga)
AP6

Typographed.

Rouletted.

1950, Sept. 26 **Unwmkd.**

Without Gum.

C64 AP6 60c deep blue 7.00 1.25

Plane over City Gate, Taipei
AP7

Jet Planes above Chung Shan Bridge
AP8

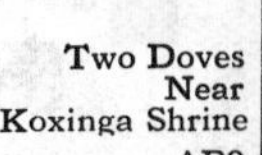

Two Doves Near Koxinga Shrine
AP9

1954 Engraved *Perf. 11½*
Without Gum

C65 AP7 $1 dark brown 4.00 35
a. Vert. pair, imperf. btwn. 250.00
C66 AP8 $1.60 olive black 3.00 25
a. Vert. pair, imperf. btwn. 165.00
b. Horiz. pair, imperf. between 120.00 120.00
C67 AP9 $5 greenish blue 5.00 50

No. C67 Surcharged in Red.

1958, Dec. 11
C68 AP9 $3.50 on $5 greenish blue 1.00 25

Sea Gull
AP10

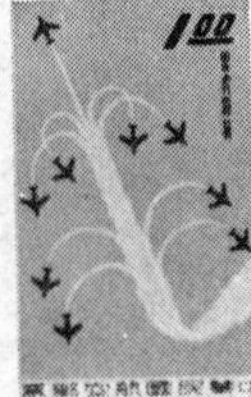

Sabre Jets in Bomb Burst Formation
AP11

1959, Mar. 20 Photo. *Perf. 13*
C69 AP10 $8 blue, gray & black 1.00 20

1960, Feb. 29 *Perf. 13* Unwmkd.

Plane Formations: $2, Loop (horiz.). $5, Diamond formation passing over grounded plane (horiz.).

C70 AP11 $1 multicolored 1.00 35
C71 " $2 " 1.00 18
C72 " $5 " 2.50 40

Issued to honor the Chinese Air Force and the "Thunder Tiger" aerobatic team.

Jet Airliner over Pitan Bridge
AP12

Designs: $6, Jet over Tropic of Cancer monument, Kiai (vert.). $10, Jet over Lion Head mountain, Sinchu (vert.).

1963, Aug. 14 Photo. *Perf. 13*
C73 AP12 $2.50 multicolored 80 8
C74 " $6 " 1.50 12
C75 " $10 " 3.00 1.00

Boeing 727 over Chilin Pavilion, Grand Hotel
AP13

Design: $8, Boeing 727 over National Palace Museum, Taipei.

1967, Apr. 1 *Perf. 13* Unwmkd.
C76 AP13 $5 multicolored 75 10
C77 " $8 " 1.00 30

Wild Geese Flying over Mountains
AP14

Designs (Wild Geese flying over): $5, The sea. $8, The land (horiz.).

1969, Aug. 14 Photo. *Perf. 13*
C78 AP14 $2.50 multicolored 40 6
C79 " $5 " 60 12
C80 " $8 " 80 20

SPECIAL DELIVERY STAMPS.

Design: Dragon in irregular oval. Stamp 8x2½ inches, divided into four parts by perforation or serrate rouletting. Prices of Nos. E1–E8 are for used parts. Complete unused strips of four are exceptionally scarce.

"Chinese Imperial Post Office" in lines, repeated to form the background which is usually lighter in color than the rest of the design.

Dragon's head facing downward. Background with period after "POSTOFFICE".

No Date.

1905 *Perf. 11.* Unwmkd.
E1 10c grass green 80.00

Serrate Roulette in Black.

E2 10c deep green 65.00

1907-10

Dragon's head facing forward. Background with no period after "POSTOFFICE".

No Date.

E3 10c light bluish green 30.00

1909-11

Background with date at bottom.

E4 10c green (Feb., 1909) 10.00
E5 10c blue grn. (Jan. 1911) 7.50

1912

"Imperial Post Office" in serifed letters repeated to form the background.

No Date. No Border. Background of 30 or 28 lines.

E6 10c green (30 lines) 15.00
a. 28 lines 17.50

Background of 35 lines of sans-serif letters. Colored Border

E8 10c green 15.00

On No. E8 the medallion in the third section has Chinese characters in the background instead of the usual English inscriptions. E6 and E8 occur with many types of four-character overprints reading "Republic of China," applied locally but unofficially at various post offices.

1913

Design: Wild Goose. Stamp 7½x2¾ inches, divided into five parts.

"Chinese Post Office" in sans-serif letters, repeated to form the background of 28 lines. With border.

Serrate Roulette in Black.

E9 10c green 85.00 6.50

Unused prices for Nos. E9–E10 are for complete strips of five parts. Used prices are for single parts.

1914

"Chinese Post Office" in antique letters, forming a background of 29 or 30 lines. No border.

Serrate Roulette in Green.

E10 10c green 25.00 75

On No. E9 the background is in sans-serif capitals, the Chinese and English inscriptions are on white tablets and the serial numbers are in black.

On No. E10 the background is in antique capitals and extends under the inscriptions. The serial numbers are in green.

NOTE:

In February, 1916, the Special Delivery Stamps were demonetized and became merely receipts without franking value. To mark this, four of the five sections of the stamp had the letters A, B, C, D either handstamped or printed on them.

SD1

Typographed.

1941 *Rouletted* Unwmkd.
Without Gum.

E11 SD1 ($2) carmine & yellow 6.00 1.25

Motorcycle Messenger
SD2

1949, July Litho. *Perf. 12½*
Without Gum.

E12 SD2 red violet 75 75
a. Rouletted 1.00 1.00

See note after No. 959.

Revenue Stamp Overprinted in Purple Brown

中華民國郵政
國內快遞費

1949 Without Gum
E13 A95 $10 greenish gray 4.00 4.00

See note after No. 962.

REGISTRATION STAMPS.

R1

Typographed.

1941 *Rouletted.* Unwmkd.
Without Gum.

F1 R1 ($1.50) green & buff 4.00 1.50

Mountain Scene
R2

1949, July Litho. *Perf. 12½*
Without Gum.

F2 R2 carmine 60 60
a. Rouletted 60 70

See note after No. 959.

Revenue Stamp Overprinted in Carmine

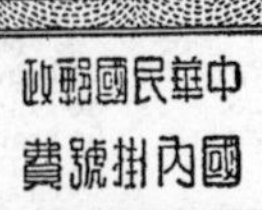

1949
F3 A95 $50 dark blue 4.00 4.00

See note after No. 962.

POSTAGE DUE STAMPS.

Regular Issue of 1902-03 Overprinted in Black

POSTAGE DUE
欠資

1904 *Perf. 14 to 15.* Unwmkd.
J1 A17 ½c chocolate 3.00 85
J2 " 1c ochre 3.00 60
J3 " 2c scarlet 3.00 1.25
J4 " 4c red brown 3.50 1.25
J5 " 5c salmon 5.00 1.25
J6 " 10c dark blue green 6.00 1.50
a. Vertical pair, imperf. between 160.00
Nos. J1-J6 (6) 23.50 6.70

D1

D2

D3

1904 Engraved
J7 D1 ½c blue 1.25 10
a. Horizontal pair, imperf. between 85.00 85.00
J8 " 1c blue 1.75 10
J9 " 2c blue 85 10
a. Horizontal pair, imperf. between 75.00 75.00
J10 " 4c blue 2.25 25
J11 " 5c " 2.75 30
J12 " 10c " 3.00 60
J13 " 20c " 7.50 2.00
J14 " 30c " 10.00 2.50
Nos. J7-J14 (8) 29.35 5.95

Arabic numeral of value at left on Nos. J12 to J14.

1911
J15 D1 1c brown 2.00 75
J16 " 2c " 3.00 1.25

The ½c, 4c, 5c and 20c in brown exist but were not issued as they arrived in China after the downfall of the Ching dynasty.

Issue of 1904 Overprinted in Red

臨時中立

1912
J19 D1 ½c blue 150.00 150.00
J20 " 4c " 250.00 200.00
J21 " 5c " 275.00 275.00
J22 " 10c " 275.00 275.00
J23 " 20c " 700.00 700.00
J24 " 30c " 700.00 700.00

Nos. J15–J16 exist with this overprint, but were not regularly issued.

1912 Overprinted in Red.
J25 D2 ½c blue 15 10
J26 " 1c brown 20 15
a. Horizontal pair, imperf. between 85.00
b. Inverted overprint 70.00
J27 " 2c brown 30 20
J28 " 4c blue 1.00 25
J29 " 5c " 50.00 35.00
J30 " 5c brown 1.00 35
a. Inverted overprint 60.00 50.00
J31 " 10c blue 2.00 50
J32 " 20c " 3.00 1.00
J33 " 30c " 6.00 2.50
Nos. J25-J33 (9) 63.65 40.05

1912 Overprinted in Black.
J34 D3 ½c blue 3.50 1.50
J35 " ½c brown 60 25

J36 D3 1c brown 50 25
a. Inverted overprint 70.00
J37 " 2c brown 1.25 50
J38 " 4c blue 2.50 75
J39 " 5c brown 2.50 1.00
a. Horizontal pair, imperf. between 135.00
J40 " 10c blue 6.00 1.75
J41 " 20c brown 12.50 5.00
J42 " 30c blue 17.50 6.00
Nos. J34–J42 (9) 46.85 17.00

D4

Printed by Waterlow & Sons.

1913, May *Perf. 14, 15*

J43 D4 ½c blue 30 10
a. Horizontal pair, imperf. between 100.00
J44 " 1c blue 60 10
J45 " 2c " 60 15
J46 " 4c " 1.50 20
J47 " 5c " 1.75 20
J48 " 10c " 3.00 50
J49 " 20c " 5.00 80
J50 " 30c " 7.50 1.25
Nos. J43–J50 (8) 20.25 3.30

Printed by the Chinese Bureau of Engraving & Printing.

1915 Re-engraved *Perf. 14*

J51 D4 ½c blue 35 5
J52 " 1c " 65 5
J53 " 2c " 65 5
J54 " 4c " 65 10
J55 " 5c " 1.00 15
J56 " 10c " 1.50 20
J57 " 20c " 3.00 25
J58 " 30c " 9.00 1.00
Nos. J51–J58 (8) 16.80 1.85

In the upper part of the stamps of type D4 there is an ornament of five marks like the letter "V". Below this is a curved label with an inscription in Chinese characters. On the 1913 stamps there are two complete background lines between the ornament and the label. The 1915 stamps show only one unbroken line at this place. There are other minute differences in the engraving of the stamps of the two issues.

D5

1932 *Perf. 14.*

J59 D5 ½c orange 8 6
J60 " 1c " 8 6
J61 " 2c " 8 6
J62 " 4c " 15 18
J63 " 5c " 15 18
J64 " 10c " 35 25
J65 " 20c " 35 25
J66 " 30c " 30 25
Nos. J59–J66 (8) 1.54 1.29

1940
Regular Stamps of 1939 Overprinted in Black or Red

暫欠
作資

J67 A57 $1 henna & dark brown (Bk) 50 50
J68 " $2 deep blue & orange brown (R) 80 80

Type of 1932.
Printed by The Commercial Press, Ltd.
Perf. 12½, 12½x13, 13.

1940-41 Engraved.

J69 D5 ½c yellow orange 5 5
J70 " 1c " 10 10
J71 " 2c " ('41) 5 5
J72 " 4c " 5 5
J73 " 5c " ('41) 8 8
J74 " 10c " ('41) 8 8
J75 " 20c " ('41) 8 8
J76 " 30c " 8 8
J77 " 50c " 8 8
J78 " $1 " 8 8
J79 " $2 " 12 12
Nos. J69–J79 (11) 85 85

D6

Thin Paper Without Gum.

1944 Typographed *Perf. 13*

J80 D6 10c bluish green 3 3
J81 " 20c light chalky blue 3 3
J82 " 40c dull rose 3 3
J83 " 50c bluish green 3 3
J84 " 60c dull blue 3 3
J85 " $1 dull rose 7 7
J86 " $2 lilac brown 8 8
Nos. J80–J86 (7) 30 30

D7

1945 Without Gum **Unwmkd.**

J87 D7 $2 rose carmine 4 4
J88 " $6 " 4 4
J89 " $8 " 4 4
J90 " $10 " 5 5
J91 " $20 " 5 5
J92 " $30 " 5 5
Nos. J87–J92 (6) 27 27

D8

Thin Paper Without Gum.

1947 Lithographed *Perf. 14*

J93 D8 $50 plum 5 5
J94 " $80 " 5 5
J95 " $100 " 5 5
J96 " $160 " 5 5
J97 " $200 " 5 5
J98 " $400 violet brown 5 5
J99 " $500 " 5 5
a. Vert. pair, imperf. between 7.00
J100 " $800 violet brown 5 5
J101 " $2000 " 5 5
Nos. J93–J101 (9) 45 45

Type of 1945, Redrawn, Surcharged with New Value in Black.

1948 Engraved. *Perf. 13½x14.*
Without Gum

J102 D7 $1000 on $20 deep claret 7 7
J103 " $2000 on $30 " 7 7
J104 " $3000 on $50 " 7 7
J105 " $4000 on $100 " 7 7
J106 " $5000 on $200 " 7 7
J107 " $10,000 on $300 " 9 9
J108 " $20,000 on $500 " 9 9
J109 " $30,000 on $1000 " 12 12
Nos. J102–J109 (8) 65 65

There are many differences in the redrawn design.

No. 627 Surcharged in Black

改作欠資
金圓
壹分
1

1949 *Perf. 12*

J110 A72 1(c) on $40 orange 8 8
J111 " 2(c) on $40 " 8 8
J112 " 5(c) on $40 " 8 8
J113 " 10(c) on $40 " 8 8
J114 " 20(c) on $40 " 8 8
J115 " 50(c) on $40 " 10 10
J116 " $1 on $40 " 10 10
J117 " $2 on $40 " 10 10
J118 " $5 on $40 " 10 10
J119 " $10 on $40 " 15 15
Nos. J110–J119 (10) 95 95

Republic of China (Taiwan)

No. 438 Surcharged in Green or Black

臺幣
肆角
欠資
40 40

1951 *Perf. 12½.* **Unwmkd.**

J120 A47 40c on 40c org. (G) 3.00 1.50
J121 " 80c on 40c " 3.00 1.50

Revenue Stamps Surcharged in Various Colors

政郵國民華中
角壹幣台資欠
10

Without Gum

1953 *Perf. 12½, 14.* **Unwmkd.**

J122 A95 10c on $50 dark blue (O) 3.00 1.00
J123 " 20c on $100 olive green (Dk Br) 3.00 1.00
J124 " 40c on $20 org. brn. 3.50 50
J125 " 80c on $500 slate green (Dk Bl) 7.00 1.00
J126 " $1 on $30 dark violet (G) 7.00 3.75
Nos. J122–J126 (5) 23.50 7.25

D9

Lithographed

1956 *Perf. 12½* **Unwmkd.**
Without Gum

J127 D9 20c rose car., & lt. bl. 15 5
J128 " 40c green & buff 15 5
J129 " 80c brown & gray 30 5
J130 " $1 ultra. & pink 30 10

No. 1197 Surcharged in Dark Violet

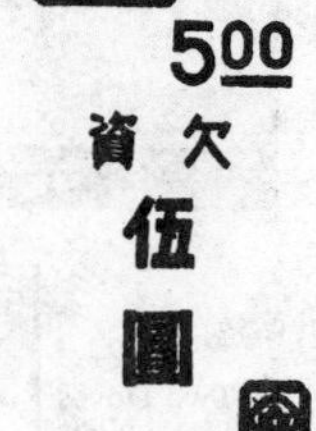

Engraved

1961, Dec. 28 *Perf. 12* **Wmk. 323**
Without Gum

J131 A135 $5 on $20 car. rose 1.00 35

Nos. 1274, 1282–1283 Surcharged in Black, Carmine Rose or Blue

1964-65 **Lithographed**

J132 A158 10c on 80c pale green 10 8
J133 " 20c on $3.60 violet blue (CR) ('65) 10 8
J134 " 40c on $4.50 verm. (B) ('65) 15 8

D10

1966-76 *Perf. 12½* **Wmk. 323**
Granite Paper; Without Gum

J135 D10 10c dk. brn. & lilac 5 4
J136 " 20c blue & yellow 5 4
J137 " 50c vio. blue & lt. blue ('70) 18 4
J138 " $1 purple & salmon 12 4
J139 " $2 grn. & lt. blue 18 5
J140 " $5 red & salmon 35 18
J141 " $10 lilac rose & pink ('76) 70 35
Nos. J135–J141 (7) 1.63 74

The 50c and $10 are gummed. The $1 and $2 were reissued with gum in 1968 and 1973 respectively.
The $10 is on ordinary paper.

PARCEL POST STAMPS

PP1

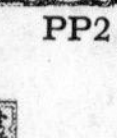
PP2

PP3

Engraved

1945-48 *Perf. 13* **Unwmkd.**
Without Gum.

Q1 PP1 $500 green 20 5
Q2 " $1000 blue 20 6

Q3 PP1 $3000 rose red 40 10
Q4 " $5000 brown 10.00 1.50
Q5 " $10,000 lilac gray 15.00 2.00
Q6 " $20,000 red orange
Nos. Q1-Q5 (5) 25.80 3.71

No. Q6 was prepared but not issued.

Perf. 12½.

Q7 PP2 $3000 red orange 35 8
Q8 " $5000 dark blue 40 10
Q9 " $10,000 violet 40 15
Q10 " $20,000 dark red 40 15

Perf. 13½

Q11 PP3 $1000 orange yellow 40 18
Q12 " $3000 blue green 50 18
Q13 " $5000 orange red 50 18
Q14 " $7000 dull blue 50 18
Q15 " $10,000 car. rose 60 18
Q16 " $30,000 olive 60 18
Q17 " $50,000 indigo 60 18
Q18 " $70,000 orange brown 65 18
Q19 " $100,000 deep plum 65 18

Denomination Tablet Without Inner Frame.

Q20 PP3 $200,000 dark green 90 30
Q21 " $300,000 pink 1.00 30
Q22 " $500,000 violet brown 1.00 40
Q23 " $3,000,000 slate blue 1.15 50
Q24 " $5,000,000 lilac 1.15 50
Q25 " $6,000,000 olive gray 1.50 60
Q26 " $8,000,000 scarlet 1.50 80
Q27 " $10,000,000 sage green 2.25 1.00
Nos. Q11-Q27 (17) 15.45 6.02

Zeros for "cents" omitted on Nos. Q23-Q27.

Parcel Post Stamps of 1945-48 Surcharged in Black or Carmine

圓拾圓金
10
圓拾圓金

1949 *Perf. 13½.* **Unwmkd.**

Q32 PP3 $10 on $3000 blue green 20 7
Q33 " $20 on $5000 orange red 20 7
Q34 " $50 on $10,000 carmine rose 20 7
Q35 " $100 on $3,000,000 slate blue (C) 28 10
Q36 " $200 on $5,000,000 lilac 40 12
Q37 " $500 on $1000 orange yellow 85 18
Q38 " $1000 on $7000 dull blue 85 25
Nos. Q32-Q38 (7) 2.98 86

Five characters in each line on Nos. Q33 to Q38.

MILITARY STAMPS.

No. 454 Overprinted in Dull Red 郵 軍

1943-44 *Perf. 12.* **Unwmkd.**

M1 A59 8c turquoise green 70 70

Nos. 383, 453-454 Overprinted in Red 郵 軍

6mm. between characters.

Perf. 14, 12½.

M2 A57 8c olive green 50 50
a. 8mm. between characters 60 60
M3 A59 8c red orange 75.00
M4 " 8c turquoise green 85 85

No. 493 Overprinted in Red 郵 軍

Perf. 13.

M5 A62 16c dull olive brown 65 20
a. Perf. 10½-11 50.00

No. M5 overprinted in black is a proof.

Stamps of 1942-44 Overprinted in Carmine or Black 郵 軍

M6 A62 50c sage green (C) 65 65
M7 " $1 rose lake (Bk) 65 65
M8 " $1 dull green (Bk) 65 65
M9 " $2 dk. bl. grn. (C) 1.20 1.20
M10 " $2 dark violet brown ('44) (Bk) 4.00 4.00

Nos. 383 and 357 Overprinted in Red 郵 軍

1944 *Perf. 12, 14.*

M11 A57 8c olive green 80 80
a. Right character inverted 50.00
M12 " 16c olive gray 3.00 3.00

Anti-Aircraft Guns
M1

Thin Paper Without Gum.

1945, Jan. 1 Typo. *Perf. 12½*

M13 M1 rose 30 40

Taiwan (Formosa)

100 Sen = 1 Yen
100 Cents = 1 Dollar

Stamps and Types of Japan (Taiwan) Overprinted in Black

中華民國
臺灣省

Lithographed.

Values in Sen and Yen.

Black Overprint.

1945 *Imperf.* **Unwmkd.**

Stamps Divided by Lines of Colored Dashes.

1 A1 3s carmine 30 25
2 " 5s blue green 40 20
3 " 10s pale blue 50 20
a. Inverted ovpt. 25.00
b. Double ovpt. 27.50
4 " 30s dark blue 75 65
5 " 40s violet 85 50
6 " 50s gray brown 50 50
7 " 1y olive green 60 65

Same Overprint on Types of Japan A99 and A100.

8 A99 5y gray green 2.50 1.50
9 A100 10y brown violet 3.50 2.00
a. Invtd. ovpt. 100.00
Nos. 1-9 (9) 9.90 6.45

The basic stamps of this issue were prepared by Japanese authorities for Taiwan use before the end of World War II when the island reverted to Chinese control. They are printed on crude buff or white wove paper. The overprint translates: "For Use in Taiwan, Chinese Republic."

A second overprinting of Nos. 2-3 was made with a different font.

China, Nos. 728-731, Surcharged in Black

限臺灣省貼用
70 錢拾柒

1946 *Perf. 14.*

10 A75 70s on $20 green 10 7
a. Inverted surcharge 125.00
11 " 1y on $30 blue 10 7
12 " 2y on $50 dk. brown 20 18
13 " 3y on $100 carmine 20 18

Issued to commemorate the convening of the Chinese National Assembly.

China Issues and Types of 1940-1946 Surcharged in Black

用貼灣臺限
錢 拾
a

Perf.

12½, 12½x13, 13, 13x12½, 14.

1946-47

14 A46 2s on 2c deep blue ('47) 5 5
15 A48 5s on 5c dull red orange 3 3
16 A39 10s on 4c pale violet 3 3
17 A48 30s on 15c brn. car. 4 4
18 A73 50s on $20 carmine ('47) 4 4
19 A37 65s on $20 bright yellow green ('47) 4 4
20 A47 1y on 20c light blue 4 4
a. Inverted surch. 50.00
21 A37 1y on $30 choc. ('47) 5 5
22 " 2y on $50 red orange ('47) 4 4
23 A73 3y on $100 dark carmine ('47) 7 7
24 " 5y on $200 olive green ('47) 7 7
25 " 10y on $500 bright blue green ('47) 10 10
26 " 20y on $700 red brown ('47) 15 15
27 " 50y on $1000 rose lake ('47) 40 40
28 " 100y on $3000 bl. ('47) 55 55
Nos. 14-28 (15) 1.70 1.70

The bottom line of the surcharge expresses the new value and consists of 2, 3 or 4 characters.

Same Surcharge on China No. 412.

1947 *Perf. 13.* **Wmk. 261**

28A A48 30s on 15c brown carmine 20.00 20.00

Type of China, 1946.

Inscribed:

貼 臺
用 灣

Engraved

1947 *Perf. 11, 11½.* **Unwmkd.**

29 A74 70c carmine 12 12
30 " $1 green 12 12
31 " $2 vermilion 12 12
32 " $3 yellow green 12 12
33 " $7 yellow orange 25 25
34 " $10 magenta 25 25
Nos. 29-34 (6) 98 98

60th birthday of Chiang Kai-shek.

Type of China, 1947.

Inscribed: 用貼灣臺

1947 *Perf. 14*

35 A76 50c deep green 15 15
36 " $3 deep blue 15 15
37 " $7.50 carmine 15 15
38 " $10 light brown 15 15
39 " $20 deep claret 15 15
Nos. 35-39 (5) 75 75

First anniversary of return of Chinese National Government to Nanking.

Dr. Sun Yat-sen
A1

1947, July 10 **Without Gum**

40 A1 $1 dark brown 5 5
41 " $2 orange brown 5 5
42 A1 $3 blue green 5 5
43 " $5 vermilion 5 5
44 " $9 deep blue 5 5
45 " $10 bright rose carmine 5 5
46 " $20 deep green 5 5
47 " $50 rose lilac 10 10
48 " $100 blue 18 18
49 " $200 dark red 15 15
Nos. 40-49 (10) 78 78

The 30c gray and $7.50 orange were not regularly issued without surcharge.

Type of 1947 Surcharged in Black

改作伍佰圓
500⁰⁰
b

1948 *Perf. 14* **Unwmkd.**

51 A1 $25 on $100 blue 40 15
52 " $500 on $7.50 orange 50 30
53 " $1000 on 30c gray 1.50 85

Stamps of China, 1943-48, Surcharged Type "a" in Black or Carmine.

1948-49 *Perf. 12½, 14*

54 A73 $5 on $70 red orange 10 10
55 A62 $10 on $3 dark yellow 12 12
56 A82 $10 on $150 dark blue (C) 10 10
57 " $20 on $250 deep lilac (C) 10 10
58 A67 $100 on $20 carmine 60.00 60.00
59 A82 $1000 on $20,000 rose pink ('49) 70 35
Nos. 54-59 (6) 61.12 60.77

The bottom line of the surcharge expresses the new value and consists of 2 or 3 characters.

Type of 1947.

1949 **Engraved.** *Perf. 14.*

63 A1 $25 olive green 15 12
64 " $5000 ochre 25 15
65 " $10,000 apple green 25 15
66 " $20,000 olive bistre 25 15
67 " $30,000 indigo 25 15
68 " $40,000 violet brown 25 15
Nos. 63-68 (6) 1.40 87

No. 42 and Type of 1947 Surcharged Type "b" in Black, Carmine Violet or Red Violet.

1949

69 A1 $300 on $3 blue green 18 12
70 " $1000 on $3 blue green (C) 40 12
71 " $2000 on $3 blue green (V) 35 25
72 " $3000 on $3 bl. green (RV) 1.00 20
73 " $3000 on $7.50 org. 11.00 80
Nos. 69-73 (5) 12.93 1.49

Stamps of China, 1940-47, Surcharged Type "a" in Black or Carmine.

Perf. 12½, 13x13½, 14.

74 A39 $2 on 2½c rose lilac (#424) 8 8
75 A72 $5 on $40 orange (#627) 6 6
76 A73 $5 on $50 purple (C) (#638) 8 8
77 " $5 on $100 dark car. (#640) 6 6
78 A57 $20 on 2c olive green (#368) 10 10
81 A63 $100 on $20 rose (#571) 12 7
82 A67 $200 on $10 dark blue (C) (#591) 20 20
84 A57 $500 on $30 dull violet (#521) 15 15
86 A62 $800 on $4 red brown (#504) 35 35

87 A67 $5000 on $10 dark blue (#591) 75 75
88 " $10,000 on $20 carmine (#592) 1.50 1.25
89 A82 $200,000 on $3000 blue (C) (#750) 25.00 15.00
Nos. 74-89 (12) 28.45 18.15

Northeastern Provinces No. 47, Surcharged in Green, Red Violet, Black or Blue

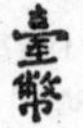

2 ★★★ 2

1949-50

91 A2 2c on $44 dark carmine rose (G) 2.00 1.00
92 " 5c on $44 dark carmine rose (RV) ('50) 2.25 1.50
a. Violet surcharge 2.50 2.00
93 " 10c on $44 dark carmine rose (RV) ('50) 4.00 90
94 " 20c on $44 dark carmine rose (Bk) ('50) 6.00 2.35
a. Double surcharge 27.50
95 " 30c on $44 dark carmine rose (Bl) ('50) 7.00 2.65
96 " 50c on $44 dark carmine rose (Bl) ('50) 12.00 5.25
Nos. 91-96 (6) 33.25 13.65

China 959a, Overprinted in Black 用貼湾臺限

Ovpt. 15mm. Wide.

1949 *Rouletted 9½.* **Unwmkd.**
97 A96 orange 15 15

China Nos. 567, 498 and 640 Surcharged Type "a" in Black.

1948-49 *Perf. 12½, 13, 14* **Unwmkd.**
98 A63 $20 on $3 red 75 20
99 A62 $50 on 50c sage green 30 10
a. Perf. 11 10.00 10.00
100 A73 $600 on $100 dark carmine 1.00 60

Bottom line of surcharge consists of 3 characters.
No. 99 has two settings of surcharge: I. Spacing 10mm. between rows of characters. II. Spacing 12mm.

Nos. 67, 47 and 68 Surcharged in Violet or Black

臺幣壹角
10

1949 *Perf. 14.*
101 A1 2c on $30,000 indigo (V) 1.75 1.50
102 " 10c on $50 rose lilac 2.50 1.25
103 " 10c on $40,000 violet brown 2.00 1.50

Numerals slightly larger on Nos. 101 and 103.
For similar surcharges on China type A82 see China Nos. 1025-1036.

AIR POST STAMP.

China No. C62a, Overprinted in Black 用貼湾臺限

Ovpt. 15mm. Wide.

1949 *Rouletted 9½* **Unwmkd.**
C1 AP5 blue green 40 40

SPECIAL DELIVERY STAMP.

China No. E12a, Overprinted in Black 用貼灣臺限

Ovpt. 12½mm. Wide.

1950 *Rouletted 9½.* **Unwmkd.**
E1 SD2 red violet 15 15

REGISTRATION STAMP.

China No. F2a Overprinted in Black 用貼灣臺限

Ovpt. 12mm. Wide.

1950 *Rouletted 9½* **Unwmkd.**
F1 R2 carmine 15 15

POSTAGE DUE STAMPS.

D1

Lithographed.

1948, Feb. 10 *Perf. 14* **Unwmkd.**
Without Gum

J1 D1 $1 blue 6 6
J2 " $3 " 6 6
J3 " $5 " 6 6
J4 " $10 " 8 8
J5 " $20 " 6 6
Nos. J1-J5 (5) 32 32

Nos. J1-J4 Surcharged in Carmine

作改
伍拾圓
5000

1948, Dec. 4
J6 D1 $50 on $1 blue 1.25 1.25
J7 " $100 on $3 " 1.25 1.25
J8 " $300 on $5 " 1.25 1.25
J9 " $500 on $10 " 2.00 2.00

Nos. 70, 72 and 64 Handstamped in Violet

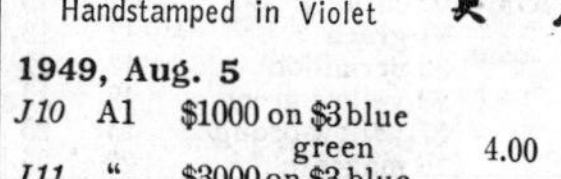

1949, Aug. 5
J10 A1 $1000 on $3 blue green 4.00 3.00
J11 " $3000 on $3 blue green 3.50 3.00
J12 " $5000 ochre 3.00 3.00

No. 48 Surcharged in Various Colors

1950
J13 A1 4c on $100 blue (Br) 1.00 75
J14 " 10c on $100 " (RV) 1.50 1.00
J15 " 20c on $100 " (Bk) 2.00 1.50
J16 " 40c on $100 " (C) 5.00 3.00
J17 " $1 on $100 " (Bl) 8.00 5.50
Nos. J13-J17 (5) 17.50 11.75

The indexes in each volume of the Scott Catalogue contain many listings which help to identify stamps.

PARCEL POST STAMPS.

Type of China, Parcel Post Stamps of 1945-48 With Added Inscription:

Engraved.

1949 *Perf. 14.* **Unwmkd.**
Q1 PP3 $100 bluish green 35.00 6
Q2 " $300 rose carmine 35.00 6
Q3 " $500 olive green 35.00 8
Q4 " $1000 slate 35.00 10
Q5 " $3000 deep plum 35.00 10
Nos. Q1-Q5 (5) 175.00 40

Chinese characters in lower corners have colorless background; denomination tablet in color.

OCCUPATION STAMPS.
Issued Under Japanese Occupation.
Kwangtung.
(kwäng'dōōng')

China No. 297 Overprinted in Black

1942 *Perf. 12½* **Unwmkd.**
1N1 A37 2c olive green 50 50
a. Inverted ovpt. 20.00

Same Overprint in Red or Black on Stamps of China, 1939-41.

Perf. 12½, 14.
1N2 A57 3c dull claret (#350) 25 25
1N3 " 8c olive green (#383) 25 25
1N4 " 10c green (#354) (R) 25 25
1N5 " 10c green (#384) (R) 25 25
1N6 " 16c olive gray (#357) 50 50
1N7 " 30c scarlet (#385) 25 25
1N8 " 50c dark blue (#386) (R) 25 25
1N9 " $1 orange brown & sepia (#387) 1.00 1.00
1N10 " $2 deep blue & yel. brown (#388) 50 50
1N11 " $5 red & slate green (#389) 1.00 1.00
1N12 " $10 dark green & dull pur. (#390) 2.00 2.00
1N13 " $20 rose lake & dark blue (#391) 1.00 1.00

Same Overprint on China Nos. 422 and 433.

Perf. 12½.
1N14 A40 1c orange 25 25
a. Inverted ovpt. 20.00 20.00
1N15 A47 20c light blue 50 50

Same Overprint on Stamps of China, 1941.

Perf. 12.
1N16 A59 1c orange 25 25
1N17 " 5c green 25 25
1N18 " 8c turquoise green 25 25
1N19 " 10c bright green 25 25
1N20 " 17c olive 50 50
1N21 " 30c scarlet 50 50
1N22 " 50c dark blue 50 50
Nos. 1N1-1N22 (22) 11.25 11.25

Stamps of China, 1939-41 Overprinted in Black

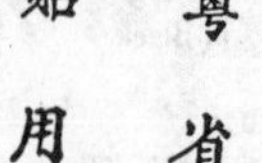

1942 *Perf. 12½, 14*
1N23 A57 2c olive grn. (#368) 25 25
1N24 " 3c dull claret (#350) 25 25
1N25 " 5c olive grn. (#352) 25 25
1N26 " 8c olive green (#353) 85.00
1N27 A57 8c olive green (#369) 30 30
1N28 " 10c green (#354) 50 50
1N29 " 16c olive gray (#357) 50 50
1N30 " 25c dark blue (#358) 50 50
1N31 " 30c scarlet (#385) 25 25
1N32 " 50c dark blue (#386) 25 25
1N33 " $1 orange brown & sepia (#387) 75 75
1N34 " $2 deep blue & yel. brn. (#388) 75 75
1N35 " $5 red & slate green (#389) 1.25 1.25
1N36 " $10 dark green & dull purple (#390) 2.00 2.00
1N37 " $20 rose lake & dark blue (#391) 2.50 2.50
Nos. 1N23-1N25, 1N27-1N37 (14) 10.30 10.30

Same Overprint on China Nos. 397-401.

1942 *Perf. 14.* **Wmk. 261**
1N38 A57 $1 orange brown & sepia 2.00 1.50
1N39 " $2 deep blue & yellow brown 2.00 1.50
1N40 " $5 red & slate grn. 2.50 2.00
1N41 " $10 dark green & dull purple 2.50 2.00
1N42 " $20 rose lake & dark blue 4.00 3.00
Nos. 1N38-1N42 (5) 13.00 10.00

Same Overprint on Stamps of China, 1941.

1942 *Perf. 12.* **Unwmkd.**
1N43 A59 2c bright ultra. 10 10
1N44 " 5c green 15 15
1N45 " 8c red orange 20 20
1N46 " 8c turquoise green 20 20
1N47 " 10c bright green 50 50
1N48 " 17c olive 50 50
1N49 " 25c rose violet 50 50
1N50 " 30c scarlet 50 50
1N51 " 50c dark blue 50 50
1N52 " $1 brown & black 1.00 1.00
1N53 " $2 blue & black 1.00 1.00
1N54 " $5 scarlet & black 1.00 1.00
1N55 " $10 green & black 1.50 1.50
1N56 " $20 rose violet & black 2.00 2.00
Nos. 1N43-1N56 (14) 9.65 9.65

China Nos. 354 and 369 Surcharged in Black

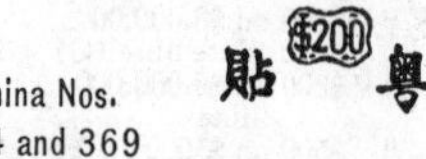

1945 *Perf. 12½* **Unwmkd.**
1N57 A57 $200 on 10c green 35.00 20.00
1N58 " $400 on 8c olive green 35.00 20.00

China No. 422 Surcharged in Black

1945
1N59 A40 $400 on 1c org. 250.00 200.00

POSTAGE DUE STAMP.

China, No. J79 Surcharged Diagonally with New Value Between Parallel Lines in Black.

1945 *Perf. 12½.* **Unwmkd.**
1NJ1 D5 $100 on $2 yellow orange 250.00 275.00
a. Inverted surch. 300.00

MENG CHIANG

(Inner Mongolia)

1941

Stamps of China Overprinted				疆 蒙 Characters 4mm. High I		疆 蒙 Characters 5mm. High II	
297	A37	2c	2N1	15	15	20	20
298	"	4c	2N2	7.00	7.00	5.00	5.00
301	"	15c	2N3	20	20	50	50
302	"	20c	2N4	60	60	75	50
303	"	25c	2N5	7.50	7.50	75	50
312	A39	½c	2N6	40	40	3.50	3.50
314	"	2½c	2N7	20	20	20	15
318	A45	13c	2N8	27.50	27.50	75	50
321	A48	30c	2N9			16.50	16.50
368	A57	2c	2N10			15	15
350	"	3c	2N11	15	15	15	15
352	"	5c	2N12	15	15	15	15
353	"	8c	2N13	15	15	25	20
369	"	8c	2N14			1.00	75
354	"	10c	2N15			30	20
357	"	16c	2N16			50	40
359	"	$1	2N17	165.00	165.00	1.75	1.75
347	"	$1	2N17A	22.50	22.50		
361	"	$5	2N18			11.00	11.00
382	"	5c	2N19			15	15
383	"	8c	2N20	20	15	11.00	11.00
384	"	10c	2N21	20	15	25	20
385	"	30c	2N22	50	20	65	50
386	"	50c	2N23	60	40	65	50
387	"	$1	2N24	2.25	2.25	3.50	3.00
388	"	$2	2N25	2.50	2.50	7.50	5.00
389	"	$5	2N26	9.00	9.00	15.00	15.00
390	"	$10	2N27	17.50	17.50	15.00	15.00
391	"	$20	2N28	25.00	25.00	20.00	20.00
394	"	10c	2N29			75	60
395	"	30c	2N30	17.50	17.50	1.00	90
396	"	50c	2N31			1.00	90
402	A39	½c	2N32			2.50	1.50
403	A40	1c	2N33	20	15	15	15
405	A39	2½c	2N34	15.00	15.00	10.00	10.00
406	A48	3c	2N35			15	15
410	A46	10c	2N36	1.25	1.00	1.00	75
413	"	17c	2N37	15.00	15.00	7.50	7.50
416	A40	25c	2N38			1.00	35
418	A48	30c	2N39	15.00	15.00	10.00	8.50
419	A47	40c	2N40	1.00	1.00	35	20
420	A40	50c	2N41	2.00	1.00	7.50	7.50
421	A39	½c	2N42	15	15	15	15
422	A40	1c	2N43	15	15	40	15
423	A46	2c	2N44	15	15		
425	A48	3c	2N45	25	25	25	15
426	A39	4c	2N46			30	15
428	A45	8c	2N47	27.50	27.50	2.00	2.00
429	A46	10c	2N48	3.50	2.50	9.00	9.00
430	A45	13c	2N49	1.00	50	1.25	1.00
431	A48	15c	2N50			50	50
432	A46	17c	2N51	50	40	60	40
433	A47	20c	2N52	60	60	60	20
434	A45	21c	2N53			60	50
435	A40	25c	2N54	60	60		
436	A46	28c	2N55			50	50
439	A40	50c	2N56	2.00	1.00	1.00	1.00

China Nos. 297-298, 302 Surcharged in Black

疆 蒙
分 壹

1942 ***Perf. 12½, 13.*** **Unwmkd.**

2N57 A37 1c on 2c olive green 50 50
2N58 " 2c on 4c green 50 40
2N59 " 10c on 20c ultramarine 7.50 7.50

Same, on China No. 313.

Perf. 14.

2N60 A40 ½c on 1c orange 1.25

Same, on Stamps of China, 1938–41

Perf. 12½.

2N61 A57 1c on 2c olive green (#368) 30 20
2N62 " 4c on 8c olive green (#353) 1.75 1.25
a. Inverted surch. 40.00 40.00
2N63 " 4c on 8c olive green (#369) 50 50
2N64 " 5c on 10c green (#354) 35 25
2N65 " 8c on 16c olive gray (#357) 60 40
2N66 " 50c on $1 henna & dark brown (#359) 1.75 1.75
a. 50c on $1 henna & dark brown (#347) 15.00 15.00
b. 50c on $1 henna & dark brown (#344) 150.00 150.00
2N67 " $1 on $2 dp. bl. & orange brown (#360) 9.00 9.00

No. 2N66b was issued without gum.

Same, on Stamps of China, 1940.

Perf. 14.

2N68 A57 4c on 8c olive green (#383) 15 15
2N69 " 15c on 30c scarlet (#385) 40 40
a. Inverted surch. 40.00 40.00
2N70 " 25c on 50c dark blue (#386) 75 75
2N71 " 50c on $1 orange brown & sepia (#387) 1.00 75
2N72 " $1 on $2 deep blue & yellow brown (#388) 2.00 1.75
2N73 " $5 on $10 dark green & dull purple (#390) 7.50 8.00
2N74 " $10 on $20 rose lake & dark blue (#391) 30.00 30.00

Same, on China No. 395.

1942 ***Perf. 14.*** **Wmk. 261**

2N75 A57 15c on 30c scarlet 17.50 17.50

Same, on China Nos. 418 and 419.

Perf. 12½, 13.

2N76 A48 15c on 30c brown carmine 7.50 7.50
2N77 A47 20c on 40c orange 1.75 1.75

Same, on Stamps of China, 1940-41.

1942 **Unwmkd.**

2N78 A40 ½c on 1c orange 10 10
2N79 A39 2c on 4c pale violet 20 15
2N80 A47 10c on 20c light blue 40 30
2N81 " 20c on 40c orange 1.75 1.50
2N82 A40 25c on 50c green 4.00 4.00

Same Surcharge on "New Peking" Prints.

Perf. 14.

2N83 A37 1c on 2c olive grn. 10 10
2N84 " 2c on 4c dull grn. 10 10
2N85 A46 5c on 10c dull vio. 20 20
2N86 A57 8c on 16c olive gray 20 20
2N87 A47 10c on 20c red brown 30 30
2N88 A48 15c on 30c brown carmine 50 50
2N89 A47 20c on 40c orange 50 50
2N90 A40 25c on 50c green 75 75
2N91 A57 50c on $1 orange brn. & sepia 1.50 1.50
2N92 " $1 on $2 deep blue & org. brown 10.00 10.00
2N93 " $5 on $10 dk. green & dull purple 12.50 12.50

The "New Peking" printings were made by the Chinese Bureau of Engraving and Printing for use in Japanese controlled areas of North China. They are on thin, poor quality paper, with dull gum or without gum and there are slight alterations in the designs.

Dragon-Carved Pillar and Doves
A1

Mining Coal
A2

Wmkd.

Characters in Circle in Sheet.

Perf. 12 x Pin-Perf. 12.

1943 **Engraved**

2N94 A1 4f deep orange 10 10
2N95 " 8f dark blue 20 20

Issued to commemorate the 5th anniversary of the Inner Mongolia post and telegraph service.

The watermark, which is 40mm. in diameter and covers four stamps, occurs three times in the sheet.

Photogravure.

1943 ***Perf. 12.*** **Unwmkd.**

2N96 A2 4f Prussian green 7 7
2N97 " 8f brown red 15 15

Issued to commemorate the 2nd anniversary of the "Greater East Asia War".

Flying Horse
A3

Yun Wang
A4

1944 ***Perf. 12½ x 12, 12 x 12½.***

2N98 A3 4f rose 10 10
2N99 A4 8f dull blue 20 20

Issued to commemorate the 5th anniversary of the founding of the Federal Autonomous Government of Mongolia, September 1, 1939.

Industrial Plant
A5

1944, Dec. 8 **Photo.** ***Perf. 12x12½***

2N100 A5 8f red brown 8 8

Issued to commemorate the 3rd anniversary of the "Greater East Asia War" and to encourage production increase.

New Peking Printings of 1942 Overprinted in Black  

Engraved

1945 ***Perf. 14.*** **Unwmkd.**

Without Gum.

2N101 A37 2c olive green 10 10
2N102 " 4c dull green 65 65
2N103 " 5c green 10 10
2N104 A57 $1 orange brown & sepia 50 50
2N105 " $2 deep blue & orange brown 2.00 2.00
2N106 " $5 red & greenish black 6.00 6.00

Same Overprint on New Peking Printings of Martyrs Issue

2N107 A40 1c orange 10 10
2N108 A45 8c deep orange 10 10
2N109 A46 10c dull violet 15 15
2N110 A47 20c red brown 15 15
2N111 A48 30c brn. carmine 10 10
2N112 A47 40c orange 10 10
2N113 A40 50c green 35 35
Nos. 2N101-2N113 (13) 10.40 10.40

Stamps of Meng Chiang, 1941 With Additional Surcharge in Red or Black 角 伍

1945

2N114 A39 10c on ½c olive black (#2N42) (R) 25 25
a. 10c on ½c olive black (#2N42, II) 75
2N115 A40 10c on 1c orange (#2N43, II) (R) 25 25
a. Without secret mark (China #313) 15.00 15.00
2N116 A37 50c on 2c olive green (#2N1, II) (Bk) 25 25
2N117 A57 50c on 2c olive green (#2N10) (Bk) 10 10
2N118 A39 50c on 4c pale violet (#2N46) (R) 25 25
2N119 A57 50c on 5c olive green (#2N12) (R) 15 15
2N120 " 50c on 5c olive green (#2N19) (R) 25 25
Nos. 2N114-2N120 (7) 1.50 1.50

Same Surcharge on Nos. 2N32 and 2N33 II.

1945 **Wmk. 261**

2N121 A39 10c on ½c olive black (R) 3.50 3.50
2N122 A40 10c on 1c org. (R) 50 50

Same Surcharge on Nos. 2N107, 2N101-2N103 and 2N108

1945 **Unwmkd.**

2N123 A40 10c on 1c orange (R) 20 20
2N124 A37 50c on 2c olive green (Bk) 15 15
2N125 " 50c on 4c dull green (R) 1.25 1.25
2N126 " 50c on 5c green 20 20
2N127 A45 $1 on 8c deep orange (R) 35 35
Nos. 2N123-2N127 (5) 2.15 2.15

NORTH CHINA

1941 **Honan** **Hopei**

STAMPS OF CHINA OVERPRINTED				南 河 I		南 河 II			北 河 I		北 河 II	
297	A37	2c	*3N1*	75	25	25	20	*4N1*	25	25	20	20
298	"	4c	*3N2*	1.10	1.00	4.00	3.00	*4N2*	30	25	15.00	15.00
301	"	15c	*3N3*	35	25	25	20	*4N3*	60	40	20	20
302	"	20c	*3N4*	1.50	25			*4N4*			30	30
303	"	25c	*3N5*			4.00	3.00	*4N5*	27.50	27.50	1.00	75
312	A39	½c	*3N6*	20	20	2.50	2.50	*4N6*	20	15	15	15
314	"	2½c	*3N7*	20	20	15	15	*4N7*	20	15	15	15
318	A45	13c	*3N8*	25.00	22.50	25	15	*4N8*	50	50	35	25
321	A48	30c	*3N9*			1.75	75	*4N9*			75	50
322	A47	40c	*3N10*			17.50	17.50					
347	A57	$1	*3N11*	17.50	17.50			*4N10*	80.00	80.00		
349	"	2c						*4N11*			15	15
350	"	3c	*3N12*	20	20	15	15	*4N12*	40	30	15	15
352	"	5c	*3N13*	20	20	15	15	*4N13*	25	25	15	15
353	"	8c	*3N14*	30	30	15	15	*4N14*	35	35	15	15
354	"	10c	*3N15*			15	15	*4N15*			15	15
357	"	16c	*3N16*			15	15	*4N16*			15	15
359	"	$1	*3N17*	125.00	125.00	2.00	1.50	*4N17*			1.25	1.00
360	"	$2						*4N18*	15.00	15.00	1.50	1.50
361	"	$5	*3N18*			20.00	20.00	*4N19*	12.50	12.50	10.00	10.00
362	"	$10						*4N20*			40.00	40.00
363	"	$20						*4N21*			125.00	125.00
368	"	2c	*3N19*			15	15	*4N22*			15	15
369	"	8c						*4N23*			40	15
382	"	5c	*3N20*			50	15	*4N24*	15	15	15	15
383	"	8c	*3N21*			15	15	*4N25*	17.50	17.50	15	15
384	"	10c	*3N22*			15	15	*4N26*	35	25	15	15
385	"	30c	*3N23*	60	40	75	20	*4N27*			15	15
386	"	50c	*3N24*	75	60	2.00	1.00	*4N28*	50	40	40	15
387	"	$1	*3N25*	2.00	1.00	20.00	15.00	*4N29*	1.50	1.00	1.00	40
388	"	$2	*3N26*	3.00	2.00	3.50	2.00	*4N30*	7.50	3.75	3.00	1.00
389	"	$5	*3N27*	4.00	4.00	15.00	15.00	*4N31*	12.50	12.50	7.50	7.50
390	"	$10	*3N28*	50.00	50.00	12.50	12.50	*4N32*	15.00	15.00	12.50	12.50
391	"	$20	*3N29*	25.00	25.00	22.50	22.50	*4N33*	22.50	22.50	20.00	20.00
392	"	5c	*3N30*			3.50	50	*4N34*			15	15
393	"	5c	*3N31*			1.50	15	*4N35*			15	15
394	"	10c						*4N36*			15	15
395	"	30c	*3N32*	3.50	1.50	2.00	60	*4N37*	75	50	25	25
396	"	50c	*3N33*			4.00		*4N38*			40	35
402	A39	½c	*3N34*			15	15	*4N39*			15	15
403	A40	1c	*3N35*	15	15	15	15	*4N40*	15	15	15	15
404	A46	2c						*4N41*			15	15
405	A39	2½c	*3N36*			2.50	1.50	*4N42*			15	15
406	A48	3c						*4N43*			15	15
410	A46	10c	*3N37*	50	15	1.00	50	*4N44*	25	15	25	25
411	A45	13c	*3N38*			15	15	*4N45*			25	25

NORTH CHINA

1941				Honan					Hopei			
STAMPS OF CHINA OVERPRINTED				河南 I		河南 II			河北 I		河北 II	
413	A46	17c	3N39	2.00	60	25	15	4N46	40	25	25	25
416	A40	25c	3N40			25	15	4N47			35	25
418	A48	30c						4N48	5.00	5.00	35	25
419	A47	40c	3N41	3.00	50	40	15	4N49	85	60	35	25
421	A39	½c	3N42	15	15	15	15	4N50	15	15	15	15
422	A40	1c	3N43	15	15	25	15	4N51	15	15	15	15
423	A46	2c	3N44	1.25	30			4N52	25	25		
425	A48	3c	3N45	25	25			4N53	25	25	15	15
426	A39	4c	3N46			15	15	4N54			25	25
428	A45	8c						4N55	50	35	25	25
429	A46	10c	3N47	7.50	2.50			4N56			25	25
430	A45	13c	3N48	2.50	75	40	15	4N57	50	35	40	40
431	A48	15c	3N49			15	15	4N58			25	25
432	A46	17c	3N50	2.50	75	15	15	4N59	65	40	35	25
433	A47	20c	3N51	7.50	2.50	15	15	4N60	65	40	25	25
434	A45	21c	3N52			15	15	4N61			25	25
435	A40	25c	3N53	75	50			4N62	65	40	40	25
436	A46	28c	3N54			15	15	4N63			25	25
1942				Nos. 3N46, 3N14,II and China No. 369 (with Honan type II overprint) with Additional Overprint in Red.					Nos. 4N54, 4N25,II, 4N14,II and 4N23 with Additional Overprint in Red.			
新嘉坡陷落紀念		4c	3N55			50	50	4N64			25	25
		8c	3N56			4.00	4.00	4N65			75	75
		8c	3N57			1.50	1.50	4N66			90	90
		8c						4N67			1.10	1.10
Issued to commemorate the fall of Singapore.												
				China Nos. 407 and 369 (both with Honan type II overprint) and Nos. 3N19 and 3N14, II with Additional Overprint in Red.					Nos. 4N22, 4N54, 4N14,II and 4N25,II with Additional Overprint in Red.			
滿洲國建國十週年紀念		2c	3N58			1.50	1.50	4N68			1.75	1.75
		4c	3N59			2.00	2.00	4N69			75	60
		8c	3N60			8.50	8.50	4N70			15.00	15.00
		8c	3N61			8.50	8.50					
		8c						4N71			1.25	1.25

Issued to commemorate the 10th anniversary of the formation of Manchukuo.

Besides the values listed on this chart many others exist on various stamps of China.

NORTH CHINA

1941

STAMPS OF CHINA OVERPRINTED			Shansi					Shantung					Supeh				
				山西 I		山西 II			山東 I		山東 II			蘇北 I		蘇北 II	
297	A37	2c	*5N1*	75	25	40	20	*6N1*	25	20	15	15	*7N1*	1.00	75	2.00	2.00
298	"	4c	*5N2*	2.50	50	35.00	15.00	*6N2*	75	30	60	40	*7N2*	7.50	7.50		
301	"	15c	*5N3*	35	15	35	20	*6N3*	50	25	15	15	*7N3*	30	25	40	30
302	"	20c						*6N4*			25	15	*7N4*			40	30
303	"	25c	*5N4*	14.00	14.00	65	30	*6N5*	50.00	50.00	75	50					
312	A39	½c	*5N5*	35	15	15	15	*6N6*	15	15	15	15	*7N5*	35	35		
314	"	2½c	*5N6*	25	25	15	15	*6N7*	15	15	15	15	*7N6*	25	25	25	25
318	A45	13c	*5N7*	40.00	40.00	25	25	*6N8*	5.00	3.00	15	15	*7N7*	40.00	40.00	25	25
321	A48	30c	*5N8*			1.00	1.00										
347	A57	$1						*6N9*	15.00	15.00			*7N8*	85.00	85.00		
349	"	2c						*6N10*			15	15					
350	"	3c	*5N9*	2.00	35	25	25	*6N11*	25	15	15	15	*7N9*	4.00	3.00	25	25
352	"	5c	*5N10*	50	25	25	25	*6N12*	15	15	15	15	*7N10*	25	25	25	25
353	"	8c	*5N11*	50	25	25	25	*6N13*	15	15	15	15	*7N11*	25	25	70	60
354	"	10c	*5N12*			40	25	*6N14*			15	15	*7N12*			25	25
357	"	16c	*5N13*			50	50	*6N15*			25	25	*7N13*			25	25
359	"	$1	*5N14*			2.50	1.50	*6N16*	100.00	100.00	2.00	2.00	*7N14*			3.00	3.00
360	"	$2	*5N15*			9.00	8.00										
361	"	$5	*5N16*			15.00	15.00	*6N17*			12.50	12.50					
368	"	2c	*5N17*			25	25	*6N18*			15	15	*7N15*			25	25
369	"	8c	*5N18*			12.50	2.00	*6N19*			15	15	*7N16*			12.50	12.50
382	"	5c	*5N19*			15	15	*6N20*			15	15	*7N17*			15	15
383	"	8c	*5N20*			25	25	*6N21*	10	10	15	15	*7N18*			15	15
384	"	10c	*5N21*	30	15	25	25	*6N22*			15	15	*7N19*	25	20	50	35
385	"	30c	*5N22*	40	25	40	40	*6N23*	75	60	25	15	*7N20*	40	35	60	35
386	"	50c	*5N23*	50	40	50	50	*6N24*	75	50	50	35	*7N21*	65	40	60	35
387	"	$1	*5N24*	2.50	1.25	9.00	2.00	*6N25*	1.75	1.25	50	40	*7N22*	4.00	2.50	10.00	10.00
388	"	$2	*5N25*	3.50	1.25	4.00	2.00	*6N26*	4.00	3.00	1.50	1.00	*7N23*	4.50	4.00	5.00	5.00
389	"	$5	*5N26*	20.00	20.00	5.00	5.00	*6N27*	10.00	9.00	5.00	3.00	*7N24*	9.00	9.00	27.50	27.50
390	"	$10	*5N27*	12.50	12.50	10.00	9.00	*6N28*	15.00	15.00	9.00	9.00	*7N25*	20.00	20.00	15.00	15.00
391	"	$20	*5N28*	15.00	15.00	15.00	15.00	*6N29*	25.00	25.00	15.00	15.00	*7N26*	25.00	25.00	22.50	22.50
392	"	5c	*5N29*			20	20	*6N30*			15	15					
393	"	5c	*5N30*			20	20	*6N31*			15	15					
394	"	10c	*5N31*			40	40	*6N32*			1.00	60	*7N27*			25	15
395	"	30c	*5N32*	20.00	20.00			*6N33*	4.00	2.50	1.00	50	*7N28*	1.25	1.00		
396	"	50c	*5N33*	1.50	65			*6N34*	1.00	75	65	30	*7N29*	1.50	1.00		
402	A39	½c	*5N34*			15	15	*6N35*			15	15	*7N30*			15	15
403	A40	1c	*5N35*	15	15	15	15	*6N36*	15	15	15	15	*7N31*	15	15	15	15
404	A46	2c	*5N36*			25	25						*7N32*			15	15
405	A39	2½c	*5N37*	75	75			*6N37*			90	60	*7N33*	5.00	5.00		
410	A46	10c	*5N38*	1.00	50			*6N38*	50	20			*7N34*	2.00	1.25		
411	A45	13c	*5N39*				25	*6N39*			25	15	*7N35*			60	40

NORTH CHINA

1941

STAMPS OF CHINA OVERPRINTED			Shansi	西 山 I		西 山 II		Shantung	東 山 I		東 山 II		Supeh	北 蘇 I		北 蘇 II	
413	A46	17c	5N40	7.50	5.00			6N40	1.25	50	65	20	7N36	20.00	17.50	40	15
416	A40	25c	5N41			35	35	6N41			25	25	7N37			40	30
418	A48	30c	5N42	20.00	20.00	20.00	20.00	6N42	5.00	4.00			7N38	1.75	1.25		
419	A47	40c	5N43	7.00	3.50	30	30	6N43	5.00	3.50	25	25	7N39	1.00	1.00	35	20
420	A40	50c	5N44	9.00	5.00	50	40	6N44			50	25	7N40	25.00	25.00		
421	A39	½c	5N45	15	15	15	15	6N45	15	15	15	15	7N41	15	15	10	10
422	A40	1c	5N46	15	15	15	15	6N46	15	15	15	15	7N42			10	10
422a	"	1c						6N47			22.50	22.50					
423	A46	2c	5N47			15	15	6N48			15	15	7N43	1.00	90		
425	A48	3c	5N48	1.00	40			6N49	25	25	40	25	7N44	25	25		
426	A39	4c	5N49			15	15	6N50			15	15	7N45			15	15
428	A45	8c	5N50	2.00	60	2.00	60	6N51	2.50	2.25	15	15					
429	A46	10c	5N51	8.00	5.00	14.00	14.00	6N52	1.00	50			7N46	10.00	9.00		
430	A45	13c	5N52	3.50	50	3.00	2.00	6N53	30	30	15	15	7N47	30	30		
431	A48	15c	5N53			40	30	6N54			15	15	7N48			30	15
432	A46	17c	5N54	50	50	40	30	6N55	30	30	15	15	7N49	40	40	40	25
433	A47	20c	5N55	50	50	40	30	6N56	40	30	15	15	7N50	60	50	25	15
434	A45	21c	5N56			40	30	6N57			15	15	7N51			25	15
435	A40	25c	5N57	75	50			6N58	50	40			7N52	60	50	75	60
436	A46	28c	5N58			50	40	6N59			25	15	7N53			20	20
439	A40	50c	5N59			2.00	75	6N60			1.25	1.25					

1942

Shansi: Nos. 5N49, 5N20, 5N11,II and 5N18,II with Additional Overprint in Red.

Shantung: Nos. 6N50, 6N13,II, 6N21,II and 6N19 with Additional Overprint in Red.

Supeh: China No. 298 and Nos. 7N45, 7N11,II and 7N16 with Additional Overprint in Red.

Overprint	Denom	Shansi		Shantung			Supeh		
坡 嘉 新 念紀落陷	4c						7N54	17.50	17.50
	4c	5N60	50 / 50	6N61	25	25	7N55	75	75
	8c	5N61	1.25 / 1.25	6N62	1.25	1.25	7N56	1.50	1.50
	8c	5N62	1.25 / 1.25	6N63	85	85	7N57	3.50	3.50
	8c	5N63	5.00 / 5.00	6N64	3.50	3.50			

Issued to commemorate the fall of Singapore.

Shansi: Nos. 5N17,II, 5N49, 5N11,II, 5N18,II and 5N20 with Additional Overprint in Red.

Shantung: Nos. 6N18, 6N50, 6N13,II, 6N19 and 6N21,II with Additional Overprint in Red.

Supeh: Nos. 7N15, 7N45, 7N11,II and 7N16 with Additional Overprint in Red.

Overprint	Denom	Shansi			Shantung			Supeh		
國建國洲滿 念紀年週十	2c	5N64	75	75	6N65	75	75	7N58	1.00	1.00
	4c	5N65	60	60	6N66	65	65	7N59	65	65
	8c	5N66	9.00	9.00	6N67	5.00	5.00	7N60	27.50	27.50
	8c	5N67	10.00	10.00	6N68	9.00	9.00	7N61	11.00	11.00
	8c	5N68	9.00	9.00	6N69	75	60			

Issued to commemorate the 10th anniversary of the formation of Manchukuo.

Besides the values listed on this chart many others exist on various stamps of China.

North China

For use in:

Honan, Hopei, Shansi, Shantung and Supeh (Northern Kiangsu).

Stamps of China, 1931-37 Surcharged North China (Hwa Pei) and Half of Original Value

北 華

分 壹

1942 *Perf. 14, 12½* **Unwmkd.**

8N1 A40 ½c on 1c org.(#313) 10 10
8N2 A37 1c on 2c olive green (#297) 15 10
8N3 " 2c on 4c green(#298) 25 10
8N4 A45 4c on 8c brown orange (#316) 60.00

Same Surcharge on Stamps of 1938-41.
Perf. 12½

8N5 A57 1c on 2c olive green (#349) 60 60
8N6 " 1c on 2c olive green (#368) 20 10
8N7 " 4c on 8c olive green (#353) 30 15
8N8 " 4c on 8c olive green (#369) 10 10
8N9 " 5c on 10c green 10 10
8N10 " 8c on 16c olive gray 40 15
8N11 " 50c on $1 henna & dark brown(#359) 75 75
8N12 " 50c on $1 henna & dark brown (#344) 150.00 150.00
8N13 " 50c on $1 henna & dark brown (#347) 15.00 15.00
8N14 " $1 on $2 deep blue & orange brown (#360) 1.50 1.50
8N15 " $1 on $2 deep blue & orange brown (#345) 5.00 5.00
8N16 " $1 on $2 deep blue & orange brown (#348) 37.50 37.50

No. 8N12 was issued without gum.

Same Surcharge on China Nos. 383-388, 390-391.
Perf. 14

8N17 A57 4c on 8c olive green 10 10
8N18 " 5c on 10c green 10 10
8N19 " 15c on 30c scarlet 10 10
a. Invtd. surch. 50.00 50.00
8N20 " 25c on 50c dark blue 15 10
8N21 " 50c on $1 orange brown & sepia 65 50
8N22 " $1 on $2 deep blue & yel. brown 1.00 90
8N23 " $5 on $10 dark green & dull purple 15.00 15.00
8N24 " $10 on $20 rose lake & dark blue 10.00 10.00

Same Surcharge on China Nos. 394-396.
Wmk. 261

8N25 A57 5c on 10c green 15 15
8N26 " 15c on 30c scarlet 40 30
8N27 " 25c on 50c dark blue 20 15

Same Surcharge on Stamps of 1940-41.
1942 *Perf. 12½, 13* **Wmk. 261**

8N28 A40 ½c on 1c orange 10 10
8N29 A40 1c on 2c deep blue 10 10
8N30 A45 4c on 8c deep orange 5.00 5.00
8N31 A46 5c on 10c dull violet 10 10
8N32 A48 15c on 30c brn. car. 35 20
8N33 A47 20c on 40c orange 20 10
8N34 A40 25c on 50c green 50 30

Unwmkd.

8N35 A40 ½c on 1c orange (#422) 10 10
a. ½c on 1c orange (#422a) 1.50 1.50
8N36 A46 1c on 2c deep blue 10 10
8N37 A39 2c on 4c pale violet 10 10
8N38 A45 4c on 8c dp. orange 10 10
8N39 A46 5c on 10c dull violet 10 10
8N40 A47 10c on 20c light blue 10 10
8N41 " 20c on 40c orange 20 15
8N42 A40 25c on 50c green 75 65

Same Surcharge on "New Peking" Prints.
Perf. 14

8N43 A37 1c on 2c olive green 10 10
8N44 " 2c on 4c dull green 10 10
a. Inverted surch. 25.00
8N45 A45 4c on 8c dp. orange 10 10
8N46 A57 8c on 16c olive gray 10 10
8N47 A47 10c on 20c red brown 15 10
8N48 A48 15c on 30c brn. car. 25 10
8N49 A47 20c on 40c orange 20 10
8N50 A40 25c on 50c green 30 15
8N51 A57 50c on $1 orange brown & sepia 20 10
8N52 " $1 on $2 deep blue & org. brown 1.25 90
8N53 " $5 on $10 dk. green & dull purple 3.50 3.50

See note after No. 2N93.

Nos. 8N44, 8N17 and 8N46 with Additional Overprint in Red

邦友 界租 還交 念紀

1943 *Perf. 14* **Unwmkd.**

8N54 A37 2c on 4c dull green 10 10
8N55 A57 4c on 8c olive green 10 10
8N56 " 8c on 16c olive gray 20 20

Issued to commemorate the return of the Foreign Concessions to China.

Nos. 8N44, 8N7 and 8N46 with Additional Overprint in Red

局總 政郵 立成 念紀年週五

1943, Aug. 15 *Perf. 14, 12½*

8N57 A37 2c on 4c dull green 10 10
8N58 A57 4c on 8c olive green 15 15
8N59 " 8c on 16c olive gray 30 30

Issued to commemorate the fifth anniversary of the North China Postal Service.

Stamps of China, 1934-41, Overprinted in Black

北 華

1943, Nov. 1

8N60 A40 1c orange (#313) 10 10
8N61 " 1c orange (#422) 10 10
8N62 A57 10c green (#354) 10 10
8N63 " $2 deep blue & yellow brown (#388) 6.00 6.00
8N64 " $5 red & greenish black (#361) 2.00 2.00
8N65 " $5 red & slate green (#389) 1.50 1.50
8N66 " $10 dark green & dull purple (#390) 6.00 6.00
8N67 " $20 rose lake & dark blue (#391) 40.00 40.00
Nos. 8N60-8N67 (8) 55.80 55.80

Same Overprint on "New Peking" Prints.

8N68 A40 1c orange 10 10
8N69 A37 2c olive green 10 10
8N70 " 4c dull green 10 10
8N71 " 5c green 10 10
8N72 A57 9c olive green 10 10
8N73 A46 10c dull violet 10 10
8N74 A57 16c olive gray 10 10
8N75 " 18c olive gray 10 10
8N76 A47 20c henna 15 10
8N77 A48 30c brown carmine 15 10
8N78 A47 40c bright orange 20 10
a. Inverted ovpt. 25.00 25.00
8N79 A40 50c green 20 10
8N80 A57 $1 orange brown & sepia 40 25
8N81 " $2 blue & org. brn. 50 30
8N82 " $5 red & slate green 75 55
8N83 " $10 dark green & dull purple 1.50 1.50
8N84 " $20 rose lake & dark blue 3.00 3.00
Nos. 8N68-8N84 (17) 7.65 6.80

See note after No. 2N93.

Nos. 8N70 and 8N62 with Additional Overprint in Red

戰 參 念紀年週一

1944, Jan. 9

8N85 A37 4c dull green 15 15
8N86 A57 10c green 15 15

Issued to commemorate the first anniversary of the declaration of war against the Allies by North China.

Nos. 8N72, 8N75, 8N79 and 8N80 with Additional Overprint in Red

會員委務政 念紀年週四

1944, Mar. 30

8N87 A57 9c olive green 15 15
8N88 " 18c olive gray 20 20
8N89 A40 50c green 40 40
8N90 A57 $1 orange brown & sepia 75 75
a. Red ovpt. inverted 20.00 20.00

Issued to commemorate the fourth anniversary of the North China Political Council.

Shanghai-Nanking Nos. 9N101-9N104 Surcharged North China (Hwa Pei) and New Value in Red or Black

華北玖分 (a) 華北壹角捌分 (b) 華北叁角陸分 (c) 華北玖角 (d)

1944 *Perf. 12½x12, 12x12½*

8N91 OS1 (*a*) 9c on 50c orange 10 10
8N92 " (*b*) 18c on $1 green (R) 15 15
a. Dble. surch. 20.00 20.00
8N93 OS2 (*c*) 36c on $2 deep blue (R) 15 15
8N94 " (*d*) 90c on $5 carmine rose 25 25

Nos. 8N72, 8N75, 8N79 and 8N80 Overprinted in Red or Blue

立成局總政郵 念紀年週六

1944, Aug. 15

8N95 A57 9c olive green 10 10
8N96 " 18c olive gray 10 10
8N97 A40 50c green 20 20
8N98 A57 $1 orange brown & sepia (Bl) 35 35

Issued to commemorate the sixth anniversary of the General Post Office Department of North China.

North China Nos. 8N76, 8N79-8N81 Overprinted in Blue or Black

席主汪 念紀典葬

1944, Dec. 5

8N99 A47 20c henna (Bl) 12 12
8N100 A40 50c green (Bl) 12 12
8N101 A57 $1 orange brown & sepia (Bl) 18 18
8N102 " $2 blue & orange brown 18 18

Issued to commemorate the death of Wang Ching-wei, puppet ruler of China.

North China Nos. 8N76, 8N79-8N81 Overprinted in Red or Black

年週二戰參 念紀

1945

8N103 A47 20c henna 12 12
8N104 A40 50c green (R) 20 20
8N105 A57 $1 orange brown & sepia 20 20
8N106 " $2 blue & orange brown 35 35

Issued to commemorate the second anniversary of the declaration of war.

Shanghai-Nanking Nos. 9N105-9N106 Surcharged in Red

華北伍角

1945 *Perf. 12x12½*

8N107 OS3 50c on $3 light orange 10 10
8N108 " $1 on $6 blue 15 15

Issued to commemorate the return of the foreign concessions in Shanghai.

Dragon Pillar OS1

Dr. Sun Yat-sen OS2

Designs: $2, Long Bridge and White Pagoda. $5, Tower in Imperial City. $10, Marble Boat, Summer Palace.

Lithographed.

1945 *Perf. 14* **Unwmkd.**

Various Papers.

8N109 OS1 $1 dull yellow 8 8
8N110 " $2 deep blue 6 6
8N111 " $5 carmine 15 15
8N112 " $10 dull green 15 15

Issued to commemorate the fifth anniversary of the North China Political Council.

1945

Without Gum; Various Papers.

8N113 OS2 $1 bistre 8 5
8N114 " $2 dark blue 12 10
8N115 " $5 terra cotta 20 15
8N116 " $10 sage green 35 25
8N117 " $20 dull violet 40 30
8N118 " $50 brown 7.50 3.75
Nos. 8N113-8N118 (6) 8.65 4.60

Nos. 8N113-8N118 without "Hwa Pei" overprint are proofs.

Wutai Mountain, Shansi OS3

Designs: $10, Kaifeng Iron Pagoda. $20, International Bridge, Tientsin. $30, Taishan Mountain, Shantung. $50, General Post Office, Peking.

1945, Aug. 15

Without Gum; Various Papers.

8N119 OS3 $5 gray green 4 4
8N120 " $10 dull brown 5 5
8N121 " $20 dull purple 7 7
8N122 " $30 slate blue 8 8
8N123 " $50 carmine 15 15
Nos. 8N119-8N123 (5) 39 39

Issued to commemorate the seventh anniversary of the North China Postal Directorate.

Shanghai and Nanking

China Nos. 299-303 Surcharged

貳角伍分 暫售 25 (a)

暫售 陸圓 6.00 (b)

1942-45 *Perf. 12½, 13½* **Unwmkd.**

9N1 A37 (*b*) $6 on 5c green 8 8
9N2 " (") $20 on 15c scarlet 6 6
9N3 " (") $500 on 15c dark green 12 12

9N4 A37 (*b*) $1000 on 20c ultramarine 12 12
9N5 " (") $1000 on 25c ultramarine 12 12

A $1000 on 20c ultramarine, No. 293, exists. Price $200.

Same Surcharge on Stamps of 1939-41.

Perf. 12½

9N6 A57 (*a*) 25c on 5c olive green (#352) 5 5
9N7 " (") 30c on 2c olive green (#368) 5 5
9N8 " (") 50c on 3c dull claret (#350) 5 5
9N9 " (") 50c on 5c olive green (#352) 5 5
9N10 " (") 50c on 8c olive green (#353) 5 5
9N11 " (*b*) $1 on 8c olive green (#353) 5 5
9N12 " (") $1 on 8c olive grn. (#369) 2.50 2.50
9N13 " (") $1 on 15c dark violet brown (#356) 5 5
9N14 " (") $1.30 on 16c olive gray (#357) 5 5
9N15 " (") $1.50 on 3c dull claret (#350) 5 5
9N16 " (") $2 on 5c olive green (#352) 5 5
9N17 " (") $2 on 10c green (#354) 5 5
9N18 " (") $3 on 15c dark violet brown (#356) 5 5
9N19 " (") $4 on 16c olive gray (#357) 5 5
9N20 " (") $5 on 15c dark violet brown (#356) 5 5
9N21 " (") $6 on 5c green (#351) 5 5
a. Perf. 14 (#371) 12.50 12.50
9N22 " (") $6 on 5c olive green (#352) 5 5
9N23 " (") $6 on 8c olive green (#353) 5 5
9N24 " (") $6 on 8c olive green (#369) 300.00 250.00
9N25 " (") $6 on 10c green (#354) 5 5
9N26 " (") $10 on 10c green (#354) 5 5
9N27 " (") $10 on 16c olive gray (#357) 5 5
9N28 " (") $20 on 3c dull claret (#350) 5 5
9N29 " (") $20 on 15c scarlet (#355) 5 5
9N30 " (") $20 on 15c dark violet brown (#356) 5 5
9N31 " (") $20 on $2 deep blue & orange brown (#360) 40 40
9N32 " (") $100 on 3c dull claret (#350) 5 5
9N33 " (") $500 on 8c olive grn. (#353) 20 20
9N34 " (") $500 on 8c olive grn. (#369) 6.00 6.00
9N35 " (") $500 on 10c green (#354) 8 8
9N36 " (") $500 on 15c scarlet (#355) 8 8
9N37 " (") $500 on 15c dark violet brown (#356) 8 8
9N38 " (") $500 on 16c olive gray (#357) 8 8
9N39 " (") $1000 on 25c dark blue (#358) 8 8
9N40 " (") $2000 on $5 red & greenish black (#361) 15 15
Nos. 9N1-9N23, 9N25-9N40 (39) 11.35 11.35

Nos. 381-391 Surcharged with Type "b."

Perf. 14

9N41 A57 $1 on 8c olive green 5 5
9N42 " $1.70 on 30c scarlet 6 6
a. Perf. 12½ 10 10
9N43 " $2 on 5c olive green 5 5
9N44 " $2 on $1 orange brown & sepia 25 25
9N45 " $3 on 8c olive green 5 5
a. $3 on 8c olive green (#383a)
b. "3" with flat top 5 5
9N46 " $6 on 5c green 7 7
9N47 " $6 on 5c olive green 7 7
9N48 " $6 on 8c olive green 7 7
9N49 " $10 on 10c green 7 7
a. Perf. 12½ 20 20
9N50 " $20 on $2 deep blue & yellow brown 10 10
9N51 " $50 on 30c scarlet 7 7
9N52 " $50 on 50c dark blue 7 7
9N53 " $50 on $5 red & slate green 10 10
9N54 " $50 on $20 rose lake & dark blue 50 50
9N55 " $100 on $10 dark green & dull purple 25 25
9N56 " $200 on $20 rose lake & dark blue 8 8
9N57 " $500 on 8c olive green 2.00 2.00
a. $500 on 8c olive green (#383a) 7.50 7.50
9N58 " $500 on 10c green 12 12
9N59 " $1000 on 30c scarlet 12 12
9N60 " $1000 on 50c dk. blue 12 12
9N61 " $1000 on $2 deep blue & yellow brown 65 65
9N62 " $2000 on $5 red & slate green 25 25

China Nos. 392-395 and 399-401 Surcharged with Type "b."

1942-45 ***Perf. 14*** **Wmk. 261**

9N63 A57 $2 on $1 orange brown & sepia (Perf. 12½) 25 25
9N64 " $6 on 5c green 7 7
9N65 " $6 on 5c olive green 7 7
9N66 " $50 on $5 red & slate green 7 7
a. Numeral tablet violet 7 7
9N67 " $100 on $10 dark green & dull purple 10 10
9N68 " $200 on $20 rose lake & dark blue 10 10
9N69 " $500 on 10c green 20 20
9N70 " $1000 on 30c scarlet 40 40
9N71 " $5000 on $10 dk. grn. & dull pur., perf. 12½ 2.50 2.50
a. Perf. 14 17.50 17.50
Nos. 9N41-9N71 (31) 8.93 8.93

Nos. 9N63 and 9N71 were not issued without surcharge. A $50 on 30c scarlet exists.

Same Surcharge on Stamps of 1940-41.

Wmk. 261

Perf. 12½, 13

9N72 A46 $30 on 2c dp. blue 30.00 30.00

A $7.50 on ½c and a $15 on 1c are known.

Unwmkd.

9N73 A39 $7.50 on ½c olive black 7 7
9N74 A40 $15 on 1c orange 7 7
a. Without secret mark 25.00 25.00
9N75 A46 $30 on 2c dp. blue 7 7
9N76 A40 $200 on 1c orange 7 7
9N77 A45 $200 on 8c deep orange 7 7
Nos. 9N73-9N77 (5) 35 35

Same Surcharge on Stamps of 1941.

Perf. 12

9N78 A59 (*a*) 5c on ½c sepia 7 7
9N79 " (") 10c on 1c orange 7 7
9N80 " (") 20c on 1c orange 7 7
9N81 " (") 40c on 5c green 7 7
9N82 " (*b*) $5 on 5c green 7 7
9N83 " (") $10 on 10c bright green 7 7
9N84 " (") $50 on ½c sepia 7 7
9N85 A59 (*b*) $50 on 1c orange 7 7
9N86 " (") $50 on 17c olive 7 7
9N87 " (") $200 on 5c green 7 7
9N88 " (") $200 on 8c turquoise green 7 7
9N89 " (") $200 on 8c red orange 7 7
9N90 " (") $500 on $5 scarlet & black 12 12
9N91 " (") $1000 on 1c org. 12 12
9N92 " (") $1000 on 25c rose violet 18 18
9N93 " (") $1000 on 30c scarlet 18 18
9N94 " (") $1000 on $2 blue & black 30 30
9N95 " (") $1000 on $10 green & black 18 18
9N96 " (") $2000 on $5 scarlet & black 35 35
Nos. 9N78-9N96 (19) 2.27 2.27

Stamps of China 1939-41 Surcharged in Red or Blue

收回租界紀念
八月一日 三十二年
貳角伍分

1943 ***Perf. 12, 12½*** **Unwmkd.**

9N97 A57 25c on 5c green 4 4
9N98 A59 50c on 8c red orange (Bl) 4 4
9N99 A57 $1 on 16c olive gray 6 6
9N100 A59 $2 on 50c dark blue 6 6

Issued to commemorate the return of the foreign concessions in Shanghai.

Wheat and Cotton
OS1

Purple Mountain, Nanking
OS2

Perf. 12½x12, 12x12½

1944 **Engraved.** **Unwmkd.**

9N101 OS1 50c orange 4 4
9N102 " $1 green 4 4
9N103 OS2 $2 deep blue 4 4
9N104 " $5 carmine rose 6 5

Issued to commemorate the fourth anniversary of the establishment of the puppet government at Nanking.

Map of Foreign Concessions in Shanghai
OS3

1944 ***Perf. 12x12½***

9N105 OS3 $3 light orange 4 6
9N106 " $6 blue 4 6

Issued to commemorate the first anniversary of the return of the foreign concessions in Shanghai.

Nos. 9N101-9N104 Surcharged in Black with Type "b."

1945, Mar. 30

9N107 OS1 $15 on 50c orange 4 4
9N108 " $30 on $1 green 4 4
9N109 OS2 $60 on $2 deep blue 4 4
9N110 " $200 on $5 carmine rose 6 8

China Nos. C31, C32, C36 and C38 Surcharged in Red, Green, Orange or Carmine

防空 1000 暫壹 仟 售圓

1945 ***Perf. 12½, 13.***

9N111 AP3 $150 on 15c gray green (R) 4 3
9N112 " $250 on 25c yellow orange (G) 4 3
9N113 " $600 on 60c deep blue (O) 8 6
9N114 " $1,000 on $1 apple green (C) 12 12

Issued as air raid precaution propaganda.

AIR POST STAMPS

China Nos. C35 and C38 Surcharged in Black

10

國內明片之航空費已付

The surcharges on Nos. 9NC1-9NC7 were in Japanese currency because all air mail then was carried by Japanese planes.

1941 ***Perf. 12½*** **Unwmkd.**

The surcharges translate: (10c) "Airmail fee for postcard within the nation has been paid." (20c) "Airmail fee for letter within the nation has been paid."

9NC1 AP3 10(s) on 50c brn. 10 10
9NC2 " 20(s) on $1 apple green 10 10

Two types of surcharge exist on No. 9NC1.

Similar Surcharge on No. C28.

1941 ***Perf. 13*** **Wmk. 261**

9NC3 AP3 20(s) on $1 apple green 3.75 3.75

Nos. C37 and C39 Surcharged

35

寄日本信函航空費已付

1941 ***Perf. 12½, 13*** **Unwmkd.**

The surcharges translate: (18c and 25c) "Airmail fee for postcard to Japan has been paid." (35c) "Airmail fee for letter to Japan has been paid."

9NC4 AP3 18(s) on 90c light olive 10 10
9NC5 " 25(s) on 90c light olive 10 10
9NC6 " 35(s) on $2 light brown 10 10

No. 9NC6 with Additional Surcharge in Red

Perf. 12½.

9NC7 AP3 60(s) on 35(s) on $2 light brown 10 10

POSTAGE DUE STAMPS

Postage Due Stamps of China 1932 Surcharged in Black

改作 壹圓 100

1945 ***Perf. 14*** **Unwmkd.**

9NJ1 D5 $1 on 2c orange 10 10

9NJ2 D5 $2 on 5c orange 10 10
9NJ3 " $5 on 10c orange 10 10
9NJ4 " $10 on 20c orange 10 10

Northeastern Provinces.

民中
國華

With the end of World War II and the collapse of Manchukuo, the Northeastern Provinces reverted to China. In many Manchurian towns and cities, the Manchukuo stamps were locally handstamped in ideograms: "Republic of China," "China Postal Service" or "Temporary Use for China." A typical example is shown above.

Dr. Sun Yat-sen
A1 A2

Typographed.
Black Surcharge.

1946, Feb. *Perf. 14* **Unwmkd.**

1	A1	50c on $5 red	5	5
2	"	50c on $10 green	5	5
3	"	$1 on $10 green	5	5
4	"	$2 on $20 brown violet	5	5
5	"	$4 on $50 brown	10	10
		Nos. 1-5 (5)	30	30

The two characters at left express the new value.

Stamps of China, 1938-41 Overprinted 用貼北東限

1946, Apr. *Perf. 12½, 13, 13½, 14*

6	A40	1c orange (#422)	5	5
7	A48	3c dp. yel. brn. (#425)	5	5
8	"	5c dull red org. (#427)	5	5
9	A57	10c green (#354)	5	5
10	"	10c green (#384)	5	5
11	A47	20c light blue (#433)	5	5
		a. Horiz. pair, imperf. between	25.00	
		Nos. 6-11 (6)	30	30

Without Gum.

1946, July **Engraved** *Perf. 14*

12	A2	5c lake	5	5
13	"	10c orange	5	5
14	"	20c yellow green	5	5
15	"	25c black brown	5	5
16	"	50c red orange	5	5
17	"	$1 blue	5	5
18	"	$2 dark violet	5	5
19	"	$2.50 indigo	5	5
20	"	$3 brown	5	5
21	"	$4 orange brown	5	5
22	"	$5 dark green	5	5
23	"	$10 crimson	5	5
24	"	$20 olive	5	5
25	"	$50 blue violet	5	5
		Nos. 12-25 (14)	70	70

Two types of $4, $10, $20 and $50: I. Character *kuo* directly left of sun emblem is open at upper and lower left corners of "box." Diagonal stroke from top center to lower right has no hook at bottom. II. Character is closed at left corners. Diagonal stroke has hook at bottom.

See also Nos. 47-52, 61-63.

China Nos. 728-731 Surcharged in Black

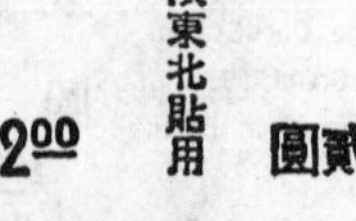

1946

26	A75	$2 on $20 green	10	10
27	"	$3 on $30 blue	10	10
28	A75	$5 on $50 dk. brown	10	10
29	"	$10 on $100 carmine	10	10

Convening of Chinese National Assembly.

Type of China, 1946.
Inscribed:
貼 東
用 北

1947 **Engraved** *Perf. 11, 11½*

30	A74	$2 carmine	10	10
31	"	$3 green	10	10
32	"	$5 vermilion	10	10
33	"	$10 yellow green	12	12
34	"	$20 yellow orange	12	12
35	"	$30 magenta	12	12
		Nos. 30-35 (6)	66	66

60th birthday of Chiang Kai-shek.

Type of China, 1947.
Inscribed: 用貼北東限

Engraved.

1947 *Perf. 14* **Unwmkd.**

36	A76	$2 deep green	10	10
37	"	$4 deep blue	10	10
38	"	$6 carmine	10	10
39	"	$10 light brown	10	10
40	"	$20 deep claret	10	10
		Nos. 36-40 (5)	50	50

First anniversary of return of Chinese National Government to Nanking.

China Nos. 644 to 646 and 634 Surcharged in Black

用貼北東限
叁 改
佰
圓 作
300圓

1947 *Perf. 12½, 14.*

41	A73	$100 on $1000 rose lake	8	7
42	"	$300 on $3000 blue	10	8
43	"	$500 on $5000 deep green & verm.	12	8
44	A37	$500 on $30 chocolate	12	12

Type of 1946.
Without Gum.

1947 **Engraved** *Perf. 14*

47	A2	$44 dark carmine rose	50	50
48	"	$100 deep green	5	5
49	"	$200 rose brown	5	5
50	"	$300 bluish green	6	6
51	"	$500 rose carmine	6	6
52	"	$1000 deep orange	8	8
		Nos. 47-52 (6)	80	80

Stamps and Types of 1946-47 Surcharged in Black or Red

壹仟伍佰圓 改
1500 作

1948 *Perf. 14* **Unwmkd.**

53	A2	$1500 on 20c yellow green	16	16
54	"	$3000 on $1 blue	10	10
55	"	$4000 on 25c black brown (R)	10	10
56	"	$8000 on 50c red orange	10	10
57	"	$10,000 on 10c orange	12	12
58	"	$50,000 on $109 dark green (R)	22	24
59	"	$100,000 on $65 dull green	20	25
60	"	$500,000 on $22 gray (R)	25	28
		Nos. 53-60 (8)	1.25	1.35

Type of 1946.
Without Gum

1949

61	A2	$22 gray	10.00
62	"	$65 dull green	11.50
63	"	$109 dark green	16.50

POSTAGE DUE STAMPS.

D1

Engraved.
Without Gum.

1947 *Perf. 14* **Unwmkd.**

J1	D1	10c dark blue	4	4
J2	"	20c "	4	4
J3	"	50c "	4	4
J4	"	$1 "	4	4
J5	"	$2 "	4	4
J6	"	$5 "	4	4
		Nos. J1-J6 (6)	24	24

Nos. J1 to J3 Surcharged in Red

拾 改
圓 作

1948

J7	D1	$10 on 10c dark blue	4	4
J8	"	$20 on 20c "	4	4
J9	"	$50 on 50c "	4	4

The surcharge reads "Changed to . . . . dollars." Characters at the left express the new value and vary on each denomination.

MILITARY STAMPS

No. 16 Surcharged in Black

郵軍
作暫
圓肆拾肆

1947 *Perf. 14.* **Unwmkd.**

M1	A2	$44 on 50c red orange	75	75

The surcharge reads: "Army Post. Temporarily for 44 dollars."

China No. M11 Overprinted in Black 用貼北東限

Thin Paper Without Gum.
Perf. 12½.

M2	M1	rose	20	20

China No. M11 Overprinted in Black 用貼北東限

M3	M1	rose	1.25	1.25

PARCEL POST STAMP.

China No. Q25 Surcharged in Black

用貼北東限
伍 改
拾
萬
圓 作

Engraved.

1948 *Perf. 13½* **Unwmkd.**
Without Gum.

Q1	PP3	$500,000 on $5,000,000 lilac	30.00

Anhwei Province

(ăn·(h)wā)

China Type A95 Handstamp Surcharged

1949, Mar. 16 **Lithographed**

1	A95	On $1000 carmine	8.00

SPECIAL DELIVERY STAMP

China Type A95 with Similar Surcharge

1949, Mar 16 **Lithographed**

E1	A95	On $500 brown	8.00

REGISTRATION STAMP

China Type A95 with Similar Surcharge

1949, Mar. 16 **Lithographed**

F1	A95	On $3000 orange	8.00

ACKNOWLEDGMENT OF RECEIPT STAMP

China Type A95 with Similar Surcharge

1949, Mar. 16 **Lithographed**

AR1	A95	On $20 red brown	8.00

Fukien Province

(fü·kyen)

Stamps of China, 1945-49, Surcharged

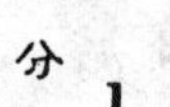

壹 郵
分 資
1

Without Gum

1949 **Engraved** *Perf. 14*

1	A82	1c on $500 bl. green	2.50	2.50
2	"	1c on $7000 light red brown	8.00	8.00
3	"	2c on $2,000,000 vermilion	1.00	75
4	"	2½c on $50,000 dp. bl.	1.50	1.50
5	A73	4c on $100 dk. car.	1.00	1.00
6	"	10c on $200 olive grn.	1.00	1.00
7	A82	10c on $3000 blue	75	75
8	"	10c on $4000 gray	90	90
9	"	10c on $6000 rose lilac	75	75
10	"	10c on $100,000 dull green	75	75
11	"	10c on $1,000,000 claret	75	75
12	"	40c on $200,000 brown violet	1.75	1.75

The surcharge on No. 2 is handstamped and in slightly larger characters.

Issue dates: No. 2, May 10; others, June.

China Nos. 973, 975-978 Overprinted 州 福

1949, June **Litho.** *Perf. 12½, 13*

13	A94	1c apple green	2.00	1.50
14	"	4c blue green	90	60
15	"	10c deep lilac	10.00	4.00
16	"	16c orange red	2.00	2.00
17	"	20c blue	4.50	3.00

Same Overprint on China No. 959, 959a

Perf. 12½, Rouletted

1949, July **Lithographed**

18	A96	orange	2.50	1.25

Same Overprint on Fukien Nos. 1, 3-4, 11 in Black or Red

1949, June **Engraved** *Perf. 14*

19	A82	1c on $500 bl. grn.	18.00	15.00
20	"	2c on $2,000,000 vermilion	3.00	2.50
21	"	2½c on $50,000 dp. bl.	3.00	2.50
22	"	10c on $4000 gray	6.00	4.50
23	"	10c on $1,000,000 claret	18.00	15.00

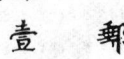

AIR POST STAMP

China No. C62 Overprinted as Nos. 13–17

Perf. 12½, Rouletted

1949, July Lithographed

C1 AP5 blue green 2.25 1.25

SPECIAL DELIVERY STAMP

China No. E12 Overprinted as Nos. 13–17

Perf. 12½, Rouletted

1949, July Lithographed

E1 SD2 red violet 2.50 1.25

REGISTRATION STAMP

China No. F2 Overprinted as Nos. 13–17

Perf. 12½, Rouletted

1949, July Lithographed

F1 R2 carmine 2.50 1.25

Hunan Province

(hü·nän)

China No. 640 Surcharged

郵資已付 湘 國內平信

1949, May Engr. ***Perf. 14***

1 A73 On $100 dk. carmine 75 75

The first printing of surcharge on No. 1 is in smaller characters.

China Nos. 797, 788, 750, 747 Surcharged

伍分 湘

1949, May Engr. ***Perf. 14***

2	A82	1c on $2,000,000 verm.	1.50	1.50
3	"	2c on $20,000 rose pink	1.50	1.50
4	"	5c on $3000 blue	1.50	1.50
5	"	10c on $500 blue green	1.50	1.50

AIR POST STAMP

China No. 790 Surcharged

湘 國內航空 付已資郵

1949, May Engr. ***Perf. 14***

C1 A82 On $40,000 green 60 60

SPECIAL DELIVERY STAMP

China No. 637 Surcharged as No. F1 in Red

1949, May Engr. ***Perf. 14***

E1 A73 On $30 dark blue 20 20

REGISTRATION STAMP

China No. 754 Surcharged

號掛內國 湘 付已資郵

1949, May Engr. ***Perf. 14***

F1 A73 On $7000 light red brown 45 45

Hupeh Province

(hü·pā, -be)

China Type A95 Surcharged

臨起華中 分壹資郵 1

1949, May Lithographed

1	A95	1c on $20 red brown	3.00	3.00
2	"	10c on $20 " "	3.00	3.00

Kansu Province

(kan·sü, gän·sü)

China No. 959 Handstamped in Purple

區青寧甘限 用貼

1949, Aug. Litho. ***Perf. 12½***

1 A96 orange 65.00

AIR POST STAMP

Same Handstamp Overprinted on China No. C62 in Red

1949, Aug. Litho. ***Perf. 12½***

C1 AP5 blue green 65.00

Counterfeits exist.

Kiangsi Province

(kyanĝ·sē, jyänĝ·sē)

China Nos. 789–791 Surcharged

郵資已付 國內平信 贛

1949 Engraved ***Perf. 14***

1	A82	On $30,000 chocolate	1.50	1.50
2	"	On $40,000 green	2.50	2.50
3	"	On $50,000 deep blue	2.50	2.50

AIR POST STAMP

Similar Surcharge on China No. 754

1949 Engraved ***Perf. 14***

C1 A82 On $7000 lt. red brn. 6.00 6.00

Third and fourth characters in right column of surcharge read "Air Mail" in Chinese on No. C1, "Registered" on Nos. F1–F2.

SPECIAL DELIVERY STAMP

Similar Surcharge on China No. 750

1949 Engraved ***Perf. 14***

E1 A82 On $3000 blue 2.25 2.25

See note below No. C1.

REGISTRATION STAMPS

Similar Surcharge on China Nos. 747 and 754

1949 Engraved ***Perf. 14***

F1	A82	On $500 blue green	2.75	2.75
F2	"	On $7000 lt. red brn.	3.50	3.50

See note below No. C1.

Stamps not listed in this Catalogue or mentioned in "For the Record" (unless recent issues) usually are revenues, locals or labels.

Kwangsi Province

(kwänĝ·sē, gwänĝ·sē)

China Nos. 811 and 818 Also Surcharged in Red

伍銀桂 分圓區

1949, May 21 Typographed

6	A62	5c on $20,000 on 10c deep green	2.75	2.75
7	"	5c on $40,000 on 20c dark olive green	4.50	4.50

China Stamps of 1946–48 Surcharged in Black or Red

a: 桂區 分2圓銀

b: 銀圓壹角貳分 桂區

1949 Engraved ***Perf. 14***

Type "a" Surcharge

8	A82	½c on $500,000 lilac rose	4.50	4.50
9	"	1c on $200,000 brown violet	1.50	1.50
10	"	2c on $300,000 yellow green	9.00	9.00
11	A73	5c on $3000 blue	1.50	1.50
12	A82	5c on $3000 "	1.50	1.50
13	"	5c on $40,000 green	1.75	1.75

Type "b" Surcharge

14	A82	13c on $50,000 deep blue (R)	1.75	1.75
15	"	13c on $50,000 dp. bl.	4.00	4.00
16	"	17c on $7000 light red brown	1.75	1.75
17	"	21c on $100,000 dull green	1.75	1.75

Shensi Province

(shen·sē)

China Nos. 747, 750 Surcharged

郵資已付 國內平信 (陝)

1949, May Engraved ***Perf. 14***

1	A82	On $500 blue green	1.75	1.75
2	"	On $3000 blue	1.75	1.75

AIR POST STAMP

Similar Surcharge on China No. 754

1949, May Engraved ***Perf. 14***

C1 A82 On $7000 lt. red brn. 2.25 2.25

SPECIAL DELIVERY STAMP

Similar Surcharge on China No. 746 in Red

1949, May Engraved ***Perf. 14***

E1 A82 On $250 deep lilac 1.75 1.75

REGISTRATION STAMPS

Similar Surcharge on China Nos. 626, 637 in Red

1949, May Typo. ***Perf. 12***

F1 A72 On $30 deep blue 3.50 3.50

Engr. ***Perf. 14***

F2 A73 On $30 dark blue 1.75 1.75

Szechwan Province.

(se′chwän′, sŭ′chwän′)

Re-engraved Issue of China, 1923, Overprinted

用貼川四限

1933 ***Perf. 14.*** **Unwmkd.**

1	A29	1c orange	50	8
2	"	5c claret	50	8
3	A30	50c deep green	1.75	40

The overprint reads "For use in Szechwan Province exclusively".

Same Overprint on Sun Yat-sen Issue of 1931-37.

Type II.

1933-34 ***Perf. 12½.***

4	A37	2c olive green	10	12
5	"	5c green	10	10
6	"	15c dark green	40	18
7	"	15c scarlet ('34)	40	45
8	"	25c ultramarine	50	12
9	"	$1 orange brown & dark brown	2.50	40
10	"	$2 blue & orange brown	5.50	90
11	"	$5 dull red & blk.	15.00	3.75
		Nos. 4-11 (8)	24.50	6.02

Same Overprint on Martyrs Issue of 1932-34.

1933 ***Perf. 14***

12	A39	½c black brown	20	10
13	A40	1c orange	10	10
14	A39	2½c rose lilac	60	30
15	A48	3c deep brown	40	10
16	A45	8c brown orange	50	10
17	A46	10c dull violet	1.00	10
18	A45	13c blue green	1.00	10
19	A46	17c brown olive	1.25	50
20	A47	20c brown red	1.25	10
21	A48	30c brown violet	1.25	10
22	A47	40c orange	3.50	25
23	A40	50c green	6.00	30
		Nos. 12-23 (12)	17.05	2.15

Stamps of China, 1947–48, Surcharged

每重貳拾公分 國內平信郵資 蓉

1949 Engraved ***Perf. 14***

24	A82	On $150 dark blue	7.00	7.00
25	"	On $250 deep lilac	7.00	7.00
26	"	On $500 blue green	1.25	1.25
27	"	On $1000 red	4.00	4.00
28	"	On $2000 vermilion	1.50	1.50
29	"	On $3000 blue	1.50	1.50
30	"	On $4000 gray	1.50	1.50
31	"	On $5000 dark brown	6.50	6.50
32	"	On $6000 rose lilac	1.50	1.50
33	"	On $7000 lt. red brn.	6.00	6.00
34	"	On $10,000 dark blue & carmine	1.50	1.50
35	"	On $20,000 rose pink	2.75	2.75
36	"	On $30,000 chocolate	1.50	1.50
37	"	On $50,000 green & dark blue	1.50	1.50
38	"	On $50,000 deep blue	1.75	1.75
39	"	On $100,000 dull yellow & olive	2.25	2.25
40	"	On $100,000 dull grn.	2.75	2.75
41	"	On $200,000 violet brown & deep blue	2.75	2.75
42	"	On $200,000 brn. vio.	2.75	2.75
43	"	On $300,000 sepia & orange brown		
44	"	On $300,000 yel. grn.	5.00	5.00
45	"	On $500,000 dark Prus. green & sepia	1.35	1.35
46	"	On $1,000,000 claret	4.25	4.25
47	"	On $2,000,000 verm.	2.75	2.75
48	"	On $3,000,000 ol. bis.	2.75	2.75
49	"	On $5,000,000 ultra.	10.00	10.00

Several of Nos. 24–49 exist with inverted surcharge and a few with bottom character of left row repeated in right row, same position.

Counterfeits exist.

China No. 737 Surcharged in Purple

蓉
郵資
貳分
2

1949 *Perf. 12½*

50 A77 2c on $500 olive green 4.25 4.25

China No. 975 Handstamp Surcharged in Purple

蓉
2½半分貳

1949 **Lithographed**

51 A94 2½c on 4c blue green 3.50 3.50

AIR POST STAMPS

China No. C55–C59, C61 Surcharged

拾每 航國
公重 空
分貳 蓉 資內

Perf. 12½, 13x12½, 14

1949, July **Unwmkd.**

C1 AP3 On $10,000 on 30c light red 1.50 1.50
a. On #C54
C2 AP4 On $10,000 on $27 bl. 2.25 2.25
a. Second surch. invtd. 75.00
b. On #C53 60.00
C3 AP3 On $20,000 on 25c light orange 2.25 2.25
C4 " On $30,000 on 90c light olive 3.00 3.00
C5 " On $50,000 on 60c bl. 15.00 15.00
C6 " On $50,000 on $1 yellow green 3.50 3.50
Nos. C1–C6 (6) 27.50 27.50

On No. C2 characters of overprint are arranged in two horizontal rows, and two of four lines are vertical.

REGISTRATION STAMPS

Stamps of China, 1944–47, Surcharged

掛號郵資 國內信函
蓉

Engr.; Typo. (A72)

1949 *Perf. 12, 13, 14*

F1 A64 On $100 yel. brown 12.00
F2 A72 On $100 dark brown 17.50
F3 A64 On $200 dark green 6.00
F4 A72 On $200 brown violet 6.00
F5 A73 On $200 olive green 35.00
F6 " On $500 brt. bl. grn. 35.00
F7 " On $700 red brown 50.00
F8 " On $5000 deep green & vermilion 30.00
Nos. F1–F8 (8) 191.50

PARCEL POST STAMP

China No. Q10 Surcharged

蓉
分壹

1949 **Engr.** *Perf. 12½*

Q1 PP2 1c on $20,000 dk. red

No. Q1 is also found with surcharged value repeated in 5 characters at top of stamp.

Tsingtau

(tsing·tou, ching·dou)

China Nos. 890, 899, 945, 894 Handstamp Surcharged in Purple Blue or Red

壹 銀
分 圓
(島青)

Engr.; Litho.

1949, May *Perf. 14, 12½*

1 A94 1c on $100 orange brown (P) 7.00 7.00
2 " 4c on $5000 light blue (P) 4.50 4.50
3 " 6c on $500 rose lilac (B) 3.50 3.50
4 " 10c on $1000 blue (R) 3.50 3.50

Yunnan Province.

(yōōn'nän'; yün'-)

Stamps of China, 1923-26, Overprinted

用貼省滇限

The overprint reads "For exclusive use in the Province of Yunnan". It was applied to prevent stamps being purchased in the depreciated currency of Yunnan and used elsewhere.

1926 *Perf. 14.* **Unwmkd.**

1 A29 ½c black brown 10 7
2 " 1c orange 12 7
3 " 1½c violet 15 12
4 " 2c yellow green 20 12
5 " 3c blue green 12 10
6 " 4c olive green 12 10
7 " 5c claret 20 10
8 " 6c red 25 15
9 " 7c violet 25 20
10 " 8c brown orange 30 28
11 " 10c dark blue 30 8
12 A30 13c brown 50 35
13 " 15c dark blue 40 35
14 " 16c olive green 50 35
15 " 20c brown red 75 15
16 " 30c brown violet 1.25 35
17 " 50c deep green 1.50 45
18 A31 $1 orange brown & sepia 3.50 1.00
19 " $2 blue & red brown 7.50 3.00
20 " $5 red & slate 40.00 35.00
Nos. 1–20 (20) 58.01 42.39

Unification Issue of China, 1929, Overprinted in Red

貼 滇
用 省

1929 *Perf. 14*

21 A35 1c brown orange 50 20
22 " 4c olive green 75 30
23 " 10c dark blue 1.50 1.00
24 " $1 dark red 22.50 20.00

Similar Overprint in Black on Sun Yat-sen Mausoleum Issue. Characters 15½-16mm. apart.

25 A36 1c brown orange 35 20
26 " 4c olive green 50 30
27 " 10c dark blue 1.25 1.00
28 " $1 dark red 12.50 10.00

London Print Issue of China, 1931-37, Overprinted

用貼省滇限

1932-34 *Perf. 12½.* **Unwmkd.**

Type I (double circle).

29 A37 1c orange 30 30
30 " 2c olive green 50 50
31 " 4c green 55 55
32 " 20c ultramarine 75 75
33 " $1 orange brown & dark brown 10.00 8.00
34 " $2 blue & orange brown 17.50 15.00
35 " $5 dull red & blk. 50.00 40.00
Nos. 29–35 (7) 79.60 65.10

Type II (single circle).

36 A37 2c olive green 15 12
37 " 4c green 50 50
38 " 5c green 35 35
39 " 15c dark green 1.75 1.25
40 " 15c scarlet ('34) 1.00 1.00
41 " 25c ultramarine 1.25 1.25
42 " $1 orange brown & dark brown 12.50 10.00
43 " $2 blue & orange brown 20.00 12.50
44 " $5 dull red & black 40.00 40.00
Nos. 36–44 (9) 77.50 71.97

Nos. 36–39, 41–44 were overprinted in London as well as in Peiping. The overprints differ in minor details. Price of London overprints (8), $350.

Tan Yuan-chang Issue of China, 1933, Overprinted

貼 滇
用 省

1933 *Perf. 14.*

45 A49 2c olive green 40 25
46 " 5c green 50 30
47 " 25c ultramarine 1.25 70
48 " $1 red 15.00 10.00

Martyrs Issue of China, 1932-34

Overprinted 用貼省滇限

1933

49 A39 ½c black brown 15 12
50 A40 1c orange 20 12
51 A39 2½c rose lilac 35 18
52 A48 3c deep brown 45 25
53 A45 8c brown orange 85 50
54 A46 10c dull violet 60 25
55 A45 13c blue green 70 25
56 A46 17c brown olive 1.30 50
57 A47 20c brown red 70 40
58 A48 30c brown violet 1.25 50
59 A47 40c orange 10.00 8.00
60 A40 50c green 10.00 8.00
Nos. 49–60 (12) 26.55 19.07

China No. 324 was overprinted with characters arranged vertically, like Sinkiang No. 114, but was not issued.

China Stamps of 1945–49 Surcharged in Black or Blue

壹 滇
省
貼
角10 用

Engr.; Litho.; Typo.

1949 *Perf. 12, 12½, 14*

61 A82 1c on $200,000 brown violet 90 90
62 " 1.2c on $40,000 green 1.25 1.25
63 A94 6c on $200 red org. 75 75
64 " 10c on $20,000 orange 75 75
65 " 12c on $50 dark Prus. grn. (Bl) 90 90
66 A72 12c on $50 greenish gray (Bl) 1.00 1.00
67 " 12c on $200 brown violet (Bl) 60 60
68 A94 30c on $20 vio. brn. 75 75
69 A82 $1.20 on $100,000 dull green 2.00 2.00

China No. 888 and 630 Surcharged

4
肆 郵
分 資
滇

1949 **Engr.** *Perf. 14*

70 A94 4c on $20 violet brown 40.00

Typo. *Perf. 12*

71 A72 12c on $200 brn. violet 65.00

Manchuria.

(măn·chōōr'ĭ·ȧ)

Kirin and Heilungkiang Issue.

Stamps of China, 1923-26, Overprinted

用貼黑吉限

The overprint reads: "For use in Ki-Hei District" the two names being abbreviated.

The intention of the overprint was to prevent the purchase of stamps in Manchuria, where the currency was depreciated, and their resale elsewhere.

1927 *Perf. 14.* **Unwmkd.**

1 A29 ½c black brown 5 5
2 " 1c orange 5 5
3 " 1½c violet 10 12
4 " 2c yellow green 15 8
5 " 3c blue green 10 10
6 " 4c olive green 15 5
7 " 5c claret 15 10
8 " 6c red 20 15
9 " 7c violet 20 18
10 " 8c brown orange 20 15
11 " 10c dark blue 20 5
12 A30 13c brown 65 30
13 " 15c dark blue 40 20
14 " 16c olive green 40 30
15 " 20c brown red 65 30
16 " 30c brown violet 65 30
17 " 50c deep green 2.50 30
18 A31 $1 orange brown & sepia 5.00 1.00
19 " $2 blue & red brown 7.50 5.00
20 " $5 red & slate 37.50 35.00
Nos. 1–20 (20) 56.80 43.78

Several values of this issue exist with inverted overprint, double overprint and in pairs with one overprint omitted. These "errors" were not regularly issued. Forgeries also exist.

Chang Tso-lin Stamps of 1928 Overprinted in Red or Blue

貼 吉
用 黑

1928 *Perf. 14*

21 A34 1c brown orange (R) 25 20
22 " 4c olive green (R) 50 30
23 " 10c dull blue (R) 1.25 1.00
24 " $1 red (Bl) 12.50 9.00

Unification Issue of China, 1929, Overprinted in Red as in 1928.

1929

25 A35 1c brown orange 50 25
26 " 4c olive green 75 50
27 " 10c dark blue 2.00 1.25
28 " $1 dark red 25.00 15.00

Similar Overprint in Black on Sun Yat-sen Mausoleum Issue of China. Characters 15-16mm. apart.

1929 *Perf. 14*

29 A36 1c brown orange 50 50
30 " 4c olive green 50 50
31 " 10c dark blue 1.25 1.00
32 " $1 dark red 15.00 9.00

Sinkiang.

(sĭn'kyăng'; shĭn'jyäng',-gyäng')

Stamps of China, 1913-19, Overprinted in Black or Red

限
新
省
貼
用
a

The first character of overprint "a" is ½ mm. out of alignment, to the left, and the overprint measures 16mm.

1915 *Perf. 14, 15.* **Unwmkd.**

1 A24 ½c black brown 18 15
2 " 1c orange 12 10
3 " 2c yellow green 18 15
4 " 3c slate green 18 15
5 " 4c scarlet 30 20
6 " 5c rose lilac 35 30
7 " 6c gray 50 30
8 " 7c violet 65 60
9 " 8c brown orange 50 45

10 A24 10c dark blue 75 75
11 A25 15c brown 80 75
12 " 16c olive green 1.50 1.25
13 " 20c brown red 1.50 1.25
14 " 30c brown violet 2.00 1.25
15 " 50c deep green 6.00 5.00
16 A26 $1 ochre & black (R) 27.50 12.50
a. Second & third characters of ovpt. transposed *1000.00*
Nos. 1-16 (16) 43.01 25.15

Stamps of China, 1913-19, Overprinted in Black or Red 限新省貼用 *b*

The five characters of overprint "b" are correctly aligned and measure 15½mm.

1916-19
17 A24 ½c black brown 10 10
18 " 1c orange 20 10
19 " 1½c violet 20 20
20 " 2c yellow green 20 10
21 " 3c slate green 20 10
22 " 4c scarlet 20 20
23 " 5c rose lilac 30 20
24 " 6c gray 35 15
25 " 7c violet 50 50
26 " 8c brown orange 20 10
27 " 10c dark blue 15 10
28 A25 13c brown 60 25
29 " 15c brown 60 30
30 " 16c olive green 30 20
31 " 20c brown red 25 20
32 " 30c brown violet 40 30
33 " 50c deep green 50 30
34 A26 $1 ochre & black (R) 3.00 75
35 " $2 dark blue & black (R) 5.00 1.50
36 " $5 scarlet & black (R) 15.00 7.50
37 " $10 yellow green & black (R) 60.00 30.00
38 " $20 yellow & black (R) 150.00 100.00
Nos. 17-38 (22) 238.25 143.15

China Nos. 243-246 Overprinted 用貼省新限

1921 ***Perf. 14***
39 A27 1c orange 50 50
40 " 3c blue green 75 75
41 " 6c gray 2.00 1.50
42 " 10c blue 15.00 15.00

Constitution Issue of China, 1923, Overprinted 貼 新 疆 用 省

1923
43 A32 1c orange 1.00 25
44 " 3c blue green 1.00 30
45 " 4c red 2.50 50
46 " 10c blue 6.00 3.00

Stamps of China, 1923-26, Overprinted Type "b" as in 1916-19, in Black or Red.

1924 **Re-engraved**
47 A29 ½c black brown 10 5
48 " 1c orange 10 5
49 " 1½c violet 10 5
50 " 2c yellow green 10 5
51 " 3c blue green 12 5
52 " 4c gray 1.00 70
53 " 5c claret 15 5
54 " 6c red 20 10
55 " 7c violet 15 10
56 " 8c orange brown 15 10
57 " 10c dark blue 15 10
58 A30 13c red brown 30 15
59 " 15c deep blue 30 20
60 " 16c olive green 35 20
61 " 20c brown red 35 12
62 " 30c brown violet 50 15
63 " 50c deep green 65 25
64 A31 $1 orange brown & sepia (R) 3.00 50
65 A31 $2 blue & red brown (R) 6.00 1.00
66 " $5 red & slate (R) 17.50 3.00
67 " $10 green & claret (R) 60.00 40.00
68 " $20 brown violet & blue (R) 85.00 65.00
Nos. 47-68 (22) 176.27 111.97
See also Nos. 69, 114.

Same Overprint on China No. 275.

1926
69 A29 4c olive green 22 8

Chang Tso-lin Stamps of China, 1928 Overprinted in Red or Blue 貼 新 用 疆

1928 ***Perf. 14***
70 A34 1c brown orange (R) 25 20
71 " 4c olive green (R) 50 45
72 " 10c dull blue (R) 1.50 1.25
73 " $1 red (Bl) 12.50 9.00

Unification Issue of China, 1929, Overprinted in Red as in 1928.

1929
74 A35 1c brown orange 60 40
75 " 4c olive green 1.00 75
76 " 10c dark blue 2.00 1.50
77 " $1 dark red 25.00 17.50

Similar Overprint in Black on Sun Yat-sen Mausoleum Issue of China.

Characters 15mm. apart

1929 ***Perf. 14***
78 A36 1c brown orange 75 30
79 " 4c olive green 1.00 50
80 " 10c dark blue 2.50 1.00
81 " $1 dark red 17.50 10.00

Stamps of Sun Yat-sen Issue of 1931-37 Overprinted 用貼省新限

1932 **Type I** ***Perf. 12½***
82 A37 1c orange 30 35
83 " 2c olive green 50 60
84 " 4c green 35 45
85 " 20c ultramarine 50 60
86 " $1 orange brown & dark brown 2.00 2.25
87 " $2 blue & org. brn. 3.00 3.25
88 " $5 dull red & black 7.00 7.50
Nos. 82-88 (7) 13.65 15.00

No. 83 was overprinted in Shanghai in 1938. The overprint differs in minor details.

1932-38 **Type II**
89 A37 2c olive green 8 10
90 " 4c green 8 10
91 " 5c green 8 10
92 " 15c dark green 20 22
93 " 15c scarlet ('34) 15 18
93A " 20c ultra. ('38) 12 35
94 " 25c ultramarine 15 18
95 " $1 orange brown & dark brown 1.00 1.10
96 " $2 blue & orange brown 1.75 2.00
97 " $5 dull red & black 5.50 5.75
Nos. 89-97 (10) 9.11 10.08

Nos. 89, 90 and 94 were overprinted in London, Peiping and Shanghai. Nos. 92, 95-97 exist with London and Peiping overprints. Nos. 91 and 93 exist with Peiping and Shanghai overprints. No. 93A is a Shanghai overprint. The overprints differ in minor details.

Tan Yuan-chang Issue of China, 1933, Overprinted as in 1928.

1933 ***Perf. 14.***
98 A49 2c olive green 28 20
99 " 5c green 75 60
100 " 25c ultramarine 1.50 1.25
101 " $1 red 15.00 12.50

Stamps of China Martyrs Issue of 1932-34 Overprinted 用貼省新限

1933-34
102 A39 ½c black brown 7 7
103 A40 1c orange 7 7
104 A39 2½c rose lilac 7 7
105 A48 3c deep brown 7 7
106 A45 8c brown orange 10 10
107 A46 10c dull violet 10 10
108 A45 13c blue green 15 15
109 A46 17c brown olive 15 15
110 A47 20c brown red 22 22
111 A48 30c brown violet 22 22
112 A47 40c orange 28 28
113 A40 50c green 32 32
Nos. 102-113 (12) 1.82 1.82

Nos. 102-113 were originally overprinted in Peiping. In 1938, Nos. 103-105, 108-112 were overprinted in Shanghai. The two overprints differ in minor details. No. 105, Shanghai overprint, is scarce. Price $35.

China No. 324 Overprinted Type "b" as in 1924.

1936 ***Perf. 14.***
114 A29 6c brown 5.00 5.00

Stamps of China, 1939-40 Overprinted in Black.

1940-45 ***Perf. 12½*** **Unwmkd.**

Type III.
115 A57 2c olive green 3 3
116 " 3c dull claret ('41) 3 3
117 " 5c green 3 3
118 " 5c olive green 3 3
119 " 8c olive green ('41) 3 3
120 " 10c green ('41) 3 3
121 " 15c scarlet 3 3
122 " 16c olive gray ('41) 5 5
123 " 25c dark blue 4 4
124 " $1 henna & dark brn. (type II) 1.50 1.50
125 " $2 deep blue & orange brn. (type I) 1.50 1.50
126 " $5 red & greenish black 6.00 6.00
Nos. 115-126 (12) 9.30 9.30

Perf. 14.

With Secret Marks.
127 A57 8c olive grn. (#383a) 5 5
a. On #383 2.50 2.50
128 " 10c green ('41) 50 50
129 " 30c scarlet ('45) 5 5
130 " 50c dark blue ('45) 5 5
131 " $1 orange brown & sepia 10 10
132 " $2 deep blue & orange brown 15 15
133 " $5 red & slate green 25 25
134 " $10 dark green & dull purple 60 60
135 " $20 rose lake & dark blue 1.10 1.10
Nos. 127-135 (9) 2.85 2.85

Wmkd. Character Yu (Post). (261)

Perf. 14.
136 A57 5c olive green 8 8
137 " 10c green 10 10
138 " 30c scarlet 15 15
139 " 50c dark blue 18 18

Martyrs Issue, 1940-41, Overprinted in Black 用貼省新限

Perf. 12, 12½, 13, 13x12, 13½x13.

1941-45 **Wmk. 261**
140 A40 1c orange 10 10
141 A39 2½c rose lilac 10 10
142 A45 8c deep orange ('45) 50 50
143 A46 10c dull violet 10 10
144 A45 13c deep yellow green 20 20
145 A46 17c brown olive 25 25
146 A40 25c red violet ('45) 35 35
147 A47 40c orange ('45) 50 50
Nos. 140-147 (8) 2.10 2.10

Unwmkd.
148 A39 ½c olive black 5 5
149 A40 1c orange ('45) 5 5
150 A46 2c deep blue ('45) 5 5
151 A48 3c deep yellow brown 5 5
152 A39 4c pale violet ('45) 5 5
153 A45 8c deep orange 5 5
154 " 13c deep yellow green ('45) 10 10
155 A48 15c brn. carmine ('45) 10 10
156 A46 17c brown olive ('45) 20 20
157 A47 20c light blue ('45) 10 10
158 A45 21c olive brown ('45) 15 15
159 A46 28c olive ('45) 15 15
160 A47 40c orange ('45) 85 85
161 A40 50c green ('45) 15 15
Nos. 148-161 (14) 2.10 2.10

Stamps of China, 1942-43 Overprinted in Carmine, Black or Red 用貼省新限

Without Gum.

1944 ***Perf. 12½, 13.***
162 A62 10c deep green (C) 4 4
163 " 20c dk. olive green (C) 4 4
164 " 25c violet brown 4 4
165 " 30c dark orange 4 4
166 " 40c red brown 4 4
167 " 50c sage green 4 4
a. Perf. 11 75 75
168 " $1 rose lake 4 4
169 " $1 dull green 4 4
170 " $1.50 deep blue (C) 4 4
171 " $2 dk. bl. green (R) 4 4
172 " $3 yellow 4 4
173 " $5 cerise 4 4
Nos. 162-173 (12) 48 48

Same Overprint on Stamps of China, 1942-43, in Black.

1944-46 ***Imperf.***
174 A57 $10 red brown 12.50 12.50
175 " $20 rose red 15 15
176 " $30 dull violet 25 25
177 " $40 rose red 30 30
178 " $50 blue ('46) 225.00 275.00
179 " $100 orange brown 50 50

Perf. 13½.
180 A57 $4 deep blue 5 5
181 " $5 lilac gray 3 3
182 " $10 red brown 5 5
183 " $20 blue green 30 30
184 " $20 rose red 15.00 15.00
185 " $30 dull violet 40 40
186 " $40 rose 50 50
187 " $50 blue 60 60
188 " $100 orange brown 15.00 15.00
Nos. 174-177, 179-188 (14) 45.63 45.63

Nos. 162 and 164 Surcharged in Black 改作壹角貳分

1944, Aug. 1
194 A62 12c on 10c deep green 8 8
195 " 24c on 25c brn. violet 10 10

Stamps of China, 1940-41, Overprinted in Black at Chengtu, Szechwan 用貼省新限

1943
196 A57 10c green (#354) 1.00 1.00
197 A47 20c lt. blue (#433) 1.00 1.00

Perf. 14 **Wmk. 261**
198 A57 50c dk. blue (#396) 1.00 1.00

China Nos. 565 and 567 Overprinted in Black 用貼省新限

1945 ***Perf. 12½*** **Unwmkd.**
200 A63 40c brown red 8 8
201 " $3 red 8 8

China Nos. 640-642, 788, 750, 753 Surcharged in Black or Red 改作伍分 用貼郵疆新限

1949 **Engraved** ***Perf. 14***
202 A73 1c on $100 dark carmine 1.50 1.50

203 A73 3c on $200 olive green (R) 1.50 1.50
204 " 5c on $500 brt. blue green (R) 1.50 1.50
205 A82 10c on $20,000 rose pink 2.25 2.25
206 " 50c on $4000 gray (R) 2.75 2.75
207 " $1 on $6000 rose lilac 6.00 6.00
Nos. 202-207 (6) 15.50 15.50

AIR POST STAMPS.

Sinkiang Nos. 53, 57, 59, 32 Overprinted in Red 空航

1932-33 ***Perf. 14.*** **Unwmkd.**

C1 A29 5c claret ('33) 75.00 50.00
C2 " 10c dark blue('33) 75.00 40.00
C3 A30 15c deep blue 650.00 150.00
C4 A25 30c brown violet 250.00 190.00

Counterfeits exist of Nos. C1-C19.

Air Post Stamps of China, 1932-37 Handstamped in Dull Red

用貼省新限

1942

C5 AP3 15c gray green 60 60
C6 " 25c orange 120.00 120.00
C7 " 30c red 50 50
C8 " 45c brown violet 60 60
C9 " 50c dark brown 5.00 5.00
C10 " 60c dark blue 60 60
C11 " 90c olive green 7.50 7.50
C12 " $1 yellow green 60 60
Nos. C5-C12 (8) 135.40 135.40

Same Handstamped Overprint on Air Post Stamps of China, 1940-41.

1942 ***Perf. 12½, 13, 13½*** **Wmk. 261**

C13 AP3 15c gray green 50 50
C14 " 25c yellow orange 50 50

1942 **Unwmkd.**

C15 AP3 25c light orange 50 50
C16 " 30c light red 60 60
C17 " 50c brown 60 60
C18 " $2 light brown 5.00 5.00
C19 " $5 lake 5.00 5.00
Nos. C15-C19 (5) 11.70 11.70

Twelve values exist with this overprint in black. Their status has not been determined. Inverted overprints exist in both red and black.

Official Perforated Characters

For use on official mail, various Sinkiang stamps were perforated with an arrangement of four Chinese characters ("For Official Business Only"). These include Nos. 1-38, 47-69, 114.

Offices in Tibet.

(tĭ·bĕt′; tĭb′ĕt)

12 Pies = 1 Anna
16 Annas = 1 Rupee

Stamps of China, Issues of 1902-10, Surcharged

分年
Three Pies

1911 ***Perf. 12 to 16.*** **Unwmkd.**

1 A17 3p on 1c ochre 1.50 1.50
a. Inverted surcharge 200.00
2 " ½a on 2c green 1.50 1.50
3 " 1a on 4c vermilion 1.50 1.50
4 " 2a on 7c maroon 2.00 2.00
5 " 2½a on 10c ultra. 3.00 3.00
6 A18 3a on 16c olive green 5.00 5.00
a. Large "S" in "Annas" 200.00
7 " 4a on 20c red brown 5.00 5.00
8 " 6a on 30c rose red 8.00 8.00
9 " 12a on 50c yel. green 20.00 20.00
10 A19 1r on $1 red & pale rose 75.00 75.00
11 " 2r on $2 red & yel. 225.00 225.00
Nos. 1-11 (11) 347.50 347.50

CHINA,
People's Republic of

LOCATION—Eastern Asia.

GOV'T.—Communist republic.

POP.—865,680,000 (est. 1977).

CAPITAL—Peking.

The communists completed their conquest of all mainland China in 1949. They established the Central Government and General Postal Administration in Peking. They ordered all but two regions to stop selling regional issues by June 30, 1950, extending validity one year from that date. The Northeast and Port Arthur-Dairen regions were exempted because their currency had a different value. These two regions stopped using separate issues at the end of 1950. Thereafter unified issues were used throughout mainland China.

After currency revaluation Mar. 1, 1955, reprints were prepared and put on sale by the Philatelic Agency in order to supply stocks of exhausted issues for collectors. Minor differences in design or paper distinguish the reprints. They are of commemorative and special issues up to the gymnastics set of 1952. Many exist canceled to order. Reprints are plentiful and inexpensive. Prices are for original issues. Reprint distinctions are footnoted.

Commemorative issues, beginning in 1949, and special issues, beginning in 1951, bear 4 numbers in lower margin: 1. Issue number. 2. Total of stamps in set. 3. Position of stamp in set. 4. Cumulative number of stamp (usually in parenthesis). A fifth number, the year of issue, was added in 1952.

The numbering system varies at times, with all numbers omitted on Nos. 938–1046.

In certain sets listings include parenthetically the position-in-set number. During some periods these parentheses in listings hold the stamp's cumulative number.

All stamps to the beginning of 1960 were issued without gum, except as noted. After that date, most stamps have gum, which is translucent and almost invisible. All issues are unwatermarked, unless otherwise noted.

100 fen = 1 yuan ($)

Prices fluctuate for most P.R.C. issues, and for Communist Regional issues. Information is inadequate or lacking about quantities printed and issued, existence of large stocks, and possible release of remainders.

Prices quoted represent averages and indicate relative values.

Lantern and Gate of Heavenly Peace

A1

Globe and Hand Holding Hammer

A2

1949, Oct. 8 **Litho.** ***Perf. 12½***

1	A1	$30 blue	1.00	1.00
2	"	$50 rose red	1.00	1.00
3	"	$100 green	1.00	1.00
4	"	$200 maroon	1.00	1.00

First session of Chinese People's Political Conference. See also Nos. 1L121–1L124.

Original Reprint

Reprints have altered ornament on lantern base. On originals, it is a full oval; in reprints, only a partial circle. Price, set, 40 cents.

1949, Nov. 16

5	A2	$100 carmine	2.00	75
6	"	$300 slate green	2.00	1.00
7	"	$500 dark blue	2.00	1.25

Asiatic and Australasian Congress of the World Federation of Trade Unions, Peking. The $100, imperf., is of dubious status. See also Nos. 1L133–1L135.

Original

Reprint

Reprints show heavier shading on index finger and thumb. Price, set, 40 cents.

Conference Hall, Peking

A3

Mao Tse-tung on Rostrum

A4

1950, Feb. 1 **Engraved** ***Perf. 14***

8	A3	$50 red	2.50	1.50
9	"	$100 blue	2.50	1.50
10	A4	$300 red brown	2.50	1.50
11	"	$500 green	2.50	1.50

Chinese People's Political Conference. See also Nos. 1L136–1L139.

Original

Reprint

Nos. 8-9: First character in top inscription shows a square, reprints an oblong.

Nos. 10-11: Originals have heavy crosshatching and lines which touch back of head and top of rostrum. Reprints have lighter lines which do not touch head or top of rostrum.

Reprints, Nos. 8-11, price 45 cents.

Gate of Heavenly Peace (same size)

A5

First Issue: Top line of shading broken at right.

1950, Feb. 10 **Litho.** ***Perf. 12½***

12	A5	$200 green	15	12
13	"	$300 brown red	15	12
14	"	$500 red	15	12
15	A5	$800 orange	2.75	12
16	"	$1000 dull violet	1.00	10
17	"	$2000 olive	1.75	12
18	"	$5000 bright pink	30	12
19	"	$8000 blue	30	1.50
20	"	$10,000 brown	30	25
		Nos. 12-20 (9)	6.85	2.57

1950, June 9 **Typographed**

Second Issue: Top line of shading extends to frame line at right.

21	A5	$1000 dull violet	10	5
22	"	$3000 red brown	10	5
23	"	$10,000 brown	10	5

中國人民郵政 貳佰圓 200

1949 Unit Issue of China Surcharged in Blue, Black, Green or Red

1950, Mar. **Litho.** ***Perf. 12½***

24	SD2	$100 on red vio. (Bl)	1.25	90
		a. Rouletted	30	30
25	R2	$200 on red (Bk)	5.00	75
		a. Rouletted	30	35
26	AP5	$300 on bl. grn. (Bk)	1.00	75
		a. Rouletted	50	60
27	A96	$500 on orange (G)	25	15
		a. Perf. 14	20.00	15.00
28	A96	$800 on orange (R)	1.00	20
		a. Rouletted	20	10
		b. Perf. 14	25.00	20.00
29	A96	$1000 on orange (Bk)	50	15
		a. Perf. 14	75	30
		Nos. 24-29 (6)	9.00	2.90

Harvesters with Ox

A6

1950, May

30	A6	$20,000 on $10,000 red	150.00	15.00

No. 30 is surcharged on an unissued stamp of East China.

Flag, Mao Tse-tung, Gate of Heavenly Peace

A7

1950, July 1 ***Perf. 14***

Yellow Stars

31	A7	$800 green & red	10.00	1.25
32	"	$1000 brown & red	10.00	2.50
33	"	$2000 dk. brown & red	10.00	3.00
34	"	$3000 dk. blue & red	10.00	3.50

Inauguration of the People's Republic, Oct. 1, 1949. See also Nos. 1L150–1L153.

Original Reprint

Originals have a single curved line in jacket button, reprints have an extra dot in button. Price, set 60 cents.

中國人民郵政 伍拾圓 ☆ 50

Sun Yat-sen Stamps of Northeastern Provinces Surcharged in Red, Black or Blue

1950, July 1 **Engraved**

35	A2	$50 on 20c yel. grn. (R)	30	4.00
36	"	$50 on 25c blk. brn. (R)	20	1.75
37	"	$50 on 50c red orange (Bk)	20	35
38	"	$100 on $2.50 indigo (R)	20	35
39	"	$100 on $3 brn. (Bk)	10.00	35
40	"	$100 on $4 org. brown, Type II (Bl)	30	1.75
		a. Type I	50.00	40.00
41	A2	$100 on $5 dk. green (Bk)	10.00	35
42	"	$100 on $10 crimson (Bl)	40	4.00
43	"	$400 on $20 olive, Type II (Bl)	40	4.00
		a. Type I	45.00	35.00
44	A2	$400 on $44 dark carmine rose (Bl)	40	1.25
45	"	$400 on $65 dull green (R)	10.00	4.00
46	"	$400 on $100 dp. grn. (R)	60	1.25
47	"	$400 on $200 rose brown (Bk)	20.00	1.25
48	"	$400 on $300 bluish green (R)	20.00	1.25
		Nos. 35-48 (14)	73.00	25.90

中國人民郵政 貳佰圓 ★★ 200

Flying Geese Type of China Surcharged in Red, Blue, Green, Brown or Black

1950, Aug. 1 ***Perf. 12½, Imperf.***

49	A97	$50 on 10c dk. blue (R)	10	12
50	"	$100 on 16c olive, imperf. (Bl)	10	12
51	"	$100 on 50c dull green, imperf. (Bl)	10	12
52	"	$200 on $1 orange (G)	10	12
53	"	$200 on $2 blue (Br)	15	20
54	"	$400 on $5 carmine rose (Bk)	20	25
55	"	$400 on $10 blue green (Bk)	20	25
56	"	$400 on $20 pur. (Bk)	1.00	50
		Nos. 49-56 (8)	1.95	1.68

Dove of Peace, by Picasso

A8

Chinese Flag and "1"

A9

1950, Aug. 1 **Engraved** ***Perf. 14***

57	A8	$400 brown	2.75	75
58	"	$800 green	2.75	1.50
59	"	$2000 blue	2.75	2.25

World Peace Campaign. See also Nos. 1L154–1L156.

Paper of originals appears bright under ultraviolet lamp. That of reprints looks dull. Price, set, 35 cents.

1950 **Engraved & Litho.**

Flag in Red & Yellow

60	A9	$100 purple	7.00	1.25
61	"	$400 red brown	7.00	1.25

62 A9 $800 green 7.00 1.50
63 " $1000 light olive 7.00 2.50
64 " $2000 blue 7.00 3.00
Nos. 60-64 (5) 35.00 9.50

First anniversary of the Chinese People's Republic. Size of $800: 38x46 mm.; others 26x32 mm.

Issue dates: No. 62, Oct. 1; others Oct. 31. See also Nos. 1L157-1L161.

Original ($800) Reprint

Reprints are a brighter red, leaves beside "1" are gray brown instead of reddish brown. On the $800 the arrangement of dots in background differs in relationship to large star. Price, set 45 cents.

(same size)

Gate of Heavenly Peace A10

"Communication" and Map of China A11

Third Issue: Cloud almost touches character at upper left. Cloud breaks inner frame line at top.

1950 Lithographed

65 A10 $100 lt. greenish bl. 10.00 *4.00*
66 " $200 green 70.00 *6.00*
67 " $300 dark carmine 65 *3.00*
68 " $400 greenish gray 90 *3.00*
69 " $500 carmine 65 *4.00*
70 " $800 orange 65 25
71 " $2000 gray olive 1.35 40
Nos. 65-71 (7) 84.20 *20.65*

Issue dates: $800, Oct. 8; $500, $2000, Dec. 1; others, Oct. 6.

1950, Nov. 1 Lithographed

72 A11 $400 green & brown 3.00 1.25
73 " $800 carmine & green 3.00 1.25

First All-China Postal Conference, Peking.

Original Reprint

Originals have 3 lines below horizontal bar between 1st & 2nd character; reprints have 4. Price, set, 30 cents.

Stalin and Mao Tse-tung—A12

1950, Dec. 1 Engraved *Perf. 14*

74 A12 $400 red 4.50 75
75 " $800 deep green 4.50 1.50
76 " $2000 dark blue 4.50 2.25

Signing of Sino-Soviet Treaty of Friendship, Alliance and Mutual Assistance. See also Nos. 1L176-1L178.

Paper of originals appears bright under ultraviolet lamp. That of reprints looks dull. Price, set 30 cents.

East China Issue of 1949 Surcharged in Red, Black, Brown or Blue

Train and Postal Runner A12a

1950, Dec. Litho. *Perf. 12½*

77 A12a $50 on $10 dp. ultra. (R) 7 3
78 " $100 on $15 orange vermilion (Bk) 10 4
a. $100 on $15 red (Bk), perf. 14 11 5
79 A12a $300 on $50 car. (Bk) 12 12
80 " $400 on $1600 violet blue (Br) 12 10
81 " $400 on $2000 brown violet (Bl) 12 6
Nos. 77-81 (5) 53 35

East China Issue of 1949 Surcharged in Red or Black

Chairman Mao A12b

1950, Dec.

82 A12b $50 on $10 ultra. (R) 5 5
83 " $400 on $15 vermilion (Bk) 5 5
84 " $400 on $2000 grn. (Bk) 5 5

(same size)

Gate of Heavenly Peace A13 A14

Fourth Issue: Similar to 3rd issue, but large cloud does not break inner frame line at top.

1950-51 Lithographed

85 A13 $100 light blue 20 50
86 " $200 dull green 35 50
87 " $300 dull lilac 25 *5.00*
88 " $400 gray green 40 50
89 " $500 carmine 20 75
90 " $800 orange 40.00 *1.00*
a. Imperf., pair 75.00
91 A13 $1000 violet 25 50
92 " $2000 olive 60.00 *2.00*
93 " $3000 brown 65 *6.00*
94 " $5000 pink 65 *6.00*
Nos. 85-94 (10) 102.95 *22.75*

Issue dates: $200, $300, $500, $800, $2000, $5000, Dec. 22, 1950; others June 8, 1951.

1951, Jan. 18 Engraved *Perf. 14*

Fifth Issue: Colored network on surface in salmon.

95 A14 $10,000 brown 50 *6.00*
96 " $20,000 olive 50 *5.00*
97 " $30,000 green 2.00 *15.00*
98 " $50,000 violet 8.00 7.50
99 " $100,000 scarlet 400.00 70.00
100 " $200,000 blue 400.00 60.00
Nos. 95-100 (6) 811.00 *163.50*

Unit Issue of China Surcharged

中國人民郵政
伍
圓
5

1951, May 2 Litho. *Perf. 12½*

101 SD2 $5 on rose lilac 25 15
102 AP5 $10 on bright green 15 8
103 R2 $15 on red 15 8
104 A96 $25 on orange 15 8

Issued for use in Northeast China, but available for use throughout China. Nos. 101-104 rouletted were sold for philatelic purposes only. Price, set, 40 cents.

Chairman Mao Tse-tung A15

1951, July 1 Engraved *Perf. 14*

105 A15 $400 chestnut 3.00 1.00
106 " $500 deep green 3.00 1.50
107 " $800 crimson 3.00 1.50

30th anniversary of the Chinese Communist Party.

Reprints are on whiter, thinner and harder paper. Price, set, 40 cents.

Picasso Dove—A16

1951, Aug. 15 *Perf. 12½*

108 A16 $400 orange brown 3.25 1.00
109 " $800 blue green 3.25 1.25
110 " $1000 dull violet 3.25 2.00

World Peace Campaign.

Reprints are perf. 14. Price, set, 40 cents.

Remittance Stamp of China Surcharged in Carmine or Black

(same size)

A17

Engraved, Commercial Press

1951, Sept. *Perf. 12½*

111 A17 $50 on $2 blue green (C) 15 40

Typo., Kang Hwa Printing Co.

Roul. 9½

112 A17 $50 on $2 gray blue (C) 25 40
113 " $50 on $5 red orange (Bk) 10 40
114 " $50 on $50 gray (C) 2.00 40

Litho., Central Trust Co.

Perf. 13

115 A17 $50 on $50 gray black (C) 10 40

Litho., Chung Hwa Book Co.

Perf. 11½

116 A17 $50 on $50 gray (C) 15 40
a. Perf. 11½x10 50 50
Nos. 111-116 (6) 2.75 2.40

National Emblem A18

1951, Oct. 1 *Perf. 14*

Engraved; Background Network Lithographed in Yellow.

117 A18 $100 Prussian blue 2.50 50
118 " $200 brown 2.50 60
119 " $400 orange 2.50 75
120 " $500 green 2.50 75
121 " $800 carmine 2.50 1.00
Nos. 117-121 (5) 12.50 3.60

Reprints exist but difficult to distinguish; paper whiter, and colors slightly brighter. Price, set, 40 cents.

Lu Hsun and Quotation A19

1951, Oct. 19 Litho. *Perf. 12½*

122 A19 $400 lilac 2.50 2.00
123 " $800 green 2.50 2.00

15th anniversary of the death of Lu Hsun (1881-1936), writer.

Original Reprint

Reprints have dot in triangle at lower right; no dot in original. Price, set, 30 cents.

Peasant Uprising, Chintien—A20

Design: Nos. 126-127, Coin of Taiping Regime and decrees of peasant government.

1951, Dec. 15 Engraved *Perf. 14*

124 A20 $400 green 4.00 1.00
125 " $800 scarlet 4.00 1.00
126 " $800 orange 4.00 1.00
127 " $1000 deep blue 4.00 1.50

Centenary of Taiping Peasant Rebellion.

Original

Reprint

Reprints of Nos. 124-125 have additional short stroke at upper left.

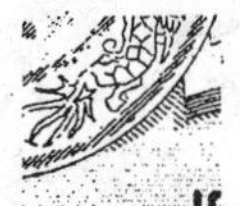
Original

Reprint

Reprints of Nos. 126-127 have two short strokes on scale near tail of right dragon on coin.
Price, Nos. 124-127, 35 cents.

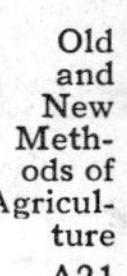

Old and New Methods of Agriculture A21

1952, Jan. 1

No.	Type	Description	Unused	Used
128	A21	$100 scarlet	2.50	85
129	"	$200 bright blue	2.50	85
130	"	$400 deep brown	2.50	85
131	"	$800 green	2.50	85

Agrarian reform.

Original

Reprint

One short horizontal line between legs of plower; 2 lines in reprints. Price set, 30 cents.

Potala Monastery, Lhasa A22

Designs: Nos. 134-135, Farmer plowing with yaks.

1952, Mar. 15 ***Perf. 12½***

No.	Type	Description	Unused	Used
132	A22	$400 vermilion	3.50	1.25
133	"	$800 claret	3.50	1.25
134	"	$800 blue green	3.50	75
135	"	$1000 dull violet	3.50	1.50

Liberation of Tibet.

Reprints, perf. 14, have a small Chinese character at lower left of the vignette which is missing in the original. Price, set, 30 cents.

Children of Four Races

A23

Hammer and Sickle on Numeral 1

A24

1952, Apr. 12 **Lithographed**

No.	Type	Description	Unused	Used
136	A23	$400 dull green	10	5
137	A23	$800 violet blue	5	5

International Child Protection Conference, Vienna.

1952, May 1

Designs: No. 139, Dove rising from worker's hand. No. 140, Dove, hammer, wheat and chimneys.

No.	Type	Description	Unused	Used
138	A24	$800 scarlet	5	5
139	"	$800 blue green	5	5
140	"	$800 orange brown	5	5

Labor Day.

Physical Exercises—A25

Stamps printed in blocks of four for each color, each block representing a specific setting-up exercise; exercises coincided with a national radio program. Where exercise positions are identical within the block, the serial number (in parenthesis) is the only means of differentiation.

1952, June 20

No.	Type	Description		Unused	Used
141	A25	$400 verm., blk. of 4		9.00	9.00
		a. Right arm forward	(1)	1.00	50
		b. Left arm forward	(2)	1.00	50
		c. as "a"	(3)	1.00	50
		d. as "b"	(4)	1.00	50
142	A25	$400 blue, blk. of 4		9.00	9.00
		a. Arms outstretched	(5)	1.00	50
		b. Knee-bend	(6)	1.00	50
		c. as "a"	(7)	1.00	50
		d. Rest	(8)	1.00	50
143	A25	$400 brown red, blk. of 4		9.00	9.00
		a. Arms forward	(9)	1.00	50
		b. Arms outstretched	(10)	1.00	50
		c. as "b"	(11)	1.00	50
		d. Rest	(12)	1.00	50
144	A25	$400 yellow green, blk. of 4		9.00	9.00
		a. Arms outstretched	(13)	1.00	50
		b. Sideways bend	(14)	1.00	50
		c. as "a"	(15)	1.00	50
		d. Hands on hips	(16)	1.00	50
145	A25	$400 red orange, blk. of 4		9.00	9.00
		a. as 144a	(17)	1.00	50
		b. Alternate toe touch	(18)	1.00	50
		c. as "a"	(19)	1.00	50
		d. Rest	(20)	1.00	50
146	A25	$400 dull blue, blk. of 4		9.00	9.00
		a. Stretch	(21)	1.00	50
		b. Toe touch	(22)	1.00	50
		c. Hands on floor	(23)	1.00	50
		d. Rest	(24)	1.00	50
147	A25	$400 org., block of 4		9.00	9.00
		a. Leg forward	(25)	1.00	50
		b. Leg extended back	(26)	1.00	50
		c. as "a"	(27)	1.00	50
		d. Rest	(28)	1.00	50
148	A25	$400 dull pur., block of 4		9.00	9.00
		a. Jumping jack	(29)	1.00	50
		b. Rest	(30)	1.00	50
		c. as "a"	(31)	1.00	50
		d. as "b"	(32)	1.00	50
149	A25	$400 yellow bister, blk. of 4		9.00	9.00
		a. Left leg raised	(33)	1.00	50
		b. Hands on hips	(34)	1.00	50
		c. Right leg raised	(35)	1.00	50
		d. as "b"	(36)	1.00	50
150	A25	$400 sky bl., blk. of 4		9.00	9.00
		a. Arms raised forward	(37)	1.00	50
		b. Arms above head	(38)	1.00	50
		c. Arms outstretched	(39)	1.00	50
		d. Rest	(40)	1.00	50
		Nos. 141-150 (10 blocks of 4)		90.00	90.00

Originals are on thin gray paper, colors darker. Reprints on thicker white paper, colors brighter. Price, set $2.

Hunting, Wei Dynasty, A.D. 386-580—A26

Designs from Murals in Cave Temples at Tunhuang, Kansu Province: No. 152, Lady attendants, Sui Dynasty, 581-617 A.D. No. 153, Gandharvas (mythology), Tang Dynasty, 618-906. No. 154, Dragon, Tang Dynasty.

1952, July 1 **Engraved**

No.	Type	Description	Unused	Used
151	A26	$800 slate green (1)	12	6
152	"	$800 chocolate (2)	12	6
153	"	$800 indigo (3)	12	6
154	"	$800 black (4)	12	6

"Glorious Mother Country," 1st series.

Marco Polo Bridge, near Peking

A27

Designs: No. 156, Cavalry passing through Great Wall. No. 157, Departure of New Fourth Army. No. 158, Mao Tsetung and Gen. Chu Teh planning counterattack.

1952, July 7 **Litho.** ***Perf. 14***

No.	Type	Description	Unused	Used
155	A27	$800 bright blue	12	6
156	"	$800 blue green	12	6
157	"	$800 plum	12	6
158	"	$800 scarlet	12	6

15th anniversary of war against Japan.

Soldier and Tanks

A28

Designs: No. 159, Soldier, sailor and airman (vert.). No. 161, Sailor and warships. No. 162, Airman and planes.

1952, Aug. 1 **Engraved** ***Perf. 12½***

No.	Type	Description	Unused	Used
159	A28	$800 carmine	12	6
160	"	$800 deep green	12	6
161	"	$800 purple	12	6
162	"	$800 orange brown	12	6

25th anniversary of People's Liberation Army.

Huai River Sluice Dam—A29

Designs: No. 164, Train on the Chengtu-Chungking Railway. No. 165, Oil refinery and derricks in the Northwest. No. 166, Mechanized state farm.

1952, Oct. 1 ***Perf. 14***

No.	Type	Description	Unused	Used
163	A29	$800 dark violet	12	6
164	"	$800 red	12	6
165	"	$800 dk. violet brown	12	6
166	"	$800 deep green	12	6

"Glorious Mother Country," 2nd series.

Doves and Globe

A30

Designs: Nos. 167-168, Picasso dove over Pacific (vert.). $2500, as No. 169.

1952, Oct. 2 ***Perf. 14***

No.	Type	Description	Unused	Used
167	A30	$400 maroon	5	4
168	"	$800 red	8	5
169	"	$800 brown orange	8	6
170	"	$2500 deep green	25	15

Peace Conference of the Asian and Pacific Regions.

Volunteers on the March—A31

Designs: No. 172, Chinese peasants loading supplies. No. 173, Volunteers attacking across river. No. 174, Meeting of Chinese and Korean troops.

1952, Oct. 25

No.	Type	Description	Unused	Used
171	A31	$800 blue green (1)	12	6
172	"	$800 vermilion (2)	12	6
173	"	$800 violet (3)	12	6
174	"	$800 lake brown (4)	12	6

2nd anniversary of Chinese Volunteers in Korea.

Woman Textile Worker

A32

Design: No. 176, Farm woman with sickle.

1953, Mar. 10

No.	Type	Description	Unused	Used
175	A32	$800 carmine	15	9
176	"	$800 emerald	15	9

International Women's Day.

Textile Worker A33 Karl Marx A34

Designs: $200, Shepherdess. $250, Stone lion. $800, Lathe operator. $1600, Coal miners. $2000, Corner tower of Forbidden City, Peking.

1953 Litho. ***Perf. 14; 12½*** **($250)**

No.	Type	Description	Unused	Used
177	A33	$50 magenta	10	10
178	"	$200 emerald	10	10
179	"	$250 ultramarine	15	15
180	"	$800 blue green	50	6
181	"	$1600 gray	35	25
182	"	$2000 red orange	45	20
		Nos. 177-182 (6)	1.65	86

Issue dates: Nos. 177-181, Mar. 25; No. 182, May 23.

1953, May 20 **Engraved** ***Perf. 14***

No.	Type	Description	Unused	Used
183	A34	$400 dark brown	15	8
184	"	$800 slate green	15	8

135th anniversary of the birth of Karl Marx (1818-1883).

Workers and Banners

A35

1953, June 25

185	A35	$400 Prussian blue	10	5
186	"	$800 carmine	20	5

7th All-China Trade Union Congress.

Picasso Dove
A36

1953, July 25

187	A36	$250 blue green	10	7
188	"	$400 orange brown	15	10
189	"	$800 purple	30	12

World Peace.

Groom, Wei Dynasty, 386–580
A37

Scenes from Tunhuang Murals: No. 191, Court Players, Wei Dynasty. No. 192, Battle Scene, Sui Dynasty, 581–617. No. 193, Ox-drawn palanquin, Tang Dynasty, 618–906.

1953, Sept. 1

190	A37	$800 deep green (1)	12	6
191	"	$800 red orange (2)	12	6
192	"	$800 Prussian blue (3)	12	6
193	"	$800 carmine (4)	12	6

"Glorious Mother Country," 3rd series.

Stalin and Mao on Kremlin Terrace—A38

Statue of Stalin at Volga-Don Canal
A39

Designs: No. 195, Lenin proclaiming Soviet power. No. 197, Stalin as orator.

1953, Oct. 5

194	A38	$800 green (1)	12	8
195	"	$800 carmine (2)	12	8
196	A39	$800 bright blue (3)	12	8
197	"	$800 orange brown (4)	12	8

35th anniversary of the Russian October Revolution.

Stamps in same designs with two additional characters meaning "Soviet" in the single-line Chinese inscription, and in different colors, were unofficially released at several small post offices in Hunan, Fukien and Canton areas in February, 1953, but were withdrawn after only a small number had been sold. Price per set, $900 unused or $500 used.

Compass, 3rd Century B.C.
A40

Designs: No. 199, Seismoscope, later Han Dynasty. No. 200, Drum cart to measure distance, Chin Dynasty. No. 201, Armillary sphere, Ming Dynasty.

1953, Dec. 1

198	A40	$800 indigo (1)	10	6
199	"	$800 dark green (2)	10	6
200	"	$800 dark slate green (3)	10	6
201	"	$800 chocolate (4)	10	6

Major inventions by ancient and medieval Chinese scientists.

"Glorious Mother Country," 4th series.

(same size)

Francois Rabelais
A41

Gate of Heavenly Peace
A42

Designs: $400, José Marti, Cuban revolutionary. $800, Chu Yuan (350–275 B.C.), philosopher. $2200, Nicolaus Copernicus, astronomer.

1953, Dec. 30

202	A41	$250 slate green (3)	10	5
203	"	$400 brown black (4)	10	5
204	"	$800 indigo (1)	10	5
205	"	$2200 chocolate (2)	10	10

1954, April 16 **Lithographed**

Sixth Issue: Inscription at upper right.

206	A42	$50 carmine	5	5
207	"	$100 light blue	7	6
208	"	$200 green	7	6
209	"	$250 ultramarine	9	8
210	"	$400 gray green	9	8
211	"	$800 orange	12	6
212	"	$1600 gray	17	8
213	"	$2000 olive	22	10
		Nos. 206-213 (8)	88	57

Textile Plant, Harbin
A43

Lenin
A44

1954, May 1 **Engraved**

Designs: $200, Tangku Harbor. $250, Tienshui-Lanchow railroad bridge, Kansu Province. $400, Heavy machine-building plant, Taiyuan, Shansi. No. 218, Automatic blast, furnace, Anshan, Manchuria. No. 219, Fushun open-cut coal mine. $2000, Automatic power plant, Northeast. $3200, Prospecting in Tayeh district, Hupeh.

214	A43	$100 brown olive	6	3
215	"	$200 blue green	6	3
216	"	$250 violet	6	3
217	"	$400 black	8	3
218	"	$800 claret	8	3
219	"	$800 indigo	12	3
220	"	$2000 red	25	15
221	"	$3200 dark brown	35	25
		Nos. 214-221 (8)	1.06	58

Economic progress.

1954, June 30 **Engraved**

Designs: $400, Lenin and Stalin Monument, Gorki (horiz.). $2000, Lenin proclaiming Soviet power.

222	A44	$400 deep green	12	8
223	"	$800 dark brown	12	12
224	"	$2000 deep carmine	12	12

30th anniversary of the death of Lenin.

Pottery Vessels, Neolithic Period, 2000 B. C.—A45

Archeological Treasures: No. 226, Stone chime, Shang Dynasty, c. 1200 B.C. No. 227, Kuo Chi Tsu-pai bronze basin, Middle Chou Dynasty, 816 B.C. No. 228, Lacquered box and wine cup, Warring States Period, 403–221 B.C.

1954, Aug. 25

225	A45	$800 brown	9	6
226	"	$800 indigo	9	6
227	"	$800 Prussian blue	9	6
228	"	$800 dark carmine	9	6

"Glorious Mother Country," 5th series.

Pipe Production, Anshan Steel Mill
A46

Stalin Statue, by Tomsky
A47

Design: $800, Rolling mill, Anshan.

1954, Oct. 1

229	A46	$400 Prussian green	10	8
230	"	$800 violet brown	10	8

1954, Oct. 15

Designs: $800, Stalin portrait. $2000, Stalin viewing hydroelectric plant.

Size: 21x45mm.

231	A47	$400 black	12	12

Size: 26x37mm.

232	A47	$800 black brown	12	12

Size: 42x26mm.

233	A47	$2000 deep red	12	12

First anniversary of the death of Stalin.

Exhibition Building, Peking—A48

1954, Nov. 7

234	A48	$800 brown, *cream*	7.50	2.00

Russian Economic and Cultural Exhibition, Peking.

Apprentices and Lathe
A49

Design: $800, Heavy machinery and workers.

1954, Dec. 15

235	A49	$400 dk. olive green	10	10
236	"	$800 bright red	10	10

Progress in technology.

Woman Worker Voting
A50

People Celebrating Opening of Congress—A51

1954, Dec. 30

237	A50	$400 deep claret	10	10
238	A51	$800 bright red	10	10

First National Congress.

Flags, Worker and Woman Holding Constitution—A52

1954, Dec. 30

239	A52	$400 brown, *buff*	10	7
240	"	$800 bright red, *yellow*	10	10

Adoption of Constitution.

High-tension Pylon
A53

1955, Feb. 25

241	A53	$800 dark Prus. blue	15	15

Development of electric power.

Factory Health Workers and Red Cross—A54

1955, June 25

Engraved; Cross Typographed

242	A54	8f dp. green & red	6.00	10

50th anniversary of Chinese Red Cross.

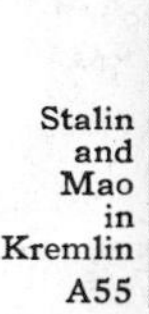

Stalin and Mao in Kremlin
A55

Soviet Specialist and Chinese Worker
A56

1955, July 25 **Engraved**

243 A55 8f brown red 7.50 20
244 A56 20f olive black 7.50 30

5th anniversary of Sino-Soviet Friendship Treaty.

Chang Heng (78–139), Astronomer
A57

Portraits of Scientists: No. 246, Tsu Chung-chih (429–500), mathematician. No. 247, Chang Sui (683–727), astronomer. No. 248, Li Shih-chen (1518–1593), physician and pharmacologist.

1955, Aug. 25 ***Perf. 14***

245 A57 8f sepia, *buff* 18 5
a. Min. sheet, sepia, *white* 70 50
246 A57 8f deep green, *buff* 18 5
a. Min. sheet, dp. grn., *white* 70 50
247 A57 8f black, *buff* 18 5
a. Min. sheet, black, *white* 70 50
248 A57 8f claret, *buff* 18 5
a. Min. sheet, claret, *white* 70 50

Miniature sheets contain one imperf. stamp each. Size: 63x90mm.

Steel Pouring Ladle
A58

1955–56 **Lithographed**

Bluish Black Frames, Multicolored Centers.

Position-in-set number in ( ).

249 A58 8f *shown* (1) 16 5
250 " 8f *High tension line* (2) 16 5
251 " 8f *Mechanized coal mining* (3) 16 5
252 " 8f *Tank cars and derricks* (4) 16 5
253 " 8f *Heavy machine shop* (5) 16 5
254 " 8f *Soldier on guard* (6) 16 5
255 " 8f *Spinning machine* (7) 16 5
256 " 8f *Workers discussing 5-year plan* (8) 16 5
257 " 8f *Combine harvester* (9) 16 5
258 " 8f *Milk production* (10) 16 5
259 " 8f *Dam* (11) 16 5
260 A58 8f *Pottery industry* (12) ('56) 16 5
261 " 8f *Truck* (13) 16 5
262 " 8f *Ship at dock* (14) 16 5
263 " 8f *Geological survey* (15) 16 5
264 " 8f *Higher education* (16) 16 5
265 " 8f *Family* (17) 16 5
266 " 8f *Workers' rest home* (18) ('56) 16 5
Nos. 249–266 (18) 2.88 90

First Five Year Plan.
Issue dates: Nos. 249–257, Oct. 1, 1955; Nos. 258–259, 261–265, Dec. 15, 1955; Nos. 260, 266, Feb. 24, 1956.

Lenin
A59

Engels
A60

1955, Dec. 15 **Engraved** ***Perf. 14***

267 A59 8f dark blue green 5.00 8
268 " 20f dk. rose carmine 5.00 20

85th anniversary of the birth of Lenin.

1955, Dec. 15

269 A60 8f deep orange 5.00 8
270 " 20f brown 5.00 20

135th anniversary of the birth of Friedrich Engels (1820–1895), German socialist.

Storming Lu Ting Bridge
A61

Crossing Great Snow Mountains
A62

1955, Dec. 30

271 A61 8f dark red 5.50 10
272 A62 8f dark blue 5.50 10

Long March of Chinese Communist army, 20th anniversary.

Miner
A63

Gate of Heavenly Peace
A64

Designs: 1f, Machinist. 2f, Airman. 2½f, Nurse. 4f, Soldier. 8f, Steel worker. 10f, Scientist. 20f, Farm woman. 50f, Sailor.

1955–56 **Lithographed** ***Perf. 14***

273 A63 ½f orange brown 5.00 8
274 " 1f purple 5.00 8
275 " 2f green 5.00 8
276 " 2½f blue ('56) 60.00 8
277 " 4f gray olive 5.00 8
278 " 8f red org. (Peking printing) 5.00 8
a. Perf. 12½ (Shanghai printing) 25.00 4.00
279 A63 10f claret ('56) 50.00 8
280 " 20f deep blue 5.00 8
281 " 50f gray 5.00 15
Nos. 273–281 (9) 145.00 79

Engraved

282 A64 $1 claret ('56) 1.50 30
283 " $2 sepia ('55) 2.75 30
284 " $5 indigo ('56) 6.00 50
285 " $10 dp. org. ('56) 14.00 4.00
286 " $20 gray violet ('56) 30.00 7.00
Nos. 282–286 (5) 54.25 12.10

Nos. 282–286 are the 7th Gate Issue.

Trucks, Mountains, Highway Map
A65

Suspension Bridge over Tatu River
A66

Design: No. 289, First truck arriving in Lhasa, and the Potala.

1956, Mar. 10 **Engraved**

287 A65 4f deep blue 12 3
288 A66 8f dark brown 12 10
289 A65 8f carmine 12 10

Completion of Sikang-Tibet and Chinghai-Tibet Highways.

Summer Palace and Marble Boat
A67

Famous Views of Imperial Peking: No. 291, Peihai Park with Jade Belt Marble Bridge. No. 292, Gate of Heavenly Peace. No. 293, Temple of Heaven. No. 294, Great Throne Hall, Forbidden City.

1956–57

290 A67 4f carmine rose (1) 10 3
291 " 4f blue green (2) 12 4
292 " 8f red org. (3) ('57) 12 6
293 " 8f Prussian blue (4) 15 6
294 " 8f yellow brown (5) 15 6
Nos. 290–294 (5) 64 25

Issue dates: No. 292, Feb. 20, 1957; others, June 15, 1956.
No. 292 exists with sun rays in background.

Salt Making
A68

Designs: No. 296, Dwelling of the Eastern Han period. No. 297, Duck hunting and harvesting. No. 298, Carriage crossing bridge.

1956, Oct. 1

295 A68 4f gray olive 12 5
296 " 4f slate blue 12 5
297 " 8f gray brown 12 5
298 " 8f sepia 12 5

Murals, Tung Han Dynasty, 250 B.C.–220 A.D., found near Chengtu.

Ancient Coins and "Save"
A69

1956, Oct. 1

299 A69 4f yellow brown 4.00 15
300 " 8f rose red 4.00 15

Promotion of saving.

Gate of Heavenly Peace
A70

Sun Yat-sen
A71

1956, Nov. 10

301 A70 4f dark green 3.50 10
302 " 8f bright red 3.50 10
303 " 16f dark carmine 3.50 10

8th National Congress of the Communist Party of China.

1956, Nov. 12

304 A71 4f brown, *cream* 5.00 15
305 " 8f deep blue, *cream* 5.00 15

90th anniversary of birth of Sun Yat-sen.

Weight Lifting
A72

Designs: No. 306, Shot put. No. 308, Track. No. 309, Soccer. No. 310, Bicycling.

1957, Mar. 20 **Litho.** ***Perf. 12½***

Hibiscus red and green; inscription in brown.

306 A72 4f deep carmine (2) 10 5
307 " 4f red lilac (5) 10 5
308 " 8f dk. blue green (1) 15 7
309 " 8f deep blue (3) 15 7
310 " 8f dp. yel. brown (4) 15 7
Nos. 306–310 (5) 65 31

First National Workers' Sports Meeting.

Truck Factory No. 1, Changchun
A73

Designs: 8f, Trucks rolling off assembly line.

1957, May 1 **Engraved** ***Perf. 14***

311 A73 4f light brown 12 7
312 " 8f slate green 12 10

China's truck industry.

Nanchang Uprising—A74

Designs: No. 314, Mao and Chu Teh at Chingkanshan. No. 315, Crossing Yellow River. No. 316, Liberation of Nanking, Apr. 23, 1949.

1957

313	A74	4f blackish violet (1)	4.00	15
314	"	4f slate green (2)	4.00	15
315	"	8f red brown (3)	4.00	15
316	"	8f deep blue (4)	4.00	15

30th anniversary of People's Liberation Army.

Issue dates: Nos. 313, 315, Aug. 10; No. 314, Aug. 30; No. 316, Dec. 30.

Congress Emblem
A75

1957, Sept. 30

317	A75	8f chocolate	4.00	10
318	"	22f indigo	4.00	10

4th International Trade Union Congress, Leipzig, Oct. 4–15.

Yangtze River Bridge
A76

Design: 20f, Road leading to and over bridge.

1957, Oct. 1

319	A76	8f scarlet	15	10
320	"	20f slate blue	15	10

Completion of Yangtze River Bridge at Wuhan.

Fireworks over Kremlin
A77

Designs: 8f, Hammer and sickle over globe and broken chain. 20f, Stylized dove and olive branch. 22f, Hands of three races holding book with Marx and Lenin. 32f, Star and pylon.

1957, Nov. 7

321	A77	4f bright red	5.00	12
322	"	8f chocolate	5.00	12
323	"	20f deep green	5.00	12
324	"	22f red brown	5.00	12
325	"	32f deep blue	5.00	12
		Nos. 321-325 (5)	25.00	60

40th anniversary of Russian October Revolution.

Map of Yellow River Basin—A78

Designs: No. 327, Sanmen Gorge dam and powerhouse. No. 328, Ocean liner on Yellow River. No. 329, Dam, irrigation canals and tree-bordered fields.

1957, Dec. 30

326	A78	4f deep orange (1)	3.00	15
327	"	4f deep blue (2)	3.00	15
328	"	8f deep lake (3)	3.00	15
329	"	8f blue green (4)	3.00	15

Yellow River control plan.

Old Man and Young Drummer
A79

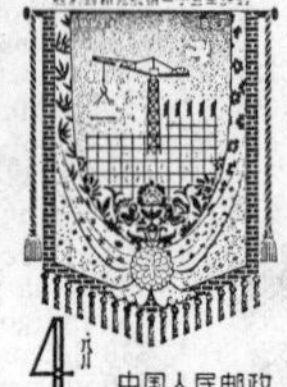

Crane, Dove and Flowers
A80

1957, Dec. 30 **Lithographed**

Multicolored

330	A79	8f *shown* (1)	20	8
331	"	8f *Plowman* (2)	20	8
332	"	8f *Woman planting tree* (3)	20	8
333	"	8f *Harvest* (4)	20	8

Agricultural cooperation.

1958, Jan. 30 **Engraved**

Designs (Congratulatory Banner and): 8f, Crane with hot ingots, cotton bolls and wheat. 16f, Train on bridge, ship and plane.

334	A80	4f emerald, *cream*	25	5
335	"	8f red, *cream*	25	5
336	"	16f ultramarine, *cream*	25	5

Fulfillment of First Five-Year Plan.

Sungyu Pagoda, Honan
A81

Trilobite, Kaoli
A82

Ancient Pagodas: No. 338, Chienhsun Pagoda, Yunnan. No. 339, Sakyamuni Pagoda, Shansi. No. 340, Flying Rainbow Pagoda, Shansi.

1958, Mar. 15 **Engraved**

337	A81	8f sepia (1)	20	8
338	"	8f Prussian blue (2)	20	8
339	"	8f maroon (3)	20	8
340	"	8f deep green (4)	20	8

1958, Apr. 15

Designs: 8f, Lufeng dinosaur. 16f, Choukoutien sino-megaceros.

341	A82	4f black	20	8
342	"	8f sepia	20	8
343	"	16f slate green	20	8

Prehistoric animals of China.

Heroes Monument
A83

1958, May 1

344	A83	8f scarlet	8.00	30
		a. Souvenir sheet	10.00	5.00

Unveiling of People's Heroes Monument, Peking. No. 344a contains one imperf. stamp, scarlet marginal inscription. Size: 87x137mm. Issued May 30.

Karl Marx
A84

Cogwheels and Factories—A85

Design: 22f, Marx Speaking to German Workers' Educational Association, London, painting by Zhukow.

1958, May 5

345	A84	8f chocolate	6.00	15
346	"	22f dark green	6.00	15

140th anniversary of the birth of Karl Marx (1818–1883).

1958, May 25

347	A85	4f brt. greenish blue	7.50	40
348	"	8f red lilac	7.50	40

8th All-China Trade Union Congress, Peking.

Dove over Globe
A86

Mother and Child
A87

1958, June 1

349	A86	8f violet blue	6.00	35
350	"	20f blue green	6.00	35

4th Congress of the International Democratic Women's Federation, Vienna, Austria, June 1958.

1958, June 1 **Lithographed**

Designs (Children): No. 352, Watering sunflowers. No. 353, Playing hide-and-seek. No. 354, Sailing toy boat.

351	A87	8f green & multi. (1)	4.50	18
352	"	8f " " (2)	4.50	18
353	"	8f " " (3)	4.50	18
354	"	8f " " (4)	4.50	18

Children's Day.

Kuan Han-ching
A88

Designs (Operas): 4f, "Dream of Butterflies." 20f, "The Riverside Pavilion."

1958, June 20 **Engraved**

355	A88	4f indigo, *cream*	7.00	25
356	"	8f brown, *cream*	7.00	25
357	"	20f black, *cream*	7.00	25
		a. Souvenir sheet of 3, *white*	80.00	12.00

700th anniversary of publication of works of Kuan Han-ching (1210–1280), dramatist. No. 357a contains 3 imperf. stamps similar to Nos. 355–357. Dark brown marginal inscription. Size: 130x100mm. Issued June 28.

Planetarium
A89

Design: 20f, Telescope and stars over Peking.

1958, June 25

358	A89	8f dark green	5.25	20
359	"	20f indigo	5.25	20

First Chinese planetarium, Peking.

Marx and Engels
A90

Wild Goose and Broadcasting Tower
A91

Design: 8f, Cover of first edition of the Communist Manifesto.

1958, July 1

360	A90	4f dark red violet	6.00	20
361	"	8f Prussian blue	6.00	20

110th anniversary of publication of the Communist Manifesto.

1958, July 10

362	A91	4f ultramarine	6.00	20
363	"	8f deep green	6.00	20

1st Conference of the Ministers of Posts and Telecommunications of Socialist Countries, Moscow, Dec. 3–17, 1957.

Peony and Doves
A92

Bronze Weather Vane
A93

Designs: 8f, Olive branch with ribbon and clouds. 22f, Atomic energy symbol over factories.

1958, July 20

364	A92	4f red	14.00	3.00
365	"	8f green	14.00	3.00
366	"	22f red brown	14.00	3.00

Congress for Disarmament and International Cooperation, Stockholm, July 17–22.

1958, Aug. 25

Designs: No. 368, Weather balloon. No. 369, Typhoon tower and weather map of Asia.

367	A93	8f yel. bister & blk. (1)	15	10
368	"	8f blue & black (2)	15	10
369	"	8f brt. grn. & blk. (3)	15	10

Meteorological services in ancient and modern China.

"5" Encircling IUS Emblem
A94

1958, Sept. 4

370	A94	8f rose lilac	4.50	10
371	"	22f deep blue green	4.50	10

5th Congress of the International Union of Students, Peking, Sept. 4–13.

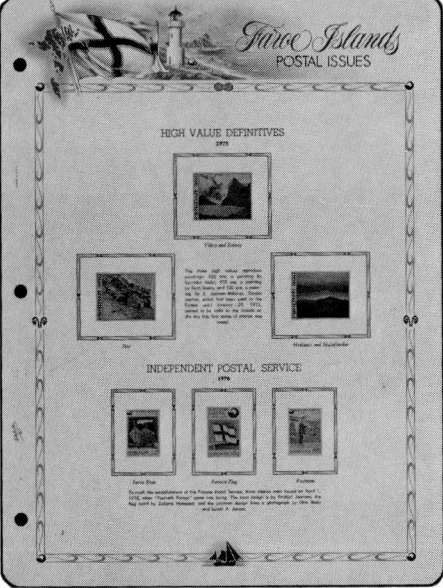

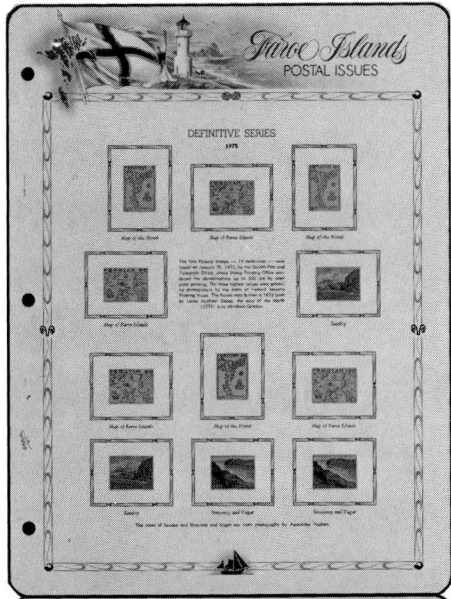

Telegraph Building, Peking
A95

1958, Sept. 29

372 A95 4f greenish black 15 8
373 " 8f rose red 15 8

Opening of Telegraph Building, Peking.

Exhibition Emblem and Exhortation
A96

Designs: No. 375, Dragon over clouds signifying "aiming high." No. 376, Flying horses, signifying "great leap forward" in production.

1958, Oct. 1

374 A96 8f slate green (1) 4.25 10
375 " 8f rose carmine (2) 4.25 10
376 " 8f red brown (3) 4.25 10

National Exhibition of Industry and Communications, Peking.

Worker and Excavator
A97

Design: 8f, Completed dam and pylon.

1958, Oct. 25

377 A97 4f dark brown 15 10
378 " 8f deep Prussian blue 25 10

Completion of the 13 Ming Tombs Reservoir.

Sputnik over Armillary Sphere
A98

Designs: 8f, Sputnik 3 in orbit. 10f, Trajectories of 3 Sputniks over earth.

1958, Oct. 30

379 A98 4f scarlet 2.50 20
380 " 8f dp. violet blue 2.50 5
381 " 10f deep green 2.50 25

Anniversary of first earth satellite launched by the USSR.

Chinese and North Korean Soldiers
A99

Designs: No. 383, Chinese soldier embracing Korean woman. No. 384, Chinese girl presenting flowers to returning soldier.

1958, Nov. 20

382 A99 8f bright purple (1) 22 10
383 " 8f chestnut (2) 22 10
384 " 8f rose carmine (3) 22 10

Return of the Chinese Volunteers from Korea.

Forest and Mountains
A100

Peony
A101

Designs: No. 386, Mounted forest patrol. No. 387, Mechanized lumbering (horiz.). No. 388, Tree-planting: "Turning the Country Green" (horiz.).

1958, Dec. 15

385 A100 8f dp. blue green (1) 25 10
386 " 8f slate green (2) 25 10
387 " 8f dark purple (3) 25 10
388 " 8f indigo (4) 25 10

Afforestation.

1958, Sept. 25 Lithographed

Designs: 3f, Lotus. 5f, Chrysanthemums.

389 A101 1½f lilac rose 7.00 10
390 " 3f blue green 7.00 10
391 " 5f deep orange 7.00 10

Atomic Reactor
A102

Design: 20f, Cyclotron.

1958, Dec. 30 Engraved

392 A102 8f deep blue 6.00 12
393 " 20f deep brown 6.00 *2.00*

Inauguration of China's first atomic reactor and cyclotron, Peking.

Children Launching Model Planes
A103

Camel Carrying Load
A104

Designs: 8f, Gliders over trees. 10f, Parachutists descending. 20f, Small monoplanes in mid-air.

1958, Dec. 30

394 A103 4f carmine 25 5
395 " 8f deep slate green 25 5
396 " 10f dark brown 25 5
397 " 20f Prussian blue 25 5

Sports-aviation publicity.

1959, Jan. 1

Designs: No. 399, Pomegranates. No. 400, Rooster. No. 401, Theatrical figure.

398 A104 8f vio. & black (1) 4.00 5
399 " 8f dp. blue green & black (2) 4.00 10
400 " 8f red & black (3) 4.00 10
401 " 8f dp. bl. & blk. (4) 4.00 10

Paper cut-outs (folk art).

Red Flag, Mao and Workers
A105

Women Workers and Atomic Model
A106

Designs: 8f, Traditional and modern blast furnaces. 10f, Steel works and workers.

1959

402 A105 4f bright red 6.50 12
403 " 8f lake 6.50 12
404 " 10f deep red 6.50 6

"Great Leap Forward" in steel production.

Issue dates: 4f, 8f, Feb. 19; 10f, May 25.

1959, Mar. 8

Design: 22f, Chinese and Soviet women holding banners dated "3.8".

405 A106 8f emerald, *cream* 40 10
406 " 22f magenta, *cream* 40 10

International Women's Day.

Natural History Museum
A107

1959, Apr. 1

407 A107 4f greenish blue 20 10
408 " 8f olive brown 20 10

Opening of Museum of Natural History, Peking.

Wheat
A108

Designs on Chinese Flag: No. 410, Rice. No. 411, Cotton bolls. No. 412, Soybeans, rapeseed and peanuts.

1959, Apr. 25

409 A108 8f red (1) 40 10
410 " 8f " (2) 40 10
411 " 8f " (3) 40 10
412 " 8f " (4) 40 10
Block of 4 (Nos. 409-412) 2.00 60

Successful harvest, 1958. Printed se-tenant in blocks of four.

Marx, Lenin and Workers
A109

Designs: 8f, Black, yellow and white fists holding banner. 22f, Steel workers parading with banners dated "5.1."

1959, May 1

413 A109 4f ultramarine 5.00 10
414 " 8f red 5.00 10
415 " 22f emerald 5.00 10

International Labor Day.

Peking Airport
A110

Design: 10f, Plane loading on runway.

1959, June 20

416 A110 8f lilac & black 5.50 10
417 " 10f olive gray & blk. 5.50 10

Opening of new Peking Airport.

Students with Marx-Lenin Banners
A111

Design: 8f, Workers with banners of Mao.

1959, July 1 Photo. *Perf. 11x11½*

418 A111 4f gray, red & dark brown 8.50 2.00
419 " 8f bister, red & dark brown 8.50 2.00

40th anniversary of the May 4th students' uprising.

Frederick Joliot-Curie
A112

Design: 22f, Three races, dove and olive branch.

1959, July 25 Engraved *Perf. 11½*

420 A112 8f violet brown 8.50 20
421 " 22f dark violet 8.50 10

10th anniversary of the World Peace Movement.

Stamp Printing Plant, Peking
A113

1959, Aug. 15 *Perf. 11x11½*

422 A113 8f deep blue green 7.00 25

Sino-Czechoslovak cooperation in stamp production.

Table Tennis
A114

1959, Aug. 30 Litho. *Perf. 14*

423 A114 4f black & blue 35 12
424 " 8f black & red 35 12

25th World Table Tennis Championships, Dortmund, German Democratic Republic.

Soviet Space Rocket
A115

1959, Sept. 10 Photo. *Perf. 11½*

425 A115 8f Prussian blue, red & black 17.50 50

Launching of first Russian space rocket, Jan. 2, 1959.

Backyard Steel Production
A116

Mao and Gate of Heavenly Peace
A117

Designs: No. 426, Sun rising over "industry and agriculture." No. 428, Farming. No. 429, Trade. No. 430, Education. No. 431, Militia. No. 432, Communal dining. No. 433, Nursery. No. 434, Care for the aged. No. 435, Health services. No. 436, Flutist; culture and sports. No. 437, Flower symbolizing unity of industry, agriculture, trade, education and armed forces.

Position-in-set number in ( ).

1959, Sept. 25 Engraved

426 A116 8f rose (1) 20 8
427 " 8f violet brown (2) 20 8
428 " 8f deep orange (3) 20 8
429 " 8f slate green (4) 20 8
430 " 8f deep blue (5) 20 8
431 " 8f olive (6) 20 8
432 " 8f indigo (7) 20 8
433 " 8f lilac rose (8) 20 8
434 " 8f gray black (9) 20 8
435 " 8f emerald (10) 20 8
436 " 8f dark violet (11) 20 8
437 " 8f red (12) 20 8
Nos. 426-437 (12) 2.40 96

First anniversary of Peoples' Communes.

1959, Sept. 28 Photo. *Perf. 11½x11*

Designs: 8f, Marx, Lenin and Kremlin. 22f, Dove over globe.

With Gum

438 A117 8f lt. brown & red 8.50 4.00
439 " 8f dull blue & red 8.50 1.00
440 " 22f bl. green & red 8.50 1.00

See note after No. 456.

National Emblem
A118

Blast Furnaces
A119

1959, Oct. 1 Lithographed *Perf. 14*

441 A118 4f pale green, red & gold 6.50 *5.00*
442 " 8f gray, red & gold 6.50 50
443 " 10f lt. bl., red & gold 6.50 30
444 " 20f pale brown, red & gold 6.50 50

Engraved and Photogravure

1959, Oct. 1 *Perf. 11½x11*

Designs: No. 446, Large coal mine. No. 447, Planer, Wuhan heavy machinery plant. No. 448, Wuhan Yangtze River Bridge. No. 449, Combine harvester. No. 450, Hsinankiang hydroelectric station. No. 451, Spinning machine. No. 452, Kirin chemical fertilizer plant.

With Gum

445 A119 8f brn. & rose red (1) 22 12
446 " 8f brown & gray (2) 22 12
447 " 8f brn. & yel. brn. (3) 22 12
448 " 8f brn. & steel bl. (4) 22 12
449 " 8f brn. & orange (5) 22 12
450 " 8f brn. & olive (6) 22 12
451 " 8f brn. & bl. grn. (7) 22 12
452 " 8f brn. & violet (8) 22 12
Nos. 445-452 (8) 1.76 96

Celebration at Gate of Heavenly Peace
A120

Mao Proclaiming Republic—A121

Designs: 10f, Workers and factory (vert.). No. 455, People rejoicing (vert.).

1959, Oct. 1 Lithographed *Perf. 14*

Inscribed: 1949-1959.

453 A120 8f cream & multi. 50 20
454 " 10f " " 50 20
455 " 20f " " 50 40

Engraved

456 A121 20f deep carmine 20.00 7.50

Nos. 438-456 commemorate 10th anniversary of the Proclamation of the People's Republic of China.

Pioneer Bugler
A122

Exhibition Emblem, Communications Symbols
A123

Designs: No. 457, Pioneers' emblem. No. 459, Schoolgirl. No. 460, Girl using rain gauge. No. 461, Boy planting tree. No. 462, Girl figure skater.

1959, Nov. 10 Photo. *Perf. 11½*

457 A122 4f red. yel. & blk. (1) 1.00 10
458 " 4f Prus. bl. & red (2) 1.00 10
459 " 8f brown & red (3) 1.00 10
460 " 8f dk. bl. & red (4) 1.00 10
461 " 8f red & green (5) 1.00 25
462 " 8f magenta & red (6) 1.00 15
Nos. 457-462 (6) 6.00 80

10th anniversary of the Young Pioneers. Black inscription on No. 457 engraved.

1959, Dec. 1 Engraved

Design: 8f, Exhibition emblem and chimneys.

463 A123 4f dark blue 15 8
464 " 8f red 15 8

Exhibition of Industry and Communications, Peking.

Palace of Nationalities
A124

Engraved, Frame Litho.

1959, Dec. 10 *Perf. 14*

465 A124 4f red & black 75 12
466 " 8f brt. green & black 75 12

Inauguration of the Cultural Palace of Nationalities, Peking.

Athletes' Monument and Track
A125

Designs: No. 468, Parachuting. No. 469, Marksmanship. No. 470, Diving. No. 471, Table tennis. No. 472, Weight lifting. No. 473, High jump. No. 474, Rowing. No. 475, Track. No. 476, Basketball. No. 477, Traditional Chinese fencing. No. 478, Motorcycling. No. 479, Gymnastics. No. 480, Bicycling. No. 481, Horsemanship. No. 482, Soccer.

1959, Dec. 28 Lithographed

467 A125 8f bister, black & gray (1) 25 8
468 " 8f dull blue, black & gray (2) 25 8
469 " 8f red brn. & blk. (3) 25 8
470 " 8f green, black & brown (4) 25 8
471 " 8f brt. grn., blk., brn. & gray (5) 25 8
472 " 8f gray, black & brown (6) 25 8
473 " 8f dull blue, black & brown (7) 25 8
474 " 8f Prus. green, black & brown (8) 25 8
475 " 8f orange, black & brown (9) 25 8
476 " 8f dull violet, black & brown (10) 25 8
477 " 8f lt. olive, black & brown (11) 25 8
478 " 8f blue, black & gray (12) 25 8
479 " 8f gray bl., blk., brn., & blue (13) 25 8
480 " 8f gray, black, brn., & violet (14) 25 8
481 " 8f red org., blk., brn., & gray (15) 25 8
482 " 8f lt. gray, blk., brn., & red (16) 25 8
Nos. 467-482 (16) 4.00 1.28

First National Sports Meeting, Peking.

Wheat and Main Pavilion
A126

Designs (Pavilion and): 8f, Meteorological symbols. 10f, Domestic animals. 20f, Fish.

1960, Jan. 20 Engr. and Litho.

Cream Background

483 A126 4f black & orange 20 10
484 " 8f black & dull blue 20 10
485 " 10f blk. & org. brown 20 10
486 " 20f blk. & greenish bl. 20 20

Opening of the National Agricultural Exhibition Halls, Peking.

With Gum

From No. 487 onward all stamps were issued with gum except as noted.

Conference Hall, Tsunyi
A127

Designs: 8f, Mao addressing conference. 10f, Crossing Chinsha River.

Engr. (4f, 10f); Photo. (8f)

1960, Jan. 25 *Perf. 11x11½*

487 A127 4f violet & blue 7.50 75
488 " 8f red & multi. 7.50 75
489 " 10f slate green 7.50 3.50

25th anniversary of the Communist Party Conference at Tsunyi.

Clara Zetkin (1857-1933)
A128

Chinese and Russian Workers
A129

Designs: 8f, Mother, child and dove. 10f, Woman tractor driver. 22f, Women of three races.

1960, Mar. 8 Photo. *Perf. 11½x11*

490 A128 4f black & multi. 25 20
491 " 8f " " 25 10
492 " 10f " " 25 20
493 " 22f " " 25 10

50th anniversary of International Women's Day.

1960, Mar. 10

Designs: 8f, Chinese and Russian flags. 10f, Chinese and Russian soldiers.

494 A129 4f dark brown 9.00 1.50
495 " 8f red, yel. & black 9.00 1.50
496 " 10f deep blue 9.00 *5.00*

10th anniversary of Sino-Soviet Treaty of Friendship. Black inscription engraved on No. 495.

Flags of Hungary and China
A130

Design: 8f, Parliament Building, Budapest.

1960, Apr. 4 *Perf. 11x11½*

497 A130 8f yellow, black, red & green 7.50 2.00
498 " 8f blue, red & blk. 7.50 2.00

15th anniversary of the liberation of Hungary.

Lenin Speaking
A131

Lunik 2, Earth and Russian Arms
A132

Designs: 8f, Portrait of Lenin. 20f, Lenin talking with Smolny Palace guard.

Engr. (4f, 20f); Engr. & Photo. (8f).

1960, April 22 *Perf. 11½x11*

499 A131 4f violet brown 7.00 1.00
500 " 8f org. red & black 7.00 3.00
501 " 20f dark brown 7.00 1.00

90th anniversary of the birth of Lenin.

1960, Apr. 30 Engraved *Perf. 11½*

Design: 10f, Lunik 3 over earth.

502 A132 8f red 3.25 20
503 " 10f green 3.25 20

Russian space flights.

Pioneers and Flags of Czechoslovakia and China
A133

View of Prague with Charles Bridge
A134

Perf. 11½x11; 11x11½

1960, May 9 Photogravure

504 A133 8f yellow & multi. 6.00 *2.25*
505 A134 8f deep green 6.00 *2.25*

15th anniversary of the liberation of Czechoslovakia.

Nostril Bouquet
A135

Designs: Various goldfish.
Position-in-set number in ( ).

1960, June 1 ***Perf. 11x11½***

Multicolored

506 A135 4f *shown* (1) 3.75 50
507 " 4f *Black-back dragon eye* (2) 3.75 50
508 " 4f *Bubble eye* (3) 3.75 50
509 " 4f *Red tiger head* (4) 3.75 50
510 " 8f *Pearl scale* (5) 3.75 50
511 " 8f *Blue dragon eye* (6) 3.75 50
512 " 8f *Skyward eye* (7) 3.75 50
513 " 8f *Red cap* (8) 3.75 50
514 " 8f *Purple cap* (9) 3.75 1.50
515 " 8f *Red head* (10) 3.75 1.50
516 " 8f *Red and white dragon eye* (11) 3.75 1.50
517 " 8f *Red dragon eye* (12) 3.75 1.50
Nos. 506-517 (12) 45.00 10.00

Sow with Litter
A136

Designs: No. 519, Pig being inoculated. No. 520, Pigs. No. 521, Pig and mechanized feeding. No. 522, Pig and bales.

1960, June 15

518 A136 8f red & black (1) 3.50 50
519 " 8f dp. grn. & blk. (2) 3.50 50
520 " 8f lilac rose & black (3) 3.50 50
521 " 8f lt. yel. green & black (4) 3.50 50
522 " 8f orange & blk. (5) 3.50 50
Nos. 518-522 (5) 17.50 2.50

Flag Inscribed "Serving the Workers"
A137

Flowers, Flags of North Korea and China
A138

Design: 8f, Inscribed stone seal.

Photogravure

1960, July 30 ***Perf. 11½x11***

523 A137 4f lt. green, red, pink & brown 7.00 1.25

Engraved and Photogravure

524 A137 8f pale blue, red & bister 7.00 1.25

3rd National Congress for Literature and Arts, Peking.

1960, Aug. 15 Photogravure

Design: 8f, Flying horse of Korea.

525 A138 8f red & multi. 7.50 2.50
526 " 8f ultra., red & indigo 7.50 2.50

15th anniversary of the liberation of Korea.

Railroad Station, Peking—A139

Design: 10f, Train arriving at station.

1960, Aug. 30 ***Perf. 11½***

527 A139 8f bl., cream & brn. 3.00 75
528 " 10f bluish green, cream & indigo 3.00 75

Opening of new Peking Railroad Station.

Girls and Flags of North Viet Nam and China
A140

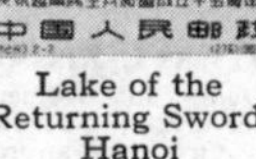

Lake of the Returning Sword, Hanoi
A141

Worker and Fresh-air Installation
A142

1960, Sept. 2 ***Perf. 11x11½, 11½x11***

529 A140 8f red & multi. 1.50 35
530 A141 8f red, gray green & gray 1.50 35

15th anniversary of the Democratic Republic of North Viet Nam.

1960, Sept. 10 ***Perf. 11½***

Designs: No. 532, Exterminator. No. 533, Window cleaning. No. 534, Medical examination of child. No. 535, Physical exercise.

531 A142 8f black & org. (1) 75 20
532 " 8f indigo & slate (2) 75 20
533 " 8f brown & blue (3) 75 20
534 " 8f maroon & ocher (4) 75 20
535 " 8f indigo & bright green (5) 75 20
Nos. 531-535 (5) 3.75 1.00

National health campaign.

Great Hall of the People—A143

Design: 10fr, Inside view.

1960, Oct. 1

536 A143 8f yellow & multi. 3.00 50
537 " 10f brown & multi. 3.00 50

Completion of the Great Hall of the People, Peking.

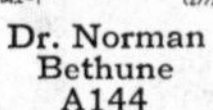

Dr. Norman Bethune
A144

Engels Addressing Congress at The Hague—A145

Design: No. 539, Dr. Bethune operating on a soldier.

Photo. (No. 538); Engr. (No. 539)

1960, Nov. 20 ***Perf. 11½x11***

538 A144 8f red & multi. 1.00 30
539 " 8f sepia 1.00 30

Dr. Norman Bethune (1890-1939), Canadian surgeon with 8th Army.

Engr. (No. 540); Photo. (No. 541).

1960, Nov. 28

Designs: 10f, Portrait of Engels.

540 A145 8f brown 12.00 2.50
541 " 10f blue & multi. 12.00 2.50

140th anniversary of the birth of Friedrich Engels (1820-1895), German Socialist.

"Hwang Shi Ba"
A146

Freighter
A147

1960-61 Photogravure

Various Chrysanthemums in Natural Colors.

542 A146 4f blue gray (1) 55 10
543 " 4f pink (2) 55 15
544 " 8f dark gray (3) 55 25
545 " 8f deep blue (4) 55 25
546 " 8f green (5) 55 10
547 " 8f magenta (6) 55 10
548 " 8f olive (7) 55 25
549 " 8f greenish blue (8) 55 10
550 " 10f gray (9) 2.00 35
551 " 10f chocolate (10) 2.00 10
552 " 20f deep blue (11) 3.25 10
553 A146 20f bright red (12) 3.25 45
554 " 22f olive bis. (13) 4.00 45
555 " 22f carmine (14) 4.00 10
556 " 30f greenish gray (15) 5.00 10
557 " 30f brt. pink (16) 5.00 10
558 " 35f deep green (17) 7.50 10
559 " 52f bright lilac rose (18) 12.50 1.25
Nos. 542-559 (18) 52.90 4.40

Issue dates: Nos. 548-550, 557-559, Dec. 10, 1960; Nos. 545-547, 554-556, Jan. 18, 1961; Nos. 542-544, Feb. 24, 1961.

1960, Dec. 15 ***Perf. 11½***

Without Gum

560 A147 8f deep blue 6.50 1.00

Launching of first 10,000-ton Chinese-built freighter.

Pantheon, Paris
A148

Design: 8f, Proclamation of the Commune.

Engraved and Photogravure

1961, Mar. 18 ***Perf. 11½x11***

561 A148 8f gray black & red 2.50 1.00
562 " 8f brown & red 2.50 1.00

90th anniversary of the Paris Commune.

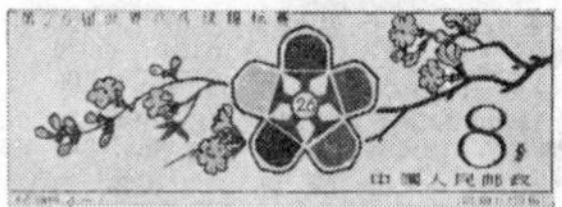

Championship Symbol and Jasmine—A149

Designs: 10f, Table tennis racket and ball; Temple of Heaven. 20f, Table tennis match. 22f, Peking workers' gymnasium.

1961, Apr. 5 Photo. ***Perf. 11***

563 A149 8f multicolored 35 8
564 " 10f " 35 8
565 " 20f " 35 8
566 " 22f " 35 25
a. Souv. sheet of 4 50.00 50.00

26th World Table Tennis Championships, Peking. No. 566a contains one each of Nos. 563-566. Red and bister marginal inscription and decoration. Size: 150x100 mm.

Jeme Tien-yow
A150

Design: 10f, Train and tunnel, Peking-Changchow Railroad.

1961, June 20 ***Perf. 11½x11***

567 A150 8f olive grn. & blk. 75 12
568 " 10f org. brn. & brn. 75 8

Centenary of the birth of Jeme Tien-yow, railroad construction engineer.

Congress Building, Shanghai—A151

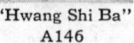

Designs: 8f, August 1st Building, Nanchang. 10f, Provisional Central Government Office, Juikin. 20f, Pagoda Hill, Yenan. 30f, Gate of Heavenly Peace, Peking.

1961, July 1 ***Perf. 11½***

569 A151 4f gold, red & claret 5.00 30
570 " 8f gold, red & blue green 5.00 30
571 " 10f gold, red & yellow brown 5.00 30
572 " 20f gold, red & ultra. 5.00 30
573 " 30f gold, red & orange red 5.00 10
Nos. 569-573 (5) 25.00 1.30

40th anniversary of the Chinese Communist Party.

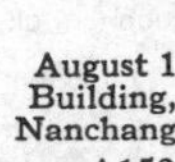

August 1 Building, Nanchang
A152

Designs: 1½f, 2f, as 1f. 3f, 4f, 5f, Trees and Sha Cho Pa Building, Juikin. 8f, 10f, 20f, Pagoda Hill, Yenan. 22f, 30f, 1059-1064.

1961-62 Engraved ***Perf. 11***
Without Gum
Size: 24x16mm

574 A152 1f violet blue 2.00 20
575 " 1½f maroon 2.00 20
576 " 2f indigo 2.00 20
577 " 3f dull violet 2.00 20
578 " 4f green 2.00 20
579 " 5f gray 2.00 5
580 " 8f sepia 2.00 5
581 " 10f brt. lilac rose 2.00 5
582 " 20f greenish blue 2.00 5
583 " 22f brown 2.00 5
584 " 30f blue 2.00 5
585 " 50f vermilion 2.00 5
Nos. 574-585 (12) 24 00 1.35

Issue dates: 1f, 1½f, 5f, July 20, 1962; others July 20, 1961. See Nos. 647-654, 1059-1064.

Flowers, Flags of Mongolia and China
A153

Design: 10f, Parliament, Ulan Bator, and statue of Sukhe Bator.

1961, July 11 Photo. ***Perf. 11x11½***

586 A153 8f crimson, ultra. & yellow 9.00 2.25
587 " 10f org., blk. & yel. 9.00 2.25

40th anniversary of the Mongolian People's Republic.

Military Museum—A154

1961, Aug. 1 ***Perf. 11½***
Engraved and Photogravure

588 A154 8f gray blue, brn. & green 6.50 15
589 " 10f gray, blk. & grn. 6.50 15

Opening of the People's Revolutionary Military Museum.

Uprising at Wuchang
A155

Sun Yat-sen
A156

Perf. 11x11½, 11½x11

1961, Oct. 10 Photogravure

590 A155 8f gray & black 7.50 20
591 A156 10f tan & black 7.50 10

50th anniversary of the 1911 Revolution.

Donkey
A157
Rejoicing Tibetans
A158

Designs: 8f, 10f, 20f, 22f, Horses; 30f, 50f, Camels. Ceramic statuettes from Tang Dynasty (618-906) graves.

1961, Nov. 10 ***Perf. 11½x11***
Statuettes in Original Colors

592 A157 4f dull blue 30 15
593 " 8f gray green 30 15
594 " 8f deep purple 30 15
595 " 10f deep blue 30 8
596 " 20f olive 30 25
597 " 22f blue green 30 10
598 " 30f red brown 30 30
599 " 50f slate 30 10
Nos. 592-599 (8) 2.40 1.28

1961, Nov. 25

Designs: 8f, Woman sower. 10f, Celebration of bumper crop. 20f, People's representatives. 30f, Tibetan children.

600 A158 4f brown & ocher 9.00 15
601 " 8f brown & light blue green 9.00 15
602 " 10f brown & yellow 9.00 15
603 " 20f brown & rose 9.00 1.00
604 " 30f brown & bluish gray 9.00 1.00
Nos. 600-604 (5) 45.00 2.45

Rebirth of the Tibetan people.

Lu Hsun
A159

1962, Feb. 26

605 A159 8f red brn. & black 20 15

80th anniversary of the birth of Lu Hsun, writer.

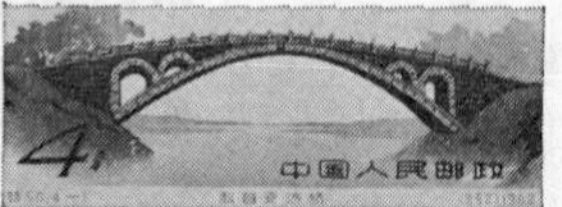

An Chi Bridge, Chao Hsien—A160

Bridges of Ancient China: 8f, Pao Tai, Soochow. 10f, Chu Pu, Kwan Hsien. 20f, Chen Yang, San Kiang.

1962, May 15 ***Perf. 11***

606 A160 4f dark gray blue 45 10
607 " 8f deep green 45 10
608 " 10f brown 45 5
609 " 20f greenish blue 45 45

Tu Fu
A161
Cranes and Bamboo
A162

Design: 4f, Tu Fu memorial pavilion, Chengtu.

1962, May 25 ***Perf. 11½x11***

610 A161 4f olive bister & black 12.00 10
611 " 8f greenish blue & black 12.00 10

Poet Tu Fu, 1,250th anniversary of birth.

1962, June 10

Designs: 10f, Two cranes in flight. 20f, Crane on rock.

612 A162 8f tan & multi. 1.25 20
613 " 10f blue & multi. 1.25 20
614 " 20f bister & multi. 1.25 20

"The Sacred Crane," from paintings by Chen Chi-fo.

Cuban Soldier and Flag
A163

Designs: 10f, Sugar cane worker. 22f, Militiaman and woman.

1962, July 10 ***Perf. 11x11½***

615 A163 8f car., rose & blk. 7.50 60
616 " 10f green & black 7.50 80
617 " 22f ultra. & black 7.50 4.50

Support of Cuba.

Torch and Map of Algeria
A164
Mei Lan-fang
A165

Design: 22f, Algerian soldiers and flag.

1962, July 10 ***Perf. 11½x11***

618 A164 8f dp. brn. & red org. 45 20
619 " 22f ocher & dp. brn. 45 30

Support of Algeria.

1962 ***Perf. 11½x11, 11x11½***

Designs (Mei Lan-fang in Women's Roles): No. 621, Beating drum. No. 622, With fan. 10f, Lady Yu with swords. 20f, With bag. 22f, Heavenly Maiden (horiz.). 30f, With spinning wheel (horiz.). 50f, Kneeling (horiz.). $3, Scene from opera "Drunken Beauty."

620 A165 4f tan & multi. 6.00 50
621 " 8f " " 6.00 60
622 " 8f gray & multi. 6.00 10
623 " 10f " " 6.00 60
624 A165 20f lt. grn. & multi. 6.00 10
625 " 22f cream & multi. 6.00 15
626 " 30f lt. blue & multi. 6.00 3.00
627 " 50f buff & multi. 6.00 4.00
Nos. 620-627 (8) 48.00 9.05

Souvenir Sheet
Perf. 11

628 A165 $3 brn. & multi. 225.00 175.00

Stage art of Mei Lan-fang, actor.

Issue dates: 4f, 8f, 10f, Aug. 8; $3, Sept. 15; others Sept. 1. Imperfs. exist. Price, set, $150.

No. 628 contains one stamp (48x58mm); Prussian blue margin with white ornamental design. Size: 108x147mm.

Flower Drum Dance, Han
A166

Folk Dances: 8f, Ordos, Mongolia. 10f, Catching shrimp, Chuang. 20f, Friend, Yi. 30f, Fiddle dance, Tibet. 50f, Tambourine dance, Uighur.

Cumulative numbers 246-251 at lower right.

1962, Oct. 15 Litho. ***Perf. 12½***
Without Gum

629 A166 4f cream & multi. 10 5
630 " 8f " " 15 5
631 " 10f " " 20 8
632 " 20f " " 35 12
633 " 30f " " 50 20
634 " 50f " " 1.00 35
Nos. 629-634 (6) 2.30 85

See Nos. 696-707.

Soldiers Storming Winter Palace—A167

Design: 8f, Lenin leading soldiers (vert.).

1962, Nov. 7 Photo. ***Perf. 11½***

635 A167 8f black & red 9.50 25
636 " 20f slate green & red 9.50 25

45th anniversary of the Russian Revolution.

Monument and Map of Albania
A168
Tsai Lun, Inventor of Papermaking
A169

Design: 10f, Albanian flag and Girl Pioneer.

1962, Nov. 28 ***Perf. 11½x11***

637 A168 8f Prus. blue & sepia 40 10
638 " 10f red, yel., & black 40 10

50th anniversary of Albanian independence.

1962, Dec. 1 ***Perf. 11½x11***

Designs: No. 640, Paper making. No. 641, Sun Szu-miao, physician. No. 642, Writing medical treatise. No. 643, Shen Ko, geologist. No. 644, Making field notes. No. 645, Kuo Shou-chin, astronomer. No. 646, Astronomical instrument.

Cumulative numbers 297–304 at lower right.

639	A169	4f multicolored	10	5
640	"	4f "	10	5
641	"	8f "	20	10
642	"	8f "	20	10
643	"	10f "	25	12
644	"	10f "	25	12
645	"	20f "	50	20
646	"	20f "	50	20
		Nos. 639-646 (8)	2.10	94

Scientists of ancient China.

Building Type of 1961

Designs: 1f, 2f, Building, Nanchang. 3f, 4f, Trees and Sha Cho Pa Building. 8f, 10f, 20f, Pagoda Hill, Yenan. 30f, Gate of Heavenly Peace, Peking.

Rough Perf. 12½

1962, Jan. Lithographed

Size: 21x16mm.

647	A152	1f ultramarine	30	5
648	"	2f greenish gray	30	5
		a. Perf. 11	30	5
649	A152	3f violet gray	30	5
650	"	4f green	30	5
		a. Perf. 14	35	10
651	A152	8f dark olive	30	5
		a. Perf. 11x11½	30	10
		b. Perf. 14	30	10
652	A152	10f brt. rose lilac	30	5
653	"	20f slate blue	30	5
		a. Perf. 11	35	15
654	A152	30f dull blue	30	5
		Nos. 647-654 (8)	2.40	40

Tank Monument, Havana
A170

Crowd in Havana—A171

Designs: No. 656, Cuban revolutionaries. No. 658, Crowd in Peking. No. 659, Cuban soldier. No. 660, Castro and Cuban flag.

Perf. 11½, 11x11½

1963, Jan. 1 Photogravure

655	A170	4f red & blk. brn.	5.00	10
656	"	4f green & black	5.00	10
657	A171	8f dull red & brn.	5.00	15
658	"	8f " " "	5.00	15
659	A170	10f ocher & black	5.00	15
660	"	10f red, bl. & black	5.00	*3.00*
		Nos. 655-660 (6)	30.00	*3.65*

4th anniversary of the Cuban revolution.

Green Dragontail
A172

Karl Marx
A173

Position-in-set number in ( ).

1963 Without Gum ***Perf. 11***

Butterflies in Natural Colors.

661	A172	4f *Tibetan clouded yellow* (1)	10	10
662	"	4f *Tritailed glory* (2)	10	10
663	"	4f *Neumogeni jungle queen* (3)	10	10
664	"	4f *Washan swordtail* (4)	10	5
665	"	4f *Striped ringlet* (5)	10	5
666	"	8f *shown* (6)	50	5
667	"	8f *Dilunulated peacock* (7)	50	5
668	"	8f *Yamfly* (8)	50	5
669	"	8f *Golden kaiser-i-hind* (9)	50	8
670	"	8f *Mushaell hairstreak* (10)	50	10
671	"	10f *Yel. org.-tip* (11)	50	5
672	"	10f *Great jay* (12)	50	5
673	"	10f *Striped punch* (13)	50	5
674	"	10f *Hainan violet-beak* (14)	50	5
675	"	10f *Omei skipper* (15)	50	5
676	"	20f *Philippines birdwing* (16)	25	5
677	"	20f *Richtofenis red apollo* (17)	25	5
678	"	22f *Blue-banded king crow* (18)	35	5
679	"	30f *Solskyi copper* (19)	40	*75*
680	"	50f *Yunnan clipper* (20)	60	*1.00*
		Nos. 661-680 (20)	7.35	*2.88*

Issue dates: Nos. 666–675, July 15; others Apr. 5.

1963, May 5 ***Perf. 11½***

Designs: No. 682, "Workers of the World, Unite" on cover of first edition of Communist Manifesto. No. 683, Marx and Engels.

Without Gum

681	A173	8f black, gold & salmon (1)	7.50	50
682	"	8f gold & red (2)	7.50	50
683	"	8f gold & choc. (3)	7.50	50

145th anniversary of birth of Karl Marx (1818–1883), German political philosopher.

Child with Top
A174

Designs (Child): No. 685, eating berries. No. 686, as traffic policeman. No. 687, with windmill. No. 688, listening to caged cricket. No. 689, with sword. No. 690, embroidering. No. 691, with umbrella. No. 692, playing with sand. No. 693, playing table tennis. No. 694, learning to add. No. 695, with kite.

1963, June 1 **Litho.** ***Perf. 12½***

Without Gum

Multicolored Designs

684	A174	4f greenish gray (1)	10	5
685	"	4f tan (2)	10	5
686	"	8f gray (3)	20	5
687	"	8f blue (4)	20	5
688	"	8f tan (5)	20	5
689	"	8f deep gray (6)	20	5
690	"	8f citron (7)	20	5
691	"	8f gray (8)	20	5
692	"	10f green (9)	25	15
693	"	10f violet (10)	25	15
694	"	20f bister (11)	45	40
695	"	20f green (12)	45	40
		Nos. 684-695 (12)	2.80	1.50

Children's Day. Imperfs. exist. Price for set, $4.

Dance Type of 1962

Folk Dances: 4f, Weavers' dance, Puyi. 8f, Kazakh. 10f, Olunchun. 20f, Labor dance, Kaochan. 30f, Reed pipe dance, Miao. 50f, Fan dance, Korea.

Cumulative numbers 261–266 at lower right.

1963, June 15 ***Perf. 12½***

Without Gum

696	A166	4f cream & multi.	7	5
697	"	8f " "	15	5
698	"	10f " "	20	8
699	"	20f " "	35	12
700	"	30f " "	60	20
701	"	50f " "	1.10	50
		Nos. 696-701 (6)	2.47	1.00

1963, June 30 **Without Gum**

Folk Dances: 4f, "Wedding Ceremony," Yu. 8f, "Encircling Mountain Forest," Pai. 10f, Long drum dance, Yao. 20f, Third day of the third month dance, Li. 30f, Knife dance, Kawa. 50f, Peacock dance, Thai.

Cumulative numbers 279–284 at lower right.

702	A166	4f cream & multi.	7	5
703	"	8f " "	15	5
704	"	10f " "	20	8
705	"	20f " "	35	12
706	"	30f " "	60	20
707	"	50f " "	1.10	50
		Nos. 702-707 (6)	2.47	1.00

Giant Panda Eating Apples
A175

Table Tennis Player
A176

Designs: No. 709, Giant panda eating bamboo shoots. 10f, Two pandas (horiz.).

1963, Aug. 5 **Photo.** ***Perf. 11½x11***

Size: 28x38mm.

708	A175	8f pale blue & black	75	25
709	"	8f " " "	75	25

Size: 50x29mm. ***Perf. 11½***

710	A175	10f olive & black	75	25

Imperfs. exist. Price, set $3.

1963, Sept. 10 **Engr.** ***Perf. 11½***

Design: No. 712, Trophies won by Chinese team.

711	A176	8f dark olive green	7.50	15
712	"	8f brown	7.50	10

27th World Table Tennis Championships.

Snub-nosed Langur
A177

Jade-green Screen Mountain
A178

Designs: 10f, Two monkeys playing. 22f, Two monkeys grooming.

Photogravure

1963, Sept. 23 ***Perf. 11½x11***

713	A177	8f gray & multi.	40	10
714	"	10f " "	40	10
715	"	22f " "	40	30

Imperfs. exist. Price, set, $2.50.

Engraved and Photogravure

1963, Oct. 15 ***Perf. 11½***

Hwang Shan Landscapes (Yellow Mountains), Anhwei Province. Nos. 724–731 horizontal.

Multicolored

716	A178	4f *shown* (1)	1.00	5
717	"	4f *"Guests Welcoming Pines"* (2)	1.00	5
718	"	4f *Pines and Rock Behind the Sea* (3)	1.00	5
719	"	4f *Terrace of Keeping Cool* (4)	1.00	5
720	"	8f *Mount of Heavenly Capital* (5)	1.00	8
721	"	8f *Mount of Scissors* (6)	1.00	8
722	"	8f *Forest of Ten Thousand Pines* (7)	1.00	8
723	"	8f *"Brush Blooming in Dream"* (8)	1.00	8
724	"	10f *Mount of Lotus Flower* (9)	1.00	12
725	"	10f *Cumulus Cloud over West Sea* (10)	1.00	12
726	"	10f *Old Pines of Hwang Shan* (11)	1.00	12
727	"	10f *"Watching the Clouds over West Sea"*	1.00	12
728	"	20f *Mount of Stalagmites* (13)	1.00	20
729	"	22f *"Stone Monkey Watching the Sea"* (14)	1.00	30
730	"	30f *Forest of Lions* (15)	1.00	60
731	"	50f *Three Fairy Tales of Pen Lai* (16)	1.00	60
		Nos. 716-731 (16)	16.00	2.70

Soccer Player
A179

Athletes and Banners—A180

Designs: No. 733, Discus, women's. No. 734, Diving, men's. No. 735, Gymnastics, women's.

Engraved and Photogravure

1963, Nov. 17 ***Perf. 11***

732	A179	8f gray, red & black (1)	4.00	15
733	"	8f gray, ultra. & black (2)	4.00	5
734	"	8f lt. green, brown & black (3)	4.00	5
735	"	8f gray, lilac rose black (4)	4.00	5

Photogravure ***Perf. 11½***

736	A180	10f red & multi. (5)	4.00	15
		Nos. 732-736 (5)	20.00	45

Games of the Newly Emerging Forces, Djakarta.

Clay Rooster and Goat
A181

Chinese Folk Toys: No. 738, Cloth camel. No. 739, Cloth tigers. No. 740, Clay ox and rider. No. 741, Cloth rabbit, wooden doll, clay roosters. No. 742, Straw rooster. No. 743, Cloth donkey and bird. No. 744, Clay lion. No. 745, Cloth tiger and tumbler doll.

1963, Dec. 10 Litho. *Perf. 11½*
Toys Multicolored; Without Gum

737 A181 4f bister (1) 8 5
738 " 4f gray (4) 8 5
739 " 4f light blue (7) 8 5
740 " 8f bister (2) 12 5
741 " 8f gray (5) 12 5
742 " 8f light blue (8) 12 5
743 " 10f bister (3) 20 10
744 " 10f gray (6) 20 10
745 " 10f light blue (9) 20 10
Nos. 737-745 (9) 1.20 60

Armed Vietnamese Family **A182** — Flags of Cuba and China **A183**

Design: No. 747, Militia with Vietnamese flag.

Photogravure
1963, Dec. 20 *Perf. 11½x11*

746 A182 8f tan, black & red 50 15
747 " 8f red & multi. 50 15

Liberation of South Viet Nam.

1964, Jan. 1

Design: No. 749, Boy waving Cuban flag.

748 A183 8f red, yellow, blue & indigo 8.75 75
749 " 8f multicolored 8.75 75

5th anniversary of the liberation of Cuba.

Woman Driving Tractor
A184

Women of the People's Commune: No. 751, harvesting. No. 752, picking cotton. No. 753, picking fruit. No. 754, reading book. No. 755, on guard duty.

1964, Mar. 8

750 A184 8f olive, pink & brown (1) 15 5
751 " 8f brn. yel. & org. (2) 15 5
752 " 8f gray & multi. (3) 15 5
753 " 8f blk., org. & bl. (4) 15 5
754 " 8f grn. & multi. (5) 15 5
755 " 8f lilac & multi. (6) 15 5
Nos. 750-755 (6) 90 30

Helpful notes abound in the "Information for Collectors" section at the front of this volume.

Chinese and African Men
A185

Design: No. 757, African drummer.

1964, Apr. 12 Photo. *Perf. 11*

756 A185 8f red & multi. 25 10
757 " 8f black & dk. brown 25 10

African Freedom Day.

Marx, Engels, Lenin and Stalin
A186

Design: No. 759, Banners and workers.

1964, May 1 *Perf. 11½*

758 A186 8f gold, red & blk. 10.00 *2.50*
759 " 8f gold, red & blk. 10.00 *2.50*

Labor Day.

Orchard, Yenan
A187

Yenan, Shrine of the Chinese Revolution: No. 761, Central Auditorium, Yang Chia Ling. No. 762, Mao's office and residence. No. 763, Auditorium, Wang Chia Ping. No. 764, Border Region Assembly Hall. No. 765, Pagoda Hill and Bridge.

1964, July 1 Photo. *Perf. 11x11½*

760 A187 8f multi. (1) 1.25 20
761 " 8f " (2) 1.25 20
762 " 8f " (3) 1.25 20
763 " 8f " (4) 1.25 20
764 " 8f " (5) 1.25 20
765 " 52f " (6) 3.00 85
Nos. 760-765 (6) 9.25 1.85

Map and Flag of Viet Nam **A188** — Alchemist's Glowing Crucible **A189**

1964, July 20 *Perf. 11½*

766 A188 8f multicolored 14.00 45

Victory in South Viet Nam.

1964, Aug. 5 *Perf. 11½x11*

Position-in-set number in ( ).

Peonies in Natural Colors

767 A189 4f *shown* (1) 40 10
768 " 4f *Night-shining jade* (2) 40 10
769 A189 8f *Pur. Kuo's cap* (3) 40 5
770 " 8f *Chao pink* (4) 40 5
771 " 8f *Yao yellow* (5) 40 10
772 " 8f *Twin beauty* (6) 40 5
773 " 8f *Ice-veiled ruby* (7) 40 5
774 " 10f *Gold-sprinkled Chinese ink* (8) 40 8
775 " 10f *Cinnabar jar* (9) 40 8
776 " 10f *Lan Tien jade* (10) 40 5
777 " 10f *Imperial robe yellow* (11) 40 8
778 " 10f *Hu red* (12) 40 8
779 " 20f *Pea green* (13) 40 10
780 " 43f *Wei purple* (14) 40 *50*
781 " 52f *Intoxicated celestial peach* (15) 40 *60*
Nos. 767-781 (15) 6.00 *2.07*

Souvenir Sheet
Perf. 11½
Without Gum

782 A189 $2 *Glorious crimson & great gold pink* 50.00 35.00

No. 782 contains one stamp (48x59mm.). Bluish gray and silver border. Size: 77x136mm.

Wine Cup **A190** — Grain Harvest **A191**

Designs: Sacrificial bronze vessels of Yin dynasty, prior to 1050 B.C.

Engraved and Photogravure
1964, Aug. 25 *Perf. 11½x11*
Frames & Inscriptions Black, Vessels Multicolored

783 A190 4f *shown* (1) 10 5
784 " 4f *Ku beaker* (2) 10 5
785 " 8f *Kuang wine urn* (3) 15 8
786 " 8f *Chia wine cup* (4) 15 8
787 " 10f *Tsun wine vessel* (5) 20 10
788 " 10f *Yu wine urn* (6) 20 10
789 " 20f *Tsun wine vessel* (7) 35 20
790 " 20f *Ceremonial cauldron* (8) 35 20
Nos. 783-790 (8) 1.60 86

1964, Sept. 26 Photogravure

Designs: No. 792, Students planting trees. No. 793, Study period. No. 794, Scientific experimentation.

791 A191 8f multicolored (1) 20 10
792 " 8f " (2) 20 10
793 " 8f " (3) 20 10
794 " 8f " (4) 20 10

Youth helping in agriculture.

Marx, Engels, Trafalgar Square, London **A192** — People with Banners **A193**

1964, Sept. 28 *Perf. 11½*

795 A192 8f red, gold & red brown *35.00 15.00*

Centenary of the First International.

1964, Oct. 1

Designs: No. 797, Gate of Heavenly Peace and Chinese flag. No. 798, People with banners, facing left.

796 A193 8f cream & multi. (1) 6.00 25
797 " 8f " " (2) 6.00 25
798 " 8f " " (3) 6.00 25
Strip of three, # 796-798 20.00 2.50
a. Souv. sheet of three 50.00 *30.00*

15th anniversary of the People's Republic. Nos. 796-798 printed se-tenant. No. 798a contains Nos. 796-798 as continuous design without separating perfs. Red and gold marginal inscription. Size: 153x114mm.

Oil Derricks
A194

Designs: 4f, Geological surveyors and truck (horiz.). 8f, "Christmas tree" and extraction accessories. 10f, Oil refinery. 20f, Tank cars (horiz.).

1964, Oct. 1

799 A194 4f lt. blue & multi. 7.00 5
800 " 8f " " 7.00 5
801 " 8f lilac & multi. 7.00 15
802 " 10f slate & multi. 7.00 5
803 " 20f brn. & multi. 7.00 1.50
Nos. 799-803 (5) 35.00 1.80

Oil industry.

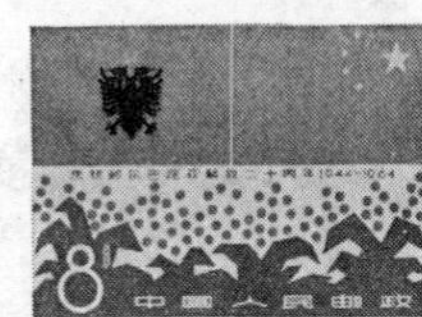

Albanian and Chinese Flags
A195

Design: 10f, Enver Hoxha and Albanian coat of arms.

1964, Nov. 29 *Perf. 11x11½*

804 A195 8f red & multi. 7.50 *75*
805 " 10f red, yel. & black 7.50 *4.00*

20th anniversary of the liberation of Albania.

Power Dam Construction
A196

Designs: No. 807, Installation of turbogenerator rotor. No. 808, Main dam. 20f, Pylon.

1964, Dec. 15 *Perf. 11½*

806 A196 4f multicolored 7.50 10
807 " 8f " 7.50 10
808 " 8f " 7.50 5
809 " 20f " 7.50 1.25

Hsin An Kiang Dam and hydroelectric power station.

Fertilizer Industry—A197

Designs (Chemical Industry): No. 811, Plastics. No. 812, Medicines. No. 813, Rubber. No. 814, Insecticides. No. 815, Industrial acids. No. 816, Industrial alkalies. No. 817, Synthetic fibers.

1964, Dec. 30 **Engr. & Photo.**

810	A197	8f red & black (1)	18	10
811	"	8f yel. grn. & blk. (2)	18	10
812	"	8f brown & black (3)	18	10
813	"	8f lilac rose & black (4)	18	10
814	"	8f blue & black (5)	18	10
815	"	8f org. & black (6)	18	10
816	"	8f violet & black (7)	18	10
817	"	8f brt. grn. & blk. (8)	18	10
		Nos. 810-817 (8)	1.44	80

Mao Studying Map
A198

Mao Tse-tung
A199

Design: No. 819, Victory at Lushan Pass.

1965, Jan. 31 **Photo.** ***Perf. 11***

818	A198	8f red & multi.	15.00
819	"	8f " "	15.00

Perf. 11½x11

820	A199	8f gold & multi.	15.00

Tsunyi Conference, 30th anniversary.

Conference Hall, Bandung—A200

Lenin
A201

1965, Apr. 18 ***Perf. 11½x11***

Design: No. 822, Asians and Africans applauding.

821	A200	8f cream & multi.	25	7
822	"	8f " "	25	8

10th anniversary of the Bandung, Indonesia, Conference, Apr. 1955.

1965, Apr. 25 ***Perf. 11½***

823	A201	8f red, choc. & sal.	17.50	*4.00*

95th anniversary of the birth of Lenin.

Chinese Player
A202

1965, Apr. 25 ***Perf. 11½***

Emerald, Gold, Red & Black

824	A202	8f *shown* (1)	15	8
825	"	8f *European woman* (2)	15	8
826	"	8f *Chinese woman* (3)	15	8
827	"	8f *European man* (4)	15	8
		Block of 4	1.00	40

28th World Table Tennis Championships, Ljubljana, Jugoslavia, Apr. 15–25. Nos. 824–827 printed se-tenant.

Climbers on Mt. Minya Konka
A203

Marx and Lenin
A204

Mountain Climbers: No. 829, on Muztagh Ata. No. 830, on Mt. Jolmo Lungma (Mt. Everest). No. 831, Women camping on Kongur Tiubie Tagh. No. 832, on Shisha Pangma.

1965, May 25 **Engr. & Photo.**

828	A203	8f bl., blk. & olive (1)	40	20
829	"	8f " " (2)	40	20
830	"	8f ultra., black & gray (3)	40	20
831	"	8f lt. bl., blk. & yel. gray (4)	40	20
832	"	8f ultra., black & gray (5)	40	20
		Nos. 828-832 (5)	2.00	1.00

Chinese mountaineering achievements, 1957–64.

1965, June 21 **Photo.** ***Perf. 11½x11***

833	A204	8f red, yel. & blk.	20.00	4.00

Postal Ministers' Congress, Peking.

Tseping Valley
A205

Chingkang Mountains, Cradle of the Chinese Revolution.

1965, July 1 ***Perf. 11x11½***

Multicolored

834	A205	4f *shown* (1)	1.50	10
835	"	8f *San Wan Tsun* (2)	1.50	10
836	"	8f *Octagon Building, Mao Ping* (3)	1.50	15
837	"	8f *River and Bridge at Lung Shih* (4)	1.50	10
838	"	8f *Ta Ching Tsun* (5)	1.50	15
839	"	10f *Bridge across the Lung Yuan* (6)	1.50	20
840	"	10f *Hwang Yang Mountain* (7)	1.50	20
841	"	52f *Chingkang Peaks* (8)	1.50	65
		Nos. 834-841 (8)	12.00	1.65

Soldiers with Books—A206

1965, Aug. 1 ***Perf. 11½***

Without Gum

Multicolored

842	A206	8f *shown* (1)	4.00	30
843	"	8f *Soldiers reading Little Red Books* (2)	4.00	30
844	"	8f *With shell and artillery* (3)	4.00	10
845	"	8f *Rifle instruction* (4)	4.00	15
846	"	8f *Sewing jacket* (5)	4.00	10
847	"	8f *Bayonet charge* (6)	4.00	3.00
848	"	8f *With banner* (7)	4.00	3.00
849	"	8f *Military band* (8)	4.00	3.00
		Nos. 842-849 (8)	32.00	9.95

People's Liberation Army. Nos. 846–849 vertical.

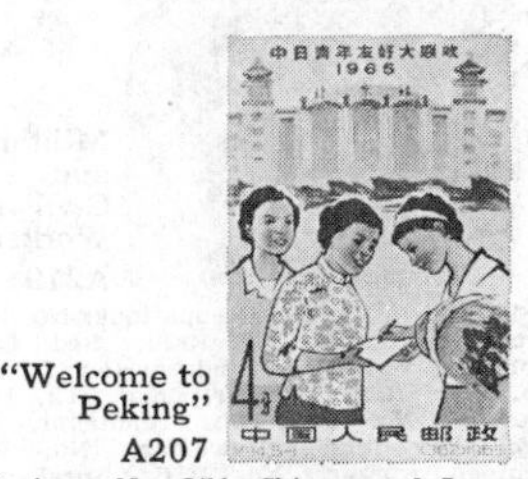

"Welcome to Peking"
A207

Designs: No. 851, Chinese and Japanese young men. No. 852, Chinese and Japanese girls. No. 853, Musical entertainment. No. 854, Emblem of meeting.

1965, Aug. 25 ***Perf. 11½x11***

850	A207	4f yellow & multi.	10	8
851	"	8f pink & multi.	15	10
852	"	8f multicolored	15	10
853	"	10f "	20	10
854	"	22f lt. blue & multi.	35	25
		Nos. 850-854 (5)	95	63

Chinese-Japanese Youth Meeting, Peking.

North Vietnamese Soldier
A208

Peoples of the World—A209

Designs: No. 856, Soldier with guns. No. 857, Soldier giving victory salute.

1965, Sept. 2 ***Perf. 11½x11***

855	A208	8f red & red brn. (1)	20	15
856	"	8f red & black (2)	20	15
857	"	8f red & vio. brn. (3)	20	15

Perf. 11½

858	A209	8f black & red (4)	20	10

Struggle of the people of Viet Nam.

Mao Tse-tung at His Desk—A210

Crossing Yellow River
A211

Victory Monument
A212

Design: No. 862, Recruits in cart.

1965, Sept. 3 ***Perf. 11***

859	A210	8f red & multi. (1)	5.50	1.00

Perf. 11x11½, 11½x11

860	A211	8f red & dk. grn. (2)	5.50	1.00
861	A212	8f red & dk. brn. (3)	5.50	1.00
862	A211	8f red & dk. grn. (4)	5.50	1.00

20th anniversary of victory over Japan.

Soccer
A213

National Games Opening Ceremonies—A214

Designs: No. 864, Archery. No. 865, Javelin. No. 866, Gymnastics. No. 867, Volleyball. No. 869, Bicycling. 20f, Diving. 22f, Hurdles. 30f, Weight lifting. 43f, Basketball.

Position-in-set number in ( ).

Perf. 11½x11, 11 (A214)

1965, Sept. 28

863	A213	4f red & multi. (1)	3.00	5
864	"	4f gray & multi. (2)	3.00	5
865	"	8f dark green & multi. (3)	3.00	5
866	"	8f lilac rose & multi. (4)	3.00	5
867	"	8f deep green & multi. (5)	3.00	5

868 A214 10f red, gold & multi. (6) 3.00 5
869 A213 10f olive & multi. (7) 3.00 5
870 " 20f ultra. & multi. (8) 3.00 5
871 " 22f org. & multi. (9) 3.00 40
872 " 30f deep blue & multi. (10) 3.00 45
873 " 43f red lilac & multi. (11) 3.00 50
Nos. 863-873 (11) 33.00 1.75

2nd National Games.

Government Building
A215

Textile Workers
A216

Designs: 4f, 20f, as 1f. 1½f, 5f, 22f, Gate of Heavenly Peace. 2f, 8f, 30f, People's Hall. 3f, 10f, 50f, Military Museum.

1965–66 ***Perf. 11½x11***

Without Gum

874 A215 1f brown 30 8
875 " 1½f red lilac 30 8
876 " 2f green 30 8
877 " 3f blue green 30 8
878 " 4f bright blue 30 8
879 " 5f vio. brown ('66) 75 8
880 " 8f rose red 30 8
881 " 10f gray olive 30 8
882 " 20f violet 30 8
883 " 22f orange 30 8
884 " 30f yellow green 30 8
885 " 50f deep blue ('66) 75 20
Nos. 874-885 (12) 4.50 1.08

1965, Nov. 30

Multicolored

886 A216 8f *shown* (1) 7.00 5
887 " 8f *Machine shop* (2) 7.00 10
888 " 8f *Welder* (3) 7.00 5
889 " 8f *Students* (4) 7.00 40
890 " 8f *Militia* (5) 7.00 40
Nos. 886-890 (5) 35.00 1.00

Women workers.

Soccer—A217

Children's Sports: No. 892, Racing. No. 893, Tobogganing and skating. No. 894, Gymnastics. No. 895, Swimming. No. 896, Rifle practice. No. 897, Jumping rope. No. 898, Table tennis.

1966, Feb. 25 ***Perf. 11***

891 A217 4f emerald & multi. (1) 7 5
892 " 4f yellow brown & multi. (2) 7 5
893 " 8f blue & multi. (3) 15 10
894 " 8f yel. & multi. (4) 15 10
895 " 8f greenish blue & multi. (5) 15 10
896 " 8f grn. & multi. (6) 15 10
897 " 10f org. & multi. (7) 20 12
898 " 52f greenish gray & multi. (8) 1.10 60
Nos. 891-898 (8) 2.04 1.22

Mobile Transformer
A218

New Industrial Machinery: No. 900, Electron microscope (vert.). No. 901, Lathe. No. 902, Vertical boring and turning machine (vert.). No. 903, Gear-grinding machine. No. 904, Hydraulic press. No. 905, Milling machine. No. 906, Electron accelerator (vert.).

Perf. 11x11½, 11½x11

1966, Mar. 30 **Engr. and Photo.**

899 A218 4f yel. & black (1) 3.50 10
900 " 8f blk. & lt. ultra (2) 3.50 10
901 " 8f sal. pink & blk. (3) 3.50 10
902 " 8f olive & black (4) 3.50 10
903 " 8f rose lilac & black (5) 3.50 10
904 " 10f gray & black (6) 3.50 50
905 " 10f bl. grn. & blk. (7) 3.50 55
906 " 22f lilac & black (8) 3.50 60
Nos. 899-906 (8) 28.00 2.15

Military and Civilian Workers
A219

Women in Various Occupations: No. 908, Train conductor. No. 909, Red Cross worker. No. 910, Kindergarten teacher. No. 911, Road sweeper. No. 912, Hairdresser. No. 913, Bus conductor. No. 914, Traveling saleswoman. No. 915, Canteen worker. No. 916, Rural mail carrier.

1966, May 10 ***Perf. 11x11½***

907 A219 8f red & multi. (1) 15 10
908 " 8f pale grn. & multi. (2) 15 10
909 " 8f yel. & multi. (3) 15 10
910 " 8f grn. & multi. (4) 15 10
911 " 8f sal. & multi. (5) 15 10
912 " 8f pale bl. & blue (6) 15 10
913 " 8f yel. & multi. (7) 15 10
914 " 8f tan & multi. (8) 15 10
915 " 8f yel. grn. & multi. (9) 15 10
916 " 8f grn. & multi. (10) 15 10
Nos. 907-916 (10) 1.50 1.00

Statue "Thunderstorm"
A220

Design: 22f, Open book and association emblem.

1966, June 27 **With Gum** ***Perf. 11***

917 A220 8f red & black 20 5
918 " 22f red, gold & yellow 50 15

Afro-Asian Writers' Association Conference, Peking.

Sun Yat-sen
A221

1966, Nov. 12 ***Perf. 11½x11***

919 A221 8f sepia & lt. buff 11.50 *5.00*

Birth centenary of Sun Yat-sen.

Athletes Holding Portrait of Mao
A222

Two Women Athletes with Little Red Book
A223

Designs: No. 921, Athletes holding Little Red Books. No. 923, Athletes reading Mao texts.

1966, Dec. 31 ***Perf. 11***

920 A222 8f red & multi. (1) 7.00 *2.00*
921 " 8f " " (2) 7.00 *2.00*

Perf. 11x11½

922 A223 8f blue & multi. (3) 7.00 *2.00*
923 " 8f " " (4) 7.00 *2.00*

1st Athletic Games of the New Emerging Nations.

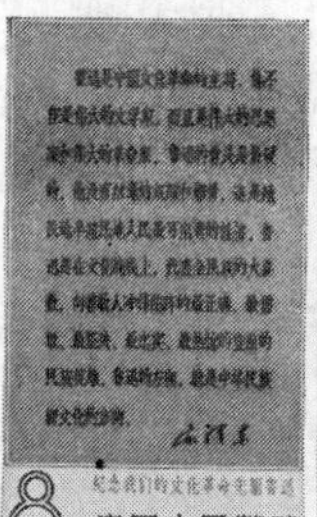

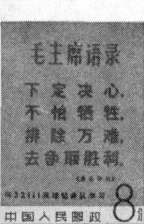

Appreciation of Lu Hsun by Mao
A224

"Be Resolute . . . ," by Mao Tse-tung
A225

Designs: No. 925, Portrait of Lu Hsun. No. 926, Lu Hsun's handwriting (3 vert. rows).

Engr. & Photo.; Photo. (No. 925)

1966, Dec. 31 ***Perf. 11½***

924 A224 8f red & black (1) 4.50 *1.50*
925 " 8f red & multi. (2) 4.50 *1.50*
926 " 8f red & black (3) 4.50 *1.50*

Lu Hsun, Revolutionary writer (1881–1936).

Perf. 11½x11, 11½ (No. 928)

1967, Mar. 10 **Photogravure**

Designs: No. 928, Drilling crew fighting natural gas fire (horiz.). No. 929, Attempt to close fire-engulfed valve.

Sizes: Nos. 927, 929, 26x38mm.; No. 928, 49x29mm.

927 A225 8f red, gold & black 4.00 1.25
928 " 8f brick red & black 4.00 1.25
929 " 8f " " 4.00 1.25

Heroic oil well firefighters.

Liu Ying-chun
A226

1967, Mar. 25 ***Perf. 11½x11***

Multicolored

930 A226 8f *shown* (1) 4.50 1.25
931 " 8f *With book by Mao* (2) 4.50 1.25
932 " 8f *Holding bridle of horse* (3) 4.50 1.25
933 " 8f *With film slide* (4) 4.50 1.25
934 " 8f *Lecturing* (5) 4.50 1.25
935 " 8f *Fatal attempt to stop runaway horse* (6) 4.50 1.25
Nos. 930-935 (6) 27.00 7.50

In memory of soldier Liu Ying-chun, hero.

Industrial Growth—A227

Design: No. 937, Banners and people facing left: agricultural growth.

1967, Apr. 15 ***Perf. 11***

936 A227 8f red & multi. 2.50 75
937 " 8f " " 2.50 75

Third Five-Year Plan.

Mao Tse-tung
A228

Thoughts of Mao
A229

1967, Apr. 20 ***Perf. 11½***

938 A228 8f red & multi. 10.00 6.00

Red & Gold

939 A229 8f *39 characters* 5.00 2.00
940 " 8f *50* " 5.00 2.00
941 " 8f *39* " *in 6 lines* 5.00 2.00
942 " 8f *53 characters* 5.00 2.00
943 " 8f *46* " 5.00 2.00
Strip of five 45.00 25.00

Gold & Red

944 A229 8f *41 characters* 5.00 2.00
945 " 8f *49* " 5.00 2.00
946 " 8f *35* " 5.00 2.00
947 " 8f *22* " 5.00 2.00
948 " 8f *29* " 5.00 2.00
Strip of five 45.00 25.00
Nos. 938-948 (11) 60.00 26.00

Thoughts of Mao Tse-tung. Nos. 939–943, Nos. 944–948 printed se-tenant in strips of 5 each.

No numbers appear below design on Nos. 938–1046.

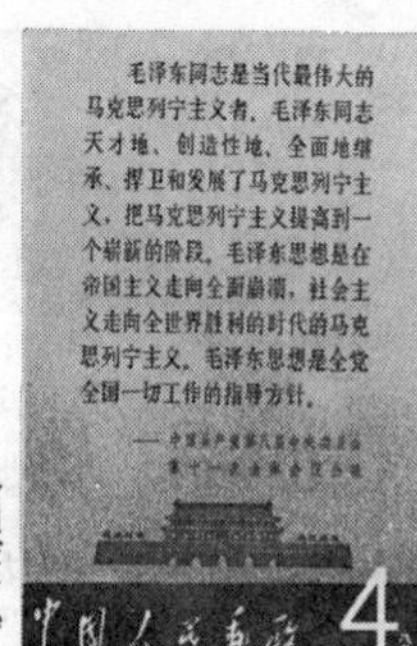

Text by Mao and Gate of Heavenly Peace
A230

Mao and Lin Piao
A231

Designs: No. 950, Mao and poem. No. 951, Mao among people of various races. No. 952, Mao facing left and Red Guards with books. No. 953, Mao with upraised right hand. No. 954, Mao leaning on rail (horiz.). 10f, Mao and Lin Piao in discussion (horiz.).

Engraved and Photogravure

1967 ***Perf. 11x11½***

Size: 36x56mm.

949	A230	4f yellow, red & maroon	9.00	2.00

Photogravure

950	A230	8f yel., brn., & red	9.00	2.00
951	"	8f yel., red & multi.	9.00	2.00
952	"	8f " "	9.00	2.00

Perf. 11

Size: 36x50, 50x36mm.

953	A231	8f black & multi.	11.00	2.00
954	"	8f " "	22.50	10.00
955	"	8f lt. blue & multi.	40.00	20.00
956	"	10f black & multi.	40.00	20.00
		Nos. 949-956 (8)	149.50	60.00

"Mao Tse-tung Our Great Teacher."
Issue dates: Nos. 949-953, May 1; Nos. 954-956, Sept. 20.

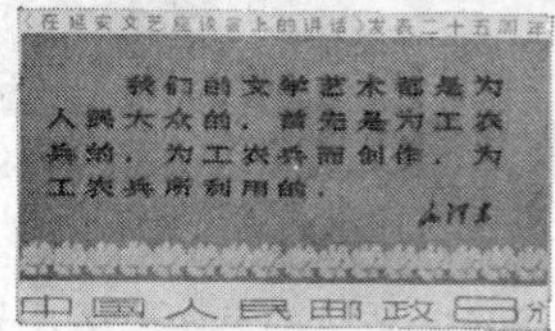

Mao Text (4 lines)—A232

Parade of Supporters—A233

Design: No. 958, Mao text (5 lines).

Engraved and Photogravure

1967, May 23 ***Perf. 11½***

957	A232	8f blk., red & yel.	15.00	*4.00*
958	"	8f " " "	15.00	*4.00*

Photogravure ***Perf. 11***

959	A233	8f multicolored	15.00	*4.00*

25th anniversary of Mao Tse-tung's "Talks on Literature and Art" in Yenan.

Mao Tse-tung
A234

1967 **Engraved** ***Perf. 11***

960	A234	4f brown	3.50	1.25
961	"	8f carmine	3.50	1.25
962	"	35f dark brown	3.50	1.25
963	"	43f vermilion	3.50	1.25
964	"	52f carmine	3.50	1.25
		Nos. 960-964 (5)	17.50	6.25

46th anniversary of Chinese Communist Party.
Issue dates: 8f, July 1, others September.

Mao, "Sun of the Revolution"—A235

Design: No. 966, Mao and people of various races.

1967, Oct. 1 ***Perf. 11½x11***

965	A235	8f multicolored	15.00	*7.50*
966	"	8f "	15.00	*7.50*

18th anniversary of the People's Republic of China.

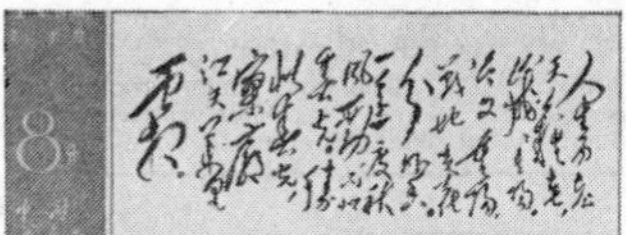

"September 9"—A236

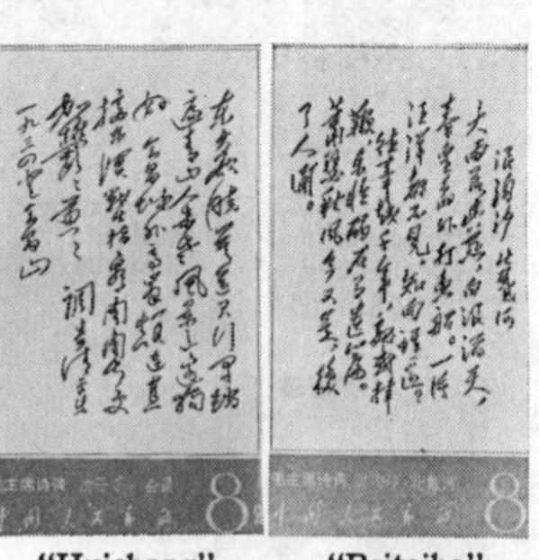

"Huichang"
A237

"Peitaiho"
A238

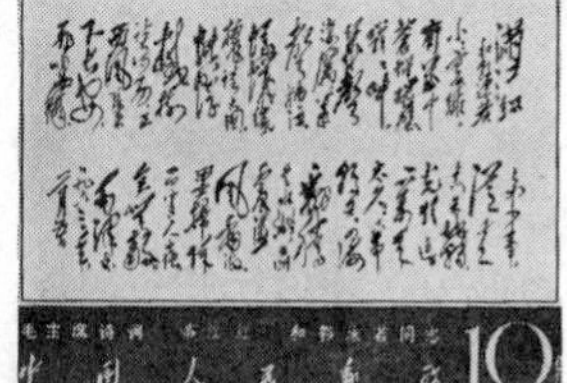

Reply to Comrade Kuo Mo-jo—A239

Mao Tse-tung Writing Poems—A240

Designs (Poems by Mao): No. 967, "The Long March." No. 968, "Liupanshan." No. 969, shown. No. 970, "The Cave of the Fairies." No. 971, "Snow." No. 972, "Lushan Pass." Nos. 973-974, shown. No. 975, "Conquest of Nanking." No. 976, "The Yellow Crane Pavilion." No. 977, "Swimming." No. 978, shown. No. 979, "Changsha."

1967-68 **Photogravure** ***Perf. 11***

Red and Yellow Frame; Poem Written in Black

Size: 79x18½mm.

967	A236	4f *9 characters, UL panel* ('68)	18.00	*6.00*
968	"	4f *11 characters, UL panel* ('68)	18.00	*6.00*

Size: 60x24mm. ***Perf. 11½***

969	A236	8f *shown, 10 characters in UL panel*	3.50	*1.00*
970	"	8f *21 characters in UL panel*	3.50	*1.00*
971	"	8f *11 characters in UL panel*	18.00	*6.00*
972	"	8f *9 characters in UL panel*	18.00	*6.00*

Size: 29x50mm.

973	A237	8f *shown*	4.00	*1.00*
974	A238	8f *shown*	18.00	*6.00*
975	"	8f *3 rows in bottom panel*	4.00	*1.00*
976	"	8f *2 rows in bottom panel*	12.50	*6.00*

Size: 52x38mm. ***Perf. 11***

977	A239	8f *3 short vert. rows, at left of poem*	12.50	*6.00*
978	"	10f *shown*	12.50	*6.00*
979	"	10f *undivided text*	4.00	*1.00*
980	A240	10f red, yellow & multi.	3.50	*6.00*
		Nos 967-980 (14)	150.00	*59.00*

Poems by Mao Tse-tung.
Issue dates: Nos. 969-970, 980, Oct. 1, 1967; Nos. 973-974, 977, May 20, 1968; others July 20, 1968.

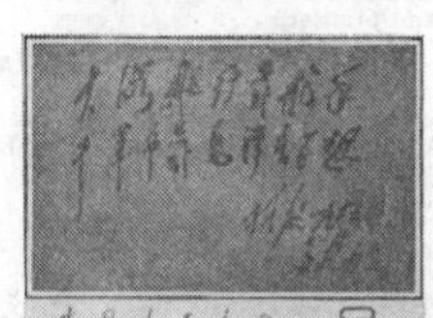

Lin Piao's Epigram on Mao Tse-tung
A241

1967, Dec. 26 **Photo.** ***Perf. 11x11½***

981	A241	8f red & gold	42.50	*4.00*

Mao and Parade of Artists—A242

"Raid on White Tiger Regiment"
A243

"Red Detachment of Women"—A244

1968 ***Perf. 11½x11; 11*** **(983, 990)**

Multicolored

982	A242	8f *shown* (56x36 mm.)	5.00	*4.00*
983	"	8f *"The Red Lantern"* (vert.)	5.00	*4.00*
984	A243	8f *shown*	5.00	*4.00*
985	"	8f *"Shachiapang" (women & soldier)*	5.00	*4.00*
986	"	8f *"On the Dock"*	5.00	*4.00*
987	"	8f *"Taking Bandits' Fort"*	5.00	*4.00*
988	A244	8f *shown*	20.00	*4.00*
989	"	8f *"The White-haired Girl"*	20.00	*4.00*
990	A242	8f *Mao with Orchestra & Chorus* (50x36 mm.)	20.00	*4.00*
		Nos. 982-990 (9)	90.00	*36.00*

Mao's direction for revolutionary literature and art.
Issue dates: Nos. 982-987, Jan. 30; Nos. 988-990, May 1.

"Unite still more closely. . ."—A245

1968, May 31 **Photo.** ***Perf. 11***

991	A245	8f red, gold & red brown	35.00	*10.00*

Mao Tse-tung's statement of support of Afro-Americans.

Listings of stamps issued since this Catalogue went to press will be found in Scott's Monthly Stamp Journal.

Statement about Cultural Revolution
A246

Directives of Chairman Mao: No. 993, Experiences of Revolutionary Committee. No. 994, Leadership role of Revolutionary Committee. No. 995, Basic principle of reform. No. 996, Purpose of Cultural Revolution.

1968, July 20 Photo. *Perf. 11½*

Red, Yellow & Brown

992 A246 8f *shown* 8.00 *5.00*
993 " 8f *5 lines over signature* 8.00 *5.00*
994 " 8f *4½ lines over signature* 8.00 *5.00*
995 " 8f *4 lines over signature* 8.00 *5.00*
996 " 8f *8 lines over signature* 8.00 *5.00*
Strip of five 130.00 *50.00*

Printed se-tenant in horizontal strips of 5 within sheet.

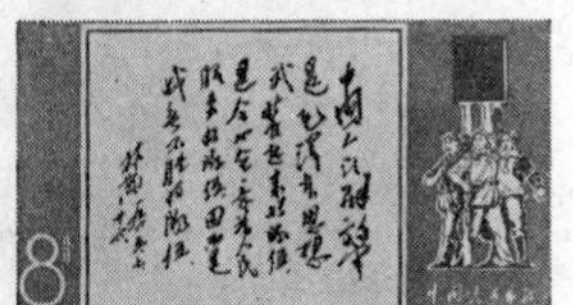

Lin Piao's Statement, July 26, 1965
A247

1968, Aug. 1 Engr. and Photo.

997 A247 8f red, gold & blk. 35.00 3.50

41st anniversary of the Chinese People's Liberation Army.

Mao Tse-tung Going to An Yuan, 1921
A248

1968, Aug. 1 *Perf. 11x11½*

998 A248 8f multicolored (with red in clouds to right of Mao) 25.00 10.00
a. Red omitted from clouds 25.00 11.00

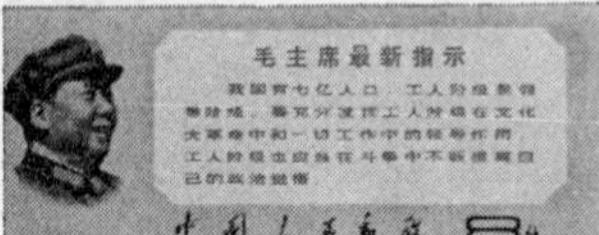

Directive of Chairman Mao—A249

1968, Nov. 30 *Perf. 11½*

999 A249 8f red & blk. brn. 30.00 *9.00*

China Map, Worker, Farmer and Soldier
A249a

1968, Nov. Photo. *Perf. 11½x11*

999A A249a 8f red, blue & bister *2000.00 2000.00*

Map inscribed: "The entire nation is red." Issued in Canton and quickly withdrawn because Taiwan appears white instead of red.

Woman, Miner and Soldier Holding Little Red Book
A250

1968, Dec. 26 *Perf. 11x11½*

1000 A250 8f multicolored 5.00 2.00

Yangtze Bridge, Nanking
A251

Road across Bridge—A252

Designs: No. 1003, Side view. 10f, Aerial view.

Litho., *Perf. 11½x11 (A251)*; Photo., *Perf. 11½ (A252)*

1969 Without Gum

1001 A251 4f multicolored *3.00 1.00*
1002 A252 8f " *3.00 1.00*
1003 " 8f " *3.00 1.00*
1004 A251 10f " *3.00 1.00*

Inauguration of Yangtze Bridge at Nanking on Dec. 29, 1968.

Singer and Pianist
A253

Designs (Piano Music from the Opera, "The Red Lantern"): No. 1006, Woman singer and pianist.

1969, Aug. Photo. *Perf. 11x11½*

Without Gum

1005 A253 8f multicolored 60 50
1006 " 8f " 60 50

Harvest
A254

1969, Oct.

Multicolored

1007 A254 4f *shown* 1.75 *1.75*
a. Brown omitted
1008 A254 8f *Two harvesters* 1.50 *1.00*
1009 " 8f *Harvesters with Little Red Books* 1.50 *1.00*
1010 " 10f *Red Cross worker examining baby* 1.50 *75*

Agriculture students.

Armed Forces and Slogan—A255

Guarding the Coast—A256

Designs: No. 1013, 43f, Snow patrol (vert.).

1969, Oct. *Perf. 11½*

1011 A255 8f red & multi. 1.00 *1.00*
a. Bayonets omitted 100.00 *100.00*
1012 A256 8f blue & multi. 1.00 *1.00*
1013 " 8f " " 1.00 *1.00*
1014 " 35f black & multi. 1.00 *1.00*
1015 " 43f " " 1.00 *1.00*
Nos. 1011-1015 (5) 5.00 *5.00*

Defense of Chen Pao-tao (Damansky Islands) in Ussuri River.

Farm Woman
A257

Designs: 8f, Foundry worker. 10f, Soldier.

1969, Dec. *Perf. 10; 11½ (#1017)*

Without Gum

1016 A257 4f verm. & dk. pur. 60 35
1017 " 8f verm. & dk. brn. 60 35
1018 " 10f verm. & black 60 35

Perforation

Nos. 1016-1018 and some succeeding issues bear two kinds of perforation: clean (Peking) and rough (Shanghai).

Building
A258

Communist Party Building, Shanghai
A259

Agriculture Building, Canton
A260

Foundry Worker
A261

Two types of 8f Gate of Heavenly Peace:
I. Strong, definite halo around sun.
II. Halo missing, white shades gradually into red.

1969-72 Photo. *Perf. 10, 11½*

Multicolored; Without Gum

1019 A258 1f *shown* 5 *40*
1020 A259 1½f *shown* 25 10
1021 A260 2f *shown* 5 *25*
1022 " 3f *1929 Party Day House, PuTien* 8 5
1023 " 4f *Mao's Home and Office, Yunnan* 10 *30*
1024 A261 5f *Woman Tractor Driver* 50 20
a. Perf. 11½ *1.50 1.50*
1025 A260 8f *Gate of Heavenly Peace*, type II 35 25
a. Type I 75 75
1026 A259 8f *Heroes Monument* 1.50 1.00
a. Perf. 11½ 3.00 2.00
1027 A260 8f *Pagoda Hill, Yenan* 7.50 *2.00*
1028 " 8f *Gate of Heavenly Peace (no sun)* 15 10
1029 " 10f *Monument, Tsu Ping* 20 *30*
1030 A259 20f *Conference Hall, Tsunyi* 6.00 *4.00*
a. Perf. 11½ *8.00 6.00*
1031 A260 20f *Highway ('72)* 30 30
1032 " 22f *Shao Shan Village, Birthplace of Mao* 35 *50*
1033 A260 35f *Conference Hall* 50 50
1034 " 43f *Chingkang Peaks* 60 50
1035 A259 50f *as 4f, different view* 5.00 3.00
1036 A260 52f *People's Hall, Peking* 80 50
1037 A261 $1 *shown ('70)* 6.00 3.00
a. Perf. 11 *7.00 4.00*
b. Perf. 11½ *7.00 4.00*
Nos. 1019-1037 (19) 30.28 *17.25*

Kin Hsün-hua
A262

Mounted Patrol
A263

1970, Jan. Without Gum *Perf. 11½*

1045 A262 8f red & gray brn. 1.75 1.75
a. 8f red & black 20.00 6.00

Death of Kin Hsün-hua in Kirin border flood.

1970, Aug. 1 Without Gum

1046 A263 8f yel. grn. & multi. 1.25 1.25
a. 8f blue green & multicolored 1.25 1.25

43rd anniversary of the People's Liberation Army.

Beginning with No. 1047 commemorative stamps carry a cumulative number in parenthesis at lower left and the year at lower right. Where such numbers help to identify, they are quoted in parenthesis.

Cpl. Yang Tse-jung A264 — Ensemble A265

1970, Aug. 1

Perf. 11½x11, 11x11½

1047 A264 8f *shown* (1) 35 35
1048 " 8f *Armed guards* (2) 35 35
1049 " 8f *Yang leaping through forest* (3) 35 35
1050 A265 8f *shown* (4) 35 35
1051 " 8f *Yang in folk costume* (5) 35 35
1052 " 8f *Four actors* (6) 35 35
Nos. 1047-1052 (6) 2.10 2.10

Scenes from opera "Taking Tiger Mountain by Strategy." Nos. 1048, 1052, horizontal.

Frontier Guard
A266

1971, Jan. Litho. ***Perf. 11½***

Without Gum

1053 A266 4f multicolored 25 25
a. Perf. 10 40 40

Second anniversary, defense of Damansky Islands (Chen Pao-tao) in Ussuri River.

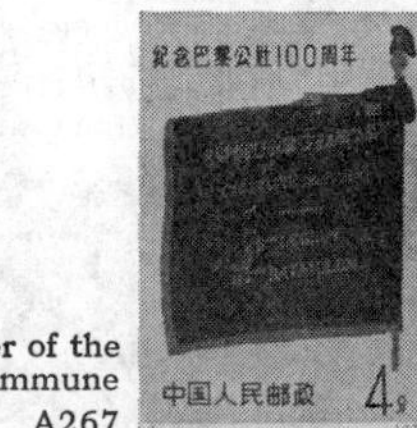

Banner of the Commune
A267

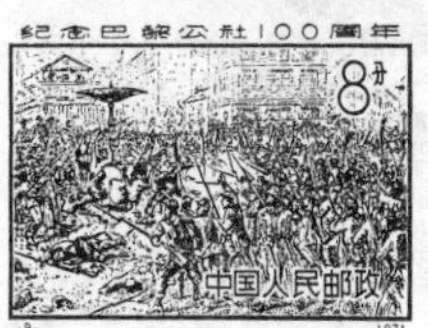

Street Battle, Paris, 1871
A268

Designs: 10f, Proclamation of the Commune. 22f, Rally.

1971, Mar. 18 Litho. and Engr.

Perf. 11½x11, 11x11½

1054 A267 4f salmon & multi. 10 10
1055 A268 8f vermilion, pink & brown 20 20
1056 A267 10f vermilion, pink & dk. brown 25 25
1057 A268 22f vermilion, pink & dk. brown 50 50

Centenary of the Paris Commune.

Redrawn Building Type of 1961

Designs: 2f, 3f, August 1 building, Nanchang. 4f, 52f, Gate of Heavenly Peace, Peking. 10f, 20f, Pagoda Hill, Yenan.

1971 Litho. ***Perf. 11x11½***

Size: 21x16mm.

1059 A152 2f slate green 1.00 1.00
1060 " 3f sepia 1.00 1.00
1061 " 4f bright pink 1.00 1.00
1062 " 10f brt. rose lilac 1.00 1.00
1063 " 20f dk. blue green 1.00 1.00
1064 " 52f orange 1.00 1.00
Nos. 1059-1064 (6) 6.00 6.00

Paper of Nos. 1059-1064 is white. That of Nos. 647-654 is toned.

Communist Party Building, Shanghai—A269

People and Factories
A270

Designs: No. 1068, Peasant Movement Training Institute. No 1069, Ching Kang Peaks. No. 1070, Conference Building, Tsunyi. No. 1071, Pagoda Hill, Yenan. No. 1073, People and People's Hall, Peking. No. 1074, People and Pagoda Hill, Yenan. 22f, Gate of Heavenly Peace, Peking.

Red and Gold Frame

1971, July 1 Photo. ***Perf. 11½***

1067 A269 4f vermilion (12) 10 10
1068 " 4f brt. green (13) 10 10
1069 " 8f greenish blue & red (14) 18 18
1070 " 8f olive black (15) 18 18
1071 " 8f bister, green & red (16) 18 18
1072 A270 8f yellow, red & multi. (18) 18 18
1073 " 8f yellow, red & multi. (19) 18 18
1074 " 8f yellow, red & multi. (20) 18 18
a. Strip of 3 (#1072-1074) 60 60
1075 A269 22f red, gold & brown (17) 60 60
Nos. 1067-1075 (9) 1.88 1.88

50th anniversary of the Chinese Communist Party. Nos. 1072-1074 printed se-tenant with continuous design.

Chinese Welcome
A271

Enver Hoxha
A272

Designs: No. 1077, Chinese and African players. No. 1078, Chinese and African girl players. 43f, Games' emblem.

1971, Nov. 3 Litho. ***Perf. 11½***

1076 A271 8f lilac rose & multicolored 20 20
1077 " 8f light yellow & multicolored 20 20
1078 " 8f dark green & multicolored 20 20
1079 " 43f green, gold & orange 1.00 1.00

Afro-Asian Table Tennis Games, Peking.

1971, Nov. 3 Photo. ***Perf. 11***

Designs: No. 1081, Party's birthplace. No. 1082, Albanian flag. 52f, Albanian partisans (horiz.).

1080 A272 8f Prussian blue & multicolored 50 50
1081 " 8f buff & multi. 50 50
1082 " 8f red, yellow & multicolored 50 50
1083 " 52f light blue & multicolored 50 50

30th anniversary of the founding of Albanian Communist Party.

Yenan Pagoda and 1942 Meeting House
A273

1972, May 23 Photogravure ***Perf. 11***

Cumulative numbers in parenthesis.

Multicolored

1084 A273 8f *shown* (33) 14 14
1085 " 8f *Uniformed choir* (34) 14 14
1086 " 8f *"Brother & Sister"* (35) 14 14
1087 " 8f *Outdoor performance* (36) 14 14
1088 " 8f *"The Red Signal Lantern"* (37) 3.00 14
1089 " 8f *Dancer from "The Red Company of Women"* (38) 14 14
Nos. 1084-1089 (6) 3.70 84

30th anniversary of the publication of the Discussions on Literature and Art at the Yenan Forum.

Various Ball Games—A274

Workers' Gymnastics
A275

1972, June 10 Multicolored

1090 A274 8f *shown* (39) 14 14
1091 A275 8f *shown* (40) 14 14
1092 " 8f *Tug of war* (41) 14 14
1093 " 8f *Mountain climbers and tents* (42) 14 14
1094 " 8f *Children diving & swimming* (43) 14 14
Nos. 1090-1094 (5) 70 70

10th anniversary of Mao Tse-tung's edict on physical culture.

Ocean Freighter Fenglei—A276

1972, July 10 Photo. ***Perf. 11½***

Multicolored

1095 A276 8f *shown* (29) 14 14
1096 " 8f *Tanker Taching No. 30* (30) 14 14
1097 " 8f *Cargo-passenger ship Changzeng* (31) 14 14
1098 " 8f *Dredger Xienfeng* (32) 14 14

Table Tennis Players' Welcome
A277

Perf. 11½x11, 11x11½

1972, Sept. 2

Multicolored

1099 A277 8f *Championship emblem* (vert.) (45) 14 14
1100 " 8f *shown* (46) 14 14
1101 " 8f *Table tennis* (47) 14 14
1102 " 22f *Women from different countries* (vert.) (48) 65 65

First Asian table tennis championships.

Wang Tsum-hu
A278

Workers on Cliffs along Canal
A279

Engraved and Photogravure

1972, Dec. 25 ***Perf. 11½x11***

1103 A278 8f multi. (44) 20 20

Wang Tsum-hu, the Iron Man, fighter for the working class.

1972, Dec. 30

Designs: No. 1105, Canal flowing through tunnel. No. 1106, Bridge. No. 1107, Canal along cliffs.

1104 A279 8f multi. (49) 15 15
1105 " 8f " (50) 15 15
1106 " 8f " (51) 15 15
1107 " 8f " (52) 15 15

Construction of Red Flag Canal, Linhsien county, Honan.

Giant Panda
A280

Woman Coal Miner
A281

Designs: Pandas in various positions. The 8f stamps are horizontal.

Perf. 11½x11, 11x11½

1973, Jan. 15 Photogravure

Designs in Black and Red

1108	A280	4f lt. yel. grn. (61)	5	5
1109	"	8f buff (59)	11	11
1110	"	8f lt. tan (60)	11	11
1111	"	10f pale green (58)	14	14
1112	"	20f pale bl. gray (57)	27	27
1113	"	43f pale lilac (62)	58	58
		Nos. 1108-1113 (6)	1.26	1.26

1973, Mar. 8 Photo. **Perf. 11½x11**

Multicolored

1114	A281	8f *shown* (63)	15	15
1115	"	8f *Committee member* (64)	15	15
1116	"	8f *Telephone line worker* (65)	15	15

International Working Women's Day. Designs are after paintings from an exhibition for 30th anniversary of the Yenan Forum on Literature and Art.

Dancing Girl

A282

Tournament Emblem

A283

1973, June 1 Photo. **Perf. 11**

Yellow & Multicolored

1117	A282	8f *shown* (86)	15	15
1118	"	8f *Musician, boy* (87)	15	15
1119	"	8f *Girl with scarf* (88)	15	15
1120	"	8f *Boy with tambourine* (89)	15	15
1121	"	8f *Girl with drum* (90)	15	15
		Nos. 1117-1121 (5)	75	75

Nos. 1117-1121 printed se-tenant.

1973, Aug. 25 Photo. **Perf. 11½**

Designs: No. 1123, Visitors from Asia, Africa and Latin America arriving by plane. No. 1124, Woman player. 22f, African, Asian and Latin American women.

1122	A283	8f multi. (91)	15	15
1123	"	8f " (92)	15	15
1124	"	8f " (93)	15	15
1125	"	22f " (94)	40	40

Asian, African and Latin American Table Tennis Friendship Invitational Tournament.

The White-haired Girl

A284

Designs: Scenes from the ballet "The White-haired Girl." Nos. 1126 and 1129 vertical.

1973, Sept. 25 Photo. **Perf. 11½**

1126	A284	8f multicolored (53)	15	15
1127	"	8f " (54)	15	15
1128	"	8f " (55)	15	15
1129	"	8f " (56)	15	15

Fair Building, Canton—A285

1973, Oct. 15 Photo. **Perf. 11**

1130	A285	8f multicolored (95)	11	11

Export Commodities Fall Fair, Canton.

Teapot with Blue Phoenix Design

A286

Designs: No. 1132, Silver pot with horse design. No. 1133, Black pottery horse. No. 1134, Woman, clay figurine. No. 1135, Carved stone pillar base. No. 1136, Galloping bronze horse. No. 1137, Bronze inkwell (toad). No. 1138, Bronze lamp, Chang Hsin Palace. No. 1139, Bronze tripod. No. 1140, Square bronze pot. 20f, Bronze wine vessel. 52f, Painted red clay tripod.

1973, Nov. 20 **Perf. 11½**

1131	A286	4f olive bister & multi. (66)	6	6
1132	"	4f vermilion & multi. (67)	6	6
1133	"	8f yellow green & multi. (68)	11	11
1134	"	8f bright rose & multi. (69)	11	11
1135	"	8f light violet & multi. (70)	11	11
1136	"	8f yellow bister & multi. (71)	11	11
1137	"	8f light blue & multi. (72)	11	11
1138	"	8f gray & multi. (73)	11	11
1139	"	10f yellow bister & multi. (74)	14	14
1140	"	10f deep orange & multi. (75)	14	14
1141	"	20f lilac & multi. (76)	27	27
1142	"	52f green & multi. (77)	75	75
		Nos. 1131-1142 (12)	2.08	2.08

Excavated works of art.

Marginal Markings

Marginal inscriptions on stamps of 1974 start at lower left with "J" for commemoratives and "T" for "special issues," followed by three numbers indicating (a) set sequence for the year, (b) total of stamps in set, and (c) number of stamp within set. At right appears the year date. Listings include the "c" number parenthetically.

Woman Gymnast

A287

Designs: No. 1144, Gymnast on rings. No. 1145, Aerial split over balance beam, woman. No. 1146, Gymnast on parallel bars. No. 1147, Uneven bars, woman. No. 1148, Gymnast on horse.

1974, Jan. 1 Photo. **Perf. 11½x11**

1143	A287	8f light green & multi. (1)	11	11
1144	"	8f light violet & multi. (2)	11	11
1145	"	8f light blue & multi. (3)	11	11
1146	"	8f salmon & multi. (4)	11	11
1147	"	8f yellow & multi. (5)	11	11
1148	A287	8f lilac rose & multi. (6)	11	11
		Nos. 1143-1148 (6)	66	66

Girls Twirling Bamboo Diabolos—A288

Designs: No. 1149, Lion Dance (vert.). No. 1150, Handstand on chairs (vert.). No. 1152, Men balancing jar. No. 1153, Plate spinning (vert.). No. 1154, Twirling umbrella (vert.).

1974, Jan. 21 **Perf. 11**

1149	A288	8f brn. & multi. (1)	11	11
1150	"	8f Prussian blue & multi. (2)	11	11
1151	"	8f lilac & multi. (3)	11	11
1152	"	8f dull blue & multi. (4)	11	11
1153	"	8f olive green & multi. (5)	11	11
1154	"	8f gray & multi. (6)	11	11
		Nos. 1149-1154 (6)	66	66

Traditional acrobatics.

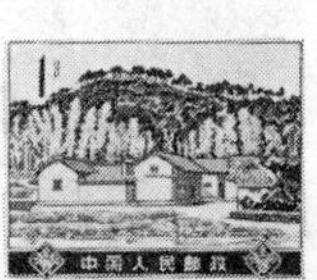

Shao Shan

A289

Transportation by Railroad

A290

Designs: 1½f, Site of 1st National Communist Party Congress. 2f, Peasant Movement Institute, Kwangchow. 3f, Headquarters of Nanchang Uprising. No. 1159, Great Hall of the People, Peking. 5f, View of Wen Chia Shih. No. 1162, Tien An Men. 10f, Tzeping in Chingkang Mountains. 20f, Site of Kutien Meeting. 22f, Tsunyi Conference site. 35f, Yenan (bridge). 43f, Hsi Pai Ho, Communist party meeting site. 50f, Fairy Cave, Lushan. 52f, Monument to People's Heroes. $2, Trucks on mountain road.

1974 Litho. **Perf. 11**

Without Gum

1155	A289	1f slate green & pale green	3	3
1156	"	1½f carmine & buff	3	3
1157	"	2f dark blue & pale green	3	3
1158	"	3f dk. olive & yel.	3	3
1159	"	4f red & yellow	6	6
1161	"	5f brown & lt. yellow	8	8
1162	"	8f dull magenta & buff	11	11
1167	"	10f blue & pink	15	15
1168	"	20f dark red & buff	30	30
1169	"	22f vio. & lt. yel.	32	30
1170	"	35f maroon & lt. yellow	52	50
1171	"	43f red brn. & buff	65	65
1172	"	50f dk. bl. & pink	*5.00*	*5.00*
1173	"	52f sepia & buff	78	75

Photogravure & Engraved

1177	A290	$1 multicolored	1.50	1.00
1178	"	$2 "	3.00	1.75
		Nos. 1155-1178 (16)	*12.59*	10.77

Capital Stadium

A290a

Design: 8f, Hotel Peking.

1974, Dec. 1 Photo. **Perf. 11**

Without Gum

1179	A290a	4f blk. & yellow green	6	*20*
1180	"	8f black & ultra.	11	11

"Veteran Secretary"

A291

Well Diggers

A292

Designs: Nos. 1183-1186 horizontal.

1974, Apr. 20 Photo. **Perf. 11**

Multicolored

1181	A291	8f *shown* (1)	11	11
1182	A292	8f *shown* (2)	11	11
1183	A291	8f *Spring hoeing* (3)	11	11
1184	"	8f *Farmers* (4)	11	11
1185	A292	8f *Farm* (5)	11	11
1186	A291	8f *Bumper crops* (6)	11	11
		Nos. 1181-1186 (6)	66	66

Paintings by farmers of Huhsien County, shown at exhibition in Peking.

Mailman on Motorcycle—A293

1974, May 15 Photo. **Perf. 11**

Multicolored

1187	A293	8f *shown* (1)	11	11
1188	"	8f *People of the world* (2)	11	11
1189	"	8f *Great Wall* (3)	11	11

Centenary of the Universal Postal Union.

Barefoot Doctor Inocculating Children—A294

Designs (Barefoot Doctors): No. 1191, Crossing stream at night to reach patient (vert.). No. 1192, Gathering herbs (vert.). No. 1193, Acupuncture treatment for farmer in the field.

Perf. 11x11½, 11½x11

1974, June 26 Photogravure

1190	A294	8f multi. (82)	11	11
1191	"	8f " (83)	11	11
1192	"	8f " (84)	11	11
1193	"	8f " (85)	11	11

Steel Worker Wang Chin-hsi—A295

1974, Sept. 30 Photo. *Perf. 11*

Designs: No. 1195, Workers studying Mao's writings around campfire. No. 1196, Drilling for oil in winter. No. 1197, Scientific industrial management. No. 1198, Oil derricks and farms. Numbered T.4.

No.	Type	Description	Unused	Used
1194	A295	8f multi. (5-1)	11	11
1195	"	8f " (5-2)	11	11
1196	"	8f " (5-3)	11	11
1197	"	8f " (5-4)	11	11
1198	"	8f " (5-5)	11	11
		Nos. 1194-1198 (5)	55	55

The workers of Taching as examples of achievement.

Members of Tachai Commune—A296

Designs: No. 1200, Farmers leveling mountains and fields in winter. No. 1201, Scientific farming. No. 1202, Trucks carrying surplus harvest. No. 1203, Young workers with banner. Numbered T.5.

1974, Sept. 30

No.	Type	Description	Unused	Used
1199	A296	8f multi. (5-1)	11	11
1200	"	8f " (5-2)	11	11
1201	"	8f " (5-3)	11	11
1202	"	8f " (5-4)	11	11
1203	"	8f " (5-5)	11	11
		Nos. 1199-1203 (5)	55	55

The farmers of Tachai as examples of achievement.

Arms of Republic and Members of Ethnic Grops—A297

Taching Steel Worker
A298

Designs: No. 1206, Tachai farm woman. No. 1207, Soldier, planes and ships. Numbered J.3.

1974, Oct. 1

No.	Type	Description	Unused	Used
1204	A297	8f multi. (1-1)	11	11
1205	A298	8f " (3-1)	11	11
1206	"	8f " (3-2)	11	11
1207	"	8f " (3-3)	11	11

People's Republic of China, 25th anniversary. Nos. 1205-1207 printed se-tenant.

Export Commodities Fair Building, Canton—A299

1974, Oct. 15

No.	Type	Description	Unused	Used
1208	A299	8f multicolored	11	11

Chinese Export Commodities Fair, Canton.

Guerrillas' Monument, Permet, Albania
A300

Albanian Patriots and Coat of Arms
A301

1974, Nov. 29 Photo. *Perf. 11½x11*

No.	Type	Description	Unused	Used
1209	A300	8f multicolored	*20*	20
1210	A301	8f "	*20*	20

Albania's liberation, 30th anniversary.

Water-cooled Generator—A302

Designs: No. 1212, Motorized rice sprouts transplanter. No. 1213, Universal cylindrical grinding machine. No. 1214, Open-air rock drill (vert.). All dated 1973.

Photogravure and Engraved

1974, Dec. 23 *Perf. 11*

No.	Type	Description	Unused	Used
1211	A302	8f vio. & multi. (78)	11	11
1212	"	8f yellow green & multi. (79)	11	11
1213	"	8f verm. & multi. (80)	11	11
1214	"	8f bl. & multi. (81)	11	11

Industrial products.

Congress Delegates—A303

Designs: No. 1216, Red flags, constitution and flowers. No. 1217, Worker, farmer and soldier, agriculture and industry. Numbered J.5.

1975, Jan. 25 Photo. *Perf. 11½*

No.	Type	Description	Unused	Used
1215	A303	8f gold & multi. (3-1)	11	11
1216	"	8f gold & multi. (3-2)	11	11
1217	"	8f gold & multi. (3-3)	11	11

Fourth National People's Congress, Peking.

Teacher Studying Revolutionary Works
A304

Designs: No. 1219, Teacher, children and horse. No. 1220, Outdoors class. No. 1221, Class held in boat. Numbered T.9.

1975, Mar. 8 Photo. *Perf. 11*

No.	Type	Description	Unused	Used
1218	A304	8f multi. (4-1)	11	11
1219	"	8f " (4-2)	11	11
1220	"	8f " (4-3)	11	11
1221	"	8f " (4-4)	11	11

Rural women teachers and for International Working Women's Day.

"Broad-sword," Encounter Position
A305

Designs: No. 1223, Exercise with 2 swords (woman). No. 1224, Graceful boxing (woman). No. 1225, Man leaping with spear. No. 1226, Woman holding cudgel. 43f, Two women with spears against man with cudgel.

1975, June 10 Photo. *Perf. 11x11½*

Size: 39x29mm.

No.	Type	Description	Unused	Used
1222	A305	8f red & multi. (6-1)	11	11
1223	"	8f red & multi. (6-2)	11	11
1224	"	8f red & multi. (6-3)	11	11
1225	"	8f red & multi. (6-4)	11	11
1226	"	8f red & multi. (6-5)	11	11

Size: 59x29mm.

No.	Type	Description	Unused	Used
1227	A305	43f red & multi. (6-6)	65	65
		Nos. 1222-1227 (6)	1.20	1.20

Wushu ("Kung Fu"), self-defense exercises. Tête bêche in sheets of 50 (5x10).

Mass Judgment and Criticisms
A306

Designs: No. 1229, Brigade leader writing wall newspaper. No. 1230, Study and criticism on battlefield (horiz.). No. 1231, Former "slave" led into battle by criticism of Lin Piao and Confucius (horiz.). Numbered T. 8.

Perf. 11½x11, 11x11½

1975, Aug. 20 Photogravure

No.	Type	Description	Unused	Used
1228	A306	8f red & multi. (4-1)	11	11
1229	"	8f " " (4-2)	11	11
1230	"	8f " " (4-3)	11	11
1231	"	8f " " (4-4)	11	11

Campaign to encourage criticism of Lin Piao and Confucius.

Athletes Studying Theory of Dictatorship of Proletariat—A307

Designs: No. 1232, Women athletes leading parade (vert.). No. 1234, Women volleyball players. No. 1235, Runner, soldier, farmer and worker (vert.). No. 1236, Young athlete and various sports. No. 1237, Athletes of various races and horse race. 35f, Children and diving tower (vert.). Numbered J. 6.

1975, Sept. 12 Photo. *Perf. 11½*

No.	Type	Description	Unused	Used
1232	A307	8f multi. (7-1)	11	11
1233	"	8f " (7-2)	11	11
1234	"	8f " (7-3)	11	11
1235	"	8f " (7-4)	11	11
1236	"	8f " (7-5)	11	11
1237	"	8f " (7-6)	11	11
1238	"	35f " (7-7)	52	50
		Nos. 1232-1238 (7)	1.18	1.16

3rd National Sports Meet.

Mountaineers
A308

Mt. Everest
A309

Design: No. 1240, Mountaineers raising Chinese flag on summit (horiz.). Numbered T.15.

Perf. 11½x11, 11x11½

1975 Photogravure

No.	Type	Description	Unused	Used
1239	A308	8f multi. (3-2)	11	11
1240	"	8f " (3-3)	11	11
1241	A309	43f " (3-1)	65	65

Chinese Mt. Everest expedition.

Agricultural Workers with Book—A310

Designs: No. 1243, Workers carrying load. No. 1244, Woman driving harvester combine. Numbered J.7.

1975, Oct. 1 *Perf. 11½*

No.	Type	Description	Unused	Used
1242	A310	8f multi. (3-1)	11	11
1243	"	8f " (3-2)	11	11
1244	"	8f " (3-3)	11	11

National Conference to promote learning from Tachai's achievements in agriculture.

Girl Giving Boy Red Scarf
A311

Designs (Children): No. 1246, Putting up wall posters criticizing Lin Piao and Confucius. No. 1247, Studying. No. 1248, Harvesting. 52f, Physical training. Numbered T.14.

1975, Dec. 1 Photo. *Perf. 11½*

No.	Type	Description	Unused	Used
1245	A311	8f multi. (5-1)	11	11
1246	"	8f " (5-2)	11	11
1247	"	8f " (5-3)	11	11
1248	"	8f " (5-4)	11	11
1249	"	52f " (5-5)	75	75
		Nos. 1245-1249 (5)	1.19	1.19

Moral, intellectual and physical progress of Chinese children.

Woman Plowing Rice Field
A312

Designs: No. 1251, Mechanized rice planting. No. 1252, Drainage and irrigation. No. 1253, Woman spraying insecticide over cotton field. No. 1254, Combine. Numbered T.13.

1975, Dec. 15 ***Perf. 11***

1250	A312	8f multi. (5-1)	11	11
1251	"	8f " (5-2)	11	11
1252	"	8f " (5-3)	11	11
1253	"	8f " (5-4)	11	11
1254	"	8f " (5-5)	11	11
		Nos. 1250-1254 (5)	55	55

Priority program of farm mechanization.

Farmland and Irrigation Canal A313

Designs of Nos. 1255-1270 numbered J.8.

1976, Feb. 20 **Photo.** ***Perf. 11½***

Multicolored

1255	A313	8f *shown* (16-1)	11	11
1256	"	8f *Irrigation canal* (16-2)	11	11
1257	"	8f *Fertilizer plant* (16-3)	11	11
1258	"	8f *Textile plant* (16-4)	11	11
1259	"	8f *Anshan Iron and Steel Co.* (16-5)	11	11
		Nos. 1255-1259 (5)	55	55

Nos. 1255-1270 commemorate fulfillment of 4th Five-year Plan.

1976, Apr. 9

Multicolored

1260	A313	8f *Coal freight trains* (16-6)	11	11
1261	"	8f *Hydroelectric station* (16-7)	11	11
1262	"	8f *Ship building* (16-8)	11	11
1263	"	8f *Oil industry* (16-9)	11	11
1264	"	8f *Pipe line and port* (16-10)	11	11
		Nos. 1260-1264 (5)	55	55

1976, June 12

Multicolored

1265	A313	8f *Train on viaduct* (16-11)	11	11
1266	"	8f *Scientific research* (16-12)	11	11
1267	"	8f *Classroom* (16-13)	11	11
1268	"	8f *Health Center* (16-14)	11	11
1269	"	8f *Apartment houses* (16-15)	11	11
1270	"	8f *Department store* (16-16)	11	11
		Nos. 1265-1270 (6)	66	66

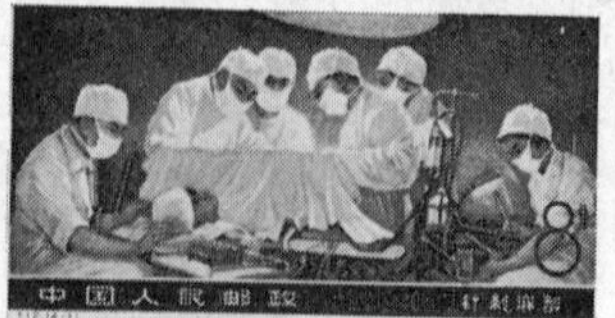

Heart Surgery with Acupuncture Anesthesia—A314

Designs (Operating Room and): No. 1272, Man driving tractor with severed arm restored. No. 1273, Man exercising broken arm in cast. No. 1274, Patient threading needle after cataract operation. Numbered T.12.

1976, Apr. 9 **Photo.** ***Perf. 11½***

1271	A314	8f brn. & multi. (4-1)	11	11
1272	A314	8f yel. green & multi. (4-2)	11	11
1273	"	8f blue green & multi. (4-3)	11	11
1274	"	8f violet blue & multi. (4-4)	11	11

Achievements in medical and health services.

Students in May 7 School—A315

Designs: No. 1276, Students as farm workers. No. 1277, Production brigade. Numbered J.9.

1976, May 7 **Photo.** ***Perf. 11½***

1275	A315	8f multi. (3-1)	11	11
1276	"	8f " (3-2)	11	11
1277	"	8f " (3-3)	11	11

10th anniversary of Chairman Mao's May 7 Directive.

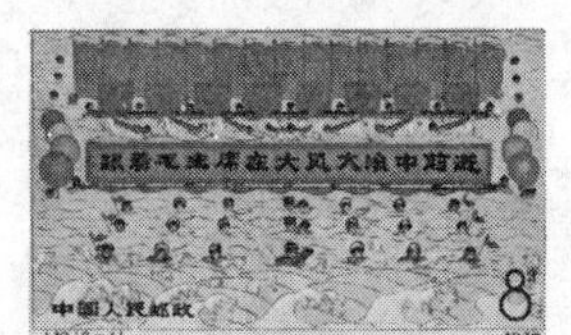

Mass Training in Swimming—A316

Designs: No. 1279, Swimmers crossing Yangtze River. No. 1280, Swimmers walking into the surf. Numbered J.10.

1976, July 16 **Photo.** ***Perf. 11½***

Size: 47x27mm.

1278	A316	8f multi. (3-1)	11	11

Size: 35x27mm.

1279	A316	8f multi. (3-2)	11	11
1280	"	8f multi. (3-3)	11	11

Chairman Mao's swim in Yangtze River, 10th anniversary.

Workers, Peasants and Soldiers Going to College—A317

Designs: No. 1282, Classroom. No. 1283, Instruction on construction site. No. 1284, Computer room. No. 1285, Graduates returning home. Numbered T.18.

1976, Sept. 6 **Photo.** ***Perf. 11½***

1281	A317	8f multi. (5-1)	11	11
1282	"	8f " (5-2)	11	11
1283	"	8f " (5-3)	11	11
1284	"	8f " (5-4)	11	11
1285	"	8f " (5-5)	11	11
		Nos. 1281-1285 (5)	55	55

Success of proletarian education system.

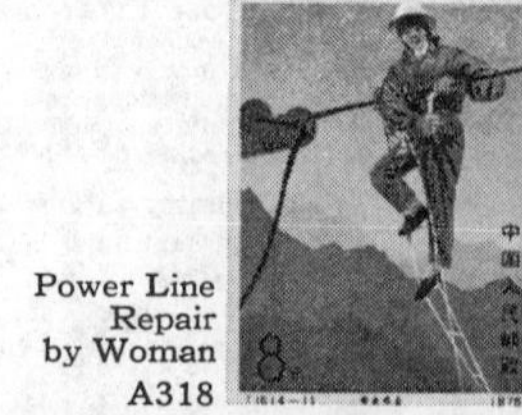

Power Line Repair by Woman A318

Designs: No. 1287, Insulator repair. No. 1288, Cherry picker. No. 1289, Transformer repair. Numbered T.16.

1976, Sept. 15

1286	A318	8f multi. (4-1)	11	11
1287	"	8f " (4-2)	11	11
1288	"	8f " (4-3)	11	11
1289	"	8f " (4-4)	11	11

Maintenance of high power lines.

Lu Hsun A319

Designs: No. 1291, Lu Hsun sick, writing in bed. No. 1292, Lu Hsun with worker, soldier and peasant. Numbered J.11.

Photogravure and Engraved

1976, Oct. 19 ***Perf. 11x11½***

1290	A319	8f multi. (3-1)	11	11
1291	"	8f " (3-2)	11	11
1292	"	8f " (3-3)	11	11

Lu Hsun (1881-1936), writer and revolutionary leader.

Old Farmer Tying Towel on Student's Head A320

Designs: No. 1294, Student teaching farm woman (horiz.). No. 1295, Students climbing mountain for new water resources. No. 1296, Student testing wheat (horiz.). 10f, Student feeding lamb. 20f, Frontier guards (horiz.). Numbered T.17.

1976, Dec. 22 **Photo.** ***Perf. 11½***

1293	A320	4f multi. (6-1)	6	6
1294	"	8f " (6-2)	11	11
1295	"	8f " (6-3)	11	11
1296	"	8f " (6-4)	11	11
1297	"	10f " (6-5)	15	15
1298	"	20f " (6-6)	30	30
		Nos. 1293-1298 (6)	84	84

Students' efforts to help poor country people.

Mao's Home, Shaoshan—A321

Designs: No. 1300, School building. No. 1301, Farmers' Association building. 10f, Railroad station. All in Shaoshan. Numbered T.11.

1976, Dec. 26 ***Perf. 11***

1299	A321	4f multi. (4-1)	6	6
1300	"	8f " (4-2)	11	11
1301	"	8f " (4-3)	11	11
1302	"	10f " (4-4)	15	15

Shaoshan, Mao's birthplace.

Chou En-lai A322

Designs: No. 1304, Chou giving report at 10th Party Congress. No. 1305, Chou with Wang Chin-hsi, famous oil worker (horiz.). No. 1306, Chou with people of Tachai, 1973 (horiz.). Numbered J.13.

1977, Jan. 8 **Photo.** ***Perf. 11½***

1303	A322	8f multi. (4-1)	11	11
1304	"	8f " (4-2)	11	11
1305	"	8f " (4-3)	11	11
1306	"	8f " (4-4)	11	11

Premier Chou En-lai (1898-1976), a founder of Chinese Communist Party, 1st death anniversary.

Liu Hu-lan, an Inspiration A323

Designs: No. 1307, Liu Hu-lan monument. No. 1308, Mao Tse-tung quotation: "A great life—a glorious death." Numbered J.12.

1977, Jan. 31

1307	A323	8f multi. (3-1)	11	11
1308	"	8f " (3-2)	11	11
1309	"	8f " (3-3)	11	11

Liu Hu-lan, Chinese heroine.

Uprising in Taiwan A324

Design: 10f, Gate of Heavenly Peace, Peking; Sun Moon Lake, Taiwan, Taiwanese people holding PRC flag. Numbered J.14.

1977, Feb. 28 **Photo.** ***Perf. 11***

1310	A324	8f multi. (2-1)	11	11
1311	"	10f " (2-2)	15	15

Uprising of the people of Taiwan, Feb. 28, 1947.

Sharpshooters—A325

Designs: No. 1313, Women horseback riders. No. 1314, Underground defense tunnel. Numbered T.10.

1977, Mar. 8 ***Perf. 11½***

1312	A325	8f multi. (3-1)	11	11
1313	"	8f " (3-2)	11	11
1314	"	8f " (3-3)	11	11

Militia women.

Forestry A326

Designs: 1f, Coal mining. 1½f, Sheepherding. 2f, Export (loading railroad car onto ship). 4f, Hydroelectric station. 5f, Fishery. 8f, Combine in field. 10f, Radio tower and mail truck. 20f, Steel production. 30f, Trucks on mountain road. 40f, Textiles. 50f, Tractor assembly line. 60f, Offshore oil rigs and birds, setting sun. 70f, Railroad bridge, Yangtze Gorge. No numbers.

1977 Photogravure *Perf. 11½*

1315	A326	1f yel. green, red & black	3	3
1316	"	1½f bl. grn., yel. grn. & brown	3	3
1317	"	2f org., bl. & blk.	4	4
1318	"	3f olive & dk. grn.	5	5
1319	"	4f lilac, orange & black	6	6
1320	"	5f light olive & ultramarine	8	8
1321	"	8f red & yellow	12	12
1322	"	10f lt. grn., orange & blue	15	15
1323	"	20fr orange, yellow & brown	30	30
1324	"	30f blue, lt. green & black	45	45
1325	"	40f multicolored	60	60
1326	"	50f citron, red & black	75	75
1327	"	60f purple, yellow & orange	90	90
1328	"	70f blue & multi.	1.05	1.00
		Nos. 1315–1328 (14)	4.61	4.56

Address by Party Committee
A327

Designs: No. 1330, Planting new rice fields. No. 1331, Farmers reading wall newspaper. No. 1332, Land reclamation. Numbered T.22.

1977, Apr. 9 *Perf. 11x11½*

1329	A327	8f multi. (4-1)	11	11
1330	"	8f " (4-2)	11	11
1331	"	8f " (4-3)	11	11
1332	"	8f " (4-4)	11	11

Building Tachai-type communities throughout China.

Worker at Microphone—A328

Designs: No. 1334, Drilling for oil during snowstorm. No. 1335, Crowd advancing under Red banner. No. 1336, Workers, industrial complex, rocket blast-off. Numbered J.15.

1977, Apr. 25 *Perf. 11*

1333	A328	8f multi. (4-1)	11	11
1334	"	8f " (4-2)	11	11
1335	"	8f " (4-3)	11	11
1336	"	8f " (4-4)	11	11

Conference on learning from Taching workers in industry.

Mongolians Hailing Anniversary
A329

Designs: 10f, Iron and steel complex, iron ore train. 20f, Cattle grazing in improved pasture. Numbered J.16.

1977, May 1 *Perf. 11x11½*

1337	A329	8f multi. (3-1)	11	11
1338	"	10f " (3-2)	15	15
1339	"	20f " (3-3)	30	30

30th anniversary of Inner Mongolian Autonomous Region.

1877 Flag of Romania and Oak Leaves
A330

Mihai Viteazu Memorial (16th Century Hero)
A331

Design: 10f, Battle of Smirdan, by N. Grigorescu. Numbered J.17.

1977, May 9 Photo. *Perf. 11*

1340	A330	8f multi. (3-1)	11	11
1341	A331	10f " (3-2)	15	15
1342	"	20f " (3-3)	30	30

Centenary of Romanian independence.

Yenan "Let 100 Flowers Bloom"
A332

Design: No. 1344, Hammer, sickle, gun and flowers; "Proletarian revolutionary literature will prosper." Numbered J.18.

1977, May, 23

1343	A332	8f green, red & gold	11	11
1344	"	8f lt. brown, red & gold	11	11

Yenan Forum on Literature and Art, 35th anniversary.

Chu Teh
A333

Designs: No. 1346, Chu Teh, last address to Congress. No. 1347, Chu Teh at his desk (horiz.). No. 1348, Chu Teh on horseback as commander of Red Army. Numbered J.19.

1977, July 6 Photo. *Perf. 11½*

1345	A333	8f multi. (4-1)	11	11
1346	"	8f " (4-2)	11	11
1347	"	8f " (4-3)	11	11
1348	"	8f " (4-4)	11	11

Chu Teh (1886–1976), Commander of Red Army, Chairman of National People's Congress.

Military under Mao's Banner
A334

Designs: No. 1350, Red Flag, Soldiers, Chingkang Mountains. No. 1351, Guerrilla fighters returning to base. No. 1352, Guerrillas crossing Yangtze. No. 1353, National defense. Numbered J.20.

1977, Aug. 1

1349	A334	8f multi. (5-1)	11	11
1350	"	8f " (5-2)	11	11
1351	"	8f " (5-3)	11	11
1352	"	8f " (5-4)	11	11
1353	"	8f " (5-5)	11	11
		Nos. 1349–1353 (5)	55	55

Liberation Army Day, 50th anniversary of People's Army.

Gate of Heavenly Peace, People and Red Flags—A335

Designs: No. 1355, People marching under Red Flag with Mao's portrait. No. 1356, People marching under Red Flag with hammer and sickle. Numbered J.23.

1977, Aug. 22 Photo. *Perf. 11½x11*

1354	A335	8f multi. (3-1)	11	11
1355	"	8f " (3-2)	11	11
1356	"	8f " (3-3)	11	11

11th National Congress of the Communist Party of China.

Chairman Mao
A336

Designs (Mao Portraits): No. 1358, as young man in Shansi. No. 1359, addressing Communist Party in Plenary Session. No. 1360, Proclaiming People's Republic at Gate of Heavenly Peace. No. 1361, at airport with Chou En-lai and Chu Teh (horiz.). No. 1362, Reviewing Army as old man. Numbered J.21.

1977, Sept. 9 Photo. *Perf. 11½*

1357	A336	8f multi. (6-1)	11	11
1358	"	8f " (6-2)	11	11
1359	"	8f " (6-3)	11	11
1360	"	8f " (6-4)	11	11
1361	"	8f " (6-5)	11	11
1362	"	8f " (6-6)	11	11
		Nos. 1357–1362 (6)	66	66

Mao-Tse-tung (1893–1976), first death anniversary.

Mao Memorial Hall—A337

Design: No. 1364, Chairman Hua's inscription. Numbered J.22.

1977, Sept. 9

1363	A337	8f lt. ultra. & multicolored	11	11
1364	"	8f lt. grn., tan & gold	11	11

Completion of Mao Memorial Hall.

Unused prices are for stamps that have been hinged.

Tractors Moving Drilling Tower
A338

Designs: No. 1366, Shui Pow Tsi oil well and women workers. No. 1367, Construction of oil pipe line, Taching, and silos. No. 1368, Tung Fang Hung oil refinery, Peking. No. 1369, Taching oil loaded into tanker in harbor. 20f, Off-shore drilling platform "Pohai No. 1." Numbered T.19.

1978, Jan. 31 Photo. *Perf. 11*

1365	A338	8f multi. (6-1)	11
1366	"	8f " (6-2)	11
1367	"	8f " (6-3)	11
1368	"	8f " (6-4)	11
1369	"	8f " (6-5)	11
1370	"	20f " (6-6)	30
		Nos. 1365–1370 (6)	85

Development of Chinese oil industry.

"Army Teaching Militia"—A339

Design: No. 1372, "Army helping with rice planting." Numbered T.23.

1978, Feb. 5 Photo. *Perf. 11*

1371	A339	8f multi. (2-1)	11
1372	"	8f " (2-2)	11

Army and people working as a family.

Red Flags, Mao Tse-tung
A340

Constitution and Red Flags
A341

Design: No. 1375, Atom symbol over symbols of agriculture and industry. All designs include Great Hall of the People, Peking, and flowers. Numbered J.24.

1978, Feb. 26

1373	A340	8f multi. (3-1)	11
1374	A341	8f " (3-2)	11
1375	A340	8f " (3-3)	11

5th National People's Congress.

Mao's Eulogy for Lei Feng
A342

Lei Feng, Studying Mao's Works
A343

Design: No. 1377, Chairman Hua's thoughts (5 lines). Numbered J.26.

1978, Mar. 5

1376	A342	8f gold & red (3-1)	11
1377	"	8f " " (3-2)	11
1378	A343	8f multi. (3-3)	11

Lei Feng (1940–1962), communist fighter; 15th anniversary of Chairman Mao's eulogy "Learn from Comrade Feng."

Hsiang Ching-yu A344 | Yang Kai-hui A345

Numbered J.27.

1978, Mar. 8

1379 A344 8f multi. (2-1) 11
1380 A345 8f " (2-2) 11

Hsiang Ching-yu, pioneer of Women's Movement, executed 1928; Yang Kai-hui, communist fighter, executed 1930.

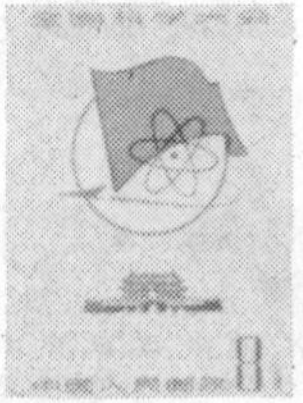

Conference Emblem
A346

Designs: No. 1382, Banners symbolizing industry, agriculture, defense and science. No. 1383, Red flag, atom symbol and globe. Numbered J.25.

1978, Mar. 18 Litho. *Perf. 11½x11*

1381 A346 8f gold & red (3-1) 11
1382 " 8f multi. (3-2) 11
1383 " 8f " (3-3) 11
a. Souvenir sheet of 3 75

National Science Conference. No. 1383a contains one each of Nos. 1381–1383 with simulated perforations; olive margin with atom symbols and inscription. Size: 140x 105mm. Sold for 50fen.

Release of Weather Balloon
A347

Weather Observations: No. 1385, Radar station, typhoon watch. No. 1386, Computer, weather maps. No. 1387, Local weather observers. No. 1388, Rockets intercepting hail clouds. Numbered T.24.

1978, Apr. 25 Photo. *Perf. 11x11½*

1384 A347 8f multi. (5-1) 11
1385 " 8f " (5-2) 11
1386 " 8f " (5-3) 11
1387 " 8f " (5-4) 11
1388 " 8f " (5-5) 11
Nos. 1384–1388 (5) 55

Galloping Horse A348 | Children Playing Soccer A349

Designs: Galloping Horses, by Hsu Pei-hung (1895–1953). 40f, 50f, 60f, 70f, $5, horiz. Numbered T.28.

Perf. 11½x11, 11x11½

1978, May 5

1389 A348 4f multi. (10-1) 5 5
1390 " 8f " (10-2) 11 11
1391 " 8f " (10-3) 11 11
1392 " 10f " (10-4) 15 15
1393 " 20f " (10-5) 30 30
1394 " 30f " (10-6) 45 45
1395 " 40f " (10-7) 60 60
1396 " 50f " (10-8) 75 75
1397 " 60f " (10-9) 90 90
1398 " 70f " (10-10) 1.05 1.00
Nos. 1389–1398 (10) 4.47 4.42

Souvenir Sheet

1399 A348 $5 multicolored 7.50

No. 1399 contains one stamp showing 4 horses (89x39mm.); black and silver margin shows floral damask pattern. Size: 147x98mm.

1978, June 1 *Perf. 11½*

Designs: No. 1401, Children on the beach. No. 1402, Little girls dancing. No. 1403, Children taking long walks. 20f, Children exercising for good health. Numbered T.21.

Size: 22x27mm.

1400 A349 8f multi. (5-2) 11
1401 " 8f " (5-3) 11
1402 " 8f " (5-4) 11
1403 " 8f " (5-5) 11

Size: 48x28mm.

1404 A349 20f multi. (5-1) 30
Nos. 1400–1404 (5) 74

Build up your health while young.

Synthetic Fiber Feeder
A350

Designs: No. 1406, Drawing out threads. No. 1407, Weaving. No. 1408, Dyeing and printing. No. 1409, Finished products. Numbered T.25.

1978, June 15 Photo. *Perf. 11½*

1405 A350 8f multi. (5-1) 11
1406 " 8f " (5-2) 11
1407 " 8f " (5-3) 11
1408 " 8f " (5-4) 11
1409 " 8f " (5-5) 11
Nos. 1405–1409 (5) 55

Chemical fiber industry. Nos. 1405–1409 printed se-tenant in continuous design.

Conference Emblem A351 | "Develop Economy and Ensure Supplies" A352

Numbered J.28.

1978, June 20 *Perf. 13*

1410 A351 8f multi. (2-1) 11
1411 A352 8f " (2-2) 11

National Conference on Learning from Taching and Tachai in Finance and Trade.

The only foreign revenue stamps listed in this Catalogue are those authorized for prepayment of postage.

New Pastures, Mongolia
A353

Designs: No. 1413, Kazakh shepherds selecting sheep for breeding. No. 1414, Mechanized shearing of sheep, Tibet, Numbered T.27.

1978, June 30 Photo. *Perf. 11½*

1412 A353 8f multi. (3-1) 11
1413 " 8f " (3-2) 11
1414 " 8f " (3-3) 11

Learning from Tachai in developing animal husbandry and new pastoral areas.

Coke Oven—A354

Designs: No. 1416, Iron furnace. No. 1417, Pouring steel. No. 1418, Steel rolling. No. 1419, Finished iron and steel products. Numbered T.26.

1978, July 22

1415 A354 8f multi. (5-1) 11
1416 " 8f " (5-2) 11
1417 " 8f " (5-3) 11
1418 " 8f " (5-4) 11
1419 " 8f " (5-5) 11
Nos. 1415–1419 (5) 55

Iron and steel industry.

Iron Fist to Prevent Revisionism A355 | Jug in Shape of Sheep A356

Designs: No. 1421, "Carrying forward revolutionary tradition." No. 1422, "Strenuous training in military skills to wipe out enemy." Numbered T.32.

1978, Aug. 1 Photo. *Perf. 11½*

1420 A355 8f multi. (3-1) 11
1421 " 8f " (3-2) 11
1422 " 8f " (3-3) 11

"Learn from Hard-boned 6th Company." (A military unit since 1939).

1978, Aug. 26

Arts and Crafts: 4f, Giant lion (toy; horiz.). No. 1425, Rhinoceros (lacquer ware; horiz). 10f, Cat (embroidery). 20f, Bag (weaving; horiz.). 30f, Teapot in shape of peacock (cloisonné). 40f, Plate with lotus, and swan-shaped box (lacquer ware; horiz.). 50f, Dragon flying in sky (ivory). 60f, Sun rising (jade; horiz.). 70f, Flight to human world (ivory). $3, Flying fairies (arts and crafts; horiz.). Numbered T.29.

1423 A356 4f multi. (10-1) 6 6
1424 " 8f " (10-2) 11 11
1425 " 8f " (10-3) 11 11
1426 " 10f " (10-4) 15 15
1427 " 20f " (10-5) 30 30
1428 " 30f " (10-6) 45 45
1429 A356 40f multi. (10-7) 60 60
1430 " 50f " (10-8) 75 75
1431 " 60f " (10-9) 90 90
1432 " 70f " (10-10) 1.05 1.00
Nos. 1423–1432 (10) 4.48 4.43

Souvenir Sheet

1433 A356 $3 multicolored 4.75

No. 1433 contains one stamp (85x36 mm.). Gold decorative margin. Size: 139x90mm.

Women, Atom Symbol, Rocket and Wheat
A357

1978, Sept. 8 Photo. *Perf. 11*

1434 A357 8f multicolored 11

4th National Women's Congress.

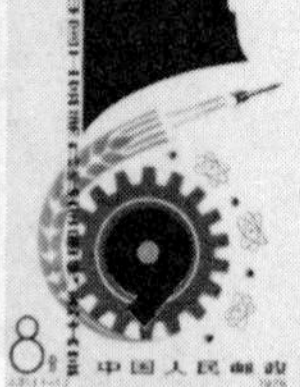

Ginseng A358 | Flag, Wheat, Cogwheel, Plane, Atom Symbols A359

Medicinal Plants: No. 1436, Horn of plenty. No. 1437, Blackberry lily. No. 1438, Balloonflower. 55f, Rhododendron dauricum. Numbered T.30.

1978, Sept. 15

1435 A358 8f multi. (5-1) 11
1436 " 8f " (5-2) 11
1437 " 8f " (5-3) 11
1438 " 8f " (5-4) 11
1439 " 55f " (5-5) 82
Nos. 1435–1439 (5) 1.26

1978, Oct. 11 Photo. *Perf. 11*

1440 A359 8f multicolored 11

9th National Trade Union Congress.

Youth League Emblem
A360

1978, Oct. 16

1441 A360 8f multicolored 11

10th National Communist Youth League Congress.

Chinese and Japanese Girls Exchanging Gifts
A361

Great Wall and Mt. Fuji
A362

1978, Oct. 22

1442	A361	8f multicolored		11
1443	A362	55f	"	82

Signing of Sino-Japanese Peace and Friendship Treaty.

Moslem, Chinese and Mongolian People
A363

Chinsha River Bridge, West Szechuan
A364

Designs: No. 1445, Loading coal at Holan Mountain. 10f, Irrigated rice fields and boxthorn. Numbered J.29.

1978, Oct. 25

1444	A363	8f multi.		(3-1)	11
1445	"	8f	"	(3-2)	11
1446	"	10f	"	(3-3)	15

20th anniversary of founding of Ningsia Moslem Autonomous Region.

1978, Nov. 1 Photo. *Perf. 11½x11*

Highway Bridges: No. 1448, Hsinhong bridge, Wuhsi. No. 1449, Chiuhsikou bridge, Fengdu. No. 1450, Chinsha River bridge, West Szechuan. 60f, Shangyeh bridge, Sanmen. $2, Hsiang-kiang River bridge. Numbered T.31.

1447	A364	8f multi.		(5-1)	12
1448	"	8f	"	(5-2)	12
1449	"	8f	"	(5-3)	12
1450	"	8f	"	(5-4)	12
1451	"	60f	"	(5-5)	90
	Nos. 1447-1451 (5)				1.38

Souvenir Sheet

1452	A364	$2 multicolored	3.20

No. 1452 contains one stamp (86x37 mm.). Ultramarine, white and gold margin shows tiny boats. Size: 145x69mm.

Mechanical Transplanting of Rice Seedlings
A365

Paintings: No. 1454, Spraying fields. No. 1455, Seed selection. No. 1456, Trade. No. 1457, Delivery of public grain in city. Numbered T.34.

1978, Nov. 30 *Perf. 11½*

1453	A365	8f multi.		(5-1)	12
1454	"	8f	"	(5-2)	12
1455	"	8f	"	(5-3)	12
1456	"	8f	"	(5-4)	12
1457	"	8f	"	(5-5)	12
	Nos. 1453-1457 (5)				60

Agricultural progress. Nos. 1453-1457 printed se-tenant in continuous design.

Dancers and Fireworks—A366

Designs: No. 1459, Industry (vert.). 10f, Agriculture (vert.). Numbered J.33.

1978, Dec. 11 Photo. *Perf. 11*

1458	A366	8f multi.		(3-1)	12
1459	"	8f	"	(3-2)	12
1460	"	10f	"	(3-3)	15

20th anniversary of Kwangsi Chuang Autonomous Region.

Miners with Pneumatic Drill
A367

Mine Development: 4f, Old Tibetan peasant reporting to surveyor. 10f, Open-cut mining with power shovel. 20f, Loaded electric train in pit. Numbered T.20.

1978, Dec. 29 Photo. & Engr.

1461	A367	4f multi.		(4-1)	6
1462	"	8f	"	(4-2)	12
1463	"	10f	"	(4-3)	15
1464	"	20f	"	(4-4)	30

Golden Pheasants Roosting on Rock
A368

Golden Pheasants: 8f, In flight. 45f, Seeking food. Numbered T.35.

1979, Jan. 25 Photo. *Perf. 11½*

1465	A368	4f multi.		(3-1)	6
1466	"	8f	"	(3-2)	12
1467	"	45f	"	(3-3)	65

AIR POST STAMPS

Mail Plane and Temple of Heaven
AP1

1951, May 1 Engraved *Perf. 12½*

C1	AP1	$1000 carmine	5	10
C2	"	$3000 green	10	10
C3	"	$5000 orange	5	15
C4	"	$10,000 violet brown & green	8	15
C5	"	$30,000 dk. bl. & brn.	70	35
		Nos. C1-C5 (5)	98	85

Planes at Airport
AP2

Designs: 28f, Plane over winding mountain highway. 35f, Plane over railroad yard. 52f, Plane over ship.

1957-58 *Perf. 14*

C6	AP2	16f indigo	10.00	5
C7	"	28f olive black	10.00	10
C8	"	35f slate	10.00	1.00
C9	"	52f Prus. blue ('58)	10.00	20

POSTAGE DUE STAMPS

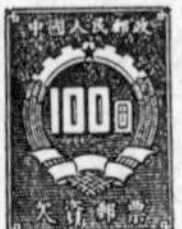

Grain and Cogwheel
D1

Numeral
D2

1950, Sept. 1 Typo. *Perf. 12½*

J1	D1	$100 steel blue	5	5
J2	"	$200 " "	5	5
J3	"	$500 " "	5	5
J4	"	$800 " "	2.00	5
J5	"	$1000 " "	15	10
J6	"	$2000 " "	15	20
J7	"	$5000 " "	10	25
J8	"	$8000 " "	10	40
J9	"	$10,000 " "	20	50
		Nos. J1-J9 (9)	2.85	1.65

1954, Aug. 18 Litho. *Perf. 14*

J10	D2	$100 red	15	8
J11	"	$200 "	15	8
J12	"	$500 "	15	8
J13	"	$800 "	5	8
J14	"	$1600 "	5	15
		Nos. J10-J14 (5)	55	47

MILITARY STAMPS

Red Star, 8-1 in Center
M1

1953, Aug. 1 Lithographed *Perf. 14*

M1	M1	$800 yellow & red (Army)	6.50	7.50
M2	"	$800 dp. purple, orange & red (Air Force)	90.00	
M3	"	$800 org., blue & red (Navy)		

The status of No. M3 is in question.

NORTHEAST CHINA

The Northeast Liberation Area included the provinces of Liaoning, Kirin, Jehol and Heilungkiang—the area generally known as Manchuria under the Japanese. The first postwar issues were local overprints on stamps of Manchukuo. In early 1946, a Ministry of Posts and Telegraphs served the areas already liberated, and in August, 1946, a Communications Committee of the Political Council was established. In June, 1947, these postal services were subordinated to the Harbin General Post Office, and this was extended to Changchun on Oct. 22, 1948, and to Mukden on Nov. 4, 1948. It was rapidly extended to cover all Manchuria.

All Stamps Issued without Gum

Mao Tse-tung
A1 A2

Lithographed

1946, Feb. *Perf. 11* Unwmkd.

1L1	A1	$1 violet	4.50	4.50
1L2	A2	$2 vermilion	25	*1.00*
1L3	"	$5 orange	25	*1.00*
		a. Booklet pane of 6	60.00	
1L4	A2	$10 blue	25	*1.00*
		a. Booklet pane of 6	60.00	

Imperfs. exist. Price, set $25.

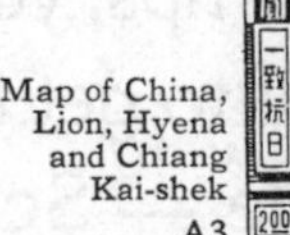

Map of China, Lion, Hyena and Chiang Kai-shek
A3

1946, Dec. 12 *Perf. 10½*

1L5	A3	$1 violet	1.50	1.50
1L6	"	$2 orange	1.50	1.50
1L7	"	$5 orange brown	3.00	3.00
1L8	"	$10 light green	6.00	6.00
		a. Imperf. pair	25.00	

10th anniversary of the capture of Chiang Kai-shek at Sian.

Railroad Workers, Chengchow
A4

1947, Feb. 7 *Perf. 10½*

1L9	A4	$1 pink	20	20
1L10	"	$2 dull green	20	20
1L11	"	$5 pink	40	40
1L12	"	$10 dull green	60	60

24th anniversary of the Chengchow railroad workers' strike and massacre.

Women (Worker, Soldier and Farmer)
A5

Wmkd. Chinese Characters in Sheet

1947, Mar. 8 *Perf. 10½x11*

1L13	A5	$5 brick red	70	70
1L14	"	$10 brown	70	70

International Women's Day, March 8.

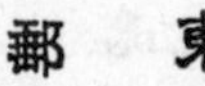

Same Overprinted in Green ("Northeast Postal Service")

北 政

1947, Mar. 18

1L15	A5	$5 brick red	2.25	2.25
1L16	"	$10 brown	2.25	2.25

Children Carrying Banner
A6

1947, Apr. 4 *Perf. 11x10½*

Granite Paper

1L17	A6	$5 rose red	1.00	1.00
1L18	"	$10 light green	50	50
1L19	"	$30 orange	1.50	1.50

Children's Day.

政 伍
拾
作 圓
50.00

Nos. 1L1-1L2 Surcharged in Red, Brown, Black, Blue or Green

1947, Apr. *Perf. 11* Unwmkd.

1L20	A1	$50 on $1 vio. (R)	12.00	10.00
		a. Brown surcharge	12.00	10.00
1L21	A2	$50 on $2 verm.	12.00	10.00
		a. Brown surcharge	12.00	10.00
1L22	A1	$100 on $1 violet	12.00	10.00
		a. Green surcharge	12.00	10.00
1L23	A2	$100 on $2 vermilion (B1)	12.00	10.00
		a. Green surcharge	12.00	10.00

Farmer and Worker
A7

Ax Severing Chain
A8

Wmkd. Chinese Characters in Sheet

1947, May 1 *Perf. 10½x11*

Granite Paper

1L24	A7	$10 orange red	30	30
1L25	"	$30 ultramarine	50	50
1L26	"	$50 gray green	80	80

Labor Day.
Exists imperf. Price, set, pairs $75.

1947, May 4 *Perf. 11*

1L27	A8	$10 bright green	60	60
1L28	"	$30 brown	70	70
1L29	"	$50 violet	80	80

28th anniversary of the students' revolt at Peking University against the 1918 peace treaty.
Exist imperf. Price, set, pairs $75.

Workers with Banner: "Oppose Imperialist Aggression"
A9

1947, May 30 *Perf. 10½x11*

Banner in Red

1L30	A9	$2 bright lilac	1.25	1.25
1L31	"	$5 bright green	1.25	1.25
1L32	"	$10 yellow	1.25	1.25
1L33	"	$20 violet	1.25	1.25
1L34	"	$30 red brown	1.25	1.25
1L35	"	$50 dark blue	1.25	1.25
1L36	"	$100 brown	1.25	1.25
		a. Souvenir sheet of 7	60.00	
		Nos. 1L30-1L36 (7)	8.75	8.75

22nd anniversary of the Shanghai-Nanking Road incident. No. 1L36a is on granite paper and contains 7 imperf. stamps similar to Nos. 1L30-1L36. Multicolored marginal inscription. Size: 215x158mm.

Nos. 1L30-1L36 exist imperf. on ordinary paper. Price, set, pairs $75.

Mao and Communist Flag
A10

1947, July 1 *Perf. 10½x11*

1L37	A10	$10 red	3.00	3.00
1L38	"	$30 bright lilac	3.00	3.00
1L39	"	$50 rose brown	7.00	7.00
1L40	"	$100 vermilion	7.00	7.00

26th anniversary of the founding of the Chinese Communist Party.

Hand Holding Rifle
A11

1947, July 7 *Perf. 10½*

1L41	A11	$10 orange	2.25	2.25
1L42	"	$30 green	2.25	2.25
1L43	"	$50 dull blue	2.25	2.25
1L44	"	$100 brown	2.25	2.25
		a. Souvenir sheet of 4	25.00	

10th anniversary of the start of Sino-Japanese War. No. 1L44a contains 4 imperf. stamps similar to Nos. 1L41-1L44. Brown marginal inscription. Size: 149x107mm.

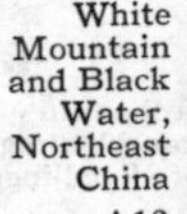

White Mountain and Black Water, Northeast China
A12

Wmkd. Zigzag Lines (141)

1947, Aug. 15 *Perf. 10½*

1L45	A12	$10 brown orange	2.00	2.00
1L46	"	$30 lt. olive green	2.00	2.00
1L47	"	$50 blue green	4.50	3.50
1L48	"	$100 sepia	4.50	3.50

2nd anniversary of the reoccupation of Northeast China and the surrender of Japan.

政 拾
作 圓
10.00

Nos. 1L1-1L2 Surcharged in Black, Red, Green or Blue

1947, Aug. 29 *Perf. 11* Unwmkd.

1L49	A1	$5 on $1 violet	17.50	17.50
		a. Red surcharge	17.50	17.50
		b. Green surcharge	17.50	17.50
1L50	A2	$10 on $2 verm.	17.50	17.50
		a. Blue surcharge	17.50	17.50
		b. Green surcharge	17.50	17.50

Map of Manchuria
A13

1947, Sept. 18 **Unwmkd.**

White Paper

1L51 A13 $10 gray green 3.00 3.00
1L52 " $20 rose lilac 3.00 3.00
1L53 " $30 black brown 7.50 7.50
1L54 " $50 carmine 7.50 7.50

16th anniversary of Japanese attack on Mukden, Sept. 18, 1931.

Northeast Political Council Offices
A14

Mao Tse-tung
(Value figures repeated)
A15

1947, Oct. 10 ***Perf. 10½***

1L55 A14 $10 yel. orange 25.00 15.00
1L56 " $20 rose red 25.00 20.00
1L57 " $100 brown 25.00 25.00

35th anniversary of the founding of the Chinese Republic.

1947, Oct. 10 White Paper ***Perf. 11***

1L58 A15 $1 brown 50 *1.50*
1L59 " $5 gray green 50 *1.50*
1L60 " $10 bright green 6.25 5.50
1L61 " $15 bluish lilac 6.25 5.50
1L62 " $20 bright rose 85 1.50
1L63 " $30 green 1.00 2.00
1L64 " $50 black brown 6.25 5.50
1L65 " $90 blue 1.00 2.00

Cream Newsprint

1L66 A15 $100 red 1.00 2.00
1L67 " $500 red orange 13.00 11.00
Nos. 1L58-1L67 (10) 36.60 *38.00*

Type A22 resembles A15, but has "YUAN" at upper right.

1947, Nov. **Redrawn**

White Paper

1L68 A15 $50 light green 75 75
1L69 " $150 red orange 1.25 1.25
1L70 " $250 bluish lilac 1.50 2.50
a. Wmkd. Chinese characters 1.50 1.50

1947, Dec. **Unwmkd.**

Newsprint

1L71 A15 $300 green 17.50 17.50
1L72 " $1,000 yellow 50 1.00
Nos. 1L68-1L72 (5) 21.50 23.00

Panel below portrait 8½x3mm. on Nos. 1L68-1L70; 7x3mm. on No. 1L58-1L67. Nos. 1L68-1L70 have different ornamental border.

Nos. 1L71-1L72 without zeros for cents.

Hand Holding Torch
A16

1947, Dec. 12 ***Perf. 11*** **Unwmkd.**

White Paper

1L73 A16 $30 rose red 2.50 1.60
1L74 " $90 dark blue 2.50 3.00
1L75 " $150 green 2.50 5.25

11th anniversary of the capture of Chiang Kai-shek at Sian.

Tomb of Gen. Li Chao-lin
A17

Globe and Banner
A18

Perf. 10½x11

1948, Mar. 9 **Unwmkd.**

1L76 A17 $30 green 5.00 6.00
a. Granite paper, wmkd. 5.00 6.00
1L77 A17 $150 violet gray 5.00 6.00
a. Granite paper, wmkd. 5.00 6.00

2nd anniversary of the assassination of Gen. Li Chao-lin, Commander of 3rd Army.

Wmkd. Chinese Characters in Sheet

1948, May 1 ***Perf. 11x10½***

1L78 A18 $50 red 5.00 5.50
1L79 " $150 green 2.50 3.50
1L80 " $250 lilac 2.00 5.00

Labor Day.

Student, Torch and Banner
A19

Perf. 10½x11

1948, May 4 **Unwmkd.**

Granite paper

1L81 A19 $50 green 4.25 3.50
1L82 " $150 brown 4.25 3.50
1L83 " $250 red 4.25 3.50

Youth Day, May 4.

Nos. 1L58, 1L61, 1L59, 1L63, 1L65, 1L2-1L4, 1L68-1L69, 1L71 Surcharged in Black, Blue, Red or Green

壹佰圓 100.00 改作

1948-49 ***Perf. 11***

1L84 A15 $100 on $1 brown purple 17.50 17.50
a. Blue surcharge 17.50 17.50
1L85 A15 $100 on $15 bluish lilac 17.50 17.50
a. Blue surcharge 17.50 17.50
1L86 A15 $300 on $5 gray green (R) 22.00 22.00
1L87 " $300 on $30 green (R) 22.00 22.00
1L88 " $300 on $90 bl. (R) 22.00 22.00
1L89 A2 $500 on $2 verm. 2.00 2.00
1L90 " $1500 on $5 org. (Bl) 2.50 2.50
1L91 " $2500 on $10 bl. (R) 3.25 3.25
1L92 A15 $500 on $50 light grn. (R, '49) 3.25 3.25
1L93 " $1500 on $150 red org. (Gr, '49) 5.50 5.50
1L94 " $2500 on $300 green ('49) 6.50 6.50
Nos. 1L84-1L94 (11) 124.00 124.00

Crane Operator
A20

Wmkd. Chinese Characters in Sheet

1948, May ***Perf. 11***

1L95 A20 $100 red & pink 50 50
1L96 A20 $300 violet brown & yellow 1.50 1.50
1L97 " $500 blue & green 1.50 1.50

6th All-China Labor Conference, Harbin.

Farmer, Worker and Soldier Saluting
A21

Mao Tse-tung
("YUAN" at upper right)
A22

Perf. 11x10½

1948, Dec. 3 **Unwmkd.**

White paper

1L98 A21 $500 vermilion 2.00 1.75
1L99 " $1500 brt. green 6.50 5.00
1L100 " $2500 brown 10.00 7.50

Liberation of Northeast China.

1949, Feb. ***Perf. 11***

1L101 A22 $300 olive 25 25
1L102 " $500 orange 2.00 1.00
1L103 " $1500 blue green 20 40
1L104 " $4500 brown 20 55
1L105 " $6500 dark blue 20 70
Nos. 1L101-1L105 (5) 2.85 2.90

See also type A15.

Workers, Globe and Flag
A23

Fields and Factories
A24

1949, May 1 ***Perf. 11½***

1L106 A23 $1000 red & dull blue 15 20
1L107 " $1500 red & pale blue 20 25
1L108 " $4500 rose & olive brown 25 30
1L109 " $6500 dull orange & green 30 40
1L110 " $10,000 maroon & ultra. 45 55
Nos. 1L106-1L110 (5) 1.35 1.70

Labor Day.

1949 ***Perf. 10, 11***

1L111 A24 $5000 Prus. blue 3.50 50
1L112 " $10,000 org. brn. 50 50
1L113 " $50,000 green 50 2.00
1L114 " $100,000 violet 50 3.00

Production in agriculture and industry.

Workers with Flags
A25

Heroes' Monument, Harbin
A26

1949, July 1 ***Perf. 11***

1L115 A25 $1500 violet, light blue & red 35 35
1L116 " $4500 dk. brn., lt. bl. & verm. 45 45
1L117 " $6500 gray, lt. blue & rose red 55 55

28th anniversary of the founding of the Chinese Communist Party.

1949, Aug. 15 ***Perf. 11½x11***

1L118 A26 $1500 brick red 35 35
1L119 " $4500 yellow green 45 45
1L120 " $6500 light blue 1.50 1.50

4th anniversary of the Reoccupation, and the surrender of Japan.

東北貼用
(enlarged)
"Northeast Postal Service"

The following commemorative issues are similar to those of the People's Republic of China, with the 4 characters shown added in different sizes and various arrangements. Reprints were also issued similar to those of the PRC.

Chinese Lantern Type of PRC, 1949

1949, Sept. 12 **Litho.** ***Perf. 12½***

1L121 A1 $1000 deep blue 3.00 1.25
1L122 " $1500 scarlet 3.00 1.25
1L123 " $3000 green 3.00 1.75
1L124 " $4500 maroon 3.00 2.00

First session of Chinese People's Political Conference.

Reprints exist. Price, set, 35 cents.

Factory
A27

1949, Oct. ***Perf. 11x10½***

1L125 A27 $1500 orange 35 30

Nos. 1L101, 1L103-1L105, 1L125 Surcharged in Black or Green

貳仟圓 2000 改作

1949, Nov. 20

1L126 A22 $2000 on $300 olive 10.00 2.50
1L127 " $2000 on $4500 purple brown (G) 45.00 10.00
1L128 " $2500 on $1500 blue green 1.00 2.50
1L129 " $2500 on $6500 blue 27.50 8.00
1L130 A27 $5000 on $1500 orange 40 50
1L131 A22 $20,000 on $4500 purple brown 25 2.25
1L132 " $35,000 on $300 olive 25 2.25
Nos. 1L126-1L132 (7) 84.40 28.00

Globe and Hammer Type of PRC

1949, Nov. 15 ***Perf. 12½***

1L133 A2 $5000 crimson 40.00 20.00
1L134 " $20,000 deep green 40.00 25.00
1L135 " $35,000 violet blue 40.00 30.00

Asiatic and Australasian Congress of the World Federation of Trade Unions, Peking.

Reprints exist. Price, set, $12.

Mao and Conference Hall Types of PRC

1950, Feb. 1 ***Perf. 14***

1L136 A3 $1000 vermilion 4.00 6.00
1L137 " $1500 deep blue 4.00 6.00
1L138 A4 $5000 dark violet brown 8.00 12.00
1L139 " $20,000 green 6.00 6.00

First session of Chinese People's Political Conference.

Reprints exist. Price, set, 30 cents.

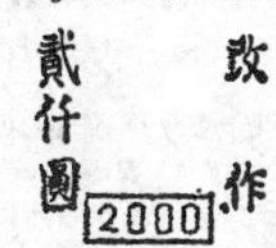

Gate of Heavenly Peace (same size)
A28

1950 *Perf. 10½*

Narrow horizontal shading

1L140	A28	$500 olive	1.50	1.00
1L141	"	$1000 orange	10	15
1L142	"	$1000 lilac rose	1.00	75
1L143	"	$2000 gray green	10	15
1L144	"	$2500 yellow	10	15
1L145	"	$5000 dp. orange	1.25	20
1L146	"	$10,000 brn. org.	1.50	1.00
1L147	"	$20,000 vio. brown	10	20
1L148	"	$35,000 deep blue	10	35
1L149	"	$50,000 brt. green	25	70
		Nos. 1L140–1L149 (10)	6.00	4.65

Flag and Mao Type of PRC

1950, July 1 *Perf. 14*

Yellow Stars

1L150	A7	$5000 grn. & red	6.00	1.00
1L151	"	$10,000 brn. & red	6.00	1.50
1L152	"	$20,000 dark brown & red	6.00	2.50
1L153	"	$30,000 dk. violet bl. & red	6.00	3.00

Inauguration of the People's Republic, Oct. 1, 1949.

Reprints exist. Price, set, 35 cents.

Picasso Dove Type of PRC

1950, Aug. 1 Engraved *Perf. 14*

1L154	A8	$2500 brown	2.00	2.00
1L155	"	$5000 green	2.00	2.00
1L156	"	$20,000 blue	2.00	2.00

World Peace Campaign.

Reprints exist. Price, set, 35 cents.

Flag Type of PRC

1950, Oct. 1 Engraved & Litho.

Flag in Red & Yellow

1L157	A9	$1000 purple	6.00	2.00
1L158	"	$2500 org. brown	6.00	2.50
1L159	"	$5000 dp. green	6.00	3.00
1L160	"	$10,000 olive	6.00	4.00
1L161	"	$20,000 blue	6.00	6.00
		Nos. 1L157–1L161 (5)	30.00	17.50

First anniversary of the Chinese People's Republic. Size of No. 1L159: 38x47mm., others 26x33mm. Reprints exist. Price, set, 35 cents.

Postal Conference Type of PRC

1950, Nov. 1 Lithographed

1L162	A11	$2500 green & dp. orange	3.00	1.00
1L163	"	$5000 car. & grn.	3.00	2.00

All-China Postal Conference, Peking.

Reprints exist. Price, set, 25 cents.

Gate of Heavenly Peace (same size)
A29

1950 *Perf. 10½*

Wide horizontal shading

1L164	A29	$5000 orange	40	1.25
1L165	"	$30,000 scarlet	25	*3.00*
1L166	"	$100,000 violet	2.00	3.00

Wmkd. Zigzag Lines (141)

1L167	A29	$250 brown	40	50
1L168	"	$500 olive	40	50
1L169	"	$1000 lilac rose	25	50
1L170	"	$2000 dull green ('51)	10	25
1L171	A29	$2500 yellow	15	25
1L172	"	$5000 orange	20	50
1L173	"	$10,000 brn. orange ('51)	30	50
1L174	"	$12,500 maroon	10	50
1L175	"	$20,000 dp. brown ('51)	30	1.00
		Nos. 1L164–1L175 (12)	4.85	*11.75*

A $50,000 green was prepared, but not issued. Price $5.00.

Stalin and Mao Tse-tung Type of PRC

Engraved

1950, Dec. 1 *Perf. 14* Unwmkd.

1L176	A12	$2500 red	1.40	1.00
1L177	"	$5000 dp. green	1.40	1.50
1L178	"	$20,000 dark blue	1.40	2.00

Signing of the Sino-Soviet Treaty of Friendship, Alliance and Mutual Assistance.

Reprints exist. Price, set, 40 cents.

PARCEL POST STAMPS

Locomotive
PP1

Lithographed

1951 *Perf. 10½, Imperf.*

1LQ1	PP1	$100,000 purple	
1LQ2	"	$300,000 brown	
1LQ3	"	$500,000 greenish blue	
1LQ4	"	$1,000,000 verm.	

PORT ARTHUR AND DAIREN

The Liaoning Postal Administration was established on April 1, 1946, in accordance with the Sino-Soviet Treaty, but was renamed one week later the Port Arthur and Dairen Postal Administration. On Apr. 3, 1947, it was combined with telecommunications and renamed the Kwantung Post and Telegraph General Administration. On May 1, 1949, the name was again changed to Port Arthur and Dairen Post and Telegraph Administration. Postal tariffs were based on local currency and both Manchukuo and Japanese stamps were overprinted for use.

Manchukuo Nos. 162 and 94 Handstamp Surcharged in Violet ("Liaoning Post")

1946, Mar. 15

2L1	A19	20f on 30f buff	40.00	40.00
2L2	A18	1y on 12f orange	25.00	25.00

Same Surcharge on Japan Nos. 260, 337, 195, 244, 263, 342 in Violet, Red or Black

1946, Apr. 1

2L3	A85	20f on 3s grn.(V)	10.00	10.00
2L4	A151	1y on 17s gray violet (R)	7.00	7.00
2L5	A57	5y on 6s car.	15.00	15.00
2L6	"	5y on 6s crim.	15.00	15.00
2L7	A88	5y on 6s orange	10.00	10.00
2L8	A154	15y on 40s dark violet	65.00	65.00
		Nos. 2L1–2L8 (8)	187.00	187.00

Surcharge sideways on Nos. 2L5–2L6.

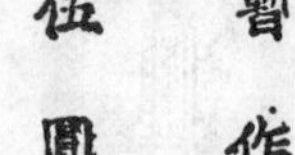

Japan Nos. 260 and 263 Surcharged

1946, Apr.

2L9	A85	1y on 3s green	75.00	
2L10	A88	5y on 6s orange	45.00	

Sha Ho Kow (suburb of Dairen) issue.

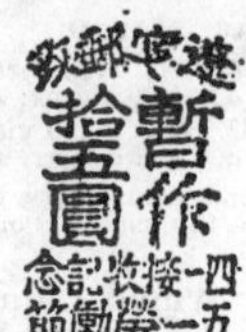

Manchukuo Nos. 84, 88 and 98 Handstamp Surcharged in Green, Red or Black

1946, May 1

2L11	A16	1y on 1f red brown (G)	17.50	17.50
2L12	A18	5y on 4f light olive green (R)	25.00	25.00
2L13	A19	15y on 30f chestnut brown	50.00	50.00

Transfer of postal administration and Labor Day.

Manchukuo Nos. 159, 86 and 94 Surcharged in Green, Red or Black

1946, July 7

2L14	A17	1y on 6f crimson rose (G)	45.00	35.00
2L15	"	5y on 2f light green (R)	70.00	55.00
2L16	A18	15y on 12f dp. org.	95.00	75.00

9th anniversary of the outbreak of war with Japan.

Manchukuo Nos. 94, 84 and 158 Surcharged in Black, Green or Red

1946, Aug. 15

2L17	A18	1y on 12f deep orange (B)	30.00	20.00
2L18	A16	5y on 1f red brown (G)	55.00	40.00
2L19	A10	15y on 5f gray black (R)	110.00	80.00

Surrender of Japan, first anniversary.

Manchukuo Nos. 159, 94 and 86 Surcharged in Green, Black or Red

1946, Oct. 10

2L20	A17	1y on 6f crimson rose (G)	25.00	20.00
2L21	A18	5y on 12f deep orange (B)	50.00	40.00
2L22	A17	15y on 2f light green (R)	95.00	80.00

35th anniversary of Chinese revolution.

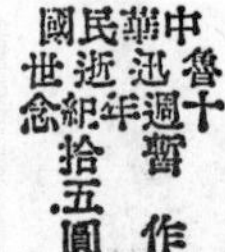

Manchukuo Nos. 84, 159 and 94 Surcharged in Black, Green or Blue

1946, Oct. 19

2L23	A16	1y on 1f red brown (B)	50.00	40.00
2L24	A17	5y on 6s crimson rose (G)	75.00	65.00
2L25	A18	15y on 12f deep orange (Bl)	120.00	90.00

10th anniversary of the death of Lu Hsun (1881–1936), writer.

Manchukuo Nos. 86, 159 and 95 Surcharged in Red, Green or Black

1947, Feb. 20

2L26	A16	1y on 2f light green (R)	45.00	35.00
2L27	A17	5y on 6s crimson rose (G)	87.50	70.00
2L28	A10	15y on 13f dark red brown	140.00	100.00

29th anniversary of the Red (USSR) Army.

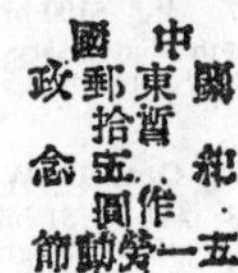

Manchukuo Nos. 86, 159 and 162 Surcharged in Red, Green or Black

1947, May 1

2L29	A17	1y on 2f light green (R)	25.00	20.00
2L30	"	5y on 6f crimson rose (G)	70.00	50.00
2L31	A19	15y on 30f buff	110.00	80.00

Labor Day.

Manchukuo Nos. 86, 88, 98 and 162 Surcharged ("Kwantung Postal Service, China")

1947, Sept. 15

2L32	A17	5y on 2f lt. grn.	30.00	25.00
2L33	A18	15y on 4f light olive green	50.00	40.00
2L34	A19	20y on 30f red brn.	75.00	60.00
2L35	"	20y on 30f buff	90.00	75.00

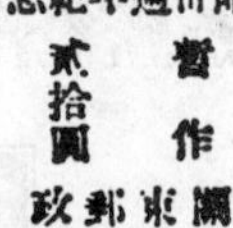

Manchukuo Nos. 86 and 159 Surcharged in Red and Green

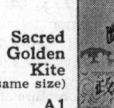

Sacred Golden Kite (same size)
A1

1948, Feb. 20

2L36	A17	10y on 2f light green (R)	95.00	95.00
2L37	"	20y on 6f crimson rose (G)	110.00	110.00
2L38	A1	100y on blue & red brown	*350.00*	*350.00*

30th anniversary of the Red (USSR) Army. No. 2L38 is on a label commemorating the 2600th anniversary of the Japanese Empire.

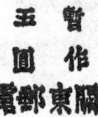

政郵華中
五 暫
圓 作
電郵東關

Japan No. 260 and Manchukuo Nos. 84, 86 and 88 Surcharged in Red, Blue or Black

1948, July

2L39	A85	5y on 3s grn. (R)	55.00	35.00
2L40	A16	10y on 1f red brown (Bl)	90.00	70.00
2L41	A17	50y on 2f lt. grn.	110.00	85.00
2L42	A18	100y on 4f lt. olive green (R)	170.00	120.00

Smaller Characters on Bottom Line

2L43	A17	10y on 2f light green (R)	70.00	70.00
2L44	A16	50y on 1f red brown	90.00	90.00

政郵東關
年週一卅念紀
壹 暫
佰 作
圓 作
節命革月十

Stamps of Manchukuo Nos. 84, 86 and 88 Surcharged in Blue, Red or Black

1948, Nov. 1

2L45	A16	10y on 1f red brown (Bl)	120.00	
2L46	A17	50y on 2f light green (R)	120.00	
2L47	A18	100y on 4f light olive green	100.00	

31st anniversary of the Russian Revolution.

年八四祝慶
模勞業農東關
念紀會大覽展
拾 暫
圓 作
電郵東關

Manchukuo Nos. 86 and 161 Surcharged in Red or Green

1948, Nov. 15

2L48	A17	10y on 2f light green (R)	
2L49	"	50y on 20f brn. (G)	

Kwantung Agricultural and Industrial Exhibition.

政郵華中

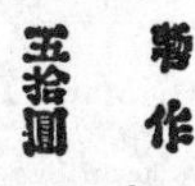

電郵東關

Manchukuo Nos. 86, 88 and 161 Surcharged in Red, Black or Green

1949, Jan.

2L50	A17	20y on 2f light green (R)	
2L51	A18	50y on 4f light olive green	
2L52	A17	100y on 20f brown (G)	

Without Gum

From No. 2L56 onward all stamps were issued without gum except as noted.

Farmer and Worker
A2

Train and Ship
A3

Ship at Dock
(No. 2L55)
A4

(No. 2L56)

1949 Litho. *Perf. 11, 11½*

2L53	A2	5y pale green	3.00	3.00
2L54	A3	10y orange	6.00	3.00
2L55	A4	50y vermilion	10.00	3.00
2L56	"	50y red (redrawn)	12.00	4.00

Issue dates: Nos. 2L56, July 7; others Apr. 1.

Worker, Flag and Means of Transport
A5

1949, May 1 *Perf. 11*

2L57	A5	10y rose pink	6.00	6.00
		a. 10y vermilion	40.00	40.00

Labor Day. No. 2L57a is from a worn plate.

Mao Tse-tung and Red Flag
A6

Heroes' Monument, Dairen
A7

1949, July 1

2L59	A6	50y red	12.50	12.50

28th anniversary of the founding of the Chinese Communist Party.

1949, Sept.

2L60	A7	10y red, blue & olive	10.00	10.00
		a. 10y red, blue & pale blue	50.00	50.00

4th anniversary of victory over Japan and opening of the Dairen Industrial Fair.

Nos. 2L53–2L54 Surcharged in Red or Black

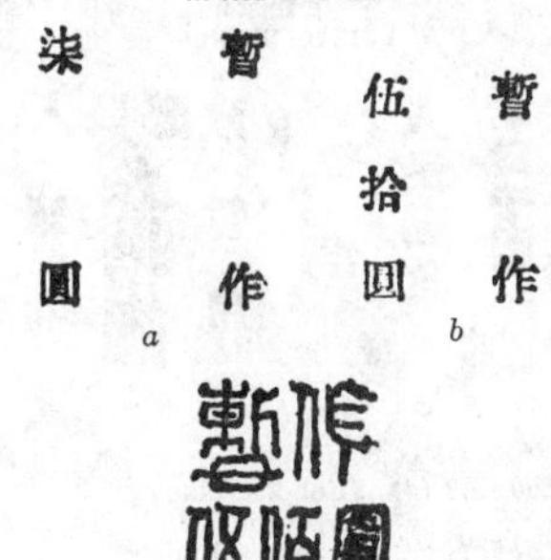

a b

c

With or Without Gum

1949, Sept.

2L62	A2 (*a*)	7y on 5y light green (R)	15.00	15.00
2L63	" (")	7y on 5y light green	15.00	15.00
2L64	" (*b*)	50y on 5y light green (R)	40.00	30.00
2L65	A3 (")	100y on 10y org.	*200.00*	*200.00*
2L66	" (*c*)	500y on 10y orange (R)	*400.00*	*400.00*
		Nos. 2L62–2L66 (5)	*670.00*	*660.00*

Size of surcharge on No. 2L63: 16x19 mm.

A 500y on 5y light green with surcharge "c" was prepared but not issued.

Stalin and Lenin
A8

1949, Nov. 7 *Perf. 11x11½*

2L68	A8	10y dull blue green (shades)	6.00	6.00

32nd anniversary of the Russian Revolution.

Workers Saluting Mao, Star and Flag
A9

1949, Nov. 16 *Perf. 11*

2L69	A9	35y dark blue, red, & yellow	8.00	8.00

Founding of the People's Republic of China.

Stalin
A10

(same size)

Gate of Heavenly Peace
A11

1949, Dec. 20 *Perf. 11½*

2L70	A10	20y dull magenta	12.00	
2L71	"	35y rose red	18.00	

70th birthday of Stalin.

1950, Mar. 10 Typo. *Perf. 10½*

2L72	A11	10y Prussian blue	2.50	1.50
2L73	"	20y dull green	2.50	1.50
2L74	"	35y red	2.25	1.00
2L75	A11	50y deep purple	2.25	1.00
2L76	"	100y lilac rose	2.25	1.00
		Nos. 2L72–2L76 (5)	11.75	6.00

NORTH CHINA

The North China Liberation Area included the provinces of Hopeh, Chahar, Shansi and Suiyuan. The original postal service, begun in the Shansi-Hopeh-Chahar Border Area in December, 1937, became the North China Postal and Telegraph Administration in May, 1949.

All Stamps Issued without Gum

Large Victory Issue

Cavalry Man Holding Nationalist Flag
A1

Perf. 10½

1946, Mar. **Wmk. Wavy Lines**

Granite Paper

Size: 34½x42mm.

3L1	A1	$1 red brown	50	50
		a. Newsprint	6.00	6.00
3L2	A1	$2 gray green	25	50
3L3	"	$4 vermilion	40	15
3L4	"	$5 violet brown	40	1.00
3L5	"	$8 violet blue	40	50
3L6	"	$10 deep carmine	80	1.00
3L7	"	$12 yellow	1.50	1.50
3L8	"	$20 light green	7.00	7.00
		Nos. 3L1–3L8 (8)	11.25	12.15

Defeat of Japan.

Small Victory Issue

Perf. 10½x10, 9½ rough

1946, May **Unwmkd.**

Granite paper

Size: 20x21mm.

3L9	A1	$1 red orange	1.00	1.00
3L10	"	$2 green	1.50	20
3L11	"	$3 light lilac	3.00	3.00
3L12	"	$5 dull purple	4.00	10
3L13	"	$8 dark blue	4.00	4.00
3L14	"	$10 rose red	1.00	1.25
3L15	"	$15 purple	*40.00*	*15.00*
3L16	"	$20 green	4.00	15
3L17	"	$30 brt. greenish bl.	1.00	*2.50*
3L18	"	$40 brt. rose lilac	2.00	*3.25*
3L19	"	$50 brown	*20.00*	25
3L20	"	$60 myrtle green	*40.00*	75

Wmkd. Wavy Lines

3L21	A1	$100 orange	1.00	*2.00*
3L22	"	$200 dull blue	1.00	*2.00*
3L23	"	$500 rose	10.00	*25.00*
		Nos. 3L9–3L23 (15)	*133.50*	*60.45*

North China Postal and Telegraph Administration

Charging Infantrymen
A2

Agriculture and Industry
A3

1949, Jan. ***Imperf.*** **Unwmkd.**

White Paper

3L24	A2	50c brown lake	65	30
3L25	"	$1 Prussian blue	65	30

Newsprint

3L26	A2	$2 apple green	65	30
3L27	"	$3 dull violet	20	30

3L28 A2 $5 brown 65 30
3L29 A3 $6 deep rose 65 30
a. White paper 75 30
3L30 A2 $10 blue green 20 30
3L31 " $12 deep carmine 65 30
Nos. 3L24-3L31 (8) 4.30 2.40

No. 3L29 issued in Peking, others in Tientsin.

Remittance Stamps of China Surcharged

$1

$3

A4

1949, Jan. Engraved *Perf. 13*

Small Central Characters

3L32 A4 50c on $50 brn. blk. 2.50 60
3L33 " $1 on $50 gray blk. 1.50 60
3L34 " $3 on $50 gray 1.50 60

Large Central Characters

3L35 A4 50c on $50 black 1.25 60
3L36 " $6 on $20 dark violet brown 1.25 50

Issued in Tientsin.

Sun Yat-sen Type A2 of Northeastern Provinces and China No. 640 Surcharged in Black, Red, Green or Blue

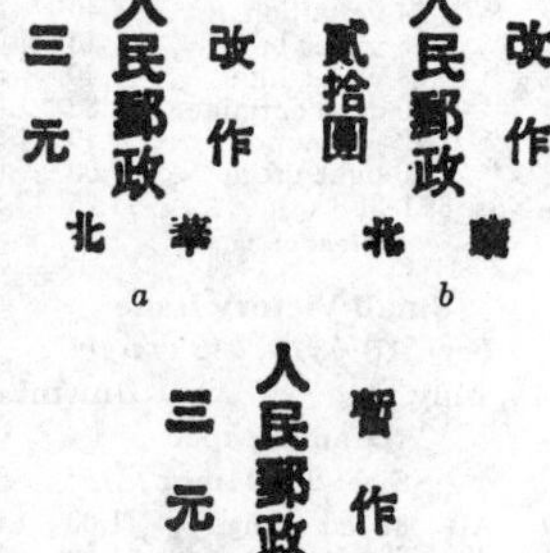

a b

c

Type "b," bottom character of left vertical row (yuan) differs. Type "c," top character of right vertical row differs.

1949, March 7 *Perf. 14*

3L37 A2 (a) 50c on 5c lake 20 *3.00*
3L38 " (") $1 on 10c orange 20 *1.00*
3L39 " (") $2 on 20c yellow green 16.00 *1.00*
a. Surch. inverted
3L40 A2 (a) $3 on 50c red org. 20 *3.00*
3L41 " (") $4 on $5 dk. grn. 2.00 *1.25*
3L42 " (") $6 on $10 crimson 60 *1.00*
3L43 " (") $10 on $300 bluish green 75 *2.00*
3L44 " (") $12 on $1 blue 75 *1.50*
3L45 " (") $18 on $3 brown 75 75
3L46 " (b) $20 on 50c red orange (Bl) 75 25
3L47 " (a) $20 on $20 olive 75 50
3L48 " (") $30 on $2.50 indigo (R) 75 *2.00*
3L49 " (") $40 on 25c black brown (R) 65 1.00
3L50 " (") $50 on $109 dark green (R) 5.00 1.00
3L51 " (b) $80 on $1 bl. (R) 7.00 35
3L52 " (a) $100 on $65 dull green (R) 10.00 50
3L53 A73 (b) $100 on $100 dark car. (Bl) 10.00 60

1949, Apr.

3L55 A2 (c) $2 on 20c yel. grn. 75 1.50
3L56 " (") $3 on 50c red org. 20 *1.00*
3L57 A2 (c) $4 on $5 dk. grn. 75 *2.00*
3L58 " (") $6 on $10 crimson 5.00 35
3L59 " (") $12 on $1 blue 35 35

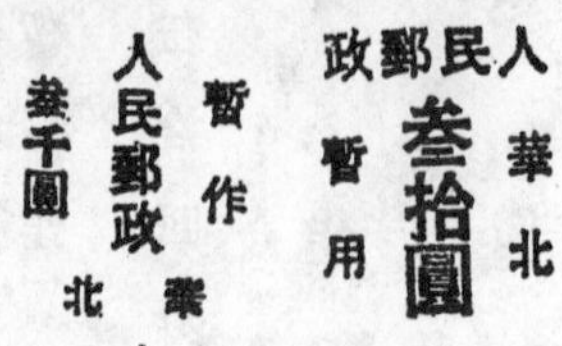

d e

1949, Apr.

3L60 A2 (d) $1 on 25c black brown (G) 15 *2.50*
3L61 " (") $10 on $300 bluish green (R) 5.00 1.75
3L62 " (") $20 on 50c red orange (G) 5.00 1.00
3L63 " (") $20 on $20 olive (R) 3.00 25
3L64 " (") $40 on 25c black brown (R) 3.00 75
3L65 " (") $50 on $109 dark green (R) 5.00 75
3L66 " (") $80 on $1 bl. (R) 3.00 75

On Stamps of China

3L67 A73 (d) $100 on $100 dk. car. (G) 8.00 2.00
3L68 " (") $300 on $700 red brn. (Bl) 6.00 60
3L69 A82 (") $500 on $500 bl. green (R) 4.00 50
3L70 " (") $3000 on $3000 blue (R) 6.00 75

On Stamps of Northeastern Provinces

1949, Aug.

3L71 A2 (e) $10 on $10 crimson (Bl) 3.00 60
3L72 " (") $30 on 20c yellow green (R) 3.00 50
3L73 " (") $50 on $44 dark car. rose (Bl) 3.00 30
3L74 " (") $100 on $3 brown (Bl) 6.00 75
3L75 " (") $200 on $4 orange brown (Bl) 8.00 2.00

On China No. 754

3L76 A82 $10 on $7000 light red brown (Bl) 6.00 2.00
Nos. 3L37-3L76 (39) 140.55 *44.15*

Overprints on Nos. 3L71 and 3L76 have 2 characters in center row.

Farmer and Worker on Globe
A5

1949, May 1 Engraved *Perf. 14*

3L77 A5 $20 crimson 1.00 50
3L78 " $40 dark blue 1.00 60
3L79 " $60 brown orange 1.00 50
3L80 " $80 dark green 1.00 1.00
3L81 " $100 purple 1.00 75
Nos. 3L77-3L81 (5) 5.00 3.35

Labor Day. Exist imperf. Price, set $4. Also issued in blocks of four, imperf. between, perf. around outer edges.

Mao Tse-tung (Chinese Numeral)
A6

Mao Tse-tung (Arabic Numeral)
A7

1949, July 1 *Perf. 14*

3L82 A6 $10 red 50 75
3L83 A7 $20 dark blue 50 15
3L84 A6 $50 orange 50 50
3L85 A7 $80 dark green 50 25
3L86 A6 $100 purple 50 50
3L87 A7 $120 olive 50 25
3L88 A6 $140 violet brown 50 1.00
Nos. 3L82-3L88 (7) 3.50 3.40

28th anniversary of the founding of the Chinese Communist Party.
Set exists imperf. Price, $15.

(same size)
Gate of Heavenly Peace
A8

Farmers and Factory
A9

1949, Nov. 26 Litho. *Perf. 12½*

3L89 A8 $50 orange 50 *2.00*
3L90 " $100 crimson 25 20
3L91 " $200 green 75 50
3L92 " $300 rose brown 2.25 50
3L93 " $400 blue 2.25 50
3L94 " $500 brown 3.50 50
3L95 " $700 violet 6.00 2.00
Nos. 3L89-3L95 (7) 15.50 *6.20*

1949, Dec. Engraved *Perf. 14*

3L96 A9 $1000 orange 2.50 10
3L97 " $3000 dark blue 25 25
3L98 " $5000 crimson 50 75
3L99 " $10,000 red brown 50 1.50

PARCEL POST STAMPS

Parcel Post Stamps of China Nos. Q23-Q27 Surcharged in Red, Black or Blue

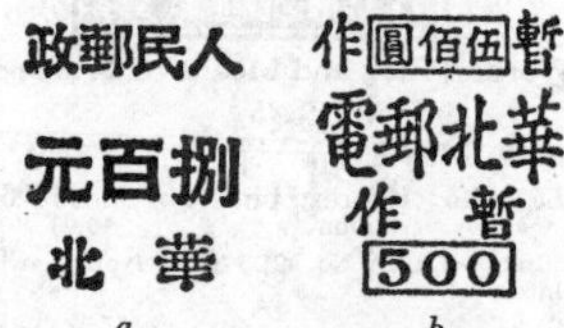

a b

1949, June

3LQ1 PP3 (a) $300 on $6,000,000 olive gray (R) 12.50
3LQ2 " (") $400 on $8,000,000 scarlet (Bl) 12.50
3LQ3 " (") $500 on $10,000,000 sage green (R) 15.00
3LQ4 " (") $800 on $5,000,000 lilac (R) 22.50
3LQ5 " (") $1000 on $3,000,000 slate blue (R) 30.00

Surcharged Type "b"

3LQ6 " (b) $500 on $3,000,000 dark blue 19.00
3LQ7 " (") $1000 on $5,000,000 vio. gray 30.00
3LQ8 " (") $3000 on $8,000,000 vermilion 42.50
3LQ9 " (") $5000 on $10,000,000 dull green 72.50
Nos. 3LQ1-3LQ9 (9) 256.50

Nos. 3LQ8-3LQ9 have large numerals unboxed.

Remittance Stamps of China (like North China Type A4) Surcharged in Black or Red

a b

Peking Surcharge (a)

1949, June Litho. *Perf. 13*

3LQ10 $6 on $5 vermilion 5.00 2.00
3LQ11 $20 on $50 gray 5.00 2.00
3LQ12 $50 on $20 dark violet brown 5.00 2.00
3LQ13 $100 on $10 olive grn. 12.00 5.00

Tientsin Surcharge (b)

Engraved *Perf. 14*

3LQ14 $20 on $1 brn. org. 5.00 3.00
a. Red surcharge 8.00 5.00
3LQ15 $30 on $2 dark green 5.00 3.00
a. Red surcharge 5.00 3.00
3LQ16 $30 on $10 olive green 5.00 3.00
a. Red surcharge 8.00 5.00
3LQ17 $100 on $10 gray grn. (R) 5.00 3.00

Lithographed *Perf. 13*

3LQ18 $50 on $5 red 5.00 3.00

Engraved *Perf. 12½*

3LQ19 $20 on $1 org. brown 12.00 8.00
3LQ20 $100 on $10 yel. green *30.00* 25.00

Typographed *Roulette 9½*

3LQ21 $30 on $2 blue green (R) 22.50 15.00

The surcharge on No. 3LQ14a is without first and last lines.

Locomotive
PP1

1949, Nov. Engraved *Perf. 14*

3LQ22 PP1 $500 crimson 5.00 7.00
3LQ23 " $1000 deep blue 12.50
3LQ24 " $2000 green 15.00
3LQ25 " $5000 deep olive 20.00
3LQ26 " $10,000 orange 35.00
3LQ27 " $20,000 red brown 90.00
3LQ28 " $50,000 brn. purple 175.00
Nos. 3LQ22-3LQ28 (7) 354.50

NORTHWEST CHINA

The Northwest China Liberation Area consisted of the provinces of Sinkiang, Tsinghai, Ningsia and the western part of Shensi. The area was first established as the Shensi-Kansu-Ningsia Border Area in October, 1936, after the Long March to Yenan. Remote Sinkiang was not included until late 1949.

All Stamps Issued without Gum

Pagoda on Yenan Hill
A1

1945, Mar. Lithographed *Imperf.*

4L1 A1 $1 green 10.00
a. Rouletted 9 20.00
4L2 A1 $5 dark blue 35.00
a. Rouletted 9 35.00
4L3 A1 $10 rose red 9.00
a. Rouletted 9 20.00
4L4 A1 $50 dull purple 4.00
4L5 " $100 yellow orange 9.00
Nos. 4L1-4L5 (5) 67.00

First issue; denomination in Chinese and Arabic. Heavy shading at top of vignette. Columns at sides.

Nos. 4L1–4L2 Surcharged in Red:

暫作三十元 (a) 暫作三十圓 (b)

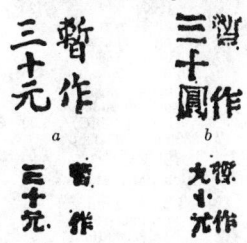

暫作三十元 (c) 暫作九十元 (d)

1946, Nov.

4L6 A1 (*a*) $30 on $1 green 10.00
4L7 " (*b*) $30 on $1 green *60.00*
a. Rectangular lower left character
4L8 A1 (*c*) $30 on $1 green 5.00
4L9 " (*b*) $60 on $1 green
4L10 " (*d*) $90 on $5 dk. bl. 10.00

Surcharges on Nos. 4L7a and 4L9 are type "b" as illustrated. Surcharge on No. 4L7 differs from "b," having lower left character as in type "a."

(same size)
Pagoda on Yenan Hill
A2 A3

1948, June

4L11 A2 $100 buff 75.00
4L12 " $300 rose pink 75
4L13 " $500 red 1.50
4L14 " $1000 blue 1.50
4L15 " $2000 yellow green 15.00
4L16 " $5000 dull purple 6.00
Nos. 4L11–4L16 (6) 99.75

Second issue; denominations in Chinese only. Many shades and proofs exist.

1948, Dec.

4L17 A3 10c yellow orange 1.00
4L18 " 20c lemon 1.00
4L19 " $1 dark blue 1.00
4L20 " $2 vermilion 1.00
4L21 " $5 pale blue green 6.00
4L22 " $10 violet 9.00
Nos. 4L17–4L22 (6) 19.00

Third issue; ornamental border at sides. Many shades exist.

Nos. 4L2 and 4L13 Surcharged in Red or Black

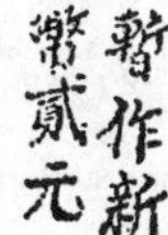

1949, Jan.

4L23 A1 $1 on $5 dark blue 18.00
4L24 A2 $2 on $500 red 6.00

Pagoda on Yenan Hill
A4

1949, May 1

4L25 A4 50c yellow to olive 15 20
4L26 " $1 dull bl. to indigo 15 20
4L27 " $3 olive yellow to orange yellow 15 20
4L28 " $5 blue green 15 20
4L29 A4 $10 vio. to dp. vio. 4.00 5.00
4L30 " $20 pink to rose red 1.00 2.00
Nos. 4L25–4L30 (6) 5.60 7.80

Fourth issue; light shading at top of vignette, columns without ornaments at sides. Many shades exist.

China Nos. 959, F2 and E12 Overprinted ("People's Post, Shensi")

人民郵政(陝)

1949, June 13 Engr. *Perf. 12½*

4L31 A96 orange 12.50 5.00
4L32 R2 carmine 15.00 7.50
4L33 SD2 red violet 15.00 10.00

Stamps of China, Sun Yat-sen Type of 1949, Overprinted in Black or Red ("People's Post, Shensi")

人民郵政 陝西

Lithographed; Engraved

1949, July 1 *Perf. 14, 12½*

4L34 A94 $10 green (887) 25 10
4L35 " $20 vio. brn. (888) 70 25
4L36 " $20 violet brown (894C) 25 10
4L37 " $50 dk. Prus. grn. (889; R) 1.00 75
4L38 " $50 green (951) 1.00 30
4L39 " $100 org. brown (890) 3.00 1.00
4L40 " $500 rose lilac (892) 4.00 1.00
4L41 " $1000 deep blue (952) (R) 9.00 25
4L42 " $2000 violet (946) (R) 9.00 3.00
4L43 " $5000 car. (953) 22.50 6.00
4L44 " $10,000 brown (954) 45.00 25.00
Nos. 4L34–4L44 (11) 95.70 37.75

Kansu-Ningsia-Tsinghai Area, Lanchow Overprints

China Nos. 959a, F2 and E12 Overprinted ("People's Post, Kansu")

人民郵政(甘)

1949, Oct. Engr. *Rouletted*

4L45 A96 orange 8.00 8.00

Perf. 12½

4L46 R2 carmine 15.00 12.00
4L47 SD2 red violet 15.00 12.00

Stamps of China, Sun Yat-sen Type of 1949, Overprinted ("People's Post, Kansu")

人民郵政(甘)

Engraved; Lithographed

1949, Oct. *Perf. 14, 12½*

4L48 A94 $10 green (887) 1.25 50
4L49 " $20 vio. brn. (888) 1.25 1.00
4L50 " $50 dk. Prus. grn. (889) 4.00 4.00
4L51 " $100 orange brown (890) 1.25 1.25
4L52 " $100 dark orange brn. (896) 2.00 2.00
4L53 " $200 red org. (891) 2.75 75
4L54 " $500 rose lilac (892) 2.75 1.00
4L55 " $1000 blue (894) 1.25 1.00
4L56 " $1000 dp. blue (898) 2.75 2.50
4L57 " $2000 violet (946) 5.00 5.00
4L58 " $5000 lt. blue (899) 10.00 10.00
4L59 " $10,000 sepia (900) 13.00 13.00
4L60 " $20,000 apple green (947) 30.00 30.00
Nos. 4L48–4L60 (13) 77.25 72.00

China Nos. 959, F2 and 791–792 Surcharged in Black or Red ("People's Post, Sinkiang")

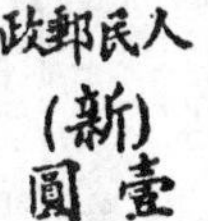

1949, Oct.

4L61 A96 $1 on orange 7.50 7.50
4L62 R2 $3 on carmine 7.50 7.50
4L63 A82 10c on $50,000 dp. blue (R) 7.50 7.50
4L64 " $1.50 on $100,000 dull grn. (R) 7.50 7.50

Northwest People's Post

Mao Tse-tung A5 Great Wall A6

1949, Oct. 15 Litho. *Imperf.*

4L65 A5 $50 rose 75 75
a. Cliché of $200 in plate of $50 75.00
4L66 A6 $100 dark blue 15 15
4L67 A5 $200 orange 75 50
4L68 A6 $400 sepia 75 35

EAST CHINA

The East China Liberation Area included the provinces of Shantung, Kiangsu, Chekiang, Anhwei and Fukien. The original postal service established in Shantung in 1941, became the East China Posts and Telegraph General Office in July, 1948.

All Stamps Issued without Gum

Mao Tse-tung A1 Transportation and Tower A2

1948, Mar. Litho. *Perf. 10½*

5L1 A1 $50 yellow orange 75 75
5L2 " $100 deep rose 2.00 1.50
5L3 " $200 dk. vio. blue 2.00 1.50
5L4 " $300 bright green 2.00 1.50
5L5 " $500 deep blue 1.00 50
5L6 " $800 vermilion 2.00 1.00
5L7 " $1000 dark blue 3.50 3.50
5L8 " $5000 rose 7.00 7.00
5L9 " $10,000 dp. carmine 15.00 15.00
Nos. 5L1–5L9 (9) 35.25 32.25

Many varieties, including unissued imperforates exist.

Perf. 9 to 11 and comp.

1949, Apr. Lithographed

5L10 A2 $1 yellow green 5 5
5L11 " $2 blue green 5 5
5L12 " $3 dull red 5 5
5L13 " $5 pale brown (ovpt. 4x4 mm.) 5 5
a. Without overprint 35.00
b. Overprint 3x3 mm. 50 50
5L14 A2 $10 ultramarine 8 8
5L15 " $13 bright violet 10 10
5L16 " $18 bright blue 10 10
5L17 " $21 vermilion 12 12
5L18 " $30 gray 15 15
5L19 " $50 crimson 20 20
5L20 " $100 olive 6.50 5.00
Nos. 5L10–5L20 (11) 7.45 5.95

Seventh anniversary of Shantung Communist Postal Administration. The overprint on the $10, character "yu" meaning "Posts," obliterates Japanese flag on tower, erroneously included in design. Two sizes of overprint exist.

Nos. 5L10–5L20 exist imperf. on different paper. Price $30.

Train and Postal Runner (1949.2.7) A3 Mao, Soldiers, Map A4

Perf. 8 to 11

1949, Apr. Lithographed

5L21 A3 $1 bright emerald 5 10
5L22 " $2 blue green 5 10
5L23 " $3 dark red 3 10
5L24 " $5 brown 3 10
5L25 " $10 ultramarine 6 10
5L26 " $13 bright violet 3 10
5L27 " $18 bright blue 3 10
5L28 " $21 vermilion 3 10
5L29 " $30 slate 15 25
5L30 " $50 crimson 25 25
5L31 " $100 olive 50 50
Nos. 5L21–5L31 (11) 1.21 1.80

Seventh anniversary of Shantung Post Office, Feb. 7. Imperf. sets were sold by the Philatelic Dept., Tientsin P.O. Price $15. See Nos. 5L69–5L76.

Perf. 9½ to 11 comp.

1949, Apr.

5L32 A4 $1 bright emerald 5 5
5L33 " $2 blue green 5 5
5L34 " $3 dull red 5 5
5L35 " $5 brown 5 5
5L36 " $10 ultramarine 5 5
5L37 " $13 bright violet 5 5
5L38 " $18 bright blue 10 10
5L39 " $21 vermilion 10 10
5L40 " $30 gray 10 10
5L41 " $50 crimson 10 10
5L42 " $100 olive 1.45 65
Nos. 5L32–5L42 (11) 1.45 1.35

Victory of Hwai-Hai (Hwaiying and Haichow). Imperf. sets were sold by the Philatelic Dept., Tientsin P.O. Price $30.

Stamps of China, Sun Yat-sen Type of 1949, Surcharged in Red or Black

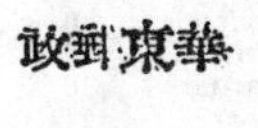
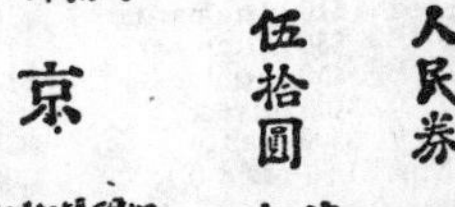

(Nanking) *a* (Wuhu) *b*

1949, May 4 Engr. *Perf. 12½*

5L43 A94 (*a*) $1 on $10 green (894A, R) 15 10
a. Perf. 13 2.00 2.00
5L44 A94 (*a*) $3 on $20 violet brown (894C) 15 10
a. Perf. 13 2.00 2.00
b. Perf. 14 4.00 4.00
c. Surch. inverted

Perf. 12½, 14

1949, May Lithographed, Engraved

5L45 A94 (*b*) $30 on $1000 dp. blue (898) 1.00 1.00
5L46 " (") $30 on $1000 blue (894) 1.00 1.00
5L47 " (") $50 on $200 org. red (897) 1.00 1.00
5L48 " (") $100 on $5000 lt. blue (899, R) 3.00 3.00
5L49 " (") $300 on $10,000 sepia (900, R) 10.00 10.00
5L50 " (") $500 on $200 org. red (897) 15.00 15.00
Nos. 5L45–5L50 (6) 31.00 31.00

Many varieties exist.

China Nos. 915a and 915 Surcharged in Green, Black or Red

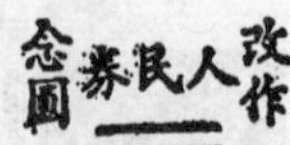

(East China)

1949, May Litho. *Perf. 12½*

5L51 A95 $5 on 50c on $20 brn., II (G) 7.00 7.00
5L52 " $10 on 50c on $20 brn., II 7.00 7.00
5L53 " $20 on 50c on $20 red brn., II (R) 7.00 7.00
a. Type I (R) 7.50 7.50

Stamps of China, Sun Yat-sen Type of 1949, Surcharged in Black or Red

政郵東華
杭
圓叁拾作暫

(Hangchow)

Engr., No. 5L57 Litho.

1949, June 25 *Perf. 14, 12½*

5L54 A94 $1 on $1 org. (886) 1.25 1.25
5L55 " $3 on $20 vio. brn. (894C, R) 75 75
5L56 " $5 on $100 orange brown (890) 1.50 1.50
5L57 " $5 on $100 dk. org. brown (896) 50 50
5L58 " $10 on $50 dk. Prus. green (889, R) 12.00 8.00
5L59 " $13 on $10 grn. (894A) 40 40
Nos. 5L54-5L59 (6) 16.40 12.40

East China Liberation Area

Maps of Shanghai and Nanking
A5

1949, May 30 Litho. *Perf. 8½ to 11*

5L60 A5 $1 orange vermilion 6 5
5L61 " $2 blue green 6 5
5L62 " $3 bright violet 6 5
5L63 " $5 violet brown 6 5
5L64 " $10 ultramarine 10 5
5L65 " $30 slate 12 15
5L66 " $50 carmine 12 15
5L67 " $100 olive 12 12
5L68 " $500 orange 35 25
Nos. 5L60-5L68 (9) 1.05 92

Liberation of Shanghai and Nanking. Many shades, paper and perforation varieties exist.

Train and Postal Runner Type Dated "1949"

1949, July-1950, Feb. *Perf. 12½, 14*

5L69 A3 $10 deep ultra. 3 5
5L70 " $15 org. verm. 3 15
a. $15 red, perf. 14 10 10
5L71 A3 $30 slate green 3 5
a. Perf. 12½ 3 10
5L72 A3 $50 carmine 10 5
5L73 " $60 blue green, perf. 14 3 10
5L74 " $100 olive, perf. 14 2.00 10
5L75 " $1600 vio. blue ('50) 75 1.00
5L76 " $2000 brown violet ('50) 1.00 1.50
Nos. 5L69-5L76 (8) 3.97 3.00

Chu Teh, Mao, Troops with Flags
A7

Mao Tse-tung
A8

1949, Aug. 17 *Perf. 12½*

5L77 A7 $70 orange 3 3
5L78 " $270 crimson 5 3
5L79 " $370 emerald 20 4
5L80 " $470 violet brown 40 4
5L81 " $570 blue 10 15
Nos. 5L77-5L81 (5) 78 29

22nd anniversary of the People's Liberation Army.

1949, Oct.

5L82 A8 $10 dark blue 2.00 50
5L83 " $15 vermilion 2.00 2.00
5L84 " $70 brown 10 5
5L85 " $100 violet brown 3 5
5L86 " $150 orange 3 5
5L87 " $200 greenish gray 3 5
5L88 " $500 gray blue 3 5
5L89 " $1000 rose 3 5
5L90 " $2000 emerald 3 10
Nos. 5L82-5L90 (9) 4.28 2.90

Stamps of China, Sun Yat-sen Type of 1949 Surcharged in Black or Red

政郵民人華中
肆佰圓 華東區
★★★★★

1949, Nov. Litho. *Perf. 12½*

5L91 A94 $400 on $200 orange red (897) 12.00 80
5L92 " $1000 on $50 greenish gray (895, R) 2.00 80
5L93 " $1200 on $100 dk. org. brown (896) 10 *1.50*
5L94 " $1600 on $20,000 apple green (947) 10 *80*
5L95 " $2000 on $1000 deep blue (952, R) 10 *80*
a. Perf. 14 *15.00*
Nos. 5L91-5L95 (5) 14.30 *4.70*

PARCEL POST STAMPS

Parcel Post Stamps of China 1945-48 Surcharged

20000
郵山
政東
貳百圓

(Shantung)

1949, Aug. 1 Engraved *Perf. 13*

5LQ1 PP1 $200 on $500 grn. 3.00 3.00
5LQ2 " $500 on $1000 bl. 4.50 4.50

Perf. 13½

5LQ3 PP3 $200 on $200,000 dark green 30.00 30.00
5LQ4 " $200 on $10,000,000 sage green 3.00 3.00
5LQ5 " $500 on $7000 dull blue 45.00 45.00
5LQ6 " $500 on $50,000 indigo 4.50 4.50
5LQ7 " $1000 on $10,000 car. rose 4.50 4.50
5LQ8 " $1000 on $100,000 dark rose brown 4.50 4.50
5LQ9 " $1000 on $300,000 pink 4.50 4.50
5LQ10 " $1000 on $500,000 vio. brown 30.00 30.00
5LQ11 " $1000 on $8,000,000 org. verm. 4.50 4.50
5LQ12 " $2000 on $5,000,000 dull violet 7.50 7.50
5LQ13 " $2000 on $6,000,000 brn. black 7.50 7.50
5LQ14 " $3000 on $30,000 olive 15.00 15.00
5LQ15 " $3000 on $70,000 org. brown 15.00 15.00
5LQ16 " $5000 on $3,000,000 dull blue 15.00 15.00
Nos. 5LQ1-5LQ16 (16) 198.00 198.00

China No. 987 Surcharged

紙印裹包 圓萬壹 圓百貳 $200 圓百伍 $500
政郵東華 圓仟壹 $1000 圓仟貳 $2000
圓萬壹 紙印裹包 圓仟伍 $5000 圓萬壹 $10,000

1949, Sept. 7 Litho. *Perf. 12½*

5LQ17 A97 $200 on $10 blue green *20.00* 9.00
5LQ18 " $500 on $10 blue green *20.00* 9.00
5LQ19 " $1000 on $10 blue green *20.00* 9.00
5LQ20 " $2000 on $10 blue green *20.00* 9.00
5LQ21 " $5000 on $10 blue green *20.00* 9.00
5LQ22 " $10,000 on $10 blue green *20.00* 9.00
Nos. 5LQ17-5LQ22 (6) *120.00* 54.00

Flying Geese Type of China, 1949, and China Nos. 984-986 Surcharged in Red or Black

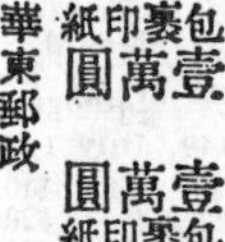

1950, Jan. 28

5LQ23 A97 $5000 on 10c blue violet (R) *50.00* 25.00
5LQ24 " $10,000 on $1 brown orange *50.00* 25.00
5LQ25 " $20,000 on $2 bl. *50.00* 25.00
5LQ26 " $50,000 on $5 car. rose *50.00* 25.00

Parcel Post Stamps of China Nos. Q1-Q4 Surcharged in Red or Black

1950, Jan. 28 Engraved *Perf. 13*

5LQ27 PP1 $5000 on $500 green (R) 50 *25.00*
5LQ28 " $10,000 on $1000 blue(R) *80.00* 25.00
5LQ29 " $20,000 on $3000 bl. green *80.00* 25.00
5LQ30 " $50,000 on $5000 org. red 16.00 25.00

CENTRAL CHINA

The Central Chinese Liberation Area included the provinces of Honan, Hupeh, Hunan and Kiangsi. The area was established between August and September, 1949, following the liberation of Hankow.

All Stamps Issued without Gum

Hupeh Postal and Telegraph Administration

Stamps of China, Sun Yat-sen Type of 1949, Surcharged ("Chinese P.O., Temporary Use")

政郵中華
用暫
100 圓壹

Engraved; Lithographed

1949, June 4 *Perf. 14, 12½*

Thin parallel lines.

6L1 A94 $1 on $200 red orange (891) 20 15
6L2 A94 $6 on $10,000 sepia (900) 20 15
6L3 " $15 on $1 org. (886) 20 15
6L4 " $30 on $100 orange brown (890) 65 50
6L5 " $30 on $100 dk. org. brown (896) 25 20
6L6 " $50 on $20 violet brown (894C) 5.00 5.00
6L7 " $80 on $1000 deep blue (898) 1.00 1.00

Thick parallel lines.

6L8 A94 $1 on $200 red orange (891) 1.00 1.00
6L9 " $3 on $5000 light blue (899) 20 20
6L10 " $10 on $500 rose lilac (892) 25 20
6L11 " $10 on $500 rose lilac (945) 1.00 75
6L12 " $50 on $20 violet brown (888) 65 65
6L13 " $50 on $20 violet brown (894C) 45 45
6L14 " $80 on $1000 blue (894) 65 65
6L15 " $80 on $1000 deep blue (898) 6.00 6.00
6L16 " $100 on $50 dk. Prus. green (899) 45 45
Nos. 6L1-6L16 (16) 18.15 17.50

Kiangsi Postal and Telegraph Administration

Central Trust Revenue Stamps of China Surcharged ("People's Post, Kiangsi")

(same size)
A1

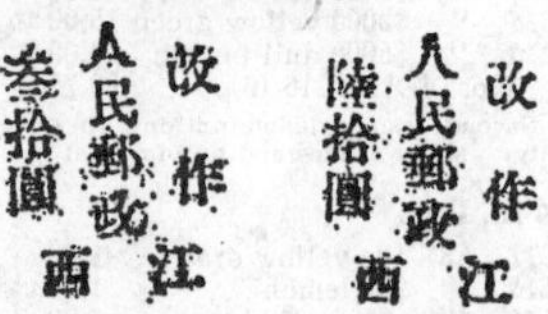

$30 $60

1949, June 20 Engr. *Perf. 12½*

6L17 A1 $3 on $30 purple 30 30
6L18 " $15 on $15 red orange 25 25
6L19 " $30 on $50 dk. blue 3.00 60
6L20 " $60 on $50 dk. blue 1.00 1.00
6L21 " $130 on $15 red org. 70 70

The $15 surcharge has 3 characters in left vertical row, the $130 surcharge has 5.

Same Surcharge on Sun Yat-sen Issues of China, 1945-49

Engraved, Litho. *Perf. 14, 12½*

6L22 A82 $1 on $250 deep lilac (746) 2.00 35
6L23 A94 $5 on $1000 deep blue (898) 2.00 60
6L24 " $5 on $2000 violet (946) 2.00 45
6L25 " $5 on $5000 light blue (899) 25 25
6L26 " $10 on $1000 blue (894) 2.00 1.25
6L27 A82 $20 on $4000 gray 35 35
6L28 A73 $30 on $100 dark carmine 2.00 1.25
6L29 A82 $30 on $20,000 rose pink 85 85
6L30 A94 $80 on $500 rose lilac (945) 85 85
6L31 " $100 on $1000 deep blue (898) 85 85
6L32 A82 $200 on $250 deep lilac 1.00 1.00
Nos. 6L17-6L32 (16) 19.40 10.90

Central China Posts and Telegraph Administration

Farmer, Soldier and Worker
A2 A3

I. Top white line of square character (yuan) at upper left does not touch left vertical stroke. No gap in shading between soldier's feet.
II. Top line connects with left vertical stroke. Gap in shading between feet.

Perf. 10 to 11½ & Comp.

1949 **Lithographed**

6L33 A2 $1 orange 4.00 4.00
6L34 " $3 brown orange 85 85
6L35 " $6 emerald 80 80
6L36 A3 $7 yellow brown 80 30
6L37 A2 $10 blue green 30 30
6L38 A3 $14 orange brown 8.00 4.00
6L39 A2 $15 ultramarine 25 10
6L40 " $30 green, I 10 15
a. Type II 10 15
6L41 A3 $35 gray blue 8.00 4.00
6L42 A2 $50 rose violet 5.50 2.75
6L43 A3 $70 deep green 25 10
6L44 A2 $80 pink 10 50
6L45 A3 $100 blue green 5 10
6L46 " $220 rose red 4.00 4.00
Nos. 6L33-6L46 (14) 33.00 21.95

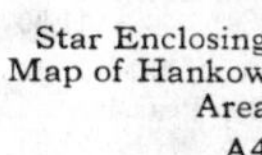

Star Enclosing Map of Hankow Area
A4

Two types of $500:
I. Thick numerals of "500". No period after "500".
II. Thin numerals and period.
Two types of $1000:
I. No period after "1000".
II. Period after "1000".

1949, July

6L48 A4 $110 orange brown 75 20
6L49 " $130 violet 50 10
6L50 " $200 deep orange 15 25
6L51 " $290 brown 15 25
6L52 " $370 dark blue 2.00 50
6L53 " $500 light blue, I 3.00 75
a. $500 blue, II 10.00 2.00
6L54 A4 $1000 dark red, I 15.00 1.00
a. $1000 dull red, II 7.50 2.00
6L55 A4 $5000 brown 5.00 3.00
6L56 " $10,000 bright pink 10.00 5.00
Nos. 6L48-6L56 (9) 36.55 11.05

Hankow River Customs Building
A5

River Wall, Wuchang
A6

Design: $290, $370, River scene, Hanyang.

1949, Aug. 16 ***Perf. 11, Imperf.***

6L57 A5 $70 green 65 50
6L58 " $220 crimson 65 50
6L59 " $290 brown 65 50
6L60 A5 $370 bright blue 65 50
6L61 A6 $500 purple 65 50
6L62 " $1000 vermilion 65 50
Nos. 6L57-6L62 (6) 3.90 3.00

Liberation of Hankow, Wuchang and Hanyang.

Nos. 6L35, 6L39 and 6L40 Surcharged in Red ("Honan People's Post")

人民幣 柒拾圓 河南省

1949, July

6L63 A2 $7 on $6 emerald 5.00 5.00
6L64 " $14 on $15 ultra. 6.50 6.50
6L65 " $70 on $30 green 10.00 10.00

Surcharge shown is for $70. The $7 has 5 characters in left column and no bottom line.

Issues of 1949 Overprinted ("Honan People's Post")

河南省 人民幣

1949, Aug.

6L66 A2 $3 brown orange 60 35
6L67 A3 $7 yellow brown 90 35
6L68 A2 $10 blue green 1.00 25
6L69 A3 $14 orange brown 1.50 75
6L70 A2 $30 yellow green (6L40a) 1.00 75
6L71 A3 $35 gray blue 1.00 65
6L72 A2 $50 rose violet 2.25 1.00
6L73 A3 $70 deep green 65 1.00
6L74 A4 $110 orange brown 3.00 3.00
6L75 A3 $220 rose red 5.00 3.00
6L76 A4 $290 brown 3.00 3.00
6L77 " $370 blue 7.50 5.00
6L78 " $500 blue, II 15.00 10.00
6L79 " $1000 dark red, I 22.50 15.00
6L80 " $5000 brown 60.00 40.00
6L81 " $10,000 bright pink 150.00 100.00
Nos. 6L66-6L81 (16) 274.90 184.10

Width of the overprint varies slightly.

Nos. 6L57-6L62 Overprinted ("Honan People's Post")

河南省 人民幣

1949, Aug. ***Perf. 11, Imperf.***

6L82 A5 $70 green 2.50 1.00
6L83 " $220 crimson 2.50 1.00
6L84 " $290 brown 2.50 1.00
6L85 " $370 bright blue 2.50 1.00
6L86 A6 $500 purple 2.50 1.00
6L87 " $1000 vermilion 2.50 2.00
Nos. 6L82-6L87 (6) 15.00 7.00

Width of overprint on Nos. 6L82-6L85, 7mm.; on Nos. 6L86-6L87, 12mm.

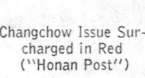

Changchow Issue Surcharged in Red ("Honan Post")

(same size)
Mao Tse-tung
A7

1949, Sept. ***Perf. 10***

6L88 A7 $290 on $30 yel. grn. 15.00 10.00
6L89 " $370 on $30 yel. grn. 25.00 15.00

Issues of 1949 Surcharged

改作 貳佰圓 200.00

1950, Jan.

6L90 A2 $200 on $1 orange 50 25
6L91 " $200 on $3 brn. org. 50 35
6L92 A2 $200 on $6 emerald 50 35
6L93 A3 $200 on $7 yel. brn. 50 35
6L94 " $200 on $14 org. brn. 50 35
6L95 " $200 on $35 gray blue 50 35
6L96 " $200 on $70 deep grn. 50 15
6L97 A2 $200 on $80 pink 50 15
6L98 A3 $200 on $220 rose red 50 15
6L99 A4 $200 on $370 blue 20 25
6L100 A3 $300 on $70 dp. green 30 20
6L101 A2 $300 on $80 pink 20 20
6L102 A3 $300 on $220 rose red 20 20
6L103 A2 $1200 on $3 brn. org. 15.00 7.50
6L104 A3 $1200 on $7 yel. brn. 2.00 40
6L105 " $1500 on $14 org. brn. 2.00 25
6L106 A2 $2100 on $1 orange 20.00 7.50
6L107 " $2100 on $6 emerald 20.00 7.50
6L108 A3 $2100 on $35 gray blue 3.50 50
6L109 A4 $5000 on $370 blue 2.00 1.25
Nos. 6L90-6L109 (20) 69.90 28.20

Two types of surcharge exist, differing in spacing of characters in top row.

PARCEL POST STAMPS

Star and Map of Hankow
PP1

1949, Nov. **Litho.** ***Perf. 11, 11½***

6LQ1 PP1 $5000 brown 1.00 1.00
6LQ2 " $10,000 scarlet 5.00 1.50
6LQ3 " $20,000 dark slate green 2.50 2.50
6LQ4 " $50,000 vermilion 1.00 5.00

SOUTH CHINA

The South China Liberation Area included the provinces of Kwantung and Kwangsi and Hainan Island. The South China Postal and Telegraph Administration was organized on or about Nov. 4, 1949.

All Stamps Issued without Gum

Pearl River Bridge, Canton
A1

1949, Nov. 4 **Litho.** ***Imperf.***

7L1 A1 $10 green 5 5
7L2 " $20 sepia 5 5
7L3 " $30 violet 5 5
7L4 " $50 carmine 5 5
7L5 " $100 ultramarine 25 15
Nos. 7L1-7L5 (5) 45 35

China Nos. 993-995 With Additional Overprint in Red ("Liberation of Swatow")

解放 暫用

1949, Nov. 9

7L6 A94 2½c on $500 rose lilac (993) 6.50 6.50
a. Handstamped 20.00 20.00
7L7 A94 2½c on $500 rose lilac (994) 12.00 12.00
a. Handstamped 20.00 20.00
7L8 A94 15c on $10 green (995) 9.00 9.00
a. Handstamped 20.00 20.00

On Unit Issues of China, 1949

7L9 A96 orange (959) 9.00 9.00
7L10 AP5 blue green (C62) 9.00 9.00
7L11 SD2 red violet (E12) 9.00 9.00
7L12 R2 carmine (F2) 9.00 9.00

On Sun Yat-sen and Flying Geese Issues of China

7L13 A94 2c orange (974) 25.00 25.00
7L14 " 4c bl. grn. (975) 250.00 225.00
7L15 " 10c dp. lilac (976) 10.00 10.00
7L16 " 20c blue (978) 12.00 12.00
7L17 A97 $1 brn. org. (984) 8.50 8.50
7L18 " $10 bl. grn. (987) 165.00 165.00
Nos. 7L6-7L18 (13) 534.00 509.00

Nos. 7L1-7L3 Surcharged in Red or Green

300

改作叁佰圓

1950, Jan.

7L19 A1 $300 on $30 vio. (R) 2.50 35
7L20 " $500 on $20 brn. (R) 2.50 35
7L21 " $800 on $30 vio. (G) 2.50 75
7L22 " $1000 on $10 gray green (R) 2.50 45
7L23 " $1000 on $20 brn. (R) 2.50 75
Nos. 7L19-7L23 (5) 12.50 2.65

SOUTHWEST CHINA

The Southwest China Liberation Area included the provinces of Kweichow, Szechwan, Yunnan, Sikang and Tibet. The Southwest Postal and Telegraph Administration was organized on or about Nov. 15, 1949 after the liberation of Kweiyang, capital of Kweichow Province.

All Stamps Issued without Gum

Chu Teh, Mao and Troops
A1

1949, Dec. **Litho.** ***Perf. 12½***

8L1 A1 $10 deep blue 1.50 1.00
8L2 " $20 rose claret 15 50
8L3 " $30 deep orange 20 50
8L4 " $50 gray green 30 50
8L5 " $100 carmine 10 50
8L6 " $200 blue 50 60
8L7 " $300 blue violet 2.00 2.00
8L8 " $500 dark gray 4.00 4.00
8L9 " $1000 pale purple 6.50 5.00
8L10 " $2000 green 22.50 17.50
8L11 " $5000 orange 50.00 40.00
Nos. 8L1-8L11 (11) 87.75 72.10

China Nos. 974-975, 984, 986-987 Surcharged ("Kweichow People's Post")

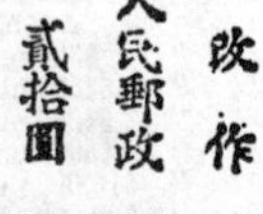

1949, Dec. 1 ***Perf. 12½***

8L12 A94 $20 on 2c orange 3.00 3.00
8L13 " $50 on 4c bl. grn. 3.00 3.00
8L14 A97 $100 on $1 brn. org. 5.00 5.00
8L15 " $400 on $5 car. rose 14.00 14.00
8L16 " $2000 on $10 blue green 35.00 35.00
Nos. 8L12-8L16 (5) 60.00 60.00

Map of China, Flag Planted in Southwest
A2

1950, Jan. **Litho.** ***Perf. 9 to 11½***

8L17 A2 $20 dark blue 10 5
8L18 " $30 green 1.25 20
8L19 " $50 red 20 10
8L20 " $100 brown 20 25

Liberation of the Southwest.

Nos. 8L5–8L6 Surcharged 圓仟貳作改

Perf. 12½

8L21 A1 $300 on $100 car. 10.00 8.00
8L22 " $500 on $100 car. 20 30
8L23 " $1200 on $100 car. 1.00 1.00
8L24 " $1500 on $200 blue 1.00 1.00
8L25 " $2000 on $200 blue 15.00 12.00
Nos. 8L21–8L25 (5) 27.20 22.30

Nos. 8L5–8L6 Overprinted ("East Szechwan") (川東)

1950, Jan.

8L26 A1 $100 carmine 4.00 4.00
8L27 " $200 blue 4.00 4.00

Nos. 8L5–8L6 Handstamp Surcharged

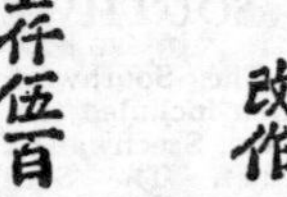

1950, Jan.

8L28 A1 $1200 on $100 car. 12.50 12.50
8L29 " $1500 on $200 blue 17.50 17.50

Many varieties, including wide and narrow settings, exist.

Nos. 8L17–8L20 Surcharged in Black or Red

叁仟圓 改作 伍仟圓
$3000 $5000

壹萬圓 貳萬圓 伍萬圓
$10,000 $20,000 $50,000

1950 *Perf. 9 to 11½*

8L30 A2 $60 on $30 grn. 20.00 10.00
8L31 " $150 on $30 grn. 20.00 10.00
8L32 " $300 on $20 dark blue (R) 2.00 2.00
8L33 " $300 on $100 brn. 20.00 10.00
8L34 " $1500 on $100 brn. 20.00 10.00
8L35 " $3000 on $50 red 3.50 3.50
8L36 " $5000 on $50 red 3.50 3.50
8L37 " $10,000 on $50 red *45.00* *20.00*
8L38 " $20,000 on $50 red 3.50 3.50
8L39 " $50,000 on $50 red 10.00 10.00
Nos. 8L30–8L39 (10) *147.50* *82.50*

Nos. 8L5–8L7 Overprinted ("West Szechwan") 川 西

1950, Jan. *Perf. 12½*

8L40 A1 $100 carmine 10.00 10.00
8L41 " $200 pale blue 10.00 10.00
8L42 " $300 blue violet 10.00 10.00

Nos. 8L4–8L7 Surcharged

蓉
圓仟貳作改
$2000

1950, Jan.

8L43 A1 $500 on $100 car. 5.00 3.00
a. Narrow spacing 35.00 35.00
8L44 A1 $800 on $100 car. 5.00 3.00
8L45 " $1000 on $50 gray green 7.00 5.00
8L46 " $2000 on $200 pale blue 12.00 8.00
8L47 A1 $3000 on $300 gray violet 25.00 20.00
Nos. 8L43–8L47 (5) 54.00 39.00

Two lines of surcharge 7mm. apart on No. 8L43, 4mm. on No. 8L43a.

China Nos. 975 and 977 Surcharged

政郵民人 政郵民人
蓉 蓉
圓百貳 圓仟壹
$200 $1000

Perf. 12½, 13 or Compound

1950, Jan.

8L48 A94 $100 on 4c bl. grn. 4.00 4.00
8L49 " $200 on 4c bl. grn. 8.00 8.00
8L50 " $800 on 16c orange red 25.00 25.00
8L51 " $1000 on 16c orange red 50.00 50.00

Unit Issue of China Overprinted ("Southwest People's Post")

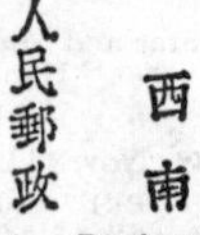

1950, Jan. **Engraved** ***Perf. 12½***

8L52 A96 orange 125.00 80.00
a. Rouletted 125.00 80.00
8L53 SD2 red violet 125.00 80.00
8L54 R2 carmine 125.00 80.00

On No. 8L54, space between overprint columns is 3mm. and right column is raised to height of left.

Nos. 8L3, 8L12–8L15 Surcharged in Black or Red

改作 捌百元

1950, Mar. ***Perf. 12½, 9 to 11½***

8L55 A1 $800 on $30 deep orange 35.00 25.00
8L56 A2 $1000 on $50 red 7.50 4.00
8L57 " $2000 on $100 brn. 10.00 6.00
8L58 " $4000 on $20 dark blue (R) 27.50 17.50
8L59 " $5000 on $30 gray green 45.00 30.00
Nos. 8L55–8L59 (5) 125.00 82.50

SHANGHAI

(See Vol. IV.)

CILICIA

(sĭ-lĭsh′ĭ-*ȧ* ; -lĭsh′*ȧ*)

LOCATION—A territory of Turkey, in southeastern Asia Minor.
GOVT.—Former French occupation.
AREA—6,238 sq. mi.
POP.—383,645.
PRINCIPAL TOWN—Seyhan.

British and French forces occupied Cilicia in 1918 and in 1919 its control was transferred to the French. Eventually part of Cilicia was assigned to the French Mandated Territory of Syria but by the Lausanne Treaty of 1923 which fixed the boundary between Syria and Turkey, Cilicia reverted to Turkey.

40 Paras = 1 Piaster

Issued under French Occupation.

The overprint on Nos. 2–93 is often found inverted, double, etc.

Numbers in parentheses are those of basic Turkish stamps.

Turkish Stamps of 1913–19 Handstamped CILICIE

Perf. 11½, 12, 12½, 13½.

1919 **Unwmkd.**

On Pictorial Issue of 1913.

2 A24 2pa red lilac (254) 80 60
3 A25 4pa dk. brown (255) 40 40
4 A27 6pa dk. blue(257) 3.00 1.75
5 A32 1¾pi slate & red brown (262) 1.00 1.00

On Issue of 1915.

6 A17 1pi blue (300) 35 35
7 A21 20pa car. rose (318) 40 40
9 A22 20pa car. rose (330) 75 75

On Commemorative Issue of 1916.

10 A41 20pa ultramarine(347) 60 60
11 " 1pi vio. & blk. (348) 70 70
12 " 5pi yellow brown & black (349) 60 60

On Issue of 1916-18.

13 A44 10pa green (424) 80 80
14 A47 50pa ultra. (428) 2.00 1.25
15 A51 25pi carmine, *straw* (434) 80 80
16 A52 50pi carmine (437) 60 60
17 " 50pi indigo (438) 7.00 7.00

On Issue of 1917.

18 A53 5pi on 2pa Prussian blue (547) 2.00 1.65

On Issue of 1919.

19 A47 50pa ultra. (555) 2.00 1.25
20 A48 2pi orange brown & indigo (556) 1.00 1.00
21 A49 5pi pale blue & black (557) 2.00 1.00

On Newspaper Stamp of 1916.

22 N3 5pa on 10pa gray green (P137) 65 45

On Semi-Postal Stamps of 1916.

23 A17 1pi blue (B19) 40 35
24 A21 20pa car. rose (B28) 50 45
25 " 1pi ultra. (B29) 2.50 2.00

Turkish Stamps of 1913–18 Handstamped CILICIE

1919

On Pictorial Issue of 1913.

31 A24 2pa red lilac (254) 20 20
32 A25 4pa dark brown (255) 75 75

On Issue of 1915.

33 A17 1pi blue (300) 50 50
34 A22 20pa carmine rose (330) 40 40

On Commemorative Issue of 1916.

35 A41 20pa ultra. (347) 55 55
36 A44 1pi violet & black (348) 50 50

On Issue of 1917.

40 A53 5pi on 2pa Prussian blue (547) 45 40

On Newspaper Stamp of 1916.

41 N3 5pa on 10pa gray green (P137) 50 50

On Semi-Postal Stamps of 1916.

42 A17 1pi blue (B19) 1.00 1.00
43 A21 20pa carmine rose (B28) 25 25

Turkish Stamps of 1913-19 Handstamped *Cilicie*

1919

On Pictorial Issue of 1913.

51 A24 2pa red lilac (254) 35 35
52 A25 4pa dark brown (255) 35 35

On Issue of 1915.

53 A17 1pi blue (300) 20 15
55 A22 5pa ochre (328) 1.25 1.00
56 " 20pa car. rose (330) 60 60

On Commemorative Issue of 1916.

57 A41 20pa ultra. (347) 50 50
58 " 1pi violet & black (348) 60 60
59 " 5pi yellow brown & black (349) 50 50

On Issue of 1916

59A A17 1pi blue (372) 22.50 13.50

On Issue of 1916-18.

60 A43 5pa orange (421) 1.00 90
61 A46 1pi dull violet (426) 60 50
63 A52 50pi green, *straw* (439) 11.50 5.00

On Issue of 1917

64 A53 5pi on 2pa Prussian blue (547) 1.85 1.35

On Newspaper Stamp of 1916.

65 N3 5pa on 10pa gray green (P137) 50 50

On Newspaper Stamp of 1919.

65A N4 5pa on 2pa olive green (P173)

On Semi-Postal Stamps of 1916.

66 A17 1pi blue (B19) 60 55
67 A19 20pa carmine (B26) 2.00 1.65
68 A21 20pa carmine rose (B28) 45.00 22.50
69 " 20pa carmine rose (B31) 60 60

Turkey No. 424 Handstamped *T.E.O. Cilicie*

1919

71 A44 10pa green 30 30

Turkish Stamps of 1913-19 Overprinted in Black, Red or Blue T. E. O. Cilicie

1919

In this setting there are various broken and wrong font letters and the letter "i" is sometimes replaced by a "t."

On Pictorial Issue of 1913.

75 A30 1pi blue (R) (260) 20 15

On Issue of 1915.

76 A21 20pa carmine rose (318) 60 70

On Commemorative Issue of 1916.

77 A41 20pa ultra. (347) 40 10
78 " 1pi violet & black (348) 30 25

On Issue of 1916-18.

79 A43 5pa orange (B1) (421) 10 10
80 A44 10pa green (424) 15 15

No.	Type	Description	Unused	Used
81	A45	20pa deep rose (Bk) (425)	40	40
82	"	20pa deep rose (Bl) (425)	12	10
83	A48	2pi orange brown & indigo (429)	20	15
83C	A49	5pi pale blue & black (R) (430)	20	15
84	A51	25pi carmine, *straw* (434)	1.85	1.35
85	A52	50pi green, *straw* (439)	30.00	22.50

On Issue of 1917.

No.	Type	Description	Unused	Used
85A	A53	5pi on 2pa Prussian blue (547)		
86	"	5pi on 2pa Prussian blue (548)	1.65	1.50

On Newspaper Stamps of 1916–19

No.	Type	Description	Unused	Used
87	N3	5pa on 10pa gray green (P137)	15	15
88	N4	5pa on 2pa olive green (P173)	10	10

On Semi-Postal Stamps of 1915–17

No.	Type	Description	Unused	Used
89	A21	20pa carmine rose (B8)		
90	"	20pa carmine rose (B28)	25	20
91	A41	10pa carmine (B42)	15	15
92	A11	10pa on 20pa violet brown (B38)	15	15
93	SP1	10pa red violet (B46)	40	30

It is understood that the Newspaper and Semi-Postal stamps overprinted "Cilicie" were used as ordinary postage stamps.

A1

Blue Surcharge.

1920 *Perf. 11½.*

No.	Type	Description	Unused	Used
98	A1	70pa on 5pa red	20	20
99	"	3½pi on 5pa red	20	20

Nos. 98-99 exist with surcharge double, inverted, double with one inverted, "OCCUPTTION," etc. Price, $1 to $2 each.

French Offices in Turkey No. 26 Surcharged — T. E. O 20 PARAS

1920 *Perf. 14x13½*

No.	Type	Description	Unused	Used
100	A3	20pa on 10c rose red	15	15
		a. "PARAS" omitted	7.50	7.50
		b. Surcharged on back	2.50	2.50

Three types of "20" exist on No. 100.

Stamps of France, 1900-17, Surcharged — O. M. F. Cilicie 5 PARAS

1920

No.	Type	Description	Unused	Used
101	A16	5pa on 2c violet brn.	10	10
102	A22	10pa on 5c green	15	15
103	"	20pa on 10c red	35	35
104	"	1pi on 25c blue	60	60
105	A20	2pi on 15c gray grn.	1.65	1.65
106	A18	5pi on 40c red & gray blue	1.50	1.50
107	"	10pi on 50c bistre brn. & lavender	2.00	2.00
108	"	50pi on 1fr claret & olive green	45.00	45.00
109	"	100pi on 5fr dark blue & buff	350.00	350.00
		Nos. 101-109 (9)	401.35	401.35

Nos. 106 to 109 surcharged in four lines.

Stamps of France, 1917, Surcharged — O. M. F. Cilicie SAND. EST 20 PARAS

1920

No.	Type	Description	Unused	Used
110	A16	5pa on 2c vio. brown	1.65	
111	A22	10pa on 5c green	1.65	
112	"	20pa on 10c red	85	
113	"	1pi on 25c blue	85	
114	A20	2pi on 15c gray grn.	3.25	
115	A18	5pi on 40c red & gray blue	25.00	
116	"	20pi on 1fr claret & olive green	42.50	
		Nos. 110-116 (7)	75.75	

On Nos. 115 and 116 "SAND. EST" is placed vertically. "Sand. Est" is an abbreviation of Sandjak de l'Est (Eastern County).

Nos. 110–116 were prepared for use, but never issued.

Stamps of France, 1900-17, Surcharged — O. M. F. Cilicie 10 PARAS

1920

No.	Type	Description	Unused	Used
117	A16	5pa on 2c violet brown	5	5
		a. Inverted surchg.	3.00	3.00
		b. Double surcharge	6.00	
		c. "Cililie"	5.00	5.00
		d. Surch. 5 pi (error)	8.00	8.00
119	A22	10pa on 5c green	8	8
		a. Inverted surcharge	3.00	3.00
		b. Surch. 5pa (error)	8.00	8.00
121	"	20pa on 10c red	8	8
		a. Inverted surcharge	3.00	3.00
		b. Surch. 10pa (error)	9.00	9.00
122	"	1pi on 25c blue	8	8
		a. Double surcharge	4.00	
		b. Inverted surcharge	3.00	3.00
123	A20	2pi on 15c gray green	20	20
		a. Double surcharge	8.00	
		b. Inverted surcharge	3.00	3.00
124	A18	5pi on 40c red & gray blue	30	30
		a. Double surcharge	12.00	
		b. Inverted surcharge	7.00	7.00
		c. "PIASRTES"	10.00	10.00
125	"	10pi on 50c bistre brown & lavender	30	30
		a. "PIASRTES"	10.00	10.00
126	"	50pi on 1fr claret & olive green	85	85
		a. "PIASRTES"	12.50	12.50
		b. Inverted surchg.	13.50	13.50
127	"	100pi on 5fr dark blue & buff	4.75	4.75
		a. "PIASRTES"	30.00	30.00
		Nos. 117-127 (9)	6.69	6.69

This surcharge has "O.M.F." in thicker letters than the preceding issues.

There were two printings of this surcharge which may be distinguished by the space of 1 or 2mm. between "Cilicie" and the numeral.

The surcharge on Nos. 119b and 121b is always inverted.

AIR POST STAMPS.

Nos. 123 and 124 Handstamped — POSTE PAR AVION

Perf. 14x13½

1920, July 15 **Unwmkd.**

No.	Type	Description	Unused	Used
C1	A20	2pi on 15c gray green	2500.00	2500.00
C2	A18	5pi on 40c red & gray blue	2500.00	2500.00
		a. "PIASRTES"		

A very limited number of Nos. C1 and C2 were used on two air mail flights between Adana and Aleppo. At a later date impressions from a new handstamp were struck "to oblige" on stamps of the regular issue of 1920 (Nos. 123, 124, 125 and 126) that were in stock at the Adana Post Office.

Counterfeits exist.

POSTAGE DUE STAMPS.

Turkish Postage Due Stamps of 1914 Handstamped.

1919 *Perf. 12.* **Unwmkd.**

Handstamped — CILICIE

No.	Type	Description	Unused	Used
J1	D1	5pa claret	1.00	80
J2	D2	20pa red	90	60
J3	D3	1pi dark blue	2.00	2.00
J4	D4	2pi slate	1.85	1.65

Handstamped — CILICIE

No.	Type	Description	Unused	Used
J5	D1	5pa claret	1.00	1.00
J6	D2	20pa red	90	90
J7	D3	1pi dark blue	2.00	2.00
J8	D4	2pi slate	1.85	1.85

Handstamped — *Cilicie*

No.	Type	Description	Unused	Used
J9	D1	5pa claret	1.00	80
J10	D2	20pa red	1.00	80
J11	D3	1pi dark blue	2.00	2.00
J12	D4	2pi slate	1.85	1.85

Postage Due Stamps of France Surcharged — O. M. F. Cilicie 2 PIASTRES

1921

No.	Type	Description	Unused	Used
J13	D2	1pi on 10c chocolate	2.50	2.50
J14	"	2pi on 20c olive green	2.50	2.50
J15	"	3pi on 30c red	2.50	2.50
J16	"	4pi on 50c violet brn.	2.50	2.50

COCHIN CHINA

(kō'chĭn chĭ'nȧ; kŏch'ĭn)

LOCATION — The southernmost state of French Indo-China in the Cambodian Peninsula.

GOVT.—French Colony.

AREA—26,476 sq. mi.

POP.—4,615,968.

CAPITAL—Saigon.

100 Centimes = 1 Franc

Surcharged in Black on Stamps of French Colonies:

5 (a) — 5 C. CH. (b) — 5 (c)

1886–87 *Perf. 14x13½* **Unwmkd.**

No.	Type	Description	Unused	Used
1	A9	(a) 5c on 25c yellow, *straw*	65.00	45.00
2	"	(b) 5c on 2c brown, *buff* ('87)	5.00	5.00
3	"	(") 5c on 25c yellow, *straw*	5.00	5.00
4	"	(c) 5c on 25c *rose* ('87)	15.00	13.50
		a. Double surcharge, one of type b	500.00	325.00
		b. Triple surcharge, two of type b	100.00	100.00
		c. Inverted surcharge		25.00

15 / 15 (d)

1888

No.	Type	Description	Unused	Used
5	A9	(d) 15c on half of 30c brown, *bistre*	13.50	

No. 5 was prepared but not issued.

The so-called Postage Due stamps were never issued.

Stamps of Cochin China were superseded by those of Indo-China in 1892.

COLOMBIA

(kō̇-lŏm'bē̇-ä)

LOCATION — On the northwest coast of South America, bordering on the Caribbean Sea and the Pacific Ocean.

GOVT.—Republic.

AREA—456,535 sq. mi. (estimated.)

POP.—25,167,500 (est. 1977).

CAPITAL—Bogotá.

In 1810 the Spanish Viceroyalty of New Granada gained its independence and with Venezuela and Ecuador formed the State of Greater Colombia. In 1832 this state split into three independent units as Venezuela, Ecuador and the Republic of New Granada. The name of the country has been successively Granadine Confederation (1858-61), United States of New Granada (1861), United States of Colombia (1861-85), Republic of Colombia (1885 to date).

100 Centavos = 1 Peso

Prices of early Colombia stamps vary according to condition. Quotations for Nos. 1–34 are for fine copies. Very fine to superb specimens sell at much higher prices, and inferior or poor copies sell at reduced prices, depending on the condition of the individual specimen.

In the earlier days many towns did not have handstamps for canceling and stamps were canceled with pen and ink. Pen cancellations, therefore, do not indicate fiscal use. (Postage stamps were not used for revenue purposes.) Prices of Nos. 1–128 are for pen-canceled specimens. Those with handstamped cancellations sell for considerably more.

Fractions of many Colombian stamps of both early and late issues are found canceled, their use to pay postage having been tolerated even though forbidden by the postal laws and regulations. Many are known to have been made for philatelic purposes.

Granadine Confederation

Coat of Arms

A1 A2

Type A1: Asterisks in frame. Wavy lines in background.

Type A2: Diamond-shaped ornaments in frame. Straight lines in background. Numerals larger.

Lithographed.

1859 *Imperf.* **Unwmkd.**

Wove Paper.

No.	Type	Description	Unused	Used
1	A1	2½c green	37.50	25.00
		a. 2½c yellow green	37.50	25.00
2	"	5c blue	24.00	17.50
		a. Tête bêche pair	1750.00	1500.00
3	"	5c violet	30.00	20.00
		a. Tête bêche pair	1750.00	1500.00
		b. "50" instead of "5"	2000.00	2200.00
4	"	10c red brown	27.50	18.00
		a. 10c buff	27.50	18.00
6	"	20c blue	27.50	20.00
		a. 20c gray blue	27.50	20.00
		b. Se-tenant with 5c	10,000.00	7500.00
		c. Tête bêche pair	8000.00	5500.00
7	"	1p carmine	22.50	30.00
		a. 1p rose	22.50	30.00
8	"	1p rose, *bluish*	175.00	

The 10c green is an essay.

Reprints of No. 7 are in brown rose or brown red. Wavy lines of background are much broken; no dividing lines between stamps.

1860 **Laid Paper.**

9 A2 5c lilac 150.00 100.00

Wove Paper.

10 A2 5c gray lilac 30.00 30.00
a. 5c lilac 30.00 30.00
11 " 10c yellow buff 25.00 22.50
a. Tête bêche pair 1500.00 1400.00
12 " 20c blue 85.00 55.00

United States of New Granada

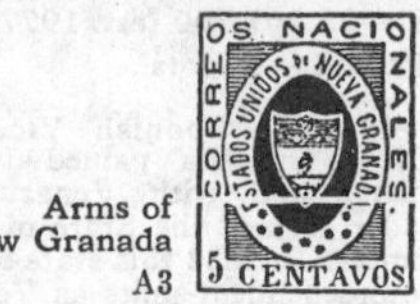

Arms of New Granada
A3

1861

13 A3 2½c black 450.00 285.00
14 " 5c yellow 100.00 65.00
a. 5c buff 100.00 65.00
16 " 10c blue 250.00 90.00
17 " 20c red 225.00 90.00
18 " 1p pink 225.00 110.00

There are 54 varieties of the 5c, 20c, and 1 peso.
Forgeries exist of Nos. 13–18.

United States of Colombia

Coat of Arms
A4 A5 A6

1862

19 A4 10c blue 90.00 60.00
20 " 20c red 900.00 375.00
21 " 50c green 125.00 90.00
22 " 1p red lilac 250.00 135.00
23 " 1p red lilac, *bluish* 1750.00 1000.00

No. 23 is on a thinner, coarser wove paper than Nos. 19-22.

1863

24 A5 5c orange 25.00 20.00
a. Star after "Cent" 30.00 22.50
25 " 10c blue 30.00 12.50
a. Period after "10" 32.50 12.50
26 " 20c red 37.50 30.00
a. Star after "Cent" 45.00 35.00
b. Transfer of 50c in stone of 20c 7500.00 4000.00

Bluish Paper.

28 A5 10c blue 27.50 15.00
a. Period after "10" 32.50 17.50
29 " 50c green 35.00 30.00
a. Star after "Cent" 40.00 35.00

Ten varieties of each.

1864 **Wove Paper.**

30 A6 5c orange 17.50 12.50
a. Tête bêche 225.00 200.00
31 " 10c blue 17.50 8.50
a. Period after 10 17.50 8.50
32 " 20c scarlet 30.00 15.00
33 " 50c green 25.00 16.50
34 " 1p red violet 200.00 100.00

Two varieties of each.

Arms of Colombia
A7 A9

A8

1865

35 A7 1c rose 7.00 5.50
a. Bluish pelure paper 10.00 7.50
36 A8 2½c *lilac* 11.00 7.00
37 A9 5c yellow 11.00 8.50
a. 5c orange 11.00 8.50
38 " 10c violet 15.00 4.50
39 " 20c blue 12.50 7.00
40 " 50c green 37.50 20.00
41 " 50c green (small figures) 30.00 12.50
42 " 1p vermilion 42.50 12.50
a. 1p rose red 42.50 12.50
b. Period after "PESO" 42.50 12.50

Ten varieties of each of the 5c, 10c, 20c, and 50c, and six varieties of the 1 peso.
No. 36 was used as a carrier stamp.

A10 A11 A12

A13 A14

A15 A16

1866 **White Wove Paper.**

45 A10 5c orange 12.50 7.00
46 A11 10c lilac 4.25 4.25
a. Pelure paper 8.50 6.50
47 A12 20c light blue 13.50 9.50
a. Pelure paper 25.00 17.50
48 A13 50c green 7.50 5.50
49 A14 1p rose red, *bluish* 30.00 25.00
a. 1p vermilion 22.50 12.50
51 A15 5p *green* 135.00 100.00
52 A16 10p *vermilion* 110.00 85.00

There are several varieties of the 1 peso having the letters "U", "N", "S" and "O" smaller.

A17

A18 A19

A20 A21

TEN CENTAVOS:
Type I: "B" of "COLOMBIA" over "V" of "CENTAVOS".
Type II: "B" of "COLOMBIA" over "VO" of "CENTAVOS".
ONE PESO:
Type I: Long thin spear heads Diagonal lines in lower part of shield.
Type II: Short thick spear heads. Horizontal and a few diagonal lines in lower part of shield.
Type III: Short thick spear heads. Crossed lines in lower part of shield. Ornaments at each side of circle are broken. (See No. 97.)

1868

53 A17 5c orange 25.00 20.00
54 A18 10c lilac (I) 1.50 90
a. 10c red violet (I) 1.50 90
b. 10c lilac (II) 1.50 90
c. 10c red violet (II) 1.50 90
d. Printed on both sides 3.25 2.00
55 A19 20c blue 2.00 1.25
56 A20 50c yellow green 2.50 1.50
57 A21 1p vermilion (II) 3.00 1.75
a. Tête bêche pair 125.00 125.00
b. 1p rose red (I) 85.00 17.50
c. 1p rose red (II) 3.00 1.75

See also Nos. 83–84, 96–97.

Counterfeits or reprints.
10c. There is a large white dot at the upper left between the circle enclosing the "X" and the ornament below.
50c. There is a shading of dots instead of dashes below the ribbon with motto. There are crossed lines in the lowest section of the shield instead of diagonal or horizontal ones.
1p. The ornaments in the lettered circle are broken. There are crossed lines in the lowest section of the shield.
These counterfeits, or reprints, are on white paper, wove and laid, on colored wove paper and in fancy colors.

A22

Two varieties.

1869-70 **Wove Paper**

59 A22 2½c *violet* 2.25 2.25
a. Laid paper ('70) 75.00 75.00
b. Laid batonné paper ('70) 30.00 30.00

Nos. 59, 59a and 59b were used as carrier stamps.
Counterfeits, or reprints, are on magenta paper wove or ribbed.

A23 A24

1870 **Wove Paper.**

62 A23 5c orange 90 90
a. 5c yellow 90 90
63 A24 25c *blue* 9.00 7.50

See also No. 89.

In the counterfeits, or reprints, of No. 63, the top of the "2" of "25" does not touch the down stroke. The counterfeits are on paper of various colors.

A25 A26

5 pesos. The ornament at the left of the "C" of "Cinco" cuts into the "C", and the shading of the flag is formed of diagonal lines.
10 pesos. The stars have extra rays between the points, and the central part of the shield has some horizontal lines of shading at each end.

1870 **Surface Colored, Chalky Paper**

64 A25 5p *green* 32.50 20.00
65 A26 10p *vermilion* 55.00 45.00

See also Nos. 77–79, 125–126.

A27

A28 A29

TEN CENTAVOS:
Type I: "S" of "CORREOS" 2¼ mm. high. First "N" of "NACIONALES" small.
Type II: "S" of "CORREOS" 2 mm. high. First "N" of "NACIONALES" wide.

1871-74 **Thin Porous Paper**

66 A27 1c green ('72) 1.75 1.75
67 " 1c rose ('73) 1.25 1.25
a. 1c carmine ('73) 1.25 1.25
68 A28 2c brown 90 90
a. 2c red brown 75 75
69 A29 10c violet (I) ('74) 1.00 90
a. 10c lilac (I) ('74) 1.00 90
b. 10c violet (II) ('74) 1.00 90
c. 10c lilac (II) ('74) 1.00 90
d. Laid paper, as #69 ('72) 30.00 30.00
e. Laid paper, as "b" ('72) 30.00 30.00

Counterfeits or reprints.
1c. The outer frame of the shield is broken near the upper left corner and the "A" of "Colombia" has no cross-bar.
2c. There are scratches across "DOS" and many white marks around the letters on the large "2".
The counterfeits, or reprints, are on white wove and bluish white laid paper.

Condor
A30

Liberty Head
A31 A32

Wove Paper.

5 pesos, re-drawn: The ornament at the left of the "C" only touches the "C", and the shading of the flag is formed of vertical and diagonal lines.
10 pesos, re-drawn: The stars are distinctly five pointed, and there is no shading in the central part of the shield.

1877

73 A30 5c purple 3.75 85
a. 5c lilac 3.75 85
74 A31 10c bistre brown 1.25 60
a. 10c red brown 1.25 60
b. 10c violet brown 1.50 60
75 A32 20c blue 1.50 90
a. 20c violet blue 7.50 3.75

77 A26 10p *rose* 30.00 15.00
78 A25 5p *light green*, redrawn 20.00 12.50
79 A26 10p *rose*, redrawn 15.00 3.50

Stamps of the issues of 1871-77 are known with private perforations of various gauges, also with sewing machine perforation.

In the counterfeits, or reprints, of the 5 pesos the ornament at the left of the "C" of "Cinco" is separated from the "C" by a black line.

In the counterfeits, or reprints, of the 10 pesos the outer line of the double circle containing "10" is broken at the top, below "OS" of "Unidos", and the vertical lines of shading contained in the double circle are very indistinct. There is a colorless dash below the loop of the "P" of "Pesos".

1876-79 Laid Paper.

80 A30 5c lilac 7.50 6.00
81 A31 10c brown 10.00 4.00
82 A32 20c blue 17.50 11.00
83 A20 50c green ('79) 20.00 12.00
84 A21 1p pale red (II) ('79) 35.00 7.00

1879 Wove Paper.

89 A24 25c green 10.00 10.00

1881 Blue Wove Paper.

93 A30 5c violet 7.50 3.50
a. 5c lilac 8.00 3.50
94 A31 10c brown 3.50 2.00
95 A32 20c blue 3.50 2.00
96 A20 50c yellow green 6.00 4.00
97 A21 1p verm. (III) 10.00 7.00

For types of 1p, see note over No. 53.

Reprints of the 10c and 20c are much worn. On the 10c the letters "TAVOS" of "CENTAVOS" often touch. On the 20c the letters "NT" of "VEINTE" touch and the left arm of the "T" is too long. Reprints of the 25c, 50c and 1p have the characteristics previously described. The reprints are on white wove or laid paper, on colored papers, and in fancy colors. Stamps on green paper exist only as reprints.

A34

A35

A36

White Wove Paper.

1 centavo: The period before "UNION" is round and there are rays between the stars and the condors.
2 centavos: The "2" s and "C" s in the corners are placed upright.
5 centavos: The last star at the right almost touches the frame.
10 centavos: The letters of the inscription are thin; there are rays between the stars and the condor.

1881 ***Imperf.***

103 A34 1c green 1.00 1.00
104 A35 2c vermilion 65 55
a. 2c rose 60 55
106 A34 5c blue 85 85
a. Printed on both sides
107 A36 10c violet 1.25 85
108 A34 20c black 2.00 1.50
Nos. 103-108 (5) 5.75 4.75

The stamps of this issue are found with perforations of various gauges, also sewing machine perforation, all of which are unofficial.

Liberty Head
A37

A37a

1881 ***Imperf.***

109 A37 1c *green* 90 75
110 " 2c *lilac rose* 90 85
111 " 5c *lilac* 1.50 1.25

Nos. 109 to 111 are found with regular or sewing machine perforation, unofficial.

Reprints:

1c. The top line of the stamp and the top frame extend to the left.

2c. There is a curved line over the scroll below the "AV" of "CENTAVOS".

5c. There are scratches across the "5" in the upper left corner.

All three values were reprinted on the three colors of paper of the originals.

Redrawn.

1 centavo: The period before "UNION" is square and the rays between the stars and the condor have been wholly or partly erased.
2 centavos: The "2" s and "C" s in the corners are placed diagonally.
5 centavos: The last star at the right touches the wing of the condor.
10 centavos: The letters of the inscription are thick; there are no rays under the stars; the last star at the right touches the wing of the condor and this wing touches the frame.

1883 ***Imperf.***

112 A34 1c green 1.25 1.25
113 A37a 2c rose 75 65
114 A34 5c blue 75 65
a. 5c ultramarine 1.00 75
b. Printed on both sides, reverse ultramarine 30.00 25.00
115 A36 10c violet 1.25 1.25

The stamps of this issue are found with regular or sewing machine perforation, privately applied.

A38

A39

1883 ***Perf. 10½, 12, 13½***

116 A38 1c gray green, *green* 65 65
a. Imperf., pair 4.00 4.00
117 A39 2c red, *rose* 60 60
a. 2c orange red, *rose* 60 60
b. 2c red, *buff* 10.00 10.00
c. Imperf., pair (#117 or 117a) 4.00 4.00
d. "DE LOS" in very small caps 10.00 10.00
118 A38 5c blue, *bluish* 1.25 1.25
a. 5c dark blue, *bluish* 1.25 1.25
b. 5c blue 1.25 1.25
c. Imperf., pair (#118 or 118a) 6.00 6.00
d. As "b," imperf., pair 8.00 8.00
119 A39 10c orange, *yellow* 1.00 1.25
a. "DE LOS" in large caps 12.50 10.00
b. Imperf., pair 6.00 6.00
120 " 20c violet, *lilac* 1.00 1.25
a. Imperf., pair 4.00 4.00
122 A38 50c brown, *buff* 1.25 1.25
a. Perf. 12 2.00 2.00
123 " 1p claret, *bluish* 2.50 1.85
a. Imperf., pair 10.00 10.00
Nos. 116-123 (7) 8.25 8.10

1886 ***Perf. 10½, 11½, 12.***

127 A38 5p brown, *straw* 5.00 4.00
a. Imperf., pair 25.00 25.00
128 " 10p *rose* 4.50 3.50
a. Imperf., pair 25.00 25.00

Republic of Colombia

A40

Simón Bolívar
A41

President Rafael Núñez
A42

1886 ***Perf. 10½ and 13½***

129 A40 1c green, *green* 60 60
a. Imperf., pair 6.00 6.00
130 A41 5c blue, *blue* 85 30
a. 5c ultra., *blue* 85 30
b. Imperf., pair (#130) 6.00 6.00
131 A42 10c orange 1.50 55
a. Imperf., pair 6.00 6.00
b. Pelure paper 2.00 75

General Antonio José de Sucre y Alcala
A43

General Antonio Nariño
A44

1887

133 A43 2c orange red, *rose* 1.00 75
a. 2c orange red, *yellow* 2.50 2.50
b. 2c orange red 7.00 7.00
c. Imperf., pair (#133) 6.00 6.00
134 A44 20c purple, *grayish* 1.75 85
a. Imperf., pair 6.00 6.00
b. Pelure paper 2.25 1.50

Impressions of No. 134 on white, blue or greenish blue paper were not regularly issued.

Arms
A45

Nariño
A46

1888

135 A45 50c brown, *buff* 90 90
a. Imperf., pair 3.50 3.50
136 " 1p claret, *bluish* 3.25 1.50
137 " 1p claret 1.50 1.25
138 " 5p orange brown 4.25 3.00
139 " 5p black 5.50 3.75
140 " 10p *rose* 5.00 3.75
Nos. 135-140 (6) 20.40 14.15

1889

141 A46 20c purple, *grayish* 85 85
a. Imperf., pair 5.00 5.00

Impressions on white, blue or greenish blue paper were not regularly issued.

Unused prices are for stamps that have been hinged.

A47

A48

A49

A50

A51

1890-91 ***Perf. 10½, 13½, 11***

142 A47 1c green, *green* 60 40
143 A48 2c orange red, *rose* 50 40
144 A49 5c blue, *greenish blue* 50 30
a. 5c deep blue, *blue* 60 30
b. Imperf., pair 3.50 3.50
146 A50 10c brown, *yellow* 45 30
147 A51 20c violet, pelure paper 1.10 1.00
Nos. 142-147 (5) 3.15 2.40

A52

A53

A54

Perf. 10½, 12, 13½, 14 to 15½.

1892 Ordinary Paper.

148 A47 1c red, *yellow* 40 30
149 A52 2c red, *rose* 2.50 2.50
150 " 2c green 25 18
a. 2c yellow green 25 18
151 A49 5c black, *buff* 85 30
152 A50 10c bistre brown, *rose* 45 30
153 A53 20c brown, *blue* 45 30
154 A45 50c violet, *violet* 75 30
155 A54 1p blue, *greenish* 90 35
156 A45 5p red, *pale rose* 3.00 1.25
157 " 10p blue 3.50 2.25
a. Thin, pale rose paper 4.25 2.75
Nos. 148-157 (10) 13.05 8.03

Nos. 148, 150-155 and 157 exist imperf. Price per pair, $5-$7.50.

A55

A55a

1895-99

158 A55 5c orange brown, *pale buff* 35 30
  a. Imperf., pair 5.00 5.00
159 " 5c red brown, *salmon* ('97) 35 30
  a. Imperf., pair 5.00 5.00
160 A53 20c yellow brown, *greenish blue* ('97) 1.00 1.00
160A " 20c brn., *buff* ('97) 17.50 11.50
161 A55a 50c red violet, *violet* ('99) 1.50 1.25

Type A55a is a redrawing of type A45. The letters of the inscriptions are slightly larger and the numerals "50" slightly smaller than in type A45.

The 20c brown on white paper is believed to be a chemical changeling.

A56

1899

162 A56 1c red, *yellow* 30 30
163 " 5c red brown, *salmon* 30 30
164 " 10c brown, *lilac rose* 75 75
165 " 50c blue, *lilac* 65 65

Cartagena Issues.

A57

1899 Blue Overprint. *Imperf.*

167 A57 5c red, *buff* 13.50 13.50
  a. Sewing machine perf. 9.00 9.00
168 A57 10c ultra., *buff* 11.50 11.50
  a. Sewing machine perf. 9.00 9.00

Nos. 168 and 168a differ slightly from the illustration.

A58

A59

A60

A61

Purple Overprint.

1899 *Sewing Machine Perf.*

170 A58 1c brown, *buff* 8.50 8.50
  a. Altered from 10c 10.00 10.00
171 A59 2c black, *buff* 8.50 8.50
  a. Altered from 10c 10.00 10.00
172 A60 5c maroon, *greenish blue* 11.50 11.50
  a. Perf. 12 11.50 11.50
  b. Without ovpt. 6.50 6.50
173 A61 10c red, *salmon* 11.50 11.50
  a. Perf. 12 11.50 11.50

Types A58 and A59 illustrate Nos. 170a and 171a, which were made from altered plates of the 10c (No. 168). Nos. 170 and 171 were made from altered plate of the 5c denomination (No. 167), show part of the top flag of the "5" and differ slightly from the illustrations.

Nos. 170-173 exist imperf. Prices about same as perf.

A62

1900 *Imperf.*

Purple Overprint

174 A62 5c red 4.50 4.50
  a. Perf. 12 6.00 6.00

A63

A64

Sewing Machine Perf.

1901 Purple Overprint.

175 A63 1c black 75 75
  a. Without overprint 2.25 2.25
  b. Double overprint 2.50 2.50
  c. Imperf., pair 2.00 2.00
  d. Inverted overprint 1.00 1.00
176 A64 2c *rose* 75 75
  a. Imperf., pair 2.00 2.00
  b. Without overprint 2.25 2.25
  c. Double overprint 2.50 2.50

A65

A66

1901 Rose Overprint

177 A65 1c blue 75 75
  a. Imperf., pair 3.00 3.00
178 A66 2c brown 75 75
  a. Imperf., pair 3.00 3.00
  b. Without overprint 75 75

A67

A68

Sewing Machine or Regular Perf. 12, 12½

1902 Magenta Overprint.

179 A67 5c violet 1.50 1.50
  a. Without overprint 1.50 1.50
  b. Double overprint 1.50 1.50
  c. Imperf., pair 3.50 3.50
180 A68 10c yellow brown 1.50 1.50
  a. Double overprint 1.50 1.50
  b. Imperf., pair 3.50 3.50
  c. Without overprint 1.50 1.50
  d. Printed on both sides 2.50 2.50

A69

A70

1902 Magenta Overprint

181 A69 5c yellow brown 90 90
  a. Without overprint 75 75
  b. Imperf., pair 2.00 2.00
182 " 10c black 90 90
  a. Without overprint 75 75
  b. Imperf., pair 5.00 5.00
183 A70 20c maroon 1.50 1.50
  b. Imperf., pair 5.00 5.00

Nos. 181-183 exist tête bêche. Price of 10c and 20c, each $17.50.

Washed copies of Nos. 167-183 are offered as "without overprint."

Barranquilla Issues.

Magdalena River A75 — Iron Quay at Sabanilla A76

La Popa Hill A77

1902-03 *Imperf.*

184 A75 2c green 1.00 1.00
185 " 2c dark blue 1.00 1.00
186 " 2c rose 15.00 15.00
187 A76 10c scarlet 50 50
188 " 10c orange 2.50 2.50
189 " 10c rose 50 50
190 " 10c maroon 50 50
191 " 10c claret 50 50
192 A77 20c violet 5.00 5.00
  a. Laid paper
193 " 20c dull blue 2.50 2.50
194 " 20c dull blue, *pink* 12.50 12.50
195 " 20c carmine rose 3.00 3.00
  Nos. 184-195 (12) 44.50 44.50

Sewing Machine Perf. and Perf. 12.

184a A75 2c green 3.25 3.25
185a " 2c dark blue 3.25 3.25
186a " 2c carmine 20.00 20.00
187a A76 10c scarlet 2.25 2.25
188a " 10c orange 7.50 7.50
189a " 10c rose 2.25 2.25
190a " 10c maroon 2.25 2.25
191a " 10c claret 2.25 2.25
192b A77 20c purple 60 60
  c. 20c lilac 60 60
193a " 20c dull blue 2.10 2.10
194a " 20c dull blue, *rose* 18.50 18.50
195b " 20c carmine rose 15.00 15.00
  Nos. 184a-195b (12) 79.20 79.20

See also Nos. 240-245.

Cruiser "Cartagena" A78

Bolívar A79

General Próspero Pinzón A80

A81

A82

1903-04 *Imperf.*

209 A78 5c blue 60 60
210 " 5c bister 90 90
211 A79 50c yellow 90 90
212 " 50c green 90 90
213 " 50c scarlet 90 90
214 " 50c carmine 90 90
  a. 50c rose 90 90
215 " 50c pale brown 90 90
216 A80 1p yellow brown 60 60
217 " 1p rose 60 60
218 " 1p blue 90 90
219 " 1p violet 12.00 12.00
220 A81 5p claret 1.50 1.50
221 " 5p pale brown 1.50 1.50
222 " 5p blue green 1.50 1.50
223 A82 10p pale green 2.00 2.00
224 " 10p claret 2.00 2.00
  Nos. 209-224 (16) 28.60 28.60

Nos. 216 and 217 measure 20½x26½mm. and No. 218, 18x24 mm.

Stamps of this issue exist with forged perforations.

Perf. 12.

209a A78 5c blue 3.75 3.75
210a " 5c bister 3.75 3.75
211a A79 50c yellow 4.25 4.25
  b. 50c orange 4.25 4.25
212a " 50c green 4.25 4.25
213a " 50c scarlet 3.25 3.25
214b " 50c rose 3.25 3.25
215a " 50c pale brown 3.25 3.25
216a A80 1p yellow brown 2.25 2.25
217a " 1p rose 2.25 2.25
218a " 1p blue 2.25 2.25
219a " 1p violet 22.50 22.50
220a A81 5p claret 7.50 7.50
221a " 5p pale brown 7.50 7.50
222a " 5p blue green 8.00 8.00
223a A82 10p pale green 8.50 8.50
224a " 10p claret 8.50 8.50
  Nos. 209a-224a (16) 95.00 95.00

Imperf.

Laid Paper.

240 A76 10c dark blue, *lilac* 75 75
241 " 10c dark blue, *bluish* 90 90
242 " 10c dark blue, *brown* 75 75
243 " 10c dark blue, *salmon* 75 75
244 " 10c dark blue, *greenish blue* 1.25 1.25
245 " 10c dark blue, *deep rose* 90 90
  Nos. 240-245 (6) 5.30 5.30

Perf. 12.

240a A76 10c dark blue, *lilac* 4.50 4.50
241a " 10c dark blue, *bluish* 3.75 3.75
242a " 10c dark blue, *brown* 4.50 4.50
243a " 10c dark blue, *salmon* 6.50 6.50
244a " 10c dk. blue, *greenish bl.* 11.50 11.50
245a " 10c dark blue, *deep rose* 4.50 4.50
  Nos. 240a-245a (6) 35.25 35.25

Medellin Issue.

A83

1902

257 A83 1c green, *straw* 15 15
  a. Imperf., pair 10.00 10.00
258 " 2c salmon, *rose* 15 15
  a. Imperf., pair 10.00 10.00
259 " 5c deep blue, *greenish* 20 20
  a. Imperf., pair 10.00 10.00
260 " 10c pale brown, *straw* 20 20
  a. Imperf., pair 10.00 10.00
261 " 20c purple, *rose* 30 30
  a. Imperf., pair 10.00 10.00
262 " 50c dull rose, *greenish* 50 50
  a. Imperf., pair 10.00 10.00
263 " 1p *yellow* 1.50 1.50
  a. Imperf., pair 25.00 25.00
264 " 5p slate, *blue* 15.00 15.00
  a. Imperf., pair 50.00 50.00
265 " 10p dark brown, *rose* 12.00 12.00
  a. Imperf., pair 50.00 50.00
  Nos. 257-265 (9) 30.00 30.00

Regular Issue.

A84

A85

A86

A87

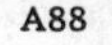
A88

A89

A90

A91

A92

1902 ***Imperf.***

266	A84	2c *rose*	20	20
267	A85	4c red, *green*	15	15
268	A86	5c green, *blue*	15	15
269	A87	10c *pink*	20	20
270	A88	20c brown, *buff*	20	20
271	A89	50c dark green, *rose*	75	75
272	A90	1p purple, *buff*	40	40
273	A91	5p green, *blue*	3.25	3.25
274	A92	10p green, *pale green*	3.50	3.50
		Nos. 266-274 (9)	8.80	8.80

Sewing Machine Perf.

266a	A84	2c *rose*	55	55
267a	A85	4c red, *green*	60	60
268a	A86	5c green, *blue*	60	60
269a	A87	10c *pink*	90	90
270a	A88	20c brown, *buff*	2.50	75
271a	A89	50c dark green, *rose*	2.50	2.50
272a	A90	1p purple, *buff*	3.00	3.00
273a	A91	5p green, *blue*	10.00	10.00
274a	A92	10p green, *pale green*	15.00	15.00
		Nos. 266a-274a (9)	35.65	33.90

1903 ***Perf. 12***

266b	A84	2c *rose*	75	75
269b	A87	10c *pink*	75	75
270b	A88	20c brown, *buff*	1.25	1.25
272b	A90	1p purple, *buff*	3.00	2.50
273b	A91	5p green, *blue*	10.00	10.00
274b	A92	10p green, *pale green*	12.50	12.50
		Nos. 266b-274b (6)	28.25	27.75

1903 ***Imperf.***

284	A85	4c blue, *green*	15	15
285	A86	5c blue, *blue*	35	35
286	A88	20c blue, *buff*	40	40
288	A89	50c blue, *rose*	75	75

Sewing Machine Perf.

284a	A85	4c blue, *green*	65	65
285a	A86	5c blue, *blue*	75	75
286a	A88	20c blue, *buff*	3.25	3.25
288a	A89	50c blue, *rose*	4.50	4.50

Perf. 12

284b	A85	4c blue, *green*	45	45
285b	A86	5c blue, *blue*	75	75
286b	A88	20c blue, *buff*	3.25	1.85
288b	A89	50c blue, *rose*	4.00	3.50

A93

1904 Pelure Paper ***Imperf.***

303	A93	½c yellow brown	45	45
304	A90	1c blue green	35	35
		a. 1c yellow green	35	35
306	A84	2c blue	30	30
307	A86	5c carmine	40	40
308	A87	10c violet	60	60
		Nos. 303-308 (5)	2.10	2.10

1904 ***Perf. 13***

303a	A93	½c yellow brown	1.85	1.50
304b	A90	1c blue green	1.35	1.25
		c. 1c yellow green	1.35	1.25
306a	A84	2c blue	1.25	1.25

Perf. 12

307a	A86	5c carmine	1.50	1.50
308a	A87	10c violet	1.50	1.50
		Nos. 303a-308a (5)	7.45	7.00

A94 A95

Pres. José Manuel Marroquín
A96

Imprint: "Lit. J. L. Arango Medellin. Col."

1904 Wove Paper ***Perf. 12***

314	A94	½c yellow	55	20
		a. Redrawn	45	15
		b. Imperf., pair	3.00	3.00
315	"	1c green	45	10
		a. Redrawn	45	10
		b. Imperf., pair	2.50	2.50
316	"	2c rose	45	10
		a. Redrawn	45	10
		b. Imperf., pair	3.00	3.00
317	"	5c blue	65	15
		a. Redrawn	60	15
		b. Imperf., pair	3.00	3.00
318	"	10c violet	90	30
		a. Imperf., pair	3.75	3.75
319	"	20c black	1.25	30
		a. Redrawn	1.25	30
		b. Imperf., pair	6.00	6.00
320	A95	1p brown	3.00	2.25
		a. Imperf., pair	10.00	10.00
321	A96	5p red & black, *yellow*	22.50	22.50
322	"	10p blue & black, *greenish*	22.50	22.50
		Nos. 314-322 (9)	52.25	48.40

On the redrawn types, the imprint is close to the base of the design instead of being spaced from it. On the redrawn 2c and 5c, the lower end of the vertical white line below "OR" of "CORREOS" forms a hook which turns to the right instead of to the left as in the originals.

See also Nos. 325-330.

A97

A98

1905 ***Imperf.***

323	A97	50p orange yellow, *pale pink*	50.00	50.00
324	A98	100p dark blue, *dark rose*	45.00	45.00

Imprint: "Lit. Nacional".

Perf. 10, 13, 13½ and Compound.

1908

325	A94	½c orange	45	15
		a. ½c yellow	60	15
		b. Imperf., pair	1.75	1.75
		c. Without imprint	5.00	5.00
326	"	1c yellow green	50	10
		a. Without imprint	50	10
		d. Imperf., pair	3.00	3.00
327	"	2c red	45	10
		a. 2c carmine	45	10
		b. Imperf., pair	3.00	3.00
328	"	5c blue	60	15
		a. Imperf., pair	5.00	5.00
329	"	10c violet	4.00	75
330	"	20c gray black	4.00	60
		Nos. 325-330 (6)	10.00	1.85

The above stamps may be easily distinguished from those of 1904 by the perforation, by the height of the design, 24mm. instead of 23mm., and by the "Lit. Nacional" imprint.

Camilo Torres
A99

Policarpa Salavarrieta
A100

Nariño
A101

Bolívar
A102

Francisco José de Caldas
A103

Francisco de Paula Santander
A104

Bolívar Demanding Liberation of Slaves
A105

Bolívar Resigning
A106

1910, Aug. **Engraved** ***Perf. 12***

331	A99	½c violet & black	60	60
		a. Center inverted	250.00	250.00
332	A100	1c deep green	60	60
333	A101	2c scarlet	60	40
334	A102	5c deep blue	75	60
335	A103	10c plum	9.00	3.50
336	A104	20c black brown	12.00	4.00
337	A105	1p dark violet	22.50	12.00
338	A106	10p claret	110.00	100.00
		Nos. 331-338 (8)	156.05	121.70

Colombian independence centenary.

Caldas
A107

Torres
A108

Nariño
A109

Santander
A110

Bolívar
A111

José María Córdoba
A112

Monument to Battle of Boyacá
A113

View of Cartagena
A114

Sucre
A115

Rufino Cuervo
A116

Antonio Ricaurte y Lozano
A117

Coat of Arms
A118

1917 Engraved. ***Perf. 14***

339	A107	½c bistre	60	15
340	A108	1c green	30	6
341	A109	2c carmine rose	30	6
342	A110	4c violet	90	45
343	A111	5c dull blue	1.35	30
344	A112	10c gray	1.10	30
345	A113	20c red	1.85	30
346	A114	50c carmine	1.85	30
347	A115	1p bright blue	6.25	60
348	A116	2p orange	6.00	90
349	A117	5p gray	18.00	6.00
350	A118	10p dark brown	35.00	10.00
		Nos. 339-350 (12)	73.50	19.42

The 1c, 5c, 10c, 50c, 2p, 5p and 10p also exist perf. 11½ and 11½ compounded with 14.

Lithographed varieties of Nos. 343, 345 and 346 are counterfeits made to defraud the government.

Imperforate copies of Nos. 339-350 are not known to have been regularly issued.

See Nos. 373-374, 400-405.

Nos. 318–319, 329–330 Surcharged in Red

Especie Provisional $ 0.00½

1918 On Issue of 1904.

351 A94 ½c on 20c black 80 45
352 " 3c on 10c violet 3.75 3.75

On Issue of 1908.

353 A94 ½c on 20c gray black 5.00 2.40
354 " 3c on 10c violet 10.00 3.50

Nos. 351 to 354 inclusive exist with surcharge reading upward or downward. On one stamp in each sheet the letter "S" in "Especie" is omitted. All denominations exist with a small zero before the decimal in the surcharge.

A119

A120

1918 Lithographed. *Perf. 13½.*

358 A119 3c red 45 15
a. Imperf., pair 6.00 6.00

1920 Engraved. *Perf. 14.*

359 A120 3c red, *orange* 20 3
a. Imperf., pair 3.75 3.75

See also Nos. 371–372.

A121

A122

A123

Perf. 10, 13½ and Compound

1920-21 Lithographed.

360 A121 ½c yellow 50 30
361 " 1c green 50 25
362 " 2c red 70 20
363 A122 3c green 45 20
a. 3c yellow green 45 20
364 A121 5c blue 60 30
365 " 10c violet 1.85 1.25
366 " 20c deep green 6.25 3.00
367 A123 50c dark red 7.00 3.50
Nos. 360–367 (8) 17.85 9.00

The tablet with "PROVISIONAL" was added separately to each design on the various lithographic stones and its position varies slightly on different stamps in the sheet. For some values there were two or more stones, on which the tablet was placed at various angles.

Nos. 360–366 exist imperf.

See also No. 375.

No. 342 Surcharged in Red

PROVICIONAL $003 — *a*
PROVISIONAL $0.03 — *b* (15mm. wide)

1921

369 A110 (*a*) 3c on 4c violet 45 30
a. Dbl. surcharge 17.50
370 " (*b*) 3c on 4c violet 3.00 1.50

See also No. 377.

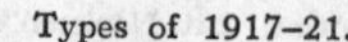
Types of 1917–21.

1923-24 Engraved. *Perf. 13½.*

371 A120 1½c chocolate 75 65
372 " 3c blue 45 10
373 A111 5c claret ('24) 1.25 15
374 A112 10c blue 2.50 35

Lithographed.

375 A121 10c dark blue 6.00 3.00
Nos. 371–375 (5) 10.95 4.25

No. 342 Surcharged in Red

PROVISIONAL $003 (18mm. wide)

1924

377 A110 3c on 4c violet 2.25 1.10
a. Double surcharge 17.50
b. Double surcharge, one inverted 17.50
c. With added surch. "3cs." in red

A124

1924–25 Litho. *Perf. 10, 10x13½*

379 A124 1c red 85 30
380 " 3c deep blue ('25) 65 30

Exist imperf. Price, each pair $5.

A125

A126

Black, Red or Green Surcharge and Overprint.

Imprint of Waterlow & Sons.

1925 *Perf. 14, 14½.*

382 A125 1c on 3c bistre brown (Bk) 22 15
383 A126 4c violet(R) 60 30
a. Inverted surch. 10.00 10.00

Imprint of American Bank Note Co.

Perf. 12.

384 A125 1c on 3c bistre brown (Bk) 3.75 3.00
a. Inverted surcharge 15.00 15.00
385 A126 4c violet (G) 45 45
a. Inverted overprint 8.00 8.00

Correos Provisional

Revenue stamps of basic types A125 and A126 were handstamped as above in violet or blue by the Cali post office in 1925, but were not authorized by the government. Denominations so overprinted are 1c, 2c, 3c, 4c and 5c.

A127

A128

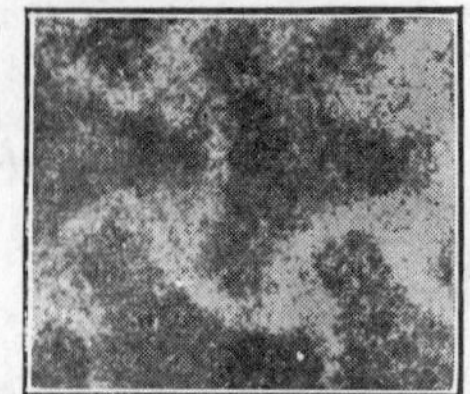
Wmk. 194

Wmkd.

Multiple Curvilinear Triangles. (194)

1926 Litho. *Perf. 10, 13½x10*

395 A127 1c gray green 45 20
396 A128 4c deep blue 45 15

Exist imperf. Price, each pair $4.

Types of 1917 and

Sabana Station
A129

Engraved.

1926–29 *Perf. 14* Unwmkd.

400 A110 4c deep blue 30 6
401 A120 8c dark blue 60 15
402 A107 30c olive bistre 4.50 85
403 A129 40c brown & yellow brown 7.50 1.25
404 A117 5p violet 7.50 90
a. Perf. 11 ('29) 7.50 2.00
405 A118 10p green 12.50 3.00
a. Perf. 11 ('29) 25.00 5.00
Nos. 400–405 (6) 32.90 6.21

Death of Bolívar
A130

1930, Dec. 17 *Perf. 12½*

408 A130 4c dark blue & black 45 30

Issued to commemorate the centenary of the death of Gen. Simón Bolívar. See also Nos. C80–C82.

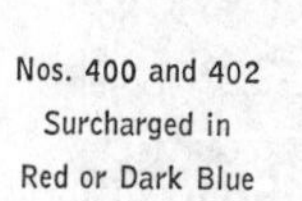
Nos. 400 and 402 Surcharged in Red or Dark Blue

1 CENTAVO

1932, Jan. 20 *Perf. 14*

409 A110 1c on 4c dp. bl. (R) 12 5
a. Inverted surcharge 8.00 8.00
410 A107 20c on 30c olive bistre (Bl) 6.25 1.25
a. Inv. surcharge 18.50
b. Dbl. surcharge 18.50

Emerald Mine
A131

Oil Wells
A132

Coffee Cultivation
A133

Platinum Mine
A134

Gold Mining
A135

Christopher Columbus
A136

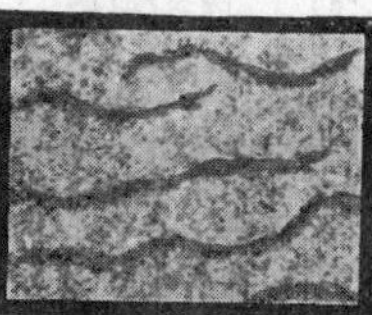
Wmk. 229

Wmkd. Wavy Lines. (229)

Imprint: "Waterlow & Sons Ltd. Londres"

1932 Engraved *Perf. 12½*

411 A131 1c green 45 3
412 A132 2c red 45 3
413 A133 5c brown 50 3
414 A134 8c blue black 2.50 50
415 A135 10c yellow 1.85 15
416 A136 20c dark blue 3.75 30
Nos. 411–416 (6) 9.50 1.04

See Nos. 441–442, 464–466a, 517.

Pedro de Heredia
A137

Coffee Picking
A138

Lithographed.

1934, Jan. 10 *Perf. 11½* Unwmkd.

417 A137 1c dark green 1.75 75
418 " 5c chocolate 1.85 75
419 " 8c dark blue 1.85 75

400th anniversary of Cartagena. See also Nos. C111–C114.

1934, Dec. Engraved *Perf. 12*

420 A138 5c brown 2.50 4

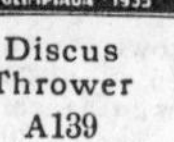
Discus Thrower
A139

Post and Telegraph Building
A145

Allegory of Olympic Games at Barranquilla—A140

Foot Race—A141

Tennis—A142

Pier at Puerto Colombia—A143

View of the Bay—A144

Designs: 2c, Soccer. 10c, Hurdling. 15c, Athlete in stadium. 18c, Baseball. 24c, Swimming. 50c, View of Barranquilla. 2p, Monument to Flag. 5p, Coat of Arms. 10p, Condor.

1935, Jan. 26 Litho. *Perf. 11½*

421	A139	2c bluish green & buff	1.50	1.50
422	"	4c deep green	1.50	1.50
423	A140	5c dark brown & yellow	2.25	1.50
		a. Horizontal pair, imperf. btwn.	225.00	
424	A141	7c dark carmine	2.00	1.75
425	A142	8c black & pink	2.00	1.75
426	A141	10c brown & blue	2.50	2.10
427	A143	12c indigo	3.00	2.75
428	A141	15c blue & red brown	5.00	3.50
429	"	18c dark violet & buff	6.00	6.00
430	A144	20c purple & green	6.00	5.00
431	"	24c bluish green & ultramarine	8.00	7.50
432	"	50c ultra. & buff	13.50	10.00
433	A145	1p drab & blue	100.00	45.00
434	"	2p dull green & gray	140.00	100.00
435	"	5p purple black & blue	300.00	250.00
436	"	10p black & gray	400.00	350.00
		Nos. 421-436 (16)	993.25	789.85

3rd National Olympic Games, Barranquilla. Counterfeits of 10p exist.

Oil Wells
A155

Gold Mining
A157

Imprint:
"American Bank Note Co."
Engraved

1935, Mar. *Perf. 12* Unwmkd.

437	A155	2c carmine rose	30	3
439	A157	10c deep orange	2.75	4

See also Nos. 468, 470, 498, 516.

No. 347 Surcharged in Black

12
CENTAVOS

1935, Aug. *Perf. 14*

440	A115	12c on 1p brt. blue	2.40	85

Types of 1932
Lithographed.
Imprint: "Lit. Nacional Bogotá"

1935–36 *Perf. 11, 11½, 12½*

441	A131	1c light green	10	3
		a. Imperf. (pair)	4.50	
442	A133	5c brown ('36)	50	3
		a. Imperf. (pair)	5.00	5.00

Simón Bolívar
A159

Tequendama Falls
A160

Wmkd. Wavy Lines. (229)

1937 Engraved *Perf. 12½*

443	A159	1c deep green	18	3
		a. Perf. 14		
444	A160	12c deep blue	1.50	1.25

See also No. 570.

Soccer Player
A161

Discus Thrower
A162

Runner
A163

1937, Jan. 4 Photo. Unwmkd.

445	A161	3c light green	1.50	1.10
446	A162	10c carmine rose	2.25	1.85
447	A163	1p black	30.00	27.50

National Olympic Games, Manizales.

Exposition Palace
A164

Stadium at Barranquilla
A165

Monument to the Colors
A166

1937, Jan. 4

448	A164	5c violet brown	60	40
449	A165	15c blue	3.75	3.50
450	A166	50c orange brown	8.00	4.75

Barranquilla National Exposition.

Stamps of 1926-37 Surcharged in Black

1
CENTAVO

1937-38 *Perf. 12½.* Unwmkd.

452	A161	1c on 3c light green	70	65
		a. Invtd. surcharge	1.75	1.75
453	A120	5c on 8c dark blue	40	35
		a. Invtd. surcharge	1.75	1.75

Wmkd. Wavy Lines. (229)

454	A160	2c on 12c deep blue	35	30
455	A134	5c on 8c blue black	40	35
		a. Invtd. surcharge	1.50	1.50
456	A160	10c on 12c deep blue ('38)	65	55
		a. Dbl. surcharge	1.75	1.75
		Nos. 452-456 (5)	2.50	2.20

Calle del Arco
A168

Entrance to Church of the Rosary
A169

Arms of Bogotá
A170

Gonzálo Jiménez de Quesada
A171

Bochica
A172

Santo Domingo Convent
A173

Mass of the Conquistadors—A174

1938, July 27 *Perf. 12½* Unwmkd.

457	A168	1c yellow green	15	15
458	A169	2c scarlet	25	18
459	A170	5c brown black	25	15
460	A171	10c brown	50	30
461	A172	15c bright blue	1.75	1.00
462	A173	20c brt. red violet	1.35	1.10
463	A174	1p red brown	18.00	16.50
		Nos. 457-463 (7)	22.25	19.38

Bogotá, 400th anniversary.

Types of 1932.
Imprint:
"Litografia Nacional Bogotá".

1938, Dec. 5 Litho. *Perf. 10½, 11*

464	A132	2c rose	60	35
465	A135	10c yellow	65	30
466	A136	20c dull blue	2.00	85
		a. 20c dk. blue, perf. 12½ ('44)	6.00	1.85

Simón Bolívar
A175

Coffee Picking
A176

Arms of Colombia
A177

Christopher Columbus
A178

Caldas
A179

Sabana Station
A180

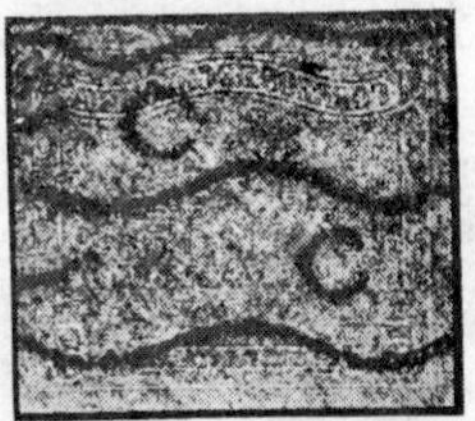
Wmk. 255

Wmkd.
Wavy Lines and C Multiple. (255)

Imprint:
"American Bank Note Co."

1939, Mar. 3 Engr. *Perf. 12*

467	A175	1c green	10	3
468	A155	2c carmine rose	10	3
469	A176	5c dull brown	10	3
470	A157	10c deep orange	60	3
471	A177	15c dull blue	90	45
472	A178	20c violet black	2.00	45
473	A179	30c olive bistre	1.50	60
474	A180	40c bistre brown	6.00	2.25
		Nos. 467-474 (8)	11.30	3.87

See also Nos. 497-499, 515, 518, 574.

General Santander
A181

Allegory
A182

General Santander
A183

Statue at Cúcuta
A184

Church at Rosario
A186

Birthplace of Santander
A185

Paya
A187

Bridge at Boyacá
A188

Death of General Santander
A189

Invasion of the Liberators
A190

Perf. 13½x13, 13½x13

Wmkd. Wavy Lines. (229)

1940, May 6 Engraved

475	A181	1c olive green	30	20
476	A182	2c dark carmine	35	25
477	A183	5c sepia	35	30
478	A184	8c carmine	75	60
479	A185	10c orange yellow	70	55
480	A186	15c dark blue	1.50	75
481	A187	20c green	1.50	90
482	A188	50c violet	3.00	3.00
483	A189	1p deep rose	7.50	6.75
484	A190	2p orange	32.50	32.50
		Nos. 475-484 (10)	48.45	45.80

Issued in commemoration of the centenary of the death of General Francisco Santander.

Tobacco Plant
A194

General Santander
A195

Garcia Rovira
A196

R. Galan
A197

Antonio Sucre
A198

Arms of Palmira
A199

Wmkd.

Wavy Lines and C Multiple. (255)

1940-43 Engraved. ***Perf. 12.***

488	A194	8c rose car. & grn.	1.00	90
489	A195	15c deep blue ('43)	45	30
490	A196	20c gray blk. ('41)	1.25	70
491	A197	40c brn. bistre ('41)	90	55
492	A198	1p black	4.00	60
		Nos. 488-492 (5)	7.60	3.05

See also Nos. 500, 554.

Lithographed.

1942, July 4 ***Perf. 11*** **Unwmkd.**

493 A199 30c claret 1.50 1.35

Issued to commemorate the 8th National Agricultural Exposition, held at Palmira.

Paradise of Isaacs, Palmira
A200

Signing Treaty of the Wisconsin
A201

1942, July 4

494 A200 50c light blue green 1.85 1.50

Issued in honor of the writer, Jorge Isaacs.

1942, Nov. 21 ***Perf. 10½***

495 A201 10c dull orange 1.25 70
  a. "2. XI. 1902" instead of "21. XI. 1902" 21.00 22.50
  b. Perf. 12 3.50 3.50

Issued in commemoration of the 40th anniversary of the signing of the Treaty of the Wisconsin, November 21, 1902.

No. 470 Surcharged in Black

5
Centavos

1944 ***Perf. 12.*** **Wmk. 255**

496 A157 5c on 10c deep orange 20 15

Counterfeits exist of No. 496 with inverted or double surcharge.

Types of 1935-41 and

National Shrine
A202

San Pedro Alejandrino
A203

Engraved.

Imprint:

"Columbian Bank Note Co."

1944-45 ***Perf. 11*** **Unwmkd.**

497	A175	1c green	20	3
498	A155	2c rose	15	3
499	A176	5c dull brown	15	3
500	A196	20c gray black	1.25	60
501	A202	30c dull olive grn. ('45)	1.25	60
502	A203	50c rose	1.25	60
		Nos. 497-502 (6)	4.25	1.89

No. 499 Surcharged in Black

1
CENTAVO

1944, Oct.

506	A176	1c on 5c dull brown	15	15
507	"	2c on 5c dull brown	18	18

Nos. 506 and 507 exist with inverted or double surcharge, created by favor.

Flag—A204

Arms—A205

Murillo Toro
A206

Hospital of St. John of God
A207

Virrey Solis
A208

A209

1944, Oct. 10 **Lithographed**

508	A204	2c ultra. & bistre	18	18
		a. Sheet of 18	4.25	
		b. Imperf., pair	10.00	
509	A205	5c ultra. & bistre	20	20
		a. Sheet of 22	6.00	
		b. Imperf., pair	10.00	
510	A206	20c black & bluish green	55	45
		a. Sheet of 8	7.50	
		b. Imperf., pair	15.00	
511	A207	40c black & red	3.50	3.50
		a. Sheet of 4	15.00	
512	A208	1p black & red	8.00	8.00
		a. Sheet of 2	17.50	
		Nos. 508-512 (5)	12.43	12.33

Souvenir Sheet.

Perforated 11x11½ all around, Stamps Imperf.

513 A209 Sheet of five 10.00 10.00

75th anniversary of General Benevolent Association of Cundinamarca. Size of No. 513: 100x87mm.

Nos. 508-513 were printed in composite sheets containing one each of Nos. 508a, 509a, 510a, 511a and 512a, and two of 513. Fifty of these were presented to government officials.

Murillo Toro
A210

San Pedro Alejandrino
A211

1944, Nov. 10 ***Perf. 11***

514 A210 5c light brown 30 22

Types of 1932-39 and A211.

Imprint:

"Litografia Nacional Bogota".

1944 **Lithographed.** ***Perf. 12½.***

515	A175	1c deep green	30	22
		a. 1c olive green	30	22
		b. Imperf., pair	2.50	2.50
516	A155	2c dark carmine	30	25
		a. Imperf., pair	2.50	2.50
517	A135	10c yellow orange	70	65
518	A179	30c gray olive	5.00	3.00
		a. Imperf., pair	30.00	
519	A211	50c rose	4.50	2.25
		Nos. 515-519 (5)	10.80	6.37

No. 469 Overprinted in Green, Blue or Red

Engraved.

1945, July 19 ***Perf. 12*** **Wmk. 255**

520	A176	5c dull brown (G)	40	10
521	"	5c dull brown (R)	40	10
522	"	5c dull brown (Bl)	40	10

Portraits are Joseph Stalin, Franklin D. Roosevelt and Winston Churchill.

Clock Tower, Cartagena
A212

1945, Nov. 15

523 A212 50c olive black 3.25 1.00

Sierra Nevada of Santa Marta
A213

Designs: 30c, Seaplane Tolima, 50c, San Sebastian Fort, Cartagena.

Lithographed.

1945, Dec. 14 ***Perf. 11*** **Unwmkd.**

524	A213	20c light green	1.10	85
525	"	30c pale blue	1.15	1.00
526	"	50c salmon pink	1.50	1.25

Issued to commemorate the 25th anniversary of the first airmail service in America, according to the inscription, but earlier services are known to have existed.

No. 442 Surcharged in Black

1
UN CENTAVO

1946, Mar. 8 ***Perf. 11x11½, 12½***

527 A133 1c on 5c brown 15 10
  a. Inverted surcharge 1.25

Gen. Antonio José de Sucre
A216

Engraved.

1946, Apr. 16 ***Perf. 12*** **Wmk. 255**

Size: 19x26½mm.

528	A216	1c brn. & turq. green	18	8
529	"	2c vio. & rose carmine	18	8

Size: 23x31mm.

530	A216	5c sepia & blue	18	5
531	"	9c dark green & red	90	75
532	"	10c ultra. & orange	75	75

533 A216 20c black & dp. orge. 80 80
534 " 30c brown red & green 75 65
535 " 40c olive black & red violet 80 70
536 " 50c dp. brn. & violet 1.25 1.00
Nos. 528-536 (9) 5.79 4.86

Map of South America A217

National Observatory A218

Lithographed.

1946, June 7 *Perf. 11* Unwmkd.
537 A217 15c ultramarine 65 50
a. Imperf. (pair) 6.00

1946, Aug.
538 A218 5c fawn 40 4
a. Imperf. (pair) 6.00
See No. 565.

Andrés Bello A219

Joaquín de Cayzedo y Cuero A220

Engraved.

1946, Sept. 3 *Perf. 12* Wmk. 255
539 A219 3c sepia 22 20
540 " 10c orange 75 50
541 " 15c slate black 80 50

Issued to commemorate the 80th anniversary of the death of Andrés Bello (1781-1865), poet and educator. See also No. C145.

1946, Sept. 20 *Perf. 12½* Wmk. 229
542 A220 2p bluish green 4.75 2.10
See also No. 568.

Type of 1945, Overprinted in Black or Green

V JUEGOS C.
A. Y DEL C.
1946

1946, Dec. 6 *Perf. 12* Wmk. 255
543 A212 50c red (Bk) 5.00 3.75
a. Dbl. overprint 25.00
544 " 50c red (G) 5.00 3.75
a. Dbl. overprint 25.00

Issued to commemorate the fifth Central American and Caribbean Championship Games.

Coffee
A221

Engraved and Lithographed.

1947, Jan. 10 *Perf. 12½* Wmk. 229
545 A221 5c multicolored 50 6

Colombian Orchid: Masdevallia Nycterina
A222

Designs (Orchids): 2c, Miltonia vexillaria. No. 548, Cattleya chocoensis. No. 549, Odontoglossum crispum. No. 550, Cattleya dowiana aurea. 10c, Cattleya labiata trianae.

Engraved and Lithographed.

1947, Feb. 7 *Perf. 12* Wmk. 255
546 A222 1c multicolored 25 15
547 " 2c " 25 18
548 " 5c " 75 15
549 " 5c " 1.85 18
550 " 5c " 1.50 18
551 " 10c " 1.65 75
Nos. 546-551 (6) 6.25 1.59

Antonio Nariño A228

Alberto Urdaneta y Urdaneta A229

Perf. 12½

1947, May 9 Litho. Unwmkd.
552 A228 5c blue, *greenish* 30 25
553 A229 10c red brown, *greenish* 40 30

Issued to commemorate the 4th Pan-American Press Congress, 1946. See also Nos. C146-C147.

Sucre Type of 1940.
Engraved.

1947 *Perf. 12.* Wmk. 255
554 A198 1p violet 2.00 60

José Celestino Mutis and José Jerónimo Triana
A230

Miguel A. Caro and Rufino J. Cuervo
A231

1947 *Perf. 12½* Wmk. 229
555 A230 25c olive green 45 38
556 A231 3p dark purple 4.00 3.75
See also Nos. 567, 569.

Metropolitan Cathedral, Plaza Bolívar, Bogotá
A232

National Capitol
A233

Ministry of Foreign Affairs
A234

A235

1948, Apr. 2
557 A232 5c black brown 15 6
558 A233 10c orange 65 65
559 A234 15c dark blue 65 65
Nos. 557-559, C148-C149 (5) 3.05 2.54

Miniature Sheet
Imperf.
560 A235 50c slate 1.85 1.85

Nos. 557-560 commemorate the 9th Pan-American Conference, Bogotá. No. 560 measures 90½x90½mm.

No. RA5A Overprinted in Black

Without Gum.

1948 *Perf. 12½* Unwmkd.
561 PT3 1c yellow orange 8 3

The letter "C" is the initial of "CORREOS".

Nos. RA33, RA24 and RA25 Overprinted in Black

CORREOS

With Gum.

1948 *Perf. 12.* Wmk. 255
562 PT6 1c olive 6 5
563 " 2c green 10 5
564 " 20c brown 30 6

Nos. 561-564 exist with inverted and double overprints.

Observatory Type of 1946.
Lithographed

1948, June 30 *Perf. 11* Unwmkd.
565 A218 5c blue 45 4

Simón Bolívar A236

Carlos Martinez Silva A237

Engraved.

1948, May 29 *Perf. 12* Wmk. 255
566 A236 15c green 45 22

Types of 1946-47.

1948 *Perf. 12½* Unwmkd.
567 A230 25c green 25 5
568 A220 2p deep green 1.10 12
569 A231 3p deep red violet 65 15

Falls Type of 1937.

1948 Wmk. 229
570 A160 10c red 10 6

Lithographed.

1948, Dec. 21 *Perf. 13½* Unwmkd.
571 A237 40c carmine 45 20

Juan de Dios Carrasquilla
A238

1949, May 20 *Perf. 12½* Wmk. 229
572 A238 5c bistre 15 6

Issued to commemorate the 75th anniversary of the foundation of the Colombian Society of Agriculture.

Julio Garavito Armero A239

Arms of Colombia A240

Engraved.

1949, Apr. 24 *Perf. 12* Wmk. 229
573 A239 4c green 30 12

Issued to honor Julio Garavito Armero (1865-1920), mathematician.

Coffee Type of 1939.
Imprint:
"American Bank Note Co."

1949, Aug. 4 Wmk. 255
574 A176 5c blue 10 3

1949, Oct. 7 *Perf. 13* Unwmkd.
575 A240 15c blue 20 6

Issued to honor the new Constitution. See also Nos. C164-C165.

Shield and Tree A241

Francisco Javier Cisneros A242

1949, Oct. 13 *Perf. 12½* Wmk. 229
576 A241 5c olive 12 3

Issued to commemorate the 4th anniversary of Colombia's first Forestry Congress and as propaganda for the government's reforestation program.

1949, Dec. 15 Photo. Unwmkd.
577 A242 50c red violet & yel. 1.10 70
578 " 50c green & violet 1.10 70
579 " 50c brown & lt. blue 1.10 70

Issued to commemorate the 50th anniversary (in 1948) of the death of Francisco Javier Cisneros.

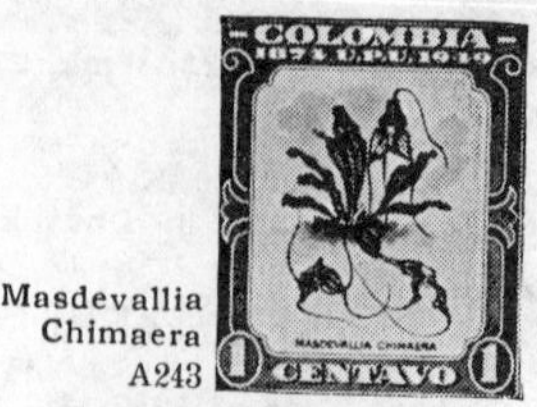

Masdevallia Chimaera
A243

Odontoglossum Crispum
A244

Eastern Hemisphere
A245

Designs: 3c, Cattleya labiata trianae. 4c, Masdevallia nycterina. 5c, Cattleya dowiana aurea. 11c, Miltonia vexillaria. 18c, Santo Domingo post office.

1950, Aug. 22 Photo. *Perf. 13*

580	A243	1c brown	22	15
581	A244	2c violet	22	15
582	A243	3c rose lilac	35	15
583	"	4c emerald	22	15
584	"	5c red orange	1.35	10
585	A244	11c red	1.10	1.00
586	"	18c ultramarine	1.00	55
		Nos. 580-586 (7)	4.46	2.25

Miniature Sheet

Imperf.

587	A245	50c orange yellow	1.35	1.35

Nos. 580-587 commemorate the 75th anniversary (in 1949) of the formation of the Universal Postal Union. No. 587 measures 91x90mm.

See No. C199.

Antonio Baraya
A246

Engraved

1950, Nov. 27 *Perf. 12½* **Unwmkd.**

588	A246	2c red	8	3

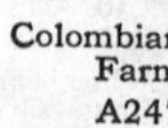

Colombian Farm
A247

1950, Dec. 28 Photo. *Perf. 11½*

589	A247	5c deep carmine & buff	35	12
590	"	5c blue green & gray	35	12
591	"	5c violet blue & gray	35	12

Issued to publicize rural life.

Arms of Bogotá
A248

Arms of Colombia
A249

Perf. 12x12½

1950, Dec. 28 Engr. **Wmkd. 255**

592	A248	5p deep green	2.75	40
593	A249	10p red orange	9.00	60

Map and Badge
A250

Guillermo Valencia
A251

Perf. 12½x13

1951, Jan. 30 Photo. **Unwmkd.**

594	A250	20c red, yel. & blue	38	15

Issued to commemorate the 60th anniversary (in 1947) of the formation of the Colombian Society of Engineers.

1951, Oct. 20 Engr. *Perf. 13x13½*

595	A251	25c black	38	18

Issued to honor Guillermo Valencia (1873-1943), newspaper founder, governor of Cauca, presidential candidate, author.

No. 468 Overprinted in Black

REVERSION
CONCESION MARES
25 Agosto 1951

1951, Dec. 11 *Perf. 12* **Wmk. 255**

596	A155	2c carmine rose	10	3

Issued to publicize the reversion of the Mares oil concession to Colombia.

Nicolas Osorio
A252

Portraits: No. 598, Pompilio Martinez. No. 599, Ezequiel Uricoechea. No. 600, Jose M. Lombana.

Engraved.

1952, Aug. 6 *Perf. 11½* **Unwmkd.**

Various Frames.

597	A252	1c deep blue	8	4
598	"	1c "	8	4
599	"	1c "	8	4
600	"	1c "	8	4

Nos. 597-600 were printed in a single sheet containing four panes of twenty-five each, separated by double rows of ornamental tabs. Although inscribed "sobretasa," the stamps were for ordinary postage.

Types of Postal Tax Stamps of 1945-50 and

Communications Building
A253 A253a

1952 *Perf. 12*

601	A253	5c ultramarine	15	6

Wmk. 255.

602	PT10	20c brown	4.50	10
603	PT6	25c dark gray	7.50	1.85
604	PT10	25c blue green	90	10
605	A253a	50c orange yel.	11.50	6.50
606	"	1p rose carmine	1.50	20
607	"	2p lilac rose	12.50	5.00
608	"	2p violet	1.50	20
		Nos. 601-608 (8)	40.05	14.01

Although inscribed "sobretasa," Nos. 601-608 were issued for ordinary postage.

Cathedral of Manizales
A254

Perf. 11½

1952, Oct. 10 Photo. **Unwmkd.**

609	A254	23c blue & gray black	25	25

Centenary of city of Manizales.

No. 555 Surcharged in Blue

1ª CONFERENCIA
19 52
LATINO-AMERICANA.
15
SIDERURGICA

1952, Oct. 30 *Perf. 12½* **Wmk. 229**

610	A230	15c on 25c olive green	38	30

Issued to publicize the Latin American Siderurgical Conference, 1952. See also No. C226.

Queen Isabella I and Monument
A255

Engraved

1953, Mar. 10 *Perf. 12½* **Unwmkd.**

611	A255	23c blue and black	38	30

Issued to commemorate the fifth centenary of the birth of Queen Isabella I of Spain.

Nos. 606 and 568 Surcharged with New Values in Dark Blue

1953, Oct. 19 **Wmk. 255**

612	A253a	40c on 1p rose car.	60	15
613	A220	50c on 2p deep green	60	15

Manuel Ancizar
A256

Portraits: 23c, José Jeronimo Triana. 30c, Manuel Ponce de Leon. 1p, Agustin Codazzi.

Perf. 12½x13

1953, Nov. Engraved **Unwmkd.**

Frames in Black.

614	A256	14c rose red	42	22
615	"	23c ultramarine	22	22
616	"	30c chocolate	45	20
617	"	1p emerald	38	18

Issued to commemorate the centenary (in 1950) of the establishment of the Chorographic Commission.

See also Nos. 687, 690, 692.

Murillo Toro and Map
A257

Engraved and Lithographed.

1953, Dec. 12 *Perf. 12* **Wmk. 255**

Black Surcharge.

618	A257	5c on 5p multi.	30	20

Issued to publicize the 2nd National Philatelic Exhibition, Bogotá, December 1953. See also No. C237.

Nos. 609 and 614 Surcharged with New Value or New Value and Ornaments.

Perf. 11½, 12½x13.

1953 **Unwmkd.**

619	A254	5c on 23c blue & gray black (C)	45	18
620	A256	5c on 14c black & rose red (Bk)	45	18

No. 614 surcharged "CINCO" in blue is listed as No. 687.

Symbolical of St. Francis Receiving Christ's Wounds
A258

1954, Apr. 23 Photo. *Perf. 11½*

621	A258	5c sepia & green	15	6

Issued to commemorate the 400th anniversary of the establishment of Colombia's first Franciscan community.

Soldier, Map and Arms
A259

1954, June 13 Engraved *Perf. 13*

622	A259	5c dull blue	20	3

Issued to commemorate the first anniversary of the assumption of the presidency by Gen. Gustavo Rojas Pinilla. See also Nos. C255, 637a.

Sports Emblem
A260

Design: 10c, Stadium and athlete holding arms of Colombia.

1954, July 18 **Unwmkd.**

623 A260 5c deep blue 35 20
624 " 10c red 55 20

Issued to publicize the 7th National Athletic Games, Cali, July 1954. See also Nos. C256–C257.

History Academy Seal
A261

1954, July 24

625 A261 5c ultra. & green 15 8

Issued to commemorate the 50th anniversary (in 1952) of the Colombian Academy of History.

Convent and Cell of St. Peter Claver
A262

1954, Sept. 9

627 A262 5c dark green 22 4
a. Souvenir sheet 1.85 1.85

Issued to commemorate the 300th anniversary of the death of St. Peter Claver.

No. 627a contains one stamp similar to No. 627, but printed in greenish black. Marginal inscriptions in black. Sheet size: 121x129½mm. See also Nos. C258–C258a.

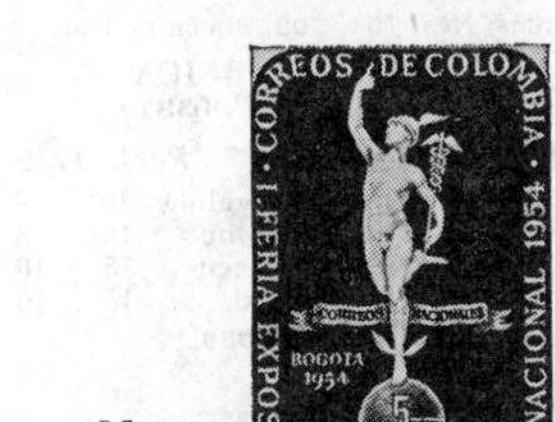

Mercury
A263

1954, Oct. 29

628 A263 5c orange 35 5

Issued to publicize the first International Fair and Exhibition, Bogotá, 1954. See Nos. C259–C260.

Tapestry Madonna
A264

College Cloister—A265

Designs: 10c, Brother Cristobal de Torres. 20c, College chapel and arms.

Perf. 12½x11½, 11½x12½

1954, Dec. 6

629 A264 5c orange & black 30 18
630 " 10c blue 35 18
631 A265 15c violet brown 45 18
632 " 20c black & brown 75 25
a. Souvenir sheet 3.00 3.00
Nos. 629–632, C263–C266 (8) 5.15 2.18

Issued to commemorate the 300th anniversary (in 1953) of the founding of the Senior College of Our Lady of the Rosary, Bogota.

No. 632a contains four stamps similar to Nos. 629–632, but printed in different colors: 5c yellow and black, 10c green, 15c dull violet, 20c black and light-blue. Marginal inscriptions in black. Sheet size: 124½x130½mm.

Steel Mill
A266

José Marti
A267

1954, Dec. 12 ***Perf. 12½x13***

633 A266 5c ultra. & black 12 6

Issued to mark the opening of the Paz del Rio steel mill, October 1954. See No. C267.

1955, Jan. 28 ***Perf. 13½x13***

634 A267 5c deep carmine 12 3

Issued to commemorate the centenary of the birth of José Marti (1853–1895), Cuban patriot. See No. C268.

Arms, Flags and Soldiers Building Bridge
A268

1955, Mar. 23 ***Perf. 12½***

635 A268 10c claret 15 5

Issued to honor Colombian soldiers who served in Korea, 1951–53. See Nos. 637a, C269.

Fleet Emblem
A269

M. S. City of Manizales and New York Skyline
A270

1955, Apr. 12 **Unwmkd.**

636 A269 15c deep green 15 5
637 A270 20c violet 25 10
a. Souvenir sheet 2.75 2.75

Issued to honor the Grand-Colombian Merchant Fleet. See Nos. C270–271a.

No. 637a contains four stamps similar to Nos. 622, 635–637, but printed in different colors: 5c blue, 10c dark carmine, 15c green, 20c purple. Marginal inscriptions in black. Sheet size: 125x131mm.

Hotel Tequendama and Church of San Diego
A271

1955, May 16 Photo. ***Perf. 11½x12***

638 A271 5c blue 12 3

See also No. C273.

Bolivar's Country Estate, Bogotá
A272

1955, Sept. 28 Engr. ***Perf. 12½***

639 A272 5c deep ultramarine 12 5

Issued to commemorate the 50th anniversary of Rotary International. See No. C274.

Belalcazar, Jiménez de Quesada and Balboa
A273

Caravels and Columbus
A274

Design: 5c, San Martin, Bolivar and Washington.

Engraved and Photogravure.

1955, Oct. 29 ***Perf. 13x12½***

640 A273 2c yellow green & brown 15 8
641 " 5c bright blue & brown 18 8
642 A274 23c light ultramarine & black 25 22
a. Souvenir sheet 3.00 3.00
Nos. 640–642, C275–C280 (9) 9.13 6.38

Issued to publicize the seventh Congress of the Postal Union of the Americas and Spain, Bogota, Oct. 12,-Nov. 9, 1955.

No. 642a contains one each of Nos. 640-642, printed in slightly different shades. It measures 120x132 mm. and is inscribed in black: "Ministerio de Comunicaciones. III Exposicion Filatelica Nacional Bogota 1955."

José Eusebio Caro
A275

1955, Nov. 29 Engr. ***Perf. 13½x13***

643 A275 5c brown 10 5

Issued to commemorate the centenary of the death of José Eusebio Caro (1817–1853), poet. See also No. C281.

Departmental Issue

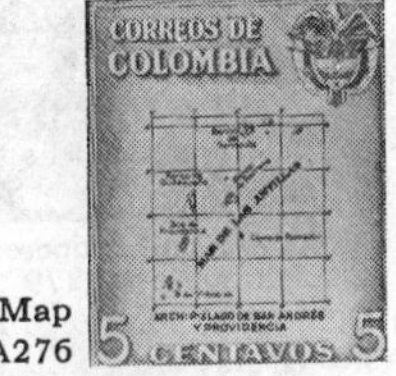

Map
A276

View of San Andres Harbor
A277

Cattle at Waterhole—A278

Designs: 2c, Docks, Atlantico. 3c, "Industry," Antioquia. 4c, Cartagena Harbor, Bolivar. No. 647, Steel Mill, Boyaca. No. 648, Cattle, Cordoba. No. 649, Map. No. 650, San Andres Harbor. No. 651, Cacao picker, Cauca. 10c, Coffee picker, Caldas. 15c, Salt Mine Chapel, Zipaquira, Cundinamarca. 20c, Tropical plants and map, Choco. 23c, Harvester, Huila. 25c, Banana Plantation, Magdalena. 30c, Gold mining, Nariño. 40c, Tobacco plantation, Santander. 50c, Oil wells, North Santander. 60c, Cotton plantation, Tolima. 1p, Sugar industry, Cauca. 3p, Amazon river at Leticia, Amazonas. 5p, Windmills and panoramic view, La Guajira. 10p, Rubber plantation, Vaupes.

Engraved; Engraved and Lithographed.

Perf. 13½x13, 13x13½, 13

1956 Engraved. Unwmkd.

Various Frames.

644 A277 2c carmine & green 10 3
645 A276 3c brown violet & black 10 3

646 A277 4c green & black 12 6
647 A276 5c dark brown & blue 15 3
648 A277 5c olive & dark violet brown 45 7
649 A276 5c blue & black 20 3
650 A277 5c carmine & greenish blue 12 3
651 " 5c olive green & red brown 20 3
652 A276 10c orange & black 50 6
653 " 15c ultra. & black 30 6
654 " 20c dark brown & blue 20 6
655 A277 23c ultra. & verm. 20 5
656 " 25c olive green & black 30 30
657 " 30c ultra. & brown 20 3
658 " 40c dull purple & red brown 25 6
659 " 50c dark green & black 28 5
660 " 60c pale brown & green 28 5
661 A278 1p magenta & greenish blue 1.50 18
662 " 2p green & red brown 1.35 25
663 " 3p carmine & black 1.25 30
664 " 5p brown & light ultramarine 3.25 1.00
665 A276 10p red brown & green 10.00 2.50
Nos. 644–665 (22) 21.30 5.26

Nos. 645, 647, 649, 652–654 measure 27x32mm. No. 665 measures 27x37 mm. See also Nos. 681–684, 685, 688–689.

Columbus and Proposed Lighthouse—A279

1956, Oct. 12 Photo. ***Perf. 12***
666 A279 3c gray black 20 8

Issued in honor of Christopher Columbus. See also Nos. C285, C306.

Altar of St. Elizabeth and Tomb of Jimenez de Quesada
A280

1956, Nov. 19 **Unwmkd.**
667 A280 5c red lilac 15 10

Issued to commemorate the 7th centenary of St. Elizabeth of Hungary, patron saint of Sante Fé de Bogotá. See No. C286.

St. Ignatius of Loyola
A281

Javier Pereira
A282

1956, Nov. 26 Engr. ***Perf. 12½x13***
668 A281 5c blue 20 5

Issued to commemorate the 400th anniversary of the death of St. Ignatius of Loyola. See No. C287.

1956, Dec. 28 ***Perf. 12*** **Unwmkd.**
669 A282 5c blue 10 5

Issued to honor 167-year-old Javier Pereira. See No. C288.

Emblem and Dairy Farm
A283

Designs: 2c, Emblem and tractor. 5c, Emblem, coffee and corn.

1957, Mar. 5 Photo. ***Perf. 14x13½***
670 A283 1c light olive green 5 5
671 " 2c light brown 5 3
672 " 5c light blue 15 5
Nos. 670–672, C292–C296 (8) 2.35 1.61

25th anniversary of the Agrarian Savings Bank of Colombia.

Arms of Military Academy and Gen. Rafael Reyes—A284

Design: 10c, Arms and Academy.

1957, July 20 Engr. ***Perf. 12½***
673 A284 5c blue 12 3
674 " 10c orange 12 3
a. Souv. sheet of 2 5.00 5.00

Issued to commemorate the 50th anniversary of the Colombian Military Academy. See Nos. C299–C300.

No. 674a contains one each of Nos. 673–674 in slightly different shades. It measures 120x131½mm. with marginal inscriptions in black.

Statue of José Matias Delgado
A285

1957, Sept. 16 Photo. ***Perf. 12***
675 A285 2c rose brown 8 8

Issued in honor of Jose Matias Delgado, liberator of El Salvador. See No. C301.

Santo Michelena, Marcos V. Crespo, P. Alcantara Herran and UPU Monument—A286

1957, Oct. 10 **Unwmkd.**
676 A286 5c green 12 12
677 " 10c gray 12 8

Issued for International Letter Writing Week and the 14th UPU Congress. See Nos. C302–C303.

St. Vincent de Paul and Children
A287

1957, Oct. 18
678 A287 1c dark olive green 7 5

Issued to commemorate the centenary of the Colombian Society of St. Vincent de Paul. See No. C304.

Fencer
A288

1957, Nov. 22 Photo. ***Perf. 12***
679 A288 4c lilac 12 12

Issued to commemorate the third South American Fencing Championship. See No. C305.

Francisco José de Caldas and Hypsometer
A289

1958, May 12 ***Perf. 12*** **Unwmkd.**
680 A289 10c black 40 12

Issued for the International Geophysical Year, 1957–58. See Nos. C309–C310.

Departmental Issue.

Type of 1956,
Designs as Before.

1958 **Engraved.** ***Perf. 13***
681 A276 3c ultra. & brown 10 3
682 " 3c olive grn. & pur. 10 3
683 " 10c green & brown 18 3
684 " 10c dk. blue & brown 18 3

Nos. 646, C291, 614, 653, 655, 616, C308, 615 and 611 Surcharged with New Value, and Old Value Obliterated, or Overprinted in Dark Blue or Green.

Perf. 12½, 12½x13, 13.

1958-59 **Unwmkd.**
685 A277 2c on 4c grn. & blk. 10 4
686 AP48 5c deep plum & multi. ('59) 10 10
687 A256 5c on 14c black & rose red ("CINCO") ('59) 45 50
688 A276 5c on 15c ultramarine & black 10 4
689 A277 5c on 23c ultramarine & vermilion (G) 20 15
690 A256 5c on 30c black & chocolate 12 8
691 AP40 10c on 25c rose violet 12 3
692 A256 20c on 23c black & ultramarine (G) ('59) 38 38
693 A255 20c on 23c blue & black ('59) 38 38
Nos. 685–693 (9) 1.95 1.70

On No. 686 the words "Correo Extra Rapido" are obliterated in dark blue.

Father Rafael Almanza and Church of San Diego, Bogota
A290

1958, Oct. 23 Photo. ***Perf. 14x13***
695 A290 10c purple 10 3

See also Nos. C313–C314.

Msgr. R. M. Carrasquilla and Church
A291

1959, Jan. 22 ***Perf. 14x13***
696 A291 10c dark red brown 12 5

Issued to commemorate the centenary of the birth of Msgr. R. M. Carrasquilla (1857–1930), rector of Our Lady of the Rosary Seminary, Bogotá. See Nos. C315–C316.

Miss Universe 1959
A292

Jorge Eliecer Gaitan
A293

1959, June 26 Photo. ***Perf. 11½***
697 A292 10c multicolored 6 5

Issued to honor Luz Marina Zuluaga, Miss Universe, 1959. See Nos. C317–C318.

Engraved

1959, July 28 ***Perf. 12x13½***
698 A293 10c on 3c gray blue (Bl) 20 5
699 " 30c rose violet 25 25

Issued in honor of Jorge Eliecer Gaitan (1898–1948), lawyer and politician.

No. 698 exists without blue surcharge. See also Nos. C319–C320.

Gen. Francisco de Paula Santander
A294

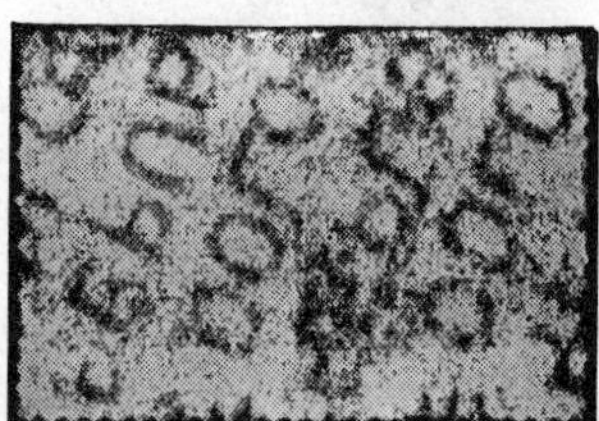

Wmk. 331

Designs: Nos. 701, 703, Simon Bolivar.

Wmkd. "REPÚBLICA DE COLOMBIA". (331)

1959 Lithographed ***Perf. 12½***
700 A294 5c brown & yellow 10 8
701 " 5c ultra. & blue 10 8
702 " 10c gray & green 15 10
703 " 10c gray & red 15 10

See also No. C389.

Capitol, Bogota
A295

1959

704 A295 2c dark blue & red brown 10 5
705 " 3c blk. brn. & lilac 10 5

Stamp of 1859 and Mail Transport by Mule
A296

Two-Toed Sloth
A297

Designs (various stamps of 1859 and): 10c, Mail boat on the Magdalena river. 25c, Train.

Photogravure

1959, Dec. 1 ***Perf. 12*** **Unwmkd.**

709 A296 5c orange & green 20 18
710 " 10c rose claret & bl. 20 18
711 " 15c car. rose & green 38 38
712 " 25c blue & red brown 38 38
Nos. 709-712, C351-C354 (8) 3.56 2.90

Centenary of Colombian postage stamps.

1960, Feb. 12 ***Perf. 12***

Designs: 10c, Alexander von Humboldt. 20c, Spider monkey.

713 A297 5c greenish blue & brown 30 10
714 " 10c black & dp. car. 45 5
715 " 20c citron & gray brown 30 3
Nos. 713-715, C357-C359 (6) 5.20 3.45

Issued to commemorate the centenary of the death of Alexander von Humboldt (1769-1859), German naturalist and geographer.

Anthurium Andreanum
A298

Lincoln Statue, Washington
A99

Flower: 20c, Espeletia grandiflora.

1960, May 10

716 A298 5c multicolored 10 8
717 " 20c brown, yellow & gray olive 15 8
Nos. 716-717, C360-C370 (13) 13.35 12.48

See also Nos. C420-C425.

Perf. 10½

1960, June 10 Litho. Wmk. 331

718 A299 20c rose lilac & black 20 7

Issued to commemorate the sesquicentennial of the birth of Abraham Lincoln (1809-1865). See also Nos. C375-C376.

Floredo House, Cradle of the Republic
A300

Arms of Santa Cruz de Mompox
A301

Design: 5c, First coins of Republic.

Perf. 12

1960, July 19 Photo. Unwmkd.

719 A301 5c green & ochre 15 10
720 A300 20c olive bistre & maroon 27 15
721 A301 20c multicolored 27 15
Nos. 719-721, C377-C385 (12) 5.61 4.83

Issued to commemorate the 150th anniversary of Colombia's independence.

St. Isidro and Farm Animals
A302

Design: 20c, Nativity by Gregorio de Arce Vasquez y Ceballos.

1960, Sept. 26 ***Perf. 12***

722 A302 10c multicolored 12 10
723 " 20c " 17 10

Issued to honor St. Isidro the Farmer, patron saint of the rural people.
See also Nos. 747, C387-C388, C439-C440.

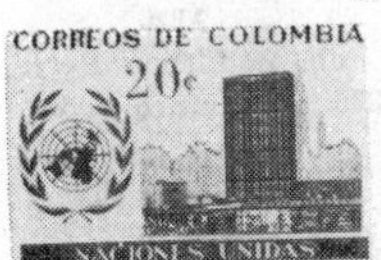

U.N. Headquarters and Emblem
A303

Perf. 11

1960, Oct. 24 Litho. Wmk. 331

724 A303 20c black & pink 18 18

Souvenir Sheet

Imperf.

725 A303 50c dark brown, bright green & black 2.50 2.50

15th anniversary of the United Nations. No. 725 contains one stamp and has dark brown marginal inscription and black number. Size: 55x48½mm.

Pan-American Highway through Colombia
A304

Alfonso Lopez
A305

Perf. 10½x11

1961, Mar. 7 Unwmkd.

726 A304 20c brown & greenish blue 70 70
Nos. 726, C390-C393 (5) 3.50 3.50

Issued to commemorate the 8th Pan-American Highway Congress, Bogota, May 20-29, 1960.

1961, Mar. 22 Photo. ***Perf. 12½***

727 A305 10c bright rose & brown 15 10
728 " 20c violet & brown 15 10

Issued to honor Alfonso Lopez (1886-1959), President of Colombia.
See Nos. C394-C396.

Cauca River Bridge, Cali
A306

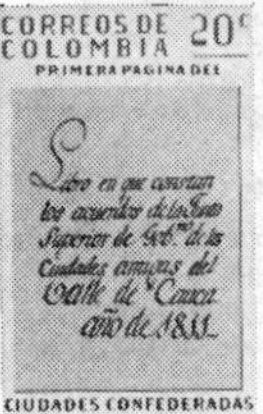

Page from Resolutions of Confederated Cities
A307

1961-62 ***Perf. 12½x13, 13½x13***

729 A306 10c red brn., blue, grn. & red ('62) 8 4
730 A307 20c pale brown & black 20 8
Nos. 729-730, C397-C401 (7) 2.31 1.22

Issued to commemorate the 50th anniversary (in 1960) of the Department of Valle del Cauca.

View of Cucuta and Arms
A308

Design: No. 732, Arms of Ocana and Pamplona.

1961, Aug. 29 ***Perf. 13x13½***

731 A308 20c blue, black, yellow & red 12 8
732 " 20c ochre, ultramarine & red 15 8

Issued to commemorate the 50th anniversary (in 1960) of the Department of North Santander. See Nos. C402-C403.

Arms of Popayan
A309

Basketball
A310

Designs: No. 734, Arms of Barranquilla. No. 735, Arms of Bucaramanga.

Perf. 12½x13

1961, Oct. 10 Unwmkd.

Arms in Multicolor

733 A309 10c blue & silver 7 3
734 " 20c blue & yellow 10 3
735 " 20c blue & gold 10 3
Nos. 733-735, C404-C408 (8) 2.27 54

Issued to honor Atlantico Department.

1961, Dec. 16 Litho. ***Perf. 13½x14***

Multicolored

736 A310 20c *shown* 12 5
737 " 20c *Runners* 12 4
738 A310 20c *Boxers* 25 10
739 " 25c *Soccer* 15 8
Nos. 736-739, C414-C418 (9) 2.78 1.12

4th Bolivarian Games, Barranquilla, 1961.

Colombian Anti-Malaria Emblem
A311

Engineers Society Emblem
A312

Design: 50c, Malaria eradication emblem and mosquito in swamp.

1962, Apr. 12 ***Perf. 12*** **Unwmkd.**

740 A311 20c lt. bistre & red 15 12
741 " 50c bistre & ultra. 22 15
Nos. 740-741, C426-C428 (5) 4.09 3.92

Issued for the World Health Organization drive to eradicate malaria.

1962, June 12 Photo. ***Perf. 11½x12***

742 A312 10c multicolored 22 22
Nos. 742, C429-C432 (5) 1.88 1.79

Issued to commemorate the 75th anniversary of the Colombian Society of Engineers.

Flags of American Nations
A313

Woman Casting Ballot and Statue of Policarpa Salavarrieta
A314

1962, June 28 ***Perf. 13***

Flags in National Colors

743 A313 25c blk. & org. verm. 12 5

Souvenir Sheet

744 A313 2.50p blk. & yel. 2.25 2.25

Issued to commemorate the 70th anniversary of the founding of the Organization of American States.
No. 744 contains one stamp, black marginal inscription. Size: 45x55mm.
See also No. C433.

Perf. 12x12½

1962, July 20 Litho. Wmk. 229

745 A314 10c light blue, gray & black 5 4

Issued to publicize women's political rights. See also Nos. 752, C434, C448-C450.

Scouts at Campfire and Tents
A315

Railroad Map of Colombia
A316

Perf. 11½x12

1962, July 28 Photo. **Unwmkd.**

746 A315 10c bright greenish blue & brown 22 22

Nos. 746, C435-C438 (5) 4.80 4.17

Issued to commemorate the 30th anniversary of the Colombian Boy Scouts.

St. Isidro Type of 1960 Redrawn

1962, Aug. 28 *Perf. 12*

747 A302 10c pink & multi. 12 4

The frame on No. 747 is solid color with white inscription similar to type AP82. See also Nos. C439-C440.

1962, Sept. 28 *Perf. 12½*

748 A316 10c black, gray, green & red 12 4

Nos. 748, C441-C444 (5) 3.04 71

Issued to publicize the progress of Colombian railroads and to commemorate the completion of the Atlantic Line from Santa Marta to Bogota.

Post Horn

A317

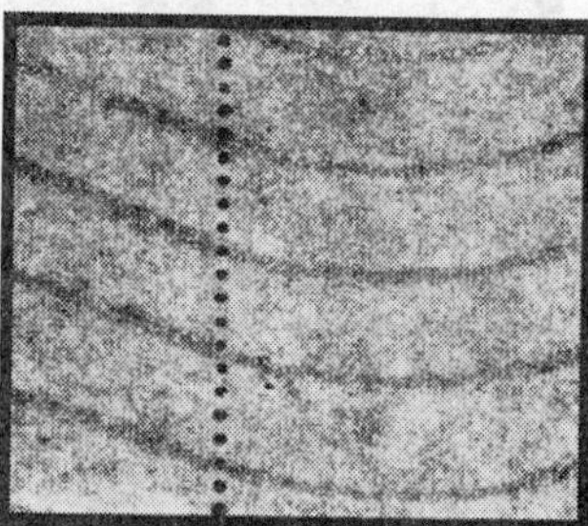

Wmk. 346

Wmkd. Parallel Curved Lines. (346)

1962, Oct. 18 Litho. *Perf. 13½x14*

749 A317 20c gold, dull gray violet & black 18 5

Issued to commemorate the 50th anniversary of the founding of the Postal Union of the Americas and Spain, UPAE. See also Nos. C445-C446.

"Virgin of the Rock"

A318

Red Cross Centenary Emblem

A319

1963, Mar. 11 **Wmk. 346**

750 A318 60c multicolored 30 5

Issued to commemorate Vatican II, the 21st Ecumenical Council of the Roman Catholic Church. See also No. C447.

1963, May 1 *Perf. 12x12½*

751 A319 5c olive bister & red 8 3

Centenary of International Red Cross.

Women's Rights Type of 1962

1963, July 11 **Wmk. 346**

752 A314 5c orange, gray & black 5 4

See also Nos. C448-C450.

Manuel Mejia J. and Flag of National Coffee Growers Assn.

A320

Perf. 12½x13

1965, Feb. 10 Engraved **Unwmkd.**

753 A320 25c rose & black 25 5

Issued to honor Manuel Mejia J. (1887-1958), banker and manager of the National Coffee Growers Association. See Nos. C464-C466.

Julio Arboleda

A321

1966, Mar. 9 Litho. *Perf. 14x13½*

754 A321 5c lt. brn., lt. yellow green & black 5 3

Issued to honor Julio Arboleda (1817-1862), writer, soldier and statesman.

Spanish Galleon, 16th Century

A322

History of Maritime Mail: 15c, Rio Hacha brigantine, 1850. 20c, Uraba canoe. 40c, Magdalena River steamship and barge, 1900. 50c, Modern motor ship and sea gull.

1966, June 16 Photo. **Unwmkd.**

755 A322 5c orange & multi. 8 3

756 " 15c car. rose, black & brown 10 5

757 " 20c brt. grn., orange & black 7 3

758 " 40c dp. bl. & multi. 18 5

759 " 50c pale bl. & multi. 38 18

Nos. 755-759 (5) 81 34

Plumed Hogfish

A323

Design: 10p, Bat ray and brittle starfish.

1966, Aug. 25 Photo. *Perf. 12½x13*

760 A323 80c multicolored 8 3

761 " 10p " 5.50 5.50

Nos. 760-761, C481-C483(5) 17.63 17.33

Arms of Venezuela, Colombia and Chile

A324

1966, Oct. 11 Litho. *Perf. 14x13½*

762 A324 40c yellow & multi. 10 3

Issued to commemorate the visits of Eduardo Frei and Raul Leoni, presidents of Chile and Venezuela. See Nos. C484-C485.

Camilo Torres, 1766-1816, Lawyer

A325

Portraits: 60c, Jorge Tadeo Lozano (1771-1816), naturalist. 1p, Francisco Antonio Zea (1776-1822), naturalist and politician.

Perf. 13½x14

1967, Jan. 18 Litho. **Unwmkd.**

763 A325 25c violet & bister 5 3

764 " 60c dk. red brown & bister 10 3

765 " 1p green & bister 50 18

Nos. 763-765, C486-C487 (5) 1.20 37

Issued to honor famous men of Colombia.

Map of South America and Arms

A326

1967, Feb. 2 Litho. *Perf. 14x13½*

766 A326 40c multicolored 18 5

767 " 60c " 20 3

Issued to publicize the Declaration of Bogota for cooperation and world peace, signed by Colombia, Chile, Ecuador, Peru and Venezuela. See No. C488.

Monochaetum Orchid and Bee

A327

Orchid: 2p, Passiflora vitifolia and butterfly.

1967, May 23 Litho. *Perf. 14*

768 A327 25c multicolored 6 3

769 " 2p " 55 55

Nos. 768-769, C489-C491 (5) 2.71 1.13

Issued to commemorate the First National Orchid Exhibition and the Topical Philatelic Flora and Fauna Exhibition, Medellin, Apr. 1967.

Lions Emblem

A328

SENA Emblem

A329

1967, July 12 Litho. *Perf. 13½x14*

770 A328 10p multicolored 2.50 65

Issued to commemorate the 50th anniversary of Lions International. See No. C492.

Lithographed and Embossed

1967, Sept. 20 **Unwmkd.**

771 A329 5p gold, brt. green & black 1.00 25

Issued to commemorate the 10th anniversary of National Apprenticeship Service, SENA. See No. C494.

Gold Diadem in Calima Style

A330

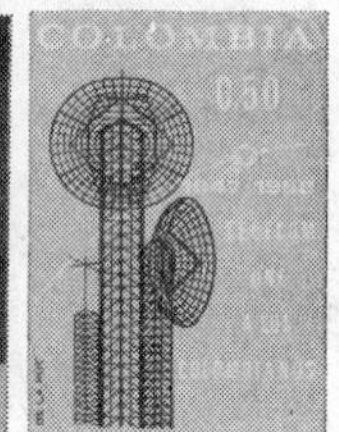

Radar Installation

A331

Pre-Columbian Art: 3p, Gold statuette, ornamental globe and bird (horiz.).

Perf. 13½x14, 14x13½

1967, Oct. 13 Photogravure

772 A330 1.60p brt. rose lilac, gold & brn. 50 15

773 " 3p dark blue, gold & brn. 65 38

Nos. 772-773, C495-C497 (5) 11.37 8.38

Issued to commemorate the meeting of the Universal Postal Union Committee on Postal Studies, Bogota, October, 1967.

1968, May 14 Litho. *Perf. 13½x14*

Design: 1p, Map of communications network.

774 A331 50c brt. yel. green, blk. & org. brn. 18 3

775 " 1p multicolored 38 3

Issued to commemorate the 20th anniversary of the National Telecommunications Service (TELECOM). See Nos. C498-C499.

The Eucharist

A332

St. Augustin, by Gregorio Vasquez

A333

1968, June 6 Litho. *Perf. 13½x14*

776 A332 60c multicolored 15 3

Issued to publicize the 39th Eucharistic Congress, Bogotá, Aug. 18-25. See Nos. C500-C501.

1968, Aug. 13 Photo. *Perf. 13*

Designs: 60c, The Gathering of Manna, by Gregorio Vasquez. 1p, The Marriage of the Virgin, by Baltazar de Figueroa. 5p, Jeweled monstrance, c. 1700. 10p, Pope Paul VI, painting by Roman Franciscan nuns.

777 A333 25c multicolored 3 3

778 " 60c " 8 3

779 " 1p " 18 3

780 " 5p " 75 15

781 " 10p " 1.00 40

a. Souv. sheet of 2 1.65 1.65

Nos. 777-781, C502-C506 (10) 7.75 2.05

Issued to commemorate the 39th Eucharistic Congress, Bogotá, Aug. 18-25. No. 781a contains two imperf. stamps similar to Nos. 780-781. Black inscription, Congress emblem in crimson and red control number in margin. Size: 90x89½mm.

Pope Paul VI

A334

Arms of National University

A335

1968, Aug. 22 Litho. *Perf. 13½x14*

782 A334 25c multicolored 12 5

Issued to commemorate the visit of Pope Paul VI to Colombia, Aug. 22–24. See Nos. C507–C509.

1968, Oct. 29 Litho. *Perf. 13½x14*

783 A335 80c multicolored 20 3

Issued to commemorate the centenary of the founding of the National University. See No. C510.

Stamp of Antioquia, 1868

A336

Institute Emblem

A337

1968, Nov. 20 Litho. *Perf. 12x12½*

784 A336 30c emerald & blue 15 3

Souvenir Sheet

785 A336 5p lt. olive & blue 2.40 2.40

Issued to commemorate the centenary of the first postage stamps of Antioquia and to publicize the 7th National Philatelic Exhibition, Medellin, Nov. 20–29. No. 785 contains one stamp; vermilion margin with white inscription and blue coat of arms and control number. Size: 59x79mm.

1969, Mar. 5 Litho. *Perf. 13½x14*

786 A337 20c multicolored 12 4

Issued to commemorate the 25th anniversary (in 1967) of the Inter-American Agricultural Sciences Institute. See No. C511.

Battle of Boyaca (Detail), by José Maria Espinosa—A338

Design: 30c, Army of liberation crossing Pisba Pass, by Francisco Antonio Caro.

1969, July 24 Litho. *Perf. 13½x14*

787 A338 20c gold & multi. 10 5
788 " 30c " 18 5

Issued to commemorate the sesquicentennial of the fight for independence. See No. C517.

"Poverty"

A339

1970, Mar. 1 Litho. *Perf. 14*

789 A339 30c blue & multi. 12 3

Issued to publicize the Colombian Institute for Family Welfare and to commemorate the 10th anniversary of the Children's Rights Law.

Greek Mask and Pre-Columbian Symbol of Literary Contest

A340

1970, Sept. 12 Litho. *Perf. 14x13½*

790 A340 30c dk. brown, red orange & ocher 6 3

Issued to publicize the 3rd Latin American Theatrical Festival of the Universities, Manizales, Sept. 12–20.

Colombian Stamps, Envelope and Emblem

A341

1970, Sept. 24 Litho. *Perf. 14x13½*

791 A341 2p brt. blue & multi. 38 5

Issued to publicize Philatelic Week.

Arms of Ibague and Discobolus

A342

1970, Oct. 13

792 A342 80c buff, emerald & sepia 25 5

9th National Games in Ibague.

St. Theresa, by Baltazar de Figueroa

A343

1970, Oct. 28 Litho. *Perf. 13½x14*

793 A343 2p multicolored 45 4

Elevation of St. Theresa (1515–1582), to Doctor of the Church. See No. C568.

Casa Cural

A344

1971, May 20 Litho. *Perf. 14x13½*

794 A344 1.10p multicolored 25 7

Fourth centenary (in 1970) of the founding of Guacari, Valle. See also No. 809.

Dancers and Music, Currulao

A345

1971 Litho. *Perf. 13½x14*

Design: 1p, Chicha Maya dancers and music.

795 A345 1p pink & multi. 42 10
796 " 1.10p lt. bl. & multi. 30 3

Souvenir Sheets

Imperf.

797 A345 Sheet of 3, multi. 1.65 1.65
- ***a.*** 2.50p Napanga 35 35
- ***b.*** 2.50p Joropo 35 35
- ***c.*** 5p Guabina 70 70

798 A345 Sheet of 3, multi. 1.85 1.85
- ***a.*** 4p Bambuco 50 50
- ***b.*** 4p Cumbia 50 50
- ***c.*** 4p Currulao 50 50

Size of Nos. 797–798: 78x110mm. Issue dates: No. 795, Dec. 20; No. 796, Aug. 5; Nos. 797–798, Aug. 10.

Constitutional Assembly, by Delgado

A346

1971, Oct. 2 *Perf. 14*

801 A346 80c multicolored 15 3

Sequicentennial of Gran Colombian Constitutional Assembly in Rosario del Cucuta. See No. C589.

Arrows Emblem

A347

1972, Feb. 24 *Perf. 13½x14*

802 A347 60c black & gray 22 3

Inter-Governmental Committee on European Migration, 20th anniversary.

Student and World Map

A348

1972, Mar. 15 *Perf. 14x13½*

803 A348 1.10p lt. grn. & brn. 20 3

20th anniversary of ICETEX, an organization which furnishes financial help for educational purposes and for technical studies abroad.

U.N. Emblem, Soldier and Frigate

A349

1972, Apr. 7

804 A349 1.20p lt. bl. & multi. 20 4

20th anniversary of the Colombian Battalion in Korea.

Mother Francisca Josefa del Castillo

A350

Handicraft

A351

1972, Apr. 6 *Perf. 13½x14*

805 A350 1.20p brn. & multi. 20 6

Tercentenary (in 1971) of the birth of Mother Francisca Josefa del Castillo, Poor Clare abbess and writer.

1972, Apr. 11

806 A351 1.10p multicolored 38 6

Colombian artisans. See Nos. C569–C571.

Maxillaria Triloris

A352

Emeralds

A353

1972, Apr. 20

807 A352 20p green & multi. 3.00 75

10th National Philatelic Exhibition, Medellin.

1972, June 16 Litho. *Perf. 13½x14*

808 A353 1.10p multicolored 45 8

Type of 1971

Design: Antonio Narifio House.

1972, June 17 *Perf. 14x13½*

809 A344 1.10p multicolored 25 4

4th centenary, town of Leyva.

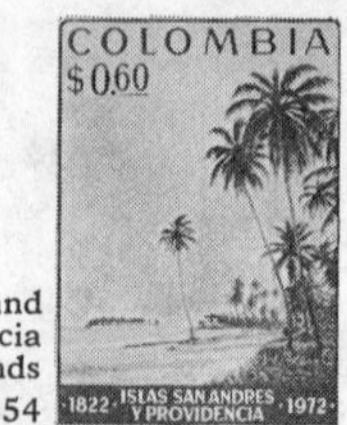

San Andres and Providencia Islands
A354

1972, June 24 *Perf. 13½x14*

810 A354 60c blue & multi. 20 3

Sesquicentennial of annexation by Colombia of San Andres and Providencia Islands.

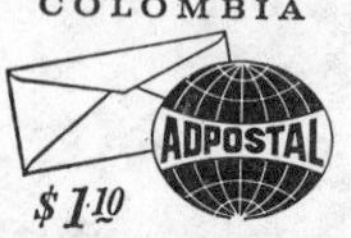

Postal Service Emblem
A355

1972, Nov. 15 Litho. *Perf. 12½x12*

811 A355 1.10p emerald 15 4

Family
A356

1972, Nov. 23

812 A356 60c orange 10 3

Social progress.

Radio League Emblem
A357

Human Figure, Tamalameque
A358

1973, Apr. 6 Litho. *Perf. 12x12½*

813 A357 60c lt. bl., ultra. & red 15 3

40th anniversary of the Colombian Radio Amateurs' League.

1973, June 15 Litho. *Perf. 13½x14*

Excavated Ceramic Artifacts: 1p, Winged urn, Tairona. 1.10p, Jug, Muisca.

814 A358 60c lt. blue & multi. 18 8
815 " 1p org. & multi. 50 5
816 " 1.10p vio. bl. & multi. 30 5
Nos. 814-816, C583-C586 (7) 3.23 78

Antonio Nariño, by José M. Espinosa
A359

Child
A360

1973, Dec. 13 Litho. *Perf. 13½x14*

817 A359 60c multicolored 15 3

Sesquicentennial of the death of General Antonio Nariño (1765–1823).

1973, Dec. 17

818 A360 1.10p multicolored 18 5

National Campaign for Children's Welfare.

Symbols of Financial Controls
A361

1973, Dec. 20 Litho. *Perf. 14x13½*

819 A361 80c ultra., ocher & black 15 5

50th anniversary of Comptroller-general's Office.

Mother Laura Montoya
A362

1974, June 18 Litho. *Perf. 13½x14*

820 A362 1p multicolored 18 3

Centenary of the birth of Mother Laura Montoya (1874–1949), founder and Mother Superior of the Missionaries of Mary Immaculata and St. Catherine of Siena.

Runner and Games' Emblem
A363

1974, July 18 Litho. *Perf. 14x13½*

821 A363 2p vermilion, yellow & brown 20 6

10th National Games, Pereira.

José Rivera
A364

1974, Aug. 3 Litho. *Perf. 14x13½*

822 A364 10p green & multi. 1.00 22

50th anniversary of the publication of "La Voragine" (The Whirlpool) by José Eustasio Rivera.

Abstract Pattern
A365

Train Emerging from Tunnel
A366

1974, Oct. 24 Litho. *Perf. 13½x14*

823 A365 1.10p multicolored 18 3

Centenary of National Insurance Co. See No. C610.

1974, Nov. 27 Litho. *Perf. 13½x14*

824 A366 1.10p multicolored 18 3

Centenary of the Antioquia railroad.

Boy, Puppy and Soccer Ball
A367

Design: 1p, Girl with racket and kitten.

1974, Dec. 9

825 A367 80c multicolored 15 5
826 " 1p " 20 8

Christmas 1974.

Gold Animal
A368

Design: 1.10p, Gold necklace.

1975, Apr. 11 Litho. *Perf. 14x13½*

827 A368 80c ultra., gold & brown 10 3
828 " 1.10p red, gold & brn. 10 3

Pre-Columbian Sinu culture artifacts. See Nos. C621–C622.

Guglielmo Marconi
A369

Santa Maria Cathedral
A370

1975, June 2 Litho. *Perf. 13½x14*

829 A369 3p multicolored 25 5

Birth centenary of Guglielmo Marconi (1874–1937), Italian electrical engineer and inventor.

1975, July 26

830 A370 80c multicolored 10 3

400th anniversary of Santa Maria City. See No. C623.

Rafael Nuñez
A371

Arms of Medellin
A372

1975, Sept. 28 Litho. *Perf. 13½x14*

831 A371 1.10p multicolored 15 3

Rafael Nuñez (1825–1894), philosopher, poet, political leader, birth sesquicentenary.

Lithographed

1975–77 *Perf. 13½x14, 12 (1.20p)*

Multicolored

832 A372 1p *shown* 25 3
833 " 1.20p *Ibagué* ('76) 15 3
834 " 1.20p *Tunja* ('76) 12 3
835 " 1.50p *Cucuta* 25 3
836 " 1.50p *Cartagena* ('76) 15 3
837 " 5p *Popayan* ('77) 30 5
838 " 5p *Barranquilla* ('77) 30 5
Nos. 832-838 (7) 1.52 25

The 1p commemorates the tercentenary of Medellin; No. 835, the centenary of Cucuta's reconstruction.

No. 827 Surcharged **$ 1.20**

1975 *Perf. 14x13½*

840 A368 1.20p on 80c multi. 15 3

Purace Indians, Cauca
A373

1976, Nov. 10 Litho. *Perf. 13½x14*

841 A373 1.50p multicolored 15 3

Callicore
A374

Designs: 5p, Morpho (butterfly). 20p, Anthurium.

1976, Nov. 17 *Perf. 12*

842 A374 3p multicolored 30 5
843 " 5p " 45 8
844 " 20p " 1.25 50

Rotary Emblem
A375

1976, Dec. 3 Litho. *Perf. 12*

845 A375 1p multicolored 12 3

Rotary Club of Colombia, 50th anniversary.

Declaration of Independence, by John Trumbull—A376

1976, Dec. 21 Litho. *Perf. 12*

846 A376 Strip of 3, multi. 5.50 3.25
a. 30p, single stamp 1.75 1.00

American Bicentennial. No. 846 printed in sheets of 4 triptychs; black control number in margin showing Bicentennial emblems and personalities of the American Revolution.

Policeman with Dog
A377

1976, Dec. 29 *Perf. 13½x14*

847 A377 1.50p multicolored 15 5

Honoring the National Police.

Nos. 831, 834, 847 Surcharged in Light Brown

1977, June Litho. *Perf. 13½x14, 12*

848	A371	2p on 1.10p multi.	20	5
849	A372	2p on 1.20p "	12	5
850	A377	2p on 1.50p "	15	5

Souvenir Sheet

Postal Museum, Bogota—A378

1977, July 27 Litho. *Perf. 14*

855 A378 25p multicolored 1.75 1.75

Postal Museum, Bogota. No. 855 contains one stamp (50x40mm.); multicolored margin shows Colombian stamps; black control number. Size: 130x105mm.

Mother and Child
A379

1977–78 Litho. *Perf. 12*

856	A379	2p multi.	10	3
857	"	2.50p " ('78)	15	3

National good nutrition plan.
Issue dates: 2p, Aug. 30. 2.50p, Jan. 26.

Jacana and Eichhornia
A380

Fidel Cano
Fundador de El Espectador

Fidel Cano, by Francisco Cano
A381

Design: 20p, Mayan cotinga and pyrostegia venusta.

1977, Sept. 6 Litho. *Perf. 14*

858	A380	10p multicolored	75	15
859	"	20p "	1.20	45
		Nos. 858-859, C644-C647 (6)	4.35	1.00

1977, Sept. 16 *Perf. 14*

860 A381 4p multicolored 25 3

90th anniversary of El Espectador, newspaper founded by Fidel Cano.

Abacus and Alphabet
A382

Cattleya Triannae
A383

1977, Sept. 16 *Perf. 13½x14*

861 A382 3p multicolored 18 3

Popular education.

1978, Apr. 18 Litho. *Perf. 12*

862 A383 2.50p multicolored 15 3

medellin 78 COLOMBIA $10

Sprinting and Games Emblem
A384

1978, June 27 Litho. *Perf. 14*

Multicolored

863	Sheet of 16	12.00	12.00
a.	A384 10p *shown*	60	30
b.	" 10p *Basketball*	60	30
c.	" 10p *Baseball*	60	30
d.	" 10p *Boxing*	60	30
e.	" 10p *Bicycling*	60	30
f.	" 10p *Fencing*	60	30
g.	" 10p *Soccer*	60	30
h.	" 10p *Gymnastics*	60	30
i.	" 10p *Judo*	60	30
j.	" 10p *Weight lifting*	60	30
k.	" 10p *Wrestling*	60	30
l.	" 10p *Swimming*	60	30
m.	" 10p *Tennis*	60	30
n.	" 10p *Target shooting*	60	30
o.	" 10p *Volleyball*	60	30
p.	" 10p *Water polo*	60	30

13th Central American and Caribbean Games, Medellin. No. 863 has black marginal inscription and control number. Size: 200x160mm.

"Sigma 2" by Alvaro Herrán
A385

1978, June 30

864 A385 8p multicolored 48 10

Chamber of Commerce, Bogota, centenary.

Gen. Tomás Cipriano de Mosquera
A386

1978, Oct. 6 Litho. *Perf. 12*

865 A386 6p multicolored 36 8

Gen. Tomás Cipriano de Mosquera (1778–1878), statesman.

SEMI-POSTAL STAMP

Girl Giving First Aid
SP1

Perf. 13½x14

1966, Apr. 26 Litho. Unwmkd.

B1	SP1	5c+5c multicolored	7	3

Issued for the Red Cross.

AIR POST STAMPS.

No. 341 Overprinted

1er.
Servicio
Postal
Aereo
6-18-19

1919 *Perf. 14.* **Unwmkd.**

C1	A109	2c carmine rose	1350.00	1000.00
		a. Numerals "1" with serifs	*3500.00*	1750.00

Used for the first experimental flight from Barranquilla to Puerto Colombia, June 18, 1919.

Issued by Compania Colombiana de Navegacion Aerea.

From 1920 to 1932 the internal airmail service of Colombia was handled by the Compania Colombiana de Navegacion Aerea (1920) and the Sociedad Colombo-Alemana de Transportes Aéreos, known familiarly as "SCADTA" (1920-1932). These organizations under government contracts operated and maintained their own post offices, and issued stamps which were the only legal franking for airmail service during this period, both in the internal and international mails. All letters had to bear government stamps as well.

Woman and Boy Watching Plane
AP1

Designs: No. C3, Clouds and small biplane at top. No. C4, Tilted plane viewed close-up from above. No. C5, Flier in plane watching biplane. No. C6, Lighthouse. No. C7, Fuselage and tail of biplane. No. C8, Condor on cliff. No. C9, Plane at rest; pilot foreground. No. C10, Ocean liner.

Lithographed.

1920, Feb. *Imperf.* **Unwmkd.**

Without Gum.

C2	AP1	10c green, red, blue, yellow & black	1500.00	1250.00
C3	"	10c blue, red & black	1500.00	1250.00
C4	"	10c yellow, red, bl. & black	2000.00	1250.00
C5	"	10c blue, red, yellow & black	1500.00	1250.00
C6	"	10c blue, green, red, yellow, & black	1500.00	1250.00
C7	"	10c green, red, blue, red brown & black	4500.00	2100.00
C8	AP1	10c brown, green, blue, red & black	2500.00	1500.00
		a. Without overprint		
C9	"	10c green, blue, red, yellow, red brown & black	1850.00	1250.00
C10	"	10c blue, yellow, green, red & black	1850.00	1250.00

Flier in Plane Watching Biplane
AP2

1920, March

C11	AP2	10c green	120.00	*300.00*

Four other 10c stamps, similar to No. C11, have two designs showing plane, mountains and water. They are printed in deep green or light brown red. Some authorities state that these four were not used regularly.

Issued by Sociedad Colombo-Alemana de Transportes Aereos (SCADTA)

Seaplane over Magdalena River
AP3

1920-21 Lithographed. *Perf. 12*

C12	AP3	10c yellow ('21)	22.50	21.00
C13	"	15c blue ('21)	21.00	20.00
C14	"	30c black, *rose*	10.00	8.50
C15	"	30c rose ('21)	16.50	15.00
C16	"	50c pale green	15.00	13.50
		Nos. C12-C16 (5)	85.00	78.00

No. C16 Handstamp Surcharged in Violet or Black:
(Illustrations of types "a" to "e" are reduced in size.)

VALOR 10 CENTAVOS
a

VALOR 10 CENTAVOS
b

Valor 10 Céntavos
c

VALOR 30 Ctvos
S.C.A.T.A
d

30¢ 30¢
e

$030
f

$030¢
g

1921

C17	AP3 (*a*)	10c on 50c	250.00	250.00
C18	" (*b*)	10c on 50c	225.00	225.00
C19	AP3 (*c*)	10c on 50c	325.00	165.00
C20	" (*b*)	30c on 50c	300.00	300.00
C21	" (*d*)	30c on 50c	450.00	165.00
C22	" (*e*)	30c on 50c	650.00	325.00
C23	" (*f*)	30c on 50c	650.00	325.00
C24	" (*g*)	30c on 50c	550.00	325.00

Plane over Magdalena River
AP4

Plane over Bogota Cathedral
AP5

1921 *Perf. 11½*

C25	AP4	5c orange yellow	3.50	3.00
C26	"	10c slate green	1.50	1.25
C27	"	15c orange brown	1.50	1.50
C28	"	20c red brown	2.50	1.85
		a. Imperf. vert., pair	*150.00*	
C29	AP4	30c green	1.75	75
C30	"	50c blue	2.10	85
C31	"	60c vermilion	27.50	12.50
C32	AP5	1p gray black	13.50	9.00
C33	"	2p rose	25.00	15.00
C34	"	3p violet	85.00	60.00
C35	"	5p olive green	275.00	250.00
		Nos. C25-C35 (11)	438.85	355.70

Exist imperf.

Nos. C16 and C12 Handstamp Surcharged
(Illustration of type "h" is reduced in size.)

VALOR 20 Ctvs.
h

30 cent.
i

1921-22 *Perf. 12*

C36	AP3 (*h*)	20c on 50c	425.00	425.00
C37	" (*i*)	30c on 10c	350.00	350.00

Seaplane over Magdalena River
AP6

Plane over Bogota Cathedral
AP7

Wmk. 116

Wmkd. Crosses and Circles (116)

1923-28 *Perf. 14x14½*

C38	AP6	5c orange yellow	75	30
C39	"	10c green	75	18
C40	"	15c carmine	80	18
C41	"	20c gray	75	15
C42	"	30c blue	75	15
C43	"	40c purple ('28)	7.50	4.50
C44	"	50c green	1.35	45
C45	"	60c brown	1.85	45
C46	"	80c olive green('28)	18.50	18.50
C47	AP7	1p black	7.50	1.10
C48	"	2p red orange	13.50	3.25
C49	"	3p violet	30.00	15.00
C50	"	5p olive green	45.00	25.00
		Nos. C38-C50 (13)	129.00	69.21

Nos. C41 and C31 Surcharged in Carmine and Dark Blue:

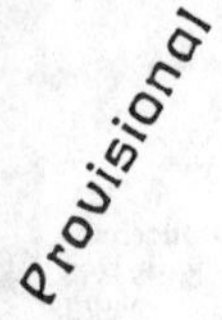

30 30 30 30
j *k*

1923

C51	AP6 (*j*)	30c on 20c gray (C)	50.00	42.50
C52	AP4 (*k*)	30c on 60c vermilion (Bl)	37.50	30.00

Nos. C41-C42 Overprinted in Black

1928 *Perf. 14x14½* **Wmk. 116**

C53	AP6	20c gray	47.50	50.00
C54	"	30c blue	45.00	47.50

Issued to commemorate the goodwill flight of Lt. Benjamin Mendez from New York to Bogota.

Magdalena River and Tolima Volcano
AP8

Columbus' Ship and Plane
AP9

Wmk. 127

Wmkd. Quatrefoils. (127)

1929, June 1 *Perf. 14*

C55	AP8	5c yellow orange	90	45
C56	"	10c red brown	75	40
C57	"	15c deep green	90	45
C58	"	20c carmine	75	25
C59	"	30c gray blue	90	30
C60	"	40c dull violet	1.25	40
C61	"	50c dark olive green	1.85	50
C62	"	60c orange brown	1.85	50
C63	"	80c green	5.50	4.25
C64	AP9	1p blue	7.50	1.75
C65	"	2p brown orange	11.50	3.25
C66	"	3p pale rose vio.	22.50	10.00
C67	"	5p olive green	60.00	22.50
		Nos. C55-C67 (13)	116.15	45.00

For International Airmail.

AP10

AP11

1929, June 1 *Perf. 14* **Wmk. 127**

C68	AP10	5c yellow orange	1.00	1.25
C69	"	10c red brown	85	1.00
C70	"	15c deep green	85	1.00

C71 AP10 20c carmine 85 1.00
C72 " 25c violet blue 85 1.00
C73 " 30c gray blue 85 1.00
C74 " 50c dark olive green 1.00 1.00
C75 " 60c brown 1.25 1.25
C76 AP11 1p blue 3.50 5.50
C77 " 2p red orange 5.50 8.00
C78 " 3p violet 75.00 80.00
C79 " 5p olive green 110.00 125.00
Nos. C68-C79 (12) 201.50 227.00

This issue was sold abroad for use on correspondence to be flown from coastal to interior points of Colombia. Cancellations are those of the country of origin rather than Colombia.

Nos. C63, C66 and C64 Surcharged in Black:

m

1830 1930
Simon Bolivar
30 cts. 30 cts.
n

1930, Dec. 15
C80 AP8 (*m*) 10c on 80c green 3.00 3.75
C81 AP9 (*n*) 20c on 3p pale rose violet 6.25 7.50
C82 " (") 30c on 1p blue 6.25 7.50

Issued to commemorate the centenary of the death of Simon Bolivar (1783-1830).

Colombian Government Issues.
Nos. C55-C67 Overprinted in Black:

CORREO AEREO
o

CORREO AEREO
p

Typographed.

1932, Jan. 1 *Perf. 14* Wmk. 127
C83 AP8 (*o*) 5c yel. orange 6.25 7.00
C84 " (") 10c red brown 1.75 55
C85 " (") 15c deep green 1.75 90
C86 " (") 20c carmine 1.25 85
C87 " (") 30c gray blue 1.25 70
C88 " (") 40c dull violet 1.85 1.10
C89 " (") 50c dark olive green 2.50 1.50
C90 " (") 60c orange brn. 1.75 1.40
C91 " (") 80c green 11.00 9.00
C92 AP9 (*p*) 1p blue 11.00 7.00
C93 " (") 2p brn. org. 22.50 14.00
C94 " (") 3p pale rose violet 37.50 42.50
C95 " (") 5p olive green 80.00 90.00
Nos. C83-C95 (13) 180.35 176.50

Coffee
AP12

Cattle
AP13

Petroleum
AP14

Bananas
AP15

Gold
AP16

Emerald
AP17

Photogravure.

1932-39 *Perf. 14* Wmk. 127
C96 AP12 5c orange & black brown 50 25
C97 AP13 10c lake & black 65 25
C98 AP14 15c blue green & violet black 40 8
C99 " 15c vermilion & violet black ('39) 2.35 12
C100 AP15 20c carmine & olive black 60 8
C101 " 20c turquoise green & olive black ('39) 3.50 25
C102 AP12 30c dark blue & black brown 1.10 12
C103 AP15 40c dark violet & olive bistre 80 12
C104 AP13 50c dark green & brownish black 2.75 60
C105 AP14 60c dark brown & black violet 60 25
C106 AP12 80c green & black brown 4.75 75
C107 AP16 1p dark blue & olive bistre 8.00 75
C108 " 2p orange brown & olive bistre 9.00 1.60
C109 AP17 3p dark violet & emerald 16.00 4.25
C110 " 5p gray black & emerald 42.50 11.00
Nos. C96-C110 (15) 93.50 20.47

Nos. C104, C106-C108 Surcharged:

1533 CARTAGENA 1933
10 10
a

1533 1933
CARTAGENA
20 centavos 20
b

1934, Jan. 5
C111 AP13 (*a*) 10(c) on 50c 2.50 3.75
C112 AP12 (") 15(c) on 80c 3.75 4.50
C113 AP16 (*b*) 20c on 1p 4.50 5.50
C114 " (") 30c on 2p 5.50 6.25

400th anniversary of Cartagena.

Nos. C100 and C103 Surcharged in Black or Carmine:

5 cts 15

1939, Jan. 15
C115 AP15 5c on 20c carmine & olive black (Bk) 38 30
C116 " 5c on 40c dark violet & olive bistre (C) 38 30
C117 " 15c on 20c carmine & olive black (Bk) 60 50
a. Double surcharge 12.50
b. Pair, one double surcharge 12.50
c. Invtd. surch. 12.50 12.50

No. CF5 Surcharged in Black.

C118 AP15 5c on 20c carmine & olive black 90 90

Nos. C102-C103 Surcharged in Black or Red

15 cts

1940, Oct. 20
C119 AP12 15c on 30c dark blue & black brown 90 55
a. Invtd. surch. 12.50
C120 AP15 15c on 40c dark violet & olive bistre (R) 1.25 65
a. Double surcharge 12.50

Pre-Columbian Monument
AP18

Symbol of Legend of El Dorado
AP19

Spanish Fortifications, Cartagena
AP20

Colonial Bogotá
AP21

Proclamation of Independence
AP22

National Library, Bogotá
AP23

Engraved.

1941, Jan. 28 *Perf. 12* Unwmkd.
C121 AP18 5c gray black 30 5
C122 AP19 10c yellow orange 30 5
C123 AP20 15c carmine rose 30 5
C124 AP21 20c yellow green 30 5
a. Imperf. vert., pair 80.00 80.00
C125 AP18 30c deep blue 30 5
C126 AP19 40c rose lake 60 5
C127 AP20 50c turq. green 60 5
C128 AP21 60c sepia 60 15
C129 AP18 80c olive black 1.50 35
C130 AP22 1p blue & black 2.00 50
C131 AP23 2p red orange & black 3.00 1.25
C132 AP22 3p vio. & black 7.50 4.75
C133 AP23 5p light green & black 15.00 13.50
Nos. C121-C133 (13) 32.30 20.85

See also Nos. C151-C163, C217-C225.

San Sebastian Fort, Cartagena
AP24

Bay of Santa Marta
AP25

Tequendama Waterfall
AP26

National Capitol, Bogotá
AP27

Lithographed.

1945, Nov. 3 *Perf. 11* Unwmkd.
C134 AP24 5c blue gray 15 8
a. Imperf., pair 12.00
C135 AP26 10c yellow orange 15 8
a. Imperf., pair 12.00
C136 AP25 15c rose 15 5
a. Imperf., pair 12.00
C137 AP24 20c lt. yel. green 18 8
a. Imperf., pair 12.00
C138 AP26 30c ultramarine 20 8
a. Imperf., pair 12.00
C139 AP25 40c claret 25 18
a. Imperf., pair 12.00
C140 AP24 50c bluish green 65 20
a. Imperf., pair 12.00
C141 AP26 60c light violet brown 1.75 1.00
a. Imperf., pair 12.00
C142 AP25 80c dk. slate grn. 2.40 1.25
a. Imperf., pair 15.00
C143 AP27 1p dark blue 3.75 1.50
a. Imperf., pair 25.00
C144 " 2p red orange 6.25 2.75
a. Imperf., pair 85.00
Nos. C134-C144 (11) 15.88 7.25

Part-perforate varieties exist for all denominations except 80c.

Bello Type of Regular Issue, 1946.
Engraved.

1946, Sept. 3 *Perf. 12* Wmk. 255
C145 A219 5c deep blue 25 20

Issued to commemorate the 80th anniversary of the death of Andrés Bello, poet and educator.

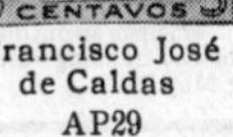

Francisco José de Caldas
AP29

Manuel del Socorro Rodriguez
AP30

Perf. 12½

1947, May 9 Litho. Unwmkd.

C146 AP29 5c deep blue, *greenish* 70 55
C147 AP30 10c red orange, *greenish* 85 75

4th Pan-American Press Congress (1946).

Chancellery Patio
AP31

Capitol, Patio Rafael Nunez
AP32

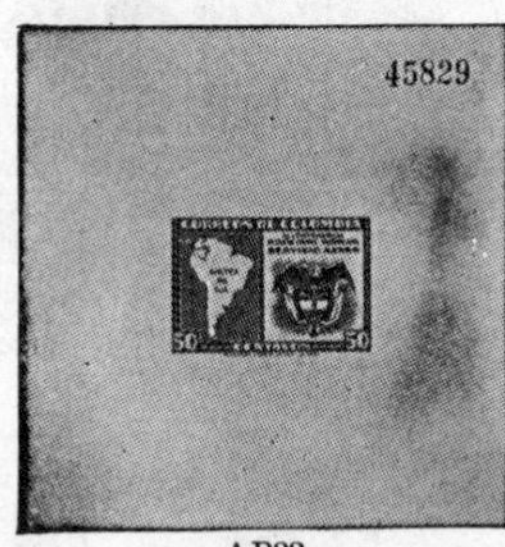

AP33

1948, Apr. 2 Engraved Wmk. 229

C148 AP31 5c dark brown 20 8
C149 AP32 15c deep blue 1.40 1.10

Miniature Sheet

Imperf.

C150 AP33 50c brown 1.85 1.85

Nos. C148–C150 commemorate the 9th Pan-American Conference, Bogotá. No. C150 measures 90½x90½mm.

Types of 1941.

1948, July 21 *Perf. 12* Unwmkd.

C151 AP18 5c orange yellow 15 3
C152 AP19 10c scarlet 18 3
C153 AP20 15c deep blue 22 3
C154 AP21 20c violet 20 5
C155 AP18 30c yellow green 25 5
C156 AP19 40c gray 45 18
C157 AP20 50c rose lake 50 15
C158 AP21 60c olive gray 70 15
C159 AP18 80c red brown 90 18
C160 AP22 1p olive green & vio. brn. 1.50 45
C161 AP23 2p deep green & brt. blue 3.00 75
C162 AP22 3p rose carmine & black 6.00 3.25
C163 AP23 5p light brown & turq. grn. 15.00 8.50
Nos. C151–C163 (13) 29.05 13.80

"Air Week" 5c Blue

The War and Air Department issued a 5c blue stamp in May, 1949, to publicize Air Week (Semana de Aviacion). The design shows a coat-of-arms, inscribed "FAC," superimposed upon an outline map of Colombia. This stamp had no franking value and its use was optional during May 16-23.

Justice and Liberty
AP34

Wing
AP35

Design: 10c, Liberty holding tablet of laws.

1949, Oct. 7 *Perf. 13* Unwmkd.

C164 AP34 5c blue green 15 3
C165 " 10c orange 15 3

Issued to honor the new Constitution.

For Domestic Postage.

1950, June 22 Litho. *Perf. 12*

C166 AP35 5c orange yellow 35 30
C167 " 10c brown red 50 38
C168 " 15c light blue 50 50
C169 " 20c light green 70 50
C170 " 30c lilac gray 1.10 35
C171 " 60c chocolate 1.65 1.65

With Network as in Parenthesis.

C172 AP35 1p gray (buff) 4.25 4.25
C173 " 2p blue (pale green) 12.00 12.50
C174 " 5p red brown (red brown) 25.00 25.00
Nos. C166–C174 (9) 46.05 45.43

No. C172 was issued both with and without network.

Nos. C151–C157 and C160–C163 Overprinted in Black **L**

1950, July 18

C175 AP18 5c orange yellow 30 18
C176 AP19 10c scarlet 30 18
C177 AP20 15c deep blue 30 18
C178 AP21 20c violet 30 20
C179 AP18 30c yellow green 38 25
C180 AP19 40c gray 45 38
C181 AP20 50c rose lake 50 45
C182 AP22 1p olive green & violet brown 2.25 2.10
C183 AP23 2p deep green & bright blue 3.50 3.50
C184 AP22 3p rose carmine & black 9.00 8.50
C185 AP23 5p light brown & turq. green 20.00 19.00
Nos. C175–C185 (11) 37.28 34.92

Nos. C151-C163 Overprinted in Black **A**

1950, July 12

C186 AP18 5c orange yellow 15 5
C187 AP19 10c scarlet 18 5
C188 AP20 15c deep blue 15 3
C189 AP21 20c violet 20 5
C190 AP18 30c yellow green 25 5
C191 AP19 40c gray 45 10
C192 AP20 50c rose lake 45 15
C193 AP21 60c olive gray 70 15
C194 AP18 80c red brown 1.25 15
C195 AP22 1p olive green & violet brown 1.85 75
C196 AP23 2p deep green & bright blue 3.25 1.50
C197 AP22 3p rose carmine & black 7.50 5.00
C198 AP23 5p light brown & turq. green 16.00 15.00
Nos. C186–C198 (13) 32.38 23.03

On Nos. C175–C198, "L" stands for LANSA, "A" for AVIANCA.

Miniature Sheet

Western Hemisphere
AP36

Imperf.

1950, Aug. 22 Photo. Unwmkd.

C199 AP36 50c gray 1.35 1.35

Issued to commemorate the 75th anniversary (in 1949) of the formation of the Universal Postal Union.

Types of 1941 Overprinted at Lower Right in Black **L**

Engraved.

1951, Sept. 15 *Perf. 12* Unwmkd.

C200 AP19 40c orange yellow 50 50
C201 AP20 50c ultramarine 65 65
C202 AP21 60c gray 90 90
C203 AP18 80c carmine rose 1.75 1.75
C204 AP22 1p red orange & red brown 2.25 2.25
C205 AP23 2p rose carmine & blue 3.50 3.50
C206 AP22 3p chocolate & emerald 9.00 10.00
C207 AP23 5p org. & gray 19.00 20.00
Nos. C200–C207 (8) 37.55 39.55

Types of 1941 Overprinted at Lower Right in Black **A**

1951–54

C208 AP19 40c org. yellow 2.00 50
C209 AP20 50c ultramarine 2.25 38
C210 AP21 60c gray 3.00 65
a. Overprint centered 1.75 65
C211 AP18 80c carmine rose 1.10 50
C212 AP22 1p red orange & red brown 4.00 38
C213 " 1p olive green & violet brown ('54) 2.10 38
C214 AP23 2p rose carmine & blue 2.50 70
C215 AP22 3p chocolate & emerald 5.00 1.00
C216 AP23 5p org. & gray 9.00 3.00
Nos. C208–C216 (9) 30.95 7.49

All values except the 2p and 3p exist without overprint.

Types of 1941.

1952, May 10 Engraved

C217 AP18 5c ultramarine 30 20
C218 AP19 10c " 30 20
C219 AP20 15c " 30 20
C220 AP21 20c " 70 30
C221 AP18 30c " 1.35 45
C222 " 5c carmine rose 30 20
C223 AP19 10c " 30 20
C224 AP21 20c " 70 30
C225 AP18 30c " 1.35 45
Nos. C217–C225 (9) 5.60 2.50

Type of 1941 Surcharged in Blue

1a CONFERENCIA 1952 SIDERURGICA LATINO AMERICANA 70 Ctvos.

1952, Oct. 30

C226 AP18 70c on 80c carmine rose 1.10 85

Issued to publicize the Latin American Siderurgical Conference, 1952.

Type of Postal Tax Stamps, 1948–50, Nos. 602 and 604 Surcharged or Overprinted in Black

CORREO 5 AEREO

1953 *Perf. 12.* Wmk. 255

C227 PT10 5c on 8c blue 10 3
C228 " 15c on 20c brown 20 3
C229 " 15c on 25c bl. green 1.25 5
C230 " 25c blue green 30 5

Many varieties of overprint or surcharge exist on Nos. C227–C231.

No. 570 Overprinted "AEREO" in Blue.

1953, Aug. *Perf. 12½* Wmk. 229

C231 A160 10c red 12 3

"Extra Rapido"

Stamps inscribed "Extra Rapido" are for use on domestic airmail carried by airlines other than AVIANCA.

No. 585 Surcharged and Overprinted "Extra Rapido" in Dark Blue

CORREO 5 EXTRA RAPIDO 5

1953 *Perf. 13* Unwmkd.

C232 A244 5c on 11c red 45 15

Capitol and Arms
AP37

Revenue Stamps Overprinted "Correo Extra-Rapido"

Gray Security Paper.

Engraved.

1953 *Perf. 12* Wmk. 255

C233 AP37 1c on 2c green 15 3
C234 " 50c red orange 17 5

AP38

Real Estate Tax Stamps Overprinted "Correo Extra-Rapido" in Black or Carmine

1953

C235 AP38 5c red orange 18 3
C236 " 20c brown (C) 18 5

On 20c, overprint is at bottom of stamp and two lines of ornaments cover real estate tax inscription at top.

Castillo y Rada and Map
AP39

Real Estate Tax Stamp Surcharged "Correo Aereo, II Exposicion Filatelica Nacional, Bogota Dicbre 1953, 15 Centavos"

Engraved and Lithographed.

1953, Dec. 12

C237 AP39 15c on 10p multi. 55 25

Issued to publicize the second National Philatelic Exhibition, Bogota, Dec. 1953.

No. RA45 Overprinted in Black — CORREO EXTRA-RAPIDO

1953

C238 PT10 10c purple 15 3

Galeras Volcano
AP40

Retreat of San Diego
AP41

Designs: 15c (C241), Las Lajas Shrine, Narino. 15c (C242), 50c, Bolivar monument. 20c, 80c, Ruiz mountain, Manizales. 40c, George Isaacs monument, Cali. 60c, Monkey Fountain, Tunja. 1p, Stadium, Medellin. 2p, Pastelillo Fort, Cartagena. 3p, Santo Domingo University gate. 5p, Las Lajas Shrine. 10p, Map of Colombia.

Perf. 13½x13, 13.

1954, Jan. 15 Engraved. Unwmkd.

C239 AP40 5c deep red violet 18 3
C240 AP41 10c black 15 3
C241 AP40 15c red orange 20 3
C242 " 15c carmine rose 15 3
C243 " 20c brown 15 3
C244 " 30c brown orange 18 3
C245 " 40c blue 15 3
C246 " 50c dark violet brown 32 3
C247 " 60c dark brown 42 3
C248 " 80c red brown 42 10

Size: 37x27mm.

Center in Black.

C249 AP41 1p deep blue 2.10 10
C250 " 2p dark green 2.50 25
C251 " 3p carmine rose 6.00 85

Size: 38x32mm., 32x38mm.

C252 AP41 5p dark green & red brown 6.75 2.10
C253 AP40 10p gray green & red orange 7.75 5.75
Nos. C239–C253 (15) 27.42 9.42

See also Nos. C307–C308.

Condor Carrying Shield
AP42

Inscribed: "Correo Extra-Rapido"

Lithographed.

1954, Apr. 23 ***Perf. 12½.***

C254 AP42 5c lilac rose 65 22

Soldier-Map-Arms Type of Regular Issue, 1954.

1954, June 13 Engraved *Perf. 13*

C255 A259 15c carmine 38 12

Issued to commemorate the first anniversary of the assumption of the presidency by General Rojas Pinilla.

See also No. C271a.

Games Type of Regular Issue, 1954.

Design: 20c, Stadium and Athlete holding arms of Colombia.

1954, July 18

C256 A260 15c chocolate 65 18
C257 " 20c deep blue green 1.35 50

7th National Games, Cali, July 1954.

Church of St. Peter Claver, Cartagena
AP45

1954, Sept. 9

C258 AP45 15c brown 35 3
a. Souvenir sheet 1.85 1.85

Issued to commemorate the 300th anniversary of the death of St. Peter Claver.

No. C258a contains one stamp similar to No. C258, but printed in red brown. Marginal inscriptions in black. Sheet size: 120½x127mm.

Mercury Type of Regular Issue, 1954.

1954, Oct. 29

C259 A263 15c deep blue 35 4

Inscribed "Extra Rapido"

C260 A263 50c scarlet 30 5

Issued to publicize the first International Fair and Exhibition, Bogotá, 1954.

Archbishop Manuel José Mosquera
AP47

Inscribed: "Correo Extra Rapido"

1954, Nov. 17

C261 AP47 2c yellow green 10 3

Issued to commemorate the centenary of the death of Archbishop Manuel José Mosquera.

Virgin of Chiquinquira
AP48

Inscribed: "Correo Extra Rapido"

Engraved and Lithographed

1954, Dec. 4

C262 AP48 5c orange brown & multicolored 12 5

See also No. C291.

College Types of Regular Issue, 1954.

Designs: 20c, Brother Cristobal de Torres. 50c, College chapel and arms.

Perf. 12½x11½, 11½x12½

1954, Dec. 6 Engraved Unwmkd.

C263 A264 15c orange & black 35 18
C264 " 20c ultramarine 60 18
C265 A265 25c dark brown 70 18
C266 " 50c black & carmine 1.65 85
a. Souvenir sheet 2.75 2.75

Issued to commemorate the 300th anniversary (in 1953) of the founding of the Senior College of Our Lady of the Rosary, Bogotá.

No. C266a contains four stamps similar to Nos. C263–C266, but printed in different colors: 15c red and black, 20c pale purple, 25c brown, 50c black and olive green. Marginal inscriptions in black. Sheet size: 124½x130½mm.

Steel Mill Type of Regular Issue.

1954, Dec. 12 ***Perf. 12½x13***

C267 A266 20c green & black 90 75

Issued to mark the opening of the Paz del Rio steel mill, October 1954.

Marti Type of Regular Issue, 1955

1955, Jan. 28 ***Perf. 13½x13***

C268 A267 15c deep green 30 8

Issued to commemorate the centenary (in 1953) of the birth of José Marti.

Korean Veterans Type of Regular Issue, 1955.

1955, Mar. 23 ***Perf. 12½***

C269 A268 20c dark green 55 25

Issued to honor Colombian soldiers who served in Korea.

Merchant Fleet Types of Regular Issue, 1955.

1955, Apr. 12 ***Perf. 12½***

C270 A269 25c black 38 5
C271 A270 50c dark green 75 50
a. Souvenir sheet 2.75 2.75

Issued to honor the Grand-Colombian Merchant Fleet.

No. C271a contains four stamps similar to Nos. C255, C269–C271, but printed in different colors; 15c lilac red, 20c olive, 25c bluish black, 50c bluish green. Marginal inscriptions in black. Sheet size: 125x131mm.

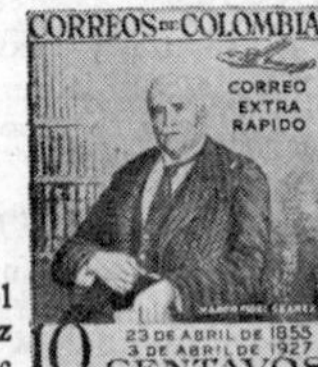

Pres. Marco Fidel Suarez
AP56

Inscribed: "Correo Extra Rapido"

1955, April 23 ***Perf. 13***

C272 AP56 10c deep blue 10 7

Issued to commemorate the centenary of the birth of Marco Fidel Suarez (1855–1927), president in 1918–1921.

Hotel-Church Type of Regular Issue, 1955.

1955, May 16 Photo. *Perf. 11½x12*

C273 A271 15c rose brown 30 3

Rotary Type of Regular Issue, 1955.

Engraved.

1955, Oct. 17 *Perf. 13* Unwmkd.

C274 A272 15c dark carmine rose 30 3

Rotary International, 50th anniversary.

O'Higgins, Santander and Sucre
AP59

Ferdinand the Catholic and Queen Isabella I
AP60

Designs: 2c, Atahualpa, Tisquesuza and Montezuma. 20c, Marti, Hidalgo and Petion. 1p, Artigas, Solano Lopez and Murillo. 2p, Abdon Calderon, Baron de Rio Branco and José de La Mar.

1955, Oct. 12 Engr. & Photo.

Inscribed: "Extra Rapido"

C275 AP59 2c dull brown & black 10 8
C276 AP60 5c dk. brn. & yel. 18 12

Regular Air Post

C277 AP59 15c rose carmine & black 22 12
C278 " 20c pale brown & black 30 8
a. Souvenir sheet of 2 3.75 3.75

Inscribed: "Extra Rapido"

C279 AP60 1p olive gray & brown 4.25 3.75
C280 " 2p violet & black 3.50 1.85
Nos. C275–C280 (6) 8.55 6.00

Issued to publicize the 7th Congress of the Postal Union of the Americas and Spain, Bogota, Oct. 12–Nov. 9, 1955.

No. C278a contains one each of Nos. C277–C278 printed in different shades. It measures 120x132mm. with marginal inscription in black: "Ministerio de Communicaciones. III Exposicion Filatelica Nacional Bogota 1955."

Caro Type of Regular Issue, 1955.

1955, Nov. 29 Engr. *Perf. 13½x13*

C281 A275 15c gray green 30 5

Issued to commemorate the centenary of the death of José Eusebio Caro, poet.

University of Salamanca
AP62

Inscribed: "Extra Rapido"

1955, Nov. 29 *Perf. 13* Unwmkd.

C282 AP62 20c dark brown 8 5

University of Salamanca, 7th centenary.

Type of Postal Tax Stamp of 1948-50 Surcharged in Black CORREO EXTRA-RAPIDO

Engraved.

1956 *Perf. 12* **Wmk. 255**

C283 PT10 2c on 8c blue 3 3

No. 617 Overprinted in Black EXTRA-RAPIDO

1956 *Perf. 12½x13* **Unwmkd.**

C284 A256 1p black & emerald 28 5

Columbus Type of Regular Issue.

1956, Oct. 11 Photo. *Perf. 12*

C285 A279 15c intense blue 38 12

Issued in honor of Christopher Columbus. See also No. C306.

St. Elizabeth Type of Regular Issue

1956, Nov. 19

C286 A280 15c red brown 35 20

Issued to commemorate the 7th centenary of St. Elizabeth of Hungary, patron saint of Santa Fé de Bogotá.

St. Ignatius Type of Regular Issue

1956, Nov. 26 Engr. *Perf. 12½x13*

C287 A281 5c brown 25 5

Issued to commemorate the 400th anniversary of the death of St. Ignatius of Loyola.

Javier Pereira
AP63

1956, Dec. 28 *Perf. 12* **Unwmkd.**

C288 AP63 20c rose carmine 20 5

Issued to honor 167-year-old Javier Pereira.

No. 649 and Type of 1941 Overprinted in Red "EXTRA RAPIDO."

1957 *Perf. 13½x13*

C289 A276 5c blue & black 10 5

Perf. 12

C290 AP23 5p orange & gray 4.25 3.00

The overprint measures 14mm.

Virgin Type of 1954.

Engraved and Lithographed

1957, May 23 *Perf. 13* **Unwmkd.**

C291 AP48 5c multicolored 7 6

Bank Type of Regular Issue, 1957.

Designs: C292, 20c, Emblem and dairy farm. 10c, Emblem and tractor. 15c, Emblem, coffee and corn. C293, Emblem, cow, horse and herd.

1957 Photo. *Perf. 14x13½*

C292	A283	5c chocolate	20	6
C293	"	5c orange	15	6
C294	"	10c green	55	50
C295	"	15c black	35	6
C296	"	20c dull red	85	80
		Nos. C292-C296 (5)	2.10	1.48

Nos. C292-C296 issued to commemorate the 25th anniversary of the founding of the Agrarian Savings Bank of Colombia.

No. C292 is inscribed "Extra Rapido."

No. C292 issued Mar. 5, others May 23.

Cyclist
AP64

1957, July 6 *Perf. 12* **Unwmkd.**

C297 AP64 2c brown 12 12
C298 " 5c ultramarine 20 20

Seventh Bicycle Tour of Colombia.

Academy Type of Regular Issue.

Designs: 15c, Coat of arms and Gen. Rafael Reyes. 20c, Coat of arms and Academy.

1957, July 20 **Engraved** *Perf. 12½*

C299 A284 15c rose carmine 18 3
C300 " 20c brown 35 3

Issued to commemorate the 50th anniversary of the Colombian Military Academy.

Delgado Type of Regular Issue, 1957.

1957, Sept. 15 Photo. *Perf. 12*

C301 A285 10c slate blue 22 15

Issued in honor of José Matías Delgado, liberator of El Salvador.

UPU Type of Regular Issue, 1957.

1957, Oct. 10

C302 A286 15c dark red brown 20 15
C303 " 25c dark blue 25 5

Issued for International Letter Writing Week and the 14th UPU Congress.

St. Vincent de Paul Type of Regular Issue, 1957.

1957, Oct. 18

C304 A287 5c rose brown 20 15

Issued to commemorate the centenary of the Colombian Society of St. Vincent de Paul.

Fencing Type of Regular Issue, 1957.

1957, Nov. 23 *Perf. 12*

C305 A288 20c dark red brown 38 38

Issued to commemorate the third South American Fencing Championship.

Columbus Type of Regular Issue, 1956, Inscribed "Extra Rapido."

1958, Jan. 8 *Perf. 12* **Unwmkd.**

C306 A279 3c dark green 3 3

Scenic Type of 1954.

Design: 25c, Las Lajas Shrine.

1958, June 20 Engr. *Perf. 13*

C307 AP40 25c dark blue 22 3
C308 " 25c rose violet 30 3

IGY Type of Regular Issue, 1958.

1958, May 12 Photo. *Perf. 12*

C309 A289 25c green 50 8

Inscribed "Extra Rapido."

C310 A289 1p purple 40 8

Nos. C309-C310 issued for the International Geophysical Year, 1957-58.

No. 659 Overprinted "AEREO" in Carmine.

1958, Oct. 16 **Engraved** *Perf. 13*

C312 A277 50c dark green & black 60 12

Almanza Type of Regular Issue, 1958.

1958, Oct. 23 Photo. *Perf. 14x13*

C313 A290 25c dark gray 30 3

Inscribed "Extra Rapido"

C314 A290 10c olive green 10 3

Carrasquilla Type of Regular Issue, 1959.

1959, Jan. 22 Photo. *Perf. 14x13*

C315 A291 25c carmine rose 18 5
C316 " 1p dark blue 75 25

Issued to commemorate the centenary of the birth (in 1857) of Msgr. R. M. Carrasquilla, rector of Our Lady of the Rosary Seminary, Bogotá.

Miss Universe Type of Regular Issue, 1959.

1959, June 26 *Perf. 11½* **Unwmkd.**

C317 A292 1.20p multi. 70 70
C318 " 5p " 24.00 24.00

Issued to honor Luz Marina Zuluaga, Miss Universe, 1959.

Gaitan Type of Regular Issue, 1959, Inscribed "Extra Rapido" and Surcharged in Black or Blue.

1959, July 28 Engr. *Perf. 12x13½*

C319 A293 2p on 1p black 70 20
C320 " 2p on 1p black (Bl) 70 20

Issued in honor of Jorge Eliecer Gaitan, (1898-1948), lawyer and politician.

The 1p black, type A293, exists without surcharge.

No. C247 Surcharged with New Value in Dark Blue; Old Value Obliterated.

1959, Aug. 24 *Perf. 13* **Unwmkd.**

C321 AP40 50c on 60c dark brown 75 38

Regular and Air Post Issues of 1948-1959 Overprinted in Black or Red UNIFICADO

1959-60

C322	A283	5c orange	40	40
C323	A287	5c rose brown ('60)	55	55
C324	A281	5c brown (R)	40	40
C325	AP41	10c black	20	3
		a. Double ovpt.	3.00	3.00
C326	A160	10c red	38	3
		a. Double ovpt.	1.50	1.50
C328	A284	15c rose carmine	30	3
		a. Inverted ovpt.	3.75	3.75
C330	AP40	20c brown	18	3
		a. Double ovpt.	1.50	1.50
C331	A284	20c brown	22	22
C332	A288	20c dark red brown ('60)	18	5
C333	AP40	25c rose violet ('60)	18	3
C334	"	25c dark blue	30	4
C335	A291	25c carmine rose	20	5
C336	A290	25c dark gray	18	4
C338	AP40	30c brown orange	18	3
C340	"	50c on 60c dark brown	25	7
C341	A291	1p dark blue	80	12
		a. Double ovpt.	3.00	3.00
C342	A292	1.20p brown, ultra., carmine & olive	75	75
C343	AP41	2p dark green & black	1.00	15
C344	"	3p carmine rose & black	3.00	45
		a. Double ovpt.	10.00	10.00
C345	"	5p dark green & red brown	4.00	50
		a. Double ovpt.	10.00	10.00
		b. Invert. ovpt.	10.00	10.00
C346	AP40	10p gray green & red orange	5.00	1.50
		Nos. C322-C346 (21)	18.65	5.47

Issued following agreement between the Colombian government and AVIANCA to unify the air postage used on all mail carried by AVIANCA.

Vertical overprint on Nos. C342 and C346.

Airmail Stamp of 1919 and Planes
AP66

Designs: 60c, No. C349a, C350a, Planes of 1919 and 1959. C349b, C350b, Stamp of 1919 and Planes.

Photogravure.

1959, Dec. 5 *Perf. 12* **Unwmkd.**

C347 AP66 35c light blue, black & red 45 8
C348 " 60c yellow green & gray 30 8

Souvenir Sheets.

C349 AP66 Sheet of two 3.25 3.25
a. 1p orange & gray 85 85
b. 1p lilac, gray & red 85 85

Inscribed "Extra Rapido"

1960, May 17

C350 AP66 Sheet of two 3.00 3.00
a. 1.50p red orange & gray 85 85
b. 1.50p olive, gray & rose 85 85

Nos. C347-C350 issued to commemorate the 40th anniversary of air post service and of the AVIANCA company.

Nos. C349-C350 measure 90x49½mm. with black marginal inscriptions.

Type of Regular Issue, 1959 and

1859 Stamp and Seaplane
AP67

Designs (various stamps of 1859 and): 10c, Map of Colombia. 25c, Pres. Mariano Ospina. 1.20p, Plane over mountains.

1959, Dec. 1 Photo. *Perf. 12*

C351 A296 25c choc. & red 50 25
C352 AP67 50c verm. & ultra. 75 65
C353 " 1.20p yellow green & carmine 1.00 85

Inscribed "Extra Rapido"

C354 A296 10c lemon & violet 15 3

Souvenir Sheet

Tête Bêche 5c Stamps of 1859
AP68

Wmkd. "REPUBLICA DE COLOMBIA". (331)

1959, Dec. 23 Litho. *Imperf.*

C355 AP68 5p, bl., *pink* 12.00 12.00

Nos. C351-C355 issued to commemorate the centenary of Colombian postage stamps.

No. C355 contains a tête bêche pair simulating the 5c blue of 1859, No. 2. Sheet sold for 5p. Size: 74½x70mm.

No. C355 exists with inscription "VALOR $5.10" instead of "VALOR $5."

35c COLOMBIA AEREO ELDORADO AEROPUERTO INTERNACIONAL BOGOTA

Eldorado Airport, Bogota
AP69

1960, Jan. 5 *Perf. 12½* **Wmk. 331**

C356 AP69 35c black & ochre 55 55
C356A " 60c vermilion & gray 50 30

Inscribed "Extra Rapido"

C356B AP69 1p Prussian blue & gray 45 45

Ant Bear
AP70

Designs: 1.30p, Armadillo. 1.45p, Parrot fish.

Photogravure

1960, Feb. 12 *Perf. 12* Unwmkd.

C357 AP70 35c sepia 1.00 12
C358 " 1.30p rose carmine & dk. brown 1.65 1.65
C359 " 1.45p light blue, bl. & yellow 1.50 1.50

Issued to commemorate the centenary of the death of Alexander von Humboldt, German naturalist and geographer (1769–1859).

Flower Type of Regular Issue, 1960

Flowers: Nos. C360, C362, C366, Passiflora mollissima. Nos. C361, C364, C367, Odontoglossum luteo purpureum. Nos. C363, C369, Anthurium andreanum. Nos. C365, C370, Stanhopea tigrina. No. C368, Espeletia grandiflora.

1960, May 10 Photo. *Perf. 12*

Flowers in Natural Colors.

C360 A298 5c dark blue 12 8
C361 " 35c maroon 38 3
C362 " 60c dark blue 90 65
C363 " 1.45p dark brown 90 90

Inscribed "Extra Rapido"

C364 A298 5c maroon 15 8
C365 " 10c brown 15 8
C366 " 1p dark blue 2.10 2.10
C367 " 1p maroon 2.10 2.10
C368 " 1p brown 2.10 2.10
C369 " 1p brown 2.10 2.10
C370 " 1p brown 2.10 2.10
Nos. C360–C370 (11) 13.10 12.32

See also Nos. C420–C425.

Fleeing Family and Uprooted Oak Emblem
AP71

Perf. 10, 11

1960, May 24 Litho. Wmk. 331

C371 AP71 60c blue green & gray 38 30

Issued to publicize World Refugee Year, July 1, 1959–June 30, 1960.

Souvenir Sheet

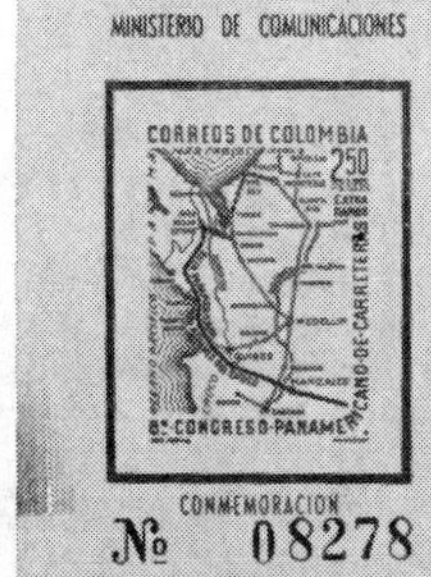

Pan-American Highway Through Colombia
AP72

1960, May 28 Lithographed *Imperf.*

C372 AP72 2.50p brown & aqua. 3.75 3.75

Issued to commemorate the 8th Pan-American Highway Congress, Bogota, May 20–29.

No. C372 measures 44x54mm. with brown marginal inscription and black control number.

Lincoln Type of Regular Issue.

1960, June 6 *Perf. 10½*

C375 A299 40c dull red brn. & black 70 70
C376 " 60c rose red & black 30 10

Issued to commemorate the sesquicentennial (in 1959) of the birth of Abraham Lincoln.

Type of Regular Issue and

Joaquin Camacho, Jorge Tadeo Lozano and Jose Miguel Pey
AP73

Designs: No. C378, Arms of Cartagena. 35c, 1.45p, Colombian flag. 60c, Andres Rosillo, Antonio Villavicencio and Joaquin Caicedo. 1p, Manuel de Bernardo Alvarez and Joaquin Gutierrez. 1.20p, Jose Antonio Galan statue. 1.30p, Front page of newspaper La Bagatela, 1811. 1.65p, Antonia Santos, Jose Acevedo y Gomez and Liborio Mejia.

Photogravure

1960, July 20 *Perf. 12* Unwmkd.

C377 AP73 5c lilac & brn. 12 10
C378 A301 5c dp. bl. green & multi. 12 10
C379 AP73 35c multicolored 18 3
C380 " 60c red brown & green 45 15
C381 " 1p vermilion & slate grn. 70 70
C382 A301 1.20p ultramarine & indigo 70 70
C383 AP73 1.30p org. & black 70 70
C384 " 1.45p multi. 1.10 1.10
C385 " 1.65p grn. & brn. 85 85
Nos. C377–C385 (9) 4.92 4.43

Souvenir Sheet

Stamps Inscribed "Extra Rapido"

Flag, Coins and Arms of Mompox and Cartagena
AP74

C386 AP74 Sheet of four 3.00 3.00
a. 50c deep claret & multicolored 50 50
b. 50c green & multicolored 50 50
c. 1p brown olive, yellow, blue & carmine 50 50
d. 1p lilac & gray 50 50

Nos. C377–C386 issued to commemorate the 150th anniversary of Colombia's independence.

No. C386 measures 90x75mm.

St. Isidro Type of Regular Issue, 1960.

Designs: 35c, No. C388a, St. Isidro and farm animals. No. C388b, Nativity.

Photogravure

1960, Sept. 26 *Perf. 12* Unwmkd.

C387 A302 35c multicolored 25 10

Souvenir Sheet

Stamps Inscribed "Extra Rapido"

C388 A302 Sheet of two 4.50 4.50
a. 1.50p multi. 1.75 1.75
b. 1.50p " 1.75 1.75

Issued to honor St. Isidro the Farmer, patron saint of the rural people. Black marginal inscription on No. C388. Size: 89½x60mm.

See also Nos. C439–C440.

Type of Regular Issue, 1959

Portrait: 35c, Simon Bolivar.

Perf. 12½

1960, Nov. 23 Litho. Wmk. 331

C389 A294 35c gray 1.25 65

Type of Regular Issue, 1961 (Pan-American Highway)

Perf. 10½x11

1961, Mar. 7 Unwmkd.

C390 A304 10c rose lilac & emerald 70 70
C391 " 20c vermilion & light blue 70 70
C392 " 30c black & emerald 70 70

Inscribed "Extra Rapido"

C393 A304 10c dark blue & emerald 70 70

Issued to commemorate the 8th Pan-American Highway Congress, Bogota, May 20–29, 1960.

Lopez Type of Regular Issue, 1961

1961, Mar. 22 Photo. *Perf. 12½*

C394 A305 35c blue & brown 45 5

Inscribed "Extra Rapido"

C395 A305 10c emerald & brown 15 10

Souvenir Sheet

C396 A305 1p lilac & brown 3.00 3.00

Issued to honor Alfonso Lopez (1886–1959), President of Colombia.

No. C396 contains one stamp with margin solidly printed in brown and lilac; colorless inscriptions, and black control number. Size: 60x75mm.

Brother Damian and San Francisco Church, Cali
AP75

Designs: No. 398, Emblem of University del Valle (vert.). 1.30p, Fine Arts School, Cali. 1.45p, Agricultural College, Palmira.

Perf. 13x13½, 13½x13

1961, Aug. 17 Photo. Unwmkd.

C397 AP75 35c violet brown & olive 38 5
C398 " 35c olive & green 30 5
C399 " 1.30p sepia & pink 60 42
C400 " 1.45p multi. 65 50

Inscribed: "Extra Rapido"

Design: 10c, View of Cali (vert.).

C401 AP75 10c brown & yel. grn. 10 8
Nos. C397–C401 (5) 2.03 1.10

Issued to commemorate the 50th anniversary (in 1960) of the department of Valle del Cauca.

View of Cucuta
AP76

1961, Aug. 29

C402 AP76 35c brown olive & green 50 5

Inscribed: "Extra Rapido"

Design: 10c, Church of the Rosary, Cucuta (vert.).

C403 AP76 10c dk. brown & gray green 15 7

Issued to commemorate the 50th anniversary (in 1960) of the department of North Santander.

Old and New Ships at Barranquilla
AP77

Arms and View of San Gil
AP78

Hotel, Popayan — AP79

Statue of Christ in Procession — AP80

Design: 1.45p, View of Velez.

Perf. 12½x13, 13x12½

1961, Oct. 10 Photo. Unwmkd.

C404 AP77 35c gold & blue 40 5
C405 AP78 35c blue green, yel. & red 50 5
C406 AP79 35c car. & brn. 50 5
C407 AP78 1.45p brn. & grn. 48 25

Inscribed: "Extra Rapido."

C408 AP80 10c brn. & yel. 12 5
Nos. C404–C408 (5) 2.00 45

Souvenir Sheets

Types of Regular and Air Post Issues

Designs, No. C409: 35c, Barranquilla arms. 40c, Popayan arms. "c," Arms and view of San Gil. "d," Holy Week in Popayan. No. C410: "a," Old and new ships at Barranquilla. "b," Hotel, Popayan. "c," Bucaramanga arms. "d," Holy Week in Popayan.

C409 Sheet of four 3.75 3.75
a. A309 35c gold & multi. 35 35
b. " 40c " " 35 35
c. AP78 1p blue, yellow & red 85 85
d. AP80 1p carmine rose & yellow 85 85

Stamps Inscribed: "Extra Rapido."

C410 Sheet of four 3.75 3.75
a. AP77 50c gold & carmine rose 35 35
b. AP79 50c gold & blue 35 35
c. A309 50c pink & multi. 85 85
d. AP80 50c blue & yellow 85 85

Nos. C404–C408 are in honor of the Atlantico Department. Nos. C409–C410 are in honor of the Departments of Atlantico, Cauca and Santander. The sheets have blue marginal inscriptions, black control numbers. Size: 90x75mm.

Nos. 713, 716 and 715 Overprinted and Surcharged 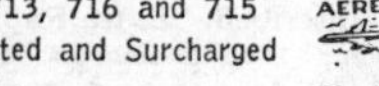

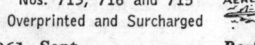

1961, Sept. ***Perf. 12***

C411 A297 5c greenish blue & brown 8 8
C412 A298 5c multicolored 10 10
C413 A297 10c on 20c citron & gray brown 10 5

"Aereo" in script on No. C412.
See also Nos. C420–425.

Sports Type of Regular Issue, 1961

Designs: No. C414, Women divers. No. C415, Tennis, mixed doubles. 1.45p, C419b, Baseball. No. C417, Torch bearer. No. C418, C419a, Bolivar statue and flags of six participating nations. No. C419c, Soccer. No. C419d, Basketball.

1961, Dec. 16 Litho. ***Perf. 13½x14***

C414 A310 35c ultra., yellow & brown 50 5
C415 " 35c car., yellow & brown 65 5
C416 " 1.45p Prussian green, yel. & brn. 75 65

Inscribed: "Extra Rapido"

C417 A310 10c carmine lake, yel. & brn. 12 5
C418 " 10c olive, yellow, blue & red 12 5
Nos. C414-C418 (5) 2.14 85

Souvenir Sheet

Stamps Inscribed: "Extra Rapido."

Imperf.

C419 Sheet of four 3.75 3.75
a. A310 50c multicolored 45 45
b. " 50c " 45 45
c. " 1p " 90 90
d. " 1p " 90 90

Issued to publicize the 4th Bolivarian Games, Barranquilla, 1961. No. C419 has black marginal inscription and control number. Size: 74x106mm.

Flower Type of 1960

Flowers: 5c, Passiflora mollissima. 10c, Espeletia grandiflora. 20c, 2p, Odontoglossum luteo purpureum. 25c, Stanhopea tigrina. 60c, Anthurium Andreanum.

Photogravure

1962, Jan. 30 ***Perf. 12*** **Unwmkd.**

Flowers in Natural Colors

C420 A298 5c gray 10 10
C421 " 10c gray blue 15 12
C422 " 20c rose lilac 15 12
C423 " 25c citron 38 15
C424 " 60c light brown 38 15

Inscribed "Extra Rapido"

C425 A298 2p salmon pink 1.85 1.85
Nos. C420-C425 (6) 3.01 2.49

Anti-Malaria Type of Regular Issue.

Designs: 40c, Colombian anti-malaria emblem. 1p, 1.45p, Malaria eradication emblem and mosquito in swamp.

1962, Apr. 12 Litho. ***Perf. 12***

C426 A311 40c yellow & red 22 15
C427 " 1.45p gray & ultra. 50 50

Inscribed "Extra Rapido"

C428 A311 1p yellow green & ultra. 3.00 3.00

Issued for the World Health Organization drive to eradicate malaria.

Type of Regular Issue, 1962 and

Abelardo Ramos and Engineering School, Cauca
AP81

Designs: 10c, Miguel Triana, Andres A. Arroyo and Monserrate shrine with cable cars. 15c, Diodoro Sanchez and first meeting place of Engineers Society. 2p, Engineers Society emblem.

1962, June 12 Photo. ***Perf. 11½x12***

C429 AP81 5c blue & dp. rose 7 7
C430 " 10c green & sepia 12 10
C431 " 15c lilac & sepia 22 15

Inscribed: "Extra Rapido"

C432 A312 2p black, yellow, red & blue 1.25 1.25

Issued to commemorate the 75th anniversary of the founding of the Colombian Society of Engineers and to publicize the Sixth National Congress of Engineers.

American States Type of 1962.

1962, June 28 Photo. ***Perf. 13***

Flags in National Colors

C433 A313 35c black & blue 38 5

Type of Regular Issue, 1962 (Women's Rights)

Perf. 12x12½

1962, July 20 Litho. Wmk. 229

C434 A314 35c ochre, gray & black 22 5

Issued to publicize women's political rights. See also Nos. C448–C450.

Scout Type of 1962.

Designs: 15c, No. C438, Scouts at campfire and tents. 40c and No. C437, Girl Scouts.

Perf. 11½x12

1962, July 26 Photo. Unwmkd.

C435 A315 15c brown & rose 20 20
C436 " 40c deep claret & pink 38 25
C437 " 1p blue & buff 1.00 50

Inscribed "Extra Rapido"

C438 A315 1p purple & yel. 3.00 3.00

Nos. C435 and C438 issued to commemorate the 30th anniversary of the Colombian Boy Scouts. Nos. C436 and C437 commemorate the 25th anniversary of the Girl Scouts.

Nativity by Gregorio Vasquez
AP82

Design: 2p, St. Isidro, similar to type A302.

Inscribed "Extra Rapido"

Photogravure

1962, Aug. 28 ***Perf. 12*** **Unwmkd.**

C439 AP82 10c gray & multi. 10 5
C440 " 2p " " 1.50 1.50

See also Nos. C387–C388.

Type of Regular Issue, 1962 and

Pres. Aquileo Parra and Magdalena River Bridge
AP83

Design: 5c, Locomotives of 1854 and 1961. 10c, Railroad map of Colombia.

1962, Sept. 28 Photo. ***Perf. 12½***

C441 AP83 5c sepia & slate green 15 5
C442 A316 10c multicolored 12 5

Engraved

C443 AP83 1p dull purple & brown 1.00 12

Inscribed: "Extra Rapido."

C444 AP83 5p blue, brown & dull grn. 1.65 45

Issued to publicize the progress of Colombian railroads and to commemorate the completion of the Atlantic Line from Santa Maria to Bogota.

UPAE Type of Regular Issue

Designs: 50c, Map of Americas and carrier pigeon. 60c, Post horn.

Perf. 13½x14

1962, Oct. 18 Litho. Wmk. 346

C445 A317 50c slate green & gold 38 15
C446 " 60c gold & plum 25 8

Issued to commemorate the 50th anniversary of the founding of the Postal Union of the Americas and Spain, UPAE.

Pope John XXIII
AP84

1963, Mar. 11

C447 AP84 60c gold, red brn., buff & red 35 5

Issued to commemorate Vatican II, the 21st Ecumenical Council of the Roman Catholic Church.

Type of Regular Issue, 1962 (Women's Rights)

1963–64 ***Perf. 12x12½***

C448 A314 5c salmon, gray & black ('64) 6 3
C449 " 45c pale grn., gray & black 30 3
C450 " 45c brt. pink, gray & black 30 3

Games Emblem
AP85

Perf. 13x14

1963, Aug. 12 Wmk. 346

C451 AP85 20c gray & multi. 22 5
C452 " 80c buff & multi. 22 5

Issued to commemorate the South American Athletic Championships (22nd for men, 12th for women), Cali, June 30–July 7.

Bolivar Statue by Arenas-Betancourt
AP86

Perf. 14x13½

1963, Aug. 30 Unwmkd.

C453 AP86 1.90p olive bister & blue 38 5

Centenary of the city of Pereira.

Tennis Player
AP87

1963, Oct. 11 ***Perf. 13½x14***

C454 AP87 55c multicolored 18 3

Issued to commemorate the 30th South American Tennis Championships, Medellin, Oct. 3–13.

Pres. John F. Kennedy and Alliance for Progress Emblem
AP88

1963, Dec. 17 Litho. ***Perf. 14x13½***

C455 AP88 10c multicolored 5 3

Issued to honor President John F. Kennedy (1917–1963).

Church of the True Cross, National Pantheon, Bogota
AP89

Design: 2p, Christ of the Martyrs, bell and tomb.

Perf. 13½x14

1964, Mar. 10 Photo. Unwmkd.

C459 AP89 1p multicolored 30 5
C460 " 2p " 50 20

View of Cartagena
AP90

1964, Mar. 18 Litho. *Perf. 14x13½*

C461 AP90 3p violet, blue, ocher & brn. 1.25 60

Issued to commemorate Cartagena's independence in 1811, Simon Bolivar's visit in 1812 and the siege of 1815.

Eleanor Roosevelt
AP91

1964, Nov. 10 Photo. *Perf. 12*

C462 AP91 20c olive & dull red brown 10 8

Issued to honor Eleanor Roosevelt (1884–1962).

Alberto Castilla and Score of "El Bunde"
AP92

1964, Nov. 10 Unwmkd.

C463 AP92 30c olive bister & Prus. grn. 10 5

Issued to honor the Department of Tolima and Maestro Alberto Castilla (1878–1937) who in 1906 founded the Tolima Conservatory of Music in Ibague.

Mejia Type of Regular Issue

Designs (Mejia portrait and): 45c, Women picking coffee. 5p, Mules carrying coffee bags. 10p, Loading coffee on freighter "Manuel Mejia."

1965, Feb. 10 Engr. *Perf. 12½x13*

C464 A320 45c brn. & black 25 3
C465 " 5p gray green & black 1.10 10
C466 " 10p ultra. & blk. 2.25 22

Issued to honor Manuel Mejia J. (1887–1958), banker and manager of the National Coffee Growers Association.

ITU Emblem
AP93

1965, Oct. 25 Photo. *Perf. 12*

C467 AP93 80c Prus. blue, lt. blue & red 20 4

Issued to commemorate the centenary of the International Telecommunication Union.

Cattleya Truanae
AP94

Pres. Manuel Murillo Toro Statue, Telegraph and Orbits
AP95

1965, Oct. 3 Litho. *Perf. 13½x14*

C468 AP94 20c yellow & multi. 8 3

Fifth Philatelic Exhibition.

1965, Nov. 1 *Perf. 13½x14, 14x13½*

Design: No. C470, Telegraph and satellites over South America (horiz.).

C469 AP95 60c multicolored 18 3
C470 " 60c " 22 3

Centenary of the telegraph in Colombia.

Junkers F-13 Seaplane, 1920
AP96

History of Colombian Aviation: 10c, Dornier Wal, 1924. 20c, Dornier Mercur, 1926. 50c, Trimotor Ford, 1932. 60c, De Havilland biplane, 1930. 1p, Douglas DC-4, 1947. 1.40p, Douglas DC-3, 1944. 2.80p, Superconstellation 1049, 1951. 3p, Boeing 720B jet, 1961.

Perf. 14x13½

1965–66 Photo. Unwmkd.

C471 AP96 5c multicolored 5 3
C472 " 10c " 5 3
C473 " 20c " 8 5
C474 " 50c " 12 5
C475 " 60c " 30 3
C476 " 1p " 38 7
C477 " 1.40p " 45 15
C478 " 2.80p " 75 30
C479 " 3p " 85 50
Nos. C471–C479 (9) 3.03 1.21

Issue dates: 5c, 60c, 3p, Dec. 13, 1965; 10c, 1p, 1.40p, July 15, 1966; 20c, 50c, 2.80p, Dec. 14, 1966.

Automobile Club Emblem and Car on Road
AP97

1966, Feb. 16 Litho. *Perf. 14x13½*

C480 AP97 20c multicolored 7 3

Issued to commemorate the 25th anniversary (in 1965) of the Automobile Club of Colombia.

Fish Type of Regular Issue, 1966.

Fish: 2p, Flying fish. 2.80p, Queen angelfish. 20p, King mackerel.

1966, Aug. 25 Photo. *Perf. 12½x13*

C481 A323 2p multicolored 30 5
C482 " 2.80p " 75 75
C483 " 20p " 11.00 11.00

Coat of Arms Type of Regular Issue, 1966

1966, Oct. 11 Litho. *Perf. 14x13½*

C484 A324 1p ultra. & multi. 35 3
C485 " 1.40p red & multi. 25 8

Issued to commemorate the visits of Eduardo Frei and Raul Leoni, presidents of Chile and Venezuela.

Portrait Type of Regular Issue

Portraits: 80c, Father Felix Restrepo Mejia, S.J. (1887—1965), theologian and scholar. 1.70p, José Joaquin Casas (1866–1951), educator and diplomat.

Perf. 13½x14

1967, Jan. 18 Litho. Unwmkd.

C486 A325 80c dark blue & bister 15 3
C487 " 1.70p blk. & bister 40 10

Famous men of Colombia.

Declaration of Bogota Type of Regular Issue

1967, Feb. 2 Litho. *Perf. 14x13½*

C488 A326 3p multicolored 45 12

See note after No. 767.

Orchid Type of Regular Issue

Orchids: 1p, Cattleya dowiana aurea (vert.). 1.20p, Masdevallia coccinea (vert.). 5p, Catasetum macrocarpum and bee.

1967, May 23 Litho. *Perf. 14*

C489 A327 1p multicolored 45 5
C490 " 1.20p " 30 5
C491 " 5p " 1.35 45
a. Souv. sheet of 3 2.40 2.40

Issued to commemorate the First National Orchid Exhibition and the Topical Philatelic Flora and Fauna Exhibition, Medellin, Apr. 1967. No. C491a contains one each of Nos. C489–C491. Gray margin with black inscription and red control number. Size: 99x149mm.

Lions Type of Regular Issue

1967, July 12 Litho. *Perf. 13½x14*

C492 A328 25c multicolored 12 5

Lions International, 50th anniversary.

"First Caesarean Section" by Grau
AP98

Perf. 14x13½

1967, Sept. 7 Litho. Unwmkd.

C493 AP98 80c multicolored 10 5

Issued to publicize the 6th Congress of Colombian Surgeons, Bogota, Sept. 25.

SENA Type of Regular Issue

Lithographed and Embossed

1967, Sept. 20 *Perf. 13½x14*

C494 A329 2p gold, verm. & blk. 55 10

Issued to commemorate the 10th anniversary of National Apprenticeship Service, SENA.

Pre-Columbian Art Type of Regular Issue

Designs: 30c, Bird pectoral. 5p Ornamental pectoral. 20p, Pitcher.

Photogravure

1967, Oct. 13 *Perf. 13½x14*

C495 A330 30c verm., gold & brown 22 5
C496 " 5p red, gold & brown 1.50 30
a. Souvenir sheet of 2 1.75 1.75
C497 A330 20p violet, gold & brown 8.50 7.50

Issued to commemorate the meeting of the Universal Postal Union Committee on Postal Studies, Bogota, October, 1967; No. C496a also commemorates the 6th National Philatelic Exhibition. No. C496a contains 2 imperf. stamps in changed colors similar to Nos. C495–C496 (30c has green background and 5 p maroon background). Gray margin with red control number. Size: 92x91mm.

Telecommunications Type of Regular Issue

Designs: 50c, Signal lights. 1p, Early Bird satellite, Southern Cross and radar.

Perf. 13½x14

1968, May 14 Litho. Unwmkd.

C498 A331 50c black, verm. & emerald 18 3
C499 " 1p ultra., yellow & gray 30 3

Issued to commemorate the 20th anniversary of the National Telecommunications Service (TELECOM).

Eucharist Type of Regular Issue

1968, June 6 Litho. *Perf. 13½x14*

C500 A332 80c rose lilac, red, yel. & black 15 3
C501 " 3p blue, red, yel. & black 45 15

Issued to publicize the 39th Eucharistic Congress, Bogotá, Aug. 18–25.

Eucharistic Congress Type of Regular Issue

Designs: 80c, The Last Supper, by Gregorio Vasquez (horiz.). 1p, St. Francis Xavier Preaching, by Gregorio Vasquez. 2p, The Dream of the Prophet Elias, by Gregorio Vasquez. 3p, Monstrance, c. 1700. 20p, Pope Paul VI, painting by Roman Franciscan nuns.

1968, Aug. 13 Photo. *Perf. 13*

C502 A333 80c multicolored 18 3
C503 " 1p " 25 3
C504 " 2p " 38 5
C505 " 3p lilac & multi. 65 5
C506 " 20p gold & multi. 4.25 1.25
Nos. C502–C506 (5) 5.71 1.41

Issued to commemorate the 39th Eucharistic Congress, Bogotá, Aug. 18–25.

Shrine of the Eucharist, Bogotá
AP99

Designs: 1.20p, Pope Paul VI giving blessing and Papal arms (vert.). 1.80p, Cathedral of Bogotá (vert.).

Perf. 14x13½, 13½x14

1968, Aug. 22 Lithographed

C507 AP99 80c multicolored 18 5
C508 " 1.20p " 22 7
C509 " 1.80p " 35 15

Visit of Pope Paul VI to Colombia.

Computer Symbols
AP100

1968, Oct. 29 Litho. *Perf. 13½x14*

C510 AP100 20c buff, carmine & green 10 3

Issued to commemorate the centenary of the National University and the First Data Processing Congress in 1967 at the University.

Agriculture Institute Type of Regular Issue

1968, Mar. 5 Litho. *Perf. 13½x14*

C511 A337 1p gray & multi. 25 3

Issued to commemorate the 25th anniversary (in 1967) of the Inter-American Agricultural Sciences Institute.

Microscope and Pen—AP101

1969, Mar. 24 Litho. *Perf. 14*

C512 AP101 5p black, yellow, verm. & pur. 90 8

Issued to commemorate the 20th anniversary (in 1968) of the University of the Andes.

Alexander von Humboldt and Andes
AP102

1969, May 3 Litho. *Perf. 14x13½*

C513 AP102 1p green & brown 20 3

Issued to commemorate the bicentenary of the birth of Alexander von Humboldt (1769–1859), German naturalist and traveler.

Map of Colombia, Amphibian Plane and Letter
AP103

Design: 1.50p, No. C516b, Globe, letter, and jet of Avianca airlines.

1969, June 18 Litho. *Perf. 14x13½*

C514 AP103 1p multi. 25 3
C515 " 1.50p " 30 10

Souvenir Sheet

Imperf.

C516 AP103 Sheet of 2 2.10 2.10
a. 5p grn. & multi. 70 70
b. 5p vio. & multi. 70 70

Issued to commemorate the 50th anniversary of the first air post flight in Colombia. No. C516 also publicizes the 8th National Philatelic Exhibition, EXFILBA 69, Barranquilla, June 18–22. No. C516 contains 2 stamps in the designs of the 1p and 1.50p; gray margin with commemorative inscription, coats of arms and red control number. Size: 92x92mm.

Independence Type of Regular Issue

1969, July 24 Litho. *Perf. 13½x14*

Design: 2.30p, Simon Bolivar, José Antonio Anzoategui, Francisco de Paula Santander and victorious army entering Bogotá, Sept. 18, 1819; painting by Ignacio Castillo Cervantes.

C517 A338 2.30p gold & multi. 45 18

Issued to commemorate the sesquicentennial of the fight for independence.

Social Security Emblem
AP104

Neurosurgeons' Congress Emblem
AP105

1969, Oct. 29 Litho. *Perf. 13½x14*

C518 AP104 20c emerald & blk. 10 4

Issued to commemorate the 20th anniversary of the Colombian Institute of Social Security.

1969, Oct. 29

C519 AP105 70c violet, red & yellow 20 3

Issued to publicize the 13th Congress of Latin-American Neurosurgeons, Bogotá.

Junkers F-13
AP106

Designs: No. C521, C522b, Globe with airlines from Bogota and Boeing jet. No. C522a, like No. C520.

1969, Nov. 28 Litho. *Perf. 14x13½*

C520 AP106 2p grn. & multi. 45 10
C521 " 3.50p ultramarine & multi. 55 25

Souvenir Sheet

Imperf.

C522 AP106 Sheet of 2 1.85 1.85
a. 3.50p lt. green & multicolored 40 40
b. 5p ultramarine & multicolored 65 65

Issued to commemorate the 50th anniversary of AVIANCA; No. C522 also publicizes the First Interamerican Philatelic Exhibition, Bogota, Nov. 28–Dec. 7.

No. C522 contains 2 imperf. stamps. Multicolored inscriptions, coat of arms, medals and red control number on light olive margin. Size: 92x90mm.

Child Mailing Letter
AP107

Design: 1.50p, Praying child and gifts.

1969, Dec. 16 Litho. *Perf. 13½x14*

C523 AP107 60c ocher & multi. 55 15
C524 " 1p multicolored 55 8
C525 " 1.50p " 55 15

Christmas 1969.

Radar Station and Pre-Columbian Head
AP108

1970, Mar. 25 Litho. *Perf. 14x13½*

C526 AP108 1p dull grn., blk. & brick red 38 3

Issued to publicize the opening of the communications satellite earth station at Chocontá in Cundinamarca Province.

Emblem of Colombian Youth Sports Institute
AP109

Art Exhibition Emblem
AP110

Design: 2.30p, Games' emblem (dove and 3 rings).

1970, Apr. 6 Litho. *Perf. 13½x14*

C527 AP109 1.50p dk. olive grn., yel. & blk. 30 18
C528 " 2.30p red & multi. 45 20

Issued to publicize the 9th National Youth Games, Ibague, July 10–20.

1970, Apr. 30 Litho. *Perf. 13½x14*

C529 AP110 30c multicolored 7 3

Issued to publicize the 2nd Biennial Art Exhibition, Medellin, May 1–June 14.

Eduardo Santos, Rural and Urban Buildings
AP111

1970, June 18 Litho. *Perf. 14x13½*

C530 AP111 1p green, yellow & black 22 3

Issued to commemorate the founding (in 1939) of the Territorial Credit Institute.

U.N. Emblem, Scales and Dove
AP112

EXFILCA Emblem
AP113

1970, June 26 *Perf. 13½x14*

C531 AP112 1.50p dk. blue, lt. bl. & yellow 25 4

25th anniversary of United Nations.

1970, Nov. Litho. *Perf. 13½x14*

C532 AP113 10p blue, gold & black 2.00 20

Issued to publicize EXFILCA 70, 2nd Interamerican Philatelic Exhibition. Caracas, Venezuela, Nov. 27–Dec. 6.

Mother Juana Ruperta in Napanga Costume and Music by Efrain Orozco
AP114

Athlete and Games Emblem
AP115

Designs: 1p, Dancers from Eastern Plains and music by Alejandro Wills. No. C535, Guabina man, woman and folk song. No. C536, Bambuco man and woman, and music. No. C537, Man and woman dancing the Cumbia, and music.

1970–71 Litho. *Perf. 13½x14*

C533 AP114 60c dp. lilac rose & multi. 45 12
C534 " 1p ultra. & multi. 42 10
C535 " 1.30p bl. & multi. 45 10
C536 " 1.30p emerald & multi. ('71) 45 10
C537 " 1.30p lilac & multi. ('71) 38 10
Nos. C533–C537 (5) 2.15 52

1971, Mar. 11

Design: 2p, Games emblem.

C542 AP115 1.50p multi. 60 38
C543 " 2p blk., orange & green 75 45

6th Pan-American Games, Cali, July 30–Aug. 13.

Gilberto Alzate Avendaño
AP116

1971, Apr. 29 Litho. *Perf. 14x13½*

C544 AP116 1p bl. & multi. 45 30

Gilberto Alzate Avendaño (1910–1960), journalist and popular leader, 10th anniversary of death.

Commemorative Medal
AP117

Lithographed and Embossed

1971, June 21 *Perf. 14x13½*

C545 AP117 1p slate green & gold 50 30

Centenary (in 1970) of the Bank of Bogota.

Olympic Center
AP118

Soccer
AP119

Designs (Games Emblem and): Nos. C546–C546c, Olympic Center. No. 547, Soccer. No. C548, Wrestling. No. C549, Bicycling. No. C550, Volleyball. No. C551, Diving (women). No. C552, Fencing. No. C553, Sailing. No. C554, Equestrian. No. C555, Jumping. No. C556, Rowing. No. C557, Cali emblem. No. C558, Basketball (women). No. C559, Stadium. No. C560, Baseball. No. C561, Hockey. No. C562, Weight lifting. No. C563, Medals. No. C564, Boxing. No. C565, Gymnastics (women). No. C566, Sharpshooting.

1971, July 16 Litho. *Perf. 13½x14*

C546 AP118 1.30p yellow & multi. 70 45
a. 1.30p green & multicolored 70 45
b. 1.30p blue & multicolored 70 45
c. 1.30p carmine & multicolored 70 45
C547 AP119 1.30p emerald & multi. 70 45
C548 " 1.30p lilac & multi. 70 45
C549 " 1.30p blue & multi. 70 45
C550 " 1.30p carmine & multi. 70 45
C551 " 1.30p blue & multi. 70 45
C552 " 1.30p carmine & multi. 70 45
C553 " 1.30p blue & multi. 70 45
C554 " 1.30p gray & multi. 70 45
C555 " 1.30p green & multi. 70 45
C556 " 1.30p bl. & multi. 70 45
C557 AP118 1.30p orange & multi. 70 45
C558 AP119 1.30p carmine & multi. 70 45
C559 AP118 1.30p light blue & multi. 70 45
C560 AP119 1.30p plum & multi. 70 45
C561 " 1.30p yel. green & multi. 70 45
C562 " 1.30p pink & multi. 70 45

C563 AP118 1.30p dp. orange & multi. 70 45
C564 AP119 1.30p plum & multi. 70 45
C565 " 1.30p lilac rose & multi. 70 45
C566 " 1.30p green & multi. 70 45
a. Sheet of 25 (Nos. C546–C566) 17.50 15.00

6th Pan American Athletic Games, Cali. First color in listings is color of emblem. No. C546b appears twice in sheet. No. C566a has marginal multicolored inscription commemorating EXFILCALI 71 Philatelic Exhibition.

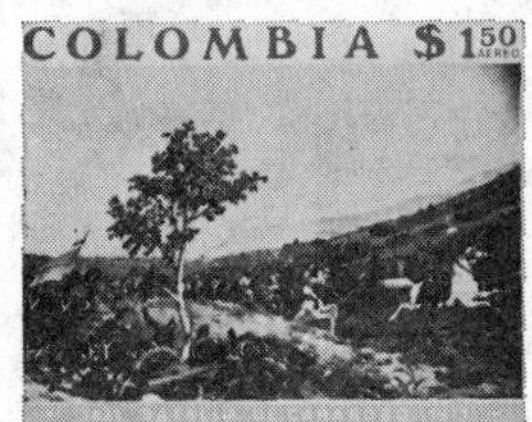

Battle of Carabobo, by Martin Tovar y Tovar—AP120

1971, Nov. 25 Litho. *Perf. 13½x14*
C567 AP120 1.50p multi. 38 15
Sesquicentennial of the Battle of Carabobo.

St. Theresa Type of Regular Issue Overprinted "AEREO"

1972 Lithographed *Perf. 13½x14*
C568 A343 2p multicolored 38 3
See note after No. 793.

Vendor
AP121

Designs: 50c, Woman wearing shawl, and woven shawl. 3p, Fruit vendor (puppet).

1971, Apr. 11 Litho. *Perf. 13½x14*
C569 AP121 50c multicolored 18 10
C570 " 1p " 22 7
C571 " 3p " 50 30
Colombian artisans.

Mormodes Rolfeanum
AP122

1972, Apr. 20 *Perf. 14x13½*
C572 AP122 1.30p multi. 45 3
7th World Orchidology Congress, Medellin.

Congo Grande Dancer
AP123

Pres. Laureano Gomez, by Ridriguez Cubillos
AP124

1972, June 21 Litho. *Perf. 13½x14*
C573 AP123 1.30p multi. 45 5
International Carnival of Barranquilla.

No. C453 Surcharged in Brown **$ 1.30**

1972, Oct. 5 Litho. *Perf. 14x13½*
C574 AP86 1.30p on 1.90p olive bister & blue 75 20

1972, Oct. 17 *Perf. 13½x14*
C575 AP124 1.30p multi. 22 3
Laureano Gomez (1898–1966), President of Colombia.

1972, Nov. 28
Design: 1.30p, Guillermo León Valencia Muñoz.
C576 AP124 1.30p multi. 27 3
Guillermo León Valencia Muñoz (1909–1971), President of Colombia.

Benito Juarez AP125 — Rebecca Fountain AP126

1972, Dec. 12 *Perf. 13½x14*
C577 AP125 1.50p multi. 25 5
Centenary of the death of Benito Juarez (1806–1872), revolutionary leader and president of Mexico.

1972, Dec. 19 Lithographed
C578 AP126 80c multicolored 42 20
C579 " 1p " 32 8

"Bucaramanga"
AP127

1972, Dec. 22 *Perf. 14x13¼*
C580 AP127 5p multicolored 75 5
350th anniversary of the founding of Bucaramanga.

Xavier University
AP128

1973, May 8 Litho. *Perf. 14x13½*
C581 AP128 1.30p lt. green & sepia 35 6
C582 " 1.50p lt. blue & sepia 35 6
350th anniversary of the founding of Xavier University in Bogotá.

Ceramic Type of Regular Issue

Excavated Ceramic Artifacts: 1p, Winged urn, Tairona. 1.30p, Woman and child, Sinu. 1.70p, Two-headed figure, Quimbaya. 3.50p, Man, Tumaco.

1973 Lithographed *Perf. 13½x14*
C583 A358 1p multicolored 50 5
C584 " 1.30p " 55 5
C585 " 1.70p " 45 20
C586 " 3.50p " 75 30
Issue dates: 1p, Oct. 11; others, June 15.

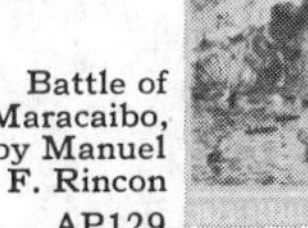

Battle of Maracaibo, by Manuel F. Rincon
AP129

1973, July 24 Litho. *Perf. 14x13½*
C587 AP129 10p bl. & multi. 2.10 12
Battle of Maracaibo, sesquicentennial.

Bank Emblem
AP130

1973, Oct. 1 Litho. *Perf. 14x13½*
C588 AP130 2p multicolored 35 5
50th anniversary of the Bank of the Republic.

No. 801 Overprinted "AEREO"

1973, Oct. 11 *Perf. 14*
C589 A346 80c multicolored 30 8

Pres. Pedro Nel Ospina, by Coroleano Leudo AP131 — Arms of Toro AP132

1973, Nov. 9 *Perf. 13½x14*
C590 AP131 1.50p multicolored 20 5
50th anniversary of the Ministry of Communications founded under Pres. Ospina.

1973, Dec. 1
C591 AP132 1p multicolored 20 5
4th centenary of the founding of Toro, Valle del Cauca.

Bolivar, Battle of Bombona
AP133

1973, Dec. 7 Litho. *Perf. 14x13½*
C592 AP133 1.30p multi. 18 6
Sesquicentennial (in 1972) of the Battle of Bombona.

Nicolaus Copernicus AP134 — Andes, Map of South America AP135

1974, Feb. 19 Litho. *Perf. 13½x14*
C593 AP134 2.50p multi. 50 12
500th anniversary of the birth of Nicolaus Copernicus (1473–1543), Polish astronomer.

1974, May 11 Litho. *Perf. 14*
C594 AP135 2p multicolored 40 6
Meeting of Communications Ministers of Members of the Andean Group, Cali, May 7–11, 1974.

Television Set
AP136

1974, July 16 Litho. *Perf. 14x13½*
C595 AP136 1.30p orange, blk. & brown 20 4
20th anniversary of Colombian television and 10th anniversary of INRAVISION, the National Institute of Radio and Television.

Championship Emblem
AP137

1974, Aug. 5 Litho. *Perf. 14x13½*
C596 AP137 4.50p multi. 38 15
2nd World Swimming Championships, Cali.

Condor—AP138

1974, Aug. 28 *Perf. 14*
C597 AP138 1.50p multi. 20 5
Bank of Colombia centenary.

UPU Envelope
AP139

1974, Sept. 9 Litho. *Perf. 14*
C598 AP139 20p multi. 2.00 25
Centenary of Universal Postal Union.

Symbol of Flight
AP140

1974, Sept. *Perf. 12x12½*
C599 AP140 20c olive 8 5

Gen. José Maria Cordoba
AP141

White-tailed Trogon, Letter
AP142

1974, Oct. 14 Litho. *Perf. 13½x14*

C609	AP141	1.30p multi.	20	3

Sesquicentennial of the Battles of Junin and Ayacucho.

Insurance Type of 1974

Design: 3p, Abstract pattern.

1974, Oct. 24 Litho. *Perf. 13½x14*

C610	A365	3p multicolored	30	8

Centenary of National Insurance Company.

Perf. 13½x14, 14x13½

1974, Nov. 14

Designs (UPU Letter and): 1.30p, Keel-billed Toucan (horiz.). 2p, Peruvian cock-of-the-rock (horiz.). 2.50p, Scarlet macaw.

C611	AP142	1p multi.	20	3
C612	"	1.30p "	22	3
C613	"	2p "	35	5
C614	"	2.50p "	25	10

Centenary of Universal Postal Union.

Forest No. 1, by Roman Roncancio—AP143

Girl with Thorn in Finger, by Gregorio Vazquez
AP144

Paintings: 3p, Women Fruit Vendors, by Miguel Diaz Vargas (1886–1956). 5p, Annunciation, Santafereña School, 17th–18th centuries.

Perf. 13½x14, 14x13½

1975, Mar. 12 Lithographed

C615	AP143	2p multicolored	45	5
C616	AP144	3p "	30	5
C617	"	4p "	38	7
C618	"	5p "	65	20

Modern and Colonial Colombian paintings.

Trees and Lake
AP145

Design: 6p, Victoria regia, Amazon River.

1975, Mar. 12 *Perf. 14x13½*

C619	AP145	1p yel. & multi.	12	3
C620	"	6p " "	48	8

Nature conservation of trees and Amazon Region.

Gold Treasure Type of 1975

Designs: 2p, Nose pendant. 10p, Alligator-shaped staff ornament.

1975, Apr. 11 Litho. *Perf. 14x13½*

C621	A368	2p grn., gold & brn.	30	5
C622	"	10p multicolored	1.50	38

Pre-Columbian Sinu Culture artifacts.

El Rodadero, Santa Maria
AP146

1975, July 26 Litho. *Perf. 14x13½*

C623	AP146	2p multicolored	18	5

400th anniversary of Santa Maria City.

Maria de J. Paramo
AP147

1975, Aug. 31 Litho. *Perf. 13½x14*

C624	AP147	4p multicolored	30	5

International Women's Year 1975. Maria de Jesus Paramo de Collazos founded first normal school for women in Bucaramanga in 1875.

"Sugar Cane"
AP148

1976, Mar. 12 Litho. *Perf. 13½x14*

C625	AP148	5p black & emerald	65	5

4th Congress of Latin-American and Caribbean sugar-exporting countries, Cali, Mar. 8–12.

View of Bogota—AP149

1976, July 2 Litho. *Perf. 12*

Blue and Multicolored

C626	AP149	10p *shown*	1.00	50
C627	"	10p *Barranquilla*	1.00	50
C628	"	10p *Cali*	1.00	50
C629	"	10p *Medellin*	1.00	50

Habitat, U.N. Conference on Human Settlements, Vancouver, Canada, May 31–June 11. Nos. C626–C629 printed se-tenant in blocks of 4, sheets of 60.

University Emblem and "90"
AP150

1976, Aug. 6 Litho. *Perf. 13½x14*

C630	AP150	5p lt. bl. & multi.	45	5

University of Colombia, 90th anniversary.

Miguel Samper
AP151

Telephone, 1895
AP152

1976, Oct. 29 Litho. *Perf. 13½x14*

C631	AP151	2p multicolored	25	5

Miguel Samper (1825–1899), economist and writer.

1976, Nov. 2

C632	AP152	3p multicolored	15	5

Centenary of first telephone call by Alexander Graham Bell, Mar. 10, 1876.

747 Jumbo Jet
AP153

1976, Dec. 3 Litho. *Perf. 12*

C633	AP153	2p multicolored	18	5

Inauguration of 747 jumbo jet service by Avianca.

Convent, Church and Plaza de San Francisco—AP154

1976, Dec. 29 Litho. *Perf. 14*

C634	AP154	6p multicolored	50	5

150th anniversary of the Congress of Panama.

Souvenir Sheet

Bank of the Republic Emblem—AP155

1977, June 6 Litho. *Perf. 14*

C635	AP155	25p multicolored	4.50	4.50

Opening of Philatelic Museum of Medellin under auspices of Banco de la Republica. No. C635 contains one stamp (50x40mm.); multicolored margin shows various orchids; black control number. Size: 130x105mm.

No. C633 Surcharged in Light Brown

1977, June Litho. *Perf. 12*

C636	AP153	3p on 2p multi.	18	5

Coffee
AP156

Coffee Grower, Pack Mule
AP157

1977–78 Litho. *Perf. 12½*

C640	AP156	3p multi.	15	5
C641	"	3.50p " ('78)	20	5

Colombian coffee.

1977, Aug. 9 Litho. *Perf. 13½x14*

C642	AP157	10p multicolored	65	5

National Federation of Coffee Growers, 50th anniversary.

Beethoven and 9th Symphony
AP158

Games' Emblem
AP159

1977, Aug. 17

C643	AP158	8p multicolored	50	5

Sesquicentennial of the death of Ludwig van Beethoven (1770–1827).

Bird Type of 1977

Tropical Birds and Plants: No. C644, Woodpecker and meriania. C645, Purple gallinule and water lilies. No. C646, Xipholaena punicea and cochlospermum orinocense. No. C647, Crowned flycatcher and jacaranda copaia.

1977, Sept. 6 Litho. *Perf. 14*

C644	A380	5p multicolored	45	8
C645	"	5p "	45	8
C646	"	10p "	75	12
C647	"	10p "	75	12

1977, Sept. 9 *Perf. 12x12½*

C648	AP159	6p multicolored	30	5

13th Central American and Caribbean Games, Medellin, 1978.

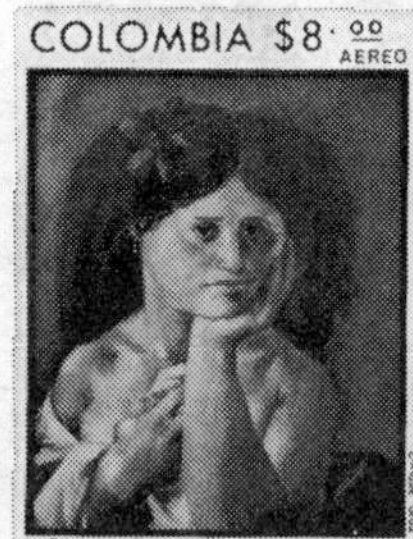

La Cayetana, by Enrique Grau
AP160

Design: No. C650, Water Nymphs, by Beatriz Gonzalez.

1977, Sept. 13 ***Perf. 14x13½***

C649	AP160	8p multicolored	50	8
C650	"	8p "	50	8

Women's suffrage, 20th anniversary.

Judge Francisco Antonio Moreno by, Joaquin Gutierrez
AP161

Design: 25p, Viceroy Manuel de Guirior.

1977, Sept. 13 ***Perf. 12***

C651	AP161	20p multi.	1.25	25
C652	"	25p "	1.50	38

Bicentenary of National Library.

Federico Lleras Acosta
AP162

Cauca University Arms
AP163

1977, Sept. 27 Litho. ***Perf. 14***

C653	AP162	5p multicolored	30	5

Dr. Federico Lleras Acosta, veterinarian and bacteriologist; birth centenary.

1977, Oct. 14

C654	AP163	5p multicolored	30	5

Sesquicentennial of the University of Cauca.

CUDECOM Building, Bogota
AP164

1977, Oct. 14

C655	AP164	1.50p multi.	10	4

Colombian Society of Engineers, 90th anniversary.

No. C612 Surcharged with New Value and Bars in Brown

1977, Dec. 3 Litho. ***Perf. 14x13½***

C656	AP142	2p on 1.30p multi.	10	5

Lost City, Tayrona Culture
AP165

Creator of Energy, by Arenas Betancourt
AP166

1978, Apr. 18 Litho. ***Perf. 12½***

C657	AP165	3.50p multi.	18	5

1978, Apr. 25 ***Perf. 12***

C658	AP166	4p blue & multi.	20	5

Sesquicentennial of Antioquia University Law School.

Column of the Slaves
AP167

Statue of Catalina, Cartagena
AP168

1978, May 9

C659	AP167	2.50p multi.	13	6

Sesquicentennial of Ocaña Convention (meeting of various political groups).

1978, May 30 Litho. ***Perf. 12***

C660	AP168	4p blk. & lt. bl.	20	5

Sesquicentennial of University of Cartagena.

Gold Pendant, Tolima
AP169

1978, July 11 Litho. ***Perf. 12x12½***

C661	AP169	3.50p multi.	18	5

Apotheosis of Spanish Language, by Luis Alberto Acuña—AP170

1978, Aug. 9 ***Perf. 14***

C662	AP170	Strip of 3, multicolored	1.90	1.90
		a. 11p, single stamp	60	60

Millennium of Spanish language. No. C662 printed in sheets of 15 (3x5). Black control number.

Presidential Guard
AP171

Figure, Muisca Culture
AP172

1978, Aug. 16 ***Perf. 13½x14***

C663	AP171	9p multicolored	50	8

Presidential Guard Battalion, 50th anniversary.

1978, Sept. 12 Litho. ***Perf. 12½***

C664	AP172	3.50p multi.	18	5

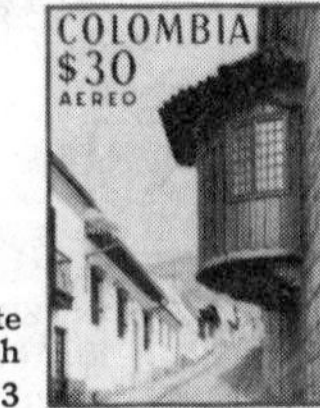

Apse of Carmelite Church
AP173

1978, Oct. 12 ***Perf. 13***

C665	AP173	30p multi.	1.50	25

Souvenir Sheet

Perf. 13½x14

C666	AP173	50p multi.	3.00	3.00

ESPAMER '78 Philatelic Exhibition, Bogota, Oct. 12–21. No. C666 contains one stamp; multicolored margin shows enlarged stamp design, ESPAMER emblem and black control number. Size: 125x95mm.

Owl, Gold Ornament, Calima
AP174

Virgin and Child, by Gregorio Vasquez
AP175

1978, Nov. 28 ***Perf. 12½***

C667	AP174	3.50p multi.	28	8

1978, Nov. 28 ***Perf. 13½x14***

C668	AP175	2.50p multi.	20	8

Christmas 1978.

AIR POST SPECIAL DELIVERY STAMPS

Post Horn and Wings
APSD1

Lithographed

1958, May 19 *Perf. 12* **Unwmkd.**

CE1 APSD1 25c dark blue & red 50 10

Same Overprinted Vertically in Red UNIFICADO

1959

CE2 APSD1 25c dark blue & red 60 12

Jet Plane and Envelope
APSD2

1963, Oct. 4 *Perf. 14*

CE3 APSD2 50c red & black 12 5

Aviation Type of Air Post Issue

History of Colombian Aviation: 80c, Boeing 727 jet, 1966.

Perf. 14x13½

1966, Dec. 14 Photo. **Unwmkd.**

CE4 AP96 80c crimson & multi. 35 8

AIR POST REGISTRATION STAMPS.

Issued by Sociedad Colombo-Alemana de Transportes Aereos (SCADTA)

No. C41 Overprinted in Red **R**

1923 *Perf. 14x14½* **Wmk. 116**

CF1 AP6 20c gray 5.00 2.50

No. C58 Overprinted in Black **R**

1929 *Perf. 14* **Wmk. 127**

CF2 AP8 20c carmine 7.50 1.75

Same Overprint on No. C71.

CF3 AP10 20c carmine 7.50 5.00

Colombian Government Issues.

Same Overprint on No. C86.

1932

CF4 AP8 20c carmine 10.00 7.00

No. C100 Overprinted **R**

CF5 AP15 20c carmine & olive black 3.25 2.25

SPECIAL DELIVERY STAMP.

Special Delivery Messenger
SD1

Engraved.

1917 *Perf. 14.* **Unwmkd.**

E1 SD1 5c gray green 2.50 2.00

REGISTRATION STAMPS.

R1

R2

Lithographed.

1865 *Imperf.* **Unwmkd.**

F1 R1 5c black 18.50 17.50
F2 R2 5c black 22.50 20.00

R3 R4

1870 White Paper.

Vertical Lines in Background.

F3 R3 5c black 3.00 3.00
F4 R4 5c black 3.00 3.00

Horizontal Lines in Background.

F5 R3 5c black 2.50 2.50
F6 R4 5c black 2.50 2.50

Reprints of Nos. F3 to F6 show either crossed lines or traces of lines in background.

R5

1881 *Imperf.*

F7 R5 10c violet 15.00 15.00
a. Sewing machine perf. 16.50 16.50
b. Perf. 11 18.50 18.50

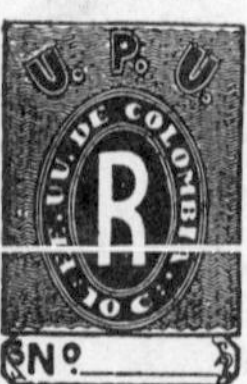

R6

1883 *Perf. 12, 13½*

F8 R6 10c red, *orange* 1.25 1.50

R7

1889–95 *Perf. 12, 13½*

F9 R7 10c red, *grayish* 90 90
F10 " 10c red, *yellowish* 1.00 1.00
F11 " 10c deep brown, *rosy buff* ('95) 90 90
F12 " 10c yellow brown, *light buff* ('92) 90 90

Nos. F9–F12 exist imperf. Prices same as for perf.

R9

1902 *Imperf.*

F13 R9 20c red brown, *blue* 1.25 1.25
a. Sewing machine perf. 1.85 1.85
b. Perf. 12 1.85 1.85

Medellin Issue.

R10

1902 *Perf. 12.*

Wove Paper.

F16 R10 10c blackish violet 4.50 4.50
a. Laid paper 4.50 4.50

Regular Issue.

1903 *Imperf.*

F17 R9 20c blue, *blue* 60 60
a. Sewing machine perf. 2.25 2.25
b. Perf. 12 2.25 2.25

R11

1904 Pelure Paper. *Imperf.*

F19 R11 10c purple 1.85 1.85
a. Sewing machine perf. 1.85 1.85
b. Perf. 12 1.85 1.85

R12

Wove Paper.

Imprint: "J. L. Arango".

1904 *Perf. 12*

F20 R12 10c purple 1.25 75
a. Imperf., pair 3.00 3.00

1909 *Perf. 10, 14, 10x14, 14x10*

Imprint: "Lit. Nacional".

F21 R12 10c purple 1.85 1.25
a. Imperf., pair 4.50 4.50

Execution at Cartagena in 1816
R13

1910, July 20 Engr. *Perf. 12*

F22 R13 10c red & black 15.00 42.50

Centenary of National Independence.

Pier at Puerto Colombia
R14

Tequendama Falls—R15

Perf. 11, 11½, 14, 11½x14

1917, Aug. 25

F23 R14 4c green & ultra. 1.50 1.35
a. Center inverted 500.00 500.00
F24 R15 10c deep blue 2.50 1.75

R16

1925 Lithographed. *Perf. 10x13½*

F25 R16 (10c) blue 2.75 1.50
a. Imperf., pair 7.00 7.00
b. Perf. 13½x10 3.50 3.50

ACKNOWLEDGMENT OF RECEIPT STAMPS.

AR1

AR2

Lithographed.

1893 *Perf. 13½.* **Unwmkd.**

H1 AR1 5c vermilion, *blue* 1.75 1.50

1894 *Perf. 12.*

H2 AR1 5c vermilion 90 65

1902–03 *Imperf.*

H3 AR2 10c blue, *blue* 25 20
a. 10c blue, *greenish blue* 25 20
b. Sewing machine perf. 1.00 1.00
c. Perf. 12 1.20 1.20

The handstamp "AR" in circle is believed to be a postmark.

AR3

AR4

1904 Pelure Paper *Imperf.*

H12 AR3 5c pale blue 50 50
a. Perf. 12 1.50 1.50

No. 307 Overprinted in Black, Green or Volet **AR**

H13 A86 5c carmine 10.00 10.00

1904 *Perf. 12.*

H16 AR4 5c blue 1.75 1.75
a. Imperf., pair 3.50 3.50

General José Acevedo y Gómez
AR5

1910, July 20 Engraved
H17 AR5 5c org. & green 6.00 7.50
Centenary of National Independence.

Sabana Station AR6 — Map of Colombia AR7

1917 *Perf. 14.*
H18 AR6 4c bistre brown 1.25 1.25
H19 AR7 5c orange brown 1.50 1.50
a. Imperf., pair 10.00

LATE FEE STAMPS.

LF1 LF2

Lithographed.

1886 *Perf. 10½.* Unwmkd.
I1 LF1 2½c *lilac* 1.25 1.00
a. Imperf., pair 6.50 6.50

1892 *Perf. 12, 13½.*
I2 LF2 2½c dark blue, *rose* 1.10 1.10
a. Imperf., pair 6.00
I3 LF2 2½c ultra., *pink* 1.50 1.50

LF3 LF4

1902 *Imperf.*
I4 LF3 5c purple *rose* 1.00 1.00
a. Perf. 12 2.00 2.00

1914 *Perf. 10, 13½.*
I6 LF4 2c violet brown 2.00 2.00
I7 " 5c blue green 2.25 2.00

Retardo   Refardo 1921

Overprints illustrated above are unauthorized and of private origin.

POSTAGE DUE STAMPS.

These are not, strictly speaking, postage due stamps but were issued to cover an additional fee, "Sobreporte", charged on mail to foreign countries with which Colombia had no postal conventions.

D1 D2 D3

Lithographed.

1866 *Imperf.* Unwmkd.
J1 D1 25c *blue* 20.00 20.00
J2 D2 50c *yellow* 20.00 20.00
J3 D3 1p *rose* 32.50 32.50

DEPARTMENT STAMPS.

These stamps are said to be for interior postage, to supersede the separate issues for the various departments.

Regular Issues Handstamped in Black, Violet, Blue or Green

Correos Departamentales

a

On Stamps of 1904.

1909 *Perf. 12.* Unwmkd.
L1 A94 ½c yellow 1.75 1.75
a. Imperf., pair 5.50 5.50
L2 A94 1c yellow green 1.75 1.75
L3 " 2c red 2.50 2.50
a. Imperf., pair 9.00 9.00
L4 A94 5c blue 2.25 2.25
L5 " 10c violet 3.75 3.75
L6 " 20c black 7.50 7.50
L7 A95 1p brown 13.50 13.50

On Stamp of 1902.

L8 A83 10p dark brown, *rose* 25.00 25.00
Nos. L1–L8 (8) 58.00 58.00

On Stamps of 1908.

Perf. 10, 13, 13½ and Compound.
L9 A94 ½c orange 1.25 1.25
a. Imperf., pair 2.50 2.50
L10 A94 1c green 1.50 1.50
a. Without imprint 1.85 1.85
L11 A94 2c red 2.50 2.50
a. Imperf., pair
L12 A94 5c blue 2.50 2.50
a. Imperf., pair 3.50 3.50
L13 A94 10c violet 3.25 3.25

On Tolima Stamp of 1888.

Perf. 10½.
L14 A23 1p red brown 7.50 7.50
Nos. L9–L14 (6) 18.50 18.50

Regular Issues Handstamped

b

On Stamps of 1904.

Perf. 12.
L15 A94 ½c yellow 1.25 1.25
L16 " 1c yellow green 1.25 1.25
L17 " 2c red 2.00 2.00
L18 " 5c blue 2.00 2.00
L19 " 10c violet 2.75 2.75
L20 " 20c black 7.00 7.00
L21 " 1p brown 13.50 13.50
Nos. L15–L21 (7) 29.75 29.75

On Stamps of 1908.

Perf. 10, 13, 13½.
L22 A94 ½c orange 1.00 1.00
L23 " 1c yellow green 4.75 4.75
L24 " 2c red 1.85 1.85
a. Imperf., pair 5.00 5.00
L25 A94 5c light blue 1.85 1.85

The handstamps on Nos. L1 to L25 are, as usual, found inverted and double.

DEPARTMENT REGISTRATION STAMPS.

Registration Stamps Handstamped like Nos. L1 to L25.

On Registration Stamp of 1904.

1909 *Perf. 12.* Unwmkd.
LF1 R12 (*a*) 10c purple 10.00 10.00
LF2 " (*b*) 10c " 10.00 10.00

On Registration Stamp of 1909.

Perf. 10, 13.
LF3 R12 (*a*) 10c purple 10.00 10.00
LF4 " (*b*) 10c " 10.00 10.00

Nos. LF1–LF4 exist imperf. Price per pair, $20.

DEPARTMENT ACKNOWLEDGMENT OF RECEIPT STAMPS.

Acknowledgment of Receipt Stamp of 1904 Handstamped like Nos. L1 to L25.

1909 *Perf. 12.* Unwmkd.
LH1 AR4 (*a*) 5c blue 12.50 12.50
a. Imperf., pair 25.00
LH2 AR4 (*b*) 5c " 12.50 12.50
a. Imperf., pair 25.00

Local Stamps for the City of Bogota.

(bō'gō-tä')

A1

Lithographed.

Pelure Paper.

1889 *Perf. 12* Unwmkd.
LX1 A1 ½c black 1.00 1.00
a. Imperf., pair 5.00 5.00

Impressions on bright blue and blue-gray paper were not regularly issued

A2 A3

White Wove Paper.

1896 *Perf. 12, 13½*
LX2 A2 ½c black 1.00 1.00

1903 *Imperf.*
LX3 A3 10c *pink* 1.65 1.65
a. Perf. 12 6.00 6.00

OFFICIAL STAMPS.

Stamps of 1917-1937 Overprinted in Black or Red:

OFICIAL   OFICIAL

a   *b*

Perf. 11, 12, 13½.

1937 Unwmkd.
O1 A131 (*a*) 1c green (Bk) 10 10
O2 A157 (") 10c deep orange (Bk) 25 15
O3 A107 (*b*) 30c olive bistre (Bk) 1.65 1.50
O4 A129 (") 40c brown & yellow brn. (Bk) 1.25 75
O5 A114 (") 50c car. (Bk) 80 60
O6 A115 (") 1p light blue (Bk) 2.10 1.75
O7 A116 (") 2p orange (Bk) 5.00 3.00
O8 A117 (") 5p gray (Bk) 18.00 15.00
O9 A118 (") 10p dark brown (Bk) 50.00 47.50

Wmkd. Wavy Lines. (229)

Perf. 12½.
O10 A132 (*a*) 2c red (Bk) 15 15
O11 A133 (") 5c brown (Bk) 12 12
O12 A160 (") 12c deep blue (R) 65 35
O13 A136 (*b*) 20c dark blue (R) 65 45
Nos. O1–O13 (13) 80.72 71.42

Tall, wrong font "I's" in OFICIAL exist on all stamps with "a" overprint.

POSTAL TAX STAMPS.

"Greatest Mother"
PT1

Lithographed.

1935, May 27 *Perf. 11½* Unwmkd.
RA1 PT1 5c olive black & scarlet 2.75 1.50

This stamp was required on all mail during Red Cross Week in 1935 (May 27–June 3) and in 1936.

Mother and Child
PT2

Perf. 10½, 10½x11.

1937, May 24 Unwmkd.
RA2 PT2 5c red 75 35

This stamp was required on all mail during Red Cross Week. The tax was for the Red Cross.

Ministry of Posts and Telegraphs Building
PT3 PT4

1939–45 Litho. *Perf. 10½, 12½*
RA3 PT3 ¼c deep blue 5 4
RA3A " ¼c dark violet brown ('45) 10 5
RA4 " ½c pink 5 4
RA5 " 1c violet 6 6
RA5A " 1c yel. org. ('45) 15 5
RA6 " 2c peacock green 38 20
RA7 " 20c light brown 1.75 75
Nos. RA3–RA7 (7) 2.54 1.19

These stamps were obligatory on all mail. The tax was for the construction of the new Communications Building.

The 25c of type PT3 and PT4 were not usable on postal matter.

See also No. 561.

Wmkd. Wavy Lines (229)

1940, Jan. 20 Engr. *Perf. 12½x13*
RA8 PT4 ¼c ultramarine 3 3
RA9 " ½c carmine 3 3
RA10 " 1c violet 3 3
RA11 " 2c blue green 12 5
RA12 " 20c brown 1.25 38
Nos. RA8–RA12 (5) 1.46 52

See note after No. RA7.

"Protection"
PT5

Wmkd.

Wavy Lines and C Multiple. (255)

1940, Apr. 25 *Perf. 12*

RA13 PT5 5c rose carmine 25 10

See also No. RA17.

Postal Tax Stamps of 1939 Surcharged in Black **$ 0,01/2 MEDIO CENTAVO**

1943 *Perf. 10½.* **Unwmkd.**

RA14 PT3 ½c on 1c violet 12 8
- *a.* Inverted surcharge 2.25

RA15 " ½c on 2c peacock green 12 8

RA16 " ½c on 20c lt. brn. 25 15

Types of 1940.

Imprint:

"Litografia Colombia Bogota S. A."

1944 **Lithographed.** *Perf. 11.*

RA17 PT5 5c dark rose 40 12

Imprint:

"Lito-Colombia Bogota-Colombia"

RA18 PT4 ¼c ultramarine 10 4

Ministry of Posts and Telegraphs Building

PT6

Engraved.

1945-48 *Perf. 12.* **Wmk. 255**

RA19 PT6 ¼c ultramarine 5 3

RA20 " ¼c sepia ('46) 5 3

RA21 " ½c carmine rose 5 3

RA22 " ½c deep magenta ('46) 5 3

RA23 " 1c violet ('46) 5 3

RA23A " 1c red org. ('46) 5 3

RA24 " 2c green ('46) 6 3

RA25 " 20c brown ('46) 30 15
- *a.* 20c red brown ('48) 15 7

Nos. RA19-RA25 (8) 66 36

These stamps were obligatory on all mail. The surtax was for the construction of the new Communications Building. See also Nos. 603, RA33.

No. 469 Overprinted in Carmine

1946, May 25

RA26 A176 5c dull brown 30 15

The surtax was for the Red Cross.

Ministry of Posts and Telegraphs Building

PT7

Lithographed.

1946 *Perf. 11* **Unwmkd.**

RA27 PT7 3c blue 10 3

No. 490 Overprinted in Carmine SOBRETASA

c

1947 *Perf. 12* **Wmk. 255**

RA28 A196 20c gray black 3.75 3.00

Arms of Colombia and Red Cross

PT8 PT9

Engraved

1947, Sept. *Perf. 12½* **Unwmkd.**

RA29 PT8 5c carmine lake 20 8

The surtax of Nos. RA29 and RA40 was for the Red Cross. See also No. RA40.

No. 466 Overprinted Type "c" in Carmine.

RA30 A136 20c dark blue 4.50 4.50

Type of 1945.

Engraved.

1947 *Perf. 12* **Wmk. 255**

RA33 PT6 1c olive bistre 4 4

Lithographed.

Black Surcharge.

1948 *Perf. 11.* **Unwmkd.**

RA36 PT9 1c on 5c light brn. 10 4

RA37 " 1c on 10c light viol. 10 4

RA38 " 1c on 25c red 10 4

RA39 " 1c on 50c ultra. 10 4

Type of 1947.

1948 *Perf. 10½*

RA40 PT8 5c vermilion 27 8

Ministry of Posts and Telegraphs Building — PT10

Mother and Child — PT11

Engraved

1948-50 *Perf. 12* **Wmk. 255**

RA41 PT10 1c rose car. ('49) 4 4

RA42 " 2c green ('50) 6 4

RA43 " 3c blue 6 4

RA44 " 5c gray 10 4

RA45 " 10c purple 25 5

Nos. RA41-RA45 (5) 51 21

A 25c stamp of type PT10 was for use on telegrams, later for regular postage. See Nos. 602, 604.

Lithographed.

1950, May 25 *Perf. 11* **Unwmkd.**

Dark Blue Surcharge.

RA46 PT11 5c on 2c gray, red, black & yellow 1.40 50
- *a.* "195" instead of "1950" 1.75 1.75
- *b.* Top bar and "19" of "1950" omit. 1.75 1.75

Marginal perforations omitted, creating 26 straight-edged copies in each sheet of 44. Surtax for Red Cross.

No. 574 Overprinted in Black **SOBRETASA**

1950, May 26 *Perf. 12* **Wmk. 255**

RA47 A176 5c blue 12 6
- *a.* Inverted ovpt. 1.25

Telegraph Stamp Surcharged in Black.

RA48 A253a 8c on 50c org. yellow 10 3

Fiscal stamps of type A253a were available for postal use after May 9, 1952. See Nos. 605-608.

Arms and Cross — PT12

Bartolome de Las Casas Aiding Youth — PT13

Engraved.

1951, May *Perf. 12½* **Unwmkd.**

RA49 PT12 5c red 20 4

RA50 PT13 5c carmine 20 4

The surtax was for the Red Cross.

No. RA43 Surcharged with New Value in Black.

1951 *Perf. 12.* **Wmk. 255**

RA51 PT10 1c on 3c blue 4 3

Type of 1951.

Engraved; Cross Lithographed.

1953 *Perf. 12½.* **Unwmkd.**

RA52 PT13 5c grn. & carmine 20 4

The surtax of Nos. RA52-RA60 was for the Red Cross.

No. C254 Overprinted with Cross and Bar in Carmine.

1954

RA53 AP42 5c lilac rose 60 30

St. Peter Claver Offering Gifts to Slaves

PT14

Engraved; Cross Typographed

1955, May 2 *Perf. 13* **Unwmkd.**

RA54 PT14 5c dp. plum & red 25 6

Issued to commemorate the 300th anniversary of the death of St. Peter Claver.

Jean Henri Dunant and Santiago Samper Brush

PT15

Photogravure;

Red Cross and "Cruz Roja" Engraved.

1956, June 1 *Perf. 13* **Unwmkd.**

RA55 PT15 5c brown & red 23 5

Nurses and Ambulances

PT16

1958, June 2 **Photo.** *Perf. 12*

RA56 PT16 5c gray & red 12 3

St. Louisa de Marillac and Church

PT17

Design: No. RA58, Henri Dunant and battle scene.

1960, Sept. 1 **Litho.** *Perf. 11*

RA57 PT17 5c brown & rose 18 8

RA58 " 5c violet blue & rose 20 8

No. RA57 issued to commemorate the 3rd centenary of the Sisters of Charity. No. RA58 issued to commemorate the centenary (in 1959) of the Red Cross idea.

Manuelita de la Cruz — PT18

Red Cross Worker and Patient — PT19

1961, Nov. 2 **Engraved** *Perf. 13*

RA59 PT18 5c dull purple & red 12 4

RA60 " 5c brown & red 12 4

Issued in memory of Red Cross Nurse Manuelita de la Cruz, who died in the line of duty during the floods of 1955. Obligatory on domestic mail for a month.

1965, Apr. 30 **Photo.** *Perf. 12*

RA61 PT19 5c bl. gray & red 8 3

Obligatory on domestic mail during May.

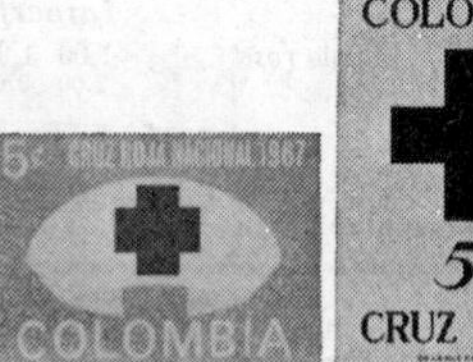

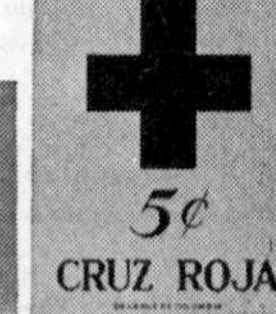

Nurse's Cap — PT20

Red Cross — PT21

1967, June 1 **Litho.** *Perf. 12*

RA62 PT20 5c brt. blue & red 5 3

1969, July 1 **Litho.** *Perf. 12x12½*

RA63 PT21 5c vio. blue & red 3 3

Child Care

PT22

1970, July 1 **Litho.** *Perf. 12½x12*

RA64 PT22 5c lt. blue & red 3 3

Antioquia

(än'tê·ō'kyä)

Originally a State, now a Department of the Republic of Colombia. Until the revolution of 1885, the separate states making up the United States of Colombia were sovereign governments in their own right. On August 4, 1886, the National Council of Bogotá, composed of two delegates from each state, adopted a new constitution which abolished the sovereign rights of states, which then became departments with governors appointed by the President of the Republic. The nine original states represented at the Bogotá Convention retained some of their previous rights, as management of their own finances, and all issued postage stamps until as late as 1904. For Panama's issues, see Panama Nos. 1-30.

Coat of Arms

A1 A2

A3 A4

Lithographed.

Wove Paper.

1868 *Imperf.* **Unwmkd.**

1 A1 2½c blue *375.00 275.00*
2 A2 5c green *285.00 175.00*
3 A3 10c lilac *800.00 375.00*
4 A4 1p red *225.00 150.00*

Reprints of Nos. 1, 3 and 4 are on a bluish white paper and all but No. 3 have scratches across the design.

A5 A6

A7 A8

A9 A10

1869

5 A5 2½c blue 2.00 1.50
6 A6 5c green 2.10 2.00
7 A7 5c green 2.10 2.00
8 A8 10c lilac 3.25 1.35
9 A9 20c brown 3.75 2.00
10 A10 1p rose red 5.25 4.75
a. 1p vermilion 10.00 8.50

Reprints of Nos. 7, 8 and 10 are on a bluish white paper; reprints of Nos. 5 and 10a on white paper. The 10c blue is believed to be a reprint.

A11

A12 A13

A14 A15

A16 A17

A18

1873

12 A11 1c yellow green 2.65 2.25
a. 1c green 2.65 2.25
13 A12 5c green 3.25 2.75
14 A13 10c lilac 12.50 10.00
15 A14 20c yellow brown 3.25 3.25
a. 20c dark brown 3.25 3.25
16 A15 50c blue 1.00 1.00
17 A16 1p vermilion 1.75 1.75
18 A17 2p *yellow* 3.00 3.00
19 A18 5p *rose* 18.50 15.00

A19 A20

Liberty Head

A21 A22

Pedro Justo Berrio

A23

1875–85

20 A19 1c *green*, unglazed ('76) 85 85
a. Glazed paper 1.40 1.40
b. 1c *light green*, laid paper ('85) 2.40 2.00
21 A19 1c black ('76) 70 70
a. Laid paper 100.00 85.00
22 A19 1c blue green ('85) 1.25 1.25
23 " 1c red lilac, laid paper ('85) 1.35 1.35
24 A20 2½c blue 1.50 1.50
a. Pelure paper ('78) *500.00 500.00*
25 A21 5c green 9.50 7.50
a. Laid paper 55.00 27.50
26 A22 5c green 9.50 7.50
a. Laid paper 55.00 27.50
27 A23 10c lilac 12.00 7.00
a. Laid paper 90.00 80.00
28 A20 10c violet, pelure paper ('78) 325.00 250.00

Arms Liberty

A24 A25

A26 A27

1878–85

29 A24 2½c bl., pelure paper 1.60 1.50
30 " 2½c green ('83) 1.35 1.35
a. Laid paper ('83) 42.50 30.00
31 A24 2½c *buff* ('85) 3.25 3.25
32 A25 5c green ('83) 1.40 1.40
a. Pelure paper 15.00 7.50
b. Laid paper ('82) 15.00 3.75
33 A25 5c violet ('83) 3.00 1.50
a. 5c blue violet ('83) 3.25 3.25
34 A26 10c violet, laid paper ('82) 65.00 22.50
35 " 10c scarlet ('83) 1.35 1.35
a. Tete beche pair 37.50 37.50
36 A27 20c brown ('83) 1.50 1.50
a. Laid paper ('82) 1.85 1.85

A28 A29

Liberty

A30

1883–85

37 A28 5c brown 2.60 1.25
a. Laid paper 85.00 45.00
38 A28 5c green ('85) 50.00 25.00
a. Laid paper ('85) 45.00 30.00
39 A28 5c yellow, laid paper ('85) 2.25 2.00
40 A29 10c blue green, laid paper 2.00 2.00
41 " 10c blue, *blue* ('85) 2.00 2.00
42 " 10c lilac, laid paper ('85) 3.75 3.75
a. Wove paper ('85) 45.00 25.00
43 A30 20c blue, laid paper ('85) 1.75 1.75

Coat of Arms

A31

1886 **Wove Paper.**

55 A31 1c green, *pink* 45 45
56 " 2½c *orange* 35 35
57 " 5c ultra., *buff* 85 45
a. 5c blue, *buff* 1.75 65
58 " 10c rose, *buff* 85 45
a. Transfer of 50c in stone of 10c 45.00 45.00
59 " 20c dark violet, *buff* 1.00 60
61 " 50c yellow brown, *buff* 1.50 1.50
62 " 1p yellow, *green* 1.75 1.50
63 " 2p green, *violet* 1.75 1.60

1887-88

64 A31 1c red, *violet* 20 20
65 " 2½c lilac, *pale lilac* 45 30
66 " 5c carmine, *buff* 65 50
67 " 5c red, *green* 1.50 1.25
68 " 10c brown, *green* 60 50

Medellin Issue.

A32

A33 A34

1888 **Type-set.**

69 A32 2½c *yellow* 9.00 9.00
70 A33 5c *yellow* 2.50 2.50
71 A34 5c red, *yellow* 2.00 2.00

Two varieties of No. 69, six of No. 70 and ten of No. 71.

A35

1889

72 A35 2½c red 3.00 3.00

Ten varieties including "eentavos".

Regular Issue.

Coat of Arms

A36 A37

A38

A39

A40

A41

1889–90 Litho. *Perf. 13½*

No.	Type	Description	Unused	Used
73	A36	1c *rose*	15	15
74	"	2½c *blue*	20	15
75	"	5c *yellow*	30	25
76	"	10c *green*	35	30
78	A37	20c blue ('90)	1.00	75
79	A38	50c violet brown ('90)	2.25	2.25
		a. Transfer of 20c in stone of 50c	60.00	60.00
80	"	50c green ('90)	1.50	1.50
81	A39	1p red ('90)	1.25	1.25
82	A40	2p *magenta* ('90)	9.50	8.00
83	A41	5p *orange red* ('90)	12.00	11.00

Nos. 73–76, 82–83 exist imperf.

The so-called "errors" of Nos. 73 to 76, printed on paper of wrong colors, are essays or, possibly, reprints. They exist perforated and imperforate.

See also No. 96.

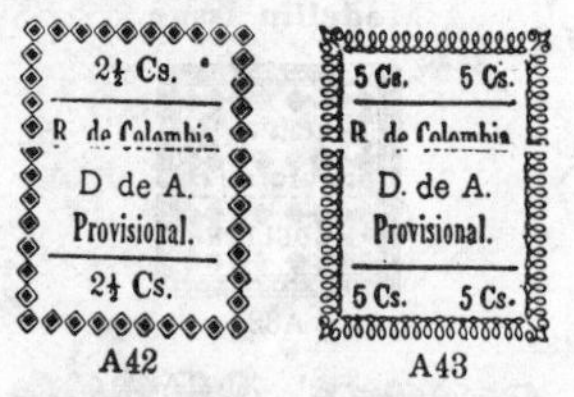
A42 A43

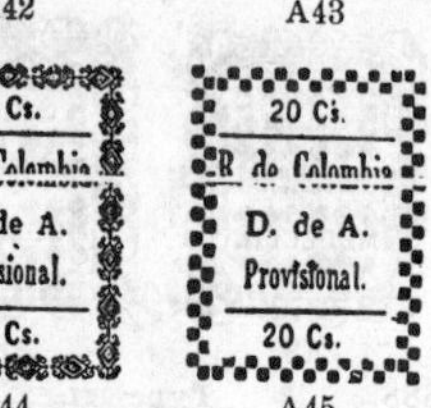
A44 A45

1890 Type-set. *Perf. 14.*

No.	Type	Description	Unused	Used
84	A42	2½c *buff*	60	60
85	A43	5c *orange*	60	60
86	A44	10c *buff*	3.25	3.25
87	"	10c *rose*	2.75	2.75
88	A45	20c *orange*	2.75	2.75

Twenty varieties of the 5c, ten of each of the other values.

A46

A47

1892 Lithographed *Perf. 13½*

No.	Type	Description	Unused	Used
89	A46	1c brown, *brownish*	40	30
90	"	2½c purple, *lilac*	35	20
92	"	5c *gray*	70	50
		a. Transfer of 2½c in stone of 5c	150.00	

1893

No.	Type	Description	Unused	Used
93	A46	1c blue	15	15
94	"	2½c green	30	22
95	"	5c vermilion	15	15
96	A36	10c pale brown	20	20

1896 *Perf. 14*

No.	Type	Description	Unused	Used
97	A47	2c gray	30	30
98	"	2c lilac rose	25	25
99	"	2½c brown	30	30
100	"	2½c steel blue	25	25
101	"	3c orange	35	30
102	"	3c olive green	25	25
103	"	5c green	15	15
104	"	5c yellow buff	20	20
105	"	10c brown violet	50	45
106	"	10c violet	50	45
107	"	20c brown orange	65	60
108	"	20c blue	1.00	85
109	"	50c gray brown	85	80
110	"	50c rose	1.25	1.25
111	"	1p blue & black	10.00	10.00
112	"	1p rose red & black	10.00	10.00
113	"	2p orange & blk.	30.00	30.00
114	"	2p dk. green & blk.	30.00	30.00
115	"	5p red vio. & blk.	35.00	35.00
116	"	5p purple & black	35.00	35.00

Nos. 115–116 with centers omitted are proofs.

General José María Córdoba
A48

1899 *Perf. 11.*

No.	Type	Description	Unused	Used
117	A48	½c greenish blue	4	6
118	"	1c slate blue	4	6
119	"	2c slate brown	4	6
120	"	3c red	4	7
121	"	4c bistre brown	4	6
122	"	5c green	4	6
123	"	10c scarlet	4	6
124	"	20c gray violet	4	6
125	"	50c olive bistre	5	9
126	"	1p greenish black	4	15
127	"	2p olive gray	4	30
		Nos. 117–127 (11)	45	1.03

Numerous part-perf. and imperf. varieties of Nos. 117-127 exist.

A49

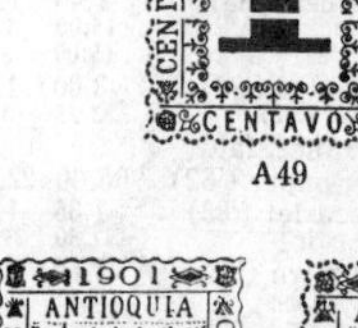
A50 A50a

1901 Type-set *Perf. 12*

No.	Type	Description	Unused	Used
128	A49	1c red	20	20
129	A50	1c ultramarine	55	55
130	"	1c bistre	50	50
130A	A50a	1c dull red	50	50
130B	"	1c ultramarine	8.00	3.50

Eight varieties of No. 128, four varieties of Nos. 129–130B.

A51

A52

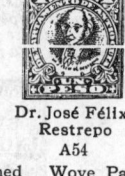

Atanasio Girardot
A53

Dr. José Félix Restrepo
A54

1902 Lithographed Wove Paper

No.	Type	Description	Unused	Used
131	A51	1c bright rose	8	8
		a. Laid paper	70	70
		b. Imperf., pair	3.00	
132	"	2c blue	8	8
		a. Transfer of 3c in stone of 2c	4.25	4.25
133	"	3c green	8	8
		a. Imperf., pair	3.00	
134	"	4c dull violet	10	10
135	A52	5c rose red	10	10
136	A53	10c rose lilac	10	10
		a. Small head	5.00	5.00
		b. 10c rose	10	10
137	"	20c gray green	20	20
138	"	30c bright rose	20	20
139	"	40c blue	20	20
140	"	50c brown, *yellow*	25	25
		Nos. 131–140 (10)	1.39	1.39

Laid Paper.

No.	Type	Description	Unused	Used
141	A54	1p purple & black	80	80
142	"	2p rose & black	80	80
143	"	5p slate blue & black	1.00	1.00

1903 Wove Paper.

No.	Type	Description	Unused	Used
143A	A51	1c blue	6	6
144	"	2c violet	7	7
		a. Imperf.	3.00	

A55

A56

Francisco Antonio Zea
A57

Custodio García Rovira
A58

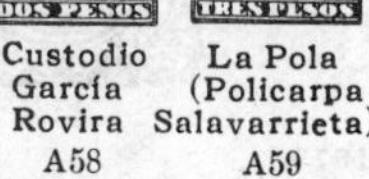
La Pola (Policarpa Salavarrieta)
A59

J. M. Restrepo
A60

José Fernández Madrid
A61

Juan del Corral
A62

1903–04

No.	Type	Description	Unused	Used
145	A55	4c yellow brown	8	8
146	"	5c blue	8	8
147	A56	10c yellow	10	7
148	"	20c purple	12	12
149	"	30c brown	55	55
150	"	40c green	55	55
151	"	50c rose	20	15
152	A57	1p olive gray	50	45
153	A58	2p purple	50	45
154	A59	3p dark blue	50	45
155	A60	4p dull red	85	65
156	A61	5p red brown	85	85
157	A62	10p scarlet	3.50	3.50
		Nos. 145–157 (13)	8.38	7.95

Nos. 145–146, 151, 153–157 exist imperf. Price by pair, $3 to $4.

Manizales Issue.

Stamps of these designs are local private post issues.

OFFICIAL STAMPS.

Stamps of 1903–04 with overprint "OFICIAL" were never issued.

REGISTRATION STAMPS.

R1

Lithographed.

1896 *Perf. 14* Unwmkd.

No.	Type	Description	Unused	Used
F1	R1	2½c rose	65	65
F2	"	2½c dull blue	65	65

Córdoba
R2

R3

1899 *Perf. 11*

No.	Type	Description	Unused	Used
F3	R2	2½c dull blue	10	10
F4	R3	10c red lilac	10	10

R4

1902 *Perf. 12*

No.	Type	Description	Unused	Used
F5	R4	10c purple, *blue*	20	20
		a. Imperf.		

ACKNOWLEDGMENT OF RECEIPT STAMPS.

AR1

Lithographed.

1902–03 *Perf. 12* Unwmkd.

No.	Type	Description	Unused	Used
H1	AR1	5c *rose*	65	65
H2	"	5c slate ('03)	15	15

AR2

Purple Handstamp.

1903 *Imperf.*

H3 AR2 10c *pink* 12.50 12.50

LATE FEE STAMPS.

Córdoba
LF1

Lithographed.

1899 *Perf. 11* Unwmkd.

I1 LF1 2½c dark green 4 8
a. Imperf., pair 2.00

LF2 LF3

1901 Type-set. *Perf. 12.*

I2 LF2 2½c red violet 65 65
a. 2½c purple 65 65
Four varieties.

1902 Lithographed

I3 LF3 2½c violet 10 10

City of Medellin

(mā'thē·yēn')

Stamps of the designs shown were not issued by any governmental agency but by the Sociedad de Mejoras Publicas.

Bolivar

(bō·lē'vär)

Originally a State, now a Department of the Republic of Colombia. (See Antioquia.)

A1

Lithographed.

1863–66 *Imperf.* Unwmkd.

1 A1 10c green *475.00* *300.00*
a. Five stars below sheild *500.00* *475.00*
2 " 10c red ('66) 20.00 20.00
a. Diagonal half used as 5c on cover 25.00
b. Five stars below shield 50.00 50.00
3 " 1p red 7.50 7.50

Fourteen varieties of each.

Coat of Arms

A2 A3

A4 A5

1873

4 A2 5c blue 2.25 2.25
5 A3 10c violet 2.50 2.50
6 A4 20c yellow green 15.00 15.00
7 A5 80c vermilion 35.00 32.50

A6

A7 A8

1874–78

8 A6 5c blue 13.50 3.50
9 A7 5c blue ('78) 4.75 3.00
10 A8 10c violet ('77) 1.25 1.00

Simón Bolívar
A9

Dated "1879".
White Wove Paper.

1879 *Perf. 12½*

11 A9 5c blue 30 30
a. Imperf., pair 1.00
12 " 10c violet 25 25
13 " 20c red 30 30
a. 20c green (error) 10.00 10.00

Bluish Laid Paper.

15 A9 5c blue 30 30
a. Imperf., pair 2.50
16 " 10c violet 2.50 2.50
a. Imperf., pair 5.00
17 " 20c red 35 35
a. Imperf., pair 2.25

Stamps of 80c and 1p on white wove paper and 1p on bluish laid paper were prepared but not placed in use.

Dated "1880".
White Wove Paper

1880 *Perf. 12½*

19 A9 5c blue 30 30
a. Imperf., pair 2.00
20 " 10c violet 35 35
a. Imperf., pair 2.00
21 " 20c red 45 45
a. 20c green (error) 12.50 12.50
23 " 80c green 2.25 2.25
24 A9 1p orange 2.50 2.50
a. Imperf., pair 6.00

Bluish Laid Paper.

25 A9 5c blue 30 30
a. Imperf., pair 1.50
26 " 10c violet 2.40 2.40
27 " 20c red 45 45
a. Imperf., pair 3.50
28 " 1p orange 275.00
a. Imperf. *300.00*

A11 A12

A13 A15

A16

Dated "1882".
White Wove Paper.

1882 *Perf. 12, 16x12*

29 A11 5c blue 35 35
30 A12 10c lilac 30 30
31 A13 20c red 45 45
33 A15 80c green 80 80
34 A16 1p orange 80 80

Nos. 29, 30 and 34 are known imperforate. They are printer's waste and were not issued through post offices.

Bolívar Bolívar
A17 A18

1882 Engraved *Perf. 12*

35 A17 5p blue & rose red 1.50 1.50
a. Imperf., pair 6.00
b. Perf. 16 5.00 5.00
c. Perf. 14 7.00 7.00
36 " 10p brown & blue 1.50 1.50
a. Imperf., pair 8.50
b. Perf. 16 5.00 5.00
c. Rouletted 10.00 10.00

Dated "1883".

1883 Litho. *Perf. 12, 16x12*

37 A11 5c blue 25 25
a. Imperf., pair 1.00
b. Perf. 12 2.75 1.25
38 A12 10c lilac 30 30
39 A13 20c red 30 30
41 A15 80c green 45 45
42 A16 1p orange 75 75
a. Perf. 16x12 2.50 2.50

1884 Dated "1884"

43 A11 5c blue 50 50
a. Perf. 12 10.00 10.00
44 A12 10c lilac 20 20
45 A13 20c red 20 20
a. Perf. 12 4.50 4.50
47 A15 80c green 30 30
a. Perf. 12 2.50 2.50
48 A16 1p orange 50 50

1885 Dated "1885"

49 A11 5c blue 15 15
50 A12 10c lilac 15 15
51 A13 20c red 15 15
53 A15 80c green 30 30
54 A16 1p orange 45 45

The note after No. 34 will also apply to imperforate stamps of the 1884-85 issues.

1891 *Perf. 14.*

55 A18 1c black 20 20
56 " 5c orange 45 45
a. Imperf., pair 1.00
57 " 10c carmine 45 45
58 " 20c blue 65 65
59 " 50c green 90 90
60 " 1p purple 1.10 1.10
Nos. 55-60 (6) 3.75 3.75

Overprinted with 7 Parallel Wavy Lines in Purple

1899

61 A18 1c black 60.00 60.00

The overprint is a control mark.

Bolívar
A19

José Fernández Madrid
A20

Manuel Rodriguez Torices
A21

José María García de Toledo
A22

1903 Laid Paper *Imperf.*

62 A19 50c dark blue, *pink* 50 50
a. Bluish paper 50 50
63 A19 50c slate green, *pink* 75 75
a. Rose paper 90 90
b. Greenish blue paper 1.75 1.75
c. Yellow paper 2.50 2.50
d. Brown paper 2.50 2.50
e. Salmon paper 6.00 6.00
64 A19 50c purple, *pink* 1.00 1.00
a. White paper 1.75 1.75
b. Brown paper 1.75 1.75
c. Greenish blue paper 1.75 1.75
d. Lilac paper 1.75 1.75
e. Rose paper 1.75 1.25
f. Yellow paper 2.50 2.50
g. Salmon paper 4.00 4.00
h. As "a," wove paper 5.00
65 A20 1p orange, *salmon* 65 65
a. Yellow paper 3.00 3.00
b. Greenish blue paper 12.00 12.00
66 A20 1p gray green, *lilac* 1.25 1.25
a. Yellow paper 6.00 6.00
b. Salmon paper 6.00 6.00
c. Green paper 6.00 6.00
d. White wove paper 10.00
67 A21 5p carmine rose, *lilac* 60 60
a. Brown paper 60 60
b. Yellow paper 90 90
c. Greenish blue paper 3.00 3.00
d. Bluish paper 5.00 5.00
e. Salmon paper 6.00 6.00
f. Rose paper 9.00 9.00
68 A22 10p dark blue, *bluish* 1.00 1.00
a. Greenish blue paper 1.00 1.00
b. Rose paper 6.00 6.00
c. Salmon paper 6.00 6.00
d. Yellow paper 6.00 6.00
e. Brown paper 6.00 6.00
f. Lilac paper 9.00 9.00
g. White paper 9.00 9.00

69 A22 10p pur., *greenish bl.* 3.75 3.75
a. Bluish paper 6.00 6.00
b. Rose paper 6.00 6.00
c. Yellow paper 6.00 6.00
d. Brown paper 6.00 6.00

Sewing Machine Perf.

Laid Paper

70 A19 50c dark blue, *pink* 65 65
a. Bluish paper 65 65
71 A19 50c slate green, *pink* 1.50 1.50
72 " 50c pur., *greenish bl.* 2.00 2.00
a. White paper 2.50 2.50
b. White wove paper 7.50
73 A20 1p orange, *salmon* 1.35 1.35
74 " 1p gray green, *lilac* 2.00 2.00
a. Yellow paper 9.00 9.00
75 A21 5p car. rose, *lilac* 2.00 2.00
a. Yellow paper 1.50 1.50
b. Brown paper 2.00 2.00
c. Bluish paper 4.00 4.00
d. White wove paper 9.00
76 A22 10p dark blue, *bluish* 2.00 2.00
a. Greenish blue paper 4.00 4.00
b. Yellow paper 6.50 6.50
c. As "b," wove paper 9.00
77 A22 10p pur., *greenish bl.* 5.00 5.00
a. Bluish paper 6.50 6.50
b. Rose paper 7.50 7.50
c. Yellow paper 10.00 10.00

José María del Castillo y Rada

A23

Manuel Anguiano

A24

Pantaleón C. Ribón

A25

1904 ***Sewing Machine Perf.***

89 A23 5c black 20 20
a. Imperf., pair 2.75 2.75
90 A24 10c brown 20 20
a. Imperf., pair 2.00 2.00
91 A25 20c red 30 30
a. Imperf., pair 5.50 5.50
92 " 20c red brown 65 65
a. Imperf., pair 6.00 6.00

A26

A28

A27

1904 ***Imperf.***

93 A26 ½c black 50 50
a. Tête bêche pair 3.00
94 A27 1c blue 1.00 1.00
95 A28 2c purple 1.25 1.25

REGISTRATION STAMPS.

Simón Bolívar

R1 R2

Lithographed.

White Wove Paper.

1879 ***Perf. 12½, 16x12.*** **Unwmkd.**

F1 R1 40c brown 85 85

Bluish Laid Paper.

F2 R1 40c brown 85 85
a. Imperf., pair 3.50

Dated "1880".

1880 **White Wove Paper.**

F3 R1 40c brown 45 45

Bluish Laid Paper.

F4 R1 40c brown 80 80
a. Imperf., pair 4.50

Dated "1882" to "1885".

White Wove Paper.

1882–85 ***Perf. 16x12***

F5 R2 40c brown (1882) 45 45
a. Perf. 12 20.00
F6 " 40c brown (1883) 35 35
a. Perf. 12 11.00
F7 " 40c brown (1884) 35 35
a. Perf. 12 11.00
F8 " 40c brown (1885) 45 45
a. Perf. 12 3.00

R3

Laid Paper.

1903 ***Imperf.***

F9 R3 20c orange, *rose* 60 60
a. Salmon paper 75 75
b. Greenish blue paper 4.00 4.00

Sewing Machine Perf.

F10 R3 20c orange, *rose* 1.00 1.00
a. Salmon paper 1.00 1.00
b. Greenish blue paper 3.00 3.00

R4

1904 **Wove Paper**

F11 R4 5c black 3.75 3.75

ACKNOWLEDGMENT OF RECEIPT STAMPS.

AR1

Lithographed

1903 ***Imperf.*** **Unwmkd.**

Laid Paper

H1 AR1 20c orange, *rose* 1.00 1.00
a. Yellow paper 1.25 1.25
b. Greenish blue paper 3.00 3.00
H2 AR1 20c dk. bl., *yellow* 1.00 1.00
a. Brown paper 1.50 1.50
b. Rose paper 1.75 1.25
c. Salmon paper 3.00 2.00
d. Greenish blue paper 3.00 2.00

Sewing Machine Perf.

H3 AR1 20c org., *greenish bl.* 6.00
a. Yellow paper 7.50
H4 AR1 20c dk. blue, *yellow* 6.00
a. Lilac paper 8.00

AR2

1904 **Wove Paper.**

H5 AR2 2c red 90 90

LATE FEE STAMPS.

LF1

Lithographed

1903 ***Imperf.*** **Unwmkd.**

Laid Paper.

I1 LF1 20c car. rose, *bluish* 50 50
I2 " 20c purple, *bluish* 40 40
a. Rose paper 1.25 1.25
b. Brown paper 1.25 1.25
c. Lilac paper 1.50 1.50
d. Yellow paper 5.00 5.00

Sewing Machine Perf.

I3 LF1 20c car. rose, *bluish* 60 60
I4 " 20c purple, *bluish* 50 50
a. Rose paper 1.25 1.25
b. Lilac paper 1.50 1.50
c. Yellow paper 5.00 5.00

Boyaca

(bō′yä·kä′)

Originally a State, now a Department of the Republic of Colombia. (See Antioquia.)

Diego Mendoza Pérez

A1

Lithographed.

1902 ***Perf. 13½*** **Unwmkd.**

Wove Paper.

1 A1 5c blue green 70 60
a. Bluish paper 65.00 65.00
b. Imperf., pair 13.50

Laid Paper.

Perf. 12

2 A1 5c green 75.00 75.00

Coat of Arms

A2 A3

General Próspero Pinzón

A4

Numeral of Value

A5

Monument of Battle of Boyacá

A6

President José Manuel Marroquin

A7

1903 **Lithographed.** ***Imperf.***

4 A2 10c dark gray 20 20
5 A3 20c red brown 35 35
6 A5 1p red 2.75 2.75
a. 1p claret 3.00 3.00
8 A6 5p *rose* 75 25
a. 5p *buff* 3.00 3.00
9 A7 10p *buff* 75 60
a. 10p *rose* 2.75
b. Tête bêche pair 7.50
Nos. 4–9 (5) 4.80 4.15

Perf. 12.

10 A2 10c dark gray 20 20
11 A3 20c red brown 45 45
12 A4 50c green 25 25
13 " 50c dull blue 1.65 1.65
14 A5 1p red 35 25
a. 1p claret 2.50 2.50
16 A6 5p *rose* 75 75
a. 5p *buff* 3.00 3.00
17 A7 10p *buff* 75 75
a. 10p *rose* 2.75
b. Tête bêche pair 10.00 7.50
Nos. 10–17 (7) 4.40 4.30

Statue of Bolívar

A8

1904

18 A8 10c orange 30 25
a. Imperf., pair 2.50 2.50

Cauca

(kou′kä)

Originally a State, now a Department of the Republic of Colombia. (See Antioquia.)

A1 A2

Handstamped.

1879 (?) ***Imperf.*** **Unwmkd.**

1 A1 (5c) black

1882

2 A2 5c violet
a. Figure in lower left corner omitted

A3 A4

1883

3 A3 (5) violet
4 A4 (5) violet

CORREOS DE LA República de Colombia DIEZ Centavos

A5 A7

1890

5 A5 5c red

Nos. 1 to 5 were sanctioned, though not authorized, by the national government.

Imperf., Sewing Machine Perf.

1902 **Typeset**

8	A7	10c *rose*	1.25	1.25
9	"	20c *orange*	90	90

Stamps of this design are believed to be of private origin and without official sanction.

Items inscribed "No hay estampillas" (No stamps available) and others inscribed "Manuel E. Jiménez" are considered by specialists to be receipt labels, not postage stamps.

Cundinamarca

(koon'dē·nä·mär'kä)

Originally a State, now a Department of the Republic of Colombia. (See Antioquia.)

Coat of Arms

A1 A2

Lithographed

1870 ***Imperf.*** **Unwmkd.**

1	A1	5c blue	2.75	2.75
2	A2	10c red	10.00	10.00

The counterfeits, or reprints, show traces of the cuts made to deface the dies.

A3 A4

A5 A6

1877–82

3	A3	10c red ('82)	2.00	2.00
		a. Laid paper ('77)	2.50	2.50
4	A4	20c green ('82)	5.00	5.00
		a. Laid paper ('77)	6.50	6.50
7	A5	50c purple ('82)	6.50	6.50
8	A6	1p brown ('82)	8.00	8.00

A7

1884

10	A7	5c blue	55	55
		a. Tête bêche pair	27.50	27.50
11	"	5c blue (redrawn)	1.25	1.25
		a. Tête bêche pair	42.50	42.50

The redrawn stamp has no period after "COLOMBIA."

10 10
CORREOS DE
CUNDINAMARCA.
(Provisionalmente.)
VALE 10 CENTAVOS.
El Admor. general.
10 10

A8

CUNDINAMARCA.
Correos provisorios.
CINCUENTA CVOS.

A9

A10

E. U. DE COLOMBIA
E. S. DE CUNDINAMARCA
SELLO PROVISORIO
CORREOS DEL ESTADO
VALE DOS REALES

A11

1883 **Typeset**

13	A8	10c *yellow*	10.00	10.00
14	A9	50c *rose*	10.00	10.00
15	A10	1p *brown*	27.50	27.50
16	A11	2r *green*	1000.00	

Typeset varieties exist: 4 of the 10c, 2 each of 50c and 1p.

Some experts doubt that No. 16 was issued. The variety without signature and watermarked "flowers" is believed to be a proof. Forgeries exist.

A12

1886 **Lithographed.**

17	A12	5c blue	65	65
18	"	10c red	3.00	3.00
19	"	10c red, *lilac*	1.50	1.50
20	"	20c green	2.50	2.50
		a. 20c yellow green	3.00	3.00
21	"	50c purple	3.50	3.50
22	"	1p orange brown	4.00	4.00

Nos. 18–20, 22, differ slightly from type A12.

Nos. 17 to 22 have been reprinted. The colors are aniline and differ from those of the original stamps. The impression is coarse and blurred.

A13 A14

3 CORREOS 3 DEPARTAMENTO DE CUNDINAMARCA REPUBLICA COLOMBIA 3 TRES CENTAVOS

Arms

A15 A16

15 CORREOS 15 DEPARTAMENTO DE CUNDINAMARCA COLOMBIA COLOMBIA 15 CENTAVOS 15

A17 A18

A19 A20

A21

1904 ***Perf. 10½, 12***

23	A13	1c orange	30	30
24	A14	2c gray blue	30	30
25	A15	3c rose	40	40
26	"	5c olive green	40	40
27	A16	10c pale brown	40	40
28	A17	15c pink	40	40
29	A18	20c blue, *green*	35	35
30	"	20c blue	70	70
31	A19	40c blue	60	65
32	"	40c blue, *buff*	15.00	15.00
33	A20	50c red violet	50	50
34	A21	1p gray green	40	40
		Nos. 23–34 (12)	19.75	19.80

Imperf.

23a	A13	1c orange	75	75
24a	A14	2c blue	75	75
		b. 2c slate	4.25	4.25
25a	A15	3c rose	1.00	1.00
26a	"	5c olive green	1.25	1.25
27a	A16	10c pale brown	1.75	1.75
28a	A17	15c pink	40	40
29a	A18	20c blue, *green*	2.00	2.00
30a	"	20c blue	1.65	1.65
31a	A19	40c blue	55	55
32a	"	40c blue, *buff*	15.00	15.00
33a	A20	50c red violet	60	60
34a	A21	1p gray green	60	60
		Nos. 23a–34a (12)	26.30	26.30

REGISTRATION STAMPS.

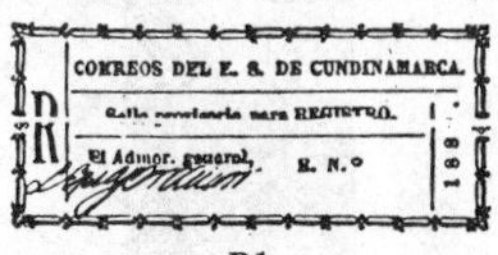

R1

1883 ***Imperf.*** **Unwmkd.**

F1	R1	*orange*	15.00	15.00

R2

1904 ***Perf. 12.***

F2	R2	10c bistre	1.00	1.00
		a. Imperf.	3.00	3.00

Magdalena

Items inscribed "No hay estampillas" (No stamps available) are considered by specialists to be not postage stamps but receipt labels.

Panama.

Issues of Panama as a state and later Department of Colombia are listed with the Republic of Panama issues (Nos. 1-30).

Santander

(sän'tän·dâr')

Originally a State, now a Department of the Republic of Colombia. (See Antioquia.)

Coat of Arms

A1 A2

Lithographed.

1884 ***Imperf.*** **Unwmkd.**

1	A1	1c blue	30	30
		a. 1c gray blue	50	50
2	A2	5c red	50	50
3	"	10c bluish purple	1.25	1.25
		a. Tête bêche pair		

No. 2 exists unofficially perforated 14.

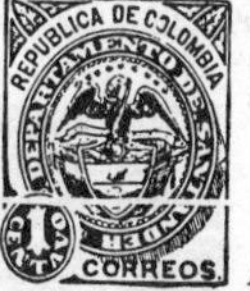

A3 A4

1886 ***Imperf.***

4	A3	1c blue	75	75
5	"	5c red	20	20
6	"	10c red violet	50	50
		a. 10c deep violet	50	50
		b. Inscribed "CINCO CENTAVOS"	15.00	15.00

The numerals in the upper corners are omitted on No. 5, while on No. 6 there are no numerals in the side panels. No. 6 exists unofficially perforated 12.

1887
7 A4 1c blue 15 15
a. 1c ultramarine 1.00 1.00
8 " 5c red 90 90
9 " 10c violet 2.75 2.75

A5

A6 A7

1889 ***Perf. 11½ and 13½.***
10 A5 1c blue 20 20
11 A6 5c red 1.00 1.00
12 A7 10c purple 50 50
a. Imperf., pair 20.00

A8 A9

1892 ***Perf. 13½***
13 A8 5c red, *rosy buff* 65 65

1895-96
14 A9 5c brown 75 75
15 " 5c yellow green ('96) 75 75

A10 A11

A12

1899 ***Perf. 10***
16 A10 1c *green* 30 30
17 A11 5c *pink* 30 30
Perf. 13½.
18 A12 10c blue 75 75
a. Perf. 12 1.00 1.00

A13

1903 ***Imperf.***
19 A13 50c red 35 35
a. 50c rose 35 35
b. "SANTENDER" 1.50 1.50
c. "Corrcos" 1.50 1.50
d. "Corceos" 1.50 1.50
e. Tête bêche pair 3.75 3.75
f. Pair, one without overprint 2.50 2.50

The overprint "Correos de Departmento Bucaramanga" on the 50c red revenue stamp has been proved to be a cancellation.

A14 A15

Arms A16 Locomotive A17

A18 A19

A20

1904 ***Imperf.***
22 A14 5c dark green 30 25
a. 5c yellow green 30 25
24 A15 10c rose 15 10
25 A16 20c brown violet 15 10
26 A17 50c yellow 20 20
27 A18 1p black 20 20
28 A19 5p dark blue 20 25
29 A20 10p carmine 40 40
Nos. 22-29 (7) 1.60 1.50

1905
30 A14 5c pale blue 30 30
31 A15 10c red brown 30 30
32 A16 20c yellow green 30 30
33 A17 50c red violet 30 30
34 A18 1p dark blue 30 30
35 A19 5p pink 40 50
36 A20 10p red 1.50 1.40
Nos. 30-36 (7) 3.40 3.40

A21

1907 ***Imperf.***
37 A21 ½c on 50c rose 45 45

Varieties and errors of spelling exist. Price, $1.50 each.

City of Cucuta

(kōō'kōō-tä)

5 cvos. A71 5 ctvos. A72

Lithographed.

"Gobierno Provisorio" at Top

1900 ***Perf. 12 Vertically.***
101 A71 1c (ctvo) *blue green* 3.25 3.25
a. "cvo." 10.00 10.00
b. "cvos." 3.50 3.50
c. "centavo' 4.00 4.00
103 A71 2c black 2.25 2.25
104 " 5c *pink* 2.25 1.50
a. Name at side (V) 6.50 3.75
105 A71 10c *pink* 2.25 1.50
a. Name at side (V) 6.50 3.75
106 A71 20c *yellow* 3.75 2.25
a. Name at side (G) 9.00 6.50
Nos. 101-106 (5) 13.75 10.75

"Gobierno Provisional" at Top
Name at Side in Black or Green

108 A72 1c (ctvo.) *blue green* (Bk) 2.75 1.00
a. "centavo" 17.50 15.00
109 A72 2c *blue green* (Bk) 1.75 1.75
110 " 5c black (G) 1.60 1.60
a. "ctvos." smaller 5.00 5.00
112 A72 10c *pink* (Bk) 1.75 1.75
113 " 20c *yellow* (G) 3.25 1.75
Nos. 106-113 (5) 11.10 7.85

Stamps of these and similar designs on white and yellow paper, with and without surcharges of ½c, 1c or 2c, are believed to have been produced without government authorization.

Tolima

(tō-lē'mä)

Originally a State, now a Department of the Republic of Colombia. (See Antioquia.)

A1

Typeset.

1870 ***Imperf.*** **Unwmkd.**

White Wove Paper.
1 A1 5c black 35.00 17.50
2 " 10c black 35.00 17.50

Printed from two settings. Setting I, ten types of 5c. Setting II, six types of 5c and four types of 10c.

Blue Laid Batonné Paper.
3 A1 5c black *700.00*

Buff Laid Batonné Paper.
4 A1 5c black 65.00 45.00

Blue Wove Paper
5 A1 5c black 35.00 17.50

Blue Vertically Laid Paper.
6 A1 5c black 60.00 35.00
a. Paper with ruled blue vertical lines

Blue Horizontally Laid Paper
7 A1 5c black 65.00 45.00

Blue Quadrille Paper.
8 A1 5c black 65.00 40.00

Ten varieties each of Nos. 3-5 and 7; 20 varieties each of Nos. 6 and 8.

Official imitations were made in 1886 from new settings of the type. There are only two varieties of each value. They are printed on blue and white paper, wove, batonné, laid, etc.

A2

A3

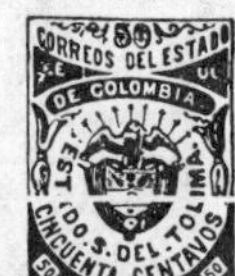
A4

A5

Yellowish White Wove Paper.

1871 **Lithographed** ***Imperf.***
9 A2 5c deep brown 1.00 1.00
a. 5c red brown 1.00 1.00
b. Value reads "CINGO" 20.00 20.00
10 A3 10c blue 3.50 3.50
11 A4 50c green 5.00 5.00
12 A5 1p carmine 8.75 8.75

The 5p stamps, type A2, are bogus varieties made from an altered die of the 5c.

The 10c, 50c and 1 peso stamps have been reprinted on bluish white wove paper. They are from new plates and most copies show traces of fine lines with which the dies had been defaced. Reprints of the 5c have a large cross at the top. The 10c on laid batonné paper is known only as a reprint.

A6

A7

A8 A9

1879 **Grayish or White Wove Paper**
14 A6 5c yellow brown 30 30
a. 5c purple brown 30 30
15 A7 10c blue 45 45
16 A8 50c green, *bluish* 45 45
a. White paper 1.10 1.10
17 A9 1p vermilion 1.75 1.75
a. 1p carmine rose 6.75 6.75

A10

1883 ***Imperf.***
18 A6 5c orange 35 35
19 A7 10c vermilion 70 70
20 A10 20c violet 1.00 1.00

Coat of Arms
A12

1884 ***Imperf.***
23 A12 1c gray 15 15
24 " 2c rose lilac 15 15
a. 2c slate 15 15
25 " 2½c dull orange 15 15
26 " 5c brown 15 15
27 " 10c blue 50 50
a. 10c slate 20 20
28 " 20c lemon 50 50
a. Laid paper 5.00 5.00
29 " 25c black 25 25
30 " 50c green 35 35

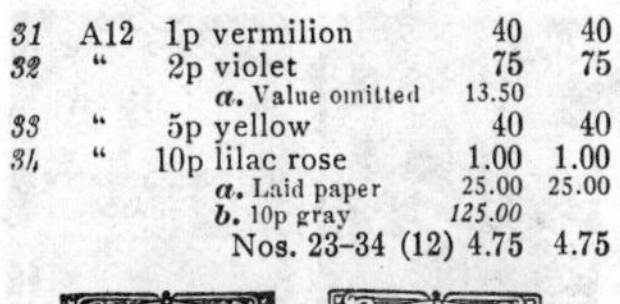

No.	Type	Description	Unused	Used
31	A12	1p vermilion	40	40
32	"	2p violet	75	75
		a. Value omitted	13.50	
33	"	5p yellow	40	40
34	"	10p lilac rose	1.00	1.00
		a. Laid paper	25.00	25.00
		b. 10p gray	125.00	
		Nos. 23-34 (12)	4.75	4.75

A13

A14

Condor with Long Wings Touching Flagstaffs
A15 A16

1886 Litho. *Perf. 10½, 11*

White Paper

No.	Type	Description	Unused	Used
36	A13	5c brown	1.00	1.00
		a. 5c yellow brown	1.00	1.00
		b. Imperf., pair	20.00	
37	A14	10c blue	3.50	3.50
		a. Imperf., pair	20.00	
38	A15	50c green	1.25	1.25
		a. Imperf., pair	20.00	
39	A16	1p vermilion	2.25	2.25
		a. Imperf., pair	30.00	

No. 38 has been reprinted in pale gray green, perforated 10½, and No. 39 in bright vermilion, perforated 11½. The impressions show many signs of wear.

Lilac Tinted Paper.

No.	Type	Description	Unused	Used
36c	A13	5c orange brown	10.00	10.00
37b	A14	10c blue	10.00	10.00
38b	A15	50c green	6.50	6.50
39b	A16	1p vermilion	5.00	5.00

A17

A18

Condor with Short Wings
A19 A20

1886 White Paper *Perf. 12*

No.	Type	Description	Unused	Used
44	A19	1c gray	5.00	5.00
		a. Imperf., pair	20.00	
45	A17	2c rose lilac	6.50	6.50
46	A18	2½c dull orange	20.00	20.00
47	A19	5c brown	9.00	9.00
		a. Imperf., pair	32.50	
48	A20	10c blue	9.00	9.00
		a. Imperf., pair	32.50	
49	"	20c lemon	6.50	6.50
		a. Tête bêche pair	90.00	
50	"	25c black	6.00	6.00
51	"	50c green	2.00	2.00
52	"	1p vermilion	4.25	4.25
		a. Imperf., pair	20.00	
53	"	2p violet	8.00	8.00
		a. Imperf., pair	25.00	
		b. Tête bêche pair	90.00	
54	"	5p orange	15.00	15.00
		a. Imperf., pair	40.00	
55	"	10p lilac rose	7.00	7.00
		a. Imperf., pair	20.00	

Condor with Long Wings, Upper Flagstaffs Omitted
A21 A22

1886 *Perf. 12, 12½, 12x11*

No.	Type	Description	Unused	Used
56	A15	2½c dull orange	65.00	65.00
		a. Imperf., pair		
		b. Transfer of 5c in stone of 2½c		
		c. Transfer of 10c in stone of 2½c		
57	A21	5c brown	7.00	7.00
		a. Imperf., pair	20.00	
		b. Transfer of 10c in stone of 5c		
		c. As "b," imperf.		
58	A14	10c ultramarine	9.00	9.00
		a. Imperf., pair	25.00	
		b. Transfer of 5c in stone of 10c		
59	A22	2p red violet	10.00	10.00
		a. Imperf., pair	32.50	
		b. Without numerals in corners, colored background, imperf.	25.00	
		c. As "b," white background	25.00	25.00
60	"	5p pale orange	17.50	17.50
		a. Imperf., pair	50.00	
		b. Bottom label inverted		
		c. Tête bêche pair		
		d. Transfer of 2p in stone of 5p		
		Imperf.		
61	A13	1c black	140.00	

No. 56 is similar to type A15, and No. 58 similar to type A14, but both have upper flag-staffs omitted.

A23

1888 *Perf. 10½.*

No.	Type	Description	Unused	Used
62	A23	5c red	15	15
		a. Imperf., pair	3.50	
63	"	10c green	50	50
		a. Imperf., pair	4.00	
64	"	50c blue	75	75
		a. Imperf., pair	6.00	6.00
65	"	1p red brown	1.25	1.25
		a. Imperf., pair	9.00	

1895 *Perf. 12, 13½*

No.	Type	Description	Unused	Used
66	A23	1c blue, *rose*	30	30
		a. Imperf., pair	9.00	
67	"	2c green, *light green*	30	30
		a. Imperf., pair	9.00	
68	"	5c red	10	10
69	"	10c green	30	30
70	"	20c blue, *yellow*	50	50
		a. Imperf., pair	10.00	
71	"	1p brown	1.50	1.50
		Nos. 66-71 (6)	3.00	3.00

'No Hay Estampillas'

Items inscribed "No hay estampillas" (No stamps available) are considered by specialists to be not postage stamps but receipt labels.

Honda Issue.

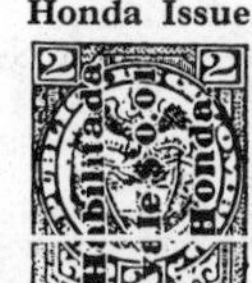

A23a

Black Surcharge.

1896 *Perf. 12*

No.	Type	Description	Unused	Used
78	A23a	1c on 2c green	32.50	32.50

Excellent counterfeits exist.

Regular Issue.

A24

A25

A26

A27

A28

A29

A30

A31

Sewing Machine or Regular

Perf. 12

1903-04 Lithographed.

No.	Type	Description	Unused	Used
79	A24	4c *green*	20	20
80	A25	10c dull blue	30	30
81	A26	20c orange	40	40
82	A27	50c *rose*	20	20
		a. 50c *buff*	20	20
84	A28	1p brown	10	10
85	A29	2p gray	10	10
86	A30	5p red	10	10
		a. Tête bêche pair	4.50	
87	A31	10p *blue*	20	20
		a. 10p *light green*	20	20
		b. 10p *green glazed*	3.25	3.25
		Nos. 79-87 (8)	1.60	1.60

Imperf.

No.	Type	Description	Unused	Used
79a	A24	4c *green*	30	30
80a	A25	10c dull blue	20	20
81a	A26	20c orange	1.00	1.00
82b	A27	50c *rose*	1.50	1.50
		c. 50c *buff*	1.50	1.00
84a	A28	1p brown	10	10
85a	A29	2p gray	10	10
86b	A30	5p red	10	10
		c. Tête bêche pair	4.50	
87c	A31	10p *blue*	2.10	2.10
		d. Tête bêche pair	4.50	
		e. A31 10p *light green*	2.10	2.10
		f. A31 10p *green glazed*	15.00	15.00
		Nos. 79a-87c (8)	5.40	5.40

COMORO ISLANDS

LOCATION—In Mozambique Channel between Madagascar and Mozambique.

GOVT.—Republic.

AREA—838 sq. mi.

POP.—262,000 (est. 1974).

CAPITAL—Moroni, Grand Comoro.

The Comoro Archipelago consists of the islands of Mayotte, Anjouan, Grand Comoro (Grande Comore) and Mohéli, which issued their own stamps as French protectorates or colonies in 1897–1914. The archipelago was attached to Madagascar from 1914 to 1946 when it became a separate French Territory. In July, 1975, Anjouan, Grand Comoro and Moheli united to declare independence as the State of Comoro. Mayotte remained French.

100 Centimes = 1 Franc

Anjouan Bay
A2

Comoro Woman Grinding Grain
A3

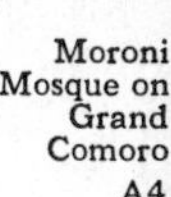

Moroni Mosque on Grand Comoro
A4

Engraved

1950 *Perf. 13* Unwmkd.

No.	Type	Description	Unused	Used
30	A2	10c blue	10	10
31	"	50c green	10	10
32	"	1fr dark olive brown	10	10
33	A3	2fr bright green	15	15
34	"	5fr purple	15	15
35	"	6fr violet brown	25	25
36	A4	7fr red	25	25
37	"	10fr dark green	25	25
38	"	11fr deep ultramarine	30	30
		Nos. 30-38 (9)	1.65	1.65

Imperforates

Most Comoro Islands stamps exist imperforate in issued and trial colors, and also in small presentation sheets in issued colors.

Military Medal Issue.

Common Design Type

1952 Engraved and Typographed

No.	Type	Description	Unused	Used
39	CD101	15fr multicolored	17.50	17.50

Mosque of Ouani, Anjouan
A5

Coelacanth
A6

1952-54 Engraved

No.	Type	Description	Unused	Used
40	A5	15fr dark brown	40	35
41	"	20fr red brown	45	40
42	A6	40fr aquamarine & indigo ('54)	8.00	6.00

FIDES Issue

Common Design Type

1956 *Perf. 13x12½* Unwmkd.

No.	Type	Description	Unused	Used
43	CD103	9fr deep violet	55	35

Human Rights Issue

Common Design Type

1958 Engraved. *Perf. 13*

No.	Type	Description	Unused	Used
44	CD105	20fr olive green & dark blue	5.50	5.50

Flower Issue

Common Design Type

Design: Colvillea.

1959 Photogravure ***Perf. 12½x12***

45 CD104 10fr multicolored 2.50 1.65

View of Dzaoudzi and Radio Symbol

A8

Design: 25fr, Radio tower and radio waves over Islands.

1960, Dec. 23 Engr. ***Perf. 13***

46 A8 20fr maroon, violet blue & green 70 60
47 " 25fr ultramarine, brown & green 85 85

Comoro radio station.

Harpa Conoidalis

A9

Sea Shells: 50c, Cypraecassis rufa. 2fr, Murex ramosus. 5fr, Turbo marmoratus. 20fr, Pterocera scorpio. 25fr, Charonia tritonis.

1962, Jan. 13 Photogravure

Shells in Natural Colors

48 A9 50c lilac & brown 30 30
49 " 1fr yellow & red 30 30
50 " 2fr pale green & pink 40 40
51 " 5fr yellow & green 80 80
52 " 20fr salmon & brown 1.85 1.85
53 " 25fr bistre & pink 2.50 2.50
Nos. 48-53, C5-C6 (8) 21.65 20.15

Wheat Emblem and Globe

A10

1963, Mar. 21 Engr. ***Perf. 13***

54 A10 20fr choc. & dark grn. 2.50 2.25

Issued for the "Freedom from Hunger" campaign of the U.N. Food and Agriculture Organization.

Red Cross Centenary Issue

Common Design Type

1963, Sept. 2 ***Perf. 13*** **Unwmkd.**

55 CD113 50fr emerald, gray & carmine 4.00 3.50

Centenary of the International Red Cross.

Human Rights Issue

Common Design Type

1963, Dec. 10 Engraved

56 CD117 15fr dark red & yellow green 4.00 3.50

Common Design Types pictured in section at front of book.

Tobacco Pouch

A13

Grand Comoro Canoe

A14

Designs: 4fr, Censer. 10fr, Carved lamp.

1963, Dec. 27 ***Perf. 13***

Size: 22x36mm.

57 A13 3fr multicolored 15 15
58 " 4fr orange, dp. claret & slate green 25 25
59 " 10fr org. brn., dk. red brown & green 50 50
Nos. 57-59, C8-C9 (5) 6.90 4.60

Philatec Issue

Common Design Type

1964, March 31

60 CD118 50fr dark blue, red & green 1.65 1.65

1964, Aug. 7 Photo. ***Perf. 13x12½***

Design: 30fr, Boutre felucca.

Size: 22x37mm.

61 A14 15fr multicolored 60 60
62 " 30fr lt. grn. & multi. 1.00 1.00

See Nos. C10-C11.

Spiny Lobster

A15

Designs: 12fr, Hammerhead shark (horiz.). 20fr, Turtle (horiz.). 25fr, Merou fish.

1965, Dec. 20 Engraved ***Perf. 13***

63 A15 1fr grn., lilac & ocher 20 20
64 " 12fr orange red, slate & gray 50 40
65 " 20fr orge. red & bl. grn. 60 50
66 " 25fr blue green, dark brown & red 70 60

Hotel Itsandra, Moroni

A16

Design: 15fr, Lake Salé, Grand Comoro.

Photogravure

1966, Dec. 19 ***Perf. 12½x13***

67 A16 15fr multicolored 40 30
68 " 25fr " 50 30

See Nos. C18-C19.

Comoro Sunbird

A17

Birds: 10fr, Malachite kingfisher. 15fr, Rothschild's fody. 30fr, Cuckoo-roller.

1967, June 20 Photo. ***Perf. 12½x13***

Size: 36x23mm.

69 A17 2fr ocher & multi. 60 60
70 " 10fr lilac & multi. 80 80
71 " 15fr yel. grn. & multi. 1.00 1.00
72 " 30fr pink & multi. 1.60 1.60
Nos. 69-72, C20-C21 (6) 7.85 5.50

WHO Anniversary Issue

Common Design Type

1968, May 4 Engraved ***Perf. 13***

73 CD126 40fr green, violet, & deep carmine 80 70

Issued for the 20th anniversary of the World Health Organization.

Surgeon-fish

A19

Design: 25fr, Imperial angelfish.

1968, Aug. 1 Engraved ***Perf. 13***

Size: 36x22mm.

74 A19 20fr vio. blue, yellow & red brown 40 40
75 " 25fr Prus. blue, dark blue & orange 50 50

See Nos. C23-C24.

Human Rights Year Issue

Common Design Type

1968, Aug. 10 Engraved ***Perf. 13***

76 CD127 60fr brown, green & orange 1.20 1.20

Msoila Prayer Rug and Praying Man

A20

Designs: Each stamp shows a different prayer position.

1969, Feb. 27 Engraved ***Perf. 13***

77 A20 20fr blue green, rose red & purple 30 25
78 " 30fr purple, rose red & blue green 40 35
79 " 45fr rose red, purple & blue green 60 50

Vanilla Flower

A21

Design: 15fr, Flower of ylang-ylang tree. 25fr, Poinsettia (country name in upper right corner).

1969-70 Photo. ***Perf. 12½x13***

Size: 36x23mm.

80 A21 10fr multicolored 25 20
81 " 15fr " 32 28
82 " 25fr " ('70) 50 35
Nos. 80-82, C26-C28 (6) 6.32 4.68

Issue dates: Nos. 80-81, Mar. 20, 1969. No. 82, Mar. 5, 1970.

ILO Issue

Common Design Type

1969, Nov. 24 Engraved ***Perf. 13***

83 CD131 5fr orange, emerald & gray 25 20

Issued for 50th anniversary of the International Labor Organization.

U.P.U. Headquarters Issue

Common Design Type

1970, May 20 Engraved ***Perf. 13***

84 CD133 65fr pur., bl. green & red brn. 1.25 80

Chiromani Costume, Anjouan

A22

Friday Mosque

A23

Design: 25fr, Bouiboui costume, Grand Comoro.

1970, Oct. 30 Photo. ***Perf. 12½x13***

85 A22 20fr green, yel. & red 40 32
86 " 25fr brn., yel. & dk. bl. 50 40

1970, Dec. 18 Engraved ***Perf. 13***

87 A23 5fr rose car., green & greenish blue 25 15
88 " 10fr dp. lilac, grn. & vio. 32 25
89 " 40fr copper red, grn. & deep brown 55 45

Great White Egret

A24

Pyrostegia Venusta

A25

Birds: 10fr, Comoro pigeon. 15fr, Green-backed heron. 25fr, Comoro blue pigeon. 35fr, Humblot's flycatcher. 40fr, Allen's gallinule.

Photogravure

1971, March 12 ***Perf. 12½x13***

90 A24 5fr multicolored 20 15
91 " 10fr yellow & multi. 28 20
92 " 15fr blue & multi. 30 22
93 " 25fr orange & multi. 45 35
94 " 35fr yel. grn. & multi. 85 60
95 " 40fr gray & multi. 1.00 80
Nos. 90-95 (6) 3.08 2.32

1971, July 19 Photo. ***Perf. 13***

Flowers: 3fr, Dogbane (horiz.). 20fr, Frangipani.

Size: 22x36, 36x22mm.

96 A25 1fr vermilion & green 15 15
97 " 3fr yellow, green & red 25 20
98 " 20fr verm. & green 70 45
Nos. 96-98, C37-C38 (5) 3.80 2.30

Lithograph Cone

A26

Sea Shells: 10fr, Pacific lettered cone. 20fr, Aulicus cone. 35fr, Polita nerita. 60fr, Snake-head cowrie.

1971, Oct. 4

99 A26 5fr lt. ultra. & multi. 20 15
100 " 10fr multicolored 25 20
101 " 20fr violet & multi. 35 30
102 " 35fr lt. blue & multi. 60 45
103 " 60fr lt. vio. & multi. 80 80
Nos. 99-103 (5) 2.20 1.90

De Gaulle Issue
Common Design Type

Designs: 20fr, Gen. de Gaulle, 1940. 35fr, Pres. de Gaulle, 1970.

104 CD134 20fr dk. car. & blk. 50 25
105 " 35fr " " " 70 55

First anniversary of the death of Charles de Gaulle (1890–1970), president of France.

Louis Pasteur, Slides, Microscope
A27

1972, Aug. 2
106 A27 65fr indigo, orange, & olive brn. 1.00 75

Sesquicentennial of the birth of Louis Pasteur (1822–1895), chemist.

Type of Air Post Issue 1971

Designs: 10fr, View of Goulaivoini. 20fr, Bay, Mitsamiouli. 35fr, Gate and fountain, Foumbouni. 50fr, View of Moroni.

1973, June 28 Photo. ***Perf. 13***
107 AP10 10fr blue & multi. 25 20
108 " 20fr grn. & multi. 40 35
109 " 35fr blue & multi. 70 65
110 " 50fr " " 85 75
Nos. 107–110, C53 (5) 4.45 3.55

Bank of Madagascar and Comoros
A28

Buildings in Moroni: 15fr, Post and Telecommunications Administration. 20fr, Prefecture.

1973, July 10 Photo. ***Perf. 13x12½***
111 A28 5fr multicolored 12 10
112 " 15fr " 22 20
113 " 20fr " 40 35

Salimata Hamissi Mosque
A29

Design: 20fr, Zaouiyat Chaduli Mosque (vert.).

Perf. 12½x13, 13x12½
1973, Oct. 20 Photogravure
114 A29 20fr multicolored 35 30
115 " 35fr " 65 60

Cheikh Mausoleum
A30

Design: 50fr, Mausoleum of President Said Mohamed Cheikh (different view).

1974, Mar. 16 Engraved ***Perf. 13***
116 A30 35fr green, olive brown & blk. 55 45
117 " 50fr green, olive brown & blk. 75 65

Koran Stand, Anjouan
A31

Designs: 15fr, Carved combs (vert.). 20fr, 3-legged table (vert.). 75fr, Sugar press.

1974, May 10 Photo. ***Perf. 12½x13***
118 A31 15fr emerald & multi. 25 20
119 " 20fr green & multi. 35 25
120 " 35fr multicolored 50 40
121 " 75fr " 90 75

UPU Emblem, Symbolic Postmark
A32

1974, Oct. 9 Engr. ***Perf. 13x12½***
122 A32 30fr multicolored 40 38

Centenary of Universal Postal Union.

Bracelet
A33

Designs: 35fr, Diadem. 120fr, Saber. 135fr, Dagger.

1975, Feb. 28 Engr. ***Perf. 13***
123 A33 20fr multicolored 35 30
124 " 35fr green & multi. 55 50
125 " 120fr blue & multi. 1.75 1.50
126 " 135fr multicolored 1.85 1.65

Mohani Village, Moheli—A34

Designs: 50fr, Djoezi Village, Moheli. 55fr, Chirazi tombs.

1975, May 26 Photo. ***Perf. 13***
127 A34 30fr vio. bl. & multi. 30 20
128 " 50fr Prus. bl. & multi. 55 40
129 " 55fr green & multi. 60 65

Skin Diver Photographing Coelacanth—A35

1975, June 27 Engr. ***Perf. 13***
130 A35 50fr multicolored 80 60

1975 coelacanth expedition.

State of Comoro

AREA—712 sq. mi.

POP.—216,587 (census 1966).

In 1978 the islands' name became the Federal and Islamic Republic of the Comoros.

Issues of 1971–75 Surcharged and Overprinted with Bars and: "ETAT COMORIEN" in Black, Silver or Red.

Tambourine Player—A36

Design: No. 153, Women dancers and tambourine players.

Printing & Perforations as Before.
A36: Photo., ***Perf. 13***

1975

Multicolored

131 A25 5fr on 1fr 6 6
132 " 5fr on 3fr 6 6
133 A17 10fr on 2fr *45* *45*
134 A28 15fr on 20fr (R) 20 15
135 A29 15fr on 20fr (S) 20 15
136 A33 15fr on 20fr 20 15
137 A31 20fr 28 20
138 A29 25fr on 35fr 35 30
139 A34 30fr 40 35
140 A30 30fr on 35fr 40 35
141 A31 30fr on 35fr 40 35
142 A33 30fr on 35fr 40 35
143 AP10 35fr 45 40
144 SP2 35fr on 35fr+10fr 45 40
145 A24 40fr 55 45
146 A34 50fr 70 60
147 A35 50fr 70 60
148 A34 50fr on 55fr (S) 70 60
149 A31 75fr 1.10 90
150 A26 75fr on 60fr (S) 1.10 90
151 A33 100fr on 120fr 1.40 1.20
152 A36 100fr blue & multi. 1.40 1.20
153 " 100fr on 150fr (S) 1.40 1.20
154 A33 200fr on 135fr 2.80 2.25
155 A32 500fr on 30fr 7.00 6.00
Nos. 131–155 (25) 23.15 19.62

Nos. 152–153 exist without overprint or surcharge. No. 155 exists with red surcharge.

Certain unlisted issues of Comoro Islands, starting in 1975, are mentioned and briefly described in "For the Record" at the back of this volume.

Comoro Flag, Map and Government Buildings
A37

1976, Nov. 18 Litho. ***Perf. 13½***
156 A37 30fr multicolored 25 15
157 " 50fr " 40 25

1st anniversary of independence.

Comoro Flag, UN Headquarters and Emblem
A38

1976, Nov. 25
158 A38 40fr multicolored 30 20
159 " 50fr " 40 25

1st anniversary of United Nations membership.

SEMI-POSTAL STAMPS
Anti-Malaria Issue
Common Design Type
Perf. 12½x12

1962, Apr. 7 Engraved **Unwmkd.**
B1 CD108 25fr+5fr brt. pink 1.75 1.75

Issued for the World Health Organization drive to eradicate malaria.

Nurse Feeding Infant
SP1

Mother and Child
SP2

1967, July 3 Engraved ***Perf. 13***
B2 SP1 25fr+5fr red, bright green & choc. 90 90

For the Red Cross.

1974, Aug. 10 Engraved ***Perf. 13***
B3 SP2 35fr+10fr red & dark brown 45 45

For the Red Cross.

AIR POST STAMPS.

Comoro Village—AP1

Comoro Men and Moroni Mosque AP2

Design: 200fr, Mosque of Ouani, Anjouan.

Engraved

1950–54 ***Perf. 13*** **Unwmkd.**

C1 AP1 50fr green & red brown 1.50 70
C2 AP2 100fr dk. brn. & red 2.50 70
C3 AP1 200fr dark green, rose brown & purple ('54) 10.00 5.00

Liberation Issue

Common Design Type

1954, June 6

C4 CD102 15fr sepia & red 12.00 10.00

10th anniversary of the liberation of France.

Madrepora Fructicosa AP3

Design: 100fr, Coral, shells and sea anemones.

Photogravure

1962, Jan. 13 ***Perf. 12½x13***

C5 AP3 100fr multicolored 3.00 3.00
C6 " 500fr multicolored 12.50 11.00

Telstar Issue

Common Design Type

1962, Dec. 5 Engraved ***Perf. 13***

C7 CD111 25fr dp. violet, dull purple & red lilac 2.75 1.50

Type of Regular Issue, 1963.

Designs: 65fr, Baskets. 200fr, Pendant.

Engraved

1963, Dec. 27 ***Perf. 13*** **Unwmkd.**

Size: 26½x48mm.

C8 A13 65fr carmine, green & ocher 2.00 1.20
C9 " 200fr greenish blue, rose lake & red 4.00 2.50

Boat Type of Regular Issue

Designs: 50fr, Mayotte pirogue. 85fr, Schooner.

1964, Aug. 7 Photo. ***Perf. 13***

Size: 27x48mm.

C10 A14 50fr multicolored 1.50 60
C11 " 85fr " 2.25 1.35

Olympic Torch and Boxers AP4 — Order of Star of Grand Comoro AP5

1964, Oct. 10 Engraved ***Perf. 13***

C12 AP4 100fr red brn., dark brn. & gray green 2.50 2.50

18th Olympic Games, Tokyo, Oct. 10–25.

1964, Dec. 10 Photo. ***Perf. 13***

C13 AP5 500fr crimson, blk., emerald & gold 10.00 6.50

ITU Issue

Common Design Type

1965, May 17 Engraved ***Perf. 13***

C14 CD120 50fr gray, greenish blue & olive 8.50 6.50

International Telecommunication Union centenary.

French Satellite A-1 Issue

Common Design Type

Designs: 25fr, Diamant rocket and launching installations. 30fr, A-1 satellite.

1966, Jan. 17 Engraved ***Perf. 13***

C15 CD121 25fr dark. purple & ultra. 2.00 2.00
C16 " 30fr dark purple & ultra. 2.50 2.50
a. Strip of 2 + label 5.00 5.00

Issued to commemorate the launching of France's first satellite, Nov. 26, 1965. No. C16a contains one each of Nos. C15–C16 and dark purple label with commemorative inscription. Each sheet contains 16 triptychs (2x8).

French Satellite D-1 Issue

Common Design Type

1966, May 16 Engraved ***Perf. 13***

C17 CD122 30fr dark green, org. & brn. 1.75 1.20

Old Gun Battery, Dzaoudzi AP6

Design: 200fr, Ksar Castle, Mutsamudu (vert.).

1966, Dec. 19 Photo. ***Perf. 13***

C18 AP6 50fr multicolored 1.00 85
C19 " 200fr " 3.50 2.00

Bird Type of Regular Issue

Birds: 75fr, Madagascar paradise flycatchers. 100fr, Blue-cheeked bee eaters.

1967, June 20 Photo. ***Perf. 13***

Size: 27x48mm.

C20 A17 75fr yellow green & multicolored 1.75 65
C21 " 100fr lt. bl. & multi. 2.10 85

Woman Skier AP7

1968, Apr. 29 Engraved ***Perf. 13***

C22 AP7 70fr brt. grn., lt. bl. & chocolate 1.20 75

Issued to commemorate the 10th Winter Olympic Games, Grenoble, France, Feb. 6–18, 1968.

Fish Type of Regular Issue

Designs: 50fr, Moorish idol. 90fr, Diagramma lineatus.

1968, Aug. 1 Engraved ***Perf. 13***

Size: 47½x27mm.

C23 A19 50fr plum, black & yellow 1.00 90
C24 " 90fr brt. green, yel. & gray green 1.75 1.35

Swimmer, Butterfly Stroke AP8

1969, Jan. 27 Photo. ***Perf. 12½***

C25 AP8 65fr verm., greenish bl. & black 1.35 1.00

Issued to commemorate the 19th Olympic Games, Mexico City, Oct. 12–27.

Flower Type of Regular Issue, 1969.

Designs: 50fr, Heliconia sp. (vert.). 85fr, Tuberose (vert.). 200fr, Orchid (angraecum eburneum; vert.).

1969, Mar. 20 Photo. ***Perf. 13***

Size: 27x48mm.

C26 A21 50fr gray & multi. 1.00 75
C27 " 85fr multicolored 1.50 1.00
C28 " 200fr dk. red & multi. 2.75 2.10

Concorde Issue

Common Design Type

1969, Apr. 17 Engraved

C29 CD129 100fr purple & brn. org. 7.50 6.00

View of EXPO, Globe and Moon AP9

Design: 90fr, Geisha, map of Japan and EXPO emblem.

1970, Sept. 13 Photo. ***Perf. 13***

C30 AP9 60fr slate & multi. 1.20 75
C31 " 90fr multicolored 1.20 75

EXPO '70 International Exposition, Osaka, Japan, Mar. 15–Sept. 13.

Sunset over Mutsamudu AP10

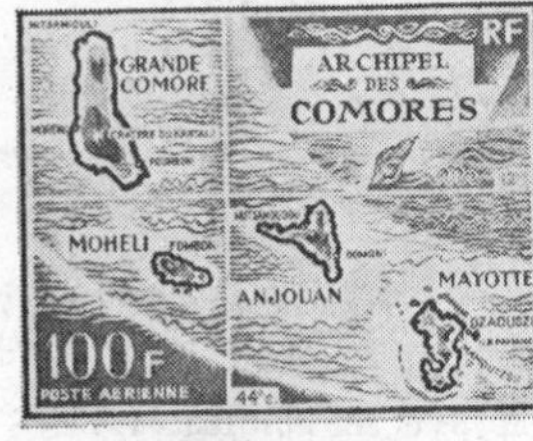

Map of Archipelago AP11

Designs: 20fr, Sada Village, Mayotte. 65fr, Old Iconi Palace, Grand Comoro. 85fr, Nioumatchoua Island, Moheli.

1971, May 3 Photo. ***Perf. 13***

C32 AP10 15fr dk. bl. & multi. 25 10
C33 " 20fr multicolored 45 25
C34 " 65fr green & multi. 90 45
C35 " 85fr blue & multi. 1.10 60

Engraved

C36 AP11 100fr brn. red, green & vio. bl. 2.00 1.00
Nos. C32–C36 (5) 4.70 2.40

See Nos. 107–110, C45–C49, C53, C62–C64.

Flower Type of Regular Issue

Flowers: 60fr, Hibiscus schizopetalus. 85fr, Acalypha sanderii.

1971, July 19 Photo. ***Perf. 13***

Size: 27x48mm.

C37 A25 60fr green, vermilion & yellow 1.20 60
C38 " 85fr green, red & yellow 1.50 90

Mural, Moroni Airport—AP12

Designs: 85fr, Mural in Arrival Hall, Moroni Airport. 100fr, View of Moroni Airport.

1972, Mar. 30 Photo. ***Perf. 13***

C39 AP12 65fr gray & multi. 60 50
C40 " 85fr " " 90 50

Engraved

C41 AP12 100fr brn., blue & slate grn. 1.50 75

New airport in Moroni.

Eiffel Tower and Moroni Telephone Exchange—AP13

Design: 75fr, Frenchman and Comoro Islander talking on telephone, radio tower and beacons.

1972, Apr. 24

C42 AP13 35fr dull red & gray 35 20

C43 AP13 75fr dk. car., violet & blue 70 35

First radio-telephone connection between France and Comoro Islands.

Underwater Spear-fishing—AP14

1972, July 5 Engraved *Perf. 13*

C44 AP14 70fr violet blue,brt. grn. & marn. 1.10 80

Types of 1971

1972, Nov. 15 Photogravure

Designs: 20fr, Cape Sima. 35fr, Bambao Palace. 40fr, Domoni Palace. 60fr, Gomajou Peninsula. 100fr, Map of Anjouan Island.

C45 AP10 20fr brn. & multi. 25 20
C46 " 35fr dark green & multi. 45 35
C47 " 40fr blue & multi. 55 40
C48 " 60fr greenish blk. & multi. 75 60

Engraved

C49 AP11 100fr maroon, bl. & slate grn. 1.50 1.00
Nos. C45-C49 (5) 3.50 2.55

Pres. Said Mohamed Cheikh AP15

1973, Mar. 16 Photo. *Perf. 13*

C50 AP15 20fr multicolored 30 25
C51 " 35fr " 50 25

President Said Mohamed Cheikh (1904–1970).

No. C24 Surcharged

120F

Mission Internationale pour l'étude du Cœlacanthe

1973, Apr. 30 Engraved *Perf. 13*

C52 A19 120fr on 90fr multi. 1.65 1.25

International Commission for Coelacanth Studies.

Map of Grand Comoro AP16

1973, June 28 Engr. *Perf. 13*

C53 AP16 135fr violet, blue & dk. brown 2.25 1.60

See Nos. C65, C68.

Karthala Volcano AP17

1973, July 16 Photo. *Perf. 13x12½*

C54 AP17 120fr multicolored 1.65 1.25

Eruption of Karthala, Sept. 1972.

Armauer G. Hansen AP18

Design: 150fr, Nicolaus Copernicus.

1973, Sept. 5 Engr. *Perf. 13*

C55 AP18 100fr brn., dk. bl. & slate green 1.65 1.25
C56 " 150fr greenish blue violet blue & chocolate 2.25 1.50

Centenary of the discovery of the Hansen bacillus, the cause of leprosy (100fr).

500th anniversary of the birth of Nicolaus Copernicus (1473–1543), Polish astronomer (150fr).

Pablo Picasso AP19

1973, Sept. 30 Photogravure

C57 AP19 200fr blk. & multi. 2.75 2.00

Souvenir Sheet

C58 AP19 100fr blk. & multi. 1.75 1.75

Pablo Picasso (1881–1973), painter. No. C58 contains one stamp; reddish brown marginal inscription. Size: 100x130mm.

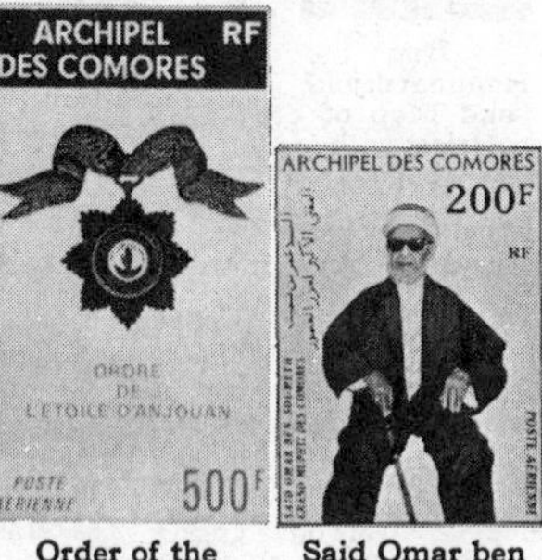

Order of the Star of Anjou AP20

Said Omar ben Soumeth AP21

1974, Jan. 7 Photo. *Perf. 13*

C59 AP20 500fr brown, blue & gold 6.00 5.00

Perf. 13x13½, 13½x13

1974, Jan. 31

Design: 135fr, Grand Mufti Said Omar (horiz.).

C60 AP21 135fr blk. & multi. 1.60 1.35
C61 " 200fr " " 2.75 1.90

Types of 1971–73

1974, Aug. 31 Photo. *Perf. 13*

Designs (Views on Mayotte): 20fr, Moya Beach. 35fr, Chiconi. 90fr, Port Mamutzu. 120fr, Map of Mayotte.

C62 AP10 20fr blue & multi. 30 20
C63 " 35fr grn. & multi. 50 40
C64 " 90fr multicolored 1.20 1.00

Engraved

C65 AP16 120fr ultra. & grn. 1.50 1.20

Jet Take-off—AP22

1975, Jan. 10 Engraved *Perf. 13*

C66 AP22 135fr multicolored 1.75 1.35

First direct route Moroni-Hahaya-Paris.

Rotary Emblem, Meeting House, Map—AP23

1975, Feb. 23 Photo. *Perf. 13*

C67 AP23 250fr multi. 3.25 2.50

Rotary International, 70th anniversary, and Moroni Rotary Club, 10th anniversary.

Map Type of 1973

Design: 230fr, Map of Moheli (horiz.).

1975, May 26 Engr. *Perf. 13*

C68 AP16 230fr ocher, olive grn. & bl. 3.25 2.50

State of Comoro

Issues of 1968–75 Surcharged and Overprinted with Bars and: "ETAT COMORIEN" in Black, Silver, Red or Orange.

Printing and Perforations as Before.

1975

Multicolored

C69 AP10 10fr on 20fr # C62 12 8
C70 AP15 20fr (S) 28 18
C71 AP10 30fr on 35fr (R) # C63 40 30
C72 AP15 35fr (S) 45 35
C73 AP10 40fr (O) 55 38
C74 A19 50fr 70 45
C75 A25 75fr on 60fr 1.10 70
C76 AP10 75fr on 60fr 1.10 70
C77 " 75fr on 65fr (O) 1.10 70
C78 AP14 75fr on 70fr 1.10 70
C79 AP11 100fr # C36 1.40 90
C80 " 100fr # C49 1.40 90
C81 AP18 100fr 1.40 90
C82 AP10 100fr on 85fr (O) 1.40 90
C83 A25 100fr on 85fr 1.40 90
C84 AP10 100fr on 90fr 1.40 90
C85 AP21 100fr on 135fr (S) 1.40 90
C86 AP22 100fr on 135fr 1.40 90
C87 AP19 200fr (S) 2.80 1.85
C88 AP21 200fr (S) 2.80 1.85
C89 AP17 200fr on 120fr 2.80 1.85
C90 AP16 200fr on 120fr 2.80 1.85
C91 " 200fr on 135fr 2.80 1.85
C92 " 200fr on 230fr 2.80 1.85
C93 AP18 400fr on 150fr 5.60 3.75
C94 AP23 400fr on 250fr 5.60 3.75
C95 AP20 500fr 7.00 4.75
Nos. C69-C95 (27) 53.10 35.09

No. C93 exists with red surcharge.

POSTAGE DUE STAMPS

Anjouan Mosque D1

Coelacanth D2

Engraved.

1950 *Perf. 14x13.* Unwmkd.

J1 D1 50c deep green 20 20
J2 " 1fr black brown 20 20

1954

J3 D2 5fr dark brown & green 15 15
J4 " 10fr gray & red brown 30 30
J5 " 20fr indigo & blue 45 45

Hibiscus D3

Designs: 2fr, 15fr, 40fr, 50fr, vertical.

1977, Nov. 19 Litho. *Perf. 13½*

Multicolored

J6 D3 1fr *shown* 3 3
J7 " 2fr *Pineapple* 3 3
J8 " 5fr *White butterfly* 6 6
J9 " 10fr *Chameleon* 10 6
J10 " 15fr *Blooming banana* 12 8
J11 " 20fr *Orchids* 15 10
J12 " 30fr *Allamanda cathartica* 25 15
J13 " 40fr *Cashews* 35 20
J14 " 50fr *Custard apple* 40 20
J15 " 100fr *Breadfruit* 80 40
J16 " 200fr *Vanilla* 1.60 80
J17 " 500fr *Ylang ylang* 4.00 2.00
Nos. J6-J17 (12) 7.89 4.11

CONGO
DEMOCRATIC REPUBLIC

(kŏng′ gō)

LOCATION — Central Africa.
GOVT.—Republic.
AREA—895,348 sq. mi. (estimated).
POP.—22,480,000 (est. 1971).
CAPITAL—Kinshasa (Leopoldville).

Congo was an independent state, founded by Leopold II of Belgium, until 1908 when it was annexed to Belgium as a colony. Congo became an independent republic in 1960. The name was changed to Republic of Zaire, Oct. 28, 1971. See Zaire in Vol. IV for later issues.

100 Centimes = 1 Franc
100 Sengi = 1 Li-Kuta,
100 Ma-Kuta = 1 Zaire (1967)

Belgian Congo Flower Issue of 1952–53 Overprinted or Surcharged **CONGO**

1960, June 6 Photo. *Perf. 11½*
Flowers in Natural Colors
Size: 21x25½mm.
Granite Paper

323 A86 10c deep plum & ochre 6 6
324 " 10c on 15c red & yel. green 10 10
a. "Congo" ovpt. omitted 10.00 10.00
325 A86 20c grn. & gray 6 6
326 " 40c green & salmon 6 5
327 " 50c on 60c blue green & pink 10 10
328 " 50c on 75c deep plum & gray 10 10
329 " 1fr car. & yel. 6 5
330 " 1.50fr violet & applegrn. 8 5
331 " 2fr olive green & buff 12 6
332 " 3fr olive green & pink 20 8
333 " 4fr chocolate & lilac 25 20
334 " 5fr deep plum & light blue grn. 25 10
335 " 6.50fr dark car. & lilac 35 10
336 " 8fr green & lt. yel. 50 20
337 " 10fr deep plum & pale olive 70 20
338 " 20fr violet blue & dull salmon 1.50 55

Overprinted **CONGO**

Size: 22x32mm.

339 A86 50fr deep plum & gray blue 8.00 3.75
340 " 100fr green & buff 13.00 6.50
Nos. 323–340 (18) 25.49 12.31

Belgian Congo Animal Issue, Nos. 306–317, Overprinted or Surcharged in Red, Blue, Black or Brown **CONGO**

341 A92 10c blue & brown (R) 6 6
342 A93 20c red orange & slate (Bl) 6 6
343 A92 40c brn. & blue (Bk) 6 6
344 A93 50c bright ultra-marine, red & sepia (R) 5 5
345 A92 1fr brown, green & black (Br) 6 5
346 A93 1.50fr black & orange yellow (R) 8 6
347 A92 2fr crimson, black & brown (Bl) 10 5
348 A93 3.50fr on 3fr black, gray & lilac rose (Bk) 18 7
349 A92 5fr brown, dk. brn. & bright green (Br) 25 10
350 A93 6.50fr blue, brown & orange yellow (R) 28 10
351 A92 8fr orange brown, olive bistre & lilac (Br) 32 25
352 A93 10fr multi. (R) 45 20
Nos. 341–352 (12) 1.95 1.11

Same Overprint on Belgian Congo No. 318.

1960

353 A94 50c golden brown, ochre & red brown 60 60

Same Overprint and Surcharge of New Value on Belgian Congo Nos. 321–322.

Inscription in French

354 A95 3.50fr on 3fr gray & red 50 50

Inscription in Flemish

355 A95 3.50fr on 3fr gray & red 50 50

Map of Congo
A93a

1960 Photogravure *Perf. 11½*

356 A93a 20c brown 8 5
357 " 50c rose red 8 3
358 " 1fr green 8 6
359 " 1.50fr red brown 12 5
360 " 2fr rose carmine 15 5
361 " 3.50fr lilac 17 8
362 " 5fr bright blue 23 12
363 " 6.50fr gray 30 15
364 " 10fr orange 50 30
365 " 20fr ultramarine 75 45
Nos. 356–365 (10) 2.46 1.34

Issued to commemorate Congo's Independence.

Flag, People and Broken Chain
A94

1961 *Perf. 11½* Unwmkd.
Flag in Blue and Yellow

366 A94 2fr rose violet 12 6
367 " 3.50fr vermilion 15 12
368 " 6.50fr yellow brown 30 15
369 " 10fr bright green 45 25
370 " 20fr carmine rose 75 55
Nos. 366–370 (5) 1.77 1.13

Issued to commemorate the signing of the Independence Agreement by Belgium, Jan. 4, 1959.

Nos. 356–365 Overprinted in Blue, Black or Red: "Conference Coquilhatville Avril Mai 1961"

1961

371 A93a 20c brown (Bl) 50 50
372 " 50c rose red (Bk) 50 50
373 " 1fr green (R) 50 50
374 " 1.50fr red brn. (Bl) 50 50
375 " 2fr rose car. (Bk) 50 50
376 " 3.50fr lilac (Bl) 50 50
377 " 5fr brt. blue (R) 50 50
378 " 6.50fr gray (R) 50 50
379 " 10fr orange (Bk) 50 50
380 " 20fr ultra. (R) 50 50
Nos. 371–380 (10) 5.00 5.00

Issued to commemorate the Coquilhatville Conference April–May, 1961.

Pres. Joseph Kasavubu
A95

Kasavubu and Map of Congo
A96

Design: 10fr, 20fr, 50fr, 100fr, Kasavubu in uniform and map.

Photogravure

1961, June 30 *Perf. 11½* Unwmkd.
Portrait and Inscription in Dark Brown

381 A95 10c yellow 8 8
382 " 20c deep rose 8 8
383 " 40c blue green 8 8
384 " 50c salmon 8 8
385 " 1fr lilac 12 8
386 " 1.50fr lt. brown 15 8
387 " 2fr bright green 15 8
388 A96 3.50fr rose pink 20 8
389 " 5fr gray 1.60 20
390 " 6.50fr ultramarine 45 8
391 " 8fr olive 50 18
392 A95 10fr lt. violet 1.20 18
393 " 20fr orange 1.20 20
394 " 50fr lt. blue 2.00 50
395 " 100fr apple green 3.00 75
Nos. 381–395 (15) 10.89 2.73

First anniversary of independence.

Nos. 381–387, 389 and 392 Overprinted: "REOUVERTURE du PARLEMENT JUILLET 1961"

1961

Portrait and Inscription in Dark Brown

396 A95 10c yellow 12 8
397 " 20c deep rose 12 8
398 " 40c blue green 12 8
399 " 50c salmon 50 35
400 " 1fr lilac 50 35
401 " 1.50fr lt. brown 1.35 1.20
402 " 2fr bright green 1.35 1.20
403 A96 5fr gray 1.35 1.20
404 A95 10fr lt. violet 1.50 1.50
Nos. 396–404 (9) 6.91 6.04

Issued to commemorate the re-opening of the Congolese parliament, July, 1961.

Dag Hammarskjold and Map of Africa with Congo
A97

Malaria Eradication Emblem and Mosquito
A98

1962, Jan. 20 Photo. *Perf. 11½*
Gray Background

405 A97 10c dark brown 5 5
406 " 20c Prussian blue 5 5
407 " 30c brown 7 7
408 " 40c dark blue 7 7
409 " 50c brown red 10 10
410 " 3fr olive green 2.85 1.90
411 " 6.50fr dark violet 85 55
412 " 8fr red brown 95 70
Nos. 405–412 (8) 4.99 3.49

Souvenir Sheets
Imperf.

413 A97 25fr black brown 4.50 4.50
a. Ovpt. in grn. 1.65 1.65

Nos. 405–413 issued in memory of Dag Hammarskjold, Secretary General of the United Nations, 1953–61.

No. 413 contains one stamp and has gold marginal inscription. Size: 65x90mm.

No 413a is overprinted "30 Juin 1962" on stamp and "2eme Anniversaire de l'Independance" on sheet margin. Issued June 30, 1962.

1962, June 15 Granite Paper

414 A98 1.50fr yellow, black & dark red 8 8
415 " 2fr yel. grn., brn. & blue green 50 23
416 " 6.50fr ultra., black & maroon 23 18

Issued for the World Health Organization drive to eradicate malaria.

Nos. 405–412 Overprinted in Blue, Purple, Black or Carmine "Paix, Travail, Austerite...., C. ADOULA 11 juillet 1962"

1962, Oct. 15
Gray Background

417 A97 10c dk. brn. (Bl) 7 3
418 " 20c Prus. blue (P) 7 3
419 " 30c brown (Bk) 7 3
420 " 40c dk. blue (C) 7 3
421 " 50c brn. red (Bl) 1.85 85
422 " 3fr olive grn. (P) 25 7
423 " 6.50fr dk. violet (Bk) 35 15
424 " 8fr red brown (C) 50 23
Nos. 417–424 (8) 3.23 1.42

Reorganization of Adoula administration.

Canceled to Order

Starting in 1963, prices in the used column are for "canceled to order" stamps. Postally used copies sell for much more.

A99

1963, Jan. 28 Engr. *Perf. 10½x13*

425 A99 2fr dull purple 1.50 1.65
426 " 4fr red 12 10
427 " 7fr dark blue 18 12
428 " 20fr slate green 35 25

Issued to commemorate Congo's first participation at the U.P.U. Congress, New Delhi, March, 1963.

Shoebill
A100

Birds: 10c, Pelicans. 20c, Crested guinea fowl (horiz.). 30c, Openbill. 40c, White-bellied storks (horiz.). 2fr, Marabou. 3fr, Greater flamingos (horiz.). 4fr, Congolese peacock. 5fr, Hartlaub ducks (horiz.). 6fr, Secretary bird. 7fr, Black-casqued hornbill (horiz.). 8fr, Sacred ibis and nest. 10fr, Crowned crane (horiz.). 20fr, Saddle-bill stork (horiz.).

Photogravure

1963 *Perf. 11½* Unwmkd.

429 A100 10c pink, ultra. & ocher 5 3
430 " 20c rose red, blue & black 5 3
431 " 30c grn., ocher & blk. 5 3

No.	Type	Description	Unused	Used
432	A100	40c gray, orge. & blk.	5	3
433	"	1fr brn., emerald & gray	5	3
434	"	2fr gray, red & indigo	1.85	60
435	"	3fr olive green, black & rose	8	5
436	"	4fr carm. rose, vio. blue & green	8	5
437	"	5fr lake, light blue & black	12	5
438	"	6fr pur., yel. & blk.	1.85	60
439	"	7fr bl. green, blk. & indigo	18	5
440	"	8fr yel., org. & blk.	20	5
441	"	10fr bl., blk. & rose	27	8
442	"	20fr citron, red & blk.	50	12
		Nos. 429-442 (14)	5.38	1.80

Cinchona Ledgeriana A101 — Red Cross Nurse A102

Designs: 10c, 30c, 5fr, Strophanthus sarmentosus.

Perf. 12½x13½, 13½x12½

1963, May 25 Engr. Unwmkd.

Cross in Red

No.	Type	Description	Unused	Used
443	A101	10c violet & dull green	5	5
444	"	20c magenta & blue	5	5
445	"	30c green & org.	5	5
446	"	40c blue & violet	6	6
447	"	5fr olive & rose claret	15	5
448	"	7fr orange & blk.	15	5
449	A102	9fr gray olive & red	20	8
450	"	20fr purple & red	2.00	1.10
		Nos. 443-450 (8)	2.71	1.49

International Red Cross centenary.

A souvenir sheet of three contains imperf. 5fr, 7fr, and 20fr stamps similar to Nos. 447, 448 and 450, but in changed colors. Marginal inscriptions in violet. Size: 109x75mm. Price $15.

Men Joining Hands and Map of Congo—A103

1963, June 29 Photo. *Perf. 11½*

No.	Type	Description	Unused	Used
451	A103	4fr multicolored	1.40	50
452	"	5fr "	12	5
453	"	9fr "	23	8
454	"	12fr "	33	15

Issued to celebrate national reconciliation.

Bulldozer and Kabambare Sewer, Leopoldville—A104

Designs: 30c, 5fr, 12fr, Excavator and blueprint. 50c, 9fr, Building Ituri road.

1963, July 1 Engraved Unwmkd.

No.	Type	Description	Unused	Used
455	A104	20c multicolored	3	3
456	"	30c "	3	3
457	"	50c "	3	3
458	A104	3fr multicolored	1.40	55
459	"	5fr "	12	5
460	"	9fr "	20	12
461	"	12fr "	27	18
		Nos. 455-461 (7)	2.08	99

Issued to publicize aid to Congo by the European Economic Community.

Leopoldville Airport N'Djili A105

Design: 5fr, 7fr, 50fr, Tail assembly and airport.

1963, Nov. 30 Photo. *Perf. 11½*

No.	Type	Description	Unused	Used
462	A105	2fr gray, yellow & red brown	5	4
463	"	5fr magenta, violet & yellow	8	8
464	"	6fr blue, yellow & dark brown	1.40	60
465	"	7fr multicolored	8	8
466	"	30fr lilac, yellow & olive	35	25
467	"	50fr multicolored	60	40
		Nos. 462-467 (6)	2.56	1.45

Issued to publicize Air Congo.

Nos. 425-428 Overprinted with Silver Frame on Three Sides and Black Inscription: "15e anniversaire/10 DECEMBRE 1948/DROITS DE L'HOMME/ 10 DECEMBRE 1963"

Engraved and Typographed

1963, Dec. 10 *Perf. 10½x13*

No.	Type	Description	Unused	Used
468	A99	2fr dull purple	6	6
469	"	4fr red	8	8
470	"	7fr dark blue	33	33
471	"	20fr slate green	35	35

15th anniversary of Universal Declaration of Human Rights.

Nos. 468-471 exist with side date panels transposed ("1963" at left, "1948" at right). Price, each $5.

Laboratory Technician and Atomic Emblem—A106

Designs: 1.50fr, 60fr, University. 8fr, 75fr, First African nuclear reactor. 25fr, 100fr, University and crest.

1964, Feb. 1 Photo. *Perf. 14x12½*

No.	Type	Description	Unused	Used
472	A106	50c multicolored	8	8
473	"	1.50fr "	8	8
474	"	8fr "	3.00	2.75
475	"	25fr "	30	23
476	"	30fr "	35	30
477	"	60fr "	60	50
478	"	75fr "	90	80
479	"	100fr "	1.15	1.00
		a. Souv. sheet of 3	4.00	4.00
		Nos. 472-479 (8)	6.46	5.74

10th anniversary of Lovanium University, Leopoldville.

No. 479a contains 3 imperf. multicolored stamps: 20fr, design as 50c; 30fr, as 8fr; 100fr. Size: 141x70mm.

Belgian Congo Issues of 1952-59 Overprinted "REPUBLIQUE DU CONGO" and Surcharged in Black on Overprinted Metallic Panels.

1964 *Perf. 11½*

No.	Type	Description	Unused	Used
480	A93	1fr on 20c red orange & slate (#307)	8	8
481	A86	2fr on 1.50fr multi. (#273)	1.60	1.40
482	A93	5fr on 6.50fr multi. (#315)	32	20
483	A86	8fr on 6.50fr multi. (#278)	40	25

Republic Issues of 1960-61 Surcharged in Black on Overprinted Metallic Rectangles or Ovals.

No.	Type	Description	Unused	Used
484	A86	1fr on 6.50fr multi. (#335)	8	8
485	A93	1fr on 20c red orange & slate (#342)	8	8
486	A86	2fr on 1.50fr multi. (#330)	8	8
487	A95	3fr on 20c deep rose & dk. brown (#382)	25	20
488	"	4fr on 40c blue grn. & dark brown (#383)	25	20
489	A93	5fr on 6.50fr multi. ("Congo" red) (#350)	33	20
		a. "Congo" black	33	20
490	A93a	6fr on 6.50fr gray (#363)	33	22
491	"	7fr on 20c brn. (#356)	38	25
		Nos. 480-491 (12)	4.18	3.24

Pole Vault A107

Sports: 7fr, 20fr, Javelin (vert.). 8fr, 100fr, Hurdling.

Photogravure

1964, July 13 *Perf. 11½* Unwmkd.

Granite Paper

No.	Type	Description	Unused	Used
492	A107	5fr gray, dk. brn. & carmine	6	5
493	"	7fr rose, violet & emerald	1.20	55
494	"	8fr orge. yel., red brn. & vio. bl.	10	5
495	"	10fr bl., vio. brn. & magenta	10	5
496	"	20fr gray grn., red brn. & verm.	25	10
497	"	100fr lilac, dark brn. & green	1.20	30
		a. Souv. sheet of 3	6.00	6.00
		Nos. 492-497 (6)	2.91	1.10

Issued to commemorate the 18th Olympic Games, Tokyo, Oct. 10-25. No. 497a contains 3 imperf. stamps (20fr orange & dark brown, pole vault; 30fr citron and dark brown, hurdling; 100fr dull green and dark brown, javelin). Dark brown marginal inscription and dull green Olympic rings. Size: 134x85mm. Sheet issued Sept. 10.

National Palace, Leopoldville A108

1964, Sept. 15 Granite Paper

No.	Type	Description	Unused	Used
498	A108	50c lilac rose & blue	3	3
499	"	1fr bl. & lilac rose	3	3
500	"	2fr brn. red & vio.	3	3
501	"	3fr emerald & red	4	3
502	"	4fr orge. & vio. bl.	4	3
503	"	5fr gray violet & emerald	4	3
504	"	6fr sepia & orge.	8	3
505	"	7fr gray olive & red brown	8	3
506	"	8fr rose red & violet blue	2.85	50
507	"	9fr violet blue & rose red	7	3
508	"	10fr brn. olive & grn.	10	3
509	"	20fr bl. & brn. orge.	15	3
510	"	30fr dark carmine rose & green	22	7
511	"	40fr ultra. & dark carmine rose	33	7
512	"	50fr brn. orge. & grn.	45	7
513	"	100fr slate & verm.	95	15
		Nos. 498-513 (16)	5.49	1.19

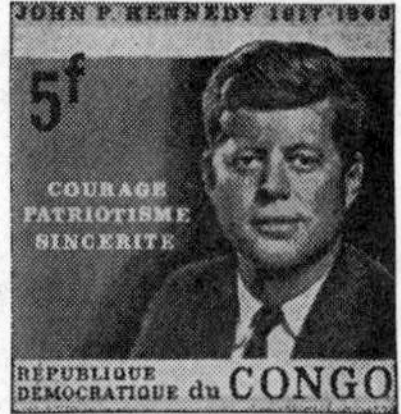

Pres. John F. Kennedy—A109

1964, Dec. 8 Photo. *Perf. 13½*

No.	Type	Description	Unused	Used
514	A109	5fr dk. bl. & black	8	3
515	"	6fr rose claret & black	8	3
516	"	9fr brown & black	10	3
517	"	30fr purple & black	42	7
518	"	40fr dull grn. & blk.	2.85	85
519	"	60fr red brn. & blk.	70	30
		Nos. 514-519 (6)	4.23	1.31

Souvenir Sheet

No.	Type	Description	Unused	Used
520	A109	150fr black & maroon	3.00	3.00

Issued in memory of Pres. John F. Kennedy (1917-63). No. 520 contains one stamp, black marginal inscription. Size: 64x76mm.

Rocket and Unisphere A110 — Basketball A111

Engraved and Typographed

1965, March 1 *Perf. 12* Unwmkd.

No.	Type	Description	Unused	Used
521	A110	50c lilac & black	4	3
522	"	1.50fr blue & lilac	4	3
523	"	2fr red brown & bright green	4	3
524	"	10fr bright green & dark red	1.00	60
525	"	18fr violet bl. & brn.	15	8
526	"	27fr rose red & grn.	33	12
527	"	40fr gray & orange	50	18
		Nos. 521-527 (7)	2.10	1.07

New York World's Fair, 1964-65.

1965, Apr. Photo. *Perf. 13½*

Designs: 6fr, 40fr, Soccer (horiz.). 15fr, 60fr, Volleyball.

No.	Type	Description	Unused	Used
528	A111	5fr black, greenish blue & ocher	4	3
529	"	6fr black, blue gray & crimson	8	5
530	"	15fr black, orange & yel. green	12	10
531	"	24fr black, rose lilac & bright grn.	30	10
532	"	40fr black, bright grn. & ultra.	1.75	60
533	"	60fr black, blue & red lilac	55	20
		Nos. 528-533 (6)	2.84	1.08

First African Games, Leopoldville, Mar. 31-Apr. 7, 1965.

Earth and Satellites A112

Designs: 9fr, 15fr, 20fr, 40fr, Satellites at left, globe at right.

Perf. 14x14½

1965, June 28 Photo. Unwmkd.

534 A112 6fr blk., sal. & vio. 8 3
535 " 9fr black, lt. green & gray 8 3
536 " 12fr orange, gray & black 10 7
537 " 15fr green, ultra. & black 13 7
538 " 18fr blk., lt. grn. & gray 1.50 42
539 " 20fr blk., sal. & vio. 22 8
540 " 30fr green, ultra. & black 33 10
541 " 40fr orange, gray & black 45 15
Nos. 534-541 (8) 2.89 95

Issued to commemorate the centenary of the International Telecommunication Union.

Congolese Paratrooper and Parachutes A113

1965, July 5 ***Perf. 13x14***

542 A113 5fr brt. blue & brn. 5 3
543 " 6fr orange & brown 5 3
544 " 7fr bl. grn. & brown 60 28
545 " 9fr brt. pink & brn. 10 8
546 " 18fr lemon & brown 18 10
Nos. 542-546 (5) 98 52

Fifth anniversary of independence.

Matadi Harbor and ICY Emblem

A114

Designs (ICY Emblem and): 8fr, 25fr, Katanga mines. 9fr, 60fr, Tshopo Dam, Stanleyville.

1965, Oct. 25 Photo. ***Perf. 13x14***

547 A114 6fr ultra., blk. & yel. 8 3
548 " 8fr orange red, black & blue 10 3
549 " 9fr blue green, black & brown orge. 10 3
550 " 12fr carmine rose, black & gray 1.15 45
551 " 25fr olive, black & rose red 27 12
552 " 60fr gray, blk. & orge. 55 15
Nos. 547-552 (6) 2.25 81

International Cooperation Year, 1965.

Soldiers Giving First Aid

A115

The Army Serving the Country: 7fr, Bridge building. 9fr, Feeding child. 19fr, Maintenance of telegraph lines. 20fr, House building. 30fr, Soldier and flag. (19fr, 20fr, 30fr, vertical.)

Perf. 12½x13, 13x12½

1965, Nov. 17

553 A115 5fr sal., brn. & red 8 3
554 " 7fr yellow & green 8 3
555 " 9fr olive & brown 10 3
556 " 19fr brt. grn. & brn. 90 55
557 " 20fr lt. blue & brn. 25 8
558 " 30fr multicolored 35 10
Nos. 553-558 (6) 1.76 82

See also Nos. 582-586.

Nos. 551-552 Overprinted with U.N. Emblem and "6e Journée Météorologique Mondiale / 23.3.66." on Metallic Strip

1966, Mar. 23 Photo. ***Perf. 13x14***

559 A114 25fr olive & black 90 55
560 " 60fr gray & black 90 80

6th World Meteorological Day.

Woman's Head and Goat

A116

Designs: 10fr, Sculptured heads. 12fr, Sitting figure and two heads (vert.). 53fr, Figure with earrings and kneeling woman with bowl (vert.).

Perf. 11½x13, 13x11½

1966, Apr. 23 Litho. Unwmkd.

561 A116 10fr red, blk. & gray 12 12
562 " 12fr grn., blk. & blue 15 15
563 " 15fr dp. blue, black & lilac 18 18
564 " 53fr dp. rose, black & vio. blue 1.50 1.25

Issued to commemorate the International Negro Arts Festival, Dakar, Senegal, Apr. 1-24.

Pres. Joseph Desiré Mobutu and Fishing Industry A117

Pres. Mobutu and: 4fr, Pyrethrum harvest. 6fr, Building industry. 8fr, Winnowing rice. 10fr, Cotton harvest. 12fr, Banana harvest. 15fr, Cacao harvest. 24fr, Pineapple harvest.

1966, May 1 Photo. ***Perf. 11½***

565 A117 2fr dark brown & dk. blue 6 6
566 " 4fr dk. brn. & org. 6 6
567 " 6fr dk. brn. & olive 95 85
568 " 8fr dk. brn. & brt. greenish blue 7 7
569 " 10fr dk. brown & brn. red 10 10
570 " 12fr dk. brn. & vio. 12 10
571 " 15fr dk. brown & lt. olive green 12 10
572 " 24fr dk. brown & lilac rose 30 20
Nos. 565-572 (8) 1.78 1.54

Souvenir Sheet

Design: Pres. Mobutu without cap, and men rolling up sleeves.

Perf. 11x11½

573 A117 Sheet of 4 1.25 1.25
a. 15fr red, blk. & ultra. 30 30

Issued to honor Lt. Gen. Joseph Desiré Mobutu, President of Congo, and to publicize the "Back to Work" campaign. No. 573 contains four stamps and flag of Congo in margin. Size: 127x94½mm.

Nos. 510-513 Overprinted

1966, June 13 ***Perf. 11½***

574 A108 30fr dark carmine rose & green 1.00 1.00
575 " 40fr ultra. & dark carmine rose 1.00 1.00
576 " 50fr brn. org. & grn. 1.10 1.10
577 " 100fr slate & verm. 1.10 1.10

Issued to commemorate the inauguration of World Health Organization Headquarters, Geneva.

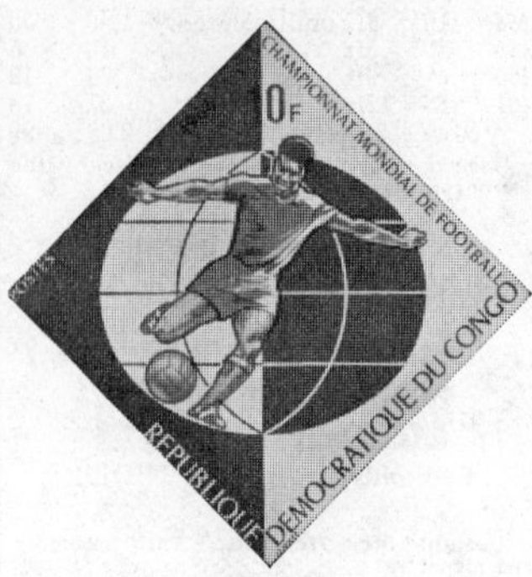

Soccer Player

A118

Designs: 30fr, Two soccer players. 50fr, Three soccer players. 60fr, Jules Rimet Cup, soccer ball and globe.

1966, July 25 Photo. ***Perf. 14***

578 A118 10fr ocher, violet & bright green 10 10
579 " 30fr brt. rose lilac, vio. & apple green 35 25
580 " 50fr apple grn., Prus. blue & tan 1.25 1.20
581 " 60fr brt. grn., dark brown & gold 65 55

Issued to commemorate the World Cup Soccer Championship, Wembley, England, July 11-30.

Army Type of 1965

The Army Serving the Country: 2fr, Soldiers giving first aid. 6fr, Feeding child. 10fr, House building (vert.). 18fr, Bridge building. 24fr, Soldier and flag (vert.).

1966, Aug. 8 ***Perf. 12½x13, 13x12½***

582 A115 2fr vermilion, indigo & red 5 3
583 " 6fr ultra. & red. brn. 8 8
584 " 10fr yel. grn. & red brown 60 55
585 " 18fr carm. rose & vio. 15 10
586 " 24fr multicolored 25 20
Nos. 582-586 (5) 1.13 96

Nos. 578-581 Overprinted in Black, Carmine or Green: "FINALE / ANGLETERRE-ALLEMAGNE / 4-2"

1966, Nov. 14 Photo. ***Perf. 14***

587 A118 10fr multi. (B or C) 22 22
588 " 30fr " (B or G) 60 60
589 " 50fr " (B or C) 95 90
590 " 60fr " (B or C) 1.25 1.00

Issued to commemorate England's victory in the World Soccer Cup Championship. The two colors of the overprint alternate in the sheets.

Souvenir Sheets

Pres. John F. Kennedy—A119

1966, Dec. 28 Engraved ***Perf. 13***

591 A119 150fr brown 4.25 4.25
592 " 150fr slate 4.25 4.25

Issued in memory of Pres. John F. Kennedy. No. 591 has slate green, No. 592 deep orange marginal design. Two imperf. sheets exist: 150fr brown with violet blue margin and 150fr slate with lilac margin. Size: 65x76mm. Price $4.25 each.

Nos. 498-503 Surcharged in Black, Red or Maroon

5 K

4e Sommet OUA
KINSHASA
du 11 au 14 - 9 - 67

1967, Sept. 11 Photo. ***Perf. 11½***

593 A108 1k on 2fr brown red & violet 8 5
a. Inverted overprint 9.00
594 A108 3k on 5fr gray vio. & emerald 15 10
595 " 5k on 4fr orange & violet blue 25 18
596 " 6.60k on 1fr bl. & lilac rose (R) 33 25
a. Inverted overprint 6.50
597 A108 9.60k on 50c lilac rose & blue 55 40
a. Inverted overprint 6.50
598 A108 9.80k on 3fr emerald & red (M) 75 55
Nos. 593-598 (6) 2.11 1.53

Souvenir Sheet

Map of Africa, Torch—A120

599 A120 50k greenish blue, black & red 2.50 2.50

Issued to commemorate the 4th meeting of the Organization for African Unity, Kinshasa (Leopoldville), Sept. 9-11. No. 599 has black marginal inscription and design in black and red. Size: 76x90mm.

Souvenir Sheet

Horn Blower and EXPO Emblem

A121

1967, Sept. 28 Engr. ***Perf. 11½***

600 A121 50k dark brown 2.85 2.85

Issued to commemorate EXPO '67, International Exhibition, Montreal, Apr. 28-Oct. 27, 1967. No. 600 has ultramarine and orange marginal inscription. Size: 90x75mm.

Nos. 565-566 and 582 Overprinted: "NOUVELLE CONSTITUTION 1967" and Surcharged with New Value on Metallic Panel in Magenta or Brown.

Perf. 11½, 12½x13

1967, Oct. 9 Photogravure

601 A117 4k on 2fr dk. brown & dk. blue (M) 25 20
602 A115 5k on 2fr verm., indigo & red (B) 30 25
603 A117 21k on 4fr dk. brown & orange (M) 1.35 1.00

Issued to commemorate the promulgation of the Constitution, June 4, 1967.

Nos. 528 and 530 Surcharged with New Value and Overprinted: "Iere Jeux Congolais / 25/6 au 2/7/1967 / Kinshasa"

1967, Oct. 16 Photo. *Perf. 13½*

604 A111 1k on 5fr multi. 12 12
605 " 9.60k on 15fr " 75 75

Issued to commemorate the First Congolese Games, Kinshasa, June 25–July 2, 1967.

No. 465 Surcharged with New Value and Overprinted: "Ier VOL BAC / ONE ELEVEN / 14/5/67"

1967, Oct. 16 *Perf. 11½*

606 A105 9.60k on 7fr multi. 1.00 25

Issued to commemorate the first flight of the BAC 111 in the service of Air Congo, May 14, 1967.

Nos. 547 and 549 Surcharged in Red or Black: "JOURNEE MONDIALE / DE L'ENFANCE / 8-10-67"

1968, Feb. 10 Photo. *Perf. 13x14*

607 A114 1k on 6fr ultra., blk. & yellow (R) 10 10
608 " 9k on 9fr bl. green, blk. & brn orange (B) 60 60

Issued for International Children's Day. The surcharge is on a rectangle printed in metallic ink.

Nos. 498, 504 and 501 Surcharged in Blue or Red: "Année Internationale / du Tourisme 24-10-1967"

1968, Feb. 10 *Perf. 11½*

609 A108 5k on 50c lilac rose & blue (Bl) 27 27
610 " 10k on 6fr sepia & orange (R) 60 60
611 " 15k on 3fr emerald & red (R) 85 85

Issued for International Tourist Year. The surcharge is on a rectangle printed in metallic ink.

Nos. 500, 498 and 502 Surcharged in Black, Violet Blue or Gold

1968, July Photo. *Perf. 11½*

612 A108 1k on 2fr brown red & violet 7 7
613 " 2k on 50c lilac rose & blue (VBl) 15 15
614 " 2k on 50c lilac rose & bl. (G) 15 15
615 " 9.60k on 4fr orange & violet blue 60 60

The surcharge on No. 612 consists of a black rectangle and new denomination in upper right corner; the surcharge on No. 613 has a violet blue rectangle with denomination printed in white on it; on No. 614 the rectangle is gold and the denomination black; on No. 615 the rectangle is black and the denomination white.

No. 565 Surcharged in White on Black Rectangle.

1968, Oct. Photo. *Perf. 11½*

616 A117 10k on 2fr dk. brn. & dark blue 60 12

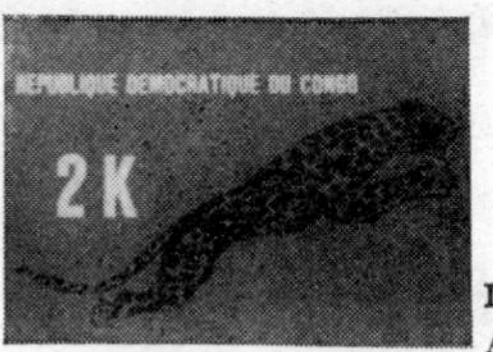

Leopard A122

1968, Nov. 5 Litho. *Perf. 10½*

617 A122 2k bright greenish blue & black 12 5
618 " 9.60k red & black 60 15

Mobutu Type of 1966 Surcharged

1968, Dec. 20 Photo. *Perf. 11½*

619 A117 15s on 2fr sepia & bright blue 3 3
620 " 1k on 6fr sepia & brown 3 3
621 " 3k on 10fr sepia & emerald 15 12
622 " 5k on 12fr sepia & orange 25 18
623 " 20k on 15fr sepia & bright green 1.00 75
624 " 50k on 24fr sepia & bright lilac 2.75 1.85
Nos. 619-624 (6) 4.21 2.96

Human Rights Flame A123

1968, Dec. 30 *Perf. 12½x13*

625 A123 2k light ultra. & bright green 12 4
626 " 9.60k green & deep carmine 55 35
627 " 10k brt. lilac & brn. 55 35
628 " 40k orange brown & purple 2.10 1.50

International Human Rights Year.

Type of 1968 Overprinted in Gold

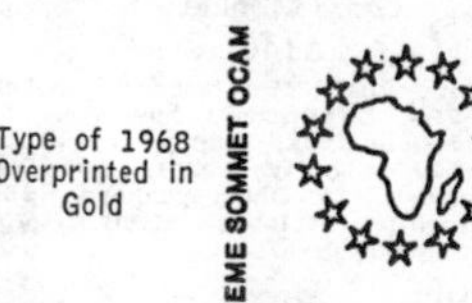

1969, Jan. 27 Photo. *Perf. 12½x13*

629 A123 2k apple green & red brown 12 6
630 " 9.60k rose & emerald 55 35
631 " 10k gray & ultra. 55 35
632 " 40k greenish blue & purple 2.10 1.50

Issued to publicize the 4th summit meeting of OCAM (Organisation Communitée Afrique et Malgache), Kinshasa, Jan. 27.

Kinshasa Fair Emblem and Cotton Boll—A124

Designs (Fair Emblem and): 6k, Copper. 9.60k, Coffee. 9.80k, Diamond. 11.60k, Oil palm fruits.

1969, May 2 Photo. *Perf. 12½x13*

633 A124 2k brt. pur., gold & red lilac 12 5
634 A124 6k green, gold & blue green 35 35
635 " 9.60k brown, gold & light brown 55 25
636 " 9.80k ultra. & gold 55 50
637 " 11.60k henna brown, gold & brn. 70 70
Nos. 633-637 (5) 2.27 1.85

Kinshasa Fair, Limete, June 30–July 21.

Fair Entrance, Emblem—A125

Designs (Fair Emblem and): 3k, Gecomin Mining Co. Pavilion. 10k, Administration Building. 25k, Pavilion of the Organization for African Unity.

1969, June 30 Photo. *Perf. 11½*

Granite Paper

638 A125 2k bright rose lilac & gold 15 12
639 " 3k blue & gold 18 15
640 " 10k light olive green & gold 50 40
641 " 25k copper red & gold 1.15 1.00

Kinshasa Fair, Limete, June 30–July 21.

Congo Arms A126

Pres. Mobutu A127

1969, July-Sept. Litho. *Perf. 14*

642 A126 10s orange & black 3 3
643 " 15s ultra. & black 3 3
644 " 30s brt. grn. & black 3 3
645 " 60s bright rose lilac & black 3 3
646 " 90s dp. bister & black 3 3

Perf. 13

647 A127 1k sky blue & multi. 3 3
648 " 2k orange & multi. 6 4
649 " 3k multicolored 9 6
650 " 5k brt. rose & multi. 15 13
651 " 6k ultra. & multi. 20 15
652 " 9.60k multicolored 35 20
653 " 10k lt. lilac & multi. 50 25
654 " 20k yellow & multi. 1.00 50
655 " 50k multicolored 2.50 1.20
656 " 100k fawn & multi. 4.50 2.25
Nos. 642-656 (15) 9.53 4.96

Well Driller, by Oscar Bonnevalle A128

Paintings: 4k, Preparation of cocoa, by Jean Van Noten. 8k, Dock workers, by Constantin Meunier. 10k, Poultry shop, by Henri Evenepoel. 15k, Steel industry, by Constantin Meunier.

Perf. 13x14, 14x13 (8k)

1969, Dec. 15 Lithographed

Size: 41x41mm.

657 A128 3k multicolored 20 17
658 " 4k " 25 20

Size: 28x41mm.

659 A128 8k multicolored 40 35

Size: 41x41mm.

660 A128 10k multicolored 55 50
661 " 15k " 1.00 75
Nos. 657-661 (5) 2.40 1.97

Issued to commemorate the 50th anniversary of the International Labor Organization.

Souvenir Sheet

Adoration of the Kings, by Rubens A129

1969, Dec. Engraved *Perf. 13*

662 A129 50k red lilac 2.50 2.50

Issued for Christmas 1969. No. 662 has blue and red lilac marginal inscription. Size: 85x85mm.

Pres. Mobutu, Map and Flag of Congo A130

1970, June 30 Litho. *Perf. 13½x13*

663 A130 10s multicolored 3 3
664 " 90s purple & multi. 3 3
665 " 1k brown & multi. 3 3
666 " 2k multicolored 9 5
667 " 7k " 38 23
668 " 10k " 55 35
669 " 20k " 1.10 75
Nos. 663-669 (7) 2.21 1.47

10th anniversary of independence.

Issues of 1964-1966 Surcharged 0,20 K

Perf. 11½, 12½x13, 13x12½

1970, Sept. 24 Photogravure

670 A108 10s on 1fr blue & lilac rose (#499) 8 6
671 " 20s on 2fr brn. red & violet (#500) 8 6
672 A117 20s on 2fr dk. brn. & dark blue (#565) 15 12
673 A108 30s on 3fr emerald & red (#501) 8 6
674 " 40s on 4fr orange & vio. blue (#502) 10 8
675 A117 40s on 4fr dk. brown & orange (#566) 15 12
676 A108 60s on 7fr gray olive & red brown (#505) 1.10 80
677 " 90s on 9fr vio. blue & rose red (#507) 1.10 80
668 A115 90s on 9fr olive & brown (#555) 15 12
679 " 1k on 7fr yellow & green (#554) 15 12
680 A108 1k on 6fr sepia & orange (#504) 15 12
681 A117 1k on 12fr dk. brown & vio. (#570) 1.10 80
682 " 2k on 24fr dk. brown & lilac rose (#572) 15 12

683 A115 2k on 24fr multi. (#586) 15 12
684 A108 3k on 30fr dk. car. rose & green (#510) 1.10 80
685 " 4k on 40fr ultra. & dk. carmine rose (#511) 15 12
686 " 5k on 50fr brn. org. & grn. (#512) 2.85 2.00
687 " 10k on 100fr slate & verm. (#513) 1.10 75
Nos. 670-687 (18) 9.89 7.17

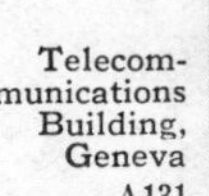
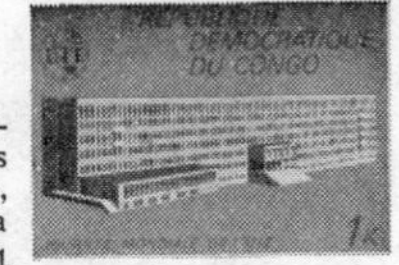

Telecommunications Building, Geneva
A131

Designs: 2k, 6.60k, U.P.U. Headquarters, Bern. 9.80k, 10k, 11k, U.N. Headquarters, New York.

1970, Oct. 24 Photo. *Perf. 11½*

688 A131 1k pink & green 5 3
689 " 2k orange & green 10 5
690 " 6.60k greenish blue & rose carmine 38 18
691 " 9.60k yel. & vio. blue 50 25
692 " 9.80k lt. ultra & brn. 55 25
693 " 10k lt. pur. & brn. 55 28
694 " 11k rose & brown 60 32
Nos. 688-694 (7) 2.73 1.36

Issued for International Telecommunications Day (1k, 9.60k); Inauguration of new Universal Postal Union Headquarters, Bern (2k, 6.60k); 25th anniversary of United Nations (9.80k, 10k, 11k).

Pres. Mobutu, Congolese Flag and Arch—A132

1970, Nov. 24 Litho. *Perf. 13*

695 A132 2k yellow & multi. 12 5
696 " 10k blue & multi. 60 28
697 " 20k red & multi. 1.25 50

Fifth anniversary of new government.

Apollo 11 in Flight
A133

Designs: 2k, Astronaut and spacecraft on moon. 7k, Pres. Mobutu decorating astronauts' wives. 10k, Pres. Mobutu with Neil A. Armstrong, Col. Edwin E. Aldrin, Jr. and Lt. Col. Michael Collins. 30k, Armstrong, Aldrin and Collins in space suits.

1970, Dec. 24 *Perf. 13x13½*

698 A133 1k blue & black 5 3
699 " 2k brt. pur. & black 9 5
700 " 7k dull org. & black 35 18
701 " 10k rose red & black 50 25
702 " 30k green & black 1.50 65
Nos. 698-702 (5) 2.49 1.16

Visit of U.S. Apollo 11 astronauts and their wives to Kinshasa.

Metopodontus 4 Savagei—A134

Designs: Various insects of Congo.

1971, Jan. 25 Photo. *Perf. 11½*

703 A134 10s dull rose & multi. 3 3
704 " 50s gray & multi. 3 3
705 " 90s multicolored 5 3
706 " 1k citron & multi. 5 3
707 " 2k gray grn. & multi. 10 5
708 " 3k lt. vio. & multi. 18 7
709 " 5k blue & multi. 40 12
710 " 10k multicolored 70 25
711 " 30k green & multi. 2.25 65
712 " 40k ocher & multi. 2.75 85
Nos. 703-712 (10) 6.54 2.11

Colotis Protomedia—A135

Designs: Various butterflies and moths of Congo.

1971, Feb. 24

713 A135 10s lt. ultra. & multi. 3 3
714 " 20s choc. & multi. 3 3
715 " 70s dp. org. & multi. 5 3
716 " 1k vio. blue & multi. 5 3
717 " 3k multicolored 18 7
718 " 5k dk. grn. & multi. 40 12
719 " 10k multicolored 55 25
720 " 15k emerald & multicolored 95 30
721 " 25k yellow & multi. 1.50 50
722 " 40k multicolored 2.65 85
Nos. 713-722 (10) 6.39 2.21

U.N. Emblem, Racial Unity
A136

1971, March 21 Photo. *Perf. 11½*

723 A136 1k lt. grn. & multi. 5 3
724 " 4k gray & multi. 17 10
725 " 5k lt. lilac & multi. 27 12
726 " 10k lt. bl. & multi. 50 25

International year against racial discrimination.

Hypericum Bequaertii
A137

Flowers: 4k, Dissotis brazzae. 20k, Begonia wollastonii. 25k, Cassia alata.

1971, May 24 Litho. *Perf. 14*

727 A137 1k multicolored 5 3
728 " 4k " 30 10
729 " 20k " 1.25 50
730 " 25k " 1.50 65

Obelisk at N'sele, Pres. Mobutu
A138

1971, May 20 Photo. *Perf. 11½*

731 A138 4k gold & multi. 22 22

4th anniversary of the People's Revolutionary Movement.

Radar Station
A139

Designs: 1k, Waves. 6k, Map of Africa with telecommunications network.

1971, June 25 Photo. *Perf. 11½*

732 A139 1k rose & multi. 5 3
733 " 3k yellow & multi. 18 7
734 " 6k lt. blue & multi. 40 12

Issued for 3rd World Telecommunications Day, May 17 (1k); opening of satellite telecommunications ground station, Kinshasa, June 30 (3k); Pan-African telecommunication system (6k).

Grass Monkeys
A140

Designs: 20s, Moustached monkeys (vert.). 70s, De Brazza's monkeys. 1k, Yellow baboons. 3k, Pygmy chimpanzee (vert.). 5k, Mangabeys (vert.). 10k, Owl-faced monkeys. 15k, Diana monkeys. 25k, Black-and-white colobus (vert.). 40k, L'Hoest's monkeys (vert.).

1971, Aug.

735 A140 10s violet & multi. 10 3
736 " 20s lt. blue & multi. 10 3
737 " 70s ocher & multi. 12 3
738 " 1k gray & multi 12 3
739 " 3k rose & multi. 25 7
740 " 5k brown & multi. 55 12
741 " 10k multicolored 1.00 25
742 " 15k " 1.50 30
743 " 25k brt. bl. & multi. 2.50 50
744 " 40k red & multi. 3.00 75
Nos. 735-744 (10) 9.24 2.11

Hotel Inter-Continental, Kinshasa
A141

1971, Oct. 2 Photogravure *Perf. 13*

745 A141 2k silver & multi. 12 4
746 " 12k gold & multi. 65 25

Man Reading
A142

Designs: 2.50k, Open book and abacus. 7k, Five letters surrounding symbolic head.

1971, Oct. 24

747 A142 50s gold, red brn., black & yel. 5 3
748 " 2.50k gold, black, dk. red & tan 15 6
749 " 7k gold, grn., yel. & black 55 18

Fight against illiteracy.

Succeeding issues are listed in Vol. IV under Zaire.

SEMI-POSTAL STAMPS

Women Carrying Food, Wheat Emblem, and Tractor
SP22

1963, Mar. 21 Photo. *Perf. 14x13*

B48 SP22 5fr+2fr lilac, violet & dark blue 18 12
B49 " 9fr+4fr ocher, gray & dk. grn. 45 25
B50 " 12fr+6fr blue, dark blue & violet 50 35
B51 " 20fr+10fr red, green & gray 2.50 2.35

Issued for the "Freedom from Hunger" campaign of the U.N. Food and Agriculture Organization.

CONGO PEOPLE'S REPUBLIC

(ex-French)

LOCATION—West Africa at equator.
GOVT.—Republic.
AREA—132,046 sq. mi.
POP.—1,440,000 (est. 1977).
CAPITAL—Brazzaville.

The former French colony of Middle Congo became a member state of the French Community Nov. 28, 1958, and achieved independence Aug. 15, 1960. For some years before 1958, the colony was joined with three other French territories to form French Equatorial Africa. Issues of Middle Congo (1907-1933) are listed under that heading.

100 Centimes = 1 Franc

Allegory of New Republic
A7

Engraved.

1959 *Perf. 13* Unwmkd.

89 A7 25fr brown, deep claret, orange & olive 45 10

Issued to commemorate the first anniversary of the proclamation of the Republic.

Imperforates

Most stamps of the Republic of the Congo exist imperforate in issued and trial colors, and also in small presentation sheets in issued colors.

C.C.T.A. Issue
Common Design Type

1960 *Perf. 13* **Unwmkd.**

90 CD106 50fr dull grn. & plum 90 80

President Fulbert Youlou A8 — Flag, Map and U.N. Emblem A9

1960

91 A8 15fr grn., black & car. 25 17
92 " 85fr indigo & carmine 1.10 50

1961, March 11 *Perf. 13*

Flag in Green, Yellow & Red

93 A9 5fr vio. brn. & dk. bl. 10 6
94 " 20fr org. & dk. blue 30 22
95 " 100fr grn. & dk. blue 1.50 1.35

Congo's admission to United Nations.

Rainbow Runner
A10

Designs (fish): 50c, 3fr, Rainbow runner. 1fr, 2fr, Sloan's viperfish. 5fr, Hatchet fish. 10fr, A deep-sea fish.

1961, Nov. 28 **Engraved**

96 A10 50c brown, olive green & salmon 6 6
97 " 1fr blue green & sepia 6 6
98 " 2fr ultra., sepia & dk. green 10 10
99 " 3fr dk. blue, green & salmon 10 10
100 " 5fr red brown, green & black 20 15
101 " 10fr blue & red brown 25 18
Nos. 96-101 (6) 77 65

Brazzaville Market
A11

1962, March 23 *Perf. 13* **Unwmkd.**

102 A11 20fr black, red & green 25 12

Common Design Types

pictured in section at front of book.

Abidjan Games Issue
Common Design Type

Designs: 20fr, Boxing. 50fr, Running, finish line.

1962, July 21 Photo. *Perf. 12½x12*

103 CD109 20fr carm., br. pink, brn. & black 28 20
104 " 50fr carm., br. pink, brn. & black 60 45

See No. C7.

African-Malgache Union Issue
Common Design Type

1962, Sept. 8

105 CD110 30fr vio., bluish grn., red & gold 55 55

Waves Around Globe
A11a

Design: 100fr, Orbit patterns around globe.

1963, Sept. 19 *Perf. 12½*

106 A11a 25fr org., grn. & ultra. 40 30
107 " 100fr light red brown, blue & plum 1.40 1.10

Issued to publicize space communications.

King Makoko's Collar
A12

Design: 15fr, Kébékébé mask.

Engraved

1963, Oct. 21 *Perf. 13* **Unwmkd.**

108 A12 10fr blk. & olive bister 15 10
109 " 15fr brn., blk., blue, yellow & red 25 12

UNESCO Emblem, Scales and Tree—A12a

1963, Dec. 10 *Perf. 13* **Unwmkd.**

110 A12a 25fr grn., dk. bl. & brn. 35 25

Issued to commemorate the 15th anniversary of the Universal Declaration of Human Rights.

Barograph and WMO Emblem
A12b

1964, Mar. 23 **Engraved**

111 A12b 50fr green, red brown & ultramarine 65 65

Fourth World Meteorological Day.

Mechanic with Machine
A13

1964, Apr. 8

112 A13 20fr greenish blue, magenta & dark brown 32 20

Training of technicians.

Corn and Tools
A14

1964, Apr. 24 *Perf. 13* **Unwmkd.**

113 A14 80fr brown, green & brown carmine 95 50

Importance of manual labor.

Diaboua Ballet
A15

Kébékébé Dance A16 — Carved Figure A17

1964, May 8 **Engraved**

114 A15 30fr multicolored 50 30
115 A16 60fr " 90 60

1964, May 22

116 A17 50fr brn. red & sepia 65 50

Classroom
A18

1964, May 26

117 A18 25fr dk. brn., red & bl. 32 20

Issued to publicize education.

Type of Air Post Issue, 1963, Inscribed: "1er ANNIVERSAIRE DE LA REVOLUTION/ FETE NATIONALE/15 AOUT 1964"

1964, Aug. 15 Photo. *Perf. 13x12*

118 AP5 20fr lt. bl., red, ocher, dark brown & bright green 27 15

Issued to commemorate the first anniversary of the revolution and the National Feast Day, Aug. 15.

Fire Squid
A19

Design: 15fr, Johnson's deep-sea angler (fish).

1964, Oct. 20 **Engraved** *Perf. 13*

119 A19 2fr verm., light green & brown 10 8
120 " 15fr violet, lt. olive green & deep claret 35 20

Cooperation Issue
Common Design Type

1964, Nov. 7 *Perf. 13* **Unwmkd.**

121 CD119 25fr car., brt. grn. & dk. brown 35 25

Communications Emblems
A20

1965, Jan. 1 Litho. *Perf. 12½x13*

122 A20 25fr olive, red brn. & black 40 25

Issued to commemorate the establishment of the national postal administration.

Sitatunga A21 — Dancer on Stilts A22

Design: 20fr, Elephant (horiz.).

1965, Mar. 15 **Engraved** *Perf. 13*

123 A21 15fr reddish brown, dull grn. & bl. 30 15
124 " 20fr black, deep blue & slate green 30 15
125 A22 85fr lilac & multi. 1.15 90

Pres. Alphonse Massamba-Debat
A23

1965–66 Photo. *Perf. 12x12½*

126 A23 20fr dark brown, grn. & yellow 25 15

127 A23 25fr brn., bl. green, emerald & black ('66) 32 15

128 " 30fr brn., bl. green, org. & black ('66) 40 20

Soccer Player
A24

Designs: 25fr, Games' emblem (map of Africa and runners). 50fr, Field ball player. 85fr, Runner. 100fr, Bicyclist.

1965, July 17 Photo. ***Perf. 12½***

Size: 28x28mm.

129 A24 25fr black, red, yellow & grn. 32 20

Size: 34x34mm.

130 A24 40fr yel. grn. & multi. 60 40

131 " 50fr red & multi. 65 40

132 " 85fr black & multi. 1.10 70

133 " 100fr yellow & multi. 1.35 85

a. Min. sheet of 5 4.75 4.75

Nos. 129–133 (5) 4.02 2.55

Issued to commemorate the First African Games, Brazzaville, July 18–25. No. 133a contains one each of Nos. 129–133. Size: 136½x169mm.

Arms of Congo
A25

1965, Nov. 15 Litho. ***Perf. 12½x13***

134 A25 20fr multicolored 28 15

Cooperative Village
A26

Design: 30fr, Gymnastic drill team with streamers.

1966, Feb. 18 ***Perf. 12½x13***

135 A26 25fr multicolored 28 15

136 " 30fr " 40 25

Sculptured Mask
A27

Designs: 30fr, Weaver, painting. 85fr, String instrument, painting (horiz.).

Perf. 13x12½, 12½x13

1966, Apr. 9 Photogravure

137 A27 30fr multicolored 40 20

138 " 85fr " 1.10 65

139 " 90fr " 1.25 70

Issued to publicize the International Negro Arts Festival, Dakar, Senegal, Apr. 1–24.

Men and Clocks
A28

1966, Apr. 15 ***Perf. 12½x12***

140 A28 70fr pale brown, ocher & dk. brown 1.10 45

Issued to publicize the introduction of the shorter work day (less lunch time, earlier quitting time).

WHO Headquarters, Geneva
A29

1966, May 3 Photo. ***Perf. 12½x13***

141 A29 50fr org. yel., violet & blue 40 25

Issued to commemorate the inauguration of the World Health Organization Headquarters, Geneva.

Church of St. Peter Claver
A30

Women's Basketball
A31

1966, June 15 Photo. ***Perf. 13x12½***

142 A30 70fr multicolored 1.10 45

1966, July 15 Engraved ***Perf. 13***

Sport: 1fr, Women's volleyball (horiz.). 3fr, Women's field ball (horiz.). 5fr, Athletes of various races. 10fr, Torch bearer. 15fr, Soccer and gold medal of First African Games.

143 A31 1fr ultra., choc. & olive 6 6

144 " 2fr choc., grn. & blue 8 6

145 " 3fr dk. grn., dk. car. & chocolate 10 8

146 " 5fr slate, emerald & chocolate 12 10

147 " 10fr dull bl., dk. grn. & violet 25 12

148 " 15fr vio., car. & choc. 30 18

Nos. 143–148 (6) 91 60

Jules Rimet Cup and Globe
A32

1966, July 15 Photo. ***Perf. 12½x12***

149 A32 30fr brt. red, gold, black & blue 50 27

Issued to commemorate the 8th World Soccer Cup Championship, Wembley, England, July 11–30.

Savorgnan de Brazza School
A33

1966, Sept. 15 Photo. ***Perf. 12½x12***

150 A33 30fr dk. pur., grn., yellow & black 40 20

Pointe-Noire Railroad Station
A34

1966, Oct. 15 Engraved ***Perf. 13***

151 A34 60fr grn., red & brn. 85 35

Student with Microscope
A35

Balumbu Mask
A36

1966, Nov. 28 Engraved ***Perf. 13***

152 A35 90fr brown, green & indigo 1.20 75

Issued to commemorate the 20th anniversary of UNESCO (United Nations Educational, Scientific and Cultural Organization).

1966, Dec. 12 Engraved ***Perf. 13***

Masks: 10fr, Kuyu. 15fr, Bakwélé. 20fr, Batéké.

153 A36 5fr carmine rose & dark brown 12 8

154 " 10fr Prus. bl. & brn. 20 12

155 " 15fr sepia, dull org. & dk. blue 25 13

156 " 20fr dp. bl. & multi. 28 15

Order of the Revolution and Map
A37

Learning the Alphabet
A38

Design: 45fr, Harvesting and loading sugar cane, and sugar mill.

Perf. 12x12½, 12½x12

1967, March 15 Photogravure

157 A37 20fr org. & multi. 28 15

158 A38 25fr blk., ocher & dark carmine 32 20

159 " 45fr blk., yel. green & light blue 55 28

Issued to honor the members of the Order of the Revolution (20fr); to publicize the literacy campaign (25fr); to publicize sugar production (45fr).

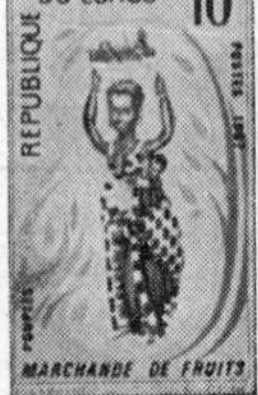

Mahatma Gandhi
A39

Fruit Vendor
A40

1967, Apr. 21 Engraved ***Perf. 13***

160 A39 90fr blue & black 1.10 60

Issued in memory of Mohandas K. Gandhi (1869–1948), Hindu nationalist leader.

1967, June Photo. ***Perf. 13x12½***

Dolls: 5fr, "Elegant Lady." 25fr, Woman pounding saka-saka. 30fr, Mother and child.

161 A40 5fr gold & multi. 12 12

162 " 10fr yel. grn. & multi. 20 15

163 " 25fr lt. ultra. & multi. 32 20

164 " 30fr multicolored 40 25

ITY Emblem, Village and Waterfall
A41

1967, July 5 Engraved ***Perf. 13***

165 A41 60fr rose claret, org. & olive green 80 50

Issued for International Tourist Year, 1967.

Symbols of Cooperation
A42

Arms of Brazzaville
A43

Europafrica Issue, 1967

1967, July 20 Photo. ***Perf. 12x12½***

166 A42 50fr multicolored 65 32

1967, Aug. 15 Litho. ***Perf. 12½x13***

167 A43 30fr yellow & multi. 45 20

Fourth anniversary of the revolution.

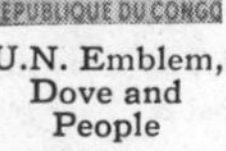

U.N. Emblem, Dove and People
A44

Boy and UNICEF Emblem
A45

1967, Oct. 24 Photo. ***Perf. 13x12½***

168 A44 90fr bl., dk. brn., red brown & yel. 1.35 70

Issued for United Nations Day, Oct. 24.

1967, Dec. 11 Engraved *Perf. 13*

169 A45 90fr maroon, black & ultra. 1.20 65

Issued to commemorate the 21st anniversary of UNICEF (United Nations International Children's Emergency Fund).

Albert Luthuli, Dove and Globe
A46

1968, Jan. 29 Engr. *Perf. 13*

170 A46 30fr brt. green & olive bister 40 25

Issued in memory of Albert Luthuli (1899–1967) of South Africa, winner of 1960 Nobel Peace Prize.

Arms of Pointe Noire
A47

1968, Feb. 20 Litho. *Perf. 12½x13*

171 A47 10fr brt. pink & multi. 15 12

Motherhood
A48

Mayombe Viaduct
A49

1968, May 25 Engraved *Perf. 13*

172 A48 15fr dk. carmine rose, sky blue & black 25 15

Issued for Mother's Day.

1968, June 24

173 A49 45fr maroon, slate green & blue 50 25

Daimler, 1889—A50

Antique Cars: 20fr, Berliet, 1897. 60fr, Peugeot, 1898. 80fr, Renault, 1900. 85fr, Fiat, 1902.

1968, July 29 Photo. *Perf. 13x12½*

174 A50 5fr ocher & multi. 15 15
175 " 20fr multicolored 30 25
176 " 60fr citron & multi. 85 45
177 " 80fr multicolored 1.10 60
178 " 85fr " 1.20 70
Nos. 174-178 (5) 3.60 2.15

Tanker, Refinery and Map of Area Served—A50a

1968, July 30 *Perf. 12½*

179 A50a 30fr multicolored 40 18

Issued to commemorate the opening of the Port Gentil (Gabon) Refinery, June 12, 1968.

U.N. Emblem and Tree of Life
A51

1968, Nov. 28 Engraved *Perf. 13*

180 A51 25fr dark green, red & deep lilac 40 18

Issued for the 20th anniversary of the World Health Organization.

Development Bank Issue
Common Design Type

1969, Sept. 10 Engraved *Perf. 13*

181 CD130 25fr carmine rose, green & ocher 35 15
182 " 30fr blue, green & ocher 40 15

Issued to commemorate the 5th anniversary of the African Development Bank.

Bicycle
A52

Designs (Bicycles and Motorcycles): 75fr, Hirondelle. 80fr, Folding bicycle. 85fr, Peugeot. 100fr, Excelsior Manxman. 150fr, Norton. 200fr, Brough Superior "Old Bill." 300fr, Matchless and N.L.G.-J.A.P.S.

1969, Oct. 6 Engraved *Perf. 13*

183 A52 50fr dk. olive, orange & rose lilac 65 32
184 " 75fr orange, rose lake & black 95 40
185 " 80fr lilac, blue & slate green 1.00 45
186 " 85fr dk. olive, gray & blue green 1.10 55
187 " 100fr blk., vio. bl., dk. brown & car. 1.25 65
188 " 150fr black, red brn. & brown olive 1.60 90
189 " 200fr bl. green, slate green & bright rose lilac 2.60 1.10
190 " 300fr black, brt. rose lilac & green 3.50 1.90
Nos. 183-190 (8) 12.65 6.27

Mayombe Train and Tourist Year Emblem
A53

Design: 40fr, Train and Mbamba Tunnel (vert.).

Perf. 13x12½, 12½x13

1969, Oct. 20 Photogravure

191 A53 40fr multicolored 55 27
192 " 60fr " 70 32

Issued for African Tourist Year.

Loutete Cement Works
A54

Designs (Loutete Cement Works): 15fr, Mixing tower (vert.). 25fr, Cable transport (vert.). 30fr, General view of plant.

1969, Dec. 10 Engraved *Perf. 13*

193 A54 10fr dark gray, rose claret & dark olive 13 8
194 " 15fr Prus. blue, red brn. & purple 18 13
195 " 25fr maroon, brown & Prus. blue 32 18
196 " 30fr violet brown, ultra. & black 35 22
a. Min. sheet of 4 1.25 1.25

Issued to publicize the cement factory at Loutete. No. 196a contains one each of Nos. 193–196. Size: 170x100mm.

ASECNA ISSUE
Common Design Type

1969, Dec. 12

197 CD132 100fr dull brown 1.35 65

Pineapple Harvest and ILO Emblem
A55

Design: 30fr, Worker at lathe and ILO emblem.

1969, Dec. 20 Engraved *Perf. 13*

198 A55 25fr blue, olive & brn. 32 18
199 " 30fr rose red, choc. & slate 35 22

Issued to commemorate the 50th anniversary of the International Labor Organization.

SOTEXCO Textile Plant, Kinsoundi
A56

Designs: 20fr, Women in spinnery. 25fr, Hand-printing textiles. 30fr, Checking woven cloth.

1970, Jan. 20

200 A56 15fr grn., blk. & lilac 18 13
201 " 20fr plum, carmine & slate green 22 13
202 " 25fr bl., slate & brn. 32 18
203 " 30fr gray, carmine rose & brown 40 18

Hotel Cosmos, Brazzaville
A57

1970, Jan. 30

204 A57 90fr slate green, blue & red brown 1.00 45

Linzolo Church
A58

Diosso Gorge
A59

Design: 90fr, Foulakari waterfall.

1970 Engraved *Perf. 13*

205 A58 25fr multicolored 32 18
206 A59 70fr " 80 35
207 " 90fr " 1.10 45

Issue dates: 25fr, Feb. 10; others, Feb. 25.

Certain unlisted issues of Congo Republic, starting in 1970, are mentioned and briefly described in "For the Record" at the back of this volume.

Volvaria Esculenta
A60

Mushrooms: 10fr, Termitomyces entolomoides. 15fr, Termitomyces microcarpus. 25fr, Termitomyces aurantiacus. 30fr, Termitomyces mammiformis. 50fr, Tremella fuciformis.

1970, Mar. 31 Photo. *Perf. 13*

208 A60 5fr Prus. blue & multi. 13 8
209 " 10fr bright carmine rose & multi. 15 12
210 " 15fr vio. blue & multi. 25 18
211 " 25fr dk. grn. & multi. 45 22
212 " 30fr purple & multi. 50 27
213 " 50fr brt. blue & multi. 70 45
Nos. 208-213 (6) 2.18 1.32

Laying Coaxial Cable
A61

Design: 30fr, Full view of rail car; 3 cable layers on railway roadbed.

1970, Apr. 30 Engraved *Perf. 13*

214 A61 25fr dk. brn. & multi. 32 18
215 " 30fr brown & multi. 40 22

Issued to publicize the laying of the coaxial cable linking Brazzaville and Pointe Noire.

U.P.U. Headquarters Issue
Common Design Type

1970, May 20

216 CD133 30fr dark purple, gray & magenta 45 22

Mother Feeding Child
A62

Dag Hammarskjold and U.N. Emblem
A63

Design: 90fr, Mother nursing infant.

1970, May 30 Photogravure

217 A62 85fr vio. bl. & multi. 1.00 55
218 " 90fr lilac & multi. 1.10 60

Issued for Mother's Day.

1970, June 20 Engraved ***Perf. 13***

Designs (U.N. Emblem and): No. 220, Trygve Lie (horiz.). No. 221, U Thant (horiz.).

219 A63 100fr scarlet, dk. red & dk. purple 1.25 75
220 " 100fr dark red, ultra. & indigo 1.25 75
221 " 100fr green, emerald & dark red 1.25 75
a. Souvenir sheet of 3 4.25 4.25

Issued to commemorate the 25th anniversary of the United Nations and to honor its Secretaries General. No. 221a contains one each of Nos. 219–221; U.N. emblem and scarlet inscriptions in margin. Size: 120½x100mm.

Brillantaisia Vogeliana
A64

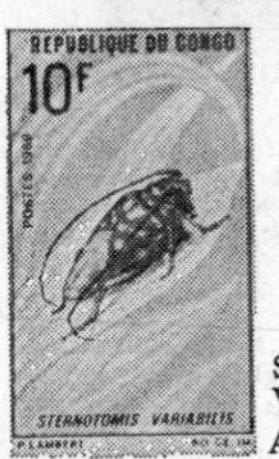

Sternotomis Variabilis
A65

Designs (Plants and Beetles): 2fr, Plectranthus decurrens. 3fr, Myrianthemum mirabile. 5fr, Connarus griffonianus. 15fr, Chelorrhina polyphemus. 20fr, Metopodontus savagei.

Perf. 12½x12, 12x12½

1970, June 30 Photogravure

222 A64 1fr dk. grn. & multi. 5 3
223 " 2fr multicolored 8 5
224 " 3fr indigo & multi. 10 6
225 " 5fr lemon & multi. 12 10
226 A65 10fr lilac & multi. 15 12
227 " 15fr orange & multi. 22 12
228 " 20fr multicolored 27 18
Nos. 222–228 (7) 99 66

Stegosaurus
A66

Prehistoric Fauna: 20fr, Dinotherium (vert.). 60fr, Brachiosaurus (vert.). 80fr, Arsinoitherium.

1970, July 20

229 A66 15fr dull green, ocher & red brown 25 15
230 " 20fr lt. blue & multi. 30 20
231 A66 60fr lt. blue & multi. 75 28
232 " 80fr lt. blue & multi. 1.10 50

Mikado 141, 1932
A67

Locomotives: 60fr, Steam locomotive 130+032, 1947. 75fr, Alsthom BB 1100, 1962. 85fr, Diesel BB BB 302, 1969.

1970, Aug. 20 Engraved ***Perf. 13***

233 A67 40fr magenta, blue green & black 60 30
234 " 60fr blk., blue & grn. 80 40
235 " 75fr red, bl. & black 1.00 45
236 " 85fr carmine, slate green & ocher 1.25 55

Cogniauxia Padolaena
A68

Green Night Adder
A69

Tropical Flowers: 2fr, Celosia cristata. 5fr, Plumeria acutifolia. 10fr, Bauhinia variegata. 15fr, Poinsettia. 20fr, Thunbergia grandiflora.

1971, Feb. 10 Photo. ***Perf. 12x12½***

237 A68 1fr lilac & multi. 8 7
238 " 2fr yellow & multi. 8 7
239 " 5fr ultra. & multi. 12 8
240 " 10fr yellow & multi. 20 13
241 " 15fr multicolored 32 18
242 " 20fr dark red & multi. 40 18
Nos. 237–242 (6) 1.20 71

Perf. 12x12½, 12½x12

1971, June 26 Photogravure

Reptiles: 10fr, African Egg-eating snake (horiz.). 15fr, Flap-necked chameleon. 20fr, Nile crocodile (horiz.). 25fr, Rock python (horiz.). 30fr, Gaboon viper. 40fr, Brown house snake (horiz.). 45fr, Jameson's mamba.

243 A69 5fr multicolored 8 8
244 " 10fr " 15 12
245 " 15fr " 25 15
246 " 20fr red & multi. 32 25
247 " 25fr green & multi. 40 32
248 " 30fr multicolored 50 40
249 " 40fr bister & multi. 50 45
250 " 45fr multicolored 65 50
Nos. 243–250 (8) 2.85 2.27

Pseudimbrasia Deyrollei—A70

Caterpillars: 15fr, Bunaea alcinoe (vert.). 20fr, Epiphora vacuna ploetzi. 25fr, Imbrasia eblis. 30fr, Imbrasia dione (vert.). 40fr, Holocera angulata.

1971, July 3 ***Perf. 13***

251 A70 10fr vermilion, black & green 20 15
252 " 15fr multicolored 25 20
253 " 20fr yel. green, black & ocher 32 28
254 " 25fr multicolored 40 32
255 " 30fr red, blk. & yel. 50 40
256 " 40fr bl., blk. & org. 75 55
Nos. 251–256 (6) 2.42 1.90

Cymothoe Sangaris
A71

Butterflies and Moths: 40fr, Papilio dardanus (vert.). 75fr, Iolaus timon. 90fr, Papilio phorcas (vert.). 100fr, Euchloron megaera.

Perf. 12½x12, 12x12½

1971, Oct. 15

257 A71 30fr yellow & multi. 50 32
258 " 40fr green & multi. 65 45
259 " 75fr multicolored 1.10 65
260 " 90fr " 1.35 90
261 " 100fr ultra & multi. 1.75 1.25
Nos. 257–261 (5) 5.35 3.57

Black and White Men Working Together
A72

1971, Oct. 30 ***Perf. 13x12½***

262 A72 50fr orange & multi. 50 25

International Year Against Racial Discrimination.

REPUBLIQUE POPULAIRE
DU CONGO
30F

Nos. 214–215 Surcharged

INAUGURATION
DE LA LIAISON COAXIALE
18-11-71

1971, Nov. 18 Engraved ***Perf. 13***

263 A61 30fr on 25fr multi. 40 25
264 " 40fr on 30fr " 50 32

Inauguration of cable service between Brazzaville and Pointe Noire. Words of surcharge arranged differently on No. 264.

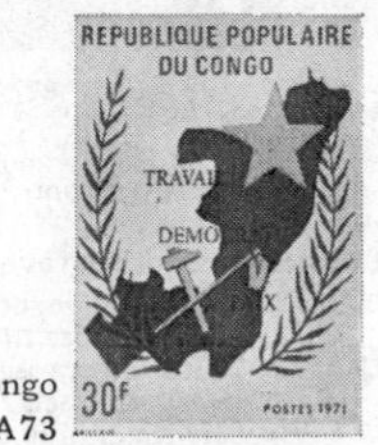

Map of Congo
A73

1971, Dec. 31 Photo. ***Perf. 12½x13***

265 A73 30fr blue & multi. 35 25
266 " 40fr yel. grn. & multi. 40 20
267 " 100fr gray & multi. 1.10 55

"Labor, Democracy, Peace."

Lion
A74

Animals: 2fr, African elephants. 3fr, Leopard. 4fr, Hippopotamus. 5fr, Gorilla (vert.). 20fr, Potto. 30fr, De Brazza's monkey. 40fr, Pygmy chimpanzee (vert.).

1972, Jan. 31 Engraved ***Perf. 13***

268 A74 1fr green & multi. 5 5
269 " 2fr dk. red & multi. 5 5
270 " 3fr red brn. & multi. 10 8
271 " 4fr violet & multi. 10 8
272 " 5fr brown & multi. 12 12
273 " 20fr orange & multi. 32 25
274 " 30fr ocher & multi. 50 28
275 A74 40fr Prus. bl. & multi. 65 45
Nos. 268–275 (8) 1.89 1.36

WHO Emblem
A75

Design: 50fr, WHO emblem (horiz.).

Perf. 12½x13, 13x12½

1973, June 30 Typographed

276 A75 40fr grn. & multi. 32 15
277 " 50fr multicolored 40 20

World Health Organization, 25th anniversary.

Kronenbourg Brewery
A76

Designs (Brewery Trademark and): 40fr, Laboratory. 75fr, Vats and controls. 85fr, Automatic control room. 100fr, Pressure room. 250fr, Bottling plant.

1973, July 15 Engr. ***Perf. 13***

278 A76 30fr red & multi. 25 15
279 " 40fr " " 32 22
280 " 75fr " " 55 32
281 " 85fr " " 80 40
282 " 100fr " " 1.10 60
283 " 250fr " " 2.10 1.10
Nos. 278–283 (6) 5.12 2.79

Kronenbourg Brewery, Brazzaville.

Golwe Locomotive, 1935
A77

Locomotives: 40fr, Diesel, 1935. 75fr, Diesel Whithcomb, 1946. 85fr, Diesel CC200.

1973, Aug. 1 Engr. ***Perf. 13***

284 A77 30fr indigo & multi. 40 25
285 " 40fr vio. bl. & multi. 50 25
286 " 75fr multicolored 90 40
287 " 85fr " 1.00 50

No. 225 Surcharged with New Value, 2 Bars, and Overprinted in Ultramarine: "SECHERESSE SOLIDARITE AFRICAINE"

1973, Aug. 16 Photo. ***Perf. 12½x12***

288 A64 100fr on 5fr multi. 80 55

African solidarity in drought emergency.

African Postal Union Issue

Common Design Type

1973, Sept. 12 Engr. ***Perf. 13***

289 CD137 100fr bl. grn., violet & brown 75 40

Bees, Beehive, Honeycomb
A78

1973, Dec. 10 Engraved ***Perf. 13***

290 A78 30fr slate green, dark red & blue 27 18
291 " 40fr slate blue, slate grn. & lt. grn. 35 18

"Work and economy."

Family, UN and FAO Emblems
A79

Designs: 40fr, Grain, UN and FAO emblems. 100fr, Grain, UN and FAO emblems (vert.).

1973, Dec. 10

292 A79 30fr dark carmine & dark brown 27 10
293 " 40fr dk. green, yellow & indigo 35 15
294 " 100fr green, brown & orange 80 50

World Food Program, 10th anniversary.

Amilcar Cabral, Cattle and Child
A80

1974, July 15 Engraved *Perf. 13*

295 A80 100fr multicolored 75 50

First death anniversary of Amilcar Cabral (1924–1973), leader of anti-Portuguese guerrilla activity in Portuguese Guinea.

Félix Eboué, Cross of Lorraine
A81

1974, Aug. 31 Litho. *Perf. 13*

296 A81 30fr blue & multi. 25 15
297 " 40fr brt. pink & multi. 35 20

Félix A. Eboué (1884–1944), Governor of Chad, first colonial governor to join Free French in WWII, 30th death anniversary.

Pineapples A82

1974, Nov. 12

Multicolored

298 A82 30fr *shown* 25 15
299 " 30fr *Bananas* 25 15
300 " 30fr *Safous* 25 15
301 " 40fr *Avocados* 35 20
302 " 40fr *Mangos* 35 20
303 " 40fr *Papaya* 35 20
304 " 40fr *Oranges* 35 20
Nos. 298-304 (7) 2.15 1.25

Charles de Gaulle and Conference Building—A83

1974, Nov. 25 Engraved *Perf. 13*

305 A83 100fr multicolored 75 50

Brazzaville Conference, 25th anniversary.

George Stephenson and Various Locomotives—A84

1974, Dec. 15

306 A84 75fr slate grn. & olive 55 35

George Stephenson (1781–1848), English inventor and railroad founder.

UDEAC Issue

Presidents and Flags of Cameroun, CAR, Congo, Gabon and Meeting Center—A84a

1974, Dec. 8 Photogravure *Perf. 13*

307 A84a 40fr gold & multi. 35 20

See note after Cameroun No. 595.
See No. C195.

Irish Setter A85

Designs: Dogs.

1974, Dec. 15 Photo. *Perf. 13x13½*

Multicolored

308 A85 30fr *shown* 35 18
309 " 40fr *Borzoi* 45 22
310 " 75fr *Pointer* 75 35
311 " 100fr *Great Dane* 1.00 55

1974, Dec. 15

Designs: Cats.

312 A85 30fr *Havana chestnut* 35 15
313 " 40fr *Red Persian* 45 18
314 " 75fr *Blue British* 75 35
315 " 100fr *African serval* 1.00 55

Labor Party Flags and People A86

Design: 40fr, Hands holding flowers and tools.

1974, Dec. 31 Engr. *Perf. 13x12½*

316 A86 30fr red & multi. 25 12
317 " 40fr red & multi. 35 18

5th anniversary of Congolese Labor Party and of introduction of red flag.

Symbols of Development—A87

U Thant and UN Headquarters—A88

Paul G. Hoffman and UN Emblem A89

Perf. 13x12½, 12½x13

1975, Feb. 28 Lithographed

318 A87 40fr multicolored 32 18
319 A88 50fr lt. bl. & multi. 35 22
320 A89 50fr yel. & multi. 35 22

National economic development.

Map of China and Mao Tse-tung—A90

1975, Mar. 9 Engraved *Perf. 13*

321 A90 75fr multicolored 60 40

25th anniversary of the People's Republic of China.

Woman Breaking Bonds, Women's Activities, Map of Congo A91

1975, June 20 Litho. *Perf. 12½*

322 A91 40fr gold & multi. 40 20

Revolutionary Union of Congolese Women, URFC, 10th anniversary.

CARA Soccer Team—A92

Design: 40fr, Team captain and manager receiving trophy (vert.).

1975, July 15 Litho. *Perf. 12½*

323 A92 30fr multicolored 27 18
324 " 40fr " 35 22

CARA team, winners of African Soccer Cup 1974.

Citroen, 1935—A93

Designs: Early autombiles.

1975, July 17 *Perf. 12*

Multicolored

325 A93 30fr *shown* 25 20
326 " 40fr *Alfa Romeo, 1911* 35 20
327 " 50fr *Rolls Royce, 1926* 40 30
328 " 75fr *Duryea, 1893* 60 45

Tipoye Transport—A94

Design: 40fr, Dugout canoe.

1975, Aug. 5

329 A94 30fr multicolored 22 13
330 " 40fr " 32 18

Traditional means of transportation.

Raising Red Flag—A95

Design: 40fr, National Conference.

1975, Aug. 15

331 A95 30fr multicolored 25 20
332 " 40fr " 35 20

2nd anniversary of installation of popular power (30fr) and 3rd anniversary of National Conference (40fr).

The only foreign revenue stamps listed in this Catalogue are those authorized for prepayment of postage.

Line Fishing A96 — Woman Pounding "Foufou" A97

Traditional Fishing: 30fr, Trap fishing (horiz.). 60fr, Spear fishing. 90fr, Net fishing (horiz.).

1975, Aug. 31 Litho. *Perf. 12*

333	A96	30fr multicolored	25	20
334	"	40fr "	35	20
335	"	60fr "	50	30
336	"	90fr "	70	50

1975, Sept. 5

Household Tasks: No. 338, Woman chopping wood. 40fr, Woman preparing manioc (horiz.).

337	A97	30fr multicolored	25	15
338	"	30fr "	25	15
339	"	40fr "	35	20

Esanga A98

Musical Instruments: 40fr, Kalakwa. 60fr, Likembe. 75fr, Ngongui.

1975, Sept. 20 *Perf. 12½*

340	A98	30fr black & brown	25	15
341	"	40fr orange & multi.	35	20
342	"	60fr green & multi.	50	35
343	"	75fr multicolored	60	40

Dzeke (Congolese) Shell Money A99

Ancient Money: No. 346, like No. 344. Nos. 345, 347, Okengo, Congolese, iron bar. 40fr, Gallic coin, c. 60 B.C. 50fr, Roman denarius, 37 B.C. 60fr, Danubian coin, 2nd century B.C. 85fr, Greek stater, 4th century B.C.

1975–76 Engr. *Perf. 13*

344	A99	30fr red & multi.	25	20
345	"	30fr violet & multi.	25	20
346	"	35fr olive & multi.	30	20
347	"	35fr dk. car. rose & multicolored	30	20
348	"	40fr Prus. bl. & brn.	35	20
349	"	50fr Prus. blue & olive	40	25
350	"	60fr dk. grn. & brn.	50	35
351	"	85fr magenta & slate green	65	40
		Nos. 344–351 (8)	3.00	2.00

Nos. 346–347 inscribed "1976" and issued Mar. 1976; others issued Oct. 5, 1975.

Moschops—A100

Pre-historic Animals: 75fr, Tyrannosaurus. 95fr, Cryptocleidus. 100fr, Stegosaurus.

1975, Oct. 15 Litho. *Perf. 13*

352	A100	55fr multicolored	45	30
353	"	75fr "	60	35
354	"	95fr "	75	50
355	"	100fr "	80	55

Albert Schweitzer A101

1975, Oct. 15 Engraved

356	A101	75fr olive, brn. & red	60	40

Albert Schweitzer (1875–1965), medical missionary, birth centenary.

Alexander Fleming A102

Designs: No. 358, André Marie Ampère. No. 359, Clement Ader.

1975, Nov. 15 Engr. *Perf. 13*

357	A102	60fr brn., green & black	50	30
358	"	95fr black, red & green	75	55
359	"	95fr red, blue & indigo	75	55

Alexander Fleming (1881–1955), developer of penicillin, 20th death anniversary; André Marie Ampère (1775–1836), physicist, bicentenary of birth; Clement Ader (1841–1925), aviation pioneer, 50th death anniversary.

U.N. Emblem "ONU" and "30"—A103

1975, Dec. 20 Engr. *Perf. 13*

360	A103	95fr car., ultra. & green	75	55

United Nations, 30th anniversary.

Women's Broken Chain—A104

Design: 60fr, Equality between man and woman, globe, IWY emblem.

1975, Dec. 20 Litho. *Perf. 12½*

361	A104	35fr magenta, ocher & gray	30	20
362	"	60fr ultra., brown & black	50	35

International Women's Year, 1975.

Pres. Marien Ngouabi, Flag and Workers—A105

Echo of the P.C.T. A106

Perf. 12½x12, 13x12½

1975, Dec. 31 Lithographed

363	A105	30fr multicolored	25	15
364	A106	35fr "	30	15

6th anniversary of the Congolese Labor Party (P.C.T.). See No. C215.

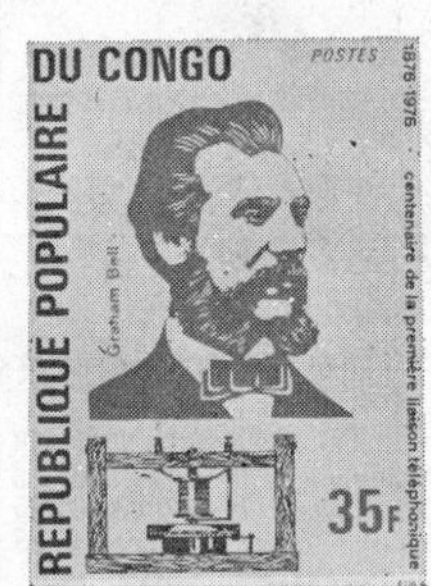

A.G. Bell and 1876 Telephone A107

1976, Apr. 25 Litho. *Perf. 12½x13*

365	A107	35fr yellow, brn. & org. brown	30	20

Centenary of first telephone call by Alexander Graham Bell, Mar. 10, 1876. See No. C229.

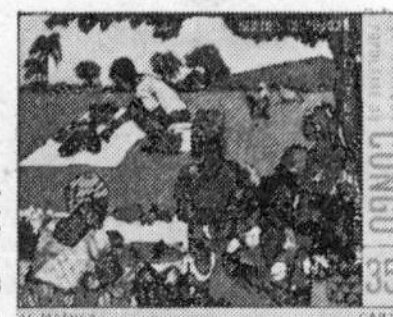

Women Selling Fruit and Vegetables A108

Design: 60fr, Market scene.

1976, Sept. 19 Litho. *Perf. 12½x13*

366	A108	35fr multicolored	30	20
367	"	60fr "	50	30

Congolese Coiffure A109

Designs: Various women's hair styles.

1976, Oct. 10 Litho. *Perf. 13*

368	A109	35fr multicolored	30	20
369	"	60fr "	50	35
370	"	95fr "	75	50
371	"	100fr "	80	55

Pole Vault, Map of Central Africa A110

Design: 95fr, Long jump and map of Central Africa.

1976, Oct. 25 *Perf. 12½*

372	A110	60fr yel. & multi.	50	35
373	"	95fr " "	75	55

Gold medalists, 1st Central African Games, Yaoundé, July 27–30, 1975.
See Nos. C230–C231.

Antelope A111

1976, Oct. 27 Litho. *Perf. 12½*

Multicolored

Size: 36x36mm.

374	A111	5fr *shown*	5	4
375	"	10fr *Buffalos*	10	5
376	"	15fr *Hippopotamus*	10	7
377	"	20fr *Wart hog*	15	10
378	"	25fr *Elephants*	20	13
		Nos. 374–378 (5)	60	39

1976, Dec. 8

Designs: Birds.

Multicolored

Size: 26x36mm.

379	A111	5fr *Saddle-bill storks*	5	4

Size: 36x36mm.

380	A111	10fr *Malachite kingfisher*	10	8
381	"	20fr *Crowned cranes*	15	12

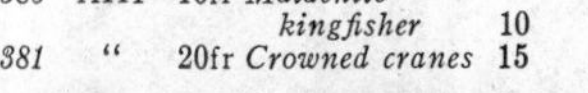

Bicycling, Map of Participants A112 — Heliotrope A113

1976, Dec. 21 Photo. *Perf. 12½x13*

Designs (Map and): 60fr, Fieldball. 80fr, Running. 95fr, Soccer.

382 A112 35fr multicolored 30 20
383 " 60fr " 50 35
384 " 80fr " 65 50
385 " 95fr " 75 55

First Central African Games, Libreville, Gabon, June–July 1976.

1976, Dec. 23 Photo. *Perf. 12½x13*

Flowers: 5fr, Water lilies. 15fr, Bird-of-paradise flower.

386 A113 5fr multicolored 5 4
387 " 10fr " 10 5
388 " 15fr " 15 10

Torch and Olive Branches
A114

1976, Dec. 25 Litho. *Perf. 12½x13*

389 A114 35fr multicolored 20 30

National Pioneer Movement.

The Spirit of '76—A115

Designs: 125fr, Pulling down George III statue. 150fr, Battle of Princeton. 175fr, Generals of Revolutionary War. 200fr, Burgoyne's surrender at Saratoga. 500fr, Battle of Lexington.

1976, Dec. 29 Litho. *Perf. 14*

390 A115 100fr multi. 90 35
391 " 125fr " 1.10 45
392 " 150fr " 1.25 50
393 " 175fr " 1.50 70
394 " 200fr " 1.65 75
Nos. 390–394 (5) 6.40 2.75

Souvenir Sheet

395 A115 500fr multi. 4.50 1.85

American Bicentennial.
No. 395 has green and blue margin, black marginal inscription. Size: 114x72 mm.

Dugout Canoe Race
A116

Design: 60fr, 2-man dugout canoes.

1977, Mar. 27 Litho. *Perf. 13x13½*

396 A116 35fr multicolored 30 20
397 " 60fr " 50 35

Dugout canoe races on Congo River.

Lilan Goua
A117

Fresh-water Fish: 15fr, Liko ko. 25fr, Liyan ga. 35fr, Mbessi. 60fr, Mongandza.

1977, June 15 Litho. *Perf. 12½*

398 A117 10fr multicolored 10 7
399 " 15fr " 15 10
400 " 25fr " 20 15
401 " 35fr " 30 20
402 " 60fr " 50 35
Nos. 398-402 (5) 1.25 87

Traditional Headdress—A118

Design: 60fr, Leopard cap.

1977, June 30 Litho. *Perf. 12½*

403 A118 35fr multicolored 30 20
404 " 60fr " 50 35

See Nos. C234–C235.

Bondjo Wrestling
A119

Designs: 40fr, 50fr, Bondjo wrestling (different). 40fr, horiz.

1977, July 15

405 A119 25fr multicolored 20 15
406 " 40fr " 30 25
407 " 50fr " 40 30

"Schwaben" LZ 10, 1911
A120

Zeppelins: 60fr, "Viktoria Luise." LZ 11, 1913. 100fr, LZ 120. 200fr, LZ 127. 300fr, "Graf Zeppelin II" LZ 130.

1977, Aug. 5 Litho. *Perf. 11*

408 A120 40fr multi. 30 15
409 " 60fr " 50 25
410 " 100fr " 80 30
411 " 200fr " 1.60 70
412 " 300fr " 2.40 1.00
Nos. 408–412 (5) 5.60 2.40

History of the Zeppelin. Exist imperf. See No. C236.

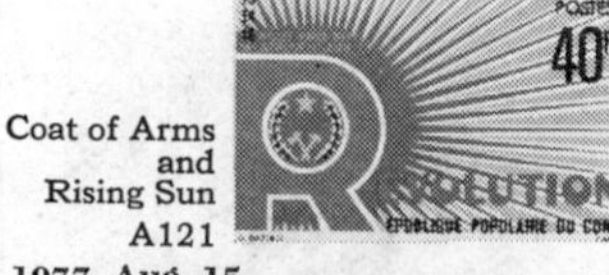

Coat of Arms and Rising Sun
A121

1977, Aug. 15

413 A121 40fr multicolored 30 25

14th anniversary of the revolution.

Victor Hugo and The Hunchback of Notre Dame—A122

Designs (Hugo and): 60fr, Les Miserables. 100fr, Les Travailleurs de la Mer (octopus).

1977, Aug. 20 Engr. *Perf. 13*

414 A122 35fr multicolored 30 20
415 " 60fr " 50 35
416 " 100fr " 80 60

Victor Hugo (1802–1885), French novelist.

Mao Tse-tung
A123

Lithographed; Gold Embossed

1977, Sept. 9 *Perf. 12x12½*

417 A123 400fr red & gold 3.25 2.50

Chairman Mao Tse-tung (1893–1976), Chinese Communist leader, first death anniversary.

Peter Paul Rubens
A124

1977, Sept. 20 Gold Embossed

418 A124 600fr gold & light blue 4.75 4.00

Peter Paul Rubens (1577–1640), painter.

Child Leading Blind Woman Across Street
A125

1977, Oct. 22 Litho. *Perf. 12½x13*

419 A125 35fr multicolored 30 20

World Health Day: To see is life.

Paul Kamba and Records
A126

1977, Oct. 29

420 A126 100fr multicolored 80 6

Paul Kamba (1912–1950), musician.

Trajan Vuia and Flying Machine
A127

Designs: 75fr, Louis Bleriot and plane. 100fr, Roland Garros and plane. 200fr, Charles Lindbergh and Spirit of St. Louis. 300fr, Tupolev Tu-144. 500fr, Lindbergh and Spirit of St. Louis over ship in Atlantic.

1977, Nov. 18 Litho. *Perf. 14*

421 A127 60fr multicolored 50 25
422 " 75fr " 60 30
423 " 100fr " 80 30
424 " 200fr " 1.60 65
425 " 300fr " 2.40 1.00
Nos. 421-425 (5) 5.90 2.50

Souvenir Sheet

426 A127 500fr multicolored 4.00 1.85

History of aviation. No. 426 has multi-colored margin showing Spirit of St. Louis at Orly Airport, Paris. Size: 117x91mm.

Elizabeth II and Prince Philip
A128

Design: 300fr, Elizabeth II wearing Crown.

1977, Dec. 21

427 A128 250fr multi. 2.00 1.00
428 " 300fr " 2.40 1.10

25th anniversary of the reign of Queen Elizabeth II. See No. C239.

King Baudouin
A129

Design: No. 430, Charles de Gaulle.

1977, Dec. 21

429	A129	200fr multi.	1.60	70
430	"	200fr "	1.60	70

King Baudouin of Belgium and Charles de Gaulle, president of France.

Ambete Sculpture
A130

Design: 85fr, Babembe sculpture.

1978, Feb. 18 Engr. *Perf. 13*

431	A130	35fr light brown & multicolored	30	20
432	"	85fr light green & multicolored	70	50

Congolese art.

St. Simon, by Rubens
A131

Rubens Paintings: 140fr, Duke of Lerma. 200fr, Madonna and Saints. 300fr, Rubens and his Wife Helena Fourment. 500fr, Farm at Laeken.

1978, Mar. 7 Litho. *Perf. 13½x14*

433	A131	60fr gold & multi.	50	25
434	"	140fr " "	1.10	45
435	"	200fr " "	1.60	70
436	"	300fr " "	2.40	1.00

Souvenir Sheet

437	A131	500fr gold & multi.	4.00	1.85

Peter Paul Rubens (1577–1640), 400th birth anniversary. No. 437 contains one stamp; multicolored margin shows entire painting. Size: 106x123mm.

Pres. Ngouabi and Microphones
A132

Designs: 60fr, Ngouabi at his desk (horiz.). 100fr, Portrait.

Perf. 12½x13, 13x12½

1978, Mar. 18 Lithographed

438	A132	35fr multicolored	30	20
439	"	60fr "	50	35
440	"	100fr "	80	60

Pres. Marien Ngouabi, first death anniversary.

Ferenc Puskas and Argentina '78 Emblem—A133

Players and Emblem: 75fr, Giacinto Facchetti. 100fr, Bobby Moore. 200fr, Raymond Kopa. 300fr, Pelé. 500fr, Franz Beckenbauer.

1978, Apr. 4 *Perf. 14x13½*

441	A133	60fr multicolored	50	25
442	"	75fr "	60	30
443	"	100fr "	80	35
444	"	200fr "	1.75	70
445	"	300fr "	2.40	1.00
		Nos. 441-445 (5)	6.05	2.60

Souvenir Sheet

446	A133	500fr multicolored	4.00	1.85

11th World Cup Soccer Championship, Argentina, June 1–25. No. 446 has light and dark blue margin showing soccer ball and net. Size: 136x100mm.

Pearl S. Buck and Chinese Women
A134

Designs: 75fr, Fridtjof Nansen, refugees and Nansen passport. 100fr, Henri Bergson, book and flame. 200fr, Alexander Fleming and Petri dish. 300fr, Gerhart Hauptmann and book. 500fr, Henri Dunant and Red Cross Station.

1978, Apr. 29

447	A134	60fr multicolored	50	25
448	"	75fr "	60	30
449	"	100fr "	80	35
450	"	200fr "	1.75	70
451	"	300fr "	2.40	1.00
		Nos. 447-451 (5)	6.05	2.60

Souvenir Sheet

452	A134	500fr multi.	4.00	1.85

Nobel Prize winners. No. 452 has multicolored margin with head of Alfred Nobel and inscribed "Nobel." Size: 119x81mm.

African Buffalos
A135

Animals and Wildlife Fund Emblem: 35fr, Okapi (vert.). 85fr, Rhinoceros. 150fr, Chimpanzee (vert.). 200fr, Hippopotamus. 300fr, Buffon's kob (vert.).

1978 *Perf. 14½*

453	A135	35fr multicolored	30	20
454	"	60fr "	50	25
455	"	85fr "	70	35
456	"	150fr "	1.20	50
457	"	200fr "	1.75	70
458	"	300fr "	2.40	1.00
		Nos. 453-458 (6)	6.85	3.00

Endangered animals.
Issue dates: 35fr, Aug. 11. Others, July 11.

Emblem, Young People, Gun and Fist
A136

1978, July 28 *Perf. 12½*

459	A136	35fr multicolored	30	20

11th World Youth Festival, Havana, July 28–Aug. 5.

Pyramids and Camels—A137

Seven Wonders of the Ancient World: 50fr, Hanging Gardens of Babylon. 60fr, Statue of Zeus, Olympia. 95fr, Colossus of Rhodes. 125fr, Mausoleum of Halicarnassus. 150fr, Temple of Artemis, Ephesus. 200fr, Lighthouse, Alexandria. 300fr, Map of Eastern Mediterranean showing locations. (50fr, 60fr, 95fr, 125fr, 200fr, vertical.)

1978, Aug. 12 Litho. *Perf. 14*

460	A137	35fr multicolored	30	15
461	"	50fr "	40	20
462	"	60fr "	50	25
463	"	95fr "	75	40
464	"	125fr "	1.00	50
465	"	150fr "	1.20	60
466	"	200fr "	1.60	75
467	"	300fr "	2.40	1.00
		Nos. 460-467 (8)	8.15	3.85

Nos. 427–428 Overprinted in Silver:
"ANNIVERSAIRE DU COURONNEMENT 1953–1978"

1978, Sept. Litho. *Perf. 14*

468	A128	250fr multi.	2.00	75
469	"	300fr "	2.40	1.00

25th anniversary of coronation of Queen Elizabeth II. See No. C244.

Kwame N'Krumah and Map of Africa—A138

1978, Sept. 23 Litho. *Perf. 13x12½*

470	A138	60fr multicolored	50	25

Kwame N'Krumah (1909–1972), president of Ghana.

Wild Boar Hunt—A139

Designs: 50fr, Fish smoking. 60fr, Hunter with spears and dog (vert.).

1978 Litho. *Perf. 12*

471	A139	35fr multicolored	35	25
472	"	50fr "	50	35
473	"	60fr "	60	40

Local hunting and fishing.
Issue dates: 35fr, 60fr, Oct. 5; 50fr, Oct. 10.

View of Kalchreut, by Dürer—A140

Paintings by Dürer: 150fr, Elspeth Tucher (vert.). 250fr, "The Great Piece of Turf" (vert.). 350fr, Self-portrait (vert.).

1978, Nov. 23 Litho. *Perf. 14*

474	A140	65fr multicolored	65	42
475	"	150fr "	1.50	1.05
476	"	250fr "	2.50	1.75
477	"	350fr "	3.50	2.50

Albrecht Dürer (1471–1528), German painter.

Basketmaker
A141

Productive Labor: 90fr, Woodcarver. 140fr, Women hoeing field.

1978, Nov. 18 Litho. *Perf. 12½*

Size: 25x36mm.

478	A141	85fr multicolored	85	60
479	"	90fr "	90	62

Size: 27x48mm.

Perf. 12

480	A141	140fr multicolored	1.40	1.00

Nos. 441–446 Overprinted in Silver:

a. "1962 VAINQUEUR:BRESIL"
b. "1966 VAINQUEUR: / GRANDE BRETAGNE"
c. "1970 VAINQUEUR: / BRESIL"
d. "1974 VAINQUEUR: / ALLEMAGNE (RFA)"
e. "1978 VAINQUEUR /: ARGENTINE"
f. "ARGENTINE–PAYS BAS 3–1 / 25 juin 1978"

1978, Nov. *Perf. 14x13½*

481	A133	(a)	60fr multi.	60	40
482	"	(b)	75fr "	75	50
483	"	(c)	100fr "	1.00	70
484	"	(d)	200fr "	2.00	1.40
485	"	(e)	300fr "	3.00	2.10
			Nos. 481-485 (5)	7.35	5.10

Souvenir Sheet

486	A133	(f)	500fr multi.	5.25

Winners, World Soccer Cup Championships 1962–1978.

SEMI-POSTAL STAMPS.

Anti-Malaria Issue

Common Design Type

Engraved

1962, Apr. 7 *Perf. 12½x12*

B3 CD108 25fr+5fr bistre 65 65

Issued for the World Health Organization drive to eradicate malaria.

Freedom from Hunger Issue

Common Design Type

1963, Mar. 21 *Perf. 13* **Unwmkd.**

B4 CD112 25fr+5fr violet blue, blue grn. & brn. 60 60

AIR POST STAMPS

Olympic Games Issue

French Equatorial Africa No. C37 Surcharged in Red Like Chad No. C1.

Engraved

1960 *Perf. 13* **Unwmkd.**

C1 AP8 250fr on 500fr greenish black, black & slate 5.50 5.50

Issued to commemorate the 17th Olympic Games, Rome, Aug. 25–Sept. 11.

Helicrysum Mechowiam—AP1

Flowers: 200fr, Cogniauxia podolaena. 500fr, Thesium tencio.

1961, Sept. 28 Engraved *Perf. 13*

C2 AP1 100fr green, lilac & yellow 1.35 95

C3 " 200fr blue green, yel. & brn. 2.65 1.20

C4 " 500fr brown red, yellow & slate green 6.00 2.65

Air Afrique Issue

Common Design Type

1961, Nov. 25 *Perf. 13* **Unwmkd.**

C5 CD107 50fr lilac rose, slate green & green 60 50

Founding of Air Afrique.

Loading Timber, Pointe-Noire Harbor—AP2

1962, June 8 Photo. *Perf. 12½x12*

C6 AP2 50fr multicolored 60 50

Issued to commemorate the opening of the International Fair and Exhibition, Pointe-Noire, June 8–11.

Abidjan Games Issue

Basketball AP3

1962, July 21 *Perf. 12x12½*

C7 AP3 100fr multicolored 1.35 95

Costus Spectabilis AP4

Design: 250fr, Mountain acanthus.

1963 *Perf. 13* **Unwmkd.**

C8 AP4 100fr multicolored 1.35 80

C9 " 250fr " 3.50 1.85

Brazzaville City Hall and Pres. Fulbert Youlou AP4a

1963, Aug. Photo. *Perf. 13x12*

C10 AP4a 100fr multi. 60.00 60.00

African Postal Union Issue

Common Design Type

1963, Sept. 8 *Perf. 12½*

C13 CD114 85fr purple, ocher & red 95 65

Air Afrique Issue, 1963

Common Design Type

Photogravure

1963, Nov. 19 *Perf. 13x12* **Unwmkd.**

C14 CD115 50fr multicolored 65 50

Liberty Place, Brazzaville—AP5

1963, Nov. 28

C15 AP5 25fr multicolored 32 25

See also No. 118.

Europafrica Issue

Common Design Type

1963, Nov. 30 *Perf. 12x13*

C16 CD116 50fr gray, yellow & dark brown 80 55

Timber Industry—AP6

1964, May 12 Engraved *Perf. 13*

C17 AP6 100fr green, brown red & blk. 1.20 70

Chiefs of State Issue

Map and Presidents of Chad, Congo, Gabon and CAR AP6a

1964, June 23 Photo. *Perf. 12½*

C18 AP6a 100fr multicolored 1.25 70

See note after Central African Republic No. C19.

Europafrica Issue, 1964

Sunburst, Wheat, Cogwheel and Globe AP7

1964, July 20 *Perf. 12x13*

C19 AP7 50fr yellow, Prussian blue & maroon 65 40

See note after Cameroun No. 402.

Hammer Thrower, Olympic Flame and Stadium—AP8

Designs (Olympic flame, stadium) and: 50fr, Weight lifter (vert.). 100fr, Badminton (vert.). 200fr, High jump.

1964, July 30 *Perf. 13* Engraved

C20 AP8 25fr vio. bl., orge. & red brown 32 15

C21 " 50fr yel. grn., orge. & red lilac 65 45

C22 " 100fr slate grn., orge. & red brown 1.25 95

C23 " 200fr crimson, orge. & deep green 2.50 1.90

a. Min. sheet of 4 5.50 5.50

Issued for the 18th Olympic Games, Tokyo, Oct. 10–25, 1964. No. C23a contains one each of Nos. C20–C23. Size: 191x99mm.

Communications Symbols AP8a

1964, Nov. 2 Litho. *Perf. 12½x13*

C24 AP8a 25fr dull rose & dark brown 40 30

See note after Chad No. C19.

Town Hall, Brazzaville—AP9

1965, Jan. 30 Photo. *Perf. 12½*

C25 AP9 100fr multicolored 1.20 65

Coupling Hooks—AP10

1965, Feb. 27 Photo. *Perf. 13x12*

C26 AP10 50fr multicolored 65 40

Economic Europe-Africa Association.

Breguet Dial Telegraph, ITU Emblem and Telstar AP11

1965, May 17 Engraved *Perf. 13*

C27 AP11 100fr dark blue, ocher & brn. 1.35 80

Issued to commemorate the centenary of the International Telecommunication Union.

Pope John XXIII and St. Peter's Cathedral—AP12

Perf. 12½x13

1965, June 26 Photo. Unwmkd.

C28 AP12 100fr golden brn. & multi. 1.20 90

Issued in memory of Pope John XXIII (1881–1963).

Pres. John F. Kennedy
AP13

Log Rolling
AP14

Portraits: 25fr on 50fr, Patrice Lumumba, premier of Congo Republic (ex-Belgian). 50fr, Sir Winston Churchill. 80fr, Barthélémy Boganda, premier of Central African Republic.

1965, June 25–26 *Perf. 12½*

C29 AP13 25fr on 50fr dark brn. & red 40 40
  a. Surch. omitted 22.50 22.50
C30 " 50fr dk. brown & yel. green 90 90
C31 " 80fr dk. brn. & bl. 1.20 1.20
C32 " 100fr dk. brown & orange yel. 1.50 1.50
  a. Min. sheet of 4 6.00 6.00

Issued to honor famous statesmen. No. C32a contains one each of Nos. C29–C32. Size: 106x143 mm.

A second miniature sheet contains one each of Nos. C29a, C30–C32. Price, $30.

1965, Aug. 14 Engraved *Perf. 13*

C33 AP14 50fr green, brn. & red brown 75 40

Issued to publicize national unity.

World Map and Symbols of Agriculture and Industry
AP15

1965, Oct. 18 Engraved *Perf. 13*

C34 AP15 50fr dk. blue, black, brn. & org. 75 50

International Cooperation Year, 1965.

Abraham Lincoln—AP16

1965, Dec. 15 Photo. *Perf. 13*

C35 AP16 90fr pink & multi. 1.10 65

Centenary of death of Abraham Lincoln.

Charles de Gaulle, Torch and Map of Africa—AP17

1966, Feb. 28 Engraved *Perf. 13*

C36 AP17 500fr dk. red, dk. grn. & dk. red brown 15.00 12.50

Issued to commemorate the 22nd anniversary of the Brazzaville Conference.

D-1 Satellite over Brazzaville Space Tracking Station
AP18

Grain, Atom Symbol and Map of Africa and Europe
AP19

1966, May 15 Engraved *Perf. 13*

C37 AP18 150fr blk., dull red & bl. green 1.85 95

1966, July 20 Photo. *Perf. 12x13*

C38 AP19 50fr multicolored 80 50

See note after Gabon No. C46.

Pres. Massamba-Debat and President's Palace
AP20

Designs: 30fr, Robespierre and storming of the Bastille. 50fr, Lenin and storming of the Winter Palace.

1966, Aug. 15 Photo. *Perf. 12x12½*

C39 AP20 25fr multicolored 28 15
C40 " 30fr " 35 15
C41 " 50fr " 60 28
  a. Souv. sheet of 3 1.50 1.50

Issued to commemorate the 3rd anniversary of the revolution. No. C41a contains one each of Nos. C39–C41. Black marginal inscription and control number. Size: 131½x160mm.

Air Afrique Issue, 1966

Common Design Type

1966, Aug. 31 Photo. *Perf. 13*

C42 CD123 30fr lilac, lemon & black 45 20

Issued to commemorate the introduction of DC-8F planes by Air Afrique.

Dr. Albert Schweitzer
AP21

1966, Sept. 4 Photo. *Perf. 12½*

C43 AP21 100fr red, black, bl. & lilac 1.25 80

Issued to honor Dr. Albert Schweitzer (1875–1965), medical missionary.

Crab, Microscope and Pagoda
AP22

1966, Dec. 26 Photo. *Perf. 13*

C44 AP22 100fr multicolored 1.20 65

Issued to commemorate the 9th International Anticancer Congress, Tokyo, Oct. 23–29.

Social Weaver
AP23

Birds: 75fr, European Bee-eater. 100fr, Lilac-breasted roller. 150fr, Regal sunbird. 200fr, Crowned cranes. 250fr, Secretary bird. 300fr, Knysna touraco.

1967 Photogravure *Perf. 13*

C45 AP23 50fr multicolored 1.00 40
C46 " 75fr " 1.35 55
C47 " 100fr " 1.65 80
C48 " 150fr " 2.00 1.10
C49 " 200fr " 2.65 1.35
C50 " 250fr " 3.50 1.75
C51 " 300fr " 4.00 2.25
  Nos. C45–C51 (7) 16.15 8.20

Issue dates: Nos. C45–C47, Feb. 13. Others, June 20.

Shackled Hands
AP24

1967, May 24 Photo. *Perf. 12½x13*

C52 AP24 500fr multi. 7.00 3.00

Issued for African Liberation Day.

Sputnik 1, Explorer 6 and Earth
AP25

Space Craft: 75fr, Ranger 6, Lunik 2 and moon. 100fr, Mars 1, Mariner 4 and Mars. 200fr, Gemini, Vostok and earth.

1967, Aug. 1 Engr. *Perf. 13*

C53 AP25 50fr purple, blue & orange brown 60 32
C54 " 75fr dk. car. & gray 90 50
C55 " 100fr red brn., Prus. bl. & ultra. 1.25 80
C56 " 200fr carmine lake, org. & blue 2.50 1.60

Space explorations.

African Postal Union Issue, 1967

Common Design Type

1967, Sept. 9 Engraved *Perf. 13*

C57 CD124 100fr verm., olive & emerald 1.20 70

Boy Scouts, Tents and Jamboree Emblem—AP26

Design: 70c, Borah Peak, Idaho; tents, Scout sign and Jamboree emblem.

1967, Sept. 29

C58 AP26 50fr brt. bl., brn. orange & red brown 55 28
C59 " 70fr dull bl., slate green & red brown 80 40

Issued to commemorate the 12th Boy Scout World Jamboree, Farragut State Park, Idaho, Aug. 1–9.

Sikorsky S-43 and Map of Africa
AP27

1967, Oct. 2 Photo. *Perf. 13*

C60 AP27 30fr multicolored 45 25

Issued to commemorate the 30th anniversary of the first airmail connection by Aeromaritime Lines from Casablanca to Pointe-Noire.

Men of Four Races Dancing on Globe
AP28

1968, Feb 8 Engraved *Perf. 13*

C61 AP28 70fr dk. brn., ultra. & emerald 90 50

Friendship among peoples.

The Oath of the Horatii, by Jacques Louis David—AP29

Paintings: 25fr, On the Barricades, by Delacroix. No. C63, Grandfather and Grandson, by Ghirlandajo (vert.). No. C64, The Demolition of the Bastille, by Hubert Robert. 200fr, Negro Woman Arranging Peonies, by Jean F. Bazille.

Perf. 12x12½, 12½x12

1968 Photogravure

C62	AP29	25fr multicolored	32	12
C63	"	30fr "	50	32
C64	"	30fr "	35	20
C65	"	100fr "	1.35	80
C66	"	200fr "	3.00	1.75
		Nos. C62-C66 (5)	5.52	3.19

Issue dates: Nos. C62, C64, Aug. 15. Nos. C63, C65-C66, Mar. 20.

See also Nos. C78-C81, C111-C115.

Early Automobile Type of Regular Issue

Designs: 150fr, Ford, 1915. 200fr, Citroën, 1922.

1968, July 29 Photo. *Perf. 13x12½*

C67	A50	150fr multicolored	2.00	1.00
C68	"	200fr lilac & multi.	2.50	1.35

Europafrica Issue

Square Knot
AP30

1968, July 20 Photo. *Perf. 13*

C69 AP30 50fr multicolored 55 25

Issued to commemorate the 5th anniversary of the economic agreement between the European Economic Community and the African and Malgache Union.

Martin Luther King, Jr.
AP31

Robert F. Kennedy
AP32

1968, Aug. 5 *Perf. 12½*

C70 AP31 50fr lt. green, Prus. grn. & black 55 25

Issued in memory of the Rev. Dr. Martin Luther King, Jr. (1929-1968), American civil rights leader.

1968, Sept. 30 Photo. *Perf. 13x12½*

C71 AP32 50fr deep carmine, apple green & black 65 32

Issued in memory of Robert F. Kennedy (1925-68), U.S. Senator and Attorney General.

Running
AP33

Olympic Rings and: 20fr, Soccer (vert.). 60fr, Boxing (vert.). 85fr, High jump.

1968, Dec. 27 Engraved *Perf. 13*

C72	AP33	5fr emerald, brt. blue & choc.	7	5
C73	"	20fr dk. blue, brown & dk. green	25	12
C74	"	60fr maroon, bright grn. & choc.	75	40
C75	"	85fr black, carmine rose & choc.	1.00	50

Issued to commemorate the 19th Olympic Games, Mexico City, Oct. 12-27.

PHILEXAFRIQUE Issue

G. De Gueidan, by Nicolas de Largillière
AP34

1968, Dec. 30 Photo. *Perf. 12½*

C76 AP34 100fr pink & multi. 1.30 1.10

Issued to publicize PHILEXAFRIQUE, Philatelic Exhibition, in Abidjan, Feb. 14-23. Printed with alternating pink label.

See also Nos. C89-C93.

2nd PHILEXAFRIQUE Issue

Common Design Type

Design: 50fr, Middle Congo No. 72 and Pointe-Noire harbor.

1969, Feb. 14 Engraved *Perf. 13*

C77 CD128 50fr carmine rose, slate green & bister brown 75 65

Issued to commemorate the opening of PHILEXAFRIQUE, Abidjan, Feb. 14.

Painting Type of 1968.

Paintings: 25fr, Battle of Rivoli, by Carle Vernet. 50fr, Battle of Marengo, by Jacques Augustin Pajou. 75fr, Battle of Friedland, by Horace Vernet. 100fr, Battle of Jena, by Charles Thevenin.

1969, May 20 Photo. *Perf. 12x12½*

C78	AP29	25fr violet blue & multi.	40	25
C79	"	50fr copper red & multi.	75	50
C80	"	75fr grn. & multi.	1.10	50
C81	"	100fr brn. & multi.	1.60	80

Bicentenary of birth of Napoleon I.

Ernesto Ché Guevara
AP35

1969, June 10 Photo. *Perf. 12½*

C82 AP35 90fr brown, orange & black 1.10 55

Issued in memory of Ernesto Ché Guevara (1928-1967), Cuban revolutionist.

Doll, Train and Space Toy
AP36

1969, June 20 Engraved *Perf. 13*

C83 AP36 100fr magenta, org. & gray 1.20 65

Issued to publicize the International Toy Fair, Nuremberg, Germany.

Europafrica Issue, 1969

Ribbon Tied Around Bar
AP37

1969, Aug. 5 Photo. *Perf. 13x12*

C84 AP37 50fr blue green, lilac & black 50 30

See note after Chad No. C11.

Armstrong, Aldrin and Collins
AP38

Painter, Poto-Poto School
AP39

Souvenir Sheet

Design: No. C85b, Blast-off from Moon.

Embossed on Gold Foil

1969, Sept. 15 *Imperf.*

C85	AP38	Sheet of 2	20.00	20.00
		a. 1000fr gold	9.00	9.00
		b. 1000fr gold	9.00	9.00

See note after Algeria No. 427. No. C85 contains one each of Nos. C85a and C85b with simulated perforations. Size: 65x52mm.

1970, Feb. 20 Engraved *Perf. 13*

Designs: 150fr, Sculpture lesson (man, infant and sculpture). 200fr, Potter working on vase.

C86	AP39	100fr multicolored	1.10	50
C87	"	150fr "	1.60	80
C88	"	200fr "	1.85	1.25

Painting Type (Philexafrique) of 1968

Paintings: 150fr, Child with Cherries, by John Russell. 200fr, Erasmus, by Hans Holbein the Younger. 250fr, "Silence" (head), by Bernardino Luini. 300fr, Scene from the Massacre of Scio, by Delacroix. 500fr, The Capture of Constantinople by the Crusaders, by Delacroix.

1970 Photogravure *Perf. 12½*

C89	AP34	150fr lilac & multi.	2.00	95
C90	"	200fr multicolored	2.40	1.20
C91	"	250fr brn. & multi.	2.65	1.50
C92	"	300fr multicolored	3.75	1.75
C93	"	500fr brn. & multi.	5.25	2.65
		Nos. C89-C93 (5)	16.05	8.05

Aurichalcite
AP40

Design: 15fr, Dioptase.

1970, Mar. 20

C94	AP40	100fr multicolored	1.10	55
C95	"	150fr "	1.75	80

Lenin
AP41

Karl Marx
AP42

Design: 75fr, Lenin, seated.

1970, June 25 Photo. *Perf. 12½*

C96	AP41	45fr green, orange & brown	50	20
C97	"	75fr violet blue, brown lake & deep claret	75	35

Issued to commemorate the centenary of the birth of Lenin (1870-1924), Russian communist leader.

1970, July 10 Engr. *Perf. 13*

Design: No. C99, Friedrich Engels.

C98	AP42	50fr emerald, dark brown & dark red	55	28
C99	"	50fr ultra., dk. brn. & dark red	55	28

Issued in memory of Karl Marx (1818-1883) and Friedrich Engels (1820-1895), German socialist writers.

Otto Lilienthal's Glider, 1891
AP43

Designs: 50fr, "Spirit of St. Louis," Lindbergh's first transatlantic solo flight, 1927. 70fr, Sputnik 1, first satellite in space. 90fr, First man on the moon, Apollo 11, 1969.

1970, Sept. 5 Engraved *Perf. 13*

C100	AP43	45fr dp. car., bl. & olive bister	55	28
C101	"	50fr emerald, slate grn. & brn.	55	32
C102	"	70fr brt. bl., olive bister & dp. carmine	80	40
C103	"	90fr brn., blue & olive gray	1.10	55

Forerunners of space exploration.

Saint on Horseback AP44

Marilyn Monroe and New York AP45

Designs from Stained Glass Windows, Brazzaville Cathedral: 150fr, Saint with staff. 250fr, The Elevation of the Host, from rose window.

1970, Dec. 10 Photo. *Perf. 12½*

C104	AP44	100fr dk. vio. blue & multi.	1.10	55
C105	"	150fr dk. vio. bl. & multi.	1.75	90
C106	"	250fr dk. vio. bl. & multi.	3.00	1.60
		a. Souvenir sheet of 3	6.00	6.00

Christmas 1970. No. C106a contains one each of Nos. C104–C106. Black marginal inscription. Size: 150x115mm.

1971, Mar. 16 Engraved *Perf. 13*

Portraits: 150fr, Martine Carol and Paris. 200fr, Erich von Stroheim and Vienna. 250fr, Sergei Eisenstein and Moscow.

C107	AP45	100fr bright green, red brown & ultra.	1.00	40
C108	"	150fr brown, brt. lilac & ultra.	1.60	60
C109	"	200fr chocolate & ultra.	2.00	90
C110	"	250fr brt. green, brn. violet & ultra.	2.40	1.00

History of motion pictures.

Painting Type of 1968

Paintings: 100fr, Christ Carrying Cross, by Paolo Veronese. 150fr, Christ on the Cross, Burgundian School, 1500 (vert.). 200fr, Descent from the Cross, by Rogier van der Weyden. 250fr, Christ Laid in the Tomb, Flemish School, 1500 (vert.). 500fr, Resurrection, by Hans Memling (vert.).

1971, April 26 Photogravure *Perf. 13*

C111	AP29	100fr grn. & multi	1.00	50
C112	"	150fr " "	1.40	65
C113	"	200fr " "	2.00	1.00
C114	"	250fr " "	2.40	1.20
C115	"	500fr " "	4.75	2.40
		Nos. C111-C115 (5)	11.55	5.75

Easter 1971.

Examination

The Catalogue editors cannot undertake to appraise, identify or pass upon genuineness or condition of stamps.

Map of Africa and Telecommunications System—AP46

1971, June 18 Photo. *Perf. 12½*

C116	AP46	70fr blue, gray & dk. brown	65	32
C117	"	85fr bl., lilac rose & dk. brn.	75	40
C118	"	90fr green, yel. & dk. brown	80	45

Pan-African telecommunications system.

Globe and Waves—AP47

1971, June 19

C119	AP47	65fr light blue & multi.	60	27

3rd World Telecommunications Day.

Japanese Mask and Play AP48

Olympic Torch and Rings AP49

Design: 150fr, Japanese and African women, symbolic leaves.

1971, June 28 Engr. *Perf. 13*

C120	AP48	75fr lilac, black & magenta	80	40
C121	"	150fr dk. brown, brn. red & red lilac	1.50	80

PHILATOKYO '71 International Stamp Exhibition, Tokyo, Apr. 20–30.

1971, July 20 Engraved *Perf. 13*

Design: 350fr, Olympic rings and various sports (horiz.).

C122	AP49	150fr brt. rose lilac, orange & slate grn.	1.60	90
C123	"	350fr bister, brt. green & violet	3.75	1.75

Pre-Olympic Year, 1971.

Scout Emblem, Japanese Dragon and African Carved Canoe—AP50

Designs (Boy Scout Emblem and): 90fr, Japanese mask and African boy (vert.). 100fr, Japanese woman and African drummer (vert.). 250fr, Congolese mask.

1971, Aug. 25

C124	AP50	85fr brt. rose lilac, Prus. blue & brown	1.00	45
C125	"	90fr dk. car., brn. & violet	1.10	50
C126	"	100fr olive gray, rose magenta & brt. green	1.25	60
C127	"	250fr brt. grn., choc. & carmine	3.00	1.40

13th Boy Scout World Jamboree, Asagiri Plain, Japan, Aug. 2–10.

Olympic Rings and Running—AP51

Designs (Olympic Rings and): 85fr, Hurdles. 90fr, Weight lifting, boxing, discus, running, javelin. 100fr, Wrestling. 150fr, Boxing.

1971, Sept. 30

C128	AP51	75fr plum, blue & dk. brn.	70	32
C129	"	85fr scarlet, slate & dk. brn.	75	35
C130	"	90fr violet bl. & dk. brown	85	45
C131	"	100fr brn. & slate	1.00	50
C132	"	150fr grn., red & dk. brn.	1.60	80
		Nos. C128-C132 (5)	4.90	2.42

75th anniversary of the first modern Olympic Games.

Congo No. C36 and de Gaulle AP52

Pres. Marien Ngouabi's Tribute to de Gaulle—AP53

Design: No. C135, Charles de Gaulle.

1971, Nov. 9

C133	AP52	500fr slate green & multi.	6.50	6.50

Lithographed; Gold Embossed

Perf. 12½

C134	AP53	1000fr gold, grn. & red	12.00	12.00
C135	"	1000fr gold, grn. & red	12.00	12.00

Charles de Gaulle (1890–1970), president of France. Nos. C134–C135 printed se-tenant.

African Postal Union Issue, 1971

Common Design Type

Design: 100fr, Allegory of Congo Republic (woman) and UAMPT Building, Brazzaville.

1971, Nov. 13 Photo. *Perf. 13x13½*

C136	CD135	100fr bl. & multi.	1.10	55

Flag of Congo Republic and "Revolution"—AP54

1971, Nov. 30

C137	AP54	100fr red & multi.	1.00	50

8th anniversary of revolution.

Workers and Flag—AP55

Design: 40fr, Flag of Congo Republic and sun.

1971, Dec 31 Photo. *Perf. 13x12½*

C138	AP55	30fr multicolored	25	12
C139	"	40fr red & multi.	35	20

2nd anniversary of founding of Congolese Labor Party (No. C138), and adoption of red flag (No. C139).

Book Year Emblem AP56

1972, June 3 Litho. *Perf. 12½*

C140	AP56	50fr red, green & yellow	40	20

International Book Year 1972.

Congolese Soccer Team—AP57

Design: No. C142, Captain of winning team and cup (vert.).

1973, Feb. 22 Photogravure *Perf. 13*

C141	AP57	100fr ultra., red & black	1.10	65
C142	"	100fr red, yellow & black	1.10	65

Girl Holding Bird, Environment Emblem AP58

1973, Mar. 5 Engraved

C143 AP58 85fr org., slate grn. & blue 65 40

U.N. Conference on Human Environment, Stockholm, Sweden, June 5–16, 1972.

Miles Davis
AP59

Designs: 140fr, Ella Fitzgerald. 160fr, Count Basie. 175fr, John Coltrane.

1973, Mar. 5 Photo. *Perf. 13x13½*

C144	AP59	125fr multi.	1.00	50
C145	"	140fr "	1.10	55
C146	"	160fr "	1.30	65
C147	"	175fr "	1.50	75

Black American jazz musicians.

Olympic Rings, Hurdling—AP60

Designs (Olympic Rings and): 150fr, Pole vault (vert.). 250fr, Wrestling.

1973, Mar. 15 Engraved *Perf. 13*

C148	AP60	100fr lilac rose & violet	1.00	50
C149	"	150fr emerald & violet	1.50	75
C150	"	250fr blue & magenta	2.50	1.35

20th Olympic Games, Munich, Aug. 26–Sept. 11, 1972.

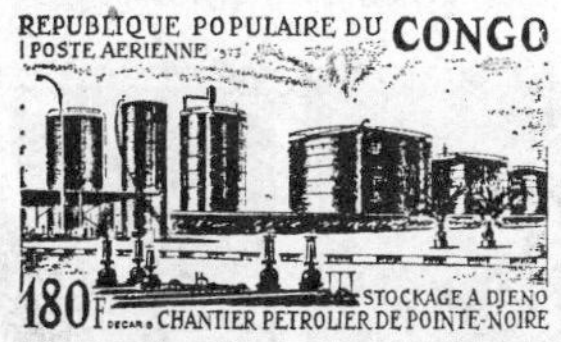

Refinery and Storage Tanks, Djéno—AP61

Designs: 230fr, Off-shore drilling platform (vert.). 240fr, Workers assembling drill (vert.). 260fr, Off-shore drilling installation.

1973, Mar. 20

C151	AP61	180fr red, blue & indigo	1.60	80
C152	"	230fr red, blue & black	2.00	1.00
C153	"	240fr red, indigo & brown	2.25	1.20
C154	"	260fr red, blue & black	2.60	1.40

Oil installations, Pointe-Noire.

Astronauts, Landing Module and Lunar Rover on Moon—AP62

1973, Mar. 31

C155 AP62 250fr multi. 2.50 1.50

Apollo 17 U.S. moon mission, Dec. 7–19, 1972.

ITU Emblem, Symbols of Communications
AP63

1973, May 24 Engr. *Perf. 13*

C156 AP63 120fr multi. 80 40

5th International Telecommunications Day.

White Horse, by Delacroix—AP64

Designs: Paintings by Eugene Delacroix.

1973, June 30 Photo. *Perf. 13*

Multicolored

C157	AP64	150fr *shown*	1.35	1.35
C158	"	250fr *Lion sleeping*	2.25	1.90
C159	"	300fr *Lion and tiger*	2.75	2.25

See Nos. C169–C171.

Copernicus and Heliocentric System—AP65

1973, June 30 Engraved

C160 AP65 50fr multicolored 45 35

500th anniversary of the birth of Nicolaus Copernicus (1473–1543), Polish astronomer.

Plane, Ship, Rocket, Village, Sun and Clouds—AP66

1973, July

C161 AP66 50fr red & multi. 40 28

Centenary of international meteorological cooperation.

Pres. Marien N'Gouabi
AP67

1973, Aug. 12 Photo. *Perf. 13*

C162	AP67	30fr multicolored	25	10
C163	"	40fr aqua & multi.	32	15
C164	"	75fr red & multi.	65	32

10th anniversary of independence.

Stamps, Album, African Woman
AP68

Designs: 40fr, No. C167, Stamps in shape of map of Congo, album, globe. No. C168, Like 30fr.

1973, Aug. 12

C165	AP68	30fr pur. & multi.	25	12
C166	"	40fr multicolored	32	15
C167	"	100fr dark brown & multi.	75	55
C168	"	100fr ocher & multi.	75	55

Nos. C165 and C168 commemorate the 10th anniversary of the revolution, Nos. C166–C167 the International Philatelic Exhibition, Brazzaville.

Painting Type of 1973 Inscribed "EUROPAFRIQUE"

Designs: Details from "Earth and Paradise," by Jan Brueghel, the Elder.

1973, Oct. 10 Photo. *Perf. 13*

Multicolored

C169	AP64	100fr *Spotted hyena*	1.00	75
C170	"	100fr *Leopard and lion*	1.00	75
C171	"	100fr *Elephant and creatures*	1.00	75

U.S. and Russian Spacecraft Docking—AP69

Design: 80fr, US and USSR spacecraft docked in space and emblems of 1975 joint space mission.

1973, Oct. 15 Engraved *Perf. 13*

C172	AP69	40fr bl., red & brn.	35	20
C173	"	80fr red, grn. & bl.	65	40

Planned joint United States and Soviet space missions.

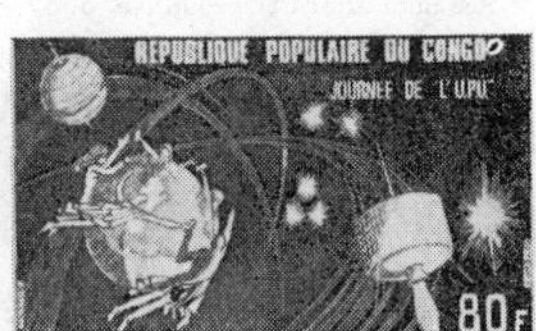

UPU Monument, Satellites, Big Dipper—AP70

1973, Nov. 20 Engraved *Perf. 13*

C174 AP70 80fr violet blue & light blue 65 35

Universal Postal Union Day.

Astronauts Working in Space—AP71

Design: 40fr, Spacecraft and Skylab docking in space.

1973, Nov. 30

C175	AP71	30fr ultra., slate grn. & choc.	25	15
C176	"	40fr mag., orange & slate grn.	35	25

Skylab, first space laboratory.

Goalkeeper, Soccer
AP72

Design: 100fr, Soccer player kicking ball.

1973, Dec. 20

C177	AP72	40fr slate green, sepia & brn.	32	25
C178	"	100fr purple, red & slate green	1.00	55

World Soccer Cup, Munich, 1974.

John F. Kennedy
AP73

1973, Dec. 20 Photo. *Perf. 12½*

C179 AP73 150fr ultra., gold & black 1.20 75

10th anniversary of the death of Pres. John F. Kennedy (1917–1963).

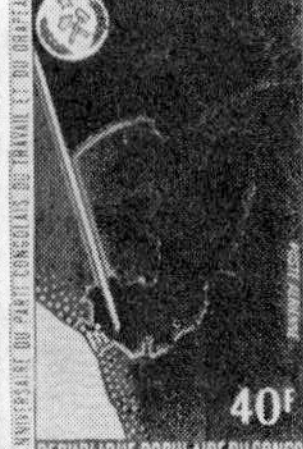

Runners AP74 — Flag over Map of Congo AP75

1973, Dec. 20 Engraved *Perf. 13*

C180	AP74	40fr slate green, red & brn.	32	25
C181	"	100fr red, slate grn. & brown	1.00	55

2nd African Games, Lagos, Nigeria.

1973, Dec. 31 Photogravure

C182 AP75 40fr deep green & multi. 32 20

4th anniversary of Congolese Labor Party and of the Congo Red Flag.

Soccer and Games Emblem
AP76

1974, June 20 Photo. *Perf. 13*

C183 AP76 250fr multi. 2.00 1.30

World Cup Soccer Championship, Munich, June 13–July 7.

Astronauts Yuri A. Gagarin and Alan B. Shepard—AP77

Designs: 30fr, Space, globe, Russian and American flags with names of astronauts who perished in space. 100fr, Alexei Leonov and Neil A. Armstrong in space and on moon.

1974, June 30 Engraved *Perf. 13*

C184 AP77 30fr red, ultra. & brown 25 15
C185 " 40fr red, bl. & brn. 35 20
C186 " 100fr car., green & brown 1.00 60

Soccer Game Superimposed on Ball
AP78

Link-up Emblem, Stages of Link-up
AP79

1974, July 31 Photo. *Perf. 13*

C187 AP78 250fr multi. 2.00 1.30

Germany's victory in World Cup Soccer Championship.

1974, Aug. 8 Engraved *Perf. 13*

Design: 300fr, Spacecraft docking over globe (horiz.).

C188 AP79 200fr purple, blue & red 1.60 1.20
C189 " 300fr multi. 2.40 1.60

Russo-American space cooperation.

Symbols of Communications, UPU Emblem—AP80

1974, Aug. 10

C190 AP80 500fr black & red 4.00 2.75

Centenary of Universal Postal Union.

Lenin and Pendulum Trace Pattern—AP81

1974, Sept. 16 Engraved *Perf. 13*

C191 AP81 150fr multi. 1.20 80

50th death anniversary of Lenin (1870–1924).

Churchill and Order of the Garter
AP82

Marconi and Wireless Telegraph
AP83

1974, Oct. 1 Litho. *Perf. 13*

C192 AP82 200fr lt. green & multi. 1.60 1.00
C193 AP83 200fr lt. ultra. & multi. 1.60 1.00

Birth centenaries of Sir Winston Churchill (1874–1965), statesman; and of Guglielmo Marconi (1874–1937), Italian electrical engineer and inventor.

No. C190 Surcharged in Violet Blue with New Value, 2 Bars and: "9 OCTOBRE 1974"

1974, Oct. 9

C194 AP80 300fr on 500fr multicolored 2.40 1.60

Universal Postal Union Day.

UDEAC Issue

Presidents and Flags of Cameroun, CAR, Gabon and Congo—AP83a

1974, Dec. 8 Photogravure *Perf. 13*

C195 AP83a 100fr gold & multi. 80 60

See note after Cameroun No. 595.

Regatta at Argenteuil, by Monet—AP84

Impressionist Paintings: 40fr, Seated Dancer, by Degas. 50fr, Girl on Swing, by Renoir. 75fr, Girl with Straw Hat, by Renoir. All vertical.

1974, Dec. 15

C196 AP84 30fr gold & multi. 35 25
C197 " 40fr " " 40 30
C198 " 50fr " " 65 50
C199 " 75fr " " 70 55

National Fair
AP85

1974, Dec. 20

C200 AP85 30fr multicolored 25 15

National Fair, Aug. 24–Sept. 8.

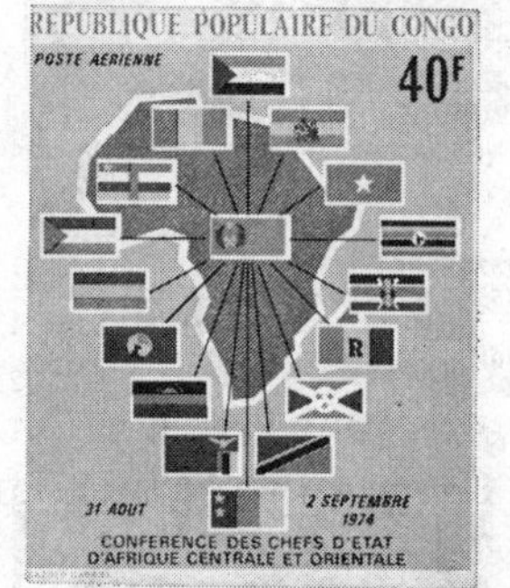

Flags of Participating Nations, Map of Africa—AP86

1974, Dec. 20 *Perf. 13*

C201 AP86 40fr ultra. & multi. 40 25

Conference of Chiefs of State of Central and East Africa, Brazzaville, Aug. 31–Sept. 2.

"Five Weeks in a Balloon," by Jules Verne
AP87

Design: 50fr, "Around the World in 80 Days," by Jules Verne.

1975, June 30 Litho. *Perf. 12½*

C202 AP87 40fr multicolored 35 20
C203 " 50fr " 40 25

Jules Verne (1828–1905), French science fiction writer, 70th death anniversary.

Paris-Brussels Train, 1890—AP88

Design: 75fr, Santa Fe, 1880.

1975, June 30

C204 AP88 50fr ocher & multi. 40 25
C205 " 75fr lt. bl. & multi. 60 35

Soyuz and Apollo-Soyuz Emblem
AP89

Design: 100fr, Apollo and emblem.

1975, July 20 Litho. *Perf. 12½*

C206 AP89 95fr orange, black & magenta 75 50
C207 " 100fr violet, blue, & black 80 60

Apollo Soyuz space test project (Russo-American space cooperation), launching July 15; link-up, July 17.

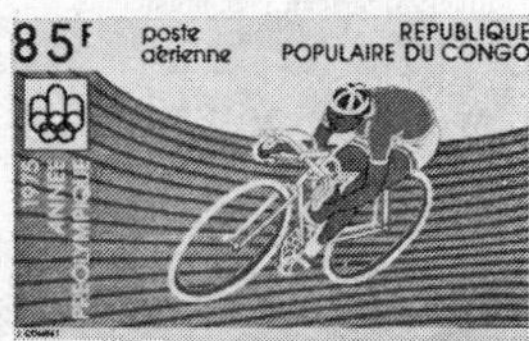

Bicycling and Montreal Olympic Emblem—AP90

Designs (Montreal Olympic Emblem and): 40fr, Boxing (vert.). 50fr, Basketball (vert.). 95fr, High jump. 100fr, Javelin. 150fr, Running.

Perf. 12½x13, 13x12½

1975, Oct. 30 Photogravure

C208 AP90 40fr multicolored 35 20
C209 " 50fr red & multi. 40 25
C210 " 85fr bl. & multi. 70 50
C211 " 95fr org. & multi. 75 55
C212 " 100fr multi. 80 60
C213 " 150fr " 1.20 90
Nos. C208–C213 (6) 4.20 3.00

Pre-Olympic Year 1975.

Map of Africa, Sports and Flags
AP91

Workers and Flag
AP92

1975, Dec. 20 Litho. *Perf. 12½*

C214 AP91 30fr multicolored 25 15

10th anniversary of first African Games, Brazzaville.

1975, Dec. 31 Litho. *Perf. 12½*

C215 AP92 60fr multicolored 50 30

6th anniversary of the Congolese Labor Party (P.C.T.).

Alphonse Fondere—AP93

Historic Ships: 5fr, like 30fr. 40fr, Hamburg, 1839. 15fr, 50fr, Gomer, 1831. 20fr, 60fr, Great Eastern, 1858. 95fr, J.M. White II, 1878.

1976 Engraved *Perf. 13*

C216	AP93	5fr multicolored	5	3
C217	"	10fr "	8	6
C218	"	15fr "	12	8
C219	"	20fr "	17	12
C220	"	30fr "	25	15
C221	"	40fr "	30	25
C222	"	50fr "	40	30
C223	"	60fr "	50	35
C224	"	95fr "	75	55
		Nos. C216-C224 (9)	2.62	1.89

Issue dates: Nos. C216-C219, May. Nos. C220-C224, Mar. 7.

Europafrica Issue 1976

Peasant Family, by Louis Le Nain
AP94

Paintings: 80fr, Boy with Top, by Jean B. Chardin. 95fr, Venus and Aeneas, by Nicolas Poussin. 100fr, The Rape of the Sabine Women, by Jacques Louis David.

1976, Mar. 20 Litho. *Perf. 12½*

C225	AP94	60fr gold & multi.	50	30
C226	"	80fr " "	65	45
C227	"	95fr " "	75	55
C228	"	100fr " "	80	60

Nos. C225-C228 printed in sheets of 8 stamps and horizontal gutter with commemorative inscription. Black control number in margin.

Telephone Type of 1976

1976, Apr. 25 Litho. *Perf. 12½x13*

C229	A107	60fr pink, maroon & crimson	50	35

Centenary of first telephone call by Alexander Graham Bell, Mar. 10, 1876.

Sports Type of 1976

Designs: 150fr, Runner and map of Central Africa. 200fr, Discus and map.

1976, Oct. 25 *Perf. 12½*

C230	A110	150fr multi.	1.20	90
C231	"	200fr "	1.60	1.10

Gold medalists, 1st Central African Games, Yaoundé, July 27-30, 1975.

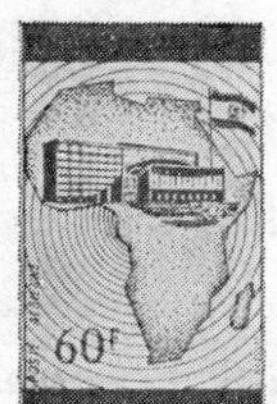

Map of Africa, Flag and OAU Headquarters
AP95

1976, Dec. 16 Typo. *Perf. 13x14*

C232	AP95	60fr multicolored	50	35

13th anniversary of the Organization for African Unity.

Europafrica Issue

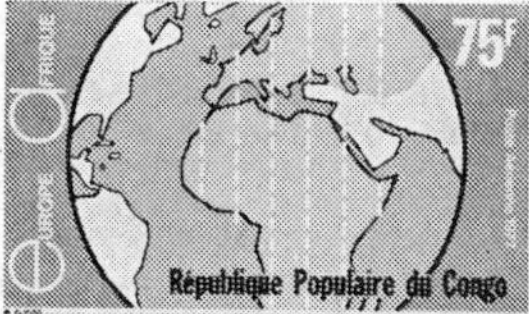

Map of Europe and Africa—AP96

1977, June 28 Litho. *Perf. 13*

C233	AP96	75fr multicolored	60	50

Headdress Type of 1977

1977, June 30 *Perf. 12½*

Designs: 250fr, Two straw caps. 300fr, Beaded cap.

C234	A118	250fr multi.	2.00	1.50
C235	"	300fr "	2.40	1.80

Zeppelin Type of 1977
Souvenir Sheet

Design: 500fr, LZ 127 over U.S. Capitol.

1977, Aug. 5 Litho. *Perf. 11*

C236	A120	500fr multi.	4.00	1.85

History of the Zeppelin.

No. C236 has multicolored margin showing parts of two Zeppelins. Size: 105x92mm. Exists imperf.

Checkerboard
AP97

1977, Aug. 20 Engr. *Perf. 13*

C237	AP97	60fr red & black	50	35

Lomé Convention on General Agreement on Tariffs and Trade (GATT).

Newton, Intelsat Satellite and Classical "Planets"—AP98

1977, Aug. 25

C238	AP98	140fr multi.	1.10	90

Isaac Newton (1642-1727), natural philosopher and mathematician, 250th death anniversary.

Elizabeth II Type of 1977
Souvenir Sheet

Design: 500fr, Royal family on balcony.

1977, Dec. 21 Litho. *Perf. 14*

C239	A128	500fr multi.	4.00	1.85

25th anniversary of the reign of Queen Elizabeth II.

Green-collared Duck
AP99

Birds: 75fr, Purple heron (vert.). 150fr, Reed warbler (vert.). 240fr, Hoopoe (vert.).

Perf. 13x12½, 12½x13

1978, May 22

C240	AP99	65fr multicolored	50	25
C241	"	75fr "	60	30
C242	"	150fr "	1.20	65
C243	"	240fr "	1.90	1.00

Souvenir Sheet

No. C239 Overprinted in Silver: "ANNIVERSAIRE DU / COURONNEMENT / 1953-1978"

1978, Sept. Litho. *Perf. 14*

C244	A128	500fr multi.	4.00	1.85

25th anniversary of coronation of Queen Elizabeth II. Size: 111x92mm.

Philexafrique II—Essen Issue
Common Design Types

Designs: No. C245, Leopard and Congo No. C243. No. C246, Eagle and Wurttemberg No. 1.

1978, Nov. 1 Litho. *Perf. 12½*

C245	CD138	100fr multi.	1.00	60
C246	CD139	100fr "	1.00	60

Nos. C245-C246 printed se-tenant.

Map of Africa Satellites
AP100

1978, Nov. 25 Engr. *Perf. 13*

C247	AP100	100fr multi.	1.00	60

Pan-African Telecommunications Network, PANAFEL.

AIR POST SEMI-POSTAL STAMPS

Hathor Pillar
SPAP1

Engraved

1964, March 9 *Perf. 13* Unwmkd.

CB1	SPAP1	10fr+5fr violet & chestnut	28	20
CB2	"	25fr+5fr orange brn. & slate green	45	35
CB3	"	50fr+5fr slate green & brown red	80	70

Issued to publicize the UNESCO world campaign to save historic monuments in Nubia.

POSTAGE DUE STAMPS

Messenger—D6

Early Transportation: 1fr, Litter. 2fr, Canoe. 5fr, Bicyclist. 10fr, Steam locomotive. 25fr, Seaplane.

Engraved

1961, Dec. 4 *Perf. 11* Unwmkd.

J34	D6	50c ultra., olive bistre & red	5	5
J35	"	1fr red brown, red & green	5	5
J36	"	2fr green, ultra., & brown	8	8
J37	"	5fr purple & gray brown	12	12
J38	D6	10fr blue, green & chocolate	28	28
J39	"	25fr blue, dk. green & dk. brown	65	65

The two types of each value in Nos. J34-J45 (early and modern transportation) were printed tête bêche, se-tenant at the base.

MH. 1521 Broussard Plane—D7

Modern transportation: 1fr, Land Rover. 2fr, River boat transporting barge. 5fr, Trailer-truck. 10fr, Diesel locomotive. 25fr, Boeing 707 jet plane.

J40	D7	50c ultra., olive bistre & red	5	5
J41	"	1fr red & green	5	5
J42	"	2fr ultra., green, & brown	8	8
J43	"	5fr purple & gray brown	12	12
J44	"	10fr dark green & chocolate	28	28
J45	"	25fr blue, dk. green & sepia	65	65
		Nos. J34-J45 (12)	2.46	2.46

See note following No. J39.

Flowers
D8

Flowers: 2fr, Phaeomeria magnifica. 5fr, Millettia laurentii. 10fr, Tuberose. 15fr, Pyrostegia venusta. 20fr, Hibiscus.

1971, Mar. 25 Photo. *Perf. 12x12½*

J46	D8	1fr multicolored	5	5
J47	"	2fr "	8	8
J48	"	5fr pink & multi.	10	10
J49	"	10fr dk. grn. & multi.	12	12
J50	"	15fr multicolored	25	25
J51	"	20fr "	40	40
		Nos. J46-J51 (6)	1.00	1.00

OFFICIAL STAMPS

Coat of Arms
O1

Typographed

1968-70 *Perf. 14x13* Unwmkd.

O1	O1	1fr multi. ('70)	5	3
O2	"	2fr " ('70)	5	5
O3	"	5fr " ('70)	10	8
O4	"	10fr " ('70)	30	18
O5	"	25fr emerald & multi.	25	10
O6	"	30fr red & multi.	30	10
O7	"	50fr multi. ('70)	90	45
O8	"	85fr " ('70)	1.60	90
O9	"	100fr " ('70)	2.00	1.10
O10	"	200fr " ('70)	3.00	2.25
		Nos. O1-O10 (10)	8.55	5.24

CORFU

(kôr·fōō'; kôr'fū)

LOCATION—An island in the Ionian Sea opposite the Greek-Albanian border.

GOVT.—A department of Greece.

AREA—245 sq. mi.

POP.—114,620 (1938).

CAPITAL—Corfu.

In 1923 Italy occupied Corfu (Kerkyra) during a controversy with Greece over the assassination of an Italian official in Epirus. Italy again occupied Corfu in 1941–43.

100 Centesimi = 1 Lira
100 Lepta = 1 Drachma

Issued under Italian Occupation

Italian Stamps of 1901-23 Overprinted **CORFÙ**

1923, Sept. 20 ***Perf. 14*** **Wmk. 140**

N1 A48 5c green 45 60
N2 " 10c claret 45 60
N3 " 15c slate 45 60
N4 A50 20c brown orange 45 60
N5 A49 30c orange brown 45 60
N6 " 50c violet 45 60
N7 " 60c blue 45 60
N8 A46 1 l brown & green 45 60
Nos. N1-N8 (8) 3.60 4.80

Italian Stamps of 1901-23 Surcharged **CORFÙ Lepta 25**

1923, Sept. 24

N9 A48 25 l on 10c claret 2.25 1.00
N10 A49 60 l on 25c blue 2.00
N11 " 70 l on 30c orange brown 2.00
N12 " 1.20d on 50c violet 1.85 1.00
N13 A46 2.40d on 1 l brown & green 1.85 1.00
N14 " 4.75d on 2 l green & orange 2.00

Nos. 10, 11 and 14 were not placed in use.

Issue for Corfu and Paxos.

Nos. N15–N34, NC1–NC12, NJ1–NJ11 and NRA1–NRA3 have been extensively counterfeited, some with forged cancellations.

Stamps of Greece, 1937-38, Overprinted in Black **CORFU**

Perf. 12x13½, 12½x12, 13½x12.

1941, June 5 **Wmk. 252**

N15 A69 5 l brown red & blue 3.00 3.00
N16 A70 10 l blue & brown red (On 397) 1.00 1.00
N17 " 10 l blue & brown red (On 413) 52.50 30.00
N18 A71 20 l black & green 1.00 1.00
N19 A72 40 l green & black 1.50 1.50
N20 A73 50 l brown & black 4.00 4.00
N21 A74 80 l indigo & yellow brown 2.00 2.00
N22 A67 1d green 2.00 2.00
N23 A84 1.50d green 10.00 10.00
N24 A75 2d ultramarine 1.50 1.00
N25 A67 3d red brown 2.00 2.00
N26 A76 5d red 2.00 2.00
N27 A77 6d olive brown 3.50 3.00
N28 A78 7d dark brown 6.00 5.00
N29 A67 8d deep blue 4.00 4.00
N30 A79 10d red brown 120.00 60.00
N31 A80 15d green 10.00 9.00
N32 A81 25d dark blue 8.00 8.00
N33 A84 30d org. brown 25.00 22.50
N34 A67 100d carmine lake 52.50 45.00
Nos. N15-N34 (20) 311.50 216.00

AIR POST STAMPS.

Greece Nos. C37 and C26 to C35, Overprinted **CORFU**

Perf.
12½x13, 13x12½, 13½x12½.

1941, June 5 **Unwmkd.**

NC1 D3 50 l dark brown 3.00 3.00
NC2 AP16 1d red 150.00 75.00
NC3 AP17 2d gray blue 3.50 3.50
NC4 AP18 5d violet 3.50 3.50
NC5 AP19 7d deep ultra. 4.00 4.00
NC6 AP20 10d bis. brown (On C26) 150.00 65.00
NC7 " 10d brn. org. (On C35) 17.50 10.00
NC8 AP21 25d rose 30.00 20.00
NC9 AP22 30d dark green 42.50 37.50
NC10 AP23 50d violet 32.50 30.00
a. Double overprint 300.00
NC11 AP24 100d brown 1000.00 500.00

On No. C36.

Serrate Roulette 13½.

NC12 D3 50 l vio. brown 25.00 20.00
a. On C36a

POSTAGE DUE STAMPS.

Postage Due Stamps of Greece, 1913-35 Overprinted **CORFU**

1941, June 5 **Unwmkd.**

Serrate Roulette 13½.

NJ1 D3 10 l carmine 1.25 1.25
NJ2 " 25 l ultramarine 1.50 1.50
NJ3 " 80 l lilac brown 175.00 60.00

Perf. 12½x13, 13½x12½.

NJ4 D3 1d light blue (On J80) 900.00 275.00
NJ5 " 2d light red 3.00 2.00
NJ6 " 5d gray 10.00 9.00
NJ7 " 10d gray green 6.00 6.00
NJ8 " 15d red brown 6.00 6.00
NJ9 " 25d light red 6.00 6.00
NJ10 " 50d orange 8.00 8.00
NJ11 " 100d slate green 275.00 160.00

POSTAL TAX STAMPS.

Greece Nos. RA61 to RA63, Overprinted **CORFU**

Perf. 13½x12

1941, June 5 **Unwmkd.**

NRA1 PT7 10 l bright rose, *pale rose* 1.00 75
NRA2 " 50 l gray green, *pale green* 1.25 1.00
NRA3 " 1d dull blue, *light blue* 7.50 6.00

Stamps overprinted "CORFU" were replaced by Italian stamps overprinted "Isole Jonie." (See Ionian Islands.)

COSTA RICA

(kŏs'tȧ rē'kȧ)

LOCATION—In Central America between Nicaragua and Panama.

GOVT.—Republic.

AREA—19,653 sq. mi.

POP.—2,010,000 (est. 1976).

CAPITAL—San José.

8 Reales = 100 Centavos = 1 Peso
100 Centimos = 1 Colón (1900)

Coat of Arms
A1

Engraved.

1863 ***Perf. 12*** **Unwmkd.**

1 A1 ½r blue 40 1.00
a. ½r light blue 40 1.00
b. Imperf. horiz. pair 85.00
c. Imperf. vert., pair
2 " 2r scarlet 1.00 1.75
3 " 4r green 6.00 6.00
4 " 1p orange 15.00 16.50

The ½r was printed from two plates. The second is in light blue with little or no sky over the mountains.

Imperforate copies of Nos. 1–2 are corner copies from poorly perforated sheets.

Nos. 1–3 Surcharged in Red or Black:

1 cto. *a* — 1 cto. *b* — 2 cts. *c* — 5 cts. U.P.U. *d* — 20 CTS U.P.U. *e*

1881–82

Red or Black Surcharge.

7 A1 (*a*) 1c on ½r blue('82) 2.00 7.00
8 " (*b*) 1c on ½r blue('82) 7.50 10.00
9 " (*c*) 2c on ½r blue 1.50 3.50
a. Double surch.
b. "Cts."
12 " (") 5c on ½r blue 5.00 6.50
a. Double surch.
13 " (*d*) 5c on ½r blue ('82) 70.00 60.00
14 " (") 10c on 2r scarlet (Bk) ('82) 35.00 40.00
15 " (*e*) 20c on 4r green ('82) 75.00 67.50

The ½r stamps surcharged "DOS CTS" were never placed in use, and are said to have been surcharged to a dealer's order.

Counterfeits exist of surcharges on Nos. 7–15.

Gen. Prospero Fernández
A6

President Bernardo Soto Alfaro
A7

1883, Jan. 1

16 A6 1c green 85 50
17 " 2c carmine 75 60
18 " 5c blue violet 1.25 50
19 " 10c orange 15.00 3.00
20 " 40c blue 75 65
Nos. 16-20 (5) 18.60 5.25

Unused copies of 40c usually lack gum.

1887

21 A7 5c blue violet 2.25 50
22 " 10c orange 1.00 60

A8 A9

1889 Black Overprint.

23 A8 1c rose 1.50 85
24 A9 5c brown 1.00 65

President Soto Alfaro
A10 A11

A12 A13

A14 A15

A16 A17

A18 A19

1889 ***Perf. 14-16 & Compound***

25 A10 1c brown 25 25
a. Horiz. pair, imperf. vert 10.00
b. Imperf. pair 30.00
c. Horiz. or vert. pair, imperf. between 32.50
26 A11 2c dark green 25 25
a. Imperf., pair 10.00
b. Vert. pair, imperf. horiz. 10.00
c. Horiz. pair, imperf. btwn. 10.00
27 A12 5c orange 40 30
a. Imperf., pair 35.00
b. Horiz. pair, imperf. btwn. 25.00
28 A13 10c red brown 25 25
a. Vert. or horiz. pair, imperf. btwn. 15.00
29 A14 20c yellow green 25 25
a. Vert. pair, imperf. horiz. 15.00
b. Horizontal pair, imperf. btwn. 15.00
30 A15 50c rose red 75 75
31 A16 1p blue 1.10 1.10
32 A17 2p dull violet 7.50 7.50
a. 2p slate 7.50 7.50

33 A18 5p olive green 25.00 22.50
34 A19 10p black 40.00 32.50
Nos. 25-34 (10) 75.75 65.65

Arms of Costa Rica
A20 A21

A22 A23

A24 A25

A26 A27

A28 A29

1892 ***Perf. 12-15 & Compound***

35 A20 1c greenish blue 20 20
36 A21 2c yellow 20 20
37 A22 5c red lilac 20 15
a. 5c violet 5.00 18
38 A23 10c light green 55 25
a. Horiz. pair, imperf. btwn.
39 A24 20c scarlet 3.50 18
a. Horiz. pair, imperf. btwn. 25.00
40 A25 50c gray blue 4.00 4.00
41 A26 1p green, *yellow* 1.10 85
42 A27 2p rose red, *pale lilac* 1.75 1.10
a. 2p brown red, *lilac* 1.75 1.10
43 A28 5p dark blue, *blue* 1.75 1.10
44 A29 10p brown, *pale buff* 4.00 4.00
a. 10p brown, *yellow* 4.00 4.00
Nos. 35-44 (10) 17.25 12.03

Imperfs. of Nos. 35-44 are proofs.

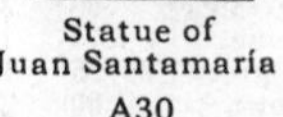

Statue of Juan Santamaría
A30

Juan Mora Fernández
A31

View of Port Limón
A32

Braulio Carillo
("Branlio" on stamp)
A33

National Theater
A34

José M. Castro
A35

Birris Bridge
A36

Juan Rafael Mora
A37

Jesús Jiménez
A38

Coat of Arms
A39

1901, Jan. ***Perf. 12-15½***

45 A30 1c green & black 25 10
46 A31 2c vermilion & black 35 15
47 A32 5c gray blue & black 30 10
a. Vert. pair, imperf. btwn. 40.00
48 A33 10c ochre & black 85 12
49 A34 20c lake & black 2.50 15
a. Vert. pair, imperf. btwn.
50 A35 50c dull lilac & dark blue 2.50 75
51 A36 1col olive bistre & black 10.00 2.00
52 A37 2col carmine rose & dark green 7.50 1.35
53 A38 5col brown & black 12.00 1.35
54 A39 10col yellow green & brown red 15.00 2.00
Nos. 45-54 (10) 51.25 8.07

The 2c exists with center inverted.

Remainders

In 1914 the government sold a large quantity of stamps at very much less than face value. The lot included most regular issues from 1901 to 1911 inclusive, postage due stamps of 1903 and official stamps of 1901-03. These stamps were cancelled with groups of thin parallel bars. They, of course, sell for much less than the prices quoted which are for stamps with regular postal cancellations.

José M. Cañas
A40

Julián Volio
A41

Eusebio Figueroa Oreamuno
A42

1903 ***Perf. 13½, 14, 15***

55 A40 4c red violet & black 1.25 60
56 A41 6c olive green & black 4.00 1.50
57 A42 25c gray lilac & brown 5.00 15

No. 49 Surcharged in Black:

1905

58 A34 1c on 20c lake & black 45 45
a. Inverted surcharge 1.75 1.75
b. Diagonal surcharge 45 45

Specimens surcharged in other colors are proofs.

Statue of Juan Santamaria
A43

Juan Mora Fernández
A44

José M. Cañas
A45

Mauro Fernández
A46

Braulio Carrillo
A47

Julián Volio
A48

Eusebio Figueroa Oreamuno
A49

José M. Castro
A50

Jesús Jiménez
A51

Juan Rafael Mora
A52

1907 ***Perf. 11x14*** **Unwmkd.**

59 A43 1c red brown & indigo 50 15
b. Perf. 14 40 15
60 A44 2c yellow green & blk. 75 20
a. Perf. 14 75 20
61 A45 4c carmine & indigo 4.50 2.00
a. Perf. 14 135.00 20.00
62 A46 5c yellow & dull blue, perf. 14 40 15
a. Perf. 11x14 2.50 30
63 A47 10c blue & black 60 25
a. Perf. 14 75 30
64 A48 20c olive green & black 5.00 1.75
a. Perf. 14 5.00 1.75
65 A49 25c gray lilac & black, perf. 14 2.00 75
a. Perf. 11x14 15.00 4.00
66 A50 50c red lilac & blue 30.00 9.00
a. Perf. 14 40.00 11.00
67 A51 1col brown & black 12.50 7.00
a. Perf. 14 15.00 8.00
68 A52 2col claret & green 50.00 27.50
a. Perf. 14 75.00 35.00
Nos. 59-68 (10) 106.25 48.75

Imperforate copies of the above set are either proofs or from unfinished sheets, which were placed on the market in London. The 1c, 2c, 5c, 20c, 50c, 1 col. and 2 col. exist with center inverted. Price, 5c, $300; others each $500.

Nos. 59-68 exist with papermaker's watermark.

Statue of Juan Santamaria
A53

Juan Mora Fernández
A54

José M. Cañas
A55

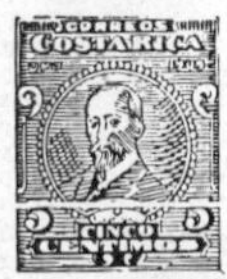

Mauro Fernández
A56

Braulio Carrillo
A57

Julián Volio
A58

Eusebio Figueroa Oreamuno
A59

Jesús Jiménez
A60

1910 ***Perf. 12.***

69 A53 1c brown 6 6
70 A54 2c deep green 15 10
71 A55 4c scarlet 10 10
72 A56 5c orange 20 6
73 A57 10c deep blue 10 8
74 A58 20c olive green 20 20
75 A59 25c deep violet 2.25 50
76 A60 1col dark brown 40 60
Nos. 69-76 (8) 3.46 1.70

Nos. 69a-73a and 72b-72c ("Cafe" ovpts.) are listed after No. 111.

No. 60a Overprinted in Red *1911*

1911 ***Perf. 14***

77 A44 2c yellow green & black 1.10 80
a. Inverted overprint 3.50 3.50
b. Double overprint, both inverted 40.00

Stamps of 1901-07 Overprinted in Red or Black **** 1911 ****

78 A30 1c green & black (R) 55 40
a. Black overprint 25.00 16.50
b. Inverted overprint
79 A43 1c red brown & indigo (Bk) 60 40
a. Inverted overprint 3.75 3.75
b. Double overprint 5.50 5.50
80 A44 2c yellow green & black (Bk) 55 35
a. Inverted overprint 2.25 2.25
b. Double overprint, one as on No. 77 12.00 12.00
c. Double overprint, one inverted 12.00 12.00
d. Pair, one stamp No. 77 20.00
e. Perf. 11x14 1.10 40

Habilitado

No. 55 Overprinted in Black

1911

81 A40 4c red violet & black 80 55

Habilitado

Stamps of 1907 Overprinted in Blue, Black or Rose

1911

Perf. 14

82 A46 5c yellow & blue (Bl) 40 20
a. "Habilitada" 2.50 2.50
b. "2911" 5.50 3.50
c. Roman "I" in "1911" 2.00 1.50
d. Double overprint 3.50 3.50
e. Inverted overprint 3.50 3.50
f. Black overprint 4.50 1.50
g. Triple overprint 4.50
h. Imperf. horizontally (pair) 25.00
83 A47 10c blue & black (Bk) 1.50 1.00
a. Roman "I" in "1911" 5.00 4.50
c. Double overprint 9.50 6.50
d. Perf. 11x14 1.10 75
84 " 10c blue & black (R), perf. 11x14 5.00 5.00
a. Roman "I" in "1911" 12.50 12.50
b. "Habilitada"
c. Perf. 14 20.00 15.00

Many counterfeits of overprint exist.

A61

A62

A63

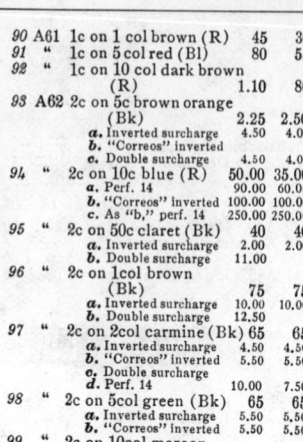

Telegraph Stamps Surcharged in Rose, Blue or Black.

1911 ***Perf. 12, 14, 14x11.***

86 A61 1c on 10c blue (R) 24 18
a. "Coereos" 7.50 5.00
b. Inverted surcharge
87 " 1c on 10c blue (Bk) 90.00 50.00
a. "Coereos"
88 " 1c on 25c violet (Bk) 18 18
a. "Coereos" 7.00 7.00
b. Pair, one without surcharge 13.50
c. Double surcharge 5.50
e. Double surcharge, one inverted 9.00
89 " 1c on 50c red brown (Bl) 35 30
a. Inverted surcharge 4.00 4.00
b. Double surcharge

90 A61 1c on 1 col brown (R) 45 30
91 " 1c on 5 col red (Bl) 80 55
92 " 1c on 10 col dark brown (R) 1.10 80
93 A62 2c on 5c brown orange (Bk) 2.25 2.50
a. Inverted surcharge 4.50 4.00
b. "Correos" inverted
c. Double surcharge 4.50 4.00
94 " 2c on 10c blue (R) 50.00 35.00
a. Perf. 14 90.00 60.00
b. "Correos" inverted 100.00 100.00
c. As "b," perf. 14 250.00 250.00
95 " 2c on 50c claret (Bk) 40 40
a. Inverted surcharge 2.00 2.00
b. Double surcharge 11.00
96 " 2c on 1col brown (Bk) 75 75
a. Inverted surcharge 10.00 10.00
b. Double surcharge 12.50
97 " 2c on 2col carmine (Bk) 65 65
a. Inverted surcharge 4.50 4.50
b. "Correos" inverted 5.50 5.50
c. Double surcharge
d. Perf. 14 10.00 7.50
98 " 2c on 5col green (Bk) 65 65
a. Inverted surcharge 5.50 5.50
b. "Correos" inverted 5.50 5.50
99 " 2c on 10col maroon (Bk) 70 70
a. "Correos" inverted 15.00
100 A63 5c on 5c orange (Bl) 30 20
a. Double surcharge 5.50 4.50
b. Inverted surcharge 5.50 4.50
c. Pair, one without surcharge 10.00
Nos. 86–100 (15) 133.82 93.16

Counterfeits exist of Nos. 87, 94 and all minor varieties.

Nos. 93–99 exist with papermaker's watermark.

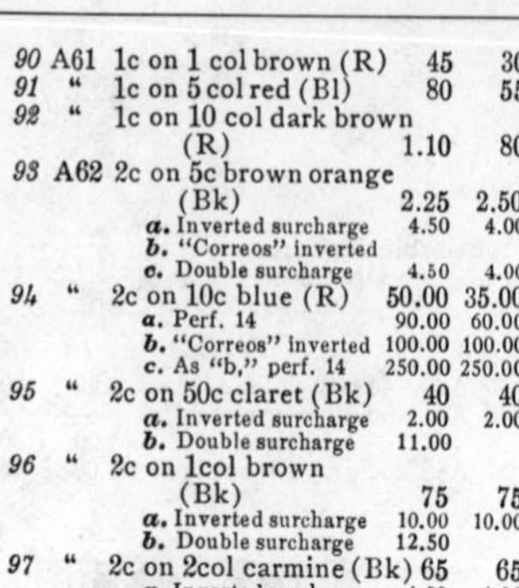

Coffee Plantation—A64

1921, June 17 Litho. *Perf. 11½*

103 A64 5c blue & black 1.35 1.10
a. Tête bêche pair 3.25 3.25
b. Imperf., pair 12.00
c. As "a," imperf. 30.00

Centenary of coffee raising in Costa Rica.

Liberty with Torch of Freedom
A65

1921 Typographed. *Perf. 11*

104 A65 5c violet 75 35
a. Imperf. 30.00

Centenary of Central American independence.

Juan Mora and Julio Acosta—A66

1921, Sept. 15 *Perf. 11½*

105 A66 2c orange & black 1.75 1.00
106 " 3c green & black 1.75 1.00
107 " 6c scarlet & black 1.75 1.25
108 " 15c dk. blue & black 5.00 4.00
109 A66 30c org. brn. & blk. 10.00 9.00
Nos. 105–109 (5) 20.25 16.25

Centenary of Central American independence. Issue requested by Costa Rican Philatelic Society. Authorized by decree calling for 2,000 of 30c and 5,000 each of other values. Many more were printed illegally including imperforates, color changes and inverted centers.

Each sheet of 20 (4x5) contains 5 tête-bêche pairs.

Simón Bolívar
A67

1921 Engraved. *Perf. 12.*

110 A67 15c deep violet 35 15

CORREOS

No. 104 Overprinted

1922

1922 ***Perf. 11***

111 A65 5c violet 50 30
a. Inverted overprint 3.00
b. Double overprint 6.00

Stamps of 1910–1921 Overprinted in Blue, Red, Black or Gold

1922 ***Perf. 12***

69a A53 1c brown (Bl) 15 10
70a A54 2c deep green (R) 20 12
71a A55 4c scarlet 25 20
72a A56 5c orange 30 20
73a A57 10c deep blue (R) 50 40
110a A67 15c deep violet (G) 1.65 1.25
Nos. 69a–110a (6) 3.05 2.27

Inverted overprints occur on all values. Counterfeits exist.

No. 72 Overprinted with Double-Lined Circle, Inscribed: "Compre Ud. Cafe de Costa Rica"

1923

72b A56 5c orange 35 25
c. "VD." for "UD." 50.00 50.00

Jesús Jiménez
A68

1923, June 18 Litho. *Perf. 11½*

112 A68 2c brown 15 15
113 " 4c green 20 15
114 " 5c blue 50 20
115 " 20c carmine 25 25
116 " 1col violet 40 35
Nos. 112–116 (5) 1.50 1.10

Issued to commemorate the centenary of the birth of President Jesús Jiménez (1823–1898).

Nos. 112 to 116 exist imperforate but were not regularly issued in that condition.

National Monument
A70

Harvesting Coffee
A71

Banana Growing
A73

General Post Office
A74

Columbus Soliciting Aid of Isabella
A75

Christopher Columbus
A76

Columbus at Cariari
A77

Map of Costa Rica
A78

Manuel M. Gutiérrez
A79

1923–26 Engraved *Perf. 12*

117 A70 1c violet 10 10
118 A71 2c yellow 30 15
119 A73 4c deep green 50 35
120 A74 5c light blue 75 10
121 " 5c yellow green ('26) 25 10
122 A75 10c red brown 1.00 20

123	A75	10c carmine rose ('26)	25	10
124	A76	12c carmine rose	2.50	1.50
125	A77	20c deep blue	2.50	1.35
126	A78	40c orange	7.50	1.50
127	A79	1col olive green	1.50	50
		Nos. 117-127 (11)	17.15	5.95

See also Nos. 151-156.

Rodrigo Arias Maldonado
A80

1924 ***Perf. 12½.***

128	A80	2c dark green	15	10
		a. Perf. 14	18	10

See No. 162.

Map of Guanacaste
A81

Mission at Nicoya
A82

1924 Lithographed. ***Perf. 12.***

129	A81	1c carmine rose	50	30
130	"	2c violet	50	30
131	"	5c green	50	30
132	"	10c orange	3.50	75
133	A82	15c light blue	1.10	65
134	"	20c gray black	1.75	1.10
135	"	25c light brown	2.50	2.00
		Nos. 129-135 (7)	10.35	5.40

Centenary of annexation of Province of Guanacaste to Costa Rica.
Exist imperf. Price, set, $40.

1925

Stamps of 1923 Surcharged:

a

b

136	A74 (*a*)	3c on 5c light blue	25	25
137	A75 (")	6c on 10c red brown	30	30
138	A78 (")	30c on 40c orange	60	50
139	A79 (*b*)	45c on 1 col olive green	1.00	50
		a. Double surcharge	25.00	

No. 124 Surcharged

=10 10=

1926

140	A76	10c on 12c carmine rose	1.50	25

College of San Luis, Cartago
A83

Chapui Asylum, San José
A84

Normal School, Heredia
A85

Ruins of Ujarrás
A86

Engraved

1926 ***Perf. 12½.*** **Unwmkd.**

143	A83	3c ultramarine	25	20
144	A84	6c dark brown	35	25
145	A85	30c deep orange	75	25
146	A86	45c black violet	1.50	60

No. 124 Surcharged in Black:

1928, Jan. 7 ***Perf. 12***

147	A76	10c on 12c carmine rose	10.00	7.50

Issued in honor of Col. Charles A. Lindbergh during his Good Will Tour of Central America.
The surcharge has been counterfeited.

No. 110 Surcharged 5 5

1928

148	A67	5(c) on 15c dp. vio.	25	12
		a. Inverted surcharge	20.00	

Type I
A88

CORREOS 5 CENTIMOS CORREOS 5 CENTIMOS
Type II Type III

CORREOS 5 CENTIMOS CORREOS 5 CENTIMOS
Type IV Type V

Surcharge Typographed (I-V) and (V) Lithographed.

1929 ***Perf. 12½***

149	A88	5c on 2col carmine (I)	12	12
		a. 5c on 2col carmine (II)	12	12
		b. 5c on 2col carmine (III)	12	12
		c. 5c on 2col carmine (IV)	12	12
		d. 5c on 2col carmine (V)	12	12

Telegraph Stamp Surcharged for Postage as in 1929, Surcharge Lithographed.

1929

150	A88	13c on 40c deep green	15	10
		a. Inverted surcharge	1.25	1.00

Excellent counterfeits exist of No. 150a.

Types of 1923-26 Issues Dated "1929"

Imprint of Waterlow & Sons.

1930 Size: 26x21½mm. ***Perf. 12½***

151	A70	1c dark violet	10	8
155	A74	5c green	10	8
156	A75	10c carmine rose	50	8

Juan Rafael Mora
A89

1931

157	A89	13c carmine rose	35	25

Seal of Costa Rica Philatelic Society ("Octubre 12 de 1932")
A90

1932, Oct. 12 ***Perf. 12***

158	A90	3c orange	25	25
159	"	5c dark green	35	35
160	"	10c carmine rose	40	40
161	"	20c dark blue	50	50

Issued to commemorate the Philatelic Exhibition of Oct. 12, 1932. See also Nos. 179-183.

Maldonado Type of 1924.

1934 ***Perf. 12½***

162	A80	3c dark green	10	8

Red Cross Nurse—A91

1935, May 31 ***Perf. 12***

163	A91	10c rose carmine	50	25

Issued in commemoration of the 50th anniversary of the founding of the Costa Rican Red Cross Society.

Air View of Cartago—A92

Miraculous Statuette and View of Cathedral
A93

Vision of 1635
A94

1935, Aug. ***Perf. 12½***

164	A92	5c green	25	15
165	A93	10c carmine	50	25
166	A92	30c orange	75	35
167	A94	45c dark violet	1.75	60
168	A93	50c blue black	3.00	1.25
		Nos. 164-168 (5)	6.25	2.60

Issued to commemorate the tercentenary of the Patron Saint, Our Lady of the Angels, of Costa Rica.

Map of Cocos Island
A95

1936, Jan. 29 ***Perf. 14, 11½ (25c)***

169	A95	4c ochre	35	15
170	"	8c dark violet	45	25
171	"	25c orange	50	25
172	"	35c brown violet	75	25
173	"	40c brown	1.00	35
174	"	50c yellow	1.00	50
175	"	2col yellow green	8.00	3.00
176	"	5col green	24.00	13.00
		Nos. 169-176 (8)	36.05	17.75

Exist imperf. Price, set, $35.

Map of Cocos Island and Ships of Columbus
A96

1936, Dec. 5 ***Perf. 12***

177	A96	5c green	20	6
178	"	10c carmine rose	20	6

Seal of Costa Rica Philatelic Society ("Diciembre 1937")—A97

1937

179	A97	2c dark brown	20	20
180	"	3c black	20	20
181	"	5c green	25	20
182	"	10c orange red	30	25

Souvenir Sheet.

Imperf.

183	A97	Sheet of four	80	80
		a. 2c dark brown	15	15
		b. 3c black	15	15
		c. 5c green	15	15
		d. 10c orange red	15	15

Issued to commemorate the Philatelic Exhibition, December, 1937. Size of No. 183: 168x101mm.

Purple Guaria Orchid, National Flower—A98

Tuna
A99

Native with Donkey Carrying Bananas
A101

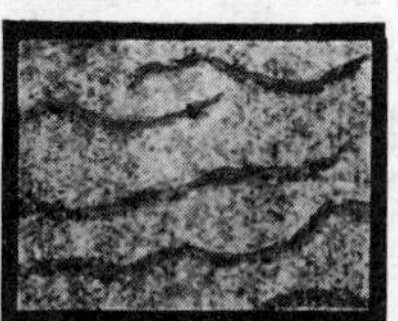

Wmk. 229

Designs: 3c, Cacao pod. 10c, Coffee harvesting.

Wmkd. Wavy Lines. (229)

1937-38 *Perf. 12½*

184	A98	1c grn. & vio. ('38)	25	6
185	"	3c chocolate ('38)	20	15

Perf. 12

Unwmkd.

186	A99	2c olive gray	30	15
187	A101	5c dark green	35	12
188	"	10c carmine rose	50	30
		Nos. 184-188 (5)	1.60	78

Nos 184-188 were issued to commemorate the National Exposition.

No. 125 Overprinted in Black **1938**

1938 *Perf. 12.* **Unwmkd.**

189	A77	20c deep blue	35	20

No. 146 Surcharged in Red:

a

b

c d

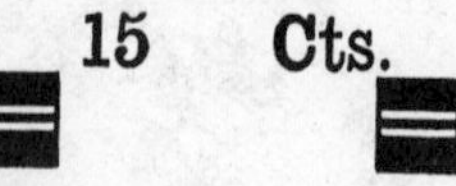

e

1940 *Perf. 12½.*

190	A86	(*a*) 15c on 45c blk. vio.	40	30
190A	"	(*b*) 15c on 45c " "	40	30
190B	"	(*c*) 15c on 45c " "	40	30
190C	"	(*d*) 15c on 45c " "	40	30
190D	"	(*e*) 15c on 45c " "	30	25
		Nos. 190-190D (5)	1.90	1.45

Allegory—A103

Overprinted "Dia Panamericano de la Salud / 2·Diciembre 1940" and Arc in Black

1940, Dec. 2 **Engraved** ***Perf. 12***

191	A103	5c green	30	20
192	"	10c rose carmine	35	25
193	"	20c deep blue	75	30
194	"	40c brown	1.25	1.00
195	"	55c orange yellow	3.00	1.25
		Nos. 191-195 (5)	5.65	3.00

Pan-American Health Day. See Nos. C46-C54.
Exist without overprint.

Stamps of 1936 Surcharged in Black:

15 CENTIMOS 15

1941 ***Perf. 14, 11½***

196	A95	15c on 25c orange	35	30
197	"	15c on 35c brn. vio.	35	30
198	"	15c on 40c brown	35	30
199	"	15c on 2 col yel. grn.	35	30
200	"	15c on 5 col green	60	55
		Nos. 196-200 (5)	2.00	1.75

Nos. 196-200 exist with surcharge inverted. Price, $5 a set.

National Stadium—A104

Engraved; Flags Typographed in National Colors

1941, May 8 ***Perf. 12½***

201	A104	5c green	1.50	35
		a. Flags omitted	35.00	
202	"	10c orange	1.25	35
203	"	15c carmine rose	2.00	50
204	"	25c dark blue	3.00	70
205	"	40c chestnut	7.00	2.00
206	"	50c purple	9.00	2.50
207	"	75c red orange	17.50	5.00
208	"	1col dark carmine	27.50	10.00
		Nos. 201-208 (8)	68.75	21.40

Issued to commemorate the Caribbean and Central American Soccer Championship. See also Nos. C57-C66, C121-C123.

No. 157 Surcharged in Black **5 Céntimos 5**

1941 ***Perf. 12***

209	A89	5c on 13c carmine rose	12	8

Cleto González Viquez
A105

1941-45 **Engraved.** ***Perf. 12½.***

210	A105	3c deep orange	12	10
210A	"	3c deep plum ('43)	12	10
210B	"	3c carmine ('45)	12	10
211	"	5c deep violet (*José Rodriguez*)	15	12
211A	"	5c brown black ('43)	12	12
		Nos. 210-211A (5)	63	54

See also No. 256.

Old University of Costa Rica
A106

New National University
A107

1941, Aug. 26 ***Perf. 12***

212	A106	5c green	40	15
213	A107	10c yellow orange	45	15
214	A106	15c lilac rose	60	15
215	A107	25c dull blue	90	35
216	A106	50c fawn	3.00	2.00
		Nos. 212-216 (5)	5.35	2.80

National University, founded in 1940. See Nos. C74-C80.

Nos. 144, 189 Surcharged in Black or Red

15 CENTIMOS 15

1942 ***Perf. 12½, 12***

217	A84	5c on 6c dark brown	25	20
218	A77	15c on 20c deep blue (R)	35	25

Torch of Freedom, "Victory" and Flags of American Nations
A108

Juan Mora Fernández
A109

1942, Sept. 25 ***Perf. 12***

219	A108	5c rose	30	15
220	"	5c yellow green	30	15
221	"	5c purple	30	15
222	"	5c deep blue	30	15
223	"	5c red orange	30	15
		Nos. 219-223 (5)	1.50	75

1943-47 **Engraved**

Designs: 2c, Bruno Carranza. 3c, Tomas Guardia. 5c, Manuel Aguilar. 15c, Francisco Morazan. 25c, Jose M. Alfaro. 50c, Francisco M. Oreamuno. 1col, Jose M. Castro. 2col, Juan Rafael Mora.

224	A109	1c red lilac	6	5
225	"	2c black	6	6
226	"	3c deep blue	6	6
227	"	5c bright blue green	12	8
		a. 5c brt. green ('47)	12	10
228	"	15c scarlet	15	6
229	"	25c bright ultra.	35	20
230	"	50c deep violet	75	50
231	"	1col black brown	2.00	1.25
232	"	2col deep orange	3.00	2.50
		Nos. 224-232 (9)	6.55	4.76

See also Nos. C81-C91A, C124-C127, C179-C181.

View of San Ramón
A118

1944, Jan. 19

233	A118	5c dark green	15	10
234	"	10c orange	20	10
235	"	15c rose pink	30	12
236	"	40c gray black	1.00	60
237	"	50c deep blue	1.25	1.00
		Nos. 233-237 (5)	2.90	1.92

Issued to commemorate the 100th anniversary of the founding of the City of San Ramón. See also Nos. C94-C102.

Nos. 220-223 Overprinted in Red or Black

La entrevista de los Presidentes De la Guardia y Picado contribuirá a afianzar la unidad Continental. 18 setiembre 1944

1944, Sept. 18

238	A108	5c yellow green (Bk)	15	12
239	"	5c purple (R)	15	12
240	"	5c deep blue (R)	15	12
241	"	5c red orange (Bk)	15	12

Issued to commemorate the amicable settlement of a boundary dispute with Panama. This overprint also exists on No. 219.

Mauro Fernández
A119

Engraved.

1945, July 21 ***Perf. 14*** **Unwmkd.**

242	A119	20c deep green	25	15

Issued to commemorate the centenary of the birth of Mauro Fernandez (1844-1905), statesman.

Coffee Harvesting
A120

1945, Oct. 9 ***Perf. 12***

243	A120	5c dk. grn. & black	15	8
244	"	10c orange & black	25	12
245	"	20c carmine rose & black	30	20

No. 242 Surcharged in Red Brown.

1946 ***Perf. 14.*** **Unwmkd.**

246	A119	15c on 20c deep green	20	12

No. 080 Overprinted in Red **CORREOS 1947**

1947, Mar. 19 ***Perf. 12***

247	A96	5c green	15	10

Cervantes
A121

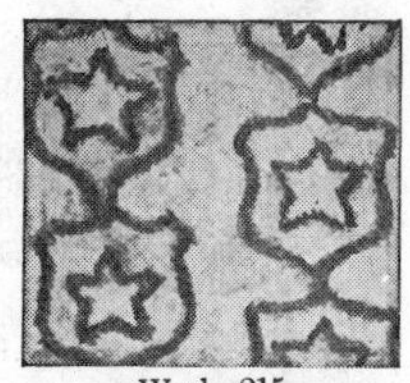

Wmk. 215

Wmkd. Small Star in Shield, Multiple. (215)

1947, Nov. 10 Engraved *Perf. 14*

249	A121	30c deep blue	30	15
250	"	55c dark carmine	50	35

Issued to commemorate the 400th anniversary of the birth of Miguel de Cervantes Saavedra, novelist, playwright and poet.

Franklin D. Roosevelt
A122

1947, Aug. 26 *Perf. 12* Unwmkd.

251	A122	5c bright green	10	10
252	"	10c carmine rose	15	12
253	"	15c ultramarine	20	18
254	"	25c orange red	25	25
255	"	50c red lilac	50	35
		Nos. 251-255, C160-C167 (13)	9.50	8.95

Small Portrait Type of 1941.

1948 *Perf. 12½.*

256	A105	3c deep ultramarine (*Bishop Bernardo A. Thiel*)	10	8

Old University of Costa Rica
A123

1953, June 25 Litho. *Perf. 12*

Black Surcharge.

257	A123	5c on 10c green	12	6

Revenue Stamp Surcharged in Red or Blue

A124

Engraved.

1955-56 *Perf. 12* Unwmkd.

258	A124	5c on 2c emerald (R)	8	6
259	"	15c on 2c emerald (Bl)	18	8
260	"	15c on 2c emerald (R) ('56)	18	8
		Nos. 258-260, C341-C344 (7)	1.59	1.17

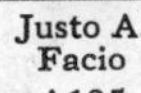

Justo A. Facio
A125

Anglo-Costa Rican Bank
A126

1960, Apr. 20 Photo. *Perf. 13½*

261	A125	10c brown red	8	6

Centenary of the birth (in 1859) of Prof. Justo A. Facio. Exists imperf.

Nos. RA12-RA15 Surcharged in Red

1963
10
CENTIMOS

1963, Mar.

262	PT3	10c on 5c dk. carmine	25	20
263	"	10c on 5c sepia	25	20
264	"	10c on 5c dull green	25	20
265	"	10c on 5c blue	25	20

1963 *Perf. 13½* Unwmkd.

266	A126	10c gray	8	6

Centenary of the Anglo-Costa Rican Bank.

Arms of San José
A127

Alberto M. Brenes Mora
A128

Coats of Arms: 35c, Cartago. 50c, Heredia. 55c, Alajuela. 65c, Guanacaste. 1col, Puntarenas. 2col, Limon.

Lithographed

1969, Sept. 14 *Perf. 14x13½*

267	A127	15c multicolored	6	4
268	"	35c "	15	10
269	"	50c gray & multi.	20	10
270	"	55c buff & multi.	25	20
271	"	65c multicolored	35	25
272	"	1col pink & multi.	60	25
273	"	2col multicolored	1.00	50
		Nos. 267-273 (7)	2.61	1.44

1976, March 1 Litho. *Perf. 10½*

274	A128	1col violet blue	25	20
		Nos. 274, C653-C657 (6)	3.53	2.71

Prof. Alberto Manuel Brenes Mora, botanist, birth centenary.

Map of Costa Rica, Reader with Book
A129

1978, July 17 Litho. *Perf. 13½*

275	A129	50c multicolored	12	10

National five-year literacy plan.

SEMI-POSTAL STAMPS.

No. 72 Surcharged in Red

+ 5c

1922 *Perf. 12.* Unwmkd.

B1	A56	5c+5c orange	1.00	40

Issued for the benefit of the Costa Rican Red Cross Society. In 1928, owing to a temporary shortage of the ordinary 5c stamp, No. B1 was placed on sale as a regular 5c stamp, the surtax being disregarded.

Discus Thrower
SP1

Trophy
SP2

Parthenon
SP3

1924 Lithographed *Imperf.*

B2	SP1	5c dark green	4.00	5.50
B3	SP2	10c carmine	4.00	5.50
B4	SP3	20c dark blue	8.50	8.00
		a. Tête bêche pair	20.00	22.50

Perf. 12.

B5	SP1	5c dark green	4.00	5.50
B6	SP2	10c carmine	4.00	5.50
B7	SP3	20c dark blue	8.50	8.00
		a. Tête bêche pair	20.00	22.50
		Nos. B2-B7 (6)	33.00	38.00

These stamps were sold at a premium of 10c each, to help defray the expenses of athletic games held at San José in December, 1924.

AIR POST STAMPS.

Airplane
AP1

Engraved

1926, June 4 *Perf. 12½* Unwmkd.

C1	AP1	20c ultramarine	2.00	50

No. 123 Overprinted

CORREO AEREO

1930, Mar. 14 *Perf. 12*

C2	A75	10c carmine rose	65	20

AP3

1930-32 *Perf. 12½*

C3	AP3	5c on 10c dk. brn. ('32)	25	10
		a. Inverted surcharge	6.00	
C4	AP3	20c on 50c ultramarine	25	20
C5	"	40c on 50c "	50	20

Telegraph Stamp Overprinted

Correo Aereo

1930, Mar. 19

C6	AP3	1col orange	1.25	30

No. O79 Surcharged in Red

1930, Mar. 11

C7	O7	8c on 1col lilac & black	75	60
C8	"	20c on 1col " "	85	75
C9	"	40c on 1col " "	2.00	1.50
C10	"	1col on 1col " "	2.25	1.85

AP6

AP7

Red Surcharge on Revenue Stamps

1931-32 *Perf. 12*

C11	AP6	2col on 2col gray green	17.50	13.50
C12	"	3col on 5col lilac brown	17.50	13.50
C13	"	5col on 10col gray black	17.50	13.50

There were two printings of this issue which were practically identical in the colors of the stamps and the surcharges.

Nos. C11 and C13 have the date "1929" on the stamp, No. C12 has "1930".

Black Overprint on Telegraph Stamp

1932, Mar. 8 *Perf. 12½*

C14	AP7	40c green	2.25	40
		a. Inverted ovpt.	13.50	

Mail Plane about to Land
AP8

Allegory of Flight
AP9

1934, Mar. 14 *Perf. 12*

C15	AP8	5c green	25	10
C16	"	10c carmine rose	25	8
C17	"	15c chocolate	60	15
C18	"	20c deep blue	65	12
C19	"	25c deep orange	85	10
C20	"	40c olive black	1.50	12
C21	"	50c gray black	1.00	25
C22	"	60c orange yellow	2.00	30
C23	"	75c dull violet	3.00	60
C24	AP9	1col deep rose	2.25	15
C25	"	2col light blue	2.50	50
C26	"	5col black	6.50	4.00
C27	"	10col red brown	11.00	7.50
		Nos. C15-C27 (13)	32.35	13.97

Stamps Nos. C15 to C27 with holes punched through were for use of government officials.

See also Nos. C216-C219.

Airplane over Poás Volcano
AP10

1937, Feb. 10

C28 AP10 1c black 12 10
C29 " 2c brown 12 10
C30 " 3c dark violet 12 10

First Fair of Costa Rica.

Punta-
renas
AP11

National
Bank
AP12

Perf. 12, 12½

1937, Dec. 15 **Unwmkd.**

C31 AP11 2c black gray 8 8
C32 " 5c green 15 12
C33 " 20c deep blue 50 40
C34 " 1.40 col olive brown 5.00 4.00

Wmkd. Wavy Lines. (229)

1938, Jan. 11 *Perf. 12½*

C35 AP12 1c purple 8 6
C36 " 3c red orange 10 6
C37 " 10c carmine rose 20 15
C38 " 75c brown 3.00 3.00

Nos. C31 to C38 were issued to commemorate the National Products Exposition held at San José in December, 1937.

Airport Administration Building, La Sabana—AP13

1940, May 2 **Engraved** **Unwmkd.**

C39 AP13 5c green 15 10
C40 " 10c rose pink 20 15
C41 " 25c light blue 25 20
C42 " 35c red brown 45 45
C43 " 60c red orange 70 70
C44 " 85c violet 2.00 1.75
C45 " 2.35col turq. green 11.00 11.00
Nos. C39–C45 (7) 14.75 14.35

Issued to commemorate the opening of the International Airport at La Sabana.

Duran Sanatorium
AP14

Overprinted "Dia Panamericano de la Salud / 2·Diciembre 1940" and Bar in Black

1940, Dec. 2 *Perf. 12*

C46 AP14 10c scarlet 20 15
C47 " 15c purple 25 25
C48 " 25c light blue 45 40
C49 AP14 35c bistre brown 70 65
C50 " 60c peacock grn. 90 90
C51 " 75c olive 1.75 1.85
C52 " 1.35col red orange 7.50 7.00
C53 " 5col sepia 27.50 27.50
C54 " 10col red lilac 55.00 55.00
Nos. C46–C54 (9) 94.25 93.70

Pan-American Health Day. Exist without overprint. Few copies of C53–C54 were sold for postal purposes, nearly all having been obtained by philatelic speculators.

No. 174 Surcharged in Black or Blue

AEREO
Aviación Panamericana
Dic. 17 1940
15 CENTIMOS 15

1940, Dec. 17 *Perf. 14*

C55 A95 15c on 50c yel. (Bk) 75 75
C56 " 30c on 50c yel. (Bl) 75 75

Issued in commemoration of Pan-American Aviation Day, proclaimed by President F. D. Roosevelt.

The 15c surcharge also exists on the 25c orange, No. 171. Price $30.

International Soccer Game at National Stadium—AP15

1941, May 8 *Perf. 12*

C57 AP15 15c red 1.25 25
C58 " 30c deep ultra. 1.50 40
C59 " 40c red brown 1.50 60
C60 " 50c purple 2.00 1.35
C61 " 60c bright green 2.50 1.50
C62 " 75c yellow orange 4.00 2.25
C63 " 1col dull violet 7.50 6.00
C64 " 1.40col rose 15.00 14.00
C65 " 2col blue green 30.00 27.50
C66 " 5col black 65.00 65.00
Nos. C57–C66 (10) 130.25 118.85

Issued to commemorate the Caribbean and Central American Soccer Championship. See also Nos. C121–C123.

Air Post Stamps of 1934 Overprinted or Surcharged in Black

Mayo 1941
Tratado Limítrofe
Costa Rica - Panamá

with New Values and Bars.

1941, June 2

C67 AP8 5c on 20c deep blue 25 20
C68 " 15c on 20c deep blue 35 25
C69 " 40c on 75c dull violet 50 35
C70 AP9 65c on 1col dp. rose 1.00 75
C71 " 1.40col on 2col light blue 5.00 4.00
C72 " 5col black 17.50 15.00
C73 " 10col red brown 20.00 20.00
Nos. C67–C73 (7) 44.60 40.55

Issued in commemoration of the settlement of the Costa Rica-Panama border dispute.

Nos. C67–C73 are found with hyphen omitted in overprint.

University Types of Regular Issue, 1941.

1941, Aug. 26 *Perf. 12*

C74 A107 15c salmon 35 15
C75 A106 30c light blue 50 20
C76 A107 40c orange 60 40
C77 A106 60c turq. green 75 65
C78 A107 1col violet 3.00 2.50
C79 A106 2col black 7.50 6.00
C80 A107 5col sepia 25.00 20.00
Nos. C74–C80 (7) 37.70 29.90

National University, founded in 1940.

Portrait Type of Regular Issue, 1943–47.

Designs: 40c, Manuel Aguilar. No. C83, Francisco Morazan. No. C83A, Jose R. De Gallegos. 50c, Jose M. Alfaro. 60c, Francisco M. Oreamuno. 65c, Jose M. Castro. 85c, Juan Rafael Mora. 1col, Jose M. Montealegre. 1.05col, Braulio Carrillo. 1.15col, Jesus Jimenez. 1.40 col, Bruno Carranza. 2col, Tomas Guardia.

1943-45 **Engraved.**

C81 A109 10c rose pink 12 8
C82 " 40c blue 30 12
C82A " 40c carmine rose ('45) 30 20
C83 " 45c magenta 45 40
C83A " 45c black ('45) 25 18
C84 " 50c turq. green 1.75 30
C84A " 50c red org. ('45) 40 30
C85 " 60c bright ultra. 60 25
C85A " 60c brt. grn. ('45) 25 20
C86 " 65c scarlet 85 40
C86A " 65c brt. ultra. ('45) 30 30
C87 " 85c deep orange 1.10 55
C87A " 85c dull purple ('45) 1.50 70
C88 " 1col black 1.60 35
C88A " 1col scarlet ('45) 60 30
C88B " 1.05col bistre brown ('45) 75 60
C89 " 1.15col red brown 2.00 1.85
C89A " 1.15col green ('45) 3.00 1.25
C90 " 1.40col deep violet 3.25 2.50
C90A " 1.40col orange yellow ('45) 1.75 1.75
C91 " 2col black 5.00 1.25
C91A " 2col olive green ('45) 1.50 50
Nos. C81–91A (22) 27.62 14.33

See also Nos. C124–C127, C179–C181.

Nos. C26–C27 Overprinted in Red or Blue

Legislacion Social
15 Setiembre 1943

1943, Sept. 16

C92 AP9 5col black (R) 4.00 3.00
C93 " 10col red brown (Bl) 7.50 5.00

Mercury and Plane
AP31

1944, Jan. 19

C94 AP31 10c red orange 20 15
C95 " 15c dark carmine 25 15
C96 " 40c bright ultra. 40 35
C97 " 45c deep red lilac 50 40
C98 " 60c turquoise green 75 70
C99 " 1col dark red brown 1.50 1.35
C100 " 1.40col gray black 10.00 9.00
C101 " 5col violet 25.00 25.00
C102 " 10col black 50.00 50.00
Nos. C94–C102 (9) 88.60 87.10

Issued to commemorate the 100th anniversary of the founding of the City of San Ramón.

Very few copies of the 5col or 10col stamps were sold for postal purposes, nearly all having been obtained by philatelic speculators.

No. C010 With Additional Overprint in Black **1944**

1944, Nov. 22

C103 AP9 1col deep rose 75 45
a. Blue ovpt. 40.00

Nos. C01-13 Overprinted in Carmine or Black

1945, Jan. 12 *Perf. 12* **Unwmkd.**

C104 AP8 5c green 85 85
C105 " 10c car. rose (Bk) 85 85
C106 " 15c chocolate 85 85
C107 " 20c deep blue 50 50
C108 AP8 25c dp. orge. (Bk) 85 85
C109 " 40c olive black 50 50
C110 " 50c gray black 85 85
C111 " 60c org. yel. (Bk) 1.35 50
C112 " 75c dull violet 1.00 85
C113 AP9 1col dp. rose (Bk) 1.00 50
C114 " 2col light blue 7.00 7.00
C115 " 5col black 9.00 9.00
C116 " 10col red brown (Bk) 12.50 12.50
Nos. C104–C116 (13) 37.10 35.60

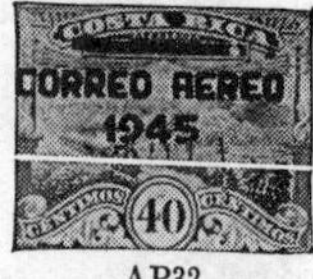

AP32

Telegraph Stamps Overprinted in Black or Carmine.

Perf. 12½

1945, Feb. 28 **Unwmkd.**

C117 AP32 40c green (C) 25 12
C118 " 50c ultramarine (C) 30 12
C119 " 1col orange (Bk) 65 40

Florence Nightingale and Edith Cavell—AP33

1945 **Engraved.**

C120 AP33 1col blk. & car. 60 25

Issued to commemorate the 60th anniversary of the Costa Rican Red Cross Society.

Soccer Type of 1941.
Inscribed: "Febrero 1946."

1946, May 13 *Perf. 12*

C121 AP15 25c green 1.50 1.10
C122 " 30c dull yellow 1.50 1.10
C123 " 55c deep blue 1.75 1.10

Portrait Type of 1943–47.

Designs: 25c, Aniceto Esquivel. 30c, Vicente Herrera. 55c, Prospero Fernandez. 75c, Bernardo Soto.

1946, May 12

C124 A109 25c blue 20 12
C125 " 30c red brown 25 20
C126 " 55c plum 40 30
C127 " 75c blue green 60 40

Hospital of St. John of God
AP38

1946, June 24 *Perf. 12½* **Unwmkd.**

Center in Black.

C128 AP38 5c yellow green 10 10
C129 " 10c dark brown 10 10
C130 " 15c carmine 10 10
C131 " 25c dark blue 20 20
C132 " 30c deep orange 40 30
C133 " 40c olive green 20 20
C134 " 50c violet 35 35
C135 " 60c dark slate green 75 70
C136 " 75c brown 60 50
a. Horiz. pair, imperf. btwn. 60.00
C137 " 1col blue 75 40
C138 " 2col brown orange 1.10 90
C139 " 3col dk. vio. brn. 2.75 2.75
C140 " 5col yellow 3.50 3.50
Nos. C128–C140 (13) 10.90 10.10

Centenary of St. John of God Hospital.

Rafael Iglesias
AP39

Designs: 3col, Ascensión Esquivel. 5col, Cleto González Viquez. 10col, Ricardo Jiménez Oreamuno.

Wmkd.
Small Star in Shield, Multiple. (215)

1947, Jan. 15 Engraved *Perf. 14*
Center in Black.

C141 AP39 2col blue 1.50 1.10
C142 " 3col deep car. 2.25 1.50
C143 " 5col dark green 3.50 2.25
C144 " 10col orange 6.50 4.00

Nos. C121 to C123 Surcharged in Black

Habilitado para
₡ 0.15
Decreto Nº 16 de
28 de abril de 1947

1947, May 5 *Perf. 12* Unwmkd.
C145 AP15 15c on 25c green 1.25 1.10
C146 " 15c on 30c dull yellow 1.25 1.10
C147 " 15c on 55c deep blue 1.25 1.10

Nos. C145-C147 exist with inverted surcharge; No. C145 with double surcharge, one inverted.

Columbus in Cariarí
AP43

1947, May 19 Engr. *Perf. 12½*
Center in Black.
C148 AP43 25c green 30 18
C149 " 30c deep ultra. 30 18
C150 " 40c red orange 40 20
C151 " 45c violet 50 35
C152 " 50c brt. carmine 60 30
C153 " 65c brown orge. 1.50 1.00
Nos. C148-C153 (6) 3.60 2.21

Nos. C84A, C85A, C127, C88A, and C88B Surcharged with New Value in Black or Red.

1947, June 3 *Perf. 12*
C154 A109 15c on 50c red orange 25 25
C155 " 15c on 60c bright green (R) 25 25
C156 " 15c on 75c blue green (R) 25 25
C157 " 15c on 1col scarlet 30 30
C158 " 15c on 1.05col bistre brown 25 25
Nos. C154-C158 (5) 1.30 1.30

Early Steam Locomotive
AP44

Engraved
1947, Nov. 10 *Perf. 12½* Unwmkd.
C159 AP44 35c blue green & black 1.00 35

Issued to commemorate the 50th anniversary of the electric railroad to the Pacific coast.

Roosevelt Type of Regular Issue.
1947, Aug. 26 *Perf. 12*
C160 A122 15c green 12 10
C161 " 30c carmine rose 18 15
C162 " 45c red brown 35 35
C163 " 65c orange yellow 40 40
C164 " 75c blue 50 40
C165 " 1col olive green 75 70
C166 " 2col black 2.00 1.85
C167 " 5col scarlet 4.00 4.00
Nos. C160-C167 (8) 8.30 7.95

National Theater
AP46

Rafael Iglesias
AP47

1948, Jan. 26 *Perf. 12½*
Center in Black.
C168 AP46 15c bright ultra. 15 10
C169 " 20c red 20 15
C170 AP47 35c dark green 30 25
C171 AP46 45c purple 40 30
C172 " 50c carmine 40 30
C173 " 75c red violet 85 80
C174 " 1col olive 1.50 1.10
C175 " 2col red brown 2.50 1.75
C176 AP47 5col orange yel. 4.25 3.50
C177 " 10col bright blue 8.50 6.75
Nos. C168-C177 (10) 19.05 15.00

50th anniversary of National Theater.

No. C150 Surcharged in Carmine

HABILITADO
PARA
₡ 0.35

1948, Apr. 21
C178 AP43 35c on 40c red orange & black 45 45

Exists with surcharge inverted.

Portrait Type of 1943-47.
Designs: 5c, Salvador Lara. 15c, Carlos Duran.

1948 Engraved *Perf. 12*
C179 A109 5c sepia 15 6
C180 " 10c olive brown 15 10
C181 " 15c violet 12 10

Nos. C88B, C120, C89A and C90A Surcharged in Carmine or Black

1824-1949
125 Aniversario
de la Anexión
Guanacaste
₡ 0.55

Perf. 12½, 12
1949, Aug. 28 Unwmkd.
C182 A109 35c on 1.05col bistre brown 25 20
C183 AP33 50c on 1col black & carmine 40 35
a. 2nd & 3rd lines both read "125 Aniversario" 7.50 7.50
C184 A109 55c on 1.15col green 65 55
C185 " 55c on 1.40col orge. yel. (Bk) 65 50

Issued to commemorate the 125th anniversary of the annexation of the province of Guanacaste.

Overprint differs on No. C183, with "Guanacaste" in capitals, and lower case "a" in "Anexión."

The variety "l" for "I" in "Anexion" is found on Nos. C182, C184 and C185.

Symbols of U.P.U.
AP48

1950, Jan. 11 Photo. *Perf. 11½*
C186 AP48 15c lilac rose 20 10
C187 " 25c chalky blue 25 10
C188 " 1col gray green 50 20

Issued to commemorate the 75th anniversary of the formation of the Universal Postal Union.

Battle of El Tejar, Cartago
AP49

Occupation of Limón
AP50

Bull (Cattle Raising)
AP51

Designs: 25c, Lucha ranch. 35c, Trenches of San Isidro Battalion. 55c and 75c, Observation post. 80c and 1col, Dr. Carlos Luis Valverde.

Inscribed: "Guerra de Liberacion Nacional 1948."

Engraved; Center Photogravure.
1950, July 20 *Perf. 12½*
Center in Black.
C189 AP49 15c bright carmine 15 8
C190 AP50 20c dull green 25 18
C191 AP49 25c dull blue 30 20
C192 " 35c chestnut 35 20
C193 " 55c lilac 70 30
C194 " 75c red orange 1.10 40
C195 AP50 80c gray 1.10 65
C196 " 1col orange yellow 1.50 75
Nos. C189-C196 (8) 5.45 2.76

Issued to commemorate the second anniversary of the War for National Liberation.

Inscribed: "Feria Nacional Agricola Ganadera e Industrial Cartago 1950."

1950, July 27
Designs: 1c, 10c, 2col, Bull. 2c, 30c and 3col, Tuna fishing. 3c and 65c, Pineapple. 5c, 50c and 5col, Bananas. 45c, 80c and 10col, Coffee picker.

Center in Black.
C197 AP51 1c bright green 10 8
C198 " 2c bright blue 10 8
C199 " 3c chocolate 10 8
C200 " 5c deep ultre 10 8
C201 " 10c green 15 8
C202 " 30c purple 30 18
C203 " 45c vermilion 35 25
C204 " 50c blue gray 50 15
C205 " 65c dark blue 60 35
C206 " 80c deep rose 1.00 80
C207 " 2col orange yellow 3.00 2.35
C208 " 3col blue 4.25 3.50
C209 " 5col carmine 9.00 7.75
C210 " 10col deep claret 10.00 9.00
Nos. C197-C210 (14) 29.55 24.73

Issued to publicize the National Agricultural, Livestock and Industrial Fair, Cartago, 1950.

Queen Isabella I and Caravels of Columbus
AP52

Engraved.
1952, Mar. 4 *Perf. 13* Unwmkd.
C211 AP52 15c carmine 10 10
C212 " 20c orange 15 15
C213 " 25c ultramarine 20 10
C214 " 55c deep green 50 40
C215 " 2col violet 1.50 75
Nos. C211-C215 (5) 2.45 1.50

Issued to commemorate the 500th anniversary of the birth of Queen Isabella I of Spain.

Mail Plane Type of 1934.
1952-53 *Perf. 12.*
C216 AP8 5c blue 12 8
C217 " 10c green 15 8
C218 " 15c carmine rose ('53) 18 8
C219 " 35c purple 50 15

Nos. C149-C151, C153 Surcharged in Red: "HABILITADO PARA CINCO CENTIMOS 1953"

1953, Apr. 24 *Perf. 12½*
Center in Black.
C220 AP43 5c on 30c deep ultramarine 1.25 1.10
C221 " 5c on 40c red orange 10 10
C222 " 5c on 45c violet 10 10
C223 " 5c on 65c brown orange 30 25

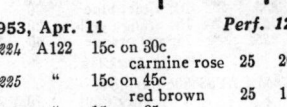

Nos. C161-C163 Surcharged in Black

15—o—15

1953, Apr. 11 *Perf. 12*
C224 A122 15c on 30c carmine rose 25 20
C225 " 15c on 45c red brown 25 15
C226 " 15c on 65c orange yellow 25 15

Refinery of Vegetable Oils and Fats
AP53

Industries: 10c, Pottery. 15c, Sugar. 20c, Soap. 25c, Lumber. 30c, Matches. 35c, Textiles. 40c, Leather. 45c, Tobacco. 50c, Preserving. 55c, Canning. 60c, General. 65c, Metals. 75c, Pharmaceuticals. 1col, Paper. 2col, Rubber. 3col, Airplane maintenance. 5col, Marble. 10col, Beer.

Engraved; Center Photogravure
1954 *Perf. 13x12½* Unwmkd.
Center in Black
C227 AP53 5c red 10 6
C228 " 10c dark blue 15 6
C229 " 15c green 12 6
C230 " 20c violet 15 10
C231 " 25c magenta 15 10
C232 " 30c purple 45 30
C233 " 35c red violet 25 12
C234 " 40c black 40 25
C235 " 45c dark green 75 35
C236 " 50c violet brown 50 15
C237 " 55c yellow 35 12
C238 " 60c brown 90 50
C239 " 65c carmine 1.10 75
C240 " 75c violet 1.65 65
C241 " 1col blue 50 30
a. Imperf., pair 50.00
C242 AP53 2col rose pink 1.50 90
C243 " 3col olive green 2.25 1.50
C244 " 5col black 3.50 1.25
C245 " 10col yellow 10.00 7.50
Nos. C227-C245 (19) 24.77 15.02

See also Nos. C252-C255A.

Globe and Rotary Emblem
AP54

Map of Costa Rica
AP55

Designs: 25c, Hand protecting boy. 40c, 2col, Hospital. 45c, Globe and palm leaves. 60c, Lighthouse.

1956, Feb. 7 Engraved. *Perf. 12*

C246 AP54 10c green 15 6
C247 " 25c dark blue 20 18
C248 " 40c dark brown 50 40
C249 " 45c bright red 35 30
C250 " 60c dark red violet 40 35
C251 " 2col yel. orange 1.00 70
Nos. C246–C251 (6) 2.60 1.99

Issued to commemorate the 50th anniversary of Rotary International (in 1955).

Industries Type of 1954

Engraved; Center Photogravure

Designs: 80c, Pharmaceuticals. Other designs as in 1954.

1956–59 Center in Black *Perf. 12*

C252 AP53 5c ultramarine 20 6
C253 " 10c violet blue 20 6
C254 " 15c orange yellow 20 6
C255 " 75c red orange 40 25

Perf. 13x12½

C255A AP53 80c purple & gray ('59) 70 60
Nos. C252–C255A (5) 1.70 1.03

1957, June 21 Engr. *Perf. 13½x13*

Designs: 10c, Map of Guanacaste. 15c, Inn. 20c, House of Santa Rosa. 25c, Gen. Jose Manuel Quiros. 30c, Old Presidential Palace. 35c, Joaquin Bernardo Calvo. 40c, Luis Molina. 45c, Gen. Jose Joaquin Mora. 50c, Gen. Jose Maria Canas. 55c, Juan Santamaria monument. 60c, National monument. 65c, Antonio Vallerriestra. 70c, Ramon Castilla y Marquesado. 75c, San Carlos fortress. 80c, Francisco Maria Oreamuno. 1col, Pres. Juan Rafael Mora.

C256 AP55 5c light blue 6 5
C257 " 10c green 10 6
C258 " 15c deep orange 8 6
C259 " 20c light brown 15 10
C260 " 25c violet blue 15 12
C261 " 30c violet 25 18
C262 " 35c carmine rose 25 18
C263 " 40c slate 25 18
C264 " 45c rose red 30 22
C265 " 50c ultramarine 30 22
C266 " 55c ochre 50 22
C267 " 60c bright carmine 40 30
C268 " 65c carmine 45 30
C269 " 70c orange yellow 60 40
C270 " 75c emerald 55 38
C271 " 80c dark brown 60 45
C272 " 1col black 65 45
Nos. C256–C272 (17) 5.64 3.87

Centenary of War of 1856–57.

Cleto Gonzalez Viquez
AP56

Highway and Gonzalez Viquez
AP57

Designs: 10c, Ricardo Jimenez Oreamuno. 20c, Puntarenas wharf and Jimenez. 35c, Post and Telegraph Bldg. and Jimenez. 55c, Pipeline and Gonzalez Viquez. 80c, National Library and Gonzalez Viquez. 1col, Electric train and Jimenez. 2col, Gonzales and Jimenez.

1959 Engraved. *Perf. 13½*

C274 AP56 5c car. & ultra. 6 6
C275 " 10c red & gray 6 6

Perf. 13½x13

C276 AP57 15c dark blue green & black 6 6
C277 " 20c carmine & brn. 15 10
C278 " 35c rose lilac & blue 20 15
C279 " 55c olive & violet 40 30
C280 " 80c ultramarine 60 50
C281 " 1col org. & maroon 60 45
C282 " 2col gray & maroon 1.50 1.25
Nos. C274–C282 (9) 3.63 2.93

Soccer
AP58

Designs: Various soccer scenes.

Photogravure.

1960, March 7 *Perf. 13½* Unwmkd.

C283 AP58 10c black 10 8
C284 " 25c ultramarine 20 15
C285 " 35c red orange 25 20
C286 " 50c red brown 30 25
C287 " 85c Pruss. green 1.00 75
C288 " 5col deep claret 3.25 3.25
Nos. C283–C288 (6) 5.10 4.68

Souvenir Sheet.

Imperf.

C289 AP58 2col blue 1.50 1.50

3rd Pan-American Soccer Games, San José, March, 1960.

Nos. C283–C288 exist imperf.

No. C289 measures 137x80mm. with black marginal inscription.

WRY Uprooted Oak Emblem
AP59

1960, Apr. 7 *Perf. 11½* Unwmkd.

Granite Paper

C290 AP59 35c violet blue, blk. & yellow 30 25
C291 " 85c black & bright pink 60 50

Issued to publicize World Refugee Year, July 1, 1959–June 30, 1960.

Banner and "OEA"
AP60

Designs: 35c, "OEA" in oval. 55c, Clasped hands. 2col, "OEA" and map of Americas. 5col, Flags forming bird. 10col, Map of Costa Rica, flags and "OEA."

1960, Aug. 15 Litho. *Perf. 10*

C292 AP60 25c blk. & multi. 20 15
a. Multi. impression sideways 30.00
C293 AP60 35c multicolored 50 45
a. Pair, imperf. between 60.00
C294 AP60 55c multicolored 75 60
C295 " 5col 4.50 4.00
C296 " 10col blk. & multi. 7.50 6.00
Nos. C292–C296 (5) 13.45 11.20

Souvenir Sheet

Imperf.

C297 AP60 2col multicolored 3.25 3.25

Nos. C292–C297 issued to commemorate the Pan-American Conference, San Jose, Aug. 15.

No. C297 measures 124x76½mm. with flags of American nations forming border.

St. Louisa de Marillac and Orphanage—AP61

St. Vincent de Paul
AP62

Designs: 25c, St. Vincent and old seminary. 50c, St. Louisa and sickroom. 1col, St. Vincent and new seminary.

1960, Oct. 26 Engr. *Perf. 14x13½*

C298 AP61 10c green 10 10
C299 " 25c carmine 10 10
C300 " 50c dark blue 35 25
C301 " 1col brown orange 60 50
C302 AP62 5col brown 3.00 2.50
Nos. C298–C302 (5) 4.15 3.45

Issued to commemorate the 300th anniversary of the deaths of St. Vincent de Paul (1581?–1660) and St. Louisa de Marillac (1591–1660). Exist imperf.

Runner—AP63

Sports: 2c, Woman swimmer. 3c, Bicyclist. 4c, Weight lifter. 5c, Woman tennis player. 10c, Boxers. 25c, Soccer player. 85c, Basketball player. 1col, Baseball batter. 5col, Romulus and Remus statue. 10col, Pistol marksman.

Perf. 13½x14

1960, Dec. 14 Photo. Unwmkd.

Designs in Black

C303 AP63 1c brt. yellow 5 5
C304 " 2c light ultra. 5 5
C305 " 3c deep rose 5 5
C306 " 4c yellow 5 5
C307 " 5c brt. yel. grn. 5 5
C308 " 10c pink 8 8
C309 " 25c lt. bl. grn. 15 15
C310 " 85c lilac 1.25 1.00
C311 " 1col gray 1.50 1.25
C312 " 10col lt. violet 12.50 10.00
Nos. C303–C312 (10) 15.73 12.73

Souvenir Sheets

Perf. 14x13½, Imperf.

C313 AP63 5col multi. 5.00 5.00

17th Olympic Games, Rome, Aug. 25–Sept. 11.

No. C313 has gold marginal inscription. Size: 100x65mm.

Nos. C303–C312 exist imperf.

No. C255 Surcharged and Overprinted in Blue or Ultramarine:

"XV Campeonato Mundial de Beisbol de Aficionados"

Engraved and Photogravure

1961, Apr. 21 *Perf. 12*

Center in Black

C314 AP53 25c on 75c red orange (Bl) 25 10
C315 " 75c red orange (U) 75 30

15th Amateur Baseball Championships.

Alberto Brenes C.
AP64

Miguel Obregon
AP65

Portraits: No. C317, Manuel Aguilar. No. C318, Agustin Gutierrez L. No. C319, Vicente Herrera.

1961, June 12 Photo. *Perf. 12*

C316 AP64 10c deep claret 8 8
C317 " 10c blue 8 8
C318 " 25c bright violet 15 12
C319 " 25c gray 15 12

First Continental Congress of Lawyers, San José, June 11–15. Exist imperf.

See also Nos. C330–C333.

1961, July 19 Litho. *Perf. 13½*

C320 AP65 10c Prus. green 6 6

Birth centenary of Prof. Miguel Obregon L. Exists imperf.

U.N. Food and Agriculture Organization
AP66

Designs: United Nations Organizations: 20c, World Health Organization. 25c, Int. Labor Organization. 30c, Int. Telecommunication Union. 35c, World Meteorological Organization. 45c, UNESCO. 85c, Int. Civil Aviation Organization. 5col, "United Nations" holding the world. 10col, Int. Bank for Reconstruction and Development.

Engraved

1961, Oct. 24 *Perf. 11½* Unwmkd.

C321 AP66 10c light green 10 10
C322 " 20c orange 20 15
C323 " 25c Prus. grn. 25 20
C324 " 30c dark blue 25 20
C325 " 35c car. rose 1.25 30
C326 " 45c violet 45 25
C327 " 85c blue 1.00 75
C328 " 10col dark slate green 7.50 6.00
Nos. C321–C328 (8) 11.00 7.95

Souvenir Sheet

Imperf.

C329 AP66 5col ultramarine 4.00 4.00

Nos. C321–C329 issued for United Nations Day, Oct. 24.

No. C329 contains one imperf. stamp and has ultramarine border and marginal inscription. Size: 100x65mm.

Portrait Type of 1961

Portraits: No. C330, Dr. José Maria Soto Alfaro. No. C331, Dr. Elias Rojas Roman. No. C332, Dr. Andres Saenz Llorente. No. C333, Dr. Juan José Ulloa Giralt.

1961 Photogravure *Perf. 13½*

C330 AP64 10c blue green 8 6
C331 " 10c violet 8 6

C332 AP64 25c dark gray 15 10
C333 " 25c deep claret 15 10

Issued to commemorate the ninth Congress of Physicians of Central America and Panama.

Nos. C229, C236 and C280 Surcharged in Black, Orange or Red.

Engraved; Center Photogravure.

1962 ***Perf. 13x12½, 13½x13***

C334 AP53 10c ("10") on 15c grn. & black 8 8
C334A " 10c ("₡ 0.10") on 15c grn. & blk. (R) 8 8
C335 " 25c on 15c green & black 15 10
C336 " 35c on 50c vio. brn. & black (O) 25 15

Engraved

C337 AP57 85c on 80c ultra. (R) 75 60
Nos. C334-C337 (5) 1.31 1.01

Nos. C324 and C282 Overprinted in Red: "II CONVENCION FILATELICA CENTROAMERICANA SETIEMBRE 1962"

1962, Sept. 12 ***Perf. 11½, 13½x13***

C338 AP66 30c dark blue 60 45
C339 AP57 2col gray & maroon 1.75 1.25

Issued to commemorate the second Central American Philatelic Convention.

Revenue Stamp Surcharged with New Values and "CORREO AEREO" in Red

1962 **Engraved** ***Perf. 12***

C341 A124 25c on 2c emerald 10 8
C342 " 35c on 2c " 15 12
C343 " 45c on 2c " 30 25
C344 " 85c on 2c " 60 50

Arms and Malaria Eradication Emblem
AP67

1963, Feb. 14 **Photo.** ***Perf. 11½***

C345 AP67 25c bright rose 15 10
C346 " 35c brown orange 20 15
C347 " 45c ultramarine 35 25
C348 " 85c blue green 60 50
C349 " 1col dark blue 75 60
Nos. C345-C349 (5) 2.05 1.60

Issued for the World Health Organization drive to eradicate malaria.

Central American Tapir
AP68

Designs: 5c, Paca. 25c, Jaguar. 30c, Ocelot. 35c, Whitetail deer. 40c, Manatee. 85c, White-throated capuchin monkey. 5col, White-lipped peccary.

Photogravure

1963, May ***Perf. 13½*** **Unwmkd.**

C354 AP68 5c yel. olive & brn. 6 6
C355 " 10c org. & slate 6 6
C356 " 25c blue & yellow 15 8
C357 " 30c light yellow grn. & brn. 30 25
C358 " 35c bister & red brown 40 20
C359 " 40c emerald & slate blue 50 35
C360 " 85c grn. & black 75 50
C361 " 5col gray green & chocolate 4.00 3.00
Nos. C354-C361 (8) 6.22 4.50

Stamp of 1863 and Packet "William Le Lacheur"
AP69

Issue of 1863 and: 2col, Recaredo Bonilla Carrillo, Postmaster, 1862-63. 3col, Burros, overland mail transport, 1839. 10col, Burro railway car.

1963, June 26 **Lithographed**

C362 AP69 25c dull rose & chalky bl. 10 8
C363 " 2col gray blue & orange 1.50 1.00
C364 " 3col bister & emerald 2.50 1.75
C365 " 10col dull green & ocher 7.50 5.00

Centenary of Costa Rica's stamps.

Souvenir Sheets

Stamps of 1863 and San José Postmark—AP70

Perf. 13½, Imperf.

1963, June 26 **Unwmkd.**

C366 AP70 5col blue, red, grn. & org. 4.00 4.00

Issued to commemorate the centenary of Costa Rica's stamps. Orange marginal inscription. Size of stamp: 29x50mm. Size of sheet: 60x100mm.

In 1968 copies of No. C366 were overprinted "2-4 Agosto 1968" and "III Exposicion Filatelica Nacional / 'Costa Rica 68'." Price $5.

Animal Type of 1963 Surcharged in Red

Designs: 10c on 1c, Little anteater. 25c on 2c, Gray fox. 35c on 3c, Armadillo. 85c on 4c, Great anteater.

1963, Sept. 14 **Photo.** ***Perf. 13½***

C367 AP68 10c on 1c bright green & orange brown 10 8
C368 " 25c on 2c orange yellow & olive green 15 8
C369 " 35c on 3c bluish grn. & brown 18 12
C370 " 85c on 4c deep rose & dark brown 45 25

No. C370 exists without surcharge. Price, $50.

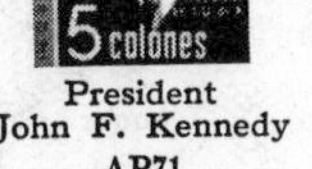

President John F. Kennedy
AP71

Ancestral Figure
AP72

Portraits—Presidents: 25c, Francisco J. Orlich, Costa Rica. 30c, Julio A. Rivera, El Salvador. 35c, Miguel Ydigoras F., Guatemala. 85c, Dr. Ramon Villeda M., Honduras. 1col, Luis A. Somoza, Nicaragua. 3col, Roberto F. Chiari, Panama.

1963, Dec. 7 ***Perf. 14*** **Unwmkd.**

Portraits in Black Brown

C371 AP71 25c violet brown 15 10
C372 " 30c brt. lilac rose 20 15
C373 " 35c ocher 25 20
C374 " 85c gray blue 60 40
C375 " 1col orange brown 60 45
C376 " 3col lt. olive grn. 3.00 2.00
C377 " 5col gray 4.00 3.00
Nos. C371-C377 (7) 8.80 6.30

Issued to commemorate the meeting of Central American Presidents with Pres. John F. Kennedy, San José, March 18-20, 1963.

1963-64 **Photo.** ***Perf. 12***

Ancient Art: 5c, Dog (horiz.). 10c, Ornamental stool (horiz.). 25c, Male figure. 30c, Ceremonial dancer. 35c, Ceramic vase. 50c, Frog. 55c, Bell. 75c, Six-limbed figure. 85c, Seated man. 90c, Bird-shaped jug. 1col, Twin human beaker (horiz.). 2col, Alligator (horiz.). 3col, Twin-tailed lizard. 5col, Figure under arch. 10col, Polished stone figure.

C378 AP72 5c lt. yel. green & Prussian green 5 5
C379 " 10c buff & dk. grn. 6 6
C380 " 25c rose & dk. brn. 12 9
C381 " 30c ochre & Pruss. green ('64) 15 8
C382 " 35c salmon & slate green 18 12
C383 " 45c light blue & dark brown 20 12
C384 " 50c dull blue & dark brn. 25 18
C385 " 55c yellow green & dk. brn. 30 18
C386 " 75c ocher & dark red brown 30 20
C387 " 85c yellow & red brown 75 50
C388 " 90c citron & red brown 1.00 50
C389 " 1col light blue & dk. brown 50 30
C390 " 2col buff & dark green 90 60
C391 " 3col yel. green & dk. brown 1.55 1.00
C392 " 5col citron & sepia 2.75 1.75
C393 " 10col rose lilac & slate grn. 4.50 4.00
Nos. C378-C393 (16) 13.56 9.73

Flags of Central American States
AP73

Alfredo Gonzalez F.
AP74

Central American Independence Issue

1964 ***Perf. 14***

C394 AP73 30c blue, gray, red & black 50 40

Nos. C381, C394 and C387 Surcharged

₡ 0.05

1964, Oct. ***Perf. 12, 14***

C395 AP72 5c on 30c ochre & Pruss. green 6 6
C396 AP73 15c on 30c blue, gray, red & black 6 6
C397 AP72 15c on 85c yellow & red brown 10 6

No. C388 Surcharged: "C 0.15 / CONFERENCIA POSTAL / DE PARIS—1864"

1964 ***Perf. 12***

C398 AP72 15c on 90c citron & red brown 12 8

Paris Postal Conference.

1965, June **Photo.** ***Perf. 12***

C399 AP74 35c dk. blue green 15 10

Issued to commemorate the 50th anniversary of the National Bank and to honor Alfredo Gonzalez F., first governor of the bank.

No. C390 Overprinted: "75 ANIVERSARIO / ASILO CHAPUI / 1890 - 1965"

1965, Aug. 14 ***Perf. 12*** **Unwmkd.**

C400 AP72 2col buff & dark green 90 65

Issued to commemorate the 75th anniversary of Chapui Asylum, San José.

Girl, FAO Emblem and Hands Holding Grain
AP75

Church of Nicoya
AP76

Designs (FAO Emblem and): 15c, Map of Costa Rica and silos (horiz.). 50c, World population chart and children. 1 col, Plane over map of Costa Rica (horiz.).

1965 **Lithographed** ***Perf. 14***

C401 AP75 15c lt. brn. & blk. 10 8
C402 " 35c black & yel. 20 15
C403 " 50c ultramarine & dark green 30 20
C404 " 1col green, black & silver 50 30

Issued for the "Freedom from Hunger" campaign of the U.N. Food and Agriculture Organization.

1965, Dec. 20 ***Perf. 13½x14***

Designs: 5c, Leonidas Briceno B. 15c, Scroll dated "25 de Julio de 1964." 35c, Map of Guanacaste and Nicoya peninsula. 50c, Dancing couple. 1col, Map showing local products.

C405 AP76 5c red brn. & blk. 5 5
C406 " 10c blue & gray 5 5
C407 " 15c bister & slate 6 6
C408 " 35c blue & slate 15 10
C409 " 50c gray & vio. bl. 25 15
C410 " 1col buff & slate 60 40
Nos. C405-C410 (6) 1.16 81

Acquisition of the Nicoya territory.

Runner and Olympic Rings
AP77

Pres. Kennedy Speaking in San José Cathedral
AP78

1965, Dec. 23 ***Perf. 13x13½***

Olympic Rings and Emblem: 10c, Bicyclists. 40c, Judo. 65c, Basketball. 80c, Soccer. 1col, Hands holding torches, and Mt. Fuji.

C411 AP77 5c bister & multi. 6 6
C412 " 10c lt. lilac & multi. 6 6

C413 AP77 40c multicolored 20 15
C414 " 65c lemon & multi. 35 20
C415 " 80c tan & multi. 50 30
C416 " 1col multicolored 65 40
a. Souv. sheet of 2 2.25 2.25
Nos. C411-C416 (6) 1.82 1.17

Issued to commemorate the 18th Olympic Games, Tokyo, Oct. 10–25, 1964. No. C416a contains two 1col stamps, one like No. C416, the other with gray background replacing yellow orange. Dark brown marginal inscription and red control number. Size: 68x93mm. Sheet also exists imperf.

Perf. 13½x13, 13x13½

1965, Dec. 23 Litho. Unwmkd.

Designs: 45c, Friendship 7 capsule circling globe, and Kennedy (horiz.). 85c, Kennedy and John, Jr. 1col, Curtis-Lee Mansion and flame from Kennedy grave, Arlington, Va.

C417 AP78 45c brt. bl. & lilac 25 20
C418 " 55c orge. & brt. bl. 35 25
C419 " 85c gray, dk. brn. & red brown 55 35
C420 " 1col multicolored 50 40
a. Souv. sheet of 2 1.50 1.50

Issued in memory of President John F. Kennedy (1917–63). No. C420a contains two 1col stamps, one like No. C420, the other with green background replacing dark blue. Dark gray marginal inscription and red control number. Size: 68x93mm. Sheet also exists imperf.

Firemen with Hoses
AP79

Designs: 5c, Fire engine "Knox" (horiz.). 10c, 1866 fire pump. 35c, Fireman's badge. 50c, Emblem and flags of Confederation of Central American Fire Brigades.

1965, March 12 Litho. *Perf. 11*

C421 AP79 5c black & red 5 5
C422 " 10c bister & red 6 5
C423 " 15c black, red brn. & red 8 6
C424 " 35c black & yellow 18 10
C425 " 50c dk. blue & red 30 15
Nos. C421-C425 (5) 67 41

Centenary of San José Fire Brigade.

Nos. C381, C383, C386 and C418-C419 Surcharged

C0.15
a

C 0.50
b

1966 Photogravure *Perf. 12*

C426 AP72 (a) 15c on 30c ocher & Prus. grn. 10 8
C427 " (") 15c on 45c lt. blue & dk. brown 10 8
C428 " (") 35c on 75c ocher & dk. red brn. 20 12

Perf. 13x13½

Lithographed

C429 AP78 (a) 35c on 55c org. & brt. blue 20 12
C430 " (b) 50c on 85c multi. 35 20
Nos. C426-C430 (5) 95 60

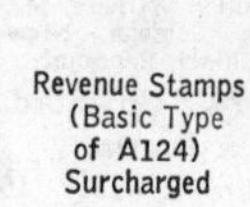

Revenue Stamps (Basic Type of A124) Surcharged

1966, Dec. Engraved *Perf. 12*

C431 A124 15c on 5c blue 10 6
C432 " 35c on 10c claret 22 12
C433 " 50c on 20c rose red 35 20

Central Bank of Costa Rica
AP80

1967, Mar. Litho. *Perf. 11*

C434 AP80 5c bright green 7 5
C435 " 15c brown 10 6
C436 " 35c scarlet 20 12

Power Lines
AP81

Telecommunications Building, San Pedro
AP82

Designs: 15c, Telephone Central. 25c, La Garita Dam. 35c, Rio Mache Reservoir. 50c, Cachi Dam.

1967, Apr. 24 Litho. *Perf. 11*

C437 AP81 5c dark gray 7 5
C438 AP82 10c bright rose 7 5
C439 AP81 15c brown orange 8 6
C440 AP82 25c bright ultra. 13 8
C441 " 35c bright green 20 10
C442 " 50c red brown 35 20
Nos. C437-C442 (6) 90 54

Electrification program.

Chondrorhyncha Aromatica
AP83

COSTA RICA
CORREO AEREO
50 CENTIMOS
XXV ANIVERSARIO

Institute Emblem
AP84

Orchids: 10c, Miltonia endresii. 15c, Stanhopea cirrhata. 25c, Trichopilia suavis. 35c, Odontoglossum schlieperianum. 50c, Cattleya skinneri. 1col, Cattleya dowiana. 2col, Odontoglossum chiriquense.

1967, June 15 Engr. *Perf. 13x13½*

Orchids in Natural Colors

C443 AP83 5c multicolored 5 5
C444 " 10c olive & multi. 9 5
C445 " 15c multicolored 10 6
C446 " 25c " 15 12
C447 AP83 35c dull violet & multi. 25 15
C448 " 50c brn. & multi. 30 20
C449 " 1col vio. & multi. 55 40
C450 " 2col dk. olive bister & multi. 1.20 80
Nos. C443-C450 (8) 2.66 1.83

Issued for the University Library.

1967, Oct. 6 Litho. *Perf. 13x13½*

C451 AP84 50c vio. blue, lt. blue & blue 20 18

Issued to commemorate the 25th anniversary of the Inter-American Agriculture Institute.

Church of Solitude
AP85

LACSA Emblem
AP86

Costa Rican Churches: 10c, Basilica of Santo Domingo, Heredia. 15c, Cathedral of Tilaran. 25c, Cathedral of Alajuela. 30c, Mercy Church. 35c, Basilica of Our Lady of Angels. 40c, Church of St. Raphael, Heredia. 45c, Ujarras ruins. 50c, Ruins of parish church, Cartago. 55c, Cathedral of San José. 65c, Parish church, Puntarenas. 75c, Church of Orosi. 80c, Cathedral of St. Isidro, the General. 85c, St. Ramon Church. 90c, Church of the Abandonned. 1col, Coronado Church. 2col, Church of St. Teresita. 3col, Parish Church, Heredia. 5col, Carmelite Church. 10col, Limon Cathedral.

1967, Dec. 15 Engr. *Perf. 12½*

C452 AP85 5c green 4 4
C453 " 10c blue 5 5
C454 " 15c lilac 6 6
C455 " 25c dull yellow 10 8
C456 " 30c org. brown 12 10
C457 " 35c light blue 15 12
C458 " 40c deep orange 15 12
C459 " 45c dull bl. green 16 15
C460 " 50c olive 18 18
C461 " 55c brown 20 18
C462 " 65c car. rose 25 20
C463 " 75c sepia 27 25
C464 " 80c yellow 35 30
C465 " 85c violet black 40 30
C466 " 90c emerald 50 40
C467 " 1col slate 35 35
C468 " 2col bright green 90 65
C469 " 3col orange 2.50 1.00
C470 " 5col violet blue 3.00 1.50
C471 " 10col carmine 4.00 3.25
Nos. C452-C471 (20) 13.73 9.28

See Nos. C561-C576.

Perf. 13x13½, 13½x13

1967, Dec. 12 Litho. & Engraved

Design: 45c, LACSA emblem and jet (horiz.). 50c, Decorated wheel and anniversary emblem.

C472 AP86 40c ultra., greenish blue & gold 15 15
C473 " 45c blk., pale grn., ultra. & gold 18 15
C474 " 50c bl. & multi. 20 18

Issued to commemorate the 20th anniversary (in 1966) of Lineas Aereas Costaricenses, LACSA, Costa Rican Airlines.

Scout Directing Traffic
AP87

Runner
AP88

Designs: 25c, Campfire under palm tree. 35c, Flag of Costa Rica, Scout flag and emblem. 50c, Encampment (horiz.). 65c, Photograph of first Scout troop (horiz.).

Lithographed and Engraved

1968, Mar. 15 *Perf. 13*

C475 AP87 15c lt. bl., blk. & light brown 10 6
C476 " 25c lt. ultra., violet blue & org. 15 10
C477 " 35c blue & multi. 22 15
C478 " 50c multicolored 27 20
C479 " 65c salmon, dark blue & brn. 40 25
Nos. C475-C479 (5) 1.14 76

Costa Rican Boy Scouts, 50th anniversary.

1968 Lithographed *Perf. 10x11*

Sports: 40c, Women's running. 55c, Boxing. 65c, Bicycling. 75c, Weight lifting. 1col, High diving. 3col, Rifle shooting.

C481 AP88 30c multicolored 12 8
C482 " 40c " 18 12
C483 " 55c " 30 20
C484 " 65c lilac & multi. 37 20
C485 " 75c multicolored 37 20
C486 " 1col " 42 30
C487 " 3col " 1.85 1.00
Nos. C481-C487 (7) 3.61 2.10

Issued to commemorate the 19th Olympic Games, Mexico City, Oct. 12–27.

Philatelic Exhibition Emblem
AP89

1969, June 5 Litho. *Perf. 11x10*

C488 AP89 35c multicolored 15 10
C489 " 40c pink & multi. 18 12
C490 " 50c lt. bl. & multi. 22 15
C491 " 2col multicolored 80 60

Issued to publicize the 4th National Philatelic Exhibition, San José, June 5–8.

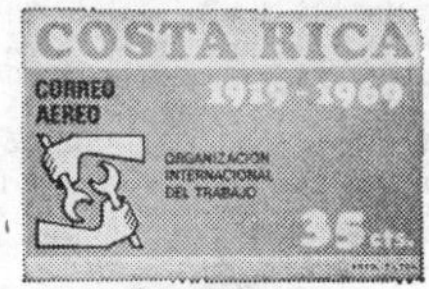

ILO Emblem
AP90

1969, Oct. 29 Litho. *Perf. 10*

C492 AP90 35c bl. grn. & blk. 18 10
C493 " 50c scarlet & blk. 27 15

Issued to commemorate the 50th anniversary of the International Labor Organization.

Soccer—AP91

Designs: 65c, Soccer ball, map of North and Central America. 85c, Soccer player. 1 col, Two players in action.

1969, Nov. 23 Litho. *Perf. 11x10*

C494 AP91 65c gray & multi. 30 20
C495 " 75c multicolored 30 20
C496 " 85c " 38 25
C497 " 1col pink & multi. 45 30

Issued to publicize the 4th Soccer Championships (CONCACAF), Nov. 23–Dec. 7.

Stylized Crab—AP92

1970, May 14 Litho. *Perf. 12½*

C498	AP92	10c black & lilac rose	3	3
C499	"	15c blk. & yel.	5	5
C500	"	50c black & brn. org.	12	10
C501	"	1.10col black & emerald	27	20

Issued to publicize the 10th Inter-American Cancer Congress, May 22–29.

Costa Rica No. 124, Magnifying Glass and Stamps AP93

Design: 2col, Father and son with stamps and album.

1970, Sept. 14 Litho. *Perf. 11*

C502	AP93	1col ultra., brn. & car. rose	24	15
C503	"	2col black, pink & ultramarine	48	40

The 5th National Philatelic Exhibition.

EXPO Emblem and Costa Rican Cart—AP94

Designs (EXPO Emblem and): 10c, Japanese floral arrangement (vert.). 35c, Pavilion and Tower of the Sun. 40c, Japanese tea ceremony. 45c, Woman picking coffee (vert.). 55c, Earth seen from moon (vert.).

1970, Oct. 22 Litho. *Perf. 13x13½*

C504	AP94	10c multicolored	6	4
C505	"	15c grn. & multi.	9	6
C506	"	35c blue & multi.	15	10
C507	"	40c gray & multi.	20	12
C508	"	45c multicolored	20	15
C509	"	55c black & multi.	20	15
		Nos. C504-C509 (6)	90	62

Issued to commemorate EXPO '70 International Exhibition, Osaka, Japan, March 15–Sept. 13.

Escazu Valley, by Margarita Bertheau—AP95

Paintings: 25c, "Irazu," by Rafael A. Garcia (vert.). 80c, Shore landscape, by Teodorico Quiros. 1col, "The Other Face," by Cesar Valverde. 2.50col, Mother and Child, by Luis Daell (vert.).

1970, Nov. 4 Litho. *Perf. 12½*

C510	AP95	25c multicolored	12	7
C511	"	45c "	12	10
C512	"	80c "	25	15
C513	"	1col "	25	20
C514	"	2.50col "	60	50
		Nos. C510-C514 (5)	1.34	1.02

Arms of Costa Rica, 1964 AP96

Various Coats of Arms, dated: 10c, Nov. 27, 1906. 15c, Sept. 29, 1848. 25c, April 21, 1840. 35c, Nov. 22, 1824. 50c, Nov. 2, 1824. 1col, March 6, 1824. 2col, May 10, 1823.

1971, Feb. 10 Litho. *Perf.14x13½*

C515	AP96	5c buff & multi.	3	3
C516	"	10c multicolored	4	3
C517	"	15c yel. & multi.	6	5
C518	"	25c pink & multi.	9	7
C519	"	35c multicolored	15	10
C520	"	50c rose & multi.	15	10
C521	"	1col beige & multi.	25	15
C522	"	2col multicolored	50	30
		Nos. C515-C522 (8)	1.27	83

National Theater AP97

1971, Apr. Litho. *Perf. 11*

C523	AP97	2col plum	50	40

Organization of American States meeting.

José Matias Delgado, Manuel José Arce AP98

Flag of Costa Rica AP99

Independence Leaders: 10c, Miguel Larreinaga and Manuel Antonio de la Cerda, Nicaragua. 15c, José Cecilio del Valle, Dionisio de Herrera, Honduras. 35c, Pablo Alvarado and Florencio del Castillo, Costa Rica. 50c, Antonio Larrazabal and Pedro Molina, Guatemala. 2col, Costa Rica coat of arms.

1971, Sept. 14 *Perf. 13*

C524	AP98	5c multicolored	3	3
C525	"	10c "	4	3
C526	"	15c gray, brown & black	6	5
C527	"	35c multicolored	15	12
C528	"	50c "	15	12
C529	AP99	1col "	25	15
C530	"	2col "	50	40
		Nos. C524-C530 (7)	1.18	90

Sesquicentennial of Central American independence.

Soccer Federation Emblem AP100 — Children of the World AP101

1971, Dec.

C531	AP100	50c multicolored	15	10
C532	"	60c "	15	10

50th anniversary of Soccer Federation of Costa Rica.

1972, Jan. 11 *Perf. 12½*

C533	AP101	50c multicolored	15	10
C534	"	1.10col red & multi.	30	25

25th anniversary (in 1971) of the United Nations International Children's Fund (UNICEF).

Tree of Guanacaste AP102

Designs: 40c, Hermitage, Liberia. 55c, Petroglyphs, Rincón Brujo. 60c, Painted head, sculpture from Curubandé (vert.).

1972, Feb. 28 *Perf. 11*

C535	AP102	20c brown, olive & brt. green	10	7
C536	"	40c brown & olive	15	10
C537	"	55c blk. & brown	15	12
C538	"	60c black, buff & vermilion	20	15

Bicentenary of the founding of the city of Liberia, Guanacaste.

Farm and Family AP103 — Inter-American Exhibitions AP104

Designs: 45c, Cattle, dairy products and meat (horiz.). 50c, Kneeling figure with plant. 10col, Farmer and map of Americas.

1972, June 30 Litho. *Perf. 12½*

C539	AP103	20c multicolored	10	7
C540	"	45c "	15	10
C541	"	50c dp. yel., grn. & black	15	10
C542	"	10col brn., orange & black	2.50	1.50

30th anniversary of the Inter-American Institute of Agricultural Sciences.

1972, Aug. 26 Litho. *Perf. 13*

C543	AP104	50c org. & brown	15	10
C544	"	2col bl. & violet	50	40

4th Interamerican Philatelic Exhibition, EXFILBRA, Rio de Janeiro, Aug. 26–Sept. 2.

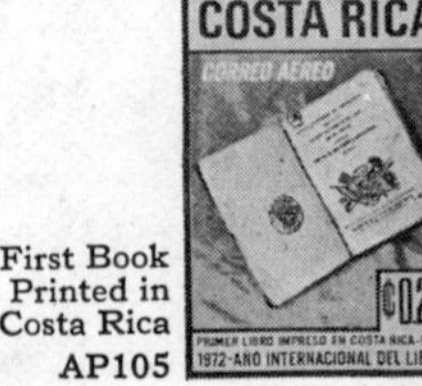

First Book Printed in Costa Rica AP105

Design: 50c, 5col, National Library (horiz.).

1972, Dec. 7 Litho. *Perf. 12½*

C545	AP105	20c bright blue	8	7
C546	"	50c gold & multi.	15	10
C547	"	75c multicolored	20	15
C548	"	5col "	1.25	1.00

International Book Year 1972.

Road to Irazú Volcano AP106

1972–73 *Perf. 11x11½, 11½x11*

Multicolored

C549	AP106	5c *like 20c*	3	3
C550	"	15c *Coco-Culebra Bay*	7	4
C551	"	20c *shown*	10	7
C552	"	25c *like 15c*	10	8
C553	"	40c *Manuel Antonio Beach*	15	10
C554	"	45c *Tourist Office emblem*	15	12
C555	"	50c *Lindora Lake*	15	12
C556	"	60c *San José P.O. (vert.)*	20	15
C557	"	80c *like 40c*	25	20
C558	"	90c *like 45c*	25	20
C559	"	1col *like 50c*	25	20
C560	"	2col *like 60c*	50	40
		Nos. C549-C560 (12)	2.20	1.71

Tourism year of the Americas.

Issue dates: 20c, 25c, 80c, 90c, 1col and 2col, Dec. 26, 1972. Others, Mar. 21, 1973.

Church Type of 1967

Designs as Before

1973, July 16 Engr. *Perf. 12½*

C561	AP85	5c slate green	6	4
C562	"	10c olive	7	5
C563	"	15c orange	8	6
C564	"	25c brown	10	8
C565	"	30c rose claret	10	8
C566	"	35c violet	12	10
C567	"	40c bright green	12	10
C568	"	45c dull yellow	15	10
C569	"	50c rose magenta	15	10
C570	"	55c blue	15	12
C571	"	65c black	20	15
C572	"	75c rose red	20	15
C573	"	80c yellow green	20	15
C574	"	85c lilac	25	20
C575	"	90c bright pink	25	20
C576	"	1col dark blue	25	20
		Nos. C561-C576 (16)	2.45	1.88

Human Rights Flame AP107 — OAS Emblem AP108

1973 Photogravure *Perf. 10½*

C577	AP107	50c black & red	15	10

25th anniversary of the Universal Declaration of Human Rights.

1973, Dec. 17 Litho. *Perf. 10½*

C578	AP108	20c dark blue & dp. carmine	10	5

25th anniversary of the Organization of American States.

Joaquin Vargas Calvo
AP109

AP110

1974, Jan. 14

Multicolored

C579 AP109 20c *shown* 10 6
C580 " 20c *Alejandro Monestel* 10 6
C581 " 20c *Julio Mata* 10 6
C582 " 60c *Julio Fonseca* 20 15
C583 " 2col *Rafael A. Chaves* 50 35
C584 " 5col *Manuel M. Gutierrez* 1.25 1.00
Nos. C579-C584 (6) 2.35 1.68

Costa Rican composers honored by the National Symphony Orchestra.

Revenue Stamps Overprinted "Habilitado para Correo Aereo"

1974, Apr. 5 Engraved *Perf. 12*

C585 AP110 50c brown 15 10
C586 " 1col violet 25 15
C587 " 2col orange 50 30
C588 " 5col olive 1.25 1.00

Telephone Building, San Pedro
AP111

EXFILMEX 74 Emblem
AP112

Designs: 65c, Rio Macho Control (horiz.). 85c, Turbines, Rio Macho Center. 1.25col, Cachi Dam and reservoir (horiz.). 2col, I.C.E. Headquarters.

1974, July 30 Litho. *Perf. 10½*

C589 AP111 50c gold & multi. 15 10
C590 " 65c " " 20 12
C591 " 85c " " 25 15
C592 " 1.25col " " 30 20
C593 " 2col " " 50 30
Nos. C589-C593 (5) 1.40 87

25th anniversary of Costa Rican Electrical Institute (I.C.E.).

1974, Aug. 22 *Perf. 13*

C594 AP112 65c green 20 15
C595 " 3col lilac rose 75 50

5th Inter-American Philatelic Exhibition, EXFILMEX-74 UPU, Mexico City, Oct. 26–Nov. 3.

Map of Costa Rica, 4-S Emblem
AP113

Design: 50c, Young harvesters and 4-S emblem.

1974, Oct. 7 Litho. *Perf. 12x11*

C596 AP113 20c bright green 10 5
C597 " 50c multicolored 15 10

25th anniversary of 4-S Clubs of Costa Rica (similar to US 4-H Clubs).

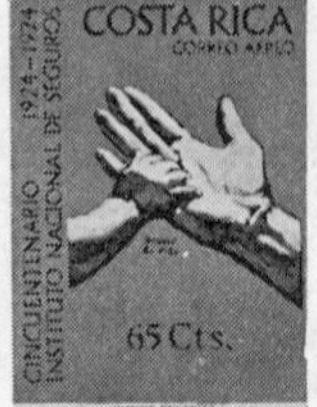

Roberto Brenes Mesen
AP114

"Life Insurance"
AP115

Designs: 85c, "Love and Death," manuscript (horiz.). 5col, Hands of writer.

1974, Oct. 14 Litho. *Perf. 10½*

C598 AP114 20c blk. & brn. 10 5
C599 " 85c black & red 25 20
C600 " 5col black & red brown 1.25 1.00

Birth centenary of Roberto Brenes Mesen, educator and writer.

1974, Oct. 30 *Perf. 14*

Designs: 20c, Ricardo Jiménez Oreamuno and Tomás Soley Güell (horiz.). 50c, Harvest Insurance (hand holding shovel; horiz.). 85c, Maritime insurance (hand holding paper boat). 1.25col, INS emblem. 2col, Workers rehabilitation (arm with crutch). 2.50col, Workers' Compensation (hand holding wrench). 20col, Fire insurance (hands protecting house).

C601 AP115 20c multi. 9 5
C602 " 50c " 15 10
C603 " 65c " 15 10
C604 " 85c " 20 15
C605 " 1.25col " 30 20
C606 " 2col " 50 30
C607 " 2.50col " 65 50
C608 " 20col " 5.00 4.00
Nos. C601-C608 (8) 7.04 5.30

Costa Rican Insurance Institute (Instituto Nacional de Seguros, INS), 50th anniversary.

WPY Emblem
AP116

Oscar J. Pinto F.
AP117

1974, Nov. 13 Litho. *Perf. 11x11½*

C609 AP116 2col vio. bl. & red 50 30

World Population Year.

1974, Dec. 2 *Perf. 13*

Designs: 50c, Alberto Montes de Oca D., champion sharpshooter. 1col, Eduardo Garnier, sports promoter. O. J. Pinto, introducer of soccer.

C610 AP117 20c gray & dk. bl. 9 5
C611 " 50c " " 15 10
C612 " 1col " " 25 15

First Central American Olympic Games, held in Guatemala, 1973.

Mormodes Buccinator
AP118

Masdevallia Ephippium
AP119

Designs: Orchids.

1975, Mar. 7 Litho. *Perf. 10½, 13½*

Multicolored

C613 AP118 25c *shown* 6 5
C614 " 25c *Gongora claviodora* 6 5
C615 AP119 25c *shown* 6 5
C616 " 25c *Encyclia spondiadum* 6 5
C617 AP118 65c *Lycaste skinnery alba* 20 15
C618 " 65c *Peristeria elata* 20 15
C619 AP119 65c *Miltonia roezelii* 20 15
C620 " 65c *Brassavola digbyana* 20 15
C621 AP118 80c *Epidendrum mirabile* 25 20
C622 " 80c *Barkeria lindleyana* 25 20
C623 AP119 80c *Cattleya skinneri* 25 20
C624 " 80c *Sobralia macrantha* 25 20
C625 AP118 1.40col *Lycaste cruenta* 35 25
C626 " 1.40col *Oncidium obryzatum* 35 25
C627 AP119 1.40col *Gongora armeniaca* 35 25
C628 " 1.40col *Sievekingia suavis* 35 25

Perf. 13½

C629 AP118 1.75col *Hexisea imbricata* 45 30
C630 " 2.15col *Warcewiczella discolor* 55 30
C631 AP119 2.50col *Oncidium kramerianum* 65 50
C632 " 3.25col *Cattleya dowiana* 85 60
Nos. C613-C632 (20) 5.94 4.30

5th National Flower Exhibition.

Stamps of same denominations printed se-tenant. Nos. C613-C628 were printed in both perforations on two different papers: dull finish and shiny. Nos. C629-C632 were printed on shiny paper.

Radio Club Emblem
AP120

Members' Flags and Emblem
AP121

Design: 2col, Federation emblem.

1975, Apr. 16 Litho. *Perf. 13½*

C633 AP120 1col blk. & red lilac 25 15
C634 AP121 1.10col multi. 30 20
C635 AP120 2col blk. & bl. 50 30

16th Central American Radio Amateurs' Convention, San José, May 2–4.

A little time given to study of the arrangement of the Scott Catalogue can make it easier to use effectively.

Nicoya Beach
AP122

Designs: 75c, Driving cattle. 1col, Colonial Church, Nicoya. 3col, Savannah riders (vert.).

1975, Aug. 1 Litho. *Perf. 13½*

C636 AP122 25c gray & multi. 6 5
C637 " 75c " " 20 20
C638 " 1col " " 25 15
C639 " 3col " " 75 60

Sesquicentennial of annexation of Nicoya District.

Costa Rica No. 158
AP123

Designs (Type A90 of 1932): No. C641, No. 159. No. C642, No. 160. No. C643, No. 161.

1975, Aug. 14 Litho. *Perf. 12*

C640 AP123 2.20col black & orange 60 50
C641 " 2.20col black & dk. green 60 50
C642 " 2.20col black & car. rose 60 50
C643 " 2.20col black & dk. blue 60 50

6th National Philatelic Exhibition, San José, Aug. 14–17. Nos. C640-C643 printed se-tenant.

IWY Emblem
AP124

1975, Oct. Litho. *Perf. 10½*

C644 AP124 40c vio. bl. & red 10 8
C645 " 1.25col black & ultra. 30 20

International Women's Year 1975.

U.N. Emblem
AP125

Designs: 60c, U.N. General Assembly (horiz.). 1.20col, U.N. Headquarters, New York.

1975, Oct. 24 *Perf. 12*

C646 AP125 10c blue & black 4 3
C647 " 60c multicolored 15 12
C648 " 1.20col " 30 20

30th anniversary of the United Nations.

The Visitation, by Jorge Gallardo
AP126

'20–30' Club Emblem
AP127

Paintings by Jorge Gallardo: 1col, Nativity and Star. 5col, St. Joseph in his Workshop, Virgin and Child.

1975, Nov. ***Perf. 10½***

C649 AP126 50c multicolored 15 10
C650 " 1col " 25 15
C651 " 5col " 1.25 1.00

Christmas 1975.

1976, Jan. 16 **Litho.** ***Perf. 12***

C652 AP127 1col multi. 25 15

'20–30' Club of Costa Rica, 20th anniversary.

Quercus Brenessi Trel
AP128

"Literary Development"
AP129

Plants: 30c, Maxillaria albertii schecht. 55c, Calathea brenesii standl. 2col, Brenesia costaricensis schlecht. 10col, Philodendron brenesii standl.

1976, March 1 ***Perf. 10½***

C653 AP128 5c multi. 3 3
C654 " 30c " 10 6
C655 " 55c " 15 12
C656 " 2col tan & multi. 50 30
C657 " 10col multi. 2.50 2.00
Nos. C653–C657 (5) 3.28 2.51

Prof. Alberto Manuel Brenes Mora, botanist, birth centenary.

1976, Apr. 9 **Litho.** ***Perf. 16***

Designs: 1.10col, Man holding book, stylized. 5col, Costa Rican flag emanating from book (horiz.).

C658 AP129 15c multi. 6 4
C659 " 1.10col " 25 20
C660 " 5col " 1.25 1.00

Publishing in Costa Rica.

Post-rider, 1839
AP130

Costa Rica No. 13, Post Office
AP131

Designs: 65c, Costa Rica No. 14 and Post Office. 85c, Costa Rica No. 15 and Post Office. 2col, UPU Monument, Bern (vert.).

1976, May 24 ***Perf. 10½***

C661 AP130 20c apple green & black 8 5
C662 AP131 50c bis. & multi. 15 10
C663 " 65c multicolored 20 15
C664 " 85c " 25 20
C665 AP130 2col blk. & lt. bl. 50 40
Nos. C661–C665 (5) 1.18 90

Centenary of Universal Postal Union (in 1974).

Nos. C662–C664 exist without the surcharges on reproductions of Nos. 13–15.

Telephones, 1876 and 1976
AP132

Designs: 2col, Wall telephone. 5col, Alexander Graham Bell.

1976, June 28

C666 AP132 1.60col lt. blue & black 40 30
C667 " 2col multi. 50 30
C668 " 5col yellow & black 1.25 1.00

Centenary of first telephone call by Alexander Graham Bell, Mar. 10, 1876.

Inverted Center Stamp of 1901 and Association Emblems—AP133

1976, Nov. 11 **Litho.** ***Perf. 10½***

C669 AP133 50c multicolored 15 10
C670 " 1col " 25 15
C671 " 2col " 50 30

Souvenir Sheet

Design: 5col, 1901 stamp between Costa Rican Philatelic Society and Interamerican Philatelic Federation emblems.

Perf. 12, Imperf.

C672 AP133 5col multi. 1.25 1.25

7th National Philatelic Exhibition and 9th Plenary Assembly of the Interamerican Philatelic Federation (FIAF), San José, Nov. 1976. No. C672 has black marginal inscription. Size: 75x60mm.

"Seeing Eye" and Map of Costa Rica
AP134

Amadeo Quiros Blanco
AP135

1976, Nov. 22 ***Perf. 16***

C673 AP134 35c blk. & blue 10 8
C674 AP135 2col multicolored 50 30

General Audit Office, 25th anniversary.

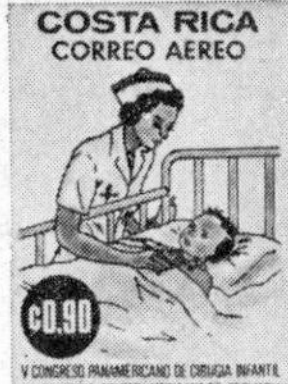

Nurse Attending Child
AP136

LACSA Circling Globe
AP137

Design: 1.10col, National Children's Hospital (horiz.).

1976, Nov. 29

C675 AP136 90c multi. 25 20
C676 " 1.10col " 30 25

5th Panamerican Congress of Pediatric Surgery and 12th Congress of Pediatrics.

1976, Dec. 1 ***Perf. 10½***

Designs: 1.20col, Route map. 3col, LACSA emblem and Costa Rican flag.

C677 AP137 1col multi. 25 15
C678 " 1.20col " 30 20
C679 " 3col " 75 50

Costa Rican Air Lines (LACSA), 30th anniversary.

Boston Tea Party
AP138

Designs: 5col, Declaration of Independence. 10col, Ringing Liberty Bell to announce Independence (vert.).

1976, Dec. 24

C680 AP138 2.20col multi. 55 40
C681 " 5col " 1.25 1.00
C682 " 10col " 2.50 2.00

American Bicentennial.

Tree of Guanacaste
AP139

Felipe J. Alvarado
AP140

Designs (Rotary Emblem and): 60c, Dr. Paul Blanco Cervantes Hospital (horiz.). 3col, Map of Costa Rica (horiz.). 10col, Paul Harris.

1977, Mar. 31 **Litho.** ***Perf. 16***

C683 AP139 40c violet blue & multi. 10 8
C684 AP140 50c black & multi. 15 10
C685 AP139 60c violet blue & multi. 15 15
C686 " 3col vio. blue & multi. 75 60
C687 AP140 10col black & multi. 2.50 2.00
Nos. C683–C687 (5) 3.65 2.93

Rotary Club of San José, 50th anniversary.

Boruca Cloth
AP141

Design: 1.50col, Painted wood ornament.

1977, Feb. 22

C688 AP141 75c multi. 20 15
C689 " 1.50col " 40 20

National Artisan and Small Industry Program.

Juana Pereira
AP142

Alonso de Anguciana de Gamboa
AP143

Designs: 1col, First Church of Our Lady of the Angels (horiz.). 1.10col, Our Lady of the Angels (gold sculpture). 1.25col, Crown of Our Lady of the Angels.

1977, June 6 **Litho.** ***Perf. 10½***

C690 AP142 50c multi. 15 10
C691 " 1col " 25 15
C692 " 1.10col " 30 20
C693 " 1.25col " 35 25

50th anniversary of the coronation of Our Lady of the Angels, patron saint of Costa Rica.

1977, July 4 **Litho.** ***Perf. 10½***

Designs: 75c, Church of Esparza. 1col, Statue of Our Lady of Candlemas. 2col, Statue of Diego de Artieda y Chirino.

C694 AP143 35c multicolored 10 8
C695 " 75c " 20 15
C696 " 1col " 25 15
C697 " 2col " 50 40

400th anniversary of the founding of Esparza.

CARE Emblem and Child
AP144

Design: 1col, CARE emblem and soybeans (horiz.).

1977, Sept. 14 **Litho.** ***Perf. 16***

C698 AP144 80c multicolored 20 15
C699 " 1col " 25 15

20th anniversary of CARE (relief organization) in Costa Rica.

Institute's Emblem
AP145

First Map of Americas, 1540
AP146

1977, Oct. 21 Litho. *Perf. 16*

C700 AP145 50c black & multi. 15 10
C701 AP146 1.40col black & multi. 35 30

Hispanic Cultural Institute of Costa Rica, 25th anniversary.

Mercy Church, by Ricardo Ulloa B.
AP147

COSTA RICA
CORREO AEREO ¢1.40

Health Ministry Emblem
AP148

Paintings: 1col, Christ, by Floria Pinto de Herrero. 5col, St. Francis and the Birds, by Louisa Gonzalez Y Saenz.

1977, Nov. 9 Litho. *Perf. 10½*

C702 AP147 50c multicolored 15 10
C703 " 1col " 25 15
C704 " 5col " 1.25 1.00

1977, Nov. 16 *Perf. 16*

C705 AP148 1.40col multi. 35 30

Creation of Ministry of Health.

Picnic
AP149

José de San Martin
AP150

Designs: 50c, Weaver. 2col, Beach scene. 5col, Fruit and vegetable market. 10col, Swans on lake.

1978, Mar. 21 Litho. *Perf. 10½*

C706 AP149 50c black & multi. 15 10
C707 " 1col black & multi. 25 15
C708 " 2col black & multi. 50 30
C709 " 5col black & multi. 1.25 1.00
C710 " 10col black & multi. 2.50 2.00
Nos. C706-C710 (5) 4.65 3.55

Conference of Latin American Tourist Organizations.

1978, Aug. 7 Litho. *Perf. 10½*

C711 AP150 5col multi. 1.25 1.00

Gen. José de San Martin (1778–1850), soldier and statesman, fought for South American independence.

Geographical Institute Emblem
AP151

University Federation Emblem
AP152

1978, Aug. 28 Litho. *Perf. 12½*

C712 AP151 5col multi. 1.20 90

Pan-American Geography and History Institute, 50th anniversary.

1978, Sept. 18 *Perf. 11*

C713 AP152 80c ultramarine 20 15

Central American University Federation, 30th anniversary.

Emblems
AP153

1978, Oct. 24 *Perf. 16*

C714 AP153 2col aqua., blk. & gold 48 35

6th Interamerican Philatelic Exhibition, Argentina 78, Buenos Aires, Oct. 1978.

Nos. C629-C631 Overprinted:
"50 Aniversario del / primer vuelo de PAN AM / en Costa Rica / 1928–1978"

1978, Nov. 1 Litho. *Perf. 13½*

C715 AP118 1.75col multi. 42 30
C716 " 2.15col " 50 38
C717 AP119 2.50col " 60 45

First Pan Am flight in Costa Rica, 50th anniversary.

Nos. C629-C631 Overprinted:
"50 Aniversario de la / visita de Lindbergh a / Costa Rica 1928–1978"

1978, Nov. 1

C718 AP118 1.75col multi. 42 30
C719 " 2.15col " 50 38
C720 AP119 2.50col " 60 45

50th anniversary of Lindbergh's visit to Costa Rica.

Nos. C603 and C607 Surcharged with New Value, 4 Bars and:
"Centenario del / Asilo Carlos / Maria Ulloa / 1878–1978"

1978, Nov. 8 *Perf. 14*

C721 AP115 50c on 65c multi. 12 10
C722 " 2col on 2.50col multi. 48 35

Asilo Carlos Maria Ulloa, birth centenary.

No. C617-C620, C630-C631 Surcharged with New Value and 4 Bars.

1978, Nov. 13 Litho. *Perf. 10½, 13½*

C723 AP118 50c on 65c 12 10
C724 " 50c on 65c 12 10
C725 AP119 50c on 65c 12 10
C726 " 50c on 65c 12 10
C727 AP118 1.20col on 2.15col 30 20
C728 AP119 2col on 2.50col 48 35
Nos. C723-C728 (6) 1.26 95

Nos. C723-C726 printed se-tenant.

AIR POST SPECIAL DELIVERY STAMPS

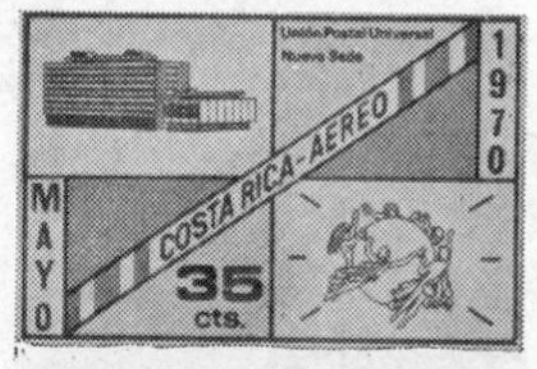

U.P.U. Headquarters and Monument, Bern
APSD1

Perf. 10x11

1970, May 20 Litho. Unwmkd.

CE1 APSD1 35c multicolored 18 10
CE2 " 60c " 30 15

Issued to commemorate the opening of the new Universal Postal Union Headquarters in Bern. The red and black label attached to the 60c is inscribed "EXPRES". Prices are for stamps with label attached.
Stamps with labels removed were used for regular airmail.

AIR POST OFFICIAL STAMPS.

Air Post Stamps of 1934
Overprinted in Red **OFICIAL**

1934 *Perf. 12.* Unwmkd.

CO1 AP8 5c green 35 35
CO2 " 10c carmine rose 35 35
CO3 " 15c chocolate 60 60
CO4 " 20c deep blue 90 90
CO5 " 25c deep orange 90 90
CO6 " 40c olive black 1.00 1.00
CO7 " 50c gray black 1.00 1.00
CO8 " 60c orange yellow 1.25 1.25
CO9 " 75c dull violet 1.25 1.25
CO10 AP9 1col deep rose 1.75 1.75
CO11 " 2col light blue 6.00 6.00
CO12 " 5col black 11.00 11.00
CO13 " 10col red brown 13.00 13.00
Nos. CO1-CO13 (13) 39.35 39.35

SPECIAL DELIVERY STAMPS

Winged Letter
SD1

Unwmkd.

1972, Mar. 20 Litho. *Perf. 11*

E1 SD1 75c brown & red 25 20
E2 " 1.50col blue & red 50 35

1973 *Perf. 11x12*

E3 SD1 75c green & red 25 20

1973, Nov. 5 Litho. *Perf. 11x11½*

E4 SD1 75c lilac & orange 25 20

Concorde
SD2

1976, May 17 Litho. *Perf. 16*

E5 SD2 1col verm. & multi. 25 20

POSTAGE DUE STAMPS.

D1

D2

Engraved

1903 *Perf. 14* Unwmkd.

Numerals in Black.

J1 D1 5c slate blue 5.50 1.35
J2 " 10c brown orange 5.50 1.00
J3 " 15c yellow green 2.25 2.25
J4 " 20c carmine 2.75 2.00
J5 " 25c slate gray 3.25 2.25
J6 " 30c brown 5.50 3.25
J7 " 40c olive bistre 5.50 3.25
J8 " 50c red violet 5.50 2.75
Nos. J1-J8 (8) 35.75 18.10

1915 Lithographed. *Perf. 12.*

J9 D2 2c orange 12 12
J10 " 4c dark blue 12 12
J11 " 8c gray green 50 50
J12 " 10c violet 20 20
J13 " 20c brown 25 25
Nos. J9-J13 (5) 1.19 1.19

OFFICIAL STAMPS.

Official stamps normally were not canceled when affixed to official mail in the 19th century. Occasionally they were canceled in a foreign country of destination. Used prices are for used stamps without cancellation or favor-canceled specimens.

Regular Issues Overprinted.
Overprinted in Red, Black, Blue or Green **Oficial**

1883-85 *Perf. 12.* Unwmkd.

O1 A6 1c green (R) 1.10 1.10
O2 " 1c green (Bk) 1.20 1.20
O3 " 2c carmine (Bk) 1.60 1.60
O4 " 2c carmine (Bl) 1.80 1.80
O5 " 5c blue violet (R) 4.25 4.25
O6 " 10c orange (G) 5.50 5.50
O7 " 40c blue (R) 5.50 5.50
Nos. O1-O7 (7) 20.95 20.95

Overprinted **OFICIAL**

1886

O8 A6 1c green (Bk) 1.50 1.50
O9 " 2c carmine (Bk) 2.50 2.50
O10 " 5c blue violet (R) 17.50 17.50
O11 " 10c orange (Bk) 17.50 17.50

Overprinted **OFICIAL**

O12 A6 1c green (Bk) 1.20 1.20
O13 " 2c carmine (Bk) 1.80 1.80
O14 " 5c blue violet (R) 13.50 13.50
O15 " 10c orange (Bk) 13.50 13.50

Nos. O8-O11 and O12-O15 exist se-tenant in vertical pairs. Price, each $75.

Overprinted in Black **Oficial**

O16 A6 5c blue violet 37.50 35.00
O17 " 10c orange 150.00 75.00

Overprinted **OFICIAL.**

1887

O18 A6 1c green 75 75
a. "OFICAL" 10.00 10.00
b. Without period 90 90
O19 " 2c carmine 70 70
a. "OFICAL" 6.00 6.00
b. Without period 90 90
O21 " 10c orange 4.25 4.25
a. "OFICAL" 6.50 6.50
b. Without period 5.00
c. Double overprint 10.00
d. "OFICAL" doubled
O22 A7 5c blue violet 2.75 2.75
a. "OFICAL" 5.00
b. Without period 3.60 3.60
O23 " 10c orange 70 70
a. "OFICAL" 3.75 3.75
b. Without period 1.25
c. Double overprint 12.50
O24 A6 40c blue 70 70
a. "OFICAL" 4.50 4.50
Nos. O18-O24 (6) 9.85 9.85

Issues of 1889–1901 Overprinted **OFICIAL**

1889 *Perf. 14, 15.*

O25 A10 1c brown 30 30
O26 A11 2c dark green 30 30
O27 A12 5c orange 30 30
O28 A13 10c red brown 30 30
O29 A14 20c yellow green 30 30
O30 A15 50c rose red 1.50 1.50
Nos. O25–O30 (6) 3.00 3.00

1892

O31 A20 1c greenish blue 35 35
O32 A21 2c yellow 35 35
O33 A22 5c violet 35 35
O34 A23 10c light green 1.50 1.50
O35 A24 20c scarlet 25 22
O36 A25 50c gray blue 70 70
Nos. O31–O36 (6) 3.50 3.47

1901–02

O37 A30 1c green & black 55 55
O38 A31 2c vermilion & black 55 55
O39 A32 5c gray blue & black 55 55
O40 A33 10c ochre & black 90 90
O41 A34 20c lake & black 1.20 1.20
O42 A35 50c lilac & dark blue 4.25 4.25
O43 A36 1col olive bistre & black 10.00 10.00
Nos. O37–O43 (7) 18.00 18.00

No. 46 Overprinted in Green **PROVISORIO OFICIAL**

1903

O44 A31 2c vermilion & black 3.50 3.50
b. "PROVISIORO" 6.00 6.00
d. Inverted overprint 6.00 6.00
f. Same as "b" inverted 12.00 12.00

Regular Issue of 1903 Overprinted **OFICIAL**

1903 *Perf. 14, 12½x14.*

O45 A40 4c red vio. & black 1.75 1.75
O46 A41 6c olive grn. & blk. 2.00 2.00
O47 A42 25c gray lilac & brown 9.00 5.00

Regular Issue of 1907 Overprinted **OFICIAL**

1908 *Perf. 14, 11x14.*

O48 A43 1c red brown & indigo 12 12
O49 A44 2c yel. grn. & black 12 12
O50 A45 4c carmine & indigo 15 15
O51 A46 5c yellow & dull blue 20 20
O52 A47 10c blue & black 1.25 1.25
O53 A49 25c gray lilac & black 25 25
O54 A50 50c red lilac & blue 40 40
O55 A51 1 col brown & black 1.00 1.00
Nos. O48–O55 (8) 3.49 3.49

The 5c, 10c and 25c exist with inverted overprint, the 4c with double impression of head.

Imperf. examples of Nos. O49 and O53 were found in 1970.

Regular Issue of 1910 Overprinted in Black **OFICIAL 15 VI·1917**

1917

O56 A56 5c orange 30 30
a. Inverted overprint 3.50 3.50
O57 A57 10c deep blue 25 25
a. Inverted overprint

O2

1920 Red Surcharge. *Perf. 12.*

O58 O2 15c on 20c olive green 50 50

O3 O4

O5 O6

1921 Black Surcharge. *Perf. 12, 14.*

O59 O3 10c on 5c orange 50 40
a. "10 CTS." invert. 22.50
O60 O4 4c carmine & indigo 45 45
a. "1291" for "1921" 15.00
O61 O5 6c on 1c red brown & indigo 50 50
O62 O6 20c on 25c gray lilac & black 50 50

Overprinted like No. O60.

O63 A50 50c red lilac & blue 2.50 2.50
O64 A51 1col brown & black 4.50 4.50
Nos. O59–O64 (6) 8.95 8.85

Nos. O60 to O64 exist with date and new values inverted, often in pairs with the normal varieties. These may be printer's waste but probably were deliberately made.

Regular Issue of 1923 Overprinted **OFICIAL**

1923 *Perf. 11½.*

O65 A68 2c brown 30 30
O66 " 4c green 15 15
O67 " 5c blue 30 30
O68 " 20c carmine 20 20
O69 " 1col violet 40 40
Nos. O65–O69 (5) 1.35 1.35

Nos. O65 to O69 exist imperforate but were not regularly issued in that condition.

O7

Engraved

1926 *Perf. 12½* **Unwmkd.**

O70 O7 2c ultramarine & black 6 6
O71 " 3c magenta & black 6 6
O72 " 4c light blue & black 8 8
O73 " 5c green & black 8 8
O74 " 6c ochre & black 8 8
O75 " 10c rose red & black 8 8
O76 " 20c olive green & black 8 8
O77 " 30c red orange & black 15 15
O78 " 45c brown & black 20 20
O79 " 1col lilac & black 30 30
Nos. O70–O79 (10) 1.17 1.17

Regular Issue of 1936 Overprinted in Black **OFICIAL**

1936 *Perf. 12.* **Unwmkd.**

O80 A96 5c green 8 8
O81 " 10c carmine rose 8 8

Type of 1926.

1937 *Perf. 12½.*

O82 O7 2c violet & black 8 8
O83 " 3c bis. brown & black 8 8
O84 " 4c rose car. & black 8 8
O85 " 5c olive green & black 8
O86 " 8c blk. brown & blk. 10
O87 " 10c rose lake & black 10
O88 " 20c indigo & black 12 12
O89 " 40c red org. & black 25 25
O90 " 55c dk. violet & black 35
O91 O7 1col brn. vio. & black 30 30
O92 " 2col gray blue & black 60 60
O93 " 5col dull yel. & blk. 3.00 3.00
O94 " 10col blue & black 15.00 15.00
Nos. O82–O94 (13) 20.14

Nine stamps of this series exist with perforated star (2c, 3c, 4c, 20c, 40c, 1col, 2col, 5col, 10col). These were issued to officials for postal purposes. Unpunched copies were sold to collectors but had no franking power. Prices for unused are for unpunched.

POSTAL TAX STAMPS

Most postal tax issues were to benefit the Children's Village and were obligatory on all mail during December.

No. C198 Surcharged in Red: "Sello de Navidad Pro-Ciudad de Los Niños 5 5"

Engraved; Center Photogravure.

1958 *Perf. 12½* **Unwmkd.**

RA1 AP51 5c on 2c bright blue & black 15 6

Similar Surcharge in Green on Type of 1954.

Design: Like No. C228, pottery.

Perf. 12

RA2 AP53 5c on 10c dark blue & black 40 8
a. Inverted surch.

Father Edward J. Flanagan PT1

Father Peralta PT2

Paintings: No. RA4, Boy by El Greco. No. RA5, Boy by Jose Ribera. No. RA6, Girl by Amadeo Modigliani.

Photogravure.

1959, Nov. 25 *Perf. 13½* **Unwmkd.**

RA3 PT1 5c green 30 8
RA4 " 5c dull gray violet 30 8
RA5 " 5c olive 30 8
RA6 " 5c lilac rose 30 8
Exist imperf.

1960 Lithographed *Perf. 14*

Designs: No. RA8, Girl by Renoir. No. RA9, Boys with cups by Velazquez. No. RA10, Singing children, sculpture by F. Zuñiga.

RA7 PT2 5c chocolate 60 8
RA8 " 5c deep orange 60 8
RA9 " 5c plum 60 8
RA10 " 5c grayish blue 60 8
Exist imperf.

No. C229 Surcharged "Sello de Navidad Pro-Ciudad de los Niños 5 5"

Engraved; Center Photogravure

1961 *Perf. 13x12½*

RA11 AP53 5c on 15c green & black 25 8

Nicolas, Son of Rubens PT3

Boys in Workshop PT4

Designs: No. RA13, Madonna by Bellini. RA14, Angel playing stringed instrument by Melozzo. RA15, Msgr. Rubén Odio H.

1962 Photogravure *Perf. 13½*

RA12 PT3 5c dark carmine 60 8
RA13 " 5c sepia 60 8
RA14 " 5c dull green 60 8
RA15 " 5c blue 60 8

Type of 1962, Inscribed "1963" Designs as before

Designs: No. RA16, Rubens' son Nicolas. No. RA17, Madonna, Bellini. No. RA18, Angel, Melozzo. No. RA19, Msgr. Rubén Odio H.

1963 Photogravure *Perf. 13½*

RA16 PT3 5c sepia 35 8
RA17 " 5c ultramarine 35 8
RA18 " 5c dark carmine 35 8
RA19 " 5c black 35 8

1964 Lithographed *Perf. 12½*

Designs: No. RA21, Two playing boys. No. RA22, Teacher and children. No. RA23, Priest with boys.

RA20 PT4 5c bright green 30 8
RA21 " 5c rose lilac 30 8
RA22 " 5c blue 30 8
RA23 " 5c brown 30 8

Brother Casiano de Madrid PT5

Christmas Ornaments PT6

Designs: No. RA25, National Children's Hospital. No. RA26, Poinsettia. No. RA27, Santa Claus with children (diamond).

1965, Dec. 10 Litho. *Perf. 10*

RA24 PT5 5c red brown 20 8
RA25 " 5c green 20 8
RA26 " 5c red 20 8
RA27 " 5c ultramarine 20 8

1966 Lithographed *Perf. 11*

Designs: No. RA29, Angel. No. RA30, Church. No. RA31, Reindeer.

RA28 PT6 5c red 20 8
RA29 " 5c lt. ultramarine 20 8
RA30 " 5c bright green 20 8
RA31 " 5c brown 20 8

General Post Office, San José PT7

1967, March Litho. *Perf. 11*

RA32 PT7 10c blue 10 6

No. RA32 was issued as a postal tax stamp to be used by organizations normally allowed free postage. On Dec. 15, 1972, it was authorized for use as an ordinary postage stamp.

Madonna and Child PT8

Star of Bethlehem, Mother and Child PT9

1967 Lithographed *Perf. 11*

RA33 PT8 5c olive green 15 5
RA34 " 5c deep lilac rose 15 5
RA35 " 5c bright blue 15 5
RA36 " 5c greenish blue 15 5

1968, Dec. Litho. *Perf. 12½*

RA37 PT9 5c gray 15 5
RA38 " 5c rose red 15 5
RA39 " 5c dark rose brown 15 5
RA40 " 5c bister brown 15 5

Madonna and Child
PT10

1969, Dec. Lithographed *Perf. 12½*

RA41	PT10	5c dark blue	3	3
RA42	"	5c orange	3	3
RA43	"	5c brown red	3	3
RA44	"	5c blue green	3	3

Christ Child and Star
PT11

1970, Dec. Litho. *Perf. 12½*

RA45	PT11	5c bright purple	3	3
RA46	"	5c lilac rose	3	3
RA47	"	5c olive	3	3
RA48	"	5c ocher	3	3

Christ Child and "PAX"
PT12

Madonna and Child
PT13

1971, Nov. 29

RA49	PT12	10c dark blue	7	3
RA50	"	10c orange	7	3
RA51	"	10c brown	7	3
RA52	"	10c green	7	3

1972, Nov. 30 *Perf. 11x11½*

RA53	PT13	10c dark blue	7	3
RA54	"	10c bright red	7	3
RA55	"	10c lilac	7	3
RA56	"	10c green	7	3

Madonna and Child
PT14

Boys Eating Cake, by Murillo
PT15

1973, Nov. 30 Litho. *Perf. 12½*

RA57	PT14	10c purple	7	3
RA58	"	10c carmine rose	7	3
RA59	"	10c gray	7	3
RA60	"	10c orange brown	7	3

1974, Nov. 25 *Perf. 13*

Paintings: No. RA62, Virgin and Child, with St. John, by Raphael. No. RA63, Maternity, by Juan R. Bonilla. No. RA64, Praying Child, by Reynolds.

RA61	PT15	10c bright pink	6	3
RA62	"	10c rose lilac	6	3
RA63	"	10c dark gray	6	3
RA64	"	10c violet blue	6	3

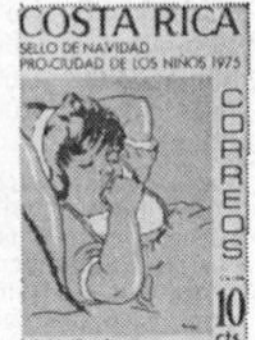

"Happy, Dreams, by Sonia Romero
PT16

Virgin and Child, by Hans Memling
PT17

Paintings: No. RA66, Virgin with Carnation, by Leonardo da Vinci. No. RA67, Children with Tortoise, by Francisco Amighetti. No. RA68, Boy with Pigeon, by Picasso.

1975, Nov. 25 Litho. *Perf. 10½*

RA65	PT16	10c gray	5	3
RA66	"	10c red lilac	5	3
RA67	"	10c orange brown	5	3
RA68	"	10c bright blue	5	3

Obligatory on all mail during December.

1976, Nov. 24 Litho. *Perf. 10½*

Paintings: No. RA70, Boy with Sombrero, by Auguste Renoir. No. RA71, Meditation (Boy), by Floria Pinto de Herrero. No. RA72, Gaston de Mezerville (boy), by Lolita Zeller de Peralta.

RA69	PT17	10c rose lilac	3	3
RA70	"	10c rose carmine	3	3
RA71	"	10c gray	3	3
RA72	"	10c violet blue	3	3

Obligatory on all mail during December.

Boy's Head, by Amparo Cruz
PT18

Boy with Kite
PT19

Paintings: No. RA74, Girl's head, by Rubens. No. RA75, Girl and infant, by Cristina Fournier. No. RA76, Mariano Goya, by Goya.

1977, Nov. Litho. *Perf. 10½*

RA73	PT18	10c gray olive	3	3
RA74	"	10c rose red	3	3
RA75	"	10c brt. ultra.	3	3
RA76	"	10c brt. rose lilac	3	3

Obligatory on all mail during December.

1978, Nov. 20 Litho. *Perf. 12½*

Designs: No. RA77, like No. RA76. Nos. RA78–RA79, Girl flying kite.

RA77	PT19	10c magenta	3	3
RA78	"	10c slate	3	3
RA79	"	10c lilac	3	3
RA80	"	10c violet blue	3	3

Obligatory on all mail during December.

Guanacaste

(gwä'nä·käs'tä)

(A province of Costa Rica)

LOCATION—On northwestern coast of Central America.

AREA—4,000 sq. mi. (approx.).

POP.—69,531 (estimated).

CAPITAL—Liberia.

Residents of Guanacaste were allowed to buy Costa Rican stamps, overprinted "Guanacaste," at a discount from face value because of the province's isolation and climate, which makes it difficult to keep mint stamps. Use was restricted to the province.

Counterfeits of most Guanacaste overprints are plentiful.

On Issue of 1883.

Overprinted Horizontally in Black **Guanacaste** 16mm.

1885 *Perf. 12* **Unwmkd.**

1	A6	1c green	3.00	3.00
		a. "Gnanacaste"	40.00	
2	"	2c carmine	2.50	2.50
		a. "Gnanacaste"	35.00	
3	"	10c orange	10.00	10.00
		a. "Gnanacaste"	50.00	

Same Overprint in Red.

4	A6	1c green	2.25	2.25
		a. "Gnanacaste"	30.00	
		b. Overprinted in black & red	75.00	
5	"	5c blue violet	12.50	2.75
		a. "Gnanacaste"	50.00	
6	"	40c blue	20.00	20.00
		a. "Gnanacaste"		

Overprinted Horizontally in Black **Guanacaste** 17½mm. *b*

7	A6	1c green	6.00	5.50
8	"	2c carmine	6.00	5.50
9	"	5c blue violet	15.00	2.75
10	"	10c orange	13.50	8.50
11	"	40c blue	32.50	27.50

Same Overprint in Red.

12	A6	5c blue violet	32.50	10.00
13	"	40c blue	*800.00*	

Overprinted Horizontally in Black **Guanacaste** 18½mm. *c*

14	A6	2c carmine	7.00	5.50
15	"	10c orange	32.50	25.00

Same Overprint in Red.

16	A6	1c green	5.50	5.50
		a. Double overprint, one in black	125.00	
17	"	5c blue violet	27.50	5.00
18	"	40c blue	37.50	37.50

Same Overprint, Vertically in Black.

19	A6	1c green	*800.00*	*800.00*
20	"	2c carmine	*500.00*	*500.00*
21	"	5c blue violet	140.00	70.00
22	"	10c orange	35.00	40.00

Guanacaste GUANACASTE GUANACASTE GUANACASTE GUANACASTE
e *f* *g* *h* *i*

Overprinted Type e, Vertically.

23	A6	1c green	80.00	80.00
24	"	2c carmine	90.00	90.00
25	"	5c blue violet	110.00	55.00
26	"	10c orange	52.50	52.50

Overprinted Type f, Vertically.

27	A6	1c green	110.00	110.00
28	"	2c carmine	110.00	110.00
29	"	5c blue violet	140.00	70.00
30	"	10c orange	52.50	52.50

Overprinted Type g, Vertically.

31	A6	1c green	*275.00*	*275.00*
32	"	2c carmine	*275.00*	*275.00*
33	"	5c blue violet	*275.00*	135.00
34	"	10c orange	120.00	120.00

Overprinted Type h, Vertically.

35	A6	1c green	120.00	120.00
36	"	2c carmine	72.50	72.50
37	"	5c blue violet	140.00	70.00
38	"	10c orange	32.50	32.50

Overprinted Type i, Vertically.

39	A6	2c carmine		
40	"	5c blue violet		
41	"	10c orange		

The authenticity of Nos. 39–41 is questioned. The 1c green also exists with overprint "1".

On Issues of 1883–87

1888–89

Overprinted Horizontally in Black **Guanacaste**

42	A7	5c blue violet	17.50	2.75
		a. "Gnanacaste"		

Overprinted Horizontally in Black **Guanacaste**

43	A7	5c blue violet	15.00	2.75

Overprinted Horizontally in Black **Guanacaste**

44	A6	2c carmine	1.75	1.75
45	A7	10c orange	1.75	1.75
		a. Invtd. ovpt.		

On Issue of 1889.

Overprinted Type b, Horizontally.

1889

47	A8	2c blue	27.50	27.50

Overprinted Type c, Vertically.

48	A8	2c blue	120.00	120.00

Overprinted Type e, Vertically.

49	A8	2c blue	55.00	55.00

Overprinted Type f, Vertically.

51	A8	2c blue	65.00	65.00

Overprinted Type g, Vertically.

52	A8	2c blue	*200.00*	*200.00*

Overprinted Type h, Vertically.

54	A8	2c blue	90.00	90.00

Dangerous counterfeits exist of Nos. 1–54.

On Nos. 25–33

Overprinted Horizontally in Black **GUANACASTE**

1890 *Perf. 14 and 15*

55	A10	1c brown	8.50	3.50
56	A11	2c dark green	3.75	2.00
57	A12	5c orange	5.50	2.00
58	A13	10c red brown	5.50	2.50
59	A14	20c yellow green	1.25	1.25
60	A15	50c rose red	2.25	2.25
		a. "GUAGACASTE"	50.00	
61	A16	1p blue	3.00	3.00
		a. "GUAGACASTE"	50.00	50.00
62	A17	2p violet	5.00	5.00
		a. "GUAGACASTE"	50.00	50.00
63	A18	5p olive green	27.50	27.50
		a. "GUAGACASTE"	60.00	60.00
		Nos. 55–63 (9)	62.25	49.00

Overprinted Horizontally in Black **GUANACASTE**

64	A10	1c brown	1.00	1.00
		a. Vert. pair, imperf. btwn.		
65	A11	2c dark green	1.00	1.00
66	A12	5c orange	1.00	1.00
67	A13	10c red brown	1.00	1.00

CRETE

(krēt)

LOCATION — An island in the Mediterranean Sea south of Greece.

GOVT.—A department of Greece.

AREA—3,235 sq. mi.

POP.—336,150 (1913).

CAPITAL—Canea.

Formerly Crete was a province of Turkey. After an extended period of civil wars, France, Great Britain, Italy and Russia intervened and declaring Crete an autonomy, placed it under the administration of Prince George of Greece as High Commissioner. In October, 1908, the Cretan Assembly voted for union with Greece and in 1913 the union was formally effected.

40 Paras = 1 Piaster
4 Metallik = 1 Grosion (1899)
100 Lepta = 1 Drachma (1900)

Issued Under Joint Administration of France, Great Britain, Italy and Russia

British Sphere of Administration. District of Heraklion (Candia).

A1

A2

Handstamped

1898 *Imperf.* **Unwmkd.**

1	A1	20pa violet	400.00	250.00

1898 Lithographed *Perf. 11½*

2	A2	10pa blue	7.50	9.00
		a. Horizontal pair, imperf. between		
		b. Imperf., pair	125.00	
3	"	20pa green	7.50	9.00
		a. Imperf., pair	125.00	

1899

4	A2	10pa brown	7.50	9.00
		a. Horizontal pair, imperf. between		
		b. Imperf., pair	125.00	
5	"	20pa rose	7.50	9.00
		a. Imperf., pair	125.00	

Counterfeits exist of Nos. 1–5.

Reprints exist of Nos. 2–5.

Russian Sphere of Administration. District of Rethymnon.

Coat of Arms

A3 A4

1899 Handstamped *Imperf.*

10	A3	1m green	9.00	6.00
11	"	2m black	9.00	6.00
12	"	2m rose	60.00	50.00
13	A4	1m blue	25.00	17.50

Nos. 10–13 exist on both wove and laid papers. Counterfeits exist.

Poseidon's Trident

A5 A5a

1899 Lithographed *Perf. 11½*

With Control Mark Overprinted in Violet.

Without Stars at Sides.

14	A5	1m orange	25.00	22.50
15	"	2m "	25.00	22.50
16	"	1gr "	25.00	22.50
17	"	1m green	25.00	22.50
18	"	2m "	25.00	22.50
19	"	1gr "	25.00	22.50
20	"	1m yellow	25.00	22.50
21	"	2m "	25.00	22.50
22	"	1gr "	25.00	22.50
23	"	1m rose	25.00	22.50
24	"	2m "	25.00	22.50
25	"	1gr "	25.00	22.50
26	"	1m violet	25.00	22.50
27	"	2m "	25.00	22.50
28	"	1gr "	25.00	22.50
29	"	1m blue	25.00	22.50
30	"	2m "	25.00	22.50
31	"	1gr "	25.00	22.50
32	"	1m black	550.00	450.00
33	"	2m "	550.00	450.00
34	"	1gr "	550.00	450.00

With Stars at Sides.

35	A5a	1m blue	9.50	8.50
36	"	2m "	9.50	8.50
37	"	1gr "	9.50	8.50
38	"	1m rose	9.50	8.50
39	"	2m "	9.50	8.50
40	"	1gr "	9.50	8.50
41	"	1m green	9.50	8.50
42	"	2m "	9.50	8.50
43	"	1gr "	9.50	8.50
44	"	1m violet	9.50	8.50
45	"	2m "	9.50	8.50
46	"	1gr "	9.50	8.50
		Nos. 35–46 (12)	114.00	102.00

Nearly all of Nos. 14 to 46 may be found without control mark, with double control marks and in various colors.

Counterfeits exist of Nos. 14–46.

Issued by the Cretan Government.

Hermes

A6

Hera

A7

Prince George of Greece

A8

Talos

A9

Minos

A10

St. George and the Dragon

A11

1900, Mar. 1 Engraved *Perf. 14*

50	A6	1l violet brown	30	15
51	A7	5l green	1.00	20
52	A8	10l red	1.10	15
53	A7	20l carmine rose	6.00	2.00

Overprinted **ΠΡΟΣΩΡΙΝΟΝ**

Red Overprint.

54	A8	25l blue	3.50	70
55	A6	50l lilac	3.75	2.75
56	A9	1d gray violet	6.50	4.50
57	A10	2d brown	15.00	12.00
58	A11	5d green & black	52.50	45.00
		Nos. 54–58 (5)	81.25	64.95

Black Overprint.

59	A8	25l blue	5.00	65
60	A6	50l lilac	3.50	2.75
61	A9	1d gray violet	6.00	4.50
		a. Inverted overprint	150.00	150.00
62	A10	2d brown	12.50	7.00
63	A11	5d green & black	47.50	40.00
		Nos. 59–63 (5)	74.50	54.90

1901 Without Overprint.

64	A6	1l bistre	*50*	50
65	A7	20l orange	2.00	50
66	A8	25l blue	9.00	1.25
67	A6	50l lilac	12.00	4.50
68	"	50l ultramarine	5.00	5.00
69	A9	1d gray violet	22.50	9.00
70	A10	2d brown	13.50	8.50
71	A11	5d green & black	25.00	22.50
		Nos. 64–71 (8)	89.50	51.75

No. 64 is a revenue stamp that was used for postage for a short time. Unused, it can only be considered as a revenue.

Types A6 to A8 in olive yellow, and types A9 to A11 in olive yellow and black are revenue stamps.

No. 66 Overprinted in Black **ΠΡΟΣΩΡΙΝΟΝ**

1901

72	A8	25l blue	10.00	75
		a. First letter of overprint inverted	35.00	35.00

No. 65 Surcharged in Black **5 5**

1904, Dec.

73	A7	5l on 20l orange	2.00	1.00
		a. Without "5" at right	5.00	5.00

Mycenaean Seal

A12

Britomartis (Cortyna Coin)

A13

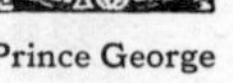

Prince George

A14

Kydon and Dog (Cydonia Coin)

A15

Triton (Itanos Coin)

A16

Ariadne (Knossos Coin)

A17

Zeus as Bull Abducting Europa (Cortyna Coin)

A18

Palace of Minos Ruins, Knossos

A19

Arkadi Monastery and Mt. Ida

A20

1905, Feb. 15

74	A12	2l dull violet	1.00	30
75	A13	5l yellow green	2.00	20
76	A14	10l red	3.50	30
77	A15	20l blue green	8.00	1.50
78	A16	25l ultramarine	6.00	75
79	A17	50l yellow brown	6.00	4.75
80	A18	1d rose carmine & deep brown	67.50	47.50
81	A19	3d orange & black	27.50	25.00
82	A20	5d olive green & black	25.00	22.50
		Nos. 74–82 (9)	146.50	102.80

The so-called revolutionary stamps of 1905 were issued for sale to collectors and, so far as can be ascertained, were of no postal value whatever.

A. T. A. Zaimis

A21

Prince George Landing at Suda

A22

1907, Aug. 28

83	A21	25l blue & black	12.00	2.25
84	A22	1d green & black	12.00	8.00

Commemorative of the administration under a High Commissioner.

Stamps of 1900-1907 Overprinted in Black **ΕΛΛΑΣ**

1908, Sept. 21

85 A6 1 l violet brown 20 20
86 A12 2 l dull violet 45 30
87 A13 5 l yellow green 90 20
88 A8 10 l red 1.35 40
89 A15 20 l blue green 2.50 1.00
90 A21 25 l blue & black 7.00 1.75
91 A17 50 l yellow brown 5.50 5.00
92 A18 1d rose carmine & deep brown 72.50 57.50
93 A10 2d brown 8.00 6.00
94 A19 3d orange & black 30.00 22.50
95 A20 5d olive grn. & blk. 22.50 21.00
Nos. 85-95 (11) 150.90 115.85

This overprint exists inverted and double, as well as with incorrect, reversed, misplaced and omitted letters. Similar errors are found on the Postage Due and Official stamps with this overprint.

Hermes by Praxiteles
A23

1908

96 A23 10 l brown red 2.50 65
a. Pair, one without overprint 8.00
b. Inverted overprint 5.00
c. Double overprint 5.00

Nos. 96 and 114 were not regularly issued without overprint.

No. 53 Surcharged ΕΛΛΑΣ ΠΡΟΣΟΡΙΝΟΝ 5 5

1909

97 A7 5 l on 20 l carmine rose 90.00 90.00

Forgeries exist of No. 97.

On No. 65

98 A7 5 l on 20 l orange 45 45
a. Inverted surcharge

Overprinted on Nos. 64, J1 ΕΛΛΑΣ ΠΡΟΣΟΡΙΝΟΝ

99 A6 1 l bistre 45 35
100 D1 1 l red 45 35

No. J4 Surcharged ΕΛΛΑΣ 2 ΠΡΟΣΩΡΙΝΟΝ

101 D1 2 l on 20 l red 75 50
a. Double surcharge 5.00
b. Inverted surcharge 5.00
c. Second letter of surch. "D" instead of "P" 18.50 18.50

No. J4 Surcharged ΕΛΛΑΣ 2 ΠΡΟΣΩΡΙΝΟΝ

102 D1 2 l on 20 l red 45 40

Overprinted in Black:
ΕΛΛΑΣ *a*
ΕΛΛΑΣ *b*
ΕΛΛΑΣ *c*

103 A23 (*a*) 10 l brown red 4.50 30
a. Inverted overprint 25.00
104 A15 (") 20 l blue green 4.50 1.00
105 A21 (*c*) 25 l blue & black 8.00 3.00
106 A17 (*a*) 50 l yellow brown 6.00 5.00
107 A22 (*b*) 1d grn. & black 15.00 9.00
108 A10 (*a*) 2d brown 11.00 10.00
109 A19 (*b*) 3d org. & black 85.00 55.00
110 A20 (") 5d olive green & black 25.00 22.50
Nos. 103-110 (8) 159.00 105.80

Stamps of 1900-08 Overprinted in Red or Black **ΕΛΛΑΣ** *d*

1909-10

111 A6 1 l violet brown 20 20
112 A12 2 l dull violet 50 25
113 A13 5 l yellow green 35 20
114 A23 10 l brown red (Bk) 70 20
115 A15 20 l blue green 5.00 50
116 A16 25 l ultramarine 5.00 60
117 A17 50 l yellow brown 7.50 5.00
118 A18 1d rose carmine & dp.brn. (Bk) 100.00 65.00
119 A19 3d orange & black 47.50 42.50
120 A20 5d olive green & black 62.50 57.50
Nos. 111-120 (10) 229.25 171.95

POSTAGE DUE STAMPS.

D1

Lithographed.

1901 *Perf. 14* **Unwmkd.**

J1 D1 1 l red 1.10 85
J2 " 5 l " 2.25 1.65
J3 " 10 l " 3.25 2.50
J4 " 20 l " 4.50 2.25
J5 " 40 l " 6.75 6.75
J6 " 50 l " 5.50 5.00
J7 " 1d " 32.50 25.00
J8 " 2d " 8.50 8.00
Nos. J1-J8 (8) 64.35 52.00

Surcharged in Black **1 ΔΡΑΧΜΗ**

1901

J9 D1 1d on 1d red 10.00 9.00

Overprinted **ΕΛΛΑΣ**

1908

J10 D1 1 l red 1.00 1.10
a. Inverted overprint 4.00 4.00
J11 " 5 l red 3.00 2.25
J12 " 10 l red 4.00 2.25
J13 " 20 l red 5.50 5.50
J14 " 40 l red 7.50 5.50
J15 " 50 l red 6.50 5.00
J16 " 1d red 125.00 125.00
J17 " 1d on 1d red 6.50 6.25
J18 " 2d red 20.00 11.00
Nos. J10-J18 (9) 179.10 163.85

Counterfeits of No. J16 exist.

Overprinted **ΕΛΛΑΣ**

1910

J19 D1 1 l red 55 55
J20 " 5 l " 2.25 2.25
J21 " 10 l " 1.65 1.65
J22 " 20 l " 7.00 5.00
J23 " 40 l " 5.00 5.00
J24 D1 50 l red 6.00 5.00
J25 " 1d " 35.00 25.00
J26 " 2d " 22.50 12.00
Nos. J19-J26 (8) 79.95 56.45

OFFICIAL STAMPS.

O1

O2

Perf. 14

1908, Jan. 14 Litho. **Unwmkd.**

O1 O1 10 l dull claret 22.50 3.50
O2 O2 30 l blue 25.00 3.75

Nos. O1-O2 exist imperf.

Overprinted **ΕΛΛΑΣ**

O3 O1 10 l dull claret 16.00 3.50
a. Inverted overprint 25.00
O4 O2 30 l blue 18.50 3.50
a. Inverted overprint 25.00

1910

Overprinted **ΕΛΛΑΣ**

O5 O1 10 l dull claret 1.35 40
O6 O2 30 l blue 1.35 40

CROATIA

(krō-ā'shĭă; shə)

LOCATION—Southeastern Europe.
GOVT.—Independent state.
AREA—44,453 sq. mi.
POP.—7,000,000 (approx.).
CAPITAL—Zagreb.

The Independent Croatian State of 1941-45 became part of the Jugoslav Federation in 1945.

100 Paras = 1 Dinar
100 Banica = 1 Kuna

Jugoslavia Nos. 143 to 148B Overprinted in Black **NEZAVISNA DRŽAVA HRVATSKA** IIIIII

Typographed.

1941, Apr. 12 *Perf. 12½* **Unwmkd.**

1 A16 50p orange 55 55
2 " 1d yellow green 55 55
3 " 1.50d red 55 55
4 " 2d deep magenta 55 55
5 " 3d dull red brown 2.25 2.25
6 " 4d ultramarine 2.25 2.25
7 " 5d dark blue 2.25 2.25
8 " 5.50d dk. vio. brn. 2.25 2.25
Nos. 1-8 (8) 11.20 11.20

The overprint exists inverted on Nos. 1-6; double on Nos. 2, 3 and 5.

Jugoslavia Nos. 142 to 154 Overprinted in Black

1941, Apr. 21

9 A16 25p black 8 8
10 " 50p orange 8 8
11 " 1d yellow green 8 8
12 " 1.50d red 8 8
13 " 2d deep magenta 10 10
14 " 3d dull red brown 10 10
15 A16 4d ultramarine 10 10
16 " 5d dark blue 20 20
17 " 5.50d dk. vio. brn. 35 35
18 " 6d slate blue 35 35
19 " 8d sepia 35 35
20 " 12d bright violet 35 35
21 " 16d dull violet 70 70
22 " 20d blue 1.00 1.00
23 " 30d bright pink 1.50 1.50
Nos. 9-23 (15) 5.42 5.42

The overprint exists inverted on Nos. 9-11, 17 and 20; double on Nos. 9, 12 and 17.

Jugoslavia Nos. 147, 148 Surcharged in Black

1941, May 16

24 A16 1d on 3d dull red brown 10 10
25 " 2d on 4d ultramarine 10 10

The overprint exists inverted and double on Nos. 24-25.

Postage Due Stamps of Jugoslavia, Nos. J28, J30 to J32, Overprinted in Black **NEZAVISNA DRŽAVA HRVATSKA FRANCO**

1941, May 17

26 D4 50p violet 10 8
27 " 2d deep blue 12 10
28 " 5d orange 18 15
29 " 10d chocolate 25 20

Counterfeit overprints on Nos. 1-29 are plentiful.

Imperforates

Nearly all Croatian stamps, from No. 30 through 80, B3 through B76, J6 through J25, O1 through O24 and RA1 through RA7 exist imperforate.

Ozalj Castle
A1

Designs: 50b, City of Jajce. 75b, Old Warasdin. 1k, Velebit Mountains. 1.50k, Zelenjak. 2k, Zagreb Cathedral. 3k, Osjek Cathedral. 4k, Drina River. No. 38, Konjica. No. 39, Zemun. 6k, Dubrovnik. 7k, Save River. 8k, Sarajevo. 10k, Plitvice. 12k, Klis Fortress, Split. 20k, Hvar. 30k, Syrmia. 50k, Senj. 100k, Banjaluka (without "F.I.").

Photogravure.

1941-43 *Perf. 11.* **Unwmkd.**

Ordinary Paper.

30 A1 25b henna 3 3
a. Tête bêche pair 10 10
31 " 50b slate blue 3 3
a. Tête bêche pair 10 10
32 " 75b dark olive green 3 3
33 " 1k Prussian green 3 3
a. Tête bêche pair 20 20
34 " 1.50k deep green 3 3
a. Tête bêche pair 20 20
35 " 2k carmine lake 3 3
a. Tête bêche pair 15 15
36 " 3k brown red 3 3
37 " 4k deep ultramarine 3 3
a. Tête bêche pair 15 15
38 " 5k black 50 3
a. Tête bêche pair 1.50 1.50
39 " 5k blue 3 3
40 " 6k light olive brown 3 3
a. Tête bêche pair 18 18
41 " 7k orange red 3 3
a. Tête bêche pair 35 35

42 A1 8k chestnut 5 3
a. Tête bêche pair 60 40
43 " 10k dark plum 15 5
a. Tête bêche pair 40 40
44 " 12k olive brown 20 10
45 " 20k golden brown 10 5
a. Tête bêche pair 50 50
46 " 30k black brown 20 10
a. Tête bêche pair 85 85
47 " 50k dark slate green 45 25
a. Tête bêche pair 3.50 3.50
48 " 100k violet 70 60
Nos. 30-48 (19) 2.68 1.54

Nos. 31, 35 and 43 exist on thin to pelure paper. Shades of all values exist.

Types of 1941 Overprinted in Brown or Green — 1941-1942 10-IV

1942, Apr. 9

49 A1 2k dark brown 10 6
50 " 5k dark carmine 15 10
51 " 10k dk. bl. green (G) 25 15

First anniversary of Croatian independence.

Banjaluka
("F.I." at upper right)
A20

1942, June 13

52 A20 100k violet 70 80

Banjaluka Philatelic Exhibition.

No. 35 Surcharged in Red Brown with New Value and Bar.

1942, June 23

53 A1 25b on 2k carmine lake 10 10
a. Tête bêche pair 35 35

Trakoscan Castle
A21

Catherine Zrinski
A23

Design: 12.50k, Citadel of Veliki Tabor.

1943

Pelure Paper

54 A21 3.50k brown carmine 20 12
55 " 12.50k violet black 30 25

No. 54 exists on ordinary paper.

1943, June 7 Engr. ***Perf. 12½***

Designs: 2k, Fran Krsto Frankopan. 3.50k, Peter Zrinski.

Various Frames.

56 A23 1k dark blue 8 8
57 " 2k dark olive green 8 8
58 " 3.50k dark red 10 10

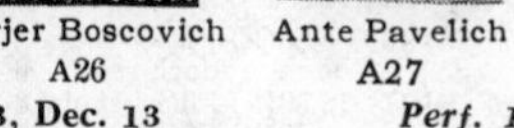

Rugjer Boscovich
A26

Ante Pavelich
A27

1943, Dec. 13 ***Perf. 11***

59 A26 3.50k copper red 15 15
60 A26 12.50k dark violet brown 20 20

Issued to honor Rugjer Boscovich (1711-1787), Serbo-Croat mathematician and physicist.

1943-44 Litho. ***Perf. 12½, 14***

61 A27 25b orange vermilion 3 3
62 " 50b Prussian blue 3 3
63 " 75b olive green 4 3
64 " 1k light green 4 3
65 " 1.50k dull gray violet 4 4
66 " 2k rose lake 4 4
67 " 3k rose brown 4 4
68 " 3.50k bright blue 4 4
a. 3.50k dk. blue, perf. 11½ 1.00 1.00
69 A27 4k bright red violet 4 4
70 " 5k ultramarine 4 4
71 " 8k org. brown 4 4
72 " 9k rose pink 4 4
73 " 10k violet brown 6 4
74 " 12k dark olive bister 6 4
75 " 12.50k gray black 6 3
76 " 18k dull brown 8 4
77 " 32k dark brown 8 4
78 " 50k greenish blue 14 10
79 " 70k orange 15 12
80 " 100k violet 25 20
Nos. 61-80 (20) 1.34 1.05

Nos. 61 and 63 measure 20½x26mm. Nos. 62 and 64-80 measure 22x27½mm.

Issue dates: 2k, 1943; No. 68a, June 13, 1943, Pavelich's birthday; others, 1944.

"Labor Day 1945"
A28

1945 Photogravure. ***Perf. 11½***

81 A28 3.50k red brown 20 30

SEMI-POSTAL STAMPS.

Types of Jugoslavia, 1941, Overprinted in Gold
"NEZAVISNA / DRZAVA / HRVATSKA"
Engraved.

1941, May 10 *Perf. 11½* Unwmkd.

B1 SP80 1.50d+1.50d bl. blk. 4.00 5.00
B2 SP81 4d+3d chocolate 4.00 5.00

Five thousand sets of Jugoslavia Nos. 142-154 were overprinted "NEZAVISNA DRZAVA HRVATSKA 10. IV. 1941" and small shield in red or blue, in 1941. Sold for double face value. Price, set, $175.

Costume of Sinj, Dalmatia
SP1

Soldiers with Arms of the Axis States
SP4

Designs (Costumes): 2k+2k, Travnik, Bosnia. 4k+4k, Turopolje, Croatia.

1941, Oct. 12 Photo. ***Perf. 10½x10***

B3 SP1 1.50k+1.50k Prussian blue & red 12 12
B4 " 2k+2k olive brown & red 20 20
B5 " 4k+4k brown lake & red 35 35

The surtax aided the Croatian Red Cross. Sheets of 20 stamps and 5 labels.

1941, Dec. 3 ***Perf. 11***

B6 SP4 4k+2k blue 1.00 1.00

The surtax was used for Croatian Volunteers in the East.

Model Plane
SP5

Model Plane
SP6

Designs: 3k+3k, Boy with model plane. 4k+4k, Model seaplane in flight.

1942, Mar. 25

B7 SP5 2k+2k sepia 15 15
B8 SP6 2.50k+2.50k dull green 25 25
B9 SP5 3k+3k brown car. 35 35
B10 SP6 4k+4k deep blue 45 45

The surtax aided the society of Croatian Wings (Hrvatska Krila).

Nos. B7-B10 were issued in sheets of 25 and in sheets of 24 plus label.

Souvenir Sheets.

SP9

Perf. 11.

B11 SP9 Sheet of two 4.50 4.50
a. 2k+8k brn. carmine 1.75 1.75
b. 3k+12k deep blue 1.75 1.75

Imperf.

B12 SP9 Sheet of two 4.50 4.50
a. 2k+8k deep blue 1.75 1.75
b. 3k+12k brn. carmine 1.75 1.75

The sheets measure 125x110mm.

To commemorate the Aviation Exposition of Zagreb. The surtax aided "Croatian Wings."

Nos. B11 and B12 exist with colors of stamps and inscriptions transposed.

Boy Trumpeters
SP10

Mother and Child
SP12

Triumphal Arch
SP11

1942, July 5 ***Perf. 11½***

B13 SP10 3k+1k lake 30 25
B14 SP11 4k+2k dark brown 30 25
B15 SP12 5k+5k deep blue green 35 35

The surtax was for national welfare. Sheets of 25.

Matthew Gubec
SP13

Ante Starcevich
SP14

SP15

1942, Nov. 22 ***Perf. 14½***

B16 SP13 3k+6k dark red 10 10
B17 SP14 4k+7k sepia 15 15

Souvenir Sheets

Perf. 12, Imperf.

B18 SP15 5k+20k dull blue 3.00 2.75

Issued to commemorate the heroes of Senj, May 9, 1937. Nos. B16-B17 were printed in sheets of 16 plus 9 labels, each bearing a hero's name. Size of No. B18: 80x95mm. The surtax aided the National Youth Society.

Sestine Peasant
SP16

Designs: 3k+1k, Slavonian peasant. 4k+2k, Bosnian peasant. 10k+5k, Dalmatian peasant. 13k+6k, Sestine peasant.

1942, Oct. 4 ***Perf. 11½***

B20 SP16 1.50k+50b orange brown & red 25 25
B21 " 3k+1k dull purple & red 25 25
B22 " 4k+2k deep blue & red 25 25
B23 " 10k+5k dark olive bistre & red 50 50
B24 " 13k+6k rose lake & red 1.20 1.20
Nos. B20-B24 (5) 2.45 2.45

The surtax aided the Croatian Red Cross. Issued in sheets of 24 stamps plus label.

Croatian Labor Corpsman
SP20

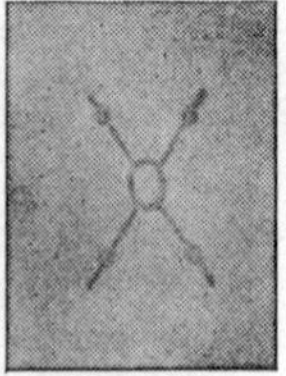

Wmk. 278

Designs: 3k+3k, Corpsman with wheelbarrow. 7k+4k, Corpsman plowing.

Wmkd.

Network Connecting Circles. (278)

1943, Jan. 17 ***Perf. 11***

B25 SP20 2(k)+1(k) olive gray & sepia 60 50

B26 SP20 3(k)+3(k) brown & sepia 60 50
B27 " 7(k)+4(k) gray blue & sepia 60 50

The surtax aided the State Labor Service (Drzavna Radna Sluzba). Issued in sheets of 9.

Arms of Zagreb and "Golden Bull"
SP23

1943, Mar. 23 **Unwmkd.**

B28 SP23 3.50k(+6.50k) brilliant ultramarine 60 60

700th anniversary of Zagreb's "Golden Bull," a Magna Carta of civic rights and privileges granted to the city in 1242 by King Bela because the Croats annihilated Tartar hordes at Grobnik.

Issued in sheets of 8 with marginal inscriptions.

Ante Pavelich
SP24

1943, Apr. 10 ***Perf. 14***

B29 SP24 5k+3k copper red 12 12
B30 " 7k+5k dark green 15 15

Surtax aided the National Youth Society.
Issued in sheets of 100, and in miniature sheets of 16 stamps and 9 labels.

Souvenir Sheets.

SP25

1943, May 17 ***Perf. 12, Imperf.***

B31 SP25 12k+8k dp. ultra. 3.00 2.75

The sheets measure 79x94mm.

Sailor at Sea of Azov
SP26

Designs: 2k+1k, Flier at Sevastopol and Rzhev. 3.50k+1.50k, Infantrymen at Stalingrad. 9k+4.50k, Panzer Division at Don River.

1943, July 1 ***Perf. 11***

B33 SP26 1k+50b green 8 7
B34 SP26 2k+1k dark red 8 7
B35 " 3.50k+1.50k dark blue 8 7
B36 " 9k+4.50k chestnut 8 7

Issued to honor the Croatian Legion which fought with the Germans in Russia.

Souvenir Sheets.

SP30

Perf. 11, Imperf.

B37 SP30 Sheet of four 60 60
a. 1k+50b dark blue 10 10
b. 2k+1k green 10 10
c. 3.50k+1.50k dark red brown 10 10
d. 9k+4.50k bluish black 10 10

The sheets measure 105x90mm. The surtax aided the Croatian Legion.

St. Mary's Church and Cistercian Cloister, Zagreb, in 1650
SP31

1943, Sept. 12 **Engr.** ***Perf. 14½***

B39 SP31 18k+9k dull gray violet 75 75

Souvenir Sheet.
Perf. 12½.

B40 SP31 18k+9k blk. brn. 2.00 2.00

Nos. B39–B40 were issued in connection with the Croatian Philatelic Society Exhibition at Zagreb. Size of No. B40: 100x131 mm.

No. B39 Overprinted in Red **HRVATSKO MORE 8. IX. 1943.**

1943, Sept. 12

B41 SP31 18k+9k dull gray violet 1.25 1.25

Return to Croatia of the Dalmatian and Croatian coasts.

Mother and Children
SP33

Nurse and Patient
SP34

1943, Oct. 3 **Litho.** ***Perf. 11***

B42 SP33 1k+50b blue green & red 8 7
B43 SP33 2k+1k brilliant carmine & red 8 8
B44 " 3.50k+1.50k bright blue & red 8 8
B45 SP34 8k+3k red brown & red 8 8
B46 " 9k+4k yellow green & red 10 10
B47 SP33 10k+5k deep violet & red 10 10
B48 SP34 12k+6k bright ultra. & red 10 10
B49 SP33 12.50k+6k dark brown & red 10 12
B50 SP34 18k+8k brown orange & red 20 18
B51 " 32k+12k dark gray & red 30 30
Nos. B42–B51 (10) 1.22 1.21

The surtax aided the Croatian Red Cross.

Post Horn and Arms
SP35

Carrier Pigeon and Plane
SP36

Mercury
SP37

Winged Wheel
SP38

1944, Feb. 3

B52 SP35 7k+3.50(k) olive bistre & red 6 6
B53 SP36 16k+8(k) blue & dark blue 8 8
B54 SP37 24k+12(k) red & rose red 18 15
B55 SP38 32k+16k gray & red 25 25

The surtax benefited communications and railway employees. Sheets of 9.

St. Sebastian
SP39

Statue of Ancient Croatian King
SP41

War Invalids
SP40

Death of King Peter Svacic, 1097
SP42

1944, Feb. 15

B56 SP39 7k+3.50(k) orange red & rose carmine 18 18
B57 SP40 16k+8k yellow green & dark green 30 30
B58 SP41 24k+12(k) yellow brown & red 30 30
B59 SP42 32k+16k blue & dark blue 30 25

The surtax aided wounded war victims. Issued in sheets of eight stamps, with marginal inscriptions and a central label picturing St. Sebastian.

Black Legion in Combat
SP43

Guarding the Drina
SP44

Jure Francetich
SP45

1944, May 22 **Photo.** ***Imperf.***

B60 SP43 3.50(k)+1.50k brown red 5 3
B61 SP44 12.50(k)+6.50k slate blue 6 4
B62 SP45 18(k)+9k olive brown 10 10

Third anniversary of Croatian independence.
The surtax aided the National Youth Society. Sheets of 20.

Perf. 14½.

B63 SP45 12.50(k)+287.50k intense black 1.75 2.00

Issued to commemorate Jure Francetich.

Labor Corpsmen Marching
SP46

Corpsman Digging
SP47

Designs: 18k+9k, Officer instructing corpsman. 32k+16k, Pavelich reviewing Labor Corps.

Perf. 11, 12½, 14½.

1944, Aug. 20 **Engraved**

B65 SP46 3.50(k)+1(k) dark red 8 6
B66 SP47 12.50(k)+6(k) sepia 8 6
B67 " 18(k)+9(k) dark blue 8 6

B68 SP47 32(k)+16(k) gray green 8 6

The surtax aided the State Labor Service (Drzavna Radna Sluzba).
Issued in sheets of 8 plus label.

Souvenir Sheet.

SP50

Perf. 12½.

B69 SP50 32(k)+16(k) dark brn., *cream* 1.50 1.75

The sheet measures 72x99mm. The surtax aided the State Labor Service.

Palm Leaf
SP51

Lithographed.

1944, Nov. 12 ***Perf. 11***

B70 SP51 2k+1k dull green & red 5 5
B71 " 3.50k+1.50k carmine lake & red 8 8
B72 " 12.50k+6k indigo & red 18 20

The surtax aided the Croatian Red Cross. Sheets of 16.

Men of Storm Division
SP52

Designs: 70k+70k, Soldiers of Storm Division in action. 100k+100k, Storm Division emblem.

Lithographed

1944 ***Perf. 11*** **Unwmkd.**

B73 SP52 50k+50k brick red 30.00 30.00
B74 " 70k+70k sepia 30.00 30.00
B75 " 100k+100k chalky blue, pale blue & deep blue 30.00 30.00

The surtax aided the First Croatian Storm Division. Sheets of 20.

Souvenir Sheet.

SP54

B76 SP54 Sheet of three 350.00 350.00
a. 50k+50k brick red
b. 70k+70k sepia
c. 100k+100k chalky blue, pale blue & deep blue

Nos. B76a to B76c are inscribed "O. A." in brick red at right below design. The sheet measures 216x132mm. The surtax aided the First Croatian Storm Division. Counterfeits exist.

Postman
SP55

Telephone Line Repairman
SP56

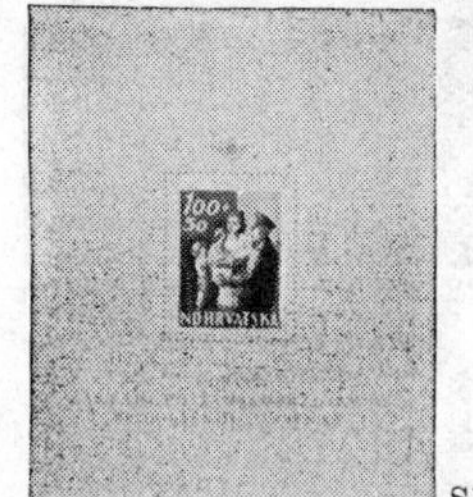

SP59

Designs; 24k+12k, Switchboard operator. 50k+25k, Postman delivering parcel.

1945 Photogravure.

B77 SP55 3.50(k)+1.50(k) slate gray 6 6
B78 SP56 12.50(k)+6(k) brown carmine 6 6
B79 " 24(k)+12(k) dark green 8 8
B80 " 50(k)+25(k) brown violet 10 10

Sheets of eight.

Souvenir Sheet.

B81 SP59 100(k)+50(k) deep brown 1.25 1.25

The surtax on Nos. B77–B81 aided employees of the P.T.T. Size of No. B81: 100x120mm.

POSTAGE DUE STAMPS.

Jugoslavia Nos. J28–J32 Overprinted in Black

NEZAVISNA DRŽAVA HRVATSKA

1941, Apr. 26 ***Perf. 12½*** **Unwmkd.**

J1 D4 50p violet 6 6
a. 50p rose violet 5.00 2.75
J2 " 1d deep magenta 6 6
J3 " 2d deep blue 7.00 6.50
J4 " 5d orange 25 25
J5 " 10d chocolate 1.25 1.00
Nos. J1–J5 (5) 8.62 7.87

The overprint on the 50p exists inverted. Counterfeit overprints exist.

Numeral of Value
D1 D2

1941, Sept. 12 **Litho.** ***Perf. 11***

J6 D1 50b carmine lake 6 8
J7 " 1k " 6 8
J8 " 2k " 18 20
J9 " 5k " 18 20
J10 " 10k " 55 60
Nos. J6–J10 (5) 1.03 1.16

Size: 24x24 mm.

1943 ***Perf. 11½, 12x12½, 12½***

J11 D2 50b light blue & gray 4 4
J12 " 1k " " 4 4
J13 " 2k " " 6 6
J14 " 4k " " 10 10
J15 " 5k " " 14 14
J16 " 6k " " 12 12
J17 " 10k blue & indigo 18 18
J18 " 15k " " 18 18
J19 " 20k " " 60 60
Nos. J11–J19 (9) 1.46 1.46

Size: 25x24¼ mm.

1942, July 30 ***Perf. 10½, 11½***

J20 D2 50b light blue & gray 6 6
J21 " 1k " " 6 6
J22 " 2k " " 10 10
J23 " 5k " " 8 8
J24 " 10k light blue & blue 40 40
J25 " 20k " " 60 60
Nos. J20–J25 (6) 1.30 1.30

OFFICIAL STAMPS.

Croatian Coat of Arms
O1 O2

Lithographed.

1942–43 ***Perf. 10½, 11½*** **Unwmkd.**

Ordinary Paper

O1 O1 25b rose lake 3 3
O2 " 50b slate black 4 3
O3 " 75b gray green 4 3
O4 " 1k orange brown 3 3
O5 " 2k turquoise blue 4 3
O6 " 3k vermilion 3 3
O7 " 4k brown violet 4 3
O8 " 5k ultramarine 6 3
a. Thin paper 5.00 5.00
O9 O1 6k bright violet 4 3
O10 " 10k light green 3 3
O11 " 12k brown rose 15 12
O12 " 20k dark blue 20 12
O13 O2 30k brown violet & gray 14 8
O14 " 40k violet black & gray 25 25
O15 " 50k brown lake & gray 35 30
O16 " 100k black & pink 40 35
Nos. O1–O16 (16) 1.87 1.47

1943–44 Thin Paper ***Perf. 11½***

O17 O1 25b claret 8 8
O18 " 50b gray 8 8
O19 " 75b dull green 8 8
O20 " 1k orange brown 8 8
O21 " 2k slate blue 8 8
O22 " 3.50k carmine rose 8 8
a. Ordinary paper 5.00 5.00
O23 O1 6k bright red violet 8 8
O24 " 12.50k deep orange 8 8
a. Ordinary paper 2.00 2.00
Nos. O17–O24 (8) 64 64

POSTAL TAX STAMPS

Nurse and Soldier
PT1

Wounded Soldier
PT2

Lithographed.

1942, Oct. 4 ***Perf. 11*** **Unwmkd.**

RA1 PT1 1k olive green & red 20 20

The tax aided the Croatian Red Cross. Issued in sheets of 24 plus label.

1943, Oct. 3

RA2 PT2 2k blue & red 25 25

The tax aided the Croatian Red Cross.

Ruins
PT3

Wounded Soldier
PT4

1944, Jan. 1 **Photo.** ***Perf. 12***

RA3 PT3 1k dark slate green 6 6
RA4 PT4 2k carmine lake 6 6
RA5 " 5k black 8 8
RA6 " 10k deep blue 15 15
RA7 " 20k brown 25 25
Nos. RA3–RA7 (5) 60 60

CUBA

(kū'bȧ)

LOCATION—The largest island of the West Indies; south of Florida.

GOVT.—Former Spanish possession.

AREA—44,206 sq. mi.

POP.—6,743,000 (est. 1960).

CAPITAL—Havana.

Formerly a Spanish possession, Cuba made several unsuccessful attempts to gain her freedom, which finally led to the intervention of the United States in 1898. In that year under the Treaty of Paris, Spain relinquished the island to the U. S. in trust for its inhabitants. In 1902 a republic was established and the Cuban Congress took over the government from the military authorities.

8 Reales Plata = 1 Peso
100 Centesimos = 1 Escudo or Peseta (1867)
1000 Milesimas = 100 Centavos = 1 Peso

Pen cancellations are common on the earlier stamps of Cuba. Stamps so cancelled sell for very much less than those with postmark cancellations.

Issued under Spanish Dominion

Used also in Puerto Rico: Nos. 1–4, 9–14, 18–21, 32–34, 35A–37, 39–41, 43–45, 47–49, 51–53.

Used only in Puerto Rico: Nos. 55–57.

Queen Isabella II
A1

Wmk. 104

Blue Paper.
Wmkd. Loops. (104)

1855 Typographed *Imperf.*

1 A1 ½r p blue green 11.50 1.50
2 " 1r p gray green 11.50 1.50
3 " 2r p carmine 60.00 6.75
4 " 2r p orange red 60.00 6.75

Nos. 2–3 also used in Philippines.

Nos. 3–4 Surcharged **Y 1/4**

1855–56

5 A1 ¼r p on 2r p car. 250.00 45.00
6 " ¼r p on 2r p orange red 350.00 90.00

Surcharged **Y 1/4**

7 A1 ¼r p on 2r p car. 250.00 45.00
a. Without fraction bar 275.00 60.00
8 " ¼r p on 2r p orange red 350.00 90.00

The "Y¼" surcharge met the "Ynterior" rate for delivery within the city of Havana.

Wmk. 105

Rough Yellowish Paper.

1856 Wmkd. Crossed Lines. (105)

9 A1 ½r p greenish blue 3.00 75
10 " 1r p green 200.00 7.50
a. 1r p emerald 210.00 10.00
11 " 2r p orange red 120.00 7.50

White Smooth Paper.

1857 **Unwmkd.**

12 A1 ½r p blue 1.50 40
13 " 1r p gray green 1.50 40
a. 1r p pale yel. green 3.25 1.00
14 " 2r p dull rose 4.50 2.25

Surcharged **Y¼**

1860

15 A1 ¼r p on 2r p dull rose 75.00 30.00
a. 1 of ¼ inverted 110.00 70.00

Queen Isabella II
A2 A3

1862–64 *Imperf.*

16 A2 ¼r p black 11.50 6.75
17 A3 ¼r p *buff* ('64) 11.00 5.25
18 " ½r p green ('64) 2.50 60
19 " ½r p green, *pale rose* ('64) 6.00 2.25
20 " 1r p blue, *salmon* ('64) 2.50 60
a. Diagonal half used as ½r on cover 40.00
21 " 2r p vermilion, *flesh* ('64) 16.50 5.25

No. 17 Overprinted in Black

1866

22 A3 ¼r p *buff* 37.50 16.50

A5 A6

1866

23 A5 5c dull violet 20.00 7.50
24 " 10c blue 1.65 85
25 " 20c green 1.25 85
26 " 40c rose 7.50 6.00

Stamps Dated "1867".

1867 *Perf. 14.*

27 A5 5c dull violet 11.50 5.25
28 " 10c blue 3.75 90
a. Imperf., pair 20.00 40.00
29 " 20c green 3.75 90
a. Imperf., pair 27.50 40.00
30 " 40c rose 6.75 5.25

Stamps Dated "1868".

1868

31 A6 5c dull violet 10.00 5.50
32 " 10c blue 2.25 1.10
a. Diagonal half used as 5c on cover 40.00
33 " 20c green 4.50 2.25
a. Diagonal half used as 10c on cover 60.00
34 " 40c rose 7.50 5.25

Nos. 31 to 34 Overprinted in Black

HABILITADO POR LA NACION.
e

1868

35 A6 5c dull violet 20.00 12.50
35A " 10c blue 20.00 12.50
36 " 20c green 20.00 12.50
37 " 40c rose 20.00 12.50

Stamps Dated "1869".

1869

38 A6 5c rose 18.50 8.50
39 " 10c red brown 3.00 1.65
a. Diagonal half used as 5c on cover 30.00
40 " 20c orange 3.75 1.65
41 " 40c dull violet 13.50 5.25

Nos. 38–41 Overprinted type "e".

42 A6 5c rose 27.50 16.50
43 " 10c red brown 22.50 13.50
44 " 20c orange 22.50 13.50
45 " 40c dull violet 27.50 16.50

"España"
A8 A9

1870 *Perf. 14*

46 A8 5c blue 75.00 22.50
47 " 10c green 1.65 50
a. Diagonal half used as 5c on cover 42.50
48 " 20c red brown 1.65 50
a. Diagonal half used as 10c on cover 45.00
49 " 40c rose 75.00 16.50

1871

50 A9 12c red lilac 11.50 4.50
a. Imperf., pair 25.00 25.00
51 " 25c ultramarine 1.65 75
a. Imperf., pair 15.00 15.00
b. Diagonal half used as 12c on cover 60.00
52 " 50c gray green 1.65 75
a. Imperf., pair 25.00 15.00
b. Diagonal half used as 25c on cover 60.00
53 " 1p pale brown 13.50 4.50
a. Imperf., pair 25.00 25.00

King Amadeo
A10

1873 *Perf. 14.*

54 A10 12½c dark green 15.00 8.00
55 " 25c gray 1.50 85
a. Diagonal half used as 12½c on cover 20.00
56 " 50c brown 85 85
a. Imperf., pair 22.50 22.50
b. Half used as 25c on cover 20.00
57 " 1p red brown 120.00 30.00
a. Diagonal half used as 50c on cover 75.00

Issues for Cuba Only

"España" Coat of Arms
A11 A12

1874

58 A11 12½c brown 6.75 3.75
59 " 25c ultramarine 65 55
a. Diagonal half used as 12½c on cover 20.00
60 " 50c deep violet 1.00 55
61 " 50c gray 1.00 55
a. Diagonal half used as 25c on cover 20.00
62 " 1p carmine 45.00 18.50
a. Imperf., pair 90.00 90.00

1875

63 A12 12½c light violet 75 40
a. Imperf., pair 25.00
64 " 25c ultramarine 40 30
a. Imperf., pair 25.00
b. Diagonal half used as 12½c on cover 22.50
65 " 50c blue green 40 30
a. Imperf., pair 25.00
b. Diagonal half used as 25c on cover 20.00
66 " 1p brown 6.00 3.75
a. 1p dark brown 6.00 3.75
b. Half used as 50c on cover 40.00

King Alfonso XII
A13 A14

1876

67 A13 12½c green 1.50 40
68 " 25c gray 50 30
a. Diagonal half used as 12½c on cover 20.00
69 " 50c ultramarine 50 30
a. Imperf., pair 7.50
70 " 1p black 5.50 2.50
a. Imperf., pair 18.50

1877

71 A14 10c light green 17.50 12.50
72 " 12½c gray 4.00 85
a. Imperf., pair 12.50
73 " 25c dark green 33 25
a. Imperf., pair 12.50
74 " 50c black 33 25
a. Imperf., pair 12.50
b. Half used as 25c on cover 20.00
75 " 1p brown 13.50 9.00
Nos. 71–75 (5) 35.66 22.85

Stamps Dated "1878".

1878

76 A14 5c blue 33 25
a. Imperf., pair 12.50
77 " 10c black 27.50 18.50
a. Imperf., pair 75.00
78 " 12½c brown bistre 1.85 85
a. 12½c gray bistre 1.25 75
b. Imperf., pair 12.50
79 " 25c deep green 25 15
a. Imperf., pair 12.50
b. Diagonal half used as 12½c on cover 12.00
80 " 50c dark blue green 25 15
a. Imperf., pair 12.50
81 " 1p carmine 5.25 4.00
a. Imperf., pair 25.00
Nos. 76–81 (6) 35.43 23.90

Stamps Dated "1879"

1879

82 A14 5c slate black 40 25
83 " 10c orange 52.50 35.00
84 " 12½c rose 40 25
85 " 25c ultramarine 33 25
a. Diagonal half used as 12½c on cover 8.00
b. Imperf., pair 25.00
86 " 50c gray 33 25
a. Diagonal half used as 25c on cover 8.00
87 " 1p olive bistre 12.00 8.00
Nos. 82–87 (6) 65.96 44.00

A15

A16

A17

1880

88 A15 5c green 25 10
89 " 10c lake 32.50 18.50
90 " 12½c gray 25 10
91 " 25c gray blue 25 10
a. Diagonal half used as 12½c on cover 12.50
92 " 50c brown 25 10
a. Half used as 25c on cover 11.50
93 " 1p yellow brown 3.75 1.85
Nos. 88–93 (6) 37.25 20.75

1881

94 A16 1c green 25 10
95 " 2c lake 15.00 11.00
96 " 2½c olive bistre 40 20
97 " 5c gray blue 25 10
98 " 10c yellow brown 25 10
99 " 20c dark brown 4.00 3.75
Nos. 94–99 (6) 20.15 15.25

1882

100 A17 1c green 25 25
101 " 2c lake 1.85 25
102 " 2½c dark brown 3.75 1.15
103 " 5c gray blue 1.85 45
a. Diagonal half used as 2½c on cover 10.00
104 " 10c olive bistre 25 10
105 " 20c red brown 40.00 18.50
Nos. 100–105 (6) 47.95 20.70

See Nos. 121–131.

Issue of 1882
Surcharged or Overprinted in Black, Blue or Red:

a

b

c

d

e

1883

106 A17 (*a*) 5 on 5c gray bl. (R) 1.00 65
- *a.* Triple surcharge
- *b.* Double surcharge 2.00 2.00
- *c.* Inverted surcharge 1.50 1.50
- *d.* Without "5" in surcharge 4.00 4.00
- *e.* Double surcharge, types "a" and "d"

107 A17 (*a*) 10 on 10c olive bister (Bl) 1.25 85
- *a.* Inverted surcharge
- *b.* Double surcharge 2.00

108 A17 (*a*) 20 on 20c red brown (Bk) 12.00 10.00
- *a.* "10" instead of "20" 30.00 30.00
- *b.* Double surcharge

109 A17 (*b*) 5 on 5c gray blue (R) 1.00 65
- *a.* Inverted surcharge 1.50 1.50
- *b.* Double surcharge 2.00

110 A17 (*b*) 10 on 10c olive bister (Bl) 1.50 90
- *a.* Inverted surcharge 1.50 1.50
- *b.* Double surcharge

111 A17 (*b*) 20 on 20c red brown (Bk) 12.00 10.00
- *a.* Double surcharge
- *b.* Double surcharge, types "b" and "c"

112 A17 (*c*) 5 on 5c gray blue (R) 1.00 75
- *a.* Inverted surcharge
- *b.* Double surcharge, types "c" and "d" 2.50

113 A17 (*c*) 10 on 10c olive bistre (Bl) 2.50 1.25
- *a.* Inverted surcharge
- *b.* Double surcharge

114 A17 (*c*) 20 on 20c red brown (Bk) 16.50 10.00
- *a.* "10" instead of "20" 55.00 55.00
- *b.* Double surcharge
- *c.* Double surcharge, types "a" and "c"

115 A17 (*d*) 5 on 5c gray blue (R) 1.00 75
- *a.* Inverted surcharge 1.25 1.25
- *b.* Double surcharge

116 A17 (*d*) 10 on 10c olive bister (Bl) 2.50 1.25
- *a.* Inverted surcharge
- *b.* Double surcharge

117 A17 (*d*) 20 on 20c red brown (Bk) 25.00 15.00
- *a.* Double surcharge, types "a" and "d"

118 A17 (*e*) 5c gray blue (R) 1.65 1.00
- *a.* Double overprint 2.25

119 A17 (*e*) 10c olive bister (Bl) 3.25 2.50
- *a.* Double overprint

120 A17 (*e*) 20c red brn. (Bk) 30.00 18.50
- *a.* Double overprint

Nos. 106-120 (15) 112.15 74.05

No. 120 has been reprinted. The overprint is handstamped instead of being press printed.

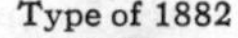
Type of 1882

1882

1st retouch

2d retouch

The differences between the stamps of 1882 and the various retouches are as follows :

Original state: The medallion is surrounded by a heavy line of color of nearly even thickness, touching the horizontal line below the word "Cuba" (or "Filipinas", as the case may be); the opening in the hair above the temple is narrow and pointed.

First retouch: The line around the medallion is thin, except at the upper right, and does not touch the horizontal line above it; the opening in the hair is slightly wider and a trifle rounded; the lock of hair above the forehead is shaped like a broad "V" and ends in a point; there is a faint white line below it, which is not found on the stamps in the original state. Owing to wear of the plate the shape of the lock of hair and the width of the white line below it vary.

Second retouch: The opening in the hair forms a semi-circle; the lock above the forehead is nearly straight, having only a slight wave, and the white line is much broader than before.

1883-86

121 A17 1c green, 2d retouch 1.50 25
122 " 2½c olive bistre 25 10
124 " 2½c violet 25 10
- *a.* 2½c red lilac ('85) 30 15
- *b.* 2½c ultramarine 25.00 12.50

125 " 5c gray blue, 1st retouch 75 8
126 " 5c gray blue, 2d retouch 2.00 1.00
- *a.* Diagonal half used as 2½c on cover 9.00

127 " 10c brn., 1st retouch 1.00 50
- *a.* Diagonal half used as 5c on cover 7.50

128 " 20c olive bistre 7.50 2.00

Nos. 121-128 (7) 13.25 4.03

1888

129 A17 2½c red brown 1.85 1.00
130 " 10c blue 1.00 60
- *a.* Diagonal half used as 5c on cover 4.00

131 " 20c brownish gray 7.50 3.00

King Alfonso XIII
A18 A19

1890-97

132 A18 1c gray brown 6.00 3.00
133 " 1c olive gray ('91) 4.00 65
134 " 1c ultramarine ('94) 1.50 25
- *a.* Imperf., pair 30.00

135 " 1c dark violet ('96) 75 17
136 " 2c slate blue 3.00 1.10
137 " 2c lilac brown ('91) 1.00 30
138 " 2c rose ('94) 8.00 1.85
- *a.* Imperf., pair 37.50

139 " 2c claret ('96) 3.75 50
140 " 2½c emerald 4.50 1.35
141 " 2½c salmon ('91) 11.50 3.00
142 " 2½c lilac ('94) 1.10 25
- *a.* Imperf., pair 37.50

143 " 2½c rose ('96) 50 15
144 " 5c olive gray 50 45
145 " 5c emerald ('91) 55 38
- *a.* Imperf., pair 22.50

146 " 5c slate blue ('96) 25 15
147 " 10c brown violet 1.35 50
148 " 10c claret ('91) 85 40
- *a.* Imperf., pair 22.50

149 " 10c emerald ('96) 1.85 15
150 " 20c dark violet 50 45
151 A18 20c ultramarine ('91) 5.25 3.00
152 " 20c red brown ('94) 8.00 3.00
- *a.* Imperf., pair 60.00

153 " 20c violet ('96) 8.50 3.75
154 " 40c org. brown ('97) 16.50 8.50
155 " 80c lilac brown ('97) 22.50 11.00

Nos. 132-155 (24) 112.20 44.30

1898

156 A19 1m orange brown 15 15
157 " 2m " 15 15
158 " 3m " 15 15
159 " 4m " 2.75 1.10
160 " 5m " 15 15
161 " 1c black violet 15 15
162 " 2c dark blue green 15 15
163 " 3c dark brown 15 15
164 " 4c orange 6.75 1.85
165 " 5c carmine rose 60 15
- *a.* Imperf., pair 25.00

166 " 6c dark blue 15 15
- *a.* Imperf., pair 25.00

167 " 8c gray brown 70 25
168 " 10c vermilion 70 25
169 " 15c slate green 2.75 25
170 " 20c maroon 40 15
171 " 40c dark lilac 1.50 25
172 " 60c black 1.85 25
173 " 80c red brown 8.50 5.25
174 " 1p yellow green 9.00 5.25
175 " 2p slate blue 13.50 5.25

Nos. 156-175 (20) 50.20 21.45

Issued under Administration of the United States.

Puerto Principe Issue.

Issues of Cuba of 1898 and 1896 Surcharged:

HABILITADO 1 cent.
a

HABILITADO 1 cents.
b

HABILITADO 2 cents.
c

HABILITADO 2 cents.
d

HABILITADO 3 cents.
e

HABILITADO 3 cents.
f

HABILITADO 5 cents.
g

HABILITADO 5 cents.
h

HABILITADO 5 cents.
i

HABILITADO 5 cents.
j

HABILITADO 3 cents.
k

HABILITADO 3 cents.
l

HABILITADO 10 cents.
m

Types a, c, d, e, f, g and h are 17½mm. high, the others are 19½mm. high.

Black Surcharge
On Nos. 156, 157, 158 and 160.

1898-99

176 (*a*) 1c on 1m orange brown 50.00 35.00
- *a.* Inverted surcharge —

177 (*b*) 1c on 1m orange brown 35.00 25.00
- *a.* Broken figure "1" 60.00 50.00
- *b.* Inverted surcharge 175.00
- *c.* Double surcharge — —
- *d.* Same as "a", inverted 225.00

178 (*c*) 2c on 2m orange brown 20.00 15.00
- *a.* Inverted surcharge 250.00 50.00

179 (*d*) 2c on 2m orange brown 35.00 22.50
- *a.* Invtd. surch. 350.00 100.00

179B (*k*) 3c on 1m orange brown 300.00 125.00
- *c.* Double surcharge — —

179D (*l*) 3c on 1m orange brown 1250.00 500.00
- *e.* Double surcharge — —

179F (*e*) 3c on 2m orange brown *1200.00*

179G (*f*) 3c on 2m orange brown — *1700.00*

180 (*e*) 3c on 3m orange brown 25.00 20.00
- *a.* Inverted surcharge 60.00

181 (*f*) 3c on 3m orange brown 70.00 50.00
- *a.* Inverted surcharge 275.00

182 (*g*) 5c on 1m orange brown 350.00 150.00
- *a.* Inverted surcharge 425.00

183 (*h*) 5c on 1m orange brown 1250.00 350.00
- *a.* Inverted surcharge 650.00

183B (*i*) 5c on 1m orange brown *4000.00*

184 (*g*) 5c on 2m orange brown 550.00 200.00

185 (*h*) 5c on 2m orange brown 1350.00 400.00

186 (*g*) 5c on 3m orange brown 150.00
- *a.* Inverted surcharge 450.00

187 (*h*) 5c on 3m orange brown 400.00
- *a.* Inverted surcharge 700.00

188 (*g*) 5c on 5m orange brown 60.00 45.00
- *a.* Inverted surcharge 400.00 150.00
- *b.* Double surcharge — —

189 (*h*) 5c on 5m orange brown 350.00 225.00
- *a.* Inverted surcharge 400.00
- *b.* Double surcharge — —

189C (*i*) 5c on 5m orange brown —

Black Surcharge on No. P25.

190 (*g*) 5c on ½m blue green 200.00 65.00
- *a.* Inverted surcharge 275.00 150.00
- *b.* Pair, one without surcharge 175.00

191 (*h*) 5c on ½m blue green 300.00 90.00
- *a.* Inverted surcharge 200.00

192 (*i*) 5c on ½m blue green 550.00 200.00
a. Double surcharge, one diagonal — *2000.00*
193 (*j*) 5c on ½m blue green 700.00 250.00

Red Surcharge on No. 161.

196 (*k*) 3c on 1c black violet 45.00 25.00
a. Inverted surcharge 90.00
197 (*l*) 3c on 1c black violet 75.00 45.00
a. Inverted surcharge 150.00
198 (*i*) 5c on 1c black violet 20.00 20.00
a. Inverted surcharge 75.00
b. Vertical surcharge —
c. Double surcharge *300.00* *300.00*
d. Double inverted surcharge —
199 (*j*) 5c on 1c black violet 50.00 40.00
a. Inverted surcharge 150.00
b. Vertical surcharge *500.00*
c. Double surcharge — *500.00*
200 (*m*) 10c on 1c black violet 20.00 *40.00*
a. Broken figure "1" 40.00 *75.00*

Black Surcharge on Nos. P26 - P30.

201 (*k*) 3c on 1m blue green 150.00 110.00
a. Inverted surcharge 200.00
b. "EENTS" 400.00 225.00
c. Same as "b", inverted 650.00
202 (*l*) 3c on 1m blue green 400.00 225.00
a. Inverted surcharge 650.00
203 (*k*) 3c on 2m blue green 550.00 200.00
a. "EENTS" 900.00 350.00
b. Inverted surcharge 500.00
c. Same as "a" inverted 700.00
204 (*l*) 3c on 2m blue green 900.00 350.00
a. Inverted surcharge 700.00
205 (*k*) 3c on 3m blue green 700.00 200.00
a. Inverted surcharge 350.00
b. "EENTS" 1000.00 350.00
c. Same as "b" inverted 700.00
206 (*l*) 3c on 3m blue green 1000.00 350.00
a. Invtd. surch. 700.00
211 (*i*) 5c on 1m blue green 1200.00
a. "EENTS" — 1800.00
212 (*j*) 5c on 1m blue green 1800.00
213 (*i*) 5c on 2m blue green 1000.00
a. "EENTS" — 1500.00
214 (*j*) 5c on 2m blue green 1500.00
215 (*i*) 5c on 3m blue green 300.00
a. "EENTS" 800.00
216 (*j*) 5c on 3m blue green — 800.00
217 (*i*) 5c on 4m blue green 1600.00 400.00
a. "EENTS" — 1100.00
b. Inverted surcharge 750.00
c. Same as "a", inverted 1400.00
218 (*j*) 5c on 4m blue green 1100.00
a. Invtd. surch. 1400.00
219 (*i*) 5c on 8m blue green 2000.00 900.00
a. Inverted surcharge 1200.00
b. "EENTS" — 1800.00
c. Same as "b", inverted 2400.00
220 (*j*) 5c on 8m blue green 1800.00
a. Invtd. surch. 2400.00

CUBA

United States Nos. 279a, 267, 279B, 268, 281a, 282C and 283a Surcharged in Black

1 c. de PESO.

Wmkd. USPS (191)

1899 ***Perf. 12.***

221 A87 1c on 1c yel. green 2.00 35
a. Vertical surch. —
222 A88 2c on 2c carmine 2.00 40
a. 2c on 2c red 2.50 35
b. "CUPA" 50.00 —
c. Invtd. surch. *1000.00* 850.00
223 A88 2½c on 2c red 1.50 50
a. 2½c on 2c carmine 2.00 2.00
224 A89 3c on 3c purple 4.00 90
a. Period between "B" and "A" 15.00 10.00
225 A91 5c on 5c blue 4.50 75
a. "CUPA" 25.00 10.00
b. "CUBA" omitted *1500.00* —
226 A94 10c on 10c brown, type I 12.00 4.50
b. "CUBA" omitted *1500.00* —
226A A94 10c on 10c brown, type II *2000.00*
Nos. 221-226 (6) 26.00 7.40

The 2½c was sold and used as a 2c stamp.

Excellent counterfeits of this and the preceding issue exist, especially inverted and double surcharges.

Issues of the Republic under U. S. Military Rule.

Statue of Columbus
A20

Royal Palms
A21

"Cuba"
A22

Ocean Liner
A23

Cane Field
A24

Wmkd. U S—C. (191C)

1899 **Engraved** ***Perf. 12***

227 A20 1c yellow green 1.25 12
228 A21 2c carmine 1.25 10
a. 2c scarlet 1.50 10
b. Booklet pane of 6 100.00
229 A22 3c purple 1.10 20
230 A23 5c blue 2.25 30
231 A24 10c brown 6.00 60
Nos. 227-231 (5) 11.85 1.32

Issues of the Republic

No. 229 Surcharged in Carmine

HABILITADO UN CENTAVO 1 OCTUBRE 1902

1902, Sept. 30

232 A22 1c on 3c purple 1.25 60
a. Inverted surcharge 17.50 17.50
b. Surcharge sideways (numeral horizontal) —
c. Double surcharge 25.00 25.00

Counterfeits of the errors are plentiful.

Re-engraved.

The re-engraved stamps of 1905-07 may be distinguished from the issue of 1899 as follows:

ORIGINAL RE-ENGRAVED

1c: The ends of the label inscribed "Centavo" are rounded instead of square.

2c: The foliate ornaments, inside the oval disks bearing the numerals of value, have been removed.

5c: Two lines forming a right angle have been added in the upper corners of the label bearing the word "Cuba".

10c: A small ball has been added to each of the square ends of the label bearing the word "Cuba".

1905 ***Perf. 12*** **Unwmkd.**

233 A20 1c green 1.00 12
234 A21 2c rose 75 10
a. Bklt. pane of 6 20.00
236 A23 5c blue 17.50 85
237 A24 10c brown 2.00 30

Maj. Gen. Antonio Maceo
A26

1907

238 A26 50c gray blue & black 85 50

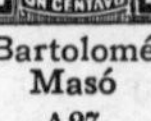

Bartolomé Masó
A27

Máximo Gómez
A28

Julio Sanguily
A29

Ignacio Agramonte
A30

Calixto García
A31

José M. Rodriquez y Rodriquez (Mayia)
A32

Carlos Roloff
A33

1910, Feb. 1

239 A27 1c green & violet 75 10
a. Center inverted 50.00 50.00
240 A28 2c carmine & green 1.25 8
a. Center inverted 250.00 250.00
241 A29 3c violet & blue 75 20
242 A30 5c blue & green 10.00 75
243 A31 8c olive & violet 75 30
244 A32 10c brown & blue 4.50 60
a. Center inverted 400.00
245 A26 50c violet & black 1.25 40
246 A33 1p slate & black 6.00 3.00
Nos. 239-246 (8) 25.25 5.43

1911-13

247 A27 1c green 50 10
248 A28 2c carmine rose 60 8
a. Bklt. pane of 6('13) 12.50
250 A30 5c ultramarine 1.25 10
251 A31 8c olive green & black 90 50
252 A33 1p black 4.00 1.50
Nos. 247-252 (5) 7.25 2.28

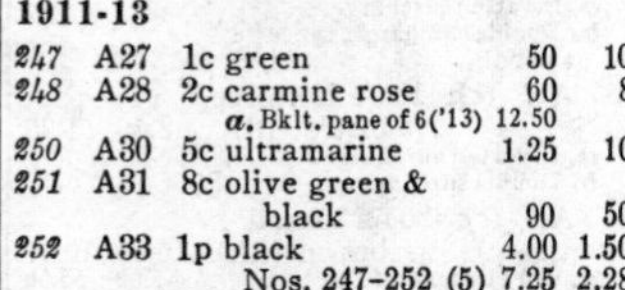

Map of Cuba
A34

1914-15

253 A34 1c green 50 6
a. Booklet pane of 6 12.50
254 " 2c carmine rose 50 5
a. Booklet pane of 6 12.50
255 " 2c red ('15) 1.00 5
a. Booklet pane of 6 12.50
256 " 3c violet 2.50 40
257 " 5c blue 3.50 25
258 " 8c olive green 2.50 75
259 " 10c brown 4.00 40
260 " 10c olive green ('15) 6.00 60
261 " 50c orange 32.50 12.50
262 " 1p gray 42.50 25.00
Nos. 253-262 (10) 95.50 40.06

Gertrudis Gómez de Avellaneda
A34a

1914

No.	Type	Description	Unused	Used
263	A34a	5c blue	9.00	4.00

Issued to commemorate the centenary of the birth of the Cuban poetess, Gertrudis Gómez de Avellaneda (1814–1873).

José Martí
A35

Máximo Gómez
A36

José de la Luz Caballero
A37

Calixto García
A38

Ignacio Agramonte
A39

Tomás Estrada Palma
A40

José A. Saco
A41

Antonio Maceo
A42

Carlos Manuel de Céspedes
A43

1917–18 *Perf. 12.* Unwmkd.

No.	Type	Description	Unused	Used
264	A35	1c blue green	65	5
		a. Booklet pane of 6	5.00	
		b. Booklet pane of 30	40.00	
265	A36	2c rose	50	5
		a. Booklet pane of 6	7.50	
		b. Booklet pane of 30	40.00	
266	"	2c light red ('18)	50	5
		a. Booklet pane of 6	7.50	
267	A37	3c violet	75	5
		a. Imperf., pair	125.00	
		b. Booklet pane of 6	6.00	
268	A38	5c deep blue	1.25	6
269	A39	8c red brown	3.00	10
270	A40	10c yellow brown	1.50	8
271	A41	20c gray green	6.00	75
272	A42	50c dull rose	7.00	75
273	A43	1p black	7.00	75
		Nos. 264–273 (10)	28.15	2.69

Wmk. 106

Wmkd. Star. (106)

1925-28 *Perf. 12.*

No.	Type	Description	Unused	Used
274	A35	1c blue green	1.25	6
		a. Booklet pane of 30	50.00	
275	A36	2c bright rose	1.00	5
		a. Bklt. pane of 6	10.00	
		b. Booklet pane of 30	50.00	
276	A38	5c deep blue	1.75	10
277	A39	8c red brown ('28)	3.50	35
278	A40	10c yel. brn. ('27)	4.00	40
279	A41	20c olive green	6.00	65
		Nos. 274–279 (6)	17.50	1.61

1926 *Imperf.*

No.	Type	Description	Unused	Used
280	A35	1c blue green	2.00	1.25
281	A36	2c bright rose	1.75	1.00
282	A38	5c deep blue	2.50	2.00

See also Nos. 304-310.

Arms of Republic
A44

1927, May 20 *Perf. 12* Unwmkd.

No.	Type	Description	Unused	Used
283	A44	25c violet	7.50	3.50

25th anniversary of the Republic.

Tomás Estrada Palma
A45

Designs: 2c, Gen. Gerardo Machado. 5c, Morro Castle. 8c, Havana Railway Station. 10c, Presidential Palace. 13c, Tobacco Plantation. 20c, Treasury Building. 30c, Sugar Mill. 50c, Havana Cathedral. 1p, Galician Clubhouse, Havana.

1928, Jan. 2 Wmk. 106

No.	Type	Description	Unused	Used
284	A45	1c deep green	40	25
285	"	2c bright rose	40	25
286	"	5c deep blue	1.25	40
287	"	8c light red brown	2.00	90
288	"	10c bistre brown	1.00	75
289	"	13c orange	1.50	75
290	"	20c olive green	2.00	80
291	"	30c dark violet	3.00	75
292	"	50c carmine rose	5.00	2.25
293	"	1p gray black	11.00	6.00
		Nos. 284–293 (10)	27.55	13.10

Sixth Pan-American Conference.

Capitol, Havana
A55

1929, May 18

No.	Type	Description	Unused	Used
294	A55	1c green	35	30
295	"	2c carmine rose	40	30
296	"	5c blue	60	35
297	"	10c bistre brown	1.25	50
298	"	20c violet	4.00	2.00
		Nos. 294–298 (5)	6.60	3.45

Opening of the Capitol, Havana.

Hurdler
A56

1930, Mar. 15 Engraved

No.	Type	Description	Unused	Used
299	A56	1c green	75	35
300	"	2c carmine	75	30
301	"	5c deep blue	1.00	30
302	"	10c bistre brown	1.50	85
303	"	20c violet	7.50	3.50
		Nos. 299–303 (5)	11.50	5.30

Issued to commemorate the second Central American Athletic Games.

Types of 1917 Portrait Issue.
Flat Plate Printing.
Engraved

1930–45 *Perf. 10, 11* Wmk. 106

No.	Type	Description	Unused	Used
304	A35	1c blue green	75	25
		a. Booklet pane of 6	7.50	
		b. Booklet pane of 30		
305	A36	2c bright rose	85.00	50.00
		a. Booklet pane of 6	600.00	
305B	A37	3c dk. rose vio. ('42)	2.50	50
		c. Booklet pane of 6	10.00	
306	A38	5c dark blue	2.50	25
306A	A39	8c red brown ('45)	2.50	40
307	A40	10c brown	2.50	40
		a. 10c yel. brn. ('35)	3.50	75
307B	A41	20c olive green ('41)	4.00	75
		Nos. 304–307 (7)	99.75	52.55

Nos. 305 and 305B were printed for booklet panes and all copies have straight edges.

Rotary Press Printing.

No.	Type	Description	Unused	Used
308	A35	1c blue green	1.00	20
309	A36	2c bright rose	1.00	20
		a. Booklet pane of 50		
310	A37	3c violet	1.50	20
		a. 3c dull violet ('38)	1.00	20
		b. 3c rose violet ('41)	75	20
		c. Bklt. pane of 50		

The flat plate stamps measure 18½x21½mm.; those from the rotary press, 19x22mm.

The Mangos of Baragua
A57

War Memorial
A61

Battle of Mal Tiempo
A58

Battle of Coliseo
A59

Maceo, Gómez and Zayas
A60

Wmk. 229

Wmkd. Wavy Lines. (229)

1933, Apr. 23 Photo. *Perf. 12½*

No.	Type	Description	Unused	Used
312	A57	3c dark brown	75	20
313	A58	5c dark blue	75	35
314	A59	10c emerald	2.50	40
315	A60	13c red	2.50	1.00
316	A61	20c black	5.00	3.00
		Nos. 312–316 (5)	11.50	4.95

Issued in commemoration of the War of Independence and the dedication of the "Soldado Invasor" monument.

Types of 1917 Issues with Carmine or Black Overprint Reading Up or Down

GOBIERNO
REVOLUCIONARIO
4-9-1933

Rotary Press Printing.
Engraved

1933, Dec. 23 *Perf. 10* Wmk. 106

No.	Type	Description	Unused	Used
317	A35	1c blue green (C)	75	30

With Additional Surcharge of New Value and Bars.

No.	Type	Description	Unused	Used
318	A37	2c on 3c violet (Bk)	75	30

Nos. 317–318 commemorate the establishment of a revolutionary junta.

Dr. Carlos J. Finlay
A62

Engraved.

1934, Dec. 3 *Perf. 10* Wmk. 106

No.	Type	Description	Unused	Used
319	A62	2c dark carmine	75	25
320	"	5c dark blue	2.00	60

Issued to commemorate the centenary of the birth of Dr. Carlos J. Finlay (1833–1915), physician-biologist who found that a mosquito transmitted yellow fever.

Pres. José Miguel Gómez
A63

Gómez Monument
A64

1936, May *Perf. 10*

No.	Type	Description	Unused	Used
322	A63	1c green	50	25
323	A64	2c carmine	1.25	40

Issued in commemoration of the unveiling of a monument to Gen. José Miguel Gómez, ex-president.

Matanzas Issue.

Map of Cuba
A65

Designs: 2c, Map of Free Zone. 4c, S. S. "Rex" in Matanzas Bay. 5c, Ships in Matanzas Bay. 8c, Caves of Bellamar. 10c, Valley of Yumuri. 20c, Yumuri River. 50c, Ships Leaving Port.

Photogravure.

Wmkd. Wavy Lines. (229)

1936, May 5 *Perf. 12½*

324	A65	1c blue green	30	20
325	"	2c red	45	25
326	"	4c claret	1.00	35
327	"	5c ultramarine	90	35
328	"	8c orange brown	2.00	80
329	"	10c emerald	1.75	75
330	"	20c brown	4.50	2.75
331	"	50c slate	7.00	4.50

Nos. 324-331, C18-C21, CE1, E8 (14) 38.70 22.45

Exist imperf. Price 20% more.

"Peace and Work"
A73

Máximo Gómez Monument
A74

"Independence"
A76

Torch
A75

"Messenger of Peace"
A77

1936, Nov. 18 *Perf. 12½*

332	A73	1c emerald	35	18
333	A74	2c crimson	45	15
334	A75	4c maroon	60	20
335	A76	5c ultramarine	2.00	75
336	A77	8c dark green	3.50	1.50

Nos. 332-336, C22-C23, E9 (8) 16.40 6.53

Maj. Gen. Máximo Gómez, birth centenary.

Sugar Cane
A78

Primitive Sugar Mill
A79

Modern Sugar Mill
A80

Wmkd. Star. (106)

1937, Oct. 2 Engraved *Perf. 10*

337	A78	1c yellow green	1.00	50
338	A79	2c red	70	30
339	A80	5c bright blue	1.00	60

Issued in commemoration of the 400th anniversary of the sugar cane industry in Cuba.

Argentine Emblem
A81

Mountain Scene (Bolivia)
A82

Arms of Brazil
A83

Canadian Scene
A84

Camilo Henriquez (Chile)
A85

Gen. Francisco de Paula Santander (Colombia)
A86

National Monument (Costa Rica)
A87

Autograph of José Marti (Cuba)
A88

Columbus Lighthouse (Dominican Republic)
A89

Juan Montalvo (Ecuador)
A90

Abraham Lincoln (United States)
A91

Quetzal and Scroll (Guatemala)
A92

Arms of Haiti
A93

Francisco Morazán (Honduras)
A94

Fleet of Columbus
A95

Engraved.

1937, Oct. 13 *Perf. 10* Wmk. 106

340	A81	1c deep green	50	50
341	A82	1c green	50	50
342	A83	2c carmine	50	50
343	A84	2c carmine	50	50
344	A85	3c violet	1.50	1.50
345	A86	3c violet	1.50	1.50
346	A87	4c bistre brown	1.25	1.25
347	A88	4c bistre brown	3.00	3.00
348	A89	5c blue	1.50	1.50
349	A90	5c blue	1.50	1.50
350	A91	8c citron	6.00	6.00
351	A92	8c citron	2.00	2.00
352	A93	10c maroon	2.00	2.00
353	A94	10c maroon	2.00	2.00
354	A95	25c rose lilac	20.00	20.00

Nos. 340-354, C24-C29, E10-E11 (23) 85.25 84.25

Nos. 340 to 354 were sold by the Cuban Post Office for three days, Oct. 13-15, during which no other stamps were sold. They were postally valid for the full face value. Proceeds from their three-day sale above 30,000 pesos were paid by the Cuban Post Office Department to the Association of American Writers and Artists. Remainders were overprinted "SVP" (Without Postal Value).

No. 283 Surcharged in Green

1937, Nov. 19 *Perf. 12* Unwmkd.

355	A44	10c on 25c violet	7.50	2.50

Centenary of Cuban railroads.

Ciboney Indian and Cigar
A96

Cigar and Globe
A97

Tobacco Plant and Cigars
A98

Wmkd. Star. (106)

1939, Aug. 28 Engraved *Perf. 10*

356	A96	1c yellow green	25	5
357	A97	2c red	50	5
358	A98	5c brt. ultramarine	1.00	20

General Calixto García
A99 A100

1939, Nov. 6 *Perf. 10, Imperf.*

359	A99	2c dark red	60	20
360	A100	5c deep blue	1.20	60

Birth centenary of General Garcia.

Gonzalo de Quesada
A101

1940, Apr. 30 Engraved *Perf. 10*

361	A101	2c rose red	1.00	50

Pan American Union, 50th anniversary.

Rotary Club Emblem, Cuban Flag and Tobacco Plant
A102

Lions Emblem, Cuban Flag and Royal Palms
A103

1940, May 18 *Perf. 10* Wmk. 106

362	A102	2c rose red	2.00	1.00

Issued in commemoration of the Rotarv International Convention held at Havana.

1940, July 23

363	A103	2c org. vermilion	2.00	1.00

Lions International Convention, Havana.

Dr. Nicolás J. Gutiérrez
A104

1940, Oct. 28

364 A104 2c org. vermilion 1.20 50
365 " 5c blue 1.50 60
  a. Sheet of four, imperf., unwmkd. 3.50 3.50
  b. As "a," black overprint ('51) 4.00 4.00

Issued in commemoration of the 100th anniversary of the publication of the first Cuban Medical Review, "El Repertorio Medico Habanero".

No. 365a measures 127x177mm. and contains two each of Nos. 364 and 365 imperforate, and upper and lower marginal inscriptions. The sheet sold for 25c.

In 1951 Nos. 365a was overprinted in black: "50 Aniversario Descubrimiento Agente Transmisor • de la Fiebre Amarilla por el Dr. Carlos J. Finlay • Honor a los Martires de la Ciencia 1901 1951." The overprint is illustrated over No. C43A, but does not include the plane and "Correo Aereo."

Major General Guillermo Moncada
A105

Moncada Riding into Battle
A106

1941, June 25

366 A105 3c dk. brown, *buff* 1.20 40
367 A106 5c bright blue 1.50 75

Issued in commemoration of the centenary of the birth of Maj. Gen. Guillermo Moncada (1841-96).

Globe Showing Western Hemisphere
A107

Maceo, Bolívar, Juárez, Lincoln and Arms of Cuba
A108

Tree of Fraternity, Havana
A110

"Labor: Wealth of America"
A109

Statue of Liberty
A111

Perf. 10, Imperf.

1942, Feb. 23 **Wmk. 106**

368 A107 1c emerald 40 12
369 A108 3c orange brown 50 15
370 A109 5c blue 90 30
371 A110 10c red violet 2.00 75
372 A111 13c red 2.00 1.00
Nos. 368-372 (5) 5.80 2.32

Issued to publicize the spirit of Democracy in the Americas.
The imperforate varieties are without gum.

Ignacio Agramonte Loynaz
A112

Rescue of Sanguily by Agramonte
A113

1942, Apr. 10 ***Perf. 10***

373 A112 3c bistre brown 90 50
374 A113 5c bright blue, *bluish* 1.75 70

Issued in commemoration of the 100th anniversary of the birth of Ignacio Agramonte Loynaz, patriot.

"Unmask the Fifth Columnists"
A114

" Be Careful, The Fifth Column is Spying on You"
A115

" Destroy it. The Fifth Column is like a Serpent"
A116

" Fulfill your Patriotic Duty by Destroying the Fifth Column"
A117

" Don't be Afraid of the Fifth Column. Attack it"
A118

1943, July 5

375 A114 1c dark blue green 40 18
376 A115 3c red 60 20
377 A116 5c bright blue 70 20
378 A117 10c dull brown 1.50 50
379 A118 13c dull rose violet 3.00 1.50
Nos. 375-379 (5) 6.20 2.58

General Eloy Alfaro and Flags of Cuba and Ecuador
A119

1943, Sept. 20

380 A119 3c green 1.25 40

Issued to commemorate the 100th anniversary of the birth of General Eloy Alfaro of Ecuador.

Retirement Security
A120

1943, Nov. 8 ***Perf. 10*** **Wmk. 106**

381 A120 1c yellow green 75 30
382 " 3c vermilion 90 30
383 " 5c bright blue 1.00 50

1944, Mar. 18

384 A120 1c brt. yellow green 75 30
385 " 3c salmon 90 30
386 " 5c light blue 1.50 75

Half the proceeds from the sale of Nos. 381-386 were used for the Communications Ministry Employees' Retirement Fund.

Portrait of Columbus
A121

Bartolomé de Las Casas
A122

First Statue of Columbus at Cárdenas
A123

Discovery of Tobacco
A124

Columbus Sights Land
A125

1944, May 19

387 A121 1c dark yellow green 30 20
388 A122 3c brown 50 20
389 A123 5c bright blue 70 30
390 A124 10c dark violet 1.50 75
391 A125 13c dark red 3.00 1.50
Nos. 387-391, C36-C37 (7) 8.25 3.65

Issued to commemorate the 450th anniversary of the discovery of America.

Major General Carlos Roloff
A126

Map of the Americas and First Brazilian Postage Stamps
A127

1944, Aug. 21

392 A126 3c violet 75 35

Issued to commemorate the 100th anniversary of the birth of Maj. Gen. Carlos Roloff.

1944, Dec. 20 **Engraved**

393 A127 3c brown orange 1.75 75

Issued to commemorate the centenary of the first postage stamps of the Americas, issued by Brazil in 1843.

Seal of the Society
A128

Luis de las Casas and
Luis Maria Penalver
A129

1945, Oct. 5 *Perf. 10* Wmk. 106

394 A128 1c yellow green 30 20
395 A129 2c scarlet 45 20

Issued to commemorate the sesquicentenary of the founding of the Economic Society of Friends of the Country.

Aged Couple—A130

1945, Dec. 27

396 A130 1c dk. yellow green 25 10
397 " 2c scarlet 40 15
398 " 5c cobalt blue 75 35

1946, Mar. 26

399 A130 1c brt. yellow green 50 25
400 " 2c salmon pink 40 25
401 " 5c light blue 60 50

See note after No. 386.

Gabriel de la Concepcion Valdés
Plácido)—A131

1946, Feb. 5

402 A131 2c scarlet 90 30

Issued to commemorate the centenary of the death of the poet Gabriel de la Concepcion Valdés.

Manuel Marquez Sterling A132
Globe and Cross A133

1946, Apr. 30

403 A132 2c scarlet 90 40

Issued to commemorate the third anniversary of the founding of the Manuel Marquez Sterling Professional School of Journalism.

1946, July 4 Engraved

404 A133 2c scarlet, *pink* 85 40

Issued in honor of the 80th anniversary of the International Red Cross.

Cow and Milkmaid
A134

Franklin D. Roosevelt
A135

1947, Feb. 20 *Perf. 10* Wmk. 106

405 A134 2c scarlet 75 30

Issued to commemorate the 1947 National Livestock Exposition.

1947, Apr. 12

406 A135 2c vermilion 50 25

Issued to commemorate the second anniversary of the death of Franklin D. Roosevelt.

Antonio Oms Sarret
and Aged Couple
A136

1947, Oct. 20

407 A136 1c dp. yellow green 20 15
408 " 2c scarlet 35 15
409 " 5c light blue 75 40

See note after No. 386.

Marta Abreu Arenabio de Estevez
A137

"Charity"
A138

Marta Abreu Monument, Santa Clara
A139

"Patriotism"
A140

1947, Nov. 29

410 A137 1c dp. yel. green 30 20
411 A138 2c scarlet 50 15
412 A139 5c bright blue 90 40
413 A140 10c dark violet 1.50 75

Issued to commemorate the centenary of the birth of Marta Abreu Arenabio de Estevez, philanthropist and humanitarian.

Armauer Hansen—A141

1948, Apr. 9

414 A141 2c rose carmine 75 30

International Leprosy Congress, Havana.

Mother and Child
A142

1948, Oct. 15 Engraved

415 A142 1c yellow green 30 20
416 " 2c scarlet 40 20
417 " 5c bright blue 85 40

See note after No. 386.

Death of José Martí
A143

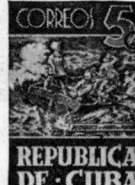

Martí Rowing to Shore
A144

Engraved.

1948, Nov. 10 *Perf. 10* Wmk. 106

418 A143 2c scarlet 35 20
419 A144 5c bright blue 80 35

Issued to commemorate (in 1945) the 50th anniversary of the death of José Martí, patriot.

Tobacco Picking
A145

Liberty Carrying Flag and Cigars
A146

Cigar and Arms of Cuba
A147

1948, Dec. 6

Size: 22½x26mm.

420 A145 1c green 15 5
421 A146 2c rose carmine 25 10
422 A147 5c bright blue 35 15

Cuba's tobacco industry.
See Nos. 445–447.

Equestrian Statue
of Gen. Antonio Maceo
A148

Sword Salute to Maceo
A149

Designs: 2c, Portrait of Maceo. 5c, Mausoleum, El Cacahual. 10c, East to West invasion. 20c, Battle of Peralejo. 50c, Declaration of Baragua. 1p, Death of Maceo at San Pedro.

1948, Dec. 15 *Perf. 12½* Wmk. 229

423 A148 1c blue green 10 8
424 " 2c red 20 6
425 " 5c blue 30 18
426 A149 8c black & brown 50 30
427 " 10c brn. & blue green 50 25
428 " 20c blue & carmine 2.50 1.25
429 " 50c carmine & ultra. 4.00 2.50
430 " 1p black & violet 7.50 3.75
Nos. 423–430 (8) 15.60 8.37

Issued to commemorate the centenary (in 1945) of the birth of General Antonio Maceo.

Symbol of Pharmacy
A150

Morro Lighthouse
A151

1948, Dec. 28 *Perf. 10*

431 A150 2c rose carmine 75 30

Issued to commemorate the First Pan-American Congress of Pharmacy, Havana, December 1948.

1949, Jan. 17 *Perf. 12½* Wmk. 229

432 A151 2c carmine 50 25

Issued to commemorate the centenary (in 1944) of the erection of the Morro Lighthouse.

Jagua Castle, Cienfuegos
A152

1949, Jan. 27 *Perf. 10* Wmk. 106

433 A152 1c yellow green 40 20
434 " 2c rose red 80 40

Issued to commemorate the 200th anniversary of the construction of Jagua Castle and the centenary of the publication of the first newspaper in Cienfuegos.

Manuel Sanguily y Garritt
A153

Map of Isle of Pines
A154

1949, Mar. 31

435 A153 2c rose red 35 20
436 " 5c blue 75 40

Issued to commemorate the centenary of the birth of Manuel Sanguily y Garritt (1848–1925), cabinet member, editor, author.

1949, Apr. 26

437 A154 5c blue 75 35

Issued to commemorate the 20th anniversary of the recognition of Cuban ownership of the Isle of Pines.

Ismael Cespedes
A155

1949, Sept. 28

438 A155 1c yellow green 35 20
439 " 2c scarlet 35 20
440 " 5c bright blue 80 40

See note after No. 386.

Gen. Enrique Collazo
A156

Enrique José Varona
A157

1950, Feb. 28 Engraved *Perf. 10*

441 A156 2c scarlet 40 20
442 " 5c bright blue 80 35

Issued to commemorate the centenary (in 1948) of the birth of General Enrique Collazo.

1950, Feb. 28

443 A157 2c scarlet 40 20
444 " 5c bright blue 80 40

Issued to commemorate the centenary of the birth of Enrique José Varona, writer and patriot.

Tobacco Types of 1948.

1950, June 20 Re-engraved

Size: 21 x 25 mm.

445 A145 1c green 40 10
446 A146 2c rose red 40 10
447 A147 5c blue 60 35

The re-engraved stamps show slight differences in many minor details.

No. 446 Overprinted in Black

BANCO NACIONAL DE CUBA
INAUGURACION
27 ABRIL
1950

1950, Apr. 27

448 A146 2c rose red 75 35

Issued to commemorate the opening of the National Bank of Cuba, April 27, 1950.

Re-engraved Tobacco Types of 1950 Overprinted in Carmine

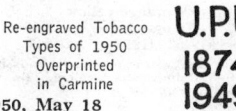

U.P.U
1874
1949

1950, May 18

449 A145 1c yellow green 25 15
450 A146 2c lilac rose 40 20
451 A147 5c light blue 75 25

75th anniversary (in 1949) of Universal Postal Union.
No. 451 exists with surcharge inverted.

Manuel Balanzategui, Antonio L. Pausa and Train Wreck
A158

Fernando Figueredo
A159

1950, Sept. 21 Engraved

452 A158 1c yellow green 35 20
453 " 2c scarlet 35 20
454 " 5c bright blue 75 40

See note after No. 386.

1951, Mar. 17 *Perf. 10* Wmk. 106

455 A159 1c green 40 15
456 " 2c scarlet 40 15
457 " 5c bright blue 75 30

Three-fourths of the proceeds from the sale of these stamps were used for the Communication Ministry Employees' Retirement Fund.
See Nos. 474, C51–C56, E15.

Miguel Teurbe Tolón and Flag
A160

Narciso Lopez
A161

Emilia Teurbe Tolón Sewing Flag
A162

Cuban Flag
A163

Engraved and Lithographed.

1951, July 3 *Perf. 13* Wmk. 229

458 A160 1c Prussian green, ultra. & red 30 15
459 A161 2c red & gray black 50 20
460 A162 5c ultra. & red 1.00 40
461 A163 10c rose violet, blue & red 1.50 60
Nos. 458-461, C41-C43, E13 (8) 10.80 3.85

Centenary of adoption of Cuba's flag.

Clara Louise Maass and Hospitals
A164

Hospitals: Lutheran Memorial, Newark, N.J. and Las Animas, Havana.

Engraved.

1951, Aug. 24 *Perf. 10* Wmk. 106

462 A164 2c scarlet 90 40

Issued to commemorate the 75th anniversary of the birth of Clara Louise Maass, (1876–1901), American nurse and martyr in yellow fever fight.

Airmail Type and

José Raul Capablanca—A165

Capablanca Club, Havana
A166

Design: 2c, Capablanca making "The Exact Play."

Perf. 13

1951, Nov. 1 Photo. Wmk. 229

463 A165 1c bl. green & org. 1.50 60
464 AP27 2c rose carmine & dark brown 2.00 1.00
465 A166 5c blk. & dp. ultra. 4.50 2.00
Nos. 463-465, C44-C46, E14 (7) 27.00 10.85

Issued to commemorate the 30th anniversary of the winning of the World Chess title by José Raul Capablanca.

Antonio Guiteras Holmes
A167

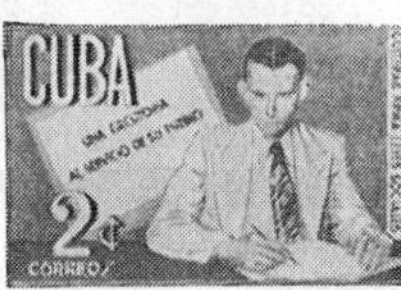

Guiteras Preparing Social Legislation
A168

Fort of the Morrillo
A169

Engraved.

1951, Oct. 22 *Perf. 10* Wmk. 106

466 A167 1c yellow green 35 15
467 A168 2c rose carmine 60 20
468 A169 5c deep blue 1.00 30
Nos. 466-468, C47-C49 (6) 5.75 2.25

Issued to commemorate the 16th anniversary of the Action of the Morrillo and to honor Antonio Guiteras Holmes, who was killed there.
Souvenir sheets containing stamps similar to Nos. 466-468, but in different colors, are listed as Nos. C49a-C49b.

Poinsettia
A170

Maj. Gen. José Maceo
A171

1951, Dec. 1 Engr. and Typo.

469 A170 1c grn. & carmine 3.00 50
470 " 2c rose car. & grn. 3.50 75

See note after No. 457. See also Nos. 498–499.

1952, Feb. 6 Engraved

471 A171 2c yellow brown 40 20
472 " 5c indigo 90 30

Issued to commemorate the centenary of the birth of Major General José Maceo.
See note after No. C49.

Queen Isabella I
A172

Receipt of Autonomy
A173

1952, Feb. 22

473 A172 2c bright red 60 20

Issued to commemorate the 500th anniversary of the birth of Queen Isabella I of Spain.
Souvenir sheets containing 2c stamps of type A172 are listed as Nos. C50a–C50b.

Type of 1951 Surcharged in Green.

1952, Mar. 18

474 A159 10c on 2c yel. brn. 1.25 50

Engraved.

1952, May 27 *Perf. 12½* Wmk. 106

Designs: 2c, Tomas Estrada Palma and Luis Estevez Romero. 5c, Barnet, Finlay, Guiteras and Nuñez. 8c, Capitol. 20c, Map, Central Highway. 50c, Sugar Mill.

Centers in Black.

475 A173 1c dark green 30 10
476 " 2c dark carmine 35 10
477 " 5c dark blue 50 15
478 " 8c dk. brn. carmine 75 20
479 " 20c dark olive green 1.75 60
480 " 50c deep orange 3.00 1.00
Nos. 475-480, C57-C60, E16 (11) 13.05 4.35

Issued to commemorate the 50th anniversary of the foundation of the Republic of Cuba.

Hands Holding Coffee Beans
A174

Designs: 2c, Map and man picking coffee beans. 5c, Farmer with pan of beans.

1952, Aug. 22 *Perf. 13½* Wmk. 229

481 A174 1c green 40 18
482 " 2c rose red 75 30
483 " 5c dark violet blue & aquamarine 1.00 40

Bicentenary of coffee cultivation.

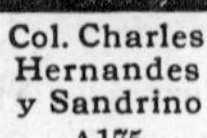

Col. Charles Hernandes y Sandrino
A175

Alonso Alvarez de la Campa
A176

1952, Oct. 7 *Perf. 10* Wmk. 106

484 A175 1c yellow green 25 15
485 " 2c scarlet 50 12
486 " 5c blue 50 20
487 " 8c black 1.50 50
488 " 10c brown red 1.50 50
489 " 20c brown 6.50 4.50
Nos. 484–489, C63–C72, E17 (17) 38.35 20.74

See note after No. 457.

Frame Engraved; Center Typographed in Black.

1952, Nov. 27

Portraits: 2c, Carlos A. Latorre. 3c, Anacleto Bermudez. 5c, Eladio G. Toledo. 8c, Angel Laborde. 10c, Jose M. Medina. 13c, Pascual Rodriguez. 20c, Carlos Verdugo.

490 A176 1c green 20 10
491 " 2c carmine 40 20
492 " 3c purple 50 20
493 " 5c blue 50 20
494 " 8c bistre brown 1.00 50
495 " 10c orange brown 90 40
496 " 13c lilac rose 1.75 60
497 " 20c olive green 2.50 1.00
Nos. 490–497, C73–C74 (10) 11.40 4.80

Issued to commemorate the 81st anniversary of the execution of eight medical students.

Christmas Type of 1951
Dated "1952-1953."
Frame Engraved; Center Typographed.

Centers: Tree.

1952, Dec. 1

498 A170 1c yellow green & carmine 4.00 1.25
499 " 3c vio. & dk. grn. 4.00 1.25

Birthplace of José Martí
A177

Marti at St. Lazarus Quarry
A178

Designs: No. 501, Court martial. No. 502, Martiano house, Havana. No. 504, El Abra ranch, Isle of Pines. No. 505, Symbols, "Marti the Poet." No. 506, Marti and Bolivar statue, Caracas. No. 507, At desk in New York. No. 508, House where revolutionary party was formed. No. 509, First issue of "Patria."

1953 Engraved. *Perf. 10.*

500 A177 1c dark green & red brown 15 8
501 " 1c dark green & red brown 15 6
502 " 3c purple & brown 30 8
503 A178 3c purple & brown 30 6
504 A177 5c deep blue & dark brown 50 20
505 A178 5c ultra. & brown 50 20
506 " 10c red brn. & blk. 1.25 40
507 " 10c dk. brn. & blk. 1.25 40
508 " 13c dark olive green & dark brown 2.00 75
509 A177 13c dark olive green & brown 2.00 1.00
Nos. 500–509, C79–C89 (21) 20.30 7.92

Centenary of birth of José Martí.

Rafael Montoro Valdez
A179

Francisco Carrera Justiz
A180

1953, Mar. 5

510 A179 3c dark violet 50 20

Issued to commemorate the centenary of the birth of Rafael Montoro Valdez, statesman.

1953, Mar. 9

511 A180 3c rose red 50 20

Issued to honor Francisco Carrera Justiz, educator and statesman.

No. 446 Surcharged with New Value.

1953, June 16

512 A146 3c on 2c rose red 40 15

Board of Accounts Bldg., Havana
A181

1953, Nov. 3 Engraved

513 A181 3c blue 40 15

Issued to publicize the First International Congress of Boards of Accounts, Havana, November 2–9, 1953.
See also Nos. C90–C91.

Miguel Coyula Llaguno
A182

Communications Association Flag
A183

Designs: 3c, 8c, Enrique Calleja Hensell. 10c, Antonio Ginard Rojas.

1954 Dated 1953.

514 A182 1c green 25 8
515 " 3c rose red 25 10
516 A183 5c blue 75 20
517 A182 8c brown carmine 1.25 50
518 " 10c brown 2.00 60
Nos. 514–518, C92–C95, E19 (10) 16.15 7.63

Nos. 515 and 517 show the same portrait, but inscriptions are arranged differently.
See note after No. 457.

José Marti
A184

Maximo Gomez
A184a

Portraits: 3c, José de la Luz Caballero. 4c, Miguel Aldama. 5c, Calixto Garcia. 8c, Ignacio Agramont. 10c, Tomas Estrada Palma. 13c, Carlos J. Finlay. 14c, Serafin Sanchez. 20c, José Antonio Saco. 50c, Antonio Maceo. 1p, Carlos Manuel de Cespedes.

1954–56 *Perf. 10.* Wmk. 106

519 A184 1c green 20 5
520 A184a 2c rose carmine 20 5
521 A184 3c violet 20 5
521A " 4c red lilac ('55) 25 6
522 A184a 5c slate blue 30 8
523 " 8c carmine lake 40 8
524 A184 10c sepia 40 8
525 " 13c orange red 75 15
525A A184a 14c gray ('56) 75 10
526 A184 20c olive 1.25 18
527 A184a 50c orange yellow 2.00 40
528 " 1p orange 3.50 60
Nos. 519–528 (12) 10.20 1.88

In 1962 the Castro government re-issued Nos. 519–520 in changed colors. On the 2c, "1833" is replaced by "?".

Maj. Gen. José M. Rodriguez
A185

Design: 5c, Gen. Rodriguez on horseback.

1954, June 8 Engraved *Perf. 12½*
Center in Dark Brown

529 A185 2c dark carmine 50 20
530 " 5c deep blue 1.00 40

Issued to commemorate the centenary of the birth of Maj. Gen. José Maria Rodriguez (in 1851).

Gen. Batista Sanatorium
A186

1954, Sept. 21 *Perf. 10* Wmk. 106

531 A186 3c deep blue 50 20

See also No. C107.

Santa Claus
A187

Maria Luisa Dolz
A188

1954, Dec. 15

532 A187 2c dk. green & car. 4.00 75
533 " 4c car. & dk. green 3.50 75

Christmas 1954.

1954, Dec. 23

534 A188 4c deep blue 50 20

Issued to commemorate the centenary of the birth of Maria Luisa Dolz, educator and defender of women's rights. See also No. C108.

Cuban Flag and Scouts Saluting
A189

1954, Dec. 27 *Perf. 12½*

535 A189 4c dark green 75 30

Issued to publicize the national patrol encampment of the Boy Scouts of Cuba.

Rotary Emblem and Paul P. Harris
A190

1955, Feb. 23 Engraved Wmk. 106

536 A190 4c blue 75 20

Rotary International, 50th anniversary.
See also No. C109.

Maj. Gen. Francisco Carrillo
A191

Portrait: 5c, Gen. Carrillo standing.

1955, Mar. 8 *Perf. 10*

537 A191 2c bright red & dark blue 40 15
538 " 5c dark blue & dark brown 75 25

Issued to commemorate the centenary of the birth of Maj. Gen. Francisco Carrillo (1851–1926).

Stamp of 1885 and Convent of San Francisco—A192

Designs (including 1855 stamp): 4c, Volanta carriage. 10c, Havana, 19th century. 14c, Captain general's residence.

1955, Apr. *Perf. 12½*

539 A192 2c lilac rose & dark greenish blue 50 20
540 " 4c ochre & dk. grn. 60 20
541 " 10c ultra. & dk. red 1.50 1.00
542 " 14c grn. & dp. org. 3.50 1.25
Nos. 539–542, C110–C113 (8) 12.20 6.15

Issued to commemorate the centenary of Cuba's first postage stamps.

Maj. Gen. Mario G. Menocal
A193

Gen. Emilio Nuñez
A194

Portraits: 10c, J. G. O. Gomez. 14c, A. Sanchez de Bustamente.

1955, June 22

543 A193 2c dark green 40 6
544 A194 4c lilac rose 50 8
545 A193 10c deep blue 75 35
546 A194 14c gray violet 1.50 50
Nos. 543–546, C114–C116, E20 (8) 11.65 5.69

See note after No. 457.

Turkey
A195

Gen. Emilio Nuñez
A196

1955, Dec. 15 Engraved

547 A195 2c slate green & dark carmine 3.75 75

548 A195 4c rose lake & bright green 3.75 60

Christmas 1955.

1955, Dec. 27

549 A196 4c claret 50 20

Issued to commemorate the centenary of the birth of Gen. Emilio Nuñez, Cuban revolutionary hero. See also Nos. C127-C128.

Francisco Cagigal de la Vega (1695-1777)
A197

Julian del Casal
A198

1956, Mar. 27 ***Perf. 12½***

552 A197 4c rose brown & slate blue 50 20

Issued to commemorate the bicentenary of the Cuban post. See also No. C129.

1956, May 2

Portraits: 4c, Luisa Perez de Zambrana. 10c, Juan Clemente Zenea. 14c, José Joaquin Palma.

Portraits in Black.

553 A198 2c green 30 10
554 " 4c rose lilac 40 12
555 " 10c blue 80 20
556 " 14c violet 1.00 25
Nos. 553-556, C131-C133, E21 (8) 7.10 2.41

See note after No. 457.

Victor Muñoz
A199

Masonic Temple, Havana
A200

1956, May 13

557 A199 4c brown & green 50 20

Issued in honor of Victor Muñoz (1873-1922), founder of Mother's Day in Cuba. See also No. C134.

1956, June 5

558 A200 4c blue 60 20

See also No. C135.

Virgin of Charity, El Cobre
A201

"The Cry of Yara"
A202

1956, Sept. 8 ***Perf. 12½***

559 A201 4c brt. blue & yel. 75 20

Issued in honor of Our Lady of Charity of Cobre, patroness of Cuba. See also No. C149.

1956, Oct. 10

560 A202 4c dk. green & brn. 50 20

Issued to commemorate Cuba's independence from Spain.

Raimundo G. Menocal
A203

The Three Wise Men
A204

1956, Dec. 3 ***Perf. 12½*** **Wmk. 106**

561 A203 4c dark brown 50 20

Issued to commemorate the centenary of the birth of Prof. Raimundo G. Menocal, physician.

1956, Dec. 1

562 A204 2c red & slate grn. 4.00 1.00
563 " 4c slate grn. & red 4.00 75

Christmas 1956.

Martin Morua Delgado
A205

Boy Scouts at Campfire
A206

1957, Jan. 30

564 A205 4c dark green 50 20

Issued to commemorate the centenary of the birth of Martin Morua Delgado, patriot.

1957, Feb. 22 ***Perf. 12½*** **Wmk. 106**

565 A206 4c slate green & red 90 35

Issued to commemorate the centenary of the birth of Lord Baden-Powell, founder of the Boy Scouts. See also No. C152.

"The Blind," by M. Vega
A207

Paintings: 4c, "The Art Critics" by M. Melero. 10c, "Volanta in Storm" by A. Menocal. 14c, "The Convalescent" by L. Romañach.

1957, Mar. **Engraved** ***Perf. 12½***

Side and Lower Inscriptions in Dark Brown.

566 A207 2c olive green 30 20
567 " 4c orange red 40 25
568 " 10c olive green 60 40
569 " 14c ultramarine 90 40
Nos. 566-569, C153-C155, E22 (8) 8.40 3.35

See note after No. 457.

Emblem of Philatelic Club of Cuba
A208

Juan F. Steegers
A209

1957, Apr. 24

570 A208 4c ochre, blue & red 60 20

Issued for Stamp Day, Apr. 24, and the National Philatelic Exhibition. See No. C156.

1957, Apr. 30

571 A209 4c blue 50 20

Issued in honor of the centenary of the birth of Juan Francisco Steegers y Perera (1856-1921), dactyloscopy pioneer. See No. C157.

Victoria Bru Sanchez
A210

Joaquin de Aguero in Battle of Jucaral
A211

1957, June 3 ***Perf. 12½*** **Wmk. 106**

572 A210 4c indigo 50 20

1957, July 4

573 A211 4c dark green 50 20

Issued to honor Joaquin de Aguero, Cuban freedom fighter and patriot. See No. C162.

Boy, Dogs and Cat
A212

Col. Rafael Manduley del Rio
A213

1957, July 17

574 A212 4c Prussian green 75 30

Issued in honor of Mrs. Jeanette Ryder, founder of the Humane Society of Cuba. See Nos. C163-C163a.

1957, July 31

575 A213 4c Prussian green 50 15

Issued to honor Col. Manduley del Rio, patriot, on the centenary of his birth (in 1856).

Palace of Justice
A214

1957, Sept. 2 **Engraved** ***Perf. 12½***

576 A214 4c blue gray 50 20

Issued to commemorate the opening of the new Palace of Justice in Havana. See also No. C165.

Generals of the Liberation
A215

1957, Sept. 26

577 A215 4c dull green & red brown 50 20
578 " 4c dull blue & red brown 50 20
579 " 4c rose & brown 50 20
580 " 4c orange yel. & brn. 50 20
581 " 4c lt. vio. & brown 50 20
Nos. 577-581 (5) 2.50 1.00

Issued to commemorate the Generals of the army of liberation.

First Publication Printed in Cuba
A216

Patio
A217

1957, Oct. 18 ***Perf. 12½*** **Wmk. 106**

582 A216 4c slate blue 50 15

Issued to publicize the José Martí National Library. See Nos. C167-C168.

1957, Nov. 19

583 A217 4c red brown & green 50 15

Issued to commemorate the centenary of the first Cuban Normal School. See also Nos. C173-C174.

Trinidad, Founded 1514
A218

Fortifications, Havana, 1611
A219

Views: 10c, Padre Pico street, Santiago de Cuba. 14c, Church of Our Lady, Camaguey.

1957, Dec. 17 **Engraved** ***Perf. 12½***

584 A218 2c brown & indigo 25 6
585 A219 4c slate green & brown 30 5
586 " 10c sepia & red 1.25 40
587 " 14c green & dk. red 1.00 20
Nos. 584-587, C175-C177, E23 (8) 7.55 2.56

See note after No. 457.

Nativity
A220

1957, Dec. 20

Center Multicolored.

588 A220 2c dark brown 3.50 1.00
589 " 4c dark slate green 3.50 75

Christmas 1957.

Dayton Hedges and Ariguanabo Textile Factory
A221

1958, Jan. 30 *Perf. 12½* Wmk. 106

590 A221 4c blue 50 15

Issued to honor Dayton Hedges, founder of Cuba's textile industry. See No. C178.

Dr. Francisco Dominguez Roldan
A222

José Ignacio Rivero y Alonso
A223

1958, Feb. 21

591 A222 4c green 50 15

Issued to honor Dr. Francisco Dominguez Roldan (1864–1942), who introduced radiotherapy and physiotherapy to Cuba.

1958, Apr. 1

592 A223 4c light olive green 50 15

Issued in honor of José Ignacio Rivero y Alonso, editor of Diario de la Marina, 1919–1944. See also No. C179.

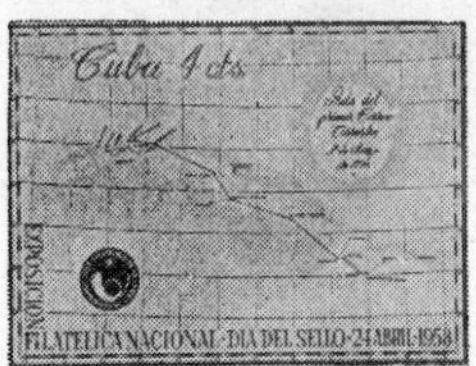

Map of Cuba and Mail Route, 1756
A224

1958, Apr. 24 ***Perf. 12½***

593 A224 4c dark green, aquamarine & buff 60 20

Issued for Stamp Day, Apr. 24 and the National Philatelic Exhibition. See No. C180.

Maj. Gen. José Miguel Gomez
A225

Nicolas Ruiz Espadero
A226

1958, June 6 *Perf. 12½* Wmk. 106

594 A225 4c slate 50 15

Issued in honor of Maj. Gen. José Miguel Gomez, President of Cuba, 1909–13. See No. C181.

1958, June 27 ***Perf. 12½***

Musicians: 4c, Ignacio Cervantes. 10c, José White. 14c, Brindis de Salas.

Indigo Emblem

595 A226 2c brown 50 10
596 " 4c dark gray 50 20
597 " 10c olive green 65 20
598 " 14c red 85 30

Physicians: 2c, Tomas Romay Chacon. 4c, Angel Arturo Aballi. 10c, Fernando Gonzalez del Valle. 14c, Vicente Antonio de Castro.

Green Emblem

599 A226 2c brown 50 10
600 " 4c gray 75 30
601 " 10c dark carmine 60 25
602 " 14c dark blue 75 30

Lawyers: 2c, Jose Maria Garcia Montes. 4c, Jose A. Gonzalez Lanuza. 10c, Juan B. Hernandez Barreiro. 14c, Pedro Gonzalez Llorente.

Red Emblem

603 A226 2c sepia 50 10
604 " 4c gray 75 30
605 A226 10c olive green 65 20
606 " 14c slate blue 85 30
Nos. 595-606 (12) 7.85 2.65

Carlos de la Torre
A227

Wmk. 321

Wmkd. "R de C" (321)

1958, Aug. 29 Engraved *Perf. 12½*

607 A227 4c violet blue 60 20

Issued to commemorate the centenary of the birth of Dr. Carlos de la Torre y Huerta (1858–1950), naturalist. See also Nos. C182–C184.

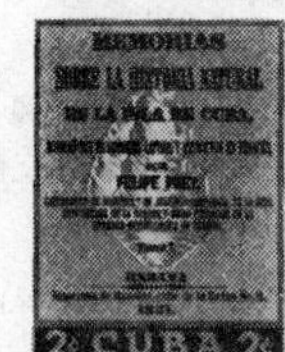

Poey's "Memorias" Title Page
A228

Felipe Poey
A229

1958, Sept. 26 Wmk. 106

608 A228 2c black & lt. violet 35 15
609 A229 4c brown black 45 15
Nos. 608-609, C185-C191, E26-E27 (11) 43.80 15.55

Issued in honor of Felipe Poey (1799–1891), naturalist.

Theodore Roosevelt
A230

Cattleyopsis Lindenii Orchid
A231

1958, Oct. 27 ***Perf. 12½***

610 A230 4c gray green 60 15

Issued to commemorate the centenary of the birth of Theodore Roosevelt. See No. C192.

Engraved & Photogravure

1958, Dec. 16 *Perf. 12½* Wmk. 321

Design: 4c, Oncidium Guibertianum Orchid.

611 A231 2c multicolored 3.50 1.00
612 " 4c " 4.00 1.00

Christmas 1958.

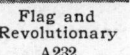

Flag and Revolutionary
A232

Gen. Adolfo Flor Crombet
A233

Engraved and Lithographed.

1959, Jan. 28 Wmk. 321

613 A232 2c car. rose & gray 30 15

Day of Liberation, Jan. 1, 1959.

1959, Mar. 18 Engr. Wmk. 106

614 A233 4c slate green 40 15

Issued in honor of General Adolfo Flor Crombet (1848-1895).

Maria Teresa Garcia Montes
A234

Carlos Manuel de Cespedes
A235

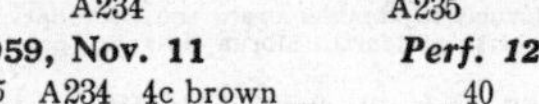

1959, Nov. 11 ***Perf. 12½***

615 A234 4c brown 40 15

Issued to honor Maria Teresa Garcia Montes (1880–1930), founder of the Musical Arts Society. See No. C198.

1959, Oct. 10 *Perf. 12½* Wmk. 106

Presidents: No. 617, Salvador Cisneros Betancourt. No. 618, Manuel de Jesus Calvar. No. 619, Bartolomé Maso. No. 620, Juan B. Spotorno. No. 621, Tomas Estrada Palma. No. 622, Francisco Javier de Céspedes. No. 623, Vicente Garcia.

616 A235 2c slate blue 40 10
617 " 2c green 40 10
618 " 2c deep violet 40 10
619 " 2c orange brown 40 10
620 " 4c dark carmine 50 20
621 " 4c deep brown 50 20
622 " 4c dark gray 50 20
623 " 4c dark violet 50 20
Nos. 616-623 (8) 3.60 1.20

Issued to honor former Cuban presidents.

No. B3 Surcharged in Red: "HABILITADO PARA / 2¢"

1960 Lithographed. Wmk. 321

624 SP2 2c on 2c+1c carmine & ultramarine 50 15

See also No. C199.

Rebel Attack on Moncada Barracks
A236

Designs: 2c, Rebels disembarking from "Granma." 10c, Battle of the Uvero. 12c, Map of Cuba and rebel ("The Invasion").

Wmkd. Interlacing Lines (320)

1960, Jan. 28 Engr. *Perf. 12½*

625 A236 1c gray olive, blue & vermilion 15 10
626 A236 2c blue, gray olive & brown 20 15
627 " 10c blue, gray olive & red 40 15
628 " 12c bright blue, brown & green 50 20
Nos. 625-628, C200-C202 (7) 4.35 1.60

First anniversary of revolution.

Stamps of 1956-59 Surcharged with New Value in Carmine or Silver

1960, Feb. 3

629 A226 1c on 4c dark gray & indigo 40 10
630 " 1c on 4c gray & green 60 25
631 " 1c on 4c gray & red 40 10
632 A227 1c on 4c violet blue 40 10
633 A231 1c on 4c multi. (S) 1.00 50
634 A233 1c on 4c slate green 35 10
635 A234 1c on 4c brown 40 10
636 A184a 2c on 14c gray 50 15
Nos. 629-636, C203-C204 (10) 5.55 2.00

Tomas Estrada Palma Statue, Havana
A237

Sailboats
A238

Statues: 2c, Mambi Victorioso (Battle of San Juan Hill), Santiago de Cuba. 10c, Marta Abreo de Estevez. 12c, Ignacio Agramonte, Camaguey.

Engraved

1960, Mar. 28 *Perf. 12½* Wmk. 321

637 A237 1c brown & dark blue 15 6
638 " 2c green & red 25 6
639 " 10c chocolate & red 60 20
640 " 12c gray olive & violet 90 30
Nos. 637-640, C206-C208 (7) 4.60 1.77

See note after No. 386

Nos. 521A, 522 and 525 Surcharged "HABILITADO / PARA / 2¢" in Violet Blue, Red or Black.

1960 *Perf. 10* Wmk. 106

641 A184 2c on 4c red lilac (VB) 50 15
642 A184a 2c on 5c slate blue (R) 60 15
643 A184 2c on 13c orange red 75 35

No. 307B Surcharged "HABILITADO / 10¢"

644 A41 10c on 20c olive grn. 50 20

Perf. 12½

1960, Sept. 22 Engr. Wmk. 321

Design: 2c, Marksman.

645 A238 1c light violet 30 20
646 " 2c orange 50 20

Issued to commemorate the 17th Olympic Games, Rome, Aug. 25–Sept. 11.
For souvenir sheet see No. C213a.

Camilo Cienfuegos and View of Escolar—A239

1960, Oct. 27 Litho. Unwmkd.

647 A239 2c brown, blue, green & red 25 10

Issued to commemorate the first anniversary of the death of Camilo Cienfuegos, revolutionary hero.

Morning Glory—A240

Tobacco and Christmas Hymn
A241

1960 Lithographed *Perf. 12½*

Flowers in Natural Colors

648 A240 1c red 50 40
649 A241 1c black & red (*Tobacco*) 75 60
650 " 1c black & red (*Mariposa*) 75 60
651 " 1c black & red (*Guaiacum*) 75 60
652 " 1c black & red (*Coffee*) 75 60
a. Block of four (1 each, #649-652) 3.50
653 A240 2c ultramarine 75 60
654 A241 2c black & ultra. (*Tobacco*) 2.25 1.75
655 " 2c black & ultra. (*Mariposa*) 2.25 1.75
656 " 2c black & ultra. (*Guaiacum*) 2.25 1.75
657 " 2c black & ultra. (*Coffee*) 2.25 1.75
a. Block of four (1 each, #654-657) 10.00
658 A240 10c ochre 2.25 1.50
659 A241 10c black & ochre (*Tobacco*) 6.00 4.00
660 " 10c black & ochre (*Mariposa*) 6.00 4.00
661 " 10c black & ochre (*Guaiacum*) 6.00 4.00
662 " 10c black & ochre (*Coffee*) 6.00 4.00
a. Block of four (1 each, #659-662) 27.50
Nos. 648-662 (15) 39.50 27.90

Issued for Christmas 1960.

Nos. 648-662 were printed in three sheets of 25. Nine stamps of type A240 form a center cross; stamps of type A241 form a block of four in each corner with the musical bars joined in an oval around the floral designs.

"Public Capital for Economic Benefit"
A242

Designs: 2c, Chart and symbols of agriculture and industry. 6c, Cogwheels.

Photogravure

1961, Jan. 10 *Perf. 11½* Unwmkd.

663 A242 1c yel., black & org. 15 5
664 " 2c blue, black & red 15 5
665 " 6c yellow, red orange & black 40 15
Nos. 663-665, C215-C218 (7) 4.20 2.15

Issued to publicize the conference of underdeveloped countries, Havana.

Jesus Menéndez and Sugar Cane
A243

1961, Jan. 22 Litho. *Perf. 12½*

666 A243 2c dk. grn. & brown 20 10

Jesus Menéndez, leader in sugar industry.

Same Overprinted in Red:
"PRIMERO DE MAYO 1961
ESTAMOS VENCIENDO"

1961, May 2

667 A243 2c dark green & brown 60 40

Issued for May Day, 1961.

Dove and U.N. Emblem
A244

1961, Apr. 12 Litho. *Perf. 12½*

668 A244 2c red brown & yellow green 30 10
669 " 10c emerald & rose lilac 50 20
a. Souvenir sheet 1.50

Issued to commemorate the 15th anniversary (in 1960) of the United Nations.

See also Nos. C222-C223.

No. 669a contains one each of Nos. 668-669, imperf. with red brown marginal inscription. Size: 107x65mm.

Maceo Stamp of 1907 and 1902 Simulated Cancel
A245

Designs: 1c, Revolutionary 10c stamp of 1874 and 1868 "cancel." 10c, Stamp of 1959 (No. 613) and "cancel."

1961, Apr. 24 Unwmkd.

670 A245 1c dull rose & dark green 25 20
671 " 2c salmon & dk. grn. 25 20
672 " 10c pale green, carmine rose & black 50 30

Issued for Stamp Day, Apr. 24.

Hand Releasing Dove
A246

1961, July 26 *Perf. 12½*

673 A246 2c black, red, yellow & gray 30 10

Issued to commemorate the 26th of July (1953) movement, Castro's revolt against Fulgencio Batista.

Burelage on back consisting of wavy lines and diagonal rows of "CUBA CORREOS" in pale salmon.

Importation Prohibited

Cuban stamps issued after No. 673 have not been listed because the embargo on trade with Cuba, proclaimed Feb. 7, 1962, by President Kennedy, prohibits the importation from any country of stamps of Cuban origin, used or unused.

SEMI-POSTAL STAMPS.

Pierre and Marie Curie
SP1

Wmkd. Star. (106)

1938, Nov. 23 Engraved *Perf. 10*

B1 SP1 2c+1c salmon 3.00 1.00
B2 " 5c+1c deep ultra. 3.00 1.25

Issued in commemoration of the 40th anniversary of the discovery of radium by Pierre and Marie Curie. The surtax was for the benefit of the International Union for the Control of Cancer.

"Agriculture" Supporting "Industry"
SP2

Perf. 12½

1959, May 7 Litho. Wmk. 321

B3 SP2 2c+1c car. & ultra. 35 15

Agricultural reforms. See Nos. 624, CB1.

Nurse—SP3

Perf. 12½, Imperf.

1959, Sept. 22 Wmk. 229

B4 SP3 2c+1c crimson rose 30 15

AIR POST STAMPS.

Seaplane over Havana Harbor
AP1

Wmkd. Star. (106)

1927, Nov. 1 Engraved *Perf. 12*

C1 AP1 5c dark blue 1.50 15

Type of 1927 Issue Overprinted

LINDBERGH
FEBRERO 1928

1928, Feb. 8

C2 AP1 5c carmine rose 2.00 1.00

No. 283 Surcharged in Red

CORREO AEREO NACIONAL
10¢ 10¢

1930, Oct. 27 Unwmkd.

C3 A44 10c on 25c violet 2.25 1.00

Airplane and Coast of Cuba
AP3

For Foreign Postage.

1931, Feb. 26 *Perf. 10* Wmk. 106

C4 AP3 5c green 25 5
C5 " 10c dark blue 40 5
C6 " 15c rose 90 30
C7 " 20c brown 1.00 6
C8 " 30c dark violet 1.25 15
C9 " 40c deep orange 3.00 40
C10 " 50c olive green 3.50 30
C11 " 1p black 5.00 85
Nos. C4-C11 (8) 15.30 2.16

See also No. C40.

Airplane
AP4

For Domestic Postage.

1931-46

C12 AP4 5c rose violet ('32) 35 6
a. 5c brown violet ('36) 35 6
C13 AP4 10c gray black 35 5
C14 " 20c carmine rose 2.50 75
C14A " 20c rose pink ('46) 1.00 20
C15 " 50c dark blue 4.00 75
Nos. C12-C15 (5) 8.20 1.81

See also No. C130.

Type of 1931 Surcharged in Black

PRIMER TREN AEREO
INTERNACIONAL. 1935
O'Meara y du Pont +10 cts.

1935, Apr. 24 *Perf. 10*

C16 AP3 10c+10c red 6.00 5.00

Imperf.

C17 AP3 10c+10c red 27.50 27.50

Matanzas Issue.

Air View of Matanzas
AP5

Designs: 10c, Airship "Macon." 20c, Airplane "The Four Winds." 50c, Air View of Fort San Severino.

Photogravure.

Wmkd. Wavy Lines. (229)

1936, May 5 *Perf. 12½*

C18 AP5 5c violet 60 40
C19 " 10c yellow orange 1.20 60
C20 " 20c green 4.00 2.75
C21 " 50c greenish slate 7.50 5.00

Exist imperf. Price 20 more.

"Lightning"
AP9

Allegory of Flight
AP10

1936, Nov. 18

C22 AP9 5c violet 3.00 75
C23 AP10 10c orange brown 3.50 1.25

Issued in commemoration of the centenary of the birth of Major General Máximo Gómez.

Flat Arch (Panama)
AP11

Carlos Antonio López (Paraguay)
AP12

Inca Gate, Cuzco (Peru)
AP13

Atlacatl (Salvador)
AP14

José Enrique Rodó (Uruguay)
AP15

Simón Bolívar (Venezuela)
AP16

Engraved.

1937, Oct. 13 *Perf. 10* Wmk. 106

C24 AP11 5c red 4.50 4.50
C25 AP12 5c red 4.50 4.50
C26 AP13 10c blue 5.00 5.00
C27 AP14 10c blue 5.00 5.00
C28 AP15 20c green 7.00 7.00
C29 AP16 20c green 7.00 7.00
Nos. C24-C29 (6) 33.00 33.00

Issued for the benefit of the Association of American Writers and Artists. See note after No. 354.

Type of 1927 Overprinted in Black

1913 1938
ROSILLO
Key West-Habana

1938, May Wmk. 106

C30 AP1 5c dark orange 5.00 1.50

Issued in commemoration of the first airplane flight from Key West to Havana, made by Domingo Rosillo, 1913.

Type of 1931-32 Overprinted

EXPERIMENTO DEL
COHETE
Postal
AÑO DE 1939

1939, Oct. 15

C31 AP4 10c emerald 25.00 7.50

Issued in connection with an experimental postal rocket flight held at Havana.

Sir Rowland Hill, Map of Cuba and First Stamps of Britain, Spanish Cuba and Republic of Cuba
AP17

1940, Nov. 28 Engr. Wmk. 106

C32 AP17 10c brown 3.50 1.25

Souvenir Sheet
Imperf.
Unwmkd.

C33 AP17 10c light brown, sheet of four 7.50 5.00
a. Single stamp 1.75 1.00

Centenary of the first postage stamp.

Sheet measures 128x178mm. Sheet sold for 60c.

No. C33 exists with each of the four stamps overprinted in black: "Exposicion de la ACNU/24 de Octubre de 1951/Dia de las Naciones" and "Historia de la Aviacion" in lower margin. Price $60.

Poet José Heredia and Palms
AP18

Heredia and Niagara Falls
AP19

1940, Dec. 30 Wmk. 106

C34 AP18 5c emerald 1.25 75
C35 AP19 10c greenish slate 2.50 1.00

Issued to commemorate the centenary of the death of José Maria Heredia y Campuzano (1803-1839), poet and patriot.

First Cuban Land Sighted by Columbus
AP20

Columbus Lighthouse
AP21

1944, May 19

C36 AP20 5c olive green 75 20
C37 AP21 10c slate black 1.50 50

Issued to commemorate the 450th anniversary of the discovery of America.

Conference of La Mejorana (Meceo, Gomez and Marti)
AP22

1948, May 21 *Perf. 12½* Wmk. 229

C38 AP22 8c orange yellow & black 2.00 75

Issued to commemorate the 50th anniversary of the start of the War of 1895.

Souvenir Sheet.
No. C33 Overprinted in Ultramarine

1948, May 21 *Imperf.* Unwmkd.

C39 AP17 10c light brown, sheet of four 7.00 6.00

The overprint is applied in the center of the four stamps, so that a portion falls on each.

Issued in honor of the American Air Mail Society Convention, Havana, May 21 to 23, 1948. The sheets sold for 60c each.

Type of 1931.

1948, June 15 *Perf. 10* Wmk. 106

C40 AP3 8c orange brown 1.25 20

Narciso Lopez Landing at Cárdenas
AP23

Flag on Cuban Fort
AP24

Flag on Morro Castle, Havana
AP25

Engraved and Lithographed.

1951, July 3 *Perf. 13* Wmk. 229

C41 AP23 5c olive green, ultramarine & red 1.00 25
C42 AP24 8c red brown, blue & red 1.50 25
C43 AP25 25c gray black, blue & red 2.50 1.25

Centenary of adoption of Cuba's flag.

Souvenir Sheet.
No. 365a Overprinted in Green.

CORREO AEREO

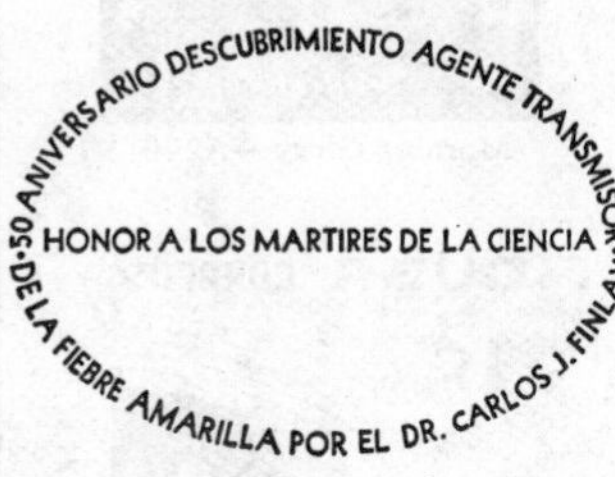

1901 1951

(Reduced Illustration of Overprint)

1951, Aug. 24 *Imperf.* Unwmkd.

C43A Sheet of four 5.00 4.50

Issued to commemorate the 50th anniversary of the discovery of the cause of yellow fever by Dr. Carlos J. Finlay, and to honor the martyrs of science.

No. C43A measures 127x177 mm. and contains two each of Nos. 364 and 365 imperforate, with upper and lower marginal inscriptions.

Resignation Play of Dr. Lasker
AP26

Capablanca Making "The Exact Play"
AP27

Design: 25c, Capablanca.

Photogravure.

1951, Nov. 1 *Perf. 13* Wmk. 229

C44 AP26 5c bl. grn. & yel. 2.50 75
C45 AP27 8c ultramarine & claret 4.00 1.00
C46 A165 25c brown & dark brown 7.50 3.00

Issued to commemorate the 30th anniversary of the winning of the World Chess title by José Raul Capablanca.

Morrillo Types of Regular Issue, 1951.

Engraved.

1951, Nov. 22 *Perf. 10* Wmk. 106

C47 A167 5c violet 80 15
C48 A168 8c deep green 1.00 20
C49 A169 25c dark brown 2.00 1.25
a. Souvenir sheet of 6, black brown, perf. 13 20.00 20.00
b. Souvenir sheet of 6, green, imperf. 75.00 75.00

Issued to commemorate the 16th anniversary of the Action of the Morrillo and to honor Antonio Guiteras Holmes who was killed there.

Nos. C49a and C49b contain one each of the 1c, 2c and 5c of types A167-A169 and of the 5c, 8c and 25c airmail stamps of types A167-A169. Marginal inscriptions are typographed in black; coat of arms engraved in color of stamps (black brown or green). Sheets are unwatermarked and measure 124x133mm

Isabella Type of Regular Issue, 1952

1952, Feb. 22

C50 A172 25c purple 2.50 1.00
  a. Souvenir sheet of 2, perf. 11 10.00 9.00
  b. Souvenir sheet of 2, imperf. 13.00 12.00

Issued to commemorate the 500th anniversary of the birth of Queen Isabella I of Spain.

Nos. C50a and C50b contain one each of a 2c of type A172 and a 25c air-mail stamp of type A172. In No. C50a, the 2c and marginal inscriptions are brown carmine; the 25c, dark blue. In No. C50b, the 2c and marginal inscriptions are dark blue; the 25c, brown carmine. Sheets measure 108x108mm.

Type of Regular Issue of 1951 Surcharged in Various Colors

5¢

AEREO

1952, Mar. 18

C51 A159 5c on 2c yel. brn. 40 15
C52 " 8c on 2c yellow brown (C) 75 10
C53 " 10c on 2c yellow brown (Bl) 75 12
C54 " 25c on 2c yellow brown (V) 1.25 80
C55 " 50c on 2c yellow brown (C) 4.00 1.75
C56 " 1p on 2c yellow brown (Bl) 10.00 6.00
Nos. C51-C56 (6) 17.15 8.92

Country School
AP32

Entrance, University of Havana
AP33

Designs: 10c, Presidential Mansion. 25c, Banknote.

Engraved.

1952, May 27 *Perf. 12½* Wmk. 106

Centers Various Shades of Green.

C57 AP32 5c dark purple 50 10
C58 AP33 8c dark red 65 15
C59 AP32 10c deep blue 1.25 20
C60 " 25c dk. vio. brn. 2.00 1.00

Issued to commemorate the 50th anniversary of the foundation of the Republic of Cuba.

Plane and Map
AP34

Agustin Parlá
AP35

Engraved

1952, July 22 *Perf. 10*

C61 AP34 8c black 75 25
  a. Souvenir sheet, 8c deep blue 5.00 5.00
  b. Souvenir sheet, 8c deep green 5.00 5.00
C62 AP35 25c ultramarine 2.00 1.00
  a. Souvenir sheet, 25c deep blue 5.00 5.00
  b. Souvenir sheet, 25c deep green 5.00 5.00

Issued to commemorate the 30th anniversary of the Key West-Mariel flight of Agustin Parla.

The four souvenir sheets are perf. 11, measure 107x95mm. and have marginal inscriptions in the same color as the stamp.

Col. Charles Hernandes y Sandrino
AP36

1952, Oct. 7

C63 AP36 5c orange 60 12
C64 " 8c brt. yel. green 75 10
C65 " 10c dark brown 1.00 25
C66 " 15c dark Prussian green 1.75 65
C67 " 20c aquamarine 2.00 85
C68 " 25c crimson 1.50 80
C69 " 30c dark violet blue 4.00 2.25
C70 " 45c rose lilac 4.00 2.75
C71 " 50c indigo 2.50 2.25
C72 " 1p bistre 7.50 4.00
Nos. C63-C72 (10) 25.60 14.02

Three-fourths of the proceeds from the sale of Nos. C63-C72 were used for the Communications Ministry Employees' Retirement Fund.

Entrance, University of Havana
AP37

F. V. Dominguez, M. Estebanez and F. Capdevila—AP38

Engraved; Centers Typographed.

1952, Nov. 27

C73 AP37 5c indigo & dark blue 90 35
C74 AP38 25c orange & dark green 2.75 1.25

Issued to commemorate the 81st anniversary of the execution of eight medical students.

AP39

Lockheed Constellation Airliners
AP40

1953, May 22 Engraved.

C75 AP39 8c orange brown 40 6
C76 " 15c scarlet 1.50 30

Typographed and Engraved

C77 AP40 2p deep green & dark brown 20.00 10.00
C78 " 5p blue & dark brown 30.00 15.00

See also Nos. C120-C121.

Page of Manifesto of Montecristi
AP42

House of Maximo Gomez
AP43

Designs: No. C79, Marti in Kingston, Jamaica. No. C80, With Workers in Tampa, Florida. No. C83, Marti addressing liberating army. No. C84, Portrait. No. C85, Dos Rios obelisk. No. C86, Marti's first tomb. No. C87, Present tomb. No. C88, Monument in Havana. No. C89, Martian forge.

1953 Engraved *Perf. 10*

C79 AP42 5c dark carmine & black 30 12
C80 " 5c dk. car. & black 30 12
C81 AP43 8c dark green & black 40 10
C82 AP42 8c dk. grn. & black 40 10
C83 AP43 10c dark blue & dark carmine 1.00 25
C84 AP42 10c dark blue & dark carmine 1.00 25
C85 " 15c violet & gray 75 50
C86 " 15c violet & gray 75 50
C87 " 25c brn. & carmine 2.00 75
C88 " 25c brn. & carmine 2.00 75
C89 AP43 50c yellow & blue 3.00 1.25
Nos. C79-C89 (11) 11.90 4.69

Issued to commemorate the centenary of the birth of José Martí.

Board of Accounts Building
AP44

Design: 25c, Plane above Board of Accounts Bldg.

1953, Nov. 3

C90 AP44 8c rose carmine 1.00 25
C91 " 25c dk. gray green 2.00 1.00

Issued to publicize the First International Congress of Boards of Account, Havana, November 2-9, 1953.

Miguel Coyula Llaguno
AP45

Antonio Ginard Rojas
AP46

Designs: 10c, Gregorio Hernandez Saez. 1p, Communications Association Flag.

1954

C92 AP45 5c dark blue 40 10
C93 AP46 8c red violet 50 15
C94 " 10c orange 1.00 25
C95 AP45 1p black 7.50 5.00

See note after No. C72.

Four-engine Plane and Cane Field
AP47

Plane and Harvesters Cutting Cane
AP48

Designs in Lower Triangle: 10c, Tractor pulling loaded wagons. 15c, Train of sugar cane. 20c, Modern mill. 25c, Evaporators. 30, Sacks of sugar. 40c, Loading sugar on ship. 45c, Ox cart. 50c, Primitive sugar mill. 1p, Alvaro Reinoso.

1954, Apr. 27 Engraved

C96 AP47 5c yellow green 50 8
C97 AP48 8c brown 1.00 8
C98 " 10c dark green 1.20 15
C99 " 15c henna brown 60 30
C100 " 20c blue 75 35
C101 " 25c scarlet 1.25 35
C102 " 30c lilac rose 1.75 40
C103 " 40c deep blue 2.25 75
C104 " 45c violet 4.50 1.50
C105 " 50c bright blue 3.00 75
C106 AP47 1p dark gray blue 6.00 1.50
Nos. C96-C106 (11) 22.80 6.21

Sanatorium Type of Regular Issue, 1954.

1954, Sept. 21 *Perf. 10* Wmk. 106

C107 A186 9c deep green 1.00 50

Dolz Type of Regular Issue, 1954.

1954, Dec. 23

C108 A188 12c carmine 1.00 50

Issued to commemorate the centenary of the birth of Maria Luisa Dolz, educator and defender of women's rights.

Rotary Type of Regular Issue, 1955.

1955, Feb. 23

C109 A190 12c carmine 1.25 40

Issued to commemorate the 50th anniversary of the founding of Rotary International.

Stamps of 1855 and 1905, Palace of Fine Arts
AP52

Designs (including 2 stamps): 12c, Plaza de la Fraternidad. 24c, View of Havana. 30c, Plaza de la Republica.

1955, Apr. 24 *Perf. 12½*

C110 AP52 8c dark greenish blue & green 75 40
C111 " 12c dark olive green & red 1.00 35
C112 " 24c dk. red & ultra. 1.35 1.00
C113 " 30c deep orange & brown 3.00 1.75

Issued to commemorate the centenary of Cuba's first postage stamps.

Mariel Bay—AP53

Views: 12c, Varadero beach. 1p, Vinales valley.

1955, June 22 Wmk. 106

C114 AP53 8c dark carmine & dk. green 75 30
C115 " 12c dark ochre & bright blue 1.00 25
C116 " 1p dark green & ochre 5.00 3.50

See note after No. C72.

Map of Crocier's 1914 Flight
AP54

Design: 30c, Jaime Gonzalez Crocier in plane.

1955, July 4 *Perf. 10*

C117 AP54 12c red & dark green 60 20
C118 " 30c dark green & magenta 2.25 60

Issued to honor Jaime Gonzalez Crocier, aviation pioneer, on the 35th anniversary of his death.

Cuban Museum, Tampa, Fla.
AP55

1955, July 1 **Engr.** *Perf. 12½*

C119 AP55 12c red & dark brown 1.10 35

Issued to commemorate the centenary of Tampa's incorporation as a town.

Lockheed Type of 1953
Typographed and Engraved

1955, Sept. 21 **Wmk. 106**

C120 AP40 2p blue & olive green 12.50 7.50
C121 " 5p deep rose & olive green 30.00 15.00

Wright Brothers' Plane and Stamps
AP56

Designs: 12c, Spirit of St. Louis. 24c, Graf Zeppelin. 30c, Constellation passenger plane. 50c, Convair jet fighter.

Engraved and Photogravure.

1955, Nov. 12 *Perf. 12½* **Wmk. 106**

Inscription and Plane in Black.

C122 AP56 8c carmine & blue 90 30
C123 " 12c yellow green & carmine 1.25 40
C124 " 24c violet & carmine 1.75 1.00
C125 " 30c blue & red orange 3.50 2.00
C126 " 50c olive green & red orange 4.50 2.25
a. Souvenir sheet of 5 20.00 20.00
Nos. C122-C126 (5) 11.90 5.95

Issued to commemorate the International Centenary Philatelic Exhibition in Havana, Nov. 12-19, 1955.

No. C126a is printed on thick paper and measures 140x178mm. It contains one each of Nos. C122-C126 with the background of each stamp printed in a different color from the perforated stamps. The sheet is inscribed in black "Republica de Cuba. Souvenir. Exposition Filatelica Internacional Centenario 1955" and "XXXII Convencion de la American Airmail Society."

"Three Friends" and Gen. Emilio Nuñez
AP57

Design: 12c, Landing on the Cuban Coast.

1955, Dec. 27 **Engraved** **Unwmkd.**

C127 AP57 8c ultramarine & dark carmine 1.00 40
C128 " 12c green & dark red brown 1.50 50

Issued to commemorate the centenary of the birth of Gen. Emilio Nuñez, Cuban revolutionary hero.

Post Type of Regular Issue, 1956.

Design: 12c, Bishop P. A. Morell de Santa Cruz (1694-1768).

1956, March 27 **Wmk. 106**

C129 A197 12c dark brown & green 90 30

Bicentenary of the Cuban post.

Plane Type of 1931-46.

1956 **Engraved** *Perf. 10*

C130 AP4 50c greenish blue 2.00 1.00

Portrait Type of Regular Issue, 1956.

1956, May 2 *Perf. 12½*

Portraits: 8c, Gen. Julio Sanguily. 12c, Gen. José Maria Aguirre. 30c, Col. Ernesto Ponts Sterling.

Portraits in Black.

C131 A198 8c brown 45 12
C132 " 12c dull yellow 90 12
C133 " 30c indigo 1.50 1.00

See note after No. C72.

Mother and Child
AP60

Masonic Temple Havana
AP61

1956, May 13 *Perf. 12½* **Wmk. 106**

C134 AP60 12c ultra. & red 80 25

Issued in honor of Mother's Day 1956.

1956, June 5

C135 AP61 12c olive green 60 20

Pigeon
AP62

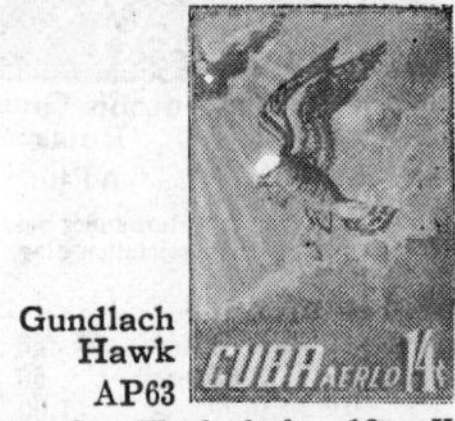

Gundlach Hawk
AP63

Birds: 8c, Wood duck. 19c, Herring gulls. 24c, White pelicans. 29c, Common merganser. 30c, Quail. 50c, Herons (great white, great blue and Wurdemann's). 1p, Northern caracara. 2p, Middle American jacana. 5p, Ivory-billed woodpecker.

1956

C136 AP62 8c blue 40 12
C137 " 12c dark blue 5.00 10
C138 AP63 14c green 1.00 20
C139 " 19c reddish brown 75 35
C140 " 24c lilac rose 90 35
C141 AP62 29c green 1.25 40
C142 " 30c dark olive bistre 1.50 50
C143 AP63 50c slate black 2.50 60
C144 " 1p dk. car. rose 4.00 1.25
C145 AP62 2p rose violet 7.50 2.50
C146 AP63 5p bright red 18.00 5.00
Nos. C136-C146 (11) 42.80 11.37

See also No. C205.

Type of 1956 Surcharged

Inauguración Edificio Club Filatélico de la República de Cuba Julio 13 de 1956.

Design: 24c, White pelicans.

1956, July 13

C147 AP63 8c on 24c dp. org. 1.00 35

Issued to commemorate the opening of the new building of the Cuba Philatelic Club, Havana, July 14, 1956.

Hubert de Blanck
AP64

Church of Our Lady of Charity
AP65

1956, July 6

C148 AP64 12c ultramarine 90 25

Issued to commemorate the centenary of the birth of Hubert de Blanck (1856-1932), composer.

1956, Sept. 8

C149 AP65 12c green & carmine 90 40
a. Souvenir sheet of 2, imperf. 6.00 4.00

Issued in honor of Our Lady of Charity of Cobre, patroness of Cuba.

No. C149a contains one each of Nos. 559 and C149 with bright blue marginal inscription and coat of arms. Size: 76x77mm. No. C149a exists with yellow of No. 559 omitted.

Benjamin Franklin
AP66

1956, Oct. 5 **Engr.** *Perf. 12½*

C150 AP66 12c red brown 1.00 40

Issued to commemorate the 250th anniversary of the birth of Benjamin Franklin.

Type of 1956 Surcharged in Blue

Design: 2p, Middle American jacana.

1956, Oct. 26 **Wmk. 106**

C151 AP62 12c on 2p dk. gray 1.50 75

Issued in honor of the 12th Inter-American Press Association Conference, Havana.

Lord Baden-Powell
AP67

1957, Feb. 22

C152 AP67 12c slate 1.50 35

Issued to commemorate the centenary of the birth of Lord Baden-Powell, founder of the Boy Scouts.

Hanabanilla Waterfall
AP68

Designs: 12c, Sierra de Cubitas. 30c, Puerto Boniato.

1957, March 29

C153 AP68 8c blue & red 75 20
C154 " 12c green & red 1.20 25
C155 " 30c olive green & dark purple 2.00 1.00

See note after No. 457.

Philatelic Club, Havana
AP69

Fingerprint
AP70

1957, Apr. 24 *Perf. 12½* **Wmk. 106**

C156 AP69 12c yellow, green & brown 1.00 25

Issued for Stamp Day, Apr. 24, and the National Philatelic Exhibition.

1957, Apr. 30

C157 AP70 12c claret brown 90 20

Issued in honor of the centenary of the birth (in 1856) of Juan Francisco Steegers y Perera, dactyloscopy pioneer.

Baseball Player
AP71

Designs: 12c, Ballerina. 24c, Girl diver. 30c, Boxers.

1957, May 17 *Perf. 12½* **Wmk. 106**

C158 AP71 8c olive green & brown 50 20
C159 " 12c pale violet & brown 1.00 20
C160 " 24c bright blue & brown 1.75 60
C161 " 30c orange & brn. 2.00 90

Issued to honor young Cuban athletes.

Joaquin de Aguero
AP72

Jeanette Ryder
AP73

1957, July 4

C162 AP72 12c indigo 90 25

Issued to honor Joaquin de Aguero, Cuban freedom fighter and patriot.

1957, July 17

C163 AP73 12c dark red brown 90 35
a. Se-tenant with No. 574 2.00 1.00

Printed in sheets of 40, containing alternate copies of Nos. 574 and C163 to honor Mrs. Jeanette Ryder, founder of the Humane Society of Cuba.

José M. de Heredia y Girard
AP74

John Robert Gregg
AP75

1957, Aug. 16 Engr. Wmk. 106

C164 AP74 8c dark blue violet 50 25

Issued in honor of the poet José Maria de Heredia y Girard (1842–1905), Cuban-born French poet.

Justice Type of Regular Issue, 1957.

1957, Sept. 2 ***Perf. 12½***

C165 A214 12c green 90 50

Opening of Palace of Justice, Havana.

1957, Oct. 1

C166 AP75 12c dark green 80 35

Issued to commemorate the 90th anniversary of the birth of John Robert Gregg, inventor of the Gregg shorthand system.

D. Figarola Caneda
AP76

José Marti National Library
AP77

1957, Oct. 18 ***Perf. 12½*** **Wmk. 106**

C167 AP76 8c ultramarine 50 20
C168 AP77 12c chocolate 90 25

Issued to publicize the José Marti National Library.

Map of Cuba and U. N. Emblem
AP78

1957, Oct. 24

C169 AP78 8c dark green & brown 75 25
C170 " 12c carmine rose & green 1.00 50
C171 " 30c indigo & bright pink 2.50 1.00

Issued for United Nations Day, 1957.

Map of Cuba and Florida
AP79

1957, Oct. 28

C172 AP79 12c dark red brown & blue 85 40

Issued to commemorate the 30th anniversary of airmail service from Key West to Havana.

Type of Regular Issue, 1957 and

Stairway and Bell Tower
AP80

Design: 12c, Facade of Normal School.

1957, Nov. 19 Engraved. ***Perf. 12½***

C173 A217 12c indigo & ochre 85 20
C174 AP80 30c dark carmine & gray 1.25 60

Issued to commemorate the centenary of the first Cuban Normal School.

View Types of Regular Issue, 1957.

Views: 8c, El Viso Fort, El Caney. 12c, Sancti Spiritus Church. 30c, Concordia Bridge, Matanzas.

1957, Dec. 17 ***Perf. 12½***

C175 A218 8c dk. gray & red 75 25
C176 A219 12c brown & gray 1.00 25
C177 A218 30c red brown & blue gray 1.50 85

See note after No. C72.

Hedges Types of Regular Issue, 1958.

Design: 8c, Dayton Hedges and Matanzas rayon factory.

1958, Jan. 30 ***Perf. 12½*** **Wmk. 106**

C178 A221 8c green 80 40

Issued to honor Dayton Hedges, founder of Cuba's textile industry.

Diario de la Marina Building
AP81

1958, April 1

C179 AP81 29c black 3.00 2.00

Issued in honor of Jose Ignacio Rivero y Alonso, editor of the newspaper, Diario de la Marina.

Map Showing Sea Mail Route, 1765
AP82

1958, Apr. 24 ***Perf. 12½*** **Wmk. 106**

C180 AP82 29c dark blue aqua. & buff 2.25 1.25

Issued for Stamp Day, Apr. 24, and the National Philatelic Exhibition.

Gen. Gomez in Battle
AP83

Snail (Polymita Picta)
AP84

1958, June 6 Engraved

C181 AP83 12c slate green 70 25

Issued in honor of Maj. Gen. José Miguel Gomez, President of Cuba, 1909-13.

1958, Aug. 29 ***Perf. 12½*** **Wmk. 321**

Fossils: 12c, Megalocnus Rodens. 30c, Ammonite.

C182 AP84 8c gray, red & yellow 1.50 75
C183 " 12c brown, *yellow green* 2.50 1.25
C184 " 30c green, *pink* 3.50 1.75

Issued to commemorate the centenary of the birth of Dr. Carlos de la Torre, naturalist.

Papilio Caiguanabus
AP85

Cuban Sea Bass
AP86

Designs: 12c, Teria gundlachia. 14c, Teria ebriola. 19c, Nathalis felicia. 29c, Butter Hamlet. 30c, Tattler.

1958, Sept. 26 ***Perf. 12½*** **Wmk. 106**

C185 AP85 8c multicolored 1.75 50
C186 " 12c emerald, blk. & orange 2.00 50
C187 " 14c multicolored 3.00 75
C188 " 19c blue, black & yellow 3.75 1.00
C189 AP86 24c multicolored 4.50 1.00
C190 " 29c blk., brown & ultra. 7.00 1.25
C191 " 30c black, yellow grn. & sepia 8.00 1.75
Nos. C185–C191 (7) 30.00 6.75

Issued in honor of Felipe Poey (1799–1891), naturalist.

Battle of San Juan Hill, 1898
AP87

Engraved.

1958, Oct. 27 ***Perf. 12½*** **Wmk. 106**

C192 AP87 12c black brown 90 30

Birth centenary of Theodore Roosevelt.

UNESCO Building, Paris
AP88

Design: 30c, "UNESCO" and map of Cuba.

1958, Nov. 7

C193 AP88 12c dk. slate grn. 1.00 40
C194 " 30c dp. ultra. 2.25 1.35

Issued to commemorate the opening of UNESCO (U. N. Educational, Scientific and Cultural Organization) Headquarters in Paris, Nov. 3.

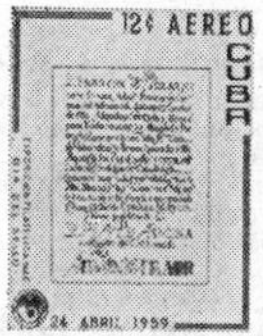

Postal Notice of 1765
AP89

Musical Arts Building
AP90

Design: 30c, Administrative postal book of St. Cristobal, Havana, 1765.

1959, Apr. 24 ***Perf. 12½*** **Wmk. 321**

C195 AP89 12c Prussian blue & sepia 75 25
C196 " 30c sepia & Prus. blue 1.25 85

Issued for Stamp Day, Apr. 24, and the National Philatelic Exhibition.

Type of 1956 Surcharged with New Value, Bar and "ASTA" Emblem in Dark Blue.

1959, Oct. 17 ***Perf. 12½*** **Wmk. 321**

C197 AP63 12c on 1p emerald 1.00 40

Issued to publicize the meeting of the American Society of Travel Agents, Oct. 17-23.

Engraved.

1959, Nov. 11 ***Perf. 12½*** **Wmk. 106**

C198 AP90 12c yellow green 90 25

Issued to commemorate the 40th anniversary of the Musical Arts Society.

No. CB1 Surcharged in Red: "HABILITADO PARA / 12c"

Engraved and Lithographed

1960 ***Perf. 12½*** **Wmk. 321**

C199 SPAP1 12c on 12c+3c carmine & green 70 35

Type of Regular Issue, 1960.

Designs: 8c, Battle of Santa Clara. 12c, Rebel forces entering Havana. 29c, Banknote changing hands ("Clandestine activities in the cities").

Engraved.

1960, Jan. 28 ***Perf. 12½*** **Wmk. 320**

C200 A236 8c blue, gray olive & salmon 60 20
C201 " 12c gray olive & ochre 1.00 20
C202 " 29c gray & carmine 1.50 60

First anniversary of the revolution.

Nos. C9 and C104 Surcharged "12c" in Red

1960, Feb. 3 Wmk. 106

C203 AP3 12c on 40c deep orange 75 30
C204 AP48 12c on 45c violet 75 30

Pigeon Type of 1956.

1960, Feb. 12 Wmk. 321

C205 AP62 12c bright blue green 50 10

Statue Type of Regular Issue, 1960.

Statues: 8c, José Marti, Matanzas. 12c, Heroes of the Cacarajicara, Pinar del Rio. 30c, Cosme de la Torriente, Isle of Pines. (horiz.).

1960, March 28 ***Perf. 12½***

C206 A237 8c gray & carmine 45 20
C207 " 12c blue & carmine 75 20
C208 " 30c violet & brown 1.50 75

See note after No. 386.

Type of 1956 and No. C33 Overprinted in Dark Blue

1960, Apr. 24 Perf. 12½ Wmk. 321

C209 AP62 8c orange yellow 30 20
C210 " 12c cerise 50 20

Souvenir Sheet

C211 AP17 Sheet of four 10.00 10.00

Nos. C209–C211 issued for Stamp Day, Apr. 24, 1960, and to publicize the National Philatelic Exhibition.

No. C211 has added marginal inscription in dark blue commemorating the centenary of the ¼r on 2r (No. 15).

Type of Olympic Games Issue, 1960.

Designs: 8c, Boxer. 12c, Runner.

Engraved

1960, Sept. 22 Perf. 12½ Wmk. 321

C212 A238 8c ultramarine 40 20
C213 " 12c carmine rose 60 40
a. Souvenir sheet of 4 3.50

Issued to commemorate the 17th Olympic Games, Rome, Aug. 25–Sept. 11. No. C213a contains one each imperf. of types of Nos. 645–646 and Nos. C212–C213 in dark blue. Red marginal inscription. Size: 78x90mm.

Airmail Stamp of 1930 and Flight Symbols of 1930, 1960
AP91

1960, Oct. 30 Litho. Unwmkd.

C214 AP91 8c multicolored 2.50 1.50

Issued to commemorate the 30th anniversary of national air mail service.

Sword and Sheaf of Wheat
AP92

Designs: 12c, Two workers (horiz.). 30c, Three maps (horiz.). 50c, Hand inscribed "Peace" in 5 languages.

Granite Paper

1961, Jan. 10 Photo. Perf. 11½

C215 AP92 8c multicolored 30 20
C216 " 12c " 45 20
C217 " 30c black & red 1.25 50
C218 " 50c black, blue & red 1.50 1.00

Issued to publicize the Conference of Underdeveloped Countries, Havana.

José Marti and "Declaration of Havana"
AP93

Background in Spanish, English or French

1961, Jan. 28 Litho. Perf. 12½

C219 AP93 8c pale green, black & red 1.00 60
C220 " 12c orange yellow, black & pale violet 1.50 1.00
C221 " 30c pale blue, black & pale brown 2.50 1.50
a. Souvenir sheet of 3 6.50 6.50
Nos. C219–C221 (9) 15.00 9.30

Declaration of Havana, Sept. 1, 1960.

Sheets of 25 are imprinted in margin "E" for Spanish, "I" for English or "F" for French.

No. C221a contains one each of Nos. C219–C221, imperf. The 8c has background in Spanish, the 12c in English and the 30c in French. Black marginal inscription. Size: 102x79mm.

U.N. Type of 1961.

1961, Apr. 12 Perf. 12½ Unwmkd.

C222 A244 8c deep carmine & yellow 30 10
C223 " 12c bright ultra. & orange 60 30
a. Souvenir sheet of 2 2.00

Issued to commemorate the 15th anniversary (in 1960) of the United Nations.

No. C223a contains one each of Nos. C222–C223, imperf. with marginal bright ultramarine inscription. Size: 107x65mm.

AIR POST SEMI-POSTAL STAMP

Farm Couple and Factory
SPAP1

Engraved and Lithographed

1959, May 7 Perf. 12½ Wmk. 321

CB1 SPAP1 12c+3c carmine & green 1.25 50

Agricultural reforms. See also No. C199.

AIR POST SPECIAL DELIVERY STAMP.

Matanzas Issue.

Matanzas Harbor
APSD1

Photogravure.

Wmkd. Wavy Lines. (229)

1936, May 5 Perf. 12½

CE1 APSD1 15c light blue 4.00 2.00

Exists imperf. Price $4.75 unused, $2.50 used.

See "Special Notices" at the front of this volume for data on the listing methods of this Catalogue, abbreviations, condition, prices and examination.

SPECIAL DELIVERY STAMPS

Issued under Administration of the United States.

U.S. No. E5 Surcharged in Red

CUBA. 10c. de PESO

Wmkd. USPS (191)

1899 Perf. 12

E1 SD3 10c on 10c blue 75.00 60.00
a. No period after "CUBA" 225.00

Issues of the Republic under U. S. Military Rule.

Special Delivery Messenger
SD2

Engraved.

Inscribed: "Immediata".

1899 Wmkd. U S—C (191C)

E2 SD2 10c orange 22.50 7.50

Issues of the Republic

Inscribed: "Inmediata".

Wmkd. U S–C (191C)

1902 Perf. 12.

E3 SD2 10c orange 1.00 50

J. B. Zayas
SD3

1910 Unwmkd.

E4 SD3 10c orange & blue 3.50 1.25
a. Center inverted 250.00

Airplane and Morro Castle
SD4

1914, Feb. 24 Perf. 12

E5 SD4 10c dark blue 5.00 75

1927 Wmkd. Star. (106)

E6 SD4 10c deep blue 4.00 35

1935 Perf. 10.

E7 SD4 10c blue 4.00 30

Matanzas Issue.

Mercury
SD5

Photogravure.

Wmkd. Wavy Lines. (229)

1936, May 5 Perf. 12½

E8 SD5 10c deep claret 3.50 1.75

Exists imperf. Price $4.25 unused, $1 used.

"Triumph of the Revolution"
SD6

1936, Nov. 18

E9 SD6 10c red orange 3.00 1.75

Issued in commemoration of the centenary of the birth of Maj. Gen. Máximo Gómez (1836-1905).

Temple of Quetzalcoatl (Mexico)
SD7

Ruben Dario (Nicaragua)
SD8

Engraved

1937, Oct. 13 Perf. 10 Wmk. 106

E10 SD7 10c deep orange 4.00 3.50
E11 SD8 10c deep orange 4.00 3.50

Issued for the benefit of the Association of American Writers and Artists. See note after No. 354.

Letter and Symbols of Transportation
SD9

1945, Oct. 30

E12 SD9 10c olive brown 1.50 20

Governor's Building, Cárdenas
SD10

Engraved and Lithographed.

1951, July 3 Perf. 13 Wmk. 229

E13 SD10 10c henna brown, ultra. & red 2.50 75

Issued to commemorate the centenary of the adoption of Cuba's flag.

Chess Type of Regular Issue, 1951

1951, Nov. 1 Photogravure

E14 A166 10c dark green & rose brown 5.00 2.50

Issued to commemorate the 30th anniversary of the winning of the World Chess title by José Raul Capablanca.

Type of Regular Issue of 1951 Surcharged in Red Violet

10¢ E. ESPECIAL

Engraved.

1952, Mar. 18 Perf. 10 Wmk. 106

E15 A159 10c on 2c yellow brown 2.25 75

Arms and Bars from National Hymn
SD12

Roseate Tern
SD13

1952, May 27 *Perf. 12½*
E16 SD12 10c deep orange & blue 2.00 75

Issued to commemorate the 50th anniversary of the founding of the Republic of Cuba.

Type of Air Post Stamps of 1952 Inscribed: "Entrega Especial"

1952, Oct. 7 *Perf. 10*
E17 AP36 10c pale olive grn. 2.00 75

Three-fourths of the proceeds from the sale of No. E17 were used for the Communications Ministry Employees' Retirement Fund.

1953, July 28
E18 SD13 10c blue 1.75 50

Gregorio Hernandez Saez
SD14

Felix Varela
SD15

1954, Feb. 23
E19 SD14 10c olive green 2.25 65

1955, June 22 *Perf. 12½*
E20 SD15 10c brn. carmine 1.75 65

See note after No. E17.

Portrait Type of Regular Issue, 1956 Inscribed: "Entrega Especial"

Portrait: 10c, Jose Jacinto Milanes.

1956, May 2 **Wmk. 106**
E21 A198 10c dark carmine rose & black 1.75 50

See note after No. E17.

Painting Type of Regular Issue, 1957, Inscribed: "Entrega Especial"

Painting: 10c, "Yesterday" by E. Garcia Cabrera.

1957, Mar. 15 Engraved *Perf. 12½*
E22 A207 10c dark brown & turquoise bl. 2.25 65

See note after No. E17.

View Type of Regular Issue, 1957, Inscribed: "Entrega Especial."

View: 10c, Independence square, Pino del Rio.

1957, Dec. 17
E23 A218 10c dk. pur. & brn. 1.50 50

See note after No. E17.

View in Havana and Messenger
SD16

1958, Jan. 10 Engraved
E24 SD16 10c blue 1.25 40
E25 " 20c green 1.50 50

See also Nos. E28, E31.

Fish Type of Air Post Issue, 1958, Inscribed "Entrega Especial."

Fish: 10c, Blackfish snapper. 20c, Mosquitofish.

1958, Sept. 26 *Perf. 12½* **Wmk. 106**
E26 AP86 10c black, blue, pink & yellow 3.00 1.50
E27 " 20c black, ultra. & pink 10.00 7.00

See note after No. C191.

Messenger Type of 1958

1960 *Perf. 12½* **Wmk. 321**
E28 SD16 10c bright violet 1.25 35

Plane Type of Air Post Issue, of 1931–46, Surcharged in Black or Red: "HABILITADO ENTREGA ESPECIAL 10¢"

1960 *Perf. 10* **Wmk. 106**
E29 AP4 10c on 20c carmine rose 1.00 40
E30 " 10c on 50c greenish blue (R) 80 35

Messenger Type of 1958

1961, June 28 *Perf. 12½* **Wmk. 321**
E31 SD16 10c orange 1.25 35

POSTAGE DUE STAMPS

Issued under Administration of the United States

Postage Due Stamps of the United States Nos. J38, J39, J41 and J42 Surcharged in Black Like Regular Issue of Same Date.

Wmkd. USPS (191)

1899 *Perf. 12.*
J1 D2 1c on 1c dp. claret 12.00 3.00
J2 " 2c on 2c dp. claret 12.00 2.50
a. Inverted surcharge 1100.00
J3 " 5c on 5c deep claret 7.50 1.75
a. "CUPA" — —
J4 " 10c on 10c dp. claret 6.50 1.00

Issues of the Republic.

D1

Engraved

1914 *Perf. 12* **Unwmkd.**
J5 D1 1c carmine rose 1.75 65
J6 " 2c " 2.00 65
J7 " 5c " 5.00 1.25

1927–28
J8 D1 1c rose red 2.00 65
J9 " 2c " 2.50 65
J10 " 5c " 6.00 85

NEWSPAPER STAMPS.

Issued under Spanish Dominion.

N1

N2

Typographed

1888 *Perf. 14* **Unwmkd.**
P1 N1 ½m black 15 15
P2 " 1m " 15 15
P3 " 2m " 15 15
P4 " 3m " 75 50
P5 N1 4m black 1.15 75
P6 " 8m " 4.50 3.00
Nos. P1–P6 (6) 6.85 4.70

1890
P7 N2 ½m red brown 40 40
P8 " 1m " 40 40
P9 " 2m " 65 50
P10 " 3m " 65 50
P11 " 4m " 4.50 1.85
P12 " 8m " 4.50 1.85
Nos. P7–P12 (6) 11.10 5.50

1892
P13 N2 ½m violet 15 15
P14 " 1m " 15 15
P15 " 2m " 15 15
P16 " 3m " 75 15
P17 " 4m " 1.85 75
P18 " 8m " 4.50 1.15
Nos. P13–P18 (6) 7.55 2.50

1894
P19 N2 ½m rose 15 15
a. Imperf., pair 15.00
P20 " 1m rose 40 15
P21 " 2m " 40 15
P22 " 3m " 1.10 50
P23 " 4m " 1.50 75
P24 " 8m " 3.00 1.50
Nos. P19–P24 (6) 6.55 3.20

1896
P25 N2 ½m blue green 15 15
P26 " 1m " 15 15
P27 " 2m " 15 15
P28 " 3m " 1.50 60
P29 " 4m " 3.00 2.50
P30 " 8m " 4.75 3.75
Nos. P25–P30 (6) 9.70 7.30

POSTAL TAX STAMPS.

Mother and Child
PT1

Nurse with Child
PT2

Wmkd. Star. (106)

1938, Dec. 1 Engraved *Perf. 10*
RA1 PT1 1c bright green 25 10

The tax benefited the National Council of Tuberculosis fund for children's hospitals. Obligatory on all mail during December and January. This note applies also to Nos. RA2–4, RA7–10, RA12–15, RA17–21.

1939, Dec. 1
RA2 PT2 1c orange vermilion 25 10

"Health" Protecting Children
PT3

Mother and Child
PT4

1940, Dec. 1
RA3 PT3 1c deep blue 25 10

1941, Dec. 1
RA4 PT4 1c olive bistre 40 10

Victory
PT5

1942–44
RA5 PT5 ½c orange 25 10
RA6 " ½c gray ('44) 30 10

Issue dates: No. RA5, July 1, 1942. No. RA6, Oct. 3, 1944.

Type of 1941 Overprinted in Black "1942"

1942, Dec. 1
RA7 PT4 1c salmon 50 20
a. Inverted ovpt. 7.50

"Health" Protecting Children
PT6

Mother and Child
PT7

1943, Dec. 1
RA8 PT6 1c brown 25 10

1949, Dec. 9
RA9 PT7 1c blue 25 10

Type of 1949 Inscribed: "1950."

1950, Dec. 1 Engraved
RA10 PT7 1c rose red 25 10

Model of Proposed Communications Building
PT8

Woman Holding Child Aloft
PT9

1951, June 5 *Perf. 10* **Wmk. 106**
RA11 PT8 1c violet 35 5

The tax was to help build a new Communications Building. This note applies also to Nos. RA16, RA34, RA43.

1951, Dec. 1
RA12 PT9 1c violet blue 25 5
RA13 " 1c brown carmine 25 5
RA14 " 1c olive bistre 25 5
RA15 " 1c deep green 25 5

Proposed Communications Building
PT10

Child
PT11

1952, Feb. 8
RA16 PT10 1c dark blue 20 5

See also Nos. RA34, RA43.

1952, Dec. 1
RA17 PT11 1c rose carmine 35 5
RA18 " 1c yellow green 35 5
RA19 " 1c blue 35 5
RA20 " 1c orange 35 5

Hands reaching for Lorraine Cross PT12

Child's Head and Lorraine Cross PT13

1953, Dec. 1 *Perf. 9½*

RA21	PT12	1c rose carmine	25	5

1954, Nov. 1 *Perf. 9½x10*

RA22	PT13	1c rose red	25	5
RA23	"	1c violet	25	5
RA24	"	1c bright blue	25	5
RA25	"	1c emerald	25	5

The tax benefited the National Council of Tuberculosis fund for children's hospitals. Obligatory on all mail during November, December, January and February. This note applies also to Nos. RA26-33, RA35-42.

Rose and Watering Can PT14

Child and Protective Hands PT15

1955, Nov. 1

RA26	PT14	1c red orange	35	10
RA27	"	1c red lilac	35	10
RA28	"	1c bright blue	35	10
RA29	"	1c orange yellow	35	10

1956, Nov. 1

RA30	PT15	1c rose red	25	5
RA31	"	1c yellow brown	25	5
RA32	"	1c bright blue	25	5
RA33	"	1c emerald	25	5

Building Type of 1952

1957, Jan. 18 *Perf. 10*

RA34	PT10	1c rose red	12	5

Mother and Child by Silvia Arrojo Fernandez PT16

National Council of Tuberculosis PT17

Engraved.

1957, Nov. 1 *Perf. 10* **Wmk. 321**

RA35	PT16	1c dull rose	35	5
RA36	"	1c bright blue	35	5
RA37	"	1c gray	35	5
RA38	"	1c emerald	35	5

1958

RA39	PT17	1c rose red	15	5
RA40	"	1c red brown	15	5
RA41	"	1c gray	15	5
RA42	"	1c emerald	15	5

Building Type of 1952

1958 **Wmk. 321**

RA43	PT10	1c rose red	12	5

CURACAO

(See Netherlands Antilles.)

CYRENAICA

(sĭr'ê-nā'ĭ-kȧ)

LOCATION — In northern Africa bordering on the Mediterranean Sea.

GOVT.—Former Italian colony.

AREA—75,340 sq. mi.

POP.—225,000 (approx. 1934).

CAPITAL—Bengasi (Benghazi).

Cyrenaica was incorporated in the kingdom of Libya in 1951.

100 Centesimi = 1 Lira
1000 Milliemes = 1 Pound (1950)

Propaganda of the Faith Issue.

Italy Nos. 143-146 Overprinted

CIRENAICA

Wmkd. Crowns. (140)

1923 *Perf. 14*

1	A68	20c olive green & brown orange	2.40	4.00
2	"	30c claret & brown orange	2.40	4.00
3	"	50c violet & brown orange	2.10	3.50
4	"	1 l bl. & brn. org.	2.10	3.50

Fascisti Issue.

Italy Nos. 159-164 Overprinted CIRENAICA in Red or Black.

1923 *Perf. 14* **Unwmkd.**

5	A69	10c dark green (R)	90	1.15
6	"	30c dark violet (R)	90	1.15
7	"	50c brown carmine	90	1.15

Wmkd. Crowns. (140)

8	A70	1 l blue	1.20	1.50
9	"	2 l brown	1.35	1.65
10	A71	5 l black & blue (R)	3.75	5.50
		Nos. 5-10 (6)	9.00	12.10

Manzoni Issue.

Italy Nos. 165-170 Overprinted in Red CIRENAICA

1924 *Perf. 14.*

11	A72	10c brown red & black	55	1.50
		a. Vertical overprint	135.00	
12	"	15c blue green & black	55	1.50
		a. Vertical ovpt.	135.00	
13	"	30c black & slate	55	1.50
		a. Dbl. ovpt., vert.	135.00	175.00
14	"	50c orange brown & black	55	1.50
		a. Vertical ovpt.	175.00	
15	"	1 l blue & black	13.50	25.00
		a. Double overprint	135.00	175.00
16	"	5 l violet & black	200.00	300.00
		Nos. 11-16 (6)	215.70	331.00

On Nos. 15 and 16 the overprint is placed vertically at the left side.

Victor Emmanuel Issue.

Italy Nos. 175-177 Overprinted CIRENAICA

1925-26 *Perf. 11* **Unwmkd.**

17	A78	60c brown carmine	30	60
18	"	1 l dark blue	30	60
19	"	1.25 l dark blue ('26)	90	1.85
		a. Perf. 13½	45.00	65.00

Saint Francis of Assisi Issue.

Italian Stamps of 1926 Overprinted CIRENAICA

1926 *Perf. 14* **Wmk. 140**

20	A79	20c gray green	60	85
21	A80	40c dark violet	60	85
22	A81	60c red brown	60	85

Overprinted in Red Cirenaica

Unwmkd.

23	A82	1.25 l dark blue, perf. 11	60	85
24	A83	5 l+2.50 l olive grn.	2.50	3.50
		Nos. 20-24 (5)	4.90	6.90

Volta Issue.

Type of Italy 1927, Overprinted Cirenaica

1927 *Perf. 14.* **Wmkd. Crown. (140)**

25	A84	20c purple	8.50	9.00
26	"	50c deep orange	75	2.25
27	"	1.25 l bright blue	1.50	3.75

No. 25 exists with overprint omitted. Price $75.

Monte Cassino Issue.

Types of 1929 Issue of Italy, Overprinted in Red or Blue CIRENAICA

1929

28	A96	20c dark green (R)	75	1.50
29	"	25c red orange (Bl)	75	1.50
30	A98	50c+10c crimson (Bl)	75	1.50
31	"	75c+15c olive brown (R)	75	1.50
32	A96	1.25 l+25c dk. vio. (R)	4.50	6.50
33	A98	5 l+1 l sapphire (R)	4.50	6.50

Overprinted in Red Cirenaica

Unwmkd.

34	A100	10 l+2 l gray brown	4.50	6.50
		Nos. 28-34 (7)	16.50	25.50

Royal Wedding Issue.

Type of Italian Stamps of 1930 Overprinted CIRENAICA

1930 **Wmkd. Crowns. (140)**

35	A101	20c yellow green	60	1.00
36	"	50c+10c deep orange	75	1.50
37	"	1.25 l+25c rose red	90	1.85

No. 35 exists with overprint omitted. Price $750.

Ferrucci Issue.

Types of Italian Stamps of 1930, Overprinted in Red or Blue Cirenaica

1930

38	A102	20c violet (R)	38	38
39	A103	25c dark green (R)	38	38
40	"	50c black (R)	38	38
41	"	1.25 l deep blue (R)	38	38
42	A104	5 l + 2 l deep carmine (Bl)	3.00	3.00
		Nos. 38-42 (5)	4.52	4.52

Virgil Issue.

Types of Italian Stamps of 1930 Overprinted in Red or Blue

CIRENAICA

1930

43	A106	15c violet black (R)	15	38
44	"	20c orange brown (Bl)	15	38
45	"	25c dark green (R)	15	38
46	"	30c light brown (Bl)	15	38
47	"	50c dull violet (R)	15	38
48	"	75c rose red (Bl)	15	38
49	"	1.25 l gray blue (R)	15	38

Unwmkd.

50	A106	5 l+1.50 l dk. vio. (R)	2.10	3.75
51	"	10 l+2.50 l olive brown (Bl)	2.10	3.75
		Nos. 43-51 (9)	5.25	10.16

Saint Anthony of Padua Issue.

Types of Italian Stamps of 1931 Overprinted in Blue or Red CIRENAICA

1931 **Wmkd. Crowns. (140)**

52	A116	20c brown (Bl)	30	60
53	"	25c green (R)	30	60
54	A118	30c gray brown (Bl)	30	60
55	"	50c dull violet (Bl)	30	60
56	A120	1.25 l slate blue (R)	30	60

Overprinted in Red or Black Cirenaica

Unwmkd.

57	A121	75c black (R)	30	60
58	A122	5 l+2.50 l dark brown (Bk)	3.50	5.50
		Nos. 52-58 (7)	5.30	9.10

Carabineer A1

1934 Photogravure **Wmk. 140**

59	A1	5c dark olive green & brown	1.25	3.00
60	"	10c brown & black	1.25	3.00
61	"	20c scarlet & indigo	1.25	3.00
62	"	50c purple & brown	1.25	3.00
63	"	60c orange brown & indigo	1.25	3.00
64	"	1.25 l dk. blue & green	1.25	3.00
		Nos. 59-64 (6)	7.50	18.00

Issued to commemorate the 2nd Colonial Art Exhibition held at Naples. See also Nos. C24-C29.

Autonomous State

Senussi Warrior A2 A3

Engraved.

1950 *Perf. 12½* **Unwmkd.**

65	A2	1m dark brown	10	15
66	"	2m rose carmine	10	15
67	"	3m orange	10	15
68	"	4m dark green	90	1.15
69	"	5m gray	15	22
70	"	8m red orange	22	30
71	"	10m purple	30	30
72	"	12m red	30	30
73	"	20m deep blue	30	38
74	A3	50m choc. & ultra.	1.50	1.85
75	"	100m blue black & carmine rose	7.50	7.50
76	"	200m violet & purple	11.00	11.00
77	"	500m dark green & orange	30.00	30.00
		Nos. 65-77 (13)	52.47	53.45

SEMI-POSTAL STAMPS

Many issues of Italy and Italian Colonies include one or more semipostal denominations. To avoid splitting sets, these issues are generally listed as regular postage unless all values carry a surtax.

Holy Year Issue.

Italian Semi-Postal Stamps of 1924 Overprinted in Black or Red

CIRENAICA

1925 *Perf. 12* **Wmk. 140**

B1	SP4	20c+10c dark green & brown	60	1.15
B2	"	30c+15c dark brown & brown	60	1.15
B3	"	50c+25c vio. & brown	60	1.15
		a. Overprint inverted		
B4	"	60c+30c deep rose & brown	60	1.15
B5	SP8	1 l+50c deep blue & violet (R)	1.50	2.25
B6	"	5 l+2.50 l org. brn. & violet (R)	2.10	3.00
		Nos. B1-B6 (6)	6.00	9.85

Colonial Institute Issue.

"Peace" Substituting Spade for Sword—SP1

1926 Typographed. ***Perf. 14.***

B7 SP1 5c+5c brown 22 45
B8 " 10c+5c olive green 22 45
B9 " 20c+5c blue green 22 45
B10 " 40c+5c brown red 22 45
B11 " 60c+5c orange 22 45
B12 " 1 l+5c blue 22 45
Nos. B7-B12 (6) 1.32 2.70

Surtax for Italian Colonial Institute.

Types of Italian Semi-Postal Stamps of 1926 Overprinted **CIRENAICA**

1927 ***Perf. 11.*** **Unwmkd.**

B13 SP10 40c+20c dark brown & black 90 1.50
B14 " 60c+30c brown red & olive brown 90 1.50
B15 " 1.25 l+60c deep blue & black 90 1.50
B16 " 5 l+2.50 l dark green & black 1.85 3.00

The surtax on these stamps was for the charitable work of the Voluntary Militia for Italian National Defense.

Allegory of Fascism and Victory SP2

1928 ***Perf. 14.*** **Wmk. 140**

B17 SP2 20c+5c blue green 50 1.00
B18 " 30c+5c red 50 1.00
B19 " 50c+10c purple 50 1.00
B20 " 1.25 l+20c dark blue 50 1.00

Issued to commemorate the 46th anniversary of the Societa Africana d'Italia. The surtax aided that society.

Types of Italian Semi-Postal Stamps of 1926 Overprinted **CIRENAICA**

1929 ***Perf. 11.*** **Unwmkd.**

B21 SP10 30c+10c red & blk. 75 1.50
B22 " 50c+20c violet & black 75 1.50
B23 " 1.25 l+50c brown & blue 1.50 2.25
B24 " 5 l+2 l olive green & black 1.50 2.25

The surtax on Nos. B21-B24 was for the charitable work of the Voluntary Militia for Italian National Defense.

Types of Italian Semi-Postal Stamps of 1926 Overprinted in Black or Red **CIRENAICA**

1930 ***Perf. 14.***

B25 SP10 30c+10c dark green & blue green (Bk) 1.50 2.25
B26 " 50c+10c dark green & violet (R) 1.50 2.25
B27 " 1.25 l+30c olive brown & red brown (R) 2.25 3.00
B28 SP10 5 l+1.50 l indigo & green (R) 11.50 20.00

The surtax on these stamps was for the charitable work of the Voluntary Militia for Italian National Defense.

Sower SP3

1930 Photogravure **Wmk. 140**

B29 SP3 50c+20c olive brown 75 1.15
B30 " 1.25 l+20c deep blue 75 1.15
B31 " 1.75 l+20c green 75 1.15
B32 " 2.55 l+50c purple 2.65 3.50
B33 " 5 l+1 l deep car. 2.65 3.50
Nos. B29-B33 (5) 7.55 10.45

Issued in commemoration of the 25th anniversary of the Italian Colonial Agricultural Institute.

The surtax was for the aid of that institution.

AIR POST STAMPS.

Prices for cancelled Air Post stamps of Cyrenaica are for "cancelled to order" copies. Postally used sell for much more.

Air Post Stamps of Tripolitania, 1931, Overprinted in Blue **Cirenaica**

1932 ***Perf. 14.*** **Wmk. 140**

C1 AP1 50c rose carmine 45 22
C2 " 60c deep orange 1.15 1.25
C3 " 80c dull violet 1.15 1.50

Air Post Stamps of Tripolitania, 1931, Overprinted in Blue **CIRENAICA**

1932

C4 AP1 50c rose carmine 38 15
C5 " 80c dull violet 1.50 2.50

This overprint was also applied to the 60c, Tripolitania No. C9. The overprinted stamp was never used in Cyrenaica, but was sold at Rome in 1943 by the Postmaster General for the Italian Colonies. Price $15.

Arab on Camel AP2

Airplane in Flight AP3

1932 Photogravure.

C6 AP2 50c purple 90 15
C7 " 75c brown rose 90 90
C8 " 80c deep blue 90 90
C9 AP3 1 l black 45 15
C10 " 2 l green 60 60
C11 " 5 l deep carmine 1.50 1.50
Nos. C6-C11 (6) 5.25 4.20

Graf Zeppelin Issue.

Zeppelin and Clouds forming Pegasus AP4

Zeppelin and Ancient Galley AP5

Zeppelin and Giant Bowman AP6

1933, Apr. 15

C12 AP4 3 l dark brown 8.00 8.00
C13 AP5 5 l purple 8.00 8.00
C14 AP6 10 l deep green 8.00 8.00
C15 AP5 12 l deep blue 8.00 8.00
C16 AP4 15 l carmine 8.00 8.00
C17 AP6 20 l black 8.00 8.00
Nos. C12-C17 (6) 48.00 48.00

North Atlantic Cruise Issue.

Airplane Squadron and Constellations AP7

1933, June 1

C18 AP7 19.75 l green & deep blue 27.50 27.50
C19 " 44.75 l red & indigo 27.50 27.50

Type of 1932 Overprinted and Surcharged

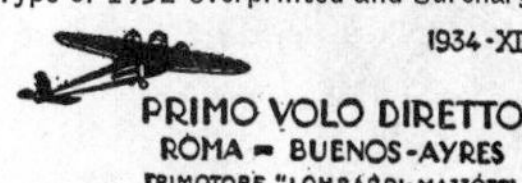

1934, Jan. 20

C20 AP3 2 l on 5 l org. brown 2.75 2.75
C21 " 3 l on 5 l yel. green 2.75 2.75
C22 " 5 l ochre 2.75 2.75
C23 " 10 l on 5 l rose 2.75 2.75

For use on mail to be carried on a special flight from Rome to Buenos Aires.

Transport Plane AP8

Venus of Cyrene AP9

1934, Oct. 9

C24 AP8 25c slate blue & orange red 1.25 1.25
C25 " 50c dark green & indigo 1.25 1.25
C26 " 75c dark brown & orange red 1.25 1.25
a. Imperf. 350.00
C27 AP9 80c orange brn. & olive green 1.25 1.25
C28 " 1 l scarlet & olive green 1.25 1.25
C29 " 2 l dk. bl. & brn. 1.25 1.25
Nos. C24-C29 (6) 7.50 7.50

Issued in commemoration of the Second Colonial Arts Exhibition held at Naples.

AIR POST SEMI-POSTAL STAMPS.

King Victor Emmanuel III SPAP1

Photogravure.

1934 ***Perf. 14.*** **Wmk. 104**

CB1 SPAP1 25c+10c gray green 1.00 1.00
CB2 " 50c+10c brown 1.00 1.00
CB3 " 75c+15c rose red 1.00 1.00
CB4 " 80c+15c brn. blk. 1.00 1.00
CB5 " 1 l+20c red brn. 1.00 1.00
CB6 " 2 l+20c brt. blue 1.00 1.00
CB7 " 3 l+25c purple 12.00 12.00
CB8 " 5 l+25c orange 12.00 12.00
CB9 " 10 l+30c deep violet 12.00 12.00
CB10 " 25 l+2 l deep green 12.00 12.00
Nos. CB1-CB10 (10) 54.00 54.00

Issued in commemoration of the 65th birthday of King Victor Emmanuel III and the non-stop flight from Rome to Mogadiscio.

AIR POST SEMI-POSTAL OFFICIAL STAMP.

Type of Air Post Semi-Postal Stamps, 1934, Overprinted Crown and "SERVIZIO DI STATO" in Black.

1934, Nov. 5 ***Perf. 14*** **Wmk. 140**

CBO1 SPAP1 25 l+2 l copper red *1500.00*

POSTAGE DUE STAMPS

D1

Engraved

1950 ***Perf. 12½*** **Unwmkd.**

J1 D1 2m dark brown 22.50 25.00
J2 " 4m deep green 22.50 25.00
J3 " 8m scarlet 22.50 25.00
J4 " 10m vermilion 22.50 25.00
J5 " 20m orange yellow 22.50 25.00
J6 " 40m deep blue 22.50 25.00
J7 " 100m dark gray 22.50 25.00
Nos. J1-J7 (7) 157.50 175.00

CZECHOSLOVAKIA

(chĕk'ô-slô-vä'kĭ-ȧ)

LOCATION—Central Europe.

GOVT.—Republic.

AREA—49,355 sq. mi.

POP.—15,030,000 (est. 1976).

CAPITAL—Prague.

The Czechoslovakian Republic consists of Bohemia, Moravia and Silesia, Slovakia and Ruthenia (Carpatho-Ukraine). In March, 1939, a German protectorate was established over Bohemia and Moravia, as well as over Slovakia which had meanwhile declared its independence. Ruthenia was incorporated in the territory of Hungary. These territories were returned to the Czechoslovak Republic in 1945, except for Ruthenia which was ceded to Russia. Czechoslovakia became a federal state on Jan. 2, 1969.

100 Haleru = 1 Koruna

Stamps of Austria overprinted "Ceskoslovenska Republika", lion and "Česko Slovensky Stat", "Provisorni Ceskoslovenska Vlada" and Arms, and "Ceskoslovenska Statni Posta" and Arms were made privately. A few of them were passed through the post but all have been pronounced unofficial and unauthorized by the Postmaster General.

During the occupation of part of Northern Hungary by the Czechoslovak forces, stamps of Hungary were overprinted "Cesko Slovenska Posta", "Ceskoslovenska Statni Posta" and Arms, and "Slovenska Posta" and Arms. These stamps were never officially issued though copies have passed the post.

Hradcany at Prague

A1

Typographed.

1918-19 *Imperf.* **Unwmkd.**

1 A1 3(h) red violet 3 3
2 " 5(h) yellow green 3 3
3 " 10(h) rose 3 3
4 " 20(h) bluish green 6 3
5 " 25(h) deep blue 12 3
  a. 25(h) ultra. 15.00
6 " 30(h) bistre 15 3
7 " 40(h) red orange 18 3
8 " 100(h) brown 40 4
9 " 200(h) ultramarine 80 4
10 " 400(h) purple 1.50 10

On the 3(h) to 40(h) the words "Posta Ceskoslovenska" are in white on a colored background; on the higher values the words are in color on a white background.

See Nos. 368, 1554, 1600.

Perf. 11½, 13½

13 A1 5(h) yellow green 10 3
  a. Perf. 11½x10½ 40 10
14 " 10(h) rose 18 4
15 " 20(h) bluish green 15 5
  a. Perf. 13½ 25 15
16 " 25(h) deep blue 20 5
  a. Perf. 11½ 75 15
20 " 200(h) ultramarine 1.50 10
Nos. 1-10, 13-16, 20 (15) 5.43 66

All values of this issue exist with various private perforations and copies have been used on letters.

The 3, 30, 40, 100 and 400h formerly listed are now known to have been privately perforated.

A2

Type II. Sun behind cathedral. Colorless foliage in foreground.

Type III. Without sun. Shaded foliage in foreground.

Type IV. No foliage in foreground. Positions of buildings changed. Letters redrawn.

1919 *Imperf.*

23 A2 1(h) dark brown (II) 4 3
25 " 5(h) blue green (IV) 15 5
27 " 15(h) red (IV) 18 15
29 " 25(h) dull violet (IV) 18 3
30 " 50(h) dull violet (II) 22 3
31 " 50(h) dark blue (IV) 18 3
32 " 60(h) orange (III) 60 15
33 " 75(h) slate (IV) 30 5
34 " 80(h) olive green (III) 35 3
36 " 120(h) gray blk. (IV) 1.00 15
38 " 300(h) dark green (III) 3.00 10
39 " 500(h) red brown (IV) 4.00 8
40 " 1000(h) violet (III) 5.00 50
  a. 1000(h) bluish violet 13.50 90
Nos. 23-40 (13) 15.20 1.38

1919-20

Perf. 11½, 13½, 13½x11½.

41 A2 1(h) dark brown (II) 4 3
42 " 5(h) blue green (IV), perf. 13½ 10 3
  a. Perf. 11½ 7.50 2.50
43 " 10(h) yel. green (IV) 10 3
  a. Imperf. 27.50 15.00
  b. Perf. 11½ 7.50 45
44 " 15(h) red (IV) 10 3
  a. Perf. 11½x10½ 13.50 2.50
  b. Perf. 11½x13½ 20.00 3.00
  c. Perf. 13½x10½ 50.00 10.00
45 " 20(h) rose (IV) 10 3
  a. Imperf. 90.00 50.00
46 " 25(h) dull violet (IV), perf. 11½ 15 3
  a. Perf. 11½x10½ 75 20
  b. Perf. 13½x10½ 5.50 2.00
47 " 30(h) red violet (IV) 15 4
  a. Imperf. 135.00 75.00
  b. Perf. 14x13½ 175.00 15.00
  c. 30 (h) dp. vio. 15 8
  d. As "c," perf. 14x13½ 200.00 15.00
  e. As "c," imperf. 135.00 75.00
50 " 60(h) orange (III) 50 15
  a. Perf. 14x13½ 6.00 1.75
53 " 120(h) gray black (IV) 7.00 1.70
Nos. 41-53 (9) 8.24 2.07

Nos. 43a, 45a and 47a were imperforate by accident and not issued in quantities as were Nos. 23 to 40.

Rouletted stamps of the preceding issues are said to have been made by a postmaster in a branch post office at Prague, or by private firms, but without authority from the Post Office Department.

The 50, 75, 80, 300, 500 and 1000h have been privately perforated.

Unlisted color varieties of types A1 and A2 were not officially released, and some are printer's waste.

Pres. Thomas Garrigue Masaryk

A4

1920 *Perf. 13½*

61 A4 125(h) gray blue 1.75 10
  a. 125(h) ultramarine 25.00 15.00
  b. Imperf. (gray blue) 17.00
  c. As "a," imperf. 35.00
62 " 500(h) slate, *grayish* 6.00 1.50
  a. Imperf. 25.00
63 " 1000(h) black brown, *brownish* 10.00 3.50
  a. Imperf. 35.00

Carrier Pigeon with Letter

A5

Czechoslovakia Breaking Chains to Freedom

A6

Hussite Priest

A7

Agriculture and Science

A8

1920 *Perf. 14*

65 A5 5(h) dark blue 3 3
  a. Perf. 13½ 45.00 15.00
  b. Imperf. 3.75
66 " 10(h) blue green 4 3
  a. Perf. 13½ 30.00 20.00
  b. Imperf. 3.75
67 " 15(h) red brown 10 3
  a. Imperf. 3.75
68 A6 20(h) rose 5 3
  a. Imperf. 3.00
69 " 25(h) lilac brown 8 5
  a. Imperf. 3.00
70 " 30(h) red violet 10 3
  a. Imperf. 3.00
71 " 40(h) red brown 15 3
  a. Tête bêche pair 2.00 1.00
  b. Perf. 13½ 50 20
  c. Imperf. 3.00
72 " 50(h) carmine 20 3
  a. Imperf. 3.00
73 " 60(h) dark blue 20 3
  a. Tête bêche pair 6.00 3.00
  b. Perf. 13½ 1.25 25
  c. Imperf. 2.00

Photogravure.

74 A7 80(h) purple 50 15
  a. Imperf. 3.00
75 " 90(h) black brown 60 30
  a. Imperf. 3.00

Typographed *Perf. 14*

76 A8 100(h) dark green 55 3
  a. Imperf. 4.50
77 " 200(h) violet 75 3
  a. Imperf. 4.50
78 " 300(h) vermilion 3.25 3
  a. Perf. 14x13½ 6.50 25
  b. Imperf. 4.50
79 " 400(h) brown 7.00 30
  a. Imperf. 22.50
80 " 500(h) deep green 8.00 10
  a. Perf. 14x13½ 40.00 4.00
  b. Imperf. 22.50
81 " 600(h) deep violet 10.00 12
  a. Perf. 14x13½ 125.00 5.00
  b. Imperf. 22.50
Nos. 65-81 (17) 31.60 1.35

No. 69 has background of horizontal lines.

1920-25 *Perf. 14*

82 A5 5(h) violet 5 3
  a. Tête bêche pair 1.50 1.25
  b. Perf. 13½ 20 20
  c. Imperf. 3.50
83 " 10(h) olive bistre 5 3
  a. Tête bêche pair 2.00 1.25
  b. Perf. 13½ 30 15
  c. Imperf. 3.50
84 " 20(h) deep orange 10 6
  a. Tête bêche pair 20.00 12.50
  b. Perf. 13½ 3.00 75
  c. Imperf. 4.50
85 " 25(h) blue green 15 5
  a. Imperf. 8.00
86 " 30(h) deep violet ('25) 3.00 6
87 A6 50(h) yellow green 20 3
  a. Tête bêche pair 30.00 20.00
  b. Perf. 13½ 6.00 1.50
  c. Imperf. 27.50
88 " 100(h) dark brown 45 3
  a. Perf. 13½ 15.00 25
  b. Imperf. 2.00
89 A6 150(h) rose 6.00 1.00
  a. Perf. 13½ 45.00 1.25
90 " 185(h) orange 1.50 6
  a. Imperf. 7.00
91 " 250(h) dark green 4.50 25
  a. Imperf. 16.50
Nos. 82-91 (10) 16.00 1.60

Type of 1920 Issue Redrawn.

Type I. Rib of leaf below "O" of POSTA is straight and extends to tip. White triangle above book is entirely at left of twig. "P" has a stubby, abnormal appendage.

Type II. Rib is extremely bent; does not reach tip. Triangle extends at right of twig. "P" like Type I.

Type III. Rib of top left leaf is broken in two. Triangle like Type II. "P" has no appendage.

1923 *Perf. 14, 14x13½*

92 A8 100(h) red, *yellow*, III, perf. 14x13½ 1.50 3
  a. Type I, perf. 14 1.50 5
  b. Type I, perf. 14x13½ 3.50 3
  c. Type II, perf. 14 2.50 3
  d. Type II, perf. 14x13½ 3.25 3
  e. Type III, perf. 14 17.00 4
93 A8 200(h) blue, *yellow*, II, perf. 14 6.50 10
  a. Type II, perf. 14x13½ 11.50 20
  b. Type III, perf. 14 12.50 25
  c. Type III, perf. 14x13½ 60.00 40
94 A8 300(h) violet, *yellow*, I, perf. 14 5.00 5
  a. Type II, perf. 14 55.00 20
  b. Type II, perf. 14x13½ 100.00 30
  c. Type III, perf. 14x13½ 9.00 4
  d. Type III, perf. 14 25.00 20

President Masaryk

A9 A10

Wmk. 107 (Vertical)

Perf. 14x13½, 13½

Wmkd. Linden Leaves. (107)

1925 **Size: 19½x23mm.** **Photo.**

95 A9 40h brown orange 1.50 5
96 " 50h olive green 2.00 3
97 " 60h red violet 3.00 3

Distinctive Marks of the Engravings.

I, II, III: Background of horizontal lines in top and bottom tablets. Inscriptions in Roman letters with serifs.

IV: Crossed horizontal and vertical lines in the tablets. Inscriptions in Antique letters without serifs.

I, II, IV: Shading of crossed diagonal lines on the shoulder at the right.

III. Shading of single lines only.

I: "T" of "Posta" over middle of "V" of "Ceskoslovenska". Three short horizontal lines in lower part of "A" of "Ceskoslovenska".

II: "T" over right arm of "V". One short line in "A".

III: "T" as in II. Blank space in lower part of "A".

IV: "T" over left arm of "V".

Engraved.

I. First Engraving.

Wmkd. Horizontally. (107)

Size: 19¾x22½mm.

98 A10 1k carmine 1.25 3
99 " 2k deep blue 3.50 4

No.	Type	Description	Unused	Used
100	A10	3k brown	8.25	10
101	"	5k blue green	3.00	18

Wmkd. Vertically. (107)

Size: 19¼x23mm.

No.	Type	Description	Unused	Used
101A	A10	1k carmine	150.00	5.00
101B	"	2k deep blue	200.00	17.50
101C	"	3k brown	425.00	17.50
101D	"	5k blue green	4.00	1.50

II. Second Engraving.

Wmkd. Horizontally. (107)

Size: 19x21½mm.

No.	Type	Description	Unused	Used
102	A10	1k carmine	75.00	25
103	"	2k deep blue	7.50	20
104	"	3k brown	8.00	25

III. Third Engraving

Size: 19-19½x21½-22mm.

Perf. 10.

No.	Type	Description	Unused	Used
105	A10	1k carmine rose	2.25	3
		a. Perf. 14	20.00	5

IV. Fourth Engraving.

Size: 19-19½x21½-22mm.

1926 ***Perf. 10, 14.***

No.	Type	Description	Unused	Used
106	A10	1k carmine rose	1.75	3
108	"	3k brown	8.50	6

See also No. 130.

Karlstein Castle
A11

1926, June 1 Engr. ***Perf. 10***

No.	Type	Description	Unused	Used
109	A11	1.20k red violet	1.50	50
110	"	1.50k carmine rose	1.25	5
111	"	2.50k dark blue	4.00	30

See also Nos. 133, 135.

Karlstein Castle
A12

Pernstein Castle
A13

Orava Castle
A14

Masaryk
A15

Strahov Monastery
A16

Hradčany at Prague
A17

Great Tatra
A18

1926–27 Engraved **Wmk. 107**

No.	Type	Description	Unused	Used
114	A13	30h gray green	2.50	20
115	A14	40h red brown	45	3
116	A15	50h deep green	60	3
117	"	60h red vio., *lilac*	1.00	4
118	A16	1.20k red violet	6.50	2.00

Perf. 13½

No.	Type	Description	Unused	Used
119	A17	2k blue	1.50	5
		a. 2k ultramarine	3.00	30
120	"	3k deep red	2.15	10
121	A18	4k brown vio. ('27)	4.00	45
122	"	5k dk. green ('27)	17.50	3.00
		Nos. 114-122 (9)	36.20	5.90

No. 116 exists in two types. The one with short, straight mustache at left sells for several times as much as that with longer wavy mustache.

See also Nos. 137–140.

Coil Stamps.

Perf. 10 Vertically.

No.	Type	Description	Unused	Used
123	A12	20h brick red	70	15
		a. Vert. pair, imperf. horiz.	175.00	
124	A13	30h gray green	35	10
		a. Vert. pair, imperf. horiz.	175.00	
125	A15	50h deep green	20	8

See also No. 141.

1927-31 ***Perf. 10.*** **Unwmkd.**

No.	Type	Description	Unused	Used
126	A13	30h gray green	40	3
127	A14	40h red brown	90	3
128	A15	50h deep green	25	3
129	"	60h red violet	40	3
130	A10	1k carmine rose	8.00	10
131	A15	1k deep red	45	4
132	A16	1.20k red violet	40	4
133	A11	1.50k carmine ('29)	55	5
134	A13	2k deep green ('29)	40	3
135	A11	2.50k dark blue	10.00	25
136	A14	3k red brown ('31)	1.00	5
		Nos. 126-136 (11)	22.75	68

No. 130 exists in two types. The one with longer mustache at left sells for several times as much as that with the short mustache.

1927-28 ***Perf. 13½***

No.	Type	Description	Unused	Used
137	A17	2k ultramarine	2.00	8
138	"	3k deep red ('28)	3.00	8
139	A18	4k brn. vio. ('28)	10.00	60
140	"	5k dk. green ('28)	7.50	45

Coil Stamp.

1927 ***Perf. 10 Vertically***

No.	Type	Description	Unused	Used
141	A12	20h brick red	75	20

Hradec Castle
A19

Town Hall, Levoča
A20

Telephone Exchange, Prague
A21

Town of Jasina
A22

Hluboka Castle
A23

Pilgrims' House at Velehrad
A24

Brno Cathedral
A25

Great Tatra
A26

Masaryk
A27

Old City Square, Prague
A28

1928, Oct. 22 ***Perf. 13½***

No.	Type	Description	Unused	Used
142	A19	30h black	10	5
143	A20	40h red brown	15	6
144	A21	50h dark green	10	5
145	A22	60h orange red	15	5
146	A23	1k carmine	15	4
147	A24	1.20k brown violet	65	35
148	A25	2k ultramarine	45	30
149	A26	2.50k dark blue	2.25	1.60
150	A27	3k dark brown	1.50	30
151	A28	5k deep violet	3.50	2.50
		Nos. 142-151 (10)	9.00	5.30

Issued in commemoration of the tenth anniversary of Czechoslovakian independence.

Coat of Arms
A29

1929–37 ***Perf. 10***

No.	Type	Description	Unused	Used
152	A29	5h dk. ultra. ('31)	5	3
153	"	10h bistre brown ('31)	5	3
154	"	20h red	5	3
155	"	25h green	8	3
156	"	30h red violet	8	3
157	"	40h dk. brown ('37)	35	3
		a. 40h red brown ('37)	75	6

Coil Stamp.

Perf. 10 Vertically.

No.	Type	Description	Unused	Used
158	A29	20h red	30	3
		Nos. 152-158 (7)	96	21

St. Wenceslas
A30

Founding St. Vitus' Cathedral
A31

Design: 3k, 5k, St. Wenceslas martyred.

1929, May 14 ***Perf. 13½***

No.	Type	Description	Unused	Used
159	A30	50h gray green	10	6
160	"	60h slate violet	15	6
161	A31	2k dull blue	1.00	23
162	A30	3k brown	1.00	25
163	"	5k brown violet	6.75	2.40
		Nos. 159-163 (5)	9.00	3.00

Millenary of the death of St. Wenceslas.

Statue of St. Wenceslas and National Museum, Prague
A33

1929 ***Perf. 10***

No.	Type	Description	Unused	Used
164	A33	2.50k deep blue	85	3

Brno Cathedral
A34

Tatra Mountain Scene
A35

Design: 5k, Old City Square, Prague.

1929, Oct. 15 ***Perf. 13½***

No.	Type	Description	Unused	Used
165	A34	3k red brown	3.00	12
166	A35	4k indigo	6.00	70
167	"	5k gray green	8.00	35

See also No. 183.

A37

Type I

Type II

Two types of 50h:

I. A white space exists across the bottom of the vignette between the coat, shirt and tie and the "HALERU" frame panel.

II. An extra frame line has been added just above the "HALERU" panel which finishes off the coat and tie shading evenly.

1930, Jan. 2 ***Perf. 10***

No.	Type	Description	Unused	Used
168	A37	50h myrtle green (II)	25	3
		a. Type I	1.00	4
169	"	60h brown violet	1.00	3
170	"	1k brown red	40	3

See also No. 234.

Coil Stamp.

1931 ***Perf. 10 Vertically***

No.	Type	Description	Unused	Used
171	A37	1k brown red	1.75	75

President Masaryk
A38

St. Nicholas' Church, Prague
A39

1930, Mar. 1 ***Perf. 13½***

No.	Type	Description	Unused	Used
175	A38	2k gray green	75	20
176	"	3k red brown	1.50	20
177	"	5k slate blue	4.00	75
178	"	10k gray black	10.00	4.75

Eightieth birthday of President Masaryk.

1931, May 15

No.	Type	Description	Unused	Used
183	A39	10k black violet	8.25	2.50

Krivoklat Castle
A40

Krumlov Castle
A42

Design: 4k, Orlik Castle.

1932, Jan. 2 ***Perf. 10***

184 A40 3.50k violet 3.50 65
185 " 4k deep blue 3.00 20
186 A42 5k gray green 3.25 20

Miroslav Tyrš
A43 A44

1932, Mar. 16

187 A43 50h yellow green 75 4
188 " 1k brown carmine 75 4
189 A44 2k dark blue 7.50 30
190 " 3k red brown 12.00 40

Issued to commemorate the centenary of the birth of Miroslav Tyrš (1832–1884), founder of the Sokol movement, and in connection with the 9th Sokol Congress.

Tyrš
A45

1933, Feb. 1

191 A45 60h dull violet 30 3

First Christian Church at Nitra
A46 A47

1933, June 20

192 A46 50h yellow green 50 5
193 A47 1k carmine rose 4.00 10

Issued in commemoration of Prince Pribina who introduced Christianity into Slovakia and founded there the first Christian church in A. D. 833.

All gutter pairs are vertical.

Friedrich Smetana
A48

1934, Mar. 26 **Engr.** ***Perf. 10***

194 A48 50h yellow green 50 3

Issued to commemorate the 50th anniversary of the death of Friedrich Smetana, Czech composer and pianist.

Consecration of Legion Colors at Kiev, Sept. 21, 1914
A49

Ensign Heyduk with Colors
A51

Legionnaires
A52

Design: 1k, Legion receiving battle flag at Bayonne.

1934, Aug. 15 ***Perf. 10***

195 A49 50h green 30 6
196 " 1k rose lake 40 5
197 A51 2k deep blue 2.25 30
198 A52 3k red brown 3.25 30

Issued in commemoration of the 20th anniversary of the Czechoslovakian Legion which fought in World War I.

Antonin Dvořák
A53

1934, Nov. 22

199 A53 50h green 40 3

Issued to commemorate the 30th anniversary of the death of Antonin Dvorák, (1841–1904), composer.

Pastoral Scene
A54

1934, Dec. 17 ***Perf. 10***

200 A54 1k claret 65 5
a. Souvenir sheet of 15 175.00 175.00
b. As "a", single stamp 8.00 7.50
201 " 2k blue 2.50 50
a. Souvenir sheet of 15 600.00 600.00
b. As "a", single stamp 30.00 30.00

Issued in commemoration of the centenary of the National Anthem.

Nos. 200a & 201a were issued in special souvenir sheets of 15 stamps each on thick paper, darker shades, perf. 13½, no gum. Words and music of the anthem at top and bottom of sheet. Forgeries exist.

President Masaryk
A55 A56

1935, Mar. 1

202 A55 50h green, *buff* 10 3
203 " 1k claret, *buff* 15 3
204 A56 2k gray blue, *buff* 2.25 15
205 " 3k brown, *buff* 3.50 20

85th birthday of President Masaryk. See No. 235.

Monument to Czech Heroes at Arras, France—A57

1935, May 4

206 A57 1k rose 50 3
207 " 2k dull blue 2.00 30

20th anniversary of the Battle of Arras.

General Milan Stefánik
A58

Sts. Cyril and Methodius
A59

1935, May 18

208 A58 50h green 20 3

1935, June 22

209 A59 50h green 15 6
210 " 1k claret 50 5
211 " 2k deep blue 1.50 20

Issued in commemoration of the millenary of the arrival in Moravia of the Apostles Cyril and Methodius.

Masaryk
A60

Statue of Macha, Prague
A61

1935, Oct. 20 ***Perf. 12½***

212 A60 1k rose lake 10 3

No. 212 exists imperforate. See No. 256.

1936, Apr. 30

213 A61 50h deep green 15 6
214 " 1k rose lake 30 6

Issued to commemorate the centenary of the death of Karel Hynek Macha (1810–1836), Bohemian poet.

Jan Amos Komensky
A61a

President Eduard Beneš
A62

Gen. Milan Stefánik
A63

1936

215 A61a 40h dark blue 10 3
216 A62 50h dull green 10 3
217 A63 60h dull violet 10 3

See Nos. 252 and 255.

Castle Palanok near Mukacevo
A64

Town of Banska Bystrica
A65

Castle at Zvikov
A66

Ruins of Castle at Strecno
A67

Castle at Cesky Raj
A68

Palace at Slavkov (Austerlitz)
A69

Statue of King George at Podebrad
A70

Town Square at Olomouc
A71

Castle Ruins at Bratislava
A72

1936, Aug. 1

218 A64 1.20k rose lilac 10 4
219 A65 1.50k carmine 10 3
220 A66 2k dark blue green 13 3
221 A67 2.50k dark blue 12 3
222 A68 3k brown 20 6
223 A69 3.50k dark violet 1.75 40
224 A70 4k dark violet 75 8
225 A71 5k green 50 8
226 A72 10k blue 2.00 25
Nos. 218-226 (9) 5.65 1.00

President Beneš
A73

Soldiers of the Czech Legion
A74

1937, Apr. 26 ***Perf. 12½*** **Unwmkd.**

227 A73 50h deep green 5 3

1937, June 15

228 A74 50h deep green 15 5
229 " 1k rose lake 30 6

Issued in commemoration of the 20th anniversary of the Battle of Zborov.

Cathedral at Prague
A75

Jan Evangelista Purkyne
A76

1937, July 1

230 A75 2k green 75 15
231 " 2.50k blue 1.25 35

Issued in commemoration of the 16th anniversary of the founding of the "Little Entente."

1937, Sept. 2

232 A76 50h slate green 20 5
233 " 1k dull rose 25 5

Issued in commemoration of the 150th anniversary of the birth of Jan Evangelista Purkyne, Czech physiologist.

Masaryk Types of 1930–35.

1937, Sept. ***Perf. 12½***

234 A37 50h black 20 3

With date "14.IX. 1937" in design.

235 A56 2k black 25 10

Issued in commemoration of the death of former President Thomas G. Masaryk on Sept. 14, 1937.

International Labor Bureau Issue.

Stamps of 1936-37 Overprinted in Violet or Black **B.I.T.1937**

1937, Oct. 6 ***Perf. 12½***

236 A73 50h deep green (Bk) 40 20
237 A65 1.50k carmine (V) 50 30
238 A66 2k deep green (V) 60 55

Bratislava Philatelic Exhibition Issue.

Souvenir Sheet.

A77

1937, Oct. 24 ***Perf. 12½***

239 A77 Sheet of two 80 80
a. 50h dark blue 30 30
b. 1k brown carmine 30 30

The sheet measures 149x110mm. The stamps show a view of Poprad Lake (50h) and the tomb of General Milan Stefanik (1k).

No. 239 overprinted 'Libération de la Tchécholovaquie, 28-X-1945" etc., was sold at a philatelic exhibition in Brussels, Belgium.

St. Barbara's Church, Kutna Hora
A79

Peregrine Falcon, Sokol Emblem
A80

1937, Dec. 4

240 A79 1.60k olive green 15 4

1938, Jan. 21

241 A80 50h deep green 30 5
242 " 1k rose lake 50 8

Issued in commemoration of the 10th International Sokol Games. Imperforate copies of No. 242 are essays. Nos. 241–242 se-tenant with labels sell slightly higher.

Legionnaires
A81

Legionnaires
A82

Legionnaire
A83

1938

243 A81 50h deep green 15 4
244 A82 50h deep green 15 5
245 A83 50h deep green 15 5

Issued to commemorate the 20th anniversary of the Battles of Bachmac, Vouziers and Doss Alto. Nos. 243–245 with label se-tenant sell for more.

Jindrich Fügner, Co-Founder of Sokol Movement
A84

1938, June 18 ***Perf. 12½***

246 A84 50h deep green 10 5
247 " 1k rose lake 20 4
248 " 2k slate blue 70 6

Issued to commemorate the 10th Sokol Summer Games. Nos. 246–248 se-tenant with labels slightly higher.

View of Pilsen
A85

Cathedral of Kosice
A86

1938, June 24

249 A85 50h deep green 15 3

Issued in connection with the Provincial Economic Council meeting at Pilsen.

1938, July 15 ***Perf. 12½***

250 A86 50h deep green 15 4

Issued in connection with the Kosice Cultural Exhibition.

Prague Philatelic Exhibition Issue.

Souvenir Sheet.

Vysehrad Castle—Hradcany
A87

1938, June 26 ***Perf. 12½***

251 A87 Sheet of two 2.50 2.50
a. 50h dark blue 1.00 1.00
b. 1k deep carmine 1.00 1.00

Issued in sheets measuring 148½x105mm.

Stefánik Type of 1936.

1938, Nov. 21

252 A63 50h deep green 10 3

Allegory of the Republic
A89

1938, Dec. 19 **Unwmkd.**

253 A89 2k light ultramarine 30 10
254 " 3k pale brown 60 15

Issued in commemoration of the 20th anniversary of Independence.

"Wir sind frei!"

Stamps of Czechoslovakia, 1918-37, overprinted with a swastika in black or red and "Wir sind frei!" were issued locally and unofficially in 1938 as Czech authorities were evacuating and German authorities arriving. They appeared in the towns of Asch, Karlsbad, Reichenberg - Maffersdorf, Rumburg, etc.

The overprint, sometimes including a surcharge or the town name (as in Karlsbad), exists on many values of postage, air post, semi-postal, postage due and newspaper stamps.

Stefánik Type of 1936.

1939 Engraved ***Perf. 12½***

255 A63 60h dark blue 9.00 10.00

Used exclusively in Slovakia.

Masaryk Type of 1935 with hyphen in Cesko - Slovensko.

1939, Apr. 23

256 A60 1k rose lake 10 3

Linden Leaves and Buds
A90

1945 Photogravure. ***Perf. 14.***

256A A90 10(h) black 3 3
257 " 30(h) yellow brown 3 3
258 " 50(h) dark green 3 3
258A " 60(h) dark blue 3 3

Engraved.

(Buds Open.)

Perf. 12½.

259 A90 60(h) blue 3 3
259A " 80(h) orange vermilion 6 5
260 " 1.20(k) rose 4 3
261 " 3(k) violet brown 5 3
262 " 5(k) green 5 3
Nos. 256A–262 (9) 35 29

Thomas G. Masaryk
A91

Coat of Arms
A92

1945-46 Photogravure. ***Perf. 12.***

262A A91 5h dull violet ('46) 8 6
262B " 10h org. yellow ('46) 8 6
262C " 20h dark brown ('46) 6 5
263 " 50h bright green 10 5
264 " 1k orange red 12 6
265 " 2k chalky blue 30 17
Nos. 262A–265 (6) 74 45

1945 ***Imperf.***

266 A92 50h olive gray 5 3
267 " 1k bright red violet 5 3
268 " 1.50k dark carmine 6 3
269 " 2k deep blue 8 3
269A " 2.40k henna brown 18 8
270 " 3k brown 6 5
270A " 4k dark slate green 10 5
271 " 6k violet blue 30 6
271A " 10k sepia 45 10
Nos. 266–271A (9) 1.33 46

Nos. 266 to 271A exist in two printings. Stamps of the first printing are on thin, hard paper in sheets of 100; those of the second printing on thick, soft wove paper in sheets of 200.

Staff Captain Ridky (British Army)
A93

Dr. Miroslav Novak (French Army)
A94

Captain Otakar Jaros (Russian Army)
A95

Staff Captain Stanislav Zimprich (Foreign Legion)
A96

Second Lieutenant Jiri Kral (French Air Force)
A97

Josef Gabcik (Parachutist)
A98

Staff Captain Alois Vasatko (Royal Air Force)
A99

Private Frantisek Adamek (British Colonial Service)
A100

Engraved

1945, Aug. 18 *Perf. 11½x12½*

272 A93 5h intense blue 3 3
273 A94 10h dark brown 3 3
274 A95 20h brick red 3 3
275 A96 25h rose red 4 3
276 A97 30h purple 8 5
277 A98 40h sepia 5 4
278 A99 50h dark olive 5 4
279 A100 60h violet 8 6
280 A93 1k carmine 5 3
281 A94 1.50k lake 6 4
282 A95 2k ultramarine 8 3
283 A96 2.50k deep violet 10 5
284 A97 3k sepia 10 5
285 A98 4k rose lilac 15 6
286 A99 5k myrtle green 27 8
287 A100 10k bright ultra. 80 20
Nos. 272–287 (16) 2.00 85

Flags of Russia, Great Britain, United States and Czechoslovakia
A101

View of Banská Bystrica
A102

Patriot Welcoming Russian Soldier, Turciansky
A103

Ruins of Castle at Sklabina
A104

Czech Patriot, Strecno
A105

1945, Aug. 29 Photo. *Perf. 10*

288 A101 1.50k bright carmine 10 8
289 A102 2k bright blue 10 10
290 A103 4k dark brown 15 25
291 A104 4.50k purple 40 25
292 A105 5k deep green 1.00 50
a. Souv. card of 5, imperf. 25.00 30.00
Nos. 288–292 (5) 1.75 1.18

National uprising against the Germans.
No. 292a contains one each of Nos. 288–292 with multicolored marginal design, on thin cardboard, ungummed. Size: 148x210mm. Sold for 50k.

General Milan Stefánik
A106

President Eduard Benes
A107

Thomas G. Masaryk
A108

1945–46 Engraved *Perf. 12, 12½*

293 A106 30h rose violet 3 3
294 A107 60h blue 10 3
295 A108 1.20(k) carmine rose 12 3
295A " 1.20(k) rose lilac ('46) 10 3
296 A106 2.40(k) rose 12 3
297 A107 3k red violet 24 3
297A A108 4k dark blue ('46) 15 3
298 " 5k Prussian green 24 3
299 A107 7k gray 25 3
300 A106 10k gray blue 60 3
300A " 20k sepia ('46) 1.25 6
Nos. 293–300A (11) 3.20 36

See also No. 325.

1945 Photogravure. *Perf. 14.*

301 A108 50h brown 3 3
302 A106 80h dark green 3 3
303 A107 1.60(k) olive green 10 3
304 A108 15k red violet 80 5

Kozina and Chod Castle, Taus
A109

Red Army Soldier
A110

Engraved.

1945, Nov. 28 *Perf. 12½*

305 A109 2.40k rose carmine 20 20
306 " 4k blue 30 20

Issued to commemorate the 250th anniversary of the death of Jan Sladky Kozina, peasant leader.

1945, Mar. 26 Litho. *Imperf.*

307 A110 2k crimson rose 50 50
308 " 5k slate black 2.00 2.00
309 " 6k ultramarine 50 50

Souvenir Sheet.

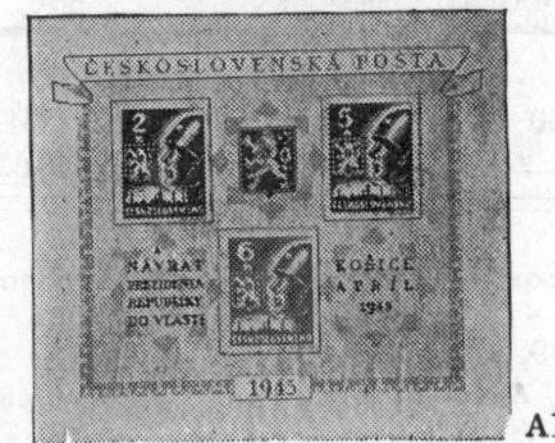

A111

1945, July 16

Gray Burelage

310 A111 Sheet of three 2.00 2.00
a. 2k crimson rose 25 25
b. 5k slate black 25 25
c. 6k ultramarine 25 25

Return of President Benes, April, 1945. Size: 137x120mm.

Clasped Hands
A112

Karel Havlícek Borovsky
A113

1945 ***Rouletted 12½***

311 A112 1.50k brown red 3.00 3.00
312 " 9k red orange 75 75
313 " 13k orange brown 1.00 1.00
314 " 20k blue 2.75 2.75

1946, July 5 **Engraved**

315 A113 1.20(k) gray black 20 15

Issued to commemorate the 90th anniversary of the death of Karel Havlicek Borovsky (1821–1856), editor and writer.

Old Town Hall, Brno
A114

Hodonin Square
A115

Perf. 12½x12, 12x12½.

1946, Aug. 3 Engraved Unwmkd.

316 A114 2.40(k) deep rose 20 6
317 A115 7.40(k) dull violet 50 4

President Eduard Benes
A116

1946, Oct. 28

318 A116 60h indigo 4 3
319 " 1.60k dull green 6 3
320 " 3k red lilac 10 3
321 " 8k sepia 30 3

Flag and Symbols
A117

Saint Adalbert
A118

1947, Jan. 1 *Perf. 12½*

322 A117 1.20(k) Prussian green 20 4
323 " 2.40(k) deep rose 20 3
324 " 4(k) deep blue 35 10

Issued to publicize Czechoslovakia's two-year reconstruction and rehabilitation program.

Stefanik Type of 1945.

1947, Nov. 5

325 A106 1k red orange 10 3

1947, Apr. 23

326 A118 1.60(k) gray 50 25
327 " 2.40(k) rose carmine 75 40
328 " 5(k) blue green 80 35

Issued to commemorate the 950th anniversary of the death of Saint Adalbert, Bishop of Prague.

Grief
A119

Allegorical Figure
A120

1947, June 10 **Engraved**

329 A119 1.20(k) black 40 20
330 " 1.60(k) slate black 40 20
331 A120 2.40(k) brown violet 60 40

Destruction of Lidice, 5th anniversary.

World Federation of Youth Symbol
A121

Thomas G. Masaryk
A122

1947, July 20

332 A121 1.20(k) violet brown 35 10
333 " 4k slate 55 15

Issued to commemorate the World Youth Festival held in Prague, July 20th to August 17, 1947.

1947, Sept. 14

334 A122 1.20(k) gray black, *buff* 30 15
335 " 4k blue black, *cream* 70 20

Death of T. G. Masaryk, 10th anniversary.

Msgr. Stefan Moyses
A123

1947, Oct. 24

336 A123 1.20k rose violet 25 10
337 " 4k deep blue 50 10

Issued to commemorate the 150th anniversary of the birth of Stefan Moyses, first Slovakian chairman of the Slavic movement.

"Freedom from Social Oppression"
A124

1947, Oct. 26 Photo. *Perf. 14*

338 A124 2.40k bright carmine 30 20
339 " 4k bright ultra. 60 20

Issued to commemorate the 30th anniversary of the Russian revolution of October, 1917.

President Eduard Benes
A125

"Czechoslovakia" Greeting Sokol Marchers
A126

1948, Feb. 15 Photogravure

Size: 17½x21½mm.

340 A125 1.50(k) brown 6 3

Size: 19x23mm.

341 A125 2k deep plum 10 3
342 " 5k bright ultra. 25 3

1948, Mar. 7 Engr. *Perf. 12½*

343 A126 1.50(k) brown 15 6
344 " 3k rose carmine 15 6
345 " 5k blue 50 8

The 11th Sokol Congress.

King Charles IV — A127 | St. Wenceslas and King Charles IV — A128

1948, Apr. 7

346 A127 1.50(k) black brown 10 5
347 A128 2(k) dark brown 10 5
348 " 3(k) brown red 25 12
349 A127 5(k) dark blue 60 20

Issued to commemorate the 600th anniversary of the foundation of Charles University, Prague.

Czech Peasants in Revolt — A129 | Jindrich Vanicek — A130

Photogravure.

1948, May 14 *Perf. 14* Unwmkd.

350 A129 1.50k dk. olive brown 15 6

Centenary of abolition of serfdom.

1948, June 10 Engraved *Perf. 12½*

Designs: 1.50k, 2k, Josef Scheiner.

351 A130 1k dark green 15 5
352 " 1.50k sepia 15 5
353 " 2k gray blue 35 8
354 " 3k claret 50 12

11th Sokol Congress, Prague, 1948.

Frantisek Palacky and F. L. Rieger — A131 | Miloslav Josef Hurban — A132

1948, June 20 Unwmkd.

355 A131 1.50k gray 20 8
356 " 3k brown carmine 20 8

Issued to commemorate the centenary of the Constituent Assembly at Kromeriz.

1948, Aug. 27 *Perf. 12½*

Designs: 3k, Ludwig Stur. 5k, Michael M. Hodza.

357 A132 1.50(k) dark brown 12 8
358 " 3(k) carmine lake 20 8
359 " 5(k) indigo 40 12

Centenary of 1848 insurrection against Hungary.

Eduard Benes — A133 | Czechoslovak Family — A134

1948, Sept. 28

360 A133 8k black 30 10

Issued in tribute to President Eduard Benes, 1884–1948.

1948, Oct. 28 *Perf. 12½x12*

361 A134 1.50k deep blue 10 10
362 " 3k rose carmine 30 18

Issued to commemorate the 30th anniversary of Czechoslovakia's Independence.

Pres. Klement Gottwald — A135 | Gottwald and Presidential Flag — A136

1948–49 *Perf. 12½.*

Size: 18⅛x23½mm.

363 A135 1.50(k) dark brown 10 3
364 " 3(k) carmine rose 25 3
a. 3(k) rose brn. 30 3
365 " 5(k) gray blue 25 3

Size: 23½x29mm.

366 A135 20(k) purple 1.25 15

See also Nos. 373, 564, 600-604.

Souvenir Sheet.

1948, Nov. 23 *Imperf.* Unwmkd.

367 A136 30k rose brown 3.00 2.00

52nd birthday of Pres. Klement Gottwald (1896–1953). Size: 67x98½mm.

Souvenir Sheet.

Hradcany Castle
A137

1948, Dec. 18

368 A137 10k dark blue violet 1.25 1.00

30th anniversary of first Czechoslovak postage stamp. Size: 79x90½mm.

Czechoslovak and Russian Workmen Shaking Hands — A138 | Lenin — A139

1948, Dec. 12 *Perf. 12½*

369 A138 3k rose carmine 24 12

Issued to commemorate the fifth anniversary of the treaty of alliance between Czechoslovakia and Russia.

1949, Jan. 21 Engraved *Perf. 12½*

370 A139 1.50(k) violet brown 24 12
371 " 5(k) deep blue 40 20

25th anniversary of the death of Lenin.

Gottwald Type of 1948
Inscribed: "UNOR 1948" and

Gottwald Addressing Meeting
A140

1949, Feb. 25 Photo. *Perf. 14*

372 A140 3k red brown 15 4

Engraved
Perf. 12½

Size: 23½x29mm.

373 A135 10k deep green 65 20

Nos. 372 and 373 were issued to commemorate the first anniversary of Klement Gottwald's speech announcing the appointment of a new government.

P. O. Hviezdoslav — A141 | Stagecoach and Train — A142

Designs (Writers): 80h, V. Vancura. 1k, J. Sverma. 2k, Julius Fucik. 4k, Jiri Wolker. 8k, Alois Jirasek.

1949 Photogravure. *Perf. 14.*

374 A141 50h violet brown 5 3
375 " 80h scarlet 8 3
376 " 1k dark olive green 8 3
377 " 2k bright blue 40 3

Engraved
Perf. 12½

378 A141 4k violet brown 40 3
379 " 8k brown black 45 3
Nos. 374-379 (6) 1.46 18

1949, May 20

Designs: 5k, Postrider and post bus. 13k, Sailing ship and plane.

380 A142 3k brown carmine 2.50 1.75
381 " 5k deep blue 60 30
382 " 13k deep green 1.25 50

Issued to commemorate the 75th anniversary of the formation of the Universal Postal Union.

Reaping
A143

Communist Emblem and Workers — A144 | Workman, Symbol of Industry — A145

Perf. 12½x12, 12x12½.

1949, May 24 Unwmkd.

383 A143 1.50k deep green 45 35
384 A144 3k brown carmine 25 20
385 A145 5k deep blue 65 35

No. 384 commemorates the ninth meeting of the Communist Party of Czechoslovakia, May 25, 1949.

Friedrich Smetana and National Theater, Prague — A146 | Aleksander Pushkin — A147

1949, June 4 *Perf. 12½x12*

386 A146 1.50k dull green 30 10
387 " 5k deep blue 70 20

Issued to commemorate the 125th anniversary of the birth of Friedrich Smetana, composer.

1949, June 6 *Perf. 12x12½*

388 A147 2k olive gray 30 20

Issued to commemorate the 150th anniversary of the birth of Aleksander S. Pushkin.

Frederic Chopin and Conservatory, Warsaw
A148

1949, June 24 *Perf. 12½x12*

389 A148 3k dark red 40 25
390 " 8k violet brown 80 45

Issued to commemorate the centenary of the death of Frederic F. Chopin.

Globe and Ribbon — A149 | Zvolen Castle — A150

1949, Aug. 20 *Perf. 12½x12*

391 A149 1.50k violet brown 30 20
392 " 5k ultramarine 60 50

Issued to publicize the 50th Prague Sample Fair, September 11–18, 1949.

Starting in 1949, commemorative stamps which are priced in italics were issued in smaller quantities than those in the balance of the set and sold at prices higher than face value.

1949, Aug. 28 *Perf. 12½*

393 A150 10k rose lake 75 5

Early Miners — A151 | Miner of Today — A152

Design: 5k, Mining Machine.

1949, Sept. 11 *Perf. 12½x12, 12½*

394 A151 1.50k sepia 1.00 90
395 A152 3k carmine rose 3.00 1.25
396 A151 5k deep blue *4.00* *1.50*

Issued to commemorate the 700th anniversary of the Czechoslovak mining industry and the 150th anniversary of the miner's laws.

Construction Workers A153

Joseph V. Stalin A154

Design: 2k, Machinist.

1949, Dec. 11 ***Perf. 12½***

397 A153 1k dark green 2.25 85
398 " 2k violet brown 1.25 40

2nd Trade Union Congress, Prague, 1949.

Cream Paper.

1949, Dec. 21 **Unwmkd.**

Design: 3k, Stalin facing left.

399 A154 1.50k greenish gray 65 40
400 " 3k claret *2.50* *1.25*

70th birthday of Joseph V. Stalin.

Skier A155 Efficiency Badge A156

Engraved, 3k Photogravure

1950, Feb. 15 ***Perf. 12½, 13½***

401 A155 1.50k gray blue *2.00* *75*
402 A156 3k violet brown, *cream* 2.00 1.20
403 A155 5k ultramarine *2.25* *1.50*

Issued to publicize the 51st Ski Championship for the Tatra cup, Feb. 15–26, 1950.

Vladimir V. Mayakovsky A157

1950, Apr. 14 **Engr.** ***Perf. 12½***

404 A157 1.50k dark brown *2.25* *95*
405 " 3k brown red 2.25 95

Issued to commemorate the 20th anniversary of the death of V. V. Mayakovsky, poet.

See also Nos. 414–417, 422–423, 432–433, 464–465, 477–478.

Soviet Tank Soldier and Hradcany A158

Designs: 2k, Hero of Labor medal. 3k, Two workers (militiamen) and Town Hall, Prague. 5k, Text of government program and heraldic lion.

1950, May 5

406 A158 1.50k gray green 30 25
407 " 2k dark brown *1.10* *75*
408 " 3k brown red 40 25
409 " 5k dark blue 55 20

Issued on the occasion of the fifth anniversary of the Czechoslovak People's Democratic Republic.

Factory and Young Couple with Tools—A159

Designs: 2k, Steam shovel. 3k, Farmer and farm scene. 5k, Three workers leaving factory.

1950, May 9 **Engraved**

410 A159 1.50k dark green 90 60
411 " 2k dark brown *1.60* *1.00*
412 " 3k rose red 40 25
413 " 5k deep blue 60 25

Canceled to Order

The government philatelic department started about 1950 to sell canceled sets of new issues. Prices in the second ("used") column are for these canceled-to-order stamps. Postally used copies are worth more.

Portrait Type of 1950

Design: S. K. Neumann.

1950, June 5 ***Perf. 12½*** **Unwmkd.**

414 A157 1.50k deep blue 18 8
415 " 3k violet brown *1.00* *90*

Issued to commemorate the 75th anniversary of the birth of Stanislav Kostka Neumann (1875–1947), journalist and poet.

1950, June 21

Design: Bozena Nemcova.

416 A157 1.50k deep blue *1.00* *90*
417 " 7k dark brown 30 15

Issued to commemorate the 130th anniversary of the birth of Bozena Nemcova (1820–1862), writer.

Liberation of Colonies A160

Designs: 2k, Allegory, Fight for Peace. 3k, Group of Students. 5k, Marching Students with flags.

1950, Aug. 14

418 A160 1.50k dark green 10 5
419 " 2k sepia *1.10* *60*
420 " 3k rose carmine 20 15
421 " 5k ultramarine 60 25

Issued to publicize the 2nd International Students World Congress, Prague, August 12–24, 1950.

Portrait Type of 1950.

Design: Zdenek Fibich.

1950, Oct. 15

422 A157 3k rose brown *90* *60*
423 " 8k gray green 35 15

Issued to commemorate the centenary of the birth of Zdenek Fibich, musician.

Miner, Soldier and Farmer A161

Czech and Soviet Soldiers—A162

1950, Oct. 6

424 A161 1.50k slate *75* *60*
425 A162 3k carmine rose 35 20

Issued to publicize Czech Army Day.

Prague Castle, 16th Century A163

Prague, 1493 A164

Designs: 3k, Prague, 1606. 5k, Prague, 1794.

1950, Oct. 21 ***Perf. 14***

426 A163 1.50k black 2.50 1.25
427 A164 2k chocolate 2.50 1.25
428 " 3k brn. carmine 2.50 1.25
429 " 5k gray 2.50 1.25
a. Block of 4 15.00 10.00

Sheets arranged in blocks of four containing one of Nos. 426 to 429. See Nos. 434–435.

Communications Symbols A165

1950, Oct. 25 ***Perf. 12½***

430 A165 1.50k chocolate 12 5
431 " 3k brown carmine *60* *30*

Issued to commemorate first anniversary of the foundation of the International League of P.T.T. Employees.

Portrait Type of 1950.

Design: J. Gregor Tajovsky.

1950, Oct. 26

432 A157 1.50k brown *75* *50*
433 " 5k deep blue 75 60

Issued to commemorate the 10th anniversary of the death of J. Gregor Tajovsky (1874–1940), Slovakian writer.

Scenic Type of 1950.

Design: Prague, 1950.

1950, Oct. 28

434 A164 1.50k indigo 30 15
a. Souvenir sheet of 4, imperf. 6.00 6.00
435 " 3k brown carmine *70* *50*

No. 434a measures 121x100 mm. and contains four copies of No. 434, imperforate, with carmine inscription in top margin.

Czech and Soviet Steel Workers A166

1950, Nov. 4 **Unwmkd.**

436 A166 1.50k chocolate 35 15
437 " 5k deep blue *85* *75*

Issued to publicize the 2nd meeting of the Union of Czechoslovak-Soviet Friendship.

Dove by Picasso A167

1951, Jan. 20 Photo. ***Perf. 14***

438 A167 2k deep blue *2.75* *2.00*
439 " 3k rose brown 2.50 1.75

Issued to commemorate the first Czechoslovak Congress of Fighters for Peace, held in Prague.

Julius Fucik A168

1951, Feb. 17 **Engr.** ***Perf. 12½***

440 A168 1.50k gray 50 35
441 " 5k gray blue *1.10* *90*

Drop Hammer A169 Installing Gear A170

1951, Feb. 24

442 A169 1.50k gray black 10 5
443 A170 3k violet brown 15 6
444 A169 4k gray blue *75* *50*

Women Machinists A171 Apprentice Miners A172

Designs: 3k, Woman tractor operator. 5k, Women of different races.

1951, Mar. 8 Photo. ***Perf. 14***

445 A171 1.50k olive brown 25 10
446 " 3k brn. carmine *1.00* *75*
447 " 5k blue 45 20

International Women's Day, Mar. 8.

1951, Apr. 12 **Engr.** ***Perf. 12½***

448 A172 1.50k gray *45* *25*
449 " 3k red brown 15 8

Plowing A173

Collective Cattle Breeding
A174

1951, Apr. 28 Photo. *Perf. 14*
450 A173 1.50k brown 60 50
451 A174 2k dark green *85* *80*

Tatra Mountain
Recreation Center—A175

Mountain Recreation Centers:
2k, Beskydy (Biskids). 3k, Krkonose (Carpathians).

1951, May 5 Engr. *Perf. 12½*
Inscribed: "ROH."
452 A175 1.50k deep green 20 8
453 " 2k dark brown *75* *60*
454 " 3k rose brown 15 8

Issued to publicize the summer opening of trade union recreation centers.

Klement Gottwald
and Joseph Stalin
A176

Factory Militiaman
A177

Red Army Soldier and Partisan
A178

Marx, Engels, Lenin and Stalin
A179

1951 *Perf. 12½* **Unwmkd.**
455 A176 1.50k olive gray 70 30
456 A177 2k red brown 18 8
457 A178 3k rose brown 35 8
458 A176 5k deep blue *2.25* *1.40*
459 A179 8k gray 75 30
Nos. 455-459 (5) *4.23* *2.16*

Issued to commemorate the 30th anniversary of the founding of the Czechoslovak Communist Party.

Antonin Dvorák
A180

Design: 1.50k, 3k, Friedrich Smetana.

1951, May 30
460 A180 1k reddish brown 12 8
461 " 1.50k olive gray *60* *25*
462 " 2k dark reddish brown 1.00 *60*
463 " 3k rose brown 12 8

International Music Festival, Prague.

Portrait Type of 1950.

1951, June 21
Portrait: Bohumir Smeral (facing right).
464 A157 1.50k dark gray *50* *45*
465 " 3k rose brown 30 15

Issued to commemorate the 10th anniversary of the death of Bohumir Smeral, political leader.

Gymnast on Rings
A181

Designs: 1.50k, Discus Thrower. 3k, Soccer. 5k, Skier.

1951, June 21
466 A181 1k dark green 75 45
467 " 1.50k dark brown 75 45
468 " 3k brown carmine 90 45
469 " 5k deep blue *2.25* *1.40*

Issued to honor the 9th Congress of the Czechoslovak Sokol Federation.

Scene from "Fall of Berlin"
A182

Scene from "The Great Citizen"
A183

1951, July 14
470 A182 80h rose brown 30 25
471 A183 1.50k dark gray 45 35
472 A182 4k gray blue *1.35* *1.10*

Issued on the occasion of the International Film Festival, Karlovy Vary, July 14–29, 1951.

Alois Jirásek
A184

"Fables and Fate"
A185

Design: 4k, Scene from "Reign of Tabor."

1951, Aug. 23 Engr. *Perf. 12½*
473 A184 1.50k gray 18 12
474 " 5k dark blue *1.75* *1.10*
Photo. *Perf. 14*
475 A185 3k dark red 27 20
476 " 4k dark brown 50 25

Issued to commemorate the centenary of the birth of Alois Jirásek, author.

Portrait Type of 1950.

Design: Josef Hybes.

1951, July 21 Engraved
477 A157 1.50k chocolate 12 8
478 " 2k rose brown *50* *40*

Issued to commemorate the centenary of the birth of Josef Hybes (1850–1921), cofounder of Czech Communist Party.

"Ostrava Region"
A186

Mining Iron Ore
A187

1951, Sept. 9
479 A186 1.50k dark brown 12 4
480 A187 3k rose brown 15 3
481 A186 5k deep blue *1.20* 75

Miner's Day, Sept. 9, 1951.

Soldiers on Parade
A188

Designs: 1k, Gunner and field gun. 1.50k, Klement Gottwald. 3k, Tankman and tank. 5k, Aviators.

Photo. (80h, 5k), Engr.
Perf. 14 (80h, 5k), 12½

1951, Oct. 6
Inscribed: "Den CS Armady 1951."
482 A188 80h olive brown 18 15
483 " 1k dark olive green 30 25
484 " 1.50k sepia 40 25
485 " 3k claret 50 25
486 " 5k blue *1.40* *1.10*
Nos. 482-486 (5) *2.78* *2.00*

Issued to publicize Army Day, Oct. 6, 1951.

Joseph Stalin and Klement Gottwald
A189

Lenin, Stalin and Soldiers
A190

1951, Nov. 3 Engraved *Perf. 12½*
487 A189 1.50k sepia 12 6
488 A190 3k red brown 12 4
489 A189 4k deep blue *90* *65*

Issued to publicize the month of Czechoslovak-Soviet friendship, 1951.

Peter Jilemnicky
A191

Ladislav Zapotocky
A192

1951, Dec. 5 **Unwmkd.**
491 A191 1.50k reddish brown 30 20
492 " 2k dull blue *65* *55*

Issued to commemorate the 50th anniversary of the birth of Peter Jilemnicky (1901–1949), writer.

1952, Jan. 12 *Perf. 11½*
493 A192 1.50k brown red 10 3
494 " 4k gray *60* *45*

Issued to commemorate the centenary of the birth of Ladislav Zapotocky, Bohemian socialist pioneer.

Jan Kollar
A193

Lenin and Lenin Hall
A194

1952, Jan. 30 *Perf. 11½* **Unwmkd.**
495 A193 3k dark carmine 10 3
496 " 5k violet blue *85* *65*

Issued to commemorate the centenary of the death of Jan Kollar (1793–1852), poet.

1952, Jan. 30 *Perf. 12½*
497 A194 1.50k rose carmine 15 3
498 " 5k deep blue *70* *50*

Issued to commemorate the 40th anniversary of the Sixth All-Russian Party Conference.

Emil Holub and African
A195

Klement Gottwald Metallurgical Plant
A196

1952, Feb. 21 *Perf. 11½*
499 A195 3k red brown 30 25
500 " 5k gray *1.75* *1.50*

Issued to commemorate the 50th anniversary ot the death of Emil Holub, explorer.

1952, Feb. 25 Photo. *Perf. 14*
Designs: 2k, Foundry. 3k, Chemical plant.
501 A196 1.50k sepia 12 8
502 " 2k red brown *1.10* *95*
503 " 3k scarlet 12 4

Student, Soldier and Worker
A197

Youths of Three Races
A198

1952, Mar. 21 *Perf. 14* **Unwmkd.**

No.	Type	Description	Unused	Used
504	A197	1.50k blue	12	6
505	A198	2k olive black	25	15
506	A197	3k lake	*90*	*80*

International Youth Day, Mar. 25, 1952.

Similar to Type of 1951.

Portrait: Otakar Sevcik.

1952, Mar. 22 Engr. *Perf. 12½*

No.	Type	Description	Unused	Used
507	A184	2k chocolate, *cream*	*50*	*45*
508	"	3k rose brown, *cream*	15	6

Issued to commemorate the centenary of the birth of Otakar Sevcik, violinist.

Jan A. Komensky
A199

Industrial and Farm Women
A200

1952, Mar. 28 Cream Paper

No.	Type	Description	Unused	Used
509	A199	1.50k dark brown	*1.35*	*75*
510	"	11k dark blue	30	10

Issued to commemorate the 360th anniversary of the birth of Jan Amos Komensky (Comenius), teacher and philosopher.

1952, Mar. 8 Cream Paper

No.	Type	Description	Unused	Used
511	A200	1.50k deep blue	*1.10*	*70*

International Women's Day Mar. 8, 1952.

Woman and Children
A201

Antifascist
A202

1952, Apr. 12 Cream Paper

No.	Type	Description	Unused	Used
512	A201	2k chocolate	*90*	*65*
513	"	3k deep claret	18	8

Issued to publicize the International Conference for the Protection of Children, Vienna, April 12-16, 1952.

1952, Apr. 11 Photo. *Perf. 14*

No.	Type	Description	Unused	Used
514	A202	1.50k red brown	12	3
515	"	2k ultramarine	*65*	*55*

Issued to publicize the Day of International Solidarity of Fighters against Fascism, April 11, 1952.

Harvester
A203

Design: 3k, Tractor and Seeders.

1952, Apr. 30

No.	Type	Description	Unused	Used
516	A203	1.50k deep blue	*80*	*65*
517	"	2k brown	20	15
518	"	3k brown red	20	15

Youths Carrying Flags
A204

1952, May 1

No.	Type	Description	Unused	Used
519	A204	3k brown red	50	40
520	"	4k dark red brown	*75*	*60*

Issued to publicize Labor Day, May 1, 1952.

Crowd Cheering Soviet Soldiers
A205

1952, May 9

No.	Type	Description	Unused	Used
521	A205	1.50k dark red	45	40
522	"	5k deep blue	*1.25*	*95*

Liberation of Czechoslovakia from German occupation, 7th anniversary.

Children
A206

J. V. Myslbek
A207

Design: 3k, "Pioneer" teaching children.

1952, May 31 Engr. *Perf. 12½*

Cream Paper.

No.	Type	Description	Unused	Used
523	A206	1.50k dark brown	10	3
524	"	2k Prus. green	*80*	*50*
525	"	3k rose brown	12	4

International Children's Day May 31, 1952.

1952, June 2

Design: 8k, Allegory, "Music."

No.	Type	Description	Unused	Used
526	A207	1.50k red brown	18	4
527	"	2k dark brown	*1.25*	*90*
528	"	8k gray green	30	5

Issued to commemorate the 30th anniversary of the death of Joseph V. Myslbek (1848–1922), sculptor.

Beethoven
A208

House of Artists
A209

1952, June 7 *Perf. 11½* **Unwmkd.**

No.	Type	Description	Unused	Used
529	A208	1.50k sepia	30	25
530	A209	3k red brown	30	25
531	A208	5k indigo	*1.20*	*95*

International Music Festival, Prague, 1952.

Lidice, Symbol of a New Life
A210

1952, June 10 *Perf. 12½*

No.	Type	Description	Unused	Used
532	A210	1.50k dk. violet brown	12	6
533	"	5k dark blue	*70*	*55*

Destruction of Lidice, 10th anniversary.

Jan Hus
A211

Bethlehem Chapel
A212

1952, July 5

No.	Type	Description	Unused	Used
534	A211	1.50k brown	10	4
535	A212	3k red brown	10	3
536	A211	5k black	*1.00*	*85*

Issued to commemorate the 550th anniversary of the installation of Jan Hus as pastor of Bethlehem Chapel, Prague.

Doctor Examining Patient
A213

Design: 2k, Doctor, Nurse, Mother and child.

1952, July 31

No.	Type	Description	Unused	Used
537	A213	1.50k dark brown	*80*	*50*
538	"	2k blue violet	10	4
539	"	3k rose brown	25	5

Czechoslovakia's Unified Health Service.

Relay Race—A214

Designs: 2k, Canoeing. 3k, Cycling. 4k, Hockey.

1952, Aug. 2 *Perf. 11½*

No.	Type	Description	Unused	Used
540	A214	1.50k dark brown	60	45
541	"	2k greenish blk.	*1.00*	*75*
542	"	3k red brown	60	45
543	"	4k deep blue	*2.75*	*2.00*

Issued to publicize Czechoslovakia's Unified Physical Education program.

F. L. Celakovski
A215

Mikulas Ales
A216

1952, Aug. 5 *Perf. 12½*

No.	Type	Description	Unused	Used
544	A215	1.50k dark brown	10	3
545	"	2k dark green	*55*	*40*

Issued to commemorate the centenary of the death of Frantisek L. Celakovski, poet and writer.

Perf. 11x11½

1952, Aug. 30 Engraved Unwmkd.

No.	Type	Description	Unused	Used
546	A216	1.50k dark gray green	40	20
547	"	6k red brown	*2.25*	*1.75*

Birth centenary of Mikulas Ales, painter.

17th Century Mining Towers
A217

Jan Zizka
A218

Designs: 1.50k, Coal Excavator. 2k, Peter Bezruc mine. 3k, Automatic coaling crane.

1952, Sept. 14 *Perf. 12½*

No.	Type	Description	Unused	Used
548	A217	1k sepia	*1.00*	*75*
549	"	1.50k dark blue	10	5
550	"	2k olive gray	10	6
551	"	3k violet brown	20	5

Issued to publicize Miners' Day, Sept. 14, 1952. No. 550 also commemorates the 85th anniversary of the birth of Peter Bezruc (Vladimir Vasek), poet.

1952, Oct. 5 Engraved *Perf. 11½*

Designs: 2k, Fraternization with Russians. 3k, Marching with flag.

Inscribed: ". . . . Armady 1952,"

No.	Type	Description	Unused	Used
552	A218	1.50k rose lake	10	3
553	"	2k olive bistre	12	4
554	"	3k dark carmine rose	15	6
555	"	4k gray	*1.20*	*90*

Issued to publicize Army Day, Oct. 5, 1952.

Souvenir Sheet.

Statues to Bulgarian Partisans and to Soviet Army—A219

1952, Oct. 18 *Perf. 12½* **Unwmkd.**

No.	Type	Description	Unused	Used
556	A219	Sheet of two	30.00	11.00
		a. 2k deep carmine	10.00	3.00
		b. 3k ultramarine	10.00	3.00

Issued to commemorate the National Philatelic Exhibition, Bratislava, Oct. 18–Nov. 2, 1952.

Danube River, Bratislava
A220

1952, Oct. 18

No.	Type	Description	Unused	Used
557	A220	1.50k dark brown	15	10

National Philatelic Exhibition, Bratislava.

Conference with Lenin and Stalin
A221

Worker and Nurse Holding Dove and Olive Branch
A222

1952, Nov. 7

No.	Type	Description	Unused	Used
558	A221	2k brown black	*70*	*55*
559	"	3k carmine	15	6

Issued to commemorate the 35th anniversary of the Russian Revolution and to publicize Czecho-slovak-Soviet friendship.

1952, Nov. 15 Photo. *Perf. 14*

No.	Type	Description	Unused	Used
560	A222	2k brown	*70*	*60*
561	"	3k red	15	3

Issued to publicize the first State Congress of the Czechoslovak Red Cross.

Matej Louda, Hussite Leader, Painted by Mikulas Ales
A223

Design: 3k, Dragon-killer Trutnov, painted by Ales.

1952, Nov. 18 Engraved *Perf. 11½*

562 A223 2k red brown 25 4
563 " 3k greenish gray 35 12

Issued to commemorate the centenary of the birth of Mikulas Ales, painter.

Gottwald Type of 1948–49.
Size: 19x24mm.

1952, June 2 *Perf. 12½* Unwmkd.

564 A135 1k dark green 8 3

"Peace" Flags
A224

Dove by Picasso
A225

1952, Dec. 12 Photo. *Perf. 14*

565 A224 3k red brown 15 3
566 " 4k deep blue *80* *70*

Issued to publicize the Congress of Nations for Peace, Vienna, Dec. 12–19, 1952.

1953, Jan. 17

Design: 4k, Czech Family.

567 A225 1.50k dark brown 10 3
568 " 4k slate blue *60* *40*

2nd Czechoslovak Peace Congress.

Smetana Museum
A226

Design: 4k, Jirásek Museum.

1953, Feb. 10 Engraved *Perf. 11½*

569 A226 1.50k dk. vio. brown 10 3
570 " 4k dark gray *1.00* *75*

Issued to commemorate the 75th anniversary of the birth of Prof. Zdenek Nejedly.

Martin Kukucin
A227

Jaroslav Vrchlicky
A228

Designs: 2k, Karel Jaromir Erben. 3k, Vaclav Matej Kramerius. 5k, Josef Dobrovsky.

1953, Feb. 28

571 A227 1k gray 5 3
572 A228 1.50k olive 10 3
573 " 2k rose lake 8 4
574 " 3k light brown 12 5
575 " 5k slate blue *1.50* *1.25*
Nos. 571–575 (5) *1.85* *1.40*

Issued to honor Czech writers and poets: 1k, 25th anniversary of death of Kukucin. 1.50k, birth centenary of Vrchlicky. 2k, centenary of completion of "Kytice" by Erben. 3k, birth bicentenary of Kramerius. 5k, birth bicentenary of Dobrovsky.

Militia
A229

Klement Gottwald
A230

Design: 8k, Portraits of Stalin and Gottwald and Peoples Assembly.

Perf. 13½x14

1953, Feb. 25 Photo. Unwmkd.

576 A229 1.50k deep blue 10 3
577 A230 3k red 15 3
578 A229 8k dark brown *1.20* *85*

Issued to commemorate the 5th anniversary of the defeat of the attempt to reinstate capitalism.

Book and Torch
A231

Design: 3k, Bedrich Vaclavek.

1953, Mar. 5 Engraved *Perf. 11½*

579 A231 1k sepia *80* *60*
580 " 3k orange brown 15 12

Issued to commemorate the 10th anniversary of the death of Bedrich Vaclavek (1897–1943), socialist writer.

Stalin Type of 1949.
Inscribed "21 XII 1879 - 5 III 1953."

1953, Mar. 12

581 A154 1.50k black 25 15

Death of Joseph Stalin, Mar. 5, 1953.

Mother and Child
A232

Girl Revolutionist
A233

1953, Mar. 8

582 A232 1.50k ultramarine 10 3
583 A233 2k brown red *50* *40*

International Women's Day.

Klement Gottwald
A234

1953, Mar. 19

584 A234 1.50k black 12 6
585 " 3k " 12 5

Souvenir Sheet.
Imperf.

586 A234 5k black 1.50 95

No. 586 measures 68x97 mm., with marginal inscriptions and laurel branch.

Nos. 584-586 commemorate the death of President Klement Gottwald, March 14, 1953.

Josef Pecka, Ladislav Zapotocky and Josef Hybes—A236

1953, Apr. 7 *Perf. 11½* Unwmkd.

587 A236 2k light violet brown 15 5

Issued to commemorate the 75th anniversary of the first congress of the Czech Social Democratic Party.

Cyclists
A237

1953, Apr. 29

588 A237 3k deep blue 45 30

Issued to commemorate the 6th International Peace Bicycle Race, Prague-Berlin-Warsaw.

Medal of "May 1, 1890"
A238

Designs: 1.50k, Lenin and Stalin. 3k, May Day Parade. 8k, Marx and Engels.

Engraved and Photogravure.

1953, Apr. 30 *Perf. 11½x11, 14*

Inscribed: "1 MAJ 1953"

589 A238 1k chocolate *1.35* *1.10*
590 " 1.50k dark gray 6 3
591 " 3k carmine lake 10 3
592 " 8k dark gray green 25 10

Issued to publicize Labor Day, May 1, 1953.

Sowing Grain
A239

Design: 7k, Reaper.

1953, May 8 Photo. *Perf. 14*

593 A239 1.50k brown 30 5
594 " 7k deep green *1.25* *1.10*

Issued to publicize the socialization of the village.

Dam
A240

Welder
A241

Design: 3k, Iron works.

1953, May 8 *Perf. 11½*

595 A240 1.50k gray *75* *45*
596 A241 2k blue gray 6 3
597 A240 3k red brown 10 3

Josef Slavik
A242

Leos Janacek
A243

1953, June 19

598 A242 75h deep gray blue *45* 8
599 A243 1.60k dark brown 85 8

Issued on the occasion of the International Music Festival, Prague, 1953.

Gottwald Type of 1948–49.

1953 *Perf. 12½, 11½*

600 A135 15h yellow green 25 3
601 " 20h dark violet brown 40 3
602 " 1k purple 65 3
603 " 3k brown carmine 15 3
604 " 3k gray 1.10 3
Nos. 600–604 (5) 2.55 15

Nos. 600-604 vary slightly in size. Nos. 600 and 602 are perf. 12½; Nos. 601, 603-604 are perf. 11½.

Pres. Antonin Zapotocky
A244

1953, June 19 Photo. *Perf. 14*

605 A244 30h violet blue 50 3
606 " 60h cerise 35 3

Julius Fucik
A245

Book and Carnation
A246

1953, Sept. 8 Engraved *Perf. 12½*

607 A245 40h dark violet brown 20 3
608 A246 60h pink *65* *35*

Issued to commemorate the 10th anniversary of the death of Julius Fucik, Communist leader executed by the Nazis.

Miner and Flag
A247

Design: 60h, Oil field and workers.

1953, Sept. 10 *Perf. 11½*

609 A247 30h gray 15 3
610 " 60h brown violet *60* *40*

Issued to publicize Miner's Day, Sept. 10, 1953.

Volleyball Game
A248

Motorcyclist
A249

Design: 60h, Woman throwing javelin.

1953, Sept. 15

611	A248	30h brown red	*2.00*	1.25
612	A249	40h dk. violet brown	2.25	60
613	A248	60h rose violet	2.25	60

Hussite Warrior — A250

Pres. Antonin Zapotocky — A251

Designs: 60h, Soldier presenting arms. 1k, Red army soldiers.

Inscribed: "Den CS Armady 1953."

1953, Oct. 8

614	A250	30h brown	20	3
615	"	60h rose lake	30	4
616	"	1k brown red	*1.10*	*1.00*

Issued to publicize Army Day, Oct. 3, 1953.

1953 ***Perf. 11½, 12½.*** **Unwmkd.**

617	A251	30h violet blue	30	3
618	"	60h carmine rose	55	3

No. 617 is perf. 11½ and measures 19x23 mm. No. 618 is perf. 12½ and measures 18¾x23¾. See also No. 780.

Charles Bridge and Prague Castle — A252

Korean and Czech Girls — A253

1953, Aug. 15 Engraved ***Perf. 11½***

619	A252	5k gray	1.75	8

1953, Oct. 11 ***Perf. 11x11½***

620	A253	30h dark brown	3.50	1.50

Issued to demonstrate Czechoslovakia's friendship with Korea.

Flags, Hradcany Castle and Kremlin

A254

Designs: 60h, Lomonosov University, Moscow. 1.20k, Lenin Ship Canal.

1953, Nov. 7

621	A254	30h dark gray	*1.75*	*1.10*
622	"	60h dark brown	1.65	1.00
623	"	1.20k ultramarine	1.75	1.65

Issued to publicize the month of Czechoslovak-Soviet friendship.

Emmy Destinn, Opera Singer — A255

National Theater, Prague — A256

Portrait: 2k, Eduard Vojan, actor.

1953, Nov. 18 ***Perf. 14***

624	A255	30h blue black	50	30
625	A256	60h brown	35	6
626	A255	2k sepia	*2.00*	*90*

Issued to commemorate the 70th anniversary of the founding of the National Theater.

Josef Manes — A257

Vaclav Hollar — A258

1953, Nov. 28 ***Perf. 11x11½***

627	A257	60h brown carmine	30	8
628	"	1.20k deep blue	*1.25*	*70*

Issued to honor Josef Manes, painter.

1953, Dec. 5

Portrait: 1.20k, Head framed, facing right.

629	A258	30h brown black	20	8
630	"	1.20k dark brown	*1.00*	*70*

Issued to honor Vaclav Hollar, artist and etcher.

Leo N. Tolstoi

A259

1953, Dec. 29 **Unwmkd.**

631	A259	60h dark green	30	12
632	"	1k chocolate	*1.35*	*75*

Issued to commemorate the 125th anniversary of the birth of Leo N. Tolstoi.

Locomotive

A260

Design: 1k, Plane loading mail.

Engraved, Center Photogravure.

1953, Dec. 29 ***Perf. 11½x11***

633	A260	60h brown orange & gray violet	30	8
634	"	1k orange brown & bright blue	*1.50*	*95*

Lenin

A261

Lenin Museum, Prague

A262

1954, Jan. 21 Engraved ***Perf. 11½***

635	A261	30h dark brown	40	20
636	A262	1.40k chocolate	*1.35*	*1.10*

Issued to commemorate the 30th anniversary of the death of Lenin.

Klement Gottwald

A263

Design: 2.40k, Revolutionist with flag.

Perf. 11x11½, 14x13½.

1954, Feb. 18

637	A263	60h dark brown	45	5
638	"	2.40k rose lake	*2.50*	*1.25*

Issued to commemorate the 25th anniversary of the fifth congress of the Communist Party in Czechoslovakia.

Gottwald Mausoleum, Prague

A264

Gottwald and Stalin

A265

Design: 1.20k, Lenin & Stalin mausoleum, Moscow.

1954, Mar. 5 ***Perf. 11½, 14x13½***

639	A264	30h olive brown	20	7
640	A265	60h deep ultra.	30	12
641	A264	1.20k rose brown	*1.35*	*1.00*

Issued to commemorate the first anniversary of the deaths of Joseph V. Stalin and Klement Gottwald.

Two Runners — A266

Group of Hikers — A267

Design: 1k, Woman swimmer.

1954, Apr. 24 ***Perf. 11½***

642	A266	30h dark brown	1.75	80
643	A267	80h dark green	*4.00*	*4.00*
644	A266	1k dk. violet blue	1.75	80

Nurse

A268

Designs: 15h, Construction worker. 40h, Postwoman. 45h, Ironworker. 50h, Soldier. 75h, Lathe operator. 80h, Textile worker. 1k, Farm woman. 1.20k, Scientist and microscope. 1.60k, Miner. 2k, Physician and baby. 2.40k, Engineer. 3k, Chemist.

Perf. 12½x12, 11½x11.

1954

645	A268	15h dark green	15	3
646	"	20h light violet	15	3
647	"	40h dark brown	25	3
648	"	45h dark gray blue	20	3
649	"	50h dark gray green	30	3
650	"	75h deep blue	25	3
651	"	80h violet brown	30	3
652	"	1k green	50	3
653	"	1.20k dark violet blue	35	3
654	"	1.60k brown black	80	3
655	"	2k orange brown	95	3
656	"	2.40k violet blue	90	3
657	"	3k carmine	1.10	5
		Nos. 645-657 (13)	6.20	41

Antonin Dvorák — A269

Prokop Divis — A270

Portraits: 40h, Leos Janacek. 60h, Bedrich Smetana.

1954, May 22 ***Perf. 11x11½***

658	A269	30h violet brown	1.00	20
659	"	40h brick red	1.35	20
660	"	60h dark blue	1.00	18

Issued to publicize the "Year of Czech Music," 1954.

1954, June 15

661	A270	30h gray	18	3
662	"	75h violet brown	*70*	*65*

Issued to commemorate the 200th anniversary of the invention of a lightning conductor by Prokop Divis.

Slovak Insurrectionist — A271

Anton P. Chekhov — A272

Design: 1.20k, Partisan woman.

1954, Aug. 28 ***Perf. 11½***

663	A271	30h brown orange	15	3
664	"	1.20k dark blue	*1.00*	*90*

Issued to commemorate the 10th anniversary of the Slovak national uprising.

1954, Sept. 24

665	A272	30h dull gray green	15	4
666	"	45h dull gray brown	*80*	*70*

Issued to commemorate the 50th anniversary of the death of Anton P. Chekhov, writer.

Soviet Representative Giving Agricultural Instruction

A273

Designs: 60h, Soviet industrial instruction. 2k, Dancers (cultural collaboration).

1954, Nov. 6 ***Perf. 11½x11***

667	A273	30h yellow brown	13	3
668	"	60h dark blue	40	4
669	"	2k vermilion	*1.35*	*1.25*

Issued to publicize the month of Czechoslovak-Soviet friendship.

Jan Neruda
A274

Portraits: 60h, Janko Jesensky. 1.60k, Jiri Wolker.

1954, Nov. 25 ***Perf. 11x11½***

670	A274	30h dark blue	80	50
671	"	60h dull red	*1.60*	*60*
672	"	1.60k sepia	80	10

Issued to honor Czechoslovak poets.

View of Telc
A275

Views: 60h, Levoca. 3k, Ceske Budejovice.

Engraved and Photogravure

1954, Dec. 10

673	A275	30h black & bistre	35	4
674	"	60h brown & bistre	45	4
675	"	3k black & bistre	*2.25*	*1.65*

Pres. Antonin Zapotocky
A276

Attacking Soldiers
A278

1954, Dec. 18 Engraved ***Perf. 11½***

676	A276	30h black brown	35	14
677	"	60h dark blue	35	14

Souvenir Sheet

Imperf.

678	A276	2k deep claret	4.00	2.00

No. 678 measures 65 x 99½ mm., with arms and quotation in dark blue on sheet margins.

Nos. 676-678 commemorate the 70th birthday of President Antonin Zapotocky.

See also Nos. 829-831.

1954, Oct. 3 ***Perf. 11½***

Design: 2k, Soldier holding child.

679	A278	60h dark green	25	3
680	"	2k dark brown	*1.60*	*1.40*

Issued to publicize Army Day, October 6, 1954.

Woman Holding Torch
A279

Comenius University Building
A280

Design: 45h, Ski jumper.

1955, Jan. 20 **Engraved**

681	A279	30h red	2.00	35

Engraved and Photogravure.

682	A279	45h black & blue	2.00	25

Issued to publicize the First National Spartacist Games, 1955.

1955, Jan. 28 Engraved ***Perf. 11½***

Design: 75h, Jan A. Komensky medal.

683	A280	60h deep green	30	3
684	"	75h chocolate	*80*	*70*

Issued to commemorate the 35th anniversary of the founding of Comenius University, Bratislava.

Czechoslovak Automobile—A281

Designs: 60h, Textile worker. 75h, Lathe operator.

1955, Mar. 15 **Unwmkd.**

685	A281	45h dull green	70	45
686	"	60h dark violet blue	30	4
687	"	75h sepia	55	4

Woman Decorating Soviet Soldier
A282

Stalin Memorial, Prague
A283

Designs: 35h, Tankman with flowers. 60h, Children greeting soldier.

1955, May 5 Engraved ***Perf. 11½***

688	A282	30h blue	15	3
689	"	35h dark brown	*80*	*60*
690	"	60h cerise	25	3

Photogravure.

691	A283	60h sepia	25	3

Issued to commemorate the 10th anniversary of Czechoslovakia's liberation.

Music and Spring
A284

Foundry Worker
A285

Design: 1k, Woman with lyre.

Engraved and Photogravure

1955, May 12

692	A284	30h black & pale blue	25	7
693	"	1k blk. & pale rose	*1.10*	*1.00*

Issued on the occasion of the International Music Festival, Prague, 1955.

1955, May 12 **Engraved**

Design: 45h, Farm workers.

694	A285	30h violet	10	3
695	"	45h green	*60*	*55*

Issued to publicize the third congress of the Trade Union Revolutionary Movement.

Woman Athlete
A286

Jakub Arbes
A287

Designs: 60h, Dancing couple. 1.60k, Athlete.

1955, June 21

696	A286	20h violet blue	*60*	*50*
697	"	60h green	25	6
698	"	1.60k red	70	30

Issued to publicize the first National Spartacist Games, Prague, June-July, 1955.

1955

Portraits: 30h, Jan Stursa. 40h, Elena Marothy-Soltesova. 60h, Josef Vaclav Sladek. 75h, Alexander Stepanovic Popov. 1.40k, Jan Holly. 1.60k, Pavel Josef Safarik.

699	A287	20h brown	18	3
700	"	30h black	18	3
701	"	40h gray green	40	7
702	"	60h black	18	3
703	"	75h claret	*1.00*	*85*
704	"	1.40k black, *cream*	50	16
705	"	1.60k dark blue	55	10
		Nos. 699-705 (7)	*2.99*	*1.27*

Issued to commemorate various anniversaries of prominent Slavs.

Girl and Boy of Two Races
A288

Costume of Ocova, Slovakia
A289

1955, July 20

706	A288	60h violet blue	30	4

Issued to commemorate the fifth World Festival of Youth in Warsaw, July 31–August 14, 1955.

1955, July 25

Regional Costumes: 75h, Detva man, Slovakia. 1.60k, Chodsko man, Bohemia. 2k, Hana woman, Moravia.

Frame and Outlines in Brown

707	A289	60h orange & rose	*7.00*	*4.75*
708	"	75h orange & lilac	*3.50*	*3.00*
709	"	1.60k blue & orange	*6.50*	*4.75*
710	"	2k yellow & rose	*8.50*	*7.00*

Carp
A290

Designs: 30h, Beetle. 35h, Gray Partridge. 1.40k, Butterfly. 1.50k, Hare.

1955, Aug. 8 **Engr. & Photo.**

711	A290	20h sepia & light blue	60	4
712	"	30h sepia & pink	35	4
713	"	35h sepia & buff	35	10
714	"	1.40k sepia & cream	*2.40*	*2.00*
715	"	1.50k sepia & lt. green	90	35
		Nos. 711-715 (5)	*4.60*	*2.53*

Tabor
A291

Designs: 45h, Prachatice. 60h, Jindrichuv Hradec.

1955, Aug. 26 **Engraved**

716	A291	30h violet brown	12	3
717	"	45h rose carmine	*60*	*55*
718	"	60h sage green	25	4

Issued to publicize the architectural beauty of the towns of Southern Bohemia.

Souvenir Sheet.

Various Views of Prague—A292

Perf. 14x13½

1955, Sept. 10 **Engraved**

719	A292	Sheet of five	20.00	20.00
		a. 30h gray black	2.25	2.25
		b. 45h gray black	2.25	2.25
		c. 60h rose lake	2.25	2.25
		d. 75h rose lake	2.25	2.25
		e. 1.60k gray black	2.25	2.25

Issued to commemorate the International Philatelic Exhibition, Prague, Sept. 10–25, 1955. Size: 145x110mm.

Sheet exists imperf., price $40.

Motorcyclists
A293

Workers, Soldier and Pioneer
A294

1955, Aug. 28

720	A293	60h violet brown	2.00	40

Issued to commemorate the 30th International Motorcycle Races at Gottwaldov, Sept. 13-18, 1955.

1955, Oct. 6 ***Perf. 11½*** **Unwmkd.**

Design: 60h, Tanks and planes.

721	A294	30h violet brown	20	4
722	"	60h slate	*1.20*	*1.10*

Army Day, Oct. 6.

Hans Christian Andersen
A295

Portraits: 40h, Friedrich von Schiller. 60h, Adam Mickiewicz. 75h, Walt Whitman.

1955, Oct. 27

723	A295	30h brown red	15	8
724	"	40h dark blue	*80*	*70*
725	"	60h deep claret	20	8
726	"	75h greenish black	35	8

Issued in honor of these four poets and to mark the 100th anniversary of the publication of Walt Whitman's "Leaves of Grass".

Railroad Bridge
A296

Designs: 30h, Train crossing bridge. 60h, Train approaching tunnel. 1.60k, Miners' housing project.

Inscribed: "Stavba Socialismu."

1955, Dec. 15

727 A296 20h dull green 15 15
728 " 30h violet brown 15 6
729 " 60h slate 20 4
730 " 1.60k carmine rose 70 10

Issued to publicize socialist public works.

Hydroelectric Plant A297 **Jewelry** A298

Designs: 10h, Miner with drill. 25h, Building construction. 30h, Harvester. 60h, Metallurgical plant.

Inscribed:
"Druhy Petilety Plan 1956–1960."

1956, Feb. 20 ***Perf. 11½x11***

731 A297 5h violet brown 15 3
732 " 10h gray black 18 3
733 " 25h dark carmine rose 40 3
734 " 30h green 20 3
735 " 60h violet blue 25 4
Nos. 731-735 (5) 1.18 16

Second Five Year Plan.

1956, Mar. 17 ***Perf. 11x11½***

Designs: 45h, Glassware. 60h, Ceramics. 75h, Textiles.

736 A298 30h gray green 30 3
737 " 45h dark blue 4.00 2.50
738 " 60h claret 25 3
739 " 75h gray 30 5

Products of Czechoslovakian industries.

Karlovy Vary (Karlsbad) A299 **"We Serve our People"** A300

Various Spas: 45h, Marianske Lazne (Marienbad). 75h, Piestany. 1.20k, Tatry Vysne Ruzbachy (Tatra Mountains).

1956, Mar. 17

740 A299 30h olive green 60 4
741 " 45h brown 80 15
742 " 75h claret 6.25 4.25
743 " 1.20k ultramarine 60 15

Issued to publicize Czechoslovakian spas.

1956, Apr. 9 Photo. ***Perf. 11x11½***

Designs: 60h, Russian War Memorial, Berlin. 1(k), Tank crewman with standard.

744 A300 30h olive brown 10 5
745 " 60h carmine rose 25 3
746 " 1(k) ultramarine 3.25 4.00

Issued to publicize the exhibition: "The Construction and Defense of our Country," Prague, April,'56.

Cyclists A301

Girl Basketball Players A302

Athletes and Olympic Rings A303

Engraved and Photogravure.

1956, Apr. 25 ***Perf. 11½*** **Unwmkd.**

747 A301 30h green & light blue 1.75 30
748 A302 45h dark blue & carmine 1.25 25
749 A303 75h brown & lemon 1.25 25

Issued to publicize the following: Ninth International Peace Cycling Race, Warsaw-Berlin-Prague, May 1-15, 1956 (No. 747). Fifth European Womens' Basketball Championship (No. 748). Summer Olympics, Melbourne, Nov. 22-Dec. 8, 1956 (No. 749).

Mozart A304 **Home Guard** A305

Designs: 45h, Josef Myslivecek. 60h, Jiri Benda. 1k, Bertramka House, Prague. 1.40k, Xaver Dusek (1731–1799) and wife Josepha. 1.60k, Nostic Theater, Prague.

1956, May 12 **Engraved**

Design in Gray Black.

750 A304 30h bistre 35 18
751 " 45h gray green 8.00 7.25
752 " 60h pale rose lilac 40 4
753 " 1k salmon 35 4
754 " 1.40k light blue 1.00 30
755 " 1.60k lemon 60 10
Nos. 750-755 (6) 10.70 7.91

Issued to commemorate the 200th anniversary of the birth of Wolfgang Amadeus Mozart and to publicize the International Music Festival in Prague.

1956, May 25

756 A305 60h violet blue 40 4

Issued to commemorate the first meeting of the Home Guard, Prague, May 25-27, 1956.

Josef Kajetan Tyl A306 **River Patrol** A307

Portraits: 20h, Ludovit Stur. 30h, Frana Sramek. 1.40k, Karel Havlicek Borovsky.

1956, June 23

757 A306 20h dull purple 24 6
758 " 30h blue 24 3
759 " 60h black 24 4
760 " 1.40k claret 2.00 1.60

Issued to honor various Czechoslovakian writers. See also Nos. 781–784, 873–876.

1956, July 8 ***Perf. 11x11½***

Design: 60h, Guard and dog.

761 A307 30h ultramarine 70 30
762 " 60h green 20 4

Issued to honor men of Frontier Guard.

Type of 1956 and

Steeplechase—A308

1956, Sept. 8 ***Perf. 11½*** **Unwmkd.**

763 A308 60h indigo & bistre 1.35 35
764 " 80h brown violet & violet 90 15
765 A303 1.20k slate & orange 70 25

Issued to publicize: Steeplechase, Pardubice, 1956 (No. 763). Marathon race, Kosice, 1956 (No. 764). Olympic Games, Melbourne, Nov. 22–Dec. 8 (No. 765).

Woman Gathering Grapes A309

Fishermen—A310

Designs: 35h, Women gathering hops. 95h, Logging.

1956, Sept. 20 **Engraved**

766 A309 30h brown lake 25 3
767 " 35h gray green 30 12
768 A310 80h dark blue 30 5
769 " 95h chocolate 1.50 1.35

Issued to publicize natural resources.

Locomotive, 1846 A311

Locomotive, 1855 A312

Locomotives: 40h, 1945. 45h, 1952. 60h, 1955. 1k, 1954.

1956, Nov. 9 ***Perf. 11½*** **Unwmkd.**

770 A311 10h brown 1.00 5
771 A312 30h gray 40 3
772 " 40h green 1.50 10
773 " 45h brn. carmine 8.50 6.50
774 " 60h indigo 40 4
775 " 1k ultramarine 60 8
Nos. 770-775 (6) 12.40 6.80

Issued to commemorate the European Timetable Conference at Prague, Nov. 9–13.

Costume of Moravia A313

Regional Costumes (women): 1.20k, Blata, Bohemia. 1.40k, Cicmany, Slovakia. 1.60k, Novohradsko, Slovakia.

1956, Dec. 15 ***Perf. 13½***

776 A313 30h brown, ultramarine & car. 1.30 40
777 " 1.20k brown, carmine & ultramarine 90 30
778 " 1.40k brown, ochre & vermilion 5.00 1.60
779 " 1.60k brown, carmine & green 1.00 40

See also Nos. 832-835.

Zapotocky Type of 1953.

1956, Oct. 7 ***Perf. 12½*** **Unwmkd.**

780 A251 30h blue 30 3

Portrait Type of 1956.

1957, Jan. 18 Engraved ***Perf. 11½***

Portraits: 15h, Ivan Olbracht. 20h, Karel Toman. 30h, F. X. Salda. 1.60k, Terezia Vansova.

Cream Paper.

781 A306 15h dark red brown 30 5
782 " 20h dark green 15 5
783 " 30h dark brown 15 4
784 " 1.60k dark blue 65 12

Issued in honor of Czechoslovakian writers.

Kolin Cathedral A315

Views: No. 786, Banska Stiavnica. No. 787, Uherske Hradiste. No. 788, Karlstein. No. 789, Charles Bridge, Prague. 1.25k, Moravska Trebova.

1957, Feb. 23

785 A315 30h dark blue gray 10 3
786 " 30h rose violet 12 3
787 " 60h deep rose 20 3
788 " 60h gray green 20 3
789 " 60h brown 20 3
790 " 1.25k gray 1.25 1.10
Nos. 785-790 (6) 2.07 1.25

Issued to commemorate anniversaries of various towns and landmarks.

Komensky Mausoleum, Naarden
A316

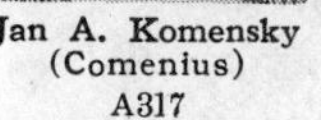

Jan A. Komensky (Comenius)
A317

Farm Woman
A318

Old Prints: 40h, Komensky teaching. 1k, Sun, moon, stars and earth.

Perf. 11½x11, 14 (A317)

1957, Mar. 28 Engraved Unwmkd.

791	A316	30h pale brown	15	8
792	"	40h dark green	15	8
793	A317	60h chocolate	*1.25*	*65*
794	A316	1k carmine rose	45	10

Issued to commemorate the 300th anniversary of the publication of "Didactica Opera Omnia" by J. A. Komensky (Comenius). No. 793 issued in sheets of four.

1957, Mar. 22 *Perf. 11½*

795	A318	30h light blue green	35	10

Issued to publicize the 3rd Congress of Agricultural Cooperatives.

Cyclists—A319

Woman Archer—A320

Boxers
A321

Rescue Team—A322

Perf. 11½x11, 11x11½

1957, Apr. 30

796	A319	30h sepia & ultra.	25	3
797	"	60h dull green & bistre	*1.75*	*95*
798	A320	60h gray & emerald	30	4
799	A321	60h sepia & orange	30	4
800	A322	60h violet & chocolate	30	4
		Nos. 796-800 (5)	*2.90*	*1.10*

Issued to publicize: 10th International Peace Cycling Race, Prague-Berlin-Warsaw (Nos. 796–797). International Archery Championships (No. 798). European Boxing Championships, Prague (No. 799). Mountain Climbing Rescue Service (No. 800).

Jan V. Stamic
A323

Musicians: No. 802, Ferdinand Laub. No. 803, Frantisek Ondricek. No. 804, Josef B. Foerster. No. 805, Vitezslav Novak. No. 806, Josef Suk.

1957, May 12 *Perf. 11½*

801	A323	60h purple	20	4
802	"	60h black	20	4
803	"	60h slate blue	20	4
804	"	60h brown	20	4
805	"	60h dull red brown	20	4
806	"	60h blue green	20	4
		Nos. 801-806 (6)	1.20	24

Spring Music Festival, Prague.

Josef Bozek
A324

School of Engineering
A325

Portraits: 60h, F. J. Gerstner. 1k, R. Skuhersky.

1957, May 25

807	A324	30h bluish black	10	3
808	"	60h gray brown	20	3
809	"	1k rose lake	30	8
810	A325	1.40k blue violet	50	8

Issued to commemorate the 250th anniversary of the School of Engineering in Prague.

Pioneer and Philatelic Symbols
A326

Design: 60h, Girl and carrier pigeon.

Engraved and Photogravure.

1957, June 8 *Perf. 11½*

811	A326	30h olive green & orange	40	10

Engraved *Perf. 13½*

812	A326	60h brown & violet blue	*1.40*	*90*

Youth Philatelic Exhibition, Pardubice.

"Grief"
A327

Motorcyclists
A328

Design: 60h, Rose, symbol of new life.

1957, June 10

813	A327	30h black	15	4
814	"	60h black & rose red	*65*	*25*

Destruction of Lidice, 15th anniversary.

1957, July 5 *Perf. 11½*

815	A328	60h dark gray & blue	60	8

32nd International Motorcycle Race.

Karel Klic
A329

Josef Ressel
A330

1957, July 5

816	A329	30h gray black	15	3
817	A330	60h violet blue	25	4

Issued to honor Karel Klic, inventor of photogravure, and Josef Ressel, inventor of the ship screw.

Chamois
A331

Gentian
A332

Designs: 30h, Brown bear. 60h, Edelweiss. 1.25k, Tatra Mountains.

1957, Aug. 28 Engr. *Perf. 11½*

Inscribed: "Tatransky Narodny Park."

818	A331	20h emerald & brownish gray	45	35
819	"	30h light blue & brown	30	3
820	A332	40h golden brown & violet blue	45	4
821	"	60h yellow & green	25	5
822	"	1.25k olive green & bistre	*2.00*	*1.25*
		Nos. 818-822 (5)	*3.45*	*1.72*

Issued to publicize the Tatra Mountains National Park. No. 822 measures 48x28½mm.

"Marycka Magdonova"
A333

Man Holding Banner of Trade Union Congress
A334

Engraved and Photogravure

1957, Sept. 15 *Perf. 11½* **Unwmkd.**

823	A333	60h black & dull red	30	3

Issued to commemorate the 90th birthday of Petr Bezruc, poet and author of "Marycka Magdonova."

1957, Sept. 28 **Engraved**

824	A334	75h rose red	35	9

Issued to publicize the fourth International Trade Union Congress, Leipzig, Oct. 4–15.

Television Transmitter and Antennas
A335

Design: 60h, Family watching television.

1957, Oct. 19 Engraved *Perf. 11½*

825	A335	40h dark blue & carmine	15	3
826	"	60h reddish brown & emerald	20	4

Issued to publicize the television industry.

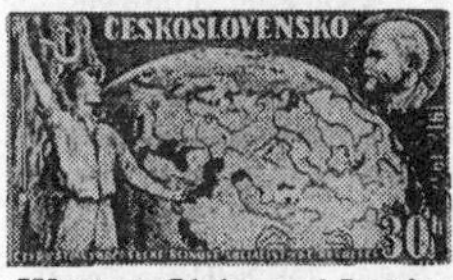

Worker, Globe and Lenin
A336

Design: 60h, Worker, factory, hammer and sickle.

1957, Nov. 7 *Perf. 12x11½*

827	A336	30h claret	12	3
828	"	60h gray blue	25	4

Russian Revolution, 40th anniversary.

Zapotocky Type of 1954 dated: 19 XII 1884 - 13 XI 1957

1957, Nov. 18 *Perf. 11½* **Unwmkd.**

829	A276	30h black	15	3
830	"	60h "	25	3

Souvenir Sheet

Imperf.

831	A276	2k black	1.00	75

Issued to commemorate the death of Pres. Antonin Zapotocky.

No. 831 measures 69x99½mm. Olive branch below stamp; no marginal inscription.

Costume Type of 1956.

Regional Costumes: 45h, Pilsen woman, Bohemia. 75h, Slovacko man, Moravia. 1.25k, Hana woman, Moravia. 1.95k, Teshinsko woman, Silesia.

1957, Dec. 18 Engraved *Perf. 13½*

832	A313	45h brown, blue & dark red	1.75	75
833	"	75h dark brown, red & green	1.35	55

834 A313 1.25k dark brown, scarlet & ochre 1.35 20
835 " 1.95k sepia, blue & vermilion *4.00* *1.50*

Radio Telescope and Observatory
A337

Meteorological Station in High Tatra
A338

Design: 75h, Sputnik 2 over Earth.

1957, Dec. 20 ***Perf. 11½***

836 A337 30h violet brown & yellow 1.75 75
837 A338 45h sepia & light blue 60 40
838 A337 75h claret & blue 3.25 1.25

International Geophysical Year, 1957–58. No. 838 also commemorates the launching of Sputnik 2, Nov. 3, 1957.

Girl Skater
A339

Litomysl Castle
A340

Designs: 40h, Canoeing. 60h, Volleyball. 80h, Parachutist. 1.60k, Soccer.

1958, Jan. 25 Engr. ***Perf. 11½x12***

839 A339 30h rose violet 35 12
840 " 40h blue 15 4
841 " 60h reddish brown 25 4
842 " 80h violet blue *1.40* *60*
843 " 1.60k bright green 70 12
Nos. 839-843 (5) *2.85* *92*

Issued to publicize various sports championship events in 1958.

1958, Feb. 10 ***Perf. 11½***

Design: 60h, Bethlehem Chapel.

844 A340 30h green 10 3
845 " 60h reddish brown 20 4

Issued to commemorate the 80th anniversary of the birth of Zdenek Nejedly, restorer of Bethlehem Chapel.

Giant Excavator
A341

Jewelry
A342

Peace Dove and : 60h, Soldiers, flame and banner (horiz.). 1.60k, Harvester and rainbow (horiz.).

1958, Feb. 25

846 A341 30h gray violet & yellow 15 3
847 " 60h gray brown & carmine 30 4
848 A341 1.60k green & dull yellow 90 10

Issued to commemorate the 10th anniversary of the "Victorious February."

Engraved and Photogravure

1958 ***Perf. 11½*** **Unwmkd.**

Designs: 45h, Dolls. 60h, Textiles. 75h, Kaplan turbine. 1.20k, Glass.

849 A342 30h rose carmine & blue 10 3
850 " 45h rose red & pale lilac 15 3
851 " 60h violet & aqua. 20 3
852 " 75h ultra. & sal. *1.40* *60*
853 " 1.20k blue green & pink 60 6
Nos. 849-853 (5) *2.45* *75*

Issued for the Universal and International Exposition at Brussels.

King George of Podebrad
A343

Design: 60h, View of Prague, 1628.

1958, May 19 **Engraved**

854 A343 30h carmine rose 15 3
855 " 60h violet blue 30 3

Issued to publicize the National Archives Exhibition, Prague, May 15–Aug. 15.

"Towards the Stars"
A344

Women of Three Races
A345

Boy, Girl and Globes
A346

1958, May 26

856 A344 30h carmine rose 60 30
857 A345 45h rose violet 20 12
858 A346 60h blue 20 5

Issued to publicize the following: The Society for Dissemination of Political and Cultural Knowledge (No. 856). The 4th Congress of the International Democratic Women's Federation (No. 857). The First World Trade Union Conference of Working Youths, held in Prague, July 14–20 (No. 858).

Grain, Hammer and Sickle
A347

Atomic Reactor—A348

Design: 45h, Map of Czechoslovakia, hammer and sickle.

1958, May 26

859 A347 30h dull red 10 3
860 " 45h green 15 3
861 A348 60h dark blue 25 4

Issued to commemorate the 11th Congress of the Czech Communist Party and the 15th anniversary of the Russo-Czechoslovakian Treaty.

Karlovy Vary—A349

Various Spas: 40h, Podebrady. 60h, Marianske Lazne. 80h, Luhacovice. 1.20k, Strbske Pleso. 1.60k, Trencianske Teplice.

1958, June 25

862 A349 30h rose claret 10 3
863 " 40h reddish brown 12 3
864 " 60h gray green 18 3
865 " 80h sepia 25 3
866 " 1.20k violet blue 40 4
867 " 1.60k light violet *1.65* *90*
Nos. 862-867 (6) *2.70* *1.06*

Telephone Operator
A350

Pres. Antonin Novotny
A351

Design: 45h, Radio transmitter.

1958, June 20

868 A350 30h blk. & brn. orge. 25 3
869 " 45h blk. & lt. green 35 12

Issued to commemorate the Conference of Postal Ministers of Communist Countries, Prague, June 30–July 9.

1958–59 ***Perf. 12½, 11½***

870 A351 30h bright violet blue 10 3
870A " 30h light violet ('59) 20 3
871 " 60h carmine rose 25 3

Redrawn.

Perf. 11½

871A A351 60h rose red ('59) 20 3

On No. 871 the top of the "6" turns down; on No. 871A it is open.

Czechoslovak Pavilion, Brussels
A352

1958, July 15 Photo. & Engraved

872 A352 1.95k light blue & bis. brown 1.10 18

Issued to mark Czechoslovakia Week at the Universal and International Exhibition at Brussels.

Portrait Type of 1956.

Portraits: 30h, Julius Fucik. 45h, G. K. Zechenter 60h, Karel Capek. 1.40k, Svatopluk Cech.

1958, Aug. 20 Engr. ***Perf. 11½***

873 A306 30h rose red 10 3
874 " 45h violet *90* *40*
875 " 60h dark blue gray 18 3
876 " 1.40k gray 40 15

Death anniversaries of four famous Czechs.

The Artist and the Muse
A353

1958, Aug. 20 ***Perf. 14***

877 A353 1.60k black 2.25 90

Issued to commemorate the 85th birthday of Max Svabinsky, artist and engraver.

Children's Hospital, Brno—A354

Designs: 60h, New Town Hall, Brno. 1k, St. Thomas Church. 1.60k, View of Brno.

1958, Sept. 6 ***Perf. 11½*** **Unwmkd.**

Size: 40x23mm.

878 A354 30h violet 10 3
879 " 60h rose red 20 3
880 " 1k brown 40 12

Perf. 14

Size: 50x28mm.

881 A354 1.60k dark slate green *2.00* *1.60*

Issued to commemorate the National Philatelic Exhibition, Brno, Sept. 9, 1958.

No. 881 sold for 3.10k, including entrance ticket to exhibition. Issued in sheets of four.

Lepiota Procera
A355

Children on Beach
A356

1958, Oct. 6 ***Perf. 14***

Mushrooms: 40h, Boletus edulis. 60h, Krombholzia rufescens. 1.40k, Amanita muscaria L. 1.60k, Armillariella mellea.

882 A355 30h dark brown, green & buff 20 6
883 " 40h violet brown & brown orange 20 12
884 " 60h black, red & buff 35 12
885 " 1.40k brown, scarlet & green 60 25
886 " 1.60k black, red brown & olive *2.40* *1.50*
Nos. 882-886 (5) *3.75* *2.05*

1958, Oct. 24 *Perf. 14* Unwmkd.

Designs: 45h, Mother, child and bird. 60h, Skier.

887 A356 30h blue, yellow & red 18 3
888 " 45h ultra. & car. 25 4
889 " 60h brown, blue & yellow 35 10

Issued to commemorate the opening of UNESCO (U.N. Educational, Scientific and Cultural Organization) Headquarters in Paris, Nov. 3.

Bozek's Steam Car of 1815
A357

Designs: 45h, "Präsident" car of 1897. 60h, "Skoda" sports car. 80h, "Tatra" sedan. 1k, "Autocar Skoda" bus. 1.25k, Trucks.

Engraved and Photogravure.

1958, Dec. 1 *Perf. 11½x11*

890 A357 30h violet black & buff 12 3
891 " 45h olive & light olive green 18 3
892 " 60h olive gray & salmon 25 3
893 " 80h claret & blue green 30 12
894 " 1k brown & light yellow green 45 12
895 " 1.25k green & buff *2.40* *80*
Nos. 890-895 (6) *3.70* *1.13*

Issued to honor the automobile industry.

Stamp of 1918 and Allegory
A358

1958, Dec. 18 Engr. *Perf. 11x11½*

896 A358 60h dark blue gray 30 5

Issued to commemorate the 40th anniversary of the first Czechoslovakian postage stamp.

Ice Hockey—A359

Sports: 30h, Girl throwing javelin. 60h, Ice hockey. 1k, Hurdling. 1.60k, Rowing. 2k, High jump.

1959, Feb. 14 *Perf. 11½x11*

897 A359 20h dark brown & gray 30 3
898 " 30h red brown & orange brown 30 3
899 " 60h dark blue & pale green 18 3
900 " 1k maroon & citron 50 4
901 " 1.60k dull violet & light blue 55 10
902 " 2k red brown & light blue *2.25* *1.25*
Nos. 897-902 (6) *4.08* *1.48*

Congress Emblem
A360

"Equality of All Races"
A361

Design: 60h, Industrial and agricultural workers and emblem.

1959, Feb. 27 *Perf. 11½*

903 A360 30h maroon & light blue 10 3
904 " 60h dk. blue & yel. 20 3

Issued to commemorate the 4th Agricultural Cooperative Congress in Prague.

1959, Mar. 23

Designs: 1k, "Peace." 2k, Mother and Child: "Freedom for Colonial People."

905 A361 60h gray green 20 5
906 " 1k gray 30 6
907 " 2k dk. gray blue *1.85* *50*

Issued to commemorate the 10th anniversary of the signing of the Universal Declaration of Human Rights.

Girl Holding Doll
A362

Frederic Joliot Curie
A363

Engraved and Photogravure.

Designs: 40h, Pioneer studying map. 60h, Pioneer with radio. 80h, Girl pioneer planting tree.

1959, Mar. 28

908 A362 30h violet blue & yellow 10 3
909 " 40h indigo & ultra. 12 3
910 " 60h black & lilac 15 3
911 " 80h brn. & lt. grn. 40 12

10th anniversary of the Pioneer organization.

1959, Apr. 17 Engraved

912 A363 60h sepia 85 15

Issued to honor Frederic Joliot Curie and the 10th anniversary of the World Peace Movement.

"Reaching for the Moon"
A364

Town Hall Pilsen
A365

1959, Apr. 17

913 A364 30h violet blue 85 25

Issued to publicize the Second Congress of the Czechoslovak Association for the Propagation of Political and Cultural knowledge.

1959, May 2

Designs: 60h, Part of steam condenser turbine. 1k, St. Bartholomew's Church, Pilsen. 1.60k, Part of lathe.

914 A365 30h light brown 10 3
915 " 60h vio. & lt. grn. 20 4
916 " 1k violet blue 40 10
917 " 1.60k black & yel. *1.50* *70*

Issued to publicize the 2nd Pilsen Stamp Exhibition in connection with the centenary of the Skoda (Lenin) armament works.

Factory and Emblem
A366

Design: 60h, Dam.

Inscribed: "IV Vseodborovy sjezd, 1959."

1959, May 13

918 A366 30h rose & yellow 12 3
919 " 60h olive gray & blue 25 4

4th Trade Union Congress.

Zvolen Castle—A367

1959, June 13

920 A367 60h gray olive & yellow 30 5

Regional Stamp Exhibition, Zvolen, 1959.

Frantisek Benda
A368

Aurel Stodola
A369

Portraits: 30h, Vaclav Kliment Klicpera. 60h, Karel V. Rais. 80h, Antonin Slavicek. 1k, Peter Bezruc.

1959, June 22 *Perf. 11½x11*

921 A368 15h violet blue 5 3
922 " 30h orange brown 10 3
923 A369 40h dull green 15 3
924 " 60h dull red brown 25 4
925 " 80h dull violet 30 6
926 A368 1k dark brown 50 6
Nos. 921-926 (6) 1.35 25

View of the Fair Grounds
A370

Designs: 60h, Fair emblem and world map. 1.60k, Pavilion "Z."

Inscribed: "Mezinarodni Veletrh Brne 6.-20.IX. 1959."

Engraved and Photogravure.

1959, July 20 *Perf. 11½* Unwmkd.

927 A370 30h lilac & yellow 12 3
928 " 60h dull blue 25 3
929 A370 1.60k dark blue & bistre 60 12

International Fair at Brno, Sept. 6–20.

Revolutionist and Flag—A371

Slovakian Fighter
A372

Design: 1.60k, Linden leaves, sun and factory.

Engraved.

1959, Aug. 29 *Perf. 11½* Unwmkd.

930 A371 30h black & rose 15 3
931 A372 60h carmine rose 25 3
932 A371 1.60k dark blue & yellow 65 6

Issued to commemorate the 15th anniversary of the national Slovakian revolution and the 40th anniversary of the Slovakian Soviet Republic.

Alpine Marmots—A373

Animals: 40h, Bison. 60h, Lynx (vert.). 1k, Wolf. 1.60k, Red deer.

Engraved and Photogravure.

1959, Sept. 25

933 A373 30h black & gray 30 3
934 " 40h dark brown & bluish green 35 8
935 " 60h brn. red & yel. 20 3
936 " 1k olive brown & blue *2.00* *95*
937 " 1.60k red brown & pink 50 10
Nos. 933-937 (5) *3.35* *1.19*

Issued to commemorate the 10th anniversary of the establishment of the Tatra National Park.

Lunik 2 Hitting Moon and Russian Flag—A374

1959, Sept. 23 *Perf. 11½*

938 A374 60h dark red & light ultramarine 60 15

Issued to commemorate the landing of the Soviet rocket on the moon, Sept. 13, 1959.

Stamp Printing Works, Peking
A375

1959, Oct. 1

939 A375 30h pale grn. & red 15 3

Issued to commemorate 10 years of Czechoslovakian - Chinese friendship.

Haydn A376

Great Spotted Woodpecker A377

Design: 3k, Charles Darwin.

1959, Oct. 16 Engr. *Perf. 11½*

940 A376 60h violet black 30 5
941 " 3k dark red brn. *1.40* *55*

150th anniversary of death of Franz Joseph Haydn, Austrian composer, and 150th anniversary of birth of Charles Darwin, English naturalist.

1959, Nov. 16 *Perf. 14*

Birds: 30h, Blue tits. 40h, Nuthatch. 60th, Golden oriole. 80h, Goldfinch. 1k, Bullfinch. 1.20k, European kingfisher.

942 A377 20h multicolored 30 12
943 " 30h " 20 12
944 " 40h " *1.50* *90*
945 " 60h " 30 10
946 " 80h " 30 15
947 " 1k " 50 20
948 " 1.20k " 60 25
Nos. 942-948 (7) *3.70* *1.84*

Nikola Tesla—A378

Designs: 30h, Alexander S. Popov. 35h, Edouard Branly. 60h, Guglielmo Marconi. 1k, Heinrich Hertz. 2k, Edwin Howard Armstrong and research tower, Alpine, N. J.

Engraved and Photogravure.

1959, Dec. 7 *Perf. 11½*

949 A378 25h black & pink *70* *10*
950 " 30h black & orange 15 4
951 " 35h blk. & lt. violet 18 4
952 " 60h black & blue 20 4
953 " 1k black & lt. green 30 6
954 " 2k black & bistre *1.75* *60*
Nos. 949-954 (6) *3.28* 88

Issued to honor inventors in the fields of telegraphy and radio.

Gymnast A379

Designs: 60h, Skier. 1.60k, Handball players.

Engraved and Photogravure.

1960, Jan. 20 *Perf. 11½*

955 A379 30h salmon pink & brown 20 3
956 " 60h light blue & black 35 8
957 " 1.60k bistre & brown 65 15

2nd Winter Spartacist Games.

1960, June 15 Unwmkd.

Designs: 30h, Two girls in "Red Ball" drill. 60h, Gymnast with stick. 1k, Three girls with hoops.

958 A379 30h lt. green & rose claret 20 3
959 " 60h pink & black 30 4
960 " 1k ochre & violet blue 50 8

Issued to commemorate the 2nd Summer Spartacist Games, Prague, June 23–July 3.

River Dredge Boat A380

Ships: 60h, River tug. 1k, Tourist steamer. 1.20k, Cargo ship "Lidice."

1960, Feb. 22 *Perf. 11½*

961 A380 30h slate green & salmon 12 3
962 " 60h maroon & pale blue 25 3
963 " 1k dk. vio. & yel. 40 4
964 " 1.20k lilac & pale green *1.20* *1.00*

Ice Hockey Players—A381

Design: 1.80k, Figure skaters.

1960, Feb. 27

965 A381 60h sepia & lt. blue 50 18
966 " 1.80k black & light green *3.50* *2.75*

Issued to commemorate the 8th Olympic Winter Games, Squaw Valley, Calif., Feb. 18-29, 1960.

1960, June 15 Unwmkd.

Designs: 1k, Running. 1.80k, Women's gymnastics. 2k, Rowing.

967 A381 1k blk. & org. 35 12
968 " 1.80k black & salmon pink 80 20
969 " 2k black & blue *2.25* *1.00*

Issued to commemorate the 17th Olympic Games, Rome, Aug. 25–Sept. 11.

Trencin Castle A382

Wmk. 341

Castles: 10h, Bezdez. 20h, Kost. 30h, Pernstein. 40h, Kremnica. 50h, Krivoklát castle. 60h, Karlstein. 1k, Smolenice. 1.60k, Kokorin.

1960-63 Engraved *Perf. 11½*

970 A382 5h gray violet 5 3
971 " 10h black 5 3
972 " 20h brown orange 10 3
973 " 30h green 15 3
974 " 40h brown 20 3
974A " 50h black ('63) 20 3
975 " 60h rose red 25 3
976 " 1k lilac 35 3
977 " 1.60k dark blue 60 3
Nos. 970-977 (9) 1.95 27

Wmkd. Striped Ovals (341)

1961, Oct.

977A A382 30h green 75 50

Lenin A383

Soldier Holding Child A384

1960, Apr. 22 Unwmkd.

978 A383 60h gray olive 40 6

90th anniversary of the birth of Lenin.

1960, May 5

Designs: No. 980, Child eating pie. No. 981, Soldier helping concentration camp victim. No. 982, Welder and factory (horiz.). No. 983, Tractor driver and farm (horiz.).

Engraved and Photogravure

979 A384 30h maroon & light blue 15 3
980 " 30h dull red 15 3
981 " 30h grn. & dull blue 15 3
982 " 60h dk. blue & buff 25 3
983 " 60h reddish brown & yel. green 25 3
Nos. 979-983 (5) 95 15

15th anniversary of liberation.

Steelworker—A385

Design: 60h, Farm woman and child.

1960, May 24

984 A385 30h maroon & gray 12 3
985 " 60h green & pale blue 20 3

Issued to publicize the 1960 parliamentary elections.

Red Cross Nurse Holding Dove—A386

Fire Fighters A387

1960, May 26 Unwmkd.

986 A386 30h brn. car. & blue 15 3
987 A387 60h dk. blue & pink 30 3

Issued to commemorate the 3rd Congress of the Czechoslovakian Red Cross (No. 986), and the 2nd Fire Fighters' Congress (No. 987).

Hand of Philatelist with Tongs and Two Stamps A388

Design: 1k, Globe and 1937 Bratislava stamp (shown in miniature on 60h).

Engraved and Photogravure

1960, July 11 *Perf. 11½*

988 A388 60h blk. & dull yel. 25 3
989 " 1k black & blue 50 5

Issued to publicize the National Stamp Exhibition, Bratislava, Sept. 24–Oct. 9.

See Nos. C49–C50.

Stalin Mine, Ostrava-Hermanovice A390

Viktorin Cornelius, Lawyer A391

Designs: 20h, Power station, Hodonin. 30h, Gottwald iron works, Kuncice. 40h, Harvester. 60h, Oil refinery.

1960, July 25

992 A390 10h blk. & pale grn. 8 3
993 " 20h maroon & light blue 12 3
994 " 30h indigo & pink 12 3
995 " 40h green & pale lilac 15 3
996 " 60h dk. blue & yel. 25 3
Nos. 992-996 (5) 72 15

Issued to publicize the new five-year plan.

1960, Aug. 23 Engraved

Portraits: 20h, Karel Matej Capek-Chod, writer. 30h, Hana Kvapilova, actress. 40h, Oskar Nedbal, composer. 60h, Otakar Ostrcil, composer.

997 A391 10h black 15 3
998 " 20h red brown 18 3
999 " 30h rose red 15 3
1000 " 40h dull green 25 3
1001 " 60h gray violet 35 4
Nos. 997-1001 (5) 1.08 16

See also Nos. 1037–41.

Skoda Sports Plane Flying Upside Down A392

1960, Aug. 28 Engr. & Photo.

1002 A392 60h vio. bl. & blue 55 7

Issued to commemorate the first aerobatic world championships, Bratislava.

Constitution and "Czechoslovakia" A393

1960, Sept. 18

1003 A393 30h violet blue & pink 15 3

Issued to commemorate the proclamation of the new socialist constitution.

Workers Reading Newspaper
A394

Man Holding Newspaper
A395

1960, Sept. 18

1004 A394 30h slate & verm. 12 3
1005 A395 60h black & rose 24 3

Issued for the Day of the Czechoslovak Press, Sept. 21, 1960, and to commemorate the 40th anniversary of the Rudé Právo paper.

Globes and Laurel—A396

1960, Sept. 18 Engraved

1006 A396 30h dark blue & bistre 15 3

Issued to commemorate the 15th anniversary of the World Federation of Trade Unions.

Black-crowned Night Heron A397 — Doronicum Clusii (Thistle) A398

Birds: 30h, Great crested grebe. 40h, Lapwing. 60h, Gray heron. 1k, Graylag goose (horiz.). 1.60k, Mallard (horiz.).

Engraved and Photogravure

1960, Oct. 24 *Perf. 11½* Unwmkd.

Designs in Black

1007 A397 25h pale violet blue 15 5
1008 " 30h pale citron 40 6
1009 " 40h pale blue 25 6
1010 " 60h pink 30 10
1011 " 1k pale yellow 40 15
1012 " 1.60k light violet *2.25* *1.00*
Nos. 1007-1012 (6) *3.75* *1.42*

1960, Nov. 21 Engraved ***Perf. 14***

Flowers: 30h, Cyclamen. 40h, Primrose. 60h, Hen-and-chickens. 1k, Gentian. 2k, Pasqueflower.

1013 A398 20h black, yellow & green 9 3
1014 " 30h black, carmine rose & green 12 3
1015 " 40h black, yellow & green 15 3
1016 A398 60h black, pink & green 25 3
1017 " 1k black, blue, vio. & green 45 3
1018 " 2k black, lilac, yel. & grn. *2.00* *1.00*
Nos. 1013-1018 (6) *3.06* *1.15*

Alfons Mucha
A399

1960, Dec. 18 Engr. *Perf. 11½x12*

1019 A399 60h dark blue gray 25 3

Issued for the Day of the Czechoslovak Postage Stamp and to commemorate the centenary of the birth of Alfons Mucha, designer of the first Czechoslovakian stamp (Type A1).

Rolling-mill Control Bridge A400 — Athletes with Flags A401

Designs: 30h, Turbo generator. 60h, Ditch-digging machine.

1961, Jan. 20 *Perf. 11½* Unwmkd.

1020 A400 20h blue 12 3
1021 " 30h rose 12 3
1022 " 60h bright green 30 3

Third Five-Year Plan.

Perf. 11x11½, 11½x11

1961, Feb. 20 Engr. & Photo.

Designs: No. 1024, Motorcycle race (horiz.). 40h, Sculling (horiz.). 60h, Ice skater. 1k, Rugby. 1.20k, Soccer. 1.60k, Long-distance runners.

1023 A401 30h rose red & blue 12 3
1024 " 30h dark blue & carmine 12 3
1025 " 40h dark gray & carmine 35 4
1026 " 60h lilac & blue 25 3
1027 " 1k ultra. & yel. 40 5
1028 " 1.20k green & buff 45 7
1029 " 1.60k sepia & salmon *1.75* *95*
Nos. 1023-1029 (7) *3.44* *1.20*

Various sports events.

Exhibition Emblem A402 — Rocket Launching A403

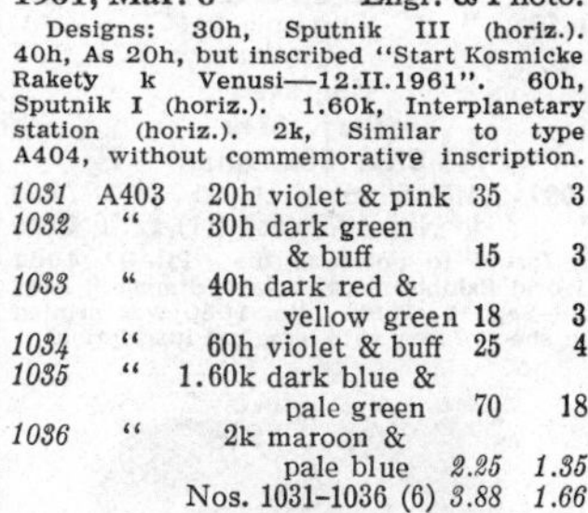

1961, Mar. 6 Engraved *Perf. 11½*

1030 A402 2k dark blue & red 1.40 8

Issued to publicize the "Praga 1962" International Stamp Exhibition, Prague, Sept. 1962.

1961, Mar. 6 Engr. & Photo.

Designs: 30h, Sputnik III (horiz.). 40h, As 20h, but inscribed "Start Kosmicke Rakety k Venusi—12.II.1961". 60h, Sputnik I (horiz.). 1.60k, Interplanetary station (horiz.). 2k, Similar to type A404, without commemorative inscription.

1031 A403 20h violet & pink 35 3
1032 " 30h dark green & buff 15 3
1033 " 40h dark red & yellow green 18 3
1034 " 60h violet & buff 25 4
1035 " 1.60k dark blue & pale green 70 18
1036 " 2k maroon & pale blue *2.25* *1.35*
Nos. 1031-1036 (6) *3.88* *1.66*

Issued to publicize Soviet space research.

Portrait Type of 1960

Portraits: No. 1037, Jindrich Mosna. No. 1038, Pavol Orszagh Hviezdoslav. No. 1039, Alois Mrstik. No. 1040, Joza Uprka. No. 1041, Josef Hora.

1961, March 27 *Perf. 11½*

1037 A391 60h green 25 3
1038 " 60h dark blue 25 3
a. "ORSZACH" instead of "ORSZAGH" 60 18
1039 " 60h dull claret 25 3
1040 " 60h gray 25 3
1041 " 60h sepia 25 3
Nos. 1037-1041 (5) 1.25 15

Man Flying into Space
A404

1961, Apr. 13 Engraved and Photo.

1042 A404 60h carmine & pale blue 25 4
1043 " 3k ultra. & yel *2.00* *65*

Issued to commemorate the first man in space, Yuri A. Gagarin, Apr. 12, 1961. See also No. 1036.

Flute Player A405 — Blast Furnace and Mine, Kladno A406

Designs: No. 1045, Dancer. 60h, Lyre player.

1961, Apr. 24 Engraved

1044 A405 30h brown black 20 3
1045 " 30h brown red 20 3
1046 " 60h violet blue 30 4

Issued to commemorate the 150th anniversary of the Prague Conservatory of Music.

1961, Apr. 24

1047 A406 3k dull red 1.25 3

Marching Workers A407 — Woman with Hammer and Sickle A408

Klement Gottwald Museum
A409

Designs: No. 1050, Lenin Museum. No. 1051, Crowd with flags. No. 1053, Man saluting Red Star.

1961, May 10

1048 A407 30h dull violet 10 3
1049 A409 30h dark blue 10 3
1050 " 30h reddish brown 10 3
1051 A407 60h vermilion 25 4
1052 A408 60h dark green 25 4
1053 " 60h carmine 25 4
Nos. 1048-1053 (6) 1.05 21

Czech Communist Party, 40th anniversary.

Puppet
A410

Designs: Various Puppets.

Engraved and Photogravure

1961, June 20 *Perf. 11½* Unwmkd.

1054 A410 30h verm. & yel. 15 3
1055 " 40h sepia & bluish grn. 15 3
1056 " 60h violet blue & salmon 25 3
1057 " 1k green & lt. blue 40 6
1058 " 1.60k maroon & pale violet *1.50* *30*
Nos. 1054-1058 (5) *2.45* *45*

Woman, Map of Africa and Flag of Czechoslovakia
A411

1961, June 26

1059 A411 60h red & blue 25 3

Issued to publicize the friendship between the people of Africa and Czechoslovakia.

Map of Europe and Fair Emblem
A412

Designs (Fair emblem and): 60h Horizontal boring machine (vert.). 1k, Scientists' meeting and nuclear physics emblem.

Engraved and Photogravure

1961, Aug. 14 ***Perf. 11½***

1060 A412 30h dark blue & pale green 15 4
1061 " 60h green & pink 25 3
1062 " 1k violet brown & light blue 40 6

Issued to publicize the International Trade Fair, Brno, Sept. 10–24.

Sugar Beet, Cup of Coffee and Bags of Sugar
A413

Charles Bridge, St. Nicholas Church and Hradcany
A414

Designs: 30h, Clover. 40h, Wheat. 60h, Hops. 1.40k, Corn. 2k, Potatoes.

1961, Sept. 18 ***Perf. 11½*** **Unwmkd.**

1063 A413 20h slate & lilac 8 3
1064 " 30h pale claret & bistre 9 3
1065 " 40h brown & orange 12 3
1066 " 60h slate green & bistre 18 3
1067 " 1.40k brown & fawn 45 6
1068 " 2k dull violet & blue *2.00* *65*
Nos. 1063-1068 (6) *2.92* *83*

1961, Sept. 25

1069 A414 60h violet blue & carmine 70 5

Issued to commemorate the 26th session of the Governor's Council of the Red Cross Societies League, Prague.

Orlik Dam and Kaplan Turbine
A415

Designs: 30h, View of Prague, flags and stamps. 40h, Hluboká Castle, river and fish. 60h, Karlovy Vary and cup. 1k, Pilsen and beer bottle. 1.20k, North Bohemia landscape and vase. 1.60k, Tatra mountains, boots, ice pick and rope. 2k, Ironworks, Ostrava Kuncice and pulley. 3k, Brno and ball bearing. 4k, Bratislava and grapes. 5k, Prague and flags.

Engraved and Photogravure

1961 ***Perf. 11½*** **Unwmkd.**

Size: 41x23mm.

1070 A415 20h gray & blue *45* *35*
1071 " 30h violet blue & red 15 10
1072 " 40h dk. blue & lt. green *45* *35*
1073 A415 60h dk. blue & yellow *45* *35*
1074 " 1k maroon & green 75 40
1075 " 1.20k green & pink *80* *55*
1076 " 1.60k brown & violet blue 90 70
1077 " 2k blk. & ochre 1.25 1.00
1078 " 3k ultra. & yel. *1.75* *1.25*
1079 " 4k purple & salmon *2.75* *1.75*

Engraved
Perf. 13½
Size: 50x29mm.

1080 A415 5k multicolored *15.00* *13.50*
Nos. 1070-1080 (11) *24.70* *20.30*

Issued to publicize the "PRAGA 1962 World Exhibition of Postage Stamps," Aug. 18–Sept. 2, 1962. No. 1080 was printed in sheet of four with marginal inscription.

Globe
A416

Engraved and Photogravure

1961, Nov. 27 ***Perf. 11½***

1081 A416 60h red & ultra. 25 3

Issued to publicize the Fifth World Congress of Trade Unions, Moscow, Dec. 4–16.

Orange Tip Butterfly
A417

Bicyclists
A418

Designs (butterflies): 20h, Zerynthia hypsipyle Sch. 30h, Apollo. 40h, Swallowtail. 60h, Peacock. 80h, Mourning cloak (Camberwell beauty). 1k, Underwing (moth). 1.60k, Red admiral. 2k, Brimstone (sulphur).

1961, Nov. 27 **Engraved**

Brown Frame and Inscriptions

1082 A417 15h blue, orange & yellow 10 6
1083 " 20h blue, yellow & red 10 10
1084 " 30h blue, carmine & green 15 10
1085 " 40h blue, ochre & carmine 30 10
1086 " 60h blue, red brn. & yel. 30 12
1087 " 80h blue, yellow, brn. & grn. 40 15
1088 " 1k pale brown, pink & blue 45 25
1089 " 1.60k multicolored 90 35
1090 " 2k blue, yellow & red *3.00* *1.20*
Nos. 1082-1090 (9) *5.70* *2.43*

Printed in sheets of ten.

Engraved and Photogravure

1962, Feb. 5 ***Perf. 11½*** **Unwmkd.**

Sports: 40h, Woman gymnast. 60h, Figure skaters. 1k, Woman bowler. 1.20k, Goalkeeper, soccer. 1.60k, Discus thrower.

1091 A418 30h black & violet blue 10 3
1092 " 40h black & yel. 15 3
1093 " 60h slate & greenish blue 20 3
1094 A418 1k black & pink 35 8
1095 A428 1.20k black & grn. 50 15
1096 A418 1.60k black & dull green *1.75* *55*
Nos. 1091-1096 (6) *3.05* *87*

Various 1962 sports events.
No. 1095 does not have the commemorative inscription.

Karel Kovarovic
A419

Frantisek Zaviska and Karel Petr
A420

Designs: 20h, Frantisek Skroup. 30h, Bozena Nemcova. 60h, View of Prague and staff of Aesculapius. 1.60k, Ladislav Celakovsky. 1.80k, Miloslav Valouch and Juraj Hronec.

1962, Feb. 26 **Engraved**

1097 A419 10h red brown 5 3
1098 " 20h violet blue 8 3
1099 " 30h brown 12 3
1100 A420 40h claret 15 6
1101 A419 60h black 25 4
1102 " 1.60k slate green 50 4
1103 A420 1.80k dark blue 65 10
Nos. 1097-1103 (7) 1.80 33

Various cultural personalities and events.

Miner and Flag—A421

1962, Mar. 19 **Engr. & Photo.**

1104 A421 60h indigo & rose 25 3

Issued to commemorate the 30th anniversary of the miners' strike at Most.

"Man Conquering Space"
A422

Soviet Spaceship Vostok 2—A423

Designs: 40h, Launching of Soviet space rocket. 80h, Multi-stage automatic rocket. 1k, Automatic station on moon. 1.60k, Television satellite.

1962, Mar. 26 **Engr. & Photo.**

1105 A422 30h dark red & light blue 12 3
1106 " 40h dark blue & salmon 18 3
1107 A423 60h dark blue & pink 30 4
1108 " 80h rose violet & lt. green 35 5
1109 A422 1k indigo & citron 45 10
1110 A423 1.60k grn. & buff *2.25* *90*
Nos. 1105-1110 (6) *3.65* *1.15*

Issued to publicize space research.

Polar Bear
A424

Zoo Animals: 30h, Chimpanzee. 60h, Camel. 1k, African and Indian elephants (horiz.). 1.40k, Leopard (horiz.). 1.60k, Przewalski horse (horiz.).

1962, Apr. 24 ***Perf. 11½*** **Unwmkd.**

Design and Inscriptions in Black

1111 A424 20h greenish blue 6 3
1112 " 30h violet 9 3
1113 " 60h orange 20 4
1114 " 1k green 35 5
1115 " 1.40k carmine rose 45 12
1116 " 1.60k light brown *1.75* *1.00*
Nos. 1111-1116 (6) *2.90* *1.27*

Child and Grieving Mother
A425

Klary's Fountain, Teplice
A426

Design: 60h, Flowers growing from ruins of Ležáky.

1962, June 9 **Engr. and Photo.**

1118 A425 30h black & red 18 3
1119 " 60h blk. & dull blue 40 3

Issued to commemorate the 20th anniversary of the destruction of Lidice and Ležáky by the Nazis.

1962, June 9

1120 A426 60h dull grn. & yel. 35 3

Issued to commemorate the 1,200th anniversary of the discovery of the medicinal springs of Teplice.

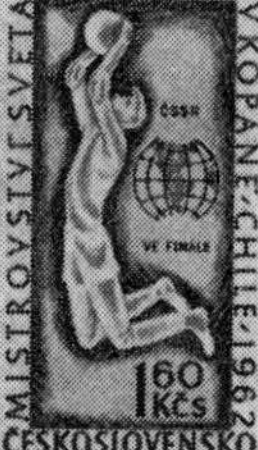

Malaria Eradication Emblem, Cross and Dove
A427

Soccer Goalkeeper
A428

Design: 3k, Dove and malaria eradication emblem.

1962, June 18 **Engr. & Photo.**

1121 A427 60h blk. & crimson 18 4
1122 " 3k dk. blue & yel. *2.00* *65*

Issued for the World Health Organization drive to eradicate malaria.

1962, June 20 *Perf. 11½* **Unwmkd.**

1123 A428 1.60k green & yel. 95 18

Issued to commemorate Czechoslovakia's participation in the World Cup Soccer Championship, Chile, May 30–June 17. See No. 1095.

Soldier in Swimming Relay Race A429 — "Agriculture" A430

1962, July 20

Designs: 40h, Soldier hurdling. 60h, Soccer player. 1k, Soldier with rifle in relay race.

1124 A429 30h green & lt. ultra. 10 3
1125 " 40h dark purple & yellow 12 3
1126 " 60h brn. & grn. 25 4
1127 " 1k dark blue & sal. pink 35 8

Issued to publicize the 2nd Summer Spartacist Games of Friendly Armies, Prague, September, 1962.

1962 Engraved *Perf. 13½*

Designs: 60h, Astronaut in capsule. 80h, Boy with flute (horiz.). 1k, Workers of three races (horiz.). 1.40k, Children dancing around tree. 1.60k, Flying bird (horiz.). 5k, View of Prague (horiz.).

1128 A430 30h multicolored 1.00 85
1129 " 60h " 60 40
a. Miniature sheet of 8 *10.00 10.00*
1130 " 80h multicolored 1.25 1.00
1131 " 1k " 1.75 1.25
1132 " 1.40k " 2.00 1.50
1133 " 1.60k " *3.50 3.00*
Nos. 1128-1133 (6) *10.10 8.00*

Souvenir Sheet

1134 A430 5k multi. *10.00 10.00*
a. Imperf. *35.00 35.00*

Issued to commemorate the "PRAGA 1962 World Exhibition of Postage Stamps," Aug. 18–Sept. 2, 1962. No. 1133 also commemorates FIP Day, Sept. 1 (Federation Internationale de Philatelie.) Printed in sheets of 10.

No. 1129a contains four stamps each of Nos. 1128–29 and two labels arranged in two rows of two se-tenant pairs of Nos. 1128–29 with a label between. Size: 170x107mm. Sold for 5k, only with ticket.

No. 1134 contains one large stamp (51x 30mm). Black marginal inscription. Size of sheet: 95x74mm. Sold only with ticket.

Children in Day Nursery and Factory A431

Sailboat and Trade Union Rest Home, Zinkovy A432

Engraved and Photogravure

1962, Oct. 29 *Perf. 11½* **Unwmkd.**

1135 A431 30h blk. & lt. blue 12 3
1136 A432 60h brown & yel. 25 3

Cruiser "Aurora" A433

1962, Nov. 7

1137 A433 30h blk. & gray bl. 12 3
1138 " 60h black & pink 22 3

Issued to commemorate the 45th anniversary of the Russian October revolution.

Cosmonaut and Worker A434

Lenin A435

1962, Nov. 7

1139 A434 30h dk. red & blue 12 3
1140 A435 60h blk. & dp. rose 22 3

40th anniversary of the U.S.S.R.

Symbolic Crane—A436

Designs: 40h, Agricultural products (vert.). 60h, Factories.

1962, Dec. 4

1141 A436 30h dk. red & yel. 10 3
1142 " 40h gray bl. & yel. 15 3
1143 " 60h blk. & dp. rose 25 6

Issued to commemorate the 12th Congress of the Communist Party of Czechoslovakia.

Ground Beetle A437 — Table Tennis A438

Beetles: 30h, Cardinal beetle. 60h, Stag beetle (vert.). 1k, Great water beetle. 1.60k, Alpine longicorn (vert.). 2k, Ground beetle (vert.).

1962, Dec. 15 Engraved *Perf. 14*

1144 A437 20h multicolored 15 3
1145 " 30h " 15 3
1146 " 60h " 20 5
1147 " 1k " 35 15
1148 " 1.60k " 55 20
1149 " 2k " *2.50 1.00*
Nos. 1144-1149 (6) *3.90 1.46*

Engraved and Photogravure

1963, Jan. *Perf. 11½*

Sports: 60h, Bicyclist. 80h, Skier. 1k, Motorcyclist. 1.20k, Weight lifter. 1.60k, Hurdler.

1150 A438 30h blk. & dp. grn. 20 3
1151 " 60h blk. & orange 25 3
1152 " 80h blk. & ultra. 35 10
1153 " 1k blk. & violet 40 20
1154 " 1.20k black & pale brown 50 30
1155 " 1.60k blk. & carmine 80 25
Nos. 1150-1155 (6) 2.50 91

Various 1963 sports events.

Industrial Plant, Laurel and Star A439 — Symbol of Child Welfare Home A440

Industrial Plant and Symbol of Growth A441

1963, Feb. 25 *Perf. 11½* **Unwmkd.**

1156 A439 30h car. & lt. blue 10 3
1157 A440 60h blk. & carmine 25 3
1158 A441 60h black & red 25 3

Issued to commemorate the 15th anniversary of the "Victorious February" and to publicize the 5th Trade Union Congress.

Artists' Guild Emblem A442 — Juraj Jánosik A443

Eduard Urx A444 — National Theater, Prague A445

Designs: No. 1163, Woman reading to children. No. 1164, Juraj Pálkovic. 1.60k, Max Svabinsky.

Engr. & Photo.; Engr. (A444)

1963, Mar. 25 *Perf. 11½* **Unwmkd.**

1159 A442 20h black & Prussian bl. 5 3
1160 A443 30h car. & lt. blue 10 3
1161 A444 30h carmine 10 3
1162 A445 60h dull red brn. & lt. blue 20 3
1163 A444 60h green 20 3
1164 " 60h black 30 3
1165 " 1.60k brown 60 6
Nos. 1159-1165 (7) 1.55 24

Various cultural personalities and events.

Boy and Girl with Flag A446 — Television Transmitter A447

Engraved and Photogravure

1963, Apr. 18 *Perf. 11½*

1166 A446 30h slate & rose red 18 3

The 4th Congress of Czechoslovak Youth.

1963, Apr. 25

Design: 40h, Television camera, mast and set (horiz.).

1167 A447 40h buff & slate 15 3
1168 " 60h dk. red & lt. bl. 25 3

Czechoslovak television, 10th anniversary.

Rocket to the Sun A448

Designs: 50h, Rockets and Sputniks leaving Earth. 60h, Spacecraft to and from Moon. 1k, 3k, Interplanetary station and Mars 1. 1.60k, Atomic rocket and Jupiter. 2k, Rocket returning from Saturn.

1963, Apr. 25

1169 A448 30h red brn. & buff 12 3
1170 " 50h slate & bluish green 18 6
1171 " 60h dk. grn. & yel. 27 3
1172 " 1k dk. gray & sal. 40 10
1173 " 1.60k gray brown & light green 65 10
1174 " 2k dk. pur. & yel. *2.00 90*
Nos. 1169-1174 (6) *3.62 1.22*

Souvenir Sheet

Imperf.

1175 A448 3k Prussian grn. & orge. red *2.25 2.25*

No. 1175 issued to commemorate the first Space Research Exhibition, Prague, Apr., 1963. Prussian green and red orange marginal inscription and design. Size: 85x70 mm.

Studio and Radio A449

Design: 1k, Globe inscribed "Peace" and aerial mast (vert.).

Engraved and Photogravure

1963, May 18 *Perf. 11½* **Unwmkd.**

1176 A449 30h chocolate & pale green 15 3
1177 " 1k bluish green & lilac 35 3

40th anniversary of Czechoslovak radio.

Tupolev Tu-104B Turbojet A450

Design: 1.80k, Ilyushin Il-18 Moskva.

1963, May 25

1178 A450 80h violet & light blue 35 3
1179 " 1.80k dk. blue & lt. green 75 3

40th anniversary of Czechoslovak airlines.

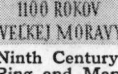

Ninth Century Ring and Map of Moravian Settlements
A451

Woman Singing
A452

Design: 1.60k, Falconer, 9th century silver disk.

1963, May 25

1180 A451 30h light green & black 15 3
1181 " 1.60k dull yellow & black 55 3

1100th anniversary of Moravian empire.

1963, May 25 Engraved

1182 A452 30h bright red 35 3

Issued to commemorate the 60th anniversary of the founding of the Moravian Teachers' Singing Club.

Kromeriz Castle and Barley
A453

Centenary Emblem, Nurse and Playing Child
A454

Engraved and Photogravure

1963, June 20 *Perf. 11½* **Unwmkd.**

1183 A453 30h slate grn. & yel. 30 3

Issued to publicize the National Agricultural Exhibition and to commemorate the 700th anniversary of Kromeriz.

1963, June 20

1184 A454 30h dk. gray & carm. 35 3

Centenary of the International Red Cross.

Bee, Honeycomb and Emblem
A455

Liberec Fair Emblem
A456

1963, June 20

1185 A455 1k brn. & yellow 40 4

Issued to publicize the 19th International Beekeepers Congress, Apimondia, 1963.

1963, July 13

1186 A456 30h blk. & dp. rose 35 3

Liberec Consumer Goods Fair.

Town Hall, Brno
A457

Cave, Moravian Karst
A458

1963, July 29

Design: 60h, Town Hall tower, Brno.

1187 A457 30h lt. bl. & maroon 10 3
1188 " 60h pink & dk. bl. 20 3

International Trade Fair, Brno.

1963, July 29

Designs: No. 1190, Trout, Hornad Valley. 60h, Great Hawk Gorge. 80h, Macocha mountains.

1189 A458 30h brn. & lt. blue 15 3
1190 " 30h dark blue & dull green 15 3
1191 " 60h green & blue 25 3
1192 " 80h sepia & pink 35 8

Blast Furnace
A459

Engraved and Photogravure

1963, Aug. 15 *Perf. 11½* **Unwmkd.**

1193 A459 60h black & bluish grn. 27 3

Issued to publicize the 30th International Congress of Iron Founders, Prague.

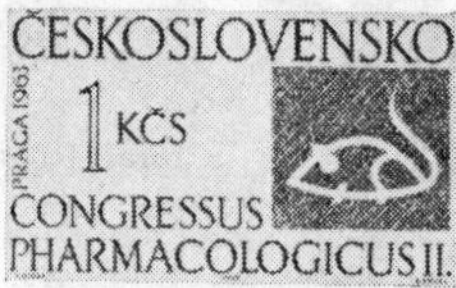

White Mouse—A460

1963, Aug. 15

1194 A460 1k black & carmine 35 3

Issued to publicize the second International Pharmacological Congress, Prague.

Farm Machinery for Underfed Nations
A461

Wooden Toys
A462

1963, Aug. 15 Engraved

1195 A461 1.60k black 60 4

Issued for the "Freedom from Hunger" campaign of the U.N. Food and Agriculture Organization.

1963, Sept. 2 Engraved *Perf. 13½*

Folk Art (Inscribed "UNESCO"): 80h, Cock and flowers. 1k, Flowers in vase. 1.20k, Janosik, Slovak hero. 1.60k, Stag. 2k, Postilion.

1196 A462 60h red & vio. bl. 20 10
1197 " 80h multicolored 30 12
1198 " 1k " 40 18
1199 " 1.20k " 50 20
1200 " 1.60k " 60 30
1201 " 2k " *2.40* *95*
Nos. 1196–1201 (6) *4.40* *1.85*

Sheets of 10.

Canoeing
A463

Tree and Star
A464

Sports: 40h, Volleyball. 60h, Wrestling. 80h, Basketball. 1k, Boxing. 1.60k, Gymnastics.

Engraved and Photogravure

1963, Oct. 26 *Perf. 11½*

1202 A463 30h indigo & green 10 3
1203 " 40h red brown & light blue 15 3
1204 " 60h brn. red & yel. 20 5
1205 " 80h dark purple & dp. org. 35 12
1206 " 1k ultra. & deep rose 40 12
1207 " 1.60k violet blue & ultra. *2.10* *1.00*
Nos. 1202–1207 (6) *3.30* *1.35*

1964 Olympic Games, Tokyo.

1963, Dec. 11 *Perf. 11½* **Unwmkd.**

Design: 60h, Star, hammer and sickle.

1208 A464 30h bister brown & light blue 10 3
1209 " 60h carmine & gray 20 3

Issued to commemorate the 20th anniversary of the Russo-Czechoslovakian Treaty.

Atom Diagrams Surrounding Head
A465

Chamois
A466

1963, Dec. 12 Engraved

1210 A465 60h dark purple 35 3

Issued to publicize the 3rd Congress of the Association for the Propagation of Scientific Knowledge.

1963, Dec. 14 *Perf. 14*

Animals: 40h, Alpine ibex. 60h, Mouflon. 1.20k, Roe deer. 1.60k, Fallow deer. 2k, Red deer.

1211 A466 30h multicolored 35 12
1212 " 40h " 50 20
1213 " 60h brown, yellow & green 65 20
1214 " 1.20k multicolored 90 20
1215 " 1.60k " 1.00 40
1216 " 2k " *4.00* *2.25*
Nos. 1211–1216 (6) *7.40* *3.37*

Figure Skating
A467

Ice Hockey
A468

Designs: 80h, Skiing (horiz.). 1k, Field ball player.

Engraved and Photogravure

1964, Jan. 20 *Perf. 11½* **Unwmkd.**

1217 A467 30h vio. bl. & yel. 10 3
1218 " 80h dk. bl. & org. 30 5
1219 " 1k brown & lilac 35 10

Issued to commemorate the International University Games (30h and 80h) and the World Field Ball Championships (1k).

1964, Jan. 20

Designs: 1.80k, Toboggan. 2k, Ski jump.

1220 A468 1k purple & pale green 60 45
1221 " 1.80k slate green & blue gray 1.15 1.00
1222 " 2k dark blue & pale green *2.75* *1.75*

Issued to commemorate the 9th Winter Olympic Games, Innsbruck, Jan. 29–Feb. 9, 1964.

Magura Rest Home, High Tatra
A469

Design: 80h, Slovak National Insurrection Rest Home, Low Tatra.

1964, Feb. 19 *Perf. 11½* **Unwmkd.**

1223 A469 60h grn. & yellow 25 3
1224 " 80h vio. bl. & pink 30 3

Skiers and Ski Lift
A470

Designs: 60h, Automobile camp, Telč. 1k, Fishing, Spis Castle. 1.80k, Lake and boats, Český Krumlov.

1964, Feb. 19 Engr. & Photo.

1225 A470 30h dark violet brown & bl. 15 3
1226 " 60h slate & car. 25 3
1227 " 1k brn. & olive 35 4
1228 " 1.80k slate green & orange 65 8

Moses, Day and Night by Michelangelo
A471

Designs: 60h, "A Midsummer Night's Dream," by Shakespeare. 1k, Man, telescope and heaven (vert.). 1.60k, King George of Podebrad (1420–71).

1964, March 20

1229 A471 40h blk. & yel. grn. 12 3
1230 " 60h slate & car. 18 3
1231 " 1k blk. & lt. blue 35 5
1232 " 1.60k black & yel. 60 15

Issued to commemorate the following: 400th anniversary of the death of Michelangelo (40h); 400th anniversary of the birth of Shakespeare (60h); 400th anniversary of the birth of Galileo (1k); 500th anniversary of the pacifist efforts of King George of Podebrad (1.60k).

Yuri A. Gagarin—A472

Astronauts: 60h, German Titov. 80h, John H. Glenn, Jr. 1k, Scott M. Carpenter (vert.). 1.20k, Pavel R. Popovich and Andrian G. Nikolayev. 1.40k, Walter M. Schirra (vert.). 1.60k, Gordon L. Cooper (vert.). 2k, Valentina Tereshkova and Valeri Bykovski (vert.).

Engraved and Photogravure

1964, Apr. 27 ***Perf. 11½*** **Unwmkd.**

Yellow Paper

1233 A472 30h blk. & vio. bl. 60 10
1234 " 60h dark green & dk. carmine 30 10
1235 " 80h dk. car. & vio. 35 10
1236 " 1k ultra. & rose violet 45 15
1237 " 1.20k vermilion & olive gray 1.00 25
1238 " 1.40k black & dull green 1.20 40
1239 " 1.60k pale purple & Pruss. grn. *2.50* *1.35*
1240 " 2k dk. blue & red 1.75 80
Nos. 1233-1240 (8) *8.15* *3.25*

World's first 10 astronauts.

Creeping Bellflower
A473

Film 'Flower' and Karlovy Vary Colonnade
A474

Flowers: 80h, Musk thistle. 1k, Chicory. 1.20k, Yellow iris. 1.60k, Gentian. 2k, Corn poppy.

1964, June 15 **Engraved** ***Perf. 14***

1241 A473 60h dark green, lilac & orge. 1.00 20
1242 " 80h black, green & red lilac 1.00 20
1243 " 1k violet blue, grn. & pink 1.00 30
1244 " 1.20k black, yellow & green 60 30
1245 " 1.60k violet & green 75 40
1246 " 2k violet, red & green *5.00* *2.00*
Nos. 1241-1246 (6) *9.35* *3.40*

Engraved and Photogravure

1964, June 20 ***Perf. 13½*** **Unwmkd.**

1247 A474 60h blk., bl. & car. 55 10

Issued to commemorate the 14th International Film Festival at Karlovy Vary, July 4–19.

Silesian Coat of Arms
A475

Young Miner of 1764
A476

1964, June 20 ***Perf. 11½***

1248 A475 30h black & yellow 25 3

Issued to commemorate the 150th anniversary of the Silesian Museum, Opava.

1964, June 20

1249 A476 60h sepia & lt. grn. 27 3

Issued to commemorate the bicentenary of the Mining School at Banska Stiavnica.

Skoda Fire Engine
A477

1964, June 20

1250 A477 60h car. rose & lt. bl. 30 3

Issued to commemorate the centenary of voluntary fire brigades in Bohemia.

Gulls, Hradcany Castle, Red Cross
A478

Human Heart
A479

1964, July 10

1251 A478 60h carmine & bluish gray 30 3

Issued to commemorate the 4th Czechoslovak Red Cross Congress at Prague.

1964, July 10

1252 A479 1.60k ultra. & car. 65 5

Issued to commemorate the 4th European Cardiological Congress at Prague.

Partisans, Girl and Factories
A480

Battle Scene, 1944
A481

Design: 60h, Partisans and flame.

Engraved and Photogravure

1964, Aug. 17 ***Perf. 11½*** **Unwmkd.**

1253 A480 30h brown & red 10 3
1254 " 60h dk. blue & red 22 3
1255 A481 60h black & red 22 3

Issued to commemorate the 20th anniversary of the Slovak National Uprising; No. 1255 commemorates the 20th anniversary of the Battles of Dukla Pass.

Hradcany at Prague
A482

Discus Thrower and Pole Vaulter
A483

Design: 5k, Charles Bridge and Hradcany.

1964, Aug. 30 ***Perf. 11½x12***

1256 A482 60h black & red 35 4

Souvenir Sheet

Engraved ***Imperf.***

1257 A482 5k deep claret 2.00 1.75

Millenium of the Hradcany, Prague.

No. 1257 measures 76x98mm.; stamp size: 30x50mm.

Engraved and Photogravure

1964, Sept. 2 ***Perf. 13½***

Designs: 60h, Bicycling (horiz.). 1k, Soccer. 1.20k, Rowing. 1.60k, Swimming (horiz.). 2.80k, Weight lifting (horiz.).

1258 A483 60h multicolored 30 12
1259 " 80h " 40 12
1260 " 1k " 50 18
1261 " 1.20k " 60 25
1262 " 1.60k " 1.00 50
1263 " 2.80k " *4.25* *2.50*
Nos. 1258-1263 (6) *7.05* *3.67*

Issued to commemorate the 18th Olympic Games, Tokyo, Oct. 10–25. Sheets of 10.

Miniature Sheet

Space Ship Voskhod I, Astronauts and Globe—A484

Engraved and Photogravure

1964, Nov. 12 ***Perf. 11½*** **Unwmkd.**

1264 A484 3k dk. blue & dull lilac, *buff* 3.50 2.75

Issued to commemorate the Russian three-manned space flight of Vladimir M. Komarov, Boris B. Yegorov and Konstantin Feoktistov, Oct. 12–13. No. 1264 contains one stamp. Size of stamp: 49x30 mm.; size of sheet: 92x66mm.

Steam Engine and Atomic Power Plant
A485

Diesel Engine "CKD Praha"
A486

1964, Nov. 16 **Engraved**

1265 A485 30h dull red brown 10 3

Engraved and Photogravure

1266 A486 60h grn. & salmon 20 3

Issued to publicize traditions and development of engineering; No. 1265 commemorates the 150th anniversary of the First Brno Engineering Works, No. 1266 honors the engineering concern CKD Praha.

European Redstart
A487

Birds: 60h, Green woodpecker. 80h, Hawfinch. 1k, Black woodpecker. 1.20k, European robin. 1.60k, European roller.

1964, Nov. 16 **Litho.** ***Perf. 10½***

1267 A487 30h multicolored 10 3
1268 " 60h blk. & multi. 20 3
1269 " 80h multicolored 30 8
1270 " 1k " 35 18
1271 " 1.20k lt. vio. blue & black 45 25
1272 " 1.60k yel. & black 75 45
Nos. 1267-1272 (6) *2.15* *1.02*

Dancer
A488

"In the Sun" Pre-school Children
A489

Designs: 60h, "Over the Obstacles," teenagers. 1k, "Movement and Beauty," woman flag twirler. 1.60k, Runners at start.

Engraved and Photogravure

1965 ***Perf. 11½*** **Unwmkd.**

1273 A488 30h red & lt. blue 15 3

Perf. 11½x12

1274 A489 30h violet blue & carmine 10 3
1275 " 60h brn. & ultra. 20 3
1276 " 1k blk. & yellow 40 6
1277 " 1.60k maroon & gray 65 20
Nos. 1273-1277 (5) 1.50 35

Issued to publicize the Third National Spartacist Games. Issue dates: No. 1273, Jan. 3. Nos. 1274–1277, May 24.

Mountain Rescue Service
A490

Arms and View, Beroun
A491

1965, Jan. 15 ***Perf. 11½*** **Unwmkd.**

Designs: No. 1279, Woman gymnast. No. 1280, Bicyclists. No. 1281, Women hurdlers.

1278 A490 60h violet & blue 25 4

1279	A490	60h maroon & ocher	25	4
1280	"	60h black & car.	25	4
1281	"	60h green & yellow	25	4

Issued to publicize: Mountain Rescue Service (No. 1278); First World Championship in Artistic Gymnastics, Prague, December 1965 (No. 1279); World Championship in Indoor Bicycling, Prague, Oct., 1965 (No. 1280); "Universiada 1965," Brno (No. 1281).

1965, Feb. 15 — Engr. and Photo.

Designs: No. 1283, Town Square, Domazlice. No. 1284, Old and new buildings, Frydek-Mystek. No. 1285, Arms and view, Lipnik. No. 1286, Fortified wall, City Hall and Arms, Policka. No. 1287, View and hops, Zatek. No. 1288, Small fortress and rose, Terezin.

1282	A491	30h vio. bl. & lt. bl.	15	3
1283	"	30h dull pur. & yel.	15	3
1284	"	30h slate & gray	15	3
1285	"	30h green & bister	15	3
1286	"	30h brown & tan	15	3
1287	"	30h dk. bl. & citron	15	3
1288	"	30h black & rose	15	3
		Nos. 1282-1288 (7)	1.05	21

Nos. 1282-87 commemorate the 700th anniversary of the founding of various Bohemian towns; No. 1288 commemorates the 20th anniversary of the liberation of the Theresienstadt (Terezin) concentration camp.

Sun's Corona—A492

Space Research: 30h, Sun. 60h, Exploration of the Moon. 1k, Twin space craft (vert.). 1.40k, Space station. 1.60k, Exploration of Mars (vert.). 2k, USSR and USA Meteorological collaboration.

Perf. 12x11½, 11½x12

1965, Mar. 15 — Engr. & Photo.

1289	A492	20h rose & red lilac	10	3
1290	"	30h rose red & yel.	12	3
1291	"	60h bluish black & yellow	22	3
1292	"	1k pur. & pale bl.	35	9
1293	"	1.40k blk. & salmon	50	14
1294	"	1.60k black & pink	60	18
1295	"	2k bluish black & light bl.	*1.20*	*1.10*
		Nos. 1289-1295 (7)	*3.09*	*1.60*

Issued to publicize space research; Nos. 1289-1290 also commemorate the International Quiet Sun Year, 1964-65.

Frantisek Ventura, Equestrian; Amsterdam, 1928
A493

Czechoslovakian Olympic Victories: 30h, Discus, Paris, 1900. 60h, Running, Helsinki, 1952. 1k, Weight lifting, Los Angeles, 1932. 1.40k, Gymnastics, Berlin, 1936. 1.60k, Double sculling, Rome, 1960. 2k, Women's gymnastics, Tokyo, 1964.

1965, Apr. 16 — *Perf. 11½x12*

1296	A493	20h choc. & gold	10	3
1297	"	30h indigo & emerald	12	3
1298	"	60h ultra. & gold	22	4
1299	"	1k red brn. & gold	40	8
1300	"	1.40k dark slate grn. & gold	75	50
1301	"	1.60k black & gold	80	50
1302	"	2k maroon & gold	90	50
		Nos. 1296-1302 (7)	3.29	1.68

Astronauts Virgil Grissom and John Young—A494

Designs: No. 1304, Alexei Leonov floating in space. No. 1305, Launching pad at Cape Kennedy, U.S.A. No. 1306, Leonov leaving space ship.

1965, Apr. 17 — *Perf. 11x11½*

1303	A494	60h slate blue & lilac rose	20	18
1304	"	60h vio. blk. & bl.	20	18
1305	"	3k slate blue & lilac rose	1.35	90
1306	"	3k vio. blk. & bl.	1.35	90

Issued to honor American and Soviet astronauts. Printed in sheets of 25; one sheet contains 20 No. 1303 and 5 No. 1305, the other sheet contains 20 No. 1304 and 5 No. 1306.

Russian Soldier, View of Prague and Guerrilla Fighters—A495

Designs: No. 1308, Blast furnace, workers and tank. 60h, Worker and factory. 1k, Worker and new constructions. 1.60k, Woman farmer, new farm buildings and machinery.

1965, May 5 — Engraved — *Perf. 13½*

1307	A495	30h dark red, black & olive	12	3
1308	"	30h multicolored	12	3
1309	"	60h violet blue, red & black	25	4
1310	"	1k deep orange, black & brn.	40	10
1311	"	1.60k yel., red & blk.	60	15
		Nos. 1307-1311 (5)	1.49	35

Issued to commemorate the 20th anniversary of liberation from the Nazis.

Slovakian Kopov Dog—A496

Dogs: 40h, German shepherd. 60h, Czech hunting dog with pheasant. 1k, Poodle. 1.60k, Czech terrier. 2k, Afghan hound.

1965, June 10 — *Perf. 12x11½*

1312	A496	30h blk. & red orge.	12	3
1313	"	40h black & yellow	18	3
1314	"	60h black & verm.	25	4
1315	"	1k black & dark carmine rose	40	8
1316	"	1.60k black & orge.	75	18
1317	"	2k black & orge.	1.00	60
		Nos. 1312-1317 (6)	2.70	96

Issued to publicize the World Dog Show at Brno and the International Dog Breeders Congress, Prague.

U.N. Headquarters Building, N.Y.
A497

Designs: 60h, U.N. Emblem and inscription. 1.60k, ICY emblem.

1965, June 24 — *Perf. 12x11½*

1318	A497	60h dark red brown & yellow	25	4
1319	"	1k ultra. & lt. bl.	40	7
1320	"	1.60k gold & dk. red	65	30

Issued to commemorate the 20th anniversary of the United Nations and for the International Cooperation Year, 1965.

Trade Union Emblem
A498

1965, June 24 — Engraved

1321	A498	60h dk. red & ultra.	25	3

Issued to commemorate the 20th anniversary of the International Trade Union Federation.

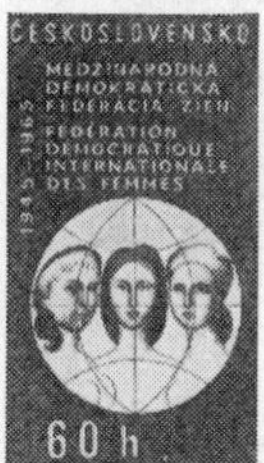

Women and Globe
A499

1965, June 24 — *Perf. 11½x12*

1322	A499	60h violet blue	25	3

Issued to commemorate the 20th anniversary of the International Women's Federation.

Children's House (Burgraves' Palace), Hradcany
A500

Matthias Tower
A501

1965, June 25 — *Perf. 11½*

1323	A500	30h slate green	20	3
1324	A501	60h dark brown	40	3

Issued to publicize the Hradcany, Prague.

Marx and Lenin
A502

1965, July 1 — Engraved and Photo.

1325	A502	60h carmine rose & gold	30	3

Issued to commemorate the 6th conference of Postal Ministers of Communist Countries, Peking, June 21-July 15.

Joseph Navratil
A503

Jan Hus
A504

Gregor Johann Mendel
A505

Costume Jewelry
A506

Bohuslav Martinu
A507

Seated Woman and University of Bratislava
A508

ITU Emblem and Communication Symbols
A509

Macromolecular Symposium Emblem
A510

Design: No. 1327, Ludwig Stur (diff. frame).

Engraved and Photogravure

1965 — *Perf. 11½* — Unwmkd.

1326	A503	30h blk. & terra cotta	18	3
1327	"	30h blk. & dull grn.	20	3
1328	A504	60h blk. & crimson	30	3
1329	A505	60h vio. blue & red	30	3
1330	A506	60h purple & gold	30	3
1331	A507	60h black. & org.	30	3
1332	A508	60h brown, *yellow*	30	3
1333	A509	1k orange & blue	45	4
1334	A510	1k blk. & dp. org.	45	5
		Nos. 1326-1334 (9)	2.78	30

No. 1326 commemorates the centenary of the death of Josef Navratil (1798-1865), painter; No. 1327, the sesquicentennial of the birth of Ludwig Stur (1815-56), Slovak author and historian; No. 1328 commemorates the 550th anniversary of the death of Jan Hus, religious reformer; No. 1329, the centenary of publication of Mendel's laws of inheritance; No. 1330 publicizes the "Jablonec 1965" costume jewelry exhibition; No. 1331, the 75th anniversary of the birth of Bohuslav Martinu (1890-1959), composer; No. 1332, the 500th anniversary of the founding of the University of Bratislava as Academia Istropolitana; No. 1333, the centenary of the International Telecommunication Union; No. 1334, the International Symposium on Macromolecular Chemistry, Prague, Sept. 1-8.

"Young Woman at her Toilette," by Titian
A512

Help for Flood Victims
A513

Rescue of Flood Victims
A514

Miniature Sheet

1965, Aug. 12

1336 A512 5k multicolored 2.75 2.00

Issued to publicize the Hradcany Art Gallery. No. 1336 contains one stamp; size of sheet: 75x97mm.

1965, Sept. 6 Engraved

1337 A513 30h violet blue 15 7

Engraved and Photogravure

1338 A514 2k dk. olive green & olive 90 45

Help for Danube flood victims in Slovakia.

Dotterel
A515

Mountain Birds: 60h, Wall creeper (vert.). 1.20k, Lesser redpoll. 1.40k, Golden eagle (vert.). 1.60k, Ring ouzel. 2k, Eurasian nutcracker (vert.).

1965, Sept. 20 Litho. *Perf. 11*

1339	A515	30h	multicolored	12	3
1340	"	60h	"	25	3
1341	"	1.20k	"	50	10
1342	"	1.40k	"	55	12
1343	"	1.60k	"	60	20
1344	"	2k	"	90	85
			Nos. 1339-1344 (6)	2.92	1.33

Levoca
A516

Coltsfoot
A517

Views of Towns: 10h, Jindrichuv Hradec. 20h, Nitra. 30h, Kosice. 40h, Hradec Králové. 50h, Telc. 60h, Ostrava. 1k, Olomouc. 1.20k, Ceske Budejovice. 1.60k, Cheb. 2k, Brno. 3k, Bratislava. 5k, Prague.

Engraved and Photogravure

1965–66 *Perf. 11½x12*

Size: 23x19mm.

1345	A516	5h black & yellow	3	3
1346	"	10h ultra. & olive bister	6	3
1347	"	20h black & lt. blue	8	3
1348	"	30h vio. bl. & lt. grn.	12	3
1348A	"	40h dark brown & lt. blue ('66)	15	3
1348B	"	50h black & ocher ('66)	20	3
1348C	"	60h red & gray ('66)	25	3
1348D	"	1k purple & pale green ('66)	45	3

Perf. 11½x11

Size: 30x23mm.

1349	A516	1.20k slate & lt. bl.	55	4
1350	"	1.60k indigo & yel.	70	3
1351	"	2k slate green & pale yel.	90	5
1352	"	3k brn. & yel.	1.35	6
1353	"	5k blk. & pink	2.50	11
		Nos. 1345-1353 (13)	7.34	53

1965, Dec. 3 Engraved *Perf. 14*

Medicinal Plants: 60h, Meadow saffron. 80h, Corn poppy. 1k, Foxglove. 1.20k, Arnica. 1.60k, Cornflower. 2k, Dog rose.

1354	A517	30h	multicolored	15	8
1355	"	60h	"	25	12
1356	"	80h	"	30	15
1357	"	1k	"	40	20
1358	"	1.20k	"	50	25
1359	"	1.60k	"	60	30
1360	"	2k	"	*3.00*	*1.50*
			Nos. 1354-1360 (7)	*5.20*	*2.60*

Strip of "Stamps"—A518

Engraved and Photogravure

1965, Dec. 18 *Perf. 11½*

1361 A518 1k dark red & gold 1.75 1.50

Issued for Stamp Day, 1965.

Romain Rolland
A519

Symbolic Musical Instruments and Names of Composers
A520

Portraits: No. 1362, Stanislav Sucharda. No. 1363, Ignac Josef Pesina. No. 1365, Donatello.

1966, Feb. 14 Engraved *Perf. 11½*

1362	A519	30h deep green	10	3
1363	"	30h violet blue	10	3
1364	"	60h rose lake	22	3
1365	"	60h brown	22	3

Issued to commemorate the following: No. 1362, centenary of birth of Stanislav Sucharda (1866–1916), sculptor; No. 1363, bicentenary of birth of Ignac Josef Pesina (1766–1808), veterinarian. No. 1364, centenary of birth of Romain Rolland (1866–1944), French writer; No. 1365, 500th anniversary of death of Donatello (1386–1466), Italian sculptor.

1966, Feb. 15 Engr. and Photo.

1366 A520 30h black & gold 35 10

Issued to commemorate the 70th anniversary of the Czech Philharmonic Orchestra.

Figure Skating Pair—A521

Designs: No. 1368, Man skater. No. 1369, Volleyball player, spiking (vert.). 1k, Volleyball player, saving (vert.). 1.60k, Woman skater. 2k, Figure skating pair.

1966, Feb. 17

1367	A521	30h dk. car. rose	15	3
1368	"	60h green	30	4
1369	"	60h car. & buff	30	4
1370	"	1k vio. & lt. blue	40	5
1371	"	1.60k brn. & yellow	60	9
1372	"	2k bl. & greenish blue	*1.65*	*40*
		Nos. 1367-1372 (6)	*3.40*	*65*

Nos. 1367–68 and 1371–72 commemorate the European Figure Skating Championships, Bratislava; Nos. 1369–70 commemorate the World Volleyball Championships.

Souvenir Sheet

Girl Dancing—A522

1966, Mar. 21 Engraved *Imperf.*

1373 A522 3k slate blue, red & med. blue 1.35 1.25

Issued to commemorate the centenary of the opera "The Bartered Bride" by Bedrich Smetana. Opening chorus "Why shouldn't we be happy. ." in margin. Size: 85x105mm.

"Ajax" 1841
A523

Locomotives: 30h, "Karlstejn" 1865. 60h, Steam engine, 1946. 1k, Steam engine with tender, 1946. 1.60k, Electric locomotive, 1964. 2k, Diesel locomotive, 1964.

1966, March 21 *Perf. 11½x11*

Buff Paper

1374	A523	20h sepia	10	3
1375	"	30h dull violet	12	3
1376	"	60h dull purple	30	3
1377	"	1k dark blue	40	7
1378	"	1.60k dk. blue green	60	20
1379	"	2k dark red	*2.10*	*90*
		Nos. 1374-1379 (6)	*3.62*	*1.26*

European Perch
A524

Fish: 30h, Brown trout (vert.). 1k, Carp. 1.20k, Northern pike. 1.40k, Grayling. 1.60k, Eel.

Perf. 13x13½, 13½x13

1966, Apr. 22 Litho. Unwmkd.

1380	A524	30h	multicolored	15	3
1381	"	60h	"	25	3
1382	"	1k	"	40	5
1383	"	1.20k	"	50	15
1384	"	1.40k	"	60	25
1385	"	1.60k	"	*2.25*	*85*
			Nos. 1380-1385 (6)	*4.15*	*1.36*

Issued to publicize the International Fishing Championships, Svit, Sept. 3–5.

WHO Headquarters, Geneva
A525

Engraved and Photogravure

1966, Apr. 25 *Perf. 12x11½*

1386 A525 1k dk. bl. & lt. blue 45 5

Issued to commemorate the inauguration of the World Health Organization Headquarters, Geneva.

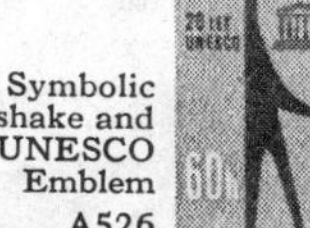

Symbolic Handshake and UNESCO Emblem
A526

1966, Apr. 25 *Perf. 11½*

1387 A526 60h bister & olive gray 25 5

Issued to commemorate the 20th anniversary of UNESCO (U.N. Educational, Scientific and Cultural Organization).

Prague Castle Issue

Belvedere Palace and St. Vitus' Cathedral
A527

Crown of St. Wenceslas, 1346
A528

Design: 60h, Madonna, altarpiece from St. George's Church.

1966, May 9 Engraved *Perf. 11½*

1388 A527 30h dark blue 18 3

Engraved and Photogravure

1389 A527 60h blk. & yel. bis. 35 4

Souvenir Sheet

Engraved

1390 A528 5k multicolored 2.50 2.50

See also Nos. 1537–1539.

Tiger Swallowtail
A529

Butterflies and Moths: 60h, Clouded sulphur. 80h, European purple emperor. 1k, Apollo. 1.20k, Burnet moth. 2k, Tiger moth.

1966, May 23 Engraved *Perf. 14*

1391	A529	30h multicolored	10	8
1392	"	60h "	20	10
1393	"	80h "	30	12
1394	"	1k "	40	15
1395	"	1.20k "	60	20
1396	"	2k "	*2.75*	*1.35*
		Nos. 1391-1396 (6)	*4.35*	*2.00*

Sheets of ten.

Flags of Russia and Czechoslovakia
A530

Designs: 60h, Rays surrounding hammer and sickle "sun." 1.60k, Girl's head and stars.

Engraved and Photogravure

1966, May 31 *Perf. 11½*

1397	A530	30h dk. bl. & crim.	12	3
1398	"	60h dk. blue & red	25	5
1399	"	1.60k red & dk. blue	60	9

Issued to commemorate the 13th Congress of the Communist Party of Czechoslovakia.

Dakota Chief
A531

Designs: 20h, Indians, canoe and tepee (horiz.). 30h, Tomahawk. 40h, Haida totem poles. 60h, Kachina, good spirit of the Hopis. 1k, Indian on horseback hunting buffalo (horiz.). 1.20k, Calumet, Dakota peace pipe.

1966, June 20 Engr. & Photo.

Size: 23x40mm.

1400	A531	20h violet blue & deep orange	10	5
1401	"	30h black & dull orange	10	5
1402	"	40h blk. & lt. blue	10	8
1403	"	60h green & yel.	30	10
1404	"	1k pur. & emerald	35	15
1405	"	1.20k violet blue & rose lilac	60	25

Engraved

Perf. 14

Size: 23x37mm.

1406	A531	1.40k multicolored	*1.80*	*50*
		Nos. 1400-1406 (7)	*3.35*	*1.18*

Issued to commemorate the centenary of the Náprstek Ethnographic Museum, Prague, and in connection with "The Indians of North America" exhibition.

Model of Molecule
A532

Engraved and Photogravure

1966, July 4 *Perf. 11½* Unwmkd.

1407	A532	60h blk. & lt. blue	20	3

Issued to commemorate the centenary of the Czechoslovak Chemical Society.

"Guernica" by Pablo Picasso
A533

1966, July 5

Size: 75x30mm.

1408	A533	60h blk. & pale bl.	1.50	1.35

30th anniversary of International Brigade in Spanish Civil War.

Sheets of 15 stamps and 5 labels inscribed "Picasso-Guernica 1937."

Pantheon, Bratislava
A534

Designs: No. 1410, Devin Castle and Ludwig Stur. No. 1411, View of Nachod. No. 1412, State Science Library, Olomouc.

1966, July 25 Engraved

1409	A534	30h dull purple	10	3
1410	"	60h dark blue	25	3
1411	"	60h green	25	3
1412	"	60h sepia	25	3

No. 1409 publicizes the Russian War Memorial, Bratislava; No. 1410, the 9th century Devin Castle as symbol of Slovak nationalism; No. 1411 commemorates the 700th anniversary of the founding of Nachod; No. 1412, the 400th anniversary of the State Science Library, Olomouc.

Atom Symbol and Sun
A535

Engraved and Photogravure

1966, Aug. 29 *Perf. 11½*

1413	A535	60h black & red	25	3

Issued to publicize Jachýmov (Joachimsthal), where pitchblende was first discovered, "cradle of the atomic age."

Brno Fair Emblem
A536

Olympia Coin and Olympic Rings
A537

1966, Aug. 29

1414	A536	60h black & red	25	3

8th International Trade Fair, Brno.

1966, Aug. 29

Design: 1k, Olympic flame, Czechoslovak flag and Olympic rings.

1415	A537	60h black & gold	25	4
1416	"	1k dk. blue & red	35	20

Issued to commemorate the 70th anniversary of the Olympic Committee.

Missile Carrier, Tank and Jet Plane
A538

1966, Aug. 31

1417	A538	60h blk. & apple grn.	25	5

Issued to commemorate the maneuvers of the armies of the Warsaw Pact countries.

Mercury
A539

Designs: 30h, Moravian silver thaler, 1620, reverse and obverse (vert.). 1.60k, Old and new buildings of Brno State Theater. 5k, International Trade Fair Administration Tower and postmark (vert.).

1966, Sept. 10

1418	A539	30h dk. red & black	10	4
1419	"	60h org. & black	20	4
1420	"	1.60k blk. & brt. grn.	60	15

Souvenir Sheet

1421	A539	5k multicolored	2.50	2.50

Issued to publicize the Brno Philatelic Exhibition, Sept. 11-25. No. 1421 contains one stamp (size: 30x40mm.). Marginal black inscription and exhibition emblem. Size: 73½x100mm.

First Meeting in Orbit—A540

Designs: 30h, Photograph of far side of Moon and Russian satellite. 60h, Photograph of Mars and Mariner 4. 80h, Soft landing on Moon. 1k, Satellite, laser beam and binary code. 1.20k, Telstar over Earth and receiving station.

Engraved and Photogravure

1966, Sept. 26 *Perf. 11½*

1422	A540	20h vio. & lt. grn.	10	3
1423	"	30h blk. & sal. pink	15	3
1424	"	60h slate & lilac	25	4
1425	"	80h dark purple & light blue	30	4
1426	"	1k black & vio.	40	15
1427	"	1.20k red & blue	*1.50*	*60*
		Nos. 1422-1427 (6)	*2.70*	*89*

Issued to publicize American and Russian achievements in space research.

Badger
A541

Game Animals: 40h, Red deer (vert.). 60h, Lynx. 80h, Hare. 1k, Red fox. 1.20k, Brown bear (vert.). 2k, Wild boar.

1966, Nov. 28 Litho. *Perf. 13½*

1428	A541	30h multicolored	12	4
1429	"	40h "	18	4
1430	"	60h "	25	4
1431	"	80h multicolored (*europaens*)	35	12
		a. 80h multi. (*europaeus*)	1.40	1.00
1432	"	1k multicolored	40	15
1433	"	1.20k "	45	18
1434	"	2k "	*2.75*	*1.20*
		Nos. 1428-1434 (7)	*4.50*	*1.77*

The sheet of 50 of the 80h contains 40 with misspelling "europaens" and 10 with "europaeus."

"Spring" by Vaclav Hollar, 1607-77
A542

Paintings: No. 1436, Portrait of Mrs. F. Wussin, by Jan Kupecký (1667-1740). No. 1437, Snow Owl by Karel Purkyne (1834-1868). No. 1438, Tulips by Vaclav Spála (1885-1964). No. 1439, Recruit by Ludovít Fulla (1902-).

1966, Dec. 8 Engraved *Perf. 14*

1435	A542	1k black	2.50	2.25
1436	"	1k multicolored	2.50	2.25
1437	"	1k "	2.50	2.25
1438	"	1k "	2.50	2.25
1439	"	1k "	*10.00*	*9.00*
		Nos. 1435-1439 (5)	*20.00*	*18.00*

Printed in sheets of 4 stamps and 2 labels. The labels in sheet of No. 1435 are inscribed "Vaclav Hollar 1607-1677" in fancy frame. Other labels are blank.

See also No. 1484.

Symbolic Bird—A543

Engraved and Photogravure

1966, Dec. 17 *Perf. 11½*

1440	A543	1k dp. bl. & yel.	85	75

Issued for Stamp Day.

Youth
A544

1967, Jan. 16 *Perf. 11½*

1441	A544	30h verm. & lt. bl.	15	4

Issued to publicize the 5th Congress of the Czechoslovak Youth Organization.

Symbolic Flower and Machinery
A545

1967, Jan. 16 Engr. & Photo.

1442	A545	30h car. & yellow	15	4

6th Trade Union Congress, Prague.

Parents with Dead Child
A545a

1967, Jan. 16 *Perf. 11½*

1442A	A545a	60h black & salmon	25	6

Issued to publicize "Peace and Freedom in Viet Nam."

View of Jihlava and Tourist Year Emblem—A546

Views and Tourist Year Emblem: 40h, Spielberg Castle and churches, Brno. 1.20k, Danube, castle and churches, Bratislava. 1.60k, Vlatava River bridges, Hradcany and churches, Prague.

1967, Feb. 13 Engraved *Perf. 11½*

Size: 40x23mm.

1443	A546	30h brown violet	12	4
1444	"	40h maroon	18	4

Size: 75x30mm.

1445	A546	1.20k violet blue	65	20
1446	"	1.60k black	*1.60*	*60*

International Tourist Year, 1967.

Black-tailed Godwit
A547

Birds: 40h, Shoveler (horiz.). 60h, Purple heron. 80h, Penduline tit. 1k, Avocet. 1.40k, Black stork. 1.60k, Tufted duck (horiz.).

1967, Feb. 20 Litho. *Perf. 13½*

1447	A547	30h multicolored	10	4
1448	"	40h "	12	5
1449	"	60h "	20	4
1450	"	80h "	30	10
1451	"	1k "	40	12
1452	"	1.40k "	60	20
1453	"	1.60k "	*2.20*	*1.20*
		Nos. 1447-1453 (7)	*3.92*	*1.75*

Solar Research and Satellite
A548

Space Research: 40h, Space craft, rocket and construction of station. 60h, Man on moon and orientation system. 1k, Exploration of solar system and rocket. 1.20k, Lunar satellites and moon photograph. 1.60k, Planned lunar architecture and moon landing.

Engraved and Photogravure

1967, March 24 *Perf. 11½*

1454	A548	30h yel. & dk. red	12	4
1455	"	40h vio. bl. & blk.	15	4
1456	"	60h lilac & green	25	5
1457	"	1k bright pink & slate	40	12
1458	"	1.20k lt. vio. & blk.	65	20
1459	"	1.60k brown lake & black	*1.00*	*60*
		Nos. 1454-1459 (6)	*2.57*	*1.05*

Gothic Painting, by Master Theodoric
A549

Designs: 40h, "Burning of Master Hus," from Litomerice Hymnal. 60h, Modern glass sculpture. 80h, "The Shepherdess and the Chimney Sweep," Andersen fairy tale, painting by J. Trnka. 1k, Section of pressure vessel from atomic power station. 1.20k, Three ceramic figurines, by P. Rada. 3k, Montreal skyline and EXPO '67 emblem.

1967, Apr. 10 Engraved *Perf. 14*

Size: 37x23mm.

1460	A549	30h multicolored	15	5
1461	"	40h "	20	10
1462	"	60h "	30	15
1463	"	80h "	45	20
1464	"	1k "	50	30
1465	"	1.20k "	*1.00*	*35*
		Nos. 1460-1465 (6)	*2.60*	*1.15*

Souvenir Sheet

Perf. 11½

Size: 40x30mm.

1466	A549	3k multicolored	1.50	1.50

Issued to commemorate EXPO '67, International Exhibition, Montreal, Apr. 28–Oct. 27, 1967. No. 1466 contains one stamp with drawing of the Czechoslovakian pavilion in the margin. Size of sheet: 96x74mm.

Canoe Race
A550

Women Playing Field Ball
A551

Designs: No. 1468, Wheels, dove and emblems of Warsaw, Berlin, Prague. 1.60k, Canoe slalom.

Perf. 12x11½, 11½x12

1967, Apr. 17 Engr. and Photo.

1467	A550	60h blk. & brt. bl.	18	8
1468	"	60h blk. & salmon	18	8
1469	A551	60h black & greenish bl.	18	8
1470	"	1.60k black & brt. violet	*1.00*	*40*

Issued to commemorate the following: No. 1467, 5th International Wild-Water Canoeing Championships; No. 1468, 20th Warsaw-Berlin-Prague Bicycle Race; No. 1469, Women's Field Ball Championships; No. 1470, 10th International Water Slalom Championships.

"Golden Street"
A552

Designs: 60h, Interior of Hall of King Wenceslas. 5k, St. Matthew, from illuminated manuscript, 11th century.

1967, May 9 *Perf. 11½x11*

1471	A552	30h rose claret	15	3
1472	"	60h bluish black	30	6

Souvenir Sheet

Perf. 11½

1473	A552	5k multicolored	2.50	2.50

Issued to publicize the Castle of Prague. No. 1473 contains one stamp with Latin marginal inscription in gold. Size: 75x95 mm.

Stylized Lyre with Flowers
A553

Old-New Synagogue, Prague
A554

Engraved and Photogravure

1967, May 10 *Perf. 11½*

1474	A553	60h dull purple & brt. green	30	6

Prague Music Festival.

1967, May 22 *Perf. 11½*

Designs: 30h, Detail from Torah curtain, 1593. 60h, Prague Printer's emblem, 1530. 1k, Mikulov jug, 1804. 1.40k, Memorial for Concentration Camp Victims 1939–45, Pincas Synagogue (menorah and tablet). 1.60k, Tombstone of David Gans, 1613.

1475	A554	30h dull red & lt. bl.	15	8
1476	"	60h black & lt. grn.	30	8
1477	"	1k dk. blue & rose lilac	50	18
1478	"	1.20k dk. brown & maroon	65	35
1479	"	1.40k black & yellow	80	35
1480	"	1.60k grn. & yellow	*3.75*	*1.60*
		Nos. 1475-1480 (6)	*6.15*	*2.64*

Issued to show Jewish relics. The items shown on the 30h, 60h and 1k are from the State Jewish Museum, Prague.

"Lidice"
A555

Prague Architecture
A556

1967, June 9 *Perf. 11½* Unwmkd.

1481	A555	30h blk. & brt. rose	15	3

Issued to commemorate the 25th anniversary of the destruction of Lidice by the Nazis.

1967, June 10 Engr. & Photo.

1482	A556	1k black & gold	40	18

Issued to publicize the 9th Congress of the International Union of Architects, Prague.

Petr Bezruc
A557

1967, June 21

1483	A557	60h dull rose & black	25	5

Issued to commemorate the centenary of the birth of Petr Bezruc, poet and writer.

Painting Type of 1966

Design: 2k, Henri Rousseau (1844–1910), self-portrait.

1967, June 22 Engr. *Perf. 11½*

1484	A542	2k multicolored	1.10	90

Issued to publicize Praga 68, World Stamp Exhibition, Prague, June 22–July 7, 1968. Printed in sheets of 4 stamps (2x2), separated by horizontal gutter with commemorative inscription and picture of National Gallery, site of Praga 68.

View of Skalitz
A558

Designs: No. 1486, Mining tower and church steeple, Pribram. No. 1487, Hands holding book and view of Presov.

1967, Aug. 21 Engr. *Perf. 11½*

1485	A558	30h violet blue	10	4
1486	"	30h slate green	10	4
1487	"	30h claret	10	4

Issued to commemorate anniversaries of the towns of Skalitz, Pribram and Presov.

Colonnade and Spring, Karlovy Vary and Communications Emblem
A559

1967, Aug. 21 Engr. and Photo.

1488	A559	30h vio. bl. & gold	35	5

Issued to commemorate the 5th Sports and Cultural Festival of the Employees of the Ministry of Communications, Karlovy Vary.

Ondrejov Conservatory and Galaxy
A560

1967, Aug. 22 Engraved

1489	A560	60h vio. bl., rose lilac & silver	60	12

Issued to commemorate the 13th International Congress of the Astronomic Union.

Orchid
A561

Flowers from the Botanical Gardens: 30h, Cobaea scandens. 40h, Lycaste deppei. 60h, Glottiphyllum davisii. 1k, Anthurium. 1.20k, Rhodocactus. 1.40k, Moth orchid.

1967, Aug. 30 Litho. *Perf. 12½*

1490	A561	20h multicolored	8	3
1491	"	30h pink & multi.	12	3
1492	"	40h multicolored	25	4
1493	"	60h lt. bl. & multi.	25	4
1494	"	1k multicolored	55	15
1495	"	1.20k lt. yel. & multi.	55	18
1496	"	1.40k multicolored	*2.00*	*55*
		Nos. 1490-1496 (7)	*3.80*	*1.02*

Red Squirrel
A562

Animals from the Tatra National Park: 60h, Wild cat. 1k, Ermine. 1.20k, Dormouse. 1.40k, Hedgehog. 1.60k, Pine marten.

Engraved and Photogravure

1967, Sept. 25 ***Perf. 11½***

1497 A562 30h black, yellow & orange 15 3
1498 " 60h black & buff 30 6
1499 " 1k blk. & lt. blue 50 15
1500 " 1.20k brown, pale green & yel. 55 18
1501 " 1.40k black, pink & yellow 70 20
1502 " 1.60k black, orange & yellow *2.25* 75
Nos. 1497-1502 (6) *4.45* *1.37*

Rockets and Weapons
A563

1967, Oct. 6 Engraved ***Perf. 11½***

1503 A563 30h slate green 20 5

Day of the Czechoslovak People's Army.

Cruiser "Aurora" Firing at Winter Palace—A564

Designs: 60h, Hammer and sickle emblems and Red Star (vert.). 1k, Hands reaching for hammer and sickle (vert.).

Engraved and Photogravure

1967, Nov. 7

1504 A564 30h blk. & dk. car. 10 3
1505 " 60h " " 20 4
1506 " 1k " " 35 10

Issued to commemorate the 50th anniversary of the Russian October Revolution.

The Conjurer, by Frantisek Tichy
A565

Paintings: 80h, Don Quixote, by Cyprian Majernik. 1k, Promenade in the Park, by Norbert Grund. 1.20k, Self-portrait, by Peter J. Brandl. 1.60k, Saints from Jan of Jeren Epitaph, by Czech Master of 1395.

1967, Nov. 13 Engr. ***Perf. 11½***

1507 A565 60h multicolored 30 20
1508 " 80h " 45 30
1509 " 1k " 50 40
1510 " 1.20k " 60 50
1511 " 1.60k " *4.75* *4.25*
Nos. 1507-1511 (5) *6.60* *5.65*

Sheets of 4. See Nos. 1589–1593, 1658–1662, 1711–1715, 1779–1783, 1847–1851, 1908–1913, 2043–2047, 2090–2093, 2147–2151.

Pres. Antonin Novotny
A566

1967, Dec. 9 Engraved ***Perf. 11½***

1512 A566 2k blue gray 60 4
1513 " 3k brown 90 6

Czechoslovakia Nos. 65, 71 and 81 of 1920—A567

1967, Dec. 18

1514 A567 1k maroon & silver 65 60

Issued for Stamp Day.

Symbolic Flag and Dates
A568

1968, Jan. 15 Engr. ***Perf. 11½***

1515 A568 30h red, dk. blue & ultramarine 15 6

50th anniversary of Czechoslovakia.

Figure Skating and Olympic Rings
A569

Designs (Olympic Rings and): 1k, Ski course. 1.60k, Toboggan chute. 2k, Ice hockey.

1968, Jan. 29 Engr. and Photo.

1516 A569 60h blk., yellow & ocher 30 7
1517 " 1k olive grn., lt. bl. & lemon 40 18
1518 " 1.60k blk., lilac & blue green 70 25
1519 " 2k blk., apple grn. & lt. bl. *1.25* 75

Issued to publicize the 10th Winter Olympic Games, Grenoble, France, Feb. 6–18.

Factories and Rising Sun
A570

Design: 60h, Workers and banner.

Engraved and Photogravure

1968, Feb. 25 ***Perf. 11½x12***

1520 A570 30h car. & dk. blue 10 4
1521 " 60h " " " 18 5

20th anniversary of February Revolution.

Map of Battle of Sokolow
A571

Human Rights Flame
A572

Engraved and Photogravure

1968, Mar. 8 ***Perf. 11½***

1522 A571 30h black, brt. bl. & carmine 18 5

Engraved

1523 A572 1k rose carmine 40 15

No. 1522 commemorates the 25th anniversary of the Battle of Sokolow, Mar. 8, 1943, against the German Army; No. 1523 commemorates the International Human Rights Year.

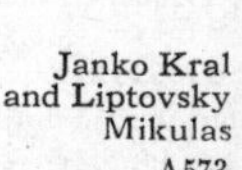

Janko Kral and Liptovsky Mikulas
A573

Karl Marx
A574

Girl's Head
A575

Arms and Allegory
A576

Head
A577

1968, Mar. 25 Engraved

1524 A573 30h green 15 3
1525 A574 30h claret 15 3

Engraved and Photogravure

1526 A575 30h dk. red & gold 15 3
1527 A576 30h dk. blue & dp. orange 15 3
1528 A577 1k multicolored 60 13
Nos. 1524-1528 (5) 1.20 25

Issued to commemorate the following: The writer Janko Kral and the Slovak town Liptovsky Mikulas (No. 1524); 150th anniversary of the birth of Karl Marx (No. 1525); centenary of the cornerstone laying of the Prague National Theater (No. 1526); 150th anniversary of the Prague National Museum (No. 1527); 20th anniversary of the World Health Organization (1k).

Symbolic Radio Waves
A578

Design: No. 1530, Symbolic television screens.

Engraved and Photogravure

1968, Apr. 29 ***Perf. 11½***

1529 A578 30h blk., carmine & vio. blue 12 6
1530 " 30h blk., carmine & vio. blue 12 6

Issued to commemorate the 45th anniversary of Czechoslovak broadcasting (No. 1529), and the 15th anniversary of television (No. 1530).

Olympic Rings, Mexican Sculpture and Gymnast
A579

Olympic Rings and: 40h, Runner and "The Sanctification of Quetzalcoatl." 60h, Netball and Mexican ornaments. 1k, Czechoslovak and Mexican Olympic emblems and carved altar. 1.60k, Soccer and ornaments. 2k, View of Hradcany, weather vane and key.

1968, Apr. 30

1531 A579 30h black, blue & carmine 10 3
1532 " 40h multicolored 20 4
1533 " 60h " 20 4
1534 " 1k " 40 15
1535 " 1.60k " 65 20
1536 " 2k blk. & multi. *2.00* 65
Nos. 1531-1536 (6) *3.55* *1.11*

Issued to publicize the 19th Olympic Games, Mexico City, Oct. 12–27.

Prague Castle Types of 1966

Designs: 30h, Tombstone of Bretislav I. 60h, Romanesque door knocker, St. Wenceslas Chapel. 5k, Head of St. Peter, mosaic from Golden Gate of St. Vitus Cathedral.

Photogravure and Engraved

1968, May 9 ***Perf. 11½***

1537 A527 30h multicolored 15 3
1538 " 60h black, red & citron 25 4

Souvenir Sheet

Engraved

1539 A528 5k multicolored 2.00 1.75

No. 1539 contains one stamp, black ornament in margin. Size: 75x94mm.

Pres. Ludvik Svoboda
A580

1968–70 Engraved *Perf. 11½*

1540 A580 30h ultramarine 10 3
1540A " 50h green ('70) 15 3
1541 " 60h maroon 20 3
1541A " 1k rose car. ('70) 30 8

Shades exist of No. 1541A.

"Business," Sculpture by Otto Gutfreund
A581

Cabaret Performer, by František Kupka
A582

Photo. & Engr.; Engr. (2k)

1968, June 5

Designs (The New Prague): 40h, Broadcasting Corporation Building. 60h, New Parliament. 1.40k, Tapestry by Jan Bauch "Prague 1787." 3k, Presidential standard.

1542 A581 30h black & multi. 9 3
1543 " 40h black & multi. 15 3
1544 " 60h dark brown & multi. 20 7
1545 " 1.40k dark brown & multi. 48 18
1546 A582 2k indigo & multi *1.75* *1.60*
1547 A581 3k blk. & multi. 1.00 70
Nos. 1542–1547 (6) *3.67* *2.61*

1968, June 21 *Perf. 11½*

Designs (The Old Prague): 30h, St. George's Basilica. 60h, Renaissance fountain. 1k, Villa America-Dvorak Museum, 18th Century building. 1.60k, Emblem from the House of Three Violins, 18th century. 2k, Josefina, by Josef Manes. 3k, Emblem of Prague, 1475.

1548 A581 30h grn., gray & yel. 9 3
1549 " 60h dk. vio., apple grn. & gold 25 4
1550 " 1k black, lt. blue & pink 35 12
1551 " 1.60k slate green & multi. 48 20
1552 A582 2k brn. & multi. *1.50* *1.35*
1553 A581 3k black, yellow, blue & pink 1.00 40
Nos. 1548–1553 (6) *3.67* *2.14*

Nos. 1542–1553 issued to publicize the Praga 68 Philatelic Exhibition. Nos. 1542–1545, 1547–1551 and 1553 issued in sheets of 15 stamps and 15 labels with Praga 68 emblem and inscription. Nos. 1546 and 1552 issued in sheets of 4 (2x2) with one horizontal label between top and bottom rows showing Praga 68 emblem.

Souvenir Sheet

View of Prague and Emblems
A583

Engraved and Photogravure

1968, June 22 *Imperf.*

1554 A583 10k multicolored 6.00 5.00

Issued for Praga 68 and to commemorate the 50th anniversary of Czechoslovak postage stamps. Type of 1918 issue and commemorative inscription in margin. Size: 75½x110mm. Sold only together with a 5k admission ticket to the Praga 68 philatelic Exhibition.

Madonna with the Rose Garlands, by Dürer
A584

1968, July 6 *Perf. 11½*

1555 A584 5k multicolored 2.75 2.50

Issued to commemorate FIP Day, July 6 (Féderation Internationale de Philatelie). Issued in sheets of 4 (2x2) with one horizontal label between, showing Praga 68 emblem.

Stage-coach on Rails
A585

Design: 1k, Steam and electric locomotives.

1968, Aug. 6 Engr. & Photo.

1556 A585 60h multicolored 25 6
1557 " 1k " 35 12

No. 1556 commemorates the 140th anniversary of the horse-drawn railroad České-Budějovice to Linz; No. 1557 commemorates the centenary of the České-Budějovice to Plzeň railroad.

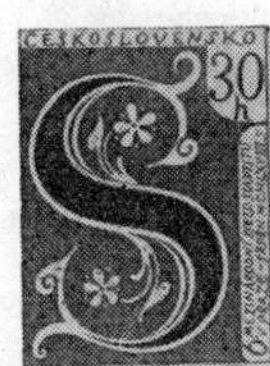

Fanciful "S"
A586

1968, Aug. 7 *Perf. 11½*

1558 A586 30h vio. blue & car. 15 3

Issued to commemorate the 6th International Slavonic Congress in Prague.

Ardspach Rocks and Ammonite
A587

Designs: 60h, Basalt formation and frog skeleton fossil. 80h, Rocks, basalt veins and polished agate. 1k, Pelecypoda (fossil shell) and Belanske Tatra mountains. 1.60k, Trilobite and Barrande rock formation.

1968, Aug. 8

1559 A587 30h blk. & citron 12 3
1560 " 60h black & rose claret 30 7
1561 " 80h blk., lt. violet & pink 35 10
1562 " 1k blk. & lt. bl. 45 17
1563 " 1.60k blk. & bis. *1.00* *60*
Nos. 1559–1563 (5) *2.22* *97*

Issued to publicize the 23rd International Geological Congress, Prague, Aug. 8–Sept. 3.

Raising Slovak Flag
A588

Design: 60h, Slovak partisans, and mountain.

1968, Sept. 9 Engraved *Perf. 11½*

1564 A588 30h ultramarine 10 3
1565 " 60h red 20 5

No. 1564 honors the Slovak National Council, No. 1565 commemorates the 120th anniversary of the Slovak national uprising.

Flowerpot, by Jiri Schlessinger (age 10)
A589

Drawings by Children in Terezin Concentration Camp: 30h, Jew and Guard, by Jiri Beutler (age 10). 60h, Butterflies, by Kitty Brunnerova (age 11).

Engraved and Photogravure

1968, Sept. 30 *Perf. 11½*

Size: 30x23mm.

1566 A589 30h black, buff & rose lilac 12 5
1567 " 60h black & multi. 25 8

Perf. 12x11½

Size: 41x23mm.

1568 A589 1k black & multi. 40 18

30th anniversary of Munich Pact.

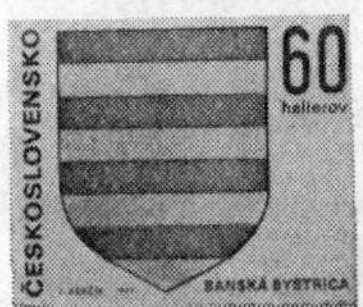

Arms of Banská Bystrica
A590

Arms of Prague
A591

Arms of Regional Capitals: No. 1570, Bratislava. No. 1571, Brno. No. 1572, České Budějovice. No. 1573, Hradec Králové. No. 1574, Košice. No. 1575, Ostrava (horse). No. 1576, Plzeň. No. 1577, Usti nad Labem.

1968, Oct. 21 *Perf. 11½*

1569 A590 60h black, red & silver 22 8
1570 " 60h black, red, silver & ultramarine 22 8
1571 " 60h black, red & silver 22 8
1572 " 60h black, red, silver & gold 22 8
1573 " 60h black, red, silver & gold 22 8
1574 " 60h black, blue, red & gold 22 8
1575 " 60h black, blue, yel. & red 22 8
1576 " 60h black, emerald, red & gold 22 8
1577 " 60h black, red, silver & gold 22 8

Perf. 11½x12

1578 A591 1k multicolored 40 15
Nos. 1569–1578 (10) 2.38 87

No. 1578 issued in sheets of 10. See also Nos. 1652–1657, 1742–1747, 1886–1888, 2000–2001.

Flag and Linden Leaves
A592

Bohemian Lion Breaking Chains (Type SP1 of 1919)

A593

Design: 60h, Map of Czechoslovakia, linden leaves, Hradcany in Prague and Castle in Bratislava.

1968, Oct. 28 *Perf. 12x11½*

1579	A592	30h deep blue & magenta	12	3
1580	"	60h black, gold, red & ultra.	25	5

Souvenir Sheet

Engraved *Perf. 11½x12*

1581	A593	5k red	2.00	2.00

Issued to commemorate the 50th anniversary of the founding of Czechoslovakia. No. 1581 has violet blue marginal inscription and red ornament. Size: 75x100mm.

Ernest Hemingway (1899–1961)

A594

Cinderlad

A595

Caricatures: 30h, Karel Capek (1890–1938), writer. 40h, George Bernard Shaw (1856–1950), writer. 60h, Maxim Gorki (1868–1930), writer. 1k, Pablo Picasso (1881–1973), painter. 1.20k, Taikan Yokoyama (1868–1958), painter. 1.40k, Charlie Chaplin (1889–1977), actor.

Engraved and Photogravure

1968, Nov. 18 *Perf. 11½x12*

1582	A594	20h black, orange & red	6	3
1583	"	30h black & multi.	15	3
1584	"	40h black, lilac & carmine	15	4
1585	"	60h black, sky blue & green	18	5
1586	"	1k black, brown & yellow	35	10
1587	"	1.20k black, dp. car. & violet	40	18
1588	"	1.40k black, brown & dp. orange	*1.50*	*55*
		Nos. 1582–1588 (7)	*2.79*	*98*

Issued to honor cultural personalities of the 20th century and UNESCO (United Nations Educational, Scientific and Cultural Organization). See Nos. 1628–1633.

Painting Type of 1967

Czechoslovakian Art: 60h, Cleopatra II, by Jan Zrzavy (1890–). 80h, Black Lake (man and horse), by Jan Preisler (1872–1918). 1.20k, Giovanni Francisci as a Volunteer, by Peter Michal Bohun (1822–1879). 1.60k, Princess Hyacinth, by Alfons Mucha (1860–1939). 3k, Madonna and Child, woodcarving, 1518, by Master Paul of Levoca.

1968, Nov. 29 Engraved *Perf. 11½*

1589	A565	60h multicolored	30	25
1590	"	80h "	45	40
1591	"	1.20k "	75	65
1592	"	1.60k "	1.00	90
1593	"	3k "	*4.00*	*3.50*
		Nos. 1589–1593 (5)	*6.50*	*5.70*

Sheets of 4.

1968, Dec. 18 Engr. and Photo.

Slovak Fairy Tales: 60h, The Proud Lady. 80h, The Ruling Knight. 1k, Good Day, Little Bench. 1.20k, The Spellbound Castle. 1.80k, The Miraculous Hunter. The designs are from illustrations by Ludovit Fulla for "Slovak Stories."

1594	A595	30h multicolored	9	5
1595	"	60h "	22	7
1596	"	80h "	30	10
1597	"	1k "	35	13
1598	"	1.20k "	45	15
1599	"	1.80k "	*2.00*	*75*
		Nos. 1594–1599 (6)	*3.41*	*1.25*

Czechoslovakia Nos. 2 and 3

A596

1968, Dec. 18

1600	A596	1k vio. blue & gold	75	65

Issued to commemorate the 50th anniversary of Czechoslovakian postage stamps.

Crescent, Cross and Lion and Sun Emblems

A597

ILO Emblem

A598

Design: 60h, 12 crosses in circles forming large cross.

Engraved and Photogravure

1969, Jan. 31 *Perf. 11½*

1601	A597	60h blk., red & gold	25	5
1602	"	1k black, ultra. & red	45	12

No. 1601 commemorates the 50th anniversary of the Czechoslovak Red Cross; No. 1602 commemorates the 50th anniversary of the League of Red Cross Societies.

1969, Jan. 31

1603	A598	1k black & gray	35	12

Issued to commemorate the 50th anniversary of the International Labor Organization.

Cheb Pistol

A599

Historical Firearms: 40h, Italian pistol with Dutch decorations, c. 1600. 60h, Wheellock rifle from Matej Kubik workshop c. 1720. 1k, Flintlock pistol, Devieuxe workshop, Liege, c. 1760. 1.40k, Dueling pistols, from Lebeda workshop, Prague, c. 1835. 1.60k, Derringer pistols, U.S.A., c. 1865.

1969, Feb. 18

1604	A599	30h black & multi.	9	3
1605	"	40h " "	12	4
1606	"	60h " "	18	6
1607	"	1k " "	30	10
1608	"	1.40k " "	42	14
1609	"	1.60k " "	*1.25*	*35*
		Nos. 1604–1609 (6)	*2.36*	*72*

Bratislava Castle, Muse and Book

A600

Designs: No. 1611, Science symbols and emblem (Brno University). No. 1612, Harp, laurel and musicians' names. No. 1613, Theatrical scene. No. 1614, Arms of Slovakia, banner and blossoms. No. 1615, School, outstretched hands and woman with linden leaves.

1969, Mar. 24 Engr. *Perf. 11½*

1610	A600	60h violet blue	25	6

Engraved and Photogravure

1611	A600	60h black, gold & slate	25	6
1612	"	60h gold, blue, black & red	25	6
1613	"	60h black & rose red	25	6
1614	"	60h rose red, silver & blue	25	6
1615	"	60h black & gold	25	6
		Nos. 1610–1615 (6)	1.50	36

Nos. 1610–1614 issued to commemorate the 50th anniversary of: Komensky University in Bratislava (#1610); Brno University (#1611); Brno Conservatory of Music (#1612); Slovak National Theater (#1613); Slovak Soviet Republic (#1614); No. 1615 commemorates the centenary of the Zniev Gymnasium (academic high school).

Baldachin-top Car and Four-seat Coupé of 1900–1905—A601

Designs: 1.60k, Laurin & Klement Voiturette, 1907, and L & K touring car with American top, 1907. 1.80k, First Prague bus, 1907, and sectionalized Skoda bus, 1967.

1969, Mar. 25

1616	A601	30h black, lilac & light green	12	3
1617	"	1.60k black, org. brn. & light blue	60	15
1618	"	1.80k multicolored	*1.75*	*1.00*

Peace, by Ladislav Guderna

A602

Engraved and Photogravure

1969, Apr. 21 *Perf. 11*

1619	A602	1.60k multicolored	70	45

Issued to commemorate the 20th anniversary of the Peace Movement. Issued in sheets of 15 stamps and 5 tabs.

Horse and Rider, by Vaclav Hollar

A603

Old Engravings of Horses: 30h, Prancing Stallion, by Hendrik Goltzius (horiz.). 80h, Groom Leading Horse, by Matthäus Merian (horiz.). 1.80k, Horse and Soldier, by Albrecht Dürer. 2.40k, Groom and Horse, by Johann E. Ridinger.

1969, Apr. 24 *Perf. 11x11½, 11½x11*

Yellowish Paper

1620	A603	30h dark brown	9	3
1621	"	80h violet brown	28	10
1622	"	1.60k slate	60	20
1623	"	1.80k sepia	65	22
1624	"	2.40k multicolored	*2.25*	*75*
		Nos. 1620–1624 (5)	*3.87*	*1.30*

M. R. Stefánik as Astronomy Professor and French General

A604

1969, May 4 Engraved *Perf. 11½*

1625	A604	60h rose claret	25	10

Issued to commemorate the 50th anniversary of the death of Gen. Milan R. Stefánik.

St. Wenceslas Pressing Wine, Mural by the Master of Litomerice

A605

Design: No. 1627, Coronation banner of the Estates, 1723, with St. Wenceslas and coats of arms of Bohemia and Czech Crown lands.

1969, May 9 Engraved *Perf. 11½*

1626	A605	3k multicolored	1.75	1.50
1627	"	3k "	1.75	1.50

Issued to publicize the art treasures of the Castle of Prague. See Nos. 1689–1690.

Caricature Type of 1968

Caricatures: 30h, Pavol Orszagh Hviezdoslav (1849–1921), Slovak writer. 40h, Gilbert K. Chesterton (1874–1936), English writer. 60h, Vladimir Mayakovski (1893–1930), Russian poet. 1k, Henri Matisse (1869–1954), French painter. 1.80k, Ales Hrdlicka (1869–1943), Czech-born American anthropologist. 2k, Franz Kafka (1883–1924), Austrian writer.

Engraved and Photogravure

1969, June 17 *Perf. 11½x12*

1628	A594	30h blk., red & bl.	9	5

1629 A594 40h black, blue & light violet 12 6
1630 " 60h black, rose & yellow 18 8
1631 " 1k blk. & multi. 30 12
1632 " 1.80k black, ultra. & ocher 54 23
1633 " 2k black, yel. & brt. green *1.75* *50*
Nos. 1628-1633 (6) *2.98* *1.04*

Issued to honor cultural personalities of the 20th century and UNESCO.

"Music," by Alfons Mucha
A606

Paintings by Mucha: 60h, "Painting." 1k, "Dance." 2.40k, "Ruby" and "Amethyst."

1969, July 14 ***Perf. 11½x11***

Size: 30x49mm.

1634 A606 30h blk. & multi. 9 3
1635 " 60h " " 18 8
1636 " 1k " " 35 12

Size: 39x51mm.

1637 A606 2.40k blk. & multi. *1.75* *1.10*

Issued to commemorate the 30th anniversary of the death of Alfons Mucha (1860-1930), painter and stamp designer (Type A1).

Pres. Svoboda and Partisans
A607

Design: No. 1639, Slovak fighters and mourners.

Engraved and Photogravure

1969, Aug. 29 ***Perf. 11***

1638 A607 30h olive green & red, *yellow* 12 3
1639 " 30h violet blue & red, *yellow* 12 3

Issued to commemorate the 25th anniversary of the Slovak uprising and of the Battle of Dukla.

Tatra Mountain Stream and Gentians
A608

Designs: 60h, Various views in Tatra Mountains. No. 1644, Mountain pass and gentians. No. 1645, Houses, Krivan Mountain and autumn crocuses.

1969, Sept. 8 Engraved ***Perf. 11***

Size: 71x33mm.

1640 A608 60h gray 18 6
1641 " 60h dark blue 18 6
1642 " 60h dull gray violet 18 6

Perf. 11½

Size: 40x23mm.

1643 A608 1.60k multicolored 48 15
1644 " 1.60k " *1.40* *60*
1645 A608 1.60k multicolored 48 15
Nos. 1640-1645 (6) *2.90* *1.08*

Issued to commemorate the 20th anniversary of the creation of the Tatra Mountains National Park. Nos. 1640-1642 are printed in sheets of 15 (3x5) with 5 labels showing mountain plants. Nos. 1643-1645 issued in sheets of 10.

Bronze Belt Ornaments
A609

Archaeological Treasures from Bohemia and Moravia: 30h, Gilt ornament with 6 masks. 1k, Jeweled earrings. 1.80k, Front and back of lead cross with Greek inscription. 2k, Gilt strap ornament with human figure.

Engraved and Photogravure

1969, Sept. 30 ***Perf. 11½x11***

1646 A609 20h gold & multi. 6 5
1647 " 30h " " 10 5
1648 " 1k red & multi. 35 16
1649 " 1.80k dull orange & multicolored 60 30
1650 " 2k gold & multi. *1.20* *40*
Nos. 1646-1650 (5) *2.31* *96*

"Mail Circling the World"
A610

1969, Oct. 1 Engraved ***Perf. 12***

1651 A610 3.20k multicolored 1.25 60

Issued to commemorate the 16th Universal Postal Union Congress, Tokyo, Oct. 1-Nov. 14. Issued in sheets of 4.

Coat of Arms Type of 1968

Engraved and Photogravure

1969, Oct. 25 ***Perf. 11½***

Multicolored

1652 A590 50h *Bardejov* 18 8
1653 " 50h *Hranice* 18 8
1654 " 50h *Kezmarok* 18 8
1655 " 50h *Krnov* 18 8
1656 " 50h *Litomerice* 18 8
1657 " 50h *Manetin* 18 8
Nos. 1652-1657 (6) 1.08 48

Painting Type of 1968

Designs: 60h, Requiem, 1944, by Frantisek Muzika. 1k, Resurrection, 1380, by the Master of the Trebon Altar. 1.60k, Crucifixion, 1950, by Vincent Hloznik. 1.80k, Girl with Doll, 1863, by Julius Bencur. 2.20k, St. Jerome, 1357-67, by Master Theodorik.

Engraved and Photogravure

1969, Nov. 25 ***Perf. 11½***

1658 A565 60h multicolored 30 25
1659 " 1k " 50 45
1660 " 1.60k " 75 65
1661 " 1.80k " 1.00 90
1662 " 2.20k " *1.50* *1.35*
Nos. 1658-1662 (5) *4.05* *3.60*

Sheets of 4.

Symbolic Sheet of Stamps—A611

1969, Dec. 18 ***Perf. 11½x12***

1663 A611 1k dk. brown, ultra. & gold 45 40

Issued for Stamp Day 1969.

Ski Jump—A612

Designs: 60h, Long distance skier. 1k, Ski jump and slope. 1.60k, Woman skier.

Engraved and Photogravure

1970, Jan. 6 ***Perf. 11½***

1664 A612 50h multicolored 15 5
1665 " 60h " 18 5
1666 " 1k " 30 10
1667 " 1.60k " *95* *40*

Issued to publicize the International Ski Championships "Tatra 1970."

Ludwig van Beethoven (1770-1827)
A613

Portraits: No. 1669, Friedrich Engels (1820-1895), German socialist. No. 1670, Maximilian Hell (1720-1792), Slovakian Jesuit and astronomer. No. 1671, Lenin (1870-1924), Russian Communist leader. No. 1672, Josef Manes (1820-1871), Czech painter. No. 1673, John Amos Comenius (1592-1670), theologian and educator.

1970, Feb. 17 Engr. ***Perf. 11x11½***

1668 A613 40h black 12 6
1669 " 40h dull red 12 6
1670 " 40h yellow brown 12 6
1671 " 40h dull red 12 6
1672 " 40h brown 12 6
1673 " 40h black 12 6
Nos. 1668-1673 (6) 72 36

Issued to commemorate the anniversaries of the birth of Beethoven, Engels, Hell, Lenin and Manes, the 300th anniversary of the death of Comenius, and to honor UNESCO.

Bells
A614

Designs: 80h, Machine tools and lathe. 1k, Folklore masks. 1.60k, Angel and Three Wise Men, 17th century icon from Koniec. 2k, View of Orlik Castle, 1787, by F. K. Wolf. 3k, "Passing through Koshu down to Mishima" from Hokusai's 36 Views of Fuji.

Engraved and Photogravure

1970, Mar. 13 ***Perf. 11½x11***

Size: 40x23mm.

1674 A614 50h multicolored 18 3
1675 " 80h " 27 5
1676 " 1k " 30 6

Size: 50x40mm.

Perf. 11½

1677 A614 1.60k multicolored 60 40
1678 " 2k " 65 45
1679 A614 3k multicolored *2.25* *1.10*
Nos. 1674-1679 (6) *4.25* *2.09*

Issued to publicize EXPO '70 International Exhibition, Osaka, Japan, March 15-Sept. 13, 1970. Nos. 1674-1676 issued in sheets of 50, Nos. 1677-1679 in sheets of 4.

Kosice Townhall, Laurel and Czechoslovak Arms
A615

1970, Apr. 5 ***Perf. 11***

1680 A615 60h slate, vermilion & gold 18 6

Issued to commemorate the 25th anniversary of the government's Kosice Program.

"The Remarkable Horse" by Josef Lada
A616

Lenin
A617

Paintings by Josef Lada: 60h, Autumn, 1955 (horiz.). 1.80k, "The Water Sprite." 2.40k, Children in Winter, 1943 (horiz.).

1970, Apr. 21 ***Perf. 11½***

1681 A616 60h black & multi. 18 10
1682 " 1k " " 35 15
1683 " 1.80k " " 60 25
1684 " 2.40k " " *1.75* *50*

1970, Apr. 22 Engr. & Photo.

Design: 60h, Lenin without cap, facing left.

1685 A617 30h dk. red & gold 9 3
1686 " 60h black & gold 18 6

Issued to commemorate the centenary of the birth of Lenin (1870-1924), Russian communist leader.

Fighters on the Barricades
A618

Design: No. 1688, Lilac, Russian tank and castle.

Engraved and Photogravure

1970, May 5 ***Perf. 11x11½***

1687 A618 30h dull purple, gold & blue 12 6
1688 " 30h dull green, gold & red 12 6

No. 1687 commemorates the 25th anniversary of the Prague uprising and No. 1688 the 25th anniversary of the liberation of Czechoslovakia from the Germans.

Prague Castle Art Type of 1969

Designs: No. 1689, Bust of St. Vitus, 1486. No. 1690, Hermes and Athena, by Bartholomy Springer (1546–1611), mural from White Tower.

1970, May 7 Engr. *Perf. 11½*

1689	A605	3k maroon & multi.	1.50	1.25
1690	"	3k lt. blue & multi.	1.50	1.25

Issued to publicize art treasures of the Castle of Prague.

Compass Rose, U.N. Headquarters and Famous Buildings of the World
A619

Engraved and Photogravure

1970, June 26 *Perf. 11*

1691	A619	1k black & multi.	30	15

Issued to commemorate the 25th anniversary of the United Nations. Issued in sheets of 15 (3x5) and 5 labels showing U.N. emblem.

Cannon from 30 Years' War and Baron Munchhausen
A620

Historical Cannons: 60h, Cannon from Hussite war and St. Barbara. 1.20k, Cannon from Prussian-Austrian war, and legendary cannoneer Javurek. 1.80k, Early 20th century cannon and spaceship "La Colombiad" (Jules Verne). 2.40k, World War I cannon and "Good Soldier Schweik."

1970, Aug. 31 *Perf. 11½*

1692	A620	30h black & multi.	9	3
1693	"	60h " "	18	5
1694	"	1.20k " "	36	10
1695	"	1.80k " "	54	22
1696	"	2.40k " "	*1.40*	*60*
		Nos. 1692–1696 (5)	*2.57*	*1.00*

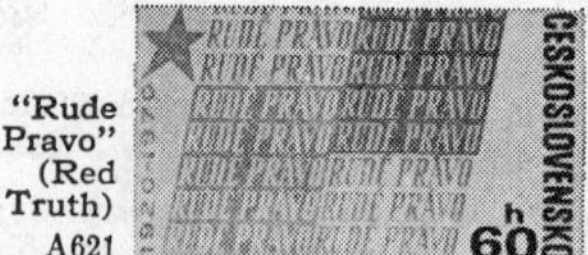

"Rude Pravo" (Red Truth)
A621

1970, Sept. 21 *Perf. 11½x11*

1697	A621	60h car. gold & blk.	18	5

Issued to commemorate the 50th anniversary of the Rude Pravo newspaper.

"Great Sun" House Sign and Old Town Tower Bridge, Prague
A622

Designs: 60h, "Blue Lion" and Town Hall Tower, Brno. 1k, Gothic corner stone and Town Hall Tower, Bratislava. 1.40k, Coat of Arms and Gothic Tower, Bratislava, and medallion. 1.60k, Moravian Eagle and Gothic Town Hall Tower, Brno. 1.80k, "Black Sun" and "Green Frog" house signs and New Town Hall, Prague.

Engr. & Photo.

1970, Sept. 23 *Perf. 11x11½*

1698	A622	40h black & multi.	12	6
1699	"	60h " "	18	10
1700	"	1k " "	30	16
1701	"	1.40k " "	*1.50*	*30*
1702	"	1.60k " "	55	24
1703	"	1.80k " "	60	28
		Nos. 1698–1703 (6)	*3.25*	*1.14*

Germany–Uruguay Semifinal Soccer Match—A623

Designs: 20h, Sundisk Games' emblem and flags of participating nations. 60h, England-Czechoslovakia match and coats of arms. 1k, Romania-Czechoslovakia match and coats of arms. 1.20k, Brazil-Italy, final match and emblems. 1.80k, Brazil-Czechoslovakia match and emblems.

1970, Oct. 29 *Perf. 11½*

1704	A623	20h black & multi.	6	3
1705	"	40h " "	12	4
1706	"	60h " "	18	5
1707	"	1k " "	35	6
1708	"	1.20k " "	45	8
1709	"	1.80k " "	*1.25*	*55*
		Nos. 1704–1709 (6)	*2.41*	*81*

Issued to commemorate the 9th World Soccer Championships for the Jules Rimet Cup, Mexico City, May 30–June 21.

Congress Emblem
A624

1970, Nov. 9 Engr. & Photo.

1710	A624	30h black, gold, ultra. & red	15	3

Congress of the Czechoslovak Socialist Youth Federation.

Painting Type of 1967

Paintings: 1k, Seated Mother, by Mikulas Galanda. 1.20k, Bridesmaid, by Karel Svolinsky. 1.40k, Walk by Night, 1944, by Frantisek Hudecek. 1.80k, Banska Bystrica Market, by Dominik Skutecky. 2.40k, Adoration of the Kings, from the Vysehrad Codex, 1085.

1970, Nov. 27 Engr. *Perf. 11½*

1711	A565	1k multicolored	40	35
1712	"	1.20k "	45	40
1713	"	1.40k "	50	45
1714	"	1.80k "	60	55
1715	"	2.40k "	*2.00*	*1.75*
		Nos. 1711–1715 (5)	*3.95*	*3.50*

Sheets of 4.

Radar
A625

Designs: 40h, Interkosmos 3, geophysical satellite. 60h, Molniya meteorological satellite. 1k, Astronaut and Vostok satellite. No. 1720, Interkosmos 4, solar research satellite. No. 1720A, Space satellite (Sputnik) over city. 1.60k, Two-stage rocket on launching pad.

Engraved and Photogravure

1970–71 *Perf. 11*

1716	A625	20h black & multi.	6	3
1717	"	40h " "	12	4
1718	"	60h " "	18	5
1719	"	1k " "	30	6
1720	"	1.20k " "	36	8
1720A	"	1.20k " " ('71)	40	9
1721	"	1.60k " "	*1.25*	*50*
		Nos. 1716–1721 (7)	*2.67*	*85*

Issued to publicize "Interkosmos," the collaboration of communist countries in various phases of space research. Issue dates: No. 1720A, Nov. 15, 1971; others, Nov. 30, 1970.

Face of Christ on Veronica's Veil
A626

Slovak Ikons, 16th–18th Centuries: 60h, Adam and Eve in the Garden (vert.). 2k, St. George and the Dragon. 2.80k, St. Michael (vert.).

1970, Dec. 17 Engraved *Perf. 11½*

Cream Paper

1722	A626	60h multicolored	25	22
1723	"	1k "	40	35
1724	"	2k "	75	65
1725	"	2.80k "	*2.00*	*1.75*

Sheets of 4.

Carrier Pigeon Type of 1920
A627

Engr. & Photo.

1970, Dec. 18 *Perf. 11x11½*

1726	A627	1k red, black & yellow green	35	30

Stamp Day.

Song of the Barricades, 1938, by Karel Stika
A628

Designs (Czech and Slovak Graphic Art): 50h, Fruit Grower's Barge, 1941, by Cyril Bouda. 60h, Moon (woman) Searching for Lilies of the Valley, 1913, by Jan Zrzavy. 1k, At the Edge of Town (working man and woman), 1931, by Koloman Sokol. 1.60k, Summer, 1641, by Vaclav Hollar. 2k, Gamekeeper and Shepherd of Orava Castle, 1847, by Peter M. Bohun.

Engraved (40h, 60h, 1k); Engraved and Photogravure (others)

1971, Jan. 28 *Perf. 11½*

1727	A628	40h brown	12	6
1728	"	50h black & multi.	15	8
1729	"	60h slate	18	10
1730	"	1k black	30	16
1731	A628	1.60k black & buff	60	24
1732	"	2k blk. & multi.	*1.35*	*35*
		Nos. 1727–1732 (6)	*2.70*	*99*

Saris Church
A629

Bell Tower, Hronsek—A630

Designs: 1k, Roofs and folk art, Horácko. 2.40k, House, Jicinsko. 3k, House and folk art, Cechy-Melnicko. 3.60k, Chrudimsko Church. 5k, Watch Tower, Cesky-Nachod. 5.40k, Baroque house, Posumavi. 6k, Cottage, Orava. 9k, Cottage, Turnovsko. 10k, Old houses, Liptov. 14k, House and wayside bell stand. 20k, Houses, Slovensko-Cicmany.

Perf. 11½x11, 11x11½

1971–72 Engr. and Photo.

1733	A630	1k blk. & multi.	30	4
1734	A629	1.60k black, dk grn. & violet	48	6
1735	A630	2k blk. & multi.	60	4
1736	A629	2.40k " "	72	6
1736A	A630	3k " " ('72)	90	8
1737	"	3.60k blk. & multi.	1.10	6
1737A	"	5k " " ('72)	1.50	12
1738	"	5.40k blk. & multi.	1.60	6
1739	"	6k " "	1.75	9
1740	"	9k " "	2.75	12
1740A	A629	10k " " ('72)	3.00	15
1741	"	14k blk. & multi.	4.25	20
1741A	"	20k " " ('72)	6.00	60
		Nos. 1733–1741A (13)	24.95	1.68

Coat of Arms Type of 1968

1971, Feb. 26 *Perf. 11½*

Multicolored

1742	A590	60h *Zilina*	22	8
1743	"	60h *Levoca*	22	8
1744	"	60h *Ceska Trebova*	22	8
1745	"	60h *Uhersky Brod*	22	8
1746	"	60h *Trutnov*	22	8
1747	"	60h *Karlovy*	22	8
		Nos. 1742–1747 (6)	1.32	48

"Fight of the Communards and Rise of the International"—A631

Design: No. 1749, World fight against racial discrimination, and "UNESCO."

1971, March 18 *Perf. 11*

1748	A631	1k multicolored	35	18
1749	"	1k "	35	18

No. 1748 commemorates the centenary of the Paris Commune. No. 1749 publicizes the Year against Racial Discrimination. Issued in sheets of 15 stamps and 5 labels.

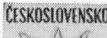

Edelweiss, Mountaineering Map and Equipment
A632

Engraved and Photogravure

1971, Apr. 27 ***Perf. 11½x11***

1750 A632 30h multicolored 15 3

50th anniversary of Slovak Alpine Club.

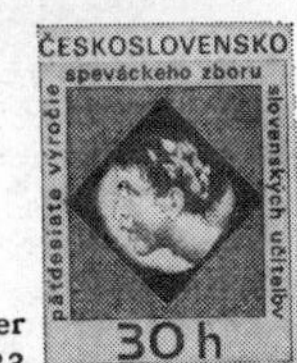

Singer
A633

1971, Apr. 27 ***Perf. 11½***

1751 A633 30h multicolored 15 3

50th anniversary of Slovak Teachers' Choir.

Abbess' Crosier, 16th Century
A634

Design: No. 1753, Allegory of Music, 16th century mural.

1971, May 9

1752 A634 3k gold & multi. 1.40 1.25
1753 " 3k black, dk. brown & buff 1.40 1.25

Art treasures of the Castle of Prague. Sheets of 4.

See also Nos. 1817–1818, 1884–1885, 1937–1938, 2040–2041, 2081–2082, 2114–2115, 2176–2177.

Lenin
A635

Designs: 40h, Hammer and sickle allegory. 60h, Raised fists. 1k, Star, hammer and sickle.

1971, May 14 ***Perf. 11***

1754 A635 30h blk., red & gold 9 3
1755 " 40h black, ultra., red & gold 12 4
1756 " 60h black, ultra., red & gold 20 5
1757 " 1k black, ultra., red & gold 35 10

50th anniversary of the Czechoslovak Communist Party.

Star, Hammer-Sickle Emblems
A636

Design: 60h, Hammer-sickle emblem, fist and people (vert.).

Perf. 11½x11, 11x11½

1971, May 24 **Engr. & Photo.**

1758 A636 30h black, red, gold & yellow 9 3
1759 " 60h black, red, gold & blue 18 8

14th Congress of Communist Party of Czechoslovakia.

Ring-necked Pheasant
A637

Designs: 60h, Rainbow trout. 80h, Mouflon. 1k, Chamois. 2k, Stag. 2.60k, Wild boar.

1971, Aug. 17 ***Perf. 11½x11***

1760 A637 20h orange & multi. 6 4
1761 " 60h lt. bl. & multi. 18 6
1762 " 80h yellow & multi. 24 6
1763 " 1k lt. grn. & multi. 30 10
1764 " 2k lilac & multi. 60 30
1765 " 2.60k bister & multi. *2.00* *65*
Nos. 1760–1765 (6) *3.38* *1.21*

World Hunting Exhibition, Budapest, Aug. 27–30.

Diesel Locomotive
A638

Gymnasts and Banners
A639

1971, Sept. 2 ***Perf. 11x11½***

1766 A638 30h lt. blue, black & red 9 3

Centenary of CKD, Prague Machine Foundry.

1971, Sept. 2 ***Perf. 11½x11***

1767 A639 30h red brn., gold & ultra. 9 3

50th anniversary of Workers' Physical Exercise Federation.

Road Intersections and Bridge
A640

1971, Sept. 2 **Engr. & Photo.**

1768 A640 1k black, gold, red & blue 35 10

14th World Highways and Bridges Congress. Sheets of 25 stamps and 25 labels printed se-tenant with continuous design.

Chinese Fairytale, by Eva Bednarova
A641

Designs: 1k, Tiger and other animals, by Mirko Hanak. 1.60k, The Miraculous Bamboo Shoot, by Yasuo Segawa (horiz.).

Perf. 11½x11, 11x11½

1971, Sept. 10

1769 A641 60h multicolored 22 5
1770 " 1k " 45 15
1771 " 1.60k " 75 45

Bratislava BIB 71 biennial exhibition of illustrations for children's books.

Apothecary Jars and Coltsfoot
A642

Designs: 60h, Jars and dog rose. 1k, Scales and adonis vernalis. 1.20k, Mortars and valerian. 1.80k, Retorts and chicory. 2.40k, Mill, mortar and henbane.

1971, Sept. 20 ***Perf. 11½x11***

Yellow Paper

1772 A642 30h multicolored 9 5
1773 " 60h " 18 8
1774 " 1k " 30 12
1775 " 1.20k " 36 16
1776 " 1.80k " 54 30
1777 " 2.40k " *1.60* *45*
Nos. 1772–1777 (6) *3.07* *1.16*

International Pharmaceutical Congress.

Painting Type of 1967

Paintings: 1k, "Waiting" (woman's head), 1967, by Imro Weiner-Král. 1.20k, Resurrection, by Master of Vyssi Brod, 14th century. 1.40k, Woman with Pitcher, by Milos Bazovsky. 1.80k, Veruna Cudova (in folk costume), by Josef Mánes. 2.40k, Detail from "Feast of the Rose Garlands," by Albrecht Dürer.

1971, Nov. 27 ***Perf. 11½***

1779 A565 1k multicolored 40 35
1780 " 1.20k " 50 45
1781 " 1.40k " 60 55
1782 " 1.80k " 75 65
1783 " 2.40k " *1.75* *1.60*
Nos. 1779–1783 (5) *4.00* *3.60*

Sheets of 4.

Workers Revolt in Krompachy, by Julius Nemcik—A643

1971, Nov. 28 ***Perf. 11x11½***

1784 A643 60h multicolored 20 10

History of the Czechoslovak Communist Party.

Wooden Dolls and Birds
A644

Folk Art and UNICEF Emblem: 80h, Jug handles, carved. 1k, Horseback rider. 1.60k, Shepherd carrying lamb. 2k, Easter eggs and rattle. 3k, "Zbojnik," folk hero.

1971, Dec. 11 ***Perf. 11½***

1785 A644 60h multicolored 25 5
1786 " 80h " 35 8
1787 " 1k " 50 12
1788 " 1.60k " 65 20
1789 " 2k " 90 40
1790 " 3k " 1.50 60
Nos. 1785–1790 (6) 4.15 1.45

25th anniversary of the United Nations International Children's Fund (UNICEF).

Runners, Parthenon, Czechoslovak Olympic Emblem
A645

Designs: 40h, Women's high jump, Olympic emblem and plan for Prague Stadium. 1.60k, Cross-country skiers, Sapporo '72 emblem and ski jump in High Tatras. 2.60k, Discus thrower, Discobolus and St. Vitus Cathedral.

1971, Dec. 16 **Engr. & Photo.**

1791 A645 30h multicolored 10 6
1792 " 40h " 13 9
1793 " 1.60k " 52 30
1794 " 2.60k " 1.35 40

75th anniversary of Czechoslovak Olympic Committee (30h, 2.60k); 20th Summer Olympic Games, Munich, Aug. 26–Sept. 10, 1972 (40h); 11th Winter Olympic Games, Sapporo, Japan, Feb. 3–13, 1972 (1.60k).

Post Horns and Lion—A646

1971, Dec. 17 ***Perf. 11x11½***

1795 A646 1k black, gold, car. & blue 33 15

Stamp Day.

Figure Skating
A647

"Ležáky"
A648

Designs (Olympic Emblems and): 50h, Ski jump. 1k, Ice hockey. 1.60k, Sledding, women's.

1972, Jan. 13 ***Perf. 11½***

1796 A647 40h purple, orange & red 13 8
1797 " 50h dk. blue, org. & red 17 8
1798 " 1k magenta, org. & red 33 18
1799 " 1.60k bl. green, org. & red *1.10* *50*

11th Winter Olympic Games, Sapporo, Japan, Feb. 3–13.

1972, Feb. 16 **Engr. & Photo.**

Designs: No. 1801, Boy's head behind barbed wire (horiz.). No. 1802, Hand rising from ruins. No. 1803, Soldier and banner (horiz.).

1800 A648 30h black, dull orange & red 10 3
1801 " 30h blk. & brn. org. 10 3
1802 " 60h blk., yel. & red 20 5
1803 " 60h slate green & multicolored 20 5

30th anniversary of: destruction of Ležáky (No. 1800) and Lidice (1802); Terezin concentration camp (No. 1801); Czechoslovak Army unit in Russia (No. 1803).

Book Year Emblem
A649

Steam and Diesel Locomotives
A650

1972, Mar. 17 ***Perf. 11½x11***

1804 A649 1k blk. & org. brn. 33 10

International Book Year 1972.

1972, Mar. 17 ***Perf. 11½x11***

1805 A650 30h multicolored 18 3

Centenary of the Kosice-Bohumin railroad.

"Pasture," by Vojtech Sedlacek
A651

Designs: 50h, Dressage, by Frantisek Tichy. 60th, Otakara Kubina, by Vaclav Fiala. 1k, The Three Kings, by Ernest Zmetak. 1.60k, Woman Dressing, by Ludovit Fulla.

Photogravure and Engraved

1972, Mar. 27 ***Perf. 11½x11***

1806 A651 40h multi. 13 5
1807 " 50h " 17 6
1808 " 60h " 20 8
1809 " 1k " 33 10
1810 " 1.60k " *1.10* *1.00*
Nos. 1806–1810 (5) *1.93* *1.29*

Czech and Slovak graphic art. 1.60k issued in sheets of 4. See also Nos. 1859–1862, 1921–1924.

Ice Hockey
A652

Design: 1k, Two players.

1972, Apr. 7 ***Perf. 11***

1811 A652 60h black & multi. 20 7
1812 " 1k " " 40 12

World and European Ice Hockey Championships, Prague.

Bicycling, Olympic Rings and Emblem
A653

1972, Apr. 7 **Multicolored**

1813 A653 50h *shown* 17 6
1814 " 1.60k *Diving, women's* 53 12
1815 " 1.80k *Canoeing* 60 15
1816 " 2k *Woman gymnast* *1.50* *60*

20th Olympic Games, Munich, Aug. 26–Sept. 11.

Prague Castle Art Type of 1971

Designs: No. 1817, Adam and Eve, column capital, St. Vitus Cathedral. No. 1818, Czech coat of arms (lion), c. 1500.

1972, May 9 ***Perf. 11½***

1817 A634 3k black & multi. *1.75* *1.50*
1818 " 3k blk., red, silver & gold 1.50 1.25

Art treasures of Castle of Prague. Sheets of 4.

Andrej Sladkovic (1820–1872), Poet
A654

Portraits: No. 1820, Janko Kral (1822–1876), poet. No. 1821, Ludmilla Podjavorinska (1872–1951), writer. No. 1822, Antonin Hudecek (1872–1941), painter. No. 1823, Frantisek Bilek (1872–1941), sculptor. No. 1824, Jan Preisler (1872–1918), painter.

Engraved and Photogravure

1972, June 14 ***Perf. 11***

1819 A654 40h pur., olive & bl. 13 5
1820 " 40h dk. green, blue & yellow 13 5
1821 " 40h black & multi. 13 5
1822 " 40h brn., grn. & bl. 13 5
1823 " 40h choc., green & orange 13 5
1824 " 40h green, slate & deep orange 13 5
Nos. 1819–1824 (6) 78 30

Men with Banners
A655

1972, June 14 ***Perf. 11x11½***

1825 A655 30h dk. violet blue, red & yellow 10 3

8th Trade Union Congress, Prague.

Art Forms of Wire
A656

Ornamental Wirework: 60h, Plane and rosette. 80h, Four-headed dragon and ornament. 1k, Locomotive and loops. 2.60k, Tray and owl.

1972, Aug. 28 ***Perf. 11½x11***

1826 A656 20h sal. & multi. 7 5
1827 " 60h multicolored 20 8
1828 " 80h pink & multi. 26 10
1829 " 1k multicolored 33 18
1830 " 2.60k rose & multi. *1.40* *50*
Nos. 1826–1830 (5) *2.26* *91*

"Jiskra"
A657

Engraved and Photogravure

1972, Sept. 27 ***Perf. 11½x11***

Size: 40x22mm.

Multicolored Design on Blue Paper

1831 A657 50h *shown* 17 5
1832 " 60h *"Mir"* 20 5
1833 " 80h *"Republika"* 26 6

Size: 48x29mm.

Perf. 11x11½

1834 A657 1k *"Kosice"* 33 10
1835 " 1.60k *"Dukla"* 53 16
1836 " 2k *"Kladno"* *2.00* *45*
Nos. 1831–1836 (6) *3.49* *87*

Czechoslovak sea-going vessels.

Hussar, 18th Century Tile
A658

1972, Oct. 24 ***Perf. 11½x11***

Multicolored

1837 A658 30h *shown* 10 6
1838 " 60h *Janissary* 20 8
1839 " 80h *St. Martin* 26 10
1840 " 1.60k *St. George* 53 15
1841 " 1.80k *Nobleman's guard* 70 20
1842 " 2.20k *Slovakian horseman* *2.00* *55*
Nos. 1837–1842 (6) *3.79* *1.14*

Horsemen from 18th–19th century tiles or enamel paintings on glass.

Worker, Flag Hoisted on Bayonet
A659

Star, Hammer and Sickle
A660

1972, Nov. 7 ***Perf. 11x11½***

1843 A659 30h gold & multi. 12 6
1844 A660 60h rose carmine & gold 24 8

55th anniversary of the Russian October Revolution (30h); 50th anniversary of the Soviet Union (60h).

Nos. 1811–1812 Overprinted in Violet Blue or Black

CSSR
MAJSTROM
SVETA

1972 ***Perf. 11***

1845 A652 60h multi. (VBl) 6.00 6.00
1846 " 1k " (Bk) 6.00 6.00

Czechoslovakia's victorious ice hockey team. The overprint on the 60h is in Czech and reads ČSSR/MISTREM/SVĚTA; the overprint on the 1k (shown) is in Slovak.

Painting Type of 1967

Designs: 1k, "Nosegay" (nudes and flowers), by Max Svabinsky. 1.20k, Struggle of St. Ladislas with Kuman nomad, anonymous, 14th century. 1.40k, Lady with Fur Hat, by Vaclav Hollar. 1.80k, Midsummer Night's Dream, 1962, by Josef Liesler. 2.40k, Pablo Picasso, self-portrait.

1972, Nov. 27 **Photo. & Engr.**

1847 A565 1k multicolored 40 35
1848 " 1.20k " 50 45
1849 " 1.40k black & cream 60 50
1850 " 1.80k multicolored 75 65
1851 " 2.40k " *3.00* *2.75*
Nos. 1847–1851 (5) *5.25* *4.70*

Sheets of 4.

Goldfinch
A661

Songbirds: 60h, Warbler feeding young cuckoo. 80h, Cuckoo. 1k, Black-billed magpie. 1.60k, Bullfinch. 3k, Song thrush.

1972, Dec. 15

Size: 30x48½mm.

1852 A661 60h yellow & multi. 24 10
1853 " 80h multicolored 32 14
1854 " 1k lt. bl. & multi. 40 16

Engraved

Size: 30x23mm.

1855 A661 1.60k multicolored 64 12
1856 " 2k " 80 16
1857 " 3k " *2.00* *70*
Nos. 1852–1857 (6) *4.40* *1.38*

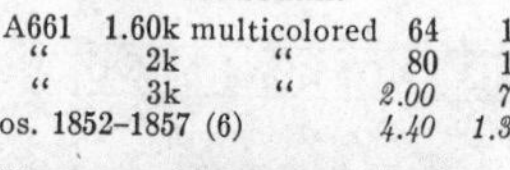

Post Horn and Allegory—A662

1972, Dec. 18 **Photo. & Engr.**

1858 A662 1k black, red lilac & gold 40 35

Stamp Day.

Art Type of 1972

1973, Jan. 25 ***Perf. 11½x11***

Designs: 30h, Flowers in Window, by Jaroslav Grus. 60h, Quest for Happiness, by Josef Balaz. 1.60k, Balloon, by Kamil Lhotak. 1.80k, Woman with Viola, by Richard Wiesner.

1859 A651 30h multicolored 12 5
1860 " 60h " 24 10
1861 " 1.60k " 64 15
1862 " 1.80k " *1.50* *50*

Czech and Slovak graphic art.

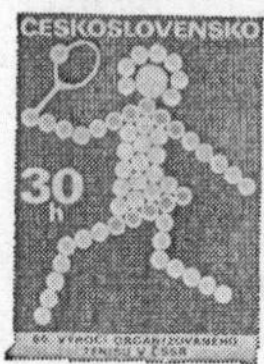

Tennis Player
A663

Figure Skater
A664

Torch and Star
A665

1973, Feb. 22 ***Perf. 11***

1863 A663 30h vio. & multi. 12 5
1864 A664 60h blk. & multi. 24 10
1865 A665 1k multicolored 40 18

80th anniversary of the tennis organization in Czechoslovakia (30h); World figure skating championships, Bratislava (60h); 3rd summer army Spartakiad of socialist countries (1k).

Star and Factories
A666

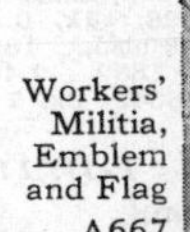

Workers' Militia, Emblem and Flag
A667

1973, Feb. 23 Photo. & Engr.

1866 A666 30h multicolored 12 5
1867 A667 60h " 24 10

25th anniversary of the Communist revolution in Czechoslovakia and of the Militia.

Capt. Jan Nalepka, Major Antonin Sochor and Laurel—A668

Designs (Torch and): 40h, Evzen Rosicky, Mirko Nespor and ivy leaves. 60h, Vlado Clementis, Karol Smidke and linden leaves. 80h, Jan Osoha, Josef Molak and oak leaves. 1k, Marie Kuderikova, Jozka Jaburkova and rose. 1.60k, Vaclav Sinkule, Eduard Urx and palm leaf.

1973, Mar. 20 *Perf. 11½x11*

Yellow Paper

1868 A668 30h blk., verm. & gold 12 5
1869 " 40h blk., verm. & green 16 7
1870 " 60h blk., verm. & gold 24 10
1871 " 80h blk., verm. & gold 32 14
1872 " 1k blk., verm. & green 40 18
1873 " 1.60k blk., verm. & silver 1.00 28
Nos. 1868-1873 (6) 2.24 82

Fighters against and victims of Fascism and Nazism during German Occupation.

Virgil I. Grissom, Edward H. White, Roger B. Chaffee—A669

Designs: 20h, Soviet planetary station "Vebera." 30h, "Intercosmos" station. 40h, Lunokhod on moon. 3.60k, Vladimir M. Komarov, Georgi T. Dobrovolsky, Vladislav N. Volkov, Victor I. Patsayev. 5k, Yuri A. Gagarin.

Photogravure and Engraved

1973, Apr. 12 *Perf. 11½x11*

Size: 40x22mm.

1874 A669 20h multicolored 8 3
1875 " 30h " 12 5
1876 " 40h " 16 7

Engraved *Perf. 11½*

Size: 49x30mm.

1877 A669 3k multicolored 1.20 54
1878 " 3.60k " 1.45 64
1879 " 5k " 3.75 3.50
Nos. 1874-1879 (6) 6.76 4.83

In memory of American and Russian astronauts.

Radio
A670

Telephone and Map of Czechoslovakia
A671

Television
A672

1973, May 1 *Perf. 11½x11*

1880 A670 30h blk. & multi. 12 5
1881 A671 30h lt. blue, pink & black 12 5
1882 A672 30h dp. bl. & multi. 12 5

Czechoslovak anniversaries: 50 years of broadcasting (No. 1880); 20 years of telephone service to all communities (No. 1881); 20 years of television (No. 1882).

Coat of Arms and Linden Branch
A673

1973, May 9 *Perf. 11x11½*

1883 A673 60h red & multi. 24 10

25th anniversary of the Constitution of May 9.

Prague Castle Art Type of 1971

Designs: No. 1884, Royal Legate, 14th century. No. 1885, Seal of King Charles IV, 1351.

1973, May 9 *Perf. 11½*

1884 A634 3k blue & multi. 1.50 1.50
1885 " 3k gold, green & dark brown 1.20 1.20

Art treasures of Castle of Prague. Sheets of 4.

Coat of Arms Type of 1968

1973, June 20

Multicolored

1886 A590 60h *Mikulov* 24 15
1887 " 60h *Zlutice* 24 15
1888 " 60h *Smolenice* 24 15

Coats of arms of Czechoslovakian cities.

Heraldic Colors of Olomouc and Moravia
A674

Anthurium
A675

1973, Aug. 23 Photo. & Engr.

1889 A674 30h multicolored 12 8

400th anniversary of University of Olomouc.

1973, Aug. 23 *Perf. 11½*

Sizes: 60h, 1k, 2k, 30x50mm.; 1.60k, 1.80k, 3.60k, 23x39mm.

Multicolored

1890 A675 60h *Tulips* 24 20
1891 " 1k *Rose* 40 35
1892 " 1.60k *shown* 65 28
1893 " 1.80k *Iris* 72 30
1894 " 2k *Chrysanthemum* 2.25 2.00
1895 " 3.60k *Cymbidium* 1.45 64
Nos. 1890-1895 (6) 5.71 3.77

Flower Show, Olomouc, Aug. 18-Sept. 2. 60h, 1k, 2k issued in sheets of 4, others in sheets of 10.

Irish Setter
A676

Designs: Hunting dogs.

1973, Sept. 5

Multicolored

1896 A676 20h *shown* 7 3
1897 " 30h *Czech terrier* 12 5
1898 " 40h *Bavarian hunting dog* 15 7
1899 " 60h *German pointer* 24 12
1900 " 1k *Cocker spaniel* 40 20
1901 " 1.60k *Dachshund* 1.20 35
Nos. 1896-1901 (6) 2.18 82

50th anniversary of the Czechoslovak United Hunting Organization.

St. John, the Baptist, by Svabinsky
A677

Works by Max Svabinsky: 60h, "August Noon" (woman). 80h, "Marriage of True Minds" (artist and muse). 1k, "Paradise Sonata I" (Adam dreaming of Eve). 2.60k, Last Judgment, stained glass window, St. Vitus Cathedral.

1973, Sept. 17 Litho. & Engr.

1902 A677 20h blk. & pale grn. 7 5
1903 " 60h black & buff 24 12

Engraved

1904 A677 80h black 32 28
1905 " 1k slate green 40 35
1906 " 2.60k multicolored 1.40 1.30
Nos. 1902-1906 (5) 2.43 2.10

Centenary of the birth of Max Svabinsky (1873-1962), artist and stamp designer. 20h and 60h issued in sheets of 25; 80h and 1k se-tenant in sheets of 4 checkerwise; 2.60k in sheets of 4.

Trade Union Emblem
A678

1973, Oct. 15 Photo. & Engr.

1907 A678 1k red, blue & yel. 40 18

8th Congress of the World Federation of Trade Unions, Varna, Bulgaria.

Painting Type of 1967

Designs: 1k, Boy from Martinique, by Antonin Pelc. 1.20k, "Fortitude" (mountaineer), by Martin Benka. 1.80k, Rembrandt, self-portrait. 2k, Pierrot, by Bohumil Kubista. 2.40k, Ilona Kubinyiova, by Peter M. Bohun. 3.60k, Virgin and Child (Veveri Madonna), c. 1350.

Photogravure and Engraved

1973, Nov. 27 *Perf. 11½*

1908 A565 1k multi., vio. bl. inscriptions 1.25 1.10
a. 1k multi., black inscriptions 3.75 3.50
1909 A565 1.20k multicolored 1.25 1.10
1910 " 1.80k " 54 50
1911 " 2k " 60 55
1912 " 2.40k " 96 85
1913 " 3.60k " 1.45 1.30
Nos. 1908-1913 (6) 6.05 5.40

Sheets of 4. Nos. 1910-1913 printed se-tenant with gold and black inscription on gutter.

Central background bluish gray on No. 1908, light bluish green on No. 1908a.

Postilion—A679

1973, Dec. 18

1914 A679 1k gold & multi. 40 16

Stamp Day 1974 and 55th anniversary of Czechoslovak postage stamps. Printed with 2 labels showing telephone and telegraph.

"CSSR"
A680

Friedrich Smetana
A681

Pablo Neruda, Chilean Flag
A682

Comecon Building, Moscow
A683

1974, Jan. 1

1915 A680 30h red, gold & ultramarine 12 3

5th anniversary of Federal Government in the Czechoslovak Socialist Republic.

1974, Jan. 4 *Perf. 11x11½*

Design: No. 1917, Josef Suk.

1916 A681 60h blk., bl. & yel. 24 12
1917 " 60h green & multi. 24 12
1918 A682 60h bl., blk. & red 24 12

Sesquicentennial of the birth of Friedrich Smetana (1824-1884), composer; centenary of the birth of Josef Suk (1874-1935), composer, and in memory of Pablo Neruda (Neftali Ricardo Reyes, 1904-1973), Chilean poet.

1974, Jan. 23

1919 A683 1k gold, red & violet blue 40 16

25th anniversary of the Council of Mutual Economic Assistance (COMECON).

Symbols of Postal Service—A684

1974, Feb. 20 *Perf. 11½*

1920 A684 3.60k multicolored 1.50 60

BRNO '74 National Stamp Exhibition, Brno, June 8–23.

Art Type of 1972

Designs: 60h, Tulips 1973, by Josef Broz. 1k, Structures 1961 (poppy and building), by Orest Dubay. 1.60k, Bird and flowers (Golden Sun-Glowing Day), by Adolf Zabransky. 1.80k, Artificial flowers, by Frantisek Gross.

1974, Feb. 21 *Perf. 11½x11*

1921	A651	60h	multicolored	24	10
1922	"	1k	"	40	16
1923	"	1.60k	"	64	24
1924	"	1.80k	"	72	28

Czech and Slovak graphic art.

Oskar Benes and Vaclav Prochazka
A685

Portraits: 40h, Milos Uher and Anton Sedlacek. 60h, Jan Hajecek and Marie Sedlackova. 80h, Jan Sverma and Albin Grznar. 1k, Jaroslav Neliba and Alois Hovorka. 1.60k, Ladislav Exnar and Ludovit Kukorelli.

Photogravure and Engraved

1974, Mar. 21 *Perf. 11½x11*

1925	A685	30h	indigo & multi.	12	3
1926	"	40h	" "	16	6
1927	"	60h	" "	24	8
1928	"	80h	" "	32	10
1929	"	1k	" "	40	14
1930	"	1.60k	" "	64	22
	Nos. 1925–1930 (6)			1.88	63

Partisan commanders and fighters.

"Water, the Source of Energy"
A686

Symbolic Designs: 1k, Importance of water for agriculture. 1.20k, Study of the oceans. 1.60k, "Hydrological Decade." 2k, Struggle for unpolluted water.

1974, Apr. 25 Engr. *Perf. 11½*

1931	A686	60h	multicolored	24	24
1932	"	1k	"	40	40
1933	"	1.20k	"	48	48
1934	"	1.60k	"	64	64
1935	"	2k	"	80	80
	Nos. 1931–1935 (5)			2.56	2.56

Hydrological Decade (UNESCO), 1965–1974. Sheets of 4.

Allegory Holding "Molniya," and Ground Station
A687

Sousaphone
A688

1974, Apr. 30 Photo. & Engr.

1936 A687 30h vio. bl. & multi. 12 6

"Intersputnik," first satellite communications ground station in Czechoslovakia.

Prague Castle Art Type of 1971

Designs: No. 1937, Golden Cock, 17th century locket. No. 1938, Glass monstrance, 1840.

1974, May 9 Engr. *Perf. 11½*

1937	A634	3k	gold & multi.	1.35	1.20
1938	"	3k	black & multi.	1.35	1.20

Art treasures of Castle of Prague. Sheets of 4.

Photogravure and Engraved

1974, May 12 *Perf. 11x11½*

Multicolored

1939	A688	20h	*shown*	8	4
1940	"	30h	*Bagpipe*	12	8
1941	"	40h	*Violin, by Martin Benka*	16	12
1942	"	1k	*Pyramid piano*	40	18
1943	"	1.60k	*Tenor quinton, 1754*	64	30
	Nos. 1939–1943 (5)			1.40	72

Prague and Bratislava Music Festivals. The 1.60k also commemorates 25th anniversary of Slovak Philharmonic Orchestra.

Child
A689

Photogravure and Engraved

1974, June 1 *Perf. 11½*

1944 A689 60h multicolored 24 12

Children's Day. Design is from illustration for children's book by Adolf Zabransky.

Globe, People and Exhibition Emblems
A690

Design: 6k, Rays and emblems symbolizing "Oneness and Mutuality."

1974, June 1

1945	A690	30h	multicolored	12	6
1946	"	6k	"	2.40	1.20

BRNO 74 National Stamp Exhibition, Brno, June 8–23. Sheets of 16 stamps and 14 labels.

Resistance Fighter
A691

Actress Holding Tragedy and Comedy Masks
A692

Photogravure and Engraved

1974, Aug. 29 *Perf. 11½*

1947 A691 30h multicolored 12 6

Slovak National Uprising, 30th anniversary.

1974, Aug. 29

1948 A692 30h red, silv. & blk. 12 6

Bratislava Academy of Music and Drama, 25th anniversary.

Slovak Girl with Flower
A693

1974, Aug. 29

1949 A693 30h multicolored 12 6

SLUK, Slovak folksong and dance ensemble, 25th anniversary.

Hero and Leander
A694

Design: 2.40k, Hero watching Leander swim the Hellespont. No. 1952, Leander reaching shore. No. 1953, Hero mourning over Leander's body. No. 1954, Hermione, Leander's sister. No. 1955, Mourning Cupid. Designs are from 17th century English tapestries in Bratislava Council Palace.

1974–76 Photo. & Engr.

1950	A694	2k	multicolored	90	80
1951	"	2.40k	"	1.10	1.00
1952	"	3k	"	1.30	1.15
1953	"	3k	"	1.30	1.15
1954	"	3.60k	"	1.60	1.40
1955	"	3.60k	"	1.60	1.40
	Nos. 1950–1955 (6)			7.80	6.90

Issue dates: Nos. 1950–1951, Sept. 25, 1974. Nos. 1952, 1954, Aug. 29, 1975. Nos. 1953, 1955, May 9, 1976.

Soldier Standing Guard, Target, 1840
A695

Painted Folk-art Targets: 60h, Landscape with Pierrot and flags, 1828. 1k, Diana crowning champion marksman, 1832. 1.60k, Still life with guitar, 1839. 2.40k, Salvo and stag in flight, 1834. 3k, Turk and giraffe, 1831.

1974, Sept. 26 *Perf. 11½*

Size: 30x50mm.

1956	A695	30h	blk & multi.	12	6
1957	"	60h	" "	24	12
1958	"	1k	" "	40	20

Engraved *Perf. 12*

Size: 40x50mm.

1959	A695	1.60k	grn. & multi.	64	55
1960	"	2.40k	sepia & multi.	96	85
1961	"	3k	multi.	1.20	1.05
	Nos. 1956–1961 (6)			3.56	2.83

UPU Emblem and Postilion—A696

Designs (UPU Emblem and): 40h, Mail coach. 60h, Railroad mail coach, 1851. 80h, Early mail truck. 1k, Czechoslovak Airlines mail plane. 1.60k, Radar.

Photogravure and Engraved

1974, Oct. 9 *Perf. 11½*

1962	A696	30h	multicolored	12	6
1963	"	40h	"	16	8
1964	"	60h	"	24	12
1965	"	80h	"	32	16
1966	"	1k	"	40	20
1967	"	1.60k	"	64	32
	Nos. 1962–1967 (6)			1.88	94

Centenary of Universal Postal Union.

Post Horn, Old Town Bridge Tower
A697

Sealed Letter
A698

Stylized Bird
A699

Postal Code Symbol
A699a

Designs: 40h, Postilion. No. 1971, Carrier pigeon. No. 1979, Map of Czechoslovakia with postal code numbers.

Photogravure and Engraved

1974, Oct. 31 *Perf. 11½x11*

1968	A697	20h	multicolored	8	5
1969	A698	30h	brn., bl. & red	12	5
1970	A697	40h	multicolored	16	5
1971	A698	60h	bl., yel. & red	24	5

Coil Stamps

1975–76 Photogravure *Perf. 14*

1976	A699	30h	bright blue	10	3
1977	"	60h	carmine	20	3
1978	A699a	30h	emerald ('76)	10	3
1979	"	60h	scarlet ('76)	20	3

Nos. 1976–1979 have black control number on back of every fifth stamp.

Ludvik Kuba, Self-portrait, 1941
A700

Paintings: 1.20k, Violinist Frantisek Ondricek, by Vaclav Brozik. 1.60k, Vase with Flowers, by Otakar Kubin. 1.80k, Woman with Pitcher, by Janko Alexy. 2.40k, Bacchanalia, c. 1635, by Karel Skreta.

1974, Nov. 27 Engraved *Perf. 11½*

1980 A700 1k multicolored 40 40
1981 " 1.20k " 48 48
1982 " 1.60k " 64 64
1983 " 1.80k " 72 72
1984 " 2.40k " 96 96
Nos. 1980-1984 (5) 3.20 3.20

Czech and Slovak art. Sheets of 4.

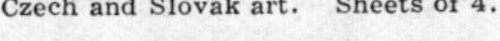

Post Horn—A701

Photogravure and Engraved

1974, Dec. 18 *Perf. 11x11½*

1985 A701 1k multicolored 40 20

Stamp Day.

Still-life with Hare, by Hollar
A702

Designs: 1k, The Lion and the Mouse, by Vaclav Hollar. 1.60k, Deer Hunt, by Philip Galle. 1.80k, Grand Hunt, by Jacques Callot.

Lithographed and Engraved

1975, Feb. 26 *Perf. 11½x11*

1988 A702 60h black & buff 24 6
1989 " 1k " " 40 10
1990 " 1.60k black & yel. 65 25
1991 " 1.80k black & buff 72 36

Hunting scenes from old engravings.

Guns Pointing at Family
A703

Young Woman and Globe
A704

Designs: 1k, Women and building on fire. 1.20k, People and roses. All designs include names of destroyed villages.

Photogravure and Engraved

1975, Feb. 26 *Perf. 11*

1992 A703 60h multicolored 24 6
1993 A703 1k multicolored 40 12
1994 " 1.20k " 48 18

Destruction of 14 villages by the Nazis, 30th anniversary.

1975, Mar. 7 *Perf. 11½x11*

1995 A704 30h red & multi. 12 3

International Women's Year 1975.

Little Queens, Moravian Folk Custom
A705

Folk Customs: 1k, Straw masks (animal heads and blackened faces), Slovak. 1.40k, The Tale of Maid Dorothea (executioner, girl, king and devil). 2k, Drowning of Morena, symbol of death and winter.

1975, Mar. 26 Engr. *Perf. 11½*

1996 A705 60h blk. & multi. 30 25
1997 " 1k " " 50 45
1998 " 1.40k " " 60 55
1999 " 2k " " 90 80

Sheets of four.

Coat of Arms Type of 1968

Photogravure & Engraved

1975, Apr. 17 *Perf. 11½*

Multicolored

2000 A590 60h *Nymburk* 24 8
2001 " 60h *Znojmo* 24 8

Coats of arms of Czechoslovakian cities.

Czech May Uprising—A706

Liberation by Soviet Army—A707

Czechoslovak-Russian Friendship—A708

1975, May 9 Photo. & Engr.

2002 A706 1k multicolored 40 15

Engraved

2003 A707 1k multicolored 40 15

Photogravure and Engraved

2004 A708 1k multicolored 40 15

30th anniversary of the May uprising of the Czech people and of liberation by the Soviet Army; 5th anniversary of the Czechoslovak-Soviet Treaty of Friendship, Cooperation and Mutual Aid.

Adolescents' Exercises—A709

Designs: 60h, Children's exercises. 1k, Men's and women's exercises.

Photogravure and Engraved

1975, June 15 *Perf. 12x11½*

2005 A709 30h lilac & multi. 12 3
2006 " 60h multicolored 26 8
2007 " 1k violet & multi. 44 15

Spartakiad 1975, Prague, June 26-29. Nos. 2005-2007 each issued in sheets of 30 stamps and 40 labels, showing different Spartakiad emblems.

Datrioides Microlepis and Sea Horse—A710

Tropical Fish (Aquarium): 1k, Beta splendens regan and pterophyllum scalare. 1.20k, Carassius auratus. 1.60k, Amphiprion percula and chaetodon sp. 2k, Pomacanthodes semicirculatus, pomocanthus maculosus and paracanthorus hepatus.

1975, June 27 *Perf. 11½*

2008 A710 60h multicolored 26 8
2009 " 1k " 44 10
2010 " 1.20k " 52 14
2011 " 1.60k " 70 16
2012 " 2k " 88 18
Nos. 2008-2012 (5) 2.80 66

Pelicans, by Nikita Charushin
A711

Book Illustrations: 30h, The Dreamer, by Lieselotte Schwarz. 40h, Hero on horseback, by Val Muntenau. 60h, Peacock, by Klaus Ensikat. 80h, Man on horseback, by Robert Dubravec.

1975, Sept. 5

2013 A711 20h multicolored 10 6
2014 " 30h " 12 8
2015 " 40h " 15 10
2016 " 60h " 26 12
2017 " 80h " 30 16
Nos. 2013-2017 (5) 93 52

Bratislava BIB 75 biennial exhibition of illustrations for children's books.

Nos. 2013-2017 issued in sheets of 25 stamps and 15 labels with designs and inscriptions in various languages.

Strakonice, 1951
A712

Designs: Motorcycles.

Photogravure and Engraved

1975, Sept. 29 *Perf. 11½*

Multicolored

2018 A712 20h *shown* 8 3
2019 " 40h *Jawa 250, 1945* 15 5
2020 A712 60h *Jawa 175, 1935* 24 8
2021 " 1k *ITAR, 1921* 44 10
2022 " 1.20k *ORION, 1903* 52 12
2023 " 1.80k *Laurin & Klement, 1898* 75 25
Nos. 2018-2023 (6) 2.18 65

Study of Short-wave Solar Radiation
A713

Soyuz-Apollo Link-up in Space
A714

Designs: 60h, Study of aurora borealis and Oréol satellite. 1k, Study of ionosphere and cosmic radiation. 2k, Copernicus, radio map of the sun and satellite.

1975, Sept. 30

2024 A713 30h multicolored 12 5
2025 " 60h yellow, rose red & violet 24 8
2026 " 1k blue, yellow & violet 44 10
2027 " 2k red, violet & yellow 88 20

Engraved

2028 A714 5k vio. & multi. 2.50 2.50
Nos. 2024-2028 (5) 4.18 2.93

International cooperation in space research. No. 2028 issued in sheets of 4.

The design of No. 2026 appears to be inverted.

Slovnaft, Petrochemical Plant—A715

Designs: 60h, Atomic power station. 1k, Construction of Prague subway. 1.20k, Construction of Friendship pipeline. 1.40k, Combine harvesters. 1.60k, Apartment house construction.

1975, Oct. 28 Photo. & Engr.

2029 A715 30h multicolored 12 5
2030 " 60h " 24 8
2031 " 1k " 44 10
2032 " 1.20k " 52 12
2033 " 1.40k " 55 14
2034 " 1.60k " 70 16
Nos. 2029-2034 (6) 2.57 65

Socialist construction, 30th anniversary. Nos. 2029-2034 printed se-tenant with labels.

Pres. Gustav Husak
A716

1975, Oct. 28 Engraved

2035 A716 30h ultramarine 12 3
2036 " 60h rose red 24 3

Prague Castle Art Type of 1971

Designs: 3k, Gold earring, 9th century. 3.60k, Arms of Premysl Dynasty and Bohemian from lid of leather case containing Bohemian crown, 14th century.

1975, Oct. 29

2040 A634 3k blk., grn., pur. & gold 1.30 1.20
2041 " 3.60k red & multi. 1.60 1.50

Art treasures of Castle of Prague. Sheets of 4.

Miniature Sheet

Ludvik Svoboda, Road Map, Buzuluk to Prague, Carnations—A717

1975, Nov. 25

2042 A717 10k multicolored 10.00 10.00

Pres. Ludvik Svoboda, 80th birthday. Size of No. 2042: 75x95mm. (stamp size: 40x55mm.). Exists imperf., price $35.

Art Type of 1967

Paintings: 1k, "May 1975" (Woman and doves for 30th anniversary of peace), by Zdenek Sklenar. 1.40k, Woman in national costume, by Eugen Nevan. 1.80k, "Liberation of Prague," by Alena Cermakova (horiz.). 2.40k, "Fire 1938" (woman raising fist), by Josef Capek. 3.40k, Old Prague, 1828, by Vincenc Morstadt.

1975, Nov. 27 Engr. *Perf. 11½*

2043 A565 1k black, buff & brown 44 40
2044 " 1.40k multicolored 60 55
2045 " 1.80k " 80 70
2046 " 2.40k " 1.00 90
2047 " 3.40k " 1.50 1.35
Nos. 2043-2047 (5) 4.34 3.90

Sheets of 4.

Carrier Pigeon—A718

Photogravure and Engraved

1975, Dec. 18 *Perf. 11½*

2048 A718 1k red & multi. 44 10

Stamp Day 1975.

Frantisek Halas A719 — Wilhelm Pieck A720

Frantisek Lexa A721 — Jindrich Jindrich A722

Ivan Krasko A723

Photogravure and Engraved

1976, Feb. 25 *Perf. 11½*

2049 A719 60h multicolored 24 8
2050 A720 60h " 24 8
2051 A721 60h " 24 8
2052 A722 60h " 24 8
2053 A723 60h " 24 8
Nos. 2049-2053 (5) 1.20 40

Anniversaries: Frantisek Halas (1901–1949), poet (No. 2049); Wilhelm Pieck (1876–1960), president of German Democratic Republic (No. 2050); Frantisek Lexa (1876–1960), professor of Egyptology (No. 2051); Jindrich Jindrich (1876–1967), composer and writer (No. 2052); Ivan Krasko (1876–1958), Slovak poet (No. 2053). No. 2051 printed in sheets of 10, others in sheets of 50.

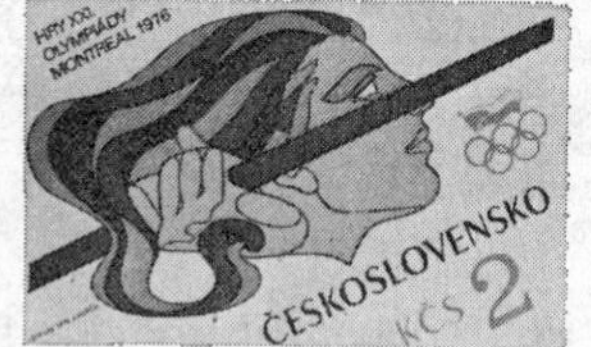

Ski Jump, Olympic Emblem A724

Designs (Winter Olympic Games Emblem and): 1.40k, Figure skating, women's. 1.60k, Ice hockey.

Photogravure and Engraved

1976, Mar. 22 *Perf. 12x11½*

2054 A724 1k gold & multi. 44 10
2055 " 1.40k " " 60 16
2056 " 1.60k " " 70 20

12th Winter Olympic Games, Innsbruck, Austria, Feb. 4–15.

Javelin and Olympic Rings—A725

Designs (Olympic Rings and): 3k, Relay race. 3.60k, Shot put.

1976, Mar. 22 *Perf. 11½*

2057 A725 2k multicolored 90 30
2058 " 3k " 1.30 45
2059 " 3.60k " 1.60 55

21st Olympic Games, Montreal, Canada, July 17–Aug. 1.

Table Tennis A726

1976, Mar. 22 *Perf. 11x12*

2060 A726 1k multicolored 44 12

European Table Tennis Championship, Prague, Mar. 26–Apr. 4.

Symbolic of Communist Party A727 — Worker, Derrick, Emblem A728

1976, Apr. 12 *Perf. 11x12*

2061 A727 30h gold & multi. 12 4
2062 A728 60h " " 24 8

15th Congress of the Communist Party of Czechoslovakia.

Radio Prague Orchestra A729 — Dancer, Violin, Tragic Mask A730

Actors A731

Folk Dancers A732

Film Festival—A733

1976, Apr. 26 *Perf. 11½*

2063 A729 20h gold & multi. 8 3
2064 A730 20h pink & multi. 8 3
2065 A731 20h lt. bl. & multi. 8 3
2066 A732 30h blk. & multi. 12 4
2067 A733 30h vio. blue, rose & green 12 4
Nos. 2063-2067 (5) 48 17

Commemorating: Czechoslovak Radio Symphony Orchestra, Prague, 50th anniversary (No. 2063); Academy of Music and Dramatic Art, Prague, 50th anniversary (No. 2064); Nova Scena Theater Company, Bratislava, 30th anniversary (No. 2065); International Folk Song and Dance Festival, Straznice, 30th anniversary (No. 2066); 20th International Film Festival, Karlovy Vary (No. 2067).

Hammer and Sickle A734 — A735

Design: 6k, Hammer and sickle (horiz.).

1976, May 14

2068 A734 30h gold, red & dark blue 12 4
2069 A735 60h gold, red & dp. carmine 24 8

Souvenir Sheet

2070 A735 6k red & multi. 2.60 2.60

Czechoslovak Communist Party, 55th anniversary. No. 2070 contains one stamp (50x30mm.); violet blue marginal inscription and gold emblem. Size: 99x90mm.

Ships in Storm, by Frans Huys (1522–1562) A736

Old Engravings of Ships: 60h, by Václav Hollar (1607–1677). 1k, by Regnier Nooms Zeeman (1623–1668). 2k, by Francois Chereau (1680–1729).

Photogravure and Engraved

1976, July 21 *Perf. 11x11½*

2071 A736 40h buff & black 16 6
2072 " 60h gray, buff & black 24 8
2073 " 1k lt. green, buff & black 44 10
2074 " 2k lt. blue, buff & black 88 30

"UNESCO" A737

1976, July 30 *Perf. 11½*

2075 A737 2k gray & multi. 88 45

30th anniversary of UNESCO. Sheets of 10.

Souvenir Sheet

Hands Holding Infant, Globe and Dove A738

1976, July 30

2076	A738	6k, sheet of 2, multicolored	9.00	8.00

European Security and Cooperation Conference, Helsinki, Finland, 2nd anniversary. No. 2076 contains 2 stamps, marginal inscription and ornamental designs in blue and black. Size: 115x165mm.

Merino Ram

A739

Couple Smoking, WHO Emblem and Skull

A740

Designs: 40h, Bern-Hana milk cow. 1.60k, Kladruby stallion Generalissimus XXVII.

Photogravure and Engraved

1976, Aug. 28 *Perf. 11½x12*

2077	A739	30h multicolored	12	4
2078	"	40h "	16	5
2079	"	1.60k "	70	16

Bountiful Earth Exhibition, Ceske Budejovice, Aug. 28–Sept. 12.

1976, Sept. 7 *Perf. 12x11½*

2080	A740	2k multicolored	88	45

Fight against smoking, World Health Organization drive against drug addiction. Printed in sheets of 10 (2x5) with WHO emblems and inscription in margin.

Prague Castle Art Type of 1971

Designs: 3k, View of Prague Castle, by F. Hoogenberghe, 1572. 3.60k, Faun and Satyr, sculptured panel, 16th century.

1976, Oct. 22 Engr. *Perf. 11½*

2081	A634	3k multicolored	1.30	1.15
2082	"	3.60k "	1.55	1.40

Art treasures of Castle of Prague.

Guernica 1937, by Imro Weiner-Kral

A741

1976, Oct. 22

2083	A741	5k multicolored	2.25	80

40th anniversary of the International Brigade in Spain.

Zebras

A472

Designs: 20h, Elephants (vert.). 30h, Cheetah. 40h, Giraffes (vert.). 60h, Rhinoceros. 3k, Bongos (vert.).

Photogravure and Engraved

Perf. 11½x11, 11x11½

1976, Nov. 3

2084	A742	10h multicolored	4	3
2085	"	20h "	8	3
2086	"	30h "	12	4
2087	"	40h "	16	5
2088	"	60h "	24	8
2089	A742	3k multicolored	1.30	35
		Nos. 2084–2089 (6)	1.94	58

African animals in Dvur Kralove Zoo.

Art Type of 1967

Paintings of Flowers: 1k, by Peter Matejka. 1.40k, by Cyril Bouda. 2k, by Jan Breughel. 3.60k, J. Rudolf Bys.

1976, Nov. 27 Engr. *Perf. 11½*

2090	A565	1k multicolored	44	40
2091	"	1.40k "	60	55
2092	"	2k "	88	80
2093	"	3.60k "	1.55	1.40

Sheets of 4. Emblem and name of Praga 1978 on horizontal gutter.

Postrider, 17th Century, and Satellites—A743

1976, Dec. 18 Photo. & Engr.

2094	A743	1k multicolored	44	12

Stamp Day 1976.

Ice Hockey

A744

Arms of Vranov

A745

Designs: 1k, Biathlon. 1.60k, Ski jump. 2k, Downhill skiing.

Photogravure and Engraved

1977, Feb. 11 *Perf. 11½*

2095	A744	60h multicolored	24	8
2096	"	1k "	44	12
2097	"	1.60k "	68	22
2098	"	2k "	88	28

6th Winter Spartakiad of Socialist Countries' Armies.

1977, Feb. 20

Designs: Coats of Arms of Czechoslovak towns.

Multicolored

2099	A745	60h *shown*	24	8
2100	"	60h *Kralupy & Vltavou*	24	8
2101	"	60h *Jicin*	24	8
2102	"	60h *Valasske Mezirici*	24	8

Window, Michna Palace

A746

Prague Renaissance Windows: 30h, Michna Palace. 40h, Thun Palace. 60h, Archbishop's Palace, Hradcany. 5k, St. Nicholas Church.

1977, Mar. 10

2103	A746	20h multicolored	8	3
2104	"	30h "	12	4
2105	"	40h "	16	5
2106	A746	60h multicolored	24	8
2107	"	5k "	2.20	1.00
		Nos. 2103–2107 (5)	2.80	1.20

PRAGA 1978 International Philatelic Exhibition, Prague, Sept. 8–17, 1978.

Children, Auxiliary Police

A747

Photogravure and Engraved

1977, Apr. 21 *Perf. 11½*

2108	A747	60h multicolored	24	8

Auxiliary Police, 25th anniversary.

Warsaw, Polish Flag, Bicyclists

A748

Congress Emblem

A749

Designs: 60h, Berlin, DDR flag, bicyclists. 1k, Prague, Czechoslovakian flag, victorious bicyclist. 1.40k, Bicyclists on highways, modern views of Berlin, Prague and Warsaw.

1977, May 7

2109	A748	30h multicolored	12	4
2110	"	60h "	24	8
2111	"	1k "	44	10
2112	"	1.40k "	60	15

30th International Bicycle Peace Race Warsaw-Prague-Berlin.

Photogravure and Engraved

1977, May 25 *Perf. 11½*

2113	A749	30h car., red & gold	12	4

9th Trade Union Congress, Prague 1977.

Prague Castle Art Type of 1971

Designs: 3k, Onyx footed bowl, 1350. 3.60k, Bronze horse, 1619.

1977, June 7 Engraved

2114	A634	3k multicolored	1.30	1.20
2115	"	3.60k "	1.60	1.50

Art treasures of Castle of Prague. Sheets of 4.

French Postrider, 19th Century, PRAGA '78 Emblem

A750

Postal Uniforms: 1k, Austrian, 1838. 2k, Austrian, late 18th century. 3.60k, Germany, early 18th century.

1977, June 8 Photo. & Engr.

2116	A750	60h multicolored	24	8
2117	"	1k "	44	10
2118	"	2k "	88	20
2119	"	3.60k "	1.50	38

PRAGA 1978 International Philatelic Exhibition, Prague, Sept. 8–17, 1978.

Nos. 2116–2119 issued in sheets of 50 and sheets of 4 with 4 labels and horizontal gutter.

Coffeepots, Porcelain Mark

A751

Mlada Boleslav Costume

A752

Czechoslovak Porcelain and Porcelain Marks: 30h, Urn. 40h, Vase. 60h, Cup and saucer, jugs. 1k, Candlestick and plate. 3k, Cup and saucer, coffeepot.

1977, June 15

2120	A751	20h multicolored	8	3
2121	"	30h "	12	4
2122	"	40h "	16	6
2123	"	60h "	24	8
2124	"	1k "	44	10
2125	"	3k "	1.30	30
		Nos. 2120–2125 (6)	2.34	61

1977, Aug. 31 Engraved *Perf. 11½*

PRAGA Emblem and Folk Costumes from: 1.60k, Vazek. 3.60k, Zavadka. 5k, Belkovice.

2126	A752	1k multicolored	44	40
2127	"	1.60k "	68	60
2128	"	3.60k "	1.55	1.40
2129	"	5k "	2.20	2.00

Issued in sheets of 10 and in sheets of 8 plus 2 labels showing PRAGA '78 emblem.

Old Woman, Devil and Spinner, by Viera Bombova

A753

Book Illustrations: 60h, Bear and tiger, by Genadij Pavlisin. 1k, Coach drawn by 4 horses (Hans Christian Andersen), by Ulf Lovgren. 2k, Bear and flamingos (Lewis Carroll), by Nicole Claveloux. 3k, King with keys, and toys, by Jiri Trnka.

1977, Sept. 9 Photo. & Engr.

2130	A753	40h multicolored	16	6
2131	"	60h "	24	8
2132	"	1k "	44	10
2133	"	2k "	88	20
2134	"	3k "	1.30	35
		Nos. 2130–2134 (5)	3.02	79

Prize-winning designs, 6th biennial exhibition of illustrations for children's books, Bratislava.

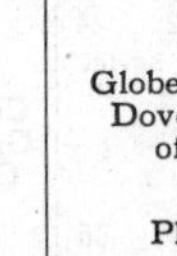

Globe, Violin, Doves, View of Prague

A754

Photogravure and Engraved

1977, Sept. 28 *Perf. 11½*

2135	A754	60h multicolored	24	8

Congress of International Music Council of UNESCO, Prague and Bratislava.

Souvenir Sheets

"For a Europe of Peace"

A755

Designs: 1.60k, "For a Europe of Cooperation." 2.40k, "For a Europe of Social Progress."

1977, Oct. 3 **Multicolored**

2136	A755	60h, sheet of 2	55	50
2137	"	1.60k, sheet of 2	1.50	1.35
2138	"	2.40k, sheet of 2	2.25	2.00

2nd European Security and Cooperation Conference, Belgrade. Nos. 2136–2138 each contain 2 stamps and 2 blue on buff inscriptions and ornaments. Size: 130x80mm.

S. P. Koroljov, Sputnik I Emblem

A756

Sailors, Cruiser Aurora

A757

Designs: 30h, Yuri A. Gagarin and Vostok I. 40h, Alexei Leonov. 1k, Neil A. Armstrong and footprint on moon. 1.60k, Construction of orbital space station.

1977, Oct. 4

2139	A756	20h	multicolored	8	3
2140	"	30h	"	12	5
2141	"	40h	"	16	6
2142	"	1k	"	44	15
2143	"	1.60k	"	68	25
		Nos. 2139–2143 (5)		1.48	54

Space research, 20th anniversary of first earth satellite.

1977, Nov. 7

2144	A757	30h multicolored	12	4

60th anniversary of Russian October Revolution.

"Russia" Arms of USSR, Kremlin

A758

"Science"

A759

1977, Nov. 7

2145	A758	30h multicolored	12	4

55th anniversary of the Union of Soviet Socialist Republics (USSR).

1977, Nov. 17

2146	A759	3k multicolored	1.35	55

Czechoslovak Academy of Science, 25th anniversary.

Art Type of 1967

Paintings: 2k, "Fear" (woman), by Jan Murdoch. 2.40k, Jan Francisci, portrait by Peter M. Bohun. 2.60k, Vaclav Hollar, self-portrait, 1647. 3k, Young Woman, 1528, by Lucas Cranach. 5k, Cleopatra, by Rubens.

1977, Nov. 27 **Engr.** ***Perf. 11½***

2147	A565	2k	multicolored	88	80
2148	"	2.40k	"	1.00	90
2149	"	2.60k	"	1.15	1.00
2150	"	3k	"	1.30	1.15
2151	"	5k	"	2.20	2.00
		Nos. 2147–2151 (5)		6.53	5.85

Sheets of 4.

View of Bratislava, by Georg Hoefnagel—A760

Design: 3.60k, Arms of Bratislava, 1436.

1977, Dec. 6

2152	A760	3k	multi.	1.30	1.15
2153	"	3.60k	"	1.55	1.40

Sheets of 4. See Nos. 2174–2175.

Stamp Pattern and Post Horn—A761

1977, Dec. 18 **Photo. & Engr.**

2154	A761	1k multicolored	45	15

Stamp Day.

Zdenek Nejedly

A762

Karl Marx

A763

Photogravure and Engraved

1978, Feb. 10 ***Perf. 11½***

2155	A762	30h	multicolored	12	4
2156	A763	40h	"	16	6

Zdenek Nejedly (1878–1962), musicologist and historian; Karl Marx (1818–1883), political philosopher.

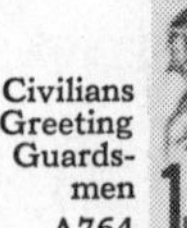

Civilians Greeting Guardsmen

A764

Intellectual, Farm Woman and Steel Worker, Flag—A765

1978, Feb. 25

2157	A764	1k	gold & multi.	45	10
2158	A765	1k	" "	45	10

30th anniversary of "Victorious February" (No. 2157), and National Front (No. 2158).

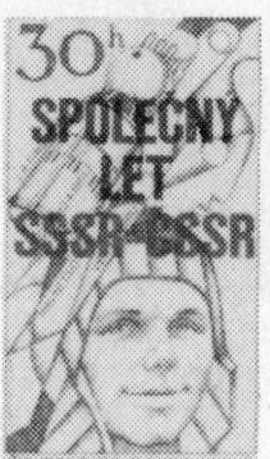

Yuri A. Gagarin and Vostok I

A766

10k Coin, 1964, and 25k Coin, 1965

A767

Design: 30h, 3.60k, like No. 2140.

Engr.; Overprint Photogravure (Blue and carmine on 30h, green and lilac rose on 3.60k)

1978, Mar. 2 ***Perf. 11½x12***

2159	A766	30h dark red	12	4
2160	"	3.60k violet blue	1.55	38

Capt. V. Remek, first Czechoslovakian cosmonaut on Russian spaceship Soyuz 28, Mar. 2–9.

1978, Mar. 14 **Photo. & Engr.**

Designs: 40h, Medal for Culture, 1972. 1.40k, Charles University medal, 1948. 3k, Ferdinand I medal, 1568. 5k, Gold florin, 1335.

2161	A767	20h	silv. & multi.	8	3
2162	"	40h	" "	16	6
2163	"	1.40k	gold & multi.	60	15
2164	"	3k	" "	1.35	55
2165	"	5k	" "	2.20	1.00
		Nos. 2161–2165 (5)		4.39	1.79

650th anniversary of Kremnica Mint.

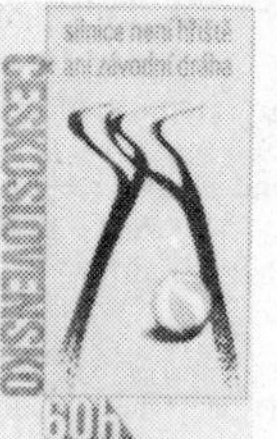

Tire Tracks and Ball

A768

Congress Emblem

A769

1978, Mar. 15

2166	A768	60h multicolored	24	8

Road safety.

Photogravure and Engraved

1978, Apr. 16 ***Perf. 11½***

2167	A769	1k multicolored	45	10

9th World Trade Union Congress, Prague 1978.

Shot Put and Praha '78 Emblem

A770

Designs: 1k, Pole vault. 3.60k, Women runners.

1978, Apr. 26

2168	A770	40h	multicolored	16	6
2169	"	1k	"	45	10
2170	"	3.60k	"	1.55	38

5th European Athletic Championships, Prague 1978.

Ice Hockey—A771

Designs: 30h, Hockey. 2k, Ice hockey play.

1978, Apr. 26

2171	A771	30h	multicolored	12	4
2172	"	60h	"	25	8
2173	"	2k	"	90	20

5th European Ice Hockey Championships and 70th anniversary of Bandy hockey.

Bratislava Type of 1977

Designs: 3k, Bratislava, 1955, by Orest Dubay. 3.60k, Fishpound Square, Bratislava, 1955, by Imro Weiner-Kral.

1978, May 9 **Engr.** ***Perf. 11½***

2174	A760	3k	multi.	1.30	1.15
2175	"	3.60k	"	1.55	1.40

Sheets of 4.

Prague Castle Art Type of 1971

Designs: 3k, King Ottokar II, detail from tomb. 3.60k, Charles IV, detail from votiv panel by Jan Ocka.

1978, May 9

2176	A634	3k	multi.	1.30	1.15
2177	"	3.60k	"	1.55	1.40

Art treasures of Castle of Prague. Sheets of 4.

Ministry of Post, Prague

A772

Photogravure and Engraved

1978, May 29 ***Perf. 12x11½***

2178	A772	60h multicolored	25	8

14th session of permanent COMECOM Commission (Ministers of Post and Telecommunications of Socialist Countries).

Palacky Bridge

A773

Prague Bridges and PRAGA '78 Emblem: 40h, Railroad bridge. 1k, Bridge of May 1. 2k, Manes Bridge. 3k, Svatopluk Cech Bridge. 5.40k, Charles Bridge.

1978, May 30

2179	A773	20h	blk. & multi.	8	3
2180	"	40h	" "	16	6
2181	"	1k	" "	45	10
2182	"	2k	" "	90	20
2183	"	3k	" "	1.30	30
2184	"	5.40k	" "	2.35	1.05
		Nos. 2179–2184 (6)		5.24	1.74

PRAGA 1978 International Philatelic Exhibition, Prague, Sept. 8–17.

St. Peter and Apostles, Clock Tower, and Emblem

A774

Town Hall Clock, Prague, by Josef Manes, and PRAGA '78 Emblem: 1k, Astronomical clock. 2k, Prague's coat of arms. 3k, Grape harvest (September). 3.60k, Libra. 10k, Arms surrounded by zodiac signs and scenes symbolic of 12 months (horiz.). 2k, 3k, 3.60k show details from design of 10k.

1978, June 20 *Perf. 11½x11*

2185	A774	40th multicolored		16	6
2186	"	1k	"	45	10
2187	"	2k	"	90	20
2188	"	3k	"	1.30	30
2189	"	3.60k	"	1.55	35
	Nos. 2185–2189 (5)			4.36	1.01

Souvenir Sheet

Perf. 12x12

2190	A774	10k multicolored	4.75	3.00

PRAGA '78 International Philatelic Exhibition, Prague, Sept. 8–17. No. 2190 contains one stamp (50x40mm.); margin design shows black clock tower and red inscription. Size: 90x125mm. Sheet exists imperf.

Folk Dancers
A775

Photogravure and Engraved

1978, July 7 *Perf. 11½x12*

2191	A775	30h multicolored	12	5

25th Folklore Festival, Vychodna.

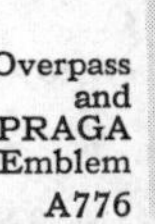

Overpass and PRAGA Emblem
A776

Designs (PRAGA Emblem and): 1k, 2k, Modern office buildings (diff.). 6k, Old and new Prague. 20k, Charles Bridge and Old Town, by Vincent Morstadt, 1828.

1978 *Perf. 12x11½*

2192	A776	60h blk. & multi.		25	8
2193	"	1k "	"	45	10
2194	"	2k "	"	90	20
2195	"	6k "	"	2.60	60

Souvenir Sheet

Engraved

2196	A776	20k multicolored	9.50

PRAGA 1978 International Philatelic Exhibition, Prague, Sept. 8–17. No. 2196 also commemorates 60th anniversary of Czechoslovak postage stamps. Size of No. 2196: 95x76mm. (stamp 61x45mm.).
Issue dates: Nos. 2192–2195, Sept. 8; No. 2196, Sept. 10.

Souvenir Sheet

Apollo's Companion, by Titian
A777

Design: No. 2197b, King Midas. Stamps show details from "Apollo Flaying Marsya" by Titian.

1978, Sept. 12 *Perf. 11½*

2197	Sheet of 2	9.50
a.	A777 10k multicolored	4.50
b.	" 10k "	4.50

Titian (1488–1576), Venetian painter. Margin of No. 2197 shows painting from which stamp designs were taken, black inscription and red PRAGA emblem. Size: 109x165mm. No. 2197 with dark blue marginal inscription "FIP" was sold only with entrance ticket to PRAGA Philatelic Exhibition.

Exhibition Hall
A778

Photogravure and Engraved

1978, Sept. 13 *Perf. 11½x11*

2198	A778	30h multicolored	12	5

22nd International Engineering Fair, Brno.

Postal Newspaper Service
A779

TV Screen, Headquarters and Logo
A780

Newspaper, Microphone
A781

Photogravure and Engraved

1978, Sept. 21 *Perf. 11½*

2199	A779	30h multicolored	12	5
2200	A780	30h "	12	5
2201	A781	30h "	12	5

25th anniversaries: Postal News Service (No. 2199); Day of the Press (No. 2200); Broadcasting and Television Day (No. 2201).

Sulky Race
A782

Pardubice Steeplechase: 10h, Falling horses and jockeys at fence. 30h, Race. 40h, Horses passing post. 1.60k, Hurdling. 4.40k, Winner.

1978, Oct. 6 *Perf. 12x11½*

2202	A782	10h multicolored		4	3
2203	"	20h	"	8	3
2204	"	30h	"	12	5
2205	"	40h	"	16	6
2206	"	1.60k	"	70	18
2207	"	4.40k	"	2.00	45
	Nos. 2202–2207 (6)			3.10	80

SEMI-POSTAL STAMPS.

Nos. B1–B123 were sold, in sets only, at 1½ times face value at the Philatelists' Window of the Prague P.O. for charity benefit. They were available for ordinary postage.

The overprints of Nos. B1–B123 have been well forged.

Austrian Stamps of 1916-18 Overprinted in Black or Blue

POŠTA ČESKOSLOVENSKÁ 1919

a

1919 *Perf. 12½.*

B1 A37 3h bright violet 10 10
B2 " 5h light green 10 10
B3 " 6h deep orange (Bl) 40 40
B4 " 6h deep orange (Bk) 800.00 750.00
B5 " 10h magenta 60 60
B6 " 12h light blue 50 50
B7 A42 15h dull red 5 5
B8 " 20h dark green 8 8
a. 20h green 50.00 40.00
B9 " 25h blue 15 15
B10 " 30h dull violet 20 20
B11 A39 40h olive green 20 20
B12 " 50h dark green 15 15
B13 " 60h deep blue 25 25
B14 " 80h orange brown 15 15
B15 " 90h red violet 50 50
B16 " 1k carmine, *yellow* (Bl) 30 30
B17 " 1k carmine, *yellow* (Bk) 55.00 55.00
B18 A40 2k light blue 2.25 2.25
B18A " 2k dark blue *2250.00 1400.00*
B19 " 3k carmine rose 35.00 25.00
B19A " 3k claret 650.00 550.00
B20 " 4k yellow green 10.00 6.00
B20A " 4k deep green 30.00 22.50
B21 " 10k violet 250.00 225.00
B21A " 10k dp. violet 350.00 275.00

The used price of No. B18A is for copies which have only a Czechoslovakian cancellation. Some of the copies of Austria No. 160 which were officially overprinted with type "a" and sold by the post office, had previously been used and lightly canceled with Austrian cancellations. These canceled-before-overprinting copies, which were postally valid, sell for about one-fourth as much.

Granite Paper.

B22 A40 2k light blue 2.25 2.25
B23 " 3k carmine rose 8.50 7.00
B24 " 4k yel. green *8000.00 8000.00*
B25 " 10k deep violet *6500.00 6500.00*

Excellent counterfeits of Nos. B1–B25 exist.

Austrian Newspaper Stamps Overprinted

POŠTA ČESKOSLOVENSKÁ 1919

b

Imperf.

On Stamp of 1908.

B26 N8 10h carmine *1000.00 900.00*

On Stamps of 1916.

B27 N9 2h brown 10 10
B28 " 4h green 15 15
B29 " 6h deep blue 13 13
B30 " 10h orange 3.50 3.00
B31 " 30h claret 1.25 1.25
Nos. B27-B31 (5) 5.13 4.63

Austrian Special Handling Stamps Overprinted in Blue or Black.

Stamps of 1916 Overprinted

POŠTA ČESKOSLOVENSKÁ 1919

c

Perf. 12½.

B32 SH1 2h claret, *yellow* (Bl) 25.00 20.00
B33 " 5h deep green, *yellow* *800.00 750.00*

Stamps of 1917 Overprinted

POŠTA ČESKOSLOVENSKÁ 1919

d

B34 SH2 2h claret, *yellow* (Bl) 8 8
a. Vert. pair, imperf. btwn. 200.00
B35 " 2h claret, *yellow* (Bk) 60.00 50.00
B36 " 5h green, *yellow* (Bk) 12 12

Austrian Air Post Stamps, Nos. C1–C3, Overprinted Type "c" Diagonally.

B37 A40 1.50k on 2k lilac 150.00 150.00
B38 " 2.50k on 3k ochre 150.00 150.00
B39 " 4k gray *500.00 450.00*

1919

Austrian Postage Due Stamps of 1908–13 Overprinted Type "b".

B40 D3 2h carmine *2500.00 2500.00*
B41 " 4h " 15.00 15.00
B42 " 6h " 8.00 6.00
B43 " 14h " 45.00 35.00
B44 " 25h " 35.00 27.50
B45 " 30h " 350.00 350.00
B46 " 50h " 600.00 525.00

Austria Nos. J49–J56 Overprinted Type "b".

B47 D4 5h rose red 10 10
B48 " 10h " 15 15
B49 " 15h " 15 15
B50 " 20h " 1.25 1.25
B51 " 25h " 80 80
B52 " 30h " 40 40
B53 " 40h " 1.00 1.00
B54 " 50h " 300.00 300.00

Austria Nos. J57–J59 Overprinted Type "a".

B55 D5 1k ultramarine 7.00 5.50
B56 " 5k " 35.00 30.00
B57 " 10k " 275.00 250.00

Austria Nos. J47–J48, J60–J63 Overprinted Type "c" Diagonally.

B58 A22 1h gray 15.00 15.00
B59 A23 15h on 2h violet 100.00 100.00
B60 A38 10h on 24h blue 75.00 75.00
B61 " 15h on 36h violet 40 40
B62 " 20h on 54h orange 75.00 75.00
B63 " 50h on 42h chocolate 40 40

Hungarian Stamps Overprinted Type "b".

Wmkd. Double Cross. (137)

1919 *Perf. 15.*

On Stamps of 1913-16.

B64 A4 1f slate *1000.00 1000.00*
B65 " 2f yellow 2.50 2.50
B66 " 3f orange 35.00 35.00
B67 " 6f olive green 3.00 3.00
B68 " 50f lake, *blue* 50 50
B69 " 60f green, *salmon* 27.50 27.50
B70 " 70f red brown *green* *1000.00 1000.00*

On Stamps of 1916.

B71 A8 10f rose 150.00 150.00
B72 " 15f violet 115.00 115.00

On Stamps of 1916-18.

B73 A9 2f brown orange 4 4
B74 " 3f red lilac 6 6
B75 " 5f green 5 5
B76 " 6f greenish blue 50 50
B77 " 10f rose red 1.50 1.50
B78 " 15f violet 20 20
B79 " 20f gray brown 7.50 7.50
B80 " 25f dull blue 60 60
B81 " 35f brown 6.50 6.50
B82 " 40f olive green 1.25 1.25

Overprinted Type "d".

B83 A10 50f red violet & lilac 70 70
B84 " 75f bright blue & pale blue 70 70
B85 " 80f yellow green & pale green 70 70
B86 " 1k red brown & claret 1.00 1.00
B87 " 2k olive brown & bistre 5.00 5.00
B88 " 3k dark violet & indigo 35.00 30.00
B89 " 5k dark brown & lt. brown 100.00 80.00
B90 " 10k violet brown & violet *725.00 650.00*

Overprinted Type "b".

On Stamps of 1918.

B91 A11 10f scarlet 10 10
B92 " 20f dark brown 10 10
B93 " 25f deep blue 2.00 60
B94 A12 40f olive green 2.00 1.50
B95 " 50f lilac 30.00 25.00

On Stamps of 1919.

B96 A13 10f red 7.50 7.50
B97 " 20f dark brown *2250.00 2250.00*

Same Overprint On Hungarian Newspaper Stamp of 1914.

Imperf.

B98 N5 (2f) orange 15 15

Same Overprint On Hungarian Special Delivery Stamp.

Perf. 15.

B99 SD1 2f gray green & red 15 15

Same Overprint On Hungarian Semi-Postal Stamps.

B100 SP3 10f+2f rose red 60 60
B101 SP4 15f+2f violet 75 75
B102 SP5 40f+2f brn. carmine 3.00 3.00
Nos. B98–B102 (5) 4.65 4.65

Hungarian Postage Due Stamps of 1903–18 Overprinted Type "b".

Wmkd. Crown in Circle. (135)

1919 *Perf. 11½, 12.*

B103 D1 50f green & black *425.00 425.00*

Wmkd. Crown. (136, 136a)

Perf. 11½, 12, 15.

B104 D1 1f green & black *350.00 350.00*
B105 " 2f " " *275.00 275.00*
B106 " 12f " " *1750.00 1750.00*
B107 " 50f " " *150.00 150.00*

Wmkd. Double Cross. (137)

Perf. 15.

On Stamps of 1914.

B110 D1 1f green & black 350.00 350.00
B111 " 2f " " 225.00 225.00
B112 " 5f " " 450.00 450.00
B113 " 12f " " *1100.00 1100.00*
B114 " 50f " " 125.00 125.00

On Stamps of 1915-18.

B115 D1 1f green & red 150.00 150.00
B116 " 2f " " 70 70
B117 " 5f " " 10.00 8.00
B118 " 6f " " 1.50 1.50
B119 " 10f green & red 40 40
a. Pair, one without overprint
B120 " 12f green & red 2.75 2.75
B121 " 15f green & red 7.25 5.25
B122 " 20f " " 1.00 1.00
B123 " 30f " " 40.00 40.00
Nos. B115–B123 (9) 213.60 209.60

Bohemian Lion Breaking its Chains SP1

Mother and Child SP2

1919 **Typographed.** **Unwmkd.**

Perf. 11½, 13½ and Compound.

Pinkish Paper.

B124 SP1 15(h) gray green 5 5
B125 " 25(h) dark brown 5 5
a. 25(h) light brown 3.50
B126 " 50(h) dark blue 5 5

Photogravure.

Yellowish Paper.

B127 SP2 75(h) slate 5 5
B128 " 100(h) brown violet 5 5
B129 " 120(h) violet, *yellow* 5 5
Nos. B124–B129 (6) 30 30

Nos. B124–B129 honor the Czecho-Slovak Legion. Nos. B124–B126 commemorate the first anniversary of Czechoslovak independence. Nos. B127–B129 were sold for the benefit of Legionnaires' orphans. Imperforates exist.

See No. 1581.

Regular Issues of Czechoslovakia Surcharged in Red:

a b

1920 *Perf. 13½.*

B130 A1 (*a*) 40(h)+20h bistre 75 75
B131 A2 (") 60(h)+20h green 75 75
B132 A4 (*b*) 125(h)+25(h) gray blue 3.50 3.50

President Masaryk SP3

Wmkd. Linden Leaves. (107)

1923 **Engraved** ***Perf. 13½x14½***

B133 SP3 50(h) gray green 50 50
B134 " 100(h) carmine 1.00 1.00
B135 " 200(h) blue 8.00 5.00
B136 " 300(h) dark brown 6.00 5.00

Issued in commemoration of the fifth anniversary of the Republic.

The monogram "CSP" (Ceskoslovenska Posta) is printed on top of the gum in brown on the back of each stamp. These stamps were sold at double their face values, the excess being given to the Red Cross and other charitable organizations.

International Olympic Congress Issue.

1925

Semi-Postal Stamps of 1923 Overprinted in Blue or Red

CONGRES OLYMP. INTERNAT. PRAHA 1925

B137 SP3 50(h) gray green (Bl) 7.50 6.00
B138 " 100(h) car. (Bl) 12.00 10.00
B139 " 200(h) blue (R) 90.00 80.00

These stamps were sold at double their face values, the excess being divided between a fund for post office clerks and the Olympic Games Committee.

Sokol Issue.

1926

Semi-Postal Stamps of 1923 Overprinted in Blue or Red

VIII. SLET VŠESOKOLSKÝ PRAHA 1926

B140 SP3 50(h) gray grn.(Bl) 7.00 5.00

B141 " 100(h) carmine(Bl) 7.00 5.00

B142 " 200(h) blue (R) 30.00 20.00
  a. Double overprint

B143 SP3 300(h) dk.brn.(R) 50.00 40.00

These stamps were sold at double their face values, the excess being given to the Congress of Sokols, June, 1926.

Midwife Presenting Newborn Child to its Father; after a Painting by Josef Manes
SP4 SP5

Engraved.

1936 *Perf. 12½* **Unwmkd.**

B144 SP4 50h+50h green 50 20

B145 SP5 1k+50h claret 1.00 50

B146 SP4 2k+50h blue 2.25 1.75

"Lullaby" by Stanislav Sucharda
SP6 SP7

1937 *Perf. 12½.*

B147 SP6 50h+50h dull green 50 50

B148 " 1k+50h rose lake 1.00 1.00

B149 SP7 2k+1k dull blue 2.00 2.00

President Masaryk and Little Girl in Native Costume
SP8

1938 *Perf. 12½*

B150 SP8 50h+50h deep green 50 50

B151 " 1k+50h rose lake 65 65

Souvenir Sheet.

Imperf.

B152 SP8 2k+3k black 4.00 4.00

No. B152 measures 72x90mm. with marginal inscriptions of "TGM" and Masaryk's signature.

Issued to commemorate the 88th anniversary of the birth of President Masaryk (1850–1937).

Souvenir Sheet.

Symbol of the Republic
SP9

1938 *Perf. 12½*

B153 SP9 2k(+8k) dark blue, sheet 3.50 3.00

Issued in sheets measuring 79x90mm. The surtax was devoted to national relief for refugees.

"Republic" and Congress Emblem
SP10

St. George Slaying the Dragon
SP11

1945 Engraved

B154 SP10 1.50(k)+1.50(k) carmine rose 20 10

B155 " 2.50(k)+2.50(k) blue 25 10

Issued to commemorate the Students' World Congress at Prague, Nov. 17, 1945.

1946

B156 SP11 2.40k+2.60k carmine rose 25 10

B157 " 4k+6k blue 50 10

Souvenir Sheet.

Imperf.

B158 SP11 4k+6k blue 75 75

No. B158 measures 70x90mm., with marginal inscriptions: "Pravda Vitezi Kveten 1945 1946." Nos. B156–B158 commemorate the 1st anniversary of Czechoslovakia's liberation. The surtax aided World War II orphans.

Souvenir Sheet.

SP13

1946, Aug. 3 *Imperf.*

B159 SP13 2.40k rose brown 75 75

Issued for the Brno National Stamp Exhibition, August, 1946.

The sheet measures 70x89mm. It was sold for 10k.

"You Went Away"
SP14

"You Remained Ours"
SP15

"You Came Back"
SP16

1946, Oct. 28 Photo. *Perf. 14*

B160 SP14 1.60k+1.40k red brown 15 12

B161 SP15 2.40k+2.60k scarlet 25 15

B162 SP16 4k+4k deep blue 50 30

The surtax was for repatriated Slovaks.

Barefoot Boy
SP17

Woman and Child
SP18

Designs: 2k+1k, Mother and child. 3k+1k, Little girl.

Engraved.

1948, Dec. 18 *Perf. 12½* **Unwmkd.**

B163 SP17 1.50(k)+1(k) rose lilac 15 8

B164 " 2(k)+1(k) deep blue 15 8

B165 " 3(k)+1(k) rose carmine 25 8

The surtax was for child welfare.

Labels alternate with stamps in sheets of Nos. B163–B165.

Inscribed: "Detem 1949."

1949, Dec. 18 *Perf. 12½*

Design: 3k+1k, Man lifting child.

B166 SP18 1.50k+50h gray *2.25* *1.25*

B167 " 3k+1k claret *3.00* *1.60*

The surtax was for child welfare.

Dove Carrying Olive Branch
SP19 SP20

1949, Dec. 18

B168 SP19 1.50k+50h claret *2.75* *1.25*

B169 SP20 3k+1k rose red *2.75* *1.25*

The surtax was for the Red Cross.

AIR POST STAMPS.

Stamps of 1918-19 Surcharged in Red, Blue or Green:

1920 *Imperf.* **Unwmkd.**

C1 A1 14k on 200(h) ultramarine (R) 12.00 12.00
  a. Inverted surcharge 60.00

C2 A2 24k on 500(h) red brown (Bl) 30.00 30.00
  a. Inverted surcharge 60.00

C3 A2 28k on 1000(h) violet (G) 25.00 25.00
  a. Inverted surcharge 60.00
  b. Double surch. 65.00

Perf. 14, 14x13½

C4 A1 14k on 200(h) ultramarine (R) 20.00 20.00
  a. Perf. 14x13½ 40.00 40.00

C5 A2 24k on 500(h) red brown (Bl) 35.00 35.00
  a. Perf. 14x13½ 55.00 55.00

C6 " 28k on 1000(h) violet (G) 35.00 35.00
  a. Inverted surcharge 70.00 70.00
  b. Perf. 14 *225.00* *225.00*

Excellent counterfeits of the overprint are known.

Stamps of 1920 Surcharged in Black or Violet:

1922, June 15

C7 A8 50(h) on 100(h) dark green (Bk) 2.50 2.50
  a. Inverted surcharge 50.00
  b. Double surcharge 45.00

C8 " 100(h) on 200(h) violet (Bk) 3.50 3.50
  a. Inverted surcharge 50.00

C9 " 250(h) on 400(h) brown (V) 8.00 8.00
  a. Inverted surcharge 50.00

Fokker Monoplane
AP3

Smolik S 19
AP4

Smolik S 19—AP5

Fokker over Prague—AP6

Engraved.

1930, Dec. 16 *Perf. 13½*

C10 AP3 50(h) deep green 10 10
  a. Perf. 12 2.00 2.00

C11 " 1k deep red 18 18
  a. Perf. 12 17.50 15.00
  b. Perf. 12x13½ 2.50 2.50

C12 AP4 2k dark green 50 30
  a. Perf. 12 12.50 12.50
  b. Perf. 13½ x12 7.50 7.50

C13 " 3k red violet 1.20 1.00

C14 AP5 4k indigo 65 60
  a. Perf. 12 5.00 5.00

C15 " 5k red brown 1.20 90
  a. Perf. 12 *500.00*

C16 AP6 10k violet blue 4.75 3.75
  a. 10k ultra. 6.00 4.50

C17 " 20k gray violet 4.75 3.00
  a. Perf. 12 4.00 3.50
  b. Perf. 13½x12 *200.00*

Nos. C10–C17 (8) 13.33 9.83

Two types exist of the 50h, 1k and 2k, and three types of the 3k, differing chiefly in the size of the printed area. A "no hill at left" variety of the 3k exists.

Imperforate copies of Nos. C10 to C17 are proofs.

Type of 1930 with hyphen in Cesko - Slovensko.

1939, Apr. 22 *Perf. 13½*

C18 AP3 30h rose lilac 10 7

Capt. Frantisek Novak
AP7

Plane over Bratislava Castle
AP8

Plane over Charles Bridge Prague
AP9

1946–47 *Perf. 12½*

C19 AP7 1.50k rose red 10 8
C20 " 5.50k dark gray blue 15 9
C21 " 9k sepia ('47) 55 6
C22 AP8 10k dull green 25 12
C23 AP7 16k violet 80 30
C24 AP8 20k light blue 1.50 60
C25 AP9 24k dark blue, *cream* 1.40 2.00
C26 " 24k rose lake 2.25 65
C27 " 50k dark gray blue 4.50 1.10
Nos. C19–C27 (9) 11.50 5.00

No. C25 was issued June 12, 1946, for use on the first Prague-New York flight.

Nos. C19 to C24, C26 and C27 Surcharged with New Value and Bars in Various Colors.

1949, Sept. 1 *Perf. 12½*

C28 AP7 1k on 1.50k rose red (Bl) 12 10
C29 " 3k on 5.50k dark gray blue (C) 18 12
C30 " 6k on 9k sepia (Br) 25 8
C31 " 7.50k on 16k vio. (C) 45 10
C32 AP8 8k on 10k dull green (G) 50 20
C33 " 12.50k on 20k light blue (Bl) 1.00 10
C34 AP9 15k on 24k rose lake (Bl) 2.00 30
C35 " 30k on 50k dk. gray blue (Bl) 2.50 75
Nos. C28–C35 (8) 7.00 1.75

Karlovy Vary (Karlsbad)
AP10

Designs: 10k, Piestany. 15k, Marienbad. 20k, Sliac.

1951, Apr. 2 Engraved *Perf. 13½*

C36 AP10 6k sage green 1.00 60
C37 " 10k deep plum 1.50 75
C38 " 15k deep ultramarine 2.25 90
C39 " 20k sepia *6.00 2.25*

View of Cesky Krumlov
AP11

Views: 1.55k, Olomouc. 2.35k, Banska Bystrica. 2.75k, Bratislava. 10k, Prague.

Perf. 11½

1955, Feb. 20 (10k) and Mar. 28

Cream Paper

C40 AP11 80h olive green 50 8
C41 " 1.55k violet brown 60 12
C42 " 2.35k violet blue 1.50 15
C43 " 2.75k rose brown 2.50 35
C44 " 10k indigo 4.00 1.25
Nos. C40–C44 (5) 9.10 1.95

Airline: Moscow-Prague-Paris
AP12

Design: 2.35k, Airline: Prague - Cairo - Beirut-Damascus.

Engraved and Photogravure.

1957, Oct. 15 *Perf. 11½* **Unwmkd.**

C45 AP12 75h ultra. & rose 65 10
C46 " 2.35k ultramarine & orange yellow 1.20 20

Planes at First Czech Aviation School, Pardubice
AP13

Design: 1.80k, Jan Kasper and flight of first Czech plane, 1909.

1959, Oct. 15

C47 AP13 1k gray & yellow 40 8
C48 " 1.80k black & pale blue 80 12

Issued to commemorate the 50th anniversary of Jan Kasper's first flight Aug. 25, 1909, at Pardubice.

Mail Coach, Plane and Arms of Bratislava
AP14

Design: 2.80k, Helicopter over Bratislava.

Engraved and Photogravure

1960, Sept. 24 *Perf. 11½* **Unwmkd.**

C49 AP14 1.60k dark blue & gray *2.00 1.00*
C50 " 2.80k green & buff *2.50 1.25*

Issued to publicize the National Stamp Exhibition, Bratislava, Sept. 24–Oct. 9.

Prague Hails Gagarin
AP15

Design: 1.80k, Gagarin, rocket and dove.

1961, June 22

C51 AP15 60h gray & carmine 20 5
C52 " 1.80k gray & blue 75 15

No. C51 commemorates Maj. Gagarin's visit to Prague, Apr. 28–29; No. C52 commemorates the first man in space, Yuri A. Gagarin, Apr. 12, 1961.

Dove and Nest of Eggs
AP16

Designs ("PRAGA" emblem and): 1.40k, Dove. 2.80k, Symbolic flower with five petals. 4.20k, Five leaves.

1962, May 14 **Engraved** *Perf. 14*

C53 AP16 80h multicolored 30 25
C54 " 1.40k black, dark red & blue 1.20 1.00
C55 " 2.80k multicolored 1.75 1.60
C56 " 4.20k " 2.75 2.50

Issued to publicize the "PRAGA 1962" World Exhibition of Postage Stamps, Aug. 18–Sept. 2, 1962.

Vostok 5 and Lt. Col. Valeri Bykovski—AP17

Design: 2.80k, Vostok VI and Lt. Valentina Tereshkova.

1963, June 26

C57 AP17 80h slate blue & pink 40 10
C58 " 2.80k dull red brn. & lt. blue 1.10 20

Issued to commemorate the space flights of Valeri Bykovski, June 14–19, and Valentina Tereshkova, first woman astronaut, June 16–19, 1963.

PRAGA 1962 Emblem, View of Prague and Plane
AP18

Designs: 60h, Istanbul '63 (Hagia Sophia). 1k, Philatec Paris 1964 (Ile de la Cité.) 1.40k, WIPA 1965 (Belvedere Palace, Vienna). 1.60k, SIPEX 1966 (Capitol, Washington). 2k, Amphilex '67 (harbor and old town, Amsterdam). 5k, PRAGA 1968 (View of Prague).

Engraved and Photogravure

1967, Oct. 30 *Perf. 11½*

Size: 30x50mm.

C59 AP18 30h choc., yellow & rose 10 5
C60 " 60h dark green, yel. & lilac 25 15
C61 " 1k blk., brick red & lt. blue 40 20
C62 " 1.40k violet, yel. & deep orange 55 28
C63 " 1.60k indigo, tan & lilac 65 35
C64 AP18 2k dark green, orange & red 80 40

Size: 40x50mm.

C65 AP18 5k multicolored *2.50 1.75*
Nos. C59–C65 (7) *5.25 3.18*

Issued to publicize the PRAGA 1968 World Stamp Exhibition, Prague, June 22–July 7, 1968. No. C59–C64 issued in sheets of 15 stamps and 15 bilingual labels. No. C65 issued in sheets of 4 stamps and one center label with commemorative inscription and airplane design.

Glider L-13
AP19

Airplanes: 60h, Sports plane L-40. 80h, Aero taxi L-200. 1k, Crop-spraying plane Z-37. 1.60k, Aerobatics trainer Z-526. 2k, Jet trainer L-29.

1967, Dec. 11 **Engr. and Photo.**

C66 AP19 30h multicolored 10 4
C67 " 60h " 22 7
C68 " 80h " 30 10
C69 " 1k " 36 12
C70 " 1.60k " 55 20
C71 " 2k " *1.25 60*
Nos. C66–C71 (6) *2.78 1.13*

Charles Bridge, Prague, and Balloon
AP20

Astronaut, Moon and Manhattan
AP21

Designs: 1k, Belvedere, fountain and early plane. 2k, Hradcany, Prague, and airship.

1968, Feb. 5 *Perf. 11½* **Unwmkd.**

C72 AP20 60h multicolored 18 6
C73 " 1k " 30 15
C74 " 2k " 60 30

Issued to publicize the PRAGA 1968 World Stamp Exhibition, Prague, June 22–July 7, 1968.

1969, July 21 **Engr. and Photo.**

Design: 3k, Lunar landing module and J. F. Kennedy Airport, New York.

C75 AP21 60h black, violet, yel. & silver 25 10
C76 " 3k blk., blue, ocher & silver 1.25 55

Issued to commemorate man's first landing on the moon, July 20, 1969, U. S. astronauts Neil A. Armstrong and Col. Edwin E. Aldrin, Jr., with Lieut. Col. Michael Collins piloting Apollo 11.

Nos. C75–C76 printed with label inscribed with names of astronauts and European date of moon landing.

TU-104A over Bitov Castle
AP22

Designs: 60h, IL-62 over Bezdez Castle. 1.40k, TU-134A over Orava Castle. 1.90k, IL-18 over Veveri Castle. 2.40k, IL-14 over Pernstejn Castle. 3.60k, TU-154 over Trencin Castle.

1973, Oct. 24 Engr. *Perf. 11½*

C77 AP22 30h multicolored 12 3
C78 " 60h " 24 8
C79 " 1.40k " 55 15
C80 " 1.90k " 75 22
C81 " 2.40k " *2.00* *50*
C82 " 3.60k " 1.50 45
Nos. C77-C82 (6) *5.16* *1.43*

50 years of Czechoslovakian aviation.

Old Water Tower and Manes Hall—AP23

Designs (Praga 1978 Emblem, Plane Silhouette and): 1.60k, Congress Hall. 2k, Powder Tower (vert.). 2.40k, Charles Bridge and Old Bridge Tower. 4k, Old Town Hall on Old Town Square (vert.). 6k, Prague Castle and St. Vitus Cathedral (vert.).

Engraved and Photogravure

1976, June 23 *Perf. 11½*

C83 AP23 60h indigo & multi. 24 8
C84 " 1.60k indigo & multi. 68 18
C85 " 2k indigo & multi. 90 20
C86 " 2.40k indigo & multi. 1.00 30
C87 " 4k indigo & multi. 1.75 45
C88 " 6k indigo & multi. 2.50 70
Nos. C83-C88 (6) 7.07 1.91

PRAGA 1978 International Philatelic Exhibition, Prague, Sept. 8–17, 1978.

Zeppelin, 1909 and 1928
AP24

Designs (PRAGA '78 Emblem and): 1k, Ader, 1890, L'Eole and Dunn, 1914. 1.60k, Jeffries-Blanchard balloon, 1785. 2k, Otto Lilienthal's glider, 1896. 4.40k, Jan Kaspar's plane, Pardubice, 1911.

Photogravure and Engraved

1977, Sept. 15 *Perf. 11½*

C89 AP24 60h multicolored 24 8
C90 " 1k " 44 10
C91 " 1.60k " 68 18
C92 " 2k " 88 25
C93 " 4.40k " 1.95 60
Nos. C89-C93 (5) 4.19 1.21

History of aviation.

Prices of premium quality never hinged stamps will be in excess of catalogue price.

SPECIAL DELIVERY STAMPS.

Doves
SD1

Typographed.

1919-20 *Imperf.* Unwmkd.

E1 SD1 2(h) red violet, *yellow* 5 5
E2 " 5(h) yellow green, *yellow* 5 5
E3 " 10(h) red brown, *yellow* ('20) 60 45

1921 White Paper.

E1a SD1 2(h) red violet 5.00
E2a " 5(h) yellow green 3.00
E3a " 10(h) red brown 75.00

It is doubted that Nos. E1a–E3a were regularly issued.

PERSONAL DELIVERY STAMPS.

PD1

Design: No. EX2, "D" in each corner.

Photogravure

1937 *Perf. 13½* Unwmkd.

EX1 PD1 50h blue 30 30
EX2 " 50h carmine 30 30

PD3

1946 *Perf. 13½*

EX3 PD3 2k deep blue 25 20

POSTAGE DUE STAMPS.

D1 D2

Typographed.

1918-20 *Imperf.* Unwmkd.

J1 D1 5(h) deep bistre 3 3
J2 " 10(h) " 4 3
J3 " 15(h) " 6 3
J4 " 20(h) " 6 3
J5 " 25(h) " 10 8
J6 " 30(h) " 6 3
J7 " 40(h) " 45 20
J8 " 50(h) " 25 3
J9 " 100(h) black brown 45 3
J10 " 250(h) orange 9.00 70
J11 " 400(h) scarlet 9.00 70
J12 " 500(h) gray green 2.00 10
J13 " 1000(h) purple 3.00 6
J14 " 2000(h) dark blue 16.00 20
Nos. J1-J14 (14) 40.50 2.25

1922 Blue Surcharge

J15 D2 20(h) on 3(h) red violet 30 15
J16 " 50(h) on 75(h) slate 75 4
J17 " 60(h) on 80(h) olive green 50 10
J18 " 100(h) on 80(h) olive green 50 4
J19 " 200(h) on 400(h) purple 80 5
Nos. J15-J19 (5) 2.85 38

1923-26 Violet Surcharge.

J20 D2 10(h) on 3(h) red violet 6 4
J21 " 20(h) on 3(h) red violet 6 4
J22 " 30(h) on 3(h) red violet 13 5
J23 " 40(h) on 3(h) red violet 20 3
J24 " 50(h) on 75(h) slate 1.00 5
J25 " 60(h) on 50(h) dark violet ('26) 1.15 65
J26 " 60(h) on 50(h) dark blue ('26) 1.50 80
J27 " 60(h) on 75(h) slate 50 6
J28 " 100(h) on 80(h) olive green 37.50 8
J29 " 100(h) on 120(h) gray black 1.00 4
J30 " 100(h) on 400(h) purple ('26) 50 6
J31 " 100(h) on 1000(h) deep violet ('26) 1.40 10
Nos. J20-J31 (12) 45.00 2.00

Nos. J15, J19, J20, J22, J23 and J30 were surcharged on stamps of type A1; others of the groups J15 to J31 were surcharged on stamps of type A2.

Postage Due Stamp of 1918-20 Surcharged in Violet **50**

1924

J32 D1 50(h) on 400(h) scarlet 1.00 5
J33 " 60(h) on 400(h) " 3.00 30
J34 " 100(h) on 400(h) " 2.00 5

Postage Due Stamps of 1918-20 Surcharged with New Values in Violet as in 1924.

1925

J35 D1 10(h) on 5(h) bistre 6 6
J36 " 20(h) on 5(h) " 6 6
J37 " 30(h) on 15(h) " 13 8
J38 " 40(h) on 15(h) " 25 4
J39 " 50(h) on 250(h) org. 1.00 4
J40 " 60(h) on 250(h) " 1.50 22
J41 " 100(h) on 250(h) " 3.00 15
Nos. J35-J41 (7) 6.00 65

Stamps of 1918-19 Surcharged with New Values in Violet as in 1922.

1926 *Perf. 14, 11½*

J42 D2 30(h) on 15(h) red 35 8
J43 " 40(h) on 15(h) red 20 8

D3 D4

Violet Surcharge.

1926 *Perf. 14*

J44 D3 30(h) on 100(h) dark green 7 3
J45 " 40(h) on 200(h) violet 8 3
J46 " 40(h) on 300(h) verm. 45 10
a. Perf. 14x13½ 25.00
J47 " 50(h) on 500(h) deep green 50 3
a. Perf. 14x13½ 2.50
J48 " 60(h) on 400(h) brown 40 6
J49 " 100(h) on 600(h) deep violet 2.50 3
a. Perf. 14x13½ 25.00 1.00
Nos. J44-J49 (6) 4.00 28

1927 Violet Surcharge.

J50 D4 100(h) dark brown 60 5
a. Perf. 13½ 200.00 8.00

Surcharged with New Value in Violet.

1927

J51 D4 40(h) on 185(h) orange 10 3
J52 " 50(h) on 20(h) car. 20 4
a. 50 (h) on 50 (h) carmine (error) 5000.00
J53 " 50(h) on 150(h) rose 30 4
a. Perf. 13½ 9.00 1.50
J54 " 60(h) on 25 (h) brown 40 15
J55 " 60(h) on 185(h) orange 40 4
J56 " 100(h) on 25(h) brown 50 4
Nos. J50-J56 (7) 2.50 39

No. J52a is known only used.

No. J12 Surcharged in Violet **200**

1927 *Imperf.*

J57 D1 200(h) on 500(h) gray green 3.50 1.75

D5 D6

1928 *Perf. 14x13½.*

J58 D5 5h dark red 5 3
J59 " 10h " 5 3
J60 " 20h " 6 3
J61 " 30h " 6 3
J62 " 40h " 6 3
J63 " 50h " 5 3
J64 " 60h " 5 3
J65 " 1k ultramarine 25 3
J66 " 2k " 45 3
J67 " 5k " 90 3
J68 " 10k " 2.00 4
J69 " 20k " 3.50 6
Nos. J58-J69 (12) 7.48 40

1946-48 Photogravure *Perf. 14*

J70 D6 10h dark blue 4 3
J71 " 20h " 6 3
J72 " 50h " 10 3
J73 " 1k carmine rose 15 3
J74 " 1.20k " 20 3
J75 " 1.50k " ('48) 40 3
J76 " 1.60k " 30 3
J77 " 2k " ('48) 30 3
J78 " 2.40k " 45 3
J79 " 3k " 75 3
J80 " 5k " 1.75 3
J81 " 6k " ('48) 2.00 3
Nos. J70-J81 (12) 6.50 36

D7 D8

1954-55 Engraved *Perf. 12½, 11½*

J82 D7 5h gray green ('55) 3 3
J83 " 10h " ('55) 4 3
J84 " 30h " 10 3
J85 " 50h " ('55) 15 3
J86 " 60h " ('55) 18 3
J87 " 95h " 40 3
J88 D8 1k violet 40 3
J89 " 1.20k " ('55) 40 3
J90 " 1.50k " 45 3
J91 " 1.60k " ('55) 50 3
J92 " 2k " 85 3
J93 " 3k " 90 3
J94 " 5k " ('55) 1.60 4
Nos. J82-J94 (13) 6.00 40

Perf. 11½ stamps are from a 1963 printing which lacks the 95h, 1.60k, and 2k.

Stylized Flower
D9

Designs: Various stylized flowers.

Engraved and Photogravure

1971-72 *Perf. 11½*

J95 D9 10h violet blue & pink ('72) 8 3
J96 " 20h vio. & lt. bl. ('72) 10 3
J97 " 30h emerald & lilac rose ('72) 10 3
J98 " 60h purple & emerald ('72) 20 3
J99 " 80h orange & violet blue ('72) 27 3

J100	D9	1k dark red & emerald ('72)	50	3
J101	"	1.20k grn. & org. ('72)	40	3
J102	"	2k blue & red ('72)	80	4
J103	"	3k blk. & yel. ('72)	95	10
J104	"	4k brown & ultra. ('72)	1.60	8
J105	"	5.40k red & lilac	2.00	10
J106	"	6k brick red & orange ('72)	2.00	12
		Nos. J95-J106 (12)	9.00	65

OFFICIAL STAMPS.

Coat of Arms
O1

Lithographed.

1945 *Perf. 10½x10.* **Unwmkd.**

O1	O1	50h deep slate green	6	5
O2	"	1k deep blue violet	8	5
O3	"	1.20k plum	15	10
O4	"	1.50k crimson rose	10	4
O5	"	2.50k bright ultramarine	15	10
O6	"	5k dark violet brown	30	20
O7	"	8k rose pink	50	35
		Nos. O1-O7 (7)	1.34	89

Redrawn.

1947 **Photogravure.** ***Perf. 14.***

O8	O1	60h red	3	3
O9	"	80h dark olive green	3	3
O10	"	1k dark lilac gray	4	3
O11	"	1.20k deep plum	8	3
O12	"	2.40k dark carmine rose	12	6
O13	"	4k bright ultramarine	20	10
O14	"	5k dark violet brown	25	12
O15	"	7.40k purple	42	20
		Nos. O8-O15 (8)	1.17	60

There are many minor changes in design, size of numerals, etc., of the redrawn stamps.

NEWSPAPER STAMPS.

Windhover
N1

Typographed.

1918-20 *Imperf.* **Unwmkd.**

P1	N1	2(h) gray green	3	3
P2	"	5(h) green ('20)	3	3
		a. 5(h) dark green	30	8
P3	"	6(h) red	25	17
P4	"	10(h) dull violet	3	3
P5	"	20(h) blue	6	3
P6	"	30(h) gray brown	15	3
P7	"	50(h) orange ('20)	25	3
P8	"	100(h) red brown ('20)	35	5
		Nos. P1-P8 (8)	1.15	40

Nos. P1 to P8 exist privately perforated.

Stamps of 1918–19 Surcharged in Violet

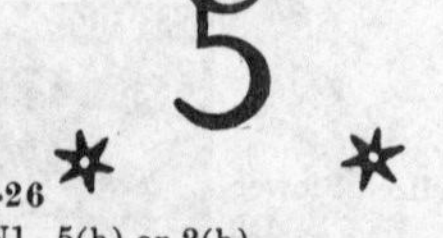

1925-26

P9	N1	5(h) on 2(h) gray green	60	30
P10	"	5(h) on 6(h) red ('26)	45	30

Special Delivery Stamps of 1918-20 Overprinted in Violet **NOVINY**

1926

P11	SD1	5(h) apple green, *yellow*	22	15
		a. 5(h) dull green, *yellow*	50	30
P12	SD1	10(h) red brown, *yellow*	15	10

With Additional Surcharge of New Value.

P13	SD1	5(h) on 2(h) red vio., *yellow*	15	3

Newspaper Stamps of 1918-19 Overprinted in Violet **O.T.**

1934

P14	N1	10(h) dull violet	5	3
P15	"	20(h) blue	5	5
P16	"	30(h) gray brown	15	10

Overprinted for use by commercial firms only.

Carrier Pigeon
N2

1937 ***Imperf.***

P17	N2	2h bistre brown	3	3
P18	"	5h dull blue	3	3
P19	"	7h red orange	3	3
P20	"	9h emerald	3	3
P21	"	10h henna brown	3	3
P22	"	12h ultramarine	5	5
P23	"	20h dark green	5	5
P24	"	50h dark brown	5	5
P25	"	1k olive gray	10	5
		Nos. P17-P25 (9)	40	35

Bratislava Philatelic Exhibition Issue.

Souvenir Sheet.

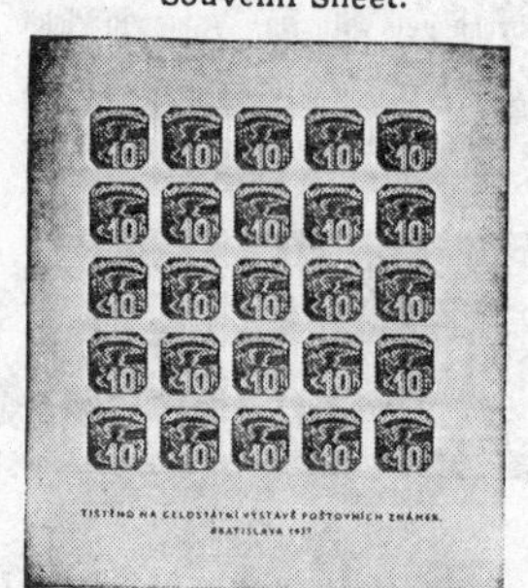

N3

1937 ***Imperf.***

P26	N3	10h henna brown, sheet of 25	2.50	2.50

Issued in sheets measuring 150x165mm.

Newspaper Delivery Boy
N4

Typographed.

1945 *Imperf.* **Unwmkd.**

P27	N4	5h dull blue	3	3
P28	"	10h red	3	3
P29	"	15h emerald	3	3
P30	"	20h dark slate green	3	3
P31	"	25h bright red violet	3	3
P32	"	30h ochre	3	3
P33	"	40h red orange	3	3
P34	"	50h brown red	6	3
P35	"	1k slate gray	10	4
P36	"	5k deep violet blue	18	10
		Nos. P27-P36 (10)	55	38

Czechoslovak Legion Post

The Czechoslovak Legion in Siberia issued these stamps for use on its mail and that of local residents. Forgeries exist.

Urn and Cathedral at Irkutsk
A1

Armored Railroad Car
A2

Sentinel
A3

Lion of Bohemia
A4

1919 **Lithographed.** ***Perf. 11½.***

1	A1	25 (k) carmine	16.50
		a. Imperf.	15.00
2	A2	50 (k) yellow green	16.50
		a. Imperf.	15.00
3	A3	1 (r) red brown	32.50
		a. Imperf.	30.00

Originals of Nos. 1–3 and 1a–3a have yellowish gum. Ungummed remainders, which were given a white gum, exist imperforate and perforated 11½ and 14. Price per set, $3.

Embossed.

Perce en Arc in Blue.

4	A4	(25k) blue & rose	2.00

Two types: (I) Six points on star-like mace head at right of goblet; large saber handle; measures 19⅓ x 24⅔ mm. (II) Five points on mace head; small saber handle; measures 20 x 25mm.

1920 No. 4 Overprinted **1920**

5	A4	(25k) blue & rose	6.50

Both types of No. 4 received overprint.

No. 5 Surcharged with New Values in Green **2**

6	A4	2 (k) blue & rose	25.00
7	"	3 (k) " "	25.00
8	"	5 (k) " "	25.00
9	"	10 (k) " "	25.00
10	"	15 (k) " "	25.00
11	"	25 (k) " "	25.00
12	"	35 (k) " "	25.00
13	"	50 (k) " "	25.00
14	"	1r " "	25.00
		Nos. 6-14 (9)	225.00

BOHEMIA AND MORAVIA

(bô·hē'mĭ·ȧ & mô·rā'vĭ·ȧ)

German Protectorate.

Stamps of Czechoslovakia, 1928-39, Overprinted in Black

BÖHMEN u. MÄHREN
ČECHY a MORAVA

Perf. 10, 12½, 12x12½.

1939, July 15 **Unwmkd.**

No.	Type	Description	Unused	Used
1	A29	5h dark ultramarine	8	12
2	"	10h brown	8	12
3	"	20h red	8	12
4	"	25h green	8	12
5	"	30h red violet	10	15
6	A61a	40h dark blue	1.75	2.10
7	A85	50h deep green	10	12
8	A63	60h dull violet	1.75	2.10
9	A60	1k rose lake (212)	35	50
10	"	1k rose lake (256)	28	50
11	A64	1.20k rose lilac	2.00	2.75
12	A65	1.50k carmine	2.00	2.75
13	A79	1.60k olive green	2.00	2.75
		a. "Mähnen"	17.50	22.50
14	A66	2k dark blue green	75	80
15	A67	2.50k dark blue	2.25	2.75
16	A68	3k brown	3.00	3.50
17	A70	4k dark violet	3.00	3.50
18	A71	5k green	3.25	4.50
19	A72	10k blue	5.00	6.50
		Nos. 1-19 (19)	27.90	35.75

The size of the overprint varies with the size of the stamps, Nos. 1 to 10 measure 17½x15½mm., Nos. 11 to 16 measure 19x18mm., Nos. 17 and 19 measure 28x17½ and No. 18 measures 23½x23mm.

Linden Leaves and Closed Buds
A1

1939-41 **Photogravure** ***Perf. 14***

No.	Type	Description	Unused	Used
20	A1	5h dark blue	3	3
21	"	10h black brown	3	3
22	"	20h crimson	3	3
23	"	25h dark blue green	13	15
24	"	30h deep plum	5	10
24A	"	30h golden brown ('41)	4	3
25	"	40h orange ('40)	10	5
26	"	50h slate green ('40)	4	3
		Nos. 20-26 (8)	45	45

See also Nos. 49-51.

Castle at Zvikov
A2

Karlstein Castle
A3

St. Barbara's Church, Kutna Hora
A4

Cathedral at Prague
A5

Brno Cathedral
A6

Town Square, Olomouc
A7

1939 **Engraved.** ***Perf. 12½.***

No.	Type	Description	Unused	Used
27	A2	40h dark blue	5	4
28	A3	50h dark blue green	4	3
29	A4	60h dull violet	4	4
30	A5	1k deep rose	4	3
31	A6	1.20k rose lilac	35	35
32	"	1.50k rose carmine	8	4
33	A7	2k dark blue green	25	6
34	"	2.50k dark blue	15	6
		Nos. 27-34 (8)	1.00	65

No. 31 measures 23½x29½mm., while No. 42 measures 18½x23mm.

Zlin—A8

Iron Works at Moravská Ostrava
A9

Prague
A10

1939-40

No.	Type	Description	Unused	Used
35	A8	3k dull rose violet	10	5
36	A9	4k slate ('40)	10	5
37	A10	5k green	1.00	15
38	"	10k light ultramarine	60	40
39	"	20k yellow brown	1.20	1.00
		Nos. 35-39 (5)	3.00	1.65

Types of 1939 and

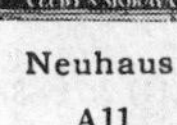

Neuhaus
A11

Lainsitz Bridge near Bechyne
A14

Pernstein Castle
A12

Samson Fountain Budweis
A15

Pardubice Castle
A13

Kromeriz
A16

Wallenstein Palace, Prague
A17

1940 **Engraved.** ***Perf. 12½***

No.	Type	Description	Unused	Used
40	A11	50h dark blue green	10	8
41	A12	80h deep blue	10	8
42	A6	1.20k violet brown	35	8
43	A13	2k gray green	10	4
44	A14	5k dark blue green	10	5
45	A15	6k brown violet	15	15
46	A16	8k slate green	15	15
47	A17	10k blue	60	15
48	A10	20k sepia	1.35	80
		Nos. 40-48 (9)	3.00	1.58

No. 42 measures 18½x23mm.; No. 31, 23½x29½mm.

Types of 1939-40.

1941

No.	Type	Description	Unused	Used
49	A1	60h violet	5	4
50	"	80h red orange	6	5
51	"	1k brown	6	3
52	A5	1.20k rose red	5	3
53	A4	1.50k lilac rose	8	4
53A	A13	2k light blue	8	10
53B	A6	2.50k ultramarine	12	10
53C	A12	3k olive	15	6
		Nos. 49-53C (8)	65	45

Nos. 49-51 show buds open. Nos. 52 and 53B measure 18¾x23½mm. and have no inscriptions below design.

Antonin Dvorák
A18

1941, Aug. 25 **Engr.** ***Perf. 12½***

No.	Type	Description	Unused	Used
54	A18	60h dull lilac	10	15
55	"	1.20k sepia	20	30

Birth centenary of Antonin Dvorák (1841-1904), composer.

Labels alternate with stamps in sheets of Nos. 54-55.

Farming Scene
A19

Factories
A20

1941, Sept. 7 **Photo.** ***Perf. 13½***

No.	Type	Description	Unused	Used
56	A19	30h dark red brown	4	6
57	"	60h dark green	4	10
58	A20	1.20k dark plum	10	20
59	"	2.50k sapphire	15	28

Issued to publicize the Prague Fair.

Nos. 52 and 53B Overprinted in Blue or Red

1942, Mar. 15 ***Perf. 12½***

No.	Type	Description	Unused	Used
60	A5	1.20k rose red (Bl)	25	35
61	A6	2.50k ultramarine (R)	40	35

Issued to commemorate the third anniversary of the Protectorate of Bohemia and Moravia.

Adolf Hitler
A21

17th Century Messenger
A22

1942 **Photogravure.** ***Perf. 14.***

Size: 17½x21½mm.

No.	Type	Description	Unused	Used
62	A21	10(h) gray black	3	3
63	"	30(h) bistre brown	3	3
64	"	40(h) slate blue	3	3
65	"	50(h) slate green	3	3
66	"	60(h) purple	3	3
67	"	80(h) orange vermilion	4	4

Engraved.

Perf. 12½

Size: 18x21mm.

No.	Type	Description	Unused	Used
68	A21	1k dull brown	5	4
69	"	1.20(k) carmine	5	3
70	"	1.50(k) claret	5	3
71	"	1.60(k) Prussian green	5	5
72	"	2k light blue	5	4
73	"	2.40(k) fawn	6	12

Size: 18½x24mm.

No.	Type	Description	Unused	Used
74	A21	2.50(k) ultramarine	5	4
75	"	3k olive green	6	4
76	"	4k bright red violet	6	4
77	"	5k myrtle green	8	4
78	"	6k claret brown	8	6
79	"	8k indigo	12	8

Size: 23½x29¾mm.

No.	Type	Description	Unused	Used
80	A21	10k dark gray green	15	10
81	"	20k gray violet	20	20
82	"	30k red	60	65
83	"	50k deep blue	80	90
		Nos. 62-83 (22)	2.70	2.65

1943, Jan. 10 **Photo.** ***Perf. 13½***

No.	Type	Description	Unused	Used
84	A22	60(h) dark rose violet	5	5

Stamp Day.

Scene from "Die Meistersinger"—A23

Richard Wagner
A24

Scene from "Siegfried"
A25

1943, May 22

No.	Type	Description	Unused	Used
85	A23	60(h) violet	5	4
86	A24	1.20(k) carmine rose	6	8
87	A25	2.50(k) deep ultra.	6	10

130th anniversary of the birth of Richard Wagner (1813-1883).

St. Vitus' Cathedral, Prague — A26

Adolf Hitler — A27

1944, Nov. 21 Engr. *Perf. 12½*

88 A26 1.50(k) dull rose brown 4 8
89 " 2.50(k) dull lilac blue 5 15

1944

90 A27 4.20(k) green 12 20

SEMI-POSTAL STAMPS.

Nurse and Wounded Soldier — SP1

Red Cross Nurse and Patient — SP2

Perf. 13½

1940, June 29 Photo. Unwmkd.

B1 SP1 60h+40h indigo 40 40
B2 " 1.20k+80h deep plum 65 60

Surtax for German Red Cross.
Labels alternate with stamps in sheets of Nos. B1–B2.

1941, Apr. 20

B3 SP2 60h+40h indigo 20 30
B4 " 1.20k+80h deep plum 20 40

Surtax for German Red Cross.
Labels alternate with stamps in sheets of Nos. B3–B4.

Old Theater, Prague — SP3

Wolfgang Amadeus Mozart — SP4

1941, Oct. 26

B5 SP3 30h+30h brown 5 5
B6 " 60h+60h Prus. green 10 10
B7 SP4 1.20k+1.20k scarlet 10 10
B8 " 2.50k+2.50k dark blue 20 30

150th anniversary of Mozart's death.
Labels alternate with stamps in sheets of Nos. B5–B8. The labels with Nos. B5–B6 show two bars of Mozart's opera "Don Giovanni." Those with Nos. B7–B8 show Mozart's piano.

Adolf Hitler — SP5

Nurse and Soldier — SP6

1942, Apr. 20 Engr. *Perf. 12½*

B9 SP5 30(h)+20(h) dull brown violet 4 4
B10 " 60(h)+40(h) dull green 4 4
B11 SP5 1.20(k)+80(h) deep claret 6 6
B12 " 2.50(k)+1.50(k) dull blue 10 16

Issued to commemorate Hitler's 53rd birthday.

1942, Sept. 4 *Perf. 13½*

B13 SP6 60h+40h deep blue 7 7
B14 " 1.20(k)+80(h) deep plum 8 8

The surtax aided the German Red Cross.

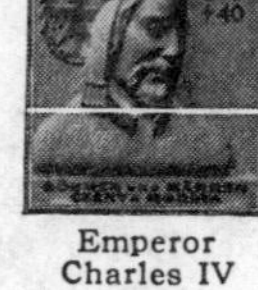

Emperor Charles IV — SP7

Peter Parler — SP8

John the Blind, King of Bohemia — SP9

Adolf Hitler — SP10

1943, Jan. 29

B15 SP7 60(h)+40(h) violet 6 5
B16 SP8 1.20(k)+80(h) car. 8 6
B17 SP9 2.50(k)+1.50(k) violet blue 12 14

The surtax was for the benefit of the German wartime winter relief.

1943, Apr. 20 Engr. *Perf. 12½*

B18 SP10 60(h)+1.40(k) dull violet 8 8
B19 " 1.20(k)+3.80(k) carmine 10 12

Issued to commemorate Hitler's 54th birthday.

Deathmask of Reinhard Heydrich — SP11

Eagle and Red Cross — SP12

1943, May 28 Photo. *Perf. 13½*

B20 SP11 60(h)+440(h) black 25 25

No. B20 exists in a miniature sheet containing a single copy. It was given to officials attending Heydrich's funeral.

1943, Sept. 16 *Perf. 13*

B21 SP12 1.20(k)+8.80(k) black & carmine 7 10

The surtax aided the German Red Cross.

Native Costumes — SP13

Nazi Emblem and Arms of Bohemia, Moravia — SP14

1944, Mar. 15 *Perf. 13½*

B22 SP13 1.20(k)+3.80(k) rose lake 10 10
B23 SP14 4.20(k)+10.80(k) golden brown 10 10
B24 SP13 10k+20k sapphire 15 20

Fifth anniversary of protectorate.

Adolf Hitler — SP15

Friedrich Smetana — SP16

1944, Apr. 20

B25 SP15 60(h)+1.40(k) olive black 4 5
B26 " 1.20(k)+3.80(k) slate green 6 10

Issued to commemorate Hitler's 55th birthday.

1944, May 12 Engr. *Perf. 12½*

B27 SP16 60(h)+1.40(k) dark gray green 4 6
B28 " 1.20(k)+3.80(k) brown carmine 10 15

Issued to commemorate the 60th anniversary of the death of Friedrich Smetana (1824-84), Czech composer and pianist.

PERSONAL DELIVERY STAMPS.

PD1

Photogravure.

1939–40 *Perf. 13½* Unwmkd.

EX1 PD1 50h indigo & bl. ('40) 40 60
EX2 " 50h carmine & rose 50 60

POSTAGE DUE STAMPS.

D1

Typographed.

1939–40 *Perf. 14* Unwmkd.

J1	D1	5h dark carmine	3	3
J2	"	10h "	3	3
J3	"	20h "	3	3
J4	"	30h "	3	3
J5	"	40h "	3	3
J6	"	50h "	4	3
J7	"	60h "	4	3
J8	"	80h "	5	3
J9	"	1k bright ultramarine	8	4
J10	"	1.20k " ('40)	15	15
J11	"	2k "	30	35
J12	"	5k "	30	35
J13	"	10k "	60	70
J14	"	20k "	1.00	1.20
		Nos. J1–J14 (14)	2.71	3.03

OFFICIAL STAMPS.

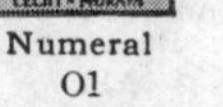

Numeral — O1

Eagle — O2

Typographed.

1941, Jan. 1 *Perf. 14* Unwmkd.

O1	O1	30h ochre	3	3
O2	"	40h indigo	3	3
O3	"	50h emerald	3	3
O4	"	60h slate green	3	3
O5	"	80h orange red	15	12
O6	"	1k red brown	5	3
O7	"	1.20k carmine	6	5
O8	"	1.50k deep plum	10	10
O9	"	2k bright blue	10	5
O10	"	3k olive	10	10
O11	"	4k red violet	20	20
O12	"	5k orange yellow	40	40
		Nos. O1–O12 (12)	1.28	1.17

1943, Feb. 15

O13	O2	30(h) bistre	3	3
O14	"	40(h) indigo	3	3
O15	"	50(h) yellow green	3	3
O16	"	60(h) deep violet	3	3
O17	"	80(h) orange red	3	3
O18	"	1k chocolate	3	4
O19	"	1.20(k) carmine	3	3
O20	"	1.50(k) brown red	4	6
O21	"	2k light blue	6	6
O22	"	3k olive	6	6
O23	"	4k red violet	8	8
O24	"	5k dark green	15	12
		Nos. O13–O24 (12)	60	60

NEWSPAPER STAMPS.

Carrier Pigeon

N1 N2

Typographed.

1939 *Imperf.* Unwmkd.

P1	N1	2h ochre	3	3
P2	"	5h ultramarine	3	3
P3	"	7h red orange	3	3
P4	"	9h emerald	3	3
P5	"	10h henna brown	4	3
P6	"	12h dark ultramarine	5	5
P7	"	20h dark green	6	10
P8	"	50h red brown	8	15
P9	"	1k greenish gray	30	35
		Nos. P1–P9 (9)	65	80

1940

No. P5 Overprinted in Black **GD-OT**

P10 N1 10h henna brown 15 25

Overprinted for use by commercial firms.

1943, Feb. 15

P11	N2	2(h) ochre	3	3
P12	"	5(h) light blue	3	3
P13	"	7(h) red orange	3	3
P14	"	9(h) emerald	3	3
P15	"	10(h) henna brown	3	3
P16	"	12(h) dark ultramarine	3	3
P17	"	20(h) dark green	4	3
P18	"	50(h) red brown	4	6
P19	"	1k slate green	4	8
		Nos. P11–P19 (9)	30	35

CARPATHO-UKRAINE
(kär·pä'thô-ū'krān)

A former province of Czechoslovakia known as Ruthenia, which in 1938 became an autonomous Czechoslovak state as a result of the Munich Agreement. On Mar. 16, 1939, it was incorporated in the Kingdom of Hungary.

100 Haleru = 1 Koruna

View of Jasina
A1

Perf. 12½

1939, Mar. 15 Engr. Unwmkd.

1 A1 3k ultramarine 2.75 *12.00*

Issued in commemoration of the inauguration of the Carpatho-Ukraine Diet, March 2, 1939.

SLOVAKIA
(slô·vä'ki·ȧ)

LOCATION—Central Europe.

GOVT.—Nominally independent republic.

AREA—14,848 sq. mi.

POP.—2,450,000.

CAPITAL—Bratislava.

Formerly a province of Czechoslovakia, Slovakia declared its independence in March, 1939. A treaty was immediately concluded with Germany guaranteeing Slovakian independence but providing for German "protection" for 25 years.

In 1945 the republic ended and Slovakia again became a part of Czechoslovakia.

100 Halierov = 1 Koruna

Czechoslovakia No. 226 Surcharged in Orange Red

Otvorenie slovenského snemu 18.I. 1939

300 h

1939, Jan. 18 *Perf. 12½* Unwmkd.

1 A72 300h on 10k blue 45 *2.75*

Issued to commemorate the opening of the Slovakian Parliament.

Stamps of Czechoslovakia, 1928-39, Overprinted in Red or Blue

Slovenský štát 1939

1939 *Perf. 10, 12½, 12x12½*

2 A29 5h dark ultra. (R) 60 60
3 " 10h brown (R) 9 9
4 " 20h red (Bl) 5 5
5 " 25h green (R) 1.40 1.40
6 " 30h red violet (Bl) 5 5
7 A61a 40h dark blue (R) 14 14
8 A73 50h deep green (R) 5 5
9 A63 50h deep green (R) 5 5
10 " 60h dull violet (R) 9 9
11 " 60h dark blue (R) 7.00 7.00
12 A60 1k rose lake (Bl) (On No. 212) 5 5

Overprinted Diagonally.

13 A64 1.20k rose lilac (Bl) 17 17
14 A65 1.50k carmine (Bl) 17 17
15 A79 1.60k olive green (Bl) 1.50 1.50
16 A66 2k dark blue green (R) 1.50 1.50
17 A67 2.50k dark blue (R) 50 50
18 A68 3k brown (R) 50 50
19 A69 3.50k dk. vio. (R) 22.50 22.50

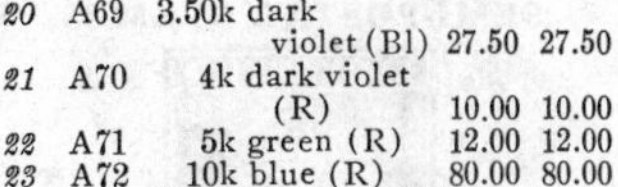

20 A69 3.50k dark violet (Bl) 27.50 27.50
21 A70 4k dark violet (R) 10.00 10.00
22 A71 5k green (R) 12.00 12.00
23 A72 10k blue (R) 80.00 80.00
Nos. 2-23 (22) 165.91 165.91

Excellent counterfeit overprints exist.

Andrej Hlinka
A1 A2

Overprinted in Red or Blue. Photogravure.

1939, Apr. *Perf. 12½* Unwmkd.

24 A1 50h dark green (R) 85 30
a. Perf. 10½ 1.50 70
b. Perf. 10½×12½ 2.00 1.60
25 " 1k dark carmine rose (Bl) 1.50 50
a. Perf. 10½ 40.00
b. Perf. 10½×12½ 4.50 2.50

1939 *Perf. 12½* Unwmkd.

26 A2 5h bright ultramarine 8 22
27 " 10h olive green 35 27
a. Perf. 10½ × 12½ 12.50 2.25
b. Perf. 10½ 17.50 3.50
28 " 20h orange red 35 27
a. Imperf. 30 30
29 " 30h deep violet 35 27
a. Imperf. 50 50
b. Perf. 10½ × 12½ 2.00 1.00
c. Perf. 10½ 2.75 1.50
30 " 50h dark green 35 27
31 " 1k dark carmine rose 60 15
32 " 2.50k bright blue 40 15
33 " 3k black brown 1.50 15
Nos. 26-33 (8) 3.98 1.75

On Nos. 32 and 33 a pearl frame surrounds the medallion. See Nos. 55-57, 69.

General Štefánik and Memorial Tomb
A3

Rev. Josef Murgas and Radio Towers
A4

1939, May *Perf. 12½*

Size: 25x20mm.

34 A3 40h dark blue 45
35 " 60h slate green 45
36 " 1k gray violet 45

Size: 30x23¾ mm.

37 A3 2k blue violet & sepia 45

Prepared to commemorate the 20th anniversary of the death of Gen. Milan Štefánik, but not issued.

1939 Unwmkd.

38 A4 60h purple 15 10
39 " 1.20k slate black 45 20

Issued in commemoration of the 10th anniversary of the death of Rev. Josef Murgas. See No. 65.

Girl Weaving
A5

Woodcutter
A6

Girl at Spring
A7

Wmk. 263

Wmkd. Double-Barred Cross Multiple. (263)

1939-44 *Perf. 12½*

40 A5 2k dark blue green 3.00 25
41 A6 4k copper brown 60 18
42 A7 5k orange red 75 25
a. Perf. 10 ('44) 60 25

Dr. Josef Tiso
A8

Presidential Residence
A9

1939-44 *Perf. 12½* Wmk. 263

43 A8 50h slate green 15 4
43A " 70h dk. red brn. ('42) 15 4
b. Perf. 10½ ('44) 15 4

See also No. 88.

1940, Mar. 14

44 A9 10k deep blue 70 50

Tatra Mountains
A10

Krivan Peak
A11

Edelweiss in the Tatra Mountains
A12

Chamois
A13

Church at Javorina
A14

1940-43 *Perf. 12½* Wmk. 263

Size: 17x21mm.

45 A10 5h dark olive green 30 5
46 A11 10h deep brown 12 5
47 A12 20h blue black 8 5
48 A13 25h olive brown 12 5
49 A14 30h chestnut brown 12 5
a. Perf. 10½ ('43) 12 5
Nos. 45-49 (5) 74 25

See Nos. 84-87, 103-107.

Hlinka Type of 1939

1940-42 *Perf. 12½* Wmk. 263

55 A2 1k dark carmine rose 30 12
56 " 2.50k bright blue ('42) 40 10
a. Perf. 10½ 40 12
57 " 3k black brown ('41) 40 10
a. Perf. 10½ 30 8

On Nos. 56 and 57 a pearl frame surrounds the medallion.

Stiavnica
A15

Lietava
A16

Spissky Hrad
A17

Bojnice
A18

1941 *Perf. 12½*

58 A15 1.20(k) rose lake 5 4
59 A16 1.50(k) rose pink 6 4
60 A17 1.60(k) royal blue 8 4
61 A18 2k dk. gray grn. 6 4

Slovakian Castles.

S. M. Daxner and Stefan Moyses
A19

Andrej Hlinka
A20

1941, May 26 Photo. Wmk. 263

62 A19 50h olive green 1.00 1.00
63 " 1k slate blue 5.00 5.00
64 " 2k black 4.00 4.00

Issued in commemoration of the 80th anniversary of the Memorandum of the Slovak Nation.

Murgas Type of 1939

1941 Wmk. 263

65 A4 60h purple 18 10

1942

69 A20 1.30k dark purple 15 5

Post Horn and Miniature Stamp
A21

Philatelist
A22

Philatelist—A23

1942, May 23

70 A21 30h dark green 60 60
71 A22 70h dark car. rose 60 60
72 A23 80h purple 60 60
73 A21 1.30k dark brown 60 60

Issued to commemorate the National Philatelic Exhibition at Bratislava.

On No. 70 the miniature stamp bears the coat-of-arms of Bratislava; on No. 73 it shows the National arms of Slovakia.

St. Stephen's Cathedral, Vienna
A24

1942, Oct. 12 *Perf. 14*

74 A24 70h blue green 75 75
75 " 1.30k olive green 75 75
76 " 2k sapphire 1.65 2.00

Issued to commemorate the European Postal Congress held in Vienna.

Slovakian Educational Society
A25

1942, Dec. 14

77 A25 70h black 10 10
78 " 1k rose red 20 25
79 " 1.30k sapphire 15 20
80 " 2k chestnut brown 20 25
81 " 3k dark green 30 30
82 " 4k dull purple 45 40
Nos. 77-82 (6) 1.40 1.50

Slovakian Educational Society, 150th anniversary.

Andrej Hlinka
A26

1943 **Wmk. 263**

83 A26 1.30k brt. ultramarine 15 10

See also Nos. 93-94A.

Types of 1939–40

1943 *Perf. 12½.* **Unwmkd.**

Size: 17x21mm.

84 A11 10h deep brown 15 10
85 A12 20h blue black 25 20
86 A13 25h olive brown 30 20
87 A14 30h chestnut brown 30 20
88 A8 70h dark red brown 20 5
Nos. 84-88 (5) 1.20 75

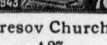

Presov Church
A27

Locomotive
A28

Railway Tunnel
A29

Viaduct
A30

1943, Sept. 5 *Perf. 14*

89 A27 70h dark rose violet 20 20
90 A28 80h sapphire 20 20
91 A29 1.30k black 20 20
92 A30 2k dark violet brown 35 35

Issued to commemorate the inauguration of the new railroad line between Presov and Strazske.

Hlinka Type of 1943 and

Ludwig Stur
A31

Martin Razus
A32

1944 **Unwmkd.**

93 A31 80h slate green 10 10
94 A32 1k brown red 18 18
94A A26 1.30k bright ultra. 20 12

Prince Pribina
A33

Designs: 70h, Prince Mojmir. 80h, Prince Ratislav. 1.30k, King Svatopluk. 2k, Prince Kocel. 3k, Prince Mojmir II. 5k, Prince Svatopluk II. 10k, Prince Braslav.

1944, Mar. 14

95 A33 50h dark green 4 5
96 " 70h lilac rose 4 5
97 " 80h red brown 6 8
98 " 1.30k bright ultra. 8 10
99 " 2k Prussian blue 16 19
100 " 3k dark brown 24 28
101 " 5k violet 42 48
102 " 10k black 1.35 1.60
Nos. 95-102 (8) 2.39 2.83

Scenic Types of 1940

Size: 18x23mm.

1944, Apr. 1 *Perf. 14*

103 A11 10h bright carmine 15 15
104 A12 20h bright blue 15 15
105 A13 25h brown red 15 15
106 A14 30h red violet 15 15
107 A10 50h deep green 15 15
Nos. 103-107 (5) 75 75

Issued to honor the 5th anniversary of Slovakia's independence.

Symbolic of National Protection
A41

President Josef Tiso
A42

1944, Oct. 6 **Wmk. 263**

108 A41 2k green 30 30
109 " 3.80k red violet 30 30

1945 **Unwmkd.**

110 A42 1k orange 55 48
111 " 1.50k brown 20 9
112 " 2k green 25 9
113 " 4k rose red 55 35
114 " 5k sapphire 55 55

Wmk. 263

115 A42 10k red violet 50 35
Nos. 110-115 (6) 2.60 1.91

To commemorate the sixth anniversary of the Republic of Slovakia's declaration of independence, March 14, 1939.

SEMI-POSTAL STAMPS.

Josef Tiso
SP1

Perf. 12½

1939, Nov. 6 **Photo.** **Wmk. 263**

B1 SP1 2.50k+2.50k royal bl. 2.50 2.50

The surtax was used for Child Welfare.

Medical Corpsman and Wounded Soldier
SP2

1941, Nov. 10

B2 SP2 50h+50h dull green 25 35
B3 " 1k+1k rose lake 35 40
B4 " 2k+1k bright blue 95 1.00

Mother and Child
SP3

Soldier and Hlinka Youth
SP4

1941, Dec. 10

B5 SP3 50h+50h dull green 40 40
B6 " 1k+1k brown 45 45
B7 " 2k+1k violet 65 65

The surtax was for the benefit of child welfare.

1942, Mar. 14

B8 SP4 70h+1k brown orange 30 35
B9 " 1.30k+1k bright blue 30 35
B10 " 2k+1k rose red 90 95

The surtax aided the Hlinka Youth Society "Hlinkova Mladez."

National Costumes

SP5 SP6 SP7

1943 *Perf. 14.*

B11 SP5 50h+50h dark slate green 15 20
B12 SP6 70h+1k deep carmine 15 20
B13 SP7 80h+2k dark blue 25 30

The surtax was for the benefit of children, the Red Cross and winter relief of the Slovakian popular party.

Infantrymen
SP8

Aviator—SP9

Tank and Gun Crew
SP10

1943, July 28

B14 SP8 70h+2k rose brown 30 30
B15 SP9 1.30k+2k sapphire 40 45
B16 SP10 2k+2k olive green 70 80

The surtax was for soldiers' welfare.

"The Slovak Language Is Our Life"— L. Stur
SP11

Slovakian National Museum
SP12

Slovakian Foundation
SP13

Slovakian Peasant
SP14

1943, Oct. 16

B17 SP11 30h+1k brown red 20 20
B18 SP12 70h+1k slate green 70 70
B19 SP13 80h+2k slate blue 20 20
B20 SP14 1.30k+2k dull brown 20 20

The surtax was for the benefit of Slovakian cultural institutions.

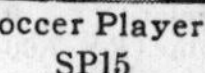

Soccer Player
SP15

Skier
SP16

Diver
SP17

Relay Race
SP18

1944, Apr. 30 **Unwmkd.**

B21	SP15	70h+70h slate green	35	40
B22	SP16	1k+1k violet	70	75
B23	SP17	1.30k+1.30k Prus. bl.	70	75
B24	SP18	2k+2k chestnut brown	70	75

Symbolic of National Protection SP19 — Children SP20

1944, Oct. 6 **Wmk. 263**

B25	SP19	70h+4k sapphire	75	75
B26	"	1.30k+4k red brown	75	75

The surtax was for the benefit of social institutions.

1944, Dec. 18

B27	SP20	2k+4k light blue	1.75	1.75
		a. Sheet of 8 + label	20.00	20.00

The surtax was to aid social work for Slovak youth.

AIR POST STAMPS.

Planes over Tatra Mountains
AP1 AP2

Perf. 12½

1939, Nov. 20 **Photo.** **Unwmkd.**

C1	AP1	30h violet	14	14
C2	"	50h dark green	14	14
C3	"	1k vermilion	20	20
C4	AP2	2k greenish black	40	40
C5	"	3k dark brown	60	60
C6	"	4k slate blue	70	70
		Nos. C1-C6 (6)	2.18	2.18

See also No. C10.

Plane in Flight
AP3

Perf. 12½

1940, Nov. 30 **Wmk. 263**

C7	AP3	5k dark violet brown	40	45
C8	"	10k gray black	35	40
C9	"	20k myrtle green	75	80

Type of 1939.

1944, Sept. 15 **Wmk. 263**

C10	AP1	1k vermilion	50	50

PERSONAL DELIVERY STAMPS

PD1

Photogravure.

1940 *Imperf.* **Wmk. 263**

EX1	PD1	50h indigo & blue	35	45
EX2	"	50h carmine & rose	35	45

POSTAGE DUE STAMPS.

D1 — Letter, Post Horn D2

Photogravure.

1939 *Perf. 12½* **Unwmkd.**

J1	D1	5h bright blue	30	35
J2	"	10h "	30	35
J3	"	20h "	30	35
J4	"	30h "	60	65
J5	"	40h "	90	60
J6	"	50h "	1.50	60
J7	"	60h "	90	60
J8	"	1k dark carmine	9.00	4.50
J9	"	2k "	9.00	1.75
J10	"	5k "	2.75	1.75
J11	"	10k "	21.00	4.50
J12	"	20k "	10.50	6.00
		Nos. J1-J12 (12)	57.05	22.00

1940-41 **Wmk. 263**

J13	D1	5h bright blue ('41)	45	45
J14	"	10h " ('41)	20	20
J15	"	20h " ('41)	20	20
J16	"	30h " ('41)	3.50	3.50
J17	"	40h " ('41)	45	45
J18	"	50h " ('41)	75	75
J19	"	60h "	75	75
J20	"	1k dark car. ('41)	90	90
J21	"	2k " " ('41)	4.50	4.50
J22	"	5k " " ('41)	2.00	2.00
J23	"	10k " " ('41)	2.50	2.50
		Nos. J13-J23 (11)	16.20	16.20

1942 *Perf. 14.* **Unwmkd.**

J24	D2	10h deep brown	7	10
J25	"	20h "	7	17
J26	"	40h "	14	17
J27	"	50h "	85	17
J28	"	60h "	17	17
J29	"	80h "	17	17
J30	"	1k rose red	20	20
J31	"	1.10k "	50	50
J32	"	1.30k "	28	17
J33	"	1.60k "	35	17
J34	"	2k "	50	17
J35	"	2.60k "	70	35
J36	"	3.50k "	1.00	75
J37	"	5k "	1.00	75
J38	"	10k "	1.75	90
		Nos. J24-J38 (15)	7.75	4.91

NEWSPAPER STAMPS.

Newspaper Stamps of Czechoslovakia, 1937, Overprinted in Red or Blue

1939, Apr. *Imperf.* **Unwmkd.**

P1	N2	2h bistre brown (Bl)	15	15
P2	"	5h dull blue (R)	10	10
P3	"	7h red orange (Bl)	15	15
P4	"	9h emerald (R)	15	15
P5	"	10h henna brown (Bl)	15	15
P6	"	12h ultramarine (R)	15	15
P7	"	20h dark green (R)	35	35
P8	"	50h dark brown (Bl)	1.25	1.25
P9	"	1k greenish gray (R)	7.25	7.25
		Nos. P1-P9 (9)	9.70	9.70

Excellent counterfeits exist of Nos. P1 to P9.

Arms of Slovakia N1 — Type Block "N" (for "Noviny"—Newspaper) N2

1939 Typographed.

P10	N1	2h ochre	12	10
P11	"	5h ultramarine	25	15
P12	"	7h red orange	25	15
P13	"	9h emerald	16	12
P14	"	10h henna brown	30	15
P15	"	12h dark ultramarine	25	15
P16	"	20h dark green	30	15
P17	"	50h red brown	40	15
P18	"	1k greenish gray	30	20
		Nos. P10-P18 (9)	2.33	1.32

1940-41 **Wmk. 263**

P20	N1	5h ultramarine	15	10
P23	"	10h henna brown	12	14
P24	"	15h bright purple ('41)	12	14
P25	"	20h dark green	25	17
P26	"	25h light blue ('41)	20	14
P27	"	40h red orange ('41)	20	14
P28	"	50h chocolate	32	14
P29	"	1k greenish gray ('41)	35	25
P30	"	2k emerald ('41)	45	35
		Nos. P20-P30 (9)	2.16	1.57

1943 Photogravure. **Unwmkd.**

P31	N2	10h green	20	20
P32	"	15h dark brown	20	20
P33	"	20h ultramarine	20	20
P34	"	50h rose red	20	20
P35	"	1k slate green	35	35
P36	"	2k intense blue	70	70
		Nos. P31-P36 (6)	1.85	1.85

DAHOMEY

(dä·hō'mā)

LOCATION—West coast of Africa.

GOVT.—Republic.

AREA—43,483 sq. mi.

POP.—3,030,000 (est. 1974).

CAPITAL—Porto-Novo.

Formerly a native kingdom including Benin, Dahomey was annexed by France in 1894. It became part of the colonial administrative unit of French West Africa in 1895. Stamps of French West Africa superseded those of Dahomey in 1945. The Republic of Dahomey was proclaimed Dec. 4, 1958.

The republic changed its name to the People's Republic of Benin on Nov. 30, 1975. See Benin for stamps issued after that date.

100 Centimes = 1 Franc

Navigation and Commerce
A1

Perf. 14x13½.

1899-1905 Typo. **Unwmkd.**

Name of Colony in Blue or Carmine.

1	A1	1c *lilac blue* ('01)	30	20
2	"	2c brown, *buff* ('04)	40	40
3	"	4c claret, *lavender* ('04)	60	60
4	"	5c yel. green ('04)	1.00	1.00
5	"	10c red ('01)	1.25	80
6	"	15c gray ('01)	80	40
7	"	20c red, *green* ('04)	5.75	4.50
8	"	25c *rose* ('99)	4.50	3.00
9	"	25c blue ('01)	5.00	4.00
10	A1	30c brown, *bistre* ('04)	6.00	4.50
11	"	40c red *straw* ('04)	6.00	5.00
12	"	50c brown, *azure* (name in red) ('01)	6.00	4.00
12A	"	50c brown, *azure* (name in blue) ('05)	10.00	7.00
13	"	75c deep violet, *orange* ('04)	25.00	22.50
14	"	1fr bronze green, *straw* ('04)	14.00	12.00
15	"	2fr violet, *rose* ('04)	35.00	32.50
16	"	5fr red lilac, *lavender* ('04)	55.00	45.00
		Nos. 1-16 (17)	176.60	147.40

Gen. Louis Faidherbe A2 — Oil Palm A3

Dr. Noel Eugène Ballay
A4

1906-07 *Perf. 13½x14.*

Name of Colony in Red or Blue.

17	A2	1c slate	20	20
18	"	2c chocolate	20	20
19	"	4c choc., *gray blue*	60	40
20	"	5c green	2.00	40
21	"	10c carmine (B)	5.00	65
22	A3	20c *azure*	4.00	3.25
23	"	25c blue, *pinkish*	4.00	3.00
24	"	30c choc., *pinkish*	5.00	3.50
25	"	35c *yellow*	30.00	4.00
26	"	45c chocolate, *greenish* ('07)	5.00	4.00
27	"	50c deep violet	6.00	5.00
28	"	75c blue, *orange*	6.00	4.00
29	A4	1fr black, *azure*	7.00	4.50
30	"	2fr blue, *pink*	40.00	40.00
31	"	5fr car., *straw* (B)	35.00	35.00
		Nos. 17-31 (15)	150.00	108.10

Stamps of 1901-05 Surcharged in Black or Carmine — **05** (*a*) **10** (*b*)

1912 *Perf. 14x13½.*

32	(*a*)	5c on 2c brown, *buff*	15	15
33	(")	5c on 4c claret, *lavender* (C)	25	25
		a. Double surcharge	65.00	
34	(")	5c on 15c gray (C)	15	15
35	(")	5c on 20c red, *green*	15	15
36	(")	5c on 25c blue (C)	20	20
		a. Inverted surcharge	60.00	
37	(")	5c on 30c brown, *bistre* (C)	30	20
38	(*b*)	10c on 40c red, *straw*	30	20
		a. Inverted surcharge	60.00	
39	(")	10c on 50c brown, *azure*, name in blue (C)	35	35
40	(")	10c on 50c brown, *azure*, name in red (C)	350.00	400.00
41	(")	10c on 75c violet, *orange*	1.75	1.75
		Nos. 32-39, 41 (9)	3.60	3.40

Two spacings between the surcharged numerals are found on Nos. 32 to 41.

Man Climbing Oil Palm
A5

1913–39 *Perf. 13½x14.*

42 A5 1c violet & black 3 3
43 " 2c chocolate & rose 5 5
44 " 4c black & brown 5 5
45 " 5c yellow green & blue green 6 6
46 " 5c violet brown & violet ('22) 6 6
47 " 10c orange red & rose 20 15
48 " 10c yellow green & blue green ('22) 6 6
49 " 10c red & olive ('25) 6 6
50 " 15c brown orange & dark violet ('17) 6 6
51 " 20c gray & chocolate 6 6
52 " 20c bluish green & green ('26) 5 5
53 " 20c magenta & black ('27) 6 6
54 " 25c ultra. & deep blue 30 20
55 " 25c violet brown & orange ('22) 10 10
56 " 30c chocolate & violet 60 60
57 " 30c red orange & rose ('22) 50 50
58 " 30c yellow & violet ('25) 6 6
59 " 30c dull green & green ('27) 6 5
60 " 35c brown & black 25 20
61 " 35c blue green & green ('38) 6 6
62 " 40c black & red orange 10 8
63 " 45c gray & ultramarine 10 10
64 " 50c chocolate & brown 1.10 1.10
65 " 50c ultramarine & blue ('22) 15 15
66 " 50c brown red & blue ('26) 6 6
67 " 55c gray green & chocolate ('38) 8 7
68 " 60c violet, *pinkish* ('25) 10 10
69 " 65c yellow brown & olive green ('26) 10 10
70 " 75c blue & violet 10 8
71 " 80c henna brown & ultramarine ('38) 7 7
72 " 85c dark blue & vermilion ('26) 18 18
73 " 90c rose & brown red ('30) 10 10
74 " 90c yellow bistre & red orange ('39) 10 6
75 " 1fr blue green & black 20 20
76 " 1fr dark blue & ultramarine ('26) 25 25
77 " 1fr yellow brown & light red ('28) 35 20
78 " 1fr dark red & red orange ('38) 20 15
79 " 1.10fr violet & bistre ('28) 65 65
80 " 1.25fr deep blue & dark brown ('33) 5.50 1.85
81 " 1.50fr dark blue & light blue ('30) 20 8
82 " 1.75fr dark brown & deep buff ('33) 1.00 75
83 " 1.75fr indigo & ultramarine ('38) 10 6
84 " 2fr yellow orange & chocolate 25 25
85 " 3fr red violet ('30) 50 40
86 " 5fr violet & dp. blue 50 45
Nos. 42–86 (45) 14.77 10.06

The 1c gray and yellow green and 5c dull red and black are Togo Nos. 193a, 196a.

Common Design Types

pictured in section at front of book.

Type of 1913 Surcharged

60 60

1922–25

87 A5 60c on 75c violet, *pinkish* 10 10
a. Double surcharge 16.50
88 " 65c on 15c brown orange & dark violet ('25) 30 30
89 " 85c on 15c brown orange & dark violet ('25) 30 30

Stamps and Type of 1913–39 Surcharged with New Value and Bars.

1924–27

90 A5 25c on 2fr orange & chocolate 10 10
91 " 90c on 75c cerise & brown red ('27) 45 45
92 " 1.25fr on 1fr dark blue & ultramarine (R) ('26) 10 10
93 " 1.50fr on 1fr dark blue & greenish blue ('27) 55 55
94 " 3fr on 5fr olivine & deep orange ('27) 2.50 2.50
95 " 10fr on 5fr blue violet & red brown ('27) 2.25 2.25
96 " 20fr on 5fr vermilion & dull green ('27) 2.25 2.25
Nos. 90–96 (7) 8.20 8.20

Colonial Exposition Issue.
Common Design Types

1931 **Engraved.** ***Perf. 12½.***

Name of Country in Black.

97 CD70 40c deep green 1.50 1.50
98 CD71 50c violet 1.50 1.50
99 CD72 90c red orange 1.50 1.50
100 CD73 1.50fr dull blue 1.50 1.50

Paris International Exposition Issue.
Common Design Types

1937 **Engraved.** ***Perf. 13.***

101 CD74 20c deep violet 25 25
102 CD75 30c dark green 30 30
103 CD76 40c carmine rose 35 35
104 CD77 50c dark brown 30 30
105 CD78 90c red 30 30
106 CD79 1.50fr ultramarine 30 30
Nos. 101–106 (6) 1.80 1.80

Souvenir Sheet.
Imperf.

107 CD77 3fr dp. blue & black 1.50 1.50

Size of No. 107: 118x99mm.

Caillié Issue.
Common Design Type

1939, Apr. 5 **Engr.** ***Perf. 12½x12***

108 CD81 90c orange brown & orange 40 40
109 " 2fr bright violet 40 40
110 " 2.25fr ultra. & dk. blue 50 50

New York World's Fair Issue.
Common Design Type

1939 **Engraved.**

111 CD82 1.25fr carmine lake 25 25
112 " 2.25fr ultramarine 25 25

Man Poling a Canoe
A7

Pile House
A8

Sailboat on Lake Nokoué
A9

Dahomey Warrior
A10

1941 ***Perf. 13.***

113 A7 2c scarlet 6 6
114 " 3c deep blue 6 6
115 " 5c brown violet 10 10
116 " 10c green 6 6
117 " 15c black 5 5
118 A8 20c violet brown 5 5
119 " 30c dark violet 10 10
120 " 40c scarlet 15 15
121 " 50c slate green 15 15
122 " 60c black 10 10
123 " 70c bright red violet 10 10
124 A9 80c brown black 12 12
125 " 1fr violet 18 18
126 " 1.30fr brown violet 20 20
127 " 1.40fr green 25 25
128 " 1.50fr bright rose 35 35
129 " 2fr brown orange 40 40
130 " 2.50fr dark blue 35 35
131 " 3fr scarlet 40 40
132 A10 5fr slate green 25 25
133 " 10fr violet brown 40 40
134 " 20fr black 65 65
Nos. 113–134 (22) 4.53 4.53

Stamps of type A8 without "RF" were issued in 1944 by the Vichy Government, but were not placed on sale in the colony.

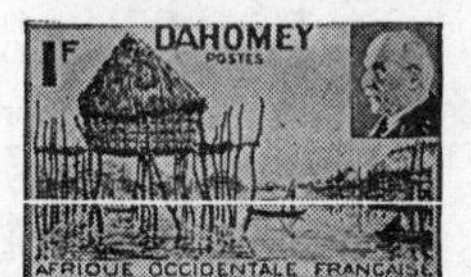

Pile House and Marshal Pétain
A11

1941 ***Perf. 12½x12.***

135 A11 1fr green 15
136 " 2.50fr blue 15

Republic

Village Ganvié—A12

Engraved

1960, Mar. 1 ***Perf. 12*** **Unwmkd.**

137 A12 25fr dark blue, brown & red 40 10

Imperforates

Most Dahomey stamps from 1960 onward exist imperforate in issued and trial colors, and also in small presentation sheets in issued colors.

C.C.T.A. Issue
Common Design Type

1960, May 16

138 CD106 5fr rose lilac & ultramarine 40 35

Issued to commemorate the 10th anniversary of the Commission for Technical Co-operation in Africa South of the Sahara (C.C.T.A.).

Emblem of the Entente
A13

Prime Minister Hubert Maga
A14

Council of the Entente Issue

1960, May 29 Photo. ***Perf. 13x13½***

139 A13 25fr multicolored 60 50

Issued to commemorate the first anniversary of the Council of the Entente (Dahomey, Ivory Coast, Niger and Upper Volta).

1960, Aug. **Engraved** ***Perf. 13***

140 A14 85fr deep claret & black 1.20 35

Issued on the occasion of Dahomey's proclamation of independence, Aug. 1, 1960.

Weaver
A15

Doves, U.N. Building and Emblem
A16

Designs: 2fr, 10fr, Wood sculptor. 3fr, 15fr, Fisherman and net (horiz.). 4fr, 20fr, Potter (horiz.).

1961, Feb. 17 **Engraved** ***Perf. 13***

141 A15 1fr rose, orange & red lilac 6 3
142 " 2fr bistre brown & chocolate 5 3
143 " 3fr green & orange 8 6
144 " 4fr olive bistre & claret 12 10
145 " 6fr rose, light violet & vermilion 12 10
146 " 10fr blue & green 25 12
147 " 15fr red lilac & vio. 27 18
148 " 20fr bluish violet & Prussian blue 40 25
Nos. 141–148 (8) 1.35 87

No. 140 Surcharged with New Value, Bars and: "Président de la République"

1961, Aug. 1

149 A14 100fr on 85fr deep claret & black 1.60 1.50

First anniversary of Independence.

1961, Sept. 20 ***Perf. 13*** **Unwmkd.**

150 A16 5fr multicolored 30 20
151 " 60fr " 90 80

Issued to commemorate the first anniversary of Dahomey's admission to the United Nations. See No. C16 and souvenir sheet No. C16a.

No. 137 Overprinted: "JEUX SPORTIFS D'ABIDJAN 24 AU 31 DECEMBRE 1961"

1961, Dec. 24

152 A12 25fr dk. blue, brown & red 50 40

Abidjan Games, Dec. 24-31.

Interior of Burned-out Fort Ouidah and Wrecked Car—A17

1962, July 31 Photo. *Perf. 12½*

153 A17 30fr multicolored 45 20
154 " 60fr " 90 50

Issued to commemorate the first anniversary of the evacuation of Fort Ouidah by the Portuguese, and its occupation by Dahomey.

African and Malgache Union Issue

Common Design Type

1962, Sept. 8 *Perf. 12½x12*

155 CD110 30fr red lilac, bluish grn., red & gold 70 30

Issued to commemorate the first anniversary of the African and Malgache Union.

Red Cross Nurses and Map

A18

Engraved

1962, Oct. 5 *Perf. 13* Unwmkd.

156 A18 5fr bl., choc. & red 10 5
157 " 20fr bl., dk. grn. & red 30 25
158 " 25fr bl., brn. & red 40 30
159 " 30fr blue, blk. & red 50 30

Ganvié Woman in Canoe A19

Peuhl Herdsman and Cattle

A20

Designs: 3fr, 65fr, Bariba chief of Nikki. 15fr, 50fr, Ouidah witch doctor, rock python. 20fr, 30fr, Nessoukoué women carrying vases on heads, Abomey. 25fr, 40fr, Dahomey girl. 60fr, Peuhl herdsman and cattle. 85fr, Ganvié woman in canoe.

1963, Feb. 18 *Perf. 13* Unwmkd.

160 A19 2fr greenish blue & violet 5 5
161 " 3fr blue & black 6 5
162 A20 5fr brn., blk. & grn. 10 6
163 A19 15fr brown, blue grn. & red brn. 25 15
164 " 20fr grn., blk. & car. 30 20
165 A20 25fr dark brown, blue & blue green 35 15
166 A19 30fr brown orange, choc. & magenta 45 20
167 A20 40fr chocolate, green & bright blue 60 30
168 A19 50fr blk., grn., brn. & red brown 75 35
169 A20 60fr chocolate, orange red & olive 85 40
170 A19 65fr orange brown & chocolate 90 50
171 " 85fr br. blue & choc. 1.25 75
Nos. 160-171 (12) 5.91 3.16

Boxers

A21

Designs: 1fr, 20fr, Soccer goalkeeper (horiz.). 2fr, 5fr, Runners.

1963, Apr. 11 Engraved

172 A21 50c green & black 4 4
173 " 1fr olive, blk. & brn. 5 5
174 " 2fr olive, blue & brn. 6 6
175 " 5fr brown, crimson & black 10 8
176 " 15fr dk. violet & brn. 25 20
177 " 20fr multicolored 40 30
Nos. 172-177 (6) 90 73

Friendship Games, Dakar, Apr. 11-21.

President's Palace, Cotonou

A22

1963, Aug. 1 Photo. *Perf. 12½x12*

178 A22 25fr multicolored 40 25

Third anniversary of independence.

Gen. Toussaint L'Ouverture

A23

U.N. Emblem, Flame and "15"

A24

1963, Nov. 18 *Perf. 12x13* Unwmkd.

179 A23 25fr multicolored 40 25
180 " 30fr " 45 30
181 " 100fr ultra., brown & red 1.50 1.00

Issued to honor Pierre Dominique Toussaint L'Ouverture (1743-1803), Haitian general, statesman and descendant of the kings of Allada (Dahomey).

1963, Dec. 10 *Perf. 12*

182 A24 4fr multicolored 8 8
183 " 6fr " 10 8
184 " 25fr " 40 30

Issued to commemorate the 15th anniversary of the Universal Declaration of Human Rights.

Somba Dance

A25

Regional Dances: 3fr, Nago dance, Pobe-Ketou (horiz.). 10fr, Dance of the baton. 15fr, Nago dance, Ouidah (horiz.). 25fr, Dance of the Sakpatassi. 30fr, Dance of the Nessouhouessi (horiz.).

1964, Aug. 8 Engraved *Perf. 13*

185 A25 2fr red, emerald & blk. 4 3
186 " 3fr dull red, bl. & grn. 6 4
187 " 10fr pur., blk. & red 15 10
188 " 15fr magenta, black & green 25 15
189 " 25fr Prussian blue, brown & orange 40 25
190 " 30fr dark red, choc. & orange 45 35
Nos. 185-190 (6) 1.35 92

Runner

A26

Design: 85fr, Bicyclist.

1964, Oct. 20 Photo. *Perf. 11*

191 A26 60fr lt. brn. & green 75 55
192 " 85fr violet blue & red lilac 1.25 90

18th Olympic Games, Tokyo, Oct. 10-25.

Cooperation Issue

Common Design Type

1964, Nov. 7 Engraved *Perf. 13*

193 CD119 25fr orge., violet & dark brown 40 25

UNICEF Emblem, Mother and Child

A27

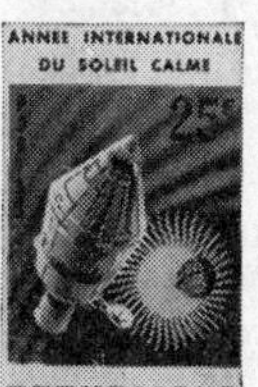

IQSY Emblem and Apollo Satellite

A28

Design: 25fr, Mother holding child in her arms.

1964, Dec. 11 *Perf. 13* Unwmkd.

194 A27 20fr yellow grn., dk. red & black 30 25
195 " 25fr blue, dark red & black 40 25

Issued for the 18th anniversary of the United Nations International Children's Emergency Fund (UNICEF).

1964, Dec. 22 Photo. *Perf. 13x12½*

Design: 100fr, IQSY emblem and Nimbus weather satellite.

196 A28 25fr green & lt. yel. 50 20
197 " 100fr dp. plum & yel. 1.50 90

International Quiet Sun Year, 1964-65.

Abomey Tapestry

A29

Designs (Abomey tapestries): 25fr, Warrior and fight scenes. 50fr, Birds and warriors (horiz.). 85fr, Animals, ship and plants (horiz.).

1965, Apr. 12 Photo. *Perf. 12½*

198 A29 20fr multicolored 30 20
199 " 25fr " 40 30
200 " 50fr " 75 50
201 " 85fr " 1.25 90
a. Min. sheet of 4 2.75 2.75

Issued to publicize the local rug weaving industry. No. 201a contains one each of Nos. 198-201. Size: 194x100mm.

Baudot Telegraph Distributor and Ader Telephone

A30

1965, May 17 Engraved *Perf. 13*

202 A30 100fr lilac, orange & black 1.50 60

Issued to commemorate the centenary of the International Telecommunication Union.

Cotonou Harbor—A31

Design: 100fr, Cotonou Harbor, denomination at left.

1965, Aug. 1 Photo. *Perf. 12½*

203 A31 25fr multicolored 45 25
204 " 100fr " 1.65 1.00

Issued to commemorate the opening of Cotonou Harbor. Nos. 203-204 printed se-tenant show a panoramic view of the harbor.

Cybium Tritor

A32

Fish: 25fr, Dentex filosus. 30fr, Atlantic sailfish. 50fr, Blackish tripletail.

1965, Sept. 20 Engraved *Perf. 13*

205 A32 10fr black & brt. blue 15 12
206 " 25fr bright blue, orange & blk. 40 30
207 " 30fr violet blue & greenish blue 45 30
208 " 50fr black, gray blue & orange 75 50

Independence Monument
A33

1965, Oct. 28 Photo. *Perf. 12x12½*
209 A33 25fr gray, blk. & red 40 20
210 " 30fr lt. ultra., black & red 45 25

October 28 Revolution, 2nd anniversary.

No. 165 Surcharged **1F**

1965, Nov. Engraved *Perf. 13*
211 A20 1fr on 25fr dk. brown, bl. & blue green 8 6

Porto Novo Cathedral
A34

Designs: 50fr, Ouidah Pro-Cathedral (vert.). 70fr, Cotonou Cathedral.

1966, March 21 Engraved *Perf. 13*
212 A34 30fr Prus. bl., vio. brn. & green 45 30
213 " 50fr vio. brn., Prus. blue & brown 75 45
214 " 70fr grn., Prus. blue & violet brn. 1.10 65

Jewelry
A35

Designs: 30fr, Architecture. 50fr, Musician. 70fr, Crucifixion, sculpture.

1966, Apr. 4 Engr. *Perf. 13*
215 A35 15fr dull red brown & black 25 15
216 " 30fr dk. brn., ultra. & brown red 45 25
217 " 50fr bright blue & dk. brown 75 40
218 " 70fr red brn. & blk. 1.10 65

Issued to commemorate the International Negro Arts Festival, Dakar, Senegal, Apr. 1–24.

Nos. 203–204 Surcharged

ACCORD DE COOPERATION
FRANCE - DAHOMEY
5e Anniversaire - 24 Avril 1966
15F

1966, Apr. 24 Photo. *Perf. 12½*
219 A31 15fr on 25fr multi. 25 15
220 " 15fr on 100fr multi. 25 15

Issued to commemorate the fifth anniversary of the Cooperation Agreement between France and Dahomey.

WHO Headquarters from the East
A36

1966, May 3 *Perf. 12½x13*
Size: 35x22½mm.
221 A36 30fr multicolored 45 30

Issued to commemorate the inauguration of the World Health Organization Headquarters, Geneva. See No. C32.

Boy Scout Signaling
A37

Designs: 10fr, Patrol standard with pennant (vert.). 30fr, Campfire and map of Dahomey (vert.). 50fr, Scouts building foot bridge.

1966, Oct. 17 Engraved *Perf. 13*
222 A37 5fr dark brown, ocher & red 10 4
223 " 10fr black, green & rose claret 15 6
224 " 30fr orange, red brn. & purple 40 25
225 " 50fr vio. bl., grn. & dark brown 70 40
a. Miniature sheet of 4 1.65 1.65

No. 225a contains one each of Nos. 222–225. Size: 168x94mm.

Clappertonia Ficifolia
A38

Lions Emblem, Dancing Children and Bird
A39

Flowers: 3fr, Hewittia sublobata. 5fr, Butterfly pea. 10fr, Water lily. 15fr, Commelina forskalaei. 30fr, Eremomastax speciosa.

1967, Feb. 20 Photo. *Perf. 12x12½*
226 A38 1fr multicolored 8 5
227 " 3fr " 12 5
228 " 5fr " 15 8
229 " 10fr " 25 10
230 " 15fr " 30 18
231 " 30fr " 60 30
Nos. 226–231 (6) 1.50 76

Nos. 170–171 Surcharged with New Value and Heavy Bar

1967, Mar. 1 Engraved *Perf. 13*
232 A19 30fr on 65fr org. brn. & chocolate 45 35
a. Double surch. 18.50
233 " 30fr on 85fr brt. bl. & chocolate 45 35
a. Double surch. 27.50
b. Invtd. surch. 27.50

1967, March 20
234 A39 100fr dull vio., deep blue & green 1.60 50

50th anniversary of Lions International.

EXPO '67 "Man in the City" Pavilion
A40

Design: 70fr, "The New Africa" exhibit.

1967, June 12 Engraved *Perf. 13*
235 A40 30fr green & choc. 45 20
236 " 70fr grn. & brn. red 1.00 65

Issued to commemorate EXPO '67, International Exhibition, Montreal, Apr. 28–Oct. 27, 1967. See No. C57 and miniature sheet No. C57a.

Europafrica Issue, 1967

Trade (Blood) Circulation, Map of Europe and Africa
A41

1967, July 20 Photo. *Perf. 12x12½*
237 A41 30fr multicolored 40 20
238 " 45fr " 65 25

Scouts Climbing Mountain, Jamboree Emblem
A42

Design: 70fr, Jamboree emblem and Scouts launching canoe.

1967, Aug. 7 Engraved *Perf. 13*
239 A42 30fr brt. blue, red brn. & slate 45 20
240 " 70fr brt. blue, slate grn. & dk. brn. 1.00 65

Issued to commemorate the 12th Boy Scout World Jamboree, Farragut State Park, Idaho, Aug. 1–9. For souvenir sheet see No. C59a.

Rhone River and Olympic Emblems
A43

Designs (Olympic Emblems and): 45fr, View of Grenoble (vert.). 100fr, Rhone Bridge, Grenoble, and Pierre de Coubertin.

1967, Sept. 2 Engraved *Perf. 13*
241 A43 30fr bister, dp. blue & green 45 20
242 " 45fr ultra., green & brown 70 25
243 " 100fr choc., green & bright blue 1.50 90
a. Miniature sheet of 3 3.25 3.25

Issued to publicize the 10th Winter Olympic Games, Grenoble, Feb. 6–18, 1968. No. 243a contains one each of Nos. 241–243. Size: 129x100mm.

Monetary Union Issue
Common Design Type

1967, Nov. 4 Engraved *Perf. 13*
244 CD125 30fr grn., dk. car. & dark brown 45 25

Issued to commemorate the 5th anniversary of the West African Monetary Union.

Cape Buffalo
A45

Animals from the Pendjari Reservation: 30fr, Lion. 45fr, Buffon's kob. 70fr, African slender-snouted crocodile. 100fr, Hippopotamus.

1968, Mar. 18 Photo. *Perf. 12½x13*
245 A45 15fr multicolored 25 15
246 " 30fr purple & multi. 45 20
247 A45 45fr blue & multi. 70 30
248 " 70fr multicolored 1.00 45
249 " 100fr " 1.50 80
Nos. 245–249 (5) 3.90 1.90

WHO Emblem
A46

1968, Apr. 22 Engraved *Perf. 13*
250 A46 30fr dk. bl., red brn. & brt. blue 45 20
251 " 70fr multicolored 1.00 55

Issued to commemorate the 20th anniversary of the World Health Organization.

Leopard
A47

Animals: 5fr, Warthog. 60fr, Spotted hyena. 75fr, Anubius baboon. 90fr, Hartebeest.

1969, Feb. 10 Photo. *Perf. 12½x12*
252 A47 5fr dk. brn. & multi. 8 5
253 " 30fr dp. ultra. & multi. 45 20
254 " 60fr dk. grn. & multi. 90 40
255 " 75fr dk. bl. & multi. 1.10 55
256 " 90fr dk. grn. & multi. 1.35 70
Nos. 252–256 (5) 3.88 1.90

Heads, Symbols of Agriculture and Science, and Globe
A48

1969, Mar. 10 Engraved *Perf. 13*
257 A48 30fr orange & multi. 45 20
258 " 70fr maroon & multi. 1.00 50

Issued to commemorate the 50th anniversary of the International Labor Organization.

Arms of Dahomey
A49

1969, June 30 Litho. *Perf. 13½x13*
259 A49 5fr yellow & multi. 8 6
260 " 30fr org. red & multi. 40 25

See also No. C101.

Development Bank Issue

Cornucopia and Bank Emblem
A50

1969, Sept. 10 Photo. *Perf. 13*
261 A50 30fr black, green & ocher 50 25

Issued to commemorate the 5th anniversary of the African Development Bank.

Europafrica Issue

Ambary (Kenaf) Industry, Cotonou
A51

Design: 45fr, Cotton industry, Parakou.

1969, Sept. 22 Litho. *Perf. 14*
262 A51 30fr multicolored 40 25
263 " 45fr " 60 30

See Nos. C105–C105a.

Sakpata Dance and Tourist Year Emblem
A52

Dances and Tourist Year Emblem: 30fr, Guelede dance. 45fr, Sato dance.

1969, Dec. 15 Litho. *Perf. 14*
264 A52 10fr multicolored 20 10
265 " 30fr " 45 20
266 " 45fr " 65 35

See No. C108.

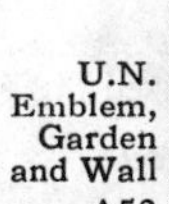

U.N. Emblem, Garden and Wall
A53

1970, Apr. 6 Engraved *Perf. 13*
267 A53 30fr ultra., red orange & slate 45 20
268 " 40fr ultra., brown & slate green 60 30

25th anniversary of the United Nations.

ASECNA Issue
Common Design Type

1970, June 1 Engraved *Perf. 13*
269 CD132 40fr red & purple 60 35

Mt. Fuji, EXPO '70 Emblem, Monorail Train
A54

1970, June 15 Litho. *Perf. 13½x14*
270 A54 5fr grn., red & vio. bl. 12 8

Issued to publicize EXPO '70 International Exhibition, Osaka, Japan, Mar. 15–Sept. 13, 1970. See Nos. C124–C125.

Alkemy, King of Ardres
A55

Designs: 40fr, Sailing ships "La Justice" and "La Concorde," Ardres, 1670. 50fr, Matheo Lopes, ambassador of the King of Ardres and his coat of arms. 200fr, Louis XIV and fleur-de-lis.

1970, July 6 Engraved *Perf. 13*
271 A55 40fr bright green, ultra. & brn. 55 22
272 " 50fr dark car., choc. & emerald 65 27
273 " 70fr gray, lemon & chocolate 90 40
274 " 200fr Prus. blue, dark car. & choc. 2.50 1.20

Issued to commemorate the 300th anniversary of the mission from the King of Ardres to the King of France, and of the audience with Louis XIV on Dec. 19, 1670.

Star of the Order of Independence
A56

Bariba Warrior
A57

1970, Aug. 1 Photo. *Perf. 12*
275 A56 30fr multicolored 35 20
276 " 40fr " 50 25

The 10th anniversary of independence.

1970, Aug. 24 *Perf. 12½x13*

Designs: 2fr, 50fr, Two horsemen. 10fr, 70fr, Horseman facing left.

277 A57 1fr yellow & multi. 6 3
278 " 2fr gray grn. & multi. 8 6
279 " 10fr blue & multi. 15 10
280 " 40fr yel. grn. & multi. 55 30
281 " 50fr gold & multi. 65 30
282 " 70fr lilac rose & multicolored 1.00 50
Nos. 277–282 (6) 2.49 1.29

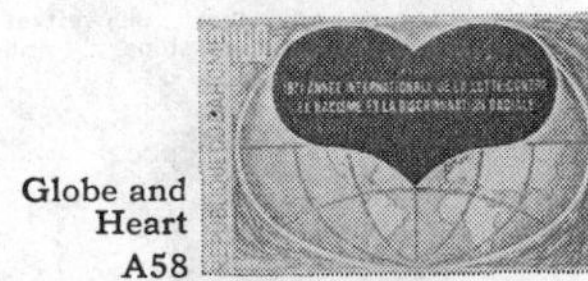

Globe and Heart
A58

Design: 40fr, Hands holding heart (vert.).

1971, June 7 Engraved *Perf. 13*
283 A58 40fr red, green & dark brown 50 30
284 " 100fr grn., red & bl. 1.10 60

International year against racial discrimination.

Ancestral Figures and Lottery Ticket
A59

King Behanzin's Emblem (1889–1894)
A60

1971, June 24 Litho. *Perf. 14*
285 A59 35fr multicolored 40 20
286 " 40fr " 50 25

4th anniversary of the National Lottery.

Photo.; Litho. (25fr, 135fr)

1971–72 *Perf. 12½*

Emblems of the Kings of Abomey: 25fr, Agoliagbo (1894–1900). 35fr, Ganyehoussou (1620–1645), bird and cup (horiz.). 100fr, Guezo (1818–1858), bull, tree and birds. 135fr, Ouegbadja (1645–1685) (horiz.). 140fr, Glèle (1858–1889), lion and sword (horiz.)

287 A60 25fr multi. ('72) 30 15
288 " 35fr green & multi. 45 20
289 " 40fr " " 50 25
290 " 100fr red & multi. 1.25 45
291 " 135fr multi. ('72) 1.40 70
292 " 140fr brown & multi. 1.75 85
Nos. 287–292 (6) 5.65 2.60

Issue dates: 25fr, 135fr, July 17, 1972. Others, Aug. 3, 1971.

Kabuki Actor, Long-distance Skiing
A61

Brahms and "Soir d'été"
A62

1972, Feb. Engraved *Perf. 13*
293 A61 35fr dk. car., brown & blue green 50 25

11th Winter Olympic Games, Sapporo, Japan, Feb. 3–13. See No. C153.

No. 268 Surcharged

1972
294 A53 35fr on 40fr multi. 45 25

1972, June 29 Engraved *Perf. 13*

Design: 65fr, Brahms, woman at piano and music (horiz.).

295 A62 30fr red brown, black & lilac 40 25
296 " 65fr red brown, black & lilac 80 50

75th anniversary of the death of Johannes Brahms (1833–1897), German composer.

The Hare and The Tortoise, by La Fontaine—A63

Fables: 35fr, The Fox and The Stork (vert.). 40fr, The Cat, The Weasel and Rabbit.

1972, Aug. 28 Engr. *Perf. 13*
297 CD136 10fr multicolored 15 10
298 " 35fr dk. red & multi. 45 25
299 " 40fr ultra. & multi. 50 30

Jean de La Fontaine (1621–1695), French fabulist.

West African Monetary Union Issue
Common Design Type

1972, Nov. 2 Engraved *Perf. 13*
300 CD136 40fr chocolate, ocher & gray 40 25

10th anniversary of West African Monetary Union.

Dr. Hansen, Microscope, Bacilli
A65

Design: 85 fr, Portrait of Dr. Hansen.

1973, May 14 Engr. *Perf. 13*
301 A65 35fr ultra., vio. brn. & brown 30 20
302 " 85fr yel. grn., bister & vermilion 75 50

Centenary of the discovery by Dr. Armauer G. Hansen of the Hansen bacillus, the cause of leprosy.

Arms of Dahomey
A66

1973, June 25 Photo. *Perf. 13*
303 A66 5fr ultra. & multi. 8 5
304 " 35fr ocher & multi. 30 15
305 " 40fr red org. & multi. 35 17

INTERPOL Emblem and Spiderweb
A67

Design: 50fr, INTERPOL emblem and communications symbols (vert.).

1973, July Engraved
306 A67 35fr verm., green & brown 35 20
307 " 50fr grn., brn. & red 50 30

50th anniversary of International Criminal Police Organization (INTERPOL).

Education in Hygiene and Nutrition
A68

Design: 100fr, Prenatal examination and care, WHO emblem.

1973, Aug. 2 Photo. *Perf. 12½x13*
308 A68 35fr multicolored 35 15
309 " 100fr " 85 50

World Health Organization, 25th anniversary.

No. 248 Surcharged with New Value, 2 Bars, and Overprinted in Red: "SECHERESSE SOLIDARITE AFRICAINE"

1973, Aug. 16
310 A45 100fr on 70fr multi. 1.20 65

African solidarity in drought emergency.

African Postal Union Issue
Common Design Type

1973, Sept. 12 Engraved *Perf. 13*
311 CD137 100fr red, purple & black 1.00 55

Epinephelus Aeneus—A69

Fish: 15fr, Drepane africana. 35fr, Pragus ehrenbergi.

1973, Sept. 18

312	A69	5fr steel bl. & indigo	12	7
313	"	15fr black & brt. blue	12	10
314	"	35fr emerald, ocher & sepia	30	15

Chameleon A70

Design: 40fr, Emblem over map of Dahomey (vert.).

1973, Nov. 30 Photo. *Perf. 13*

315	A70	35fr olive & multi.	35	20
316	"	40fr multicolored	40	30

1st anniversary of the Oct. 26 revolution.

The Chameleon in the Tree—A71

Designs: 5fr, The elephant, the hen and the dog (vert.). 10fr, The sparrowhawk and the dog (vert.). 25fr, The chameleon in the tree. 40fr, The eagle, the viper and the hen.

1974, Feb. 14 Photo. *Perf. 13*

317	A71	5fr emerald & multi.	8	5
318	"	10fr slate bl. & multi.	10	7
319	"	25fr " " "	20	15
320	"	40fr lt. bl. & multi.	35	17

Folktales of Dahomey.

German Shepherd—A72

1974, Apr. 25 Photo. *Perf. 13*

Multicolored

321	A72	40fr *shown*	35	20
322	"	50fr *Boxer*	40	25
323	"	100fr *Saluki*	85	60

Council Issue

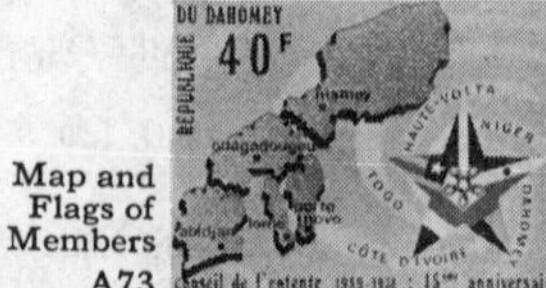

Map and Flags of Members A73

1974, May 29 Photo. *Perf. 13x12½*

324	A73	40fr blue & multi.	35	20

15th anniversary of the Council of Accord.

Certain unlisted issues of Dahomey, starting in 1974, are mentioned and briefly described in "For the Record" at the back of this volume.

Locomotive 232, 1911—A74

Designs: Locomotives.

1974, Sept. 2 Photo. *Perf. 13x12½*

Multicolored

325	A74	35fr *shown*	30	20
326	"	40fr *Freight, 1877*	35	20
327	"	100fr *Crampton, 1849*	85	60
328	"	200fr *Stephenson, 1846*	1.65	1.25

Globe, Money, People in Bank A75

1974, Oct. 31 Engraved *Perf. 13*

329	A75	35fr multicolored	35	20

World Savings Day.

Dompago Dance, Hissi Tribe A76

Flags of Dahomey and Nigeria over Africa A77

Folk Dances: 25fr, Fetish Dance, Vaudou-Tchinan. 40fr, Bamboo Dance, Agbehoun. 100fr, Somba Dance, Sandoua (horiz.).

1975, Aug. 4 Litho. *Perf. 12*

330	A76	10fr yellow & multi.	12	6
331	"	25fr dk. grn. & multi.	20	12
332	"	40fr red & multi.	32	22
333	"	100fr multicolored	85	50

1975, Aug. 11 Photo. *Perf. 12½x13*

Design: 100fr, Arrows connecting maps of Dahomey and Nigeria (horiz.).

334	A77	65fr multicolored	55	35
335	"	100fr grn. & multi.	85	55

Year of intensified cooperation between Dahomey and Nigeria.

Map, Pylons, Emblem—A78

Benin Electric Community Emblem and Pylon A79

1975, Aug. 18

336	A78	40fr multicolored	35	25
337	A79	150fr "	1.25	85

Benin Electric Community and Ghana-Togo-Dahomey cooperation.

Map of Dahomey, Rising Sun A80

Albert Schweitzer, Nurse, Patient A81

1975, Aug. 25 Photo. *Perf. 12½x13*

338	A80	35fr multicolored	28	15

Cooperation Year for the creation of a new Dahoman society.

1975, Sept. 22 Engr. *Perf. 13*

339	A81	200fr olive, green & red brown	1.65	1.10

Birth centenary of Albert Schweitzer (1875–1965), medical missionary and musician.

Woman Speaking on Telephone, IWY Emblem A82

Design: 150fr, International Women's Year emblem and linked rings.

1975, Oct. 20 Engr. *Perf. 12½x13*

340	A82	50fr Prus. blue & lilac	40	25
341	"	150fr emerald, brn.& orange	1.25	65

International Women's Year 1975.
Later issues are listed under Benin.

SEMI-POSTAL STAMPS.

Regular Issue of 1913 Surcharged in Red **+5c**

1915 *Perf. 14x13½.* **Unwmkd.**

B1 A5 10c+5c orange red & rose 35 25

Curie Issue
Common Design Type

1938 *Perf. 13*

B2 CD80 1.75fr+50c bright ultramarine 3.25 3.25

French Revolution Issue
Common Design Type

Name and Value Typo. in Black.

1939 Photogravure.

B3 CD83 45(c)+25(c) green 2.50 2.50
B4 " 70(c)+30(c) brown 2.50 2.50
B5 " 90(c)+35(c) red orange 2.50 2.50
B6 " 1.25fr+1fr rose pink 2.50 2.50
B7 " 2.25fr+2fr blue 2.50 2.50
Nos. B3-B7 (5) 12.50 12.50

Postage Stamps of 1913-38 Surcharged in Black **SECOURS +1 fr. NATIONAL**

1941 *Perf. 13½x14.*

B8 A5 50c+1fr brown red & blue 30 30
B9 " 80c+2fr henna brown & ultramarine 2.25 2.25
B10 " 1.50fr+2fr dark blue & light blue 2.50 2.50
B11 " 2fr+3fr yellow orange & chocolate 2.50 2.50

Common Design Type and

Radio Operator
SP1

Senegalese Artillerymen
SP2

1941 Photogravure. *Perf. 13½.*

B12 SP1 1f+1fr red 40
B13 CD86 1.50fr+3fr claret 40
B14 SP2 2.50fr+1fr blue 40

The surtax was for the defense of the colonies.

Stamps of type A11 surcharged "OEUVRES COLONIALES" and new values were issued in 1944 by the Vichy Government, but were not placed on sale in the colony.

Republic

Anti-Malaria Issue
Common Design Type

1962, Apr. 7 Engr. *Perf. 12½x12*

B15 CD108 25fr+5fr org. brn. 60 60

Issued for the World Health Organization drive to eradicate malaria.

Freedom from Hunger Issue
Common Design Type

1963, Mar. 21 *Perf. 13* **Unwmkd.**

B16 CD112 25fr+5fr olive, brn. red & brown 55 55

AIR POST STAMPS.
Common Design Type
Engraved.

1940 *Perf. 12½* **Unwmkd.**

C1 CD85 1.90fr ultramarine 8 8
C2 " 2.90fr dark red 8 8
C3 " 4.50fr dark gray green 15 15
C4 " 4.90fr yellow bistre 25 25
C5 " 6.90fr deep orange 40 40
Nos. C1-C5 (5) 96 96

Common Design Types

1942

C6 CD88 50c carmine & blue 8
C7 " 1fr brown & black 10
C8 " 2fr dark green & red brown 12
C9 " 3fr dk. blue & scarlet 30
C10 " 5fr vio. & brown red 25

Frame Engr., Center Typo.

C11 CD89 10fr ultramarine, indigo & orange 25
C12 " 20fr rose carmine, magenta & gray black 30
C13 " 50fr yellow green, dull green & deep blue 65 65
Nos. C6-C13 (8) 2.05

There is doubt whether Nos. C6-C12 were officially placed in use.

Republic

Somba House—AP4

Design: 500fr, Royal Court of Abomey.

Engraved

1960, Apr. 1 *Perf. 13* **Unwmkd.**

C14 AP4 100fr indigo, ochre & vio. brn. 1.50 45
C15 " 500fr bistre brown, brown red & dark green 7.00 1.25

Type of Regular Issue, 1961.

1961, Sept. 20

C16 A16 200fr multicolored 3.25 2.75
a. Souvenir sheet of three 4.75 4.75

Issued to commemorate the first anniversary of Dahomey's admission to the United Nations. No. C16a contains one each of Nos. 150-151 and C16. Bistre marginal inscription. Size: 129x85mm.

Air Afrique Issue
Common Design Type

1962, Feb. 17 *Perf. 13*

C17 CD107 25fr ultra., black & orange brown 55 45

Issued to commemorate the founding of Air Afrique (African Airlines).

Palace of the African and Malgache Union, Cotonou
AP5

1963, July 27 Photo. *Perf. 13x12*

C18 AP5 250fr dk. & lt. blue, ocher & grn. 3.50 2.00

Issued to commemorate the assembly of chiefs of state of the African and Malgache Union held at Cotonou in July.

African Postal Union Issue
Common Design Type

1963, Sept. 8 *Perf. 12½* **Unwmkd.**

C19 CD114 25fr bright blue, ocher & red 45 30

See note after Cameroun No. C47.

Boeing 707—AP6

Designs (Boeing 707): 200fr, On the ground. 300fr, Over Cotonou airport. 500fr, In the air.

1963, Oct. 25 Engraved *Perf. 13*

C20 AP6 100fr dark purple, grn. & bis. 1.25 40
C21 " 200fr violet, brown orge. & grn. 2.50 1.25
C22 " 300fr blue, red brn. & brt. grn. 3.50 1.75
C23 " 500fr brn. orge., dk. brn. & yel. green 6.00 2.50

Priests Carrying Funerary Boat, Isis Temple, Philae
AP7

1964, March 9 *Perf. 13* **Unwmkd.**

C24 AP7 25fr violet blue & brown 70 50

Issued to publicize the UNESCO world campaign to save historic monuments in Nubia.

Weather Map and Symbols
AP8

1965, Mar. 23 Photo. *Perf. 12½*

C25 AP8 50fr multicolored 80 50

Fifth World Meteorological Day.

ICY Emblem and Men of Various Races—AP9

1965, June 26 Engraved *Perf. 13*

C26 AP9 25fr dull purple, maroon & grn. 40 20
C27 " 85fr dp. blue, maroon & slate grn. 1.25 80

International Cooperation Year, 1965.

Winston Churchill
AP10

1965, June 15 Photo. *Perf. 12½*

C28 AP10 100fr multi. 1.65 1.25

Issued in memory of Sir Winston Churchill (1874-1965), statesman and World War II leader.

Abraham Lincoln—AP11

1965, July 15 *Perf. 13*

C29 AP11 100fr multi. 1.65 1.25

Centenary of death of Abraham Lincoln.

John F. Kennedy and Arms of Dahomey
AP12

1965, Nov. 22 Photo. *Perf. 12½*

C30 AP12 100fr deep green & black 1.65 1.25

Issued in memory of President John F. Kennedy (1917-63).

Dr. Albert Schweitzer and Patients
AP13

1966, Jan. 17 Photo. *Perf. 12½*

C31 AP13 100fr multi. 1.65 1.25

Issued in memory of Dr. Albert Schweitzer (1875-1965), medical missionary, theologian and musician.

WHO Type of Regular Issue

Design: 100fr, WHO Headquarters from the West.

1966, May 3 *Perf. 13* **Unwmkd.**

Size: 47x28mm.

C32 A36 100fr ultra., yellow & black 1.65 1.00

Issued to commemorate the inauguration of the World Health Organization Headquarters, Geneva.

Pygmy Goose
AP14

Broad-billed Rollers
AP15

Birds: 100fr, Firey-breasted bush-shrike. 250fr, Emerald cuckoos. 500fr, Emerald starling.

1966-67 *Perf. 12½*

C33	AP14	50fr multicolored	1.00	40
C34	"	100fr "	1.75	65
C35	AP15	200fr multi. ('67)	3.25	1.35
C36	"	250fr multi. ('67)	4.00	1.85
C37	AP14	500fr multicolored	7.00	3.50
		Nos. C33-C37 (5)	17.00	7.75

Issue dates: 50fr, 100fr, 500fr, June 13, 1966. Others, Jan. 20, 1967.

Industrial Symbols
AP16

1966, July 21 **Photo.** *Perf. 12x13*

C38	AP16	100fr multi.	1.50	90

3rd anniversary of agreement between European Economic Community and the African and Malagache Union.

Pope Paul VI and St. Peter's, Rome—AP17

Pope Paul VI and U.N. General Assembly
AP18

Design: 70fr, Pope Paul VI and view of New York City.

1966, Aug. 22 **Engraved** *Perf. 13*

C39	AP17	50fr brt. grn., rose car. & org. brown	75	40
C40	"	70fr dk. bl., slate grn. & lake	1.00	60
C41	AP18	100fr dk. grn., brn. vio. & slate blue	1.50	1.00
		a. Min. sheet of 3	3.50	3.50

Issued to commemorate Pope Paul's appeal for peace before the U.N. General Assembly, Oct. 4, 1965. No. C41a contains one each of Nos. C39-C41. Size: 178x100mm.

Air Afrique Issue, 1966
Common Design Type

1966, Aug. 31 **Photo.** *Perf. 12½*

C42	CD123	30fr dark violet, black & gray	50	25

Issued to commemorate the introduction of DC-8F planes by Air Afrique.

"Science"—AP20

Designs: 45fr, "Art" (carved female statue, vert.). 100fr, "Education" (book and letters).

1966, Nov. 4 **Engraved** *Perf. 13*

C43	AP20	30fr magenta, ultra. & vio. brn.	40	25
C44	"	45fr maroon & grn.	70	40
C45	"	100fr blk., maroon & bright blue	1.50	90
		a. Min. sheet of 3	3.00	3.00

Issued to commemorate the 20th anniversary of UNESCO (United Nations Educational, Scientific and Cultural Organization). No. C45a contains one each of Nos. C43-C45 Size: 169x100mm.

Madonna by Alessio Baldovinetti
AP21

Designs: 50fr, Nativity after 15th century Beaune tapestry. 100fr, Adoration of the Shepherds, by José Ribera.

1966, Dec. 25 **Photo.** *Perf. 12½x12*

C46	AP21	50fr multicolored	2.25	1.35
C47	"	100fr "	4.00	2.75
C48	"	200fr "	6.75	5.00

Christmas 1966.
See Nos. C95-C96, C109-C115.

1967, Apr. 10 *Perf. 12½x12*

Paintings by Ingres: No. C49, Self-portrait, 1804. No. C50, Oedipus and the Sphinx.

C49	AP21	100fr multicolored	2.00	1.50
C50	"	100fr "	2.00	1.50

Issued to commemorate the centenary of the death of Jean Auguste Dominique Ingres (1780-1867), French painter.

Three-master Suzanne—AP22

Windjammers: 45fr, Three-master Esmeralda (vert.). 80fr, Schooner Marie Alice (vert.). 100fr, Four-master Antonin.

1967, May 8 *Perf. 13*

C51	AP22	30fr multicolored	50	25
C52	"	45fr "	70	45
C53	"	80fr "	1.20	60
C54	"	100fr "	1.50	85

Nos. C29-C30 Surcharged

29 MAI 1967
50e Anniversaire
de la naissance
de
John F. Kennedy

125F

1967, May 29 **Photo.** *Perf. 13, 12½*

C55	AP11	125fr on 100fr multi.	2.00	1.00
		a. Surch. invtd.	22.50	
C56	AP12	125fr on 100fr dp. grn. & blk.	2.00	1.00
		a. Surch. invtd.	25.00	

Issued to commemorate the 50th anniversary of the birth of President John F. Kennedy.

EXPO '67 "Man In Space" Pavilion
AP23

1967, June 12 **Engraved** *Perf. 13*

C57	AP23	100fr dull red & Prus. blue	1.50	85
		a. Min. sheet of 3	3.25	3.25

Issued to commemorate EXPO '67, International Exhibition, Montreal, Apr. 28-Oct. 27, 1967. No. C57a contains one each of Nos. 235-236 and C57. Size: 149x100mm.

Europafrica Issue, 1967

Konrad Adenauer, by Oscar Kokoschká
AP24

1967, July 19 **Photo.** *Perf. 12½x12*

C58	AP24	70fr multicolored	1.25	90
		a. Souv. sheet of 4	5.00	5.00

Issued in memory of Konrad Adenauer (1876-1967), chancellor of West Germany (1949-1963). No. C58a contains 4 No. C58. Dark gray marginal inscription. Size: 140x158mm.

Jamboree Emblem, Ropes and World Map
AP25

1967, Aug. 7 **Engr.** *Perf. 13*

C59	AP25	100fr lilac, slate grn. & dp. blue	1.50	90
		a. Souv. sheet of 3	3.75	3.50

Issued to commemorate the 12th Boy Scout World Jamboree, Farragut State Park, Idaho, Aug. 1-9. No. C59a contains one each of Nos. 239-240 and C59. Bright blue marginal inscription. Size: 149x100mm.

No. C48 Surcharged in Red

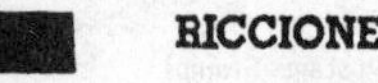

RICCIONE
150F
12-29
Août
1967

1967, Aug. 12 **Photo.** *Perf. 12½x12*

C60	AP21	150fr on 200fr multi.	2.50	2.00
		a. "150F" omitted	110.00	110.00

Issued to publicize the Riccione, Italy, Stamp Exhibition.

African Postal Union Issue, 1967
Common Design Type

1967, Sept. 9 **Engraved** *Perf. 13*

C61	CD124	100fr red, brt. lilac & emerald	1.50	1.00

Charles de Gaulle
AP26

1967, Nov. 21 **Photo.** *Perf. 12½x13*

C62	AP26	100fr multicolored	2.50	2.00
		a. Souv. sheet of 4	10.00	10.00

Issued to honor Pres. Charles de Gaulle of France on the occasion of Pres. Christophe Soglo's state visit to Paris, Nov. 1967. No. C62a contains 4 No. C62. Black marginal inscription. Size: 140x161 mm.

Madonna, by Matthias Grunewald
AP27

Paintings: 50fr, Holy Family by the Master of St. Sebastian (horiz.). 100fr, Adoration of the Magi by Ulrich Apt the Elder. 200fr, Annunciation, by Matthias Grunewald.

1967, Dec. 11 Photo. ***Perf. 12½***

C63	AP27	30fr multicolored	35	25
C64	"	50fr "	70	40
C65	"	100fr "	1.50	90
C66	"	200fr "	3.00	1.40

Christmas 1967.

Venus de Milo and Mariner 5 AP28

Gutenberg Monument, Strasbourg Cathedral AP29

Design: No. C68, Venus de Milo and Venus 4 Rocket.

1968, Feb. 17 Photo. ***Perf. 13***

C67	AP28	70fr greenish blue & multi.	1.25	60
C68	"	70fr deep blue & multi.	1.25	60
		a. Souv. sheet of 2	2.50	2.50

Issued to commemorate the explorations of the planet Venus, Oct. 18–19, 1967. No. C68a contains one each of Nos. C67–C68. Black marginal inscription. Size: 106x96mm.

1968, May 20 Litho. ***Perf. 14x13½***

Design: 100fr, Gutenberg Monument, Mainz, and Gutenberg press.

C69	AP29	45fr green & org.	70	35
C70	"	100fr dk. & lt. bl.	1.35	65
		a. Souv. sheet of 2	2.25	2.25

Issued to commemorate the 500th anniversary of the death of Johann Gutenberg, inventor of printing from movable type. No. C70a contains one each of Nos. C69–C70. Marginal inscription in green and dark blue. Size: 130x100mm.

Martin Luther King, Jr. AP30

Designs: 30fr, "We must meet hate with creative love" in French, English and German. 100fr, Full-face portrait.

Perf. 12½, 13½x13

1968, June 17 Photogravure

Size: 26x46mm.

C71	AP30	30fr red brown, yel. & black	40	20

Size: 26x37mm.

C72	AP30	55fr multicolored	70	40
C73	"	100fr "	1.25	65
		a. Min. sheet of 3	2.75	2.75

Issued in memory of the Rev. Dr. Martin Luther King, Jr. (1929–1968), American civil rights leader. No. C73a contains one each of Nos. C71–C73. Size: 150x114mm.

Robert Schuman—AP31

Designs: 45fr, Alcide de Gasperi. 70fr, Konrad Adenauer.

1968, July 20 Photo. ***Perf. 13***

C74	AP31	30fr deep yellow, blk. & green	40	20
C75	"	45fr orange, dark brn. & olive	60	30
C76	"	70fr multi.	1.00	45

Issued to commemorate the 5th anniversary of the economic agreement between the European Economic Community and the African and Malgache Union.

Battle of Montebello, by Henri Philippoteaux AP32

Paintings: 45fr, 2nd Zouave Regiment at Magenta, by Riballier. 70fr, Battle of Magenta, by Louis Eugène Charpentier. 100fr, Battle of Solferino, by Charpentier.

1968, Aug. 12 ***Perf. 12½x12***

C77	AP32	30fr multicolored	45	20
C78	"	45fr "	70	30
C79	"	70fr "	1.00	50
C80	"	100fr "	1.50	75

Issued for the Red Cross.

Mail Truck in Village—AP33

Designs: 45fr, Mail truck stopping at rural post office. 55fr, Mail truck at river bank. 70fr, Mail truck and train.

1968, Oct. 7 Photo. ***Perf. 13x12½***

C81	AP33	30fr multicolored	30	20
C82	"	45fr "	60	30
C83	"	55fr "	70	40
C84	"	70fr "	85	50

Aztec Stadium, Mexico City AP34

Designs (Olympic Rings and); 45fr, Ball player, Mayan sculpture (vert.). 70fr, Wrestler, sculpture from Uxpanapan (vert.). 150fr, Olympic Stadium, Mexico City.

1968, Nov. 20 Engraved ***Perf. 13***

C85	AP34	30fr deep claret & slate green	45	20
C86	"	45fr ultra. & dark rose brown	60	25
C87	AP34	70fr slate green & dark brown	90	40
C88	"	150fr dk. carmine & dark brown	2.10	1.00
		a. Min. sheet of 4	4.50	4.50

Issued to commemorate the 19th Olympic Games, Mexico City, Oct. 12–27.

No. C88a contains one each of Nos. C85–C88. It is folded down the vertical gutter separating Nos. C85–C86 se-tenant at left and Nos. C87–C88 se-tenant at right. Size: 235x102mm.

The Annunciation, by Foujita AP35

Paintings by Foujita: 30fr, Nativity (horiz.). 100fr, The Virgin and Child. 200fr, The Baptism of Christ.

Perf. 12x12½, 12½x12

1968, Nov. 25 Photogravure

C89	AP35	30fr multicolored	50	20
C90	"	70fr "	90	45
C91	"	100fr "	1.50	65
C92	"	200fr "	3.00	1.35

Christmas 1968.

PHILEXAFRIQUE Issue

Painting: 100fr, Diderot, by Louis Michel Vanloo.

1968, Dec. 16 ***Perf. 12½x12***

C93	AP35	100fr multicolored	1.50	1.00

Issued to publicize PHILEXAFRIQUE, Philatelic Exhibition in Abidjan, Feb. 14–23. Printed with alternating bluish violet label.

2nd PHILEXAFRIQUE Issue

Common Design Type

Design: 50fr, Dahomey No. 119 and aerial view of Cotonou.

1969, Feb. 14 Engraved ***Perf. 13***

C94	CD128	50fr bl., brn. & pur.	75	60

Issued to commemorate the opening of PHILEXAFRIQUE, Feb. 14.

Type of Painting (Christmas) Issue, 1966

Paintings: No. C95, Virgin of the Rocks, by Leonardo da Vinci. No. C96, Virgin with the Scales, by Cesare da Sesto.

1969, Mar. 17 Photo. ***Perf. 12½x12***

C95	AP21	100fr vio. & multi.	1.35	65
C96	"	100fr grn. & multi.	1.35	65

Issued to commemorate the 450th anniversary of the death of Leonardo da Vinci (1452–1519).

General Bonaparte, by Jacques Louis David AP36

Paintings: 60fr, Napoleon I in 1809, by Robert J. Lefevre. 75fr, Napoleon on the Battlefield of Eylau, by Antoine Jean Gros (horiz.). 200fr, Gen. Bonaparte at Arcole, by Gros.

1969, Apr. 14 Photo. ***Perf. 12½x12***

C97	AP36	30fr multicolored	1.20	85
C98	"	60fr "	1.75	1.25
C99	"	75fr "	2.50	1.65
C100	"	200fr "	5.50	3.25

Bicentenary of the birth of Napoleon I.

Arms Type of Regular Issue, 1969

1969, June 30 Litho. ***Perf. 13½x13***

C101	A49	50fr multicolored	60	30

Apollo 8 Trip Around the Moon AP37

Embossed on Gold Foil

1969, July ***Die-cut Perf. 10½***

C102	AP37	1000fr gold	15.00	15.00

Issued to commemorate the U.S. Apollo 8 mission, which put the first men into orbit around the moon, Dec. 21–27, 1968.

ALUNISSAGE APOLLO XI JUILLET 1969

Nos. C67–C68 Surcharged

125F

1969, Aug. 1 Photo. ***Perf. 13***

C103	AP28	125fr on 70fr greenish blue & multi.	2.00	1.00
C104	"	125fr on 70fr dp. bl. & multi.	2.00	1.00

Issued to commemorate man's first landing on the moon, July 20, 1969; U. S. astronauts Neil A. Armstrong and Col. Edwin E. Aldrin, Jr., with Lieut. Col. Michael Collins piloting Apollo 11.

Europafrica Issue

Type of Regular Issue, 1969

Design: 100fr, Oil palm industry, Cotonou.

1969, Sept. 22 Litho. ***Perf. 14***

C105	A51	100fr multicolored	1.25	65
		a. Souv. sheet of 3	2.25	2.25

No. C105a contains one each of Nos. 262–263 and C105. Black marginal inscription. Size: 107½x148mm.

Dahomey Rotary Emblem AP38

1969, Sept. 25 ***Perf. 14x13½***

C106	AP38	50fr multicolored	75	40

Issued to honor Rotary International.

No. C33 Surcharged

10F

1969, Nov. 15 Photo. *Perf. 12½*
C107 AP14 10fr on 50fr multi. 12 6

Dance Type of Regular Issue

Design: 70fr, Teke dance and Tourist Year emblem.

1969, Dec. 15 Litho. *Perf. 14*
C108 A52 70fr multicolored 90 40

Painting Type of 1966

Paintings: 30fr, Annunciation, by Vrancke van der Stockt. 45fr, Nativity, Swabian School (horiz.). 110fr, Madonna and Child, by the Master of the Gold Brocade. 200fr, Adoration of the Kings, Antwerp School.

Perf. 12½x12, 12x12½

1969, Dec. 20
C109 AP21 30fr multicolored 50 35
C110 " 45fr red & multi. 75 50
C111 " 110fr multicolored 2.00 1.20
C112 " 200fr " 3.50 2.25

Christmas 1969.

1969, Dec. 27 *Perf. 12½x12*

Paintings: No. C113, The Artist's Studio (detail), by Gustave Courbet. No. C114, Self-portrait with Gold Chain, by Rembrandt. 150fr, Hendrickje Stoffels, by Rembrandt.

C113 AP21 100fr red & multi. 1.25 75
C114 " 100fr grn. & multi. 1.25 75
C115 " 150fr multicolored 2.00 1.00

Franklin D. Roosevelt
AP39

Astronauts, Rocket and U.S. Flag
AP40

1970, Feb. Photo. *Perf. 12½*
C116 AP39 100fr ultra., yellow grn. & blk. 1.25 50

Issued to commemorate the 25th anniversary of the death of Pres. Franklin Delano Roosevelt (1882–1945).

1970, Mar. 9 Photo. *Perf. 12½*

Designs: 50fr, Astronauts riding rocket through space. 70fr, Astronauts in landing module approaching moon. 110fr, Astronauts planting U.S. flag on moon.

C117 AP40 30fr multicolored 40 25

Souvenir Sheet

C118 AP40 Sheet of 4 3.50 3.50
a. 50fr violet blue & multi. 60 60
b. 70fr " " " 85 85
c. 110fr " " " 1.25 1.25

See note after No. C104. No. C118 contains one each of Nos. C117, C118a, C118b and C118c; violet blue marginal inscription in French, German and English. Size: 120x157mm.

Walt Whitman and Dahoman Huts
AP41

1970, Apr. 30 Engraved *Perf. 13*
C119 AP41 100fr Prus. blue, brown & emerald 1.25 50

Issued to honor Walt Whitman (1818–1892), American poet.

No. C117 Surcharged in Silver with New Value, Heavy Bar and:
"APOLLO XIII / SOLIDARITE / SPATIALE / INTERNATIONALE"

1970, May 15 Photo. *Perf. 12½*
C120 AP40 40fr on 30fr multi. 65 65

The flight of Apollo 13.

Soccer Players and Globe—AP42

Designs: 50fr, Goalkeeper catching ball. 200fr, Players kicking ball.

1970, May 19
C121 AP42 40fr multicolored 60 35
C122 " 50fr " 70 40
C123 " 200fr " 3.00 1.40

Issued to publicize the 9th World Soccer Championships for the Jules Rimet Cup, Mexico City, May 30–June 21, 1970.

EXPO '70 Type of Regular Issue

Designs (EXPO '70 Emblems and): 70fr, Dahomey pavilion. 120fr, Mt. Fuji, temple and torii.

1970, June 15 Litho. *Perf. 13½x14*
C124 A54 70fr yellow, red & dark violet 85 40
C125 " 120fr yel., red & grn. 1.50 75

Issued to publicize EXPO '70 International Exhibition Osaka, Japan, Mar. 15–Sept. 13, 1970.

No. C123 Surcharged with New Value and Overprinted:
"Bresil-Italie / 4–1"

1970, July 13 Photo. *Perf. 12½*
C126 AP42 100fr on 200fr multi. 1.50 65

Issued to commemorate Brazil's victory in the 9th World Soccer Championships, Mexico City.

Mercury, Map of Africa and Europe
AP43

Ludwig van Beethoven
AP44

Europafrica Issue, 1970

1970, July 20 Photo. *Perf. 12x13*
C127 AP43 40fr multicolored 50 30
C128 " 70fr " 85 40

1970, Sept. 21 Litho. *Perf. 14x13½*
C129 AP44 90fr bright blue & vio. black 1.25 50
C130 " 110fr yellow green & dk. brown 1.35 70

Issued to commemorate the bicentenary of the birth of Ludwig van Beethoven (1770–1827), composer.

Symbols of Learning
AP45

1970, Nov. 6 Photo. *Perf. 12½*
C131 AP45 100fr multi. 1.25 50

Issued to commemorate the laying of the foundation stone for the University at Calavi.

Annunciation, Rhenish School, c.1340
AP46

Paintings of Rhenish School, circa 1340: 70fr, Nativity. 110fr, Adoration of the Kings. 200fr, Presentation at the Temple.

1970, Nov. 9 *Perf. 12½x12*
C132 AP46 40fr gold & multi. 50 25
C133 " 70fr " " 90 35
C134 " 110fr " " 1.35 60
C135 " 200fr " " 2.75 1.10

Christmas 1970.

Charles de Gaulle, Arc de Triomphe and Flag
AP47

Design: 500fr, de Gaulle as old man and Notre Dame Cathedral, Paris.

1971, March 15 Photo. *Perf. 12½*
C136 AP47 40fr multicolored 60 30
C137 " 500fr " 6.00 3.00

In memory of Gen. Charles de Gaulle (1890–1970), President of France.

L' Indifférent, by Watteau
AP48

Painting: No. C139, Woman playing stringed instrument, by Watteau.

1971, May 3 Photo. *Perf. 13*
C138 AP48 100fr red brown & multi. 1.20 80
C139 " 100fr red brown & multi. 1.20 80

250th death anniversary of Jean Antoine Watteau (1684–1721), French painter.

1971, May 29 Photo. *Perf. 13*

Dürer Paintings: 100fr, Self-portrait, 1498. 200fr, Self-portrait, 1500.

C140 AP48 100fr blue green & multi. 1.20 80
C141 " 200fr dark green & multi. 2.75 1.60

500th anniversary of the birth of Albrecht Dürer (1471–1528), German painter and engraver. See Nos. C151–C152, C174–C175.

Johannes Kepler and Diagram
AP49

Designs: 200fr, Kepler, trajectories, satellite and rocket.

1971, July 12 Engraved *Perf. 13*
C142 AP49 40fr brt. rose lilac, black & violet blue 50 25
C143 " 200fr red, black & dark blue 2.75 1.20

400th anniversary of the birth of Johannes Kepler (1571–1630), German astronomer.

Europafrica Issue

Jet Plane, Maps of Europe and Africa—AP50

Designs: 100fr, Ocean liner, maps of Europe and Africa.

1971, July 19 Photo. *Perf. 12½x12*
C144 AP50 50fr black, lt. blue & orange 60 30
C145 " 100fr multicolored 1.20 60

African Postal Union Issue, 1971

Common Design Type

Design: 100fr, Dahomey coat of arms and UAMPT building, Brazzaville, Congo.

1971, Nov. 13 *Perf. 13x13½*
C146 CD135 100fr bl. & multi. 1.20 60

Flight into Egypt, by Van Dyke
AP51

Paintings: 40fr, Adoration of the Shepherds, by the Master of the Hausbuch, c. 1500 (vert.). 70fr, Adoration of the Kings, by Holbein the Elder (vert.). 200fr, The Birth of Christ, by Dürer.

1971, Nov. 22 *Perf. 13*
C147 AP51 40fr gold & multi. 50 25
C148 " 70fr " " 90 45

C149 AP51 100fr gold & multi. 1.20 50
C150 " 200fr " " 2.40 1.20

Christmas 1971.

Painting Type of 1971 Inscribed: "25e ANNIVERSAIRE DE L'UNICEF"

Paintings: 40fr, Prince Balthazar, by Velasquez. 100fr, Infanta Margarita Maria, by Velázquez.

1971, Dec. 11

C151 AP48 40fr gold & multi. 50 30
C152 " 100fr " " 1.20 50

25th anniversary of the United Nations International Children's Fund (UNICEF).

Olympic Games Type of Regular Issue

Design: 150fr, Sapporo '72 emblem, ski jump and stork flying.

1972, Feb. Engraved *Perf. 13*

C153 A61 150fr brn., dp. rose lilac & blue 2.00 1.00

11th Winter Olympic Games, Sapporo, Japan, Feb. 3–13.

Boy Scout and Scout Flag
AP52

Designs: 40fr, Scout playing marimba. 100fr, Scouts doing farm work.

1972, Mar. 19 Photo. *Perf. 13*

Size: 26x35mm.

C154 AP52 35fr multicolored 30 20
C155 " 40fr " 50 25

Size: 26x46mm.

C156 AP52 100fr yel. & multi. 1.20 60
a. Souvenir sheet of 3 2.25 2.25

World Boy Scout Seminar, Cotonou, March 1972. No. C156a contains Nos. C154–C156 with perf. 12½. Red marginal inscription and black control number. Size: 150x115mm.

Workers Training Institute and Friedrich Naumann—AP53

Design: 250fr, Workers Training Institute and Pres. Theodor Heuss of Germany.

1972, Mar. 29 Photo. *Perf. 13x12*

C157 AP53 100fr brt. rose, blk. & violet 1.10 55
C158 " 250fr blue, black & violet 3.00 1.25

Laying of foundation stone for National Workers Training Institute.

Mosaic Floor, St. Mark's, Venice—AP54

12th Century Mosaics from St. Mark's Basilica: 40fr, Roosters carrying fox on a pole. 65fr, Noah sending out dove.

1972, Apr. 10 *Perf. 13*

C159 AP54 35fr gold & multi. 50 30
C160 " 40fr " " 60 40
C161 " 65fr " " 90 60

UNESCO campaign to save Venice.

Neapolitan and Dahoman Dancers
AP55

1972, May 3 *Perf. 13½x13*

C162 AP55 100fr multi. 1.20 70

12th Philatelic Exhibition, Naples.

Running, German Eagle, Olympic Rings
AP56

Designs (Olympic Rings and): 85fr, High jump and Glyptothek, Munich. 150fr, Shot put and Propylaeum, Munich.

1972, June 12 Engraved *Perf. 13*

C163 AP56 20fr ultra., green & brown 25 15
C164 " 85fr brown, green & ultra. 90 40
C165 " 150fr green, brown & ultra. 1.75 90
a. Miniature sheet of 3 3.50 3.50

20th Olympic Games, Munich, Aug. 26–Sept. 10. No. C165a contains one each of Nos. C163–C165. Size: 130x99mm.

Louis Blériot and his Plane—AP57

1972, June 26

C166 AP57 100fr vio., claret & brt. bl. 1.20 65

Birth centenary of Louis Blériot (1872–1936), French aviation pioneer.

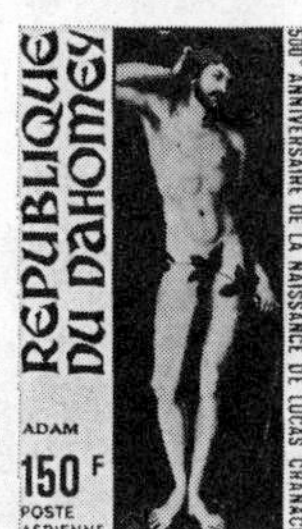

Adam, by Lucas Cranach
AP58

Design: 200fr, Eve, by Lucas Cranach.

1972, Oct. 24 Photogravure

C167 AP58 150fr multi. 2.00 1.00
C168 " 200fr " 2.50 1.10

500th anniversary of the birth of Lucas Cranach (1472–1553), German painter.

Pauline Borghese, by Canova
AP59

1972, Nov. 8

C169 AP59 250fr multi. 3.00 1.50

Sesquicentennial of the death of Antonio Canova (1757–1822), Italian sculptor.

Nos. C163–C165 Overprinted:

a. 5.00m.–10.00m. / VIREN / 2 MEDAILLES D'OR
b. HAUTEUR DAMES / MEYFARTH / MEDAILLE D'OR
c. POIDS / KOMAR / MEDAILLE D'OR

1972, Nov. 13 Engraved *Perf. 13*

C170 AP56 (*a*) 20fr multi. 30 20
C171 " (*b*) 85fr " 1.00 50
C172 " (*c*) 150fr " 2.00 1.10
a. Miniature sheet of 3 3.75 3.75

Gold medal winners in 20th Olympic Games: Lasse Viren, Finland, 5,000m. and 10,000m. races (20fr); Ulrike Meyfarth, Germany, women's high jump (85fr); Wladyslaw Komar, Poland, shot put (150fr).

Louis Pasteur
AP60

1972, Nov. 30

C173 AP60 100fr brt. grn., lilac & brn. 1.20 65

Sesquicentennial of the birth of Louis Pasteur (1822–1895), chemist and bacteriologist.

Painting Type of 1971

Paintings by Georges de La Tour: 35fr, Vielle player. 150fr, The Newborn (horiz.).

1972, Dec. 11 Photogravure

C174 AP48 35fr multicolored 42 20
C175 " 150fr " 2.00 1.10

320th death anniversary of Georges de La Tour (1593–1652), French painter.

Annunciation, School of Agnolo Gaddi
AP61

Paintings: 125fr, Nativity, by Simone dei Crocifissi. 140fr, Adoration of the Shepherds, by Giovanni di Pietro. 250fr, Adoration of the Kings, by Giotto.

1972, Dec. 15

C176 AP61 35fr gold & multi. 40 20
C177 " 125fr " " 1.20 60
C178 " 140fr " " 1.60 80
C179 " 250fr " " 2.60 1.50

Christmas 1972. See Nos. C195–C198, C218, C223, C225–C226.

Statue of St. Teresa, Basilica of Lisieux—AP62

Design: 100fr, St. Teresa, roses, and globe (vert.).

1973, May 14 Photo. *Perf. 13*

C180 AP62 40fr black, gold & light ultra. 40 25
C181 " 100fr gold & multi. 1.00 55

Centenary of the birth of St. Teresa of Lisieux (Therese Martin, 1873–97), Carmelite nun.

Scouts, African Scout Emblem—AP63

Designs (African Scout Emblem and): 20fr, Lord Baden-Powell (vert.). 40fr, Scouts building bridge.

1973, July 2 Engraved *Perf. 13*

C182 AP63 15fr blue, green & chocolate 15 10
C183 " 20fr olive & Prus. blue 20 15
C184 " 40fr green, Prus. bl. & brown 40 20
a. Souvenir sheet of 3 85 85

24th Boy Scout World Conference, Nairobi, Kenya, July 16–21. No. C184a contains 3 stamps similar to Nos. C182–C184 in changed colors (15fr in ultramarine, slate green and chocolate; 20fr in chocolate, ultramarine and indigo; 40fr in slate green, indigo and chocolate). Ultramarine marginal inscription and border. Size: 180x100 mm.

Copernicus, Venera and Mariner Satellites—AP64

Design: 125fr, Copernicus, sun, earth and moon (vert.).

1973, Aug. 20 Engr. *Perf. 13*

C185 AP64 65fr blk., dk. brn. & orange 80 45
C186 " 125fr bl., slate grn. & purple 1.25 65

500th anniversary of the birth of Nicolaus Copernicus (1473–1543), Polish astronomer.

Head and City Hall, Brussels
AP64a

1973, Sept. 17 Engraved *Perf. 13*

C187 AP64a 100fr blk., Prus. blue & dk. green 90 60

African Weeks, Brussels, Sept. 15–30, 1973.

WMO Emblem, World Weather Map—AP65

1973, Sept. 25

C188 AP65 100fr olive grn. & lt. brown 1.00 60

Centenary of international meteorological cooperation.

Europafrica Issue

"EUROPAFRIQUE"—AP66

Design: 40fr, similar to 35fr.

1973, Oct. 1 Engraved *Perf. 13*

C189 AP66 35fr multicolored 35 20
C190 " 40fr blue, sepia & ultra. 40 30

John F. Kennedy AP67

1973, Oct. 18

C191 AP67 200fr blue green, violet & slate grn. 2.00 1.20
a. Souvenir sheet 2.50 2.50

10th anniversary of the death of President John F. Kennedy (1917–1963). No. C191a contains one stamp in changed colors (bright blue, magenta & brown). Magenta marginal inscription and border. Size: 140x109mm.

Soccer—AP68

Designs: 40fr, Two soccer players. 100fr, Three soccer players.

1973, Nov. 19 Engr. *Perf. 13*

C192 AP68 35fr multicolored 30 20
C193 " 40fr " 40 25
C194 " 100fr " 90 65

World Soccer Cup, Munich 1974.

Painting Type of 1972

Designs: 35fr, Annunciation, by Dirk Bouts. 100fr, Nativity, by Giotto. 150fr, Adoration of the Kings, by Botticelli. 200fr, Adoration of the Shepherds, by Jacopo Bassano (horiz.).

1973, Dec. 20 Photo. *Perf. 13*

C195 AP61 35fr gold & multi. 35 25
C196 " 100fr " " 1.00 60
C197 " 150fr " " 1.50 1.00
C198 " 200fr " " 2.00 1.30

Christmas 1973.

No. C188 Surcharged in Violet with New Value and: "OPERATION SKYLAB / 1973–1974"

1974, Feb. 4 Engraved *Perf. 13*

C199 AP65 200fr on 100fr multi. 1.75 1.25

Skylab U.S. space missions, 1973–74.

Skiers, Snowflake, Olympic Rings AP69

1974, Feb. 25 Engraved *Perf. 13*

C200 AP69 100fr vio.bl., brn. & brt. bl. 90 65

50th anniversary of first Winter Olympic Games, Chamonix, France.

Marie Curie AP70

Designs: 50fr, Lenin. 150fr, Churchill.

1974, June 7 Engr. *Perf. 13*

C201 AP70 50fr dark red & brt. lilac 45 30
C202 " 125fr olive & dull red 1.10 75
C203 " 150fr brt. lilac & Prus. blue 1.35 90

50th anniversary of the death of Lenin (50fr); 40th anniversary of the death of Marie Sklodowska Curie (125fr); centenary of the birth of Winston Churchill (150fr).

Bishop, Persian, 18th Century AP71 **Frederic Chopin AP72**

Design: 200fr, Queen, Siamese chess piece, 19th century.

1974, June 14 Photo. *Perf. 12½x13*

C204 AP71 50fr org. & multi. 50 35
C205 " 200fr brt. green & multi. 1.75 1.25

21st Chess Olympiad, Nice, June 6–30, 1974.

1974, June 24 Engr. *Perf. 13*

Design: No. C207, Ludwig van Beethoven.

C206 AP72 150fr black & copper red 1.25 90
C207 " 150fr black & copper red 1.25 90

Famous musicians, Frederic Chopin (1810–1849) and Ludwig van Beethoven (1770–1827).

Astronaut on Moon, and Earth AP73

1974, July 10 Engraved *Perf. 13*

C208 AP73 150fr multi. 1.25 1.00

5th anniversary of the first moon walk.

Nos. C182–C183 Surcharged and Overprinted in Black or Red: "XIe JAMBOREE PANARABE DE BATROUN-LIBAN"

1974, July 19

C209 AP63 100fr on 15fr multi. 75 45
C210 " 140fr on 20fr multi. (R) 1.20 75

11th Pan-Arab Jamboree, Batrun, Lebanon, Aug. 1974. Overprint includes 2 bars over old denomination; 2-line overprint on No. C209, 3 lines on No. C210.

Nos. C193–C194 Overprinted and Surcharged with New Value and Two Bars: "R F A 2 / HOLLANDE 1"

1974, July 26 Engraved *Perf. 13*

C211 AP68 100fr on 40fr 80 35
C212 " 150fr on 100fr 1.20 55

World Cup Soccer Championship, 1974, victory of German Federal Republic.

Earth and UPU Emblem—AP74

Designs (UPU Emblem and): 65fr, Concorde in flight. 125fr, French railroad car, c. 1860. 200fr, African drummer and Renault mail truck, pre-1939.

1974, Aug. 5 Engraved *Perf. 13*

C213 AP74 35fr rose claret & violet 30 10
C214 " 65fr Prus. green & claret 60 20
C215 " 125fr multicolored 1.10 42
C216 " 200fr " 1.75 70

Centenary of Universal Postal Union.

Painting Type of 1972 and

Lion of Belfort by Frederic A. Bartholdi—AP75

Painting: 250fr, Girl with Falcon, by Philippe de Champaigne.

1974, Aug. 20 Engraved *Perf. 13*

C217 AP75 100fr rose brown 1.00 35
C218 AP61 250fr multi. 2.50 1.00

Rhamphorhynchus—AP76

Prehistoric Animals: 150fr, Stegosaurus. 200fr, Tyrannosaurus.

1974, Sept. 23 Photogravure

C219 AP76 35fr multicolored 30 12
C220 " 150fr " 1.20 55
C221 " 200fr " 1.50 70

Europafrica Issue

Globe, Cogwheel, Emblem—AP77

1974, Dec. 20 Typo. *Perf. 13*

C222 AP77 250fr red & multi. 2.50 1.00

Printed tête bêche in sheets of 10.

Christmas Type of 1972 and

Nativity, by Martin Schongauer AP78

Paintings: 35fr, Annunciation, by Schongauer. 100fr, Virgin in Rose Arbor, by Schongauer. 250fr, Virgin and Child, with St. John the Baptist, by Botticelli.

1974, Dec. 23 Photo. *Perf. 13*

C223 AP61 35fr gold & multi. 30 15
C224 AP78 40fr " " 40 25
C225 AP61 100fr " " 1.00 35
C226 " 250fr " " 2.50 1.00

Apollo and Soyuz Spacecraft AP79

Designs: 200fr, American and Russian flags, rocket take-off. 500fr, Apollo-Soyuz link-up.

1975, July 16 Litho. *Perf. 12½*

C227 AP79 35fr multicolored 30 15
C228 " 200fr vio. bl., red & blue 1.60 70
C229 " 500fr violet blue, indigo & red 4.00 2.25

Apollo Soyuz space test project (Russo-American cooperation); launching July 15; link-up, July 17.

Nos. C227–C228 Surcharged in Silver or Black: "RENCONTRE / APOLLO-SOYOUZ / 17 Juil. 1975"

1975, July 17 Litho. *Perf. 12½*

C230	AP79	100fr on 35fr (S)	80	35
C231	"	300fr on 200fr	2.40	1.00

Apollo-Soyuz link-up in space, July 17, 1975.

ARPHILA Emblem, "Stamps" and Head of Ceres—AP80

1975, Aug. 22 Engr. *Perf. 13*

C232	AP80	100fr blk., bl. & lilac	90	35

ARPHILA 75, International Philatelic Exhibition, Paris, June 6–16.

Holy Family, by Michelangelo AP81 — Infantry and Stars AP82

Europafrica Issue

1975, Sept. 29 Litho. *Perf. 12*

C233	AP81	300fr gold & multi.	2.75	1.00

1975, Nov. 18 Engr. *Perf. 13*

Designs (Stars and): 135fr, Drummers and fifer. 300fr, Artillery with cannon. 500fr, Cavalry.

C234	AP82	75fr grn., car. & purple	60	25
C235	"	135fr bl., magenta & sepia	1.10	45
C236	"	300fr vio. bl., verm. & choc.	2.40	1.00
C237	"	500fr verm., dk. grn. & brn.	4.00	1.75

American bicentennial.

Diving and Olympic Rings AP83

Design: 250fr, Soccer and Olympic rings.

1975, Nov. 24

C238	AP83	40fr vio., greenish bl. & ol. brn.	35	15
C239	"	250fr red, emerald & brown	2.00	90

Pre-Olympic Year 1975.

AIR POST SEMI-POSTAL STAMPS.

V1

POUR LA PROTECTION DE L'ENFANCE INDIGENE
A.O.F.
DAHOMEY 2fr +6fr

V2

V3

V4

Stamps of the preceding designs were issued in 1942 by the Vichy Government, but were not placed in use in the colony.

AIR POST PARCEL POST STAMPS

Nos. C20–C23, C14 Surcharged in Black or Red

300F

COLIS POSTAUX

1967-69 Engraved *Perf. 13*

CQ1	AP6	200fr on 200fr multi.	4.00	2.50
CQ2	"	300fr on 100fr multi.	5.00	4.00
CQ3	"	500fr on 300fr multi.	9.00	6.00
CQ4	"	1000fr on 500fr multi.	17.50	14.00
CQ5	AP4	5000fr on 100fr multi. (R) ('69)	70.00	00.00
		Nos. CQ1–CQ5 (5)	105.50	96.50

On No. CQ5, "Colis Postaux" is at top, bar at right.

POSTAGE DUE STAMPS.

Dahomey Natives D1

Numeral of Value D2

Typographed.

1906 *Perf. 14x13½.* Unwmkd.

J1	D1	5c green, *greenish*	85	85
J2	"	10c red brown	1.40	1.40
J3	"	15c dark blue	3.00	3.00
J4	"	20c *yellow*	1.85	1.85
J5	"	30c red, *straw*	2.00	2.00
J6	"	50c violet	7.00	7.00
J7	"	60c *buff*	4.00	4.00
J8	"	1fr *pinkish*	10.00	10.00
		Nos. J1–J8 (8)	30.10	30.10

1914

J9	D2	5c green	6	6
J10	"	10c rose	10	10
J11	"	15c gray	15	15
J12	"	20c brown	15	15
J13	"	30c blue	20	20
J14	"	50c black	40	40
J15	"	60c orange	60	40
J16	"	1fr violet	55	55
		Nos. J9–J16 (8)	2.21	2.01

1927

Type of 1914 Issue Surcharged **2F.**

J17	D2	2fr on 1fr lilac rose	1.10	1.25
J18	"	3fr on 1fr orange brown	1.25	1.25

Carved Mask D3

1941 Engraved *Perf. 14x13*

J19	D3	5c black	3	3
J20	"	10c lilac rose	4	4
J21	"	15c dark blue	4	4
J22	"	20c bright yellow green	6	6
J23	"	30c orange	8	8
J24	"	50c violet brown	17	17
J25	"	60c slate green	20	20
J26	"	1fr rose red	30	30
J27	"	2fr yellow	35	35
J28	"	3fr dark purple	40	40
		Nos. J19–J28 (10)	1.67	1.67

Stamps of type D3 with value numerals replacing "RF" at upper left corner were issued in 1943-44 by the Vichy Government, but were not placed on sale in the colony.

Republic

Panther and Man—D4

Perf. 14x13½

1963, July 22 Typo. Unwmkd.

J29	D4	1fr grn. & rose claret	5	5
J30	"	2fr brn. & emerald	8	8
J31	"	5fr orge. & vio. blue	12	12
J32	"	10fr magenta & blk.	25	25
J33	"	20fr vio. blue & orge.	30	30
		Nos. J29–J33 (5)	80	80

Mail Boat—D5

Designs: No. J35, Heliograph. No. J36, Morse receiver. No. J37, Mailman on bicycle. No. J38, Early telephone. No. J39, Autorail. No. J40, Mail truck. No. J41, Radio tower. No. J42, DC-8F jet plane. No. J43, Early Bird communications satellite.

1967, Oct. 24 Engraved *Perf. 11*

J34	D5	1fr brn., dull pur. & bl.	8	8
J35	"	1fr dull pur., brn. & bl.	8	8
J36	"	3fr dk. brn., dk. green & orange	12	12
J37	"	3fr dk. grn., dk. brown & orange	12	12
J38	"	5fr olive bister, lilac & bl.	15	15
J39	"	5fr lilac, olive bister & bl.	15	15
J40	"	10fr brown orange, violet & green	25	25
J41	"	10fr vio., brn. org. & grn.	25	25
J42	"	30fr Prus. bl., maroon & violet	50	50
J43	"	30fr vio., Prus. blue & maroon	50	50
		Nos. J34–J43 (10)	2.20	2.20

The two designs of each value in Nos. J34–J43 were printed tête bêche, se-tenant at the base.

PARCEL POST STAMPS

Nos. 141–146 and 148 Surcharged **COLIS POSTAUX** **5F**

Engraved

1967, Jan. *Perf. 13* Unwmkd.

Q1	A15	5fr on 1fr multi.	10	10
Q2	"	10fr on 2fr "	20	20
Q3	"	20fr on 6fr "	40	40
Q4	"	25fr on 3fr "	50	50
Q5	"	30fr on 4fr "	60	60
Q6	"	50fr on 10fr "	1.00	1.00
		a. "20" instead of "50"	57.50	
Q7	"	100fr on 20fr multi.	2.00	2.00
		Nos. Q1–Q7 (7)	4.80	4.80

The surcharge is arranged to fit the shape of the stamp.

No. Q6a occurred once on the sheet of the 50fr on 10fr.

DALMATIA

(dăl·mā'shĭ·*ȧ*; -sh*ȧ*)

LOCATION—A promontory in the northwestern part of the Balkan Peninsula, together with several small islands in the Adriatic Sea.

GOVT.—Part of the former Austro-Hungarian crownland of the same name.

AREA—113 sq. mi.

POP.—18,719 (1921).

CAPITAL—Zara.

Stamps were issued during Italian occupation. This territory was subsequently annexed by Italy.

100 Centesimi = 1 Corona = 1 Lira

Issued under Italian Occupation.

Italy No. 87 Surcharged — **una corona**

Wmkd. Crown. (140)

1919, May 1 — ***Perf. 14***

1 A46 1 cor on 1 l brown & green 50 65

Italian Stamps of 1906-08 Surcharged — **5 centesimi di corona** *a*

1921–22

2 A48 5c on 5c green 15 15
3 " 10c on 10c claret 15 15
4 A49 25c on 25c blue ('22) 40 65
5 " 50c on 50c vio. ('22) 50 70

Italian Stamps of 1901-10 Surcharged — **1 corona** *b*

6 A46 1cor on 1 l brown & green ('22) 65 90
7 " 5cor on 5 l blue & rose ('22) 4.00 5.50
8 A51 10cor on 10 l gray grn. & red ('22) 6.50 9.00
Nos. 1-8 (8) 12.85 17.70

Surcharges similar to these but differing in style or arrangement of type were used in Austria under Italian occupation.

SPECIAL DELIVERY STAMPS.

Italian Special Delivery Stamp No. E1 Surcharged — **25 centesimi di corona**

Wmkd. Crowns. (140)

1921 — ***Perf. 14***

E1 SD1 25c on 25c rose red 35 45
a. Double surcharge 13.50 13.50

Italian Special Delivery Stamp Surcharged — **LIRE 1,20 DI CORONA**

1922

E2 SD2 1.20 l on 1.20 l blue & rose 20.00

No. E2 was not placed in use.

POSTAGE DUE STAMPS.

Italian Postage Due Stamps Surcharged types "a" or "b"

Wmkd. Crown. (140)

1922 — ***Perf. 14.***

J1 D3 (*a*) 50c on 50c buff & magenta 50 70
J2 " (*b*) 1cor on 1 l blue & red 65 1.10
J3 " (") 2cor on 2 l bl. & red 2.50 3.50
J4 " (") 5cor on 5 l bl. & red 4.00 6.25

DANISH WEST INDIES

LOCATION—A group of islands in the West Indies, lying east of Puerto Rico.

GOVT.—A former Danish colony.

AREA—132 sq. mi.

POP.—27,086 (1911).

CAPITAL—Charlotte Amalie.

The United States bought these islands in 1917 and they became the U. S. Virgin Islands, using U. S. stamps and currency.

100 Cents = 1 Dollar
100 Bits = 1 Franc (1905)

Coat of Arms
A1

Wmk. 111

Yellowish Paper.
With Yellow Burelage.
Wmkd. Small Crown (111)

1855 Typographed ***Imperf.***

1 A1 3c dark carmine, brown gum 130.00 130.00
a. 3c dark carmine, yellow gum 180.00 180.00
b. 3c dark carmine, white gum 700.00

No. 1b is known only unused.

No. 1 was reprinted in carmine, unwatermarked, in 1930. Price $120.

A second (1942) reprint of No. 1 in rose carmine, unwatermarked, has printed on the back across each horizontal row: "Nytryk 1942. G. A. Hagemann: Danmarks og Dansk Vestindiens Frimaerker, Bind 2." Price $60.

White Paper. Yellow Burelage.

1866

2 A1 3c rose 50.00 42.50
a. 3c rose carmine 50.00 42.50

1872–73 ***Perf. 12½***

3 A1 3c rose 110.00 130.00
a. 3c rose carmine 110.00 130.00

Without Burelage.

4 A1 4c dull blue ('73) 200.00 300.00
a. Imperf. (pair) 675.00 800.00
b. Horiz. pair, imperf. vert. 600.00 700.00

No. 4 was reprinted in 1930 in ultramarine, unwatermarked and imperf. Price $120.

A second (1942) reprint of No. 4 in blue, unwatermarked and imperf., has printing on the back like the 1942 reprint of No. 1. Price $60.

Numeral of Value
A2

NORMAL FRAME

INVERTED FRAME

The arabesques in the corners have a main stem and a branch. When the frame is in normal position, in the upper left corner the branch leaves the main stem half way between two little leaflets. In the lower right corner the branch starts at the foot of the second leaflet. When the frame is inverted the corner designs are, of course, transposed.

Wmk. 112

White Wove Paper,
Varying from Thin to Thick.
Perf. 14x13½

1873–96 **Wmkd. Crown. (112)**

5 A2 1c green & brown red 16.00 12.50
a. 1c green & rose lilac 25.00 20.00
b. 1c green & red violet 25.00 20.00
c. 1c green & violet 52.50 52.50
d. 1c green & claret 16.00 12.50
e. Inverted frame 16.00 12.50
6 " 3c blue & carmine 20.00 11.00
a. 3c dull blue & rose 20.00 11.00
b. 3c dull blue & red 20.00 11.00
c. 3c blue & lake 20.00 11.00
d. Imperf. (pair) 500.00
e. Inverted frame 20.00 10.00
7 " 4c brown & dull blue 14.00 15.00
a. 4c brown & bright blue 14.00 15.00
b. 4c brown & ultra. 130.00 100.00
c. Diagonal half used as 2c on cover 150.00
d. Inverted frame 325.00 300.00
8 " 5c green & gray 20.00 13.00
a. 5c green & dark gray 20.00 13.00
b. Inverted frame 20.00 13.00
9 " 7c lilac & orange 22.50 45.00
a. 7c lilac & yellow 50.00 60.00
b. Inverted frame 40.00 60.00
10 " 10c blue & brown 20.00 13.00
a. 10c blue & black brown 20.00 13.00
b. Period between "t" & "s" of "cents" 30.00 18.00
c. Inverted frame 20.00 13.00
11 " 12c red lilac & yel. grn. 25.00 27.50
a. 12c lilac & dp. grn. 55.00 50.00
12 " 14c lilac & green 450.00 500.00
a. Inverted frame 1250.00 1400.00
13 " 50c violet 75.00 90.00
a. 50c gray violet 100.00 125.00

Nos. 9 and 13 Surcharged in Black

I CENT *a* — **10 CENTS 1895** *b*

1887–95

14 A2 (*a*) 1c on 7c lilac & orange 50.00 65.00
a. 1c on 7c lilac & yellow 90.00 110.00
b. Double surcharge 200.00 250.00
c. Inverted frame 85.00 95.00
d. Triple surcharge ——
e. Pair, one without surch. ——
15 " (*b*) 10c on 50c violet ('95) 17.00 20.00

Type of 1873

1896–1901 ***Perf. 13***

16 A2 1c green & red violet ('98) 10.00 10.00
a. Normal frame 225.00 225.00
17 A2 3c bl. & lake ('98) 10.00 10.00
a. Normal frame 200.00 180.00
18 " 4c bistre & dull blue ('01) 10.00 10.00
a. Diagonal half used as 2c on cover 25.00
b. Inverted frame 50.00 50.00
19 " 5c green & gray 27.50 25.00
a. Normal frame 450.00 425.00
20 " 10c blue & brown ('01) 60.00 72.50
a. Inverted frame 650.00 850.00
b. Period between "t" and "s" of "cents" 70.00 82.50
Nos. 16-20 (5) 117.50 127.50

Arms
A5

1900

21 A5 1c light green 1.30 1.30
22 " 5c light blue 7.50 7.50

See also Nos. 29–30.

Nos. 6a, 17, 20 Surcharged:

2 CENTS 1902 *c* — **8 Cents 1902** *d*

Surcharge "c" in Black

1902 ***Perf. 14x13½***

23 A2 2c on 3c blue & carmine 325.00 350.00
a. "2" in date with straight tail 350.00 375.00
b. Normal frame 1000.00

Perf. 13

24 A2 2c on 3c blue & lake 6.50 8.00
a. "2" in date with straight tail 8.50 11.00
b. Dated "1901" 325.00 375.00
c. Normal frame 180.00 225.00
d. Dk. green surch. 900.00
e. As "d" & "a" 1100.00
f. As "d" & "c" ——
25 " 8c on 10c blue & brown 16.00 22.50
a. "2" with straight tail 18.00 25.00
b. On No. 20b 20.00 27.50
c. Inverted frame 250.00 275.00

Surcharge "d" in Black

27 A2 2c on 3c blue & lake 7.00 8.50
a. Normal frame 200.00 225.00
28 " 8c on 10c bl. & brn. 7.50 7.50
a. On No. 20b 14.00 14.00
b. Inverted frame 180.00 190.00

Wmk. 113

1903 **Wmkd. Crown (113)**

29 A5 2c carmine 7.50 7.50
30 " 8c brown 18.00 20.00

King Christian IX
A8

St. Thomas Harbor
A9

1905 Typographed *Perf. 13*

31	A8	5b green	5.50	3.00
32	"	10b red	5.50	3.00
33	"	20b green & blue	10.00	9.00
34	"	25b ultramarine	9.00	8.00
35	"	40b red & gray	7.50	7.00
36	"	50b yellow & gray	8.00	9.00

Frame Typo., Center Engraved
Wmkd. Two Crowns. (113)
Perf. 12

37	A9	1fr green & blue	14.00	20.00
38	"	2fr org. red & brn.	27.50	40.00
39	"	5fr yellow & brown	70.00	125.00
		Nos. 31-36 (6)	157.00	224.00

Nos. 18, 22, 30 Surcharged in Black

5
BIT
1905

Wmkd. Crown. (112)

1905 *Perf. 13*

40	A2	5b on 4c bistre & dull blue	14.00	27.50
		a. Inverted frame	30.00	42.50
41	A5	5b on 5c light blue	8.50	17.50

Wmkd. Crown. (113)

42	A5	5b on 8c brown	8.50	17.50

King Frederik VIII
A10

Frame Typo., Center Engraved

1908 *Perf. 13* **Wmk. 113**

43	A10	5b green	2.00	85
44	"	10b red	2.00	85
45	"	15b violet & brown	4.00	4.00
46	"	20b green & blue	20.00	14.00
47	"	25b blue & dk. blue	1.75	1.20
48	"	30b claret & slate	30.00	18.00
49	"	40b vermilion & gray	3.00	5.50
50	"	50b yellow & brown	3.75	6.50
		Nos. 43-50 (8)	66.50	50.90

King Christian X
A11

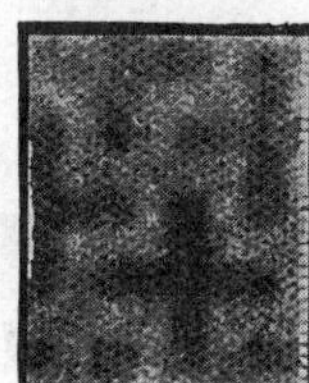

Wmk. 114

Wmkd. Multiple Crosses. (114)

1915-17 *Perf. 14x14½*

51	A11	5b yellow green	1.75	4.00
52	"	10b red	1.75	35.00
53	"	15b lilac & red brown	2.25	35.00
54	"	20b green & blue	2.25	35.00
55	"	25b blue & dark blue	2.25	8.00
56	"	30b claret & black	2.25	35.00
57	"	40b orange & black	2.25	35.00
58	"	50b yellow & brown	2.25	35.00
		Nos. 51-58 (8)	17.00	222.00

Forged and favor cancellations exist.

POSTAGE DUE STAMPS.

Royal Cipher, "Christian 9 Rex"
D1

Lithographed

1902 *Perf. 11½* **Unwmkd.**

J1	D1	1c dark blue	4.50	9.00
J2	"	4c "	7.00	11.00
J3	"	6c "	22.50	35.00
J4	"	10c "	17.50	25.00

There are five types of each value. On the 4c they may be distinguished by differences in the figures "4"; on the other values the differences are minute.

It was not the custom to cancel these stamps. Copies without gum have probably been used.

Counterfeits of Nos. J1–J4 exist.

D2

1905-13 *Perf. 13*

J5	D2	5b red & gray	3.00	5.00
J6	"	20b " "	9.00	13.00
J7	"	30b " "	4.00	6.00
J8	"	50b red & gray	8.00	11.00
		a. Perf. 14x14½ ('13)	15.00	55.00
		b. Perf. 11½	180.00	

All values of this issue are known imperforate, but were not regularly issued.

Counterfeits of Nos. J5–J8 exist.

Danish West Indies stamps were replaced by those of the United States in 1917, after the U.S. bought the islands.

DANZIG

(dăn[t]'sĭg ; dăn'zĭg)

LOCATION—In northern Europe bordering on the Baltic Sea.

GOVT.—Former free city and state.

AREA—754 sq. mi.

POP.— 407,000 (approx. 1939).

CAPITAL—Danzig.

Established as a "Free City and State" under the protection of the League of Nations in 1920, Danzig was seized by Germany in 1939. It became a Polish province in 1945.

100 Pfennig = 1 Gulden (1923)
100 Pfennig = 1 Mark

Used Prices of 1920–23

are for favor-canceled stamps unless otherwise noted. Postally used copies bring higher prices.

German Stamps of 1906-20 Overprinted in Black

Danzig

Wmkd. Lozenges. (125)

1920 *Perf. 14, 14½, 15x14½*

1	A16	5pf green	20	18
2	"	10pf carmine rose	20	18
3	A22	15pf violet brown	20	18
4	A16	20pf blue violet	20	18
5	"	30pf orange & black, *buff*	20	18
6	"	40pf carmine rose	20	18
7	"	50pf purple & black, *buff*	20	18
8	A17	1m red	55	55
9	"	1.25m green	55	55
10	"	1.50m yellow brown	75	80
11	A21	2m blue	75	1.10
		a. Double ovpt.	700.00	
12	"	2.50m lilac rose	2.10	3.00
13	A19	3m black violet	3.75	5.75
14	A16	4m black & rose	3.75	4.50
15	A20	5m slate & carmine	85	1.40
		a. Center inverted	4500.00	
		b. Invtd. ovpt.		7500.00
		Nos. 1-15 (15)	14.45	18.91

The 5pf brown, 10pf orange and 40pf lake and black with this overprint were not regularly issued. Price for trio, $850.

"Germania"
A1

German Stamps of 1906-20
Surcharged in Violet, Red, Green or Brown.

1920

19	A1	5pf on 30pf orange & black, *buff* (V)	14	12
20	"	10pf on 20pf blue violet (R)	14	12
		a. Double surch.	125.00	125.00
21	"	25pf on 30pf orange & black, *buff* (G)	14	12
		a. Inverted surcharge	125.00	125.00
22	"	60pf on 30pf orange & black, *buff* (Br)	45	45
		a. Double surch.	125.00	160.00
23	"	80pf on 30pf orange & black, *buff* (V)	45	45

A2

A3

A4

A5

A6

A7

Surcharged in Black, Red, Blue or Green

Gray Burelage with Points Up.

25	A2	1m on 30pf orange & black, *buff* (Bk)	1.00	1.40
		a. Pair, one without surcharge		
		d. Double surch.		
26	A3	1¼m on 3pf brn. (R)	1.00	1.40
27	A4	2m on 35pf red brown (Bl)	1.00	1.40
		d. Surch. omitted	85.00	85.00
28	A5	3m on 7½pf org. (G)	1.00	1.40
29	A6	5m on 2pf gray (R)	1.00	1.40
30	A7	10m on 7½pf orange (Bk)	5.25	7.25
		d. Double surcharge	67.50	

All values exist without burelage and with double burelage.

Gray Burelage with Points Down.

26a	A3	1¼m on 3pf brown	22.50	25.00
27a	A4	2m on 35pf red brown	350.00	200.00
28a	A5	3m on 7½pf orange	10.00	9.00
29a	A6	5m on 2pf gray	10.00	20.00
30a	A7	10m on 7½pf orange	6.25	6.75

Violet Burelage with Points Up.

25b	A2	1m on 30pf orange & black, *buff*	35.00	32.50
26b	A3	1¼m on 3pf brown	4.25	5.00
27b	A4	2m on 35pf red brown	14.00	16.00
28b	A5	3m on 7½pf orange	1.40	1.40
29b	A6	5m on 2pf gray	1.40	1.40
30b	A7	10m on 7½pf orange	1.40	1.40

Violet Burelage with Points Down.

25c	A2	1m on 30pf orange & black, *buff*	1.25	1.50
26c	A3	1¼m on 3pf brown	4.25	7.25
27c	A4	2m on 35pf red brown	16.00	25.00
28c	A5	3m on 7½pf orange	47.50	55.00
29c	A6	5m on 2pf gray	4.25	5.50
30c	A7	10m on 7½pf orange	16.00	22.00

Excellent counterfeits of the surcharges are known.

German Stamps of 1906-20 Overprinted in Blue

1920

31	A22	2pf gray	145.00	170.00
32	"	2½pf gray	210.00	250.00
33	A16	3pf brown	13.50	15.00
		a. Dbl. overprint	75.00	75.00
34	"	5pf green	20	25
		a. Double overprint	45.00	45.00
35	A22	7½pf orange	45.00	50.00
36	A16	10pf carmine	4.25	4.75
		a. Dbl. overprint	100.00	
37	A22	15pf dark violet	35	45
		a. "Danzig" omitted	25.00	
		b. Double overprint	45.00	
38	A16	20pf blue violet	35	45

Overprinted in Carmine or Blue.

39	A16	25pf orange & black, *yellow*	35	45
40	"	30pf orange & black, *buff*	60.00	70.00
42	"	40pf lake & black	1.75	2.00
		a. Inverted overprint		
		b. Double ovpt.		
43	"	50pf purple & blk., *buff*	210.00	250.00
44	"	60pf magenta (Bl)	*1900.00*	*2250.00*
45	"	75pf green & blk.	35	45
46	"	80pf lake & black, *rose*	2.75	3.25
47	A17	1m carmine	*800.00*	*925.00*

Overprinted in Carmine

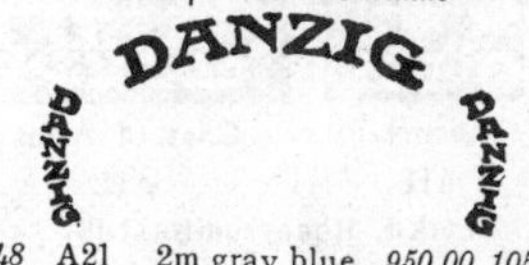

48	A21	2m gray blue	*950.00*	*1050.00*
		a. Dbl. ovpt.		

Counterfeit overprints of Nos. 31 to 48 exist.

Nos. 44, 47 and 48 were issued in small quantities and usually affixed directly to the mail by the postal clerk.

Hanseatic Trading Ship
A8 A9

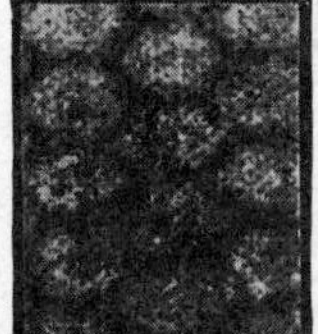

Wmk. 108

Serrate Roulette 13½.

Wmkd. Honeycomb. (108)

1921, Jan. 31 Typographed

49 A8 5(pf) brown & violet 28 30
50 " 10(pf) orange & dark violet 28 30
51 " 25(pf) green & carmine rose 55 60
52 " 40(pf) carmine rose 2.50 3.25
53 " 80(pf) ultramarine 35 40
54 A9 1m carmine rose & black 1.25 1.75
55 " 2m dark blue & dark green 3.50 4.50
56 " 3m black & greenish blue 1.25 1.75
57 " 5m indigo & rose red 1.25 1.75
58 " 10m dark green & brown org. 2.25 5.00
Nos. 49-58 (10) 13.46 19.60

Issued in commemoration of the Constitution.

Nos. 49 and 50 with center in red instead of violet and Nos. 49, 50 and 54 with center inverted are probably proofs. All values of this issue exist imperforate but are not known to have been regularly issued in that condition.

1921, Mar. 11 *Perf. 14*

59 A8 25(pf) green & carmine rose 70 80
60 " 40(pf) carmine rose 90 1.00
61 " 80(pf) ultramarine 5.25 6.00

No. 45 Surcharged in Black

A10

1921, May 6 **Wmk. 125**

62 A10 60pf on 75pf green & black 50 60
a. Double surcharge 72.50 72.50

Arms

A11

Coat of Arms

A12

Wmkd. Honeycomb. (108)

(Vertical or Horizontal.)

1921-22 *Perf. 14*

63 A11 5(pf) orange 18 20
64 " 10(pf) dark brown 12 14
65 " 15(pf) green 12 14
66 " 20(pf) slate 12 14
67 " 25(pf) dark green 14 16
68 " 30(pf) blue & carmine 18 25
a. Center inverted 35.00
69 " 40(pf) green & car. 12 14
a. Center inverted 35.00
70 " 50(pf) dark green & carmine 12 14
71 " 60(pf) carmine 12 27
72 " 80(pf) black & car. 18 40

Paper With Faint Gray Network.

73 A11 1m org. & carmine 12 14
a. Center inverted 35.00
74 " 1.20m blue violet 90 85
75 " 2m gray & carmine 2.10 2.40
76 " 3m vio. & carmine 7.00 9.50

Serrate Roulette 13½

77 A12 5m green, red & black 1.20 2.00
78 " 9m rose, red & orange ('22) 3.50 6.00
79 " 10m ultramarine, red & black 1.20 2.00
80 A12 20m red & black 1.20 2.00
Nos. 63-80 (18) 18.62 26.87

In this and succeeding issues the mark values usually have the face of the paper covered with a gray network. This network is often very faint and occasionally is omitted.

Nos. 64, 66, 69-76 exist imperf. Price, each $15.

See Nos. 81-93, 99-105.

Type of 1921 and

Coat of Arms

A13 A13a

1922 *Perf. 14* **Wmk. 108**

81 A11 75(pf) deep violet 12 15
82 " 80(pf) green 12 15
83 " 1.25m violet & carmine 12 15
84 " 1.50m slate gray 17 15
85 " 2m carmine rose 12 15
86 " 2.40m dark brown & carmine 55 80
87 " 3m carmine lake 17 18
88 " 4m dark blue 55 80
89 " 5m deep green 14 20
90 " 6m carmine lake 9 17
a. 6m carmine rose, wmk. 109 horiz. (error) *2250.00*
91 " 8m light blue 35 60
92 " 10m orange 14 20
93 " 20m orange brown 14 22
94 A13 50m gold & carmine 1.75 3.00
a. 50m gold & red 8.75 11.50
95 A13a 100m metallic green & red 3.25 4.00
Nos. 81-95 (15) 7.78 10.92

No. 95 has buff instead of gray network.

Nos. 81-83, 85-86, 88 exist imperf. Price, each $15.

Nos. 94-95 exist imperf. Price, each $45.

Nos. 87, 88 and 91 Surcharged in Black or Carmine

6

l

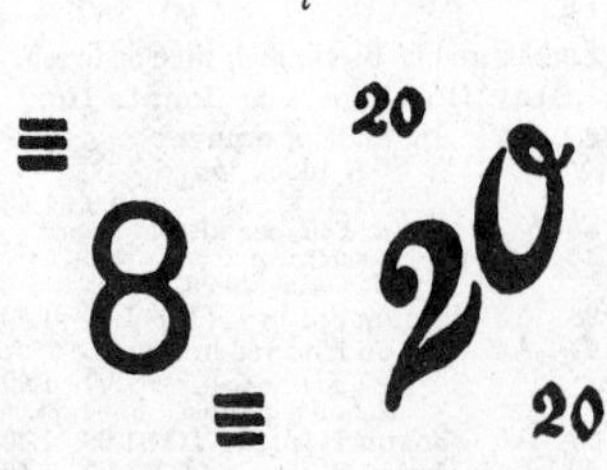

m *n*

1922

96 A11 (*l*) 6m on 3m carmine lake 18 15
a. Dbl. surch.
97 " (*m*) 8m on 4m dark blue 22 50
a. Dbl. surch. 60.00 67.50
98 " (*n*) 20m on 8m light blue (C) 28 40

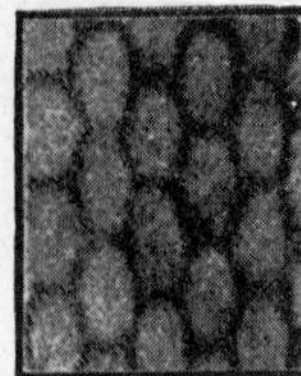

Wmk. 109

Wmkd. Webbing. (109)

(Vertical or Horizontal.)

1922-23 *Perf. 14*

99 A11 4m dark blue 14 20
100 " 5m dark green 14 20
102 " 10m orange 14 20
103 " 20m orange brown 14 20

Paper Without Network.

104 A11 40m pale blue 16 20
105 A11 80m red 16 20
Nos. 99-105 (6) 88 1.20

Nos. 104-105 exist imperf. Price, each $15.

Coat of Arms

A15 A15a

Coat of Arms

A16

1923 *Perf. 14*

Paper With Gray Network.

106 A15 50m pale blue & red 14 20
107 A15a 100m dk. green & red 14 20
108 " 150m violet & red 14 20
109 A16 250m violet & red 22 25
110 " 500m gray black & red 22 25
111 " 1000m brown & red 22 25
112 " 5000m silver & red 1.40 *4.00*

Paper Without Network.

113 A15 50m pale blue 16 20
114 A15a 100m deep green 16 20
115 A15 200m orange 16 20
Nos. 106-115 (10) 2.96 *5.95*

Nos. 109-112 exist imperf. Price, each $22.50.

Nos. 113-115 exist imperf. Price, each $15.

A17

1923 *Perf. 14*

Paper With Gray Network.

117 A17 250m violet & red 16 20
118 " 300m bl. grn. & red 14 22
119 " 500m gray & red 16 20
120 " 1000m brown & red 16 20
121 " 3000m violet & red 16 20
123 A16 10,000m orange & red 35 40
124 " 20,000m pale blue & red 55 60
125 " 50,000m green & red 35 60
Nos. 117-125 (8) 2.03 2.62

Nos. 117-125 exist imperf. Price, each $15.

Surcharged in Red

100 000

1923, Aug. 14

126 A16 100,000m on 20,000m pale bl. & red 1.25 4.00

1923 *Perf. 14*

Paper Without Network.

127 A17 1000m brown 16 20
129 " 5000m rose 16 20
131 " 20,000m pale blue 16 20
132 " 50,000m green 16 20

Paper With Gray Network.

133 A17 100,000m deep blue 16 20
134 " 250,000m violet 16 20
135 " 500,000m slate 16 20
Nos. 127-135 (7) 1.12 1.40

Nos. 126-135 exist imperf.

Abbreviations.

th=(tausend) thousand
mil=million

Stamps of Preceding Issues Surcharged

100
Tausend

1923 *Perf. 14*

Paper Without Network.

137 A15 40th m on 200m orange 50 *1.25*
a. Double surcharge 55.00
138 " 100th m on 200m orange 50 *1.25*
139 " 250th m on 200m orange 5.25 *11.50*
140 A15a 400th m on 100m deep green 28 40
141 A17 500th m on 50,000m green 28 40
142 " 1 mil m on 10,000m orange 2.50 *5.25*

The surcharges on Nos. 140 to 142 differ in details from those on Nos. 137 to 139.

Type of 1923 Surcharged

10
Millionen

Paper With Gray Network.

143 A16 10mil m on 1,000,000m orange 35 40
Nos. 137-143 (7) 9.66 *20.45*

Nos. 142-143 exist imperf. Price, each $15.

Type of 1923 Surcharged

1
Million

Perf. 14.

Paper Without Network.

144 A17 1 mil m on 10,000m rose 22 32
145 " 2 mil m on 10,000m rose 22 32
146 " 3 mil m on 10,000m rose 22 32
147 " 5 mil m on 10,000m rose 22 32
b. Dbl. surch. 60.00
148 " 10 mil m on 10,000m gray lilac 28 35
149 " 20 mil m on 10,000m gray lilac 28 35
150 " 25 mil m on 10,000m gray lilac 22 35

151 A17 40 mil m on 10,000m gray lilac 22 35
a. Double surcharge 55.00
152 A17 50 mil m on 10,000m gray lilac 22 35

Type of 1923 Surcharged in Red

300 Millionen

153 A17 100 mil m on 10,000 m gray lilac 22 35
154 " 300 mil m on 10,000 m gray lilac 22 35
155 " 500 mil m on 10,000 m gray lilac 22 35
Nos. 144-155 (12) 2.76 4.08

Nos. 144-147 exist imperf. Price, each $15.
Nos. 153-155 exist imperf. Price, each $17.50.

Types of 1923 Surcharged

10 Pfennige

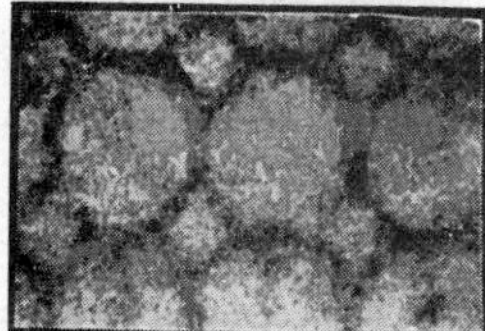

Wmk. 110

Wmkd. Octagons. (110)

1923 ***Perf. 14***

156 A15 5pf on 50m rose 55 45
157 " 10pf on 50m rose 55 45
158 A15a 20pf on 100m rose 55 45
159 A15 25pf on 50m rose 5.25 8.00
160 " 30pf on 50m rose 2.25 1.75
161 A15a 40pf on 100m rose 2.25 2.00
162 " 50pf on 100m rose 2.75 2.75
163 " 75pf on 100m rose 8.75 11.50

Type of 1923 Surcharged

2 Gulden

164 A16 1g on 1 mil m rose 5.25 5.50
165 " 2g on 1 mil m rose 13.00 16.00
166 " 3g on 1 mil m rose 32.50 45.00
167 " 5g on 1 mil m rose 32.50 45.00
Nos. 156-167 (12) 106.15 138.85

Coat of Arms
A19

Wmkd. Webbing. (109)

1924-37 ***Perf. 14***

168 A19 3(pf) brown, *yellowish* ('36) 1.40 70
a. 3(pf) dp. brown, *white* ('27) 2.75 70
170 A19 5(pf) orange, *yellowish* ('36) 2.25 20
a. White paper 2.50 20
b. Bklt. pane of 10
c. Tête bêche pair 225.00
d. Syncopated perf., #170 ('37) 14.00 7.25
e. Syncopated perf., #170a ('32) 25.00 7.25
171 A19 7(pf) yellow green ('33) 1.20 1.35
172 " 8(pf) yellow green ('37) 2.75 3.50
173 A19 10(pf) green, *yellowish* ('36) 4.75 20
a. White paper 5.25 20
b. Bklt. pane of 10
c. 10(pf) bl. grn., *yellowish* ('37) 5.25 30
d. Tête bêche pair 225.00
e. Syncopated perf., #173 ('37) 27.50 10.00
f. Syncopated perf., #173a ('32) 35.00 12.00
g. Syncopated perf., #173c ('37) 11.50 11.00
175 A19 15(pf) gray 1.90 30
176 " 15(pf) red, *yellowish* ('36) 2.25 8
a. White paper ('25) 2.50 10
b. Bklt. pane of 10
177 A19 20(pf) carmine & red 2.10 14
178 " 20(pf) gray ('35) 1.75 1.60
179 " 25(pf) slate & red 12.00 45
180 " 25(pf) carmine ('35) 16.00 60
181 " 30(pf) green & red 4.50 20
182 " 30(pf) dk. violet ('35) 2.10 3.25
183 " 35(pf) ultra. ('25) 1.60 70
184 " 40(pf) dk. blue & blue 4.50 20
185 " 40(pf) yellow brown & red ('35) 9.00 14.00
186 " 40(pf) dark blue ('35) 1.75 1.60
a. Imperf. 32.50
187 A19 50(pf) blue & red 10.50 90
a. Yellowish paper ('36) 7.75 3.25
188 A19 55(pf) plum & scarlet ('37) 5.25 6.25
189 " 60(pf) dark green & red ('35) 6.25 12.00
190 " 70(pf) yellow green & red ('35) 2.10 2.40
191 " 75(pf) violet & red 3.50 2.40
a. Yellowish paper ('36) 3.00 3.25
192 A19 80(pf) dk. org. brown & red ('35) 2.75 4.00
Nos. 168-192 (23) 102.15 57.02

The 5pf and 10pf with syncopated perforations (Netherlands type C) are coils.
See also Nos. 225-232.

Oliva Castle and Cathedral
A20

St. Mary's Church
A23

Council Chamber on the Langenmarkt
A24

Wmk. 125

Designs: 2g, Mottlau River and Krantor. 3g, View of Zoppot.

Wmkd. Lozenges. (125)

1924-32 Engraved. ***Perf. 14.***

193 A20 1g yellow green & black 32.50 26.00
Parcel post cancel 14.00
194 " 1g orange & gray black ('25) 21.00 1.40
a. 1g red orange & black ('32) 25.00 5.25
Parcel post cancel 1.00
195 " 2g red violet & black 55.00 55.00
Parcel post cancel 40.00
196 A20 2g rose & black ('25) 3.25 3.25
Parcel post cancel 2.25
197 " 3g dk. blue & black 3.50 3.25
Parcel post cancel 2.00
198 A23 5g brn. red & black 3.50 3.50
Parcel post cancel 2.00
199 A24 10g dk. brn. & blk. 27.50 40.00
Parcel post cancel 30.00
Nos. 193-199 (7) 146.25 132.40

See also No. 233.

Stamps of 1924-25 Overprinted in Black, Violet or Red

1920
15. November
1930

Wmkd. Webbing. (109)

1930, Nov. 15 **Typographed**

200 A19 5(pf) orange 2.10 1.75
201 " 10(pf) yel. grn. (V) 3.50 2.50
202 " 15(pf) red 4.50 4.00
203 " 20(pf) car. & red 2.10 2.40
204 " 25(pf) slate & red 5.25 4.00
205 " 30(pf) green & red 8.75 14.00
206 " 35(pf) ultra. (R) 35.00 45.00
207 " 40(pf) dark blue & blue (R) 10.50 14.00
208 " 50 (pf) dp. bl. & red 35.00 45.00
209 " 75(pf) violet & red 35.00 45.00

Wmkd. Lozenges. (125)

Engraved.

210 A20 1g orange & black (R) 35.00 45.00
Nos. 200-210 (11) 176.70 222.65

10th anniversary of the Free State. Counterfeits exist.

Nos. 171 and 183 Surcharged in Red Blue or Green

w *x*

1934-36

211 A19 (*w*) 6(pf) on 7(pf) yel. green (R) 1.00 1.20
212 " (") 8(pf) on 7(pf) yellow green (Bl) ('35) 2.10 2.75
213 " (") 8(pf) on 7(pf) yellow green (R) ('36) 1.40 1.75
214 " (") 8(pf) on 7(pf) yellow green (G) ('36) 1.00 1.20
215 " (*x*) 30(pf) on 35(pf) ultra. (Bl) 10.50 14.00
Nos. 211-215 (5) 16.00 20.90

Bathing Beach, Brösen
A25

View of Brösen Beach
A26

War Memorial at Brösen
A27

Skyline of Danzig
A28

Wmkd. Webbing. (109)

1936, June 23 **Typo.** ***Perf. 14***

216 A25 10pf deep green 85 80
217 A26 25pf rose red 1.40 1.80
218 A27 40pf bright blue 2.25 3.00

Village of Brösen, 125th anniversary. Exist imperf. Price of set, $110.

1937, Mar. 27

219 A28 10(pf) dark blue 90 1.10
220 " 15(pf) violet brown 1.25 1.35

Air Defense League.

Danzig Philatelic Exhibition Issue.

Souvenir Sheet.

St. Mary's Church
A29

1937, June 6 ***Perf. 14*** **Wmk. 109**

221 A29 50pf dk. green, sheet 1.75 3.25

Issued for the Danzig Philatelic Exhibition, June 6-8, 1937. Sheet measures 149x104mm.

Arthur Schopenhauer
A30 A31

Design: 40(pf), Full-face portrait, white hair.

Perf. 14

1938, Feb. 22 **Photo.** **Unwmkd.**

222 A30 15(pf) dull blue 1.75 2.00
223 A31 25(pf) sepia 5.00 5.00
224 " 40(pf) org. verm. 2.10 2.50

Issued in commemoration of the 150th anniversary of the birth of Schopenhauer.

Wmk. 237

Type of 1924-35.

Wmkd. Swastikas. (237)

1938-39 Typographed *Perf. 14*

225 A19 3(pf) brown 55 *4.50*
226 " 5(pf) orange 1.00 70
a. Booklet pane of 10
b. Syncopated perf. 2.25 4.75
227 A19 8(pf) yellow green 4.25 *10.00*
228 " 10(pf) blue green 1.25 60
a. Booklet pane of 10
b. Syncopated perf. 2.75 6.00
229 A19 15(pf) scarlet 3.00 4.75
a. Booklet pane of 10
230 A19 25(pf) carmine 3.00 4.75
231 " 40(pf) dark blue 3.00 4.75
232 " 50(pf) bright blue & red ('39) 3.00 4.75

Engraved.

233 A20 1g red orange & black 6.25 8.75
Nos. 225-233 (9) 25.30 *43.55*

No. 233 measures 32½x21¼mm; No. 194, 31x21mm.

Nos. 226b and 228b are coils with Netherlands type C perforation.

Knights in Tournament, 1500
A33

French Leaving Danzig, 1814
A35

Designs: 10(pf), Signing of Danzig-Sweden neutrality treaty, 1630. 25(pf), Battle of Weichselmünde, 1577.

Photogravure.

1939, Jan. 7 *Perf. 14* **Unwmkd.**

234 A33 5(pf) dark green 1.25 1.75
235 " 10(pf) copper brown 1.40 2.25
236 A35 15(pf) slate black 1.75 2.75
237 " 25(pf) brown violet 2.10 3.50

Stamp Day.

Scientists Issue.

Gregor Mendel
A37

Designs: 15(pf), Dr. Robert Koch. 25(pf), Wilhelm Roentgen.

1939, Apr. 29 Photo. *Perf. 13x14*

238 A37 10(pf) copper brown 75 80
239 " 15(pf) indigo 1.00 1.00
240 " 25(pf) dk. olive grn. 1.40 2.00

Issued in honor of the achievements of Mendel, Koch and Roentgen.

Issued under German Administration

Stamps of Danzig, 1925-39, Surcharged in Black:

Rpf 4 Deutsches Reich Rpf 4 — *a*

Rpf 4 Deutsches Reich Rpf 4 — *b*

1 Reichsmark

Deutsches Reich — *c*

Wmkd. Webbing. (109)

1939 *Perf. 14.*

241 A19 (*b*) 4rpf on 35(pf) ultramarine 95 1.10
242 " (") 12rpf on 7(pf) yel. green 1.00 1.20
243 " (*a*) 20rpf gray 3.25 3.50

Wmkd. Swastikas. (237)

244 A19 (*a*) 3rpf brown 95 1.10
245 " (") 5rpf orange 95 1.10
246 " (") 8rpf yel. green 1.50 1.85
247 " (") 10rpf blue green 2.10 2.40
248 " (") 15rpf scarlet 3.25 3.50
249 " (") 25rpf carmine 2.60 3.00
250 " (") 30rpf dark violet 1.90 2.25
251 " (") 40rpf dark blue 2.60 3.00
252 " (") 50rpf bright blue & red 3.50 4.00
253 A20 (*c*) 1rm on 1g red orange & black 14.00 16.00

Wmkd. Lozenges. (125)

254 A20 (*c*) 2rm on 2g rose & black 22.50 26.00
Nos. 241-254 (14) 61.05 70.00

Nos. 241 to 254 were valid throughout Germany.

SEMI-POSTAL STAMPS.

St. George and Dragon
SP1

Wmkd. Honeycomb. (108)

Size: 19x22 mm.

1921, Oct. 16 Typo. *Perf. 14*

B1 SP1 30pf+30pf green & orange 35 45
B2 " 60pf+60pf rose & orange 1.00 1.20

Size: 25x30 mm.

Serrate Roulette 13½.

B3 SP1 1.20m+1.20m dark blue & orange 1.75 2.00

Aged Pensioner
SP2

Wmkd. Webbing. (109)

Paper With Gray Network.

1923, Mar. *Perf. 14*

B4 SP2 50m+20m lake 18 30
B5 " 100m+30m red violet 18 30

Philatelic Exhibition Issue.

Neptune Fountain
SP3

Various Frames.

1929, July 7 Engr. **Unwmkd.**

B6 SP3 10(pf) yellow green & gray 2.25 2.40
B7 " 15(pf) car. & gray 2.25 2.40
B8 " 25(pf) ultramarine & gray 7.75 6.50
a. 25 (pf) vio. blue & black 62.50 80.00

These stamps were sold exclusively at the Danzig Philatelic Exhibition, June 7th to 14th, 1929. They were sold at double their face values, the excess being for the aid of the exhibition.

Regular Issue of 1924-25 Surcharged in Black

5 W. H. W.

1934, Jan. 15 **Wmk. 109**

B9 A19 5(pf)+5(pf) orange 10.50 12.00
B10 " 10(pf)+5(pf) yellow green 25.00 27.50
B11 " 15(pf)+5(pf) car. 14.00 16.00

Surtax for winter welfare. Counterfeits exist.

Stock Tower
SP4

George Hall
SP6

City Gate, 16th Century
SP5

1935, Dec. 16 Typo. *Perf. 14*

B12 SP4 5(pf)+5pf orange 85 80
B13 SP5 10(pf)+5pf green 1.25 1.35
B14 SP6 15(pf)+10pf scarlet 2.60 2.50

Surtax for winter welfare.

Milk Can Tower
SP7

Frauentor
SP8

Krantor
SP9

Langgarter Gate
SP10

High Gate
SP11

1936, Nov. 25

B15 SP7 10pf+5pf dk. blue 1.40 1.50
a. Imperf. 52.50
B16 SP8 15pf+5pf dull grn. 1.40 1.50
B17 SP9 25pf+10pf red brn. 1.75 2.00
B18 SP10 40pf+20pf brown & red brown 2.60 3.00
B19 SP11 50pf+20pf blue & dark blue 3.50 4.00
Nos. B15-B19 (5) 10.65 12.00

Surtax for winter welfare.

SP12

SP13

1937, Oct. 30

B20 SP12 25(pf)+25(pf) dark carmine 3.50 4.75
B21 SP13 40(pf)+40(pf) blue & red 3.50 4.75
a. Souvenir sheet of two 14.00 16.00

Founding of Danzig community at Magdeburg.

No. B21a contains one each of Nos. B20-B21 with marginal inscriptions including "1937." Size: 146x105mm.

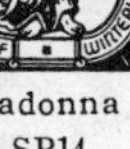

Madonna
SP14

Mercury
SP15

Weather Vane, Town Hall
SP16

Neptune Fountain
SP17

St. George and Dragon
SP18

1937, Dec. 13

No.	Type	Description	Unused	Used
B23	SP14	5pf+5pf brt. violet	1.40	1.60
B24	SP15	10pf+5pf dk. brown	3.50	4.00
B25	SP16	15pf+5pf blue & yellow brown	4.25	4.75
B26	SP17	25pf+10pf blue green & green	4.50	5.25
B27	SP18	40pf+25pf bright carmine & blue	7.75	8.75
		Nos. B23-B27 (5)	21.40	24.35

Surtax for winter welfare. Designs are from frieze of the Artushof.

"Peter von Danzig" Yacht Race
SP19

Ships: 10+5pf, Dredger Fu Shing. 15+10pf, S. S. Columbus. 25+10pf, S. S. City of Danzig. 40+15pf, Peter von Danzig, 1472.

1938, Nov. 28 Photo. Unwmkd.

No.	Type	Description	Unused	Used
B28	SP19	5(pf)+5(pf) dk. blue green	1.50	1.85
B29	"	10(pf)+5(pf) golden brown	2.00	2.25
B30	"	15(pf)+10(pf) olive green	2.25	2.50
B31	"	25(pf)+10(pf) indigo	3.00	3.50
B32	"	40(pf)+15(pf) violet brown	3.50	4.00
		Nos. B28-B32 (5)	12.25	14.10

Surtax for winter welfare.

AIR POST STAMPS.

AP1

AP2

No. 6 Surcharged in Blue or Carmine.

Wmkd. Lozenges. (125)

1920, Sept. 29 ***Perf. 14***

No.	Type	Description	Unused	Used
C1	AP1	40(pf) on 40pf carmine rose (Bl)	1.75	2.40
		a. Double surcharge	250.00	250.00
C2	AP1	60(pf) on 40pf carmine rose (C)	1.75	2.40
		a. Double surcharge	250.00	250.00
C3	AP2	1m on 40pf carmine rose (Bl)	1.75	2.40

Plane faces left on No. C2.

Plane over Danzig
AP3 AP4

Wmkd. Honeycomb. (108)

1921-22 Typographed. ***Perf. 14.***

No.	Type	Description	Unused	Used
C4	AP3	40(pf) blue green	28	40
C5	"	60(pf) dark violet	28	40
C6	"	1m carmine	28	40
C7	"	2m orange brown	28	40

Serrate Roulette 13½.

Size: 34½x23mm.

No.	Type	Description	Unused	Used
C8	AP4	5m violet blue	80	1.10
C9	"	10m deep green ('22)	1.65	2.50
		Nos. C4-C9 (6)	3.57	5.20

Nos. C4-C9 exist imperf. Price, each $45.

Wmkd. Webbing. (109)

1923 ***Perf. 14.***

No.	Type	Description	Unused	Used
C10	AP3	40(pf) blue green	35	*1.35*
C11	"	60(pf) dark violet	35	*1.35*
		a. Double impression	75.00	
C12	"	1m carmine	35	*1.35*
C13	"	2m orange brown	35	*1.35*
C14	"	25m pale blue	35	45

Serrate Roulette 13½.

Size: 34½x23mm.

No.	Type	Description	Unused	Used
C15	AP4	5m violet blue	35	55
C16	"	10m deep green	35	55

Paper With Gray Network.

No.	Type	Description	Unused	Used
C17	AP4	20m orange brown	35	55

Size: 40x23mm.

No.	Type	Description	Unused	Used
C18	AP4	50m orange	35	55
C19	"	100m red	35	55
C20	"	250m dark brown	35	55
C21	"	500m carmine rose	35	55
		Nos. C10-C21 (12)	4.20	*9.70*

Nos. C14, C18-C21 exist imperf. Price, each $35.

Post Horn and Airplanes
AP5

1923, Oct. 18 ***Perf. 14***

Paper Without Network.

No.	Type	Description	Unused	Used
C22	AP5	250,000m scarlet	40	1.00
C23	"	500,000m scarlet	40	1.00

Exist imperf. Price, each $27.50.

Surcharged **2 Millionen**

No.	Type	Description	Unused	Used
C24	AP5	2mil m on 100,000m scarlet	40	80
C25	"	5mil m on 50,000m scarlet	40	80
		b. Cliché of 10,000m in sheet of 50,000m	20.00	40.00

Exist imperf. Price, each $45.

Nos. C24 and C25 were not regularly issued without surcharge, although copies have been passed through the post. Price, uncanceled, each $7.50.

Plane over Danzig
AP6 AP7

1924

No.	Type	Description	Unused	Used
C26	AP6	10(pf) vermilion	17.50	2.50
C27	"	20(pf) carmine rose	1.50	1.25
C28	"	40(pf) olive brown	3.50	2.00
C29	"	1g deep green	3.50	2.00
C30	AP7	2½g violet brown	25.00	30.00
		Nos. C26-C30 (5)	51.00	37.75

Nos. C26-C30 exist imperf. Price of Nos. C26-C29 $45 each; No. C30, $110.

Regular Issue of 1924 Surcharged in Various Colors

10 ▬▬ 10
Luftpost-Ausstellung
1932

1932 Wmkd. Lozenges. (125)

No.	Type	Description	Unused	Used
C31	A20	10(pf) on 1g yellow grn. & blk. (G)	9.75	9.50
C32	"	15(pf) on 2g red vio. & blk. (V)	9.75	9.50
C33	"	20(pf) on 3g dark blue & black (Bl)	9.75	9.50
C34	A23	25(pf) on 5g brown red & black (R)	9.75	9.50
C35	A24	30(pf) on 10g dark brn. & blk. (Br)	9.75	9.50
		Nos. C31-C35 (5)	48.75	47.50

Issued in connection with the International Air Post Exhibition of 1932. The surcharges were variously arranged to suit the shapes and designs of the stamps. The stamps were sold at double their surcharged values, the excess being donated to the exhibition funds.

Airplane
AP8 AP9

1935 Wmkd. Webbing. (109)

No.	Type	Description	Unused	Used
C36	AP8	10pf scarlet	1.75	33
C37	"	15pf yellow	2.10	1.20
C38	"	25pf dark green	1.75	1.20
C39	"	50pf gray blue	7.75	7.25
C40	AP9	1g magenta	4.25	*10.50*
		Nos. C36-C40 (5)	17.60	*20.48*

See also Nos. C42-C45.

Souvenir Sheet

St. Mary's Church—AP10

1937, June 6 ***Perf. 14***

No.	Type	Description	Unused	Used
C41	AP10	50pf dk. blue	1.85	3.25

Issued for the Danzig Philatelic Exhibition, June 6-8, 1937. Size: 149x104mm.

Type of 1935.

1938-39 Wmkd. Swastikas. (237)

No.	Type	Description	Unused	Used
C42	AP8	10pf scarlet	2.10	5.50
C43	"	15pf yellow ('39)	2.50	6.00
C44	AP8	25pf dark green	2.50	6.00
C45	"	50pf gray blue ('39)	7.00	15.00

POSTAGE DUE STAMPS.

Danzig Coat of Arms
D1 D2

Wmkd. Honeycomb. (108)

1921-22 Typographed. ***Perf. 14***

Paper Without Network.

No.	Type	Description	Unused	Used
J1	D1	10(pf) deep violet	28	30
J2	"	20(pf) deep violet	28	30
J3	"	40(pf) deep violet	28	30
J4	"	60(pf) deep violet	28	30
J5	"	75(pf) dp. vio. ('22)	28	30
J6	"	80(pf) deep violet	28	30
J7	"	120(pf) deep violet	28	30
J8	"	200(pf) dp. vio. ('22)	85	90
J9	"	240(pf) deep violet	28	30
J10	"	300(pf) dp. vio. ('22)	85	90
J11	"	400(pf) deep violet	85	90
J12	"	500(pf) deep violet	85	90
J13	"	800(pf) dp. vio. ('22)	85	90
J14	"	20m dp. vio. ('22)	85	90
		Nos. J1-J14 (14)	7.34	7.80

Nos. J1-J14 exist imperf. Price, each $13.50.

1923 Wmkd. Webbing. (109)

No.	Type	Description	Unused	Used
J15	D1	100(pf) deep violet	40	55
J16	"	200(pf) "	2.25	3.00
J17	"	300(pf) "	40	55
J18	"	400(pf) "	40	55
J19	"	500(pf) "	40	55
J20	"	800(pf) "	60	75
J21	"	10m "	40	55
J22	"	20m "	40	55
J23	"	50m "	40	55

Paper With Gray Network.

No.	Type	Description	Unused	Used
J24	D1	100m deep violet	35	40
J25	"	500m deep violet	35	40
		Nos. J15-J25 (11)	6.35	8.40

Nos. J22-J25 exist imperf. Price, each $11.50.

Nos. J22-J23 and type of 1923 Surcharged **10000**

1923, Oct. 1

Paper Without Network.

No.	Type	Description	Unused	Used
J26	D1	5000(m) on 50m	28	32
J27	"	10,000(m) on 20m	28	32
J28	"	50,000(m) on 500m	28	32
J29	"	100,000(m) on 20m	75	85

On No. J26 the numerals of the surcharge are all of the larger size.

A 1000(m) on 100m deep violet was prepared but not issued. Price, $110.

Nos. J26-J28 exist imperf. Price, each $22.50.

1923-28 Wmkd. Octagons. (110)

No.	Type	Description	Unused	Used
J30	D2	5(pf) blue & black	60	50
J31	"	10(pf) " "	55	40
J32	"	15(pf) " "	80	70
J33	"	20(pf) " "	1.20	1.10
J34	"	30(pf) " "	7.00	70
J35	"	40(pf) " "	2.00	1.75
J36	"	50(pf) " "	2.00	50
J37	"	60(pf) " "	12.50	12.50
J38	"	100(pf) " "	16.00	5.25
J39	"	3g blue & carmine	7.75	17.50
		a. "Guldeu" instead of "Gulden"	225.00	
		Nos. J30-J39 (10)	50.40	40.90

Used prices of Nos. J30-J39 are for postally used copies.

Postage Due Stamps of 1923 Issue Surcharged in Red

5

1932, Dec. 20

J40	D2	5(pf) on 40(pf) blue & black	1.90	4.50
J41	"	10(pf) on 60(pf) blue & black	32.50	4.00
J42	"	20(pf) on 100(pf) blue & black	1.90	3.50

Type of 1923.

Wmkd. Swastikas. (237)

1938-39 ***Perf. 14.***

J43	D2	10(pf) bl. & blk. ('39)	1.35	*8.75*
J44	"	30(pf) blue & black	2.00	*13.00*
J45	"	40(pf) bl. & blk. ('39)	6.25	*26.00*
J46	"	60(pf) blue & black ('39)	7.00	*27.50*
J47	"	100(pf) blue & black	8.75	*27.50*
		Nos. J43-J47 (5)	25.35	*102.75*

OFFICIAL STAMPS.

Regular Issues of 1921-22 Overprinted

D M
a

Wmkd. Honeycomb. (108)

1921-22 ***Perf. 14x14½.***

O1	A11	5(pf) orange	22	25
O2	"	10(pf) dark brown	12	18
		a. Invtd. ovpt.	67.50	
O3	"	15(pf) green	12	18
O4	"	20(pf) slate	12	18
O5	"	25(pf) dark green	12	18
O6	"	30(pf) blue & carmine	35	45
O7	"	40(pf) green & carmine	14	18
O8	"	50(pf) dk. grn. & car.	14	18
O9	"	60(pf) carmine	14	18
O10	"	75(pf) deep violet ('22)	18	22
O11	"	80(pf) black & carmine	95	1.20
O12	"	80(pf) green ('22)	18	22

Paper With Faint Gray Network

O14	A11	1m org. & carmine	12	18
O15	"	1.20m blue violet	95	1.20
O16	"	1.25m vio. & car. ('22)	18	22
O17	"	1.50m slate gray ('22)	18	22
O18	"	2m gray & car.	12.00	15.00
		a. Invtd. ovpt.		
O19	"	2m car. rose ('22)	18	22
O20	"	2.40m dark brown & carmine ('22)	1.40	2.00
O21	"	3m violet & car.	9.75	13.00
O22	"	3m car. lake ('22)	18	22
O23	"	4m dark blue ('22)	1.40	2.00
O24	"	5m deep green ('22)	18	22
O25	"	6m car. lake ('22)	18	22
O26	"	10m orange ('22)	18	22
O27	"	20m org. brown ('22)	18	22
		Nos. O1-O27 (26)	29.84	38.74

Double overprints exist on Nos. O1-O2, O5-O7, O10 and O12. Price, each $17.50.

Same Overprint on No. 96

O28	A11	6m on 3m carmine lake	22	45
		a. Inverted overprint	30.00	

No. 77 Overprinted

1922 ***Serrate Roulette 13½***

O29	A12	5m grn., red & blk.	3.50	4.75

Nos. 99-103, 106-107 Overprinted Type "a"

Wmkd. Webbing. (109)

1923 ***Perf. 14***

O30	A11	4m dark blue	18	20
O31	"	5m dark green	18	35
O32	"	10m orange	18	20
O33	"	20m orange brown	18	20
O34	A15	50m pale blue & red	18	20
O35	A15a	100m dk. green & red	18	20

Nos. 113-115, 118-120 Overprinted Type "a"

O36	A15	50m pale blue	18	27
		a. Inverted overprint	27.50	
O37	A15a	100m dark green	18	22
O38	A15	200m orange	18	22
		a. Inverted overprint	27.50	

Paper With Gray Network.

O39	A17	300m bl. green & red	18	20
O40	"	500m gray & red	18	27
O41	"	1000m brown & red	18	27
		Nos. O30-O41 (12)	2.16	2.80

Regular Issue of 1924-25 Overprinted

Dienst-marke

1924-25 ***Perf. 14x14½***

O42	A19	5(pf) orange	1.75	1.25
O43	"	10(pf) yellow green	1.75	1.25
O44	"	15(pf) gray	1.75	1.25
O45	"	15(pf) red ('25)	16.00	7.25
O46	"	20(pf) car. & red	1.50	1.20
O47	"	25(pf) slate & red	17.50	16.00
O48	"	30(pf) green & red	2.25	2.00
O49	"	35(pf) ultra. ('25)	42.50	40.00
O50	"	40(pf) dark blue & dull blue	5.50	6.25
O51	"	50(pf) dp. bl. & red	17.50	20.00
O52	"	75(pf) violet & red	35.00	*62.50*
		Nos. O42-O52 (11)	143.00	*158.95*

Double overprints exist on Nos. O42-O44, O47, O50-O52. Price, each $65.

DENMARK

(děn'märk)

LOCATION—Denmark occupies the northern part of a peninsula which separates the North and Baltic Seas, and includes the surrounding islands.

GOVT.—Kingdom.

AREA—16,629 sq. mi.

POP.—5,150,000 (est. 1975).

CAPITAL—Copenhagen.

96 Skilling = 1 Rigsbank Daler

100 Ore = 1 Krone (1875)

> Prices of early Denmark stamps vary according to condition. Quotations for Nos. 1-15 are for fine copies. Very fine to superb specimens sell at much higher prices, and inferior or poor copies sell at reduced prices, depending on the condition of the individual specimen.

Numeral and Inscription of Value — A1

Royal Emblems — A2

Wmk. 111

Wmkd. Small Crown. (111)

1851 Typographed. ***Imperf.***

With Yellow Brown Burelage.

1	A1	2rs blue	*2400.00*	1000.00
		a. First printing	*4250.00*	*1750.00*
2	A2	4rs brown	475.00	30.00
		a. First printing	525.00	32.50
		b. 4rs yel. brown	550.00	45.00

The first printing of Nos. 1 and 2 had the burelage printed from a copper plate, giving a clear impression with the lines in slight relief. The subsequent impressions had the burelage typographed, with the lines fainter and not rising above the surface of the paper.

Nos. 1-2 were reprinted in 1885 and 1901 on heavy yellowish paper, unwatermarked and imperforate, with a brown burelage. No. 1 was also reprinted without burelage, on both yellowish and white paper. Price for least costly reprint of No. 1, $40.

No. 2 was reprinted in 1951 in 10 shades with "Colour Specimen 1951" printed on the back. It was also reprinted in 1961 in 2 shades without burelage and with "Farve Nytryk 1961" printed on the back. Price for least costly reprint of No. 2, $8.50.

Dotting in Spandrels — A3

Wavy Lines in Spandrels — A4

1854-57

3	A3	2s blue ('55)	80.00	45.00
4	"	4s brown	175.00	9.00
		a. 4s yellow brown	175.00	9.00
5	"	8s green ('57)	275.00	50.00
		a. 8s yellow green	275.00	50.00
6	"	16s gray lilac ('57)	350.00	100.00

1858-62

7	A4	4s brown	45.00	5.00
		a. 4s yellow brown	45.00	5.00
		b. Wmk. 112 ('62)	45.00	6.00
8	"	8s green	250.00	55.00

Nos. 2 to 8 inclusive are known with unofficial perforation 12 or 13, and Nos. 4, 5, 7 and 8 with unofficial roulette 9½.

Nos. 3, 6-8 were reprinted in 1885 on heavy yellowish paper, unwatermarked, imperforate and without burelage. Nos. 4-5 were reprinted in 1924 on white paper, unwatermarked, imperforate, gummed and without burelage. Price for No. 3, $9; Nos. 4-5, each $85; No. 6, $15; Nos. 7-8, each $7.50.

Wmk. 112

Wmkd. Crown. (112)

1863 ***Rouletted 11***

9	A4	4s brown	60.00	11.00
		a. 4s deep brown	60.00	11.00
10	A3	16s violet	700.00	350.00

Royal Emblems — A5

1864-68 ***Perf. 13.***

11	A5	2s blue ('65)	55.00	25.00
		a. Imperf., (pair)	250.00	300.00
		b. Perf. 12½	175.00	100.00
12	"	3s red violet ('65)	70.00	35.00
		a. Imperf., (pair)	300.00	
		b. Perf. 12½	175.00	110.00
13	"	4s red	45.00	6.00
		a. Imperf., (pair)	180.00	300.00
14	"	8s bistre ('68)	325.00	60.00
		a. Imperf., (pair)	650.00	
		b. Perf. 12½	325.00	120.00
15	"	16s olive green	325.00	75.00
		a. Imperf., (pair)	800.00	
		b. Perf. 12½	600.00	450.00

Nos. 11-15 were reprinted in 1886 on heavy yellowish paper, unwatermarked, imperforate and without gum. The reprints of all values except the 4s were printed in two vertical rows of six, inverted with respect to each other, so that horizontal pairs are always tête bêche. Price $8 each.

Nos. 13 and 15 were reprinted in 1942 with printing on the back across each horizontal row: "Nytryk 1942. G. A. Hagemann: Danmarks og Vestindiens Frimaerker, Bind 2." Price, $50 each.

A6

NORMAL FRAME

INVERTED FRAME

The arabesques in the corners have a main stem and a branch. When the frame is in normal position, in the upper left corner the branch leaves the main stem half way between two little leaflets. In the lower right corner the branch starts at the foot of the second leaflet. When the frame is inverted the corner designs are, of course, transposed.

1870-71 ***Perf. 14x13½*** **Wmk. 112**

Paper Varying from Thin to Thick.

16	A6	2s gray & ultramarine ('71)	65.00	20.00
		a. 2s gray & blue	55.00	18.00
		b. Imperf., (pair)	225.00	
		c. Inverted frame	600.00	225.00
17	"	3s gray & bright lilac ('71)	95.00	47.50
		a. Imperf., (pair)	225.00	
		b. Inverted frame	1000.00	600.00
18	"	4s gray & carmine	75.00	10.00
		a. Imperf., (pair)	225.00	
		b. Inverted frame	650.00	90.00
19	"	8s gray & brown ('71)	130.00	47.50
		a. Imperf., (pair)	275.00	
		b. Inverted frame	750.00	450.00
20	"	16s gray & green ('71)	180.00	85.00
		a. Imperf., (pair)	375.00	
		b. Inverted frame	1000.00	750.00

Perf. 12½.

21	A6	2s gray & bl. ('71)	1000.00	1200.00
22	"	4s gray & carmine	110.00	60.00
24	"	48s brown & lilac	375.00	150.00
		a. Imperf., (pair)	700.00	
		b. Inverted frame	1600.00	850.00

Nos. 16-20, 24 were reprinted in 1886 on thin white paper, unwatermarked, imperforate and without gum. These were printed in sheets of 10 in which 1 stamp has the normal frame (price $22.50 each and 9 the inverted (price $9 each; No. 24, $12).

1875-79 ***Perf. 14x13½.***

25	A6	3ö gray blue & gray	8.50	4.50
		a. First "A" of "DANMARK" missing	37.50	55.00
		b. Imperf.		
		c. Inverted frame	8.50	4.50

26 A6 4ö slate & blue 6.00 15
a. 4ö gray & blue 6.00 15
b. 4ö slate & ultramarine 30.00 4.00
c. 4ö gray & ultramarine 30.00 4.00
d. Imperf., (pair) 250.00
e. Inverted frame 9.00 15
27 " 5ö rose & bl. ('79) 25.00 35.00
a. Ball of lower curve of large "5" missing 110.00 150.00
b. Inverted frame 700.00 1000.00
28 " 8ö slate & carmine 8.50 12
a. 8ö gray & car. 20.00 65
b. Imperf., (pair) 275.00
c. Inverted frame 10.00 12
29 " 12ö slate & dull lake 9.00 1.50
a. 12ö gray & bright lilac 40.00 8.00
b. 12ö gray & dull magenta 9.00 1.50
c. Inverted frame 9.00 1.50
30 " 16ö slate & brown 37.50 1.50
a. 16ö lt. gray & brn. 50.00 9.00
b. Inverted frame 37.50 1.50
31 " 20ö rose & gray 45.00 9.00
a. 20ö car. & gray 45.00 9.00
b. Inverted frame 45.00 9.00
32 " 25ö gray & green 37.50 9.00
a. Inverted frame 45.00 17.50
33 " 50ö brown & violet 45.00 10.00
a. 50ö brown & blue violet 200.00 42.50
b. Inverted frame 52.50 16.50
34 " 100ö gray & orange ('77) 57.50 16.00
a. Imperf., (pair) 300.00
b. Inverted frame 90.00 30.00

The stamps of this issue on thin semi-transparent paper are far scarcer than those on thicker paper.

See also Nos. 41-42, 44, 46-47, 50-52.

Arms
A7

Two types of numerals in corners: ⑤ ⑤

1882

Small Corner Numerals.

35 A7 5ö green 80.00 32.50
37 " 20ö blue 110.00 14.00

1884-85

Larger Corner Numerals.

38 A7 5ö green 10.00 1.50
a. Imperf.
39 " 10ö carmine ('85) 10.00 85
a. Small numerals in corners 450.00 400.00
b. Imperf., pair 250.00
c. Pair, Nos. 39, 39a 500.00 600.00
40 " 20ö blue 13.00 80
a. Pair, Nos. 37, 40 400.00 600.00
b. Imperf., pair 2500.00

Stamps with large corner numerals have white line around crown and lower oval touches frame.

The plate of the 10 ore, No. 39, was damaged and three clichés in the bottom row were replaced by clichés for post cards, which had small numerals in the corners, making the variety No. 39a.

Two clichés with small numerals were inserted in the plate of No. 40.

Wmkd. Crown. (112)

1895-1901 *Perf. 13.*

41 A6 3ö blue & gray 5.50 1.80
b. Inverted frame 7.00 1.80
42 " 4ö slate & blue ('96) 3.75 12
a. Inverted frame 4.50 12
43 A7 5ö green 7.00 60
44 A6 8ö slate & carmine 4.50 10
a. Inverted frame 4.50 10
45 A7 10ö rose carmine 8.00 60
46 A6 12ö slate & dull lake 5.00 1.50
a. Inverted frame 12.00 1.75
47 " 16ö slate & brown 17.50 3.00
a. Inverted frame 22.50 3.00
48 A7 20ö blue 8.00 1.50
49 " 24ö brown ('01) 10.00 4.50
50 A6 25ö gray & grn. ('98) 45.00 6.50
a. Inverted frame 45.00 7.50
51 A6 50ö brown & violet ('97) 37.50 9.00
a. Inverted frame 52.50 16.00
52 " 100ö slate & orange 37.50 14.00
a. Inverted frame 40.00 14.00

1902-04 Wmkd. Crown. (113)

41c A6 3ö blue & gray 2.50 1.50
d. Invtd. frame 40.00 17.50
42b A6 4ö slate & blue 11.00 4.50
c. Invtd. frame 40.00 17.50
43a A7 5ö green 2.00 12
44d A6 8ö slate & carmine 180.00 140.00
45a A7 10ö rose carmine 2.00 12
48a " 20ö blue 8.00 1.50
50b A6 25ö gray & green 11.00 3.25
c. Invtd. frame 55.00 20.00
51b A6 50ö brown & violet 16.00 7.00
c. Invtd. frame 130.00 50.00
52b A6 100ö slate & orange 17.50 6.00
c. Invtd. frame 140.00 50.00

Wmk. 113

1902 Wmkd. Crown. (113)

53 A7 1ö orange 50 40
a. Imperf., pair 250.00
54 " 15ö lilac 7.00 25
a. Imperf., pair

Nos. 44d, 44, 49 Surcharged:

4 ØRE
a

15 15 ØRE
b

1904-12 Wmkd. Crown. (113)

55 A6 (a) 4ö on 8ö slate & carmine 2.00 2.00
a. Wmk. 112 ('12) 17.50 30.00
b. As "a", inverted frame

Wmkd. Crown. (112)

56 A7 (b) 15ö on 24ö brown 2.75 2.75
a. Short "15" at right 17.50 30.00

Numeral of Value
A10

King Christian IX
A11

King Frederik VIII
A12

Wmkd. Crown. (113)

1905-17 Typographed. *Perf. 13.*

57 A10 1ö orange ('06) 1.50 12
58 " 2ö carmine 1.50 10
a. Perf. 14x14½ ('17) 2.00 2.00
59 " 3ö gray 2.50 12
60 " 4ö dull blue 2.50 12
a. Perf. 14x14½ ('17) 8.00 8.00
61 " 5ö dp. green ('12) 3.00 8
62 " 10ö deep rose ('12) 3.50 10
63 " 15ö lilac 8.50 15
64 " 20ö dark blue ('12) 22.50 50
Nos. 57-64 (8) 45.50 1.29

The three wavy lines in design A10 are symbolical of the three waters which separate the principal Danish islands.

See also Nos. 85-96.

1904-05 Engraved.

65 A11 10ö scarlet 2.25 8
66 " 20ö blue 10.00 50
67 " 25ö brown ('05) 12.50 1.50
68 " 50ö dull vio. ('05) 25.00 22.50
69 A11 100ö ochre ('05) 18.00 18.00
Nos. 65-69 (5) 67.75 42.58

1905-06 Re-engraved.

70 A11 5ö green 3.00 10
71 " 10ö scarlet ('06) 10.00 10

The re-engraved stamps are much clearer than the originals, and the decoration on the king's left breast has been removed.

1907-12

72 A12 5ö green 75 8
a. Imperf.
73 " 10ö red 1.50 6
a. Imperf.
74 " 20ö indigo 3.25 15
a. 20ö bright blue ('11) 5.00 35
75 " 25ö olive brown 5.50 25
76 " 35ö dp. orange ('12) 5.00 2.50
77 " 50ö claret 17.50 2.25
78 " 100ö bistre brown 45.00 1.00
Nos. 72-78 (7) 78.50 6.29

Nos. 47, 31 and O9 Surcharged:

Dark Blue Surcharge.

1912 Wmkd. Crown. (112) *Perf. 13.*

79 A6 (c) 35ö on 16ö slate & brown 11.00 16.00
a. Inverted frame 140.00 170.00

Perf. 14x13½.

80 A6 (c) 35ö on 20ö rose & gray 10.00 12.00
a. Inverted frame 50.00 70.00

Black Surcharge.

81 O1 (d) 35ö on 32ö green 13.00 20.00

General Post Office, Copenhagen
A15

Wmkd. Two Crowns. (113)

1912 Engraved *Perf. 13*

82 A15 5kr dark red 300.00 75.00
See No. 135.

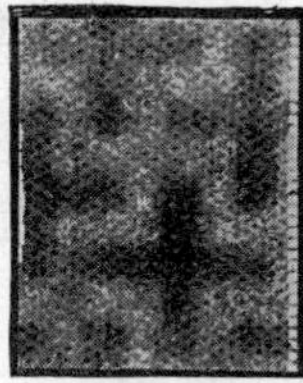

Wmk. 114

Wmkd. Multiple Crosses. (114)

1913-30 Typo. *Perf. 14x14½*

85 A10 1ö deep orange ('14) 20 12
a. Booklet pane of 6, (2 No. 85, 2 No. 91 + 2 labels) 9.00
86 " 2ö carmine ('13) 40 12
a. Imperf., (pair) 225.00 400.00
b. Booklet pane, 4 + 2 labels 9.00
87 " 3ö gray ('13) 1.30 12
88 " 4ö blue ('13) 2.50 12
a. Half used as 2ö on cover 800.00
89 " 5ö dark brown ('21) 40 6
a. Imperf., (pair) 275.00
b. Booklet pane, 4 + 2 labels 6.00
90 A10 5ö light green ('30) 65 10
a. Booklet pane, 4 + 2 labels 5.00
b. Booklet pane of 50
91 " 7ö apple green ('26) 1.75 18
a. Booklet pane, 4 + 2 labels 7.50
92 " 7ö dark violet ('30) 3.25 1.30
93 " 8ö gray ('21) 3.00 60
94 " 10ö green ('21) 50 6
a. Imperf., (pair) 350.00
b. Booklet pane, 4 + 2 labels 8.00
95 " 10ö bistre brn. ('30) 1.00 10
a. Booklet pane, 4 + 2 labels 5.00
b. Booklet pane of 50
96 " 12ö violet ('26) 6.50 80
Nos. 85-96 (12) 21.45 3.68

No. 88a was used with No. 97 in Faroe Islands Jan. 3-23, 1919.

King Christian X
A16 A17

1913-28 Typo. *Perf. 14x14½*

97 A16 5ö green 70 6
a. Booklet pane of 4 12.50
98 " 7ö orange ('18) 1.75 40
99 " 8ö dark gray ('20) 4.00 1.25
100 " 10ö red 50 6
a. Imperf., (pair) 300.00
b. Booklet pane of 4 12.50
101 " 12ö gray green ('18) 5.50 5.00
102 " 15ö violet 70 6
103 " 20ö deep blue 2.50 10
104 " 20ö brown ('21) 50 6
105 " 20ö red ('26) 1.60 15
106 " 25ö dark brown 4.00 20
107 " 25ö brn. & blk. ('20) 20.00 1.50
108 " 25ö red ('22) 2.00 30
109 " 25ö yel. green ('25) 1.70 25
110 " 27ö vermilion & blk. ('18) 18.00 20.00
111 " 30ö grn. & blk. ('18) 5.00 50
112 " 30ö orange ('21) 1.50 50
113 " 30ö dark blue ('25) 1.80 35
114 " 35ö orange 5.50 55
115 " 35ö yel. & blk. ('19) 2.50 50
116 " 40ö violet & blk. ('18) 5.00 45
117 " 40ö gray blue & black ('20) 8.00 80
118 " 40ö dark blue ('22) 3.50 1.00
119 " 40ö orange ('25) 1.80 35
120 " 50ö claret 12.50 1.60
121 " 50ö claret & black ('19) 25.00 30
122 " 50ö light gray ('22) 3.00 10
a. 50ö dark gray ('21) 16.00 50
123 " 60ö brn. & bl. ('19) 11.00 50
a. 60ö brn. & ultra. ('19) 40.00 5.00
124 " 60ö greenish bl. ('21) 3.50 45
125 " 70ö brown & green ('20) 5.50 35
126 " 80ö blue green ('15) 25.00 10.00
127 " 90ö brown & red ('20) 5.50 40
128 " 1kr brn. & blue ('22) 20.00 65
129 " 2kr gray & claret ('25) 40.00 4.50
130 " 5kr vio. & brn. ('27) 7.50 5.00
131 " 10kr vermilion & yellow green ('28) 200.00 50.00
Nos. 97-131 (35) 456.55 108.24

No. 97 surcharged "2 ORE" is Faroe Islands No. 1.

Nos. 87 and 98, 89 and 94, 89 and 104, 90 and 95, 97 and 103, 100 and 102 exist se-tenant in coils for use in vending machines.

1913-20 **Engraved**

132 A17 1kr yellow brown 40.00 25
133 " 2kr gray 50.00 2.50
134 " 5kr purple ('20) 10.00 2.50

G.P.O. Type of 1912

Engraved

1915 *Perf. 14x14½* **Wmk. 114**

135	A15	5kr dark red ('15)	325.00	75.00

Nos. 46 and O10 Surcharged in Black

DANMARK 80 ØRE POSTFRIM.

e

Typographed

Perf. 13

1915 **Wmkd. Crown. (112)**

136	A6 (*c*)	80ö on 12ö slate & dull lake	30.00	50.00
		a. Invtd. frame	275.00	450.00
137	O1 (*e*)	80ö on 8ö carmine	32.50	60.00
		a. "POSTERIM"	50.00	90.00

POSTFRIM.

Newspaper Stamps Surcharged ØRE 27 ØRE

DANMARK

On Issue of 1907.

1918 *Perf. 13* **Wmkd. Crown. (113)**

138	N1	27ö on 1ö olive	100.00	140.00
139	"	27ö on 5ö blue	100.00	140.00
140	"	27ö on 7ö car.	100.00	140.00
141	"	27ö on 10ö dp. lilac	100.00	140.00
142	"	27ö on 68ö yellow brown	8.00	14.00
143	"	27ö on 5kr rose & yellow green	5.00	7.00
144	"	27ö on 10kr bistre & blue	7.00	13.00
		Nos. 138-144 (7)	420.00	594.00

On Issue of 1914-15.

Wmkd. Multiple Crosses. (114)

Perf. 14x14½.

145	N1	27ö on 1ö olive gray	3.25	5.00
146	"	27ö on 5ö blue	9.00	13.00
147	"	27ö on 7ö rose	3.25	3.25
148	"	27ö on 8ö green	5.00	8.00
149	"	27ö on 10ö deep lilac	4.00	5.00
150	"	27ö on 20ö green	4.00	6.00
151	"	27ö on 29ö org. yel.	4.00	5.00
152	"	27ö on 38ö orange	22.50	30.00
153	"	27ö on 41ö yel. brn.	6.00	10.00
154	"	27ö on 1kr blue grn. & maroon	3.25	2.50
		Nos. 145-154 (10)	64.25	87.75

Kronborg Castle
A20

Sonderborg Castle
A21

Roskilde Cathedral
A22

Perf. 14½x14, 14x14½

1920, Oct. 5 Typographed

156	A20	10ö red	2.50	25
157	A21	20ö slate	2.50	15
158	A22	40ö dark brown	8.00	4.00

This issue was to commemorate the reunion of Northern Schleswig with Denmark.

1921

159	A20	10ö green	2.50	25
160	A22	40ö dark blue	25.00	4.50

Stamps of 1918 Surcharged in Blue 8 8

1921-22

161	A16	8ö on 7ö orange ('22)	1.75	1.75
162	"	8ö on 12ö gray grn.	2.50	2.50

No. 87 Surcharged 8

1921

163	A10	8ö on 3ö gray	2.00	2.00

King Christian X
A23

King Christian IV
A24

A25

A26

1924, Dec. 1 *Perf. 14x14½.*

164	A23	10ö green	4.75	1.50
165	A24	10ö green	4.75	1.50
166	A25	10ö green	4.75	1.50
167	A26	10ö green	4.75	1.50
168	A23	15ö violet	4.75	1.50
169	A24	15ö violet	4.75	1.50
170	A25	15ö violet	4.75	1.50
171	A26	15ö violet	4.75	1.50
172	A23	20ö dark brown	4.75	1.50
173	A24	20ö dark brown	4.75	1.50
174	A25	20ö dark brown	4.75	1.50
175	A26	20ö dark brown	4.75	1.50
		3 Blocks of 4, #164-175	72.50	67.50
		Nos. 164-175 (12)	57.00	18.00

Issued to commemorate the 300th anniversary of the Danish postal service.

The sheets of each value are composed of stamps of types A23, A24, A25 and A26, arranged in groups of four as illustrated.

Stamps of 1921-22 Surcharged:

20 20 *k* — 20 ■ 20 ■ *l*

1926

176	A16 (*k*)	20ö on 30ö org.	3.25	3.25
177	" (*l*)	20ö on 40ö dk. bl.	4.00	4.00

A27

A28

1926, Mar. 11 *Perf. 14x14½.*

178	A27	10ö dull green	1.00	12
179	A28	20ö dark red	1.20	10
180	"	30ö dark blue	6.00	40

Issued in commemoration of the 75th anniversary of the introduction of postage stamps in Denmark.

Stamps of 1913-26 Surcharged in Blue or Black

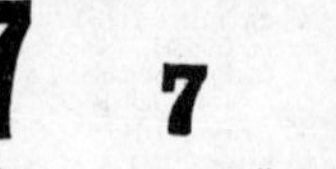
7 *m* — 7 7 *n*

1926-27 *Perf. 14x14½.*

181	A10 (*m*)	7ö on 8ö gray (Bl)	1.75	1.75
182	A16 (*n*)	7ö on 27ö verm. & black	4.75	6.00
183	A16 (*n*)	7ö on 20ö red ('27)	70	35
184	" (")	12ö on 15ö violet	2.25	2.25

Surcharged on Official Stamps of 1914-23.

185	O1 (*e*)	7ö on 1ö orange	3.50	5.00
186	" (")	7ö on 3ö gray	8.50	13.00
187	" (")	7ö on 4ö blue	3.50	5.00
188	" (")	7ö on 5ö green	40.00	50.00
189	" (")	7ö on 10ö green	5.00	5.50
190	" (")	7ö on 15ö violet	3.50	4.00
191	" (")	7ö on 20ö indigo	14.00	18.00
		a. Double surcharge	*300.00*	
		Nos. 181-191 (11)	87.45	110.85

Caravel
A30

King Christian X
A31

1927 Typographed. *Perf. 14x14½.*

192	A30	15ö red	2.75	6
193	"	20ö gray	2.75	15
194	"	25ö light blue	1.00	10
195	"	30ö ochre	1.00	10
196	"	35ö red brown	4.25	15
197	"	40ö yellow green	4.25	10
		Nos. 192-197 (6)	16.00	66

See also Nos. 232-238J.

1930, Sept. 26

210	A31	5ö apple green	1.20	10
		a. Booklet pane, 4 + 2 labels	8.50	
211	"	7ö violet	4.25	1.75
212	"	8ö dark gray	17.00	5.00
213	"	10ö yellow brown	2.25	12
		a. Booklet pane, 4 + 2 labels	11.00	
214	"	15ö red	2.25	12
215	"	20ö light gray	14.00	1.75
216	"	25ö light blue	7.00	20
217	"	30ö yellow buff	7.00	40
218	"	35ö red brown	7.00	1.00
219	"	40ö deep green	7.00	45
		Nos. 210-219 (10)	68.95	10.89

60th birthday of King Christian X.

DANMARK 1 ØRE ØRE POSTFRIMÆRKE

Wavy Lines and Numeral of Value
A32

Type of 1905-12 Issue.

Engraved, Redrawn

1933-40 *Perf. 13* **Unwmkd.**

220	A32	1ö gray black	5	3
221	"	2ö scarlet	10	5
222	"	4ö blue	50	15
223	"	5ö yellow green	1.00	8
		a. 5ö gray green	11.00	12.00
		b. Tête bêche pair	10.00	9.00
		c. Booklet pane of 4	4.50	
		d. Booklet pane of 4, (1 No. 223a & 3 No. B6)	13.00	
224	"	5ö rose lake ('38)	3	3
		a. Booklet pane of 4	25	
		b. Booklet pane of 10	75	
224C	"	6ö orange ('40)	35	6
225	"	7ö violet	2.25	20
226	"	7ö yel. green ('38)	2.25	30
226A	"	7ö light brown ('40)	40	15
227	"	8ö gray	65	15
227A	"	8ö yellow green ('40)	45	10
228	"	10ö yellow orange	9.00	6
		a. Tête bêche pair	22.50	14.00
		b. Booklet pane of 4	40.00	
229	"	10ö light brown ('37)	6.00	10
		a. Booklet pane of 4	27.50	
		b. Booklet pane of 4, (1 No. 229 & 3 No. B7)	12.00	
230	A32	10ö violet ('38)	55	3
		a. Booklet pane of 4	2.50	
		b. Bklt. pane of 4, (2 No. 230 & 2 No. B10)	3.25	
		Nos. 220-230 (14)	23.58	1.49

The stamps of 1905-12 were typographed. They had a solid background with groups of small hearts below the heraldic lions in the upper corners and below "DA" and "RK" of "DANMARK". The numerals of value were enclosed in single-lined ovals.

The 1933-40 stamps are line-engraved and have a background of crossed lines. The hearts have been removed and the numerals of value are now in double-lined ovals. Two types exist of some values.

The 1ö, No. 220, was issued on fluorescent paper in 1969.

No. 230 with wide margins is from booklet pane No. 230b.

Of the tête bêche pairs, those with gutters are twice as plentiful. Prices are for the less costly.

Surcharges of 20, 50 and 60öre on Nos. 220, 224 and 224C are listed as Faroe Islands Nos. 2-3, 5-6.

See also Nos. 318, 333, 382, 416, 437-437A, 493-498.

Certain Tête Bêche

pairs of 1938-55 issues which reached the market in 1971, and were not regularly issued, are not listed. This group comprises 24 different major-number vertical pairs of types A32, A47, A61 and SP3 (13 with gutters, 11 without), and pairs of some minor numbers and shades. They were removed from booklet pane sheets.

Type of 1927 Issue.

1933-34 **Engraved.** ***Perf. 13***

Type I.

Type I—Two columns of squares between sail and left frame line.

232	A30	20ö gray	7.00	12
233	"	25ö blue	30.00	4.75
234	"	25ö brown ('34)	20.00	12
235	"	30ö orange yellow	2.25	1.00
236	"	30ö blue ('34)	2.00	12
237	"	35ö violet	1.40	18
238	"	40ö yellow green	2.50	15
		Nos. 232-238 (7)	65.15	6.44

Type II.

Type II—One column of squares between sail and left frame line.

1933-40

238A	A30	15ö deep red	1.40	6
		k. Booklet pane of 4	7.00	
		l. Booklet pane of 4, (1 No. 238A, 3 No. B8)	20.00	
238B	A30	15ö yel. green ('40)	3.00	6
238C	"	20ö gray black ('39)	4.50	12
238D	"	20ö red ('40)	90	5
238E	"	25ö deep brown ('39)	1.00	10
238F	"	30ö blue ('39)	3.50	15
238G	"	30ö orange ('40)	90	10
238H	"	35ö violet ('40)	1.25	25
238I	"	40ö yel. green ('39)	7.50	25
238J	"	40ö blue ('40)	1.50	12
		Nos. 238A-238J (10)	25.45	1.26

Nos. 232-238J, engraved, have cross-hatched background. Nos. 192-197, typographed, have solid background.

No. 238A surcharged 20ore is listed as Faroe Islands No. 4.

King Christian X
A33

1934-41 ***Perf. 13***

239	A33	50ö gray	1.20	10
240	"	60ö blue green	2.75	12
240A	"	75ö dark blue ('41)	80	10
241	"	1k light brown	3.50	10
242	"	2k dull red	6.50	50
243	"	5k violet	12.50	2.25
		Nos. 239-243 (6)	27.25	3.17

Nos. 233, 235 Surcharged in Black 4

1934, June 9

244	A30	4ö on 25ö blue	50	15
245	"	10ö on 30ö orange yellow	3.00	1.50

"The Ugly Duckling"
A34

Hans Christian Andersen
A35

"The Little Mermaid"
A36

1935, Oct. 4 *Perf. 13*

246 A34 5ö light green 4.00 10
a. Tête bêche pair 11.00 8.00
b. Bklt. pane of 4 17.50
247 A35 7ö dull violet 2.50 60
248 A36 10ö orange 5.00 10
a. Tête bêche pair 14.00 11.00
b. Bklt. pane of 4 22.50
249 A35 15ö red 13.00 10
a. Tête bêche pair 32.50 17.50
b. Bklt. pane of 4 65.00
250 " 20ö gray 10.00 60
251 " 30ö dull blue 3.25 25
Nos. 246-251 (6) 37.75 1.75

Issued to commemorate the centenary of the publication of the earliest installment of Hans Christian Andersen's "Fairy Tales."

Note on tête bêche pair prices after No. 230 applies to Nos. 246a, 248a and 249a.

Nikolai Church
A37

Hans Tausen
A38

Ribe Cathedral
A39

1936 *Perf. 13*

252 A37 5ö green 2.00 10
a. Bklt. pane of 4 10.00
253 " 7ö violet 2.00 60
254 A38 10ö light brown 2.25 10
a. Bklt. pane of 4 11.00
255 " 15ö dull rose 2.75 10
256 A39 30ö blue 12.00 65
Nos. 252-256 (5) 21.00 1.55

Issued in commemoration of the 400th anniversary of the Church Reformation in Denmark.

No. 229 Overprinted in Blue

K.P.K.
17.-26. SEPT.
19 37

1937, Sept. 17

257 A32 10ö light brown 2.50 2.50

Issued in commemoration of the Jubilee Exhibition held by the Copenhagen Philatelic Club on the occasion of their 50th anniversary. The stamps were on sale at the Exhibition only, each holder of a ticket of admission (1kr.) being entitled to purchase 20 stamps at face value, and each holder of a season ticket (5kr.) being entitled to purchase 100 stamps.

Yacht and Summer Palace, Marselisborg
A40

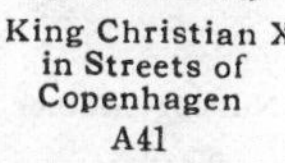

King Christian X in Streets of Copenhagen
A41

Equestrian Statue of King Frederik V and Amalienborg Palace
A42

1937, May 15 *Perf. 13*

258 A40 5ö green 2.00 25
a. Bklt. pane of 4 10.00
259 A41 10ö brown 2.00 10
a. Bklt. pane of 4 10.00
260 A42 15ö scarlet 1.75 10
a. Bklt. pane of 4 13.00
261 A41 30ö blue 11.00 1.25

Issued in commemoration of the 25th anniversary of the accession to the throne of King Christian X.

Emancipation Column, Copenhagen
A43

1938, June 20 *Perf. 13*

262 A43 15ö scarlet 75 12

Issued to commemorate the 150th anniversary of the abolition of serfdom in Denmark.

No. 223 Overprinted in Red on Alternate Stamps

D.F.U.
FRIM-UDST.
19 38

1938, Sept. 2

263 A32 5ö yel. green (pair) 4.00 4.25

10th Danish Philatelic Exhibition.

Bertel Thorvaldsen
A44

Statue of Jason
A45

1938, Nov. 17 Engr. *Perf. 13*

264 A44 5ö rose lake 60 15
265 A45 10ö purple 60 12
266 A44 30ö dark blue 2.00 35

The return to Denmark in 1838 of Bertel Thorvaldsen, Danish sculptor.

Stamps of 1933-39 Surcharged with New Values in Black:

6 *a*   15 *b*   20 *c*

1940

267 A32 (*a*) 6ö on 7ö yellow green 25 25
268 " (") 6ö on 8ö gray 45 45
269 A30 (*b*) 15ö on 40ö yel. grn. (On No. 238) 2.00 2.25
270 " (") 15ö on 40ö yel. grn. (On No. 238I) 1.50 1.30
271 " (*c*) 20ö on 15ö deep red 90 8
272 " (*b*) 40ö on 30ö bl. (On No. 238F) 1.25 30
Nos. 267-272 (6) 6.35 4.63

Bering's Ship
A46

1941, Nov. 27 Engr. *Perf. 13*

277 A46 10ö dark violet 50 20
278 " 20ö red brown 75 50
279 " 40ö dark blue 75 35

Issued in commemoration of the 200th anniversary of the death of Vitus Bering, explorer.

King Christian X
A47

1942-46 *Perf. 13* **Unwmkd.**

280 A47 10ö violet 25 3
a. Booklet pane of 4 1.25
281 " 15ö yellow green 30 6
a. Booklet pane of 4 1.50
282 " 20ö red 30 3
283 " 25ö brown ('43) 30 6
284 " 30ö orange 30 6
285 " 35ö bright red violet ('44) 35 15
a. 35ö brt. lilac rose ('45) 3.00 1.00
286 " 40ö blue ('43) 35 4
286A " 45ö olive brown ('46) 60 10
286B " 50ö gray ('45) 55 6
287 " 60ö bluish green ('44) 55 6
287A " 75ö dark blue ('46) 60 10
Nos. 280-287A (11) 4.45 75

Round Tower
A48

Condor Plane
A49

1942, Nov. 27

288 A48 10ö violet 20 10

Issued to commemorate the 300th anniversary of the Round Tower, Copenhagen.

1943, Oct. 29

289 A49 20ö red 25 10

Issued to commemorate the 25th anniversary of the Danish Aviation Company (Det Danske Luftfartsselskab).

Ejby Church
A50

Designs: 15ö, Oesterlars Church. 20ö, Hvidbjerg Church.

1944 **Engraved.** *Perf. 13*

290 A50 10ö violet 20 12
291 " 15ö yellow green 60 60
292 " 20ö red 25 12

Ole Roemer
A53

King Christian X
A54

1944, Sept. 25

293 A53 20ö henna brown 40 20

Issued to commemorate the 300th anniversary of the birth of Ole Roemer, astronomer.

1945, Sept. 26

294 A54 10ö lilac 20 10
295 " 20ö red 25 10
296 " 40ö deep blue 50 15

75th birthday of King Christian X.

Small State Seal
A55

Tycho Brahe
A56

1946-47 *Perf. 13* **Unwmkd.**

297 A55 1k brown 40 3
298 " 2k red ('47) 80 5
299 " 5k dull blue 2.00 6

Nos. 297-299 issued on ordinary and fluorescent paper.

See also Nos. 395-400, 441A-444D, 499-506.

1946, Dec. 14 **Engraved**

300 A56 20(ö) dark red 30 10

Issued to commemorate the 400th anniversary of the birth of Tycho Brahe, astronomer.

First Danish Locomotive
A57

Modern Steam Locomotive
A58

Diesel Locomotive
A59

1947, June 27

301 A57 15(ö) steel blue 50 20
302 A58 20(ö) red 50 15
303 A59 40(ö) deep blue 1.00 50

Issued to commemorate the centenary of the inauguration of the Danish State Railways.

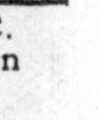

Jacob C. Jacobsen
A60

King Frederik IX
A61

1947, Nov. 10 *Perf. 13*

304 A60 20(ö) dark red 30 12

Issued to commemorate the 60th anniversary of the death of Jacob Christian Jacobsen, founder of the Glyptothek Art Museum, Copenhagen.

1948-50 *Perf. 13* **Unwmkd.**

Three types among 15ö, 20ö, 30ö:

I. Background of horizontal lines. No outline at left for cheek and ear. King's uniform textured in strong lines.

II. Background of vertical and horizontal lines. Contour of cheek and ear at left. Uniform same.

III. Background and facial contour lines as in II. Uniform lines double and thinner.

306 A61 15(ö) green (II) 50 6
a. Type III ('49) 50 6
b. Bklt. pane of 4 2.50

307 A61 20(ö) dk. red (I) 50 6
a. Type III ('49) 50 6
308 " 25(ö) light brown 80 10
309 " 30(ö) orange (II) 7.50 10
a. Type III ('50) 7.50 10
310 " 40(ö) dull blue ('49) 2.25 45
311 " 45(ö) olive ('50) 85 10
312 " 50(ö) gray ('49) 85 10
313 " 60(ö) greenish blue ('50) 85 6
314 " 75(ö) lilac rose ('50) 65 6
Nos. 306-314 (9) 14.75 1.09

See also Nos. 319-326, 334-341, 354.

Legislative Assembly, 1849
A62

Symbol of U.P.U.
A63

1949, June 5

315 A62 20(ö) red brown 45 10

Issued to commemorate the centenary of the adoption of the Danish constitution.

1949, Oct. 9

316 A63 40ö dull blue 80 40

Issued to commemorate the 75th anniversary of the formation of the Universal Postal Union.

Kalundborg Radio Station and Masts
A64

1950, Apr. 1 Engr. *Perf. 13*

317 A64 20ö brown red 40 15

Issued to commemorate the 25th anniversary of radio broadcasting in Denmark.

Types of 1933-50.

1950-51 *Perf. 13* **Unwmkd.**

318 A32 10ö green 4 3
a. Booklet pane of 4 25
b. Booklet pane of 6 35
c. Booklet pane of 8 40
319 A61 15(ö) lilac 35 3
a. Bklt. pane of 4 1.75
b. 15(ö) gray lilac 65 3
320 " 20(ö) light brown 30 3
321 " 25(ö) dark red 90 3
322 " 35(ö) gray green ('51) 75 10
323 " 40(ö) gray 75 6
324 " 50(ö) dark blue 1.25 10
325 " 55(ö) brown ('51) 5.00 2.00
326 " 70(ö) deep green 1.50 6
Nos. 318-326 (9) 10.84 2.44

Warship of 1701
A65

Hans Christian Oersted
A66

1951, Feb. 26 Engr. *Perf. 13*

327 A65 25(ö) dark red 90 15
328 " 50(ö) deep blue 3.00 1.50

Issued to commemorate the 250th anniversary of the foundation of the Naval Officers' College.

1951, Mar. 9 **Unwmkd.**

329 A66 50(ö) blue 1.60 45

Issued to commemorate the centenary of the death of Hans Christian Oersted, physicist.

Post Chaise ("Ball Post")
A67

Marine Rescue
A68

1951, Apr. 1 *Perf. 13*

330 A67 15(ö) purple 1.00 10
331 " 25(ö) henna brown 1.00 10

Issued to commemorate the centenary of Denmark's first postage stamp.

1952, Mar. 26

332 A68 25(ö) red brown 40 10

Issued to commemorate the centenary of the foundation of the Danish Lifesaving Service.

Types of 1933-50.

1952-53 *Perf. 13*

333 A32 12(ö) lt. yellow green 35 3
334 A61 25(ö) light blue 1.00 10
335 " 30(ö) brown red 60 3
336 " 50(ö) aquamarine ('53) 40 6
337 " 60(ö) deep blue ('53) 70 6
338 " 65(ö) gray ('53) 50 10
339 " 80(ö) orange ('53) 60 6
340 " 90(ö) olive ('53) 1.50 6
341 " 95(ö) red org. ('53) 1.00 25
Nos. 333-341 (9) 6.65 75

Jelling Runic Stone
A69

Designs: 15(ö), Vikings' camp, Trelleborg. 20(ö), Church of Kalundborg. 30(ö), Nyborg castle. 60(ö), Goose tower, Vordinborg.

1953-56 *Perf. 13*

342 A69 10(ö) deep green 15 5
343 " 15(ö) light rose violet 15 5
344 " 20(ö) brown 20 8
345 " 30(ö) red ('54) 25 8
346 " 60(ö) deep blue ('54) 40 12

Designs: 10(ö), Manor house, Spottrup. 15(ö), Hammershus castle ruins. 20(ö), Copenhagen stock exchange. 30(ö), Statue of Frederik V, Amalienborg. 60(ö), Soldier statue at Fredericia.

347 A69 10(ö) green ('54) 15 5
348 " 15(ö) lilac ('55) 15 5
349 " 20(ö) brown ('55) 20 8
350 " 30(ö) red ('55) 25 8
351 " 60(ö) deep blue ('56) 60 12
Nos. 342-351 (10) 2.50 76

Nos. 342-351 were issued to commemorate the 1000th anniversary of the Kingdom of Denmark. Each stamp represents a different century.

Telegraph Equipment of 1854
A70

King Frederik V
A71

1954, Feb. 2 *Perf. 13*

352 A70 30(ö) red brown 45 12

Issued to commemorate the centenary of the telegraph in Denmark.

1954, Mar. 31

353 A71 30(ö) dark red 75 10

Issued to commemorate the 200th anniversary of the founding of the Royal Academy of Fine Arts.

Type of 1948-50

1955, Apr. 27

354 A61 25(ö) lilac 30 5

Nos. 224C and 226A Surcharged with New Value in Black. Nos. 307 and 321 Surcharged with New Value and 4 Bars.

1955-56

355 A32 5ö on 6ö orange 10 4
356 " 5ö on 7ö light brown 10 8
357 A61 30(ö) on 20(ö) dark red (I) 30 5
a. Type III 50 10
b. Double surch. 375.00 375.00
358 " 30(ö) on 25(ö) dark red ('56) 65 6
a. Double surch.

Sören Kierkegaard—A72

Ellehammer's Plane—A73

1955, Nov. 11 **Unwmkd.**

359 A72 30(ö) dark red 50 10

Issued to commemorate the 100th anniversary of the death of Sören Kierkegaard, philosopher and theologian.

1956, Sept. 12 **Engraved**

360 A73 30ö dull red 60 10

Issued to commemorate the 50th anniversary of the first flight made by Jacob Christian Hansen Ellehammer in a heavier-than-air craft.

Northern Countries Issue.

Whooper Swans
A74

1956, Oct. 30 *Perf. 13*

361 A74 30ö rose red 3.00 20
362 " 60ö ultramarine 1.25 75

Issued to emphasize the close bonds among the northern countries: Denmark, Finland, Iceland, Norway and Sweden.

Prince's Palace
A75

Harvester
A76

Design: 60ö, Sun God's Chariot.

1957, May 15 **Unwmkd.**

363 A75 30ö dull red 1.75 10
364 " 60ö dark blue 1.00 45

Issued to commemorate the 150th anniversary of the National Museum.

1958, Sept. 4 Engr. *Perf. 13*

365 A76 30ö terra cotta 30 6

Centenary of the Royal Veterinary and Agricultural College.

King Frederik IX
A77

Ballet Dancer
A78

1959, Mar. 11

366 A77 30ö rose red 80 8
367 " 35ö rose lilac 60 45
368 " 60ö ultramarine 50 15

King Frederik's 60th birthday.

1959, May 16

369 A78 35ö rose lilac 25 8

Issued to publicize the Danish Ballet and Music Festival, May 17-31. See also Nos. 401, 422.

No. 319 Surcharged

30
Verdensflygtningeåret 1959-60

1960, Apr. 7

370 A61 30ö on 15ö purple 25 12

Issued to publicize World Refugee Year, July 1, 1959–June 30, 1960.

Seeder and Farm
A79

Designs: 30ö, Harvester combine. 60ö, Plow.

1960, Apr. 28 Engr. *Perf. 13*

371 A79 12ö green 15 5
372 " 30ö dull red 20 6
373 " 60ö dark blue 60 15

King Frederik IX and Queen Ingrid
A80

1960, May 24 **Unwmkd.**

374 A80 30ö dull red 85 8
375 " 60ö blue 65 25

Issued to commemorate the 25th anniversary of the marriage of King Frederik IX and Queen Ingrid.

Bascule Light
A81

Niels R. Finsen
A82

1960, June 8 **Engraved**

376 A81 30ö dull red 30 6

Issued to commemorate the 400th anniversary of the Lighthouse Service.

1960, Aug. 1 *Perf. 13*

377 A82 30ö dark red 30 6

Issued to commemorate the centenary of the birth of Dr. Niels R. Finsen, physician and scientist.

Nursing Mother
A83

DC-8 Airliner
A84

1960, Aug. 16 **Unwmkd.**

378 A83 60ö ultramarine 70 25

Issued to commemorate the 10th meeting of the regional committee for Europe of the World Health Organization, Copenhagen, Aug. 16–20.

Europa Issue, 1960

Common Design Type

1960, Sept. 19 *Perf. 13*

Size: 28x21mm.

379 CD3 60ö ultramarine 45 20

SAS Issue

1961, Feb. 24

380 A84 60ö ultramarine 40 20

Issued to commemorate the 10th anniversary of the Scandinavian Airlines System, SAS.

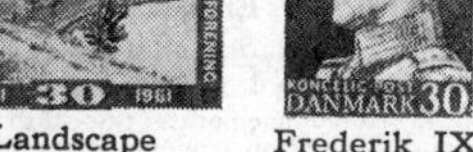

Landscape A85 — Frederik IX A86

1961, Apr. 21 *Perf. 13*

381 A85 30ö copper brown 25 8

Issued to commemorate the 50th anniversary of Denmark's Society of Nature Lovers.

Fluorescent Paper

as well as ordinary paper, was used in printing many definitive and commemorative stamps, starting in 1962. These include No. 220; the 15, 20, 25, 30, 35 (Nos. 386 and 387), 50 and 60ö, 1.20k, 1.50k and 25k definitives of following set, and Nos. 297–299, 318, 318a–b, 333, 380, 401–427, 429–435, 438–439, 493, 543, 548, B30.

Only fluorescent paper was used for Nos. 436–437, 437A and 440 onward; in semi-postals from B31 onward.

1961–63 **Engraved** *Perf. 13*

382 A32 15ö green ('63) 20 3
383 A86 20ö brown 55 5
384 " 25ö brown ('63) 30 3
385 " 30ö rose red 55 3
386 " 35ö olive green 1.00 25
387 " 35ö rose red ('63) 30 3
388 " 40ö gray 30 5
389 " 50ö aquamarine 30 6
390 " 60ö ultramarine 35 6
391 " 70ö green 1.25 10
392 " 80ö red orange 60 5
393 " 90ö olive bistre 1.75 12
394 " 95ö claret ('63) 60 30
Nos. 382–394 (13) 8.05 1.16

See also Nos. 417–419, 438–441.

State Seal Type of 1946–47

1962–65

395 A55 1.10k lilac ('65) 1.50 35
396 " 1.20k gray 1.00 6
397 " 1.25k orange 1.00 8
398 " 1.30k green ('65) 1.00 20
399 " 1.50k red lilac 75 6
400 " 25k yellow green 9.00 65
Nos. 395–400 (6) 14.25 1.40

Dancer Type of 1959

Inscribed "15-31 MAJ"

1962, Apr. 26

401 A78 60ö ultramarine 50 18

Issued to publicize the Danish Ballet and Music Festival, May 15–31. No. 369 is dated "17-31 MAJ."

Old Mill A87 — M.S. Selandia A88

1962, May 10 *Perf. 13* **Unwmkd.**

402 A87 10ö red brown 10 5

Issued to commemorate the centenary of the abolition of mill monopolies.

1962, June 14 **Engraved**

403 A88 60ö dark blue 2.75 2.25

Issued to commemorate the 50th anniversary of M.S. Selandia, the first Diesel ship.

Violin Scroll, Leaves, Lights and Balloon—A89

1962, Aug. 31

404 A89 35ö rose violet 30 6

Issued to commemorate the 150th anniversary of the birth of Georg Carstensen, founder of Tivoli amusement park, Copenhagen.

Cliffs on Möen Island A90 — Germinating Wheat A91

1962, Nov. 22

405 A90 20ö pale brown 15 5

Issued to publicize preservation of natural treasures and landmarks.

1963, Mar. 21 **Engraved**

406 A91 35ö terra cotta 30 8

Issued for the "Freedom from Hunger" campaign of the U.N. Food and Agriculture Organization.

Railroad Wheel, Tire Tracks, Waves and Swallow A92 — Sailing Vessel, Coach, Postilions and Globe A93

1963, May 14 *Perf. 13* **Unwmkd.**

407 A92 15ö green 15 6

Issued to commemorate the inauguration of the "Bird Flight Line" railroad link between Denmark and Germany.

1963, May 27

408 A93 60ö dark blue 50 15

Issued to commemorate the centenary of the first International Postal Conference, Paris, 1863.

Niels Bohr and Atom Diagram A94 — Early Public School Drawn on Slate A95

1963, Nov. 21 **Engraved**

409 A94 35ö red brown 30 7
410 " 60ö dark blue 55 15

Issued to commemorate the 50th anniversary of Prof. Niels Bohr's (1885–1962) atom theory.

1964, June 19 *Perf. 13* **Unwmkd.**

411 A95 35ö red brown 30 6

Issued to commemorate the 150th anniversary of the royal decrees for the public school system.

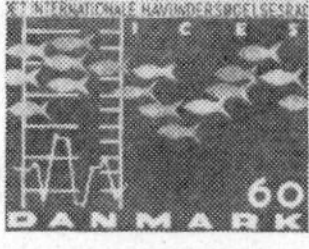

Fish and Chart A96 — Danish Watermarks and Perforations A97

1964, Sept. 7 **Engraved**

412 A96 60ö violet blue 45 15

Issued to commemorate the Conference of the International Council for the Exploration of the Sea, Copenhagen.

1964, Oct. 10 *Perf. 13*

413 A97 35ö pink 35 8

Issued for the 25th anniversary of Stamp Day and to publicize the Odense Stamp Exhibition, Oct. 10–11.

Landscape A98 — Calculator, Ledger and Inkwell A99

1964, Nov. 12 **Engraved**

414 A98 25ö brown 20 6

Issued to publicize preservation of natural treasures and landmarks.

1965, Mar. 8 **Unwmkd.**

415 A99 15ö lt. olive green 15 6

Issued to commemorate the centenary of the first Business School in Denmark.

Types of 1933 and 1961

1965, May 15 **Engraved** *Perf. 13*

416 A32 25ö apple green 18 3
417 A86 40ö brown 25 3
a. Bklt. pane of 4 1.25
418 " 50ö rose red 25 3
419 " 80ö ultramarine 60 5

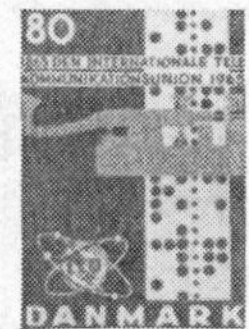

ITU Emblem, Telegraph Key and Teletype Paper A100 — Carl Nielsen A101

1965, May 17

420 A100 80ö dark blue 60 15

Issued to commemorate the centenary of the International Telecommunication Union.

1965, June 9 **Engraved**

421 A101 50ö brown red 25 6

Issued to commemorate the centenary of the birth of Carl Nielsen (1865–1931), composer.

Dancer Type of 1959

Inscribed "15-31 MAJ"

1965, Sept. 23

422 A78 50ö rose red 30 8

Issued to publicize the Danish Ballet and Music Festival, May 15–31.

Bogo Windmill A102 — Mylius Dalgas Surveying Wasteland A103

1965, Nov. 10 **Engraved** *Perf. 13*

423 A102 40ö brown 25 8

Issued to publicize the preservation of natural treasures and landmarks.

1966, Feb. 24

424 A103 25ö olive green 15 5

Issued to commemorate the centenary of the Danish Heath Society (reclamation of wastelands), founded by Enrico Mylius Dalgas.

Christen Kold A104

1966, March 29 *Perf. 13*

425 A104 50ö dull red 30 6

Issued to commemorate the 150th anniversary of the birth of Christen Kold (1816–70), educator.

Poorhouse, Copenhagen A105 — Holte Allée, Bregentved A106

Dolmen (Grave) in Jutland A107

1966 **Unwmkd.**

426 A105 50ö dull red 30 6
427 A106 80ö dark blue 50 15
428 A107 1.50k dk. slate grn. 1.00 15

Nos. 426–428 issued to publicize preservation of national treasures and ancient monuments. Issue dates: 50ö, May 12; 80ö, June 16; 1.50k, Nov. 24.

Georg Jensen by Ejnar Nielsen A108 — Music Bar and Instruments A109

1966, Aug. 31 **Engr.** *Perf. 13*

429 A108 80ö dark blue 50 15

Issued to commemorate the centenary of the birth of Georg Jensen, silversmith.

1967, Jan. 9

430 A109 50ö dark red 30 6

Issued to commemorate the centenary of the Royal Danish Academy of Music.

Cogwheels, and Broken Customs Duty Ribbon
A110

1967, Mar. 2

431 A110 80ö dark blue 50 15

Issued to publicize the European Free Trade Association. Industrial tariffs were abolished Dec. 31, 1966, among EFTA members: Austria, Denmark, Finland, Great Britain, Norway, Portugal, Sweden and Switzerland.

Windmill and Medieval Fortress
A111

Designs: 40ö, Ship's rigging and baroque house front. 50ö, Old Town Hall. 80ö, New building construction.

1967 Engraved *Perf. 13*

432	A111	25ö green	15	8
433	"	40ö sepia	25	8
434	"	50ö red brown	30	8
435	"	80ö dark blue	85	25

The 800th anniversary of Copenhagen.
Issue dates: Nos. 432–433, Apr. 6; Nos. 434–435, May 11.

Princess Margrethe and Prince Henri
A112

1967, June 10

436 A112 50ö red 40 10

Issued to commemorate the marriage of Crown Princess Margrethe and Prince Henri de Monpezat.

Types of 1933–1961

1967–71 Engraved *Perf. 13*

437	A32	30ö dark green	15	4
437A	"	40ö orange ('71)	14	5
438	A86	50ö brown	25	6
		a. Booklet pane of 4	1.25	
439	A86	60ö rose red	30	5
		a. Booklet pane of 4	1.50	
		b. Booklet pane of 6	2.00	
		c. Booklet pane of 8	2.50	
440	A86	80ö green	40	4
441	"	90ö ultramarine	50	4
441A	A55	1.20k Prus. green ('71)	45	10
442	"	2.20k orange	1.80	10
443	"	2.80k gray	1.80	10
444	"	2.90k rose violet	1.25	10
444A	"	3k dark slate green ('69)	1.10	10
444B	"	3.10k plum ('70)	1.25	18
444C	"	4k gray ('69)	1.50	10
444D	"	4.10k olive ('70)	1.60	18
		Nos. 437–444D (14)	12.49	1.24

Issue dates: Nos. 437–441, June 30, 1967; Nos. 442–443, July 8, 1967; No. 444, Apr. 29, 1968; Nos. 444A, 444C, Aug. 28, 1969; Nos. 444B, 444D, Aug. 27, 1970; Nos. 437A, 441A, June 24, 1971.

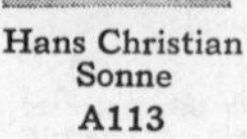

Hans Christian Sonne
A113

Cross-anchor and Porpoise
A114

1967, Sept. 21

445 A113 60ö red 30 10

Issued to commemorate the 150th anniversary of the birth of Hans Christian Sonne, pioneer of the cooperative movement in Denmark.

1967, Nov. 9 Engraved *Perf. 13*

446 A114 90ö dark blue 50 18

Issued to commemorate the centenary of the Danish Seamen's Church in Foreign Ports.

Esbjerg Harbor
A115

Koldinghus
A116

1968, Apr. 24

447 A115 30ö dk. yel. green 25 6

Centenary of Esbjerg Harbor.

1968, June 13

448 A116 60ö copper red 30 6

700th anniversary of Koldinghus Castle.

Shipbuilding Industry
A117

Sower
A118

Designs: 50ö, Chemical industry. 60ö, Electric power. 90ö, Engineering.

1968, Oct. 24 Engraved *Perf. 13*

449	A117	30ö green	15	6
450	"	50ö brown	25	6
451	"	60ö red brown	30	6
452	"	90ö dark blue	50	25

Issued to publicize Danish industries.

1969, Jan. 29

453 A118 30ö gray green 20 8

Issued to commemorate the 200th anniversary of the Royal Agricultural Society of Denmark.

Five Ancient Ships
A119

Frederik IX
A120

Nordic Cooperation Issue

1969, Feb. 28 Engraved *Perf. 13*

454	A119	60ö brown red	30	8
455	"	90ö blue	60	40

Issued to commemorate the 50th anniversary of the Nordic Society and to commemorate the centenary of postal cooperation among the northern countries: Denmark, Finland, Iceland, Norway and Sweden. The design is taken from a coin found at the site of Birka, an ancient Swedish town.

1969, Mar. 11

456	A120	50ö sepia	30	6
457	"	60ö dull red	30	6

70th birthday of King Frederik IX.

Europa Issue, 1969
Common Design Type

1969, Apr. 28

Size: 28x20mm.

458 CD12 90ö chalky blue 50 25

Kronborg Castle
A121

Danish Flag
A122

1969, May 22 Engraved *Perf. 13*

459 A121 50ö brown 25 10

Issued to commemorate the 50th anniversary of the association of Danes living abroad.

1969, June 12

460 A122 60ö bluish black, red & gray 40 8

Issued to commemorate the 750th anniversary of the fall of the Dannebrog (Danish flag) from heaven.

Martin Andersen Nexø
A123

Niels Stensen
A124

1969, Aug. 28

461 A123 80ö deep green 40 15

Issued to commemorate the centenary of the birth of Martin Andersen Nexø (1869–1954), novelist.

1969, Sept. 25

462 A124 1k deep brown 50 15

Issued to commemorate the 300th anniversary of the publication of Niels Stensen's geological work "On Solid Bodies."

Abstract Design
A125

Symbolic Design
A126

1969, Nov. 10 Engraved *Perf. 13*

463 A125 60ö rose, red & ultra. 30 6

1969, Nov. 20

464 A126 30ö olive green 20 8

Issued to commemorate the centenary of the birth of Valdemar Poulsen (1869–1942), electrical engineer and inventor.

Post Office Bank
A127

School Safety Patrol
A128

1970, Jan. 15 Engraved *Perf. 13*

465 A127 60ö dk. red & org. 20 6

Issued to commemorate the 50th anniversary of post office banking service.

1970, Feb. 19

466 A128 50ö brown 20 10

Issued to publicize road safety.

Candle in Window
A129

Deer
A130

1970, May 4 Engraved *Perf. 13*

467 A129 50ö slate, dull blue & yellow 20 10

Issued to commemorate the 25th anniversary of liberation from the Germans.

1970, May 28

468 A130 60ö yellow green, red & brown 20 8

Tercentenary of Jaegersborg Deer Park.

Elephant Figurehead, 1741
A131

"The Homecoming" by Povl Christensen
A132

1970, June 15 *Perf. 11½*

469 A131 30ö multicolored 15 8

Royal Naval Museum, tercentenary.

1970, June 15 *Perf. 13*

470 A132 60ö org., dull vio. & olive green 20 8

Issued to commemorate the 50th anniversary of the union of North Schleswig and Denmark.

Electromagnet
A133

1970, Aug. 13 Engraved

471 A133 80ö gray green 40 12

Issued to commemorate the 150th anniversary of Hans Christian Oersted's discovery of electromagnetism.

Bronze Age Ship
A134

Ships: 50ö, Viking shipbuilding, from Bayeux tapestry. 60ö, Thuroe schooner with topgallant. 90ö, Tanker.

1970, Sept. 24

472	A134	30ö ocher & brown	15	8
473	"	50ö brown red & rose brown	20	8
474	"	60ö gray olive & red brown	30	8
475	"	90ö bl. grn. & ultra.	50	40

U.N. Emblem
A135

1970, Oct. 22 Engraved *Perf. 13*

476 A135 90ö bl., grn. & red 40 30

25th anniversary of the United Nations.

Bertel Thorvaldsen
A136

Mathilde Fibiger
A137

1970, Nov. 19

477 A136 2k slate blue 70 18

Issued to commemorate the bicentenary of the birth of Bertel Thorvaldsen (1768–1844), sculptor.

1971, Feb. 25

478 A137 80ö olive green 30 12

Danish Women's Association centenary.

Refugees
A138

Hans Egede
A139

1971, March 26 Engr. *Perf. 13*

479 A138 50ö brown 20 8
480 " 60ö brown red 25 8

Joint northern campaign for the benefit of refugees.

1971, May 27

481 A139 1k brown 35 15

250th anniversary of arrival of Hans Egede in Greenland and beginning of its colonization.

Swimming
A140

Designs: 50ö, Gymnastics. 60ö, Soccer. 90ö, Sailing.

1971, Oct. 14

482 A140 30ö blue & green 15 8
483 " 50ö dk. red & brown 25 8
484 " 60ö gray, yellow & dark blue 30 8
485 " 90ö ultra., pale grn. & violet 45 25

Georg Brandes
A141

1971, Nov. 11 Engr. *Perf. 13*

486 A141 90ö dark blue 45 20

Centenary of first lectures given by Georg Brandes (1842–1927), writer and literary critic.

Sugar Production
A142

1972, Jan. 27

487 A142 80ö slate green 30 10

Centenary of Danish sugar production.

King Frederik IX
A143

1972, Mar. 11 Engr. *Perf. 13*

488 A143 60ö red brown 25 8

In memory of King Frederik IX (1899–1972).

Abstract Design
A144

1972, Mar. 11

489 A144 1.20k brt. rose lilac, blue gray & brown 40 18

Centenary of the Danish Meteorological Institute.

Nikolai F. S. Grundtvig
A145

Locomotive, 1847, Ferry, Travelers
A146

1972, May 4 Engraved *Perf. 13*

490 A145 1k sepia 35 15

Centenary of the death of Nikolai Frederik Severin Grundtvig (1783–1872), theologian and poet.

1972, June 26

491 A146 70ö rose red 25 10

125th anniversary of Danish State Railways.

Rebild Hills
A147

"Tinker Turned Politician"
A148

1972, June 26

492 A147 1k blue, slate green & maroon 35 18

Types of 1933–46

1972–78 Engraved *Perf. 13*

493 A32 20ö slate blue ('74) 7 3
494 " 50ö sepia ('74) 18 3
495 " 60ö apple grn. ('76) 22 3
496 " 60ö gray ('78) 22 3
497 " 70ö red 25 3
498 " 70ö apple green ('77) 25 8
499 A55 2.50k orange 90 15
500 A55 2.80k olive ('75) 1.00 18
501 " 3.50k lilac 1.25 10
502 " 4.50k olive 1.60 10
503 " 6k vio. blk. ('76) 2.10 45
504 " 7k red lilac ('78) 2.50 60
505 " 9k brn. olive ('77) 3.25 1.00
506 " 10k lemon ('76) 3.50 75
Nos. 493-506 (14) 17.29 3.56

1972, Sept. 14

507 A148 70ö dark red 25 10

250th anniversary of the comedies of Ludvig Holberg (1684–1754) on the Danish stage.

WHO Building, Copenhagen
A149

1972, Sept. 14

508 A149 2k blue, black & lt. red brown 70 30

Opening of World Health Organization Building, Copenhagen.

Bridge Across Little Belt
A150

Aeroskobing House c. 1740
A151

Designs (Diagrams): 60ö, Hanstholm Harbor. 70ö, Lim Fjord Tunnel. 90ö, Knudshoved Harbor.

1972, Oct. 19 Engraved *Perf. 13*

509 A150 40ö dark green 15 8
510 " 60ö dark brown 20 8
511 " 70ö dark red 25 8
512 " 90ö dk. blue green 30 12

Highway engineering.

1972, Nov. 23

Danish Architecture: 60ö, East Bornholm farmhouse, 17th century (horiz.). 70ö, House, Christianshavn, c. 1710. 1.20k, Hvide Sande farmhouse, c. 1810 (horiz.).

Size: 20x28mm., 27x20mm.

513 A151 40ö red, brn. & blk. 15 8
514 " 60ö black, violet blue & green 21 8

Size: 18x37mm., 36x20mm.

515 A151 70ö red, dark red & black 25 8
516 " 1.20k dark brown, red & green 45 16

Johannes V. Jensen
A152

Guard Rails and Cogwheels
A153

1973, Feb. 22 Engraved *Perf. 13*

517 A152 90ö green 30 12

Centenary of the birth of Johannes Vilhelm Jensen (1873–1950), lyric poet and novelist.

1973, Mar. 22

518 A153 50ö sepia 18 7

Centenary of first Danish Factory Act for labor protection.

P. C. Abildgaard
A154

Rhododendron
A155

1973, Mar. 22

519 A154 1k dull blue 35 15

Bicentenary of Royal Veterinary College, Christianshaven, founded by Prof. P. C. Abildgaard.

1973, Apr. 26

Design: 70ö, Dronningen of Denmark rose.

520 A155 60ö brn., grn. & vio. 21 8
521 " 70ö dark red, rose & green 25 8

Centenary of the founding of the Horticultural Society of Denmark.

Nordic Cooperation Issue 1973

Nordic House, Reykjavik
A156

1973, June 26 Engr. *Perf. 13*

522 A156 70ö multicolored 25 10
523 " 1k " 50 15

A century of postal cooperation among Denmark, Finland, Iceland, Norway and Sweden, and in connection with the Nordic Postal Conference, Reykjavik.

Sextant, Stella Nova and Cassiopeia
A157

St. Mark, from 11th Century Book of Dalby
A158

1973, Oct. 18 Engraved *Perf. 13*

524 A157 2k dark blue 70 30

400th anniversary of the publication of "De Nova Stella," by Tycho Brahe.

1973, Oct. 18 Photo. *Perf. 14x14½*

525 A158 120ö buff & multi. 60 30

300th anniversary of Royal Library.

Devil and Gossips, Fanefjord Church, 1480
A159

Frescoes: No. 527, Queen Esther and King Ahasuerus, Tirsted Church, c.1400. No. 528, Miraculous Harvest, Jetsmark Church, c.1474. No. 529, Jesus carrying cross, and wearing crown of thorns, Biersted Church, c.1400. No. 530, Creation of Eve, Fanefjord Church, c.1480.

1973, Nov. 28 Engr. *Perf. 13*

Cream Paper

526 A159 70ö dk. red, yellow & green 50 15
527 " 70ö dk. red, yellow & green 50 15
528 " 70ö dk. red, yellow & green 50 15

529 A159 70ö dk. red, yellow & green 50 15
530 " 70ö dk. red, yellow & green 50 15
a. Booklet pane of 10 5.00
Nos. 526-530 (5) 2.50 75

Nos. 526-530 printed se-tenant in sheets of 50 (5x10). No. 530a contains 2 each of Nos. 526-530.

Blood Donors A160 — Queen Margrethe A161

1974, Jan. 24

531 A160 90ö purple & red 32 15
"Blood Saves Lives."

1974-78 Engraved Perf. 13

532 A161 60ö brown 22 10
533 " 60ö orange 22 3
534 " 70ö red 25 3
535 " 70ö dark brown 25 3
536 " 80ö green 30 15
537 " 80ö dp. brown ('76) 30 3
538 " 90ö red lilac 32 4
539 " 90ö dull red 32 3
540 " 90ö slate green ('76) 32 3
541 " 100ö dp. ultramarine 35 5
542 " 100ö gray ('75) 35 5
543 " 100ö red ('76) 35 5
544 " 100ö brown ('77) 35 5
545 " 110ö orange ('78) 40 5
546 " 120ö slate 45 6
547 " 120ö red ('77) 45 6
548 " 130ö ultra. ('75) 48 15
549 " 150ö vio. blue ('78) 48 8
550 " 180ö slate green ('77) 65 10
Nos. 532-550 (19) 6.81 1.17

Pantomime Theater A162

1974, May 16

552 A162 100ö indigo 35 15

Centenary of the Pantomime Theater, Tivoli.

Hverringe A163

Views: 60ö, Norre Lyndelse, Carl Nielsen's childhood home. 70ö, Odense, Hans Chr. Andersen's childhood home. 90ö, Hesselagergaard (vert.). 120ö, Hindsholm.

1974, June 20 Engr. Perf. 13

553 A163 50ö brown & multi. 18 8
554 " 60ö slate green & multicolored 22 8
555 " 70ö red brown & multicolored 25 8
556 " 90ö dark green & maroon 32 8
557 " 120ö red orange & dark green 45 12
Nos. 553-557 (5) 1.42 44

Emblem, Runner with Map A164 — Iris A165

Design: 80ö, Compass.

1974, Aug. 22 Engr. Perf. 13

558 A164 70ö dk. blue & brn. 25 10
559 " 80ö brn. & vio. bl. 30 20

World Orienteering Championships 1974.

1974, Sept. 19

Design: 120ö, Purple orchid.

560 A165 90ö brn., vio. blue & slate green 32 15
561 " 120ö indigo, lilac & slate green 45 12

Copenhagen Botanical Garden centenary.

Mailman, 1624, and Postilion, 1780 A166

Carrier Pigeon A167

Design: 90ö, Balloon and sailing ships.

1974, Oct. 9 Engraved Perf. 13

562 A166 70ö lemon & dk. brn. 25 10
563 " 90ö dull grn. & sepia 32 10
564 A167 120ö dark blue 45 12

350th anniversary of Danish Post Office (70ö, 90ö) and centenary of Universal Postal Union (120ö).

Souvenir Sheet

Ferslew's Essays, 1849 and 1852—A168

Engr. & Photo.

1975, Feb. 27 Perf. 13

565 A168 Sheet of 4, multi. 5.00 5.50
a. 70ö *Coat of arms* 1.20 1.30
b. 80ö *King Frederik VII* 1.20 1.30
c. 90ö *King Frederik VII* 1.20 1.30
d. 100ö *Mercury* 1.20 1.30

HAFNIA 76 International Stamp Exhibition, Copenhagen, Aug. 20-29, 1976. Size of No. 565: 68x93mm. Sold for 5k.

See No. 585.

Early Radio Equipment A169 — Flora Danica Plate A170

1975, Mar. 20 Engr. Perf. 13

566 A169 90ö dull red 40 10

Danish broadcasting, 50th anniversary.

1975, May 22

Danish China: 90ö, Flora Danica tureen. 130ö, Vase and tea caddy, blue fluted china.

567 A170 50ö slate green 18 8
568 " 90ö brown red 40 8
569 " 130ö violet blue 48 30

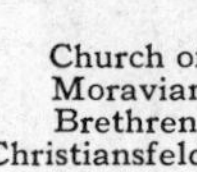

Church of Moravian Brethren, Christiansfeld A171

Designs: 120ö, Kongsgaard farmhouse, Lejre. 150ö, Anna Queenstraede, Helsingor (vert.).

1975, June 19

570 A171 70ö sepia 25 14
571 " 120ö olive green 50 15
572 " 150ö violet black 52 15

European Architectural Heritage Year 1975.

Hans Christian Andersen A172 — Watchman's Square, Abenra A173

Designs: 70ö, Numbskull Jack, drawing by Vilh. Pedersen. 130ö, The Marshking's Daughter, drawing by L. Frohlich.

1975, Aug. 28 Engr. Perf. 13

573 A172 70ö brown & black 25 14
574 " 90ö brn. red & dk. brown 60 10
575 " 130ö bl. blk. & sepia 48 30

Hans Christian Andersen (1805-1875), writer, death centenary.

1975, Sept. 25

Designs: 90ö, Haderslev Cathedral (vert.). 100ö, Mögeltönder Polder. 120ö, Mouth of Vidaaen at Höjer Floodgates.

576 A173 70ö multicolored 25 14
577 " 90ö " 32 10
578 " 100ö " 36 10
579 " 120ö " 44 20

European Kingfisher A174

Designs: 70ö, Hedgehog. 90ö, Cats. 130ö, Avocets. 200ö, Otter.

1975, Oct. 23 Engr. Perf. 13

580 A174 50ö violet black 18 8
581 " 70ö black 25 14
582 " 90ö brown 32 10
583 " 130ö bluish black 48 22
584 " 200ö brown black 72 32
Nos. 580-584 (5) 1.95 86

Protected animals, and for the centenary of the Danish Society for the Prevention of Cruelty to Animals (90ö).

Souvenir Sheet

HAFNIA Type of 1974

1975, Nov. 20 Engr. & Photo.

585 A168 Sheet of 4, multi. 3.50 4.00
a. 50ö buff & brown, No. 2 80 90
b. 70ö buff, brown & blue, No. 1 80 90
c. 90ö buff, blue & brown, No. 11 80 90
d. 130ö olive, brown & buff, No. 19 80 90

HAFNIA 76 International Stamp Exhibition, Copenhagen, Aug. 20-29, 1976. Size of No. 585: 68x93mm. Sold for 5k.

Copenhagen, Center A175

View from Round Tower A176

Copenhagen, Views: 100ö, Central Station, interior. 130ö, Harbor.

1976, Mar. 25 Engr. Perf. 12½

586 A175 60ö multicolored 22 10
587 A176 80ö " 30 10
588 " 100ö " 35 10
589 A175 130ö " 48 30

Postilion, by Otto Bache A177 — Emil Chr. Hansen, Physiologist, in Laboratory A178

1976, June 17 Engr. Perf. 12½

590 A177 130ö multicolored 1.00 90

Souvenir Sheet

591 A177 130ö multicolored 11.00 12.50

HAFNIA 76 International Stamp Exhibition, Copenhagen, Aug. 20-29. No. 591 contains one stamp similar to No. 590 with design continuous into sheet margin. Sheet shows painting "A String of Horses Outside an Inn" of which No. 590 shows a detail. Black marginal inscription and HAFNIA emblem. Size: 103x81mm. Sheet sold for 15k including exhibition ticket.

1976, Sept. 23 Engr. Perf. 13

592 A178 100ö orange red 35 10

Carlsberg Foundation (art and science), centenary.

Glass Blower Molding Glass A179 — Five Water Lilies A180

Danish Glass Production: 80ö, Finished glass removed from pipe. 130ö, Glass cut off from foot. 150ö, Glass blown up in mold.

1976, Nov. 18 Engr. Perf. 13

593 A179 60ö slate 22 15
594 " 80ö dark brown 30 14
595 " 130ö dark blue 48 30
596 " 150ö red brown 52 20

Photogravure and Engraved

1977, Feb. 2 Perf. 12½

597 A180 100ö bright green & multicolored 40 15
598 " 130ö ultramarine & multicolored 52 30

Nordic countries cooperation for protection of the environment and 25th Session of Nordic Council, Helsinki, Feb. 19.

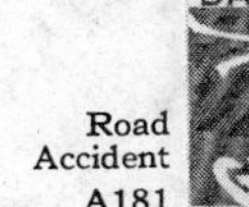

Road Accident
A181

1977, Mar. 24 Engr. *Perf. 12½*

599	A181	100ö brown red	40	15

Road Safety Traffic Act, May 1, 1977.

Europa Issue 1977

Allinge
A182

Design: 1.30k, View, Ringsted.

1977, May 2 Engr. *Perf. 12½*

600	A182	1k dull red	40	15
601	"	1.30k dark blue	52	35

Kongeåen
A183

Landscapes, Southern Jutland: 90ö, Skallingen. 150ö, Tørskind. 200ö, Jelling.

1977, June 30 Engr. *Perf. 12½*

602	A183	60ö multicolored	22	15
603	"	90ö "	32	15
604	"	150ö "	55	20
605	"	200ö "	70	30

See Nos. 616–619.

Hammers and Horseshoes
A184

Globe Flower
A185

Designs: 1k, Chisel, square and plane. 1.30k, Trowel, ceiling brush and folding ruler.

1977, Sept. 22 Engr. *Perf. 12½*

606	A184	80ö dark brown	28	14
607	"	1k red	35	15
608	"	1.30k violet blue	52	30

Danish crafts.

1977, Nov. 17 Engr. *Perf. 12½*

Design: 1.50k, Cnidium dubium.

609	A185	1k multicolored	35	15
610	"	1.50k "	55	20

Endangered flora.

Handball
A186

1978, Jan. 19 *Perf. 12½*

611	A186	1.20k red	42	16

Men's World Handball Championships.

Christian IV, Frederiksborg Castle
A187

Frederiksborg Museum
A188

1978, Mar. 16

612	A187	1.20k brown red	42	16
613	A188	1.80k black	65	24

Frederiksborg Museum, centenary.

Europa Issue

Jens Bang's House, Aalborg
A189

Frederiksborg Castle, Ground Plan and Elevation
A190

1978, May 11 Engr. *Perf. 12½*

614	A189	1.20k red	42	16
615	A190	1.50k dark blue & violet blue	52	20

Landscape Type of 1977

Landscapes, Central Jutland: 70ö, Kongenshus Memorial Park. 120ö, Post Office, Old Town in Aarhus. 150ö, Lignite fields, Soby. 180ö, Church wall, Stadil Church.

1978, June 15 Engr. *Perf. 12½*

616	A183	70ö multicolored	25	12
617	"	120ö "	42	16
618	"	150ö "	52	20
619	"	180ö "	65	25

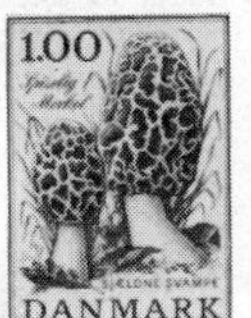

Boats in Harbor
A191

Edible Morel
A192

Designs: 1k, Eel traps. 1.80k, Boats in berth. 2.50k, Drying nets.

1978, Sept. 7 Engr. *Perf. 12½*

620	A191	70ö olive gray	28	12
621	"	1k reddish brown	40	15
622	"	1.80k slate	72	25
623	"	2.50k sepia	1.00	40

Danish fishing industry.

1978, Nov. 16 Engr. *Perf. 12½*

Design: 1.20k, Satan's mushroom.

624	A192	1k sepia	40	15
625	"	1.20k dull red	48	16

SEMI-POSTAL STAMPS.

Nos. 159, 157 Surcharged in Red **+ 5 +**

Wmkd. Multiple Crosses. (114)

1921, June 17 *Perf. 14½x14*

B1 A20 10ö+ 5ö green 20.00 20.00

B2 A21 20ö+10ö slate 25.00 25.00

Crown and Staff of Aesculapius SP1

Dybbol Mill SP2

1929, Aug. 1 **Engraved**

B3 SP1 10ö yellow green 6.00 6.00
a. Bklt. pane of 2 15.00

B4 " 15ö brick red 6.00 6.00
a. Bklt. pane of 2 15.00

B5 " 25ö deep blue 27.50 27.50
a. Bklt. pane of 2 75.00

These stamps were sold at a premium of 5 öre each for benefit of the Danish Cancer Committee.

1937, Jan. 20 *Perf. 13* **Unwmkd.**

B6 SP2 5(ö)+5(ö) green 1.00 1.00

B7 " 10(ö)+5(ö) lt. brn. 2.75 2.75

B8 " 15(ö)+5(ö) carmine 2.75 2.75

The surtax was for a fund in memory of H. P. Hanssen, statesman.

Nos. 223a and B6, Nos. 229 and B7, Nos. 238A and B8 are found se-tenant in booklets. For booklet panes, see Nos. 223d, 229b and 238e.

Queen Alexandrine SP3

Princesses Ingrid and Margrethe SP4

1939–41 *Perf. 13*

B9 SP3 5ö+3ö rose lake & red ('41) 20 20
a. Booklet pane of 4 1.00 1.00

B10 " 10ö+5ö dark violet & red 35 20

B11 " 15ö+5ö scarlet & red 50 45

The surtax was for the Danish Red Cross.

Nos. 230 and B10 have been issued se-tenant in booklets. See No. 230b. In this pane No. 230 measures 23½x31mm. from perf. to perf.

1941-43

B12 SP4 10(ö)+5(ö) dark violet 35 20
a. Bklt. pane of 10 6.00

B13 " 20(ö)+5(ö) red ('43) 35 25

The surtax was for the Children's Charity Fund.

No. 288 Surcharged in Red **+ 5**

1944, May 11

B14 A48 10ö + 5ö violet 18 18
a. Bklt. pane of 10 8.00

The surtax was for the Danish Red Cross.

Symbols of Freedom SP5

Explosions at Rail Junction SP6

Danish Flag SP7

Princess Anne-Marie SP8

1947, May 4 **Engr.** *Perf. 13*

B15 SP5 15(ö)+5(ö) green 50 50

B16 SP6 20(ö)+5(ö) dark red 50 50

B17 SP7 40(ö)+5(ö) dp. blue 1.10 1.10

Issued in memory of the Danish struggle for liberty and the liberation of Denmark. The surtax was for the Liberty Fund.

1950, Oct. 19 **Unwmkd.**

B18 SP8 25ö+5ö rose brown 60 60

The surtax was for the National Children's Welfare Association.

S. S. Jutlandia SP9

1951, Sept. 13 *Perf. 13*

B19 SP9 25(ö)+5(ö) red 85 80

The surtax was for the Red Cross.

No. 335 Surcharged in Black **NL + 10**

1953, Feb. 13

B20 A61 30(ö)+10(ö) brn. red 2.25 2.25

The surtax was for flood relief in the Netherlands.

Stone Memorial SP10

1953, Mar. 26 *Perf. 13*

B21 SP10 30(ö)+5(ö) dk. red 1.75 1.50

The surtax was for cultural work of the Danish Border Union.

Nos. B15 and B16 Surcharged with New Value and Ornamental Screen in Black

1955, Feb. 17

B22 SP5 20(ö)+5(ö) on 15(ö) +5(ö) green 1.75 1.75

B23 SP6 30(ö)+5(ö) on 20(ö) +5(ö) dark red 1.75 1.75

The surtax was for the Liberty Fund.

No. 341 Surcharged **30 + 5 Ungarns-hjælpen**

1957, Mar. 25

B24 A61 30ö+5ö on 95ö red orange 60 60

The surtax went to the Danish Red Cross for aid to Hungary.

No. 335 Surcharged: "Gronlandsfonden + 10"

1959, Feb. 23

B25 A61 30ö+10ö brown red 1.25 1.25

The surtax was for the Greenland Fund.

Globe Encircled by Red Cross Flags SP11

Queen Ingrid SP12

1959, June 24 **Engr.** *Perf. 13*

B26 SP11 30ö+5ö rose red 60 40

B27 " 60ö+5ö light ultra. & carmine 1.10 90

Issued to commemorate the centenary of the International Red Cross idea. The surtax was for the Red Cross. Crosses photogravure on No. B27.

1960, Oct. 25 **Unwmkd.**

B28 SP12 30ö+10ö dark red 1.00 1.00

Issued to commemorate Queen Ingrid's 25th anniversary as a Girl Scout. The surtax was for the Scouts' fund for needy and sick children.

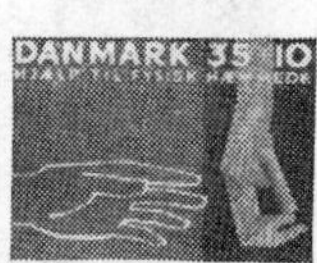

African Mother and Child SP13

Healthy and Crippled Hands SP14

1962, May 24

B29 SP13 30ö+10ö dark red 1.10 1.10

Issued to aid underdeveloped countries.

1963, June 24 *Perf. 13*

B30 SP14 35ö+10ö dark red 1.75 1.75

The surtax was for the benefit of the Cripples' Foundation.

Old Bridge at Danish-German Border SP15

1964, May 28 **Engraved**

B31 SP15 35ö+10ö henna brn. 1.50 1.50

The surtax was for the Danish Border Union.

Princesses Margrethe, Benedikte and Anne-Marie SP16

Happy Child SP17

1964, Aug. 24

B32 SP16 35ö+10ö dull red 90 90

B33 " 60ö+10ö dark blue & red 1.75 1.75

The surtax was for the Red Cross.

1965, Oct. 21 **Engr.** *Perf. 13*

B34 SP17 50ö+10ö brick red 75 75

The surtax was for the National Children's Welfare Association.

"Red Cross" in 32 Languages and Red Cross, Red Lion and Sun, and Red Crescent Emblems SP18

1966, Jan. 20 **Engraved** *Perf. 13*

B35 SP18 50ö+10ö red 60 60

Engraved and Photogravure

B36 SP18 80ö+10ö dark blue & red 1.00 1.00

The surtax was for the Red Cross.

"Refugees 66" SP19

Symbolic Rose SP20

1966, Oct. 24 **Engraved** *Perf. 13*

B37 SP19 40ö+10ö sepia 1.25 1.25

B38 " 50ö+10ö rose red 1.25 1.25

B39 " 80ö+10ö blue 2.25 2.25

The surtax was for aid to refugees.

1967, Oct. 12

B40 SP20 60ö+10ö brown red 55 55

The surcharge was for the Salvation Army.

Two Greenland Boys in Round Tower SP21

1968, Sept. 12 **Engraved** *Perf. 13*

B41 SP21 60ö+10ö dark red 1.00 1.00

The surtax was for child welfare work in Greenland.

Princess Margrethe and Prince Henrik with Prince Frederik SP22

1969, Dec. 11

B42 SP22 50ö+10ö brn. & red 60 60
B43 " 60ö+10ö brown red & red 60 60

The surtax was for the Danish Red Cross.

Child Seeking Help
SP23

1970, Mar. 13

B44 SP23 60ö+10ö brown red 65 65

Surtax for "Save the Children Fund."

Child
SP24

1971, Apr. 29 Engraved *Perf. 13*

B45 SP24 60ö+10ö copper red 55 55

Surtax was for the National Children's Welfare Association.

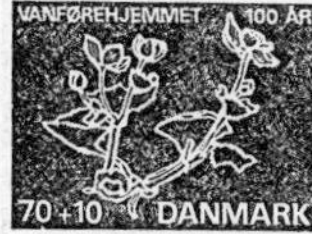

Marsh Marigold
SP25

1972, Aug. 17

B46 SP25 70ö+10ö grn. & yel. 50 50

Centenary of the Society and Home for the Disabled.

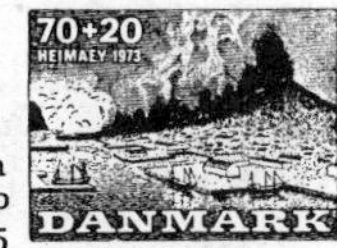

Heimaey Town and Volcano
SP26

1973, Oct. 17 Engraved *Perf. 13*

B47 SP26 70ö+20ö violet blue & red 60 60

The surtax was for the victims of the eruption of Heimaey Volcano, Jan. 23, 1973.

Queen Margrethe, IWY Emblem
SP27

1975, Mar. 20 Engr. *Perf. 13*

B48 SP27 90ö+20ö red & buff 75 75

International Women's Year 1975. Surtax was for a foundation to benefit women primarily in Greenland and Faroe Islands.

Skuldelev I
SP28

Ships: 90ö+20ö, Thingvalla, emigrant steamer. 100ö+20ö, Liner Frederick VIII, c. 1930. 130ö+20ö, Three-master Danmark.

1976, Jan. 22 Engr. *Perf. 13*

B49 SP28 70+20ö olive brown 70 70
B50 " 90+20ö brick red 90 90
B51 " 100+20ö olive green 90 90
B52 " 130+20ö vio. blue 1.00 1.00

Bicentenary of American Declaration of Independence.

People and Red Cross
SP29

Invalid in Wheelchair
SP30

1976, Feb. 26 Engr. *Perf. 13*

B53 SP29 100ö+20ö red & black 44 44
B54 " 130ö+20ö blue, red & black 55 55

Centenary of Danish Red Cross.

1976, May 6 Engr. *Perf. 13*

B55 SP30 100ö+20ö vermilion & black 44 44

The surtax was for the Foundation to Aid the Disabled.

Mother and Child
SP31

Anti-Cancer Campaign
SP32

1977, Mar. 24 Engr. *Perf. 12½*

B56 SP31 1k+20ö multi. 48 48

Danish Society for the Mentally Handicapped, 25th anniversary. Surtax was for the Society.

1978, Oct. 12 Engr. *Perf. 13*

B57 SP32 120ö+20ö red 50 50

Danish Anti-Cancer Campaign, 50th anniversary. Surtax was for campaign.

AIR POST STAMPS.

Airplane and Plowman
AP1

Towers of Copenhagen
AP2

Wmkd. Multiple Crosses. (114)

1925–29 Typo. *Perf. 12x12½*

C1 AP1 10ö yellow green 18.00 18.00
C2 " 15ö violet ('26) 30.00 30.00
C3 " 25ö scarlet 25.00 25.00
C4 " 50ö light gray ('29) 75.00 75.00
C5 " 1kr chocolate ('29) 70.00 70.00
Nos. C1–C5 (5) 218.00 218.00

Perf. 13

1934, June 9 Engr. **Unwmkd.**

C6 AP2 10ö orange 1.25 1.25
C7 " 15ö red 4.50 4.50
C8 " 20ö Prussian blue 4.50 4.50
C9 " 50ö olive black 4.50 4.50
C10 " 1kr brown 12.50 12.00
Nos. C6–C10 (5) 26.75 26.75

LATE FEE STAMPS

Numeral
LF1

Coat of Arms
LF2

Wmkd. Multiple Crosses. (114)

1923 Typographed *Perf. 14x14½*

I1 LF1 10ö green 3.25 90
a. Double ovpt.

No. I1 was, at first, not a postage stamp but represented a tax for the services of the post office clerks in filling out postal forms and writing addresses. In 1923 it was put into use as a Late Fee stamp.

1926–31

I2 LF2 10ö green 1.50 25
I3 " 10ö brown ('31) 1.25 25

Engraved

1934 *Perf. 13* **Unwmkd.**

I4 LF2 5ö green 25 8
I5 " 10ö orange 25 10

POSTAGE DUE STAMPS.

Regular Issues of 1913-20 Overprinted **PORTO**

Wmkd. Multiple Crosses. (114)

1921, May 1 *Perf. 14x14½*

J1 A10 1ö deep orange 1.50 1.00
J2 A16 5ö green 1.80 1.10
J3 " 7ö orange 1.50 1.00
J4 " 10ö red 9.00 5.50
J5 " 20ö deep blue 4.00 2.00
J6 " 25ö brown & black 5.50 2.25
J7 " 50ö claret & black 3.25 85
Nos. J1–J7 (7) 26.55 13.70

Same Overprint in Dark Blue On Military Stamp of 1917

1921, Nov. 23

J8 A16 10ö red 4.75 3.50
a. "S" inverted 110.00 110.00

Numeral of Value
D1

Typographed (Solid Panel).

1921-30 *Perf. 14x14½.*

J9 D1 1ö orange ('22) 35 35
J10 " 4ö blue ('25) 1.20 1.20
J11 " 5ö brown ('22) 75 35
J12 " 5ö light green ('30) 60 35
J13 " 7ö apple green ('27) 7.00 7.00
J14 " 7ö dark violet ('30) 10.00 10.00
J15 " 10ö yellow green ('22) 70 20
J16 " 10ö light brown ('30) 70 20
J17 " 20ö greenish blue ('21) 1.10 45
a. Double impression 1300.00
J18 " 20ö gray ('30) 2.00 60
J19 " 25ö scarlet ('23) 1.75 60
J20 " 25ö violet ('26) 1.75 1.00
J21 " 25ö light blue ('30) 2.00 1.50
J22 " 1kr dark blue ('21) 15.00 5.50
J23 " 1kr brown & dark blue ('25) 6.00 2.25
J24 " 5kr purple ('25) 14.00 5.50
Nos. J9–J24 (16) 64.90 37.05

Engraved (Lined Panel).

1934–55 *Perf. 13* **Unwmkd.**

J25 D1 1ö slate 10 10
J26 " 2ö carmine 10 10
J27 " 5ö yellow green 10 6
J28 " 6ö dark olive ('41) 30 12
J29 " 8ö magenta ('50) 2.00 2.00
J30 " 10ö orange 12 6
J31 " 12ö deep ultra. ('55) 30 25
J32 " 15ö violet ('37) 25 6
J33 " 20ö gray 15 6
J34 " 25ö blue 20 8
J35 " 30ö green ('53) 25 10
J36 " 40ö claret ('49) 30 18
J37 " 1k brown 60 12
Nos. J25–J37 (13) 4.77 3.29

No. 96 Surcharged in Black **PORTO 15**

1934 *Perf. 14x14½* **Wmk. 114**

J38 A10 15ö on 12ö violet 1.10 40

MILITARY STAMPS.

Nos. 97 and 100 Overprinted in Blue **S F**

Wmkd. Multiple Crosses. (114)

1917 *Perf. 14x14½.*

M1 A16 5ö green 12.00 14.00
a. "S" inverted 175.00 200.00
M2 " 10ö red 8.00 9.00
a. "S" inverted 100.00 110.00

The letters "S F" are the initials of "Soldater Frimaerke" (Soldier's Stamp).

OFFICIAL STAMPS.

Small State Seal
O1

Wmkd. Crown. (112)

1871 Typographed *Perf. 14x13½*

O1 O1 2s blue 70.00 45.00
a. 2s ultramarine 70.00 45.00
b. Imperf., pair 250.00
O2 " 4s carmine 40.00 10.00
a. Imperf., pair 250.00
O3 " 16s green 200.00 130.00
a. Imperf., pair 350.00

Perf. 12½.

O4 O1 4s carmine 1400.00 140.00
O5 " 16s green 225.00 175.00

Nos. O1, O2 and O3 were reprinted in 1886 upon white wove paper, unwatermarked and imperforate. Price $9 each.

1875 *Perf. 14x13½.*

O6 O1 3ö violet 3.00 9.00
O7 " 4ö greenish blue 4.00 1.75
O8 " 8ö carmine 2.75 65
a. Imperf., pair
O9 " 32ö green 12.00 12.00

1899-02 *Perf. 13.*

O9A O1 3ö red lilac ('02) 2.75 2.75
c. Imperf., pair 375.00
O9B " 4ö blue 1.25 1.25
O10 " 8ö carmine 9.00 9.00

1902-06 **Wmkd. Crown. (113)**

O11 O1 1ö orange 1.40 1.40
O12 " 3ö red lilac ('06) 1.00 1.00
O13 " 4ö blue ('03) 1.20 1.20
O14 " 5ö green 75 35
O15 " 10ö carmine 1.20 80
Nos. O11-O15 (5) 5.55 4.75

Wmkd. Multiple Crosses. (114)

1914-23 *Perf. 14x14½.*

O16 O1 1ö orange 1.25 1.25
O17 " 3ö gray ('18) 3.50 4.00
O18 " 4ö blue ('16) 18.00 18.00
O19 " 5ö green ('15) 70 25
O20 " 5ö chocolate ('23) 3.75 5.50
O21 " 10ö red ('17) 2.75 1.00
O22 " 10ö green ('21) 1.10 70
O23 " 15ö violet ('19) 16.00 16.00
O24 " 20ö indigo ('20) 4.50 3.50
Nos. O16-O24 (9) 51.55 50.20

The use of Official stamps was discontinued April 1, 1924.

NEWSPAPER STAMPS.

Numeral of Value
N1

Wmkd. Crown. (113)

1907 Typographed *Perf. 13*

P1 N1 1ö olive 2.25 1.00
P2 " 5ö blue 9.00 6.00
P3 " 7ö carmine 4.00 35
P4 " 10ö deep lilac 6.00 1.50
P5 " 20ö green 6.00 35
P6 " 38ö orange 10.00 45
P7 " 68ö yellow brown 14.00 6.50
P8 " 1kr blue green & claret 7.00 45
P9 " 5kr rose & yellow green 35.00 9.00
P10 " 10kr bistre & blue 50.00 8.00
Nos. P1-P10 (10) 143.25 33.60

Wmkd. Multiple Crosses. (114)

1914-15 *Perf. 14x14½.*

P11 N1 1ö olive gray 2.25 35
P12 " 5ö blue 10.00 3.00
P13 " 7ö rose 4.50 35
P14 " 8ö green ('15) 7.00 40
P15 " 10ö deep lilac 8.00 35
P16 " 20ö green 90.00 1.00
a. Imperf., pair 400.00
P17 " 29ö org. yel. ('15) 15.00 85
P18 " 38ö orange 1200.00 55.00
P19 " 41ö yellow brown ('15) 11.00 70
P20 " 1kr blue green & maroon 20.00 40
Nos. P11-P17, P19-P20 (9) 167.75 7.40

PARCEL POST STAMPS.

These stamps were for use on postal packets sent by the Esbjerg-Fanö Ferry Service.

Regular Issues of 1913-30 Overprinted

POSTFÆRGE

Wmkd. Multiple Crosses. (114)

1919-41 *Perf. 14x14½.*

Q1 A10 10ö green ('22) 10.00 6.50
Q2 " 10ö bis. brown ('30) 9.00 3.50
Q3 A16 10ö red 25.00 25.00
a. "POSFAERGE" 125.00 125.00
Q4 " 15ö violet 11.00 11.00
a. "POSFAERGE" 110.00 110.00
Q5 " 30ö orange ('22) 9.00 8.50
Q6 " 30ö dark blue ('26) 2.75 3.00
Q7 " 50ö claret & black ('20) 80.00 80.00
Q8 " 50ö light gray ('22) 17.50 4.00
a. 50ö dark gray ('22) 42.50 42.50
Q9 " 1kr brown & blue ('24) 27.50 9.00
Q9A " 5kr vio. & brn. ('41) 2.75 2.50
Q10 " 10kr vermilion & green ('30) 75.00 75.00

Engraved.

Q11 A17 1kr yellow brown 70.00 70.00
a. "POSFFAERGE" 1100.00 1100.00
Nos. Q1-Q11 (12) 339.50 298.00

Overprinted on Regular Issue of 1927-30.

1927-30

Q12 A30 15ö red ('27) 11.00 6.00
Q13 " 30ö ochre ('27) 11.00 7.50
Q14 " 40ö yellow green ('30) 11.00 4.50

Overprinted on Regular Issues of 1933-40.

1936-42 *Perf. 13* **Unwmkd.**

Q15 A32 5ö rose lake ('42) 10 10
Q16 " 10ö yellow orange 14.00 14.00
Q17 " 10ö lt. brown ('38) 1.25 1.25
Q18 " 10ö purple ('39) 30 30
Q19 A30 15ö deep red 75 75
Q20 " 30ö blue, I 3.75 3.25
Q21 " 30ö blue, II ('40) 5.00 6.00
Q22 " 30ö orange, II ('42) 60 60
Q23 " 40ö yel. green, I 3.75 3.75
Q24 " 40ö yellow green, II ('40) 5.00 6.00
Q25 " 40ö blue, II ('42) 60 60
Q26 A33 50ö gray 1.00 1.00
Q27 " 1k light brown 85 80
Nos. Q15-Q27 (13) 36.95 38.40

Overprinted on
Nos. 284, 286 and 286B

1945

Q28 A47 30ö orange 75 70
Q29 " 40ö blue 75 70
Q30 " 50ö gray 90 70

Overprinted on
Nos. 318, 309, 310, 312 and 297.

1949-53

Q31 A32 10ö green ('53) 30 30
Q32 A61 30(ö) orange 1.25 1.25
Q33 " 40(ö) dull blue 1.00 1.00
Q34 " 50(ö) gray ('50) 2.50 1.40
Q35 A55 1k brown ('50) 1.00 60
Nos. Q31-Q35 (5) 6.05 4.55

Overprinted on Nos.
335, 323, 336, 326 and 397.

1955-65

Q36 A61 30(ö) brown red 75 75
Q37 " 40(ö) gray 60 50
Q38 " 50(ö) aquamarine 70 70
Q39 " 70(ö) deep green 70 70
Q40 A55 1.25k orange ('65) 3.00 3.00
Nos. Q36-Q40 (5) 5.75 5.65

Overprinted on Nos. 417 and 419.

1967 Engraved *Perf. 13*

Q41 A86 40ö brown 45 45
Q42 " 80ö ultramarine 55 55

Nos. 224, 438, 441, 297-299 Overprinted

POSTFÆRGE

1967-74 Engraved *Perf. 13*

Q43 A32 5ö rose lake 10 10
Q44 A86 50ö brown ('74) 40 40
Q45 " 90ö ultra. ('70) 50 50
Q46 A55 1k brown 60 60
Q47 " 2k red ('72) 80 80
Q48 " 5k dull blue ('72) 1.75 1.75
Nos. Q43-Q48 (6) 4.15 4.15

Nos. Q44-Q45, Q47-Q48 are on fluorescent paper.

Overprinted on No. 544

1975, Feb. 27

Q49 A161 100ö dp. ultra. 40 40

Prices of premium quality never hinged stamps will be in excess of catalogue price.

DIEGO-SUAREZ

(dyā'gō swä'räs)

LOCATION—A town at the northern end of Madagascar.

GOVT.—Former French colony.

POP.—12,237.

From 1885 to 1896 Diégo-Suarez, (Antsirane), a French naval base, was a separate colony and issued its own stamps. These were succeeded by stamps of Madagascar.

100 Centimes = 1 Franc

Stamps of French Colonies Handstamp Surcharged in Violet

1890 *Perf. 14x13½.* **Unwmkd.**

1 A9 15c on 1c *blue* 90.00 25.00
2 " 15c on 5c green, *greenish* 225.00 25.00
3 " 15c on 10c *lavender* 90.00 25.00
4 " 15c on 20c red, *green* 225.00 25.00
5 " 15c on 25c *rose* 40.00 15.00

This surcharge is found inverted, double, etc. Counterfeits exist.

Ship Flying French Flag
A2

Symbolical of Union of France and Madagascar
A3 A4

France
A5

1890 **Lithographed.** ***Imperf.***

6 A2 1c black 375.00 110.00
7 A3 5c " 375.00 75.00
8 A4 15c " 100.00 30.00
9 A5 25c " 100.00 45.00

A6

1891

10 A6 5c black 70.00 30.00

Excellent counterfeits exist of Nos. 6 to 10.

Stamps of French Colonies Surcharged in Red or Black:

a

b

1892 ***Perf. 14x13½***

11 A9 (*a*) 5c on 10c *lavender* (R) 55.00 30.00
a. Inverted surcharge 135.00 110.00
12 " (*b*) 5c on 20c red, *green* 55.00 20.00
a. Inverted surcharge 135.00 100.00

Stamps of French Colonies Overprinted in Black or Red

c

1892

13 A9 1c *blue* (R) 10.00 5.00
a. Inverted overprint 10.00
14 " 2c brown, *buff* 10.00 5.00
a. Inverted overprint 10.00
15 " 4c claret, *lavender* 15.00 10.00
16 " 5c green, *greenish* 30.00 25.00
a. Inverted overprint 30.00 30.00
17 " 10c *lavender* 10.00 8.00
a. Inverted overprint 7.50
18 " 15c blue 10.00 5.00
19 " 20c red, *green* 10.00 7.00
20 " 25c *rose* 9.00 5.00
a. Inverted overprint 10.00 5.00
21 " 30c brown, *bistre* (R) 450.00 325.00
a. Inverted overprint 450.00 325.00
22 " 35c *yellow* 500.00 275.00
a. Inverted overprint 500.00 275.00
23 " 75c carmine, *rose* 20.00 15.00
24 " 1fr bronze green, *straw* (R) 20.00 15.00
a. Double overprint

Navigation and Commerce
A10 A11

1892 **Typographed.**

Name of Colony in Blue or Carmine.

25 A10 1c *blue* 75 75
26 " 2c brown, *buff* 75 75
27 " 4c claret, *lavender* 60 40
28 " 5c green, *greenish* 1.25 1.00
29 " 10c *lavender* 2.00 1.00
30 " 15c blue, quadrille paper 2.85 2.50
31 " 20c red, *green* 5.00 4.00
32 " 25c *rose* 4.50 4.00
33 " 30c brown, *bistre* 5.50 4.00
34 " 40c red, *straw* 7.50 5.00
35 " 50c carmine, *rose* 16.00 8.00
36 " 75c violet, *orange* 12.00 9.00
37 " 1fr bronze green, *straw* 17.50 10.00
Nos. 25-37 (13) 76.20 50.40

1894

38 A11 1c *blue* 20 20
39 " 2c brown, *buff* 1.00 75
40 " 4c claret, *lavender* 1.00 75
41 " 5c green, *greenish* 1.65 1.25
42 " 10c *lavender* 1.65 1.25
43 " 15c blue, quadrille paper 1.65 1.25
44 A11 20c red, *green* 3.00 2.40
45 " 25c *rose* 2.40 1.25
46 " 30c brown, *bistre* 2.40 1.40
47 " 40c red, *straw* 2.40 1.40
48 " 50c carmine, *rose* 4.00 3.00
49 " 75c violet, *orange* 1.85 1.25
50 " 1fr bronze green, *straw* 5.00 4.00
Nos. 38-50 (13) 28.20 20.15

Bisected stamps of type A11 are mentioned in note after Madagascar No. 62.

POSTAGE DUE STAMPS.

D1

D2

Lithographed.

1891 ***Imperf.*** **Unwmkd.**

J1 D1 5c violet 40.00 15.00
J2 D2 50c black 40.00 15.00

Excellent counterfeits exist of Nos. J1 and J2.

Postage Due Stamps of French Colonies Overprinted Type "c" in Black

1892

J3 D1 1c black 35.00 20.00
J4 " 2c black 35.00 20.00
a. Inverted overprint 30.00 15.00
J5 " 3c black 30.00 15.00
J6 " 4c " 30.00 15.00
J7 " 5c " 30.00 15.00
J8 " 10c black 12.00 10.00
a. Inverted overprint 15.00 15.00
J9 " 15c black 12.00 10.00
a. Double overprint 15.00 15.00
J10 " 20c black 60.00 40.00
J11 " 30c black 30.00 20.00
a. Inverted overprint 25.00 22.50
J12 " 60c black 450.00 200.00
J13 " 1fr brown 650.00 450.00

DJIBOUTI

(jē'bōō'tē')

LOCATION—East Africa.

GOVT.—Republic.

AREA—8,800 sq. mi.

POP.—300,000 (est. 1977).

CAPITAL—Djibouti.

The French Territory of the Afars and Issas became the Republic of Djibouti June 27, 1977. For 1894–1902 issues with "Djibouti" or "DJ", see Somali Coast.

Afars and Issas Issues of 1972–1977 Overprinted and Surcharged with Bars and "REPUBLIQUE DE DJIBOUTI" in Black, Dark Green, Blue or Brown

Printing and Perforations as Before

1977

Multicolored

439 A63 1fr on 4fr (#358; B) 5 5
440 A81 2fr on 5fr (#433; B) 5 5
441 A75 5fr on 20fr (#421; B) 5 5
442 A70 8fr (#380; B) 12 8
443 A71 20fr (#387; DG) 20 15
444 A81 30fr (#434; B) 35 25
445 A71 40fr (#388; DG) 45 35
446 " 45fr (#389; Bl) 50 40
447 A78 45fr (#428; B) 50 40
448 A72 50fr (#394; B) 55 40
449 A71 60fr (#391; Br) 65 50
450 A79 70fr (#430; B) 85 60
451 A81 70fr (#435; B) 85 60
452 A74 100fr (#418; B) 1.10 85
453 A72 150fr (#399; B) 1.75 1.35
454 A76 200fr (#422; B) 2.25 1.50
455 A80 200fr (#432; B) 2.40 1.75
456 A74 300fr (#419; B) 3.50 2.50
Nos. 439-456, C106-C108 (21) 23.37 16.93

Map and Flag of Djibouti
A83

Water Pipe
A84

Design: 65fr, Map and flag of Djibouti, map of Africa (horiz.).

1977, June 27 **Litho.** ***Perf. 12½***

457 A83 45fr multicolored 50 40
458 " 65fr " 75 55

Independence, June 27.

1977, July 4

Designs: 10fr, Headrest (horiz.). 25fr, Pitcher.

459 A84 10fr multicolored 10 8
460 " 20fr " 20 15
461 " 25fr " 30 22

Ostrich
A85

Design: 100fr, Weaver.

1977, Aug. 11 **Litho.** ***Perf. 12½***

462 A85 90fr multicolored 1.00 75
463 " 100fr " 1.10 85

Snail
A86

Designs: 15fr, Fiddler crab. 50fr, Klipspringers. 70fr, Green turtle. 80fr, Priacanthus hamrur (fish). 150fr, Dolphinfish.

1977 **Litho.** ***Perf. 12½***

464 A86 15fr multicolored 15 10
465 " 45fr " 50 40
466 " 50fr " 55 40
467 " 70fr " 85 60
468 " 80fr " 90 70
469 " 150fr " 1.75 1.25
Nos. 464-469 (6) 4.70 3.45

Issue dates: 45fr, 70fr, 80fr, Sept. 14. Others, Dec. 5.

Pres. Hassan Gouled Aptidon and Djibouti Flag
A87

1978, Feb. 12 **Litho.** ***Perf. 13***

470 A87 65fr multicolored 75 50

Charaxes Hansali A88 — Necklace A89

Butterflies: 20fr, Colias electo. 25fr, Acraea chilo. 150fr, Junonia hierta.

1978, Mar. 13 Litho. *Perf. 12½x13*

471	A88	5fr multicolored		5	4
472	"	20fr	"	20	15
473	"	25fr	"	30	22
474	"	150fr	"	1.75	1.25

1978, May 29 Litho. *Perf. 12½x13*

Design: 55fr, Necklace (different).

475	A89	45fr pink & multi.	50	35
476	"	55fr blue & multi.	60	40

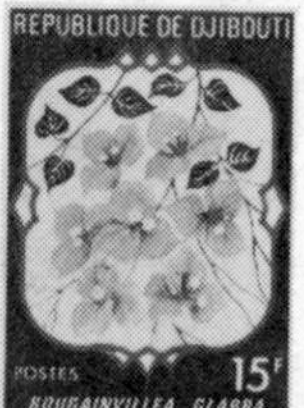

Bougainvillea A90

Flowers: 35fr, Hibiscus schizopetalus. 250fr, Caesalpinia pulcherrima.

1978, July 10 Photo. *Perf. 12½x13*

477	A90	15fr multicolored		18	15
478	"	35fr	"	40	30
479	"	250fr	"	2.75	2.25

Charonia Nodifera—A91

Sea Shell: 80fr, Charonia variegata.

1978, Oct. 9 Litho. *Perf. 13*

480	A91	10fr multicolored		15	10
481	"	80fr	"	1.20	80

Chaetodon A92

Fish: 30fr, Yellow surgeonfish. 40fr, Harlequinfish.

1978, Nov. 20 Litho. *Perf. 13x12½*

482	A92	8fr multicolored		12	8
483	"	30fr	"	45	30
484	"	40fr	"	60	40

AIR POST STAMPS

Afars and Issas Nos. C104–C105, C103 Overprinted with Bars and "REPUBLIQUE DE DJIBOUTI" in Brown or Black

1977 Engraved *Perf. 13*

C106	AP37	55fr multi. (Br)	60	45
C107	"	75fr multi.	85	65

Litho. *Perf. 12*

C108	AP36	500fr multi.	5.75	4.00

Map of Djibouti, Dove, UN Emblem—AP38

1977, Oct. 19 Photo. *Perf. 13*

C109	AP38	300fr multi.	3.50	2.25

Djibouti's admission to the United Nations.

Marcel Brochet MB 101, 1955—AP39

Designs: 85fr, Tiger Moth, 1960. 200fr, Rallye-Commodore, 1973.

1978, Feb. 27 Litho. *Perf. 13*

C110	AP39	60fr multicolored		65	45
C111	"	85fr	"	90	60
C112	"	200fr	"	2.25	1.50

Djibouti Aero Club.

Old Man, by Rubens AP40

Design: 500fr, Hippopotamus Hunt, by Rubens (horiz.).

1978, Apr. 24 Photo. *Perf. 13*

C113	AP40	50fr multicolored		55	40
C114	"	500fr	"	5.50	4.00

Peter Paul Rubens (1577–1640), 400th birth anniversary.

Player Holding Soccer Cup AP41

Design: 300fr, Soccer player, map of South America with Argentina, Cup and emblem.

1978, June 20 Litho. *Perf. 13*

C115	AP41	100fr multi.		1.10	75
C116	"	300fr	"	3.25	2.50

11th World Cup Soccer Championship, Argentina, June 1–25.

Nos. C115–C116 Overprinted:
a. ARGENTINE / CHAMPION 1978
b. ARGENTINE / HOLLANDE / 3–1

1978, Aug. 20 Litho. *Perf. 13*

C117	AP41	(*a*) 100fr multi.		1.10	75
C118	"	(*b*) 300fr	"	3.25	2.50

Argentina's victory in 1978 Soccer Championship.

Tahitian Women, by Gauguin—AP42

Young Hare, by Dürer AP43

Perf. 13x12½, 12½x13

1978, Sept. 25 Lithographed

C119	AP42	100fr multi.		1.10	75
C120	AP43	250fr	"	2.75	2.00

Paul Gauguin (1848–1903) and Albrecht Dürer (1471–1528), painters.

Philexafrique II—Essen Issue

Common Design Types

Designs: No. C121, Lynx and Djibouti No. 456. No. C122, Jay and Brunswick No. 3.

1978, Dec. 13 Litho. *Perf. 13x12½*

C121	CD138	90fr multi.		1.00	70
C122	CD139	90fr	"	1.00	70

Nos. C121–C122 printed se-tenant.

UPU Emblem, Map of Djibouti, Dove AP44

1978, Dec. 18 Engr. *Perf. 13*

C123	AP44	200fr multi.	3.00	2.00

Centenary of Congress of Paris.

Common Design Types
pictured in section at front of book.

DOMINICAN REPUBLIC

(dô·mĭn′ĭ·kăn rê·pŭb′lĭk)

LOCATION — The republic comprises about two-thirds of the island of Hispaniola in the West Indies.

GOVT.—Republic.

AREA—18,700 sq. mi.

POP.—5,000,000 (est. 1977).

CAPITAL—Santo Domingo (formerly Ciudad Trujillo).

8 Reales = 1 Peso

100 Centavos = 1 Peso (1880)

100 Centimos = 1 Franco (1883)

100 Centavos = 1 Peso (1885)

> Prices of early Dominican Republic stamps vary according to condition. Quotations for Nos. 1–31 are for fine copies. Very fine to superb specimens sell at much higher prices, and inferior or poor copies sell at reduced prices, depending on the condition of the individual specimen.

Coat of Arms
A1 A2

Typographed

1865 *Imperf.* **Unwmkd.**

Wove Paper.

1	A1	½r *rose*	175.00	175.00
2	"	1r *deep green*	425.00	425.00

Twelve varieties of each.

Laid Paper.

3	A2	½r *pale green*	275.00	250.00
4	"	1r *straw*	725.00	625.00

Twelve varieties of the ½r, ten varieties of the 1r.

A3 A4

1866 Laid Paper **Unwmkd.**

5	A3	½r *straw*	90.00	80.00
6	"	1r *pale green*	350.00	350.00
7	A4	1r *pale green*	80.00	75.00

Nos. 5–8 have 21 varieties (sheets of 21).

Wmk. 115

Wmkd. Diamonds. (115)

8	A3	1r *pale green*	1200.00	1200.00

1866–67 Wove Paper. **Unwmkd.**

9	A3	½r *rose* ('67)	25.00	25.00
10	"	1r *pale green*	50.00	45.00
		a. Inscription double, top and bottom	*250.00*	*250.00*
11	"	1r *blue* ('67)	22.50	20.00
		a. 1r *light blue* ('67)	22.50	20.00
		b. No space between "Un" and "real"	150.00	125.00
		c. Without inscription at top & bottom	175.00	150.00
		d. Inscriptions invtd., top & bottom		

1867–71 Pelure Paper.

13	A3	½r *rose*	50.00	50.00
15	"	½r *lavender* ('68)	80.00	80.00
		a. Without inscription at top and bottom		400.00
		b. Double inscriptions one inverted		*300.00*
16	"	½r *greenish gray* ('68)	80.00	80.00
18	"	½r *olive* ('69)	*1000.00*	*1000.00*
23	"	1r *lavender*	75.00	75.00
24	A4	1r *rose* ('68)	75.00	75.00
25	"	1r *magenta* ('69)	*550.00*	*550.00*
26	"	1r *salmon* ('71)	75.00	75.00

1870–73 Ordinary Paper.

27	A3	½r *magenta*	450.00	450.00
28	"	½r blue, *rose* (black inscription) ('71)	30.00	30.00
		a. Blue inscription	250.00	250.00
		b. Without inscription at top and bottom		
29	"	½r *yellow* ('73)	15.00	15.00
		a. Without inscription at top and bottom	225.00	225.00
30	A4	1r *violet* ('73)	15.00	15.00
		a. Without inscription at top and bottom	250.00	250.00
31	"	1r *dark green*	32.50	32.50

Nos. 9–31 have 21 varieties (sheets of 21). Nos. 29 and 30 are known pin-perforated, unofficially.

Bisects are known of several of the early 1r stamps.

Coat of Arms
A5 A6

1879 *Perf. 12½x13*

32	A5	½r violet	1.25	1.25
		a. Imperf., pair	4.00	4.00
		b. Horiz. pair, imperf. vert.	12.50	
33	"	½r violet, *bluish*	1.25	1.25
		a. Imperf., pair	4.00	4.00
34	"	1r carmine	1.25	1.25
		a. Imperf., pair	4.00	4.00
		b. Perf. 13	4.00	4.00
		c. Perf. 13x12½	4.50	4.50
35	"	1r carmine, *salmon*	1.25	1.25
		a. Imperf., pair	4.00	4.00

In 1891 15 stamps of 1879–83 were surcharged "U P U," new values and crossed diagonal lines.

Rouletted in Color

1880 Typographed

36	A6	1c green	70	50
		a. Broken "T"	6.00	5.00
		b. Laid paper	30.00	30.00
37	"	2c red	55	50
		a. Pelure paper	20.00	20.00
		b. Laid paper	22.50	22.50
38	"	5c blue	65	40
39	"	10c rose	1.35	50
40	"	20c brown	80	55
41	"	25c violet	1.20	80
42	"	50c orange	1.50	1.10
43	"	75c ultramarine	2.00	1.50
		a. Laid paper	20.00	20.00
44	"	1p gold	2.75	2.50
		a. Laid paper	27.50	27.50
		b. Double impression	22.50	22.50
		Nos. 36–44 (9)	11.50	8.35

1881 Network Covering Stamp.

45	A6	1c green	45	35
		a. Broken "T"	4.00	3.00
46	"	2c red	50	40
47	"	5c blue	55	35
48	"	10c rose	70	45
49	"	20c brown	70	50
50	"	25c violet	90	70
51	"	50c orange	1.00	75
52	"	75c ultramarine	2.50	1.75
53	"	1p gold	3.50	3.25
		Nos. 45–53 (9)	10.80	8.50

Preceding Issues Surcharged with Value in New Currency:

5 céntimos. (*a*) 5 céntimos (*b*)

5 céntimos. (*c*) 1 franco. (*d*)

1 Franco. (*e*) 1 franco (*f*)

1 franco, 25 céntimos. (*g*)

5 francos. (*h*) 5 francos (*i*)

1883 Without Network.

54	(*a*)	5c on 1c green	1.00	85
		a. Broken "T" in "CENTAVO"	6.00	6.00
		b. Inverted surcharge	14.00	14.00
		c. Surcharged "25 céntimos"	40.00	40.00
		d. Surcharged "10 céntimos"	17.50	17.50
55	(*b*)	5c on 1c green	7.00	3.00
		a. Broken "T" in "CENTAVO"	17.50	17.50
		b. Double surch.	75.00	
		c. Inverted surcharge	45.00	45.00
56	(*c*)	5c on 1c green	6.00	3.00
		a. Broken "T" in "CENTAVO"	17.50	17.50
		b. Surcharged "10 céntimos"	22.50	22.50
		c. Surcharged "25 céntimos"	27.50	27.50
57	(*a*)	10c on 2c red	2.50	2.25
		a. Inverted surcharge	20.00	20.00
		d. Surcharged "5 céntimos"	35.00	35.00
		e. Surcharged "25 céntimos"	60.00	60.00
58	(*c*)	10c on 2c red	2.50	2.25
		a. "Céntimso"		
		b. Inverted surcharge	30.00	30.00
		c. Surcharged "25 céntimos"	50.00	50.00
		d. "10" omitted	50.00	
59	(*a*)	25c on 5c blue	2.75	2.25
		a. Surcharged "5 céntimos"	37.50	
		b. Surcharged "10 céntimos"	32.50	32.50
		c. Surcharged "50 céntimos."	55.00	55.00
		d. Inverted surcharge	27.50	27.50
60	(*c*)	25c on 5c blue	2.75	2.50
		a. Inverted surcharge	32.50	27.50
		b. Surcharged "10 céntimos"	32.50	27.50
		e. "25" omitted	70.00	
		f. Surcharged on back		75.00
61	(*a*)	50c on 10c rose	10.00	6.00
		a. Inverted surcharge	32.50	30.00
62	(*c*)	50c on 10c rose	15.00	9.00
		a. Inverted surcharge	40.00	40.00
63	(*d*)	1fr on 20c brown	7.00	7.00
64	(*e*)	1fr on 20c brown	8.50	7.50
		a. Comma after "Franco,"	20.00	20.00
65	(*f*)	1fr on 20c brown	9.50	8.50
		a. Inverted surcharge		70.00
66	(*g*)	1fr 25c on 25c violet	9.00	9.00
		a. Inverted surcharge	45.00	45.00
67	(")	2fr 50c on 50c orange	7.00	7.00
		a. Inverted surcharge	25.00	22.50
68	(")	3fr 75c on 75c ultra.	11.00	11.00
		b. Inverted surcharge	40.00	40.00
		c. Laid paper	40.00	40.00
70	(*i*)	5fr on 1p gold	275.00	275.00
		a. "s" of "francos" inverted	375.00	375.00

With Network.

71	(*a*)	5c on 1c green	1.75	1.75
		a. Broken "T" in "CENTAVO"	5.00	5.00
		b. Inverted surcharge	15.00	15.00
		c. Double surch.	12.50	12.50
		d. Surcharged "25 céntimos"	27.50	27.50
		e. "5" omitted	60.00	60.00
72	(*b*)	5c on 1c green	8.00	3.00
		a. Broken "T" in "CENTAVO"	22.50	10.00
		b. Inverted surcharge	25.00	25.00
73	(*c*)	5c on 1c green	10.00	5.00
		a. Broken "T" in "CENTAVO"	20.00	9.00
		b. Surcharged "10 céntimos"	25.00	20.00
		c. Surcharged "25 céntimos"	45.00	
74	(*a*)	10c on 2c red	2.25	1.75
		a. Surcharged "5 céntimos"	35.00	32.50
		b. Surcharged "25 céntimos"	50.00	50.00
		c. "10" omitted	45.00	
75	(*c*)	10c on 2c red	1.50	1.25
		a. Inverted surcharge	17.50	10.00
76	(*a*)	25c on 5c blue	4.00	2.50
		a. Surcharged "10 céntimos"	65.00	
		b. Surcharged "5 céntimos"	45.00	
		c. Surcharged "50 céntimos"	55.00	
77	(*c*)	25c on 5c blue	30.00	15.00
		a. Inverted surcharge		
		b. Surcharged on back		
78	(*a*)	50c on 10c rose	10.00	3.75
		a. Inverted surcharge	17.50	12.50
		b. Surcharged "25 céntimos"	50.00	
79	(*c*)	50c on 10c rose	12.50	4.00
		a. Inverted surcharge	40.00	
80	(*d*)	1fr on 20c brown	6.50	6.50
81	(*e*)	1fr on 20c brown	7.50	7.50
		a. Comma after "Franco,"	25.00	25.00
		b. Inverted surcharge	60.00	
82	(*f*)	1fr on 20c brown	9.00	9.00
83	(*g*)	1fr 25c on 25c violet	20.00	15.00
		a. Inverted surcharge	50.00	
84	(")	2fr 50c on 50c orange	10.00	9.00
		a. Inverted surcharge	25.00	20.00
85	(")	3fr 75c on 75c ultra.	17.50	17.50
86	(*h*)	5fr on 1p gold	70.00	70.00
		a. Invert. surcharge		
87	(*i*)	5fr on 1p gold	75.00	75.00

Many minor varieties exist in Nos. 54–87: accent on "i" of "centimos"; "5" with straight top; "1" with straight serif.

Coat of Arms
A7 A7a

1885–91 Engraved *Perf. 12*

88	A7	1c green	50	30
89	"	2c vermilion	50	30
90	"	5c blue	80	30
91	A7a	10c orange	1.25	40
92	"	20c dark brown	1.35	55
93	"	50c violet ('91)	3.75	2.25
94	A7	1p carmine ('91)	7.50	6.25
95	"	2p red brown ('91)	10.00	8.00
		Nos. 88–95 (8)	25.65	18.35

Nos. 93, 94 and 95 were issued without gum.

Imperf. varieties are proofs.

Coat of Arms
A8

1895-97 ***Perf. 12½x14***

No.	Type	Description	Unused	Used
96	A8	1c green	70	40
		a. Perf. 14 ('97)	80	45
97	"	2c orange red	70	40
		a. Perf. 14 ('97)	2.75	60
98	"	5c blue	70	45
		a. Perf. 14 ('97)	80	50
99	"	10c orange	80	60
		a. Perf. 14 ('97)	90	65

Nos. 96 to 99 are known imperforate but were not issued in this condition.

Columbus Mausoleum Issue.

Voyage of Diego Méndez from Jamaica—A9

Enriquillo's Revolt
A10

Sarcophagus of Columbus
A11

"Española" Guarding Remains of Columbus
A12

Toscanelli Replying to Columbus
A13

Bartolomé de las Casas Defending Indians
A14

Columbus at Salamanca
A15

Columbus' Mausoleum
A16

1899, Feb. 27 **Litho.** ***Perf. 11½***

No.	Type	Description	Unused	Used
100	A9	1c brown violet	3.25	2.75
		a. Imperf., pair	5.00	
102	A10	2c rose red	90	55
		a. Imperf., pair	3.00	
103	A11	5c blue	1.00	55
		a. Imperf., pair	3.00	
104	A12	10c orange	2.00	1.10
		a. Tête bêche pair	30.00	30.00
		b. Imperf., pair	3.00	
105	A13	20c brown	3.25	3.25
		a. Imperf., pair	5.00	
106	A14	50c yellow green	3.25	3.25
		a. Tête bêche pair	50.00	50.00
		b. Imperf., pair	9.00	
		c. as "a," imperf.	90.00	
107	A15	1p *gray blue*	9.00	8.00
		a. Imperf., pair	22.50	
108	A16	2p bistre brown	17.50	17.50
		a. Imperf., pair	35.00	

1900, Jan.

No.	Type	Description	Unused	Used
109	A11	¼c black	50	50
		a. Imperf., pair	1.75	2.25
110	A15	½c black	50	50
		b. Imperf., pair	1.75	2.25
110A	A9	1c gray green	65	55
		c. Imperf., pair	3.00	
		Nos. 100-110A (11)	41.80	38.50

Nos. 100-110A were issued to raise funds for a Columbus mausoleum.

Map of Hispaniola
A17

Coat of Arms
A18

1900, Oct. 21 ***Perf. 14*** **Unwmkd.**

No.	Type	Description	Unused	Used
111	A17	¼c dark blue	55	35
112	"	½c rose	55	35
113	"	1c olive green	55	35
114	"	2c deep green	55	35
115	"	5c red brown	55	35
		a. Vertical pair, imperf. between	15.00	

Perf. 12.

No.	Type	Description	Unused	Used
116	A17	10c orange	60	35
117	"	20c lilac	2.25	2.00
		a. 20c rose (error)	5.00	5.00
118	"	50c black	1.75	1.75
119	"	1p brown	2.00	1.75
		Nos. 111-119 (9)	9.35	7.60

Several varieties in design are known in this issue. They were deliberately made. Counterfeits of Nos. 111-119 abound.

1901-06 **Typographed** ***Perf. 14***

No.	Type	Description	Unused	Used
120	A18	½c carmine & violet	40	35
121	"	½c black & orange('05)	70	50
122	"	½c green & black ('06)	50	25
123	"	1c olive green & violet	45	15
124	"	1c black & ultra. ('05)	80	45
125	"	1c car. & blk. ('06)	50	30
126	"	2c deep green & violet	45	20
127	"	2c black & violet ('05)	80	35
128	"	2c orange brown & black ('06)	45	15
129	"	5c org. brn. & violet	45	25
130	"	5c blk. & claret ('05)	1.00	55
131	"	5c blue & black ('06)	50	30
132	"	10c orange & violet	50	30
133	"	10c black & grn. ('05)	1.50	80
134	"	10c red violet & black ('06)	50	30
135	"	20c brn. violet & vio.	1.00	60
136	"	20c black & olive('05)	3.25	2.75
137	"	20c olive green & black ('06)	2.25	1.50
138	"	50c gray black & violet	3.00	2.25
139	"	50c black & red brown ('05)	17.50	10.00
140	"	50c brn. & black ('06)	2.75	2.75
141	"	1p brown & violet	7.50	5.50
142	"	1p blk. & gray('05)	110.00	110.00
143	"	1p violet & black('06)	6.00	5.00
		Nos. 120-143 (24)	162.75	145.55

Issue dates: Nov. 15, 1901, May 11, 1905, Aug. 17, 1906.

See also Nos. 172-176.

Francisco Sánchez
A19

Juan Pablo Duarte
A20

Ramón Mella
A21

Ft. Santo Domingo
A22

1902, Feb. 25 **Engraved** ***Perf. 12***

No.	Type	Description	Unused	Used
144	A19	1c dark green & black	35	35
		a. Center inverted	2.25	
145	A20	2c scarlet & black	35	35
		a. Center inverted	2.25	
146	"	5c blue & black	35	35
		a. Center inverted	2.25	
147	A19	10c orange & black	35	35
148	A21	12c purple & black	35	35
		a. Center inverted	2.25	
149	"	20c rose & black	35	35
		a. Center inverted	2.25	
150	A22	50c brown & black	50	50
		a. Center inverted	2.25	
		Nos. 144-150 (7)	2.60	2.60

400th anniversary of Santo Domingo. Imperforate varieties of Nos. 144 to 150 were never sold to the public.

Nos. 138, 141 Surcharged in Black

2
dos cts

1904, Aug.

No.	Type	Description	Unused	Used
151	A18	2c on 50c black & violet	4.00	4.00
		a. Inverted surcharge	12.00	12.00
152	"	2c on 1p brn. & vio.	4.50	4.25
		a. Inverted surcharge	10.00	10.00
		b. "2" omitted	32.50	32.50
		c. As "b," inverted	65.00	65.00
153	"	5c on 50c blk. & vio.	1.25	1.25
		a. Inverted surcharge	4.00	4.00
154	"	5c on 1p brown & violet	1.75	1.75
		a. Inverted surcharge	4.00	4.00
155	"	10c on 50c black & violet	2.75	2.75
		a. Inverted surcharge	10.00	10.00
156	"	10c on 1p brown & violet	2.75	2.75
		a. Inverted surcharge	4.00	4.00
		Nos. 151-156 (6)	17.00	16.75

Official Stamps of 1902 Overprinted

16 de Agosto
1904

Red Overprint.

1904, Aug. 16

No.	Type	Description	Unused	Used
157	O1	5c dark blue & black	2.00	1.50
		a. Inverted overprint	2.75	2.75

Black Overprint.

No.	Type	Description	Unused	Used
158	O1	2c scarlet & black	2.50	2.25
		a. Inverted overprint	2.75	2.75
159	"	5c dk. blue & black	350.00	350.00
160	"	10c yel. green & black	2.25	2.25
		a. Inverted overprint	6.50	6.50

Surcharged

16 de Agosto
1 1904 1

No.	Type	Description	Unused	Used
161	O1	1c on 20c yellow & black	2.00	2.00
		a. Inverted surcharge	3.25	3.25

Nos. J1-J2 Surcharged or Overprinted

REPUBLICA DOMINICANA
1
CENTAVOS
CORREOS

Surcharged "CENTAVOS".

1904-05 **Black Surcharge.**

No.	Type	Description	Unused	Used
162	D1	1c on 2c olive gray	60.00	60.00
		a. "entavos"		
		b. "Dominican"	150.00	150.00
		c. "Centavo"	150.00	150.00

Carmine Surcharge or Overprint.

No.	Type	Description	Unused	Used
163	D1	1c on 2c olive gray	1.25	85
		a. Inverted surcharge	1.50	1.50
		b. "Domihicana"	8.50	8.50
		c. Same as "b" inverted	25.00	25.00
		d. "Dominican"	8.00	8.00
		e. "Centavos" omitted	25.00	25.00
		g. "entavos"	17.50	
163F	"	1c on 4c olive gray	15.00	3.50
164	"	2c olive gray	45	25
		a. "Domihicana"	5.50	5.50
		b. Inverted overprint	1.25	1.25
		c. Same as "a" inverted	14.00	14.00
		d. "Dominican"	3.50	3.50
		e. "Centavos" omitted	8.00	5.00
		f. "entavos"	6.00	6.00
		g. Same as "f" inverted	17.50	17.50
		h. as "d," inverted	17.50	17.50

Surcharged "CENTAVO".

No.	Type	Description	Unused	Used
165	D1	1c on 4c olive gray	30	30
		a. "Domihicana"	6.00	6.00
		c. Inverted surcharge	1.25	1.25
		d. "1" omitted	14.00	14.00
		e. Same as "a" invtd.	22.50	22.50
		f. Same as "d" invtd.	32.50	32.50
		g. Double surcharge	22.50	22.50

No. 92 Surcharged in Red

DOS
1905
CENTAVOS

1905, Apr. 4

No.	Type	Description	Unused	Used
166	A7a	2c on 20c dark brown	2.75	2.75
		a. Inverted surcharge	11.00	11.00
167	"	5c on 20c dark brown	1.50	1.25
		a. Inverted surcharge	14.00	14.00
		b. Double surcharge	17.50	17.50
168	"	10c on 20c dark brown	3.00	3.00

Nos. 166-168 exist with inverted "A" for "V" in "CENTAVOS" in surcharge.

Nos. J2, J4, J3 Surcharged:

REPUBLICA DOMINICANA. UN centavo.

REPUBLICA DOMINICANA. DOS centavos.

1906, Jan. 16 ***Perf. 14***

Red Surcharge.

No.	Type	Description	Unused	Used
169	D1	1c on 4c olive gray	60	35
		a. Inverted surcharge	10.00	10.00

1906, May 1

Black Surcharge.

170 D1 1c on 10c olive gray 65 35
a. Inverted surcharge 10.00 10.00
b. Double surcharge 14.00 14.00
c. "OMINICANA" 15.00 15.00
171 " 2c on 5c olive gray 65 35
a. Inverted surcharge 10.00 10.00

The varieties small "C" or small "A" in "REPUBLICA" are found on Nos. 169, 170 and 171.

Arms Type of 1901–06.

Wmk. 116

Wmkd. Crosses and Circles. (116)

1907-10

172 A18 ½c green & blk. ('08) 35 20
173 " 1c carmine & black 35 15
174 " 2c orange brown & black 35 15
175 " 5c blue & black 45 30
176 " 10c red violet & black ('10) 4.00 1.00
Nos. 172–176 (5) 5.50 1.80

No. 06 Overprinted in Red **HABILITADO 1911**

Perf. 13½x14, 13½x13

1911, July 11

177 O2 2c scarlet & black 70 50
a. "HABILITAOO" 7.50 6.00
b. Inverted overprint 17.50
c. Double overprint 17.50

Coat of Arms A23 — Juan Pablo Duarte A24

1911-13 ***Perf. 14.***

Center in Black

178 A23 ½c orange ('13) 15 12
179 " 1c green 15 12
180 " 2c carmine 15 10
181 " 5c gray blue ('13) 30 15
182 " 10c red violet 70 35
183 " 20c olive green 4.00 2.75
184 " 50c yel. brown ('12) 1.50 1.50
185 " 1p violet ('12) 2.50 2.25
Nos. 178–185 (8) 9.45 7.34

See Nos. 230–232.

1914, Apr. 13 ***Perf. 13x14***

Background Red, White and Blue.

186 A24 ½c orange & black 45 40
187 " 1c green & black 45 40
188 " 2c rose & black 45 40
189 " 5c slate & black 50 45
190 " 10c magenta & black 60 55
191 " 20c olive grn. & blk. 1.50 1.50
192 " 50c brown & black 2.25 2.25
193 " 1p dull lilac & black 3.00 2.75
Nos. 186–193 (8) 9.20 8.70

To commemorate the centenary of the birth of Juan Pablo Duarte (1813–1876), patriot and revolutionary.

Official Stamps of 1909–12 Surcharged in Violet or Overprinted in Red:

Habilitado Habilitado

1915

MEDIO CENTAVO **1915**
a *b*

1915, Feb. ***Perf. 13½x13, 13½x14***

194 O2 (*a*) ½c on 20c orange & black 45 35
a. Inverted surcharge 5.00
b. Double surcharge 7.50
c. "Habilitado" omitted 3.50
195 " (*b*) 1c blue green & black 50 30
a. Inverted overprint 4.00
b. Double overprint 5.00
c. Overprinted "1915" only 12.50
196 " (") 2c scarlet & black 55 30
a. Inverted overprint 4.00
b. Double overprint 6.00
c. Overprinted "1915" only 8.50
d. "1915" double
197 " (") 5c dark blue & black 60 30
a. Inverted overprint 5.00
b. Double overprint 7.50
c. Double overprint, one inverted 25.00
d. Overprinted "1915" only 7.50
198 " (") 10c yellow green & black 1.75 1.75
a. Inverted overprint 5.00
199 " (") 20c orange & black 5.00 4.50
a. "Habilitado" omitted
Nos. 194–199 (6) 8.85 7.50

Nos. 194, 196–198 are known with both perforations. Nos. 195 and 199 are only perf. 13½x13.

The variety capital "I" for "1" in "Habilitado" occurs once in each sheet in all denominations.

A25

Type of 1911–13 Redrawn Overprinted "1915" in Red. Lithographed.

1915 ***Perf. 11½*** **Unwmkd.**

TWO CENTAVOS:
Type I. "DOS" in small letters.
Type II. "DOS" in larger letters with white dot at each end of the word.

200 A25 ½c violet & black 45 25
a. Imperf., pair 2.50
201 " 1c yellow brown & black 40 12
a. Imperf., pair 3.00
b. Vert. pair, imperf. horiz. 7.00
c. Horiz. pair, imperf. vert. 7.00
202 " 2c olive green & black (I) 1.50 35
a. Imperf., pair 2.75
203 " 2c olive green & black (II) 1.25 25
a. Center omitted 70.00
b. Frame omitted 70.00
c. Imperf., pair 4.00
d. Horiz. pair, imperf. vert. 8.00
204 " 5c magenta & black 1.50 35
a. Pair, one without overprint 50.00
b. Imperf., pair 3.00
205 " 10c gray blue & black 1.50 45
a. Imperf., pair 3.25
b. Horiz. pair, imperf. vert. 35.00
206 A25 20c rose red & black 3.50 1.00
a. Imperf., pair 6.00
207 " 50c green & black 5.00 2.75
a. Imperf., pair 15.00
208 " 1p orange & black 9.00 5.50
a. Imperf., pair 22.50
Nos. 200–208 (9) 24.10 11.02

Type of 1915 Overprinted "1916" in Red.

1916

209 A25 ½c violet & black 45 15
a. Imperf., pair 20.00
210 " 1c green & black 1.00 15
a. Imperf., pair 20.00

Type of 1915 Overprinted "1917" in Red.

1917-19

213 A25 ½c red lilac & black 70 25
a. Horizontal pair, imperf. between 35.00 35.00
214 " 1c yellow green & black 80 10
215 " 2c olive green & black 60 10
a. Imperf., pair 30.00
216 " 5c magenta & black 7.00 70

Type of 1915 Overprinted "1919" in Red

1919

219 A25 2c olive green & black 3.50 15

Type of 1915 Overprinted "1920" in Red.

1920-27

220 A25 ½c lilac rose & black 40 25
a. Horizontal pair, imperf. between 25.00 25.00
b. Inverted overprint
c. Double overprint
d. Double overprint, one inverted
221 " 1c yel. green & blk. 35 12
a. Overprint omitted 60.00
222 " 2c olive green & black 35 8
a. Vertical pair, imperf. between 27.50
223 " 5c deep rose & black 3.25 40
224 " 10c blue & black 2.00 25
225 " 20c rose red & black ('27) 3.00 50
226 " 50c green & black ('27) 27.50 9.00
Nos. 220–226 (7) 36.85 10.60

Type of 1915 Overprinted "1921" in Red.

1921

227 A25 1c yellow green & black 1.00 30
a. Horizontal pair, imperf. between 32.50 32.50
b. Imperf., pair 32.50 32.50
228 " 2c olive green & black 2.00 40

Redrawn Design of 1915 without Overprint

1922

230 A25 1c green 40 12
231 " 2c carmine (II) 85 12
232 " 5c blue 1.75 30

Arms of Dominican Republic
A26 — A27

Second Redrawing.

TEN CENTAVOS:
Type I. Numerals 2 mm. high. "DIEZ" in thick letters with large white dot at each end.
Type II. Numerals 3 mm. high. "DIEZ" in thin letters with white dot with colored center at each end.

1924-27

233 A26 1c green 35 10
a. Vertical pair, imperf. between 32.50 32.50
234 " 2c red 40 10
235 " 5c blue 40 12
236 " 10c pale blue & black (I) ('26) 5.50 1.35
236A " 10c pale blue & black (II) 14.00 75
236B " 50c gray green & black ('26) 27.50 20.00
237 " 1p org. & black ('27) 9.00 7.00
Nos. 233–237 (7) 57.15 29.42

In the second redrawing the shield has a flat top and the design differs in many details from the stamps of 1911–13 and 1915–22.

1927

238 A27 ½c lilac rose & black 20 10

Exhibition Pavilion
A28

1927 ***Perf. 12.*** **Unwmkd.**

239 A28 2c carmine 90 50
240 " 5c ultramarine 1.00 50

Issued to commemorate the National and West Indian Exhibition at Santiago de los Caballeros.

Ruins of Columbus' Fortress
A29

1928

241 A29 ½c lilac rose 35 30
242 " 1c deep green 40 15
a. Horizontal pair, imperf. between 20.00
243 " 2c red 40 15
244 " 5c dark blue 1.25 35
245 " 10c light blue 1.25 35
246 " 20c rose 1.50 40
247 " 50c yellow green 8.00 5.00
248 " 1p orange yellow 14.00 11.00
Nos. 241–248 (8) 27.15 17.70

Reprints exist of 1c, 2c and 10c.

Horacio Vasquez A30 — **Convent of San Ignacio de Loyola** A31

1929

249 A30 ½c dull rose 50 25
a. Imperf., pair 11.00
250 " 1c gray green 50 20
a. Imperf., pair 11.00
251 " 2c red 60 20
a. Imperf., pair 8.50
252 " 5c dk. ultramarine 1.00 30
a. Imperf., pair 12.00

253 A30 10c pale blue 1.50 45
Nos. 249-253 (5) 4.10 1.40

Issued in commemoration of the signing of the "Frontier" treaty between the Dominican Republic and Haiti.

1930, May 1 ***Perf. 11½***

254 A31 ½c red brown 60 50
a. Imperf., pair 35.00 35.00
255 " 1c deep green 60 15
256 " 2c vermilion 60 15
257 " 5c deep blue 1.35 45
258 " 10c light blue 2.50 1.00
Nos. 254-258 (5) 5.65 2.25

Cathedral of Santo Domingo, First Church in America
A32

1931 ***Perf. 12.***

260 A32 1c deep green 70 20
a. Imperf., pair 40.00
261 A32 2c scarlet 70 20
a. Imperf., pair 40.00
262 A32 3c violet 80 15
263 " 7c dark blue 1.50 25
264 " 8c bistre 2.50 85
265 " 10c light blue 3.75 1.00
a. Imperf., pair 30.00
Nos. 260-265 (6) 9.95 2.65

Fernando Arturo de Merino As Archbishop A33 — As President A34

Tomb of Merino
A35

Cathedral of Santo Domingo
A36

1933, Feb. 27 Engraved ***Perf. 14***

266 A35 ½c light violet 35 30
267 A33 1c yellow green 40 20
268 A34 2c light red 90 75
269 A33 3c deep violet 50 20
270 A35 5c dark blue 60 30
271 A34 7c ultramarine 1.20 50
272 A35 8c dark green 1.35 75
273 A33 10c orange yellow 1.10 40
274 A34 20c carmine rose 2.00 1.25
275 A36 50c lemon 7.00 5.00
276 " 1p dark brown 20.00 12.50
Nos. 266-276 (11) 35.40 22.15

Issued in commemoration of the centenary of the birth of Fernando Arturo de Meriño (1833-1906)

Tower of Homage, Ozama Fortress
A37

1932 Lithographed ***Perf. 12***

278 A37 1c green 45 15
279 " 3c violet 65 10

Issue dates: 1c, July 2; 3c, June 22.

"CORREOS" added at left.

1933, May 28

283 A37 1c dark green 50 15

President Rafael L. Trujillo
A38 A39

1933, Aug. 16 Engraved ***Perf. 14***

286 A38 1c yellow green & black 70 30
287 A39 3c deep violet & black 80 25
288 A38 7c ultra. & black 2.25 75

Commemorating the 42nd anniversary of the birth of President Rafael Leonidas Trujillo Molina.

San Rafael Bridge
A40

1934 Lithographed. ***Perf. 12.***

289 A40 ½c dull violet 65 30
290 " 1c dark green 85 20
291 " 3c violet 1.20 12

Opening of San Rafael Bridge.

Trujillo Bridge
A41

1934

292 A41 ½c red brown 70 20
293 " 1c green 1.00 12
294 " 3c purple 1.35 15

Issued in commemoration of the opening of the General Trujillo Bridge near Ciudad Trujillo.

Ramfis Bridge
A42

1935, Apr. 6

295 A42 1c green 55 12
296 " 3c yellow brown 60 12
297 A42 5c brown violet 1.25 55
298 " 10c rose 2.50 1.20

Issued in commemoration of the opening of the Ramfis Bridge over the Higuamo River.

President Trujillo—A43

A44

A45

1935 ***Perf. 11***

299 A43 3c yellow & brown 40 20
300 A44 5c orange red, blue, red & bistre 45 15
301 A45 7c ultramarine, blue, red & brown 70 15
302 A44 10c red violet, blue, red & bistre 90 15

Issued in commemoration of the ratification of a treaty setting the frontier between Dominican Republic and Haiti.

National Palace—A46

1935, Apr. 1 ***Perf. 11½***

303 A46 25c yellow orange 2.50 18

Issued for obligatory use on all mail addressed to the president and cabinet ministers.

Post Office, Santiago
A47

1936

304 A47 ½c bright violet 45 15
305 " 1c green 45 12

Issue dates: ½c, Jan. 14; 1c, Jan. 4.

George Washington Ave., Ciudad Trujillo
A48

1936, Feb. 22

306 A48 ½c brown & violet brown 45 35
a. Imperf. (pair) 40.00
307 " 2c carmine & brown 45 20
308 " 3c yellow orange & red brown 80 25
309 " 7c ultramarine, blue & brown 1.00 60
a. Imperf. (pair) 40.00

Issued in commemoration of the dedication of George Washington Avenue, Ciudad Trujillo.

José Nuñez de Cáceres
A49

Felix M. del Monte
A55

Proposed National Library
A56

Designs: 1c, Gen. Gregorio Luperon. 2c, Emiliano Tejera. 3c, President Trujillo. 5c, Jose Reyes. 7c, Gen. Antonio Duverge. 25c, Francisco J. Peynado. 30c, Salome Urena. 50c, Gen. Jose M. Cabral. 1p, Manuel de Jesus Galvan. 2p, Gaston F. Deligne.

Engraved.

1936 ***Perf. 13½, 14.*** **Unwmkd.**

310 A49 ½c dull violet 35 20
311 " 1c dark green 25 10
312 " 2c carmine 25 15
313 " 3c violet 30 10
314 " 5c deep ultra. 45 30
315 " 7c slate blue 80 55
316 A55 10c orange 90 40
317 A56 20c olive green 3.00 2.00
318 A55 25c gray violet 2.50 2.00
319 " 30c scarlet 3.75 3.00
320 " 50c black brown 5.00 3.50
321 " 1p black 10.00 8.00
322 " 2p yellow brown 27.50 25.00
Nos. 310-322 (13) 56.05 45.30

The funds derived from the sale of these stamps were returned to the National Treasury Fund for the erection of a building for the National Library and Archives.

Issue dates: 3c, 7c, Mar. 18; others, May 22.

President Trujillo and Obelisk
A62

1937, Jan. 11 Litho. ***Perf. 11½***

323 A62 1c green 30 10
324 " 3c violet 60 15
325 " 7c blue & turquoise blue 1.35 40

Issued in commemoration of the first anniversary of naming Ciudad Trujillo.

Discus Thrower and Flag
A63

1937, Aug. 14

Flag in Red and Blue.

326 A63 1c dark green 10.00 75
327 " 3c violet 12.50 75
328 " 7c dark blue 22.50 3.50

Issued in commemoration of the First National Olympic Games, August 16, 1937.

Symbolical of Peace, Labor and Progress—A64

1937, Sept. 18 ***Perf. 12***

329 A64 3c purple 50 12

"8th Year of the Benefactor."

Monument to Father F. X. Billini
A65

1937, Dec. 29

330 A65 ½c deep orange 25 10
331 " 5c purple 65 18

Issued in commemoration of the centenary of the birth of Father Francisco Xavier Billini (1837–1890).

Globe and Torch of Liberty
A66

1938, Feb. 22 ***Perf. 11½***

332 A66 1c green 40 10
333 " 3c purple 65 10
334 " 10c orange 1.20 30

Issued in commemoration of the 150th anniversary of the Constitution of the United States of America.

Pledge of Trinitarians, City Gate and National Flag
A67

1938, July 16 ***Perf. 12***

335 A67 1c green, red & dark blue 55 30
336 " 3c purple, red & blue 70 25
337 " 10c org., red & blue 1.35 60

Issued in commemoration of the Trinitarians and patriots, Francisco Del Rosario Sanchez, Ramon Matias Mella and Juan Pablo Duarte, who helped free their country from foreign domination.

Seal of the University of Santo Domingo
A68

1938, Oct. 28

338 A68 ½c orange 35 18
339 " 1c dp. grn. & lt. grn. 45 15
340 " 3c purple & pale violet 55 12
341 " 7c dp. blue & lt. blue 85 35

Issued in commemoration of the fourth centenary of the founding of the University of Santo Domingo, on October 28, 1538.

Trylon and Perisphere, Flag and Proposed Columbus Lighthouse—A69

1939, Apr. 30 Litho. ***Perf. 12***

Flag in Blue and Red.

342 A69 ½c red orange & orange 45 15
343 " 1c green & light green 50 20
344 " 3c purple & pale violet 55 18
345 " 10c orange & yellow 1.65 65
Nos. 342-345, C33 (5) 4.65 1.93

New York World's Fair.

José Trujillo Valdez
A70

1939 Typographed

346 A70 ½c black & pale gray 35 20
347 " 1c black & yel. grn. 40 15
348 " 3c black & yellow brown 45 15
349 " 7c blk. & dp. ultra. 1.00 60
350 " 10c black & bright red violet 1.75 50
Nos. 346-350 (5) 3.95 1.60

Issued in commemoration of the fourth anniversary of the death of José Trujillo Valdez (1863–1935), father of President Trujillo Molina.

Map of the Americas and Flags of 21 American Republics
A71

Sir Rowland Hill
A72

1940, Apr. 14 Litho. ***Perf. 11½***

Flags in National Colors

351 A71 1c deep green 35 15
352 " 2c carmine 50 18
353 " 3c red violet 75 10
354 " 10c orange 1.35 30
355 " 1p chestnut 17.50 11.00
Nos. 351-355 (5) 20.45 11.73

Issued in commemoration of the 50th anniversary of the founding of the Pan American Union.

1940, May 6 ***Perf. 12***

356 A72 3c brt. red violet & rose lilac 10.00 50
357 " 7c dark blue & light blue 18.00 1.75

Centenary of first postage stamp.

Julia Molina Trujillo—A73

1940, May 26

358 A73 1c green, light green & dark green 40 12
359 " 2c bright red, buff & deep rose 50 15
360 " 3c orange, dull orange & brown orange 65 12
361 " 7c blue, pale blue & dark blue 1.50 50

Issued in commemoration of Mother's Day.

Map of Caribbean
A74

1940, June 6 ***Perf. 11½***

362 A74 3c bright carmine & pale rose 55 15
363 " 7c dark blue & light blue 1.00 25
364 " 1p yellow green & pale green 9.00 5.00

Issued in commemoration of the second Inter-American Caribbean Conference held at Ciudad Trujillo, May 31 to June 6.

Marion Military Hospital
A75

1940, Dec. 24

365 A75 ½c chestnut & fawn 35 25

Fortress, Ciudad Trujillo
A76

Statue of Columbus, Ciudad Trujillo
A77

1941

366 A76 1c dark green & light green 20 8
367 A77 2c bright red & rose 25 12
368 " 10c orange brown & buff 85 15

Issue dates: 1c, Mar. 27; others, Apr. 7.

Sánchez, Duarte, Mella and Trujillo—A78

1941, May 16

369 A78 3c bright red lilac & red violet 35 12
370 " 4c bright red, crimson & pale rose 45 15
371 " 13c dk. blue & lt. bl. 1.00 30
372 " 15c orange brn. & buff 2.25 1.00
373 " 17c light blue, blue & pale blue 2.25 1.10
374 " 1p orange, yellow brown & pale orange 8.50 4.00
375 " 2p light gray & pale gray 17.50 8.00
Nos. 369-375 (7) 32.30 14.67

Issued in commemoration of the Trujillo-Hull Treaty signed September 24, 1940 and effective April 1, 1941.

Bastion of February
A79

1941, Oct. 20

376 A79 5c bright blue & light blue 75 30

School, Torch of Knowledge, Pres. Trujillo—A80

1941

377 A80 ½c chestnut & fawn 30 12
378 " 1c dk. grn. & lt. grn. 40 15

Education campaign.
Issue dates: ½c, Dec. 12, 1c, Dec. 2.

Reserve Bank of Dominican Republic
A81

1942 **Unwmkd.**

379 A81 5c light brown & buff 50 15
380 " 17c dp. blue & light blue 1.25 50

Issued to commemorate the founding of the Reserve Bank, October 24, 1941.

Representation of Transportation
A82

1942, Aug. 15

381 A82 3c dark brown, green, yellow & light blue 55 10
382 " 15c purple, green, yellow & lt. blue 1.35 40

Issued in commemoration of the 8th anniversary of the Day of Posts and Telegraph.

Virgin of Altagracia
A83

1942, Aug. 15

383 A83 ½c gray & pale gray 1.25 12
384 " 1c deep green & light green 2.25 10
385 " 3c bright red lilac & lilac 7.50 8
386 " 5c dark violet brown & vio. brown 2.75 12
387 " 10c rose pink & pink 8.00 30
388 " 15c deep blue & light blue 9.00 35
Nos. 383-388 (6) 30.75 1.07

Issued to commemorate the 20th anniversary of the coronation of Our Lady of Altagracia.

Bananas A84 Cows A85

1942-43

389 A84 3c dark brown & green ('43) 65 15
390 " 4c vermilion & black ('43) 70 25
391 A85 5c deep blue & copper brown 65 15
392 " 15c dark purple & blue green 1.25 50

Emblems of Dominican and Trujillista Parties
A86

1943, Jan.

393 A86 3c orange 55 10
394 " 4c dark red 75 20
395 " 13c bright red lilac 1.35 25
396 " 1p light blue 6.00 2.25

Issued in commemoration of the re-election of President Rafael Trujillo Molina, May 16, 1942.

Model Market, Ciudad Trujillo
A87

1944

397 A87 2c dark brown & buff 25 15

Bastion of Feb. 27 and National Flag
A88

1944, Feb. 27 **Unwmkd.**

Flag in Dark Blue and Carmine.

398 A88 ½c ochre 12 8
399 " 1c yellow green 12 8
400 " 2c scarlet 20 10
401 " 3c bright red violet 25 10
402 " 5c yellow orange 30 12
403 " 7c bright blue 40 25
404 " 10c orange brown 60 25
405 " 20c olive green 1.00 65
406 " 50c light blue 2.50 1.75
Nos. 398-406, C46-C48 (12) 10.34 6.20

Souvenir Sheet.

Imperf.

407 Sheet of twelve, multi. 80.00 75.00
a. Single stamp 4.00 4.00

Centenary of Independence.
No. 407 contains one each of Nos. 398-406, C46-C48 with simulated perforations. Inscribed in brown: "Serie Conmemorativa del Centenario de la Republica 27 de Febrero." Size: 141x205mm.

Battlefield and Nurse with Child
A90

1944, Aug. 1

408 A90 1c dark blue green, buff & carmine 20 8
a. Vertical pair, imperf. between 10.00
b. Horiz. pair, imperf. vert. 10.00
409 " 2c dark brown, buff & carmine 40 15
410 " 3c bright blue, buff & carmine 40 8
411 " 10c rose carmine, buff & carmine 80 20

Issued to honor the 80th anniversary of the International Red Cross.

Municipal Building, San Cristóbal A91 Emblem of Communications A92

Lithographed.

1945, Jan. 10 ***Perf. 12*** **Unwmkd.**

412 A91 ½c blue & light blue 10 10
413 " 1c dark green & green 15 8
414 " 2c red orange & orange 15 10
415 " 3c dark brown & brown 20 12
416 " 10c ultra. & gray blue 70 20
Nos. 412-416 (5) 1.30 60

Centenary of the constitution.

1945, Sept. 1

Center in Dark Blue and Carmine.

417 A92 3c orange 20 8
418 " 20c yellow green 1.20 25
419 A92 50c light blue 2.25 85
Nos. 417-419, C53-C56 (7) 5.65 2.28

Palace of Justice, Ciudad Trujillo
A93

1946 ***Perf. 11½.***

420 A93 3c dark red brown & buff 30 10

Map of Hispaniola
A94

1946, Aug. 4 ***Perf. 12***

421 A94 10c rose brown, yellow, lilac, blue, red, & green 60 25

Issued to commemorate the 450th anniversary of the founding of Santo Domingo. See also Nos. C62-C63.

Waterfall of Jimenoa—A95

1946-47

Center Multicolored

422 A95 1c yellow green ('47) 20 8
423 " 2c carmine ('47) 20 10
424 " 3c deep blue 25 8
425 " 13c red violet ('47) 60 35
426 " 20c chocolate, ('47) 1.25 30
427 " 50c orange ('47) 2.50 1.35
Nos. 422-427, C64-C67 (10) 9.60 5.91

Executive Palace
A96

1948, Feb. 27

428 A96 1c yellow green 12 8
429 " 3c deep blue 18 8

See also Nos. C68-C69.

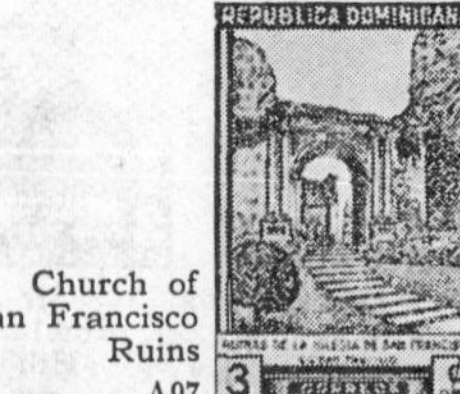

Church of San Francisco Ruins
A97

1949, Apr. 13 ***Perf. 11½***

430 A97 1c dark green & pale green 15 6
431 " 3c deep blue & pale blue 20 8
Nos. 430-431, C70-C73 (6) 2.55 1.46

Gen. Pedro Santana A98 Pigeon and Globe A99

1949, Aug. 10

432 A98 3c deep blue & blue 20 8

Issued to commemorate the centenary of the Battle of Las Carreras. See No. C74.

1949, Sept. 15

Center and Inscriptions in Brown.

433 A99 1c green & pale green 18 12
434 " 2c yel. green & yel. 22 8
435 " 5c blue & pale blue 30 10
436 " 7c dark violet blue & pale blue 60 20

Issued to commemorate the 75th anniversary of the formation of the Universal Postal Union.

Hotel Jimani—A100

Hotels: 1c, 2c, Hamaca. 5c, Montana. 15c, San Cristobal. 20c, Maguana.

1950-52

437 A100 ½c orange brown & buff 10 6
438 " 1c deep green & green ('51) 15 8
439 " 2c red orange & salmon ('52) 15 8
440 " 5c blue & light blue 30 8
441 " 15c dp. org. & yel. 65 12
442 " 20c lilac & rose lilac 1.25 20
443 " 1p choc. & yellow 5.00 2.00
Nos. 437-443, C75-C76 (9) 10.50 4.74

The ½c, 15c and 20c exist imperf.

Ruins of Church and Hospital of San Nicolas de Bari
A101

School of Medicine A102 Queen Isabella I A103

1950, Oct. 2

444 A101 2c dark green & rose brown 25 8
445 A102 5c violet blue & orange brown 35 10

18th Pan-American Health Conference. Exist imperf. See No. C77.

1951, Oct. 12

446 A103 5c dark blue & red brown 35 10

500th anniversary of the birth of Queen Isabella I of Spain. Exists imperf.

Dr. Salvador B. Gautier Hospital
A104

1952, Aug.

447 A104 1c dark green 12 6
448 " 2c red 18 6
449 " 5c violet blue 35 10
Nos. 447-449, C78-C79 (5) 3.25 2.37

Columbus Lighthouse and Flags of 21 Republics
A105

1953, Jan. 6 Engraved *Perf. 13*

450 A105 2c dark green 18 6
451 " 5c deep blue 25 8
452 " 10c deep carmine 45 25
Nos. 450-452, C80-C86 (10) 7.93 6.39

Miniature sheet containing Nos. 450-452 and C80-C86 is listed as No. C86a.

Treasury Building, Ciudad Trujillo
A106

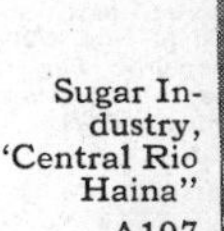

Sugar Industry, "Central Rio Haina"
A107

1953 Lithographed. *Perf. 11½.*

453 A106 ½c brown 8 6
454 " 2c dark blue 10 8
455 A107 5c blue & vio. brn. 20 8
456 A106 15c orange 75 25

José Marti
A108

Monument to the Peace of Trujillo
A109

1954 *Perf. 12½.*

457 A108 10c deep blue & dark brown 45 18

Centenary of the birth of José Marti (1853-1895), Cuban patriot.

1954, May 25

458 A109 2c green 8 6
459 " 7c blue 25 8
460 " 20c orange 80 15

See also No. 493.

Rotary Emblem
A110

1955, Feb. 23 *Perf. 12*

461 A110 7c deep blue 55 20

50th anniversary, Rotary International. See No. C90.

Gen. Rafael L. Trujillo
A111

Designs: 4c, Trujillo in civilian clothes. 7c, Trujillo statue. 10c, Symbols of culture and prosperity.

1955, May 16 Engr. *Perf. 13½x13*

462 A111 2c red 15 6
463 " 4c light olive green 25 8
464 " 7c indigo 30 12
465 " 10c brown 55 20
Nos. 462-465, C91-C93 (7) 3.40 1.58

25th anniversary of the Trujillo era.

General Rafael L. Trujillo
A112

Angelita Trujillo
A113

1955, Dec. 20 *Perf. 13* Unwmkd.

466 A112 7c deep claret 35 12
467 " 10c dark blue 55 18

See also No. C94.

1955, Dec. 20 Litho. *Perf. 12½*

468 A113 10c blue & ultramarine 55 18

Nos. 466-468 were issued to publicize the International Fair of Peace and Brotherhood in Ciudad Trujillo, Dec. 1955.

Airport
A114

1956, Apr. 6 *Perf. 12½*

469 A114 1c brown 12 8
470 " 2c red orange 18 8

Issued to commemorate the third Caribbean conference of the International Civil Aviation Organization. See No. C95.

Cedar
A115

See also No. 493.

1956, Dec. 8 *Perf. 11½x12*

471 A115 5c car. rose & green 30 10
472 " 6c red violet & green 35 15

Issued to publicize the reforestation program. See No. C96.

Fair Emblem
A116

Fanny Blankers-Koen, Netherlands
A117

1957, Jan. 10 *Perf. 12½*

473 A116 7c blue, light brown & vermilion 35 15

Issued to publicize the 2nd International Livestock Show, Ciudad Trujillo, Jan. 10-20, 1957. Exists imperf.

Engraved & Lithographed

1957, Jan. 24 *Perf. 11½*

Olympic Winners and Flags: 2c, Jesse Owens, United States. 3c, Kee Chung Sohn, Japan. 5c, Lord Burghley, England. 7c, Bob Mathias, United States.

Flags in National Colors.

474 A117 1c brown, light blue, violet & maroon 8 6
475 " 2c dark brown, light blue & violet 12 10
476 " 3c red lilac & red 20 10
477 " 5c red orange & vio. 28 15
478 " 7c green & violet 40 20
Nos. 474-478, C97-C99 (8) 2.26 1.76

To commemorate the 16th Olympic Games, Melbourne, Nov. 22-Dec. 8, 1956. Exist imperf.

Miniature sheets of 5 exist, perf. and imperf., containing one each of Nos. 474-478. Sheets measure 169 x 86 mm. and have no marginal inscriptions. Price, 2 sheets, perf. and imperf., $6.

Lars Hall, Sweden, Pentathlon
A118

Olympic Winners and Flags: 2c, Betty Cuthbert, Australia, 100 & 200 meter dash. 3c, Egil Danielsen, Norway, javelin. 5c, Alain Mimoun, France, marathon. 7c, Norman Read, New Zealand, 50 km. walk.

Perf. 13½

1957, July 18 Photo. Unwmkd.

Flags in National Colors.

479 A118 1c brown & brt. blue 7 6
480 A118 2c orange vermilion & dark blue 10 8
481 " 3c dark blue 12 10
482 " 5c olive & dark blue 25 15
483 " 7c rose brown & dark blue 40 20
Nos. 479-483, C100-C102 (8) 2.09 1.74

Issued in honor of the 1956 Olympic winners. Exist imperf.

Miniature sheets of 8 exist, perf. and imperf., containing one each of Nos. 479-483 and C100-C102. The center label in these sheets is printed in two forms: Olympic gold medal or Olympic flag. Sheets measure 140x140mm. Price, 4 sheets, perf. and imperf., medal and flag, $18.

A third set of similar miniature sheets (perf. and imperf.) with center label showing an incorrect version of the Dominican Republic flag (colors transposed) was printed. These sheets are said to have been briefly sold on the first day, then withdrawn as the misprint was discovered. Price, 2 sheets, perf. & imperf., $110.

Gerald Ouellette, Canada, Small Bore Rifle, Prone—A119

Ron Delaney, Ireland, 1,500 Meter Run—A120

Olympic Winners and Flags: 3c, Tenley Albright, United States, figure skating. 5c, Joaquin Capilla, Mexico, platform diving. 7c, Ercole Baldini, Italy, individual road race (cycling).

Engraved and Lithographed

1957, Nov. 12 *Perf. 13½*

Flags in National Colors

484 A119 1c red brown 6 6
485 A120 2c gray brown 8 8
486 A119 3c violet 12 10
487 A120 5c red orange 20 15
488 A119 7c Prussian green 25 18
Nos. 484-488, C103-C105 (8) 1.96 1.67

Issued in honor of the 1956 Olympic winners. Exist imperf.

Miniature sheets of 5 exist, perf. and imperf., containing one each of Nos. 484-488. Sheets have no marginal inscriptions. Price, 2 sheets, perf. and imperf., $5.50.

Mahogany Flower
A121

1957-58 Lithographed *Perf. 12½*

489 A121 2c green & maroon 12 8

Perf. 12

490 A121 4c lilac & rose ('58) 18 12
491 " 7c ultra. & gray grn. 35 12
492 " 25c brn. & orge. ('58) 85 35

Sizes: No. 489, 25x29¼mm.; Nos. 490-492, 24x28¾mm. In 1959, the 2c was reissued in size 24¼x28½mm. with slightly different tones of green and maroon.

Issue dates: 2c, Oct. 24; 7c, Nov. 6; 4c and 25c, Apr. 7, 1958.

Type of 1954, Redrawn

Perf. 12x11½

1957, June 12 Unwmkd.

493 A109 7c bright blue 45 12

On No. 493 the "$" is smaller, the shading of the sky and steps stronger and the letters in "Correos" shorter and bolder.

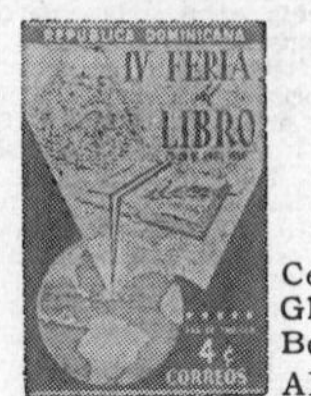

Cervantes, Globe and Book A122

1958, Apr. 23 Litho. *Perf. 12½*

494 A122 4c yellow green 15 6
495 " 7c red lilac 20 10
496 " 10c light olive brown 35 15

Fourth Book Fair, Apr. 23–28. Exist imperf.

Gen. Rafael L. Trujillo A123

1958, Aug. 16 *Perf. 12*

497 A123 2c red lilac & yellow 6 6
498 " 4c green & yellow 15 8
499 " 7c brown & yellow 25 12
a. Souv. sheet of 3 60 50

Issued to commemorate the 25th anniversary of Gen. Trujillo's designation as "Benefactor of his country."

No. 499a measures 152x101mm and contains one each of Nos. 497–499, imperf. Brown marginal inscription.

S. S. Rhadames A124

1958, Oct. 27 *Perf. 12½*

500 A124 7c bright blue 40 18

Day of the Dominican Merchant Marine. Exists imperf.

Shozo Sasahara, Japan, Featherweight Wrestling A125

Olympic Winners and Flags: 1c, Gillian Sheen, England, fencing (vert.). 2c, Milton Campbell, United States, decathlon (vert.). 5c, Madeleine Berthod, Switzerland, downhill skiing. 7c, Murray Rose, Australia, 400 & 1,500 meter freestyle.

1958, Oct. 30 Photo. *Perf. 13½*

Flags in National Colors

501 A125 1c rose, indigo & ultramarine 7 7
502 " 2c brown & blue 9 9

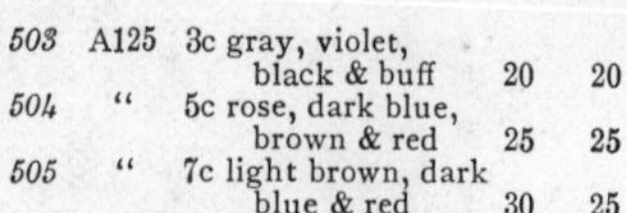

503 A125 3c gray, violet, black & buff 20 20
504 " 5c rose, dark blue, brown & red 25 25
505 " 7c light brown, dark blue & red 30 25
Nos. 501-505, C106-C108 (8) 2.21 2.16

To honor 1956 Olympic winners. Exist imperf.

Miniature sheets of 5 exist, perf. and imperf. containing one each of Nos. 501–505. Size: 140x119½mm. Price, 2 sheets, perf. and imperf., $3.

Globe and Symbolic Fire A126

1958, Nov. 3 Litho. *Perf. 11½*

506 A126 7c blue & deep car. 25 15

Issued to commemorate the opening of UNESCO (U. N. Educational, Scientific and Cultural Organization) Headquarters in Paris, Nov. 3.

Dominican Republic Pavilion, Brussels Fair A127

1958, Dec. 9 *Perf. 12½* Unwmkd.

507 A127 7c blue green 30 15

Issued for the Universal and International Exposition at Brussels. See Nos. C109–C110a.

Gen. Trujillo Placing Wreath on Altar of the Nation A128

1959, July 10 *Perf. 12*

508 A128 9c brown, green, red & gold 30 15
a. Souv. sheet 40 40

Issued to commemorate the 29th anniversary of the Trujillo regime.

No. 508a contains one 9c, imperf. Size: 141x90mm.

Lt. Leonidas Rhadames Trujillo, Team Captain A129

Jamaican Polo Team A130

Design: 10c, Lt. Trujillo on polo pony.

1959, May 15

509 A129 2c violet 15 10
510 A130 7c yellow brown 40 20
511 " 10c green 45 30

Jamaica-Dominican Republic polo match at Ciudad Trujillo.
See also No. C111.

Symbolical of Census A131

1959, Aug. 15 Litho. *Perf. 12½*

Flag in Ultramarine and Red.

512 A131 1c blue & black 12 10
513 " 9c green & black 30 25
514 " 13c orange & black 50 35

Issued to publicize the 1960 census.

Trujillo Stadium A132

1959, Aug. 27

515 A132 9c green & gray 45 25

Issued to publicize the 3rd Pan American Games Chicago, Aug. 27–Sept. 7.

Charles V A133

1959, Oct. 12 *Perf. 12* Unwmkd.

516 A133 5c bright pink 20 10
517 " 9c violet blue 30 15

Issued to commemorate the 400th anniversary of the death of Charles V (1500–1558), Holy Roman Emperor.

Rhadames Bridge A134

Designs: 1c and No. 520, Different view of bridge.

1959–60 Lithographed. *Perf. 12*

518 A134 1c green & gray ('60) 12 10
519 " 2c ultra. & gray 20 12
520 A134 2c red & gray ('60) 20 10
521 " 5c brown & dull red brown 30 18

Issue dates: No. 519, Oct. 22; 5c, Nov. 30; 1c and No. 520, Feb. 6, 1960.

Sosua Refugee Settlement and WRY Emblem—A135

1960, Apr. 7 *Perf. 12½*

Center in Gray

522 A135 5c red brown & yellow green 15 10
523 " 9c car. & light blue 30 15
524 " 13c orange & green 40 25
Nos. 522-524, C113-C114 (5) 2.05 1.50

Issued to publicize World Refugee Year, July 1, 1959–June 30, 1960.

Sholam Takhti, Iran, Lightweight Wrestling—A136

Olympic Winners: 2c, Mauru Furukawa, Japan, 200 meter breast stroke. 3c, Mildred McDaniel, U.S.A., high jump. 5c, Terence Spinks, England, featherweight boxing. 7c, Carlo Pavesi, Italy, fencing.

Perf. 13½

1960, Sept. 14 Photo. Unwmkd.

Flags in National Colors

525 A136 1c red, yellow green & black 5 5
526 " 2c orange, greenish blue & brown 6 6
527 " 3c henna brown & blue 10 10
528 " 5c brown & ultra. 15 12
529 " 7c green, blue & rose brown 20 20
Nos. 525-529, C115-C117 (8) 1.71 1.53

Issued to commemorate the 17th Olympic Games, Rome, Aug. 25–Sept. 11. Exist imperf.

Miniature sheets of 5 exist, perf. and imperf., containing one each of Nos. 525–529, and a Dominican Republic flag in national colors. Sheet size: 160x121mm. Price, 2 sheets, perf. and imperf., $3.75.

Post Office, Ciudad Trujillo A137

1960, Aug. 26 Litho. *Perf. 11½x12*

530 A137 2c ultra. & gray 15 10

Exists imperf.

Cattle—A138

1960, Aug. 30

531 A138 9c carmine & gray 35 18

Issued to publicize the Agricultural and Industrial Fair, San Juan de la Maguana.

Nos. 518, 490–491, 453, 427 Surcharged in Red, Black or Blue

HABILITADO
PARA
2¢

1960–61 ***Perf. 12***

536 A134 2c on 1c green & gray (R) 20 10
537 A121 9c on 4c lilac & rose 70 15
a. Inverted surcharge 30.00
538 A121 9c on 7c ultramarine & gray green (R) ('61) 70 20
539 A106 36c on ½c brown ('61) 2.00 80
a. Inverted surcharge 25.00
540 A95 1p on 50c multicolored (B1) ('61) 4.50 2.25
Nos. 536–540 (5) 8.10 3.50

Trujillo Memorial
A139

Coffee and Cacao
A140

1961 ***Perf. 11½*** **Unwmkd.**

548 A139 1c brown 12 5
549 " 2c green 15 5
550 " 4c rose lilac 45 40
551 " 5c light blue 35 12
552 " 9c red orange 45 30
Nos. 548–552 (5) 1.52 92

Issued in memory of Gen. Rafael L. Trujillo (1891–1961).

1961, Dec. 30 Litho. ***Perf. 12½***

553 A140 1c blue green 5 5
554 " 2c orange brown 6 5
555 " 4c violet 12 8
556 " 5c blue 15 8
557 " 9c gray 25 8
Nos. 553–557, C118–C119 (7) 1.88 1.59

Exist imperf.

Dagger Pointing at Mosquito
A141

1962, Apr. 29 Photo. ***Perf. 12***

558 A141 10c bright pink & red lilac 25 18
559 " 20c pale brown & brown 50 45
560 " 25c pale green & yellow green 65 50
Nos. 558–560, B39–B40, C120–C121, CB24–CB25 (9) 4.60 4.13

Issued for the World Health Organization drive to eradicate malaria.

Broken Fetters and Laurel
A142

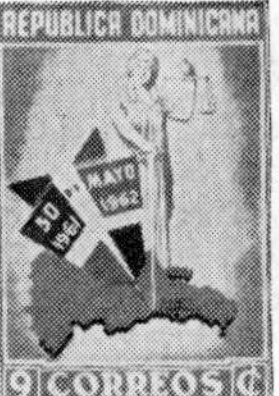

"Justice" and Map of Dominican Republic
A143

Farm, Factory and Flag
A144

Design: 20c, Flag, torch and inscription.

1962, May 30 Litho. ***Perf. 12½***

561 A142 1c grn., yel., ultra. & red 12 8
562 A143 9c bistre, ultra. & red 40 18
563 A142 20c lt. blue, ultra. & red 70 35
a. Souv. sheet of 3 1.50 1.50
564 A143 1p lilac, ultra. & red 3.50 2.25
Nos. 561–564, C122–C123 (6) 6.62 4.16

First anniversary of end of Trujillo era. Exist imperf.

No. 563a contains one each of Nos. 561–563, imperf. with ultramarine inscription on pink background. Size: 154x91mm.

1962, May 22

565 A144 1c ultra., red & grn. 5 4
566 " 2c ultra., & red 8 5
567 " 3c ultra., red & brn. 10 6
568 " 5c ultra., red & blue 15 8
569 " 15c ultra., red & orge. 30 20
Nos. 565–569 (5) 68 43

Map and Laurel
A145

1962, June 14 **Lithographed**

570 A145 1c black 35 18

Issued to honor the martyrs of June 1959 revolution.

Western Hemisphere and Carrier Pigeon
A146

Archbishop Adolfo Alejandro Nouel
A147

1962, Oct. 23 ***Perf. 12½*** **Unwmkd.**

571 A146 2c rose red 12 6
572 " 9c orange 35 15
573 " 14c blue green 40 25
Nos. 571–573, C124–C125 (5) 1.87 1.21

Issued to commemorate the 50th anniversary of the founding of the Postal Union of the Americas and Spain, UPAE.

1962, Dec. 18

574 A147 2c blue green & dull blue 8 5
575 " 9c org. & red brn. 35 15
576 " 13c maroon & vio. brown 45 20
Nos. 574–576, C126–C127 (5) 1.93 1.20

Issued to commemorate the centenary of the birth of Archbishop Adolfo Alejandro Nouel, President of Dominican Republic in 1911.

Globe, Banner and Emblems
A148

1963, Apr. 15 ***Perf. 11½*** **Unwmkd.**

Banner in Dark Blue & Red

577 A148 2c green 6 5
578 " 5c brt. rose lilac 15 10
579 " 9c orange 25 18
Nos. 577–579, B41–B43 (6) 1.00 84

Issued for the "Freedom from Hunger" campaign of the U.N. Food and Agriculture Organization.

Juan Pablo Duarte
A149

Designs: 7c, Francisco Sanchez. 9c, Ramon Mella.

1963, July 7 Litho. ***Perf. 12x11½***

580 A149 2c ultramarine 6 5
581 " 7c dull green 18 15
582 " 9c red lilac 25 18

Issued to commemorate the 120th anniversary of separation from Haiti. See also No. C128.

Ulises F. Espaillat, Benigno F. de Rojas and Pedro F. Bono
A150

Designs: 4c, Generals Santiago Rodriguez, José Cabrera and Benito Moncion. 5c, Capotillo monument. 9c, Generals Gaspar Polanco, Gregorio Luperon and José A. Salcedo.

1963, Aug. 16 ***Perf. 11½*** **Unwmkd.**

583 A150 2c green 8 5
584 " 4c red orange 12 8
585 " 5c brown 15 10
586 " 9c bright blue 25 18
a. Souv. sheet of 4 1.00 1.00

Issued to commemorate the centenary of the Restoration. No. 586a contains 4 imperf. stamps similar to Nos. 583–586. Brown marginal inscription. Size: 229x106½mm.

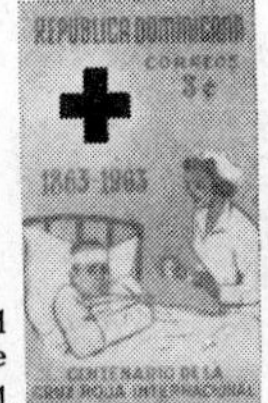

Patient and Nurse
A151

1963, Oct. 25 ***Perf. 12½*** **Unwmkd.**

587 A151 3c gray & carmine 10 6
588 " 6c emerald & red 20 12

Centenary of International Red Cross. Exist imperf. See No. C129.

Scales, Globe and UNESCO Emblem
A152

1963, Dec. 10 **Lithographed**

589 A152 6c pink & dp. pink 18 12
590 " 50c light grn. & grn. 1.10 85

Universal Declaration of Human Rights, 15th anniversary. Exist imperf. See also Nos. C130–C131.

Ramses II Battling the Hittites (from Abu Simbel)—A153

Design: 6c, Two heads of Ramses II.

1964, March 8 ***Perf. 12½*** **Unwmkd.**

591 A153 3c pale pink & vermilion 10 8
592 " 6c pale bl. & ultra. 20 15
593 " 9c pale rose & red brown 30 20
Nos. 591–593, C132–C133 (5) 1.35 1.03

Issued to publicize the UNESCO world campaign to save historic monuments in Nubia.

Maximo Gomez
A154

Palm Chat
A155

1964, Apr. 30 **Lithographed**

594 A154 2c lt. blue & blue 6 6
595 " 6c dull pink & dull claret 18 12

Issued to commemorate the bicentenary of the founding of the town of Bani.

1964, June 8 ***Perf. 12½*** **Unwmkd.**

Design: 6c, Hispaniolan parrot.

Size: 27x37½mm.

596 A155 3c ultra., brn. & yel. 15 12
597 " 6c gray & multi. 30 18

See also Nos. 602–604, C134.

Rocket Leaving Earth
A156

Designs: 1c, Launching of rocket (vert.). 3c, Space capsule orbiting earth. 6c, As 2c.

1964, July 28 **Lithographed**

598 A156 1c sky blue 9 7
599 " 2c emerald 12 8
600 " 3c blue 15 12
601 " 6c sky blue 30 15
Nos. 598–601, C135–C136 (6) 1.56 1.02

Issued to commemorate the conquest of space.

Bird Type of 1964

Designs: 1c, Narrow-billed tody. 2c, Hispaniolan emerald hummingbird. 6c, Hispaniolan trogon.

1964, Nov. 7 *Perf. 11½*

Size: 26x37mm.

Birds in Natural Colors

602	A155	1c bright pink	10	9
603	"	2c dark brown	12	9
604	"	6c blue	25	18

Universal Postal Union and United Nations Emblems
A157

1964, Dec. 5 Litho. *Perf. 12½*

605	A157	1c red	7	5
606	"	4c green	18	10
607	"	5c orange	20	12

Issued to commemorate the 15th Universal Postal Union Congress, Vienna, Austria, May–June 1964. See also No. C138.

International Cooperation Year Emblem—A158

1965, Feb. 16 *Perf. 12½* Unwmkd.

608	A158	2c lt. blue & ultra.	6	5
609	"	3c emerald & dk. grn.	8	6
610	"	6c salmon pink & red	18	10

Issued to publicize the United Nations International Cooperation Year. See No. C139.

Virgin of Altagracia A159 — Flags of 21 American Nations A160

Design: 2c, Hands holding lily.

1965, Mar. 18 *Perf. 12½* Unwmkd.

611	A159	2c green, emerald & deep rose	12	8
612	"	6c multicolored	45	35

Issued to commemorate the Fourth Mariological Congress and the Eleventh International Marian Congress. No. 612 exists imperf. See No. C140.

1965, Apr. 14 Litho. *Perf. 11½*

613	A160	2c brn., yel. & multi.	6	5
614	"	6c red lilac & multi.	18	12

Organization of American States.

Stamp of 1865 (No. 1)
A161

1965, Dec. 28 Litho. *Perf. 12½*

615	A161	1c pink, buff & blk.	8	6
616	"	2c blue, buff & blk.	10	7
617	"	6c emerald, buff & black	20	15
		a. Souv. sheet of 2	1.75	1.75
		Nos. 615-617, C142-C143 (5)	1.13	93

Issued to commemorate the centenary of the first Dominican postage stamps. No. 617a shows replicas of Nos. 1–2. Bright blue marginal inscription. Size: 100x65 mm. Sold for 50c.

WHO Headquarters, Geneva
A162

1966, May 21 Litho. *Perf. 12½*

618	A162	6c blue	18	10
619	"	10c red lilac	30	18

Issued to commemorate the inauguration of World Health Organization Headquarters, Geneva.

Man Holding Map of Republic
A163

1966, May 23

620	A163	2c blk. & brt. green	6	4
621	"	6c blk. & dp. orange	18	10

Issued to publicize the general elections, June 1, 1966.

Ascia Monuste A164 — National Altar A165

1966 Lithographed *Perf. 12½*

Various Butterflies in Natural Colors

Size: 31x21mm.

622	A164	1c blue & vio. blue	4	4
623	"	2c lt. grn. & brt. grn.	6	5
624	"	3c lt. gray & gray	9	5
625	"	6c pink & magenta	18	10
626	"	8c buff & brown	25	12
		Nos. 622-626, C146-C148 (8)	5.27	3.11

Issue dates: 1c, Sept. 7; 3c, Sept. 11; others, Nov. 8.

1967, Jan. 18 Litho. *Perf. 11½*

627	A165	1c bright blue	3	3
628	"	2c carmine rose	4	4
629	"	3c emerald	6	5
630	"	4c gray	8	6
631	"	5c orange yellow	10	8
632	"	6c orange	12	10
		Nos. 627-632, C149-C151 (9)	1.33	1.06

Map of Republic and Emblem
A166

1967, Mar. 30 Litho. *Perf. 12½*

633	A166	2c yel., bl. & black	7	5
634	"	6c org., bl. & black	20	10
635	"	10c emerald, blue & black	35	18

Development Year, 1967.

Rook and Knight
A167

1967, June 23 Litho. *Perf. 12½*

636	A167	25c multicolored	70	50

Issued to commemorate the 5th Central American Chess Championships, Santo Domingo. See also Nos. C152–C152a.

Alliance for Progress A168 — Institute Emblem A169

1967, Sept. 16 Litho. *Perf. 12½*

637	A168	1c bright green	4	4

Issued to commemorate the 6th anniversary of the Alliance for Progress. See Nos. C153–C154.

1967, Oct. 7

638	A169	3c bright green	9	7
639	"	6c salmon pink	18	12

Issued to commemorate the 25th anniversary of the Inter-American Agriculture Institute. See also No. C155.

Globe and Satellite
A170

1968, June 15 Typo. *Perf. 12*

640	A170	6c black & multi.	25	20

Issued to commemorate World Meteorological Day, Mar. 23. See Nos. C156–C157.

Boxers
A171

1968, June 29

641	A171	6c rose red & deep claret	20	18

Issued to commemorate the fight between Carlos Ortiz, Puerto Rico, and Teo Cruz, Dominican Republic, for the World Lightweight Boxing Championship. See Nos. C158–C159.

Lions Emblem
A172

1968, Aug. 9 Litho. *Perf. 11½*

642	A172	6c brown & multi.	18	10

Issued to commemorate the 50th anniversary (in 1967) of Lions International. See No. C160.

Wrestling and Olympic Emblem
A173

Designs (Olympic Emblem and): 6c, Running. 25c, Boxing.

1968, Nov. 12 Litho. *Perf. 11½*

643	A173	1c sky blue & multi.	8	5
644	"	6c pale grn. & multi.	20	12
645	"	25c pale lilac & multi.	85	45
		Nos. 643-645, C161-C162 (5)	2.58	1.77

Issued to commemorate the 19th Olympic Games, Mexico City, Oct. 12–27.

Map of Americas and House A174 — Stool in Human Form A175

1969, Jan. 25 Litho. *Perf. 12½*

646	A174	6c bright blue, light blue & green	20	12

Issued to publicize the 7th Inter-American Conference for Savings and Loans, Santo Domingo, Jan. 25–31. See No. C163.

1969, Jan. 31 Litho. *Perf. 12½*

Taino Art: 2c, Wood carved mother figure (vert.). 3c, Face carved on 3-cornered stone. 4c, Stone hatchet (vert.). 5c, Clay pot.

647	A175	1c yel., org. & black	5	4
648	"	2c lt. grn., grn. & blk.	7	5
649	"	3c citron, olive & bright green	10	6
650	"	4c lt. lilac, lilac & bright green	15	7
651	"	5c yel., org. & brown	18	8
		Nos. 647-651, C164-C166 (8)	1.60	97

Taino art flourished in the West Indies at the time of Columbus.

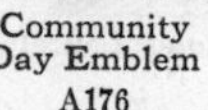

Community Day Emblem A176 — COTAL Emblem A177

Headquarters Building and COTAL Emblem
A178

1969, Mar. 25 Litho. *Perf. 12½*

652 A176 6c dull green & gold 20 10

Issued for Community Development Day, March 22.

1969, May 25 Litho. *Perf. 12½*

Design: 2c, Boy and COTAL emblem.

653 A177 1c lt. & dk. blue & red 3 3
654 " 2c emerald & dark green 6 4
655 A178 6c verm. & pink 18 10

Issued to publicize the 12th Congress of the Confederation of Latin American Tourist Organizations (COTAL), Santo Domingo, May 25–29.
See No. C167.

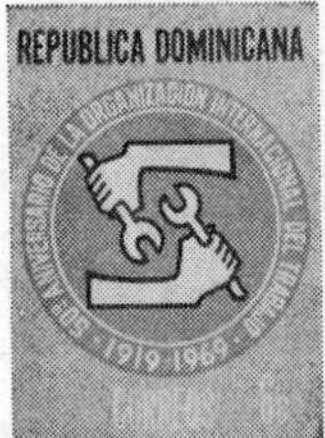

ILO Emblem A179 — Sliding into Base A180

1969, June 27 Litho. *Perf. 12½*

656 A179 6c lt. greenish blue, greenish blue & black 40 10

Issued to commemorate the 50th anniversary of the International Labor Organization. See No. C168.

1969, Aug. 15 Litho. *Perf. 12½*

Designs: 1c, Catching a fly ball. 2c, View of Cibao Stadium (horiz.).

Size: 21x31mm. (1c, 3c); 43x30mm. (2c).

657 A180 1c green & gray 8 5
658 " 2c green & lt. green 10 8
659 " 3c pur. & red brown 12 10
Nos. 657-659, C169-C171 (6) 4.00 2.66

Issued to publicize the 17th World Amateur Baseball Championships, Santo Domingo.

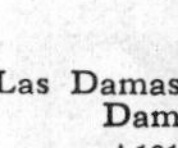

Las Damas Dam
A181

Tavera Dam—A182

Designs: 2c, Las Damas hydroelectric station (vert.). 6c, Arroyo Hondo substation.

1969 Lithographed *Perf. 12*

660 A181 2c green & multi. 6 4
661 " 3c dk. blue & multi. 9 5
662 " 6c bright rose lilac 18 10
663 A182 6c multicolored 18 10
Nos. 660-663, C172-C173 (6) 1.11 59

Issued to publicize the national electrification plan.

Issue dates: Nos. 660–662, Sept. 15. No. 663, Oct. 15.

Juan Pablo Duarte A183 — Map of Republic, People, Census Emblem A184

1970, Jan. 26 Litho. *Perf. 12*

664 A183 1c emerald & dk. grn. 5 3
665 " 2c salmon pink & deep carmine 6 4
666 " 3c brt. pink & plum 9 5
667 " 6c blue & vio. blue 18 10
Nos. 664-667, C174 (5) 68 40

Issued for Duarte Day in memory of Juan Pablo Duarte (1813–1876), liberator.

1970, Feb. 6 *Perf. 11*

Design: 6c, Census emblem and inscription.

668 A184 5c emerald & black 15 8
669 " 6c ultramarine & bl. 18 10

Census of 1970. See No. C175.

Abelardo Rodriguez Urdaneta
A185

"One of Many"
A186

1970, Feb. 20 Litho. *Perf. 12½*

670 A185 3c ultramarine 9 6
671 A186 6c grn. & yel. green 18 10

Issued to honor Abelardo Rodriguez Urdaneta, sculptor. See No. C176.

Masonic Symbols
A187

1970, Mar. 2

672 A187 6c green 18 10

Issued to publicize the 8th Inter-American Masonic Conference, Santo Domingo, Mar. 1–7. See No. C177.

Communications Satellite—A188

1970, May 25 Litho. *Perf. 12½*

673 A188 20c olive & gray 65 40

Issued for World Telecommunications Day. See No. C178.

U.P.U. Headquarters, Bern
A189

1970, June 5 *Perf. 11*

674 A189 6c gray & brown 18 10

Issued to commemorate the inauguration of the new Universal Postal Union Headquarters in Bern. See No. C179.

Education Year Emblem A190 — Pedro Alejandrino Pina A191

1970, June 26 Litho. *Perf. 12½*

675 A190 4c rose lilac 12 6

Issued for International Education Year, 1970. See No. C180.

1970, Aug. 24 Litho. *Perf. 12½*

676 A191 6c lt. red brn. & blk. 18 10

Issued to commemorate the 150th anniversary of the birth and the centenary of the death of Pedro Alejandrino Pina (1820–70), author.

Children Reading
A192

1970, Oct. 12 Litho. *Perf. 12½*

677 A192 5c dull green 15 8

Issued to publicize the First World Exhibition of Books and Culture Festival, Santo Domingo, Oct. 11–Dec. 11. See Nos. C181–C182.

Virgin of Altagracia A193 — Manuel Rodriguez Objio A194

1971, Jan. 20 Litho. *Perf. 12½*

678 A193 3c multicolored 15 10

Inauguration of the Basilica of Our Lady of Altagracia. See No. C184.

1971, June 18 Litho. *Perf. 11*

679 A194 6c light blue 18 10

Centenary of the death of Manuel Rodriguez Objio (1838–1871), poet.

Boxing and Canoeing
A195

Design: 5c, Basketball.

1971, Sept. 10

680 A195 2c brown & orange 8 6
681 " 5c brown & lt. green 18 10

2nd National Games. See No. C186.

Goat and Fruit
A196

Designs: 2c, Cow and goose. 3c, Cacao and horse. 6c, Bananas, coffee and pig.

1971, Sept. 29 *Perf. 12½*

682 A196 1c brown & multi. 3 3
683 " 2c plum & multi. 6 3
684 " 3c green & multi. 9 5
685 " 6c blue & multi. 18 10
Nos. 682-685, C187 (5) 96 66

6th National agriculture and livestock census.

José Nuñez de Cáceres—A197 — Shepherds and Star—A198

1971, Dec. 1 *Perf. 11*

686 A197 6c lt. blue, lilac & dark blue 18 10

Sesquicentennial of first national independence. See No. C188.

1971, Dec. 10 *Perf. 12½*

687 A198 6c blue, brn. & yel. 20 12

Christmas 1971. See No. C189.

UNICEF Emblem, Child on Beach
A199

1971, Dec. 14 Litho. *Perf. 11*

688 A199 6c gray bl. & multi. 18 10

25th anniversary of the United Nations International Children's Fund (UNICEF). See No. C190.

Book Year Emblem
A200

Taino Mask
A201

1972, Jan. 25 *Perf. 12½*

689 A200 1c grn., ultra. & red 4 4

690 " 2c brn., ultra. & red 6 4

International Book Year 1972. See No. C191.

1972, May 10 Litho. *Perf. 11*

Taino Art: 4c, Ladle and amulet. 6c, Human figure.

691 A201 2c pink & multi. 6 4

692 " 4c blk., bl. & ocher 12 6

693 " 6c gray & multi. 18 10

Nos. 691-693, C194-C196 (6) 1.51 82

Taino art. See note after No. 651.

Globe
A202

1972, May 17 *Perf. 12½*

694 A202 6c blue & multi. 18 10

4th World Telecommunications Day. See No. C197.

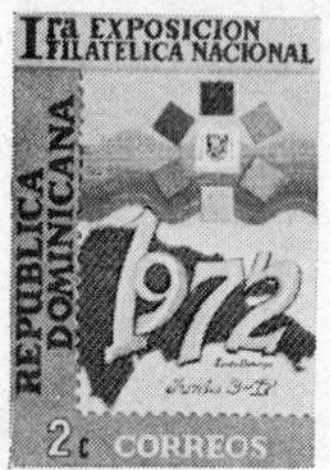

"1972," Stamps and Map of Dominican Republic
A203

1972, June 3

695 A203 2c green & multi. 6 4

First National Philatelic Exhibition, Santo Domingo, June 3-17. See No. C198.

Basketball
A204

1972, Aug. 25 Litho. *Perf. 12½*

696 A204 2c blue & multi. 10 7

20th Olympic Games, Munich, Aug. 26–Sept. 11. See No. C199.

Club Emblem
A205

1972, Sept. 29 Litho. *Perf. 10½*

697 A205 1c lt. green & multi. 3 3

50th anniversary of the Club Activo 20-30 Internacional. See No. C200.

Emilio A. Morel
A206

1972, Oct. 20 *Perf. 12½*

698 A206 6c bright pink & multicolored 18 10

Emilio A. Morel (1884-1958), poet and journalist. See No. C201.

Central Bank Building
A207

Design: 5c, One peso note.

1972, Oct. 23

699 A207 1c black & multi. 3 3

700 " 5c red, blk. & grn. 15 8

25th anniversary of Central Bank. See No. C202.

Holy Family
A208

Poinsettia
A209

1972, Nov. 21

701 A208 2c rose lilac, purple & gold 8 6

702 A209 6c red & multi. 20 12

Christmas 1972. See No. C203.

Mail Box and Student
A210

1972, Dec. 15

703 A210 2c rose red 6 3

704 " 6c blue 18 10

705 " 10c emerald 30 15

Publicity for correspondence schools.

Tavera Dam
A211

1973, Feb. 26 Litho. *Perf. 12½*

706 A211 10c multicolored 30 15

Inauguration of the Tavera Dam.

Various Sports—A212

1973, Mar. 30 *Perf. 13½x13*

707 A212 2c brn., yel. & grn., block of 4 30 20

a. Upper left 6 4

b. Upper right 6 4

c. Lower left 6 4

d. Lower right 6 4

708 A212 25c dk. green & yel. green, block of 4 3.25 1.50

a. Upper left 65 32

b. Upper right 65 32

c. Lower left 65 32

d. Lower right 65 32

Nos. 707-708, C204-C205 (4 blocks of 4) 5.75 3.00

Publicity for the 12th Central American and Caribbean Games, Santo Domingo, Summer 1974.

Christ Carrying the Cross
A213

Design: 6c, Belfry of Church of Our Lady of Carmen (vert.).

1973, Apr. 18 Litho. *Perf. 10½*

709 A213 2c multicolored 10 6

710 " 6c " 20 15

Holy Week, 1973. See No. C206.

WMO Emblem, Weather Satellite, "Weather"
A214

Mask, Cibao
A215

1973, Aug. 10 Litho. *Perf. 13½x13*

711 A214 6c magenta & multi. 18 12

Centenary of international meteorological cooperation. See No. C208.

1973, Oct. 12 Litho. *Perf. 10½*

Multicolored

712 A215 1c *Maguey drum* (horiz.) 3 3

713 " 2c *Carved amber* (horiz.) 6 4

714 " 4c *shown* 12 8

715 " 6c *Pottery* 18 12

Nos. 712-715, C210-C211 (6) 90 62

Opening of Museum of Mankind in Santo Domingo.

Nativity
A216

Design: 6c, Stained glass window (vert.).

Perf. 13½x13, 13x13½

1973, Nov. 26

716 A216 2c blk., bl. & yellow 8 6

717 " 6c rose & multi. 20 15

Christmas 1973. See No. C212.
No. 717 exists imperf.

Dominican Scout Emblem
A217

Design: 5c, Scouts and flag.

1973, Dec. 7 Lithographed *Perf. 12*

Size: 35x35mm.

718 A217 1c ultra. & multi. 3 3

Size: 26x36mm.

719 A217 5c black & multi. 15 10

50th anniversary of Dominican Republic Boy Scouts. See No. C213.

Sports Palace, Basketball Players
A218

Design: 6c, Bicyclist and race track.

1974, Feb. 25 Litho. *Perf. 13½*

720 A218 2c red brn. & multi. 8 6

721 " 6c yellow & multi. 20 15

12th Central American and Caribbean Games, Santo Domingo, 1974. See Nos. C214-C215.

Bell Tower, Cathedral of Santo Domingo
A219

Mater Dolorosa
A220

1974, June 27 Litho. *Perf. 13½*

722 A219 2c multicolored 8 6

723 A220 6c " 20 15

Holy Week 1974. See No. C216.

Francisco del Rosario Sanchez Bridge—A221

1974, July 12 *Perf. 12*

724 A221 6c multicolored 18 12

See No. C217.

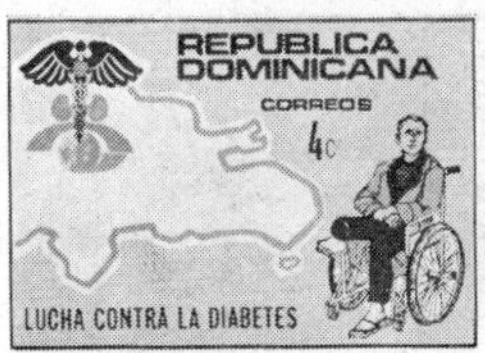

Map, Emblem and Patient A222

Design: 5c, Map of Dominican Republic, diabetics' emblem and pancreas.

1974, Aug. 22 Litho. *Perf. 13*

725 A222 4c blue & multi. 12 8
726 " 5c yel. grn. & multi. 12 10

Fight against diabetes. See Nos. C218–C219.

Train and UPU Emblem A223

Design: 6c, Mail coach and UPU emblem.

1974, Oct. 9 Litho. *Perf. 13½*

727 A223 2c blue & multi. 6 4
728 " 6c brown & multi. 18 12

Centenary of Universal Postal Union. See Nos. C220–C221a.

Golfers A224

Design: 2c, Championship emblem and badge of Dominican Golf Association (horiz.).

Perf. 13x13½, 13½x13

1974, Oct. 24

729 A224 2c yellow & black 8 6
730 " 6c blue & multi. 20 15

World Amateur Golf Championships. See Nos. C222–C223.

Christmas Decorations A225

Virgin and Child A226

1974, Dec. 3 Litho. *Perf. 12*

731 A225 2c multicolored 8 6
732 A226 6c " 20 15

Christmas 1974. See No. C224.

Tomatoes, FAO Emblem A227

1974, Dec. 5

Multicolored

733 A227 2c *shown* 6 4
734 " 3c *Avocados* 9 6
735 " 5c *Coconuts* 15 10

World Food Program, 10th anniversary. See No. C225.

Fernando A. Defillo A228

Tower, Our Lady of the Rosary Convent A229

1975, Feb. 14 Litho. *Perf. 13½x13*

736 A228 1c dull brown 3 3
737 " 6c dull green 18 12

Dr. Fernando A. Defillo (1874–1949), physician.

1975, Mar. 26 Litho. *Perf. 13½*

Design: 2c, Jesus saying "I am the Resurrection and the Life."

738 A229 2c brown & multi. 6 4
739 " 6c multicolored 18 12

Holy Week 1975. See No. C226.

Hands (Steel Beams) with Symbols of Agriculture, Industry A230

1975, May 19 Litho. *Perf. 10½x10*

740 A230 6c dull blue & multi. 18 12

16th Assembly of the Governors of the International Development Bank, Santo Domingo, May 1975. See No. C228.

Satellite Tracking Station A231

1975, June 21 Litho. *Perf. 13½*

741 A231 5c multicolored 15 10

Opening of first earth satellite tracking station in Dominican Republic. See No. C229.

Apollo A232

Design: 4c, Soyuz.

1975, July 24

Size: 35x25mm.

742 A232 1c blue & multi. 3 3
743 " 4c vio. blue & multi. 12 8

Apollo Soyuz space test project (Russo-American cooperation), launching July 15; link-up, July 17. See No. C230.

Father Rafael C. Castellanos A233

1975, Aug. 6 Litho. *Perf. 12*

744 A233 6c brown & buff 18 12

Father Rafael C. Castellanos (1875–1934), first Apostolic Administrator in Dominican Republic, birth centenary.

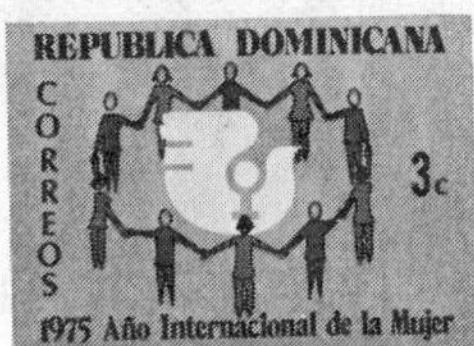

Women and Men Around IWY Emblem A234

1975, Aug. 6 *Perf. 13*

745 A234 3c orange & multi. 9 6

International Women's Year 1975.

Guacanagarix A235

Basketball A236

Indian Chiefs: 2c, Guarionex. 3c, Caonabo. 4c, Bohechio. 5c, Cayacoa. 6c, Anacona (woman). 9c, Hatuey.

1975, Sept. 27 Litho. *Perf. 12*

746 A235 1c yellow & multi. 3 3
747 " 2c salmon & multi. 6 4
748 " 3c vio. bl. & multi. 9 6
749 " 4c green & multi. 12 8
750 " 5c blue & multi. 15 10
751 " 6c violet & multi. 18 12
752 " 9c rose & multi. 27 18
Nos. 746-752, C231-C233 (10) 1.65 1.11

1975, Oct. 24 Litho. *Perf. 12*

Design: 6c, Baseball and Games' emblem.

753 A236 2c pink & multi. 8 6
754 " 6c orange & multi. 20 15

7th Pan-American Games, Mexico City, Oct. 13–26. See Nos. C234–C235.

Carolers A237

Design: 6c, Dominican nativity with farmers and shepherds.

1975, Dec. 12 Litho. *Perf. 13x13½*

755 A237 2c yellow & multi. 6 4
756 " 6c blue & multi. 18 12

Christmas 1975. See No. C236.

Abudefdul Marginatus—A238

1976, Jan. 23 Litho. *Perf. 13*

Multicolored

757 A238 10c *shown* 30 20
758 " 10c *Snakefish* 30 20
759 " 10c *Squirrelfish* 30 20
760 " 10c *Angelfish* 30 20
761 " 10c *Porgy* 30 20
Nos. 757-761 (5) 1.50 1.00

Nos. 757–761 printed se-tenant.

Ascension, by J. Priego A239

"Separacion Dominicana" and Adm. Cambiaso A240

Design: 2c, Mary Magdalene, by Enrique Godoy.

1976, Apr. 14 Litho. *Perf. 13½*

762 A239 2c blue & multi. 8 6
763 " 6c yellow & multi. 20 10

Holy Week 1976. See No. C238.

1976, Apr. 15 *Perf. 13½x13*

764 A240 20c multicolored 60 40

Naval Battle off Tortuga, Apr. 15, 1844.

Maps of US and Dominican Republic A241

Design: 9c, Maps within cogwheels.

1976, May 29 Litho. *Perf. 13½*

765 A241 6c vio. bl. & multi. 18 8
766 " 9c " " 28 12

American Bicentennial. See Nos. C239–C240.

Flags of Dominican Republic and Spain
A242

1976, May 31

767 A242 6c multicolored 18 8

Visit of King Juan Carlos I and Queen Sofia of Spain. See No. C241.

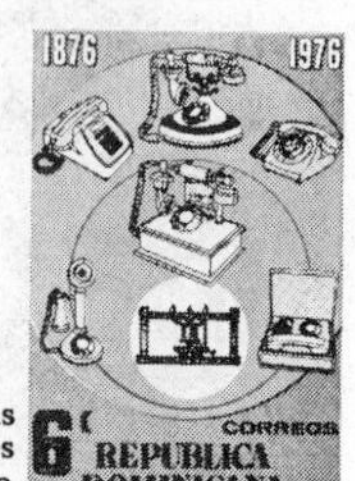

Various Telephones
A243

1976, July 15 ***Perf. 12x12½***

768 A243 6c multicolored 18 8

Centenary of first telephone call by Alexander Graham Bell, Mar. 10, 1876. See No. C242.

Vision of Duarte, by Luis Desangles
A244

Juan Pablo Duarte, by Rhadames Mejia
A245

1976, July 20 Litho. ***Perf. 13x13½***

769 A244 2c multicolored 6 3

Perf. 13½

770 A245 6c multicolored 18 8

Juan Pablo Duarte, liberation hero, death centenary. See Nos. C243–C244.

Fire Hydrant
A246

Design: 6c, Firemen's emblem.

1976, Sept. 13 Litho. ***Perf. 12***

771 A246 4c multicolored 12 6
772 " 6c " 18 8

Honoring firemen. Nos. 771–772 inscribed "Corrreos". See No. C245.

Radio and Atom Symbols
A247

1976, Oct. 8 Lithographed ***Perf. 13½***

773 A247 6c red & black 18 8

Dominican Radio Club, 50th anniversary. See No. C246.

Spain, Central and South America, Galleon
A248

1976, Oct. 22 Litho. ***Perf. 13½***

774 A248 6c multicolored 18 8

Spanish heritage. See No. C247.

Boxing and Montreal Emblem
A249

Design: 3c, Weight lifting.

1976, Oct. 22 ***Perf. 12***

775 A249 2c blue & multi. 6 3
776 " 3c multicolored 9 4

21st Olympic Games, Montreal, Canada, July 17–Aug. 1. See Nos. C248–C249.

Virgin and Child
A250

Three Kings
A251

1976, Dec. 8 Litho. ***Perf. 13½***

777 A250 2c multicolored 6 3
778 A251 6c " 18 12

Christmas 1976. See No. C250.

Cable Car and Beach Scenes
A252

1977, Jan. 7

779 A252 6c multicolored 18 12

Tourist publicity. See Nos. C251–C253.

Championship Emblem
A253

1977, Mar. 4 Litho. ***Perf. 13½***

780 A253 3c rose & multi. 10 6
781 " 5c yellow & multi. 15 10

10th Central American and Caribbean Children's and Young People's Swimming Championships, Santo Domingo. See Nos. C254–C255.

Christ Carrying Cross
A254

Design: 6c, Head with crown of thorns.

1977, Apr. 18 Litho. ***Perf. 13½x13***

782 A254 2c multicolored 6 3
783 " 6c black & rose 18 8

Holy Week 1977. See No. C256.

Doves, Lions Emblem
A255

1977, May 6 ***Perf. 13½x13***

784 A255 2c lt. blue & multi. 6 3
785 " 6c salmon & multi. 18 8

12th annual Dominican Republic Lions Convention. See No. C257.

Battle Scene
A256

1977, June 15 Litho. ***Perf. 13x13½***

786 A256 20c multicolored 60 40

Dominican Navy.

Water Lily
A257

Designs: 4c, "Flor de Mayo" (orchid). 6c, Sebesten.

1977, Aug. 19 Litho. ***Perf. 12***

787 A257 2c multicolored 6 3
788 " 4c " 12 6
789 " 6c " 18 8
Nos. 787-789, C259-C260 (5) 1.57 97

National Botanical Garden.

Chart and Computers
A258

1977 Litho. ***Perf. 13***

790 A258 6c multicolored 18 8

7th Interamerican Statistics Conference. See No. C261.

Solenodon Paradoxus
A259

Design: 20c, Iguana and Congress emblem.

1977, Dec. 29 Litho. ***Perf. 13***

791 A259 6c multicolored 18 8
792 " 20c " 60 40

8th Pan-American Veterinary and Zootechnical Congress. See Nos. C262–C263.

Main Gate, Casa del Cordon, 1503
A260

Crown of Thorns, Tools at the Cross
A261

1978, Jan. 19 ***Perf. 13x13½***

Size: 26x36mm.

793 A260 6c multicolored 18 8

Spanish heritage. See No. C264.

1978, Mar. 21 Litho. ***Perf. 12***

Design: 6c, Head of Jesus with crown of thorns.

Size: 22x33mm.

794 A261 2c multicolored 6 3
795 " 6c slate 18 8

Holy Week 1978. See Nos. C265–C266.

Cardinal Octavio A. Beras Rojas
A262

Pres. Manuel de Troncoso
A263

1978, May 5 Litho. ***Perf. 13***

796 A262 6c multicolored 18 8

First Cardinal from Dominican Republic, consecrated May 24, 1976. See No. C268.

1978, June 12 Litho. ***Perf. 13½***

797 A263 2c blk., rose & brn. 6 3
798 " 6c blk., gray & brn. 18 8

Manuel de Jesus Troncoso de la Concha (1878–1955), president of Dominican Republic 1940–1942.

Father Juan N. Zegri y Moreno
A264

1978, July 11 Litho. ***Perf. 13x13½***

799	A264	6c multicolored	18	8

Congregation of the Merciful Sisters of Charity, centenary. See No. C273.

Boxing and Games' Emblem
A265

Design: 6c, Weight lifting.

1978, July 21 ***Perf. 12***

800	A265	2c multicolored	6	3
801	"	6c "	18	8

13th Central American and Caribbean Games, Medellin, Colombia. See Nos. C274–C275.

Sun over Landscape
A266

Ships of Columbus, Map of Dominican Republic
A267

Design: 6c, Sun over beach and boat.

1978, Sept. 12 Litho. ***Perf. 12***

802	A266	2c multicolored	6	3
803	"	6c "	18	8

Tourist publicity. See Nos. C280–C281.

1978, Oct. 12 Litho. ***Perf. 13½***

804	A267	2c multicolored	6	3

Spanish heritage. See No. C282.

Dove, Lamp, Poinsettia
A268

Design: 6c, Dominican family and star (vert.).

1978, Dec. 5 Litho. ***Perf. 12***

805	A268	2c multicolored	6	3
806	"	6c "	18	8

Christmas 1978. See No. C284.

Questions?
Comment?
Corrections?
Help us serve you better. Let us know what you think by filling out our questionnaire at the front of this book.

Want more information from an advertiser? Use the handy Reader Service Card in back of the yellow pages.

SEMI-POSTAL STAMPS

Nos. 474-478 Surcharged in Red

+2¢

Engraved and Lithographed.

1957, Feb. 8 ***Perf. 11½*** **Unwmkd.**

Flags in National Colors

B1 A117 1c+2c brown, light blue, violet & maroon 10 10
B2 " 2c+2c dark brown, light blue & violet 10 10
B3 " 3c+2c red lilac & red 15 15
B4 " 5c+2c red orange & violet 20 20
B5 " 7c+2c green & violet 30 30
Nos. B1-B5, CB1-CB3 (8) 2.40 2.40

The surtax was to aid Hungarian refugees. A similar 25c surcharge was applied to the miniature sheets described in the footnote following No. 478. Price, 2 sheets, perf. and imperf., $17.50.

Nos. 479-483 Surcharged in Red Orange

1957, Sept. 9 **Photo.** ***Perf. 13½***

Flags in National Colors

B6 A118 1c+2c brown, & bright blue 18 15
B7 " 2c+2c orange verm. & dark blue 25 20
B8 " 3c+2c dark blue 30 30
B9 " 5c+2c olive & dark blue 45 30
B10 " 7c+2c rose brown & dark blue 55 40
Nos. B6-B10, CB4-CB6 (8) 3.58 3.15

Issued to commemorate the centenary of the birth of Lord Baden Powell and the 50th anniversary of the Scout Movement. The surtax was for the Dominican Republic Boy Scouts.

A similar 5c surcharge was applied to the miniature sheets described in the footnote following No. 483. Price, 4 sheets, perf. and imperf., medal and flag, $35.

Types of Olympic Regular Issue, 1957, Surcharged in Carmine

+2¢ +2¢

REFUGIADOS REFUGIADOS
a *b*

1958, May 26 **Engr. & Litho.**

Flags in National Colors

Pink Paper

B11 A119 (*a*) 1c+2c red brn. 25 25
B12 " (*b*) 1c+2c red brn. 25 25
B13 A120 (*a*) 2c+2c gray brown 30 30
B14 " (*b*) 2c+2c gray brown 30 30
B15 A119 (*a*) 3c+2c violet 30 30
B16 " (*b*) 3c+2c violet 30 30
B17 A120 (*a*) 5c+2c red org. 40 40
B18 " (*b*) 5c+2c red org. 40 40
B19 A119 (*a*) 7c+2c Prussian green 50 50
B20 " (*b*) 7c+2c Prussian green 50 50
Nos. B11-B20, CB7-CB12 (16) 6.50 6.50

The surtax was for the United Nations Relief and Works Agency for Palestine Refugees.

A similar 5c surcharge, plus marginal United Nations emblem and "UNRWA," was applied to the miniature sheets described in the footnote following No. 488. Price, 4 sheets, perf. and imperf., $30.

Nos. 501-505 Surcharged

Perf. 13½

1959, Apr. 13 **Photo.** **Unwmkd.**

Flags in National Colors

B21 A125 1c+2c rose, indigo & ultramarine 35 35
B22 " 2c+2c brown & blue 45 45
B23 " 3c+2c gray, violet, black & buff 50 50
B24 " 5c+2c rose, dark blue, brown & red 60 60
B25 " 7c+2c light brown, dark blue & red 65 65
Nos. B21-B25, CB13-CB15 (8) 5.40 5.40

International Geophysical Year, 1957-58.

A similar 5c surcharge was applied to the miniature sheets described in the footnote following No. 505. Price, 2 sheets, perf. and imperf., $22.50.

Type of 1957 Surcharged in Red

Engraved and Lithographed

1959, Sept. 10 ***Imperf.*** **Unwmkd.**

Flags in National Colors

B26 A117 1c+2c brown, light blue, violet & maroon 15 15
B27 " 2c+2c dark brown, lt. blue & violet 18 18
B28 " 3c+2c red lilac & red 20 20
B29 " 5c+2c red orange & violet 25 25
B30 " 7c+2c green & violet 35 35
Nos. B26-B30, CB16-CB18 (8) 2.58 2.58

3rd Pan American Games, Chicago, Aug. 27-Sept. 7, 1959.

World Refugee Year Issue

Nos. 522-524 Surcharged in Red

1960, Apr. 7 **Litho.** ***Perf. 12½***

Center in Gray

B31 A135 5c+5c red brown & yellow green 25 25
B32 " 9c+5c carmine & light blue 30 30
B33 " 13c+5c orange & green 60 60
Nos. B31-B33, CB19-CB20 (5) 2.00 2.00

Issued to publicize World Refugee Year, July 1, 1959-June 30, 1960. The surtax was for aid to refugees.

Souvenir sheets exist perf. and imperf., containing one each of Nos. B31-B33 and CB19-CB20. Size: 152x99mm. Black marginal inscription. Price, 2 sheets, perf. and imperf., $10.

Nos. 525-529 Surcharged: "XV ANIVERSARIO DE LA UNESCO +2c"

1962, Jan. 8 **Photo.** ***Perf. 13½***

Flags in National Colors

B34 A136 1c+2c red, yellow green & black 8 8
B35 " 2c+2c orange, greenish blue & brown 10 10
B36 " 3c+2c henna brown & blue 12 12
B37 " 5c+2c brown & ultra. 18 18
B38 A136 7c+2c green, blue & rose brown 20 20
Nos. B34-B38, CB21-CB23 (8) 2.08 2.08

Issued to commemorate the 15th anniversary (in 1961) of UNESCO (U.N. Educational, Scientific and Cultural Organization).

A similar 5c surcharge was applied to the miniature sheets described in the footnote following No. 529. Price, 2 sheets, perf. and imperf., $7.50.

Anti-Malaria Type of Regular Issue, 1962

1962, Apr. 29 **Litho.** ***Perf. 12***

B39 A141 10c+2c br. pink & red lilac 30 25
B40 " 20c+2c pale brown & brown 50 40

Issued for the World Health Organization drive to eradicate malaria.

Type of Regular Issue, 1963

1963, Apr. 15 ***Perf. 11½*** **Unwmkd.**

Banner in Dark Blue & Red

B41 A148 2c+1c green 6 6
B42 " 5c+2c brt. rose lilac 18 15
B43 " 9c+2c orange 30 30

Issued for the "Freedom from Hunger" campaign of the U.N. Food and Agriculture organization. A souvenir sheet contains three imperf. stamps similar to Nos. B41-B43. Dark blue marginal inscription. Size: 172x102mm. Price, $1.25.

Nos. 591-593 Surcharged

1964, March 8 ***Perf. 12½***

B44 A153 3c+2c pale pink & vermilion 12 12
B45 " 6c+2c pale blue & ultramarine 18 18
B46 " 9c+2c pale rose & red brown 24 24
Nos. B44-B46, CB26-CB27 (5) 1.19 1.19

Issued to publicize the UNESCO world campaign to save historic monuments in Nubia.

Nos. 622-626 Surcharged

PRO DAMNIFICADOS CICLON INES

1966, Dec. 9 **Litho.** ***Perf. 12½***

Size: 31x21mm.

B47 A164 1c+2c multicolored 6 5
B48 " 2c+2c " 8 6
B49 " 3c+2c " 10 8
B50 " 6c+4c " 20 16
B51 " 8c+4c " 24 20
Nos. B47-B51, CB28-CB30 (8) 4.43 4.30

The surtax was for victims of hurricane Inez.

AIR POST STAMPS

Map of Hispaniola—AP1

Perf. 11½

1928, May 31 **Litho.** **Unwmkd.**

C1 AP1 10c deep ultra. 6.00 3.25

1930

C2 AP1 10c ochre 4.00 3.25
a. Vertical pair imperf. between 800.00
C3 " 15c scarlet 7.00 4.50
C4 " 20c dull green 3.25 50
C5 " 30c violet 7.00 5.00

Nos. C2 to C5 have only "CENTAVOS" in lower panel. Dates of issue: 10c, 20c, Jan. 24; 15c, 30c, Feb. 14.

1930

C6 AP1 10c light blue 1.75 1.00
C7 " 15c blue green 4.00 1.25
C8 AP1 20c yellow brown 4.00 60
a. Imperf. vertically (pair) 400.00
C9 " 30c chocolate 7.00 1.75

Dates of issue: 10c, 15c, 20c, Sept.; 30c, Oct.

Batwing Sundial Erected in 1753
AP2

1931-33 ***Perf. 12***

C10 AP2 10c carmine 4.00 60
C11 " 10c light blue ('32) 2.00 55
C12 " 10c dk. grn. ('33) 6.50 2.25
C13 " 15c rose lilac 3.50 60
C14 " 20c dark blue 6.50 1.50
a. Numerals reading up at left and down at right 6.75 2.25
b. Imperf., pair 300.00
C15 " 30c green 3.00 40
C16 " 50c red brown 6.50 90
C17 " 1p deep orange 11.00 3.00
Nos. C10-C17 (8) 43.00 9.80

Issue dates: Aug. 16, 1931; July 2, 1932; May 28, 1933.

Airplane and Ozama Fortress
AP3

1933, Nov. 20

C18 AP3 10c dark blue 4.00 65

Airplane and Trujillo Bridge
AP4

1934, Sept. 20

C19 AP4 10c dark blue 3.50 65

Symbolic of Flight
AP5

1935, Apr. 29

C20 AP5 10c light blue & dark blue 2.75 60

AP6

1936, Feb. 11 ***Perf. 11½***

C21 AP6 10c dark blue & turquoise blue 3.25 60

Allegory of Flight
AP7

1936, Oct. 17

C22 AP7 10c dark blue, blue & turquoise blue 3.00 45

Macorís Airport
AP8

1937, Oct. 22

C23 AP8 10c green 1.25 18

Fleet of Columbus
AP9

Air Fleet
AP10

Proposed Columbus Lighthouse
AP11

1937, Nov. 9 ***Perf. 12***

C24 AP9 10c rose red 2.50 1.50
C25 AP10 15c purple 2.00 1.00
C26 AP11 20c dark blue & light blue 2.00 1.00
C27 AP10 25c red violet 3.00 1.25
C28 AP11 30c yellow green 2.75 1.00
C29 AP10 50c brown 5.50 1.50
C30 AP11 75c dark olive green 12.50 12.00
C31 AP9 1p orange 8.50 3.00
Nos. C24-C31 (8) 38.75 22.25

Issued in commemoration of the goodwill flight to all American countries by the planes "Colon", "Pinta", "Niña" and "Santa Maria".

Pan American Clipper
AP12

1938, July 30

C32 AP12 10c green 1.25 20

Trylon and Perisphere, Plane and Proposed Columbus Lighthouse—AP13

1939, Apr. 30

C33 AP13 10c green & light green 1.50 75

New York World's Fair.

Airplane
AP14

1939, Oct. 18

C34 AP14 10c green & deep green 1.75 25
a. Pair, imperf. between 500.00

Proposed Columbus Lighthouse, Plane and Caravels—AP15

Christopher Columbus and Proposed Lighthouse
AP16

Proposed Lighthouse
AP17

Christopher Columbus
AP18

Caravel—AP19

1940, Oct. 12

C35 AP15 10c sapphire & light blue 75 60
C36 AP16 15c orange brown & brown 1.15 90
C37 AP17 20c rose red & red 1.15 90
C38 AP18 25c bright red lilac & red violet 1.15 50
C39 AP19 50c green & light green 2.25 1.80
Nos. C35-C39 (5) 6.45 4.70

Discovery of America by Columbus and proposed Columbus memorial lighthouse in Dominican Republic.

Posts and Telegraph Building, San Cristobal
AP20

1941, Feb. 21

C40 AP20 10c bright red lilac & pale lilac rose 65 25

Globe, Wing and Letter
AP21

1942, Feb. 13

C41 AP21 10c dk. vio. brn. 80 8
C42 " 75c deep orange 5.00 3.00

Plane
AP22

1943, Sept. 1

C43 AP22 10c bright red lilac 60 12
C44 " 20c deep blue & blue 70 18
C45 " 25c yellow olive 7.00 3.75

Plane, Flag, Coat of Arms and Torch of Liberty
AP23

1944, Feb. 27 ***Perf. 11½***

Flag in Gray, Dark Blue, Carmine

C46 AP23 10c multicolored 60 12
C47 " 20c " 75 20
C48 " 1p " 3.50 2.50

Centenary of Independence. See No. 407 for souvenir sheet listing.

Communications Building, Ciudad Trujillo
AP24

1944, Nov. 12 **Litho.** ***Perf. 12***

C49 AP24 9c yel. grn. & blue 30 12
C50 " 13c dull brown & rose carmine 35 8
C51 " 25c orange & dull red 60 12
b. Vert. pair, imperf. between 75.00
C52 " 30c black & ultra. 1.25 1.10

Twenty booklets of 100 (25 panes of 4) of the 25c were issued. Single panes are unknown to experts.

Emblem of Communications
AP25

1945, Sept. 1

Center in Dark Blue and Carmine.

C53 AP25 7c deep yellow green 30 35
C54 " 12c red orange 35 25
C55 " 13c deep blue 45 20
C56 " 25c orange brown 90 30

AP26

Flags and National Anthem
AP27

Lithographed.

1946, Feb. 27 ***Perf. 12*** **Unwmkd.**

Center in Dark Blue, Deep Carmine and Black.

C57 AP26 10c carmine 70 50
C58 " 15c blue 1.25 90
C59 " 20c chocolate 1.50 90
C60 " 35c orange 1.75 80
C61 AP27 1p green, yellow grn. & citron 15.00 12.50
Nos. C57-C61 (5) 20.20 15.60

Nos. C57-C61 exist imperf.

Map of Hispaniola
AP28

1946, Aug. 4

C62 AP28 10c multicolored 50 20
C63 " 13c " 85 20

See note after No. 421.

Waterfall of Jimenoa
AP29

1947, Mar. 18 Lithographed

Center Multicolored.

C64 AP29 18c light blue 75 75
C65 " 23c carmine 85 85
C66 " 50c red violet 1.25 70
C67 " 75c chocolate 1.75 1.35

Executive Palace
AP30

1948, Feb. 27

C68 AP30 37c orange brown 1.00 1.00
C69 " 1p orange yellow 3.00 2.00

Church of San Francisco Ruins
AP31

Las Carreras Monument
AP32

1949 *Perf. 11½* Unwmkd.

C70 AP31 7c olive green & pale olive green 20 15
C71 " 10c orange brown & buff 25 12
C72 " 15c bright rose & pale pink 75 35
C73 " 20c green & pale green 1.00 70

Issue dates: 10c, Apr. 4; others, Apr. 13.

1949, Aug. 10

C74 AP32 10c red & pink 35 8

Issued to commemorate the centenary of the Battle of Las Carreras.

Hotel Montana
AP33

Design: 37c, Hotel San Cristobal.

1950, Sept.

C75 AP33 12c dark blue & blue 40 12
C76 " 37c carmine & pink 2.50 2.00

Map, Plane and Caduceus
AP34

1950, Oct. 2

C77 AP34 12c orange brown & yellow 60 15

The 13th Pan-American Health Conference. Exists imperf.

Dr. Salvador B. Gautier Hospital
AP35

1952, Aug.

C78 AP35 23c deep blue 85 80
C79 " 29c carmine 1.75 1.35

Columbus Lighthouse and Plane
AP36

Ano Mariano Initials in Monogram
AP37

1953, Jan. 6 Engraved *Perf. 13*

C80 AP36 12c ochre 35 25
C81 " 14c dark blue 40 35
C82 " 20c black brown 65 60
C83 " 23c deep plum 80 65
C84 " 25c dark blue 85 70
C85 " 29c deep green 1.00 70
C86 " 1p red brown 3.00 2.75
a. Miniature sheet of 10 10.00 10.00
Nos. C80–C86 (7) 7.05 6.00

No. C86a is lithographed and contains one each of Nos. 450–452 and C80–C86, in slightly different shades. Sheet measures 190x130mm. and is imperf. with simulated perforations printed in dark blue. No marginal inscriptions.

A miniature sheet similar to No. C86a, but measuring 200x163mm. and in folder, exists. Price, $60.

1954, Aug. 21 Litho. *Perf. 11½*

C87 AP37 8c claret 25 15
C88 " 11c blue 35 10
C89 " 33c brown orange 1.00 65

Marian Year. Nos. C87–C89 exist imperf.

Rotary Type of Regular Issue, 1955.

1955, Feb. 23 *Perf. 12*

C90 A110 11c rose red 40 20

Rotary International, 50th anniversary.

Flags
AP39

Portraits of General Hector B. Trujillo: 25c, In civilian clothes. 33c, In uniform.

Engraved.

1955, May 16 *Perf. 13½x13*

C91 AP39 11c blue, yellow & carmine 45 12
C92 " 25c rose violet 70 40
C93 " 33c orange brown 1.00 60

The center of No. C91 is lithographed. Issued to commemorate the 25th anniversary of the inauguration of the Trujillo era.

Fair Type of Regular Issue, 1955

1955, Dec. 20 *Perf. 13* Unwmkd.

C94 A112 11c vermilion 40 12

Issued to publicize the International Fair of Peace and Brotherhood in Ciudad Trujillo, Dec. 1955.

ICAO Type of Regular Issue, 1956.

1956, Apr. 6 Litho. *Perf. 12½*

C95 A114 11c ultramarine 35 12

Issued to commemorate the third Caribbean conference of the International Civil Aviation Organization.

Tree Type of Regular Issue, 1956.

Design: 13c, Mahogany tree.

1956, Dec. 8 Litho. *Perf. 11½x12*

C96 A115 13c orange & green 45 18

Issued to publicize the reforestation program.

Type of Regular Issue, 1957.

Olympic Winners and Flags: 11c, Paavo Nurmi, Finland. 16c, Ugo Frigerio, Italy. 17c, Mildred Didrikson ("Didrickson" on stamp), United States.

Engraved and Lithographed.

1957, Jan. 24 *Perf. 11½* Unwmkd.

Flags in National Colors

C97 A117 11c ultramarine & red orange 28 25
C98 " 16c carmine & light green 40 40
C99 " 17c black, violet & red 50 50

Issued to commemorate the 16th Olympic Games, Melbourne, Nov. 22–Dec. 8, 1956. Exist imperf.

Souvenir sheets of 3 exist, perf. and imperf., containing one each of Nos. C97–C99. Sheets measure 169x86mm., with Olympic flag and motto on left margin. Price, 2 sheets, perf. and imperf., $5.

Type of Regular Issue, 1957.

Olympic Winners and Flags: 11c, Robert Morrow, United States, 100 & 200 meter dash. 16c, Chris Brasher, England, steeplechase. 17c, A. Ferreira Da Silva, Brazil, hop, step and jump.

1957, July 18 Photo. *Perf. 13½*

Flags in National Colors

C100 A118 11c yellow green & dark blue 30 30
C101 " 16c lilac & dark blue 40 40
C102 " 17c brown & blue green 45 45

1956 Olympic winners. Exist imperf.

See note on miniature sheets following No. 483.

Types of Regular Issue, 1957.

Olympic Winners and Flags: 11c, Hans Winkler, Germany, individual jumping. 16c, Alfred Oerter, United States, discus throw. 17c, Shirley Strickland, Australia, 800 meter hurdles.

Engraved and Lithographed.

Flags in National Colors

1957, Nov. 12 *Perf. 13½* Unwmkd.

C103 A119 11c ultramarine 30 25
C104 A120 16c rose carmine 45 40
C105 A119 17c claret 50 45

1956 Olympic winners. Exist imperf.

Miniature sheets of 3 exist, perf. and imperf., containing one each of Nos. C103–C105. Sheets have no marginal inscriptions. Price, 2 sheets, perf. and imperf., $5.50.

Type of Regular Issue, 1958.

Olympic Winners and Flags: 11c, Charles Jenkins, 400 & 800 meter run, and Thomas Courtney, 1,600 meter relay, United States. 16c, Field hockey team, India. 17c, Yachting team, Sweden.

Photogravure.

1958, Oct. 30 *Perf. 13½* Unwmkd.

Flags in National Colors

C106 A125 11c blue, olive & brown 35 35
C107 " 16c light green, orange & dark blue 45 45
C108 " 17c vermilion, blue & yellow 50 50

1956 Olympic winners. Exist imperf.

Miniature sheets of 3 exist, perf. and imperf., containing one each of Nos. C106–C108. Size: 140x78½mm. Price, 2 sheets, perf. and imperf., $3.

Fair Type of Regular Issue, 1958.

1958, Dec. 9 Litho. *Perf. 12½*

C109 A127 9c gray 30 20
C110 " 25c light violet 75 45
a. Souvenir Sheet of 3, imperf. 1.50 1.25

No. C110a contains one each of Nos. C109-C110 and 507 and measures 137x72½mm. Black marginal inscription.

Issued for the Universal and International Exposition at Brussels.

Polo Type of Regular Issue, 1959

Design: 11c, Dominican polo team.

1959, May 15 *Perf. 12*

C111 A130 11c orange 45 40

Jamaica-Dominican Republic polo match at Ciudad Trujillo.

"San Cristobal" Plane
AP42

Lithographed.

1960, Feb. 25 *Perf. 11½* Unwmkd.

C112 AP42 13c orange, blue, green & gray 45 25

Dominican Civil Aviation.

Children and WRY Emblem
AP43

1960, Apr. 7 *Perf. 12½*

C113 AP43 10c plum, gray & green 55 45
C114 " 13c gray & green 65 55

Issued to publicize World Refugee Year, July 1, 1959–June 30, 1960.

Olympic Type of Regular Issue.

Olympic Winners: 11c, Pat McCormick, U.S.A., diving. 16c, Mithat Bayrack, Turkey, welterweight wrestling. 17c, Ursula Happe, Germany, 200 meter breast stroke.

Photogravure

1960, Sept. 14 *Perf. 13½*

Flags in National Colors

C115 A136 11c blue, gray & brown 30 25
C116 " 16c red, brown & olive 40 35
C117 " 17c black, blue & ochre 45 40

Issued to commemorate the 17th Olympic Games, Rome, Aug. 25–Sept. 11. Exist imperf.

Miniature sheets of 3 exist, perf. and imperf., containing one each of Nos. C115–C117, with no marginal inscription. Size: 160x76mm. Price, 2 sheets, perf. and imperf., $3.75.

Coffee-Cacao Type of Regular Issue, 1961

1961, Dec. 30 Litho. *Perf. 12½*

C118 A140 13c orange verm. 40 40
C119 " 33c bright yellow 85 85

Exist imperf.

Anti-Malaria Type of Regular Issue, 1962

1962, Apr. 29 *Perf. 12* Unwmkd.

C120 A141 13c pink & red 35 30

C121 A141 33c orange & deep orange 75 75

Issued for the World Health Organization drive to eradicate malaria.

Type of Regular Issue, 1962.

Designs: 13c, Broken fetters and laurel. 50c, Flag, torch and inscription.

1962, May 30 ***Perf. 12½***

C122 A142 13c brn., yel., olive, ultra. & red 40 30
C123 " 50c rose lilac, ultra. & red 1.50 1.00

First anniversary, end of Trujillo era. No. C122 exists imperf.

UPAE Type of Regular Issue, 1962

1962, Oct. 23 ***Perf. 12½***

C124 A146 13c bright blue 40 25
C125 " 22c dull red brn. 60 50

Issued to commemorate the 50th anniversary of the founding of the Postal Union of the Americas and Spain, UPAE. Exist imperf.

Nouel Type of Regular Issue, 1962

Design: Frame altered with rosary and cross surrounding portrait.

1962, Dec. 18

C126 A147 13c bl. & pale bl. 40 25
C127 " 25c violet & pale violet 65 55
a. Souv. sheet 1.25 1.25

Birth centenary of Archbishop Adolfo Alejandro Nouel, president of Republic in 1911. Exist imperf.

No. C127a contains one each of Nos. C126–C127 imperf. Pale violet margin with blue inscription. Size: 153x93mm.

Sanchez, Duarte, Mella
AP44

1963, July 7 Litho. ***Perf. 11½x12***

C128 AP44 15c orange 40 30

Issued to commemorate the 120th anniversary of separation from Haiti.

World Map
AP45

1963, Oct. 25 ***Perf. 12½*** **Unwmkd.**

C129 AP45 10c gray & car. 40 35

Centenary of International Red Cross. Exists imperf.

Human Rights Type of Regular Issue, 1963

1963, Dec. 10 **Lithographed**

C130 A152 7c fawn & red brn. 30 25
C131 " 10c light blue & blue 35 25

15th anniversary, Universal Declaration of Human Rights. Exist imperf.

Ramses II Battling the Hittites (from Abu Simbel)
AP46

1964, March 8 ***Perf. 12½***

C132 AP46 10c bright violet 35 25
C133 " 13c yellow 40 35

UNESCO world campaign to save historic monuments in Nubia. Exist imperf.

Striated Woodpecker—AP47

1964, June 8 **Lithographed**

C134 AP47 10c multicolored 40 30

Type of Space Issue, 1964

Designs: 7c, Rocket leaving earth. 10c, Space capsule orbiting earth.

1964, July 28 ***Perf. 12½*** **Unwmkd.**

C135 A156 7c bright green 40 25
C136 " 10c violet blue 50 35
a. Souv. sheet 5.00 5.00

Issued to commemorate the conquest of space.

No. C136a contains 7c and 10c stamps similar to Nos. C135–C136 with gray border, violet blue inscription and simulated perforation. Size: 149x82mm.

Pres. John F. Kennedy
AP48

1964, Nov. 22 ***Perf. 11½***

C137 AP48 10c buff & dk. brn. 50 35

Issued in memory of President John F. Kennedy (1917–63). Sheets of 10 (5x2) with brown marginal inscription and date and sheets of 50.

U.P.U. Type of Regular Issue

1964, Dec. 5 Litho. ***Perf. 12½***

C138 A157 7c blue 20 18

Issued to commemorate the 15th Universal Postal Union Congress, Vienna, Austria, May–June, 1964.

ICY Type of Regular Issue, 1965

1965, Feb. 16 ***Perf. 12½*** **Unwmkd.**

C139 A158 10c lilac & violet 35 30

Issued to publicize the United Nations International Cooperation Year.

Basilica of Our Lady of Altagracia
AP49

1965, Mar. 18 ***Perf. 12½*** **Unwmkd.**

C140 AP49 10c multicolored 40 30

Issued to commemorate the Fourth Mariological Congress and the Eleventh International Marian Congress.

Abraham Lincoln
AP50

1965, Apr. 15 Litho. ***Perf. 12½***

C141 AP50 17c bright blue 50 35

Issued to commemorate the centenary of the death of Abraham Lincoln.

Stamp Centenary Type of Regular Issue, 1965

Design: Stamp of 1865, (No. 2).

1965, Dec. 28 Litho. ***Perf. 12½***

C142 A161 7c violet, light green & black 35 30
C143 " 10c yellow, light green & black 40 35

Issued to commemorate the centenary of the first Dominican postage stamps.

ITU Emblem, Old and New Communication Equipment
AP51

1966, Apr. 6 Litho. ***Perf. 12½***

C144 AP51 28c pink & car. 80 60
C145 " 45c bright green & green 1.25 1.00

Issued to commemorate the centenary (in 1965) of the International Telecommunication Union.

Butterfly Type of Regular Issue

1966, Nov. 8 Litho. ***Perf. 12½***

Various Butterflies in Natural Colors

Size: 35x24mm.

C146 A164 10c lt. vio. & vio. 40 25
C147 " 50c orange & dp. orange 1.75 1.00
C148 " 75c pink & rose red 2.50 1.50

Altar Type of Regular Issue

1967, Jan. 18 Litho. ***Perf. 11½***

C149 A165 7c light olive grn. 20 15
C150 " 10c lilac 25 20
C151 " 20c yellow brown 45 35

Chess Type of Regular Issue

Design: 10c, Pawn and Bishop.

1967, June 23 Litho. ***Perf. 12½***

C152 A167 10c olive, lt. olive & black 40 30
a. Souv. sheet 90 90

Issued to commemorate the 5th Central American Chess Championships, Santo Domingo. No. C152a contains 2 imperf. stamps similar to Nos. 636 and C152. Gray chessboard design in margin with map of Dominican Republic and black inscription. Size: 117x76mm.

Alliance for Progress Type of Regular Issue

1967, Sept. 16 Litho. ***Perf. 12½***

C153 A168 8c gray 22 15
C154 " 10c blue 28 18

Alliance for Progress, 6th anniversary.

Cornucopia and Emblem
AP52

Latin American Flags
AP53

1967, Oct. 7

C155 AP52 12c multicolored 30 20

Issued to commemorate the 25th anniversary of the Inter-American Agriculture Institute.

Satellite Type of Regular Issue

1968, June 15 Typo. ***Perf. 12***

C156 A170 10c dp. bl. & multi. 40 30
C157 " 15c purple & multi. 55 40

World Meteorological Day, Mar. 23.

Boxing Type of Regular Issue

Designs: Two views of boxing match.

1968, June 29

C158 A171 7c org. yel. & grn. 25 15
C159 " 10c gray & blue 35 20

See note after No. 641.

Lions Type of Regular Issue

1968, Aug. 9 Litho. ***Perf. 11½***

C160 A172 10c ultra. & multi. 30 20

Issued to commemorate the 50th anniversary (in 1967) of Lions International.

Olympic Type of Regular Issue

Designs (Olympic Emblem and): 10c, Weight lifting. 33c, Pistol shooting.

1968, Nov. 12 Litho. ***Perf. 11½***

C161 A173 10c buff & multi. 35 30
C162 " 33c pink & multi. 1.10 85

Issued to commemorate the 19th Olympic Games, Mexico City, Oct. 12–27.

1969, Jan. 25 Litho. ***Perf. 12½***

C163 AP53 10c pink & multi. 30 18

Issued to publicize the 7th Inter-American Savings and Loan Conference, Santo Domingo, Jan. 25–31.

Taino Art Type of Regular Issue

Taino Art: 7c, Various spatulas with human heads (vert.). 10c, Female torso forming drinking vessel. 20c, Vase with human head (vert.).

1969, Jan. 31 Litho. ***Perf. 12½***

C164 A175 7c lt. blue, blue & lemon 20 12
C165 " 10c pink, vermilion & brown 35 20
C166 " 20c yel., org. & brn. 50 35

COTAL Type of Regular Issue

Design: 10c, Airport of the Americas and COTAL emblem.

1969, May 25 Litho. ***Perf. 12½***

C167 A178 10c brn. & pale fawn 25 18

See note after No. 655.

ILO Type of Regular Issue

1969, June 27 Litho. ***Perf. 12½***

C168 A179 10c rose, red & blk. 25 18

Issued to commemorate the 50th anniversary of the International Labor Organization.

Baseball Type of Regular Issue

Designs: 7c, Bleachers, Tetelo Vargas Stadium (horiz.). 10c, Batter, catcher and umpire. 1p, Quisqueya Stadium (horiz.).

1969, Aug. 15 Litho. ***Perf. 12½***

Size: 43x30mm. (7c, 1p); 21x31mm. (10c).

C169 A180 7c magenta & orange 30 18
C170 " 10c maroon & rose red 40 25
C171 " 1p violet blue & brown 3.00 2.00

Issued to publicize the 17th World Amateur Baseball Championships.

Electrification Types of Regular Issue

Design: No. C172, Rio Haina steam plant. No. C173, Valdesa Dam.

1969 **Lithographed** ***Perf. 12***

C172 A181 10c org. vermilion 30 15
C173 A182 10c multicolored 30 15

Issued to publicize the national electrification plan.

Issue dates: No C172, Sept. 15; No. C173, Oct. 15.

Duarte Type of Regular Issue

1970, Jan. 26 Litho. ***Perf. 12***

C174 A183 10c brn. & dk. brn. 30 18

Issued for Duarte Day in memory of Juan Pablo Duarte (1813–1876), liberator.

Census Type of Regular Issue

Design: 10c, Buildings and census emblem.

1970, Feb. 6 *Perf. 11*

C175 A184 10c lt. bl. & multi. 35 25

Issued to publicize the 1970 census.

Sculpture Type of Regular Issue

Design: 10c, The Prisoner, by Abelardo Rodriguez Urdaneta (vert.).

1970, Feb. 20 Litho. *Perf. 12½*

C176 A186 10c bluish gray 30 20

Issued to honor Abelardo Rodriguez Urdaneta, sculptor.

Masonic Type of Regular Issue

1970, Mar. 2

C177 A187 10c brown 25 18

The 8th Inter-American Masonic Conference, Santo Domingo, Mar. 1–7.

Satellite Type of Regular Issue

1970, May 25 Litho. *Perf. 12½*

C178 A188 7c blue & gray 25 20

World Telecommunications Day.

U.P.U. Type of Regular Issue

1970, June 5 *Perf. 11*

C179 A189 10c yellow & brown 20 18

Inauguration of new Universal Postal Union headquarters, Bern.

Education Year Type of Regular Issue

1970, June 26 Litho. *Perf. 12½*

C180 A190 15c bright pink 30 25

International Education Year, 1970.

Dancers AP54

Album, Globe and Emblem AP55

Design: 10c, U.N. emblem and wheel.

1970, Oct. 12 Litho. *Perf. 12½*

C181 AP54 7c blue & multi. 20 12
C182 " 10c pink & multi. 30 18

Issued to publicize the First World Exhibition of Books and Culture Festival, Santo Domingo, Oct. 11–Dec. 11.

1970, Oct. 26 Litho. *Perf. 11*

C183 AP55 10c multicolored 30 20

Issued to publicize EXFILCA 70, 2nd Interamerican Philatelic Exhibition, Caracas, Venezuela, Nov. 27–Dec. 6.

Basilica of Our Lady of Altagracia AP56

1971, Jan. 20 Litho. *Perf. 12½*

C184 AP56 17c multicolored 55 35

Inauguration of the Basilica of Our Lady of Altagracia.

Map of Dominican Republic, CARE Package AP57

1971, May 28 Litho. *Perf. 12½*

C185 AP57 10c blue & green 25 18

25th anniversary of CARE, a U.S.-Canadian Cooperative for American Relief Everywhere.

Sports Type of Regular Issue

Design: 7c, Volleyball.

1971, Sept. 10 *Perf. 11*

C186 A195 7c lilac & gray 25 15

2nd National Games.

Animal Type of Regular Issue

Design: 25c, Cock and grain.

1971, Sept. 29 *Perf. 12½*

C187 A196 25c black & multi. 60 45

6th National agriculture and livestock census.

Independence Type of Regular Issue

Design: 10c, Dominican-Colombian flag of 1821.

1971, Dec. 1 *Perf. 11*

C188 A197 10c violet blue, yellow & red 25 18

Sesquicentennial of first national independence.

Christmas Type of Regular Issue

Design: 10c, Bell, 1493.

1971, Dec. 10 *Perf. 12½*

C189 A198 10c red, grn. & yel. 25 18

Christmas 1971.

UNICEF Type of Regular Issue

Design: 15c, UNICEF emblem and child on beach.

1971, Dec. *Perf. 11*

C190 A199 15c multicolored 35 27

25th anniversary of the United Nations International Children's Fund (UNICEF).

Book Year Type of Regular Issue

1972, Jan. 25 Litho. *Perf. 12½*

C191 A200 12c lilac, dark blue & red 30 22

International Book Year 1972.

Magnifying Glass over Peru on Map of Americas AP58

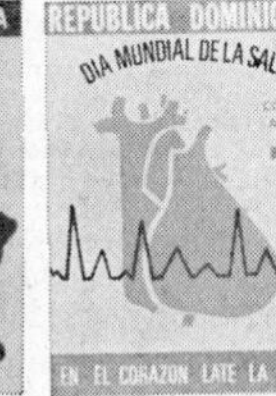

"Your Heart is your Health" AP59

1972, Mar. 7 Litho. *Perf. 12*

C192 AP58 10c blue & multi. 35 25

EXFILIMA '71, 3rd Inter-American Philatelic Exposition, Lima, Peru, Nov. 6–14, 1971.

1972, Apr. 27 Litho. *Perf. 11*

C193 AP59 7c red & multi. 20 12

World Health Day.

Taino Art Type of 1972

Taino Art: 8c, Ritual vessel showing human figures. 10c, Trumpet (shell). 25c, Carved vomiting spoons. All horiz.

1972, May 10 Litho. *Perf. 11*

C194 A201 8c multicolored 20 12
C195 " 10c lt. bl. & multi. 30 15
C196 " 25c multicolored 65 35

Telecommunications Type of Regular Issue

1972, May 17 *Perf. 12½*

C197 A202 21c yellow & multi. 50 30

4th World Telecommunications Day.

Exhibition Type of Regular Issue

1972, June 3

C198 A203 33c org. & multi. 90 50

First National Philatelic Exhibition, Santo Domingo, June 3–17.

Olympic Type of Regular Issue.

Design: 33c, Running.

1972, Aug. 25 Litho. *Perf. 12½*

C199 A204 33c yel. & multi. 1.00 60

20th Olympic Games, Munich, Aug. 26–Sept. 11.

Club Type of Regular Issue

1972, Sept. 29 Litho. *Perf. 10½*

C200 A205 20c blue & multi. 50 30

50th anniversary of the Club Activo 20–30 Internacional.

Morel Type of Regular Issue

1972, Oct. 20 Litho. *Perf. 12½*

C201 A206 10c multicolored 25 15

Emilio A. Morel (1884–1958), poet and journalist.

Bank Type of Regular Issue

Design: 25c, Silver coin, 1947, and entrance to the Mint.

1972, Oct. 23

C202 A207 25c ocher & multi. 60 35

25th anniversary of the Central Bank.

"La Navidad" Fortress, 1492 AP60

1972, Nov. 21 Litho. *Perf. 12½*

C203 AP60 10c multicolored 20 14

Christmas 1972.

Sports Type of Regular Issue

Designs: Various sports.

1973, Mar. 30 Litho. *Perf. 13½x13*

C204 A212 8c blk. & lt. blue, block of 4 1.00 60
a. Upper left 20 12
b. Upper right 20 12
c. Lower left 20 12
d. Lower right 20 12
C205 A212 10c dk. bl. & lilac rose, block of 4 1.20 70
a. Upper left 25 14
b. Upper right 25 14
c. Lower left 25 14
d. Lower right 25 14

Publicity for the 12th Central American and Caribbean Games, Santo Domingo, Summer 1974.

Easter Type 1973

Design: 10c, Belfry of Church of Our Lady of Help.

1973, Apr. 18 Litho. *Perf. 10½*

C206 A213 10c multicolored 30 15

Holy Week 1973.

North and South America on Globe AP61

1973, May 29 Litho. *Perf. 12*

C207 AP61 7c multicolored 21 15

Pan-American Health Organization, 70th anniversary (in 1972).

WMO Type of Regular Issue

1973, Aug. 10 Litho. *Perf. 13½x13*

C208 A214 7c green & multi. 21 15

Centenary of international meteorological cooperation.

INTERPOL Emblem Police Scientist AP62

1973, Sept. 28 Litho. *Perf. 10½*

C209 AP62 10c violet blue, bl. & emerald 30 20

50th anniversary of International Criminal Police Organization.

Handicraft Type of Regular Issue

1973, Oct. 12

Multicolored

C210 A215 7c *Sailing ship, mosaic* 21 15
C211 " 10c *Maracas rattles* (horiz.) 30 20

Opening of Museum of Mankind in Santo Domingo.

Christmas Type of Regular Issue

Design: 10c, Angels adoring Christ Child.

1973, Nov. 26 Litho. *Perf. 13½x13*

C212 A216 10c multicolored 30 20

Christmas 1973.

Scout Type of Regular Issue

Design: 21c, Scouts cooking and Lord Baden-Powell.

1973, Dec. 7 Litho. *Perf. 12*

C213 A217 21c red & multi. 63 42

50th anniversary of Dominican Republic Boy Scouts.

Sport Type of Regular Issue

Designs: 10c, Olympic swimming pool and diver. 25c, Olympic Stadium, soccer and discus.

1974, Feb. 25 Litho. *Perf. 13½*

C214 A218 10c blue & multi. 30 20
C215 " 25c multicolored 75 50

12th Central American and Caribbean Games, Santo Domingo, 1974.

The Last Supper AP63

1974, June 27 Litho. *Perf. 13½*

C216 AP63 10c multicolored 30 20

Holy Week 1974.

Bridge Type of 1974

Design: 10c, Higuamo Bridge.

1974, July 12 *Perf. 12*

C217 A221 10c multicolored 30 20

Diabetes Type of 1974

Designs (Map of Dominican Republic, Diabetes' Emblem and): 7c, Kidney. 33c, Eye and heart.

1974, Aug. 22 Litho. *Perf. 13*

C218 A222 7c yellow & multi. 22 15
C219 " 33c lt. bl. & multi. 1.00 65

Fight against diabetes.

UPU Type of 1974

Designs (UPU Emblem and): 7c, Ships. 33c, Jet.

1974, Oct. 9 Litho. *Perf. 13½*

C220 A223 7c grn. & multi. 22 15
C221 " 33c red & multi. 1.00 35
a. Souvenir sheet of 4 1.50 1.50

Centenary of Universal Postal Union. No. C221a contains one each of Nos. 727–728 and C220–C221 forming continuous design. Red marginal inscription. Size: 120x91mm.

Golfers and Championship Emblem
AP64

Design: 20c, Golfer and Golf Association emblem.

1974, Oct. 24 Litho. *Perf. 13x13½*

C222 AP64 10c grn. & multi. 35 25
C223 " 20c " " 65 45

World Amateur Golf Championships.

Hand Holding Dove
AP65

1974, Dec. 3 Litho. *Perf. 12*

C224 AP65 10c multicolored 30 20

Christmas 1974.

FAO Type of 1974

Design: 10c, Bee, beehive and barrel of honey.

1974, Dec. 5

C225 A227 10c multicolored 30 20

World Food Program, 10th anniversary.

Chrismon, Lamb, Candle and Palm
AP66

Spain No. 1, España 75 Emblem
AP67

1975, Mar. 26 Litho. *Perf. 13½*

C226 AP66 10c gold & multi. 30 20

Holy Week 1975.

1975, Apr. 10

C227 AP67 12 red, yel. & blk. 36 25

España 75, International Philatelic Exhibition, Madrid, Apr. 4–13.

Development Bank Type of 1975

1975, May 19 Litho. *Perf. 10½x10*

C228 A230 10c rose carmine & multicolored 30 20

16th Assembly of the Governors of the International Development Bank, Santo Domingo, May 1975.

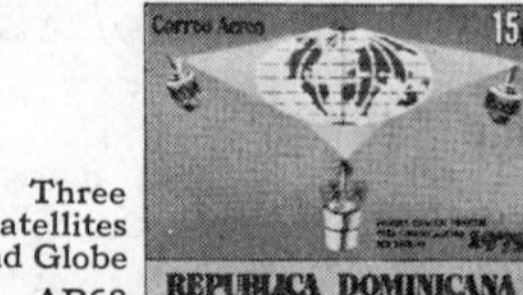

Three Satellites and Globe
AP68

1975, June 21 Litho. *Perf. 13½*

C229 AP68 15c multicolored 45 30

Opening of first earth satellite tracking station in Dominican Republic.

Apollo Type of 1975

Design: 2p, Apollo-Soyuz link-up over earth.

1975, July 24 *Perf. 13*

Size: 42x28mm.

C230 A232 2p multicolored 4.00 2.50

Apollo Soyuz space test project (Russo-American cooperation), launching July 15; link-up, July 17.

Indian Chief Type of 1975

Designs: 7c, Mayobanex. 8c, Cotubanama and Juan de Esquivel. 10c, Enriquillo and Mencia.

1975, Sept. 27 Litho. *Perf. 12*

C231 A235 7c lt. grn. & multi. 21 14
C232 " 8c org. & multi. 24 16
C233 " 10c gray & multi. 30 20

Volleyball
AP69

Design: 10c, Weight lifting and Games' emblem.

1975, Oct. 24 Litho. *Perf. 12*

C234 AP69 7c blue & multi. 25 20
C235 " 10c multicolored 35 25

7th Pan-American Games, Mexico City, Oct. 13–26.

Christmas Type of 1975

Design: 10c, Dove and peace message.

1975, Dec. 12 Litho. *Perf. 13x13½*

C236 A237 10c yel. & multi. 30 20

Christmas 1975.

Valdesia Dam—AP70

1976, Jan. 26 Litho. *Perf. 13*

C237 AP70 10c multicolored 30 20

Holy Week Type 1976

Design: 10c, Crucifixion, by Eliezer Castillo.

1976, Apr. 14 Litho. *Perf. 13½*

C238 A239 10c multicolored 30 20

Holy Week 1976.

Bicentennial Type of 1976 and

George Washington, Independence Hall
AP71

Design: 10c, Hands holding maps of US and Dominican Republic.

1976, May 29 Litho. *Perf. 13½*

C239 A241 10c vio. bl., grn. & black 30 20
C240 AP71 75c black & org. 2.25 1.50

American Bicentennial; No. C240 also for Interphil 76 International Philatelic Exhibition, Philadelphia, Pa., May 29–June 6.

King Juan Carlos I and Queen Sofia
AP72

1976, May 31

C241 AP72 21c multicolored 65 42

Visit of King Juan Carlos I and Queen Sofia of Spain.

Telephone Type of 1976

Design: 10c, Alexander Graham Bell and telephones, 1876 and 1976.

1976

C242 A243 10c multicolored 30 20

Centenary of first telephone call by Alexander Graham Bell, Mar. 10, 1876.

Duarte Types of 1976

Designs: 10c, Scroll with Duarte letter and Dominican flag. 33c, Duarte leaving for Exile, by E. Godoy.

1976, July 20 Litho. *Perf. 13½*

C243 A245 10c blue & multi. 30 20

Perf. 13x13½

C244 A244 33c brn. & multi. 1.00 65

Juan Pablo Duarte, liberation hero, death centenary.

Fire Engine
AP73

1976, Sept. 13 Litho. *Perf. 12*

C245 AP73 10c multicolored 30 20

Honoring firemen.

Radio Club Type of 1976

1976, Oct. 8 Lithographed *Perf. 13½*

C246 A247 10c blue & black 30 20

Dominican Radio Club, 50th anniversary.

Various People
AP74

1976, Oct. 15 Litho. *Perf. 13½*

C247 AP74 21c multicolored 65 42

Spanish heritage.

Olympic Games Type of 1976

Design (Montreal Olympic Games Emblem and): 10c, Running. 25c, Basketball.

1976, Oct. 22 *Perf. 12*

C248 A249 10c ocher & multi. 30 20
C249 " 25c green & multi. 75 50

21st Olympic Games, Montreal, Canada, July 17–Aug. 1.

Christmas Type of 1976

Design: 10c, Angel with bells.

1976, Dec. 8 Litho. *Perf. 13½*

C250 A251 10c multicolored 30 20

Tourist Activities
AP75

Designs: 12c, Angling and hotel. 25c, Horseback riding and waterfall (vert.).

1977, Jan. 7

Size: 36x36mm.

C251 AP75 10c multicolored 30 20

Size: 34x25½, 25½x34mm.

C252 AP75 12c multicolored 36 25
C253 " 25c " 75 50

Tourist publicity.

Championship Type of 1977

1977, Mar. 4 Litho. *Perf. 13½*

C254 A253 10c yellow green & multi. 30 20
C255 " 25c light brown & multicolored 75 50

10th Central American and Caribbean Children's and Young People's Swimming Championships, Santo Domingo.

Holy Week Type 1977

Design: 10c, Belfry and open book.

1977, Apr. 15 Litho. *Perf. 13½x13*

C256 A254 10c multicolored 30 20

Holy Week 1977.

Lions Type of 1977

1977, May 6 *Perf. 13½x13*

C257 A255 7c light green & multicolored 21 15

12th annual Dominican Republic Lions Convention.

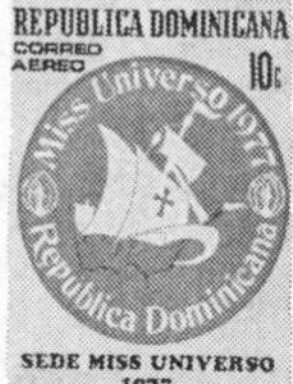

Caravel under Sail
AP76

1977, July 16 Litho. *Perf. 13*

C258 AP76 10c multicolored 30 20

Miss Universe Contest, held in Dominican Republic.

Melon Cactus
AP77

Design: 33c, Coccothrinax (tree).

1977, Aug. 19 Litho. *Perf. 12*

C259 AP77 7c multicolored 21 15
C260 " 33c " 1.00 65

National Botanical Garden.

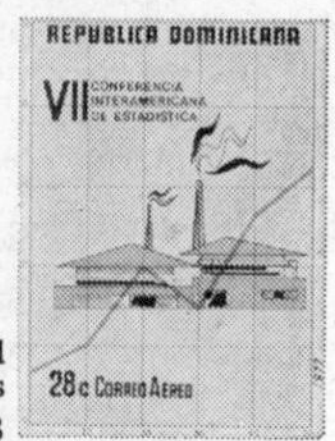

Chart and Factories
AP78

1977 Litho. *Perf. 13x13½*

C261 AP78 28c multicolored 85 55

7th Interamerican Statistics Conference.

Animal Type of 1977

Designs (Congress Emblem and): 10c, "Dorado," red Roman stud bull. 25c, Flamingo (vert.).

1977, Dec. 29 Litho. *Perf. 13*

C262 A259 10c multicolored 30 20
C263 " 25c " 75 50

8th Pan-American Veterinary and Zootechnical Congress.

Spanish Heritage Type of 1978

Design: 21c, Window, Casa del Tostado, 16th century.

1978, Jan. 19 *Perf. 13x13½*

Size: 28x41mm.

C264 A260 21c multicolored 65 42

Holy Week Type, 1978

Designs: 7c, Facade, Santo Domingo Cathedral. 10c, Facade of Dominican Convent.

1978, Mar. 21 Litho. *Perf. 12*

Size: 27x36mm.

C265 A261 7c multicolored 22 14
C266 " 10c " 30 20

Holy Week 1978.

Schooner Duarte
AP79

1978, Apr. 15 Litho. *Perf. 13½*

C267 AP79 7c multicolored 22 14

Dominican naval forces training ship.

Cardinal Type of 1978

1978, May 5 Litho. *Perf. 13*

C268 A262 10c multicolored 30 20

Octavio A. Beras Rojas, first Cardinal from Dominican Republic.

Antenna
AP80

1978, May 17 Litho. *Perf. 13½*

C269 AP80 25c silver & multi. 75 50

10th World Telecommunications Day.

No. C1 and Map
AP81

1978, June 6

C270 AP81 10c multicolored 30 20

50th anniversary of first Dominican Republic airmail stamp.

Globe, Soccer Ball, Emblem
AP82

Crown, Cross and Rosary Emblem
AP83

Design: 33c, Soccer field, Argentina '78 emblem and globe.

1978, June 29

C271 AP82 12c multicolored 36 25
C272 " 33c " 1.00 65

11th World Cup Soccer Championship, Argentina, June 1-25.

1978, July 11 *Perf. 13x13½*

C273 AP83 21c multicolored 62 42

Congregation of the Merciful Sisters of Charity, centenary.

Sports Type of 1978

Designs (Games' Emblem and): 7c, Baseball (vert.). 10c, Soccer (vert.).

1978, July 21 Litho. *Perf. 13½*

C274 A265 7c multicolored 22 14
C275 " 10c " 30 20

13th Central American and Caribbean Games, Medellin, Colombia.

Wright Brothers and Glider, 1902
AP84

Designs: 7c, Diagrams of Flyer I and jet (vert.). 13c, Diagram of air flow over wing. 45c, Flyer I over world map.

1978, Aug. 8 *Perf. 12*

C276 AP84 7c multicolored 22 14
C277 " 10c " 30 20
C278 " 13c " 40 25
C279 " 45c " 1.35 90

75th anniversary of first powered flight.

Tourist Type of 1978

Designs: 7c, Sun and musical instruments. 10c, Sun and plane over Santo Domingo.

1978, Sept. 12 Litho. *Perf. 12*

C280 A266 7c multicolored 22 14
C281 " 10c " 30 20

Tourist publicity.

People and Globe
AP85

1978, Oct. 12 Litho. *Perf. 13½*

C282 AP85 21c multicolored 65 22

Spanish heritage.

Dominican Republic and UN Flags
AP86

1978, Oct. 23 *Perf. 12*

C283 AP86 33c multicolored 1.00 35

33rd anniversary of the United Nations.

Statue of the Virgin
AP87

1978, Dec. 5 Litho. *Perf. 12*

C284 AP87 10c multicolored 30 20

Christmas 1978.

AIR POST SEMI-POSTAL STAMPS

Nos. C97-C99 Surcharged in Red

Engraved and Lithographed.

1957, Feb. 8 *Perf. 11½* Unwmkd.

Flags in National Colors

CB1 A117 11c+2c ultramarine & red orange 40 40
CB2 " 16c+2c carmine & light green 55 55
CB3 " 17c+2c black, violet & red 60 60

The surtax was to aid Hungarian refugees. A similar 25c surcharge was applied to the souvenir sheets described in the footnote following No. C99. Price, 2 sheets, perf. and imperf., $17.50.

Nos. C100-C102 Surcharged in Red Orange

1957, Sept. 9 Photo. *Perf. 13½*

Flags in National Colors

CB4 A118 11c+2c yellow green & dark blue 50 45
CB5 " 16c+2c lilac & dark blue 65 65
CB6 " 17c+2c brown & blue green 70 70

See note after No. B10.

A similar 5c surcharge was applied to the miniature sheets described in the footnote following No. 483. Price, 4 sheets, perf. and imperf., medal and flag, $35.

Types of Olympic Air Post Stamps, 1957, Surcharged in Carmine

+2¢ +2¢

REFUGIADOS REFUGIADOS
a *b*

Engraved and Lithographed

1958, May 26 *Perf. 13½*

Flags in National Colors

Pink Paper

CB7 A119 (*a*) 11c+2c ultra. 40 40
CB8 " (*b*) 11c+2c ultra. 40 40
CB9 A120 (*a*) 16c+2c rose carmine 50 50
CB10 " (*b*) 16c+2c rose carmine 50 50
CB11 A119 (*a*) 17c+2c claret 60 60
CB12 " (*b*) 17c+2c claret 60 60
Nos. CB7-CB12 (6) 3.00 3.00

The surtax was for the United Nations Relief and Works Agency for Palestine Refugees.

A similar 5c surcharge, plus marginal United Nations emblem and "UNRWA," was applied to the miniature sheets described in the footnote following No. C105. Price, 4 sheets, perf. and imperf., $30.

Nos. C106-C108 Surcharged

Photogravure.

1959, Apr. 13 *Perf. 13½* Unwmkd.

Flags in National Colors

CB13 A125 11c+2c blue, olive & brown 70 70

CB14 A125 16c+2c light green, orange & dark blue 90 90
CB15 " 17c+2c vermilion blue & yellow 1.25 1.25

Issued for the International Geophysical Year.

A similar 5c surcharge was applied to the miniature sheets described in the footnote following No. C108. Price, 2 sheets, perf. and imperf., $25.

Type of Regular Issue 1957 Surcharged in Red

Engraved and Lithographed

1959, Sept. 10 ***Imperf.***

Flags in National Colors

CB16 A117 11c+2c ultramarine & red orange 40 40
CB17 " 16c+2c carmine & light green 50 50
CB18 " 17c+2c black, violet & red 55 55

Issued for the 3rd Pan American Games, Chicago, Aug. 27-Sept. 7, 1959.

World Refugee Year Issue.

Nos. C113-C114 Surcharged in Red

1960, Apr. 7 Litho. ***Perf. 12½***

CB19 AP43 10c+5c plum, gray & green 40 40
CB20 " 13c+5c gray & green 45 45

For souvenir sheets see note after No. B33.

Nos. C115-C117 Surcharged: "XV ANIVERSARIO DE LA UNESCO +2c"

Photogravure

1962, Jan. 8 ***Perf. 13½*** **Unwmkd.**

Flags in National Colors

CB21 A136 11c+2c blue, gray & brown 35 35
CB22 " 16c+2c red, brown & olive 50 50
CB23 " 17c+2c black, blue & ochre 55 55

See note after No. B38.

A similar 5c surcharge was applied to the miniature sheets described in the footnote following No. C117. Price, 2 sheets, perf. and imperf., $7.50.

Anti-Malaria Type of Regular Issue, 1962.

1962, Apr. 29 Litho. ***Perf. 12***

CB24 A141 13c+2c pink & red 40 40
CB25 " 33c+2c orange & deep orange 90 90

Issued for the World Health Organization drive to eradicate malaria. Souvenir sheets exist, perf. and imperf. containing one each of Nos. B39-B40, CB24-CB25 and a 25c+2c pale green and yellow green. Dark brown marginal inscription. Size: 169x102mm.

Nos. C132-C133 Surcharged

1964. March 8

CB26 AP46 10c+2c brt. vio. 30 30
CB27 " 13c+2c yellow 35 35

Issued to publicize the UNESCO world campaign to save historic monuments in Nubia.

Nos. C146-C148 Surcharged Like Semi-Postal Issue B47-B51

1966, Dec. 9 **Litho.** ***Perf. 12½***

Size: 35x24mm.

CB28 A164 10c+5c multi. 35 35
CB29 " 50c+10c " 1.40 1.40
CB30 " 75c+10c " 2.00 2.00

Surtax for victims of hurricane Inez.

AIR POST OFFICIAL STAMPS.

OAP1

Typographed.

Blue Overprint.

1930, Dec. 3 ***Perf. 12*** **Unwmkd.**

CO1 OAP1 10c light blue 17.50 15.00
a. Pair, one without overprint 1250.00
CO2 " 20c orange 17.50 15.00

SPECIAL DELIVERY STAMPS.

Biplane

SD1

Lithographed.

1920 ***Perf. 11½.*** **Unwmkd.**

E1 SD1 10c deep ultra. 4.50 1.25
a. Imperf., pair

Special Delivery Messenger

SD2

1925

E2 SD2 10c dark blue 7.00 2.00

SD3

1927

E3 SD3 10c red brown 5.50 1.35
a. "E EXPRESO" at top 40.00 35.00

Type of 1927.

1941 **Redrawn.**

E4 SD3 10c yellow green 2.50 85
E5 " 10c dark blue green 2.00 60

The redrawn design differs slightly from SD3.

Issue dates: E4, Mar. 27; E5, Aug. 7.

Emblem of Communications

SD4

1945, Sept. 1 ***Perf. 12***

E6 SD4 10c rose carmine, carmine & dark blue 65 30

1950 **Lithographed.** **Unwmkd.**

E7 SD5 10c multicolored 65 30
Exists imperf.

Modern Communications System

SD6

1956, Aug. 18 ***Perf. 11½***

E8 SD6 25c green 1.00 50

Carrier Pigeon

SD7

1967 **Lithographed** ***Perf. 11½***

E9 SD7 25c light blue 90 40

Carrier Pigeon, Globe

SD8

1978, Aug. 2 **Litho.** ***Perf. 13½***

E10 SD8 25c multicolored 75 40

INSURED LETTER STAMPS.

Merino Issue of 1933 Surcharged in Red or Black

PRIMA
VALORES DECLARADOS
SERVICIO INTERIOR
8
CENTAVOS

1935, Feb. 1 ***Perf. 14.*** **Unwmkd.**

G1 A34 8c on 7c ultra. (R) 90 30
a. Invtd. surcharge 20.00
G2 A33 15c on 10c orange yellow (R) 75 20
a. Invtd. surcharge 20.00
G3 A35 30c on 8c dk.grn.(R) 1.75 65
G4 A34 45c on 20c carmine rose (Bk) 2.50 70
G5 A36 70c on 50c lemon(R) 5.50 1.25
Nos. G1-G5 (5) 11.40 3.10

Merino Issue of 1933 Surcharged in Red

PRIMA
VALORES DECLARADOS
SERVICIO INTERIOR
8
CENTAVOS

1940

G6 A35 8c on ½c light violet 1.50 1.00
G7 A34 8c on 7c ultramarine 1.50 1.00

Coat of Arms

IL1

1940-45 **Lithographed.** ***Perf. 11½***

Arms in Black

G8 IL1 8c brown red 70 10
a. 8c dk. red, no shading on inner frame 70 12
G9 IL1 15c deep orange ('45) 80 20
G10 " 30c dk. green ('41) 1.10 20
a. 30c yellow green 1.10 20
G11 IL1 45c ultra. ('44) 1.75 50
G12 " 70c olive brn. ('44) 2.50 45
Nos. G8-G12 (5) 6.85 1.45

Redrawn Type of 1940-45.

1952-53 **Arms in Black.**

G13 IL1 8c carmine lake ('53) 60 25
G14 " 15c red orange ('53) 1.25 40
G15 " 70c dp. brn. carmine 3.50 1.50

Larger and bolder numerals on 8c and 15c. Smaller and bolder "70." There are many other minor differences in the design.

1954 **Type of 1940-45**

Arms in Black, 15x16mm.

G16 IL1 10c carmine 40 20

Coat of Arms

IL2

Lithographed.

1955-69 ***Perf. 11½*** **Unwmkd.**

Arms in Black, 13½x11½mm.

G17 IL2 10c carmine rose 40 12
G18 " 15c red orange ('56) 1.75 1.00
G19 " 20c red orange ('58) 85 45
a. 20c orange ('69) 85 45
b. 20c orange, retouched ('69) 2.00 1.00
G20 IL2 30c dk. green ('55) 1.00 25
G21 " 40c dk. green ('58) 1.50 1.00
a. 40c light yellow green ('62) 1.00 75
G22 IL2 45c ultra. ('56) 2.75 1.25
G23 " 70c dp. brn. car. ('56) 3.00 2.00
Nos. G17-G23 (7) 11.25 6.07

On No. G19b the horizontal shading lines of shield are omitted.

Type of 1940-45

Second Redrawing

1963 ***Perf. 12½***

Arms in Black, 17x16mm.

G24 IL1 10c red orange 40 30
G25 " 20c orange 60 60

Third Redrawing

1966 **Lithographed** ***Perf. 12½***

Arms in Black, 14x14mm.

G26 IL1 10c violet 40 30
G27 " 40c orange 1.75 1.25

Type of 1955-62

1968 **Lithographed** ***Perf. 11½***

Arms in Black, 13½x11½mm.

G28 IL2 20c red 1.00 60
G29 " 60c yellow 2.25 1.50

1973-76 **Lithographed** ***Perf. 12½***

Arms in Black, 11x11mm.

G30 IL2 10c carmine rose ('76) 30 20
G31 " 20c yellow 70 50
G32 " 20c orange ('76) 60 30
G33 " 40c yellow green 1.40 90
a. 40c green ('76) 1.20 60
G34 IL2 70c blue 2.25 1.50

1973 ***Perf. 11½***

Arms in Black, 13½x11½mm.

G35 IL2 10c dark violet 40 25

1978, Aug. 9 ***Perf. 10½***

Arms in Black, 11x11mm.

G36 IL2 10c rose magenta 30 20
G37 " 40c bright green 1.20 60

POSTAGE DUE STAMPS.

Numeral of Value
D1

Typographed.

1901 ***Perf. 14.*** **Unwmkd.**

J1 D1 2 (c) olive gray 30 15
J2 " 4 (c) " 40 20
J3 " 5 (c) " 75 30
J4 " 10 (c) " 1.50 75

Wmkd. Crosses and Circles. (116)

1909

J5 D1 2 (c) olive gray 25 15
J6 " 4 (c) " 30 20
J7 " 6 (c) " 75 50
J8 " 10 (c) " 2.50 1.50

1913

J9 D1 2 (c) olive green 25 15
J10 " 4 (c) " 30 20
J11 " 6 (c) " 40 25
J12 " 10 (c) " 60 45

Lithographed.

1922 ***Perf. 11½.*** **Unwmkd.**

J13 D1 1(c) olive green 25 25

Numeral of Value
D2 D3

1942

J14 D2 1c dark red & pale pink 12 8
J15 " 2c dark blue & pale blue 18 10
J16 " 4c dark green & pale green 18 12
J17 " 6c brown & buff 25 20
J18 " 8c yellow orange & pale yellow 30 25
J19 " 10c magenta & pale pink 40 35
Nos. J14–J19 (6) 1.43 1.10

1959

Size: 20½x25mm.

J20 D2 2c dark blue 35 20

1960–66 Lithographed ***Perf. 11½***

Size: 21x25½mm.

J21 D3 1c dark carmine rose 50 50
J22 " 2c dark blue ('66) 35 35
J23 " 4c green 1.50 1.50

OFFICIAL STAMPS.

Bastion of February 27
O1

Lithographed

1902, Feb. 25 ***Perf. 12*** **Unwmkd.**

O1 O1 2c scarlet & black 30 20
O2 " 5c dark blue & black 35 25
O3 " 10c yellow green & black 50 30
O4 " 20c yellow & black 60 40
a. Imperf., pair 9.00

Bastion of February 27
O2

Columbus Lighthouse
O3

Wmkd. Crosses and Circles. (116)

Typographed

1909–12 ***Perf. 13½x13, 13½x14***

O5 O2 1c blue green & black 20 20
O6 " 2c scarlet & black 25 25
O7 " 5c dark blue & black 35 30
O8 " 10c yellow green & black ('12) 75 50
O9 " 20c org. & black ('12) 1.25 75
Nos. O5–O9 (5) 2.80 2.00

The 2c and 5c are found in both perforations; 1c and 20c only perf. 13½x13; 10c only perf. 13½x14.

1928 ***Perf. 12.*** **Unwmkd.**

O10 O3 1c green 10 8
O11 " 2c red 12 10
O12 " 5c ultramarine 20 15
O13 " 10c light blue 25 20
O14 " 20c orange 40 30
Nos. O10–O14 (5) 1.07 83

Proposed Columbus Lighthouse
O4

1937 Lithographed. ***Perf. 11½.***

O15 O4 3c dark purple 30 15
O16 " 7c indigo & blue 40 30
O17 " 10c orange yellow 60 40

Proposed Columbus Lighthouse
O5

1939–41

O18 O5 1c deep green & light green 8 6
O19 " 2c crimson & pale pink 12 8
O20 " 3c purple & lt. violet 15 8
O21 " 5c dark blue & light blue ('40) 35 18
O21A " 5c light blue ('41) 70 10
O22 " 7c bright blue & light blue ('41) 40 15
O23 " 10c yellow orange & pale orange ('41) 40 20
O24 " 20c brown orange & buff ('41) 1.25 40
O25 " 50c bright red lilac & pale lilac ('41) 2.00 1.00
Nos. O18–O25 (9) 5.45 2.25

Type of 1939.

1950 Redrawn.

O26 O5 50c deep carmine & rose 1.50 75

The numerals "50" measure 3mm., and are close to left and right frames; numerals measure 4mm. on No. O25. There are other minor differences.

Denominations in "Centavos Oro."

1950

O27 O5 5c light blue 15 10
O28 " 10c yellow & pale yellow 30 20
O29 " 20c dull orange brown & buff 60 45

Letters of top inscription are 1½mm. high.

Type of 1939-41.
Second Redrawing.
Denominations in "Centavos Oro."

1958 ***Perf. 11½*** **Unwmkd.**

O30 O5 7c blue & light blue 20 10
O31 " 20c yellow brown & buff 50 35
O32 " 50c red lilac & bright pink 1.25 85

The letters of top inscription are 2mm. high, the trees at base of monument have been redrawn, etc. On No. O32 the numerals are similar to No. O26.

POSTAL TAX STAMPS.

Santo Domingo after Hurricane
PT1

Hurricane's Effect on Capital
PT2

Lithographed.

1930, Dec. ***Perf. 12.*** **Unwmkd.**

RA1 PT1 1c green & rose 20 15
a. Tête bêche pair 1.50 1.50
RA2 " 2c red & rose 25 20
a. Tête bêche pair 2.00 1.75
RA3 PT2 5c ultra. & rose 35 25
a. Tête bêche pair 2.00 2.00
RA4 " 10c yellow & rose 45 40
a. Tête bêche pair 2.25 2.25

Imperf.

RA5 PT1 1c green & rose 35 25
a. Tête bêche pair 1.75 1.75
RA6 " 2c red & rose 45 30
a. Tête bêche pair 1.75 1.75
RA7 PT2 5c ultra. & rose 65 50
a. Tête bêche pair 2.00 2.00
RA8 " 10c yellow & rose 80 60
a. Tête bêche pair 2.50 2.50
Nos. RA1–RA8 (8) 3.50 2.65

PT2a

Overprinted or Surcharged in Black.

1932, Dec. 20 ***Perf. 12***

Cross in Red

RA8B PT2a 1c yel. green 50 50
RA8C " 3c on 2c violet 60 60
RA8D " 5c blue 1.75 1.50
RA8E " 7c on 10c turq. blue 2.75 2.50

Obligatory on all first class mail from Dec. 20, 1932, until Jan. 5, 1933. The tax benefited the Red Cross.

Dr. Martos Sanatorium
PT3

Nurse and Child
PT4

1944, Apr. 1 Litho. ***Perf. 11½***

RA9 PT3 1c deep blue, slate blue & red 25 10

1947, Apr. 1 **Unwmkd.**

RA10 PT4 1c deep blue, pale blue & car. 25 10

Sanatorium of the Holy Help
PT5

1949, Apr. 1

RA11 PT5 1c deep blue, pale blue & car. 25 10

Youth Holding Banner
PT6

"Suffer Little Children to Come Unto Me"
PT7

1950, Apr. 1 ***Perf. 11½***

RA12 PT6 1c deep blue, pale bl. & carmine 25 10

1950, Dec. 1 ***Perf. 12, 12½***

Size: 22½ x 32mm.

RA13 PT7 1c light blue & pale blue 40 12

Vertical line centering side borders merges into dots toward the bottom. See also Nos. RA13A, RA17, RA19, RA26, RA32, RA35.

The tax was for child welfare.

1951, Dec. 1 Redrawn

RA13A PT7 1c light blue & pale blue 1.00 25

In the redrawn stamp, the standing child, a blonde in No. RA13, is changed to a brunette; more foliage has been added above child's head and to branches showing in upper right corner. Vertical dashes in side borders.

Tuberculosis Sanatorium, Santiago—PT8

1952, Apr. 1 Litho. ***Perf. 11½***

RA14 PT8 1c light blue & carmine 25 10

Sword, Serpent and Crab
PT9

1953, Feb. 1 ***Perf. 12.*** **Unwmkd.**

RA15 PT9 1c carmine 30 12

The tax was for the Dominican League Against Cancer. See also Nos. RA18, RA21, RA43, RA46, RA51, RA56, RA61, RA67, RA72, RA76, RA82.

Tuberculosis Dispensary for Children—PT10

1953, Apr. 1 Litho. *Perf. 12½*

RA16 PT10 1c deep blue, pale bl. & red 25 10

Jesus Type of 1950
Second Redrawing

1953, Dec. 1 *Perf. 11½*

Size: 22x31mm.

RA17 PT7 1c blue 45 15

Solid shading in sky reduced to a few scattered dots. Girl's left arm indicated. Rough white dots in side borders.

Cancer Type of 1952

1954, Oct. 1 Redrawn *Perf. 12½*

RA18 PT9 1c rose carmine 20 10
a. 1c red orange ('61) 30 12
b. 1c carmine ('70) 50 20

Upper right serif of numeral "1" eliminated; diagonal line added through "C" and period removed; sword extended, placing top on a line with top of "1." Dots of background screen arranged diagonally. Many other differences.

The tax was for the Dominican League Against Cancer. No. RA18a exists imperf.

On No. RA18b background screen eliminates white outline of crab.

Jesus Type of 1950

1954, Dec. 1 Third Redrawing

Size: 23x32¾mm.

RA19 PT7 1c bright blue 40 20

Center completely screened. Girl's left hand shown, resting on Jesus' knee. Tiny white horizontal rectangles in side borders.

Lorraine Cross as Bell Clapper
PT11

1955, Apr. 1 Litho. *Perf. 11½x12*

RA20 PT11 1c black, yellow & red 25 10

Cancer Type of 1952.
Second Redrawing.

1956, Oct. 1 *Perf. 12½*

RA21 PT9 1c carmine 35 15
a. 1c red orange ('64) 45 20

Similar to No. RA18, but dots of background screen arranged in vertical and horizontal rows. Outlines of central device, lettering and frame clearly delineated. "C" of "¢" smaller. Upper claw in solid color.

TB Dispensary Type of 1953

1954, Apr. 1 Redrawn

RA22 PT10 1c blue & red 25 10
a. Red (cross) omitted 50.00

No. RA22 has third color omitted; clouds added; bolder letters and numerals.

Angelita Trujillo PT12 — Lorraine Cross PT13

1955, Dec. 1 *Perf. 12½* Unwmkd.

RA23 PT12 1c violet 25 12

The tax was for child welfare.

1956, Apr. 1 Litho. *Perf. 11½*

RA24 PT13 1c black, green, lemon & red 18 8

The tax was for the Anti-Tuberculosis League. Inscribed: B.C.G. (Bacillus Calmette-Guerin).

Children PT14 — Lorraine Cross PT15

1957, Apr. 1

RA25 PT14 1c red, black, yel., green & blue 18 8

Jesus Type of 1950
Fourth Redrawing.

1956, Dec. 1 *Perf. 12* Unwmkd.

Size: 21¾x31¼mm.

RA26 PT7 1c blue 25 10

Thin white lines around numeral boxes. Girl's bouquet touches Jesus' sleeve. Tiny white squares or rectangles in side borders. Foliage at either side of "Era de Trujillo" panel.

1958, Apr. 1 Litho. *Perf. 12½*

RA27 PT15 1c brown carmine & red 15 10

Type of 1958 Inscribed "1959"

1959, Apr. 1

RA28 PT15 1c brown carmine & red 18 12

Lorraine Cross PT16 — Lorraine Cross PT17

1960, Apr. 1 Litho. *Perf. 12*

RA29 PT16 1c bl., pale yellow & red 25 15

The tax was for the Anti-Tuberculosis League.

1961, Apr. 1 *Perf. 11½* Unwmkd.

RA30 PT17 1c blue & red 15 8

The tax was for the Anti-Tuberculosis League.

Maria de los Angeles M. de Trujillo and Housing Project
PT18

1961, Aug. 1 Lithographed *Perf. 12*

RA31 PT18 1c carmine rose 25 12

The tax was for aid to the needy.
Nos. RA31–RA33 exist imperf.

Jesus Type of 1950
Fifth Redrawing

1961, Dec. 1 *Perf. 12½* Unwmkd.

RA32 PT7 1c blue 20 10

No. RA32 is similar to No. RA19, but "Era de Trujillo" has been replaced by a solid color panel.

Type of 1961 Dated "1962."

1962, Apr. 1 *Perf. 12½*

RA33 PT17 1c blue & red 15 8

The tax was for the Anti-Tuberculosis League.

Man's Chest and Lorraine Cross PT19 — Hibiscus PT20

1963, Apr. 1 *Perf. 12x11½*

RA34 PT19 1c lt. ultra. & red 25 12

Jesus Type of 1950
Sixth Redrawing

1963, Dec. 1 *Perf. 11½*

Size: 21¾x32mm.

RA35 PT7 1c blue 20 8
a. 1c dp. bl. ('64) 20 10

No. RA35 is similar to No. RA26, but "Era de Trujillo" panel has been omitted.

1966, Apr. 1 Litho. *Perf. 11½*

RA36 PT20 1c emerald & car. 15 8

The tax was for the Anti-Tuberculosis League.

Domingoa Nodosa PT21 — Civil Defense Emblem PT22

1967, Apr. 1 Litho. *Perf. 12½*

RA37 PT21 1c lilac & red 15 8

The tax was for the Anti-Tuberculosis League.

1967, July 1 Litho. *Rouletted 13*

RA38 PT22 1c multicolored 25 18

The tax was for the Civil Defense Organization.

Boy, School and Yule Bells PT23 — Hand Holding Invalid PT24

1967, Dec. 1 Litho. *Perf. 12½*

RA39 PT23 1c rose red & pink 25 12

1968 *Perf. 11*

RA40 PT23 1c vermilion 30 18

No. RA40 has screened background; No. RA39, smooth background.

The tax was for child welfare.

See Nos. RA49A, RA52, RA57, RA62, RA68, RA73, RA77, RA81.

1968, Mar. 19 Litho. *Perf. 12½*

RA41 PT24 1c green & yellow 15 8
a. 1c olive green & deep yellow, perf. 11½x12 ('69) 15 8

The tax was for the rehabilitation of the handicapped. See Nos. RA47, RA50, RA54.

Dogbane PT25 — Schoolyard and Torch PT26

1968, Apr. 25 Litho. *Perf. 12½*

RA42 PT25 1c emerald, yellow & red 8 4

The tax was for the Anti-Tuberculosis League. See Nos. RA45, RA49.

Redrawn Cancer Type of 1955

1968, Oct. 1 Litho. *Perf. 12*

RA43 PT9 1c emerald 12 8

The tax was for the Dominican League against Cancer.

1969, Feb. 1 Litho. *Perf. 12½*

RA44 PT26 1c light blue 8 4

Issued for Education Year 1969.

Flower Type of 1968

Design: No. RA45, Violets.

1969, Apr. 25 Litho. *Perf. 12½*

RA45 PT25 1c emerald, lilac & red 12 8

The tax was for the Anti-Tuberculosis League.

Redrawn Cancer Type of 1955

1969, Oct. 1 Litho. *Perf. 11*

RA46 PT9 1c brt. rose lilac 12 3

The tax was for the Dominican League against Cancer.

Invalid Type of 1968

1970, Mar. 2 *Perf. 12½*

RA47 PT24 1c blue 15 10

The tax was for the rehabilitation of the handicapped.

Book, Sun and Education Year Emblem PT27 — Communications Emblem PT28

1970, Feb. 6 *Perf. 11*

RA48 PT27 1c bright pink 8 4

International Education Year.

Flower Type of 1968

Design: 1c, Eleanthus capitatus; cross in upper left corner, denomination in lower right.

1970, Apr. 30 *Perf. 11*

RA49 PT25 1c emerald, red & yellow 15 8

Tax for Anti-Tuberculosis League.

Boy Type of 1967

1970, Dec. 1 *Perf. 12½*

RA49A PT23 1c orange 25 20

1971, Jan. 2 Litho. *Perf. 11*

Size: 17½x20½mm.

RA49B PT28 1c vio. bl. & red (white frame) 15 10

Tax was for Postal and Telegraph Communications School.

See Nos. RA53, RA58, RA63, RA69, RA78.

Invalid Type of 1968

1971, Mar. 1 Litho. *Perf. 11*

RA50 PT24 1c brt. rose lilac 15 8

Tax was for rehabilitation of the handicapped.

Cancer Type of 1952
Third Redrawing

1971, Oct. 1 *Perf. 11½*

RA51 PT9 1c dp. yellow green 18 10

Background of No. RA51 appears white and design stands out. No. RA43 has greenish background and design appears faint. Numeral "1" on No. RA51 is 3½mm. high, on No. RA43 it is 3mm.

Boy Type of 1967

1971, Dec. 1 Litho. *Perf. 11*

RA52 PT23 1c green 20 10

Communications Type of 1971

1972, Jan. 3 Litho. *Perf. 12½*

Size: 19x22mm.

RA53 PT28 1c dk. blue & red (blue frame) 15 8

Tax was for the Postal and Telegraph Communications School.

Invalid Type of 1968

1972, Mar. 1 Litho. *Perf. 11½*

RA54 PT24 1c brown 15 10

Orchid
PT29

1972, Apr. 2 *Perf. 11*

RA55 PT29 1c lt. green, red & yellow 20 10

Tax was for the Anti-Tuberculosis League.

Redrawn Cancer Type of 1954–58

1972, Oct. 2 *Perf. 12½*

RA56 PT9 1c orange 18 10

Tax was for Dominican League against Cancer.

Boy Type of 1967

1972, Dec. 1 *Perf. 12*

RA57 PT23 1c violet 15 10

Tax was for child welfare.

Communications Type of 1971

1973, Jan. 2 *Perf. 10½*

Size: 19x22mm.

RA58 PT28 1c dark blue & red (red frame) 10 8

Tax was for Postal and Telegraph Communications School.

Invalid
PT30

Hibiscus
PT31

1973, Mar. 1 Litho. *Perf. 12½*

Size: 21x25mm.

RA59 PT30 1c olive 15 8

Tax was for the Dominican Rehabilitation Association. See Nos. RA66, RA70, RA74, RA79.

1973, Apr. 17 Litho. *Perf. 10½*

RA60 PT31 1c multicolored 15 8

Tax was for Anti-Tuberculosis League. Exists imperf.

Cancer Type of 1952 Redrawn and "1973" Added

1973, Oct. 1 *Perf. 13½*

RA61 PT9 1c olive green 8 6

Tax was for Dominican League Against Cancer.

Boy Type of 1967

1973, Dec. 1 Litho. *Perf. 13x13½*

RA62 PT23 1c blue 15 10

Communications Type of 1971

1973, Nov. 3 *Perf. 10½*

Size: 19x22mm.

RA63 PT28 1c blue & red (lt. grn. frame) 8 6

Tax was for Postal and Telegraph Communications School. Exists imperf.

Invalid Type of 1972

1974, Mar. 1 Litho. *Perf. 10½*

Size: 22x27½mm.

RA66 PT30 1c lt. ultramarine 15 12

See note after No. RA59.

Cancer Type of 1952 Redrawn and "1974" Added

1974, Oct. 1 *Perf. 12*

RA67 PT9 1c orange 6 5

Tax was for Dominican League Against Cancer.

Boy Type of 1967

1974, Dec. 2 Litho. *Perf. 11½*

RA68 PT23 1c dk. brn. & buff 6 5

Communications Type of 1971

1974, Nov. 13 *Perf. 10½*

RA69 PT28 1c blue & red (yel. frame) 6 5

Invalid Type of 1972 Dated "1975"

1975, Mar. 1 *Perf. 13½x13*

Size: 21x32mm.

RA70 PT30 1c olive brown 6 5

Tax was for the Dominican Rehabilitation Association.

Catteeyopsis
Rosea
PT32

Oncidium
Colochilum
PT33

1975, Apr. 1 *Perf. 12*

RA71 PT32 1c blue & multi. 6 5

Tax was for Anti-Tuberculosis League.

Cancer Type of 1952 Redrawn and "1975" Added

1975, Oct. 1 Litho. *Perf. 12*

RA72 PT9 1c violet blue 10 5

Tax was for Dominican League Against Cancer. Exists imperf.

Boy Type of 1967

1975, Dec. 1 Litho. *Perf. 12*

RA73 PT23 1c red orange 10 5

Tax was for child welfare.

Invalid Type of 1973 Dated "1976"

1976, Mar. 1 Litho. *Perf. 12*

Size: 21x31mm.

RA74 PT30 1c ultramarine 10 5

Tax was for Dominican Rehabilitation Association.

1976, Apr. 6 *Perf. 13x13½*

RA75 PT33 1c green & multi. 10 5

Tax was for Anti-Tuberculosis League. See No. RA80, RA84.

Cancer Type of 1952 Redrawn and "1976" Added

1976, Oct. 1 Litho. *Perf. 13½*

RA76 PT9 1c green 10 5

Tax was for Dominican League Against Cancer.

Boy Type of 1967

1976, Dec. 1 Litho. *Perf. 13½*

RA77 PT23 1c purple 10 5

Tax was for child welfare.

Communications Type of 1971

1977, Jan. 7 Litho. *Perf. 10½*

Size: 19x22mm.

RA78 PT28 1c blue & red (lilac frame) 10 5

Tax was for Postal and Telegraph Communications School.

Invalid Type of 1973 Dated "1977"

1977, Mar. 11 *Perf. 12*

Size: 21x31mm.

RA79 PT30 1c ultramarine 10 5

Tax was for Dominican Rehabilitation Association.

Orchid Type of 1976 Dated "1977"

Orchid: Oncidium variegatum.

1977, Apr. 22 Litho. *Perf. 13½*

RA80 PT33 1c multicolored 10 5

Tax was for Anti-Tuberculosis League.

Boy Type of 1967

1977, Dec. 27 Litho. *Perf. 12*

RA81 PT23 1c emerald 8 3

Tax was for child welfare.

Cancer Type of 1952 Redrawn and "1977" Added

1978, Oct. 2 Litho. *Perf. 13½*

RA82 PT9 1c lilac rose 8 3

Tax was for Dominican League Against Cancer.

Mother, Child
and Holly
PT34

1978, Dec. 1 Litho. *Perf. 13½*

RA83 PT34 1c green 8 3

Tax was for child welfare.

Orchid Type of 1973 Dated "1978"

Flower: Yellow alder.

1978 Litho. *Perf. 13½*

RA84 PT33 1c light blue & multicolored 8 3

Tax was for Anti-Tuberculosis League.

POSTAL TAX AIR POST STAMPS.

Postal Tax Stamps Surcharged in Red or Gold

HABILITADO PARA
CORREO AEREO
+5

1930, Dec. 3 *Perf. 12* Unwmkd.

RAC1 PT2 5c+5c black & rose (R) 15.00 15.00
- *a.* Tête bêche pair 125.00
- *b.* "Habilitado Para" missing 50.00

RAC2 " 10c+10c black & rose (R) 15.00 15.00
- *a.* Tête bêche pair 125.00
- *b.* "Habilitado Para" missing 50.00
- *c.* Gold surch. 150.00 150.00
- *d.* As "c," tête bêche pair 500.00
- *e.* As "c," "Habilitado Para" missing 200.00

Nos. RAC1–RAC2 were on sale only on Dec. 3, 1930.

RAC4 PT2 5c+5c ultramarine & rose (R) 7.00 7.00
- *a.* Tête bêche pair 60.00
- *b.* Inverted surcharge 45.00
- *c.* Tête bêche pair, inverted surcharge 750.00
- *d.* Pair, one without surcharge 250.00
- *e.* "Habilitado Para" missing 15.00

RAC5 " 10c+10c yellow & rose (G) 6.00 6.00
- *a.* Tête bêche pair 50.00
- *b.* "Habilitado Para" missing 17.50

Imperf.

RAC6 PT2 5c+5c ultramarine & rose (R) 7.00 7.00
- *a.* Tête bêche pair 60.00
- *b.* "Habilitado Para" missing 17.50

RAC7 " 10c+10c yellow & rose (G) 7.00 7.00
- *a.* Tête bêche pair 60.00
- *b.* "Habilitado Para" missing 17.50

It was obligatory to use Nos. RA1 to RA8 and RAC1 and RAC7 on all postal matter, in amounts equal to the ordinary postage.

This surtax was for the aid of sufferers from the hurricane of Sept. 3rd, 1930.

Nos. RAC1 to RAC7 have been reprinted.

No. 261 Overprinted in Green

CORREO AEREO INTERNO

1933, Oct. 11

RAC8 A32 2c scarlet 35 25
- *a.* Double overprint 12.50
- *b.* Pair, one without ovpt. 450.00

By official decree a copy of this stamp, in addition to the regular postage, had to be used on every letter, etc., sent by the internal air post service.

DUTCH INDIES

(See Netherlands Indies.)

DUTCH NEW GUINEA

(See Netherlands New Guinea.)

EASTERN RUMELIA

(ĕs'tĕrn rōō·mē'lĭ·ȧ; -mēl'yȧ)

(South Bulgaria)

LOCATION—In southern Bulgaria.

GOVT.—A former autonomous unit of the Turkish Empire.

CAPITAL—Philippopolis (Plovdiv).

In 1885 the province of Eastern Rumelia revolted against Turkish rule and united with Bulgaria, adopting the new name of South Bulgaria. This union was assured by the Treaty of Bucharest in 1886, following the war between Serbia and Bulgaria.

40 Paras = 1 Piastre

Counterfeits of all overprints are plentiful.

A1

A2

A3

Stamps of Turkey, 1876-84, Overprinted in Blue.

1880 *Perf. 13½* **Unwmkd.**

No.	Type	Description	Unused	Used
1	A1	½pi on 20pa yellow green	20.00	20.00
2	"	2pi on 2pi yellow brown	*50.00*	
3	A2	10pa black & rose	*25.00*	
4	"	20pa violet & green	22.50	22.50
5	"	1pi black & blue	*70.00*	
6	"	2pi black & buff	50.00	50.00
7	"	5pi red & blue	125.00	125.00
8	A3	10pa blk. & red lilac	*15.00*	

Nos. 2, 3, 5 and 8 were not placed in use.

Inverted and double overprints of all values exist.

Same, with Extra Overprint "R. O."

No.	Type	Description	Unused	Used
9	A3	10pa black & red lilac	25.00	25.00

Crescent and Turkish Inscriptions of Value

A4

1881 Typographed *Perf. 13½*

No.	Type	Description	Unused	Used
10	A4	5pa black & olive	1.25	40
11	"	10pa black & green	2.00	40
12	"	20pa black & rose	20	40
13	"	1pi black & blue	2.00	1.50
14	"	5pi rose & blue	12.00	15.00

Tête bêche pairs, imperforates and all perf. 11½ copies of Nos. 10 to 14 were not placed in use, and were found only in the remainder stock. This is true also of a 10pa cliché in the 20pa plate, and of a cliché of Turkey No. 63 in the 1pi plate.

1884 *Perf. 11½, 13½*

No.	Type	Description	Unused	Used
15	A4	5pa lilac & pale lilac	20	20
16	"	10pa green & pale green	8	20
17	"	20pa carmine & pale rose	20	
18	"	1pi blue & pale blue	20	
19	"	5pi brown & pale brown	*100.00*	

No. 17–19 were not placed in use.

Nos. 15 to 19 imperf. are from the remainder stock.

South Bulgaria.

Counterfeits of all overprints are plentiful.

Nos. 10 to 14 Overprinted in Two Types:

a

b

Type a: Four toes on each foot.
Type b: Three toes on each foot.

1885 *Perf. 13½.* **Unwmkd.**

Blue Overprint.

No.	Type	Description	Unused	Used
20	A4	5pa black & olive	*75.00*	*75.00*
21	"	10pa black & green	*225.00*	*225.00*
22	"	20pa black & rose	75.00	75.00
23	"	1pi black & blue	8.00	10.00
24	"	5pi rose & blue	200.00	200.00

Black Overprint.

No.	Type	Description	Unused	Used
25	A4	1pi black & blue	10.00	13.50
26	"	5pi rose & blue	200.00	200.00

Same Overprint on Nos. 15 to 17.

Perf. 11½, 13½

Blue Overprint.

No.	Type	Description	Unused	Used
27	A4	5pa lilac & pale lilac, perf. 11½	4.00	10.00
		a. Perf. 13½	12.50	12.50
28	"	10pa green & pale green	4.00	10.00
29	"	20pa carmine & pale rose	45.00	60.00

Black Overprint.

No.	Type	Description	Unused	Used
30	A4	5pa lilac & pale lilac	7.50	10.00
31	"	10pa green & pale green	8.00	10.00
32	"	20pa carmine & pale rose	7.50	10.00

Nos. 10 to 14 Handstamped in Black in Two Types:

a

b

Type a: First letter at top circular.
Type b: First letter at top oval.

1885 *Perf. 13½*

No.	Type	Description	Unused	Used
33	A4	5pa black & olive	*300.00*	
34	"	10pa black & green	*300.00*	
35	"	20pa black & rose	35.00	40.00
36	"	1pi black & blue	20.00	25.00
		a. On Turkey No. 63 (error)		
37	"	5pi rose & blue	*300.00*	*325.00*

Same Handstamp in Black on Nos. 15 to 17.

Perf. 11½, 13½.

No.	Type	Description	Unused	Used
38	A4	5pa lilac & pale lilac, perf. 13½	7.50	10.00
		a. Perf. 11½	75.00	100.00
39	"	10pa green & pale green	6.00	7.50
40	"	20pa carmine & pale rose	6.00	8.00

Nos. 20 to 40 exist with inverted and double handstamps. Overprints in unlisted colors are proofs.

The stamps of South Bulgaria were superseded in 1886 by those of Bulgaria.

EASTERN SILESIA

(ĕs'tĕrn sĭ·lē'shĭ·ȧ; -shȧ)

LOCATION—In central Europe.

GOVT.—Former Austrian crownland.

AREA—1,987 sq. mi.

POP.—680,422 (estimated 1920).

CAPITAL—Troppau.

After World War I, this territory was occupied by Czechoslovakia and eventually was divided between Poland and Czechoslovakia, the dividing line running through Teschen.

100 Heller = 1 Krone
100 Fennigi = 1 Marka

Plebiscite Issues.

Stamps of Czechoslovakia 1918-20, Overprinted in Black, Blue, Violet or Red **SO 1920**

1920 *Imperf.* **Unwmkd.**

No.	Type	Description	Unused	Used
1	A2	1(h) dark brown	30	30
2	A1	3(h) red violet	10	10
3	A2	5(h) blue green	30.00	25.00
4	"	15(h) red	12.50	8.00
5	A1	20(h) blue green	10	10
6	A2	25(h) dull violet	1.25	75
7	A1	30(h) bistre (R)	25	15
8	"	40(h) red orange	30	20
9	A2	50(h) dull violet	40	30
10	"	50(h) dark blue	1.60	1.35
11	"	60(h) orange (Bl)	1.00	75
12	"	75(h) slate (R)	40	40
13	"	80(h) olive green (R)	40	35
14	A1	100(h) brown	60	50
15	A2	120(h) gray blk. (R)	2.50	1.25
16	A1	200(h) ultramarine (R)	1.60	1.25
17	A2	300(h) green (R)	2.50	2.00
18	A1	400(h) purple (R)	2.00	1.35
20	A2	500(h) red brown (Bl)	6.00	4.50
		a. Black overprint	10.00	8.00
21	"	1000(h) violet (Bl)	10.00	6.00
		a. Black ovpt.	150.00	150.00
		Nos. 1-21 (20)	73.80	54.60

Perf. 11½, 14

No.	Type	Description	Unused	Used
22	A2	1(h) dark brown	5	5
23	"	5(h) blue green	10	10
24	"	10(h) yellow green	10	10
		a. Imperf.	*275.00*	*200.00*
25	"	15(h) red	10	12
26	"	20(h) rose	30	30
		a. Imperf.	*325.00*	*250.00*
27	"	25(h) dull violet	30	30
28	"	30(h) red violet (Bl)	30	30
29	"	60(h) orange (Bl)	40	40
30	A1	200(h) ultra. (R)	4.00	3.00
		Nos. 22-30 (9)	5.65	4.67

The letters "S. O." are the initials of "Silésie Orientale".

Forged cancellations are found on Nos. 1-30.

Overprinted **19 SO 20**

No.	Type	Description	Unused	Used
31	A4	500(h) slate, *grayish* (C)		75.00
32	"	1000(h) black brown, *brownish* (V)		75.00

Excellent counterfeits of this overprint exist.

Stamps of Poland, 1919, Overprinted **S. O. 1920.**

1920 *Perf. 11½*

No.	Type	Description	Unused	Used
41	A10	5f green	4	4
42	"	10f red brown	5	5
43	"	15f light red	5	5
44	A11	25f olive green	5	5
45	"	50f blue green	5	5

Overprinted **S. O. 1920.**

No.	Type	Description	Unused	Used
46	A17	1k deep green	5	5
47	"	1.50k brown	5	5
48	"	2k dark blue	5	5
49	A18	2.50k dull violet	5	5
50	A19	5k slate blue	6	6
		Nos. 41-50 (10)	50	50

SPECIAL DELIVERY STAMPS.

Czechoslovakia Special Delivery Stamps Overprinted **S O 19 20**

1920 *Imperf.* **Unwmkd.**

Blue Overprint.

No.	Type	Description	Unused	Used
E1	SD1	2(h) red violet, *yellow*	5	5
		a. Black overprint	1.00	1.00
E2	"	5(h) yellow green, *yellow*	10	8
		a. Black overprint	6.50	6.50

POSTAGE DUE STAMPS.

Czechoslovakia Postage Due Stamps Overprinted In Blue or Red **SO 1920**

1920 *Imperf.* **Unwmkd.**

No.	Type	Description	Unused	Used
J1	D1	5(h) deep bistre (Bl)	10	10
		a. Black ovpt.	65.00	50.00
J2	"	10(h) deep bistre	10	10
J3	"	15(h) "	10	10
J4	"	20(h) "	10	10
J5	"	25(h) "	15	20
J6	"	30(h) "	15	20
J7	"	40(h) "	40	40
J8	"	50(h) "	40	40
J9	"	100(h) black brown (R)	70	70
J10	"	500(h) gray green (R)	3.50	3.00
J11	"	1000(h) purple (R)	8.00	7.00
		Nos. J1-J11 (11)	13.70	12.30

Forged cancellations exist.

NEWSPAPER STAMPS.

Czechoslovakia Newspaper Stamps Overprinted in Black **SO 1920**

1920 *Imperf.* **Unwmkd.**

No.	Type	Description	Unused	Used
P1	N1	2(h) gray green	10	10
P2	"	6(h) red	10	10
P3	"	10(h) dull violet	40	40
P4	"	20(h) blue	40	40
P5	"	30(h) gray brown	40	40
		Nos. P1-P5 (5)	1.40	1.40

ECUADOR

(ĕk′wȧ·dôr)

LOCATION — On the northwest coast of South America, bordering on the Pacific Ocean.

GOVT.—Republic.

AREA—116,270 sq. mi. (approx.).

POP.—7,560,000 (est. 1977).

CAPITAL—Quito.

The Republic of Ecuador was so constituted on May 11, 1830, after the Civil War which separated the original members of the Republic of Colombia, founded by Simón Bolívar, by uniting the Presidency of Quito with the Viceroyalty of New Granada, and the Captaincy of Venezuela. The Presidency of Quito became the Republic of Ecuador.

8 Reales = 1 Peso
100 Centavos = 1 Sucre (1881)

Coat of Arms
A1 A2

Typographed.
Quadrille Paper.

1865 ***Imperf.*** **Unwmkd.**

1 A1 1r yellow 17.50 12.50

1865–66 **Wove paper**

2 A1 ½r ultramarine 8.00 8.00
a. ½r gray blue 8.00 8.00
b. Batonné paper 12.50 12.50
c. Blue paper 35.00 35.00
3 " 1r buff 10.00 10.00
a. 1r orange buff 12.00 11.00
4 " 1r yellow 8.00 8.00
a. 1r olive yellow 12.00 10.00
b. Laid paper 85.00 70.00
c. Diagonal half used as ½r on cover 125.00
d. Batonné paper 15.00 15.00
5 " 1r green 100.00 30.00
a. Diagonal half used as ½r on cover 125.00
6 A2 4r red ('66) 150.00 85.00
a. 4r red brown 150.00 85.00
b. Arms in circle 150.00 85.00
c. Printed on both sides 300.00
d. Half used as 2r on cover 600.00

Letter paper embossed with arms of Ecuador was used in printing a number of sheets of Nos. 2, 4–6.

Papermakers' watermarks are known on No. 2 ("Bath" and crown) and No. 4 ("Rolland Freres").

On the 4r the oval holding the coat of arms is usually 13½–14mm. wide, but on about one-fifth of the stamps in the sheet it is 15–15½mm. wide, almost a circle.

The 2r, 8r and 12r, type A1, are bogus.

Proofs of the ½r, type A1, are known in black and green.

An essay of type A2 shows the condor's head facing right.

1871–72 **Blue-surface Paper**

7 A1 ½r ultramarine 15.00 12.50
8 " 1r yellow 100.00 45.00

Reprints of types A1 and A2 differ in color from originals, have a different sheet makeup and lack gum. Type A1 reprints usually have a double frameline at left. All stamps on blue paper with horizontal blue lines are reprints.

Coat of Arms
A3 A4

Lithographed

1872 **White Paper** ***Perf. 11***

9 A3 ½r blue 9.00 2.50
10 A4 1r yellow 10.00 3.00
11 A3 1p rose 2.00 *10.00*

The 1r surcharged 4c is fraudulent.

Coat of Arms
A5 A6

A7 A8

A9 A10

1881, Nov. 1 **Engraved** ***Perf. 12***

12 A5 1c yellow brown 8 8
13 A6 2c lake 12 12
14 A7 5c blue 2.50 35
15 A8 10c orange 12 12
16 A9 20c gray violet 15 15
17 A10 50c blue green 35 *1.20*
Nos. 12–17 (6) 3.32 *2.02*

The 1c surcharged 3c, and 20c surcharged 5c are fraudulent.

No. 17 Surcharged in Black

DIEZ
CENTAVOS

1883, April

18 A10 10c on 50c blue grn. 17.50 17.50
a. Double surcharge

A12 A13

A14 A15

1887

19 A12 1c blue green 30 15
20 A13 2c vermilion 50 15
21 A14 5c blue 1.50 30
22 A15 80c olive green 3.00 *7.50*

President Juan Flores
A16

1892

23 A16 1c orange 10 10
24 " 2c dark brown 10 10
25 " 5c vermilion 10 10
26 " 10c green 10 10
27 " 20c red brown 10 10
28 " 50c maroon 10 *40*
29 " 1s blue 20 *1.00*
30 " 5s purple 50 *1.50*
Nos. 23–30 (8) 1.30 *3.40*

The issues of 1892, 1894, 1895 and 1896 were printed by the Hamilton Bank Note Co., New York, to the order of N. F. Seebeck, who held a contract for stamps with the government of Ecuador.

No. 30 in green is said to be an essay or color trial.

Nos. 29 and 30 Surcharged in Black

5 CENTAVOS

1893

Surcharge Measures 25½x2½ mm.

31 A16 5c on 1s blue 1.50 1.50
32 " 5c on 5s purple 3.50 3.50
a. Double surcharge

Surcharge Measures 24x2¼ mm.

33 A16 5c on 1s blue 1.25 1.25
a. Double surcharge, one inverted
34 " 5c on 5s purple 5.00 5.00
a. Double surcharge, one inverted

Nos. 28–30 Surcharged in Black

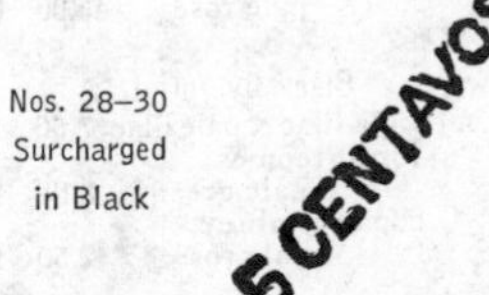

35 A16 5c on 50c maroon 50 50
a. Inverted surch. 2.00
36 " 5c on 1s blue 75 75
37 " 5c on 5s purple 3.50 3.50

President Juan Flores A19 — President Vicente Rocafuerte A20

38 A19 5c on 5s lake 75 65

It is stated that No. 38 was used exclusively as a postage stamp and not for telegrams.

1894 **Dated 1894.** ***Perf. 12.***

Various Frames

39 A20 1c blue 20 20
40 " 2c yellow brown 20 20
41 " 5c green 25 20
b. Perf. 14 3.00 1.25
42 " 10c vermilion 40 30
43 " 20c black 60 35
44 " 50c orange 2.50 1.00
45 " 1s carmine 4.00 2.00
46 " 5s dark blue 6.00 5.00
Nos. 39–46 (8) 14.15 9.25

1895 **Same, Dated "1895".**

47 A20 1c blue 50 45
48 " 2c yellow brown 50 45
49 " 5c green 40 25
50 " 10c vermilion 40 20
51 " 20c black 60 55
52 " 50c orange 2.25 1.00
53 " 1s carmine 10.00 4.00
54 " 5s dark blue 5.00 1.85
Nos. 47–54 (8) 19.65 8.75

Reprints of the 2c, 10c, 50c, 1s and 5s of the 1894–95 issues are generally on thick paper. Original issues are on thin to medium thick paper. To distinguish reprints from originals, a comparison of paper thickness, paper color, gum, printing clarity and direction of paper weave is necessary. Price 10 cents each.

Coat of Arms
A21 A22

A23 A24

A25 A26

A27 A28

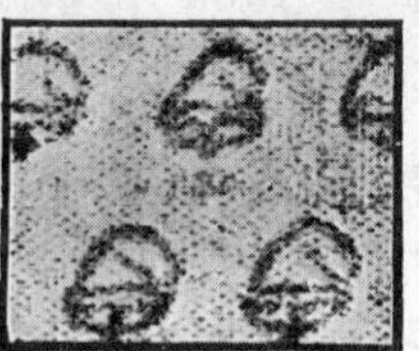

Wmk. 117

1896 **Wmkd. Liberty Cap. (117)**

55 A21 1c dark green 50 45
56 A22 2c red 50 20
57 A23 5c blue 50 20
58 A24 10c bistre brown 40 *50*
59 A25 20c orange 70 *1.00*
60 A26 50c dark blue 1.25 *2.00*
61 A27 1s yellow brown 2.50 *2.50*
62 A28 5s violet 5.00 *4.00*
Nos. 55–62 (8) 11.35 *10.85*

Unwmkd.

62A A21 1c dark green 60 20
62B A22 2c red 60 20
62C A23 5c blue 60 20
62D A24 10c bistre brown 50 *1.00*
62E A25 20c orange 3.75 *4.00*
62F A26 50c dark blue 50 *2.00*
62G A27 1s yellow brown 3.50 *6.00*
62H A28 5s violet 3.75 *4.00*
Nos. 62A–62H (8) 13.80 *17.60*

Reprints of Nos. 55–62H are on very thick paper, with paper weave direction vertical. Price 10 cents each.

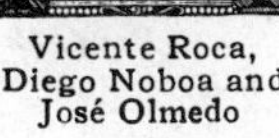

Vicente Roca, Diego Noboa and José Olmedo
A28a

General Juan Francisco Elizalde
A28b

Lithographed

1896, Oct. 9 *Perf. 11½* **Unwmkd.**

63 A28a 1c rose 35 35
64 A28b 2c blue 35 35
65 A28a 5c green 40 40
66 A28b 10c ochre 40 40
67 A28a 20c red 50 *1.00*
68 A28b 50c violet 75 *1.50*
69 A28a 1s orange 1.50 *2.00*
Nos. 63-69 (7) 4.25 *6.00*

Issued in commemoration of the success of the Liberal Party in 1845 and 1895.

Coat of Arms
A29 A30

Black Surcharge.

1896, Nov. *Perf. 12*

70 A29 1c on 1c vermilion, "1893-1894" 35 30
a. Inverted surcharge 1.25 1.25
b. Double surcharge 4.00 4.00
71 " 2c on 2c blue, "1893-1894" 1.00 1.00
a. Invtd. surcharge 2.00 2.00
72 " 5c on 10c orange, "1887-1888" 30 25
a. Inverted surcharge 1.00 1.00
b. Double surcharge 2.50 2.50
c. Surcharged "2 cts" 50 50
d. "1893-1894" 3.00 3.00
73 " 10c on 4c brown, "1887-1888" 65 60
a. Inverted surcharge 1.00 1.00
b. Double surcharge 2.00 2.00
c. Double surcharge, one inverted
d. Surcharged "1 cto" 1.65 1.65
e. "1891-1892" 7.50 7.50

Similar surcharges of type A29 include: Dated "1887–1888"—1c on 1c blue green, 1c on 2c red, 1c on 4c brown, 1c on 10c yellow; 2c on 2c red, 2c on 10c yellow; 10c on 1c green. Dated "1891–1892"—1c on 1c blue green, 1c on 4c brown. Dated "1893–1894"—2c on 10c yellow; 10c on 1c vermilion, 10c on 10s black.

Wmkd. Liberty Cap. (117)

Surcharge in Black or Red

1896, Oct.

74 A30 5c on 20c orange 7.50 6.00
76 " 10c on 50c dk. bl. (R) 7.50 6.00
a. Double surcharge

The surcharge is diagonal, horizontal, or vertical.

Overprinted

On Issue of 1894.

1897 **Unwmkd.**

77 A20 1c blue 1.00 80
78 " 2c yellow brown 75 50
79 A20 5c green 35 30
80 " 10c vermilion 1.25 1.00
81 " 20c black 1.35 1.25
82 " 50c orange 3.50 1.00
83 " 1s carmine 9.00 2.50
84 " 5s dark blue 40.00 35.00
Nos. 77-84 (8) 57.20 42.35

On Issue of 1895.

85 A20 1c blue 2.75 2.75
86 " 2c yellow brown 1.10 1.10
87 " 5c green 80 60
88 " 10c vermilion 3.25 3.25
89 " 20c black 1.10 1.10
90 " 50c orange 15.00 7.00
91 " 1s carmine 7.00 4.00
92 " 5s dark blue 7.00 7.00
Nos. 85-92 (8) 38.00 26.80

Overprinted

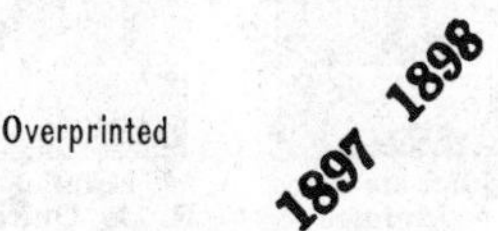

On Issue of 1894.

93 A20 1c blue 85 60
94 " 2c yellow brown 60 50
95 " 5c green 25 15
96 " 10c vermilion 2.00 1.25
97 " 20c black 2.00 1.25
98 " 50c orange 4.00 1.75
99 " 1s carmine 7.00 4.50
100 " 5s dark blue 50.00 45.00
Nos. 93-100 (8) 66.70 55.00

On Issue of 1895.

101 A20 1c blue 2.00 80
102 " 2c yellow brown 80 80
103 " 5c green 1.00 70
104 " 10c vermilion 3.75 2.50
105 " 20c black 3.00 80
106 " 50c orange 1.25 85
107 " 1s carmine 5.00 4.00
108 " 5s dark blue 6.00 5.00
Nos. 101-108 (8) 22.80 15.45

Overprints on Nos. 77–108 are to be found reading upward from left to right and downward from left to right, as well as inverted.

Overprinted **1897 Y 1898**

1897 On Issue of 1894.

109 A20 10c vermilion *40.00 40.00*

On Issue of 1895.

110 A20 2c yellow brown *35.00 35.00*
111 " 1s carmine *40.00 40.00*
112 " 5s dark blue *40.00 35.00*

Nos. 56, 59 Overprinted

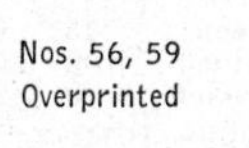

1897, June **Wmk. 117**

113 A22 2c red 30.00 30.00
114 A25 20c orange 32.50 32.50

Many forged overprints on Nos. 77–114 exist, made on original stamps and reprints.

Same Overprint on Stamps or Types of 1896.

1897 *Perf. 11½.* **Unwmkd.**

115 A28a 1c rose 1.25 1.25
116 A28b 2c blue 1.00 1.00
117 " 10c ochre 1.00 1.00
118 A28a 1s yellow 3.00 3.00

No. 63 Overprinted

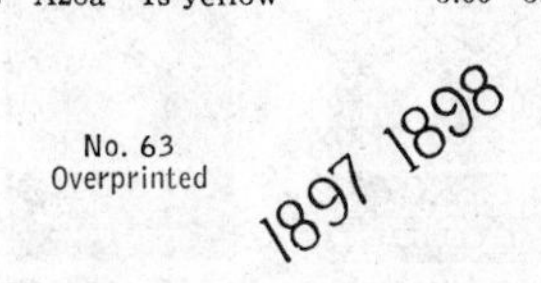

1897

119 A28a 1c rose 50 50

Nos. 63–66 Overprinted in Black

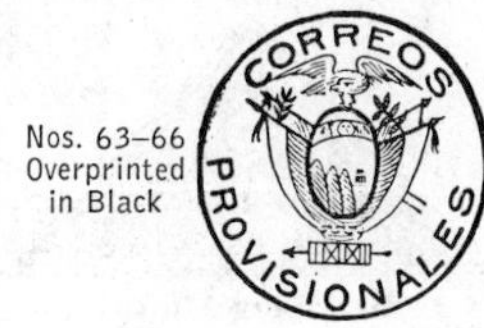

1897

122 A28a 1c rose 2.25 2.25
a. Inverted overprint 3.00 3.00
123 A28b 2c blue 2.25 2.25
a. Inverted overprint 3.00 3.00
124 A28a 5c green 2.25 2.25
a. Inverted overprint 3.00 3.00
125 A28b 10c ochre 2.25 2.25
a. Double overprint 5.00 5.00
b. Inverted overprint 3.00 3.00

The 20c, 50c and 1s with this overprint in black and all values of the issue overprinted in blue are reprints.

Coat of Arms
A33

1897, June 23 **Engr.** *Perf. 14–16*

127 A33 1c dark yellow green 10 10
128 " 2c orange red 10 10
129 " 5c lake 15 15
130 " 10c dark brown 15 15
131 " 20c yellow 30 *50*
132 " 50c dull blue 30 *80*
133 " 1s gray 40 *1.00*
134 " 5s dark lilac 70 *1.50*
Nos. 127-134 (8) 2.20 *4.30*

A34 A35

1899, May

135 A34 1c on 2c orange red 1.50 50
136 A35 5c on 10c brown 1.00 35
a. Double surcharge

Luis Vargas Torres
A36

Abdón Calderón
A37

Juan Montalvo
A38

José Mejia
A39

Santa Cruz y Espejo
A40

Pedro Carbo
A41

José Joaquín Olmedo
A42

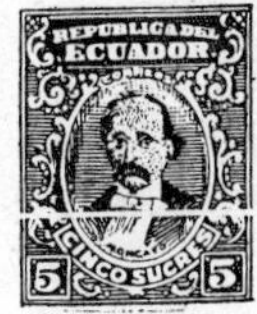

Pedro Moncayo
A43

1899 *Perf. 12½–16*

137 A36 1c gray blue & black 12 10
a. Imperf. vertically
138 A37 2c brown lilac & black 15 10
139 A38 5c lake & black 20 10
140 A39 10c violet & black 20 10
141 A40 20c green & black 20 12
142 A41 50c lilac rose & black 75 60
143 A42 1s ochre & black 3.00 2.00
144 A43 5s lilac & black 6.00 5.00
Nos. 137-144 (8) 10.62 8.12

1901

145 A36 1c scarlet & black 12 10
146 A37 2c green & black 15 10
147 A38 5c gray lilac & black 15 8
148 A39 10c deep blue & black 15 12
149 A40 20c gray & black 20 15
150 A41 50c light blue & black 75 60
151 A42 1s brown & black 3.00 2.00
152 A43 5s gray blk. & blk. 5.00 4.00
Nos. 145-152 (8) 9.52 7.15

In July, 1902, following the theft of a quantity of stamps during a fire at Guayaquil, the Government authorized the governors of the provinces to handstamp their stocks. Many varieties of these handstamps exist.

Other control marks were used in 1907.

A44

Surcharged on Revenue Stamp Dated 1901-1902.

1903-06 *Perf. 14, 15.*

153 A44 1c on 5c gray lilac ('06) 20 20
154 " 1c on 20c gray ('06) 3.00 2.50
155 " 1c on 25c yellow 30 20
a. Double surcharge
156 " 1c on 1s blue ('06) 25.00 20.00
157 " 3c on 5c gray lilac ('06) 3.00 2.00
158 " 3c on 20c gray ('06) 7.50 6.00
159 " 3c on 25c yel. ('06) 7.50 6.00
159A " 3c on 1s blue ('06) 75 75
Nos. 153-159A (8) 47.25 37.65

Counterfeits are plentiful. See Nos. 191–197.

Capt. Abdón Calderón
A45 A46

1904, July 31 *Perf. 12*

160 A45 1c red & black 25 25
161 " 2c blue & black 25 25
162 A46 5c yellow & black 1.25 85
163 A45 10c red & black 2.50 75
164 " 20c blue & black 6.00 2.00
165 A46 50c yellow & black 42.50 32.50
Nos. 160-165 (6) 52.75 36.60

Issued in commemoration of the centenary of the birth of Abdón Calderón, 1804–1904.

President Vicente Roca
A47

President Diego Noboa
A48

President Francisco Robles
A49

President José M. Urvina
A50

President García Moreno
A51

President Jerónimo Carrión
A52

President Javier Espinoza
A53

President Antonio Borrero
A54

1907, July *Perf. 14, 15*

166	A47	1c red & black	18	12
167	A48	2c pale blue & black	25	15
168	A49	3c orange & black	35	15
169	A50	5c lilac rose & black	50	12
170	A51	10c deep blue & blk.	1.50	18
171	A52	20c yel. green & blk.	2.00	25
172	A53	50c violet & black	4.00	60
173	A54	1s green & black	6.00	1.50
		Nos. 166-173 (8)	14.78	3.07

The stamps of the 1907 issue frequently have control marks similar to those found on the 1899 and 1901 issues. These marks were applied to distinguish the stamps issued in the various provinces and to serve as a check on local officials.

Locomotive
A55

García Moreno
A56

Gen. Eloy Alfaro
A57

Abelardo Moncayo
A58

Archer Harman
A59

James Sivewright
A60

Mt. Chimborazo
A61

1908

174	A55	1c red brown	1.00	1.50
175	A56	2c blue & black	1.50	1.00
176	A57	5c claret & black	3.00	2.50
177	A58	10c ochre & black	2.00	2.00
178	A59	20c green & black	2.00	3.00
179	A60	50c gray & black	2.00	3.00
180	A61	1s black	4.00	5.00
		Nos. 174-180 (7)	15.50	18.00

Issued in commemoration of the opening of the Guayaquil-Quito Railway.

José Mejía Vallejo
A62

Francisco J. E. Santa Cruz y Espejo
A63

Francisco Ascásubi
A64

Juan Salinas
A65

Juan Pio de Montúfar
A66

Carlos de Montúfar
A67

Juan de Dios Morales
A68

Manuel R. de Quiroga
A69

Principal Exposition Building
A70

1909 *Perf. 12.*

181	A62	1c green	20	40
182	A63	2c blue	20	40
183	A64	3c orange	20	50
184	A65	5c claret	20	50
185	A66	10c yellow brown	25	50
186	A67	20c gray	25	75
187	A68	50c vermilion	25	75
188	A69	1s olive green	25	1.00
189	A70	5s violet	75	2.00
		Nos. 181-189 (9)	2.55	6.80

National Exposition of 1909.

Surcharged CINCO CENTAVOS

1909

190	A68	5c on 50c vermilion	60	60

Revenue Stamps Surcharged as in 1903.

1910 *Perf. 14, 15*

Stamps Dated 1905-1906.

191	A44	1c on 5c green	75	75
192	"	5c on 20c blue	3.00	1.00
193	"	5c on 25c violet	5.00	2.00

Stamps Dated 1907-1908.

194	A44	1c on 5c green	15	10
195	"	5c on 20c blue	6.00	5.00
196	"	5c on 25c violet	20	20

Stamp Dated 1909—1910

197	A44	5c on 20c blue	*27.50*	*27.50*

President Roca
A71

President Noboa
A72

President Robles
A73

President Urvina
A74

President Moreno
A75

President Borrero
A76

1911-28 *Perf. 12.*

198	A71	1c scarlet & black	15	8
199	"	1c orange ('16)	12	8
200	"	1c light blue ('25)	12	8
201	A72	2c blue & black	35	8
202	"	2c green ('16)	12	8
203	"	2c dark violet ('25)	12	8
204	A73	3c org. & blk. ('13)	1.10	35
205	"	3c black ('15)	15	8
206	A74	5c scarlet & black	50	8
207	"	5c violet ('15)	18	8
208	"	5c rose ('25)	18	8
209	"	5c dark brown ('28)	25	8
210	A75	10c deep blue & black	75	8
211	"	10c deep blue ('15)	75	20
212	"	10c yellow green ('25)	20	8
213	"	10c black ('28)	60	10
214	A76	1s green & black	4.00	1.25
215	"	1s orange & black ('27)	2.50	25
		Nos. 198-215 (18)	12.14	3.19

A77

1912 *Perf. 14, 15*

216	A77	1c on 1s green	50	50
217	"	2c on 2s carmine	70	70
218	"	2c on 5s dull blue	70	70
219	"	2c on 10s yellow	1.50	1.25
		a. Inverted surcharge	3.00	3.00

No. 216 exists with narrow "V" and small "U" in "UN" and Nos. 217, 218 and 219 with "D" with serifs or small "O" in "DOS".

Enrique Váldez
A78

Jerónimo Carrión
A79

Javier Espinoza
A80

1915-17 *Perf. 12*

220	A78	4c red & black	18	8
221	A79	20c grn. & blk. ('17)	1.75	25
222	A80	50c deep violet & black	3.00	50

Olmedo

A86

Monument to "Fathers of the Country"

A95

Laurel Wreath and Star

A104

Designs: 2c, Rafael Ximena. 3c, Roca. 4c, Luis F. Viviero. 5c, Luis Febres Cordero. 6c, Francisco Lavayen. 7c, Jorge Antonio de Elizalde. 8c, Baltazar Garcia. 9c, Jose de Antepara. 15c, Luis Urdaneta. 20c, Jose M. Villamil. 30c, Miguel Letamendi. 40c, Gregorio Escobedo. 50c, Gen. Antonio Jose de Sucre. 60c, Juan Illingworth. 70c, Roca. 80c, Rocafuerte. 1s, Simon Bolivar.

1920

223	A86	1c yellow green	20	10
224	"	2c carmine	15	15
225	"	3c yellow brown	15	15
226	"	4c myrtle green	25	20
227	"	5c pale blue	25	10
228	"	6c red orange	40	40
229	"	7c brown	1.00	75
230	"	8c apple green	50	30
231	"	9c lake	80	60
232	A95	10c light blue	75	15
233	A86	15c dark gray	1.00	50
234	"	20c dark violet	1.00	25
235	"	30c bright violet	2.00	1.25
236	"	40c dark brown	2.50	2.00
237	"	50c dark green	2.25	50
238	"	60c dark blue	3.00	2.00
239	"	70c gray	5.00	3.50
240	"	80c orange yellow	4.00	3.50
241	A104	90c green	5.00	3.50
242	A86	1s pale blue	9.00	6.00
		Nos. 223-242 (20)	39.20	25.90

Nos. 223 to 242 were issued in commemoration of the centenary of the independence of Guayaquil.

Postal Tax Stamp of 1924 Overprinted **POSTAL**

1925

259	PT6	20c bistre brown	1.25	50

Stamps of 1915–25 Overprinted in Black or Red (Upright or Inverted) QUITO 1926 ESMERALDAS

1926

260	A71	1c light blue	2.50	2.50
261	A72	2c dark violet	2.50	2.50
262	A73	3c black (R)	2.50	2.50
263	A86	4c myrtle green	2.50	2.50
264	A74	5c rose	2.50	2.50
265	A75	10c yellow green	2.50	2.50
		Nos. 260-265 (6)	15.00	15.00

Quito-Esmeraldas railway opening.

Postal Tax Stamps of 1920-24 Overprinted **POSTAL**

1927

266	PT6	1c olive green	15	8
		a. "POSTAI"	1.50	1.00
		b. Double overprint	1.50	1.00
		c. Inverted overprint	1.50	1.00
267	PT6	2c deep green	15	8
		a. "POSTAI"	1.50	1.00
		b. Double overprint	1.50	1.00
268	"	20c bistre brown	90	12
		a. "POSTAI"	10.00	6.00

Quito Post Office

A109

1927, June

269	A109	5c orange	15	8
270	"	10c dark green	20	12
271	"	20c violet	40	20

Opening of new Quito P.O.

Postal Tax Stamp of 1924 Overprinted **POSTAL** in Dark Blue.

1928

273	PT6	20c bistre brown	25	8
		a. Double overprint, one inverted	1.50	60

A110

Nos. 235, 239–240 Overprinted in Red Brown and Surcharged in Dark Blue.

1928, July 8

274	A110	10c on 30c violet	2.00	2.00
		a. Surch. invtd.		
275	"	50c on 70c gray	2.50	2.50
276	"	1s on 80c org. yel.	3.00	3.00
		a. Surch. invtd.		

Quito-Cayambe railway opening.

Stamps of 1920 Surcharged ASAMBLEA NCNAL. 1928 5 CTVOS.

1928, Oct. 9

277	A86	1c on 1c yel. grn.	8.00	8.00
278	"	1c on 2c carmine	12	12
279	"	2c on 3c yel. brn.	85	85
		a. Double surcharge, one reading up	5.00	5.00
280	"	2c on 4c myrtle green	65	65
281	"	2c on 5c light blue	25	25
		a. Double surcharge	5.00	5.00
282	"	2c on 7c brown	11.00	11.00
283	"	5c on 6c red orange	15	15
		a. "5 ctvos." omitted	5.00	
284	"	10c on 7c brown	50	50
285	"	20c on 8c apple green	15	15
		a. Double surcharge		
286	A95	40c on 10c blue	1.00	1.00
287	A86	40c on 15c dark gray	40	40
288	"	50c on 20c dark violet	8.00	8.00
289	"	1s on 40c dk. brn.	1.75	1.75
290	"	5s on 50c dk. green	2.25	2.00
291	"	10s on 60c dark blue	9.00	8.00

With Additional Surcharge in Red **0.10**

292	A86	10c on 2c on 7c brown	15	15
		a. Red surcharge double	5.00	5.00
		Nos. 277-292 (16)	44.22	42.97

National Assembly of 1928.
Counterfeit overprints exist of Nos. 277–291.

A111

A112

Surcharged in Various Colors

1928, Oct. 31 *Perf. 14*

293	A111	5c on 20c gray lilac (Bk)	1.00	75
294	"	10c on 20c gray lilac (R)	1.00	75
295	"	20c on 1s green (O)	1.00	75
296	"	50c on 1s green (Bl)	1.25	60
297	"	1s on 1s green (V)	1.50	75
298	"	5s on 2s red (G)	5.00	4.00
299	"	10s on 2s red (Br)	6.00	6.00
		a. Black surcharge	7.00	7.00
		Nos. 293-299 (7)	16.75	13.60

Quito-Otavalo railway opening.

Postal Tax Stamp of 1924 Overprinted in Red **POSTAL**

1929 *Perf. 12.*

302	PT6	2c deep green	6	6

There are two types of overprint on No. 302 differing slightly.

1929 Red Overprint.

303	A112	1c dark blue	8	6
		a. Overprint reading down	8	6

See also Nos. 586–587.

Plowing

A113

Cultivating Cacao

A114

Cacao Pod

A115

Growing Tobacco

A116

Exportation of Fruits

A117

Landscape—A118

Loading Sugar Cane

A119

Scene in Quito

A120

Scene in Quito

A121

Olmedo

A122

Sucre

A123

Bolívar

A124

Monument to Simón Bolívar

A125

1930, Aug. 1 *Perf. 12½*

No.	Type	Description	Unused	Used
304	A113	1c yellow & carmine	20	10
305	A114	2c yellow & green	20	10
306	A115	5c deep green & violet brown	20	12
307	A116	6c yellow & red	30	12
308	A117	10c orange & olive green	30	15
309	A118	16c red & yellow green	40	30
310	A119	20c ultramarine & yellow	45	18
311	A120	40c orange & sepia	50	18
312	A121	50c orange & sepia	65	18
313	A122	1s deep green & black	1.50	25
314	A123	2s dark blue & black	3.00	50
315	A124	5s dark violet & black	6.00	75
316	A125	10s carmine rose & black	20.00	5.00
		Nos. 304-316 (13)	33.70	7.93

Centenary of founding of republic.

A126 A127

1933 Red Overprint. *Perf. 15.*

No.	Type	Description	Unused	Used
317	A126	10c olive brown	18	12

Blue Overprint.

No.	Type	Description	Unused	Used
318	A127	10c olive brown	18	8
		a. Inverted overprint	4.00	4.00

Nos. 307, 309 Surcharged in Black

1933 *Perf. 12½*

No.	Type	Description	Unused	Used
319	A116	5c on 6c yellow & red	20	10
320	A118	10c on 16c red & yellow green	25	10
		a. Inverted ovpt.	4.00	4.00

Landscape
A128

Mt. Chimborazo
A129

1934-45 *Perf. 12.*

No.	Type	Description	Unused	Used
321	A128	5c violet	15	5
322	"	5c blue	15	5
323	"	5c dark brown	15	5
323A	"	5c slate black ('45)	15	5
324	"	10c rose	15	5
325	"	10c dark green	15	5
326	"	10c brown	15	5
327	"	10c orange	15	5
328	"	10c olive green	15	5
329	"	10c gray black ('35)	20	5
329A	"	10c red lilac ('44)	15	5

Perf. 14.

No.	Type	Description	Unused	Used
330	A129	1s carmine rose	1.50	60
		Nos. 321-330 (12)	3.20	1.15

Stamps of 1930 Surcharged or Overprinted in various colors similar to:

INAUGURACION MONUMENTO A BOLIVAR

QUITO, 24 DE JULIO DE 1935

1935 *Perf. 12½.*

No.	Type	Description	Unused	Used
331	A116	5c on 6c yellow & red (Bl)	30	15
332	"	10c on 6c yellow & red (G)	35	15
333	A119	20c ultra. & yel. (R)	40	20
334	A120	40c orange & sepia (G)	50	30
335	A121	50c orange & sepia (G)	70	50
336	A124	1s on 5s dark violet & black (Gold)	2.00	90
337	"	2s on 5s dark violet & black (Gold)	3.00	1.35
338	A125	5s on 10s car. rose & black (Bl)	5.00	3.25
		Nos. 331-338, C35-C38 (12)	28.25	22.80

Unveiling of a monument to Bolivar at Quito, July 24, 1935.

The five-stamp Sociedad Colombista Panamericana series of 1935 and five airmail stamps of a similar design are not recognized by this Catalogue as having been issued primarily for postal purposes.

Telegraph Stamp Overprinted Diagonally in Red **POSTAL**

1935 *Perf. 14½*

No.	Type	Description	Unused	Used
339	A126	10c olive brown	12	8

Map of Galápagos Islands
A130

Galapagos Land Iguana
A131

Galápagos Tortoise
A132

Charles R. Darwin
A133

Columbus
A134

Island Scene
A135

1936 *Perf. 14.*

No.	Type	Description	Unused	Used
340	A130	2c black	20	10
341	A131	5c olive green	30	15
342	A132	10c brown	50	15
343	A133	20c dark violet	50	20
344	A134	1s dark carmine	1.00	50
345	A135	2s dark blue	2.00	1.00
		Nos. 340-345 (6)	4.50	2.10

Issued to commemorate the centenary of the visit of Charles Darwin to the Galápagos Islands, September 17, 1835.

Tobacco Stamp Overprinted in Black

POSTAL

1936 *Rouletted 7.*

No.	Type	Description	Unused	Used
346	PT7	1c rose red	10	8
		a. Horiz. pair, imperf. vertical		
		b. Double surcharge		

No. 346 is similar to type PT7 but does not include "CASA CORREOS".

Louis Godin, Charles M. de la Condamine and Pierre Bouguer
A136

Portraits: 5c, 20c, Antonio Ulloa, La Condamine and Jorge Juan.

1936 **Engraved.** *Perf. 12½*

No.	Type	Description	Unused	Used
347	A136	2c deep blue	8	8
348	"	5c dark green	10	8
349	"	10c deep orange	12	8
350	"	20c violet	30	15
351	"	50c dark red	60	35
		Nos. 347-351, C39-C42 (9)	3.10	1.46

Bicentenary of Geodesical Mission to Quito.

Independence Monument
A137

1936 *Perf. 13½x14.*

No.	Type	Description	Unused	Used
352	A137	2c green	1.25	30
353	"	5c dark violet	1.25	30
354	"	10c carmine rose	1.25	35
355	"	20c black	1.25	50
356	"	50c blue	2.00	1.50
357	"	1s dark red	2.50	1.75
		Nos. 352-357, C43-C50 (14)	41.75	36.45

Issued to commemorate the first International Philatelic Exhibition at Quito.

Coat of Arms
A138

Overprint in Black or Red

1937 *Perf. 12½*

No.	Type	Description	Unused	Used
359	A138	5c olive green	20	10
360	"	10c dark blue (R)	20	10

Andean Landscape
A139

Atahualpa, the Last Inca
A140

Hat Weavers
A141

Coast Landscape
A142

Gold Washing
A143

1937, Aug. 19 *Perf. 11½*

No.	Type	Description	Unused	Used
361	A139	2c green	10	8
362	A140	5c deep rose	15	8
363	A141	10c blue	20	5
364	A142	20c deep rose	50	25
365	A143	1s olive green	75	35
		Nos. 361-365 (5)	1.70	81

"Liberty" Carrying Flag of Ecuador
A144

Engraved and Lithographed

1938, Feb. 22 *Perf. 12*

Center Multicolored

No.	Type	Description	Unused	Used
366	A144	2c blue	15	10
367	"	5c violet	18	10
368	"	10c black	25	10
369	"	20c brown	30	15
370	"	50c black	45	18
371	"	1s olive black	75	35
372	"	2s dark brown	1.50	50
		Nos. 366-372, C57-C63 (14)	8.03	2.98

U.S. Constitution, 150th anniversary.

Winged Figure Holding Globe
A145

Cactus and Winged Wheel
A146

"Communications"
A147

"Construction"
A148

Engraved.

1938, Oct. 30 *Perf. 13, 13x13½*

373 A145 10c brt. ultramarine 10 6
374 A146 50c deep red violet 18 12
375 A147 1s copper red 40 10
376 A148 2s dark green 60 10

Progress of Ecuador Exhibition.

Parade of Athletes
A149

Runner
A150

Basketball
A151

Wrestlers
A152

Diver
A153

1939, Mar. *Perf. 12*

377 A149 5c carmine rose 2.50 50
378 A150 10c deep blue 2.75 60
379 A151 50c gray olive 3.50 75
380 A152 1s dull violet 6.00 75
381 A153 2s dull olive green 9.50 1.00
Nos. 377-381, C65-C69 (10) 48.00 5.45

First Bolivarian Games (1938), La Paz.

Dolores Mission
A154

Trylon and Perisphere
A155

1939, June 16 *Perf. 12½x13*

382 A154 2c blue green 6 6
383 " 5c rose red 10 6
384 " 10c ultramarine 15 6
385 " 50c yellow brown 40 25
386 " 1s black 70 25
387 " 2s purple 1.20 25
Nos. 382-387, C73-C79 (13) 4.43 1.83

Golden Gate International Exposition.

1939, June 30

388 A155 2c light olive green 6 5
389 " 5c red orange 12 5
390 A155 10c ultramarine 15 6
391 " 50c slate gray 50 15
392 " 1s rose carmine 75 18
393 " 2s black brown 1.25 20
Nos. 388-393, C80-C86 (13) 4.70 1.28

New York World's Fair.

Flags of the 21 American Republics
A156

Francisco J. E. Santa Cruz y Espejo
A157

1940 *Perf. 12.*

394 A156 5c deep rose & black 10 8
395 " 10c dark blue & black 15 8
396 " 50c Prussian green & black 35 15
397 " 1s deep violet & black 60 30
Nos. 394-397, C87-C90 (8) 4.05 1.60

Pan American Union, 50th anniversary.

1941, Dec. 15

398 A157 30c blue 25 8
399 " 1s red orange 65 15

Issued to commemorate the Exposition of Journalism held under the auspices of the National Newspaper Men's Union. See Nos. C91-C92.

Francisco de Orellana
A158

Gonzalo Pizarro
A159

View of Guayaquil—A160

View of Quito—A161

1942, Jan. 30

400 A158 10c sepia 15 8
401 A159 40c deep rose 30 10
402 A160 1s violet 45 15
403 A161 2s dark blue 85 35
Nos. 400-403, C93-C96 (8) 5.70 2.31

Issued to commemorate the 400th anniversary of the discovery and exploration of the Amazon River by Francisco de Orellana.

Remigio Crespo Toral
A162

Alfredo Baquerizo Moreno
A163

1942 *Perf. 13½*

404 A162 10c green 10 6
405 " 50c brown 25 10

See also No. C97.

1942

406 A163 10c green 10 6

Mt. Chimborazo
A164

1942-47 *Perf. 12*

407 A164 30c red brown 15 6
407A " 30c light blue ('43) 15 6
407B " 30c red orange ('44) 15 6
407C " 30c green ('47) 15 6

View of Guayaquil
A165

1942-44

408 A165 20c red 10 6
408A " 20c deep blue ('44) 10 6

Gen. Eloy Alfaro
A166

Devil's Nose
A167

Designs: 30c, Military College. 1s, Montecristi, Alfaro's birthplace.

1942

409 A166 10c dark rose & black 20 8
410 A167 20c olive black & red brown 20 10
411 " 30c olive gray & green 30 12
412 " 1s slate & salmon 60 25
Nos. 409-412, C98-C101 (8) 4.80 3.50

Issued to commemorate the centenary of the birth of President Alfaro (1842-1903).

Nos. 370-372
Overprinted in Red Brown

BIENVENIDO — WALLACE

Abril 15 — 1943

1943, Apr. 15 *Perf. 11½*

413 A144 50c multicolored 50 50
414 " 1s " 1.00 1.00
415 " 2s " 1.50 1.50
Nos. 413-415, C102-C104 (6) 5.80 5.80

Visit of Vice-President Henry A. Wallace of the United States.

"30 Centavos"
A170

Black Surcharge.

1943 *Perf. 12½*

416 A170 30c on 50c red brown 12 6
a. Without bars 15 8

Map Showing United States and Ecuador
A171

1943, Oct. 9 *Perf. 12*

417 A171 10c dull violet 25 20
418 " 20c red brown 25 20
419 " 30c orange 30 25
420 " 50c olive green 35 25
421 " 1s deep violet 50 35
422 " 10s olive bistre 5.00 3.00
Nos. 417-422, C114-C118 (11) 16.30 12.75

Issued to commemorate the good will tour of President Arroyo del Rio in 1942.

1944, Feb. 7

423 A171 10c yellow green 15 12
424 " 20c rose pink 20 15
425 " 30c dark gray brown 25 18
426 " 50c deep red lilac 40 30
427 " 1s olive gray 50 35
428 " 10s red orange 5.00 3.00
Nos. 423-428, C119-C123 (11) 11.40 8.05

No. 385
Surcharged in Black

30
Centavos

1944 *Perf. 12½x13* **Unwmkd.**

429 A154 30c on 50c yel. brn. 20 8

Archbishop Federico González Suárez
A172

Government Palace, Quito
A173

1944 *Perf. 12*

430 A172 10c deep blue 15 8
431 " 20c green 20 8
432 " 30c dk. vio. brown 30 6
433 " 1s dull violet 60 20
Nos. 430-433, C124-C127 (8) 5.00 3.22

Birth centenary of Archbishop Federico Gonzalez Suarez.

Air Post Stamps
Nos. C76 and C83
Surcharged in Black

POSTAL
30
Centavos

1944 *Perf. 12½x13*

434 AP15 30c on 50c rose violet 12 6
435 AP16 30c on 50c slate green 12 6

Nos. 382 and 388
Surcharged in Black

CINCO
Centavos

1944-45

436 A154 5c on 2c blue green 10 6
a. Double surcharge
437 A155 5c on 2c light olive green ('45) 10 6

1944 Engraved *Perf. 11*

438 A173 10c dark green 15 6

439 " 30c blue 15 6

Symbol of the Red Cross
A174

1945, Apr. 25 *Perf. 12*

Cross in Rose.

440 A174 30c bistre brown 75 25

441 " 1s red brown 90 30

442 " 5s turquoise grn. 2.00 1.00

443 " 10s scarlet 5.00 3.00

Nos. 440–443, C131–C134 (8) 17.90 11.95

International Red Cross, 80th anniversary.

Nos. 370 to 372
Overprinted in Dark Blue and Gold

★
LOOR A CHILE
OCTUBRE 2 1945

1945, Oct. 2 *Perf. 11½*

Center Multicolored.

444 A144 50c black 40 25
a. Double overprint

445 " 1s olive black 50 35

446 " 2s dark brown 1.00 75

Nos. 444–446, C139–C141 (6) 4.35 3.70

Visit of Pres. Juan Antonio Rios of Chile.

General Antonio José de Sucre
A175

1945, Nov. 14 Engraved *Perf. 12*

447 A175 10c olive 6 6

448 " 20c red brown 12 10

449 " 40c olive gray 15 12

450 " 1s dark green 30 25

451 " 2s sepia 70 40

Nos. 447–451, C142–C146 (10) 4.78 3.48

150th anniversary of birth of Gen. Antonio José de Sucre.

No. 438 Surcharged in Blue

¢
VEINTE
CENTAVOS

1945 *Perf. 11*

452 A173 20c on 10c dark green 15 8
a. Fancy bar omitted

Map of Pan-American Highway and Arms of Loja
A176

1946, Apr. 22 Engraved *Perf. 12*

453 A176 20c red brown 12 8

454 " 30c bright green 18 12

455 " 1s bright ultra. 25 25

456 " 5s deep red lilac 1.50 1.00

457 " 10s scarlet 3.25 2.50

Nos. 453–457, C147–C151 (10) 10.75 6.95

Torch of Democracy
A177

Popular Suffrage
A178

Flag of Ecuador
A179

Pres. José M. Velasco Ibarra
A180

1946, Aug. 9 *Perf. 12½* **Unwmkd.**

458 A177 5c dark blue 6 6

459 A178 10c Prussian green 10 6

460 A179 20c carmine 25 10

461 A180 30c chocolate 35 15

Nos. 458–461, C152–C155 (8) 2.56 1.37

Issued to commemorate the 2nd anniversary of the Revolution of May 28, 1944.

"30 Ctvs."
A181
Black Surcharge.

1946

462 A181 30c on 50c red brown 12 6

Nos. CO13–CO14
With Additional Overprint in Black

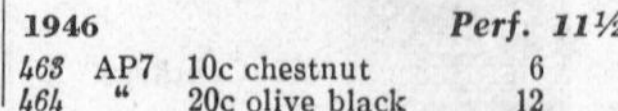

1946 *Perf. 11½*

463 AP7 10c chestnut 6 6

464 " 20c olive black 12 8

Instructor and Student
A182

1946, Sept. 16 *Perf. 12½*

465 A182 10c deep blue 15 10

466 " 20c chocolate 15 10

467 " 30c dark green 20 12

468 " 50c bluish black 35 15

469 " 1s dark red 60 20

470 " 10s dark violet 4.00 1.00

Nos. 465–470, C156–C160 (11) 11.05 4.42

Campaign for adult education.

Mariana de Jesus Paredes y Flores
A183

Urn
A184

1946, Nov. 28

471 A183 10c black brown 18 10

472 " 20c green 25 12

473 " 30c purple 25 15

474 A184 1s rose brown 65 35

Nos. 471–474, C161–C164 (8) 5.28 3.62

Issued to commemorate the 300th anniversary of the death of the Blessed Mariana de Jesus Paredes y Flores.

Pres. Vicente Rocafuerte
A185

Jesuits' Church Quito
A186

F.J.E. de Santa Cruz y Espejo
A187

1947, Nov. 27 *Perf. 12*

475 A185 5c reddish brown 8 6

476 " 10c sepia 8 6

477 " 15c gray black 10 6

478 A186 20c reddish brown 15 6

479 " 30c red violet 15 8

480 " 40c bright ultra. 25 15

481 A187 45c dark slate green 30 15

482 " 50c olive black 35 18

483 " 80c orange red 40 15

Nos. 475–483, C165–C171 (16) 3.86 1.95

Type of 1946,
Overprinted "POSTAL" in Black but
Without Additional Surcharge.

1948 Engraved.

484 A181 10c orange 60 8

Andrés Bello
A188

Flagship of Columbus
A189

1948, Apr. 21 *Perf. 13*

485 A188 20c light blue 15 8

486 " 30c rose carmine 20 10

487 " 40c blue green 25 12

488 " 1s black brown 50 20

Nos. 485–488, C172–C174 (7) 2.50 1.35

83rd anniversary of the death of Andrés Bello (1781–1865), educator.

No. 480
Overprinted
in Black

CONFERENCIA
ECONOMICA
GRANCOLOMBIANA
MAYO 24 DE 1.948

1948, May 24 *Perf. 12*

489 A186 40c bright ultramarine 25 20

See also No. C175.

1948 *Perf. 14*

490 A189 10c dark blue green 15 6

491 " 20c brown 25 8

492 " 30c dark purple 30 8

493 " 50c deep claret 40 10

494 " 1s ultramarine 50 15

495 " 5s carmine 1.75 35

Nos. 490–495, C176–C180 (11) 8.00 2.92

Issued to publicize the proposed Columbus Memorial Lighthouse near Ciudad Trujillo, Dominican Republic.

Feria Nacional
1948

No. 483
Overprinted
in Blue

ECUADOR
de hoy y del
MAÑANA

1948 *Perf. 12*

"MANANA" Reading Down.

496 A187 80c orange red 25 15

Issued to publicize the National Fair of Today and Tomorrrow, 1948. See No. C181.

Telegrafo I in Flight
A190

Book and Pen
A191

1948 Engraved. *Perf. 12½*

497 A190 30c red orange 20 8

498 " 40c rose lilac 20 8

499 " 60c violet blue 20 10

500 " 1s brown red 30 12

501 " 3s brown 85 30

502 " 5s gray black 1.25 45

Nos. 497–502, C182–C187 (12) 6.65 4.13

25th anniversary (in 1945) of the first postal flight in Ecuador.

1948, Oct. 12 *Perf. 14* **Unwmkd.**

503	A191	10c deep claret	10	6
504	"	20c brown	15	8
505	"	30c dark green	20	10
506	"	50c red	25	12
507	"	1s purple	35	15
508	"	10s dull blue	3.50	50
		Nos. 503-508, C188-C192 (11)	8.25	3.31

Campaign for adult education.

Franklin D. Roosevelt and Two of "Four Freedoms"
A192 A193

1948, Oct. 24 *Perf. 12½*

509	A192	10c rose brn. & gray	15	15
510	"	20c brn. olive & blue	20	15
511	A193	30c olive bister & carmine rose	30	20
512	"	40c red violet & sepia	40	20
513	"	1s orange brown & carmine	50	40
		Nos. 509-513, C193-C197 (10)	4.65	2.28

Issued in tribute to Franklin D. Roosevelt (1882-1945).

Maldonado and Map
A194

Riobamba Aqueduct
A195

Maldonado on Bank of Riobamba
A196

Pedro V. Maldonado
A197

1948, Nov. 17 **Engraved** **Unwmkd.**

514	A194	5c gray black & vermilion	20	8
515	A195	10c carmine & gray black	25	8
516	A196	30c bistre brown & ultramarine	30	12
517	A195	40c sage green & violet	35	12
518	A194	50c green & carmine	40	15
519	A197	1s brown & slate blue	50	20
		Nos. 514-519, C198-C201 (10)	4.00	1.75

Bicentenary of the death of Pedro Vicente Maldonado, geographer.

A198

Miguel de Cervantes Saavedra
A199

1949, May 2 *Perf. 12½x12*

520	A198	30c dark carmine rose & dp. ultra.	20	12
521	A199	60c bis. & brn. vio.	35	15
522	A198	1s green & rose carmine	50	20
523	A199	2s gray black & red brown	1.25	30
524	A198	5s choc. & aqua.	2.00	60
		Nos. 520-524, C202-C206 (10)	9.45	3.07

Issued to commemorate the 400th anniversary of the birth of Miguel de Cervantes Saavedra, novelist, playwright and poet.

No. 480 Surcharged in Carmine

II CONGRESO
Junio 1949

0.10
Eucarístico Ncl.

1949, June 15 *Perf. 12*

525	A186	10c on 40c bright ultramarine	20	8
526	"	20c on 40c bright ultramarine	25	10
		a. Double surcharge		
527	"	30c on 40c bright ultramarine	30	12
		Nos. 525-527, C207-C209 (6)	1.50	1.05

Issued to commemorate the Second National Eucharistic Congress, Quito, June, 1949.

No. 526 exists se-tenant with No. 527

Monument on Equator
A200

Arms of Ecuador
R1

1949, June **Engr.** *Perf. 12½x12*

528	A200	10c deep plum	15	6

No. 542 Surcharged in Black and Carmine

0.30
75 ANIVERSARIO
U.
P.
U.

1949 *Perf. 12x12½*

529	A203	10c on 50c green	20	15
530	"	20c on 50c "	30	15
531	A203	30c on 50c green	50	15
		Nos. 529-531, C210-C213 (7)	4.35	2.55

Universal Postal Union, 75th anniversary.

Consular Service Stamps Surcharged in Black

POSTAL
20 ctvs.

1949 *Perf. 12*

532	R1	20c on 25c red brown	10	6
533	"	30c on 50c gray	10	6

Nos. RA49A and RA55 Overprinted in Black

POSTAL
a

1950 *Perf. 12.* **Unwmkd.**

534	PT18	5c green	10	6
535	PT21	5c blue	10	6

Overprint 15 mm. on No. 534.

Nos. 528 and 517 to 519 Overprinted or Surcharged

ALFABETIZACION

in Black or Carmine.

1950, Feb. 10 *Perf. 12½x12*

536	A200	10c deep plum	12	8

Perf. 12½

537	A195	20c on 40c sage green & violet	15	8
538	"	30c on 40c sage green & violet	20	10
539	A194	50c green & carmine	25	12
540	A197	1s brown & slate blue (C)	35	12

No. C220 Overprinted Type "a" in Carmine.
Perf. 11
Overprint 15 mm. long.

541	AP28	10s violet	2.50	1.00
		Nos. 536-541, C216-C220 (11)	7.92	3.70

Nos. 536 to 541 were issued to publicize adult education.

San Pablo Lake
A203

Perf. 12x12½

1950, May **Engraved** **Unwmkd.**

542	A203	50c green	15	8

Consular Service Stamp Surcharged "CORREOS" and New Value Vertically in Black.

1950 *Perf. 12*

544	R1	30c on 50c gray	15	8

Coat of Arms
R2

Consular Service Stamps Overprinted or Surcharged in Black.

POSTAL
20 Ctvs. 20
b

POSTAL
c

CORREOS
d

50
ctvs.
POSTAL
e

1951 *Perf. 12.* **Unwmkd.**

545	R1(*b*)	5c on 10c carmine rose	8	6
546	" (*c*)	10c carmine rose	10	6
547	" (*d*)	10c carmine rose	10	6
548	" (*b*)	20c on 25c red brown	10	6
549	" (")	30c on 50c gray	12	6
550	R2(")	40c on 25c blue	12	6
551	" (*e*)	50c on 25c blue	20	6
		Nos. 545-551 (7)	82	42

Surcharge on No. 545 expressed: "5 ctvs." Small (lower case) "c" in "ctvs." on No. 550.

Consular Service Stamps Surcharged in Black

CAMPAÑA
Alfabetización
20 Ctvs. 20

1951

552	R2	20c on 25c blue	12	8
553	"	30c on 25c blue	15	10

Adult education. See Nos. C225-C226.

Consular Service Stamp Surcharged Type "e" in Black.

1951

554	R2	"$0,30" on 50c carmine rose	15

Reliquary of St. Mariana and Vatican
A204

Perf. 12½x12

1952, Feb. **Engraved** **Unwmkd.**

555	A204	10c emerald & red brown	15	8
556	"	20c dp. blue & pur.	20	12
557	"	30c carmine & blue green	35	15
		Nos. 555-557, C227-C230 (7)	3.20	1.23

Issued to publicize the canonization of Mariana de Jesus Paredes y Flores.

Presidents
Galo Plaza and Harry Truman
A205

Design: 2s, Pres. Plaza addressing U. S. Congress.

1952, Mar. 26 ***Perf. 12***

558 A205 1s rose carmine & gray black 40 20
559 " 2s dull blue & sepia 80 25

Issued to commemorate the 1951 visit of Pres. Galo Plaza y Lasso to the United States. See Nos. C231–C232.

R3

Fiscal Stamps Surcharged or Overprinted Type "c" Horizontally in Carmine or Black.

Engraved.

1952 ***Perf. 12.*** **Unwmkd.**

560 R3 20c on 30(c) deep blue (C) 12 6
561 " 30(c) deep blue 15 6

Diagonal Overprint.

562 A138 50(c) purple 20 6

Pres. José M. Urvina, Slave and "Liberty"
A206

Lithographed.

1952 ***Hyphen-hole Perf. 7x6½***

563 A206 20c red & green 25 6
564 " 30c red & violet blue 30 8
565 " 50c blue & carmine 50 10
Nos. 563–565, C236–C239 (7) 5.05 1.74

Issued to commemorate the centenary of the abolition of slavery in Ecuador.

Consular Service Stamps Surcharged in Black

POSTAL
10
Centavos
f

1952-53 ***Perf. 12.*** **Unwmkd.**

566 R1 10c on 20s blue ('53) 8 6
567 " 20c on 10s gray ('53) 10 6
568 " 20c on 20s blue 10 6
569 " 30c on 10s gray ('53) 12 6
570 " 30c on 20s blue 12 6
Nos. 566-570 (5) 52 30

Similar surcharges of 60c and 90c on the 20s blue are said to be bogus.

Teacher and Students
A207

New Citizens Voting
A208

Designs: 10c, Instructor with student. 30c, Teaching the alphabet.

1953, Apr. 13 **Engraved**

571 A207 5c light blue 25 6
572 " 10c dark car. rose 30 6
573 A208 20c bright brown orange 40 8
574 " 30c deep red lilac 60 10
Nos. 571–574, C240–C241 (6) 3.20 60

1952 adult education campaign.

A209

Cuicocha Lagoon
A210

Black Surcharge.

1953

575 A209 40c on 50c purple 40 8

1953 **Engraved.** ***Perf. 13x12½.***

Designs: 10c, Equatorial Line monument. 20c, Quininde countryside. 30c, Tomebamba river. 40c, La Chilintosa rock. 50c, Iliniza Mountains.

Frames in Black.

576 A210 5c bright blue 8 6
577 " 10c bright green 8 6
578 " 20c purple 12 6
579 " 30c brown 15 6
580 " 40c orange 20 6
581 " 50c deep carmine 50 8
Nos. 576-581 (6) 1.13 38

Carlos Maria Cardinal de la Torre and Arches
A211

1954, Jan. **Photo.** ***Perf. 8½***

582 A211 30c black & vermilion 15 6
583 " 50c black & rose lilac 20 8
Nos. 582–583, C253–C255 (5) 1.30 66

Issued to commemorate the first anniversary of the elevation of Archbishop de la Torre to Cardinal.

Queen Isabella I
A212

1954, Apr. 22

584 A212 30c black & gray 15 8
585 " 50c blk. brn. & yel. 20 10
Nos. 584–585, C256–C260 (7) 1.95 1.46

Issued to commemorate the 500th anniversary of the birth of Queen Isabella I (1451–1504) of Spain.

Type of 1929; "POSTAL" Overprint Larger, No Letterspacing.

1954–55 ***Perf. 12*** **Unwmkd.**

586 A112 5c olive green ('55) 15 6
587 " 10c orange 20 6

The normal overprint on Nos. 586–587 reads up. It also exists reading down.

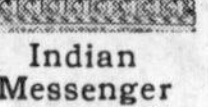

Indian Messenger
A213

Products of Ecuador
A214

1954, Aug. 2 **Litho.** ***Perf. 11***

588 A213 30c dark brown 15 6

Issued to publicize the Day of the Postal Employee. See also No. C263.

1954, Sept. 24 **Photogravure**

589 A214 10c orange 12 6
590 " 20c vermilion 18 6
591 " 30c rose pink 25 6
592 " 40c dark gray green 35 8
593 " 50c yellow brown 50 10
Nos. 589-593 (5) 1.40 36

José Abel Castillo
A215

Babahoyo River Los Rios
A216

Perf. 11½x11

1955, Oct. 19 **Engraved** **Unwmkd.**

594 A215 30c olive bistre 12 6
595 " 50c dark gray 15 8
Nos. 594–595, C282–C286 (7) 2.72 1.60

Issued to commemorate the 30th anniversary of the first flight of the "Telegrafo I" and to honor José Abel Castillo, aviation pioneer.

1955–56 **Photogravure** ***Perf. 13***

Designs: 5c, Palms, Esmeraldas. 10c, Fishermen, Manabi. 30c, Guayaquil, Guayas. 50c, Pital River, El Oro. 70c, Cactus, Galapagos Isls. 80c, Orchids, Napo-Pastaza. 1s, Aguacate Mission, Zamora-Chinchipe. 2s, Jibaro Indian, Morona-Santiago.

596 A216 5c yellow green ('56) 5 5
597 " 10c blue ('56) 6 5
598 " 20c brown 8 5
599 " 30c dark gray 10 6
600 " 50c blue green 15 6
601 " 70c olive ('56) 20 8
602 " 80c deep violet ('56) 50 10
603 " 1s orange ('56) 30 12
604 " 2s rose red ('56) 60 20
Nos. 596-604 (9) 2.04 77

See also Nos. 620–630, 670, C288–C297, C310–C311.

Brother Juan Adam Schwarz, S. J.
A217

1956, Aug. 27 **Engraved** ***Perf. 13½***

605 A217 5c yellow green 6 6
606 " 10c orange red 8 6
607 " 20c light violet 10 6
608 A217 30c dark green 10 6
609 " 40c blue 12 6
610 " 50c deep ultramarine 20 6
611 " 70c orange 30 8
Nos. 605–611, C302–C305 (11) 2.36 1.59

Issued to commemorate the bicentennial of printing in Ecuador and in honor of Brother Juan Adam Schwarz, S.J.

Andres Hurtado de Mendoza
A218

Gil Ramirez Davalos
A219

Designs: 20c, Brother Vincent Solano.

1957, Apr. 7 ***Perf. 12*** **Unwmkd.**

612 A218 5c dark blue, *pink* 6 5
613 A219 10c green, *greenish* 8 5
614 A218 20c chocolate, *buff* 10 5
a. Souvenir sheet of 4 50 50
Nos. 612–614, C312–C314 (6) 89 53

Issued to commemorate the fourth centenary of the founding of Cuenca.

No. 614a contains two 5c gray and two 20c brown red stamps in designs similar to Nos. 612 and 614. It was printed on white ungummed paper, is imperf. and is inscribed "II Exposicion Filatelica Nacional, Cuenca, 11 al 20 de Abril de 1957." Size: 140x120mm.

Francisco Marcos, Gen. Pedro Alcantara Herran and Santos Michelena
A220

1957, Sept. 5 **Engr.** ***Perf. 14½x14***

615 A220 40c yellow 10 5
616 " 50c ultramarine 12 6
617 " 2s dark red 45 25

7th Postal Congress of the Americas and Spain (in 1955).

Souvenir Sheets

Various Railroad Scenes
A221

Lithographed.

1957 ***Perf. 10½x11***

618 A221 Sheet of five 20c 60 50
619 " Sheet of five 30c 60 50

Issued to commemorate the opening of the Quito-Ibarra-San Lorenzo railroad.

Nos. 618–619 measure 118x110mm. with ultramarine inscriptions and contain 2 orange yellow, 1 ultramarine and 2 carmine stamps, each in a different design.

Scenic Type of 1955–56.

Designs as before, except: 40c, Cactus, Galapagos Islands. No. 629, San Pablo, Imbabura.

1957-58 Photogravure. ***Perf. 13***

620 A216 5c light blue 4 4
621 " 10c brown 4 4
622 " 20c crimson rose 5 4
623 " 20c yellow green 5 4
624 " 30c rose red 5 4
625 " 40c chalky blue 40 5
626 " 50c light violet 12 5
627 " 90c brt. ultramarine 40 8
628 " 1s dark brown 18 10
629 " 1s gray black ('58) 20 10
630 " 2s brown 50 20
Nos. 620-630 (11) 2.03 78

Blue and Yellow Macaw
A222

Birds: 20c, Red-breasted toucan. 30c, Condor. 40c, Black-tailed and sword-tailed hummingbirds.

Perf. 13½x13

1958, Jan. 7 Litho. **Unwmkd.**

Birds in Natural Colors.

634 A222 10c red brown 15 5
635 " 20c dark gray 20 6
636 " 30c brt. yellow green 30 10
637 " 40c red orange 35 12

Carlos Sanz de Santamaria
A223

Richard M. Nixon and Flags
A224

Design: No. 640, Dr. Ramon Villeda Morales and flags. 2.20s, José Carlos de Macedo Soares and horizontal flags.

1958 ***Perf. 12***

Flags in Red, Blue, Yellow & Green.

638 A223 1.80s dull violet 35 20
639 A224 2s dark green 50 20
640 " 2s dark brown 40 20
641 A223 2.20s black brown 50 20

No. 638 commemorates the visit of Colombia's Foreign Minister Dr. Carlos Sanz de Santamaria to Ecuador.

No. 639 commemorates the visit of U. S. Vice President Richard M. Nixon to Ecuador, May 9-10.

No. 640 commemorates the visit of President Ramon Villeda Morales of Honduras.

No. 641 commemorates the visit of Brazil's Foreign Minister José Carlos de Macedo Soares to Ecuador. See Nos. C419–C421.

Locomotive of 1908
A225

Garcia Moreno, Jose Caamano, L. Plaza and Eloi Alfaro
A226

Design: 50c, Diesel locomotive.

Perf. 13½x14, 14

1958, Aug. 9 Photo. **Unwmkd.**

642 A225 30c brown black 12 6
643 " 50c dark carmine 20 10
644 A226 5s dark brown 1.00 70

Issued to commemorate the 50th anniversary of the Guayaquil-Quito railroad.

Cardinal
A227

Birds: 30c, Andean cock-of-the-rock. 50c, Glossy cowbird. 60c, Red-fronted Amazon.

1958 Lithographed. ***Perf. 13½x13***

Birds in Natural Colors.

645 A227 20c bluish green, black & red 15 6
646 " 30c buff, black & bright blue 18 6
647 " 50c orange, black & green 25 8
648 " 60c pale rose, black & bluish green 30 12

UNESCO Building and Eiffel Tower, Paris
A228

1958, Nov. 3 Engraved ***Perf. 12½***

649 A228 80c brown 30 15

Issued to commemorate the opening of UNESCO (U. N. Educational, Scientific and Cultural Organization) Headquarters in Paris, Nov. 3.

Globe and Satellites
A229

Virgin of Quito
A230

1958, Dec. 20 Photo. ***Perf. 14x13½***

650 A229 1.80s dark blue 1.50 50

Issued to commemorate the International Geophysical Year, 1957–58.

1959, Sept. 8 ***Perf. 13*** **Unwmkd.**

651 A230 5c olive green 6 5
652 " 10c yellow brown 8 5
653 A230 20c purple 10 6
654 " 30c ultramarine 12 6
655 " 80c dark carmine rose 20 10
Nos. 651-655 (5) 56 32

See also No. C290.

Uprooted Oak Emblem
A231

1960, Apr. 7 Litho. ***Perf. 14x13***

656 A231 80c rose carmine & green 25 15

Issued to publicize World Refugee Year, July 1, 1959–June 30, 1960.

Great Anteater and Arms
A232

Animals: 40c, Tapir and map. 80c, Spectacled bear and arms. 1s, Puma and map.

1960, May 14 Photo. ***Perf. 13***

657 A232 20c orange, green & black 8 6
658 " 40c yellow green, blue green & brown 15 8
659 " 80c blue, black & red brown 30 15
660 " 1s Prussian blue, plum & ochre 50 20

Issued to commemorate the 4th centenary of the founding of the city of Baeza.

See also Nos. 676–679.

Hotel Quito
A233

Designs: No. 662, Dormitory, Catholic University. No. 663, Dormitory, Central University. No. 664, Airport, Quito. No. 665, Overpass on Highway to Quito. No. 666, Security Bank. No. 667, Ministry of Foreign Affairs. No. 668, Government Palace. No. 669, Legislative Palace.

Perf. 11x11½

1960, Aug. 8 Engraved **Unwmkd.**

661 A233 1s dark purple & reddish brown 15 10
662 " 1s dark blue & brown 15 10
663 " 1s black & red 15 10
664 " 1s dark blue & ultramarine 15 10
665 " 1s dark purple & dk. car. rose 15 10
666 " 1s black & olive bistre 15 10
667 " 1s dark purple & turquoise 15 10
668 " 1s dark blue & green 15 10
669 " 1s black & violet 15 10
Nos. 661-669 (9) 1.35 90

11th Inter-American Conference, Quito.

Souvenir Sheet

Type of Regular Issue, 1955–56.

Design: Orchids, Napo-Pastaza.

1960 Photogravure ***Perf. 13***

Yellow Paper.

670 A216 Sheet of two 30 30
a. 80c deep violet 15 15
b. 90c deep green 15 15

Issued to commemorate the 25th anniversary of Asociacion Filatelica Ecuatoriana. Marginal inscription in silver. Size: 85x55mm. Exists with silver inscription omitted.

"Freedom of Expression"
A234

Manabi Bridge
A235

Designs: 10c, "Freedom to vote." 20c, "Freedom to work." 30c, Coins, "Monetary stability."

1960, Aug. 29 Litho. ***Perf. 13***

671 A234 5c dark blue 5 4
672 " 10c light violet 5 4
673 " 20c orange 8 4
674 " 30c bluish green 10 4
675 A235 40c brown & bluish green 12 5
Nos. 671-675 (5) 40 21

Issued to publicize the achievements of President Camilo Ponce Enriquez. See Nos. C370–C374.

Animal Type of 1960.

Animals: 10c, Collared peccary. 20c, Kinkajou. 80c, Jaguars. 1s, Mountain coati.

Photogravure

1961, July 13 ***Perf. 13*** **Unwmkd.**

676 A232 10c green, rose red & black 8 5
677 " 20c violet, greenish blue & brown 10 7
678 " 80c red orange, dull yel. & black 25 12
679 " 1s brown, bright grn. & org. 40 20

Issued to commemorate the 400th anniversary of the founding of the city of Tena.

Graphium Pausianus
A236

Butterflies: 30c, Papilio torquatus leptalea. 50c, Graphium molops molops. 80c, Battus lycidas.

1961, July 13 Litho. ***Perf. 13½***

680 A236 20c pink & multi. 6 5
681 " 30c lt. ultramarine & multi. 10 6
682 " 50c org. & multi. 15 10
683 " 80c blue green & multicolored 25 15

See also Nos. 711–713.

1961

Estación de Biología Marítima de Galápagos

Galapagos Islands Nos. L1–L3 Overprinted in Black or Red

XXXXXXXXXXXX

1961, Oct. 31 Photo. ***Perf. 12***

684 A1 20c dark brown 20 6
685 A2 50c violet 20 8
686 A1 1s dk. olive grn. (R) 40 15
Nos. 684-686, C389-C391 (6) 2.15 1.54

Issued to commemorate the establishment of maritime biological stations on Galapagos Islands by UNESCO.

"The overprint illustration is from the 50c. It is arranged differently on 20c and 1s. See also Nos. C389–C391.

Daniel Enrique Proano School
A237

Designs: 60c, Loja-Zamora highway (vert.). 80c, Aguirre Abad College, Guayaquil. 1s, Army quarters, Quito.

Perf. 11x11½, 11½x11

1962, Jan. 10 Engr. Unwmkd.

687 A237 50c dull blue & black 10 5
688 " 60c olive green & black 15 6
689 " 80c org. red & black 20 8
690 " 1s rose lake & blk. 25 10

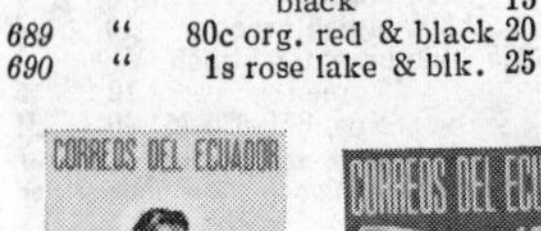

Pres. Arosemena, Flags of Ecuador, U.S.
A238

Protection for The Family
A239

Designs (Arosemena and): 10c, Flags of Ecuador. 20c, Flags of Ecuador and Panama.

1963, July 1 Litho. *Perf. 14*

691 A238 10c buff & multi. 6 5
692 " 20c multicolored 8 5
693 " 60c " 12 6
Nos. 691-693, C409-C411 (6) 1.21 96

Issued to commemorate Pres. Carlos J. Arosemena's friendship trip, July 1962.

1963, July 9 *Perf. 14* **Unwmkd.**

694 A239 10c ultra., red, gray & black 6 5

Issued to commemorate the 25th anniversary of Social Insurance. See No. C413.

No. 655 Overprinted or Surcharged in Black or Blue

1961 DIA DEL EMPLEADO POSTAL 10

1963 Photogravure *Perf. 13*

695 A230 10c on 80c dark carmine rose 5 5
696 " 20c on 80c dark carmine rose 6 5
697 " 50c on 80c dark carmine rose 10 6
698 " 60c on 80c dark car. rose (Bl) 15 8
699 " 80c dark carmine rose 20 10
Nos. 695-699 (5) 56 34

Nos. 661-669 Surcharged **0,10** XXXXX

1964, Apr. 20 Engr. *Perf. 11x11½*

700 A233 10c on 1s dk. pur. & reddish brn. 8 4
701 " 10c on 1s dk. pur. & turquoise 8 4
702 " 20c on 1s dk. blue & brown 10 4
703 " 20c on 1s dark blue & green 10 4
704 " 30c on 1s dk. pur. & dk. carm. rose 12 5
705 A233 40c on 1s black & olive bister 12 5
706 " 60c on 1s blk. & red 20 6
707 " 80c on 1s dk. blue & ultramarine 24 8
708 " 80c on 1s blk. & vio. 24 8
Nos. 700-708 (9) 1.28 48

No. 656 Overprinted in Black or Light Ultramarine **1961**

1964 Lithographed *Perf. 14x13*

709 A231 80c rose car. & grn. 2.00 50

Butterfly Type of 1961

Butterflies: Same as on Nos. 680, 682-683.

1964, June Litho. *Perf. 13½*

711 A236 20c bright green & multicolored 6 5
712 " 50c salmon pink & multicolored 10 6
713 " 80c lt. red brown & multicolored 20 8

Alliance for Progress Emblem, Agriculture and Industry
A240

Designs: 50c, Emblem, gear wheels, mountain and seashore. 80c, Emblem, banana worker, fish, factory and ship.

1964, Aug. 26 *Perf. 12* **Unwmkd.**

715 A240 40c bister brn. & vio. 15 6
716 " 50c red orge. & blk. 25 8
717 " 80c blue & dk. brn. 30 15

Issued to publicize the Alliance for Progress which aims to stimulate economic growth and raise living standards in Latin America.

No. 650 Overprinted in Red **FARO DE COLON**

1964 Photogravure *Perf. 14x13½*

718 A229 1.80s dark blue 3.00 1.50

No. 656 Overprinted

(Reduced Size)
Overprint covers four stamps

1964, July Litho. *Perf. 14x13*

719 A231 80c rose carmine & green (block of 4) 3.00 1.50

Organization of American States.

World Map and Banana Tree
A241

1964, Oct. 26 *Perf. 12½x12*

720 A241 50c dk. brn., gray & gray olive 8 6
721 " 80c black, orange & gray olive 12 8

Issued to publicize the Banana Conference, Oct.-Nov. 1964. See Nos. C427-C428a.

King Philip II of Spain and Map of Upper Amazon River
A242

Designs (Map and): 20c, Juan de Salinas de Loyola. 30c, Hernando de Santillan.

1964, Dec. 6 Litho. *Perf. 13½*

722 A242 10c rose, blk. & buff 5 4
723 " 20c blue green, blk. & buff 6 5
724 " 30c blue, blk. & buff 6 6

Issued to commemorate the 4th centenary of the establishment of the Royal High Court in Quito.

Pole Vaulting
A243

1964, Dec. 16 *Perf. 14x13½*

725 A243 80c vio. bl., yel. grn. & brown 20 10

Issued to commemorate the 18th Olympic Games, Tokyo, Oct. 10-25. See also Nos. C432-C434.

Peter Fleming and Two-toed Sloth
A244

Designs: 20c, James Elliot and armadillo. 30c, T. Edward McCully, Jr., and squirrel. 40c, Roger Youderian and deer. 60c, Nathaniel (Nate) Saint and plane over Napo River.

1965 *Perf. 13½* **Unwmkd.**

726 A244 20c emerald & multi. 4 4
727 " 30c yellow & multi. 5 4
728 " 40c lilac & multi. 6 5
729 " 60c multicolored 10 8
730 " 80c " 15 10
Nos. 726-730 (5) 40 31

Issued in memory of five American Protestant missionaries, killed by the Auca Indians, Jan. 8, 1956. Issue dates: 80c, May 11; others, July 8.

Juan B. Vázquez and Benigno Malo College
A245

1965, June 6 Litho. *Perf. 14*

731 A245 20c black, yellow & violet blue 4 4
732 " 60c black, red, yel. & violet blue 8 6
733 A245 80c black, emerald, yel. & vio. blue 10 8

Issued to commemorate the centenary (in 1964) of the founding of Benigno Malo National College.

National Anthem, Juan Leon Mera and Antonio Neumane
A246

1965, Aug. 10 Litho. *Perf. 13½*

734 A246 50c pink & black 8 6
735 " 80c lt. green & blk. 12 10
736 " 5s bister & black 60 45
737 " 10s lt. ultra. & blk. 1.10 90

Issued to commemorate the centenary of the national anthem. The name of the poet Juan Leon Mera is misspelled on the stamps.

Torch and Athletes (Shot Put, Discus, Javelin and Hammer Throw)
A247

Torch and Athletes: 50c, 1s, Runners. 60c, 1.50s, Soccer.

1965, Nov. 20 *Perf. 12x12½*

738 A247 40c orge., gold & blk. 5 4
739 " 50c orange verm., gold & black 6 5
740 " 60c blue, gold & blk. 10 6
741 " 80c bright yel. grn., gold & black 12 6
742 " 1s light violet, gold & black 15 10
743 " 1.50s bright pink, gold & black 20 18
Nos. 738-743, C435-C440 (12) 2.98 2.47

Issued to publicize the 5th Bolivarian Games, held at Guayaquil and Quito.

Stamps of 1865
A248

1965, Dec. 30 Litho. *Perf. 13½*

Stamps of 1865 in Yellow, Ultramarine & Green

744 A248 80c rose red 12 8
745 " 1.30s rose lilac 18 15
746 " 2s chocolate 30 20
747 " 4s black 50 35
a. Souv. sheet of 4 1.25 1.25

Issued to commemorate the centenary of Ecuadorian postage stamps. No. 747a contains four imperf. stamps similar to Nos. 744-747. Dark blue marginal inscription and black control number. Size: 140x125 mm.

Certain unlisted issues of Ecuador of 1966-69 are mentioned and briefly described in "For the Record" at the back of this volume.

Pavonine Quetzal — A249

Bust of Peñaherrera, Central University, Quito — A250

Birds: 50c, Blue-crowned motmot. 60c, Paradise tanager. 80c, Wire-tailed manakin.

1966, June 17 Litho. *Perf. 13½*

Birds in Natural Colors

748 A249 40c dull rose & blk. 6 5
749 " 50c salmon & blk. 6 5
750 " 60c lt. ocher & blk. 8 6
751 " 80c lt. blue & black 10 8
Nos. 748-751, C441-C448 (12) 2.85 2.39

Various Surcharges on Issues of 1956-66

1967-68

752 AP72 30c on 1.10s multi. (C337) 4 4
753 AP66 40c on 1.70s yellow brown (C292) 5 4
754 A247 40c on 3.50s lt. vio., gold & black (C438) 5 4
755 A246 50c on 5s bister & black (736) ('68) 6 5
756 A247 80c on 1.50s bright pink, gold & black (743) 10 6
757 A249 80c on 2.50s lt. yel. green & multi. (C445) 10 6
758 " 1s on 4s gray & multi. (C447) 12 10
759 AP66 1.30s on 1.90s olive (C293) 15 12
760 A246 2s on 10s lt. ultra. & black (737) ('68) 25 18
Nos. 752-760, C449-C450 (11) 1.12 85

The surcharge on Nos. 754-755, 757 and 759-760 includes "Resello." The obliteration of old denomination and arrangement of surcharges differ on each stamp.

Perf. 12x12½, 12½x12

1967, Dec. 29 Lithographed

Designs: 50c, Law books. 80c, Open book and laurel (horiz.).

761 A250 50c brt. green & blk. 6 5
762 " 60c rose & black 7 6
763 " 80c rose lilac & blk. 8 6
Nos. 761-763, C451-C452 (5) 56 44

Issued to commemorate the centenary (in 1964) of the birth of Dr. Victor Manuel Peñaherrera (1864-1932), author of the civil and criminal codes of Ecuador.

Otto Arosemena Gomez — A251

Lions Emblem — A252

1968, May 9 Litho. *Perf. 13½x14*

Design: 1s, Page from the Constitution.

764 A251 80c lilac & multi. 8 6
765 " 1s multicolored 10 8

First anniversary of the administration of Pres. Otto Arosemena Gomez. See Nos. C453-C454.

1968, May 24 Litho. *Perf. 13½x14*

766 A252 80c multicolored 8 6
767 " 1.30s " 14 10
768 " 2s pink & multi. 20 15
a. Souv. sheet of 1 3.50 3.50

Issued to commemorate the 50th anniversary (in 1967) of Lions International.

No. 768a contains one 5s stamp (size: 39x49mm.). Violet blue marginal inscriptions and red control numbers. Size: 71x104mm. Exists imperf.

Nos. C331 and C326 Surcharged in Violet and Dark Blue

RESELLO
$ 0,40
$ 0,50
a

RESELLO
b

1969, Jan. 10 *Perf. 11½, 14x13½*

769 AP79 (*a*) 40c on 1.30s green & brn. red (V) 4 4
770 AP76 (*b*) 50c on 1.30s dk. grn. & lt. brn (DBl) 5 5

Type of 1958 Surcharged and Overprinted in Plum and Black

RESELLO
$ 0,50

Design: Ignacio Luis Arcaya, Foreign Minister of Venezuela.

1969, Mar. Litho. *Perf. 12*

Flags in Red, Blue and Yellow.

771 A223 50c on 2s sepia 5 5
772 " 80c on 2s " 8 6
773 " 1s on 2s " 10 8
774 " 2s " 20 15
Nos. 771-774, C455-C457 (7) 81 70

Nos. 771-774 were not issued without overprint. The obliteration of old denomination on No. 772 is a small square around a star. Overprint is plum, except for the black small coat of arms on right flag.

Map of Ecuador and Oriental Region — A253

Surcharge Typographed in Dark Blue, Red Brown, Black or Lilac

1969 Lithographed *Perf. 14*

775 A253 20c on 30c multi. (DBl) 3 3
776 " 40c on 30c multi. (RBr) 4 4
777 " 50c on 30c multi. (DBl) 5 5
778 " 60c on 30c multi. (DBl) 6 6
779 " 80c on 30c multi. (Bk) 8 8
780 " 1s on 30c multi. (L) 10 10
781 " 1.30s on 30c multi. (Bk) 13 10
782 " 1.50s on 30c multi. (Bk) 15 12
783 A253 2s on 30c multi. (DBl) 20 18
784 " 3s on 30c multi. (DBl) 30 25
785 " 4s on 30c multi. (Bk) 20 15
786 " 5s on 30c multi. (Bk) 25 20
Nos. 775-786 (12) 1.59 1.36

Nos. 775-786 were not issued without surcharge.

M. L. King, John and Robert Kennedy — A254

Thecla Coronata — A255

1969-70 Typographed *Perf. 12½*

787 A254 4s black, blue, green & buff 40 15

Perf. 13½

788 A254 4s black, lt. blue & green ('70) 40 15

In memory of John F. Kennedy, Robert F. Kennedy and Martin Luther King, Jr.

1970 Lithographed *Perf. 12½*

Butterflies: 20c, Papilio zabreus. 30c, Heliconius chestertoni. 40c, Papilio pausanias. 50c, Pereute leucodrosime. 60c, Metamorpha dido. 80c, Morpho cypris. 1s, Catagramma astarte.

789 A255 10c buff & multi. 3 3
790 " 20c lt. grn. & multi. 3 3
791 " 30c pink & multi. 3 3
792 " 40c lt. blue & multi. 4 3
793 " 50c gold & multi. 5 4
794 " 60c salmon & multi. 6 5
795 " 80c silver & multi. 8 6
796 " 1s lt. grn. & multi. 10 8
Nos. 789-796, C461-C462 (10) 70 58

Same, White Background

1970 *Perf. 13½*

797 A255 10c multicolored 3 3
798 " 20c " 3 3
799 " 30c " 3 3
800 " 40c " 4 3
801 " 50c " 5 4
802 " 60c " 6 5
803 " 80c " 8 6
804 " 1s " 10 8
Nos. 797-804, C463-C464 (10) 70 58

Surcharged Revenue Stamps

A256 A257

1970, June 16 Litho. *Perf. 14*

Red Surcharge

805 A256 1s on 1s lt. blue 10 4
806 " 1.30s on 1s " 13 6
807 " 1.50s on 1s " 15 8
808 " 2s on 1s " 20 10
809 " 5s on 1s " 50 20
810 " 10s on 1s " 1.00 40
Nos. 805-810 (6) 2.08 88

1970 Typographed *Perf. 12*

Black Surcharge

811 A257 60c on 1s violet 6 4
812 " 80c on 1s " 8 4
813 " 1s on 1s " 10 4
814 " 1.10s on 1s " 11 4
815 " 1.30s on 1s " 13 4
816 " 1.50s on 1s " 15 4
817 " 2s on 1s " 20 5
818 A257 2.20s on 1s violet 22 5
819 " 3s on 1s " 30 8
Nos. 811-819 (9) 1.35 42

1970

820 A257 1.10s on 2s green 11 4
821 " 1.30s on 2s " 13 4
822 " 1.50s on 2s " 15 4
823 " 2s on 2s " 20 5
824 " 3.40s on 2s " 34 8
825 " 5s on 2s " 50 12
826 " 10s on 2s " 1.00 25
827 " 20s on 2s " 2.00 45
828 " 50s on 2s " 5.00 1.20
Nos. 820-828 (9) 9.43 2.27

1970

829 A257 3s on 5s blue 30 8
830 " 5s on 5s " 50 12
831 " 10s on 40s orange 1.00 25

Arms of Zamora Chinchipe — A258

Flags of Ecuador and Chile — A259

Design: 1s, Arms and flag of Esmeraldas.

1971 Lithographed *Perf. 10½*

832 A258 50c pale yel. & multi. 5 3
833 " 1s salmon & multi. 10 8
Nos. 832-833, C465-C469 (7) 2.28 1.76

1971, Sept. *Perf. 12½*

840 A259 1.30s black & multi. 13 10

Visit of Pres. Salvador Allende of Chile, Aug. 24. See Nos. C481-C482.

Ismael Pérez Pazmiño — A260

1971, Sept. 16 *Perf. 12x11½*

841 A260 1s green & multi. 10 8

50th anniversary of "El Universo," newspaper founded by Ismael Pérez Pazmiño. See Nos. C485-C486.

CARE Package — A261

Flags of Ecuador and Argentina — A262

1971-72 *Perf. 12½*

842 A261 30c lilac ('72) 3 3
843 " 40c emerald ('72) 4 3
844 " 50c blue 5 3
845 " 60c carmine 5 3
846 " 80c lt. brown ('72) 8 4
Nos. 842-846 (5) 25 16

25th anniversary of CARE, a U.S.-Canadian Cooperative for American Relief Everywhere.

1972 *Perf. 11½*

847 A262 1s black & multi. 10 8

Visit of Lt. Gen. Alejandro Agustin Lanusse, president of Argentina, Jan. 25. See Nos. C491-C492.

Jesus Giving Keys to St. Peter, by Miguel de Santiago
A263

Ecuadorian Paintings: 1.10s, Virgin of Mercy, Quito School. 2s, Virgin Mary, by Manuel Samaniego.

1972, Apr. 24 Litho. *Perf. 14x13½*

848 A263 50c black & multi. 5 3
849 " 1.10s " " 11 10
850 " 2s " " 20 15
a. Souv. sheet of 3 40 40
Nos. 848-850, C494-C495 (5) 1.66 1.28

No. 850a contains 3 imperf. stamps similar to Nos. 848-850. Blue marginal inscription. Size: 129x110mm.

1972, May 4

Ecuadorian Statues: 50c, Our Lady of Sorrow, by Caspicara. 1.10s, Nativity. Quito School (horiz.). 2s, Virgin of Quito, anonymous.

851 A263 50c black & multi 5 3
852 " 1.10s " " 11 10
853 " 2s " " 20 15
a. Souv. sheet of 3 40 40
Nos. 851-853, C496-C497 (5) 1.66 1.28

Letters of "Ecuador" 3mm. high on Nos. 851-853, 7mm. high on Nos. 848-850. No. 853a contains 3 imperf. stamps similar to Nos. 851-853. Blue marginal inscription. Size. 129x110mm.

Gen. Juan Ignacio Pareja
A264

Designs: 40c, Juan José Flores. 50c, Leon de Febres Cordero. 60c, Ignacio Torres. 70c, Francisco de Paula Santander. 1s, José M. Cordova.

1972, May 24 *Perf. 12½*

854 A264 30c blue & multi. 3 3
855 " 40c " " 4 3
856 " 50c " " 5 4
857 " 60c " " 6 5
858 " 70c " " 7 5
859 " 1s " " 10 8
Nos. 854-859, C498-C503 (12) 4.68 3.58

Sesquicentennial of the Battle of Pichincha and the liberation of Quito.

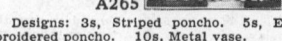

Woman Wearing Poncho
A265

Designs: 3s, Striped poncho. 5s, Embroidered poncho. 10s, Metal vase.

1972, July Photo. *Perf. 13*

860 A265 2s multicolored 20 15
861 " 3s " 30 25
862 " 5s " 50 20
863 " 10s dp. bl. & multi. 1.00 50
a. Souvenir sheet of 4 2.25 2.25
Nos. 860-863, C504-C507 (8) 4.00 2.65

Handicraft of Ecuador. No. 863a contains 4 imperf. stamps similar to Nos. 860-863. Gray green marginal inscription and ornament. Black control number. Size 104x164mm.

Sucre Statue, Santo Domingo
A266

Radar Station
A267

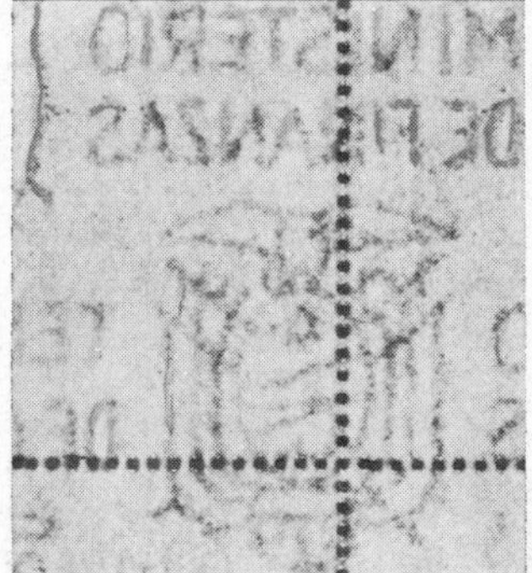

Wmk. 367

Wmkd. Liberty Cap, Emblem and Inscription (367)

1972, Dec. 6 Litho. *Perf. 11½*

Designs: 1.80s, San Agustin Convent. 2.30s, Plaza de la Independencia. 2.50s, Bolivar statue, La Alameda. 4.75s, Chapel door.

864 A266 1.20s yel. & multi. 12 10
865 " 1.80s " " 18 15
866 " 2.30s " " 23 20
867 " 2.50s " " 25 22
868 " 4.75s " " 48 30
Nos. 864-868, C518-C524 (12) 5.41 4.25

Sesquicentennial of the Battle of Pichincha.

1973, Apr. 5 Litho. *Perf. 11½*

869 A267 1s multicolored 18 12

Inauguration of earth telecommunications station, Oct. 19, 1972.

Blue-footed Boobies
A268

1973 Lithographed *Perf. 11½x12*

Multicolored

870 A268 30c *shown* 6 4
871 " 40c *Blue-faced booby* 8 5
872 " 50c *Oyster-catcher* 10 6
873 " 60c *California sea lions* 12 8
874 " 70c *Galapagos giant tortoise* 14 10
875 " 1s *California sea lion* 18 12
Nos. 870-875, C527-C528 (8) 1.22 72

Elevation of Galapagos Islands to a province of Ecuador.

Issue dates: 50c, Oct. 3; others Aug. 16.

Black-chinned Mountain Tanager
A269

Birds of Ecuador: 2s, Moriche oriole. 3s, Toucan barbet (vert.). 5s, Masked crimson tanager (vert.). 10s, Blue-necked tanager (vert.).

Perf. 11x11½, 11½x11

1973, Dec. 6 Litho. Unwmkd.

876 A269 1s brick red & multi. 12 6
877 " 2s lt. blue & multi. 24 12
878 " 3s lt. green & multi. 36 18
879 " 5s pale lilac & multi. 60 30
880 " 10s pale yel. green & multi. 1.20 60
Nos. 876-880 (5) 2.52 1.26

Two souvenir sheets exist: one contains 2 imperf. stamps similar to Nos. 876-877 with yellow margin and black inscription; the other 3 stamps similar to Nos. 878-880; gray margin and black inscription including "Aereo." Both sheets dated "1972." Size: 143x84mm.

Marco T. Varea, Botanist
A270

Portraits: 60c, Pio Jaramillo Alvarado, writer. 70c, Prof. Luciano Andrade M. No. 883, Marco T. Varea, botanist. No. 884, Dr. Juan Modesto Carbo Noboa, medical researcher. No. 885, Alfredo J. Valenzuela. No. 886, Capt. Edmundo Chiriboga G. 1.20s, Francisco Campos R., scientist. 1.80s, Luis Vernaza Lazarte, philanthropist.

1974 *Perf. 12x11½* Unwmkd.

881 A270 60c crimson rose 8 4
882 " 70c lilac 10 5
883 " 1s ultramarine 12 6
884 " 1s orange 12 6
885 " 1s emerald 12 6
886 " 1s brown 12 6
887 " 1.20s apple green 15 8
889 " 1.80s light blue 22 12
Nos. 881-889 (8) 1.03 53

Arcade
A271

Designs: 30c, Monastery, entrance. 40c, Church. 50c, View of Church through gate (vert.). 60c, Chapel (vert.). 70c, Church and cemetery (vert.).

Perf. 11½x12, 12x11½

1975, Feb. 4 Lithographed

896 A271 20c yellow & multi. 3 3
897 " 30c " " 4 3
898 " 40c " " 5 3
899 " 50c " " 6 3
900 " 60c " " 8 4
901 " 70c " " 10 5
Nos. 896-901 (6) 36 21

Colonial Monastery, Tilipulo, Cotopaxi Province.

Angel Polibio Chaves, Founder of Bolivar Province
A272

Portrait: No. 903, Emilio Estrada Ycaza (1916-1961), archeologist.

1975 Litho. *Perf. 12x11½*

902 A272 80c vio. bl. & lt. bl. 10 6
903 " 80c verm. & pink 10 6

Issue dates: No. 902, Feb. 21; No. 903, Mar. 25.

R. Rodriguez Palacios and A. Duran Quintero
A273

"Woman of Action"
A274

1975, Apr. 1 Litho. *Perf. 12x11½*

910 A273 1s multicolored 12 6

Meeting of the Ministers for Public Works of Ecuador and Colombia, July 27, 1973.

See Nos. C547-C548.

1975, June

Design: No. 912, 1s, "Woman of Peace."

911 A274 1s yellow & multi. 12 6
912 " 1s blue & multi. 12 6

International Women's Year 1975.

Planes, Soldier and Ship
A275

1975, July 9 *Perf. 11½x12*

913 A275 2s multicolored 24 12

Three years of National Revolutionary Government.

Hurdling
A276

Designs: Modern sports drawn Inca style.

1975, Sept. 11 Litho. *Perf. 11½*

914 A276 20c *shown* 3 3
915 " 20c *Chess* 3 3
916 " 30c *Basketball* 4 3
917 " 30c *Boxing* 4 3
918 " 40c *Bicycling* 5 3
919 " 40c *Steeplechase* 5 3
920 " 50c *Soccer* 6 3
921 " 50c *Fencing* 6 3
922 " 60c *Golf* 7 4
923 " 60c *Vaulting* 7 4
924 " 70c *Judo (standing)* 8 4
925 " 70c *Wrestling* 8 4
926 " 80c *Swimming* 10 5
927 " 80c *Weight lifting* 10 5

928 A276 1s *Table tennis* 12 6
929 " 1s *Paddle ball* 12 6
Nos. 914-929, C554-C558 (21) 2.79 1.46

3rd Ecuadorian Games.

Genciana
A277

Designs: Ecuadorian plants.

Perf. 12x11½, 11½x12

1975, Nov. 18 **Lithographed**

Multicolored

930 A277 20c *Orchid* (vert.) 3 3
931 " 30c *shown* 4 3
932 " 40c *Bromeliaceae cactaceae* (vert.) 5 3
933 " 50c *Orchid* 6 3
934 " 60c *Orchid* 7 4
935 " 80c *Flowering cactus* 10 5
936 " 1s *Orchid* 12 6
Nos. 930-936, C559-C563 (12) 2.31 1.19

Venus, Chorrera Culture
A278

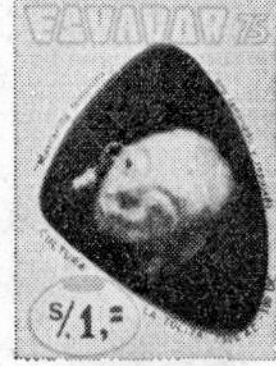

Female Mask, Tolita Culture
A279

Designs: 30c, Venus, Valdivia Culture. 40c, Seated man, Chorrera Culture. 50c, Man with poncho, Panzaleo Culture (late). 60c, Mythical head, Cashaloma Culture. 80c, Musician, Tolita Culture. No. 943, Chief Priest, Manteña Culture. No. 945, Ornament, Tolita Culture. No. 946, Angry mask, Tolita Culture.

1976, Feb. 12 **Litho.** ***Perf. 11½***

937 A278 20c multicolored 3 3
938 " 30c " 4 3
939 " 40c " 5 3
940 " 50c " 6 3
941 " 60c " 7 4
942 " 80c " 10 5
943 " 1s " 12 6
944 A279 1s " 12 6
945 " 1s " 12 6
946 " 1s " 12 6
Nos. 937-946, C568-C572 (15) 2.67 1.37

Archaeological artifacts.

Strawberries
A280

Carlos Amable Ortiz (1859-1937)
A281

1976, Mar. 30

947 A280 1s blue & multi. 12 6

25th Flower and Fruit Festival, Ambato. See Nos. C573-C574.

1976, Mar. 15 **Litho.** ***Perf. 11½***

Portraits: No. 949, Sixto Maria Duran (1875-1947). No. 950, Segundo Cueva Celi (1901-1969). No. 951, Cristobal Ojeda Davila (1910-1952). No. 952, Luis Alberto Valencia (1918-1970).

948 A281 1s verm. & multi. 12 6
949 A281 1s orange & multi. 12 6
950 " 1s lt. grn. & multi. 12 6
951 " 1s blue & multi. 12 6
952 " 1s lt. brn. & multi. 12 6
Nos. 948-952 (5) 60 30

Ecuadorian composers and musicians.

Institute Emblem
A282

1977, Aug. 15 **Litho.** ***Perf. 11½x12***

953 A282 2s multicolored 24 12

11th General Assembly of Pan-American Institute of Geography and History, Quito, Aug. 15-30. See Nos. C597-C597a.

Hands Holding Rotary Emblem
A283

José Peralta
A284

1977, Aug. 31 **Litho.** ***Perf. 12***

954 A283 1s multicolored 12 6
955 " 2s " 24 12

Souvenir Sheets

Imperf.

956 A283 5s multicolored 70 50
957 " 10s " 1.40 75

Rotary Club of Guayaquil, 50th anniversary. Nos. 956-957 have black control numbers. Size: 90x115mm.

1977 **Litho.** ***Perf. 11½***

Design: 2.40s, Peralta statue.

958 A284 1.80s multicolored 22 10
959 " 2.40s " 28 14

José Peralta (1855-1937), writer, 40th death anniversary. See No. C609.

Blue-faced Booby
A285

Galapagos Birds: 1.80s, Red-footed booby. 2.40s, Blue-footed boobies. 3.40s, Gull. 4.40s, Galapagos hawk. 5.40s, Map of Galapagos Islands and boobies (vert.).

Perf. 11½x12, 12x11½

1977, Nov. 29 **Lithographed**

960 A285 1.20s multicolored 14 6
961 " 1.80s " 22 10
962 " 2.40s " 28 14
963 " 3.40s " 40 20
964 " 4.40s " 52 25
965 " 5.40s " 65 28
Nos. 960-965 (6) 2.21 1.03

Dr. Corral Moscoso Hospital, Cuenca
A286

1978, Apr. 12 **Litho.** ***Perf. 11½x12***

966 A286 3s multicolored 36 18

Inauguration (in 1977) of Dr. Vicente Corral Moscoso Regional Hospital, Cuenca. See Nos. C613-C614.

Surveyor Plane over Ecuador
A287

Latin-American Lions Emblem
A288

1978, Apr. 12 **Litho.** ***Perf. 11½***

967 A287 6s multicolored 72 35

Military Geographical Institute, 50th anniversary. See Nos. C619-C620.

1978

968 A288 3s multicolored 36 18
969 " 4.20s " 50 25

7th meeting of Latin American Lions, Jan. 25-29. See Nos. C621-C623.

70th Anniversary Emblem
A289

1978, Sept. **Litho.** ***Perf. 11½***

970 A289 4.20s gray & multi. 50 25

70th anniversary of Filanbanco (Philanthropic Bank). See No. C626.

Goalmouth and Net—A290

Designs: 1.80s, "Gauchito" and Games emblem (vert.). 4.40s, "Gauchito" (vert.).

1978, Nov. 1 **Litho.** ***Perf. 12***

971 A290 1.20s multicolored 14 6
972 " 1.80s " 22 10
973 " 4.40s " 52 25
Nos. 971-973, C627-C629 (6) 3.13 1.53

11th World Cup Soccer Championship, Argentina, June 1-25.

SEMI-POSTAL STAMPS.

Nos. 423-428
Surcharged in Carmine or Blue:

Hospital

Méndez + $ 0,50

1944, May 9 *Perf. 12* Unwmkd.

B1	A171	10c+10c yellow green (C)	35	25
B2	"	20c+20c rose pink	40	30
B3	"	30c+20c dk. gray brn.	40	35
B4	"	50c+20c dp. red lilac	60	45
B5	"	1s+50c olive gray (C)	1.00	85
B6	"	10s+2s red orange	4.00	2.50
		Nos. B1-B6 (6)	6.75	4.70

The surtax aided Mendez Hospital.

AIR POST STAMPS.

In 1928-30, the internal airmail service of Ecuador was handled by the Sociedad Colombo-Alemana de Transportes Aereos ("SCADTA") under government sanction. During this period SCADTA issued stamps which were the only legal franking for airmail service except that handled under contract with Pan American-Grace Airways. SCADTA issues are Nos. C1-C6, C16-C25.

Colombia Air Post Stamps of 1923 Surcharged in Carmine

ECUADOR
PROVISIONAL
50 50

"Provisional" at 45° Angle.
Perf. 14x14½

1928, Aug. 28 Wmk. 116

C1	AP6	50c on 10c green	100.00	75.00
C2	"	75c on 15c car.	250.00	150.00
C3	"	1s on 20c gray	75.00	50.00
C4	"	1½s on 30c blue	60.00	35.00
C5	"	3s on 60c brown	100.00	60.00
		Nos. C1-C5 (5)	585.00	370.00

"Provisional" at 41° Angle.

1929, Mar. 20

C1a	AP6	50c on 10c green	125.00	125.00
C2a	"	75c on 15c carmine	150.00	150.00
C3a	"	1s on 20c gray	125.00	150.00

Same with "Cts."
Between Surcharged Numerals

C6	AP6	50c on 10c green	*1100.00*	*800.00*

A 75c on 15c carmine with "Cts." between the surcharged numerals exists. There is no evidence that it was regularly issued or used.

Plane over River Guayas
AP1

Engraved.

1929, May 5 *Perf. 12* Unwmkd.

C8	AP1	2c black	15	10
C9	"	5c carmine rose	15	10
C10	"	10c deep brown	20	6
C11	"	20c dark violet	30	8
C12	"	50c deep green	1.00	35
C13	"	1s dark blue	3.00	1.75
C14	"	5s orange yellow	10.00	9.00
C15	AP1	10s orange red	55.00	55.00
		Nos. C8-C15 (8)	70.30	66.94

Issued to commemorate the establishing of commercial air service in Ecuador. The stamps were available for all forms of postal service and were largely used for franking ordinary letters.

Nos. C13-C15 show numerals in color on white background. Counterfeits of No. C15 exist.

See Nos. C26-C31.

Quito Cathedral
AP2

Mount Chimborazo
AP3

Lithographed.

1929, Apr. 1 *Perf. 14* Wmk. 127

C16	AP2	50c red brown	2.50	2.50
C17	"	75c green	2.50	2.50
C18	"	1s rose	3.50	2.50
C19	"	1½s gray blue	3.50	3.00
C20	"	2s violet	12.50	10.00
C21	"	3s brown	12.50	10.00
C22	AP3	5s light blue	40.00	30.00
C23	"	10s light red	85.00	65.00
C24	"	15s violet	150.00	125.00
C25	"	25s olive green	200.00	150.00
		Nos. C16-C25 (10)	512.00	400.50

Plane Type of 1929
Engraved.

1930-44 *Perf. 12.* Unwmkd.

C26	AP1	1s carmine lake	3.00	50
C27	"	1s green ('44)	50	12
C28	"	5s olive green	4.00	3.25
C29	"	5s purple ('44)	1.00	12
C30	"	10s black	12.00	3.00
C31	"	10s brt. ultra. ('44)	2.00	12
		Nos. C26-C31 (6)	22.50	7.11

Nos. C26-C31 show numerals in color on white background.

Overprinted in Various Colors.

AP4

1930, June 4

C32	AP4	1s car. lake (Bk)	15.00	15.00
		a. Double overprint (R Br+Bk)	85.00	
C33	"	5s olive green (Bl)	15.00	15.00
C34	"	10s black (R Br)	15.00	15.00

Issued to commemorate the flight of Capt. Benjamin Mendez from Bogota to Quito, bearing a crown of flowers for the tomb of Grand Marshal Sucre.

Air Post Official Stamps of 1929-30
Overprinted in Various Colors

INAUGURACION
MONUMENTO
A BOLIVAR
QUITO, 24 DE
JULIO DE 1935

or Surcharged Similarly
in Upper & Lower Case

1935, July 24

C35	AP1	50c dp. grn. (Bl)	6.00	6.00
C36	"	50c olive brown (R)	6.00	6.00
C37	"	1s on 5s olive green (Bk)	6.00	6.00
		a. Double surcharge	100.00	
C38	"	2s on 10s black (R)	6.00	6.00

Issued to commemorate the unveiling of a monument to Bolivar at Quito, July 24th, 1935.

Geodesical Mission Issue

Nos. 349-351
Overprinted
in Blue or Black

AÉREO

1936, July 3 *Perf. 12½*

C39	A136	10c dp. orge. (Bl)	30	10
C40	"	20c violet (Bk)	30	10
C41	"	50c dark red (Bl)	50	12

Charles M. de la Condamine and Pedro Maldonado
AP5

C42	AP5	70c black	80	40

Bicentenary of Geodesical Mission visit to Quito.

Philatelic Exhibition Issue

Type of Regular Issue Overprinted "AEREA"

1936, Oct. 20 *Perf. 13½x14*

C43	A137	2c rose	5.00	5.00
C44	"	5c brown orange	5.00	5.00
C45	"	10c brown	5.00	5.00
C46	"	20c ultramarine	5.00	5.00
C47	"	50c red violet	5.00	5.00
C48	"	1s green	5.00	5.00
		Nos. C43-C48 (6)	30.00	30.00

Condor and Plane—AP6
Perf. 13½

C49	AP6	70c orange brown	1.00	75
C50	"	1s dull violet	1.25	1.00

Nos. C43-C50 were issued to commemorate the first International Philatelic Exhibition at Quito.

Condor over "El Altar"
AP7

1937-46 *Perf. 11½, 12*

C51	AP7	10c chestnut	8	5
C52	"	20c olive black	15	6
C53	"	40c rose carmine ('46)	15	6
C54	"	70c black brown	20	15
C55	"	1s gray black	30	25
C56	"	2s dark violet	75	35
		Nos. C51-C56 (6)	1.63	92

Issue dates: 40c, Oct. 7, 1946; others, Aug. 19, 1937.

Portrait of Washington, American Eagle and Flags
AP8

Engraved and Lithographed.

1938, Feb. 22 *Perf. 12*

Center Multicolored.

C57	AP8	2c brown	10	10
C58	"	5c black	10	10
C59	"	10c brown	15	10
C60	"	20c dark blue	25	10
C61	"	50c violet	60	20
C62	"	1s black	1.00	25
C63	"	2s violet	2.25	65
		Nos. C57-C63 (7)	4.45	1.50

Issued in commemoration of the 150th anniversary of the Constitution of the United States of America.

In 1947, Nos. C61 to C63 were overprinted in dark blue: "Primero la Patria!" and plane. These revolutionary propaganda stamps were later renounced by decree.

No. RA35
Surcharged in Red

AEREO
SEDTA
0,65

1938, Nov. 16 *Perf. 13½*

C64	PT12	65c on 3c ultramarine	15	10

A national airmail concession was given to the Sociedad Ecuatoriano de Transportes Aereos (SEDTA)) in July, 1938. No. RA35 was surcharged for SEDTA postal requirements. SEDTA operated through 1940.

Army Horseman
AP9

Woman Runner
AP10

Tennis
AP11

Boxing
AP12

Olympic Fire
AP13

1939, Mar. Engraved *Perf. 12*

C65	AP9	5c light green	1.00	15
C66	AP10	10c salmon	1.25	25
C67	AP11	50c reddish brown	5.50	25
C68	AP12	1s black brown	6.00	40
C69	AP13	2s rose carmine	10.00	80
		Nos. C65-C69 (5)	23.75	1.85

First Bolivarian Games (1938), La Paz.

Plane over Chimborazo
AP14

1939, May 1 *Perf. 13x12½*

C70	AP14	1s yellow brown	30	6
C71	"	2s rose violet	60	6
C72	"	5s black	1.65	10

Golden Gate Bridge and Mountain Peak
AP15

Empire State Building and Mountain Peak
AP16

1939 ***Perf. 12½x13***

C73 AP15 2c black 6 6
C74 " 5c rose red 6 6
C75 " 10c indigo 10 8
C76 " 50c rose violet 15 15
C77 " 1s chocolate 20 15
C78 " 2s yellow brown 40 15
C79 " 5s emerald 85 25
Nos. C73-C79 (7) 1.82 90

Golden Gate International Exposition.

1939

C80 AP16 2c brown orange 6 6
C81 " 5c dark carmine 6 6
C82 " 10c indigo 10 6
C83 " 50c slate green 15 8
C84 " 1s deep orange 25 8
C85 " 2s dark red violet 40 15
C86 " 5s dark gray 85 10
Nos. C80-C86 (7) 1.87 59

New York World's Fair.

Map of the Americas and Airplane
AP17

Francisco J. E. Santa Cruz y Espejo
AP18

1940, July 9

C87 AP17 10c red org. & blue 20 6
C88 " 70c sepia & blue 25 6
C89 " 1s copper brown & blue 40 12
C90 " 10s black & blue 2.00 75

Pan American Union, 50th anniversary.

1941, Dec. 15

C91 AP18 3s rose carmine 1.50 20
C92 " 10s yellow orange 3.00 40

See note after No. 399.

Old Map of South America Showing Amazon River
AP19

Panoramic View of Amazon River
AP20

Designs: 70c, Gonzalo de Pineda. 5s, Painting of the expedition.

1942, Jan. 30

C93 AP19 40c black & buff 35 18
C94 " 70c olive 75 15
C95 AP20 2s dark green 1.00 40
C96 AP19 5s rose 1.85 90

See note after No. 403.

Remigio Crespo Toral
AP21

1942, Sept. 1 ***Perf. 13½***

C97 AP21 10c dull violet 35 10

Gen. Eloy Alfaro
AP22

Devil's Nose
AP23

Designs: 3s, Military College. 5s, Montecristi, Alfaro's birthplace.

1943, Feb. 16 ***Perf. 12***

C98 AP22 70c dark rose & black 50 30
C99 AP23 1s olive black & red brown 60 60
C100 " 3s olive gray & green 1.00 90
C101 " 5s slate & salmon 1.40 1.15

Issued to commemorate the centenary of the birth of President Alfaro (1842-1903).

Nos. C61-C63 Overprinted in Red Brown
BIENVENIDO — WALLACE
Abril 15 — 1943

1943, Apr. 15 ***Perf. 11½***

Center Multicolored.

C102 AP8 50c violet 70 70
C103 " 1s black 85 85
C104 " 2s violet 1.25 1.25

Issued to commemorate the visit of Vice-President Henry A. Wallace of the United States.

Nos. 374-376 Overprinted
"AEREO LOOR A BOLIVIA
JUNIO 11—1943"
(like Nos. C111-C113).

1943, June 11 ***Perf. 13***

C105 A146 50c deep red violet 25 25
C106 A147 1s copper red 35 35
C107 A148 2s dark green 55 50

Issued to commemorate the visit of President Enrique Penaranda of Bolivia.
Vertical overprints on Nos. C105-C106.

Nos. 374-376 Overprinted
"AEREO LOOR A PARAGUAY
JULIO 5—1943"
(like Nos. C111-C113).

1943, July 5

C108 A146 50c deep red violet 25 25
a. Double ovpt. 30.00
C109 A147 1s copper red 35 35
C110 A148 2s dark green 55 40

Issued to commemorate the visit of President Higinio Morinigo of Paraguay.
Vertical overprints on Nos. C108-C109.

Nos. 374-376 Overprinted in Black

AEREO

LOOR A VENEZUELA

JULIO 23 — 1943

1943, July 23

C111 A146 50c deep red violet 25 25
C112 A147 1s copper red 40 40
C113 A148 2s dark green 55 40

Issued to commemorate the visit of President Isaias Medina Angarita of Venezuela.
Vertical overprint on Nos. C111-C112.
See also Nos. C105-C110.

President Arroyo del Rio Addressing U.S. Congress
AP26

1943, Oct. 9 ***Perf. 12***

C114 AP26 50c dark brown 50 50
C115 " 70c bright rose 65 60
C116 " 3s dark blue 75 65
C117 " 5s dark green 1.75 1.00
C118 " 10s olive black 6.00 5.75
Nos. C114-C118 (5) 9.65 8.50

Issued to commemorate the good will tour of President Arroyo del Rio in 1942.

1944, Feb. 7

C119 AP26 50c deep red lilac 50 45
C120 " 70c red brown 75 50
C121 " 3s turquoise grn. 75 50
C122 " 5s bright ultra. 1.25 1.00
C123 " 10s scarlet 1.65 1.50
Nos. C119-C123 (5) 4.90 3.95

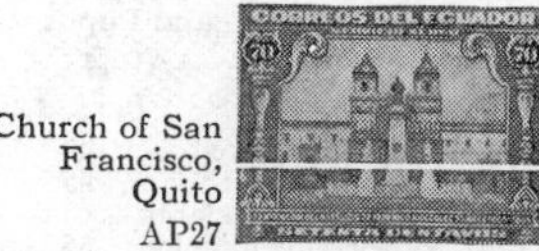

Church of San Francisco, Quito
AP27

1944, Feb. 13

C124 AP27 70c turquoise grn. 55 50
C125 " 1s olive 55 50
C126 " 3s red orange 1.00 80
C127 " 5s carmine rose 1.65 1.00

See note after No. 433.

Government Palace, Quito
AP28

1944 **Engraved** ***Perf. 11***

C128 AP28 3s orange 50 10
C129 " 5s dark brown 75 10
C130 " 10s dark red 1.50 12

See also No. C221.

Symbol of the Red Cross
AP29

1945, Apr. 25 ***Perf. 12*** **Unwmkd.**

Cross in Rose.

C131 AP29 2s deep blue 1.00 90
C132 " 3s green 1.25 1.00
C133 " 5s dark violet 2.00 1.50
C134 " 10s carmine rose 5.00 4.00

Issued to commemorate the 80th anniversary of the founding of the International Red Cross.

No. RA55 Surcharged in Black

AEREO
40
Ctvs.

1945, June 8

C135 PT21 40c on 5c blue 20 10
a. Double surcharge 9.00

Counterfeits exist.

Nos. C128 to C130 Overprinted in Green

V
SETIEMBRE 5
1945

1945, Sept. 6 ***Perf. 11***

C136 AP28 3s orange 70 70
a. Inverted ovpt. 25.00
b. Double ovpt. 25.00
C137 " 5s dark brown 90 90
C138 " 10s dark red 2.75 2.75

Nos. C61-C63
Overprinted in Dark Blue and Gold

LOOR A CHILE
OCTUBRE 2 1945

1945, Oct. 2 ***Perf. 12***

Center Multicolored.

C139 AP8 50c violet 75 75
C140 " 1s black 85 80
C141 " 2s violet 85 80

Visit of Pres. Juan Antonio Rios of Chile.

Monument to Liberty
AP30

Map of Pan-American Highway and Arms of Cuenca
AP31

1945, Nov. 14 **Engraved.**

C142 AP30 30c blue 20 15
C143 " 40c rose carmine 25 15
C144 " 1s dull violet 50 40
C145 " 3s gray black 1.00 85
C146 " 5s purple brown 1.50 1.00
Nos. C142-C146 (5) 3.45 2.55

Issued to commemorate the 150th anniversary of the birth of General Antonio José de Sucre.

1946, Apr. 22 **Unwmkd.**

C147 AP31 1s carmine rose 50 45
C148 " 2s violet 70 60
C149 " 3s turquoise grn. 1.00 55
C150 " 5s red orange 1.25 75
C151 " 10s dark blue 2.00 65
Nos. C147-C151 (5) 5.45 3.00

Revolution Types of Regular Issue

1946, Aug. 9 ***Perf. 12½***

C152 A177 40c deep claret 10 10
C153 A178 1s sepia 25 10
C154 A179 2s indigo 60 25
C155 A180 3s olive green 85 55

Issued to commemorate the 2nd anniversary of the Revolution of May 28, 1944.

National Union of Periodicals, Initials and Quill Pen
AP36

1946, Sept. 16

C156 AP36 50c dull purple 40 35
C157 " 70c dark green 45 40
C158 " 3s red 75 50
C159 " 5s indigo 1.00 65
C160 " 10s chocolate 3.00 85
Nos. C156-C160 (5) 5.60 2.75

Issued to publicize a campaign for adult education.

The Blessed Mariana Teaching Children
AP37

"Lily of Quito"
AP38

1946, Nov. 28 **Unwmkd.**

C161 AP37 40c chocolate 45 15
C162 " 60c deep blue 55 50
C163 AP38 3s orange yel. 1.10 1.00
C164 " 5s green 1.85 1.25

Issued to commemorate the 300th anniversary of the death of the Blessed Mariana de Jesus Paredes y Flores.

Juan de Velasco
AP39

Riobamba Irrigation Canal
AP40

1947, Nov. 27 ***Perf. 12***

C165 AP39 60c dark green 15 8
C166 " 70c purple 20 8
C167 " 1s black brown 20 6
C168 " 1.10s carmine rose 20 18
C169 AP40 1.30s deep blue 25 20
C170 " 1.90s olive bistre 50 25
C171 " 2s olive green 50 15
Nos. C165-C171 (7) 2.00 1.00

Andrés Bello
AP41

Christopher Columbus
AP42

1948, Apr. 21 ***Perf. 13***

C172 AP41 60c magenta 30 15
C173 " 1.30s dark blue green 60 35
C174 " 1.90s dk. rose carmine 50 35

No. C166 Overprinted in Black

CONFERENCIA
ECONOMICA
GRANCOLOMBIANA
MAYO 24 DE 1.948

1948, May 24 ***Perf. 12***

C175 AP39 70c purple 50 45

1948, May 26 ***Perf. 14***

C176 AP42 50c olive green 20 20
C177 " 70c rose carmine 30 30
C178 AP42 3s ultramarine 65 60
C179 " 5s brown 1.25 50
C180 " 10s deep violet 2.25 50
Nos. C176-C180 (5) 4.65 2.10

See note after No. 495.

No. C169 Overprinted in Carmine

Feria Nacional
1948
de hoy y del
ECUADOR
MAÑANA

1948, Aug. 26 ***Perf. 12*** **Unwmkd.**

C181 AP40 1.30s deep blue 45 45

Issued to publicize the National Fair of Today and Tomorrow, 1948.

Elia Liut and Telegrafo I
AP43

Teacher and Pupils
AP44

1948, Sept. 10 ***Perf. 12½***

C182 AP43 60c rose red 40 35
C183 " 1s green 45 40
C184 " 1.30s deep claret 45 45
C185 " 1.90s deep violet 50 45
C186 " 2s dark brown 60 55
C187 " 5s blue 1.25 80
Nos. C182-C187 (6) 3.65 3.00

Issued to commemorate the 25th anniversary (in 1945) of the first postal flight in Ecuador.

1948, Oct. 12 ***Perf. 14***

C188 AP44 50c violet 40 35
C189 " 70c deep blue 40 35
C190 " 3s dark green 60 55
C191 " 5s red 80 40
C192 " 10s brown 1.50 65
Nos. C188-C192 (5) 3.70 2.30

Campaign for adult education.

Franklin D. Roosevelt and Two of "Four Freedoms"
AP45 AP46

1948, Oct. 24 ***Perf. 12½***

C193 AP45 60c emerald & orange brown 20 18
C194 " 1s carmine rose & slate 25 20
C195 AP46 1.50s green & red brown 40 30
C196 " 2s red & black 90 25
C197 " 5s ultra. & blk. 1.35 25
Nos. C193-C197 (5) 3.10 1.18

Issued in tribute to Franklin D. Roosevelt, 1882-1945.

Maldonado Types of Regular Issue

1948, Nov. 17

C198 A196 60c deep orange & rose carmine 40 15
C199 A197 90c red & gray black 40 15
C200 A196 1.30s purple & deep orange 60 35
C201 A197 2s deep blue & dull green 60 35

See note after No. 519.

Juan Montalvo and Cervantes
AP47

Don Quixote
AP48

1949, May 2 **Engr.** ***Perf. 12½x12***

C202 AP47 1.30s olive brown & ultramarine 50 50
C203 AP48 1.90s green & rose carmine 40 40
C204 AP47 3s violet & orange brown 50 40
C205 AP48 5s red & gray black 1.50 20
C206 AP47 10s red lilac & aquamarine 2.25 20
Nos. C202-C206 (5) 5.15 1.70

Issued to commemorate the 400th anniversary of the birth of Miguel de Cervantes Saavedra, novelist, playwright and poet, and the 60th anniversary of the death of Juan Montalvo (1832-1889), Ecuadorean writer.

No. C168 Surcharged in Blue

II CONGRESO
Junio 1949
Eucarístico Ncl.
50 —— 50

1949, June 15 ***Perf. 12***

C207 AP39 50c on 1.10s carmine rose 20 20
C208 " 60c on 1.10s carmine rose 25 25
C209 " 90c on 1.10s carmine rose 30 30

Issued to commemorate the Second Eucharistic Congress, Quito, June 1949.

No. C128 Surcharged in Black

75 Aniversario
* U. P. U. *
60 centavos 60

1949, Oct. 11 ***Perf. 11***

C210 AP28 60c on 3s orange 60 50
a. Double surcharge 20.00
C211 " 90c on 3s orange 55 35
C212 " 1s on 3s " 70 55
C213 " 2s on 3s " 1.50 70

"SUCRE(S)" in capitals on Nos. C212-C213.
Issued to commemorate the 75th anniversary of the formation of the Universal Postal Union.

AP49

Black Surcharge.

1950 ***Perf. 12*** **Unwmkd.**

C214 AP49 60c on 50c gray 15 6
a. Double surcharge 17.50

No. C170 Surcharged with New Value in Black.

C215 AP40 90c on 1.90s olive bistre 35 15

Nos. C168, C128-C129 and Type of 1944 Surcharged or Overprinted
ALFABETIZACION
in Black or Carmine.

1950, Feb. 10 ***Perf. 12***

C216 AP39 50c on 1.10s carmine rose 25 20
C217 " 70c on 1.10s carmine rose 30 25

Perf. 11

C218 AP28 3s orange 70 60
C219 AP28 5s dk. brn. (C) 1.10 70
C220 " 10s violet (C) 2.00 45
Nos. C216-C220 (5) 4.35 2.20

Issued to publicize adult education.

Govt. Palace Type of 1944

1950, May 15 **Engr.** ***Perf. 11***

C221 AP28 10s violet 1.25 10

No. C169 Surcharged with New Value in Black.

1950 ***Perf. 12***

C222 AP40 90c on 1.30s deep blue 25 6

See No. C235.

Nos. C128-C129 Overprinted in Black

20.000 Cruce
Linea Ecuatorial
PANAGRA
26-Julio-1951

1951, July 28 ***Perf. 11*** **Unwmkd.**

C223 AP28 3s orange 80 80
C224 " 5s dark brown 1.35 1.10

Issued to commemorate the 20,000th crossing of the equator by Pan American-Grace Airways planes.

Nos. C202-C203 Surcharged in Black

CAMPANA
Alfabetización
60 Ctvs. 60
a

CAMPAÑA
ALFABETIZACION
1,00 Sucre 1,00
b

1951 ***Perf. 12½x12*** **Unwmkd.**

C225 AP47 (*a*) 60c on 1.30s olive brn. & ultra. 25 15

C226 AP48 (*b*) 1s on 1.90s green & rose carmine 25 15
a. Inverted surcharge 15.00

Issued to publicize adult education.

St. Mariana de Jesus
AP50

1952, Feb. 15 Engraved.

C227	AP50	60c plum & aquamarine	55	25
C228	"	90c dark green & light ultra.	60	20
C229	"	1s carmine & dark green	65	25
C230	"	2s indigo & rose lilac	70	18

Issued to publicize the canonization of Mariana de Jesus Paredes y Flores.

Presidents
Galo Plaza and Harry Truman
AP51

Design: 5s, Pres. Plaza addressing U. S. Congress.

1952, Mar. 26 ***Perf. 12***

C231	AP51	3s lilac & blue green	70	60
C232	"	5s red brown & olive gray	1.35	1.25
		a. Souvenir sheet	4.00	4.00

No. C232a measures 126 x 61 mm., and contains one each of Nos. C231 and C232, with marginal inscriptions in lilac and red brown.
Issued to commemorate the 1951 visit of Pres. Galo Plaza y Lasso to the United States.

Consular Service Stamps Surcharged "AEREO" and New Value in Black.

1952 ***Perf. 12*** **Unwmkd.**

C233	R2	60c on 1s green	12	8
C234	"	1s on 1s "	18	10

Type R2 illustrated above No. 545.

No. C169 Surcharged with New Value in Carmine.

C235	AP40	90c on 1.30s deep blue	15	8

See No. C222.

Pres. José M. Urvina and Allegory of Freedom
AP52

Torch of Knowledge
AP53

Hyphen-hole Perf. 7x6½

1952, Nov. 18 **Lithographed.**

C236	AP52	60c rose red & blue	1.00	45
C237	AP52	90c lilac & red	1.00	50
C238	"	1s orange & green	1.00	25
C239	"	2s red brown & blue	1.00	30

Issued to commemorate the centenary of the abolition of slavery in Ecuador.

Engraved.

Design: 2s, Aged couple studying alphabet.

1953, Apr. 13 ***Perf. 12*** **Unwmkd.**

C240	AP53	1s dark blue	65	15
C241	"	2s red orange	1.00	15

1952 adult education campaign.

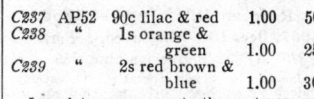

Globe Showing Part of Western Hemisphere
AP54

1953, June 5 ***Perf. 12½x12***

C242	AP54	60c orange yellow	35	30
C243	"	90c dark blue	40	35
C244	"	3s carmine	80	50

Issued to publicize the crossing of the equator by the Pan-American highway.

Consular Service Stamps Surcharged in Black

AEREO
1
SUCRE
a

AEREO 1 SUCRE
b

1953-54 ***Perf. 12.***

C245	R1 (*a*)	60c on 2s brown	25	8
C246	R2 (")	60c on 5s sepia ('54)	25	8
C247	" (")	70c on 5s sepia ('54)	30	15
C248	" (")	90c on 50c carmine rose ('54)	35	8
C249	R1 (*b*)	1s on 2s brown	35	15
C250	" (*a*)	1s on 2s brown ('54)	35	10
C251	" (")	2s on 2s brown ('54)	60	18
C252	" (")	3s on 5s violet ('54)	90	25
		Nos. C245-C252 (8)	3.35	1.07

The surcharge reads upward on Nos. C250-C252.

Carlos Maria Cardinal de la Torre
AP55

Queen Isabella I
AP56

1954, Jan. 13 Photo. ***Perf. 8½.***

Center in Black.

C253	AP55	60c rose lilac	20	10
C254	"	90c green	30	12
C255	"	3s orange	45	30

Issued to commemorate the first anniversary of the elevation of Archbishop de la Torre to Cardinal.

1954, April 22

C256	AP56	60c dark green & green	12	12
C257	"	90c lilac rose	18	18
C258	"	1s black & pale lilac	20	18
C259	"	2s black brown & pale blue	35	30
C260	AP56	5s black brown & buff	75	50
		Nos. C256-C260 (5)	1.60	1.28

See note after No. 585.

Post Office, Guayaquil—AP57

Engraved.

1954, May 19 ***Perf. 12½x12.***

Black Surcharge

C261	AP57	80c on 20c red	25	20
C262	"	1s on 20c red	30	20

Issued to commemorate the 25th anniversary of Pan American-Grace Airways' operation in Ecuador.

Plane, Gateway and Wheel
AP58

Lithographed

1954, Aug. 2 ***Perf. 11*** **Unwmkd.**

C263	AP58	80c blue	12	10

Issued to publicize the Day of the Postal Employee.

San Pablo Lagoon
AP59

1954, Sept. 24 **Photogravure**

C264	AP59	60c orange	10	6
C265	"	70c rose pink	15	6
C266	"	90c deep green	20	8
C267	"	1s dk. gray grn.	25	8
C268	"	2s blue	40	12
C269	"	3s yellow brown	50	20
		Nos. C264-C269 (6)	1.60	60

Glorification of Abdon Calderon Garaicoa
AP60

Capt. Calderon
AP61

1954, Oct. 1

C270	AP60	80c rose pink	25	18
C271	AP61	90c blue	25	18

Issued to commemorate the 150th anniversary of the birth of Capt. Abdon Calderon Garaicoa.

El Cebollar College
AP62

Brother Miguel Instructing Boys
AP63

Designs: 90c, Francisco Febres Cordero (Brother Miguel). 2.50s, Tomb of Brother Miguel. 3s, Monument to Brother Miguel.

1954, Dec. 3 ***Perf. 11*** **Unwmkd.**

C272	AP62	70c dark green	15	8
C273	AP63	80c dark brown	20	10
C274	"	90c dark gray blue	20	10
C275	"	2.50s indigo	35	25
C276	AP62	3s lilac rose	60	45
		Nos. C272-C276 (5)	1.50	98

Issued to commemorate the centenary of the birth of Francisco Febres Cordero (Brother Miguel).

No. C221 Surcharged in Various Colors

E. M. P. 1955

$ 1,00

1955, May 25

C277	AP28	1s on 10s violet (Bk)	25	15
C278	"	1.70s on 10s vio. (C)	40	20
C279	"	4.20s on 10s violet (Br)	85	75

Denomination in larger type on No. C279.
Issued to publicize the National Exhibition of Daily Periodicals.

"La Rotonda," Guayaquil, and Rotary Emblem
AP64

Design: 90c, Eugenio Espejo hospital, Quito, and Rotary emblem.

1955, July 9 Engraved ***Perf. 12½***

C280	AP64	80c dark brown	45	40
C281	"	90c dark green	50	45

Issued to commemorate the 50th anniversary of the founding of Rotary International.

José Abel Castillo
AP65

Design:
2s, 5s, José Abel Castillo and Map of Ecuador.

1955, Oct. 19 ***Perf. 11x11½***

C282	AP65	60c chocolate	35	18
C283	"	90c lt. olive green	35	18
C284	"	1s lilac	40	15
C285	"	2s vermilion	45	25
C286	"	5s ultramarine	90	70
		Nos. C282-C286 (5)	2.45	1.46

See note after No. 595.

No. C29 Surcharged in Black.

1
X SUCRE X

1955, Oct. 24 *Perf. 12*
C287 AP1 1s on 5s purple 35 30

A similar surcharge on No. C29, set in two lines with letters 5mm. high and no X's or black-out line of squares, was privately applied.

San Pablo, Imbabura
AP66

Designs: 50s, Rumichaca Caves. 1.30s, Virgin of Quito. 1.50s, Cotopaxi Volcano. 1.70s, Tungurahua Volcano, Tungurahua. 1.90s, Guanacos. 2.40s, Mat market. 2.50s, Ruins at Incapirca. 4.20s, El Carmen, Cuenca, Azuay. 4.80s, Santo Domingo Church.

1956, Jan. 2 Photo. *Perf. 13*
C288 AP66 50c slate blue 40 10
C289 " 1s ultramarine 40 12
C290 " 1.30s crimson 45 18
C291 " 1.50s deep green 35 12
C292 " 1.70s yellow brown 25 15
C293 " 1.90s olive 40 35
C294 " 2.40s red orange 45 35
C295 " 2.50s violet 45 35
C296 " 4.20s black 60 50
C297 " 4.80s yellow orange 75 65
Nos. C288-C297 (10) 4.50 2.87

See also Nos. C310-C311.

Honorato Vazquez
AP67

Title Page of First Book
AP68

1956, May 28 Engraved
Various Portraits.
C298 AP67 1s yellow green 25 15
C299 " 1.50s red 35 25
C300 " 1.70s bright blue 30 25
C301 " 1.90s slate blue 35 25

Birth centenary (in 1955) of Honorato Vazquez, statesman.

1956, Aug. 27 *Perf. 13½* Unwmkd.
C302 AP68 1s black 20 15
C303 " 1.70s slate blue 25 20
C304 " 2s black brown 40 30
C305 " 3s reddish brown 55 50

Bicentenary of printing in Ecuador.

Hands Reaching for U.N. Emblem
AP69

1956, Oct. 24 *Perf. 14*
C307 AP69 1.70s red orange 75 30

Issued to commemorate the tenth anniversary of the United Nations (in 1955).
See also No. C319.

Coat of Arms and Basketball Player
AP70

Designs: 1.70s, Map of South America with flags and girl basketball players.

Photogravure.

1956, Dec. 28 *Perf. 14½x14*
C308 AP70 1s red lilac 30 12
C309 " 1.70s deep green 55 20

Issued to commemorate the 6th South American Women's Basketball Championship, August 1956.

Scenic Type of 1956.

1957, Jan. 2 *Perf. 13*
C310 AP66 50c blue green 20 8
C311 " 1s orange 30 12

Type of Regular Issue, 1957

Designs: 50c, Map of Cuenca, 16th century. 80c, Cathedral of Cuenca. 1s, Modern City Hall.

Photogravure.

1957, Apr. 7 *Perf. 12* Unwmkd.
C312 A219 50c brown, *cream* 15 8
a. Souvenir sheet of 4 1.00 1.00
C313 " 80c red, *bluish* 20 18
C314 " 1s purple, *yellow* 30 12
a. Souvenir sheet of 3 1.50 1.50

Issued to commemorate the fourth centenary of the founding of Cuenca.

No. C312a contains four imperf. 50c stamps similar to No. 613, but inscribed "AEREO" and printed in green. The sheet measures 140x120mm. and is printed on white ungummed paper. It is inscribed "IV Reunion de Consulta de la Comision del Instituto Panamericano de Geografia e Historia, Cuenca 4 al 12 de Abril de 1957."

No. C314a contains three imperf. stamps in designs similar to Nos. C312-C314, but with colors changed to orange (50c), brown (80c), violet (1s). The sheet measures 140x120mm. and is printed on white ungummed paper. It is inscribed "III Congreso de Ingenieros y Arquitectos del Ecuador, Cuenca, 6 al 9 de Abril de 1957."

Gabriela Mistral
AP71

Arms of Espejo, Carchi
AP72

Lithographed.

1957, Sept. 18 *Perf. 14* Unwmkd.
C315 AP71 2s light blue, black & red 30 20

Issued to honor Gabriela Mistral (1889-1957), Chilean poet and educator.
See also Nos. C406-C407.

Province of Carchi.

1957, Nov. 16 *Perf. 14½x13½*

Arms of Cantons: 2s, Montufar. 4.20s, Tulcan.

Coat of Arms Multicolored.
C316 AP72 1s carmine 20 15
C317 " 2s black 25 20
C318 " 4.20s ultramarine 65 55

See also Nos. C334-C337, C355-C364, C392-C395.

Redrawn U.N. Type of 1956.

1957, Dec. 10 Engraved. *Perf. 14*
C319 AP69 2s greenish blue 50 45

Issued to honor the United Nations. Dates, as on No. C307, are omitted; inscribed: "Homenaje a las Naciones Unidas."

Mater Dolorosa, San Gabriel College
AP73

Rafael Maria Arizaga
AP74

Design: Nos. C321 & 1s, Door of San Gabriel College, Quito.

1958, Apr. 27 Engraved. *Perf. 14*
C320 AP73 30c rose claret, *deep rose* 25 15
C321 " 30c rose claret, *deep rose* 25 15
C322 " 1s dark blue, *light blue* 25 15
C323 " 1.70s dark blue, *light blue* 30 25

Issued to commemorate the 50th anniversary of the miracle of San Gabriel College, Quito.

Issued in 2 sheets of 50. One sheet contains alternate copies of Nos. C320-C321, the other Nos. C322-C323.

1958, July 21 Lithographed
C324 AP74 1s multicolored 20 15

Issued to commemorate the centenary of the birth of Rafael Maria Arizaga (1858-1933), writer.
See also Nos. C343, C350, C412.

Daule River Bridge
AP75

Engraved.

1958, July 25 *Perf. 13½x14*
C325 AP75 1.30s green 25 20

Issued to commemorate the opening of the River Daule bridge in Guayas province.
See also Nos. C367-C369.

Basketball Player
AP76

Symbolical of the Eucharist
AP77

Photogravure

1958, Sept. 1 *Perf. 14x13½*
C326 AP76 1.30s dark green & light brown 60 50

South American basketball championships.

1958, Sept. 25 Litho. Unwmkd.

Design: 60c, Cathedral of Guayaquil.
C327 AP77 10c violet & buff 6 5
C328 " 60c orange & violet brown 12 8
C329 " 1s brown & light blue 18 12

Souvenir Sheet

Symbolical of the Eucharist
AP78

Perf. 13½x14
C330 AP78 Sheet of four 1.00 1.00
a. 40c dark blue (any position) 20 20

Nos. C327-C330 issued to commemorate the 3rd National Eucharistic Congress.
No. C330 measures 115 x 88½mm.

Stamps of 1865 and 1920
AP79

Designs: 2s, Stamps of 1920 and 1948. 4.20s, Municipal museum and library.

Photogravure.

1958, Oct. 8 *Perf. 11½* Unwmkd.
Granite Paper
C331 AP79 1.30s green & brown red 35 30
C332 " 2s blue & violet 60 40
C333 " 4.20s dark brown 1.10 80

Issued to publicize the National Philatelic Exposition (EXFIGUA), Guayaquil, Oct. 4-14.

Coat of Arms Type of 1957.
Province of Imbabura.

Arms of Cantons: 50c, Cotacachi. 60c, Antonio Ante. 80c, Otalvo. 1.10s, Ibarra.

Lithographed.

1958, Nov. 9 *Perf. 14½x13½*
Coats of Arms Multicolored.
C334 AP72 50c black & red 10 8
C335 " 60c black, blue & red 15 8
C336 " 80c black & yel. 20 10
C337 " 1.10s black & red 25 12

Charles V
AP80

Paul Rivet
AP81

Engraved & Photogravure
Perf. 14x13½

1958, Dec. 12 Unwmkd.
C338 AP80 2s brown red & dark brown 30 25
C339 " 4.20s dark gray & red brown 65 60

Issued to commemorate the 400th anniversary of the death of Charles V, Holy Roman Emperor.

1958, Dec. 29 Photo. *Perf. 11½*
Granite Paper.
C340 AP81 1s brown 15 12

Issued in honor of Paul Rivet (1876-1958), French anthropologist.

1959, May 6

Portrait: 2s, Alexander von Humboldt.

C341 AP81 2s slate 30 15

Issued to commemorate the centenary of the death of Alexander von Humboldt, German naturalist and geographer.

Front Page of "El Telegrafo"
AP82

1959, Feb. Litho. *Perf. 13½*

C342 AP82 1.30s blue green & black 25 18

Issued to commemorate the 75th anniversary of Ecuador's oldest newspaper.

Portrait Type of 1958

Portrait: José Luis Tamayo.

1959, June 26 *Perf. 14* Unwmkd.

Portrait Multicolored.

C343 AP74 1.30s light green, blue & salmon 25 18

Issued to commemorate the centenary of the birth of José Luis Tamayo (1858–1947), lawyer.

El Sagrario and House of Manuela Canizares
AP83

Condor
AP84

Designs: 80c, Hall at San Agustin. 1s, First words of the constitutional act. 2s, Entrance to Cuartel Real. 4.20s, Allegory of Liberty.

Photogravure.

1959, Aug. 28 *Perf. 14* Unwmkd.

C344 AP83 20c ultramarine & light brown 6 6
C345 " 80c bright blue & deep orange 12 8
C346 " 1s dark red & dark olive 15 12
C347 AP84 1.30s bright blue & orange 25 15
C348 " 2s ultramarine & orange brown 25 20
C349 " 4.20s scarlet & bright blue 60 55
Nos. C344–C349 (6) 1.43 1.16

Sesquicentennial of the revolution.

Portrait Type of 1958

Portrait: 1s, Alfredo Baquerizo Moreno.

1959, Sept. 26 Litho. *Perf. 14*

C350 AP74 1s gray, red & salmon 18 12

Issued to commemorate the centenary of the birth of Alfredo Baquerizo Moreno (1859–1951), statesman.

Pope Pius XII
AP85

1959, Oct. 9 *Perf. 14½* Unwmkd.

C351 AP85 1.30s multicolored 30 25

Issued in memory of Pope Pius XII.

Flags of Argentina, Bolivia, Brazil, Guatemala, Haiti, Mexico and Peru
AP86

Flags of: 80c, Chile, Costa Rica, Cuba, Dominican Republic, Panama, Paraguay, United States. 1.30s, Colombia, Ecuador, Honduras, Nicaragua, Salvador, Uruguay, Venezuela.

1959, Oct. 12 *Perf. 13½.*

C352 AP86 50c multicolored 15 10
C353 " 80c yel., red & bl. 20 18
C354 " 1.30s multicolored 30 25

Organization of American States.

Coat of Arms Type of 1957
Province of Pichincha.

Arms of Cantons: 10c, Rumiñahui. 40c, Pedro Moncayo. 1s, Mejia. 1.30s, Cayambe. 4.20s, Quito.

Lithographed.

1959–60 *Perf. 14½x13½* Unwmkd.

Coat of Arms Multicolored.

C355 AP72 10c black & dark red ('60) 6 6
C356 " 40c blk. & yellow 10 6
C357 " 1s black & brown ('60) 15 10
C358 " 1.30s black & green ('60) 25 15
C359 " 4.20s black & org. 60 50
Nos. C355–C359 (5) 1.16 87

Province of Cotopaxi.

Arms of Cantons: 40c, Pangua. 60c, Pujili. 70c, Saquisili. 1s, Salcedo. 1.30s, Latacunga.

1960

Coat of Arms Multicolored

C360 AP72 40c black & car. 6 6
C361 " 60c black & blue 10 6
C362 " 70c blk. & turq. 15 6
C363 " 1s black & red orange 18 10
C364 " 1.30s black & org. 20 10
Nos. C360–C364 (5) 69 38

Flags of American Nations
AP87

1960, Feb. 23 *Perf. 13x12½*

C365 AP87 1.30s multcolored 20 15
C366 " 2s " 30 25

Issued to commemorate the 11th Inter-American Conference, Feb. 1960.

Bridge Type of 1958.

Bridges: No. C367, Juntas. No. C368, Saracay. 2s, Railroad bridge, Ambato.

1960 Lithographed *Perf. 13½*

C367 AP75 1.30s chocolate 20 15

Photo. *Perf. 12½*

C368 AP75 1.30s emerald 20 10
C369 " 2s brown 25 20

Building of three new bridges.

Bahia-Chone Road
AP88

Pres. Camilo Ponce Enriquez
AP89

Designs: 4.20s, Public Works Building, Cuenca. 5s, El Coca airport. 10s, New Harbor, Guayaquil.

1960, Aug. Litho. *Perf. 14*

C370 AP88 1.30s black & dull yellow 20 12
C371 " 4.20s rose carmine & light green 45 40
C372 " 5s dark brown & yellow 70 50
C373 " 10s dark blue & blue 1.20 1.00

Perf. 11x11½

C374 AP80 2s orange brown & black 2.25 50
Nos. C370–C374 (5) 4.80 2.52

Nos. C370–C374 issued to publicize the achievements of Pres. Camilo Ponce Enriquez (1956–1960).

Issue dates: Nos. C370–C373, Aug. 24. No. C374, Aug. 31.

Red Cross Building, Quito and Henri Dunant—AP90

1960, Oct. 5 *Perf. 13x14* Unwmkd.

C375 AP90 2s rose violet & carmine 50 25

Centenary (in 1959) of Red Cross idea.

El Belen Church, Quito
AP91

1961, Jan. 14 *Perf. 12½*

C376 AP91 3s multicolored 50 35

Issued to commemorate Ecuador's participation in the 1960 Barcelona Philatelic Congress.

Map of Ecuador and Amazon River System
AP92

1961, Feb. 27 Litho. *Perf. 10½*

C377 AP92 80c salmon, claret & green 25 20
C378 " 1.30s gray, slate & green 30 25
C379 " 2s beige, red & green 40 30

Issued to commemorate Amazon Week, and the 132nd anniversary of the Battle of Tarqui against Peru.

Juan Montalvo, Juan Leon Mera, Juan Benigno Vela
AP93

Hugo Ortiz G.
AP94

1961, Apr. 13 *Perf. 13* Unwmkd.

C380 AP93 1.30s salmon & black 25 15

Centenary of Tungurahua province.

1961, May 25 *Perf. 14x14½*

Design: No. C382, Ortiz monument.

C381 AP94 1.30s greenish blue, black & yellow 25 15
C382 " 1.30s greenish blue, purple, olive & brown 25 15

Issued in memory of Lieutenant Hugo Ortiz G., killed in battle Aug. 2, 1941.

Condor and Airplane Stamp of 1936
AP95

Designs: 1.30s, Map of South America and stamp of 1865. 2s, Bolivar monument stamp of 1930.

Perf. 10½

1961, May 25 Litho. Unwmkd.

Size: 41x28mm.

C383 AP95 80c orange & violet 25 20

Size: 41x34mm.

C384 AP95 1.30s blue, yellow, olive & carmine 35 30

Size: 40½x37mm.

C385 AP95 2s carmine rose & black 45 40

Issued to publicize the Third National Philatelic Exhibition, Quito, May 25–June 3, 1961.

Arms of Los Rios and Egret
AP96

1961, May 27 ***Perf. 14½x13½***
Coat of Arms Multicolored

C386 AP96 2s blue & black 35 25

Centenary (in 1960) of Los Rios province.

Gabriel Garcia Moreno
AP97

Remigio Crespo Toral
AP98

1961, Sept. 24 ***Perf. 12*** **Unwmkd.**

C387 AP97 1s blue, brown & buff 25 15

Issued to commemorate the centenary of the restoration of national integrity.

1961, Nov. 3 ***Perf. 14*** **Unwmkd.**

C388 AP98 50c multicolored 12 8

Issued to commemorate the centenary of the birth of Remigio Crespo Toral, poet laureate of Ecuador.

Galapagos Islands Nos. LC1–LC3 Overprinted in Black or Red: "Estacion de Biologia Maritima de Galapagos" and "UNESCO 1961" (Similarly to Nos. 684–686).

1961, Oct. 31 **Photo.** ***Perf. 12***

C389 A1 1s deep blue 30 30
a. "de Galápagos" on top line 1.50 1.50
C390 A1 1.80s rose violet 35 30
a. UNESCO emblem omitted 1.00 1.00
C391 A1 4.20s black (R) 70 65

Issued to commemorate the establishment of maritime biological stations on Galapagos Islands by UNESCO.

Coat of Arms Type of 1957.
Province of Tungurahua.

Arms of Cantons: 50c, Pillaro. 1s, Pelileo. 1.30s, Baños. 2s, Ambato.

Perf. 14½x13½

1962, Mar. 30 **Litho.** **Unwmkd.**
Coats of Arms Multicolored

C392 AP72 50c black 10 6
C393 " 1s " 15 12
C394 " 1.30s " 20 15
C395 " 2s " 30 25

Pres. Arosemena and Prince Philip, Arms of Ecuador and Great Britain and Equator Monument
AP99

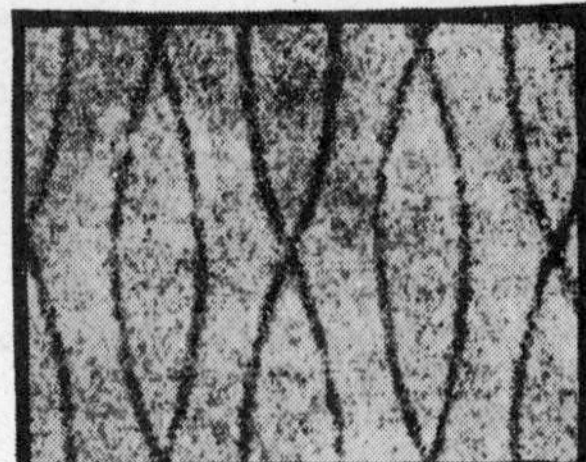

Wmk. 340

Wmkd. Alternating Interlaced Wavy Lines. (340)

1962, Feb. 17 ***Perf. 14x13½***

C396 AP99 1.30s blue, sepia, red & yel. 25 20
C397 " 2s multicolored 35 25

Issued to commemorate the visit of Prince Philip, Duke of Edinburgh, to Ecuador, Feb. 17–20, 1962.

Mountain Farming
AP100

Lithographed

1963, Mar. 21 ***Perf. 12½*** **Unwmkd.**

C398 AP100 30c emerald, yel. & blk. 10 10
C399 " 3s dull red, grn. & orge. 45 40
C400 " 4.20s blue, black & yellow 60 50

Issued for the "Freedom from Hunger" campaign of the U.N. Food and Agriculture Organization.

Mosquito and Malaria Eradication Emblem
AP101

1963, Apr. 17 ***Perf. 12½*** **Unwmkd.**

C401 AP101 50c dull yel., car. rose & blk. 10 10
C402 " 80c brt. grn., car. rose & blk. 15 12
C403 " 2s brt. pink, dp. claret & black 35 35

Issued for the World Health Organization drive to eradicate malaria.

Stagecoach and Jet Plane
AP102

1963, May 7 **Lithographed**

C404 AP102 2s orge. & car. rose 30 25
C405 AP102 4.20s claret & ultra. 55 50

Issued to commemorate the centenary of the first International Postal Conference, Paris, 1863.

Type of 1957 Inscribed "Islas Galapagos," Surcharged with New Value and Overprinted "Ecuador" in Black or Red.

1963, June 19 ***Perf. 14*** **Unwmkd.**

C406 AP71 5s on 2s gray, dk. blue & red 60 50
C407 " 10s on 2s gray, dark blue & red (R) 1.20 1.00

The basic 2s exists without surcharge and overprint. No. C407 exists with "ECUADOR" omitted, and with both "ECUADOR" and "10 SUCRES" double.

No. C375 Overprinted: "1863–1963/Centenario/de la Fundación/de la Cruz Roja/Internacional"

Photogravure

1963, June 21 ***Perf. 13x14***

C408 AP90 2s rose violet & carmine 35 30

Issued to commemorate the centenary of the founding of the International Red Cross.

Type of Regular Issue, 1963.

Designs (Arosemena and): 70c, Flags of Ecuador. 2s, Flags of Ecuador and Panama. 4s, Flags of Ecuador and U.S.

1963, July 1 **Lithographed** ***Perf. 14***

C409 A238 70c pale blue & multicolored 10 10
C410 " 2s pink & multi. 25 20
C411 " 4s light blue & multicolored 60 50

Issued to commemorate Pres. Arosemena's friendship trip, July 1962.

Portrait Type of 1958

Portrait: 2s, Dr. Mariano Cueva.

Lithographed

1963, July 4 ***Perf. 14*** **Unwmkd.**

C412 AP74 2s lt. grn. & multi. 25 20

Issued to commemorate the 150th anniversary of the birth of Dr. Mariano Cueva (1812–1882).

Social Insurance Symbol
AP103

Mother and Child
AP104

1963, July 9 **Lithographed**

C413 AP103 10s brn., bl., gray & ocher 1.00 90

12th anniversary of Social Insurance.

1963, July 28 ***Perf. 12½***

C414 AP104 1.30s org., dark bl. & blk. 25 20
C415 " 5s gray, red & brown 60 50

Issued to publicize the 7th Pan-American and South American Pediatrics Congresses, Quito.

Simon Bolivar Airport, Guayaquil
AP105

1963, July 25 ***Perf. 14***

C416 AP105 60c gray 8 8
C417 " 70c dull green 12 10
C418 " 5s brown violet 50 45

Issued to commemorate the opening of Simon Bolivar Airport, Guayaquil, July 15, 1962.

Nos. 638, 640–641 Overprinted "AEREO"

1964 ***Perf. 12***
Flags in National Colors

C419 A223 1.80s dull violet 60 50
C420 A224 2s dark brown 60 50
C421 A223 2.20s black brown 60 50

On 1.80s and 2.20s, "AEREO" is vertical, reading down.

No. 650 Overprinted in Gold: "FARO DE COLON / AEREO"

1964 **Photo.** ***Perf. 14x13½***

C422 A229 1.80s dark blue *3.00* 1.75

Nos. C352–C354 Overprinted **1961**

1964 **Lithographed** ***Perf. 13½***

C423 AP86 50c blue & multi. *75* *40*
C424 " 80c yel. & multi. *75* *40*
C425 " 1.30s pale green & multi. *75* *40*

No. C307 Overprinted: "DECLARACION / DERECHOS HUMANOS / 1964 / XV-ANIV"

Engraved

1964, Sept. 29 ***Perf. 14*** **Unwmkd.**

C426 AP69 1.70s red orange 25 20

Issued to commemorate the 15th anniversary (in 1963) of the Universal Declaration of Human Rights.

Banana Type of Regular Issue

1964, Oct. 26 **Litho.** ***Perf. 12½x12***

C427 A241 4.20s blk., bister & gray olive 50 45
C428 " 10s blk., scarlet & gray olive 95 85
a. Souv. sheet of 4 2.00 2.00

Issued to publicize the Banana Conference, Oct.–Nov. 1964. No. C428a contains four imperf. stamps similar to Nos. 720–721 and C427–C428. Pale blue margin with black inscription and red control number. Size: 120x95mm.

John F. Kennedy, Flag-draped Coffin and John Jr.
AP106

1964, Nov. 22 **Litho.** ***Perf. 14***

C429 AP106 4.20s multicolored 1.00 80
C430 " 5s " 1.25 1.00
C431 " 10s " 2.00 1.50
a. Souv. sheet of 3 10.00 10.00

Issued in memory of President John F. Kennedy (1917–63).

No. C431a contains stamps similar to Nos. C429–C431, imperf. Pale lilac margin with brown and white inscriptions. Red control number. Size: 114x130mm.

Olympic Type of Regular Issue

Designs: 1.30s, Gymnast (vert.). 1.80s, Hurdler. 2s, Basketball.

Perf. 13½x14, 14x13½

1964, Dec. 16 **Unwmkd.**

C432 A243 1.30s violet blue, verm. & brn. 25 20
C433 " 1.80s violet blue & multi. 30 25

C434 A243 2s red & multi. 35 30
a. Souv. sheet of 4 4.00 4.00

18th Olympic Games, Tokyo, Oct. 10–25.

No. C434a contains stamps similar to Nos. 725 and C432–C434, imperf. Pale olive margin with black and white inscriptions and red control number. Size: 139x107mm.

Sports Type of Regular Issue, 1965

Torch and Athletes: 2s, 3s, Diver, gymnast, wrestlers and weight lifter. 2.50s, 4s, Bicyclists. 3.50s, 5s, Jumpers.

1965, Nov. 20 Litho. *Perf. 12x12½*

C435 A247 2s bl., gold & blk. 25 18
C436 " 2.50s orange, gold & black 30 25
C437 " 3s bright pink, gold & black 35 30
C438 " 3.50s light violet, gold & black 40 35
C439 " 4s brt. yel. grn., gold & black 45 40
C440 " 5s red orange, gold & black 55 50
a. Souv. sheet of 12 5.00 5.00
Nos. C435–C440 (6) 2.30 1.98

Issued to commemorate the 5th Bolivarian Games, held at Guayaquil and Quito. No. C440a contains 12 imperf. stamps similar to Nos. 738–743 and C435–C440. Black and red inscriptions. Size: 215x129mm.

Bird Type of Regular Issue

Birds: 1s, Yellow grosbeak. 1.30s, Black-headed parrot. 1.50s, Scarlet tanager. 2s, Sapphire quail-dove. 2.50s, Violet-tailed sylph. 3s, Lemon-throated barbet. 4s, Yellow-tailed oriole. 10s, Collared puffbird.

1966, June 17 Litho. *Perf. 13½*

Birds in Natural Colors

C441 A249 1s lt. red brown & black 10 8
C442 " 1.30s pink & black 15 10
C443 " 1.50s pale green & black 15 12
C444 " 2s salmon & blk. 20 15
C445 " 2.50s lt. yel. green & black 25 20
C446 " 3s salmon & blk. 30 25
C447 " 4s gray & black 40 35
C448 " 10s beige & blk. 1.00 90
Nos. C441–C448 (8) 2.55 2.15

Nos. C436 and C443 Surcharged

1967

C449 A247 80c on 2.50s orange, gold & black 10 8
C450 A249 80c on 1.50s multi. 10 8

Old denomination on No. C449 is obliterated with heavy bar; the surcharge on No. C450 includes "Resello" and an ornament over old denomination.

Peñaherrera Monument, Quito
AP107

Design: 2s, Peñaherrera statue.

1967, Dec. 29 Litho. *Perf. 12x12½*

C451 AP107 1.30s blk. & org. 15 12
C452 " 2s black & lt. ultra. 20 15

See note after No. 763.

Arosemena Type of Regular Issue, 1968

Designs: 1.30s, Inauguration of Pres. Arosemena. 2s, Pres. Arosemena speaking in Punta del Este.

1968, May 9 Litho. *Perf. 13½x14*

C453 A251 1.30s multicolored 15 12
C454 " 2s " 20 18

First anniversary of administration of Pres. Otto Arosemena Gomez.

No. C448 Surcharged in Plum, Dark Blue or Green

RESELLO

$ 0,80

1969, Jan. 9 Litho. *Perf. 13½*

Bird in Natural Colors

C455 A249 80c on 10s beige (P) 8 8
C456 " 1s on 10s " (DBl) 10 10
C457 " 2s on 10s " (G) 20 18

"Operation Friendship"
AP108

1969–70 Typo. *Perf. 13½*

C458 AP108 2s yellow, black, red & lt. blue 20 18
a. 2s yel., blk., car. & bl., perf. 12½ 20 18
C459 AP108 2s bl., blk., car. & yel. ('70) 20 18

Friendship campaign. Medallion background on Nos. C458 and C458a is blue; on No. C459, yellow.

No. 639 Surcharged in Gold "S/. 5 AEREO" and Bar

1969, Nov. 25 Litho. *Perf. 12*

C460 A224 5s on 2s multi. 1.25 75

Butterfly Type of Regular Issue

Butterflies: 1.30s, Morpho peleides. 1.50s, Anartia amathea.

1970 Lithographed *Perf. 12½*

C461 A255 1.30s multicolored 13 11
C462 " 1.50s pink & multi. 15 12

Same, White Background

1970 *Perf. 13½*

C463 A255 1.30s multicolored 13 11
C464 " 1.50s " 15 12

Arms Type of Regular Issue

Provincial Arms and Flags: 1.30s, El Oro. 2s, Loja. 3s, Manabi. 5s, Pichincha. 10s, Guayas.

1971 Lithographed *Perf. 10½*

C465 A258 1.30s pink & multi. 13 10
C466 " 2s multicolored 20 15
C467 " 3s " 30 25
C468 " 5s " 50 40
C469 " 10s " 1.00 75
Nos. C465–C469 (5) 2.13 1.65

Presentation of the Virgin
AP109

Pres. Allende and Chilean Flag
AP110

Art of Quito: 1.50s, Blessed Anne at Prayer. 2s, St. Theresa de Jesus. 2.50s, Altar of Carmen (horiz.). 3s, Descent from the Cross. 4s, Christ of St. Mariana de Jesus. 5s, Shrine of St. Anthony. 10s, Cross of San Diego.

1971 *Perf. 11½*

Inscriptions in Black

C473 AP109 1.30s multi. 13 10
C474 " 1.50s " 15 12
C475 " 2s " 20 15
C476 " 2.50s " 25 20
C477 " 3s " 30 25
C478 " 4s " 40 30
C479 " 5s " 50 40
C480 " 10s " 1.00 75
Nos. C473–C480 (8) 2.93 2.27

Design: 2.10s, Pres. José M. Velasco Ibarra of Ecuador, Pres. Salvador Allende of Chile and national flags.

1971, Aug. 24 *Perf. 12½*

C481 AP110 2s multicolored 20 15
C482 " 2.10s " 21 16

Visit of Pres. Salvador Allende of Chile, Aug. 24.

Globe and Emblem
AP111

1971

C483 AP111 5s black 50 40
C484 " 5.50s dull purple & black 55 45

Opening of Postal Museum, Aug. 24, 1971.

Pazmiño Type of Regular Issue

1971, Sept. 16 *Perf. 12x11½*

C485 A260 1.50s grn. & multi. 15 12
C486 " 2.50s " " 25 20

50th anniversary of "El Universo," newspaper founded by Ismael Pérez Pazmiño.

Map of Americas
AP112

Designs: 10s, Converging roads and map. 20s, Map of Americas and Equator. 50s, Mountain road and monument on Equator.

1971 *Perf. 11½*

C487 AP112 5s org. & multi. 50 45
C488 " 10s org. & black 1.00 90
C489 " 20s black, blue & brt. rose 2.00 1.80
C490 " 50s blue, black & gray 5.00 4.00

11th Pan-American Road Congress.
Issue dates: 5s, 10s, 50s, Nov. 15; 20s, Nov. 22.

Arms of Ecuador and Argentina
AP113

Design: 5s, Presidents José M. Velasco Ibarra and Alejandro Agustin Lanusse.

1972

C491 AP113 3s blk. & multi. 30 27
C492 " 5s " " 50 40

Visit of Lt. Gen. Alejandro Agustin Lanusse, president of Argentina, Jan. 25.

Flame, Scales, Map of Americas
AP114

1972, Apr. 24 Litho. *Perf. 12½*

C493 AP114 1.30s blue & red 13 10

17th Conference of the Interamerican Federation of Lawyers, Quito, Apr. 24.

Religious Paintings Type of Regular Issue

Ecuadorian Paintings: 3s, Virgin of the Flowers, by Miguel de Santiago. 10s, Virgin of the Rosary, by Quito School.

1972, Apr. 24 *Perf. 14x13½*

C494 A263 3s black & multi. 30 25
C495 " 10s " " 1.00 75
a. Souv. sheet of 2 1.40 1.40

No. C495a contains one each of Nos. C494–C495. Blue marginal inscription. Size: 98x110½mm. Exists imperf.

1972, May 4

Ecuadorian Statues: 3s, St. Dominic, Quito School. 10s, St. Rosa of Lima, by Bernardo de Legarda.

C496 A263 3s black & multi. 30 25
C497 " 10s " " 1.00 75
a. Souv. sheet of 2 1.40 1.40

No. C497a contains one each of Nos. C496–C497. Blue marginal inscription. Size: 98x110½mm. Exists imperf. Letters of "Ecuador" 3mm. high on Nos. C496–C497, 7mm. high on Nos. C494–C495.

Portrait Type of Regular Issue

Designs (Generals, from Paintings): 1.30s, José Maria Saenz. 3s, Tomás Wright. 4s, Antonio Farfan. 5s, Antonio José de Sucre. 10s, Simon Bolivar. 20s, Arms of Ecuador.

1972, May 24

C498 A264 1.30s blue & multi. 13 10
C499 " 3s " " 30 25
C500 " 4s " " 40 30
C501 " 5s " " 50 40
C502 " 10s " " 1.00 75
C503 " 20s " " 2.00 1.50
Nos. C498–C503 (6) 4.33 3.30

Sesquicentennial of the Battle of Pichincha and the liberation of Quito.

Artisan Type of Regular Issue

Designs: 2s, Woman wearing flowered poncho. 3s, Striped poncho. 5s, Poncho with roses. 10s, Gold sunburst sculpture.

1972, July Photo. *Perf. 13*

C504 A265 2s multicolored 20 15
C505 " 3s " 30 25
C506 " 5s " 50 40
C507 " 10s orange red & multicolored 1.00 75
a. Souvenir sheet of 4 2.25 2.25

Handicraft of Ecuador. No. C507a contains one each of Nos. C504–C507. Pale claret marginal inscription and ornament. Black control number. Size 104x164mm.

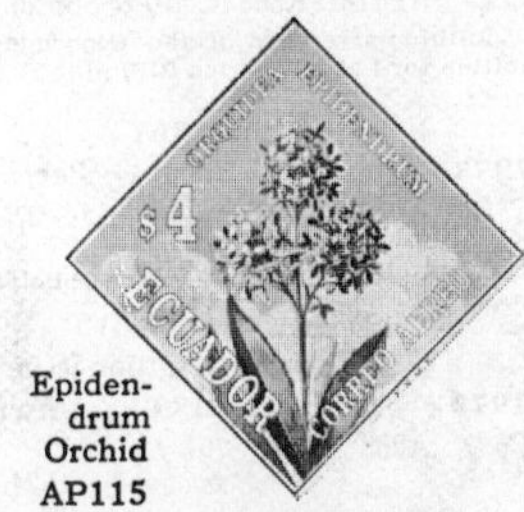

Epidendrum Orchid
AP115

1972 Photogravure *Perf. 12½*

Multicolored; Flowers in Natural Colors

C508	AP115	4s *shown*	40	30
C509	"	6s *Canna*	60	45
C510	"	10s *Jimson weed*	1.00	75
		a. Souv. sheet of 3	2.25	2.25

No. C510a contains one each of Nos. C508–C510. Blue marginal inscription and ornaments. Black control number. Size: 166x106mm. Exists imperf.

Oil Drilling Towers
AP116

Coat of Arms
AP117

1972, Oct. 17 Litho. *Perf. 11½*

C511	AP116	1.30s blue & multi.	13	10

Ecuadorian oil industry.

1972, Nov. 18 Litho. *Perf. 11½*

Arms Multicolored

C512	AP117	2s black	20	15
C513	"	3s "	30	25
C514	"	4s "	40	30
C515	"	4.50s "	45	35
C516	"	6.30s "	63	50
C517	"	6.90s "	69	55
		Nos. C512–C517 (6)	2.67	2.10

Pichincha Type of Regular Issue

Designs: 2.40s, Corridor, San Agustin. 4.50s, La Merced Convent. 5.50s, Column base. 6.30s, Chapter Hall, San Agustin. 6.90s, Interior, San Agustin. 7.40s, Crucifixion, Cantuña Chapel. 7.90s, Decorated ceiling, San Agustin.

1972, Dec. 6 Wmk. 367

C518	A266	2.40s yel. & multi.	25	18
C519	"	4.50s " "	45	35
C520	"	5.50s " "	55	45
C521	"	6.30s " "	65	50
C522	"	6.90s " "	70	55
C523	"	7.40s " "	75	60
C524	"	7.90s " "	80	65
		Nos. C518–C524 (7)	4.15	3.28

Sesquicentennial of the Battle of Pichincha.

UN Emblem AP118 — OAS Emblem AP119

1973, Mar. 23 Litho. Unwmkd.

Perf. 11½

C525	AP118	1.30s lt. bl. & blk.	20	10

25th anniversary of the Economic Committee for Latin America (CEPAL).

Wmk. 367

1973, Apr. 14 Litho. *Perf. 11½*

C526	AP119	1.50s multi.	27	14
		a. Unwmkd.		

Day of the Americas and "Philately for Peace."

Bird Type of Regular Issue

1973 *Perf. 11½x11* Unwmkd.

C527	A268	1.30s *Blue-footed booby*	24	12
C528	A268	3s *Brown pelican*	30	15

Elevation of Galapagos Islands to a province of Ecuador.

Presidents Lara and Caldera
AP120

1973, June 15 Wmk. 367

C529	AP120	3s multicolored	55	28

Visit of Pres. Rafael Caldera of Venezuela, Feb. 5–7.

Silver Coin, 1934
AP121

Globe, OPEC Emblem, Oil Derrick
AP122

Ecuadorian Coins: 10s, Silver coin, obverse. 50s, Gold coin, 1928.

Perf. 14

1973, Dec. 14 Photo. Unwmkd.

C530	AP121	5s multicolored	50	25
C531	"	10s "	1.00	50
C532	"	50s "	5.00	2.50
		a. Souvenir sheet of 3	6.75	6.75

No. C532a contains one each of Nos. C530–C532; light blue margin with gold and black inscription, coat of arms and control numbers. Dated "1972." Size: 115x 88mm. Exists imperf.

A gold marginal overprint was applied in 1974 to No. C532a (perf. and imperf.): "X Campeonato Mundial de Football / Munich—1974".

A carmine overprint was applied in 1974 to No. C532a (perf. and imperf.): "Seminario de Telecommunicaciones Rurales, / Septiembre—1974 / Quito—Ecuador" and ITU emblem.

1974, June 15 Litho. *Perf. 11½*

C533	AP122	2s multicolored	24	12

Meeting of Organization of Oil Exporting Countries, Quito, June 15–24.

Ecuadorian Flag, UPU Emblem
AP123

1974, July 15 Litho. *Perf. 11½*

C534	AP123	1.30s multi.	15	8

Centenary of Universal Postal Union.

Teodoro Wolf
AP124

Capt. Edmundo Chiriboga
AP125

1974 Lithographed *Perf. 12x11½*

C535	AP124	1.30s blk. & ultra.	15	8
C536	AP125	1.50s gray	18	8

Teodoro Wolf, geographer; Edmundo Chiriboga, national hero. Issue dates, No. C535, Nov. 29; No. C536, Dec. 4.

Congress Emblem
AP126

1974, Dec. 8 Litho. *Perf. 11½x12*

C537	AP126	5s blue & multi.	60	30

8th Inter-American Postmasters' Congress, Quito.

Map of Americas and Coat of Arms
AP127

Manuel J. Calle, Journalist
AP128

1975, Feb. 1 *Perf. 12x11½*

C538	AP127	3s black & multi.	35	18

EXFIGUA Stamp Exhibition and 5th General Assembly of Federacion Inter-Americana de Filatelia, Guayaquil, Nov. 1973.

1975 *Perf. 12x11½*

Portraits: No. C540, Leopoldo Benites V., president of U.N. General Assembly, 1973–74; No. C541, Adofo H. Simmonds G. (1892–1969), journalists; No. C542, Juan de Dios Martinez Mera, President of Ecuador, birth centenary.

C539	AP128	5s lilac rose	60	30
C540	"	5s gray	60	30
C541	"	5s violet	60	30
C542	"	5s blk. & rose red	60	30

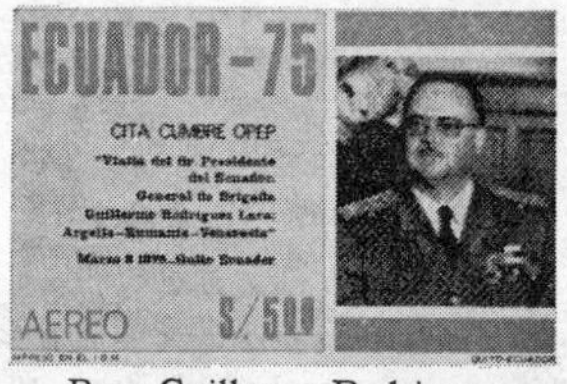

Pres. Guillermo Rodriguez Lara—AP129

1975 *Perf. 12* Unwmkd.

C546	AP129	5s verm. & black	60	30

State visit of Pres. Guillermo Rodriguez Lara to Algeria, Romania and Venezuela.

Meeting Type of 1975

Designs: 1.50s, Rafael Rodriguez Palacio and Argelino Duran Quintero meeting at border in Ruichacha. 2s, Signing border agreement.

1975, Apr. 1 Litho. *Perf. 12x11½*

C547	A273	1.50s multicolored	18	10
C548	"	2s "	24	12

Meeting of the Ministers for Public Works of Ecuador and Colombia, July 27, 1973.

Sacred Heart (Painting)
AP130

Quito Cathedral
AP131

Design: 2s, Monstrance.

1975, Apr. 28 Litho. *Perf. 12x11½*

C549	AP130	1.30s yel. & multi.	15	8
C550	"	2s bl. & multi.	24	12
C551	AP131	3s multi.	36	18

3rd Bolivarian Eucharistic Congress, Quito, June 9–16, 1974.

J. Delgado Panchana with Trophy
AP132

J. Delgado Panchana Swimming
AP133

Perf. 12x11½, 11½x12

1975, June 12 Unwmkd.

C552	AP132	1.30s bl. & multi.	15	8
C553	AP133	3s blk. & multi.	36	18

Jorge Delgado Panchana. South American swimming champion, 1971 and 1974.

Sports Type of 1975

1975, Sept. 11 Litho. *Perf. 11½*

C554	A276	1.30s *Tennis*	15	8
C555	"	2s *Target shooting*	24	12
C556	"	2.80s *Volleyball*	34	16
C557	"	3s *Raft with sails*	36	18
C558	"	5s *Mask*	60	30
		Nos. C554–C558 (5)	1.69	84

3rd Ecuadorian Games.

Flower Type of 1975

1975, Nov. 18 Litho. *Perf. 11½x12*

C559	A277	1.30s *Pitcairnia pungens*	16	8
C560	"	2s *Scarlet sage*	24	12
C561	"	3s *Amaryllis*	36	18
C562	"	4s *Opuntia quitense*	48	24
C563	"	5s *Amaryllis*	60	30
		Nos. C559–C563 (5)	1.84	92

Tail Assemblies and Emblem
AP134

Planes over Map of Ecuador
AP135

1975, Dec. 17 Litho. *Perf. 11½*

C564 AP134 1.30s bl. & multi. 16 8
C565 AP135 3s multicolored 36 18

TAME, Military Transport Airline, 13th anniversary.

Benalcázar Statue
AP136

1976, Feb. 6 Litho. *Perf. 11½*

C566 AP136 2s multicolored 24 12
C567 " 3s " 36 18

Sebastián de Benalcázar (1495–1550), Spanish conquistador, founder of Quito.

Archaeology Type of 1975

Designs: 1.30s, Seated man, Carchi Culture. 2s, Funerary urn, Tuncahuan Culture. 3s, Priest, Bahia de Caraquez Culture. 4s, Snail's shell, Cuasmal Culture. 5s, Bowl supported by figurines, Guangala Culture.

1976, Feb. 12 Litho. *Perf. 11½*

C568 A278 1.30s multicolored 16 8
C569 " 2s " 24 12
C570 " 3s " 36 18
C571 " 4s " 48 24
C572 " 5s " 60 30
Nos. C568–C572 (5) 1.84 92

Archaeological artifacts.

Fruit Type of 1976

Designs: 2s, Apples. 5s, Rose.

1976, Mar. 30

C573 A280 2s blue & multi. 24 12
C574 " 5s " " 60 30

25th Flower and Fruit Festival, Ambato.

Lufthansa Jet
AP137

1976, June 25 Litho. *Perf. 12*

C575 AP137 10s bl. & multi. 1.20 75

Lufthansa, 50th anniversary.

An imperf. 20s miniature sheet exists, similar to No. C575 enlarged, with overprinted black bar covering line below "Lufthansa." Size: 90x115mm.

Projected Post Office, Quito
AP138

Fruit Peddler
AP139

1976, Aug. 10 Litho. *Perf. 12*

C576 AP138 5s blk. & multi. 60 30

Design for new General Post Office, Quito.

1976, July 25

Designs: No. C578, Longshoreman. No. C579, Cerros del Carmen and Santa Ana, hills of Guayaquil (horiz.). No. C580, Sebastián de Belalcázar. No. C581, Francisco de Orellana. No. C582, Chief Guayas and his wife Quila.

C577 AP139 1.30s red & multi. 16 8
C578 " 1.30s " " 16 8
C579 " 1.30s " " 16 8
C580 " 2s " " 24 12
C581 " 2s " " 24 12
C582 " 2s " " 24 12
Nos. C577–C582 (6) 1.20 60

Founding of Quayaquil, 441st anniversary.

Emblem and Laurel
AP140

1976, Aug. 9

C583 AP140 1.30s yel. & multi. 16 8

Bolivarian Society of Ecuador, 50th anniversary.

Western Hemisphere and Equator Monument
AP141

Congress Emblem
AP142

1976, Sept. 6

C584 AP141 2s multicolored 24 12

Souvenir Sheet
Imperf.

C585 AP141 5s multicolored *3.00* *3.00*

3rd Conference of Pan-American Transport Ministers, Quito, Sept. 6–11. No. C585 contains design similar to No. C584 with black denomination and red control number in margin. Size: 95x114mm.

1976, Sept. 27 Litho. *Perf. 11½*

C586 AP142 1.30s bl. & multi. 16 8
C587 " 3s bl. & multi. 36 18

Souvenir Sheet
Imperf.

C588 AP142 10s bl. & multi. 1.50 1.50

10th Inter-American Congress of the Construction Industry, Quito, Sept. 27–30. No. C588 has black control number. Size: 89x115mm.

George Washington
AP143

Design: 5s, Naval battle, Sept. 23, 1779, in which the Bonhomme Richard, commanded by John Paul Jones, defeated and captured the Serapis, British man-of-war, off Yorkshire coast (horiz.).

1976, Oct. 18 Litho. *Perf. 12*

C589 AP143 3s blk. & multi. 36 18
C590 " 5s red brn. & yel. 60 30

American Bicentennial.

Dr. Hideyo Noguchi
AP144

Luis Cordero
AP145

1976 Litho. *Perf. 11½*

C591 AP144 3s yel. & multi. 36 18

Dr. Hideyo Noguchi (1876–1928), bacteriologist (at Rockefeller Institute), birth centenary. A 10s imperf. miniature sheet in same design exists with red control number and without "Aereo." Size: 95x114 mm.

1976, Dec. Litho. *Perf. 11½*

C592 AP145 2s multicolored 24 12

Luis Cordero (1833–1912), president of Ecuador.

Mariuxi Febres Cordero
AP146

1976, Dec. *Perf. 11½*

C593 AP146 3s multicolored 36 18

Mariuxi Febres Cordero, South American swimming champion.

Flags and Monument
AP147

1976, Nov. 9 *Perf. 12*

C594 AP147 3s multicolored 36 18

Miniature Sheet
Imperf.

C595 AP147 5s multicolored 70 70

2nd Meeting of the Agriculture Ministers of the Andean Countries, Quito, Nov. 8–10. No. C595 has red control number. Size: 95x115mm.

See "Special Notices" at the front of this volume for data on the listing methods of this Catalogue, abbreviations, condition, prices and examination.

Sister Catalina
AP148

Congress Hall, Quito
AP149

1977, June 17 Litho. *Perf. 12x11½*

C596 AP148 1.30s black & pale sal. 16 8

Sister Catalina de Jesus Herrera (1717–1795), writer.

1977, Aug. 15 Litho. *Perf. 12x11½*

C597 AP149 5s multicolored 60 30
a. 10s souvenir sheet 1.30

11th General Assembly of Pan-American Institute of Geography and History, Quito, Aug. 15–30. No. C597a contains the designs of types A282 and AP149 without denominations and with simulated perforations; black and blue inscriptions, black control number. Size: 90x115mm.

Pres. Alfonso López Michelsen, Flag of Colombia—AP150

Designs: 5s, Pres. López M. of Colombia, Pres. Alfredo Povedo B. of Ecuador and aide. 7s, as 5s (vert.). 9s, 10s, Presidents with aides.

1977 *Perf. 12*

C598 AP150 2.60s multi. 30 15
C599 " 5s " 60 30
C600 " 7s " 85 42
C601 " 9s " 1.10 55

Imperf.

C602 AP150 10s multi. 1.30

Meeting of the Presidents of Ecuador and Colombia and Declaration of Putumayo, Feb. 25, 1977. Nos. C598–C602 are overprinted in multiple fluorescent, colorless rows: INSTITUTO GEOGRAFICO MILITAR GOBIERNO DEL ECUADOR. No. C602 has black control number. Size: 115x91mm.

Ceramic Figure, Tolita Culture
AP151

Designs: 9s, Divine Shepherdess, sculpture by Bernardo de Legarda. 11s, The Fruit Seller, sculpture by Legarda. 20s, Sun God, pre-Columbian gold mask.

1977, Aug. 24 *Perf. 12*

C603 AP151 7s gold & multi. 85 42
C604 " 9s " " 1.10 55
C605 " 11s " " 1.32 68

Souvenir Sheet
Gold Embossed *Imperf.*

C606 AP151 20s vio. bl., blk. & gold 2.60

Central Bank of Ecuador, 50th anniversary. No. C606 has black control number. Size: 89x115mm. Nos. C603–C605 overprinted like Nos. C598–C602.

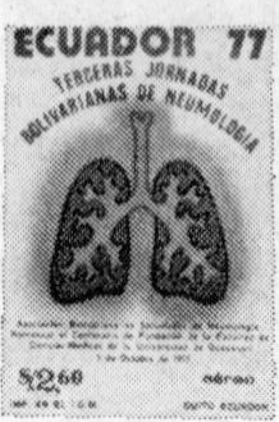

Lungs AP152

Brother Miguel, St. Peter's, Rome AP153

1977, Oct. 5 Litho. ***Perf. 12x11½***

C607 AP152 2.60s multi. 32 15

3rd Congress of the Bolivarian Pneumonic Society and centenary of the founding of the medical faculty of the University of Guayaquil.

1977

C608 AP153 2.60s multi. 32 15

Beatification of Brother Miguel.

Peralta Type of 1977

Design: 2.60s, Titles of works by Peralta and his bookmark.

1977 ***Perf. 11½***

C609 A284 2.60s multicolored 32 15

José Peralta (1855–1937), writer, 40th death anniversary.

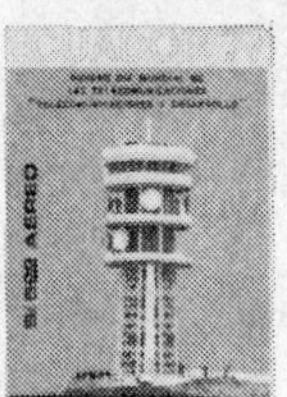

Broadcast Tower AP154

Remigio Romero y Cordero AP155

1977, Dec. 2 Litho. ***Perf. 12x11½***

C610 AP154 5s multicolored 60 30

9th World Telecommunications Day.

1978, Mar. 2 Litho. ***Perf. 12½x11½***

C611 AP155 3s multi. 36 18
C612 " 10.60s " 1.25 60

Imperf.

C612A AP155 10s multi. 1.20 65

Remigio Romero y Cordero (1895–1967), poet.

No. C612A contains a vignette similar to Nos. C611–C612, poem and black control number. Size: 90x114mm.

Dr. Vicente Corral Moscoso AP156

Faces AP157

Design: 5s, Hospital emblem with Caduceus.

1978, Apr. 12 Litho. ***Imperf.***

C613 AP156 5s multicolored 75 35

Perf. 12x11½

C614 AP156 7.60s multi. 90 45

Inauguration (in 1977) of Dr. Vicente Corral Moscoso Regional Hospital, Cuenca.

No. C613 has black control number. Size: 89x114mm.

1978, Mar. 17

Designs: 9s, Emblems and flags of Ecuador. 10s, 11s, Hands reaching for light.

C615 AP157 7s multicolored 85 42
C616 " 9s " 1.10 55
C617 " 11s " 1.35 65

Imperf.

C618 AP157 10s multi. 1.20 65

Ecuadorian Social Security Institute, 50th anniversary.

No. C618 has black control number. Size: 89x114mm.

Geographical Institute Type of 1978

Design: 7.60s, Plane over map of Ecuador with mountains.

1978, Apr. 12 Litho. ***Perf. 11½***

C619 A287 7.60s multicolored 90 45

Imperf.

C620 A287 10s multicolored 1.20 65

Military Geographical Institute, 50th anniversary. No. C620 contains 2 vignettes with simulated perforations in designs of Nos. 967 and C619, Institute emblem, black control number. Size: 115x89mm.

Lions Type of 1978

1978 ***Perf. 11½***

C621 A288 5s multicolored 60 30
C622 " 6.20s " 75 38

Imperf.

C623 A288 10s multicolored 1.20 65

7th meeting of Latin American Lions, Jan. 25–29. No. C623 contains a vignette similar to Nos. C621–C622, inscriptions and black control number. Size: 115x90mm.

San Martin AP158

1978, Apr. 13 Litho. ***Perf. 12***

C624 AP158 10.60s multi. 1.30 65

Imperf.

C625 AP158 10s multi. 1.20 65

Gen. José de San Martin (1778–1850), soldier and statesman. No. C625 contains a vignette similar to No. C624, inscriptions and black control number. Size: 115x90mm.

Bank Type of 1978

Design: 5s, Bank emblem.

1978, Sept. Litho. ***Perf. 11½***

C626 A289 5s gray & multi. 60 30

70th anniversary of Filanbanco (Philanthropic Bank).

Soccer Type of 1978

Designs: 2.60s, "Gauchito" and Games' emblem. 5s, "Gauchito." 7s, Soccer ball. 9s, Games' emblem (vert.). 10s, Games' emblem.

1978, Nov. 1 ***Perf. 12***

C627 A290 2.60s multicolored 30 15
C628 " 7s " 85 42
C629 " 9s " 1.10 55

Imperf.

C630 A290 5s black & blue 60 30
C631 " 10s " " 1.20 65

11th World Cup Soccer Championship, Argentina, June 1–25. Nos. C630–C631 have black control numbers. Size: 115x90mm.

Bernardo O'Higgins AP159

Old Men of Vilcabamba AP160

1978 Litho. ***Perf. 12x11½***

C632 AP159 10.60s multi. 1.30 65

Imperf.

C633 AP159 10s multi. 1.20 65

Gen. Bernardo O'Higgins (1778–1842), Chilean soldier and statesman. No. C633 contains a vignette similar to No. C632, inscriptions and black control number. Size: 115x90mm.

1978 ***Perf. 12x11½***

C634 AP160 5s multicolored 60 30

Vilcabamba, valley of longevity.

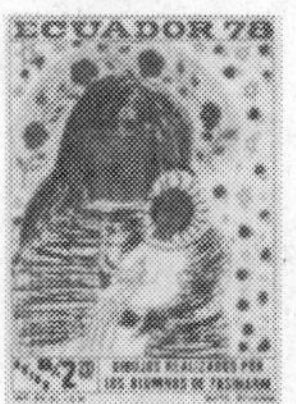

Hubert H. Humphrey AP161

Virgin and Child AP162

1978 Litho. ***Perf. 12x11½***

C635 AP161 5s multicolored 60 30

Hubert H. Humphrey (1911–1978), Vice President of the U.S.

1978

Children's Drawings: 4.60s, Holy Family. 6.20s, Candle and children.

C636 AP162 2.20s multi. 26 12
C637 " 4.60s " 55 28
C638 " 6.20s " 75 38

Christmas 1978.

Village, by Anibal Villacis AP163

Ecuadorian Painters: No. C640, Mountain Village, by Gilberto Almeida. No. C641, Bay, by Roura Oxandaberro. No. C642, Abstract, by Luis Molinari. No. C643, Statue, by Oswaldo Viteri. No. C644, Tools, by Enrique Tabara.

1978 ***Perf. 12***

C639 AP163 5s multicolored 60 30
C640 " 5s " 60 30
C641 " 5s " 60 30
C642 " 5s " 60 30
C643 " 5s " 60 30
C644 " 5s " 60 30
Nos. C639–C644 (6) 3.60 1.80

AIR POST SEMI-POSTAL STAMPS.

Nos. C119-C123
Surcharged in Blue or Red:

Hospital
Méndez + $ 0,50

1944, May 9 *Perf. 12* **Unwmkd.**

CB1	AP26	50c+50c deep red lilac	4.00	4.00
CB2	"	70c+30c red brn.	4.00	4.00
CB3	"	3s+50c turquoise green (R)	4.00	4.00
CB4	"	5s+1s brt. ultra. (R)	4.00	4.00
CB5	"	10s+2s scarlet	4.00	4.00
		Nos. CB1-CB5 (5)	20.00	20.00

The surtax aided Mendez Hospital.

AIR POST REGISTRATION STAMPS.

Issued by Sociedad Colombo-Alemana de Transportes Aereos (SCADTA)

Nos. C3 and C3a
Overprinted "R" in Carmine.

1928-29 *Perf. 14x14½* **Wmk. 116**

CF1	AP6	1s on 20c gray (#C3)	175.00	150.00
		a. 1s on 20c gray (C3a)	200.00	175.00

No. C18 Overprinted "R" in Black.

1929 *Perf. 14* **Wmk. 127**

CF2	AP2	1s rose	75.00	60.00

AIR POST OFFICIAL STAMPS.

Air Post Stamps of 1929 Overprinted in Red or Black **OFICIAL**

1929, May *Perf. 12* **Unwmkd.**

CO1	AP1	2c black (R)	50	50
CO2	"	5c carmine rose	50	50
CO3	"	10c deep brown	50	50
CO4	"	20c dark violet	50	50
CO5	"	50c deep green	1.50	1.35
CO6	"	1s dark blue	1.65	1.50
		a. Invtd. ovpt.	225.00	
CO7	"	5s org. yellow	6.50	6.50
CO8	"	10s orange red	125.00	110.00
		Nos. CO1-CO8 (8)	136.65	121.35

Establishment of commercial air service in Ecuador.
Counterfeits of No. CO8 exist.

1930, Jan. 9

CO9	AP1	50c olive brown	1.50	1.35
CO10	"	1s carmine lake	2.50	2.00
CO11	"	5s olive green	5.00	5.00
CO12	"	10s black	10.00	10.00

Air Post Stamps of 1937
Overprinted in Black **OFICIAL**

1937, Aug. 19 *Perf. 11½*

CO13	AP7	10c chestnut	20	20
CO14	"	20c olive black	25	20
CO15	"	70c black brown	30	20
CO16	"	1s gray black	35	20
CO17	"	2s dark violet	50	40
		Nos. CO13-CO17 (5)	1.60	1.20

No. C79
Overprinted in Black **OFICIAL**

1940, Aug. 1 *Perf. 12½x13*

CO18	AP15	5s emerald	70	65

Nos. C352-C354 Overprinted:
"1961 oficial"

1964 *Perf. 13½*

CO19	AP86	50c blue & multi.	1.00	1.00
CO20	AP86	80c yel. & multi.	1.00	1.00
CO21	"	1.30s pale green & multi.	1.00	1.00

SPECIAL DELIVERY STAMPS.

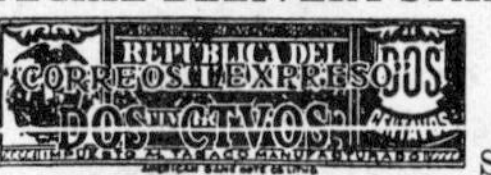

SD1

1928 *Perf. 12.* **Unwmkd.**

E1	SD1	2c on 2c blue	1.50	5.00
E2	"	5c on 2c blue	2.00	5.00
E3	"	10c on 2c blue	2.00	5.00
		a. "10 CENTAVOS" inverted	7.50	15.00
E4	"	20c on 2c blue	2.50	5.00
E5	"	50c on 2c blue	2.50	5.00
		Nos. E1-E5 (5)	10.50	25.00

No. RA49A
Surcharged in Red **EXPRESO 20 Ctvs.**

1945

E6	PT18	20c on 5c green	15	10

LATE FEE STAMP.

No. RA49A
Surcharged in Black **U. H. 10 Ctvs.**

1945 *Perf. 12.* **Unwmkd.**

I1	PT18	10c on 5c green	15	12

POSTAGE DUE STAMPS.

Numeral
D1

Coat of Arms
D2

Wmkd. Liberty Cap. (117)

1896 **Engraved** *Perf. 12*

J1	D1	1c blue green	1.25	2.00
J2	"	2c "	40	1.00
J3	"	5c "	1.25	1.25
J4	"	10c "	85	1.50
J5	"	20c "	35	2.00
J6	"	50c "	30	2.50
J7	"	100c "	60	5.00
		Nos. J1-J7 (7)	5.00	15.25

Reprints are on very thick paper with distinct watermark and vertical paper-weave direction. Price 5c each.

Unwmkd.

J8	D1	1c blue green	1.75	4.00
J9	"	2c "	1.75	4.00
J10	"	5c "	1.75	4.00
J11	"	10c "	1.75	4.00
J12	"	20c "	2.25	5.00
J13	"	50c "	3.00	7.00
J14	"	100c "	4.00	10.00
		Nos. J8-J14 (7)	16.25	38.00

1929

J15	D2	5c deep blue	10	8
J16	"	10c orange yellow	15	12
J17	"	20c red	25	25

Numeral
D3

Lithographed

1958, Nov. *Perf. 13½* **Unwmkd.**

J18	D3	10c bright lilac	3	3
J19	"	50c emerald	6	6
J20	"	1s maroon	15	15
J21	"	2s red	25	25

OFFICIAL STAMPS.

Regular Issues of 1881 and 1887 Handstamped in Black

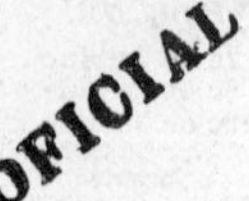

1886 *Perf. 12* **Unwmkd.**

O1	A5	1c yellow brown	50	50
O2	A6	2c lake	75	75
O3	A7	5c blue	1.25	1.25
O4	A8	10c orange	1.00	1.00
O5	A9	20c gray violet	1.00	1.00
O6	A10	50c blue green	4.00	3.50
		Nos. O1-O6 (6)	8.50	8.00

1887

O7	A12	1c green	75	75
O8	A13	2c vermillion	75	75
O9	A14	5c blue	1.00	1.00
O10	A15	80c olive green	4.00	3.00

Nos. O1 to O10 are known with red handstamp but these are believed to be speculative.

The overprint on the 1886–87 issues is handstamped and is found in various positions.

Flores O1

Arms O1a

1892 Carmine Overprint.

O11	O1	1c ultramarine	8	25
O12	"	2c "	8	25
O13	"	5c "	8	25
O14	"	10c "	8	20
O15	"	20c "	8	10
O16	"	50c "	8	50
O17	"	1s "	25	50
		Nos. O11-O17 (7)	73	2.05

1894

O18	O1a	1c slate green (R)	2.50	
O19	"	2c lake (Bk)	2.50	

Nos. O18 and O19 were not placed in use.

Rocafuerte O2

Dated 1894.

1894 Carmine Overprint

O20	O2	1c gray black	25	50
O21	"	2c "	25	25
O22	"	5c "	25	25
O23	"	10c "	10	20
O24	"	20c "	30	25
O25	"	50c "	1.50	1.50
O26	"	1s "	2.00	2.00
		Nos. O20-O26 (7)	4.65	4.95

Dated 1895

1895 Carmine Overprint.

O27	O2	1c gray black	2.25	2.25
O28	"	2c "	3.00	3.00
O29	"	5c "	50	50
O30	O2	10c gray black	3.00	3.00
O31	"	20c "	5.00	5.00
O32	"	50c "	7.50	7.50
O33	"	1s "	1.50	1.50
		Nos. O27-O33 (7)	22.75	22.75

Reprints of 1894-95 issues are on very thick paper with paper weave found both horizontal and vertical for all denominations. Generally they are blacker than originals.

Overprinted FRANQUEO OFICIAL in Carmine.

1896 **Wmkd. Liberty Cap. (117)**

O34	A21	1c olive bistre	35	35
O35	A22	2c "	35	35
O36	A23	5c "	35	35
O37	A24	10c "	35	35
O38	A25	20c "	35	35
O39	A26	50c "	35	35
O40	A27	1s "	1.00	75
O41	A28	5s "	1.75	1.65
		Nos. O34-O41 (8)	4.85	4.50

Reprints of Nos. O34-O41 are on thick paper with vertical paper weave direction.

Unwmkd.

O42	A21	1c olive bistre	1.00	1.00
O43	A22	2c "	1.00	1.00
O44	A23	5c "	1.00	70
O45	A24	10c "	75	60
O46	A25	20c "	1.00	1.00
O47	A26	50c "	1.00	1.50
O48	A27	1s "	2.00	1.25
O49	A28	5s "	3.00	2.25
		Nos. O42-O49 (8)	10.75	9.30

Reprints of Nos. O42-O49 all have overprint in black. Price 3c each.

Issue of 1894 Overprinted 1897 1898

1897–98

O50	O2	1c gray black	5.00	5.00
O51	"	2c "	6.00	6.00
O52	"	5c "	50.00	50.00
O53	"	10c "	6.00	6.00
O54	"	20c "	2.75	1.75
O55	"	50c "	10.00	10.00
O56	"	1s "	15.00	15.00
		Nos. O50-O56 (7)	94.75	93.75

Issue of 1894 Overprinted 1897 1898

O57	O2	1c gray black	1.50	1.50
O58	"	2c "	3.50	1.25
O59	"	5c "	6.00	6.00
O60	"	10c "	50.00	50.00
O61	"	20c "	1.50	1.50
O62	"	50c "	5.00	5.00
O63	"	1s "	65.00	65.00
		Nos. O57-O63 (7)	133.50	130.25

Issue of 1894 Overprinted 1897 Y 1898

O64	O2	1c gray black	8.00	8.00
O65	"	2c "	8.00	8.00
O66	"	5c "	8.00	8.00
O67	"	10c "	8.00	8.00
O68	"	20c "	8.00	8.00
O69	"	50c "	8.00	8.00
O70	"	1s "	8.00	8.00
		Nos. O64-O70 (7)	56.00	56.00

Issue of 1895 Overprinted in Black 1897 1898

O71	O2	1c gray black	3.00	3.00
O72	"	2c "	2.00	2.00
O73	"	5c "	3.00	3.00
O74	O2	10c gray black	3.00	3.00
O75	"	20c "	5.00	5.00
O76	"	50c "	22.50	
O77	"	1s "	45.00	45.00
		Nos. O71-O77 (7)	83.50	

Issue of 1895 Overprinted 1897 1898

O78	O2	1c gray black	1.25	1.25
O79	"	2c "	90	90
O80	"	5c "	2.50	2.50
O81	"	10c "	90	90
O82	"	20c "	1.00	60
O83	"	50c "	2.00	75
O84	"	1s "	7.50	7.50
		Nos. O78-O84 (7)	16.05	14.40

Issue of 1895 Overprinted 1897 Y 1898

O85	O2	1c gray black	40.00	40.00
O86	"	2c "	1.25	1.25
O87	"	5c "	95	75
O88	"	10c "	35.00	35.00
O89	"	20c "	60.00	60.00
O90	"	50c "	15.00	15.00
O91	"	1s "	75.00	75.00
		Nos. O85-O91 (7)	227.20	227.00

Many forged overprints of Nos. O50–O91 exist, made on the original stamps and reprints.

O3

Black Surcharge.

1898–99 *Perf. 15, 16*

O92	O3	5c on 50c lilac	30	30
		a. Inverted surcharge	1.50	1.50
O93	"	10c on 20s orange	85	85
		a. Double surcharge	2.25	2.25
O94	"	10c on 50c lilac	75.00	75.00
O95	"	20c on 50c lilac	2.50	2.50
O96	"	20c on 50s green	2.25	2.25
		Nos. O92-O96 (5)	80.90	80.90

Green Surcharge.

O97	O3	5c on 50c lilac	1.25	1.25
		a. Double surcharge	2.00	
		b. Double surcharge, black and green	6.50	
		c. Same as "b", black surcharge inverted	2.00	

1899 Red Surcharge.

O98	O3	5c on 50c lilac	1.25	1.25
		a. Double surcharge	2.00	
		b. Double surcharge, black and red	2.50	
O99	"	20c on 50s green	2.50	2.50
		a. Inverted surcharge	5.00	
		b. Double surcharge, red and black	8.00	

Similar Surcharge. Value in Words in Two Lines. Black Surcharge.

O100	O3	1c on 5c blue	27.50	

Red Surcharge

O101	O3	2c on 5c blue	40.00	
O102	"	4c on 20c blue	35.00	

Types of Regular Issue of 1899 Overprinted in Black

OFICIAL

1899 *Perf. 14, 15*

O103	A37	2c orange & black	30	20
O104	A39	10c " "	30	20
O105	A40	20c " "	30	25
O106	A41	50c " "	30	25

OFICIAL

The above overprint was applied to remainders of the postage stamps of 1904 with the idea of increasing their salability. They were never regularly in use as official stamps.

Regular Issue of 1911-13 Overprinted in Black

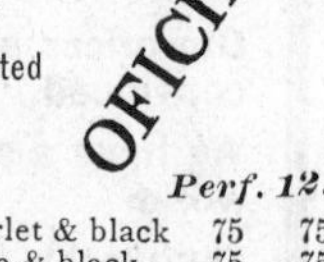

1913 *Perf. 12.*

O107	A71	1c scarlet & black	75	75
O108	A72	2c blue & black	75	75
O109	A73	3c orange & black	40	35
O110	A74	5c scarlet & black	1.00	75
O111	A75	10c blue & black	1.00	30
		Nos. O107-O111 (5)	3.90	2.90

Regular Issue of 1911-13 Overprinted OFICIAL

Overprint 22x3½ mm.

1916-17

O112	A72	2c blue & black	7.50	7.50
O113	A74	5c scarlet & black	7.50	7.50
O114	A75	10c blue & black	4.50	4.50

Overprint 25x4 mm.

O115	A71	1c scarlet & black	75	75
O116	A72	2c blue & black	1.00	1.00
		a. Invtd. ovpt.	1.50	1.50
O117	A73	3c orange & black	60	60
O118	A74	5c scarlet & black	1.00	1.00
O119	A75	10c blue & black	1.00	50
		Nos. O115-O119 (5)	4.35	3.85

Same Overprint On Regular Issue of 1915-17.

O120	A71	1c orange	30	30
O121	A72	2c green	30	30
O122	A73	3c black	50	40
O123	A78	4c red & black	50	50
		a. Invtd. ovpt.	1.00	
O124	A74	5c violet	30	25
O125	A75	10c blue	55	55
O126	A79	20c green & black	3.50	3.50
		Nos. O120-O126 (7)	5.95	5.80

Regular Issues of 1911-17 Overprinted in Black or Red

O127	A71	1c orange	20	15
O128	A72	2c green	20	20
O129	A73	3c black (Bk)	15	10
O130	"	3c black (R)	20	20
		a. Inverted overprint		
O131	A78	4c red & black	20	10
O132	A74	5c violet	35	20
O133	A75	10c blue & black	1.00	50
O134	"	10c blue	20	20
O135	A79	20c green & black	1.00	40
		Nos. O127-O135 (9)	3.50	2.05

Regular Issue of 1920 Overprinted **OFICIAL**

1920

O136	A86	1c green	15	15
		a. Inverted overprint	2.00	2.00
O137	"	2c carmine	12	12
O138	"	3c yellow brown	15	15
O139	"	4c dark green	20	20
		a. Inverted overprint	2.00	3.00
O140	"	5c blue	20	20
O141	"	6c orange	15	15
O142	"	7c brown	20	20
O143	"	8c yellow green	25	25

O144 A86 9c red 35 35
O145 A95 10c blue 20 20
O146 A86 15c gray 1.00 1.00
O147 " 20c deep violet 1.25 1.10
O148 " 30c violet 1.40 1.20
O149 " 40c dark brown 2.00 1.00
O150 " 50c dark green 1.25 1.25
O151 " 60c dark blue 1.50 1.50
O152 " 70c gray 1.50 1.50
O153 " 80c yellow 1.75 1.75
O154 A104 90c green 2.00 2.00
O155 A86 1s blue 3.00 3.00
Nos. O136-O155 (20) 18.62 17.27

Nos. O136 to O155 were issued in commemoration of the centenary of the independence of Guayaquil.

Stamps of 1911 Overprinted — OFICIAL

1922
O156 A71 1c scarlet & black 75 30
O157 A72 2c blue & black 35 30

Revenue Stamps of 1919-1920 Overprinted like Nos. O156 and O157

1924
O158 PT3 1c dark blue 40 30
O159 " 2c green 2.00 1.25

Regular Issues of 1911-17 Overprinted — OFICIAL

1924
O160 A71 1c orange 1.50 1.50
a. Inverted overprint 2.50

Overprinted in Black or Red — OFICIAL

O161 A72 2c green 10 10
O162 A73 3c black (R) 12 12
O163 A78 4c red & black 25 25
O164 A74 5c violet 30 15
O165 A75 10c deep blue 25 20
O166 A76 1s green & black 85 85
Nos. O160-O166 (7) 3.37 3.17

No. O106 with Additional Overprint — Acuerdo No 4.228

1924 *Perf. 14, 15*
O167 A41 50c orange & black 85 85

Nos. O160 to O167 inclusive exist with inverted overprint.

No. 199 Overprinted — OFICIAL

1924 *Perf. 12*
O168 A71 1c orange 1.00 1.00

Regular Issues of 1911-25 Overprinted — OFICIAL

1925
O169 A71 1c scarlet & black 1.50 70
a. Invtd. ovpt. 1.50
O170 A71 1c orange 15 15
a. Invtd. ovpt. 1.00
O171 A72 2c green 15 15
a. Invtd. ovpt. 1.00
O172 A73 3c black (Bk) 25 25
O173 " 3c black (R) 30 30
O174 A78 4c red & black 15 15
O175 A74 5c violet 25 25
O176 " 5c rose 25 25
O177 A75 10c deep blue 15 15
Nos. O169-O177 (9) 3.15 2.35

Regular Issues of 1916-25 Overprinted Vertically Up or Down — OFICIAL

1927, Oct.
O178 A71 1c orange 15 15
O179 A86 2c carmine 15 12
O180 " 3c yellow brown 15 12
O181 " 4c myrtle green 15 12
O182 " 5c pale blue 15 15
O183 A75 10c yellow green 15 12
Nos. O178-O183 (6) 90 78

Regular Issues of 1920-27 Overprinted — OFICIAL

1928
O184 A71 1c light blue 15 12
O185 A86 2c carmine 15 12
O186 " 3c yellow brown 15 15
a. Invtd. ovpt. 1.00
O187 " 4c myrtle green 15 15
O188 " 5c light blue 15 15
O189 A75 10c yellow green 15 15
O190 A109 20c violet 15 15
a. Ovpt. reading up 1.00
Nos. O184-O190 (7) 1.05 99

The overprint is placed vertically reading down on No. O190.

Regular Issue of 1936 Overprinted in Black — OFICIAL

1936 *Perf. 14.*
O191 A131 5c olive green 8 6
O192 A132 10c brown 10 8
O193 A133 20c dark violet 12 10
O194 A134 1s dark carmine 30 25
O195 A135 2s dark blue 50 40
Nos. O191-O195 (5) 1.10 89

Regular Postage Stamps of 1937 Overprinted in Black — OFICIAL

1937 *Perf. 11½*
O196 A139 2c green 5 5
O197 A140 5c deep rose 6 6
O198 A141 10c blue 8 6
O199 A142 20c deep rose 10 8
O200 A143 1s olive green 25 20
Nos. O196-O200 (5) 54 45

Tobacco Stamp, Overprinted in Black
CORRESPONDENCIA OFICIAL

1946 *Rouletted.* **Unwmkd.**
O201 PT7 1c rose red 6 6

Communications Building, Quito
O4

Lithographed.

1947 *Perf. 11* **Unwmkd.**
O202 O4 30c brown 15 10
O203 " 30c greenish blue 15 10
a. Imperf., pair
O204 " 30c purple 15 10

Nos. O202 to O204 overprinted "Primero la Patria!" and plane in dark blue are said to be essays.

No. 719 with Additional Diagonal Overprint: — oficial

1964 *Perf. 14x13*
O205 A231 80c rose car. & grn. (block of 4) 2.25 2.25

The "OEA" overprint covers four stamps, the "oficial" overprint is applied to every stamp.

A set of 20 imperforate items in the above Roosevelt design, some overprinted with the initials of various government ministries, was released in 1949. Later that year a set of eight miniature sheets, bearing the same design plus a marginal inscription, "Presidencia (or Vicepresidencia) de la Republica," and a frame-line were released. In the editors' opinion, information justifying the listing of these issues has not been received.

POSTAL TAX STAMPS.

Roca
PT1

1920 *Perf. 12.* **Unwmkd.**
RA1 PT1 1c orange 30 10

PT2 PT3

RA2 PT2 1c red & blue 20 10
a. "de" inverted 2.00 2.00
b. Double overprint 2.00 60
c. Inverted overprint 2.00 60
RA3 PT3 1c deep blue 30 10
a. Inverted ovpt. 1.25 1.00
b. Double ovpt. 1.25 1.00

PT4 PT5

Red or Black Surcharge or Overprint.

Stamp Dated 1911-1912.
RA4 PT4 20c deep blue 27.50 12.00

Stamp Dated 1913-1914.
RA5 PT4 20c deep blue (R) 1.50 50

Stamp Dated 1917-1918.
RA6 PT4 20c olive green (R) 1.75 60
a. Dated 1919-20 9.00
RA7 PT5 1c on 2c green 30 12

Stamp Dated 1911-1912.
RA8 PT5 1c on 5c green 25 10
a. Double surcharge

Stamp Dated 1913-1914.
RA9 PT5 1c on 5c green 2.50 50
a. Double surcharge 3.00 2.00

On Nos. RA7, RA8 and RA9 the surcharge is found reading upward or downward.

Post Office
PT6

1920-24 **Engraved.**
RA10 PT6 1c olive green 10 4
RA11 " 2c deep green 20 10
RA12 " 20c bistre brown ('24) 75 15
RA13 " 2s violet 3.00 3.00
RA14 " 5s blue 5.00 5.00
Nos. RA10-RA14 (5) 9.05 8.29

Revenue Stamps of 1917-18 Surcharged Vertically in Red reading up or down — Casa de Correos VEINTE CTS. 1921—1922

1921-22
RA15 PT5 20c on 1c dark blue 20.00 3.00
RA16 " 20c on 2c green 20.00 3.00

No. RA12 Surcharged in Green — DOS CENTAVOS — 2 —

1924
RA17 PT6 2c on 20c bistre brown 20 10
a. Invtd. surch. 2.00 2.00
b. Dbl. surch. 3.00 3.00

PT7

1924 *Rouletted 7*
RA18 PT7 1c rose red 25 15
a. Inverted overprint 1.50

Similar Design, Eagle at left
Perf. 12
RA19 PT7 2c blue 30 12
a. Inverted overprint 1.50 1.00

PT8

Inscribed "Timbre Fiscal".

1924
RA20 PT8 1c yellow 1.00 75
RA21 " 2c dark blue 40 20

Inscribed "Region Oriental".
RA22 PT8 1c yellow 35 15
RA23 " 2c dark blue 35 30

Overprint on No. RA22 reads down or up.

Revenue Stamp Overprinted in Blue — CASA de Correos y Telegrafos de Guayaquil

1934
RA24 2c green 15 10
a. Blue overprint inverted 2.00 1.50
b. Blue overprint double, one inverted 2.50 1.50

Postage Stamp of 1930 Overprinted in Red

Perf. 12½.

RA25 A119 20c ultra. & yel. 25 20

Telegraph Stamp Overprinted in Red, like No. RA24, and Surcharged diagonally in Black

2 ctvos.

1934 ***Perf. 14***

RA26 2c on 10c olive brown 15 10
a. Double surcharge 2.00

Overprint Blue, Surcharge Red.

RA27 2c on 10c olive brown 15 10

PT9

PT10

1934–36 ***Perf. 12.***

RA28 PT9 2c green 12 5
a. Both overprints in red ('36) 12 5

Postal Tax stamp of 1920–24, overprinted in red "POSTAL" has been again overprinted "CASA de Correos y Teleg. de Guayaquil" in black.

Symbols of Post and Telegraph Service
PT11

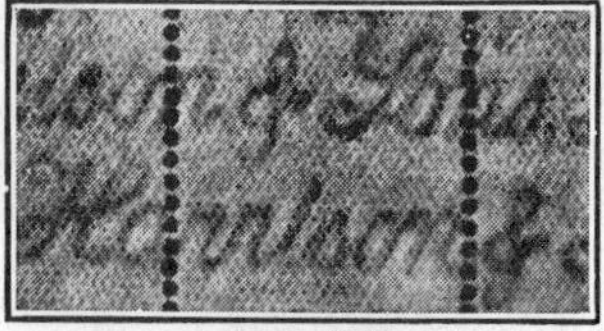

Wmk. 233

Photogravure.
Wmkd.
"Harrison & Sons, London" in Script Letters. (233)

1934 ***Perf. 14½x14.***

RA29 PT10 2c yellow green 8 5

Issued to pay a postal tax of 2c for the rebuilding of the General Post Office at Guayaquil.

1935

RA30 PT11 20c claret 15 10

Issued to pay a postal tax of 20c for the rebuilding of the General Post Office at Guayaquil.

No. RA29 Surcharged in Red and Overprinted in Black

3 ctvs,
Seguro Social del Campesino Quito, 16 de Otbre-1935

1935

RA31 PT10 3c on 2c yellow green 15 10
a. Double surcharge

Issued for the Social and Rural Workers' Insurance Fund.

Tobacco Stamp Surcharged in Black

Seguro Social del Campesino 3 ctvs

1936 ***Rouletted 7.*** **Unwmkd.**

RA32 PT7 3c on 1c rose red 15 10
a. Lines of words reversed 18 12
b. Imperf. vertically (pair)

Issued for the Social and Rural Workers' Insurance Fund.

No. 310 Overprinted in Black

Casa de Correos y Telégrafos de Guayaquil

1936 ***Perf. 12½***

RA33 A119 20c ultramarine & yellow 15 8
a. Double overprint

Tobacco Stamp Surcharged in Black

SEGURO SOCIAL DEL CAMPESINO 3 ctvs.

1936 ***Rouletted 7***

RA34 PT7 3c on 1c rose red 10 5

Issued for the Social and Rural Workers' Insurance Fund.

PT12

PT13

Worker

1936 **Engraved** ***Perf. 13½***

RA35 PT12 3c ultramarine 10 5

Issued for the Social and Rural Workers' Insurance Fund.

Surcharged in Black.

1936

RA36 PT13 5c on 3c ultra. 10 5

This combines the 2c for the rebuilding of the post office with the 3c for the Social and Rural Workers' Insurance Fund.

National Defense Issue.

Tobacco Stamp, Surcharged in Black.

TIMBRE PATRIOTICO DIEZ CENTAVOS

1936 ***Rouletted 7.***

RA37 PT7 10c on 1c rose 18 6
a. Double surch.

Symbolical of Defense
PT14

1937–42 ***Perf. 13½***

RA38 PT14 10c deep blue 20 8

A 1s violet and 2s green exist in type PT14.

PT15

Overprinted or Surcharged in Black.

1937–42 **Engr. & Typo.** ***Perf. 13½***

RA39 PT15 5c light brn. & red 20 8
d. Invert. ovpt. 3.50

Perf. 12, 11½.

RA39A PT15 20c on 5c rose pink & red ('42) 7.50
RA39B " 20c on 1s yel. brn. & red ('42) 7.50
RA39C " 20c on 2s grn. & red ('42) 7.50

A 50c dark blue and red exists in type PT15.

5 5

No. RA38 Surcharged in Red

POSTAL ADICIONAL

1937 **Engraved** ***Perf. 12½***

RA40 PT14 5c on 10c deep blue 15 8

Map of Ecuador
PT16

1938 ***Perf. 14x13½.***

RA41 PT16 5c carmine rose 18 8

Issued for the Social and Rural Workers' Insurance Fund.

No. C42 Surcharged in Red

20 20
CASA DE CORREOS Y TELEGRAFOS DE GUAYAQUIL
20 20

1938 ***Perf. 12½.***

RA42 AP5 20c on 70c black 30 10

No. 307 Surcharged in Red

CAMPAÑA CONTRA EL CANCER
5 5

1938

RA43 A116 5c on 6c yel. & red 15 6

This stamp was obligatory on all mail from Nov. 23rd to 30th, 1938. The tax was for the International Union for the Control of Cancer.

Tobacco Stamp, Surcharged in Black

POSTAL ADICIONAL CINCO CENTAVOS

1939 ***Rouletted.***

RA44 PT7 5c on 1c rose 12 5
a. Double surcharge
b. Triple surcharge

Tobacco Stamp, Surcharged in Blue

CASAS DE CORREOS Y TELEGRAFOS CINCO CENTAVOS

1940

RA45 PT7 5c on 1c rose red 10 5
a. Double surcharge 1.00 1.00

No. 370 Surcharged in Carmine

CASA DE CORREOS y TELEGRAFOS DE GUAYAQUIL
20 20

1940 ***Perf. 11½.***

RA46 A144 20c on 50c black & multicolored 15 10
a. Double surcharge, one inverted

Tobacco Stamp, Surcharged in Black

TIMBRE PATRIOTICO VEINTE CENTAVOS

1940 ***Rouletted***

RA47 PT7 20c on 1c rose red 15 7

Farmer Plowing
PT17

Communication Symbols
PT18

1940 ***Perf. 13x13½.***

RA48 PT17 5c carmine rose 10 5

1940–43 ***Perf. 12.***

RA49 PT18 5c copper brown 8 5
RA49A " 5c green ('43) 8 5

Pursuit Planes
PT19

1941 ***Perf. 11½x13***

RA50 PT19 20c ultramarine 25 6

The tax was used for national defense.

Warrior Shielding Women
PT20

1942–46 **Engraved** ***Perf. 12***

RA51 PT20 20c dark blue 18 6
RA51A " 40c black brown ('46) 18 8

The tax was used for national defense.
A 20c carmine, 20c brown and 30c gray exist lithographed in type PT20.

No. 370 Surcharged in Carmine

CASA DE CORREOS y TELEGRAFOS DE GUAYAQUIL
VEINTE CENTAVOS

1942 ***Perf. 11½***

RA52 A144 20c on 50c black & multicolored 25 15
a. Double surch. 2.50

No. RA35
Surcharged in Red

ADICIONAL
CINCO
CENTAVOS

1943 *Perf. 13½.*
RA53 PT12 5c on 3c ultra. 10 4

No. RA53
with Additional
Surcharge in Black

5 Centavos
CASA DE
CORREOS
DE GQUIL.
y

1943
RA54 PT12 5c on 5c on 3c ultramarine 10 4

Peons
PT21

1943 *Perf. 12*
RA55 PT21 5c blue 8 4
The tax was for farm workers.

Revenue Stamp
(as No. RA64)
Overprinted in Black

TIMBRE
PATRIOTICO

1943 *Perf. 12½*
RA56 20c red orange 6.00 35

Revenue Stamp
(as No. RA64)
Surcharged in Black

TIMBRE PATRIOTICO
VEINTE CENTAVOS

1943 *Perf. 12*
RA57 20c on 10c orange 55 10
a. Double surch.

Coat of Arms
PT22

1943 *Perf. 12½*
RA58 PT22 20c orange red 12 5
The tax was for national defense.

No. RA58
Surcharged in Black

30
Centavos

1944
RA59 PT22 30c on 20c org. red 15 5
a. Double surcharge

Consular Service
Stamps
Surcharged
in Black

TIMBRE
ESCOLAR
20 ctvs. 20

1951 *Perf. 12.* **Unwmkd.**
RA60 R1 20c on 1s red 10 4
RA61 " 20c on 2s brown 10 4
RA62 " 20c on 5s violet 10 4

Teacher and Pupils in Schoolyard
PT23

PT24

1952 Engraved. *Perf. 13*
RA63 PT23 20c blue green 12 4

Revenue Stamp Overprinted
"PATRIOTICO / SANITARIO"

1952 *Perf. 12*
RA64 PT24 40(c) olive green 15 6

Woman Holding Flag
PT25

PT26

1953 *Perf. 12½.*
RA65 PT25 40c ultramarine 15 5

Telegraph Stamp Surcharged
"ESCOLAR 20 Centavos" in Black

1954 *Perf. 13.* **Unwmkd.**
RA66 PT26 20c on 30c red brown 12 4

Revenue Stamps Surcharged or
Overprinted Horizontally in Black
"PRO TURISMO 1954"

1954 *Perf. 12* **Unwmkd.**
RA67 R2 10c on 25c blue 10 4
RA68 R3 10c on 50c orange red 10 4
RA69 " 10c carmine 10 4

PT27

Telegraph Stamp Surcharged
"Pro-Turismo 1954 10 ctvs. 10"
in Black

1954 *Perf. 13*
RA70 PT27 10c on 30c red brn. 10 3

Revenue Stamp
Overprinted in Black

ESCOLAR

1954 *Perf. 12*
RA71 R3 20c olive black 10 3

Consular Service
Stamp
Surcharged in Black

0,20 0,20
ESCOLAR
Veinte centavos

1954
RA72 R1 20c on 10s gray 10 3

Young Student at Desk
PT28

Globe, Ship and Plane
PT29

Imprint:
"Heraclio Fournier.—Vitoria"

1954 Photo. *Perf. 11*
RA73 PT28 20c rose pink 10 4
See also No. RA76.

1954 Engraved *Perf. 12*
RA74 PT29 10c deep magenta 12 5

Soldier Kissing Flag
PT30

1955 Photogravure. *Perf. 11*
RA75 PT30 40c blue 10 4
See also No. RA77.

Types of 1954-55 Redrawn.
Imprint:
"Thomas de la Rue & Co. Ltd."

1957 *Perf. 13* **Unwmkd.**
RA76 PT28 20c rose pink 10 4
Perf. 14x14½
RA77 PT30 40c blue 12 4
No. RA77 is inscribed "Republica del Ecuador."

AIR POST POSTAL TAX STAMPS.

No. 438
Surcharged
in Black
or Carmine

FOMENTO-AERO-
COMUNICACIONES
20 Ctvs.

1945 *Perf. 11.* **Unwmkd.**
RAC1 A173 20c on 10c dark green 25 6
a. Pair, one without surch. 45.00
RAC2 " 20c on 10c dark green (C) 25 6
Obligatory on letters and parcel post carried on planes in the domestic service.

Liberty, Mercury and Planes
PTAP1

1946 **Engraved.** *Perf. 12.*
RAC3 PTAP1 20c org. brn. 25 15

Galapagos Islands
(Columbus Archipelago)

Issued for use in the Galapagos Islands, a province of Ecuador, but were commonly used throughout the country.

Sea Lions
A1

Map
A2

Design: 1s, Marine iguana.

Photogravure.

1957, July 15 *Perf. 12* **Unwmkd.**
L1 A1 20c dark brown 30 15
L2 A2 50c violet 20 15
L3 A1 1s dark olive green 80 40

Issued to commemorate the 125th anniversary of Ecuador's possession of the Galapagos Islands, and to publicize the islands.

AIR POST STAMPS

Type of Regular Issue, 1957.

Designs: 1s, Santa Cruz Island. 1.80s, Map of Galapagos archipelago. 4.20s, Galapagos giant tortoise.

Photogravure.

1957, July 19 *Perf. 12* **Unwmkd.**
LC1 A1 1s deep blue 25 15
LC2 " 1.80s rose violet 50 25
LC3 " 4.20s black 1.25 60

Issued to commemorate the 125th anniversary of Ecuador's possession of the Galapagos Islands and to publicize the islands.

Redrawn Type of Ecuador, 1956

1959, Jan. 3 **Engraved.** *Perf. 14*
LC4 AP69 2s light olive green 75 50

Issued to honor the United Nations.
See note after No. C407.

EGYPT

(ē'jĭpt)

LOCATION—In northern Africa, bordering on the Mediterranean and the Red Sea.

GOVT.—Republic.

AREA—386,198 sq. mi.

POP.—38,740,000 (est. 1977).

CAPITAL—Cairo.

Modern Egypt was a part of Turkey until 1914 when a British Protectorate was declared over the country and the Khedive was deposed in favor of Hussein Kamil under the title of Sultan. In 1922 the protectorate ended and the reigning sultan was declared king of the new monarchy. Egypt became a republic on June 18, 1953. Egypt merged with Syria in 1958 to form the United Arab Republic. Syria left this union in 1961. In 1971 Egypt took the name of Arab Republic of Egypt.

40 Paras = 1 Piastre
1000 Milliemes = 100 Piastres = 1 Pound (1888)
1000 Milliemes = 1 Pound

Turkish Suzerainty

Turkish Inscriptions
A1

A2

A3

A4

A5

A6

A7

Wmk. 118

Surcharged in Black

Wmkd. Pyramid and Star. (118)
Perf. 12½, 12½x13, 13x12½.

1866 Lithographed

1 A1 5pa slate green 11.00 11.00
- *a.* Imperf. 50.00 50.00
- *b.* Imperf. vertically, pair 225.00
- *c.* Imperf. horizontally, pair 200.00

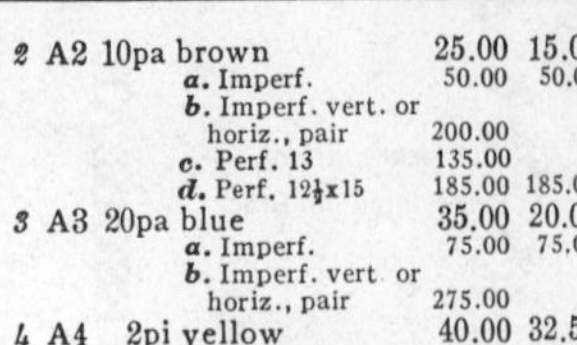

2 A2 10pa brown 25.00 15.00
- *a.* Imperf. 50.00 50.00
- *b.* Imperf. vert. or horiz., pair 200.00
- *c.* Perf. 13 135.00
- *d.* Perf. 12½x15 185.00 185.00

3 A3 20pa blue 35.00 20.00
- *a.* Imperf. 75.00 75.00
- *b.* Imperf. vert. or horiz., pair 275.00

4 A4 2pi yellow 40.00 32.50
- *a.* Imperf. 60.00 60.00
- *b.* Imperf. vert. or horiz., pair 200.00 200.00
- *c.* Perf. 12½x15 80.00 80.00
- *d.* Diagonal half used as 1 pi on cover 400.00

5 A5 5pi rose 175.00 150.00
- *a.* Imperf. 225.00 225.00
- *b.* Imperf. vert. or horiz., pair *650.00*
- *d.* Inscription of 10 pi, imperf. 350.00
- *e.* Perf. 12½x15 250.00 250.00
- *f.* Same as "d" perf. 12½x15 450.00 450.00

6 A6 10pi slate blue 200.00 200.00
- *a.* Imperf. 200.00 200.00
- *b.* Imperf. vert. or horiz., pair *1000.00 1000.00*

Unwmkd.

Typographed

7 A7 1pi rose lilac 22.50 4.00
- *a.* Imperf. 32.50 32.50
- *b.* Imperf. vert. or horiz., pair 225.00

Single imperforates of types A1–A10 are sometimes simulated by trimming wide-margined copies of perforated stamps.

Proofs of Nos. 1–7 are on smooth white paper, unwatermarked and imperforate. Proofs of No. 7 are on thinner paper than No. 7a.

Sphinx and Pyramid
A8

Wmk. 119

Wmkd. Crescent and Star. (119)

1867 Litho. *Perf. 15x12½*

8 A8 5pa orange 6.00 2.75
- *a.* Imperf. 22.50 22.50
- *b.* Imperf. vert. or horiz., pair 100.00

9 " 10pa lilac 20.00 4.25
- *a.* 10pa violet 20.00 4.25
- *b.* Half used as 5pa on newspaper piece 350.00

11 " 20pa blue green 20.00 4.50
- *a.* 20pa yellow green 22.50 4.25
- *b.* Imperf.

13 " 1pi rose red 3.50 1.00
- *a.* Imperf. 17.50 17.50
- *b.* Imperf. vertically, pair 100.00 100.00
- *c.* Half used as 20pa on cover 350.00
- *d.* Rouletted 10.00

14 " 2pi blue 35.00 7.50
- *a.* Imperf. 50.00
- *b.* Imperf. vert., pair
- *c.* Diagonal half used as 1pi on cover
- *d.* Perf. 12½

15 " 5pi brown 150.00 65.00

There are four types of each value, so placed that any block of four contains all four types.

A9

A10

Typographed by the Government at Boulac

Clear Impressions.
Thick Opaque Paper.

Perf. 12½x13½, Clean-cut.

1872 Wmk. 119

19 A9 5pa brown 6.00 3.75
20 " 10pa lilac 6.00 2.50
21 " 20pa blue 11.00 2.75
- *e.* Imperforate 20.00

22 " 1pi rose red 13.00 45
- *e.* Imperforate 17.50
- *h.* Half used as 20pa on cover 100.00
- *i.* Horiz. pair, imperf. between

23 " 2pi dull yellow 27.50 2.75
24 " 2½pi dull violet 25.00 4.00
25 " 5pi green 75.00 13.00
- *j.* Tete beche pair

Perf. 13½, Clean-cut.

19a A9 5pa brown 9.00 6.50
20a " 10pa dull lilac 3.50 2.25
21a " 20pa blue 17.50 7.00
22a " 1pi rose red 25.00 2.25
23a " 2pi dull yellow 9.00 2.75
24a " 2½pi dull violet 300.00 110.00
25a " 5pi green 125.00 27.50

Lithographed

21m A9 20pa blue, perf. 12½x13½ 35.00 15.00
21n " 20pa blue, perf. 13½ 70.00 27.50
21p " 20pa blue, imperf. 70.00
22m " 1pi rose red, perf. 12½x13½ 85.00 1.65
22n " 1pi rose red, perf. 13½ 125.00 2.50

Typographed

Blurred Impressions.
Thinner Paper.

Wmkd. Crescent and Star. (119)

1874-75 *Perf. 12½, Rough.*

26 A10 5pa brown ('75) 5.00 2.25
- *e.* Imperforate 35.00
- *f.* Imperforate horiz., pair 85.00 90.00
- *g.* Tête bêche pair 35.00 35.00

20b A9 10pa gray lilac 4.00 2.25
- *g.* Tête bêche pair 150.00 150.00

21b " 20pa gray blue 22.50 2.50
- *k.* Half used as 10pa on cover 300.00

22b " 1pi vermilion 3.00 70
- *f.* Imperforate 6.00 6.00
- *g.* Tête bêche pair 60.00 60.00

23b " 2pi yellow 25.00 3.00
- *j.* Tête bêche pair 350.00 350.00

24b " 2½pi deep violet 4.00 2.25
- *e.* Imperforate 17.50 17.50
- *f.* Tête bêche pair 300.00 300.00

25b " 5pi yellow green 27.50 9.00
- *e.* Imperforate 17.50

No. 26f normally occurs tête-bêche.

Perf. 13½x12½, Rough.

26c A10 5pa brown 3.00 2.25
- *j.* Tête bêche pair 30.00 30.00

20c A9 10pa gray lilac 5.00 2.25
- *j.* Tête bêche pair 150.00 150.00

21c " 20pa gray blue 3.00 2.25
- *h.* Pair, imperf. between 200.00

22c " 1pi vermilion 9.00 85
- *j.* Tête bêche pair 250.00 250.00

23c " 2pi yellow 3.50 3.00
- *g.* Tête bêche pair 300.00 300.00
- *k.* Half used as 1pi on cover *700.00*

Perf. 12½x13½, Rough.

23d A9 2pi yellow ('75) 14.00 4.75
- *h.* Tête bêche pair

24d " 2½pi deep violet ('75) 12.00 8.00
- *j.* Tête bêche pair 600.00 600.00

25d " 5pi yellow green ('75) 175.00 125.00

Stamp of 1872-75 Surcharged in Black

PARAS 5

Perf. 12½, 12½x13½, Rough

1879, Jan. 1

27 A9 5pa on 2½pi dull violet 4.50 5.00
- *a.* Imperf. 27.50 27.50
- *b.* Tête bêche pair *1750.00 1750.00*
- *c.* Inverted surcharge 32.50 32.50
- *d.* Perf. 12½x13½ 4.50 5.00
- *e.* As "d," tête bêche pair
- *f.* As "c," perf. 12½x13½ 47.50 47.50

28 A9 10pa on 2½pi dull violet 4.50 5.00
- *a.* Imperf. 37.50 37.50
- *b.* Tête bêche pair 850.00 850.00
- *c.* Inverted surcharge 32.50 32.50
- *d.* Perf. 12½x13½ 8.00 8.00
- *e.* As "c," perf. 12½x13½ 50.00 50.00

A11

A12

A13

A14

A15

A16

1879-93 Typo. *Perf. 14x13½*

29 A11 5pa brown 20 15
30 A12 10pa violet 20.00 2.75
31 " 10pa lilac rose ('81) 32.50 3.25
32 " 10pa gray ('82) 8.00 65
33 " 10pa green ('84) 18 12
34 A13 20pa ultramarine 45.00 1.00
35 " 20pa rose ('84) 5.00 35
36 A14 1pi rose 12.50 20
37 " 1pi ultra. ('84) 1.50 8
38 A15 2pi orange yellow 11.00 30
39 " 2pi org. brn. ('93) 5.00 30
40 A16 5pi green 55.00 4.50
41 " 5pi gray ('84) 7.00 35
Nos. 29-41 (13) 202.88 14.00

Imperf. examples of Nos. 29–31, 35–38 and 40 are proofs.

A17

1884, Feb. 1

42 A17 20pa on 5pi green 7.50 75
- *a.* Inverted surcharge 25.00 25.00

A18

A19

A20

1888

43 A18 1m brown 25 5
44 A19 2m green 45 6
45 A20 5m carmine rose 90 5

Imperf. examples of Nos. 43–45 are proofs.

A21

A22

1889-93

46 A21 3m maroon ('92) 2.00 70
47 " 3m orange ('93) 1.10 15
48 A22 10pi purple 10.00 45

Nos. 37, 39, 41, 43 to 45, 47 and 48 exist on both ordinary and chalky paper.

A23

1906 Chalk-surfaced Paper.

49 A23 4m brown red 1.25 50

Boats on Nile A24 — Cleopatra A25

Ras-el-Tin Palace A26 — Giza Pyramids A27

Sphinx A28 — Colossi of Thebes A29

Pylon of Karnak and Temple of Khonsu A30 — Citadel at Cairo A31

Rock Temple of Abu Simbel A32 — Aswan Dam A33

Perf. 13½x14

1914, Jan. 8 Wmk. 119

Chalk-surfaced Paper

50 A24 1m olive brown 10 8
51 A25 2m deep green 25 12
52 A26 3m orange 40 15
53 A27 4m red 75 35
54 A28 5m lake 50 4
 a. Bklt. pane of 6
55 A29 10m dark blue 1.00 8

Perf. 14

56 A30 20m olive green 2.50 12
57 A31 50m red violet 4.00 40
58 A32 100m black 7.50 40
59 A33 200m plum 15.00 70
 Nos. 50-59 (10) 32.00 2.44

All values of this issue exist imperforate on both watermarked and unwatermarked paper but are not known to have been issued in that condition.

See also Nos. 61-72.

British Protectorate

No. 52 Surcharged

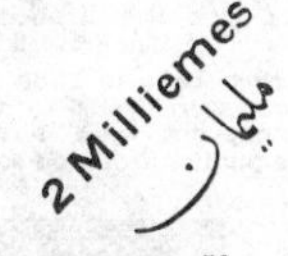

1915, Oct. 15

60 A26 2m on 3m orange 50 50
 a. Inverted surcharge 85.00 85.00

Scenic Types of 1914 and

Statue of Ramses II

A34 A35

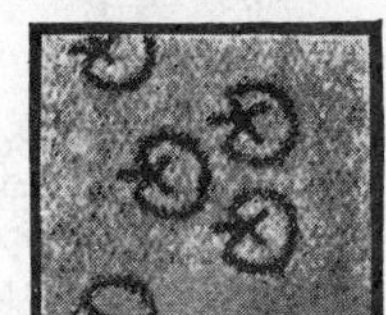

Wmk. 120

Wmkd. Triple Crescent and Star. (120)

1921-22 *Perf. 13½x14*

Chalk-surfaced Paper

61 A24 1m olive brown 12 7
62 A25 2m deep green 1.00 1.00
63 " 2m red ('22) 30 20
64 A26 3m orange 75 30
65 A27 4m green ('22) 1.25 1.00
66 A28 5m lake 45 6
67 " 5m pink 75 6
 a. Booklet pane of 6
68 A29 10m deep blue 1.75 10
69 " 10m lake ('22) 1.25 25
70 A34 15m indigo ('22) 1.00 15
71 A35 15m indigo ('22) 7.50 70

Perf. 14

72 A30 20m olive green 2.50 12
73 A31 50m maroon 5.00 25
74 A32 100m black 15.00 2.25
 Nos. 61-74 (14) 38.62 6.51

Independent Kingdom

Stamps of 1921-22 Overprinted

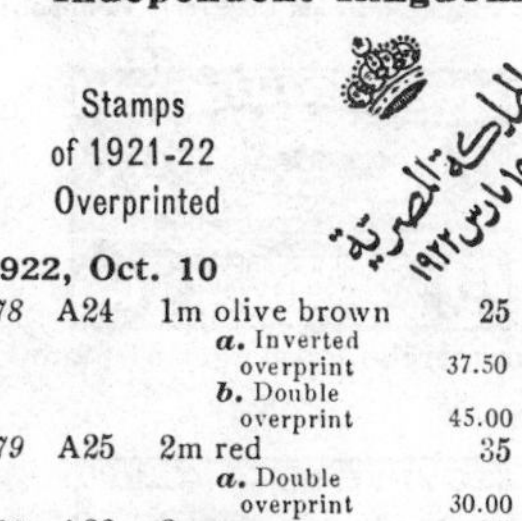

1922, Oct. 10

78 A24 1m olive brown 25 12
 a. Inverted overprint 37.50 37.50
 b. Double overprint 45.00 45.00
79 A25 2m red 35 10
 a. Double overprint 30.00 30.00
80 A26 3m orange 75 35
81 A27 4m green 50 35
 a. Double ovpt. 60.00
 b. Inverted ovpt.
82 A28 5m pink 50 5
83 A29 10m lake 75 6
84 A34 15m indigo 1.75 10
85 A35 15m indigo 1.00 20

Perf. 14

86 A30 20m olive green 1.75 15
 a. Inverted overprint 60.00 60.00
 b. Double overprint 50.00 50.00
87 A31 50m maroon 2.25 18
 a. Inverted overprint 250.00 250.00
 b. Double overprint
88 A32 100m black 8.00 50
 a. Inverted overprint 135.00 135.00
 b. Double overprint 135.00 135.00
 Nos. 78-88 (11) 17.85 2.16

Same Overprint on Nos. 58-59

Wmkd. Crescent and Star (119)

90 A32 100m black 45.00 30.00
91 A33 200m plum 7.50 50
 a. Inverted overprint 200.00

Nos. 78-91 were issued to commemorate the proclamation of the Egyptian monarchy.

The overprint signifies "The Egyptian Kingdom, March 15, 1922". It exists in four types, one lithographed and three typographed on Nos 78-87, but lithographed only on Nos. 88-91.

King Fuad

A36 A37

Wmkd. Triple Crescent and Star. (120)

Size 18x22½ mm.

1923-24 Photo. *Perf. 13½*

92 A36 1m orange 6 6
93 " 2m black 12 6
94 " 3m brown 30 18
95 " 4m yellow green 30 15
96 " 5m orange brown 12 4
 a. Imperf., pair 25.00
97 " 10m rose 30 5
98 " 15m ultramarine 45 5
 a. Imperf., pair 80.00

Perf. 14

Size 22x28 mm.

99 A36 20m dark green 1.00 8
100 " 50m myrtle green 2.75 8
101 " 100m red violet 4.50 20
102 " 200m violet ('24) 10.00 80
 a. Imperf., pair 150.00
103 A37 £1 ultramarine & dark violet ('24) 65.00 8.50
 a. Imperf., pair 425.00
 Nos. 92-103 (12) 84.00 10.25

Thoth Carving Name of King Fuad A38

1925, Apr. Litho. *Perf. 11*

105 A38 5m brown 4.00 4.00
106 " 10m rose 4.00 4.00
107 " 15m ultramarine 4.00 4.00

International Geographical Congress, Cairo.

Nos. 106-107 exist with both white and yellowish gum.

Oxen Plowing A39

Wmk. 195

Wmkd. Multiple Crown and Arabic F. (195)

1926 *Perf. 13x13½*

108 A39 5m light brown 85 70
109 " 10m bright rose 85 70
110 " 15m deep blue 85 70
111 " 50m Prussian grn. 3.00 2.50
112 " 100m brown violet 5.50 5.00
113 " 200m bright violet 10.00 9.00
 Nos. 108-113 (6) 21.05 18.60

Issued to commemorate the 12th Agricultural and Industrial Exhibition at Gezira. "F" in watermark stands for Fuad.

King Fuad A40

Perf. 14x14½

1926, Apr. 2 Photo. **Wmk. 120**

114 A40 50pi brown violet & red violet 35.00 5.50

58th birthday of King Fuad.

Nos. 111-113 Surcharged **5 MILLIEMES**

Perf. 13x13½

1926, Aug. 24 Wmk. 195

115 A39 5m on 50m Prussian green 80 70
116 " 10m on 100m brn. vio. 80 70
117 " 15m on 200m brt. vio. 80 70
 a. Dbl. surcharge 125.00

Ship of Hatshepsut—A41

1926, Dec. 9 Litho. *Perf. 13x13½*

118 A41 5m brown & black 1.50 85
119 " 10m deep red & black 1.50 1.00
120 " 15m deep blue & black 1.50 1.00

International Navigation Congress, Cairo.

Nos. 118-120, 114 Overprinted

PORT FOUAD
a

PORT FOUAD
b

1926, Dec. 21

121 A41 (*a*) 5m brn. & blk. 65.00 50.00
122 " (") 10m deep red & black 65.00 50.00
123 " (") 15m deep blue & black 65.00 50.00

Perf. 14x14½ **Wmk. 120**

124 A40 (*b*) 50pi brn. violet & red vio. 750.00 700.00

Inauguration of Port Fuad opposite Port Said.

Nos. 121-123 have a block over "Le Caire" at lower left.

Forgeries of Nos. 121-124 exist.

Branch of Cotton
A42

Perf. 13x13½

1927, Jan. 25 **Wmk. 195**

125 A42 5m dark brown & slate green 1.00 85
126 " 10m deep red & slate green 1.50 1.00
127 " 15m deep blue & slate green 1.50 1.00

International Cotton Congress, Cairo.

King Fuad
A43 A44

A45

A46

Photogravure.

1927-37 ***Perf. 13x13½*** **Wmk. 195**

128 A43 1m orange 10 4
129 " 2m black 15 4
130 " 3m olive brown 15 8
131 " 3m deep green ('30) 25 6
132 " 4m yellow green 45 15
133 " 4m brown ('30) 50 20
134 " 4m deep green ('34) 75 18
135 " 5m dk. red brown ('29) 25 3
a. Booklet pane of 6
b. 5m chestnut 30 3
136 A43 10m dark red ('29) 60 3
a. 10m orange red 90 6
b. Booklet pane of 6
137 " 10m purple ('34) 1.30 8
138 " 13m car. rose ('32) 50 12
139 " 15m ultramarine 1.00 4
a. Booklet pane of 6
140 " 15m dk. vio. ('34) 2.00 5
141 " 20m ultra. ('34) 3.00 8

Early printings of Nos. 128, 129, 130, 132, 135, 136 and 139 were from plates with screen of vertical dots in the vignette; later printings show screen of diagonal dots.

Perf. 13½x14

142 A44 20m olive green 1.00 5
143 " 20m ultra. ('32) 2.25 6
144 " 40m olive brown ('32) 1.25 6
145 " 50m Prussian green 1.00 3
a. 50m greenish blue 1.50 3
146 " 100m brown violet 2.75 6
a. 100m claret 3.00 8
147 " 200m deep violet 4.00 25

Printings of Nos. 142, 145 and 146, made in 1929 and later, were from new plates with stronger mpressions and darker colors.

Lithographed; Center Photogravure.

Perf. 13x13½

148 A45 500m choc. & Pruss. blue ('32) 30.00 4.00
a. Entirely photogravure 30.00 4.00
149 A46 £1 dk. grn. & org. brn. ('37) 35.00 5.00
a. Entirely photogravure 35.00 5.00
Nos. 128-149 (22) 88.25 10.69

Statue of Amenhotep, Son of Hapu
A47

1927, Dec. 29 **Photo.** ***Perf. 13½x13***

150 A47 5m orange brown 45 40
151 " 10m copper red 85 55
152 " 15m dark blue 1.00 65

Statistical Congress, Cairo.

Imhotep — A48
Mohammed Ali Pasha — A49

1928, Dec. 15

153 A48 5m orange brown 40 35
154 A49 10m copper red 40 35

Issued to commemorate the International Congress of Medicine at Cairo and the centenary of the Faculty of Medicine at Cairo.

Prince Farouk
A50

1929, Feb. 11 **Lithographed**

155 A50 5m chocolate & gray 1.00 1.00
156 " 10m dull red & gray 1.00 1.00
157 " 15m ultra. & gray 1.00 1.00
158 " 20m Prussian blue & gray 1.00 1.00

Ninth birthday of Prince Farouk.

1929

155a A50 5m chocolate & black 60.00 60.00
156a " 10m dull red & brown 60.00 60.00
157a " 15m ultramarine & brown 60.00 60.00
158a " 20m Prussian blue & brown 60.00 60.00

Nos. 155a to 158a are trial color proofs. They were sent to the Universal Postal Union, but were never placed on sale to the public, although some are known used.

Tomb Fresco at El-Bersheh
A51

1931, Feb. 15 ***Perf. 13x13½***

163 A51 5m brown 70 60
164 " 10m copper red 80 60
165 " 15m dark blue 1.00 75

Issued to commemorate the 14th Agricultural and Industrial Exhibition, Cairo.

Nos. 114 and 103 Surcharged with Bars and

MILLS 50 ملیما ٥٠
a

MILLS 100 مليم ١٠٠
b

1932 ***Perf. 14x14½*** **Wmk. 120**

166 A40 (*a*) 50m on 50pi brn. violet & red violet 3.50 1.25

Perf. 14

167 A37 (*b*) 100m on £1 ultra. & dark vio. 100.00 90.00

Locomotive of 1852
A52

Designs (Locomotives): 13m, Of 1859. 15m, Of 1862. 20m, Of 1932.

Perf. 13x13½

1933, Jan. 19 **Litho.** **Wmk. 195**

168 A52 5m brown & black 2.50 1.50
169 " 13m dull red & black 8.00 6.00
170 " 15m purple & blk. 8.00 6.00
171 " 20m deep blue & black 8.00 6.00

International Railroad Congress, Heliopolis.

Commercial Passenger Airplane
A56

Dornier Do-X—A57

Graf Zeppelin
A58

1933, Dec. 20 **Photogravure**

172 A56 5m brown 3.25 1.50
173 " 10m bright violet 8.00 6.00
174 A57 13m brn. carmine 10.00 6.00
175 " 15m violet 8.00 6.00
176 A58 20m blue 12.00 10.00
Nos. 172-176 (5) 41.25 29.50

International Aviation Congress, Cairo.

Khedive Ismail Pasha
A59 A60

1934, Feb. 1 ***Perf. 13½***

177 A59 1m deep orange 15 15
178 " 2m black 20 15
179 " 3m brown 20 20
180 " 4m blue green 30 30
181 " 5m red brown 30 15
182 " 10m violet 60 25
183 " 13m copper red 90 60
184 " 15m dull violet 70 25
185 " 20m ultramarine 1.00 40
186 " 50m Prussian blue 3.00 40
187 " 100m olive green 6.50 60
188 " 200m deep violet 15.00 2.50

Perf. 13½x13

189 A60 50pi brown 70.00 35.00
190 " £1 Prus. blue 110.00 55.00
Nos. 177-190 (14) 208.85 95.95

10th Congress of Universal Postal Union, Cairo.

King Fuad
A61

1936-37 ***Perf. 13½***

191 A61 1m dull orange 12 4
192 " 2m black 25 4
193 " 4m dark green 30 10
194 " 5m chestnut 25 3
a. Booklet pane of 6
195 " 10m purple ('37) 60 10
196 " 15m brown violet 85 8
197 " 20m sapphire 1.00 10
Nos. 191-197 (7) 3.37 49

Entrance to Agricultural Building
A62

Agricultural Building
A63

Design: 15m, 20m, Industrial Building.

1936, Feb. 15 ***Perf. 13½x13***

198 A62 5m brown 55 50

Perf. 13x13½

199 A63 10m violet 80 75
200 " 13m copper red 1.10 1.00
201 " 15m dark violet 80 75
202 " 20m blue 2.00 2.00
Nos. 198-202 (5) 5.25 5.00

Issued to commemorate the 15th Agricultural and Industrial Exhibition, Cairo.

Signing of Treaty—A65

1936, Dec. 22 ***Perf. 11***

203 A65 5m brown 45 40
204 " 15m dark violet 55 50
205 " 20m sapphire 80 70

Signing of Anglo-Egyptian Treaty, Aug. 26, 1936.

King Farouk
A66

Medal for Montreux Conference
A67

1937-44 ***Perf. 13x13½*** **Wmk. 195**

206 A66 1m brown orange 4 3
207 " 2m vermilion 5 4
208 " 3m brown 5 3
209 " 4m green 10 5
210 " 5m red brown 10 3
a. Booklet pane of 6 75
211 " 6m light yellow green ('40) 20 3
a. Booklet pane of 6 1.00
212 " 10m purple 20 3
a. Booklet pane of 6 3.00
213 " 13m rose carmine 20 12
214 " 15m dark violet brown 25 3
a. Booklet pane of 6 3.00
215 " 20m blue 30 3
216 " 20m lilac gray ('44) 35 6
Nos. 206-216 (11) 1.84 48

1937, Oct. 15 ***Perf. 13½x13***

217 A67 5m red brown 35 30
218 " 15m dark violet 65 50
219 " 20m sapphire 75 60

Issued in commemoration of the International Treaty signed at Montreux, Switzerland, under which foreign privileges in Egypt were to end in 1949.

Eye of Ré
A68

1937, Dec. 8 ***Perf. 13x13½***

220 A68 5m brown 60 55
221 " 15m dark violet 65 60
222 " 20m sapphire 65 60

15th Ophthalmological Congress, Cairo, December, 1937.

King Farouk, Queen Farida—A69

1938, Jan. 20 ***Perf. 11***

223 A69 5m red brown 2.75 2.50

Royal wedding of King Farouk and Farida Zulficar.

Inscribed: "11 Fevrier 1938"

1938, Feb. 11

224 A69 £1 green & sepia 85.00 80.00

King Farouk's 18th birthday.

Cotton Picker
A70

1938, Jan. 26 ***Perf. 13½x13***

225 A70 5m red brown 65 60
226 " 15m dark violet 1.35 1.25
227 " 20m sapphire 1.10 1.00

Issued to commemorate the 18th International Cotton Congress at Cairo.

Pyramids of Giza and Colossus of Thebes—A71

1938, Feb. 1 ***Perf. 13x13½***

228 A71 5m red brown 80 75
229 " 15m dark violet 1.10 1.00
230 " 20m sapphire 1.25 1.00

International Telecommunication Conference, Cairo.

Branch of Hydnocarpus—A72

1938, Mar. 21 ***Perf. 13x13½***

231 A72 5m red brown 85 50
232 " 15m dark violet 85 70
233 " 20m sapphire 85 70

International Leprosy Congress, Cairo.

King Farouk and Pyramids
A73

King Farouk
A74 A75

Backgrounds: 40m, Hussan Mosque. 50m, Cairo Citadel. 100m, Aswan Dam. 200m, Cairo University.

1939-46 **Photo.** ***Perf. 14x13½***

234 A73 30m gray 35 3
a. 30m slate gray 30 3
234B " 30m olive green ('46) 35 4
235 " 40m dark brown 50 3
236 " 50m Prussian green 55 3
237 " 100m brown violet 80 4
238 " 200m dark violet 2.00 8

Perf. 13½x13

239 A74 50pi green & sepia 3.50 50
240 A75 £1 deep blue & dark brown 7.50 70
Nos. 234-240 (8) 15.55 1.45

For £1 with A77 portrait, see No. 269D. See Nos. 267-269D.

King Fuad
A76

King Farouk
A77

1944, Apr. 28 ***Perf. 13½x13***

241 A76 10m dark violet 20 20

Issued to commemorate the eighth anniversary of the death of King Fuad.

1944-50 ***Perf. 13x13½*** **Wmk. 195**

242 A77 1m yel. brown ('45) 6 3
243 " 2m red orange ('45) 6 3
244 " 3m sepia ('46) 20 15
245 " 4m deep green ('45) 25 20
a. Booklet pane of 6
246 A77 5m red brown ('46) 10 3
247 " 10m deep violet 18 3
b. Booklet pane of 6
247A A77 13m rose red ('50) 60 25
248 " 15m dark violet ('45) 20 3
249 " 17m olive green 25 8
250 " 20m dark gray ('45) 30 6
251 " 22m deep blue ('45) 40 10
a. Booklet pane of 6
Nos. 242-251 (11) 2.60 98

King Farouk
A78

Khedive Ismail Pasha
A79

1945, Feb. 10 ***Perf. 13½x13***

252 A78 10m deep violet 20 20

25th birthday of King Farouk.

1945, Mar. 2 **Photogravure**

253 A79 10m dark olive 20 20

50th anniversary of death of Khedive Ismail Pasha.

Flags of Arab Nations
A80

1945, July 29

254 A80 10m violet 12 12
255 " 22m deep yellow green 30 30

League of Arab Nations Conference, Cairo, Mar. 22, 1945.

Flags of Egypt and Saudi Arabia
A81

Perf. 13x13½

1946, Jan. 10 **Wmk. 195**

256 A81 10m deep yellow green 15 15

Visit of King Ibn Saud, Jan., 1946.

Citadel, Cairo
A82

1946, Aug. 9

257 A82 10m yellow brown & deep yellow green 25 25

Withdrawal of British troops from Cairo Citadel, Aug. 9, 1946.

King Farouk and Inchas Palace, Cairo
A83

Portraits: 2m, Prince Abdullah, Yemen. 3m, Pres. Bechara el-Khoury, Lebanon. 4m, King Abdul Aziz ibn Saud, Saudi Arabia. 5m, King Faisal II, Iraq. 10m, Amir Abdullah ibn Hussein, Jordan. 15m, Pres. Shukri el Kouatly, Syria.

1946, Nov. 9

258 A83 1m deep yellow green 8 8
259 " 2m sepia 8 8
260 " 3m deep blue 10 10
261 " 4m brown orange 12 12
262 " 5m brown red 15 15
263 " 10m dark gray 18 18
264 " 15m deep violet 20 20
Nos. 258-264 (7) 91 91

Issued to commemorate the Arab League Congress at Cairo, May 28, 1946.

Parliament Building, Cairo
A84

1947, Apr. 7 **Photogravure**

265 A84 10m green 18 18

Issued to commemorate the 36th conference of the Interparliamentary Union, April, 1947.

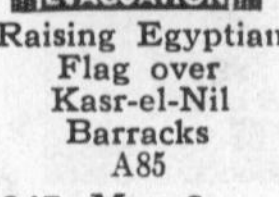

Raising Egyptian Flag over Kasr-el-Nil Barracks
A85

King Farouk
A85a

1947, May 6 *Perf. 13½x13*

266 A85 10m deep plum & yellow green 15 15

Issued to commemorate the withdrawal of British troops from the Nile Delta.

Farouk Types 1939 Redrawn

1947-51 *Perf. 14x31½* **Wmk. 195**

267 A73 30m olive green 30 3
268 " 40m dark brown 40 4
269 " 50m Prussian green ('48) 55 5
269A " 100m dark brown violet ('49) 1.65 8
269B " 200m dark violet('49) 4.00 20

Perf. 13½13

269C A85a 50pi green & sepia ('51) 10.00 3.75
269D A75 £1 dp. bl. & dk. brn. ('50) 22.50 2.00
Nos. 267-269D (7) 39.40 6.15

The king faces slightly to the left and clouds have been added in the sky on Nos. 267-269B. Backgrounds as in 1939-46 issue. Portrait on £1 as on type A77.

Field and Branch of Cotton
A86

Map and Infantry Column
A87

Perf. 13½x13

1948, Apr. 1 **Wmk. 195**

270 A86 10m olive green 30 25

Issued to commemorate the International Cotton Congress held at Cairo in April, 1948.

1948, June 15 *Perf. 11½x11*

271 A87 10m green 35 35

Arrival of Egyptian troops at Gaza, May 15, 1948.

Ibrahim Pasha
A88

1948, Nov. 10 *Perf. 13x13½*

272 A88 10m brown red & deep green 25 25

Issued to commemorate the centenary of the death of Ibrahim Pasha (1789-1848).

Statue, "The Nile"
A89

Protection of Industry and Agriculture
A90

Perf. 13x13½

1949, Mar. 1 **Photo.** **Wmk. 195**

273 A89 1m dark green 10 10
274 " 10m purple 20 20
275 " 17m crimson 25 25
276 " 22m deep blue 30 30

Perf. 11½x11

277 A90 30m dark brown 40 40
Nos. 273-277 (5) 1.25 1.25

Souvenir Sheets.

Photogravure and Lithographed.

Imperf.

278 A89 Sheet of 4 1.25 1.25
a. 1m red brown
b. 10m dark brown
c. 17m brown orange
d. 22m dark Prussian green

279 A90 Sheet of 2 1.75 1.75
a. 10m violet gray
b. 30m red orange

Nos. 273-279 were issued to publicize the 16th Agricultural and Industrial Exposition, Cairo.

No. 278 has frame and marginal inscriptions in dark green. Size: 127x104½ mm.

No. 279 has frame and marginal inscriptions in dark violet. Size: 108x123 mm.

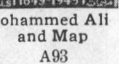

Mohammed Ali and Map
A93

Globe
A94

Perf. 11½x11

1949, Aug. 2 **Photo.** **Wmk. 195**

280 A93 10m orange brown & green 25 25

Centenary of death of Mohammed Ali.

1949, Oct. 9 *Perf. 13½x13*

281 A94 10m rose brown 35 30
282 " 22m violet 60 50
283 " 30m dull blue 80 70

75th anniversary of the formation of the Universal Postal Union.

Scales of Justice
A95

1949, Oct. 14 *Perf. 13x13½*

284 A95 10m deep olive green 20 20

Issued to commemorate the end of the Mixed Judiciary System, Oct. 14, 1949.

Desert Scene
A96

1950, Dec. 27

285 A96 10m violet & red brown 25 25

Issued to commemorate the opening of the Fuad I Institute of the Desert.

Fuad I University
A97

1950, Dec. 27

286 A97 22m dp. grn. & claret 35 35

Issued to commemorate the 25th anniversary of the founding of Fuad I University.

Globe and Khedive Ismail Pasha
A98

1950, Dec. 27

287 A98 30m claret & deep green 40 40

75th anniversary of Royal Geographic Society of Egypt.

Picking Cotton
A99

1951, Feb. 24

290 A99 10m olive green 20 20

International Cotton Congress, 1951.

King Farouk and Queen Narriman
A100

1951, May 6 **Photo.** *Perf. 11x11½*

291 A100 10m green & red brown 1.00 1.00
a. Souvenir sheet 1.35 1.35

Issued to commemorate the marriage of King Farouk and Narriman Sadek, May 6, 1951.

No. 291a was issued in sheets measuring 129x112 mm., with ornamental border and inscriptions in gray and black.

Stadium Entrance
A101

Arms of Alexandria and Olympic Emblem
A102

King Farouk
A103

1951, Oct. 5 *Perf. 13x13½, 13½x13*

292 A101 10m brown 50 50
293 A102 22m deep green 90 90
294 A103 30m bl. & dp. grn. 1.00 1.00
a. Souvenir sheet 5.00 5.00

Issued to publicize the first Mediterranean Games, Alexandria, Oct. 5-20, 1951.

No. 294a measures 189x117mm., and contains one each of Nos. 292-294 with ornamental frame and background in buff.

Winged Figure and Map
A105

Designs: 22m, King Farouk and Map. 30m, King Farouk and Flag.

Dated "16 Oct. 1951."

1952, Feb. 11 *Perf. 13½x13*

296 A105 10m deep green 50 50
297 " 22m plum & dp. grn. 90 90
298 " 30m green & brown 1.00 1.00
a. Souv. sheet 5.00 5.00

Issued to commemorate the abrogation of the Anglo-Egyptian treaty.

No. 298a measures 134 x 113mm., and contains one each of Nos. 296 to 298, with ornamental border and Arabic inscriptions in gray.

Stamps of 1937-51 Overprinted in Various Colors

ملك مصر والسودان
١٦ اكتوبر سنة ١٩٥١

Perf. 13x13½

1952, Jan. 17 **Wmk. 195**

299 A77 1m yellow brown 10 8
300 " 2m red orange (Bl) 10 8
301 A66 3m brown (Bl) 12 10
302 A77 4m deep green (RV) 12 8
303 A66 6m lt. yel. grn.(RV) 30 15
304 A77 10m deep violet (C) 20 4
305 " 13m rose red (Bl) 25 15
306 " 15m dark violet (C) 60 22
307 " 17m olive green (C) 90 15
308 " 20m dark gray (RV) 1.00 15
309 " 22m deep blue (C) 1.50 80

No. 244, the 3m sepia, exists with this overprint but was not regularly issued or used.

Same Overprint, 24½mm. Wide on Nos. 267 to 269B.

Perf. 14x13½

310 A73 30m olive green 55 8
a. Dk. blue overprint 35 6

311 A73 40m dark brown (G) 50 18
312 " 50m Pruss. grn. (C) 65 10
313 " 100m dark brown violet (C) 1.00 25
314 " 200m dark violet (C) 2.50 30

Same Overprint, 19mm. Wide, on Nos. 269C–269D.

Perf. 13½x13.

315 A85a 50pi green & sepia (C) 8.50 3.50
316 A75 £1 deep blue & dark brown (Bl) 18.00 3.75
Nos. 299–316 (18) 36.89 10.16

The overprint translates: King of Egypt and the Sudan, Oct. 16, 1951.

Egyptian Flag
A106

Perf. 13½x13

1952, May 6 Photo. Wmk. 195

317 A106 10m orange yellow, deep blue & deep green 25 25
a. Souvenir sheet 85 85

Issued to commemorate the birth of Crown Prince Ahmed Fuad, January 16, 1952.

No. 317a measures 115½ x 137½mm., with ornamental border and Arabic inscriptions in deep blue, salmon and green.

"Dawn of New Era"
A107

Symbolical of Egypt Freed
A108

Designs: 10m, "Egypt" with raised sword. 22m, Citizens marching with flag.

Perf. 13x13½, 13½x13

1952, Nov. 23

Dated: "23 Juillet 1952."

318 A107 4m deep green & orange 10 10
319 " 10m deep green & copper brown 15 15
320 A108 17m brown orange & deep green 25 25
321 " 22m chocolate & deep green 35 35

Change of government, July 23, 1952.

Republic

Farmer
A109

Soldier
A110

Mosque of Sultan Hassan
A111

Queen Nefertiti
A112

1953–56 ***Perf. 13x13½***

322 A109 1m red brown 5 3
323 " 2m dark lilac 6 4
324 " 3m bright blue 6 4
325 " 4m dark green 6 4
326 A110 10m dark brown ("*Defence*") 12 6
327 " 10m dark brown ("*Defense*") 8 3
328 " 15m gray 15 3
329 " 17m dark greenish blue 18 6
330 " 20m purple 18 6

Perf. 13½.

331 A111 30m dull green 20 4
332 " 32m bright blue 25 10
333 " 35m violet ('55) 40 5
334 " 37m golden brown ('56) 50 8
335 " 40m red brown 30 4
336 " 50m violet brown 45 5
337 A112 100m henna brown 75 10
338 " 200m dark greenish blue 1.25 20
339 " 500m purple 3.00 90
340 " £1 dark green, black & red 6.00 70
Nos. 322–340 (19) 14.04 2.65

Nos. 327–330 are inscribed "Defense." See No. 490.

Nos. 206, 208 and 211 Overprinted in Black with Three Bars to Obliterate Portrait.

1953 ***Perf. 13x13½***

342 A66 1m brown orange 2.25 2.25
343 " 3m brown 8 6
344 " 6m light yellow green 8 6

Same Overprint on Stamps of 1939–51

Perf. 13x13½, 13½x13.

345 A77 1m yellow brown 6 6
346 " 2m red orange 6 6
347 " 3m sepia 6 6
348 " 4m deep green 8 6
349 " 10m deep violet 12 10
350 " 13m rose red 18 15
351 " 15m dark violet 18 10
352 " 17m olive green 20 15
353 " 20m dark gray 25 12
354 " 22m deep blue 30 25
355 A73 30m olive green (#267) 35 18
356 " 50m Prussian green (#269) 50 20
357 " 100m dark brown violet (#269A) 75 25
358 " 200m dk.vio. (#269B) 2.50 35
359 A85a 50pi green & sepia 4.50 1.00
360 A75 £1 deep blue & dark brown (#269D) 9.00 1.35
Nos. 345–360 (16) 19.09 4.44

Same Overprint on Nos. 299-309, 311 and 314.

360A A77 1m yellow brown 1.50 1.50
360B " 2m red orange 25 20
360C A66 3m brown 1.50 1.50
360D A77 4m deep green 1.50 1.50
360E A66 6m lt. yel. green 2.00 1.50
361 A77 10m deep violet 1.00 1.00
362 " 13m rose red 50 30
362A " 15m dark violet 6.00 6.00
362B " 17m olive green 6.00 6.00
362C " 20m dark gray 6.00 6.00
362D " 22m deep blue 22.50 22.50
363 A73 40m dark brown 60 35
364 " 200m dark violet 2.50 50
Nos. 360A–364 (13) 51.85 48.85

Practically all values of Nos. 342-364 exist with double overprint.

Symbols of Electronic Progress
A113

1953, Nov. 23 Photo. *Perf. 13x13½*

365 A113 10m bright blue 25 25

Electronics Exposition, Cairo, Nov. 23.

Crowd Acclaiming the Republic
A114

Farmer
A115

Design: 30m, Crowd, flag and eagle.

Perf. 13½x13

1954, June 18 Wmk. 195

366 A114 10m brown 15 15
367 " 30m deep blue 35 35

Issued to commemorate the first anniversary of the proclamation of the republic.

1954-55 ***Perf. 13x13½.***

368 A115 1m red brown 5 3
369 " 2m dark lilac 5 3
370 " 3m bright blue 6 4
371 " 4m dark green ('55) 6 6
372 " 5m deep carmine ('55) 12 8
Nos. 368–372 (5) 34 24

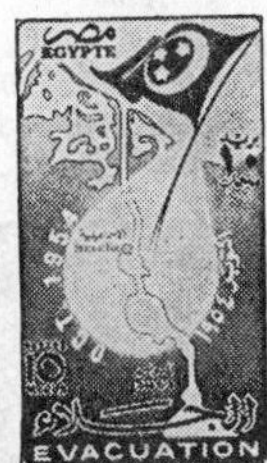

Egyptian Flag and Map
A116

Globe
A117

Design: 35m, Bugler, soldier and map.

1954, Nov. 4 ***Perf. 13½x13***

373 A116 10m rose violet & green 15 15
374 " 35m vermilion, black & blue green 50 50

Issued to commemorate the agreement of Oct. 19, 1954, with Great Britain for the evacuation of the Suez Canal zone by British troops.

Arab Postal Union Issue.

1955, Jan. 1

375 A117 5m yellow brown 10 10
376 " 10m green 20 20
377 " 37m violet 60 60

Issued to commemorate the founding of the Arab Postal Union, July 1, 1954.

Paul P. Harris and Rotary Emblem
A118

Design: 35m, Globe, wings and Rotary emblem.

Perf. 13½x13

1955, Feb. 23 Wmk. 195

378 A118 10m claret 30 15
379 " 35m blue 60 40

Issued to commemorate the 50th anniversary of the founding of Rotary International.

Nos. 375-377 Overprinted مؤتمر البريد العربي القاهرة-١٥/٣/١٩٥٥

1955, Nov. 1

381 A117 5m yellow brown 10 10
382 " 10m green 20 20
383 " 37m violet 55 55

Issued to commemorate the Arab Postal Union Congress held at Cairo, March 15, 1955.

Map of Africa and Asia, Olive Branch and Rings
A119

Globe, Torch, Dove and Olive Branch
A120

Perf. 13x13½, 13½x13

1956, July 29

384 A119 10m chestnut & green 20 15
385 A120 35m orange yellow & dull purple 45 40

Afro-Asian Festival, Cairo, July, 1956.

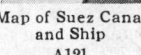

Map of Suez Canal and Ship
A121

Queen Nefertiti
A122

Perf. 11½x11

1956, Sept. 26 **Wmk. 195**

386 A121 10m blue & buff 30 25

Nationalization of the Suez Canal, July 26, 1956. See also No. 393.

1956, Oct. 15 ***Perf. 13½x13***

387 A122 10m dark green 45 45

Issued to publicize the International Museum Week (UNESCO), Oct. 8-14.

Egyptians Defending Port Said
A123

1956, Dec. 20 Litho. ***Perf. 11x11½***

388 A123 10m brown violet 25 20

Issued in honor of the defenders of Port Said.

No. 388 Overprinted in Carmine Rose

EVACUATION 22·12·56

1957, Jan. 14

389 A123 10m brown violet 25 20

Issued to commemorate the evacuation of Port Said by British and French troops, Dec. 22, 1956.

Old and New Trains
A124

1957, Jan. 30 Photo. ***Perf. 13x13½***

390 A124 10m red violet & gray 18 15

Issued to commemorate the 100th anniversary of the Egyptian Railway System (in 1956).

Mother and Children
A125

1957, Mar. 21

391 A125 10m crimson 18 15

Mother's Day, 1957.

Battle Scene
A126

Perf. 13x13½

1957, Mar. 28 **Wmk. 195**

392 A126 10m bright blue 15 15

Issued to commemorate the 150th anniversary of the victory over the British at Rosetta.

Type of 1956;
New Inscriptions in English

1957, Apr. 15 ***Perf. 11½x11***

393 A121 100m blue & yellow green 80 65

Issued to commemorate the reopening of the Suez Canal.

No. 393 is inscribed: "Nationalisation of Suez Canal Co. Guarantees Freedom of Navigation" and "Reopening 1957".

Map of Gaza Strip
A127

Perf. 13½x13

1957, May 4 Photo. **Wmk. 195**

394 A127 10m Prussian blue 20 18

"Gaza Part of Arab Nation."

Al Azhar University
A128

1957, Apr. 27 ***Perf. 13x13½***

New Arabic Date in Red.

395	A128	10m bright violet	15	15
396	"	15m violet brown	20	20
397	"	20m dark gray	25	25

Millenary of Al Azhar University, Cairo.

Shepheard's Hotel, Cairo
A129

Gate, Palace and Eagle
A130

Perf. 13½x13

1957, July 20 **Wmk. 195**

398 A129 10m bright violet 15 12

Reopening of Shepheard's Hotel, Cairo.

Wmk. 315

Wmkd. Multiple Eagle (315)

1957, July 22 ***Perf. 11½x11***

399 A130 10m yellow & brown 15 12

First meeting of New National Assembly.

Amasis I in Battle of Avaris, 1580 B. C.—A131

Designs: No. 401, Sultan Saladin, Hitteen, 1187 A. D. No. 402, Louis IX of France in chains, Mansourah, 1250 (vertical). No. 403, Map of Middle East, Ein Galout, 1260. No. 404, Port Said, 1956.

Inscribed:
"Egypt Tomb of Aggressors 1957"

Perf. 13x13½, 13½x13

1957, July 26

400	A131	10m carmine rose	18	10
401	"	10m dark olive green	18	10
402	"	10m brown violet	18	10
403	"	10m greenish blue	18	10
404	"	10m yellow brown	18	10
		Nos. 400-404 (5)	90	50

No. 400 exists with Wmk. 195.

Ahmed Arabi Speaking to the Khedive—A132

Perf. 13x13½

1957, Sept. 16 **Wmk. 315**

405 A132 10m deep violet 15 12

75th anniversary of Arabi Revolution.

Hafez Ibrahim
A133

Portrait: No. 407, Ahmed Shawky.

1957, Oct. 14 ***Perf. 13½x13***

406	A133	10m dull red brown	15	12
407	"	10m olive green	15	12

Nos. 406-407 are printed se-tenant in sheets of 50. Issued to commemorate the 25th anniversary of the deaths of Hafez Ibrahim and Ahmed Shawky, poets.

MiG and Ilyushin Planes—A134

Design: No. 409, Viscount plane.

1957, Dec. 19 ***Perf. 13x13½***

408	A134	10m ultramarine	15	12
409	"	10m green	15	12

Issued to commemorate the 25th anniversaries of the Egyptian Air Force and of Misrair, the Egyptian airline. Nos. 408-409 printed se-tenant.

Pyramids, Dove and Globe—A135

1957, Dec. 26 Photo. **Wmk. 315**

410	A135	5m brown orange	10	8
411	"	10m green	15	12
412	"	15m bright violet	20	20

Issued to publicize the Afro-Asian Peoples Conference, Cairo, Dec. 26—Jan. 2.

Farmer's Wife
A136

Ramses II
A137

1957-58 ***Perf. 13½*** **Wmk. 315**

413	A136	1m blue green ('58)	5	
414	A137	10m violet	12	8

"Industry"
A138

Wmk. 318

Wmkd. Multiple Eagle and "Misr" (318)

1958

415	A136	1m light blue green	5	4
416	A138	5m brown	6	4
417	A137	10m violet	12	4

See also Nos. 438-444, 474-488.

Cyclists
A139

Mustafa Kamel
A140

Perf. 13½x13

1958, Jan. 12 **Wmk. 315**

418 A139 10m light red brown 18 15

Issued to publicize the fifth International Bicycle Race, Egypt, Jan. 12-26.

1958, Feb. 10 Photo. **Wmk. 318**

419 A140 10m blue gray 18 15

Issued to commemorate the 50th anniversary of the death of Mustafa Kamel, orator and politician.

United Arab Republic

Linked Maps of Egypt and Syria A141 — Cotton A142

Perf. 11½x11

1958, Mar. 22 **Wmk. 318**

436 A141 10m yellow & green 15 12

Birth of United Arab Republic. See No. C90.

1958, Apr. 5 ***Perf. 13½x13***

437 A142 10m Prussian blue 15 12

Issued for the International Fair for Egyptian Cotton, April, 1958.

Types of 1957–58 Inscribed "U.A.R. EGYPT" and

Princess Nofret A143

Designs: 1m, Farmer's wife. 2m, Ibn-Tulun's Mosque. 4m, 14th century glass lamp (design lacks "1963" of A217). 5m. "Industry" (factories and cogwheel). 10m, Ramses II. 35m, "Commerce" (eagle, ship and cargo).

1958 ***Perf. 13½x14***

438 A136 1m crimson 5 3
439 A138 2m blue 5 4
440 A143 3m dark red brown 5 3
441 A217 4m green 5 3
442 A138 5m brown 6 4
443 A137 10m violet 12 3
444 A138 35m light ultra. 80 5
Nos. 438–444 (7) 1.18 25

See Nos. 474–488, 532–535.

Qasim Amin A144 — Doves, Broken Chain and Globe A145

1958, Apr. 23 ***Perf. 13½x13***

445 A144 10m deep blue 18 12

50th anniversary of the death of Qasim Amin, author of "Emancipation of Women."

1958, June 18

446 A145 10m violet 15 10

Issued on the fifth anniversary of the republic to publicize the struggle of peoples and individuals for freedom.

Cement Industry A146

Industries: No. 448, Textile. No. 449, Iron & steel. No. 450, Petroleum (Oil). No. 451, Electricity and fertilizers.

Perf. 13½x13

1958, July 23 **Photo.** **Wmk. 318**

447 A146 10m red brown 15 10
448 " 10m blue green 15 10
449 " 10m bright red 15 10
450 " 10m olive green 15 10
451 " 10m dark blue 15 10
Nos. 447–451 (5) 75 50

Nos. 447–451 are printed in one sheet of 25 in vertical rows of five.

Souvenir Sheet

U. A. R. Flag—A147

1958, July 23 ***Imperf.***

452 A147 50m green, deep carmine & black 10.00 10.00

No. 452 measures 80½x75½mm. with black marginal inscription. Nos. 447–452 issued on the 6th anniversary of the Revolution of July 23, 1952.

Sayed Darwich A148 — Hand Holding Torch, Broken Chain and Flag A149

1958, Sept. 15 ***Perf. 13½x13***

453 A148 10m violet brown 12 10

Issued to commemorate the 35th anniversary of the death of Sayed Darwich, Arab composer.

1958, Oct. 14 **Photo.** **Wmk. 318**

454 A149 10m carmine rose 12 10

Establishment of the Republic of Iraq.

Maps and Cogwheels A150

1958, Dec. 8 ***Perf. 13x13½***

455 A150 10m blue 18 10

Issued to publicize the Economic Conference of Afro-Asian Countries, Cairo, Dec. 8.

Overprinted in Red in English and Arabic in 3 Lines: "Industrial and Agricultural Production Fair."

1958, Dec. 9

456 A150 10m light red brown 18 10

Issued to publicize the Industrial and Agricultural Production Fair, Cairo, Dec. 9.

Dr. Mahmoud Azmy and U.N. Emblem—A151

1958, Dec. 10

457 A151 10m dull violet 20 15
458 " 35m green 55 45

Tenth anniversary of the signing of the Universal Declaration of Human Rights.

University Building, Sphinx, "Education" and God Thoth A152

1958, Dec. 21 **Photo.** **Wmk. 318**

459 A152 10m greenish black 12 10

50th anniversary of Cairo University.

No. 337 Surcharged

الجمهورية العربية المتحدة ═ ٥٥

UAR ═ 55

1959, Jan. 20 ***Perf. 13½*** **Wmk. 195**

460 A112 55m on 100m henna brown 45 30

Arms of U.A.R. A154

Emblem A153

1959, Feb. 2 ***Perf. 13x13½***

461 A153 10m light olive green 12 10

Afro-Asian Youth Conference, Cairo, Feb. 2.

Perf. 13½x13

1959, Feb. 22 **Photo.** **Wmk. 318**

462 A154 10m green, black & red 12 10

First anniversary, United Arab Republic.

Nile Hilton Hotel A155

1959, Feb. 22 ***Perf. 13x13½***

463 A155 10m dark gray 12 10

Opening of the Nile Hilton Hotel, Cairo.

Globe, Radio and Telegraph—A156

1959, Mar. 1

464 A156 10m violet 12 10

Arab Union of Telecommunications.

United Arab States Issue

Flags of U. A. R. and Yemen A157

1959, Mar. 8

465 A157 10m slate green, carmine & black 12 10

First anniversary of United Arab States.

Oil Derrick and Pipe Line A158

Perf. 13½x13

1959, Apr. 16 **Litho.** **Wmk. 318**

466 A158 10m light blue & dark blue 12 8

First Arab Petroleum Congress, Cairo.

Railroad A159

Designs: No. 468, Bus on highway. No. 469, River barge. No. 470, Ocean liner. No. 471, Telecommunications on map. No. 472, Stamp printing building, Heliopolis.

1959, July 23 **Photo.** ***Perf. 13x13½***

Frame in Gray.

467 A159 10m maroon 7 7
468 " 10m green 7 7
469 " 10m violet 7 7
470 " 10m dark blue 8 8
471 " 10m dull purple 8 8

472 A159 10m scarlet 8 8

Nos. 467-472 (6) 45 45

An imperf. souvenir sheet, issued with this set, commemorates the seventh anniversary of the Egyptian revolution of 1952. The sheet carries a single 50m green and red stamp, 57x32mm., picturing a ship, train, plane and motorcycle mail carrier. Marginal Arabic inscriptions in black; size: 80x74mm. The government printed 140,000 of this sheet and sold it only if the buyer also bought five sets of Nos. 467–472.

Globe, Swallows and Map
A160

1959, Aug. 8 ***Perf. 13½x13***

473 A160 10m maroon 10 8

Issued to commemorate the convention of the Association of Arab Emigrants in the United States.

Types of 1953–58 without "Egypt" and

St. Simon's Gate, Bosra, Syria
A161

Wmk. 328

Designs: 1m, Farmer's wife. 2m, Ibn-Tulun's Mosque. 3m, Princess Nofret. 4m, 14th century glass lamp (design lacks "1963" of A217). 5m, "Industry" (factories and cogwheel). 10m, Ramses II. 15m, Omayyad Mosque, Damascus. 20m, Lotus vase, Tutankhamen treasure. 35m, Eagle, ship and cargo. 40m, Scribe statue. 45m, Saladin's citadel, Aleppo. 55m, Eagle, cotton and wheat. 60m, Dam and factory. 100m, Eagle, hand, cotton and grain. 200m, Palmyra ruins, Syria. 500m, Queen Nefertiti, inscribed "UAR" (no ovpt.).

Wmkd. U A R. (328)

Photogravure.

1959–60 ***Perf. 13½x14, 14x13½.***

474 A136 1m vermilion 3 3
475 A138 2m deep blue ('60) 4 4
476 A143 3m maroon 4 4
477 A217 4m green ('60) 4 4
478 A138 5m black ('60) 5 4
479 A137 10m dark olive green 10 3
480 A138 15m deep claret 15 4
481 " 20m crimson ('60) 20 5
482 A161 30m brown violet 30 6
483 A138 35m light violet blue ('60) 40 6
484 A143 40m sepia 60 8
485 A161 45m lilac gray ('60) 1.00 8
486 A138 55m brt. blue green 1.00 8
487 " 60m deep purple ('60) 60 8
488 " 100m orange & slate green ('60) 1.50 10
489 A161 200m light blue & maroon 2.50 10
490 A112 500m dark gray & red ('60) 5.00 30
Nos. 474–490 (17) 13.55 1.25

Shield and Cogwheel
A162

Perf. 13½x13

1959, Oct. 20 Photo. **Wmk. 328**

491 A162 10m brt. car. rose 12 8

Issued for Army Day, 1959.

Cairo Museum—A163

1959, Nov. 18 ***Perf. 13x13½***

492 A163 10m olive gray 12 8

Centenary of Cairo museum.

Abu Simbel Temple of Ramses II
A164

1959, Dec. 22 ***Perf. 11x11½***

493 A164 10m light red brown, *pinkish* 25 20

Issued as propaganda to save historic monuments in Nubia threatened by the construction of Aswan High Dam.

Postrider, 12th century
A165

1960, Jan. 2 ***Perf. 13x13½***

494 A165 10m dark blue 12 8

Issued for Post Day, Jan. 2.

Hydroelectric Power Station, Aswan Dam—A166

1960, Jan. 9

495 A166 10m violet black 15 8

Issued to commemorate the inauguration of the Aswan Dam hydroelectric power station, Jan. 9.

Arabic and English Description of Aswan High Dam—A167

Architect's Drawing of Aswan High Dam—A168

1960, Jan. 9 ***Perf. 11x11½***

496 A167 10m claret 15 8
497 A168 35m claret 45 25

Issued to commemorate the start of work on the Aswan High Dam. Nos. 496–497 printed se-tenant vertically in sheet.

Symbols of Agriculture and Industry
A169

Arms and Flag
A170

1960. Jan. 16 ***Perf. 13½x13***

498 A169 10m gray green & slate green 12 8

Industrial and Agricultural Fair, Cairo.

1960, Feb. 22 Photo. **Wmk. 328**

499 A170 10m green, black & red 12 8

Issued to commemorate the 2nd anniversary of the proclamation of the United Arab Republic.

No. 340 Overprinted "UAR" in English and Arabic in Red

1960 ***Perf. 13½*** **Wmk. 195**

500 A112 £1 dark green, black & red 8.00 1.00
a. Double ovpt. *50.00*

"Art"
A171

Perf. 13½x13

1960, Mar. 1 **Wmk. 328**

501 A171 10m brown 12 8

Issued to publicize the 3rd Biennial Exhibition of Fine Arts in Alexandria.

Arab League Center, Cairo—A172

1960, Mar. 22 Photo. ***Perf. 13x13½***

502 A172 10m dull green & black 12 8

Opening of Arab League Center and Arab Postal Museum, Cairo.

Refugees Pointing to Map of Palestine—A173

1960, Apr. 7

503 A173 10m orange vermilion 10 8
504 " 35m Prussian blue 35 30

Issued to publicize World Refugee Year, July 1, 1959–June 30, 1960.

Weight Lifter
A174

Stadium, Cairo—A175

Sports: No. 506, Basketball. No. 507, Soccer. No. 508, Fencing. No. 509, Rowing. 30m, Steeplechase (horiz.). 35m, Swimming (horiz.)

Perf. 13½x13

1960, July 23 Photo. **Wmk. 328**

505 A174 5m gray 5 5
506 " 5m brown 5 5
507 " 5m deep claret 10 5
508 " 10m bright carmine 15 5
509 " 10m gray green 15 5
510 " 30m purple 35 15
511 " 35m dark blue 45 20
Nos. 505–511 (7) 1.30 60

Souvenir Sheet

Imperf.

512 A175 100m car. & brn. 1.25 75

Nos. 505–511 issued to commemorate the 17th Olympic Games, Rome, Aug. 25–Sept. 11.

Nos. 505–509 are printed in one sheet of 25 in vertical rows of five.

No. 512 measures 80x75mm, with black marginal inscription.

Dove and U.N. Emblem
A176

Design: 35m, Lights surrounding U.N. emblem (horiz.).

Perf. 13½x13

1960, Oct. 24 **Wmk. 328**

513 A176 10m purple 10 8
514 " 35m bright rose 30 25

15th anniversary of United Nations.

Abu Simbel Temple of Queen Nefertari—A177

Perf. 11x11½

1960, Nov. 14 Photo. **Wmk. 328**

515 A177 10m ocher, *buff* 25 20

Issued as propaganda to save historic monuments in Nubia and in connection with the UNESCO meeting, Paris, Nov. 14.

Model Post Office A178

1961, Jan. 2 *Perf. 13x13½*

516 A178 10m brt. car. rose 12 8

Issued for Post Day, Jan. 2.

Eagle, Fasces and Victory Wreath A179

Wheat and Globe Surrounded by Flags A180

1961, Feb. 22 *Perf. 13½x13*

517 A179 10m dull violet 12 8

3rd anniversary of United Arab Republic.

1961, March 21 **Wmk. 328**

518 A180 10m vermilion 12 8

Issued to publicize the International Agricultural Exhibition, Cairo, March 21–April 20.

Patrice Lumumba and Map A181

Reading Braille and WHO Emblem A182

1961, March 30 *Perf. 13½x13*

519 A181 10m black 12 8

Issued for Africa Day, Apr. 15 and to commemorate the 3rd Conference of Independent African States, Cairo, March 25–31.

1961, Apr. 6 Photogravure

520 A182 10m red brown 12 8

World Health Organization Day. See No. B21.

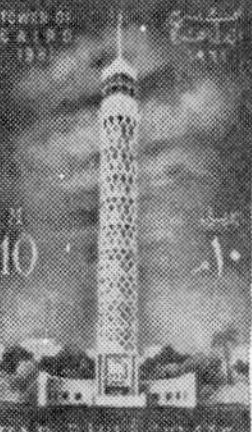

Tower of Cairo A183

Arab Woman and Son, Palestine Map A184

1961, Apr. 11 *Perf. 13½x13*

521 A183 10m greenish blue 12 8

Issued to commemorate the opening of the 600-foot Tower of Cairo, on island of Gizireh. See also No. C95.

1961, May 15 **Wmk. 328**

522 A184 10m bright green 15 8

Issued for Palestine Day.

Symbols of Industry and Electricity A185

Chart and Workers—A186

Designs: No. 524, New buildings and family. No. 525, Ship, train, bus and radio. No. 526, Dam, cotton and field. No. 527, Hand holding candle and family.

Photogravure

1961, July 23 *Perf. 13x13½*

523	A185	10m deep carmine	8	3
524	"	10m bright blue	8	3
525	"	10m dk. vio. brown	8	3
526	"	35m dark green	28	5
527	"	35m bright purple	28	6
		Nos. 523-527 (5)	80	20

Souvenir Sheet

Imperf.

528 A186 100m red brown 1.25 1.25

Nos. 523–528 issued to commemorate the ninth anniversary of the revolution. No. 528 has pale brown border with black inscription. Size: 82x75mm.

Map of Suez Canal and Ships A187

Perf. 11½x11

1961, July 26 **Unwmkd.**

529 A187 10m olive 12 8

Fifth anniversary of the nationalization of the Suez Canal Company.

Various Enterprises of Misr Bank A188

Perf. 13x13½

1961, Aug. 22 **Wmk. 328**

530 A188 10m red brown, *pinkish* 12 8

The 41st anniversary of Misr Bank.

Flag, Ship's Wheel and Battleship A189

1961, Aug. 29 Photo. *Perf. 13½x13*

531 A189 10m deep blue 12 8

Issued for Navy Day.

Eagle of Saladin over Cairo A190

U.N. Emblem, Book, Cogwheel and Corn A191

Type A143 of 1958 Redrawn and Type A190

1961, Aug. 31 *Perf. 11½* **Unwmkd.**

Designs: 1m, Farmer's wife. 4m, 14th century glass lamp. 35m, "Commerce."

532	A143	1m blue	3	3
533	"	4m olive	5	3
534	A190	10m purple	10	3
535	A143	35m slate blue	30	6

Smaller of two Arabic inscriptions in new positions: 1m, at right above Egyptian numeral; 4m, upward to spot beside waist of lamp; 35m, upper left corner below "UAR." On 4m, "UAR" is 2mm. deep instead of 1mm. "Egypt" omitted as in 1959–60.

Perf. 13½x13

1961, Oct. 24 Photo. **Wmk. 328**

Design: 35m, Globe and cogwheel (horiz.).

536 A191 10m black & ochre 10 8
537 " 35m blue green & brown 30 25

Issued to honor the United Nations' Technical Assistance Program and to commemorate the 16th anniversary of the United Nations.

Trajan's Kiosk, Philae—A192

1961, Nov. 4 *Perf. 11½* **Unwmkd.**

Size: 60x27mm.

538 A192 10m deep violet blue 25 20

Issued to commemorate the 15th anniversary of UNESCO, and to publicize UNESCO's help in safeguarding the monuments of Nubia.

Palette, Brushes and Map of Mediterranean A193

Atom and Educational Symbols A194

1961, Dec. 14 *Perf. 13½* **Wmk. 328**

539 A193 10m dark red brown 12 8

Issued to publicize the 4th Biennial Exhibition of Fine Arts in Alexandria.

1961, Dec. 18

540 A194 10m dull purple 12 8

Issued to publicize Education Day.

Arms of U.A.R. A195

1961, Dec. 23 *Perf. 11½* **Unwmkd.**

541 A195 10m br. pink, br. green & black 12 8

Issued to commemorate Victory Day.

Sphinx at Giza A196

1961, Dec. 27 *Perf. 11x11½*

542 A196 10m black 12 8

Issued to publicize the "Sound and Light" Project, the installation of floodlights and sound equipment at the site of the Pyramids and Sphinx.

Post Office Printing Plant, Nasser City—A197

1962, Jan. 2 Photo. *Perf. 11½x11*
543 A197 10m dark brown 12 8
Issued for Post Day, Jan. 2.

Map of Africa, King Mohammed V of Morocco and Flags
A198

1962, Jan. 4 *Perf. 11x11½*
544 A198 10m indigo 12 8
Issued to commemorate the first anniversary of the African Charter, Casablanca.

Girl Scout Saluting and Emblem
A199

Perf. 13x13½

1962, Feb. 22 Wmk. 328
545 A199 10m bright blue 15 10
Egyptian Girl Scouts' 25th anniversary.

Arab Refugees, Flag and Map
A200

Mother and Child
A201

1962, March 7 *Perf. 13½x13*
546 A200 10m dark slate green 12 8
Issued to commemorate the 5th anniversary of the liberation of the Gaza Strip.

1962, March 21 Photogravure
547 A201 10m dark violet brown 12 8
Issued for Arab Mother's Day, March 21.

Map of Africa and Post Horn
A202

1962, Apr. 23 Wmk. 328
548 A202 10m crimson & ochre 12 8
549 " 50m dp. blue & ochre 40 30
Establishment of African Postal Union.

Cadets on Parade and Academy Emblem—A203

1962, June 18 *Perf. 13x13½*
550 A203 10m green 12 8
Issued to commemorate the 150th anniversary of the Egyptian Military Academy.

Malaria Eradication Emblem
A204

Theodor Bilharz
A205

1962, June 20 *Perf. 13½x13*
551 A204 10m dk. brn. & red 12 8
552 " 35m dk. grn. & blue 30 28
Issued for the World Health Organization drive to eradicate malaria.

1962, June 24 *Perf. 11x11½*
553 A205 10m brown orange 12 8
Issued to commemorate the centenary of the death of Dr. Theodor Bilharz (1825–1862), German physician who first described bilharziasis, an endemic disease in Egypt.

Patrice Lumumba and Map of Africa
A206

Hand on Charter
A207

Wmk. 342

Watermarked Coat of Arms, Multiple (342)

1962, July 1 Photogravure
554 A206 10m rose & red 12 8
Issued in memory of Patrice Lumumba (1925–61), Premier of Congo.

1962, July 10 *Perf. 11x11½*
555 A207 10m bright blue & dark brown 12 8
Proclamation of the National Charter.

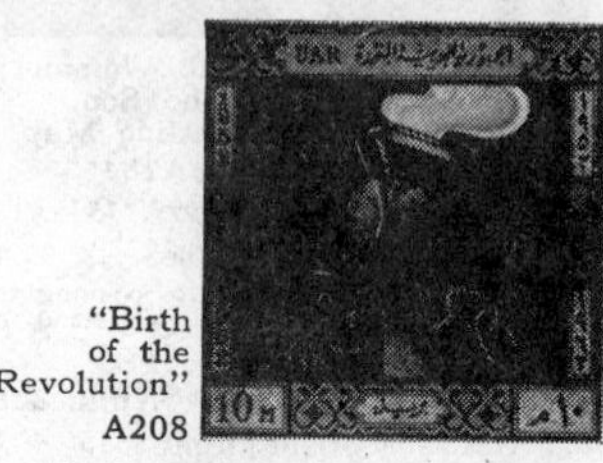

"Birth of the Revolution"
A208

Symbolic Designs: No. 557, Proclamation (Scroll and book). No. 558, Agricultural Reform (Farm and crescent). No. 559, Bandung Conference (Dove, globe and olive branch). No. 560, Birth of UAR (Eagle and flag). No. 561, Industrialization (cogwheel, factory, ship and bus). No. 562, Aswan High Dam. No. 563, Social Revolution (Modern buildings and emblem). 100m, Arms of UAR, emblems of Afro-Asian and African countries and United Nations emblem.

1962, July 23 *Perf. 11½*
556 A208 10m brown, dark red brown & pink 15 8
557 " 10m dark blue & sepia 15 8
558 " 10m sepia & brt. bl. 15 8
559 " 10m olive & dark ultramarine 15 8
560 " 10m grn., blk. & red 15 8
561 " 10m brown orange & indigo 15 8
562 " 10m brown orange & violet blk. 15 8
563 " 10m orange & black 15 9
Nos. 556-563 (8) 1.20 65

Souvenir Sheets

Perf. 11½, Imperf.
564 A208 100m green, pink, red & black 1.25 1.00
Issued to commemorate the tenth anniversary of the revolution. No 564 contains one stamp; green marginal inscription. Size: 71x79mm.

Mahmoud Moukhtar, Museum and Sculpture—A209

1962, July 24 *Perf. 11½x11*
565 A209 10m light violet blue & olive 10 8
Issued to commemorate the opening of the Moukhtar Museum, Island of Gezireh. The sculpture is "La Vestale de Secrets" by Moukhtar.

Flag of Algeria and Map of Africa Showing Algeria
A210

1962, Aug. 15 *Perf. 11x11½*
566 A210 10m multicolored 12 8
Algeria's independence, July 1, 1962.

Rocket, Arms of U.A.R. and Atom Symbol
A211

1962, Sept. 1 Photo. Wmk. 342
567 A211 10m bright green, red & black 12 8
Launching of U.A.R. rockets.

Rifle and Target—A212

Map of Africa, Table Tennis Paddle, Net and Ball—A213

1962, Sept. 18 *Perf. 11½*
568 A212 5m grn., blk. & red 5 5
569 A213 5m grn., blk & red 6 5
570 A212 10m bistre, blue & dark green 12 10
571 A213 10m bistre, blue & dark green 12 10
572 A212 35m dp. ultra., red & black 40 30
573 A213 35m dp. ultra., red & black 40 30
Nos. 568-573 (6) 1.15 90
Issued to commemorate the 38th World Shooting Championships and the First African Table Tennis Tournament. Types A212 and A213 are printed se-tenant at the base in sheets of 70.

Dag Hammarskjold and U.N. Emblem—A214

Perf. 11½x11

1962, Oct. 24 Photo. Wmk. 342

Portrait in Slate Blue
574 A214 5m deep lilac 5 4
575 " 10m olive 12 8
576 " 35m dp. ultramarine 30 30
Issued to honor Dag Hammarskjold, Secretary General of the United Nations, 1953–61, and to commemorate the 17th anniversary of the United Nations.

Condition is the all-important factor of price. Prices quoted are for stamps in fine condition.

Queen Nefertari Crowned by Isis and Hathor
A215

1962, Oct. 31 *Perf. 11½*

577 A215 10m blue & ochre 15 15

Issued to publicize the UNESCO campaign to safeguard the monuments of Nubia.

Jet Trainer, Hawker Hart Biplane and College Emblem
A216

1962. Nov. 2 *Perf. 11½x11*

578 A216 10m blue, dark blue & crimson 12 8

25th anniversary of Air Force College.

14th Century Glass Lamp and "1963"
A217

Yemen Flag and Hand with Torch
A218

1963, Feb. 20 *Perf. 11x11½*

579 A217 4m dark brown, green & carm. 6 4

Issued for use on greeting cards. See also nos. 441, 477.

1963, Mar. 14 Photo. Wmk. 342

580 A218 10m olive & brt. car. 10 8

Establishment of Yemen Arab Republic.

Tennis Player, Pyramids and Globe
A219

Perf. 11½x11

1963, Mar. 20 **Unwmkd.**

581 A219 10m gray, blk. & brn. 10 8

Issued to commemorate the International Lawn Tennis Championships, Cairo.

Cow, U.N. and F.A.O. Emblems
A220

Designs: 10m, Corn, wheat and emblems (vert.). 35m, Wheat, corn and emblems.

Perf. 11½x11, 11x11½

1963, Mar. 21 **Wmk. 342**

582 A220 5m violet & dp. orge. 5 4
583 " 10m ultra. & yellow 10 8
584 " 35m blue, yel. & blk. 30 28

Issued for the "Freedom from Hunger" campaign of the U.N. Food and Agriculture Organization.

Centenary Emblem
A221

Design: 35m, Globe and emblem.

Perf. 11x11½

1963, May 8 **Unwmkd.**

585 A221 10m light blue, red & maroon 10 8
586 " 35m light blue & red 30 25

Centenary of the Red Cross.

Arab Socialist Union Emblem
A222

Design: 50m, Tools, torch and symbol of National Charter.

Photogravure

1963, July 23 ***Perf. 11½*** **Wmk. 342**

587 A222 10m slate & rose pink 10 8

Souvenir Sheets

Perf. 11½, Imperf.

588 A222 50m violet blue & orange yellow 1.00 1.00

Issued to commemorate the 11th anniversary of the revolution and to publicize the Arab Socialist Union. No. 588 contains one stamp, violet blue marginal inscription. Size: 69x80mm.

Television Station, Cairo, and Screen
A223

1963, Aug. 1 ***Perf. 11½x11***

589 A223 10m dark blue & yel. 10 8

Issued to publicize the 2nd International Television Festival, Alexandria, Sept. 1–10.

Queen Nefertari
A224

Swimmer and Map of Suez Canal
A225

Designs: 10m, Great Hypostyle Hall, Abu Simbel. 35m, Ramses in moonlight.

Photogravure

1963, Oct. 1 ***Perf. 11*** **Wmk. 342**

Size: 25x42mm. (5m, 35m); 28x61mm. (10m)

590 A224 5m brt. vio. bl. & yel. 5 4
591 " 10m gray, black & red orange 10 8
592 " 35m orge. yel. & blk. 30 28

Issued to publicize the UNESCO world campaign to save historic monuments in Nubia.

1963, Oct. 15

593 A225 10m blue & salmon rose 10 8

Issued to commemorate the International Suez Canal Swimming Championship.

Ministry of Agriculture—A226

Perf. 11½x11

1963, Nov. 20 **Wmk. 342**

594 A226 10m multicolored 10 8

Issued to commemorate the 50th anniversary of the Ministry of Agriculture.

Modern Building and Map of Africa and Asia—A227

1963, Dec. 7

595 A227 10m multicolored 10 8

Afro-Asian Housing Congress, Dec. 7–12.

Scales, Globe, UN Emblem—A228

1963, Dec. 10

596 A228 5m dark grn. & yel. 8 4
597 " 10m blue, gray & blk. 15 8
598 " 35m rose red, pink & red 40 28

Issued to commemorate the 15th anniversary of the Universal Declaration of Human Rights.

Sculpture, Arms of Alexandria and Palette with Flags
A229

1963, Dec. 12 ***Perf. 11x11½***

599 A229 10m pale blue, dark blue & brown 10 8

Issued to publicize the 5th Biennial Exhibition of Fine Arts in Alexandria.

Lion and Nile Hilton Hotel
A230

Vase, 13th Century
A231

Pharaoh Userkaf (5th Dynasty)
A232

Designs: 1m, Vase, 14th century. 2m, Ivory headrest. 3m, Pharaonic calcite boat. 4m, Minaret and gate. 5m, Nile and Aswan High Dam. 10m, Eagle of Saladin over pyramids. 15m, Window, Ibn Tulun's mosque. No 608, Mitwalli Gate, Cairo. 35m, Nefertari. 40m, Tower Hotel. 55m, Sultan Hassan's Mosque. 60m, Courtyard, Al Azhar University. 200m, Head of Ramses II. 500m, Funerary mask of Tutankhamen.

Photogravure

1964–67 ***Perf. 11*** **Unwmkd.**

Size: Nos. 608, 612, 19x24mm.; others, 24x29mm.

600 A231 1m citron & ultra. 5 3
601 A230 2m magenta & bister 10 5
602 " 3m salmon, org. & bl. 10 5
603 A235 4m ocher, black & ultramarine 25 10
604 A230 5m brown & brt. bl. 10 10
a. 5m brown & dark blue 10 10
605 A231 10m green, dark brn. & lt. brown 10 10
606 A230 15m ultra. & yellow 10 8
607 " 20m brn. orge. & blk. 15 8
608 A231 20m light olive green ('67) 25 8
609 " 30m yellow & brn. 35 10
610 " 35m salmon, ocher & ultramarine 30 10
611 " 40m ultra. & yellow 35 10
612 " 55m brt. red lilac ('67) 50 20
613 " 60m greenish blue & yellow brown 45 20

Wmk. 342

614 A232 100m dark violet brn. & slate 1.00 25
615 " 200m bluish black & & yel. brown 2.50 50
616 " 500m ultramarine & deep orange 4.50 1.00
Nos. 600-616 (17) 11.15 3.12

Nos. 603 and N107 lack the vertically arranged dates which appear at lower right on No. 619.

HSN Commission Emblem
A233

Perf. 11x11½

1964, Jan. 10 Wmk. 342

617 A233 10m dull blue, dark blue & yellow 10 5

Issued to commemorate the first conference of the Commission of Health, Sanitation and Nutrition.

Arab League Emblem—A234

1964, Jan. 13 ***Perf. 11***

618 A234 10m brt. grn. & blk. 10 5

Issued to commemorate the first meeting of the Heads of State of the Arab League, Cairo, January.

Minaret at Night
A235

1964 ***Perf. 11*** **Unwmkd.**

619 A235 4m emerald, blk. & red 8 3

Issued for use on greeting cards. See also No. 603.

Old and New Dwellings and Map of Nubia—A236

Perf. 11½x11

1964, Feb. 27 Photo. Wmk. 342

620 A236 10m dull vio. & yel. 10 8

Resettlement of Nubian population.

Map of Africa and Asia and Train
A237

1964, March 21

621 A237 10m dull blue, dark blue & yellow 8 8

Asian Railway Conference, Cairo, Mar. 21.

Ikhnaton and Nefertiti with Children
A238

1964, Mar. 21 ***Perf. 11x11½***

622 A238 10m dk. brn. & ultra. 8 8

Issued for Arab Mother's Day, March 21.

Arab Postal Union Emblem
A239

World Health Organization Emblem
A240

1964, Apr. 1 Photo. Wmk. 342

623 A239 10m orange brown & blue, *salmon* 8 8

Issued to commemorate the 10th anniversary of the Permanent Office of the Arab Postal Union.

1964, Apr. 7

624 A240 10m dark blue & red 8 8

World Health Day (Anti-Tuberculosis).

Statue of Liberty, World's Fair Pavilion and Pyramids
A241

1964, Apr. 22 ***Perf. 11½x11***

625 A241 10m bright green & olive, *grayish* 8 8

New York World's Fair, 1964–65.

Nile and Aswan High Dam
A242

1964, May 15 ***Perf. 11½*** **Unwmkd.**

626 A242 10m black & blue 8 8

The diversion of the Nile.

"Land Reclamation"—A243

Design: No. 628, "Electricity," Aswan High Dam hydroelectric station.

1964, July 23 ***Perf. 11½***

627 A243 10m yel. & emerald 8 8
628 " 10m green & black 8 8

Issued to publicize land reclamation and hydroelectric power due to the Aswan High Dam.

An imperf. souvenir sheet, issued July 23, contains two 50m black and blue stamps showing Aswan High Dam before and after diversion of the Nile. Black portrait of President Nasser and blue inscription in margin. Size of stamps: 42x26 mm.; size of sheet: 104x81mm. Price $2.25.

Map of Africa and 34 Flags
A244

1964, July 17 Photogravure

629 A244 10m brown, bright blue & black 8 8

Issued to commemorate the Assembly of Heads of State and Government of the Organization for African Unity at Cairo in July.

Jamboree Emblem—A245

Design: No. 631, Emblem of Air Scouts.

1964, Aug. 28 ***Perf. 11½*** **Unwmkd.**

630 A245 10m red, grn. & blk. 12 8
631 " 10m green & red 12 8

The 6th Pan Arab Jamboree, Alexandria.

Flag of Algeria—A246

1964, Sept. 5 ***Perf. 11½x11***

Flags in Original Colors

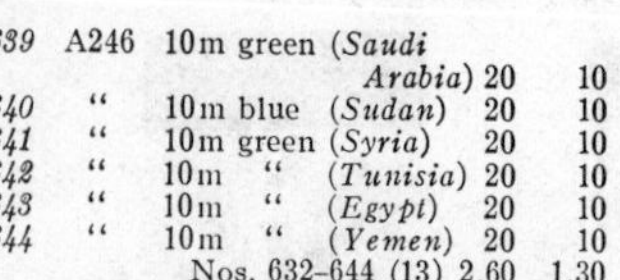

632 A246 10m green (*Algeria*) 20 10
633 " 10m " (*Iraq*) 20 10
634 " 10m " (*Jordan*) 20 10
635 " 10m " (*Kuwait*) 20 10
636 " 10m " (*Lebanon*) 20 10
637 " 10m " (*Libya*) 20 10
638 " 10m " (*Morocco*) 20 10
639 A246 10m green (*Saudi Arabia*) 20 10
640 " 10m blue (*Sudan*) 20 10
641 " 10m green (*Syria*) 20 10
642 " 10m " (*Tunisia*) 20 10
643 " 10m " (*Egypt*) 20 10
644 " 10m " (*Yemen*) 20 10
Nos. 632–644 (13) 2.60 1.30

Issued to commemorate the second meeting of the Heads of State of the Arab League, Alexandria, Sept. 1964.

World Map, Dove, Olive Branches and Pyramids—A247

1964, Oct. 5 ***Perf. 11½***

645 A247 10m slate bl. & yel. 8 8

Issued to commemorate the Conference of Heads of State of Non-Aligned Countries, Cairo, Oct. 1964.

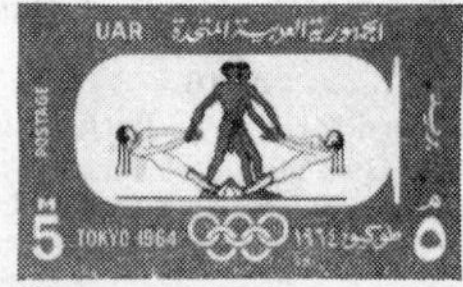

Pharaonic Athletes—A248

Designs from ancient decorations: 10m, Four athletes (vert.). 35m, Wrestlers (vert.). 50m, Pharaoh in chariot hunting.

Perf. 11½x11, 11x11½

1964, Oct. 10 Photo. Unwmkd.

Sizes: 39x22mm., 22x39mm.

646 A248 5m lt. grn. & orge. 4 4
647 " 10m slate blue & light brown 8 8
648 " 35m dull violet & light brown 38 35

Size: 58x24mm.

649 A248 50m ultra. & brn. orange 40 40

18th Olympic Games Tokyo, Oct. 10–25.

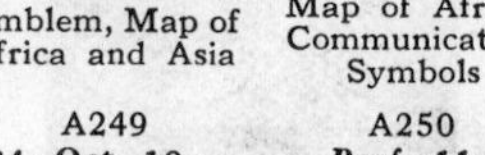

Emblem, Map of Africa and Asia
A249

Map of Africa, Communication Symbols
A250

1964, Oct. 10 ***Perf. 11x11½***

650 A249 10m vio. & yellow 8 8

First Afro-Asian Medical Congress.

1964, Oct. 24

651 A250 10m green & black 8 8

Issued to commemorate the Pan-African and Malagasy Posts and Telecommunications Congress, Cairo, Oct. 24–Nov. 6.

God Horus and Facade, Nefertari Temple, Abu Simbel—A251

Ramses II
A252

Designs: 35m, A god holding rope of life, Abu Simbel. 50m, Isis of Kalabsha (horiz.).

1964, Oct. 24 ***Perf. 11½, 11x11½***

652	A251	5m greenish blue & yel. brown	10	4
653	A252	10m sepia & bright yellow	20	5
654	A251	35m brown orange & indigo	60	35

Souvenir Sheet
Imperf.

655	A252	50m olive & violet black	75	75

Issued to publicize the "Save the Monuments of Nubia" campaign. No. 655 contains one horizontal stamp; violet black and olive marginal inscription. Size: 106x63mm.

Emblems of Cooperation, Rural Handicraft and Women's Work
A253

Perf. 11½x11

1964, Dec. 8 Photo. **Unwmkd.**

656	A253	10m yellow & dk. bl.	8	8

Issued to commemorate the 25th anniversary of the Ministry of Social Affairs.

United Nations and UNESCO Emblems, Pyramids
A254

Minaret, Mardani Mosque
A255

1964, Dec. 24 ***Perf. 11x11½***

657	A254	10m ultra. & yellow	8	8

Issued for UNESCO Day.

1965, Jan. 20 Photo. ***Perf. 11***

658	A255	4m blue & dk. brn.	3	3

Issued for use on greeting cards.

Police Emblem over City
A256

Oil Derrick and Emblem
A257

Perf. 11x11½

1965, Jan. 25 **Wmk. 342**

659	A256	10m black & yellow	8	8

Issued for Police Day.

1965, Mar. 16 Photogravure

660	A257	10m dk. brn. & yel.	8	8

Issued to publicize the 5th Arab Petroleum Congress and the 2nd Arab Petroleum Exhibition.

Flags and Emblem of the Arab League
A258

Red Crescent and WHO Emblem
A259

Design: 20m, Arab League emblem (horiz.).

1965, Mar. 22 **Wmk. 342**

661	A258	10m grn., red & blk.	15	15
662	"	20m ultra. & brn.	16	15

20th anniversary of the Arab League.

1965, Apr. 7 Photogravure

663	A259	10m blue & crimson	8	8

Issued to commemorate World Health Day (Smallpox: Constant Alert).

Dagger in Map of Palestine
A260

1965, Apr. 9 ***Perf. 11x11½***

664	A260	10m black & red	8	8

Deir Yassin massacre, Apr. 9, 1948.

ITU Emblem, Old and New Communication Equipment
A261

1965, May 17 ***Perf. 11½x11***

665	A261	5m vio. blk. & yel.	4	4
666	"	10m red & yellow	8	5
667	"	35m dk. blue, ultra. & yellow	28	25

Issued to commemorate the centenary of the International Telecommunication Union.

Library Aflame and Lamp
A262

1965, June 7 Photo. **Wmk. 342**

668	A262	10m blk., grn. & red	8	5

Issued to commemorate the burning of the Library of Algiers, June 7, 1962.

Sheik Mohammed Abdo
A263

1965, July 11 ***Perf. 11x11½***

669	A263	10m Prus. blue & bister brown	6	5

Issued to commemorate the 60th anniversary of the death of Mohammed Abdo (1850-1905), Mufti of Egypt.

Pouring Ladle (Heavy Industry)
A264

President Gamal Abdel Nasser and Emblems of Arab League, African Unity Organization, Afro-Asian Countries and United Nations
A265

1965, July 23 ***Perf. 11½***

Designs: No. 670, Search for off-shore oil. No. 672, Housing, construction in Nassar City (diamond shaped).

670	A264	10m indigo & lt. bl.	10	10
671	"	10m brown & yellow	10	10
672	A264	10m yel. brn. & blk.	10	10
673	A265	100m lt. grn. & blk.	1.75	1.75

13th anniversary of the revolution.

The 100m was printed in sheets of six, consisting of two singles and two vertical pairs. Margins and gutters contain multiple UAR coat of arms in light green. Size: 240x330mm.

4th Pan Arab Games Emblem
A266

Map and Emblems of Previous Games
A267

Designs: No. 675, Swimmers Zeitun and Abd el Gelil and arms of Alexandria. 35m, Race horse "Saadoon."

Perf. 11½x11; 11½ (#676)

1965, Sept. 2 Photo. **Wmk. 342**

674	A266	5m blue & red	3	3
675	"	10m deep blue & dark brown	15	10
676	A267	10m org. brown & deep blue	15	10
677	A266	35m green & brown	28	25

Issued to publicize the 4th Pan Arab Games, Cairo, Sept. 2-11. No. 675 commemorates the long-distance swimming competition at Alexandria, a part of the Games.

Map of Arab Countries, Emblem of Arab League and Broken Chain—A268

1965, Sept. 13 Photo. ***Perf. 11½***

678	A268	10m brown & yellow	6	5

Issued to commemorate the Third Arab Summit Conference, Casablanca, Sept. 13.

Land Forces Emblem and Sun
A269

Perf. 11x11½

1965, Oct. 20 Wmk. 342

679 A269 10m bister brown & black 6 5

Issued for Land Forces Day.

Map of Africa, Torch and Olive Branches—A270

1965, Oct. 21 *Perf. 11½*

680 A270 10m dull purple & carmine rose 6 5

Issued to commemorate the Assembly of Heads of State of the Organization for African Unity.

Ramses II, Abu Simbel, and ICY Emblem
A271

Pillars, Philae, and U.N. Emblem
A272

Designs: 35m, Two Ramses II statues, Abu Simbel and UNESCO emblem. 50m, Cartouche of Ramses II and ICY emblem (horiz.).

Photogravure

1965, Oct. 24 *Perf. 11½* **Wmk. 342**

681	A271	5m yel. & slate grn.	10	10
682	A272	10m blue & black	35	15
683	A271	35m dk. vio. & yel.	75	25

Souvenir Sheet

Imperf.

684 A272 50m brt. ultra. & dark brown 1.25 1.00

Issued to publicize the international cooperation in saving the Nubian monuments. No. 684 also commemorates the 20th anniversary of the United Nations. No. 684 contains one stamp (42x25m.) and has marginal inscription in bright ultramarine and dark brown. Size: 105x63mm.

Al-Maqrizi, Buildings and Books
A273

Perf. 11½x11

1965, Nov. 20 Photo. Wmk. 342

685 A273 10m olive & dk. slate green 6 5

Issued to commemorate the 600th anniversary of the birth of Ahmed Al-Maqrizi (1365–1442), historian.

Flag of U.A.R., Arms of Alexandria and Art Symbols—A274

1965, Dec. 16 *Perf. 11x11½*

686 A274 10m multicolored 6 5

Issued to publicize the 6th Biennial Exhibition of Fine Arts in Alexandria, Dec. 16, 1965–March 31, 1966.

Parchment Letter, Carrier Pigeon and Postrider—A275

1966, Jan. 2 *Perf. 11½* **Wmk. 342**

687 A275 10m multicolored 10 10

Post Day, Jan. 2. See Nos. CB1–CB2.

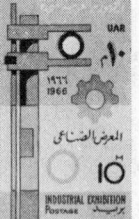

Lamp and Arch
A276

Exhibition Poster
A277

1966, Jan. 10 *Perf. 11* **Unwmkd.**

688 A276 4m vio. & dp. orange 3 3

Issued for use on greeting cards.

Perf. 11x11½

1966, Jan. 27 Wmk. 342

689 A277 10m lt. blue & black 6 5

Industrial Exhibition, Jan. 29–Feb.

Arab League Emblem
A278

Printed Page and Torch
A279

1966, March 22 Photo. Wmk. 342

690 A278 10m brt. yel. & pur. 6 5

Arab Publicity Week, March 22–28.

1966, March 25 *Perf. 11x11½*

691 A279 10m deep orange & slate blue 6 5

Centenary of the national press.

Traffic Signal at Night
A280

Hands Holding Torch, Flags of U.A.R. and Iraq
A281

1966, May 4 Photo. Wmk. 342

692 A280 10m green & red 6 5

Issued for Traffic Day.

1966. May 26 *Perf. 11x11½*

693 A281 10m dp. claret, rose red & brt. green 6 5

Friendship between U.A.R. and Iraq.

Workers and U.N. Emblem
A282

Perf. 11½x11

1966, June 1 Photo. Wmk. 342

694	A282	5m blue green & blk.	3	3
695	"	10m bright rose lilac & green	6	5
696	"	35m orange & black	28	25

Issued to commemorate the 50th session of the International Labor Organization.

Mobilization Dept. Emblem, People and City
A283

1966, June 30 *Perf. 11x11½*

697 A283 10m dull purple & brown 6 5

Population sample, May 31–June 16.

"Salah el Din," Crane and Cogwheel
A284

Present-day Basket Dance and Pharaonic Dance—A285

Designs: No. 699, Transfer of first stones of Abu Simbel. No. 700, Development of Sinai (map of Red Sea area and Sinai Peninsula). No. 701, El Maadi Hospital and nurse with patient.

Perf. 11½

1966, July 23 Photo. Wmk. 342

698	A284	10m org. & multi.	10	10
699	"	10m bright green & multi.	10	10
700	"	10m yel. & multi.	10	10
701	"	10m lt. blue & multi.	10	10

Souvenir Sheet

Imperf.

702 A285 100m multicolored 1.00 1.00

Issued to commemorate the 14th anniversary of the revolution. No. 702 contains one stamp. Size: 115x67mm.

Suez Canal Headquarters, Ships and Map of Canal—A286

1966, July 26 *Perf. 11½*

703 A286 10m bl. & crimson 15 10

Issued to commemorate the 10th anniversary of the nationalization of the Suez Canal.

Cotton, Farmers with Plow and Tractor
A287

Designs: 10m, Rice. 35m, Onions.

Perf. 11½x11

1966, Sept. 9 Photo. Wmk. 342

704	A287	5m purple & lt. blue	3	3
705	"	10m emerald & yel. brown	10	10
706	"	35m blue & orange	28	25

Issued for Farmer's Day.

WHO Headquarters, Geneva
A288

Designs: 10m, U.N. refugee emblem. 35m, UNICEF emblem.

Perf. 11½x11

1966, Oct. 24 Wmk. 342

707 A288 5m olive & brt. pur. 3 3
708 " 10m org. & brt. pur. 10 10
709 " 35m lt. bl. & brt. pur. 28 25

21st anniversary of the United Nations.

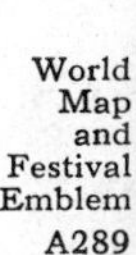

World Map and Festival Emblem
A289

1966, Nov. 8 Photogravure

710 A289 10m brt. pur. & yel. 6 5

Issued to publicize the 5th International Television Festival, Nov. 1–10.

Arms of UAR, Rocket and Pylon
A290

1966, Dec. 23 *Perf. 11½* Wmk. 342

711 A290 10m bright green & car. rose 10 10

Issued for Victory Day.

Jackal
A291

Design: 35m, Alabaster head from Tutankhamen treasure.

1967, Jan. 2 Photogravure

712 A291 10m slate, yel. & brn. 25 20
713 " 35m blue, dark vio. & ocher 45 45

Issued for Post Day, Jan. 2.

Carnations
A292

Workers Planting Tree
A293

1967, Jan. 10 *Perf. 11* Unwmkd.

714 A292 4m citron & purple 5 3

Issued for use on greeting cards.

Perf. 11x11½

1967, Mar. 15 Wmk. 342

715 A293 10m bright green & black violet 8 5

Issued to publicize the Tree Festival.

Gamal el-Dine el-Afaghani and Arab League Emblem
A294

1967, Mar. 22 Photo. Wmk. 342

716 A294 10m dp. green & dk. brown 8 5

Arab Publicity Week, March 22–28.

Census Emblem, Man, Woman and Factory—A295

1967, Apr. 23 *Perf. 11½x11*

717 A295 10m blk. & dp. org. 8 5

First industrial census.

Brickmaking Fresco, Tomb of Rekhmire, Thebes, 1504–1450 B.C.—A296

1967, May 1 Photo. Wmk. 342

718 A296 10m olive & orange 8 5

Issued for Labor Day, 1967.

Ramses II and Queen Nefertari
A297

Design: 35m, Shooting geese, frieze from tomb of Atet at Meidum, c. 2724 B. C.

Perf. 11½x11

1967, June 7 Photo. Wmk. 342

719 A297 10m multicolored 25 20
720 " 35m dk. grn. & org. 45 45
Nos. 719-720, C113-C115 (5) 3.20 1.85

Issued for International Tourist Year, 1967.

President Nasser, Crowd and Map of Palestine
A298

1967, June 22 *Perf. 11½*

721 A298 10m dp. orange, yel. & olive 45 30

Issued to publicize Arab solidarity for "the defense of Palestine."

Souvenir Sheet

National Products—A299

1967, July 23 *Imperf.* Wmk. 342

722 A299 100m multicolored 90 90

Issued to commemorate the 15th anniversary of the revolution. No. 722 contains one stamp with yellow, green and brown margin. Size: 111½x66mm.

Salama Higazi
A300

Perf. 11x11½

1967, Oct. 14 Photo. Wmk. 342

723 A300 20m brn. & dk. blue 12 8

Issued to commemorate the 50th anniversary of the death of Salama Higazi, pioneer of Egyptian lyric stage.

Stag on Ceramic Disk
A301

Design: 55m, Apse showing Christ in Glory, Madonna and Saints, Coptic Museum, and UNESCO Emblem.

1967, Oct. 24 *Perf. 11½*

724 A301 20m dull rose & dark blue 12 8
725 " 55m dk. slate grn. & yellow 45 25

Issued to commemorate the 22nd anniversary of the United Nations. See No. C117.

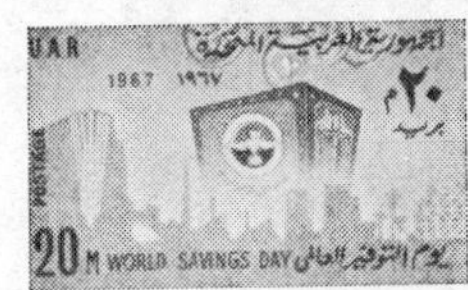

Savings Bank and Postal Authority Emblems—A302

1967, Oct. 31 *Perf. 11½x11*

726 A302 20m salmon pink & dark blue 12 8

International Savings Day.

Rose
A303

Photogravure

1967, Dec. 15 *Perf. 11* Unwmkd.

727 A303 5m grn. & rose lilac 5 3

Issued for use on greeting cards.

Pharaonic Dress
A304

Aswan High Dam and Power Lines
A305

Designs: Various pharaonic dresses from temple decorations.

Perf 11x11½

1968, Jan. 2 Wmk. 342

728 A304 20m brown, green & buff 25 10
729 " 55m lt. grn., yellow & sepia 75 25
730 " 80m dk. brown, bl. & brt. rose 1.25 50

Issued for Post Day, Jan. 2.

1968, Jan. 9

731 A305 20m yellow, blue & dk. brown 10 8

Issued to commemorate the first electricity generated by the Aswan Hydroelectric Station.

Alabaster Vessel, Tutankhamen Treasure
A306

Girl, Moon and Paint Brushes
A308

Capital of Coptic Limestone Pillar
A307

Perf. 11x11½, 11½

1968, Jan. 20 Photo. Wmk. 342

732 A306 20m dk. ultra., yel. & brown 15 10
733 A307 80m lt. green, dk. purple & olive green 40 35

2nd International Festival of Museums.

1968, Feb. 15 ***Perf. 11x11½***

734 A308 20m brt. bl. & black 10 8

Issued to publicize the 7th Biennial Exhibition of Fine Arts, Alexandria, Feb. 15.

Cattle and Veterinarian
A309

Perf. 11½x11

1968, May 4 Photo. **Wmk. 342**

735 A309 20m brown, yellow & green 10 8

8th Arab Veterinary Congress, Cairo.

Human Rights Flame
A310

Perf. 11x11½

1968, July 1 Photo. **Wmk. 342**

736 A310 20m citron, crimson & green 12 8

737 " 60m sky blue, crim. & green 36 30

International Human Rights Year, 1968.

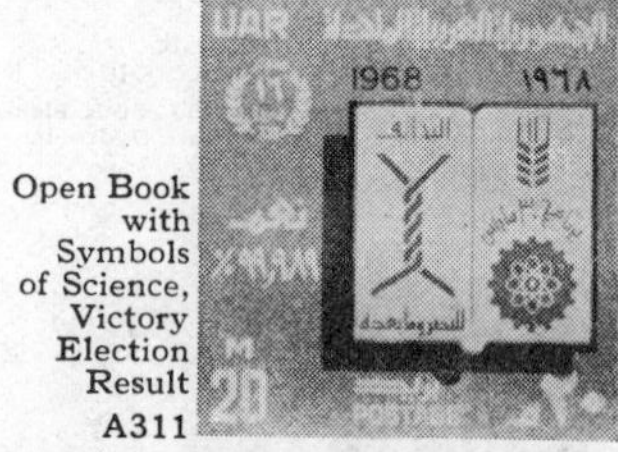

Open Book with Symbols of Science, Victory Election Result
A311

Workers, Cogwheel with Coat of Arms and Open Book
A312

1968, July 23 ***Perf. 11½***

738 A311 20m rose red & slate green 12 8

Souvenir Sheet

Imperf.

739 A312 100m lt. green, org. & purple 1.00 1.00

16th anniversary of the revolution.
No. 739 has orange marginal inscription and the ornaments. Size: 116x68mm.

Imhotep and WHO Emblem—A313

Design: No. 741, Avicenna and WHO emblem.

Perf. 11½x11

1968, Sept. 1 Photo. **Wmk. 342**

740 A313 20m bl., yel. & brn. 30 10

741 " 20m yel., blue & brn. 30 10

Issued to commemorate the 20th anniversary of the World Health Organization. Nos. 740–741 printed in checkerboard sheets of 50 (5x10).

Table Tennis
A314

Perf. 11x11½

1968, Sept. 20 Photo. **Wmk. 342**

742 A314 20m light green & dark brown 12 8

First Mediterranean Table Tennis Tournament, Alexandria, Sept. 20–27.

Factories and Fair Emblem
A315

1968, Oct. 20 ***Perf. 11½*** **Wmk. 342**

743 A315 20m blue gray, red & slate blue 12 8

Cairo International Industrial Fair.

Temples of Philae—A316

Refugees, Map of Palestine, Refugee Year Emblem
A317

Design: 55m, Temple at Philae and UNESCO emblem.

1968, Oct. 24 **Photogravure**

744 A316 20m multicolored 12 8

745 A317 30m " 25 20

746 " 55m lt. blue, yellow & black 50 26

Issued for United Nations Day, Oct. 24.

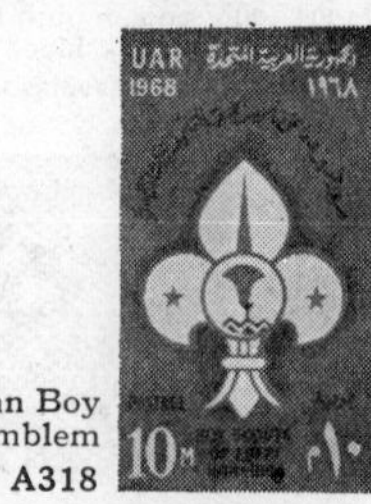

Egyptian Boy Scout Emblem
A318

1968, Nov. 1

747 A318 10m dull orange & violet blue 6 4

50th anniversary of Egyptian Boy Scouts.

Pharaonic Sports
A319

Design: 30m, Pharaonic sports (different).

1968, Nov. 1

748 A319 20m pale olive, pale salm. & black 12 8

749 " 30m pale blue, buff & purple 18 15

Issued to commemorate the 19th Olympic Games, Mexico City, Oct. 12–27.

Aly Moubarak
A320

Lotus
A321

1968, Nov. 9 ***Perf. 11½***

750 A320 20m green, brown & bister 25 8

Issued to honor Aly Moubarak (1823–1893), founder of the modern educational system in Egypt.

1968, Dec. 11 Photo. **Wmk. 342**

751 A321 5m brt. blue, green & yellow 10 3

Issued for use on greeting cards.

Son of Ramses III
A322

Hefni Nassef
A323

Pharaonic Dress: No. 753, Ramses III. No. 754, Girl carrying basket on her head. 55m, Queen of the New Empire in transparent dress.

1969, Jan. 2 Photo. ***Perf. 11½***

752 A322 5m blue & multi. 20 5

753 " 20m " " 25 10

754 " 20m " " 30 15

755 " 55m " " 70 35

Issued for Post Day, Jan. 2.

Perf. 11x11½

1969, Mar. 2 Photo. **Wmk. 342**

Portrait: No. 757, Mohammed Farid.

756 A323 20m purple & brown 30 10

757 " 20m emerald & brn. 30 10

Issued to commemorate the 50th anniversaries of the death of Hefni Nassef (1860–1919) writer and government worker, and of Mohammed Farid (1867–1919), lawyer and Speaker of the Nationalist Party. Nos. 756–757 printed se-tenant in sheets of 50 (10x5).

Teacher and Children
A324

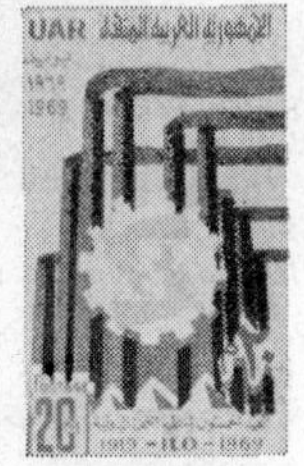

ILO Emblem and Factory Chimneys
A325

1969, Mar. 2 ***Perf. 11x11½***

758 A324 20m multicolored 25 8

Arab Teacher's Day.

1969, Apr. 11 Photo. **Wmk. 342**

759 A325 20m brown, ultra. & carmine 25 8

Issued to commemorate the 50th anniversary of the International Labor Organization.

Flag of Algeria, Africa Day and Tourist Year Emblems—A326

Wmk. 342

1969, May 25 Litho. ***Perf. 11½x11***

Flags in Original Colors

760 A326 10m green (*Algeria*) 20 12

761 " 10m " (*Botswana*) 20 12

762 " 10m " (*Burundi*) 20 12

763 " 10m " (*Cameroun*) 20 12

764 " 10m blue (*Cent. Afr. Rep.*) 20 12

765 " 10m blue (*Chad*) 20 12

766 " 10m " (*Congo, ex-Belgian*) 20 12

767 " 10m green (*Congo, ex-French*) 20 12

768 " 10m green (*Dahomey*) 20 12

769 " 10m blue (*Equatorial Guinea*) 20 12

770 " 10m blue (*Ethiopia*) 20 12

771 " 10m " (*Gabon*) 20 12

772 " 10m green (*Gambia*) 20 12

773 " 10m " (*Ghana*) 20 12

774 " 10m " (*Guinea*) 20 12

775 " 10m " (*Ivory Coast*) 20 12

776 " 10m green (*Kenya*) 20 12

777 " 10m " (*Lesotho*) 20 12

778 " 10m blue (*Liberia*) 20 12

779 " 10m green (*Libya*) 20 12

780 " 10m " (*Malagasy*) 20 12

781 " 10m " (*Malawi*) 20 12

782 " 10m " (*Mali*) 20 12

783 " 10m " (*Mauritania*) 20 12

784 " 10m blue (*Mauritius*) 20 12

785 " 10m green (*Morocco*) 20 12

786 " 10m " (*Niger*) 20 12

787 " 10m " (*Nigeria*) 20 12

788 " 10m green (*Rwanda*) 20 12

789 " 10m " (*Senegal*) 20 12

790 " 10m " (*Sierra Leone*) 20 12

791 " 10m green (*Somalia*) 20 12

792 " 10m blue (*Sudan*) 20 12

793 A326 10m vio. (*Swaziland*) 20 12
794 " 10m bl. (*Tanzania*) 20 12
795 " 10m green (*Togo*) 20 12
796 " 10m " (*Tunisia*) 20 12
797 " 10m black (*Uganda*) 20 12
798 " 10m green (*Egypt*) 20 12
799 " 10m " (*Upper Volta*) 20 12
800 " 10m blue (*Zambia*) 20 12
Nos. 760-800 (41) 8.20 4.92

Year of African Tourism, 1969.

El Fetouh Gate, Cairo
A327

Sculptures from the Egyptian Museum, Cairo—A328

Millenary of Cairo—A329

Designs: No. 802, Al Azhar University. No. 803, The Citadel. No. 805, Sculptures, Coptic Museum. No. 806, Glass plate and vase, Fatimid dynasty, Islamic Museum. No. 807a, Islamic coin. No. 807b, Fatimist era jewelry. No. 807c, Copper vase. No. 807d, Coins and plaque.

Perf. 11½x11

1969, July 23 Photo. Wmk. 342

801 A327 10m dark brown & multi. 10 4
802 " 10m green & multi. 10 4
803 " 10m blue & multi. 10 4

Perf. 11½

804 A328 20m yellow green & multi. 25 10
805 " 20m dp. ultra. & multi. 25 10
806 " 20m brown & multi. 25 10
Nos. 801-806 (6) 1.05 42

Souvenir Sheet

807 A329 Souv. sheet of 4 1.25 1.25
a. 20m dark blue & multicolored 18 12
b. 20m lilac & multicolored 18 12
c. 20m yel. & multi. 18 12
d. 20m dark green & multicolored 18 12

Issued to commemorate the millenium of the founding of Cairo. No. 807 has pale lilac margin and dark blue inscription. Size: 128x70mm.

African Development Bank Emblem
A330

Perf. 11x11½

1969, Sept. 10 Photo. Wmk. 342

808 A330 20m emerald, yellow & violet 25 8

Issued to publicize the 5th anniversary of the African Development Bank.

Pharaonic Boat and UN Emblem
A331

Temple of Philae Inundated and UNESCO Emblem
A332

Design: 5m, King and Queen from Abu Simbel Temple and UNESCO Emblem (size: 21x38mm.).

Perf. 11x11½, 11½x11

1969, Oct. 24 Photo. Wmk. 342

809 A332 5m brown & multi. 5 3
810 A331 20m yellow & ultra. 25 8

Perf. 11½

811 A332 55m yellow & multi. 45 22

Issued for United Nations Day.

Ships of 1869 and 1967 and Maps of Africa and Suez Canal—A333

1969, Nov. 15 *Perf. 11½x11*

812 A333 20m lt. blue & multi. 25 8

Centenary of the Suez Canal.

Cairo Opera House and Performance of Aida—A334

1969, Nov. 15

813 A334 20m multicolored 25 8

Centenary of the Cairo Opera House.

Crowd with Egyptian and Revolutionary Flags—A335

1969, Nov. 15 *Perf. 11½x11*

814 A335 20m brt. green, dull lilac & red 25 8

Revolution of 1919.

Ancient Arithmetic and Computer Cards—A336

Perf. 11½x11

1969, Dec. 17 Photo. Wmk. 342

815 A336 20m multicolored 25 8

Issued to publicize the International Congress for Scientific Accounting, Cairo, Dec. 17–19.

Poinsettia
A337

Sakkara Step Pyramid
A338

El Fetouh Gate, Cairo
A339

Fountain, Sultan Hassan Mosque, Cairo
A340

King Khafre (Ruled c. 2850 B.C.)
A341

1969, Dec. 24 *Perf. 11* **Unwmkd.**

816 A337 5m yel., grn. & car. 3 3

Issued for use on greeting cards.

Photo.; Engr. (20m, 55m)

Unwmkd.; Wmk. 342 (20m, £1)

1969–70 *Perf. 11*

Designs: 5m, Al Azhar Mosque. 10m, Luxor Temple. 50m, Qaitbay Fort, Alexandria.

817 A338 1m multi. ('70) 3 3
818 " 5m " ('70) 3 3
819 " 10m " ('70) 6 4
820 A339 20m dark brown 40 8
821 A338 50m multi. ('70) 30 20
822 A340 55m slate green 75 22

Perf. 11½

Photo. and Engr.

823 A341 £1 orange & slate green ('70) 5.00 4.00
Nos. 817-823 (7) 6.57 4.60

See Nos. 889–891, 893–897, 899, 901–902, 904.

Veiled Women, by Mahmoud Said
A342

Perf. 11x11½

1970, Jan. 2 Photo. Wmk. 342

Size: 45x89mm.

824 A342 100m blue & multi. 1.75 45

Post Day, Jan. 2. Sheet of 8 with two panes of 4.

Parliament, Scales, Globe and Laurel—A343

1970, Feb. 2 *Perf. 11½x11*

825 A343 20m blue, violet blue & ocher 25 8

Issued to publicize the International Conference of Parliamentarians on the Middle East Crisis, Cairo, Feb. 2–5.

Map of Arab League Countries, Flag and Emblem—A344

Perf. 11½x11

1970, Mar. 22 Photo. Wmk. 342

826 A344 30m brn. orange, grn. & dk. purple 25 12

Issued to commemorate the 25th anniversary of the Arab League. See No. B42.

Mena House and Sheraton Hotel
A345

1970, Mar. 23

827 A345 20m olive, org. & bl. 25 8

Issued to commemorate the centenary of Mena House and the inauguration of the Cairo Sheraton Hotel.

Manufacture of Medicine—A346

1970, Apr. 20

828 A346 20m brn., yel. & blue 25 8

Issued to commemorate the 30th anniversary of the production of medicines in Egypt.

Mermaid
A347

1970, Apr. 20 ***Perf. 11x11½***

829 A347 20m orange, black & ultramarine 25 8

Issued to publicize the 8th Biennial Exhibition of Fine Arts, Alexandria, March 12.

Misr Bank and Talaat Harb
A348

ITU Emblem
A349

1970, May 7 Photo. **Wmk. 342**

830 A348 20m multicolored 25 8

50th anniversary of Misr Bank.

1970, May 17 ***Perf. 11x11½***

831 A349 20m dk. brn., yellow & dull blue 25 8

World Telecommunications Day.

U.P.U. Head-quarters, Bern
A350

1970, May 20 ***Perf. 11½x11***

832 A350 20m multicolored 25 8

Issued to commemorate the inauguration of the new Universal Postal Union Headquarters in Bern. See No. C128.

Basketball Player and Map of Africa
A351

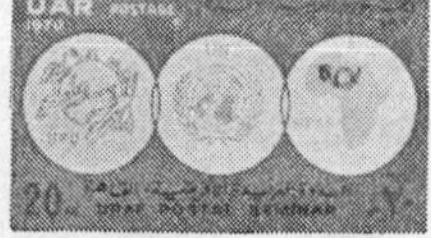

U.P.U., U.N. and U.P.A.F. Emblems
A352

Designs: No. 834, Soccer player, map of Africa and cup (horiz.).

Perf. 11x11½, 11½x11

1970, May 25 Photo. **Wmk. 342**

833 A351 20m lt. blue, yellow & brown 25 8
834 " 20m yellow & multi. 25 8
835 A352 20m ocher, green & black 25 8

Issued for Africa Day. No. 833 also commemorates the 5th African basketball championship for men; No. 834 the annual African Soccer championship and No. 835 publicizes the African Postal Union seminar.

Fist and Freed Bird
A353

1970, July 23 Photo. ***Perf. 11***

836 A353 20m lt. green, orange & black 25 8

Souvenir Sheet

Imperf.

837 A353 100m lt. blue, deep org. & blk. 1.00 45

Issued to commemorate the 18th anniversary of the revolution. No. 837 contains one stamp; U.N. emblem, Scales of Justice and orange commemorative inscription in margin. Size: 110x70mm.

Al Aqsa Mosque on Fire—A354

1970, Aug. 21 ***Perf. 11*** **Wmk. 342**

838 A354 20m multicolored 25 8
839 " 60m brt. bl. & multi. 50 24

First anniversary of the burning of Al Aqsa Mosque, Jerusalem.

Standardization Emblems
A355

1970, Oct. 14 ***Perf. 11*** **Wmk. 342**

840 A355 20m yellow, ultra. & green 25 8

Issued to commemorate World Standards Day and the 25th anniversary of the International Standardization Organization, ISO.

U.N. Emblem, Scales and Dove
A356

Temple at Philae
A357

Child, Education Year and U.N. Emblems
A358

Designs: 10m, U.N. emblem. No. 845, Second Temple at Philae (denomination at left).

Perf. 11 (5m), 11½ (others)

1970, Oct. 24 Photo. **Wmk. 342**

841 A356 5m lt. bl., rose lilac & slate 10 10
842 A357 10m yellow, brown & light blue 15 10
843 A358 20m slate & multi. 25 15
844 A357 55m brn., bl. & ocher 45 25
845 " 55m " " " 45 25
Strip of 3 (#842, 844–845) 1.05 60
Nos. 841–845, B43 (6) 1.90 1.05

Issued to commemorate the 25th anniversary of the United Nations. No. 843 also commemorates International Education Year; Nos. 842, 844–845 commemorate the work of UNESCO in saving the Temples of Philae; Nos. 842, 844–845 printed se-tenant in sheets of 35 (15 No. 842 and 10 each Nos. 844–845). Nos. 844–845 show continuous picture of the Temples at Philae.

Gamal Abdel Nasser
A359

1970, Nov. 6 ***Perf. 11*** **Wmk. 342**

846 A359 5m sky blue & black 8 3
847 " 20m gray grn. & blk. 25 8

Issued in memory of Gamal Abdel Nasser (1918–1970), President of Egypt. See Nos. C129–C130.

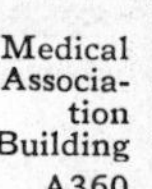

Medical Association Building
A360

Designs: No. 849, Old and new National Library. No. 850, Egyptian Credo (Nasser quotation). No. 851, Engineering Society, old and new buildings. No. 852, Government Printing Offices, old and new buildings.

1970, Dec. 20 Photo. ***Perf. 11***

848 A360 20m yel., grn. & brn. 25 8
849 " 20m grn. & multi. 25 8
850 " 20m lt. bl. & brown 25 8
851 " 20m bl., yel. & brn. 25 8
852 " 20m " " " 25 8
Nos. 848–852 (5) 1.25 40

Nos. 848–852 printed se-tenant in sheets of 50 (5x10) commemorate: 50th anniversary of Egyptian Medical Association (No. 848); centenary of National Library (No. 849); Egyptian Engineering Association (No. 851) sesquicentennial of Government Printing Offices (No. 852).

Map and Flags of UAR, Libya, Sudan
A361

1970, Dec. 27 ***Perf. 11½***

853 A361 20m lt. green, car. & black 25 8

Signing of the Charter of Tripoli affirming the unity of UAR, Libya and the Sudan, Dec. 27, 1970.

Qalawun Minaret
A362

Designs (Minarets): 10m, As Saleh. 20m, Isna. 55m, Al Hakim.

1971, Jan. 2 ***Perf. 11*** **Wmk. 342**

854 A362 5m green & multi. 5 3
855 " 10m " " 15 4
856 " 20m " " 25 8
857 " 55m " " 55 20
Strip of 4 (Nos. 854–857) + label 1.00 35

Post Day, 1971. Nos. 854–857 printed se-tenant in sheets of 40 stamps and 10 blue and yellow labels.

See Nos. 905–908, 932–935.

Gamal Abdel Nasser
A363

Photogravure and Engraved

1971 ***Perf. 11½*** **Wmk. 342**

858 A363 200m brn. violet & dark blue 2.50 1.00
859 " 500m blue & black 6.00 2.75

Souvenir Sheet

Design: Portrait facing right.

Imperf.

860 A363 Sheet of 2 6.00 3.75
a. 100m light green & black 3.00 1.00
b. 200m blue & black 2.25 1.75

No. 860 commemorates inauguration of the Aswan High Dam, which is shown in margin. Green and blue marginal inscription. Size: 134x79mm.

Issue dates: No. 860, Jan. 15; Nos. 858–859, Feb. 1.

See No. 903.

Cotton and Globe
A364

1971, Mar. 6 Photo. *Perf. 11½x11*
861 A364 20m light green, blue & brown 25 10
Egyptian cotton.

Arab Countries, and Arab Postal Union Emblem
A365

1971, Mar. 6 Wmk. 342
862 A365 20m lt. blue, orange & slate green 25 10
9th Arab Postal Congress, Cairo, March 6–25. See No. C131.

Cairo Fair Emblem
A366

1971, Mar. 6 *Perf. 11x11½*
863 A366 20m plum, black & orange 25 10
Cairo International Fair, March 2–23.

Nesy Ra, Apers Papyrus and WHO Emblem—A367

Perf. 11½x11

1971, Apr. 30 Photo. Wmk. 342
864 A367 20m yellow bister & purple 25 10
World Health Organization Day.

Gamal Abdel Nasser
A368

1971, May 1 *Perf. 11*
865 A368 20m pur. & bl. gray 12 8
866 " 55m blue & purple 33 20

Map of Africa, Telecommunications Symbols
A369

1971, May 17 *Perf. 11½x11*
867 A369 20m bl. & multi. 25 10
Pan-African telecommunications system.

Wheelwright
A370

Hand Holding Wheat and Laurel
A371

Candle Lighting Africa—A372

Perf. 11x11½

1971, July 23 Photo. Wmk. 342
868 A370 20m yel. & multi. 25 8
869 A371 20m tan, green & ocher 25 8

Souvenir Sheet
Imperf.
870 A372 100m blue & multi. 1.00 60
19th anniversary of the July Revolution. No. 870 contains one stamp with simulated perforations in gold and with blue marginal inscription. Portrait of Pres. Nasser in margin. Size: 115x70mm.

Arab Postal Union Emblem
A373

1971, Aug. 3 *Perf. 11½*
871 A373 20m blk., yel. & grn. 25 8
25th anniversary of the Conference of Sofar, Lebanon, establishing the Arab Postal Union. See No. C135.

Arab Republic of Egypt

Three Links
A374

Perf. 11½x11

1971, Sept. 28 Photo. Wmk. 342
872 A374 20m gray, org. brn. & black 25 10
Confederation of Arab Republics (Egypt, Syria and Libya). See No. C136.

Gamal Abdel Nasser
A375

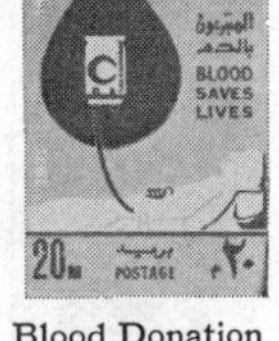

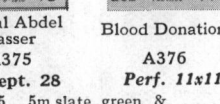

Blood Donation
A376

1971, Sept. 28 *Perf. 11x11½*
873 A375 5m slate green & violet brown 3 3
874 " 20m violet brown & ultra. 12 8
875 " 30m ultra. & brown 18 12
876 " 55m brn. & emerald 33 20
First anniversary of the death of President Gamal Abdel Nasser.

1971, Oct. 24
877 A376 20m green & carmine 25 8
"Blood Saves Lives."

Princess Nursing Child, UNICEF Emblem
A377

Submerged Pillar, Philae, UNESCO Emblem
A379

Equality Year Emblem
A378

Perf. 11x11½, 11½x11

1971, Oct. 24 Photo. Wmk. 342
878 A377 5m buff, black & orange brown 5 3
879 A378 20m red brn., green, yel. & black 25 8
880 A379 55m black, lt. blue, yel. & brown 50 20
United Nations Day. No. 878 honors U.N. International Children's Fund; No. 879 for International Year Against Racial Discrimination; No. 880 honors U.N. Educational, Scientific and Cultural Organization. See No. C137.

Postal Traffic Center, Alexandria
A380

1971, Oct. 31 *Perf. 11½x11*
881 A380 20m blue & bister 25 8
Opening of Postal Traffic Center in Alexandria.

Sunflower
A381

Abdalla El Nadim
A382

1971, Nov. 13 *Perf. 11*
882 A381 5m lt. blue & multi. 10 5
For use on greeting cards.

1971, Nov. 14 *Perf. 11x11½*
883 A382 20m green & brown 25 10
Abdalla El Nadim (1845–1896), journalist, publisher, connected with Orabi Revolution.

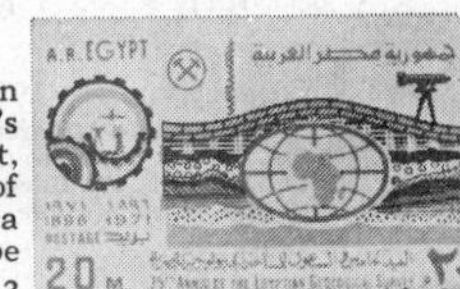

Section of Earth's Crust, Map of Africa on Globe
A383

1971, Nov. 27 *Perf. 11½x11*
884 A383 20m ultra., yellow & brown 25 10
75th anniversary of Egyptian Geological Survey and International Conference, Nov. 27–Dec. 1.

Postal Union Emblem, Letter and Dove
A384

Design: 55m, African Postal Union emblem and letter.

1971, Dec. 2
885 A384 5m multicolored 5 3
886 " 20m olive, black & orange 25 8
887 " 55m red, blk. & blue 50 20
10th anniversary of African Postal Union. See No. C138.

Money and Safe Deposit Box
A385

1971, Dec. 23 *Perf. 11½*
888 A385 20m rose, brn. & grn. 25 8
70th anniversary of Postal Savings Bank.

Types of 1969–70, 1971 Inscribed "A. R. Egypt" and

Ramses II
A385a

Designs as before and: No. 894, King Citi I. No. 897, Queen Nefertari. No. 900, Sphinx and Middle Pyramid. 100m, Cairo Mosque. 200m, Head of Pharaoh Userkaf.

Photogravure

1972–76 ***Perf. 11*** **Unwmkd.**

889	A338	1m multicolored	3	3
890	"	1m dk. brn. ('73)	3	3
891	"	5m multicolored	3	3
892	A385a	5m olive ('73)	3	3
892A	"	5m olive, wmk. 342 ('76)	3	3
893	A338	10m multicolored	7	5
894	"	10m lt. brn. ('73)	5	3
895	A339	20m olive	40	20
896	"	20m purple ('73)	10	3
897	A338	50m multicolored	33	22
898	A385a	50m dull bl. ('73)	25	15
899	A340	55m red lilac	36	24

Perf. 11½ **Wmk. 342**

900	A340	55m green ('74)	75	40
901	A339	100m lt. blue, dp. org. & black	50	35

Photogravure and Engraved

902	A341	200m yellow green & brown	1.00	70
903	A363	500m blue & choc.	2.30	1.50
904	A341	£1 orange & slate green	4.60	3.50
		Nos. 889-904 (17)	10.86	7.52

Minaret Type of 1971

Designs: 5m, West Minaret, Nasser Mosque. 20m, East Minaret, Nasser Mosque. 30m, Minaret, Al Gawli Mosque. 55m, Minaret, Ibn Tulun Mosque.

Photogravure

1972, Jan. 2 ***Perf. 11*** **Wmk. 342**

905	A362	5m dk. grn. & multi.	3	3
906	"	20m " "	14	9
907	"	30m " "	20	14
908	"	55m " "	36	25
		Strip of 4 (Nos. 905-908) + label	73	51

Post Day, 1972. Nos. 905-908 printed se-tenant in sheets of 40 stamps and 10 blue and yellow labels.

Police Emblem and Activities
A386

1972, Jan. 25 ***Perf. 11½***

909	A386	20m dull blue, brown & yellow	25	9

Police Day 1972.

UNESCO, U.N. and Book Year Emblems
A387

1972, Jan. 25 ***Perf. 11x11½***

910	A387	20m lt. yel. grn., vio. blue & yellow	25	9

International Book Year 1972.

Alexandria Biennale
A388

1972, Feb. 15 ***Perf. 11½*** **Wmk. 342**

911	A388	20m black, brt. rose & yellow	14	9

9th Biennial Exhibition of Fine Arts, Alexandria, March, 1972.

Fair Emblem
A389

Abdel Moniem Riad
390

1972, March 5 ***Perf. 11x11½***

912	A389	20m blue, orange & yellow green	25	9

International Cairo Fair.

1972, Mar. 21 **Photo.** **Wmk. 342**

913	A390	20m blue & brown	25	9

In memory of Brig. Gen. Abdel Moniem Riad (1919–1969), military hero.

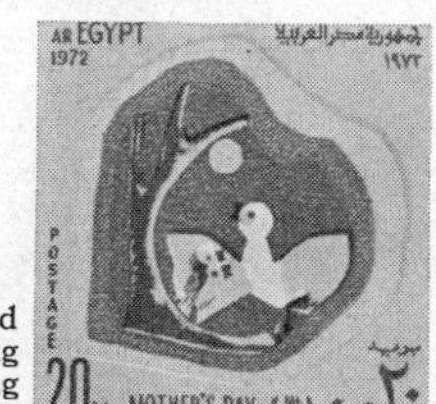

Bird Feeding Young
A391

1972, Mar. 21 ***Perf. 11½***

914	A391	20m yel. & multi.	25	9

Mother's Day.

Tutankhamen
A392

Design: 55m, Back of chair with king's name and symbols of eternity.

1972, May 22 **Unwmkd.**

915	A392	20m gray, black & ocher	50	20
916	"	55m purple & yel.	1.00	30

50th anniversary of the discovery of the tomb of Tutankhamen by Howard Carter and Lord Carnarvon. See Nos. C142-C144.

Queen Nefertiti
A393

Perf. 11½

1972, May 22 **Photo.** **Wmk. 342**

917	A393	20m red, blk. & gold	10	7

50th anniversary of the Society of the Friends of Art.

Map of Africa
A394

1972, May 25 ***Perf. 11x11½***

918	A394	20m pur., bl. & brn.	25	7

Africa Day.

Atom Symbol, "Faith and Science"
A395

Design: No. 920, Egyptian coat of arms.

1972, July 23 ***Perf. 11½***

919	A395	20m bl., claret & blk.	15	7
920	"	20m olive grn., gold & black	15	7

20th anniversary of the revolution.

Boxing, Olympic and Motion Emblems—A396

Designs (Olympic and Motion Emblems and): 10m, Wrestling. 20m, Basketball.

1972, Aug. 17 ***Perf. 11½x11***

921	A396	5m blue & multi.	3	3
922	"	10m yellow & multi.	5	4
923	"	20m verm. & multi.	10	7
		Nos. 921-923, C149-C152 (7)	1.01	66

20th Olympic Games, Munich, Aug. 26–Sept. 11.

Flag of Confederation of Arab Republics—A397

1972, Sept. 1 ***Perf. 11½*** **Wmk. 342**

924	A397	20m carmine, bister & black	15	7

First anniversary of Confederation of Arab Republics.

Red Crescent, TB and UN Emblems
A398

Heart and WHO Emblem
A399

Refugees, UNRWA Emblem, Map of Palestine—A400

Design: 55m, Inundated Temple of Philae, UNESCO emblem.

1972, Oct. 24 **Photo.** ***Perf. 11x11½***

925	A398	10m brn. orange, red & blue	5	3

Perf. 11½

926	A399	20m grn., yel. & blk.	10	7

Perf. 11

927	A400	30m lt. blue, purple & lt. brown	15	10

Perf. 11½

928	A399	55m brown, gold & bluish gray	27	18

United Nations Day. No. 925 commemorates the 14th Regional Tuberculosis Conference, Cairo, 1972; No. 926 is for World Health Month; No. 927 publicizes aid to refugees and No. 928 the U.N. campaign to save the Temples at Philae.

Morning Glory
A401

1972, Oct. 24 ***Perf. 11***

929	A401	10m yel., lilac & green	5	3

For use on greeting cards.

"Seeing Eye"
A402

1972, Nov. 30 ***Perf. 11½***

930	A402	20m multicolored	15	7

Social Work Day.

Sculling Race, View of Luxor—A403

1972, Dec. 17 ***Perf. 11*** **Wmk. 342**

931	A403	20m blue & brown	10	7

Third Nile International Rowing Festival, Dec. 1972.

Minaret Type of 1971

Minarets: 10m, Al Maridani, 1338. 20m, Bashtak, 1337. 30m, Qusun, 1330. 55m, Al Gashankir, 1306.

1973, Jan. 2

Frame in Brt. Yel. Green

932	A362	10m multicolored	5	3
933	"	20m "	10	7
934	"	30m "	15	10
935	"	55m "	27	18
		Strip of 4 (#932–935) + label	57	38

Post Day, 1973. Nos. 932–935 printed se-tenant in sheets of 40 stamps and 10 yellow and green labels.

Cairo Fair Emblem

A404

Perf. 11½x11

1973, Mar. 21 Photo. Wmk. 342

936 A404 20m gray & multi. 10 7

International Cairo Fair.

Family

A405

1973, Mar. 21 ***Perf. 11x11½***

937 A405 20m multicolored 10 7

Family planning.

Sania Girls' School and Hoda Sharawi

A406

Perf. 11½x11

1973, July 15 Photo. Wmk. 342

938 A406 20m ultra., green & brown 10 7

Centenary of education for girls and 50th anniversary of the Egyptian Women's Union, founded by Hoda Sharawi.

Rifaa el Tahtawi

A407

1973, July 15 ***Perf. 11x11½***

939 A407 20m brt. green, olive & brown 10 7

Centenary of the death of Rifaa el Tahtawi, champion of democracy and principal of language school.

Omar Makram

A408

Abdel Rahman al Gabarti, Historian

A409

"Reconstruction and Battle"—A410

Design: No. 941, Mohamed Korayem, martyr.

1973, July 23

940	A408	20m yel. green, blue & brown	10	7
941	"	20m lt. green, blue & brown	10	7
942	A409	20m ocher & brown	10	7

Souvenir Sheet

Imperf.

943 A410 110m gold, blue & black 1.00 1.00

21st anniversary of the revolution establishing the republic. No. 943 contains one stamp and has gold marginal inscription. Size: 97x102mm.

Grain, Cow, FAO Emblem

A411

Perf. 11½x11

1973, Oct. 24 Wmk. 342

944 A411 10m brn., dk. blue & yellow green 5 4

10th anniversary of the World Food Organization.

Inundated Temples at Philae

A412

1973, Oct. 24 ***Perf. 11½***

945 A412 55m bl., pur. & org. 40 18

UNESCO campaign to save the temples at Philae.

Bank Building

A413

1973, Oct. 24

946 A413 20m brown orange, green & black 10 8

75th anniversary of the National Bank of Egypt.

Rose

A414

1973, Oct. 24 ***Perf. 11***

947 A414 10m blue & multi. 5 3

For use on greeting cards.

Human Rights Flame

A415

Taha Hussein

A416

Perf. 11x11½

1973, Dec. 8 Photo. Wmk. 342

948 A415 20m yel. green, dk. bl. & carmine 10 8

25th anniversary of the Universal Declaration of Human Rights.

1973, Dec. 10

949 A416 20m dk. bl., brown & emerald 10 8

In memory of Dr. Taha Hussein (1893–1973), "Father of Education" in Egypt, writer, philosopher.

Pres. Sadat, Flag and Battle of Oct. 6—A417

1973, Dec. 23 ***Perf. 11x11½***

950 A417 20m yel., blk. & red 1.00 60

Crossing of Suez Canal by Egyptian forces, Oct. 6, 1973.

WPY Emblem and Chart

A418

Cairo Fair Emblem

A419

1974, Mar. 21 ***Perf. 11*** **Wmk. 342**

951 A418 55m orange, green & dark blue 28 18

World Population Year.

1974, Mar. 21 Photogravure

952 A419 20m blue & multi. 15 8

Cairo International Fair.

Nurse and Medal of Angels of Ramadan 10

A420

1974, May 15 ***Perf. 11½***

953 A420 55m multicolored 28 18

Nurses' and World Hospital Day.

Workers, Relief Carving from Queen Tee's Tomb, Sakhara—A421

1974, May 15 ***Perf. 11***

954 A421 20m yel., blue & brn. 15 8

Workers' Day.

Pres. Sadat, Troops Crossing Suez Canal

A422

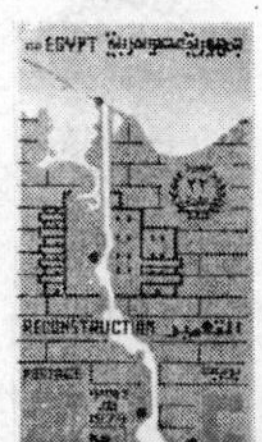

"Reconstruction," Map of Suez Canal and New Building

A423

Sheet of Aluminum
A424

Design: 110m, Pres. Sadat's "October Working Paper," symbols of science and development.

1974, July 23 Photo. ***Perf. 11x11½***

955 A422 20m multicolored 10 8
956 A423 20m bl., gold & blk. 10 8

Perf. 11½

957 A424 20m plum & silver 10 8

Souvenir Sheet

Imperf.

958 A424 110m green & multi. 55 55

22nd anniversary of the revolution establishing the republic and for the end of the October War. No. 958 contains one stamp (52x59mm.). Gold and green marginal inscription. Size: 72½x108mm.

Pres. Sadat and Flag—A425

Perf. 11x11½

1974, Oct. 6 **Wmk. 342**

959 A425 20m yel., blk. & red 50 20

First anniversary of Battle of Oct. 6.

Palette and Brushes
A426

1974, Oct. 6 ***Perf. 11½***

960 A426 30m pur., yel. & blk. 15 12

6th Exhibition of Plastic Art.

Teachers and Pupils
A427

1974, Oct. 6 ***Perf. 11x11½***

961 A427 20m multicolored 10 8

Teachers' Day.

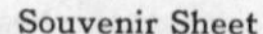

Souvenir Sheet

UPU Monument, Bern—A428

1974, Oct. 6 ***Imperf.***

962 A428 110m gold & multi. 1.00 1.00

Centenary of Universal Postal Union. No. 962 contains one stamp, yellow green marginal inscription. Size: 75x100mm.

Emblems, Cogwheel and Calipers—A429

Refugee Camp under Attack and UN Refugee Organization Emblem
A430

Child and UNICEF Emblem
A431

Temple of Philae
A432

1974, Oct. 24 ***Perf. 11½, 11x11½***

963 A429 10m blk., bl. & yel. 5 4
964 A430 20m dp. orange, blue & black 10 8
965 A431 30m grn., bl. & brn. 15 12
966 A432 55m blk., bl. & yel. 35 18

United Nations Day. World Standards Day (10m); Palestinian refugee repatriation (20m); Family Planning (30m); Campaign to save Temple of Philae (55m).

Calla Lily
A433

1974, Nov. 7 ***Perf. 11***

967 A433 10m ultra. & multi. 5 4

For use on greeting cards.

10m-coins, Smoke-stacks and Grain
A434

1974, Nov. 7 ***Perf. 11½x11***

968 A434 20m yel. green, dark blue & silver 10 8

International Savings Day.

Organization Emblem and Medical Services
A435

1974, Nov. 7 ***Perf. 11½***

969 A435 30m vio., red & gold 15 12

Health Insurance Organization, 10th anniversary.

Mustafa Lutfy El Manfalouty
A436

Abbas Mahmoud El Akkad
A437

Perf. 11x11½

1974, Dec. 8 Photo. **Wmk. 342**

970 A436 20m bl. blk. & brn. 15 8
971 A437 20m brn. & bl. blk. 15 8

Arab writers; Mustafa Lutfy El Manfalouty (1876–1924) and Abbas Mahmoud El Akkad (1889–1964). Nos. 970–971 printed se-tenant in sheets of 50.

Goddess Maat Facing God Thoth—A438

Fish-shaped Vase—A439

Pharaonic Golden Vase
A440

Sign of Life, Mirror
A441

Perf. 11½

1975, Jan. 2 Photo. Wmk. 342

972 A438 20m silver & multi. 20 10
973 A439 30m multicolored 25 15
974 A440 55m " 35 25
975 A441 110m blue & multi. 75 50

Post Day 1975. Egyptian art works from 12th–5th centuries B.C.

Om Kolthoum
A442

Perf. 11½

1975, Mar. 3 Photo. Unwmkd.

976 A442 20m brown 20 12

In memory of Om Kolthoum, singer.

Crescent, Globe, Al Aqsa and Kaaba
A443

Cairo Fair Emblem
A444

1975, Mar. 25

977 A443 20m multicolored 10 8

Mohammed's Birthday.

Perf. 11x11½

1975, Mar. 25 **Wmk. 342**

978 A444 20m multicolored 10 8

International Cairo Fair.

Kasr El Ainy Hospital WHO Emblem
A445

Perf. 11½x11

1975, May 7 Photo. **Wmk. 342**

979 A445 20m dk. brn. & bl. 10 8

World Health Organization Day.

Children Reading Book
A446

Children and Line Graph
A447

1975, May 7 *Perf. 11x11½*

980 A446 20m multicolored 10 8
981 A447 20m " 10 8

Science Day.

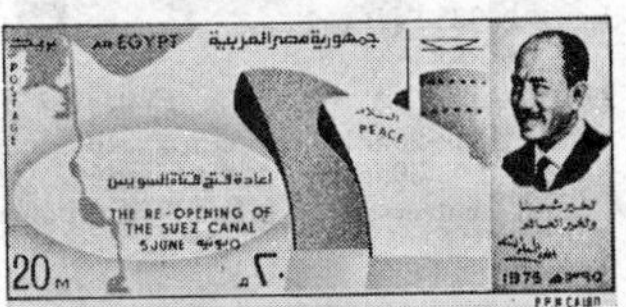

Suez Canal, Globe, Ships, Pres. Sadat—A448

1975, June 5 *Perf. 11½*

982 A448 20m bl., brn. & black 35 20

Reopening of the Suez Canal, June 5. See Nos. C166-C167.

Belmabgoknis Flowers
A449

1975, July 30 Photo. **Wmk. 342**

983 A449 10m green & blue 5 3

For use on greeting cards.

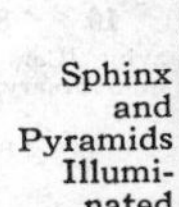

Sphinx and Pyramids Illuminated
A450

Rural Electrification
A451

Map of Egypt with Tourist Sites—A452

1975, July 23

984 A450 20m blk., org. & grn. 15 8
985 A451 20m dk. bl. & brown 15 8

Perf. 11

986 A452 110m multicolored 1.00 1.00

23rd anniversary of the revolution establishing the republic. No. 986 printed in sheets of 6 (2x3). Size: 71x80mm.

Volleyball
A453

1975, Aug. 2 Photo. *Perf. 11x11½*

Orange & Green

987 A453 20m *shown* 10 8
988 " 20m *Running* 10 8
989 " 20m *Torch and flag bearers* 10 8
990 " 20m *Basketball* 10 8
991 " 20m *Soccer* 10 8
Nos. 987-991 (5) 50 40

6th Arab School Tournament. Nos. 987-991 printed se-tenant in sheets of 50.

Egyptian Flag and Tanks
A454

Perf. 11½

1975 Photo. **Unwmkd.**

992 A454 20m multicolored 10 8

Two-line Arabic Inscription in Bottom Panel, "M" over "20"

992A A454 20m multicolored 10 8

No. 992 commemorates 2nd anniversary of Battle of Oct. 6, "The Spark;" No. 992A, the International Symposium on War of October 1973, Cairo University, Oct. 27-31.

Issue dates: No. 992, Oct. 6. No. 992A, Oct. 24.

Arrows Pointing to Fluke, and Emblems
A455

Submerged Wall and Sculpture, UNESCO Emblem
A456

Perf. 11x11½

1975, Oct. 24 **Wmk. 342**

993 A455 20m multicolored 10 8
994 A456 55m " 75 30

United Nations Day. 20m publicizes International Conference on Schistosomiasis (Bilharziasis); 55m commemorates UNESCO help in saving temples at Philae. See Nos. C169-C170.

Pharaonic Gate, University Emblem
A457

Al Biruni
A458

1975, Nov. 15 Photo. **Wmk. 342**

995 A457 20m multicolored 10 8

Ain Shams University, 25th anniversary.

1975, Dec. 23 Photo. *Perf. 11x11½*

Designs: No. 997, Al Farabi and lute. No. 998, Al Kanady, book and compass.

996 A458 20m bl., brn. & grn. 10 8
997 " 20m " " " 10 8
998 " 20m " " " 10 8

Arab philosophers.

Ibex (Prow)
A459

Designs (from Tutankhamen's Tomb): 30m, Lioness. 55m, Cow's head (Goddess Hawthor). 110m, Hippopotamus' head (God Horus).

1976, Jan. 2 *Perf. 11½* **Unwmkd.**

999 A459 20m multicolored 25 15

Wmk. 342

1000 A459 30m brown, gold & ultramarine 50 30
1001 " 55m multicolored 50 35
1002 " 110m " 1.00 75

Post Day 1976.

Lake, Aswan Dam, Industry and Agriculture—A460

Perf. 11½x11

1976, Jan. 27 Photo. **Wmk. 342**

1003 A460 20m multicolored 10 8

Filling of lake formed by Aswan High Dam.

Fair Emblem
A461

Commemorative Medal
A462

1976, Mar. 15 *Perf. 11x11½*

1004 A461 20m org. & purple 10 8

9th International Cairo Fair, Mar. 8-27.

1976, Mar. 15 **Wmk. 342**

1005 A462 20m olive, yellow & black 10 8

11th Biennial Exhibition of Fine Arts, Alexandria.

Hands Shielding Invalid
A463

1976, Apr. 7 Photo. *Perf. 11½*

1006 A463 20m dk. green, lt. grn. & yel. 10 8

Founding of Faithfulness and Hope Society.

Eye and WHO Emblem
A464

1976, Apr. 7

1007 A464 20m dk. brn., yel. & green 10 8

World Health Day: "Foresight prevents blindness."

Pres. Sadat, Legal Department Emblem
A465

Perf. 11½x11

1976, May 15 Photo. **Wmk. 342**

1008 A465 20m olive & multi. 10 8

Centenary of State Legal Department.

Scales of Justice A466

1976, May 15 *Perf. 11x11½*

1009 A466 20m car., black & green 10 8

5th anniversary of Rectification Movement.

Al-Ahram Front Page, First Issue A467

Perf. 11½x11

1976, June 25 Photo. Wmk. 342

1010 A467 20m bis. & multi. 10 8

Centenary of Al-Ahram newspaper.

World Map, Pres. Sadat and Emblems—A468

1976, July 23 *Perf. 11x11½*

1011 A468 20m bl., blk. & yel. 10 8

Souvenir Sheet

Imperf.

1012 A468 110m blue, black & yellow 1.00 75

24th anniversary of the revolution. No. 1012 shows design of No. 1011 enlarged to fill entire area. Size: 85x76mm.

Scarborough Lily A469

1976, Sept. 10 Photo. *Perf. 11*

1013 A469 10m multicolored 5 4

For use on greeting cards.

Reconstruction of Sinai by Irrigation—A470

Abu Redice Oil Wells and Refinery A471

Unknown Soldier, Memorial Pyramid for October War—A472

1976, Oct. 6 *Perf. 11x11½*

1014 A470 20m multicolored 10 8
1015 A471 20m " 10 8
1016 A472 110m green, blue & black 1.00 1.00

October War (crossing of Suez Canal), 3rd anniversary. Size of No. 1016: 65x77 mm.

Papyrus with Children's Animal Story—A473

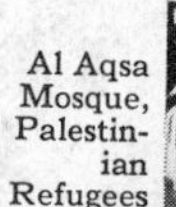

Al Aqsa Mosque, Palestinian Refugees A474

Designs: 55m, Isis, from Philae Temple, UNESCO emblem (vert.). 110m, UNESCO emblem and "30".

Perf. 11½, 11½x11

1976, Oct. 24 Photo. Wmk. 342

1017 A473 20m dk. bl., bister & brown 10 8
1018 A474 30m brn., grn. & black 15 12
1019 A473 55m dark blue & bister 28 18
1020 A474 110m lt. grn., violet blue & red 1.00 35

30th anniversary of UNESCO.

Census Chart A475

1976, Nov. 22 Photo. *Perf. 11½x11*

1021 A475 20m multicolored 10 8

10th General Population and Housing Census.

Nile and Commemorative Medal—A476

Ikhnaton A477

1976, Nov. 22 *Perf. 11x11½*

1022 A476 20m grn. & brown 10 8

Geographical Society of Egypt, centenary (in 1975).

1977, Jan. 2 Photo. *Perf. 11x11½*

Designs: 30m, Ikhnaton's daughter. 55m, Nefertiti, Ikhnaton's wife. 110m, Ikhnaton, front view.

1023 A477 20m multicolored 20 15
1024 " 30m " 25 20
1025 " 55m " 50 30
1026 " 110m " 1.00 75

Post Day 1977.

Policeman, Emblem and Emergency Car—A478

Wmk. 342

1977, Feb. 25 Photo. *Perf. 11½x11*

1027 A478 20m multicolored 20 8

Police Day.

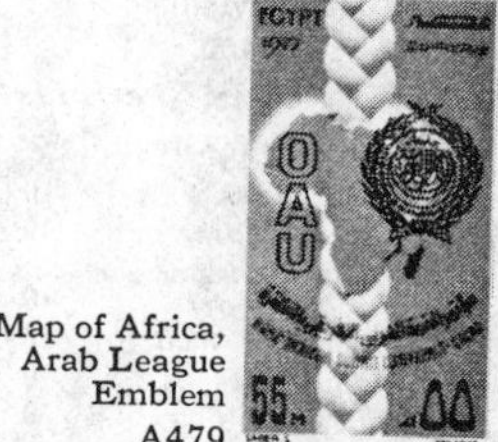

Map of Africa, Arab League Emblem A479

1977, Mar. 7 *Perf. 11x11½*

1028 A479 55m multicolored 28 18

First Afro-Arab Summit Conference, Cairo.

Fair Emblem, Pharaonic Ship—A480

1977, Mar. 7 *Perf. 11½x11*

1029 A480 20m green, black & red 20 8

10th International Cairo Fair.

King Faisal A481

1977, Mar. 22 Photo. *Perf. 11x11½*

1030 A481 20m indigo & brn. 10 8

King Faisal Ben Abdel-Aziz Al Saud of Saudi Arabia (1906–1975).

Healthy and Crippled Children A482

1977, Apr. 12 Wmk. 342

1031 A482 20m multicolored 10 8

National campaign to fight poliomyelitis.

APU Emblem, Members' Flags A483

1977, Apr. 12 *Perf. 11½*

1032 A483 20m blue & multi. 10 8
1033 " 30m gray & multi. 15 12

25th anniversary of Arab Postal Union (APU).

Children's Village A484

Perf. 11½x11

1977, May 7 Photo. Wmk. 342

1034 A484 20m multicolored 10 8
1035 " 55m " 28 18

Inauguration of Children's Village, Cairo.

Loom, Spindle and Factory A485

1977, May 7

1036 A485 20m multicolored 10 8

Egyptian Spinning and Weaving Company, El Mehalla el Kobra, 50th anniversary.

Satellite, Globe, ITU Emblem A486

1977, May 17 *Perf. 11x11½*

1037 A486 110m dark blue & multi. 1.00 75

World Telecommunications Day.

Flag and "25"
A487

Egyptian Flag and Eagle—A488

Wmk. 342

1977, July 23 Photo. ***Perf. 11½x11***

1038 A487 20m silver, carmine & black 20 8

Perf. 11x11½

1039 A488 110m multicolored 75 35

25th anniversary of July 23rd Revolution. No. 1039 printed in sheets of six. Size: 75x83mm.

Saad Zaghloul — A489

Archbishop Capucci, Map of Palestine — A490

Perf. 11x11½

1977, Aug. 23 Photo. **Wmk. 342**

1040 A489 20m dark green & dark brown 20 8

Saad Zaghloul, leader of 1919 Revolution, 50th death anniversary.

1977, Sept. 1

1041 A490 45m emerald & bl. 45 18

Palestinian Archbishop Hilarion Capucci, jailed by Israel in 1974.

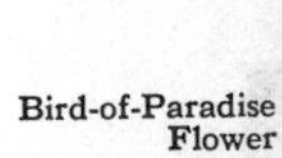

Bird-of-Paradise Flower
A491

1977, Sept. 3

1042 A491 10m multicolored 10 4

For use on greeting cards.

Proclamation Greening the Land
A492

Wmk. 342

1977, Sept. 25 Photo. ***Perf. 11x11½***

1043 A492 20m multicolored 20 8

Agrarian Reform Law, 25th anniversary.

Soldier, Tanks, Medal of Oct. 6
A493

Anwar El Sadat—A494

1977, Oct. 6 ***Perf. 11½x11***

1044 A493 20m multicolored 20 8

Unwmkd. ***Perf. 11***

1045 A494 140m dk. brn., gold & red 1.40 1.40

Crossing of Suez Canal, 4th anniversary. No. 1045 printed in sheets of 16.

Refugees Looking at Al Aqsa Mosque
A495

Goddess Taueret and Spirit of Flight (Horus)
A496

Mural Relief, Temple of Philae
A497

Wmk. 342

1977, Oct. 24 Photo. ***Perf. 11***

1046 A495 45m green, red & black 22 16

1047 A496 55m dp. bl. & yel. 28 18

1048 A497 140m olive bister & dark brown 70 48

United Nations Day.

Electric Trains, First Egyptian Locomotive
A498

1977, Oct. 22

1049 A498 20m multicolored 10 8

125th anniversary of Egyptian railroads.

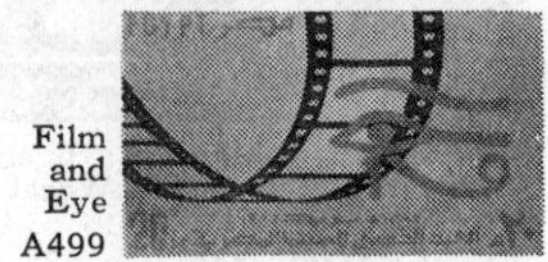

Film and Eye
A499

1977, Nov. 16 ***Perf. 11½x11***

1050 A499 20m gray, black & gold 10 8

50th anniversary of Egyptian cinema.

Natural Gas Well and Refinery
A500

1977, Nov. 17 **Photogravure**

1051 A500 20m multicolored 10 8

National Oil Festival, celebrating the acquisition of Sinai oil wells.

Pres. Sadat and Dome of the Rock—A501

Wmk. 342

1977, Dec. 31 Photo. ***Perf. 11½x11***

1052 A501 20m grn., brn.& blk. 10 8

1053 " 140m grn., blk.& brn. 70 48

Pres. Sadat's peace mission to Israel.

Ramses II
A502

Design: 45m, Queen Nefertari, bas-relief.

1978, Jan. 2 ***Perf. 11½***

1054 A502 20m green, black & gold 10 8

1055 " 45m orange, black & olive 22 16

Post Day 1978.

Water Wheels, Fayum
A503

Flying Duck, from Floor in Ikhnaton's Palace—A504

Designs: 5m, Birdhouse. 10m, Statue of Horus. 20m, Al Rifa'i Mosque, Cairo. 50m, Monastery, Wadi al-Natrun. 55m, Ruins of Edfu Temple. 85m, Medum pyramid. 100m, Facade, El Morsi Mosque, Alexandria. 200m, Column, Alexandria, and Sphinx. 500m, Arabian stallion.

Wmk. 342

1978 ***Perf. 11½***

1056 A503 1m slate blue 3 3
1057 " 5m bister brown 3 3
1058 " 10m bright green 5 3
1059 " 20m dark brown 10 8
1060 " 50m bright blue 25 15
1061 " 55m olive 28 18
1062 " 85m deep purple 42 30
1063 " 100m brown 50 40
1064 " 200m bl. & indigo 1.00 80

Perf. 11½x11

1065 A504 500m multi. 2.50
1066 " £1 " 5.00
Nos. 1056-1066 (11) 10.16

Issue dates: Nos. 1065-1066, Feb. 27. Others, July 23.

Fair Emblem and Wheat
A505

1978, Mar. 15 ***Perf. 11½***

1072 A505 20m multicolored 10 8

11th Cairo International Fair, Mar. 11-25.

Emblem, Kasr El Ainy School
A506

1978, Mar. 18 ***Perf. 11½x11***

1073 A506 20m lt. blue, black & gold 10 8

Kasr El Ainy School of Medicine, 150th anniversary.

Soldiers and Emblem — A507

Youssef El Sebai — A508

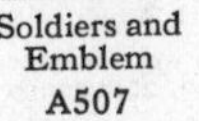

1978, Mar. 30 ***Perf. 11x11½***

1074 A507 20m multicolored 10 8
1075 A508 20m bister brown 10 8

Nos. 1069–1070 printed se-tenant.
Youssef El Sebai, newspaper editor, assassinated on Cyprus and in memory of the commandos killed in raid on Cyprus.

Biennale Medal, Statue for Entrance to Port Said
A509

1978, Apr. 1 ***Perf. 11½***

1076 A509 20m blue, green & black 10 8

12th Biennial Exhibition of Fine Arts, Alexandria.

Child with Smallpox, UN Emblem
A510

1978, Apr. 7 Photo. ***Perf. 11½***

1077 A510 20m multicolored 10 8

Eradication of smallpox.

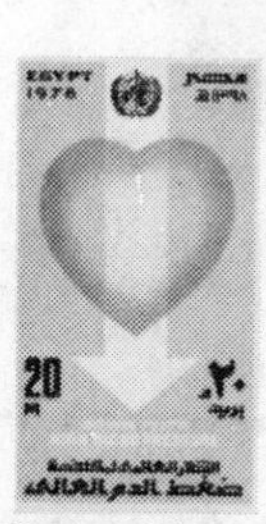

Heart and Arrow, UN Emblem
A511

Anwar El Sadat
A512

1978, Apr. 7 **Wmk. 342**

1078 A511 20m multicolored 10 8

Fight against hypertension.

1978, May 15 Photo. ***Perf. 11½x11***

1079 A512 20m green, brown & gold 10 8

7th anniversary of Rectification Movement.

Social Security Emblem—A513

1978, May 16 ***Perf. 11***

1080 A513 20m light green & dark brown 10 8

General Organization of Insurance and Pensions (Social Security), 25th anniversary.

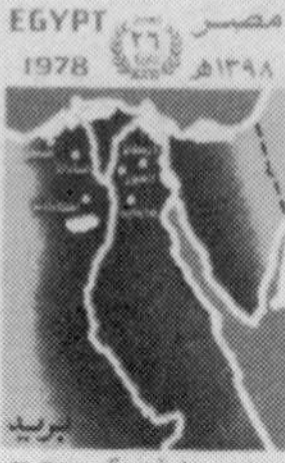

New Cities on Map of Egypt
A514

Map of Egypt and Sudan, Wheat
A515

Wmk. 342

1978, July 23 Photo. ***Perf. 11½***

1081 A514 20m multicolored 10 8
1082 A515 45m " 22 16

26th anniversary of July 23rd revolution.

Symbols of Egyptian Ministries
A516

1978, Aug. 28 Photo. ***Perf. 11½x11***

1083 A516 20m multicolored 10 8

Centenary of Egyptian Ministerial System.

Pres. Nasser and "Spirit of Egypt" Showing Way—A517

1978, Oct. 6 Photo. ***Perf. 11x11½***

1084 A517 20m multicolored 10 8

Crossing of Suez Canal, 5th anniversary.

Human Rights Emblem
A518

Dove and Human Rights Emblem
A520

Kobet al Sakra Mosque, Refugee Camp
A519

Design: 55m, Temple at Biga and UNESCO emblem (horiz.).

Perf. 11, 11½ (45m)

1978, Oct. 24 Photo. **Wmk. 342**

1085 A518 20m multicolored 10 8
1086 A519 45m " 22 16
1087 A518 55m " 28 18
1088 A520 140m " 70 48

United Nations Day.

Pilgrims, Mt. Arafat and Holy Kaaba—A521

1978, Nov. 7 Photo. ***Perf. 11***

1089 A521 45m multicolored 22 16

Pilgrimage to Mecca.

Tahtib Horse Dance
A522

1978, Nov. 7

1090 A522 10m multicolored 5 4
1091 " 20m " 10 8

U.N. Emblem, Globe and Grain
A523

1978, Nov. 11 Photo ***Perf. 11½***

1092 A523 20m green, dk. blue & yellow 10 8

Technical Cooperation Among Developing Countries Conference, Buenos Aires, Argentina, Sept. 1978.

Pipes, Map and Emblem of Sumed Pipeline—A524

1978, Nov. 11

1093 A524 20m brown, blue & yellow 10 8

Inauguration of Sumed pipeline from Suez to Alexandria, 1st anniversary.

Mastheads
A525

Abu el Walid
A526

1978, Dec. 24 ***Perf. 11x11½***

1094 A525 20m brn. & black 10 8

150th anniversary of the newspaper El Wakea el Masriya.

1978, Dec. 24

1095 A526 45m brt. green & indigo 22 18

800th death anniversary of Abu el Walid ibn Rashid.

Helwan Observatory and Sky—A527

1978, Dec. 30 **Wmk. 342**

1096 A527 20m multicolored 10 8

Helwan Observatory, 75th anniversary.

Second Daughter of Ramses II
A528

Ramses Statues, Abu Simbel, and Cartouches
A529

1979, Jan. 2 Photo. ***Perf. 11***

1097 A528 20m brn. & yellow 10 8

Perf. 11½x11

1098 A529 140m multicolored 70 48

Post Day 1978.

SEMI-POSTAL STAMPS.

Princess Ferial
SP1

Wmkd. Multiple Crown and Arabic F. (195)

1940, May 17 Photo. *Perf. 13½x14*
B1 SP1 5m+5m copper brown 50 45

No. B1 Overprinted in Green **1943** ١٩٤٣

1943, Nov. 17
B2 SP1 5m+5m copper brown 4.50 4.00
a. Arabic date "1493" 100.00 100.00

The surtax on Nos. B1 and B2 was for the children's fund.

First Postage Stamp of Egypt
SP2

Khedive Ismail Pasha
SP3

Designs: 17m+17m, King Fuad. 22m+22m, King Farouk.

Perf. 13x13½

1946, Feb. 28 Wmk. 195
B3 SP2 1m+1m gray 10 10
B4 SP3 10m+10m violet 15 15
B5 " 17m+17m brown 25 25
B6 " 22m+22m yellow green 30 30
a. Souvenir sheet, perf. 8½ 30.00 25.00
b. As "a," imperf. 30.00 25.00

Issued to commemorate the 80th anniversary of Egypt's first postage stamp.

Nos. B6a and B6b measure 129x171mm. and contain one each of Nos. B3 to B6, with inscriptions in top and bottom margins.

Goddess Hathor, King Men-kau-Re (Mycerinus) and Jackal-headed Goddess
SP7

Ramesseum, Thebes—SP8

Queen Nefertiti
SP9

Funerary Mask of King Tutankhamen
SP10

Perf. 13½x13

1947, Mar. 9 Wmk. 195
B9 SP7 5m+ 5m slate 25 25
B10 SP8 15m+15m deep blue 50 40
B11 SP9 30m+30m henna brown 70 70
B12 SP10 50m+50m brown 1.00 1.00

Issued to commemorate the International Exposition of Contemporary Art, Cairo.

Boy Scout Emblem
SP11

Scout Emblems: 20m+10m, Sea Scouts. 35m+15m, Air Explorers.

Photogravure.

1956, July 25 *Perf. 13½x13*
B13 SP11 10m+10m green 35 30
B14 " 20m+10m ultra. 50 45
B15 " 35m+15m blue 70 65

Issued to commemorate the 2nd Arab Scout Jamboree, Alexandria-Aboukir, 1956.

Souvenir sheets, perf. and imperf., contain one each of Nos. B13-B15. Size: 118x158mm. Price $300 each.

Ambulance
SP12

1957, May 13 *Perf. 13x13½*
B16 SP12 10m+5m rose red 20 18

Issued to commemorate the 50th anniversary of the Public Aid Society.

United Arab Republic

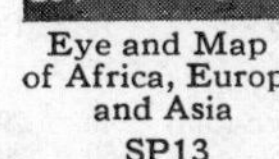

Eye and Map of Africa, Europe and Asia
SP13

Postal Emblem
SP14

Perf. 13½x13

1958, Mar. 1 Photo. Wmk. 318
B17 SP13 10m+5m orange 60 60

Issued to commemorate the First Afro-Asian Congress of Ophthalmology, Cairo.

The surtax was for centers to aid the blind.

1959, Jan. 2
B18 SP14 10m+5m blue green, red & black 15 12

Issued for Post Day, Jan. 2. The surtax went to the social fund for postal employees.

Children and U. N. Emblem
SP15

Arab League Building, Cairo, and Emblem
SP16

1959, Oct. 24 Wmk. 328
B19 SP15 10m+5m brown lake 20 12
B20 " 35m+10m dark blue 40 35

Issued for International Children's Day and to honor UNICEF.

Braille Type of Regular Issue, 1961.

1961, Apr. 6 *Perf. 13½x13*
B21 A182 35m+15m yel. & brn. 50 50

World Health Organization Day.

1962, Mar. 22 Photo. Wmk. 328
B22 SP16 10m+5m gray 25 25

Arab Publicity Week, Mar. 22–28.

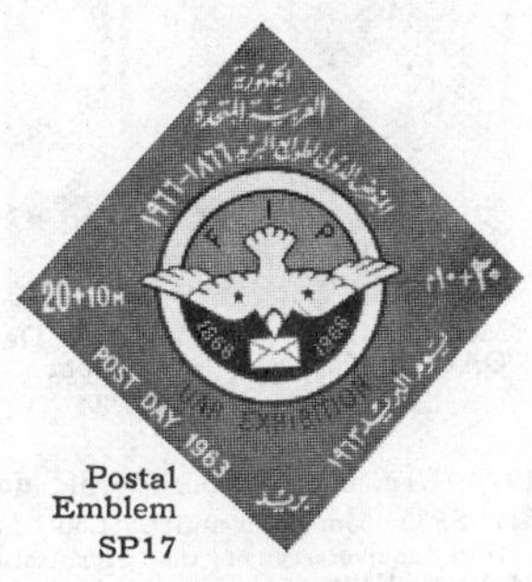

Postal Emblem
SP17

Stamp of 1866—SP18

1963, Jan. 2 *Perf. 11½* Wmk. 342
B23 SP17 20m+10m brt. green, red & black 50 50
B24 SP18 40m+20m black & brown orange 75 75
B25 " 40m+20m brn. orange & black 75 75

Issued for Post Day, Jan. 2 and to publicize the 1966 exhibition of the Federation International de Philatelie. Nos. B24–B25 printed se-tenant.

Arms of U.A.R. and Pyramids
SP19

1964, Jan. 2 *Perf. 11* Wmk. 342
B26 SP19 10m+5m orge. yel. & green 1.00 75
B27 " 80m+40m greenish blue & black 2.00 1.50
B28 " 115m+55m orange brn. & black 2.50 2.00

Issued for Post Day. Jan. 2.

Type of 1963 and

Postal Emblem—SP20

Designs: No. B30, Emblem of Postal Secondary School. 80m+40m, Postal emblem, gearwheel and laurel wreath.

Photogravure

1965, Jan. 2 *Perf. 11½* Unwmkd.
B29 SP20 10m+5m light green & carmine 12 12
B30 " 10m+5m ultraviolet, carm. & black 12 12
B31 SP18 80m+40m rose, brt. green & black 95 95

Issued for Post Day, Jan. 2. No. B31 also publicizes the Stamp Centenary Exhibition.

Souvenir Sheet

Stamps of Egypt, 1866—SP21

1966, Jan. 2 *Imperf.* Wmk. 342
B32 SP21 140m+60m black, slate blue & rose 2.00 2.00

Issued for Post Day, 1966, and to commemorate the centenary of the first Egyptian postage stamps. Size: 105x62mm.

Pharaonic "Mediator"
SP22

Design: 115m+40, Pharaonic guard.

1967, Jan. 2 *Perf. 11½* Wmk. 342

B33 SP22 80m+20m multi. 1.25 1.00
B34 " 115m+40m " 2.50 1.50

Issued for Post Day, Jan. 2.

Grand Canal, Doges' Palace, Venice, and Santa Maria del Fiore, Florence—SP23

Design: 115m+30m, Piazetta and Campanile, Venice, and Palazzo Vecchio, Florence.

Perf. 11½x11

1967, Dec. 9 Photo. Wmk. 342

B35 SP23 80m+20m grn., yel. & brown 65 65
B36 " 115m+30m olive, yel. & slate blue 1.00 1.00

The surtax was to help save the cultural monuments of Venice and Florence, damaged in the 1966 floods.

Boy and Girl SP24 **Emblem and Flags of Arab League SP25**

Design: No. B38, Five children and arch.

Perf. 11

1968, Dec. 11 Photo. Wmk. 342

B37 SP24 20m+10m car., blue & light brown 18 18
B38 " 20m+10m vio. blue, sepia & light green 18 18

Issued for Children's Day and to commemorate the 22nd anniversary of UNICEF (United Nations Children's Fund).

1969, Mar. 22 *Perf. 11x11½*

B39 SP25 20m+10m multi. 35 18

Arab Publicity Week, March 22-28.

Refugee Family SP26

Perf. 11½

1969, Oct. 24 Photo. Wmk. 342

B40 SP26 30m+10m multi. 35 18

Issued for United Nations Day.

Men of Three Races, Human Rights Emblem SP27

1970, Mar. 21 *Perf. 11½x11*

B41 SP27 20m+10m multi. 25 18

Issued to publicize the International Day for the Elimination of Racial Discrimination.

Arab League Type of Regular Issue

1970, Mar. 22 Wmk. 342

B42 A344 20m+10m blue, grn. & brown 25 18

25th anniversary of Arab League.

Map of Palestine and Refugees SP28

Perf. 11½x11

1970, Oct. 24 Photo. Wmk. 342

B43 SP28 20m+10m multi. 50 20

Issued to commemorate the 25th anniversary of the United Nations and to draw attention to the plight of the Palestinian refugees.

Arab Republic of Egypt

Blind Girl, WHO and Society Emblems SP29

1973, Oct. 24 Photo. *Perf. 11x11½*

B44 SP29 20m+10m bl. & gold 25 15

25th anniversary of the World Health Organization and for the Light and Hope Society, which educates and helps blind girls.

Map of Africa, OAU Emblem SP30 **Social Work Day Emblem SP31**

Perf. 11x11½

1973, Dec. 8 Photo. Wmk. 342

B45 SP30 55m+20m multi. 1.50 1.50

10th anniversary of the Organization for African Unity.

1973, Dec. 8

B46 SP31 20m+10m multi. 25 15

Social Work Day.

Jehane al Sadat Consoling Wounded Man—SP32

1974, Mar. 21 *Perf. 11* Wmk. 342

B47 SP32 20m+10m multi. 15 15

Faithfulness and Hope Society.

AIR POST STAMPS.

Mail Plane in Flight AP1

Wmkd. Multiple Crown and Arabic F. (195)

Photogravure.

1926, Mar. 10 *Perf. 13x13½.*

C1 AP1 27m deep violet 9.00 7.50

1929, July 17

C2 AP1 27m orange brown 3.00 2.75

Zeppelin Issue.

No. C2 Surcharged in Blue or Violet

GRAF ZEPPELIN
AVRIL 1931
50
جراف تسبلن
ابريل ١٩٣١
٥٠

1931, Apr. 6

C3 AP1 50m on 27m orange brown (Bl) 20.00 20.00
a. "1951" instead of "1931" 35.00 35.00
C4 " 100m on 27m orange brown (V) 20.00 20.00

Airplane over Giza Pyramids AP2

1933-38 Lithographed *Perf. 13x13½*

C5 AP2 1m orange & black 10 8
C6 " 2m gray & black 1.00 55
C7 " 2m orange red & black ('38) 80 75
C8 " 3m olive brown & black 20 20
C9 " 4m green & black 50 45
C10 " 5m dp. brn. & black 35 10
C11 " 6m dark green & black 70 65
C12 " 7m dark blue & black 45 45
C13 " 8m violet & black 25 15
C14 " 9m deep red & black 80 80
C15 " 10m violet & brown 50 15
C16 " 20m dark green & brown 35 10
C17 " 30m dull blue & brown 50 20
C18 " 40m deep red & brn. 5.00 12
C19 " 50m orange & brown 4.50 12
C20 " 60m gray & brown 2.00 20
C21 " 70m dark blue & blue green 1.50 20
C22 " 80m olive brown & blue green 1.50 20
C23 " 90m orange & blue green 1.75 20
C24 " 100m violet & blue green 2.25 25
C25 " 200m deep red & blue green 5.00 50
Nos. C5-C25 (21) 30.00 6.42

Type of 1933.

1941-43 Photogravure

C34 AP2 5m copper brown ('43) 15 12
C35 " 10m violet 40 20
C36 " 25m dark violet brown ('43) 40 20
C37 " 30m green 50 20

No. C37 Overprinted in Black

مؤتمر الملاحة الجوية الدولى للشرق الأوسط

Le Caire 1946 - ١٩٤٦ القاهرة

1946, Oct. 1

C38 AP2 30m green 40 20
a. Double overprint 100.00 100.00
b. Inverted overprint 125.00 125.00

Issued to commemorate the Middle East International Air Navigation Congress, Cairo, October 1946.

King Farouk, Delta Dam and DC-3 Plane—AP3

Perf. 13x13½

1947, Feb. 19 Photo. Wmk. 195

C39 AP3 2m red orange 10 4
C40 " 3m dark brown 10 10
C41 " 5m red brown 10 10
C42 " 7m dp. yel. orange 12 12
C43 " 8m green 15 10
C44 " 10m violet 15 8
C45 " 20m bright blue 25 15
C46 " 30m brown violet 35 18
C47 " 40m carmine rose 50 20
C48 " 50m Prussian green 60 25
C49 " 100m olive green 1.00 45
C50 " 200m dark gray 2.00 1.25
Nos. C39-C50 (12) 5.42 3.02

Nos. C49 and C50 Surcharged in Black

Mills
13
مليم
١٣
S.A.I.D.E.
23-8-1948 ١٩٤٨

1948, Aug. 23

C51 AP3 13m on 100m olive green 45 45
C52 " 22m on 200m dark gray 55 55
a. Date omitted

Issued to commemorate the inaugural flights of "Services Aeriens Internationaux d'Egypte" from Cairo to Athens and Rome, August 23, 1948.

Nos. C39 to C50 Overprinted in Various Colors

ملك مصر والسودان
١٦ اكتوبر سنة ١٩٥١

Overprint 27mm. Wide.

1952, Jan. *Perf. 13x13½* Wmk. 195

C53 AP3 2m red orange (Bl) 8 8
C54 " 3m dk. brn. (RV) 10 10
C55 " 5m red brown 12 10
C56 " 7m dp. yel. org (Bl) 25 25
C57 " 8m green (RV) 18 18
C58 " 10m violet (G) 25 25
C59 " 20m brt. blue (RV) 1.25 1.00
C60 " 30m brown violet (G) 50 40
a. Dark green overprint
C61 AP3 40m carmine rose 1.65 80
a. Brown overprint 1.65 1.25
C62 AP3 50m Prussian green (RV) 1.00 1.00
C63 " 100m olive green 2.00 1.85
C64 " 200m dark gray (RV) 3.25 3.25
Nos. C53-C64 (12) 10.63 9.26

See note after No. 316.

Delta Dam and Douglas DC-3 AP4

1953 Photogravure.

C65 AP4 5m red brown 10 8
C66 " 15m olive green 18 15

Nos. C39-C49 Overprinted in Black with Three Bars to Obliterate Portrait.

1953

C67 AP3 2m red orange 20 20
C68 " 3m dark brown 40 40
C69 " 5m red brown 10 10
C70 " 7m dp. yel. orange 15 15
C71 " 8m green 20 20
C72 " 10m violet 6.00 6.00
C73 " 20m bright blue 25 20
C74 " 30m brown violet 40 35
C75 " 40m carmine rose 45 45
C76 " 50m Prussian green 60 55
C77 " 100m olive green 1.00 1.00
Nos. C67–C77 (11) 9.75 9.60

Nos. C53–C64 Overprinted in Black with Three Bars to Obliterate Portrait.

1953

C78 AP3 2m red orange 8 8
C79 " 3m dark brown 12 12
C80 " 5m red brown 8 8
C81 " 7m dp. yel. orange 3.00 3.00
C82 " 8m green 18 18
C83 " 10m violet 25 25
C84 " 20m bright blue 12.00 12.00
C85 " 30m brown violet 35 35
C86 " 40m carmine rose 13.00 13.00
C87 " 50m Prussian green 50 45
C88 " 100m olive green 75 75
C89 " 200m dark gray 2.00 1.75
Nos. C78–C89 (12) 32.31 32.01

Practically all values of Nos. C67-C89 exist with double overprint.

United Arab Republic

Type of Regular Issue

Perf. 11½x11

1958, March 22 Photo. Wmk. 318

C90 A141 15m ultra. & red brn. 20 20

Birth of United Arab Republic.

Pyramids at Giza
AP5

Al Azhar University
AP6

Designs: 15m, Colossi of Memnon, Thebes. 90m, St. Catherine Monastery, Mt. Sinai.

1959–60 ***Perf. 13x13½*** **Wmk. 328**

C91 AP5 5m bright red 5 5
C92 " 15m dark dull violet 15 15
C93 AP6 60m dark green 50 50
C94 AP5 90m brn. car. ('60) 1.00 40

Nos. C91–C93 exist imperf. See also Nos. C101, C105.

Type of Regular Issue, Redrawn (Tower of Cairo)

1961, May 1 ***Perf. 13½x13***

C95 A183 50m bright blue 40 35

Top inscription has been replaced by two airplanes.

Weather Vane, Anemometer and U.N. World Meteorological Organization Emblem—AP7

Perf. 11½x11

1962, Mar. 23 Photo. Unwmkd.

C96 AP7 60m yellow & deep blue 50 50

2nd World Meteorological Day, Mar. 23.

Patrice Lumumba and Map of Africa
AP8

Perf. 13½x13

1962, July 1 Wmk. 328

C97 AP8 35m multicolored 30 30

Issued in memory of Patrice Lumumba (1925–61), Premier of Congo.

Maritime Station, Alexandria
AP9

Designs: 30m, International Airport, Cairo. 40m, Railroad Station, Luxor.

1963, Mar. 18 ***Perf. 13x13½***

C98 AP9 20m dark brown 16 12
C99 " 30m carmine rose 25 20
C100 " 40m black 35 30

Type of 1959–60 and

Temple of Queen Nefertari, Abu Simbel—AP10

Arch and Tower of Cairo
AP11

Designs: 80m, Al Azhar University seen through arch. 140m, Ramses II, Abu Simbel.

Perf. 11½x11, 11x11½

1963, Oct. 24 Photo. Wmk. 342

C101 AP6 80m violet black & brt. blue 3.00 50
C102 AP10 115m brown & yel. 95 70
C103 " 140m pale vio., blk. & orge. red 1.15 90

Unwmkd.

C104 AP11 50m yel. brn. & brt. blue ('64) 50 40
C105 AP6 80m vio. bl. & lt. blue ('65) 2.50 50

Weather Vane, Anemometer and WMO Emblem—AP12

Perf. 11½x11

1965, Mar. 23 Wmk. 342

C106 AP12 80m dark blue & rose lilac 65 50

Fifth World Meteorological Day.

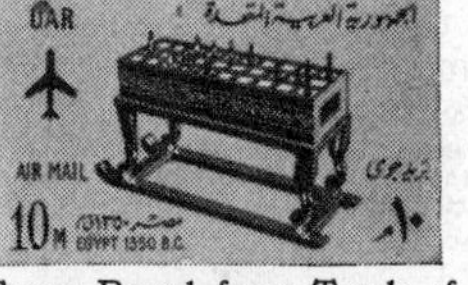

Game Board from Tomb of Tutankhamen—AP13

1965, July 1 Photo. Unwmkd.

C107 AP13 10m yel. & dk. bl. 6 5

Temples at Abu Simbel—AP14

1966, Apr. 28 ***Perf. 11½*** **Wmk. 342**

C108 AP14 20m multicolored 12 10
C109 " 80m " 48 35

Issued to commemorate the transfer of the temples of Abu Simbel to a hilltop, 1963–66.

Scout Camp and Jamboree Emblem—AP15

1966, Aug. 10 ***Perf. 11½x11***

C110 AP15 20m olive & rose 12 10

Issued to commemorate the 7th Pan-Arab Boy Scout Jamboree, Good Daim, Libya, Aug. 12.

St. Catherine Monastery, Mt. Sinai
AP16

1966, Nov. 30 Photo. Wmk. 342

C111 AP16 80m multicolored 48 35

Issued to commemorate the 1400th anniversary of St. Catherine Monastery, Sinai.

Cairo Airport
AP17

1967, Apr. 26 ***Perf. 11½x11***

C112 AP17 20m sky blue, slate green & lt. brown 12 10

Hotel El Alamein and Map of Nile Delta
AP18

Designs: 80m, The Virgin's Tree, Virgin Mary and Child. 115m, Fishing in the Red Sea.

1967, June 7 ***Perf. 11½*** **Wmk. 342**

C113 AP18 20m dull purple, slate green & dull org. 20 10
C114 " 80m blue & multi. 80 35
C115 " 115m brown, orange & blue 1.50 75

Issued for International Tourist Year, 1967.

Oil Derricks, Map of Egypt—AP19

1967, July 23 Photogravure

C116 AP19 50m orange & bluish black 30 26

15th anniversary of the revolution.

Type of Regular Issue, 1967

Design: 80m, Back of Tutankhamen's throne and UNESCO emblem.

1967, Oct. 24 ***Perf. 11½*** **Wmk. 342**

C117 A301 80m blue & yellow 48 35

22nd anniversary of the United Nations.

Koran—AP20

1968, Mar. 25 ***Perf. 11½*** **Wmk. 342**

C118 AP20 30m lilac, bl. & yel. 50 15
C119 " 80m lilac, bl. & yel. 1.00 35

Issued to commemorate the 1400th anniversary of the Koran. Nos. C118–C119 are printed in miniature sheets of 4 containing 2 each of Nos. C118–C119, decorative border and gutters. Size: 240x158 mm.

St. Mark and St. Mark's Cathedral—AP21

1968, June 25 ***Perf. 11½*** **Wmk. 342**

C120 AP21 80m brt. grn., dk. brown & dp. carmine 48 35

Issued to commemorate the 1900th anniversary of the martyrdom of St. Mark and to commemorate the consecration of St. Mark's Cathedral, Cairo.

Map of United Arab Airlines and Boeing 707—AP22

Design: No. C122, Ilyushin 18 and routes of United Arab Airlines.

1968-69 Photo. ***Perf. 11½x11***

C121 AP22 55m blue, ocher & carmine 33 26
C122 " 55m blue, yel. & vio. black ('69) 33 26

Issued to commemorate the first flights of a Boeing 707 (No. C121) and an Ilyushin 18 (No. C122) for United Arab Airlines.

Mahatma Gandhi, Arms of India and UAR AP23 — **Imam El Boukhary AP24**

1969, Sept. 10 ***Perf. 11x11½***

C123 AP23 80m lt. blue, ocher & brown 65 35

Issued to commemorate the centenary of the birth of Mohandas K. Gandhi (1869–1948), leader in India's fight for independence.

1969, Dec. 27 Photo. **Wmk. 342**

C124 AP24 30m light olive & dark brown 18 15

Issued to commemorate the 1100th anniversary of the death of the Imam El Boukhary (824–870), philosopher and writer.

Azzahir Beybars Mosque AP25

1969, Dec. 27 Engr. ***Perf. 11½x11***

C125 AP25 30m red lilac 18 15

700th anniversary of the founding of the Azzahir Beybars Mosque, Cairo.

Lenin AP26

Perf. 11x11½

1970, Apr. 22 Photo. **Wmk. 342**

C126 AP26 80m lt. grn. & brn. 48 35

Issued to commemorate the centenary of the birth of Lenin (1870–1924).

Phantom Fighters and Destroyed Factory—AP27

1970, May 1 ***Perf. 11½x11***

C127 AP27 80m yel., green & dk. vio. brn. 75 35

Issued to commemorate the destruction of the Abu-Zaabal factory by Israeli planes.

U.P.U. Type of Regular Issue

1970, May 20 Photo. **Wmk. 342**

C128 A350 80m multicolored 48 35

Issued to commemorate the inauguration of the new Universal Postal Union Headquarters in Bern.

Nasser and Burial Mosque AP28

1970, Nov. 6 ***Perf. 11*** **Wmk. 342**

C129 AP28 30m olive & black 18 15
C130 " 80m brown & black 48 35

Issued in memory of Gamal Abdel Nasser (1918–1970), President of Egypt.

Postal Congress Type of Regular Issue

Perf. 11½x11

1971, Mar. 6 Photo. **Wmk. 342**

C131 A365 30m lt. olive, orange & slate green 18 15

9th Arab Postal Congress, Cairo, March 6–25.

Nasser, El Rifaei and Sultan Hussein Mosques—AP29

Designs: 85m, Nasser and Ramses Square, Cairo. 110m, Nasser, Sphinx and pyramids.

Perf. 11½x11

1971, July 1 Photo. **Wmk. 342**

C132 AP29 30m multicolored 50 15
C133 " 85m " 1.25 35
C134 " 110m " 1.75 50

APU Type of Regular Issue

1971, Aug. 3 ***Perf. 11½*** **Wmk. 342**

C135 A373 30m brn., yel. & bl. 18 15

25th anniversary of the Conference of Sofar, Lebanon, establishing the Arab Postal Union.

Arab Republic of Egypt

Confederation Type of Regular Issue

Perf. 11½x11

1971, Sept. 28 Photo. **Wmk. 342**

C136 A374 30m gray, slate green & dk. purple 18 12

Confederation of Arab Republics (Egypt, Syria and Libya).

Al Aqsa Mosque and Woman AP30

Perf. 11½

1971, Oct. 24 Photo. **Wmk. 342**

C137 AP30 30m bl., yel., brn. & green 18 12

25th anniversary of the United Nations (in 1970) and for the return of Palestinian refugees.

Postal Union Type of Regular Issue

Design: 30m, African Postal Union emblem and letter.

1971, Dec. 2 ***Perf. 11½x11***

C138 A384 30m green, black & blue 18 12

10th anniversary of African Postal Union.

Aida, Triumphal March AP31

1971, Dec. 23 ***Perf. 11½*** **Wmk. 342**

C139 AP31 110m dk. brn., yel. & slate grn. 70 40

Centenary of the first performance of the opera Aida, by Giuseppe Verdi.

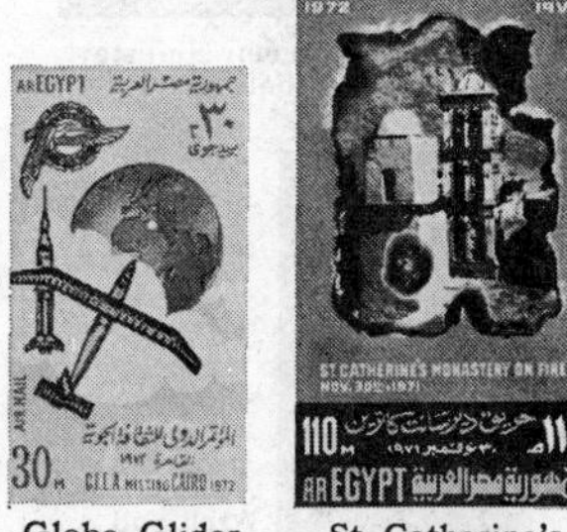

Globe, Glider, Rocket Club Emblem AP32 — **St. Catherine's Monastery on Fire AP33**

1972, Feb. 11 ***Perf. 11x11½***

C140 AP32 30m blue, ocher & yellow 18 12

International Aerospace Education Conference, Cairo, Jan. 11–13.

Perf. 11½x11

1972, Feb. 15 **Unwmkd.**

C141 AP33 110m dp. car., org. & black 70 40

The burning of St. Catherine's Monastery in Sinai Desert, Nov. 30, 1971.

Tutankhamen in Garden AP34

Tutankhamen, from 2nd Sarcophagus—AP35

Design: No. C143, Ankhesenamun.

1972, May 22 Photo. ***Perf. 11½***

C142 AP34 110m brn. orange, bl. & grn. 1.00 35
C143 " 110m brn. orange, bl. & grn. 1.00 35

Souvenir Sheet

Imperf.

C144 AP35 200m gold & multi. 3.50 3.50

50th anniversary of the discovery of the tomb of Tutankhamen. Nos. C142–C143 printed se-tenant in sheets of 50. The continuous design is from a painted ivory plaque on lid of a coffer.

No. C144 has blue inscription and gold scarab ornaments in margin. Size: 97x102 mm.

Souvenir Sheet

Flag of Confederation of Arab Republics—AP36

1972, July 23 Photo. ***Imperf.***

C145 AP36 110m gold, dp. car. & black 1.00 1.00

20th anniversary of the revolution. No. C145 has gold commemorative inscription and black portraits of Presidents Nasser and Anwar El Sadat in margin. Size: 107x69 mm.

Temples at Abu Simbel
AP37

Designs: 30m, Al Azhar Mosque and St. George's Church. 110m, Pyramids at Giza.

1972 *Perf. 11½x11* **Wmk. 342**

C146 AP37 30m bl. brn. & buff 15 10
C147 " 85m blue, brown & ocher 45 30
C148 " 110m multicolored 56 32

Issue dates: Nos. C146, C148, Nov. 22; No. C147, Aug. 1.

Olympic Type of Regular Issue

Designs (Olympic and Motion Emblems and): No. C149, Handball. No. C150, Weight lifting. 50m, Swimming. 55m, Gymnastics. All vertical.

1972, Aug. 17 *Perf. 11x11½*

C149 A396 30m multicolored 15 10
C150 " 30m yel. & multi. 15 10
C151 " 50m blue & multi. 25 16
C152 " 55m multicolored 28 16

Champollion, Rosetta Stone, Hieroglyphics—AP38

1972, Oct. 16

C153 AP38 110m gold, green & black 1.25 50

Sesquicentennial of the deciphering of Egyptian hieroglyphics by Jean-François Champollion.

World Map, Telephone, Radar, ITU Emblem—AP39

1973, Mar. 21 **Photo.** *Perf. 11*

C154 AP39 30m lt. bl., dk. blue & black 15 10

5th World Telecommunications Day.

Karnak Temple, Luxor
AP40

Hand Dripping Blood and Falling Plane
AP41

1973, Mar. 21

C155 AP40 110m dp. ultra., blk.&rose 1.00 70

Sound and light at Karnak.

1973, May 1 *Perf. 11x11½*

C156 AP41 110m multi. 1.50 75

Israeli attack on Libyan civilian plane, Feb. 1973.

WMO Emblem, Weather Vane
AP42

1973, Oct. 24 *Perf. 11x11½*

C157 AP42 110m blue, gold & purple 1.00 50

Centenary of international meteorological cooperation.

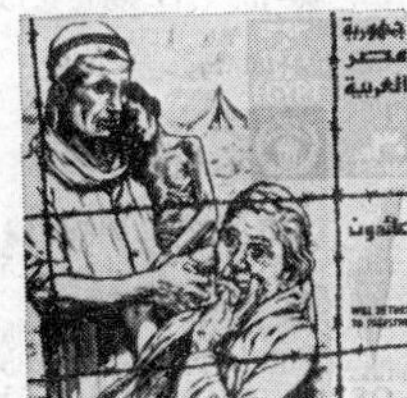

Refugees, Map of Palestine
AP43

1973, Oct. 24 *Perf. 11½*

C158 AP43 30m dark brown, yel. & blue 35 25

Plight of Palestinian refugees.

INTERPOL Emblem
AP44

Postal and UPU Emblems
AP45

Perf. 11x11½

1973, Dec. 8 **Photo.** **Wmk. 342**

C159 AP44 110m blk. & multi. 55 28

50th anniversary of the International Criminal Police Organization.

1974, Jan. 2 *Perf. 11* **Unwmkd.**

Designs (UPU Emblems and): 30m, Arab Postal Union emblem. 55m, African Postal Union emblem. 110m, Universal Postal Union emblem.

Size: 26x46½mm.

C160 AP45 20m gray, red & black 10 8
C161 " 30m salmon, blk. & purple 15 10
C162 " 55m emerald, blk. & bright magenta 70 25

Size: 37x37½mm. *Perf. 11½*

C163 AP45 110m lt. blue, blk. & gold 1.00 50

Post Day 1974.

Solar Bark of Khufu (Cheops)
AP46

Photogravure

1974, Mar. 21 *Perf. 11½* **Wmk. 342**

C164 AP46 110m blue, gold & brown 1.00 50

Solar Bark Museum.

Hotel Meridien
AP47

1974, Oct. 6 *Perf. 11½x11*

C165 AP47 110m multi. 1.00 50

Opening of Hotel Meridien, Cairo.

Suez Canal Type of 1975

1975, June 5 *Perf. 11½*

C166 A448 30m bl., yel. green & indigo 40 25
C167 " 110m indigo & blue 1.25 50

Reopening of the Suez Canal, June 5.

Irrigation Commission Emblem
AP48

1975, July 20

C168 AP48 110m orange & dk. green 1.00 50

9th International Congress on Irrigation and Drainage, Moscow, and 25th anniversary of the International Commission on Irrigation and Drainage.

Refugees and UNWRA Emblem—AP49

Woman and IWY Emblem
AP50

Perf. 11x11½

1975, Oct. 24 **Photo.** **Wmk. 342**

C169 AP49 30m multicolored 15 12

Unwmkd.

C170 AP50 110m olive, orange & black 1.00 50

United Nations Day. 30m publicizes U.N. help for refugees; 110m is for International Women's Year 1975.

Step Pyramid, Sakhara, and Entrance Gate
AP51

Designs: 45m, Plane over Giza Pyramids. 140m, Plane over boats on Nile.

Perf. 11½x11

1977, Nov. 15 **Photo.** **Wmk. 342**

C171 AP51 45m yel. & brn. 22 16
C172 " 115m bl. & brown 60 30
C173 " 140m bl. & purple 70 48

Flyer and U.N. ICAO Emblem
AP52

Wmk. 342

1978, Dec. 30 **Photo.** *Perf. 11x11½*

C174 AP52 140m blue, black & brown 70 55

75th anniversary of 1st powered flight.

AIR POST SEMI-POSTAL STAMPS

United Arab Republic

Pharaonic Mail Carriers and Papyrus Plants
SPAP1

Design: 115m+55m, Jet plane, world map and stamp of Egypt, 1926 (No. C1).

Photogravure

1966, Jan. 2 *Perf. 11½* Wmk. 342

CB1	SPAP1	80m+40m yel., grn., brn., lilac & blue	80	70
CB2	"	115m+55m blue, yel. & lilac	1.00	85

Issued for Post Day, Jan. 2. Nos. CB1-CB2 printed se-tenant in sheets of 28.

SPECIAL DELIVERY STAMPS.

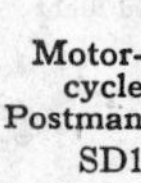

Motor-cycle Postman
SD1

Wmkd.
Multiple Crown and Arabic F. (195)

1926, Nov. 28 Photo. *Perf. 13x13½*

E1	SD1	20m dark green	4.50	2.00

1929, Sept.

E2	SD1	20m brown red & black	70	40

Inscribed "Postes Expres."

1943-44 Lithographed

E3	SD1	26m brown red & gray black	90	90
E4	"	40m dull brown & pale gray ('44)	60	30

No. E4 Overprinted in Black ملك مصر والسودان ١٦ اكتوبر سنة ١٩٥١

Overprint 27mm. Wide.

1952, Jan.

E5	SD1	40m dull brown & pale gray	55	45

See note after No. 316.

POSTAGE DUE STAMPS.

D1

D2

Wmkd. Crescent and Star. (119)

1884, Jan. 1 Litho. *Perf. 10½*

J1	D1	10pa red	8.50	1.50
		a. Imperf. vert., pair	100.00	
J2	"	20pa red	15.00	3.00
J3	"	1pi red	25.00	6.00
J4	"	2pi red	37.50	3.00
J5	"	5pi red	7.50	6.50

1886, Aug. 1 Unwmkd.

J6	D1	10pa red	2.50	1.00
		a. Imperf. vert., pair	60.00	60.00
J7	"	20pa red	60.00	9.00
J8	"	1pi red	2.00	85
J9	"	2pi red	2.00	35

1888, Jan. 1 *Perf. 11½*

J10	D2	2m green	1.25	75
		a. Horiz. pair, imperf. between	60.00	
J11	"	5m rose red	2.00	75
J12	"	1pi blue	20.00	7.00
J13	"	2pi yellow	15.00	3.00
J14	"	5pi gray	60.00	40.00
		a. Period after "PIASTRES"	85.00	60.00
		Nos. J10-J14 (5)	98.25	51.50

Excellent counterfeits of J1 to J14 are plentiful. There are four types of each of Nos. J1 to J14, so placed that any block of four contains all four types.

D3

D4

Typographed.

1889 *Perf. 14x13½* Wmk. 119

J15	D3	2m green	60	10
		a. Half used as 1m on cover		4.00
J16	"	4m maroon	40	8
J17	"	1pi ultramarine	75	8
J18	"	2pi orange	1.00	25

Nos. J15-J18 exist on both ordinary and chalky paper. Imperf. examples of Nos. J15-J17 are proofs.

Black Surcharge.

1898

J19	D4	3m on 2pi orange	25	25
		a. Inverted surch.	25.00	25.00
		b. Double surcharge	85.00	85.00
		c. Pair, one without surcharge	140.00	

There are two types of this surcharge. In one type, the spacing between the last two Arabic characters at the right is 2mm. In the other type, this spacing is 3mm., and there is an added sign on top of the second character from the right.

D5

D6

Wmkd.
Triple Crescent and Star. (120)

1921 *Perf. 14x13½*

J20	D5	2m green	35	35
J21	"	4m vermilion	1.35	70
J22	D6	10m deep blue	1.25	90

1921-22

J23	D5	2m vermilion	25	15
J24	"	4m green	25	15
J25	D6	10m lake ('22)	30	10

Nos. J18, J23-J25 Overprinted

1922, Oct. 10 Wmk. 119

J26	D3	2pi orange	3.00	1.00
		a. Ovpt. right side up	6.00	4.50

Wmk. 120

J27	D5	2m vermilion	35	25
J28	"	4m green	60	50
J29	D6	10m lake	1.00	60

Overprint on Nos. J26-J29 is inverted.

Arabic Numeral
D7

Wmkd.
Multiple Crown and Arabic F. (195)

1927-56 Lithographed *Perf. 13x13½*

Size: 18x22½ mm.

J30	D7	2m slate	25	15
J31	"	2m orange ('38)	25	15
J32	"	4m green	40	15
J33	"	4m olive brown ('32)	80	20
J34	"	5m brown	80	30
J35	"	6m gray green ('41)	50	20
J36	"	8m brown violet	50	25
J37	"	10m brick red ('29)	65	25
		a. 10m deep red	75	35
J38	"	12m rose lake ('41)	75	25
J38A	"	20m dark red ('56)	1.50	75

Perf. 13½x14

Size: 22x28 mm.

J39	D7	30m purple	3.50	1.50
		Nos. J30-J39 (11)	9.90	4.15

Postage Due Stamps and Type of 1927 Overprinted in Various Colors ملك مصر والسودان ١٦ اكتوبر سنة ١٩٥١

1952, Jan. 16 *Perf. 13x13½*

J40	D7	2m orange (Bl)	15	15
J41	"	4m green	30	30
J42	"	6m gray green (RV)	35	35
J43	"	8m brown violet (Bl)	40	35
J44	"	10m dull rose (Bl)	75	35
		a. 10m brown red (Bk)	65	40
J45	"	12m rose lake (Bl)	50	30

Perf. 14

J46	D7	30m purple (C)	1.50	55
		Nos. J40-J46 (7)	3.95	2.35

See note after No. 316.

United Arab Republic

1960 *Perf. 13x13½* Wmk. 318

Size: 18x22½ mm.

J47	D7	2m orange	45	15
J48	"	4m light green	55	20
J49	"	6m green	75	25
J50	"	8m brown violet	55	35
J51	"	12m rose brown	1.00	50
J52	"	20m dull rose brown	1.50	50

Perf. 14

Size: 22x28 mm.

J53	D7	30m violet	5.00	1.00
		Nos. J47-J53 (7)	9.80	2.95

1962 *Perf. 13x13½* Wmk. 328

Size: 18x22½mm.

J54	D7	2m salmon	15	10
J55	"	4m light green	25	10
J56	"	10m red brown	50	15
J57	"	12m rose brown	80	60
J58	"	20m dull rose brown	1.65	1.00

Perf. 14

Size: 22x28mm.

J59	D7	30m light violet	2.00	1.75
		Nos. J54-J59 (6)	5.35	3.70

D8

Photogravure

1965 *Perf. 11* Unwmkd.

J60	D8	2m org. & vio. black	10	10
J61	"	8m lt. bl. & dk. blue	15	15
J62	"	10m yellow & emerald	15	15
J63	"	20m lt. bl. & vio. blk.	20	15
J64	"	40m orange & emerald	35	20
		Nos. J60-J64 (5)	95	75

A little time given to study of the arrangement of the Scott Catalogue can make it easier to use effectively.

MILITARY STAMPS

From November 1, 1932 to February 29, 1936 members of the British Forces in Egypt were permitted to send letters to Great Britain at reduced rates. Special seals were used in place of Egyptian stamps. These seals were replaced by special stamps March 1, 1936.

Fuad Type of 1927.
Inscribed "Army Post".
Wmkd.
Multiple Crown and Arabic F. (195)

1936, Mar. 1 Photo. *Perf. 13½x14*

M1	A44	3m green	40	15
M2	"	10m carmine	1.25	30

King Farouk
M1

1939, Dec. 16 *Perf. 13x13½*

M3	M1	3m green	45	3.00
M4	"	10m carmine rose	1.25	20

United Arab Republic

Arms of UAR and Military Emblems
M2

Perf. 11x11½

1971, Apr. 15 Photo. Wmk. 342

M5	M2	10m purple	10	10

OFFICIAL STAMPS.

O1

Wmkd. Crescent and Star. (119)

1893, Jan. 1 Typo. *Perf. 14x13½*

O1	O1	orange brown	25	15

No. O1 exists on ordinary and chalky paper.

Imperf. examples of No. O1 are proofs.

Regular Issues of 1884-93 Overprinted **O.H.H.S.** اميري

1907

O2	A18	1m brown	10	6
O3	A19	2m green	15	6
		a. Double ovpt.		
O4	A21	3m orange	20	6
O5	A20	5m carmine rose	25	4
O6	A14	1pi ultramarine	35	6
O7	A16	5pi gray	2.50	20
		Nos. O2-O7 (6)	3.55	48

Imperf. examples of Nos. O2-O3, O5-O7 are proofs.

Overprinted **O.H.H.S.**

1913

O8	A20	5m carmine rose	25	15
		a. Inverted overprint	55.00	27.50
		b. No period after "S"	5.00	2.75

Regular Issues Overprinted **O.H.H.S.** اميرى

1914-15 On Issues of 1888-1906

O9	A19	2m green	25	20
		a. Inverted ovpt.	9.00	9.00
		b. Dbl. ovpt.	200.00	200.00
		c. No period after "S"	3.00	3.00

O10	A23	4m brown red	25	20
		a. Inverted ovpt.	85.00	85.00

On Issue of 1914.

O11	A24	1m olive brown	15	12
		a. No period after "S"	2.00	2.00
O12	A26	3m orange	20	15
		a. No period after "S"	4.00	4.00
O13	A28	5m lake	25	8
		a. No period after "S"	3.00	3.00
		b. Two periods after "S"	3.00	3.00
		Nos. O9-O13 (5)	1.10	75

Regular Issues Overprinted

O.H.H.S.
أميرى

On Issues of 1888–1906

1915, Oct.

O14	A19	2m green	15	12
		a. Inverted overprint	7.00	7.00
		b. Double overprint	9.00	
O15	A23	4m brown red	30	15

On Issue of 1914.

O16	A28	5m lake	30	18
		a. Pair, one without ovpt.	90.00	

On Issue of 1921-22.

1922 Wmk. 120

O17	A24	1m olive brown	3.00	1.25
		a. Two periods after "S"	175.00	
O18	A25	2m red	3.00	1.25
O19	A26	3m orange	70.00	65.00
O20	A28	5m pink	3.00	1.25
		a. Double ovpt.	90.00	

Regular Issues of 1921–22 Overprinted

O.H.E.M.S.
الحكومة
الملكية المصرية

1922

O21	A24	1m olive brown	30	25
		a. Two periods after "S"	25.00	
O22	A25	2m red	35	30
O23	A26	3m orange	1.00	80
O24	A27	4m green	1.75	1.50
		a. Two periods after "H", none after "S"	75.00	75.00
O25	A28	5m pink	50	25
		a. Two periods after "H", none after "S"	35.00	35.00
O26	A29	10m deep blue	1.25	1.00
O27	A34	15m indigo	1.50	1.25
O28	A35	15m indigo	60.00	50.00
		a. Two periods after "H", none after "S"	225.00	225.00
O29	A31	50m maroon	5.00	3.75
		Nos. O21-O29 (9)	71.65	59.10

1923

O30	A29	10m lake	1.50	1.25
		a. Two periods after "H", none after "S"	50.00	50.00

Regular Issue of 1923 Overprinted in Black or Red

أميرى

1924 *Perf. 13½x14*

O31	A36	1m orange	60	20
O32	"	2m gray (R)	75	45
O33	"	3m brown	1.00	70
O34	"	4m yellow green	1.50	90
O35	"	5m orange brown	60	30
O36	"	10m rose	1.25	45
O37	"	15m ultramarine	1.50	60

Perf. 14

O38	A36	50m myrtle green	3.75	1.50
		Nos. O31-O38 (8)	10.95	5.10

O2 O3

Wmkd.
Multiple Crown and Arabic F. (195)

1926–35 Litho. *Perf. 13x13½*

Size 18½x22mm.

O39	O2	1m light orange	6	6
O40	"	2m black	6	6
O41	"	3m olive brown	8	8
O42	"	4m light green	10	8
O43	"	5m brown	15	6
O44	"	10m dull red	50	8
O45	"	10m bright violet ('34)	25	8
O46	"	15m deep blue	60	10
O47	"	15m brown violet ('34)	30	8
O48	"	20m deep blue ('35)	40	10

Perf. 13½

Size 22½x27½ mm.

O49	O2	20m olive green	1.00	20
O50	"	50m myrtle green	1.00	15
		Nos. O39-O50 (12)	4.50	1.13

1938, Dec. Size 22½x19mm.

O51	O3	1m orange	4	4
O52	"	2m red	6	6
O53	"	3m olive brown	8	8
O54	"	4m yellow green	10	8
O55	"	5m brown	10	6
O56	"	10m bright violet	12	8
O57	"	15m rose violet	18	10
O58	"	20m blue	20	12

Perf. 14x13½.

Size 26½x22 mm.

O59	O3	50m myrtle green	40	15
		Nos. O51-O59 (9)	1.28	77

Nos. O51 to O59 Overprinted in Various Colors

ملك مصر والسودان
١٦ اكتوبر سنة ١٩٥١

Overprint 19mm. Wide.

1952, Jan. *Perf. 13x13½*

O60	O3	1m orange (Br)	4	4
O61	"	2m red	4	4
O62	"	3m olive brown (Bl)	5	5
O63	"	4m yellow green (Bl)	5	5
O64	"	5m brown (Bl)	5	4
O65	"	10m bright violet (Bl)	10	8
O66	"	15m rose violet (Bl)	15	12
O67	"	20m blue	20	20

Overprint 24½mm. Wide.

Perf. 14x13½.

O68	O3	50m myrtle green (RV)	50	45
		Nos. O60-O68 (9)	1.21	1.11

See note after No. 316.

United Arab Republic

Numeral O4 — Arms of U.A.R. O5

Perf. 13x13½

1959 Lithographed Wmk. 318

O69	O4	10m brown violet	45	8
O70	"	35m chalky blue	90	12

1962-63 Wmk. 328

O71	O4	1m orange ('63)	3	3
O72	"	4m yellow grn. ('63)	3	3
O73	"	5m brown	4	4
O74	"	10m dark brown	4	4
O75	"	35m dark blue	26	26
O76	"	50m green	40	40
O77	"	100m violet ('63)	80	40
O78	"	200m rose red ('63)	1.60	80
O79	"	500m gray ('63)	4.00	2.00
		Nos. O71-O79 (9)	7.20	4.00

Photogravure

1966–68 *Perf. 11½x11* Unwmkd.

O80	O5	1m ultramarine	3	3
O81	"	4m brown	3	3
O82	"	5m olive	3	3
O83	"	10m brown black	5	5
O84	"	20m magenta	10	10
O85	"	35m dark purple	18	18
O86	"	50m orange	25	25
O87	"	55m dark purple	28	28

Wmk. 342

O88	O5	100m brt. green & brick red	50	40
O89	"	200m blue & brick red	1.00	75
O90	"	500m olive & brick red	2.50	2.00
		Nos. O80-O90 (11)	4.95	4.10

1969 Wmk. 342

O91	O5	10m magenta	6	6

Arab Republic of Egypt

Arms of Egypt
O6

Perf. 11

1972, June 30 Photo. Wmk. 342

O92	O6	1m blk. & vio. blue	3	3
		a. 1m black & light blue ('75)	3	3
O93	O6	10m blk. & carmine	5	5
		a. 10m black & rose red ('76)	5	5
O94	O6	20m black & olive	10	10
O95	"	50m black & orange	25	25
O96	"	55m black & purple	27	27
		Nos. O92-O96 (5)	70	70

1973, Apr. 15

O97	O6	20m lilac & sepia	10	10
		a. 20m purple & lt. brown ('76)	10	10

OCCUPATION STAMPS
For Use in Palestine.

فلسطين

Nos. 208, 211 and 213 Overprinted in Green or Black

PALESTINE
a

Perf. 13x13½

1948, May 15 Wmk. 195

N1	A66	3m brown	12	12
N2	"	6m light yellow green (Bk)	15	15
N3	"	13m rose carmine	18	18

Same Overprint in Red, Green or Black on Stamps of Egypt, 1939–46.

Perf. 13x13½, 13½x13

N4	A77	1m yel. brown (G)	12	12
N5	"	2m red orange (G)	12	12
N6	"	4m deep green	12	12
N7	"	5m red brown (Bk)	15	15
N8	"	10m deep violet	18	18
N9	"	15m dark violet	18	18
N10	"	17m olive green	20	20
N11	"	20m dark gray	25	25
N12	"	22m deep blue	30	30
N13	A74	50pi green & sepia	4.00	4.00
N14	A75	£1 deep blue & dark brown	8.00	8.00

The two lines of the overprint are more widely separated on Nos. N13 and N14.

Nos. 267–269, 237 and 238 Overprinted in Red

فلسطين

PALESTINE
b

Perf. 14x13½.

N15	A73	30m olive green	35	35
N16	"	40m dark brown	45	45
N17	"	50m Prussian green	60	60
N18	"	100m brown violet	1.75	1.75
N19	"	200m dark violet	3.50	3.50
		Nos. N1-N19 (19)	20.72	20.72

The surcharge is arranged to fit the size of the stamps.

Nos. N1-N19 Overprinted in Black with Three Bars to Obliterate Portrait

Perf. 13x13½, 13½x13, 14x13½

1953 Wmk. 195

N20	A77	1m yellow brown	5	5
N21	"	2m red orange	5	5
N22	A66	3m brown	8	8
N23	A77	4m deep green	8	8
N24	"	5m red brown	10	10
N25	A66	6m lt. yellow green	12	12
N26	A77	10m deep violet	15	15
N27	A66	13m rose carmine	20	20
N28	A77	15m dark violet	20	20
N29	"	17m olive green	25	25
N30	"	20m dark gray	30	30
N31	"	22m deep blue	35	35
N32	A73	30m olive green	45	45
N33	"	40m dark brown	60	60
N34	"	50m Prussian green	90	90
N35	"	100m brown violet	1.50	1.50
N36	"	200m dark violet	2.75	2.75
N37	A74	50pi green & sepia	7.00	7.00
N38	A75	£1 deep blue & dark brown	12.00	12.00
		Nos. N20-N38 (19)	27.13	27.13

Regular Issue of 1953–55 Overprinted Type "a" in Blue or Red

1954-55 *Perf. 13x13½*

N39	A115	1m red brown	4	4
N40	"	2m dark lilac	5	5
N41	"	3m bright blue (R)	6	6
N42	"	4m dark green (R)	8	8
N43	"	5m deep carmine	10	10
N44	A110	10m dark brown	12	12
N45	"	15m gray (R)	15	15

N46 A110 17m dark greenish blue (R) 15 15
N47 " 20m purple (R) ('54) 18 18

فلسطين

Nos. 331–333 and 335–340 Overprinted in Blue or Red

PALESTINE
c

1955-56 *Perf. 13½.*

N48 A111 30m dull green (R) 20 20
N49 " 32m brt. blue (R) 25 25
N50 " 35m violet (R) 25 25
N51 " 40m red brown 40 40
N52 " 50m violet brown 45 45
N53 A112 100m henna brown 1.00 1.00
N54 " 200m dark greenish blue (R) 2.25 2.25
N55 " 500m purple (R) 5.00 5.00
N56 " £1 dark green, black & red (R) ('56) 10.00 10.00
Nos. N39–N56 (18) 20.73 20.73

Type of 1957 Overprinted in Red

فلسطين
PALESTINE
d

1957 *Perf. 13½x13* **Wmk. 195**

N57 A127 10m blue green 1.00 1.00

Nos. 414-417 Overprinted Type "d" in Red.

1957-58 *Perf. 13½* **Wmk. 315**

N58 A138 10m violet 15 15

Wmk. 318

N59 A136 1m light blue green ('58) 6 6
N60 A137 5m brown ('58) 8 8
N61 A138 10m violet ('58) 15 15

United Arab Republic

Nos. 438–444 Overprinted Type "d" in Red or Green

Photogravure.

1958 *Perf. 13½x14* **Wmk. 318**

N62 A136 1m crimson 5 5
N63 A137 2m blue 5 5
N64 A143 3m dk. red brn. (G) 5 5
N65 A217 4m green 6 6
N66 A137 5m brown 10 10
N67 A138 10m violet 10 10
N68 A137 35m light ultra. 40 40
Nos. N62–N68 (7) 81 81

Same Overprint in Red on Freedom Struggle Type of 1958

1958 *Perf. 13½x13*

N69 A145 10m dark brown 1.00 1.00

Same Overprint in Green on Declaration of Human Rights Type of 1958.

1958 *Perf. 13x13½*

N70 A151 10m rose violet 1.00 1.00
N71 " 35m red brown 1.50 1.50

No. 460 Overprinted Type "d" in Green

1959 *Perf. 13½* **Wmk. 195**

N72 A112 55m on 100m henna brown 75 75

"PALESTINE" Added in English and Arabic to Stamps of Egypt

World Refugee Year Type

1960 *Perf. 13x13½* **Wmk. 328**

N73 A173 10m orange brown 10 10
N74 " 35m dark blue gray 30 30

Type of Regular Issue 1959–60

1960 *Perf. 13½x14*

N75 A143 1m brown orange 5 5
N76 " 4m olive gray 5 5
N77 " 5m dark dull purple 6 6
N78 " 10m dark olive green 12 12

Palestine Day Type

1961, May 15 *Perf. 13½x13*

N79 A184 10m purple 12 12

WHO Day Type

1961 *Perf. 13½x13* **Wmk. 328**

N80 A182 10m blue 15 15

U.N.T.A.P. Type

1961, Oct. 24

N81 A191 10m dk. blue & org. 10 10
N82 " 35m verm. & black 30 30

Education Day Type

1961, Dec. 18 Photo. *Perf. 13½*

N83 A194 10m red brown 10 10

Victory Day Type

1961, Dec. 23 *Perf. 11½* **Unwmkd.**

N84 A195 10m brn. org. & brn. 12 12

Gaza Strip Type

Perf. 13½x13

1962, March 7 **Wmk. 328**

N85 A200 10m red brown 10 10

Arab Publicity Week Type

1962, March 22 *Perf. 13½x13*

N86 SP16 10m dark purple 10 10

Anti-Malaria Type

1962, June 20 Photogravure

N87 A204 10m brown & dark carmine rose 10 10
N88 " 35m black & yellow 30 30

Hammarskjold Type

Perf. 11½x11

1962, Oct. 24 **Wmk. 342**

Portrait in Slate Blue

N89 A214 5m bright rose 6 6
N90 " 10m brown 15 15
N91 " 35m blue 35 35

Lamp Type of Regular Issue

Perf. 11x11½

1963, Feb. 20 **Unwmkd.**

N92 A217 4m dark brown, orange & ultra. 6 6

"Freedom from Hunger" Type

Perf. 11½x11, 11x11½

1963, Mar. 21 **Wmk. 342**

N93 A220 5m light green & deep orange 5 5
N94 " 10m olive & yellow 8 8
N95 " 35m dull purple, yellow & black 28 28

Red Cross Centenary Type

Designs: 10m, Centenary emblem, bottom panel added. 35m, Globe and emblem, top and bottom panels added.

Perf. 11x11½

1963, May 8 **Unwmkd.**

N96 A221 10m dk. bl. & crimson 8 8
N97 " 35m crimson & dk. bl. 28 28

"Save Abu Simbel" Type, 1963

1963, Oct. 15 *Perf. 11* **Wmk. 342**

N98 A224 5m black & yellow 5 5
N99 " 10m gray, blk. & yel. 8 8
N100 " 35m org. yel. & vio. 28 28

Human Rights Type, 1963

1963, Dec. 10 Photo. *Perf. 11½x11*

N101 A228 5m dk. brown & yel. 5 5
N102 " 10m deep claret, gray & black 8 8
N103 " 35m lt. green, pale green & black 28 28

Types of Regular Issue, 1964

1964 *Perf. 11* **Unwmkd.**

N104 A231 1m citron & lt. violet 5 5
N105 A230 2m orange & slate 5 5
N106 " 3m blue & ocher 5 5
N107 A235 4m olive gray, olive, brown & rose 5 5
N108 A230 5m rose & bright bl. 10 10
a. 5m rose & dk. blue 1.00 1.00
N109 A231 10m olive, rose & brn. 8 8
N110 A230 15m lilac & yellow 20 20
N111 " 20m brn. blk. & olive 10 10
N112 A231 30m dp. orange & indigo 15 15
N113 " 35m buff, ocher & emerald 18 18
N114 " 40m ultra. & emerald 20 20
N115 " 60m greenish blue & brown orange 40 40

Wmk. 342

N116 A232 100m bluish black & yellow brn. 50 50
Nos. N104–N116 (13) 2.11 2.11

Arab League Council Type, 1964

1964, Jan. 13 Photogravure

N117 A234 10m olive & black 5 5

Minaret Type, 1964

1964 *Perf. 11* **Unwmkd.**

N118 A235 4m olive, red brown & red 5 5

Arab Postal Union Type, 1964

1964, Apr. 1 *Perf. 11* **Wmk. 342**

N119 A239 10m emerald & ultra., *lt. grn.* 8 8

WHO Type, 1964

1964, Apr. 7

N120 A240 10m vio. blk. & red 8 8

Minaret Type, 1965

1965, Jan. 20 *Perf. 11* **Unwmkd.**

N121 A255 4m grn. & dk. brn. 6 6

Arab League Type, 1965

1965, Mar. 22 *Perf. 11* **Wmk. 342**

N122 A258 10m grn., red & blk. 8 8
N123 " 20m green & brn. 16 16

World Health Day Type, 1965

1965, Apr. 7 *Perf. 11* **Wmk. 342**

N124 A259 10m brt. grn. & crim. 8 8

Massacre Type, 1965

1965, Apr. 9 Photogravure

N125 A260 10m slate bl. & red 12 12

ITU Type, 1965

1965, May 17 *Perf. 11* **Wmk. 342**

N126 A261 5m slate grn., slate blue & yel. 5 5
N127 " 10m carmine, rose red & gray 8 8
N128 " 35m vio. bl., ultra. & yellow 28 28

United Nations Type, 1966

Designs: 5m, WHO Headquarters Building, Geneva. 10m, U.N. Refugee emblem. 35m, UNICEF emblem.

1966, Oct. 24 *Perf. 11* **Wmk. 342**

N129 A288 5m rose & brt. pur. 5 5
N130 " 10m yellow brown & brt. purple 6 6
N131 " 35m bright green & brt. purple 28 28

Victory Day Type, 1966

Photogravure

1966, Dec. 23 *Perf. 11½* **Wmk. 342**

N132 A290 10m olive & car. rose 6 6

Arab Publicity Week Type, 1967

Perf. 11x11½

1967, Mar. 22 Photo. **Wmk. 342**

N133 A294 10m vio. bl. & brn. 6 6

Labor Day Type, 1967

Perf. 11½x11

1967, May 1 Photo. **Wmk. 342**

N134 A296 10m olive & sepia 6 6

OCCUPATION AIR POST STAMPS.

Nos. C39–C50 Overprinted Type "b" in Black, Carmine or Red.

Perf. 13x13½

1948, May 15 **Wmk. 195**

NC1 AP3 2m red orange (Bk) 12 12
NC2 " 3m dark brown (C) 12 12
NC3 " 5m red brown (Bk) 12 12
NC4 " 7m deep yellow orange (Bk) 15 15
NC5 " 8m green (C) 15 15
NC6 " 10m violet 18 18
NC7 " 20m bright blue 25 25
NC8 " 30m brn. vio. (Bk) 35 35
NC9 " 40m car. rose (Bk) 50 50
NC10 " 50m Prussian green 75 75
NC11 " 100m olive green 1.25 1.25
NC12 " 200m dark gray 2.50 2.50
Nos. NC1–NC12 (12) 6.44 6.44

Nos. NC1-NC12 Overprinted in Black with Three Bars to Obliterate Portrait

1953

NC13 AP3 2m red orange 75 75
NC14 " 3m dark brown 15 15
NC15 " 5m red brown 3.00 3.00
NC16 " 7m dp. yel. org. 30 30
NC17 " 8m green 60 60
NC18 " 10m violet 25 25
NC19 " 20m bright blue 40 40
NC20 " 30m brown violet 35 35
NC21 " 40m carmine rose 45 45
NC22 " 50m Prus. green 75 75
NC23 " 100m olive green 3.00 3.00
NC24 " 200m dark gray 2.25 2.25
Nos. NC13–NC24 (12) 12.25 12.25

Nos. NC1-NC3, NC6, NC10, NC11 with Additional Overprint in Various Colors

ملك مصر والسودان
١٦ أكتوبر سنة ١٩٥١

Overprinted in Black with Three Bars to Obliterate Portrait

NC25 AP3 2m red orange (Bk+Bl) 10 10
NC26 " 3m dark brown (Bk+RV) 2.00 2.00
NC27 " 5m red brown (Bk) 12 10
NC28 " 10m violet (R+G) 2.50 2.50
NC29 " 50m Prussian green (R+RV) 1.50 1.50
NC30 " 100m olive green (R+Bk) 8.50 8.50
Nos. NC25–NC30 (6) 14.72 14.70

Nos. C65-C66 Overprinted Type "b" in Black or Red

1955 *Perf. 13x13½* **Wmk. 195**

NC31 AP4 5m red brown 75 75
NC32 " 15m olive green (R) 1.00 1.00

United Arab Republic

"PALESTINE" Added in Arabic and English to Air Post Stamps.

Type of 1963

Perf. 11½x11

1963, Oct. 24 Photo. **Wmk. 342**

NC33 AP6 80m blk. & brt. bl. 1.00 65
NC34 AP10 115m black & yel. 1.50 95
NC35 " 140m blue, ultra. & orge. red 2.00 1.15

Cairo Tower Type, 1964

Perf. 11x11½

1964, Nov. 2 **Unwmkd.**

NC36 AP11 50m dull vio. & light blue 40 40

World Meteorological Day Type

1965, Mar. 23 *Perf. 11* **Wmk. 342**

NC37 AP12 80m dk. bl. & orge. 65 65

Type of Regular Issue, 1965
(Game Board)

1965, July 1 Photo. *Perf. 11*

NC38 AP13 10m brn. orange & bright green 6 6

OCCUPATION SPECIAL DELIVERY STAMP.

No. E4 Overprinted Type "b" in Carmine.

1948 *Perf. 13x13½.* **Wmk. 195**

NE1 SD1 40m dull brown & pale gray 45 45

OCCUPATION POSTAGE DUE STAMPS.

Postage Due Stamps of Egypt, 1927-41, Overprinted Type "a" in Black or Rose.

1948 *Perf. 13x13½.* **Wmk. 195**

NJ1	D7	2m orange	5	5
NJ2	"	4m green (R)	5	5
NJ3	"	6m gray green	6	6
NJ4	"	8m brown violet	8	8
NJ5	"	10m brick red	10	10
NJ6	"	12m rose lake	12	12

Overprinted Type "b" in Red.
Perf. 14.
Size: 22x28mm.

NJ7	D7	30m purple	30	30
		Nos. NJ1-NJ7 (7)	76	76

ELOBEY, ANNOBON AND CORISCO

(å·lō'bå, än'ô·bōn' & kô·rïs'kō)

LOCATION — A group of islands near the Guinea Coast of western Africa.

GOVT. — Spanish colonial possessions administered as part of the Continental Guinea District. A second district under the same governor-general included Fernando Po.

AREA—13¾ sq. mi.

POP.—2,950 (estimated 1910).

CAPITAL—Santa Isabel.

100 Centimos = 1 Peseta

King Alfonso XIII
A1

Typographed.

Control Numbers on Back

1903 *Perf. 14* **Unwmkd.**

1	A1	¼c carmine	75	35
2	"	½c dark violet	75	35
3	"	1c black	75	35
4	"	2c red	75	35
5	"	3c dark green	75	35
6	"	4c dark blue green	75	35
7	"	5c violet	75	35
8	"	10c rose lake	1.50	1.00
9	"	15c orange buff	4.50	1.00
10	"	25c dark blue	7.50	3.00
11	"	50c red brown	10.00	4.50
12	"	75c black brown	10.00	6.00
13	"	1p orange red	15.00	8.00
14	"	2p chocolate	37.50	20.00
15	"	3p dp. olive grn.	55.00	25.00
16	"	4p claret	120.00	37.50
17	"	5p blue green	135.00	37.50
18	"	10p dull blue	275.00	52.50
		Nos. 1-18 (18)	676.25	198.45

Same as A1, Dated "1905".

1905 **Control Numbers on Back**

19	A1	1c carmine	1.50	45
20	"	2c deep violet	6.00	45
21	A1	3c black	1.50	45
22	"	4c dull red	1.50	45
23	"	5c deep green	1.50	45
24	"	10c blue green	5.25	65
25	"	15c violet	6.00	2.50
26	"	25c rose lake	6.00	2.50
27	"	50c orange buff	10.00	3.75
28	"	75c dark blue	10.00	3.75
29	"	1p red brown	21.00	9.00
30	"	2p black brown	22.50	12.00
31	"	3p orange red	22.50	12.00
32	"	4p dark brown	150.00	52.50
33	"	5p bronze green	150.00	52.50
34	"	10p claret	425.00	140.00
		Nos. 19-34 (16)	840.25	293.40

Nos. 19-22 Surcharged in Black or Red

1906
10 CÉNTS.

1906

35	A1	10c on 1c rose (Bk)	7.50	3.00
		a. Inverted surcharge	7.50	3.00
		b. Value omitted	15.00	6.50
		c. Frame omitted	8.00	3.50
		d. Double surcharge	7.50	3.00
		e. Surcharged "15 cents"	15.00	6.50
		f. Surcharged "25 cents"	20.00	9.00
		g. Surcharged "50 cents"	20.00	9.00
		h. "1906" omitted	8.00	3.50
36	"	15c on 2c deep violet (R)	7.50	3.00
		a. Frame omitted	8.00	3.00
		b. Surcharged "25 cents"	11.00	4.50
		c. Inverted surcharge	7.50	3.00
		d. Double surcharge	7.50	3.50
36E	"	15c on 2c deep violet (Bk)	8.00	2.50
37	"	25c on 3c black (R)	7.50	3.50
		a. Inverted surcharge	7.50	3.50
		b. Double surcharge	7.50	3.50
		c. Surcharged "15 cents"	8.00	5.00
		d. Surcharged "50 cents"	12.50	5.00
37E	"	25c on 3c black (Bk)	8.00	3.50
		f. Inverted surcharge	8.00	3.50
		g. Surcharged "15 cents"	8.00	5.00
		h. Surcharged "10 cents"	12.50	3.50
38	"	50c on 4c red (Bk)	7.50	3.50
		a. Inverted surcharge	7.50	3.50
		b. Value omitted	18.00	8.50
		c. Frame omitted	8.00	3.50
		e. Double surcharge	7.50	3.50
		f. "1906" omitted	8.00	3.50
		g. Surcharged "10 cents"	15.00	6.50
		h. Surcharged "25 cents"	15.00	6.50
		Nos. 35-38 (6)	46.00	19.00

Eight other surcharges were prepared but not issued: 10c on 50c, 75c, 1p, 2p and 3p; 15c on 50c and 5p; 50c on 5c.

King Alfonso XIII
A2

1907 **Control Numbers on Back**

39	A2	1c dark violet	75	60
40	"	2c black	75	60
41	"	3c red orange	75	60
42	"	4c dark green	75	60
43	"	5c blue green	75	60
44	"	10c violet	8.50	3.50
45	"	15c carmine	3.00	1.10
46	"	25c orange	3.00	1.10
47	"	50c blue	3.00	1.10
48	"	75c brown	9.00	1.85
49	"	1p black brown	15.00	3.50
50	"	2p orange red	20.00	5.25
51	"	3p dark brown	20.00	5.25
52	"	4p bronze green	20.00	5.25
53	"	5p claret	27.50	5.25
54	"	10p rose	60.00	15.00
		Nos. 39-54 (16)	192.75	51.15

Stamps of 1907 Surcharged

HABILITADO
PARA
05CTMS

1908-09 Black Surcharge.

55	A2	5c on 3c red orange ('09)	2.00	1.00
56	"	5c on 4c dark green ('09)	2.00	1.00
57	"	5c on 10c violet	4.25	4.25
58	"	25c on 10c violet	25.00	15.00

1910 Red Surcharge.

59	A2	5c on 1c dark violet	2.00	1.00
60	"	5c on 2c black	2.00	1.00

Nos. 55-60 exist with surcharge inverted (price each $10 unused, $7.50 used); with double surcharge, one black, one red (price $15 each); with "PARA" omitted (price each $15 unused, $7.50 used).

The same 5c surcharge was also applied to Nos. 45-54, but these were not issued. Price $10 each.

In 1909, stamps of Spanish Guinea replaced those of Elobey, Annobon and Corisco.

1909
CORREOS
10 cen de peseta

Revenue stamps surcharged as above were unauthorized although some were postally used.

EPIRUS

(ê·pī'rŭs)

LOCATION—Southeastern Europe comprising parts of Greece and Albania.

This territory formerly belonged to Turkey but is now divided between Greece and Albania. The northern part of the Greek section, now a part of Albania, set up a provisional government during 1912–13 and issued postage stamps but it collapsed in 1916, following Greek occupation. The name "Epirus" is taken from the Greek word meaning "Mainland."

100 Lepta = 1 Drachma

Chimarra Issue.

Double-headed Eagle, Skull and Crossbones
A1

Handstamped. Without Gum.

1914 (Feb.) *Imperf.* **Unwmkd.**

Control Mark in Blue.

1	A1	1 l black & blue		
2	"	5 l blue & red		
3	"	10 l red & black		
4	"	25 l blue & red		
		Nos. 1-4 (4)	*400.00*	*300.00*

All values exist without control mark. This mark is a solid blue oval, about 12x8 mm., containing the colorless Greek letters "ΣΠ," the first two letters of Spiromilios, the Chimarra commander.

All four exist with value inverted and the 1, 5 and 10 l with value double.

Some students question the official character of this issue. Counterfeits are plentiful.

Provisional Government Issues

Infantryman with Rifle
A2 A3

Serrate Roulette 13½

1914 (March) **Lithographed**

5	A2	1 l orange	75	75
6	"	5 l green	50	50
7	A3	10 l carmine	50	50
8	"	25 l deep blue	50	50
9	A2	50 l brown	2.00	2.00
10	"	1d violet	3.00	3.00
11	"	2d black	15.00	10.00
12	"	5d gray green	13.50	10.00
		Nos. 5-12 (8)	35.75	27.25

Turkish stamps surcharged "Epirus Autonomous" and new values in Greek were on sale for a few days in Argyrokastron (Gjinokaster).

Flag of Epirus
A5

1914 (Aug.)

15	A5	1 l brown & blue	65	65
16	"	5 l green & blue	65	65
17	"	10 l rose red & blue	90	90
18	"	25 l dark blue & blue	1.25	1.25
19	"	50 l violet & blue	1.25	1.25
20	"	1d carmine & blue	3.25	3.25
21	"	2d orange & blue	1.25	1.25
22	"	5d dk. green & blue	3.25	3.25
		Nos. 15-22 (8)	12.45	12.45

Koritsa Issue.

A7

1914

26	A7	25 l dark blue & bl.	4.00	4.50
27	"	50 l violet & blue	5.00	6.00

Chimarra Issue.

1911-23 Issues of Greece Overprinted

ΕΛΛΗΝΙΚΗ
1914
ΧΕΙΜΑΡΡΑ

1914 (Aug.)

34	A24	1 l green	3.75	2.75
35	A25	2 l carmine	3.75	2.75
36	A24	3 l vermilion	3.75	2.75
37	A26	5 l green	5.50	4.00
38	A24	10 l carmine	8.00	6.25
39	A25	20 l slate	11.00	9.00
40	"	25 l blue	15.00	12.50
41	A26	50 l violet brown	18.50	16.50
		Nos. 34-41 (8)	69.25	56.50

The 2 l and 3 l are engraved stamps of the 1911–21 issue, the others are lithographed stamps of the 1912–23 issue.

Overprint reads: "Greek Chimarra 1914".

Stamps of this issue are with or without a black monogram (S.S., for S. Spiromilios) in manuscript. Counterfeits are plentiful.

Foreign postal stationery (stamped envelopes, postal cards and air letter sheets) lies beyond the scope of this Catalogue which is limited to adhesive postage stamps.

Stamps of the following designs were not regularly issued for postal purposes in the opinion of the editors.

ΛΕΠΤΑ 5
ΚΟΡΥΤΣΑ

Three varieties, 1914

Six varieties, 1914

Seven varieties, 1914.

Fifteen varieties, 1914.

Four varieties, 1920.

OCCUPATION STAMPS.

Issued under Greek Occupation.

Greek Occupation Stamps of 1913 Overprinted Horizontally

Β. ΗΠΕΙΡΟΣ

Serrate Roulette 13½.

1914-15 Black Overprint. **Unwmkd.**

N1	O1	1 l brown	90	90
N2	O2	2 l red	90	90
		b. 2 l rose	2.00	2.00
N4	O2	3 l orange	90	90
N5	O1	5 l green	1.20	1.20
N6	"	10 l rose red	1.65	1.65
N7	"	20 l violet	3.75	3.75
N8	O2	25 l pale blue	4.25	4.25
N9	O1	30 l gray green	13.50	12.00
N10	O2	40 l indigo	13.50	12.00
N11	O1	50 l dark blue	13.50	12.00
N12	O2	1d violet brown	37.50	30.00
		Nos. N1-N12 (11)	91.55	79.55

The overprint exists double on 4 denominations (1 l, 2 l red, 3 l and 1d); inverted on 7 (1 l, 2 l red, 3 l, 5 l, 10 l, 20 l and 1d). Prices twice or triple normal copies.

Red Overprint.

N1a	1 l brown	2.00
N2a	2 l red	2.00
N4a	3 l orange	2.00
N5a	5 l green	2.00

Nos. N1a–N5a were not issued. Exist canceled.

Regular Issues of Greece, 1911–23, Overprinted

Β. ΗΠΕΙΡΟΣ

On Issue of 1911-21

1916 **Engraved.**

N17	A24	3 l vermilion	2.00	2.00
N18	A26	30 l carmine rose	30.00	30.00
N19	A27	1d ultramarine	45.00	40.00
N20	"	2d vermilion	60.00	55.00
N21	"	3d carmine rose	60.00	55.00
N22	"	5d ultramarine	135.00	125.00
		a. Double overprint	135.00	125.00
		Nos. N17-N22 (6)	332.00	307.00

On Issue of 1912-23.

1916 **Lithographed**

N23	A24	1 l green	1.40	1.40
N24	A25	2 l carmine	1.40	1.40
N25	A24	3 l vermilion	1.40	1.40
N26	A26	5 l green	1.40	1.40
N27	A24	10 l carmine	3.25	3.25
N28	A25	20 l slate	5.00	5.00
N29	"	25 l blue	5.25	5.25
N30	A26	30 l rose	9.00	9.00
N31	A25	40 l indigo	9.00	9.00
N32	A26	50 l violet brown	9.00	9.00
		Nos. N23-N32 (10)	46.10	46.10

In each sheet there are two varieties in the overprint: the "I" in "Epirus" omitted and an inverted "L" in place of the first letter of the word.

Counterfeits exist of Nos. N1–N32.

Postage stamps issued in 1940–41, during Greek occupation, are listed under Greece.

EQUATORIAL GUINEA

LOCATION—Gulf of Guinea, West Africa.
GOVT.—Republic.
AREA—10,832 sq. mi.
POP.—310,000 (est. 1974).
CAPITAL—Malabo.

The Spanish provinces Fernando Po and Rio Muni united and became independent as the Republic of Equatorial Guinea, Oct. 12, 1968.

100 Centimos = 1 Peseta

Clasped Hands and Laurel

A1

Pres. Francisco Macias Nguema

A2

Photogravure

1968, Oct. 12 ***Perf. 13*** **Unwmkd.**

1	A1	1p deep blue, gold & sepia	8	8
2	"	1.50p dark green, gold & brown	8	8
3	"	6p copper red, gold & brown	30	12

Issued to commemorate the attainment of independence, Oct. 12, 1968.

1970, Jan. 27 ***Perf. 13x12½***

4	A2	50c dull orange, brown & crimson	8	8
5	"	1p pink, green & lilac	8	8
6	"	1.50p pale olive, brown & blue green	8	8
7	"	2p buff, green & olive	10	8
8	"	2.50p pale green, dk. grn. & dark blue	20	10
9	"	10p bister, Prus. blue & violet brown	1.15	20
10	"	25p gray, blk. & brn.	2.25	40
		Nos. 4-10 (7)	3.94	1.02

Pres. Macias Nguema and Cock

A3

1971, Apr. **Photogravure** ***Perf. 13***

11	A3	3p light blue & multi.	10	10
12	"	5p buff & multi.	30	10
13	"	10p pale lilac & multi.	50	20
14	"	25p pale grn. & multi.	90	50

2nd anniversary of independence, Oct. 12, 1970.

Torch, Bow and Arrows—A4

1972 **Photogravure** ***Perf. 11½***

15	A4	50p ocher & multi.	2.50	70

"3rd Triumphal Year."

Certain unlisted issues of Equatorial Guinea, starting in 1972, are mentioned and briefly described in "For the Record" at the back of this volume.

SPECIAL DELIVERY STAMPS

Archer with Crossbow—SD1

1971, Oct. 12 Photo. ***Perf. 12½x13***

E1	SD1	4p blue & multi.	20	10
E2	"	8p rose & multi.	40	12

3rd anniversary of independence.

ERITREA

(ĕr'ē-trā'ä)

LOCATION—In northeast Africa, bordering on the Red Sea.
GOVT.—Former Italian Colony.
AREA—15,754 sq. mi. (1936).
POP.—600,573 (1931).
CAPITAL—Asmara.

Eritrea was incorporated as a State of Italian East Africa in 1936.

100 Centesimi = 1 Lira

Stamps of Italy Overprinted

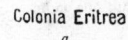

Colonia Eritrea

a

b

Wmk. 140

Wmkd. Crown (140)

1892 ***Perf. 14.***

Overprinted Type "a" in Black.

1	A6	1c bronze green	1.40	45
		a. Invtd. overprint	175.00	120.00
		b. Double ovpt.	300.00	
2	A7	2c orange brown	45	27
		a. Invtd. overprint	300.00	200.00
		b. Double ovpt.	325.00	
3	A33	5c green	12.00	1.60
		a. Inverted ovpt.	*1750.00*	*1250.00*

Overprinted Type "b" in Black.

4	A17	10c claret	7.00	65
5	"	20c orange	40.00	75
6	"	25c blue	100.00	6.00
7	A25	40c brown	1.60	1.35
8	A26	45c slate green	2.00	1.60
9	A27	60c violet	2.25	2.00
10	A28	1 l brown & yellow	4.00	3.50
11	A38	5 l blue & rose	120.00	57.50

1895-99

Overprinted type "a" in Black.

12	A39	1c brown ('99)	2.00	2.00
13	A40	2c org. brown ('99)	35	35
14	A41	5c green	35	35
		a. Inverted ovpt.	*450.00*	*1150.00*

Overprinted type "b" in Black.

15	A34	10c claret ('98)	50	40
16	A35	20c orange	65	50
17	A36	25c blue	1.00	80
18	A37	45c olive green	2.25	2.75

Overprinted type "a" in Black.

1903-28

19	A42	1c brown	12	12
		a. Inverted ovpt.	18.50	18.50
20	A43	2c orange brown	12	12
21	A44	5c blue green	7.00	27
22	A45	10c claret	7.50	18
23	"	20c orange	38	18
24	"	25c blue	60.00	2.25
		a. Double ovpt.	90.00	90.00
25	"	40c brown	35.00	2.50
26	"	45c olive green	65	65
27	"	50c violet	30.00	2.25
28	A46	75c dark red & rose ('28)	2.25	1.20
29	"	1 l brown & green	55	35
30	"	1.25 l bl. & ultra. ('28)	1.85	45
31	"	2 l dark green & orange ('25)	2.50	2.50
32	"	2.50 l dark green & org. ('28)	14.00	3.50
33	"	5 l blue & rose	3.00	1.50
		Nos. 19-33 (15)	164.92	18.02

Surcharged in Black

Colonia Eritrea
C. 15

1905

34	A45	15c on 20c orange	4.00	45

Overprinted type "a" in Black

1908-28

35	A48	5c green	12	12
36	"	10c claret ('09)	12	12
37	"	15c slate ('20)	55	45
38	A49	20c green ('25)	60	70
39	"	20c lilac brown ('28)	55	55
40	"	25c blue ('09)	25	12
41	"	30c gray ('25)	60	70
42	"	40c brown ('16)	5.50	2.75
43	"	50c violet ('16)	75	27
44	"	60c brn. car. ('18)	1.35	1.50
45	"	60c brn. orge. ('28)	17.50	22.50
46	A51	10 l gray green & red ('16)	72.50	90.00
		Nos. 35-46 (12)	100.39	119.78

See also No. 53.

Government Building at Massaua

A1 A2

Engraved.

1910-29 ***Perf. 13½*** **Unwmkd.**

47	A1	15c slate	30.00	1.40
		a. Perf. 11 ('29)	20.00	13.50
48	A2	25c dark blue	70	65
		a. Perf. 12		

Farmer Plowing
A3 A4

1914–28

49 A3 5c green 27 27
a. Perf. 11 ('28) 135.00 15.00
50 A4 10c carmine 70 35
a. Perf. 11 ('28) 12.50 5.00
b. Perf. 13½x14 3.75 1.35

No. 47 Surcharged in Red or Black

Cent. 5

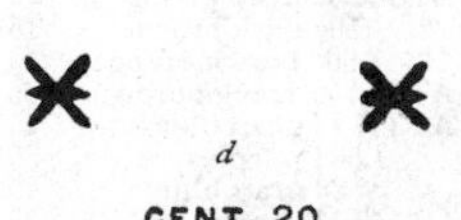

d

CENT. 20

e

1916

51 A1 (*d*) 5c on 15c slate (R) 2.75 3.25
52 " (*e*) 20c on 15c slate 22 15
a. "CEN" for "CENT" 4.50 4.50
b. "CENT" omitted 22.50 22.50
c. "ENT" 4.50 4.50

Italy No. 113 Overprinted in Black **ERITREA** *f*

1921 ***Perf. 14.*** **Wmk. 140**

53 A50 20c brown orange 55 75

Victory Issue.

Italian Victory Stamps of 1921 Overprinted type "f" 13mm. long.

1922

54 A64 5c olive green 45 60
55 " 10c red 45 60
56 " 15c slate green 60 85
57 " 25c ultramarine 75 1.00

Somalia Nos. 10–16 Overprinted **ERITREA** *g*

In Black and Bars over Original Values,

1922 **Wmkd. Crowns. (140)**

58 A1 2c on 1b brown 1.00 1.15
59 " 5c on 2b blue green 1.00 1.00
60 A2 10c on 1a claret 1.00 30
61 " 15c on 2a brn. orange 1.00 40
62 " 25c on 2½a blue 1.00 40
63 " 50c on 5a yellow 2.00 65
a. "ERITREA" double 135.00
64 " 1 l on 10a lilac 2.65 2.25
a. "ERITREA" double 100.00 100.00
Nos. 58-64 (7) 9.65 6.15

See Nos. 81–87.

Propagation of the Faith Issue.

Italy Nos. 143–146 Overprinted **ERITREA**

1923

65 A68 20c olive green & brown orange 2.40 4.00
66 " 30c claret & brown orange 2.40 4.00
67 " 50c violet & brown orange 2.10 3.50
68 " 1 l blue & brown orange 2.10 3.50

Fascisti Issue.

Italy Nos. 159–164 Overprinted in Red or Black

ERITREA *j*

1923 ***Perf. 14*** **Unwmkd.**

69 A69 10c dark green (R) 75 1.10
70 " 30c dark violet (R) 75 1.10
71 " 50c brown carmine 75 1.10

Wmkd. Crowns. (140)

72 A70 1 l blue 1.00 1.50
73 " 2 l brown 1.10 1.65
74 A71 5 l black & blue (R) 3.75 5.50
Nos. 69-74 (6) 8.10 11.95

Manzoni Issue.

Italy Nos. 165-170 Overprinted **ERITREA** in Red.

1924 ***Perf. 14.***

75 A72 10c brown red & blk. 50 1.50
76 " 15c bl. grn. & black 50 1.50
77 " 30c black & slate 50 1.50
78 " 50c orange brown & black 50 1.50
79 " 1 l blue & black 13.50 24.00
80 " 5 l violet & blk. 210.00 300.00
Nos. 75-80 (6) 225.50 330.00

On Nos. 79 and 80 the overprint is placed vertically at the left side.

Somalia Nos. 10-16 Overprinted type "g" in Blue or Red.

1924

Bars over Original Values.

81 A1 2c on 1b brown 3.00 3.25
82 " 5c on 2b blue green (R) 1.85 2.25
83 A2 10c on 1a rose red 45 45
84 " 15c on 2a brown orange 45 45
a. Pair, one without "ERITREA" 200.00
85 " 25c on 2½a blue (R) 65 50
a. Double surch. 100.00
86 " 50c on 5a yellow 3.00 90
87 " 1 l on 10a lilac (R) 3.75 3.75
Nos. 81-87 (7) 13.15 11.55

Stamps of Italy, 1901–08 Overprinted type "j" in Black.

1924

88 A42 1c brown 75 1.10
a. Inverted ovpt. 60.00
89 A43 2c orange brown 38 50
90 A48 5c green 90 70

Victor Emmanuel Issue.

Italy Nos. 175–177 Overprinted **ERITREA** *k*

1925–26 ***Perf. 11*** **Unwmkd.**

91 A78 60c brown carmine 30 60
a. Perf. 13½ 1.50 2.25
92 " 1 l dark blue 22 50
a. Perf. 13½ 7500.00 1500.00

Perf. 13½

93 A78 1.25 l dark blue ('26) 50 90
a. Perf. 11 90 1.50

Saint Francis of Assisi Issue.

Italian Stamps of 1926 Overprinted

ERITREA

1926 ***Perf. 14*** **Wmk. 140**

94 A79 20c gray green 55 90
95 A80 40c dark violet 55 90
96 A81 60c red brown 55 90

Overprinted in Red **Eritrea**

Perf. 11 **Unwmkd.**

97 A82 1.25 l dark blue 55 90

Perf. 14

98 A83 5 l + 2.50 l olive green 2.50 3.50
Nos. 94-98 (5) 4.70 7.10

Italian Stamps of 1926 Overprinted type "f" in Black.

1926 ***Perf. 14.*** **Wmk. 140**

99 A46 75c dark red & rose 2.25 1.00
a. Double ovpt. 60.00
100 " 1.25 l blue & ultra. 2.00 40
101 " 2.50 l dark green & orange 15.00 3.25

Volta Issue.

Type of Italy, 1927, Overprinted **Eritrea** *o*

1927

102 A84 20c purple 1.50 1.85
103 " 50c deep orange 1.50 1.85
a. Double overprint 20.00
104 " 1.25 l bright blue 3.75 4.50

Italian Stamps of 1925-28 Overprinted type "a" in Black.

1928-29

105 A86 7½c lt. brown ('29) 2.75 3.25
106 " 50c bright violet 2.75 2.75

Italian Stamps of 1927-28 Overprinted type "f."

1928-29

107 A86 50c bright violet 5.25 6.25

Perf. 11. **Unwmkd.**

107A A85 1.75 l deep brown 3.75 1.75

Italy No. 192 Overprinted type "o."

1928 ***Perf. 14*** **Wmk. 140**

108 A85 50c brown & slate 75 35

Monte Cassino Issue.

Types of 1929 Issue of Italy Overprinted in Red or Blue ERITREA

1929 ***Perf. 14.***

109 A96 20c dark green (R) 75 1.50
110 " 25c red orange (Bl) 75 1.50
111 A98 50c+10c crimson (Bl) 75 1.50
112 " 75c+15c olive brown (R) 75 1.50
113 A96 1.25 l+25c dark violet (R) 4.50 6.75
114 A98 5 l+1 l sapphire (R) 4.50 6.75

Overprinted in Red **Eritrea**

Unwmkd.

115 A100 10 l+2 l gray brown 4.50 6.75
Nos. 109-115 (7) 16.56 26.25

Royal Wedding Issue.

Type of Italian Stamps of 1930 Overprinted ERITREA

1930 **Wmk. 140**

116 A101 20c yellow green 60 90
117 " 50c+10c deep orange 75 1.50
118 " 1.25 l+25c rose red 1.00 2.00

Lancer
A5

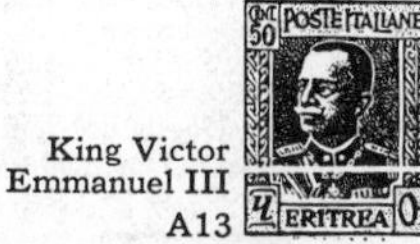

Scene in Massaua
A6

Designs: 2c, 35c, Lancer. 5c, 10c, Postman. 15c, Lineman. 25c, Askari (infantryman). 2 l, Railroad viaduct. 5 l, Asmara Deghe Selam. 10 l, Camels.

Lithographed

1930 ***Perf. 14*** **Wmk. 140**

119 A5 2c bright blue & black 20 20
120 " 5c dark violet & black 20 20
121 " 10c yel. brown & black 20 20
122 " 15c dark green & black 20 20
123 " 25c gray green & black 20 13
124 " 35c red brown & black 50 65
125 A6 1 l dark blue & black 15 13
126 " 2 l chocolate & black 1.50 90
127 " 5 l olive grn. & blk. 2.10 2.50
128 " 10 l dull blue & black 2.75 3.75
Nos. 119-128 (10) 8.00 8.86

Ferrucci Issue.

Types of Italian Stamps of 1930 Overprinted type "f" in Red or Blue.

1930

129 A102 20c violet (R) 35 35
130 A103 25c dark green (R) 35 35
131 " 50c black (R) 35 35
132 " 1.25 l deep blue (R) 35 35
133 A104 5 l + 2 l deep carmine (Bl) 2.75 2.75
Nos. 129-133 (5) 4.15 4.15

Virgil Issue.

Types of Italian Stamps of 1930 Overprinted in Red or Blue

ERITREA

1930 **Photogravure.**

134 A106 15c violet black 15 35
135 " 20c orange brown 15 35
136 " 25c dark green 15 35
137 " 30c light brown 15 35
138 " 50c dull violet 15 35
139 " 75c rose red 15 35
140 " 1.25 l gray blue 15 35

Engraved.

Unwmkd.

141 A106 5 l+1.50 l dk. violet 1.85 3.75
142 " 10 l+2.50 l olive brn. 1.85 3.75
Nos. 134-142 (9) 4.75 9.95

Saint Anthony of Padua Issue.

Types of Italian Stamps of 1931 Overprinted type "f" in Blue, Red or Black

1931 **Photogravure.** **Wmk. 140**

143 A116 20c brown (Bl) 30 60
144 " 25c green (R) 30 60
145 A118 30c gray brown (Bl) 30 60
146 " 50c dull violet (Bl) 30 60
147 A120 1.25 l slate blue (R) 30 60

Engraved.

Unwmkd.

148 A121 75c black (R) 30 60
149 A122 5 l + 2.50 l dark brown (Bk) 3.00 5.25
Nos. 143-149 (7) 4.80 8.85

King Victor Emmanuel III
A13

1931 **Photo.** **Wmkd. Crown. (140)**

150 A13 7½c olive brown 22 22
151 " 20c slate blue & car. 15 15
152 " 30c olive green & brown violet 22 15
153 " 40c bl. & yel. green 22 15
154 " 50c bistre brown & olive 15 15
155 " 75c carmine rose 50 15
156 " 1.25 l violet & indigo 1.00 15
157 " 2.50 l dull green 2.00 38
Nos. 150-157 (8) 4.46 1.50

Camel
A14

Temple Ruins
A18

Designs: 2c, 10, Camel. 5c, 15c, Shark fishery. 25c, Baobab tree. 35c, Pastoral scene. 2 l, African elephant. 5 l, Eritrean man. 10 l, Eritrean woman.

1934 Photo. Wmkd. Crowns. (140)

158 A14 2c deep blue 20 20
159 " 5c black 20 20
160 " 10c brown 20 15
161 " 15c orange brown 30 22
162 " 25c gray green 30 15
163 " 35c purple 45 50
164 A18 1 l dark blue gray 22 15
165 A14 2 l olive black 2.75 38
166 A18 5 l carmine rose 2.00 45
167 " 10 l red orange 2.25 60
Nos. 158–167 (10) 8.87 3.00

Abruzzi Issue.

Types of 1934 Issue Overprinted in Black or Red ONORANZE AL DUCA DEGLI ABRUZZI

1934

168 A14 10c dull blue (R) 2.25 2.25
169 " 15c blue 1.50 2.25
170 " 35c green (R) 1.50 2.25
171 A18 1 l copper red 1.50 2.25
172 A14 2 l rose red 3.75 3.75
173 A18 5 l purple (R) 2.25 3.75
174 " 10 l olive green (R) 2.25 3.75
Nos. 168–174 (7) 15.00 20.25

Grant's Gazelle
A22

1934 Photogravure

175 A22 5c olive grn. & brn. 1.25 2.50
176 " 10c yellow brown & black 1.25 2.50
177 " 20c scarlet & indigo 1.25 2.50
178 " 50c dk. vio. & brn. 1.25 2.50
179 " 60c orange brown & indigo 1.25 2.50
180 " 1.25 l dk. blue & grn. 1.25 2.50
Nos. 175–180 (6) 7.50 15.00

Second Colonial Arts Exhibition, Naples. See also Nos. C1–C6.

SEMI-POSTAL STAMPS.

Many issues of Italy and Italian Colonies include one or more semipostal denominations. To avoid splitting sets, these issues are generally listed as regular postage, airmail, etc., unless all values carry a surtax.

Italy Nos. B1–B3 Overprinted type "f."

1915-16 ***Perf. 14.*** **Wmk. 140**

B1 SP1 10c+5c rose 55 85
a. "EPITREA" 3.00 3.50
b. Inverted ovpt. 150.00 150.00
B2 SP2 15c+5c slate 3.00 3.50
B3 " 20c+5c orange 1.00 1.25
a. "EPITREA" 4.50 5.25
b. Inverted overprint 37.50 37.50
c. Pair, one without ovpt. 600.00

No. B2 Surcharged **20**

1916

B4 SP2 20c on 15c+5c slate 3.00 3.50
a. "EPITREA" 18.00 16.50
b. Pair, one without overprint 175.00

Counterfeits exist of the minor varieties of Nos. B1, B3–B4.

Holy Year Issue.

Italy Nos. B20–B25 Overprinted in Black or Red

ERITREA

1925 ***Perf. 12***

B5 SP4 20c+10c dark green & brown 60 1.10
B6 " 30c+15c dark brown & brown 60 1.10
a. Double overprint
B7 " 50c+25c vio. & brn. 60 1.10
B8 " 60c+30c deep rose & brown 60 1.10
a. Inverted overprint
B9 SP8 1 l+50c deep blue & violet (R) 1.35 2.25
B10 " 5 l+2.50 l orange brown & violet (R) 1.75 3.00
Nos. B5–B10 (6) 5.50 9.65

Colonial Institute Issue.

"Peace" Substituting Spade for Sword
SP1

1926 Typographed ***Perf. 14***

B11 SP1 5c+5c brown 22 45
B12 " 10c+5c olive green 22 45
B13 " 20c+5c blue green 22 45
B14 " 40c+5c brown red 22 45
B15 " 60c+5c orange 22 45
B16 " 1 l+5c blue 22 45
Nos. B11–B16 (6) 1.32 2.70

The surtax of 5c on each stamp was for the Italian Colonial Institute.

Types of Italian Semi-Postal Stamps of 1926 Overprinted type "k."

1927 ***Perf. 11½*** **Unwmkd.**

B17 SP10 40c+20c dark brown & black 90 1.50
B18 " 60c+30c brown red & olive brown 90 1.50
B19 " 1.25 l+60c deep blue & black 90 1.50
B20 " 5 l+2.50 l dark green & black 1.75 3.00

The surtax on these stamps was for the charitable work of the Voluntary Militia for Italian National Defense.

Fascism and Victory
SP2

Typographed.

1928 ***Perf. 14.*** **Wmk. 140**

B21 SP2 20c+5c blue green 50 90
B22 " 30c+5c red 50 90
B23 SP2 50c+10c purple 50 90
B24 " 1.25 l+20c dark blue 50 90

The surtax was for the Society Africana d'Italia, whose 46th anniversary was commemorated by the issue.

Types of Italian Semi-Postal Stamps of 1928 Overprinted type "f."

1929 ***Perf. 11.*** **Unwmkd.**

B25 SP10 30c+10c red & black 75 1.50
B26 " 50c+20c violet & black 75 1.50
B27 " 1.25 l+50c brown & blue 1.35 2.25
B28 " 5 l+2 l olive green & blk. 1.35 2.25

The surtax was for the charitable work of the Voluntary Militia for Italian National Defense.

Types of Italian Semi-Postal Stamps of 1929 Overprinted type "f" in Black or Red.

1930 ***Perf. 14.***

B29 SP10 30c+10c dark green & blue green (Bk) 1.50 2.25
B30 " 50c+10c dark green & violet (R) 1.50 2.25
B31 " 1.25 l+30c olive brown & red brown (R) 2.25 3.00
B32 " 5 l+1.50 l indigo & green (R) 12.00 20.00

The surtax was for the charitable work of the Voluntary Militia for Italian National Defense.

Agriculture
SP3

1930 Photogravure **Wmk. 140**

B33 SP3 50c+20c olive brown 65 1.15
B34 " 1.25 l+20c deep blue 65 1.15
B35 " 1.75 l+20c green 65 1.15
B36 " 2.55 l+50c purple 2.50 3.50
B37 " 5 l+1 l deep car. 2.50 3.50
Nos. B33–B37 (5) 6.95 10.45

Italian Colonial Agricultural Institute, 25th anniversary. The surtax aided that institution.

AIR POST STAMPS

Desert Scene—AP1

Design: 80c, 1 l, 2 l, Plane and globe.

Wmkd. Crowns. (140)

1934 Photogravure. ***Perf. 14.***

C1 AP1 25c slate blue & orange red 1.25 2.25
C2 " 50c green & indigo 1.25 2.25
C3 " 75c brn. & org. red 1.25 2.25
C4 " 80c orange brown & olive green 1.25 2.25
C5 " 1 l scarlet & olive green 1.25 2.25
C6 " 2 l dk. blue & brown 1.25 2.25
Nos. C1–C6 (6) 7.50 13.50

Second Colonial Arts Exhibition, Naples.

Plowing
AP3

Plane and Cacti
AP6

Designs: 25c, 1.50 l, Plowing. 50c, 2 l, Plane over mountain pass. 60c, 5 l, Plane and trees. 75c, 10 l, Plane and cacti. 1 l, 3 l, Bridge.

1936 Photogravure.

C7 AP3 25c deep green 22 30
C8 " 50c dark brown 15 15
C9 " 60c brown orange 45 60
C10 AP6 75c orange brown 30 15
C11 AP3 1 l deep blue 15 15
C12 " 1.50 l purple 30 15
C13 " 2 l gray blue 45 22
C14 " 3 l copper red 4.25 1.75
C15 " 5 l green 3.00 45
C16 AP6 10 l rose red 8.50 60
Nos. C7–C16 (10) 17.77 4.52

AIR POST SEMI-POSTAL STAMPS.

King Victor Emmanuel III
SPAP1

Photogravure.

1934 ***Perf. 14*** **Wmk. 140**

CB1 SPAP1 25c+10c gray green 1.50 1.50
CB2 " 50c+10c brown 1.50 1.50
CB3 " 75c+15c rose red 1.50 1.50
CB4 " 80c+15c black brown 1.50 1.50
CB5 " 1 l+20c red brn. 1.50 1.50
CB6 " 2 l+20c bright blue 1.50 1.50
CB7 " 3 l+25c purple 12.00 12.00
CB8 " 5 l+25c orange 12.00 12.00
CB9 " 10 l+30c dp. vio. 12.00 12.00
CB10 " 25 l+2 l deep green 12.00 12.00
Nos. CB1–CB10 (10) 57.00 57.00

Issued in commemoration of the 65th birthday of King Victor Emmanuel III and the nonstop flight from Rome to Mogadiscio. Used prices are for stamps canceled to order.

AIR POST SEMI-POSTAL OFFICIAL STAMP.

Type of Air Post Semi-Postal Stamps, 1934, Overprinted Crown and "SERVIZIO DI STATO" in Black.

1934 ***Perf. 14.*** **Wmk. 140**

CBO1 SPAP1 25 l+2 l copper red 1500.00

SPECIAL DELIVERY STAMPS.

Special Delivery Stamps of Italy, Overprinted type "a."

1907 ***Perf. 14*** **Wmk. 140**

E1 SD1 25c rose red 2.75 2.75
a. Double ovpt.

1909

E2 SD2 30c blue & rose 22.50 25.00

1920

E3 SD1 50c dull red 75 75

"Italia"
SD1

1924 Engraved. Unwmkd.
E4 SD1 60c dark red & brn. 1.85 2.25
a. Perf. 13½ 2.75 2.75
E5 " 2 l dark blue & red 3.25 3.75

Nos. E4 and E5
Surcharged in Dark Blue or Red:

70 ٧٠
v
2,50 ٢,٥٠
w

1926
E6 SD1 (v) 70c on 60c dark red & brown (Bl) 2.00 2.25
E7 " (w) 2.50 l on 2 l dark blue & red (R) 3.25 3.75

Type of 1924 Surcharged
in Blue or Black:

1927-35 *Perf. 11*
E8 SD1 1.25 l on 60c dark red & brown (Bl) 2.00 35
a. Perf. 14 (Bl) ('35) 70.00 3.50
b. Perf. 11 (Bk) ('35) 250.00 5.50
c. Perf. 14 (Bk) ('35) 1850.00 135.00

AUTHORIZED DELIVERY STAMP.

Authorized Delivery Stamp of Italy,
No. EY2, Overprinted Type "f" in Black.

1939-41 *Perf. 14* Wmk. 140
EY1 AD2 10c dk. brn. ('41) 25
a. 10c reddish brown 15.00 22.50

On No. EY1a, which was used in Eritrea, the overprint hits the figures "10." On No. EY1, which was sold in Rome, the overprint falls above the 10's.

POSTAGE DUE STAMPS.

Postage Due Stamps of Italy
Overprinted type "a" at Top

1903 *Perf. 14* Wmk. 140
J1 D3 5c buff & magenta 5.25 6.00
a. Double overprint 35.00
J2 D3 10c buff & magenta 1.00 1.35
J3 " 20c " " 1.00 1.35
J4 " 30c " " 1.35 1.75
J5 " 40c " " 4.50 6.00
J6 " 50c " " 6.50 8.00
J7 " 60c " " 2.25 3.50
J8 " 1 l blue & magenta 2.25 70
J9 " 2 l " " 2.50 3.75
J10 " 5 l " " 21.00 24.00
J11 " 10 l " " *550.00* 32.50

Same with Overprint at Bottom

1920-22
J1b D3 5c buff & magenta 35 50
c. Numeral and ovpt. inverted 22.50
J2a " 10c buff & magenta 45 75
J3a " 20c " " 52.50 45.00
J4a " 30c " " 5.50 6.00
J5a " 40c " " 2.75 3.75
J6a " 50c " " 2.75 3.75
J7a " 60c " " 5.50 7.50
J8a " 1 l blue & magenta 8.50 10.00
J9a " 2 l " " *400.00* *350.00*
J10a D3 5 l blue & magenta 37.50 42.50
J11a " 10 l " " 3.00 5.25

1903 Wmk. 140
J12 D4 50 l yellow 90.00 45.00
J13 " 100 l blue 42.50 13.50

1927
J14 D3 60c buff & brown 11.00 13.50

Postage Due Stamps of Italy, 1934,
Overprinted type "j" in Black.

1934
J15 D6 5c brown 30 38
J16 " 10c blue 30 38
J17 " 20c rose red 45 50
a. Inverted ovpt. 75.00
J18 " 25c green 45 50
J19 " 30c red orange 60 75
J20 " 40c black brown 60 75
J21 " 50c violet 60 30
J22 " 60c black 75 1.10
J23 D7 1 l red orange 75 30
J24 " 2 l green 10.00 13.50
J25 " 5 l violet 13.00 16.50
J26 " 10 l blue 15.00 17.50
J27 " 20 l carmine rose 20.00 22.50
Nos. J15-J27 (13) 62.80 74.96

PARCEL POST STAMPS.

These stamps were used by affixing them to the way bill so that one half remained on it following the parcel, the other half staying on the receipt given the sender. Most used halves are right halves. Complete stamps were obtainable canceled, probably to order. Both unused and used prices are for complete stamps.

Parcel Post Stamps of Italy, 1914-17,
Overprinted type "j" in Black
on Each Half.

1916 *Perf. 13½.* Wmk. 140
Q1 PP2 5c brown 30.00 35.00
Q2 " 10c deep blue *1250.00* *1350.00*
Q3 " 25c red 32.50 40.00
Q4 " 50c orange 4.50 6.00
Q5 " 1 l violet 4.50 6.00
Q6 " 2 l green 3.00 4.50
Q7 " 3 l bistre 45.00 52.50
Q8 " 4 l slate 52.50 60.00

Halves Used

Q1	2.00	Q5	25
Q2	30.00	Q6	30
Q3	1.00	Q7	2.00
Q4	20	Q8	2.00

Overprinted type "f" on Each Half.

1917-24
Q9 PP2 5c brown 75 1.10
Q10 " 10c deep blue 45 75
Q11 " 20c black 45 75
Q12 " 25c red 45 75
Q13 " 50c orange 75 1.10
Q14 " 1 l violet 75 1.10
Q15 " 2 l green 75 1.10
Q16 " 3 l bistre 1.25 1.85
Q17 " 4 l slate 1.85 2.50
Q18 " 10 l rose lilac ('24) 15.00 17.50
Q19 " 12 l red brown ('24) 45.00 52.50
Q20 " 15 l olive green ('24) 45.00 52.50
Q21 " 20 l brn. vio. ('24) 52.50 60.00
Nos. Q9-Q21 (13) 164.95 193.50

Halves Used

Q9	10	Q16	10
Q10	10	Q17	12
Q11	10	Q18	40
Q12	10	Q19	75
Q13	10	Q20	1.25
Q14	10	Q21	2.00
Q15	10		

Parcel Post Stamps of Italy, 1927-39,
Overprinted type "f" on Each Half.

1927-37
Q21A PP3 10c dp. bl. ('37) *2000.00* 150.00
Q22 " 25c red ('37) 165.00 4.50
Q23 " 30c ultra. ('29) 22 45
Q24 " 50c orange ('36) 165.00 4.50
Q25 " 60c red ('29) 22 45
Q26 " 1 l brn. vio. ('36) 80.00 1.85
a. 1 l lilac 90.00 1.85
Q27 PP3 2 l green ('36) 17.50 2.50
Q28 " 3 l bistre 45 1.25
Q29 " 4 l gray 60 1.85
Q30 " 10 l rose lilac ('36) 60.00 67.50
Q31 PP3 20 l lilac brown ('36) 75.00 80.00
Nos. Q22-Q31 (10) 563.99 164.85

Halves Used

Q21A	8.00	Q26a	30
Q22	20	Q27	30
Q23	20	Q28	20
Q24	20	Q29	20
Q25	20	Q30	75
Q26	30	Q31	1.50

ESTONIA

(ĕs·tō'nĭ·ȧ)

LOCATION—In Northern Europe, bordering on the Baltic Sea and the Gulf of Finland.

GOVT.—Former independent republic.

AREA—18,353 sq. mi.

POP.—1,126,413 (1940).

CAPITAL—Tallinn.

Formerly a part of Russia, Estonia declared its independence in 1918. In 1940 it was incorporated in the Union of Soviet Socialist Republics.

100 Kopecks = 1 Ruble
100 Penni = 1 Mark (1919)
100 Sents = 1 Kroon (1928)

A1

A2

Lithographed.

1918-19 *Imperf.* Unwmkd.
1 A1 5k pale red 20 20
2 " 15k bright blue 20 20
a. Perf. 11½ 10.00 10.00
3 A2 35p gray brown ('19) 45 45
a. Printed on both sides 75.00
4 " 70p olive green ('19) 75 75

Nos. 1-4 exist privately perforated.

Russian Stamps
of 1909-17
Handstamped in
Violet or Black

1919 *Perf. 14, 14½x15, 13½.*
8 A14 1k orange *1000.00* *1000.00*
9 " 2k green 15.00 15.00
10 " 3k red 20.00 20.00
11 " 5k claret 20.00 20.00
12 A15 10k dk. blue (Bk) 25.00 25.00
13 " 10k dark blue 45.00 45.00
14 A14 10k on 7k light blue (Bk) *250.00* *250.00*
15 A11 15k red brown & blue 25.00 25.00
16 " 25k grn. & violet 25.00 25.00
17 " 35k red brown & green *500.00* *500.00*
18 A8 50k violet & green 60.00 60.00
19 A9 1r pale brown, brown & orange 75.00 75.00
20 A13 10r scarlet, yellow & gray *1200.00* *1200.00*

Imperf.

21 A14 1k orange 20.00 20.00
22 " 2k green *250.00* *250.00*
23 " 3k red 30.00 30.00
24 A9 1r pale brown, brown & red orange *200.00* *200.00*
25 A12 3½r maroon & green 150.00 150.00
26 A13 5r dk. bl., grn. & pale bl. *250.00* *250.00*

This overprint has been extensively counterfeited.
No. 20 is always creased.

Gulls
A3

1919, May 13 *Imperf.*
27 A3 5p yellow 75 75

A4

A5

A6

A7

Viking Ship
A8

1919-20 *Perf. 11½*
28 A4 10p green 20 20

Imperf.

29 A4 5p orange 5 5
30 " 10p green 5 5
31 A5 15p rose 15 15
32 A6 35p blue 15 15
33 A7 70p dull violet ('20) 15 15
34 A8 1m blue & black brown 20 20
a. Gray granite paper ('20) 20 20
35 " 5m yellow & black 25 30
a. Gray granite paper ('20) 75 20
b. Inverted center (white paper) *300.00* *300.00*
36 " 15m yellow green & violet ('20) 1.50 65
37 " 25m ultra. & blk. brn. ('20) 1.75 1.10
Nos. 28-37 (10) 4.45 3.00

See also Nos. 76-77.

Skyline of Tallinn
A9

1920-24 *Imperf.* Pelure Paper
39 A9 25p green 30 5
40 " 25p yellow ('24) 30 10
41 " 35p rose 40 10
42 " 50p green ('21) 20 10
43 " 1m vermilion 85 15
44 " 2m blue 60 20
45 " 2m ultramarine 40 15
46 " 2.50m blue 80 12
Nos. 39-46 (8) 3.85 97

Nos. 39 to 46 with sewing machine perforation are unofficial.

Stamps of 1919-20 Surcharged

1 Mk.
a

2 Mk.
b

1920 *Imperf.*
55 A5 (a) 1m on 15p rose 20 15

56	A9	(a) 1m on 35p rose	20	15
57	A7	(b) 2m on 70p dull violet	40	20

Weaver
A10

Blacksmith
A11

1922–23 Typographed. *Imperf.*

58	A10	½m orange ('23)	1.35	1.25
59	"	1m brown ('23)	2.00	1.20
60	"	2m yellow green	2.25	1.25
61	"	2½m claret	2.25	2.00
62	A11	5m rose	3.00	1.35
63	"	9m red ('23)	6.50	3.25
64	"	10m deep blue	3.50	1.50
		Nos. 58-64 (7)	20.85	11.80

1922-25 *Perf. 14.*

65	A10	½m orange ('23)	60	8
66	"	1m brown ('23)	1.20	4
67	"	2m yellow green	1.75	4
68	"	2½m claret	2.50	4
69	"	3m bl. green ('24)	1.50	10
70	A11	5m rose	2.50	6
71	"	9m red ('23)	2.00	30
72	"	10m deep blue	2.00	4
73	"	12m red ('25)	3.25	80
74	"	15m plum ('25)	2.75	40
75	"	20m ultra. ('25)	7.00	20
		Nos. 65-75 (11)	27.05	2.10

See also No. 89.

Viking Ship Type of 1920.

1922, June 8 *Perf. 14x13½*

76	A8	15m yellow green & violet	3.50	15
77	"	25m ultramarine & black brown	5.00	1.00

Map of Estonia
A13

1923–24

Paper with Lilac Network.

78	A13	100m olive green & blue	12.50	70

Paper with Buff Network.

79	A13	300m brown & blue ('24)	20.00	3.00

National Theater, Tallinn
A14

1924, Dec. 9 *Perf. 14x13½.*

Paper with Blue Network.

81	A14	30m violet & black	4.00	1.50

Paper with Rose Network.

82	A14	70m carmine rose & black	6.75	1.25

Vanemuine Theater, Tartu
A15

1927, Oct. 25

Paper with Lilac Network.

83	A15	40m deep blue & olive brown	3.75	50

Stamps of 1922–25 Surcharged in New Currency in Red or Black

1918 24/II 1928

S. S.

1928 *Perf. 14.*

84	A10	2s yellow green	60	15
85	A11	5s rose red	60	15
86	"	10s deep blue	1.00	15
		a. Imperf. (pair)	*300.00*	*250.00*
87	"	15s plum	2.00	35
88	"	20s ultramarine	1.75	45
		Nos. 84-88 (5)	5.95	1.25

10th anniversary of independence.

3rd Philatelic Exhibition Issue

Blacksmith Type of 1922–23.

1928, July 6

89	A11	10m gray	2.00	1.25
		a. Imperf., pair		

Sold only at Tallinn Philatelic Exhibition.

Arms
A16

Paper with Network as in Parenthesis.

1928-35 *Perf. 14, 14½x14.*

90	A16	1s dark gray (blue)	25	4
91	"	2s yellow green (orange)	25	3
92	"	4s green (brown) ('29)	60	6
93	"	5s red (green)	40	4
		a. 5 feet on lowest lion	15.00	10.00
		b. Booklet pane of 6		
94	A16	8s violet (buff) ('29)	1.25	10
95	"	10s light blue (lilac)	1.00	3
		a. Booklet pane of 6		
96	"	12s crimson (green)	1.25	6
97	"	15s yellow (blue)	1.25	4
98	"	15s car. (gray) ('35)	6.00	20
99	"	20s slate blue (red)	1.75	4
100	"	25s red violet (green) ('29)	4.50	8
101	"	25s blue (brn.) ('35)	6.50	20
102	"	40s red orange (blue) ('29)	3.50	20
103	"	60s gray (brn.) ('29)	4.50	20
104	"	80s brown (blue) ('29)	6.00	60
		Nos. 90-104 (15)	39.00	1.92

A 1940 printing of the 1s is on thick, gray-toned laid paper. Price, $3.

Types of 1924 Issues Surcharged:

KROON 1 KROON
a

2 KROONI 2
b

3 KROONI 3
c

1930, Sept. 1 *Perf. 14x13½.*

Paper with Green Network.

105	A14	(a) 1k on 70m carmine & black	3.50	2.00

Paper with Rose Network.

106	A13	(b) 2k on 300m brown & blue	8.00	4.00

Paper with Blue Network.

107	A13	(c) 3k on 300m brown & blue	17.50	12.50

University Observatory
A17

University of Tartu
A18

Paper with Network as in Parenthesis.

1932, June 1 *Perf. 14.*

108	A17	5(s) red (yellow)	3.00	35
109	A18	10(s) lt. blue (lilac)	1.60	10
110	A17	12(s) carmine (blue)	5.00	1.00
111	A18	20(s) dark blue (green)	5.00	15

University of Tartu tercentenary.

Narva Falls
A19

Ancient Bard Playing Harp
A20

1933, Apr. 1 Photo. *Perf. 14x13½.*

112	A19	1k gray black	3.25	25

See also No. 149.

Paper with Network as in Parenthesis.

1933, May 29 Typo. *Perf. 14*

113	A20	2(s) green (orange)	1.00	20
114	"	5(s) red (green)	1.50	20
115	"	10(s) blue (lilac)	2.50	12

Tenth National Singing Festival.

Woman Harvester
A21

President Konstantin Päts
A22

1935, Mar. 1 Engr. *Perf. 13½.*

116	A21	3k black brown	80	60

1936-40 Typographed. *Perf. 14.*

117	A22	1(s) chocolate	40	8
118	"	2(s) yellow green	40	5
119	"	3(s) dp. org. ('40)	2.50	1.25
120	"	4(s) rose violet	60	10
121	"	5(s) light blue green	40	5
122	"	6(s) rose lake	40	10
123	"	6(s) dp. green ('40)	10.00	10.00
124	"	10(s) greenish blue	80	5
125	"	15(s) crimson rose ('37)	1.75	8
126	"	15(s) deep blue ('40)	3.25	20
127	"	18(s) deep car. ('39)	10.00	3.25
128	"	20(s) bright violet	1.25	4
129	"	25(s) dark blue ('38)	4.00	7
130	"	30(s) bistre ('38)	4.50	25
131	"	30(s) ultra. ('39)	6.00	25
132	"	50(s) orange brown	2.50	20
133	"	60(s) bright pink	4.75	60
		Nos. 117-133 (17)	53.50	16.62

St. Brigitta Convent Entrance
A23

Ruins of Convent, Pirita River
A24

Front View of Convent
A25

Seal of Convent
A26

Paper with Network as in Parenthesis.

1936, June 10 *Perf. 13½.*

134	A23	5s green (buff)	40	10
135	A24	10s blue (lilac)	60	15
136	A25	15s red (orange)	75	75
137	A26	25s ultra. (brown)	1.35	1.35

St. Brigitta Convent, 500th anniversary.

Harbor at Tallinn
A27

1938, Apr. 11 Engraved *Perf. 14*

138	A27	2k blue	55	1.50

Friedrich R. Faehlmann
A28

Friedrich R. Kreutzwald
A29

1938 Typographed. *Perf. 13½.*

139	A28	5s dark green	40	20
140	A29	10s deep brown	60	20
141	"	15s dark carmine	1.00	60
142	A28	25s ultramarine	1.50	1.30
		a. Sheet of four	8.00	12.50

Society of Estonian Scholars centenary.

No. 142a contains one each of Nos. 139–142, with inscription in top margin. Size: 89x138mm.

Hospital at Pärnu
A30

Seashore Hotel
A31

1939, June 20 Typographed

144	A30	5(s) dark green	55	10
145	A31	10(s) deep red violet	55	8
146	A30	18(s) dark carmine	1.75	1.75
147	A31	30(s) deep blue	2.50	1.75
		a. Sheet of four	10.00	17.50

Centenary of health resort and baths at Pärnu.

No. 147a contains one each of Nos. 144–147, with inscription at left. Size: 137x 90mm.

Narva Falls Type of 1933.

1940, Apr. 15 Engraved

149	A19	1k slate green	40	1.50

The sky consists of heavy horizontal lines and the background consists of horizontal and vertical lines.

Carrier Pigeon and Plane
A32

1940, July 30 **Typographed**

150	A32	3(s) red orange	18	15
151	"	10(s) purple	18	7
152	"	15(s) rose brown	18	7
153	"	30(s) dark blue	1.50	85

Centenary of the first postage stamp.

SEMI-POSTAL STAMPS.

Assisting Wounded Soldier
SP1

Offering Aid to Wounded Hero
SP2

Lithographed

1920, June *Imperf.* **Unwmkd.**

B1	SP1	35p+10p red & olive green	20	25
B2	SP2	70p+15p deep blue & brown	20	25

Surcharged ✻ 2 Mk ✻

1920

B3	SP1	1m on 35p+10p red & olive green	40	25
B4	SP2	2m on 70p+15p deep blue & brown	40	25

Nurse and Wounded Soldier
SP3

1921, Aug. 1 ***Imperf.***

B5	SP3	2½ (3½)m orange, brown & carmine	75	1.10
B6	"	5 (7)m ultramarine, brown & carmine	75	1.10

1922, Apr. 26 ***Perf. 13½x14***

B7	SP3	2½(3½)m orange, brown & carmine	1.25	1.65
		a. Vert. pair, imperf. horiz.	8.00	10.00
B8	SP3	5(7)m ultramarine, brown & carmine	1.25	1.65
		a. Vert. pair, imperf. horiz.	8.00	10.00

Nos. B5–B8 Overprinted **Aita hädalist.**

1923 ***Imperf.***

B9	SP3	2½(3½)m	17.50	22.50
B10	"	5(7)m	20.00	25.00

Perf. 13½x14.

B11	SP3	2½(3½)m	25.00	30.00
		a. Vert. pair, imperf. horiz.	80.00	100.00
B12	SP3	5(7)m	30.00	35.00
		a. Vert. pair, imperf. horiz.	80.00	100.00

Excellent forgeries are plentiful.

Nos. B7 and B8 Surcharged **5 5** **6 6**

1926, June 15

B13	SP3	5(6)m on 2½(3½)m	1.75	1.50
		a. Vert. pair, imperf. horiz.	10.00	12.50
B14	SP3	10(12)m on 5(7)m	2.50	2.00
		a. Vert. pair, imperf. horiz.	10.00	12.50

Nos. B5–B14 had the franking value of the lower figure. They were sold for the higher figure, the excess going to the Red Cross Society.

Kuressaare Castle
SP4

Tartu Cathedral
SP5

Parliament Building, Tallinn
SP6

Narva Fortress
SP7

View of Tallinn
SP8

Wmk. 207

Reduced illustration. Watermark covers a large part of sheet.

Laid Paper.

Wmkd. Arms of Finland in the Sheet. (207)

1927, Nov. 19 **Typo.** ***Perf. 14½x14***

B15	SP4	5m+5m blue green & olive, *grayish*	40	60
B16	SP5	10m+10m deep blue & brown, *cream*	40	60
B17	SP6	12m+12m rose red & olive green, *bluish*	40	60

Perf. 14x13½

B18	SP7	20m+20m blue & chocolate, *gray*	60	1.25
B19	SP8	40m+40m orange brown & slate, *buff*	75	1.25
		Nos. B15–B19 (5)	2.55	4.30

The money derived from the surtax was donated to the Committee for the commemoration of War for Liberation.

Red Cross Issue.

Symbolical of Succor to Injured
SP9

Symbolical of "Light of Hope"
SP10

1931, Aug. 1 ***Perf. 13½*** **Unwmkd.**

B20	SP9	2s+3s green & carmine	3.00	3.00
B21	SP10	5s+3s red & car.	3.00	3.00
B22	"	10s+3s light blue & carmine	3.00	3.00
B23	SP9	20s+3s dark blue & carmine	7.50	7.50

Nurse and Child
SP11

Lorraine Cross and Flower
SP13

Taagepera Sanatorium
SP12

Paper with Network as in Parenthesis.

1933, Oct. 1 ***Perf. 14, 14½.***

B24	SP11	5s+3s vermilion (green)	3.50	3.00
B25	SP12	10s+3s light blue & red (violet)	3.50	3.00
B26	SP13	12s+3s rose & red (green)	5.00	4.00
B27	SP12	20s+3s dark blue & red (orange)	8.00	7.00

The surtax was for a fund to combat tuberculosis.

Arms of Narva
SP14

Arms of Pärnu
SP15

Arms of Tartu
SP16

Arms of Tallinn
SP17

Paper with Network as in Parenthesis.

1936, Feb. 1 ***Perf. 13½***

B28	SP14	10s+10s green & ultra. (gray)	2.50	3.00
B29	SP15	15s+15s carmine & blue (gray)	3.00	4.00
B30	SP16	25s+25s gray blue & red (brown)	4.00	4.75
B31	SP17	50s+50s black & dull orange (olive)	8.00	13.50

Arms of Paide
SP18

Arms of Rakvere
SP19

Arms of Valga
SP20

Arms of Viljandi
SP21

Paper with Network as in Parenthesis.

1937, Jan. 2

B32	SP18	10(s)+10(s) green (gray)	2.50	3.25
B33	SP19	15(s)+15(s) red brown (gray)	2.50	3.25
B34	SP20	25(s)+25(s) dark blue (lilac)	3.50	4.75
B35	SP21	50(s)+50(s) dark violet (gray)	7.50	9.00

Arms of Baltiski
SP22

Arms of Vöru
SP23

Arms of Haapsalu
SP24

Arms of Kuressaare
SP25

Designs are the armorial bearings of various cities.

1938, Jan. 21

Paper with Gray Network.

B36	SP22	10(s)+10(s) dark brown	2.50	2.50
B37	SP23	15(s)+15(s) carmine & green	3.00	3.25
B38	SP24	25(s)+25(s) dark blue & carmine	4.00	4.75
B39	SP25	50(s)+50(s) black & orange yellow	10.00	14.00
		a. Sheet of four	20.00	25.00

No. B39a measures 106x150 mm. and contains one each of Nos. B36 to B39, with marginal inscriptions. Issued in connection with the annual Charity Ball held at Tallinn, January 2, 1938.

Arms of Viljandi
SP27

Arms of Pärnu
SP28

Arms of Tartu
SP29

Arms of Harju
SP30

Designs are the armorial bearings of various districts.

1939, Jan. 10

Paper with Gray Network.

B41	SP27	10(s)+10(s) dark blue green	2.50	2.75
B42	SP28	15(s)+15(s) car.	3.00	3.25
B43	SP29	25(s)+25(s) dark blue	5.00	6.00
B44	SP30	50(s)+50(s) brown lake	10.00	20.00
		a. Sheet of four	22.50	35.00

No. B44a measures 90x138mm., and contains one each of Nos. B41 to B44, with marginal inscriptions.

Arms of Võru
SP32

Arms of Järva
SP33

Arms of Lääne
SP34

Arms of Saare
SP35

Paper with Gray Network.

1940, Jan. 2 Typo. *Perf. 13½*

B46	SP32	10(s)+10(s) deep grn. & ultra.	1.75	2.00
B47	SP33	15(s)+15(s) dark car. & ultra.	2.25	3.25
B48	SP34	25(s)+25(s) dark blue & scarlet	2.75	4.75
B49	SP35	50(s)+50(s) ocher & ultra.	6.00	15.00

AIR POST STAMPS.

Airplane
AP1

Typographed.

1920, Mar. 13 *Imperf.* Unwmkd.

C1	AP1	5m yellow, blue & black	1.75	1.75

No. C1 Overprinted "1923" in Red.

1923, Oct. 1

C2	AP1	5m multicolored	5.00	6.00

No. C1 Surcharged in Red

1923, Oct. 1

C3	AP1	15m on 5m multi.	6.00	7.00

Pairs of No. C1 Surcharged in Black or Red

45 Marka

1923

1923, Oct.

C4	AP1	10m on 5m+5m (B)	10.00	12.50
C5	"	20m on 5m+5m (R)	20.00	25.00
C6	"	45m on 5m+5m (R)	50.00	65.00

Rough Perf. 11½.

C7	AP1	10m on 5m+5m (B)	*150.00*	*175.00*
C8	"	20m on 5m+5m (R)	*85.00*	*110.00*

The pairs comprising Nos. C7 and C8 are imperforate between. Forged surcharges and perforations abound.

Monoplane in Flight—AP2

Designs: Various views of planes in flight.

1924, Feb. 12 ***Imperf.***

C9	AP2	5m yellow & black	1.25	2.00
C10	"	10m blue & black	1.25	1.50
C11	"	15m red & black	1.25	2.25
C12	"	20m green & black	1.25	2.00
C13	"	45m violet & black	1.25	3.00
		Nos. C9-C13 (5)	6.25	10.75

The paper is covered with a faint network in pale shades of the frame colors. There are four varieties of the frames and five of the pictures.

1925, July 15 ***Perf. 13½.***

C14	AP2	5m yellow & black	75	1.25
C15	"	10m blue & black	75	1.25
C16	"	15m red & black	75	2.00
C17	"	20m green & black	50	1.25
C18	"	45m violet & black	1.25	2.25
		Nos. C14-C18 (5)	4.00	8.00

Counterfeits of Nos. C1 to C18 are plentiful.

OCCUPATION STAMPS.

Issued under German Occupation.

For Use in Tartu (Dorpat)

Russian Stamps of 1909-12 Surcharged

20 Pfg.

1918 ***Perf. 14x14½*** **Unwmkd.**

N1	A15	20pf on 10k dk. blue	20.00	25.00
N2	A8	40pf on 20k blue & carmine	20.00	25.00

Forged overprints exist.

Estonian Arms and Swastika
OS1

Perf. 11½

1941, Aug. Typo. **Unwmkd.**

N3	OS1	15k brown	5.00	6.50
N4	"	20k green	5.00	6.00
N5	"	30k dark blue	10.00	7.25

Exist imperf. Price $60.

Nos. N3-N5 were issued on both ordinary paper with colorless gum and thick chalky paper with yellow gum. Same prices.

SEMI-POSTAL STAMPS

Mountain Tower, Tallinn
OSP1

Designs: 20k+20k, Stone Bridge, Tartu (horiz.). 30k+30k, Narva Castle (horiz.). 50k+50k, Tallinn view (horiz.). 60k+60k, Tartu University. 100k+100k, Narva Castle, close view.

Paper with Gray Network

Perf. 11½

1941, Sept. 29 Photo. **Unwmkd.**

NB1	OSP11	5k+15k dk. brn.	20	*1.00*
NB2	"	20k+20k red lilac	20	*1.00*
NB3	"	30k+30k dk. bl.	20	*1.00*
NB4	"	50k+50k bluish green	20	*1.00*
NB5	"	60k+60k carmine	20	*1.00*
NB6	"	100k+100k gray	35	*1.00*
		Nos. NB1-NB6 (6)	1.35	*6.00*

Nos. NB1-NB6 exist imperf. Price, set unused $14, used $30.

A miniature sheet containing one each of Nos. NB1-NB6, imperf., exists in various colors. It was not postally valid.

ETHIOPIA

(ē'thi-ō'pi-ȧ)

(Abyssinia)

LOCATION—In northeastern Africa.
GOVT.—Former monarchy.
AREA—398,350 sq. mi.
POP.—28,930,000 (est. 1977).
CAPITAL—Addis Ababa.

16 Guerche = 1 Menelik Dollar
or 1 Maria Theresa Dollar
100 Centimes = 1 Franc (1905)
40 Paras = 1 Piastre (1908)
16 Mehalek = 1 Thaler or Talari (1928)
100 Centimes = 1 Thaler (1936)
100 Cents = 1 Ethiopian Dollar (1946)
100 Cents = 1 Birr (1978)

Excellent forgeries of Nos. 1-86 exist.

Menelik II
A1

Lion of Judah
A2

Typographed

1894 ***Perf. 14x13½*** **Unwmkd.**

1	A1	¼g green	1.75	1.75
2	"	½g red	1.00	1.10
3	"	1g blue	1.00	1.10
4	"	2g dark brown	1.00	1.00
5	A2	4g lilac brown	1.00	1.00
6	"	8g violet	1.00	1.00
7	A2	16g black	1.25	1.25
		Nos. 1-7 (7)	8.00	8.20

For 4g, 8g and 16g stamps of type A1, see Nos. J3a, J4a, and J7a.

Nos. 1-7 Handstamped in Violet, Blue or Black

Ethiopie

1901

8	A1	¼g green	6.00	6.00
9	"	½g red	6.00	6.00
10	"	1g blue	6.00	6.00
11	"	2g dark brown	6.00	6.00
12	A2	4g lilac brown	7.50	7.50
13	"	8g violet	9.00	9.00
14	"	16g black	10.00	10.00
		Nos. 8-14 (7)	50.50	50.50

Two types of overprint on Nos. 8-14: 9½mm. and 8½mm. wide.

Handstamped in Violet, Blue or Black

ቦስጣ።

1902

15	A1	¼g green	3.00	3.00
16	"	½g red	3.00	3.00
17	"	1g blue	4.50	4.50
18	"	2g dark brown	4.50	4.50
19	A2	4g lilac brown	7.50	7.50
20	"	8g violet	10.00	10.00
21	"	16g black	20.00	20.00
		Nos. 15-21 (7)	52.50	52.50

The handstamp reads "Bosta" (Post).

Handstamped in Violet, Blue or Black

መልክት።

1903

22	A1	¼g green	3.00	3.00
		a. On stamp No. 15		
23	"	½g red	3.00	3.00
24	"	1g blue	4.50	4.50
		a. On stamp No. 17		
25	"	2g dark brown	6.00	6.00
26	A2	4g lilac brown	6.00	6.00
27	"	8g violet	12.00	12.00
28	"	16g black	18.00	18.00
		Nos. 22-28 (7)	52.50	52.50

The handstamp reads "Malekt." (Message).

Handstamped in Violet or Blue

ምልክት

1904

36	A1	¼g green	6.00	6.00
37	"	½g red	6.00	6.00
38	"	1g blue	7.50	7.50
39	"	2g dark brown	9.00	9.00
40	A2	4g lilac brown	12.00	12.00
41	"	8g violet	20.00	20.00
42	"	16g black	30.00	30.00
		Nos. 36-42 (7)	90.50	90.50

The handstamp reads "Malekt." (Message).

Preceding Issues Surcharged with New Values in French Currency in Blue, Violet, Rose or Black:

05 (a) 1,60 (b)

1905

On Nos. 1 to 7.

43	A1	(a)	5c on ¼g green	4.50	4.50
44	"	(")	10c on ½g red	4.50	4.50
45	"	(")	20c on 1g blue	4.50	4.50
46	"	(")	40c on 2g dark brown	6.00	6.00
47	A2	(")	80c on 4g lilac brown	9.00	9.00
48	"	(b)	1.60fr on 8g vio.	12.00	12.00
49	"	(")	3.20fr on 16g blk.	18.00	18.00
			Nos. 43-49 (7)	58.50	58.50

On No. 8.

50	A1	(a)	5c on ¼g green	50.00	50.00

On Nos. 15 to 20.

51	A1	(a)	5c on ¼g green	9.00	9.00
51B	"	(")	10c on ½g red	185.00	185.00
51C	"	(")	20c on 1g blue	*15.00*	
51D	"	(")	40c on 2g dark brown	*50.00*	

51E A2 (*a*) 80c on 4g lilac brown 70.00
51F " (*b*)1.60fr on 8g vio. 100.00

On Nos. 22, 24 & 26.

52 A1 (*a*) 5c on ¼g grn. 25.00 25.00
52B " (") 20c on 1g blue 35.00
52D A2 (") 80c on 4g lilac brown 100.00

On No. 36.

53 A1 (*a*) 5c on ¼g green 22.50 22.50

The status of Nos. 51C–51F, 52B–52D is questioned.

5%m (*c*) — 5 centimes. (*d*)

On No. 2.

54 A1 (*c*) 5c on half of ½g red 3.00 3.00

On Nos. 15 & 21.

54B A1 (*c*) 5c on ¼g green 35.00 35.00
55 A2 (*d*) 5c on 16g black 70.00 70.00

On No. 28.

56 A2 (*d*) 5c on 16g black 70.00 70.00

The overprints and surcharges on Nos. 8 to 56 inclusive were handstamped, the work being very roughly done. Apparently any color of ink that was at hand was used. It is not at all improbable that other varieties may exist.

As is usual with handstamped overprints and surcharges there are many inverted and double.

Surcharged with New Values in Various Colors and ምኒልክ in Violet.

1906, Jan. 1

57 A1 5c on ¼g green 4.50 4.50
58 " 10c on ½g red 6.00 6.00
59 " 20c on 1g blue 6.00 6.00
60 " 40c on 2g dark brown 6.00 6.00
61 A2 80c on 4g lilac brown 7.50 7.50
62 " 1.60fr on 8g violet 9.00 9.00
63 " 3.20fr on 16g black 27.50 27.50
Nos. 57-63 (7) 66.50 66.50

Two types of the 4-character overprint ("Menelik"): 15x3½mm. and 16½x4½ mm.

Surcharged with New Values and ምኒልክ። in Violet.

1906, July 1

64 A1 5c on ¼g green 4.50 4.50
a. Surcharged "20" 30.00 30.00
65 " 10c on ½g red 4.50 4.50
66 " 20c on 1g blue 7.50 7.50
67 " 40c on 2g dark brown 7.50 7.50
68 A2 80c on 4g lilac brown 9.00 9.00
69 " 1.60fr on 8g violet 10.00 12.00
70 " 3.20fr on 16g black 27.50 32.50
Nos. 64-70 (7) 70.50 77.50

The control overprint reads "Menelik."

Surcharged in Violet: ዳግማዊ። ዳግማዊ።

☆1/2☆ (*e*) ✳ 1.✳ (*f*)

1907, July 1

71 A1 (*e*) ¼ on ¼g green 4.50 4.50
72 " (") ½ on ½g red 4.50 4.50
73 " (*f*) 1 on 1g blue 6.00 6.00
74 " (") 2 on 2g dark brown 7.50 7.50
a. Surcharged "40" 37.50
75 A2 (*f*) 4 on 4g lilac brown 7.50 7.50
a. Surcharged "80" 37.50
76 " (") 8 on 8g violet 10.00 10.00
77 " (") 16 on 16g black 15.00 15.00
Nos. 71-77 (7) 55.00 55.00

Nos. 71–72 are also found with stars farther away from figures.

The control overprint reads "Dagmawi" ("Second"), meaning Emperor Menelik II.

Nos. 2, 23 Surcharged in Blue — PIASTRE

1908, Mar. 25

78 A1 1pi on ½g red (#2) 4.50 4.50
79 " 1pi on ½g red (#23) 150.00 125.00

The surcharges on Nos. 57 to 79 are handstamped and are found double, inverted, etc.

Surcharged in Black — 1/4 piastre

1908, Nov. 1

80 A1 ¼p on ¼g green 1.00 1.00
81 " ½p on ½g red 1.00 1.00
82 " 1p on 1g blue 1.25 1.25
83 " 2p on 2g dark brown 2.00 2.00
84 A2 4p on 4g lilac brown 2.50 2.50
85 " 8p on 8g violet 6.50 6.50
86 " 16p on 16g black 10.00 10.00
Nos. 80-86 (7) 24.25 24.25

Surcharges on Nos. 80–85 are found double, inverted, etc.

King Solomon's Throne
A3

Menelik in Native Costume
A4

Menelik in Royal Dress
A5

1909, Mar. 27 *Perf. 11½*

87 A3 ¼g blue green 50 40
88 " ½g rose 50 40
89 " 1g green & orange 2.00 1.00
90 A4 2g blue 2.00 1.50
91 " 4g grn. & carmine 3.00 2.50
92 A5 8g vermilion & deep green 5.00 3.75
93 " 16g verm. & car. 7.50 6.25
Nos. 87-93 (7) 20.50 15.80

Nos. 1–7 Handstamped and Surcharged in ms. — AFF EXCEP FAUTE TIMB

1911, Oct. 1 *Perf. 14x13½*

94 A1 ¼g on ¼g green 65.00 32.50
95 " ½g on ½g red 65.00 32.50
96 " 1g on 1g blue 65.00 32.50
97 " 2g on 2g dk. brn. 65.00 32.50
98 A2 4g on 4g lilac brown 65.00 32.50
99 " 8g on 8g violet 65.00 32.50
100 " 16g on 16g black 65.00 32.50
Nos. 94-100 (7) 455.00 227.50

Nos. 94–100 are provisionals used at Dire-Dawa for 5 days. The overprint is abbreviated from "Affranchissement Exceptionnel Faute Timbres" (Special Franking Lacking Stamps). Nos. 94–100 exist without ms. surcharge. Forgeries exist.

Stamps of 1909 Handstamped in Violet or Black:

ተፈሪ፡ ፬የካቲት ፲፱፻፱። 11-2-1917 (*g*)

ዘውዲቱ፡ ፬የካቲት ፲፱፻፱። 11-2-1917 (*h*)

1917, Mar. 30 *Perf. 11½*

101 A3 (*g*) ¼g blue green (V) 2.00 2.00
102 " (") ½g rose (V) 2.00 2.00
104 A4 (*h*) 2g blue (Bk) 3.00 3.00
105 " (") 4g green & carmine (Bk) 5.00 5.00
106 A5 (") 8g vermilion & dp. grn. (Bk) 8.00 8.00
107 " (") 16g vermilion & carmine (Bk) 15.00 15.00
Nos. 101-107 (6) 35.00 35.00

Coronation of Empress Zauditu.

Nos. 101–107 exist with overprint inverted and Nos. 101–106 with it double.

Stamps of 1909 Overprinted in Blue, Black or Red:

ተፈሪ ። ፬የካቲት፡ ፲፱፻፱። 11/2/1917 (*i*)

ዘውዲቱ ። ፬የካቲት፡ ፲፱፻፱። 11/2/1917 (*j*)

1917, Apr. 5

108 A3 (*i*) ¼g blue green (Bl) 20 15
109 " (") ½g rose (Bl) 25 20
110 " (") 1g green & orange (Bl) 1.50 1.50
111 A4 (") 2g blue (R) 42.50 45.00
112 " (*j*) 2g blue (Bk) 30 25
113 " (") 4g green & carmine (Bl) 60 60
a. Black overprint 7.50 7.50
114 A5 (*j*) 8g vermilion & deep green (Bl) 50 50
115 " (") 16g vermilion & carmine (Bl) 80 80
Nos. 108-115 (8) 46.65 49.00

Coronation of Empress Zauditu.

Nos. 108–115 all exist with double overprint and inverted overprint. Nos. 108, 112, 113, 114 and 115 exist with double overprint, one inverted, and various combinations.

Preceding Issue with Additional Surcharge

1/4 (*k*) 1/2 (*l*) 1 (*m*) 2 (*n*)

1917, May 28

116 A5 (*k*) ¼g on 8g vermilion & deep green 2.00 2.00
117 " (*l*) ½g on 8g vermilion & deep green 2.00 2.00
118 " (*m*) 1g on 16g vermilion & carmine 5.00 5.00
119 " (*n*) 2g on 16g vermilion & carmine 5.00 5.00

Nos. 116 to 119 all exist with the numerals double and inverted and No. 116 with the Amharic surcharge double.

Sommering's Gazelle
A6

Ras Tafari
A9

Cathedral of St. George—A12

Empress Waizeri Zauditu
A18

Designs: ¼g, Giraffes. ½g, Leopard. 2g, Ras Tafari. 4g, Regent Tafari. 8g, White rhinoceros. 12g, Somali ostriches. 1t, African elephant. 2t, Water buffalo. 3t, Lions. 5t, 10t, Empress Zauditu.

1919, June 16 Typo. *Perf. 11½.*

120 A6 ⅛g violet and brown 4 4
121 " ¼g blue green & drab 4 4
122 " ½g scarlet & olive green 5 4
123 A9 1g rose lilac & gray green 6 5
124 " 2g dp. ultra. & fawn 6 6
125 " 4g turquoise blue & orange 10 10
126 A12 6g light blue & orange 10 10
127 " 8g olive green & black brown 15 12
128 " 12g red violet & gray 25 20
129 " 1t rose & gray black 40 30
130 " 2t black & brown 1.50 1.00
131 " 3t grn. & dp. org. 2.00 1.00
132 A18 4t brn. & lilac rose 2.25 2.00
133 " 5t carmine & gray 3.00 3.00
134 " 10t gray green & bistre 4.50 4.00
Nos. 120-134 (15) 14.50 12.05

Reprints differ slightly in color from originals. Reprints exist imperf. and some values with inverted centers. Price for set, unused or canceled, $1.50.

No. 132 Surcharged in Blue

፬ ግርሽ ።
4guerches

1919, Oct.

135 A18 4g on 4t brown & lilac rose 90 90

The Amharic surcharge indicates the new value and, therefore, varies on Nos. 135 to 154. There are numerous defective letters and figures, several types of the "2" of "½," the errors "guerhce," "gnerche," etc.

Stamps of 1919 Surcharged

አንድ ፡
ግርሽ ።
1 guerche

1921–22

136 A6 ⅛g on ⅛g violet & brown ('22) 50 50
137 " 1g on ¼g green & drab 50 50
138 A9 2g on 1g lilac brown & gray grn. ('22) 75 75
139 A18 2g on 4t brown & lilac rose ('22) 17.50 17.50
140 A6 2½g on ⅛g scarlet & olive green 75 75
141 A9 4g on 2g ultra. & fawn ('22) 75 75
Nos. 136–141 (6) 20.75 20.75

Stamps and Type of 1919 Surcharged

፩ ግርሽ ፡
1 guerche

1925–28

142 A12 ⅛g on 1t rose & gray blk. ('26) 75 75
a. Without colon ('28) 10.00 10.00
143 A18 ⅛g on 5t carmine & gray ('26) 40 40
144 A12 1g on 6g blue & org. 40 40
145 " 1g on 12g lilac & gray 27.50 27.50
146 " 1g on 3t green & org. ('26) 12.50 12.50
147 A18 1g on 10t gray green & bister ('26) 50 50
Nos. 142–147 (6) 42.05 42.05

On No. 142 the surcharge is at the left side of the stamp, reading upward. On No. 142a it is at the right, reading downward. The two surcharges are from different, though similar, settings. On No. 146 the surcharge is at the right, reading upward. See note following No. 154.

There are also many irregularly produced settings in imitation of Nos. 136–154 which differ slightly from the originals.

Type of 1919 Surcharged

፩ ግርሽ ፡

= 1 guerche =

1926

147A A12 1g on 12g lilac & gray 35.00 35.00
b. Vertical bars at lower right corner 37.50

Stamps of 1919 Surcharged

አንድ ፡ ፡ ግርሽ ፡

1 guerche 

1926

148 A12 ½g on 8g olive green & black brown 1.00 1.00
149 " 1g on 6g blue & orange 15.00 15.00
150 " 1g on 12g lilac & gray 27.50 27.50

Stamps of 1919 Surcharged

የግርሽ ፡ አላድ ፡

1/2 guerche 

1927

151 A12 ½g on 8g olive green & black brown 75 75
152 " 1g on 6g blue & orange 20.00 20.00
153 " 1g on 12g lilac & gray 90 90
154 " 1g on 3t green & orange 35.00 35.00

Many varieties of surcharge, such as double, inverted, lines transposed or omitted, and inverted "2" in "½," exist on Nos. 136–154.

Ras Tafari
A22

Empress Zauditu
A23

1928, Sept. 5 Typo. *Perf. 13½x14*

155 A22 ⅛m orange & light blue 60 50
156 A23 ¼m indigo & red orange 40 40
157 A22 ½m gray green & black 60 50
158 A23 1m dark carmine & black 40 30
159 A22 2m dark blue & black 40 30
160 A23 4m yellow & olive 40 30
161 A22 8m violet & olive 1.00 75
162 A23 1t orange brown & violet 1.25 1.00
163 A22 2t green & bistre 1.75 1.75
164 A23 3t chocolate & green 2.50 2.00
Nos. 155–164 (10) 9.30 7.80

Preceding Issue Overprinted in Black, Violet or Red

፲፱፻፳
ፖ፡ ቴ፡ ቴ፡
የተመረቀበት፡
ቀን፡ መታበቢያ፡

1928, Sept. 1

165 A22 ⅛m orange & light blue (Bk) 60 50
166 A23 ¼m indigo & red orange (V) 60 50
167 A22 ½m gray green & black (V) 60 50
168 A23 1m dark carmine & black (V) 60 50
169 A22 2m dark blue & black (R) 60 50
170 A23 4m yellow & olive (Bk) 60 50
171 A22 8m violet & olive (R) 60 50
172 A23 1t orange brown & violet (Bk) 60 50
173 A22 2t grn. & bistre (R) 1.00 75
174 A23 3t chocolate & green (R) 1.50 1.25
Nos. 165–174 (10) 7.30 6.00

Opening of General Post Office, Addis Ababa.

Stamps of 1928 Issue Handstamped in Violet, Red or Black

ንጉሥ፡ ተፈሪ፡
NEGOUS TEFERI

1928, Oct. 7

175 A22 ⅛m orange & light blue (V) 90 90
176 " ½m gray green & black (R) 90 90
177 " 2m dark blue & black (R) 90 90
178 " 8m violet & olive (Bk) 90 90
179 " 2t green & bistre (V) 90 90
Nos. 175–179 (5) 4.50 4.50

Crowning of Regent Tafari Makonen as Negus on Oct. 7, 1928.

Nos. 175–177 exist with overprint vertical.

Stamps of 1928 Overprinted in Red or Green

ቀዳማዊ
ኃይለ ሥላሴ
መጋቢት ፳፭ ቀን
፲፱፻፳፪

HAYLE SELASSIE 1er
3 Avril 1930

1930, Apr. 3

180 A22 ⅛m orange & light blue (R) 20 15
181 A23 ¼m indigo & red org. (G) 25 20
182 A22 ½m gray green & black (R) 20 15
183 A23 1m dark carmine & black (G) 25 20
184 A22 2m dark blue & black (R) 25 20
185 A23 4m yel. & olive (R) 40 30
186 A22 8m vio. & olive (R) 75 75
187 A23 1t orange brown & violet (R) 1.75 1.75
188 A22 2t green & bistre (R) 2.25 2.25
189 A23 3t chocolate & green (R) 3.00 3.00
Nos. 180–189 (10) 9.30 8.95

Issued in commemoration of the proclamation of the Negus Tafari as King of Kings of Abyssinia under the name "Haile Selassie I."

A similar overprint, set in four vertical lines, was printed on all denominations of the 1928 issue. It was not considered satisfactory and was rejected. The trial impressions were not placed on sale to the public, but some copies reached private hands and have been passed through the post.

Stamps of 1928 Overprinted in Red or Olive Brown

ቀዳማዊ ፡
ኃይለ ፡ ሥላሴ ፡
መጋቢት ፡ ፳፭ ፡ ቀን ፡
፲፱፻፳፪

HAILE SELASSIE 1er
3 Avril 1930

1930, Apr. 3

190 A22 ⅛m orange & light blue 25 20
191 A23 ¼m indigo & red orange (OB) 25 25
192 A22 ½m gray green & black 25 20
193 A23 1m dark carmine & black (OB) 25 25
194 A22 2m dark blue & black 25 25
195 A23 4m yellow & olive 50 50
196 A22 8m violet & olive 75 75
197 A23 1t orange brown & violet 1.75 1.75
198 A22 2t green & bistre 2.25 2.25
199 A23 3t chocolate & green 3.00 3.00
Nos. 190–199 (10) 9.50 9.40

Issued in commemoration of the proclamation of the Negus Tafari as Emperor Haile Selassie I.

All stamps of this series exist with "H" of "HAILE" omitted.

Stamps of 1928 Handstamped in Violet or Red

ሥላሴ ፡
ቀዳማዊ ኃይለ
ንጉሠ ነገሥት
፳፫
ጥቅምት፡
፲፱፻፳፫

1930, Nov. 2

200 A22 ⅛m orange & light blue (V) 30 25
201 A23 ¼m indigo & red orange (V) 30 25
202 A22 ½m gray green & black (R) 30 25
203 A23 1m dark carmine & black (V) 30 25
204 A22 2m dark blue & black (R) 30 25
205 A23 4m yellow & olive (V) 30 25
206 A22 8m violet & olive (V or R) 75 75
207 A23 1t orange brown & violet (V) 1.00 1.00
208 A22 2t green & bistre (V or R) 1.50 1.50
209 A23 3t choc. & green (V or R) 2.25 2.25
Nos. 200–209 (10) 7.30 7.00

Issued in commemoration of the cornation of the Emperor Haile Selassie I, November 2nd, 1930.

Haile Selassie Coronation Monument, Symbols of Empire
A24

1930, Nov. Engraved *Perf. 12½*

210 A24 1g orange 20 20
211 " 2g ultramarine 20 20
212 " 4g violet 20 20
213 " 8g dull green 35 30
214 " 1t brown 50 50
215 " 3t green 75 75
216 " 5t red brown 75 75
Nos. 210–216 (7) 2.95 2.90

Coronation of Emperor Haile Selassie I.

Reprints of Nos. 210 to 216 exist. Paper is thinner and gum whiter than the originals. Price 7c each.

Stamps of 1928 Surcharged in Green, Red or Blue

የመሐለቅ ፰ተኛ

1/8 Mehalek

የመሐለቅ ግማሽ — Type I
የመሐለቅ ፰ተኛ — Type II

1931, Mar. 20 *Perf. 13½x14.*

217 A23 ⅛m on 1m dark carmine & black (G) 30 30
218 A22 ⅛m on 2m dark blue & black (R) 30 30

219 A23 ⅛m on 4m yellow & olive (G) 30 30
220 " ¼m on 1m dark carmine & black (Bl) 30 30
221 A22 ¼m on 2m dark blue & black (R) 75 75
222 A23 ¼m on 4m yellow & olive (G) 75 75
225 " ½m on 1m dark carmine & black (Bl) 75 75
226 A22 ½m on 2m dark blue & black (R) 75 75
227 A23 ½m on 4m yellow & olive (G)(II) 75 75
a. ½m on 4m yellow & olive (I) 7.50 7.50
228 " ½m on 3t chocolate & green (R) 5.00 5.00
230 A22 1m on 2m dark blue & black (R) 1.00 1.00
Nos. 217–230 (11) 10.95 10.95

The ½m on 1/8m orange and light blue and ½m on ¼m indigo and red orange were clandestinely printed and never sold at the post office.

No. 230 with double surcharge in red and blue is a color trial.

Ras Makonnen
A25

Empress Menen
A27

View of Hawash River and Railroad Bridge—A26

Designs: 2g, 8g, Haile Selassie I (profile). 4g, 1t, Statue of Menelik II. 3t, Empress Menen (full face). 5t, Haile Selassie I (full face).

Perf. 12½, 12x12½, 12½x12.

1931, June 27 **Engraved**

232 A25 ⅛g red 15 15
233 A26 ¼g olive green 15 15
234 A25 ½g dark violet 20 15
235 A27 1g red orange 20 20
236 " 2g ultramarine 25 25
237 A25 4g violet 35 35
238 A27 8g blue green 1.10 1.10
239 A25 1t chocolate 2.00 2.00
240 A27 3t yellow green 3.25 3.25
241 " 5t red brown 5.00 5.00
Nos. 232–241 (10) 12.65 12.60

Reprints of Nos. 232 to 241 are on thinner and whiter paper than the originals. Price 5c each.

Stamps of 1931 Surcharged in Blue or Carmine similar to cut

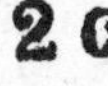

2 c

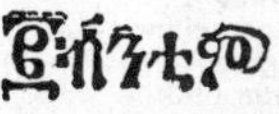

1936 ***Perf. 12x12½, 12½x12.***

242 A25 1c on ⅛g red 1.10 75
243 A26 2c on ¼g olive green (C) 1.10 75
244 A25 3c on ½g dk. vio. 1.10 85
245 A27 5c on 1g red org. 2.00 1.25
246 " 10c on 2g ultra. (C) 2.50 1.50
Nos. 242–246 (5) 7.80 5.10

Haile Selassie I
A32 A33

Lithographed

1942, Mar. 23 ***Perf. 14x13½***

247 A32 4c light blue green, indigo & black 50 40
248 " 10c rose, indigo & black 1.50 85
249 " 20c deep ultramarine, indigo & black 3.00 1.25

1942–43 **Unwmkd.**

250 A33 4c light blue green & indigo 30 20
251 " 8c yel. org. & indigo 40 20
252 " 10c rose & indigo 55 30
253 " 12c dull violet & indigo 65 35
254 " 20c deep ultramarine & indigo 1.00 50
255 " 25c dull green & indigo ('43) 1.50 75
256 " 50c dull brown & indigo ('43) 2.25 1.25
257 " 60c lilac & indigo ('43) 3.00 1.75
Nos. 250–257 (8) 9.65 5.30

Nos. 250–254 Surcharged in Black or Brown

ኦበሊስክ፡
OBELISK
3 Nov. 1943

፫
3

1943, Nov. 3

258 A33 5c on 4c light blue green & indigo 20.00 20.00
259 " 10c on 8c yellow orange & indigo 20.00 20.00
260 " 15c on 10c rose & indigo 20.00 20.00
261 " 20c on 12c dull violet & indigo (Br) 20.00 20.00
262 " 30c on 20c dp. ultra. & indigo (Br) 20.00 20.00
Nos. 258–262 (5) 100.00 100.00

Restoration of the Obelisk in Myazzia Place, Addis Ababa, and the 14th anniversary of the coronation of Emperor Haile Selassie I.

On No. 262, "3" is surcharged on "2" of "20" to make "30."

Palace of Menelik II
A34

Menelik II
A35

Statue
A36

Designs: 50c, Mausoleum. 65c, Menelik II (with scepter).

1944, Dec. 31 **Litho.** ***Perf. 10½***

263 A34 5c green 75 60
264 A35 10c red lilac 1.25 90
265 A36 20c deep blue 1.75 1.50
266 A34 50c dull purple 2.50 1.50
267 A35 65c bistre brown 4.25 2.25
Nos. 263–267 (5) 10.50 6.75

Issued to commemorate the centenary of the birth of Emperor Menelik II, August 18, 1844.

Unissued Semi-Postal Stamps Overprinted in Carmine:

Nurse and Baby
A39

ድ ል

V

Various Designs
Inscribed "Croix Rouge".

1945, Aug. 7 **Photo.** ***Perf. 11½***

268 A39 5c bright green 60 60
269 " 10c bright red 60 60
270 " 25c bright blue 60 60
271 " 50c dk. yellow brown 2.50 2.50
272 " 1t bright violet 4.00 4.00
Nos. 268–272 (5) 8.30 8.30

Nos. 268 to 272 without overprint were ordered printed in Switzerland before Ethiopia fell to the invading Italians, so were not delivered to Addis Ababa. After that country's liberation, the set was overprinted "V" and issued for ordinary postage. These stamps exist without overprint, but were not so issued. Price $1.25.

See Nos. B36–B40.

Lion of Judah
A44

Menelik II
A45

Mail Transport, Old and New
A46

Designs: 50c, Old Post Office, Addis Ababa. 70c, Menelik II and Haile Selassie I.

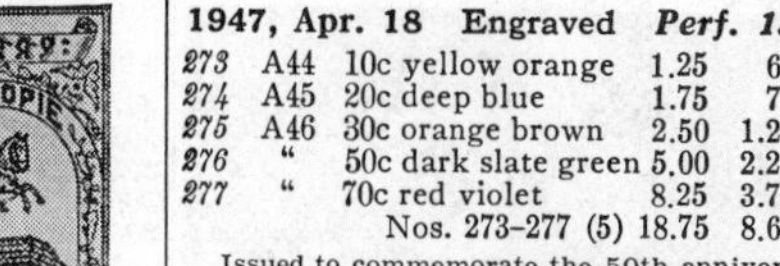

1947, Apr. 18 **Engraved** ***Perf. 13***

273 A44 10c yellow orange 1.25 60
274 A45 20c deep blue 1.75 75
275 A46 30c orange brown 2.50 1.25
276 " 50c dark slate green 5.00 2.25
277 " 70c red violet 8.25 3.75
Nos. 273–277 (5) 18.75 8.60

Issued to commemorate the 50th anniversary of Ethiopia's postal system.

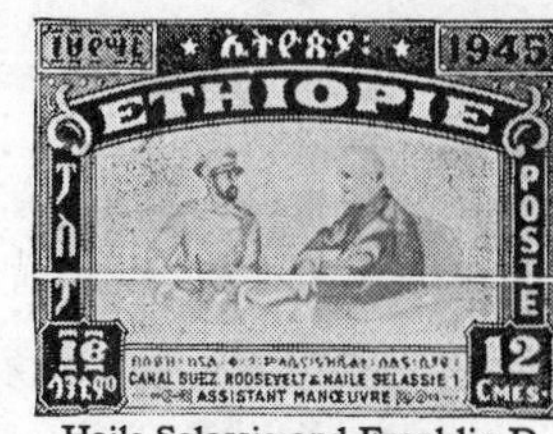

Haile Selassie and Franklin D. Roosevelt—A49

Design: 65c, Roosevelt and U. S. Flags.

Engraved and Photogravure.

1947, May 23 ***Perf. 12½*** **Unwmkd.**

278 A49 12c carmine lake & blue green 50 25
279 " 25c dk. blue & rose 1.00 50
280 " 65c black, red & deep blue 2.00 1.25
Nos. 278–280, C21–C22 (5) 18.00 14.00

Negus Sahle Selassie—A50

Negus Sahle Selassie
A52

Design: 30c, View of Ankober.

1947, May 1 **Engraved** ***Perf. 13***

281 A50 20c deep blue 1.00 50
282 " 30c dark purple 1.50 75
283 A52 $1 deep green 3.75 2.00

150th anniversary of Selassie dynasty.

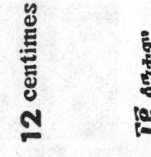

No. 255 Surcharged in Orange

12 centimes

1947, July 14 ***Perf. 14x13½***

284 A33 12c on 25c dull green & indigo 22.50 22.50

Amba Alaguie—A53

Wmk. 282

Designs: 2c, Trinity Church. 4c, Debra Sina. 5c, Mecan, near Achanguie. 8c, Lake Tana. 12c, 15c, Parliament Building, Addis Ababa. 20c, Aiba, near Mai Cheo. 30c, Bahr Bridge over Blue Nile. 60c, 70c, Canoe on Lake Tana. $1, Omo Falls. $3, Mt. Alamata. $5, Ras Dashan Mountains.

Wmkd.
Ethiopian Star and Amharic Characters, Multiple. (282)

1947-53 Engraved *Perf. 13x13½*

285	A53	1c rose violet	10	5
286	"	2c blue violet	15	8
287	"	4c green	25	12
288	"	5c dark green	25	12
289	"	8c deep orange	40	20
290	"	12c red	50	20
290A	"	15c dk. olive brn. ('53)	45	20
291	"	20c blue	75	30
292	"	30c orange brown	1.25	40
292A	"	60c red ('51)	1.50	70
293	"	70c rose lilac	2.25	65
294	"	$1 dk. car. rose	4.50	75
295	"	$3 bright blue	12.00	2.50
296	"	$5 olive	15.00	4.50
		Nos. 285-296 (14)	39.35	10.77

Issue dates: 15c, May 25, 1953; 60c, Feb. 10, 1951; others, Aug. 23, 1947.

Empress Waizero Menen and Emperor Haile Selassie I
A54

1949, May 5 *Perf. 13* Wmk. 282

297	A54	20c blue	80	50
298	"	30c yellow orange	80	65
299	"	50c purple	2.00	1.00
300	"	80c green	2.75	1.25
301	"	$1 red	4.50	2.00
		Nos. 297-301 (5)	10.85	5.40

Central ornaments differ on each denomination.

Issued to commemorate the eighth anniversary of Ethiopia's liberation from Italian occupation.

Dejach Balcha Hospital—A55

Abuna Petros
A56

Designs: 20c, Haile Selassie raising flag. 30c, Lion of Judah statue. 50c, Empress Waizero Menen, Haile Selassie and building.

Perf. 13x13½, 13½x13.

1950, Nov. 2 Engr. Wmk. 282

302	A55	5c purple	50	30
303	A56	10c deep plum	1.25	60
304	"	20c deep carmine	1.50	75
305	"	30c green	2.75	1.25
306	A55	50c deep blue	5.00	2.75
		Nos. 302-306 (5)	11.00	5.65

Issued to commemorate the 20th anniversary of the coronation of Emperor Haile Selassie and Empress Menen.

Abbaye Bridge
A57

1951, Jan. 1 *Perf. 14* Unwmkd.

308	A57	5c dark green & dark brown	2.00	15
309	"	10c dp. orange & blk.	3.00	25
310	"	15c deep blue & orange brown	3.75	35
311	"	30c olive & lilac rose	6.00	55
312	"	60c brown & dp. bl.	10.00	1.25
313	"	80c purple & green	15.00	1.75
		Nos. 308-313 (6)	39.75	4.30

Issued to commemorate the opening of the Abbaye Bridge over the Blue Nile.

Tomb of Ras Makonnen
A58

1951, Mar. 2
Center in Black.

314	A58	5c dark green	80	20
315	"	10c deep ultramarine	1.00	25
316	"	15c blue	1.25	30
317	"	30c claret	3.75	1.00
318	"	80c rose carmine	5.00	1.50
319	"	$1 orange brown	7.00	1.75
		Nos. 314-319 (6)	18.80	5.00

55th anniversary of the Battle of Adwa.

Emperor Haile Selassie I
A59

1952, July 23 *Perf. 13½*

320	A59	5c dark green	30	12
321	"	10c red orange	50	18
322	"	15c black	75	25
323	"	25c ultramarine	1.00	35
324	"	30c violet	1.25	50
325	"	50c rose red	1.75	85
326	"	65c chocolate	3.00	1.10
		Nos. 320-326 (7)	8.55	3.35

60th birthday of Haile Selassie I.

Open Road to Sea
A60

Designs: 25c, 50c, Road and broken chain. 65c, Map. 80c, Allegory: Reunion. $1, Haile Selassie raising flag. $2, Ethiopian flag and seascape. $3, Haile Selassie addressing League of Nations.

Engraved.

1952, Sept. 11 *Perf. 13* Wmk. 282

327	A60	15c brown carmine	1.00	35
328	"	25c red brown	1.25	55
329	"	30c yellow brown	2.00	85
330	"	50c purple	2.75	1.10
331	"	65c gray	4.00	1.40
332	"	80c blue green	5.00	1.75
333	"	$1 rose carmine	7.50	2.50
334	"	$2 deep blue	15.00	4.00
335	"	$3 magenta	25.00	7.50
		Nos. 327-335 (9)	63.50	20.00

Issued to celebrate Ethiopia's federation with Eritrea, effected Sept. 11, 1952.

Haile Selassie and New Ethiopian Port
A61

Design: 15c, 30c, Haile Selassie on deck of ship.

1953, Oct. 4

337	A61	10c red & dark brn.	1.25	60
338	"	15c blue & dark grn.	1.75	60
339	"	25c org. & dk. brn.	2.25	1.00
340	"	30c red brown & dark green	4.00	1.50
341	"	50c pur. & dk. brn.	7.00	2.50
		Nos. 337-341 (5)	16.25	6.20

Issued to commemorate the first anniversary of the federation of Ethiopia and Eritrea.

Princess Tsahai at a Sickbed
A62

Perf. 13x13½

1955, July 8 Engr. Wmk. 282
Cross Typographed in Red

342	A62	15c choc. & ultra.	1.00	40
343	"	20c green & orange	1.50	60
344	"	30c ultra. & green	2.50	60

Issued to commemorate the 20th anniversary of the founding of the Ethiopian Red Cross.

Promulgating the Constitution
A63

Bishops' Consecration by Archbishop
A64

Designs: 25c, Kagnew Battalion. 35c, Reunion with the Motherland. 50c, "Progress." 65c, Empress Waizero Menen and Emperor Haile Selassie I.

Engraved.

1955, Nov. 3 *Perf. 12½* Unwmkd.

345	A63	5c grn. & chocolate	50	20
346	A64	20c carmine & green	90	30
347	"	25c magenta & gray	1.25	45
348	A63	35c brn. & red org.	1.50	50
349	A64	50c dark brown & ultramarine	2.50	90
350	"	65c violet & carmine	3.50	1.10
		Nos. 345-350 (6)	10.15	3.45

Issued to commemorate the silver jubilee of the coronation of Emperor Haile Selassie I and Empress Waizero Menen.

Emperor Haile Selassie and Fair Emblem
A65

1955, Nov. 5 Wmk. 282

351	A65	5c green & olive green	50	15
352	"	10c carmine & deep ultramarine	75	20
353	"	15c violet black & green	1.00	30
354	"	50c magenta & red brown	1.50	70

Silver Jubilee Fair, Addis Ababa.

Nos. 291 and 292A Overprinted

የዓለም ስደተኞች ዓመት
World Refugee Year
1959-1960

1960, Apr. 7 *Perf. 13x13½*

355	A53	20c blue	50	35
356	"	60c red	1.00	65

Issued to publicize World Refugee Year, July 1, 1959–June 30, 1960.

Map of Africa, "Liberty" and Haile Selassie
A66

Emperor Haile Selassie
A67

Perf. 13½

1960, June 14 Engr. Unwmkd.

357	A66	20c orange & green	75	75
358	"	80c orange & violet	1.75	75
359	"	$1 orange & maroon	2.00	1.00

Issued to commemorate the 2nd Conference of Independent African States at Tunis. Issued in sheets of 10.

1960, Nov. 2 *Perf. 14* Wmk. 282

360	A67	10c brown & blue	40	12
361	"	25c violet & emerald	75	35
362	"	50c dark blue & orange yellow	1.50	1.00
363	"	65c slate green & salmon pink	2.00	1.10
364	"	$1 indigo & rose violet	3.00	1.10
		Nos. 360-364 (5)	7.65	3.67

Issued to commemorate the 30th anniversary of the coronation of Emperor Haile Selassie I.

Africa Hall, U.N. Economic Commission for Africa
A68

1961, Apr. 15 ***Perf. 14*** **Wmk. 282**
365 A68 80c ultramarine 1.25 65

Issued for Africa Freedom Day, Apr. 15. Issued in sheets of 10.

Map of Ethiopia, Olive Branch and Emperor Haile Selassie I
A69

1961, May 5 ***Perf. 13x13½***
366 A69 20c green 30 20
367 " 30c violet blue 45 30
368 " $1 brown 1.50 80

Issued to commemorate the 20th anniversary of Ethiopia's liberation from Italian occupation.

African Wild Ass
A70

Designs: 15c, Eland. 25c, Elephant. 35c, Giraffe. 50c, Beisa. $1, Lion.

1961, June 16 ***Perf. 14*** **Wmk. 282**
369 A70 5c black & emerald 18 5
370 " 15c red brown & grn. 30 5
371 " 25c sepia & emerald 40 15
372 " 35c light red brown & green 50 20
373 " 50c brown red & emerald 65 45
374 " $1 red brown & green 1.65 80
Nos. 369-374 (6) 3.68 1.70

Issued in sheets of 10.

Emperor Haile Selassie I and Empress Waizero Menen
A71

1961, July 27 ***Perf. 11*** **Unwmkd.**
375 A71 10c green 45 25
376 " 50c violet blue 90 55
377 " $1 carmine rose 1.50 1.00

Issued to commemorate the golden wedding anniversary of the Emperor and Empress.

Warlike Horsemanship (Guks)
A72

Designs: 15c, Hockey. 20c, Bicycling. 30c, Soccer. 50c, Marathon runner, Olympic winner, 1960.

Photogravure and Engraved

1962, Jan. 14 ***Perf. 12x11½***
378 A72 10c yel. green & car. 18 5
379 " 15c pink & dk. brown 25 8
380 " 20c red & black 35 12
381 " 30c ultramarine & dull purple 55 20
382 " 50c yellow & green 90 30
Nos. 378-382 (5) 2.23 75

Issued to commemorate the Third Africa Football (soccer) Cup, Addis Ababa, Jan. 14-22.

Malaria Eradication Emblem, World Map and Mosquito
A73

Engraved

1962, Apr. 7 ***Perf. 13½*** **Wmk. 282**
383 A73 15c black 25 12
384 " 30c purple 40 25
385 " 60c red brown 1.00 60

Issued for the World Health Organization drive to eradicate malaria.

Abyssinian Ground Hornbill
A74

Birds: 15c, Abyssinian roller. 30c, Bataleur (vert.). 50c, Double-toothed barbet (vert.). $1, Didric cuckoo.

Photogravure

1962, May 5 ***Perf. 11½*** **Unwmkd.**

Granite Paper
386 A74 5c multicolored 25 10
387 " 15c emerald, brown & ultramarine 45 20
388 " 30c light brown, black & red 75 25
389 " 50c multicolored 1.35 55
390 " $1 " 2.75 90
Nos. 386-390 (5) 5.55 2.00

See also Nos. C77-C81, C97-C101, C107-C111.

Assab Hospital
A75

Designs: 15c, School at Assab. 20c, Church at Massawa. 50c, Mosque at Massawa. 60c, Assab port.

Engraved

1962, Sept. 11 ***Perf. 13½*** **Wmk. 282**
391 A75 3c purple 20 4
392 " 15c dark blue 25 12
393 " 20c green 30 14
394 " 50c brown 60 30
395 " 60c carmine rose 90 40
Nos. 391-395 (5) 2.25 1.00

Issued to commemorate the tenth anniversary of the Federation of Ethiopia and Eritrea.

King Bazen, Madonna and Stars over Bethlehem—A76

Designs: 15c, Ezana, obelisks and temple. 20c, Kaleb and sailing fleet. 50c, Lalibela, rock-church and frescoes (vert.). 60c, Yekuno Amlak and priests preaching in village. 75c, Zara Yacob and procession around tree. $1, Lebna Dengel and tournament.

Photogravure

1962, Nov. 2 ***Perf. 14½*** **Unwmkd.**
396 A76 10c multicolored 20 10
397 " 15c " 30 10
398 " 20c " 35 15
399 " 50c " 70 25
400 " 60c " 75 40
401 " 75c " 1.00 60
402 " $1 " 1.50 90
Nos. 396-402 (7) 4.80 2.50

Issued on the 32nd anniversary of the coronation of Emperor Haile Selassie I and to commemorate ancient kings and saints.

Map of Ethiopian Telephone Network
A77

Wheat Emblem
A78

Designs: 50c, Radio mast and waves. 60c, Telegraph pole and rising sun.

Perf. 13½x14

1963, Jan. 1 **Engraved** **Wmk. 282**
403 A77 10c dark red 40 15
404 " 50c ultramarine 90 40
405 " 60c brown 1.25 50

Issued to commemorate the 10th anniversary of the Imperial Board of Telecommunications.

1963, Mar. 21 ***Perf. 13½*** **Unwmkd.**
406 A78 5c deep rose 12 6
407 " 10c rose carmine 18 10
408 " 15c violet blue 30 15
409 " 30c emerald 45 30

Issued for the "Freedom from Hunger" campaign of the U.N. Food and Agriculture Organization.

Abuna Salama
A79

Queen of Sheba
A80

Spiritual Leaders: 15c, Abuna Aregawi. 30c, Abuna Tekle Haimanot. 40c. Yared. 60c, Zara Yacob.

1964, Jan. 3 ***Perf. 13½*** **Unwmkd.**
410 A79 10c blue 20 10
411 " 15c dark green 25 15
412 " 30c brown red 50 35
413 " 40c dark blue 90 50
414 " 60c brown 1.25 1.00
Nos. 410-414 (5) 3.10 2.10

1964, March 2 **Photo.** ***Perf. 11½***

Ethiopian Queens: 15c, Helen. 50c, Seble Wongel. 60c, Mentiwab. 80c, Taitu, consort of Menelik II.

Granite Paper
415 A80 10c multicolored 30 10
416 " 15c " 50 15
417 " 50c " 90 40
418 " 60c " 1.25 60
419 A80 80c multicolored 1.75 75
Nos. 415-419 (5) 4.70 2.00

Priest Teaching Alphabet to Children
A81

Eleanor Roosevelt
A82

Designs: 10c, Classroom. 15c, Woman learning to read (vert.). 40c, Students in chemistry laboratory (vert.). 60c, Graduation procession (vert.).

1964, June 1 ***Perf. 11½*** **Unwmkd.**

Granite Paper
420 A81 5c brown 15 7
421 " 10c emerald 15 10
422 " 15c rose violet 20 14
423 " 40c violet blue 60 25
424 " 60c dark purple 1.00 40
Nos. 420-424 (5) 2.10 96

Issued to publicize education.

1964, Oct. 11 **Photogravure**

Granite Paper

Portrait in Slate Blue
425 A82 10c yellow bister 15 8
426 " 60c orange brown 80 50
427 " 80c green & gold 1.00 70

Issued to honor Eleanor Roosevelt (1884-1962).

King Serse Dengel and View of Gondar, 1563
A83

Ethiopian Leaders: 10c, King Fasiladas and Gondar in 1632. 20c, King Yassu the Great and Gondar in 1682. 25c, Emperor Theodore II and map of Ethiopia. 60c, Emperor John IV and Battle of Gura, 1876. 80c, Emperor Menelik II and Battle of Adwa, 1896.

1964, Dec. 12 **Photo.** ***Perf. 14½x14***
428 A83 5c multicolored 10 4
429 " 10c " 15 6
430 " 20c " 30 15
431 " 25c " 50 20
432 " 60c " 1.00 45
433 " 80c " 1.25 60
Nos. 428-433 (6) 3.30 1.50

Ethiopian Rose
A84

Flowers: 10c, Kosso tree. 25c, St.-John's-wort. 35c, Parrot's-beak. 60c, Maskal daisy.

1965, Mar. 30 ***Perf. 12x13½***
434 A84 5c multicolored 10 5
435 " 10c " 15 5
436 " 25c " 50 15
437 " 35c " 75 25
438 " 60c grn., yel. & orge. 1.00 40
Nos. 434-438 (5) 2.50 90

ITU Emblem, Old and New Communication Symbols
A85

Perf. 13½x14½

1965, May 17 Litho. Unwmkd.

439 A85 5c blue, indigo & yel. 15 6
440 " 10c blue, indigo & org. 22 10
441 " 60c blue, indigo & lilac rose 85 45

Issued to commemorate the centenary of the International Telecommunication Union.

Laboratory
A86

Designs: 5c, Textile spinning mill. 10c, Sugar factory. 20c, Mountain road. 25c, Autobus. 30c, Diesel locomotive and bridge. 35c, Railroad station, Addis Ababa.

1965, July 19 Photo. *Perf. 11½*

Granite Paper

Portrait in Black

442 A86 3c sepia 8 3
443 " 5c dull purple & buff 10 5
444 " 10c black & gray 12 5
445 " 20c grn. & pale yel. 25 10
446 " 25c dk. brown & yel. 35 15
447 " 30c maroon & gray 50 25
448 " 35c dark blue & gray 65 30
Nos. 442-448 (7) 2.05 93

ICY Emblem
A87

1965, Oct. 24 *Perf. 11½* Unwmkd.

Granite Paper

449 A87 10c bl. & red brown 20 10
450 " 50c dp. bl. & red. brn. 75 40
451 " 80c violet blue & red brown 1.00 60

International Cooperation Year, 1965.

National Bank Emblem
A88

Designs: 10c, Commercial Bank emblem. 60c, National and Commercial Bank buildings.

1965, Nov. 2 Photo. *Perf. 13*

452 A88 10c deep carmine, black & indigo 35 10
453 " 30c ultra., black & indigo 65 20
454 " 60c black, yellow & indigo 95 40

Issued to publicize the National and Commercial Banks of Ethiopia.

"Light and Peace" Press Building
A89

1966, Apr. 5 Engraved *Perf. 13*

455 A89 5c pink & black 8 4
456 " 15c lt. yel. grn. & blk. 27 12
457 " 30c org. yellow & blk. 55 25

Issued to commemorate the opening of the "Light and Peace" Printing Press building.

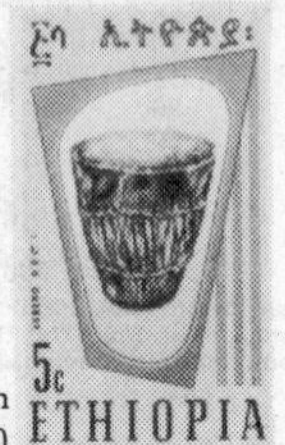

Kebero Drum
A90

Musical Instruments: 10c, Begena harp. 35c, Mesenko guitar. 50c, Krar lyre. 60c, Washent flutes.

1966, Sept. 9 Photo. *Perf. 13½*

458 A90 5c brt. green & black 10 5
459 " 10c dull blue & black 15 8
460 " 35c orange & black 55 25
461 " 50c yellow & black 80 35
462 " 60c rose car. & black 1.00 45
Nos. 458-462 (5) 2.60 1.18

Emperor Haile Selassie—A91

1966, Nov. 1 *Perf. 12* Unwmkd.

463 A91 10c blk., gold & grn. 15 5
464 " 15c blk., gold & dp. carmine 25 10
465 " 40c black & gold 70 50

Issued to commemorate 50 years of leadership of Emperor Haile Selassie.

UNESCO Emblem and Map of Africa
A92

Lithographed

1966, Nov. 30 *Perf. 13½* Wmk. 282

466 A92 15c bl., car. & black 35 10
467 " 60c olive, brown & dark blue 90 45

Issued to commemorate the 20th anniversary of UNESCO (United Nations Educational, Scientific and Cultural Organization).

WHO Headquarters, Geneva
A93

1966, Nov. 30

468 A93 5c olive, ultramarine & brown 20 5
469 " 40c brown, purple & emerald 65 30

Issued to commemorate the opening of World Health Organization Headquarters, Geneva.

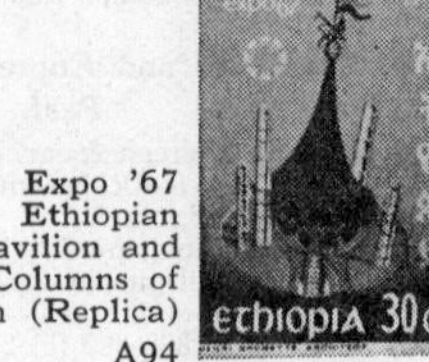

Expo '67 Ethiopian Pavilion and Columns of Axum (Replica)
A94

Perf. 12x13½

1967, May 2 Photo. Unwmkd.

470 A94 30c brt. bl. & multi. 60 20
471 " 45c multicolored 75 25
472 " 80c gray & multi. 1.50 50

Issued to commemorate EXPO '67, International Exhibition, Montreal, Apr. 28-Oct. 27, 1967.

Diesel Train and Map—A95

1967, June 7 Photo. *Perf. 12*

473 A95 15c multicolored 30 15
474 " 30c " 60 25
475 " 50c " 1.00 30

Issued to commemorate the 50th anniversary of the Djibouti-Addis Ababa railroad.

Papilionidae Aethiops
A96

Various Butterflies.

Perf. 13½x13

1967, June 30 Photo. Unwmkd.

476 A96 5c buff & multi. 10 5
477 " 10c lilac & multi. 20 6
478 " 20c multicolored 35 15
479 " 35c blue & multi. 60 20
480 " 40c multicolored 75 25
Nos. 476-480 (5) 2.00 71

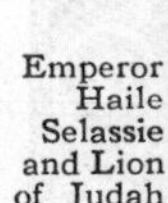

Emperor Haile Selassie and Lion of Judah
A97

1967, July 21 *Perf. 11½*

Granite Paper

481 A97 10c dark brown, emerald & gold 25 6
482 " 15c dk. brown, yel. & gold 40 9
483 " $1 dk. brown, red & gold 1.75 75

Souvenir Sheet

484 A97 $1 dark brown, purple & gold 3.50 2.75

Issued to commemorate the 75th birthday of Emperor Haile Selassie. No. 484 contains one stamp; brown marginal inscription. Size 120x75mm.

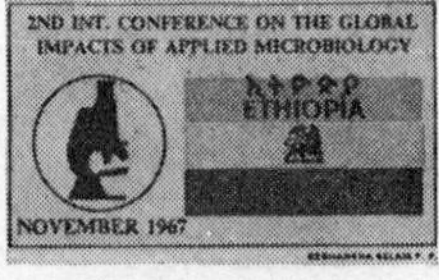

Microscope and Ethiopian Flag
A98

1967, Nov. 6 Litho. *Perf. 13*

Flag in Grn., Yel., Red & Blk.

485 A98 5c blue 15 5
486 " 30c ocher 45 20
487 " $1 violet 1.50 60

Issued to commemorate the 2nd International Conference on the Global Impact of Applied Microbiology, Addis Ababa, Nov. 6-12.

Wall Painting from Debre Berhan Selassie Church, Gondar, 17th Century—A99

Designs (ITY Emblem and): 25c, Votive throne from Atsbe Dera, 4th Century B.C. (vert.). 35c, Prehistoric cave painting, Harar Province. 50c, Prehistoric stone tools, Melke Kontoure (vert.).

1967, Nov. 20 Photo. *Perf. 14½*

488 A99 15c multicolored 30 20
489 " 25c yellow green, buff & black 50 30
490 " 35c grn., brn. & blk. 70 40
491 " 50c yellow & black 90 50

International Tourist Year, 1967.

Processional Bronze Cross, Biet-Maryam Church
A100

Emperor Theodore
A101

Crosses of Lalibela: 10c, Processional copper cross. 15c, Copper cross, Biet-Maryam church. 20c, Lalibela-style cross. 50c, Chiseled copper cross, Madhani Alem church.

1967, Dec. 7 Photo. *Perf. 14½*

Crosses in Silver

492 A100 5c yellow & black 8 4
493 " 10c red orange & blk. 15 6
494 " 15c violet & black 25 10
495 " 20c brt. rose & blk. 30 15
496 " 50c org. yel. & black 90 40
Nos. 492-496 (5) 1.68 75

Perf. 14x13½

1968, Apr. 18 Litho. Unwmkd.

Designs: 20c, Emperor Theodore and lions (horiz.). 50c, Imperial crown.

497 A101 10c lt. violet, ocher & brown 15 6
498 " 20c lilac, brown & dark violet 30 15
499 " 50c dk. green, org. & rose claret 85 30

Issued to commemorate the centenary of the death of the Emperor Theodore (1818?-1868).

Human Rights Flame
A102

1968, May 31 ***Perf. 14½*** **Unwmkd.**

500 A102 15c pink, red & blk. 30 30
501 " $1 light blue, brt. blue & black 1.50 1.50

International Human Rights Year, 1968.

Shah Riza Pahlavi, Emperor and Flags—A103

1968, June 3 **Litho.** ***Perf. 13½***

502 A103 5c multicolored 12 12
503 " 15c " 25 25
504 " 30c " 70 70

Issued to commemorate the visit of Shah Mohammed Riza Pahlavi of Iran.

Emperor Haile Selassie Appealing to League of Nations, 1935

A104

Designs: 35c, African Unity Building and map of Africa. $1, World map, symbolizing international relations.

1968, July 22 **Photo.** ***Perf. 14x13½***

505 A104 15c blue, red, black & gold 25 25
506 " 35c black, emerald, red & gold 55 55
507 " $1 dark blue, lilac, black & gold 1.75 1.75

Ethiopia's struggle for peace.

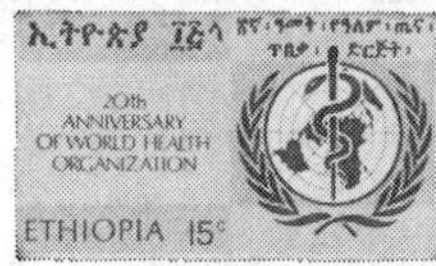

WHO Emblem

A105

Perf. 14x13½

1968, Aug. 30 **Litho.** **Unwmkd.**

508 A105 15c brt. green & blk. 25 25
509 " 60c red lilac & blk. 90 90

Issued to commemorate the 20th anniversary of the World Health Organization.

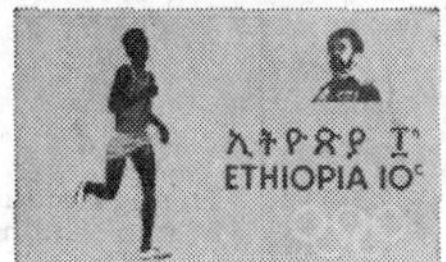

Running

A106

Designs: 15c, Soccer. 20c, Boxing. 40c, Basketball. 50c, Bicycling.

1968, Oct. 12 ***Perf. 11½***

510 A106 10c lt. green & multi. 15 15
511 " 15c brt. vio. & multi. 25 25
512 " 20c blue & multi. 30 30
513 " 40c multicolored 60 60
514 " 50c beige & multi. 90 90
Nos. 510-514 (5) 2.20 2.20

Issued to commemorate the 19th Olympic Games, Mexico City, Oct. 12-27.

Arrussi Woman

A107

Regional Costumes: 15c, Man from Gemu Gefa. 20c, Gojam man. 30c, Kefa man. 35c, Harer woman. 50c, Ilubabor grass coat. 60c, Woman from Eritrea.

Perf. 13½x13

1968, Dec. 10 **Photo.** **Unwmkd.**

515 A107 5c silver & multi. 7 7
516 " 15c " " 15 15
517 " 20c " " 20 20
518 " 30c " " 30 30
519 " 35c " " 35 35
520 " 50c " " 60 60
521 " 60c " " 85 85
Nos. 515-521 (7) 2.52 2.52

See Nos. 575-581.

Message Stick and Amharic Postal Emblem—A108

1969, Mar. 10 **Litho.** ***Perf. 14***

522 A108 10c emerald, black & brown 20 20
523 " 15c yel., blk. & brn. 30 30
524 " 35c multicolored 75 75

Issued to commemorate the 75th anniversary of Ethiopian postal service.

ILO Emblem

A109

1969, Apr. 11 **Litho.** ***Perf. 14½***

525 A109 15c orange & black 30 30
526 " 60c emerald & blk. 1.25 1.25

Issued to commemorate the 50th anniversary of the International Labor Organization.

Dove, Red Cross, Crescent, Lion and Sun Emblems—A110

1969, May 8 ***Perf. 13*** **Wmk. 282**

527 A110 5c lt. ultramarine, black & red 8 8
528 " 15c lt. ultramarine, green & red 25 25
529 A110 30c lt. ultra., violet blue & red 50 50

Issued to commemorate the 50th anniversary of the League of Red Cross Societies.

Endybis Silver Coin, 3rd Century

A111

Ancient Ethiopian Coins: 10c, Gold coin of Ezana, 4th century. 15c, Gold coin of Kaleb, 6th century. 30c, Bronze coin of Armah, 7th century. 40c, Bronze coin of Wazena, 7th century. 50c, Silver coin of Gersem, 8th century.

1969, June 19 **Photo.** ***Perf. 14½***

530 A111 5c ultramarine, black & silver 10 10
531 " 10c bright red, black & gold 18 18
532 " 15c brn., black & gold 30 30
533 " 30c dp. carmine, black & bronze 60 60
534 " 40c dk. green, black & bronze 70 70
535 " 50c dp. violet, black & silver 90 90
Nos. 530-535 (6) 2.78 2.78

Zebras and Tourist Year Emblem

A112

Designs: 10c, Camping. 15c, Fishing. 20c, Water skiing. 25c, Mountaineering (vert.).

Perf. 13x13½, 13½x13

1969, Aug. 29 **Litho.** **Unwmkd.**

536 A112 5c multicolored 10 10
537 " 10c " 15 15
538 " 15c " 25 25
539 " 20c " 40 40
540 " 25c " 50 50
Nos. 536-540 (5) 1.40 1.40

International Year of African Tourism.

Stylized Bird and U.N. Emblem

A113

Designs: 30c, Stylized flowers, U.N. and peace emblems (vert.). 60c, Stylized bird, U.N. emblem and plane.

1969, Oct. 24 ***Perf. 11½*** **Unwmkd.**

541 A113 10c lt. blue & multi. 15 15
542 " 30c " " " 45 45
543 " 60c " " " 1.00 1.00

25th anniversary of the United Nations.

See "Special Notices" at the front of this volume for data on the listing methods of this Catalogue, abbreviations, condition, prices and examination.

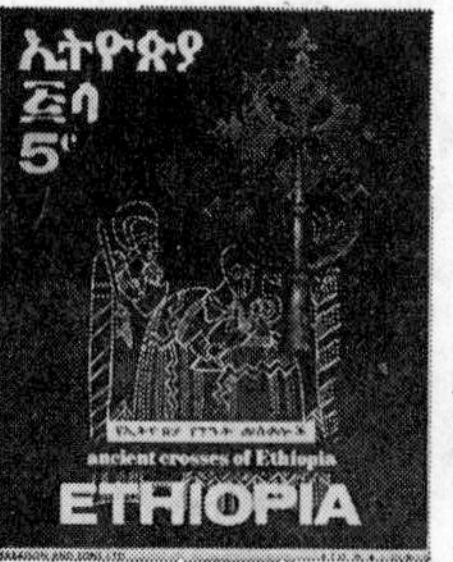

Ancient Cross and Holy Family

A114

Designs: Various ancient crosses.

Photogravure

1969, Dec. 10 ***Perf. 14½x13½***

544 A114 5c blk., yel. & dk. bl. 10 10
545 " 10c black & yellow 15 15
546 " 25c blk., yel. & green 45 45
547 " 60c black & ocher 1.00 1.00

Ancient Figurines—A115

Ancient Ethiopian Pottery: 20c, Vases, Yeha period, 4th-3rd centuries B.C. 25c, Vases and jugs, Axum, 4th-6th centuries A.D. 35c, Bird-shaped jug and jugs, Matara, 4th-6th centuries A.D. 60c, Decorated pottery, Adulis, 6th-7th centuries A.D.

1970, Feb. 6 **Photo.** ***Perf. 14½***

548 A115 10c black & multi. 15 15
549 " 20c " " 30 30
550 " 25c " " 35 35
551 " 35c " " 50 50
552 " 60c " " 90 90
Nos. 548-552 (5) 2.20 2.20

Medhane Alem Church—A116

Rock Churches of Lalibela, 12th-13th Centuries: 10c, Bieta Emmanuel. 15c, The four Rock Churches of Lalibela. 20c, Bieta Mariam. 50c, Bieta Giorgis.

1970, Apr. 15 ***Perf. 13*** **Unwmkd.**

553 A116 5c brown & multi. 8 8
554 " 10c " " 15 15
555 " 15c " " 30 30
556 " 20c " " 35 35
557 " 50c " " 75 75
Nos. 553-557 (5) 1.63 1.63

Sailfish Tang

A117

Tropical Fish: 10c, Undulate triggerfish. 15c, Orange butterflyfish. 25c, Butterflyfish. 50c, Imperial Angelfish.

1970, June 19 **Photo.** ***Perf. 12½***

558 A117 5c multicolored 10 10

No.	Type	Description	Unused	Used
559	A117	10c multicolored	15	15
560	"	15c "	25	25
561	"	25c "	50	50
562	"	50c "	85	85
		Nos. 558-562 (5)	1.85	1.85

Education Year Emblem
A118

1970, Aug. 14 ***Perf. 13½*** **Unwmkd.**

No.	Type	Description	Unused	Used
563	A118	10c multicolored	15	15
564	"	20c gold, ultramarine & emerald	35	35
565	"	50c gold, emerald & orange	75	75

Issued for International Education Year.

Map of Africa
A119

Designs: 30c, Flag of Organization of African Unity. 40c, OAU Headquarters, Addis Ababa.

1970, Sept. 21 Photo. ***Perf. 13½***

No.	Type	Description	Unused	Used
566	A119	20c multicolored	27	27
567	"	30c "	40	40
568	"	40c green & multi.	60	60

Organization of African Unity.

Emperor Haile Selassie
A120

1970, Oct. 30 ***Perf. 14½*** **Unwmkd.**

No.	Type	Description	Unused	Used
569	A120	15c Prus. bl. & multi.	18	18
570	"	50c multicolored	65	65
571	"	60c "	1.00	1.00

Issued to commemorate the 40th anniversary of the coronation of Emperor Haile Selassie I.

Posts, Telecommunications and G.P.O. Buildings—A121

1970, Dec. 30 Litho. ***Perf. 13½***

No.	Type	Description	Unused	Used
572	A121	10c verm. & multi.	18	18
573	"	50c brown & multi.	80	80
574	"	80c multicolored	1.10	1.10

Opening of new Posts, Telecommunications and General Post Office buildings.

Costume Type of 1968

Regional Costumes: 5c, Warrior from Begemedir and Semain. 10c, Woman from Bale. 15c, Warrior from Wolega. 20c, Woman from Showa. 25c, Man from Sidamo. 40c, Woman from Tigre. 50c, Man from Wello.

1971, Feb. 17 Photo. ***Perf. 11½***

Granite Paper

No.	Type	Description	Unused	Used
575	A107	5c gold & multi.	8	8
576	"	10c " "	15	15
577	"	15c " "	25	25
578	"	20c " "	30	30
579	"	25c " "	40	40
580	"	40c " "	50	50
581	"	50c " "	80	80
		Nos. 575-581 (7)	2.48	2.48

Plane's Tail with Emblem
A122

Designs: 10c, Ethiopian scenes. 20c, Nose of Boeing 707. 60c, Pilots in cockpit, and engine. 80c, Globe with routes shown.

1971, Apr. 8 ***Perf. 14½x14***

No.	Type	Description	Unused	Used
582	A122	5c multicolored	8	8
583	"	10c "	15	15
584	"	20c "	30	30
585	"	60c "	85	85
586	"	80c "	1.10	1.10
		Nos. 582-586 (5)	2.48	2.48

Ethiopian Airlines, 25th anniversary.

Fountain of Life, 15th Century Gospel Book
A123

Ethiopian Paintings: 10c, King David, 15th century manuscript. 25c, St. George, 17th century painting on canvas. 50c, King Lalibela, 18th century painting on wood. 60c, Yared singing before King Kaleb, mural in Axum Cathedral, 18th century.

1971, June 15 Photo. ***Perf. 11½***

Granite Paper

No.	Type	Description	Unused	Used
587	A123	5c tan & multi.	8	8
588	"	10c pale sal. & multi.	15	15
589	"	25c lemon & multi.	30	30
590	"	50c yellow & multi.	65	65
591	"	60c gray & multi.	1.00	1.00
		Nos. 587-591 (5)	2.18	2.18

Black and White Heads, Globes
A124

Designs: 60c, Black and white hand holding globe. 80c, Four races, globes.

1971, Aug. 31 **Unwmkd.**

No.	Type	Description	Unused	Used
592	A124	10c org., red brown & black	20	20
593	"	60c grn., bl. & blk.	65	65
594	"	80c blue, org., yel. & black	1.10	1.10

International Year Against Racial Discrimination.

Emperor Menelik II and Reading of Treaty of Ucciali
A125

Contemporary Paintings: 30c, Menelik II on horseback gathering the tribes. 50c, Ethiopians and Italians in Battle of Adwa. 60c, Menelik II at head of his army.

1971, Oct. 20 Litho. ***Perf. 13½***

No.	Type	Description	Unused	Used
595	A125	10c multicolored	20	20
596	"	30c "	35	35
597	"	50c "	65	65
598	"	60c "	1.00	1.00

75th anniversary of victory of Adwa over the Italians, March 1, 1896.

Haile Selassie Broadcasting and Map of Ethiopia
A126

Designs: 5c, Two telephones, 1897, Menelik II and Ras Makonnen. 30c, Ethiopians around television set. 40c, Telephone microwave circuits. 60c, Map of Africa on globe and telephone dial.

1971, Nov. 2

No.	Type	Description	Unused	Used
599	A126	5c brown & multi.	6	6
600	"	10c yellow & multi.	12	12
601	"	30c vio. bl. & multi.	40	40
602	"	40c black & multi.	55	55
603	"	60c vio. bl. & multi.	90	90
		Nos. 599-603 (5)	2.03	2.03

75th anniversary of telecommunications in Ethiopia.

UNICEF Emblem, Mother and Child
A127

Designs (UNICEF Emblem and): 10c, Children drinking milk. 15c, Man holding sick child. 30c, Kindergarten class. 50c, Father and son.

1971, Dec. 15 **Unwmkd.**

No.	Type	Description	Unused	Used
604	A127	5c yellow & multi.	8	8
605	"	10c pale brn. & multi.	15	15
606	"	15c rose & multi.	22	22
607	"	30c violet & multi.	45	45
608	"	50c green & multi.	75	75
		Nos. 604-608 (5)	1.65	1.65

25th anniversary of the United Nations International Children's Fund (UNICEF).

Nos. 445-448 Overprinted

U.N. SECURITY COUNCIL
FIRST MEETING
IN AFRICA 1972

1972, Jan. 28 Photo. ***Perf. 11***

Portrait in Black

No.	Type	Description	Unused	Used
609	A86	20c green & pale yel.	30	30
610	"	25c dk. brn. & yellow	45	45
611	"	30c maroon & gray	65	65
612	"	35c dk. blue & gray	80	80

First meeting of U.N. Security Council in Africa.

River Boat on Lake Haik—A128

1972, Feb. 7 Litho. ***Perf. 11½***

Granite Paper; Multicolored

No.	Type	Description	Unused	Used
613	A128	10c *shown*	15	15
614	"	20c *Boats on Lake Abaya*	30	30
615	"	30c *on Lake Tana*	50	50
616	"	60c *on Baro River*	1.00	1.00

Proclamation of Cyrus the Great
A129

1972, Mar. 28 Photo. ***Perf. 14x14½***

No.	Type	Description	Unused	Used
617	A129	10c red & multi.	15	15
618	"	60c emerald & multi.	90	90
619	"	80c gray & multi.	1.25	1.25

2500th anniversary of the founding of the Persian empire by Cyrus the Great.

Houses, Sidamo Province
A130

Ethiopian Architecture: 10c, Tigre Province. 20c, Eritrea Province. 40c, Addis Ababa. 80c, Shoa Province.

1972, Apr. 11 Litho. ***Perf. 13½***

No.	Type	Description	Unused	Used
620	A130	5c black & multi.	8	8
621	"	10c blk., gray & brn.	15	15
622	"	20c black & multi.	30	30
623	"	40c black, blue green & brown	60	60
624	"	80c black, brown & red brown	1.15	1.15
		Nos. 620-624 (5)	2.28	2.28

Hands Holding Map of Ethiopia
A131

Designs: 10c, Hands shielding Ethiopians. 25c, Map of Africa, hands reaching for African Unity emblem. 50c, Brown and white hands clasped, U.N. emblem. 60c, Hands protecting dove. Each denomination shows different portrait of the Emperor.

Perf. 14½x14

1972, July 21 Litho. **Unwmkd.**

No.	Type	Description	Unused	Used
625	A131	5c scarlet & multi.	7	7
626	"	10c ultra. & multi.	13	13
627	"	25c vio. bl. & multi.	33	33
628	"	50c lt. blue & multi.	65	65

No.	Type	Description	Unused	Used
629	A131	60c brown & multi.	80	80
		Nos. 625-629 (5)	1.98	1.98

80th birthday of Emperor Haile Selassie.

Running, Flags of Mexico, Japan, Italy
A132

1972, Aug. 25 *Perf. 13½x13*

Multicolored

No.	Type	Description	Unused	Used
630	A132	10c *shown*	13	13
631	"	30c *Soccer*	40	40
632	"	50c *Bicycling*	65	65
633	"	60c *Boxing*	80	80

20th Olympic Games, Munich, Germany, Aug. 26–Sept. 11.

Open Bible, Cross and Orbit
A133

Designs: 50c, First and 1972 headquarters of the British and Foreign Bible Society (vert.). 80c, First Amharic Bible.

1972, Sept. 25 Photo. *Perf. 13½*

No.	Type	Description	Unused	Used
634	A133	20c dp. red & multi.	27	27
635	"	50c " " "	65	65
636	"	80c " " "	1.00	1.00

United Bible Societies World Assembly, Addis Ababa, Sept. 1972.

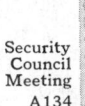

Security Council Meeting
A134

Designs: 60c, Building where Security Council met. 80c, Map of Africa with flags of participating members.

1972, Nov. 1 Litho. *Perf. 13½*

No.	Type	Description	Unused	Used
637	A134	10c light blue & violet blue	13	13
638	"	60c multicolored	75	75
639	"	80c "	1.00	1.00

First United Nations Security Council meeting, Addis Ababa, Jan. 28–Feb. 4, 1972.

Fish in Polluted Sea
A135

Designs: 30c, Fisherman, beacon, family. 80c, Polluted seashore.

1973, Feb. 23 Photo. *Perf. 13½*

No.	Type	Description	Unused	Used
640	A135	20c gold & multi.	30	30
641	"	30c " "	45	45
642	"	80c " "	1.25	1.25

World message from the sea, Ethiopian anti-pollution campaign.

INTERPOL and Ethiopian Police Emblems
A136

Designs: 50c, INTERPOL emblem and General Secretariat, Paris. 60c, INTERPOL emblem.

1973, Mar. 20 Photo. *Perf. 13½*

No.	Type	Description	Unused	Used
643	A136	40c dull org. & blk.	60	60
644	"	50c blue, blk. & yel.	75	75
645	"	60c dk. car. & black	90	90

50th anniversary of International Criminal Police Organization (INTERPOL).

Virgin of Emperor Zara Yaqob
A137

Ethiopian Art: 15c, Crucifixion, Zara Yaqob period. 30c, Virgin and Child, from Entoto Mariam Church. 40c, Christ, contemporary mosaic. 80c, The Evangelists, contemporary bas-relief.

1973, May 15 Photo. *Perf. 11½*

Granite Paper

No.	Type	Description	Unused	Used
646	A137	5c brown & multi.	7	7
647	"	15c dp. blue & multi.	20	20
648	"	30c gray grn. & multi.	40	40
649	"	40c multicolored	50	50
650	"	80c slate & multi.	1.10	1.10
		Nos. 646-650 (5)	2.27	2.27

Free African States in 1963 and 1973
A138

Designs (Map of Africa and): 10c, Flags of OAU members. 20c, Symbols of progress. 40c, Dove and people. 80c, Emblems of various UN agencies.

1973 May 25 *Perf. 14½x14*

No.	Type	Description	Unused	Used
651	A138	5c red & multi.	8	8
652	"	10c ol. gray & multi.	17	17
653	"	20c green & multi.	33	33
654	"	40c sepia & multi.	65	65
655	"	80c lt. blue & multi.	1.35	1.35
		Nos. 651-655 (5)	2.58	2.58

Organization for African Unity, 10th anniversary.

Scouts Saluting Ethiopian and Scout Flags
A139

Designs: 15c, Road and road sign. 30c, Girl Scout reading to old man. 40c, Scout and disabled people. 60c, Ethiopian Boy Scout.

1973, July 10 Photo. *Perf. 11½*

Granite Paper

No.	Type	Description	Unused	Used
656	A139	5c blue & multi.	7	7
657	"	15c lt. grn. & multi.	20	20
658	"	30c yellow & multi.	42	42
659	"	40c crimson & multi.	55	55
660	"	60c violet & multi.	85	85
		Nos. 656-660 (5)	2.09	2.09

24th Boy Scout World Conference, Nairobi, Kenya, July 16–21.

WMO Emblem
A140

Designs: 50c, WMO emblem and anemometer. 60c, Weather satellite over earth, and WMO emblem.

1973, Sept. 4 Photo. *Perf. 13½*

No.	Type	Description	Unused	Used
661	A140	40c black, blue & dull blue	50	50
662	"	50c dull bl. & black	60	60
663	A140	60c dull bl. & multi.	80	80

Centenary of international meteorological cooperation.

Prince Makonnen, Duke of Harer
A141

Human Rights Flame
A142

Designs: 5c, Old wall of Harer. 20c, Operating room. 40c, Boy Scouts learning first aid, and hospital. 80c, Prince Makonnen and hospital.

1973, Nov. 1 *Perf. 14½* **Unwmkd.**

No.	Type	Description	Unused	Used
664	A141	5c gray & multi.	5	5
665	"	10c red brn. & multi.	10	10
666	"	20c green & multi.	25	25
667	"	40c brn. red & multi.	50	50
668	"	80c ultra. & multi.	1.00	1.00
		Nos. 664-668 (5)	1.90	1.90

Opening of Prince Makonnen Memorial Hospital.

Perf. 11½

1973, Nov. 16 Photo. **Unwmkd.**

Granite Paper

No.	Type	Description	Unused	Used
669	A142	40c yellow, gold & dark green	50	50
670	"	50c lt. green, gold & dark green	60	60
671	"	60c orange, gold & dark green	80	80

25th anniversary of the Universal Declaration of Human Rights.

Emperor Haile Selassie
A143

1973, Nov. 5 Photo. *Perf. 11½*

No.	Type	Description	Unused	Used
672	A143	5c yellow & multi.	5	3
673	"	10c brt. bl. & multi.	12	5
674	"	15c green & multi.	18	7
675	"	20c dull yel. & multi.	25	10
676	"	25c multicolored	30	13
677	"	30c "	35	15
678	"	35c "	42	17
679	"	40c ultra. & multi.	48	20
680	"	45c multicolored	55	22
681	"	50c orange & multi.	60	25
682	"	55c magenta & multi.	65	28
683	"	60c multicolored	70	30
684	"	70c red org. & multi.	85	35
685	"	90c brt. vio. & multi.	1.10	45
686	"	$1 multicolored	1.20	50
687	"	$2 org. & multi.	2.35	1.00
688	"	$3 multicolored	3.50	1.50
689	"	$5 "	6.00	2.50
		Nos. 672-689 (18)	19.65	8.25

Wicker Furniture
A144

Designs: Various wicker baskets, wall hangings, dinnerware.

1974, Jan. 31 Photo. *Perf. 11½*

Granite Paper

No.	Type	Description	Unused	Used
690	A144	5c vio. bl. & multi.	5	5
691	"	10c " " "	10	10
692	"	30c " " "	30	30
693	"	50c " " "	50	50
694	"	60c " " "	60	60
		Nos. 690-694 (5)	1.55	1.55

Cow, Calf, Syringe
A145

Designs: 15c, Inoculation of cattle. 20c, Bullock and syringe. 50c, Laboratory technician, cow's head, syringe. 60c, Map of Ethiopia, cattle, syringe.

1974, Feb. 20 Litho. *Perf. 13½x13*

No.	Type	Description	Unused	Used
695	A145	5c sepia & multi.	5	5
696	"	15c ultra. & multi.	15	15
697	"	20c " "	20	20
698	"	50c orange & multi.	50	50
699	"	60c gold & multi.	60	60
		Nos. 695-699 (5)	1.50	1.50

Campaign against cattle plague.

Umbrella Makers
A146

Designs: 30c, Weaving. 50c, Child care. 60c, Foundation headquarters.

1974, Apr. 17 Photo. *Perf. 14½*

No.	Type	Description	Unused	Used
700	A146	10c lt. lilac & multi.	10	10
701	"	30c multicolored	30	30
702	"	50c "	50	50
703	"	60c blue & multi.	60	60

20th anniversary of Haile Selassie I Foundation.

Ceremonial Robe
A147

Designs: Ceremonial robes.

1974, June 26 Lithographed *Perf. 13*

No.	Type	Description	Unused	Used
704	A147	15c multicolored	15	15
705	"	25c ocher & multi.	25	25
706	"	35c green & multi.	35	35
707	"	40c lt. brn. & multi.	40	40
708	"	60c gray & multi.	60	60
		Nos. 704-708 (5)	1.75	1.75

World Population Statistics
A148

Designs: 50c, "Larger families—lower living standard." 60c, Rising population graph.

1974, Aug. 19 Photo. *Perf. 14½*

709	A148	40c yellow & multi.	40	40
710	"	50c violet & multi.	50	50
711	"	60c green & multi.	60	60

World Population Year 1974.

UPU Emblem, Letter Carrier's Staff
A149

Celebration Around "Damara" Pillar
A150

Designs (UPU Emblem and): 50c, Letters and flags. 60c, Globe. 70c, Headquarters, Bern.

1974, Oct. 9 Photo. *Perf. 11½*

Granite Paper

712	A149	15c yellow & multi.	15	15
713	"	50c multicolored	50	50
714	"	60c ultra. & multi.	60	60
715	"	70c multicolored	70	70

Centenary of Universal Postal Union.

1974, Dec. 17 Photo. *Perf. 14x14½*

Designs: 5c, Site of Gishen Mariam Monastery. 20c, Cross and festivities. 80c, Torch (Chibos) Parade.

716	A150	5c yellow & multi.	5	5
717	"	10c " "	10	10
718	"	20c " "	20	20
719	"	80c " "	80	80

Meskel Festival, Sept. 26–27, commemorating the finding in the 4th century of the True Cross, of which a fragment is kept at Gishen Mariam Monastery in Wollo Province.

Precis Clelia
A151

Adoration of the Kings
A152

Butterflies: 25c, Charaxes achaemenes. 45c, Papilio dardanus. 50c, Charaxes druceanus. 60c, Papilio demodocus.

1975, Feb. 18 Photo. *Perf. 12x12½*

720	A151	10c silver & multi.	10	10
721	"	25c gold & multi.	25	25
722	"	45c pur. & multi.	45	45
723	"	50c grn. & multi.	50	50
724	"	60c brt. bl. & multi.	60	60
		Nos. 720–724 (5)	1.90	1.90

1975, Apr. 23 Photo. *Perf. 11½*

Designs: 10c, Baptism of Jesus. 15c, Jesus teaching in the Temple. 30c, Jesus giving sight to the blind. 40c, Crucifixion. 80c, Resurrection.

Granite Paper

725	A152	5c brown & multi.	5	5
726	"	10c black & multi.	10	10
727	"	15c dk. brn. & multi.	15	15
728	"	30c " " "	30	30
729	"	40c black & multi.	40	40
730	"	80c slate & multi.	80	80
		Nos. 725–730 (6)	1.80	1.80

Murals from Ethiopian churches.

Warthog
A153

Designs: Wild animals.

1975, May 27 Photo. *Perf. 11½*

Multicolored; Granite Paper

731	A153	5c *shown*	5	5
732	"	10c *Aardvark*	10	10
733	"	20c *Semien wolf*	20	20
734	"	40c *Gelada baboon*	40	40
735	"	80c *Civet*	80	80
		Nos. 731–735 (5)	1.55	1.55

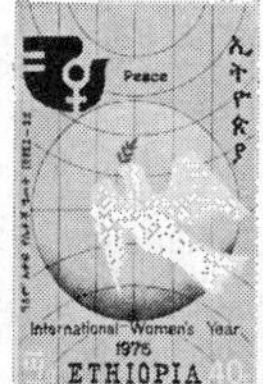

"Peace," Dove, Globe, IWY Emblem
A154

Designs (IWY Emblem and): 50c, Symbols of development. 90c, Equality between men and women.

1975, June 30 Litho. *Perf. 14x14½*

736	A154	40c blue & black	40	40
737	"	50c sal. & multi.	50	50
738	"	90c multicolored	90	90

International Women's Year 1975.

Postal Museum
A155

Designs: Various interior views of Postal Museum.

1975, Aug. 19 Photo. *Perf. 13x12½*

739	A155	10c ocher & multi.	10	10
740	"	30c pink & multi.	30	30
741	"	60c multicolored	60	60
742	"	70c lt. grn. & multi.	70	70

Ethiopian National Postal Museum, opening.

Map of Ethiopia and Sun
A156

1975, Sept. 11 Photo. *Perf. 11½*

Granite Paper

743	A156	5c lilac & multi.	5	5
744	"	10c ultra. & multi.	10	10
745	"	25c brown & multi.	25	25
746	"	50c yellow & multi.	50	50
747	"	90c brt. grn. & multi.	90	90
		Nos. 743–747 (5)	1.80	1.80

1st anniversary of Ethiopia Tikdem (Socialism).

U.N. Emblem
A157

1975, Oct. 24 Photo. *Perf. 11½*

748	A157	40c lilac & multi.	40	40
749	"	50c multicolored	50	50
750	"	90c blue & multi.	90	90

United Nations, 30th anniversary.

Ilubabor Hair Style
A158

Delphinium Wellbyi
A159

Regional Hair Styles: 15c, Arusi. 20c, Eritrea. 30c, Bale. 35c, Kefa. 50c, Begemdir. 60c, Shewa.

1975, Dec. 15 Photo. *Perf. 11½*

751	A158	5c multicolored	5	5
752	"	15c "	15	15
753	"	20c "	20	20
754	"	30c "	30	30
755	"	35c "	35	35
756	"	50c "	50	50
757	"	60c "	60	60
		Nos. 751–757 (7)	2.15	2.15

See Nos. 832–838.

1976, Jan. 15 Photo. *Perf. 11½*

Flowers: 10c, Plectocephalus varians. 20c, Brachystelma asmarensis (horiz.). 40c, Ceropegia inflata. 80c, Erythrina brucei.

758	A159	5c multicolored	5	5
759	"	10c "	10	10
760	"	20c "	20	20
761	"	40c "	40	40
762	"	80c "	80	80
		Nos. 758–762 (5)	1.55	1.55

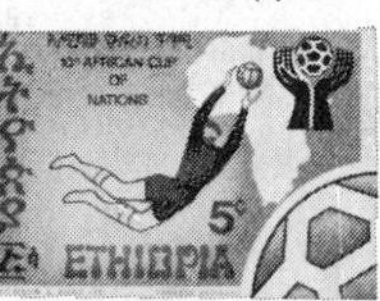

Goalkeeper, Map of Africa, Games' Emblem
A160

Designs: Various scenes from soccer, map of Africa and ball.

1976, Feb. 27 Photo. *Perf. 14½*

763	A160	5c org. & multi.	5	5
764	"	10c yel. & multi.	10	10
765	"	25c lilac & multi.	25	25
766	"	50c green & multi.	50	50
767	"	90c bright green & multicolored	90	90
		Nos. 763–767 (5)	1.80	1.80

10th African Cup of Nations, Addis Ababa and Dire Dawa, Feb. 29–Mar. 14.

Telephones, 1876 and 1976
A161

Ethiopian Jewelry
A162

Designs: 60c, Alexander Graham Bell. 90c, Transmission tower.

1976, Mar. 10 Litho. *Perf. 12x13½*

768	A161	30c light ocher & multicolored	30	30
769	"	60c emerald & multicolored	60	60
770	"	90c vermilion, black & buff	90	90

Centenary of first telephone call by Alexander Graham Bell, Mar. 10, 1876.

Granite Paper

1976, May 14 Photo. *Perf. 11½*

Designs: Women wearing various kinds of Ethiopian jewelry.

771	A162	5c blue & multi.	5	5
772	"	10c plum & multi.	10	10
773	"	20c gray & multi.	20	20
774	"	40c green & multi.	40	40
775	"	80c org. & multi.	80	80
		Nos. 771–775 (5)	1.55	1.55

Boxing
A163

Hands Holding Map of Ethiopia
A164

Designs (Montreal Olympic Emblem and): 80c, Runner and maple leaf. 90c, Bicycling.

1976, July 15 Litho. *Perf. 12½x12*

776	A163	10c multicolored	10	10
777	"	80c brt. red, black & green	80	80
778	"	90c brt. red & multi.	90	90

21st Olympic Games, Montreal, Canada, July 17–Aug. 1.

1976, Aug. 5 Photo. *Perf. 14½*

779	A164	5c rose & multi.	5	5
780	"	10c olive & multi.	10	10
781	"	25c orange & multi.	25	25
782	"	50c multicolored	50	50
783	"	90c dk. bl. & multi.	90	90
		Nos. 779–783 (5)	1.80	1.80

Development through cooperation.

Revolution Emblem: Eye and Map
A165

1976, Sept. 9 Photo. *Perf. 13½*

784	A165	5c multicolored	5	5
785	"	10c "	10	10
786	"	25c "	25	25
787	"	50c yellow & multi.	50	50
788	"	90c green & multi.	90	90
		Nos. 784–788 (5)	1.80	1.80

2nd anniversary of the revolution (Tikdem).

Sunburst Around Crest
A166

Plane Over Man with Donkey
A167

1976, Sept. 13 Photo. *Perf. 11½*

789	A166	5c grn. gold & blk.	5	3
790	"	10c org., gold & blk.	10	5
791	"	15c greenish blue, gold & black	15	8
792	"	20c lilac, gold & blk.	20	10
793	"	25c brt. green, gold & black	25	12
794	"	30c car., gold & blk.	30	15
795	"	35c yellow, gold & black	35	18

No.	Type	Description	Unused	Used
796	A166	40c olive, gold & blk.	40	20
797	"	45c brt. grn., gold & black	45	22
798	"	50c car. rose, gold & black	50	25
799	"	55c ultra., gold & blk.	55	28
800	"	60c fawn, gold & blk.	60	30
801	"	70c rose, gold & blk.	70	35
802	"	90c bl., gold & blk.	90	45
803	"	$1 dull grn., gold & black	1.00	50
804	"	$2 gray, gold & black	2.00	1.00
805	"	$3 brn. vio., gold & black	3.00	1.50
806	"	$5 slate bl., gold & black	5.00	2.50
		Nos. 789-806 (18)	16.50	8.26

1976, Oct. 28 Litho. *Perf. 12x12½*

Designs: 10c, Globe showing routes. 25c, Crew and passengers forming star. 50c, Propeller and jet engine. 90c, Airplanes surrounding map of Ethiopia.

No.	Type	Description	Unused	Used
807	A167	5c dull bl. & multi.	5	5
808	"	10c lilac & multi.	10	10
809	"	25c multicolored	25	25
810	"	50c orange & multi.	50	50
811	"	90c olive & multi.	90	90
		Nos. 807-811 (5)	1.80	1.80

Ethiopian Airlines, 30th anniversary.

Tortoises

A168

Hand Holding Makeshift Hammer

A169

Reptiles: 20c, Chameleon. 30c, Python. 40c, Monitor lizard. 80c, Nile crocodiles.

1976, Dec. 15 Photo. *Perf. 14½*

No.	Type	Description	Unused	Used
812	A168	10c multicolored	10	10
813	"	20c "	20	20
814	"	30c "	30	30
815	"	40c "	40	40
816	"	80c "	80	80
		Nos. 812-816 (5)	1.80	1.80

1977, Jan. 20 Litho. *Perf. 12½*

Designs: 5c, Hands holding bowl and plane dropping food. 45c, Infant with empty bowl, and bank note. 60c, Map of affected area, footprints and tire tracks. 80c, Film strip, camera and Ethiopian sitting between eggshells.

No.	Type	Description	Unused	Used
817	A169	5c multicolored	5	5
818	"	10c "	10	10
819	"	45c "	45	45
820	"	60c "	60	60
821	"	80c "	80	80
		Nos. 817-821 (5)	2.00	2.00

Ethiopian Relief and Rehabilitation Commission for drought and disaster areas.

Elephant and Ruins, Axum, 7th Century

A170

Designs: 10c, Ibex and temple, 5th century, B.C., Yeha. 25c, Megalithic dolmen and pottery, Sourre Kabanawa. 50c, Awash Valley, stone axe, Acheulean period. 80c, Omo Valley, hominid jawbone.

1977, Mar. 15 Photo. *Perf. 13½*

No.	Type	Description	Unused	Used
822	A170	5c gold & multi.	5	5
823	"	10c " "	10	10
824	"	25c " "	25	25
825	"	50c " "	50	50
826	"	80c " "	80	80
		Nos. 822-826 (5)	1.70	1.70

Archaeological sites and finds in Ethiopia.

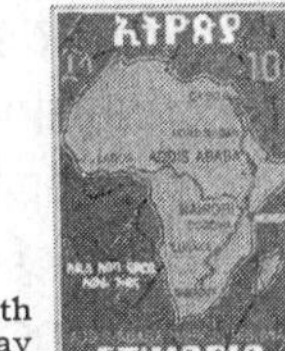

Map of Africa with Trans-East Highway

A171

1977, Mar. 30 *Perf. 14*

No.	Type	Description	Unused	Used
827	A171	10c gold & multi.	10	10
828	"	20c " "	20	20
829	"	40c " "	40	40
830	"	50c " "	50	50
831	"	60c " "	60	60
		Nos. 827-831 (5)	1.80	1.80

Addis Ababa to Nairobi Highway and projected highways to Cairo, Egypt, and Gaborone, Botswana.

Hairstyle Type of 1975

Regional Hairstyles: 5c, Wollega. 10c, Gojjam. 15c, Tigre. 20c, Harrar. 25c, Gemu Gofa. 40c, Sidamo. 50c, Wollo.

1977, Apr. 28 Photo. *Perf. 11½*

No.	Type	Description	Unused	Used
832	A158	5c multicolored	5	5
833	"	10c "	10	10
834	"	15c "	15	15
835	"	20c "	20	20
836	"	25c "	25	25
837	"	40c "	40	40
838	"	50c "	50	50
		Nos. 832-838 (7)	1.65	1.65

Addis Ababa

A172

Towns of Ethiopia: 10c, Asmara. 25c, Harer. 50c, Jima. 90c, Dese.

1977, June 20 Photo. *Perf. 14½*

No.	Type	Description	Unused	Used
839	A172	5c silver & multi.	5	5
840	"	10c " "	10	10
841	"	25c " "	25	25
842	"	50c " "	50	50
843	"	90c " "	90	90
		Nos. 839-843 (5)	1.80	1.80

Terebratula Abyssinica

A173

Fractured Imperial Crown

A174

Fossil Shells: 10c, Terebratula subalata. 25c, Cuculloea lefeburiaua. 50c, Ostrea plicatissima. 90c, Trigonia cousobrina.

1977, Aug. 15 Photo. *Perf. 14x13½*

No.	Type	Description	Unused	Used
844	A173	5c multicolored	5	5
845	"	10c "	10	10
846	"	25c "	25	25
847	"	50c "	50	50
848	"	90c "	90	90
		Nos. 844-848 (5)	1.80	1.80

1977, Sept. 9 Litho. *Perf. 15*

Designs: 10c, Symbol of the Revolution (spade, axe, torch). 25c, Warriors, hammer and sickle, map of Ethiopia. 60c, Soldier, farmer and map. 80c, Map and emblem of revolutionary government.

No.	Type	Description	Unused	Used
849	A174	5c multicolored	5	5
850	"	10c "	10	10
851	"	25c "	25	25
852	"	60c "	60	60
853	"	80c "	80	80
		Nos. 849-853 (5)	1.80	1.80

Third anniversary of the revolution.

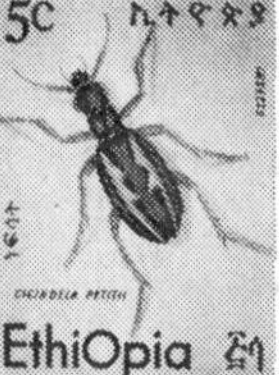

Cicindela Petitii

A175

Lenin, Globe, Map of Ethiopia and Emblem

A176

Insects: 10c, Heliocopris dillonii. 25c, Poekilocerus vignaudii. 50c, Pepsis heros. 90c, Pepsis dedjaz.

1977, Sept. 30 Photo. *Perf. 14x13½*

No.	Type	Description	Unused	Used
854	A175	5c multicolored	5	5
855	"	10c "	10	10
856	"	25c "	25	25
857	"	50c "	50	50
858	"	90c "	90	90
		Nos. 854-858 (5)	1.80	1.80

1977, Nov. 15 Litho. *Perf. 12*

No.	Type	Description	Unused	Used
859	A176	5c orange & multi.	5	5
860	"	10c multicolored	10	10
861	"	25c salmon & multi.	25	25
862	"	50c lt. bl. & multi.	50	50
863	"	90c yellow & multi.	90	90
		Nos. 859-863 (5)	1.80	1.80

60th anniversary of Russian October Revolution.

Chondrostoma Dilloni

A177

Salt-water Fish: 10c, Ostracion cubicus. 25c, Serranus summana. 50c, Serranus luti. 90c, Tetraodon maculatus.

1978, Jan. 20 Litho. *Perf. 15½*

No.	Type	Description	Unused	Used
864	A177	5c multicolored	5	5
865	"	10c "	10	10
866	"	25c "	25	25
867	"	50c "	50	50
868	"	90c "	90	90
		Nos. 864-868 (5)	1.80	1.80

Cattle

A178

Domestic Animals: 10c, Mules. 25c, Goats. 50c, Dromedaries. 90c, Horses.

1978, Mar. 27 Litho. *Perf. 13½x14*

No.	Type	Description	Unused	Used
869	A178	5c yel. & multi.	5	5
870	"	10c multicolored	10	10
871	"	25c grn. & multi.	25	25
872	"	50c verm. & multi.	50	50
873	"	90c ultra. & multi.	90	90
		Nos. 869-873 (5)	1.80	1.80

Foreign postal stationery (stamped envelopes, postal cards and air letter sheets) lies beyond the scope of this Catalogue which is limited to adhesive postage stamps.

Weapons and Shield, Map of Ethiopia

A179

Bronze Ibex, 5th Century B.C.

A180

Designs: (Map of Ethiopia and): 10c, Civilian fighters. 25c, Map of Africa. 60c, Soldiers. 80c, Red Cross nurse and wounded man.

1978, May Litho. *Perf. 15½*

No.	Type	Description	Unused	Used
874	A179	5c multicolored	5	5
875	"	10c "	10	10
876	"	25c "	25	25
877	"	60c "	60	60
878	"	80c "	80	80
		Nos. 874-878 (5)	1.80	1.80

"Call of the Motherland."

1978, June 21 Litho. *Perf. 15½*

Ancient Bronzes: 10c, Lion, Yeha, 5th century B.C. (horiz.). 25c, Lamp with ibex attacked by dog, Matara, 1st century B.C. 50c, Goat, Axum, 3rd century A.D. (horiz.). 90c, Ax, chisel and sickle, Yeha, 5th–4th centuries B.C.

No.	Type	Description	Unused	Used
879	A180	5c multicolored	5	5
880	"	10c "	10	10
881	"	25c "	25	25
882	"	50c "	50	50
883	"	90c "	90	90
		Nos. 879-883 (5)	1.80	1.80

Globe and Argentina '78 Emblem

A181

Designs (Argentina '78 Emblem and): 20c, Soccer player kicking ball. 30c, Two players embracing, net and ball. 55c, World map and ball. 70c, Soccer field (vert.).

Perf. 14x13½, 13½x14

1978, July 19 Lithographed

No.	Type	Description	Unused	Used
884	A181	5c multicolored	5	5
885	"	20c "	20	20
886	"	30c "	30	30
887	"	55c "	55	55
888	"	70c "	70	70
		Nos. 884-888 (5)	1.80	1.80

11th World Cup Soccer Championship, Argentina, June 1–25.

Map of Africa, Oppressed African

A182

Designs (Map of Africa and): 10c, Policeman pointing gun. 25c, Sniper with gun. 60c, African caught in net. 80c, Head of free man.

1978, Aug. 25 *Perf. 12½x13½*

No.	Type	Description	Unused	Used
889	A182	5c multicolored	5	5
890	"	10c "	10	10
891	"	25c "	25	25
892	"	60c "	60	60
893	"	80c "	80	80
		Nos. 889-893 (5)	1.80	1.80

Namibia Day.

Soldiers, Guerrilla and Jets
A183

Design: $1, People looking toward sun, crushing snake, flags.

1978, Sept. 8 Photo. ***Perf. 14***

894	A183	80c multicolored	80	80
895	"	$1 "	1.00	1.00

4th anniversary of revolution.

Hand and Globe with Tools
A184

Designs: 15c, Symbols of energy, communications, education, medicine, agriculture and industry. 25c, Cogwheels and world map. 60c, Globe and hands passing wrench. 70c, Flying geese and turtle over globe.

1978, Nov. 10 Litho. ***Perf. 12x12½***

896	A184	10c multicolored	10	10
897	"	15c "	15	15
898	"	25c "	25	25
899	"	60c "	60	60
900	"	70c "	70	70
		Nos. 896-900 (5)	1.80	1.80

Technical Cooperation Among Developing Countries Conference, Buenos Aires, Argentina, Sept. 1978.

Human Rights Emblem
A185

1978, Dec. 7 Photo. ***Perf. 12½x13½***

901	A185	5c multicolored	5	5
902	"	15c "	15	15
903	"	25c "	25	25
904	"	35c "	35	35
905	"	1b "	1.00	1.00
		Nos. 901-905 (5)	1.80	1.80

Declaration of Human Rights, 30th anniversary.

Broken Chain, Anti-Apartheid Emblem
A186

Stele from Osole
A187

1978, Dec. 28 Litho. ***Perf. 12½x12***

906	A186	5c multicolored	5	5
907	"	20c "	20	20
908	"	30c "	30	30
909	"	55c "	55	55
910	"	70c "	70	70
		Nos. 906-910 (5)	1.80	1.80

Anti-Apartheid Year.

1979, Jan. 25 ***Perf. 14***

Ancient Carved Stones, Soddo Region: 10c, Anthropomorphous stele, Gorashino. 25c, Leaning stone, Wado. 60c, Round stones, Ambeut. 80c, Bas-relief, Tiya.

911	A187	5c multicolored	5	5
912	"	10c "	10	10
913	"	25c "	25	25
914	"	60c "	60	60
915	"	80c "	80	80
		Nos. 911-915 (5)	1.80	1.80

SEMI-POSTAL STAMPS.

Types of 1931, Overprinted in Red at Upper Left ✚

Perf. 12x12½, 12½x12.

1936, Feb. 25 **Unwmkd.**

No.	Type	Description	Unused	Used
B1	A27	1g light green	35	30
B2	"	2g rose	35	30
B3	A25	4g blue	35	30
B4	A27	8g brown	50	50
B5	A25	1t purple	50	50
		Nos. B1-B5 (5)	2.05	1.90

Nos. B1-B5 were sold at twice face value, the surtax going to the Red Cross.

Nos. 289, 290 and 292 to 294 Surcharged in Blue

EXPOSITION 1949 +8c

Perf. 13x13½

1949, June 13 **Wmk. 282**

No.	Type	Description	Unused	Used
B6	A53	8c+8c deep orange	75	60
B7	"	12c+5c red	75	60
B8	"	30c+15c org. brown	1.50	1.25
B9	"	70c+70c rose lilac	10.00	7.00
B10	"	$1+80c dk. car. rose	11.50	10.00
		Nos. B6-B10 (5)	24.50	19.45

Type A39 Surcharged in Carmine ✚ + 10 ct.

Photogravure.

1950, May 8 *Perf. 11½* **Unwmkd.**

Various Designs

Inscribed "Croix Rouge"

No.	Type	Description	Unused	Used
B11	A39	5c+10c bright green	75	60
B12	"	10c+10c bright red	1.25	65
B13	"	25c+10c bright blue	2.00	2.00
B14	"	50c+10c dark yellow brown	5.50	3.75
B15	"	1t+10c brt. violet	7.50	5.00
		Nos. B11-B15 (5)	17.00	12.00

The surtax was for the Red Cross.

Nos. B6-B10 Overprinted in Black 1951

Perf. 13x13½

1951, Nov. 17 **Wmk. 282**

No.	Type	Description	Unused	Used
B16	A53	8c+8c deep orange	60	50
B17	"	12c+5c red	60	50
B18	"	30c+15c org. brown	90	75
B19	"	70c+70c rose lilac	7.50	6.25
B20	"	$1+80c dark carmine rose	11.00	7.50
		Nos. B16-B20 (5)	20.60	15.50

Tree, Staff and Snake SP1

Engraved

1951, Nov. 25 *Perf. 13* **Wmk. 282**

Lower Panel in Red.

No.	Type	Description	Unused	Used
B21	SP1	5c+2c deep blue green	30	15
B22	"	10c+3c orange	40	25
B23	"	15c+3c deep blue	50	40
B24	SP1	30c+5c red	1.25	85
B25	"	50c+7c red brown	2.50	1.75
B26	"	$1+10c purple	4.50	2.75
		Nos. B21-B26 (6)	9.45	6.15

The surtax was for anti-tuberculosis work.

1958, Dec. 1

Lower Panel in Red

No.	Type	Description	Unused	Used
B27	SP1	20c+3c dull purple	40	30
B28	"	25c+4c emerald	50	35
B29	"	35c+5c rose violet	60	40
B30	"	60c+7c violet blue	1.25	80
B31	"	65c+7c violet	3.00	1.75
B32	"	80c+9c car. rose	4.00	2.50
		Nos. B27-B32 (6)	9.75	6.10

The surtax was for anti-tuberculosis work.

Nos. B27-B32 were the only stamps on sale from Dec. 1-25, 1958.

Type of Regular Issue, 1955, Surcharged

RED CROSS CENTENARY 1859-1959 +2c

Engraved; Cross Typographed in Red

1959, May 30 **Wmk. 282**

No.	Type	Description	Unused	Used
B33	A62	15c+2c olive bistre & rose red	50	50
B34	"	20c+3c violet & emerald	60	60
B35	"	30c+5c rose carmine & greenish bl.	1.00	1.00

Issued to commemorate the centenary of the International Red Cross idea. The surtax was for the Red Cross.

Type A39 Surcharged

Silver Jubilee 1960 + 5 ct.

Perf. 11½

1960, May 7 **Photo.** **Unwmkd.**

No.	Type	Description	Unused	Used
B36	A39	5c+1c bright green	35	25
B37	"	10c+2c bright red	45	30
B38	"	25c+3c bright blue	90	65
B39	"	50c+4c dk. yel. brn.	1.35	1.00
B40	"	1t+5c bright violet	2.50	1.80
		Nos. B36-B40 (5)	5.55	4.00

25th anniversary of Ethiopian Red Cross.

Crippled Boy on Crutches SP2

Engraved

1963, July 23 *Perf. 13½* **Wmk. 282**

No.	Type	Description	Unused	Used
B41	SP2	10c+2c ultramarine	25	20
B42	"	15c+3c red	35	25
B43	"	50c+5c bright grn.	1.00	75
B44	"	60c+5c red lilac	1.50	1.00

The surtax was to aid the disabled.

AIR POST STAMPS.

Regular Issue of 1928 Handstamped in Violet, Red, Black or Green

Perf. 13½x14

1929, Aug. 17 **Unwmkd.**

No.	Type	Description	Unused	Used
C1	A22	⅛m orange & light blue	60	75
C2	A23	¼m indigo & red orange	60	75
C3	A22	½m gray green & black	60	75
C4	A23	1m dk. car. & black	60	75
C5	A22	2m dark blue & black	75	90
C6	A23	4m yellow & olive	75	90
C7	A22	8m violet & olive	75	90
C8	A23	1t orange brown & violet	75	90
C9	A22	2t green & bistre	90	1.20
C10	A23	3t choc. & green	90	1.20
		Nos. C1-C10 (10)	7.20	9.00

The overprint signifies "16 August 1929 —Airplane of the Ethiopian Government." The stamps commemorate the arrival at Addis Ababa of the first air mail carried by an airplane of the Ethiopian Government. There are three types of the overprint: (I) 19½mm. high; "colon" at right of bottom word. (II) 20mm. high; same "colon." (III) 19½-mm. high; no "colon." Many errors exist.

Symbols of Empire, Airplane and Map AP1

931, June 17 **Engr.** *Perf. 12½*

No.	Type	Description	Unused	Used
C11	AP1	1g orange red	20	30
C12	"	2g ultramarine	25	35
C13	"	4g violet	30	50
C14	"	8g blue green	70	1.00
C15	"	1t olive brown	1.30	35
C16	"	2t carmine	2.50	4.00
C17	"	3t yellow green	3.75	5.50
		Nos. C11-C17 (7)	9.00	12.00

Nos. C11 to C17 exist imperforate.

Reprints of C11 to C17 exist. Paper is thinner and gum whiter than the originals. Reprints usually sell at about one-tenth of above prices.

Nos. 250, 255 and 257 Surcharged in Black

20 - 4 - 39

a

AERIENNE
REPRISE POSTE
ETHIOPIENNE
29/12/46
Eth. Doll. 0,50

b

Perf. 14x13½

1947, Mar. 20 **Unwmkd.**

No.	Type	Description	Unused	Used
C18	A33 (a)	12c on 4c light blue green & indigo	25.00	22.50
C19	" (b)	50c on 25c dull green & indigo	25.00	22.50
a.		"26·12·46"	75.00	
C20	A33 (b)	$2 on 60c lilac & indigo	50.00	37.50
a.		"26·12·46"	100.00	

Resumption of airmail service, Dec. 29, 1946.

Franklin D. Roosevelt AP2

Design: $2, Haile Selassie.

Engraved and Photogravure.

1947, May 23 *Perf. 12½*

No.	Type	Description	Unused	Used
C21	AP2	$1 dark purple & sepia	6.00	4.50
C22	"	$2 carmine & deep blue	8.50	7.50

Farmer Plowing AP3

Designs: 10c, 25c, Zoquala, extinct volcano. 30c, 35c, Tesissat Falls, Abai River. 65c, 70c, Amba Alaguie. $1, Sacala, source of Nile. $3, Gorgora and Dembia, Lake Tana. $5, Magdala, former capital. $10, Ras Dashan, mountain peak.

Engraved

1947-55 *Perf. 13x13½* **Wmk. 282**

No.	Type	Description	Unused	Used
C23	AP3	8c purple brown	25	12
C24	"	10c bright green	25	12
C25	"	25c dull purple ('52)	40	20
C26	"	30c orange yellow	60	15
C27	"	35c blue ('55)	60	30
C28	"	65c purple ('51)	90	50
C29	"	70c red	1.50	55
C30	"	$1 deep blue	1.75	75
C31	"	$3 rose lilac	7.50	4.50
C32	"	$5 red brown	12.50	6.25
C33	"	$10 rose violet	22.50	15.00
		Nos. C23-C33 (11)	48.75	28.44

U. P. U. Monument, Bern—AP4

1950, Apr. 3 *Perf. 12½* **Unwmkd.**

No.	Type	Description	Unused	Used
C34	AP4	5c green & red	30	20
C35	"	15c dark slate green & carmine	40	30
C36	"	25c org. yel. & grn.	45	30
C37	"	50c car. & ultra.	1.00	65

Issued to commemorate the 75th anniversary of the formation of the Universal Postal Union.

Convair Plane over Mountains AP5

Engraved and Lithographed

1955, Dec. 30 *Perf. 12½* **Unwmkd.**

Center Multicolored

No.	Type	Description	Unused	Used
C38	AP5	10c gray green	40	25
C39	"	15c carmine	50	30
C40	"	20c violet	75	40

10th anniversary of Ethiopian Airlines.

Promulgating the Constitution AP6

Perf. 14x13½

1956, July 16 **Engr.** **Wmk. 282**

No.	Type	Description	Unused	Used
C41	AP6	10c reddish brown & ultramarine	35	25

C42 AP6 15c dark carmine rose & olive green 45 25
C43 " 20c blue & orange red 60 40
C44 " 25c purple & green 75 45
C45 " 30c dark green & red brown 1.00 65
Nos. C41-C45 (5) 3.15 2.00

25th anniversary of the constitution.

Aksum
AP7

Ancient Capitals: 10c, Lalibela. 15c, Gondar. 20c, Mekele. 25c, Ankober.

1957, Feb. 7 ***Perf. 14***

Centers in Green.

C46 AP7 5c red brown 40 20
C47 " 10c rose carmine 40 20
C48 " 15c red orange 50 25
C49 " 20c ultramarine 75 35
C50 " 25c claret 1.00 50
Nos. C46-C50 (5) 3.05 1.50

Amharic "A"
AP8

Designs: Various Amharic characters and views of Addis Ababa. The characters, arranged by values, spell Addis Ababa.

1957, Feb. 14 **Engraved**

Amharic Letters in Scarlet.

C51 AP8 5c ultramarine, *salmon pink* 15 10
C52 " 10c olive green, *pink* 25 20
C53 " 15c dull purple, *yellow* 35 20
C54 " 20c green, *buff* 50 30
C55 " 25c plum, *pale blue* 80 35
C56 " 30c red, *pale green* 1.00 40
Nos. C51-C56 (6) 3.05 1.55

70th anniversary of Addis Ababa.

Map, Rock Church at Lalibela and Obelisk—AP9

1958, April 15 ***Perf. 13½*** **Wmk. 282**

C57 AP9 10c green 35 15
C58 " 20c rose red 50 30
C59 " 30c bright blue 85 35

Issued to commemorate the conference of Independent African States, Accra, April 15–22.

Map of Africa and U. N. Emblem
AP10

1958, Dec. 29 ***Perf. 13***

C60 AP10 5c emerald 25 8
C61 " 20c carmine rose 40 25
C62 AP10 25c ultramarine 50 40
C63 " 50c pale purple 1.00 55

Issued to commemorate the first session of the United Nations Economic Conference for Africa, opened in Addis Ababa Dec. 29.

Nos. C23-29 Overprinted

የአየር ፖስት ፴ኛ ዓመት
30th Airmail Ann.
1929 - 1959

Perf. 13x13½

1959, Aug. 16 Engraved Wmk. 282

C64 AP3 8c purple brown 30 20
C65 " 10c bright green 40 25
C66 " 25c dull purple 50 35
C67 " 30c orange yellow 60 40
C68 " 35c blue 75 45
C69 " 65c purple 1.00 70
C70 " 70c red 1.25 90
Nos. C64-C70 (7) 4.80 3.25

30th anniversary of Ethiopian airmail service.

Ethiopian Soldier and Map of Congo
AP11

Globe with Map of Africa
AP12

Photogravure

1962, July 23 ***Perf. 11½*** **Unwmkd.**

Granite Paper

C71 AP11 15c orange, blue, brn. & green 30 15
C72 " 50c purple, blue, brn. & green 70 45
C73 " 60c red, blue, brn. & green 1.00 50

Issued to commemorate the second anniversary of the Ethiopian contingent of the United Nations forces in the Congo and in honor of the 70th birthday of Emperor Haile Selassie.

1963, May 22 **Granite Paper**

C74 AP12 10c magenta & black 30 15
C75 " 40c emerald & black 70 35
C76 " 60c blue & black 1.00 50

Issued to commemorate the conference of African heads of state for African Unity, Addis Ababa.

Bird Type of Regular Issue, 1962

Birds: 10c, Black-headed forest oriole. 15c, Broad-tailed paradise whydah (vert.). 20c, Lammergeier (vert.). 50c, White-checked touraco. 80c, Purple indigo bird.

1963, Sept. 12 ***Perf. 11½***

Granite Paper

C77 A74 10c multicolored 20 12
C78 " 15c " 25 18
C79 " 20c bl., blk. & ocher 45 25
C80 " 50c lemon & multi. 75 45
C81 " 80c ultra., blk.& brn. 1.50 75
Nos. C77-C81 (5) 3.15 1.75

Swimming
AP13

Sport: 10c, Basketball (vert.). 15c, Javelin. 80c, Soccer game in stadium.

Perf. 14x13½

1964, Sept. 15 Litho. Unwmkd.

C82 AP13 5c multicolored 10 15
C83 " 10c " 15 15
C84 " 15c " 30 30
C85 " 80c " 1.25 60

18th Olympic Games, Tokyo, Oct. 10–25.

Queen Elizabeth II and Emperor Haile Selassie
AP14

1965, Feb. 1 **Photo.** ***Perf. 11½***

Granite Paper

C86 AP14 5c multicolored 12 5
C87 " 35c " 45 25
C88 " 60c " 75 40

Issued to commemorate the visit of Queen Elizabeth II of Great Britain, Feb. 1–8.

Koka Dam and Power Plant
AP15

Designs: 15c, Sugar cane field. 50c, Blue Nile bridge. 60c, Gondar castles. 80c, Coffee tree. $1, Cattle at water hole. $3, Camels at well. $5, Ethiopian Air Lines jet plane.

1965, July 19 ***Perf. 11½*** **Unwmkd.**

Granite Paper

Portrait in Black

C89 AP15 15c vio. brn. & buff 20 15
C90 " 40c vio. bl. & lt. bl. 50 30
C91 " 50c grn. & lt. blue 60 35
C92 " 60c claret & yellow 75 45
C93 " 80c grn., yel. & red 90 50
C94 " $1 brn. & lt. blue 1.10 60
C95 " $3 claret & pink 3.50 1.65
C96 " $5 ultra. & lt. bl. 7.50 3.00
Nos. C89-C96 (8) 15.05 7.00

Bird Type of Regular Issue, 1962

Birds: 10c, White-collared kingfisher. 15c, Blue-breasted bee-eater. 25c, African paradise flycatcher. 40c, Village weaver. 60c, White-collared pigeon.

1966, Feb. 15 **Photo.** ***Perf. 11½***

Granite Paper

C97 A74 10c dull yel. & multi. 20 15
C98 " 15c lt. blue & multi. 30 15
C99 " 25c gray & multi. 50 20
C100 " 40c pink & multi. 80 30
C101 " 60c multicolored 1.20 40
Nos. C97-C101 (5) 3.00 1.20

Black Rhinoceros—AP16

Animals: 10c, Leopard. 20c, Black-and-white colobus (monkey). 30c, Mountain nyala. 60c, Nubian ibex.

1966, June 20 **Litho.** ***Perf. 13***

C102 AP16 5c deep green, black & gray 15 7
C103 " 10c green, black & ocher 20 10
C104 " 20c citron, black & green 40 15
C105 " 30c yel. grn., blk. & ocher 60 18
C106 AP16 60c yel. grn., blk. & dark brn. 1.25 30
Nos. C102-C106 (5) 2.60 80

Bird Type of Regular Issue, 1962

Birds: 10c, Blue-winged goose (vert.). 15c, Yellow-billed duck. 20c, Wattled ibis. 25c, Striped swallow. 40c, Black-winged lovebird (vert.).

1967, Sept. 29 **Photo.** ***Perf. 11½***

Granite Paper

C107 A74 10c lt. ultra. & multi. 20 15
C108 " 15c green & multi. 25 15
C109 " 20c yellow & multi. 30 15
C110 " 25c salmon & multi. 50 15
C111 " 40c pink & multi. 1.00 40
Nos. C107-C111 (5) 2.25 1.00

SPECIAL DELIVERY STAMPS.

Motorcycle Messenger
SD1

Addis Ababa Post Office
SD2

Engraved.

1947, Apr. 24 ***Perf. 13*** **Unwmkd.**

E1 SD1 30c orange brown 60 50
E2 SD2 50c blue 2.00 1.50

1954-62 **Wmk. 282**

E3 SD1 30c org. brown ('62) 1.00 75
E4 SD2 50c blue 90 50

POSTAGE DUE STAMPS.

Menelik II
D1

Perf. 14x13½

1896, June 10 **Unwmkd.**

Black Overprint.

J1 D1 ¼g green 1.00
J2 " ½g red 1.00
J3 " 4g lilac brown 60
a. Without overprint 60
J4 " 8g violet 60
a. Without overprint 60

Red Overprint.

J5 D1 1g blue 1.00
J6 " 2g dark brown 1.00
J7 " 16g black 60
a. Without overprint 60
Nos. J1-J7 (7) 5.80

Regular Issue of 1894
Handstamped in Various Colors:

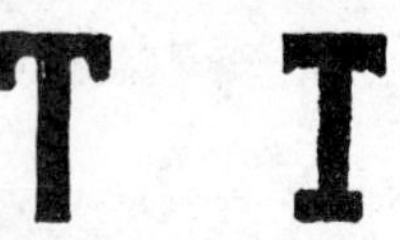

a *b*

1905, Jan. 1

J8 A1 (*a*) ¼g green 6.00 6.00
J9 " (") ½g red 6.00 6.00

J10 A1 (*a*) 1g blue 6.00 6.00
J11 " (") 2g dark brown 6.00 6.00
J12 A2 (") 4g lilac brown 6.00 6.00
J13 " (") 8g violet 9.00 9.00
J14 " (") 16g black 20.00 20.00
J15 A1 (*b*) ¼g green 6.00 6.00
J16 " (") ½g red 6.00 6.00
J17 " (") 1g blue 6.00 6.00
J18 " (") 2g dark brown 6.00 6.00
J19 A2 (") 4g lilac brown 6.00 6.00
J20 " (") 8g violet 9.00 9.00
J21 " (") 16g black 20.00 20.00
Nos. J8–J21 (14) 118.00 118.00

Excellent forgeries of Nos. J8–J42 exist.

Regular Issue of 1894 Handstamped in Blue or Violet

TAXE A PERCEVOIR T

1906, July 1

J22 A1 ¼g green 5.00 5.00
J23 " ½g red 5.00 5.00
J24 " 1g blue 5.00 5.00
J25 " 2g dark brown 5.00 5.00
J26 A2 4g lilac brown 5.00 5.00
J27 " 8g violet 7.50 7.50
J28 " 16g black 12.50 12.50
Nos. J22–J28 (7) 45.00 45.00

Nos. J22, J24, J25 and J26 exist with inverted overprint, also No. J22 with double overprint.

With Additional Surcharge of Value Handstamped as on Regular Issue of 1907.

1907, July 1

J29 A1 (*e*) ¼ on ¼g green 10.00 10.00
J30 " (") ½ on ½g red 10.00 10.00
J31 " (*f*) 1 on 1g blue 10.00 10.00
J32 " (") 2 on 2g dark brown 10.00 10.00
J33 A2 (") 4 on 4g lilac brown 10.00 10.00
J34 " (") 8 on 8g violet 10.00 10.00
J35 " (") 16 on 16g black 14.00 14.00
Nos. J29–J35 (7) 74.00 74.00

Nos. J30, J31, J32 and J33 exist with inverted surcharge.

Regular Issue of 1894 Handstamped in Black

1908, Dec. 1

J36 A1 ¼g green 75 40
J37 " ½g red 75 50
J38 " 1g blue 75 50
J39 " 2g dark brown 80 70
J40 A2 4g lilac brown 1.25 1.25
J41 " 8g violet 2.50 2.75
J42 " 16g black 7.00 5.50
Nos. J36–J42 (7) 13.80 11.60

Nos. J36 to J42 exist with inverted overprint and Nos. J36, J37, J38 and J40 with double overprint.

Same Handstamp on Regular Issue of 1909.

1912, Dec. 1 *Perf. 11½*

J43 A3 ¼g blue green 75 55
J44 " ½g rose 1.00 65
J45 " 1g green & orange 2.00 1.65
J46 A4 2g blue 2.50 2.00
J47 " 4g grn. & carmine 3.50 2.75
J48 A5 8g verm. & dp. grn. 5.00 4.25
J49 " 16g verm. & car. 12.00 9.00
Nos. J43–J49 (7) 26.75 20.85

Nos. J43 to J49, all exist with inverted overprint.

Same Handstamp on Regular Issue of 1919 in Blue Black

1925–27 *Perf. 11½*

J50 A6 ⅛g violet & brown *12.00 12.00*
J51 " ¼g bl. green & drab *12.00 12.00*
J52 " ½g scarlet & olive green *12.00 12.00*
J53 A9 1g rose lilac & gray green 2.50 2.50
J54 " 2g dp. ultra. & fawn *12.00 12.00*

Same Handstamp on Nos. 110 and 112.

1930 (?)

J55 A3 (*i*) 1g grn. & org. *12.00 12.00*
J56 A4 (*j*) 2g blue *12.00 12.00*

D2

Lithographed.

1951, Apr. 2 *Perf. 11½* **Unwmkd.**

J57 D2 1c emerald 20 10
J58 " 5c rose red 25 15
J59 " 10c violet 40 20
J60 " 20c ochre 50 30
J61 " 50c brt. ultramarine 1.00 75
J62 " $1 rose lilac 1.75 1.50
Nos. J57–J62 (6) 4.10 3.00

OCCUPATION STAMPS.

Issued under Italian Occupation.

100 Centesimi = 1 Lira

Victor Emmanuel III

OS1

Emperor Victor Emmanuel

OS2

Wmk. 140

1936 Wmkd. Crowns. (140) *Perf. 14*

N1 OS1 10c orange brown 30 30
N2 " 20c purple 40 30
N3 OS2 25c dark green 22 22
N4 " 30c dark brown 30 30
N5 " 50c rose carmine 22 15
N6 OS1 75c deep orange 40 30
N7 " 1.25l deep blue 1.00 50
Nos. N1–N7 (7) 2.84 2.07

For later issues see Italian East Africa.

The first price column gives the catalogue value of an unused stamp, the second that of a used stamp.

FAR EASTERN REPUBLIC

(fär ēs'tērn rê·pŭb'lĭk)

LOCATION—In Siberia east of Lake Baikal.
GOVT.—Republic.
AREA—900,745 sq. mi.
POP.—1,560,000 (approx. 1920)
CAPITAL—Chita.

A short-lived independent government was established here in 1920.

100 Kopecks = 1 Ruble

Vladivostok Issue.

Russian Stamps Surcharged or Overprinted:

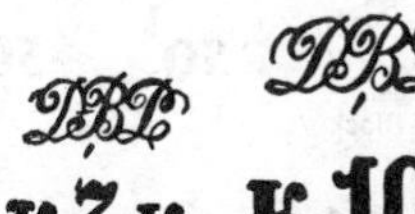

a

b c

On Stamps of 1909–17.

Perf. 14, 14½x15, 13½.

1920 **Unwmkd.**

2 A14 (*a*) 2k green 8.00 8.00
3 " (") 3k red 5.00 5.00
4 A11 (*b*) 3k on 35k red brown & green 8.00 8.00
5 A15 (*a*) 4k carmine 6.00 6.00
6 A11 (*b*) 4k on 70k brown & orange 4.00 4.00
8 " (") 7k on 15k red brn. & blue 2.00 2.00
  a. Inverted surcharge 35.00
  b. Pair, one overprinted "DBP" only
9 A15 (*a*) 10k dark blue 50.00 50.00
  a. Overprint on back 100.00
10 A12 (*c*) 10k on 3½r maroon & lt. green 16.00 16.00
11 A11 (*a*) 14k blue & rose 16.00 16.00
12 " (") 15k red brown & blue 7.50 7.50
13 A8 (") 20k blue & car. 55.00 55.00
14 A11 (*b*) 20k on 14k blue & rose 4.00 4.00
  a. Surch. on back 40.00
15 " (*a*) 25k grn. & vio. 10.00 10.00
16 " (") 35k red brown & green 27.50 27.50
17 A8 (") 50k brown violet & green 10.00 10.00
18 A9 (") 1r pale brown, dark brown & orange 250.00 250.00

On Stamps of 1917.

Imperf.

21 A14 (*a*) 1k orange 7.50 7.50
22 " (") 2k gray green 3.00 3.00
23 " (") 3k red 10.00 10.00
25 A11 (*b*) 7k on 15k red brown & deep blue 3.00 3.00
  a. Pair, one without surcharge
  b. Pair, one overprinted "DBP" only
26 A12 (*c*) 10k on 3½r maroon & light green 7.50 7.50
27 A9 (*a*) 1r pale brown, brown & red orange 10.00 10.00

On Stamps of Siberia 1919.

Perf. 14, 14½x15.

30 A14 (*a*) 35k on 2k green 4.00 4.00
  a. "DBP" on back 45.00 45.00

Imperf.

31 A14 (*a*) 35k on 2k green 9.00 9.00
32 " (") 70k on 1k orange 4.50 4.50

Counterfeit surcharges and overprints abound.

Postal Savings Stamps Surcharged for Postal Use.

A1

Wmk. 171

Wmkd. Diamonds. (171)

Perf. 14½x15.

35 A1 (*b*) 1k on 5k green, *buff* 8.00 8.00
36 " (") 2k on 10k brown, *buff* 12.00 12.00

The letters on these stamps resembling "DBP," are the Russian initials of "Dalni Vostochini Respoublika" (Far Eastern Republic).

Chita Issue.

A2

A2a

Typographed.

1921 *Imperf.* **Unwmkd.**

38 A2 2k gray green 1.00 1.00
39 A2a 4k rose 1.00 1.00
40 A2 5k claret 1.25 1.25
41 A2a 10k blue 2.00 2.00

Blagoveshchensk Issue.

A3

1921 Lithographed *Imperf.*

42 A3 2r red 3.50 4.00
43 " 3r dark green 3.50 4.00
44 " 5r dark blue 3.50 4.00
  a. Tête bêche pair 35.00 40.00
45 " 15r dark brown 3.50 4.00
46 " 30r dark violet 3.50 4.00
  a. Tête bêche pair 40.00 45.00
Nos. 42–46 (5) 17.50 20.00

Remainders of Nos. 42–46 were canceled in colored crayon or by typographed bars. These sell for half of foregoing prices.

Chita Issue.

A4

A5

1922 Lithographed. *Imperf.*

49 A4 1k orange 75 1.25
50 " 3k dull red 50 60
51 A5 4k deep rose & buff 50 60
52 A4 5k orange brown 1.25 60
53 " 7k light blue 1.25 2.00
a. Perf. 11½ 1.25 2.00
b. Rouletted 9 2.00 3.00
c. Perf. 11½x rouletted 4.00 4.00
54 A5 10k dk. blue & red 60 1.00
55 A4 15k dull rose 75 1.25
56 A5 20k blue & red 75 1.25
57 " 30k grn. & red orange 1.00 1.50
58 " 50k blk. & red orange 1.50 2.25
Nos. 49-58 (10) 8.85 12.30

The 4k exists with "4" omitted.

Vladivostok Issue.

Stamps of 1921 Overprinted in Red

1917
7-XI
1922

1922 *Imperf.*

62 A2 2k gray green 10.00 12.50
a. Inverted overprint 35.00
63 A2a 4k rose 10.00 12.50
a. Inverted overprint 60.00
b. Double overprint 50.00
64 A2 5k claret 12.50 17.50
a. Inverted overprint 60.00
b. Double overprint 50.00
65 A2a 10k blue 12.50 17.50
a. Inverted overprint 125.00

Issued to commemorate the fifth anniversary of the Russian revolution of November, 1917.

Once in the setting the figures "22" of 1922 have the bottom stroke curved instead of straight. Price $15 apiece.

Vladivostok Issue.

Russian Stamps of 1922-23 Surcharged in Black or Red

Д. В.
коп. 1 коп.
ЗОЛОТОМ

1923 *Imperf.*

66 A50 1k on 100r red 50 50
a. Invtd. surch. 45.00
67 " 2k on 70r violet 50 50
68 A49 5k on 10r blue (R) 50 50
69 A50 10k on 50r brown 75 75
a. Invtd. surch. 30.00

Perf. 14½x15.

70 A50 1k on 100r red 75 75
Nos. 66-70 (5) 3.00 3.00

OCCUPATION STAMPS.

Issued under Occupation of General Semenov. Chita Issue.

Russian Stamps of 1909-12 Surcharged:

Р. 1 Р.
a

2р.50к. Р. 5 Р.
b *c*

1920 *Perf. 14, 14x15½* Unwmkd.

N1 A15 (*a*) 1r on 4k car. 22.50 30.00
N2 A8 (*b*) 2r 50k on 20k blue & carmine 22.50 30.00
N3 A14 (*c*) 5r on 5k claret 12.50 20.00
a. Double surch. 25.00
N4 A11 (*a*) 10r on 70k brown & orange 22.50 30.00

FAROE ISLANDS

(The Faroes)

LOCATION—North Atlantic Ocean.
GOVT.—Self-governing part of Kingdom of Denmark.
AREA—540 sq. mi.
POP.—40,000 (1975).
CAPITAL—Thorshavn.

100 Ore = 1 Krone

Denmark No. 97 Handstamp Surcharged

2
ØRE

1919, Jan. Typo. *Perf. 14x14½*

1 A16 2ö on 5ö green 550.00 350.00

Counterfeits of surcharge exist.

Denmark No. 88a, the bisect, was used with Denmark No. 97 in Faroe Islands Jan. 3-23, 1919.

Denmark Nos. 220, 224, 238A, 224C Surcharged in Blue or Black

50 ≡ 50
b

20 |||| 20
c

20
d

1940-41 Engraved *Perf. 13*

2 A32 (*b*) 20(ö) on 1ö gray black (Bl) ('41) 55.00 55.00
3 " (*c*) 20(ö) on 5ö rose lake (Bl) ('41) 50.00 25.00
4 A30 (*d*) 20(ö) on 15ö deep red (Bk) 70.00 14.00
5 A32 (*b*) 50(ö) on 5ö rose lake (Bk) 200.00 70.00
6 " (") 60(ö) on 6ö org. (Bk) 140.00 140.00
Nos. 2-6 (5) 515.00 304.00

Nos. 2-6 were issued during British administration.

Map of Islands, 1673
A1

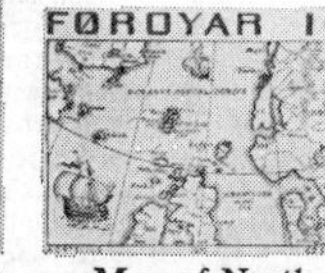

Map of North Atlantic, 1573
A2

West Coast, Sandoy
A3

Vidoy and Svinoy, by Eyvindur Mohr
A4

Designs: 50ö, 90ö, like 5ö. 60ö, 80ö, 120ö, like 10ö. 200ö, like 70ö. 250ö, 300ö, View of Streymoy and Vagar. 450ö, Houses, Nes, by Ruth Smith. 500ö, View of Hvitanes and Skalafjordur, by S. Joensen-Mikines.

Perf. 13

1975, Jan. 30 Engr. Unwmkd.

7 A1 5ö sepia 3 3
8 A2 10ö emerald & dk. blue 4 4
9 A1 50ö grayish green 18 18
10 A2 60ö brown & dk. blue 22 22
11 A3 70ö vio. bl. & slate grn. 25 25
12 A2 80ö ocher & dk. blue 30 30
13 A1 90ö red brown 32 32
14 A2 120ö brt. bl. & dk. blue 45 45
15 A3 200ö vio. bl. & slate grn. 70 70
16 " 250ö multicolored 90 90
17 " 300ö " 1.10 1.10

Photo. *Perf. 12½x13*

18 A4 350ö multicolored 1.25 1.25
19 " 450ö " 1.60 1.60
20 " 500ö " 1.75 1.75
Nos. 7-20 (14) 9.09 9.09

Faroe Boat
A5

Faroe Flag
A6

Faroe Mailman
A7

Engr.; Litho. (A6)

1976, Apr. 1 *Perf. 12½x13, 12 (A6)*

21 A5 125ö copper red 46 46
22 A6 160ö multicolored 60 60
23 A7 800ö olive 2.80 2.80

Faroe Islands independent Postal service, Apr. 1, 1976.

Motor Fishing Boat
A8

Faroese Fishing Vessels and Map of Islands: 125ö, Inland fishing cutter. 160ö, Modern seine fishing vessel. 600ö, Deep-sea fishing trawler.

1977, Apr. 28 Photo. *Perf. 14½x14*

24 A8 100ö green & black 35 35
25 " 125ö carmine & black 45 45
26 " 160ö blue & black 60 60
27 " 600ö brown & black 2.10 2.10

Common Snipe
A9

Birds: 180ö, Oystercatcher. 250ö, Whimbrel.

Photogravure & Engraved

1977, Sept. 29 *Perf. 14½x14*

28 A9 70ö multicolored 25 25
29 " 180ö " 62 62
30 " 250ö " 90 90

See "Special Notices" at the front of this volume for data on the listing methods of this Catalogue, abbreviations, condition, prices and examination.

North Coast, Puffins
A10

Mykines Village
A11

Mykines Island: 140ö, Tilled fields and coast. 150ö, Aerial view. 180ö, Map.

Perf. 13x13½, 13½x13

1978, Jan. 26 Photogravure

Size: 21x28mm., 28x21mm.

31 A10 100ö multicolored 35 35
32 A11 130ö " 45 45
33 " 140ö " 48 48
34 A10 150ö " 52 52

Size: 37x26mm. ***Perf. 14½x14***

35 A11 180ö multicolored 65 65
Nos. 31-35 (5) 2.45 2.45

Gannets
A12

Old Library
A13

Sea Birds: 180ö, Puffins. 400ö, Guillemots.

Lithographed and Engraved

1978, Apr. 13 *Perf. 12x12½*

36 A12 140ö multicolored 48 48
37 " 180ö " 65 65
38 " 400ö " 1.40 1.40

1978, Dec. 7 *Perf. 13*

Design: 180ö, New Library.

39 A13 140ö gray green & light green 48 48
40 " 180ö brown & buff 65 65

Completion of New Library Building.

Girl Guide, Tent and Fire
A14

1978, Dec. 7 Photo. *Perf. 13½*

41 A14 140ö multicolored 48 48

Faroese Girl Guides, 50th anniversary.

FERNANDO PO

(fĕr·năn′dō pō′)

LOCATION—An island in the Gulf of Guinea off west Africa.

GOVT.—Province of Spain.

AREA—800 sq. mi.

POP.—62,612 (1960).

CAPITAL—Santa Isabel.

Together with the islands of Elobey, Annobon and Corisco, Fernando Po came under the administration of Spanish Guinea. Postage stamps of Spanish Guinea were used until 1960.

The provinces of Fernando Po and Rio Muni united Oct. 12, 1968, to form the Republic of Equatorial Guinea.

100 Centimos = 1 Escudo = 2.50 Pesetas
100 Centimos = 1 Peseta
1000 Milesimas = 100 Centavos = 1 Peso (1882)

Queen Isabella II A1 — King Alfonso XII A2

Typographed.

1868 *Perf. 14* Unwmkd.

No.	Type	Description	Unused	Used
1	A1	20c brown	400.00	150.00

Forgeries exist.

1879 Centimos de Peseta.

No.	Type	Description	Unused	Used
2	A2	5c green	45.00	7.50
3	"	10c rose	45.00	7.50
4	"	50c blue	45.00	7.50

1882-89 Centavos de Peso.

No.	Type	Description	Unused	Used
5	A2	1c green	15.00	3.75
6	"	2c rose	17.50	5.25
7	"	5c gray blue	40.00	6.75
8	"	10c dark brown ('89)	47.50	5.25

Nos. 5–7 Handstamp Surcharged in Blue, Black or Violet

a

1884–95

No.	Type	Description	Unused	Used
9	A2	50c on 1c green ('95)	45.00	12.00
11	"	50c on 2c rose	24.00	4.50
12	"	50c on 5c blue ('87)	45.00	13.50

Inverted and double surcharges exist.

King Alfonso XIII A4

1894–97 *Perf. 14*

No.	Type	Description	Unused	Used
13	A4	⅛c slate ('96)	20.00	2.75
14	"	2c rose ('96)	15.00	1.85
15	"	5c blue green ('97)	15.00	1.85
16	"	6c dark violet ('96)	13.50	2.25
17	"	10c brn. violet ('94)	90.00	22.50
18	"	10c lake ('95)	25.00	5.00
19	"	10c orge. brn. ('96)	11.00	1.90
20	"	12½c dark brown ('96)	12.00	2.25
21	"	20c slate blue ('96)	12.00	2.25
22	"	25c claret ('96)	20.00	2.25
		Nos. 13-22 (10)	233.50	44.85

Stamps of 1894–97 Handstamped in Blue, Black or Red

b c

Type "b" Surcharge

1896–98

No.	Type	Description	Unused	Used
23	A4	5c on 2c rose (Bl)	17.50	3.75
24	"	5c on 10c brown violet (Bl)	50.00	10.00
25	"	5c on 12½c brn. (Bl)	13.50	3.50
a.		Black surcharge	13.50	3.50

Type "c" Surcharge

No.	Type	Description	Unused	Used
26	A4	5c on ⅛c slate (Bk)	8.50	4.50
27	"	5c on 2c rose (Bl)	8.50	4.50
a.		Black surcharge	8.50	4.50
28	A4	5c on 5c green (R)	47.50	12.00
29	"	5c on 6c dk. vio. (R)	9.00	8.00
a.		Violet surcharge	10.00	9.00
30	A4	5c on 10c orange brown (Bk)	60.00	15.00
31	"	5c on 12½c brn. (R)	16.50	6.00
32	"	5c on 20c slate blue (R)	15.00	5.25
33	"	5c on 25c claret (Bk)	15.00	6.00
a.		Blue surcharge	15.00	6.00

Type "a" Surcharge

1898–99

No.	Type	Description	Unused	Used
34	A4	50c on 2c rose (Bl)	25.00	6.25
35	"	50c on 10c brown violet (Bl)	55.00	15.00
36	"	50c on 10c lake (Bl)	60.00	15.00
37	"	50c on 10c orange brown (Bl)	55.00	15.00
38	"	50c on 12½c brown (Bk)	47.50	10.00

The "a" surcharge also exists on 1/8c, 5c and 25c.

Arms

A5 A6

Revenue Stamps Handstamped in Blue

1897–98 *Imperf.*

No.	Type	Description	Unused	Used
39	A5	5c on 10c rose	22.50	9.00
40	A6	10c rose	27.50	12.50

A7

Arms—A8

A9

A9a

Revenue Stamps Handstamped in Black or Red

1899 *Imperf.*

No.	Type	Description	Unused	Used
41	A7	15c on 10c green	27.50	13.50
a.		Blue surcharge, vertical	27.50	13.50
42	A8	10c on 25c green	80.00	35.00
43	A9	15c on 25c green	100.00	47.50
43A	A9a	15c on 25c grn. (R)	350.00	275.00
b.		Black surcharge	350.00	275.00

Surcharge on No. 41 is either horizontal, inverted or vertical.

On No. 42 "CORREOS" is overprinted in red.

King Alfonso XIII A10

1899 *Perf. 14*

No.	Type	Description	Unused	Used
44	A10	1m orange brown	3.00	75
45	"	2m "	3.00	75
46	"	3m "	3.00	75
47	"	4m "	3.00	75
48	"	5m "	3.00	75
49	"	1c black violet	3.00	75
50	"	2c dark blue green	3.00	75
51	"	3c dark brown	3.00	75
52	"	4c orange	9.00	1.50
53	"	5c carmine rose	3.00	75
54	"	6c dark blue	3.00	75
55	"	8c gray brown	9.00	75
56	"	10c vermilion	6.00	75
57	"	15c slate green	6.00	75
58	"	20c maroon	16.50	1.50
59	"	40c violet	100.00	15.00
60	"	60c black	100.00	15.00
61	"	80c red brown	100.00	15.00
62	"	1p yellow green	325.00	75.00
63	"	2p slate blue	325.00	75.00
		Nos. 44-63 (20)	1026.50	207.75

Nos. 44-63 exist imperf. Price for set, $1,400.

1900 Surcharged type "a",

No.	Type	Description	Unused	Used
64	A10	50c on 20c maroon	15.00	3.75
a.		Blue surcharge	17.50	4.50

Surcharged type "b".

No.	Type	Description	Unused	Used
64B	A10	5c on 20c maroon	75.00	7.50

Surcharged type "c".

No.	Type	Description	Unused	Used
65	A10	5c on 20c maroon	16.50	3.75

Dated "1900"

1900

No.	Type	Description	Unused	Used
66	A10	1m black	4.50	75
67	"	2m "	4.50	75
68	A10	3m black	4.50	75
69	"	4m "	4.50	75
70	"	5m "	4.50	75
71	"	1c green	4.50	75
72	"	2c violet	4.50	75
73	"	3c rose	4.50	75
74	"	4c black brown	4.50	75
75	"	5c blue	4.50	75
76	"	6c orange	4.50	1.50
77	"	8c bronze green	4.50	1.50
78	"	10c claret	4.50	75
79	"	15c dark violet	4.50	75
80	"	20c olive brown	4.50	75
81	"	40c brown	10.00	1.50
82	"	60c green	20.00	1.50
83	"	80c dark blue	20.00	3.00
84	"	1p red brown	100.00	17.50
85	"	2p orange	150.00	37.50
		Nos. 66-85 (20)	367.50	73.75

Nos. 66–85 exist imperf.

A11 A12

Revenue Stamps Overprinted or Surcharged with Handstamp in Red or Black

1900 *Imperf.*

No.	Type	Description	Unused	Used
86	A11	10c blue (R)	22.50	10.00
87	A12	5c on 10c blue	27.50	16.50

Nos. 52 and 80 Surcharged type "a" in Violet or Black.

1900

No.	Type	Description	Unused	Used
88	A10	50c on 4c orange (V)	18.50	5.25
a.		Green surcharge	30.00	15.00
88B	"	50c on 20c olive brown	15.00	6.75

A13 A14

1901 *Perf. 14*

No.	Type	Description	Unused	Used
89	A13	1c black	3.00	75
90	"	2c orange brown	3.00	75
91	"	3c dark violet	3.00	75
92	"	4c light violet	3.00	75
93	"	5c orange red	1.85	75
94	"	10c violet brown	1.85	75
95	"	25c deep blue	1.85	75
96	"	50c claret	3.00	75
97	"	75c dark brown	2.25	75
98	"	1p blue green	30.00	4.50
99	"	2p red brown	30.00	6.75
100	"	3p olive green	30.00	10.00
101	"	4p dull red	30.00	10.00
102	"	5p dark green	37.50	10.00
103	"	10p buff	80.00	22.50
		Nos. 89-103 (15)	260.30	70.50

Dated "1902"

1902 Control Numbers on Back.

No.	Type	Description	Unused	Used
104	A13	5c dark green	3.00	45
105	"	10c slate	3.00	45
106	"	25c claret	6.75	1.10
107	"	50c violet brown	15.00	3.00
108	"	75c light violet	15.00	3.00
109	"	1p carmine rose	20.00	4.50
110	"	2p olive green	37.50	10.00
111	"	5p orange red	55.00	20.00
		Nos. 104-111 (8)	155.25	42.50

Nos. 104–111 exist imperf. Price for set, $425.

1903 *Perf. 14*

Control Numbers on Back

No.	Type	Description	Unused	Used
112	A14	¼c dark violet	45	30
113	"	½c black	45	30

No.	Type	Description	Unused	Used
114	A14	1c scarlet	45	30
115	"	2c dark green	45	30
116	"	3c blue green	45	30
117	"	4c violet	45	30
118	"	5c rose lake	60	30
119	"	10c orange buff	75	38
120	"	15c blue green	3.00	1.10
121	"	25c red brown	3.25	1.50
122	"	50c black brown	5.25	2.50
123	"	75c carmine	15.00	4.00
124	"	1p dark brown	25.00	6.00
125	"	2p dk. olive grn.	30.00	8.00
126	"	3p claret	30.00	8.00
127	"	4p dark blue	40.00	13.50
128	"	5p deep dull blue	55.00	15.00
129	"	10p dull red	120.00	24.00
		Nos. 112–129 (18)	330.55	86.08

Dated "1905"

1905 Control Numbers on Back.

No.	Type	Description	Unused	Used
136	A14	1c deep violet	45	35
137	"	2c black	45	35
138	"	3c vermilion	45	35
139	"	4c deep green	45	35
140	"	5c blue green	60	35
141	"	10c violet	1.85	55
142	"	15c carmine lake	1.85	55
143	"	25c orange buff	11.50	1.50
144	"	50c green	9.00	2.25
145	"	75c red brown	10.00	6.00
146	"	1p dp. gray brn.	11.50	6.00
147	"	2p carmine	22.50	9.00
148	"	3p deep brown	32.50	10.00
149	"	4p bronze green	40.00	12.50
150	"	5p claret	62.50	18.50
151	"	10p deep blue	100.00	27.50
		Nos. 136–151 (16)	305.60	96.10

King Alfonso XIII
A15

1907 Control Numbers on Back.

No.	Type	Description	Unused	Used
152	A15	1c blue black	30	35
153	"	2c carmine rose	30	10
154	"	3c deep violet	30	10
155	"	4c black	30	10
156	"	5c orange buff	38	30
157	"	10c maroon	1.85	55
158	"	15c bronze green	60	30
159	"	25c dark brown	21.00	8.00
160	"	50c blue green	38	22
161	"	75c vermilion	45	22
162	"	1p dull blue	2.50	55
163	"	2p brown	9.00	3.00
164	"	3p lake	9.00	3.00
165	"	4p violet	9.00	3.00
166	"	5p black brown	9.00	3.00
167	"	10p orange brown	9.00	3.00
		Nos. 152–167 (16)	73.36	25.79

No. 157 Handstamp Surcharged in Black or Blue

HABILITADO
PARA
05CTMS

1908

No.	Type	Description	Unused	Used
168	A15	5c on 10c maroon (Bk)	2.50	1.25
169	"	5c on 10c maroon (Bl)	8.50	4.25

The surcharge on Nos. 168–169 exists inverted, double and otherwise.

Seville-Barcelona Issue of Spain, 1929, Overprinted FERNANDO POO in Blue or Red

1929 *Perf. 11.*

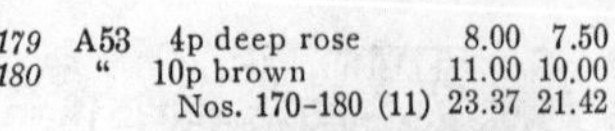

No.	Type	Description	Unused	Used
170	A52	5c rose lake	22	22
171	A53	10c green (R)	22	22
		a. Perf. 14	60	50
172	A50	15c Prussian blue (R)	22	22
173	A51	20c purple (R)	22	22
174	A50	25c bright rose	22	22
175	A52	30c black brown	22	22
176	A53	40c dark blue (R)	45	45
177	A51	50c deep orange	75	65
178	A52	1p blue black (R)	1.85	1.50
179	A53	4p deep rose	8.00	7.50
180	"	10p brown	11.00	10.00
		Nos. 170–180 (11)	23.37	21.42

Virgin Mary
A16

Photogravure

1960 *Perf. 13x12½* **Unwmkd.**

No.	Type	Description	Unused	Used
181	A16	25c dull gray violet	8	8
182	"	50c brown olive	8	8
183	"	75c violet brown	8	8
184	"	1p orange vermilion	8	8
185	"	1.50p light blue green	8	8
186	"	2p red lilac	8	8
187	"	3p dark blue	3.75	75
188	"	5p light red brown	38	9
189	"	10p lt. olive green	75	22
		Nos. 181–189 (9)	5.36	1.54

Tricorn and Windmill from "The Three-Cornered Hat" by Falla
A17

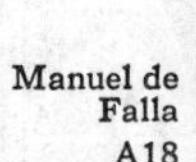

Manuel de Falla
A18

1960 *Perf. 13x12½, 12½x13*

No.	Type	Description	Unused	Used
190	A17	35c slate green	8	3
191	A18	80c Prussian green	8	4

Issued to honor Manuel de Falla (1876–1946), Spanish composer.

See Nos. B1–B2.

Map of Fernando Po
A19

General Franco
A20

Designs: 70c, Santa Isabel Cathedral.

Perf. 13x12½, 12½x13

1961, Oct. 1 Photo. **Unwmkd.**

No.	Type	Description	Unused	Used
192	A19	25c gray violet	8	3
193	A20	50c olive brown	8	4
194	A19	70c bright green	8	4
195	A20	1p red orange	10	4

Issued to commemorate the 25th anniversary of the nomination of Gen. Francisco Franco as Chief of State.

Ocean Liner
A21

Design: 50c, S.S. San Francisco.

1962, July 10 *Perf. 12½x13*

No.	Type	Description	Unused	Used
196	A21	25c dull violet	10	3
197	"	50c gray olive	10	3
198	"	1p orange brown	10	6

Mailman
A22

Mail Transport Symbols
A23

Perf. 13x12½, 12½x13

1962, Nov. 23 **Unwmkd.**

No.	Type	Description	Unused	Used
199	A22	15c dark green	10	3
200	A23	35c lilac rose	10	3
201	A22	1p brown	10	4

Issued for Stamp Day.

Fetish
A24

1963, Jan. 29 *Perf. 13x12½*

No.	Type	Description	Unused	Used
202	A24	50c olive gray	5	3
203	"	1p deep magenta	6	4

Issued to help the victims of the Seville flood.

Nuns
A25

Design: 50c, Nun and child (vert.).

Perf. 12½x13, 13x12½

1963, July 6 Photo. **Unwmkd.**

No.	Type	Description	Unused	Used
204	A25	25c bright lilac	6	3
205	"	50c dull green	6	3
206	"	1p red orange	10	4

Issued for child welfare.

Child and Arms
A26

1963, July 12 *Perf. 12½x13*

No.	Type	Description	Unused	Used
207	A26	50c brown olive	4	4
208	"	1p carmine rose	6	6

Issued for Barcelona flood relief.

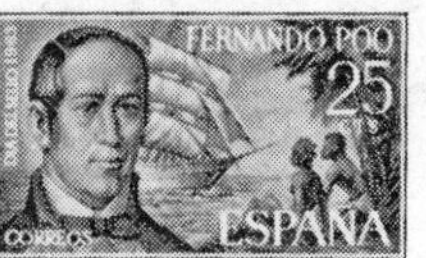

Governor Chacon
A27

Orange Blossoms
A28

Men in Dugout Canoe
A29

1964, Mar. 6 *Perf. 12½x13, 13x12½*

No.	Type	Description	Unused	Used
209	A27	25c violet black	6	3
210	A28	50c dark olive	6	3
211	A27	1p brown red	10	6

Issued for Stamp Day 1963.

1964, June 1 Photo. *Perf. 13x12½*

Design: 50c, Pineapple.

No.	Type	Description	Unused	Used
212	A29	25c purple	4	4
213	A28	50c dull olive	4	4
214	A29	1p deep claret	7	5

Issued for child welfare.

Ring-necked Francolin
A30

1964, July 1

Designs: 15c, 70c, 3p, Ring-necked francolin. 25c, 1p, 5p, Two mallards. 50c, 1.50p, 10p, Head of great blue touraco.

No.	Type	Description	Unused	Used
215	A30	15c chestnut	4	3
216	"	25c dull violet	4	3
217	"	50c dark olive green	4	3
218	"	70c green	8	3
219	"	1p brown orange	10	3
220	"	1.50p greenish blue	22	6
221	"	3p violet blue	75	15
222	"	5p dull purple	2.25	30
223	"	10p bright green	3.50	75
		Nos. 215–223 (9)	7.02	1.41

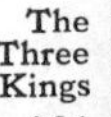

The Three Kings
A31

Designs: 50c, 1.50p, Caspar (vert.).

Perf. 13x12½, 12½x13

1964, Nov. 23 **Unwmkd.**

No.	Type	Description	Unused	Used
224	A31	50c green	3	3
225	"	1p orge. vermilion	5	5
226	"	1.50p deep green	22	8
227	"	3p ultramarine	2.25	1.35

Issued for Stamp Day, 1964.

Boy
A32

Woman Fruit Picker
A33

Design: 1.50p, Girl learning to write, and church.

1964, Mar. 1 Photo. *Perf. 13x12½*

228 A32 50c indigo 3 3
229 A33 1p dark red 6 4
230 " 1.50p greenish blue 17 6

Issued to commemorate 25 years of peace.

Plectrocnemia Cruciata
A34

Design: 1p, Metopodontus savagei (horiz.).

Perf. 13x12½, 12½x13

1965, June 1 Photo. **Unwmkd.**

231 A34 50c slate green 3 3
232 " 1p rose red 6 4
233 " 1.50p Prussian blue 15 6

Issued for child welfare.

Pole Vault
A35

Arms of Fernando Po
A36

Perf. 12½x13, 13x12½

1965, Nov. 23 Photo. **Unwmkd.**

234 A35 50c yellow green 3 3
235 A36 1p brt. org. brown 6 4
236 A35 1.50p bright blue 15 6

Issued for Stamp Day, 1965.

White and Negro Children Reading
A37

Design: 1.50p, St. Elizabeth of Hungary (vert.).

Perf. 12½x13, 13x12½

1966, June 1 Photo. **Unwmkd.**

237 A37 50c dark green 3 3
238 " 1p brown red 6 4
239 " 1.50p dark blue 15 6

Issued for child welfare.

White-nosed Monkey
A38

Designs: 40c, 4p, Head of moustached monkey (vert.).

1966, Nov. 23 Photo. *Perf. 13*

240 A38 10c dk. blue & yel. 3 3
241 " 40c lt. brown, blue & black 3 3
242 " 1.50p olive bister, brn. org. & black 10 10
243 " 4p slate grn., brn. org. & black 25 25

Issued for Stamp Day, 1966.

Flowers
A39

Designs: 40c, 4p, Six flowers.

1967, June 1 Photo. *Perf. 13*

244 A39 10c brt. carmine & pale green 3 3
245 " 40c red brown & org. 3 3
246 " 1.50p red lilac & lt. red brown 10 10
247 " 4p dk. bl. & lt. grn. 25 25

Issued for child welfare.

Linsang
A40

Designs: 1.50p, Needle-clawed galago (vert.). 3.50p, Fraser's scaly-tailed flying squirrel.

1967, Nov. 23 Photo. *Perf. 13*

248 A40 1p black & bister 15 8
249 " 1.50p brown & olive 15 8
250 " 3.50p rose lake & dull green 25 25

Issued for Stamp Day 1967.

Stamp of 1868, No. 1, and Arms of San Carlos—A41

Designs: 1.50p, Fernando Po No. 1 and arms of Santa Isabel. 2.50p, Fernando Po No. 1 and arms of Fernando Po.

1968, Feb. 4 Photo. *Perf. 13*

251 A41 1p brt. plum & brn. orange 15 13
252 " 1.50p dp. blue & brown orange 15 13
253 " 2.50p brown & brown orange 25 25

Centenary of the first postage stamp.

Zodiac Issue

Libra
A42

Signs of the Zodiac: 1.50p, Leo. 2.50p, Aquarius.

1968, Apr. 25 Photo. *Perf. 13*

254 A42 1p brt. magenta, *light yellow* 15 13
255 " 1.50p brown, *pink* 15 13
256 " 2.50p dk. vio., *yellow* 25 25

Issued for child welfare.

SEMI-POSTAL STAMPS

Types of Regular Issue, 1960

Designs: 10c+5c, Manuel de Falla. 15c+5c, Dancers from "Love, the Magician."

Perf. 12½x13, 13x12½

1960 Photogravure **Unwmkd.**

B1 A18 10c+5c maroon 10 5
B2 A17 15c+5c dark brown & bistre 10 5

The surtax was for child welfare.

Whale
SP1

Design: 20c+5c, 50c+20c, Harpooning whale.

1961 *Perf. 12½x13*

B3 SP1 10c+5c rose brown 6 5
B4 " 20c+5c dark slate green 6 5
B5 " 30c+10c olive brown 8 5
B6 " 50c+20c dark brown 22 4

Issued for Stamp Day, 1960.

Hand Blessing Woman
SP2

Design: 25c+10c, Boy making sign of the cross, and crucifix.

1961, June 21 *Perf. 13x12½*

B7 SP2 10c+5c rose brown 4 3
B8 " 25c+10c gray violet 6 3
B9 " 80c+20c dark green 10 4

The surtax was for child welfare.

Ethiopian Tortoise
SP3

Design: 25c+10c, 1p+10c, Native carriers, palms and shore.

1961, Nov. 23 *Perf. 12½x13*

B10 SP3 10c+5c rose red 4 3
B11 " 25c+10c dk. purple 4 3
B12 " 30c+10c violet brn. 5 3
B13 " 1p+10c red orange 8 4

Issued for Stamp Day 1961.

FEZZAN

(See Libya, Occupation Stamps).

FINLAND

(fĭn'lănd)

(Suomi)

LOCATION—In northern Europe bordering on the Gulfs of Bothnia and Finland.

GOVT.—Republic.

AREA—130,119 sq. mi. (excluding water area).

POP.—4,740,000 (est. 1977).

CAPITAL—Helsinki (Helsingfors).

Finland was a Grand Duchy of the Russian Empire from 1809 until December, 1917, when it declared its independence.

100 Kopecks = 1 Ruble
100 Pennia = 1 Markka (1866)

Issues under Russian Empire.

Prices of early Finland stamps vary according to condition. Quotations for Nos. 1–3B are for fine copies. Used prices are for pen-canceled copies. Very fine to superb specimens sell at much higher prices, and inferior or poor copies sell at reduced prices, depending on the condition of the individual specimen.

Coat of Arms
A1

Typographed.

1856 *Imperf.* **Unwmkd.**

Small Pearls in Post Horns.

Wove Paper.

1 A1 5k blue *4000.00* 900.00
Pen and town cancellation 1250.00
Town cancellation 2000.00
a. Tête bêche pair *20,000.00*
As "a," pen and town cancellation *25,000.00*

2 " 10k rose 4000.00 275.00
Pen and town cancellation 475.00
Town cancellation 650.00
a. Tête bêche pair *15,000.00*
As "a," pen and town cancellation *18,000.00*

1858

Wide Vertically Laid Paper

2C A1 10k rose 750.00
Pen and town cancellation 1000.00
Town cancellation 1300.00
d. Tête bêche pair

The wide vertically laid paper has 13–14 distinct lines per 2 cm. The 10k rose also exists on a narrow laid paper with lines sometimes indistinct. Price, 60 per cent of that for a wide laid paper example.

A 5k blue with small pearls exists on narrow vertically laid paper.

Stamps on diagonally laid paper are envelope cut squares.

Large Pearls in Post Horns.

Wove Paper.

3 A1 5k blue *3500.00* 800.00
Pen and town cancellation 1100.00
Town cancellation 1600.00
a. Tête bêche pair *18,000.00*
As "a," pen and town cancellation *22,500.00*

1859

Wide Vertically Laid Paper

3B A1 5k blue *7000.00*
Pen and town cancellation *8000.00*

Reprints of Nos. 2 and 3, made in 1862, are on brownish paper, on vertically laid paper, and in tête bêche pairs on normal and vertically laid paper. Reprints of 1871, 1881 and 1893 are on yellowish or white paper. Price for least costly of each, $45.

In 1956, Nos. 2 and 3 were reprinted for the Centenary with post horn watermark and gum. Price, $30 each.

Coat of Arms
A2

Serpentine Roulette 7½, 8

1860

Nos. 4–13, with serpentine roulette, are seldom in perfect condition. Usually some of the "teeth" are missing. In average condition, one or two teeth are gone. Prices are for average specimens. Copies with all teeth intact sell for many times more.

Four types of indentation are noted:

I. Depth 1–1¼mm.

II. Depth 1½–1¾mm.

III. Depth 2–2¼mm.

IV. Shovel-shaped teeth. Depth 1¼–1½mm.

Wove Paper.

4 A2 5k blue, *bluish*, roulette I 200.00 45.00
a. Roulette II 225.00 50.00
b. Imperf. vert.

5 " 10k rose, *pale rose*, roulette I 175.00 20.00
a. Roulette II 250.00 25.00

A3

A4

1866–74 ***Serpentine Roulette***

6 A3 5p pur. brown, *lilac*, roulette I ('73) 125.00 40.00
a. Roulette II 750.00
b. 5p red brown, *lilac*, roulette III ('71) 125.00 40.00

7 " 8p *green*, roulette III ('67) 100.00 37.50
a. Ribbed paper, roulette III ('72) 450.00 100.00
b. Roulette II ('74) 120.00 40.00
c. As "b," ribbed paper ('74) 140.00 45.00
d. Roulette I ('73) 200.00 55.00
e. As "d," ribbed paper 450.00 130.00
f. Serp. roulette 10½ ('67) *4500.00*

8 " 10p *yellow*, roulette III ('70) 175.00 45.00
a. 10p *buff*, roulette II 275.00 65.00
b. 10p *buff*, roulette I ('73) 225.00 75.00

9 " 20p blue, *blue*, roulette III 100.00 12.50
a. Roulette II 110.00 15.00
b. Roulette I ('73) 275.00 27.50
c. Roulette IV ('74) *850.00 300.00*
d. Imperf. horiz. *200.00*
e. Printed on both sides (40p blue on back) *5500.00*

10 " 40p rose, *lilac rose*, roulette III 140.00 14.00
a. Ribbed paper, roulette III ('73) 225.00 27.50
b. Roulette II 150.00 15.00
c. As "b," ribbed paper ('73) 150.00 17.50
d. Roulette I 325.00 25.00
e. As "d," ribbed paper 250.00 20.00
f. Roulette IV *600.00*
g. As "f," ribbed paper *1500.00*
h. Serp. roulette 10½ *4500.00*

11 A4 1m yel. brown, roulette III ('67) 700.00 250.00
a. Roulette II 1100.00 375.00
b. Final "A" of "MARKKA" covered by color spot 850.00 300.00

Nos. 7f and 10h are also known in compound serpentine roulette 10½ and 7½.

Nos. 4 to 11 were reprinted in 1893 on thick wove paper. Colors differ from originals. Roulette type IV. Price for Nos. 4–10, each $25. Price for No. 11, $42.50.

Thin or Thick Laid Paper.

12 A3 5p red brown, *lilac*, roulette III 110.00 35.00
a. Roulette II 125.00 35.00
b. Roulette I 110.00 35.00
d. 5p *buff*, roul. III (error) *4500.00*
e. Tête bêche pair *9000.00*

13 " 10p *buff*, roulette III 160.00 42.50
a. 10p *yellow*, roulette II 200.00 55.00
b. 10p *yellow*, roulette I 750.00 140.00
c. 10p red brown, *lilac*, roul. III (error) *4000.00 2500.00*

A5

A6

1875 ***Perf. 14x13½***

16 A5 32p lake 1200.00 400.00

1875–81 ***Perf. 11***

17 A5 2p gray 42.50 45.00
18 " 5p orange 110.00 10.00
a. 5p yellow 120.00 17.50
19 A5 8p blue green 130.00 55.00
a. 8p yellow green 140.00 70.00
20 A5 10p brown ('81) 225.00 45.00
21 " 20p ultramarine 90.00 2.00
a. 20p blue 90.00 2.25
b. 20p Prussian blue 190.00 25.00
c. Tête bêche pair 2750.00 1800.00
22 A5 25p carmine ('79) 110.00 10.00
a. 25p rose 125.00 25.00
23 A5 32p carmine 190.00 25.00
a. 32p rose 250.00 37.50
24 A5 1m violet ('77) 325.00 100.00

A souvenir card was issued in 1974 for NORDIA 1975 reproducing a block of four of the unissued "1 MARKKAA" design.

Nos. 19 and 23 were reprinted in 1893, perf. 12½. Price $17.50 each.

1881–83 ***Perf. 12½***

25 A5 2p gray 11.00 12.00
a. Imperf., pair 150.00
26 A5 5p orange 32.50 5.50
a. Tête bêche pair 3500.00 3000.00
b. Imperf. vert., pair 150.00 150.00
c. Imperf. horiz., pair 175.00
27 A5 10p brown 70.00 12.50
28 " 20p ultramarine 25.00 1.50
a. 20p blue 27.50 1.50
b. Tête bêche pair 2250.00 1500.00
c. Imperf., pair 100.00
29 A5 25p rose 37.50 6.00
a. 25p carmine 37.50 6.00
b. Tête bêche pair 4000.00 4500.00
30 A5 1m violet ('82) 200.00 35.00

Nos. 27–29 were reprinted in 1893 in deeper shades, perf. 12½. Price $35 each.

1881 ***Perf. 11x12½***

26d A5 5p orange 225.00 65.00
27a " 10p brown 550.00 200.00
28d " 20p ultramarine 300.00 30.00
28e " 20p blue 300.00 30.00
29c " 25p rose 300.00 75.00
29d " 25p carmine 300.00 75.00
30a " 1m violet 800.00

1881 ***Perf. 12½x11***

26e A5 5p orange 225.00 65.00
27b " 10p brown 550.00 200.00
28f " 20p ultramarine 300.00 30.00
28g " 20p blue 300.00 30.00
29e " 25p rose 300.00 75.00
29f " 25p carmine 300.00 75.00

1885 ***Perf. 12½.***

31 A5 5p emerald 20.00 45
a. 5p yellow green 20.00 45
b. Tête bêche pr. 4000.00 3750.00
32 " 10p carmine 25.00 2.00
a. 10p rose 25.00 2.00
33 " 20p orange 20.00 30
a. 20p yellow 27.50 3.25
b. Tête bêche pr. 3000.00 2500.00
34 " 25p ultramarine 40.00 1.20
a. 25p blue 40.00 1.00
35 " 1m gray & rose 16.00 12.50
36 " 5m green & rose 325.00 250.00
37 " 10m brown & rose 400.00 350.00

1889–92 ***Perf. 12½***

38 A6 2p slate ('90) 60 60
39 " 5p green ('90) 20.00 18
40 " 10p carmine ('90) 25.00 30
a. 10p rose ('90) 25.00 30
41 " 20p orange ('92) 20.00 18
a. 20p yellow ('90) 25.00 1.00
42 " 25p ultra. ('91) 30.00 30
a. 25p blue 35.00 50
43 " 1m slate & rose ('92) 3.50 1.50
a. 1m brownish gray & rose ('90) 30.00 2.50
44 " 5m grn. & rose ('90) 37.50 42.50
45 " 10m brn. & rose ('90) 45.00 55.00

The 2p slate, perf. 14x13, is believed to be an essay.

See also Nos. 60–63.

Imperial Arms of Russia

A7 A8 A9

A10

A11

Wmk. 168

Laid Paper.

Wmkd.

Wavy Lines and Letters. (168)

1891–92 ***Perf. 14½x15***

46 A7 1k orange yellow 4.00 4.75
47 " 2k green 5.00 6.00
48 " 3k carmine 7.00 10.00
49 A8 4k rose 10.00 11.00
50 A7 7k dark blue 5.00 1.75
51 A8 10k dark blue 14.00 7.00
52 A9 14k blue & rose 14.00 12.00
53 A8 20k blue & carmine 11.00 11.00
54 A9 35k violet & green 17.50 22.50
55 A8 50k violet & green 20.00 18.00

Perf. 13½.

56 A10 1r brown & orange 65.00 55.00
57 A11 3½r black & gray 200.00 250.00
a. 3½r black & yellow *(error) 5500.00 5000.00*
58 " 7r blk. & yellow 160.00 150.00
Nos. 46–58 (13) 528.50 559.00

Forgeries of Nos. 57, 57a, 58 exist.

Type of 1889–90.

Wove Paper.

1895–96 ***Perf. 14x13*** **Unwmkd.**

60 A6 5p green 65 15
61 " 10p rose 65 15
a. Imperf. 70.00 70.00
62 " 20p orange 65 15
a. Imperf. 65.00 65.00
63 " 25p ultramarine 1.00 30
a. 25p blue 1.00 30
b. Imperf. 75.00 75.00

A12 A13 A14

A15

1901 Lithographed *Perf. 14½x15*

Chalky Paper.

64 A12 2p yellow 3.00 1.75
65 " 5p green 11.00 30
66 A13 10p carmine 16.00 50
67 A12 20p dark blue 27.50 25
68 A14 1m violet & green 125.00 4.00

Perf. 13½.

69 A15 10m black & gray 200.00 120.00
Nos. 64-69 (6) 382.50 126.80

Imperf. sheets of 10p and 20p, stolen during production, were privately perforated 11½ to defraud the P.O. Uncanceled imperfs. of Nos. 65-68 are believed to be proofs.

Types of 1901 Redrawn.

No. 64.

No. 70.

2p. On No. 64, the "2" below "II" is shifted slightly leftward. On No. 70, the "2" is centered below "II."

No. 65.

No. 71.

5p. On No. 65, the frame lines are very close. On No. 71, a clear white space separates them.

Nos. 66, 67.

Nos. 72, 73.

10p, 20p. On Nos. 66-67, the horizontal central background lines are faint and broken. On Nos. 72-73, they are clear and solid, though still thin.
20p. On No. 67, "H" close to "2" with period midway. On No. 73 they are slightly separated with period close to "H".

No. 68.

Nos. 74, 74a.

1m. On No. 68, the "1" following "MARKKA" lacks serif at base. On Nos. 74-74a, this "1" has serif.

No. 69.

No. 75.

10m. On No. 69, the serifs of "M" and "A" in top and bottom panels do not touch. On No. 75, the serifs join.

1901-14 Typo. *Perf. 14, 14½x15*

Ordinary Paper.

70 A12 2p orange 90 90
a. Imperf. *275.00 300.00*
71 " 5p green 1.40 20
b. Imperf. 80.00 80.00
72 A13 10p carmine 70 10
a. Imperf. 80.00 80.00
b. Background inverted 17.50 75
73 A12 20p dark blue 60 10
a. Imperf. 80.00 80.00
74 A14 1m lilac & green, perf. 14 ('14) 1.00 25
a. 1m vio. & bl. grn., perf. 14½x15 ('02) 8.00 30
b. Imperf. 100.00 100.00
Nos. 70-74 (5) 4.60 1.55

Perf. 13½.

75 A15 10m black & drab ('03) 100.00 22.50

A16

A17

A18

1911-16 *Perf. 14, 14½x15*

77 A16 2p orange 12 15
78 " 5p green 12 6
a. Imperf. 80.00 65.00
b. Perf. 14½x15 160.00 20.00
79 A17 10p rose 25 5
a. Imperf. 60.00 60.00
b. Perf. 14½x15 1.25 85
80 A16 20p deep blue 30 5
a. Imperf. 40.00 40.00
81 A18 40p violet & blue 15 10
a. Perf. 14½x15 1000.00 850.00
Nos. 77-81 (5) 94 41

There are three minor types of No. 79.

Perf. 14½

82 A15 10m blk. & greenish gray ('16) 80.00 90.00
a. Horiz. pair, imperf. vert. 1000.00

Republic.

Helsinki Issue.

Arms of the Republic
A19

Two types of the 40p.
Type I—Thin figures of value.
Type II—Thick figures of value.

Perf. 14, 14½x15

1917-29 Unwmkd.

83 A19 5p green 15 8
84 " 5p gray ('19) 15 8
85 " 10p rose 15 8
a. Imperf. 175.00 175.00
86 " 10p green ('19) 90 10
a. Perf. 14½x15 700.00
87 " 10p light blue ('21) 15 8
88 " 20p buff 15 8
89 " 20p rose ('20) 50 10
90 " 20p brown ('24) 35 35
91 " 25p blue 30 10
92 " 25p light brown ('19) 18 10
93 " 30p green ('23) 30 25
94 " 40p violet (I) 15 8
a. Perf. 14½x15 150.00 4.00
95 " 40p blue green (II) ('29) 15 35
a. Type I ('24) 6.00 70
96 " 50p orange brown 25 8
97 " 50p deep blue ('19) 3.00 12
a. Perf. 14½x15 400.00
98 " 50p green ('21) 15 10
99 " 60p red violet ('21) 30 8
a. Imperf. 55.00 55.00
100 " 75p yellow ('21) 15 25
101 " 1m dull rose & blk. 9.00 10
102 " 1m red orange 15 *5.00*
103 " 1⅓m blue green & red violet ('29) 15 12
104 " 2m green & black 2.25 30
105 " 2m dark blue & indigo ('22) 50 8
106 " 3m blue & black ('21) 42.50 18
107 " 5m red violet & black 20.00 15
108 " 10m brown & gray black, perf. 14 75 65
a. 10m lt. brown & blk., perf. 14½x15 ('29) 5.00 *100.00*
110 " 25m dull red & yellow ('21) 70 *7.00*
Nos. 83-108, 110 (27) 83.43 *16.04*

Copies of a 2½p gray of this type exist. They are proofs from the original die which were distributed through the Universal Postal Union. No plate was made for this denomination.

See also Nos. 127-140, 143-152.

Vasa Issue

A20

1918 Lithographed. *Perf. 11½.*

111 A20 5p green 40 55
112 " 10p red 30 45
113 " 30p slate 50 1.10
114 " 40p brown violet 30 55
115 " 50p orange brown 50 1.25
116 " 70p gray brown 2.25 4.00
117 " 1m red & gray 50 75
118 " 5m red violet & gray 55.00 80.00
Nos. 111-118 (8) 59.75 88.65

Nos. 111-118 exist imperforate but were not regularly issued in that condition.
Sheet margin copies, perf. on 3 sides, imperf. on margin side, were sold by post office.

Stamps and Type of 1917-29 Surcharged
50
50 50

1919 *Perf. 14*

119 A19 10p on 5p green 30 18
120 " 20p on 10p rose 30 18
121 " 50p on 25p blue 60 30
122 " 75p on 20p orange 20 20

Stamps and Type of 1917-29 Surcharged:

30 P (*a*) 1½ M (*b*)

1921

123 A19 (*a*) 30p on 10p green 65 15
124 " (") 60p on 40p red violet 2.00 40
125 " (") 90p on 20p rose 15 20
126 " (*b*) 1½m on 50p blue 50 18
a. Thin "2" in "½" 6.50 70
b. Imperf. 120.00 150.00

Wmk. 121

Arms Type of 1917-29.

Wmkd. Multiple Swastika. (121)

1925-29 *Perf. 14, 14½x15*

127 A19 10p ultramarine ('27) 60 75
128 " 20p brown 60 75
129 " 25p brn. org. ('29) 1.50 *16.00*
130 " 30p yellow green 15 18
131 " 40p blue green (I) 2.00 10
a. Type II 3.50 15
132 " 50p gray green ('27) 50 15
133 " 60p red violet 15 20
134 " 1m deep orange 4.00 15
135 " 1⅓m blue green & red violet 7.00 12
136 " 2m dark blue & indigo 35 18
137 " 3m chalky bl. & blk. 1.10 20
138 " 5m red violet & black 35 15
139 " 10m light brown & black ('27) 4.00 5.50
140 " 25m deep orange & yellow ('27) 18.00 *200.00*
Nos. 127-140 (14) 40.30 *224.43*

A21

Wmk. 208

Wmkd. Post Horn. (208)

1927, Dec. 6 Typo. *Perf. 14*

141 A21 1½m deep violet 15 25
142 " 2m deep blue 25 1.00

Issued in commemoration of the tenth anniversary of Finnish independence.

Arms Type of 1917-29.

Perf. 14½x15

1927-29 Wmk. 208

143 A19 20p light brown ('29) 80 *3.50*
144 " 40p bl. grn. (II) ('28) 15 15
145 " 50p gray green ('28) 15 20
146 " 1m deep orange 15 15
a. Imperf. 100.00 100.00
b. Perf. 14 1.50 15
147 " 1⅓m blue green & red vio. ('28) 3.25 15
a. Perf. 14 200.00 3.50
148 " 2m dark blue & indigo ('28) 15 30
149 " 3m chalky blue & black 15 20
a. Perf. 14 2.75 2.00
150 " 5m red violet & black ('28) 15 20
151 " 10m lt. brn. & black 70 *13.00*
152 " 25m brn. org. & yel. 70 *32.50*
Nos. 143-152 (10) 6.35 *50.35*

Philatelic Exhibition Issue.

A22

Overprint in Black

1928, Nov. 10 Litho. Wmk. 208

153 A22 1m deep orange 7.50 12.00
154 " 1½m blue green & red violet 7.50 12.00

Nos. 153 and 154 were sold exclusively at the Helsinki Philatelic Exhibition, Nov. 10-18, 1928, and were valid only during that period.

S. S. "Bore" Leaving Turku
A23

Turku Cathedral
A24

Turku Castle
A25

Typographed

1929, May 22 *Perf. 14* Wmk. 208

155 A23 1m olive green 1.75 1.50
156 A24 1½m chocolate 3.50 1.75
157 A25 2m dark gray 50 1.50

Issued to commemorate the 700th anniversary of the founding of the city of Turku (Abo).

A26

1930–46 *Perf. 14* **Unwmkd.**

No.	Type	Description	Unused	Used
158	A26	5p chocolate	10	10
159	"	10p dull violet	10	10
160	"	20p yellow green	25	25
161	"	25p yellow brown	10	10
		a. Booklet pane of 4	40	
162	A26	40p blue green	2.50	25
163	"	50p yellow	40	25
164	"	50p blue green ('32)	10	6
		a. Booklet pane of 4	40	
		b. Imperf.	70.00	70.00
165	A26	60p dark gray	25	20
165A	"	75p dp. org. ('42)	10	10
166	"	1m red orange	30	8
		a. Booklet pane of 4	1.20	
166B	A26	1m yel. grn. ('42)	20	10
167	"	1.20m crimson	35	50
168	"	1.25m yellow ('32)	10	6
		a. Booklet pane of 4	40	
169	A26	1½m red violet	4.00	10
170	"	1½m carmine ('32)	20	10
170A	"	1½m slate ('40)	12	8
170B	"	1.75m org. yel. ('40)	75	15
171	"	2m indigo	25	15
172	"	2m dp. violet ('32)	9.00	8
173	"	2m carmine ('36)	25	8
		a. Booklet pane of 4	1.00	
173B	A26	2m yel. org. ('42)	25	10
173C	"	2m blue green ('45)	25	10
174	"	2½m brt. blue ('32)	1.75	15
174A	"	2½m carmine ('42)	20	8
174B	"	2.75m rose violet('40)	12	8
175	"	3m olive black	20.00	15
		a. Double foot on lion	250.00	100.00
175B	A26	3m carmine ('45)	30	10
175C	"	3m yellow ('45)	30	35
176	"	3½m brt. blue ('36)	5.00	15
176A	"	3½m olive ('42)	20	8
176B	"	4m olive ('45)	25	8
176C	"	4½m sapphire ('42)	20	20
176D	"	5m sapphire ('45)	30	10
176E	"	5m purple ('45)	30	15
		j. Imperf.	80.00	80.00
176F	A26	5m yellow ('46)	30	5
		k. Imperf.	25.00	25.00
176G	A26	6m carmine ('45)	30	15
		m. Imperf.	80.00	80.00
176H	A26	8m purple ('46)	20	10
176I	"	10m sapphire ('45)	50	5
		Nos. 158–176I (38)	50.14	5.11

See also Nos. 257–262, 270–274, 291–296, 302–304.

Stamps of types A26–A29 overprinted "ITA KARJALA" are listed under Karelia, Nos. N1–N15.

Castle in Savonlinna

A27

Lake Saima

A28

Woodchopper

A29

1930 **Engraved**

No.	Type	Description	Unused	Used
177	A27	5m blue	30	6
178	A28	10m gray lilac	47.50	2.00
179	A29	25m black brown	1.75	12

See also Nos. 205 and 305.

Elias Lönnrot

A30

Seal of Finnish Literary Society

A31

1931, Jan. 1 **Typographed**

No.	Type	Description	Unused	Used
180	A30	1m olive brown	3.50	2.00
181	A31	1½m dull blue	10.00	2.00

Centenary of Finnish Literary Society.

A32

1931, Feb. 28

No.	Type	Description	Unused	Used
182	A32	1½m red	2.50	4.00
183	"	2m blue	2.50	4.00

75th anniversary of first use of postage stamps in Finland.

Nos. 162-163 Surcharged

50 PEN.

1932, Jan.

No.	Type	Description	Unused	Used
195	A26	50p on 40p bl. grn.	1.20	15
196	"	1.25m on 50p yellow	3.00	50

President P. E. Svinhufvud

A33

Alexis Kivi

A34

1931, Dec. 15

No.	Type	Description	Unused	Used
197	A33	2m gray blue & blk.	1.75	1.50

Issued to commemorate the 70th birthday of President Pehr Eyvind Svinhufvud.

Lake Saima Type of 1930.

1932–43 **Re-engraved**

No.	Type	Description	Unused	Used
205	A28	10m red violet ('43)	75	10
		a. 10m dark violet	20.00	70

On Nos. 205 and 205a the lines of the islands, the clouds and the foilage are much deeper and stronger than on No. 178.

1934, Oct. 10 **Typographed**

No.	Type	Description	Unused	Used
206	A34	2m red violet	2.00	1.50

Issued in commemoration of the centenary of the birth of Alexis Kivi, Finnish poet (1834–1872).

Bards Reciting the "Kalevala"

A35

Goddess Louhi, As Eagle Seizing Magic Mill

A36

Kullervo

A37

1935, Feb. 28 **Engraved**

No.	Type	Description	Unused	Used
207	A35	1¼m brown lake	1.50	1.20
208	A36	2m black	2.00	50
209	A37	2½m blue	4.00	1.20

Issued to commemorate the centenary of the publication of the "Kalevala" (Finnish National Epic).

No. 170 Surcharged in Black

2 MARKKAA

1937, Feb.

No.	Type	Description	Unused	Used
212	A26	2m on 1½m carmine	4.00	40

Field Marshal Gustaf Mannerheim

A38

Swede-Finn Co-operation in Colonization

A39

1937, June 4 **Photo.** ***Perf. 14***

No.	Type	Description	Unused	Used
213	A38	2m ultramarine	75	50

Issued in commemoration of the 70th birthday of Field Marshal Baron Carl Gustaf Mannerheim, June 4th, 1937.

1938, June 1

No.	Type	Description	Unused	Used
214	A39	3½m dark brown	1.50	1.00

Tercentenary of the colonization of Delaware by Swedes and Finns.

Early Post Office

A40

Designs: 1¼m, Mail delivery in 1700. 2m, Modern mail plane. 3½m, Helsinki post office.

1938, Sept. 6 **Photo.** ***Perf. 14***

No.	Type	Description	Unused	Used
215	A40	50p green	35	35
		a. Bklt. pane of 3	5.00	
216	"	1¼m dark blue	90	80
		a. Bklt. pane of 2	6.50	
217	"	2m scarlet	1.20	50
		a. Bklt. pane of 2	8.75	
218	"	3½m slate black	4.50	3.00
		a. Bklt. pane of 2	22.00	

Issued in commemoration of the 300th anniversary of the Finnish Postal System.

Post Office, Helsinki

A44

1939–42 **Photogravure**

No.	Type	Description	Unused	Used
219	A44	4m brown black	18	12

Engraved

No.	Type	Description	Unused	Used
219A	A44	7m black brown ('42)	50	10
219B	"	9m rose lake ('42)	50	10

See also No. 248.

University of Helsinki

A45

1940, May 1 **Photogravure**

No.	Type	Description	Unused	Used
220	A45	2m deep blue & blue	75	50

Issued in commemoration of the 300th anniversary of the founding of the University of Helsinki.

Nos. 168 and 173 Surcharged in Black

mk 1:75

1940, June 16 **Typographed**

No.	Type	Description	Unused	Used
221	A26	1.75m on 1.25m yel.	1.00	70
222	"	2.75m on 2m carmine	2.50	30

President Kallio Reviewing Military Band

A46

1941, May 24 **Engraved**

No.	Type	Description	Unused	Used
223	A46	2.75m black	75	45

Issued in memory of President Kyösti Kallio (1873–1940).

Castle at Viborg

A47

1941, Aug. 30 **Typographed**

No.	Type	Description	Unused	Used
224	A47	1.75m yellow orange	50	60
225	"	2.75m rose violet	50	60
226	"	3.50m blue	85	1.00

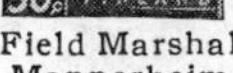

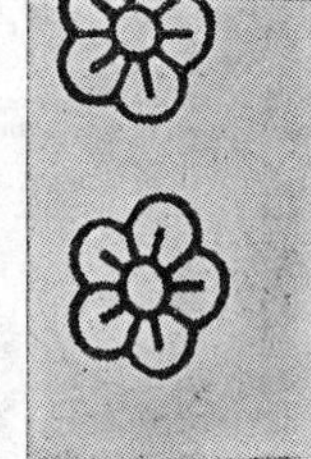

Field Marshal Mannerheim

A48

Wmk. 273

Wmkd. Roses. (273)

1941, Dec. 31 **Engraved** ***Perf. 14***

No.	Type	Description	Unused	Used
227	A48	50p dull green	40	50
228	"	1.75m deep brown	50	60
229	"	2m dark red	40	45
230	"	2.75m dull violet brown	60	80
231	"	3.50m deep blue	45	45
232	"	5m slate blue	45	45
		Nos. 227–232 (6)	2.80	3.25

President Risto Ryti

A49

No.	Type	Description	Unused	Used
233	A49	50p dull green	40	50
234	"	1.75m deep brown	50	60
235	"	2m dark red	40	45
236	"	2.75m dull violet brn.	60	80
237	"	3.50m deep blue	45	45
238	"	5m slate blue	45	45
		Nos. 233–238 (6)	2.80	3.25

Types A48–A49 overprinted "ITA KARJALA" are listed under Karelia, Nos. N16–N27.

Häme Bridge, Tampere
A50

South Harbor, Helsinki
A51

1942 **Unwmkd.**

239 A50 50m dull brown vio. 1.50 8
240 A51 100m indigo 2.50 20

See also No. 350.

Altar and Open Bible
A52

17th Century Printer
A53

1942, Oct. 10

241 A52 2.75m dark brown 35 50
242 A53 3.50m violet blue 55 1.10

Issued to commemorate the 300th anniversary of the printing of the first Bible in Finnish, 1642.

No. 174B Surcharged in Black

3½mk

1943, Feb. 1

243 A26 3.50m on 2.75m rose violet 15 15

Minna Canth
A54

1944, Mar. 20

244 A54 3.50m dark olive green 30 45

Issued to commemorate the centenary of the birth of Minna Canth (1844–96), author and playwright.

President P. E. Svinhufvud
A55

K. J. Stahlberg
A56

1944, Aug. 1

245 A55 3.50m black 25 40

Death of President Svinhufvud (1861–1944).

1945, May 16 **Engraved** ***Perf. 14***

246 A56 3.50m brown violet 20 25

80th birthday of Dr. K. J. Stahlberg.

Castle in Savonlinna
A57

Jean Sibelius
A58

1945, Sept. 4

247 A57 15m lilac rose 1.00 15
248 A44 20m sepia 1.20 8

For a 35m of type A57, see No. 280.

1945, Dec. 8

249 A58 5m dark slate green 18 25

80th birthday of Jean Sibelius (1865–1957), composer.

No. 176E Surcharged with New Value and Bars in Black.

1946, Mar. 16

250 A26 8(m) on 5m purple 12 15

Victorious Athletes
A59

Lighthouse at Uto
A60

1946, June 1 **Engraved** ***Perf. 13½***

251 A59 8m brown violet 20 20

Issued to commemorate the 3rd Sports Festival, Helsinki, June 27–30, 1946.

1946, Sept. 19

252 A60 8m deep violet 20 20

Issued to commemorate the 250th anniversary of the Finnish Department of Pilots and Lighthouses.

Post Bus
A61

1946–47 ***Perf. 14*** **Unwmkd.**

253 A61 16m gray black 25 50
253A " 30m gray black ('47) 70 15

Old Town Hall, Porvoo
A62

Cathedral, Porvoo
A63

1946, Dec. 3

254 A62 5m gray black 20 25
255 A63 8m deep claret 20 25

Issued to commemorate the 600th anniversary of the founding of the city of Porvoo (Borga).

Waterfront, Tammisaari
A64

1946, Dec. 14

256 A64 8m greenish black 20 25

Issued to commemorate the 400th anniversary of the founding of the town of Tammisaari (Ekenas).

Lion Type of 1930.

1947 **Typographed** ***Perf. 14***

257 A26 2½m dark green 12 8
258 " 3m slate gray 20 8
259 " 6m deep orange 65 12
260 " 7m carmine 20 10
261 " 10m purple 2.00 8
262 " 12m deep blue 1.00 8
Nos. 257-262 (6) 4.17 54

Pres. Juho K. Paasikivi
A65

Postal Savings Emblem
A66

1947, Mar. 15 **Engraved**

263 A65 10m gray black 20 25

1947, Apr. 1

264 A66 10m brown violet 20 25

Issued to commemorate the 60th anniversary of the foundation of the Finnish Postal Savings Bank.

Ilmarinen, the Plowman
A67

Girl and Boy Athletes
A68

1947, June 2

265 A67 10m gray black 20 25

Issued to mark the second year of peace following World War II.

1947, June 2

266 A68 10m bright blue 25 30

Issued to commemorate the Finnish Athletic Festival, Helsingfors, June 29–July 3, 1947.

Wheat and Savings Bank Association Emblem
A69

Sower
A70

1947, Aug. 21

267 A69 10m red brown 20 25

Issued to commemorate the 125th anniversary of the Finnish Savings Bank Association.

1947, Nov. 1

268 A70 10m gray black 20 25

Issued to commemorate the 50th anniversary of Finnish Agricultural Societies.

Koli Mountain and Lake Pielisjärvi
A71

Statue of Michael Agricola
A72

1947, Nov. 1

269 A71 10m indigo 20 25

Issued to commemorate the 60th anniversary of the Finnish Touring Association.

Lion Type of 1930.

1948 **Typographed.** ***Perf. 14***

270 A26 3m dark green 70 8
271 " 6m yellow green 60 30
272 " 9m carmine 20 8
273 " 15m dark blue 2.00 8
274 " 24m brown lake 65 18
Nos. 270-274 (5) 4.15 72

No. 261 Surcharged with New Value and Bars in Black.

1948, Feb. 9

275 A26 12(m) on 10m pur. 1.00 18

1948, Oct. 2 **Engraved** ***Perf. 14***

Design: 12m, Agricola translating New Testament.

276 A72 7m rose violet 55 1.00
277 " 12m gray blue 55 1.00

Issued to commemorate the 400th anniversary of publication of the Finnish translation of the New Testament, by Michael Agricola.

Sveaborg Fortress
A73

Post Rider
A74

1948, Oct. 15

278 A73 12m deep green 1.00 1.00

Issued to commemorate the 200th anniversary of the construction of Sveaborg Fortress on the Gulf of Finland.

1948, Oct. 27

279 A74 12m green 14.00 20.00

Issued to commemorate the Helsinki Philatelic Exhibition. Sold only at exhibition, for 62m of which 50m was entrance fee.

1949 **Castle Type of 1945.**

280 A57 35m violet 3.00 15

Sawmill and Cellulose Plant
A75

Pine Tree and Globe
A76

Woman with Torch
A77

1949, June 15

281	A75	9m brown	1.25	1.50
282	A76	15m dull green	1.25	1.50

Issued to publicize the Third World Forestry Congress, Helsinki, July 10-20, 1949.

1949, July 16 Engraved *Perf. 14*

283	A77	5m dull green	2.50	*8.00*
284	"	15m red (*Worker*)	2.50	*8.00*

Issued to commemorate the 50th anniversary of the Finnish labor movement.

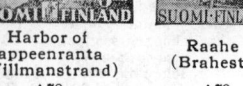

Harbor of Lappeenranta (Willmanstrand)
A78

Raahe (Brahestad)
A79

1949

285	A78	5m dark blue green	35	25
286	A79	9m brown carmine	65	50
287	A78	15m bright blue (*Kristiinan-kaupunki*)	75	45

Issued to commemorate the 300th anniversary of the founding of Willmanstrand, Brahestad and Kristinestad (Kristiinan-kaupunki).

Issue dates: 5m, Aug. 6; 9m, Aug. 13; 15m, July 30.

Technical High School Badge
A80

Hannes Gebhard
A81

1949, Sept. 13

288	A80	15m ultramarine	60	50

Issued to commemorate the centenary of the founding of the technical school.

1949, Oct. 2

289	A81	15m dull green	60	50

Issued to commemorate the 50th anniversary of the establishment of Finnish cooperatives.

Finnish Lake Country
A82

1949, Oct. 8

290	A82	15m blue	60	55

Issued to commemorate the 75th anniversary of the formation of the Universal Postal Union.

Lion Type of 1930

1950 Typographed *Perf. 14.*

291	A26	8m bright green	40	65
292	"	9m red orange	25	18
293	"	10m violet brown	3.00	10
294	"	12m scarlet	25	8
295	"	15m plum	7.00	10
296	"	20m deep blue	3.75	10
		Nos. 291-296 (6)	14.65	1.21

Forsell's Map of Old Helsinki
A83

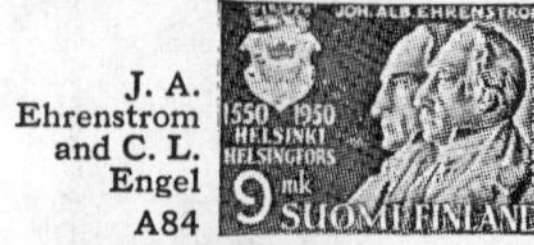

J. A. Ehrenstrom and C. L. Engel
A84

City Hall
A85

1950, June 11 Engraved

297	A83	5m emerald	25	25
298	A84	9m brown	50	60
299	A85	15m deep blue	45	25

Issued to commemorate the 400th anniversary of the founding of Helsinki.

J. K. Paasikivi
A86

View of Kajaani
A87

1950, Nov. 27

300	A86	20m deep ultramarine	45	25

80th birthday of Pres. J. K. Paasikivi.

1951, July 7 *Perf. 14* Unwmkd.

301	A87	20m red brown	45	25

Tercentenary of Kajaani.

Lion and Chopper Types of 1930

1952 Typographed

302	A26	10m emerald	1.25	15
303	"	15m red	2.25	12
304	"	25m blue	1.75	10

Engraved

305	A29	40m black brown	1.00	12

Arms of Pietarsaari
A88

Rooftops of Vaasa
A89

1952, June 19 *Perf. 14* Unwmkd.

306	A88	25m blue	55	45

Issued to commemorate the 300th anniversary of the founding of Pietarsaari (Jacobstad).

1952, Aug. 3

307	A89	25m brown	55	45

Centenary of the burning of Vaasa.

Chess Symbols
A90

1952, Aug. 10

308	A90	25m gray	1.00	1.00

Issued to publicize the 10th Chess Olympics, Helsinki, Aug. 10-31, 1952.

Torch Bearers
A91

1953, Jan. 27

309	A91	25m blue	55	45

Issued to commemorate the centenary of the temperance movement in Finland.

Air View of Hamina (Fredrikshamn)
A92

Ivar Wilskman
A93

1953, June 20

310	A92	25m dark gray green	55	45

Tercentenary of Hamina.

1954, Feb. 26

311	A93	25m blue	55	45

Issued to commemorate the centenary of the birth of Prof. Ivar Wilskman, "father of gymnastics in Finland."

Arms of Finland
A94

"In the Outer Archipelago"
A95

1954-59 ***Perf. 11½***

312	A94	1m red brown ('55)	35	8
313	"	2m green ('55)	35	8
314	"	3m deep orange	35	8
314A	"	4m gray ('58)	30	8
315	"	5m violet blue	80	8
316	"	10m blue green	80	5
		a. Bklt. pane of 5 (vert. strip)	12.00	
317	"	15m rose red	2.00	5
318	"	15m yel. orange ('57)	2.50	8
319	"	20m rose lilac	3.00	10
320	"	20m rose red ('56)	1.00	5
321	"	25m deep blue	2.75	5
322	"	25m rose lilac ('59)	3.00	8
323	"	30m light ultra. ('56)	1.00	5
		Nos. 312-323 (13)	18.20	91

See Nos. 398, 400-405A, 457-459, 461A-462, 464-464B.

1954, July 21 ***Perf. 14***

324	A95	25m black	55	45

Issued to commemorate the centenary of the birth of Albert Edelfelt, painter.

J. J. Nervander
A96

Composite of Finnish Public Buildings
A97

1955, Feb. 23

325	A96	25m blue	60	45

Issued to commemorate the 150th anniversary of the birth of J. J. Nervander, astronomer and poet.

1955, Mar. 20 Engraved *Perf. 14*

326	A97	25m gray	15.00	15.00

Sold for 125m, which included the price of admission to the National Postage Stamp Exhibition, Helsinki, March 30 to April 3, 1955.

Bishop Henrik with Foot on Lalli, his Murderer
A98

Conference Hall, Helsinki
A99

Design: 25m, Arrival of Bishop Henrik and monks.

1955, May 19

327	A98	15m rose brown	75	50
328	"	25m green	75	50

Issued to commemorate the 800th anniversary of the adoption of Christianity in Finland.

1955, Aug. 25

329	A99	25m bluish green	90	60

Issued to commemorate the 44th conference of the Interparliamentarian Union, Helsinki, Aug. 25-31, 1955.

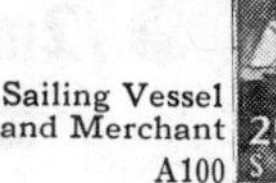

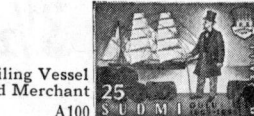

Sailing Vessel and Merchant
A100

1955, Sept. 2

330	A100	25m sepia	90	60

350th anniversary of founding of Oulu.

Town Hall, Lahti
A101

Radio Sender and Map of Finland
A102

1955, Nov. 1 ***Perf. 14x13½***

331	A101	25m violet blue	90	60

50th anniversary of founding of Lahti.

1955, Dec. 10 ***Perf. 14***

Designs: 15m, Otto Nyberg. 25m, Telegraph wires and pines under snow.

Inscribed:
Lennatin 1855-1955 Telegrafen.

332	A102	10m green	75	50
333	"	15m dull violet	75	50
334	"	25m light ultra.	75	50

Issued to commemorate the centenary of the telegraph in Finland.

Lighthouse and Porkkala Peninsula
A103

1956, Jan. 26 ***Perf. 14*** **Unwmkd.**

335 A103 25m greenish blue 55 45

Issued to commemorate the return of the Porkkala Region to Finland by Russia, Jan. 1956.

Church at Lammi
A104

Designs: 40m, House of Parliament. 60m, Fortress of Olavinlinna (Olofsborg).

1956–57 ***Perf. 11½***

336 A104 30m gray olive 75 15
337 " 40m dull purple 1.25 15
338 " 50m gray olive ('57) 2.00 15
338A " 60m pale pur. ('57) 2.50 15

See Nos. 406–408A.

Johan V. Snellman
A105

Gymnast and Athletes
A106

1956, May 12 **Engraved** ***Perf. 14***

339 A105 25m dark violet brown 55 45

Issued to commemorate the 150th anniversary of the birth of Johan V. Snellman (1806–1881), statesman.

1956, June 28

340 A106 30m violet blue 90 50

Issued to commemorate the Finnish Gymnastic and Sports Games, Helsinki, June 28–July 1, 1956.

A107

Rouletted

1956, July 7 **Typo.** **Wmk. 208**

341 A107 30m deep ultra. 3.00 4.00
a. Tête bêche pair 6.00 8.00
b. Pane of 10 32.50 47.50

Issued to publicize the FINLANDIA Philatelic Exhibition, Helsinki, July 7–15, 1956.

Printed in sheets containing four 2x5 panes, with white margins around each group. The stamps in each double row are printed tete-beche, making the position of the watermark differ in the vertical row of each pane of ten.

Sold for 155m, price including entrance ticket to exhibition.

Town Hall at Vasa
A108

Engraved.

1956, Oct. 2 ***Perf. 14*** **Unwmkd.**

342 A108 30m bright blue 60 45

350th anniversary of Vasa.

Northern Countries Issue.

Whooper Swans
A108a

1956, Oct. 30 ***Perf. 12½***

343 A108a 20m rose red 2.50 75
344 " 30m ultramarine 4.00 75

See footnote after Denmark No. 362.

University Clinic, Helsinki
A109

Scout Sign, Emblem and Globe
A110

1956, Dec. 17 ***Perf. 11½***

345 A109 30m dull green 75 45

Issued to commemorate the bicentenary of public health service in Finland.

1957, Feb. 22 ***Perf. 14***

346 A110 30m ultramarine 75 45

50th anniversary of Boy Scouts.

Arms Holding Hammers and Laurel
A111

"Lex" from Seal of Parliament
A112

Design: 20m, Factories and cogwheel.

1957, Apr. 15 **Engraved** ***Perf. 13½***

347 A111 20m dark blue 55 45
348 " 30m carmine 55 45

Issued to commemorate the 50th anniversaries of the Central Federation of Finnish Employers (No. 347) and of the Finnish Trade Union Movement (No. 348).

1957, May 23 ***Perf. 14***

349 A112 30m olive gray 70 45

Issued to commemorate the 50th anniversary of the Finnish parliament.

Harbor Type of 1942.

1957 ***Perf. 14*** **Unwmkd.**

350 A51 100m greenish blue 1.50 15

Ida Aalberg
A114

Arms of Finland
A115

1957, Dec. 4 ***Perf. 14***

351 A114 30m violet gray & maroon 60 45

Issued to commemorate the centenary of the birth of Ida Aalberg, Finnish actress.

1957, Dec. 6 ***Perf. 11½***

352 A115 30m blue 75 45

Issued to commemorate the 40th anniversary of Finland's independence.

Jean Sibelius
A116

Ski Jump
A117

1957, Dec. 8 ***Perf. 14***

353 A116 30m black 75 45

Issued in memory of Jean Sibelius (1865–1957), composer.

1958, Feb. 1 **Engraved** ***Perf. 11½***

Design: 30m, Skier (vertical).

354 A117 20m slate green 75 60
355 " 30m blue 90 45

Issued to publicize the Nordic championships of the International Ski Federation, Lahti.

"March of the Bjorneborgienses," by Edelfelt
A118

South Harbor, Helsinki
A119

1958, Mar. 8

356 A118 30m violet gray 75 45

Issued to commemorate the 400th anniversary of the founding of Pori (Bjorneborg).

1958, June 2 ***Perf. 11½*** **Unwmkd.**

357 A119 100m bluish green 6.00 15

See No. 410.

Seal of Jyväsky lä Lyceum
A120

1958, Oct. 1 ***Perf. 11½***

358 A120 30m rose carmine 1.00 25

Issued to commemorate the centenary of the founding of the first Finnish secondary school.

Chrismon and Globe
A121

Diet at Porvoo, 1809
A122

1959, Jan. 19

359 A121 30m dull violet 60 25

Issued to commemorate the centenary of the Finnish Missionary Society.

1959, Mar. 22 ***Perf. 11½***

360 A122 30m dark blue gray 80 25

Issued to commemorate the 150th anniversary of the inauguration of the Diet at Porvoo.

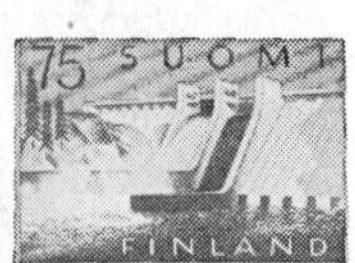

Saw Cutting Log
A123

Pyhakoski Power Station
A124

Design: 30m, Forest.

1959, May 13 **Engraved**

361 A123 10m reddish brown 55 45
362 " 30m green 80 45

No. 361 commemorates the centenary of the establishment of the first steam sawmill in Finland; No. 362, the centenary of the Department of Forestry.

1959, May 24

363 A124 75m gray 1.10 15

See No. 409.

Oil Lamp
A125

Woman Gymnast
A126

1959, Dec. 19

364 A125 30m blue 60 45

Issued to commemorate the centenary of the liberation of the country trade.

1959, Nov. 14 **Unwmkd.**

365 A126 30m rose lilac 80 45

Issued to honor Finnish women's gymnastics and the centenary of the birth of Elin Oihonna Kallio, pioneer of Finnish women's physical education.

Arms of Six New Towns
A127

1960, Jan. 2 ***Perf. 14***

366 A127 30m light violet 60 25

Issued to commemorate the founding of new towns in Finland: Hyvinkaa, Kouvola, Riihimaki, Rovaniemi, Salo and Seinajoki.

Type of 1860 Issue
A128

Typographed

1960, Mar. 25 ***Rouletted 4½***

367 A128 30m blue & gray 5.50 5.50

Issued to commemorate the centenary of Finland's serpentine roulette stamps, and in connection with HELSINKI 1960, 40th anniversary exhibition of the Federation of Philatelic Societies of Finland, March 25–31. Sold only at the exhibition for 150m including entrance ticket.

Mother and Child, Waiting Crowd and Uprooted Oak Emblem
A129

1960, Apr. 7 Engraved *Perf. 11½*

368 A129 30m rose claret 50 35
369 " 40m dark blue 50 35

Issued to publicize World Refugee Year, July 1, 1959–June 30, 1960.

Johan Gadolin A130 — Hj. Nortamo A131

1960, June 4 *Perf. 11½*

370 A130 30m dark brown 55 30

Issued to commemorate the bicentennary of the birth of Johan Gadolin, chemist.

1960, June 13 Unwmkd.

371 A131 30m gray green 55 30

Issued to commemorate the centenary of the birth of Hj. Nortamo (Hjalmar Nordberg), writer.

Symbolic Tree and Cuckoo
A132

1960, June 18

372 A132 30m vermilion 60 30

Karelian National Festival, Helsinki, June 18–19.

Geodetic Instrument A133 — Urho Kekkonen A134

Design: 30m, Aurora borealis and globe.

1960, July 26 *Perf. 13½* Unwmkd.

373 A133 10m blue & pale brown 60 25
374 " 30m vermilion & rose carmine 70 25

Issued to publicize the 12th General Assembly of the International Union of Geodesy and Geophysics, Helsinki.

1960, Sept. 3 Engraved *Perf. 11½*

375 A134 30m violet blue 1.00 25

Issued to honor President Urho Kekkonen on his 60th birthday.

Europa Issue, 1960

Common Design Type

1960, Sept. 19 *Perf. 13½*

Size: 30½x21mm.

376 CD3 30m dark blue & Prus. blue 65 30
377 CD3 40m dark brown & plum 65 30

A 30m gray similar to No. 376 was printed with simulated perforations in a non-valid souvenir sheet privately released in London for STAMPEX 1961.

Uno Cygnaeus A135 — "Pommern" and Arms of Mariehamn A136

1960, Oct. 13 *Perf. 11½*

378 A135 30m dull violet 55 30

Issued to commemorate the 150th anniversary of the birth of Pastor Uno Cygnaeus, founder of elementary schools.

1961, Feb. 21 *Perf. 11½*

379 A136 30m greenish blue 75 30

Centenary of the founding of Mariehamn.

Lake and Rowboat
A137

Turku Castle
A138

1961 Engraved Unwmkd.

380 A137 5m green 25 10
381 A138 125m slate green 3.50 25

See also Nos. 399, 411.

Postal Savings Bank Emblem A139 — Symbol of Standardization A140

1961, May 24

382 A139 30m Prussian green 55 30

Issued to commemorate the 75th anniversary of Finland's Postal Savings Bank.

Lithographed

1961, June 5 *Perf. 14x13½*

383 A140 30m dk. slate green & orange 55 30

Issued to commemorate the meeting of the International Organization for Standardization, ISO, Helsinki, June 5.

Juhani Aho
A141

Engraved

1961, Sept. 11 *Perf. 11½* Unwmkd.

384 A141 30m red brown 55 30

Issued to commemorate the centenary of the birth of Juhani Aho (1861–1921), writer.

Various Buildings
A142

1961, Oct. 16 *Perf. 11½*

385 A142 30m slate 55 30

Issued to commemorate 150 years of the Central Board of Buildings.

Arvid Jarnefelt
A143

1961, Nov. 16

386 A143 30m deep claret 55 30

Issued to commemorate the centenary of the birth of Arvid Jarnefelt, writer.

Bank of Finland A144 — First Finnish Locomotive A145

1961, Dec. 12 Engraved *Perf. 11½*

387 A144 30m brown violet 55 30

150th anniversary of Bank of Finland.

1962, Jan. 31 *Perf. 11½* Unwmkd.

Designs: 30m, Steam locomotive and timber car. 40m, Diesel locomotive and passenger train.

388 A145 10m gray green 75 30
389 " 30m violet blue 75 30
390 " 40m dull red brown 1.00 30

Centenary of the Finnish State Railways.

Mora Stone
A146

1962, Feb. 15

391 A146 30m gray brown 55 30

Issued to commemorate 600 years of political rights of the Finnish people.

Senate Place, Helsinki
A147

1962, Apr. 8 *Perf. 11½* Unwmkd.

392 A147 30m violet brown 55 30

Issued to commemorate the sesquicentennial of the proclamation of Helsinki as capital of Finland.

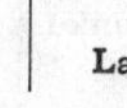

Common Design Types pictured in section at front of book.

Customs Emblem A148 — Staff of Mercury A149

1962, Apr. 11

393 A148 30m red 55 30

Issued to commemorate the sesquicentennial of the Finnish Board of Customs.

1962, May 21 Engraved

394 A149 30m bluish green 55 30

Issued to commemorate the centenary of the first commercial bank in Finland.

Santeri Alkio A150 — Finnish Labor Emblem and Conveyor Belt A151

1962, June 17 *Perf. 11½* Unwmkd.

395 A150 30m brown carmine 55 30

Issued to commemorate the centenary of the birth of Santeri Alkio, writer and pioneer of the young people's societies in Finland.

1962, Oct. 19

396 A151 30m chocolate 55 30

National production progress.

Survey Plane and Compass
A152

1962, Nov. 14

397 A152 30m yellow green 55 30

Issued to commemorate the 150th anniversary of the Finnish Land Survey Board.

Types of 1954–61 and

Log Floating
A153

Parainen Bridge
A154

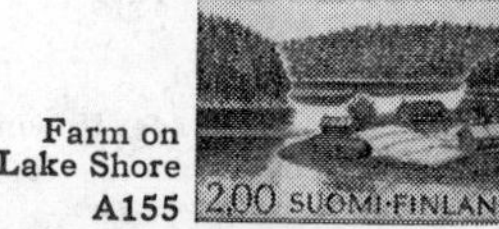

Farm on Lake Shore
A155

Ristikallio in Kuusamo—A156

Designs: 40p, House of Parliament. 50p, Church at Lammi. 60p, 65p, Fortress of Olavinlinna. 2.50m, Aerial view of Punkaharju.

1963-67 Engraved *Perf. 11½*

398 A94 5p violet blue 6 3
a. Booklet pane of 2 (vert. pair) 15.00
b. Bklt. pane of 2 (horiz. pair) 12.50
399 A137 5p green 15 3
400 A94 10p blue green 8 3
a. Booklet pane of 2 (vert. pair) 15.00
401 A94 15p yellow orange 35 3
402 " 20p rose red 15 3
a. Booklet pane of 1 15.00
b. Bklt. pane of 3 (2 No. 400, 1 No. 402+label; horiz. strip) 22.50
c. Bklt. pane of 5 (2 No. 398, 2 No. 400, 1 No. 402; horiz. strip) 4.00
403 A94 25p rose lilac 20 3
404 " 30p light ultra. 1.25 3
404A " 30p blue gray ('65) 20 3
405 " 35p blue 35 3
405A " 40p ultra. ('67) 40 4
406 A104 40p dull purple 35 10
407 " 50p gray olive 30 3
408 " 60p pale purple 35 10
408A " 65p pale pur. ('67) 40 8
409 A124 75p gray 50 5
410 A119 1m bluish green 55 3
411 A138 1.25m slate green 70 8
412 A153 1.50m dk. greenish gray 85 8
413 A154 1.75m blue 1.00 8
414 A155 2m green ('64) 1.10 8
414A " 2.50m ultra. & yel. ('67) 1.40 25
415 A156 5m dk. slate grn. ('64) 2.75 60
Nos. 398-415 (22) 13.44 1.87

Pennia denominations expressed: "0,05", "0,10", etc.
Four stamps of type A94 (5p, 10p, 20p, 25p) come in two types: I. Four vertical lines in "O" of SUOMI. II. Three lines in "O."
See also Nos. 457-464B.

Mother and Child
A157

1963, Mar. 21 *Perf. 11½* Unwmkd.

416 A157 40p red brown 65 30

Issued for the "Freedom from Hunger" campaign of the U.N. Food and Agriculture Organization.

"Christ Today"
A158

Design: 10p, Crown of thorns and medieval cross of consecration.

1963, July 30 Engraved *Perf. 11½*

417 A158 10p maroon 50 25
418 " 30p dark green 70 30

Issued to commemorate the 4th assembly of the Lutheran World Federation, Helsinki, July 30-Aug. 8.

Europa Issue, 1963
Common Design Type

1963, Sept. 16
Size: 30x20mm.

419 CD6 40p red lilac 70 35

Assembly Building, Helsinki
A159

1963, Sept. 18

420 A159 30p violet blue 55 30

Issued to commemorate the centenary of the Representative Assembly of Finland.

Convair Metropolitan
A160

M. A. Castrén
A161

Design: 40p, Caravelle jetliner.

1963, Nov. 1

421 A160 35p slate green 60 20
422 " 40p brt. ultramarine 60 20

40th anniversary of Finnish air traffic.

1963, Dec. 2 Unwmkd.

423 A161 35p violet blue 80 20

Issued to commemorate the 150th anniversary of the birth of Matthias Alexander Castrén (1813-52), ethnologist and philologist.

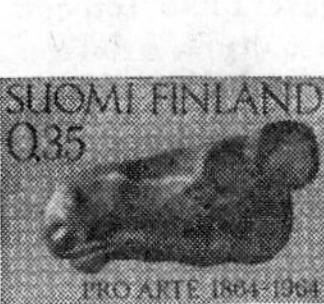
Stone Elk's Head, 2000 B.C.
A162

Emil Nestor Setälä
A163

1964, Feb. 5 Litho. *Perf. 11½*

424 A162 35p ocher & slate green 80 20

Issued to commemorate the centenary of the Finnish Artists' Association. The soapstone sculpture was found at Huittinen.

1964, Feb. 27 Engraved

425 A163 35p dark red brown 80 20

Issued to commemorate the centenary of the birth of Emil Nestor Setälä (1864-1946), philologist, minister of education and foreign affairs and chancellor of Abo University.

Staff of Aesculapius
A164

1964, June 13 *Perf. 11½* Unwmkd.

426 A164 40p slate green 50 20

Issued to commemorate the 18th General Assembly of the World Medical Association, Helsinki, June 13-19, 1964.

Ice Hockey
A165

1965, Jan. 4 Engraved

427 A165 35p dark blue 60 20

Issued to publicize the World Ice Hockey Championships, Finland, March 3-14, 1965.

Design from Centenary Medal
A166

1965, Feb. 6 *Perf. 11½* Unwmkd.

428 A166 35p olive gray 60 20

Issued to commemorate the centenary of communal self-government in Finland.

K. J. Stahlberg and "Lex" by W. Runeberg
A167

1965, Mar. 22 Engraved

429 A167 35p brown 60 20

Issued to commemorate the centenary of the birth of Kaarlo Juho Stahlberg (1865-1952), first President of Finland.

International Cooperation Year Emblem
A168

1965, Apr. 2 Lithographed *Perf. 14*

430 A168 40p bister, dull red, black & green 60 20

U.N. International Cooperation Year.

"Fratricide" by Gallen-Kallela
A169

Sibelius, Piano and Score
A170

Design: 35p, Girl's Head by Akseli Gallen-Kallela.

1965, Aug. 26 *Perf. 13½x14*

431 A169 25p multicolored 1.10 45
432 " 35p " 1.10 45

Issued to commemorate the centenary of the birth of the painter Aksell Gallen-Kallela.

1965, May 15 Engraved *Perf. 11½*
Design: 35p, Musical score and bird.

433 A170 25p violet 80 30
434 " 35p dull green 80 30

Issued to commemorate the centenary of the birth of Jean Sibelius (1865-1957), composer.

Antenna for Satellite Telecommunication
A171

"Winter Day" by Pekka Halonen
A172

1965, May 17

435 A171 35p blue 75 30

Issued to commemorate the centenary of the International Telecommunication Union.

Perf. 14x13½

1965, Sept. 23 Litho. Unwmkd.

436 A172 35p gold & multi. 1.10 30

Issued to commemorate the centenary of the birth of the painter Pekka Halonen.

Europa Issue, 1965
Common Design Type
Engraved and Lithographed

1965, Sept. 27 *Perf. 13½x14*

437 CD8 40p bister, red brn., dk. blue & grn. 75 30

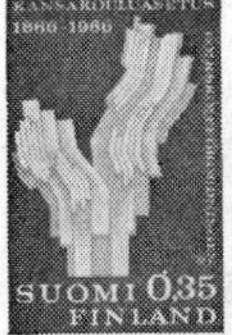
"Growth"
A173

Old Post Office
A174

1966, May 11 Litho. *Perf. 14*

438 A173 35p vio. blue & blue 50 20

Issued to commemorate the centenary of the promulgation of the Elementary School Decree.

1966, June 11 Litho. *Perf. 14*

439 A174 35p ocher, yel., dk. blue & black 5.50 5.50

Issued to commemorate the centenary of the first postage stamps in Finnish currency, and in connection with the NORDIA Stamp Exhibition, Helsinki, June 11-15. The stamp was sold only to buyers of a 1.25m exhibition entrance ticket.

UNESCO Emblem and World Map
A175

Finnish Police Emblem
A176

Lithographed and Engraved

1966, Oct. 9 *Perf. 14*

440 A175 40p grn., yel., blk. & brn. orange 50 25

Issued to commemorate the 20th anniversary of UNESCO (United Nations Educational, Scientific and Cultural Organization).

1966, Oct. 15

441 A176 35p dp. ultra., blk. & silver 60 25

Issued to honor the Finnish police.

Insurance Sesquicentennial Medal
A177

Engraved and Photogravure

1966, Oct. 28 *Perf. 14*

442 A177 35p maroon, olive & black 60 25

Issued to commemorate the 150th anniversary of the Finnish insurance system.

UNICEF Emblem
A178

1966, Nov. 14

443 A178 15p lt. ultra., purple & green 40 25

Issued to publicize the activities of UNICEF (United Nations Children's Emergency Fund).

"FINEFTA," Finnish Flag and Circle
A179

1967, Feb. 15 Engraved *Perf. 14*

444 A179 40p ultramarine 75 25

Issued to publicize the European Free Trade Association, EFTA. See note after Denmark No. 431.

Windmill and Arms of Uusikaupunki
A180

Mannerheim Monument by Aimo Tukiainen
A181

Lithographed and Engraved

1967, Apr. 19 *Perf. 14*

445 A180 40p multicolored 55 25

Issued to commemorate the 350th anniversary of Uusikaupunki (Nystad).

1967, June 4 *Perf. 14*

446 A181 40p violet & multi. 55 25

Issued to commemorate the centenary of the birth of Field Marshal Carl Gustav Emil Mannerheim.

Double Mortise Corner
A182

Watermark of Thomasböle Paper Mill
A183

Lithographed and Photogravure

1967, June 16

447 A182 40p multicolored 55 25

Issued to honor Finnish settlers in Sweden.

Lithographed and Engraved

1967, Sept. 6 *Perf. 14*

448 A183 40p olive & black 55 25

Issued to commemorate the 300th anniversary of the Finnish paper industry.

Martin Luther, by Lucas Cranach
A184

Photogravure and Engraved

1967, Nov. 4 *Perf. 14*

449 A184 40p bister & brown 55 25

450th anniversary of the Reformation.

"Wood and Water" Globe and Flag
A185

Designs (Globe, Flag and): 25p, Flying swan. 40p, Ear of wheat.

1967, Dec. 5 *Perf. 11½*

450 A185 20p green & blue 55 25
451 " 25p ultra. & blue 55 25
452 " 40p magenta & blue 55 25

Issued to commemorate the 50th anniversary of Finland's independence.

Zachris Topelius and Blue Bird
A186

1968, Jan. 14 Litho. *Perf. 14*

453 A186 25p blue & multi. 55 25

Issued to commemorate the 150th anniversary of the birth of Zachris Topelius (1818–1898), writer and educator.

Skiers and Ski Lift
A187

1968, Feb. 19 Photo. *Perf. 14*

454 A187 25p multicolored 75 30

Issued to publicize Winter Tourism in Finland.

Paper Making, by Hannes Autere
A188

Wmk. 363

Wmkd. Tree Stump (363)

1968, Mar. 12 Lithographed

455 A188 45p dark red, brown & orange 55 25

Issued to publicize the Finnish paper industry and to commemorate the 150th anniversary of the oldest Finnish paper mill, Tervakoski, whose own watermark was used for this stamp.

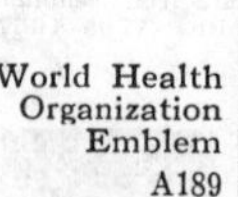

World Health Organization Emblem
A189

Lithographed and Photogravure

1968, Apr. 6 *Perf. 14* Unwmkd.

456 A189 40p red orange, dk. blue & gold 55 25

To honor World Health Organization.

Lion Type of 1954–58 and

Market Place and Mermaid Fountain, Helsinki
A190

Keuru Wooden Church, 1758
A191

Häme Bridge, Tampere—A192

Finnish Arms from Grave of King Gustav Vasa, 1581
A194

Designs: 25p, Post bus. 30p, Aquarium-Planetarium, Tampere. No. 463, P.O., Tampere. No. 465, National Museum, Helsinki (vert.). No. 467A, like 70p. 1.30m, Helsinki railroad station.

Engr. (type A94); Litho. (#465 & type A190); Engr. & Litho. (others).

***Perf. 11½; 12½* (type A190); *14* (#465, 470A); *13½* (#470).**

1968–78

457	A94	1p lt. red brn.	25	5
458	"	2p gray green	15	3
459	"	4p gray	25	5
460	A192	25p multi. ('71)	30	6
461	A191	30p " ('71)	75	15
461A	A94	35p dull org. ('74)	25	6
		b. Bklt. pane of 4 (# 398, # 461A, # 400, # 464A) + label	1.25	
462	A94	40p orange ('73)	25	3
		a. Bklt. pane of 3 (2 # 404A, # 462) + 2 labels	3.50	
463	A192	40p multi. ('73)	35	6
464	A94	50p lt. ultra. ('70)	30	3
		c. Bklt. pane of 5 (#401, #403, #464, 2 #398) + 5 labels	5.00	
464A	A94	50p rose lake ('74)	30	3
		d. Bklt. pane of 4 (#400, 2 #402, #464A) + label	70	
464B	A94	60p blue ('73)	35	4
465	A191	60p multi. ('73)	35	4
466	A190	70p multi. ('73)	40	5
467	A191	80p multi. ('70)	60	10
467A	A190	80p multi. ('76)	45	10
468	A192	90p "	70	10
469	A191	1.30m " ('71)	90	12
470	A194	10m " ('74)	5.50	1.25
470A	"	20m multi. ('78)	11.00	2.50
		Nos. 457–470A (19)	23.40	4.85

Infantry Monument, Vaasa
A195

Camping Ground
A196

Designs: 25p, War Memorial (cross), Hietaniemi Cemetery. 40p, Soldier, 1968.

1968, June 4 Photo. *Perf. 14*

471 A195 20p lt. vio. & multi. 50 25
472 " 25p lt. bl. & multi. 50 25
473 " 40p orange & multi. 50 25

To honor Finnish national defense.

1968, June 10 Lithographed

474 A196 25p multicolored 70 25

Issued to publicize Finland for summer vacations.

Paper, Pulp and Pine
A197

Mustola Lock, Saima Canal
A198

Lithographed and Embossed

1968, July 2 *Perf. 14* Unwmkd.

475 A197 40p multicolored 55 25

Finnish wood industry.

1968, Aug. 5 Litho. *Perf. 14*

476 A198 40p multicolored 55 25

Opening of the Saima Canal.

Oskar Merikanto and Pipe Organ
A199

1968, Aug. 5 Unwmkd.

477 A199 40p violet, silver & light brown 55 25

Issued to commemorate the centenary of the birth of Oskar Merikanto, composer.

Ships in Harbor and Emblem of Central Chamber of Commerce
A200

Welder
A201

1968, Sept. 13 Litho. *Perf. 14*

478 A200 40p light blue, brt. blue & black 55 25

Issued to publicize economic development and to commemorate the 50th anniversary of the Central Chamber of Commerce of Finland.

1968, Oct. 11 Lithographed *Perf. 14*

479 A201 40p blue & multi. 55 25

Finnish metal industry.

Lyre, Students' Emblem
A202

Five Ancient Ships
A203

Lithographed and Engraved

1968, Nov. 24 *Perf. 14*

480 A202 40p ultra., violet blue & gold 55 25

Issued to publicize the work of the student unions in Finnish social life.

Nordic Cooperation Issue

1968, Feb. 28 Engraved *Perf. 11½*

481 A203 40p lt. ultramarine 55 25

See footnote after Denmark No. 455.

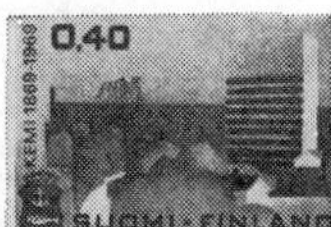

Town Hall and Arms of Kemi
A203a

1969, Mar. 5 Photo. ***Perf. 14***

482 A203a 40p multicolored 55 25

Centenary of the town of Kemi.

Europa Issue, 1969
Common Design Type

1969, Apr. 28 Photo. ***Perf. 14***
Size: 30x20mm.

483 CD12 40p dull rose, vio. bl. & dark blue 1.00 30

I.L.O. Emblem A204 — Armas Järnefelt A205

Lithographed and Engraved

1969, June 2 ***Perf. 11½***

484 A204 40p deep rose & violet blue 55 25

Issued to commemorate the 50th anniversary of the International Labor Organization.

1969, Aug. 14 Photo. ***Perf. 14***

485 A205 40p multicolored 55 25

Centenary of the birth of Armas Järnefelt (1869–1958), composer and conductor. Portrait on stamp by Vilho Sjöström.

Emblems and Flag A206 — Johannes Linnankoski A207

1969, Sept. 19 Photo. ***Perf. 14***

486 A206 40p lt. blue, black, green & lilac 55 25

Issued to publicize the importance of National and International Fairs in Finnish economy.

1969, Oct. 18 Lithographed

487 A207 40p dark brown red & multi. 55 25

Issued to commemorate the centenary of the birth of Johannes Linnankoski (1869–1913), writer.

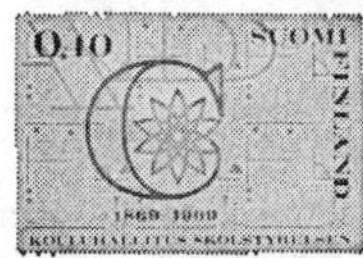

Educational Symbols
A208

Lithographed and Engraved

1969, Nov. 24 ***Perf. 11½***

488 A208 40p gray, vio. & grn. 55 25

Centenary of the Central School Board.

DC-8-62 CF Plane and Helsinki Airport
A209

1969, Dec. 22 Photo. ***Perf. 14***

489 A209 25p sky bl. & multi. 55 25

Golden Eagle
A210

1970, Feb. 10 Litho. ***Perf. 14***

490 A210 30p multicolored 1.10 30

Year of Nature Conservation, 1970.

Swatches in Shape of Factories
A211

1970, Mar. 9 Litho. ***Perf. 14***

491 A211 50p multicolored 55 25

Finnish textile industry.

Molecule Diagram and Factories A212 — UNESCO Emblem and Lenin A213

Atom Diagram and Laurel A214 — U.N. Emblem and Globe A215

1970, Mar. 26 Photo. ***Perf. 14***

492 A212 50p multicolored 55 25

Finnish chemical industry.

1970 Litho. and Engraved

493 A213 30p gold & multi. 75 25
494 A214 30p red & multi. 55 25

Photogravure and Gold Embossed

495 A215 50p blue, violet blue & gold 55 25

Issued to commemorate the 25th anniversary of the United Nations. No. 493 also publicizes the UNESCO-sponsored Lenin Symposium, Tampere, Apr. 6–10. No. 494 also publicizes the Nuclear Data Conference of the Atomic Energy Commission, Otaniemi (Helsinki), June 15–19.

Issue dates: No. 493, Apr. 6; No. 494, June 15; No. 495, Oct. 24.

Handicapped Volleyball Player A216 — Meeting of Auroraseura Society A217

1970, June 27 Litho. ***Perf. 14***

496 A216 50p org., red & blk. 55 25

Issued to publicize the position of handicapped civilians and war veterans in society and their potential contributions to it.

1970, Aug. 15 Photo. ***Perf. 14***

497 A217 50p multicolored 55 25

Issued to commemorate the 200th anniversary of the Auroraseura Society, dedicated to the study of Finnish history, geography, economy and language. The design of the stamp is after a painting by Eero Jarnefelt.

Uusikaarlepyy Arms, Church and 17th Century Building—A218 — Urho Kekkonen, Medal by Aimo Tukiainen A219

Design: No. 499, Arms of Kokkola, harbor, Sports Palace and 17th century building.

1970 ***Perf. 14***

498 A218 50p multicolored 55 25
499 " 50p " 55 25

Issued to commemorate the 350th anniversaries of the towns of Uusikaarlepyy and Kokkola. Issue dates: No. 498, Aug. 21; No. 499, Sept. 17.

1970, Sept. 3 Litho. & Engr.

500 A219 50p ultra., silver & black 55 25

70th birthday of Pres. Urho Kekkonen.

Globe, Maps of U.S., Finland, U.S.S.R.—A220 — Pres. Paasikivi by Essi Renavall A221

Lithographed and Gold Embossed

1970, Nov. 2

501 A220 50p black, blue, pink & gold 70 25

Issued to publicize the Strategic Arms Limitation Talks (SALT) between the U.S. and U.S.S.R., Helsinki, Nov. 2–Dec. 18.

1970, Nov. 27 Photo. ***Perf. 14***

502 A221 50p gold, bright blue & slate 55 25

Centenary of the birth of Juho Kusti Paasikivi (1870–1956), President of Finland.

Cogwheels
A222

1971, Jan. 28 Litho. ***Perf. 14***

503 A222 50p multicolored 55 25

Finnish industry.

Europa Issue, 1971
Common Design Type

1971, May 3 Litho. ***Perf. 14***
Size: 30x20mm.

504 CD14 50p dp. rose, yellow & black 75 25

Tornio Church A223 — Front Page, January 15, 1771 A224

1971, May 12 Litho. ***Perf. 14***

505 A223 50p multicolored 55 25

350th anniversary of the town of Tornio.

1971, June 1 Litho. ***Perf. 14***

506 A224 50p multicolored 55 25

Bicentenary of the Finnish press.

Athletes in Helsinki Stadium
A225

Design: 50p, Running and javelin in Helsinki Stadium.

1971, July 5 Lithographed *Perf. 14*

507 A225 30p multicolored 1.10 30
508 " 50p " 1.10 30

European Athletic Championships.

Sailboats
A226

1971, July 14

509 A226 50p multicolored 1.00 30

International Lightning Class Championships, Helsinki, July 14–Aug. 1.

Silver Tea Pot, Guild's Emblem, Tools
A227

1971, Aug. 6

510 A227 50p lilac & multi. 55 25

600th anniversary of Finnish goldsmiths' art.

"Plastic Buttons and Houses"
A228

Photogravure and Embossed

1971, Oct. 20 ***Perf. 14***

511 A228 50p multicolored 55 25

Finnish plastics industry.

Europa Issue 1972

Common Design Type

1972, May 2 **Litho.** ***Perf. 14***

Size: 20x30mm.

512 CD15 30p dk. red & multi. 75 30
513 " 50p lt. brn. & multi. 1.00 30

Finnish National Theater
A229

1972, May 22 **Litho.** ***Perf. 14***

514 A229 50p lt. vio. & multi. 55 25

Centenary of the Finnish National Theater, founded by Kaarlo and Emilie Bergbom.

Globe, U.S. and U.S.S.R. Flags
A230

1972, June 2

515 A230 50p multicolored 55 25

Strategic Arms Limitation Talks (SALT), final meeting, Helsinki, Mar. 28–May 26; treaty signed, Moscow, May 26.

Map and Arms of Aland
A231

Training Ship Suomen Joutsen
A232

1972, June 9

516 A231 50p multicolored 55 25

50th anniversary of first Provincial Meeting of Aland.

1972, June 19

517 A232 50p orange & multi. 75 30

Tall Ships' Race 1972, Helsinki, Aug. 20.

Costume from Perni, 12th Century
A233

Circle Surrounding Map of Europe
A234

1972, Nov. 19 **Litho.** ***Perf. 13***

Multicolored

518 A233 50p *shown* 45 20
519 " 50p *Married couple, Tenhola, 18th century* 45 20
520 A233 50p *Girl, Nastola, 19th century* 45 20
521 " 50p *Man, Voyni, 19th century* 45 20
522 " 50p *Lapps, Inari, 19th century* 45 20
a. Booklet pane of 10 4.50
Nos. 518-522 (5) 2.25 1.00

Regional costumes. Nos. 518–522 printed se-tenant.

No. 522a contains 2 each of Nos. 518–522.

See Nos. 533–537.

1972, Dec. 11 ***Perf. 14x13½***

523 A234 50p multicolored 1.10 30

Preparatory Conference on European Security and Cooperation.

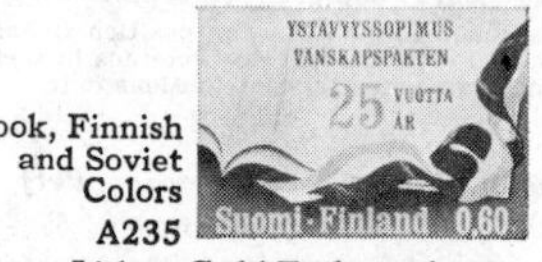

Book, Finnish and Soviet Colors
A235

Litho.; Gold Embossed

1973, Apr. 6 ***Perf. 14***

524 A235 60p gold & multi. 55 25

25th anniversary of the Soviet-Finnish Treaty of Friendship.

Pres. Kyösti Kallio
A236

1973, Apr. 10 **Litho.** ***Perf. 13***

525 A236 60p multicolored 55 25

Centenary of the birth of Kyösti Kallio (1873–1940), president of Finland.

Europa Issue 1973

Common Design Type

1973, Apr. 30 **Photo.** ***Perf. 14***

Size: 31x21mm.

526 CD16 60p blue, brt. blue & emerald 70 25

Nordic Cooperation Issue

Nordic House, Reykjavik
A236a

1973, June 26 **Engr.** ***Perf. 12½***

527 A236a 60p multicolored 75 25
528 " 70p " 75 25

A century of postal cooperation among Denmark, Finland, Iceland, Norway and Sweden, and in connection with the Nordic Postal Conference, Reykjavik.

Map of Europe, "EUROPA" as a Maze
A237

Litho., Embossed

1973, July 3 ***Perf. 13***

529 A237 70p multicolored 55 25

Conference for European Security and Cooperation, Helsinki, July 1973.

Paddling
A238

Radiosonde, WMO Emblem
A239

1973, July 18 **Litho.** ***Perf. 14***

530 A238 60p multicolored 65 25

Canoeing World Championships, Tampere, July 26–29.

1973, Aug. 6 **Litho.** ***Perf. 14***

531 A239 60p multicolored 55 25

Centenary of international meteorological cooperation.

Eliel Saarinen and Design for Parliament, Helsinki
A240

1973, Aug. 20 ***Perf. 12½x13***

532 A240 60p multicolored 55 25

Centenary of the birth of Eliel Saarinen (1873–1950), architect.

Costume Type of 1972

1973, Oct. 10 **Litho.** ***Perf. 13***

Multicolored

533 A233 60p *Woman, Kaukola* 40 15
534 " 60p *Woman, Jaaski* 40 15
535 " 60p *Married couple, Koivisto* 40 15
536 " 60p *Mother and son, Sakyla* 40 15
537 " 60p *Girl, Hainavesi* 40 15
Nos. 533-537 (5) 2.00 75

Regional costumes. Nos. 533–537 printed se-tenant.

DC10–30 Jet
A241

1973, Nov. 1 **Litho.** ***Perf. 14***

538 A241 60p multicolored 55 25

50th anniversary of regular air service, Finnair.

Santa Claus in Reindeer Sleigh
A242

1973, Nov. 15 **Litho.** ***Perf. 14***

539 A242 30p multicolored 75 25

Christmas 1973.

"The Barber of Seville"
A243

1973, Nov. 21

540 A243 60p multicolored 55 25

Centenary of opera in Finland.

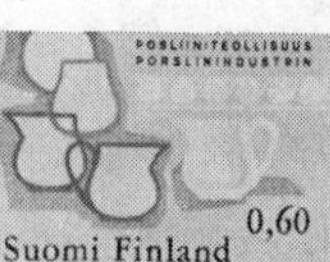

Production of Porcelain Jug
A244

Nurmi, by Waino Aaltonen
A245

1973, Nov. 23

541 A244 60p blue & multi. 55 25

Finnish porcelain.

1973, Dec. 11

542 A245 60p multicolored 65 25

Paavo Nurmi (1897–1973), runner, Olympic winner, 1920–1924–1928.

Arms, Map and Harbor of Hanko
A246

1974, Jan. 10 **Litho.** ***Perf. 14***

543 A246 60p blue & multi. 55 25

Centenary of the town of Hanko.

Ice Hockey
A247

1974, Mar. 5 Lithographed ***Perf. 14***

544 A247 60p multicolored 55 25

European and World Ice Hockey Championships, held in Finland.

Seagulls (7 Baltic States)
A248

1974, Mar. 18 ***Perf. 12½***

545 A248 60p multicolored 55 25

Protection of marine environment of the Baltic Sea.

Goddess of Freedom, by Waino Aaltonen
A249

Ilmari Kianto and Old Pine
A250

Europa Issue, 1974

1974, Apr. 29 **Litho.** ***Perf. 13x12½***

546 A249 70p multicolored 65 30

1974, May 7 ***Perf. 13***

547 A250 60p multicolored 55 25

Ilmari Kianto (1874–1970), writer.

Society Emblem, Symbol
A251

Lithographed and Embossed

1974, June 12 *Perf. 13½x14*

548 A251 60p gold & multi. 55 25

Centenary of Adult Education.

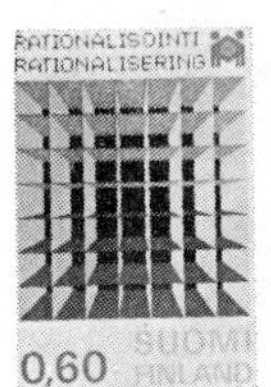

Grid
A252

UPU Emblem
A253

1974, June 14 Litho. *Perf. 14x13½*

549 A252 60p multicolored 55 25

Rationalization Year in Finland, dedicated to economic and business improvements.

1974, Oct. 10 Litho. *Perf. 13½x14*

550 A253 60p multicolored 55 25
551 " 70p " 55 25

Centenary of Universal Postal Union.

Elves Distributing Gifts
A254

Concrete Bridge and Granite Bridge, Aunessilta
A255

1974, Nov. 16 Litho. *Perf. 14x13½*

552 A254 35p multicolored 75 25

Christmas 1974.

Lithographed and Engraved

1974, Dec. 17 *Perf. 14*

553 A255 60p multicolored 55 25

Royal Finnish Directorate of Roads and Waterways, 175th anniversary.

Coat of Arms, 1581
A256

Chimneyless Log Sauna
A256a

Cheese Frames
A257

Carved Wooden Distaffs
A258

Kirvu Weather Vane
A258a

Design: 1.50m, Wood-carved high drinking bowl, 1542.

Perf. 11½; 14 (2m)

1975–79 Engraved

555 A256 10p red lilac ('78) 6 3
a. Bklt. pane of 4 (#555, 2 #557, #561 + label 60
556 A256 20p olive ('77) 12 3
557 " 30p carmine ('77) 18 3
558 " 40p orange 22 3
559 " 50p green ('76) 28 3
560 " 60p blue 35 3
561 " 70p sepia 40 3
562 " 80p dull red & blue green ('76) 45 3
563 " 90p violet ('77) 50 3
564 " 1.10m yellow ('79) 60 8
565 " 1.20m dk. blue ('79) 65 10
566 A258 1.50m multi. ('76) 85 10

Lithographed

567 A256a 2m multi. ('77) 1.15 25

Lithographed and Engraved

568 A257 2.50m multi. ('76) 1.40 25
569 A258 4.50m " ('76) 2.50 35
570 A258a 5m " ('77) 2.80 35
Nos. 555-570 (16) 12.51 1.75

Finland No. 16
A259

Girl Combing Hair, by Magnus Enckell
A260

Lithographed and Typographed

1975, Apr. 26 *Perf. 13*

571 A259 70p multicolored 2.75 2.75

Nordia 75 Philatelic Exhibition, Helsinki, Apr. 26–May 1. Sold only at exhibition for 3m including entrance ticket.

Europa Issue 1975

Design: 90p, Washerwoman, by Tyko Sallinen (1879–1955).

1975, Apr. 28 Litho. *Perf. 13x12½*

572 A260 70p gray & multi. 65 25
573 " 90p tan & multi. 65 25

Balance of Justice, Sword of Legality
A261

Rescue Boat and Sinking Ship
A262

1975, May 7 *Perf. 14*

574 A261 70p vio. bl. & multi. 50 15

Sesquicentennial of State Economy Comptroller's Office.

1975, June 2 Litho. *Perf. 14*

575 A262 70p multicolored 50 15

12th International Salvage Conference, Finland, stressing importance of coordinating sea, air and communications resources in salvage operations.

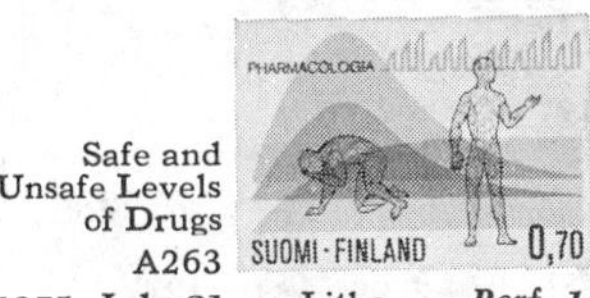

Safe and Unsafe Levels of Drugs
A263

1975, July 21 Litho. *Perf. 14*

576 A263 70p multicolored 50 15

Importance of pharmacological studies and for the 6th International Pharmacology Congress, Helsinki.

Olavinlinna Castle
A264

1975, July 29 *Perf. 13*

577 A264 70p multicolored 50 15

500th anniversary of Olavinlinna Castle.

Swallows over Finlandia Hall
A265

"Men and Women Working for Peace"
A266

1975, July 30

578 A265 90p multicolored 55 25

European Security and Cooperation Conference, Helsinki, July 30–Aug. 1. (The swallows of the design represent freedom, mobility and continuity.)

1975, Oct. 24 Litho. *Perf. 13x12½*

579 A266 70p multicolored 50 15

International Women's Year 1975.

"Continuity and Growth"
A267

Boys as Three Kings and Herod
A268

1975, Oct. 29 *Perf. 13*

580 A267 70p brn. & multi. 50 15

Industrial Art and for the centenary of the Finnish Society of Industrial Art.

1975, Nov. 8 *Perf. 14*

581 A268 40p blue & multi. 35 15

Christmas 1975.

Top Border of State Debenture
A269

Lithographed and Engraved

1976, Jan. 9 *Perf. 11½*

582 A269 80p multicolored 45 15

Centenary of State Treasury.

Glider over Lake Region
A270

1976, Jan. 13 Litho. *Perf. 14*

583 A270 80p multicolored 45 15

15th World Glider Championships, Rayskala, June 13–27.

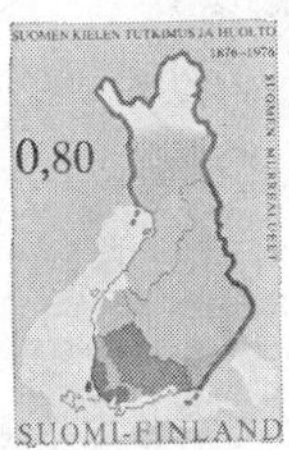

Heikki Klemetti
A271

1976, Feb. 14 Litho. *Perf. 13*

584 A271 80p green & multi. 45 15

Prof. Heikki Klemetti (1876–1953), musician and writer, birth centenary.

Map with Areas of Different Dialects
A272

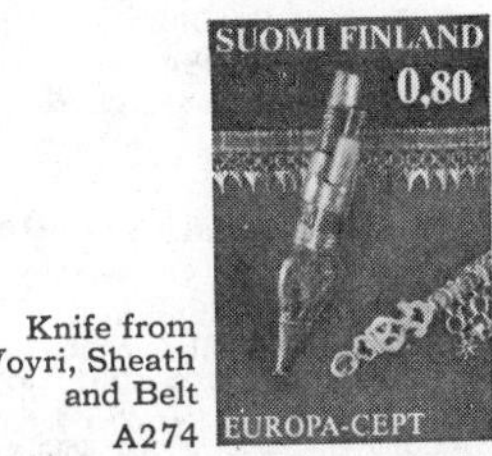

Aino Ackté, by Albert Edelfelt
A273

1976, Mar. 10 Litho. *Perf. 13*

585 A272 80p multicolored 45 15

Finnish Language Society, centenary.

1976, Apr. 23

586 A273 70p yellow & multi. 40 15

Aino Ackté (1876–1944), opera singer, birth centenary.

Europa Issue 1976

Knife from Voyri, Sheath and Belt
A274

1976, May 3 Litho. *Perf. 13*

587 A274 80p vio. bl. & multi. 45 15

Radio and Television
A275

1976, Sept. 9 Litho. *Perf. 13*

588 A275 80p multicolored 45 15

Radio broadcasting in Finland, 50th anniversary.

Christmas Morning Ride to Church
A276

1976, Oct. 23 **Litho.** ***Perf. 14***

589 A276 50p multicolored 30 15

Christmas 1976.

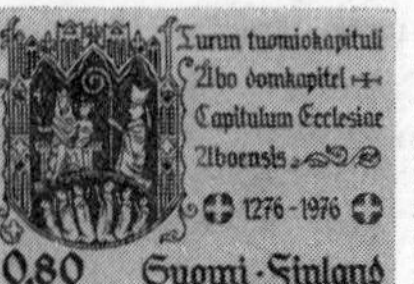

Turku Chapter Seal (Virgin and Child)
A277

1976, Nov. 1 **Litho.** ***Perf. 12½***

590 A277 80p buff, brn. & red 45 15

700th anniversary of the Cathedral Chapter of Turku.

Alvar Aalto, Finlandia Hall, Helsinki
A278

1976, Nov. 4

591 A278 80p multicolored 45 15

Hugo Alvar Henrik Aalto (1898–1976), architect.

Ice Dancers
A280

Five Water Lilies
A281

1977, Jan. 25 **Litho.** ***Perf. 13***

592 A280 90p multicolored 50 25

European Figure Skating Championships, Finland, Jan. 25–29.

Photogravure and Engraved

1977, Feb. 2 ***Perf. 12½***

593 A281 90p bright green & multicolored 50 25
594 " 1m ultra. & multi. 55 35

Nordic countries cooperation for protection of the environment and 25th Session of Nordic Council, Helsinki, Feb. 19.

Icebreaker Rescuing Merchantman
A282

1977, Mar. 2 **Litho.** ***Perf. 13***

595 A282 90p multicolored 50 25

Winter navigation between Finland and Sweden, centenary.

Nuclear Reactor
A283

1977, Mar. 3 ***Perf. 12½x13***

596 A283 90p multicolored 50 25

Opening of nuclear power station on Hästholmen Island.

Europa Issue 1977

Autumn Landscape, Northern Finland
A284

1977, May 2 **Litho.** ***Perf. 12½x13***

597 A284 90p multicolored 50 25

Tree, Birds and Nest
A285

Orthodox Church, Valamo Cloister
A286

1977, May 4 ***Perf. 13x12½***

598 A285 90p multicolored 50 25

75th anniversary of cooperative banks.

1977, May 31 **Litho.** ***Perf. 14***

599 A286 90p multicolored 50 25

Consecration festival of new Orthodox Church at Valamo Cloister, Heinävesi; 800th anniversary of introduction of orthodoxy in Karelia and of founding of Valamo Cloister.

Paavo Ruotsalainen
A287

1977, July 8 **Litho.** ***Perf. 13***

600 A287 90p multicolored 50 25

Paavo Ruotsalainen (1777–1852), lay leader of Pietists in Finland.

People Fleeing Fire and Water
A288

Volleyball
A289

1977, Sept. 14 **Litho.** ***Perf. 14***

601 A288 90p multicolored 50 25

Civil defense for security.

1977, Sept. 15

602 A289 90p multicolored 50 25

European Women's Volleyball Championships, Finland, Sept. 29–Oct. 2.

Children Bringing Water for Sauna
A290

1977, Oct. 25

603 A290 50p multicolored 30 15

Christmas 1977.

Finnish Flag
A291

Wall Telephone, 1880, New Telephone
A292

1977, Dec. 5 **Litho.** ***Perf. 14***

Size: 31x21mm.

604 A291 80p multicolored 50 25

Size: 37x25mm. ***Perf. 13***

605 A291 1m multicolored 55 25

60th anniversary of Finland's declaration of independence.

1977, Dec. 9 ***Perf. 14***

606 A292 1m multicolored 55 25

Centenary of first telephone in Finland.

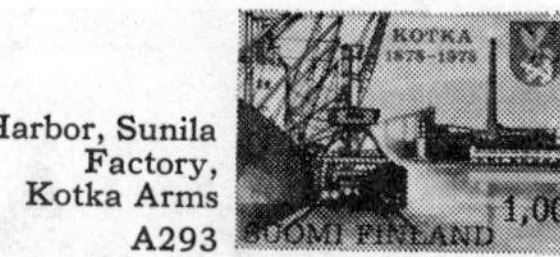

Harbor, Sunila Factory, Kotka Arms
A293

1978, Jan. 2 **Litho.** ***Perf. 14***

607 A293 1m multicolored 55 25

Centenary of founding of Kotka.

Europa Issue 1978

Paimio Sanitarium by Alvar Aalto
A294

Design: 1.20m, Hvittrask studio house, 1902 (horiz.).

1978, May 2 **Litho.** ***Perf. 13***

608 A294 1m multicolored 55 25
609 " 1.20m " 65 30

Rural Bus Service
A295

1978, June 8 **Litho.** ***Perf. 14***

610 A295 1m multicolored 55 25

Eino Leino and Eagle
A296

1978, July 6 **Litho.** ***Perf. 13***

611 A296 1m multicolored 55 25

Eino Leino (1878–1926), poet.

Function Theory and Rhythmical Lines
A297

1978, Aug. 15 **Litho.** ***Perf. 14***

612 A297 1m multicolored 55 25

ICM 78, International Congress of Mathematicians, Helsinki, Aug. 15–23.

Child Feeding Birds
A298

1978, Oct. 23 **Litho.** ***Perf. 14***

613 A298 50p multicolored 28 12

Christmas 1978.

Child, Flowers, IYC Emblem
A299

1979, Jan. 2 **Litho.** ***Perf. 13***

614 A299 1.10m multicolored 60 28

International Year of the Child.

SEMI-POSTAL STAMPS

Arms
SP1 1M+50 P

Typographed.

1922, May 15 *Perf. 14* **Unwmkd.**

B1 SP1 1m+50p gray & red 70 3.50
a. Perf. 13x13½ 4.00

Red Cross Standard SP2 — Symbolic SP3 — Ship of Mercy SP4

1930, Feb. 6

B2 SP2 1m+10p red orange & red 1.75 5.00
B3 SP3 1½m+15p grayish green & red 1.50 5.00
B4 SP4 2m+20p dark blue & red 2.75 13.00

The surtax on this and subsequent similar issues was for the benefit of the Red Cross Society of Finland.

Church in Hattula SP5 — SP8

Designs: 1½m+15p, Castle of Hameenlinna. 2m+20p, Fortress of Viipuri.

1931, Jan. 1 **Engraved**

Cross in Red.

B5 SP5 1m+10p gray green 2.75 6.50
B6 " 1½m+15p lilac brn. 6.50 6.50
B7 " 2m+20p dull blue 1.50 8.50

Typographed.

1931, Oct. 15 *Rouletted 4, 5*

B8 SP8 1m+4m black 22.50 27.50

The surtax was to assist the Postal Museum of Finland in purchasing the Richard Granberg collection of entire envelopes.

Helsinki University Library SP9 — Nikolai Church at Helsinki SP10

Design: 2½m+25p, Parliament Building, Helsinki.

1932, Jan. 1 *Perf. 14*

B9 SP9 1¼m+10p olive bistre & red 1.75 7.50
B10 SP10 2m+20p deep violet & red 1.00 3.50
B11 SP9 2½m+25p light blue & red 1.50 11.00

Bishop Magnus Tawast SP12 — Michael Agricola SP13

Design: 2½m+25p, Isacus Rothovius.

1933, Jan. 20 **Engraved**

B12 SP12 1¼m+10p black brown & red 2.00 2.50
B13 SP13 2m+20p brown violet & red 75 1.00
B14 " 2½m+25p indigo & red 75 1.00

Evert Horn SP15

Designs: 2m+20p, Torsten Stalhandske. 2½m+25p, Jakob (Lazy Jake) de la Gardie.

1934, Jan. **Cross in Red.**

B15 SP15 1¼m+10p brown 90 1.00
B16 " 2m+20p gray lilac 1.50 2.00
B17 " 2½m+25p gray 90 1.00

Mathias Calonius SP18 — Robert Henrik Rehbinder SP21

Designs: 2m+20p, Henrik C. Porthan. 2½m+25p, Anders Chydenius.

1935, Jan. 1 **Cross in Red.**

B18 SP18 1¼m+15p brown 60 80
B19 " 2m+20p gray lilac 1.00 1.50
B20 " 2½m+25p gray blue 60 80

1936, Jan. 1

Designs: 2m+20p, Count Gustaf Mauritz Armfelt. 2½m+25p, Count Arvid Bernard Horn.

Cross in Red.

B21 SP21 1¼m+15p dark brown 75 1.00
B22 " 2m+20p violet brown 3.00 3.50
B23 " 2½m+25p blue 75 1.00

The "Uusimaa" SP24 — The "Turunmaa" SP25

Design: 3½m+35p, The "Hameenmaa."

1937, Jan. 1 **Cross in Red.**

B24 SP24 1¼m+15p brown 1.00 1.00
B25 SP25 2m+20p brown lake 17.50 3.50
B26 SP24 3½m+35p indigo 80 1.25

Aukuste Makipeska SP27 — Skiing SP31

Designs: 1¼m+15p, Robert Isidor Orn. 2m+20p, Edward Bergenheim. 3½m+35p, Johan Mauritz Nordenstam.

1938, Jan. 5 **Engraved**

Cross in Red

B27 SP27 50p+5p dark green 70 90
B28 " 1¼m+15p dk. brown 1.00 1.20
B29 " 2m+20p rose lake 9.00 3.00
B30 " 3½m+35p dark blue 90 1.20

1938, Jan. 18

Designs: 2+1m, Ski jumper. 3.50+1.50m, Skier.

B31 SP31 1.25(m)+75(p) slate green 5.00 9.00
B32 " 2(m)+1(m) dark carmine 5.00 9.00
B33 " 3.50(m)+1.50(m) dark blue 5.00 9.00

Issued to commemorate the ski championships held at Lahti.

Soldier—SP34

1938, May 16

B34 SP34 2m+½m blue 1.75 1.75

Issued to commemorate the victory of the White Army over the Red Guards. The surtax was for the benefit of the members of the Union of the Finnish Front.

Battlefield at Solferino SP35

1939, Jan. 2 **Cross in Scarlet.**

B35 SP35 50p+5p dark green 75 80
B36 " 1¼m+15p dk. brown 75 80
B37 " 2m+20p lake 17.50 3.50
B38 " 3½m+35p dark blue 80 90

Issued in commemoration of the 75th anniversary of the founding of the International Red Cross Society.

Soldiers with Crossbows SP36 — Arms of Finland SP40

Designs: 1¼m+15p, Cavalryman. 2m+20p, Soldier of Charles XII of Sweden. 3½m+35p, Officer and soldier of War with Russia, 1808–1809.

1940, Jan. 3 **Cross in Red.**

B39 SP36 50p+5p dark green 70 1.00
B40 " 1¼m+15p dk. brown 1.00 1.25
B41 " 2m+20p lake 1.00 1.25
B42 " 3½m+35p dp. ultra. 90 1.10

The surtax aided the Finnish Red Cross.

1940, Feb. 15 **Lithographed**

B43 SP40 2m+2m indigo 45 75

The surtax was given to a fund for the preservation of neutrality.

Mason SP41 — Soldier's Emblem SP45

Designs: 1.75m+15p, Farmer plowing. 2.75m+25p, Mother and child. 3.50m+35p, Finnish flag.

1941, Jan. 2 **Engraved**

Cross in Red.

B44 SP41 50p+5p green 30 50
B45 " 1.75m+15p brown 1.00 1.20
B46 " 2.75m+25p brown carmine 5.00 5.00
B47 " 3.50m+35p dp. ultra. 75 1.00

See also Nos. B65–B68.

1941, May 24 **Unwmkd.**

B48 SP45 2.75m+25p bright ultramarine 55 50

The surtax was for the aid of the soldiers who fought in the Russo-Finnish War.

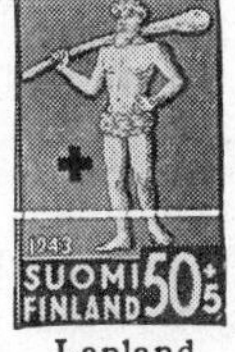

Aaland Arms SP46 — Lapland Arms SP51

Designs: Coats of Arms—1.75m+15p, Nyland. 2.75m+25p, Finland's first arms. 3.50m+35p, Karelia. 4.75m+45p, Satakunta.

1942, Jan. 2 *Perf. 14*

Cross in Red.

B49 SP46 50p+5p green 40 50
B50 " 1.75m+15p brown 1.00 1.25
B51 " 2.75m+25p dark red 1.25 1.50
B52 " 3.50m+35p deep ultramarine 1.25 1.25
B53 " 4.75m+45p dark slate green 90 1.25
Nos. B49-B53 (5) 4.80 5.75

The surtax aided the Finnish Red Cross.

1943, Jan. 6 **Inscribed "1943."**

Designs: Coats of Arms—2m+20p, Hame. 3.50m+35p, Eastern Bothnia. 4.50m+45p, Savo.

Cross in Red.

B54 SP51 50p+5p green 25 50
B55 " 2m+20p brown 60 1.00
B56 " 3.50m+35p dark red 60 1.00
B57 " 4.50m+45p bright ultramarine 1.00 2.00

The surtax aided the Finnish Red Cross.

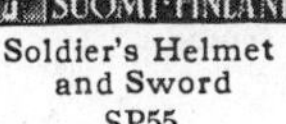

Soldier's Helmet and Sword SP55 — Mother and Children SP56

1943, Feb. 1 *Perf. 13*

B58 SP55 2m+50p dark brn. 30 40
B59 SP56 3.50m+1m brown red 30 40

The surtax was for national welfare.

Red Cross Train
SP57

Designs: 2m+50p, Ambulance. 3.50m+75p, Red Cross Hospital, Helsinki. 4.50m+1m, Hospital plane.

Inscribed "1944"

1944, Jan. 2 *Perf. 14*

Cross in Red.

B60 SP57 50p+25p green 25 25
B61 " 2m+50p sepia 25 35
B62 " 3.50m+75p verm. 25 35
B63 " 4.50m+1m bright ultramarine 70 1.00

The surtax aided the Finnish Red Cross.

Symbols of Peace SP61 — Wrestling SP62

1944, Dec. 1

B64 SP61 3.50m+1.50m dark red brown 20 25

The surtax was for national welfare.

Types of 1941 Inscribed "1945."
Photogravure and Engraved.

1945, May 2 Cross in Red.

B65 SP41 1m+25p green 20 25
B66 " 2m+50p brown 20 25
B67 " 3.50m+75p brown carmine 20 25
B68 " 4.50m+1m dp. ultra. 45 45

The surtax was for the Finnish Red Cross.

1945, Apr. 16 Engraved *Perf. 13½*

Designs: 2+1m, Gymnast. 3.50+1.75m, Runner. 4.50+2.25m, Skier. 7+3.50m, Javelin thrower.

B69 SP62 1(m)+50p bluish green 25 50
B70 " 2(m)+1(m) deep red 25 50
B71 " 3.50(m)+1.75(m) dull violet 25 50
B72 " 4.50(m)+2.25(m) ultramarine 25 50
B73 " 7(m)+3.50(m) dull brown 45 90
Nos. B69-B73 (5) 1.45 2.90

Fishing SP67 — Nurse and Children SP71

Designs: 3+75p, Churning. 5+1.25m, Reaping. 10+2.50m, Logging.

Engraved; Cross Typo. in Red

1946, Jan. 7

B74 SP67 1(m)+25(p) dull green 35 35
B75 " 3(m)+75(p) lilac brown 20 20
B76 " 5(m)+1.25(m) rose red 20 20
a. Red Cross omitted 250.00
B77 SP67 10(m)+2.50(m) ultramarine 25 25

The surtax was for the Finnish Red Cross.

1946, Sept. 2 Engraved

Design: 8+2m, Doctor examining infant.

B78 SP71 5(m)+1m green 20 25
B79 " 8(m)+2m brn. vio. 20 30

The surtax was for the prevention of tuberculosis.

Nos. B78 and B79 Surcharged with New Values in Black.

1947, Apr. 1

B80 SP71 6(m)+1(m) on 5(m)+1m green 20 40
B81 " 10(m)+2(m) on 8(m)+2m brown violet 30 50

The surtax was for the prevention of tuberculosis.

Medical Examination of Infants
SP73 — SP74

Designs: 10+2.50m, Infant held by the feet. 12+3m, Mme. Alli Paasikivi and a child. 20+5m, Infant standing.

1947, Sept. 15 Engraved

B82 SP73 2.50m+1m green 25 40
B83 SP74 6m+1.50m dk. red 30 70
B84 " 10m+2.50m red brown 25 70
B85 SP73 12m+3m deep blue 30 60
B86 SP74 20m+5m dark red violet 30 75
Nos. B82-B86 (5) 1.40 3.15

The surtax was for the prevention of tuberculosis.

Zachris Topelius
SP78

Designs: 7+2m, Fredrik Pacius. 12+3m, Johan L. Runeberg. 20+5m, Fredrik Cygnaeus.

Engraved; Cross Typo. in Red

1948, May 10 *Perf. 14* Unwmkd.

B87 SP78 3m+1m green 20 35
B88 " 7m+2m rose red 20 40
B89 " 12m+3m bright blue 50 60
B90 " 20m+5m dark violet 30 65

The surtax was for the Finnish Red Cross.

Nos. B83, B84 and B86 Surcharged with New Values and Bars in Black.

1948, Sept. 13 Engr. *Perf. 13½*

B91 SP74 7m+2m on 6m+1.50m dark red 1.10 1.25
B92 " 15m+3m on 10m+2.50m red brown 30 90
B93 " 24m+6m on 20m+5m dark red violet 35 1.25

The surtax was for the prevention of tuberculosis.

Tying Birch Boughs SP79 — Wood Anemone SP83

Designs: 9+3m, Bathers in Sauna house. 15+5m, Rural bath house. 30+10m, Cold plunge in lake.

Engraved; Cross Typo. in Red

1949, May 5 *Perf. 13½x14*

B94 SP79 5m+2m dull green 30 40
B95 " 9m+3m dk. car. 30 40
B96 " 15m+5m deep blue 40 80
B97 " 30m+10m dark violet brown 50 1.00

The surtax was for the Finnish Red Cross.

1949, June 2 Engraved

Designs: 9+3m, Wild rose. 15+5m, Coltsfoot.

Inscribed: "1949"

B98 SP83 5m+2m green 30 35
B99 " 9m+3m carmine 30 35
B100 " 15m+5m olive bistre 40 50

The surtax was for the prevention of tuberculosis.

Similar to Type of 1949.

Designs: 5+2m, Water lily. 9+3m, Pasqueflower. 15+5m, Bell flower cluster.

1950, Apr. 1 Inscribed: "1950."

B101 SP83 5m+2m emerald 1.75 1.75
B102 " 9m+3m rose car. 40 60
B103 " 15m+5m blue 60 70

The surtax was for the prevention of tuberculosis.

Hospital Entrance, Helsinki SP84 — Blood Donor's Medal SP86

Design: 12+3m, Giving blood.

Engraved; Cross Typo. in Red

1951, Mar. 17 *Perf. 14* Unwmkd.

B104 SP84 7m+2m chocolate 35 50
B105 " 12m+3m blue violet 35 50
B106 SP86 20m+5m carmine 1.10 1.25

The surtax was for the Finnish Red Cross.

Capercaillie
SP87

Designs: 12m+3m, European cranes. 20m+5m, Caspian terns.

1951, Oct. 26 Engraved

B107 SP87 7m+2m dark green 1.10 1.25
B108 " 12m+3m rose brown 1.00 1.10
B109 " 20m+5m blue 1.00 1.10

The surtax was for the prevention of tuberculosis.

Diver SP88 — Soccer Players SP89

Designs: 20m+3m, Stadum, Helsinki. 25m+4m, Runners.

1951-52

Inscribed: "XV Olympia 1952."

B110 SP88 12m+2m rose car. 45 60
B111 SP89 15m+2m green ('52) 45 60
B112 SP88 20m+3m deep blue 45 60
B113 SP89 25m+4m brown('52) 45 60

Issued to publicize the XV Olympic Games, Helsinki, 1952. The surtax was to help finance the games.

Margin blocks of four of each denomination were cut from regular or perf.-through-margin sheets and pasted by the selvage, overlapping, in a printed folder to create a kind of souvenir booklet. Price $8.

Field Marshal Mannerheim SP90 — Great Titmouse SP91

Engraved; Cross Typo. in Red

1952, Mar. 4

B114 SP90 10m+2m gray 80 90
B115 " 15m+3m rose violet 80 90
B116 " 25m+5m blue 1.00 1.00

The surtax was for the Red Cross.

1952, Dec. 4 Engraved

Designs: 15m+3m, Spotted flycatchers and nest. 25m+5m, Swift.

B117 SP91 10m+2m green 75 75
B118 " 15m+3m plum 1.00 1.00
B119 " 25m+5m deep blue 1.25 1.10

The surtax was for the prevention of tuberculosis.

European Red Squirrel SP92 — Children Receiving Parcel from Welfare Worker SP93

Designs: 15m+3m, Brown bear. 25m+5m, European elk.

Engraved.

1953, Nov. 16 *Perf. 14* Unwmkd.

B120 SP92 10m+2m red brown 75 1.00
B121 " 15m+3m violet 80 1.00
B122 " 25m+5m dk. green 1.25 1.10

The surtax was for the prevention of tuberculosis.

Engraved; Cross Typographed in Red

1954, Mar. 8 *Perf. 11½*

Designs: 15m+3m, Aged woman knitting. 25m+5m, Blind basket-maker and dog.

B123 SP93 10m+2m dark olive green 1.00 1.00
B124 " 15m+3m dark blue 1.00 1.00
B125 " 25m+5m dk. brown 1.00 1.00

The surtax was for the Finnish Red Cross.

Bumblebees and Dandelions SP94 — European Perch SP95

Designs: 15m+3m, Butterfly. 25m+5m, Dragonfly.

Engraved; Cross Typographed in Red

1954, Dec. 7 ***Perf. 14***

B126 SP94 10m+2m brown 1.00 1.00
B127 " 15m+3m carmine 1.00 1.00
B128 " 25m+5m blue 1.00 1.00

The surtax was for the prevention of tuberculosis.

Engraved; Cross Typographed in Red

1955, Sept. 26 ***Perf. 14***

Designs: 15m+3m, Northern pike. 25m+5m, Atlantic salmon.

B129 SP95 10(m)+2(m) dull green 90 75
B130 " 15(m)+3(m) violet brown 90 75
B131 " 25(m)+5(m) dark blue 1.00 1.00

The surtax was for the Anti-Tuberculosis Society.

Gen. von Dobeln in Battle of Juthas, 1808
SP96

Waxwing
SP97

Illustrations by Albert Edelfelter from J. L. Runeberg's "Tales of Ensign Stal": 15(m)+3(m), Col. J. Z. Duncker holding flag. 25(m)+5(m), Son of fallen Soldier.

Engraved; Cross Typographed in Red.

1955, Nov. 24

B132 SP96 10(m)+2(m) deep ultramarine 60 60
B133 " 15(m)+3(m) dark red brown 75 75
B134 " 25(m)+5(m) green 1.00 1.00

The surtax was for the Red Cross.

Engraved; Cross Typographed in Red.

Birds: 20m+3m, Eagle owl. 30m+5m, Mute swan.

1956, Sept. 25 ***Perf. 11½***

B135 SP97 10m+2m dull red brown 75 60
B136 " 20m+3m blue green 75 70
B137 " 30m+5m blue 1.00 90

The surtax was for the Anti-Tuberculosis Society.

Pekka Aulin
SP98

Wolverine (Glutton)
SP99

Portraits: 10m+2m, Leonard von Pfaler. 20m+3m, Gustaf Johansson. 30m+5m, Viktor Magnus von Born.

Engraved; Cross Typographed in Red.

1956, Nov. 26 **Unwmkd.**

B138 SP98 5m+1m grayish green 40 30
B139 " 10m+2m brown 55 45
B140 " 20m+3m magenta 80 60
B141 " 30m+5m lt. ultra. 1.00 70

The surtax was for the Red Cross.

Engraved; Cross Typographed in Red

1957, Sept. 5 ***Perf. 11½***

Designs: 20m+3m, Lynx. 30m+5m, Reindeer.

B142 SP99 10m+2m dull pur. 60 60
B143 " 20m+3m sepia 75 60
B144 " 30m+5m dk. blue 1.00 80

The surtax was for the Anti-Tuberculosis Society. See also Nos. B160–B165.

Red Cross Flag
SP100

Raspberry
SP101

1957, Nov. 25 **Engraved** ***Perf. 14***

Cross in Red.

B145 SP100 10m+2m olive green 1.10 1.00
B146 " 20m+3m maroon 1.10 1.00
B147 " 30m+5m dull bl. 1.10 1.00

Issued to commemorate the 80th anniversary of the Finnish Red Cross.

Type of 1952.

Flowers: 10m+2m, Lily of the valley. 20m+3m, Red clover. 30m+5m, Hepatica.

Engraved; Cross Typographed in Red

1958, May 5 ***Perf. 14*** **Unwmkd.**

B148 SP91 10m+2m green 75 75
B149 " 20m+3m lilac rose 75 75
B150 " 30m+5m ultra. 1.00 1.00

The surtax was for the Anti-Tuberculosis Society.

Engraved; Cross Typographed in Red.

1958, Nov. 20 ***Perf. 11½***

Designs: 20m+3m, Cowberry. 30m+5m, Blueberry.

B151 SP101 10m+2m orange 90 80
B152 " 20m+3m red 1.00 90
B153 " 30m+5m dk. blue 1.10 1.00

The surtax was for the Red Cross.

Daisy
SP102

Reindeer
SP103

Designs: 20m+5m, Primrose. 30m+5m, Cornflower.

Engraved; Cross Typographed in Red.

1959, Sept. 7 **Unwmkd.**

B154 SP102 10m+2m green 1.10 70
B155 " 20m+3m light brown 1.20 75
B156 " 30m+5m blue 1.30 1.00

The surtax was for the Anti-Tuberculosis Society.

Engraved; Cross Typographed in Red

1960, Nov. 24 ***Perf. 11½***

Designs: 20m+3m, Lapp and lasso. 30m+5m, Mountains.

B157 SP103 10m+2m dark gray 75 75
B158 " 20m+3m gray violet 80 80
B159 " 30m+5m rose violet 1.30 1.10

The surtax was for the Red Cross.

Animal Type of 1957.

Designs: 10m+2m, Muskrat. 20m+3m, Otter. 30m+5m, Seal.

Engr.; Cross at right, Typo. in Red

1961, Sept. 4

B160 SP99 10m+2m brown carmine 70 60
B161 " 20m+3m slate blue 80 70
B162 " 30m+5m blue green 1.10 90

The surtax was for the Anti-Tuberculosis Society.

Animal Type of 1957.

Designs: 10m+2m, Hare. 20m+3m, Pine marten. 30m+5m, Ermine.

Engraved; Cross Typographed in Red

1962, Oct. 1

B163 SP99 10m+2m gray 70 60
B164 " 20m+3m dull red brown 80 70
B165 " 30m+5m vio. bl. 1.10 90

The surtax was for the Anti-Tuberculosis Society.

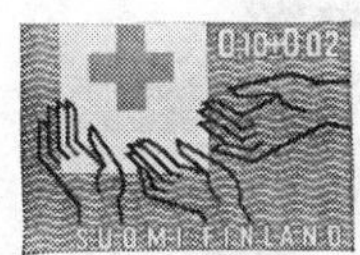

Cross and Outstretched Hands
SP104

Engraved; Cross Typographed in Red

1963, May 8 ***Perf. 11½*** **Unwmkd.**

B166 SP104 10p+2p red. brn. 75 70
B167 " 20p+3p violet 80 75
B168 " 30p+5p green 1.10 1.00

The surtax was for the Red Cross.

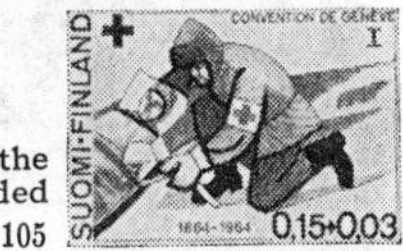

Attending the Wounded
SP105

Red Cross Activities: 25p+4p, Hospital ship. 35p+5p, Prisoner-of-war health examination. 40p+7p, Gift parcel distribution.

Engraved; Cross Typographed in Red

1964, May 26 ***Perf. 11½***

B169 SP105 15p+3p vio. blue 50 40
B170 " 25p+4p green 60 50
B171 " 35p+5p vio. brn. 70 70
B172 " 40p+7p dk. olive green 1.00 1.00

The surtax was for the Red Cross.

Finnish Spitz
SP106

Artificial Respiration
SP107

Designs: 25p+4p, Karelian bear dog. 35p+5p, Finnish hunting dog.

Engraved; Cross Typographed in Red

1965, May 10 ***Perf. 11½***

B173 AP106 15p+3p orge. brn. 80 70
B174 " 25p+4p black 1.00 75
B175 " 35p+5p gray brn. 1.10 90

Surtax for Anti-Tuberculosis Society.

1966, May 7 Lithographed ***Perf. 14***

First Aid: 25p+4p, Skin diver rescuing occupants of submerged car. 35p+5p, Helicopter rescue in winter.

B176 SP107 15p+3p multi. 60 50
B177 " 25p+4p " 75 55
B178 " 35p+5p " 1.00 75

The surtax was for the Red Cross.

Birch
SP108

Horse-drawn Ambulance
SP109

Trees: 25p+4p, Pine. 40p+7p, Spruce.

1967, May 12 **Litho.** ***Perf. 14***

B179 SP108 20p+3p multi. 50 40
B180 " 25p+4p " 50 40
B181 " 40p+7p " 70 70

Surtax for Anti-Tuberculosis Society. See Nos. B185–B187.

1967, Nov. 24 **Litho.** ***Perf. 14***

Designs: 25p+4p, Ambulance, 1967. 40p+7p, Red Cross.

Cross in Red

B182 SP109 20p+3p dull yel., grn. & blk. 45 30
B183 " 25p+4p violet & black 55 50
B184 " 40p+7p dk. grn., blk. & dk. bl. 75 60

The surtax was for the Red Cross.

Tree Type of 1967

Trees: 20p+3p, Juniper. 25+4p, Aspen. 40p+7p, Chokecherry.

1969, May 12 **Litho.** ***Perf. 14***

B185 SP108 20p+3p multi. 45 35
B186 " 25p+4p " 50 45
B187 " 40p+7p " 60 55

Surtax for Anti-Tuberculosis Society.

"On the Lapp's Magic Rock"
SP110

Designs: 30p+6p, Juhani blowing horn on Impivaara Rock (vert.). 50+10p, The Pale Maiden. The designs are from illustrations by Askeli Gallen-Kallelas for "The Seven Brothers" by Aleksis Kivi.

1970, May 8 **Litho.** ***Perf. 14***

B188 SP110 25p+5p multi. 50 30
B189 " 30p+6p " 50 35
B190 " 50p+10p " 60 50

The surtax was for the Red Cross.

Cutting and Loading Timber
SP111

Designs: 30p+6p, Floating logs downstream. 50p+10p, Sorting logs at sawmill.

1971, Apr. 25 **Litho.** ***Perf. 14***

B191 SP111 25p+5p multi. 50 35
B192 " 30p+6p " 50 45
B193 " 50p+10p " 60 50

Surtax for Anti-Tuberculosis Society.

Blood Donor and Nurse
SP112

Designs: 30p+6p, Blood research (microscope, slides; vert.). 50p+10p, Blood transfusion.

1972, Oct. 23

B194 AP112 25p+5p multi. 50 40
B195 " 30p+6p " 50 45
B196 " 50p+10p " 60 60

Surtax was for the Red Cross.

Girl with Lamb, by Hugo Simberg
SP113

Paintings: 40p+10p, Summer Evening, by Vilho Sjöström. 60p+15p, Woman at Mountain Fountain, by Juho Rissanen.

1973, Sept. 12 Litho. *Perf. 13x12½*

B197 SP113	30p+5p multi.		50	40
B198 "	40p+10p	"	50	50
B199 "	60p+15p	"	75	75

Surtax was for the Red Cross. Birth centenaries of featured artists.

Morel
SP114

Mushrooms: 50p+10p, Chanterelle. 60p+15p, Boletus edulis.

1974, Sept. 24 Litho. *Perf. 12½x13*

B200 SP114	35p+5p	multi.	50	40
B201 "	50p+10p	"	50	50
B202 "	60p+15p	"	70	70

Finnish Red Cross.

Echo, by Ellen Thesleff (1869–1954)
SP115

Paintings: 60p+15p, Hilda Wiik, by Maria Wiik (1853–1928). 70p+20p, At Home (old woman in chair), by Helene Schjerfbeck (1862–1946).

1975, Sept. 30 Litho. *Perf. 13x12½*

B203 SP115	40p+10p multi.	50	40
B204 "	60p+15p multi.	55	45
B205 "	70p+20p multi.	65	60

Finnish Red Cross. In honor of International Women's Year paintings by women artists were chosen.

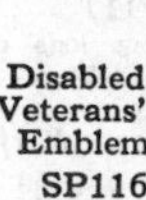

Disabled Veterans' Emblem
SP116

Lithographed and Photogravure

1976, Jan. 15 ***Perf. 14***

B206 SP116	70p+30p multi.	75	75

The surtax was for hospitals for disabled war veterans.

Wedding Procession
SP117

Designs: 70p+15p, Wedding dance (vert.). 80p+20p, Bride, groom, matron and pastor at wedding dinner.

1976, Sept. 15 Litho. *Perf. 13*

B207 SP117	50p+10p	multi.	35	30
B208 "	70p+15p	"	50	50
B209 "	80p+20p	"	55	55

Surtax for Anti-Tuberculosis Society.

Disaster Relief
SP118

Designs: 80p+15p, Community work. 90p+20p, Blood transfusion service.

1977, Jan. 19 Litho. *Perf. 14*

B210 SP118	50p+10p	multi.	35	30
B211 "	80p+15p	"	55	50
B212 "	90p+20p	"	65	55

Finnish Red Cross centenary.

Long-distance Skiing
SP119

Design: 1m+50p, Ski jump.

1977, Oct. 5 Litho. *Perf. 13*

B213 SP119	80p+40p	multi.	65	60
B214 "	1m+50p	"	85	75

Surtax was for World Ski Championships, Lahti, Feb. 17–26, 1978.

Saffron Milkcap
SP120

Edible Mushrooms: 80p+15p, Parasol mushrooms (vert.). 1m+20p, Gypsy mushrooms.

1978, Sept. 13 Litho. *Perf. 13*

B215 SP120	50p+10p	multi.	35	30
B216 "	80p+15p	"	55	50
B217 "	1m+20p	"	65	60

Surtax was for Red Cross.

AIR POST STAMPS.

No. 178 Overprinted in Red

ZEPPELIN 1930

1930, Sept. 24 *Perf. 14* Unwmkd.

C1 A28 10m gray lilac		110.00	120.00
	a. "1830" for "1930"	1600.00	1700.00

Issued Sept. 24, 1930; overprinted expressly for use on mail carried in "Graf Zeppelin" on her return flight from Finland to Germany on Sept. 24, 1930, after which trip the stamps ceased to be valid for postage. Forgeries of Nos. C1 and C1a are almost always on No. 205, rather than No. 178.

Douglas DC-2
AP1

1944 Engraved

C2 AP1	3.50m dark brown	35	45

Issued to commemorate the 20th anniversary of Air Transport Service, 1923-43.

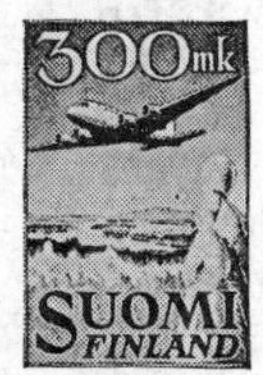

Douglas DC-6 Over Winter Landscape
AP2

1950, Feb. 13

C3 AP2	300m blue	3.50	2.00

Available also for ordinary postage.

Type of 1950 Redrawn

1958, Jan. 20 *Perf. 11½*

C4 AP2	300(m) blue	6.00	1.00

On No. C4 "mk" is omitted.

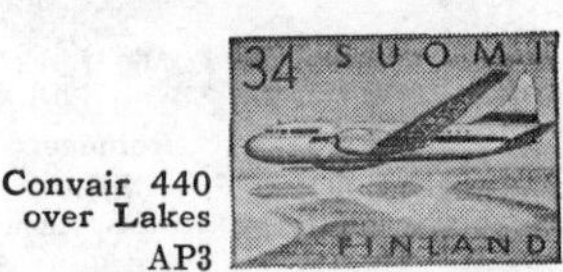

Convair 440 over Lakes
AP3

1958, Oct. 31 *Perf. 11½* Unwmkd.

C5 AP3	34m blue	90	45

No. C5 Surcharged with New Value and Bars

1959, Apr. 5

C6 AP3	45m on 34m blue	1.50	1.25

1959, Nov. 2

C7 AP3	45m blue	90	30

1963, Feb. 15

C8 AP3	45p blue	35	15

DC-6 Type of 1950

1963, Oct. 10

C9 AP2	3m blue	1.75	35

Convair Type of 1958

1970, July 15

C10 AP3	57p ultramarine	40	12

MILITARY STAMPS.

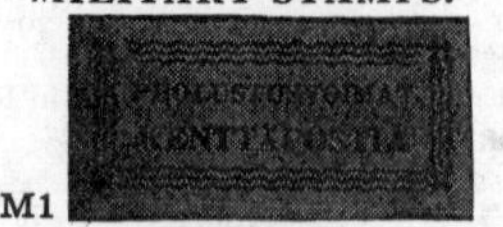

M1

Typographed.

1941, Nov. 1 *Imperf.* Unwmkd.

M1 M1	(4m) *dark orange*	20	40

No. M1 has simulated roulette printed in black.

Type of 1930-46 Overprinted in Black

KENTTÄ-POSTI FÄLTPOST

1943, Oct. 16 *Perf. 14*

M2 A26	2m deep orange	15	30
M3 "	3½m greenish blue	15	25

Post Horn and Sword
M2

1943 Size: 29½x19½mm.

M4 M2	(2m) green	15	25
M5 "	(3m) rose violet	15	30

1944 Size: 20x16mm.

M6 M2	(2m) green	15	25
M7 "	(3m) rose violet	15	25

Post Horns and Arms of Finland
M3

1963, Sept. 26 Litho. *Perf. 14*

M8 M3	violet blue	*125.00*	*130.00*

Used during maneuvers Sept. 30–Oct. 5, 1963. Valid from Sept. 26.

PARCEL POST STAMPS

AUTOPAKETTI
0025290
1 mk
No 6 BILPAKET

PP1

Wmkd. Rose & Triangles Multiple

Rouletted 6 on 2 or 3 Sides

1949–50 Typographed

Q1	PP1	1m brt. grn. & blk.	1.00	3.50
Q2	"	5m red & black	5.00	6.00
Q3	"	20m orange & black	7.50	7.50
Q4	"	50m bl. & blk. ('50)	2.50	6.00
Q5	"	100m brn. & blk. ('50)	2.50	6.00
		Nos. Q1-Q5 (5)	18.50	29.00

Mail Bus
PP2

Engraved

1952–58 *Perf. 14* Unwmkd.

Q6	PP2	5m carmine rose	50	80
Q7	"	20m orange	70	1.50
Q8	"	50m blue ('54)	1.10	2.50
Q9	"	100m brown ('58)	2.00	4.00

Mail Bus
PP3

1963 *Perf. 12*

Q10	PP3	5p red & black	25	25
Q11	"	20p orange & black	25	25
Q12	"	50p blue & black	30	30
Q13	"	1m brown & black	60	75

Nos. Q1–Q13 were issued only in booklets: panes of 6 for Nos. Q1–Q5, 10 for Nos. Q6–Q9 and 5 for Nos. Q10–Q13.

Used prices are for regular postal or mail-bus cancels. Pen strokes, cutting or other cancels sell for half as much.

FIUME

(fyōō'mȧ)

LOCATION—A city and surrounding territory on the Adriatic Sea.

GOVT.—Formerly a part of Italy.

AREA—8 sq. mi.

POP.—44,956 (estimated 1924).

Formerly a port of Hungary, Fiume was claimed by Jugoslavia and Italy following World War I. During the discussion, the poet, Gabriele d'Annunzio, organized his legionnaires and seized Fiume, together with the islands of Arbe, Carnaro and Veglia, in the name of Italy. Jugoslavia recognized Italy's claim and the city was annexed in January, 1924.

100 Filler = 1 Korona
100 Centesimi = 1 Corona (1919)
100 Centesimi = 1 Lira

Hungarian Stamps of 1916-18 Overprinted FIUME

Wmkd. Double Cross. (137)

1918 *Perf. 15*

On Stamps of 1916.

White Numerals.

1	A8	10f rose	30.00	10.00
2	"	15f violet	17.50	6.50

Nos. 1–2 overprints are handstamped.

On Stamps of 1916–18.

Colored Numerals.

3	A9	2f brown orange	40	20
4	"	3f red violet	40	20
5	"	5f green	40	20
6	"	6f greenish blue	40	20
7	"	10f rose red	30.00	8.00
8	"	15f violet	40	20
9	"	20f gray brown	40	20
10	"	25f deep blue	65	40
11	"	35f brown	85	60
12	"	40f olive green	8.00	2.00

White Numerals

13	A10	50f red violet & lilac	80	50
14	"	75f bright blue & pale blue	2.00	60
15	"	80f green & pale green	80	50
16	"	1k red brown & claret	8.00	2.00
17	"	2k olive brn. & bis.	60	50
18	"	3k dark violet & indigo	4.00	2.00
19	"	5k dark brown & light brown	10.00	5.00
20	"	10k violet brown & violet	90.00	60.00

Inverted or double overprints exist on most of Nos. 4–15.

On Stamps of 1918.

21	A11	10f scarlet	50	25
22	"	20f dark brown	50	20
23	A12	40f olive green	6.00	1.50

The overprint on Nos. 3–23 was applied both by press and handstamp. Prices are for the less costly. Prices of Nos. 7, 12, 20 and 23 are for handstamps.

Forgeries of Nos. 1–23 abound.

A1 A2

Postage Due Stamps of Hungary, 1915-20 Overprinted and Surcharged in Black.

1919, Jan.

24	A1	45f on 6f green & red	2.25	60
25	"	45f on 20f " "	2.25	60

Hungarian Savings Bank Stamp Surcharged in Black.

1919, Jan. 29

26	A2	15f on 10f dk. violet	2.25	60

"Italy"
A3

Italian Flag on Clock-Tower in Fiume
A4

"Revolution"
A5

Sailor Raising Italian Flag at Fiume (1918)
A6

Lithographed.

1919 *Perf. 11½* **Unwmkd.**

27	A3	2c dull blue	15	15
28	"	3c gray brown	15	15
29	"	5c yellow green	15	15
30	A4	10c rose	15	15
31	"	15c violet	15	15
32	"	20c green	15	15
33	A5	25c dark blue	15	15
34	A6	30c deep violet	15	15
35	A5	40c brown	22	22
36	"	45c orange	15	15
37	A6	50c yellow green	15	15
38	"	60c claret	15	15
39	"	1cor brown orange	15	15
40	"	2cor bright blue	22	15
41	"	3cor orange red	22	15
42	"	5cor deep brown	22	22
43	"	10cor olive green	1.50	1.00
		Nos. 27–43 (17)	4.18	3.54

The earlier printings of January and February are on thin grayish paper and in sheets of 70. A March printing is on semi-transparent white paper, also in sheets of 70. An April printing is on white paper of medium thickness and in sheets of 100. Part-perforate examples of most of this series are known.

A7

A8

A9

A10

1919 *Perf. 11½*

46	A7	5c yellow green	15	15
47	A8	10c rose	15	15
48	A9	30c violet	22	15
49	A10	40c yellow brown	60	40
50	"	45c orange	22	15
51	A9	50c yellow green	22	15
52	"	60c claret	22	15
	a.	Perf. 13x12½	22.50	22.50
53	A9	10cor olive green	1.15	75
	a.	Perf. 13x12½	22.50	15.00
	b.	Perf. 10½	22.50	15.00
		Nos. 46–53 (8)	2.93	2.05

Five other denominations—25c, 1cor, 2cor, 3cor and 5cor—were not officially issued. Some copies of the 25c are known canceled.

Stamps of 1919 Handstamp Surcharged FRANCO 5

1919–20

58	A4	5c on 20c green ('20)	15	15
59	A10	5c on 25c blue	15	15
60	A5	10c on 45c orange	15	15
61	A9	15c on 30c violet ('20)	15	15
62	A10	15c on 45c orange	15	15
63	A9	15c on 60c claret ('20)	15	15
64	A6	25c on 50c yellow green ('20)	1.00	55
65	A9	25c on 50c yellow green ('20)	15	15
66	A6	55c on 1cor brn. org.	1.15	60
67	"	55c on 2cor brt. blue	1.15	85
68	"	55c on 3cor org. red	1.20	85
69	"	55c on 5cor dp. brn.	1.20	85
70	A9	55c on 10cor olive green	1.35	1.25
		Nos. 58–70 (13)	8.10	6.00

Semi-Postal Stamps of 1919 Surcharged:

Valore globale Cent. 5
a

Valore globale Cent. 45
b

1919–20

73	SP6	(a)	5c on 5c green	15	15
74	"	(")	10c on 10c rose	15	15
75	"	(")	15c on 15c gray	15	15
76	"	(")	20c on 20c orange	15	15
77	SP9	(")	25c on 25c bl. ('20)	15	15
78	SP7	(b)	45c on 45c olive green	15	15
79	"	(")	60c on 60c rose	15	15
80	"	(")	80c on 80c violet	15	15
81	"	(")	1cor on 1cor slate	15	15
82	SP8	(a)	2cor on 2cor red brown	30	30
83	"	(")	3cor on 3cor black brown	60	60
84	"	(")	5cor on 5cor yellow brown	90	90
85	"	(")	10cor on 10cor dark violet ('20)	30	30
			Nos. 73–85 (13)	3.45	3.45

Double or inverted surcharges, or imperf. varieties, exist on most of Nos. 73–85.

There were three settings of the surcharges on Nos. 73–85 except No. 77 which is known only with one setting.

Gabriele d'Annunzio
A11

Severing the Gordian Knot
A12

Pale Buff Background.

1920, Sept. 12 Typo. *Perf. 11½*

86	A11	5c green	15	15
87	"	10c carmine	15	15
88	"	15c dark gray	15	15
89	"	20c orange	22	15
90	"	25c dark blue	38	15
91	"	30c red brown	45	15
92	"	45c olive gray	55	15
93	"	50c lilac	55	15
94	"	55c bistre	60	15
95	"	1 l black	1.00	45
96	"	2 l red violet	2.75	75
97	"	3 l dark green	2.75	1.15
98	"	5 l brown	2.75	1.15
99	"	10 l gray violet	3.00	1.65
		Nos. 86–99 (14)	15.45	6.50

Counterfeits of Nos. 86 to 99 are plentiful.

1920, Sept. 12

Designs: 10c, Ancient emblem of Fiume. 20c Head of "Fiume." 25c, Hands holding daggers.

100	A12	5c green	10.00	3.75
101	"	10c deep rose	2.25	75
102	"	20c brown orange	3.00	75
103	"	25c dark blue	15.00	6.00

These stamps were issued to mark the anniversary of the occupation of Fiume by d'Annunzio. They were available for franking the correspondence of the legionnaires on the day of issue only, Sept. 12, 1920

Counterfeits of Nos. 100 to 103 are plentiful.

Commemorative Stamps of 1920 Overprinted in Black or Red and New Values — Reggenza Italiana del Carnaro

1920, Nov. 20

104	A12	1c on 5c green	15	15
105	"	2c on 25c blue (R)	15	15
106	"	5c green	15	15
107	"	10c rose	15	15
108	"	15c on 10c rose	15	15
109	"	15c on 20c brn. orange	15	15
110	"	15c on 25c blue (R)	22	22
111	"	20c brown orange	15	15
112	"	25c blue (R)	15	15
113	"	25c blue (Bk)	37.50	22.50
114	"	25c on 10c rose	1.50	1.00
115	"	50c on 20c brn. org.	15	15
116	"	55c on 5c green	10	10
117	"	1 l on 10c rose	1.85	1.15
118	"	1 l on 25c blue (R)	165.00	67.50
119	"	2 l on 5c green	3.75	1.85
120	"	5 l on 10c rose	30.00	3.75
121	"	10 l on 20c brown orange	100.00	25.00
		Nos. 104-121 (18)	341.27	124.42

The Fiume Legionnaires of d'Annunzio occupied the islands of Arbe and Veglia in the Gulf of Carnaro from Nov. 13, 1920, until Jan. 5, 1921.

Varieties of overprint or surcharge exist for most of Nos. 104–121.

Same Overprint with **ARBE** at top

1920

122	A12	5c green	75	45
123	"	10c rose	1.50	75
124	"	20c brown orange	2.25	1.00
125	"	25c deep blue	7.50	3.50
126	"	50c on 20c brn. org.	3.00	1.50
127	"	55c on 5c green	3.00	1.50
		Nos. 122–127 (6)	18.00	8.70

The overprint on Nos. 122–125 comes in two widths: 11mm. and 14mm. Prices are for the 11mm. width.

Same Overprint with **VEGLIA** at top.

1920

128	A12	5c green	75	45
129	"	10c rose	1.50	75
130	"	20c brown orange	2.25	1.00
131	"	25c deep blue	7.50	3.50
132	"	50c on 20c brn. org.	3.00	1.50
133	"	55c on 5c green	3.00	1.50
		Nos. 128–133 (6)	18.00	8.70

The overprint on Nos. 128–131 comes in two widths: 17mm. and 19mm. Prices are for the 17mm. width.

Nos. 122–133 exist with double and inverted overprints.

Counterfeits of these overprints exist.

Stamps of 1920 Overprinted — Governo Provvisorio

1921, Feb. 2

Pale Buff Background.

134	A11	5c green	15	15
135	"	10c carmine	15	15
136	"	15c dark gray	15	15
137	"	20c orange	15	15
138	"	25c dark blue	15	15
139	"	30c red brown	22	15
140	"	45c olive gray	22	15
141	"	50c lilac	22	15
142	"	55c bistre	30	15
143	"	1 l black	25.00	25.00

144 A11 2 l red violet 1.00 60
145 " 3 l dark green 1.85 1.50
146 " 5 l brown 1.85 60
147 " 10 l gray violet 2.75 2.50

With Additional Surcharge LIRE UNA

148 A11 1 l on 30c red brown 45 22
Nos. 134-148 (15) 34.61 31.77

Most of Nos. 134-143, 148 and E10-E11 exist with inverted or double overprint.
See Nos. E10-E11.

First Constituent Assembly.

24 - IV - 1921

Semi-Postal Stamps of 1919 Overprinted

1921, Apr. 24

149 SP6 5c blue green 45 15
150 " 10c rose 38 15
151 " 15c gray 38 15
152 " 20c orange 38 15
153 SP7 45c olive green 55 30
154 " 60c carmine rose 70 55
155 " 80c bright violet 90 70

With Additional Overprint "L".

156 SP7 1 l on 1cor dark slate 1.25 75
157 SP8 2 l on 2cor red brown 4.00 22
158 " 3 l on 3cor blk. brn. 8.50 5.25
159 " 5 l on 5cor yel. brn. 10.00 30
160 " 10 l on 10cor dk. vio. 11.00 8.50
Nos. 149-160 (12) 38.49 17.17

The overprint exists inverted on several denominations.

Second Constituent Assembly.

"Constitution" Issue of 1921 With Additional Overprint "1922".

1922

161 SP6 5c blue green 1.10 22
162 " 10c rose 15 22
163 " 15c gray 2.25 30
164 " 20c orange 15 22
165 SP7 45c olive green 15 22
166 " 60c carmine rose 15 22
167 " 80c bright violet 15 22
168 " 1 l on 1 cor dark slate 15 22
169 SP8 2 l on 2 cor red brown 15 22
170 " 3 l on 3 cor blk. brn. 22 30
171 " 5 l on 5 cor yel. brn. 30 30
Nos. 161-171 (11) 4.92 2.66

Nos. 161-171 have the overprint in heavier type than Nos. 149-160 and "IV" in Roman instead of sans-serif numerals.
The overprint exists inverted or double on almost all values.

Venetian Ship
A16

Roman Arch
A17

St. Vitus
A18

Rostral Column
A19

1923, Mar. *Perf. 11½*

Pale Buff Background.

172 A16 5c blue green 15 15
173 " 10c violet 15 15
174 " 15c brown 15 15
175 A17 20c orange red 15 15
176 " 25c dark gray 15 15
177 " 30c dark green 15 15
178 A18 50c dull blue 15 15
179 " 60c rose 15 15
180 " 1 l dark blue 15 15
181 A19 2 l violet brown 1.50 38
182 " 3 l olive bistre 9.00 3.50
183 " 5 l yellow brown 3.75 90
Nos. 172-183 (12) 15.60 6.13

Stamps of 1923 Overprinted REGNO D'ITALIA

1924

Pale Buff Background.

184 A16 5c blue green 15 22
185 " 10c violet 15 22
186 " 15c brown 15 22
187 A17 20c orange red 15 22
188 " 25c dark gray 15 22
189 " 30c dark green 15 22
190 A18 50c dull blue 15 22
191 " 60c red 15 22
192 " 1 l dark blue 15 22
193 A19 2 l violet brown 50 65
194 " 3 l olive 1.10 1.25
195 " 5 l yellow brown 1.35 1.65
Nos. 184-195 (12) 4.30 5.53

The overprint exists inverted on almost all values.

Stamps of 1923 Overprinted

22 Febb. 1924

1924

Pale Buff Background.

196 A16 5c blue green 15 22
197 " 10c violet 15 22
198 " 15c brown 15 22
199 A17 20c orange red 15 22
200 " 25c dark gray 15 22
201 " 30c dark green 15 22
202 A18 50c dull blue 15 22
203 " 60c red 15 22
204 " 1 l dark blue 15 22
205 A19 2 l violet brown 45 60
206 " 3 l olive 60 75
207 " 5 l yellow brown 60 75
Nos. 196-207 (12) 3.00 4.08

Postage stamps of Fiume were superseded by stamps of Italy.

SEMI-POSTAL STAMPS.

Semi-Postal Stamps of Hungary, 1916-17. Overprinted FIUME

Wmkd. Double Cross. (137)

1918 *Perf. 15*

B1 SP3 10f+2f rose 90 38
a. Inverted overprint 15.00 7.50
B2 SP4 15f+2f dull violet 90 30
a. Inverted overprint 11.00 5.00
B3 SP5 40f+2f brown car. 1.25 55
a. Inverted overprint 11.00 5.00

Examples of Nos. B1-B3 with overprint hand-stamped sell for higher prices.

Statue of Romulus and Remus Being Suckled by Wolf
SP6

Venetian Galley
SP7

Church of St. Mark's, Venice
SP8

Typographed.

1919 *Perf. 11½* **Unwmkd.**

B4 SP6 5c+5 l blue green 2.25 1.00
B5 " 10c+5 l rose 2.25 1.00
B6 " 15c+5 l dark gray 2.25 1.00
B7 " 20c+5 l orange 2.25 1.00
B8 SP7 45c+5 l olive green 2.25 1.00
B9 " 60c+5 l car. rose 2.25 1.00
B10 " 80c+5 l brt. violet 2.25 1.00
B11 " 1cor+5 l dark slate 2.25 1.00
B12 SP8 2cor+5 l red brown 2.25 1.00
B13 " 3cor+5 l black brown 2.25 1.00
B14 " 5cor+5 l yel. brown 2.25 1.00
B15 " 10cor+5 l dark violet 2.25 1.00
Nos. B4-B15 (12) 27.00 12.00

Nos. B4 to B15 were issued in commemoration of the 200th day of peace. The surtax aided Fiume students in Italy. "Posta di Fiume" is printed on the back of Nos. B4-B16.

Dr. Antonio Grossich
SP9

1919, Sept. 20

B16 SP9 25c + 2 l blue 22 15

The surtax benefited the Dr. Grossich Foundation.

SPECIAL DELIVERY STAMPS

Special Delivery Stamp of Hungary, 1916, Overprinted FIUME

1918 *Perf. 15* **Wmk. 137**

E1 SD1 2f gray green & red 22 15

No. E1 with overprint handstamped sells for more.

SD3

Typographed.

1920 *Perf. 11½* **Unwmkd.**

E2 SD3 30c slate blue 55 22
E3 " 50c rose 55 22

Nos. 102 and 100 Surcharged Reggenza Italiana del Carnaro 50 50 ESPRESSO

1920

E4 A12 30c on 20c brown orange 35.00 10.00
E5 " 50c on 5c green 9.00 3.00

Same Surcharge with **ARBE** at top.

E6 A12 30c on 20c brown orange 42.50 13.00
E7 " 50c on 5c green 18.50 5.25

Overprint on Nos. E6-E7 is 11mm. wide.

Same Surcharge with **VEGLIA** at top.

E8 A12 30c on 20c brown orange 42.50 13.00
E9 " 50c on 5c green 18.50 5.25

Overprint on Nos. E8-E9 is 17mm. wide.

Nos. E2 and E3 Overprinted Governo Provvisorio

1921

E10 SD3 30c slate blue 55 22
E11 " 50c rose 55 22

Fiume in 16th Century
SD4

1923 *Perf. 11, 11½.*

E12 SD4 60c rose & buff 15 15
E13 " 2 l dark blue & buff 22 30

Stamps of 1923 Overprinted

1924

E14 SD4 60c carmine & buff 15 22
E15 " 2 l dark blue & buff 22 30

Overprinted

22 Febbraio 1924

E16 SD4 60c carmine & buff 15 22
E17 " 2 l dark blue & buff 22 30

POSTAGE DUE STAMPS.

Postage Due Stamps of Hungary, 1915-1916, Overprinted FIUME

1918 *Perf. 15* **Wmk. 137**

J1 D1 6f green & black 60.00 15.00
J2 " 12f " " 52.50 15.00
J3 " 50f " " 30.00 7.50
J4 " 1f green & red 7.50 3.75
J5 " 2f " " 22 15
J6 " 5f " " 3.00 1.15
J7 " 6f " " 22 15
J8 " 10f " " 4.50 2.25
J9 " 12f " " 22 15
J10 " 15f " " 6.00 3.75

J11 D1 20f green & red 30 15
J12 " 30f " " 6.00 3.00

The overprint on Nos. J1–J12 was applied both by press and handstamp. Prices are for the less costly. Inverted and double overprints exist. Excellent forgeries exist.

Eagle
D2

Typographed

1919 ***Perf. 11½.*** **Unwmkd.**

J13 D2 2c brown 15 15
J14 " 5c brown 15 15

Semi-Postal Stamps of 1919 with Overprint "Valore Globale" Surcharged:

Segnatasse

L. 0.02

a

1921

J15 SP6 2c on 15c gray 30 30
J16 " 4c on 10c rose 15 15
J17 SP9 5c on 25c blue 15 15
J18 SP6 6c on 20c orange 15 15
J19 " 10c on 20c orange 55 45

Surcharged:

Segnatasse

L. 0.20

b

J20 SP7 20c on 45c olive green 38 38
J21 " 30c on 1cor dark slate 38 45
J22 " 40c on 80c violet 22 22
J23 " 50c on 60c carmine 30 30
J24 " 60c on 45c olive green 38 38
J25 " 80c on 45c olive green 38 38

Surcharged type "a."

J26 SP8 1 l on 2 cor red brn. 75 75
Nos. J15–J26 (12) 4.09 4.06

See note below No. 85 regarding settings of "Valore Globale" overprint.

NEWSPAPER STAMPS.

Newspaper Stamp of Hungary, 1914, Overprinted FIUME

1918 ***Imperf.*** **Wmk. 137**

P1 N5 (2f) orange 22 15

No. P1 with overprint handstamped sells for more.

Eagle
N1

1919 ***Perf. 11½*** **Unwmkd.**

P2 N1 2c deep buff 22 22

Re-engraved

P3 N1 2c deep buff 38 38

In the re-engraved stamp the top of the "2" is rounder and broader, the feet of the eagle show clearly and the diamond at bottom has six lines instead of five.

Steamer
N2

1920

P4 N2 1c gray green 15 15

No. P4 exists imperf.

See note on FIUME-KUPA Zone, Italian Occupation, after Jugoslavia No. NJ22.

FRANCE

(frâns)

LOCATION—Western Europe.
GOVT.—Republic.
AREA—212,918 sq. mi.
POP.—53,080,000 (est. 1977).
CAPITAL—Paris.

100 Centimes = 1 Franc

Prices of early French stamps vary according to condition. Quotations for Nos. 1–48 are for fine copies. Very fine to superb specimens sell at much higher prices, and inferior or poor copies sell at reduced prices, depending on the condition of the individual specimen.

Ceres
A1

FORTY CENTIMES.

4 Type I. 4 Type II.

Typographed

1849–50 ***Imperf.*** **Unwmkd.**

1 A1 10c bistre, *yellowish* ('50) 800.00 225.00
a. 10c dk. bistre, *yellowish* 1000.00 250.00
b. 10c greenish bis. 2000.00 450.00
c. Tête bêche pr. *35,000.00* *7000.00*
2 " 15c yellow green, *greenish* ('50) 6000.00 750.00
a. 15c green, *greenish* 6000.00 750.00
b. Tête bêche pair *85,000.00*
3 " 20c black, *yellowish* 225.00 35.00
a. 20c black 300.00 45.00
b. 20c black, *buff* 1350.00 275.00
c. Tête bêche pair 3250.00 3000.00
4 " 20c dark blue 750.00
a. 20c blue, *bluish* 900.00
b. 20c blue, *yellowish* 1100.00
c. Tête bêche pair *20,000.00*
6 " 25c light blue, *bluish* 2250.00 27.50
a. 25c blue, *bluish* ('50) 2750.00 45.00
b. 25c blue, *yellowish* 2500.00 40.00
c. Tête bêche pr. *70,000.00* *5500.00*
7 " 40c org., *yellowish* (I) ('50) 1200.00 325.00
a. 40c orange vermilion, *yellowish* (I) 1400.00 400.00
b. 40c orange, *yellowish* (II) *9500.00* *2400.00*
c. Pair, types I and II *15,000.00* *4500.00*
8 A1 1fr dull org. red *20,000.00* *9000.00*
a. 1fr verm., *yellowish* *30,000.00* *10,000.00*
b. Tête bêche pair *150,000.00* *100,000.00*
c. 1fr pale verm. ("Vervelle") *8500.00*
9 " 1fr dk. carmine, *yellowish* 3500.00 650.00
a. Tête bêche pair *70,000.00* *12,000.00*
b. 1fr brown carmine *7000.00* 1000.00
c. 1fr lt. carmine *4000.00* 800.00

No. 4, which lacks gum, was not issued due to a rate change to 25c after the stamps were prepared.

An ungummed sheet of No. 8c was found in 1895 among the effects of Anatole A. Hulot, the printer. It was sold to Ernest Vervelle, a Parisian dealer, by whose name the stamps are known.

Nos. 1, 4, 6, 7 and 13 are of similar designs and colors to French Colonies Nos. 9, 11, 12, 14, and 8. There are numerous shades of each. They can seldom be correctly allocated except by the cancellations.

See Nos. 329–329e, 612–613, 624.

1862 **Re-issue.**

1d A1 10c bistre 250.00
2d " 15c yellow green 300.00
3d " 20c black, *yellowish* 210.00
4d " 20c blue 210.00
6d " 25c blue 210.00
7d " 40c orange (I) 250.00
7e " 40c orange (II) 8000.00
9d " 1fr pale lake 300.00

The re-issues are in lighter colors and on whiter paper than the originals. An official imitation of the essay, 25c on 20c blue, was made at the same time as the re-issues. Price $5,000.

President Louis Napoleon
A2

Emperor Napoleon III
A3

1852

10 A2 10c pale bistre, *yellowish* *12,000.00* 350.00
a. 10c dark bistre, *yellowish* *13,000.00* 400.00
11 " 25c blue, *bluish* 1250.00 35.00

1862 **Re-issue.**

10b A2 10c bistre 275.00
11a " 25c blue 210.00

The re-issues are in lighter colors and on whiter paper than the originals.

1853–60 ***Imperf.***

Die I. The curl above the forehead directly below "R" of "EMPIRE" is made up of two lines very close together, often appearing to form a single thick line. There is no shading across the neck.

Die II. The curl is made of two distinct, more widely separated lines. There are lines of shading across the upper neck.

12 A3 1c olive green, *pale blue* (II) ('60) 75.00 50.00
a. 1c bronze green, *pale bluish* 85.00 60.00
13 " 5c green, *greenish* (I) ('54) 325.00 50.00
14 " 10c bistre, *yellowish* (I) 225.00 5.00
a. 10c yellow, *yellowish* (I) 1350.00 65.00
b. 10c bistre brown, *yellowish* (I) 325.00 15.00
c. 10c bistre, *yellowish* (II) ('60) 325.00 22.50
15 " 20c blue, *bluish* (I) ('54) 110.00 85
a. 20c dk. blue, *bluish* (I) 165.00 1.35
b. 20c milky blue (I) 225.00 10.00
c. 20c blue, *lilac* (I) *2500.00* 70.00
d. 20c blue, *bluish* (II) ('60) 250.00 3.50
e. As "d," tête bêche pair *60,000.00*
16 " 20c blue, *greenish* (I) *3250.00* 140.00
a. 20c blue, *greenish* (II) *3250.00* 185.00
17 " 25c bl., *bluish* (I) 1100.00 200.00
18 A3 40c org., *yellowish* (I) 1150.00 10.00
a. 40c orange vermilion, *yellowish* 1400.00 18.50
19 A3 80c lake, *yellowish* (I) ('54) 1000.00 35.00
a. Tête bêche pair *110,000.00* *7000.00*
20 A3 80c rose, *pinkish* (I) ('60) 700.00 37.50
a. Tête bêche pair *22,500.00* *5500.00*
21 A3 1fr lake, *yellowish* (I) 2000.00 1600.00
a. Tête bêche pair *135,000.00* *62,500.00*

Most values of the 1853–60 issue are known unofficially rouletted, pin-perf., perf. 7 and percé en scie.

1862 **Re-issue.**

17c A3 25c blue (I) 200.00
20c " 80c rose (I) 1000.00
21c " 1fr lake (I) 800.00
d. Tête bêche pair 9000.00

The re-issues are in lighter colors and on whiter paper than the originals.

1862-71 ***Perf. 14x13½***

22 A3 1c olive green, *pale blue* (II) 40.00 25.00
a. 1c bronze green, *pale blue* (II) 50.00 27.50
23 " 5c yellow green, *greenish* (I) 80.00 5.50
a. 5c dp. green, *greenish* (I) 100.00 7.25
24 " 5c green, *pale blue* ('71) (I) 425.00 52.50
25 " 10c bistre, *yellowish* (II) 400.00 2.50
a. 10c yellow brn., *yellowish* (II) 450.00 3.00
26 " 20c blue, *bluish* (II) 85.00 50
a. Tête bêche pair (II) 2000.00 800.00
27 " 40c orange, *yellowish* (I) 525.00 3.50
28 " 80c rose, *pinkish* (I) 450.00 27.50
a. 80c bright rose, *pinkish* (I) 550.00 40.00
b. Tête bêche pair (I) *6500.00* 2250.00

Napoleon III
A4 A5

Napoleon III
A6

1863–70 ***Perf. 14x13½***

29 A4 1c bronze green, *pale blue* ('70) 11.00 8.00
a. 1c olive green, *pale blue* 13.50 9.00
b. Imperf. 1000.00
30 " 2c red brn., *yellowish* 27.50 16.50
a. Imperf. 200.00
31 " 4c gray 75.00 32.50
a. Tête bêche pair *6000.00* *5000.00*
b. Imperf. 150.00
32 A5 10c bister, *yellowish* ('67) 125.00 3.00
a. Imperf. 150.00
33 " 20c blue, *bluish* ('67) 70.00 90
a. Imperf. 275.00
34 " 30c brown, *yellowish* ('67) 285.00 12.50
a. 30c dark brown, *yellowish* 450.00 20.00
c. Imperf. 150.00
35 " 40c orange, *yellowish* ('68) 325.00 8.00
a. 40c pale orange, *yellowish* 375.00 9.00
b. Imperf. 210.00

36 A5 80c rose, *pinkish* ('68) 300.00 13.50
  a. 80c car., *yellowish* 375.00 20.00
  b. Imperf. 450.00

37 A6 5fr gray lilac, *lavender* ('69) 3250.00 650.00
  a. "5" and "F" omitted 32,500.00
  b. Imperf. 6250.00

No. 33 exists in two types, differing in the size of the dots at either side of POSTES.

On No. 37, the "5" and "F" vary in height from 3¾mm. to 4½mm. All known copies of No. 37a are more or less damaged.

The imperforate varieties of Nos. 29–36 constitute the "Rothschild Issue," said to have been authorized exclusively for the banker to use on his correspondence. Used copies exist.

No. 29 was reprinted in 1887 by authority of Granet, Minister of Posts. The reprints show a yellowish shade under the ultraviolet lamp. Price $850.

Ceres

A7 A8

A9 Type I A10 Type II

A11 Type III

Bordeaux Issue. Lithographed.

On the lithographed stamps, except for type I of the 20c, the shading on the cheek and neck is in lines or dashes, not in dots. On the typographed stamps the shading is in dots.

The 2c, 10c and 20c (types II and III) occur in two or more types. The most easily distinguishable are:

2c—Type A. To the left of and within the top of the left "2" are lines of shading composed of dots.

2c—Type B. These lines of dots are replaced by solid lines.

10c—Type A. The inner frame lines are of the same thickness as all other frame lines.

10c—Type B. The inner frame lines are much thicker than the others.

Three Types of the 20c.

A9—Type I. The inscriptions in the upper and lower labels are small and there is quite a space between the upper label and the circle containing the head. There is also very little shading under the eye and in the neck.

A10—Type II. The inscriptions in the labels are similar to those of the first type, the shading under the eye and in the neck is heavier and the upper label and circle almost touch.

A11—Type III. The inscriptions in the labels are much larger than those of the two preceding types, and are similar to those of the other values of the same type in the set.

1870–71 *Imperf.*

38 A7 1c olive green, *pale blue* 52.50 52.50
  a. 1c bronze green, *pale blue* 72.50 72.50

39 " 2c red brown, *yellowish* (B) 140.00 140.00
  a. 2c brick red, *yellowish* (B) 800.00 600.00
  b. 2c maroon, *yellowish* (B) 1100.00 750.00
  c. 2c chocolate, *yellowish* (A) 750.00 700.00

40 " 4c gray 165.00 165.00

41 A8 5c green, *greenish* 150.00 90.00
  a. 5c yellow green, *greenish* 185.00 135.00
  b. 5c emerald, *greenish* 1300.00 650.00

42 " 10c bistre, *yellowish* (A) 500.00 45.00
  a. 10c bistre, *yellowish* (B) 550.00 60.00

43 A9 20c blue, *bluish* (I) 5250.00 450.00
  a. 20c dark blue, *bluish* (I) 6250.00 625.00

44 A10 20c bl., *bluish* (II) 550.00 35.00
  a. 20c dark blue, *bluish* (II) 700.00 80.00
  b. 20c ultramar., *bluish* (II) 11,500.00 2500.00

45 A11 20c blue, *bluish* (III) ('71) 550.00 13.50
  a. 20c ultramarine, *bluish* (III) 1400.00 450.00

46 A8 30c brn., *yellowish* 250.00 210.00
  a. 30c black brown, *yellowish* 1000.00 525.00

47 " 40c orange, *yellowish* 275.00 80.00
  a. 40c yellow orange, *yellowish* 275.00 80.00
  b. 40c red orange, *yellowish* 550.00 150.00
  c. 40c scarlet, *yellowish* 3500.00 1400.00

48 " 80c rose, *pinkish* 325.00 185.00
  a. 80c dull rose, *pinkish* 375.00 200.00

All values of the 1870 issue are known rouletted, pin-perf. and perf. 14, unofficially.

A12
Blue Surcharge

1871 Typographed. ***Perf. 14x13½.***

49 A12 10(c) on 10c bister 1000.00

No. 49 was never placed in use. Counterfeits exist.

Ceres

A13 A14

Two types of the 40c as in the 1849–50 issue.

1870–73 Typo. ***Perf. 14x13½***

50 A7 1c olive green, *pale blue* 17.50 8.50
  a. 1c bronze green, *pale blue* ('72) 22.50 9.50

51 " 2c red brown, *yellowish* ('72) 35.00 8.00

52 " 4c gray ('72) 135.00 20.00

53 " 5c yellow green, *pale blue* ('72) 60.00 4.50
  a. 5c green 70.00 7.50

54 A13 10c bis., *yellowish* 200.00 37.50
  a. Tête bêche pair 2250.00 1250.00

55 " 10c bistre, *rose* ('73) 125.00 5.50
  a. Tête bêche pair 1750.00 1000.00

56 " 15c bistre, *yellowish* ('71) 125.00 2.50
  a. Tête bêche pr. 14,000.00 3500.00

57 " 20c dull blue, *bluish* 100.00 4.50
  a. 20c bright blue, *bluish* 120.00 6.00
  b. Tête bêche pair 1650.00 800.00

58 " 25c blue, *bluish* ('71) 45.00 65
  a. 25c dark bl., *bluish* 50.00 85
  b. Tête bêche pair 2500.00 1500.00

59 " 40c orange, *yellowish* (I) 240.00 3.50
  a. 40c orange yellow, *yellowish* (I) 275.00 4.00
  b. 40c orange, *yellowish* (II) 1400.00 110.00
  c. 40c orange yellow, *yellowish* (II) 1400.00 110.00
  d. Pair, types I and II 2500.00 325.00

No. 58 exists in three main plate varieties, differing in one or another of the flower-like corner ornaments.

Nos. 54, 57 and 58 were reprinted imperf. in 1887. See note after No. 37.

1872-75 Larger Numerals.

60 A14 10c bistre, *rose* ('75) 125.00 5.50
  a. Cliché of 15c in plate of 10c 1750.00 2000.00
  b. As "a," se-tenant with #60 2500.00 2750.00

61 A14 15c bistre ('73) 125.00 2.25

62 " 30c brn., *yellowish* 200.00 3.25

63 " 80c rose, *pinkish* 250.00 8.50

Peace and Commerce ("Type Sage")
A15

Type I. The "N" of "INV" is under the "B" of "REPUBLIQUE".

Type II. The "N" of "INV" is under the "U" of "REPUBLIQUE".

1876-78 Type I.

64 A15 1c green, *greenish* 65.00 35.00
  a. Imperf. 125.00

65 " 2c grn., *greenish* 625.00 185.00
  a. Imperf. 750.00

66 " 4c green, *greenish* 60.00 27.50
  a. Imperf. 135.00

67 " 5c green, *greenish* 275.00 27.50
  a. Imperf. 400.00

68 " 10c green, *greenish* 325.00 15.00
  a. Imperf. 375.00

69 " 15c gray lilac, *grayish* 325.00 11.00
  a. Imperf. 375.00

70 " 20c red brown, *straw* 240.00 10.00
  a. Imperf. 250.00

71 " 20c blue, *bluish* 8500.00

72 " 25c ultra., *bluish* 2750.00 55.00

73 " 30c brn., *yellowish* 165.00 5.00
  a. Imperf. 200.00

74 " 40c red, *straw* ('78) 165.00 20.00
  a. Imperf. 200.00

75 " 75c carmine, *rose* 325.00 8.00
  a. Imperf. 350.00

76 " 1fr bronze green, *straw* 250.00 6.50
  a. Imperf. 325.00

No. 71 was never put into use.

The reprints of No. 71 are of the second type. They are imperforate or with forged perforation.

1876-77 Type II.

77 A15 2c green, *greenish* 45.00 12.00

78 " 5c green, *greenish* 12.00 20
  a. Imperf. 135.00

79 " 10c grn., *greenish* 575.00 175.00

80 " 15c gray lilac, *grayish* 225.00 85

81 " 25c ultra., *bluish* 185.00 20
  a. 25c blue, *bluish* 185.00 40
  b. Pair, types I & II 12,000.00 5000.00
  c. Imperf. 300.00

82 " 30c yellow brown, *yellowish* 20.00 40
  a. 30c brown, *yellowish* 22.50 40

83 " 75c carmine, *rose* ('77) 750.00 60.00

84 " 1fr bronze green, *straw* ('77) 32.50 3.00
  a. Imperf. 450.00

1877-80

86 A15 1c *lilac blue* 1.35 30
  a. 1c *gray blue* 1.35 40
  b. Imperf. 67.50

87 " 1c *Prussian blue* ('80) 3750.00 2100.00

88 " 2c brown, *straw* 2.00 50
  a. 2c brown, *yellow* 2.50 1.00
  b. Imperf. 67.50

89 " 3c yellow, *straw* ('78) 90.00 30.00
  a. Imperf. 125.00

90 " 4c claret, *lavender* 1.85 1.00
  a. 4c violet brown, *lavender* 2.50 1.25
  b. Imperf. 67.50

91 " 10c *lavender* 16.50 45
  a. 10c *rose lilac* 18.50 65
  b. 10c *lilac* 18.50 65
  c. Imperf. 75.00

92 " 15c blue ('78) 10.00 20
  a. Imperf. 80.00
  b. 15c blue, *bluish* 165.00 2.00

93 " 25c *red* ('78) 350.00 15.00
  a. Imperf. 550.00

94 A15 35c *yellow* ('78) 200.00 20.00
  a. 35c *yellow orange* 225.00 22.50
  b. Imperf. 250.00

95 " 40c red, *straw* ('80) 26.50 90
  a. Imperf. 210.00

96 " 5fr vio., *lavender* 250.00 50.00
  a. 5fr red lilac, *lavender* 275.00 60.00
  b. Imperf. 625.00

1879-90

97 A15 3c gray, *grayish* ('80) 1.35 70
  a. Imperf. 67.50

98 " 20c red, *yel. green* 17.50 1.65
  a. 20c red, *deep green* ('84) 20.00 1.85
  b. Imperf. 75.00

99 " 25c yellow, *straw* 135.00 2.50
  a. Imperf. 240.00

100 " 25c *pale rose* ('86) 17.50 40
  a. Imperf. 100.00

101 " 50c rose, *rose* ('90) 60.00 65
  a. 50c carmine, *rose* 65.00 65

102 " 75c deep violet, *orange* ('90) 85.00 20.00
  a. 75c deep violet, *yellow* 90.00 22.50

1892 Quadrille Paper

103 A15 15c blue 5.50 20
  a. Imperf. 110.00

1898–1900 Ordinary Paper

104 A15 5c yellow green 7.00 20
  a. Imperf. 85.00

Type I.

105 A15 5c yellow green 4.50 40
  a. Imperf. 160.00

106 " 10c *lavender* 8.00 1.40
  a. Imperf. 185.00

107 " 50c carmine, *rose* 60.00 20.00

108 " 2fr brn., *azure* ('00) 52.50 22.50
  b. Imperf. 2000.00

See also No. 226.

Reprints of A15, type II, were made in 1887 and left imperf. See note after No. 37. Price for set of 27, $2,750.

Liberty, Equality and Fraternity
A16

"The Rights of Man"
A17

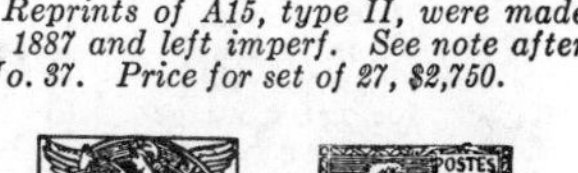

Liberty and Peace
A18

1900–29 ***Perf. 14x13½***

109 A16 1c gray 18 5
  a. Imperf. 21.00

110 " 2c violet brown 18 5
  a. Imperf. 35.00

111 " 3c orange 30 5
  a. 3c red 7.00 2.00
  b. Imperf. 27.50

112 " 4c yellow brown 1.50 30
  a. Imperf. 80.00

113 " 5c green 45 5
  a. Imperf. 55.00
  b. Bklt. pane of 10 20.00

114 " 7½c lilac ('26) 30 15

115 " 10c lilac ('29) 3.00 10

116 A17 10c carmine 20.00 40
  a. Numerals printed separately 22.50 7.00
  b. Imperf., #116 or 116a 200.00

117 " 15c orange 5.00 15
  a. Imperf. 150.00

118 " 20c brown violet 55.00 5.50

119 " 25c blue 90.00 70
  a. Numerals printed separately 100.00 5.00
  b. Imperf., #119 or 119a 350.00

120 " 30c violet 65.00 3.50

121 A18 40c red & pale blue 9.50 25
  a. Imperf. 140.00

122 " 45c grn. & blue ('06) 10.00 60
  a. Imperf. 150.00

123 A18 50c bistre brown & lavender 80.00 50
a. Imperf. 250.00
124 " 60c vio.& ultra.('20) 50 20
a. Imperf. 210.00
125 " 1fr claret & olive green 18.50 15
a. Imperf. 150.00
126 " 2fr gray violet & yellow 600.00 35.00
a. Imperf. *2250.00*
127 " 2fr orange & pale blue ('20) 16.50 20
a. Imperf. 325.00
128 " 3fr vio.& blue ('25) 17.50 3.50
129 " 3fr bright violet & rose ('27) 35.00 70
a. Imperf. 165.00
130 " 5fr dk. blue & buff 45.00 1.85
a. Imperf. 675.00
131 " 10fr green & red ('26) 80.00 8.00
132 " 20fr magenta & green ('26) 165.00 14.00
Nos. 109-132 (24) 1318.41 75.95

In the 10c and 25c values, the first printings show the numerals to have been impressed by a second operation, whereas, in later printings, the numerals were inserted in the plates. Two operations were used for all 20c and 30c, and one operation for the 15c.

No. 114 was issued precanceled only. Prices for precanceled stamps in first column are for those which have not been through the post and have original gum. Prices in the second column are for postally used, gumless stamps.

See also No. P7.

Flat Plate & Rotary Press

The following stamps were printed by both flat plate and rotary press: Nos. 109-113, 144-146, 163, 166, 168, 170, 177-178, 185, 192 and P7.

"Rights of Man"—A19

Sower A20

1902

133 A19 10c rose red 17.50 18
a. Imperf. 185.00
134 " 15c pale red 5.00 15
a. Imperf. 300.00
135 " 20c brown violet 65.00 9.00
a. Imperf. 325.00
136 " 25c blue 75.00 80
137 " 30c lilac 185.00 7.25
a. Imperf. 625.00
Nos. 133-137 (5) 347.50 17.38

1903-38

138 A20 10c rose 5.50 6
a. Imperf. 80.00
139 " 15c slate green 1.50 5
a. Imperf. 80.00
b. Booklet pane of 10 18.50
140 " 20c violet brown 50.00 70
a. Imperf. 100.00
141 " 25c dull blue 60.00 65
a. Imperf. 110.00
142 " 30c violet 140.00 3.25
a. Imperf. 300.00
143 " 45c light violet ('26) 2.75 40
144 " 50c dull blue ('21) 15.00 20
a. Imperf. 42.50
145 " 50c gray green ('26) 2.50 15
a. Imperf. 75.00
146 " 50c vermilion ('26) 10 5
a. Booklet pane of 10 4.50
b. Imperf. 55.00
147 " 50c greenish blue ('38) 30 5
a. Imperf. 37.50
148 " 60c light violet ('24) 2.50 60
149 " 65c rose ('24) 1.10 50
a. Imperf. 110.00
150 " 65c gray green ('27) 3.00 60
151 " 75c rose lilac ('26) 1.75 20
a. Imperf. 300.00
152 " 80c vermilion ('26) 45.00 4.75
153 " 85c vermilion ('24) 11.00 30
154 A20 1fr dull blue ('26) 3.50 5
Nos. 138-154 (17) 345.50 12.56

See also Nos. 941, 942A.

Sower, Ground under Feet A21

Sower, no Ground under Feet A22

1906

With Ground Under Feet of Figure

155 A21 10c red 2.75 45
a. Imperf., pair 175.00

1906-37

TEN AND THIRTY-FIVE CENTIMES.

Type I. Numerals and letters of the inscriptions thin.

Type II. Numerals and letters thicker.

No Ground Under the Feet.

156 A22 1c olive bistre ('33) 8 8
157 " 2c dark green ('33) 6 6
158 " 3c vermilion ('33) 6 6
159 " 5c green 60 5
a. Imperf., pair 20.00
b. Bklt. pane of 10 17.50
160 " 5c orange ('21) 1.20 5
a. Bklt. pane of 10 18.50
161 " 5c cerise ('34) 6 6
162 " 10c red (II) 55 5
a. Imperf., pair 20.00
b. 10c red (I) ('06) 6.00 20
c. Booklet pane of 10 (I) 65.00
d. Booklet pane of 10 (II) 50.00
e. Booklet pane of 6 (II) 135.00
163 " 10c green (II) ('21) 30 5
a. 10c green (I) ('27) 17.50 16.50
b. Booklet pane of 10 (II) 9.00
c. Booklet pane of 10 (I) 200.00
164 " 10c ultramarine ('32) 7 7
165 " 15c red brown ('26) 12 3
a. Booklet pane of 10 17.50
166 " 20c brown 1.65 10
a. Imperf., pair 37.50
167 " 20c red violet ('26) 13 3
a. Bklt. pane of 10 4.25
168 " 25c blue 70 5
a. Bklt. pane of 10 18.50
b. Imperf., pair 35.00
169 " 25c brown ('27) 10 5
170 " 30c orange 9.00 50
a. Imperf., pair 125.00
171 " 30c red ('21) 5.50 1.10
172 " 30c cerise ('25) 40 8
a. Booklet pane of 10 5.50
173 " 30c light blue ('25) 1.00 5
a. Bklt. pane of 10 12.50
174 " 30c copper red ('37) 15 5
a. Booklet pane of 10 4.00
175 " 35c violet (II) ('26) 8.50 35
a. Imperf., pair 125.00
b. 35c vio. (I) ('06) 100.00 2.50
176 " 35c green ('37) 70 20
177 " 40c olive ('25) 50 8
b. Bklt. pane of 10 20.00
178 " 40c vermilion ('26) 1.15 12
a. Bklt. pane of 10 15.00
179 " 40c violet ('27) 1.75 10
180 " 40c lt. ultra. ('28) 1.00 5
181 " 1.05fr vermilion ('25) 4.75 1.65
182 " 1.10fr cerise ('27) 7.50 75
183 " 1.40fr cerise ('26) 11.00 7.00
184 " 2fr Prussian green ('31) 6.50 30
Nos. 156-184 (29) 65.08 13.17

The 10c and 35c, type I, were slightly retouched by adding thin white outlines to the sack of grain, the underside of the right arm and the back of the skirt. It is difficult to distinguish the retouches except on clearly-printed copies. The white outlines were made stronger on the stamps of type II.

Stamps of types A16, A18, A20 and A22 were printed in 1916-20 on paper of poor quality, usually grayish and containing bits of fiber. This is called G. C. (Grande Consommation) paper.

Nos. 160, 162b, 163, 175b and 176 also exist imperf.

See also Nos. 241-241b, P8.

Louis Pasteur A23

1923-26

185 A23 10c green 25 6
a. Booklet pane of 10 4.25
186 " 15c green ('24) 40 7
187 " 20c green ('26) 1.00 15
188 " 30c red 20 15
189 " 30c green ('26) 25 10
190 " 45c red ('24) 1.00 65
191 " 50c blue 1.50 20
192 " 75c blue ('24) 1.40 25
a. Imperf., pair 200.00
193 " 90c red ('26) 6.00 1.50
194 " 1fr blue ('25) 12.00 8
195 " 1.25fr blue ('26) 12.00 3.25
196 " 1.50fr blue ('26) 4.00 10
Nos. 185-196 (12) 40.00 6.56

Nos. 185, 188 and 191 were issued to commemorate the centenary of the birth of Pasteur.

No. 125 Overprinted in Blue: CONGRES PHILATELIQUE DE BORDEAUX 1923

1923, June 15

197 A18 1fr claret & olive green 300.00 300.00

Allegory of Olympic Games at Paris A24

The Trophy A25

Milo of Crotona A26

Victorious Athlete A27

Perf. 14x13½, 13½x14

1924, Apr. 1

198 A24 10c gray green & yellow green 80 30
199 A25 25c rose & dark rose 1.00 12
200 A26 30c brown red & black 8.00 5.50
201 A27 50c ultra. & dk. blue 9.50 90

8th Olympic Games, Paris. Exist imperf.

Pierre de Ronsard A28

1924, Oct. 6 ***Perf. 14x13½***

219 A28 75c blue, *bluish* 50 40

Issued to commemorate the 400th anniversary of the birth of Pierre de Ronsard, poet (1524-1585).

"Light and Liberty" Allegory—A29

Majolica Vase A30

Potter Decorating Vase—A31

Terrace of Château—A32

1924-25 ***Perf. 14x13½, 13½x14.***

220 A29 10c dark green & yellow ('25) 35 25
221 A30 15c indigo & green ('25) 35 25
a. Imperf. 115.00
222 A31 25c violet brown & garnet 45 15
223 A32 25c gray blue & violet ('25) 55 25
224 A31 75c indigo & ultramarine 1.85 75
225 A29 75c dark blue & lt. blue ('25) 8.00 3.00
a. Imperf. 115.00
Nos. 220-225 (6) 11.55 4.65

Issued to commemorate the International Exhibition of Decorative Modern Arts at Paris, 1925.

Philatelic Exhibition Issue.

Souvenir Sheet.

A32a

1925, May 2 *Perf. 14x13½*

226 A32a 5fr carmine (A15, type II) sheet of four 625.00 525.00
- *a.* Imperf. sheet 4000.00
- *b.* Single stamp, perf. 100.00 70.00
- *c.* Single stamp, imperf. 800.00

Issued in sheets measuring 140x220 mm.

These were not on sale at post offices but solely at the International Philatelic Exhibition, Paris, May, 1925.

Stamps of 1907-26 Surcharged **=25c**

1926-27

227 A22 25c on 30c light blue 10 6
228 " 25c on 35c violet 10 8
- *a.* Double surcharge 100.00

229 A20 50c on 60c light violet ('27) 70 25
230 " 50c on 65c rose ('27) 45 10
231 A23 50c on 75c blue 1.20 20
232 A20 50c on 80c vermilion ('27) 45 30
233 " 50c on 85c verm. ('27) 40 12
234 A22 50c on 1.05fr verm. ('27) 1.10 20
235 A23 50c on 1.25fr blue 75 20
236 A20 55c on 60c lt. vio. 90.00 35.00
238 A22 90c on 1.05fr verm. 3.75 1.85
240 " 1.10fr on 1.40fr cerise 65 20
Nos. 227-240 (12) 99.65 38.56

No. 236 is known only precanceled. See second note after No. 132.

Nos. 229, 230, 234, 238 and 240 have three bars instead of two. The 55c surcharge has thinner, larger numerals and a rounded "c." Width, including bars, is 17mm., instead of 13mm.

Strasbourg Exhibition Issue.

Souvenir Sheet.

A32b

1927, June 4

241 A32b Sheet of two 625.00 525.00
- *a.* 5fr light ultra. (A22) 210.00 185.00
- *b.* 10fr carmine rose (A22) 210.00 185.00

Issued in sheets measuring 111x140mm. Sold at the Strasbourg Philatelic Exhibition as souvenirs.

Marcelin Berthleot
A33

1927, Sept. 7

242 A33 90c dull rose 35 12

Issued to commemorate the centenary of the birth of Marcelin Berthelot (1827-1907), chemist and statesman.

Lafayette, Washington, S. S. Paris and Airplane "Spirit of St. Louis"
A34

1927, Sept. 15

243 A34 90c dull red 60 40
- *a.* Value omitted 1000.00

244 " 1.50fr deep blue 1.40 60
- *a.* Value omitted 600.00

Visit of American Legionnaires to France, September, 1927. Exist imperf.

Joan of Arc
A35

1929, Mar.

245 A35 50c dull blue 30 6
- *a.* Booklet pane of 10 5.00
- *b.* Imperf. 65.00

Issued in commemoration of the 500th anniversary of the relief of Orleans by the French forces led by Joan of Arc.

Le Havre Exhibition Issue.

A36

Blue Overprint.

1929, May 18

246 A36 2fr orange & pale blue 375.00 275.00

No. 246 was sold exclusively at the International Philatelic Exhibition, Le Havre, May, 1929. Sold for 7fr, which included a 5fr admission ticket.

Excellent counterfeits of No. 246 exist.

Reims Cathedral
A37

Dies I, II & III. Die IV

Die I Die II Die III

3fr—Die I. The window of the first turret on the left is made of two lines. The horizontal line of the frame surrounding 3F is not continuous.

3fr—Die II. Same as Die I but the line under 3F is continuous.

3fr—Die III. Same as Die II but there is a deeply cut line separating 3 and F.

3fr—Die IV. The window of the first turret on the left is made of three lines.

Mont-Saint-Michel
A38

Die I. Die II.

5fr—Die I. The line at the top of the spire is broken.

5fr—Die II. The line is unbroken.

Port of La Rochelle
A39

Dies I & II. Die III.

10fr—Die I. The top of the "E" of "POSTES" has a serif. The oval of shading inside the "0" of "10 fr" and the outer oval are broken at their bases.

10fr—Die II. The same top has no serif. Interior and exterior of "0" broken as in Die I.

10fr—Die III. Top of "E" has no serif. Interior and exterior of "0" complete.

Pont du Gard, Nimes
A40

Dies I & II.

Die III.

20fr—Die I. Shading of the first complete arch in the left middle tier is made of horizontal lines. Size 36 x 20¾ mm. Perf. 13½.

20fr—Die II. Same, size 35½ x 21 mm. Perf. 11.

20fr—Die III. Shading of same arch is made of three diagonal lines. Thin paper. Perf. 13.

Engraved.

1929-33 *Perf. 11, 13, 13½*

247 A37 3fr dark gray ('30) (I) 70.00 1.85
247A " 3fr dark gray ('30) (II) 115.00 3.75
247B " 3fr dark gray ('30) (III) 300.00 14.00
248 " 3fr bluish slate ('31) (IV) 70.00 1.85
249 A38 5fr brown ('30) (I) 18.00 1.00
250 " 5fr brown ('31) (II) 16.00 20
251 A39 10fr lt. ultra. (I) 85.00 10.00
251A " 10fr ultra. (II) 100.00 16.50
252 " 10fr dark ultramarine ('31) (III) 75.00 4.25
253 A40 20fr red brn. (I) 185.00 25.00
254 " 20fr bright red brown ('33) (II) 750.00 150.00
254A " 20fr orange brown ('31) (III) 175.00 22.50

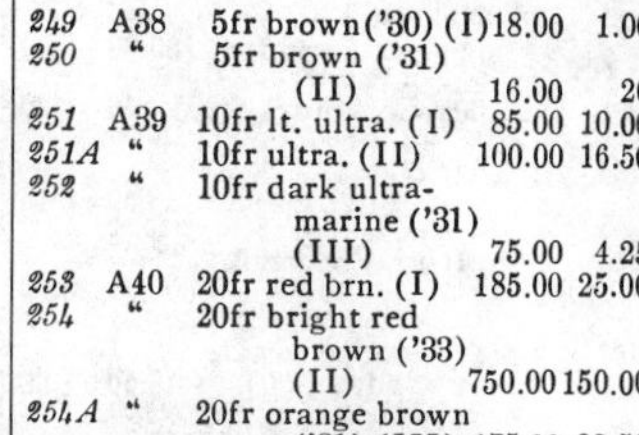

View of Algiers
A41

1929, Jan. 1 Typographed

255 A41 50c blue & rose red 1.35 12

Issued in commemoration of the centenary of the first French settlement in Algeria.

Nos. 146 and 196 Overprinted **CONGRÈS DU B. I. T. 1930**

1930, Apr. 23 *Perf. 14x13½*

256 A20 50c vermilion 1.10 90
257 A23 1.50fr blue 10.00 8.50

International Labor Bureau, 48th Congress, Paris.

Colonial Exposition Issue.

Fachi Woman
A42

French Colonials
A43

1930-31 Typo. *Perf. 14x13½*

258 A42 15c gray black 15 5
259 " 40c dark brown 50 10
260 " 50c dark red 15 5
- *a.* Booklet pane of 10 6.00

261 " 1.50fr deep blue 7.25 20

Photogravure.

Perf. 13½.

262 A43 1.50fr deep blue ('31) 21.00 50
Nos. 258-262 (5) 29.05 90

Arc de Triomphe
A44

Peace with Olive Branch
A45

1931 Engraved *Perf. 13*

263 A44 2fr red brown 21.00 20

1932-39 Typo. *Perf. 14x13½*

264 A45 30c deep green 25 6
265 " 40c bright violet 10 3
266 " 45c yellow brown 85 45
267 " 50c rose red 8 3
- *a.* Imperf., pair 35.00
- *b.* Booklet pane of 10 3.50

268 " 55c dull violet ('37) 40 8
269 " 60c ochre ('37) 10 5
270 " 65c violet brown 30 8
271 " 65c brt. ultra. ('37) 12 3
- *a.* Booklet pane of 10 4.50

272 " 75c olive green 12 6
273 " 80c orange ('38) 8 6
274 " 90c dark red 22.50 1.10
275 " 90c bright green ('38) 6 6

276 A45 90c ultramarine('38) 15 3
a. Booklet pane of 10 5.50
277 " 1fr orange 55 5
278 " 1fr rose pink ('38) 85 8
279 " 1.25fr brown olive 40.00 1.50
280 " 1.25fr rose car. ('39) 1.25 60
281 " 1.40fr bright red violet ('39) 3.50 2.00
282 " 1.50fr deep blue 10 7
283 " 1.75fr magenta 2.25 5
Nos. 264-283 (20) 73.61 6.47

The 50c is found in 4 types, differing in the lines below belt and size of "c."

Le Puy-en-Velay—A46

1933 Engraved *Perf. 13*

290 A46 90c rose 2.50 25

Aristide Briand A47 Paul Doumer A48

Victor Hugo A49

1933, Dec. 11 Typo. *Perf. 14x13½*

291 A47 30c blue green 15.00 5.00
292 A48 75c red violet 18.50 30
293 A49 1.25fr claret 1.35 30

Dove and Olive Branch A50 Joseph Marie Jacquard A51

1934, Feb. 20

294 A50 1.50fr ultra. 37.50 7.50

1934, Mar. 14 Engr. *Perf. 14x13*

295 A51 40c blue 1.50 50

Issued to commemorate the centenary of the death of Joseph Marie Jacquard (1752–1834), inventor of an improved loom for figured weaving.

Jacques Cartier A52

1934, July 18 *Perf. 13*

296 A52 75c rose lilac 16.50 75
297 " 1.50fr blue 35.00 1.50

Issued to commemorate the 400th anniversary of Carter's discovery of Canada.

No. 279 Surcharged

50c

1934, Nov. *Perf. 14x13½*

298 A45 50c on 1.25fr brown olive 2.50 20

Breton River Scene A53

1935, Feb. Engraved *Perf. 13*

299 A53 2fr blue green 25.00 25

S. S. Normandie—A54

1935, April

300 A54 1.50fr dark blue 12.00 65
a. 1.50fr lt. blue ('36) 47.50 8.50
b. 1.50fr blue green ('36) 1250.00

Issued in commemoration of the maiden voyage of the transatlantic steamship, the "Normandie".

Benjamin Delessert A55

1935, May 20

301 A55 75c blue green 16.50 45

Issued in commemoration of the opening of the International Savings Bank Congress, May 20, 1935.

View of St. Trophime at Arles A56 Victor Hugo A57

1935, May 3

302 A56 3.50fr dark brown 25.00 1.65

1935, May 30 *Perf. 14x13*

303 A57 1.25fr magenta 1.85 65

Victor Hugo (1802–1885), 50th anniversary of death.

Cardinal Richelieu A58 Jacques Callot A59

1935, June 12 *Perf. 13*

304 A58 1.50fr deep rose 16.50 75

Issued in commemoration of the tercentenary of the founding of the French Academy by Cardinal Richelieu.

1935, Nov. *Perf. 14x13*

305 A59 75c red 11.00 20

Issued in commemoration of the 300th anniversary of the death of Jacques Callot, engraver.

André Marie Ampère A60

1936, Feb. 27 *Perf. 13*

306 A60 75c brown 16.50 50

Issued to commemorate the centenary of the death of André Marie Ampère (1775–1836), scientist. (Portrait by Louis Boilly.)

Windmill at Fontvielle, Immortalized by Daudet—A61

1936, Apr. 27

307 A61 2fr ultramarine 1.35 10

Issued in commemoration of the 70th anniversary of the publication, in 1866, of Alphonse Daudet's "Lettres de mon Moulin".

Pilâtre de Rozier and his Balloon A62

1936, June 4

308 A62 75c Prussian blue 17.50 1.10

Issued in commemoration of the 150th anniversary of the death of Jean Joseph Pilâtre de Rozier, balloonist.

Rouget de Lisle A63

"La Marseillaise" A64

1936, June 27

309 A63 20c Prussian green 90 40
310 A64 40c dark brown 3.75 1.25

Centenary of the death of Claude Joseph Rouget de Lisle, composer of "La Marseillaise."

Canadian War Memorial at Vimy Ridge—A65

1936, July 26

311 A65 75c henna brown 7.00 85
312 " 1.50fr dull blue 12.50 9.00

Issued to commemorate the unveiling of the Canadian War Memorial at Vimy Ridge, July 26, 1936.

Jean Léon Jaurès A66

Jean Jaurès A67

1936, July 30

313 A66 40c red brown 1.75 35
314 A67 1.50fr ultramarine 9.00 1.10

Issued in commemoration of the assassination of Jean Léon Jaurès (1859–1914), socialist and politician.

Herald A68 Allegory of Exposition A69

1936, Sept. 15 Typo. *Perf. 14x13½*

315 A68 20c bright violet 12 8
316 " 30c Prussian green 1.00 35
317 " 40c ultramarine 30 10
318 " 50c red orange 18 5
319 A69 90c carmine 7.50 5.50
320 " 1.50fr ultramarine 13.50 1.00
Nos. 315-320 (6) 22.60 7.08

Publicity for the 1937 Paris Exposition.

"Peace" A70

1936, Oct. 1 Engr. *Perf. 13*

321 A70 1.50fr blue 13.50 65

Skiing A71

1937, Jan. 18

322 A71 1.50fr dark blue 6.50 55

Issued in commemoration of the International Ski Meet at Chamonix—Mont Blanc.

Pierre Corneille, Portrait by Charles Le Brun A72

1937, Feb. 15

323 A72 75c brown carmine 1.00 40

Issued to commemorate the 300th anniversary of the publication of "Le Cid."

Paris Exposition Issue.

Exposition Allegory—A73

1937, Mar. 15

324	A73	1.50fr turquoise bl.	1.35	45

Jean Mermoz A74

Memorial to Mermoz A75

1937, Apr. 27

325	A74	30c dark slate green	30	20
326	A75	3fr dark violet	5.00	1.85
		a. 3fr violet	5.00	1.85

Issued in honor of aviator Jean Mermoz (1901–36).

Electric Train A76

Streamlined Locomotive A77

1937, May 31

327	A76	30c dark green	60	50
328	A77	1.50fr dark ultra.	7.50	4.50

13th International Railroad Congress.

International Philatelic Exhibition Issue.

Souvenir Sheet

A77a

Ceres Type of 1849–50.

1937, June 18 Typo. *Perf. 14x13½*

329	A77a	Sheet of four (A1)	175.00	150.00
		a. 5c ultramarine & dark brown	32.50	32.50
		b. 15c red & rose red	32.50	32.50
		c. 30c ultramarine & rose red	32.50	32.50
		d. 50c red & dark brown	32.50	32.50
		e. Imperf. sheet of four	*1500.00*	

Issued in sheets measuring 150x220mm. The sheets were sold only at the exhibition in Paris, a ticket of admission being required for each sheet purchased.

René Descartes, by Frans Hals A78

1937, June Engraved *Perf. 13*

Inscribed: "Discours sur la Méthode."

330	A78	90c copper red	70	50

Inscribed "Discours de la Méthode"

331	A78	90c copper red	1.35	50

Issued in commemoration of the third centenary of the publication of "Discours de la Méthode" by René Descartes.

France Congratulating U.S.A. A79

1937, Sept. 17

332	A79	1.75fr ultramarine	1.25	80

Issued to commemorate the 150th anniversary of the Constitution of the United States of America.

No. 277 Surcharged in Red

80c

1937, Oct. *Perf. 14x13½*

333	A45	80c on 1fr orange	40	30
		a. Inverted surch.	240.00	

Mountain Road at Iseran A80

1937, Oct. 4 Engraved *Perf. 13*

334	A80	90c dark green	30	15

Issued in commemoration of the opening of the mountain road at Iseran, Savoy.

Ceres A81

1938–40 Typo. *Perf. 14x13½*

335	A81	1.75fr dark ultramarine	85	15
336	"	2fr car. rose ('39)	20	5
337	"	2.25fr ultra. ('39)	3.25	12
338	"	2.50fr green ('39)	1.40	8
339	"	2.50fr violet blue('40)	70	25
340	"	3fr rose lilac ('39)	60	5
		Nos. 335–340 (6)	7.00	70

Léon Gambetta A82

1938, Apr. 2 Engraved *Perf. 13*

341	A82	55c dark violet	35	30

Issued in commemoration of the centenary of the birth of Léon Gambetta (1838-1882), lawyer and statesman.

Arc de Triomphe of Orange A82a

Miners A83

Keep and Gate of Vincennes A86

Palace of the Popes, Avignon A84

Medieval Walls of Carcassonne A85

Port of St. Malo—A87

1938

342	A82a	2fr brown black	1.00	85
343	A83	2.15fr violet brown	90	20
344	A84	3fr carmine brn.	6.00	1.75
345	A85	5fr deep ultra.	40	20
346	A86	10fr brown, *blue*	1.50	1.00
347	A87	20fr dark blue green	32.50	8.50
		Nos. 342–347 (6)	42.30	12.50

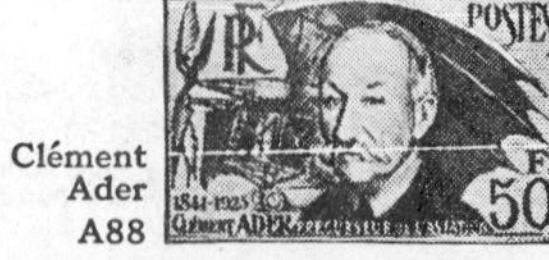

Clément Ader A88

1938, June 16

348	A88	50fr ultramarine (thin paper)	90.00	50.00
		a. 50fr dk. ultra. (thick paper)	100.00	65.00

Issued in honor of Clément Ader, air pioneer.

Soccer Players A89

1938, June 1

349	A89	1.75fr dark ultra.	6.00	3.25

World Cup Soccer Championship.

Costume of Champagne Region A90

Jean de La Fontaine A91

1938, June 13

350	A90	1.75fr dark ultra.	3.25	1.65

Issued in commemoration of the tercentenary of the birth of Dom Pierre Pérignon, discoverer of the champagne process.

1938, July 8

351	A91	55c dark blue green	50	30

Issued to honor Jean de La Fontaine (1621-1695) the fabulist.

Seal of Friendship and Peace, Victoria Tower and Arc de Triomphe—A92

1938, July 19

352	A92	1.75fr ultramarine	85	60

Issued in honor of the visit of King George VI and Queen Elizabeth of Great Britain to France.

Mercury A93

Paul Cézanne, Self-portrait A95

1938–42 Typo. *Perf. 14x13½*

353	A93	1c dark brown ('39)	5	3
354	"	2c slate green ('39)	5	3
355	"	5c rose	5	3
356	"	10c ultramarine	5	3
357	"	15c red orange	4	3
358	"	15c orange brown ('39)	30	10
359	"	20c red violet	4	3
360	"	25c blue green	6	3
361	"	30c rose red ('39)	5	3
362	"	40c dark violet ('39)	5	3
363	"	45c light green ('39)	45	25
364	"	50c deep blue ('39)	1.75	6
365	"	50c dark green ('41)	25	8
366	"	50c greenish blue ('42)	6	3
367	"	60c red orange ('39)	15	8

368 A93 70c magenta ('39) 20 7
369 " 75c dark orange brown ('39) 3.50 1.00
Nos. 353–369 (17) 7.10 1.94

No. 366 exists imperforate. See also Nos. 455–458.

1939, Mar. 15 Engr. ***Perf. 13***
370 A95 2.25fr Prus. blue 3.25 1.40

Issued in commemoration of the centenary of the birth of Paul Cézanne (1839–1906), painter.

Georges Clemenceau and Battleship Clemenceau—A96

1939, Apr. 18
371 A96 90c ultramarine 40 35

Issued to commemorate the laying of the keel of the warship "Clemenceau" January 17, 1939.

Statue of Liberty, French Pavilion, Trylon and Perisphere—A97

1939-40
372 A97 2.25fr ultramarine 2.75 1.35
373 " 2.50fr ultra. ('40) 2.40 1.60

New York World's Fair.

Joseph Nicéphore Niepce and Louis Jacques Mandé Daguerre A98

1939. Apr. 24
374 A98 2.25fr dark blue 3.50 2.00

Centenary of photography.

Iris A99 Pumping Station at Marly A100

1939–44 Typo. ***Perf. 14x13½***
375 A99 80c red brown ('40) 10 6
376 " 80c yellow green ('44) 5 4
377 " 1fr green 30 5
378 " 1fr crimson ('40) 8 3
a. Bklt. pane of 10 3.00
379 " 1fr greenish blue ('44) 6 6
380 " 1.20fr violet ('44) 6 5
381 " 1.30fr ultramarine ('40) 12 10
382 " 1.50fr red orange ('41) 25 15
383 " 1.50fr henna brown ('44) 6 5
384 " 2fr violet brown ('44) 6 5
385 " 2.40fr carmine rose ('44) 12 8
386 " 3fr orange ('44) 8 6
387 " 4fr ultramarine ('44) 10 10
Nos. 375–387 (13) 1.44 88

1939 Engraved. ***Perf. 13.***
388 A100 2.25fr bright ultra. 4.00 1.35

Issued in commemoration of France's participation in the International Water Exposition at Liège.

St. Gregory of Tours A101

1939, June 10
389 A101 90c red 55 40

Issued to commemorate the 14th centenary of the birth of St. Gregory of Tours, historian and bishop.

"The Oath of the Tennis Court" by Jacques David—A102

1939, June 20
390 A102 90c deep slate green 40 30

150th anniversary of French Revolution.

Cathedral of Strasbourg A103

1939, June 23
391 A103 70c brown carmine 55 35

Issued to commemorate the 500th anniversary of the completion of Strasbourg Cathedral.

Porte Chaussée, Verdun—A104

1939, June 23
392 A104 90c black brown 75 55

Issued to commemorate the 23rd anniversary of the Battle of Verdun.

View of Pau A105

1939, Aug. 25
393 A105 90c bright rose, *gray blue* 90 45

Maid of Languedoc A106

Bridge at Lyons A107

1939
394 A106 70c black, *blue* 35 30
395 A107 90c dull brown violet 35 30

Imperforates

Nearly all French stamps issued from 1940 onward exist imperforate. Officially 20 sheets, ranging from 25 to 100 subjects, were left imperforate.

Georges Guynemer A108

1940, Nov. 7
396 A108 50fr ultramarine 7.25 4.50

Issued in honor of Georges Guynemer (1894-1917), World War I ace.

Stamps of 1938-39 Surcharged in Carmine **1F**

1940-41 ***Perf. 14x13½.***
397 A81 1fr on 1.75fr dk. ultra. 5 5
398 " 1fr on 2.25fr ultramarine ('41) 5 5
399 " 1fr on 2.50fr green ('41) 6 6

Stamps of 1932-39 Surcharged in Carmine, Red or Black **= 1F**

Perf. 13, 14x13½.
400 A22 30c on 35c green (C) ('41) 8 8
401 A45 50c on 55c dull violet (C) ('41) 8 8
a. Invtd. surch. 240.00
402 " 50c on 65c brt. ultra. (C) ('41) 6 6
a. Invtd. surch. 165.00
403 " 50c on 75c olive green (C) ('41) 5 5
404 A93 50c on 75c dark orange brown (C) ('41) 10 10
405 A45 50c on 80c orange (C) ('41) 10 10
406 " 50c on 90c ultra. (C) ('41) 5 5
a. Invtd. surch. 90.00
b. "05" instead of "50" 2250.00 2250.00
407 " 1fr on 1.25fr rose carmine (Bk) ('41) 10 10
408 " 1fr on 1.40fr bright red violet (R) ('41) 10 10
a. Dble. surch. 325.00
409 " 1fr on 1.50fr dark blue (C) ('41) 15 15
410 A83 1fr on 2.15fr violet brown (C) 8 8
411 A85 2.50fr on 5fr dp. ultra. (C) ('41) 18 18
a. Dble. surch. 100.00 60.00
412 A86 5fr on 10fr brown, *bl.* (C) ('41) 1.60 1.60
413 A87 10fr on 20fr dark blue green (C) ('41) 70 70
414 A88 20fr on 50fr dk. ultra. (#348a) (C) ('41) 25.00 25.00
a. 20fr on 50fr ultra., thin paper (#348) 26.50 26.50
Nos. 400–414 (15) 28.43 28.43

Marshal Pétain A109 Frédéric Mistral A110

1941 ***Perf. 13.***
415 A109 40c red brown 35 30
416 " 80c turquoise blue 50 45
417 " 1fr red 15 15
418 " 2.50fr deep ultra. 80 80

1941, Feb. 20 ***Perf. 14x13***
419 A110 1fr brown lake 15 15

Issued in honor of Frédéric Mistral, poet and Nobel prize winner for literature in 1904.

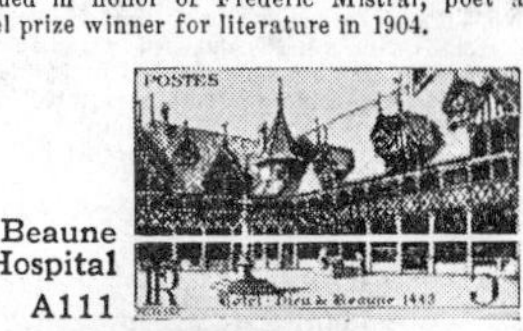

Beaune Hospital A111

View of Angers A112

Ramparts of St. Louis, Aiguesmortes A113

1941
420 A111 5fr brown black 20 10
421 A112 10fr dark violet 15 10
422 A113 20fr brown black 60 55

1942

Inscribed "Postes Francaises". Imprint: "FELTESSE" at right.
423 A111 15fr brown lake 25 20

Marshal Pétain
A114 A115

Marshal Pétain
A116 A117

Marshal Pétain A118

1941–42 Typo. *Perf. 14x13½*

No.	Type	Description	Unused	Used
427	A114	20c lilac ('42)	5	5
428	"	30c rose red	5	5
429	"	40c ultramarine	10	10
431	A115	50c deep green	5	5
432	"	60c violet ('42)	6	6
433	"	70c sapphire ('42)	6	6
434	"	70c orange ('42)	8	8
435	"	80c brown	8	8
436	"	80c emerald ('42)	8	8
437	"	1fr rose red	6	6
438	"	1.20fr red brown ('42)	5	5
439	A116	1.50fr rose	6	6
440	"	1.50fr dull red brown ('42)	5	5
		a. Booklet pane of 10	1.75	
441	"	2fr blue green ('42)	5	5
443	"	2.40fr rose red ('42)	10	6
444	"	2.50fr ultramarine	40	23
445	"	3fr orange	5	5
446	A115	4fr ultra. ('42)	8	6
447	"	4.50fr dark green ('42)	35	20
		Nos. 427–447 (19)	1.86	1.48

Nos. 431 to 438 measure 16½ x 20½ mm.

No. 440 was forged by the French Underground ("Defense de la France") and used to frank clandestine journals, etc., from February to June, 1944. The forgeries were ungummed, both perforated 11½ and imperforate, with a back handstamp covering six stamps and including the words: "Atelier des Faux."

1942 Engraved. *Perf. 14x13.*

No.	Type	Description	Unused	Used
448	A115	4fr bright ultramarine	18	12
449	"	4.50fr dark green	12	10
450	A117	5fr Prussian green	6	5
		Perf. 13		
451	A118	50fr black	2.00	1.50

Nos. 448 and 449 measure 18x21½mm.

Jules Massenet A119

Stendhal (Marie Henri Beyle) A120

1942, June 22 *Perf. 14x13*

No.	Type	Description	Unused	Used
452	A119	4fr Prussian green	20	15

Issued to commemorate the centenary of the birth of Jules Massenet (1842–1912), composer.

1942, Sept. 14 *Perf. 13*

No.	Type	Description	Unused	Used
453	A120	4fr black brown & orange red	35	35

Issued to commemorate the centenary of the death of Stendhal (1783–1842), writer.

André Blondel A121

Town-Hall Belfry, Arras A122

1942, Sept. 14

No.	Type	Description	Unused	Used
454	A121	4fr dull blue	30	30

Issued in honor of André Eugène Blondel (1863–1938), physicist.

Mercury Type of 1938–42 Inscribed "Postes Françaises".

1942 *Perf. 14x13½*

No.	Type	Description	Unused	Used
455	A93	10c ultramarine	6	5
456	"	30c rose red	6	5
457	A93	40c dark violet	6	5
458	"	50c turquoise blue	6	5

1942, Dec. 8 Engraved *Perf. 13*

No.	Type	Description	Unused	Used
459	A122	10fr green	18	12

Coats of Arms.

Lyon A123

Brittany A124

Provence A125

Ile de France A126

1943 Typographed. *Perf. 14x13½*

No.	Type	Description	Unused	Used
460	A123	5fr violet blue, org., red orange & blk.	15	8
461	A124	10fr ochre & black	20	12
462	A125	15fr violet blue, org., red & black	1.25	1.10
463	A126	20fr violet blue, org., & dull brown	85	70

Antoine Lavoisier A127

1943, July 5 Engr. *Perf. 14x13*

No.	Type	Description	Unused	Used
464	A127	4fr ultramarine	15	15

Issued to commemorate the 200th anniversary of the birth of Lavoisier (1743-94), French scientist.

Lake Lerie and Meije Dauphiné Alps—A128

1943, July 5 *Perf. 13*

No.	Type	Description	Unused	Used
465	A128	20fr dull gray green	45	45

Nicolas Rolin, Guigone de Salins and Hospital of Beaune—A129

1943, July 21

No.	Type	Description	Unused	Used
466	A129	4fr blue	30	30

Issued to commemorate the 500th anniversary of the founding of the Hospital of Beaune.

Coats of Arms.

Flanders A130

Languedoc A131

Orléans A132

Normandy A133

1944, Mar. 27 Typo. *Perf. 14x13½*

No.	Type	Description	Unused	Used
467	A130	5fr vermilion, orange & black	8	6
468	A131	10fr brown, black, dull red & yellow	12	7
469	A132	15fr brown, bright ultra. & orange	55	50
470	A133	20fr ultramarine, dull red orange & black	60	60

Edouard Branly A134

Early Postal Car A135

1944, Feb. 21 Engraved *Perf. 14x13*

No.	Type	Description	Unused	Used
471	A134	4fr ultramarine	15	10

Issued to commemorate the centenary of the birth of Edouard Branly, electrical inventor.

1944, June 10 *Perf. 13*

No.	Type	Description	Unused	Used
472	A135	1.50fr dark blue grn.	12	12

Issued to commemorate the centenary of France's traveling postal service.

Chateau de Chenonceaux A136

Claude Chappe A137

1944, June 10

No.	Type	Description	Unused	Used
473	A136	15fr lilac brown	35	35
		a. 15fr blk. brn.	2.50	2.50
		b. 15fr black	21.00	

1944, Aug. 14 *Perf. 14x13*

No.	Type	Description	Unused	Used
474	A137	4fr dark ultramarine	15	15

Issued to commemorate the 150th anniversary of the invention of an optical telegraph by Claude Chappe (1763–1805).

Gallic Cock A138

Marianne A139

1944 Lithograped *Perf. 12*

No.	Type	Description	Unused	Used
477	A138	10c yellow green	6	6
478	"	30c dark rose violet	10	10
479	"	40c blue	6	6
480	"	50c dark red	6	6
481	A139	60c olive brown	10	10
482	"	70c rose lilac	6	6
483	"	80c yellow green	30	30
484	"	1fr violet	5	5
485	"	1.20fr deep carmine	5	5
486	"	1.50fr deep blue	5	5
487	A138	2fr indigo	5	5
488	A139	2.40fr red orange	50	50
489	"	3fr deep blue green	12	12
490	"	4fr greenish blue	12	12
491	"	4.50fr black	12	12
492	"	5fr violet blue	1.50	1.50
493	A138	10fr violet	1.40	1.40
494	"	15fr olive brown	1.40	1.40
495	A138	20fr dk. slate green	1.50	1.50
		Nos. 477–495 (19)	7.60	7.60

Nos. 477–495 were issued first in Corsica after the Allied landing, and released in Paris Nov. 15, 1944.

Chateau de Chenonceaux—A140

1944, Oct. 30 Engraved *Perf. 13*

No.	Type	Description	Unused	Used
496	A140	25fr black	35	35

Thomas Robert Bugeaud A141

1944, Nov. 20

No.	Type	Description	Unused	Used
497	A141	4fr myrtle green	15	15

Issued to commemorate the 100th anniversary of the Battle of Isly, August 14th, 1844.

Church of St. Denis A142

1944, Nov. 20

No.	Type	Description	Unused	Used
498	A142	2.40fr brown carmine	12	12

Issued to commemorate the 800th anniversary of the Church of St. Denis.

Type of 1938-42, Overprinted in Black RF Inscribed "Postes Francaises"

1944 *Perf. 14x13½.*

No.	Type	Description	Unused	Used
499	A93	10c ultramarine	5	5
500	"	30c rose red	5	5
501	"	40c dark violet	5	5
502	"	50c greenish blue	5	5

The overprint "RF" in various forms, with or without Lorraine Cross, was also applied to stamps of the French State at Lyon and fourteen other cities.

French Forces of the Interior and Symbol of Liberation A143

1945, Jan.

No.	Type	Description	Unused	Used
503	A143	4fr dark ultramarine	10	8

Issued to commemorate the Liberation.

Stamps of the above design, and of one incorporating "FRANCE" in the top panel, were printed by photogravure in England during World War II upon order of the Free French Government. They were not issued. There are three values in each design; 25c green, 1fr red, 2.50fr blue. Price: set, above design, $135; set inscribed "FRANCE," $300.

Marianne
A144

Perf. 11½x12½.

1944-45 Engraved Unwmkd.

505	A144	10c ultramarine	4	3
506	"	30c bistre	4	3
507	"	40c indigo	4	3
508	"	50c red orange	4	3
509	"	60c chalky blue	4	3
510	"	70c sepia	4	4
511	"	80c deep green	4	3
512	"	1fr lilac	4	3
513	"	1.20fr dark olive green	4	4
514	"	1.50fr rose ('44)	5	4
515	"	2fr dark brown	6	5
516	"	2.40fr red	6	6
517	"	3fr bright olive green	6	5
518	"	4fr bright ultra.	5	5
519	"	4.50fr slate gray	10	6
520	"	5fr bright orange	10	6
521	"	10fr yellow green	12	10
522	"	15fr lake	25	25
523	"	20fr brown orange	75	45
523A	"	50fr deep purple	2.00	1.35
		Nos. 505-523A (20)	3.96	2.81

The 2.40fr exists imperf. in a miniature sheet of 4 which was not issued.

Coat of Arms A145 Ceres A146 Marianne A147

1945-47 Typo. *Perf. 14x13½.*

524	A145	10c brown black	5	3
525	"	30c dark blue green	5	5
526	"	40c lilac rose	10	10
527	"	50c violet blue	5	3
528	A146	60c brt. ultra.	10	10
530	"	80c bright green	5	3
531	"	90c dull green('46)	50	20
532	"	1fr rose red	5	3
533	"	1.20fr brown black	10	10
534	"	1.50fr rose lilac	6	6
535	A147	1.50fr rose pink	5	3
536	"	2fr myrtle green	5	3
536A	A146	2fr light blue green ('46)	7	7
537	A147	2.40fr scarlet	15	8
538	A146	2.50fr brown ('46)	10	6
539	A147	3fr sepia	4	3
540	"	3fr deep rose ('46)	6	3
541	"	4fr ultramarine	8	6
541A	"	4fr violet ('46)	8	5
541B	"	4.50fr ultra. ('47)	6	3
542	"	5fr light green	10	4
542A	"	5fr rose pink ('47)	6	4
543	"	6fr brt. ultra.	15	8
544	"	6fr crimson rose ('46)	10	5
545	"	10fr red orange	13	10
546	"	10fr ultra. ('46)	27	15
547	"	15fr brt. red violet	1.00	55
		Nos. 524-547 (27)	3.66	2.23

No. 531 is known only precanceled. See second note after No. 132.

Due to a reduction of the domestic postage rate, No. 542A was sold for 4.50fr.

See also Nos. 576 to 580, 594 to 602, 614, 615, 650 to 654.

Engraved.

1945-46 *Perf. 14x13*

548	A147	4fr dark blue	5	5
549	"	10fr deep blue ('46)	25	6
550	"	15fr bright red violet ('46)	1.50	30
551	"	20fr blue green ('46)	60	10
552	"	25fr red ('46)	1.50	30
		Nos. 548-552 (5)	3.90	81

Marianne
A148

1945 Engraved *Perf. 13*

553	A148	20fr dark green	70	35
554	"	25fr violet	1.20	70
555	"	50fr red brown	1.00	55
556	"	100fr brt. rose car.	2.75	1.65

CFA

French stamps inscribed or surcharged "CFA" and new value are listed under Réunion in Vol. IV.

Arms of Metz A149 Arms of Strasbourg A150

1945, Mar. 3 *Perf. 14x13*

557	A149	2.40fr dark blue	8	8
558	A150	4fr black brown	8	8

Liberation of Metz and Strasbourg.

Costumes of Alsace and Lorraine and Cathedrals of Strasbourg and Metz—A151

1945, May 16 *Perf. 13*

559	A151	4fr henna brown	15	15

Liberation of Alsace and Lorraine.

World Map Showing French Possessions—A152

1945, Sept. 17

560	A152	2fr Prussian blue	10	10

No. B193 Surcharged with New Value in Black.

1946 *Perf. 14x13½*

561	SP147	3fr on 2fr+1fr red orange	5	5

Coats of Arms.

Corsica A153 Alsace A154

Lorraine A155 County of Nice A156

Typographed.

1946 *Perf. 14x13½.* Unwmkd.

562	A153	10c dp. ultra. & blk.	5	3
563	A154	30c black, red orange & yellow	6	5
564	A155	50c brn., yel. & red	6	5
565	A156	60c red, ultramarine & black	8	6

Reaching for "Peace" A157 Holding the Dove of Peace A158

1946, July 29 Engraved *Perf. 13*

566	A157	3fr Prussian green	7	5
567	A158	10fr dark blue	15	10

Peace Conference of Paris, 1946.

Vézelay
A159

Luxembourg Palace
A160

Rocamadour
A161

Pointe du Raz, Finistère
A162

1946 *Perf. 13.* Unwmkd.

568	A159	5fr rose violet	10	8
569	A160	10fr dark blue	12	8
570	A161	15fr dark violet brown	40	10
571	A162	20fr slate gray	20	6

See also Nos. 591-592.

Globe and Wreath
A163

1946, Nov.

572	A163	10fr dark blue	25	25

Issued to honor the general conference of the United Nations Educational, Scientific and Cultural Organization, Paris, 1946.

Cannes
A164

Stanislas Square, Nancy
A165

1946-48 Engraved *Perf. 13*

573	A164	6fr rose red	20	12
574	A165	25fr black brown	30	8
575	"	25fr dk. blue ('48)	1.00	30

Ceres & Marianne Types of 1945.

Typographed.

1947 *Perf. 14x13½* Unwmkd.

576	A146	1.30fr dull blue	17	10
577	A147	3fr green	15	3
578	"	3.50fr brown red	15	8
579	"	5fr blue	12	3
580	"	6fr carmine	10	3
		Nos. 576-580 (5)	69	27

Colonnade of the Louvre
A166

La Conciergerie, Paris Prison
A167

La Cité, Oldest Section of Paris
A168

Place de la Concorde
A169

1947, May 7 Engraved *Perf. 13*

581	A166	3.50fr chocolate	30	30
582	A167	4.50fr dark slate gray	30	30
583	A168	6fr red	50	50
584	A169	10fr bright ultra.	50	50

Issued to commemorate the 12th Congress of the Universal Postal Union, Paris, May 7 to July 7, 1947.

Auguste Pavie A170 François Fénelon A171

1947, May 30

585 A170 4.50fr sepia 15 15

Issued to commemorate the centenary of the birth of Auguste Pavie, French pioneer in Laos.

1947, July 12

586 A171 4.50fr chocolate 17 17

Issued to honor Francois de Salignac de la Mothe-Fénelon, prelate and writer.

Fleur-de-Lis and Double Carrick Bend A172

1947, Aug. 2 **Unwmkd.**

587 A172 5fr brown 20 20

Issued to commemorate the 6th World Boy Scout Jamboree held at Moisson, August 9th to 18th, 1947.

Captured Patriot A173 View of Conques A174

1947, Nov. 10 Engraved *Perf. 13*

588 A173 5fr sepia 18 18

No. 576 Surcharged in Carmine.

1947, Nov. Typo. *Perf. 14x13½*

589 A146 1fr on 1.30fr dull bl. 10 10

1947, Dec. 18 Engraved *Perf. 13*

590 A174 15fr henna brown 35 15

Types of 1946-47.

1948 Re-engraved.

591	A160	12fr rose carmine	18	18
592	"	15fr bright red	18	18
593	A174	18fr dark blue	30	15

"FRANCE" substituted for inscriptions "RF" and "REPUBLIQUE FRANCAISE."

Marianne Type of 1945.

1948–49 Typo. *Perf. 14x13½*

594	A147	2.50fr brown	1.35	85
595	"	3fr lilac rose	15	6
596	"	4fr light blue green	25	6
597	"	4fr brown orange	40	15
598	"	5fr light blue green	20	3
599	"	8fr blue	20	6
600	"	10fr bright violet	25	3
601	"	12fr ultra. ('49)	45	6
602	"	15fr crimson rose ('49)	50	3
		a. Bklt. pane of 10	35.00	
		Nos. 594-602 (9)	3.75	1.33

No. 594 known only precanceled. See second note after No. 132.

François René de Chateau-briand A175

1948, July 3 Engraved *Perf. 13*

603 A175 18fr dark blue 35 25

Issued to commemorate the centenary of the death of Vicomte de Chateaubriand (1768–1848).

Philippe François M. de Hautecloque (Gen. Jacques Leclerc)—A176

1948, July 3

604 A176 6fr gray black 15 15

See also Nos. 692-692A.

Chaillot Palace A177

A178

1948, Sept. 21

605	A177	12fr carmine rose	30	30
606	A178	18fr indigo	35	35

Issued to commemorate the meeting of the United Nations General Assembly, Paris, 1948.

Genissiat Dam A179 Paul Langevin A180

1948, Sept. 21

607 A179 12fr carmine rose 35 30

1948, Nov. 17 *Perf. 14x13*

Design: 8fr, Jean Perrin.

608	A180	5fr dark brown carmine	15	12
609	"	8fr dark greenish blue	15	12

Issued to commemorate the placing of the ashes of physicists Paul Langevin (1872–1946) and Jean Perrin (1870–1942) in the Pantheon.

No. 544 Surcharged with New Value and Bars in Black.

1949, Jan. *Perf. 14x13½*

610 A147 5fr on 6fr crimson rose 10 7

Arctic Scene A181

1949, May 2 *Perf. 13*

611 A181 15fr indigo 45 45

Issued to publicize French polar explorations.

Types of 1849 and 1945.

1949, May 9 Engraved *Imperf.*

612	A1	15fr red	2.75	2.75
		a. Strip of 4 (1 each Nos. 612 to 615)+label	12.50	12.50
613	"	25fr deep blue	2.75	2.75

Perf. 14x13

614	A147	15fr red	2.75	2.75
615	"	25fr deep blue	2.75	2.75

Printed in sheets containing a horizontal row of ten each of Nos. 612 to 615, the imperforate and perforated stamps separated by a row of labels.

Nos. 612 to 615 were issued to commemorate the centenary of the first French postage stamps.

Arms of Burgundy A182

Designs (Arms): 50c, Guyenne (Aquitania). 1fr, Savoy. 2fr, Auvergne. 4fr, Anjou.

1949, May 11 Typo. *Perf. 14x13½*

616	A182	10c blue, red & yellow	6	3
617	"	50c blue, red & yellow	8	4
618	"	1fr brown & red	8	4
619	"	2fr green, yel. & red	15	4
620	"	4fr blue, red & yel.	27	10
		Nos. 616-620 (5)	64	25

See also Nos. 659-663, 694-699, 733-739, 782-785.

Collegiate Church of St. Barnard and Dauphiné Arms—A183

1949, May 14 Engraved *Perf. 13*

621 A183 12fr red brown 30 20

Issued to commemorate the 600th anniversary of France's acquisition of the Dauphiné region.

U.S. and French Flags, Plane and Steamship—A184

1949, May 14

622 A184 25fr blue & carmine 60 50

Issued to publicize Franco-American friendship.

Cloister of St. Wandrille Abbey A185

1949, May 18

623 A185 25fr deep ultramarine 30 8

See also No. 649.

Type of 1849 Inscribed "1849–1949" in Lower Margin.

1949, June 1

624	A1	10fr brown orange	37.50	37.50
		a. Sheet of 10	400.00	400.00

Issued to commemorate the centenary of the first French postage stamp.

No. 624 has wide margins, measuring 40 x 52 mm., from perforation to perforation. Sold for 110 francs which included cost of admission to the Centenary International Exhibition, Paris, June 1949.

Claude Chappe A186 Jean Racine A187

Designs: 15fr, François Arago and André M. Ampère. 25fr, Emile Baudot. 50fr, Gen. Gustave A. Ferrié.

Inscribed: "C.I.T.T. PARIS 1949".

1949, June 13 *Perf. 13* Unwmkd.

625	A186	10fr vermilion	75	50
626	"	15fr sepia	1.35	50
627	"	25fr deep claret	2.40	2.00
628	"	50fr deep blue	3.00	1.50

Issued to publicize the International Telegraph and Telephone Conference, Paris, May–July 1949.

1949

629 A187 12fr sepia 30 30

Issued to commemorate the 250th anniversary of the death of Jean Racine, dramatist.

Abbey of St. Bertrand de Comminges A188

Meuse Valley, Ardennes A189

Mt. Gerbier de Jonc, Vivarais A190

1949 Engraved.

630	A188	20fr dark red	25	6
631	A189	40fr Prussian grn.	1.40	10
632	A190	50fr sepia	1.00	8

A191

1949, Oct. 18

633 A191 15fr deep carmine 30 25

Issued to commemorate the 50th anniversary of the Assembly of Presidents of Chambers of Commerce of the French Union.

U.P.U. Allegory A192

1949, Nov. 7

634	A192	5fr dark green	25	20
635	"	15fr deep carmine	40	30
636	"	25fr deep blue	1.00	60

Issued to commemorate the 75th anniversary of the formation of the Universal Postal Union.

Raymond Poincaré
A193

François Rabelais
A195

Charles Péguy and Cathedral at Chartres—A194

1950, May 27 ***Perf. 13*** **Unwmkd.**

637 A193 15fr indigo 35 30

1950, June

638 A194 12fr dark brown 30 30
639 A195 12fr red brown 30 30

Chateau of Chateaudun
A196

1950, Nov. 25

640 A196 8fr chocolate & bistre brown 30 30

Madame Récamier
A197

Marie de Sévigné
A198

1950

641 A197 12fr dark green 35 35
642 A198 15fr ultramarine 35 35

Palace of Fontainbleau
A199

1951, Jan. 20

643 A199 12fr dark brown 35 35

Jules Ferry
A200

Jean-Baptiste de la Salle
A202

Hands Holding Shuttle
A201

1951, Mar. 17

644 A200 15fr bright red 50 45

1951, Apr. 9

645 A201 25fr deep ultramarine 90 80

Issued to publicize the International Textile Exposition at Lille, April–May, 1951.

1951, Apr. 28

646 A202 15fr chocolate 35 35

Issued to commemorate the 300th anniversary of the birth of Jean-Baptiste de la Salle, educator and saint.

Map and Anchor
A203

1951, May 12

647 A203 15fr deep ultramarine 50 40

Issued to commemorate the 50th anniversary of the creation of the French colonial troops.

Vincent d'Indy
A204

1951, May 15

648 A204 25fr deep green 1.75 1.10

Issued to commemorate the centenary of the birth of Vincent d'Indy, composer.

Abbey Type of 1949.

1951

649 A185 30fr bright blue 3.50 2.25

Marianne Type of 1945–47.

1951 Typographed. ***Perf. 14x13½***

650 A147 5fr dull violet 40 3
651 " 6fr green 3.50 27
652 " 12fr red orange 45 4
653 " 15fr ultramarine 25 6
a. Booklet pane of 10 4.25
654 " 18fr cerise 5.50 40
Nos. 650–654 (5) 10.10 80

Professors Nocard, Bouley and Chauveau; Gate at Lyons School—A205

1951, June 8 Engraved ***Perf. 13***

655 A205 12fr red violet 60 50

Issued to honor Veterinary Medicine.

Gen. Picqué, Cols. Roussin and Villemin; Val de Grace Dome
A206

1951, June 17 **Unwmkd.**

656 A206 15fr red brown 65 40

Issued to honor Military Medicine.

St. Nicholas, by Jean Didier
A207

1951, June 23

657 A207 15fr indigo, deep claret & orange 55 40

Chateau Bontemps, Arbois
A208

1951, June 23

658 A208 30fr indigo 65 10

Arms Type of 1949

Arms of: 10c, Artois. 50c, Limousin. 1fr, Béarn. 2fr, Touraine. 3fr, Franche-Comté.

1951, June Typo. ***Perf. 14x13½***

659 A182 10c red, violet blue & yellow 6 3
660 " 50c green, red & blk. 15 8
661 " 1fr blue, red & yel. 18 6
662 " 2fr violet blue, red & yellow 30 5
663 " 3fr red, violet blue & yellow 80 17
Nos. 659–663 (5) 1.49 39

Seal of Paris
A209

Maurice Noguès and Globe
A210

Engraved

1951, July 7 ***Perf. 13*** **Unwmkd.**

664 A209 15fr deep blue, dark brown & red 55 35

Issued to commemorate the 2,000th anniversary of the founding of Paris.

1951, Oct. 13

665 A210 12fr indigo & blue 60 45

Issued to honor Maurice Nogues, aviation pioneer.

Charles Baudelaire
A211

Poets: 12fr, Paul Verlaine. 15fr, Arthur Rimbaud.

1951, Oct. 27

666 A211 8fr purple 30 30
667 " 12fr gray 45 45
668 " 15fr deep green 55 55

Georges Clemenceau
A212

1951, Nov. 11

669 A212 15fr black brown 30 30

Issued to commemorate the centenary of the birth of Georges Clemenceau.

Chateau du Clos, Vougeot
A213

1951, Nov. 17

670 A213 30fr black brown & brown 1.65 85

Chaillot Palace and Eiffel Tower
A214

1951, Nov. 6

671 A214 18fr red 80 60
672 " 30fr deep ultra. 1.00 70

Issued to publicize the opening of the Geneva Assembly of the United Nations, Paris, Nov. 6, 1951.

Observatory, Pic du Midi
A215

Abbaye aux Hommes, Caen
A216

1951, Dec. 22

673 A215 40fr violet 2.00 12
674 A216 50fr black brown 1.85 8

Marshal Jean de Lattre de Tassigny—A217

1952, May 8 ***Perf. 13*** **Unwmkd.**

675 A217 15fr violet brown 80 30

Issued to honor Marshal Jean de Lattre de Tassigny, 1890–1952.

See also No. 717.

Gate of France, Vaucouleurs
A218

1952, May 11

676 A218 12fr brown black 1.50 90

Flags and Monument at Narvik, Norway
A219

1952, May 28

677 A219 30fr violet blue 2.25 1.10

Issued to commemorate the 12th anniversary of the Battle of Narvik, May 27, 1940.

Chateau de Chambord
A220

1952, May 30

678 A220 20fr dark purple 45 8

Assembly Hall, Strasbourg
A221

1952, May 31

679 A221 30fr dark green 7.00 4.50

Issued to honor the Council of Europe.

Monument, Bir-Hacheim Cemetery
A222

1952, June 14

680 A222 30fr rose lake 2.50 1.60

Issued to commemorate the 10th anniversary of the defense of Bir-Hacheim.

Abbey of the Holy Cross, Poitiers
A223

1952, June 21

681 A223 15fr bright red 35 30

Issued to commemorate the 14th centenary of the foundation of the Abbey of the Holy Cross at Poitiers.

Leonardo da Vinci, Amboise Chateau and La Signoria, Florence—A224

1952, July 9

682 A224 30fr deep ultra. 5.00 3.00

Issued to commemorate the 500th anniversary of the birth of Leonardo da Vinci.

Garabit Viaduct
A225

1952, July 5

683 A225 15fr dark blue 50 40

Sword and Military Medals, 1852-1952
A226

Dr. René Laënnec
A227

1952, July 5

684 A226 15fr chocolate, green & yellow 50 40

Issued to commemorate the centenary of the creation of the Military Medal.

1952, Nov. 7

685 A227 12fr dark green 45 35

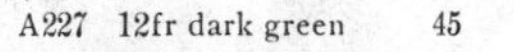

Versailles Gate, Painted by Utrillo
A228

1952, Dec. 20

686 A228 18fr violet brown 1.50 1.10

Publicity for the restoration of Versailles Palace. See also No. 728.

Mannequin
A229

1953, Apr. 24 ***Perf. 13*** **Unwmkd.**

687 A229 30fr blue black & rose violet 70 25

Issued to publicize the dressmaking industry of France.

Gargantua of François Rabelais
A230

Célimène from The Misanthrope
A231

Figaro, from the Barber of Seville
A232

Hernani of Victor Hugo
A233

1953

688 A230 6fr deep plum & carmine 12 10
689 A231 8fr indigo & ultra. 15 10
690 A232 12fr violet brown & dark green 15 6
691 A233 18fr violet brown & black brown 60 30

Type of 1948
Inscribed "Général Leclerc Maréchal de France"

1953-54

692 A176 8fr red brown 60 45
692A " 12fr dark green & gray grn. ('54) 1.85 1.10

Issued to honor the memory of General Jacques Leclerc.

Map and Cyclists, 1903-1953
A234

1953, July 26

693 A234 12fr red brown, ultramarine & black 60 50

Issued to commemorate the 50th anniversary of the inauguration of the Bicycle Tour of France.

Arms Type of 1949.

Coats of Arms: 50c, Picardy. 70c, Gascony. 80c, Berri. 1fr, Poitou. 2fr, Champagne. 3fr, Dauphiné.

1953 Typographed. ***Perf. 14x13½***

694 A182 50c blue, yellow & red 30 20
695 " 70c red, blue & yellow 30 20
696 " 80c blue, red & yellow 30 20
697 " 1fr blk., red & yellow 12 6
698 " 2fr brn., blue & yel. 12 6
699 " 3fr red, blue & yellow 35 8
Nos. 694-699 (6) 1.49 80

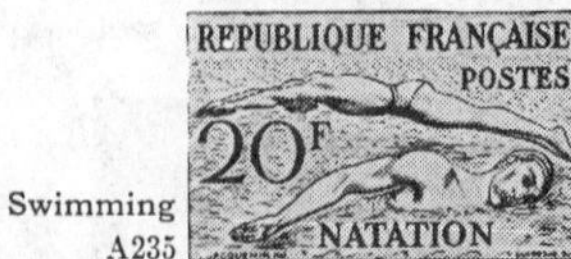

Swimming
A235

Sports: 25fr, Track. 30fr, Fencing. 40fr, Canoe racing. 50fr, Rowing. 75fr, Equestrian.

1953, Nov. 28 Engr. ***Perf. 13***

700 A235 20fr carmine & dark brown 65 8
701 A235 25fr dark green & dark brown 1.40 15
702 " 30fr ultramarine & dark brown 65 10
703 " 40fr chocolate & indigo 1.85 15
704 " 50fr blue green & dark brown 2.00 8
705 " 75fr org. & claret 13.50 7.50
Nos. 700-705 (6) 20.05 8.06

No. 654 Surcharged with New Value and Bars in Black.

1954 ***Perf. 14x13½***

706 A147 15fr on 18fr cerise 1.00 15

Farm Woman
A236

Gallic Cock
A237

1954 Typographed

707 A236 4fr blue 25 5
708 " 8fr brown red 4.00 30
709 A237 12fr cerise 2.50 35
710 " 24fr blue green 9.00 3.00

Nos. 707-710 are known only precanceled. See also Nos. 833-834, 840-844, 910-913, 939 and 952-955. See second note after No. 132.

Tapestry and Gobelin Workshop
A238

Entrance to Exhibition Park
A239

Designs: 30fr, Book manufacture. 40fr, Porcelain and glassware. 50fr, Jewelry and metalsmith's work. 75fr, Flowers and perfumes.

1954, May 6 Engr. ***Perf. 13***

711 A238 25fr red brown, carmine & black brown 2.40 10
712 " 30fr dark green & lilac gray 35 6
713 " 40fr dark brown, violet brown & orange brown 55 8
714 " 50fr bright ultra., dull green & orange brown 60 6
715 " 75fr deep carmine & magenta 3.75 30
Nos. 711-715 (5) 7.65 60

1954, May 22

716 A239 15fr blue & dark carmine 40 30

Issued to commemorate the 50th anniversary of the founding of the Fair of Paris.

De Lattre Type of 1952

1954, June 5

717 A217 12fr violet blue & indigo 1.85 1.00

Allied Landings
A240

1954, June 5

718 A240 15fr scarlet & ultra. 45 30

The 10th anniversary of the liberation.

View of Lourdes
A241

Street Corner, Quimper
A242

Views: 8fr, Seine valley, Les Andelys. 10fr, Beach at Royan. 18fr, Cheverny Chateau. 20fr, Beach, Gulf of Ajaccio.

1954

719 A241 6fr ultramarine, indigo & dark green 20 10
720 " 8fr bright blue & dark green 10 6
721 " 10fr aquamarine & orange brown 12 5
722 A242 12fr rose violet & dark violet 12 5
723 A241 18fr blue, dark green & indigo 50 27
724 " 20fr black brown, blue green & red brown 40 7
Nos. 719-724 (6) 1.44 60

See also No. 873.

Abbey Ruins, Jumièges
A243

St. Philibert Abbey, Tournus
A244

1954, June 13

725 A243 12fr violet blue, indigo & dark green 1.20 90

13th centenary of Abbey of Jumièges.

1954, June 18

726 A244 30fr indigo & blue 7.00 4.00

Issued to publicize the first conference of the International Center of Romance Studies.

View of Stenay
A245

1954, June 26

727 A245 15fr dark brown & orange brown 90 55

Issued to commemorate the 300th anniversary of the acquisition of Stenay by France.

Versailles Type of 1952

1954, July 10

728 A228 18fr dp. bl., indigo & vio. brn. 5.00 2.75

Villandry Chateau
A246

1954, July 17

729 A246 18fr dark blue & dk. blue green 4.50 3.00

Napoleon Awarding Legion of Honor Decoration—A247

1954, Aug. 14

730 A247 12fr scarlet 1.35 60

Issued to commemorate the 150th anniversary of the first Legion of Honor awards at Camp de Boulogne.

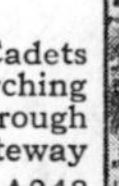

Cadets Marching Through Gateway
A248

1954, Aug. 1

731 A248 15fr violet gray, dark bl. & carmine 1.35 60

Issued to commemorate the 150th anniversary of the founding of the Military School of Saint-Cyr.

Allegory
A249

Duke de Saint-Simon
A250

1954, Oct. 4

732 A249 30fr indigo & choc. 7.00 4.50

Issued to publicize the fact that the metric system was first introduced in France.

Arms Type of 1949

Arms: 50c, Maine. 70c, Navarre. 80c, Nivernais. 1fr, Bourbonnais. 2fr, Angoumois. 3fr, Aunis. 5fr, Saintonge.

1954 Typographed. *Perf. 14x13½*

733 A182 50c multicolored 12 7
734 " 70c grn., red & yel. 12 10
735 " 80c blue, red & yel 22 15
736 " 1fr red, blue & yel. 10 6
737 " 2fr black, red & yel. 7 3
738 " 3fr brown, red & yel. 5 3
739 " 5fr blue & yellow 10 3
Nos. 733-739 (7) 78 47

1955, Feb. 5 Engr. *Perf. 13*

740 A250 12fr dark brown & violet brown 90 60

Issued to commemorate the 200th anniversary of the death of Louis de Rouvroy, Duke de Saint-Simon (1675-1755).

Allegory and Rotary Emblem
A251

Marianne
A252

1955, Feb. 23

741 A251 30fr violet blue, blue & orange 90 70

Issued to commemorate the 50th anniversary of the founding of Rotary International.

1955-59 Typo. *Perf. 14x13½*

751 A252 6fr terra cotta 2.75 1.85
752 " 12fr green 1.85 1.35
a. Bklt. pane of 10+2 labels 22.50
753 " 15fr carmine 30 3
a. Bklt. pane of 10 4.50
754 " 18fr green ('58) 30 6
755 " 20fr ultra. ('57) 30 3
a. Bklt. pane of 10 4.00
756 " 25fr rose red ('59) 60 3
a. Bklt. pane of 8 5.00
b. Bklt. pane of 10 4.75
Nos. 751-756 (6) 6.10 3.35

No. 751 was issued in coils of 1,000.
No. 752 was issued in panes of 10 stamps and two labels with marginal instructions for folding to form a booklet.
Nos. 754-755 are found in two types, distinguished by the numerals. On the 18fr there is no serif at base of "1" on the earlier type.

Philippe Lebon, Inventor of Illuminating Gas—A253

Inventors: 10fr, Barthélemy Thimonnier, sewing machine. 12fr, Nicolas Appert, canned foods. 18fr, Dr. E. H. St. Claire Deville, aluminum. 25fr, Pierre Martin, steel making. 30fr, Bernigaud de Chardonnet, rayon.

1955, Mar. 5 Engraved

757 A253 5fr dark violet blue & blue 65 35
758 " 10fr dark brown & orange brown 65 35
759 " 12fr dark green 80 60
760 " 18fr dark violet blue & indigo 2.00 1.50
761 " 25fr dark brownish pur. & violet 2.25 1.10
762 " 30fr rose carmine & scarlet 2.25 1.10
Nos. 757-762 (6) 8.60 5.00

St. Stephen Bridge, Limoges
A254

1955, Mar. 26 *Perf. 13* Unwmkd.

763 A254 12fr yellow brown & dark violet brown 1.25 85

Gloved Model in Place de la Concorde
A255

1955, Mar. 26

764 A255 25fr black brown, violet blue & black 65 10

Issued to publicize French glove manufacturing.

Jean Pierre Claris de Florian
A256

1955, Apr. 2

765 A256 12fr blue green 70 45

200th anniversary of the birth of Jean Pierre Claris de Florian, fabulist.

Eiffel Tower and Television Antennas
A257

1955, Apr. 16

766 A257 15fr indigo & ultra. 55 35

Issued to publicize French advancement in television.

Wire Fence and Guard Tower
A258

1955, Apr. 23

767 A258 12fr dark gray blue & brown black 55 45

Issued to commemorate the 10th anniversary of the liberation of concentration camps.

Electric Train
A259

1955, May 11

768 A259 12fr black brown & slate blue 75 50

Issued to publicize the electrification of the Valenciennes-Thionville railroad line.

Jacquemart of Moulins
A260

1955, May 28

769 A260 12fr black brown 1.10 60

Jules Verne and Nautilus
A261

1955, June 3

770 261 30fr indigo 5.75 4.50

Issued to commemorate the 50th anniversary of the death of Jules Verne.

Auguste and Louis Lumière and Motion Picture Projector
A262

1955, June 12

771 A262 30fr rose brown 4.50 3.25

Issued to commemorate the 60th anniversary of the invention of motion pictures.

Jacques Coeur and His Mansion at Bourges
A263

1955, June 18

772 A263 12fr violet 2.25 1.25

Issued to commemorate the 5th centenary of the death of Jacques Coeur (1395?–1456), French merchant.

Corvette "La Capricieuse"
A264

1955, July 9

773 A264 30fr aqua. & dk. bl. 5.50 3.50

Issued to commemorate the centenary of the voyage of La Capricieuse to Canada.

Bordeaux
A265

Designs: 8fr, Marseilles. 10fr, Nice. 12fr, Valentre bridge, Cahors. 18fr, Uzerche. 25fr, Fortifications, Brouage.

1955, Oct. 15

774 A265 6fr carmine lake 7 5
775 " 8fr indigo 8 5
776 " 10fr deep ultramarine 10 5
777 " 12fr violet & brown 10 5
778 " 18fr bluish green & indigo 35 8
779 " 25fr orange brown & red brown 30 5
Nos. 774–779 (6) 1.00 33

See Nos. 838–839.

Mount Pelée, Martinique
A266

1955, Nov. 1

780 A266 20fr dark & light purple 35 5

Gérard de Nerval
A267

1955, Nov. 11

781 A267 12fr lake & sepia 55 35

Issued to commemorate the centenary of the death of Gérard de Nerval (Labrunie), author.

Arms Type of 1949.

Arms of: 50c, County of Foix. 70c, Marche. 80c, Roussillon. 1fr, Comtat Venaissin.

Perf. 14x13½

1955, Nov. 19 Typo. **Unwmkd.**

782 A182 50c multicolored 5 4
783 " 70c red, blue & yellow 6 4
784 " 80c brn., yel. & red 6 4
785 " 1fr bl., red & yellow 5 5

Concentration Camp Victim and Monument
A268

Belfry at Douai
A269

1956, Jan. 14 Engr. *Perf. 13*

786 A268 15fr brown black & red brown 25 25

No. 786 shows the national memorial for Nazi deportation victims erected at the Natzwiller Struthof concentration camp in Alsace.

1956, Feb. 11

787 A269 15fr ultramarine & indigo 30 30

Col. Emil Driant
A270

1956, Feb. 21

788 A270 15fr dark blue 30 30

Issued to commemorate the 40th anniversary of the death of Col. Emil Driant during the battle of Verdun.

Trench Fighting
A271

1956, Mar. 3

789 A271 30fr indigo & dk. olive 1.10 70

40th anniversary of Battle of Verdun.

Jean Henri Fabre, Entomology
A272

Scientists: 15fr, Charles Tellier, Refrigeration. 18fr, Camille Flammarion, Popular Astronomy. 30fr, Paul Sabatier, Catalytic Chemistry.

1956, Apr. 7

790 A272 12fr violet brown & orange brown 40 35
791 " 15fr violet blue & intense black 60 35
792 " 18fr bright ultra. 1.75 1.10
793 " 30fr Prussian green & dk. green 1.85 1.10

Grand Trianon, Versailles
A273

1956, Apr. 14

794 A273 12fr violet brown & gray green 1.40 90

Symbols of Latin American and French Culture
A274

1956, Apr. 21

795 A274 30fr brown & red brown 1.85 1.25

Issued in recognition of the friendship between France and Latin America.

"The Smile of Reims" and Botticelli's "Spring"
A275

1956, May 5

796 A275 12fr black & green 90 40

Issued to emphasize the cultural and artistic kinship of Reims and Florence.

Leprosarium and Maltese Cross
A276

1956, May 12

797 A276 12fr sepia, red brown & red 45 30

Issued in honor of the Knights of Malta.

St. Yves de Treguier
A277

1956, May 19

798 A277 15fr bluish gray & black 35 30

Issued in honor of St. Yves, patron saint of lawyers.

Marshal Franchet d'Esperey
A278

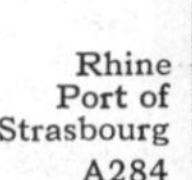

Miners Monument
A279

1956, May 26

799 A278 30fr deep claret 1.00 60

Issued to commemorate the centenary of the birth of Marshal Louis Franchet d'Esperey.

1956, June 2

800 A279 12fr violet brown 40 30

Issued to commemorate the 100th anniversary of the town Montceau-les-Mines.

Basketball
A280

"Rebuilding Europe"
A281

Sports: 40fr, Pelota (Jai alai). 50fr, Rugby. 75fr, Mountain climbing.

1956, July 7

801 A280 30fr gray violet & black 45 10
802 " 40fr brown & violet brown 55 20
803 " 50fr rose violet & violet 60 6
804 " 75fr indigo, green & blue 1.50 60

Europa Issue.

Perf. 13½x14

1956, Sept. 15 Typo. **Unwmkd.**

805 A281 15fr rose & rose lake 80 10

Engraved.

Perf. 13

806 A281 30fr light blue violet blue 2.40 45

Issued to symbolize the cooperation among the six countries comprising the Coal and Steel Community.

No. 805 measures 21x35½mm., No. 806 measures 22x35½mm.

Dam at Donzère-Mondragon
A282

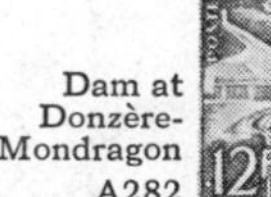

Cable Railway to Pic du Midi
A283

Rhine Port of Strasbourg
A284

1956, Oct. 6 Engraved *Perf. 13*

807 A282 12fr gray violet & violet brown 55 45
808 A283 18fr indigo 1.00 55
809 A284 30fr indigo & dk. bl. 1.75 1.00

French technical achievements.

Antoine-Augustin Parmentier
A285

1956, Oct. 27

810 A285 12fr brown red & brown 50 30

Issued in honor of A. A. Parmentier, nutrition chemist, who popularized the potato in France.

Petrarch—A286

Portraits: 12fr, J. B. Lully. 15fr, J. J. Rousseau. 18fr, Benjamin Franklin. 20fr, Frederic Chopin. 30fr, Vincent van Gogh.

1956, Nov. 10

811 A286 8fr green 40 30
812 " 12fr claret 40 30
813 " 15fr dark red 60 40
814 " 18fr ultramarine 2.25 1.40
815 " 20fr bright violet 2.25 70
816 " 30fr bright greenish blue 2.25 1.40
Nos. 811-816 (6) 8.15 4.50

Issued in honor of famous men who lived in France.

Pierre de Coubertin and Olympic Stadium—A287

1956, Nov. 24

817 A287 30fr dark blue gray & purple 1.35 85

Issued in honor of Baron Pierre de Coubertin, founder of the modern Olympic Games.

Homing Pigeon
A288

1957, Jan. 12

818 A288 15fr deep ultramarine, indigo & red brown 40 30

Victor Schoelcher
A289

1957, Feb. 16 **Engraved**

819 A289 18fr lilac rose 40 30

Issued in honor of Victor Schoelcher, who freed the slaves in the French Colonies.

Sèvres Porcelain
A290

1957, Mar. 23 ***Perf. 13*** **Unwmkd.**

820 A290 30fr ultra. & vio. bl. 60 45

Issued to commemorate the the bicentenary of the porcelain works at Sèvres (in 1956).

Gaston Planté and Storage Battery
A291

Designs: 12fr, Antoine Béclère and X-ray apparatus. 18fr, Octave Terrillon, autoclave, microscope and surgical instruments. 30fr, Etienne Oemichen and early helicopter.

1957, Apr. 13

821 A291 8fr gray black & deep claret 40 40
822 " 12fr dark blue, black & emerald 40 40
823 " 18fr rose red & magenta 1.35 1.35
824 " 30fr green & slate green 1.65 1.65

Uzès Chateau
A292

1957, Apr. 27

825 A292 12fr slate blue & bistre brown 30 20

Jean Moulin A293 — Le Quesnoy A294

Portraits: 10fr, Honoré d'Estienne d'Orves. 12fr, Robert Keller. 18fr, Pierre Brossolette. 20fr, Jean-Baptiste Lebas.

1957, May 18

826 A293 8fr violet brown 45 35
827 " 10fr black & violet blue 35 35
828 " 12fr brown & slate green 50 30
829 " 18fr purple & black 1.50 1.10
830 " 20fr Prussian blue & dark blue 70 40
Nos. 826-830 (5) 3.50 2.50

Issued in honor of the heroes of the French Underground of World War II.

See also Nos. 879-882, 915-919, 959-963, 990-993.

1957, June 1

831 A294 8fr dark slate green 10 8

See also No. 837.

Symbols of Justice
A295

1957, June 1

832 A295 12fr sepia & ultra. 25 25

Issued to commemorate the 150th anniversary of the French Cour des Comptes.

Farm Woman Type of 1954.

1957-59 ***Perf. 14x13½***

833 A236 6fr orange 10 5
833A " 10fr bright grn. ('59) 60 8
834 " 12fr red lilac 20 10

Nos. 833-834 issued without precancellation.

Symbols of Public Works
A296

1957, June 20 **Engr.** ***Perf. 13***

835 A296 30fr slate green, brown & ochre 50 40

Brest
A297

1957, July 6

836 A297 12fr gray green & brown olive 55 40

Scenic Types of 1955, 1957.

Designs: 15fr, Le Quesnoy. 35fr, Bordeaux. 70fr, Valentre bridge, Cahors.

1957, July 19 **Unwmkd.**

837 A294 15fr dark blue green & sepia 12 4
838 A265 35fr dark blue green & slate green 85 25
839 " 70fr black & dull green 2.25 60

Gallic Cock Type of 1954.

1957 **Typo.** ***Perf. 14x13½***

840 A237 5fr olive bistre 25 6
841 " 10fr bright blue 35 12
842 " 15fr plum 90 45
843 " 30fr bright red 2.50 75
844 " 45fr green 15.00 6.00
Nos. 840-844 (5) 19.00 7.38

Nos. 840-844 are known only precanceled. See second note after No. 132.

Leo Lagrange and Stadium
A298

1957, Aug. 31 **Engr.** ***Perf. 13***

845 A298 18fr lilac gray & black 40 30

Issued to commemorate the International University Games, Paris, Aug. 31-Sept. 8.

"United Europe" A299 — Auguste Comte A300

1957, Sept. 16

846 A299 20fr red brown & green 30 10
847 " 35fr dark brown & blue 60 30

Issued to publicize a united Europe for peace and prosperity.

1957, Sept. 14

848 A300 35fr brown red & sepia 70 70

Issued to commemorate the centenary of the death of Auguste Comte, mathematician and philosopher.

Roman Amphitheater, Lyon
A301

1957, Oct. 5 ***Perf. 13***

849 A301 20fr brown orange & brown violet 45 30

Issued to commemorate the 2,000th anniversary of the founding of Lyon.

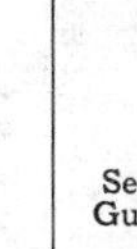

Sens River, Guadeloupe
A302

Beynac-Cazenac, Dordogne A303 — Nicolaus Copernicus A304

Designs: 10fr, Elysee Palace. 25fr, Chateau de Valencay, Indre. 35fr, Rouen Cathedral. 50fr, Roman Ruins, Saint-Remy. 65fr, Evian-les-Bains.

1957, Oct. 19

850 A302 8fr green & light brown 10 8
851 " 10fr dark olive bistre & violet brown 8 5
852 A303 18fr indigo & dark brown 20 5
853 A302 25fr blue gray & violet brown 22 8
854 A303 35fr carmine rose & lake 35 5
855 A302 50fr olive green & olive bistre 35 5
856 " 65fr dark blue & indigo 70 8
Nos. 850-856 (7) 2.00 44

See also Nos. 907-909.

1957, Nov. 9 **Engraved** ***Perf. 13***

Portraits: 10fr, Michelangelo. 12fr, Miguel de Cervantes. 15fr, Rembrandt. 18fr, Isaac Newton. 25fr, Mozart. 35fr, Johann Wolfgang von Goethe.

857 A304 8fr dark brown 35 20
858 " 10fr dark green 35 30
859 " 12fr dark purple 45 40
860 " 15fr brown & orange brown 45 30
861 " 18fr deep blue 1.10 70
862 " 25fr lilac & claret 80 40
863 " 35fr blue 1.20 1.00
Nos. 857-863 (7) 4.70 3.30

Louis Jacques Thénard
A305

1957, Nov. 30 **Unwmkd.**

864 A305 15fr olive bistre & greenish black 35 35

Issued to commemorate the centenary of the death of L. J. Thenard, chemist, and the founding of the Charitable Society of the Friends of Science.

Dr. Philippe Pinel
A306

Joseph Louis Lagrange
A307

Doctors' Portraits: 12fr, Fernand Widal. 15fr, Charles Nicolle. 35fr, René Leriche.

1958, Jan. 25

865 A306 8fr brown olive 50 35
866 " 12fr bright violet blue 50 35
867 " 15fr deep blue 50 40
868 " 35fr black 1.00 55

Issued in honor of famous French physicians.

1958, Feb. 15 ***Perf. 13***

Portraits: 12fr, Urbain Jean Joseph Leverrier. 15fr, Jean Bernard Leon Foucault. 35fr, Claude Louis Berthollet.

869 A307 8fr blue green & violet blue 50 40
870 " 12fr sepia & gray 50 40
871 " 15fr slate grn. & grn. 85 50
872 " 35fr maroon & copper red 1.25 75

Issued to honor French scientists.

Lourdes Type of 1954.

1958

873 A241 20fr greenish blue & olive 30 8

Le Havre
A308

Maubeuge
A309

Designs: 18fr, Saint-Die. 25fr, Sete.

1958, Mar. 29 Engr. ***Perf. 13***

874 A308 12fr olive green & carmine rose 35 35
875 A309 15fr bright purple & brown 55 40
876 " 18fr ultramarine & indigo 50 40
877 A308 25fr dark blue, blue green & brown 60 55

Reconstruction of war-damaged cities.

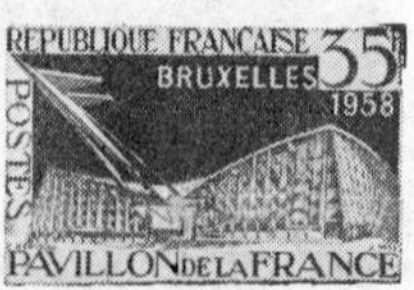

French Pavilion, Brussels
A310

1958, Apr. 12

878 A310 35fr brown, dark green & blue 40 30

Issued for the Universal and International Exposition at Brussels.

Heroes Type of 1957.

Portraits: 8fr, Jean Cavaillès. 12fr, Fred Scamaroni. 15fr, Simone Michel-Levy. 20fr, Jacques Bingen.

1958, Apr. 19

879 A293 8fr violet & black 30 25
880 " 12fr ultra. & green 30 25
881 " 15fr brown & gray 1.25 75
882 " 20fr olive & ultra. 1.00 75

Issued in honor of the heroes of the French Underground in World War II.

Bowling
A311

Sports: 15fr, Naval joust. 18fr, Archery (vert.). 25fr, Breton wrestling (vert.).

1958, Apr. 26

883 A311 12fr rose & brown 45 40
884 " 15fr blue, olive gray & green 45 30
885 " 18fr green & brown 80 55
886 " 25fr brown & indigo 80 50

Senlis Cathedral
A312

1958, May 17

887 A312 15fr ultramarine & indigo 35 35

Bayeux Tapestry Horsemen
A313

1958, June 21

888 A313 15fr blue & carmine 50 30

Europa Issue, 1958

Common Design Type

Size: 22x36mm.

1958, Sept. 13 Engraved ***Perf. 13***

889 CD1 20fr rose red 60 10
890 " 35fr ultramarine 70 24

Foix Chateau
A314

1958, Oct. 11

891 A314 15fr ultramarine, green & olive brown 25 10

Common Design Types pictured in section at front of book.

City Halls, Paris and Rome
A315

1958, Oct. 11

892 A315 35fr gray, greenish blue & rose red 60 40

Issued to publicize the cultural ties between Rome and Paris and the need for European unity.

UNESCO Building, Paris
A316

Design: 35fr, Different view of building.

1958, Nov. 1 ***Perf. 13***

893 A316 20fr greenish blue & olive bistre 25 15
894 " 35fr dark slate green & red orange 30 30

Issued to commemorate the opening of UNESCO (U.N. Educational, Scientific and Cultural Organization) Headquarters in Paris, Nov. 3.

Soldier's Grave in Wheat Field
A317

Arms of Marseilles
A318

1958, Nov. 11

895 A317 15fr dark green & ultramarine 25 20

Issued to commemorate the 40th anniversary of the World War I armistice.

1958–59 Typo. ***Perf. 14x13½***

Arms (Cities): 70c, Lyon. 80c, Toulouse. 1fr, Bordeaux. 2fr, Nice. 3fr, Nantes. 5fr, Lille. 15fr, Algiers.

896 A318 50c dk. blue & ultra. 5 5
897 " 70c multicolored 4 5
898 " 80c red, blue & yellow 5 5
899 " 1fr dark blue, yellow & red 6 4
900 " 2fr dark blue, red & green 6 5
901 " 3fr multicolored 6 5
902 " 5fr dark brn. & red 6 5
903 " 15fr multi. ('59) 17 6
Nos. 896–903 (8) 55 40

See also Nos. 938, 940, 973, 1040–1042, 1091–1095, 1142–1144.

Arc de Triomphe and Flowers
A319

1959, Jan. 17 Engraved ***Perf. 13***

904 A319 15fr brown, blue, green, claret & red 25 15

Paris Flower Festival.

Symbols of Learning and Medal
A320

1959, Jan. 24 ***Perf. 13***

905 A320 20fr lake, black & violet 20 15

Issued to commemorate the sesquicentennial of the Palm Leaf Medal of the French Academy.

Charles de Foucauld
A321

1959, Jan. 31

906 A321 50fr deep brown, blue & maroon 80 65

Issued to honor Father Charles de Foucauld, explorer and missionary of the Sahara.

Type of 1957

Designs: 30fr, Elysee Palace. 85fr, Evian-les Bains. 100fr, Sens River, Guadeloupe.

1959, Feb. 10

907 A302 30fr dark slate green 70 8
908 " 85fr deep claret 1.50 10
909 " 100fr deep violet 2.75 8

Gallic Cock Type of 1954.

1959 Typographed. ***Perf. 14x13½***

910 A237 8fr violet 35 6
911 " 20fr yellow green 90 35
912 " 40fr henna brown 4.50 2.50
913 " 55fr emerald 12.00 8.50

Nos. 910–913 were issued with precancellation. See second note after No. 132.

Miners' Tools and School
A322

1959, Apr. 11 Engr. ***Perf. 13***

914 A322 20fr red, black & blue 25 20

Issued to commemorate the 175th anniversary of the National Mining School.

Heroes Type of 1957.

Portraits: No. 915, The five martyrs of the Buffon school. No. 916, Yvonne Le Roux. No. 917, Médéric-Védy. No. 918, Louis Martin-Bret. 30fr, Gaston Moutardier.

1959, Apr. 25 Engr. ***Perf. 13***

915 A293 15fr black & violet 35 25
916 " 15fr magenta & rose violet 45 35
917 " 20fr green & greenish blue 45 35
918 " 20fr orange brown & brown 70 45
919 " 30fr magenta & vio. 75 50
Nos. 915–919 (5) 2.70 1.90

Dam at Foum el Gherza
A323

Marcoule Atomic Center
A324

Designs: 30fr, Oil field at Hassi Messaoud, Sahara. 50fr, C. N. I. T. Building (Centre National des Industries et des Techniques).

1959, May 23

920 A323 15fr olive & greenish blue 25 25
921 A324 20fr bright carmine & red brown 45 30
922 " 30fr dark blue, brown & green 40 30
923 A323 50fr olive green & slate blue 55 35

Issued to publicize French technical achievements.

Marceline Desbordes-Valmore
A325

1959, June 20

924 A325 30fr blue, brown & green 30 25

Issued to commemorate the centenary of the death of Marceline Desbordes-Valmore, poet.

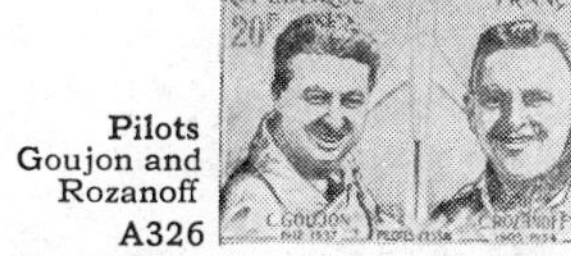

Pilots Goujon and Rozanoff
A326

1959, June 13

925 A326 20fr light blue & orange brown 30 30

Issued in honor of Charles Goujon and Col. Constantin Rozanoff, test pilots.

Tancarville Bridge
A327

1959, Aug. 1 Engr. *Perf. 13*

926 A327 30fr dark blue, brown & olive 30 20

Marianne and Ship of State
A328

Jean Jaures
A329

1959, July Typo. *Perf. 14x13½*

927 A328 25fr black & red 40 3

See also No. 942.

1959, Sept. 12 Engr. *Perf. 13*

928 A329 50fr chocolate 40 35

Issued to commemorate the centenary of the birth of Jean Jaures, socialist leader.

Europa Issue, 1959
Common Design Type

1959, Sept. 19

Size: 22x36mm

929 CD2 25fr bright green 40 15
930 " 50fr bright violet 60 25

Blood Donors
A330

1959, Oct. 17 Engraved

931 A330 20fr magenta & gray 20 15

French-Spanish Handshake
A331

1959, Oct. 24 *Perf. 13*

932 A331 50fr blue, rose carmine & orange 55 40

Issued to commemorate the 300th anniversary of the signing of the Treaty of the Pyrenees.

Polio Victim Holding Crutches
A332

Henri Bergson
A333

1959, Oct. 31

933 A332 20fr dark blue 20 18

Vaccination against poliomyelitis.

1959, Nov. 7

934 A333 50fr light red brown 45 35

Issued to commemorate the centenary of the birth of Henri Bergson, philosopher.

Avesnes-sur-Helpe
A334

Design: 30fr, Perpignan.

1959, Nov. 14

935 A334 20fr sepia & blue 20 15
936 " 30fr brown, deep claret & blue 30 20

New NATO Headquarters, Paris
A335

1959, Dec. 12

937 A335 50fr green, brown & ultramarine 1.00 65

Issued to commemorate the 10th anniversary of the North Atlantic Treaty Organization.

Types of 1958–59 and

Farm Woman
A336

Sower
A337

Designs: 5c, Arms of Lille. 15c, Arms of Algiers. 25c, Marianne and Ship of State.

Typographed.

1960–61 ***Perf. 14x13½*** **Unwmkd.**

938 A318 5c dk. brn. & red 5.25 6
939 A336 10c bright green 20 3
940 A318 15c red, ultramarine, yellow & green 20 5
941 A337 20c greenish blue & carmine rose 20 3
942 A328 25c vermilion & ultramarine 1.85 3
b. Bklt. pane of 8 20.00
c. Bklt. pane of 10 25.00
942A A337 30c gray & ultra. ('61) 1.60 30
Nos. 938–942A (6) 9.30 50

Earlier stamps of Farm Woman type (A336), but with no decimals in denominations, are listed as Nos. 707–708, 833–834 (A236). Nos. 938–942A are in the New Franc currency (100 old francs equal 1 New Franc).

Laon Cathedral
A338

Kerrata Gorge
A339

Designs: 30c, Fougères Chateau. 50c, Mosque, Tlemcen. 65c, Sioule Valley. 85c, Chaumont Viaduct. 1fr, Cilaos Church, Reunion.

1960, Jan. 16 Engr. *Perf. 13*

943 A338 15c blue & indigo 20 8
944 " 30c blue, sepia & green 55 6
945 A339 45c bright violet & olive gray 50 6
946 " 50c slate green & light claret 55 4
947 A338 65c slate green, blue & black brn. 55 17
948 " 85c blue, sepia & green 85 10
949 A339 1fr violet blue, blue & green 80 4
Nos. 943–949 (7) 4.00 55

Pierre de Nolhac
A340

1960, Feb. 13

950 A340 20c black & gray 30 20

Issued to commemorate the centenary of the birth of Pierre de Nolhac, curator of Versailles and historian.

Museum of Art and Industry, Saint-Etienne
A341

1960, Feb. 20

951 A341 30c brown, carmine & slate 40 30

Gallic Cock Type of 1954.

1960 Typographed. ***Perf. 14x13½***

952 A237 8c violet 85 6
953 " 20c yellow green 2.50 20
954 " 40c henna brown 5.00 1.50
955 " 55c emerald 14.00 9.00

Nos. 952–955 were issued only precanceled. See second note after No. 132.

View of Cannes
A342

1960, Mar. 5 Engr. *Perf. 13*

956 A342 50c red brown & light green 1.00 65

Issued to commemorate the meeting of European municipal administrators, Cannes, March, 1960.

Woman of Savoy and Alps
A343

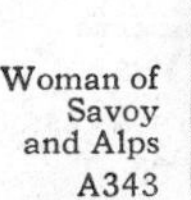

Woman of Nice and Shore
A344

1960 ***Perf. 13*** **Unwmkd.**

957 A343 30c slate green 50 30
958 A344 50c brown, yellow & rose 60 40

Issued to commemorate the centenary of the annexation of Nice and Savoy.

Heroes Type of 1957.

Portraits: No. 959, Edmund Debeaumarché. No. 960, Pierre Massé. No. 961, Maurice Ripoche. No. 962, Leonce Vieljeux. 50c, Abbé René Bonpain.

1960, Mar. 26

959 A293 20c bistre & black 1.25 75
960 " 20c pink & rose claret 1.25 75
961 " 30c violet & bright violet 1.25 75
962 " 30c slate blue & bright blue 1.40 1.00
963 " 50c slate green & red brown 2.00 1.40
Nos. 959–963 (5) 7.15 4.65

Issued in honor of the heroes of the French Underground of World War II.

"Education" and Children
A345

1960, May 21 Engraved *Perf. 13*

964 A345 20c rose lilac, purple & blk. 25 15

Issued to commemorate the 150th anniversary of the first secondary school in Strasbourg.

Blois Chateau
A346

View of La Bourboule
A347

1960, May

965 A346 30c dark blue, sepia & green 50 35

966 A347 50c olive brown, car. & green 60 40

Lorraine Cross
A348

Marianne
A349

1960, June 18

967 A348 20c red brown, dark brown & yellow green 25 20

Issued to commemorate the 20th anniversary of the French Resistance Movement in World War II.

Typographed

1960, June 18 ***Perf. 14x13½***

968 A349 25c lake & gray 18 5
a. Bklt. pane of 8 2.75
b. Bklt. pane of 10 3.00

Jean Bouin and Stadium
A350

1960, July 9 Engraved ***Perf. 13***

969 A350 20c blue, magenta & olive gray 25 18

Issued to commemorate the 17th Olympic Games, Rome, Aug. 25–Sept. 11.

Europa Issue, 1960.
Common Design Type

1960, Sept. 17 ***Perf. 13***

Size: 36x22mm.

970 CD3 25c green & bluish green 25 8

971 " 50c maroon & red lilac 40 20

Lisieux Basilica
A351

1960, Sept. 24 ***Perf. 13***

972 A351 15c blue, gray & black 25 20

Arms Type of 1958–59.
Design: Arms of Oran.

Typographed

1960, Oct. 15 ***Perf. 14x13½***

973 A318 5c red, blue, yellow & emerald 20 5

Madame de Staël by François Gerard
A352

1960, Oct. 22 Engraved ***Perf. 13***

974 A352 30c dull claret & brown 35 25

Issued to honor Madame de Staël (1766–1817), writer.

Gen. J. B. E. Estienne
A353

1960, Nov. 5

975 A353 15c light lilac & blk. 20 20

Issued to commemorate the centenary of the birth of Gen. Jean Baptiste Eugene Estienne.

Marc Sangnier and Youth Hostel at Bierville
A354

1960, Nov. 5

976 A354 20c blue, black & lilac 20 15

Issued to honor Marc Sangnier, founder of the French League for Youth Hostels.

Badge of Order of Liberation
A355

1960, Nov. 14 Engraved ***Perf. 13***

977 A355 20c black & bright green 30 18

Order of Liberation, 20th anniversary.

Lapwings
A356

Birds: 30c, Puffin. 45c, European teal. 50c, European bee-eaters.

1960, Nov. 12

978 A356 20c multicolored 35 20
979 " 30c " 35 20
980 " 45c " 80 70
981 " 50c " 70 35

Issued to publicize wildlife protection.

André Honnorat
A357

1960, Nov. 19

982 A357 30c blue, blk. & grn. 35 20

Issued to honor André Honnorat, statesman, fighter against tuberculosis and founder of the University City of Paris, an international students' community.

St. Barbara and Medieval View of School
A358

1960, Dec. 3 Engraved

983 A358 30c red, blue & olive brown 40 30

Issued to commemorate the 500th anniversary of St. Barbara School, Paris.

"Mediterranean" by Aristide Maillol
A359

Marianne by Cocteau
A360

1961, Feb. 18 ***Perf. 13*** **Unwmkd.**

984 A359 20c carmine & indigo 25 15

Issued to commemorate the centenary of the birth of Aristide Maillol, sculptor.

1961, Feb. 23

985 A360 20c blue & carmine 12 3

A second type has an extra inverted-V-shaped mark (a blue flag top) at right of hair tip. Price unused $2, used 50 cents.

Paris Airport, Orly
A361

1961, Feb. 25

986 A361 50c black, dark blue, & bluish green 55 35

Issued to commemorate the inauguration of new facilities at Orly airport.

George Méliès and Motion Picture Screen
A362

1961, March 11

987 A362 50c purple, indigo & olive bistre 75 55

Issued to commemorate the centenary of the birth of George Méliès, motion picture pioneer.

Jean Baptiste Henri Lacordaire
A363

1961, Mar. 25 ***Perf. 13***

988 A363 30c light brown & black 30 25

Issued to commemorate the centenary of the death of the Dominican monk Lacordaire, orator and liberal Catholic leader.

Jean Nicot
A364

1961, Mar. 25

989 A364 30c green, red brown & red 30 22

Issued to commemorate the fourth centenary of the introduction of the use of tobacco in Europe.

Heroes Type of 1957.

Portraits: No. 990, Jacques Renouvin. No. 991, Lionel Dubray. No. 992, Paul Gateaud. No. 993, Mère Elisabeth.

1961, Apr. 22

990 A293 20c blue & lilac 45 35
991 " 20c gray green & blue 70 45
992 " 30c brown orange & black 45 35
993 " 30c violet & black 1.10 70

Bagnoles-de-l'Orne
A365

1961, May 6

994 A365 20c olive, ochre, blue & green 25 20

Dove, Olive Branch and Federation Emblem
A366

1961, May 6

995 A366 50c bright blue, green & maroon 40 30

World Federation of Ex-Service Men.

Deauville in 19th Century
A367

1961, May 13 Engraved

996 A367 50c rose claret 80 70

Centenary of Deauville.

La Champmeslé
A368

Mont-Dore, Snowflake and Cable Car
A369

French actors: No. 998, Talma. No. 999, Rachel. No. 1000, Gérard Philipe. No. 1001, Raimu.

1961, June 10 *Perf. 13* Unwmkd.

Dark Carmine Frame

997	A368	20c chocolate & yellow green	30	25
998	"	30c brown & crimson	40	30
999	"	30c yellow green & slate grn.	40	30
1000	"	50c olive & chocolate	70	45
1001	"	50c blue green & red brown	70	50
		Nos. 997-1001 (5)	2.50	1.80

Issued to honor great French actors and in connection with the Fifth World Congress of the International Federation of Actors.

1961, July 1

1002	A369	20c orange & rose lilac	25	15

Pierre Fauchard A370 — St. Theobald's Church, Thann A371

1961, July 1

1003	A370	50c dark green & black	50	35

Issued to commemorate the bicentenary of the death of Pierre Fauchard, first surgeon dentist.

1961, July 1

1004	A371	20c slate green, violet & brn.	55	35

800th anniversary of Thann.

Europa Issue, 1961

Common Design Type

1961, Sept. 16 *Perf. 13*

Size: 35x22mm.

1005	CD4	25c vermilion	17	8
1006	"	50c ultramarine	32	20

Saint-Paul, Maritime Alps A372

Designs: 30c, Beach and sailboats, Arcachon. 45c, Sully-sur-Loire Chateau. 50c, View of Cognac. 65c, Rance Valley and Dinan. 85c, City hall and Rodin's Burghers, Calais. 1fr, Roman gates of Lodi, Medea, Algeria.

1961, Oct. 9 Engraved *Perf. 13*

1007	A372	15c blue & purple	10	6
1008	"	30c ultra., slate green & light brown	20	10
1009	"	45c violet blue, red brown & green	30	5
1010	"	50c green, Prussian blue & slate	30	5
1011	"	65c red brown, slate green & blue	40	10
1012	"	85c slate green, slate & red brown	60	10
1013	"	1fr dk. blue, slate & bistre	2.00	8
		Nos. 1007-1013 (7)	3.90	54

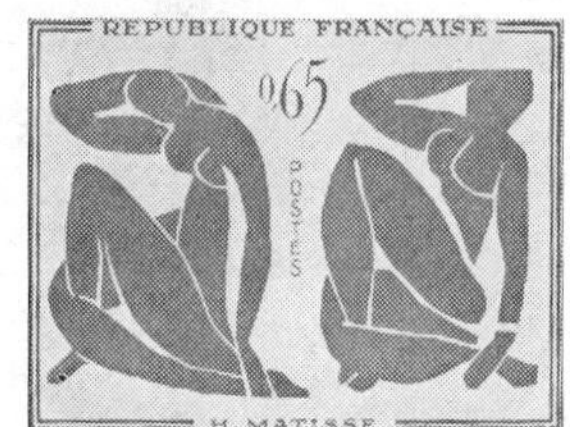

Blue Nudes, by Matisse—A373

Paintings: 50c, "The Messenger," by Braque. 85c, "The Cardplayers," by Cézanne. 1fr, "The 14th July," by Roger de La Fresnaye.

1961, Nov. 10 *Perf. 13x12*

1014	A373	50c dark brown, blue, black & gray	2.75	1.65
1015	"	65c green, violet, & ultra.	3.25	2.00
1016	"	85c black, brown, red & olive	3.00	2.40
1017	"	1fr multicolored	4.00	3.00

Liner France A374

1962, Jan. 11 Engraved *Perf. 13*

1018	A374	30c dark blue, blk. & car.	30	30

New French liner France.

Skier Going Downhill A375 — Maurice Bourdet A376

Design: 50c, Slalom.

1962, Jan. 27 *Perf. 13*

1019	A375	30c ultra. & dark violet blue	30	25
1020	"	50c dark green, blue & lilac	50	35

Issued to publicize the World Ski Championships, Chamonix, Feb. 1962.

1962, Feb. 17

1021	A376	30c slate	30	25

Issued to commemorate the 60th anniversary of the birth of Maurice Bourdet, radio commentator and resistance hero.

Pierre-Fidele Bretonneau A377

1962, Feb. 17

1022	A377	50c bright lilac & blue	45	35

Issued to commemorate the centenary of the death of Pierre-Fidele Bretonneau, physician.

Chateau and Bridge, Laval, Mayenne A378 — Gallic Cock A379

1962, Feb. 24

1023	A378	20c bistre brown & slate green	25	15

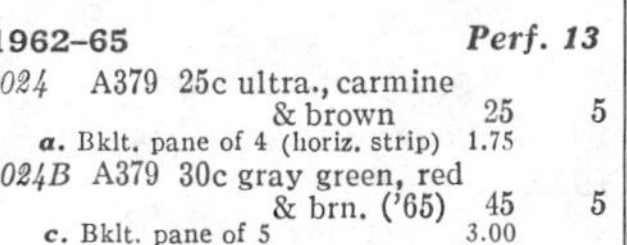

1962-65 *Perf. 13*

1024	A379	25c ultra., carmine & brown	25	5
		a. Bklt. pane of 4 (horiz. strip)	1.75	
1024B	A379	30c gray green, red & brn. ('65)	45	5
		c. Bklt. pane of 5	3.00	
		d. Bklt. pane of 10	6.00	

No. 1024 was also issued on experimental luminescent paper in 1963.

Ramparts of Vannes A380

Dunkirk A381

Paris Beach, Le Touquet A381a

1962 Engraved *Perf. 13*

1025	A380	30c dark blue	40	25
1026	A381	95c green, bistre & red lilac	1.10	16
1027	A381a	1fr grn., red brn. & blue	70	5

No. 1026 commemorates the 300th anniversary of Dunkirk.

Stage Setting and Globe A382

1962, Mar. 24 Unwmkd.

1028	A382	50c slate grn., ocher & magenta	50	35

International Day of the Theater, Mar. 27.

Memorial to Fighting France, Mont Valerien A383

Resistance Heroes' Monument, Vercors A384

Design: 50c, Ile de Sein monument.

1962, Apr. 7

1029	A383	20c olive & slate green	35	20
1030	A384	30c bluish black	40	30
1031	"	50c blue & indigo	45	45

Issued to publicize memorials for the French Underground in World War II.

Malaria Eradication Emblem and Swamp A385 — Nurses with Child and Hospital A386

1962, Apr. 14 Engraved

1032	A385	50c dark blue & dark red	45	40

Issued for the World Health Organization drive to eradicate malaria.

1962, May 5 *Perf. 13* Unwmkd.

1033	A386	30c blue grn., gray & red brown	25	25

National Hospital Week, May 5-12.

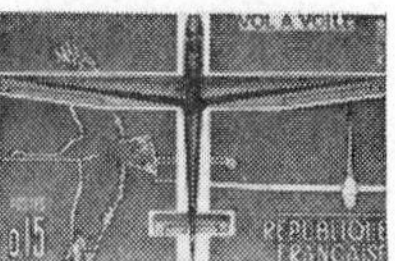

Glider—A387

Design: 20c, Planes showing development of aviation.

1962, May 12

1034	A387	15c orange red & brown	15	12
1035	"	20c lilac rose & rose claret	20	18

Issued to publicize sports aviation.

School Emblem
A388

1962, May 19 Engraved

1036 A388 50c maroon, ochre & dk. violet 60 50

Issued to commemorate the centenary of the Watchmaker's School at Besançon.

Louis XIV and Workers Showing Modern Gobelin—A389

1962, May 26 *Perf. 13* **Unwmkd.**

1037 A389 50c olive, slate grn. & carmine 55 40

Issued to commemorate the 300th anniversary of the Gobelin tapestry works, Paris.

Blaise Pascal—A390

1962, May 26

1038 A390 50c slate grn. & deep orange 55 50

Issued to commemorate 300th anniversary of the death of Blaise Pascal (1623–1662), mathematician, scientist and philosopher.

Palace of Justice, Rennes
A391

1962, June 12

1039 A391 30c blk., grayish blue & grn. 40 30

Arms Type of 1958–59

Arms: 5c, Amiens. 10c, Troyes. 15c, Nevers.

1962–63 Typo. *Perf. 14x13½*

1040 A318 5c verm., ultra. & yellow 7 4
1041 " 10c red, ultra. & yellow ('63) 5 4
1042 " 15c verm., ultra. & yellow 8 4

Phosphor Tagging

In 1970 France began to experiment with luminescence. Phosphor bars have been added to Nos. 1041, 1143, 1231, 1231C, 1292A–1294B, 1494–1498, 1563–1579B.

Rose
A392

Design: 30c, Old-fashioned rose.

1962, Sept. 8 Engraved *Perf. 13*

1043 A392 20c olive, grn. & br. carmine 25 20
1044 " 30c dk. slate grn., olive & car. 40 30

Europa Issue, 1962
Common Design Type

1962, Sept. 15

Size: 36x22mm.

1045 CD5 25c violet 20 8
1046 " 50c henna brown 40 20

Space Communications Center, Pleumeur-Bodou, France—A394

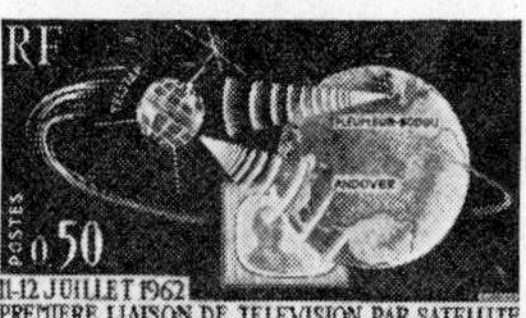

Telstar, Earth and Television Set
A395

1962, Sept. 29 Engraved *Perf. 13*

1047 A394 25c gray, yellow & green 20 10
1048 A395 50c dark blue, grn. & ultra. 40 30

Issued to commemorate the first television connection of the United States and Europe through the Telstar satellite, July 11–12.

"Bonjour Monsieur Courbet" by Gustave Courbet—A396

Paintings: 65c, "Madame Manet on Blue Sofa," by Edouard Manet. 1fr, "Guards officer on horseback," by Theodore Géricault (vert.).

1962, Nov. 9 *Perf. 13x12, 12x13*

1049 A396 50c multicolored 3.25 2.00
1050 " 65c " 2.25 1.75
1051 " 1fr " 4.00 3.25

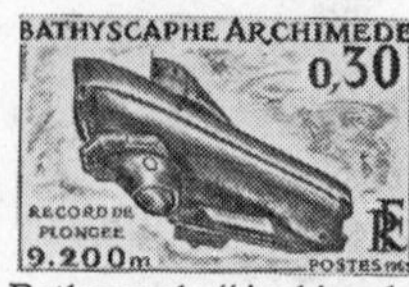

Bathyscaph "Archimede"
A397

1963, Jan. 26 *Perf. 13* **Unwmkd.**

1052 A397 30c dk. blue & blk. 30 25

French deep-sea explorations.

Flowers and Nantes Chateau
A398

1963, Feb. 11

1053 A398 30c vio. bl., carm. & slate green 30 25

Nantes flower festival.

St. Peter, Window at St. Foy de Conches—A399

Design: 50c, Jacob Wrestling with the Angel, by Delacroix.

1963, Mar. 2 *Perf. 12x13*

1054 A399 50c multicolored 3.00 2.40
1055 " 1fr " 6.50 5.00

See also Nos. 1076–1077.

Hungry Woman and Wheat Emblem
A400

1963, Mar. 21 Engraved *Perf. 13*

1056 A400 50c slate grn. & brn. 50 40

Issued for the "Freedom from Hunger" campaign of the U.N. Food and Agriculture Organization.

Cemetery and Memorial, Glières

A401

Design: 50c, Memorial, Ile de la Cité, Paris.

1963, Mar. 23 *Perf. 13* **Unwmkd.**

1057 A401 30c dk. brn. & olive 35 35
1058 " 50c indigo 40 40

Issued to commemorate the heroes of the resistance against the Nazis.

Beethoven, Birthplace at Bonn and Rhine
A402

Designs: No. 1060, Emile Verhaeren, memorial at Roisin and residence. No. 1061, Giuseppe Mazzini, Marcus Aurelius statue and Via Appia, Rome. No. 1062, Emile Mayrisch, Colpach Chateau and blast furnace, Esch. No. 1063, Hugo de Groot, Palace of Peace, The Hague and St. Agatha Church, Delft.

1963, Apr. 27 *Perf. 13* **Unwmkd.**

1059 A402 20c ocher, slate & bright green 30 30
1060 " 20c purple, black & maroon 30 30
1061 " 20c maroon, slate & olive 30 30
1062 " 20c maroon, dark brown & ocher 30 30
1063 " 30c dark brown, violet & ocher 40 40
Nos. 1059–1063 (5) 1.60 1.60

Issued to honor famous men of the European Common Market countries.

Hotel des Postes and Stagecoach, 1863
A403

1963, May 4

1064 A403 50c grayish black 40 30

Issued to commemorate the first International Postal Conference, Paris, 1863.

Lycée Louis-le-Grand, Belvédère, Panthéon and St. Étienne du Mont Church
A404

1963, May 18

1065 A404 30c slate green 25 20

Issued to commemorate the 400th anniversary of the Jesuit Clermont secondary school, named after Louis XIV.

St. Peter's Church and Ramparts, Caen
A405

1963, June 1 *Perf. 13* **Unwmkd.**

1066 A405 30c gray blue & brown 30 25

Radio Telescope, Nançay—A406

1963, June 8 Engraved

1067 A406 50c dark blue & dk. brown 35 30

Amboise Chateau
A407

Saint-Flour
A408

Designs: 50c, Côte d'Azur Varoise. 85c, Vittel. 95c, Moissac.

1963, June 15

1068 A407 30c slate, green & bister 20 5
1069 " 50c dark green, dk. blue & henna brn. 40 5
1070 A408 60c ultra., dark green & henna brn. 45 15
1071 A407 85c dk. grn., yel. grn. & brn. 80 15
1072 A408 95c dark brown & black 70 20
Nos. 1068-1072 (5) 2.55 60

Water Skiing Slalom
A409

1963, Aug. 31 *Perf. 13* **Unwmkd.**

1073 A409 30c slate green, blk. & car. 25 15

Issued to commemorate the World Water Skiing Championships, Vichy.

Europa Issue, 1963
Common Design Type

1963, Sept. 14

Size: 36x22mm.

1074 CD6 25c red brown 25 18
1075 " 50c green 45 24

Type of 1963

Designs: 85c, "The Married Couple of the Eiffel Tower" by Marc Chagall. 95c, "The Fur Merchants," window, Chartres Cathedral.

1963, Nov. 9 Engraved *Perf. 12x13*

1076 A399 85c multicolored 2.00 1.25
1077 " 95c " 1.00 75

Philatec Issue
Common Design Type

1963, Dec. 14 *Perf. 13* **Unwmkd.**

1078 CD118 25c dk. gray, slate green & dk. carmine 20 6

Radio and Television Center, Paris
A411

1963, Dec. 15 Engraved

1079 A411 20c orange brown, slate & olive 15 8

Fire Brigade Insignia, Symbols of Fire, Water and Civilian Defense
A412

1964, Feb. 8 Engraved *Perf. 13*

1082 A412 30c bl., org. & red 20 18

Issued to honor the fire brigades and civilian defense corps.

Handicapped Laboratory Technician
A413

1964, Feb. 22 *Perf. 13* **Unwmkd.**

1083 A413 30c green, red brown & brn. 20 15

Rehabilitation of the handicapped.

John II the Good (1319-64) by Girard d'Orleans
A414

1964, Apr. 25 *Perf. 12x13*

1084 A414 1fr multicolored 3.25 1.75

The lack of a price for a listed item does not necessarily indicate rarity.

Stamp of 1900
A415

Mechanized Mail Handling
A416

Designs: No. 1086, Stamp of 1900, Type A17. No. 1088, Telecommunications.

1964, May 9 *Perf. 13*

1085 A415 25c bister & dk. car. 25 25
1086 " 25c bister & blue 25 25
1087 A416 30c black, blue & orange brn. 25 25
1088 " 30c blk., car. rose & bluish grn. 25 25
a. Strip of 4 (1 each Nos. 1085-88 + label) 1.10 1.10

Printed in sheets of 20 stamps, containing five No. 1088a. The label shows the Philatec emblem in green.

Type of Semi-Postal Issue, 1959 with "25e ANNIVERSAIRE" added

1964, May 9

1089 SP208 25c multicolored 20 12

25th anniversary, night airmail service.

Madonna and Child from Rose Window of Notre Dame
A417

1964, May 23 *Perf. 12x13*

1090 A417 60c multicolored 75 60

Issued to commemorate the 800th anniversary of Notre Dame Cathedral, Paris.

Arms Type of 1958-59

Arms: 1c, Niort. 2c, Guéret. 12c, Agen. 18c, Saint-Denis, Réunion. 30c, Paris.

1964-65 Typo. *Perf. 14x13½*

1091 A318 1c vio. blue & yel. 3 3
1092 " 2c emerald, vio. bl. & yellow 3 3
1093 " 12c blk., red & yel. 10 3
1094 " 18c multicolored 14 8
1095 " 30c vio. bl. & red ('65) 25 4
a. Bklt. pane of 10 5.00
Nos. 1091-1096 (5) 55 21

Gallic Coin
A418
Perf. 13½x14

1964-66 Typographed **Unwmkd.**

1096 A418 10c emerald & bister 90 5
1097 " 15c org. & bister ('66) 45 5
1098 A418 25c lilac & brown 50 10
1099 " 50c bright bl. & brn. 75 15

Nos. 1096-1099 are known only precanceled. See second note after No. 132. See Nos. 1240-1242, 1315-1318, 1421-1424.

Postrider, Rocket and Radar Equipment—A419

1964, June 5 Engraved *Perf. 13*

1100 A419 1fr brown, dk. red & dark blue 15.00 15.00

Sold for 4fr, including 3fr admission to PHILATEC. Issued in sheets of 8 stamps and 8 labels (2x8 subjects with labels in horizontal rows 1, 4, 5, 8; stamps in rows 2, 3, 6, 7). Commemorative inscriptions on side margins.

Caesar's Tower, Provins
A420

Chapel of Notre Dame du Haut, Ronchamp—A421

1964-65

1101 A421 40c slate grn., dk. brn. & brn. ('65) 30 6
1102 A420 70c slate, green & carmine 45 6
1103 A421 1.25fr brt. bl., slate grn. & olive 1.00 35

The 40c was issued in vertical coils in 1971. Every 10th coil stamp has a red control number printed twice on the back.

Georges Mandel
A422

Judo
A423

1964, July 4 *Perf. 13* **Unwmkd.**

1104 A422 30c violet brown 25 25

Issued to commemorate the 20th anniversary of the death of Georges Mandel (1885-1944), Cabinet minister, executed by the Nazis.

1964, July 4

1105 A423 50c dark blue & violet brown 35 20

Issued to publicize the 18th Olympic Games, Tokyo, Oct. 10-25, 1964.

Champlevé Enamel from Limoges, 12th Century—A424

Design: No. 1107, The Lady (Claude Le Viste ?) with the Unicorn, 15th century tapestry.

1964 ***Perf. 12x13***

1106 A424 1fr multicolored 2.50 1.35
1107 " 1fr " 90 70

No. 1106 shows part of an enamel sepulchral plate portraying Geoffrey IV, Count of Anjou and Le Maine (1113–1151), who was called Geoffrey Plantagenet.

Issue dates: No. 1106, July 4. No. 1107, Oct. 31.

Paris Taxis Carrying Soldiers to Front, 1914
A425

1964, Sept. 5 ***Perf. 13*** **Unwmkd.**

1108 A425 30c black, bl. & red 35 20

50th anniversary of Battle of the Marne.

Europa Issue, 1964
Common Design Type

1964, Sept. 12 Engraved
Size: 22x36mm.

1109 CD7 25c dk. car., dp. ocher & grn. 20 10
1110 " 50c vio., yel. grn. & dk. car. 40 20

Cooperation Issue
Common Design Type

1964, Nov. 6 ***Perf. 13*** **Unwmkd.**

1111 CD119 25c red brown, dk. brn. & dk. bl. 20 10

Joux Chateau
A427

1965, Feb. 6 Engraved

1112 A427 1.30fr reddish brn., brn. red & dark brn. 80 15

"The English Girl from the Star" by Toulouse-Lautrec—A428

St. Paul on the Damascus Road, Window, Cathedral of Sens
A429

Leaving for the Hunt
A430

Apocalypse Tapestry, 14th Century
A431

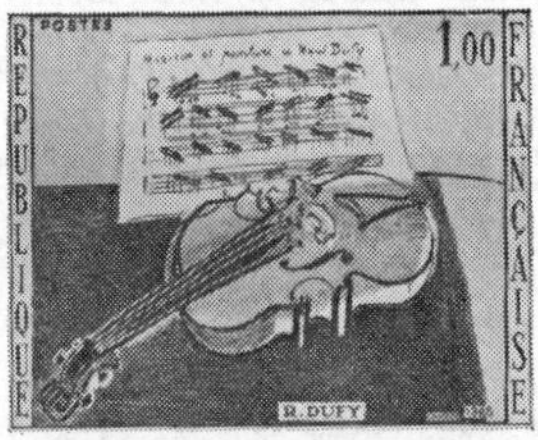

"The Red Violin" by Raoul Dufy
A432

Designs: No. 1115, "August" miniature of Book of Hours of Jean de France, Duc de Berry ("Les Très Riches Heures du Duc de Berry"), painted by Flemish brothers, Pol, Hermant and Jannequin Limbourg, 1411–16. No. 1116, Scene from oldest existing set of French tapestries, showing the Winepress of the Wrath of God (Revelations 14: 19–20).

1965 ***Perf. 12x13, 13x12***

1113 A428 1fr multicolored 75 60
1114 A429 1fr " 55 45
1115 A430 1fr " 50 40
1116 A431 1fr " 50 40
1117 A432 1fr blk., pink & car. 50 40
Nos. 1113–1117 (5) 2.80 2.25

No. 1114 issued to commemorate the 800th anniversary of the Cathedral of Sens.

Dates of issue: No. 1113, Mar. 12. No. 1114, June 5. No. 1115, Sept. 25. No. 1116, Oct. 30. No. 1117, Nov. 6.

Paris Parade of Returning Deportees, 1945
A433

1965, Apr. 1 ***Perf. 13*** **Unwmkd.**

1118 A433 40c Prussian green 40 30

Issued to commemorate the 20th anniversary of the return of people deported during World War II.

House of Youth and Culture, Troyes
A434

1965, Apr. 10 Engraved

1119 A434 25c indigo, brown & dk. green 30 15

Issued to publicize the 20th anniversary of the establishment of recreational cultural centers for young people.

Woman Carrying Flowers
A435

Flags of France, USA, USSR and Great Britain Crushing Swastika
A436

1965, Apr. 24 ***Perf. 13*** **Unwmkd.**

1120 A435 60c dark green, deep orge. & verm. 40 30

Issued to publicize the tourist Campaign of Welcome and Amiability.

1965, May 8

1121 A436 40c black, carmine & ultra. 30 15

Issued to commemorate the 20th anniversary of victory in World War II.

Telegraph Key, Syncom Satellite and Pleumeur-Bodou Station
A437

1965, May 17

1122 A437 60c dark blue, brn. & black 40 30

Issued to commemorate the centenary of the International Telecommunication Union.

Croix de Guerre
A438

1965, May 22 Engraved

1123 A438 40c red, brown & bright green 30 25

Issued to commemorate the 50th anniversary of the Croix de Guerre medal.

Cathedral of Bourges
A439

Moustiers-Sainte-Marie
A440

Views: 30c, Road and tunnel, Mont Blanc. 60c, Aix-les-Bains, sailboat. 75c, Tarn Gorge, Lozère mountains. 95c, Vendée River, man poling boat, and windmill. 1fr, Prehistoric stone monuments, Carnac.

1965, June–July

1124 A439 30c bl., vio. bl. & brown violet 30 6
1125 " 40c gray blue & reddish brn. 30 18
1126 A440 50c green, blue gray & bister 35 6
1127 A439 60c blue & red brn. 40 10
1128 " 75c brown, blue & green 80 40
1129 A440 95c brn., grn. & bl. 70 15
1130 " 1fr gray, green & brown 65 6
Nos. 1124–1130 (7) 3.50 1.01

No. 1124 was issued July 17 to commemorate the opening of the Mont Blanc Tunnel. No. 1125 (Bourges Cathedral) was issued in connection with the French Philatelic Societies Federation Congress, held at Bourges.

Europa Issue, 1965
Common Design Type

1965, Sept. 25 ***Perf. 13***
Size: 36x22mm.

1131 CD8 30c red 25 6
1132 " 60c gray 40 25

Planting Seedling
A441

Etienne Régnault, "Le Taureau" and Coast of Reunion
A442

1965, Oct. 2

1133 A441 25c slate green, yel. grn. & red brn. 18 12

National reforestation campaign.

1965, Oct. 2

1134 A442 30c indigo & dark carmine 20 10

Tercentenary of settlement of Reunion.

Atomic Reactor and Diagram, Symbols of Industry, Agriculture and Medicine

A443

1965, Oct. 9

1135 A443 60c brt. bl. & blk. 40 30

Issued to commemorate the 20th anniversary of the Atomic Energy Commission.

Air Academy and Emblem

A444

1965, Nov. 6 ***Perf. 13***

1136 A444 25c dk. bl. & green 15 10

Issued to commemorate the 50th anniversary of the Air Academy, Salon-de-Provence.

French Satellite A-1 Issue

Common Design Type

Design: 60c, A-1 satellite.

1965, Nov. 30 Engraved ***Perf. 13***

1137 CD121 30c Prus. blue, brt. blue & blk. 20 20

1138 " 60c black, Prus. bl. & brt. blue 40 30

a. Strip of 2 + label 65

Issued to commemorate the launching of France's first satellite, Nov. 26, 1965. No. 1138a contains one each of Nos. 1137-1138 and bright blue label with commemorative inscription. Each sheet contains 16 triptychs (2x8).

Arms of Auch

A446

Arms (Cities): 20c, Saint-Lô. 25c, Mont-de-Marsan.

Typo.; Photo. (20c)

1966 ***Perf. 14x13; 14 (20c)***

1142 A446 5c blue & red 5 3

1143 " 20c vio. bl., silver, gold & red 10 3

1144 " 25c red brn. & ultra. 18 6

The 5c and 20c were issued in sheets and in vertical coils. In the coils, every 10th stamp has a red control number on the back.

French Satellite D-1 Issue

Common Design Type

1966, Feb. 18 Engraved ***Perf. 13***

1148 CD122 60c blue blk., grn. & claret 35 30

Launching of the D-1 satellite at Hammaguir, Algeria, Feb. 17, 1966.

Horses from Bronze Vessel of Vix

A448

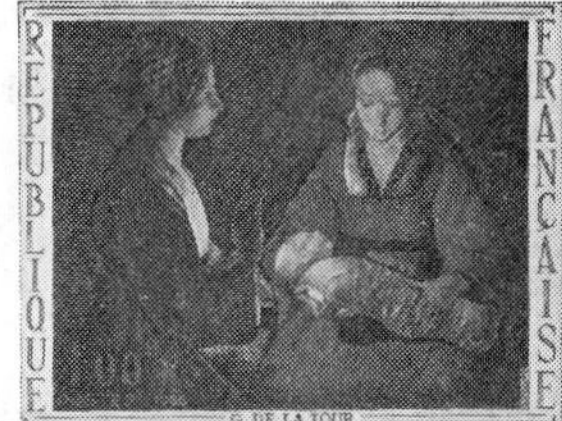

"The Newborn" by Georges de La Tour

A449

The Baptism of Judas (4th Century Bishop of Jerusalem)

A450

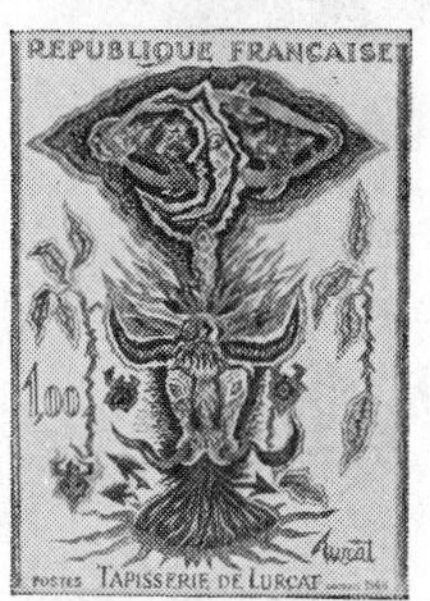

"The Moon and the Bull" Tapestry by Jean Lurçat

A451

"Crispin and Scapin" by Honoré Daumier

A452

1966 ***Perf. 13x12, 12x13***

1149 A448 1fr multicolored 50 40

1150 A449 1fr " 50 40

1151 A450 1fr " 50 40

1152 A451 1fr multicolored 55 45

1153 A452 1fr " 55 45

Nos. 1149-1153 (5) 2.60 2.10

The design of No. 1149 is a detail from a 6th century B.C. vessel, found in 1953 in a grave near Vix, Cote d'Or.

The design of No. 1151 is from a stained glass window in the 13th century Sainte-Chapelle, Paris.

Issue dates: No. 1149, Mar. 26. No. 1150, June 25. No. 1151, Oct. 22. No. 1152, Nov. 19. No. 1153, Dec. 10.

Chessboard, Knight, Emblems for King and Queen

A453

St. Michael Slaying the Dragon

A455

Rhone Bridge, Pont-Saint-Esprit

A454

1966, Apr. 2 Engraved ***Perf. 13***

1154 A453 60c sepia, gray & dk. vio. blue 50 30

Issued to publicize the Chess Festival.

1966, Apr. 23 ***Perf. 13*** **Unwmkd.**

1155 A454 25c blk. & dull blue 20 12

1966, Apr. 30 Litho. and Engr.

1156 A455 25c multicolored 25 10

Millenium of Mont-Saint-Michel.

Stanislas Leszczynski, Lunéville Chateau

A456

1966, May 6 Engraved

1157 A456 25c slate, green & brown 18 12

Issued to commemorate the 200th anniversary of the reunion of Lorraine and Bar (Barrois) with France.

St. Andrew's and Sèvre River, Niort

A457

1966, May 28 Engraved ***Perf. 13***

1158 A457 40c bright blue, indigo & grn. 35 20

Bernard Le Bovier de Fontenelle and 1666 Meeting Room

A458

1966, June 4

1159 A458 60c dark carmine rose & brown 40 25

300th anniversary, Académie des Sciences.

William the Conqueror, Castle and Norman Ships—A459

1966, June 4

1160 A459 60c brown red & deep blue 45 30

900th anniversary of Battle of Hastings.

Tracks, Globe and Eiffel Tower

A460

1966, June 11

1161 A460 60c dark brn., car. & dull blue 35 25

19th International Railroad Congress.

Oléron Bridge

A461

1966, June 20

1162 A461 25c Prussian blue, brown & blue 20 10

Issued to commemorate the opening of Oléron Bridge, connecting Oléron Island in the Bay of Biscay with the French mainland.

Europa Issue, 1966

Common Design Type

1966, Sept. 24 Engraved ***Perf. 13***

Size: 22x36mm.

1163 CD9 30c Prussian blue 20 6

1164 " 60c red 35 20

Vercingetorix at Gergovie, 52 B.C.

A462

Bishop Remi Baptizing King Clovis, 496 A.D.
A463

Design: 60c, Charlemagne attending school (page holding book for crowned king).

1966, Nov. 5 ***Perf. 13***

1165	A462	40c choc., green & gray blue	25	15
1166	A463	40c dk. red brown & black	25	15
1167	"	60c purple, rose car. & brown	40	20

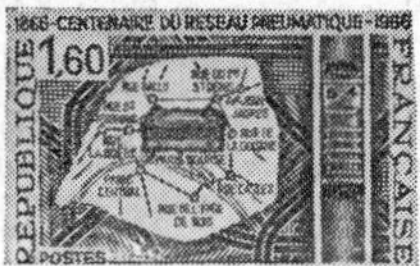

Map of Pneumatic Post and Tube
A464

1966, Nov. 11

1168	A464	1.60fr maroon & indigo	1.10	60

Centenary of Paris pneumatic post system.

Val Chateau
A465

1966, Nov. 19 **Engraved** ***Perf. 13***

1169	A465	2.30fr dark blue, slate grn. & brown	1.50	12

Rançe Power Station
A466

1966, Dec. 3

1170	A466	60c dk. blue, slate grn. & brown	40	20

Issued to publicize the tidal power station in the estuary of the Rance River on the English Channel.

European Broadcasting Union Emblem
A467

1967, Mar. 4 **Engraved** ***Perf. 13***

1171	A467	40c dk. blue & rose brown	25	20

Issued to publicize the 3rd International Congress of the European Broadcasting Union, Paris, March 8-22.

"Father Juniet's Gig" by Henri Rousseau—A468

Francois I by Jean Clouet
A469

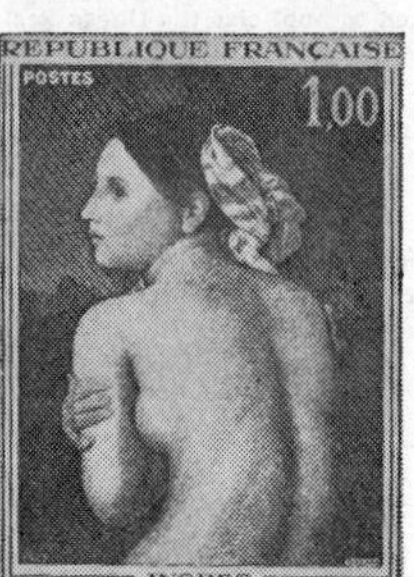

The Bather, by Jean-Dominique Ingres
A470

St. Eloi, the Goldsmith, at Work
A471

1967 **Engr.** ***Perf. 13x12, 12x13***

1172	A468	1fr multicolored	60	50
1173	A469	1fr "	60	50
1174	A470	1fr "	60	50
1175	A471	1fr "	60	50

The design of No. 1175 is from a 16th century stained glass window in the Church of Sainte Madeleine, Troyes.

Issue dates: No. 1172, Apr. 15. No. 1173, July 1. No. 1174, Sept. 9. No. 1175, Oct. 7.

Snow Crystal and Olympic Rings
A472

1967, Apr. 22 **Photogravure** ***Perf. 13***

1176	A472	60c brt. & lt. blue & red	40	20

Issued to publicize the 10th Winter Olympic Games, Grenoble, Feb. 6-18, 1968.

French Pavilion, EXPO '67
A473

1967, Apr. 22 **Engraved**

1177	A473	60c dull blue & blue green	40	20

Issued to commemorate the International Exhibition EXPO '67, Montreal, Apr. 28-Oct. 27, 1967.

Europa Issue, 1967
Common Design Type

1967, Apr. 29
Size: 22x36mm.

1178	CD10	30c blue & gray	20	8
1179	"	60c brn. & lt. blue	35	22

Great Bridge, Bordeaux—A474

1967, May 8

1180	A474	25c olive, black & brown	20	10

Nungesser, Coli and "L'Oiseau Blanc"
A475

1967, May 8

1181	A475	40c slate, dark & lt. brown	30	20

Issued to commemorate the 40th anniversary of the attempted transatlantic flight of Charles Nungesser and François Coil, French aviators.

Goüin House, Tours
A476

1967, May 13 **Engraved** ***Perf. 13***

1182	A476	40c vio. blue, red brown & red	30	20

Issued to publicize the Congress of the Federation of French Philatelic Societies in Tours.

Ramon and Alfort Veterinary School
A477

1967, May 27

1183	A477	25c brown, dp. blue & yel. green	20	12

Issued to commemorate the 200th anniversary of the Alfort Veterinary School and to honor Professor Gaston Ramon (1886-1963).

Robert Esnault-Pelterie, Diamant Rocket and A-1 Satellite—A478

1967, May 27

1184	A478	60c slate & vio. bl.	40	25

Issued to honor Robert Esnault-Pelterie (1881-1957), aviation and space expert.

City Hall, Saint-Quentin
A479

Saint-Germain-en-Laye
A480

Views: 60c, Clock Tower, Vire. 75c, Beach, La Baule, Brittany. 95c, Harbor, Boulogne-sur-Mer. 1fr, Rodez Cathedral. 1.50fr, Morlaix; old houses, grotesque carving, viaduct.

1967

1185	A479	50c bl., slate blue & brown	30	6
1186	"	60c dp. bl., slate bl. & dk. red brn.	35	8
1187	A480	70c rose car., red brown & blue	45	5
1188	"	75c multicolored	45	27
1189	"	95c sky blue, lilac & slate grn.	55	27
1190	A479	1fr indigo & blue gray	55	5
1191	"	1.50fr brt. bl., brt. grn. & red brown	85	20
		Nos. 1185-1191 (7)	3.50	98

Issue Dates: 1fr, 1.50fr, June 10; 70c, June 17; 50c, 60c, 95c, July 8; 75c, July 24.

Orchids
A481

Cross of Lorraine, Soldiers and Sailors
A483

Scales of Justice, City and Harbor
A482

1967, July 29 Engr. *Perf. 13*

1192 A481 40c dp. carmine, brt. pink & pur. 25 18

Orleans flower festival.

1967, Sept. 4

1193 A482 60c dk. plum, dull blue & ocher 35 20

Issued to publicize the 9th International Accountancy Congress, Paris, Sept. 6–12.

1967, Oct. 7 Engraved *Perf. 13*

1194 A483 25c brn., dp. ultra. & blue 17 10

Issued to commemorate the 25th anniversary of the Battle of Bir Hacheim.

Marie Curie, Bowl Glowing with Radium
A484

1967, Oct. 23 Engr. *Perf. 13*

1195 A484 60c dk. bl. & ultra. 35 30

Issued to commemorate the centenary of the birth of Marie Curie (1867–1934), scientist who discovered radium and polonium, Nobel prize winner for physics and chemistry.

Lions Emblem
A485

Marianne (by Cheffer)
A486

1967, Oct. 28

1196 A485 40c dark carmine & violet blue 30 15

50th anniversary of Lions International.

1967, Nov. 4 Engraved

1197 A486 25c dark blue 65 15
1198 " 30c bright lilac 75 3
a. Bklt. pane of 5 4.75
b. Bklt. pane of 10 9.50

Coils (vertical) of Nos. 1197 and 1231 show a red number on the back of every 10th stamp.

See Nos. 1230–1231C.

King Philip II (Philip Augustus) at Battle of Bouvines
A487

Designs: No. 1200, Election of Hugh Capet as King (horiz.). 60c, King Louis IX (St. Louis) holding audience for the poor.

1967, Nov. 13 Engraved *Perf. 13*

1199 A487 40c gray & black 25 15
1200 " 40c steel bl. & ultra. 25 15
1201 " 60c green & dark red brown 35 15

Commemorative Medal
A488

1968, Jan. 6 Engraved *Perf. 13*

1202 A488 40c dk. slate green & bister 25 15

Issued to commemorate the 50th anniversary of postal checking service.

Various Road Signs
A489

1968, Feb. 24

1203 A489 25c lilac, red & dk. blue green 15 12

Issued to publicize road safety.

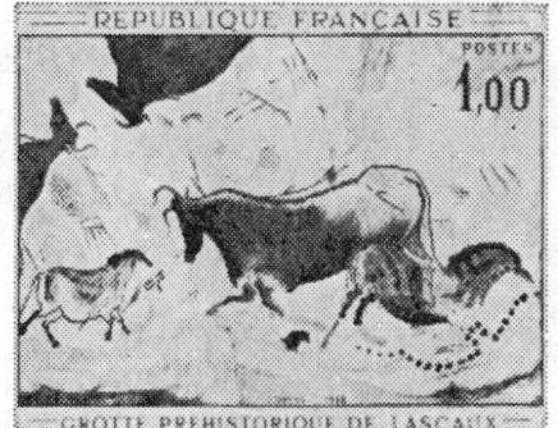
Prehistoric Paintings, Lascaux Cave—A490

"Arearea" (Merriment) by Paul Gauguin—A491

The Dance, by Emile Antoine Bourdelle
A492

Portrait of the Model, by Auguste Renoir
A493

1968 Engr. *Perf. 13x12, 12x13*

1204 A490 1fr multicolored 60 50
1205 A491 1fr " 75 50
1206 A492 1fr carmine & gray olive 75 50
1207 A493 1fr multicolored 75 50

Issue dates: No. 1204, Apr. 13. No. 1205, Sept. 21. No. 1206, Oct. 26. No. 1207, Nov. 9.

Audio-visual Institute, Royan
A494

1968, Apr. 13 *Perf. 13*

1208 A494 40c slate grn., brn. & Prus. blue 25 12

Issued to publicize the 5th Conference for World Cooperation with the theme of teaching living languages by audio-visual means.

Europa Issue, 1968
Common Design Type

1968, Apr. 27

Size: 36x22mm.

1209 CD11 30c brt. red lilac & ocher 20 8
1210 " 60c brown & lake 35 25

Alain René Le Sage
A495

1968, May 4

1211 A495 40c bl. & rose vio. 25 12

Issued to commemorate the 300th anniversary of the birth of Alain René Le Sage (1668–1747), novelist and playwright.

Chateau de Langeais
A496

1968, May 4

1212 A496 60c slate blue, grn. & red brown 35 20

Pierre Larousse
A497

1968, May 11 Engraved *Perf. 13*

1213 A497 40c rose vio. & brn. 25 8

Issued to honor Pierre Larousse (1817–1875), grammarian, lexicographer and encyclopedist.

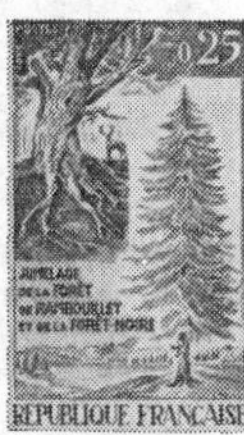
Gnarled Trunk and Fir Tree
A498

1968, May 18 Engraved *Perf. 13*

1214 A498 25c greenish blue, brn. & green 18 12

Issued to commemorate the twinning of Rambouillet Forest in France and the Black Forest in Germany.

Map of Papal Enclave, Valréas, and John XXII Receiving Homage—A499

1968, May 25

1215 A499 60c brn., bister brn. & purple 40 30

Issued to commemorate the 650th anniversary of the papal enclave at Valréas.

Louis XIV, Arms of France and Flanders
A500

1968, June 29

1216 A500 40c rose carmine, gray & lemon 30 12

Issued to commemorate the 300th anniversary of the Treaty of Aachen which reunited Flanders with France.

Martrou Bridge, Rochefort
A501

1968, July 20

1217 A501 25c sky blue, blk. & dk. red brn. 18 10

Letord Lorraine Bimotor Plane over Map of France—A502

1968, Aug. 17 Engraved *Perf. 13*

1218 A502 25c bright blue, indigo & red 20 12

Issued to commemorate the 50th anniversary of the first regularly scheduled air mail route in France from Paris to St. Nazaire.

Tower de Constance, Aigues-Mortes

A503

1968, Aug. 31

1219 A503 25c red brn., sky bl. & olive bister 20 10

Bicentenary of the release of Huguenot prisoners from the Tower de Constance, Aigues-Mortes.

Cathedral and Pont Vieux, Beziers

A504

1968, Sept. 7 Engraved *Perf. 13*

1220 A504 40c indigo, bister & green 25 10

"Victory" over White Tower of Salonika

A505

1968, Sept. 28

1221 A505 40c red lilac & plum 25 10

Issued to commemorate the 50th anniversary of the armistice on the eastern front in World War I, Sept. 29, 1918.

Louis XV, Arms of France and Corsica

A506

1968, Oct. 5 *Perf. 13*

1222 A506 25c ultramarine, green & blk. 20 10

Issued to commemorate the 200th anniversary of the return of Corsica to France.

Relay Race

A507

1968, Oct. 12

1223 A507 40c ultra., brt. green & olive brown 35 30

Issued to commemorate the 19th Olympic Games, Mexico City, Oct. 12–27.

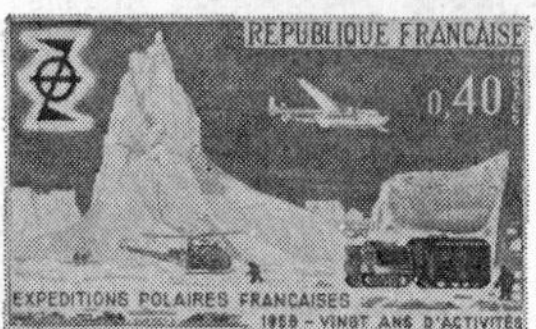

Polar Camp with Helicopter, Plane and Snocat Tractor—A508

1968, Oct. 19

1224 A508 40c Prus. blue, lt. greenish blue & brown red 35 18

20 years of French Polar expeditions.

Leon Bailby, Paris Opera Staircase and Hospital Beds

A509

"Victory" over Arc de Triomphe and Eternal Flame

A510

1968, Oct. 26

1225 A509 40c ocher & maroon 30 20

Issued to publicize the 50th anniversary of the "Little White Beds" children's hospital fund.

1968, Nov. 9 Engraved *Perf. 13*

1226 A510 25c dark car. rose & deep blue 15 10

Issued to commemorate the 50th anniversary of the armistice which ended World War I.

Death of Bertrand Du Guesclin at Chateauneuf-de-Randon, 1380

A511

1968, Nov. 16

Designs: No. 1228, King Philip IV (the Fair) and first States-General assembly, 1302 (horiz.). 60c, Joan of Arc leaving Vaucouleurs, 1429.

1227 A511 40c copper red, grn. & gray 25 12

1228 " 40c green, ultra. & brown 25 12

1229 " 60c vio. blue, slate blue & bister 35 20

See also No. 1260.

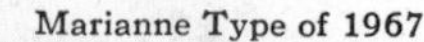

Marianne Type of 1967

1969–70 Engraved *Perf. 13*

1230 A486 30c green 30 5
- *a.* Bklt. pane of 10 4.00

1231 " 40c deep carmine 35 3
- *a.* Bklt. pane of 5 (horiz. strip) 3.25
- *b.* Bklt. pane of 10 3.50
- *d.* With label ('70) 75 30

Typographed *Perf. 14x13*

1231C A486 30c blue green 11 3

No. 1231d was issued in sheets of 50 with alternating labels showing coat of arms of Perigueux, arranged checkerwise, to commemorate the inauguration of the Perigueux stamp printing plant.

The 40c coil is noted after No. 1198.

Church of Brou, Bourg-en-Bresse

A512

Views: 80c, Vouglans Dam, Jura. 85c, Chateau de Chantilly. 1.15fr, Sailboats in La Trinité-sur-Mer harbor.

1969 Engraved *Perf. 13*

1232 A512 45c olive, blue & red brown 35 7

1233 " 80c olive bister, brn. red & dark brown 55 8

1234 " 85c slate grn., dull blue & gray 55 30

1235 " 1.15fr brt. bl., gray grn. & brn. 70 40

"February" Bas-relief from Amiens Cathedral

A513

Philip the Good, by Roger van der Weyden

A514

Sts. Savin and Cyprian before Ladicius, Mural, St. Savin, Vienne—A515

The Circus, by Georges Seurat

A515a

1969 *Perf. 12x13*

1236 A513 1fr dk. grn. & brn. 75 50

1237 A514 1fr multicolored 75 50

1238 A515 1fr " 75 50

1239 A515a 1fr " 75 50

Issue dates: No. 1236, Feb. 22; No. 1237, May 3; No. 1238, June 28; No. 1239, Nov. 8.

Gallic Coin Type of 1964–66

1969 Typographed *Perf. 13½x14*

1240 A418 22c brt. grn. & vio. 30 5

1241 " 35c red & ultra. 65 18

1242 " 70c ultramarine & red brown 2.00 85

Nos. 1240–1242 are known only precanceled. See note after No. 132.

Hautefort Chateau

A516

1969, Apr. 5 Engraved *Perf. 13*

1243 A516 70c blue, slate & bister 50 20

Irises

A517

1969, Apr. 12 Photogravure

1244 A517 45c multicolored 35 20

Issued to publicize the 3rd International Flower Show, Paris, Apr. 23–Oct. 5.

Europa Issue, 1969

Common Design Type

1969, Apr. 26 Engraved *Perf. 13*

Size: 36x22mm.

1245 CD12 40c carmine rose 25 7

1246 " 70c Prussian blue 45 25

Albert Thomas and Thomas Memorial, Geneva

A518

1969, May 10 Engraved *Perf. 13*

1247 A518 70c brn., olive bister & indigo 45 20

Issued to commemorate the 50th anniversary of the International Labor Organization and to honor Albert Thomas (1878–1932), director of the ILO 1920–1932.

Garigliano Battle Scene, 1944
A519

1969, May 10

1248 A519 45c black & violet 35 15

Issued to commemorate the 25th anniversary of the Battle of the Garigliano against the Germans.

Chateau du Marché, Chalons-sur-Marne
A520

Parachutists over Normandy Beach
A521

1969, May 24

1249 A520 45c bister, dull blue & green 30 15

Federation of French Philatelic Societies, 42nd congress.

1969, May 31

1250 A521 45c dk. bl. & vio. bl. 30 15

Issued to commemorate the 25th anniversary of the landing of Special Air Service and Free French commandos in Normandy, June 6, 1944.

Monument of the French Resistance, Mt. Mouchet
A522

1969, June 7

1251 A522 45c dk. green, slate, & indigo 30 15

Issued to commemorate the 25th anniversary of the battle of Mt. Mouchet between French resistance fighters and the Germans, June 2 and 10, 1944.

French Troops Landing in Provence
A523

1969, Aug. 23 Engraved ***Perf. 13***

1252 A523 45c slate & black brown 30 20

Issued to commemorate the 25th anniversary of the landing of French and American forces in Provence, Aug. 15, 1944.

Russian and French Aviators
A524

1969, Oct. 18 Engraved ***Perf. 13***

1253 A524 45c slate, deep blue & carmine 30 25

Issued to honor the French aviators of the Normandy-Neman Squadron who fought on the Russian Front, 1942–45.

Kayak on Isère River
A525

1969, Aug. 2 Engraved ***Perf. 13***

1254 A525 70c orange brown, olive & dark blue 60 20

Issued to commemorate the International Canoe and Kayak Championships, Bourg-Saint-Maurice, Savoy, July 31–Aug. 6.

Napoleon as Young Officer and his Birthplace, Ajaccio—A526

1969, Aug. 16

1255 A526 70c bright greenish blue, olive & rose violet 60 25

Issued to commemorate the 200th anniversary of the birth of Napoleon Bonaparte (1769–1821).

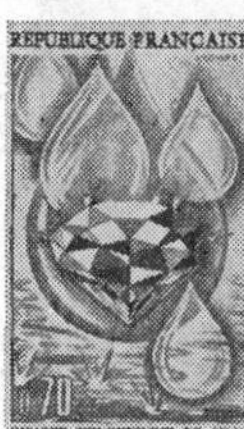

Drops of Water and Diamond
A527

Mediterranean Mouflon
A528

1969, Sept. 27

1256 A527 70c black, dp. blue & brt. green 50 25

European Water Charter.

1969, Oct. 11

1257 A528 45c olive, black & orange brown 35 25

Issued to publicize wildlife protection.

Central School of Arts and Crafts
A529

1969, Oct. 18

1258 A529 70c dk. green, yel. grn. & orange 50 25

Issued to commemorate the inauguration of the Central School of Arts and Crafts at Chatenay-Malabry.

Nuclear Submarine "Le Redoutable"
A530

1969, Oct. 25

1259 A530 70c dp. blue, green & slate green 50 24

Type of 1968 and

Henri IV and Edict of Nantes
A531

Designs: No. 1260, Pierre Terrail de Bayard wounded at Battle of Brescia (after a painting in Versailles). No. 1262, Louis XI, Charles the Bold and map of France.

1969, Nov. 8 Engraved ***Perf. 13***

1260 A511 80c brown, bister & black 55 20

1261 A531 80c black & vio. bl. 55 20

1262 " 80c olive, dp. green & dk. red brn. 55 20

"Firecrest" and Alain Gerbault
A532

1970, Jan. 10 Engraved ***Perf. 13***

1263 A532 70c indigo, bright blue & gray 60 20

Issued to commemorate the 40th anniversary of the completion of Alain Gerbault's trip around the world aboard the "Firecrest," 1923–29.

Gendarmery Emblem, Mountain Climber, Helicopter, Motorcyclists and Motorboat—A533

1970, Jan. 31

1264 A533 45c slate green, dk. blue & brown 40 18

Issued to honor the National Gendarmery, founded 1791.

Field Ball Player
A534

1970, Feb. 21 Engraved ***Perf. 13***

1265 A534 80c slate green 65 25

Issued to publicize the 7th International Field Ball Games, Feb. 26–March 8.

Alphonse Juin and Church of the Invalides—A535

1970, Feb. 28

1266 A535 45c gray blue & dark brown 45 15

Issued to honor Marshal Alphonse Pierre Juin (1888–1967), military leader.

Aerotrain
A536

1970, Mar. 7

1267 A536 80c purple & gray 55 30

Issued to publicize the introduction of the aerotrain, which reaches a speed of 320 miles per hour.

Pierre Joseph Pelletier, Joseph Bienaimé Caventou, Quinine Formula and Cell—A537

1970, Mar. 21 Engraved ***Perf. 13***

1268 A537 50c slate green, sky bl. & dp. car. 45 15

Discovery of quinine, 150th anniversary.

Pink Flamingos
A538

Diamant B Rocket and Radar
A539

1970, Mar. 21

1269 A538 45c olive, gray & pink 45 15

European Nature Conservation Year, 1970.

1970, Mar. 28

1270 A539 45c bright green 35 15

Issued to publicize the space center in Guyana and the launching of the Diamant B rocket, Mar. 10, 1970.

Europa Issue, 1970

Common Design Type

1970, May 2 Engraved *Perf. 13*

Size: 36x22mm.

1271 CD13 40c deep carmine 25 8
1272 " 80c sky blue 50 25

Annunciation, by Primitive Painter of Savoy, 1480
A540

The Triumph of Flora, by Jean Baptiste Carpeaux—A541

Diana Returning from the Hunt, by François Boucher—A542

Dancer with Bouquet, by Edgar Degas
A543

1970 *Perf. 12x13, 13x12*

1273 A540 1fr multicolored 80 50
1274 A541 1fr red brown 80 50
1275 A542 1fr multicolored 80 50
1276 A543 1fr " 80 50

Issue dates: No. 1273, May 9. No. 1274, July 4. No. 1275, Oct. 10. No. 1276, Nov. 14.

Arms of Lens, Miner's Lamp and Pit Head
A544

1970, May 16 Engraved *Perf 13*

1277 A544 40c scarlet 30 12

Issued to publicize the 43rd National Congress of the Federation of French Philatelic Societies, Lens, May 14–21.

Diamond Rock, Martinique
A545

Haute Provence Observatory and Spiral Nebula
A546

Designs: 95c, Chancelade Abbey, Dordogne. 1fr, Gosier Islet, Guadeloupe.

1970, June 20 Engraved *Perf. 13*

1278 A545 50c slate grn., brt. bl. & plum 35 8
1279 " 95c lt. olive, car. & brown 60 40
1280 " 1fr slate grn., brt. blue & dk. car. rose 60 8
1281 A546 1.30fr dk. blue, vio. blue & dark green 80 40

Hand Reaching for Freedom
A547

Handicapped Javelin Thrower
A548

1970, June 27

1282 A547 45c vio. blue, blue & bister 30 12

Liberation of concentration camps, 25th anniversary.

1970, June 27

1283 A548 45c rose car., ultra. & emerald 35 15

Issued to publicize the International Games of the Handicapped, St. Etienne, June 1970.

Pole Vault
A549

1970, Sept. 11 Engraved *Perf. 13*

1284 A549 45c carmine, blue & indigo 35 15

Issued to publicize the First European Junior Athletic Championships, Colombes, Sept. 11–13.

Royal Salt Works, Arc-et-Senans
A550

1970, Sept. 26

1285 A550 80c blue, brown & dark green 60 25

Issued to publicize the restoration of the 18th century Royal Salt Works buildings, by Claude Nicolas Ledoux (1736–1806) at Arc-et-Senans, for use as a center for studies of all aspects of future human life.

Armand Jean du Plessis, Duc de Richelieu—A551

Designs: No. 1287, Battle of Fontenoy, 1745. No. 1288, Louis XIV and Versailles.

1970, Oct. 17 Engraved *Perf. 13*

1286 A551 45c black, slate & carmine rose 35 20
1287 " 45c orange, brown & indigo 35 20
1288 " 45c slate green, lemon & org. brown 35 20

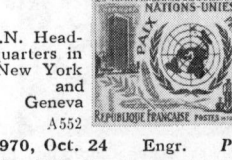

U.N. Headquarters in New York and Geneva
A552

1970, Oct. 24 Engr. *Perf. 13*

1289 A552 80c olive, dp. ultra. & dk. purple 60 30

25th anniversary of the United Nations.

View of Bordeaux and France No. 43—A553

1970, Nov. 7

1290 A553 80c violet blue & gray blue 65 40

Centenary of the Bordeaux issue.

Col. Denfert-Rochereau and Lion of Belfort, by Frederic A. Bartholdi—A554

1970, Nov. 14

1291 A554 45c dark blue, olive & red brown 35 18

Centenary of the siege of Belfort during Franco-Prussian War.

Marianne (by Bequet)
A555

1971–74 Typographed *Perf. 14x13*

1292 A555 45c sky blue 25 6
1292A " 60c green ('74) 70 4

Engraved *Perf. 13*

1293 A555 50c rose carmine 25 4
  a. Bklt. pane of 5 (horiz. strip) 1.50
  b. Bklt. pane of 10 3.00
1294 A555 60c green ('74) 1.20 10
  a. Booklet pane of 10 12.50
1294B A555 80c car. rose ('74) 50 5
  c. Booklet pane of 5 2.50
  d. Booklet pane of 10 5.00

Nos. 1294 and 1294B issued also in vertical coils with control number on back of every 10th stamp.

No. 1293 issued only in booklets and in vertical coils with red control number on back of every 10th stamp.

See Nos. 1494–1498.

St. Matthew, Sculpture from Strasbourg Cathedral
A556

Winnower, by François Millet
A557

The Dreamer, by Georges Rouault
A558

1971 Engraved *Perf. 12x13*

1295 A556 1fr dark red brown 80 50
1296 A557 1fr multicolored 80 50
1297 A558 1fr " 80 50

Issue dates: No. 1295, Jan. 23; No. 1296, Apr. 3; No. 1297, June 5.

Figure Skating Pair—A560

1971, Feb. 20 Engraved *Perf. 13*

1299 A560 80c vio. bl., slate & aquamarine 65 35

World Figure Skating Championships, Lyons, Feb. 23–28.

Underwater Exploration A561

1971, March 6

1300 A561 80c blue black & blue green 65 25

International Exhibition of Ocean Exploration, Bordeaux, March 9–14.

Cape Horn Clipper "Antoinette" and Solidor Castle, Saint-Malo A562

1971, Apr. 10 Engraved *Perf. 13*

1301 A562 80c bl., pur. & slate 65 40

Pyrenean Chamois A563

1971, Apr. 24 Engraved *Perf. 13*

1302 A563 65c bl., dk. brn. & brown olive 55 25

National Park of Western Pyrenees.

Europa Issue, 1971

Common Design Type and

Santa Maria della Salute, Venice A564

1971, May 8 Engraved *Perf. 13*

1303 A564 50c blue gray & olive bister 40 10

Size: 36x22mm.

1304 CD14 80c rose lilac 55 24

Cardinal, Nobleman and Lawyer—A565

Storming of the Bastille—A566

Design: No. 1306, Battle of Valmy.

1971

1305 A565 45c blue, rose red & purple 40 15
1306 " 45c bl., olive bister & brn. red 40 20
1307 A566 65c dark brown, gray blue & magenta 50 30

No. 1305 commemorates the opening of the Estates General, May 5, 1789; No. 1306, Battle of Valmy (Sept. 20, 1792) between French and Prussian armies; 65c, Storming of the Bastille, Paris, July 14, 1789.

Issue dates: No. 1305, May 8; No. 1306, Sept. 18; 65c, July 10.

Grenoble A568

1971, May 29 Engraved *Perf. 13*

1308 A568 50c ocher, lilac & rose red 25 12

44th National Congress of the Federation of French Philatelic Societies, Grenoble, May 30–31.

"Rural Family Aid" Shedding Light on Village A569

1971, June 5

1309 A569 40c vio., bl. & green 25 12

Aid for rural families.

Chateau and Fort de Sedan A570

Pont d'Arc, Ardèche Gorge A571

Views: 60c, Sainte Chapelle, Riom. 65c, Fountain and tower, Dole. 90c, Tower and street, Riquewihr.

1971 Engraved *Perf. 13*

1310 A571 60c black, green & blue 35 8
1311 " 65c lilac, ocher & black 40 8
1312 " 90c grn., vio. brn. & red brn. 50 8
1313 A570 1.10fr slate green, Prus. blue & brown 60 18
1314 A571 1.40fr slate green, blue & dk. brown 80 10
Nos. 1310–1314 (5) 2.65 52

Issue dates: 60c, June 19; 65c, 90c, July 3; 1.10fr, 1.40fr, June 12.

Gallic Coin Type of 1964–66

1971, July 1 Typo. *Perf. 13½x14*

1315 A418 26c lilac & brown 20 5
1316 " 30c light brown & brown 30 10
1317 " 45c dull green & brown 80 15
1318 " 90c red & brown 90 30

Nos. 1315–1318 are known only precanceled. See second paragraph after No. 132.

Bourbon Palace A572

1971, Aug. 28 Engraved *Perf. 13*

1319 A572 90c violet blue 65 25

59th Conference of the Interparliamentary Union.

Embroidery and Tool Making A573

1971, Oct. 16

1320 A573 90c brn. red, brt. lilac & claret 80 25

40th anniversary of the first assembly of presidents of artisans' guilds.

Reunion Chameleon A574

1971, Nov. 6 Photo. *Perf. 13*

1321 A574 60c brown, yellow, green & black 1.00 45

Nature protection.

De Gaulle Issue

Common Design Type and

De Gaulle in Brazzaville, 1944 A576

Designs: No. 1324, De Gaulle entering Paris, 1944. No. 1325, Pres. de Gaulle, 1970.

1971, Nov. 9 Engraved

1322 CD134 50c black 30 15
1323 A576 50c ultramarine 30 15
1324 A576 50c rose red 30 15
1325 CD134 50c black 30 15
a. Strip of 4 + label 1.35 90

First anniversary of the death of Charles de Gaulle (1890–1970). Nos. 1322–1325 printed se-tenant in sheets of 20 containing 5 strips of 4 plus label with Cross of Lorraine and inscription.

Antoine Portal and first Session of Academy—A577

1971, Nov. 13

1326 A577 45c dark purple & magenta 35 20

Sesquicentennial of the founding of the National Academy of Medicine; Baron Antoine Portal was first president.

L'Etude, by Jean Honoré Fragonard A578

Women in Garden, by Claude Monet A579

St. Peter Presenting Pierre de Bourbon, by Maitre de Moulins A580

Boats, by André Derain—A581

1972 Engr. *Perf. 12x13, 13x12*

1327 A578 1fr black & multi. 80 50
1328 A579 1fr slate green & multicolored 80 50
1329 A580 2fr dark brown & multicolored 2.25 70
1330 A581 2fr yel. & multi. 2.40 70

Issue dates: No. 1327, Jan. 22; No. 1328, June 17; No. 1329, Oct. 14; No. 1330, Dec. 16.

Map of South Indian Ocean, Penguin and Ships
A582

1972, Jan. 29 *Perf. 13*

1331 A582 90c blk., bl. & ocher 1.00 40

Bicentenary of discovery of the Crozet and Kerguelen Islands.

Slalom and Olympic Emblems
A583

1972, Feb. 7

1332 A583 90c dark olive & dp. carmine 80 35

11th Winter Olympic Games, Sapporo, Japan, Feb. 3–13.

Hearts, U.N. Emblem, Caduceus and Pacemaker—A584

1972, Apr. 8 Engr. *Perf. 13*

1333 A584 45c dark carmine, orange & gray 45 25

"Your heart is your health," world health month.

Red Deer, Sologne Plateau
A585

Charlieu Abbey
A585a

Bazoches-du-Morvand Chateau
A586

Saint-Just Cathedral, Narbonne
A587

1972 *Perf. 13*

1334 A585 1fr ocher & red brn. 65 10
1335 A585a 1.20fr slate & dull brown 70 12
1336 A586 2fr slate green, blk. & red brn. 1.00 10
1337 A587 3.50fr blue, gray olive & car. rose 2.00 25

Issue dates: 1fr, Sept. 10; 1.20fr, Apr. 29; 2fr, Sept. 9; 3.50fr, Apr. 8.

Eagle Owl
A588

Design: 60c, Salmon (horiz.).

1972

1338 A588 60c green, indigo & brt. blue 80 45
1339 " 65c slate, olive brn. & sepia 80 45

Nature protection. Issue dates: 60c, May 27; 65c, Apr. 15.

Europa Issue 1972

Common Design Type and

Aix-la-Chapelle Cathedral
A589

1972, Apr. 22 Engr. *Perf. 13*

1340 A589 50c yel., vio. brn. & dk. olive 35 10

Photogravure
Size: 22x36mm.

1341 CD15 90c red orange & multicolored 70 25

Bouquet Made of Hearts and Blood Donors' Emblem
A590

Newfoundlander "Côte d'Emeraude"
A591

1972, May 5 Engraved

1342 A590 40c red 35 15

20th anniversary of the Blood Donors Association of Post and Telecommunications Employees.

1972, May 6

1343 A591 90c org., vio. blue & slate green 80 35

Cathedral, Saint-Brieuc
A592

1972, May 20

1344 A592 50c lilac rose 30 12

45th Congress of the Federation of French Philatelic Societies, Saint-Brieuc, May 21–22.

Hand Holding Symbol of Postal Code
A593

1972, June 3 Typo. *Perf. 14x13*

1345 A593 30c grn., blk. & car. 20 5
1346 " 50c car., blk. & yel. 25 6

Introduction of postal code system.

Old and New Communications
A594

1972, July 1 Engraved *Perf. 13*

1347 A594 45c slate & vio. bl. 30 12

21st International Congress of P.T.T. (Post, Telegraph and Telephone) Employees, Paris, July 1–7.

Hurdler and Olympic Rings
A595

1972, July 8

1348 A595 1fr deep olive 80 30

20th Olympic Games, Munich, Aug. 26–Sept. 11.

Hikers and Mt. Aigoual
A596

Bicyclist
A597

1972, July 15 Photo. *Perf. 13*

1349 A596 40c brt. rose & multi. 1.35 40

International Year of Tourism and 25th anniversary of the National Hikers Association.

1972, July 22 Engraved

1350 A597 1fr gray, brown & lilac 1.60 60

World Bicycling Championships, Marseille, July 29–Aug. 2.

"Incroyables and Merveilleuse," 1794
A598

Designs: 60c, Bonaparte at the Arcole Bridge. 65c, Egyptian expedition (soldiers and scientists finding antiquities; pyramids in background).

1972 Engraved *Perf. 13*

1351 A598 45c olive, dk. green & car. rose 35 20
1352 " 60c red, black & indigo 45 25
1353 " 65c ocher, ultra. & chocolate 50 25

French history. Issue dates: 45c, Oct. 7; 60c, 65c, Nov. 11.

Champollion, Rosetta Stone with Key Inscription—A599

1972, Oct. 14

1354 A599 90c vio. blue, brn. red & black 70 30

Sesquicentennial of the deciphering of hieroglyphs by Jean-François Champollion.

St. Teresa, Portal of Notre Dame of Alençon
A600

1973, Jan. 6 Engraved *Perf. 13*

1355 A600 1fr Prussian blue & indigo 90 25

Centenary of the birth of St. Teresa of Lisieux, the Little Flower (Thérèse Martin, 1873–1897), Carmelite nun.

Anthurium (Martinique)
A601

1973, Jan. 20 Photogravure

1356 A601 50c gray & multi. 36 10

Colors of France and Germany Interlaced—A602

1973, Jan. 22

Size: 48x27mm.

1357 A602 50c multicolored 35 15

10th anniversary of the Franco-German Cooperation Treaty. See Germany No. 1101.

Polish Immigrants—A603

1973, Feb. 3 Engraved *Perf. 13*

1358 A603 40c slate green, dp. car. & brown 36 15

50th anniversary of Polish immigration into France, 1921–1923.

Last Supper, St. Austremoine Church, Issoire
A604

Kneeling Woman, by Charles Le Brun
A605

Angel, Wood, Moutier-D'Ahun
A606

Lady Playing Archlute, by Antoine Watteau
A607

1973 Engraved *Perf. 12x13*

1359 A604 2fr brn. & multi. 1.65 75
1360 A605 2fr dk. red & yel. 1.65 75
1361 A606 2fr olive brown & vio. brn. 1.65 75
1362 A607 2fr black & multi. 1.65 75

Issue dates: No. 1359, Feb. 10; No. 1360, Apr. 28; No. 1361, May 26; No. 1362, Sept. 22.

Tuileries Palace, Telephone Relays
A608

Oil Tanker, Francis I Lock
A609

Airbus A300-B
A610

1973

1363 A608 45c ultra., slate grn. & bister 40 12
1364 A609 90c plum, blk. & bl. 55 20
1365 A610 3fr dk. green, blue & black 2.25 1.25

French technical achievements.
Issue dates: 45c, May 15; 90c, Oct. 27; 3fr, Apr. 7.

Europa Issue 1973

Common Design Type and

City Hall, Brussels, CEPT Emblem
A611

1973, Apr. 14 Engr. *Perf. 13*

1366 A611 50c bright pink & chocolate 35 10

Photogravure

Size: 36x22mm.

1367 CD16 90c slate green & multicolored 55 30

Masonic Lodge Emblem
A612

1973, May 12 Engr. *Perf. 13*

1368 A612 90c magenta & violet blue 65 30

Bicentenary of the Free Masons of France.

Guadeloupe Raccoon
A613

White Storks
A614

1973

1369 A613 40c lilac, sepia & olive 30 15
1370 A614 60c black, aqua. & orange red 50 30

Nature protection.
Issue dates: 40c, June 23; 60c, May 12.

Tourist Issue

Doubs Waterfall
A615

Clos-Lucé, Amboise
A617

Palace of Dukes of Burgundy, Dijon
A616

Design: 90c, Gien Chateau.

1973 Engraved *Perf. 13*

1371 A615 60c multicolored 35 10
1372 A616 65c red & purple 40 15
1373 " 90c Prus. bl., indigo & brown 55 10
1374 A617 1fr ocher, blue & slate green 55 10

Issue dates: 60c, Sept. 8; 65c, May 19; 90c, Aug. 18; 1fr, June 23.

Academy Emblem
A618

1973, May 26

1375 A618 1fr lilac, slate green & red 65 25

50th anniversary of the Academy of Overseas Sciences.

Racing Car and Clocks
A619

1973, June 2

1376 A619 60c dk. brn. & blue 45 25

50th anniversary of the 24-hour automobile race at Le Mans.

Five-master France II—A620

1973, June 9

1377 A620 90c ultra., Prussian blue & indigo 60 20

Tower and Square, Toulouse
A621

1973, June 9

1378 A621 50c pur. & red brn. 40 12

46th Congress of the Federation of French Philatelic Societies, Toulouse, June 9–12.

Dr. Armauer G. Hansen
A622

Ducretet and his Transmission Diagram
A623

1973, Sept. 29 Engraved *Perf. 13*

1379 A622 45c green, dk. olive & ocher 35 12

Centenary of the discovery of the Hansen bacillus, the cause of leprosy.

1973, Oct. 6

1380 A623 1fr yellow green & magenta 65 25

75th anniversary of the first transmission of radio signals from the Eiffel Tower to the Pantheon by Eugene Ducretet (1844–1915).

Molière as Sganarelle
A624

1973, Oct. 20

1381 A624 1fr dark red & olive brown 65 25

Tercentenary of the death of Molière (Jean-Baptiste Poquelin; 1622–1673), playwright and actor.

Pierre Bourgoin and Philippe Kieffer
A625

1973, Oct. 27

1382 A625 1fr red, rose claret & violet blue 60 25

Pierre Bourgoin (1907–70), and Philippe Kieffer (1899–1963), heroes of the Free French forces in World War II.

Napoleon, Jean Portalis and Palace of Justice, Paris—A626

Exhibition Halls—A627

The Coronation of Napoleon, by Jean Louis David
A628

1973 Engraved ***Perf. 13***

1383 A626 45c blue, chocolate & gray 30 12
1384 A627 60c olive, slate grn. & brown 40 18
1385 A628 1fr slate grn., olive & claret 60 30

History of France. No. 1383 commemorates the preparation of the Code Napoleon; No. 1384, Napoleon's encouragement of industry and No. 1385 his coronation. Issue dates: 45c, Nov. 3; 60c, Nov. 24; 1fr, Nov. 12.

Eternal Flame, Arc de Triomphe
A629

Weather Vane
A630

1973, Nov. 10

1386 A629 40c purple, violet blue & red 30 15

50th anniversary of the Eternal Flame at the Arc de Triomphe, Paris.

1973, Dec. 1

1387 A630 65c ultra., black & green 40 20

50th anniversary of the Department of Agriculture.

Human Rights Flame and Man
A631

Postal Museum
A632

1973, Dec. 8 Engraved ***Perf. 13***

1388 A631 45c car., org. & blk. 30 10

25th anniversary of the Universal Declaration of Human Rights.

1973, Dec. 19

1389 A632 50c maroon & bister 35 10

Opening of new post and philately museum, Paris.

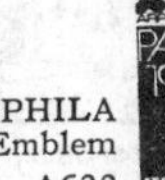

ARPHILA 75 Emblem
A633

1974, Jan. 19 Engraved ***Perf. 13***

1390 A633 50c brown, blue & bright lilac 30 8

ARPHILA 75 Philatelic Exhibition, Paris, June 1975.

Concorde over Charles de Gaulle Airport
A634

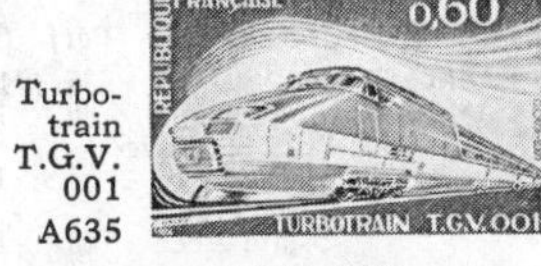

Turbo-train T.G.V. 001
A635

Phenix Nuclear Power Station
A636

1974 Engraved ***Perf. 13***

1391 A634 60c purple & olive gray 50 25
1392 A635 60c multicolored 75 25
1393 A636 65c " 35 15

French technical achievements.
Issue dates: No. 1391, Mar. 18; No. 1392, Aug. 31; 65c, Sept. 21.

Cardinal Richelieu, by Philippe de Champaigne—A637

Painting by Joan Miró—A638

Canal du Loing, by Alfred Sisley
A639

"In Honor of Nicolas Fouquet," Tapestry by Georges Mathieu
A640

Engr.; Photo. (#1395, 1397)

1974 ***Perf. 12x13, 13x12***

1394 A637 2fr multicolored 1.25 75
1395 A638 2fr " 1.25 75
1396 A639 2fr " 1.25 75
1397 A640 2fr " 1.25 75

Nos. 1394–1397 are printed in sheets of 25 with alternating labels publicizing "ARPHILA 75," Paris, June 6–16, 1975.
Issue dates: No. 1394, Mar. 23; No. 1395, Sept. 14; No. 1396, Nov. 9; No. 1397, Nov. 16.

French Alps and Gentian
A641

1974, Mar. 30 Engr. ***Perf. 13***

1398 A641 65c vio., bl. & gray 45 25

Centenary of the French Alpine Club.

Europa Issue 1974

"Age of Bronze," by Auguste Rodin
A642

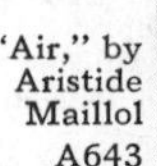

"Air," by Aristide Maillol
A643

1974, Apr. 20 ***Perf. 13***

1399 A642 50c brt. rose lilac & black 30 8
1400 A643 90c olive & brown 60 30

Sea Rescue—A644

1974, Apr. 27

1401 A644 90c multicolored 60 25

Reorganized sea rescue organization.

Council Building, View of Strasbourg and Emblem—A645

1974, May 4 Engr. ***Perf. 13***

1402 A645 45c indigo, bister & blue 30 12

25th anniversary of the Council of Europe.

Tourist Issue

View of Salers
A646

Basilica of St. Nicolas de Porte
A647

Seashell over Corsica
A648

Design: 1.10fr, View of Lot Valley.

1974 Engraved *Perf. 13*

1403	A646	65c yellow green & chocolate	30	15
1404	"	1.10fr choc. & slate green	50	25
1405	A647	2fr gray & lilac	90	5
1406	A648	3fr multicolored	1.50	20

Issue dates: 65c, June 22; 1.10fr, Sept. 7; 2fr, Oct. 12; 3fr, May 11.

Bison
A649

Giant Armadillo of Guyana
A650

1974

1407	A649	40c bister, choc. & blue	40	10
1408	A650	65c slate, olive & green	40	20

Nature protection.
Issue dates: No. 1407, May 25; No. 1408, Oct. 19.

Americans Landing in Normandy and Arms of Normandy—A651

General Marie-Pierre Koenig
A652

Order of the French Resistance
A653

1974

1409	A651	45c green, rose & indigo	30	12
1410	A652	1fr multicolored	55	25
1411	A653	1fr "	70	30

30th anniversary of the liberation of France from the Nazis. Design of No. 1410 includes diagram of battle of Bir-Hakeim and Free French and Bir-Hakeim memorials.
Issue dates, 45c, June 8; No. 1410, May 25. No. 1411, Nov. 23. See No. B478.

Pfister House, 16th Century, Colmar
A654

1974, June 1

1412	A654	50c multicolored	30	8

47th Congress of the Federation of French Philatelic Societies, Colmar, May 30–June 4.

Chess
A655

1974, June 8

1413	A655	1fr dk. brn. & multi.	60	30

21st Chess Olympiad, Nice, June 6–30.

Facade with Statue of Louis XIV, and 1675 Medal
A656

1974, June 15

1414	A656	40c indigo, blue & brown	30	10

300th anniversary of the founding of the Hotel des Invalides (Home for poor and sick officers and soldiers).

Peacocks Holding Letter, and Globe—A657

1974, Oct. 5 Engraved *Perf. 13*

1415	A657	1.20fr ultra., dp. grn. & dk. car.	65	40

Centenary of Universal Postal Union.

Copernicus and Heliocentric System—A658

1974, Oct. 12

1416	A658	1.20fr multicolored	60	35

500th anniversary of the birth of Nicolaus Copernicus (1473–1543), Polish astronomer.

Tourist Issue

Palace of Justice, Rouen
A659

Saint-Pol-de-Leon
A660

Chateau de Rochechouart
A661

1975 Engraved *Perf. 13*

1417	A659	85c multicolored	30	15
1418	A660	1.20fr blue, bister & choc.	50	10
1419	A661	1.40fr brown, indigo & green	60	15

Issue dates: 85c, Jan. 25; 1.20fr, Jan. 18; 1.40fr, Jan. 11.

Snowy Egret
A662

Gallic Coin
A663

1975, Feb. 15 Engraved *Perf. 13*

1420	A662	70c brt. blue & bis.	45	20

Nature protection.

1975, Feb. 16 Typo. *Perf. 13½x14*

1421	A663	42c orange & mag.	40	15
1422	"	48c lt. blue & red brown	50	15
1423	"	70c brt. pink & red	80	25
1424	"	1.35fr lt. grn. & brn.	1.10	50

Nos. 1421–1424 are known only precanceled. See second note after No. 132. See Nos. 1460–1463, 1487–1490.

The Eye—A664

Ionic Capital—A665

Graphic Art—A666

Ceres—A667

1975 Engraved *Perf. 13*

1425	A664	1fr red, purple & orange	60	25
1426	A665	2fr grn., slate grn. & magenta	1.10	40
1427	A666	3fr dk. carmine & olive green	1.60	65
1428	A667	4fr red, slate grn. & bister	2.25	90

Souvenir Sheet

1429	Sheet of 4	11.00	11.00
a.	2fr A664 dp. car. & slate blue	1.25	1.25
b.	3fr A665 brt. bl., slate blue & deep carmine	1.75	1.75
c.	4fr A666 slate blue, bright blue & plum	2.50	2.50
d.	6fr A667 bright blue, slate blue & plum	3.50	3.50

ARPHILA 75, International Philatelic Exhibition, Paris, June 6–16. No. 1429 has ornamental border and commemorative inscription. Size: 150x143mm. Issue dates: 1fr, Mar. 1; 2fr, Mar. 22; 3fr, Apr. 19; 4fr, May 17; souvenir sheet, Apr. 2.

Pres. Georges Pompidou
A668

Paul as Harlequin, by Picasso
A669

1975, Apr. 3 Engraved *Perf. 13*

1430	A668	80c black & gray	35	12

Georges Pompidou (1911–74), President of France, 1969–74.

Europa Issue 1975

1975, Apr. 26 Photo. *Perf. 13*

Design: 1.20fr, Woman on Balcony, by Kees van Dongen (horiz.).

1431	A669	80c multicolored	45	12
1432	"	1.20fr "	60	20

Machines, Globe, Emblem
A670

1975, May 3 Engraved

1433	A670	1.20fr bl., blk. & red	60	25

World Machine Tool Exhibition, Paris, June 17–26.

Senate Assembly Hall
A671

1975, May 24 Engraved *Perf. 13*

1434 A671 1.20fr olive & dark carmine 60 25

Centenary of the Senate of the Republic.

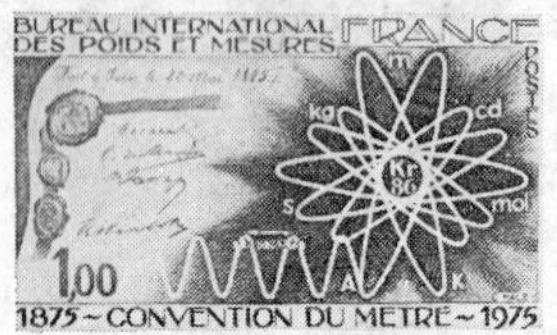

Meter Convention Document, Atom Diagram and Waves—A672

1975, May 31

1435 A672 1fr multicolored 50 20

Centenary of International Meter Convention, Paris, 1875.

Metro Regional Train
A673

"Gazelle" Helicopter
A674

1975

1436	A673	1fr indigo & brt. bl.	70	20
1437	A674	1.30fr violet blue & green	60	30

French technical achievements.

Issue dates: 1fr, June 21; 1.30fr, May 31.

Youth and Flasks, Symbols of Study and Growth
A675

1975, June 21

1438 A675 70c red. pur. & blk. 35 15

Student Health Foundation.

People's Theater, Bussang, and Maurice Pottecher—A676

1975, Aug. 9 Engraved *Perf. 13*

1439 A676 85c multicolored 35 20

80th anniversary of the People's Theater at Bussang, founded by Maurice Pottecher.

Regions of France

Central France A677

Aquitaine A678

Limousin A679

Picardy A680

Burgundy A681

Loire A682

Guyana A683

Auvergne A684

Poitou-Charentes A685

Southern Pyrenees—A686

Pas-de-Calais
A687

1975–76 Engraved *Perf. 13*

1440	A677	25c blue & yellow green	15	10
1441	A678	60c multicolored	30	10
1442	A679	70c "	40	15
1443	A680	85c bl., green & orange	40	20
1444	A681	1fr red, yellow & maroon	45	15
1445	A682	1.15fr blue, bister & green	60	20
1446	A683	1.25fr multi.	55	10
1447	A684	1.30fr dk. bl. & red	65	25
1448	A685	1.90fr slate, olive & Prus. blue	1.00	30
1449	A686	2.20fr multi.	1.00	40
1450	A687	2.80fr car., blue & black	1.35	50
		Nos. 1440-1450 (11)	6.85	2.45

Issue dates—1975: 85c, Nov. 15; 1fr, Oct. 25; 1.15fr, Sept. 6; 1.30fr, Oct. 4; 1.90fr, Dec. 6; 2.80fr, Dec. 13. 1976: 25c, Jan. 31; 2.20fr, Jan. 10; 60c, May 22; 70c, May 29; 125fr, Oct. 16.

French Flag, F.-H. Manhes, Jean Verneau, Pierre Kaan
A690

1975, Sept. 27

1453 A690 1fr multicolored 50 20

Liberation of concentration camps, 30th anniversary. F.-H. Manhes (1889–1959), Jean Verneau (1890–1944) and Pierre Kaan (1903–1945) were French resistance leaders, imprisoned in concentration camps.

Monument, by Joseph Riviere
A691

1975, Oct. 11

1454 A691 70c multicolored 35 15

Land Mine Demolition Service, 30th anniversary. Monument was erected in Alsace to honor land mine victims.

Symbols of Suburban Living
A692

1975, Oct. 18

1455 A692 1.70fr brown, blue & green 90 30

Creation of new towns.

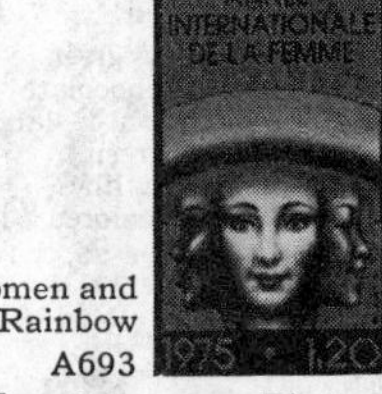

Women and Rainbow
A693

1975, Nov. 8 Photogravure

1456 A693 1.20fr silver & multi. 55 30

International Women's Year 1975.

Saint-Nazaire Bridge
A694

1975, Nov. 8 Engraved

1457 A694 1.40fr bl., indigo & green 75 15

French and Russian Flags
A695

Frigate Melpomene
A696

1975, Nov. 22

1458 A695 1.20fr blue, red & ocher 60 30

Franco-Soviet diplomatic relations, 50th anniversary.

1975, Dec. 6

1459 A696 90c multicolored 40 25

Gallic Coin Type of 1975

1976, Jan. 1 Typo. *Perf. 13½x14*

1460	A663	50c lt. green & brown	40	15
1461	"	60c lilac & brn.	55	20
1462	"	90c org. & brn.	80	35
1463	"	1.60fr vio. & brn.	1.40	55

Nos. 1460–1463 are known only precanceled. See second note after No. 132.

Lintel, St. Genis des Fontaines Church—A697

Venus of Brassempouy (Paleolithic)
A698

"The Joy of Life," by Robert Delaunay—A699

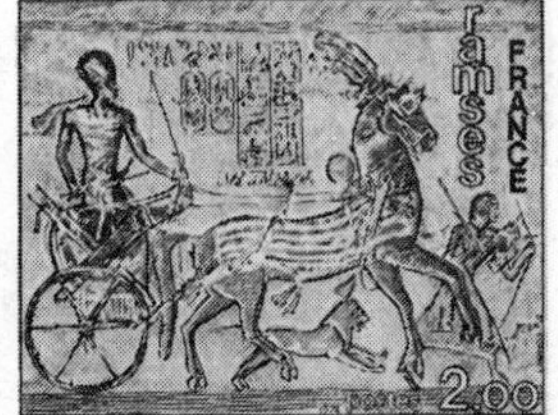

Ramses II, from Abu Simbel Temple, Egypt—A700

Still Life, by Maurice de Vlaminck—A701

1976 Engr. *Perf. 13*

1464 A697 2fr bl. & slate bl. 1.00 60
1465 A698 2fr dk. brn. & yel. 1.00 60

Photo. *Perf. 12½x13*

1466 A699 2fr multicolored 1.00 50

Engr. *Perf. 13x12½*

1467 A700 2fr multicolored 1.00 50

Perf. 13

1468 A701 2fr multicolored 1.00 50
Nos. 1464–1468 (5) 5.00 2.70

Issue dates: No. 1464, Jan. 24; No. 1465, Mar. 6; No. 1466, July 24; No. 1467, Sept. 4; No. 1468, Dec. 18.

Tourist Issue

Chateau Fort de Bonaguil
A702

Lodève Cathedral
A703

Biarritz
A704

Thiers
A705

Ussel
A706

Chateau de Malmaison
A707

1976 Engraved *Perf. 13*

1469 A702 1fr multicolored 50 8
1470 A703 1.10fr violet blue 55 15
1471 A704 1.40fr multicolored 70 17
1472 A705 1.70fr " 85 15
1473 A706 2fr " 1.00 10
1474 A707 3fr " 1.50 12
Nos. 1469–1474 (6) 5.10 77

Issue dates: 1fr, 2fr, July 10; 1.10fr, Nov. 13; 1.40fr, Sept. 25; 1.70fr, Oct. 9; 3fr, Apr. 10.

Destroyers, Association Emblem
A708

1976, Apr. 24

1475 A708 1fr vio. bl., magenta & lemon 50 20

Naval Reserve Officers Association, 50th anniversary.

Gate, Rouen
A709

Young Person
A710

1976, Apr. 24

1476 A709 80c olive gray & salmon 40 15

49th Congress of the Federation of French Philatelic Societies, Rouen, Apr. 23–May 2.

1976, Apr. 27

1477 A710 60c bl. grn., indigo & carmine 30 12

JUVAROUEN 76, International Youth Philatelic Exhibition, Rouen, Apr. 25–May 2.

Europa Issue 1976

Ceramic Pitcher, Strasbourg, 18th Century
A711

Design: 1.20fr, Sevres porcelain plate and CEPT emblem.

1976, May 8 Photo. *Perf. 13*

1478 A711 80c multicolored 40 15
1479 " 1.20fr " 60 25

Count de Vergennes and Benjamin Franklin—A712

1976, May 15 Engr. *Perf. 13*

1480 A712 1.20fr multicolored 60 25

American Bicentennial.

Battle of Verdun Memorial
A713

Communication
A714

1976, June 12 Engraved

1481 A713 1fr multicolored 50 20

Battle of Verdun, 60th anniversary.

1976, June 12 Photogravure

1482 A714 1.20fr multicolored 60 25

Troncais Forest
A715

Cross of Lorraine
A716

1976, June 19 Engraved

1483 A715 70c green & multi. 35 18

Protection of the environment.

1976, June 19

1484 A716 1fr multicolored 50 20

Association of Free French, 30th anniversary.

Symphonie Communications Satellite
A717

1976, June 26 Photogravure

1485 A717 1.40fr multicolored 70 30

French technical achievements.

Gallic Coin Type of 1975

1976, July 1 Typo. *Perf. 13½x14*

1487 A663 52c vermilion & dk. brown 40 15
1488 " 62c vio. & dk. brn. 40 25
1489 " 95c tan & dk. brn. 60 30
1490 " 1.70fr dark blue & dk. brn. 1.00 45

Nos. 1487–1490 are known only precanceled. See second note after No. 132.

Paris Summer Festival
A719

1976, July 10 Engraved

1491 A719 1fr multicolored 50 20

Summer festival in Tuileries Gardens, Paris.

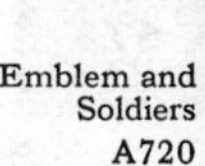

Emblem and Soldiers
A720

1976, July 8

1492 A720 1fr blk., dp. blue & magenta 50 20

Officers Reserve Corps, centenary.

Sailing
A721

1976, July 17

1493 A721 1.20fr blue, black & violet 60 25

21st Olympic Games, Montreal, Canada, July 17–Aug. 1.

Marianne Type of 1971–74

1976 Typographed *Perf. 14x13*

1494 A555 80c green 40 4

Engraved *Perf. 13*

1495 A555 80c green 40 4
a. Booklet pane of 10 4.00
1496 A555 1fr carmine rose 50 5
a. Booklet pane of 5 2.50
b. Booklet pane of 10 5.00

No. 1495 issued in booklets only. "POSTES" 6mm. long on Nos. 1292A and 1494; 4mm. on others.

Nos. 1494 and 1496 were issued untagged in 1977.

Coil Stamps

1976, Aug. 1 Engr. *Perf. 13 Horiz.*

1497 A555 80c green 40 15
1498 " 1fr carmine rose 50 10

Red control number on back of every 10th stamp.

Woman's Head, by Jean Carzou—A722

1976, Sept. 18 Engr. *Perf. 13x12½*

1499 A722 2fr multicolored 1.00 50

Old and New Telephones—A723

1976, Sept. 25 Engr. *Perf. 13*

1500 A723 1fr multicolored 50 12

Centenary of first telephone call by Alexander Graham Bell, Mar. 10, 1876.

Festival Emblem and Trophy, Pyrenees, Hercules and Pyrène A724

Police Emblem A725

1976, Oct. 2

1501 A724 1.40fr multicolored 70 30

10th International Tourist Film Festival, Tarbes, Oct. 4–10.

1976, Oct. 9 Engr. *Perf. 13*

1502 A725 1.10fr ultra., red & olive 55 20

National Police, help and protection.

Atomic Particle Accelerator, Diagram—A726

1976, Oct. 22 Photogravure

1503 A726 1.40fr multicolored 70 25

European Center for Nuclear Research (CERN).

"Exhibitions" A727

1976, Nov. 20 Engr. *Perf. 13*

1504 A727 1.50fr multicolored 75 20

Trade Fairs and Exhibitions.

Abstract Design A728

1976, Nov. 27 Photogravure

1505 A728 1.10fr multicolored 55 20

Customs Service.

Atlantic Museum, Port Louis—A729

1976, Dec. 4 Engraved

1506 A729 1.45fr greenish blue & olive 75 30

Regions of France

Réunion A730

Martinique A731

Franche-Comté A732

Brittany A733

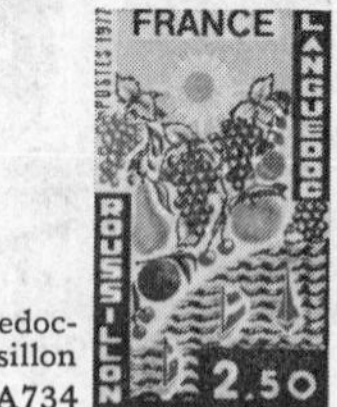

Languedoc-Roussillon A734

Rhône-Alps A735

Champagne-Ardennes A736

Alsace A737

Photo. (1.45fr, 1.50fr, 2.50fr); Engr.

1977 *Perf. 13*

1507 A730 1.45fr green & lilac rose 75 20
1508 A731 1.50fr multicolored 75 20
1509 A732 2.10fr " 1.05 25
1510 A733 2.40fr " 1.20 20
1511 A734 2.50fr " 1.25 30
1512 A735 2.75fr Pruss. blue 1.40 40
1513 A736 3.20fr multi. 1.60 50
1514 A737 3.90fr " 1.95 65
Nos. 1507–1514 (8) 9.95 2.70

Issue dates: 1.45fr, Feb. 5; 1.50fr, Jan. 29; 2.10fr, Jan. 8; 2.40fr, Feb. 19; 2.50fr, Jan. 15; 2.75fr, Jan. 22; 3.20fr, Apr. 16; 3.90fr, Feb. 26.

Pompidou Cultural Center—A738

1977, Feb. 5 Engr. *Perf. 13*

1515 A738 1fr multicolored 50 12

Inauguration of the Georges Pompidou National Center for Art and Culture, Paris.

Dunkirk Harbor A739

1977, Feb. 12

1516 A739 50c multicolored 25 8

Expansion of Dunkirk harbor facilities.

Bridge at Mantes, by Corot—A740

Virgin and Child, by Rubens A741

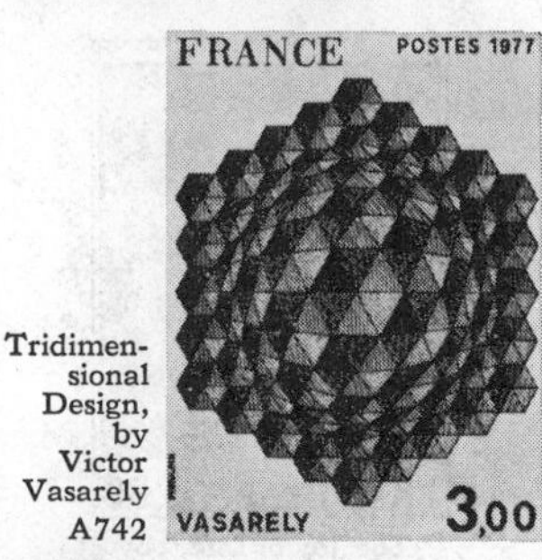

Tridimensional Design, by Victor Vasarely A742

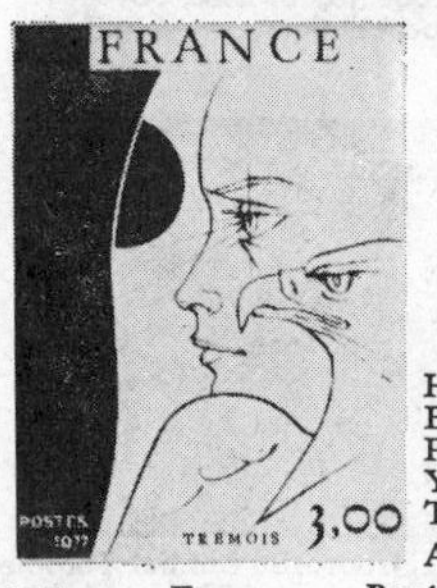

Head and Eagle, by Pierre-Yves Tremois A743

1977 Engr. *Perf. 13x12½*

1517 A740 2fr multicolored 1.00 40

Perf. 12x13

1518 A741 2fr multicolored 1.00 35

Perf. 12½x13

1519 A742 3fr ultra. & slate green 1.50 55

Photogravure

1520 A743 3fr dk. red & blk. 1.50 50

Issue dates: No. 1517, Feb. 12; No. 1518, Nov. 5; No. 1519, Apr. 7; No. 1520, Sept. 17.

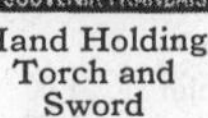

Hand Holding Torch and Sword A744

Pisces A745

1977, Mar. 5 Engr. *Perf. 13*

1521 A744 80c ultra. & multi. 40 15

"France remembers its dead."

1977–78 Engraved *Perf. 13*

Zodiac Signs: 58c, Cancer. 61c, Sagittarius. 68c, Taurus. 73c, Aries. 78c, Libra. 1.05fr, Scorpio. 1.15fr, Capricorn. 1.25fr, Leo. 1.85fr, Aquarius. 2fr, Virgo. 2.10fr, Gemini.

1522 A745 54c violet blue 28 10
1523 " 58c emerald 30 10

1524 A745 61c bright blue 30 10
1525 " 68c deep brown 35 15
1526 " 73c rose car. 36 12
1527 " 78c vermilion 40 10
1528 " 1.05fr bright lilac 52 20
1529 " 1.15fr orange 58 15
1530 " 1.25fr lt. olive grn. 60 10
1531 " 1.85fr slate green 92 35
1532 " 2fr blue green 1.00 30
1533 " 2.10fr lilac rose 1.05 10
Nos. 1522–1533 (12) 6.66 1.87

Issue dates: 54c, 68c, 1.05fr, 1.85fr, Apr. 1, 1977. Others, 1978.

Nos. 1522–1533 are known only precanceled. See second note after No. 132.

Europa Issue

Village in Provence
A746

Design: 1.40fr, Brittany port.

1977, Apr. 23

1534 A746 1fr multicolored 50 10
1535 " 1.40fr " 70 20

Flowers and Gardening
A747

1977, Apr. 23 Engr. ***Perf. 13***

1536 A747 1.70fr multicolored 85 30

National Horticulture Society, centenary.

Symbolic Flower
A748

1977, May 7

1537 A748 1.40fr multicolored 70 25

International Flower Show, Nantes, May 12–23.

Battle of Cambray
A749

1977, May 14

1538 A749 80c multicolored 40 12

300th anniversary of the capture of Cambray and the incorporation of Cambresis District into France.

Carmes Church, School, Map of France
A750

Modern Constructions
A751

1977, May 14

1539 A750 1.10fr multicolored 55 15

Catholic Institutes in France.

1977, May 21

1540 A751 1.10fr multicolored 55 15

European Federation of the Construction Industry.

Annecy Castle
A752

1977, May 28

1541 A752 1fr multicolored 50 15

Congress of the Federation of French Philatelic Societies, Annecy, May 28–30.

Tourist Issue

Abbey, Pont-à-Mousson
A753

Abbey Tower, Saint-Amand-les-Eaux
A754

Collegiate Church of Dorat
A755

Fontenay Abbey
A756

Bayeux Cathedral
A757

Chateau de Vitré
A758

1977 Engraved ***Perf. 13***

1542 A753 1.25fr multicolored 62 12
1543 A754 1.40fr " 70 10
1544 A755 1.45fr " 72 20
1545 A756 1.50fr " 75 20
1546 A757 1.90fr blk. & yel. 95 25
1547 A758 2.40fr " 1.20 8
Nos. 1542–1547 (6) 4.94 95

Issue dates: 1.25fr, Oct. 1; 1.40fr, Sept. 17; 1.45fr, July 16; 1.50fr, June 4; 1.90fr, July 9; 2.40fr, Sept. 24.

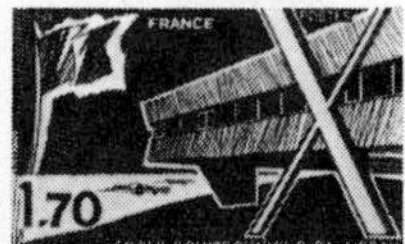

Polytechnic School and "X"
A759

1977, June 4 Engr. ***Perf. 13***

1548 A759 1.70fr multicolored 85 25

Relocation at Palaiseau of Polytechnic School, founded 1794.

Soccer and Cup—A760

1977, June 11

1549 A760 80c multicolored 40 12

Soccer Cup of France, 60th anniversary.

De Gaulle Memorial
A761

Stylized Map of France
A762

Photogravure & Embossed

1977, June 18

1550 A761 1fr gold & multi. 50 10

5th anniversary of dedication of De Gaulle memorial at Colombey-les-Deux-Eglises.

1977, June 18 Engr. ***Perf. 13***

1551 A762 1.10fr ultra. & red 55 20

French Junior Chamber of Commerce.

Battle of Nancy
A763

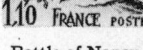

Arms of Burgundy
A764

1977, June 25

1552 A763 1.10fr bl. & slate 55 20

Battle of Nancy between the Dukes of Burgundy and Lorraine, 500th anniversary.

1977, July 2

1553 A764 1.25fr olive brn. & slate green 62 20

Annexation of Burgundy by the French Crown, 500th anniversary.

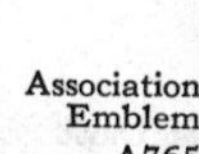

Association Emblem
A765

1977, July 8

1554 A765 1.40fr ultra., olive & red 70 20

French-speaking Parliamentary Association.

Red Cicada
A766

1977, Sept. 10 Photo. ***Perf. 13***

1555 A766 80c multicolored 40 15

Nature protection.

French Handicrafts
A767

1977, Oct. 1 Engraved ***Perf. 13***

1556 A767 1.40fr multicolored 70 20

French craftsmen.

Industry and Agriculture
A768

1977, Oct. 22

1557 A768 80c brn. & olive 40 15

Economic and Social Council, 30th anniversary.

Table Tennis
A769

1977, Dec. 17 Engr. ***Perf. 13***

1558 A769 1.10fr multicolored 55 18

French Table Tennis Federation, 50th anniversary, and French team, gold medal winner, Birmingham.

Abstract, by Roger Excoffon—A770

1977, Dec. 17 ***Perf. 13x12½***

1559 A770 3fr multicolored 1.50 50

Sabine, after David
A771

1977–78 Engraved *Perf. 13*

1560	A771	1c slate	3	3
1561	"	2c bright violet	3	3
1562	"	5c slate green	3	3
1563	"	10c red brown	5	3
1564	"	15c Prus. blue	8	3
1565	"	20c bright green	10	3
1566	"	30c orange	15	4
1567	"	50c red lilac	25	4
1568	"	80c green	40	4
		a. Bklt. pane of 10	4.00	
1569	A771	80c olive	40	4
1570	"	1fr red	50	5
		a. Bklt. pane of 5	2.50	
		b. Bklt. pane of 10	5.00	
1571	A771	1fr green	50	5
1572	"	1.20fr red	60	5
		a. Bklt. pane of 5	3.00	
1573	A771	1.40fr bright blue	70	8
1574	"	1.70fr greenish bl.	85	7
1575	"	2fr emerald	1.00	6
1576	"	2.10fr lilac rose	1.10	10
1577	"	3fr dark brown	1.50	12
		Nos. 1560–1577 (18)	8.27	92

Issue dates: Nos. 1568, 1570 Dec. 17, 1977. Others, 1978.

Coil Stamps

1978 *Perf. 13 Horiz.*

1578	A771	80c bright green	40	4
1579	"	1fr " "	50	5
1579A	"	1fr bright red	50	5
1579B	"	1.20fr " "	60	5

Percheron, by Jacques Birr
A772

Osprey
A773

1978 Photo. *Perf. 13*

1580	A772	1.70fr multicolored	85	20

Engraved

1581	A773	1.80fr multicolored	90	25

Nature protection.
Issue dates: 1.70fr, Jan. 7; 1.80fr, Oct. 14.

Examination

The Catalogue editors cannot undertake to appraise, identify or pass upon genuineness or condition of stamps.

Tournament, 1662, Etching
A774

Institut de France and Pont des Arts, Paris, by Bernard Buffet
A776

Horses, by Yves Brayer—A777

1978 Engr. *Perf. 12x13*

1582	A774	2fr black	1.00	35

Perf. 13x12

1584	A776	3fr multicolored	1.50	45
1585	A777	3fr multicolored	1.50	45

Issue dates: 2fr, Jan. 14; No. 1584, Feb. 4; No. 1585, Dec. 9.

Communications School and Tower
A778

1978, Jan. 19 Engr. *Perf. 13*

1586	A778	80c Prussian blue	40	15

National Telecommunications School, centenary.

Swedish and French Flags, Map of Saint Barthelemy—A779

1978, Jan. 19

1587	A779	1.10fr multicolored	55	15

Centenary of the reunion with France of Saint Barthelemy Island, West Indies.

Regions of France

Ile de France
A780

Tanker, Refinery, Flower, Upper Normandy
A781

Lower Normandy
A782

1978 Photo. *Perf. 13*

1588	A780	1fr red, bl. & blk.	50	15

Engr.

1589	A781	1.40fr multicolored	70	15

Photogravure

1590	A782	1.70fr multi.	85	20

Issue dates. 1fr, Mar. 4; 1.40fr, Jan. 21; 1.70fr, Mar. 31.

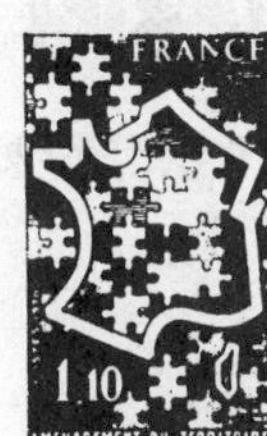

Stylized Map of France
A788

Young Stamp Collector
A789

1978, Feb. 11 Engr. *Perf. 13*

1596	A788	1.10fr vio. & grn.	55	15

Program of administrative changes, 15th anniversary.

1978, Feb. 25

1597	A789	80c multicolored	40	12

JUVEXNIORT, Youth Philatelic Exhibition, Niort, Feb. 25–March 5.

Tourist Issue

Verdon Gorge
A790

Saint-Saturnin Church
A792

Pont Neuf, Paris
A791

Our Lady of Bec-Hellouin Abbey
A793

Chateau D'Esquelbecq
A794

Aubazine Abbey
A795

Fontevraud Abbey
A796

1978 Engraved *Perf. 13*

1598	A790	50c multicolored	25	8
1599	A791	80c "	40	7
1600	A792	1fr black	50	8
1601	A793	1.10fr multicolored	55	15
1602	A794	1.10fr "	55	12
1603	A795	1.25fr car. & brn.	60	15
1604	A796	1.70fr multicolored	85	15
		Nos. 1598–1604 (7)	3.70	80

Issue dates: 1.25fr, Feb. 18; 50c, Mar. 6; No. 1601, Mar. 26; 80c, May 27; 1fr, June 10; 1.70fr, June 3; No. 1602, June 17.

Fish and Underwater Flora
A797

1978, Apr. 15 Photo. *Perf. 13*

1605	A797	1.25fr multicolored	60	20

Port Cros National Park, 15th anniversary.

Flowers, Butterflies and Houses
A798

1978, Apr. 22 Engr. *Perf. 13*

1606	A798	1.70fr multicolored	85	18

50th anniversary of the beautification of France campaign.

Hands Shielding Source of Heat and Light—A799

1978, Apr. 22

1607 A799 1fr multicolored 50 10

Energy conservation.

World War I Memorial near Lens A800

Fountain of the Innocents, Paris A801

1978, May 6

1608 A800 2fr lemon & magenta 1.00 25

Colline Notre Dame de Lorette memorial of World War I.

Europa Issue 1978

Design: 1.40fr, Flower Park Fountain, Paris.

1978, May 6

1609 A801 1fr multicolored 50 8
1610 " 1.40fr " 70 17

Maurois Palace, Troyes A802

1978, May 13

1611 A802 1fr multicolored 50 15

51st Congress of the Federation of French Philatelic Societies, Troyes, May 13–15.

Roland Garros Tennis Court and Player—A803

1978, May 27

1612 A803 1fr multicolored 50 13

Roland Garros Tennis Court, 50th anniversary.

Hand and Plant A804

Printing Office Emblem—A805

1978, Sept. 9 Engr. ***Perf. 13***

1613 A804 1.30fr brn., red & green 65 15

Encouragement of handicrafts.

1978, Sept. 23

1614 A805 1fr multicolored 50 15

National Printing Office, established 1538.

Fortress, Besançon, and Collegiate Church, Dole A806

Valenciennes and Maubeuge A807

1978

1615 A806 1.20fr multicolored 60 15
1616 A807 1.20fr " 60 15

Reunion of Franche-Comté and Valenciennes and Maubeuge with France, 300th anniversary.

Issue dates: No. 1615, Sept. 23, No. 1616, Sept. 30.

Sower Type of 1906–1937 and Academy Emblem A808

Gymnasts, Strasbourg Cathedral, Storks A809

1978, Oct. 7

1617 A808 1fr multicolored 50 15

Academy of Philately, 50th anniversary.

1978, Oct. 21

1618 A809 1fr multicolored 50 15

19th World Gymnastics Championships, Strasbourg, Oct. 23–26.

Various Sports A810

Polish Veterans' Monument A811

1978, Oct. 21

1619 A810 1fr multicolored 50 15

Sports for all.

1978, Nov. 11

1620 A811 1.70fr multicolored 85 20

Polish veterans of World War II.

Railroad Car and Monument, Compiègne Forest, Rethondes—A812

1978, Nov. 11 Engr. ***Perf. 13***

1621 A812 1.20fr indigo 60 15

60th anniversary of World War I armistice.

Handicapped People A813

1978, Nov. 18

1622 A813 1fr multicolored 50 15

Rehabilitation of the handicapped.

Human Rights Emblem A814

1978, Dec. 9 Engr. ***Perf. 13***

1623 A814 1.70fr dark brown & blue 85 20

30th anniversary of Universal Declaration of Human Rights.

Child and IYC Emblem A815

1979, Jan. 6 Engr. ***Perf. 13***

1624 A815 1.70fr multi. 85 20

International Year of the Child.

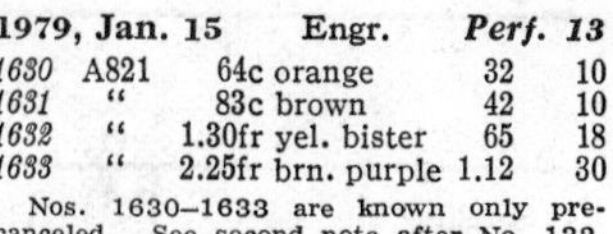

"Music," 15th Century Miniature A816

1979, Jan. 13 ***Perf. 13x12½***

1625 A816 2fr multicolored 1.00 25

Orange Agaric A821

Mushrooms: 83c, Death trumpet. 1.30fr, Olive wood pleurotus. 2.25fr, Cauliflower claveria.

1979, Jan. 15 Engr. ***Perf. 13***

1630 A821 64c orange 32 10
1631 " 83c brown 42 10
1632 " 1.30fr yel. bister 65 18
1633 " 2.25fr brn. purple 1.12 30

Nos. 1630–1633 are known only precanceled. See second note after No. 132.

Victor Segalen A822

1979, Jan. 20

1634 A822 1.50fr multicolored 75 20

Victor Segalen (1878–1919), physician, explorer and writer.

Hibiscus and Palms A823

1979, Feb. 3

1635 A823 35c multicolored 18 6

International Flower Festival, Martinique.

Buddha, Stupas, Temple of Borobudur A824

1979, Feb. 24

1636 A824 1.80fr olive & slate green 90 22

Save the Temple of Borobudur, Java, campaign.

F. POULBOT 1879 1979

POSTES

1.30 FRANCE

Boy, by Poulbot A825

1979, Mar. 24 **Photogravure**

1637 A825 1.20fr multicolored 60 15

Francisque Poulbot (1879–1946).

INDEX of Commemorative Issues

SEMI-POSTAL STAMPS.

SP1

SP2

Red Surcharge on No. B1

Typographed

1914 *Perf. 14x13½* **Unwmkd.**

B1	SP1	10c+5c red	2.75	2.00
B2	SP2	10c+5c red	22.50	2.50
		a. Bklt. pane of 10	300.00	

Issue dates: No. B1, Aug. 11; No. B2, Sept. 10.

Widow at Grave SP3

War Orphans SP4

Woman Plowing SP5

"Trench of Bayonets" SP6

Lion of Belfort SP7

"La Marseillaise" SP8

1917-19

B3	SP3	2c+3c violet brown	2.00	2.00
B4	SP4	5c+5c green ('19)	7.00	4.00
B5	SP5	15c+10c gray grn.	16.50	14.00
B6	"	25c+15c deep blue	70.00	40.00
B7	SP6	35c+25c slate & violet	120.00	90.00
B8	SP7	50c+50c pale brown & dk. brown	160.00	135.00
B9	SP8	1fr+1fr claret & maroon	285.00	225.00
B10	"	5fr+5fr deep blue & black	1400.00	800.00
		Nos. B3-B10 (8)	2060.50	1310.00

Hospital Ship and Field Hospital SP9

1918, Aug.

B11	SP9	15c+5c slate & red	80.00	27.50

Semi-Postal Stamps of 1917-19 Surcharged **+5c** **=**

1922, Sept. 1

B12	SP3	2c+1c violet brown	10	10
B13	SP4	5c+2½c green	25	20
B14	SP5	15c+5c gray green	40	35
B15	"	25c+5c deep blue	75	60
B16	SP6	35c+5c slate & violet	2.50	1.35
B17	SP7	50c+10c pale brown & dark brown	6.00	3.50
		a. Pair, one without surcharge		
B18	SP8	1fr+25c claret & maroon	10.00	7.00
B19	"	5fr+1fr bl. & black	80.00	60.00
		Nos. B12-B19 (8)	100.00	73.10

Style and arrangement of surcharge differs for each denomination.

Types of 1917-19.

1926-27

B20	SP3	2c+1c violet brown	30	30
B21	SP7	50c+10c olive brown & dark brown	12.00	2.25
B22	SP8	1fr+25c deep rose & red brown	18.50	9.50
B23	"	5fr+1fr slate blue & black	60.00	40.00

Sinking Fund Issues.

Types of Regular Issues of 1903-07 Surcharged in Red or Blue

Caisse d'Amortissement +10c

1927, Sept. 26

B24	A22	40c+10c lt. blue (R)	3.50	2.50
B25	A20	50c+25c green (Bl)	5.00	4.00

Type of Regular Issue of 1923 Surcharged in Black

C A

+50c

B26	A23	1.50fr+50c orange	5.00	4.00

Industry and Agriculture SP10

1928, May **Engraved** *Perf. 13½*

B27	SP10	1.50fr+8.50fr dull blue	110.00	110.00
		a. 1.50fr+8.50fr blue green	300.00	300.00

Types of 1903-23 Issues Surcharged as in 1927.

1928, Oct. 1 *Perf. 14x13½*

B28	A22	40c+10c gray lilac (R)	8.00	7.00
B29	A20	50c+25c orange brown (Bl)	18.50	15.00
B30	A23	1.50fr+50c rose lilac (Bk)	25.00	20.00

Types of 1903-23 Issues Surcharged as in 1927.

1929, Oct. 1

B31	A22	40c+10c green	15.00	10.00
B32	A20	50c+25c lilac rose	18.50	15.00
B33	A23	1.50fr+50c chestnut	32.50	20.00

"The Smile of Reims" SP11

1930, Mar. 15 **Engraved** *Perf. 13*

B34	SP11	1.50fr+3.50fr red violet	60.00	60.00
		a. Bklt. pane of 4	275.00	275.00

Types of 1903-07 Issues Surcharged

Caisse d'Amortissement +10c

1930, Oct. 1 *Perf. 14x13½*

B35	A22	40c+10c cerise	15.00	9.00
B36	A20	50c+25c gray brown	25.00	18.50
B37	A22	1.50fr+50c violet	40.00	25.00

Allegory, French Provinces SP12

1931, Mar. 1 *Perf. 13*

B38	SP12	1.50fr+3.50fr green	110.00	110.00

Types of 1903-07 Issues Surcharged

Caisse d'Amortissement +10c

1931, Oct. 1 *Perf. 14x13½*

B39	A22	40c+10c olive green	30.00	25.00
B40	A20	50c+25c gray violet	75.00	55.00
B41	A22	1.50fr+50c deep red	75.00	55.00

"France" Giving Aid to an Intellectual SP13

Symbolic of Music SP14

1935, Dec. 9 **Engraved** *Perf. 13*

B42	SP13	50c+10c ultra.	3.50	1.65
B43	SP14	50c+2fr dull red	42.50	30.00

The surtax was for the aid of distressed and exiled intellectuals.

Statue of Liberty SP15

Children of the Unemployed SP16

1936-37

B44	SP15	50c+25c dark blue ('37)	3.75	2.75
B45	"	75c+50c violet	7.00	5.00

The surtax was for the aid of political refugees.

1936, May

B46	SP16	50c+10c copper red	5.00	3.75

The surtax was for the aid of children of the unemployed.

Type of 1935 Semi-Postal Surcharged in Black **+20c**

1936, Nov.

B47	SP14	20c on 50c+2fr dull red	3.25	2.50

Jacques Callot SP17

Anatole France (Jacques Anatole Thibault) SP18

Hector Berlioz SP19

Victor Hugo SP20

Auguste Rodin SP21

Louis Pasteur SP22

1936-37 **Engraved**

B48	SP17	20c+10c brn. car.	2.50	2.00
B49	SP18	30c+10c emerald ('37)	2.50	1.75
B50	SP19	40c+10c emerald	2.50	2.00
B51	SP20	50c+10c copper red	4.00	2.00
B52	SP21	90c+10c rose red ('37)	5.00	3.50
B53	SP22	1.50fr+50c dp. ultra.	16.50	10.00
		Nos. B48-B53 (6)	33.00	21.25

The surtax was used for relief of unemployed intellectuals.

1938

B54	SP18	30c+10c brn. car.	2.00	1.75
B55	SP17	35c+10c dull grn.	3.00	2.00
B56	SP19	55c+10c dull vio.	4.50	2.00
B57	SP20	65c+10c ultra.	4.50	2.00
B58	SP21	1fr+10c car. lake	4.50	2.00
B59	SP22	1.75fr+25c dp. blue	7.50	3.25
		Nos. B54-B59 (6)	26.00	13.00

Tug of War
SP23

Foot Race
SP24

Hiking
SP25

1937, June 16

B60 SP23 20c+10c brown 2.00 1.75
B61 SP24 40c+10c red brn. 2.00 1.75
B62 SP25 50c+10c black brown 2.00 1.75

The surtax was for the Recreation Fund of the employees of the Post, Telephone and Telegraph.

Pierre Loti
(Louis Marie Julien Viaud)
SP26

1937, Aug.

B63 SP26 50c+20c rose car. 3.25 2.25

The surtax was for the Pierre Loti Monument Fund.

"France" and Infant
SP27

1937–39

B64 SP27 65c+25c brn. violet 1.25 90
B65 " 90c+30c peacock blue ('39) 1.10 85

The surtax was used for public health work.

Winged Victory of Samothrace
SP28

Jean Charcot
SP29

1937, Aug.

B66 SP28 30c blue green 70.00 32.50
B67 " 55c red 70.00 32.50

On sale at the Louvre for 2.50 fr. The surtax of 1.65 fr. was for the benefit of the Louvre Museum.

1938-39

B68 SP29 65c+35c dark blue green 1.00 1.00
B69 " 90c+35c bright red violet ('39) 7.25 5.50

The surtax was for the benefit of French seamen.

Palace of Versailles
SP30

1938, May 9

B70 SP30 1.75fr+75c deep blue 15.00 11.00

Issued in commemoration of the National Exposition of Painting and Sculpture at Versailles. The surtax was for the benefit of the Versailles Concert Society.

French Soldier
SP31

Monument
SP32

1938, May 16

B71 SP31 55c+70c brown violet 2.85 2.50
B72 " 65c+1.10fr peacock blue 2.85 2.50

The surtax was for a fund to erect a monument to the glory of the French Infantrymen.

1938, May 25

B73 SP32 55c+45c vermilion 8.50 6.50

The surtax was for a fund to erect a monument in honor of the Army Medical Corps.

Reims Cathedral
SP33

"France" Welcoming Her Sons
SP34

1938, July 10

B74 SP33 65c+35c ultra. 6.50 5.50

Issued to commemorate the completion of the reconstruction of Reims Cathedral, July 10, 1938.

1938, Aug. 8

B75 SP34 65c+60c rose car. 4.00 2.75

The surtax was for the benefit of French volunteers repatriated from Spain.

Curie Issue
Common Design Type

1938, Sept. 1

B76 CD80 1.75fr+50c deep ultramarine 6.00 4.50

Victory Parade Passing Arc de Triomphe
SP36

1938, Oct. 8

B77 SP36 65c+35c brown carmine 4.25 3.25

20th anniversary of the Armistice.

Student and Nurse—SP37

1938, Dec. 1

B78 SP37 65c+60c peacock bl. 4.25 3.25

The surtax was for Student Relief.

Blind Man and Radio
SP38

1938, Dec.

B79 SP38 90c+25c brn. violet 3.75 2.75

The surtax was used to help provide radios for the blind.

Civilian Facing Firing Squad
SP39

Red Cross Nurse
SP40

1939, Feb. 1

B80 SP39 90c+35c blk. brown 4.50 3.50

The surtax was used to erect a monument to civilian victims of World War I.

1939, Mar. 24

B81 SP40 90c+35c dark slate green, turquoise blue & red 4.00 3.00

Issued in commemoration of the 75th anniversary of the founding of the International Red Cross Society.

Army Engineer—SP41

1939, Apr. 3

B82 SP41 70c+50c verm. 4.50 4.00

Issued in honor of the Army Engineering Corps. The surtax was used to erect a monument to those members who died in World War I.

Ministry of Post, Telegraph and Telephone
SP42

1939, Apr. 8

B83 SP42 90c+35c turquoise blue 8.00 5.50

The surtax was used to aid orphans of employees of the postal system. Issued to commemorate the opening of the new building for the Ministry of Post, Telegraph and Telephones.

Mother and Child
SP43

Eiffel Tower
SP44

1939, Apr. 24

B84 SP43 90c+35c red 2.00 1.50

The surtax was used to aid children of the unemployed.

1939, May 5

B85 SP44 90c+50c red vio. 4.50 3.00

Issued in commemoration of the 50th anniversary of the Eiffel Tower. The surtax was used for celebration festivities.

Puvis de Chavannes
SP45

Claude Debussy
SP46

Honoré de Balzac
SP47

Claude Bernard
SP48

1939–40

B86	SP45	40c+10c verm.	1.35	1.25
B87	SP46	70c+10c brown violet	1.50	1.25
B87A	"	80c+10c brown violet ('40)	1.10	1.10
B88	SP47	90c+10c bright red violet	1.75	1.40
B88A	"	1fr+10c bright red violet ('40)	1.10	1.10
B89	SP48	2.25fr+25c bright ultramarine	3.50	2.25
B89A	"	2.50fr+25c bright ultra. ('40)	1.10	1.10
		Nos. B86-B89A (7)	11.40	9.45

The surtax was used to aid unemployed intellectuals.

Mothers and Children
SP49 SP50

1939, June 15

B90	SP49	70c+80c blue, green & violet	2.25	2.25
B91	SP50	90c+60c dark brown, dull vio. & brn.	2.25	2.25

The surtax was used to aid France's repopulation campaign.

"The Letter" by Jean Honoré Fragonard
SP51

Statue of Widow and Children
SP52

1939, July 6

B92	SP51	40c+60c brown, sepia & pur.	3.25	2.50

The surtax was used for the Postal Museum.

1939, July 20

B93	SP52	70c+30c brown violet	4.50	3.25

The surtax was for the benefit of French seamen.

French Soldier
SP53

Colonial Trooper
SP54

1940, Feb. 15

B94	SP53	40c+60c sepia	90	70
B95	SP54	1fr+50c turquoise blue	90	70

The surtax was used to assist the families of mobilized men.

World Map Showing French Possessions
SP55

1940, Apr. 15

B96	SP55	1fr+25c scarlet	2.25	1.50

Marshal Joseph J.C. Joffre
SP56

Marshal Ferdinand Foch
SP57

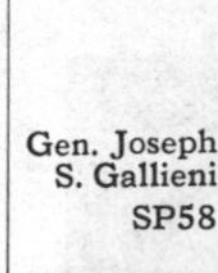

Gen. Joseph S. Gallieni
SP58

Woman Plowing
SP59

1940, May 1

B97	SP56	80c+45c choc.	1.40	1.40
B98	SP57	1fr+50c dk. vio.	1.40	1.40
B99	SP58	1.50fr+50c brn. red	1.40	1.35
B100	SP59	2.50fr+50c indigo & dull blue	1.50	1.00

The surtax was used for war charities.

Doctor, Nurse, Soldier and Family
SP60

Nurse and Wounded Soldier
SP61

1940, May 12

B101	SP60	80c+1fr dark green & red	2.75	2.75
B102	SP61	1fr+2fr sepia & red	2.75	2.75

The surtax was used for the Red Cross.

Nurse with Injured Children
SP62

1940, Nov. 12

B103	SP62	1fr+2fr sepia	60	50

The surtax was used for victims of the war.

Wheat Harvest
SP63

Sowing
SP64

Picking Grapes
SP65

Grazing Cattle
SP66

1940, Dec. 2

B104	SP63	80c+2fr brown black	1.25	1.00
B105	SP64	1fr+2fr chestnut	1.25	1.00
B106	SP65	1.50fr+2fr bright violet	1.25	1.00
B107	SP66	2.50fr+2fr deep green	1.25	1.00

The surtax was for national relief.

Prisoners of War
SP67 SP68

1941, Jan. 1

B108	SP67	80c+5fr dk. green	1.00	1.00
B109	SP68	1fr+5fr rose brn.	1.00	1.00

The surtax was for prisoners of war.

Science Fighting Cancer
SP69

1941, Feb. 20

B110	SP69	2.50fr+50c slate black & brown	1.00	1.00

The surtax was used for the control of cancer.

Type of 1941 Surcharged "+10c" in Blue.

1941, Mar. 4

B111	A109	1fr+10c crimson	15	15

Men Hauling Coal
SP70

"France" Aiding Needy Man
SP71

1941

B112	SP70	1fr+2fr sepia	70	50
B113	SP71	2.50fr+7.50fr dark blue	1.00	85

The surtax was for Marshal Pétain's National Relief Fund.

Liner Pasteur
SP72

Red Surcharge

1941, July 17

B114	SP72	1fr+1fr on 70c dark blue green	15	15

World Map, Mercator Projection
SP73

1941

B115	SP73	1fr+1fr multi.	50	45

Fisherman
SP74

1941, Oct. 23

B116 SP74 1fr+9fr dark blue green 90 90

Surtax for benefit of French seamen.

Arms of Various Cities.

Nancy
SP75

Lille
SP76

Rouen
SP77

Bordeaux
SP78

Toulouse
SP79

Clermont-Ferrand
SP80

Marseilles
SP81

Lyon
SP82

Rennes
SP83

Reims
SP84

Montpellier
SP85

Paris
SP86

1941 ***Perf. 14x13.***

B117 SP75 20c+30c brown black 1.50 1.50
B118 SP76 40c+60c orange brown 1.50 1.50
B119 SP77 50c+70c greenish blue 1.50 1.50
B120 SP78 70c+80c rose violet 1.50 1.50
B121 SP79 80c+1fr dp. rose 1.50 1.50

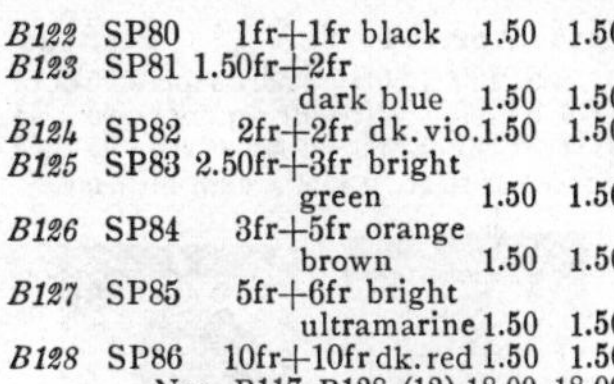

B122 SP80 1fr+1fr black 1.50 1.50
B123 SP81 1.50fr+2fr dark blue 1.50 1.50
B124 SP82 2fr+2fr dk. vio. 1.50 1.50
B125 SP83 2.50fr+3fr bright green 1.50 1.50
B126 SP84 3fr+5fr orange brown 1.50 1.50
B127 SP85 5fr+6fr bright ultramarine 1.50 1.50
B128 SP86 10fr+10fr dk. red 1.50 1.50
Nos. B117-B128 (12) 18.00 18.00

Count de La Pérouse
SP87

1942, Mar. 23 ***Perf. 13***

B129 SP87 2.50fr+7.50fr ultramarine 80 80

Issued to commemorate the 200th anniversary of the birth of Jean Francois de Galaup de La Pérouse, (1741–1788), French navigator and explorer. The surtax was for National Relief.

Planes over Fields
SP88

1942, Apr. 4

B130 SP88 1.50fr+3.50fr light violet 35 35

The surtax was for the benefit of French airmen and their families.

Alexis Chabrier
SP89

1942, May 18

B131 SP89 2fr+3fr sepia 75 75

Emmanuel Chabrier (1841–1894), composer, birth centenary. The surtax was for works of charity among musicians.

Symbolical of French Colonial Empire
SP90

1942, May 18

B132 SP90 1.50fr+8.50fr black 65 65

The surtax was for National Relief.

Jean de Vienne
SP91

1942, June 16

B133 SP91 1.50fr+8.50fr sepia 80 80

Issued in commemoration of the 600th anniversary of the birth of Jean de Vienne, first admiral of France. The surtax was for the benefit of French seamen.

Type of Regular Issue, 1941 Surcharged in Carmine

+ 50

S N

1942, Sept. 10 ***Perf. 14x13½***

B134 A116 1.50fr+50c bright ultramarine 10 10

The surtax was for national relief ("Secours National").

Arms of Various Cities.

Chambéry
SP92

La Rochelle
SP93

Poitiers
SP94

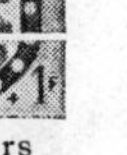

Orléans
SP95

Grenoble
SP96

Angers
SP97

Dijon
SP98

Limoges
SP99

Le Havre
SP100

Nantes
SP101

Nice
SP102

St. Etienne
SP103

Engraved.

1942, Oct. ***Perf. 14x13*** **Unwmkd.**

B135 SP92 50c+60c black 1.50 1.50
B136 SP93 60c+70c greenish blue 1.50 1.50
B137 SP94 80c+1fr rose 1.50 1.50
B138 SP95 1fr+1.30fr dark green 1.50 1.50
B139 SP96 1.20fr+1.50fr rose violet 1.50 1.50
B140 SP97 1.50fr+1.80fr slate blue 1.50 1.50

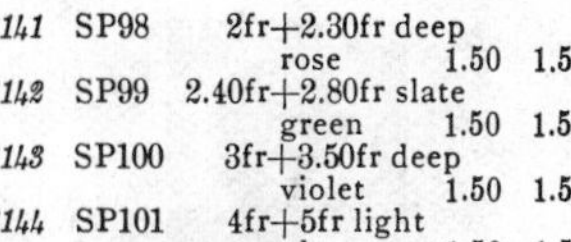

B141 SP98 2fr+2.30fr deep rose 1.50 1.50
B142 SP99 2.40fr+2.80fr slate green 1.50 1.50
B143 SP100 3fr+3.50fr deep violet 1.50 1.50
B144 SP101 4fr+5fr light ultra. 1.50 1.50
B145 SP102 4.50fr+6fr red 1.50 1.50
B146 SP103 5fr+7fr bright red violet 1.50 1.50
Nos. B135-B146 (12) 18.00 18.00

The surtax was for national relief.

Tricolor Legion—SP104

1942, Oct. 12 ***Perf. 13***

B147 SP104 1.20+8.80fr dark blue 2.50 2.50
a. Vert. strip of 3 (1 each Nos. B147, B148 + albino impression) 7.50 7.50
B148 " 1.20+8.80fr crimson 2.50 2.50

These stamps were printed in sheets of 20 stamps and 5 albino impressions arranged: 2 horizontal rows of 5 dark blue stamps, 1 row of 5 albino impressions, and 2 rows of 5 crimson stamps.

Marshal Henri Philippe Pétain
SP105 SP106

1943, Feb. 8

B149 SP105 1fr+10fr rose red 3.00 3.00
a. Strip of 4 (1 each Nos. B149-B152 + label) 13.50 13.50
B150 " 1fr+10fr blue 3.00 3.00
B151 SP106 2fr+12fr rose red 3.00 3.00
B152 " 2fr+12fr blue 3.00 3.00

The surtax was for national relief. Printed in sheets of 20, the 10 blue stamps at left, the 10 rose red at right, separated by a vertical row of five white labels bearing a tri-colored battle-ax.

Marshal Pétain
SP107

"Work"
SP108

"Family"
SP109

"State"
SP110

Marshal Pétain
SP111

1943, June 7

B153 SP107 1.20fr+1.40fr dull violet 7.00 7.00
a. Strip of 5 (1 each Nos. B153 to B157) 37.50 37.50
B154 SP108 1.50fr+2.50fr red 7.00 7.00
B155 SP109 2.40fr+7fr brown 7.00 7.00
B156 SP110 4fr+10fr dark violet 7.00 7.00
B157 SP111 5fr+15fr red brown 7.00 7.00
Nos. B153–B157 (5) 35.00 35.00

Issued to commemorate Pétain's 87th birthday. The surtax was for national relief.
Printed in sheets of 25 (5x5). Each horizontal strip includes the five values, arranged by denomination.

Civilians Under Air Attack
SP112

Civilians Doing Farm Work
SP113

Prisoner's Family Doing Farm Work
SP114

1943, Aug. 23

B158 SP112 1.50fr+3.50fr black 55 55

Surtax was for bomb victims at Billancourt, Dunkirk, Lorient, Saint-Nazaire.

1943, Sept. 27

B159 SP113 1.50fr+8.50fr sepia 60 60
B160 SP114 2.40fr+7.60fr dark green 60 60

The surtax was for families of war prisoners.

Michel de Montaigne
SP115

Picardy Costume
SP121

Designs: 1.20fr+1.50fr, Francois Clouet. 1.50fr+3fr, Ambrose Paré. 2.40fr+4fr, Chevalier Pierre de Bayard. 4fr+6fr, Duke of Sully. 5fr+10fr, Henri IV.

1943, Oct. 2

B161 SP115 60c+80c Prussian green 1.25 1.25
B162 " 1.20fr+1.50fr blk. 1.25 1.25
B163 " 1.50fr+3fr deep ultramarine 1.25 1.25
B164 " 2.40fr+4fr red 1.25 1.25
B165 SP115 4fr+6fr dull brown red 1.25 1.25
B166 " 5fr+10fr dull green 1.25 1.25
Nos. B161–B166 (6) 7.50 7.50

The surtax was for national relief. Issued to honor famous 16th century Frenchmen.

1943, Dec. 27

Designs: 18th Century Costumes: 1.20fr+2fr, Brittany. 1.50fr+4fr, Ile de France. 2.40+5fr, Burgundy. 4fr+6fr, Auvergne. 5fr+7fr, Provence.

B167 SP121 60c+1.30fr sepia 1.40 1.40
B168 " 1.20fr+2fr lt. vio. 1.40 1.40
B169 " 1.50fr+4fr turq. blue 1.40 1.40
B170 " 2.40fr+5fr rose carmine 1.40 1.40
B171 " 4fr+6fr chalky blue 1.40 1.40
B172 " 5fr+7fr red 1.40 1.40
Nos. B167–B172 (6) 8.40 8.40

The surtax was for national relief.

Admiral Tourville
SP127

Charles Gounod
SP128

1944, Feb. 21

B173 SP127 4fr+6fr dull red brown 60 60

Issued to commemorate the 300th anniversary of the birth of Admiral Anne-Hilarion de Cotentin Tourville (1642–1701).

1944, Mar. 27 *Perf. 14x13*

B174 SP128 1.50fr+3.50fr sepia 20 20

Issued to commemorate the 50th anniversary of the death of Charles Gounod, composer (1818–1893).

Marshal Pétain
SP129

Farming
SP130

Industry
SP131

1944, Apr. 24 *Perf. 13*

B175 SP129 1.50fr+3.50fr sepia 2.75 2.75
B176 SP130 2fr+3fr dp. ultra. 55 55
B177 SP131 4fr+6fr rose red 55 55

Marshal Henri Pétain's 88th birthday.

Modern Streamliner and 19th Century Train
SP132

Molière (Jean-Baptiste Poquelin)
SP133

1944, Aug. 14

B178 SP132 4fr+6fr black 30 30

Issued to commemorate the centenary of the Paris-Rouen, Paris-Orléans railroad.

1944, July 31

Designs: 80c+2.20fr, Jules Hardouin Mansart. 1.20fr+2.80fr, Blaise Pascal. 1.50fr+3.50fr, Louis II of Bourbon. 2fr+4fr, Jean-Baptiste Colbert. 4fr+6fr, Louis XIV.

B179 SP133 50c+1.50fr rose carmine 55 55
B180 " 80c+2.20fr dark green 55 55
B181 " 1.20fr+2.80fr black 55 55
B182 " 1.50fr+3.50fr bright ultramarine 55 55
B183 " 2fr+4fr dull brown red 55 55
B184 " 4fr+6fr red 55 55
Nos. B179–B184 (6) 3.30 3.30

Noted 17th century Frenchmen.

French Cathedrals.

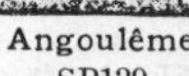

Angoulême
SP139

Chartres
SP140

Amiens
SP141

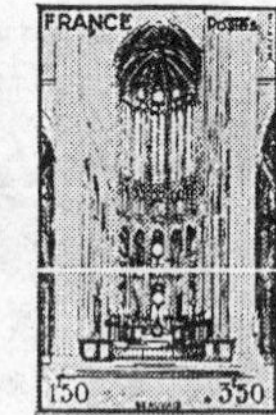

Beauvais
SP142

Albi
SP143

1944, Nov. 20

B185 SP139 50c+1.50fr black 15 15
B186 SP140 80c+2.20fr rose violet 20 20
B187 SP141 1.20fr+2.80fr brown carmine 33 33
B188 SP142 1.50fr+3.50fr deep blue 38 38
B189 SP143 4fr+6fr orge. red 40 40
Nos. B185–B189 (5) 1.46 1.46

Coat of Arms of Renouard de Villayer
SP144

Sarah Bernhardt
SP145

1944, Dec. 9 **Engraved**

B190 SP144 1.50fr+3.50fr deep brown 10 10

Stamp Day.

1945, May 16 *Perf. 13* **Unwmkd.**

B191 SP145 4fr+1fr dark violet brown 15 15

Issued to commemorate the 100th anniversary of the birth of Sarah Bernhardt, actress.

War Victims
SP146

Tuberculosis Patient
SP147

1945, May 16

B192 SP146 4fr+6fr dark violet brown 10 10

The surtax was for war victims of the P.T.T.

1945, May 16 Typo. *Perf. 14x13½*

B193 SP147 2fr+1fr red orange 5 5

The surtax was for the aid of tuberculosis victims.

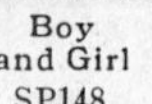

Boy and Girl
SP148

Burning of Oradour Church
SP149

1945, July 9 Engraved *Perf. 13*

B194 SP148 4fr+2fr Prussian green 12 12

The surtax was used for child welfare.

1945, Oct. 13

B195 SP149 4fr+2fr sepia 15 15

Destruction of Oradour, June, 1944.

Louis XI and Post Rider
SP150

1945, Oct. 13

B196 SP150 2fr+3fr dp. ultra. 18 18

Stamp Day.

Ruins of Dunkirk
SP151

Ruins of Rouen—SP152

Ruins of Caen—SP153

Ruins of Saint-Malo
SP154

1945, Nov. 5

B197	SP151	1.50fr+1.50fr red brown	12	12
B198	SP152	2fr+2fr violet	12	12
B199	SP153	2.40fr+2.60fr blue	12	12
B200	SP154	4fr+4fr black	12	12

The surtax was to aid the suffering residents of Dunkirk, Rouen, Caen and Saint Malo.

Alfred Fournier
SP155

Henri Becquerel
SP156

1946, Feb. 4 Engraved *Perf. 13*

B201	SP155	2fr+3fr red brown	15	15
B202	SP156	2fr+3fr violet	15	15

Issued to raise funds for the fight against veneral disease (B201) and for the struggle against cancer (B202).

No. B202 commemorated the 50th anniversary of the discovery of radio-activity by Henri Becquerel.

See also No. B221.

Church of the Invalides, Paris—SP157

1946, Mar. 11

B203 SP157 4fr+6fr red brown 22 22

The surtax was to aid disabled war veterans.

French Warships
SP158

1946, Apr. 8

B204 SP158 2fr+3fr gray black 20 20

The surtax was for naval charities.

"The Letter" by Jean Siméon Chardin
SP159

Fouquet de la Varane
SP160

1946, May 25

B205 SP159 2fr+3fr brown red 35 35

The surtax was used for the Postal Museum.

1946, June 29

B206 SP160 3fr+2fr sepia 35 35

Stamp Day.

François Villon
SP161

Designs: 3fr+1fr, Jean Fouquet. 4fr+3fr, Philippe de Commynes. 5fr+4fr, Joan of Arc. 6fr+5fr, Jean de Gerson. 10fr+6fr, Charles VII.

1946, Oct. 28

B207	SP161	2fr+1fr dark Prus. green	70	70
B208	"	3fr+1fr dark blue violet	70	70
B209	"	4fr+3fr henna brown	70	20
B210	"	5fr+4fr ultra.	70	70
B211	"	6fr+5fr sepia	70	70
B212	"	10fr+6fr red	70	70
		Nos. B207-B212 (6)	4.20	4.20

Church of St. Sernin, Toulouse
SP167

Notre Dame du Port, Clermont-Ferrand
SP168

Cathedral of St. Front, Perigueux
SP169

Cathedral of St. Julien, Le Mans
SP170

Cathedral of Notre Dame, Paris
SP171

François Michel le Tellier de Louvois
SP172

1947 Engraved

B213	SP167	1fr+1fr car. rose	15	15
B214	SP168	3fr+2fr dark blue violet	17	17
B215	SP169	4fr+3fr henna brown	35	35
B216	SP170	6fr+4fr dp. blue	60	60
B217	SP171	10fr+6fr dark gray green	75	75
		Nos. B213-B217 (5)	2.02	2.02

1947, Mar. 15

B218 SP172 4.50fr+5.50fr car. rose 1.20 1.20

Stamp Day, March 15, 1947.

Submarine Pens, Shipyard and Monument
SP173

1947, Aug. 2

B219 SP173 6fr+4fr bluish black 20 15

Issued to commemorate the British commando raid on the Nazi U-boat base at St. Nazaire, 1942.

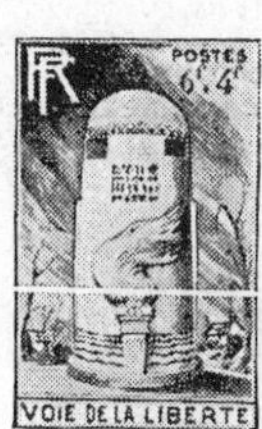

Liberty Highway Marker
SP174

Louis Braille
SP175

1947, Sept. 5

B220 SP174 6fr+4fr dark green 30 30

The surtax was to help defray maintenance costs of the Liberty Highway.

Fournier Type of 1946

1947, Oct. 20

B221 SP155 2fr+3fr indigo 30 30

1948, Jan. 19

B222 SP175 6fr+4fr purple 30 30

Etienne Arago
SP176

Alphonse de Lamartine
SP177

1948, Mar. 6

B223 SP176 6fr+4fr blk. brn. 40 40

Stamp Day, March 6–7, 1948.

1948, Apr. 5 Engraved *Perf. 13*

Designs: 3fr+2fr, Alexandre A. Ledru-Rollin. 4fr+3fr, Louis Blanc. 5fr+4fr, Albert (Alexandre Martin). 6fr+5fr, Pierre J. Proudhon. 10fr+6fr, Louis Auguste Blanqui. 15fr+7fr, Armand Barbés. 20fr+8fr, Dennis A. Affre.

B224	SP177	1fr+1fr dark green	60	60
B225	"	3fr+2fr henna brown	80	80
B226	"	4fr+3fr vio. brown	80	80
B227	"	5fr+4fr light blue green	1.00	1.00
B228	"	6fr+5fr indigo	1.00	1.00
B229	"	10fr+6fr car. rose	1.00	1.00
B230	"	15fr+7fr slate blk.	2.00	2.00
B231	"	20fr+8fr purple	2.50	2.50
		Nos. B224-B231 (8)	9.70	9.70

Centenary of the Revolution of 1848.

Dr. Léon Charles Albert Calmette
SP178

1948, June 18

B232 SP178 6fr+4fr dark greenish blue 23 20

Issued to mark the first International Congress on the Calmette-Guerin bacillus vaccine.

Farmer
SP179

Designs: 5fr+3fr, Fisherman. 8fr+4fr, Miner. 10fr+6fr, Metal worker.

1949, Feb. 14

B233	SP179	3fr+1fr claret	25	15
B234	"	5fr+3fr dark blue	30	20
B235	"	8fr+4fr indigo	45	35
B236	"	10fr+6fr dark red	60	40

Étienne François de Choiseul and Post Cart
SP180

Baron de la Brède et de Montesquieu
SP181

1949, Mar. 26

B237 SP180 15fr+5fr dark green 1.10 1.10

Stamp Day, March 26–27, 1949.

1949, Nov. 14

Designs: 8fr+2fr, Voltaire. 10fr+3fr, Antoine Watteau. 12fr+4fr, Georges de Buffon. 15fr+5fr, Joseph F. Dupleix. 25fr+10fr, A. R. J. Turgot.

B238 SP181 5fr+1fr dk. green 2.75 2.75
B239 " 8fr+2fr indigo 2.75 2.75
B240 " 10fr+3fr brown red 2.75 2.75
B241 " 12fr+4fr purple 2.75 2.75
B242 " 15fr+5fr rose carmine 3.25 3.25
B243 " 25fr+10fr ultra. 3.75 3.75
Nos. B238–B243 (6) 18.00 18.00

"Spring"
SP182

Designs: 8fr+2fr, Summer. 12fr+3fr, Autumn. 15fr+4fr, Winter.

1949, Dec. 19

B244 SP182 5fr+1fr green 1.35 1.35
B245 " 8fr+2fr yel. org. 1.35 1.35
B246 " 12fr+3fr purple 1.75 1.75
B247 " 15fr+4fr dp. blue 1.75 1.75

Postman
SP183

1950, Mar. 11

B248 SP183 12fr+3fr dp. bl. 3.00 2.25

Stamp Day, March 11–12, 1950.

André de Chénier
SP184

Alexandre Brongniart, Bust by Houdon
SP185

Portraits: 8fr+3fr, J. L. David. 10fr+4fr, Lazare Carnot. 12fr+5fr, G. J. Danton. 15fr+6fr, Maximilian Robespierre. 20fr+10fr, Louis Hoche.

1950, July 10 Engraved *Perf. 13*

Frames in Indigo.

B249 SP184 5fr+2fr brown violet 5.00 5.00
B250 " 8fr+3fr black brown 5.00 5.00
B251 " 10fr+4fr lake 5.00 5.00
B252 " 12fr+5fr red brn. 5.50 5.50
B253 " 15fr+6fr dk. grn. 5.50 5.50
B254 " 20fr+10fr dark violet blue 6.00 6.00
Nos. B249–B254 (6) 32.00 32.00

1950, Dec. 22

Design: 15fr–3fr, "L'Amour" by Etienne M. Falconet.

B255 SP185 8fr+2fr indigo & carmine 2.75 2.75
B256 " 15fr+3fr red brn. & carmine 2.75 2.75

The surtax was for the Red Cross.

Mail Car Interior
SP186

Alfred de Musset
SP187

1951, Mar. 10 *Perf. 13* Unwmkd.

B257 SP186 12fr+3fr lilac gray 2.75 2.75

Stamp Day, March 10–11, 1951.

1951, June 2

Designs: 8fr+2fr, Eugène Delacroix. 10fr+3fr, J.-L. Gay-Lussac. 12fr+4fr, Robert Surcouf. 15fr+5fr, C. M. Talleyrand. 30fr+10fr, Napoleon I.

Frames in Dark Brown.

B258 SP187 5fr+1fr dk. grn. 5.00 5.00
B259 " 8fr+2fr vio. brn. 5.50 5.50
B260 " 10fr+3fr greenish black 5.50 5.50
B261 " 12fr+4fr dark violet brown 5.50 5.50
B262 " 15fr+5fr brn. car. 5.50 5.50
B263 " 30fr+10fr indigo 8.00 8.00
Nos. B258–B263 (6) 35.00 35.00

Child at Prayer by Le Maître de Moulins
SP188

18th Century Child by Quentin de la Tour
SP189

1951, Dec. 15

Cross in Red.

B264 SP188 12fr+3fr dark brown 3.00 3.00
B265 SP189 15fr+5fr deep ultramarine 3.00 3.00

The surtax was for the Red Cross.

Stagecoach of 1844
SP190

1952, Mar. 8 *Perf. 13*

B266 SP190 12fr+3fr dp. grn. 3.25 2.75

Stamp Day, March 8, 1952.

Gustave Flaubert
SP191

Portraits: 12fr+3fr, Edouard Manet. 15fr+4fr, Camille Saint-Saens. 18fr+5fr, Henri Poincaré. 20fr+6fr, Georges-Eugene Haussmann. 30fr+7fr, Adolphe Thiers.

1952, Oct. 18

Frames in Dark Brown.

B267 SP191 8fr+2fr indigo 4.50 4.50
B268 " 12fr+3fr violet blue 4.50 4.50
B269 " 15fr+4fr dk. grn. 4.50 4.50
B270 " 18fr+5fr dk. brn. 4.50 4.50
B271 " 20fr+6fr car. 5.00 5.00
B272 " 30fr+7fr purple 5.00 5.00
Nos. B267–B272 (6) 28.00 28.00

Cupid from Diana Fountain Versailles
SP192

Design: 15fr+5fr, Similar detail, cupid facing left.

1952, Dec. 13

Cross in Red.

B273 SP192 12fr+3fr dark green 3.25 3.25
B274 " 15fr+5fr indigo 3.25 3.25
a. Bklt. pane 10 47.50

The surtax was for the Red Cross.

Count d'Argenson
SP193

St. Bernard
SP194

1953, Mar. 14

B275 SP193 12fr+3fr dp. blue 3.00 3.00

Issued to commemorate the Day of the Stamp. The surtax was for the Red Cross.

1953, July 9

Portraits: 12fr+3fr, Olivier de Serres. 15fr+4fr, Jean Philippe Rameau. 18fr+5fr, Gaspard Monge. 20fr+6fr, Jules Michelet. 30fr+7fr, Marshal Hubert Lyautey.

B276 SP194 8fr+2fr ultra. 4.50 4.50
B277 " 12fr+3fr dark grn. 4.50 4.50
B278 " 15fr+4fr brn. car. 5.00 5.00
B279 " 18fr+5fr dark blue 5.00 5.00
B280 " 20fr+6fr dk. pur. 5.00 5.00
B281 " 30fr+7fr brown 6.00 6.00
Nos. B276–B281 (6) 30.00 30.00

The surtax was for the Red Cross.

Madame Vigée-Lebrun and her Daughter
SP195

Count Antoine de La Vallette
SP196

Design: 15fr+5fr, "The Return from Baptism," by Louis Le Nain.

1953, Dec. 12

Cross in Red

B282 SP195 12fr+3fr red brn. 5.00 5.00
a. Bklt. pane (4 #B282, 4 #B283 with gutter btwn.) 45.00
B283 SP195 15fr+5fr indigo 6.00 6.00

The surtax was for the Red Cross.

1954, Mar. 20 Engraved *Perf. 13*

B284 SP196 12fr+3fr deep green & chocolate 4.50 4.00

Stamp Day, March 20, 1954.

Louis IX
SP197

"The Sick Child," by Eugene Carrière
SP198

Portraits: 15fr+5fr, Jacques Benigne Bossuet. 18fr+6fr, Sadi Carnot. 20fr+7fr, Antoine Bourdelle. 25fr+8fr, Dr. Emile Roux. 30fr+10fr, Paul Valéry.

1954, July 10

B285 SP197 12fr+4fr dp. bl. 17.50 17.50
B286 " 15fr+5fr purple 17.50 17.50
B287 " 18fr+6fr dk. brn. 17.50 17.50
B288 " 20fr+7fr crimson 18.50 18.50
B289 " 25fr+8fr indigo 18.50 18.50
B290 " 30fr+10fr deep claret 18.50 18.50
Nos. B285–B290 (6) 108.00 108.00

See also Nos. B303–B308 and B312–B317.

1954, Dec. 18

Design: 15fr+5fr, "Young Girl with Doves," by Jean Baptiste Greuze.

Cross in Red

B291 SP198 12fr+3fr violet gray & indigo 5.00 5.00
a. Bklt. pane (4 #B291, 4 #B292 with gutter btwn.) 45.00
B292 SP198 15fr+5fr dark brown & orange brown 6.00 6.00

No. B291a was issued to commemorate the 90th anniversary of the Red Cross. The gutter between panes is inscribed in red.

The surtax was for the Red Cross.

Balloon Post, 1870
SP199

1955, Mar. 19 ***Perf. 13*** **Unwmkd.**

B293 SP199 12fr+3fr dark greenish blue, violet brown & olive green 5.50 4.00

Stamp Day, March 19–20, 1955.

King Philip II
SP200

Child with Cage by Pigalle
SP201

Portraits: 15fr+6fr, Francois de Malherbé. 18fr+7fr, Sebastien de Vauban. 25fr+8fr, Charles G. de Vergennes. 30fr+9fr, Pierre S. de Laplace. 50fr+15fr, Pierre Auguste Renoir.

1955, June 11

B294	SP200	12fr+5fr bright purple	13.50	13.50
B295	"	15fr+6fr deep bl.	13.50	13.50
B296	"	18fr+7fr dp. grn.	14.00	14.00
B297	"	25fr+8fr gray	14.00	14.00
B298	"	30fr+9fr rose brn.	14.00	14.00
B299	"	50fr+15fr blue green	14.00	14.00
		Nos. B294–B299 (6)	83.00	83.00

See also Nos. B321–B326.

1955, Dec. 17

Design: 15fr+5fr, Child with Goose, by Boethus of Chalcedon.

Cross in Red.

B300	SP201	12fr+3fr claret	3.00	3.00
B301	"	15fr+5fr dk. blue	3.00	3.00
		a. Booklet pane of 10	30.00	

The surtax was for the Red Cross.

Francois of Taxis
SP202

1956, Mar. 17 **Engraved** ***Perf. 13***

B302 SP202 12fr+3fr ultramarine, green & dark brown 1.85 1.85

Stamp Day, March 17–18, 1956.

Portrait Type of 1954.

Portraits: No. 303, Guillaume Budé. No. B304, Jean Goujon. No. B305, Samuel de Champlain. No. B306, Jean Simeon Chardin. No. B307, Maurice Barrès. No. B308, Maurice Ravel.

1956, June 9 ***Perf. 13***

B303	SP197	12fr+3fr sapphire	3.00	3.00
B304	"	12fr+3fr lilac gray	3.00	3.00
B305	"	12fr+3fr brt. red	3.00	3.00
B306	"	15fr+5fr green	3.00	3.00
B307	"	15fr+5fr vio. brn.	3.50	3.50
B308	"	15fr+5fr dp. vio.	3.50	3.50
		Nos. B303–B308 (6)	19.00	19.00

Peasant Boy by Le Nain
SP203

Design: 15fr+5fr, Gilles by Watteau.

1956, Dec. 8 **Unwmkd.**

Cross in Red

B309 SP203 12fr+3fr olive gray 1.75 1.75
a. Bklt. pane (4 #B309, 4 #B310 with gutter btwn.) 15.00
B310 SP203 15fr+5fr rose lake 1.75 1.75

The surtax was for the Red Cross.

Blind Man and Beggar, Engraving by Jacques Callot
SP205

Design: 20fr+8fr, Women beggars.

Genoese Felucca, 1750
SP204

1957, Mar. 16 ***Perf. 13***

B311 SP204 12fr+3fr bluish gray & brn. black 1.65 1.40

Issued to commemorate the Day of the Stamp, March 16, 1957, and to honor the Maritime Postal Service.

Portrait Type of 1954

1957, June 15

Portraits: No. B312, Jean de Joinville. No. B313, Bernard Palissy. No. B314, Quentin de la Tour. No. B315, Hugues Félicité Robert de Lamennais. No. B316, George Sand. No. B317, Jules Guesde.

B312	SP197	12fr+3fr olive gray & olive grn.	2.25	2.25
B313	"	12fr+3fr greenish black & greenish bl.	2.40	2.40
B314	"	15fr+5fr claret & bright red	2.50	2.50
B315	"	15fr+5fr ultra. & indigo	2.50	2.50
B316	"	18fr+7fr greenish black & dark green	2.75	2.75
B317	"	18fr+7fr dark violet brown & red brown	2.75	2.75
		Nos. B312–B317 (6)	15.15	15.15

1957, Dec. 7 **Engraved** ***Perf. 13***

B318 SP205 15fr+7fr ultra. & red 1.75 1.75
a. Bklt. pane (4 #B318, 4 #B319 with gutter btwn.) 15.00
B319 SP205 20fr+8fr dark violet brown & red 1.75 1.75

The surtax was for the Red Cross.

Motorized Mail Distribution
SP206

1958, Mar. 15

B320 SP206 15fr+5fr olive gray, olive green & red brown 1.10 1.00

Stamp Day, Mar. 15.

Portrait Type of 1955.

Portraits: No. B321, Joachim du Bellay. No. B322, Jean Bart. No. B323, Denis Diderot. No. B324, Gustave Courbet. 20fr+8fr, J. B. Carpeaux. 35fr+15fr, Toulouse-Lautrec.

1958, June 7 **Engraved** ***Perf. 13***

B321	SP200	12fr+4fr yel. grn.	1.50	1.50
B322	"	12fr+4fr dk. blue	1.50	1.50
B323	SP200	15fr+5fr dull claret	1.50	1.50
B324	"	15fr+5fr ultra.	1.50	1.50
B325	"	20fr+8fr brt. red	2.00	2.00
B326	"	35fr+15fr green	2.00	2.00
		Nos. B321–B326 (6)	10.00	10.00

St. Vincent de Paul
SP207

Portrait: 20fr+8fr, J. H. Dunant.

1958, Dec. 6 **Unwmkd.**

Cross in Carmine.

B327 SP207 15fr+7fr grayish green 1.00 1.00
a. Bklt. pane (4 #B327, 4 #B328 with gutter btwn.) 8.50
B328 SP207 20fr+8fr violet 1.00 1.00

The surtax was for the Red Cross.

Plane Landing at Night
SP208

1959, Mar. 21

B329 SP208 20fr+5fr slate green, black & rose 60 60

Issued for the Day of the Stamp, March 21, and to publicize night air mail service. The surtax was for the Red Cross.
See also No. 1089.

Geoffroi de Villehardouin and Ships
SP209

Designs: No. B331, André Le Nôtre and formal garden. No. B332, Jean Le Rond d'Alembert, books and wheel. No. B333, David d'Angers, statue and building. No. B334, M. F. X. Bichat and torch. No. B335, Frédéric Auguste Bartholdi, Statue of Liberty and Lion of Belfort.

1959, June 13 **Engraved** ***Perf. 13***

B330	SP209	15fr+5fr violet blue	1.10	1.10
B331	"	15fr+5fr dark slate green	1.10	1.10
B332	"	20fr+10fr olive bistre	1.40	1.40
B333	"	20fr+10fr dark gray	1.40	1.40
B334	"	30fr+10fr dark car. rose	1.50	1.50
B335	"	30fr+10fr orange brown	1.50	1.50
		Nos. B330–B335 (6)	8.00	8.00

The surtax was for the Red Cross.

No. 927 Surcharged **FREJUS +5f**

1959, Dec. **Typo.** ***Perf. 14x13½***

B336 A328 25fr+5fr black & red 35 35

The surtax was for the flood victims at Frejus.

Charles Michel de l'Épée
SP210

Design: 25fr+10fr, Valentin Hauy.

1959, Dec. 5 **Engraved** ***Perf. 13***

Cross in Carmine

B337 SP210 20fr+10fr black & claret 1.00 1.00
a. Bklt. pane (4 #B337, 4 #B338 with gutter btwn.) 8.50
B338 SP210 25fr+10fr dark blue & black 1.00 1.00

The surtax was for the Red Cross.

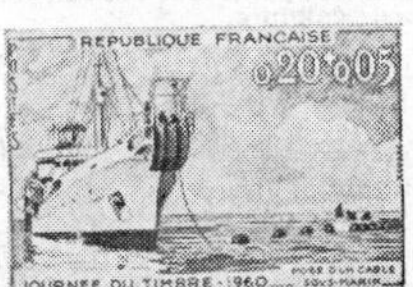

Ship Laying Underwater Cable
SP211

1960, Mar. 12

B339 SP211 20c+5c greenish blue & dark blue 90 90

Issued for the Day of the Stamp. The surtax went to the Red Cross.

Refugee Girl Amid Ruins
SP212

1960, Apr. 7

B340 SP212 25c+10c green, brown & indigo 40 35

Issued to publicize World Refugee Year, July 1, 1959–June 30, 1960. The surtax was for aid to refugees.

Michel de L'Hospital
SP213

Designs: No. B342, Henri de la Tour D'Auvergne, Viscount of Turenne. No. B343, Nicolas Boileau (Despreaux). No. B344, Jean-Martin Charcot, M.D. No. B345, Georges Bizet. 50c+15c, Edgar Degás.

1960, June 11 **Engraved** ***Perf. 13***

B341	SP213	10c+5c purple & rose carmine	2.00	2.00
B342	"	20c+10c olive & violet brn.	2.25	2.25
B343	"	20c+10c Prus. green & deep yellow green	2.40	2.40
B344	"	30c+10c rose carmine & rose red	2.40	2.40

B345 SP213 30c+10c dk. blue & violet blue 2.40 2.40
B346 " 50c+15c slate blue & gray 2.65 2.65
Nos. B341-B346 (6) 14.10 14.10

The surtax was for the Red Cross.
See also Nos. B350-B355.

Staff of the Brotherhood of St. Martin
SP214

Letter Carrier, Paris 1760
SP215

Design: 25c+10c, St. Martin, 16th century wood sculpture.

1960, Dec. 3 *Perf. 13* Unwmkd.

B347 SP214 20c+10c rose claret & red 1.50 1.50
a. Bklt. pane (4 #B347, 4 #B348 with gutter btwn.) 12.50
B348 SP214 25c+10c light ultra. & red 1.50 1.50

The surtax was for the Red Cross.

1961, March 18 *Perf. 13*

B349 SP215 20c+5c slate grn. brown & red 40 35

Stamp Day. Surtax for Red Cross.

Famous Men Type of 1960

Designs: 15+5c, Bertrand Du Guesclin. B351, Pierre Puget. B352, Charles Coulomb. 30+10c, Antoine Drouot. 45c+10c, Honoré Daumier. 50+15c, Guillaume Apollinaire.

1961, May 20 Engraved

B350 SP213 15c+5c red brown & black 1.65 1.65
B351 " 20c+10c dk. green & lt. blue 1.65 1.65
B352 " 20c+10c vermilion & rose car. 1.65 1.65
B353 " 30c+10c black & brown orange 1.65 1.65
B354 " 45c+10c chocolate & dk. green 1.85 1.85
B355 " 50c+15c dk. car. rose & violet 1.85 1.85
Nos. B350-B355 (6) 10.30 10.30

"Love" by Rouault
SP216

Medieval Royal Messenger
SP217

Designs from "Miserere" by Georges Rouault: 25c+10c, "The Blind Consoles the Seeing."

1961, Dec. 2 *Perf. 13*

B356 SP216 20c+10c brown, black & red 1.65 1.65
a. Bklt. pane (4 #B356, 4 #B357 with gutter btwn.) 14.00
B357 SP216 25c+10c brown, black & red 1.65 1.65

The surtax was for the Red Cross.

1962, March 17

B358 SP217 20c+5c rose red, blue & sepia 55 45

Stamp Day. Surtax for Red Cross.

Denis Papin, Scientist
SP218

Rosalie Fragonard by Fragonard
SP219

Portraits: No. B360, Edme Bouchardon, sculptor. No. B361, Joseph Lakanal, educator. 30c+10c, Gustave Charpentier, composer. 45c+15c, Edouard Estaunié, writer. 50c+20c, Hyacinthe Vincent, physician and bacteriologist.

1962, June 2 Engraved

B359 SP218 15c+5c bluish grn. & dk. gray 1.10 1.10
B360 " 20c+10c claret & brown 1.10 1.10
B361 " 20c+10c gray & slate 1.65 1.65
B362 " 30c+10c br. blue & indigo 1.65 1.65
B363 " 45c+15c orange brn. & choc. 1.65 1.25
B364 " 50c+20c greenish blue & black 2.00 2.00
Nos. B359-B364 (6) 9.15 9.15

The surtax was for the Red Cross.

1962, Dec. 8

Design: 25c+10c, Child dressed as Pierrot.

Cross in Red

B365 SP219 20c+10c reddish brown 90 90
a. Bklt. pane (4 #B365, 4 #B366 with gutter btwn.) 7.50
B366 SP219 25c+10c dull grn. 90 90

The surtax was for the Red Cross.

Jacques Amyot, Classical Scholar
SP220

Portraits: 30c+10c, Pierre de Marivaux, playwright. 50c+20c, Jacques Daviel, surgeon.

1963, Feb. 23 *Perf. 13* Unwmkd.

B367 SP220 20c+10c maroon, gray & purple 80 80
B368 " 30c+10c Prussian grn. & maroon 80 80
B369 " 50c+20c ultra., ocher & olive 1.00 1.00

The surtax was for the Red Cross.

Roman Chariot
SP221

1963, March 16 Engraved

B370 SP221 20c+5c brn. orge. & vio. brown 35 35

Stamp Day. Surtax for Red Cross.

Étienne Méhul, Composer
SP222

Designs: 30c+10c, Nicolas-Louis Vauquelin, chemist. 50c+20c, Alfred de Vigny, poet.

1963, May 25 *Perf. 13* Unwmkd.

B371 SP222 20c+10c dp. blue, dk. brown & deep orange 1.00 1.00
B372 " 30c+10c magenta, gray olive & black 1.00 1.00
B373 " 50c+20c slate, black & brn. 1.40 1.40

The surtax was for the Red Cross.

"Child with Grapes" by David d'Angers and Centenary Emblem
SP223

Design: 25c+10c, "The Fifer," by Edouard Manet.

1963, Dec. 9 *Perf. 13* Unwmkd.

B374 SP223 20c+10c blk. & red 60 60
a. Bklt. pane (4 #B374, 4 #B375 with gutter btwn.) 5.25
B375 SP223 25c+10c slate green & red 60 60

Issued to commemorate the centenary of the International and the French Red Cross. The surtax was for the Red Cross.

Post Rider, 18th Century
SP224

1964, March 14 Engraved

B376 SP224 20c+5c Prus. grn. 30 25

Issued for Stamp Day.

Resistance Memorial by Watkin, Luxembourg Gardens
SP225

De Gaulle's 1940 Poster "A Tous les Francais"
SP226

Allied Troops Landing in Normandy and Provence—SP227

Designs: 20c+5c, "Deportation," concentration camp with watchtower and barbed wire. No. B380, Street fighting in Paris and Strasbourg.

1964 Engraved *Perf. 13*

B377 SP225 20c+5c slate black 25 25

Perf. 12x13

B378 SP226 25c+5c dark red, blue, red & blk. 50 50

Perf. 13

B379 SP227 30c+5c black, blue & orange brn. 30 30
B380 " 30c+5c orge. brn., claret & black 40 40
B381 SP225 50c+5c dark green 45 45
Nos. B377-B381 (5) 1.90 1.90

Issued to commemorate the 20th anniversary of liberation from the Nazis.
Issue dates: Nos. B377, B381, Mar. 21; No. B378, June 18; No. B379, June 6; No. B380, Aug. 22.

President René Coty
SP229

Jean Nicolas Corvisart
SP230

Portraits: No. B383, John Calvin. No. B384, Pope Sylvester II (Gerbert).

1964 *Perf. 13* Unwmkd.

B382 SP229 30c+10c dp. claret & black 35 35
B383 " 30c+10c dk. grn., blk. & brown 40 40
B384 " 30c+10c slate & claret 40 40

The surtax was for the Red Cross.
Issue dates: No. B382, Apr. 25; No. B383, May 25; No. B384, June 1.

1964, Dec. 12 Engraved

Portrait; 25c+10c, Dominique Larrey.

Cross in Carmine

B385 SP230 20c+10c black 40 25
a. Bklt. pane (4 # B385, 4 # B386 with gutter btwn.) 3.50
B386 SP230 25c+10c black 40 25

Issued to honor Jean Nicolas Corvisart (1755-1821), physician of Napoleon I, and Dominique Larrey (1766-1842), Chief Surgeon of the Imperial Armies. The surtax was for the Red Cross.

Paul Dukas, Composer
SP231

Portraits: No. B387, Duke François de La Rochefoucauld, writer. No. B388, Nicolas Poussin, painter. No. B389, Duke Charles of Orléans, poet.

1965, Feb. Engraved *Perf. 13*

B387 SP231 30c+10c orge. brn. & dark blue 50 50
B388 " 30c+10c car. & dk. red brown 50 50
B389 " 40c+10c dark red brn., dk. red & Pruss. blue 55 55
B390 " 40c+10c dk. brn. & slate blue 55 55

The surtax was for the Red Cross.
Nos. B387 and B390 were issued Feb. 13; Nos. B388-B389 were issued Feb. 20.

Packet "La Guienne"
SP232

1965, Mar. 29 *Perf. 13* Unwmkd.

B391 SP232 25c+10c ultra., black & slate green 50 50

Issued for Stamp Day, 1965. "La Guienne" was used for transatlantic mail service. Surtax was for the Red Cross.

Infant with Spoon by Auguste Renoir
SP233

Design: 30c+10c, Coco Writing (Renoir's daughter Claude).

1965, Dec. 11 Engraved *Perf. 13*
Cross in Carmine

B392 SP233 25c+10c slate 30 25
a. Bklt. pane (4 # B392, 4 # B393 with gutter btwn.) 2.75
B393 SP233 30c+10c dull red brown 35 25

The surtax was for the Red Cross.

Francois Mansart and Carnavalet Palace, Paris—SP234

Designs: No. B395, St. Pierre Fourier and Basilica of St. Pierre Fourier, Mirecourt. No. B396, Marcel Proust and St. Hilaire Bridge, Illiers. No. B397, Gabriel Fauré, monument and score of "Penelope." No. B398, Elie Metchnikoff, microscope and Pasteur Institute. No. B399, Hippolyte Taine and birthplace.

1966 Engraved *Perf. 13*

B394 SP234 30c+10c dk. red brn. & green 30 30
B395 " 30c+10c black & gray green 30 30
B396 " 30c+10c indigo, sepia & green 30 30
B397 " 30c+10c bister brn. & indigo 30 30
B398 " 30c+10c black & dull brown 30 30
B399 " 30c+10c green & olive brown 30 30
Nos. B394-B399 (6) 1.80 1.80

The surtax was for the Red Cross.
Issue dates: Nos. B394-B396, Feb. 12. Others, June 25.

Engraver Cutting Die and Tools
SP235

1966, March 19 Engraved *Perf. 13*

B400 SP235 25c+10c slate, dk. brn. & dp. org. 35 35

Stamp Day. Surtax for Red Cross.

Angel of Victory, Verdun Fortress, Marching Troops
SP236

First Aid on Battlefield, 1859
SP237

1966, May 28 *Perf. 13*

B401 SP236 30c+5c Prus. bl., ultra. & dk. bl. 30 30

Victory of Verdun, 50th anniversary.

1966, Dec. 10 Engraved *Perf. 13*

Design: 30c+10c, Nurse giving first aid to child, 1966.

Cross in Carmine

B402 SP237 25c+10c green 40 40
a. Bklt. pane (4 # B402, 4 # B403 with gutter btwn.) 3.25
B403 SP237 30c+10c slate 40 40

The surtax was for the Red Cross.

Emile Zola
SP238

Letter Carrier, 1865
SP239

Portraits: No. B405, Beaumarchais (pen name of Pierre Augustin Caron). No. B406, St. Francois de Sales (1567-1622). No. B407, Albert Camus (1913-1960).

1967 Engraved *Perf. 13*

B404 SP238 30c+10c slate blue & blue 30 30
B405 " 30c+10c rose brn. & lilac 30 30
B406 " 30c+10c dull vio. & purple 30 30
B407 " 30c+10c brown & dull claret 30 30

The surtax was for the Red Cross.
Issue dates: Nos. B404-B405, Feb. 4. Others, June 24.

1967, Apr. 8

B408 SP239 25c+10c indigo, green & red 30 30

Issued for Stamp Day.

Ivory Flute Player
SP240

Ski Jump and Long Distance Skiing
SP241

Design: 30c+10c, Violin player, ivory carving.

1967, Dec. 16 Engraved *Perf. 13*
Cross in Carmine

B409 SP240 25c+10c dull vio. & lt. brown 35 35
a. Bklt. pane (4 # B409, 4 # B410 with gutter btwn.) 3.25
B410 SP240 30c+10c green & lt. brown 35 35

The surtax was for the Red Cross.

1968, Jan. 27

Designs: 40c+10c, Ice hockey. 60c+20c, Olympic flame and snowflakes. 75c+25c, Woman figure skater. 95c+35c, Slalom.

B411 SP241 30c+10c verm., gray & brown 25 25
B412 " 40c+10c lilac, lemon & bright magenta 30 30
B413 " 60c+20c dk. green, org. & brt. vio. 45 45
B414 " 75c+25c brt. pink, yel. grn. & blk. 65 65
B415 " 95c+35c bl., brt. pink & red brn. 85 85
Nos. B411-B415 (5) 2.50 2.50

Issued for the 10th Winter Olympic Games, Grenoble, Feb. 6-18.

Rural Mailman, 1830
SP242

1968, Mar. 16 Engraved *Perf. 13*

B416 SP242 25c+10c bl. gray, ultra. & red 35 35

Issued for Stamp Day.

François Couperin, Composer, and Instruments
SP243

Portraits: No. B418, Gen. Louis Desaix de Veygoux (1768-1800) and scene showing his death at the Battle of Marengo, Italy. No. B419, Saint-Pol-Roux (pen name of Paul-Pierre Roux, 1861-1940), Christ on the Cross and ruins of Camaret-sur-Mer. No. B420, Paul Claudel (poet and diplomat, 1868-1955) and Joan of Arc at the stake.

1968 Engraved *Perf. 13*

B417 SP243 30c+10c purple & rose lilac 35 35
B418 " 30c+10c dk. green & brown 35 35
B419 " 30c+10c copper red & olive bister 35 35
B420 " 30c+10c dark brown & lilac 35 35

Issue dates: Nos. B417-B418, Mar. 23; Nos. B419-B420, July 6.

Spring, by Nicolas Mignard
SP244

Designs (Paintings by Nicolas Mignard): 30c+10c, Fall. No. B423, Summer. No. B424, Winter.

1968-69 Engraved *Perf. 13*
Cross in Carmine

B421 SP244 25c+10c purple & slate blue 35 35
a. Bklt. pane (4 # B421, 4 # B422 with gutter btwn.) 3.00
B422 SP244 30c+10c brown & rose carmine 35 35
B423 " 40c+15c dk. brn. & brn. ('69) 50 50
a. Bklt. pane (4 # B423, 4 # B424 with gutter btwn.) 4.00
B424 SP244 40c+15c purple & Prus. blue ('69) 50 50

The surtax was for the Red Cross.

Mailmen's Omnibus, 1881
SP245

1969, Mar. 15 Engraved *Perf. 13*

B425 SP245 30c+10c brown, green & black 35 30

Issued for Stamp Day.

Gen. Francois Marceau
SP246

Portraits: No. B427, Charles Augustin Sainte-Beuve (1804-1869), writer. No. B428, Albert Roussel (1869-1937), musician. No. B429, Marshal Jean Lannes (1769-1809). No. B430, Georges Cuvier (1769-1832), naturalist. No. B431, André Gide, (1869-1951), writer.

1969

B426 SP246 50c+10c brn. red 50 50
B427 " 50c+10c slate blue 50 50
B428 " 50c+10c deep violet blue 50 50
B429 " 50c+10c choc. 50 50
B430 " 50c+10c dp. plum 50 50
B431 " 50c+10c bl. green 50 50
Nos. B426-B431 (6) 3.00 3.00

The surtax was for the Red Cross.
Issue dates: Nos. B426-B428, Mar. 24. No. B429, May 10, Nos. B430-B431, May 17.

Gen. Jacques Leclerc, La Madeleine and Battle—SP247

1969, Aug. 23 Engraved *Perf. 13*

B432 SP247 45c+10c slate & olive 40 35

Issued to commemorate the 25th anniversary of the liberation of Paris, Aug. 25, 1944.

Same Inscribed
"Liberation de Strasbourg"

1969, Nov. 22 Engraved *Perf. 13*

B433 SP247 70c+10c brown, choc. & olive 60 50

Issued to commemorate the 25th anniversary of the liberation of Strasbourg.

Philibert Delorme, Architect, and Chateau d'Anet—SP248

Designs: No. B435, Louis Le Vau (1612–1670), architect, and Vaux-le-Vicomte Chateau, Paris. No. B436, Prosper Merimée (1803–1870), writer, and Carmen. No. B437, Alexandre Dumas (1820–1870), writer, and Three Musketeers. No. B438, Edouard Branly (1844–1940), physicist, electric circuit and convent of the Carmes, Paris. No. B439, Maurice de Broglie (1875–1960), physicist, and X-ray spectrograph.

1970 **Engraved** ***Perf. 13***

B434	SP248	40c+10c slate grn.	45	45
B435	"	40c+10c dk. car.	45	45
B436	"	40c+10c Prus. bl.	45	45
B437	"	40c+10c vio. blue	45	45
B438	"	40c+10c dp. brn.	45	45
B439	"	40c+10c dk. gray	45	45
		Nos. B434-B439 (6)	2.70	2.70

The surtax was for the Red Cross.
Issue dates: No. B434–B436, Feb. 14; Nos. B437–B439, Apr. 11.

City Mailman, 1830
SP249

"Life and Death"
SP250

1970, Mar. 14

B440	SP249	40c+10c black, ultra. & dark carmine rose	55	30

Issued for Stamp Day.

1970, Apr. 4

B441	SP250	40c+10c brt. bl., olive & carmine rose	35	30

Issued to publicize the fight against cancer in connection with Health Day, Apr. 7.

Marshal de Lattre de Tassigny
SP251

1970, May 8 **Engraved** ***Perf. 13***

B442	SP251	40c+10c slate & violet blue	40	35

Issued to commemorate the 25th anniversary of the entry into Berlin of French troops under Marshal Jean de Lattre de Tassigny, May 8, 1945.

Lord and Lady, Dissay Chapel Fresco
SP252

Design: No. B444, Angel holding whips, from fresco in Dissay Castle Chapel, Vienne, c. 1500.

1970, Dec. 12 **Engraved** ***Perf. 13***

Cross in Carmine

B443	SP252	40c+15c green	1.00	90
		a. Bklt. pane (4 # B443, 4 # B444 with gutter btwn.)	8.50	
B444	SP252	40c+15c copper red	1.00	90

The surtax was for the Red Cross.

Daniel-Francois Auber and "Fra Diavolo" Music
SP253

Designs: No. B446, Gen. Charles Diego Brosset (1898–1944), and Basilica of Fourvière. No. B447, Victor Grignard (1871–1935), chemist, and Nobel Prize medal. No. B448, Henri Farman (1874–1958) and plane. No. B449, Gen. Charles Georges Delestraint (1879–1945) and scroll. No. B450, Jean Eugène Robert-Houdin (1805–1871) and magician's act.

1971 **Engraved** ***Perf. 13***

B445	SP253	50c+10c brn. vio. & brown	1.20	1.00
B446	"	50c+10c dk. slate green & olive gray	1.20	1.00
B447	"	50c+10c brown red & olive	1.20	1.00
B448	"	50c+10c violet blue & violet	1.20	1.00
B449	"	50c+10c purple & claret	1.20	1.00
B450	"	50c+10c slate grn. & blue green	1.20	1.00
		Nos. B445-B450 (6)	7.20	6.00

The surtax was for the Red Cross.
Issue dates: Nos. B445–B446, Mar. 6. No. B447, May 8. No. B448, May 29. Nos. B449–B450, Oct. 16.

Army Post Office, 1914–1918
SP254

1971, March 27 **Engr.** ***Perf. 13***

B451	SP254	50c+10c olive, brown & blue	60	40

Stamp Day, 1971.

Girl with Dog, by Greuze
SP255

Aristide Bergès (1833–1904)
SP256

Design: 50c+10c, "The Dead Bird," by Jean-Baptiste Greuze (1725–1805).

1971, Dec. 11

Cross in Carmine

B452	SP255	30c+10c vio. blue	85	85
		a. Bklt. pane (4 # B452, 4 # B453 with gutter btwn.)	7.50	
B453	SP255	50c+10c dp. car.	85	85

The surtax was for the Red Cross.

1972 **Engraved** ***Perf. 13***

Portraits: No. B455, Paul de Chomedey (1612–1676), founder of Montreal, and arms of Neuville-sur-Vanne. No. B456, Edouard Belin (1876–1963), inventor. No. B457, Louis Blériot (1872–1936), aviation pioneer. No. B458, Adm. François Joseph, Count de Grasse (1722–1788), hero of the American Revolution. No. B459, Théophile Gautier (1811–1872), writer.

B454	SP256	50c+10c black & green	1.00	1.00
B455	"	50c+10c black & blue	1.00	1.00
B456	"	50c+10c black & lilac rose	1.00	1.00
B457	"	50c+10c red & black	1.00	1.00
B458	"	50c+10c orange & black	1.25	1.25
B459	"	50c+10c black & brown	1.25	1.25
		Nos. B454-B459 (6)	6.50	6.50

The surtax was for the Red Cross.
Issue dates: Nos. B454–B455, Feb. 19; No. B456, June 24; No. B457, July 1; Nos. B458–B459, Sept. 9.

Rural Mailman, 1894
SP257

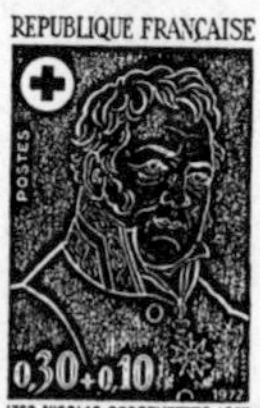

Nicolas Desgenettes
SP258

1972, Mar. 18 **Engr.** ***Perf. 13***

B460	SP257	50c+10c bl., yel. & olive gray	60	50

Stamp Day 1972.

1972, Dec. 16 **Engraved** ***Perf. 13***

Designs: 30c+10c, René Nicolas Dufriche, Baron Desgenettes, M.D. (1762–1837). 50c+10c, François Joseph Broussais, M.D. (1772–1838).

B461	SP258	30c+10c slate green & red	75	65
		a. Bklt. pane (4 # B461, 4 # B462 with gutter btwn.)	6.25	
B462	SP258	50c+10c red	75	65

The surtax was for the Red Cross.

Gaspard de Coligny
SP259

Portraits: No. B463, Gaspard de Coligny (1519–1572), admiral and Huguenot leader. No. B464, Ernest Renan (1823–1892), philologist and historian. No. B465, Alberto Santos Dumont (1873–1932), Brazilian aviator. No. B466, Gabrielle-Sidonie Colette (1873–1954), writer. No. B467, René Duguay-Trouin (1673–1736), naval commander. No. B468, Louis Pasteur (1822–1895), chemist, bacteriologist. No. B469, Tony Garnier (1869–1948), architect.

1973 **Engraved** ***Perf. 13***

B463	SP259	50c+10c multi.	90	80
B464	"	50c+10c "	90	80
B465	"	50c+10c "	90	80
B466	"	50c+10c "	90	80
B467	"	50c+10c "	90	80
B468	"	50c+10c "	1.00	1.00
B469	"	50c+10c "	1.00	1.00
		Nos. B463-B469 (7)	6.50	6.00

Issue dates: No. B463, Feb. 17; No. B464, Apr. 28; No. B465, May 26; No. B466, June 2; No. B467, June 9; No. B468, Oct. 6; No. B469, Nov. 17.

Mail Coach, 1835
SP260

1973, Mar. 24 **Engraved** ***Perf. 13***

B470	SP260	50c+10c greenish blue	45	35

Stamp Day, 1973.

Mary Magdalene
SP261

St. Louis-Marie de Montfort
SP262

Design: 50c+10c, Mourning woman. Designs are from 15th century Tomb of Tonnerre.

1973, Dec. 1

B471	SP261	30c+10c slate green & red	40	40
		a. Bklt. pane (4 # B471, 4 # B472 with gutter btwn.)	4.00	
B472	SP261	50c+10c dk. gray & red	60	60

Surtax was for the Red Cross.

1974, Feb. 23 **Engraved** ***Perf. 13***

Portraits: No. B474, Francis Poulenc (1899–1963), composer. No. B475, Jules Barbey d'Aurevilly (1808–1889), writer. No. B476, Jean Giraudoux (1882–1944), writer.

B473	SP262	50c+10c multi.	1.25	1.25
B474	"	50c+10c "	85	85
B475	"	80c+15c "	85	85
B476	"	80c+15c "	85	85

Issue dates: No. B473, Mar. 9; No. B474, July 20; Nos. B475–B476, Nov. 16.

Automatically Sorted Letters
SP263

1974, Mar. 9 **Engraved** ***Perf. 13***

B477	SP263	50c+10c multi.	40	35

Stamp Day 1974. Automatic letter sorting center, Orleans-la-Source, opened Jan. 30, 1973.

Order of Liberation and 5 Honored Cities—SP264

1974, June 15 **Engraved** ***Perf. 13***

B478	SP264	1fr+10c multi.	66	65

30th anniversary of liberation from the Nazis.

"Summer" SP265 — "Winter" SP266

Designs: B481, "Spring" (girl on swing). B482, "Fall" (umbrella and rabbits).

1974, Nov. 30 **Engr.** ***Perf. 13***

B479 SP265 60c+15c multi. 45 35
a. Bklt. pane (4 # B479, 4 # B480 with gutter btwn.) 4.25
B480 SP266 80c+15c multi. 55 45

1975, Nov. 29

B481 SP265 60c+15c multi. 45 35
a. Booklet pane (4 # B481, 4 # B482 with gutter btwn.) 4.25
B482 SP266 80c+20c multi. 55 45

Surtax was for the Red Cross.

Dr. Albert Schweitzer SP267

Edmond Michelet SP268

André Siegfried and Map SP269

Portraits: No. B483, Albert Schweitzer (1875–1965), medical missionary, birth centenary. No. B484, Edmond Michelet (1899–1970), Resistance hero, statesman. No. B485, Robert Schuman (1886–1963), promoter of United Europe. No. B486, Eugene Thomas (1903–1969), minister of PTT. No. B487, André Siegfried (1875–1959), political science professor, writer, birth centenary.

1975 **Engraved** ***Perf. 13***

B483 SP267 80c+20c multi. 60 60
B484 SP268 80c+20c blue & indigo 60 60
B485 " 80c+20c blk. & indigo 60 60
B486 " 80c+20c black & slate 60 60
B487 SP269 80c+20c blk. & blue 60 60
Nos. B483-B487(5) 3.00 3.00

Issue dates: No. B483, Jan. 11; No. B484, Feb. 22; No. B485, May 10; No. B486, June 28; No. B487, Nov. 15.

Second Republic Mailman's Badge SP270

1975, Mar. 8 **Photogravure**

B488 SP270 80c+20c multi. 55 50

Stamp Day.

"Sage" Type of 1876 SP271

Marshal A. J. de Moncey SP272

1976, Mar. 13 **Engr.** ***Perf. 13***

B489 SP271 80c+20c black & lilac 50 50

Stamp Day 1976.

1976 **Engraved** ***Perf. 13***

Designs: No. B491, Max Jacob (1876–1944), Dadaist writer, by Picasso. No. B492, Jean Mounet-Sully (1841–1916), actor. No. B493, Gen. Pierre Daumesnil (1776–1832). No. B494, Eugène Fromentin (1820–1876), painter.

B490 SP272 80c+20c multi. 52 50
B491 " 80c+20c red brn. & olive 52 50
B492 " 80c+20c multi. 52 50
B493 " 1fr+20c " 60 55
B494 " 1fr+20c " 60 55
Nos. B490-B494 (5) 2.76 2.60

Issue dates: No. B490, May 22; No. B491, July 22. No. B492, Aug. 28; No. B493, Sept. 4; No. B494, Sept. 25.

Anna de Noailles SP273

St. Barbara SP274

1976, Nov. 6 **Engr.** ***Perf. 13***

B495 SP273 1fr+20c multi. 60 55

Anna de Noailles (1876–1933), writer and poet.

1976, Nov. 20

Design: 1fr+25c, Cimmerian Sibyl. Sculptures from Brou Cathedral.

Cross in Carmine

B496 SP274 80c+20c violet 52 45
a. Booklet pane (4 # B496, 4 # B497 with gutter between) 4.75
B497 SP274 1fr+25c dk. brn. 62 55

Surtax was for the Red Cross.

Marckolsheim Relay Station Sign SP275

1977, Mar. 26 **Engr.** ***Perf. 13***

B498 SP275 1fr+20c multi. 60 55

Stamp Day.

Edouard Herriot, Statesman and Writer SP276

Christmas Figurine, Provence SP277

Designs: No. B500, Abbé Breuil (1877–1961), archaeologist. No. B501, Guillaume de Machault (1305–1377), poet and composer. No. B502, Charles Cros (1842–1888).

1977 **Engraved** ***Perf. 13***

B499 SP276 1fr+20c multi. 60 55
B500 " 1fr+20c " 60 55
B501 " 1fr+20c " 60 55
B502 " 1fr+20c " 60 55

Issue dates: No. B499, Oct. 8; No. B500, Oct. 15; No. B501, Nov. 12; No. B502, Dec. 3.

1977, Nov. 26

Design: 1fr+25c, Christmas figurine (woman), Provence.

B503 SP277 80c+20c red & indigo 52 45
a. Booklet pane (4 # B503, 4 # B504 with gutter between) 4.75
B504 SP277 1fr+25c red & slate green 62 55

Surtax was for the Red Cross.

Marie Noël, Writer SP278

Mail Collection, 1900 SP279

Designs: No. B506, Georges Bernanos (1888–1948), writer. No. B507, Leo Tolstoi (1828–1910), Russian writer. No. B508, Charles Marie Leconte de Lisle (1818–1894), poet. No. B509, Voltaire (1694–1778) and Jean Jacques Rousseau (1712–1778). No. B510, Claude Bernard (1813–1878), physiologist.

1978 **Engraved** ***Perf. 13***

B505 SP278 1fr+20c multi. 60 40
B506 " 1fr+20c " 60 40
B507 " 1fr+20c " 60 40
B508 " 1fr+20c " 60 40
B509 " 1fr+20c " 60 40
B510 " 1fr+20c " 60 40
Nos. B505-B510 (6) 3.60 2.40

Issue dates: No. B505, Feb. 11; No. B506, Feb. 18; No. B507, Apr. 15; No. B508, Mar. 26; No. B509, July 1; No. B510, Sept. 16.

1978, Apr. 8 **Engr.** ***Perf. 13***

B511 SP279 1fr+20c multi. 60 40

Stamp Day 1978.

The Hare and the Tortoise SP280

Design: 1.20fr+30c, The City Rat and the Country Rat.

1978, Dec. 2 **Engr.** ***Perf. 13***

B512 SP280 1fr+25c multi. 62 40
a. Booklet pane (4 # B512, 4 # B513 with gutter between) 5.75
B513 SP280 1.20fr+30c multi. 75 50

Surtax was for the Red Cross.

Marshal de Berchény SP281

1979, Jan. 13 **Engr.** ***Perf. 13***

B514 SP281 1.20fr+30c multi. 75 40

Marshal Ladislas de Berchény (1689–1778).

General Post Office, from 1908 Post Card—SP282

1979, Mar. 10 **Engr.** ***Perf. 13***

B520 SP282 1.20fr+30c multi. 60 35

Stamp Day 1979.

AIR POST STAMPS.

Nos. 127, 130 Overprinted in Dark Blue or Black **Poste Aérienne**

Perf. 14x13½

1927, June 25 **Unwmkd.**

C1 A18 2fr org.&bl. (DB) 175.00 160.00
C2 " 5fr dark blue & buff (Bk) 175.00 160.00

These stamps were on sale only at the International Aviation Exhibition at Marseilles, June, 1927. One set could be purchased by each holder of an admission ticket. Excellent counterfeits exist.

Nos. 242, 196 Surcharged **10 FR.**

1928, Aug. 23

C3 A33 10fr on 90c dull rose 1750.00 1750.00
a. Inverted surcharge *10,000.00 10,000.00*
b. Space between "10" and bars 6½mm. *3000.00 3000.00*
C4 A23 10fr on 1.50fr bl. 8000.00 8000.00
a. Space between "10" and bars 6½mm. *10,000.00 10,000.00*

Nos. C3–C4 received their surcharge in New York by order of the French consul-general. They were for use in paying the 10fr fee for letters leaving the liner Ile de France on a catapulted hydroplane when the ship was one day off the coast of France on its eastward voyage.

The normal space between "10" and bars is 4½mm., but on 10 stamps in each pane of 50 the space is 6½mm. Counterfeits exist.

View of Marseille, Church of Notre Dame at Left
AP1

1930–31 **Engraved** ***Perf. 13***

C5 AP1 1.50fr dp. carmine 15.00 1.25
C6 " 1.50fr dark blue ('31) 15.00 75
a. 1.50fr ultramarine 27.50 10.00
b. With perf. initials (EIPA 30) 425.00 325.00

No. C6a was sold at the International Air Post Exhibition, Paris, Nov. 6–20, 1930, at face value plus 5 francs, the price of admission. Most of the stamps of the first printing were perforated "EIPA30".

Blériot's Monoplane—AP2

1934, Sept. 1 ***Perf. 13***

C7 AP2 2.25fr violet 20.00 4.00

Issued in commemoration of the first flight across the English Channel, by Louis Blériot.

Plane over Paris
AP3

1930

C8 AP3 85c deep green 1.85 42
C9 " 1.50fr blue 5.50 2.25
C10 " 2.25fr violet 13.50 4.50
C11 " 2.50fr rose 13.50 4.50
C12 " 3fr ultramarine 4.25 30
C13 " 3.50fr orange brown 37.50 7.50
C14 AP3 50fr emerald 750.00 225.00
a. 50fr dp. grn. 1100.00 500.00
Nos. C8–C14 (7) 826.10 244.47

Monoplane over Paris—AP4

Paper with Red Network Overprint

1936, July 10 ***Perf. 12½***

C15 AP4 50fr ultramarine 675.00 210.00

Airplane and Galleon
AP5

Airplane and Globe
AP6

1936, Aug. 17 ***Perf. 13***

C16 AP5 1.50fr dark ultra. 12.50 1.75
C17 AP6 10fr Prussian green 325.00 90.00

Issued in commemoration of the 100th air mail flight across the South Atlantic Ocean.

Centaur and Plane
AP7

Iris
AP8

Zeus Carrying Hebe
AP9

Chariot of the Sun
AP10

1946–47 **Engraved** **Unwmkd.**

C18 AP7 40fr dark green 50 12
C19 AP8 50fr rose pink 50 8
C20 AP9 100fr dark blue ('47) 1.35 25
C21 AP10 200fr red 2.10 50

Ile de la Cité, Paris, and Gull
AP11

1947, May 7

C22 AP11 500fr dk. Prussian green 27.50 22.00

Universal Postal Union 12th Congress, Paris, May 7–July 7, 1947.

View of Lille
AP12

Air View of Paris—AP13

Designs: 200fr, Bordeaux. 300fr, Lyon. 500fr, Marseille.

1949-50 ***Perf. 13.*** **Unwmkd.**

C23 AP12 100fr sepia 85 10
C24 " 200fr dark blue green 5.50 60
C25 " 300fr purple 12.50 8.00
C26 " 500fr bright red 30.00 2.75
C27 AP13 1000fr sepia & blk., *blue* ('50) 80.00 15.00
Nos. C23–C27 (5) 128.85 26.45

Alexander III Bridge and Petit Palais, Paris—AP14

1949, June 13

C28 AP14 100fr brown carmine 5.00 3.75

Issued to publicize the International Telegraph and Telephone Conference, Paris, May–July 1949.

Jet Plane, Mystère IV
AP15

Planes: 200fr, Noratlas. 500fr, Miles Magister. 1000fr, Provence.

1954, Jan. 16

C29 AP15 100fr red brown & blue 1.25 8
C30 " 200fr black brown & violet blue 3.75 12
C31 AP15 500fr carmine & orange 100.00 10.00
C32 " 1000fr violet brown, blue green & indigo 90.00 10.00

Maryse Bastié and Plane
AP16

1955, June 4 ***Perf. 13*** **Unwmkd.**

C33 AP16 50fr deep plum & rose pink 6.75 4.50

Issued to honor Maryse Bastié, 1898-1952.

Caravelle—AP17

Designs: 300fr, Morane Saulnier 760 "Paris." 1000fr, Alouette helicopter.

1957-59 **Engraved.** ***Perf. 13***

C34 AP17 300fr slate green, greenish blue & sepia ('59) 4.25 1.75
C35 " 500fr deep ultramarine & black 17.50 1.75
C36 " 1000fr lilac, olive black & black ('58) 45.00 21.00

Types of 1954-59.

Planes: 2fr, Noratlas. 3fr, MS760, Paris. 5fr, Caravelle. 10fr, Alouette helicopter.

1960, Jan. 11

C37 AP15 2fr violet blue & ultra. 1.85 8
a. 2fr ultramarine 3.00 18
C38 AP17 3fr slate green, greenish blue & sepia 2.50 8
C39 " 5fr deep ultramarine & black 4.25 40
C40 " 10fr lilac, olive black & black 10.00 1.35

Type of 1957–59.

Design: 2fr, Jet plane, Mystère 20.

1965, June 12 **Engraved** ***Perf. 13***

C41 AP17 2fr slate blue & indigo 1.60 8

Concorde Issue

Common Design Type

1969, Mar. 2 **Engraved** ***Perf. 13***

C42 CD129 1fr indigo & bright blue 2.75 35

Issued to commemorate the first flight of the prototype Concorde plane at Toulouse, March 1, 1969.

Jean Mermoz, Antoine de Saint-Exupéry and Concorde—AP19

1970, Sept. 19 **Engraved** ***Perf. 13***

C43 AP19 20fr blue & indigo 9.00 1.25

Issued to honor Jean Mermoz (1901–1936) and the writer Antoine de Saint-Exupéry (1900–1944), aviators and air mail pioneers.

Balloon, Gare d'Austerlitz, Paris
AP20

1971, Jan. 16 Engraved *Perf. 13*

C44 AP20 95c bl., vio. bl., org. & slate grn. 1.50 1.10

Centenary of the balloon post from besieged Paris, 1870-71.

Didier Daurat, Raymond Vanier and Plane Landing at Night—AP21

1971, Apr. 17 Engraved *Perf. 13*

C45 AP21 5fr Prus. blue, black & light green 2.25 25

Honoring Didier Daurat (1891-1969) and Raymond Vanier (1895-1965), aviation pioneers.

Hélène Boucher, Maryse Hilsz and Caudron-Renault and Moth-Morane Planes—AP22

Design: 15fr, Henri Guillaumet, Paul Codos, Latécoère 521, Guillaumet's crashed plane in Andes, skyscrapers.

1972-73 Engraved *Perf. 13*

C46 AP22 10fr plum, red & slate 5.00 75
C47 " 15fr dp. car., gray & brn. ('73) 7.00 1.10

Hélène Boucher (1908-1934) and Maryse Hilsz (1901-1946), aviation pioneers.

Henri Guillaumet (1902-1940) and Paul Codos (1896-1960), aviation pioneers.

Issue dates: 10fr, June 10, 1972; 15fr, Feb. 24, 1973.

Concorde
AP23

1976, Jan. 10 Engr. *Perf. 13*

C48 AP23 1.70fr brt. bl., red & black 1.00 50

First flight of supersonic jet Concorde from Paris to Rio de Janeiro, Jan. 21.

Planes over the Atlantic, New York-Paris—AP24

1977, June 4 Engr. *Perf. 13*

C49 AP24 1.90fr multi. 1.00 50

First transatlantic flight by Charles A. Lindbergh from New York to Paris, 50th anniversary, and first attempted westbound flight by French aviators Charles Nungesser and Francois Coli.

Plane over Flight Route
AP25

1978, Oct. 14 Engr. *Perf. 13*

C50 AP25 1.50fr multicolored 75 35

75th anniversary of first airmail route from Villacoublay to Pauillac, Gironde.

AIR POST SEMI-POSTAL STAMPS.

Antoine de Saint-Exupéry
SPAP1

Col. Jean Dagnaux
SPAP2

Engraved

1948 *Perf. 13* Unwmkd.

CB1 SPAP1 50fr+30fr violet brown 1.00 1.00
CB2 SPAP2 100fr+70fr dark blue 2.00 1.50

Modern Plane and Ader's "Eole"
SPAP3

1948, Feb.

CB3 SPAP3 40fr+10fr dark blue 85 75

Issued to commemorate the 50th anniversary of the flight of Clément Ader's plane, the Eole, in 1897.

POSTAGE DUE STAMPS.

D1

D2

Lithographed

1859-70 *Imperf.* Unwmkd.

J1 D1 10c black *5000.00* 135.00
J2 " 15c black ('70) 85.00 140.00

In the lithographed stamps the central bar of the "E" of "CENTIMES" is very short, and the accent on "a" slants at an angle of 30°, for the 10c and 17° for the 15c, while on the typographed the central bar of the "E" is almost as wide as the top and bottom bars and the accent on the "a" slants at an angle of 47°.

No. J2 is known rouletted unofficially.

1859-78 Typographed.

J3 D1 10c black 14.00 7.50
J4 " 15c black ('63) 15.00 7.00
J5 " 20c black ('77) *1350.00*
J6 " 25c black ('71) 60.00 22.50
J7 " 30c black ('78) 100.00 65.00
J8 " 40c blue ('71) 185.00 225.00
 a. 40c ultramarine *2750.00 3500.00*
 b. 40c Prussian blue *1250.00*
J9 " 60c yellow ('71) 275.00 *700.00*
J10 D1 60c blue ('78) 37.50 *65.00*
 a. 60c dark blue 300.00 325.00
J10B " 60c black *1350.00*

The 20c and 60c black were never put into use.

Nos. J3, J4, J6, J8 and J9 are known rouletted unofficially and Nos. J4, J6, J7 and J10 pin-perf. unofficially.

1882-92 *Perf. 14x13½*

J11 D2 1c black 25 25
J12 " 2c " 6.50 7.00
J13 " 3c " 7.00 7.50
J14 " 4c " 10.00 8.50
J15 " 5c " 25.00 6.75
J16 " 10c " 22.50 60
J17 " 15c " 14.00 3.50
J18 " 20c " 65.00 40.00
J19 " 30c " 45.00 60
J20 " 40c " 27.50 15.00
J21 " 50c " ('92) 140.00 60.00
J22 " 60c " ('84) 140.00 16.50
J23 " 1fr " 200.00 125.00
J24 " 2fr " ('84) 375.00 250.00
J25 " 5fr " ('84) 700.00 575.00

Excellent counterfeits exist of Nos. J23-J25.

1884

J26 D2 1fr brown 115.00 35.00
J27 " 2fr " 80.00 60.00
J28 " 5fr " 135.00 110.00

1893-1941

J29 D2 5c blue ('94) 15 5
J30 " 10c brown 15 6
J31 " 15c light green ('94) 4.00 40
J32 " 20c olive green ('06) 1.00 15
J33 " 25c rose ('23) 1.40 90
J34 " 30c red ('94) 15 5
J35 " 30c orange red ('94) 250.00 25.00
J36 " 40c rose ('25) 3.25 1.10
J37 " 45c green ('24) 1.40 70
J38 " 50c brown violet ('95) 15 8
 a. 50c lilac 15 8
J39 " 60c blue green ('25) 25 12
J40 " 1fr rose, *straw* ('96) 250.00 150.00
J41 " 1fr red brn., *straw* ('20) 60 5
J42 " 1fr red brown ('35) 18 8
J43 " 2fr red orange ('10) 90.00 25.00
J44 " 2fr bright violet ('26) 15 10
J45 " 3fr magenta ('26) 20 12
J45A " 5fr red orange ('41) 70 60

D3

D4

1908-25

J46 D3 1c olive green 30 10
J47 " 10c violet 30 8
 a. Imperf., pair 125.00
J48 " 20c bistre ('19) 3.00 15
J49 " 30c bistre ('09) 1.35 15
J50 " 50c red ('09) 110.00 25.00
J51 " 60c red ('25) 60 35
 Nos. J46-J51 (6) 115.55 25.83

"Recouvrements" stamps were used to recover charges due on undelivered or refused mail which was returned to the sender.

Nos. J49-J50 Surcharged **20c.**

1917

J52 D3 20c on 30c bistre 4.00 1.25
J53 " 40c on 50c red 4.00 80
 a. Double surch. 85.00

In Jan. 1917 several values of the current issue of postage stamps were handstamped "T" in a triangle and used as postage due stamps.

Recouvrements Stamps of 1908-25 Surcharged **50**

1926

J54 D3 50c on 10c lilac 1.65 75
J55 " 60c on 1c olive green 2.50 1.25
J56 " 1fr on 60c red 7.50 2.75
J57 " 2fr on 60c red 7.50 3.25

1927-31

J58 D4 1c olive green ('28) 40 22
J59 D3 10c rose ('31) 60 15
J60 " 30c bistre 1.20 5
J61 " 60c red 1.00 7
J62 " 1fr violet 4.75 90
J63 " 1fr Prus. green ('31) 6.00 20
J64 " 2fr blue 16.00 6.50
J65 " 2fr olive brn. ('31) 50.00 7.00
 Nos. J58-J65 (8) 80.45 15.09

Nos. J62 to J65 have the numerals of value double-lined.

Nos. J64, J62 Surcharged in Red or Black

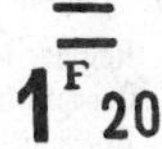

1929

J66 D4 1.20fr on 2fr blue 9.00 2.50
J67 " 5fr on 1fr violet (Bk) 13.50 2.50

No. J61 Surcharged **UN FRANC**

1931

J68 D4 1fr on 60c red 3.50 50

Sheaves of Wheat
D5 D6

Typographed.

1943-46 *Perf. 14x13½.* Unwmkd.

J69 D5 10c sepia 5 3
J70 " 30c bright red violet 5 4
J71 " 50c blue green 6 3
J72 " 1fr bright ultramarine 5 3
J73 " 1.50fr rose red 10 6
J74 " 2fr turquoise blue 7 5
J75 " 3fr brown orange 7 5
J76 " 4fr deep violet ('45) 1.65 1.00
J77 " 5fr bright pink 20 15
J78 " 10fr red orange ('45) 1.35 20
J79 " 20fr olive bis. ('46) 2.40 35
 Nos. J69-J79 (11) 6.05 1.99

Type of 1943.
Inscribed "Timbre Taxe."

1946-53

J80 D5 10c sepia ('47) 1.00 60
J81 " 30c brt. red vio. ('47) 85 60
J82 " 50c blue green ('47) 3.25 1.65
J83 " 1fr bright ultra. ('47) 5 5
J85 " 2fr turquoise blue 6 6
J86 " 3fr brown orange 6 5
J87 " 4fr deep violet 10 7
J88 " 5fr bright pink ('47) 10 5
J89 " 10fr red orange ('47) 18 5
J90 " 20fr olive bistre ('47) 75 15
J91 " 50fr dark green ('50) 1.75 8
J92 " 100fr deep green ('53) 20.00 1.10
 Nos. J80-J92 (12) 28.15 4.51

1960 Typographed. *Perf. 14x13½*

J93 D6 5c bright pink 1.00 20
J94 " 10c red orange 1.25 25
J95 " 20c olive bistre 1.85 20
J96 " 50c dark green 6.00 60
J97 " 1fr deep green 15.00 75
 Nos. J93-J97 (5) 25.10 2.00

Corn Poppy
D7

Flowers: 5c, Centaury. 10c, Gentian. 20c, Violets. 30c, Forget-me-not. 40c, Columbine. 50c, Clover. 1fr, Soldanel.

1964-71 Typo. *Perf. 14x13½*

J98 D7 5c car. rose, red & green ('65) 5 5
J99 " 10c carmine rose, brt. blue & green ('65) 5 5
J100 " 15c brn., green & red 6 6
J101 " 20c dk. green, green & vio. ('71) 8 5

J102 D7 30c brn., ultra. & grn. 14 6
J103 " 40c dk. grn., scarlet & yel. ('71) 18 6
J104 " 50c violet blue, car. & grn. ('65) 22 8
J105 " 1fr violet blue, lilac & green ('65) 45 12
Nos. J98-J105 (8) 1.23 53

MILITARY STAMPS

Regular Issue Overprinted in Black or Red **F. M.**

1901-39 ***Perf. 14x13½*** **Unwmkd.**

M1 A17 15c orange ('01) 40.00 5.00
a. Inverted overprint 85.00 45.00
b. Imperf., pair 165.00
M2 A19 15c pale red ('03) 25.00 3.00
M3 A20 15c slate green ('04) 25.00 3.50
a. No period after "M" 45.00 17.50
b. Imperf., pair 165.00
M4 " 10c rose ('06) 16.50 4.50
a. No period after "M" 45.00 20.00
b. Imperf., pair 140.00
M5 A22 10c red ('07) 40 15
a. Inverted overprint 45.00 35.00
b. Imperf., pair 100.00
M6 A20 50c vermilion ('29) 2.00 50
a. No period after "M" 25.00 9.00
b. Period in front of F 25.00 9.00
M7 A45 50c rose red ('34) 80 15
a. No period after "M" 5.00 3.00
b. Invtd. ovpt. 30.00 20.00
M8 " 65c brt. ultra. (R) ('38) 15 15
a. No period after "M" 15.00 11.00
M9 " 90c ultra. (R) ('39) 25 25

"F. M." are initials of Franchise Militaire (Military Frank). See No. S1.

M1

Flag—M2

1946-47 **Typographed.**

M10 M1 dark green 55 35
M11 " rose red ('47) 18 5

Nos. M10-M11 were valid also in the French colonies.

1964, July 20 ***Perf. 13x14***

M12 M2 multicolored 30 20

OFFICIAL STAMPS

For the Council of Europe.

For use only on mail posted in the post office in the Council of Europe Building, Strasbourg.

France No. 854 Overprinted: "CONSEIL DE L'EUROPE."

Engraved.

1958, Jan. 14 ***Perf. 13*** **Unwmkd.**

1O1 A303 35fr carmine rose & lake 1.85 3.00

Council of Europe Flag O1

1958-59

Flag in Ultramarine.

1O2 O1 8fr red orange & brown violet 20 20
1O3 " 20fr yel. & lt. brown 35 25
1O4 " 25fr lilac rose & slate green ('59) 50 35
1O5 " 35fr red 65 60
1O6 " 50fr lilac rose ('59) 1.35 1.35
Nos. 1O2-1O6 (5) 3.05 2.75

1963, Jan. 3

Flag in Ultramarine

1O7 O1 20c yellow & lt. brown 35 25
1O8 " 25c lilac rose & slate green 75 65
1O9 " 50c lilac rose 1.15 1.00

1965-71

Flag in Ultramarine & Yellow

1O10 O1 25c vermilion, yellow & slate green 40 35
1O11 " 30c vermilion & yellow 40 35
1O12 " 40c verm., yel. & gray ('69) 35 35
1O13 " 50c red, yellow & green ('71) 45 40
1O14 " 60c verm., yel. & vio. 60 50
1O15 " 70c verm., yellow & dk. brn. ('69) 1.65 1.25
Nos. 1O10-1O15 (6) 3.85 3.20

Issue dates: 25c, 30c, 60c, Jan. 16, 1965. 50c, Feb. 20, 1971. Others, Mar. 24, 1969.

Type of 1958 Inscribed "FRANCE"

1975-76 **Engraved** ***Perf. 13***

Flag in Ultramarine & Yellow

1O16 O1 60c org., yel. & emerald 35 30
1O17 " 80c yellow & magenta 45 40
1O18 " 1fr carmine, yellow & gray olive ('76) 85 75
1O19 " 1.20fr org., yel. & blue 85 75

Issue dates: 1fr, Oct. 16, 1976. Others, Nov. 22, 1975.

New Council Headquarters, Strasbourg O2

1977, Jan. 22 **Engr.** ***Perf. 13***

1O20 O2 80c car. & multi. 35 28
1O21 " 1fr brn. & multi. 42 32
1O22 " 1.40fr gray & multi. 65 50

Human Rights Emblem in Upper Left Corner

1978, Oct. 14

1O23 O2 1.20fr red lilac & multicolored 60 35
1O24 " 1.70fr blue & multi. 85 60

30th anniversary of the Universal Declaration of Human Rights.

For the United Nations Educational, Scientific and Cultural Organization

For use only on mail posted in the post office in the UNESCO Building, Paris.

Khmer Buddha and Hermes by Praxiteles
O1

Engraved

1961-65 ***Perf. 13*** **Unwmkd.**

2O1 O1 20c dark gray, olive bistre & blue 30 25
2O2 " 25c blk., lake & grn. 35 30
2O3 " 30c chocolate & bister brown ('65) 40 35
2O4 " 50c black, red & violet blue 1.00 75
2O5 " 60c greenish bl., red brn. & rose lilac ('65) 65 60
Nos. 2O1-2O5 (5) 2.70 2.25

Book and Globe
O2

1966, Dec. 17

2O6 O2 25c gray 25 25
2O7 " 30c dark red 30 30
2O8 " 60c green 55 55

20th anniversary of UNESCO.

Human Rights Flame
O3

1969-71 **Engraved** ***Perf. 13***

2O9 O3 30c slate green, red & deep brown 20 20
2O10 " 40c dk. car. rose, red & dp. brn. 30 30
2O11 " 50c ultra., carmine & brn. ('71) 40 40
2O12 " 70c pur., red & slate 1.65 1.10

Universal Declaration of Human Rights.

Type of 1969 Inscribed "FRANCE"

1975, Nov. 15 **Engr.** ***Perf. 13***

2O13 O3 60c grn., red & dark brown 35 30
2O14 " 80c ocher, red & red brown 45 40
2O15 " 1.20fr indigo, red & brown 85 75

O4

1976-78 **Engr.** ***Perf. 13***

2O16 O4 80c multicolored 35 28
2O17 " 1fr " 42 32
2O18 " 1.20fr " ('78) 60 35
2O19 " 1.40fr " 65 50
2O20 " 1.70fr " ('78) 85 60
Nos. 2O16-2O20 (5) 2.87 2.05

Issue dates: 1.20fr, 1.70fr, Oct. 14, 1978. Others, Oct. 23, 1976.

NEWSPAPER STAMPS.

Coat of Arms
N1

Typographed.

1868 ***Imperf.*** **Unwmkd.**

P1 N1 2c lilac 175.00 40.00
P2 " 2c(+2c) blue 325.00 175.00

Perf. 12½.

P3 N1 2c lilac 25.00 14.00
P4 " 2c(+4c) rose 85.00 60.00
P5 " 2c(+2c) blue 37.50 20.00
P6 " 5c lilac 650.00 375.00

Nos. P2, P4, and P5 were sold for face plus an added fiscal charge indicated in parenthesis. Nos. P1, P3 and P6 were used simply as fiscals.

The 2c rose and 5c lilac imperforate and the 5c rose and 5c blue, both imperforate and perforated, were never put into use.

Nos. P1-P6 were reprinted for the 1913 Ghent Exhibition and the 1937 Paris Exhibition (PEXIP).

No. 109 Surcharged in Red **1/2 centime**

1919 ***Perf. 14x13½***

P7 A16 ½c on 1c gray 12 12
a. Inverted surcharge 225.00 150.00

No. 156 Surcharged.

1933

P8 A22 ½c on 1c olive bistre 25 25

FRANCHISE STAMP.

No. 276 Overprinted "F".

1939 ***Perf. 14x13½*** **Unwmkd.**

S1 A45 90c ultramarine 1.85 1.85
a. Period after "F" 16.50 16.50

No. S1 was for the use of Spanish refugee soldiers in France. "F" stands for "Fugitives."

OCCUPATION STAMPS.

Issued under German Occupation.

(Alsace and Lorraine).

O1

Perf. 13½x14.

1870 **Typographed** **Unwmkd.**

Network with Points Up.

N1 O1 1c olive green 52.50 110.00
N2 " 2c red brown 100.00 135.00
a. 2c dark brown 125.00 165.00
N3 " 4c gray 95.00 65.00
N4 " 5c yellow green 62.50 10.00
N5 " 10c yellow brown 30.00 3.50
a. 10c bistre brn. 57.50 5.00
b. Network lemon yellow 72.50 8.50
N6 " 20c ultramarine 65.00 10.00
N7 " 25c brown 125.00 67.50
a. 25c black brown 165.00 100.00

There are three varieties of the 4c and two of the 10c, differing in the position of the figures of value, and several other setting varieties.

Network with Points Down.

N8	O1	1c olive green	300.00	800.00
N9	"	2c red brown	150.00	700.00
N10	"	4c gray	165.00	125.00
N11	"	5c yellow grn.	2500.00	325.00
N12	"	10c bistre	80.00	10.00
		a. Network lemon yellow	275.00	75.00
N13	O1	20c ultramarine	225.00	115.00
N14	"	25c brown	475.00	250.00

Official imitations have the network with points downward. The "P" of "Postes" is 2½mm. from the border in the imitations and 3mm. in the originals. The word "Postes" measures 12¾ to 13mm. on the imitations, and from 11 to 12½mm. on the originals.

The imitations are perf. 13½x14½; originals, perf. 13½x14¼.

The stamps for Alsace and Lorraine were replaced by stamps of the German Empire on Jan. 1, 1872.

German Stamps of 1905–16 Surcharged:

3 Cent. (a) 1 F (b)

✱ 1F.25 Cent. ✱ (c)

Wmkd. Lozenges. (125)

1916 *Perf. 14, 14½.*

N15	A16 (a)	3c on 3pf brown	15	15
N16	" (")	5c on 5pf green	15	18
N17	A22 (")	8c on 7½pf orange	38	55
N18	A16 (")	10c on 10pf car.	25	25
N19	A22 (")	15c on 15pf yellow brown	15	15
N20	A16 (")	25c on 20pf blue	38	38
		a. 25c on 20pf ultramarine	45	45
N21	" (")	40c on 30pf orange & black, *buff*	30	38
N22	" (")	50c on 40pf lake & black	38	50
N23	" (")	75c on 60pf magenta	75	1.10
N24	" (b)	1fr on 80pf lake & black, *rose*	1.25	1.75
N25	A17 (c)	1fr 25c on 1m carmine	7.50	7.50
		a. Double surcharge	100.00	
N26	A21 (")	2fr 50c on 2m gray blue	6.25	7.50
		a. Double surcharge	90.00	
		Nos. N15–N26 (12)	17.89	20.39

These stamps were also used in parts of Belgium occupied by the German forces.

Alsace.

Issued under German Occupation.

Stamps of Germany 1933-36 Overprinted in Black **Elsaß**

Wmkd. Swastikas. (237)

1940 *Perf. 14*

N27	A64	3(pf) olive bistre	15	30
N28	"	4(pf) dull blue	25	55
N29	"	5(pf) bright green	15	35
N30	"	6(pf) dark green	15	35
N31	"	8(pf) vermilion	15	35
N32	"	10(pf) chocolate	15	35
N33	"	12(pf) deep carmine	25	50
N34	"	15(pf) maroon	35	80
N35	"	20(pf) bright blue	35	80
N36	"	25(pf) ultramarine	40	90
N37	"	30(pf) olive green	50	1.10
N38	"	40(pf) red violet	50	1.10
N39	"	50(pf) dark green & black	90	1.80
N40	"	60(pf) claret & blk.	1.15	2.00
N41	"	80(pf) dark blue & black	1.25	2.10
N42	"	100(pf) orange & blk.	1.90	3.65
		Nos. N27–N42 (16)	8.55	17.00

Lorraine.

Issued under German Occupation.

Stamps of Germany 1933-36 Overprinted in Black **Lothringen**

Wmkd. Swastikas. (237)

1940 *Perf. 14.*

N43	A64	3(pf) olive bistre	18	65
N44	"	4(pf) dull blue	25	65
N45	"	5(pf) bright green	18	65
N46	"	6(pf) dark green	18	28
N47	"	8(pf) vermilion	18	65
N48	"	10(pf) chocolate	18	55
N49	"	12(pf) deep carmine	25	45
N50	"	15(pf) maroon	45	75
		a. Inverted surcharge	120.00	
N51	A64	20(pf) bright blue	45	80
N52	"	25(pf) ultramarine	50	80
N53	"	30(pf) olive green	65	1.00
N54	"	40(pf) red violet	65	1.00
N55	"	50(pf) dark green & black	1.10	1.50
N56	"	60(pf) claret & black	1.35	1.85
N57	"	80(pf) dark blue & black	1.65	2.65
N58	"	100(pf) orange & blk.	1.85	3.25
		Nos. N43–N58 (16)	10.05	17.48

Besetztes Gebiet Nordfrankreich

These three words, in a rectangular frame covering two stamps, were handstamped in black on Nos. 267, 367 and 369 and used in the Dunkerque region in July-August, 1940. The German commander of Dunkerque authorized the overprint.

Issued jointly by the Allied Military Government of the United States and Great Britain, for civilian use.

Arc de Triomphe O2

Lithographed

1944 *Perf. 11* Unwmkd.

2N1	O2	5c bright red violet	5	5
2N2	"	10c light gray	5	5
2N3	"	25c brown	5	5
2N4	"	50c olive bistre	5	5
2N5	"	1fr peacock green	5	5
2N6	"	1.50fr rose pink	4	4
2N7	"	2.50fr purple	7	7
2N8	"	4fr ultramarine	4	4
2N9	"	5fr black	7	7
2N10	"	10fr yellow orange	8.50	8.00
		Nos. 2N1-2N10 (10)	8.97	8.47

1945

Numerals Printed in Black.

2N11	O2	30c orange	6	6
2N12	"	40c pale gray	6	6
2N13	"	50c olive bistre	6	6
2N14	"	60c violet	6	6
2N15	"	80c emerald	6	6
2N16	"	1.20fr brown	6	6
2N17	"	1.50fr vermilion	6	6
2N18	"	2fr yellow	6	6
2N19	"	2.40fr dark rose	6	6
2N20	"	3fr bright red violet	6	6
		Nos. 2N11–2N20 (10)	60	60

FRENCH OFFICES ABROAD

OFFICES IN CHINA

Prior to 1923 several of the world powers maintained their own post offices in China for the purpose of sending and receiving overseas mail. French offices were maintained in Canton, Hoi Hao (Hoihow), Kwangchowan (Kouang-tchéou-wan), Mongtseu (Mong-tseu), Packhoi (Pakhoi), Tong King (Tchongking), Yunnan Fou (Yunnanfu).

100 Centimes = 1 Franc
100 Cents = 1 Piastre

Peace and Commerce A1

Stamps of France Overprinted in Red or Black.

Perf. 14x13½.

1894–1900 Unwmkd.

1	A1	5c grn., *greenish* (R)	1.00	75
2	"	5c yellow green, I (R) ('00)	1.00	50
		a. Type II	15.00	7.50
3	"	10c *lavender*, I (R)	2.00	75
		a. Type II	6.25	5.00
4	"	15c blue (R)	2.50	85
5	"	20c red, *green*	2.00	1.00
6	"	25c *rose* (R)	1.75	50
7	"	30c brn., *bistre*	1.75	1.50
8	"	40c red, *straw*	2.50	2.00
9	"	50c carmine, *rose*, I	6.25	5.00
		a. Red overprint	18.00	
		b. Type II (Bk)	5.00	3.00
10	"	75c deep violet, *orange* (R)	30.00	18.50
11	"	1fr bronze green, *straw*	5.00	1.50
		a. Double overprint	110.00	
12	"	2fr brown, *azure* ('00)	12.50	8.50
12A	"	5fr red lilac, *lavender*	27.50	16.50
		b. Red overprint	125.00	

Surcharged in Black **Chine 25**

13	A1	25c on 1fr bronze, green, *straw*	25.00	16.50

Surcharged in Red **Chine 2 Cents**

1901

14	A1	2c on 25c *rose*	425.00	125.00
15	"	4c on 25c "	375.00	125.00
16	"	6c on 25c "	450.00	185.00
17	"	16c on 25c "	130.00	80.00
		a. Black surcharge		2750.00

Stamps of Indo-China Surcharged in Black **CHINE 二之五仙**

1902–04

18	A3	1c *lilac blue*	75	50
19	"	2c brown, *buff*	1.25	1.00
20	"	4c claret, *lavender*	1.00	75
21	"	5c yellow green	1.25	1.00
22	"	10c red	1.00	1.00
23	"	15c gray	1.50	1.50
24	"	20c red, *green*	2.75	2.25
25	"	25c *rose*	3.50	2.50
26	"	25c blue ('04)	3.00	2.25
27	"	30c brown, *bistre*	2.00	1.50
28	"	40c red, *straw*	8.00	7.50
29	"	50c carmine, *rose*	22.50	18.50
30	"	50c brown, *azure* ('04)	3.75	3.00
31	A3	75c violet, *orange*	12.50	8.50
32	"	1fr bronze grn., *straw*	15.00	11.00
33	"	5fr red lilac, *lavender*	35.00	27.50
		Nos. 18–33 (16)	115.25	90.25

The Chinese characters surcharged on Nos. 18–33 are the Chinese equivalents of the French values and therefore differ on each denomination. Another printing of these stamps was made in 1904 which differs from the first one principally in the size and shape of the letters in "CHINE", particularly the "H" which is much thinner in the second printing. Prices are for the less expensive variety. Many varieties of surcharge exist.

Liberty, Equality and Fraternity A3

"Rights of Man" A4

A5

1902-03 Typographed.

34	A3	5c green	60	60
35	A4	10c rose red ('03)	60	60
36	"	15c pale red	1.00	60
37	"	20c brn. violet ('03)	2.00	2.00
38	"	25c blue ('03)	1.50	60
39	"	30c lilac ('03)	1.75	1.75
40	A5	40c red & pale blue	4.25	4.25
41	"	50c bistre brown & lavender	5.50	4.25
42	"	1fr claret & olive green	7.50	3.75
43	"	2fr gray violet & yellow	18.50	12.50
44	"	5fr dark blue & buff	27.50	18.50
		Nos. 34–44 (11)	70.70	49.40

Surcharged in Black **5**

1903

45	A4	5c on 15c pale red	6.25	3.00
		a. Invtd. surcharge	27.50	27.50

Stamps of Indo-China, 1904–06, Surcharged as Nos. 18 to 33 in Black.

1904–05

46	A4	1c olive green	50	50
47	"	2c violet brown, *buff*	50	50
47A	"	4c claret, *bluish*	575.00	350.00
48	"	5c deep green	1.00	1.00
49	"	10c carmine	1.00	1.00
50	"	15c org. brown, *blue*	1.00	1.00
51	"	20c red, *green*	3.75	3.75
52	"	25c deep blue	2.00	1.25
53	"	40c *bluish*	1.75	1.25
54	"	1fr pale green	165.00	110.00
55	"	2fr brown, *orange*	12.50	8.50
56	"	10fr org. brn., *green*	80.00	67.50
		Nos. 46–56 (12)	844.00	546.25

Many varieties of the surcharge exist on Nos. 46–55.

Stamps of 1902-03 Surcharged in Black **2 CENTS 仙二**

1907

57	A3	2c on 5c green	12	12
58	A4	4c on 10c rose red	12	12
		a. Pair, one without surcharge	25.00	
59	"	6c on 15c pale red	50	25
60	"	8c on 20c brn. violet	1.50	1.10
		a. "8" inverted	18.50	18.50
61	"	10c on 25c blue	12	12
62	A5	20c on 50c bistre brown & lavender	75	75
		a. Double surcharge		
		b. Triple surch.	100.00	100.00
63	"	40c on 1fr claret & olive green	7.50	5.00

64 A5 2pi on 5fr dark blue & buff 8.00 5.00
a. Double surcharge 550.00 550.00
Nos. 57-64 (8) 18.61 12.46

Stamps of 1902-03 Surcharged in Black — 2 CENTS 分二

1911-22

65 A3 2c on 5c green 30 7
66 A4 4c on 10c rose red 45 12
67 " 6c on 15c orange 75 30
68 " 8c on 20c brn. violet 50 18
69 " 10c on 25c blue ('21) 60 30
70 " 20c on 50c blue ('22) 21.00 20.00
71 A5 40c on 1fr claret & olive green 1.10 50

No. 44 Surcharged — 2 $ 圓二

73 A5 $2 on 5fr blue & buff ('22) 80.00 65.00
Nos. 65-73 (8) 104.70 86.47

Types of 1902-03 Surcharged in Black — 2 CENTS 分二

1922

75 A3 1c on 5c orange 1.25 75
76 A4 2c on 10c green 2.50 1.25
77 " 3c on 15c orange 3.75 3.00
78 " 4c on 20c red brown 5.00 3.75
79 " 5c on 25c dk. violet 2.50 1.25
80 " 6c on 30c red 5.00 3.75
82 " 10c on 50c blue 5.00 3.75
83 A5 20c on 1fr claret & olivegreen 12.50 10.00
84 " 40c on 2fr orange & pale blue 12.50 10.00
85 " $1 on 5fr dark blue & buff 75.00 75.00
Nos. 75-85 (10) 125.00 112.50

POSTAGE DUE STAMPS.

Postage Due Stamps of France Handstamped in Red or Black — Chine

Perf. 14x13½.

1901-07 **Unwmkd.**

J1 D2 5c light blue (R) 1.50 1.25
J2 " 10c chocolate (R) 3.00 2.50
J3 " 15c light green (R) 3.00 2.50
J4 " 20c olive green (R) ('07) 2.50 2.50
J5 " 30c carmine 5.00 3.75
J6 " 50c lilac 5.00 3.75
Nos. J1-J6 (6) 20.00 16.25

Stamps of 1894-1900 Handstamped in Carmine — A PERCEVOIR

1903

J7 A1 5c yel. green *1350.00* 500.00
a. Purple handstamp *1350.00* 500.00
b. 5c green, *greenish* *2750.00*
J8 A1 10c *lavender* *3000.00* *2500.00*
a. Purple handstamp *3000.00* *2500.00*
J9 A1 15c blue *1350.00* 400.00
a. Purple handstamp *1350.00* 400.00
J10 A1 30c brn., *bister* *800.00* 42.50
a. Purple handstamp *800.00* 42.50

Same Handstamp on Stamps of 1902-03 in Carmine

1903

J14 A3 5c green *800.00* *400.00*
a. Purple handstamp *800.00* *400.00*
J15 A4 10c rose red 325.00 75.00
a. Purple handstamp 325.00 75.00
J16 A4 15c pale red 350.00 80.00
a. Purple handstamp 350.00 80.00

Stamps of 1894-1900 Handstamped in Carmine — A PERCEVOIR

1903

J20 A1 5c yel. green *950.00* 175.00
a. Purple handstamp *950.00* 175.00
b. 5c green, *greenish* *2750.00*
J21 A1 10c *lavender* *3000.00* *2500.00*
a. Purple handstamp *3000.00* *2500.00*
J22 A1 15c blue 550.00 42.50
a. Purple handstamp 550.00 42.50
J23 A1 30c brn., *bister* 225.00 37.50
a. Purple handstamp 225.00 37.50

Same Handstamp on Stamps of 1902-03 in Carmine or Purple

1903

J27 A3 5c green (C) 550.00 225.00
a. Purple handstamp 550.00 225.00
J28 A4 10c rose red (C) 160.00 22.50
a. Purple handstamp 160.00 22.50
J29 A4 15c pale red (C) 300.00 25.00
a. Purple handstamp 300.00 25.00
J30 A4 30c lilac (P) *3000.00* *2500.00*

The handstamps on Nos. J7-J30 are found inverted, double, etc.

The cancellations on these stamps should have dates between Sept. 1, and Nov. 30, 1903, to be genuine.

Postage Due Stamps of France 1893-1910 Surcharged in Black — 2 CENTS 分二

1911

J33 D2 2c on 5c blue 65 45
a. Double surch. 25.00 25.00
J34 " 4c on 10c chocolate 50 45
a. Double surch. 25.00 25.00
J35 " 8c on 20c olive green 75 70
a. Double surch. 25.00 25.00
J36 " 20c on 50c lilac 90 70

1922

J37 D2 1c on 5c blue 30.00 27.50
J38 " 2c on 10c brown 42.50 37.50
J39 " 4c on 20c olive grn. 42.50 37.50
J40 " 10c on 50c brn. vio. 42.50 37.50

CANTON

Stamps of Indo-China, 1892-1900, Overprinted in Red — CANTON 州廣

1901 ***Perf. 14x13½.*** **Unwmkd.**

1 A3 1c *lilac blue* 75 75
1A " 2c brown, *buff* 75 75
2 " 4c claret, *lavender* 1.00 1.00
2A " 5c grn., *greenish* 210.00 210.00
3 " 5c yellow green 1.00 1.00
4 " 10c *lavender* 2.00 2.00
5 " 15c blue, quadrille paper 1.25 1.25
6 " 15c gray 2.00 2.00
a. Dbl. overprint 10.00
7 " 20c red, *green* 3.75 3.75
8 " 25c *rose* 3.75 3.75
9 " 30c brown, *bistre* 7.50 7.50
10 " 40c red, *straw* 10.00 10.00
11 " 50c carmine, *rose* 12.50 12.50
12 " 75c deep violet, *orange* 16.50 16.50
13 " 1fr bronze green, *straw* 12.50 12.50
14 " 5fr red lilac, *lavender* 110.00 110.00
Nos. 1-14 (16) 395.25 395.25

The Chinese characters in the overprint on Nos. 1-14 read "Canton." On Nos. 15-64, they restate the denomination of the basic stamp.

Surcharged in Black — CANTON 仙六

1903-04

15 A3 1c *lilac blue* 1.25 1.25
16 " 2c brown, *buff* 1.25 1.25
17 " 4c claret, *lavender* 1.25 1.25
18 " 5c yellow green 1.00 75
19 A3 10c rose red 1.00 75
20 " 15c gray 1.25 1.00
21 " 20c red, *green* 6.25 6.25
22 " 25c blue 2.75 2.00
23 " 25c *rose* ('04) 2.75 1.75
24 " 30c brown, *bistre* 7.50 6.25
25 " 40c red, *straw* 21.00 15.00
26 " 50c carmine, *rose* 160.00 135.00
27 " 50c brown, *azure* ('04) 32.50 30.00
28 " 75c dp. vio., *orange* 32.50 30.00
a. "INDO-CHINE" inverted *15,000.00*
29 A3 1fr bronze green, *straw* 30.00 30.00
30 " 5fr red lilac, *lavender* 30.00 30.00
Nos. 15-30 (16) 332.25 292.50

Many varieties of the surcharge exist on Nos. 15-30.

Stamps of Indo-China, 1892-1906, Surcharged in Red or Black — CANTON 花銀八厘

A second printing of the 1906 surcharges of Canton, Hoi Hao, Kwangchowan, Mongtseu, Packhoi, Tong King and Yunnan Fou was made in 1908. The inks are grayish instead of full black and vermilion instead of carmine. Prices are for the cheaper variety which usually is the second printing.

The 4c and 50c of the 1892 issue of Indo-China are known with this surcharge and similarly surcharged for other cities in China. The surcharges on these two stamps are always inverted. It is stated that they were irregularly produced and never issued.

1906

31 A4 1c olive green (R) 75 75
32 " 2c violet brown, *buff* 75 75
33 " 4c claret, *bluish* (R) 75 75
34 " 5c deep green (R) 1.00 75
35 " 10c carmine 1.25 1.00
36 " 15c orange brn., *blue* 1.50 1.50
37 " 20c red, *green* 1.00 1.00
38 " 25c deep blue 1.00 1.00
39 " 30c pale brown 1.50 1.25
40 " 35c *yellow* (R) 1.00 50
41 " 40c *bluish* (R) 1.25 1.25
42 " 50c bistre brown 2.00 2.00
43 A3 75c deep violet, *orange* (R) 21.00 21.00
44 A4 1fr pale green 5.00 5.00
45 " 2fr brn., *org.* (R) 15.00 12.50
46 A3 5fr red lilac, *lavender* 32.50 30.00
47 A4 10fr orange brown, *green* 30.00 30.00
Nos. 31-47 (17) 117.25 111.00

The surcharge exists inverted on 1c, 25c and 1fr.

Stamps of Indo-China, 1907, Surcharged "CANTON", and Chinese Characters, in Red or Blue.

1908

48 A5 1c olive brown & black 50 50
49 " 2c brown & black 50 50
50 " 4c blue & black 75 50
51 " 5c green & black 75 50
52 " 10c red & black (Bl) 75 25
53 " 15c violet & black 1.25 1.25
54 A6 20c violet & black 1.25 1.25
55 " 25c blue & black 1.25 1.25
56 " 30c brown & black 2.50 2.50
57 " 35c olive grn. & blk. 2.50 2.50
58 " 40c brown & black 3.00 3.00
59 " 50c car. & black (Bl) 3.75 3.00
60 A7 75c vermilion & black (Bl) 3.75 3.75
61 A8 1fr carmine & black (Bl) 6.25 6.25
62 A9 2fr green & black 15.00 13.50
63 A10 5fr blue & black 18.50 17.50
64 A11 10fr purple & black 37.50 32.50
Nos. 48-64 (17) 99.75 91.00

Nos. 48-64 Surcharged with New Values in Cents or Piastres in Black, Red or Blue

1919

65 A5 2/5c on 1c 50 50
66 " 4/5c on 2c 50 50
67 " 13/5c on 4c (R) 50 50
68 " 2c on 5c 50 50
69 A5 4c on 10c (Bl) 50 50
a. Chinese "2" instead of "4" 7.00 7.00
70 " 6c on 15c 75 50
71 A6 8c on 20c 75 75
72 " 10c on 25c 1.00 50
73 " 12c on 30c 1.00 50
a. Double surcharge 37.50 37.50
74 " 14c on 35c 1.00 50
a. Closed "4" 3.00 3.00
75 " 16c on 40c 1.00 75
76 " 20c on 50c (Bl) 1.00 75
77 A7 30c on 75c (Bl) 1.00 50
78 A8 40c on 1fr (Bl) 3.75 2.25
79 A9 80c on 2fr (R) 3.75 3.75
80 A10 2pi on 5fr (R) 5.00 4.00
81 A11 4pi on 10fr (R) 5.00 5.00
Nos. 65-81 (17) 27.50 22.25

HOI HAO

Stamps of Indo-China Overprinted in Red — HOI HAO 州瓊

1901 ***Perf. 14x13½.*** **Unwmkd.**

1 A3 1c *lilac blue* 1.25 1.25
2 " 2c brown, *buff* 1.25 1.25
3 " 4c claret, *lavender* 1.25 1.25
4 " 5c yellow green 1.25 1.25
5 " 10c *lavender* 1.75 1.75
6 " 15c blue 700.00 300.00
7 " 15c gray 75 75
8 " 20c red, *green* 5.00 5.00
9 " 25c *rose* 2.50 2.50
10 " 30c brown, *bistre* 10.00 8.50
11 " 40c red, *straw* 10.00 8.50
12 " 50c carmine, *rose* 15.00 12.50
13 " 75c deep violet, *orange* 85.00 75.00
14 " 1fr bronze green, *straw* 300.00 300.00
15 " 5fr red lilac, *lavender* 250.00 235.00
Nos. 1-15 (15) 1385.00 954.50

The Chinese characters in the overprint on Nos. 1-15 read "Hoi Hao." On Nos. 16-66, they restate the denomination of the basic stamp.

Surcharged in Black — HOI HAO 仙六

1903-04

16 A3 1c *lilac blue* 38 38
17 " 2c brown, *buff* 38 38
18 " 4c claret, *lavender* 75 75
19 " 5c yellow green 75 75
20 " 10c red 75 75
21 " 15c gray 60 60
22 " 20c red, *green* 2.00 2.00
23 " 25c blue 1.00 1.00
24 " 25c *rose* ('04) 85 85
25 " 30c brown, *bistre* 1.25 1.25
26 " 40c red, *straw* 15.00 15.00
27 " 50c carmine, *rose* 15.00 15.00
28 " 50c brn., *azure* ('04) 42.50 42.50
29 " 75c dp. violet, *orange* 15.00 15.00
a. "INDO-CHINE" inverted *10,000.00*
30 " 1fr bronze green, *straw* 15.00 15.00
31 " 5fr red lilac, *lavender* 75.00 75.00
Nos. 16-31 (16) 186.21 186.21

Many varieties of the surcharge exist on Nos. 1-31.

Stamps of Indo-China, 1892-1906, Surcharged in Red or Black — HOI HAO 花銀八厘

1906

32 A4 1c olive green (R) 75 75
33 " 2c violet brown, *buff* 75 75
34 " 4c claret, *bluish* (R) 1.00 1.00
35 " 5c deep green (R) 1.50 1.50
36 " 10c carmine 1.50 1.50
37 " 15c orange brn., *blue* 1.60 1.60
38 " 20c red, *green* 1.60 1.60
39 " 25c deep blue 1.85 1.85
40 " 30c pale brown 1.85 1.85
41 " 35c *yellow* (R) 2.50 2.50
42 " 40c *bluish* (R) 3.75 3.75
43 " 50c gray brown 5.00 5.00

44 A3 75c deep violet, *orange* (R) 16.00 16.00
45 A4 1fr pale green 15.00 15.00
46 " 2fr brn., *orange* (R) 15.00 15.00
47 A3 5fr red lilac, *lavender* 50.00 50.00
48 A4 10fr orange brown, *green* 55.00 55.00
Nos. 32-48 (17) 174.65 174.65

Stamps of Indo-China, 1907, Surcharged "HOI HAO" and Chinese Characters, in Red or Blue.

1908

49 A5 1c ol. brn. & black 25 25
50 " 2c brown & black 25 25
51 " 4c blue & black 50 50
52 " 5c green & black 60 60
53 " 10c red & black (Bl) 75 75
54 " 15c violet & black 1.60 1.60
55 A6 20c violet & black 2.50 2.50
56 " 25c blue & black 2.50 2.50
57 " 30c brown & black 2.50 2.50
58 " 35c olive grn. & blk. 2.50 2.50
59 " 40c brown & black 2.00 2.00
61 " 50c car. & black (Bl) 2.75 2.75
62 A7 75c vermilion & black (Bl) 3.00 3.00
63 A8 1fr car. & blk. (Bl) 6.75 6.75
64 A9 2fr green & black 15.00 15.00
65 A10 5fr blue & black 25.00 25.00
66 A11 10fr purple & black 37.50 37.50
Nos. 49-66 (17) 105.95 105.95

Issue of 1908 Surcharged with New Values in Cents or Piastres in Black, Red or Blue.

1919

67 A5 2/5c on 1c olive brown & black 38 38
68 " 4/5c on 2c yellow brown & black 38 38
69 " 1 3/5c on 4c blue & black (R) 50 50
70 " 2c on 5c grn. & black 38 38
71 " 4c on 10c red & black (Bl) 60 60
a. Chinese "2" instead of "4" 1.75 1.75
72 " 6c on 15c vio. & blk. 60 60
73 A6 8c on 20c vio. & blk. 75 75
a. "S" of "CENTS" omitted 35.00 35.00
74 " 10c on 25c blue & blk. 2.00 2.00
75 " 12c on 30c brn. & blk. 50 50
76 " 14c on 35c olive green & black 60 60
a. Closed "4" 5.00 5.00
77 " 16c on 40c yellow brown & black 50 50
79 " 20c on 50c carmine & black (Bl) 75 75
80 A7 30c on 75c vermilion & black (Bl) 1.25 1.25
81 A8 40c on 1fr carmine & black (Bl) 3.25 3.25
82 A9 80c on 2fr green & black (R) 7.50 7.50
83 A10 2pi on 5fr blue & black (R) 21.00 21.00
a. Triple surcharge of new value 150.00
84 A11 4pi on 10fr purple & black (R) 90.00 90.00
Nos. 67-84 (17) 130.94 130.94

KWANGCHOWAN

A Chinese Territory leased to France, 1898 to 1945.

Stamps of Indo-China, 1892-1906, Surcharged in Red or Black

Kouang Tchéou-Wan

花銀八厘

1906 *Perf. 14x13½* **Unwmkd.**

1 A4 1c olive green (R) 1.10 1.10
2 " 2c violet brown, *buff* 1.10 1.10
3 " 4c claret, *bluish* (R) 1.50 1.50
4 " 5c deep green (R) 1.50 1.50
5 " 10c carmine 1.50 1.50
6 " 15c orange brown, *blue* 2.00 2.00
7 " 20c red, *green* 1.50 1.50
8 A4 25c deep blue 1.50 1.50
9 " 30c pale brown 1.50 1.50
10 " 35c *yellow* (R) 1.50 1.50
11 " 40c *bluish* (R) 1.50 1.50
12 " 50c bistre brown 6.25 6.25
13 A3 75c deep violet, *orange* (R) 8.50 8.50
14 A4 1fr pale green 10.00 10.00
15 " 2fr brown, *orange* (R) 10.00 10.00
16 A3 5fr red lilac, *lavender* 67.50 67.50
17 A4 10fr orange brown, *green* 80.00 80.00
Nos. 1-17 (17) 198.45 198.45

Various varieties of the surcharge exist on Nos. 2-10.

Stamps of Indo-China, 1907, Surcharged "KOUANG-TCHEOU" and Value in Chinese in Red or Blue.

1908

18 A5 1c olive brown & blk. 18 18
19 " 2c brown & black 18 18
20 " 4c blue & black 25 25
21 " 5c green & black 25 25
22 " 10c red & black (Bl) 18 18
23 " 15c violet & black 80 80
24 A6 20c violet & black 1.50 1.50
25 " 25c blue & black 1.60 1.60
26 " 30c brown & black 2.50 2.50
27 " 35c olive green & black 3.75 3.75
28 " 40c brown & black 3.75 3.75
30 " 50c carmine & black (Bl) 3.75 3.75
31 A7 75c vermilion & black (Bl) 3.75 3.75
32 A8 1fr carmine & black (Bl) 6.25 6.25
33 A9 2fr green & black 15.00 15.00
34 A10 5fr blue & black 25.00 25.00
35 A11 10fr purple & black 37.50 37.50
a. Double surch. 250.00 250.00
b. Triple surch. 250.00 250.00
Nos. 18-35 (17) 106.19 106.19

The Chinese characters overprinted on Nos. 1 to 35 repeat the denomination of the basic stamp.

Issue of 1908 Surcharged with New Values in Cents or Piastres in Black, Red or Blue.

1919

36 A5 2/5c on 1c olive brown & black 18 18
37 " 4/5c on 2c yellow brown & black 18 18
38 " 1 3/5c on 4c blue & black (R) 30 20
39 " 2c on 5c green & black 30 25
a. "2 CENTS" inverted 21.00
40 " 4c on 10c red & black (Bl) 1.00 50
41 " 6c on 15c vio. & blk. 25 15
42 A6 8c on 20c vio. & blk. 1.50 1.25
43 " 10c on 25c bl. & blk. 3.75 3.50
44 " 12c on 30c brn. & blk. 38 30
45 " 14c on 35c olive green & black 90 65
a. Closed "4" 10.00 8.50
46 " 16c on 40c yellow brown & black 38 20
48 " 20c on 50c carmine & black (Bl) 55 45
49 A7 30c on 75c vermilion & black (Bl) 2.10 2.00
50 A8 40c on 1fr carmine & black (Bl) 2.50 2.10
a. "40 CENTS" inverted
51 A9 80c on 2fr green & black (R) 3.75 1.75
52 A10 2pi on 5fr blue & black (R) 67.50 65.00
53 A11 4pi on 10fr purple & black (R) 8.00 7.50
Nos. 36-53 (17) 93.52 86.16

Stamps of Indo-China, 1922-23, Overprinted in Black, Red or Blue KOUANG-TCHEOU

1923

54 A12 1/10c black & salmon (Bl) 8 8
55 A12 1/5c deep blue & black (R) 8 8
a. Black ovpt. 30.00
56 " 2/5c olive brown & black (R) 10 10
57 " 4/5c brt. rose & black 10 10
58 " 1c yellow brown & black (Bl) 15 15
59 " 2c gray green & black (R) 25 25
60 " 3c vio. & blk. (R) 25 25
61 " 4c orange & black 25 25
62 " 5c carmine & black 25 25
63 A13 6c dull red & black 30 30
64 " 7c olive grn. & blk. 25 25
65 " 8c black (R) 50 50
66 " 9c yellow & black 50 50
67 " 10c blue & black 50 50
68 " 11c violet & black 50 50
69 " 12c brown & black 50 50
70 " 15c orange & black 75 75
71 " 20c blue & black, *straw* (R) 50 50
72 " 40c vermilion & black, *bluish* (Bl) 1.00 1.00
73 " 1pi blue green & blk., *greenish* 3.00 3.00
74 " 2pi violet brown & black, *pinkish* (Bl) 3.75 3.75
Nos. 54-74 (21) 13.56 13.56

Indo-China Stamps of 1927 Overprinted in Black or Red KOUANG-TCHÉOU

1927

75 A14 1/10c light olive green (R) 6 6
76 " 1/5c yellow 8 8
77 " 2/5c light blue (R) 12 12
78 " 4/5c deep brown 15 15
79 " 1c orange 12 12
80 " 2c blue green (R) 25 25
81 " 3c indigo (R) 25 25
82 " 4c lilac rose 25 25
83 " 5c deep violet 25 25
84 A15 6c deep red 30 30
85 " 7c light brown 30 30
86 " 8c gray green (R) 30 30
87 " 9c red violet 38 30
88 " 10c light blue (R) 38 30
89 " 11c orange 38 30
90 " 12c myrtle green (R) 38 30
91 A16 15c dull rose & olive brown 85 85
92 " 20c vio. & slate (R) 85 85
93 A17 25c orange brown & lilac rose 85 85
94 " 30c deep blue & olive gray (R) 50 42
95 A18 40c verm. & lt. blue 42 33
96 " 50c light green & slate (R) 60 50
97 A19 1pi dark blue, black & yellow (R) 1.50 1.50
98 " 2pi red, deep blue & orange (R) 1.50 1.50
a. Double ovpt. 30.00
Nos. 75-98 (24) 11.02 10.43

Stamps of Indo-China, 1931-41, Overprinted in Black or Red KOUANG-TCHÉOU

1937-41 *Perf. 13, 13½*

99 A20 1/10c Prussian blue 5 5
100 " 1/5c lake 6 6
101 " 2/5c orange red 8 8
102 " 1/2c red brown 10 10
103 " 4/5c dark violet 10 10
104 " 1c black brown 8 8
105 " 2c dark green 8 8
a. Inverted ovpt. 55.00
106 A21 3c dark green 18 18
107 " 3c yel. brn. ('41) 8 8
108 " 4c dark blue (R) 30 30
109 " 4c dark green ('41) 12 12
110 " 4c yel. orge. ('41) 60 60
111 " 5c deep violet 25 25
112 " 5c deep green ('41) 12 12
113 " 6c orange red 12 12
114 " 7c black (R) ('41) 10 10
115 " 8c rose lake ('41) 12 12
116 A21 9c black, *yellow* (R) ('41) 12 12
d. Black ovpt. 2.50 2.50
117 A22 10c dark blue (R) 38 38
118 " 10c ultramarine, *pink* (R) ('41) 12 12
119 " 15c dark blue (R) 15 15
120 " 18c blue (R) ('41) 8 8
121 " 20c rose 15 15
122 " 21c olive green 12 12
123 " 22c green ('41) 12 12
124 " 25c deep violet 1.00 1.00
125 " 25c dk. bl. (R) ('41) 12 12
126 " 30c orange brown 15 15
127 A23 50c dark brown 25 25
128 " 60c dull violet 25 25
129 " 70c lt. bl. (R) ('41) 10 10
130 " 1pi yellow green 55 55
131 " 2pi red 55 55
Nos. 99-131 (33) 6.75 6.75

Colonial Arts Exhibition Issue.

Common Design Type

Souvenir Sheet.

1937 **Engraved.** ***Imperf.***

132 CD79 30c green & sepia 1.85 1.85

Sheet size: 118x99mm.

New York World's Fair Issue.

Common Design Type

1939 ***Perf. 12½x12*** **Unwmkd.**

133 CD82 13c carmine lake 25 25
134 " 23c ultramarine 25 25

Petain Issue.

Indo-China Nos. 209-209A Overprinted "KOUANG TCHEOU" in Blue or Red.

1941 **Engraved** ***Perf. 12½x12***

135 A27a 10c carmine lake (B) 12
136 " 25c blue (R) 12

Nos. 135-136 were issued by the Vichy government, and were not placed on sale in Kwangchowan. This is also true of 16 stamps of Indo-China types A20-A23 without "RF" and overprinted "KOUANG-TCHEOU."

SEMI-POSTAL STAMPS.

French Revolution Issue

Common Design Type

Photogravure.

1939 ***Perf. 13.*** **Unwmkd.**

Name and Value Typo. in Black.

B1 CD83 6c+2c green 2.00 2.00
B2 " 7c+3c brown 2.00 2.00
B3 " 9c+4c red orange 2.00 2.00
B4 " 13c+10c rose pink 2.00 2.00
B5 " 23c+20c blue 2.00 2.00
Nos. B1-B5 (5) 10.00 10.00

Indo-China Nos. B19A and B19C Overprinted "KOUANG-TCHEOU" in Blue or Red, and Common Design Type

1941 **Photogravure** ***Perf. 13½***

B6 SP1 10c+10c red (B) 18
B7 CD86 15c+30c maroon & carmine 18
B8 SP2 25c+10c blue (R) 30

Nos. B6-B8 were issued by the Vichy government, and were not placed on sale in Kwangchowan.

Nos. 135-136 were surcharged "OEUVRES COLONIALES" and surtax (including change of denomination of the 25c to 5c). These were issued in 1944 by the Vichy government, and not placed on sale in Kwangchowan.

Common Design Types

pictured in section at front of book.

AIR POST SEMI-POSTAL STAMPS.

Stamps of Indo-China types V4, V5 and V6 overprinted "KOUANG-TCHEOU" and type of Cameroons V10 inscribed "KOUANG-TCHEOU" were issued in 1942 by the Vichy Government, but were not placed on sale in the territory.

MONGTSEU
(Mengtsz)

Stamps of Indo-China Surcharged in Black **MONGTZE** 仙 六

1903-04 *Perf. 14x13½.* **Unwmkd.**

1 A3 1c *lilac blue* 2.25 2.25
2 " 2c brown, *buff* 1.85 1.85
3 " 4c claret, *lavender* 1.85 1.85
4 " 5c yellow green 2.25 2.25
5 " 10c red 2.50 2.50
6 " 15c gray 3.00 3.00
7 " 20c red, *green* 3.00 3.00
7C " 25c *rose* 275.00 275.00
8 " 25c blue 3.50 3.50
9 " 30c brown, *bistre* 3.50 3.50
10 " 40c red, *straw* 25.00 25.00
11 " 50c carmine, *rose* 135.00 135.00
12 " 50c brown, *azure* ('04) 37.50 37.50
13 " 75c dp. vio., *orange* 35.00 35.00
a. "INDO-CHINE" inverted 15,000.00
14 " 1fr bronze green, *straw* 35.00 35.00
15 " 5fr red lilac, *lavender* 35.00 35.00
Nos. 1-15 (16) 601.20 601.20

Many varieties of the surcharge exist on Nos. 1-15.

Stamps of Indo-China, 1892-1906, Surcharged in Red or Black **Mong-Tseu** 花銀八厘

1906

16 A4 1c olive green (R) 75 75
17 " 2c violet brown, *buff* 75 75
18 " 4c claret, *bluish* (R) 75 75
19 " 5c deep green (R) 75 75
20 " 10c carmine 75 75
21 " 15c orange brown, *blue* 1.00 1.00
22 " 20c red, *green* 1.50 1.50
23 " 25c deep blue 1.50 1.50
24 " 30c pale brown 2.50 2.50
25 " 35c *yellow* (R) 1.75 1.75
26 " 40c *bluish* (R) 1.75 1.75
27 " 50c bistre brown 6.25 6.25
28 A3 75c deep violet, *orange* (R) 16.00 16.00
a. "INDO-CHINE" inverted 16,500.00
29 A4 1fr pale green 7.50 7.50
30 " 2fr brn., *orange* (R) 18.50 18.50
31 A3 5fr red lilac, *lavender* 37.50 37.50
32 A4 10fr orange brown, *green* 50.00 50.00
a. Chinese characters inverted 675.00 675.00
Nos. 16-32 (17) 149.50 149.50

Inverted varieties of the surcharge exist on Nos. 19, 22 and 32.

Stamps of Indo-China, 1907, Surcharged "MONGTSEU" and Value in Chinese in Red or Blue.

1908

33 A5 1c olive brown & blk. 25 25
34 " 2c brown & black 25 25
35 " 4c blue & black 25 25
36 " 5c green & black 50 50
37 " 10c red & black (Bl) 1.00 1.00
38 " 15c violet & black 1.00 1.00
39 A6 20c violet & black 1.50 1.50
40 " 25c blue & black 2.00 2.00
41 " 30c brown & black 1.25 1.25
42 " 35c olive grn. & black 1.50 1.50
43 " 40c brown & black 1.50 1.50
45 " 50c car. & black (Bl) 1.50 1.50
46 A7 75c vermilion & black (Bl) 3.75 3.75
47 A8 1fr car. & black (Bl) 3.75 3.75
48 A9 2fr green & black 5.00 5.00
49 A10 5fr blue & black 42.50 42.50
50 A11 10fr purple & black 42.50 42.50
Nos. 33-50 (17) 110.00 110.00

The Chinese characters overprinted on Nos. 1 to 50 repeat the denomination of the basic stamp.

Issue of 1908 Surcharged with New Values in Cents or Piastres in Black, Red or Blue.

1919

51 A5 2/5c on 1c olive brown & black 25 25
52 " 4/5c on 2c yellow brown & black 25 25
53 " 1 3/5c on 4c blue & black (R) 75 75
54 " 2c on 5c green & black 50 50
55 " 4c on 10c red & black (Bl) 1.00 1.00
56 " 6c on 15c vio. & black 1.00 1.00
57 A6 8c on 20c vio. & black 1.25 1.25
58 " 10c on 25c bl. & black 1.25 1.25
59 " 12c on 30c brn. & blk. 1.25 1.25
60 " 14c on 35c olive green & black 1.25 1.25
a. Closed "4" 5.00 5.00
61 " 16c on 40c yellow brown & black 1.25 1.25
63 " 20c on 50c carmine & black (Bl) 1.25 1.25
64 A7 30c on 75c vermilion & black (Bl) 1.25 1.25
65 A8 40c on 1fr carmine & black (Bl) 3.00 3.00
66 A9 80c on 2fr green & black (R) 2.00 2.00
a. Triple surcharge, one inverted 140.00 140.00
67 A10 2pi on 5fr blue & black (R) 55.00 55.00
a. Triple surcharge, one inverted 160.00 160.00
b. Double surch. 160.00 160.00
68 A11 4pi on 10fr purple & black (R) 7.50 7.50
Nos. 51-68 (17) 80.00 80.00

PAKHOI

Stamps of Indo-China Surcharged in Black **PACKHOI** 仙 六

1903-04 *Perf. 14x13½* **Unwmkd.**

1 A3 1c *lilac blue* 3.00 3.00
2 " 2c brown, *buff* 2.25 2.25
3 " 4c claret, *lavender* 1.50 1.50
4 " 5c yellow green 1.50 1.50
5 " 10c red 1.25 1.25
6 " 15c gray 1.25 1.25
7 " 20c red, *green* 2.50 2.50
8 " 25c blue 2.50 2.50
9 " 25c *rose* ('04) 1.50 1.50
10 " 30c brown, *bistre* 2.75 2.75
11 " 40c red, *straw* 21.00 21.00
12 " 50c carmine, *rose* 150.00 150.00
13 " 50c brn., *azure* ('04) 25.00 25.00
14 " 75c dp. violet, *orange* 25.00 25.00
a. "INDO-CHINE" inverted 12,500.00
15 " 1fr bronze green, *straw* 27.50 27.50
16 " 5fr red lilac, *lavender* 42.50 42.50
Nos. 1-16 (16) 311.00 311.00

Many varieties of the surcharge exist on Nos. 1-16.

Stamps of Indo-China 1892-1906, Surcharged in Red or Black **PAK-HOI** 花銀八厘

1906

17 A4 1c olive green (R) 60 60
18 " 2c violet brown, *buff* 60 60
19 " 4c claret, *bluish* (R) 60 60
20 " 5c deep green (R) 60 60
21 " 10c carmine 60 60
22 " 15c org. brown, *blue* 2.10 2.10
23 " 20c red, *green* 1.50 1.50
24 " 25c deep blue 1.50 1.50
25 " 30c pale brown 1.50 1.50
26 " 35c *yellow* (R) 1.50 1.50
27 " 40c *bluish* (R) 1.35 1.35
28 " 50c bistre brown 2.10 2.10
29 A3 75c deep violet, *orange* (R) 20.00 20.00
30 A4 1fr pale green 12.50 12.50
31 A4 2fr brn., *orange* (R) 17.50 17.50
32 A3 5fr red lilac, *lavender* 40.00 40.00
33 A4 10fr orange brown, *green* 45.00 45.00
Nos. 17-33 (17) 149.55 149.55

Various varieties of the surcharge exist on Nos. 17-24.

Stamps of Indo-China, 1907, Surcharged "PAKHOI" and Value in Chinese in Red or Blue.

1908

34 A5 1c olive brn. & blk. 18 18
35 " 2c brown & black 25 25
36 " 4c blue & black 30 30
37 " 5c green & black 50 50
38 " 10c red & black (Bl) 50 50
39 " 15c violet & black 75 75
40 A6 20c violet & black 75 75
41 " 25c blue & black 75 75
42 " 30c brown & black 1.25 1.25
43 " 35c olive grn. & blk. 1.25 1.25
44 " 40c brown & black 1.25 1.25
46 " 50c car. & blk. (Bl) 1.25 1.25
47 A7 75c vermilion & black (Bl) 2.25 2.25
48 A8 1fr carmine & black (Bl) 2.50 2.50
49 A9 2fr green & black 7.50 7.50
50 A10 5fr blue & black 37.50 37.50
51 A11 10fr purple & black 62.50 62.50
Nos. 34-51 (17) 121.23 121.23

The Chinese characters overprinted on Nos. 1 to 51 repeat the denomination of the basic stamps.

Issue of 1908 Surcharged with New Values in Cents or Piastres in Black, Red or Blue.

1919

52 A5 2/5c on 1c olive brown & black 30 30
a. "PAK-HOI" and Chinese double 50.00 50.00
53 " 4/5c on 2c yellow brown & black 30 30
54 " 1 3/5c on 4c blue & black (R) 30 30
55 " 2c on 5c grn. & black 50 50
56 " 4c on 10c red & black (Bl) 1.25 1.25
57 " 6c on 15c vio. & blk. 30 30
58 A6 8c on 20c vio. & blk. 1.00 1.00
59 " 10c on 25c bl. & blk. 1.25 1.25
60 " 12c on 30c brn. & blk. 60 60
a. "12 CENTS" double 50.00 50.00
61 " 14c on 35c olive green & black 30 30
a. Closed "4" 4.00 4.00
62 " 16c on 40c yellow brown & black 80 80
64 " 20c on 50c carmine & black (Bl) 55 55
65 A7 30c on 75c vermilion & black (Bl) 55 55
66 A8 40c on 1fr carmine & black (Bl) 4.00 4.00
67 A9 80c on 2fr green & black (R) 1.25 1.25
68 A10 2pi on 5fr blue & black (R) 3.75 3.75
69 A11 4pi on 10fr purple & black (R) 7.50 7.50
Nos. 52-69 (17) 24.50 24.50

TCHONGKING
(Chungking)

Stamps of Indo-China Surcharged in Black **TCHONGKING** 仙 六

1903-04 *Perf. 14x13½* **Unwmkd.**

1 A3 1c *lilac blue* 1.50 1.50
2 " 2c brown, *buff* 1.50 1.50
3 " 4c claret, *lavender* 1.50 1.50
4 " 5c yellow green 1.50 1.50
5 " 10c red 1.50 1.50
6 " 15c gray 1.50 1.50
7 " 20c red, *green* 1.50 1.50
8 " 25c blue 17.50 17.50
9 " 25c *rose* ('04) 2.25 2.25
10 " 30c brown, *bistre* 3.50 3.50
11 " 40c red, *straw* 18.50 18.50
12 " 50c carmine, *rose* 100.00 100.00
13 A3 50c brn., *azure* ('04) 55.00 55.00
14 " 75c violet, *orange* 17.50 17.50
15 " 1fr bronze green, *straw* 18.50 18.50
16 " 5fr red lilac, *lavender* 30.00 30.00
Nos. 1-16 (16) 273.25 273.25

Many varieties of the surcharge exist on Nos. 1-14.

Stamps of Indo-China and French China, issued in 1902 with similar overprint, but without Chinese characters, were not officially authorized.

Stamps of Indo-China, 1892-1906, Surcharged in Red or Black **Tch'ong K'ing** 花銀八厘

1906

17 A4 1c olive green (R) 85 85
18 " 2c violet brown, *buff* 85 85
19 " 4c claret, *bluish* (R) 85 85
20 " 5c deep green (R) 85 85
21 " 10c carmine 85 85
22 " 15c orange brown, *blue* 2.50 2.50
23 " 20c red, *green* 85 85
24 " 25c deep blue 1.50 1.50
25 " 30c pale brown 1.35 1.35
26 " 35c *yellow* (R) 1.35 1.35
27 " 40c *bluish* (R) 2.75 2.75
28 " 50c bistre brown 2.75 2.75
29 A3 75c deep violet, *orange* (R) 15.00 15.00
30 A4 1fr pale green 10.00 10.00
31 " 2fr brown, *orange* (R) 10.00 10.00
32 A3 5fr red lilac, *lavender* 47.50 47.50
33 A4 10fr orange brown, *green* 55.00 55.00
Nos. 17-33 (17) 154.80 154.80

Variety "T" omitted in surcharge occurs once in each sheet of Nos. 17-33. Other surcharge varieties exist, such as inverted surcharge on 1c and 2c.

Stamps of Indo-China, 1907, Surcharged "TCHONGKING" and Value in Chinese in Red or Blue.

1908

34 A5 1c olive brown & black 12 12
35 " 2c brown & black 18 18
36 " 4c blue & black 25 25
37 " 5c green & black 60 60
38 " 10c red & black (Bl) 85 85
39 " 15c violet & black 1.15 1.15
40 A6 20c violet & black 1.25 1.25
41 " 25c blue & black 1.25 1.25
42 " 30c brown & black 1.35 1.35
43 " 35c olive green & black 2.25 2.25
44 " 40c brown & black 5.50 5.50
45 " 50c carmine & black (Bl) 3.75 3.75
46 A7 75c vermilion & black (Bl) 3.75 3.75
47 A8 1fr carmine & black (Bl) 3.75 3.75
48 A9 2fr green & black 37.50 37.50
49 A10 5fr blue & black 11.00 11.00
50 A11 10fr pur. & black 125.00 125.00
Nos. 34-50 (17) 199.50 199.50

The Chinese characters overprinted on Nos. 1 to 50 repeat the denomination of the basic stamp.

Issue of 1908 Surcharged with New Values in Cents or Piastres in Black, Red or Blue.

1919

51 A5 2/5c on 1c olive brown & black 25 18
52 " 4/5c on 2c yellow brown & black 25 25
53 " 1 3/5c on 4c blue & black (R) 50 38
54 " 2c on 5c grn. & blk. 30 30
55 " 4c on 10c red & black (Bl) 30 25
56 " 6c on 15c vio. & blk. 30 18
57 A6 8c on 20c vio. & blk. 30 18
58 " 10c on 25c bl. & black 50 50
59 " 12c on 30c brn. & blk. 60 50

60 A6 14c on 35c olive green & black 60 30
a. Closed "4" 5.50 4.25
61 " 16c on 40c yellow brown & black 85 60
a. "16 CENTS" dbl. 37.50 37.50
62 " 20c on 50c carmine & black (Bl) 3.75 3.75
63 A7 30c on 75c vermilion & black (Bl) 75 50
64 A8 40c on 1fr carmine & black (Bl) 85 85
65 A9 80c on 2fr green & black (R) 1.75 1.60
66 A10 2pi on 5fr blue & black (R) 2.25 2.25
67 A11 4pi on 10fr purple & black (R) 2.25 2.25
Nos. 51-67 (17) 16.35 14.82

YUNNAN FOU

(Formerly Yunnan Sen, later known as Kunming)

Stamps of Indo-China Surcharged in Black

YUNNANSEN
仙六

1903-04 ***Perf. 14x13½.*** **Unwmkd.**

1 A3 1c *lilac blue* 3.00 2.50
2 " 2c brown, *buff* 2.25 2.25
3 " 4c claret, *lavender* 2.25 2.00
4 " 5c yellow green 2.25 1.75
5 " 10c red 2.25 1.75
6 " 15c gray 2.50 2.25
7 " 20c red, *green* 3.00 2.50
8 " 25c blue 3.00 2.50
9 " 30c brown, *bistre* 3.00 3.00
10 " 40c red, *straw* 27.50 17.50
11 " 50c carmine, *rose* 175.00 150.00
12 " 50c brown, *azure* ('04) 75.00 75.00
13 " 75c deep violet, *orange* 21.00 18.50
a. "INDO-CHINE" inverted 13,500.00
14 " 1fr bronze green, *straw* 21.00 18.50
15 " 5fr red lilac, *lavender* 30.00 30.00
Nos. 1-15 (15) 373.00 330.00

The Chinese characters overprinted on Nos. 1 to 15 repeat the denomination of the basic stamp.

Many varieties of the surcharge exist on Nos. 1-15.

Stamps of Indo-China, 1892-1906, Surcharged in Red or Black

Yunnan-Fou

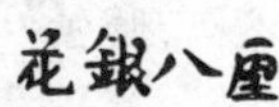

1906 ***Perf. 14x13½.*** **Unwmkd.**

17 A4 1c olive green (R) 1.00 1.00
18 " 2c vio. brown, *buff* 1.00 1.00
19 " 4c claret, *bluish* (R) 1.50 1.50
20 " 5c deep green (R) 1.50 1.50
21 " 10c carmine 1.50 1.50
22 " 15c org. brown, *blue* 2.00 2.00
23 " 20c red, *green* 1.75 1.75
24 " 25c deep blue 1.75 1.75
25 " 30c pale brown 1.75 1.75
26 " 35c *yellow* (R) 2.25 2.25
27 " 40c *bluish* (R) 2.50 2.50
28 " 50c bistre brown 2.50 2.50
29 A3 75c deep violet, *orange* (R) 18.50 18.50
30 A4 1fr pale green 10.00 10.00
31 " 2fr brown, *orange* (R) 10.00 10.00
32 A3 5fr red lilac, *lavender* 27.50 27.50
33 A4 10fr orange brown, *green* 30.00 30.00
Nos. 17-33 (17) 117.00 117.00

Various varieties of the surcharge exist on Nos. 18, 20, 21 and 27.

Stamps of Indo-China, 1907, Surcharged "YUNNANFOU", and Value in Chinese in Red or Blue.

1908

34 A5 1c olive brown & blk. 30 30
35 " 2c brown & black 30 30
36 A5 4c blue & black 30 30
37 " 5c green & black 60 30
38 " 10c red & black (Bl) 30 30
39 " 15c violet & black 1.75 1.25
40 A6 20c violet & black 1.75 1.25
41 " 25c blue & black 1.75 1.35
42 " 30c brown & black 2.10 1.85
43 " 35c olive grn. & blk. 2.10 1.85
44 " 40c brown & black 3.00 3.00
45 " 50c carmine & black (Bl) 3.00 3.00
46 A7 75c vermilion & black (Bl) 3.75 3.25
47 A8 1fr carmine & black (Bl) 5.50 5.00
48 A9 2fr green & black 8.50 8.50
a. "YUNANNFOU" 1000.00 1000.00
49 A10 5fr blue & black 20.00 17.50
a "YUNANNFOU" 1000.00 1000.00
50 A11 10fr purple & black 37.50 37.50
a. "YUNANNFOU" 1000.00 1000.00
Nos. 34-50 (17) 92.50 86.80

The Chinese characters overprinted on Nos. 17 to 50 repeat the denomination of the basic stamp.

1919

Issue of 1908 Surcharged with New Values in Cents or Piastres in Black, Red or Blue.

51 A5 2/5c on 1c olive brown & black 30 25
a. New value double 42.50
52 " 4/5c on 2c yellow brown & black 55 42
53 " 1 3/5c on 4c blue & black (R) 55 50
54 " 2c on 5c grn. & blk. 42 30
a. Triple surcharge 75.00
55 " 4c on 10c red & black (Bl) 42 30
56 " 6c on 15c violet & black 42 30
57 A6 8c on 20c violet & black 75 55
58 " 10c on 25c blue & black 1.10 85
59 " 12c on 30c brown & black 85 60
60 " 14c on 35c olive green & black 1.80 1.50
a. Closed "4" 40.00 40.00
61 " 16c on 40c yellow brn. & black 1.80 1.50
62 " 20c on 50c carmine & black (Bl) 85 65
63 A7 30c on 75c vermilion & black (Bl) 1.80 1.50
64 A8 40c on 1fr carmine & black (Bl) 2.10 1.85
65 A9 80c on 2fr green & black (R) 3.50 3.50
a. Triple surch., one inverted 90.00
66 A10 2pi on 5fr blue & black (R) 18.50 18.50
67 A11 4pi on 10fr purple & black (R) 5.00 5.00
Nos. 51-67 (17) 40.71 38.07

OFFICES IN CRETE

Austria, France, Italy and Great Britain maintained their own post offices in Crete during the period when that country was an autonomous state.

100 CENTIMES=1 FRANC

Liberty, Equality and Fraternity

A1

"Rights of Man"

A2

Liberty and Peace (Symbolized by Olive Branch)

A3

Typographed.

1902-03 ***Perf. 14x13½.*** **Unwmkd.**

1 A1 1c gray 75 75
2 " 2c violet brown 75 75
3 " 3c red orange 75 75
4 " 4c yellow brown 75 75
5 " 5c green 50 38
6 A2 10c rose red 1.00 60
7 " 15c pale red ('03) 1.00 75
8 " 20c brn. violet ('03) 1.25 1.00
9 " 25c blue ('03) 1.50 1.25
10 " 30c lilac ('03) 2.00 1.75
11 A3 40c red & pale blue 3.75 2.75
12 " 50c bistre brown & lavender 6.00 3.50
13 " 1fr claret & olive green 8.50 7.50
14 " 2fr gray violet & yellow 11.00 8.50
15 " 5fr dark blue & buff 16.00 12.50
Nos. 1-15 (15) 55.50 43.48

A4

A5

Black Surcharge.

1903

16 A4 1pi on 25c blue 10.00 10.00
17 A5 2pi on 50c bistre brown & lavender 18.50 18.50
18 " 4pi on 1fr claret & olive green 32.50 30.00
19 " 8pi on 2fr gray violet & yellow 50.00 40.00
20 " 20pi on 5fr dark blue & buff 67.50 50.00
Nos. 16-20 (5) 178.50 148.50

OFFICES IN EGYPT

French post offices formerly maintained in Alexandria and Port Said.

100 CENTIMES=1 FRANC

ALEXANDRIA

A1

French Stamps Overprinted in Red, Blue or Black.

Perf. 14x13½

1899-1900 **Unwmkd.**

1 A1 1c *lilac blue* (R) 40 40
a. Double overprint 30.00
b. Triple overprint 30.00
2 " 2c brown, *buff* (Bl) 60 60
3 " 3c gray, *grayish* (Bl) 85 40
4 A1 4c claret, *lavender* (Bl) 60 60
5 " 5c yellow green, (I) (R) 1.00 85
a. Type II (R) 47.50 35.00
6 " 10c *lavender*, (I) (R) 2.00 1.85
a. Type II (R) 16.50 10.00
7 " 15c blue (R) 2.00 1.25
8 " 20c red, *green* 4.00 2.25
a. Double ovpt. 12.00
9 " 25c *rose* (R) 1.75 1.00
a. Inverted overprint 17.50
b. Double overprint, one inverted 30.00
10 " 30c brown, *bistre* 5.00 3.00
11 " 40c red, *straw* 4.00 4.00
12 " 50c carmine, *rose* (II) 7.00 5.00
a. Type I 50.00 5.00
13 " 1fr bronze green, *straw* 7.00 5.00
14 " 2fr brown, *azure* ('00) 30.00 27.50
15 " 5fr red lilac, *lavender* 40.00 40.00
Nos. 1-15 (15) 106.20 93.70

A2

A3

A4

1902-03

16 A2 1c gray 8 8
17 " 2c violet brown 15 10
18 " 3c red orange 15 9
19 " 4c yellow brown 17 10
20 " 5c green 30 15
21 A3 10c rose red 45 15
22 " 15c orange 30 20
a. 15c pale red ('03) 50 40
23 " 20c brown violet ('03) 50 25
24 " 25c blue ('03) 20 4
25 " 30c violet ('03) 1.75 1.00
26 A4 40c red & pale blue 1.35 65
27 " 50c bistre brown & lavender 2.00 75
28 " 1fr claret & olive green 2.25 75
29 " 2fr gray vio. & yel. 4.50 3.75
30 " 5fr dark blue & buff 6.00 5.00
Nos. 16-30 (15) 20.15 13.06

The 2c, 5c, 10c, 20c and 25c exist imperf. Price, each $15.

See also Nos. 77-86.

Stamps of 1902-03 Surcharged Locally in Black **4 Mill.**

1921

31 A2 2m on 5c green 1.65 1.00
32 " 3m on 3c red orange 1.85 1.35
a. Larger numeral 20.00 17.50
33 A3 4m on 10c rose 1.25 1.00
34 A2 5m on 1c dark gray 1.65 1.40
35 " 5m on 4c yellow brn. 1.65 1.65
36 A3 6m on 15c orange 85 85
a. Larger numeral 17.50 17.50
37 " 8m on 20c brn. vio. 1.25 1.10
a. Larger numeral 10.00 10.00
38 " 10m on 25c blue 60 40
a. Inverted surcharge 7.00 7.00
b. Double surcharge 7.00 7.00
39 " 12m on 30c violet 5.00 4.50
40 A2 15m on 2c violet brn. 1.85 1.50

Surcharged **15 Mill.**

41 A4 15m on 40c red & pale blue 5.00 4.00
42 " 15m on 50c bistre brn. & lavender 2.00 2.00
43 " 30m on 1fr claret & olive green 65.00 57.50

44 A4 60m on 2fr gray violet & yellow 85.00 85.00
a. Larger numeral 165.00 165.00
45 " 150m on 5fr dark blue & buff 120.00 120.00

Port Said Nos. 20 and 19 Surcharged like Nos. 32 and 40.

45A A2 3m on 3c red orge. 32.50 32.50
46 " 15m on 2c vio. brn. 32.50 32.50

Alexandria No. 28 Surcharged with Two New Values.

1921

46A A4 30m on 15m on 1fr claret & olive green 325.00 325.00

The surcharge "15 Mill." was made in error and is cancelled by a bar.

The surcharges were lithographed on Nos. 31, 33, 38, 39 and 42 and typographed on the other stamps of the 1921 issue. Nos. 34, 36 and 37 were surcharged by both methods.

Alexandria Stamps of 1902-03 Surcharged in Paris — 2 MILLIEMES

1921-23

47 A2 1m on 1c gray 70 70
48 " 2m on 5c green 40 40
49 A3 4m on 10c rose 1.00 90
50 " 4m on 10c green ('23) 60 50
51 A2 5m on 3c red orange ('23) 2.00 1.65
52 A3 6m on 15c orange 50 45
53 " 8m on 20c brn. violet 30 25
54 " 10m on 25c blue 30 25
55 " 10m on 30c violet 90 80
56 " 15m on 50c blue ('23) 80 50

Surcharged — 15 MILLIÈMES

57 A4 15m on 50c bistre brown & lavender 90 80
58 " 30m on 1fr claret & olive green 80 55
59 " 60m on 2fr gray vio. & yellow *700.00 700.00*
60 " 60m on 2fr orange & pale blue ('23) 4.00 2.50
61 " 150m on 5fr blue & buff 3.25 2.25
Nos. 47-58, 60-61 (14) 16.45 12.50

Stamps and Types of 1902-03 Surcharged with New Values and Bars in Black.

1925

62 A2 1m on 1c gray 20 20
63 " 2m on 5c orange 20 20
64 " 2m on 5c green 50 50
65 A3 4m on 10c green 20 20
66 A2 5m on 3c red orange 20 20
67 A3 6m on 15c orange 30 30
68 " 8m on 20c brn. vio. 20 20
69 " 10m on 25c blue 10 10
70 " 15m on 50c blue 40 35
71 A4 30m on 1fr claret & olive green 40 35
72 " 60m on 2fr orange & pale blue 1.20 1.00
73 " 150m on 5fr dark blue & buff 1.10 90
Nos. 62-73 (12) 5.00 4.50

Types of 1902-03 Issue.

1927-28

77 A2 3m orange ('28) 50 45
81 A3 15m slate blue 50 45
82 " 20m rose lilac ('28) 1.50 1.00
84 A4 50m orange & blue 3.50 2.75
85 " 100m slate blue & buff 4.00 2.85
86 " 250m gray grn. & red 7.00 5.25
Nos. 77-86 (6) 17.00 12.75

SEMI-POSTAL STAMPS.

Regular Issue of 1902-03 Surcharged in Carmine — +5c

1915 *Perf. 14x13½.* **Unwmkd.**

B1 A3 10c+5c rose 20 20

Sinking Fund Issue.

Type of 1902-03 Issue Surcharged in Blue or Black — +5 Mm Caisse d'Amortissement

1927-30

B2 A3 15m+5m dp. orange 65 65
B3 " 15m+5m red violet ('28) 1.20 1.20
a. 15m+5m violet ('30) 2.50 2.50

Type of 1902-03 Issue Surcharged as in 1927-28.

1929

B4 A3 15m+5m fawn 1.85 1.85

POSTAGE DUE STAMPS.

Postage Due Stamps of France, 1893-1920, Surcharged in Paris in Black — 2 MILLIEMES

1922 *Perf. 14x13½.* **Unwmkd.**

J1 D2 2m on 5c blue 50 50
J2 " 4m on 10c brown 50 50
J3 " 10m on 30c rose red 50 50
J4 " 15m on 50c brown violet 70 70
J5 " 30m on 1fr red brown, *straw* 1.35 1.35
Nos. J1-J5 (5) 3.55 3.55

D3

1928 Typographed.

J6 D3 1m slate 70 70
J7 " 2m light blue 45 45
J8 " 4m lilac rose 55 55
J9 " 5m gray green 50 50
J10 " 10m light red 55 55
J11 " 20m violet brown 45 45
J12 " 30m green 1.35 1.35
J13 " 40m light violet 1.00 1.00
Nos. J6-J13 (8) 5.55 5.55

Nos. J6 to J13 were also available for use in Port Said.

PORT SAID

A1

Stamps of France Overprinted in Red, Blue or Black.

Perf. 14x13½.

1899-1900 **Unwmkd.**

1 A1 1c *lilac blue* (R) 55 40
2 " 2c brown, *buff* (Bl) 65 60
3 " 3c gray, *grayish* (Bl) 85 60
4 " 4c claret, *lavender* (Bl) 85 60
5 " 5c yel. grn. (I) (R) 2.25 1.65
a. Type II (R) 17.50 4.00
6 " 10c *lavender* (I) (R) 3.00 3.00
a. Type II (R) 22.50 15.00
7 " 15c blue (R) 3.00 2.00
8 " 20c red, *green* 4.00 2.00
9 " 25c *rose* (R) 3.00 60
a. Double overprint 45.00
10 " 30c brown, *bistre* 3.00 2.25
a. Inverted overprint 40.00
11 " 40c red, *straw* 4.00 2.35
12 " 50c carmine, *rose* (II) 6.00 4.00
a. Type I 100.00 35.00
b. Dbl. ovpt. (II) 65.00
13 " 1fr bronze green, *straw* 8.00 5.00
14 " 2fr brn., *azure* ('00) 25.00 16.50
15 A1 5fr red lilac, *lavender* 37.50 27.50
Nos. 1-15 (15) 101.65 69.05

Regular Issue Surcharged in Red — PORT SAID VINGT CINQ

1899

16 A1 25c on 10c *lavender* 50.00 10.00

With Additional Surcharge "25."

17 A1 25c on 10c *lavender* 150.00 60.00

A2

A3

A4

1902-03 Typographed.

18 A2 1c gray 20 15
19 " 2c violet brown 20 15
20 " 3c red orange 20 15
21 " 4c yellow brown 30 20
22 " 5c blue green 30 25
a. 5c yellow green 1.00 85
23 A3 10c rose red 50 25
24 " 15c pale red ('03) 70 40
a. 15c orange 70 40
25 " 20c brown violet ('03) 60 30
26 " 25c blue ('03) 70 40
27 " 30c violet ('03) 1.65 1.25
28 A4 40c red & pale blue 1.50 1.00
29 " 50c bistre brown & lavender 2.25 1.35
30 " 1fr claret & olive green 2.50 2.00
31 " 2fr gray vio. & yellow 4.00 3.75
32 " 5fr dark blue & buff 9.00 8.50
Nos. 18-32 (15) 24.60 20.10

See Nos. 83-92.

Stamps of 1902-03 Surcharged Locally — 2 Milliemes

1921

33 A2 2m on 5c green 2.35 2.35
a. Inverted surcharge 12.00 12.00
34 A3 4m on 10c rose 2.35 2.35
a. Inverted surcharge 12.00 12.00
35 A2 5m on 1c gray 2.50 2.50
a. Inverted surcharge 16.50 16.50
b. "5" inverted 200.00 200.00
c. Surcharged "2 Milliemes" 13.50 13.00
36 " 5m on 2c violet brown 4.00 4.00
a. Surcharged "2 Milliemes" 16.50 16.50
b. Same as "a", inverted 27.50 27.50
37 " 5m on 3c red orange 3.00 3.00
a. Inverted surcharge 12.00 12.00
b. On Alexandria #18 110.00 110.00
38 " 5m on 4c yel. brn. 2.50 2.50
a. Inverted surcharge 17.50 17.50
39 " 10m on 2c violet brown 3.00 3.00
40 " 10m on 4c yel. brn. 7.00 7.00
a. Inverted surcharge 17.50 17.50
41 A3 10m on 25c blue 2.00 2.00
a. Inverted surcharge 15.00 15.00
42 " 12m on 30c violet 13.50 13.50
43 A2 15m on 4c yel. brn. 2.35 2.35
a. Inverted surcharge 16.50 16.50
44 A3 15m on 15c pale red 15.00 15.00
a. Inverted surcharge 25.00 25.00
45 " 15m on 20c brn. vio. 15.00 15.00
a. Inverted surcharge 27.50 27.50
46 A4 30m on 50c bistre brn. & lavender 120.00 120.00
47 A4 60m on 50c bistre brn. & lavender 125.00 125.00
48 " 150m on 50c bistre brn. & lavender 150.00 150.00

Nos. 46, 47 and 48 have a bar between the numerals and "Milliemes", which is in capital letters.

Same Surcharge on Stamps of French Offices in Turkey, 1902-03.

49 A2 2m on 2c vio. brn. 25.00 25.00
50 " 5m on 1c gray 25.00 25.00
a. "5" inverted 200.00 200.00

Stamps of 1902-03 Surcharged — 15 MILLIEMES

51 A4 15m on 40c red & pale blue 16.50 16.00
a. "MILLtEMES" 40.00 40.00
52 " 15m on 50c bistre brn. & lavender 25.00 25.00
a. "MILLtEMES" 100.00 100.00
b. Bar below 15 17.50 17.50
53 " 30m on 1fr claret & olive green 90.00 90.00
a. "MILLtEMES" 250.00 250.00
54 " 60m on 2fr gray violet & yellow 30.00 30.00
a. "MILLtEMES" 110.00 110.00
55 " 150m on 5fr dark blue & buff 90.00 90.00
a. "MILLtEMES" 250.00 250.00

Stamps of 1902-03 Surcharged in Paris — 2 MILLIEMES

1921-23

56 A2 1m on 1c gray 30 30
57 " 2m on 5c green 30 30
58 A3 4m on 10c rose 85 85
59 A2 5m on 3c red orange 2.75 2.75
60 A3 6m on 15c orange 90 90
a. 6m on 15c pale red 4.00 4.00
61 " 8m on 20c brown violet 60 60
62 " 10m on 25c blue 1.00 1.00
63 " 10m on 30c violet 1.75 1.75
64 " 15m on 50c blue 1.50 1.50

Surcharged — 15 MILLIÈMES

65 A4 15m on 50c bistre brown & lavender 1.50 1.50
66 " 30m on 1fr claret & olive green 1.75 1.75
67 " 60m on 2fr gray violet & yellow 37.50 37.50
68 " 60m on 2fr orange & pale blue 2.65 2.65
69 " 150m on 5fr blue & buff 2.35 2.35
Nos. 56-69 (14) 55.70 55.70

Stamps and Types of 1902-03 Surcharged with New Values and Bars

1925

70 A2 1m on 1c gray 20 20
71 " 2m on 5c green 20 20
72 A3 4m on 10c rose red 20 20
73 A2 5m on 3c red orange 20 20
74 A3 6m on 15c orange 20 20
75 " 8m on 20c brn. vio. 20 20
76 " 10m on 25c blue 30 30
77 " 15m on 50c blue 30 30
78 A4 30m on 1fr claret & olive green 40 40
79 " 60m on 2fr orange & pale blue 55 55
80 " 150m on 5fr dark blue & buff 75 75
Nos. 70-80 (11) 3.50 3.50

Types of 1902-03 Issue.

1927-28

83 A2 3m orange ('28) 40 40
87 A3 15m slate blue 45 45
88 " 20m rose lilac ('28) 60 60
90 A4 50m orange & blue 75 75
91 " 100m slate blue & buff 1.10 1.10
92 " 250m gray green & red 2.25 2.25
Nos. 83-92 (6) 5.55 5.55

SEMI-POSTAL STAMPS.

Regular Issue of 1902-03 Surcharged in Carmine **+5c**

1915 *Perf. 14x13½.* Unwmkd.

B1 A3 10c+5c rose 65 65

Sinking Fund Issue.

Type of 1902-03 Issue Surcharged in Blue or Black **+5 Mm** Caisse d'Amortissement

1927-30

B2 A3 15m+5m deep orange (Bl) 65 65
B3 " 15m+5m red violet ('28) 65 65
a. 15m+5m violet ('30) 1.50 1.50
B4 " 15m+5m fawn ('29) 75 75

POSTAGE DUE STAMPS.

Postage Due Stamps of France, 1893–1906, Surcharged Locally in Black **15 Millièmes**

1921 *Perf. 14x13½.* **Unwmkd.**

J1 D2 12m on 10c brown 16.50 16.50
J2 " 15m on 5c blue 18.50 18.50
J3 " 30m on 20c olive green 23.50 23.50
a. Invtd. surch. 150.00 150.00
J4 " 30m on 50c red violet *1350.00 1350.00*

Same Surcharged in Red or Blue **4 MILLIEMES**

1921

J5 D2 2m on 5c blue (R) 16.50 16.50
a. Blue surcharge 110.00 110.00
J6 " 4m on 10c brn. (Bl) 18.50 18.50
a. Surcharged "15 Millièmes" 225.00 225.00
J7 " 10m on 30c red (Bl) 16.50 16.50
a. Inverted surcharge 35.00 35.00
J8 " 15m on 50c brown violet (Bl) 23.50 23.50
a. Inverted surch. 40.00 40.00

Nos. J5–J8 exist with second "M" in "Milliemes" inverted, also with final "S" omitted.

Alexandria Nos. J6–J13 were also available for use in Port Said.

French Offices In Morocco

See French Morocco.

FRENCH OFFICES IN TURKISH EMPIRE (Levant)

Various powers maintained post offices in the Turkish Empire before World War I by authority of treaties which ended with the signing of the Treaty of Lausanne in 1923. The foreign post offices were closed Oct. 27, 1923.

100 CENTIMES=1 FRANC
25 CENTIMES=40 PARAS=1 PIASTRE

A1

Stamps of France Surcharged in Black or Red.
Perf. 14x13½.

1885–1901 Unwmkd.

1 A1 1pi on 25c yellow, *straw* ('85) 150.00 4.00
a. Inverted surch. 900.00 375.00
2 " 1pi on 25c *rose* (R) ('86) 60 20
a. Inverted surch. 70.00 55.00
3 " 2pi on 50c carmine, *rose* (II) ('90) 5.50 50
a. Type I ('01) 110.00 11.00
4 " 3pi on 75c carmine, *rose* ('85) 8.00 3.50
5 " 4pi on 1fr bronze green, *straw* ('85) 6.00 2.00
6 " 8pi on 2fr brown, *azure* ('00) 11.00 7.00
7 " 20pi on 5fr red lilac, *lavender* ('90) 27.50 13.50

A2

A3

A4

A5

A6

Typographed.

1902–07 *Perf. 14x13½.*

21 A2 1c gray 12 8
22 " 2c violet brown 18 15
23 " 3c red orange 15 15
24 " 4c yellow brown 45 40
a. Imperf., pair 20.00
25 A2 5c green ('06) 25 15
26 A3 10c rose red 30 12
27 " 15c pale red ('03) 65 40
28 " 20c brown violet ('03) 65 40
29 " 25c blue ('07) 17.50 15.00
a. Imperf., pair 165.00
30 A3 30c lilac ('03) 1.20 60
31 A4 40c red & pale blue 1.20 60
32 " 50c bistre brown & lavender ('07) 60.00 55.00
a. Imperf., pair 400.00
33 A4 1fr claret & olive green ('07) 150.00 150.00
a. Imperf., pair 450.00

Black Surcharge.

34 A5 1pi on 25c blue ('03) 25 4
a. Second "1" omitted 9.00 8.50
b. Double surch. 13.50 10.00
35 A6 2pi on 50c bistre brn. & lavender 50 20
36 " 4pi on 1fr claret & olive green 80 50
a. Imperf., pair 275.00
37 A6 8pi on 2fr gray violet & yellow 6.00 3.75
38 A6 20pi on 5fr dark blue & buff 1.35 1.00
Nos. 21–38 (18) 241.55 228.54

Nos. 29, 32–33 were used during the early part of 1907 in the French Offices at Harrar and Diredawa, Ethiopia. Djibouti and Port Said stamps were also used.

No. 27 Surcharged in Green **1 Piastre Beyrouth**

1905

39 A3 1pi on 15c pale red 550.00 100.00
a. "Piastte" *2000.00 325.00*

Stamps of France 1900-21 Surcharged:

1 PIASTRE 30 PARAS *a* — **20 PARAS** *b* — **15 PIASTRES** *c*

1921-22

40 A22 (*a*) 30pa on 5c green 20 15
41 " (") 30pa on 5c orange 20 15
42 " (*b*) 1pi 20pa on 10c red 25 20
43 " (") 1pi 20pa on 10c grn. 25 15
44 " (") 3pi 30pa on 25c blue 25 10
45 " (") 4pi 20pa on 30c orange 25 15
a. "4" omitted
46 A20 (") 7pi 20pa on 50c blue 20 10
47 A18 (*c*) 15pi on 1fr claret & olive green 40 30
48 " (") 30pi on 2fr orange & pale blue 3.75 2.25
49 " (") 75pi on 5fr dark blue & buff 2.35 1.00
Nos. 40-49 (10) 8.10 4.55

Stamps of France, 1903-07, Handstamped **3 PIASTRES 30 PARAS**

1923

52 A22 1pi 20pa on 10c red 16.50 16.50
54 A20 3pi 30pa on 15c gray green 7.50 7.50
55 A22 7pi 20pa on 35c vio. 7.50 7.50
a. 1pi 20pa on 35c violet (error) 250.00 250.00
b. Double surch. 40.00

CAVALLE
(Cavalla)

A1

A2

Stamps of France Overprinted or Surcharged in Red, Blue or Black
Perf. 14x13½.

1893–1900 Unwmkd.

1 A1 5c green, *greenish* (R) 5.00 4.00
a. Double overprint 12.00
2 " 5c yellow green (I) ('00) (R) 5.00 4.00
3 " 10c *lavender* (II) (Bl) 6.00 5.00
a. 10c *lavender* (I) 55.00 50.00
4 " 15c blue (R) 7.00 6.00
5 A2 1pi on 25c *rose* (Bl) 8.00 7.00
6 " 2pi on 50c carmine, *rose* (Bl) 27.50 20.00
7 " 4pi on 1fr bronze green, *straw* (R) 35.00 25.00
8 " 8pi on 2fr brown, *azure* ('00) (Bk) 32.50 30.00
Nos. 1-8 (8) 126.00 101.00

A3

A4

A5

A6

1902-03

9 A3 5c green 40 30
10 A4 10c rose red ('03) 50 40
11 " 15c orange 60 40
a. 15c pale red ('03) 2.50 2.50

Surcharged in Black.

12 A5 1pi on 25c blue 1.00 60
13 A6 2pi on 50c bistre brn. & lavender 1.85 1.40
14 " 4pi on 1fr claret & olive green 3.00 2.35
15 " 8pi on 2fr gray violet & yellow 4.75 4.50
Nos. 9-15 (7) 12.10 9.95

DEDEAGH
(Dedeagatch)

A1

A2

Stamps of France Overprinted or Surcharged in Red, Blue or Black.
Perf. 14x13½.

1893-1900 Unwmkd.

1 A1 5c green, *greenish* (II) (R) 4.00 3.00
2 " 5c yellow green (I) ('00) (R) 4.00 4.00
3 " 10c *lavender* (II) (Bl) 6.00 5.00
a. Type I 12.00 8.00
4 " 15c blue (R) 8.00 5.00
5 A2 1pi on 25c *rose* (Bl 10.00 8.00
6 " 2pi on 50c carmine, *rose* (Bl) 16.50 13.50
7 " 4pi on 1fr bronze green, *straw* (R) 20.00 13.50
8 " 8pi on 2fr brown, *azure* ('00) (Bk) 30.00 25.00
Nos. 1-8 (8) 98.50 77.00

A3

A4

A5

A6

1902–03

9 A3 5c green 30 25
10 A4 10c rose red ('03) 40 25
11 " 15c orange 70 30

Black Surcharge.

15 A5 1pi on 25c blue ('03) 80 40
16 A6 2pi on 50c bistre brown & lavender 1.85 1.50
a. Double surcharge 40.00
17 " 4pi on 1fr claret & olive green 4.00 3.50
18 " 8pi on 2fr gray violet & yellow 6.00 5.00
Nos. 9-18 (7) 14.05 11.20

PORT LAGOS

A1

A2

Stamps of France Overprinted or Surcharged in Red or Blue.

1893 ***Perf. 14x13½*** **Unwmkd.**

1 A1 5c green, *greenish* (R) 8.00 6.00
2 " 10c *lavender* (Bl) 14.00 9.00
3 " 15c blue (R) 27.50 22.50
4 A2 1pi on 25c *rose* 20.00 18.50
5 " 2pi on 50c carmine, *rose* (Bl) 45.00 35.00
6 " 4pi on 1fr bronze green, *straw* (R) 35.00 32.50

VATHY

(Samos)

A1

A2

Stamps of France Overprinted or Surcharged in Red, Blue or Black.

Perf. 14x13½

1894-1900 **Unwmkd.**

1 A1 5c green, *greenish* (R) 3.50 3.00
2 " 5c yellow green (I) ('00) (R) 3.50 3.00
a. Type II 27.50 20.00
3 " 10c *lavender* (I)(Bl) 4.50 4.50
a. Type II 15.00 10.00
4 " 15c blue (R) 5.00 5.00
5 A2 1pi on 25c *rose* (Bl) 5.75 4.50
6 " 2pi on 50c carmine, *rose* (Bl) 12.00 11.00
7 " 4pi on 1fr bronze green, *straw* (R) 12.00 12.00
8 " 8pi on 2fr brown, *azure* ('00) (Bk) 27.50 27.50
9 " 20pi on 5fr lilac, *lavender* ('00) (Bk) 45.00 40.00
Nos. 1-9 (9) 118.75 110.50

OFFICES IN ZANZIBAR

Until 1906 France maintained post offices in the Sultanate of Zanzibar, but in that year Great Britain assumed direct control over this protectorate and the French withdrew their postal system.

16 ANNAS=1 RUPEE

A1

A2

Stamps of France Surcharged in Red, Blue or Black.

1894-96 ***Perf. 14x13½*** **Unwmkd.**

1 A1 ½a on 5c green, *greenish* (R) 1.50 1.00
2 " 1a on 10c *lavender* (Bl) 4.00 3.00
3 " 1½a on 15c blue ('96) (R) 7.00 6.00
a. "ANNAS" 35.00 35.00
4 " 2a on 20c red, *green* ('96) (Bk) 4.00 3.00
5 " 2½a on 25c *rose* (Bl) 2.50 1.50
a. Double surcharge 15.00
6 " 3a on 30c brown, *bistre* ('96) (Bk) 6.00 5.00
7 " 4a on 40c red, *straw* ('96) (Bk) 6.50 5.50
8 " 5a on 50c carmine, *rose* (Bl) 9.50 8.00
9 " 7½a on 75c violet, *orange* ('96) (R) 150.00 140.00
10 " 10a on 1fr bronze green, *straw* (R) 14.00 12.00
11 " 50a on 5fr red lilac, *lavender* ('96) (Bk) 120.00 110.00

1894

12 A2 ½a & 5c on 1c *lilac blue* (R) 70.00 60.00
13 " 1a & 10c on 3c gray, *grayish* (R) 65.00 65.00
14 " 2½a & 25c on 4c claret, *lavender* (Bk) 100.00 100.00
15 " 5a & 50c on 20c red, *green* (Bk) 100.00 100.00
16 " 10a & 1fr on 40c red, *straw* (Bk) 175.00 175.00

There are two distinct types of the figures 5c, four of the 25c and three of each of the others of this series.

A3

Surcharged in Red, Blue or Black.

1896-1900

17 A3 ½a on 5c green, *greenish* (R) 2.00 2.00
18 " ½a on 5c yellow green (I) (R) 2.25 2.00
a. Type II 2.25 2.00
19 " 1a on 10c *lavender* (II) (Bl) 2.50 2.00
a. Type I 3.50 3.50
20 " 1½a on 15c blue (R) 1.65 1.40
21 " 2a on 20c red, *green* (Bk) 1.65 1.40
a. "ZANZIBAR" double 27.50 27.50
b. "ZANZIBAR" triple 35.00
22 " 2½a on 25c *rose* (Bl) 1.65 1.40
23 " 3a on 30c brown, *bistre* (Bk) 2.25 2.25
24 " 4a on 40c red, *straw* (Bk) 1.85 1.85
25 " 5a on 50c rose, *rose* (II) (Bl) 11.00 8.00
a. Type I 30.00 28.50
26 " 10a on 1fr bronze grn., *straw* (R) 5.00 4.00
27 " 20a on 2fr brown, *azure* (Bk) 7.00 6.50
a. "ZANZIBAS" 250.00 250.00
28 " 50a on 5fr lilac, *lavender* (Bk) 15.00 13.50
a. "ZANZIBAS" *850.00 850.00*
Nos. 17-28 (12) 53.80 46.30

A4

A5

1897

29 A4 2½a & 25c on ½a on 5c green, *greenish* 300.00 70.00
30 " 2½a & 25c on 1a on 10c *lavender* 1000.00 300.00
31 " 2½a & 25c on 1½a on 15c blue 1000.00 300.00
32 A5 5a & 50c on 3a on 30c brown, *bistre* 1000.00 300.00
33 " 5a & 50c on 4a on 40c red, *straw* 1000.00 300.00

PosteFrance 2½ Annas 25c. ZANZIBAR
A6

PosteFrance 5 Annas 50c. ZANZIBAR
A7

Printed on the Margins of Sheets of French Stamps.

1897

34 A6 2½a & 25c green, *greenish* 525.00
35 " 2½a & 25c *lavender* 850.00
36 " 2½a & 25c blue 850.00
37 A7 5a & 50c brn., *bis.* 850.00
38 " 5a & 50c red, *straw* 850.00

There are several varieties of figures in the above surcharges.

A8

A9

A10

Surcharged in Red or Black.

1902-03

39 A8 ½a on 5c green (R) 1.50 1.20
40 A9 1a on 10c rose red ('03) 2.00 1.85
41 " 1½a on 15c pale red ('03) 4.00 3.75
42 " 2a on 20c brown violet ('03) 5.00 4.00
43 " 2½a on 25c blue ('03) 4.50 4.00
44 " 3a on 30c lilac ('03) 4.00 3.50
a. 5a on 30c (error) 90.00 90.00
45 A10 4a on 40c red & pale blue 7.00 6.50
46 " 5a on 50c bistre brn. & lavender 5.00 4.50
47 " 10a on 1fr claret & olive green 9.00 8.00
48 " 20a on 2fr gray violet & yellow 17.50 17.50
49 " 50a on 5fr dark blue & buff 25.00 25.00
Nos. 39-49 (11) 84.50 79.80

Nos. 23-24
Surcharged in Black:

25 ▬ 2½ *a*   50 ▬ 5 *b*

1 fr ▬ 10 *c*

1904

50 A3(*a*) 25(c) & 2½(a) on 4a on 40c red, *straw* 400.00
51 " (*b*) 50(c) & 5(a) on 3a on 30c brown, *bistre* 450.00
52 A3 (*b*) 50(c) & 5(a) on 4a on 40c red, *straw* 450.00
53 " (*c*) 1fr & 10(a) on 3a on 30c brown, *bistre* 650.00
54 " (") 1fr & 10(a) on 4a on 40c red, *straw* 700.00

Stamps of 1902-03 Issue Surcharged in Red or Black:

2 25 *d*   25c 2½ *e*

50c 1 fr

cinq *f*   dix *g*

55 A8(*d*) 25(c) & 2(a) on ½a on 5c green (R) 35.00
56 A9(*e*) 25c & 2½(a) on 1a on 10c rose red 40.00
a. Inverted surcharge 400.00
57 "(") 25c & 2½(a) on 3c on 30c lilac 650.00
a. Inverted surcharge 700.00
b. Double surcharge, both inverted 1000.00
58 " (*f*) 50c & 5(a) on 3a on 30c lilac 450.00
59 " (*g*) 1fr & 10(a) on 3a on 30c lilac 525.00

Postage Due Stamps of 1897 Issue With Various Surcharges.

Overprinted "Timbre" in Red.

60 D1 ½a on 5c blue 140.00

Overprinted "Affrancht" in Black.

61 D1 1a on 10c brown 140.00

With Red Bars Across "CHIFFRE" and "TAXE"

62 D1 1½a on 15c green 275.00

The illustrations are not exact reproductions of the new surcharges but are merely intended to show their relative positions and general styles.

POSTAGE DUE STAMPS.

D1

Stamps of France Surcharged in Red, Blue or Black.

1897 ***Perf. 14x13½.*** **Unwmkd.**

J1 D1 ½a on 5c blue (R) 5.00 3.25
J2 " 1a on 10c brown (Bl) 5.00 2.75
a. Inverted surcharge 40.00 40.00
J3 " 1½a on 15c green (R) 7.00 3.75
J4 " 3a on 30c carmine (Bk) 8.00 5.75
J5 " 5a on 50c lilac (Bl) 7.00 5.00
a. 2½a on 50c lilac (Bl) 325.00 325.00
Nos. J1-J5 (5) 32.00 20.50

Methods and style of listing are detailed in "Special Notices" at the front of this volume.

FRENCH COLONIES

From 1859 to 1906 and in 1944 and 1945 special stamps were issued for use in all French Colonies which did not have stamps of their own.

100 CENTIMES=1 FRANC

Perforations: Nos. 1–45 are known variously perforated unofficially.

Gum: Many of Nos. 1-45 were issued without gum. Some were gummed locally.

Reprints: Nos. 1-7, 9-12, 24, 26-42, 44 and 45 were reprinted officially in 1887. These reprints are ungummed and the colors of both design and paper are deeper or brighter than the originals. Price for Nos. 1-6, $30 each.

> Prices of early French Colonies stamps vary according to condition. Quotations for Nos. 1–23 are for fine copies. Very fine to superb specimens sell at much higher prices, and inferior or poor copies sell at reduced prices, depending on the condition of the individual specimen.

Eagle and Crown
A1

Typographed.

1859–65 *Imperf.* Unwmkd.

No.	Type	Description	Unused	Used
1	A1	1c olive green, *pale blue* ('62)	10.00	11.00
2	"	5c yellow green, *greenish* ('62)	11.00	9.00
3	"	10c bistre, *yellowish*	13.00	4.50
		a. Pair, one sideways	500.00	250.00
4	"	20c blue, *bluish* ('65)	16.00	9.00
5	"	40c orange, *yellowish*	10.00	5.50
6	"	80c carmine rose, *pinkish* ('65)	35.00	32.50

Napoleon III
A2 A3

Ceres Napoleon III
A4 A5

1871–72 *Imperf.*

No.	Type	Description	Unused	Used
7	A2	1c olive green, *pale blue* ('72)	40.00	32.50
8	A3	5c yellow green, *greenish* ('72)	450.00	325.00
9	A4	10c bistre, *yellowish*	175.00	80.00
		a. Tête bêche pair	16,500.00	12,500.00
10	"	15c bistre, *yellowish* ('72)	150.00	9.00
11	"	20c blue, *bluish*	275.00	80.00
		a. Tête bêche pair		9000.00
12	"	25c blue, *bluish* ('72)	90.00	9.00
13	A5	30c brown, *yellowish*	80.00	22.50
14	A4	40c orange, *yellowish* (I)	130.00	9.00
		a. Type II	1600.00	300.00
		b. Pair, types I & II	3750.00	900.00
15	A5	80c rose, *pinkish*	450.00	65.00

For types I and II of 40c see illustrations over No. 1 of France.

Ceres
A6 A7

1872–77 *Imperf.*

No.	Type	Description	Unused	Used
16	A6	1c olive green, *pale blue* ('73)	10.00	11.00
17	"	2c red brown, *yellowish*	275.00	325.00
18	"	4c gray ('76)	*5500.00*	325.00
19	"	5c green, *pale blue*	10.00	7.00
20	A7	10c bistre, *rose* ('76)	110.00	9.00
21	"	15c bistre ('77)	300.00	70.00
22	"	30c brown, *yellowish*	55.00	12.00
23	"	80c rose, *pinkish* ('73)	225.00	90.00

No. 17 was used only in Cochin China, 1876-77. Excellent forgeries of Nos. 17 and 18 exist.

With reference to the stamps of France and French Colonies in the same designs and colors see the note after France No. 9.

Peace and Commerce Commerce
A8 A9

1877–78 Type I. *Imperf.*

No.	Type	Description	Unused	Used
24	A8	1c green, *greenish*	18.50	22.50
25	"	4c green, *greenish*	11.00	9.00
26	"	30c brown, *yellowish* ('78)	22.50	22.50
27	"	40c verm., *straw*	16.50	14.00
28	"	75c carmine, *rose* ('78)	45.00	40.00
29	"	1fr bronze green, *straw*	20.00	11.00

Type II.

No.	Type	Description	Unused	Used
30	A8	2c green, *greenish*	9.00	7.00
31	"	5c green, *greenish*	13.50	3.50
32	"	10c green, *greenish*	55.00	7.00
33	"	15c gray, *grayish*	150.00	50.00
34	"	20c red brown, *straw*	40.00	4.00
35	"	25c ultra., *bluish*	25.00	7.00
		a. 25c blue, *bluish* ('78)	*3500.00*	120.00
36	"	35c violet black, *orange* ('78)	27.50	17.50

1878–80 Type II.

No.	Type	Description	Unused	Used
38	A8	1c *lilac blue*	13.50	13.50
39	"	2c brown, *buff*	11.00	9.00
40	"	4c claret, *lavender*	15.00	15.00
41	"	10c *lavender* ('79)	60.00	14.00
42	"	15c blue ('79)	22.50	9.00
43	"	20c red, *green* ('79)	50.00	9.00
44	"	25c *red* ('79)	300.00	225.00
45	"	25c yellow, *straw* ('80)	325.00	20.00

No. 44 was used only in Mayotte, Nossi-Bé and New Caledonia. Forgeries exist.

The 3c yellow, 3c gray, 15c yellow, 20c blue, 25c rose and 5fr lilac were printed together with the reprints, and were never issued.

1881-86 *Perf. 14x13½.*

No.	Type	Description	Unused	Used
46	A9	1c *lilac blue*	1.10	1.10
47	"	2c brown, *buff*	1.35	1.35
48	"	4c claret, *lavender*	1.35	1.35
49	"	5c green, *greenish*	1.50	85
50	"	10c *lavender*	3.00	1.85
51	"	15c blue	4.50	85
52	"	20c red, *yellow grn.*	14.00	6.25
53	"	25c yellow, *straw*	4.00	1.65
54	"	25c *rose* ('86)	4.00	85
55	"	30c brown, *bistre*	12.00	8.00
56	A9	35c violet black, *yellow orange*	14.00	12.00
		a. 35c violet black, *yellow*	17.50	12.00
57	"	40c vermilion, *straw*	16.00	11.00
58	"	75c carmine, *rose*	32.50	20.00
59	"	1fr bronze green, *straw*	22.50	13.50

Nos. 46–59 exist imperforate. They are proofs and were not used for postage, except the 10c.

For stamps of type A9 surcharged with numerals see: Cochin China, Diego Suarez, Gabon, Madagascar, Nossi Be, New Caledonia, Reunion, Senegal, Tahiti.

SEMI-POSTAL STAMPS.

Resistance Fighters
SP1

Lithographed.

1943 *Rouletted* Unwmkd.

No.	Type	Description	Unused	Used
B1	SP1	1.50fr+98.50fr indigo & gray	10.00	10.00

The surtax was for the benefit of patriots and the French Committee of Liberation.

No. B1 was printed in sheets of 10 (5x2) with adjoining labels for each stamp. The label shows the Lorraine cross in indigo in a gray frame.

Colonies Offering Aid to France
SP2

1943 *Perf. 12*

No.	Type	Description	Unused	Used
B2	SP2	9fr+41fr red violet	40	40

The surtax was for the benefit of French Patriots.

Patriots and Map of France
SP3

1943

No.	Type	Description	Unused	Used
B3	SP3	50c+4.50fr yellow green	35	40
B4	"	1.50fr+8.50fr cerise	35	40
B5	"	3fr+12fr greenish blue	35	40
B6	"	5fr+15fr olive gray	35	40

The surtax was for the aid of combatants and patriots.

Refugee Family
SP4

1943

No.	Type	Description	Unused	Used
B7	SP4	10fr+40fr dull blue	1.50	1.75

The surtax was for refugee relief work.

Woman and Child with Wing
SP5

1944

No.	Type	Description	Unused	Used
B8	SP5	10fr+40fr greenish black	1.80	2.00

The surtax was for the general benefit of aviation.

Nos. B1–B8 were originally prepared for use in the French Colonies, but after the landing of Free French troops in Corsica they were used there and later also in Southern France. They became valid throughout France in November 1944.

POSTAGE DUE STAMPS.

D1

Typographed.

1884-85 *Imperf.* Unwmkd.

No.	Type	Description	Unused	Used
J1	D1	1c black	1.40	1.40
J2	"	2c "	1.40	1.40
J3	"	3c "	1.40	1.40
J4	"	4c "	1.65	1.25
J5	"	5c "	2.00	1.65
J6	"	10c "	3.00	2.50
J7	"	15c "	5.00	3.00
J8	"	20c "	5.00	4.00
J9	"	30c "	6.00	3.00
J10	"	40c "	8.00	3.00
J11	"	60c "	15.00	8.00
J12	"	1fr brown	12.00	10.00
		a. 1fr black	135.00	
J13	"	2fr brown	10.00	8.00
		a. 2fr black	135.00	
J14	"	5fr brown	35.00	32.50
		a. 5fr black	175.00	

Nos. J12a, J13a and J14a were not regularly issued.

1894-1906

No.	Type	Description	Unused	Used
J15	D1	5c pale blue	25	25
J16	"	10c gray brown	25	25
J17	"	15c pale green	25	25
J18	"	20c olive green ('06)	25	25
J19	"	30c carmine	50	30
J20	"	50c lilac	50	40
J21	"	60c brown, *buff*	1.50	85
		a. 60c dark violet, *buff*	1.50	85
J22	"	1fr red, *buff*	2.00	1.35
		a. 1fr rose, *buff*	7.50	7.25
		Nos. J15–J22 (8)	5.50	3.90

D2

1945 Lithographed *Perf. 12*

No.	Type	Description	Unused	Used
J23	D2	10c slate blue	5	5
J24	"	15c yellow green	5	5
J25	"	25c deep orange	6	6
J26	"	50c greenish black	25	25
J27	"	60c copper brown	25	25
J28	"	1fr deep red lilac	10	10
J29	"	2fr red	25	25
J30	"	4fr slate gray	60	60
J31	"	5fr bright ultramarine	60	60
J32	"	10fr purple	3.00	2.50
J33	"	20fr dull brown	1.25	1.35
J34	"	50fr deep green	1.65	2.00
		Nos. J23–J34 (12)	8.11	8.06

FRENCH CONGO

(frĕnch kŏng'gō)

LOCATION—Central Africa.

GOVT.—French possession.

French Congo was originally a separate colony, but was joined in 1888 to Gabon and placed under one commissioner-general with a lieutenant-governor presiding in Gabon and another in French Congo. In 1894 the military holdings in Ubangi were attached to French Congo, and in 1900 the Chad military protectorate was added. Postal service was not established in Ubangi or Chad, however, at that time. In 1906 Gabon and Middle Congo were separated and French Congo ceased to exist as such. Chad and Ubangi remained attached to Middle Congo as the joint dependency of "Ubangi—Chari—Chad," and Middle Congo stamps were used there.

Issues of the Republic of the Congo are listed under Congo Republic (ex-French).

100 Centimes = 1 Franc

Stamps of French Colonies Surcharged Horizontally in Red or Black

Congo français
5c.

1891 ***Perf. 14x13½.*** **Unwmkd.**

1 A9 5c on 1c *lilac blue* (R) 2000.00 1650.00
2 " 5c on 1c *lilac blue* 60.00 30.00
  a. Double surcharge 60.00 60.00
3 " 5c on 15c blue 100.00 45.00
  a. Double surcharge 110.00 70.00
5 " 5c on 25c *rose* 32.50 10.00
  a. Inverted surcharge 60.00 25.00

1891–92

First "O" of "Congo" is a Capital, "Francais" with Capital "F".

6 A9 5c on 20c red, *green* 350.00 165.00
7 " 5c on 25c *rose* 32.50 10.00
  a. Surch. vert. 35.00 11.00
8 " 10c on 25c *rose* 55.00 17.50
  a. Inverted surcharge 50.00 20.00
  b. Surch. vert. 55.00 17.50
  c. First "o" of "Congo" small 50.00 17.50
  d. Double surcharge 80.00 35.00
9 " 10c on 40c red, *straw* 800.00 135.00
10 " 15c on 25c *rose* 50.00 12.00
  a. Surch. vert. 50.00 12.00
  b. Inverted surcharge 55.00 25.00
  c. Double surch. 70.00 35.00

First "O" of Congo small. Surcharge Vertical, Reading Down or Up. No period.

11 A9 5c on 25c *rose* 25.00 7.50
12 " 10c on 25c *rose* 40.00 12.00
13 " 15c on 25c *rose* 35.00 10.00

Postage Due Stamps of French Colonies Surcharged in Red or Black Reading Down or Up

Congo français
Timbres poste
10 c

1892 ***Imperf.***

14 D1 5c on 5c black (R) 45.00 35.00
15 " 5c on 20c black (R) 45.00 35.00
16 " 5c on 30c black (R) 55.00 50.00
17 " 10c on 1fr brown 50.00 35.00
  a. Double surcharge 50.00 35.00
  b. Surch. horiz. 450.00

Excellent counterfeits of Nos. 1-17 exist.

Navigation and Commerce
A3

1892–1900 Typo. ***Perf. 14x13½***

Colony Name in Blue or Carmine

18 A3 1c *lilac blue* 40 40
19 " 2c brown, *buff* 60 60
  a. Name double 45.00 30.00
20 " 4c claret, *lavender* 60 60
  a. Name in black and in blue 45.00 30.00
21 " 5c green, *greenish* 1.40 1.40
22 " 10c *lavender* 5.00 3.00
  a. Name double 150.00 135.00
23 " 10c red ('00) 60 40
24 " 15c blue, quadrille paper 14.00 4.50
25 " 15c gray ('00) 2.50 1.85
26 " 20c red, *green* 7.00 4.50
27 " 25c *rose* 6.00 4.50
28 " 25c blue ('00) 3.25 2.50
29 " 30c brown, *bistre* 7.00 4.50
30 " 40c red, *straw* 13.00 9.00
31 " 50c carmine, *rose* 14.00 9.00
32 " 50c brown, *azure* ('00) 2.85 2.50
  a. Name double 165.00 165.00
33 " 75c dp. vio., *orange* 11.00 9.00
34 " 1fr bronze green, *straw* 15.00 9.00
Nos. 18-34 (17) 104.20 67.25

Leopard
A4

Bakalois Woman
A5

Coconut Grove
A6

Wmk. 122

Wmkd. Thistle Branch. (122)

1900 ***Perf. 11***

35 A4 1c brown violet & gray lilac 15 10
  a. Background inverted 13.50 13.50
36 " 2c brown & orange 15 10
  a. 2c dark red & red 50.00
  b. Imperf., pair 20.00 20.00
37 " 4c scarlet & gray blue 30 10
  a. 4c dark red & red 250.00
  b. Background inverted 15.00 15.00
38 " 5c green & gray green 40 10
  a. Imperf. pair 40.00 40.00
39 " 10c dark red & red 1.65 60
  a. Imperf., pair 40.00 40.00
40 " 15c dull violet & olive green 40 20
  a. Imperf., pair 30.00 30.00

Wmk. 123

Wmkd. Rose Branch. (123)

41 A5 20c yel. grn. & org. 40 20
42 " 25c blue & pale blue 40 30
43 " 30c car. rose & org. 85 40
44 " 40c orange brown & bright green 1.00 50
  a. Imperf., pair 30.00 30.00
  b. Center inverted 37.50 37.50
45 " 50c gray violet & lilac 1.40 1.25
46 " 75c red violet & org. 3.75 2.25
  a. Imperf., pair 30.00 30.00

Wmk. 124

Wmkd. Olive Branch. (124)

47 A6 1fr gray lilac & olive 5.00 4.00
  a. Center inverted 85.00 85.00
  b. Imperf., pair 37.50 37.50
48 " 2fr carmine & brown 10.00 6.00
  a. Imperf., pair 65.00 65.00
49 " 5fr brown orange & gray 22.50 20.00
  a. 5fr ochre & gray 200.00 200.00
  b. Center inverted 125.00 125.00
  c. Wmk. 123 90.00
  d. Imperf., pair 165.00 165.00
Nos. 35-49 (15) 48.35 36.10

Nos. 26 and 29 Surcharged in Black

Valeur
15

1900 ***Perf. 14x13½*** **Unwmkd.**

50 A3 5c on 20c red, *green* 2500.00
51 " 15c on 30c brown, *bis.* 1000.00
  a. Dbl. surch. 2250.00

Nos. 43 and 48 Surcharged in Black:

5c
a

0,10
b

1903 ***Perf. 11*** **Wmk. 123**

52 A5 (a) 5c on 30c carmine rose & org. 110.00 50.00
  a. Inverted surcharge 650.00

Wmk. 124

53 A6 (b) 10c on 2fr carmine & brown 140.00 55.00
  a. Inverted surcharge 650.00

Counterfeits of the preceding surcharges are known.

FRENCH EQUATORIAL AFRICA

(frĕnch ē'kwȧ-tō'rĭ-ăl ăf'rĭ-kȧ)

LOCATION—North of Belgian Congo and south of Libya.

GOVT.—Former French Colony.

AREA—959,256 square miles.

POP.—4,491,785.

CAPITAL—Brazzaville.

In 1910 Gabon and Middle Congo, with its military dependencies, were politically united as French Equatorial Africa. The component colonies were granted administrative autonomy. In 1915 Ubangi-Chari-Chad was made an autonomous civilian colony and in 1920 Chad was made a civil colony. In 1934 the four colonies were administratively united as one colony, but this federation was not completed until 1936. Each colony had its own postal administration until 1936 when they were united. The postal issues of the former colonial subdivisions are listed under the names of those colonies.

In 1958, French Equatorial Africa was divided into four republics: Chad, Congo, Gabon and Central African Republic (formerly Ubangi-Chari).

100 Centimes = 1 Franc

Stamps of Gabon, 1932, Overprinted "Afrique Equatoriale Francaise" and Bars Similar to "a" and "b" in Black

Perf. 13x13½, 13½x13.

1936 **Unwmkd.**

1 A16 1(c) brown violet 6 6
2 " 2(c) black, *rose* 6 6
3 " 4(c) green 23 18
4 " 5(c) greenish blue 20 10
5 " 10(c) red, *yellow* 25 10
6 A17 40(c) brown violet 55 20
7 " 50(c) red brown 45 20
8 " 1fr yellow green, *blue* 11.00 4.00
9 A18 1.50fr dull blue 70 15
10 " 2fr brown red 6.00 3.00
Nos. 1-10 (10) 19.50 8.05

Stamps of Middle Congo, 1933 Overprinted in Black:

AFRIQUE
ÉQUATORIALE
FRANÇAISE

a

AFRIQUE ÉQUATORIALE
FRANÇAISE

b

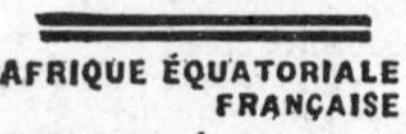

AFRIQUE EQUATORIALE
FRANÇAISE

c

1936

11 A4 (b) 1(c) light brown 7 7
12 " (") 2(c) dull blue 8 8
13 " (") 4(c) olive green 15 6
14 " (") 5(c) red violet 15 10
15 " (") 10(c) slate 45 35
16 " (") 15(c) dark violet 45 35
17 " (") 20(c) red, *pink* 25 20
18 " (") 25(c) orange 1.00 60

19 A5 (*a*) 40(c) org. brown 1.00 60
20 " (*c*) 50(c) black violet 65 60
21 " (") 75(c) black, *pink* 1.40 1.00
22 " (*a*) 90(c) carmine 90 60
23 " (*c*) 1.50fr dark blue 50 40
24 A6 (*a*) 5fr slate blue 17.50 11.00
25 " (") 10fr black 10.00 8.00
26 " (") 20fr dk. brown 11.00 8.00
Nos. 11-26 (16) 45.55 32.01

Paris International Exposition Issue.
Common Design Types

1937, Apr. 15 Engraved. ***Perf. 13.***
27 CD74 20c dark violet 85 85
28 CD75 30c dark green 85 85
29 CD76 40c carmine rose 85 85
30 CD77 50c dk. brn. & blue 50 50
31 CD78 90c red 85 85
32 CD79 1.50fr ultramarine 85 85
Nos. 27-32 (6) 4.75 4.75

Logging on Loeme River
A1

People of Chad
A2

Pierre Savorgnan de Brazza
A3

Emile Gentil
A4

Paul Crampel
A5

Governor Victor Liotard
A6

Two types of 25c:
I. Wide numerals (4mm.).
II. Narrow numerals (3½mm.).

1937-40 Photo. ***Perf. 13½x13***
33 A1 1c brown & yellow 5 4
34 " 2c violet & green 6 6
35 " 3c blue & yellow ('40) 6 6
36 " 4c magenta & blue 6 6
37 " 5c dk. & lt. green 5 5
38 A2 10c magenta & blue 5 5
39 " 15c blue & buff 5 5
40 " 20c brown & yellow 10 5
41 " 25c copper red & blue (I) 15 6
a. Type II 30 20
42 A3 30c gray green & green 10 10
43 " 30c chalky blue, indigo & buff ('40) 6 6
44 A2 35c deep green & yellow ('38) 30 18
45 A3 40c copper red & blue 5 5
46 " 45c dark blue & light green 1.35 85
47 " 45c deep green & yellow green ('40) 12 12
48 " 50c brown & yellow 8 5
49 " 55c purple & blue ('38) 15 10
50 " 60c maroon & gray blue ('40) 8 8
51 A4 65c dark blue & light green 8 5
52 " 70c deep violet & buff ('40) 12 12
53 " 75c olive black & dull yellow 1.65 1.00
54 " 80c brn. & yel. ('38) 10 6
55 " 90c copper red & buff 10 6
56 " 1fr dark violet & light green 50 20
57 A3 1fr cerise & dull orange ('38) 70 15
58 A4 1fr blue green & slate green ('40) 12 12
59 A5 1.25fr copper red & buff 40 40
60 " 1.40fr dark brown & pale green ('40) 12 12
61 " 1.50fr dk. & lt. blue 40 25
62 " 1.60fr deep violet & buff ('40) 13 13
63 " 1.75fr brown & yellow 45 25
64 A4 1.75fr blue & light blue ('38) 10 8
65 A5 2fr dk. & lt. green 50 25
66 A6 2.15fr brown, violet & yellow ('38) 15 6
67 " 2.25fr blue & light blue ('39) 30 30
68 " 2.50fr rose lake & buff ('40) 12 12
69 " 3fr dark blue & buff 15 8
70 " 5fr dk. & lt. green 40 30
71 " 10fr dark violet & blue 75 50
72 " 20fr olive black & dull yellow 80 65
Nos. 33-72 (40) 11.06 7.32

Colonial Arts Exhibition Issue
Souvenir Sheet.
Common Design Type

1937 ***Imperf.***
73 CD79 3fr red brown 2.10 2.10
Sheet size: 111x99mm.

Count Louis Edouard Bouet-Willaumez and His Ship "La Malouine"—A7

1938, Dec. 5 ***Perf. 13½.***
74 A7 65c gray brown 40 40
75 " 1fr deep rose 40 40
76 " 1.75fr blue 60 60
77 " 2fr dull violet 60 60

Issued in commemoration of the centenary of Gabon.

New York World's Fair Issue.
Common Design Type

1939, May 10 Engr. ***Perf. 12½x12***
78 CD82 1.25fr carmine lake 60 60
79 " 2.25fr ultramarine 60 60

Common Design Types
pictured in section at front of book.

Libreville View and Marshal Petain
A7a

1941 Engraved ***Perf. 12½x12***
79A A7a 1fr bluish green 45
79B " 2.50fr blue 45

Nos. 79A-79B were issued by the Vichy government, and were not placed on sale in the colony. This is also true of four stamps of types A2, A3 and A5 without "RF" monogram released in 1943-44.

Stamps of 1936-40, Overprinted in Carmine or Black:

AFRIQUE FRANÇAISE
LIBRE
a

LIBRE
b

1940-41 ***Perf. 13½x13***
80 A1 (*a*) 1c brown & yellow (C) 25 25
81 " (") 2c violet & green (C) 30 30
82 " (") 3c blue & yellow (C) 30 30
83 A4 (*b*) 4c olive green (Bk) (No. 13) 3.75 3.00
84 A1 (*a*) 5c dk. green & lt. green (C) 30 30
85 A2 (") 10c magenta & blue (Bk) 45 45
86 " (") 15c blue & buff (C) 40 40
87 " (") 20c brown & yellow (C) 50 50
88 " (") 25c copper red & blue (Bk) 1.85 1.85
89 A3 (*b*) 30c gray green & green (C) 4.00 3.25
90 " (") 30c gray green & green (Bk) ('41) 60 40
91 " (") 30c chalky blue, indigo & buff (C) ('41) 3.75 3.25
92 " (") 30c chalky blue, indigo & buff (Bk) ('41) 2.25 2.25
93 A2 (*a*) 35c deep green & yellow (C) 40 40
94 A3 (*b*) 40c copper red & blue (Bk) 20 15
a. Double overprint 18.00
95 " (") 45c deep green & yellow green (C) 25 20
96 " (") 45c deep green & yellow green (Bk) ('41) 20 15
a. Double overprint 3.50 3.50
97 " (") 50c brown & yellow (C) 1.65 1.35
98 " (") 50c brown & yellow (Bk) ('41) 90 80
a. Double overprint 30.00
99 " (") 55c purple & blue (C) 30 25
100 " (") 55c purple & blue (Bk) ('41) 20 15
a. Double overprint 5.00 5.00
b. Double, one inverted 18.00
101 " (") 60c maroon & gray blue (Bk) 15 10
102 A4 (") 65c dark blue & light green (Bk) 20 20
a. Double overprint 18.00
103 A4 (*b*) 70c deep violet & buff (Bk) 22 18
a. Double overprint 3.50 3.50
104 " (") 75c olive black & dull yel. (Bk) 12.50 12.50
105 " (") 80c brown & yellow (Bk) 12 10
a. Double overprint 18.00
106 " (") 90c copper red & buff (Bk) 30 30
a. Double overprint 18.00
b. Double, one inverted 18.00
107 " (") 1fr blue green & slate green (Bk) 2.00 1.40
108 " (") 1fr blue green & slate green (C) ('41) 1.75 1.75
109 A3 (") 1fr cerise & dull orange (Bk) 50 35
110 A5 (") 1.40fr dark brown & pale green (Bk) 10 7
a. Double overprint 3.00 3.00
111 " (") 1.50fr dark blue & light blue (Bk) 20 20
a. Double overprint 5.00 5.00
112 " (") 1.60fr deep violet & buff (Bk) 15 10
113 " (") 1.75fr brown & yellow (Bk) 40 22
114 A6 (") 2.15fr brown, violet & yel. (Bk) 25 15
a. Double overprint 3.00 3.00
115 " (") 2.25fr blue & light blue (C) 40 40
a. Double overprint 5.00 5.00
116 " (") 2.25fr blue & light blue (Bk) ('41) 50 45
a. Double overprint 18.00
117 " (") 2.50fr rose lake & buff (Bk) 25 25
a. Double overprint 18.00
118 " (") 3fr dark blue & buff (C) 40 40
119 " (") 3fr dark blue & buff (Bk) ('41) 60 50
a. Double overprint 4.00 4.00
120 " (") 5fr dark green & light green (C) 1.00 1.00
121 " (") 5fr dark green & light green (Bk) ('41) 40.00 20.00
122 " (") 10fr dark violet & blue (C) 55 50
123 " (") 10fr dark violet & blue (Bk) ('41) 27.50 20.00
a. Double overprint
124 " (") 20fr olive black & dull yellow (C) 55 55
125 " (") 20fr olive black & dull yellow (Bk) ('41) 2.75 2.75
Nos. 80-125 (46) 116.14 84.37

Nos. 48, 51 Surcharged in Black or Carmine

LIBRE
75 c

1940
126 A3 75c on 50c brown & yellow (Bk) 8 8
a. Double surcharge
127 A4 1fr on 65c dark blue & light green (C) 6 5
a. Double surcharge 3.50

Middle Congo No. 67
Overprinted in Carmine:

AFRIQUE FRANÇAISE
LIBRE

Perf. 13½

128 A4 4c olive green 16.50 14.00

Stamps of 1940
With Additional
Overprint in Black **24-10-40**

1940			*Perf. 13½x13*	
129	A4	80c brn. & yellow	5.50	4.50
		a. Overprint without "2"	15.00	
130	"	1fr blue green & slate green	5.50	4.50
131	A3	1fr cerise & dull orange	5.50	4.50
132	A5	1.50fr dark blue & light blue	5.50	4.50

These stamps were sold affixed to post cards and at a slight increase over face value to cover the cost of the cards.

Issued to commemorate the arrival of General de Gaulle in Brazzaville, capital of Free France, October 24, 1940.

Stamps of 1937-40
Overprinted in Black **Afrique Française Libre**

1941				
133	A1	1c brown & yellow	40	40
134	"	2c violet & green	40	40
135	"	3c blue & yellow	40	40
136	"	5c dk. & lt. green	40	40
137	A2	10c magenta & blue	40	40
138	"	15c blue & buff	40	40
139	"	20c brown & yellow	40	40
140	"	25c copper red & blue	85	85
141	"	35c dp. green & yel.	85	85
		a. Double overprint	8.50	
		Nos. 133-141 (9)	4.50	4.50

There are two settings of the overprint on Nos. 133 to 141 and C10. The first has a space of 1mm. between lines of the overprint, the second has space of 2 mm.

Phoenix
A8

1941		Photogravure	*Perf. 14x14½*	
142	A8	5c brown	4	4
143	"	10c dark blue	5	5
144	"	25c emerald	5	5
145	"	30c deep orange	8	10
146	"	40c dark slate green	10	10
147	"	80c red brown	10	10
148	"	1fr deep red lilac	10	10
149	"	1.50fr bright red	8	8
150	"	2fr gray	12	10
151	"	2.50fr bright ultramarine	10	8
152	"	4fr dull violet	20	7
153	"	5fr yellow bistre	12	12
154	"	10fr deep brown	20	15
155	"	20fr deep green	35	25
		Nos. 142-155 (14)	1.69	1.39

Eboue Issue.
Common Design Type
Engraved.

1945		*Perf. 13.*	**Unwmkd.**	
156	CD91	2fr black	6	6
157	"	25fr Prussian green	60	60

Nos. 156 and 157 exist imperforate.

Nos. 142, 144 and 151
Surcharged with New Values and Bars
in Red, Carmine or Black.

1946			*Perf. 14x14½*	
158	A8	50c on 5c brown (R)	15	15
159	"	60c on 5c " (R)	15	15
160	"	70c on 5c brown (R)	10	10
161	"	1.20fr on 5c " (C)	10	10
162	"	2.40fr on 25c emerald	20	20
163	"	3fr on 25c "	40	40
164	"	4.50fr on 25c "	35	35
165	"	15fr on 2.50fr bright ultramarine (C)	35	35
		Nos. 158-165 (8)	1.80	1.80

Black Rhinoceros and Rock Python
A9

Jungle Scene
A10

Mountainous Shore Line
A11

Gabon Forest
A12

Niger Boatman
A13

Young Bacongo Woman
A14
Engraved.

1946		*Perf. 12½*	**Unwmkd.**	
166	A9	10c deep blue	4	4
167	"	30c violet black	5	5
168	"	40c deep orange	5	5
169	A10	50c violet blue	5	5
170	"	60c dark carmine	10	10
171	"	80c dk. olive green	8	8
172	A11	1fr deep orange	5	5
173	"	1.20fr deep claret	20	20
174	"	1.50fr dark green	35	27
175	A12	2fr dk. violet brown	6	6
176	"	3fr rose carmine	5	5
177	"	3.60fr red brown	70	65
178	"	4fr deep blue	10	8
179	A13	5fr dark brown	25	6
180	"	6fr deep blue	15	10
181	"	10fr black	25	5
182	A14	15fr brown	55	5
183	"	20fr deep claret	35	5
184	A14	25fr black	50	5
		Nos. 166-184 (19)	3.93	2.09

Imperforates

Most French Equatorial Africa stamps from 1951 onward exist imperforate in issued and trial colors, and also in small presentation sheets in issued colors.

Pierre Savorgnan de Brazza
A15

1951, Nov. 5 *Perf. 13*

185 A15 10fr indigo & dark grn. 35 7

Issued to commemorate the centenary of the birth of Pierre Savorgnan de Brazza, explorer.

Military Medal Issue.
Common Design Type
Engraved and Typographed.

1952, Dec. 1 *Perf. 13*

186 CD101 15fr multicolored 2.00 1.50

Lt. Gov. Adolphe L. Cureau—A16

1954, Sept. 20 Engraved

187 A16 15fr olive green & red brown 60 20

Savannah Monitor—A17

1955, May 2 **Unwmkd.**

188 A17 8fr dark green & claret 55 20

Issued in connection with the International Exhibition for Wildlife Protection, Paris, May 1955.

FIDES Issue.

Boali Waterfall and Power Plant, Ubangi-Chari
A18

Designs: 10fr, Cotton, Chad. 15fr, Brazzaville Hospital, Middle Congo. 20fr, Libreville Harbor, Gabon.

1956, Apr. 25			*Perf. 13x12½*	
189	A18	5fr dark brown & claret	10	8
190	"	10fr black & bluish green	15	10
191	"	15fr indigo & gray violet	20	5
192	"	20fr dark red & red orange	25	8

See note after Common Design Type CD103.

Coffee Issue.

Coffee
A19

1956, Oct. Engraved *Perf. 13*

193 A19 10fr brown violet & violet blue 30 10

Leprosarium at Mayumba and Maltese Cross—A20

1957, Mar. 11

194 A20 15fr green, blue green & red 60 20

Issued in honor of the Knights of Malta.

Giant Eland
A21

Animals: 2fr, Lions. 3fr, Elephant. 4fr, Greater kudu. (3fr and 4fr vertical.)

1957, Nov. 4				
195	A21	1fr green & brown	10	10
196	"	2fr Prussian green & olive green	10	10
197	"	3fr green, gray & blue	10	10
198	"	4fr maroon & gray	10	10

WHO Building, Brazzaville
A22

1958, May 19 Engraved. *Perf. 13*

199 A22 20fr dark green & orange brown 35 30

Issued to commemorate the 10th anniversary of the World Health Organization.

Flower Issue
Common Design Type

Design: 10fr, Euadania. 25fr, Spathodea.

1958, July 7		Photo.	*Perf. 12x12½*	
200	CD104	10fr dark violet, yellow & green	20	12
201	"	25fr grn., yel. & red	40	15

Human Rights Issue
Common Design Type

1958, Dec. 10 Engraved. *Perf. 13*

202 CD105 20fr Prussian green & dark blue 65 50

SEMI-POSTAL STAMPS.
Common Design Type

1938, Oct. 24 Engraved.

B1 CD80 1.75fr+50c bright ultramarine 6.50 6.50

Stamps of 1937-38
Surcharged in Black or Red **+35c**

1938, Nov. 7 *Perf. 13x13½*

B2 A4 65c+35c dark blue & light green (R) 75 60

B3 A4 1.75fr+50c blue & light blue (Bk) 75 60

The surtax was for welfare.

French Revolution Issue
Common Design Type
Name and Value Typo. in Black.

1939, July 5 Photogravure.

B4 CD83 45(c)+25(c) green 5.00 5.00
B5 " 70(c)+30(c) brown 5.00 5.00
B6 " 90(c)+35(c) red orange 5.00 5.00
B7 " 1.25fr+1fr rose pink 5.00 5.00
B8 " 2.25fr+2fr blue 5.00 5.00
Nos. B4-B8, CB1 (6) 33.50 33.50

Issued to commemorate the 150th anniversary of the French Revolution. The surtax was used for the defense of the colonies.

Common Design Type and

Native Artilleryman SP1 — Gabon Infantryman SP2

1941 Photogravure *Perf. 13½*

B8A SP1 1fr+1fr red 90
B8B CD86 1.50fr+3fr maroon 90
B8C SP2 2.50fr+1fr blue 90

Nos. B8A-B8C were issued by the Vichy government and not placed on sale in the colony.

Nos. 79A-79B were surcharged "OEUVRES COLONIALES" and surtax (including change of denomination of the 2.50fr to 50c). These were issued in 1944 by the Vichy government and not placed on sale in the colony.

Brazza and Stanley Pool SP3

1941 Photogravure. *Perf. 14½x14.*

B9 SP3 1fr+2fr dark brown & red 20 20

The surtax was for a monument to Pierre Savorgnan de Brazza.

Regular Stamps of 1937-39 Surcharged in Red

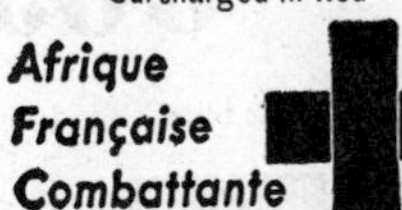

Afrique
Française
Combattante
+ 50 fr.

1943, June 28 *Perf. 13½x13*

B10 A6 2.25fr+50fr blue & light blue 4.00 4.00
B11 " 10fr+100fr dark violet & blue 12.00 12.00

Nos. 129 and 132 with additional Surcharge in Carmine

LIBÉRATION
+ 10 fr.

1944

B12 A4 80c+10fr brown & yellow 5.00 5.00
B13 A5 1.50fr+15fr dark blue & light blue 5.00 5.00

Same Surcharge printed Vertically on Stamps of 1941.

Perf. 14x14½.

B14 A8 5c+10fr brown 2.50 2.50
B15 " 10c+10fr dark blue 2.50 2.50
B16 " 25c+10fr emerald 2.50 2.50
B17 " 30c+10fr dp. org. 2.50 2.50
B18 " 40c+10fr dark slate green 2.50 2.50
B19 " 1fr+10fr deep red lilac 2.50 2.50
B20 " 2fr+20fr gray 2.50 2.50
B21 " 2.50fr+25fr bright ultramarine 2.50 2.50
Nos. B12-B21 (10) 30.00 30.00

Nos. 129 and 132 with additional Surcharge in Carmine

RÉSISTANCE
+ 10 fr.

1944 *Perf. 13½x13*

B22 A4 80c+10fr brown & yellow 5.00 5.00
B23 A5 1.50fr+15fr dark blue & light blue 5.00 5.00

Same Surcharge printed Vertically on Stamps of 1941.

Perf. 14x14½

B24 A8 5c+10fr brown 2.25 2.25
B25 " 10c+10fr dark blue 2.25 2.25
B26 " 25c+10fr emerald 2.25 2.25
B27 " 30c+10fr dp. org. 2.25 2.25
B28 " 40c+10fr dark slate green 2.25 2.25
B29 " 1fr+10fr deep red lilac 2.25 2.25
B30 " 2fr+20fr gray 2.25 2.25
B31 " 2.50fr+25fr bright ultramarine 2.25 2.25
B32 " 4fr+40fr dull violet 2.25 2.25
B33 " 5fr+50fr yellow bistre 2.25 2.25
B34 " 10fr+100fr dp. brn. 2.25 2.25
B35 " 20fr+200fr dp.grn. 2.25 2.25
Nos. B22-B35 (14) 37.00 37.00

Nos. B12 to B35 were issued to raise funds for the Committee to Aid the Fighting Men and Patriots of France.

Red Cross Issue
Common Design Type

1944 Photogravure. *Perf. 14½x14*

B38 CD90 5fr+20fr royal blue 30 30

The surtax was for the French Red Cross and national relief.

Tropical Medicine Issue
Common Design Type

1950, May 15 Engraved. *Perf. 13*

B39 CD100 10fr+2fr dark blue green & violet brown 1.75 1.75

The surtax was for charitable work.

AIR POST STAMPS.

Hydroplane over Pointe-Noire
AP1

Trimotor over Stanley Pool
AP2

Photogravure.

1937 *Perf. 13½* **Unwmkd.**

C1 AP1 1.50fr olive black & yellow 8 8
C2 " 2fr magenta & blue 12 12
C3 " 2.50fr green & buff 15 15
C4 " 3.75fr brown & light green 15 15
C5 AP2 4.50fr copper red & blue 15 15
C6 " 6.50fr blue & light green 35 35
C7 " 8.50fr red brown & yellow 35 35
C8 " 10.75fr violet & light green 35 35
Nos. C1-C8 (8) 1.70 1.70

V4

Stamps of types AP1 and AP2 without "R F" and stamp of the design shown above were issued in 1943 and 1944 by the Vichy Government, but were not placed on sale in the colony.

Nos. C1, C3-C7 Overprinted in Black

Afrique Française
Libre

1940-41

C9 AP1 1.50fr ('41) 100.00 90.00
a. Double overprint
C10 " 2.50fr 35 35
a. Double overprint 50.00
C11 " 3.75fr ('41) 90.00 85.00
C12 AP2 4.50fr 45 45
a. Double overprint 50.00 50.00
C13 " 6.50fr 75 75
C14 " 8.50fr 45 45

No. C8 Surcharged in Carmine

Afrique Française
Libre
50 fr.

C15 AP2 50fr on 10.75fr 3.00 3.00

No. C3 Surcharged in Black

Afrique Française
Libre
10F

C16 AP1 10fr on 2.50fr ('41) 45.00 40.00
Nos. C9-C16 (8) 240.00 220.00

Counterfeits of Nos. C9 and C11 exist. See note following No. 141.

Common Design Type

1941 Photogravure *Perf. 14½x14*

C17 CD87 1fr dark orange 20 15
C18 " 1.50fr bright red 25 20
C19 " 5fr brown red 45 25
C20 " 10fr black 45 25
C21 " 25fr ultramarine 50 30
C22 " 50fr dark green 30 20
C23 " 100fr plum 55 40
Nos. C17-C23 (7) 2.70 1.75

Victory Issue
Common Design Type
Engraved.

1946, May 8 *Perf. 12½* **Unwmkd.**

C24 CD92 8fr lilac rose 30 30

Chad to Rhine Issue
Common Design Types

1946, June 6

C25 CD93 5fr dark violet 25 25
C26 CD94 10fr slate green 25 25
C27 CD95 15fr deep blue 45 45
C28 CD96 20fr red orange 55 55
C29 CD97 25fr sepia 60 60
C30 CD98 50fr brown carmine 70 70
Nos. C25-C30 (6) 2.80 2.80

Palms and Village—AP3

Village and Waterfront—AP4

Bearers in Jungle—AP5

1946 Engraved. *Perf. 13.*

C31 AP3 50fr red brown 90 25
C32 AP4 100fr greenish black 1.60 35
C33 AP5 200fr deep blue 3.00 55

UPU Issue
Common Design Type

1949, July 4

C34 CD99 25fr green 3.50 3.50

Brazza Holding Map—AP6

1951, Nov. 5

C35 AP6 15fr brown, indigo & red 50 10

Issued to commemorate the centenary of the birth of Pierre Savorgnan de Brazza, explorer.

Archbishop Augouard and St. Anne Cathedral, Brazzaville
AP7

1952, Dec. 1

C36 AP7 15fr olive green, dark brown & violet brown 1.25 85

Issued to commemorate the centenary of the birth of Archbishop Philippe-Prosper Augouard.

Anhingas—AP8

1953, Feb. 16

C37 AP8 500fr greenish black, black & slate 12.00 1.60

Liberation Issue
Common Design Type

1954, June 6

C38 CD102 15fr violet & violet brn. 1.20 1.20

Log Rafts—AP9

Designs: 100fr, Fishing boats and nets, Lake Chad. 200fr, Age of mechanization.

1955, Jan. 24		**Engraved**	
C39	AP9 50fr indigo, brown & dark green	70	13
C40	" 100fr aquamarine, dark green & black brown	2.00	20
C41	" 200fr red & deep plum	3.00	50

Gov. Gen. Félix Eboué, View of Brazzaville and the Pantheon
AP10

1955, Apr. 30 ***Perf. 13*** **Unwmkd.**

C42 AP10 15fr sepia, brown & slate blue 1.20 75

Gen. Louis Faidherbé and African Sharpshooter—AP11

1957, July 20

C43 AP11 15fr sepia & orange vermilion 75 65

Centenary of French African Troops.

AIR POST SEMI-POSTAL STAMPS.

French Revolution Issue
Common Design Type
Photogravure.

1939 ***Perf. 13.*** **Unwmkd.**

Name and Value Typo. in Orange.

CB1 CD83 4.50fr+4fr brown black 8.50 8.50

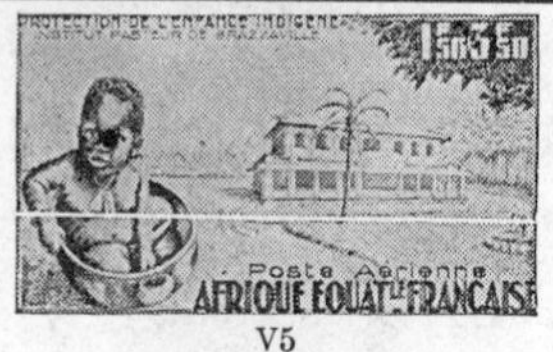
V5

V6

V7

Stamps of the designs shown above and stamp of Cameroun type V10 inscribed "Afrique Equatoriale Frcaise" were issued in 1942 by the Vichy Government, but were not placed on sale in the colony.

No. C8 Surcharged in Red

1943, June 28 ***Perf. 13½***

CB2 AP2 10.75fr+200fr violet & light green 65.00 65.00

Counterfeits exist.

POSTAGE DUE STAMPS.

Numeral of Value on Equatorial Butterfly
D1 D2

Photogravure.

1937	***Perf. 13***		**Unwmkd.**
J1	D1 5c reddish purple & light blue	4	4
J2	" 10c copper red & buff	6	6
J3	" 20c dark green & green	6	6
J4	" 25c red brown & buff	5	5
J5	" 30c copper red & light blue	10	10
J6	" 45c magenta & yellow green	18	18
J7	" 50c dark olive green & buff	15	15
J8	" 60c reddish purple & yellow	25	25
J9	" 1fr brown & yellow	28	28
J10	" 2fr dark blue & buff	45	45
J11	" 3fr red brown & light green	45	45
	Nos. J1-J11 (11)	2.07	2.07

1947	**Engraved.**		
J12	D2 10c red	10	10
J13	" 30c deep orange	10	10
J14	" 50c greenish black	10	10
J15	" 1fr carmine	10	10
J16	" 2fr emerald	10	10
J17	" 3fr deep red lilac	12	12
J18	" 4fr deep ultramarine	12	12
J19	" 5fr red brown	25	25
J20	" 10fr peacock blue	35	35
J21	" 20fr sepia	45	45
	Nos. J12-J21 (10)	1.79	1.79

FRENCH GUIANA

(frĕnch gē-ä'nȧ)

LOCATION — On the northeast coast of South America bordering on the Atlantic Ocean.

GOVT.—Former French colony.

AREA—34,740 sq. mi.

POP.—28,537 (1946).

CAPITAL—Cayenne.

Formerly a colony, French Guiana became an overseas department of France in 1946.

100 Centimes = 1 Franc

Stamps of French Colonies Surcharged in Black

Déc. 1886.
GUY. FRANÇ.
0f 05
a

1886, Dec. ***Imperf.*** **Unwmkd.**

1	A8 5c on 2c green, *greenish*	175.00	175.00
	b. No "f" after "O"	225.00	225.00
	Perf. 14x13½.		
2	A9 5c on 2c brown, *buff*	200.00	200.00
	b. No "f" after "O"	150.00	135.00

Two types of No. 1: Surcharge 12mm. high, and surcharge 10½mm. high.

Avril 1887. — GUY FRANÇ 0f 20 *b*   Avril 1887. — GUY FRANÇ. 0f 25 *c*

Date Line Reads "^Vril 1887"

1887, Apr. ***Imperf.***

4 A8 20c on 35c *orange* 16.50 16.50

Date Line Reads "Avril 1887"

5	A8 5c on 2c green, *greenish*	40.00	35.00
6	" 20c on 35c *orange*	100.00	90.00
7	A7 25c on 30c brown, *yellowish*	13.50	12.50

Variety "small 'f' omitted" occurs on Nos. 5–7.

French Colonies Nos. 22 and 26 Surcharged:

DÉC. 1887.
GUY. FRANÇ.
5c
d

8	A7 5c on 30c brown, *yellowish*	45.00	40.00
	a. Double surcharge	150.00	150.00
	b. Inverted surcharge	300.00	300.00
	c. Pair, one without surcharge	150.00	150.00
9	A8 5c on 30c brown, *yellowish*	500.00	450.00

French Colonies Nos. 22 and 28 Surcharged:

Février 1888 — GUY. FRANÇ 5 *e*   Février 1888 — GUY. FRANÇ 10 *f*

1888

10	A7 (*e*) 5c on 30c brn., *yellowish*	47.50	45.00
	b. Double surcharge	150.00	150.00
	c. Inverted surcharge	150.00	150.00
11	A8 (*f*) 10c on 75c carmine, *rose*	70.00	70.00

Stamps of French Colonies Overprinted in Black

GUYANE.

1892, Feb. 20 ***Imperf.***

12	A8 2c green, *greenish*	300.00	300.00
13	A7 30c brown, *yellowish*	45.00	40.00
14	A8 35c *orange*	850.00	650.00
15	" 40c red, *straw*	40.00	35.00
16	" 75c carmine, *rose*	45.00	35.00
	a. Inverted overprint	110.00	100.00
17	" 1fr bronze green, *straw*	55.00	50.00
	a. Inverted overprint	150.00	150.00

1892	***Perf. 14x13½***		
18	A9 1c *lilac blue*	14.00	9.00
19	" 2c brown, *buff*	11.00	9.00
20	" 4c claret, *lavender*	11.00	10.00
21	" 5c green, *greenish*	11.00	10.00
	a. Inverted overprint	35.00	35.00
	b. Double overprint	35.00	
22	" 10c *lavender*	16.50	13.50
	a. Inverted overprint	16.50	13.50
23	" 15c blue	15.00	13.50
24	" 20c red, *green*	14.00	13.50
25	" 25c *rose*	22.50	10.00
26	" 30c brown, *bistre*	13.50	10.00
27	" 35c *orange*	60.00	60.00
28	" 40c red, *straw*	45.00	35.00
	a. Inverted overprint	50.00	40.00
29	" 75c carmine, *rose*	40.00	35.00
30	" 1fr bronze green, *straw*	70.00	60.00

French Colonies No. 51 Surcharged

GUYANE. DÉC. 92. 0f05

1892, Dec.

31 A9 5c on 15c blue 7.50 7.00

Navigation and Commerce
A12

1892–1904 **Typographed**

Name of Colony in Blue or Carmine.

32	A12 1c *lilac blue*	40	40
33	" 2c brown, *buff*	20	20
34	" 4c claret, *lavender*	40	20
	a. "GÜYANE" double	55.00	55.00
35	" 5c green, *greenish*	2.75	2.25
36	" 5c yellow green ('04)	20	10
37	" 10c *lavender*	2.25	1.00
38	" 10c red ('00)	1.35	40
39	" 15c blue, quadrille paper	8.00	60

40 A12 15c gray, *light gray* ('00) 35.00 27.50
41 " 20c red, *green* 6.00 3.75
42 " 25c *rose* 4.00 85
43 " 25c blue ('00) 4.50 4.50
44 " 30c brown, *bistre* 5.00 4.00
45 " 40c red, *straw* 5.00 4.00
46 " 50c carmine, *rose* 8.00 4.00
47 " 50c brown, *azure* ('00) 6.00 4.75
48 " 75c deep violet, *orange* 11.00 6.00
49 " 1fr bronze green, *straw* 4.00 3.00
50 " 2fr violet, *rose* ('02) 70.00 1.85
Nos. 32-50 (19) 174.05 69.35

Great Anteater
A13

Washing Gold
A14

Palm Grove at Cayenne—A15

1905-28

51 A13 1c black 5 5
52 " 2c blue 6 6
53 " 4c red brown 10 10
54 " 5c green 20 12
55 " 5c orange ('22) 5 5
56 " 10c rose 10 5
57 " 10c green ('22) 8 8
58 " 10c red, *bluish* ('25) 6 6
59 " 15c violet 28 25
60 A14 20c red brown 8 6
61 " 25c blue 38 15
62 " 25c violet ('22) 15 12
63 " 30c black 25 15
64 " 30c rose ('22) 6 6
65 " 30c red orange ('25) 8 8
66 " 30c dark green, *greenish* ('28) 15 15
67 " 35c *yellow* ('06) 10 5
68 " 40c rose 10 6
69 " 40c black ('22) 15 12
70 " 45c olive ('07) 15 7
71 " 50c violet 80 60
72 " 50c blue ('22) 10 8
73 " 50c gray ('25) 10 8
74 " 60c lilac, *rose* ('25) 10 10
75 " 65c myrtle grn. ('26) 12 10
76 " 75c green 15 15
77 " 85c magenta ('26) 10 8
78 A15 1fr rose 8 7
79 " 1fr blue, *bluish* ('25) 10 8
80 " 1fr blue, *yellow green* ('28) 65 65
81 " 1.10fr light red ('28) 25 25
82 " 2fr blue 15 8
83 " 2fr orange red, *yellow* ('26) 35 30
84 " 5fr black 1.50 1.25
85 " 10fr green, *yellow* ('24) 4.00 3.75
a. Printed on both sides 15.00 15.00
86 " 20fr brown lake ('24) 4.75 4.50
Nos. 51-86 (36) 15.93 14.01

Issue of 1892 Surcharged in Black or Carmine

05 *j* **10** *k*

1912

87 A12 (*j*) 5c on 2c brown, *buff* 15 15
88 " (") 5c on 4c claret, *lavender* (C) 10 10
89 A12 (*j*) 5c on 20c red, *green* 15 15
90 " (") 5c on 25c *rose* (C) 60 60
91 " (") 5c on 30c brown, *bistre* (C) 30 30
92 " (*k*) 10c on 40c red, *straw* 15 15
93 " (") 10c on 50c carmine, *rose* 55 55
a. Double surcharge 110.00
Nos. 87-93 (7) 2.00 2.00

Two spacings between the surcharged numerals are found on Nos. 87 to 93.

No. 59 Surcharged in Various Colors **0,01** =

1922

94 A13 1c on 15c violet(Bk) 8 8
95 " 2c on 15c " (Bl) 8 8
a. Inverted surch. 17.50
96 " 4c on 15c violet (G) 8 8
a. Double surch. 17.50
97 " 5c on 15c violet (R) 8 8

Type of 1905-28 Surcharged in Blue

VINGT FRANCS VINGT FRANCS

1923

98 A15 10fr on 1fr green, *yellow* 4.00 4.00
99 " 20fr on 5fr lilac, *rose* 4.00 4.00

Stamps and Types of 1905-28 Surcharged with New Value and Bars in Black or Red.

1924-27

100 A13 25c on 15c violet('25) 10 10
a. Triple surch. 20.00
101 A15 25c on 2fr blue ('24) 10 10
a. Double surcharge 25.00
b. Triple surcharge 27.50
102 A14 65c on 45c olive (R) ('25) 15 15
103 " 85c on 45c olive (R) ('25) 20 20
104 " 90c on 75c red ('27) 20 20
105 A15 1.05fr on 2fr light yellow brown ('27) 25 25
106 " 1.25fr on 1fr ultra. (R) ('26) 20 20
107 " 1.50fr on 1fr light blue ('27) 30 30
108 " 3fr on 5fr violet ('27) 30 30
a. No period after "F" 2.50 2.50
Nos. 100-108 (9) 1.80 1.80

Carib Archer
A16

Shooting Rapids, Maroni River
A17

Government Building, Cayenne
A18

1929-40 *Perf. 13½ x 14.*

109 A16 1c gray lilac & greenish blue 6 6
110 " 2c dark red & blue green 4 4
111 " 3c gray lilac & greenish blue ('40) 5 5
112 " 4c olive brown & red violet 7 7
113 " 5c Prussian blue & red orange 6 6
114 " 10c magenta & brown 6 6
115 " 15c yellow brown & red orange 6 6
116 " 20c dark blue & olive green 10 10
117 " 25c dk. red & dk. brn. 10 10

Perf. 14 x 13½.

118 A17 30c dull & lt. green 12 12
119 " 30c green & brown ('40) 5 5
120 " 35c Prussian green & olive green ('38) 15 15
121 " 40c orange brown & olive gray 5 5
122 " 45c grn. & dk. brn. 20 20
123 " 45c olive green & light green ('40) 10 10
124 " 50c dark blue & olive gray 10 10
125 " 55c violet blue & carmine ('38) 18 18
126 " 60c salmon & green ('40) 8 6
127 " 65c salmon & green 15 15
128 " 70c indigo & slate blue ('40) 12 12
129 " 75c indigo & slate blue 30 30
130 " 80c black & violet blue ('38) 12 12
131 " 90c dark red & vermilion 12 12
132 " 90c red violet & brown ('39) 12 12
133 " 1fr lt. vio. & brn. 20 20
134 " 1fr carmine & light red ('38) 60 27
135 " 1fr black & violet blue ('40) 8 6
136 A18 1.05fr vermilion & olivine 1.50 1.20
137 " 1.10fr olive brown & red violet 1.50 1.20
138 " 1.25fr black brown & blue green ('33) 15 17
139 " 1.25fr rose & light red ('39) 12 12
140 " 1.40fr olive brown & red violet ('40) 12 10
141 " 1.50fr dark blue & light blue 10 10
142 " 1.60fr olive brown & blue green ('40) 12 10
143 " 1.75fr brown red & black brown ('33) 45 40
144 " 1.75fr violet blue ('38) 13 13
145 " 2fr dark green & rose red 10 10
146 " 2.25fr violet blue ('39) 12 10
147 " 2.50fr copper red & brown ('40) 10 10
148 " 3fr brown red & red violet 10 10
149 " 5fr dull violet & yellow green 12 10
150 " 10fr olive gray & deep ultramarine 18 12
151 " 20fr indigo & verm. 25 25
Nos. 109-151 (43) 8.60 7.46

Colonial Exposition Issue.
Common Design Types
Name of Country Printed in Black.

1931 Engraved. *Perf. 12½.*

152 CD70 40c deep green 1.25 1.25
153 CD71 50c violet 1.25 1.25
154 CD72 90c red orange 1.25 1.25
155 CD73 1.50fr dull blue 1.25 1.25

Recapture of Cayenne by d'Estrées, 1676
A19

Products of French Guiana
A20

1935, Oct. 21 *Perf. 13*

156 A19 40c gray brown 1.50 1.00
157 " 50c dull red 3.00 1.85
158 " 1.50fr ultramarine 1.50 1.25
159 A20 1.75fr lilac rose 4.00 3.50
160 " 5fr brown 3.50 2.50
161 " 10fr blue green 3.50 2.50
Nos. 156-161 (6) 17.00 12.60

Issued to commemorate the tercentenary of the founding of French possessions in the West Indies.

Paris International Exposition Issue.
Common Design Types

1937, Apr. 15

162 CD74 20c deep violet 25 25
163 CD75 30c dark green 25 25
164 CD76 40c carmine rose 25 25
165 CD77 50c dark brown 25 25
166 CD78 90c red 25 25
167 CD79 1.50fr ultramarine 25 25
Nos. 162-167 (6) 1.50 1.50

Colonial Arts Exhibition Issue
Souvenir Sheet.
Common Design Type

1937 *Imperf.*

168 CD75 3fr violet 1.40 1.40
Sheet size: 118x99mm.

New York World's Fair Issue
Common Design Type
Engraved.

1939, May 10 *Perf. 12½x12*

169 CD82 1.25fr carmine lake 30 30
170 " 2.25fr ultramarine 30 30

View of Cayenne and Marshal Petain
A21a

1941 Engraved *Perf. 12½x12*

170A A21a 1fr deep lilac 12
170B " 2.50fr blue 12

Nos. 170A-170B were issued by the Vichy government and were not placed on sale in the colony. This is also true of three stamps of types A16-A18 without "RF" released in 1944.

Common Design Types pictured in section at front of book.

Eboue Issue.
Common Design Type

1945 Engraved. *Perf. 13.*

171	CD91	2fr black	10	10
172	"	25fr Prussian green	20	15

This issue exists imperforate.

Arms of Cayenne
A22

1945 Lithographed *Perf. 12*

173	A22	10c deep gray violet	6	6
174	"	30c brown orange	6	6
175	"	40c light blue	6	6
176	"	50c violet brown	6	6
177	"	60c orange yellow	6	6
178	"	70c pale brown	8	8
179	"	80c light green	7	7
180	"	1fr blue	10	10
181	"	1.20fr bright violet	7	7
182	"	1.50fr deep orange	15	15
183	"	2fr black	13	13
184	"	2.40fr red	13	13
185	"	3fr pink	15	15
186	"	4fr deep ultramarine	20	20
187	"	4.50fr dp. yel. green	20	20
188	"	5fr orange brown	22	22
189	"	10fr dark violet	22	22
190	"	15fr rose carmine	20	20
191	"	20fr olive green	25	25
		Nos. 173-191 (19)	2.47	2.47

Hammock
A23

Guiana Girl
A26

Maroni River Bank
A24

Inini Scene
A25

Toucans
A27

Parrots—A28
Engraved

1947, June 2 *Perf. 13.* **Unwmkd.**

192	A23	10c dark blue green	6	6
193	"	30c bright red	6	6
194	"	50c dark violet brown	6	6
195	A24	60c greenish black	8	6
196	"	1fr red brown	8	6
197	"	1.50fr black brown	10	7
198	A25	2fr deep yellow green	12	10
199	"	2.50fr deep ultramarine	12	10
200	"	3fr red brown	15	12
201	A26	4fr black brown	30	27
202	"	5fr deep blue	30	27
203	"	6fr red brown	30	27
204	A27	10fr deep ultra.	1.25	1.00
205	"	15fr black brown	1.35	1.00
206	"	20fr red brown	1.75	1.50
207	A28	25fr brt. blue green	2.25	2.00
208	"	40fr black brown	2.25	2.00
		Nos. 192-208 (17)	10.58	9.00

SEMI-POSTAL STAMPS.

Regular Issue of 1905–28 Surcharged in Red

1915 *Perf. 13½x14.* **Unwmkd.**

B1	A13	10c+5c rose	4.50	3.00
		a. Inverted surcharge	35.00	25.00
		b. Double surcharge	25.00	22.50

Regular Issue of 1905–28 Surcharged in Rose

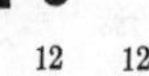

B2	A13	10c+5c rose	12	12

Curie Issue
Common Design Type

1938 *Perf. 13.*

B3	CD80	1.75fr+50c bright ultramarine	3.00	3.00

French Revolution Issue
Common Design Type

1939 Photogravure

Name and Value in Black.

B4	CD83	45(c) +25(c) grn.	3.00	3.00
B5	"	70(c)+30(c) brn.	3.00	3.00
B6	"	90(c)+35(c) red orange	3.00	3.00
B7	"	1.25fr+1fr rose pink	3.00	3.00
B8	"	2.25fr+2fr blue	3.00	3.00
		Nos. B4-B8, CB1 (6)	20.00	20.00

Common Design Type and

Colonial Infantryman
SP1

Colonial Policeman
SP2

1941 Photogravure *Perf. 13½*

B9	SP1	1fr+1fr red	25	
B10	CD86	1.50fr+3fr maroon	30	
B11	SP2	2.50fr+1fr blue	25	

Nos. B9–B11 were issued by the Vichy government, and were not placed on sale in the colony.

Nos. 170A–170B were surcharged "OEUVRES COLONIALES" and surtax (including change of denomination of the 2.50fr to 50c). These were issued in 1944 by the Vichy government, and not placed on sale in the colony.

Red Cross Issue
Common Design Type

1944 *Perf. 14½x14.*

B12	CD90	5fr+20fr dark copper brown	15	15

The surtax was for the French Red Cross and national relief.

AIR POST STAMPS.

Cayenne—AP1
Photogravure.

1933, Nov. 20 *Perf. 13½* **Unwmkd.**

C1	AP1	50c orange brown	10	10
C2	"	1fr yellow green	6	6
C3	"	1.50fr dark blue	10	10
C4	"	2fr orange	10	10
C5	"	3fr black	10	10
C6	"	5fr violet	10	10
C7	"	10fr olive green	10	10
C8	"	20fr scarlet	15	15
		Nos. C1-C8 (8)	81	81

V4

V5

Stamp of type AP1 without "RF" and stamps of the designs shown above were issued in 1942 and 1944 by the Vichy Government, but were not placed on sale in the colony.

Common Design Type

1945 Photo. *Perf. 14½x14*

C9	CD87	50fr dark green	35	35
C10	"	100fr plum	60	60

Victory Issue
Common Design Type

1946, May 8 Engraved. *Perf. 12½.*

C11	CD92	8fr black	40	40

Issued to commemorate the European victory of the Allied Nations in World War II.

Chad to Rhine Issue
Common Design Types

1946, June 6

C12	CD93	5fr dark slate blue	20	20
C13	CD94	10fr lilac rose	20	20
C14	CD95	15fr dk. vio. brown	30	30
C15	CD96	20fr dark slate green	35	35
C16	CD97	25fr violet brown	35	35
C17	CD98	50fr bright lilac	40	40
		Nos. C12-C17 (6)	1.80	1.80

Eagles—AP2

Tapir
AP3

Toucans—AP4

1947, June 2 Engraved. *Perf. 13*

C18	AP2	50fr deep green	4.50	4.50
C19	AP3	100fr red brown	5.00	5.00
C20	AP4	200fr dark gray blue	8.00	8.00

AIR POST SEMI-POSTAL STAMP
French Revolution Issue
Common Design Type
Photogravure

1939, July 5 *Perf. 13* **Unwmkd.**

Name & Value Typo. in Orange

CB1	CD83	5fr+4fr brown black	5.00	5.00

V6

Stamps of the design shown above and stamp of Cameroun type V10 inscribed "Guyane Francaise" were issued in 1942 by the Vichy Government, but were not placed on sale in the colony.

POSTAGE DUE STAMPS.

Postage Due Stamps of France, 1893–1926, Overprinted **GUYANE FRANÇAISE**

1925-27 *Perf. 14x13½.* **Unwmkd.**

J1	D2	5c light blue	5	5
J2	"	10c brown	8	8
J3	"	20c olive green	10	10
J4	"	50c violet brown	23	18
J5	"	3fr magenta ('27)	2.50	2.25

Surcharged in Black

GUYANE FRANÇAISE 25 centimes à percevoir

No.	Type	Description	Unused	Used
J6	D2	15c on 20c olive green	8	8
		a. Blue surcharge	15.00	
J7	D2	25c on 5c light blue	13	10
J8	"	30c on 20c olive green	18	10
J9	"	45c on 10c brown	12	10
J10	"	60c on 5c light blue	22	22
J11	"	1fr on 20c olive green	40	30
J12	"	2fr on 50c violet brown	40	40
		Nos. J1-J12 (12)	4.49	3.96

Royal Palms
D3

Guiana Girl
D4

1929, Oct. 14 Typo. *Perf. 13½x14*

No.	Type	Description	Unused	Used
J13	D3	5c indigo & Prussian blue	8	8
J14	"	10c bistre brown & Prussian green	6	6
J15	"	20c green & rose red	5	5
J16	"	30c olive brown & rose red	6	6
J17	"	50c vio. & olive brn.	10	10
J18	"	60c brown red & olive brown	20	20
J19	D4	1fr deep blue & orange brown	35	35
J20	"	2fr brown red & bluish green	50	50
J21	"	3fr violet & black	85	85
		Nos. J13-J21 (9)	2.25	2.25

D5

1947, June 2 Engr. *Perf. 14x13*

No.	Type	Description	Unused	Used
J22	D5	10c dark carmine rose	5	5
J23	"	30c dull green	5	5
J24	"	50c black	7	7
J25	"	1fr bright ultramarine	7	7
J26	"	2fr dark brown red	10	10
J27	"	3fr deep violet	10	10
J28	"	4fr red	18	18
J29	"	5fr brown violet	20	20
J30	"	10fr blue green	45	45
J31	"	20fr lilac rose	50	50
		Nos. J22-J31 (10)	1.77	1.77

FRENCH GUINEA

(frĕnch gĭn'ĭ)

LOCATION—On the coast of West Africa, between Portuguese Guinea and Sierra Leone.

GOVT.—Former French colony.

AREA—89,436 sq. mi.

POP.—2,058,442 (est. 1941).

CAPITAL—Conakry.

French Guinea stamps were replaced by those of French West Africa around 1944–45. French Guinea became the Republic of Guinea Oct. 2, 1958. See "Guinea" for issues of the republic.

100 Centimes = 1 Franc.

Navigation and Commerce — A1

Fulah Shepherd — A2

Perf. 14x13½.

1892-1900 Typographed. Unwmkd.

Name of Colony in Blue or Carmine

No.	Type	Description	Unused	Used
1	A1	1c *lilac blue*	40	40
2	"	2c brown, *buff*	40	40
3	"	4c claret, *lavender*	60	60
4	"	5c green, *greenish*	2.25	2.00
5	"	10c *lavender*	1.65	1.00
6	"	10c red ('00)	14.00	10.00
7	"	15c blue, quadrille paper	1.85	1.25
8	"	15c gray, *light gray* ('00)	40.00	35.00
9	"	20c red, *green*	5.00	4.00
10	"	25c *rose*	3.00	2.35
11	"	25c blue ('00)	6.00	5.00
12	"	30c brown, *bistre*	10.00	8.00
13	"	40c red, *straw*	10.00	7.00
		a. "GUINEE FRANCAISE" double	125.00	125.00
14	"	50c carmine, *rose*	14.00	7.50
15	"	50c brown, *azure* ('00)	8.00	7.00
16	"	75c deep violet, *orange*	17.50	15.00
17	"	1fr bronze green, *straw*	13.50	11.50
		Nos. 1-17 (17)	148.15	118.00

1904

No.	Type	Description	Unused	Used
18	A2	1c *yellow green*	20	12
19	"	2c violet brown, *buff*	20	18
20	"	4c carmine, *blue*	40	30
21	"	5c green, *greenish*	40	30
22	"	10c carmine	80	30
23	"	15c violet, *rose*	2.00	1.25
24	"	20c carmine, *green*	4.00	3.25
25	"	25c blue	4.00	3.25
26	"	30c brown	7.00	6.00
27	"	40c red, *straw*	9.00	7.00
28	"	50c brown, *azure*	9.00	8.00
29	"	75c green, *orange*	10.00	10.00
30	"	1fr bronze green, *straw*	13.50	11.50
31	"	2fr red, *orange*	30.00	27.50
32	"	5fr green, *yellow green*	40.00	37.50
		Nos. 18-32 (15)	130.50	116.45

Gen. Louis Faidherbé
A3

Oil Palm
A4

Dr. Noel Eugène Ballay
A5

1906-07

Name of Colony in Red or Blue.

No.	Type	Description	Unused	Used
33	A3	1c gray	10	10
34	"	2c brown	20	15
35	"	4c brown, *blue*	30	25
36	"	5c green	1.00	75
37	"	10c carmine (B)	5.00	60
38	A4	20c *blue*	1.00	75
39	"	25c blue, *pinkish*	2.25	1.85
40	"	30c brown, *pinkish*	1.40	1.10
41	"	35c *yellow*	60	40
42	"	45c chocolate, *greenish gray*	1.00	90
43	"	50c deep violet	3.25	2.75
44	"	75c blue, *orange*	1.00	1.00
45	A5	1fr black, *azure*	7.00	5.50
46	"	2fr blue, *pink*	14.00	12.00
47	"	5fr car., *straw* (B)	17.50	17.50
		Nos. 33-47 (15)	55.60	45.60

Regular Issues Surcharged in Black or Carmine

05 (a) 10 (b)

1912

On Issue of 1892–1900

Surcharged Type *a*

No.	Type	Description	Unused	Used
48	A1	5c on 2c brown, *buff*	30	30
49	"	5c on 4c claret, *lavender* (C)	15	15
50	"	5c on 15c blue (C)	17	17
51	"	5c on 20c red, *green*	1.00	1.00
52	"	5c on 30c brown, *bistre* (C)	1.20	1.20

Surcharged Type *b*

No.	Type	Description	Unused	Used
53	A1	10c on 40c red, *straw*	40	40
54	"	10c on 75c deep violet, *orange*	1.85	1.85
		a. Double surcharge, inverted	50.00	

On Issue of 1904.

Surcharged Type *a*

No.	Type	Description	Unused	Used
55	A2	5c on 2c violet brown, *buff*	20	20
		a. Pair, one without surcharge		
56	"	5c on 4c car., *blue*	20	20
57	"	5c on 15c violet, *rose*	25	25
58	"	5c on 20c carmine, *green*	25	25
59	"	5c on 25c blue (C)	25	25
60	"	5c on 30c brown (C)	25	25

Surcharged Type *b*

No.	Type	Description	Unused	Used
61	A2	10c on 40c red, *straw*	30	30
62	"	10c on 50c brown, *azure* (C)	85	85
		Nos. 48-62 (15)	7.62	7.62

Two spacings between the surcharged numerals are found on Nos. 48 to 62.

Ford at Kitim
A6

1913–33 *Perf. 13½x14*

No.	Type	Description	Unused	Used
63	A6	1c violet & blue	4	4
64	"	2c brn. & vio. brown	4	4
65	"	4c gray & black	5	5
66	"	5c yellow green & blue green	5	5
		a. Booklet pane of 4		
67	"	5c brown violet & green ('22)	5	5
68	"	10c red orange & rose	6	6
		a. Booklet pane of 4		
69	"	10c yellow green & blue green ('22)	5	5
70	"	10c vio. & verm. ('25)	6	5
71	"	15c violet brown & rose ('16)	5	5
72	"	15c gray green & yel. grn. ('25)	5	5
73	"	15c red brown & rose lilac ('27)	12	7
74	"	20c brown & violet	5	5
75	"	20c green & blue green ('26)	15	10
76	"	20c brown red & brown ('27)	7	6
77	"	25c ultra. & blue	18	18
78	"	25c blk. & vio. ('22)	15	8
79	"	30c violet brown & green	10	10
80	"	30c red orange & rose ('22)	6	6
81	"	30c rose red & green ('25)	5	5
82	"	30c dull green & blue green ('28)	45	33
83	"	35c blue & rose	6	6
84	"	40c green & gray	18	10
85	"	45c brown & red	25	18
86	"	50c ultra. & black	1.65	90
87	"	50c ultramarine & blue ('22)	12	7
88	"	50c yellow brown & olive ('25)	6	5
89	"	60c violet, *pinkish* ('25)	5	5
90	"	65c yellow brown & slate blue ('26)	35	33
91	"	75c red & ultramarine	40	25
92	"	75c indigo & dull blue ('25)	10	10
93	"	75c magenta & yellow green ('27)	45	25
94	"	85c olive green & red brown ('26)	12	12
95	"	90c brown red & rose ('30)	1.65	1.40
96	"	1fr violet & black	22	20
97	"	1.10fr violet & olive brown ('28)	1.75	1.75
98	"	1.25fr violet & yellow brown ('33)	45	30
99	"	1.50fr dark blue & lt. blue ('30)	1.10	75
100	"	1.75fr olive brown & violet ('33)	50	45
101	"	2fr org. & vio. brn.	70	20
102	"	3fr red violet ('30)	2.00	1.25
103	"	5fr black & violet	3.00	2.50
104	"	5fr dull blue & black ('22)	60	55
		Nos. 63-104 (42)	17.64	13.38

Nos. 66 and 68 exist on both ordinary and chalky paper, No. 71 on chalky paper only.

Type of 1913–33 Surcharged

60 = 60

1922

No.	Type	Description	Unused	Used
105	A6	60c on 75c violet, *pinkish*	10	10

Stamps and Type of 1913-33 Surcharged with New Value and Bars.

1924-27

No.	Type	Description	Unused	Used
106	A6	25c on 2fr orange & brown (R) ('24)	7	7
107	"	25c on 5fr dull blue & black ('24)	8	8
108	"	65c on 75c rose & ultra. ('25)	25	25
109	"	85c on 75c rose & ultra. ('25)	25	25
110	"	90c on 75c brown red & cerise ('27)	45	45
111	"	1.25fr on 1fr dark blue & ultramarine ('26)	8	8
112	"	1.50fr on 1fr deep blue & light blue ('27)	42	42
113	"	3fr on 5fr magenta & slate ('27)	1.10	1.10
114	"	10fr on 5fr blue & blue green, *bluish* ('27)	2.50	2.50
115	"	20fr on 5fr rose lilac & brown olive, *pinkish* ('27)	5.00	5.00
		Nos. 106-115 (10)	10.20	10.20

Colonial Exposition Issue.

Common Design Types

1931 Engraved. *Perf. 12½.*

Name of Country in Black.

No.	Type	Description	Unused	Used
116	CD70	40c deep green	1.10	1.00
117	CD71	50c violet	1.10	1.00
118	CD72	90c red orange	1.00	80
119	CD73	1.50fr dull blue	80	50

Paris International Exposition Issue.

Common Design Types

1937 *Perf. 13.*

No.	Type	Description	Unused	Used
120	CD74	20c deep violet	40	40
121	CD75	30c dark green	40	40
122	CD76	40c carmine rose	40	40
123	CD77	50c dark brown	40	40
124	CD78	90c red	40	40
125	CD79	1.50fr ultramarine	40	40
		Nos. 120-125 (6)	2.40	2.40

Colonial Arts Exhibition Issue.

Souvenir Sheet.

Common Design Type

1937 *Imperf.*

No.	Type	Description	Unused	Used
126	CD76	3fr Prussian green	1.35	1.35

Sheet size: 118x99mm.

Guinea Village—A7

Hausa Basket Workers—A8

Forest Waterfall—A9

Guinea Women A10

1938-40 *Perf. 13*

No.	Type	Description	Unused	Used
128	A7	2c vermilion	3	3
129	"	3c ultramarine	4	4
130	"	4c green	5	5
131	"	5c rose carmine	5	5
132	"	10c peacock blue	5	5
133	"	15c violet brown	5	5
134	A8	20c dark carmine	5	5
135	"	25c peacock blue	7	7
136	"	30c ultramarine	7	7
137	"	35c green	7	7
138	"	40c black brn. ('40)	6	6
139	"	45c dark green ('40)	10	10
140	"	50c red brown	7	7
141	A9	55c dark ultramarine	10	10
142	"	60c dark ultra. ('40)	25	25
143	"	65c green	12	10
144	"	70c green ('40)	25	25
145	"	80c rose violet	10	10
146	"	90c rose violet ('39)	25	25
147	"	1fr orange red	60	40
148	"	1fr brn. black ('40)	8	8
149	"	1.25fr orange red ('39)	30	30
150	"	1.40fr brown ('40)	33	33
151	"	1.50fr brown	60	40
152	A10	1.60fr orange red ('40)	20	20
153	"	1.75fr ultramarine	12	10
154	"	2fr magenta	30	12
155	"	2.25fr brt. ultra. ('39)	35	35
156	"	2.50fr brown black ('40)	25	25
157	"	3fr peacock blue	7	7
158	"	5fr rose violet	20	10
159	"	10fr slate green	20	15
160	"	20fr chocolate	50	30
		Nos. 128-160 (33)	5.93	4.96

Caillié Issue

Common Design Type

1939 Engraved *Perf. 12½x12*

No.	Type	Description	Unused	Used
161	CD81	90c orange brown & orange	20	20
162	"	2fr bright violet	25	25
163	"	2.25fr ultramarine & dark blue	20	20

Issued to commemorate the centenary of the death of René Caillié, French explorer.

New York World's Fair Issue.

Common Design Type

1939

No.	Type	Description	Unused	Used
164	CD82	1.25fr carmine lake	25	25
165	"	2.25fr ultramarine	25	25

Ford at Kitim and Marshal Petain A11

1941 *Perf. 12x12½.*

No.	Type	Description	Unused	Used
166	A11	1fr green	10	10
167	"	2.50fr deep blue	10	10

Nos. 166-167 were issued by the Vichy government. Seven stamps of types A7-A10 without "RF" are also Vichy issues (1943-44), but are believed not to have been placed on sale in the colony.

Stamps of French Guinea were followed by those of French West Africa.

Common Design Types pictured in section at front of book.

SEMI-POSTAL STAMPS.

Regular Issue of 1913 Surcharged in Red

1915 *Perf. 13½x14.* Unwmkd.

No.	Type	Description	Unused	Used
B1	A6	10c+5c orange & rose	30	12

No. B1 exists on both ordinary and chalky paper.

Curie Issue

Common Design Type

1938 Engraved. *Perf. 13.*

No.	Type	Description	Unused	Used
B2	CD80	1.75fr+50c bright ultramarine	2.75	2.75

French Revolution Issue

Common Design Type

1939 Photogravure.

Name and Value Typo. in Black.

No.	Type	Description	Unused	Used
B3	CD83	45(c)+25(c) green	1.85	1.85
B4	"	70(c)+30(c) brown	1.85	1.85
B5	"	90(c)+35(c) red orange	1.85	1.85
B6	"	1.25fr+1fr rose pink	1.85	1.85
B7	"	2.25fr+2fr blue	1.85	1.85
		Nos. B3-B7 (5)	9.25	9.25

Stamps of 1938, Surcharged in Black

SECOURS
+ 1 fr.
NATIONAL

1941 *Perf. 13.* Unwmkd.

No.	Type	Description	Unused	Used
B8	A8	50c+1fr red brown	20	20
B9	A9	80c+2fr rose violet	1.65	1.65
B10	"	1.50fr+2fr brown	1.65	1.65
B11	A10	2fr+3fr magenta	1.65	1.65

Common Design Type and

Senegalese Soldier SP1

Colonial Infantryman SP2

1941 *Perf. 13* Unwmkd.

No.	Type	Description	Unused
B12	SP1	1fr+1fr red	25
B13	CD86	1.50fr+3fr maroon	25
B14	SP2	2.50fr+1fr blue	25

Nos. B12-B14 were issued by the Vichy government, and were not placed on sale in the colony.

Nos. 166-167 were surcharged "OEUVRES COLONIALES" and surtax (including change of denomination of the 2.50fr to 50c). These were issued in 1944 by the Vichy government and not placed on sale in the colony.

AIR POST STAMPS.

Common Design Type

Engraved.

1940 *Perf. 12½x12.* Unwmkd.

No.	Type	Description	Unused	Used
C1	CD85	1.90fr ultramarine	8	8
C2	"	2.90fr dark red	12	12
C3	"	4.50fr dk. gray green	15	15
C4	"	4.90fr yellow bistre	20	20
C5	"	6.90fr deep orange	25	25
		Nos. C1-C5 (5)	80	80

Common Design Types

1942 Engraved.

No.	Type	Description	Unused	Used
C6	CD88	50c carmine & blue	5	
C7	"	1fr brown & black	6	
C8	"	2fr dark green & red brown	8	
C9	"	3fr dark blue & scarlet	9	
C10	"	5fr violet & brown red	15	

Frame Engraved, Center Typographed.

No.	Type	Description	Unused	Used
C11	CD89	10fr ultramarine, indigo & violet	15	
C12	CD89	20fr rose carmine, magenta & gray blue	18	
C13	"	50fr yellow green, dull green & gray black	35	60
		Nos. C6-C13 (8)	1.11	

There is doubt whether Nos. C6-C12 were officially placed in use.

AIR POST SEMI-POSTAL STAMPS.

Stamps of types of Dahomey V1, V2 and V3, and of Cameroun V10, inscribed "Guinée", "Guinée Frcaise" or "Guinée Française," were issued in 1942 by the Vichy Government, but were not placed on sale in the colony.

POSTAGE DUE STAMPS.

Fulah Woman D1

Heads and Coast D2

Typographed.

1905 *Perf. 14x13½* Unwmkd.

No.	Type	Description	Unused	Used
J1	D1	5c blue	40	40
J2	"	10c brown	60	60
J3	"	15c green	1.50	1.00
J4	"	30c rose	1.75	85
J5	"	50c black	3.00	2.25
J6	"	60c dull orange	4.00	3.00
J7	"	1fr violet	13.50	12.50
		Nos. J1-J7 (7)	24.75	20.60

1906-08

No.	Type	Description	Unused	Used
J8	D2	5c green, *greenish* ('08)	6.00	4.00
J9	"	10c violet brown ('08)	2.00	1.50
J10	"	15c dark blue ('08)	1.00	1.00
J11	"	20c *yellow*	1.00	1.00
J12	"	30c red, *straw* ('08)	9.00	7.50
J13	"	50c violet ('08)	8.00	7.00
J14	"	60c black, *buff* ('08)	7.00	6.00
J15	"	1fr *pinkish* ('08)	4.00	4.00
		Nos. J8-J15 (8)	38.00	32.00

D3

D4

1914

No.	Type	Description	Unused	Used
J16	D3	5c green	6	6
J17	"	10c rose	6	6
J18	"	15c gray	8	8
J19	"	20c brown	8	8
J20	"	30c blue	10	10
J21	"	50c black	15	15
J22	"	60c orange	45	45
J23	"	1fr violet	45	45
		Nos. J16-J23 (8)	1.43	1.43

Type of 1914 Issue Surcharged **2F.**

1927

No.	Type	Description	Unused	Used
J24	D3	2fr on 1fr lilac rose	1.65	1.65
J25	"	3fr on 1fr org. brown	1.65	1.65

1938 Engraved.

No.	Type	Description	Unused	Used
J26	D4	5c dark violet	4	4
J27	"	10c carmine	4	4
J28	"	15c green	5	5
J29	"	20c red brown	5	5
J30	"	30c rose violet	8	8
J31	"	50c chocolate	8	8
J32	"	60c peacock blue	9	9
J33	"	1fr vermilion	13	13
J34	"	2fr ultramarine	25	25
J35	"	3fr black	25	25
		Nos. J26-J35 (10)	1.06	1.06

A 10c of type D4 without "RF" was issued in 1944 by the Vichy Government, but was not placed on sale in the colony.

FRENCH INDIA

(frĕnch ĭn'dĭ-ȧ)

LOCATION—East coast of India bordering on Bay of Bengal.

GOVT.—Former French Territory.

AREA—196 sq. mi.

POP.—323,295 (1941).

CAPITAL—Pondichéry.

French India was an administrative unit comprising the five settlements of Chandernagor, Karikal, Mahé, Pondichéry and Yanaon. These united with India in 1949 and 1954.

100 Centimes = 1 Franc

24 Caches = 1 Fanon (1923)

8 Fanons = 1 Rupie

Navigation and Commerce
A1

A2

Perf. 14x13½.

1892-1907 Typographed. Unwmkd.

Colony Name in Blue or Carmine

No.	Type	Description	Unused	Used
1	A1	1c *lilac blue*	40	40
2	"	2c brown, *buff*	40	40
3	"	4c claret, *lavender*	60	60
4	"	5c green, *greenish*	1.25	85
5	"	10c *lavender*	2.50	1.00
6	"	10c red ('00)	85	60
7	"	15c blue, quadrille paper	2.50	1.65
8	"	15c gray, *light gray* ('00)	8.00	8.00
9	"	20c red, *green*	1.50	1.00
10	"	25c *rose*	1.00	60
11	"	25c blue ('00)	3.50	2.75
12	"	30c brown, *bistre*	12.50	12.00
13	"	35c *yellow* ('06)	3.50	1.25
14	"	40c red, *straw*	1.60	1.20
15	"	45c *gray green* ('07)	85	40
16	"	50c carmine, *rose*	1.50	1.20
17	"	50c brown, *azure* ('00)	2.50	2.00
18	"	75c deep violet, *orange*	2.00	2.00
19	"	1fr bronze green, *straw*	2.50	2.25
		Nos. 1-19 (19)	49.45	40.15

Nos. 10 and 16 Surcharged in Carmine or Black **0,05**

1903

No.	Type	Description	Unused	Used
20	A1	5c on 25c *rose*	110.00	65.00
21	"	10c on 25c *rose*	110.00	75.00
22	"	15c on 25c *rose*	40.00	40.00
23	"	40c on 50c carmine, *rose* (Bk)	185.00	140.00

Counterfeits of Nos. 20-23 abound.

1903

No.	Type	Description	Unused	Used
24	A2	5c gray blue & black	6.00	6.00

Brahma
A5

Kali Temple near Pondichéry
A6

1914-22 *Perf. 13½x14, 14x13½*

No.	Type	Description	Unused	Used
25	A5	1c gray & black	6	6
26	"	2c brn. vio. & black	8	8
27	"	2c green & brown violet ('22)	10	10
28	"	3c brown & black	10	10
29	"	4c orange & black	12	12
30	"	5c blue green & black	15	15
31	"	5c violet brown & black ('22)	10	10
32	"	10c deep rose & black	12	12
33	"	10c green & black ('22)	15	15
34	"	15c violet & black	18	18
35	"	20c orange red & black	35	35
36	"	25c blue & black	40	40
37	"	25c ultramarine & terra cotta ('22)	15	15
38	"	30c ultra. & black	35	35
39	"	30c rose & black ('22)	20	20
40	A6	35c chocolate & black	35	35
41	"	40c orange red & black	35	35
42	"	45c blue green & black	35	35
43	"	50c deep rose & black	20	20
44	"	50c ultramarine & blue ('22)	20	20
45	"	75c blue & black	60	60
46	"	1fr yellow & black	60	60
47	"	2fr violet & black	1.25	1.25
48	"	5fr ultra. & black	45	45
49	"	5fr rose & black ('22)	70	70
		Nos. 25-49 (25)	7.66	7.66

No. 34 Surcharged **0,01 ≡** in Various Colors.

1922

No.	Type	Description	Unused	Used
50	A5	1c on 15c (Bk)	10	10
51	"	2c on 15c (Bl)	10	10
52	"	5c on 15c (R)	10	10

Stamps and Types of 1914-22 Surcharged with New Values in Caches, Fanons and Rupies in Black, Red or Blue:

1 FANON

2 CACHES

12 CACHES

3

ROUPIES

1923-28

No.	Type	Description	Unused	Used
54	A5	1ca on 1c gray & black (R)	9	8
55	"	2ca on 5c violet brown & black	13	13
		a. Horizontal pair, imperf. between		
56	"	3ca on 3c brown & black	13	13
57	"	4ca on 4c orange & black	15	13
58	"	6ca on 10c green & black	20	20
59	A6	6ca on 45c blue green & black (R)	15	15
60	A5	10ca on 20c deep red & blue green ('28)	60	60
61	"	12ca on 15c violet & black	20	20
62	"	15ca on 20c orange & black	20	20
63	A6	16ca on 35c light blue & yellow brown ('28)	55	55
64	A5	18ca on 30c rose & black	20	20
65	A6	20ca on 45c green & dull red ('28)	30	30
66	A5	1fa on 25c deep green & rose red ('28)	65	65
67	A6	1fa 3ca on 35c chocolate & black (Bl)	20	20
68	"	1fa 6ca on 40c orange & black (R)	20	20
69	"	1fa 12ca on 50c ultra. & blue (Bl)	20	20
70	"	1fa 12ca on 75c blue & black (Bl)	20	20
		a. Double surch.	40.00	
71	"	1fa 16ca on 75c brown red & green ('28)	90	70
72	A5	2fa 9ca on 25c ultramarine & terra cotta (Bl)	40	23
73	A6	2fa 12ca on 1f violet & dark brown ('28)	50	50
74	"	3fa 3ca on 1fr yellow & black (R)	45	45
		a. Double surch.	40.00	
75	"	6fa 6ca on 2fr violet & black (Bl)	1.40	1.00
76	"	1r on 1fr green & deep blue (R) ('26)	2.00	2.00
77	"	2r on 5fr rose & black (R)	2.00	1.65
		a. Double surch.	40.00	
78	"	3r on 2fr gray & blue violet (R) ('26)	4.50	3.00
79	"	5r on 5fr rose & black, *greenish* ('26)	5.00	4.00
		Nos. 54-79 (26)	21.50	17.85

Nos. 60, 63, 66 and 73 have the original value obliterated by bars.

A7

A8

1929

No.	Type	Description	Unused	Used
80	A7	1ca dark gray & black	8	8
81	"	2ca vio. brn. & black	8	8
82	"	3ca brown & black	8	8
83	"	4ca orange & black	10	8
84	"	6ca gray green & green	10	8
85	"	10ca brn., red & grn.	12	12
86	A8	12ca grn. & lt. green	12	10
87	A7	16ca bright blue & black	18	15
88	"	18ca brown red & vermilion	18	15
89	"	20ca dark blue & green, *bluish*	15	12
90	A8	1fa gray green & rose red	15	12
91	"	1fa 6ca red orange & black	15	12
92	"	1fa 12ca deep blue & ultramarine	15	12
93	"	1fa 16ca rose red & green	15	13
94	"	2fa 12ca bright violet & brown	20	15
95	"	6fa 6ca dull violet & black	17	15
96	"	1r gray green & deep blue	20	12
97	"	2r rose & black	30	20
98	"	3r light gray & gray lilac	60	40
99	"	5r rose & black, *greenish*	85	45
		Nos. 80-99 (20)	4.11	3.00

Colonial Exposition Issue.

Common Design Types

1931 Engraved. *Perf. 12½.*

No.	Type	Description	Unused	Used
100	CD70	10ca deep green	85	85
101	CD71	12ca violet	85	85
102	CD72	18ca red orange	85	85
103	CD73	1fa 12ca dull blue	85	85

Paris International Exposition Issue.

Common Design Types

1937 *Perf. 13.*

No.	Type	Description	Unused	Used
104	CD74	8ca deep violet	35	35
105	CD75	12ca dark green	35	35
106	CD76	16ca carmine rose	35	35
107	CD77	20ca dark brown	35	35
108	CD78	1fa 12ca red	35	35
109	CD79	2fa 12ca ultra.	35	35
		Nos. 104-109 (6)	2.10	2.10

Colonial Arts Exhibition Issue.

Souvenir Sheet.

Common Design Type

1937 *Imperf.*

No.	Type	Description	Unused	Used
110	CD79	5fa red violet	1.50	1.50

Sheet size: 118x99mm.

New York World's Fair Issue.

Common Design Type

1939 Engraved *Perf. 12½x12*

No.	Type	Description	Unused	Used
111	CD82	1fa 12ca carmine lake	35	35
112	"	2fa 12ca ultramarine	55	55

Temple near Pondichéry and Marshal Petain—A9

1941 Engraved *Perf. 12½x12*

No.	Type	Description	Unused	Used
112A	A9	1fa 16ca car. & red	10	
112B	"	4fa 4ca blue	10	

Nos. 112A-112B were issued by the Vichy government, and were not placed on sale in French India.

Stamps of 1923 Overprinted in Carmine or Blue:

FRANCE LIBRE — a

FRANCE LIBRE — b

Perf. 13½x14, 14x13½.

1941 Unwmkd.

No.	Type	Description	Unused	Used
113	A5 (a)	15ca on 20c orange & black (C)	20.00	20.00
114	" (")	18ca on 30c rose & black (C)	50	50
115	A6 (a)	1fa 3ca on 35c chocolate & black (C)	25.00	25.00
		a. Horiz. ovpt.	20.00	20.00
116	A5 (b)	2fa 9ca on 25c ultramarine & terra cotta (Bl)	375.00	325.00
		a. Ovpt. "a" (Bl)	400.00	325.00
		b. Ovpt. "b" (C)	550.00	

Common Design Types

pictured in section at front of book.

Stamps of 1929
Overprinted in Carmine or Blue.

No.	Type	Description	Unused	Used
117	A7 (a)	2ca violet brown & black (C)	2.00	1.85
118	" (")	3ca brown & black (C)	60	60
119	" (")	4ca orange & black (C)	1.85	1.65
120	" (")	6ca gray green & green (C)	40	40
121	" (")	10ca brown red & green (Bl)	60	50
122	A8 (")	12ca green & light green (C)	60	50
123	A7 (")	16ca bright blue & black (C)	40	40
123A	" (")	18ca brown red & vermilion (Bl)	250.00	185.00
124	" (")	20ca dark blue & green, *bluish* (C)	60	50
125	A8 (")	1fa gray green & rose red (Bl)	60	40
126	" (")	1fa 6ca red orange & black (C)	60	40
127	" (")	1fa 12ca deep blue & ultra. (C)	1.25	1.00
128	" (")	1fa 16ca rose red & green (C)	60	40
129	" (")	2fa 12ca bright violet & brown (C)	60	40
130	" (")	6fa 6ca dull violet & black (C)	60	50
131	" (")	1r gray green & deep blue (C)	60	40
132	" (")	2r rose & black (C)	60	40
133	" (")	3r light gray & gray lilac (C)	60	50
134	" (")	5r rose & black, *greenish* (C)	2.00	1.25
		Nos. 113-115, 117-123, 124-134 (21)	60.00	57.55

Same Overprints on Paris Exposition Issue of 1937.

Perf. 13.

No.	Type	Description	Unused	Used
135	CD74 (b)	8ca deep violet (C)	2.00	2.00
135A	" (")	8ca deep violet (Bl)	75.00	75.00
135B	" (a)	8ca deep violet (C)	40.00	40.00
135C	" (")	8ca deep violet (Bl)	70.00	65.00
136	CD75 (")	12ca dark green (C)	1.00	1.00
137	CD76 (")	16ca carmine rose (Bl)	1.00	1.00
138	CD78 (")	1fa 12ca red (Bl)	1.00	1.00
139	CD79 (")	2fa 12ca ultra. (C)	1.00	1.00
		Nos. 135-139 (8)	191.00	186.00

Inverted overprints exist.

Souvenir Sheet

No. 110 Overprinted "FRANCE LIBRE" Diagonally in Blue Violet

Two types of overprint:
I. Overprint 37mm. With serifs.
II. Overprint 24mm., as type "a" shown above No. 113. No serifs.

1941 ***Imperf.*** **Unwmkd.**

No.	Type	Description	Unused	Used
140	CD79	5fa red violet (I)	250.00	210.00
		a. Type II	300.00	275.00

Overprinted on New York World's Fair Issue, 1939.

Perf. 12½x12.

No.	Type	Description	Unused	Used
141	CD82 (a)	1fa 12ca carmine lake (Bl)	85	85
142	" (")	2fa 12ca ultra. (C)	85	85

Lotus Flowers
A10

Photogravure

1942 ***Perf. 14x14½*** **Unwmkd.**

No.	Type	Description	Unused	Used
143	A10	2ca brown	10	10
144	"	3ca dark blue	10	10
145	"	4ca emerald	10	10
146	"	6ca dark orange	10	10
147	"	12ca greenish black	10	10
148	"	16ca rose violet	10	10
149	"	20ca dark red brown	15	12
150	"	1fa bright red	20	15
151	"	1fa 18ca slate black	20	15
152	"	6fa 6ca brt. ultra.	25	15
153	"	1r dull violet	20	18
154	"	2r bistre	40	30
155	"	3r chocolate	50	40
156	"	5r dark green	50	45
		Nos. 143-156 (14)	3.00	2.50

Stamps of 1923-39 Overprinted in Blue or Carmine

FRANCE LIBRE
c

FRANCE LIBRE
d

Perf. 13½x14, 14x13½.

1942-43

Overprinted on No. 64

No.	Type	Description	Unused	Used
156A	A5 (c)	18ca on 30c rose & black (B)	100.00	70.00

Overprinted on Stamps of 1929

No.	Type	Description	Unused	Used
157	A7 (c)	2ca violet brown & black (C)	20	20
		a. Black overprint	15.00	15.00
158	" (")	3ca brown & black (C)	30	30
159	" (")	6ca gray green & green (Bl)	30	30
160	A8 (d)	12ca green & light green (Bl)	60	60
161	A7 (c)	16ca bright blue & black (C)	30	30
162	" (")	18ca brown red & vermilion (Bl)	30	30
163	" (")	20ca dark blue & green, *bluish* (Bl) ('43)	1.50	1.25
164	" (")	20ca dark blue & green, *bluish* (C)	30	30
165	A8 (d)	1fa gray green & rose red (Bl)	20	20
166	" (")	1fa 6ca red orange & black (C)	50	50
167	" (")	1fa 12ca deep blue & ultra. (C)	40	40
168	" (")	1fa 16ca rose red & green (Bl)	20	20
169	" (")	2fa 12ca bright violet & brown (Bl)	10.00	10.00
170	" (")	2fa 12ca bright violet & brown (C)	50	50
171	A8 (d)	6fa 6ca dull violet & black (C)	85	85
172	" (")	1r gray green & deep blue (C)	1.65	1.65
173	" (")	2r rose & black (C)	1.25	1.25
174	" (")	3r light gray & gray lilac (C)	1.25	1.25
175	" (")	3r light gray & gray lilac (Bl) ('43)	45.00	40.00
176	" (")	5r rose & black, *greenish* (C)	1.35	1.35
		Nos. 156A-176 (21)	166.95	131.70

Same Overprints on Paris International Exposition Issue of 1937.

Perf. 13.

No.	Type	Description	Unused	Used
177	CD74 (c)	8ca deep violet (Bl)	2.00	1.40
178	CD75 (d)	12ca dark green (Bl)	1.65	1.65
179	CD76 (")	16ca carmine rose (Bl)	500.00	375.00
180	CD78 (")	1fa 12ca red (Bl)	25	25
181	CD79 (")	2fa 12ca ultramarine (C)	90	80

Same Overprint on New York World's Fair Issue, 1939.

Perf. 12½x12.

No.	Type	Description	Unused	Used
182	CD82 (d)	1fa 12ca carmine lake (Bl)	40	40
183	" (")	2fa 12ca ultramarine (C)	1.00	1.00

No. 87 Surcharged in Carmine

FRANCE LIBRE
2 fa 9 ca

1942-43 ***Perf. 13½x14***

No.	Type	Description	Unused	Used
184	A7	1ca on 16ca	20.00	12.00
185	"	4ca on 16ca ('43)	20.00	12.00
186	"	10ca on 16ca	12.00	4.00
187	"	15ca on 16ca	10.00	4.00
188	"	1fa 3ca on 16ca ('43)	20.00	10.00
189	"	2fa 9ca on 16ca ('43)	16.50	10.00
190	"	3fa 3ca on 16ca ('43)	12.00	5.00
		Nos. 184-190 (7)	110.50	57.00

Nos. 95-99 Surcharged in Carmine

FRANCE LIBRE
1 cache

1943 ***Perf. 14x13½.***

No.	Type	Description	Unused	Used
191	A8	1ca on 6fa 6ca dull violet & black	3.50	2.50
192	"	4ca on 6fa 6ca dull violet & black	4.50	4.00
193	"	10ca on 6fa 6ca dull violet & black	85	20
194	"	15ca on 6fa 6ca dull violet & black	1.25	50
195	"	1fa 3ca on 6fa 6ca dull violet & black	2.00	85
196	"	2fa 9ca on 6fa 6ca dull violet & black	2.00	1.10
197	"	3fa 3ca on 6fa 6ca dull violet & black	2.00	1.10
198	"	1ca on 1r gray green & deep blue	1.00	1.00
199	"	2ca on 1r gray green & deep blue	20	20
200	"	4ca on 1r gray green & deep blue	20	20
201	A8	6ca on 2r rose & black	20	20
202	"	10ca on 2r rose & black	40	40
203	"	12ca on 2r rose & black	20	20
204	"	15ca on 3r light gray & gray lilac	20	20
205	"	16ca on 3r light gray & gray lilac	20	20
206	"	1fa 3ca on 3r light gray & gray lilac	20	20
207	"	1fa 6ca on 5r rose & black, *greenish*	40	40
208	"	1fa 12ca on 5r rose & black, *greenish*	40	20
209	"	1fa 16ca on 5r rose & black, *greenish*	40	40
		Nos. 191-209 (19)	20.10	14.05

In 1943, twenty-seven stamps were overprinted in red or dark blue, "FRANCE TOUJOURS" and a Lorraine Cross within a circle measuring 17¾mm. in diameter. The stamps overprinted were 19 denominations of the regular 1929 postage series, plus Nos. 104 to 109 and Nos. 111 and 112. Of each stamp, 200 were overprinted.

No. 95 Surcharged in Carmine with New Value and Bars.

1943 ***Perf. 14x13½.*** **Unwmkd.**

No.	Type	Description	Unused	Used
209A	A8	1ca on 6fa 6ca	7.00	5.00
209B	"	4ca on 6fa 6ca	7.00	5.00
209C	"	10ca on 6fa 6ca	2.00	1.50
209D	"	15ca on 6fa 6ca	2.00	1.50
209E	"	1fa 3ca on 6fa 6ca	6.00	5.00
209F	"	2fa 9ca on 6fa 6ca	6.50	5.00
209G	"	3fa 3ca on 6fa 6ca	6.50	5.00
		Nos. 209A-209G (7)	37.00	28.00

Eboue Issue.

Common Design Type

1945 **Engraved.** ***Perf. 13.***

No.	Type	Description	Unused	Used
210	CD91	3fa 8ca black	10	10
211	"	5r 1fa 16ca Prussian green	30	30

Nos. 210 and 211 exist imperforate.

Apsaras
A11

Brahman Ascetic
A12

Designs: 6ca, 8ca, 10ca, Dvarabalagar. 12ca, 15ca, 1fa, Vishnu. 1fa 6ca, 2fa, 2fa 2ca, Dvarabalagar (foot raised). 2fa 12ca, 3fa, 5fa, Temple Guardian. 7fa 12ca, 1r 2fa, 1r 4fa 12ca, Tigoupalagar.

1948 Photogravure ***Perf. 13x13½***

No.	Type	Description	Unused	Used
212	A11	1ca dark olive green	4	4
213	"	2ca orange brown	6	6
214	"	4ca violet, *cream*	6	6
215	"	6ca yellow orange	15	8
216	"	8ca gray black	30	25
217	"	10ca dull yellow green, *pale green*	28	28
218	"	12ca violet brown	12	9
219	"	15ca Prussian green	12	12
220	"	1fa violet, *pale rose*	25	15
221	"	1fa 6ca brown red	20	20
222	"	2fa dark green	20	12
223	"	2fa 2ca blue, *cream*	35	25
224	"	2fa 12ca brown	40	35
225	"	3fa deep orange	75	45
226	"	5fa red violet, *rose*	55	50
227	"	7fa 12ca dark brown	50	45
228	"	1r 2fa brown black	1.35	1.35
229	"	1r 4fa 12ca olive green	1.40	1.35
		Nos. 212-229 (18)	7.08	6.15

1952

No.	Type	Description	Unused	Used
230	A12	18ca rose red	25	25
231	"	1fa 15ca violet blue	75	75
232	"	4fa olive green	75	75

Military Medal Issue.
Common Design Type

1952 Engr. and Typo. ***Perf. 13***
233 CD101 1fa multicolored 85 85

SEMI-POSTAL STAMPS.

Regular Issue of 1914 Surcharged in Red ✚ 5c

1915 ***Perf. 14x13½*** **Unwmkd.**
B1 A5 10c+5c rose & black 30 30
a. Inverted surch. 20.00 20.00

There were two printings of this surcharge; in the first it was placed at the bottom of the stamp, in the second it was near the top.

Regular Issue of 1914 Surcharged in Red 5 ✚

1916
B2 A5 10c+5c rose & black 4.00 4.00
a. Inverted surch. 17.50 17.50
b. Double surch. 20.00 20.00

Surcharged ✚ 5 C

B3 A5 10c+5c rose & black 55 55

Surcharged 5 C

B4 A5 10c+5c rose & black 20 20

Surcharged ✚ 5c

B5 A5 10c+5c rose & black 30 30

Curie Issue
Common Design Type

1938 **Engraved.** ***Perf. 13.***
B6 CD80 2fa12ca+20ca bright ultramarine 3.50 3.50

French Revolution Issue
Common Design Type

1939 **Photogravure.**
Name and Value Typo. in Black.
B7 CD83 18ca+10ca green 2.00 2.00
B8 " 1fa 6ca+12ca brown 2.00 2.00
B9 " 1fa 12ca+16ca red orange 2.00 2.00
B10 " 1fa 16ca+1fa16ca rose pink 2.00 2.00
B11 " 2fa 12ca+3fa blue 2.00 2.00
Nos. B7-B11 (5) 10.00 10.00

Common Design Type and

Non-Commissioned Officer, Native Guard
SP1

Sepoy
SP2

1941 Photogravure ***Perf. 13½***
B12 SP1 1fa 16ca+1fa 16ca red 20
B13 CD86 2fa 12ca+5fa maroon 20
B13A SP2 4fa 4ca+1fa 16ca blue 20

Nos. B12–B13A were issued by the Vichy government, and were not placed on sale in French India.

Nos. 112A–112B were surcharged "OEUVRES COLONIALES" and surtax (including change of denomination of the 4fa 4ca to 20ca). These were issued in 1944 by the Vichy government and were not placed on sale in French India.

Red Cross Issue
Common Design Type

1944 Photogravure. ***Perf. 14½x14.***
B14 CD90 3fa+1r 4fa dark olive brown 20 20

The surtax was for the French Red Cross and national relief.

Tropical Medicine Issue
Common Design Type

1950 **Engraved.** ***Perf. 13.***
B15 CD100 1fa+10ca indigo & deep blue 60 60

The surtax was for charitable work.

AIR POST STAMPS.

Common Design Type
Photogravure.

1942 ***Perf. 14½x14.*** **Unwmkd.**
C1 CD87 4fa dark orange 20 15
C2 " 1r bright red 20 20
C3 " 2r brown red 30 30
C4 " 5r black 40 40
C5 " 8r ultramarine 70 55
C6 " 10r dark green 70 60
Nos. C1-C6 (6) 2.50 2.20

Victory Issue
Common Design Type

1946 **Engraved.** ***Perf. 12½***
C7 CD92 4fa dark blue green 25 25

Issued to commemorate the European Victory of the Allied Nations in World War II.

Chad to Rhine Issue
Common Design Types

1946, June 6
C8 CD93 2fa 12ca olive bistre 25 25
C9 CD94 5fa dark blue 25 25
C10 CD95 7fa 12ca dark purple 35 35
C11 CD96 1r 2fa green 35 35
C12 CD97 1r 4fa 12ca dk. car. 35 35
C13 CD98 3r 1fa violet brown 35 35
Nos. C8-C13 (6) 1.90 1.90

A 3r ultramarine and red, picturing the Temple of Chindambaram, was sold at Paris June 7 to July 8, 1948, but not placed on sale in the colony.

Bas-relief Figure of Goddess
AP1

Wing and Temple AP2
Bird over Palms AP3

Perf. 12x13, 13x12.

1949 Photogravure **Unwmkd.**
C14 AP1 1r yellow & plum 1.50 1.00
C15 AP2 2r grn. & dk. grn. 2.50 2.00
C16 AP3 5r light blue & violet brown 7.00 6.50

UPU Issue
Common Design Type

1949 Engraved ***Perf. 13***
C17 CD99 6fa lilac rose 2.25 2.25

Issued to commemorate the 75th anniversary of the formation of the Universal Postal Union.

Liberation Issue
Common Design Type

1954, June 6
C18 CD102 1fa sepia & violet brown 1.50 1.50

AIR POST SEMI-POSTAL STAMPS.

V4

Stamps of the above design and of Cameroun type V10 inscribed "Etabts Frcais dans l'Inde" were issued in 1942 by the Vichy Government, but were not placed on sale in French India.

POSTAGE DUE STAMPS.

Postage Due Stamps of France, 1893–1941.

Surcharged **6 CACHES** like Regular Issue in Black, Blue or Red.

1923 ***Perf. 14x13½.*** **Unwmkd.**
J1 D2 6ca on 10c brown (Bl) 25 25
J2 " 12ca on 25c rose (Bk) 25 25
J3 " 15ca on 20c olive green (R) 25 25
J4 " 1fa 6ca on 30c red (Bl) 35 35
J5 " 1fa 12ca on 50c brown violet (Bl) 40 40
J6 " 1fa 15ca on 5c blue(Bk) 50 50
J7 " 3fa 3ca on 1fr red brn., *straw* (Bl) 85 85
Nos. J1-J7 (7) 2.85 2.85

Types of Postage Due Stamps of French Colonies, 1884-85, Surcharged with New Values as in 1923 in Red or Black. Bars over Original Values.

1928
J8 D1 4ca on 20c gray lilac 20 20
J9 D1 1fa on 30c orange 40 40
J10 " 1fa 16ca on 5c blue black (R) 50 50
J11 " 3fa on 1f light green 85 85

D3

D4

1929 Typographed
J12 D3 4ca deep red 10 10
J13 " 6ca blue 10 10
J14 " 12ca green 10 10
J15 " 1fa brown 15 15
J16 " 1fa 12ca lilac gray 25 25
J17 " 1fa 16ca buff 30 30
J18 " 3fa lilac 50 50
Nos. J12-J18 (7) 1.50 1.50

Photogravure.

1948 ***Perf. 13x13½.*** **Unwmkd.**
J19 D4 1ca dark violet 5 5
J20 " 2ca dark brown 5 5
J21 " 6ca blue green 8 8
J22 " 12ca deep orange 10 10
J23 " 1fa dark carmine rose 10 10
J24 " 1fa 12ca brown 15 15
J25 " 2fa dark slate blue 20 20
J26 " 2fa 12ca henna brown 30 30
J27 " 5fa dark olive green 60 60
J28 " 1r dark blue violet 75 75
Nos. J19-J28 (10) 2.38 2.38

FRENCH MOROCCO

(frĕnch mô-rŏk'ō)

LOCATION—Northwest coast of Africa.
GOVT.—Former French Protectorate.
AREA—153,870 sq. mi.
POP.—8,340,000 (estimated 1954).
CAPITAL—Rabat.

French Morocco was a French Protectorate from 1912 until 1956 when it, along with the Spanish and Tangier zones of Morocco, became the independent country, Morocco.

Stamps inscribed "Tanger" were for use in the international zone of Tangier in northern Morocco.

100 Centimos = 1 Peseta
100 Centimes = 1 franc (1917)

French Offices in Morocco

A1

A2

Stamps of France Surcharged in Red or Black.
Perf. 14x13½.

1891-1900 **Unwmkd.**
1 A1 5c on 5c green, *greenish* (R) 2.50 1.25
a. Imperf., pair 40.00
2 " 5c on 5c yellow green (I) (R) ('99) 10.00 10.00
a. Type II 10.00 8.00
3 " 10c on 10c *lavender* (II) (R) 10.00 1.00
a. Type I 12.00 6.00
b. 10c on 25c *rose* 350.00
4 " 20c on 20c red, *green* 12.00 10.00
5 " 25c on 25c *rose* (R) 7.50 30
a. Double surcharge 60.00
b. Imperf., pair 45.00
6 " 50c on 50c carmine, *rose*(II) 37.50 12.00
a. Type I 165.00 100.00

7 A1 1p on 1fr bronze green, *straw* 35.00 22.50
8 " 2p on 2fr brown, *azure* (Bk) ('00) 100.00 85.00
Nos. 1-8 (8) 214.50 142.05

No. 3b was never sent to Morocco.

France Nos. J15-J16
Overprinted in Carmine.

1893

9 A2 5c black 850.00 350.00
10 " 10c black 750.00 225.00

Counterfeits exist.

A3

A4

A5

Surcharged in Red or Black.

1902-10

11 A3 1c on 1c gray (R) ('08) 20 10
a. Surcharge omitted
12 " 2c on 2c vio. brn. ('08) 35 25
13 " 3c on 3c red org. ('08) 35 25
14 " 4c on 4c yellow brown ('08) 3.75 2.50
15 " 5c on 5c green (R) 1.50 30
a. Double surch. 60.00
16 A4 10c on 10c rose red ('03) 1.00 20
a. Surcharge omitted
17 " 20c on 20c brown violet ('03) 8.00 4.50
18 " 25c on 25c blue ('03) 8.00 50
19 " 35c on 35c vio. ('10) 13.50 9.00
20 A5 50c on 50c bis. brn. & lavender ('03) 12.50 3.50
21 " 1p on 1fr claret & olive grn. ('03) 35.00 25.00
22 " 2p on 2fr gray violet & yellow ('03) 40.00 25.00
Nos. 11-22 (12) 124.15 71.10

Nos. 11-14 exist spelled CFNTIMOS or GENTIMOS.
The 25c on 25c with surcharge omitted is listed as No. 81a.

Postage Due Stamps
Nos. J1-J2
Handstamped

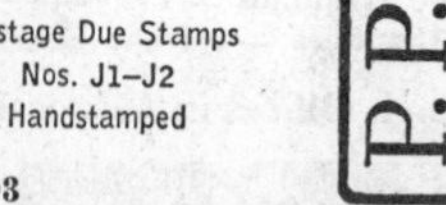

1903

24 D2 5c on 5c light blue 425.00
25 " 10c on 10c chocolate 850.00

Nos. 24 and 25 were used only on Oct. 10, 1903. Used copies were not canceled, the overprint serving as a cancelation.
Counterfeits exist.

Types of 1902-10 Issue
Surcharged in
Red or Blue

1
سنتيم

1911-17

26 A3 1c on 1c gray (R) 5 5
27 " 2c on 2c violet brown 10 10
28 " 3c on 3c orange 10 8
29 " 5c on 5c green (R) 15 6
30 A4 10c on 10c rose 7 6
a. Imperf., pair 90.00
31 " 15c on 15c orange ('17) 75 65
32 " 20c on 20c brn. violet 1.00 85
33 " 25c on 25c blue (R) 60 20
34 " 35c on 35c violet (R) 2.25 1.00
35 A5 40c on 40c red & pale blue ('17) 1.85 1.85
36 " 50c on 50c bis. brown & lavender (R) 8.00 5.25
37 A5 1p on 1fr claret & olive green 5.25 2.00
Nos. 26-37 (12) 20.17 12.15

Stamps of this design were issued by the Cherifien posts in 1912-13. The Administration Cherifienne des Postes, Telegraphes et Telephones was formed in 1911 under French guidance.

French Protectorate

A6

A7

A8

Issue of 1911-17
Overprinted "Protectorat Francais"

1914-21

38 A6 1c on 1c gray 10 5
39 " 2c on 2c violet brown 10 6
40 " 3c on 3c orange 25 20
41 " 5c on 5c green 8 5
a. New value omitted 90.00 90.00
42 A7 10c on 10c rose 8 5
a. New value omitted 140.00 140.00
43 " 15c on 15c org. ('17) 10 5
a. New value omitted 25.00 25.00
44 " 20c on 20c brown violet 1.50 70
a. "Protectorat Francais" double 100.00 100.00
45 " 25c on 25c blue 40 5
a. New value omitted 90.00 90.00
46 " 25c on 25c violet ('21) 25 6
a. "Protectorat Francais" omitted 13.50 13.50
b. "Protectorat Francais" double 50.00 50.00
c. "Protectorat Francais" double (R+Bk) 45.00 45.00
47 " 30c on 30c violet ('21) 4.50 3.75
48 " 35c on 35c violet 1.65 60
49 A8 40c on 40c red & pale blue 5.00 3.00
a. New value omitted 90.00 90.00
50 " 45c on 45c green & blue ('21) 14.00 11.00
51 " 50c on 50c bistre brown & lavender 25 8
a. "Protectorat Francais" inverted 35.00 25.00
b. "Protectorat Francais" double
52 " 1p on 1fr claret & olive green 50 6
a. "Protectorat Francais" inverted 90.00 80.00
b. New value double 45.00 45.00
c. New value double, one inverted 45.00 45.00
53 " 2p on 2fr gray violet & yellow 1.20 40
a. New value omitted 50.00 50.00
b. "Protectorat Francais" omitted 30.00 30.00
c. New value double
d. New value double, one inverted
54 " 5p on 5fr dark blue & buff 4.00 2.00
Nos. 38-54 (17) 33.96 22.16

Tower of Hassan, Rabat
A9

Mosque of the Andalusians, Fez
A10

City Gate, Chella
A11

Koutoubiah, Marrakesh
A12

Bab Mansour, Meknés
A13

Remains of Hadrian's Temple
A14

Engraved.

1917 *Perf. 13½x14, 14x13½*

55 A9 1c greenish gray 8 8
56 " 2c brown lilac 15 8
57 " 3c orange brown 10 10
a. Imperf., pair 27.50 27.50
58 A10 5c yellow green 6 6
59 " 10c rose red 8 6
60 " 15c dark gray 6 5
a. Imperf., pair 18.50 18.50
61 A11 20c red brown 1.20 1.00
62 " 25c dull blue 1.00 15
63 " 30c gray violet 1.20 85
64 A12 35c orange 1.00 60
65 " 40c ultramarine 25 18
66 " 45c gray green 6.00 3.50
67 A13 50c dark brown 2.25 1.00
a. Imperf., pair 20.00 20.00
68 A13 1fr slate 2.65 1.35
a. Imperf., pair 16.50 16.50
69 A14 2fr black brown 90.00 42.50
70 " 5fr dark gray green 17.50 14.00
71 " 10fr black 17.50 15.00
Nos. 55-71 (17) 141.08 80.56

See note following No. 115.
See Nos. 93-105.

Types of the 1902-10 Issue
Overprinted **TANGER**

1918-24 *Perf. 14x13½.*

72 A3 1c gray 10 10
73 " 2c violet brown 10 10
74 " 3c red orange 15 15
75 " 5c green 20 15
76 " 5c orange ('23) 40 40
77 A4 10c rose 20 20
78 " 10c green ('24) 15 15
79 " 15c orange 35 35
80 " 20c violet brown 60 60
81 " 25c blue 85 50
a. "TANGER" omitted 150.00 110.00
82 " 30c red orange ('24) 90 60
83 " 35c violet 1.00 60
84 A5 40c red & pale blue 1.00 60
85 " 50c bistre brown & lavender 9.00 5.00
86 A4 50c blue 6.00 4.00
87 A5 1fr claret & olive green 3.00 1.50
88 " 2fr orange & pale bl. ('24) 30.00 27.50
89 " 5fr dark blue & buff ('24) 27.50 22.50
Nos. 72-89 (18) 81.50 65.00

Types of 1917 and

Tower of Hassan, Rabat
A15

Bab Mansour, Meknès
A16

Scene in Volubilis
A17

1923-27 Photo. *Perf. 13½*

90 A15 1c olive green 5 5
91 " 2c brown violet 5 5
92 " 3c yellow brown 5 5
93 A10 5c orange 6 6
94 " 10c yellow green 6 5
95 " 15c dark gray 6 5
96 A11 20c red brown 6 5
97 " 20c red violet ('27) 15 15
98 " 25c ultramarine 6 6
99 " 30c deep red 6 6
100 " 30c turq. blue ('27) 22 10
101 A12 35c violet 8 8
102 " 40c orange red 5 5
103 " 45c deep green 6 6
104 A16 50c dull turquoise 5 5
105 A12 50c dark olive green ('27) 20 5
106 A16 60c lilac 12 10
107 " 75c red violet ('27) 12 12
108 " 1fr deep brown 13 13
109 " 1.05fr red brown ('27) 50 40
110 " 1.40fr dull rose ('27) 18 13
111 " 1.50fr turq. blue ('27) 25 6
112 A17 2fr olive brown 40 30
113 " 3fr deep red ('27) 40 40
114 " 5fr dark gray green 1.25 85

115 A17 10fr black 3.50 2.00
Nos. 90–115 (26) 8.17 5.51

Nos. 90–110, 112–115 exist imperf.

The stamps of 1917 were line engraved. Those of 1923–27 were printed by photogravure and have in the margin at lower right the imprint "Helio Vaugirard".

No. 102 Surcharged in Black

15c 15c

1930

120 A12 15c on 40c orange red 40 40

Nos. 100, 106 and 110 Surcharged in Blue Similarly to No. 176.

1931

121 A11 25c on 30c turq. blue 80 80
a. Inverted surch. 27.50 22.50
122 A16 50c on 60c lilac 20 5
a. Inverted surch. 30.00 25.00
123 " 1fr on 1.40fr rose 60 40
a. Inverted surch. 30.00 25.00

Old Treasure House and Tribunal, Tangier
A18

Roadstead at Agadir
A19

Post Office at Casablanca
A20

Moulay Idriss of the Zehroun
A21

Kasbah of the Oudayas, Rabat
A22

Court of the Medersa el Attarine at Fez
A23

Saadiens' Tombs at Marrakesh
A25

Kasbah of Si Madani el Glaoui at Ouarzazat—A24

1933–34 Engraved Perf. 13

124 A18 1c olive black 4 4
125 " 2c red violet 6 6
126 A19 3c dark brown 6 6
127 " 5c brown red 6 6
128 A20 10c blue green 10 6
129 " 15c black 6 6
130 " 20c red brown 6 6
131 A21 25c dark blue 10 6
132 " 30c emerald 10 5
133 " 40c black brown 10 6
134 A22 45c brown violet 8 8
135 " 50c dark blue green 10 4
a. Booklet pane of 10
136 " 65c brown red 6 6
a. Booklet pane of 10
137 A23 75c red violet 6 6
138 " 90c orange red 8 5
139 " 1fr deep brown 30 7
140 " 1.25fr black ('34) 30 10
141 A24 1.50fr ultramarine 15 5
142 " 1.75fr myrtle green ('34) 8 7
143 " 2fr yellow brown 70 5
144 " 3fr carmine rose 15.00 2.35
145 A25 5fr red brown 2.00 30
146 " 10fr black 2.75 2.00
147 " 20fr bluish gray 2.75 2.25
Nos. 124–147 (24) 25.15 8.10

No. 135 Surcharged in Red

40c

1939

148 A22 40c on 50c dark blue green 5 5

Mosque of Salé
A26

Sefrou
A27

Cedars
A28

Goatherd
A29

Ramparts of Salé
A30

Scimitar-horned Oryxes
A31

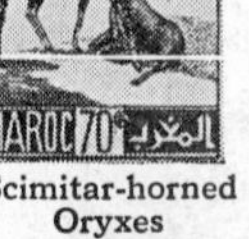

Fez
A33

Valley of Draa
A32

1939–42

149 A26 1c rose violet 3 3
150 A27 2c emerald 5 5
151 " 3c ultramarine 5 5
152 A26 5c dark blue green 5 5
153 A27 10c bright red violet 6 6
154 A28 15c dark green 5 5
155 " 20c black brown 5 5
156 A29 30c deep blue 5 5
157 " 40c chocolate 5 6
158 " 45c Prussian green 13 15
159 A30 50c rose red 27 20
159A " 50c Prussian green ('40) 5 6
160 " 60c turquoise blue 30 20
160A " 60c chocolate ('40) 5 5
161 A31 70c dark violet 5 5
162 A32 75c greenish black 5 5
163 " 80c peacock blue ('40) 5 5
163A " 80c dark green ('42) 5 5
164 A30 90c ultramarine 5 5
165 A28 1fr chocolate 5 5
165A A32 1.20fr rose violet ('42) 7 7
166 " 1.25fr henna brown 15 12
167 " 1.40fr rose violet 6 6
168 A30 1.50fr copper red ('40) 6 6
168A " 1.50fr rose ('42) 6 6
169 A33 2fr Prussian green 6 6
170 " 2.25fr dark blue 8 8
170A A26 2.40fr red ('42) 5 5
171 " 2.50fr scarlet 15 12
171A " 2.50fr deep blue ('40) 18 10
172 A33 3fr black brown 5 5
172A A26 4fr dp. ultra. ('42) 5 5
172B A32 4.50fr greenish black ('42) 10 10
173 A31 5fr dark blue 13 8
174 " 10fr red 23 23
174A " 15fr Prussian green ('42) 1.25 1.10
175 " 20fr dk. vio. brown 50 45
Nos. 149–175 (37) 4.77 4.25

See also Nos. 197–219.

No. 136 Surcharged in Black

35c

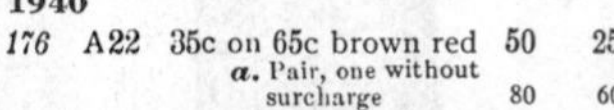

1940

176 A22 35c on 65c brown red 50 25
a. Pair, one without surcharge 80 60

The surcharge was applied on alternate rows in the sheet, making pairs, one stamp with a surcharge and one without. This was done to make a pair equal 1 franc, the new rate.

One Aim Alone—Victory
A34

Tower of Hassan, Rabat
A35

1943 Lithographed Perf. 12.

177 A34 1.50fr deep blue 4 4

1943

178 A35 10c rose lilac 4 4
179 " 30c blue 4 4
180 " 40c lake 4 4
181 " 50c blue green 4 4
182 " 60c dark violet brown 4 4
183 " 70c rose violet 4 4
184 " 80c gray green 4 4
185 " 1fr carmine lake 4 4
186 " 1.20fr violet 4 4
187 " 1.50fr red 4 4
188 " 2fr light blue green 8 5
189 " 2.40fr carmine rose 6 5
190 " 3fr olive brown 8 5
191 " 4fr dark ultramarine 6 5
192 " 4.50fr slate black 6 5
193 " 5fr dull blue 8 6
194 " 10fr orange brown 10 6
195 " 15fr slate green 40 10
196 " 20fr deep plum 42 10
Nos. 178-196 (19) 1.74 97

Types of 1939-42.
Perf. 13½x14, 14x13½.

1945-47 Typographed. Unwmkd.

197 A27 10c red violet 6 6
199 A29 40c chocolate 6 6
200 A30 50c Prussian green 6 6
203 A28 1fr chocolate ('46) 6 6
204 A32 1.20fr vio. brn. ('46) 6 6
205 A27 1.30fr blue ('47) 15 12
206 A30 1.50fr deep red 6 6
207 A33 2fr Prussian green 6 6
209 " 3fr black brown 6 6
210 A29 3.50fr dark red ('47) 12 8
212 A31 4.50fr magenta ('47) 7 6
214 " 5fr indigo 12 12
215 A32 6fr chalky blue ('46) 6 6
216 A31 10fr red 35 25
217 " 15fr Prussian green 45 20
218 " 20fr dk. vio. brown 70 40
219 " 25fr black brown 70 70
Nos. 197–219 (17) 3.20 2.47

The Terraces
A37

Mountain District
A39

Fortress
A38

Marrakesh
A40

Gardens of Fez—A41

Ouarzazat District
A42

Engraved.

1947–48 *Perf. 13* **Unwmkd.**

No.	Type	Description	Unused	Used
221	A37	10c black brown	5	4
222	"	30c bright red	6	6
223	"	50c bright greenish blue	6	4
224	"	60c bright red violet	6	5
225	A38	1fr black	6	5
226	"	1.50fr blue	6	5
227	A39	2fr bright green	10	6
228	"	3fr brown red	6	6
229	A40	4fr dark blue violet	7	6
230	A41	5fr dark green	20	18
231	A40	6fr crimson	7	5
232	A41	10fr deep blue ('47)	12	6
233	A42	15fr dark green ('47)	30	10
234	"	20fr henna brn. ('47)	25	6
235	"	25fr purple ('47)	60	20
		Nos. 221–235 (15)	2.12	1.12

1948-49

No.	Type	Description	Unused	Used
236	A37	30c purple	4	4
237	A38	2fr violet brown ('49)	6	5
238	A40	4fr green	7	5
239	A41	8fr orange ('49)	18	8
240	"	10fr blue	18	6
241	A42	10fr carmine rose	20	6
242	A38	12fr red	25	5
243	A42	18fr deep blue	27	25
		Nos. 236–243 (8)	1.25	64

No. 175 Surcharged with New Value and Wavy Lines in Carmine.

1948

No.	Type	Description	Unused	Used
244	A31	8fr on 20fr dark violet brown	20	15

Fortified Oasis—A43

Walled City—A44

1949

No.	Type	Description	Unused	Used
245	A43	5fr blue green	10	5
246	A44	15fr red	22	5
247	"	25fr ultramarine	45	7

See also No. 300.

Detail, Gate of Oudayas, Rabat
A45

Nejjarine Fountain, Fez
A46

Garden, Meknes
A47

1949 *Perf. 14x13*

No.	Type	Description	Unused	Used
248	A45	10c black	4	4
249	"	50c rose brown	10	10
250	"	1fr blue violet	6	6
251	A46	2fr dark carmine rose	6	6
252	"	3fr dark blue	6	5
253	"	5fr bright green	12	5
254	A47	8fr dark blue green	18	4
255	"	10fr bright red	18	4
		Nos. 248–255 (8)	80	44

Postal Administration Building, Meknes
A48

1949, Oct. *Perf. 13*

No.	Type	Description	Unused	Used
256	A48	5fr dark green	60	60
257	"	15fr deep carmine	80	80
258	"	25fr deep blue	1.00	1.00

Issued to commemorate the 75th anniversary of the formation of the Universal Postal Union.

Todra Valley
A49

1950

No.	Type	Description	Unused	Used
259	A49	35fr red brown	35	6
260	"	50fr indigo	35	5

See also No. 270.

Nos. 204 and 205 Surcharged in Black or Blue

1fr

1950 *Perf. 14x13½, 13½x14*

No.	Type	Description	Unused	Used
261	A32	1fr on 1.20fr violet brown (Bk)	6	6
262	A27	1fr on 1.30fr blue (Bl)	6	6

The surcharge is transposed and spaced to fit the design on No. 262.

No. 231 Surcharged with New Value and Wavy Lines in Black.

1951 *Perf. 13*

No.	Type	Description	Unused	Used
263	A40	5fr on 6fr crimson	10	6

Statue of Gen. Jacques Leclerc
A50

1951, Apr. 28 **Engraved**

No.	Type	Description	Unused	Used
264	A50	10fr blue green	45	45
265	"	15fr deep carmine	45	45
266	"	25fr indigo	70	70

Issued to commemorate the unveiling of a monument to Gen. Leclerc at Casablanca, April 28, 1951. See No. C39.

Loustau Hospital, Oujda
A51

Designs: 15fr, New Hospital, Meknes. 25fr, New Hospital, Rabat.

1951

No.	Type	Description	Unused	Used
267	A51	10fr indigo & purple	40	40
268	"	15fr Prussian green & red brown	45	45
269	"	25fr dark brown & indigo	50	50

Todra Valley Type of 1950.

1951

No.	Type	Description	Unused	Used
270	A49	30fr ultramarine	40	10

Pigeons at Fountain
A52

Karaouine Mosque, Fez
A53

Patio, Oudayas
A54

Oudayas Point, Rabat
A55

Patio of Old House
A56

MAROC MAROC
Type I (No. 275) Type II (No. 276)

Perf. 14x13, 13.

1951–53 **Engraved.** **Unwmkd.**

No.	Type	Description	Unused	Used
271	A52	5fr magenta ('52)	8	4
272	A53	6fr blue green ('52)	10	5
273	A52	8fr brown ('52)	9	8
273A	A53	10fr rose red ('53)	15	5
274	"	12fr deep ultra. ('52)	20	6
275	A54	15fr red brown (I)	90	6
276	"	15fr red brown (II)	30	5
277	A55	15fr purple ('52)	35	5
278	"	18fr red ('52)	40	28
279	A56	20fr dp. greenish blue ('52)	30	15
		Nos. 271–279 (10)	2.87	87

See also Nos. 297–299.

8th-10th Century Capital
A57

Casablanca Monument
A58

Capitals: 20fr, XIIth Century. 25fr, XIIIth–XVIth Century. 50fr, XVIIth Century.

1952, Apr. 5 *Perf. 13*

No.	Type	Description	Unused	Used
280	A57	15fr deep blue	1.00	1.00
281	"	20fr red	1.00	1.00
282	"	25fr purple	1.00	1.00
283	"	50fr deep green	1.00	1.00

1952, Sept. 22 **Engr. & Typo.**

No.	Type	Description	Unused	Used
284	A58	15fr multicolored	90	70

Issued to commemorate the centenary of the creation of the French Military Medal.

Daggers of South Morocco
A59

Post Rider and Public Letter-writer
A60

Designs: 20fr and 25fr, Antique brooches.

1953, Mar. 27 **Engraved.**

No.	Type	Description	Unused	Used
285	A59	15fr dark carmine rose	90	90
286	"	20fr violet brown	90	90
287	"	25fr dark blue	90	90

See No. C46.

1953, May 16

No.	Type	Description	Unused	Used
288	A60	15fr violet brown	60	60

Stamp Day, May 16, 1953.

Bine el Ouidane Dam
A61

1953, Nov. 3 *Perf. 13*

No.	Type	Description	Unused	Used
290	A61	15fr indigo	60	55

See also No. 295.

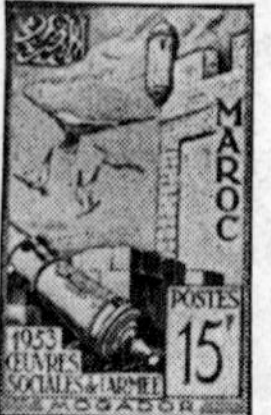

Mogador Fortress
A62

Design: 30fr, Moorish knights.

1953, Dec. 4

No.	Type	Description	Unused	Used
291	A62	15fr green	65	65
292	"	30fr red brown	65	65

Issued to aid Army Welfare Work.

Nos. 226 and 243 Surcharged with New Value and Wavy Lines in Black.

1954

293	A38	1fr on 1.50fr blue	8	8
294	A42	15fr on 18fr deep blue	23	23

Dam Type of 1953.

1954, Mar. 8

295	A61	15fr red brown & indigo	30	12

Station of Rural Automobile Post

A63

1954, Apr. 10

296	A63	15fr dark blue green	40	40

Stamp Day, April 10, 1954.

Types of 1951–53

1954 Engraved. *Perf. 14x13*

297	A52	15fr dark blue green	20	5

Typographed.

298	A52	5fr magenta	20	15
299	A55	15fr rose violet	30	25

Walled City Type of 1949

1954 Engraved. *Perf. 13*

300	A44	25fr purple	40	20

Marshal Lyautey at Rabat — A64

Lyautey, Builder of Cities — A65

Designs: 15fr, Marshal Lyautey at Khenifra. 50fr, Hubert Lyautey, Marshal of France.

1954, Nov. 17

301	A64	5fr indigo	1.00	1.00
302	"	15fr dark green	1.00	1.00
303	A65	30fr rose brown	1.50	1.50
304	"	50fr dark red brown	1.50	1.50

Issued to commemorate the centenary of the birth of Marshal Hubert Lyautey.

Franco-Moslem Education

A66

Moslem Student at Blackboard

A67

Designs: 30fr, Moslem school at Camp Boulhaut. 50fr, Moulay Idriss College at Fez.

1955, Apr. 16 *Perf. 13* Unwmkd.

305	A66	5fr indigo	50	50
306	A67	15fr rose lake	50	50
307	A66	30fr chocolate	75	65
308	A67	50fr dark blue green	85	85

Issued to publicize Franco-Moslem solidarity.

Map and Rotary Emblem

A68

1955, June 11

309	A68	15fr blue & orange brown	60	40

Issued to commemorate the 50th anniversary of the founding of Rotary International.

Post Office, Mazagan

A69

1955, May 24

310	A69	15fr red	25	25

Stamp Day.

Bab el Chorfa, Fez — A70

Mahakma (Courthouse), Casablanca — A71

Fortress, Safi

A72

Designs: 50c, 1fr, 2fr, Mrissa Gate, Salé. 10fr, 12fr, 15fr, Minaret at Rabat. 30fr, Menara Garden, Marrakesh. 40fr, Tafraout Village. 50fr, Portuguese cistern, Mazagan. 75fr, Garden of Oudaya, Rabat.

1955 *Perf. 13½x13, 13x13½, 13*

311	A70	50c brown violet	3	3
312	"	1fr blue	4	4
313	"	2fr red lilac	4	4
314	"	3fr bluish black	5	4
315	"	5fr vermilion	20	17
316	"	6fr green	7	6
317	"	8fr orange brown	20	20
318	"	10fr violet brown	50	10
319	"	12fr greenish blue	10	5
320	"	15fr magenta	40	4
321	A71	18fr dark green	50	40
322	"	20fr brown lake	20	5
323	A72	25fr bright ultramarine	90	10
324	"	30fr green	85	20
325	"	40fr orange red	35	10
326	"	50fr black brown	2.00	8
327	A71	75fr greenish blue	60	30
		Nos. 311-327 (17)	7.03	2.00

Succeeding issues, released under the Kingdom, are listed under Morocco in Vol. III.

SEMI-POSTAL STAMPS.

French Protectorate

No. 30 Surcharged in Red — ✚ 5c

1914 *Perf. 14x13½* Unwmkd.

B1	A4	10c+5c on 10c rose	6500.00	5750.00

No. B1 is known only with inverted surcharge.

Same Surcharge on No. 42 with "Protectorat Francais".

B2	A7	10c+5c on 10c rose	1.00	1.00
		a. Double surcharge	30.00	30.00
		b. Inverted surcharge	40.00	40.00
		c. "c" omitted	17.50	17.50

On Nos. B1 and B2 the cross is set up from pieces of metal (quads), the horizontal bar being made from two long pieces, the vertical bar from two short pieces. Each cross in the setting of twenty-five differs from the others.

No. 30 Handstamp Surcharged in Red — + 5c

B3	A4	10c+5c on 10c rose	650.00	500.00

No. B3 was issued at Oujda. The surcharge ink is water-soluble.

No. 42 Surcharged in Vermilion or Carmine — + 5c

B4	A7	10c+5c on 10c rose (V)	5.00	5.00
		a. Double surcharge	37.50	32.50
		b. Inverted surcharge	45.00	35.00
		c. Double surcharge, one inverted	40.00	35.00
B5	"	10c+5c on 10c rose (C)	110.00	110.00

On Nos. B4 and B5 the horizontal bar of the cross is single and not as thick as on Nos. B1 and B2.

No. B5 was sold largely at Casablanca.

SP1

SP2

1915 Carmine Surcharge.

B6	SP1	5c+5c green	70	60
		a. Inverted surcharge	50.00	50.00

No. B6 was not issued without the Red Cross surcharge.

B7	SP2	10c+5c rose	85	85

No. B7 was used in Tangier.

SP3

SP4

France No. B2 Overprinted in Black.

B8	SP3	10c+5c red	2.00	2.00

1917 Carmine Surcharge.

B9	SP4	10c+5c on 10c rose	85	85

On No. B9 the horizontal bar of the cross is made from a single, thick piece of metal.

Marshal Hubert Lyautey

SP5

1935, May 15 Photo. *Perf. 13x13½*

B10	SP5	50c+50c red	4.00	4.00
B11	"	1fr+1fr dark green	4.00	4.00
B12	"	5fr+1fr blk. brn.	20.00	20.00

Stamps of 1933–34 Surcharged in Blue or Red — O.S.E. +3 c

1938 *Perf. 13.*

B13	A18	2c+2c red violet (Bl)	1.75	1.75
B14	A19	3c+3c dark brown (Bl)	1.75	1.75
B15	A20	20c+20c red brown (Bl)	1.75	1.75
B16	A21	40c+40c black brown (R)	1.75	1.75
B17	A22	65c+65c brown red (Bl)	1.75	1.75
B18	A23	1.25fr+1.25fr black (R)	1.75	1.75
B19	A24	2fr+2fr yellow brown (Bl)	1.75	1.75
B20	A25	5fr+5fr red brown (Bl)	1.75	1.75
		Nos. B13-B20 (8)	14.00	14.00

Stamps of 1939 Surcharged in Black

+2f

Enfants de France au Maroc

1942

B21	A29	45c+2fr Prussian green	1.50	1.50
B22	A30	90c+4fr ultra.	1.50	1.50
B23	A32	1.25fr+6fr henna brown	1.50	1.50
B24	A26	2.50fr+8fr scarlet	1.50	1.50

The arrangement of the surcharge differs slightly on each denomination.

No. 207 Surcharged in Black

AIDEZ LES TUBERCULEUX +1f

1945 *Perf. 13½x14* Unwmkd.

B26	A33	2fr+1fr Prussian green	5	5

Mausoleum of Marshal Lyautey

SP7

Statue of Marshal Lyautey

SP8

1945 Lithographed *Perf. 11½*

B27	SP7	2fr+3fr dark blue	8	8

The surtax was for French works of solidarity.

3f

No. B26 Surcharged in Red

1946 *Perf. 13½x14*

B28	A33	3fr(+1fr) on 2fr+1fr Prussian green	6	6

Engraved.

1946, Dec. 16 *Perf. 13½x14, 13*

B29 SP8 2fr+10fr black 40 40
B30 " 3fr+15fr copper red 50 50
B31 " 10fr+20fr bright blue 90 90

The surtax was for works of solidarity.

JOURNÉE
DU
TIMBRE
1947

No. 212
Surcharged in
Rose Violet

+5F50

1947, Mar. 15 *Perf. 13½x14*

B32 A31 4.50fr+5.50fr magenta 50 50

Stamp Day, 1947.

Map and Symbols of Prosperity from Phosphates
SP9

1947 *Perf. 13*

B33 SP9 4.50fr+5.50fr green 22 22

Issued to commemorate the 25th anniversary of the exploitations of the Cherifien Office of Phosphates.

Power
SP10

Health
SP11

1948, Feb. 9

B34 SP10 6fr+ 9fr red brown 60 60
B35 SP11 10fr+20fr dp. ultra. 60 60

The surtax was for combined works of Franco-Moroccan solidarity.

Type of Regular Issue of 1923, Inscribed: "Journée du Timbre 1948."

1948, Mar. 6

B36 A16 6fr+4fr red brown 30 30

Stamp Day, Mar. 6, 1948.

Battleship off Moroccan Coast
SP12

1948, Aug.

B37 SP12 6fr+9fr purple 55 55

The surtax was for naval charities.

Wheat Field near Meknès
SP13

Designs: 2fr+5fr, Olive grove, Taroudant. 3fr+7fr, Net and coastal view. 5fr+10fr, Aguedal Gardens, Marrakesh.

1949, Apr. 12 Engraved Unwmkd.

Inscribed: "SOLIDARITÉ 1948."

B38 SP13 1fr+2fr orange 30 30
B39 " 2fr+5fr carmine 30 30
B40 " 3fr+7fr peacock blue 30 30
B41 " 5fr+10fr dark brown violet 30 30
a. Sheet of four 6.00 6.00
Nos. B38-B41, CB31-CB34 (8) 3.20 3.00

No. B41a contains one each of Nos. B38-B41. Size: 120x96mm.

Gazelle Hunter, from 1899 Local Stamp—SP14

1949, May 1

B42 SP14 10fr+5fr chocolate & carmine rose 40 40

Stamp Day and 50th anniversary of Mazagan-Marrakesh local postage stamp.

Moroccan Soldiers and Flag
SP15

Rug Weaving
SP16

1949

B43 SP15 10fr+10fr bright red 50 50

The surtax was for Army Welfare Work.

1950, Apr. 11

Designs: 2fr+5fr, Pottery making. 3fr+7fr, Bookbinding. 5fr+10fr, Copper work.

Inscribed: "SOLIDARITE 1949."

B44 SP16 1fr+2fr deep carmine 70 70
B45 " 2fr+5fr dark greenish blue 70 70
B46 " 3fr+7fr dark purple 70 70
B47 " 5fr+10fr red brown 70 70
a. Sheet of four 6.00 4.00
Nos. B44-B47, CB36-CB39 (8) 4.40 4.40

No. B47a contains one each of Nos. B44-B47. Size: 95½x120½mm.

Ruins of Sala Colonia at Chella
SP17

1950, Sept. 25 Engraved. *Perf. 13*

B48 SP17 10fr+10fr deep magenta 50 50
B49 " 15fr+15fr indigo 50 50

The surtax was for Army Welfare Work.

AIR POST STAMPS.
French Protectorate

Biplane over Casablanca
AP1

Photogravure.

1922-27 *Perf. 13½* Unwmkd.

C1 AP1 5c deep orange ('27) 5 5
a. Imperf., pair 25.00
C2 " 25c deep ultramarine 20 10
a. Imperf., pair 37.50
C3 " 50c greenish blue 5 5
a. Imperf., pair 27.50
C4 " 75c deep blue 25.00 4.75
a. Imperf., pair 300.00
C5 " 75c deep green 5 5
a. Imperf., pair 35.00
C6 " 80c vio. brown ('27) 40 12
a. Imperf., pair 27.50
C7 " 1fr vermilion 5 5
a. Imperf., pair 30.00
C8 " 1.40fr brown lake ('27) 50 30
C9 " 1.90fr deep blue ('27) 60 40
C10 " 2fr black violet 25 20
a. 2fr deep violet 30 25
b. Imperf., pair 90.00
C11 " 3fr gray black ('27) 70 30
Nos. C1-C11 (11) 27.85 6.37

The 25c, 50c, 75c deep green and 1fr each were printed in two or three types, differing in frameline thickness, or hyphen in "Helio-Vaugirard" imprint.

Nos. C8-C9 Surcharged in Blue or Black

1fr

1931, Apr. 10

C12 AP1 1fr on 1.40fr (B) 60 60
a. Inverted surcharge 125.00 125.00
C13 " 1.50fr on 1.90fr (Bk) 60 60

Rabat and Tower of Hassan
AP2

Casablanca—AP3

1933, Jan. Engraved

C14 AP2 50c dark blue 17 17
C15 " 80c orange brown 12 6
C16 " 1.50fr brown red 15 6
C17 AP3 2.50fr carmine rose 1.50 20
C18 " 5fr violet 80 60
C19 " 10fr blue green 27 25
Nos. C14-C19 (6) 3.01 1.34

Storks and Minaret, Chella
AP4

Plane and Map of Morocco
AP5

1939-40 *Perf. 13*

C20 AP4 80c Prussian green 5 5
C21 " 1fr dark red 5 5
C22 AP5 1.90fr ultramarine 5 6
C23 " 2fr red violet ('40) 6 5
C24 " 3fr chocolate 6 6
C25 AP4 5fr violet 35 35
C26 AP5 10fr turquoise blue 20 20
Nos. C20-C26 (7) 82 82

Plane over Oasis
AP6

1944 Lithographed *Perf. 11½*

C27 AP6 50c Prussian green 6 4
C28 " 2fr ultramarine 6 5
C29 " 5fr scarlet 10 10
C30 " 10fr violet 10 10
C31 " 50fr black 30 30
C32 " 100fr deep blue & red 85 85
Nos. C27-C32 (6) 1.47 1.44

Plane—AP7

1945 Engraved *Perf. 13*

C33 AP7 50fr sepia 30 30

Moulay Idriss
AP8

La Medina—AP9

1947-48

C34 AP8 9fr dk. rose car. 10 6
C35 " 40fr dark blue 30 6
C36 " 50fr deep claret ('47) 30 8
C37 AP9 100fr deep greenish blue 1.00 30
C38 " 200fr henna brown 1.75 60
Nos. C34-C38 (5) 3.45 1.10

Leclerc Type of Regular Issue

1951, Apr. 28

C39 A50 50fr purple 70 70

Issued to commemorate the unveiling of a monument to Gen. Leclerc at Casablanca, April 28, 1951.

Kasbah of the Oudayas, Rabat
AP11

1951, May 22

C40	AP11	300fr purple	9.00	5.00

Ben Smine Sanatorium
AP12

1951, June 4

C41	AP12	50fr purple & Prussian green	1.00	1.00

Fortifications, Chella
AP13

Plane Near Marrakesh
AP14

Fort, Anti-Atlas Mountains
AP15

View of Fez
AP16

1952, Apr. 19 *Perf. 13* **Unwmkd.**

C42	AP13	10fr blue green	20	8
C43	AP14	40fr red	50	18
C44	AP15	100fr brown	1.35	20
C45	AP16	200fr purple	4.00	1.35

Antique Brooches
AP17

1953, Mar. 27

C46	AP17	50fr dark green	1.00	1.00

"City" of the Agdal, Meknes
AP18

Designs: 20fr, Yakoub el Mansour, Rabat. 40fr, Ainchock, Casablanca. 50fr, El Aliya, Fedala.

1954, Mar. 8

C47	AP18	10fr olive brown	70	70
C48	"	20fr purple	70	70
C49	"	40fr red brown	80	80
C50	"	50fr deep green	90	90

Franco-Moroccan solidarity.

Naval Vessel and Sailboat
AP19

Village in the Anti-Atlas
AP20

"Ksar es Souk," Rabat and Plane
AP21

1954, Oct. 18

C51	AP19	15fr dark blue green	60	60
C52	"	30fr violet blue	65	65

1955, July 25 Engraved. *Perf. 13*

Designs: 200fr, Estuary of Bou Regreg, Rabat and Plane.

C53	AP20	100fr bright violet	80	10
C54	"	200fr bright carmine	1.50	40
C55	AP21	500fr greenish blue	4.00	1.85

AIR POST SEMI-POSTAL STAMPS.

French Protectorate

Moorish Tribesmen
SPAP1

Designs: 25c, Moor plowing with camel and burro. 50c, Caravan nearing Saffi. 75c, Walls, Marrakesh. 80c, Sheep grazing at Azrou. 1fr, Gate at Fez. 1.50fr, Aerial view of Tangier. 2fr, Aerial view of Casablanca. 3fr, Storks on old wall, Rabat. 5fr, Moorish fete.

Perf. 13½

1928, July 26 Photo. **Unwmkd.**

CB1	SPAP1	5c deep blue	1.50	1.50
CB2	"	25c brn. orange	1.50	1.50
CB3	"	50c red	1.50	1.50
CB4	"	75c org. brown	1.50	1.50
CB5	"	80c olive green	1.50	1.50
CB6	"	1fr orange	1.50	1.50
CB7	"	1.50fr Pruss. blue	1.50	1.50
CB8	"	2fr deep brown	1.50	1.50
CB9	"	3fr deep violet	1.50	1.50
CB10	SPAP1	5fr brn. black	1.50	1.50
		Nos. CB1–CB10 (10)	15.00	15.00

These stamps were sold in sets only and at double their face value. The money received for the surtax was divided among charitable and social organizations. The stamps were not sold at post offices but solely by subscription to the Moroccan Postal Administration.

Stamps of 1928

Overprinted **Tanger** in Red or Blue.

1929, Feb. 1

CB11	SPAP1	5c dp. blue (R)	1.50	1.50
CB12	"	25c brn.org. (Bl)	1.50	1.50
CB13	"	50c red (Bl)	1.50	1.50
CB14	"	75c orgbrn. (Bl)	1.50	1.50
CB15	"	80c olive green (R)	1.50	1.50
CB16	"	1fr orange (Bl)	1.50	1.50
CB17	"	1.50fr Prus. bl. (R)	1.50	1.50
CB18	"	2fr dp. brn. (R)	1.50	1.50
CB19	"	3fr dp. vio. (R)	1.50	1.50
CB20	"	5fr brn. blk. (R)	1.50	1.50
		Nos. CB11–CB20 (10)	15.00	15.00

These stamps were sold at double their face values and only in Tangier. The surtax benefited various charities.

Marshal Hubert Lyautey
SPAP10

1935, May 15 *Perf. 13½*

CB21	SPAP10	1.50fr+1.50fr blue	10.00	9.00

Nos. C14, C19 Surcharged in Red **O.S.E. +50 c**

1938 *Perf. 13*

CB22	AP2	50c+50c dk. blue	2.00	2.00
CB23	AP3	10fr+10fr blue green	2.00	2.00

Plane over Oasis
SPAP11

Statue of Marshal Lyautey
SPAP12

1944 Lithographed *Perf. 11½*

CB23A	SPAP11	1.50fr+98.50fr red, dp. bl. & black	55	55

The surtax was for charity among the liberated French.

No. C29 Surcharged in Black

+ 5F
18 Juin 1940
‡
18 Juin 1946

1946, June 18 *Perf. 11*

CB24	AP6	5fr+5fr scarlet	25	25

Issued to commemorate the 6th anniversary of the appeal made by Gen. Charles de Gaulle, June 18, 1940. The surtax was for the Free French Association of Morocco.

1946, Dec. Engraved. *Perf. 13*

CB25	SPAP12	10fr+30fr dark green	55	55

The surtax was for works of solidarity.

Replenishing Stocks of Food
SPAP13

Agriculture
SPAP14

1948, Feb. 9 **Unwmkd.**

CB26	SPAP13	9fr+16fr deep green	70	70
CB27	SPAP14	20fr+35fr brown	70	70

The surtax was for combined works of Franco-Moroccan solidarity.

Tomb of Marshal Hubert Lyautey
SPAP15

1948, May 18 *Perf. 13*

CB28	SPAP15	10fr+25fr dark green	40	40

Lyautey Exposition, Paris, June, 1948.

P. T. T. Clubhouse
SPAP16

1948, June 7 **Engraved**

CB29	SPAP16	6fr+34fr dark green	75	75
CB30	"	9fr+51fr red brown	75	75

The surtax was used for the Moroccan P. T. T. employees vacation colony at Ifrane.

View of Agadir
SPAP17

Plane over Globe
SPAP18

Designs: 6fr+9fr, Fez. 9fr+16fr, Atlas Mountains. 15fr+25fr, Valley of Draa.

1949, Apr. 12 *Perf. 13*

Inscribed: "SOLIDARITÉ 1948."

CB31	SPAP17	5fr+5fr dark green	50	45
CB32	"	6fr+9fr orange red	50	45
CB33	"	9fr+16fr black brown	50	45

CB34 SPAP17 15fr+25fr indigo 50 45
a. Sheet of four 6.00 6.00

No. CB34a contains one each of Nos. CB31–CB34. Size: 96x120mm.

1950, Mar. 11 **Engr. and Typo.**

CB35 SPAP18 15fr+10fr blue green & carmine 50 50

Issued to commemorate the "Day of the Stamp," March 11–12, 1950, and to mark the 25th anniversary of the first air post link between Casablanca and Dakar.

Scenes and Map: Northwest Corner
SPAP19

Designs (quarters of map): 6fr+9fr, Northeast. 9fr+16fr, Southwest. 15fr+25fr, Southeast.

1950, Apr. 11 **Engraved**

Inscribed: "SOLIDARITÉ 1949."

CB36 SPAP19 5fr+5fr deep ultramarine 40 40
CB37 " 6fr+9fr Prussian green 40 40
CB38 " 9fr+16fr dark brown 40 40
CB39 " 15fr+25fr brown red 40 40
a. Sheet of four 6.00 6.00

No. CB39a contains one each of Nos. CB36–CB39. Size: 120½x95½mm.

Arch of Triumph of Caracalla at Volubilis
SPAP20

1950, Sept. 25 **Unwmkd.**

CB40 SPAP20 10fr+10fr sepia 40 40
CB41 " 15fr+15fr blue green 40 40

The surtax was for Army Welfare Work.

Casablanca Post Office and First Air Post Stamp—SPAP21

1952, Mar. 8 ***Perf. 13***

CB42 SPAP21 15fr+5fr red brown & deep green 1.35 1.35

Issued to publicize the "Day of the Stamp," March 8, 1952, and to commemorate the 30th anniversary of French Morocco's first air post stamp.

POSTAGE DUE STAMPS.

French Offices in Morocco

Postage Due Stamps and Types of France Surcharged in Red or Black
5 CENTIMOS

1896 ***Perf. 14x13½.*** **Unwmkd.**

On Stamps of 1891-93.

J1 D2 5c on 5c lt. blue (R) 1.50 1.00
J2 " 10c on 10c choc. (R) 3.00 1.00
J3 D2 30c on 30c carmine 6.00 4.50
a. Pair, one without surcharge
J4 " 50c on 50c lilac 6.50 3.50
a. "S" of "CENTIMOS" omitted 10.00
J5 " 1p on 1fr lilac brown 115.00 90.00

1909-10

On Stamps of 1908-10.

J6 D3 1c on 1c olive grn. (R) 50 50
J7 " 10c on 10c violet 11.00 10.00
J8 " 30c on 30c bistre 12.50 12.50
J9 " 50c on 50c red 18.50 18.50

Postage Due Stamps of France Surcharged in Red or Blue
5

1911

On Stamps of 1893-96.

J10 D2 5c on 5c blue (R) 1.00 1.00
J11 " 10c on 10c choc. (R) 3.00 3.00
a. Double surch. 35.00 35.00
J12 " 50c on 50c lilac (Bl) 3.50 3.50

On Stamps of 1908-10.

J13 D3 1c on 1c olive green (R) 40 40
J14 " 10c on 10c violet (R) 1.65 1.65
J15 " 30c on 30c bistre (R) 2.00 2.00
J16 " 50c on 50c red (Bl) 3.75 3.75
Nos. J10–J16 (7) 15.30 15.30

French Protectorate

D4

D5

1915–17

Type of 1911 Issue Overprinted "Protectorat Francais".

J17 D4 1c on 1c black 5 5
a. New value double 40.00
J18 " 5c on 5c blue 25 25
J19 " 10c on 10c chocolate 50 50
J20 " 20c on 20c olive green 50 45
J21 " 30c on 30c rose red 1.35 1.25
J22 " 50c on 50c vio. brown 2.50 1.20
Nos. J17–J22 (6) 5.15 3.70

Nos. J13 to J16 With Additional Overprint "Protectorat Francais".

1915

J23 D3 1c on 1c olive green 20 20
J24 " 10c on 10c violet 65 55
J25 " 30c on 30c bistre 75 65
J26 " 50c on 50c red 85 75

1917–26 **Typographed**

J27 D5 1c black 5 5
J28 " 5c deep blue 5 5
J29 " 10c brown 6 6
J30 " 20c olive green 45 30
J31 " 30c rose 7 7
J32 " 50c lilac brown 7 7
J33 " 1fr red brown, *straw* ('26) 20 15
J34 " 2fr violet ('26) 45 20
Nos. J27–J34 (8) 1.40 95

Postage Due Stamps of France, 1882-1906 Overprinted **TANGER**

1918

J35 D2 1c black 15 15
J36 " 5c blue 25 25
J37 " 10c chocolate 40 40
J38 " 15c green 1.25 1.25
J39 " 20c olive green 1.25 1.25
J40 " 30c rose red 3.00 3.00
J41 " 50c violet brown 4.75 4.75
Nos. J35–J41 (7) 11.05 11.05

Postage Due Stamps of France, 1908-19 Overprinted **TANGER**

1918

J42 D3 1c olive green 15 15
J43 " 10c violet 35 35
J44 " 20c bistre 2.00 2.00
J45 " 40c red 4.50 4.50

Nos. J31 and J29 Surcharged **50c**

1944 ***Perf. 14x13½*** **Unwmkd.**

J46 D5 50c on 30c rose 1.00 1.00
J47 " 1fr on 10c brown 1.50 1.25
J48 " 3fr on 10c brown 3.00 2.35

Type of 1917–1926

1945-52 **Typographed.**

J49 D5 1fr brown lake ('47) 25 20
J50 " 2fr rose lilac ('47) 30 20
J51 " 3fr ultramarine 10 8
J52 " 4fr red orange 10 8
J53 " 5fr green 25 10
J54 " 10fr yellow brown 20 10
J55 " 20fr carmine ('50) 45 30
J56 " 30fr dull brown ('52) 85 60
Nos. J49–J56 (8) 2.50 1.66

PARCEL POST STAMPS.

French Protectorate

PP1

1917 ***Perf. 13½x14*** **Unwmkd.**

Q1 PP1 5c green 20 10
Q2 " 10c carmine 20 15
Q3 " 20c lilac brown 20 15
Q4 " 25c blue 40 25
Q5 " 40c dark brown 60 25
Q6 " 50c red orange 1.00 25
Q7 " 75c pale slate 1.25 75
Q8 " 1f ultramarine 1.65 15
Q9 " 2f gray 2.50 20
Q10 " 5f violet 3.25 25
Q11 " 10f black 4.00 25
Nos. Q1–Q11 (11) 15.25 2.75

FRENCH POLYNESIA

(French Oceania)

LOCATION—South Pacific Ocean.
GOVT.—French Overseas Territory.
AREA—1,544 sq. mi.
POP.—137,382 (1977).
CAPITAL—Papeete.

In 1903 various French Establishments in the South Pacific were united to form a single colony. Most important of the island groups are the Society Islands, Marquesas Islands, the Tuamotu group and the Gambier, Austral and Rapa Islands. Tahiti, largest of the Society group, ranks first in importance.

100 Centimes = 1 Franc

Navigation and Commerce
A1

Perf. 14x13½.

1892–1907 **Typographed** **Unwmkd.**

Name of Colony in Blue or Carmine.

1 A1 1c *lilac blue* 40 40
2 " 2c brown, *buff* 60 60
3 " 4c claret, *lavender* 1.00 85
4 " 5c green, *greenish* 2.50 1.65
5 " 5c yellow green ('06) 50 30
6 " 10c *lavender* 5.00 3.00
7 " 10c red ('00) 50 30
8 " 15c blue, quadrille paper 4.00 2.00
9 " 15c gray, *light gray* ('00) 1.00 60
10 " 20c red, *green* 3.00 1.60
11 " 25c *rose* 10.00 6.00
12 " 25c blue ('00) 2.50 1.50
13 " 30c brown, *bistre* 3.25 2.40
14 " 35c *yellow* ('06) 1.00 75
15 " 40c red, *straw* 22.50 16.00
16 " 45c *gray green* ('07) 60 60
17 " 50c carmine, *rose* 1.40 1.00
18 " 50c brown, *azure* ('00) 55.00 47.50
19 " 75c deep violet, *orange* 2.25 1.60
20 " 1fr bronze green, *straw* 3.25 2.50
Nos. 1–20 (20) 120.25 91.15

Tahitian Girl A2 Kanakas A3

Fautaua Valley
A4

1913-30

21 A2 1c violet & brown 6 6
22 " 2c brown & black 6 6
23 " 4c orange & blue 8 8
24 " 5c green & yellow green 10 10
25 " 5c blue & black ('22) 6 6
26 " 10c rose & orange 18 15
27 " 10c blue green & yellow green ('22) 10 10
28 " 10c orange red & brown red, *bluish* ('26) 30 30
29 " 15c org. & blk. ('15) 12 12
a. Imperf., pair 10.00
30 " 20c black & violet 10 10
a. Imperf., pair 15.00
31 " 20c green & blue green ('26) 10 10
32 " 20c brown red & dark brown ('27) 20 20
33 A3 25c ultramarine & blue 10 8
34 " 25c violet & rose ('22) 10 10
35 " 30c gray & brown 60 60
a. Imperf., pair 35.00
36 " 30c rose & red orange ('22) 22 22
37 " 30c black & red orange ('26) 10 10
38 " 30c slate blue & blue green ('27) 30 30
39 " 35c green & rose 12 10
40 " 40c black & green 15 12
41 " 45c orange & red 15 15
42 " 50c dark brown & black 2.25 2.00
43 " 50c ultramarine & blue ('22) 10 10
44 " 50c gray & blue violet ('26) 15 15
45 " 60c green & black ('26) 8 8

46 A3 65c olive brown & red violet ('27) 30 30
47 " 75c vio. brn. & vio. 35 30
48 " 90c brown red & rose ('30) 3.75 3.75
49 A4 1fr rose & black 40 40
50 " 1.10fr violet & dark brown ('28) 30 30
51 " 1.40fr bistre brown & violet ('29) 90 90
52 " 1.50fr indigo & blue ('30) 3.75 3.75
53 " 2fr dark brown & green 85 75
54 " 5fr violet & blue 2.50 1.85
Nos. 21-54 (34) 18.98 17.83

No. 7 Overprinted **EFO 1915**

1915
55 A1 10c red 55 45
a. Inverted overprint 17.50 17.50

No. 29 Surcharged **10**

1916
56 A2 10c on 15c orange & black 20 20

Nos. 22, 41 and 29 Surcharged **05 1921**

1921
57 A2 5c on 2c brown & black 5.50 5.50
58 A3 10c on 45c orange & red 5.00 5.00
59 A2 25c on 15c orange & black 90 90

On No. 58 the new value and date are set wide apart and without bar.

Types of 1913-30 Issue Surcharged **60**

1923-27
60 A3 60c on 75c blue & brn. 10 10
61 A4 65c on 1fr dark blue & olive (R) ('25) 30 30
62 " 85c on 1fr dark blue & olive (R) ('25) 30 30
63 A3 90c on 75c brown red & cerise ('27) 20 20

No. 26 Surcharged **45 c. 1924**

1924
64 A2 45c on 10c rose & orange 35 35
a. Inverted surch. 85.00 85.00

Stamps and Type of 1913-30 Surcharged with New Value and Bars

1924-27
65 A4 25c on 2fr dark brown & green 20 20
66 " 25c on 5fr violet & bl. 20 20
67 " 1.25fr on 1fr dark blue & ultramarine (R) ('26) 20 20
68 " 1.50fr on 1fr dark blue & light blue ('27) 30 30
69 " 20fr on 5fr orange & brt. vio. ('27) 5.50 4.00
Nos. 65-69 (5) 6.40 4.90

Surcharged **TROIS FRANCS**

1926
70 A4 3fr on 5fr gray & blue (Bk) 30 30
71 " 10fr on 5fr green & black (R) 1.00 85

Papetoai Bay, Moorea
A5

1929, Mar. 25
72 A5 3fr green & dark brn. 2.00 2.00
73 " 5fr light blue & dark brown 3.50 3.50
74 " 10fr light red & dark brown 8.00 8.00
75 " 20fr lilac & dk. brown 11.00 11.00

Colonial Exposition Issue.
Common Design Types

1931, Apr. 13 Engr. *Perf. 12½*
Name of Country Printed in Black.
76 CD70 40c deep green 1.00 1.00
77 CD71 50c violet 1.00 1.00
78 CD72 90c red orange 1.00 1.00
79 CD73 1.50fr dull blue 1.25 1.25

Spear Fishing
A12

Tahitian Girl
A13

Idols
A14

Photogravure.

1934-39 *Perf. 13½, 13½x13*
80 A12 1c gray black 4 4
81 " 2c claret 4 4
82 " 3c light blue ('39) 5 5
83 " 4c orange 10 10
84 " 5c violet 12 12
85 " 10c dark brown 5 5
86 " 15c green 7 7
87 " 20c red 8 8
88 A13 25c gray blue 7 7
89 " 30c yellow green 25 25
90 " 30c orange brown ('39) 6 6
91 A14 35c deep green ('38) 70 70
92 A13 40c red violet 5 5
93 " 45c brown orange 1.35 1.35
94 " 45c dark green ('39) 20 20
95 " 50c violet 6 6
96 " 55c blue ('38) 90 90
97 " 60c black ('39) 8 8
98 " 65c brown 60 60
99 " 70c bright pink ('39) 12 12
100 " 75c olive green 1.10 1.10
101 " 80c violet brown ('38) 15 15
102 " 90c rose red 12 12
103 A14 1fr red brown 5 5
104 " 1.25fr brown violet 1.25 1.25
105 " 1.25fr rose red ('39) 10 10
106 " 1.40fr org. yel. ('39) 12 12
107 " 1.50fr blue 13 13
108 " 1.60fr dull violet ('39) 12 12
109 " 1.75fr olive 1.00 1.00
110 " 2fr red 10 10
111 " 2.25fr deep blue ('39) 12 12
112 " 2.50fr black ('39) 12 12
113 " 3fr brn. org. ('39) 12 12
114 " 5fr red violet ('39) 10 10
115 " 10fr dark green ('39) 45 45
116 " 20fr dark brown ('39) 75 75
Nos. 80-116 (37) 10.89 10.89

Common Design Types pictured in section at front of book.

Paris International Exposition Issue.
Common Design Types

1937 Engraved. *Perf. 13.*
117 CD74 20c deep violet 35 35
118 CD75 30c dark green 35 35
119 CD76 40c carmine rose 40 40
120 CD77 50c dark brown & blue 40 40
121 CD78 90c red 40 40
122 CD79 1.50fr ultramarine 40 40
Nos. 117-122 (6) 2.30 2.30

Colonial Arts Exhibition Issue.
Souvenir Sheet.
Common Design Type

1937 *Imperf.*
123 CD78 3fr emerald 1.50 1.50
Sheet size: 118x99mm.

New York World's Fair Issue.
Common Design Type

1939, May 10 Engr. *Perf. 12½x12*
124 CD82 1.25fr carmine lake 40 40
125 " 2.25fr ultramarine 40 40

Fautaua Valley and Marshal Petain
A15a

1941 Engraved *Perf. 12½x12*
125A A15a 1fr bluish green 12
125B " 2.50fr deep blue 12

Nos. 125A-125B were issued by the Vichy government, and were not placed on sale in the colony. This is also true of five stamps of types A12-A14 without "RF" released in 1942-44.

Stamps of 1929-39 Overprinted in Black or Red
FRANCE LIBRE

1941 *Perf. 14x13½, 13½x13*
126 A14 1fr red brown (Bk) 80 80
127 " 2.50fr black (R) 1.00 80
128 A5 3fr green & dark brown (R) 1.00 1.00
129 A14 3fr brn. org. (Bk) 1.25 1.00
130 A5 5fr light blue & dark brown (R) 1.65 1.65
131 A14 5fr red violet (Bk) 1.25 1.00
132 A5 10fr light red & dark brown (R) 2.25 2.25
133 A14 10fr dark green (R) 9.00 9.00
134 A5 20fr lilac & dark brown (R) 17.50 17.50
135 A14 20fr dark brown (R) 8.00 8.00
Nos. 126-135 (10) 43.70 43.00

Ancient Double Canoe
A16

1942 Photo. *Perf. 14½x14*
136 A16 5c dark brown 5 5
137 " 10c dark gray blue 6 6
138 " 25c emerald 6 6
139 " 30c red orange 6 6
140 " 40c dark slate green 6 6
141 " 80c red brown 8 8
142 " 1fr rose violet 6 6
143 " 1.50fr bright red 12 10
144 " 2fr gray black 12 12
145 " 2.50fr bright ultra. 40 35
146 " 4fr dull violet 20 17
147 " 5fr bistre 20 17
148 " 10fr deep brown 25 22
149 " 20fr deep green 25 20
Nos. 136-149 (14) 1.97 1.76

Eboue Issue.
Common Design Type

1945 Engraved *Perf. 13*
150 CD91 2fr black 12 12
151 " 25fr Prussian green 35 35
Nos. 150 and 151 exist imperforate.

Nos. 136, 138 and 145 Surcharged with New Values and Bars in Carmine or Black.

1946 *Perf. 14½x14.*
152 A16 50c on 5c (C) 12 12
153 " 60c on 5c (C) 12 12
154 " 70c on 5c (C) 12 12
155 " 1.20fr on 5c (C) 12 12
156 " 2.40fr on 25c (Bk) 12 12
157 " 3fr on 25c (Bk) 12 12
158 " 4.50fr on 25c (Bk) 33 33
159 " 15fr on 2.50fr (C) 45 45
Nos. 152-159 (8) 1.50 1.50

Coast of Mooréa
A17

Fisherman and Catch
A18

Tahitian Girl
A20

House at Faa
A19

Island of Borabora
A21

Island Women
A22

Engraved.

1948 *Perf. 13* **Unwmkd.**
160 A17 10c brown 5 4
161 " 30c blue green 6 6
162 " 40c deep blue 6 6
163 A18 50c red brown 6 6
164 " 60c dark brown olive 6 6
165 " 80c bright blue 6 6
166 A19 1fr red brown 8 8
167 " 1.20fr slate 10 8
168 " 1.50fr deep ultramarine 12 10
169 A20 2fr sepia 15 15
170 " 2.40fr red brown 22 22

171 A20 3fr purple 2.00 40
172 " 4fr blue black 22 22
173 A21 5fr sepia 35 30
174 " 6fr steel blue 35 30
175 " 10fr dk. brn. olive 55 25
176 A22 15fr vermilion 1.10 85
177 " 20fr slate 1.20 70
178 " 25fr sepia 1.20 80
Nos. 160-178 (19) 7.99 4.79

Imperforates

Most French Polynesia stamps from 1948 onward exist imperforate in issued and trial colors, and also in small presentation sheets in issued colors.

Military Medal Issue.

Common Design Type

Engraved and Typographed.

1952, Dec. 1

179 CD101 3fr black, green, yel. & purple 1.85 1.85

Girl of Borabora A23

Girl Playing Guitar A24

1955, Sept. 26 **Engraved**

180 A23 9fr dark brown, black & red 4.00 3.00

FIDES Issue.

Common Design Type

Design: 3fr, Dry dock at Papeete.

1956, Oct. 22 Engr. *Perf. 13x12½*

181 CD103 3fr greenish blue 50 45

1958, Nov. 3 *Perf. 13* Unwmkd.

Design: 4fr, 7fr, 9fr, Man with headdress. 10fr, 20fr, Girl with shells on beach.

182 A24 10c green & reddish brown 20 15
183 " 25c slate green, claret & carmine 25 20
184 " 1fr bright blue, brown & red orange 30 25
185 " 2fr brown, violet brown & violet 35 30
186 " 4fr slate green & orange yellow 40 35
187 " 7fr red brown, green & orange 75 65
188 " 9fr violet brown, grn. & orange 1.00 70
189 " 10fr dark blue, brown & carmine 1.25 60
190 " 20fr purple, rose red & brown 1.75 1.25
Nos. 182-190 (9) 6.25 4.45

See Nos. 302-304.

Human Rights Issue

Common Design Type

1958, Dec. 10

191 CD105 7fr dark gray & dark blue 5.00 5.00

Flower Issue

Common Design Type

Design: 4fr, Breadfruit.

1959, Jan. Photo. *Perf. 12½x12*

192 CD104 4fr multicolored 2.00 1.50

Spear Fishing A25

Tahitian Dancers A26

1960, May 16 Engraved *Perf. 13*

193 A25 5fr green, brown & lilac 50 40
194 A26 17fr ultramarine, bright green & red brown 1.60 1.10

Post Office, Papeete A27

1960, Dec. 15 *Perf. 13* Unwmkd.

195 A27 16fr green, blue & claret 1.35 85

Saraca Indica A28

Design: 25fr, Hibiscus.

1962, July 12 Photo. *Perf. 13*

196 A28 15fr multicolored 3.00 1.65
197 " 25fr " 4.00 2.50

Map of Australia and South Pacific—A29

1962, July 18 *Perf. 13x12*

198 A29 20fr multicolored 3.50 2.25

Issued to commemorate the Fifth South Pacific Conference, Pago Pago, July 1962.

Spined Squirrelfish—A30

Fish: 10fr, One-spot butterflyfish. 30fr, Radiate lionfish. 40fr, Horned boxfish.

1962, Dec. 15 Engraved *Perf. 13*

199 A30 5fr black, magenta & bister 1.00 45
200 " 10fr multicolored 1.50 65
201 " 30fr " 3.00 1.85
202 " 40fr " 4.50 3.00

South Pacific Games Issue

Soccer A30a

Design: 50fr, Throwing the javelin.

1963, Aug. 29 Photo. *Perf. 12½*

203 A30a 20fr brt. ultra. & brn. 2.50 1.50
204 " 50fr bright carmine rose & ultra. 4.00 2.50

Issued to publicize the South Pacific Games, Suva, Aug. 29-Sept. 7.

Red Cross Centenary Issue

Common Design Type

1963, Sept. 2 Engraved *Perf. 13*

205 CD113 15fr vio. brn., gray & carmine 3.50 3.50

International Red Cross centenary.

Human Rights Issue

Common Design Type

1963, Dec. 10 *Perf. 13* Unwmkd.

206 CD117 7fr green & violet blue 4.50 4.00

Philatec Issue

Common Design Type

1964, Apr. 9 *Perf. 13* Unwmkd.

207 CD118 25fr grn., dk. slate green & red 4.50 4.00

Tahitian Dancer A31

1964, May 14 Engraved *Perf. 13*

208 A31 1fr multicolored 25 20
209 " 3fr deep claret, blk. & orange 40 35

Soldiers, Truck and Battle Flag A32

1964, July 10 Photo. *Perf. 12½*

210 A32 5fr multicolored 90 45

Issued to honor the Tahitian Volunteers of the Pacific Battalion. See No. C31.

Tuamotu Scene A33

Views: 4fr, Borabora. 7fr, Papeete Harbor. 8fr, Paul Gauguin's tomb, Marquesas. 20fr, Mangareva, Gambier Islands.

1964, Dec. 1 Litho. *Perf. 12½x13*

211 A33 2fr multicolored 25 20
212 " 4fr " 40 30
213 " 7fr " 70 50
214 " 8fr " 80 50
215 " 20fr " 1.85 1.25
Nos. 211-215, C32 (6) 5.60 3.65

Painting from a School Dining Room A34

1965, Nov. 29 Engraved *Perf. 13*

216 A34 20fr dk. brown, slate grn. & dk. car. 2.50 1.50

Issued to publicize the School Canteen Program. See No. C38.

Outrigger Canoe on Lagoon A35

Ships: 11fr, Large cruising yacht (vert.). 12fr, Motorboat for sport fishing. 14fr, Outrigger canoes with sails. 19fr, Schooner (vert.). 22fr, Modern coaster "Oiseau des Isles II."

1966, Aug. 30 Engraved *Perf. 13*

217 A35 10fr brt. ultramarine, emerald & maroon 70 35
218 " 11fr maroon, dk. blue & slate green 80 55
219 " 12fr emerald, dk. bl. & red lilac 1.00 60
220 " 14fr brown, blue & slate green 1.20 75
221 " 19fr scarlet, slate grn. & dp. blue 1.40 75
222 " 22fr multicolored 2.00 1.00
Nos. 217-222 (6) 7.10 4.00

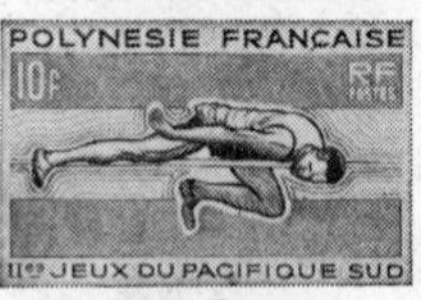

High Jump A36

Designs: 20fr, Pole vault (vert.). 40fr, Women's basketball (vert.). 60fr, Hurdling.

1966, Dec. 15 Engraved *Perf. 13*

223 A36 10fr dk. red, lemon & black 60 35
224 " 20fr blue, emerald & black 1.20 75
225 " 40fr emerald, bright pink & black 2.25 1.40
226 " 60fr dull yellow, bl. & black 3.00 2.50

Issued to commemorate the Second South Pacific Games, Nouméa, New Caledonia, Dec. 8-18.

Poi Pounder A37 — Javelin Throwing A38

1967, June 15 Engraved *Perf. 13*

227 A37 50fr orange & black 3.50 2.50

Issued to commemorate the 50th anniversary of the Society for Oceanic Studies.

1967, July 11

Designs: 5fr, Spring dance (horiz.). 15fr, Horse race (horiz.). 16fr, Fruit carriers' race. 21fr, Canoe race (horiz.).

228	A38	5fr multicolored	50	25
229	"	13fr "	85	35
230	"	15fr "	90	50
231	"	16fr "	1.00	60
232	"	21fr "	1.65	85
		Nos. 228-232 (5)	4.90	2.55

Issued to publicize the July Festival.

Earring A39

Art of the Marquesas Islands: 10fr, Carved mother-of-pearl. 15fr, Decorated canoe paddle. 23fr, Oil vessel. 25fr, Carved stilt stirrups. 30fr, Fan handles. 35fr, Tattooed man. 50fr, Tikis.

1967-68 Engraved *Perf. 13*

233	A39	10fr dp. claret, dull red & ultra. ('68)	60	40
234	"	15fr blk. & emerald ('68)	90	55
235	"	20fr olive gray, dk. car. & lt. bl.	1.20	70
236	"	23fr dk. brn., ocher & blue ('68)	1.35	75
237	"	25fr dk. brown, dk. blue & lilac	1.50	90
238	"	30fr brn. & red lilac	1.85	1.35
239	"	35fr ultra. & dark brown ('68)	2.25	1.50
240	"	50fr brn., slate grn. & light blue	3.00	2.00
		Nos. 233-240 (8)	12.65	8.15

Issue dates: 20fr, 25fr, 30fr, 50fr, Dec. 19, 1967; others Feb. 28, 1968.

WHO Anniversary Issue

Common Design Type

1968, May 4 Engraved *Perf. 13*

241	CD126	15fr bl. grn., maroon & deep violet	80	60
242	"	16fr orange, lilac & blue green	90	60

Issued for the 20th anniversary of the World Health Organization.

Human Rights Year Issue

Common Design Type

1968, Aug. 10 Engraved *Perf. 13*

243	CD127	15fr bl., red & brn.	90	45
244	"	16fr brown, bright pink & ultra.	1.20	75

Tiare Apetahi A40

Flower: 17fr, Tiare Tahiti.

1969, Mar. 27 Photo. *Perf. 12½x13*

245	A40	9fr multicolored	70	40
246	"	17fr "	1.20	50

Runner A41

Designs: 9fr, Boxer (horiz.). 17fr, High jump. 22fr, Long jump.

1969, Aug. 13 Engraved *Perf. 13*

247	A41	9fr bl., vio. & sepia	60	40
248	"	17fr red, sepia & claret	90	50
249	"	18fr blue, brown olive & claret	1.35	70
250	"	22fr brt. grn. & choc.	1.75	1.00

Issued to publicize the 3rd South Pacific Games, Port Moresby, Papua and New Guinea, Aug. 13-23.

ILO Issue

Common Design Type

1969, Nov. 24 Engraved *Perf. 13*

251	CD131	17fr orange, emerald & olive	1.10	50
252	"	18fr orange, dk. brn. & vio. blue	1.35	65

Territorial Assembly A42

Buildings: 14fr, Governor's Residence. 17fr, House of Tourism. 18fr, Maeva Hotel. 24fr, Taharaa Hotel.

1969, Dec. 22 Photo. *Perf. 12½x12*

253	A42	13fr black & multi.	60	30
254	"	14fr " "	80	40
255	"	17fr " "	1.00	50
256	"	18fr " "	1.25	60
257	"	24fr " "	1.40	70
		Nos. 253-257 (5)	5.05	2.50

Stone Figure with Globe A43

Designs: 40fr, Globe, plane, map of Polynesia and men holding "PATA" sign (horiz.). 60fr, Polynesian carrying globe.

1970, Apr. 7 Engraved *Perf. 13*

258	A43	20fr deep plum, gray & blue	1.20	50
259	"	40fr emerald, rose lilac & ultra.	2.75	1.20
260	"	60fr red brown, blue & dark brown	3.50	1.75

Issued to publicize the 1970 Pacific Area Travel Association Congress (PATA).

U.P.U. Headquarters Issue

Common Design Type

1970, May 20 Engraved *Perf. 13*

261	CD133	18fr maroon, purple & brown	1.20	50
262	"	20fr lilac rose, olive & indigo	1.40	70

Night Fishing—A44

1971, May 11 Photo. *Perf. 13*

263 A44 10fr multicolored 90 50

See Nos. C71-C73.

Flowers A45

Designs: Various flowers. 12fr is horiz.

Perf. 12½x13, 13x12½

1971, Aug. 27

264	A45	8fr multicolored	60	40
265	"	12fr "	1.00	60
266	"	22fr "	1.40	75

Day of a Thousand Flowers.

Water-skiing Slalom—A46

Designs: 20fr, Water-skiing, jump (vert.). 40fr, Figure water-skiing.

1971, Oct. 11 Engraved *Perf. 13*

267	A46	10fr greenish bl., dk. red & brown	70	40
268	"	20fr car., emerald & brown	1.40	70
269	"	40fr brn., grn. & lilac	2.40	1.35

World water-skiing championships, Oct. 1971.

De Gaulle Issue

Common Design Type

Designs: 30fr, Gen. de Gaulle, 1940. 50fr, Pres. de Gaulle, 1970.

1971, Nov. 9 Engraved *Perf. 13*

270	CD134	30fr red lilac & blk.	2.00	1.20
271	"	50fr " " "	3.00	1.65

First anniversary of the death of Charles de Gaulle (1890-1970), president of France.

Map of Tahiti and Jerusalem Cross A47

1971, Dec. 18 Photo. *Perf. 13x12½*

272 A47 28fr lt. bl. & multi. 1.75 85

2nd rally of French Boy Scouts and Guides, Taravao, French Polynesia.

"Alcoholism" A48 — Mother and Child A49

1972, Mar. 24 Photo. *Perf. 13*

273 A48 20fr brown & multi. 1.20 90

Fight against alcoholism.

1973, Sept. 26 Photo. *Perf. 12½x13*

274 A49 28fr pale yel. & multi. 1.40 90

Day nursery.

Polynesian Golfer A50

Design: 24fr, Atimaono Golf Course.

1974, Feb. 27 Photogravure *Perf. 13*

275	A50	16fr multicolored	90	70
276	"	24fr "	1.50	90

Atimaono Golf Course.

Hand Throwing Life Preserver to Puppy—A51

1974, May 9 Photo. *Perf. 13*

277 A51 21fr brt. bl. & multi. 1.00 60

Society for the Protection of Animals.

Around a Fire, on the Beach A52

Polynesian Views: 2fr, Lagoons and mountains. 6fr, Pebble divers. 10fr, Lonely Mountain and flowers (vert.). 15fr, Sailing ship at sunset. 20fr, Lagoon and mountain.

1974, May 22

278	A52	2fr multicolored	12	8
279	"	5fr "	22	17
280	"	6fr "	35	25
281	"	10fr "	45	35
282	"	15fr "	80	45
283	"	20fr "	1.00	60
		Nos. 278-283 (6)	2.94	1.90

Polynesian Woman and UPU Emblem
A53

Lion, Sun and Emblem
A54

1974, Oct. 9 Engraved *Perf. 13*

284	A53	65fr multicolored	2.00	1.75

Centenary of Universal Postal Union.

1975, June 17 Photogravure

285	A54	26fr multicolored	1.00	60

15th anniversary of Lions International in Tahiti.

Fish and Leaf—A55

1975, July 9 Litho. *Perf. 12*

286	A55	19fr dp. ultra. & grn.	70	40

Polynesian Association for the Protection of Nature.

Pompidou Type of France 1975

1976, Feb. 16 Engr. *Perf. 13*

287	A668	49fr dk. vio. & blk.	1.50	1.00

Georges Pompidou (1911–74), President of France (1965–74).

Alain Gerbault and Sailboat
A56

1976, May 25 Photo. *Perf. 13*

288	A56	90fr multicolored	2.25	1.50

50th anniversary of Alain Gerbault's arrival in Bora Bora.

Turtle
A57

Design: 42fr, Hand protecting bird.

1976, June 24 Litho. *Perf. 12½*

289	A57	18fr multicolored	50	25
290	"	42fr "	1.10	65

World Ecology Day.

A. G. Bell, Telephone, Radar and Satellite—A58

1976, Sept. 15 Engr. *Perf. 13*

291	A58	37fr multicolored	1.00	60

Centenary of first telephone call by Alexander Graham Bell, Mar. 10, 1876.

Marquesas Dugout Canoe—A59

Dugout Canoes from: 30fr, Raiatea. 75fr, Tahiti. 100fr, Tuamotu.

1976, Dec. 16 Litho. *Perf. 13x12½*

292	A59	25fr multicolored	75	40
293	"	30fr "	85	45
294	"	75fr "	2.00	1.00
295	"	100fr "	2.40	1.40

Sailing Ship—A60

Designs: Various sailing vessels.

1977, Dec. 22 Litho. *Perf. 13*

296	A60	20fr multicolored	45	35
297	"	50fr "	1.00	75
298	"	85fr "	1.85	1.20
299	"	120fr "	2.75	1.75

Hibiscus
A61

Girl with Shells on Beach
A62

Designs: 10fr, Vanda orchids. 16fr, Pua (fagraea berteriana). 22fr, Gardenia.

1978–79 Photo. *Perf. 12½x13*

300	A61	10fr multicolored	20	15
301	"	13fr "	25	20
302	"	16fr "	32	25
303	"	22fr "	45	32

Issue dates: Nos. 301–302, Aug. 23, 1978; Nos. 300, 303, Jan. 25, 1979.

1978, Nov. 3 Engr. *Perf. 13*

Designs (as type A24 with "1958 1978" added): 28fr, Man with headdress. 36fr, Girl playing guitar.

304	A62	20fr multicolored	40	30
305	"	28fr "	55	40
306	"	36fr "	72	55
		a. Souvenir sheet of 3	2.00	2.00

20th anniversary of stamps inscribed: Polynesie Francaise. No. 306a contains Nos. 304–306; dark brown marginal inscription and design. Size: 130x100mm.

Tahiti—A63

Ships: 30fr, Monowai. 75fr, Tahitien. 100fr, Mariposa.

1978, Dec. 29 Litho. *Perf. 13x12½*

307	A63	15fr multicolored	30	22
308	"	30fr "	60	45
309	"	75fr "	1.50	1.10
310	"	100fr "	2.00	1.50

Porites Coral
A64

Design: 37fr, Montipora coral.

1979, Feb. 15 *Perf. 13x12½*

311	A64	32fr multicolored	65	48
312	"	37fr "	75	55

Raiatea
A65

Landscapes: 1fr, Moon over Bora Bora. 2fr, Mountain peaks, Ua Pu. 3fr, Sunset over Motu Tapu. 5fr, Motu Beach. 6fr, Palm and hut, Tuamotu.

1979, Mar. 8 *Perf. 13x13½*

313	A65	1fr multicolored	3	3
314	"	2fr "	4	3
315	"	3fr "	6	5
316	"	4fr "	8	6
317	"	5fr "	10	8
318	"	6fr "	12	10
		Nos. 313–318 (6)	43	35

SEMI-POSTAL STAMPS.

Nos. 55 and 26 Surcharged in Red ✚ 5c

1915 *Perf. 14x13½* **Unwmkd.**

B1 A1 10c+5c red 4.50 4.50
  a. "e" instead of "c" 10.00 10.00
  b. Inverted surcharge 25.00 25.00
B2 A2 10c+5c rose & orange 1.85 1.85
  a. "e" instead of "c" 7.50 7.50
  b. "c" inverted 7.50 7.50
  c. Inverted surcharge 22.50 22.50

Surcharged in Carmine ✚ 5c

B3 A2 10c+5c rose & orange 55 55
  a. "e" instead of "c" 4.50 4.50
  b. Inverted surcharge 25.00 25.00

Surcharged in Carmine ✚ 5c

1916

B4 A2 10c+5c rose & orange 55 55

Curie Issue
Common Design Type

1938 Engraved. *Perf. 13*

B5 CD80 1.75fr+50c bright ultramarine 3.75 3.75

French Revolution Issue
Common Design Type

1939 Photogravure
Name and Value Typo. in Black.

B6 CD83 45(c)+25(c) grn. 2.75 2.75
B7 " 70(c)+30(c) brn. 2.75 2.75
B8 " 90(c)+35(c) red orange 2.75 2.75
B9 " 1.25fr+1fr rose pink 2.75 2.75
B10 " 2.25fr+2fr blue 2.75 2.75
Nos. B6-B10, CB1 (6) 19.75 19.75

Common Design Type and

Marine Officer
SP1

"L'Astrolabe"
SP2

1941 Photogravure *Perf. 13½*

B11 SP1 1fr+1fr red 35
B12 CD86 1.50fr+3fr maroon 35
B12A SP2 2.50fr+1fr blue 35

Nos. B11-B12A were issued by the Vichy government, and were not placed on sale in the colony.

Nos. 125A-125B were surcharged "OEUVRES COLONIALES" and surtax (including change of denomination of the 2.50fr to 50c). These were issued in 1944 by the Vichy government and not placed on sale in the colony.

Red Cross Issue
Common Design Type

1944 Photogravure. *Perf. 14½x14.*

B13 CD90 5fr+20fr peacock blue 15 15

The surtax was for the French Red Cross and national relief.

Tropical Medicine Issue
Common Design Type

1950 Engraved. *Perf. 13.*

B14 CD100 10fr+2fr dk. blue grn. & dk. grn. 75 75

The surtax was for charitable work.

AIR POST STAMPS.

Seaplane in Flight
AP1

Photogravure.

1934, Nov. 5 *Perf. 13½* **Unwmkd.**

C1 AP1 5fr green 10 10

V4

Stamps of type AP1 without "RF" monogram and stamp of the above design were issued in 1944 by the Vichy Government, but were not placed on sale in the colony.

No. C1 Overprinted in Red

FRANCE LIBRE

1941

C2 AP1 5fr green 70 70

Common Design Type

1942 *Perf. 14½x14.*

C3 CD87 1fr dark orange 15 15
C4 " 1.50fr bright red 15 15
C5 " 5fr brown red 20 20
C6 " 10fr black 45 45
C7 " 25fr ultramarine 50 50
C8 " 50fr dark green 35 35
C9 " 100fr plum 50 40
Nos. C3-C9 (7) 2.30 2.20

Victory Issue
Common Design Type

1946, May 8 Engr. *Perf. 12½*

C10 CD92 8fr dark green 45 45

Issued to commemorate the European Victory of the Allied Nations in World War II.

Chad to Rhine Issue
Common Design Types

1946, June 6

C11 CD93 5fr red orange 40 40
C12 CD94 10fr dark olive bistre 40 40
C13 CD95 15fr dk. yel. green 40 40
C14 CD96 20fr carmine 40 40
C15 CD97 25fr dark rose violet 40 40
C16 CD98 50fr black 70 70
Nos. C11-C16 (6) 2.70 2.70

Shearwater and Moorea Landscape
AP2

Fishermen—AP3

Shearwater over Maupiti Shoreline
AP4

1948, Mar. 1 *Perf. 13* **Unwmkd.**

C17 AP2 50fr red brown 5.50 5.50
C18 AP3 100fr purple 5.00 3.00
C19 AP4 200fr blue green 12.00 9.00

UPU Issue
Common Design Type

1949

C20 CD99 10fr deep blue 3.25 3.25

Gauguin's "Nafea faaipoipo"
AP5

1953, Sept. 24

C21 AP5 14fr dark brown, dark gray green & red 30.00 30.00

Issued to commemorate the 50th anniversary of the death of Paul Gauguin.

Liberation Issue
Common Design Type

1954, June 6

C22 CD102 3fr dk. greenish bl. & bl. grn. 1.10 1.10

Bahia Peak, Borabora—AP6

1955, Sept. 26 *Perf. 13* **Unwmkd.**

C23 AP6 13fr indigo & blue 2.00 1.65

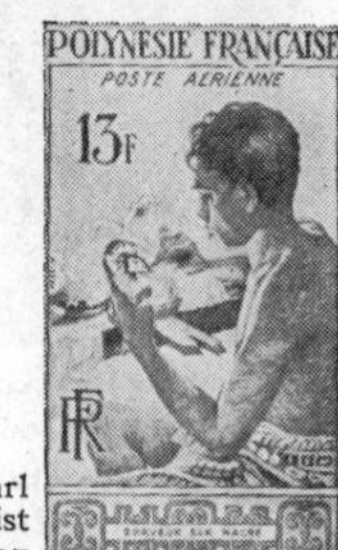

Mother-of-Pearl Artist
AP7

Designs: 50fr, "Women of Tahiti," Gauguin (horiz.). 100fr, "The White Horse," Gauguin. 200fr, Night fishing at Moorea (horiz.).

1958, Nov. 3 Engr. *Perf. 13*

C24 AP7 13fr multicolored 1.50 70
C25 " 50fr " 5.00 1.75
C26 " 100fr " 8.50 4.00
C27 " 200fr lilac & slate 11.00 4.00

Airport, Papeete—AP8

1960, Dec. 15

C28 AP8 13fr rose lilac, vio., & yel. green 1.25 75

Telstar Issue
Common Design Type

1962, Dec. 5 *Perf. 13*

C29 CD111 50fr red lilac, maroon & violet blue 4.00 2.50

Tahitian Dancer
AP10

1964, May 14 Photo. *Perf. 13*

C30 AP10 15fr multicolored 1.20 75

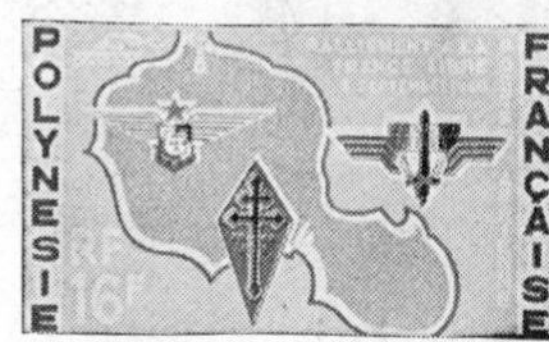

Map of Tahiti and Free French Emblems—AP11

1964, July 10 **Unwmkd.**

C31 AP11 16fr multicolored 4.00 1.60

Issued to commemorate the rallying of French Polynesia to the Free French cause.

Moorea Scene—AP12

1964, Dec. 1 Litho. *Perf. 13*

C32 AP12 23fr multicolored 1.60 90

ITU Issue
Common Design Type

1965, May 17 Engraved *Perf. 13*

C33 CD120 50fr violet, red brn. & blue 15.00 9.00

Issued to commemorate the centenary of the International Telecommunication Union.

Paul Gauguin—AP13

Design: 25fr, Gauguin Museum (stylized). 40fr, Primitive statues at Gauguin Museum.

1965 Engraved ***Perf. 13***

C34 AP13 25fr olive green 2.50 1.20
C35 " 40fr blue green 3.50 1.75
C36 " 75fr brt. red brn. 7.00 4.00

Opening of Gauguin Museum, Papeete.

Skin Diver with Spear Gun—AP14

1965, Sept. 1 Engraved ***Perf. 13***

C37 AP14 50fr red brn., dull blue & dk. green 20.00 15.00

World Championships in Underwater Fishing, Tuamotu Archipelago, Sept. 1965.

Painting from a School Dining Room
AP15

Radio Tower, Globe and Palm
AP16

1965, Nov. 29

C38 AP15 80fr brn., blue, dull blue & red 6.50 3.50

School Canteen Program.

1965, Dec. 29 Engraved ***Perf. 13***

C39 AP16 60fr orange, green & dk. brn. 5.00 3.00

50th anniversary of the first radio link between Tahiti and France.

French Satellite A-1 Issue

Common Design Type

Designs: 7fr, Diamant Rocket and launching installations. 10fr, A-1 satellite.

1966, Feb. 7

C40 CD121 7fr choc., dp. green & lilac 2.00 2.00
C41 " 10fr lilac, dp. green & dk. brown 2.50 2.50
a. Strip of 2 + label 4.75 4.75

Issued to commemorate the launching of France's first satellite, Nov. 26, 1965. No. C41a contains one each of Nos. C40-C41 and dark brown label with commemorative inscription. Each sheet contains 16 triptychs (2x8).

French Satellite D-1 Issue

Common Design Type

1966, May 10 Engraved ***Perf. 13***

C42 CD122 20fr brown, bright grn. & claret 2.50 1.20

Papeete Harbor—AP17

1966, June 30 Photo. ***Perf. 13***

C43 AP17 50fr multicolored 5.00 2.00

"Vive Tahiti" by A. Benichou
AP18

1966, Nov. 28 Photo. ***Perf. 13***

C44 AP18 13fr multicolored 1.50 70

Explorer's Ship and Canoe—AP19

Designs: 60fr, Polynesian costume and ship. 80fr, Louis Antoine de Bougainville (vert.).

1968 Engraved ***Perf. 13***

C45 AP19 40fr green, blue & ocher 2.50 1.35
C46 " 60fr brt. blue, org. & black 3.50 2.00
C47 " 80fr red lilac, sal. & lake 4.50 2.50
a. Souv. sheet of 3 11.50 11.50

Issued to commemorate the 200th anniversary of the discovery of Tahiti by Louis Antoine de Bougainville. No. C47a contains one each of Nos. C45-C47. Ocher marginal inscription. Size: 174x99mm.

The Meal, by Paul Gauguin—AP20

1968, July 30 Photo. ***Perf. 12x12½***

C48 AP20 200fr multi. 15.00 10.00

See also Nos. C63-C67, C78-C82, C89-C93, C98.

Shot Put
AP21

PATA 1970 Poster
AP22

1968, Oct. 12 Engraved ***Perf. 13***

C49 AP21 35fr dark car. rose & brt. grn. 3.50 1.65

Issued to commemorate the 19th Olympic Games, Mexico City, Oct. 12-27.

Concorde Issue

Common Design Type

1969, Apr. 17

C50 CD129 40fr red brown & car. rose 8.00 5.50

1969, July 9 Photo. ***Perf. 12½x13***

C51 AP22 25fr blue & multi. 1.75 75

Issued to publicize PATA 1970 (Pacific Area Travel Association Congress), Tahiti.

Underwater Fishing
AP23

Design: 52fr, Hand holding fish made up of flags (vert.).

1969, Aug. 5 Photo. ***Perf. 13***

C52 AP23 48fr blk., greenish blue & red lilac 2.75 1.60
C53 " 52fr bl., blk. & red 3.75 2.00

Issued to publicize the World Underwater Fishing Championships.

Gen. Bonaparte as Commander of the Army in Italy, by Jean Sebastien Rouillard
AP24

1969, Oct. 15 Photo. ***Perf. 12½x12***

C54 AP24 100fr car. & multi. 30.00 25.00

Bicentenary of the birth of Napoleon Bonaparte (1769-1821).

Eiffel Tower, Torii and EXPO Emblem
AP25

Pearl Diver Descending, and Basket
AP26

Design: 30fr, Mount Fuji, Tower of the Sun and EXPO emblem (horiz.).

1970, Sept. 15 Photo. ***Perf. 13***

C55 AP25 30fr multicolored 2.50 1.20
C56 " 50fr " 4.50 2.40

EXPO '70 International Exposition, Osaka, Japan, Mar. 15-Sept. 13.

1970, Sept. 30 Engraved ***Perf. 13***

Designs: 5fr, Diver collecting oysters. 18fr, Implantation into oyster (horiz.). 27fr, Open oyster with pearl. 50fr, Woman with mother of pearl jewelry.

C57 AP26 2fr slate, greenish bl. & red brn. 30 15
C58 " 5fr greenish blue, ultra. & org. 50 25
C59 " 18fr slate, magenta & orange 1.20 60
C60 " 27fr brt. pink, brn. & dull lilac 1.85 1.00
C61 " 50fr gray, red brn. & orange 3.25 1.75
Nos. C57-C61 (5) 7.10 3.75

Pearl industry of French Polynesia.

The Thinker, by Auguste Rodin and Education Year Emblem—AP27

1970, Oct. 15 Engraved ***Perf. 13***

C62 AP27 50fr blue, indigo & terra cotta 3.50 1.75

International Education Year.

Painting Type of 1968

Paintings by Artists Living in Polynesia: 20fr, Woman on the Beach, by Yves de Saint-Front. 40fr, Abstract, by Frank Fay. 60fr, Woman and Shells, by Jean Guillois. 80fr, Hut under Palms, by Jean Masson. 100fr, Polynesian Girl, by Jean-Charles Bouloc (vert.).

Perf. 12x12½, 12½x12

1970, Dec. 14 Photogravure

C63 AP20 20fr brn. & multi. 2.00 1.00
C64 " 40fr " " 4.00 2.00
C65 " 60fr " " 5.00 2.50
C66 " 80fr " " 6.50 3.00
C67 " 100fr " " 8.50 4.50
Nos. C63-C67 (5) 26.00 13.00

South Pacific Games Emblem
AP28

1971, Jan. 26 *Perf. 12½*

C68 AP28 20fr ultra.&multi. 1.20 60

Publicity for 4th South Pacific Games, held in Papeete, Sept. 8–19, 1971.

Memorial Flame
AP29

1971, March 19 Photo. *Perf. 12½*

C69 AP29 5fr multicolored 1.10 70

In memory of Charles de Gaulle.

Soldier and Badge—AP30

1971, Apr. 21

C70 AP30 25fr multicolored 3.00 2.00

30th anniversary of departure of Tahitian volunteers to serve in World War II.

Water Sports Type of Regular Issue

Designs: 15fr, Surfing (vert.). 16fr, Skin diving (vert.). 20fr, Water-skiing with kite.

1971, May 11 Photo. *Perf. 13*

C71	A44	15fr	multicolored	90	50
C72	"	16fr	"	1.00	60
C73	"	20fr	"	1.20	70

Sailing
AP31

Designs: 18fr, Golf. 27fr, Archery. 53fr, Tennis.

1971, Sept. 8 *Perf. 12½*

C74	AP31	15fr	multicolored	85	55
C75	"	18fr	"	1.25	75
C76	"	27fr	"	1.75	90
C77	"	53fr	"	3.25	1.50
	a. Souvenir sheet of 4			7.50	7.50

4th South Pacific Games, Papeete, Sept. 8–19. No. C77a contains one each of Nos. C74–C77. Black marginal inscription. Size: 136x169mm.

Painting Type of 1968

Paintings by Artists Living in Polynesia: 20fr, Hut and Palms, by Isabelle Wolf. 40fr, Palms on Shore, by André Dobrowolski. 60fr, Polynesian Woman, by Françoise Séli (vert.). 80fr, Holy Family, by Pierre Heymann (vert.). 100fr, Crowd, by Nicolai Michoutouchkine.

1971, Dec. 15 Photo. *Perf. 13*

C78	AP20	20fr	multicolored	1.50	80
C79	"	40fr	"	2.00	1.20
C80	"	60fr	"	3.50	2.50
C81	"	80fr	"	5.00	3.50
C82	"	100fr	"	6.00	4.00
	Nos. C78–C82 (5)			18.00	12.00

Papeete Harbor—AP32

1972, Jan. 13

C83 AP32 28fr violet & multi. 1.75 85

Free port of Papeete, 10th anniversary.

Figure Skating and Dragon
AP33

1972, Jan. 25 Engraved *Perf. 13*

C84 AP33 20fr ultra., lake & brt. green 1.50 65

11th Winter Olympic Games, Sapporo, Japan, Feb. 3–13.

South Pacific Commission Headquarters, Noumea—AP34

1972, Feb. 5 Photogravure *Perf. 13*

C85 AP34 21fr blue & multi. 1.20 60

South Pacific Commission, 25th anniversary.

Festival Emblem
AP35

1972, May 9 Engr. *Perf. 13*

C86 AP35 36fr org., bl. & grn. 2.00 1.00

South Pacific Festival of Arts, Fiji, May 6–20.

Kon Tiki and Route, Callao to Tahiti—AP36

1972, Aug. 18 Photo. *Perf. 13*

C87 AP36 16fr dk. & lt. blue, blk. & org. 1.50 75

25th anniversary of the arrival of the raft Kon Tiki in Tahiti.

Charles de Gaulle and Memorial
AP37

1972, Dec. 9 Engraved *Perf. 13*

C88 AP37 100fr slate 8.00 5.00

Gen. Charles de Gaulle (1890–1970), president of France.

Painting Type of 1968

Paintings by Artists Living in Polynesia; 20fr, Horses, by Georges Bovy. 40fr, Sailboats, by Ruy Juventin (vert.). 60fr, Harbor, by André Brooke. 80fr, Farmers, by Daniel Adam (vert.). 100fr, Dancers, by Aloysius Pilioko (vert.).

1972, Dec. 14 Photogravure

C89	AP20	20fr	gold & multi.	1.50	75
C90	"	40fr	" "	2.00	1.20
C91	"	60fr	" "	3.50	3.00
C92	"	80fr	dk. grn., buff & dk. brn.	5.00	4.00
C93	"	100fr	gold & multi.	6.00	5.00
	Nos. C89–C93 (5)			18.00	13.95

St. Teresa and Lisieux Basilica
AP38

1973, Jan. 23 Engraved *Perf. 13*

C94 AP38 85fr multicolored 6.00 3.50

Centenary of the birth of St. Teresa of Lisieux (1873–1897), Carmelite nun.

Nicolaus Copernicus—AP39

1973, Mar. 7 Engraved *Perf. 13*

C95 AP39 100fr brn., vio. bl. & red lilac 6.50 4.00

500th anniversary of the birth of Nicolaus Copernicus (1473–1543), Polish astronomer.

Plane over Tahiti—AP40

1973, Apr. 3 Photo. *Perf. 13*

C96 AP40 80fr ultra., gold & light green 4.50 3.00

Air France's World Tour via Tahiti.

DC-10 at Papeete Airport—AP41

1973, May 18 Engraved *Perf. 13*

C97 AP41 20fr blue, ultra. & slate green 1.20 60

Start of DC-10 service.

Painting Type of 1968

Design: 200fr, "Ta Matete" (seated women), by Paul Gauguin.

1973, June 7 Photo. *Perf. 13*

C98 AP20 200fr multi. 10.00 6.00

70th anniversary of the death of Paul Gauguin (1848–1903), painter.

Pierre Loti and Characters from his Books—AP42

1973, July 4 Engraved *Perf. 13*

C99 AP42 60fr multicolored 3.00 1.75

50th anniversary of the death of Pierre Loti (1850–1923), French naval officer and writer.

"Sun," by Jean Francois Favre
AP43

Paintings by Artists Living in Polynesia: 40fr, Woman with Flowers, by Eliane de Gennes. 60fr, Seascape, by Alain Sidet. 80fr, Crowded Bus, by Francois Ravello. 100fr, Stylized Boats, by Jackie Bourdin (horiz.).

1973, Dec. 13 Photo. *Perf. 13*

C100	AP43	20fr	gold & multi.	1.00	75
C101	"	40fr	" "	2.00	1.20
C102	"	60fr	" "	3.00	2.50
C103	"	80fr	" "	4.50	3.00
C104	"	100fr	" "	5.50	4.50
	Nos. C100–C104 (5)			16.00	11.95

Bird, Fish, Flower and Water
AP44

1974, June 12 Photo. *Perf. 13*

C105 AP44 12fr blue & multi. 75 35

Nature protection.

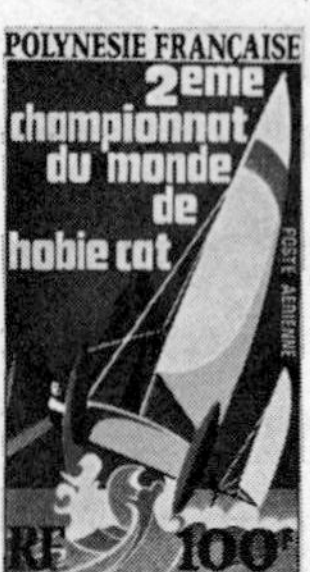

Catamaran under Sail
AP45

1974, July 22 Engraved *Perf. 13*

C106 AP45 100fr multi. 4.00 2.00

2nd Catamaran World Championships.

Still-life, by Rosine Temarui-Masson
AP46

Paintings by Artists Living in Polynesia: 40fr, Palms and House on Beach, by Marcel Chardon. 60fr, Man, by Marie-Françoise Avril. 80fr, Polynesian Woman, by Henriette Robin. 100fr, Lagoon by Moonlight, by David Farsi (horiz.).

1974, Dec. 12 Photogravure *Perf. 13*

C107 AP46 20fr gold & multi. 80 60
C108 " 40fr " " 1.20 80
C109 " 60fr " " 2.50 1.75
C110 " 80fr " " 3.50 2.40
C111 " 100fr " " 5.00 3.00
Nos. C107-C111 (5) 13.00 8.55

See also Nos. C122-C126.

Polynesian Gods of Travel—AP47

Designs: 75fr, Tourville hydroplane, 1929. 100fr, Passengers leaving plane.

1975, Feb. 7 Engraved *Perf. 13*

C112 AP47 50fr sepia, purple & brown 2.00 1.00
C113 " 75fr green, blue & red 3.00 1.50
C114 " 100fr green, sepia & carmine 4.00 2.00

Fifty years of Tahitian aviation.

French Ceres Stamp and Woman
AP48

1975, May 29 Engr. *Perf. 13*

C115 AP48 32fr verm., brown & black 1.20 70

ARPHILA 75 International Philatelic Exhibition, Paris, June 6-16.

Shot Put and Games' Emblem
AP50

Designs: 30fr, Volleyball. 40fr, Women's swimming.

1975, Aug. 1 Photo. *Perf. 13*

C117 AP50 25fr dark red & multi. 90 50
C118 " 30fr emerald & multi. 1.10 60
C119 " 40fr vio. blue & multi. 1.35 75

5th South Pacific Games, Guam, Aug. 1-10.

Flowers, Athlete, View of Montreal
AP51

1975, Oct. 15 Engr. *Perf. 13*

C120 AP51 44fr brt. bl., verm. & black 1.50 1.00

Pre-Olympic Year 1975.

U.P.U. Emblem, Jet and Letters—AP52

1975, Nov. 5 Engr. *Perf. 13*

C121 AP52 100fr brn., bl. & olive 3.50 2.00

World Universal Postal Union Day.

Paintings Type of 1974

Paintings by Artists Living in Polynesia: 20fr, Beach Scene, by R. Marcel Marius (horiz.). 40fr, Roofs with TV antennas, by M. Anglade (horiz.). 60fr, Street scene with bus, by J. Day (horiz.). 80fr, Tropical waters (fish), by J. Steimetz. 100fr, Women, by A. van der Heyde.

1975, Dec. 17 Litho. *Perf. 13*

C122 AP46 20fr gold & multi. 80 50
C123 " 40fr " " 1.20 70
C124 " 60fr " " 2.00 1.25
C125 " 80fr " " 2.75 1.75
C126 " 100fr " " 3.25 2.25
Nos. C122-C126 (5) 10.00 6.45

Concorde—AP53

1976, Jan. 21 Engr. *Perf. 13*

C127 AP53 100fr car., blue & indigo 4.00 3.50

First commercial flight of supersonic jet Concorde from Paris to Rio de Janeiro, Jan. 21.

Adm. Rodney, Count de la Perouse, "Barfleur" and "Triomphant" in Battle—AP54

Design: 31fr, Count de Grasse and Lord Graves, "Ville de Paris" and "Le Terible" in Chesapeake Bay Battle.

1976, Apr. 15 Engr. *Perf. 13*

C128 AP54 24fr greenish blue, lt. brn. & blk. 65 30
C129 " 31fr magenta, red & lt. brn. 85 50

American Bicentennial.

King Pomaré I
AP55

Portraits: 21fr, King Pomaré II. 26fr, Queen Pomaré IV. 30fr, King Pomaré V.

1976, Apr. 28 Litho. *Perf. 12½*

C130 AP55 18fr olive & multi. 45 20
C131 " 21fr multicolored 65 30
C132 " 26fr gray & multi. 80 35
C133 " 30fr plum & multi. 90 45

Pomaré Dynasty. See Nos. C141-C144.

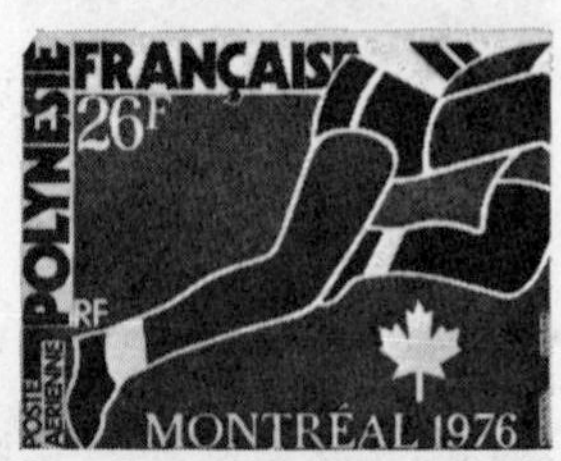

Running and Maple Leaf—AP56

Designs: 34fr, Long jump (vert.). 50fr, Olympic flame and flowers.

1976, July 19 Engr. *Perf. 13*

C134 AP56 26fr ultra. & multi. 60 35
C135 " 34fr " " 90 55
C136 " 50fr " " 1.00 75
a. Miniature sheet of 3 2.75 2.75

21st Olympic Games, Montreal, Canada, July 17-Aug. 1. No. C136a contains one each of Nos. C134-C136. Size: 180x100 mm.

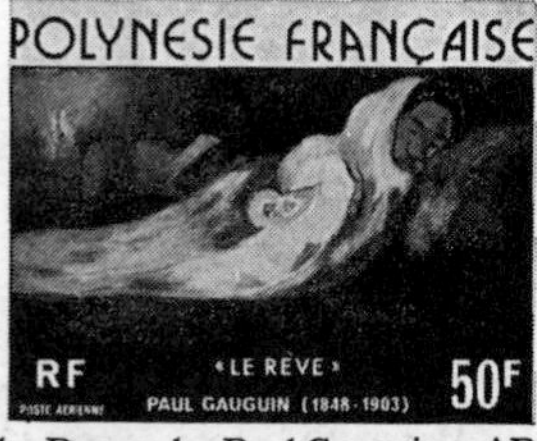

The Dream, by Paul Gauguin—AP57

1976, Oct. 17 Photo. *Perf. 13*

C137 AP57 50fr multi. 1.85 1.20

Murex Steeriae AP58   Pocillopora AP59

Sea Shells: 27fr, Conus Gauguini. 35fr, Conus marchionatus.

1977, Mar. 14 Photo. *Perf. 12½x13*

C138 AP58 25fr violet blue & multi. 60 25
C139 " 27fr ultra. & multi. 75 35
C140 " 35fr blue & multi. 1.00 40

See Nos. C156-C158.

Royalty Type of 1976

Portraits: 19fr, King Maputeoa, Mangareva. 33fr, King Camatoa V, Raiatea. 39fr, Queen Vaekehu, Marquesas. 43fr, King Teurarii III, Rurutu.

1977, Apr. 19 Litho. *Perf. 12½*

C141 AP55 19fr dull red & multi. 40 30
C142 " 33fr dark blue & multi. 75 55
C143 " 39fr ultra. & multi. 85 65
C144 " 43fr grn. & multi. 90 70

Polynesian rulers.

Perf. 13x12½, 12½x13

1977, May 23 Photogravure

Design: 25fr, Acropora (horiz.).

C145 AP59 25fr multicolored 55 40
C146 " 33fr " 75 55

3rd Symposium on Coral Reefs, Miami, Fla. See Nos. C162-C163.

De Gaulle Memorial AP60   Tahitian Dancer AP61

Photogravure and Embossed

1977, June 18 *Perf. 13*
C147 AP60 40fr gold & multi. 90 65

5th anniversary of dedication of De Gaulle memorial at Colombey-les-Deux-Eglises.

1977, July 14 Litho. *Perf. 12½*
C148 AP61 27fr multicolored 60 45

Charles A. Lindbergh and Spirit of St. Louis—AP62

1977, Aug. 18 Litho. *Perf. 12½*
C149 AP62 28fr multicolored 60 45

Charles A. Lindbergh's solo transatlantic flight from New York to Paris, 50th anniversary.

Mahoe AP63 — Palms on Shore AP64

Design: 12fr, Frangipani.

1977, Sept. 15 Photo. *Perf. 12½x13*
C150 AP63 8fr multicolored 15 10
C151 " 12fr " 25 20

1977, Nov. 8 Photo. *Perf. 12½x13*
C152 AP64 32fr multicolored 70 50

Ecology, protection of trees.

Rubens' Son Albert AP65

1977, Nov. 28 Engr. *Perf. 13*
C153 AP65 100fr greenish blk. & rose claret 2.25 1.60

Peter Paul Rubens (1577–1640), painter, 400th birth anniversary.

Capt. Cook and "Discovery"—AP66

Design: 39fr, Capt. Cook and "Resolution."

1978, Jan. 20 Engr. *Perf. 13*
C154 AP66 33fr multicolored 75 55
C155 " 39fr " 85 65

Bicentenary of Capt. James Cook's arrival in Hawaii.

Shell Type of 1977

Sea Shells: 22fr, Erosaria obvelata. 24fr, Cypraea ventriculus. 31fr, Lambis robusta.

1978, Apr. 13 Photo. *Perf. 13½x13*
C156 AP58 22fr bright blue & multi. 45 35
C157 " 24fr bright blue & multi. 48 35
C158 " 31fr bright blue & multi. 65 45

Tahitian Woman and Boy, by Gauguin AP67

1978, May 7 *Perf. 13*
C159 AP67 50fr multi. 1.00 75

Paul Gauguin (1848–1903), 75th death anniversary.

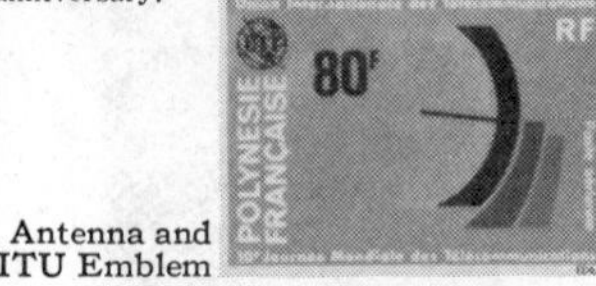

Antenna and ITU Emblem AP68

1978, May 17 Litho. *Perf. 13*
C160 AP68 80fr gray & multi. 1.60 1.20

10th World Telecommunications Day.

Soccer and Argentina '78 Emblem AP69

1978, June 1
C161 AP69 28fr multicolored 56 40

11th World Cup Soccer Championship, Argentina, June 1–25.

Coral Type of 1977

Designs: 26fr, Fungia (horiz.). 34fr, Millepora.

Perf. 13x12½, 12½x13

1978, July 13 Photogravure
C162 AP59 26fr multicolored 52 35
C163 " 34fr " 68 50

Radar Antenna, Polynesian Woman AP70

1978, Sept. 5 Engr. *Perf. 13*
C164 AP70 50fr bl. & black 1.00 75

Papenoo earth station.

Bird and Rainbow over Island—AP71

1978, Oct. 5 Photogravure
C165 AP71 23fr multicolored 46 35

Nature protection.

Nos. C154–C155 Overprinted in Black or Violet Blue: '"1779–1979" / BICENTENAIRE / DE LA / MORT DE'

1979, Feb. 14 Engr. *Perf. 13*
C166 AP66 33fr multi. 65 50
C167 " 39fr " (VBl) 80 60

Bicentenary of Capt. Cook's death. On No. C167 date is last line of overprint.

AIR POST SEMI-POSTAL STAMP.

French Revolution Issue
Common Design Type
Photogravure.

1939, July 5 *Perf. 13* **Unwmkd.**
Name and Value Typo. in Orange.
CB1 CD83 5fr+4fr brown black 6.00 6.00

V5

Stamps of the above design and of Cameroun type V10 inscribed "Etabts Frcais de l'Océanie" were issued in 1942 by the Vichy Government, but were not placed on sale in the colony.

POSTAGE DUE STAMPS.

Postage Due Stamps of French Colonies, 1894-1906, Overprinted

Établissements Français de l'Océanie

1926-27 *Perf. 14x13½* **Unwmkd.**
J1 D1 5c light blue 10 10
J2 " 10c brown 15 15
J3 " 20c olive green 20 20
J4 " 30c dull red 20 20
J5 " 40c rose 30 30
J6 " 60c blue green 30 30
J7 " 1fr red brown, *straw* 40 40
J8 " 3fr magenta ('27) 1.50 1.50

With Additional Surcharge of New Value

J9 D1 2fr on 1fr orange red 60 60
Nos. J1-J9 (9) 3.75 3.75

Fautaua Falls, Tahiti D2 — Tahitian Youth D3

1929 Typographed *Perf. 13½x14*
J10 D2 5c light blue & dark brown 12 12
J11 " 10c vermilion & green 10 10
J12 " 30c dark brown & dark red 22 22
J13 " 50c yellow green & dark brown 10 10
J14 " 60c dull violet & yellow green 55 55
J15 D3 1fr Prussian blue & red violet 30 30
J16 " 2fr brown red & dark brown 15 15
J17 " 3fr blue violet & blue green 20 20
Nos. J10-J17 (8) 1.74 1.74

D4 — Polynesian Club D5

1948 Engraved. *Perf. 14x13.*
J18 D4 10c bright blue green 4 4
J19 " 30c black brown 5 5
J20 " 50c dark carmine rose 6 6
J21 " 1fr ultramarine 8 8
J22 " 2fr dark blue green 10 10
J23 " 3fr red 20 20
J24 " 4fr violet 30 30
J25 " 5fr lilac rose 35 35
J26 " 10fr slate 75 75
J27 " 20fr red brown 1.00 1.00
Nos. J18-J27 (10) 2.93 2.93

1958 *Perf. 14x13* **Unwmkd.**
J28 D5 1fr dark brown & green 20 20
J29 " 3fr bluish black & henna brown 30 30
J30 " 5fr brown & ultra. 35 35

OFFICIAL STAMPS

Bread-fruit O1

Polynesian Fruits: 2fr, 3fr, 5fr, like 1fr. 7fr, 8fr, 10fr, 15fr, "Vi Tahiti." 19fr, 20fr, 25fr, 35fr, Avocados. 50fr, 100fr, 200fr, Mangos.

1977, June 9 Litho. *Perf. 12½*
O1 O1 1fr ultra. & multi. 3 3
O2 " 2fr " " 4 4
O3 " 3fr " " 6 4
O4 " 5fr " " 10 8
O5 " 7fr red & multi. 15 10
O6 " 8fr " " 20 15
O7 " 10fr " " 25 20
O8 " 15fr " " 35 25
O9 " 19fr black & multi. 40 30
O10 " 20fr " " 45 35
O11 " 25fr " " 55 40
O12 " 35fr " " 70 55
O13 " 50fr " " 1.10 80
O14 " 100fr red & multi. 2.25 1.50
O15 " 200fr ultra. & multi. 4.50 3.25
Nos. O1-O15 (15) 11.13 8.04

FRENCH SOUTHERN and ANTARCTIC TERRITORIES

AREA—9,000 sq. mi.
POP.—191 (1978).

Formerly dependencies of Madagascar, these areas, comprising the Kerguelen Archipelago; St. Paul, Amsterdam and Crozet Islands and Adelie Land in Antarctica, achieved territorial status on Aug. 6, 1955.

100 Centimes = 1 Franc

Madagascar No. 289 Overprinted in Red:

TERRES AUSTRALES ET
ANTARCTIQUES FRANÇAISES

Engraved.

1955, Oct. 28 *Perf. 13* Unwmkd.

1 A25 15f dark green & deep ultramarine 27.50 27.50

Rockhopper Penguins, Crozet Archipelago—A1

New Amsterdam
A2

Design: 10fr, 15fr, Elephant seal.

1956, Apr. 25 Engr. *Perf. 13*

2 A1 50c dk. bl., sepia & yel. 50 55
3 " 1fr ultramarine, orange & gray 50 55
4 A2 5fr blue & dp. ultra. 1.10 1.25
5 " 8fr gray violet & dark brown 9.50 10.00
6 " 10fr indigo 1.65 1.75
7 " 15fr indigo & brn. vio. 1.85 2.10
Nos. 2–7 (6) 15.10 16.20

Polar Observation
A3

1957, Oct. 11

8 A3 5fr black & violet 3.75 3.75
9 " 10fr rose red 3.75 3.75
10 " 15fr dark blue 3.75 3.75

International Geophysical Year, 1957–58.

Imperforates

Most stamps of this French possession exist imperforate in issued and trial colors, and also in small presentation sheets in issued colors.

Flower Issue

Common Design Type

Design: Pringlea (horiz.).

1959 Photogravure. *Perf. 12½x12*

11 CD104 10fr salmon, green & yellow 2.50 2.50

Common Design Types

pictured in section at front of book.

Light-mantled Sooty Albatross
A4

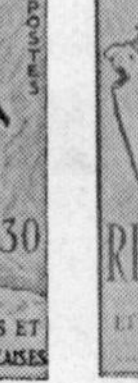

Coat of Arms
A5

Designs: 40c, Skua (horiz.). 12fr, King shag.

1959, Sept. 14 Engraved. *Perf. 13*

12 A4 30c blue, green & red brown 45 45
13 " 40c black, dull red brown & blue 45 45
14 " 12fr lt. blue & black 2.25 2.25

Typographed
Perf. 13x14

15 A5 20fr ultramarine, light blue & yellow 7.50 7.50

Sheathbills
A6

Designs: 4fr, Sea leopard (horiz.). 25fr, Weddell seal at Kerguélen (horiz.). 85fr, King penguin.

1960, Dec. 15 Engraved *Perf. 13*

16 A6 2fr greenish blue, gray & choc. 70 70
17 " 4fr blue, dark brown & dark green 70 70
18 " 25fr slate green, bistre brown & black 2.75 2.75
19 " 85fr greenish blue, org. & black 10.00 10.00

Yves-Joseph de Kerguélen-Trémarec—A7

1960, Nov. 22

20 A7 25fr red orange, dark blue & brown 9.50 9.50

Issued to honor Yves-Joseph de Kerguélen-Trémarec, discoverer of the Kerguélen Archipelago.

Charcot, Compass Rose and "Pourquoi-pas?"
A8

1961, Dec. 26 *Perf. 13* Unwmkd.

21 A8 25fr brown, green & red 10.00 10.00

Issued to commemorate the 25th anniversary of the death of Commander Jean Charcot, Antarctic explorer.

Elephant Seals Fighting
A9

1963, Feb. 11 Engraved *Perf. 13*

22 A9 8fr dark blue, black & claret 2.75 2.75

See No. C4.

Penguins and Camp on Crozet Island
A10

Design: 20fr, Research station and IQSY emblem.

1963, Dec. 16 *Perf. 13* Unwmkd.

23 A10 5fr blk., red brown & Prussian blue 6.25 6.25
24 " 20fr violet, slate & red brown 35.00 35.00

Issued to publicize the International Quiet Sun Year, 1964–65. See No. C6.

Great Blue Whale
A11

Black-browed Albatross
A12

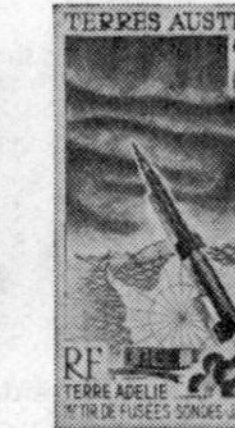

Aurora Australis, Map of Antarctica and Rocket
A13

Designs: 10fr, Cape pigeons. 12fr, Phylica trees, Amsterdam Island. 15fr, Killer whale (orca).

1966–69 Engraved *Perf. 13*

25 A11 5fr brt. bl. & indigo 3.00 3.00
26 A12 10fr slate, indigo & olive brown ('69) 7.00 7.00
27 A11 12fr brt. blue, slate green & lemon ('69) 7.00 7.00
27A " 15fr olive, dk. blue & indigo ('69) 3.75 3.75
28 A12 20fr slate, olive & orange ('68) 42.50 42.50
Nos. 25–28 (5) 63.25 63.25

Issue dates: 5fr, Dec. 12, 1966; 20fr, Jan. 31, 1968; 10fr, 12fr, Jan. 6, 1969; 15fr, Dec. 21, 1969.

1967, March 4 Engraved *Perf. 13*

29 A13 20fr magenta, blue & black 5.75 5.75

Issued to commemorate the launching of the first space rocket from Adelie Land, January, 1967.

Dumont D'Urville
A14

1968, Jan. 20

30 A14 30fr lt. ultra., dark bl. & dk. brn. 10.00 10.00

Jules Sébastien César Dumont D'Urville (1790–1842), French naval commander and South Seas explorer.

WHO Anniversary Issue

Common Design Type

1968, May 4 Engraved *Perf. 13*

31 CD126 30fr red, yel. & blue 6.00 6.00

Issued for the 20th anniversary of the World Health Organization.

Human Rights Year Issue

Common Design Type

1968, Aug. 10 Engraved *Perf. 13*

32 CD127 30fr greenish blue, red & brown 7.00 7.00

Polar Camp with Helicopter, Plane and Snocat Tractor
A15

1969, Mar. 17 Engraved *Perf. 13*

33 A15 25fr Prus. blue, lt. greenish blue & brown red 4.50 4.50

20 years of French Polar expeditions.

ILO Issue

Common Design Type

1970, Jan. 1 Engraved *Perf. 13*

35 CD131 20fr orange, dk. blue & brown 2.50 2.50

U.P.U. Headquarters Issue

Common Design Type

1970, May 20 Engraved *Perf. 13*

36 CD133 50fr blue, plum & olive bister 5.00 5.00

Ice Fish—A16

Fish: Nos. 38–43, Antarctic cods, various species. 135fr, Zanchlorhynchus spinifer.

1971 Engraved *Perf. 13*

37 A16 5fr brt. green, indigo & orange 40 40
38 " 10fr reddish brown & deep violet 60 60
39 " 20fr deep claret, brt. green & orange 1.00 1.00
40 " 22fr purple, brn. olive & magenta 80 80
41 " 25fr grn., indigo & org. 1.25 1.25
42 " 30fr sepia, gray & blue violet 1.85 1.85
43 " 35fr slate green, dk. brn. & ocher 1.40 1.40
44 " 135fr Prus. bl., dp. org. & olive green 3.50 3.50
Nos. 37–44 (8) 10.80 10.80

Issue dates: Nos. 37–39, 41–42, Jan. 1; Nos. 40, 43–44, Dec. 22.

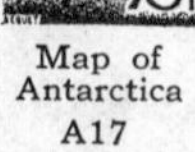

Map of Antarctica A17 | Microzetia Mirabilis A18

1971, Dec. 22

45	A17	75fr red	30.00	30.00

Tenth anniversary of the Antarctic Treaty pledging peaceful uses of and scientific co-operation in Antarctica.

1972

Insects: 15fr, Christiansenia dreuxi. 22f, Phtirocoris antarcticus. 30fr, Antarctophytosus atriceps. 40fr, Paractora drenxi. 140fr, Pringleophaga Kerguelenensis.

46	A18	15fr claret orange & brown	85	85
47	"	22fr violet blue, slate grn. & yel.	1.10	1.10
48	"	25fr green, rose lilac & purple	1.10	1.10
49	"	30fr bl. & multi.	1.50	1.50
50	"	40fr dk. brown, ocher & black	1.85	1.85
51	"	140fr blue, emerald & brown	4.50	4.50
		Nos. 46-51 (6)	10.90	10.90

Issue dates: Nos. 48, 50–51, Jan. 3; Nos. 46–47, 49, Dec. 16.

De Gaulle Issue
Common Design Type

Designs: 50fr, Gen. de Gaulle, 1940. 100fr, Pres. de Gaulle, 1970.

1972, Feb. 1 Engraved *Perf. 13*

52	CD134	50fr brt. grn. & blk.	1.50	1.50
53	"	100fr " " "	3.25	3.25

First anniversary of death of Charles de Gaulle (1890–1970), president of France.

Kerguelen Cabbage A19

Designs: 61fr, Azorella selago (horiz.). 87fr, Acaena ascendens (horiz.).

1972–73

54	A19	45fr dull red, ultra. & slate green	1.85	1.85
55	"	61fr multi. ('73)	1.50	1.50
56	"	87fr " ('73)	1.85	1.85

Issue dates: 45fr, Dec. 18, 1972; others, Dec. 13, 1973.

Mailship Sapmer and Map of Amsterdam Island—A20

1974, Dec. 31 Engraved *Perf. 13*

57	A20	75fr blue, black & dark brown	1.65	1.65

25th anniversary of postal service.

Antarctic Tern A21

Designs: 50c, Antarctic petrel. 90c, Sea lioness. 1fr, Weddell seal. 1.20fr, Kerguelen cormorant (vert.). 1.40fr, Gentoo penguin (vert.).

1976, Jan. Engraved *Perf. 13*

58	A21	40c multicolored	38	38
59	"	50c "	50	50
60	"	90c "	70	70
61	"	1fr "	75	75
62	"	1.20fr "	1.00	1.00
63	"	1.40fr "	1.15	1.15
		Nos. 58-63 (6)	4.48	4.48

James Clark Ross A22 | James Cook A23

Design: 30c, Climbing Mount Ross.

1976, Dec. 16 Engr. *Perf. 13*

64	A22	30c multicolored	80	80
65	"	3fr "	3.25	3.25

First climbing of Mount Ross, Kerguelen Island, by James Clark Ross, Jan. 5, 1875.

1976, Dec. 16

66	A23	70c multicolored	2.50	2.50

Bicentenary of Capt. Cook's voyage past Kerguelen Island. See No. C46.

Commerson's Dolphins A24

Design: 1.10fr, Blue whale.

1977, Feb. 1 Engraved *Perf. 13*

67	A24	1.10fr blue & indigo	75	75
68	"	1.50fr multicolored	1.25	1.25

Macrocystis Algae—A25

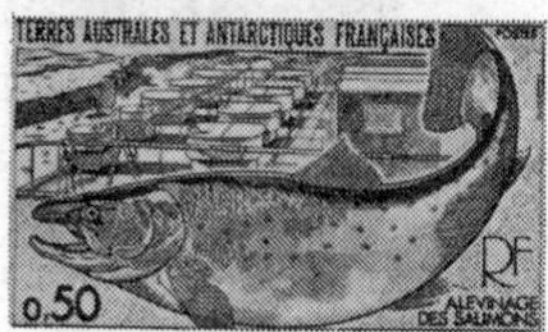

Salmon Hatchery—A26

Magga Dan—A27

Designs: 70c, Durvillea algae. 90c, Albatross. 1fr, Underwater sampling and scientists (vert.). 1.40fr, Thala Dan and penguins.

1977, Dec. 20 Engr. *Perf. 13*

69	A25	40c olive brown & bister	20	20
70	A26	50c dk. bl. & pur.	25	25
71	A25	70c black, green & brown	38	38
72	A26	90c grn., brt. blue & brown	45	45
73	A27	1fr slate	65	65
74	"	1.20fr multicolored	75	75
75	"	1.40fr "	85	85
		Nos. 69-75 (7)	3.53	3.53

See Nos. 77–79.

Explorer with French and Expedition Flags A28

1977, Dec. 24

76	A28	1.90fr multicolored	1.25	1.25

French Polar expeditions, 1947–48, 30th anniversary.

Types of 1977

Designs: 40c, E. E. Forbin. 50c, P. H. Jeanne D'Arc and helicopter. 1.40fr, Kerguelen cormorant.

1979, Jan. 1 Engr. *Perf. 13*

77	A27	40c black & blue	20	20
78	"	50c " "	25	25
79	A26	1.40fr multicolored	70	70

R. Rallier du Baty A29

1979, Jan. 1

80	A29	1.20fr citron & indigo	60	60

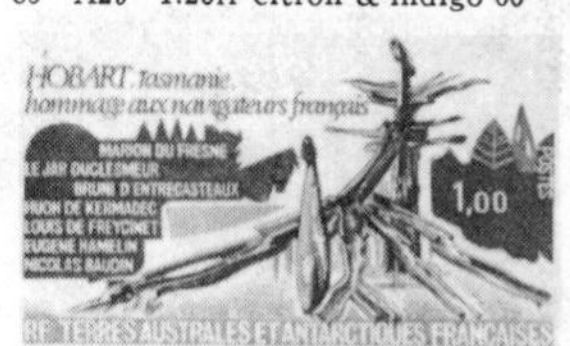

French Navigators Monument, Hobart—A30

1979, Jan. 1

81	A30	1fr multicolored	50	50

French navigators and explorers.

AIR POST STAMPS

Emperor Penguins and Map of Antarctica—AP1

Engraved

1956, April 25 ***Perf. 13*** **Unwmkd.**

C1 AP1 50fr light olive green & dk. green 35.00 35.00
C2 " 100fr dull blue & indigo 35.00 35.00

Wandering Albatross—AP2

1959, Sept. 14

C3 AP2 200fr brown red, blue & black 22.50 22.50

Adélie Penguins—AP3

1963, Feb. 11 ***Perf. 13*** **Unwmkd.**

C4 AP3 50fr black, dark blue & dp. claret 22.50 22.50

Telstar Issue

Common Design Type

1963, Feb. 11

C5 CD111 50fr deep blue, olive & green 17.50 17.50

Radio Towers, Adelie Penguins and IQSY Emblem AP4

1963, Dec. 16 Engraved

C6 AP4 100fr blue, verm. & black 62.50 62.50

International Quiet Sun Year, 1964–65.

Discovery of Adelie Land—AP5

1965, Jan. 20 Engraved ***Perf. 13***

C7 AP5 50fr blue & indigo 50.00 50.00

125th anniversary of the discovery of Adelie Land by Dumont d'Urville.

ITU Issue

Common Design Type

1965, May 17 ***Perf. 13*** **Unwmkd.**

C8 CD120 30fr Prussian blue, sepia & dark car. rose 140.00 110.00

Issued to commemorate the centenary of the International Telecommunication Union.

French Satellite A-1 Issue

Common Design Type

Designs: 25fr, Diamant rocket and launching installations. 30fr, A-1 satellite.

1966, Mar. 2 Engraved ***Perf. 13***

C9 CD121 25fr dk. grn., choc. & slate 15.00 15.00
C10 " 30fr chocolate, slate & dk. green 15.00 15.00
a. Strip of 2 + label 32.50 32.50

Issued to commemorate the launching of France's first satellite, Nov. 26, 1965. No. C10a contains one each of Nos. C9–C10 and label with dark green commemorative inscription. Each sheet contains 16 triptychs (2x8).

French Satellite D-1 Issue

Common Design Type

1966, Mar. 27

C11 CD122 50fr dark purple, lilac & org. 25.00 25.00

Issued to commemorate the launching of the D-1 satellite at Hammaguir, Algeria, Feb. 17, 1966.

Ionospheric Research Pylon, Adelie Land AP6

1966, Dec. 12

C12 AP6 25fr plum, blue & dark brown 14.00 14.00

Port aux Français, Emperor Penguin and Explorer—AP7

Design: 40fr, Aerial view of Saint Paul Island.

1968–69 Engraved ***Perf. 13***

C13 AP7 40fr brt. blue & dk. gray ('69) 5.00 5.00
C14 " 50fr lt. ultra., dk. grn. & black 13.50 13.50

Kerguelen Island and Rocket AP8

Design: 30fr, Adelie Land.

1968, Apr. 22 Engraved ***Perf. 13***

C15 AP8 25fr slate grn., dk. brn. & Prus. blue 10.00 10.00
C16 AP8 30fr dk. brn., slate green & Prus. blue 10.00 10.00
a. Strip of 2+label 22.50 22.50

Issued to commemorate space explorations with Dragon rockets, 1967–68. No. C16a contains one each of Nos. C15–C16 and label with slate green and dark brown commemorative inscription.

Eiffel Tower, Antarctic Research Station, Ship from Paris Arms and Albatross AP9

1969, Jan. 13

C17 AP9 50fr bright blue 7.50 7.50

Issued to commemorate the 5th Consultative Meeting of the Antarctic Treaty Powers, Paris, Nov. 18, 1968.

Concorde Issue

Common Design Type

1969, Apr. 17

C18 CD129 85fr indigo & bl. 20.00 20.00

Map of Amsterdam Island AP10

Map of Kerguelen Island—AP11

Coat of Arms AP12

Designs: 50fr, Possession Island. 200fr, Point Geology Archipelago.

1969–71 Engraved ***Perf. 13***

C19 AP10 30fr brown ('70) 3.00 3.00
C20 AP11 50fr slate grn., bl. & dk. red ('70) 4.25 4.25
C21 " 100fr blue & black 6.25 6.25
C22 AP10 200fr slate grn., brn. & Prus. blue ('71) 10.00 10.00
C23 AP12 500fr peacock blue 17.50 17.50
Nos. C19–C23 (5) 41.00 41.00

The 30fr commemorates the 20th anniversary of the Amsterdam Island Meteorological Station.

Issue dates: 30fr, Mar. 27, 1970; 50fr, Dec. 22, 1970; 100fr, 500fr, Dec. 21, 1969; 200fr, Jan. 1, 1971.

Port-aux-Français, 1970—AP13

Design: 40fr, Port-aux-Français, 1950.

1971, Mar. 9 Engraved ***Perf. 13***

C24 AP13 40fr blue, ocher & slate green 2.75 2.75
C25 " 50fr blue, brn. olive & slate grn. 4.25 4.25
a. Strip of 2+label 7.50 7.50

20th anniversary of Port-aux-Français on Kerguelen Island. No. C25a contains one each of Nos. C24–C25 and label with blue and brown olive commemorative inscription.

Marquis de Castries Taking Possession of Crozet Island, 1772—AP14

Design: 250fr, Fleur-de-lis flag raising on Kerguelen Island.

1972 Engraved ***Perf. 13***

C26 AP14 100fr black 5.00 5.00
C27 " 250fr blk. & dk. brn. 8.50 8.50

Bicentenary of the discovery of the Crozet and Kerguelen Islands. Issue dates: 100fr, Jan. 24; 250fr, Feb. 23.

M. S. Galliéni—AP15

1973, Jan. 25 Engr. ***Perf. 13***

C28 AP15 100fr black & blue 12.50 12.50

Exploration voyages of the Galliéni.

"Le Mascarin," 1772—AP16

Sailing Ships: 145fr, "L'Astrolabe," 1840. 150fr, "Le Rolland," 1774. 185fr, "La Victoire," 1522.

1973, Dec. 13 Engraved *Perf. 13*

C29	AP16	120fr brown olive	2.00	2.00
C30	"	145fr brt. ultra.	2.50	2.50
C31	"	150fr slate	2.75	2.75
C32	"	185fr ocher	3.00	3.00

Ships used in exploring Antarctica.
See Nos. C37–C38.

Alfred Faure Base—AP17

Design: Nos. C33–C35 show panoramic view of Alfred Faure Base.

1974, Jan. 7 Engraved *Perf. 13*

C33	AP17	75fr Prus. bl., ultra. & brown	2.35	2.35
C34	"	110fr Prus. blue, ultra. & brown	3.00	3.00
C35	"	150fr Prus. blue, ultra. & brown	4.00	4.00
		Triptych (Nos. C33–C35)	10.00	10.00

10th anniversary of the Alfred Faure Antarctic Base. Nos. C33–C35 printed se-tenant.

Penguin, Map of Antarctica, Letters
AP18

1974, Oct. 9 Engraved *Perf. 13*

C36	AP18	150fr multicolored	3.00	3.00

Centenary of Universal Postal Union.

Ship Type of 1973

Designs: 100fr, "Le Français." 200fr, "Pourquoi-pas?"

1974, Dec. 16 Engraved *Perf. 13*

C37	AP16	100fr bright blue	1.50	1.50
C38	"	200fr dk. car. rose	3.00	3.00

Ships used in exploring Antarctica.

Rockets over Kerguelen Islands—AP19

Design: 90fr, Northern lights over map of northern coast of Russia.

1975, Jan. 26 Engraved *Perf. 13*

C39	AP19	45fr pur. & multi.	1.50	1.50
C40	"	90fr " "	1.50	1.50
		a. Strip of 2 + label	3.25	3.25

Franco-Soviet magnetosphere research. No. C40a contains one each of Nos. C39–C40, and label with red inscription and indigo design. Sheets contain 5 No. C40a.

"La Curieuse"—AP20

Ships: 2.70fr, Commandant Charcot. 4fr, Marion-Dufresne.

1976, Jan. Engraved *Perf. 13*

C41	AP20	1.90fr multi.	1.50	1.50
C42	"	2.70fr "	2.25	2.25
C43	"	4fr red & multi.	3.00	3.00

Dumont D'Urville Base, 1956—AP21

Design: 4fr, Dumont D'Urville Base, 1976, Adelie Land.

1976, Jan.

C44	AP21	1.20fr multicolored	1.00	1.00
C45	"	4fr "	3.25	3.25
		a. Strip of 2 + label	4.50	4.50

20th anniversary of the Dumont D'Urville Antarctic Base. No. C45a contains one each of Nos. C44–C45 and label with map of Antarctica and penguins.

Capt. Cook's Ships Passing Kerguelen Island—AP22

1976, Dec. 31 Engr. *Perf. 13*

C46	AP22	3.50fr slate & blue	3.75	3.75

Bicentenary of Capt. Cook's voyage past Kerguelen Island.

Sea Lion and Cub
AP23

1977–79 Engr. *Perf. 13*

C47	AP23	4fr dk. blue & green ('79)	2.00	2.00
C48	"	10fr multicolored	9.00	9.00

Satellite Survey, Kerguelen—AP24

Designs: 70c, Geophysical laboratory. 1.90fr, Satellite and Kerguelen tracking station. 3fr, Satellites, Adelie Land.

1977–79 Engr. *Perf. 13*

C49	AP24	70c multicolored	35	35
C50	"	1.90fr "	95	95
C51	"	2.70fr "	2.10	2.10
C52	"	3fr "	2.50	2.50

Issue dates: 3fr, Dec. 20, 1977; 2.70fr, Jan. 4, 1978; 70c, 1.90fr, Jan. 1, 1979.

Elephant Seals
AP25

1979, Jan. 1

C53	AP25	10fr multicolored	5.00	5.00

Challenger—AP26

1979, Jan. 1

C54	AP26	2.70fr blk. & bl.	1.35	1.35

Antarctic expeditions to Crozet and Kerguelen Islands, 1972–1976.

FRENCH SUDAN

(frĕnch sōō·dăn′; -dän′)

LOCATION—In northwest Africa, north of French Guinea and Ivory Coast.

GOVT.—Former French Colony.

AREA—590,966 sq. mi.

POP.—3,794,270 (1941).

CAPITAL—Bamako.

In 1899 French Sudan was abolished as a separate colony and was divided among Dahomey, French Guinea, Ivory Coast, Senegal and Senegambia and Niger. Issues for French Sudan were resumed in 1921.

From 1906 to 1921 a part of this territory was known as Upper Senegal and Niger. A part of Upper Volta was added in 1933. See Mali.

100 Centimes = 1 Franc

Navigation and Commerce
A1 A2

Stamps of French Colonies, Surcharged in Black.

1894 *Perf. 14x13½* Unwmkd.

1	A1	15c on 75c carmine, *rose*	1650.00	1150.00
2	"	25c on 1fr bronze green, *straw*	1650.00	950.00

The imperforate stamp like No. 1 was made privately in Paris from a fragment of the lithographic stone which had been used in the Colony for surcharging No. 1.

Counterfeit surcharges exist.

1894–1900 Typographed

Name of colony in Blue or Carmine.

3	A2	1c *lilac blue*	65	65
4	"	2c brown, *buff*	85	85
5	"	4c claret, *lavender*	1.50	1.25
6	"	5c green, *greenish*	2.50	2.00
7	"	10c *lavender*	5.50	5.50
8	"	10c red ('00)	1.25	1.25
9	"	15c blue, quadrille paper	1.50	1.25
10	"	15c gray, *light gray* ('00)	2.25	2.25
11	"	20c red, *green*	9.00	8.50
12	"	25c *rose*	9.00	8.00
13	"	25c blue ('00)	2.00	2.00
14	"	30c brown, *bistre*	15.00	12.00
15	"	40c red, *straw*	11.00	8.50
16	"	50c carmine, *rose*	18.50	16.50
17	"	50c brown, *azure* ('00)	3.75	3.75
18	"	75c deep violet, *orange*	13.50	13.50
19	"	1fr bronze green, *straw*	2.50	2.50
		Nos. 3–19 (17)	100.25	90.25

Camel and Rider
A3

Stamps of Upper Senegal and Niger Overprinted in Black.

1921–30 *Perf. 13½x14*

21	A3	1c brn. vio. & violet	6	6
22	"	2c dark gray & dull violet	6	6

23 A3 4c black & blue 6 6
24 " 5c olive brown & dark brown 6 6
25 " 10c yellow green & blue green 8 8
26 " 10c red violet & blue ('25) 6 6
27 " 15c red brown & orange 10 10
28 " 15c yellow green & deep green ('25) 6 6
29 " 15c orange brown & violet ('27) 18 18
30 " 20c brn. vio. & black 8 8
31 " 25c black & blue green 6 6
a. Booklet pane of 4
32 " 30c red orange & rose 10 10
33 " 30c blue green & black ('26) 8 8
34 " 30c dull green & blue green ('28) 40 40
35 " 35c rose & violet 6 6
36 " 40c gray & rose 20 17
37 " 45c blue & olive brown 12 12
38 " 50c ultramarine & blue 20 20
39 " 50c red orange & blue ('26) 12 8
40 " 60c violet, *pinkish* ('26) 6 6
41 " 65c bistre & pale blue ('28) 22 22
42 " 75c org. & olive brn. 20 20
43 " 90c brown red & pink ('30) 1.65 1.65
44 " 1fr dark brown & dull violet 25 15
45 " 1.10fr gray lilac & red violet ('28) 40 40
46 " 1.50fr deep blue & blue ('30) 1.75 1.75
47 " 2fr green & blue 70 55
48 " 3fr red violet ('30) 3.00 3.00
a. Double overprint 47.50
49 " 5fr violet & black 1.65 1.35
Nos. 21-49 (29) 12.02 11.40

Type of 1921 Surcharged **60 = 60**

1922
50 A3 60c on 75c violet, *pinkish* 10 10

Stamps and Type of 1921-30 Surcharged with New Values and Bars.

1925-27
51 A3 25c on 45c blue & olive brown ('25) 15 15
52 " 65c on 75c orange & olive brown ('25) 25 25
53 " 85c on 2fr green & blue ('25) 40 30
54 " 85c on 5fr violet & black ('25) 40 30
55 " 90c on 75c brown red & salmon pink ('27) 60 30
56 " 1.25fr on 1fr deep blue & light blue (R) ('26) 25 25
57 " 1.50fr on 1fr dp. blue & ultramarine ('27) 25 25
58 " 3fr on 5fr dull red & brn. org. ('27) 1.10 60
59 " 10fr on 5fr brown red & blue green ('27) 5.50 5.00
60 " 20fr on 5fr violet & vermilion ('27) 7.00 6.00
Nos. 51-60 (10) 15.90 13.40

Sudanese Woman
A4

Entrance to the Residency at Djenné
A5

Sudanese Boatman
A6

1931-40 **Typo.** ***Perf. 13x14.***
61 A4 1c dark red & black 5 5
62 " 2c dp. blue & orange 6 6
63 " 3c dark red & black ('40) 6 6
64 " 4c gray lilac & rose 6 6
65 " 5c indigo & green 8 8
66 " 10c olive green & rose 6 6
67 " 15c black & brt. violet 6 6
68 " 20c henna brown & light blue 6 6
69 " 25c red violet & light red 6 6
70 A5 30c green & lt. green 12 8
71 " 30c dark blue & red orange ('40) 6 6
72 " 35c olive green & green ('38) 10 8
73 " 40c olive green & pink 6 6
74 " 45c dark blue & red orange 15 12
75 " 45c olive green & green ('40) 8 8
76 " 50c red & black 6 6
77 " 55c ultramarine & carmine ('38) 10 10
78 " 60c bright blue & brown ('40) 10 10
79 " 65c brt. vio. & black 8 8
80 " 70c violet blue & car. rose ('40) 12 12
81 " 75c bright blue & olive brown 45 20
82 " 80c carmine & brown ('38) 7 7
83 " 90c deep red & red orange 10 10
84 " 90c bright violet & slate black ('39) 10 10
85 " 1fr indigo & green 2.35 25
86 " 1fr rose red ('38) 1.00 15
87 " 1fr carmine & brown ('40) 7 7
88 A6 1.25fr violet & dull violet ('33) 15 12
89 " 1.25fr red ('39) 12 12
90 " 1.40fr bright violet & black ('40) 12 12
91 " 1.50fr dk. blue & ultra. 8 8
92 " 1.60fr brown & deep blue ('40) 12 12
93 " 1.75fr dark brown & deep blue ('33) 6 5
94 " 1.75fr violet blue ('38) 8 7
95 " 2fr org. brn. & green 8 7
96 " 2.25fr violet blue & ultramarine ('39) 18 18
97 " 2.50fr light brown ('40) 20 20
98 " 3fr Prussian green & brown 8 8
99 " 5fr red & black 40 20
100 " 10fr dull blue & green 50 50
101 " 20fr red violet & brown 60 60
Nos. 61-101 (41) 8.49 4.94

Colonial Exposition Issue.

Common Design Types

1931 **Engraved** ***Perf. 12½***

Name of Country Printed in Black.

102 CD70 40c deep green 75 75
103 CD71 50c violet 75 75
104 CD72 90c red orange 75 75
105 CD73 1.50fr dull blue 75 75

Paris International Exposition Issue.

Common Design Types

1937 ***Perf. 13.***
106 CD74 20c deep violet 35 35
107 CD75 30c dark green 35 35
108 CD76 40c carmine rose 35 35
109 CD77 50c dark brown 35 35
110 CD78 90c red 35 35
111 CD79 1.50fr ultramarine 35 35
Nos. 106-111 (6) 2.10 2.10

Colonial Arts Exhibition Issue.

Souvenir Sheet.

Common Design Type

1937 **Engraved** ***Imperf.***
112 CD77 3fr magenta & blk. 1.35 1.35
Sheet size: 118x99mm.

Caillie Issue

Common Design Type

1939 ***Perf. 12½x12.***
113 CD81 90c org. brn. & org. 20 20
114 " 2fr bright violet 20 20
115 " 2.25fr ultramarine & dark blue 20 20

Centenary of the death of René Caillié (1799-1838), French explorer.

New York World's Fair Issue.

Common Design Type

1939, May 10
116 CD82 1.25fr carmine lake 22 22
117 " 2.25fr ultramarine 22 22

Entrance to the Residency at Djenné and Marshal Pétain
A7

1941 **Engraved** ***Perf. 12x12½.***
118 A7 1fr green 10 10
119 " 2.50fr blue 10 10

Stamps of types A4 and A5 without "RF" were issued in 1943 and 1944 by the Vichy Government, but were not placed on sale in the colony.

Stamps of French Sudan were superseded by those of French West Africa.

SEMI-POSTAL STAMPS.

Curie Issue

Common Design Type

Engraved.

1938 ***Perf. 13*** **Unwmkd.**
B1 CD80 1.75fr+50c bright ultramarine 3.50 3.50

French Revolution Issue

Common Design Type

1939 **Photogravure.**

Name and Value Typo. in Black.

B2 CD83 45(c)+25(c) green 2.25 2.25
B3 " 70(c)+30(c) brown 2.25 2.25
B4 " 90(c)+35(c) red orange 2.25 2.25
B5 " 1.25fr+1fr rose pink 2.25 2.25
B6 " 2.25fr+2fr blue 2.25 2.25
Nos. B2-B6 (5) 11.25 11.25

Stamps of 1931-40, Surcharged in Black or Red **SECOURS + 1 fr. NATIONAL**

1941 ***Perf. 13x14***
B7 A5 50c+1fr red & black (R) 25 25
B8 " 80c+2fr carmine & brown (Bk) 2.50 2.50
B9 A6 1.50fr+2fr dark blue & ultra. (Bk) 2.50 2.50
B10 " 2fr+3fr orange brown & green (Bk) 2.50 2.50

Common Design Type and

Native Officer
SP1

Aviation Officer
SP2

1941 **Photogravure** ***Perf. 13½***
B11 SP1 1fr+1fr red 22
B12 CD86 1.50fr+3fr claret 22
B13 SP2 2.50fr+1fr blue 22

The surtax was for the defense of the colonies.

Nos. B11-B13 were issued by the Vichy government and were not placed on sale in the colony.

Stamps of type A7, surcharged "OEUVRES COLONIALES" and new values, were issued in 1944 by the Vichy Government, but were not placed on sale in the colony.

AIR POST STAMPS.

Common Design Type

Engraved.

1940 ***Perf. 12½x12.*** **Unwmkd.**
C1 CD85 1.90fr ultramarine 10 10
C2 " 2.90fr dark red 10 10
C3 " 4.50fr dark gray green 25 25
C4 " 4.90fr yellow bistre 20 20
C5 " 6.90fr deep orange 20 20
Nos. C1-C5 (5) 85 85

Common Design Types

1942
C6 CD88 50c carmine & blue 6 15
C7 " 1fr brown & black 7
C8 " 2fr dark green & red brown 8
C9 " 3fr dark blue & scarlet 10
C10 " 5fr vio. & brn. red 15

Frame Engraved,
Center Typographed.

C11 CD89 10fr ultramarine, indigo & gray black 13
C12 " 20fr rose carmine, magenta & light violet 15
C13 " 50fr yellow green, dull green & dull blue 40 60
Nos. C6-C13 (8) 1.14

There is doubt whether Nos. C7-C12 were officially placed in use.

AIR POST SEMI-POSTAL STAMPS.

Stamps of type of Dahomey V1, V2, V3 and V4 inscribed "Soudan Frcais", "Soudan" or "Soudan Francais" were issued in 1942 by the Vichy Government, but were not placed on sale in the colony.

POSTAGE DUE STAMPS.

D1

D2

Postage Due Stamps of Upper Senegal and Niger Overprinted in Black.

Typographed.

1921		*Perf. 14x13½*	Unwmkd.	
J1	D1	5c green	10	10
J2	"	10c rose	20	20
J3	"	15c gray	20	20
J4	"	20c brown	20	20
J5	"	30c blue	25	25
J6	"	50c black	50	50
J7	"	60c orange	50	50
J8	"	1fr violet	55	55
		Nos. J1-J8 (8)	2.50	2.50

Type of 1921 Issue Surcharged **2F.**

1927				
J9	D1	2fr on 1fr lilac rose	1.35	1.35
J10	"	3fr on 1fr orange brown	1.35	1.35

1931				
J11	D2	5c green	6	6
J12	"	10c rose	6	6
J13	"	15c gray	7	7
J14	"	20c dark brown	10	10
J15	"	30c dark blue	10	10
J16	"	50c black	10	10
J17	"	60c deep orange	20	20
J18	"	1fr violet	30	30
J19	"	2fr lilac rose	30	30
J20	"	3fr red brown	30	30
		Nos. J11-J20 (10)	1.59	1.59

FRENCH WEST AFRICA

(frĕnch wĕst' ăf'rĭ-kȧ)

LOCATION—Northwestern Africa.

GOVT.—Former French colonial administrative unit.

AREA—1,821,768 sq. mi.

POP.—18,777,163 (est.).

CAPITAL—Dakar.

French West Africa comprised the former colonies of Senegal, French Guinea, Ivory Coast, Dahomey, French Sudan, Mauritania, Niger and Upper Volta.

In 1958, these former colonies became republics, eventually issuing their own stamps. Until the republic issues appeared, stamps of French West Africa continued in use. The Senegal and Sudanese Republics issued stamps jointly as the Federation of Mali, starting in 1959.

50 fr.

Senegal No. 156 Surcharged in Red

1943		*Perf. 12½x12.*	Unwmkd.	
1	A30	1.50fr on 65c dark violet	10	10
2	"	5.50fr on 65c dark violet	15	15
3	"	50fr on 65c dark violet	85	45

Mauritania No. 91 Surcharged in Red

5 fr.

1944			*Perf. 13*	
4	A7	3.50fr on 65c deep green	9	8
5	"	4fr on 65c "	9	8
6	"	5fr on 65c "	30	20
7	"	10fr on 65c "	30	20
		Nos. 1-7 (7)	1.88	1.26

Common Design Types pictured in section at front of book.

Senegal Nos. 143, 148 and 188 Surcharged with New Values in Black or Orange.

1944		*Perf. 12½x12*		
8	A29	1.50fr on 15c black (O)	10	10
9	"	4.50fr on 15c black (O)	25	25
10	"	5.50fr on 2c brown	40	30
11	"	10fr on 15c black (O)	60	45
12	CD81	20fr on 90c orange brown & orange	45	25
13	"	50fr on 90c orange brown & orange	1.25	90

Mauritania No. 109 Surcharged in Black.

14	A6	15fr on 90c orange brown & orange	20	13
		Nos. 8-14 (7)	3.25	2.38

Eboue Issue.

Common Design Type

1945		Engraved	*Perf. 13*	
15	CD91	2fr black	10	10
16	"	25fr Prussian green	60	60

Nos. 15 and 16 exist imperforate.

Colonial Soldiers
A1

1945		Lithographed	*Perf. 12*	
17	A1	10c indigo & buff	6	4
18	"	30c olive & yellow	6	5
19	"	40c blue & buff	6	6
20	"	50c red orange & gray	6	6
21	"	60c olive brown & blue	6	6
22	"	70c magenta & citron	10	10
23	"	80c blue green & pale lemon	10	8
24	"	1fr brown violet & citron	5	5
25	"	1.20fr gray brown & citron	90	90
26	"	1.50fr chocolate & pink	5	5
27	"	2fr ochre & gray	15	10
28	"	2.40fr red & gray	30	25
29	"	3fr brown red & yellowish	8	5
30	"	4fr ultra. & pink	10	8
31	"	4.50fr orange brown & yellowish	8	8
32	"	5fr dark purple & yellowish	8	6
33	"	10fr olive green & pink	35	6
34	"	15fr orange & yellow	75	30
35	"	20fr slate green & greenish	75	28
		Nos. 17-35 (19)	4.14	2.71

Rifle Dance, Mauritania
A2

Shelling Coconuts, Togo
A6

Bamako Dike, French Sudan
A3

Trading Canoe, Niger River
A4

Oasis of Bilma, Niger
A5

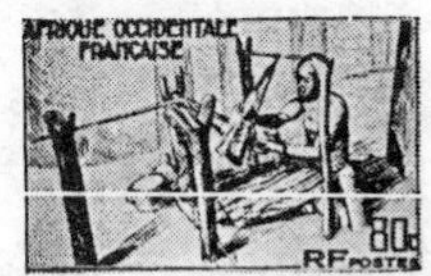

Kouandé Weaving, Dahomey
A7

Donkey Caravan, Senegal
A8

Crocodile and Hippopotamus, Ivory Coast
A9

Bamako Fountain, French Sudan
A11

Gathering Coconuts, French Guinea
A10

Peul Woman of Djenné
A12

Bamako Market
A13

Dahomey Laborer
A14

Woman of Mauritania
A15

Fula Woman, French Guinea
A16

Djenné Mosque, French Sudan
A17

Monorail Train, Senegal
A18

Agni Woman, Ivory Coast
A19

Azwa Women at Niger River
A20

Engraved.

1947		*Perf. 12½*	Unwmkd.	
36	A2	10c blue	3	3
37	A3	30c red brown	4	4
38	A4	40c gray green	4	4
39	A5	50c red brown	4	4
40	A6	60c gray black	15	15
41	A7	80c brown violet	15	15
42	A8	1fr maroon	6	6
43	A9	1.20fr dark blue green	30	30
44	A10	1.50fr ultramarine	35	30
45	A11	2fr red orange	6	6
46	A12	3fr chocolate	15	8
47	A13	3.60fr brown red	35	35
48	A14	4fr deep blue	6	6
49	A15	5fr dark gray green	10	5
50	A16	6fr dark blue	12	6
51	A17	10fr brown red	25	6
52	A18	15fr sepia	35	5
53	A19	20fr chocolate	35	5
54	A20	25fr greenish black	60	7
		Nos. 36-54 (19)	3.55	2.00

Types of 1947.

1948 Re-engraved.

55 A6 60c brown olive 18 7
56 A12 3fr chocolate 7 5

Nos. 40 and 46 are inscribed "TOGO" in lower margin. Inscription omitted on Nos. 55 and 56.

Imperforates

Most stamps of French West Africa from 1949 onward exist imperforate in issued and trial colors, and also in small presentation sheets in issued colors.

Military Medal Issue.

Common Design Type

Engraved and Typographed.

1952, Dec. 1 *Perf. 13*

57 CD101 15fr black, grn., yel. & black brown 1.65 1.65

Treich Laplène and Map
A21

1952, Dec. 1 Engraved

58 A21 40fr brown lake 65 7

Issued to honor Marcel Treich Laplene, a leading contributor to the development of Ivory Coast.

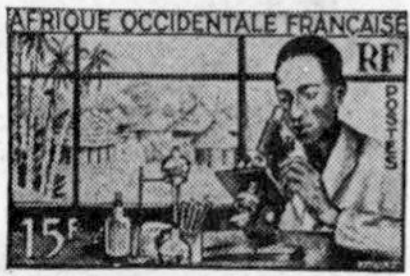

Medical Laboratory
A22

1953, Nov. 18

59 A22 15fr brown, dark blue grn. & blk. brn. 40 5

Couple Feeding Antelopes
A23

1954, Sept. 20

60 A23 25fr multicolored 45 5

Gov. Noel Eugène Ballay
A24

1954, Nov. 29

61 A24 8fr indigo & brown 40 15

Chimpanzee
A25

Giant Pangolin
A26

1955, May 2 *Perf. 13* **Unwmkd.**

62 A25 5fr dark gray & dark brown 40 15
63 A26 8fr dark brown & blue green 30 15

Issued in connection with the International Exhibition for Wildlife Protection, Paris, May 1955.

Map, Symbols of Industry, Rotary Emblem
A27

1955, July 4

64 A27 15fr dark blue 30 20

Issued to commemorate the 50th anniversary of the founding of Rotary International.

FIDES Issue

Mossi Railroad Upper Volta
A28

Designs: 1fr, Date grove, Mauritania. 2fr, Milo Bridge, French Guinea. 4fr, Cattle raising, Niger. 15fr, Farm machinery and landscape, Senegal. 17fr, Woman and Sansanding River, French Sudan. 20fr, Palm oil production, Dahomey. 30fr, Road construction, Ivory Coast.

1956 Engraved *Perf. 13x12½*

65 A28 1fr dark green & dark blue green 25 25
66 " 2fr dark blue green & blue 25 25
67 " 3fr dark brown & red brown 30 25
68 " 4fr dark carmine rose 35 30
69 " 15fr indigo & ultra. 35 10
70 " 17fr dark blue & indigo 40 25
71 " 20fr rose lake 40 25
72 " 30fr dark purple & claret 40 25
Nos. 65-72 (8) 2.70 1.90

See note after Cameroun No. 329.

Coffee Issue.

Coffee
A28a

1956, Oct. 22 *Perf. 13*

73 A28a 15fr dark blue green 20 5

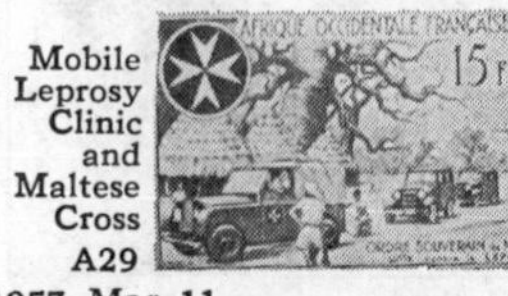

Mobile Leprosy Clinic and Maltese Cross
A29

1957, Mar. 11

74 A29 15fr dull red brown, purple & red 50 20

Issued in honor of the Knights of Malta.

Map of Africa
A30

1958, Feb. *Perf. 13* **Unwmkd.**

75 A30 20fr greenish blue, black & dull red brown 45 25

Issued to publicize the sixth International Congress for African Tourism at Dakar.

"Africa" and Communications Symbols
A31

1958, Mar. 15 Engraved

76 A31 15fr orange, ultramarine & chocolate 40 25

Stamp Day. See No. 86.

Abidjan Bridge
A32

1958, Mar. 15

77 A32 20fr dark slate green & greenish blue 45 10

Bananas
A33

1958, May 19 *Perf. 13*

78 A33 20fr rose lilac, dark green & olive 35 10

Flower Issue

Common Design Type

Designs: 10fr, Gloriosa. 25fr, Adenopus. 30fr, Cyrtosperma. 40fr, Cistanche. 65fr, Crinum Moorei.

1958-59 Photogravure. *Perf. 12x12½*

79 CD104 10fr multicolored 20 10
80 " 25fr red, yellow & green ('59) 30 10
81 " 30fr multicolored 40 30
82 " 40fr blk. brn., grn. & yel. ('59) 50 40
83 " 65fr multicolored 80 40
Nos. 79-83 (5) 2.20 1.30

Moro Naba Sagha and Map
A34

1958, Nov. 1 Engraved *Perf. 13*

84 A34 20fr olive brown, carmine & violet 30 25

Issued to commemorate the 10th anniversary of the reestablishment of the Upper Volta territory.

Human Rights Issue

Common Design Type

1958, Dec. 10

85 CD105 20fr maroon & dk. bl. 65 65

Type of 1958 Redrawn.

1959, Mar. 21 Engraved *Perf. 13*

86 A31 20fr red, greenish bl. & slate grn. 75 60

Name of country omitted on No. 86; "RF" replaced by "CF," inscribed "Dakar-Abidjan."

Stamp Day.

SEMI-POSTAL STAMPS.

Red Cross Issue

Common Design Type

Photogravure.

1944 *Perf. 14½x14.* **Unwmkd.**

B1 CD90 5fr+20fr plum 1.25 1.25

The surtax was for the French Red Cross and national relief.

Type of France, 1945, Overprinted in Black **A O F**

1945 Engraved. *Perf. 13.*

B2 SP150 2fr+3fr orange red 12 12

Tropical Medicine Issue

Common Design Type

1950, May 15 *Perf. 13*

B3 CD100 10fr+2fr red brown & sepia 2.00 2.00

The surtax was for charitable work.

AIR POST STAMPS.

Common Design Type

Photogravure.

1945 *Perf. 14½x14* **Unwmkd.**

C1 CD87 5.50fr ultramarine 20 20
C2 " 50fr dark green 1.10 15
C3 " 100fr plum 1.10 15

Victory Issue

Common Design Type

1946, May 8 Engr. *Perf. 12½*

C4 CD92 8fr violet 25 25

Chad to Rhine Issue

Common Design Types

1946, June 6

C5 CD93 5fr brown carmine 45 45
C6 CD94 10fr deep blue 45 45
C7 CD95 15fr bright violet 60 60
C8 CD96 20fr dark slate green 60 60
C9 CD97 25fr olive brown 75 75
C10 CD98 50fr brown 1.10 1.10
Nos. C5-C10 (6) 3.95 3.95

Antoine de Saint-Exupéry, Map and Natives
AP1

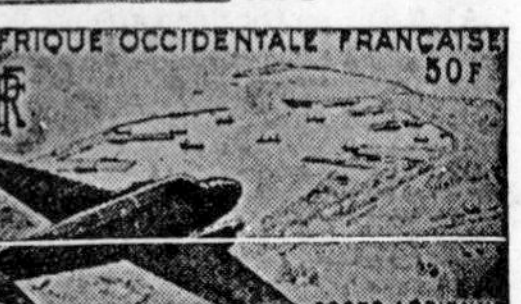

Plane over Dakar—AP2

Great White Egrets in Flight—AP3

Natives and Phantom Plane—AP4

1947, Mar. 24 Engraved

No.	Type	Description	Unused	Used
C11	AP1	8fr red brown	20	15
C12	AP2	50fr rose violet	90	20
C13	AP3	100fr ultramarine	3.50	1.25
C14	AP4	200fr slate gray	3.00	1.25

UPU Issue
Common Design Type

1949, July 4 *Perf. 13*

No.	Type	Description	Unused	Used
C15	CD99	25fr multicolored	3.00	3.00

Vridi Canal, Abidjan—AP5

1951, Nov. 5 *Perf. 13* Unwmkd.

No.	Type	Description	Unused	Used
C16	AP5	500fr red orange, blue green & deep ultramarine	8.00	1.25

Liberation Issue
Common Design Type

1954, June 6

No.	Type	Description	Unused	Used
C17	CD102	15fr indigo & ultramarine	1.50	1.50

Logging—AP6

Designs: 100fr, Radiotelephone exchange. 200fr, Baobab trees.

1954, Sept. 20

No.	Type	Description	Unused	Used
C18	AP6	50fr olive green & orange brown	75	10
C19	"	100fr indigo, dark brown & dark green	1.35	20
C20	"	200fr blue green, greenish black & brown lake	4.00	75

Gen. Louis Faidherbé and African Sharpshooter
AP7

1957, July 20 *Perf. 13* Unwmkd.

No.	Type	Description	Unused	Used
C21	AP7	15fr indigo & blue	60	60

Centenary of French African troops.

Gorée Island and Woman—AP8

Designs: 20fr, Map with planes and ships. 25fr, Village and modern city. 40fr, Seat of Council of French West Africa. 50fr, Worker, ship and peanut plant. 100fr, Bay of N'Gor.

1958, March 15 Engraved

No.	Type	Description	Unused	Used
C22	AP8	15fr black brown, green & violet	40	30
C23	"	20fr blk. brn., dk. bl. & red brown	40	30
C24	"	25fr black violet, bistre & green	40	30
C25	"	40fr dark blue, brown & green	40	30
C26	"	50fr vio., brn. & grn.	70	30
C27	"	100fr brn., bl.& grn.	1.25	30
		a. Souvenir sheet	3.75	4.00
		Nos. C22–C27 (6)	3.55	1.80

Issued to commemorate the centenary of Dakar.

No. C27a measures 185x125mm. and contains one each of Nos. C22–C27, with picture of old Dakar in center and inscribed: "Centenaire de Dakar."

Woman Playing Native Harp
AP9

1958, Dec. 1 *Perf. 13* Unwmkd.

No.	Type	Description	Unused	Used
C28	AP9	20fr red brown, black & gray	40	25

Issued in connection with the inauguration of Nouakchot as capital of Mauritania.

POSTAGE DUE STAMPS.

D1

Engraved.

1947 *Perf. 13* Unwmkd.

No.	Type	Description	Unused	Used
J1	D1	10c red	8	8
J2	"	30c deep orange	8	8
J3	"	50c greenish black	10	10
J4	"	1fr carmine	10	10
J5	"	2fr emerald	10	10
J6	"	3fr red lilac	15	15
J7	"	4fr deep ultramarine	20	20
J8	"	5fr red brown	40	40
J9	"	10fr peacock blue	70	70
J10	"	20fr sepia	90	90
		Nos. J1–J10 (10)	2.81	2.81

OFFICIAL STAMPS

Mask
O1

Typographed.

1958 *Perf. 14x13* Unwmkd.

Various Masks.

No.	Type	Description	Unused	Used
O1	O1	1fr dark brown red	20	20
O2	"	3fr bright green	20	20
O3	"	5fr crimson rose	15	6
O4	"	10fr light ultramarine	15	6
O5	"	20fr bright red	20	6
O6	"	25fr purple	30	6
O7	"	30fr green	40	30
O8	"	45fr gray black	50	30
O9	"	50fr dark red	70	15
O10	"	65fr bright ultra.	90	30
O11	"	100fr olive bistre	1.60	20
O12	"	200fr deep green	3.75	65
		Nos. O1–O12 (12)	9.05	2.54

FUNCHAL

(fōō·shäl')

LOCATION—A city and administrative district in the Madeira island group in the Atlantic Ocean northwest of Africa.

GOVT.—A part of the Republic of Portugal.

POP.—150,574 (1900).

Postage stamps of Funchal were superseded by those of Madeira. These, in turn, were displaced by the stamps of Portugal.

1000 Reis=1 Milreis

King Carlos

A1 A2

Perf. 11½, 12½, 13½

1892–93 Typographed Unwmkd.

No.	Type	Description	Unused	Used
1	A1	5r yellow	1.25	1.00
		a. Half used as 2½r on cover		25.00
		b. Perf. 11½	5.00	4.00
2	"	10r red violet	1.20	1.10
3	"	15r chocolate	2.50	1.50
4	"	20r lavender	3.00	1.50
		a. Perf. 13½	5.25	4.00
5	"	25r dark green	2.50	1.25
6	"	50r ultramarine	3.00	1.00
		a. Perf. 13½	6.00	1.50
7	"	75r carmine	6.00	5.00
8	"	80r yellow green	6.00	5.50
		a. Perf. 13½	12.50	10.00
9	"	100r brown, *yellow* ('93)	3.75	2.75
		a. Diagonal half used as 50r on cover		
10	"	150r carmine, *rose* ('93)	20.00	17.50
11	"	200r dark blue, *blue* ('93)	27.50	20.00
12	"	300r dark blue, *salmon* ('93)	30.00	20.00

The reprints of this issue have shiny white gum and clean-cut perforation 13½. The shades differ from those of the originals and the uncolored paper is thin. Price $1.50 each.

1897–1905 *Perf. 12*

Name and Value in Black except Nos. 25 and 34.

No.	Type	Description	Unused	Used
13	A2	2½r gray	20	20
14	"	5r orange	25	22
15	"	10r light green	25	22
16	"	15r brown	2.50	1.75
17	"	15r gray green ('99)	1.50	1.25
18	"	20r gray violet	60	40
19	"	25r sea green	1.25	33
20	"	25r carmine rose ('99)	35	25
		a. Booklet pane of 6		
21	"	50r dark blue	1.75	60
		a. Perf. 12½	8.25	2.00
22	"	50r ultramarine ('05)	45	35
23	"	65r slate blue ('98)	45	35
24	"	75r rose	60	45
25	A2	75r brown & red, *yellow* ('05)	1.00	1.50
26	"	80r violet	60	45
27	"	100r dark blue, *blue*	60	45
		a. Diagonal half used as 50r on cover		
28	"	115r orange brown, *pink* ('98)	75	75
29	"	130r gray brown, *buff* ('98)	75	60
30	"	150r light brown, *buff*	75	60
31	"	180r slate, *pinkish* ('98)	1.00	1.00
32	"	200r red violet, *pale lilac*	1.50	1.50
33	"	300r blue, *rose*	2.00	1.50
34	"	500r black & red, *blue*	1.50	1.10
		a. Perf. 12½	5.50	4.00
		Nos. 13–34 (22)	20.60	15.82

Addenda

For the Record

Index

Number Changes

Advertisements

ADDENDA

These stamps were received too late for inclusion in their proper places in the Catalogue. Later issues will be found listed in Scott's Chronicle of New Issues which appears in Scott's Monthly Stamp Journal. U.S. and Canada subscription price $8.50 for 1 year (12 issues); 2 years $15.50; 3 years $22. $10 per year additional for subscriptions outside U.S. and Canada (by air). Cash with order.

Address Scott's Monthly Stamp Journal, Subscription Dept., P.O. Box 925, Farmingdale, N. Y. 11737.

AFGHANISTAN

Nour Mohammad Taraki
A356

1978, Dec. Litho. ***Perf. 12***

955 A356 12af multicolored 35 30

Nour Mohammad Taraki, founder of People's Democratic Party of Afghanistan, installation as president.

Woman Breaking Chain
A357

1979, Mar. Litho. ***Perf. 11***

956 A357 14af red & ultra. *60*

Women's Day. Inscribed "POSSTES."

ALBANIA

Enver Hoxha
A389

1978, Oct. 16 Litho. ***Perf. 12x12½***

1874 A389 80q red & multi. 40 12
1875 " 1.20 l " " 60 25
1876 " 2.40 l " " 1.20 50

Miniature Sheet

Perf. 12½ on 2 sides x imperf.

1877 A389 2.20 l red & multi. 1.20

70th birthday of Enver Hoxha, First Secretary of Central Committee of the Communist Party of Albania. Size of No. 1877: 67x88½mm.

The first price column gives the catalogue value of an unused stamp, the second that of a used stamp.

Woman and Wheat
A390

Designs: 25q, Woman with egg crates. 80q, Shepherd and sheep. 2.60 l, Milkmaid and cows.

1978, Dec. 15 ***Perf. 12x12½***

1878 A390 15q multicolored 8 3
1879 " 25q " 12 5
1880 " 80q " 40 12
1881 " 2.60 l " 1.25 45

ALGERIA

Pres. Boumediène—A225

1979, Jan. 7 Photo. ***Perf. 12x11½***

624 A225 60c grn., red & brn. 30 15

Houari Boumediène, president of Algeria 1965–1978.

Torch and Books
A226

1979, Jan. 27 Photo. ***Perf. 11½***

625 A226 60c multicolored 30 15

National Front of Liberation Party Congress.

Pres. Boumediène—A227

1979, Feb. 4 Photo. ***Perf. 11½***

626 A227 1.40d multicolored 70 35

40 days after death of Pres. Houari Boumediène.

Proclamation of New President
A228

1979, Feb. 10

627 A228 2d multicolored 1.00 50

Election of Pres. Chadli Bendjedid.

AIR POST STAMP

Storks and Plane
AP7

1979, Mar. 24 Photo. ***Perf. 11½***

C19 AP7 10d multicolored 5.00 2.50

ANDORRA

Spanish Administration

Young Woman
A38

Designs: 5p, Young man. 12p, Bridegroom and bride riding mule.

1978, Feb. 14 Photo. ***Perf. 13***

108 A38 3p multicolored 10 6
109 " 5p " 15 10
110 " 12p " 36 24

French Administration

Pyrenean Chamois
A118

White Partridges
A119

1979, Mar. 26 Engr. ***Perf. 13***

267 A118 1fr multicolored 50 40

1979, Apr. 9 Photo. ***Perf. 13***

268 A119 1.20fr multicolored 60 48

Nature protection.

ARGENTINA

Buildings Type of 1978

Design: 40p, Historic City Hall, Salta (vert.). No. 1161B, Historic City Hall, Buenos Aires (horiz.). 800p, Ruins of Jesuit Mission.

1978, Dec. Photo. ***Perf. 13½***

1161A A540 40p gray blue & black 12 3
1161B " 50p citron & blk. 15 3

1979, Mar. 20

1173 A540 800p rose lilac & black 1.80

San Martin Type of 1978

1979 **Engraved** **Wmk. 365**

1198 A553 2000p greenish black 4.00

Numeral Type of 1978

1978–79

1208 A558 180p blue & ultra. 55
1209 " 200p blue & ultra. 40

Slope at Chacabuco, by Pedro Subercaseaux—A565

Painting: 1000p, The Embrace of Maipu (San Martin and O'Higgins), by Pedro Subercaseaux (vert.).

1978, Dec. 16 Litho. ***Perf. 13½***

1227 A565 500p multi. 1.00
1228 " 1000p " 2.00

José de San Martin, 200th birth anniversary.

Adolfo Alsina
A566

Design: No. 1230, Mariano Moreno.

1979, Jan. 20

1229 A566 200p lt. bl. & blk. 40
1230 " 200p yellow, red & black 40

Aldolfo Alsina (1829–1877), political leader, vice-president; Mariano Moreno (1778–1811), lawyer, educator, political leader.

Argentina No. 37 and UPU Emblem—A567

1979, Jan. 20

1231 A567 200p multicolored 40

Centenary of Argentina's UPU membership.

Still-life, by Cárcova
A568

Painting: 300p, The Laundresses, by Faustino Brughetti.

1979, Mar. 3

1232 A568 200p multicolored 40
1233 " 300p " 60

Ernesto de la Cárcova (1866–1927) and Faustino Brughetti (1877–1956), Argentine painters.

Balcarce Earth Station
A569

1979, Mar. 3

1234 A569 200p multicolored 40

Third Interamerican Telecommunications Conference, Buenos Aires, March 5–9.

AUSTRIA

Figure Skater
A515

1979, Mar. 7 Photo. ***Perf. 14x13½***

1113 A515 4s multicolored 58 40

World Ice Skating Championships, Vienna.

Steamer Franz I
A516

Designs: 2.50s, Tugboat Linz. 3s, Passenger ship Theodor Körner.

1979, Mar. 13 Engr. ***Perf. 13½***

1114 A516 1.50s violet blue 22 15
1115 " 2.50s sepia 38 25
1116 " 3s magenta 45 30

First Danube Steamship Company, 150th anniversary.

Fashion Design, by Theo Zasche, 1900
A517

Photogravure and Engraved

1979, Mar. 26 ***Perf. 13x13½***

1117 A517 2.50s multicolored 38 25

50th International Fashion Week, Vienna.

Wiener Neustadt Cathedral
A518

1979, Mar. 27 Engr. ***Perf. 13½***

1118 A518 4s violet blue 58 40

Cathedral of Wiener Neustadt, 700th anniversary.

Teacher and Pupils, by Franz A. Zauner
A519

Population Chart and Barock Angel
A520

Photogravure and Engraved

1979, Mar. 30 ***Perf. 14x13½***

1119 A519 2.50s multicolored 38 25

Education of the deaf in Austria, 200th anniversary.

1979, Apr. 6

1120 A520 2.50s multicolored 38 25

Austrian Central Statistical Bureau, 150th anniversary.

Laurenz Koschier
A521

Diesel Motor
A522

Europa Issue, 1979

1979, May 4

1121 A521 6s ocher & purple 90 60

1979, May 4 Photogravure

1122 A522 6s multicolored 90 60

13th CIMAC Congress (International Organization for Internal Combustion Machines).

Arms of Ried, Schärding and Braunau
A523

Photogravure and Engraved

1979, June 1 ***Perf. 13½x14***

1123 A523 3s multicolored 45 30

200th anniversary of Innviertel District.

Flood and City
A524

1979, June 1 ***Perf. 14x13½***

1124 A524 2.50s multicolored 38 25

Flood prevention.

BELGIUM

Tyll Eulenspiegel, Lay Action Emblem
A417

European Parliament Emblem
A418

1979, Mar. 3 Photo. ***Perf. 11½***

1024 A417 4.50fr multicolored 32 6

10th anniversary of Lay Action Centers.

1979, Mar. 3

1025 A418 8fr multicolored 56 12

European Parliament, first direct elections, June 7–10.

St. Michael Banishing Lucifer
A419

1979, Mar. 17 Photo. & Engr.

1026 A419 4.50fr rose red & black 32 6
1027 " 8fr bright green & black 56 12

Millennium of Brussels.

NATO Emblem and Monument
A420

1979, Mar. 31 Photogravure

1028 A420 30fr multicolored 2.10 50

North Atlantic Treaty Organization, 30th anniversary.

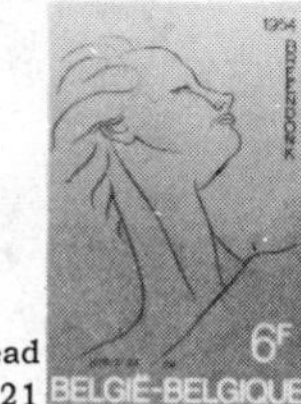

Prisoner's Head
A421

1979, Apr. 7 Photo. & Engr.

1029 A421 6fr orange & blk. 42 8

25th anniversary of the National Political Prisoners' Monument at Breendonk.

SEMI-POSTAL STAMPS

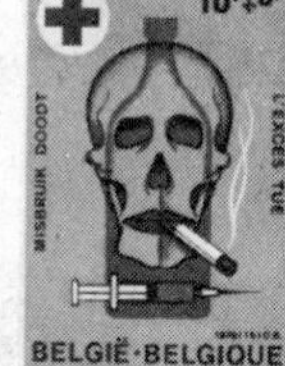

Young People Giving First Aid
SP446

Skull with Bottle, Cigarette, Syringe
SP447

1979, Feb. 10 Photo. ***Perf. 11½***

B976 SP446 8fr+3fr multi. 78 78
B977 SP447 16fr+8fr " 1.70 1.70

Belgian Red Cross.

BENIN

IYC Emblem
A116

Designs: 20fr, Globe as balloon carrying children. 50fr, Children of various races surrounding globe.

1979, Feb. 20 Litho. *Perf. 12x13*

420 A116 10fr multicolored 10 10
421 " 20fr " 20 20
422 " 50fr " 50 50

International Year of the Child.

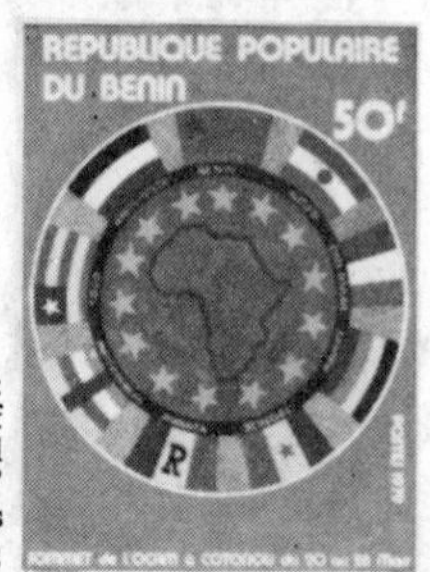

Emblem: Map of Africa and Members' Flags
A118

Designs: 60fr, Map of Benin and flags. 80fr, OCAM flag and map of Africa showing member states.

1979, Mar. 20 Litho. *Perf. 12x13*

427 A118 50fr multicolored 50 50
428 " 60fr " 60 60
429 " 80fr " 80 80

OCAM Summit Conference, Cotonou, Mar. 20–28.

BOLIVIA

Jesus and Children
A218

1979, Feb. 20 Litho. *Perf. 13½*

629 A218 8b multicolored 1.40 25

International Year of the Child.

Antofagasta Cancel **A219** — **Eduardo Abaroa, and Chain** **A220**

Designs: 1b, La Chimba cancel. 1.50b, Mejillones cancel. 5.50b, View of Antofagasta (horiz.). 6.50b, Woman in chains, symbolizing captive province. 8b, Map of Antofagasta Province, 1876. 10b, Arms of province.

1979, Mar. 23 Litho. *Perf. 10½*

630 A219 50c buff & black 10 3
631 " 1b pink & black 18 3
632 " 1.50b pale green & black 28 6

Perf. 13½

633 A220 5.50b multicolored 95 25
634 " 6.50b " 1.20 28
635 " 7b " 1.25 28
636 " 8b " 1.40 35
637 " 10b " 1.75 48
Nos. 630–637 (8) 7.11 1.76

Centenary of loss of Antofagasta coastal area to Chile.

Emblem and Map of Bolivia **A221** — **Gymnast** **A222**

1979, Mar. 26 *Perf. 13½x13*

638 A221 3b multicolored 55 12

Radio Club of Bolivia.

Perf. 13x13½, 13½x13

1979, Mar. 27

Design: 6.50b, Runner and Games emblem (horiz.).

639 A222 6.50b multicolored 1.20 28
640 " 10b " 1.75 48

Southern Cross Sports Games, Bolivia, Nov. 3–12, 1978.

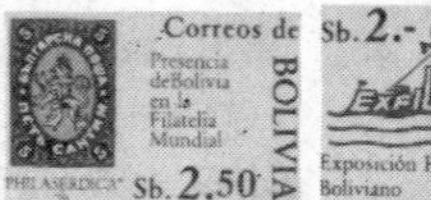

Bulgaria No. 1 **A223** — **EXFILMAR Emblem** **A224**

1979, Mar. 30 *Perf. 10½*

641 A223 2.50b multicolored 45 12

PHILASERDICA '79 International Philatelic Exhibition, Sofia, Bulgaria, May 18–27.

1979, Apr. 2

642 A224 2b multicolored 36 8

Bolivian Maritime Philatelic Exhibition, La Paz, Nov. 18–28.

BRAZIL

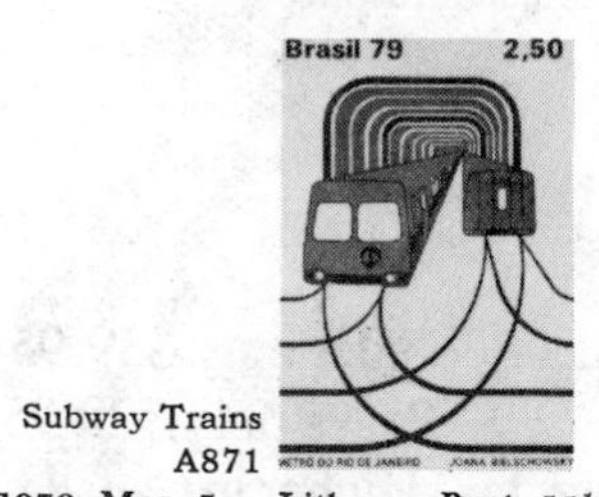

Subway Trains
A871

1979, Mar. 5 Litho. *Perf. 11½*

1601 A871 2.50cr multicolored 30 15

Inauguration of Rio de Janeiro's subway system.

Old and New Post Offices—A872

Designs: No. 1603, Old and new mail boxes. No. 1604, Manual and automatic mail sorting. No. 1605, Old and new planes. No. 1606, Telegraph and telex machine. No. 1607, Mailmen's uniforms.

1979, Mar. 20 Litho. *Perf. 11x11½*

1602 A872 2.50cr multicolored 30 15
1603 " 2.50cr " 30 15
1604 " 2.50cr " 30 15
1605 " 2.50cr " 30 15
1606 A872 2.50cr multicolored 30 15
1607 " 2.50cr " 30 15
Nos. 1602–1607 (6) 1.80 90

10th anniversary of the new Post and Telegraph Department, and 18th Universal Postal Union Congress, Rio de Janeiro, Sept.–Oct., 1979.

BURUNDI

Virgin and Child, by Rubens
A86

Paintings of the Virgin and Child by: 13fr, Rubens. 17fr, Solario. 27fr, Tiepolo. 31fr, Gerard David. 40fr, Bellini.

1979, Feb. Photo. *Perf. 14x13*

543 A86 13fr multicolored 40
544 " 17fr " 50
545 " 27fr " 80
546 " 31fr " 95
547 " 40fr " 1.20
Nos. 543–547 (5) 3.85

Christmas 1978. See No. C270.

AIR POST STAMPS

Type of 1979

1979, Feb. Photo. *Perf. 14x13½*

C270 Sheet of 5, multi. 4.00
a. A86 13fr *like* #543 40
b. " 17fr *like* #544 50
c. " 27fr *like* #545 80
d. " 31fr *like* #546 95
e. " 40fr *like* #547 1.20

Christmas 1978. No. C270 has green, gold and black margin. Size: 114x120mm.

CAMEROUN

Pres. Ahidjo, Giscard D'Estaing, Flags of Cameroun and France—A173

1979, Feb. 8 Photo. *Perf. 13*

651 A173 60fr multicolored 60 40

Visit of Pres. Valery Giscard D'Estaing of France to Cameroun.

Human Rights Emblem, Globe, Scroll and African—A174

1979, Feb. 11 Litho. *Perf. 12x12½*

652 A174 5fr multicolored 5 3

Universal Declaration of Human Rights, 30th anniversary (in 1978). See No. C278.

AIR POST STAMP

Human Rights Type of 1979

1979, Feb. 11 Litho. *Perf. 12x12½*

C278 A174 500fr multi. 5.00 4.00

Universal Declaration of Human Rights, 30th anniversary (in 1978).

CAPE VERDE

Freighter Cabo Verde—A38

1978, Oct. Litho. *Perf. 14*

391 A38 1e multicolored 20

First ship of Cape Verde merchant marine.

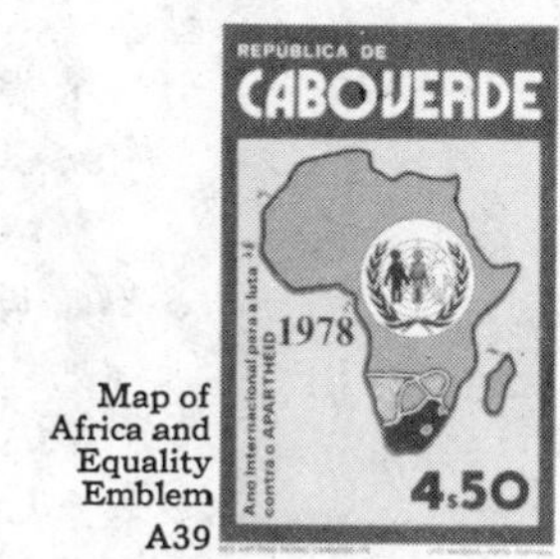

Map of Africa and Equality Emblem
A39

1978

392 A39 4.50e multicolored 90

Anti-Apartheid Year.

Human Rights Emblem
A40

1978, Dec. 10 Litho. *Perf. 14*

393 A40 1.50e multicolored 30
394 " 2e " 40

Universal Declaration of Human Rights, 30th anniversary.

CENTRAL AFRICA

Catherine Bokassa
A113

Design: 60fr, Emperor Bokassa.

1978, Dec. 4 Litho. *Perf. 13*

364	A113	40fr multicolored	40	20
365	"	60fr "	60	30

First anniversary of coronation. See No. C202.

Rowland Hill, Letter Scale and G.B. No. 1—A114

Designs (Rowland Hill and): 50fr, U.S. No. 1, mailman on bicycle. 60fr, Austria No. P4 and 19th century mailman. 80fr, Switzerland No. 2L1, postilion and mail-coach.

1978, Dec. 9 Litho. *Perf. 13½*

366	A114	40fr multicolored	40	20
367	"	50fr "	50	25
368	"	60fr "	60	30
369	"	80fr "	80	40
		Nos. 366–369, C203–C204	5.30	2.65

Sir Rowland Hill (1795–1879), originator of penny postage.

Nos. 303–307 Overprinted in Silver: "VAINQUEUR : ARGENTINE"

1978, Dec. 27

370	A97	50fr multicolored	50	25
371	"	60fr "	60	30
372	"	100fr "	1.00	50
373	"	200fr "	2.00	1.00
374	"	300fr "	3.00	1.50
		Nos. 370–374 (5)	7.10	3.55

Souvenir Sheet

No. 308 Overprinted in Silver: "ARGENTINE – PAYS BAS 3–1 / 25 juin 1978"

375	A97	500fr multicolored	5.00	2.50

Argentina's victory in World Cup Soccer Championship 1978.

Children Painting and Dutch Portrait—A115

Designs (UNICEF, Eagle Emblems and): 50fr, Eskimo children skiing, and ski jump. 60fr, Children with toy racing car, and Carl Benz with early car model. 80fr, Children launching rocket, and Intelsat.

1979, Mar. 6 Litho. *Perf. 13½*

376	A115	40fr multicolored	40	20
377	"	50fr "	50	25
378	"	60fr "	60	30
379	"	80fr "	80	40
		Nos. 376-379, C206–C207 (6)	5.30	2.65

International Year of the Child.

AIR POST STAMPS

Bokassa Type 1978

Design: 150fr, Catherine and Jean Bedel Bokassa (horiz.).

1978, Dec. 4 Litho. *Perf. 13*

C202	A113	150fr multi.	1.50	75

First anniversary of coronation. A 1000fr gold embossed souvenir sheet showing Emperor Bokassa exists.

Rowland Hill Type of 1978

Designs (Rowland Hill and): 100fr, Mailman and Tuscany No. 23. 200fr, Balloon and France No. 1. 500fr, Central Africa Nos. 1–2.

1978, Dec. 27

C203	A114	100fr multi.	1.00	50
C204	"	200fr "	2.00	1.00

Souvenir Sheet

C205	A114	500fr multi.	5.00	2.50

Sir Rowland Hill (1795–1879), originator of penny postage. No. C205 contains one stamp (37½x39mm.); multicolored margin shows Penny Black. Size: 83x85mm. 1500fr gold embossed stamp and souvenir sheet exist.

IYC Type of 1979

Designs (UNICEF, Eagle Emblems and): 100fr, Chinese girl flying kites and German Do-X flying boat, 1929. 200fr, Boys playing leapfrog, hurdler and Olympic emblem. 500fr, Child with abacus and Albert Einstein with his equation.

1979, Mar. 6 *Perf. 13½*

C206	A115	100fr multi.	1.00	50
C207	"	200fr "	2.00	1.00

Souvenir Sheet

C208	A115	500fr multi.	5.00	2.50

International Year of the Child. No. C208 contains one stamp (56x33mm.); multicolored margin shows various spacecraft. Size: 110x79mm. 1500fr gold embossed stamp and souvenir sheet exist.

CHAD

AIR POST STAMPS

Antoine de Saint-Exupéry—AP69

Designs: 50fr, Wilbur and Orville Wright and Flyer. 80fr, Hugo Junkers and his plane. 100fr, Gen. Italo Balbo and his plane. 120fr, Concorde. 500fr, Wilbur and Orville Wright and Flyer.

1978, Oct. 25 Litho. *Perf. 13½*

C232	AP69	40fr multicolored	40	20
C233	"	50fr "	50	25
C234	"	80fr "	80	40
C235	"	100fr "	1.00	50
C236	"	120fr "	1.20	60
		Nos. C232–C236 (5)	3.90	1.95

Souvenir Sheet

C237	AP69	500fr multi.	5.50	

History of aviation and 75th anniversary of 1st powered flight. No. C237 has multicolored margin showing Concorde in flight. Size: 104x99mm.

Philexafrique II—Essen Issue
Common Design Types

Designs: No. C238, Rhinoceros and Chad No. C6. No. C239, Kingfisher and Mecklenburg-Strelitz No. 1.

1978, Nov. 1 *Perf. 12½*

C238	CD138	100fr multi.	1.00	50
C239	CD139	100fr "	1.00	50

Nos. C238–C239 printed se-tenant.

CHILE

No. 477 Surcharged in Bright Green

1979 Litho. *Perf. 13x14*

533	A253	3.50p on 10c gray green	28	

Examination

The Catalogue editors cannot undertake to appraise, identify or pass upon genuineness or condition of stamps.

Flags of Chile and Salvation Army A284

1979, Mar. 17 Litho. *Perf. 14½*

534	A284	10p multicolored	80	

Salvation Army in Chile, 70th anniversary.

Pope Paul VI A285

1979, Mar. 30

535	A285	11p multicolored	88	

In memory of Pope Paul VI (1897–1978).

CHINA

Lu Hao-tung A438

Yellow Jade Brush Holder A439

Wmk. 323

1979, Mar. 29 Engr. *Perf. 13x12½*

2148	A438	$2 blue	10	8

Lu Hao-tung (1868–1895), revolutionist.

Unwmkd.

1979, Apr. 12 Photo. *Perf. 12*

Ancient Brush Washers: $5, White jade, Ming Dynasty. $8, Dark green jade, Ch'ing Dynasty. $10, Bluish jade, Ch'ing Dynasty. All horiz.

Granite Paper

2149	A439	$2 multicolored	10	8
2150	"	$5 "	25	20
2151	"	$8 "	40	32
2152	"	$10 "	50	40

People's Republic

Albert Einstein and his Equation A369

1979, Mar. 14 Photo. *Perf. 11½x11*

1468	A369	8f brown, gold & black	12	

Albert Einstein (1879–1955), theoretical physicist.

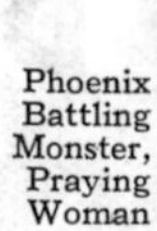

Phoenix Battling Monster, Praying Woman A370

Design: 60f, Man riding dragon to heaven. Designs from silk paintings found in Changsha tomb, Warring States Period (475–221 B.C.). Numbered T.33.

1979, Mar. 29 *Perf. 11*

1469	A370	8f multi. (2-1)	12	
1470	"	60f " (2-2)	90	

COLOMBIA

AIR POST STAMP

Bull Ring, Cathedral, Manizales AP176

1979, Jan. 6 Litho. *Perf. 14*

C669	AP176	7p multicolored	56	15

Manizales Fair.

CONGO REPUBLIC

Heart and Charts A142

1978, Dec. 16 Engr. *Perf. 13*

487	A142	100fr multicolored	1.00	70

Fight against hypertension.

Party Emblem and Road—A143

1978, Dec. 31 Litho. *Perf. 12½x12*

488	A143	60fr multicolored	60	40

Congolese Labor Party, 9th anniversary.

Capt. Cook, Polynesians and House—A144

Designs: 150fr, Island scene. 250fr, Polynesian longboats. 350fr, Capt. Cook's ships off Hawaii.

1979, Jan. ***Perf. 14½***

489	A144	65fr multicolored	65	42
490	"	150fr "	1.50	1.05
491	"	250fr "	2.50	1.75
492	"	350fr "	3.50	2.50

Capt. James Cook (1728–1779), 250th birth anniversary.

Pres. Marien Ngouabi
A145

1979, Mar. 18 **Litho.** ***Perf. 12***

493	A145	35fr multicolored	35	22
494	"	60fr "	60	40

2nd anniversary of assassination of President Ngouabi.

COSTA RICA

AIR POST STAMPS

Star over Map of Costa Rica
AP154

"Flying Men", Chorotega
AP155

1978, Nov. 13 ***Perf. 10½***

C729	AP154	50c bl. & black	12	10
C730	"	1col rose lilac & black	24	18
C731	"	5col org. & blk.	1.20	85

Christmas 1978. Nos. C729–C731 printed in sheets of 100 and se-tenant in sheets of 15 (3x5).

1978, Nov. 20 ***Perf. 11½***

Designs: 1.20col, Oviedo giving his History of Indies to Duke of Calabria (horiz.). 10col, Lord of Oviedo's coat of arms.

C732	AP155	85c multi.	20	15
C733	"	1.20col black & lt. blue	30	20
C734	"	10col multi.	2.40	1.75

500th birth anniversary of Gonzalo Fernandez de Oviedo, first chronicler of Spanish Indies.

Mgr. Domingo Rivas
AP156

San José Cathedral
AP157

1978, Dec. 6 ***Perf. 16***

C735	AP156	1col black & indigo	24	18

Perf. 13½

C736	AP157	20col multi.	4.80	3.50

Centenary of the Cathedral of San José.

CZECHOSLOVAKIA

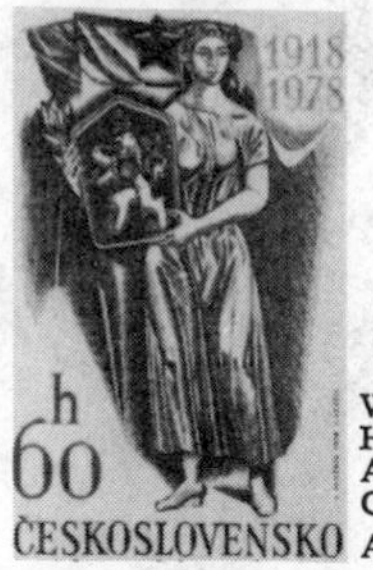

Woman Holding Arms of Czechoslovakia
A783

Photogravure and Engraved

1978, Oct. 28 ***Perf. 11½***

2208	A783	60h multicolored	25	10

60th anniversary of independence.

Art Type of 1974

Paintings: 2.40k, Flowers, by Jakub Bohdan (1660–1724). 3k, The Dream of Salas, by Ludovit Fulla (1902–) (horiz.). 3.60k, Apostle with Censer, Master of the Spissko Capitals (c. 1480–1490).

1978, Nov. 27 **Engraved**

2209	A700	2.40k multi.	1.05	25
2210	"	3k "	1.30	30
2211	"	3.60k "	1.60	30

Slovak National Gallery, 30th anniversary.

Musicians, by Jan Könyves
A784

Slovak Ceramics: 30h, Janosik on Horseback, by Jozef Franko. 40h, Woman in Folk Costume, by Michal Polasko. 1k, Three Girls Singing, by Ignac Bizmayer. 1.60k, Janosik Dancing, by Ferdis Kostka.

Photogravure and Engraved

1978, Dec. 5 ***Perf. 11½x12***

2212	A784	20h multicolored	8	3
2213	"	30h "	12	5
2214	"	40h "	16	6
2215	"	1k "	45	10
2216	"	1.60k "	70	18
		Nos. 2212–2216 (5)	1.51	42

Alfons Mucha and his Design for 1918 Issue—A785

1978, Dec. 18 ***Perf. 11½***

2217	A785	1k multicolored	45	10

60th Stamp Day.

DENMARK

Telephones
A193

1979, Jan. 25 **Engr.** ***Perf. 12½***

626	A193	1.20k dull red	48	16

Centenary of Danish telephone.

SEMI-POSTAL STAMP

Child and IYC Emblem
SP33

1979, Jan. 25 **Engr.** ***Perf. 12½***

B58	SP33	1.20k+20ö red & brown	55	55

International Year of the Child.

DJIBOUTI

Alsthom BB 1201 at Dock—A93

Locomotives: 55fr, Steam locomotive 231. 60fr, Steam locomotive 130 and map of route. 75fr, Diesel.

1979, Jan. 29 **Litho.** ***Perf. 13***

485	A93	40fr multicolored	60	40
486	"	55fr "	82	55
487	"	60fr "	90	60
488	"	75fr "	1.12	75

Djibouti-Addis Ababa railroad.

Children and IYC Emblem—A94

Design: 200fr, Mother and child, IYC emblem.

1979, Feb. 26 **Litho.** ***Perf. 13***

489	A94	20fr multicolored	30	20
490	"	200fr "	3.00	2.00

International Year of the Child.

Plane over Ardoukoba Volcano—A95

Design: 30fr, Helicopter over Ardoukoba Volcano (vert.).

1979, Mar. 19

491	A95	30fr multicolored	45	30
492	"	90fr "	1.35	60

DOMINICAN REPUBLIC

Starving Child, ICY Emblem
A269

1979, Feb. 26 **Litho.** ***Perf. 12***

807	A269	2c orange & black	6	3

International Year of the Child. See Nos. C287–C289.

AIR POST STAMPS

Pope John Paul II
AP88

1979, Jan. 25 **Litho.** ***Perf. 13½***

C285	AP88	10c multicolored	30	20

Visit of Pope John Paul II to the Dominican Republic, Jan. 25–26.

Map of Beata Island
AP89

1979, Jan. 25 ***Perf. 12***

C286	AP89	10c multicolored	30	20

First expedition of radio amateurs to Beata Island.

Year of the Child Type, 1979

Designs (ICY Emblem and): 7c, Children reading book. 10c, Symbolic head and protective hands. 33c, Hands and jars.

1979, Feb. 26

C287	A269	7c multicolored	20	14
C288	"	10c "	30	20
C289	"	33c "	1.00	65

International Year of the Child.

POSTAL TAX STAMP

University Seal
PT35

1979, Feb. 10 **Litho.** ***Perf. 13½***

RA85	PT35	2c ultra. & gray	10	3

450th anniversary of University of Santo Domingo.

ECUADOR

Symbols for Male and Female
A291

1979, Mar. Litho. ***Perf. 12x11½***

974	A291	3.40s multicolored	40	20

Inter-American Women's Commission, 50th anniversary.

AIR POST STAMPS

House and Monument
AP164

Design: 3.40s, Monument (vert.).

1979 Litho. ***Perf. 12***

C645	AP164	2.40s multi.	30	15
C646	"	3.40s "	40	18

Imperf.

C647	AP164	10s multi.	1.20

Sesquicentennial of Battle of Portete and Tarqui. No. C647 contains vignettes similar to Nos. C645–C646; inscriptions and black control number. Size: 115x90mm.

EGYPT

Book, Reader and Globe
A530

Wmk. 342

1979, Feb. 1 Photo. ***Perf. 11½x11***

1099	A530	20m yellow green & brown	10	10

Cairo 11th International Book Fair.

Wheat, Globe, Fair Emblem—A531

Perf. 11x11½

1979, Mar. 17 Photo. **Unwmkd.**

1100	A531	20m blue, orange & black	10	10

12th Cairo International Fair, March–Apr.

Skull, Poppy, Agency Emblem—A532

1979, Mar. 20 ***Perf. 11***

1101	A532	70m multicolored	35	35

Anti-Narcotics General Administration, 50th anniversary.

Isis Holding Horus
A533

1979, Mar. 21

1102	A533	140m multicolored	70	70

Mother's Day.

World Map and Book—A534

Perf. 11x11½

1979, Mar. 22 **Wmk. 342**

1103	A534	45m yellow, blue & brown	22	22

Cultural achievements of the Arabs.

ETHIOPIA

Cotton and Shemma Valley
A188

Shemma Industry: 10c, Women spinning cotton yarn. 20c, Man reeling cotton. 65c, Weaver. 80c, Cotton garments.

1979, Mar. 15 Litho. ***Perf. 15½***

916	A188	5c multicolored	5	5
917	"	10c "	10	10
918	"	20c "	20	20
919	"	65c "	65	65
920	"	80c "	80	80
		Nos. 916–920 (5)	1.80	1.80

FAROE ISLANDS

Ram
A15

Lithographed and Engraved

1979, Mar. 19 ***Perf. 12***

42	A15	25k multicolored	10.00

FINLAND

Runner
A300

1979, Feb. 7 Litho. ***Perf. 14***

615	A300	1.10m multicolored	60	28

8th Orienteering World Championships, Finland, Sept. 1–4.

FRANCE

Tourist Issue

Steenvorde Windmill
A828

Wall Painting, Niaux Cave
A829

Royal Palace, Perpignan
A830

1979 Engraved ***Perf. 13***

1640	A828	1.20fr multicolored	60	20
1641	A829	1.50fr "	75	25

Issue dates: 1.20fr, May 12; 1.50fr, July 9.

1979, Apr. 21

1642	A830	1.70fr multicolored	85	42

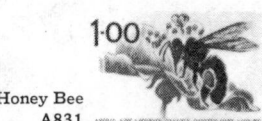

Honey Bee
A831

1979, Mar. 31 Engr. ***Perf. 13***

1643	A831	1fr multicolored	50	25

Nature protection.

St. Germain des Prés Abbey
A832

1979, Apr. 21

1644	A832	1.40fr multicolored	70	35

Europa Issue 1979

Simoun Mail Monoplanes, 1935, and Map of Mail Routes—A833

Design: 1.70fr, Floating spheres used on Seine during siege of Paris, 1870.

1979, Apr. 28

1645	A833	1.20fr multicolored	60	30
1646	"	1.70fr "	85	42

Ship and View of Nantes
A834

1979, May 5 Engr. ***Perf. 13***

1647	A834	1.20fr multicolored	60	20

52nd National Congress of French Philatelic Societies, Nantes, May 5–7.

Royal Palace, 1789
A835

1979, May 19

1648	A835	1fr violet & purple	50	18

European Elections
A836

1979, May 19 Photo. ***Perf. 13***

1649	A836	1.20fr multicolored	60	20

European Parliament, first direct elections, June 10.

Joan of Arc Monument
A837

1979, May 24 **Engraved**

1650	A837	1.70fr multicolored	85	30

Joan of Arc, the Maid of Orleans (1412–1431).

SEMI-POSTAL STAMP

Type of 1979

Design: No. B515, Leon Jouhaux (1879–1954), labor leader.

1979, May 12 Engr. ***Perf. 13***

B515	SP281	1.20fr+30c multi.	75	40

FOR THE RECORD

The items recorded here appeared on the stamp market in the 1960's and '70s, and have not been listed in the Scott Standard Catalogue. They are arranged chronologically and briefly described.

CONTENTS

AFGHANISTAN

Sets exist perf., imperf.

1963

GANEFO Games, Djakarta. *Sept. 3.* 2, 3, 4, 5, 10p, 9af; airmail, 300, 500p (8v). 2 souvenir sheets, 250, 300p.

Red Cross centenary. *Oct. 9.* 2, 3, 4, 5, 10p; airmail, 100, 200p, 4, 6af (9v). 2 souvenir sheets, 3, 4af.

Nubian Monuments Protection. *Nov. 16.* 100, 150, 200, 250, 500p; airmail, 5, 7.50, 10af (8v).

1964

Women's Day. *Jan. 5.* 2, 3, 4, 5, 10p (5v).

Afghan Boy and Girl Scouts. *Jan. 5.* 2, 3, 4, 5, 10p; airmail, 2af x 2, 2.50, 3, 4, 5, 12af (12v). 4 souvenir sheets, 5, 6x2, 10 af.

Children and Young People. *Jan. 22.* 2, 3, 4, 5, 10p; airmail, 200, 300p (7v).

Afghan Red Crescent Society. *Feb. 8.* 100, 200p, 2.50, 3.50af; airmail, 100p, 5, 7.50af (7v).

Teachers' Day. *Mar. 3.* 2, 3, 4, 5, 10p; airmail, 1.50, 2, 3, 3.50af (9v). 2 souvenir sheets, 4, 6af.

United Nations Day. *Mar. 9.* 2, 3, 4, 5, 10p; airmail, 100p, 2, 3af (8v). 2 souvenir sheets, 4, 5af, imperf.

Declaration of Human Rights, 15th anniversary. *Mar. 9.* Same values and sheets as United Nations Day set, each with 50p surcharge (8v).

UNICEF (United Nations Children's Fund). *Mar. 15.* 100, 150, 200, 250p; airmail, 5, 7.50, 10af (7v).

Fight Against Malaria. *Mar. 15.* 2, 3, 4, 5p; semi-postal, 4p+10p; airmail, 2, 5, 10af (8v). 2 souvenir sheets, 2af, perf.; 5af, imperf.

BHUTAN

1966

King Jigme Wangchuk, Coins, 40th anniversary of accession. *July 1.* Gold foil embossed. 10, 25, 50ch, 1, 1.30, 2, 3, 4, 5nu (9v).

Abominable Snowman (Yeti). *Oct. 12.* 1, 2, 3, 4, 5, 15, 30, 40, 50ch. *Nov. 15.* 1.25, 2.50, 3, 5, 6, 7nu (15v).

1967

Nos. 19–21, 38–39, 63–67 overprinted "Air Mail" in straight or curved lines. *Jan. 10.* (20v).

Flowers, *Feb. 9.* 3, 5, 7, 10, 50ch, 1, 2.50, 4, 5nu (9v).

Boy Scouts of Bhutan. *Mar. 28.* Perf., imperf. 5, 10, 15, 50ch, 1.25, 4nu (6v). Souvenir sheet of 2 (1.25, 4nu).

EXPO '67. *May 15.* Nos. 50–52 overprinted (3v). Souvenir sheet of 2 (1.50, 2.50nu) perf., imperf.

Churchill and Battle of Britain. *June 26.* Perf., imperf. 45ch, 2, 4nu (3v). Souvenir sheet of 2 (2, 4nu).

World Boy Scout Jamboree, Idaho. *Aug. 1.* Boy Scouts of Bhutan issue overprinted "World Jamboree/Idaho, U.S.A./Aug. 1–9/67." (6v and sheet).

Girl Scouts of Bhutan. *Sept. 18.* Perf., imperf. 5, 10, 15ch, 1.50, 2.50, 5nu (6v). Souvenir sheet of 2 (2.50, 5nu).

Astronauts. *Oct. 30.* Imperf., tridimensional. 3, 5, 7, 10, 15, 30, 50ch, 1.25nu; airmail, 2.50, 4, 5, 9nu (12v). 3 souvenir sheets of 4 (3, 5, 7, 10ch; 15, 30, 50ch, 1.25nu; 2.50, 4, 5, 9nu).

1968

Pheasants. *Jan. 20.* Perf., imperf. 1, 2, 4, 8, 15ch, 2, 4nu; *Apr. 23.* 5, 7, 9nu (10v).

10th Winter Olympics, Grenoble. Abominable Snowman issue of 1966 overprinted (2 types). *Feb. 16.* Perf., imperf. 40ch, 1.25, 3, 6nu (4v).

Mythological Creatures. *Mar. 14.* 2, 3, 4, 5, 15, 20, 30, 50ch, 1.25, 2nu; airmail, 1.50, 2.50, 4, 5, 10nu (15v).

Butterflies, *May 20.* Imperf., tridimensional. 15, 50ch, 1.25, 2nu; airmail, 3, 4, 5, 6nu (8v). 2 souvenir sheets of 4 (15, 50ch, 1.25, 2nu; 3, 4, 5, 6nu).

Paintings (relief printed). *July 8.* Imperf. 2, 4, 5, 10, 45, 80ch, 1.05, 1.40, 2, 3, 4, 5nu; *Aug. 28:* airmail, 1.50, 2.50, 6, 8nu (16v). (van Gogh, Millet, Monet, Corot). 4 souvenir sheets of 4 (2, 4, 5, 10ch; 45, 80ch, 1.05, 1.40nu; 2, 3, 4, 5nu; 1.50, 2.50, 6, 8nu).

19th Summer Olympics, Mexico City. *Oct. 1.* Perf., imperf. 5, 45, 60, 80ch, 1.05, 2, 3, 5nu (8v). Souvenir sheet of 2 (1.05, 5nu).

International Human Rights Year. *Nov. 12.* (Black and gold overprint on unissued gold foil coin set, 3 sizes) 15, 35ch, 9nu (3v).

Flood Relief. *Dec. 7.* Summer Olympics issue surcharged 5ch+5ch, 80ch+25ch, 2nu+50ch (3v).

Birds of Bhutan. *Dec. 7.* 2, 3, 4, 5, 15ch; *Dec. 28:* 20, 30, 50ch 1.25, 2nu; *Jan. 29, 1969:* Airmail, 1.50, 2.50, 4, 5, 10nu (15v).

1969

Fish. *Feb. 27.* Imperf., tridimensional. 15, 20, 30ch; airmail, 5, 6, 7nu (6v). Souvenir sheet of 4 (30ch, 5, 6, 7nu).

Insects. *Apr. 10.* Imperf., tridimensional. 10, 75ch, 1.25, 2nu; airmail, 3, 4, 5, 6nu (8v). 2 Souvenir sheets of 4 (10, 75ch, 1.25, 2nu; 3, 4, 5, 6nu).

Universal Postal Union, admission of Bhutan. *May 2.* Perf., imperf. 5, 10, 15, 45, 60ch, 1.05, 1.40, 4nu (8v).

History of Steel Making (printed on steel foil). Imperf. *June 2:* 2, 5, 15, 45, 75ch. 1.50, 1.75, 2nu; airmail, 3, 4, 5, 6nu (12v). *June 30.* 6 souvenir sheets of 2 (2, 45ch; 5, 15ch; 75ch, 2nu; 1.50, 1.7nu; 3, 6nu; 4, 5nu).

Birds, *Aug. 5.* Imperf., tridimensional. 15, 50ch, 1.25, 2nu; airmail, 3, 4, 5, 6nu (8v). *Aug. 28;* 2 souvenir sheets of 4 (15, 50ch, 1.25, 2nu; 3, 4, 5, 6nu).

Buddhist Prayer Banners (printed on silk). *Sept. 30.* Imperf. 15, 75ch, 2, 5, 6nu (5v). Souvenir sheet of 3 (75ch, 5, 6nu) perf., imperf.

Apollo 11 Moon Landing. *Nov. 3.* Imperf., tridimensional. 3, 5, 15, 20, 25, 45, 50ch, 1.75nu; airmail, 3, 4, 5, 6nu (12v). *Nov. 20.* 3 souvenir sheets of 4 (3, 5, 15, 20ch; 25, 45, 50ch, 1.75nu; 3, 4, 5, 6nu).

1970

Paintings, *Jan. 19.* Imperf., tridimensional. 5, 10,

15ch, 2.75nu; airmail, 3, 4, 5, 6nu (8v). (Clouet, van Eyck, David, Homer, Rubens, Gentileschi, Ghirlandaio, Raphael). 2 souvenir sheets of 4 (5, 10, 15ch, 2.75nu; 3, 4, 5, 6nu).

Flowers, paintings (relief printed). *May 6,* Imperf. 2, 3, 5, 10, 15, 75ch, 1, 1.40nu; *May 28.* Airmail, 80, 90ch, 1.10, 1.40, 1.60, 1.70, 3, 3.50nu (16v). (van Gogh, Redon, Kiyoteru Kuroda, Renoir, Monet, La Tour, Oudot). 4 souvenir sheets of 4 (2, 3, 5, 10ch; 15, 75ch, 1, 1.40nu; 80, 90ch, 1.10, 1.40nu; 1.60, 1.70, 3, 3.50nu).

Preceding Issues Surcharged, *June.*
Mythological Creatures issue of 1968. 5ch x 6; 20ch x 3.
No. 14 (Freedom from Hunger). 20ch.
Nos. 63–67 (Animals). 20ch x 5.
Abominable Snowman issue of 1966. 20ch x 6.
Flower issue of 1967. 20ch x 2.
Boy Scout issue of 1967. 20ch x 2.
Churchill. Battle of Britain issue of 1967. 20ch x 2.
Pheasant issue of 1968. 20ch x 3.
Birds issue of 1968. 20ch x 9.
UPU issue of 1969. 20ch x 3.

Animals, Imperf., tridimensional. *Sept. 17:* 5, 10, 20, 25, 30, 40, 65, 75, 85ch; *Oct. 15:* airmail. 2, 3, 4, 5nu (13v).

Space Conquest. Imperf., tridimensional. *Nov. 9:* 2, 5, 15, 25, 30, 50, 75ch, 1.50nu; *Nov. 30:* airmail, 2, 3, 6, 7nu (12v). 3 souvenir sheets of 4 (2, 5, 15, 25ch; 30, 50, 75ch, 1.50nu; 2, 3, 6, 7nu).

1971

History of Sculpture (plastic bas-relief sculptures from antiquity to Modigliani). *Mar.* Imperf. 10, 75ch, 1.25, 2nu; airmail, 3, 4, 5, 6nu (8v). 2 souvenir sheets of 4 (10, 75ch, 1.25, 2nu; 3, 4, 5, 6nu).

Apollo 15 and Lunokhod 1. *Mar. 20.* Imperf., tridimensional. 10ch, 1.70nu; airmail, 2.50, 4nu (4v). Souvenir sheet of 4 (10ch, 1.70, 2.50, 4nu).

Antique Cars. Imperf. *May 20:* 2, 5, 10, 15, 20, 30, 60ch; *June 10:* 75, 85ch, 1, 1.20, 1.55, 1.80, 2, 2.50nu; *July 5:* 4, 6, 7, 9, 10nu (20v).

Preceding Issues Surcharged. *July 1.*
Nos. 22–23, 55ch on 1.30nu, 90ch on 2nu.
Nos. 65–66, 55ch on 3nu, 90ch on 4nu.
Boy Scout issue of 1967, 90ch on 4nu.
Pheasant issue of 1968, 55ch on 5nu, 90ch on 9nu.
Mythology issue of 1968, 55ch on 4nu.
Olympic issue of 1968, 90ch on 1.05nu.
Birds issue of 1968, 90ch on 2nu.
UPU issue of 1969, 55ch on 60ch.
UPU issue of 1970, 90ch on 2.50nu.
Space issue of 1971 (Apollo 15), 90ch on 1.70nu.

1972

Paintings (relief printed). Imperf. *Jan. 29:* 15, 20, 90ch, 2.50nu; *Feb. 28:* airmail, 1.70, 4.60, 5.40, 6nu (8v). (Renoir, Manet, da Vinci, Millet, Rousseau, Gauguin, Degas, Guillaumin) 2 souvenir sheets of 4 (15, 20, 90ch, 2.50nu; 1.70, 4.60, 5.40, 6nu).

Famous Men (plastic bas-reliefs). *Apr. 22.* Imperf. 10, 15, 55ch; airmail; 2, 6, 8nu (6v). (Gandhi, J.F. Kennedy, Churchill, de Gaulle, Pope John XXIII, Eisenhower). Souvenir sheet of 4 (55ch, 2, 6, 8nu).

International Book Year. *May 15.* 2, 3, 5, 20ch (4v).

20th Summer Olympics, Munich. *June 6.* 10, 15, 20, 30, 45ch; airmail, 35ch. 1.35, 7nu (8v). Souvenir sheet of 3 (35ch, 1.35, 7nu) perf., imperf.

Apollo 16 (rockets and astronauts). *Sept. 1.* Imperf., tridimensional. 15, 20, 90ch, 2.50nu; airmail, 1.70, 4.60, 5.40, 6nu (8v). 2 souvenir sheets of (15, 20, 90ch, 2.50nu; 1.70, 4.60, 5.40, 6nu).

Dogs. *Oct. 5.* Perf., imperf. 5, 10, 15, 25, 55ch, 8nu, souvenir sheet of 2 (55ch, 8nu); *Jan. 1, 1973.* 2, 3, 15, 20, 30, 99ch, 2.50, 4nu, souvenir sheet of 3 (99ch, 2.50, 4nu); *Jan. 15.* Airmail souvenir sheet, 18nu. (14v).

1973

Roses (scented paper). *Jan. 30.* 15, 25, 30ch, 3nu; airmail, 6, 7nu (6v). Souvenir sheet of 2 (6, 7nu) perf., imperf.

Apollo 17 (astronauts on moon). *Feb. 23.* Imperf., tridimensional. 10, 15, 55ch, 2nu; airmail, 7, 9nu (6v). Souvenir sheet of 4 (10, 15, 55ch, 2nu); circular souvenir sheet of 2 (7, 9nu).

Folk Songs, on Record. *Apr. 15.* 10, 25ch, 1.25, 7, 8nu; airmail, 3, 9nu (7v).

King Jigme Dorji Wangchuk, memorial. *May 2.* Gold foil, 10, 25ch, 3nu; airmail, 6, 8nu (5v). Souvenir sheet of 2 (6, 8nu).

Mushrooms, *Sept. 25.* Imperf., tridimensional. 15, 25, 30ch, 3nu; airmail. 6, 7nu (6v). Souvenir sheet of 4 (15, 25, 30ch, 3nu) and of 2 (6, 7nu).

INDIPEX Philatelic Exhibition (Bhutanese mail service scenes). *Nov. 14.* 5, 10, 15, 25ch. 1.25, 3nu, airmail, 5, 6nu (8v). Souvenir sheet of 2 (5, 6nu).

1974

Reading and Writing, paintings. *Feb. 15.* 1, 2, 3, 5, 10, 15, 25, 50, 60, 80ch, 1, 1.25nu (12v). (Fragonard, Carpaccio, Liotard, Holbein, Terborch).

CAMBODIA (Khmer)

1972

20th Summer Olympics, Munich. *Nov. 2.* Gold foil, airmail, 900r x 4 (4v). 2 souvenir sheets of 2, 900r x 2.

Apollo 16. *Nov. 2.* Gold foil, airmail 900r x 2. (2v). Souvenir sheet of 2 (900r x 2) perf., imperf.

1973

World Cup Soccer Championships. Gold foil, airmail, 900r x 4 (4v).

1974

John F. Kennedy and Apollo 11 Astronauts on Moon. Gold foil, airmail, 1100r x 2 (2v). Souvenir sheet of 2 (1100r x 2).

Copernicus, 500th birth anniversary. Gold foil, airmail, 1200r. Souvenir sheet, 1200r.

UPU Centenary. Gold foil, airmail, 1200r x 2 (2v). Souvenir sheet, 1200r.

1975

World Cup Soccer Championships. *Feb.* 1, 5, 10, 25r; airmail, 50, 100, 150, 200, 250r (9v). 9 imperf. souvenir sheets; same with simulated perforations; 2 sheets, 200, 250r, perf. Gold foil, airmail, 1200r, same, souvenir sheet.

21st Summer Olympics, Montreal, 1976 (ancient and modern sports). 1, 5, 10, 25r; airmail, 50, 100, 150, 200, 250r (9v). 9 imperf. souvenir sheets; same with simulated perforations. 2 souvenir sheets, 200, 250r, perf. Gold foil, airmail, 1200r.

UPU Centenary. *April 12.* (Second issue) 15, 20, 70, 160, 180, 235r, airmail 500, 1000, 2000r (9v). 9 imperf. souvenir sheets; same with simulated perforations. 2 souvenir sheets, 1000, 2000r. Gold foil embossed, airmail, perf., imperf. 1000r x 2 (train & plane). Same, souvenir sheet, 1200r (Chinese junks).

CAMEROUN

1977

Winter Olympics, 1976, Innsbruck. *Aug. 10.* 40, 50fr; airmail, 140, 200, 350fr (5v). Airmail souvenir sheet, 500fr.

Apollo-Soyuz Project. *Aug. 10.* 40, 60fr; airmail, 100, 250, 350fr (5v). Airmail souvenir sheet, 500fr.

CHAD

1970

Apollo Program. *May.* 40fr; airmail, 15, 25fr (3v). Souvenir sheet, 50fr.

Napoleon. *June 12.* Perf., imperf. airmail, 10, 25, 32fr, se-tenant in sheets of 6 (3v). Souvenir sheet, 40fr. Gold foil, 10fr and souvenir sheet.

World Cup Soccer Championships, Mexico. *July 2.* Perf., imperf. 1, 4, 5fr x 2 (4v). Souvenir sheet; 15fr.

EXPO '70, Osaka, Japan (Japanese prints). *July.* Perf., imperf. 50c, 1, 2fr, se-tenant in sheets of 6 (3v).

19th Summer Olympics and 1970 Soccer Cup, Mexico. *July 1.* Airmail 5fr. Souvenir sheet, 15fr. Gold foil, 5 fr. Souvenir sheet, 5fr.

Christmas, paintings. *Aug. 19.* Perf., imperf. 3, 25fr; airmail, 32fr (3v). (Virgin and Child by Solario, Dürer, Fouquet).

Paintings, flowers and woman (Iba N'Diaye). *Aug. 28.*Airmail, 250 fr × 2.

20th Summer Olympics, Munich, 1972. *Sept.* 3, 8, 20fr; airmail, 10, 35fr (5v). Souvenir sheet, 40fr.

Apollo 11 and 12. *Sept.* Imperf. airmail gold foil, 25fr and souvenir sheet.

20th Summer Olympics, Munich, *Oct. 14.* Imperf. gold foil, 10fr and airmail souvenir sheet.

Napoleon II. *July 23.* 10fr, se-tenant with label. Souvenir sheet, 40fr. Embossed gold foil, 10fr perf., imperf. Same, 2 souvenir sheets. 10fr, perf., imperf.

French Royalty. *1970–71.* Perf., imperf. About 70 stamps and souvenir sheets showing paintings against gold background. Various denominations, both postage and airmail, printed se-tenant.

1971

11th Winter Olympics, Sapporo, 1972 (Kiyonaga paintings). *Feb. 16.* Perf., imperf. 50c, 1, 2fr (3v).

Flowers, paintings. *Apr. 28.* Perf., imperf. 1, 4, 5fr, printed se-tenant (3v). (Rubens, Van Os, Brueghel).

Space Exploration and John F. Kennedy. *Feb. 16.* Perf., imperf. 8, 10fr; airmail, 35fr (3v). Souvenir sheet, 40fr.

Olympic Games (sport and culture). *Apr. 28.* Perf., imperf. 15, 20fr; airmail, 25fr (3v). Airmail souvenir sheet, 50fr.

Peace and Sciences. *July 5.* Embossed gold foil. Perf. and imperf., 10fr and souvenir sheet, 10fr.

Christmas. *July 17.* Nos. 205–210 overprinted "Noel/ 1971" in gold (6v).

20th Summer Olympics, Munich. Soccer Cup issue of 1970 overprinted in gold. Airmail souvenir sheets: 15fr; 5fr × 2 and 2 labels.

11th Winter Olympics, Sapporo. *July 17.* EXPO '70 and Winter Olympic issues of 1971 overprinted in gold (6v).

1972–73

Soccer World Champions, Great Britain, 1966. Gold foil, 5fr and souvenir sheet, 5fr.

Summer Olympics, Munich. *June 24.* Nos. 181–204 overprinted (24v).

Wild Animals. *Nov.* Airmail, 20, 30, 100, 130, 150fr (5v). Souvenir sheet, 200fr.

20th Summer Olympics, Munich.

Olympic Flame and Athletes: *1973.* 20, 30, 50fr; airmail, 100, 130, 150fr (6v). Souvenir sheet, 200 fr.

Athletes and Abstract White Drawings of Athletes in Background: *1973.* 25, 40, 50, 75fr; airmail, 100, 150fr (6v). Souvenir sheet, 250fr.

Music, paintings. *Apr.* 30, 70, 100fr; airmail, 125, 150fr (5v). (Costa, Oudry, Saraceni, Metsu). Souvenir sheet, 300fr.

Easter. *Apr.* 60, 120fr; airmail, 40, 150, 250fr (5v). Souvenir sheet, 400fr.

Modern Trains. 10, 40, 50, 150, 200fr (5v). Souvenir sheet, 300fr.

Domestic Animals (sheep, dromedaries, cats, dogs, horses). 20, 30fr; airmail, 100, 130, 150fr (5v).

Horses, paintings. 20, 60, 100, 150fr (4v). (Gericault, Potter, Stubbs, Vernet). Souvenir sheet, 500fr.

Aircraft, Airmail, 5, 25, 70, 150, 200fr (5v). Souvenir sheet, 350fr.

Christmas, paintings. 30, 40, 55fr; airmail, 60, 250fr (5v). (Lotto, Tintoretto, Schongauer, Barocci, Lochner, Memling). Souvenir sheet, 400fr.

COMORO ISLANDS

Most sets exist perf., imperf.

1975

Apollo-Soyuz Space Issue. 10, 30, 50fr; airmail 100, 200, 400fr (6v). Souvenir sheet, 500fr. Embossed gold foil, airmail, 1500fr, same souvenir sheet, 1500fr.

1976

American Bicentennial. *Jan. 15.* 15, 25, 35, 40, 75fr; airmail 500fr (6v). Airmail souvenir sheet, 400fr. Embossed on gold foil, airmail, 1000fr, same, souvenir sheet, 1500fr.

12th Winter Olympics, Innsbruck. *Mar 30.* 5, 30, 35, 50fr; airmail, 200, 400fr (6v). Airmail souvenir sheet, 500fr. Embossed on gold foil, airmail, 1000fr, same airmail souvenir sheet, 1000fr.

21st Summer Olympics, Montreal. *Mar. 30.* 20, 25, 40, 75fr; airmail, 100, 500fr (6v). Airmail souvenir sheet, 400fr.

Telephone Centenary, *July 1.* 10, 25, 75fr; airmail, 100, 200, 500fr (6v). 2 airmail souvenir sheets, 400, 500fr.

American Bicentennial, Project Viking III. *Nov. 23.* 5, 10, 25, 35, 100fr; airmail, 500fr (6v). **Project Viking IV.** Embossed on gold foil, airmail, 1500fr (Pioneer and rocket). Same, airmail souvenir sheet, 1500fr (Mars landing vehicle).

United Nations Postal Administration, 25th anniversary. *Nov. 25.* 15, 30, 50, 75fr; airmail, 200, 400fr (6v). Airmail souvenir sheet, 500fr.

American Bicentennial, Civil War Battles. *Dec. 30.* 10, 30, 50fr; airmail, 100, 200, 400fr (6v). Airmail souvenir sheet, 500fr. Embossed on gold foil, airmail, 1500fr (Kennedy, moon landing). Same, airmail souvenir sheet, 1000fr (Abraham Lincoln).

Endangered Species. *Dec. 30.* 15, 20, 35, 40, 75fr; airmail, 400fr (6v). Airmail souvenir sheet, 500fr.

1977

Endangered Species. *Apr. 14.* 10, 30, 40, 50fr; airmail, 200, 400fr (6v). Airmail souvenir sheet, 500fr.

Airships and Railroads. *Apr. 14.* 20, 25, 50, 75fr; airmail, 200, 500fr (6v). Airmail souvenir sheet, 500fr.

Nobel Prize, 75th anniversary. *July 7.* 30, 40, 50, 100fr; airmail, 200, 400fr (6v). Airmail souvenir sheet, 500fr.

Peter Paul Rubens, 400th birth anniversary. *July 7.* 20, 25, 50, 75fr; airmail, 200, 500fr (6v). Airmail souvenir sheet, 500fr (self-portrait).

Silver Jubilee QEII. *July 7.* Embossed on gold foil, airmail, 500fr. Same, 2 airmail souvenir sheets, 500, 1000fr.

Fish, various local species. 30, 40, 50, 100fr; airmail, 200, 400fr (6v). Airmail souvenir sheet, 500fr.

Space Ships and Vehicles. 30, 50, 75, 100fr; airmail. 200, 400fr (6v). Airmail souvenir sheet, 500fr.

Concorde, "Paris-New-York-22 nov, 1977" overprinted in gold on UNPA 25th anniversary, 200fr airmail.

Fairy Tales. 15, 30, 35, 40, 50fr; airmail, 400fr (6v) (Hansel & Gretel, Alice in Wonderland, Pinocchio, Good Little Henri, Peter and the Wolf, 1001 Nights).

1978

Birds. *Feb. 6.* 15, 20, 35, 40, 75fr; airmail, 400fr (6v). Airmail souvenir sheet, 500fr.

World Cup Soccer, Argentina '78. *Feb. 6.* 30, 50, 75, 100fr; airmail, 200, 400fr (6v). Airmail souvenir sheet, 500fr. Embossed on gold foil, airmail, 1000fr. Same, airmail souvenir sheet, 1000fr.

Famous Composers. *Apr. 5.* 30, 40, 50, 100fr; airmail, 200, 400fr (6v). Airmail souvenir sheet, 500fr.

Albrecht Dürer, 450th death anniversary. *Apr. 5.* 20, 25, 50, 75fr; airmail, 200, 500fr (6v). Airmail souvenir sheet, 500fr.
Aug. 20, 30, 40fr; airmail, 100, 200, 400fr (6v). 3 airmail souvenir sheets, 500, 1000, 1500fr.

QE II Coronation, 25th anniversary. *May 25.* 10, 25, 40, 100fr; airmail, 200, 500fr (6v). Airmail souvenir sheet, 500fr. Embossed on gold foil, airmail, 500, 1000fr. Same, 2 souvenir sheets, 1000fr.

Butterflies. *May 8.* 15, 20, 30, 50, 75fr; airmail, 400fr (6v). Airmail souvenir sheet, 500fr.

World Telecommunications, 10th anniversary. *June.* 30, 50, 75, 100fr; airmail, 200, 400fr (6v).

History of Aviation. *June.* 30, 50, 75, 100fr; airmail, 200, 400fr (6v). Airmail souvenir sheet, 500fr.

Peter Paul Rubens, 400th anniversary. *June.* 10, 25, 35, 50, 75fr; airmail, 500fr (6v). 3 airmail souvenir sheets, 400, 1000, 1500fr.

Rowland Hill. *Aug.* 20, 30, 40, 75fr; airmail, 200, 400fr (6v). Airmail souvenir sheet, 500fr.

World Cup Soccer. *Sept.* Overprinted "Rep. Fed. Islamique / des Comores / 1 Argentine / 2 Hollande / 3 Bresil." 30, 50, 75, 100fr; airmail 200, 400fr (6v). Airmail souvenir sheet, 500fr.

Europe-Africa. *Sept.* 10, 25, 35, 50fr; airmail, 100, 500fr (6v). Airmail souvenir sheet, 500fr.

CONGO PEOPLE'S REPUBLIC

1970

Paintings. *Feb.* 3, 40fr; airmail, 25fr (3v). (Fragonard, Boucher).

Olympic Games. *Feb.* 2, 5, 15, 50fr (4v). Airmail souvenir sheet, 100fr.

Kennedys, King and Space. *Feb.* 1, 10, 20, 30fr (4v).

1971

13th World Boy Scout Jamboree, Japan. *July 14.* Gold foil, airmail, 1000fr and silver foil souvenir sheet of 4 (90fr × 4).

1977

History of Aviation, famous fliers. 60, 75, 100, 200, 300fr (5v). Souvenir sheet, 500fr.

Peter Paul Rubens, 400th birth anniversary. **Mao Tse-tung,** 1st anniversary of death. *Sept.* Embossed gold foil, 400, 600fr (2v).

Famous Persons. *Dec.* 200, 200, 250, 300fr (4v) (Baudouin, de Gaulle, QEII Silver Jubilee (2)). Airmail souvenir sheet, 500fr (QEII and Royal Family).

DAHOMEY

1974

World Cup Soccer Championships, Munich. *July 16.* Airmail, 35, 40, 100, 200, 300fr (5v). Souvenir sheet, 500fr. Embossed gold foil. 1000fr, same souvenir sheet.

UPU centenary. *Aug. 5.* Airmail, 50, 100, 125, 150, 200fr (5v). Souvenir sheet, 500fr. 6 souvenir sheets with simulated perforations. Airmail gold foil 1000fr, same souvenir sheet.

Conquest of Solar System's Planets. *Oct. 31.* Perf., imperf. Airmail 50, 100, 150, 200fr (4v). 4 souvenir sheets with simulated perforations. Souvenir sheet, 500fr.

World Soccer Champions, Germany. *Nov.* Perf., imperf. Airmail 100, 125, 150, 300fr (4v). 4 souvenir sheets with simulated perforations. Souvenir sheet, 500fr. Embossed gold foil, perf., imperf., 1000fr and 4 souvenir sheets.

ECUADOR

1966

International Telecommunication Union, centenary. *Jan. 27.* Perf., imperf. 10c × 2, 80c; airmail, 1.50, 3, 4s (6v). 2 souvenir sheets of 3 (10, 80c, 3s; 10c, 1.50, 4s).

Space Exploration. *Jan. 27.* 10c, 1s; airmail, 1.30, 2, 2.50, 3.50s (6v). Souvenir sheet of 3 (10c, 1.30, 3.50s) perf., imperf.

Dante and Galileo. 10, 80c; airmail, 2, 3s (4v). Souvenir sheet of 3 (10, 80c, 3s) perf., imperf.

Pope Paul VI. 10c; airmail, 1.30, 3.50s (3v). Souvenir sheet of 3 (10c, 1.30, 3.50s) perf., imperf.

Famous Men. *June 24.* 10c, 1s; airmail, 1.50, 2.50, 4s (5v). (Hammarskjold, Churchill, Schweitzer, J. F. Kennedy). Souvenir sheet of 3 (10c, 1.50, 4s).

Olympic Games. (Greek athletes, classic period). *June 27.* 10c × 2, 80c; airmail, 1.30, 3, 3.50s (6v). 2 souvenir sheets of 3 (10c, 1.30, 3.50s; 10, 80c, 3s) perf., imperf.

Winter Olympics, 1924–1968. 10c, 1s; airmail, 1.50, 2, 2.50, 4s (6v). Souvenir sheet of 3 (10c, 1.50, 4s) perf., imperf.

French-American Space Research. 10c; airmail, 1.50, 4s (3v). Souvenir sheet of 3 (10c, 1.50, 4s) perf., imperf.

Italian Space Research. 10c; airmail, 1.30, 3.50s (3v). Souvenir sheet of 3 (10c, 1.30, 3.50s) perf., imperf.

Moon Exploration. 10, 80c, 1s; airmail, 2, 2.50, 3s (6v). Souvenir sheet of 3 (10, 80c, 3s) perf., imperf.

1967

19th Summer Olympics, Mexico. *Mar. 13.* 10c, 1s; airmail, 1.30, 2, 2.50, 3.50s (6v). Souvenir sheet of 3 (10c, 1.30, 3.50s) perf., imperf. Diamond-shaped; 10c × 2, 80c; airmail, 1.50, 3, 4s (6v). 2 souvenir sheets of 3 (10c, 1.50, 4s; 10, 80c, 3s) perf., imperf.

National Eucharistic Congress, 4th. *May 10.* 10, 60, 80c, 1s; airmail, 1.50, 2s (6v). Souvenir sheet, 10s perf., imperf.

Madonnas, paintings. *May.* 10, 40, 50c; airmail, 1.30, 2.50, 3s (6v). (Reni, van Hemesen, Memling, Dürer, Raphael, Murillo).

Women, paintings. *Sept. 9.* 10c, 1s; airmail, 1.50, 2, 2.50, 4s (6v). (van der Weyden, Rubens, Dürer, Gainsborough, Manet, Raphael). Souvenir sheet of 3 (10c, 1.50, 4s) perf., imperf.

John F. Kennedy, 50th birth anniversary. *Sept. 11.* 10c × 2, 80c; airmail, 1.30, 3, 3.50s (6v). 2 souvenir sheets of 3 (10, 80c, 3s; 10c, 1.30, 3.50s) perf., imperf.

Christmas. *Dec. 29.* 10c × 2, 40, 50, 60c; airmail, 2.50s (6v).

1968

Christian Local Art. *Jan. 19.* 10, 80c, 1s; airmail, 1.30, 1.50, 2s (6v). Souvenir sheet of 3 (3, 3.50, 4s) perf., imperf.

Tourist Year (9th COTAL Congress). *Apr. 1.* 20, 30, 40, 50, 60, 80c, 1s; airmail, 1.30, 1.50, 2s (10v).

1969

Pope Paul VI, Latin American visit and **39th International Eucharistic Congress.** Bogota, 40, 60c, 1s; airmail, 1.30, 2s (5v). Souvenir sheets of 2 (1, 2s) and 3 (40, 60c, 1.30s); imperf.

Guayaquil University Centenary, religious paintings with university coat of arms ovptd. in silver. 40, 60c, 1s; airmail, 1.30, 2s (5v). (van der Weyden, Raphael, Veronese). Souvenir sheets of 3 (40, 60c, 2s) and 2 (1, 2s) imperf.

EQUATORIAL GUINEA

Most sets exist perf., imperf.
Most imperf. sets have surface colored paper

1972

Apollo 15. *Jan. 28.* 1, 3, 5, 8, 10p; airmail, 15, 25p (7v). 3 airmail semi-postal souvenir sheets 25p+200p, perf.; 50p+250p, imperf.; gold foil, 200p+25p, perf., 200p+50p, imperf.

11th Winter Olympics, Sapporo. *Feb. 3.* 1, 2, 3, 5, 8p; airmail, 15, 50p (7v). 2 airmail semi-postal souvenir sheets, 200p+25p, perf.; 250p+50p, imperf.; gold foil, 200p+25p, perf., 200p+50p, imperf., 2 each.

Christmas; paintings. *1971.* 1, 3, 5, 8, 10p; airmail, 15, 25p (7v). 2 airmail semi-postal souvenir sheets 25p+200p, perf.; 50p+200p, imperf. (Virgin and Child by da Vinci, Murillo, Raphael, Mabuse, van der Weyden, Dürer), gold foil, 200p+25p, perf., 250p+50p, imperf.

Easter. *Apr. 28.* 1, 3, 5, 8, 10p; airmail, 15, 25p (7v). 2 souvenir sheets (25, 200p), perf., semi-postal 250p+50p, imperf., gold foil airmail semi-postal 200p+25p, perf., 250+50p, imperf., 2 each with designs by Velazquez and El Greco.

20th Summer Olympics, Munich (sports; inscribed "Augsburgo"). *May 5.* 1, 2, 3, 5, 8p; airmail, 15, 50p (7v). 2 airmail semi-postal souvenir sheets 200p+25p, perf.; 250p+50p, imperf. Presentation folder with gold foil airmail semi-postal 200p+25p, perf., 200p+50p, imperf.

Gold Medal Winners, Sapporo. *May 25.* 1, 2, 3, 5, 8p; airmail, 15, 50p (7v). Airmail souvenir sheet, 250p+50p, imperf.; souvenir sheet of 2 (25, 200p) perf. Gold foil, 200p+25p, perf., 250p+50p, imperf., 6 each.

Black Gold Medal Winners, Munich. *June 26.* 1, 2, 3, 5, 8p; airmail, 15, 50p (7v). 2 airmail semi-postal souvenir sheets 200p+25p, perf.; 250p+50p, imperf. Gold foil, 200p+25p, perf., 250p+50p, imperf., 9 each.

Olympic Games, Regatta in Kiel & Oberschleissheim. *July 25.* 1, 2, 3, 5, 8p; airmail, 15, 50p (7v). 2 airmail semi-postal souvenir sheets 200p+25p, perf.; 250p+50p, imperf. Gold foil, 200p+25p, perf., 250p+50p, imperf., 2 each.

1972 Munich Olympics. *Aug. 10.* 1, 2, 3, 5, 8p; airmail, 15, 50p (7v). 2 airmail semi-postal souvenir sheets 200p+25p, perf.; 250p+50p, imperf. *Aug. 17.* 10 gold foil sheets, 200p+25p each, perf. Same, 10 imperf. sheets, 250p+50p each.

Olympic Equestrian Events. *Aug. 24.* 1, 2, 3, 5, 8p; airmail, 15, 50, 50p (7v). 2 airmail semi-postal souvenir sheets 200p+25p, perf.; 250p+50p, imperf. Gold foil souvenir sheets, 200p+25p, perf. Same, imperf. sheets, 250p+50p, 8 each. 2 stamps, 200p+25p, perf., 250p+50p, imperf. 3 sheets of 2, 200p+25p (2 perf., 1 imperf.)

Japanese Railroad centenary (locomotives). *Sept. 21.* 1, 3, 5, 8, 10p; airmail, 15, 25p (7v). 2 airmail semi-postal souvenir sheets 200p+25p, perf.; 250p+50p, imperf. 11 gold foil souvenir sheets of 1; (200p+25p, perf. (9), 200p+25p, imperf. (2). 2 sheets of 2, each 200p+25p. perf., imperf.

Gold Medal Winners, Munich Games. *Oct. 30.* 1, 2, 3, 5, 8p; airmail, 15, 50p (7v). 2 airmail semi-postal souvenir sheets 200p+25p, perf.; 250p+50p, imperf. 4 gold foil souvenir sheets, 200p+25p, perf., 250p+50p, imperf., 2 each.

Christmas and 500th birth anniversary of Lucas Cranach. (Madonnas and Christmas seals). *Nov. 22.* 1, 3, 5, 8, 10p; airmail, 15, 25p (7v). (Giotto, Schongauer, Fouquet, de Morales, Fini, David, Sassetta). 2 airmail semi-postal souvenir sheets, 200p+25p, perf., 250+50p, imperf. Gold foil souvenir sheets, 200p+25p (6), perf., 250p+50p (6) imperf. Souvenir sheets of 2, 200p+25p, perf., imperf. Ovptd. stamp 200p+25p.

American and Russian astronaut memorial. *Dec. 14.* 1, 3, 5, 8, 10p; airmail, 15, 25p (7v). 2 airmail semi-postal souvenir sheets 200p+25p, perf.; 250p+50p, imperf. Gold foil ovptd. "Apollo 16 and 17" 200p+25p, perf., 250p+50p, imperf., 2 each.

1973

Trans-Atlantic Yacht Race. *Jan. 22.* 1, 2, 3, 5, 8p; airmail, 15, 50p (7v). 2 airmail semi-postal souvenir sheets 200p+25p, perf.; 250p+50p, imperf.

Renoir paintings. *Feb. 22.* 1, 2, 3, 5, 8p; airmail, 15, 50p (7v). 2 airmail semi-postal souvenir sheets 25p+200p, perf.; 50p+250p, imperf. Golf foil, 200p+25p, perf., 250p+50p, imperf.

Conquest of Venus (spacecraft). *Mar. 22.* 1, 3, 5, 8, 10p; airmail, 15, 25p (7v). 2 airmail semi-postal souvenir sheets 200p+25p, perf.; 250p+50p, imperf.

Apollo Flights 11–17. *Mar. 22.* 18 gold foil airmail semi-postal souvenir sheets: 14 sheets of 1 (7 × 200p+25p, perf.; 7 × 250p+50p, imperf.); 4 sheets of 2, 200p+25p, perf., 250p+50p, imperf. 2 each.

National Workers Party. *April.* 1, 1.50, 2, 4, 5p (5v).

Independence, 4th anniversary. *April.* 1.50, 2, 3, 4, 5p (5v).

Easter, paintings. *Apr. 25.* 1, 3, 5, 8, 10p; airmail, 15, 25p (7v). (Verrocchio, Perugino, Tintoretto, Witz, Pontormo). 2 airmail semi-postal souvenir sheets 200p+25p, perf.; 250p+50p, imperf. Gold foil issue of 1972 ovptd. 4 sheets, 200p+25p, perf., 250p+50p, imperf. 2 each.

Copernicus. 500th birth anniversary (US and USSR space explorations). *May 15.* 4 gold foil airmail semi-postal souvenir sheets, 200p+25p, perf.; 250p+50p, imperf., 2 each.

Tour de France bicycle race. 59th. *May 22.* 1, 2, 3, 5, 8p; airmail, 15, 50p (7v). 2 airmail semi-postal souvenir sheets 200p+25p, perf.; 250p+50p, imperf.

Paintings. *June 29.* 1, 2, 3, 5, 8p; airmail, 15, 50p (7v). 2 airmail semi-postal souvenir sheets 200p+25p, perf.; 250p+50p, imperf.

World Cup Soccer Championships, Munich, 1974. *Aug. 30.* 5, 10, 15, 20, 25, 55, 60c; airmail, 5, 70p (9v). 2 airmail souvenir sheets, 130p, perf.; 200p, imperf.

Rubens paintings. *Sept. 23.* 1, 2, 3, 5, 8p; airmail, 15, 50p (7v). 2 souvenir sheets of 2 (200, 25p perf.; 250, 50p imperf.).

New Currency: Ekuele.

World Cup Soccer Championships, Munich, 1974. *Oct. 24.* 2 Gold foil souvenir sheets 130e × 2, perf.; 200e × 2, imperf. 2 souvenir sheets of 2, 130p, perf., 200p, imperf.

Christmas, paintings. *Oct. 30.* 1, 3, 5, 8, 10p; airmail, 15, 25p (7v). (Nativity by, van der Weyden, Bosco, de Carvajal, Mabuse, Lucas Jordon, P. Goecke, Maino, Fabriano, Lochner). 2 airmail semi-postal souvenir sheets 200p+25p, perf.; 250p+50p, imperf.

Apollo Program and J. F. Kennedy. *Nov. 10.* Gold foil airmail semi-postal 200p+25p, perf.; 250p+50p, imperf. and souvenir sheets (same).

World Cup Soccer (famous players). *Nov. 20.* 30, 35, 40, 45, 50, 65, 70c; airmail, 8, 60p (9v). 2 souvenir sheets, 130p, perf., 200p, imperf.

Princess Anne's Wedding. *Dec. 17.* Gold foil airmail souvenir sheets, 2 sheets of 1, 250e each; 1 sheet of 2, 250e × 2, perf., imperf.

Pablo Picasso Memorial (Blue Period paintings). *Dec. 20.* 30, 35, 40, 45, 50c; airmail, 8, 60e (7v). 2 souvenir sheets, 130e, perf.; 200e, imperf.

1974

Copernicus, 500th birth anniversary. *Feb. 8.* 5, 10, 15, 20c, 4e, airmail, 10, 70e (7v). 2 souvenir sheets 130e, perf.; 200e, imperf. *Apr. 10.* 8 gold foil souvenir sheets: 130e (3), perf.; 200e (3), imperf., 250e, perf., 300e, imperf. 4 souvenir sheets of 2, 250e, perf., 250e, imperf; 2 each.

World Cup Soccer Championships (final games) Munich. *Feb. 28.* 75, 80, 85, 90, 95c, 1, 1.25e; airmail, 10, 50e (9v). 2 souvenir sheets, 130e, perf.; 200e, imperf.

Easter, paintings. *Mar. 27.* 1, 3, 5, 8, 10p; airmail, 15, 25p (7v). (Fra Angelico, Castagno, Allori, Multscher, della Francesca, Pleydenwurff, Correggio). 2 airmail semi-postal souvenir sheets 200p+25p, perf.; 250p+50p, imperf.

Holy Year 1975 (famous churches). *Apr. 11.* 5, 10, 15, 20c, 3.50e; airmail, 10, 70e (7v). 2 souvenir sheets 130e, perf., 200e, imperf.

World Cup Soccer (contemporary players). *Apr. 30.* 1.50, 1.75, 2, 2.25, 2.50, 3, 3.50e; airmail, 10, 60e (9v). 2 souvenir sheets of 2, 65e × 2, perf.; 100e × 2, imperf.

UPU centenary (transportation from messenger to rocket). *May 30.* 60, 70, 80c, 1, 1.50e; airmail, 30, 50e (7v). 2 souvenir sheets, 225e, perf.; 150e × 2, imperf. *June 8.* 2 airmail deluxe souvenir sheets, 130e. 1 sheet of 2, 130e, perf.

Picasso Memorial (Pink Period paintings). *June 28.* 55, 60, 65, 70, 75c; airmail, 10, 50e (7v). 2 souvenir sheets 130e, perf.; 200e, imperf.

World Cup Soccer Championships. *July 8.* 6 gold foil airmail souvenir sheets: 4 sheets of 1, 130e (2), 250e (2); 2 sheets of 2, 130e × 2, 250e × 2.

Aleksander Solzhenitsyn. *July 25.* Gold foil airmail souvenir sheets, 250e perf., 300e imperf.

Opening of American West. *July 30.* 30, 35, 40, 45, 50c; airmail, 8, 60p (7v). 2 souvenir sheets 130p, perf.; 200p, imperf.

Flowers. *Aug. 20.* 5, 10, 15, 20, 25c, 1, 3, 5, 8, 10p; airmail, 5, 15, 25, 70p (14v). 4 souvenir sheets: 130p; 200p; 2 semi-postal, 200p+25p, 250p+50p.

Christmas. *Sept. 16.* 60, 70, 80c, 1, 1.50e; airmail, 30, 50e (7v). 2 souvenir sheets, 225e, perf.; 300e, imperf.

Barcelona soccer team, 75th anniversary. *Sept. 25.* 1, 3, 5, 8, 10e; airmail, 15, 60e (7v, miniature sheet of 7 plus label). 2 souvenir sheets 200e, perf.; 300e, imperf. 4 gold foil airmail souvenir sheets, 200e each, perf. and imperf.

UPU centenary and ESPANA 75. *Oct. 9.* 1.25, 1.50, 1.75, 2, 2.25e; airmail, 35, 60e (7v). 2 airmail souvenir sheets 225e, perf., 300e, imperf. *Oct. 14.* Gold foil sheets, 250e, 300e, 250e × 2 perf., imperf.

Nature protection, Australian animals: *Oct. 25.* 80, 85, 90, 95c. 1e; airmail, 15, 40e (7v). 2 souvenir sheets 130e, perf.; 200e, imperf. **African animals:** *Nov. 6.* 55, 60, 65, 70, 75c; airmail, 10, 70e (7v). 2 souvenir sheets 130e, perf.; 200e, imperf. **Australian and South American Birds:** *Nov. 26.* 1.25, 1.50, 1.75, 2, 2.25, 2.50, 2.75, 3, 3.50, 4p; airmail, 20, 25, 30, 35p (14v). 4 souvenir sheets 130p × 2, perf.; 200p × 2, imperf. **Endangered Species:** *Dec. 17.* 10, 15, 20, 25, 30, 35, 40, 45, 50, 55, 60c, 1, 2e; airmail, 10, 70e (15v se-tenant in sheet of 15).

Monkeys, various species. *Dec. 27.* Se-tenant in sheets of 16. 5, 10, 15, 20, 25, 30, 35, 40, 45, 50, 55, 60c, 1, 2e; airmail 10, 70e (16v).

Cats, various species. *Dec. 27.* Se-tenant in sheets of 16. 5, 10, 15, 20, 25, 30, 35, 40, 45, 50, 55, 60c, 1, 2e; airmail 10, 70e (16v).

Fish, various species. *Dec. 27.* Se-tenant in sheets of 16. 5, 10, 15, 20, 25, 30, 35, 40, 45, 50, 55, 60c, 1, 2e; airmail 10, 70e (16v).

Butterflies, various species. *Dec. 27.* Se-tenant in sheets of 16. 5, 10, 15, 20, 25, 30, 35, 40, 45, 50, 55, 60c, 1, 2e; airmail 10, 70e (16v).

1975

Picasso Memorial (Paintings from last period). *Jan. 27.* 5, 10, 15, 20, 25c; airmail, 5, 70e (7v). 2 souvenir sheets 130e, perf.; 200e, imperf.

ARPHILA 75 Philatelic Exhibition Paris. *Jan. 27.* 8 gold foil airmail souvenir sheets, 3 sheets of 1, 250e, 1 sheet of 2, 250e, perf.; 3 sheets of 1, 300e; 1 sheet of 2, 300e, imperf.

Easter and Holy Year 1975. *Feb. 15.* 60, 70, 80c, 1, 1.50e; airmail, 30, 50e (7v). 2 airmail souvenir sheets 225e, perf.; 300e, imperf.

12th Winter Olympics, Innsbruck, 1976. *Mar. 10.* 5, 10, 15, 20, 25, 30, 35, 40, 45c, 25, 70e (11v). 2 souvenir sheets 130e, perf.; 200e, imperf. 2 gold foil souvenir sheets, 1 sheet of 1, 250e, 1 sheet of 2, 250e × 2.

Don Quixote. *Apr. 4.* 30, 35, 40, 45, 50c; airmail, 25, 60e (7v). 2 souvenir sheets 130e, perf.; 200e, imperf.

American Bicentennial. *April 30.* (First Issue) 5, 20, 40, 75c, 2, 5, 8e; airmail 25, 30e (9v). Airmail souvenir sheets, 130e, perf., 200e, imperf.

April 30. (Second Issue) 10, 30, 50c, 1, 3, 6, 10e; airmail, 12, 40e (9v). 2 airmail souvenir sheets, 130e, perf., 200e, imperf.

July 4. (Presidents) 5, 10, 20, 30, 40, 50, 75c, 1, 2, 3, 5, 6, 8, 10e; airmail, 12, 25, 30, 40e (18v). 4 airmail souvenir sheets, 225e × 2, perf., 300e × 2, imperf. Embossed gold foil 6 souvenir sheets airmail 200e × 2, 200e (2) perf., 300e × 2, 300e (2) imperf.

Bull Fight. *May 26.* 80, 85, 90, 95c, 8e; airmail, 35, 40e (7v). 2 airmail souvenir sheets, 130e, perf., 200e, imperf.

Apollo-Soyuz Space Project. *June 20.* 1, 2, 3, 5, 5.50, 7, 7.50, 9, 15e; airmail, 20, 30e (11v). 2 airmail souvenir sheets, 225e, perf., 300e, imperf.

Apollo-Soyuz Space Project. *July 17.* Airmail souvenir sheet, 250e, perf.

Famous Painters, Nudes. *Aug. 10.* Se-tenant in sheets of 16. 5, 10, 15, 20, 25, 30, 35, 40, 45, 50, 55, 60c, 1, 2e; airmail 10, 70e (16v). (Egyptian, Greek, Roman, Indian art, Goes, Dürer, Liss, Beniort, Renoir, Gauguin, Stenlen, Picasso, Modigliani, Matisse, Padua). Airmail souvenir sheetlets embossed gold foil, 10 × 200p +25p, perf., 10 × 250p+50p, imperf.

Conquerors of the Seas. *Sept. 5.* 30, 35, 40, 45, 50, 55, 60, 65, 70, 75c; airmail 8, 10, 50, 60p (14v). 4 airmail souvenir sheets, 130p, perf., 200p, imperf., 2 each.

Christmas and Holy Year 1975. *Oct.* 60, 70, 80c, 1, 1.50e; airmail 30, 50e (7v) (Jordan, Barocci, Vereycke, Rubens, Mengs, Del Castillo, Cavedone). 2 airmail souvenir sheets, 225e, perf., 300e, imperf. Embossed gold foil, 4 souvenir sheets, 200e, perf., 300e, imperf. 2 gold foil miniature sheets of 2, 200e+200e, perf., 300e+300e, imperf.

President Macias, I.W.Y. *Dec. 25.* 1.50, 3, 3.50, 5, 7, 10e; airmail 100, 300e (8v). 2 airmail souvenir sheets (world events), 100 (U.S., Yorktown 2c), 300e, imperf.

1976

Uniforms, Cavalry. *Feb. 2.* 5, 10, 15, 20, 25c; airmail, 5, 70p (7v). 2 airmail souvenir sheets, 130p, perf., 200p, imperf.

12th Winter Olympics, Innsbruck '76. *Feb.* 50, 55, 60, 65, 70, 75, 80, 85, 90e; airmail 35, 60e (11v). 2 airmail souvenir sheets, 130e, perf., 200e, imperf.

21st Summer Olympics Montreal '76. Ancient to Modern Games. *Feb.* 50, 60, 70, 80, 90c; airmail 35, 60e (7v). 2 souvenir sheets airmail, 225e, perf., 300e, imperf.

21st Summer Olympics Montreal '76 *Mar. 5.* 50, 60, 70, 80, 90c; airmail 30, 60e (7v). 2 airmail souvenir sheets 225e, perf., 300e, imperf. 4 embossed gold foil airmail souvenir sheets, 250e, perf., 300e, imperf. 2 miniature sheets of 2, 250e×2, perf., 300e×2, imperf.

U.N. 30th Anniversary. *June.* Airmail souvenir sheet, 250e, perf.

El Greco, paintings. *Apr. 5.* 1, 3, 5, 8, 10e; airmail, 15, 25e (7v). 2 airmail semipostal souvenir sheets, 200+25e, perf., 250+50e, imperf.

21st Summer Olympics, Montreal, modern games. *May 7.* 50, 55, 60, 65, 70, 75, 80, 85, 90c; airmail, 35, 60e (11v). 2 airmail souvenir sheets, 225e, perf., 300e, imperf. 4 embossed on gold foil souvenir sheets, 250e, perf., 300e, imperf. (2 each). 2 miniature sheets of 2, 250e × 2, perf., 300e × 2, imperf.

Contemporary Automobiles, *June 10.* 1, 3, 5, 8, 10p; airmail, 15, 25p (7v). 2 airmail semipostal souvenir sheets, 200+25p, perf., 250+50p, imperf.

Nature Protection, European Animals. *July 1.* 5, 10, 15, 20, 25c; airmail, 5, 70p (7v). 2 airmail souvenir sheets, 130p, perf., 200p, imperf. **Asian Animals.** *Sept. 20.* 30, 35, 40, 45c, 8p; airmail 50c, 60p (7v). 2 airmail souvenir sheets, 130p, perf., 200p, imperf. **Asian Birds.** *Sept. 20.* 55, 60, 65, 70, 75c; airmail, 10, 50p (7v). 2 airmail souvenir sheets, 130p, perf., 200p, imperf. **European Birds.** *Sept. 20.* 5, 10, 15, 20, 25c; airmail, 5, 70p (7v). 2 airmail souvenir sheets, 130p, perf., 200p, imperf. **North American Birds.** *Sept. 20.* 80, 85, 90, 95c, 1p; airmail, 15, 40p (7v). 2 airmail souvenir sheets, 130p, perf., 200p, imperf.

Motorcycle Aces. *July 22.* 1e × 2, 2e × 2, 3e × 2, 4e × 2, 5e × 2, 10e × 2, 30e × 2, 40e × 2 (16v) in se-tenant blocks of 8 different values.

21st Summer Olympics, Montreal. *Aug.* 7, 10, 25e se-tenant strip of 3; airmail, 200e (4v). Airmail souvenir sheet, 300e, imperf.

Flowers. *Aug. 16.* **South America.** 30, 35, 40, 45, 50c;

airmail, 8, 60p (7v). 2 airmail souvenir sheets, 130p, perf., 200p, imperf. **Oceania.** 80, 85, 90, 95c, 1p; airmail, 15, 40p (7v). 2 airmail souvenir sheets, 130p, perf., 200p, imperf.

1977

Butterflies. *Jan.* 80, 85, 90, 95c, 8e; airmail, 35, 40e (7v). 2 airmail souvenir sheets, 130e, perf., 200e, imperf.

Madrid Real, 75th anniversary. *Jan.* 2, 4, 5, 8, 10, 15e; airmail, 20, 35, 150e (9v).

Ancient Carriages. *Feb.* 5, 10, 15, 20, 25, 30, 35, 40, 45, 50, 55, 60c, 1, 2e; airmail, 10, 70e (16v).

Chinese Art. *Feb.* 60, 70, 80c, 1, 1.50e; airmail, 30. 50e (7v). 2 airmail souvenir sheets, 130e, perf., 200e, imperf.

African Masks. *Mar.* 5, 10, 15, 20, 25c; airmail, 5, 70e (7v). 2 airmail souvenir sheets, 130e, perf., 200e, imperf.

North American Animals., 1.25, 1.50, 1.75, 2, 2.25e; airmail, 20, 50e (7v). 2 airmail souvenir sheets, 130e, perf., 200e, imperf.

World Championship Soccer, Argentina '78. *July 25.*

Famous Players. 2, 4, 5, 8, 10, 15e; airmail, 20, 35e (8v). 2 airmail souvenir sheets, 150e, perf., 250e, imperf.

Famous Teams. 2, 4, 5, 8, 10, 15e; airmail, 20, 35e (8v se-tenant). 2 gold foil embossed souvenir sheets, 500e (Amphilex '77, Cutty Sark, Concorde); airmail, 500e (World Cup).

Napoleon. *Aug. 20.*

Life and Battle Scenes. 5, 10, 15, 20, 25, 30, 35, 40, 45, 50, 55, 60c, 1, 2e; airmail, 10, 70e (se-tenant in sheet of 16).

Military Uniforms. 5, 10, 15, 20, 25, 30, 35, 40, 45, 50, 55, 60c, 1, 2e; airmail, 10, 70e (se-tenant in sheet of 16).

South American Animals, *Aug.* 2.50, 2.75, 3, 3.50, 4e; airmail, 25, 35e (7v). 2 airmail souvenir sheets, 130e, perf., 200e imperf.

U.S.S.R. Space Program, 20th anniversary. *Dec. 15.* 2, 4, 5, 8, 10, 15e; airmail, 20, 35e (8v). 2 airmail souvenir sheets, 150e, imperf., 250e, perf.

1978

Ancient Sailing Ships. *Jan. 6.* 5, 10, 15, 20, 25c; airmail, 5, 70e, also 5, 10, 20, 25, 70e (12v). 4 airmail souvenir sheets, 150, 225e, perf., 250, 300e, imperf. Gold foil embossed airmail souvenir sheets, 500e, perf., imperf.

Pre-Olympics '80. *Jan. 17.*

Winter Games, Lake Placid. 5, 10, 20, 25e; airmail, 70e (5v). 2 airmail souvenir sheets, 150e, perf., 250e, imperf. Gold foil embossed airmail souvenir sheet, 500e, perf., imperf.

Summer Games, Moscow. 2, 3, 5, 8, 10, 15e; airmail, 30, 50e (8v). 2 airmail souvenir sheets, 150e, perf., 250e, imperf. Gold foil embossed airmail souvenir sheet, 500e perf., imperf.

Summer Water Games, Talinn. 5, 10, 20, 25e; airmail, 70e (5v). 2 airmail souvenir sheets, 150e, perf., 250e, imperf. Gold foil embossed airmail souvenir sheet, 500e, perf., imperf.

QE II Coronation, 25th anniversary. *Apr. 25.* 2, 5, 8, 10, 12, 15e; airmail, 30, 50e (8v). 2 airmail souvenir sheets, 150e perf., 250e imperf.

English Knights of 1200–1350 A.D. *Apr. 25.* 5, 10, 15, 20, 25e; airmail, 15, 70e (7v). 2 airmail souvenir sheets, 130e perf., 250e imperf.

Old Locomotives. *Aug.* 1, 2, 3, 5, 10e; airmail, 25, 70e (7v). 2 airmail souvenir sheets, 150e perf., 250e imperf.

Prehistoric Animals. *Aug.* 30, 35, 40, 45, 50e; airmail, 25, 60e (7v). Airmail souvenir sheet, 130e.

Souvenir Sheets. *Aug.* Airmail: **Francisco Goya,** "Maja Vestida," 150e; **Peter Paul Rubens—UNICEF,** 250e; **Europa—CEPT—Eurphila, 78,** 250e; **30th International Stamp Fair, Riccione,** 150e; **1978 Events.** Sheet of 3, QE II Coronation, 150e; CEPT, 250e and World Cup Soccer, Argentina '78 and Spain '82, 150e; Christmas, Titian painting, "The Virgin," 150e.

INDEX and IDENTIFIER

See also Addenda and For the Record